THE OXFORD ENGLISH DICTIONARY

SECOND EDITION

THE OXFORD ENGLISH DICTIONARY

First Edited by

JAMES A. H. MURRAY, HENRY BRADLEY, W. A. CRAIGIE
and C. T. ONIONS

COMBINED WITH

A SUPPLEMENT TO THE OXFORD ENGLISH DICTIONARY

Edited by

R. W. BURCHFIELD

AND RESET WITH CORRECTIONS, REVISIONS
AND ADDITIONAL VOCABULARY

THE OXFORD ENGLISH DICTIONARY

SECOND EDITION

Prepared by

J. A. SIMPSON *and* E. S. C. WEINER

VOLUME XII

Poise–Quelt

CLARENDON PRESS · OXFORD

Oxford University Press, Great Clarendon Street, Oxford OX2 6DP
Oxford New York
Athens Auckland Bangkok Bogotá Buenos Aires Calcutta
Cape Town Chennai Dar es Salaam Delhi Florence Hong Kong Istanbul
Karachi Kuala Lumpur Madrid Melbourne Mexico City Mumbai
Nairobi Paris São Paulo Singapore Taipei Tokyo Toronto Warsaw
and associated companies in
Berlin Ibadan

Oxford is a registered trade mark of Oxford University Press

First published 1989
Reprinted 1991 (with corrections), 1998

British Library Cataloguing in Publication Data
Oxford English dictionary.—2nd ed.
1. English language—Dictionaries
I. Simpson, J. A. (John Andrew), 1953-
II. Weiner, Edmund S. C., 1950-
423
ISBN 0-19-861224-9 (vol. XII)
ISBN 0-19-861186-2 (set)

Library of Congress Cataloging-in-Publication Data
The Oxford English dictionary.—2nd ed.
prepared by J. A. Simpson and E. S. C. Weiner
Bibliography: p.
ISBN 0-19-861224-9 (vol. XII)
ISBN 0-19-861186-2 (set)
1. English language—Dictionaries. I. Simpson, J. A.
II. Weiner, E. S. C. III. Oxford University Press.
PE1625.087 1989
423—dc19 88-5330

Data capture by ICC, Fort Washington, Pa.
Text-processing by Oxford University Press
Typesetting by Pindar Graphics Origination, Scarborough, N. Yorks.
Manufactured in the United States of America by
World Color Book Services, Taunton, Mass.

KEY TO THE PRONUNCIATION

THE pronunciations given are those in use in the educated speech of southern England (the so-called 'Received Standard'), and the keywords given are to be understood as pronounced in such speech.

I. *Consonants*

b, d, f, k, l, m, n, p, t, v, z *have their usual English values*

g as in *go* (gəʊ)
h ... *ho!* (həʊ)
r ... *run* (rʌn), *terrier* ('tɛrɪə(r))
(r) ... *her* (hɜː(r))
s ... *see* (siː), *success* (sək'sɛs)
w ... *wear* (wɛə(r))
hw ... *when* (hwɛn)
j ... *yes* (jɛs)

θ as in *thin* (θɪn), *bath* (bɑːθ)
ð ... *then* (ðɛn), *bathe* (beɪð)
ʃ ... *shop* (ʃɒp), *dish* (dɪʃ)
tʃ ... *chop* (tʃɒp), *ditch* (dɪtʃ)
ʒ ... *vision* ('vɪʒən), *déjeuner* (deʒøne)
dʒ ... *judge* (dʒʌdʒ)
ŋ ... *singing* ('sɪŋɪŋ), *think* (θiŋk)
ŋg ... *finger* ('fɪŋgə(r))

(FOREIGN AND NON-SOUTHERN)

ʎ as in It. *serraglio* (ser'raʎo)
ɲ ... Fr. *cognac* (kɔɲak)
x ... Ger. *ach* (ax), Sc. *loch* (lɒx), Sp. *frijoles* (fri'xoles)
ç ... Ger. *ich* (ɪç), Sc. *nicht* (nɪçt)
ɣ ... North Ger. *sagen* ('zaːɣən)
c ... Afrikaans *baardmannetjie* ('baːrtmanəci)
ɥ ... Fr. *cuisine* (kɥizin)

Symbols in parentheses are used to denote elements that may be omitted either by individual speakers or in particular phonetic contexts: e.g. *bottle* ('bɒt(ə)l), *Mercian* ('mɜːʃ(ɪ)ən), *suit* (s(j)uːt), *impromptu* (ɪm'prɒm(p)tjuː), *father* ('fɑːðə(r)).

II. *Vowels and Diphthongs*

SHORT

ɪ as in *pit* (pɪt), *-ness*, (-nɪs)
ɛ ... *pet* (pɛt), Fr. *sept* (sɛt)
æ ... *pat* (pæt)
ʌ ... *putt* (pʌt)
ɒ ... *pot* (pɒt)
ʊ ... *put* (pʊt)
ə ... *another* (ə'nʌðə(r))
(ə) ... *beaten* ('biːt(ə)n)
i ... Fr. *si* (si)
e ... Fr. *bébé* (bebe)
a ... Fr. *mari* (mari)
ɑ ... Fr. *bâtiment* (bɑtimɑ̃)
ɔ ... Fr. *homme* (ɔm)
o ... Fr. *eau* (o)
ø ... Fr. *peu* (pø)
œ ... Fr. *boeuf* (bœf) *coeur* (kœr)
u ... Fr. *douce* (dus)
ʏ ... Ger. *Müller* ('mʏlər)
y ... Fr. *du* (dy)

LONG

iː as in *bean* (biːn)
ɑː ... *barn* (bɑːn)
ɔː ... *born* (bɔːn)
uː ... *boon* (buːn)
ɜː ... *burn* (bɜːn)
eː ... Ger. *Schnee* (ʃneː)
ɛː ... Ger. *Fähre* ('fɛːrə)
aː ... Ger. *Tag* (taːk)
oː ... Ger. *Sohn* (zoːn)
øː ... Ger. *Goethe* ('gøːtə)
yː ... Ger. *grün* (gryːn)

NASAL

ɛ̃, æ̃ as in Fr. *fin* (fɛ̃, fæ̃)
ɑ̃ ... Fr. *franc* (frɑ̃)
ɔ̃ ... Fr. *bon* (bɔ̃)
œ̃ ... Fr. *un* (œ̃)

DIPHTHONGS, etc.

eɪ as in *bay* (beɪ)
aɪ ... *buy* (baɪ)
ɔɪ ... *boy* (bɔɪ)
əʊ ... *no* (nəʊ)
aʊ ... *now* (naʊ)
ɪə ... *peer* (pɪə(r))
ɛə ... *pair* (pɛə(r))
ʊə ... *tour* (tʊə(r))
ɔə ... *boar* (bɔə(r))

aɪə as in *fiery* ('faɪərɪ)
aʊə ... *sour* (saʊə(r))

The incidence of main stress is shown by a superior stress mark (') preceding the stressed syllable, and a secondary stress by an inferior stress mark (ˌ), e.g. *pronunciation* (prəˌnʌnsɪ'eɪʃ(ə)n).

For further explanation of the transcription used, see *General Explanations*, Volume I.

LIST OF ABBREVIATIONS, SIGNS, ETC.

Some abbreviations listed here in italics are also in certain cases printed in roman type, and vice versa.

a. (in Etym.)	adoption of, adopted from
a (as *a* 1850)	*ante*, 'before', 'not later than'
a.	adjective
abbrev.	abbreviation (of)
abl.	ablative
absol.	absolute, -ly
Abstr.	(in titles) *Abstract, -s*
acc.	accusative
Acct.	(in titles) *Account*
A.D.	*Anno Domini*
ad. (in Etym.)	adaptation of
Add.	Addenda
adj.	adjective
Adv.	(in titles) *Advance, -d, -s*
adv.	adverb
advb.	adverbial, -ly
Advt.	advertisement
Aeronaut.	(as label) in Aeronautics; (in titles) *Aeronautic, -al, -s*
AF., AFr.	Anglo-French
Afr.	Africa, -n
Agric.	(as label) in Agriculture; (in titles) *Agriculture, -al*
Alb.	Albanian
Amer.	American
Amer. Ind.	American Indian
Anat.	(as label) in Anatomy; (in titles) *Anatomy, -ical*
Anc.	(in titles) *Ancient*
Anglo-Ind.	Anglo-Indian
Anglo-Ir.	Anglo-Irish
Ann.	Annals
Anthrop., Anthropol.	(as label) in Anthropology; (in titles) *Anthropology, -ical*
Antiq.	(as label) in Antiquities; (in titles) *Antiquity*
aphet.	aphetic, aphetized
app.	apparently
Appl.	(in titles) *Applied*
Applic.	(in titles) *Application, -s*
appos.	appositive, -ly
Arab.	Arabic
Aram.	Aramaic
Arch.	in Architecture
arch.	archaic
Archæol.	in Archæology
Archit.	(as label) in Architecture; (in titles) *Architecture, -al*
Arm.	Armenian
assoc.	association
Astr.	in Astronomy
Astrol.	in Astrology
Astron.	(in titles) *Astronomy, -ical*
Astronaut.	(in titles) *Astronautic, -s*
attrib.	attributive, -ly
Austral.	Australian
Autobiogr.	(in titles) *Autobiography, -ical*
A.V.	Authorized Version
B.C.	Before Christ
B.C.	(in titles) British Columbia
bef.	before
Bibliogr.	(as label) in Bibliography; (in titles) *Bibliography, -ical*
Biochem.	(as label) in Biochemistry; (in titles) *Biochemistry, -ical*
Biol.	(as label) in Biology; (in titles) *Biology, -ical*
Bk.	*Book*
Bot.	(as label) in Botany; (in titles) *Botany, -ical*
Bp.	Bishop
Brit.	(in titles) *Britain, British*
Bulg.	Bulgarian
Bull.	(in titles) *Bulletin*
c (as *c* 1700)	*circa*, 'about'
c. (as 19th c.)	century
Cal.	(in titles) *Calendar*
Cambr.	(in titles) *Cambridge*
Canad.	Canadian
Cat.	Catalan
catachr.	catachrestically
Catal.	(in titles) *Catalogue*
Celt.	Celtic
Cent.	(in titles) *Century, Central*
Cent. Dict.	*Century Dictionary*
Cf., cf.	*confer*, 'compare'
Ch.	Church
Chem.	(as label) in Chemistry; (in titles) *Chemistry, -ical*
Chr.	(in titles) *Christian*
Chron.	(in titles) *Chronicle*
Chronol.	(in titles) *Chronology, -ical*
Cinemat., Cinematogr.	in Cinematography
Clin.	(in titles) *Clinical*
cl. L.	classical Latin
cogn. w.	cognate with
Col.	(in titles) *Colonel, Colony*
Coll.	(in titles) *Collection*
collect.	collective, -ly
colloq.	colloquial, -ly
comb.	combined, -ing
Comb.	Combinations
Comm.	in Commercial usage
Communic.	in Communications
comp.	compound, composition
Compan.	(in titles) *Companion*
compar.	comparative
compl.	complement
Compl.	(in titles) *Complete*
Conc.	(in titles) *Concise*
Conch.	in Conchology
concr.	concrete, -ly
Conf.	(in titles) *Conference*
Congr.	(in titles) *Congress*
conj.	conjunction
cons.	consonant
const.	construction, construed with
contr.	contrast (with)
Contrib.	(in titles) *Contribution*
Corr.	(in titles) *Correspondence*
corresp.	corresponding (to)
Cotgr.	R. Cotgrave, *Dictionarie of the French and English Tongues*
cpd.	compound
Crit.	(in titles) *Criticism, Critical*
Cryst.	in Crystallography
Cycl.	(in titles) *Cyclopædia, -ic*
Cytol.	(in titles) *Cytology, -ical*
Da.	Danish
D.A.	*Dictionary of Americanisms*
D.A.E.	*Dictionary of American English*
dat.	dative
D.C.	District of Columbia
Deb.	(in titles) *Debate, -s*
def.	definite, -ition
dem.	demonstrative
deriv.	derivative, -ation
derog.	derogatory
Descr.	(in titles) *Description, -tive*
Devel.	(in titles) *Development, -al*
Diagn.	(in titles) *Diagnosis, Diagnostic*
dial.	dialect, -al
Dict.	Dictionary; *spec.*, the *Oxford English Dictionary*
dim.	diminutive
Dis.	(in titles) *Disease*
Diss.	(in titles) *Dissertation*
D.O.S.T.	*Dictionary of the Older Scottish Tongue*
Du.	Dutch
E.	East
Eccl.	(as label) in Ecclesiastical usage; (in titles) *Ecclesiastical*
Ecol.	in Ecology
Econ.	(as label) in Economics; (in titles) *Economy, -ics*
ed.	edition
E.D.D.	*English Dialect Dictionary*
Edin.	(in titles) *Edinburgh*
Educ.	(as label) in Education; (in titles) *Education, -al*
EE.	Early English
e.g.	*exempli gratia*, 'for example'
Electr.	(as label) in Electricity; (in titles) *Electricity, -ical*
Electron.	(in titles) *Electronic, -s*
Elem.	(in titles) *Element, -ary*
ellipt.	elliptical, -ly
Embryol.	in Embryology
e.midl.	east midland (dialect)
Encycl.	(in titles) *Encyclopædia, -ic*
Eng.	England, English
Engin.	in Engineering
Ent.	in Entomology
Entomol.	(in titles) *Entomology, -logical*
erron.	erroneous, -ly
esp.	especially
Ess.	(in titles) *Essay, -s*
et al.	*et alii*, 'and others'
etc.	et cetera
Ethnol.	in Ethnology
etym.	etymology
euphem.	euphemistically
Exam.	(in titles) *Examination*
exc.	except
Exerc.	(in titles) *Exercise, -s*
Exper.	(in titles) *Experiment, -al*
Explor.	(in titles) *Exploration, -s*
f.	feminine
f. (in Etym.)	formed on
f. (in subordinate entries)	form of
F.	French
fem. (*rarely* f.)	feminine
fig.	figurative, -ly
Finn.	Finnish
fl.	*floruit*, 'flourished'
Found.	(in titles) *Foundation, -s*
Fr.	French
freq.	frequent, -ly
Fris.	Frisian
Fund.	(in titles) *Fundamental, -s*
Funk or *Funk's Stand. Dict.*	*Funk and Wagnalls Standard Dictionary*
G.	German
Gael.	Gaelic
Gaz.	(in titles) *Gazette*
gen.	genitive
gen.	general, -ly
Geogr.	(as label) in Geography; (in titles) *Geography, -ical*

attrib., of or pertaining to such a person or letter; **poison** (also **poisons, poisons'**) **register**, a register of the names of those to whom a poison or poisons have been made available; **poison-ring**, a ring by which poison was communicated in the grasp of the hand; **poison-tower**, a chamber in which the poisonous fumes are condensed in arsenic works; **poison-vent**, a channel through which the fumes pass into the *poison-tower*.

1930 D. L. SAYERS *Strong Poison* i. 12 She signed the *poison-book in the name of Mary Slater, and the handwriting has been identified as that of the prisoner. **1943** G. GREENE *Ministry of Fear* I. iii. 33 We'll look into the poison books. **1947** A. CHRISTIE *Labours of Hercules* ii. 62, I never said anything about the missing arsenic. I even cooked the poison book! **1950** 'A. GILBERT' *Is she Dead Too?* iii. 46 He had brought a prescription that required..a drug only to be obtained by signing the Poison Book. **1978** J. SYMONS *Blackheath Poisonings* III. 152 His poison book's all in order, and there's this entry in it for arsenic. **1898** 'R. BOLDREWOOD' *Rom. Canvas Town* 61 All this time the *poison-cart was kept going. **1826** MRS. HEMANS *Forest Sanct.* I. xx, I flung it back, as guilt's own *poison-cup. **1839** URE *Dict. Arts* 56 According to the quality of the *poison-flour [previously called 'arsenic meal'] it yields from ¾ to ⅞ of its weight of the glass or enamel. **1915** H. W. WILSON *Great War* IV. 336/2 After the great chemical experiment with *poison gas in April, the Germans had been able to advance to the manor-house. *Ibid.*, The Duke of Würtemberg..had apparently become convinced, after his poison-gas victory in April, that chemical methods of making war were the most successful. **1922** D. H. LAWRENCE *Fantasia of Unconscious* xi. 207 The problem of the future is a question of the strongest poison-gas. **1924** T. HARDY *Winter Words* (1928) 171 After two thousand years of mass We've got as far as poison-gas. **1970** R. STETLER *Battle of Bogside* 179 President Johnson..called a press conference to deny the poison gas charge. **1970** G. JACKSON *Let.* 4 Apr. in *Soledad Brother* (1971) 211 An enemy that would starve his body,.. chain his body,..and poison-gas it. **1975** tr. *Melchior's Sleeper Agent* (1976) II. 39 Stacks of incendiary bombs and poison gas projectiles. **1926** S. LEWIS *Mantrap* x. 117 The *poison-green tufted velvet couch. **1937** [see *candy-pink* s.v. CANDY *sb.*[1] 2]. **1975** P. G. WINSLOW *Death of Angel* x. 212 He drives a poison-green two-seater. **1883** R. HALDANE *Workshop Receipts* Ser. II. 372/1 The unhairing in lime-pits is done..with the so-called '*poison-lime'. **1937** E. E. EVANS-PRITCHARD *Witchcraft, Oracles & Magic among Azande* 10 The principal Zande oracles are: (*a*) *benge*, *poison oracle, which operates through the administration of strychnine to fowls, and formerly to human beings also. **1955** M. GLUCKMAN *Custom & Conflict in Africa* iv. 88 Each question is framed to allow of a 'yes' or 'no' answer to the problem, thus: 'if X is the witch who is making my son ill, poison-oracle, kill the chicken; if X is not the witch, poison-oracle, spare the chicken'. **1972** M. D. McLEOD in Singer & Street *Zande Themes* 167 The Zande clearly considered the rubbing-board oracle less accurate than both the termite oracle and the poison oracle. **1914** *N.Y. World* 11 Mar. 5/1 Women..crowded the Union County Court room..hoping to hear some plausible elucidation of the '*poison pen' mystery. **1929** M. LIEF *Hangover* 302 The King of the Tabloids sat in his counting-house counting up the two and a half million circulation gained through the blood and scandal shed by..poison-pen letters. **1935** D. L. SAYERS *Gaudy Night* v. 100 Isn't our poison-pen rather silly to get all her spelling right? **1956** A. WILSON *Anglo-Saxon Attitudes* II. iii. 388 To all the other clergymen she was busy addressing poison-pen letters. **1973** J. THOMSON *Death Cap* vii. 93 She had seemed..a perfect front runner in the poison-pen stakes, the classic example of the embittered spinster. **1975** D. LODGE *Changing Places* iii. 124 I've had what I believe is called a poison-pen letter from Euphoria, an anonymous letter. **1936** COOK & LAWALL *Remington's Pract. Pharm.* (ed. 8) lxxxiv. 1357 The *poison register must be always open for inspection by the proper authorities. **1978** J. SYMONS *Blackheath Poisonings* III. 150 He sent.. Sergeant Miles to look at the poison registers. **1877** W. JONES *Finger-ring* 433 A *poison ring of curious construction is described by Mr. Fairholt. **1907** *Yesterday's Shopping* (1969) 499 In the case of Poisons being required it is absolutely necessary..that the *Poisons Register be signed at the time of purchase. **1957** *Encycl. Brit.* XVII. 693/1 These poisons in their uncompounded form may only be supplied to persons known to the pharmacist and their sale must be recorded in the poisons' register. **1958** H. G. MOSS *Retail Pharmacist's Handbk.* xxiii. 360 Certain professional and trade users may obtain First Schedule poisons on a signed order instead of attending and signing the Poisons Register. **1971** GILBERT & SHARP *Pharmaceuticals* xi. 140 First Schedule poisons may be sold without any prescription, but only if the purchaser is known to the pharmacist and signs the Poisons Register. **1839** URE *Dict. Arts* 55 A vertical section of the *poison tower. *Ibid.* 823 There are poison towers and extensive condensing chambers attached. *Ibid.* 56 Pipes leading to the *poison vent.

b. *esp.* in names of plants (or parts of them) having poisonous qualities: **poison-ash** = *poison-sumac*; **poison-bay**, *Illicium floridanum* (N.O. *Magnoliaceæ*), the leaves of which are reputed poisonous; **poison-berry**, any plant (or its fruit) of the genus *Cestrum* (N.O. *Solanaceæ*), of the West Indies and Brazil; also, 'the boraginaceous shrub *Bourreria succulenta*' (*Cent. Dict.*); **poison-bulb**, one of several South African bulbous plants belonging to the family Amaryllidaceæ, esp. *Boophane disticha*; **poison-bush**, (*a*) a poisonous species of *Euphorbia*; (*b*) a West Indian shrub, *Thevetia neriifolia* (N.O. *Apocynaceæ*); (*c*) *Austral.*, one of several plants bearing leaves harmful to cattle, esp. a species of *Gastrolobium*; **poison-dogwood**, **poison-elder** = *poison-sumac*; **poison-flag**, an American species of Iris (*I. versicolor*); **poison-hemlock** *U.S.*, the common hemlock, *Conium maculatum*; **poison-ivy**, one of several trailing or climbing North American shrubs belonging to the genus *Rhus* (or *Toxicodendron*), esp. *R. toxicodendron* (or *T. toxicaria*), bearing leaves resembling ivy, and greenish flowers followed by white berries, and producing inflammation of the skin and other reactions when touched; also *fig.*, an unpleasant person; **poison-nut**, (*a*) the violently poisonous seed of *Tanghinia venenifera* (N.O. *Apocynaceæ*), used by the natives of Madagascar in trial by ordeal; also the tree; (*b*) = NUX VOMICA (Webster 1864); **poison-oak**, the low-growing variety of *Rhus Toxicodendron* (see *poison-ivy*); also the allied *R. diversiloba* of Pacific N. America, which has similar properties; **poison-pea**, *Swainsona Greyana* (see next); **poison-plant**, name in Australia for several leguminous plants whose leaves are poisonous to cattle, as species of *Gastrolobium*, *Swainsona Greyana*, and *Lotus australis*; also, a name used for various plants harmful to man or livestock; **poison-root** (of Carolina), *Æsculus pavia*, the twigs and roots of which were used to stupify fish; **poison-sumac**, *Rhus vernix* or *Toxicodendron vernis*, a tall N. American shrub with pinnate leaves, also called *poison-ash* or *poison-elder*, and having properties resembling those of the allied *poison-ivy*; **poison vine**, (*a*) a climbing plant of Mediterranean regions, *Periploca græca* (N.O. *Asclepiadaceæ*), having poisonous milky juice (also called *milkvine*); (*b*) = *poison-ivy*; **poison-weed** = *poison-ivy*; **poison-withe**: see quot. See also POISON-TREE, POISONWOOD.

1760 J. LEE *Introd. Bot.* App. 323 *Poison Ash, *Rhus.* **1763** W. LEWIS *Comm. Phil. Techn.* 330 Mr. Catesby.. describes one, called there the poison-ash, from whose trunk flows a liquid, black as ink. **1866** *Treas. Bot.* 619 In Alabama ..*I*[*llicium*] *floridanum*..has..acquired the name of *Poison-bay. **1756** P. BROWNE *Jamaica* (1789) 173 Blue *Poison Berries... The nightingales are said to feed upon the berries of this shrub, which are reckoned very poisonous. **1822** W. BURCHELL *Trav. Interior S. Africa* I. xxi. 539 Plants of *Amaryllis toxicaria* were..very abundant. .. This plant is well known to the Bushmen, on account of the virulent poison contained in its bulb. It is also known to the Colonists and Hottentots, by the name of *Gift-bol* (*Poison-bulb). **1866** *Treas. Bot.* 181 *B*[*uphane*] *toxicaria* is called the Poison Bulb, and is said to be fatal to cattle. **1966** E. PALMER *Plains of Camdeboo* v. 82 The Poison Bulb, with its innocent blue-green fan of leaves, that they [*sc.* Bushmen] pounded for its deadly juice. **1760** J. LEE *Introd. Bot.* App. 323 *Poison Bush, *Euphorbia.* **1871** KINGSLEY *At Last* i, It proved to be *Thevetia neriifolia*... This was the first..warning which we got not to meddle rashly with 'poison-bush'. **1889** J. H. MAIDEN *Useful Native Plants Austral.* 129 *Gastrolobium* spp... These plants are dangerous to stock and are hence called '*Poison Bushes'. Large numbers of cattle are lost annually in Western Australia through eating them. **1927** M. M. BENNETT *Christison of Lammermoor* xx. 185 There were quicksands and the dreaded poison-bush, *Gastrolobium grandiflorum.* **1965** *Austral. Encycl.* VII. 157/2 Many species of *Gastrolobium* have, and nearly all species deserve, the name poison-bush or poison-plant. **1814** J. BIGELOW *Florula Bostoniensis* 72 *Rhus vernix.* *Poison dogwood. Swamp Sumach... Grows in bunches in wet swamps. **1958** Poison-dogwood [see *poison-elder*]. **1822** A. EATON *Man. Bot.* (ed. 3) 428 *Rhus vernix*, poison sumach, *poison elder... Berries green, at length whitish. **1866** *Treas. Bot.* 979 Poison Sumach or Poison Elder, is a tall shrub with pinnate leaves. **1958** G. A. PETRIDES *Field Guide to Trees & Shrubs* 84 Names in common use, such as Poison-elder or Poison-dogwood, usually refer to Poison Sumac. **1845–50** MRS. LINCOLN *Lect. Bot.* 140 Species of Iris, one of which, the common blue flag,..is sometimes called *Poison flag. *Ibid.* 151 *Poison hemlock, (Conium,) water parsnip,..water cowbane, are among the poisonous plants of this tribe. **1784** *Mem. Amer. Acad.* I. 422 *Poison Ivy..produces the same kind of inflammations and eruptions..as the poison wood tree. **1832** W. D. WILLIAMSON *Hist. State Maine* I. 130 Poison Ivy..is a dangerous medicine. **1857** GRAY *First Less. Bot.* (1866) 34 By these rootlets..the Ivy of Europe, and our Poison Rhus,—here called Poison Ivy,—fasten themselves firmly to walls. **1883** C. PHELPS in *Harper's Mag.* Jan. 282/2 The poison-ivy was gorgeous with a fatal beauty. **1891** M. E. FREEMAN *N. England Nun* 191 [She] saw Joseph Tenney's face through branches of pink dog-bane and over masses of poison-ivy. **1935** M. DE LA ROCHE *Young Renny* xxvi. 265 Bright-coloured tendrils of poison ivy stretched toward their path. **1939** 'B. GRAY' *Miss Dynamite* xvi. 179 So this is the charming little prairie flower that Norman's fallen in love with!.. Primrose, my foot! Her name's Poison Ivy! **1963** W. BLUNT *Of Flowers & Village* 29 We mayn't have these growing wild in England, nor the American poison ivy. **1971** *Rhodora* LXXIII. 76 More than 350,000 cases of poison-ivy dermatitis are estimated for the United States per year. **1976** F. GREENLAND *Misericordia Drop* II. viii. 138 Those amiable characters, my personal poison ivy, who so conscientiously compile our Code of Procedure. **1857** HENFREY *Bot.* §512 The seeds of..the Madagascar *Poison-nut are very deadly. **1743** J. CLAYTON *Flora Virginica* 33 *Rhus*... *Poison-Oak. **1760** J. LEE *Introd. Bot.* App. 323 Poison Oak, *Rhus.* **1883** STEVENSON *Silverado Sq.* 42 An abominable shrub or weed called poison-oak, whose very neighbourhood is venomous to some. **1905** G. E. COLE *Early Oregon* 29 Having been poisoned with poison oak so that I was completely blind, the others advised me to return. **1958** G. A. PETRIDES *Field Guide to Trees & Shrubs* 81 Some authorities believe differences between the several forms of Poison-oak and Poison-ivy are inconsequential. **1971** *Rhodora* LXXIII. 523 As the finer particles become less prevalent, the soil becomes more conducive to the growth of poison-oak. **1884** MILLER *Plant-n.*, *Swainsona Greyana*, Darling River Pea, Horse-poison-plant,..or *Poison Pea, of Australia. **1866** *Treas. Bot.* 521 A number of the species of this [*Gastrolobium*] and of allied genera are known in Western Australia as *Poison plants; and farmers lose annually a large number of cattle through their eating the foliage. *Ibid.* 522 Dr. Harvey says the worst of the Poison-plants is *G*[*astrolobium*] *bilobum*. **1881** F. OATES *Metabele Land & Victoria Falls* xi. 243 The 'poison plant', growing low, and bearing a yellow plum-like fruit, was gathered on one occasion near the waggon-track. **1927** J. MASEFIELD *Sard Harker* III. 121 Dangling from the boughs, there were strings of withered poison-ivy... He dodged the poison-plant. **1965** Poison-plant [see *poison-bush*]. **1712** PETIVER in *Phil. Trans.* XXVII. 424 Carolina *Poyson Root... Castaneæ Equinæ facie. Arbor..flore galeato spicato. **1817** A. EATON *Man. Bot.* 34 *Rhus... vernix*, (*poison sumach) glabrous panicle few-flowered. **1820** J. C. GILLELAND *Ohio & Mississippi Pilot* 261 Sumach... Most common in bottoms that are rich or at least moderately so... *R*[*hus*] *pumilum* (poison sumach). **1832** W. D. WILLIAMSON *Hist. State Maine* I. 118 The poison Sumach occurs in the western, but very seldom, if ever, in the eastern part of the State. **1866** Poison-sumach [see *poison elder*]. **1901** C. T. MOHR *Plant Life Alabama* 600 Poison Sumach, Poison Elder... Alleghenian, Carolinian, and Louisianian areas. **1978** *Washington Post* 4 Aug. (Weekend Suppl.) 27/2 Poison ivy, poison sumac, and some species of baneberry have white fruits and are poisonous. **1709** J. LAWSON *New Voyage to Carolina* 101 The *Poison Vine is so called, because it colours the Hands of those who handle it. **1803** A. ELLICOTT *Jrnl.* viii. 212 My journey up the river was disagreeable and painful, being blistered by the rhus radicans (poison vine) from head to feet. **1891** M. E. RYAN *Told in Hills* II. i. 24 Here and there a poison-vine flashed back defiance under its crimson banners. **1935** *Yale Review* Sept. 174, I hear them [*sc.* horses] snortin' up the land where the pizen-vines grow around the sycamore stumps. **1624** CAPT. SMITH *Virginia* 170 The poysoned weed [in the Bermudas] is much in shape like our English Iuy. *margin*, The *poison weed. **1856** L. J. F. JAEGER *Jrnl.* 20 Sept. in *Publ. Hist. Soc. S. Calif.* (1928) XIV. 128, 2 of the mules died at the Tinajas Altas—I think they ate some of the *poison weed also. **1693** *Phil. Trans.* XVII. 619 The *Poyson-Wyth of Barbados, which is a kind of Bryony.

B. *adj.* **1.** Poisonous, poisoned, envenomed. *Obs.* exc. as coinciding with the attrib. use of the sb. in 4 a.

1530 TINDALE *Wks.* (Parker Soc.) I. 17 With what poison, deadly, and venomous hate hateth a man his enemy. *Ibid.* 18 To make him of so poison a nature. **1531** *Ibid.* II. 143 Ye have chewed and mingled it with your poison spittle. **1533** MORE *Answ. Poysoned Bk.* Wks. 1063/2 A crosse.., the beholdynge wherof deuowred and destroyed the venome of al the poyson serpentes. **1769** E. BANCROFT *Guiana* 257 Their arms are..poison arrows. **1822** SHELLEY *Scenes fr. Faust* ii. 78 They dart forth polypus-antennae, To blister with their poison spume The wanderer. **1897** MARY KINGSLEY *W. Africa* 464 If he claims the ordeal,..he usually has to take a poison drink.

2. Wicked, dangerous; hateful, objectionable. *U.S. dial.*

1839 C. F. BRIGGS *Adventures of Harry Franco* I. 18 'I presume there's no occasion for hurrying,' said the driver. 'Yes there is though, you pisen critter,' said a passenger. **1850** 'M. TENSAS' *Odd Leaves from Life of Louisiana 'Swamp Doctor'* 152 Lizey Johnson's middle darter, Prinsanna,..left her husband in the state of Georgy, and kum to Luzaanny an' got marred to a nother man, the pisen varmint, to do sich as that and her own lawful husband. **1880** 'MARK TWAIN' *Tramp Abroad* 225 B'long to a *church*! Why boss he's ben the pizenest kind of a Free-will Babtis' for forty year. They ain't no pizener ones 'n' what *he* is.

C. *adv.* Intensely, extremely. Chiefly *U.S. dial.*

1840 C. F. HOFFMAN *Greyslaer* I. 61 The night was pison cold, I tell ye. **1884** 'MARK TWAIN' *Huck. Finn* xxvii. 275 The funeral sermon was very good, but pison long and tiresome. **1892** R. L. STEVENSON Let. 31 Jan. in *Wks.* (1923) XXXIII. 23 This is a poison bad world for the romancer, this Anglo Saxon world. **1894** 'MARK TWAIN' *Pudd'nhead Wilson* xiv. 194 You's got to be pison good, en let him see it. **1926** in H. Wentworth *Amer. Dial. Dict.* (1944) 464/2 Pizen-neat.

poison ('pɔɪz(ə)n), *v.* Forms: see the sb.; also 4 **poisone**, 5 **poysn, -yn, poysne, poysyn, (posyn)**, 6 **poisin**. [ME. *poison-en*, a. OF. *poisonn-er* to give to drink (cf. mod.F. *empoisonner* to poison), f. *poison* POISON, or refashioned from an OF. **poisnier*:—L. *pōtiōn-āre* to give (any one) to drink, to drug, f. *pōtiō-nem* drink, poisonous draught, POTION. So Pr. *pozionar*, Sp. *ponzoñar*.]

1. a. *trans.* To administer poison to; to introduce poison into the system of (man or animal); to kill or injure by means of poison, poisonous gases, etc.

13.. *Coer de L.* 2732 He leet taken alle the cors..And caste into the watyr off our welle, Us to poyson and to quelle. **13..** *E.E. Allit. P.* B. 1095 Poysened & parlatyk & pyned in fyres. *c* **1380** WYCLIF *Wks.* (1880) 333 þe pope & þe emperour myȝte priuely be poysined bi suche fadres. **1387** TREVISA *Higden* (Rolls) VII. 303 He was i-poysened wiþ venym þat was i-doo in his chalys. *c* **1400** MAUNDEV. (Roxb.) vi. 19 þis same sowdan was puysond at Damasc. **1483** *Cath. Angl.* 295/1 To Puson, *toxicare.* **1526** *Pilgr. Perf.* (W. de W. 1531) 234 b, Lyke as the worme yᵗ is crusshed or poysoned. **1560** DAUS tr. *Sleidane's Comm.* 260 b, The Pope hireth men to poyson other. **1676** ETHEREDGE *Man of Mode* III. iii, *Sir Fop.* I sat near one of 'em..and was almost Poison'd with a pair of Cordivant Gloves he wears. *Lov.* Oh!.. How I hate the smell! **1697** DRYDEN *Virg. Georg.* III. 813 The Water-

Snake..lyes poyson'd in his Bed. **1786** W. THOMSON *Watson's Philip III* (1839) 327 He was charged with having poisoned the queen. **1802** R. ANDERSON *Cumberld. Ball.* 35 Peer Jemmy was puzzen'd, they say, by a black. **1879** FROUDE *Cæsar* 119 Boys of ten years had learnt the art of poisoning their fathers.

b. To produce morbid effects in (the blood, a wound, a limb, etc.) by impregnation or infusion of poison, decomposing organic matter, ptomaine, etc. Cf. *blood-poisoning* in POISONING *vbl. sb.* b.

1605 SHAKS. *Lear* III. vi. 70 Tooth that poysons if it bite. **1635** J. HAYWARD tr. *Biondi's Banish'd Virg.* 203 The raw nocturnall ayre that had poysoned the wound. **1899** J. HUTCHINSON in *Arch. Surg.* I. No. 38. 157 Mrs. M —— had been pushing back the nail-fold at the root of the nail with a penknife and had as she suspected poisoned it. *a* **1907** *Mod.* His hand was poisoned by being pierced with an old nail. The bite of some insects may poison the blood. A foot poisoned by the action of a dye-stuff on an excoriated part.

2. To impregnate, taint, or infect (air, water, etc.) with poison so as to render it poisonous or baneful; to charge or smear (a weapon) with poison. See also POISONED *ppl. a.* 2.

c **1375** *Sc. Leg. Saints* xxxiii. (*George*) 62 Thru.. corrupcion Of þe ayre þat he wald poyson. **1548** ELYOT, *Inficere pocula veneno*, to poison the drynk, to put poyson in the cuppe. **1552** HULOET, Poyson a place wyth carrayne, *funesto*. **1553** T. WILSON *Rhet.* (1580) 127 As if one should poison a Conduite hedde, or a River, from whence all menne fetche their water. **1612** WEBSTER *White Devil* Wks. (Rtldg.) 36/2 To have poison'd his prayer-book, or a pair of beads, The pummel of his saddle,..Or the handle of his racket. **1697** DRYDEN *Virg. Georg.* III. 725 A Plague..Pois'ning the Standing Lakes, and Pools Impure. **1851** MAYNE REID *Scalp Hunt.* xxvii, Indians..engaged in poisoning the points of their arrows.

3. *fig.* **a.** To corrupt, pervert morally; to turn to error or evil, influence perversely.

1395 PURVEY *Remonstr.* (1851) 99 It is feynid now that symple prestis wolen poisone men with gastli venym, that is, errour othir eresie. **1550** J. COKE *Eng. & Fr. Heralds* §68 Eij b, Monster de Labright..whose ancetours you poysoned with money causyng them to be traytours to Englande. **1604** SHAKS. *Oth.* I. iii. 112 Did you, by indirect, and forced courses Subdue, and poyson this yong Maides affections? **1701** ROWE *Amb. Step-Moth.* II. ii. 787 Hast thou not With thy false Arts poyson'd his Peoples Loyalty? **1868** FREEMAN *Norm. Conq.* II. vii. 137 There was another voice at the royal ear, ever ready to poison the royal mind.

b. To prove destructive or fatal to (an action, state, condition, etc.).

1605 SHAKS. *Lear* II. iv. 39 Meeting heere the other Messenger, Whose welcome I perceiu'd had poison'd mine. **1687** BOYLE *Martyrd. Theodora* ix, The deadly draught.. poysoned not his [Socrates'] reputation,..but that of his accusers and his judges. **1697** DRYDEN *Virg. Past.* VII. 40 Lest his ill Arts or his malicious Tongue Shou'd poison, or bewitch my growing Song. **1765** FOOTE *Commissary* I. Wks. 1799 II. 15 The slightest suspicion wou'd poison your project. **1894** HALL CAINE *Manxman* III. x, Tom could not deny himself a word of bitterness to poison the pleasure.

4. *transf.* **a.** To render (a thing) foul and unfit for its purpose by some noxious or deleterious addition or application.

1500–20 DUNBAR *Poems* lix. 9 That fulle dismemberit hes my meter, And poysound it with strang salpeter. *a* **1693** LUDLOW *Mem.* (1771) 31 Confessing that he had accordingly poisoned the two cannon and the Harquebuz that was broken. **1706** PHILLIPS, To *Poison a Piece*, a Term in Gunnery. See To Cloy and to Nail. **1765** *Museum Rust.* III. 284 Some..were exactly level, so as to be quite poisoned with the wet, which could not drain off. **1816** VANDERSTRAETEN *Impr. Agric.* 6 The land will be poisoned with noxious roots and plants. **1884** C. G. W. LOCK *Workshop Receipts* Ser. III. 66/2 They pronounced it to be full of arsenic and antimony; so..that their furnaces were, as they said, 'poisoned', and rendered unfit for refining.

b. *Chem.* Of a substance: to reduce or destroy the activity of (a catalyst, or occas. an electrode). Cf. POISON *sb.* 2 c.

1913 in C. Ellis *Hydrogenation Oils* (1914) 311 The use of chlorine would 'poison' the catalyst. **1921** G. G. HENDERSON *Catalysis in Industr. Chem.* iv. 72 Infinitesimal quantities of chlorine, bromine or iodine absolutely poison the metal, the presence of even a minute trace of bromine in phenol, for instance, preventing the latter being changed into cyclohexanol. **1937** *Jrnl. Inst. Electr. Engineers* LXXX. 198/2 An antimony electrode..lends itself particularly well to the recording of hydrogen-ion concentration, since this electrode is 'poisoned' by very few substances. **1965** H. H. WILLARD et al. *Instrumental Methods Chem. Analysis* (ed. 4) xxii. 588 The quinhydrone electrode is quickly prepared, develops its potential rapidly, and is not readily poisoned. **1972** *Times* 27 Sept. 20/3 Lead contaminants in fuel tend to 'poison' catalytic elements that help burn exhaust more completely in a converter mounted in the exhaust pipe. **1974** BANDTOCK & HANSON *Success in Chem.* xiv. 318 Vanadium (v) oxide is a reasonably efficient catalyst for the oxidation of sulphur dioxide and is not readily poisoned.

c. *Nuclear Sci.* To act as a poison in (a nuclear reactor or fuel). Also occas., to add a poison to (a reactor). Cf. POISON *sb.* 2 d.

1945 H. D. SMYTH *Gen. Acct. Devel. Atomic Energy Mil. Purposes* viii. 80 Other fission products are being produced also. These consist typically of unstable and relatively unfamiliar nuclei so that it was originally impossible to predict how great an undesirable effect they would have on the multiplication constant. Such deleterious effects are called poisoning. **1948** C. PINCHER *Into Atomic Age* 38 Fragments from the split uranium 235 atoms collect in the slugs and..are said to 'poison' the uranium. **1960** WEHR & RICHARDS *Physics of Atom* xi. 328 This radioactivity is due principally to the fission products which poisoned the fuel element. **1968** F. KERTESZ *Lang. Nucl. Sci.* (Oak Ridge Nat. Lab. TM 2367) 23 Nuclear jargon is filled with gloomy, funereal terms: fuel elements are transported in coffins and reactors are poisoned to control them.

5. *Saltworks.* (See quots.)

1885 HOLLAND *Chesh. Gloss.*, *Poisoning*,..said of a pan when some ingredient is put into it to make the brine work differently. **1894** BARING-GOULD *Queen of L.* II. 16 A little glue or soft soap is put into the brine—this is called 'poisoning' it—to collect the impurities.

poisonable (ˈpɔɪzənəb(ə)l), *a.* [f. prec. + -ABLE.]

†**1.** Having the property of poisoning; poisonous. *Obs.*

c **1470** HENRYSON *Orpheus & Eurydice* 313 (Bann. MS.) Thy meit wennome, thy drink is pvsonable. *c* **1550** R. BIESTON *Bayte Fortune* B iv, Three thinges there be to man as venim poysonable. *a* **1598** ROLLOCK *Lect. Passion*, etc. (1616) 551 The drinking of deadly and poysonable things. **1645** USSHER *Body Div.* (1647) 368 Without the which they may be hurtfull and poisonable unto us. *c* **1720** W. GIBSON *Farrier's Guide* II. liv. (1738) 207 The biting of a mad Dog, is not so poisonable as is generally supposed.

2. Capable of being poisoned; subject to poison.

1846 in WORCESTER. **1871** SIR J. PAGET in *Mem. & Lett.* iii. 246 My blood and textures regained the state they had before..and I became again more poisonable.

†**ˈpoisonal**, *a.* *Obs. rare.* [See -AL[1] I.] Poisonous.

a **1660** *Contemp. Hist. Irel.* (Ir. Arch. Soc.) I. 132 That prejudicious and poysonall peace. *Ibid.* III. 85.

poisoned (ˈpɔɪz(ə)nd), *ppl. a.* [f. POISON *v.* + -ED[1].]

1. Of men or animals: Affected with, sickened with, or killed by poison.

c **1300** *Cursor M.* 21056 (Edin.) Þe pussund [*v. rr.* puisund, poysoned] men he raisid raþe Þat war stan-dede for suilc a drinc. *c* **1440** *Promp. Parv.* 407/1 Poysenyd, *intoxicatus, virulentus.* **1483** *Cath. Angl.* 295/1 Pusond, *toxicatus, venenatus.* **1898** *Allbutt's Syst. Med.* V. 887 In certain poisoned conditions of blood..fatty degeneration of the muscular fibres of the heart may be very extensive. **1899** *Ibid.* VIII. 641 There is a distinct history of a poisoned wound.

b. *fig.* Affected with moral poison; corrupted.

1578 LYTE *Dodoens* III. lxxx. 430 A Pharisee, who maketh a glorious and beautifull shewe, but inwardly is of a corrupt and poysoned nature.

2. Impregnated, imbued, charged, or smeared with poison.

1470–85 MALORY *Arthur* XVIII. iii. 729 And soo it befelle ..a good knyght..to take a poysond Appel. **1600** J. PORY tr. *Leo's Africa* Introd. 27 Which causeth them to shoote poisoned arrowes. **1605** SHAKS. *Macb.* I. vii. 11 This euen-handed Iustice Commends th' Ingredience of our poyson'd Challice To our owne lips. **1725** DE FOE *Voy. round World* (1840) 89 For fear of poisoned arrows.

b. *fig.* Charged with moral poison.

1567 *Reg. Privy Council Scot.* I. 537 That the youtheid be nocht infectit be poysonit doctrine. **1611** BIBLE *Transl. Pref.* 3 The Scripture is..a Physi[ci]ons-shop of preseruatiues against poisoned heresies. **1741** MIDDLETON *Cicero* II. x. 391 The flatteries and poisoned honors of the Senate.

†**3.** Endowed with poison; venomous. *Obs.*

1533 MORE *Answ. Poysoned Bk.* Wks. 1063/2 Al yᵉ poysoned serpentes of hell. **1579** LYLY *Euphues* (Arb.) 124 Taken out of the heade of the poysoned Dragon. **1582** STANYHURST *Æneis* II. (Arb.) 58 The owtpeaking from weeds of poysoned adder.

†**b.** *fig.* Full of moral poison; envenomed, malignant. *Obs.*

1508 DUNBAR *Flyting* 70 It salbe blawin owt, How that thow, poysonit pelor, gat thy paikis. **1588** *Marprel. Epist.* (Arb.) 3 Right poysond, persecuting and terrible priests.

poisoner (ˈpɔɪzənə(r)). [f. POISON *v.* + -ER[1].]

a. One who or that which poisons (*lit.* and *fig.*).

1382 WYCLIF *Rev.* xxii. 15 Houndes, and venym doers [*gl.* or poyseners], and vnchaast men. **1482** *Monk of Evesham* (Arb.) 83 They that were posynners and posynyd folke. **1563** WINȜET *Four Scoir Thre Quest.* Wks. 1888 I. 52 Poysonnaris of the peple of God. **1611** SHAKS. *Wint. T.* I. ii. 352, I must be the poysoner Of good Polixenes. **1693** DRYDEN *Juvenal* VI. (1697) 159 So many Mischiefs were in one combin'd; So much one single Pois'ner cost Mankind. **1868** FREEMAN *Norm. Conq.* II. ix. 413 Having..stooped to the trade of a secret poisoner. **1889** *Century Mag.* Aug. 510 The cobra surpasses as a poisoner all of our American snakes. **1893** *Daily News* 28 Feb. 5/1 It renders the animal proof against the attacks of the poisoner microbe.

b. A cook, esp. for large numbers. *joc.* (*Austral.* and *N.Z.*).

1905 E. C. BULEY *Austral. Life in Town & Country* 23 The shearers' cook is always a competent man and supplies his clients with the best fare obtainable, utterly 'belying' the name of 'poisoner', usually bestowed upon him. **1936** A. RUSSELL *Gone Nomad* 14, I had to take my turn..as 'slushy' to 'Doughboy' Terry, the cook—'camp poisoner', as we affectionately called him. **1969** L. HADOW *Full Cycle* 208 'I'm not much good at cooking but I'll try.' 'Never you mind about that. Up north we've got the best poisoners in the country.'

Hence **ˈpoisoneress** (*rare*), a female poisoner.

1598 GRENEWEY *Tacitus' Ann.* XIII. iv. 183 Nero.. commanded the poisoneresse [Agrippina] to be put to death. **1611** COTGR., *Empoisonneresse*, a poisonneresse, a woman that impoisons.

ˈpoisonful, *a.* *Obs.* or *dial.* [f. POISON *sb.* + -FUL.] Full of or containing poison; poisonous, venomous, deadly, baneful. **a.** *lit.*

1554 BECON *Supplic.* Wks. 1563 II. III. 22 Vnto these vnwholsome and pestilent and poysonfull Pastures the dryue the shepe. **1596** RALEIGH *Discov. Gviana* 26 There breed diuers poysonfull wormes and serpents. **1615** W. LAWSON *Country Housew. Gard.* (1626) 45 Poysonfull smoke. **1643** TRAPP *Comm. Gen.* xlv. 7 He makes of a poisonfull viper, a wholesome triacle. **1693** I. MATHER *Cases Consc.* (1862) 262 The vulgar Error concerning the Basilisks killing with the Look of his Poysonful Eye. [**1855** ROBINSON *Whitby Gloss.* s.v., 'The house was parfitly puzzomful'.]

b. *fig.* Poisonous to the mind or morals.

1520 WHITINTON *Vulg.* (1527) 22 (20) What is so detestable to a man as this poysonfull couetyse? **1534** —— *Tullyes Offices* I. (1540) 20 Mischevous and poysonfull flaterers. **1662** HIBBERT *Body Div.* I. 233 They vented their damnable and poisonful doctrine. **1679** C. NESSE *Antid. agst. Popery* 157 This is such a poisonful position.

Hence †**ˈpoisonfully** *adv.*, venomously.

1599 *Broughton's Let.* vii. 20 Marrow, verely serpentine and viperous,..poysonfully sprinkling his Grace.

poisoning (ˈpɔɪzənɪŋ), *vbl. sb.* [f. POISON *v.* + -ING[1].] **a.** The action of the verb POISON.

c **1440** *Promp. Parv.* 407/1 Poysenynge, *intoxicacio.* **1548** UDALL, etc. *Erasm. Par. Mark* v. 30 b, Treasons and poysoninges, with the practise of art Magike or sorcery. **1626** BACON *Sylva* §915 Poisoning of air is no less dangerous than poisoning of water. **1631** *Star Chamb. Cases* (Camden) 10 A poysoninge of my Lord's honor with the Duke, with the King, and with the rest of the nobility. **1769** BLACKSTONE *Comm.* IV. iii. 34 In case of murder by poisoning, a man may be a principal felon, by preparing and laying the poison.

b. As the second element in combinations with words denoting (*a*) the agent or medium, as ***beer-, food-, fungus-, phosphorus-poisoning***, (*b*) the object, as **blood-poisoning**: see BLOOD *sb.* 21.

1897 Phosphorus poisoning [see PHOSPHORUS 4]. **1900** *Westm. Gaz.* 1 Dec. 6/2 The number of persons..who have been or are suffering from beer-poisoning amounts to about 1,200. **1902** *Daily Chron.* 18 Sept. 3/4 The microbe.. discovered by Dr. Klein in the Welbeck food-poisoning cases. **1904** *Westm. Gaz.* 6 Oct. 10/1 A very considerable number of the cases of fungus-poisoning recorded annually.

ˈpoisoning, *ppl. a.* [f. as prec. + -ING[2].] That poisons; poisonous.

1604 F. HERING *Mod. Defence* 24 The poysoning quality of Arsenicke. **1828** A. JOLLY *Sunday Serv.* (1840) 246 Temporal quiet often proves intoxicating and poisoning by its..pleasures. **1847** EMERSON *Poems, Woodnotes* II. 69 Whom the city's poisoning spleen Made not pale, or fat, or lean.

ˈpoisonless, *a. rare.* [f. POISON *sb.* + -LESS.] Free from poison.

1608 TOPSELL *Serpents* 272 Their [English spiders'] byting is poysonlesse. **1654** W. JENKYN *Fun. Serm.* 11 Not only poisonlesse but wholsome. **1895** C. F. NICHOLS in *Review of Rev.* Mar. 292 A commune..would require..to be poisonless, at least with regard to virulent..disease.

†**ˈpoisonly**, *adv.* *Obs. rare*⁻¹. [f. POISON *a.* + -LY[2].] Poisonously, after the manner of poison.

1562 J. HEYWOOD *Prov. & Epigr.* (1867) 214 Thy prophesy poysonly to the pricke goth.

†**ˈpoisonment.** *Obs. rare*⁻¹. [f. POISON *v.* + -MENT: cf. F. *empoisonnement.*] The act of poisoning; in quot., a means of poisoning, poison.

c **1470** HARDING *Chron.* ccx. v, Some in his sherte put oft tyme venemyng, And some in meate and drinke great poysonement; Some in his hose, by great ymagenement.

poisonous (ˈpɔɪzənəs), *a.* [f. POISON *sb.* + -OUS.]

1. Containing or of the nature of poison; having the quality or properties of a poison; venomous.

1573–80 BARET *Alv.* P 546 Poisonous. Venemous, full of poison, stinking, of an euill taste, *virulentus.* **1665** DRYDEN & HOWARD *Ind. Queen* III. i, Yet we destroy the poisonous viper's young. **1697** DRYDEN *Virg. Georg.* II. 209 Nor pois'nous Aconite is here produc'd. **1726** LEONI *Alberti's Archit.* I. 15/2 A Steam..so poysonous, that..it..infected all Asia. **1866** *Treas. Bot.* 109 The Deadly Nightshade... All parts of the plant are poisonous. *Ibid.*, When taken in large or poisonous doses.

2. *fig.* **a.** Morally destructive or corrupting; conveying an evil influence; malevolent, malignant. Also in trivial use, unpleasant, nasty.

a **1586** SIDNEY *Astr. & Stella* civ, Enuious wits, what hath bene mine offence, That with such poysonous care my lookes you marke? **1660** *Trial Regic.* 14 Many Poysonous Opinions having gone abroad. **1817** SHELLEY *Rev. Islam* IX. xv, The falsehood of their poisonous lips. **1904** BENSON *Challoners* xiii, Yes, it is nonsense... It is poisonous, suicidal nonsense. **1906** *Daily Chron.* 6 Mar. 4/7 'Awfully', 'rotten'—and 'poisonous', which is rapidly superseding both—are probably the most ill-used words in the English language as it is spoken. **1912** E. PUGH *Harry the Cockney* xi. 121 Foolish habit to think at any time, Weaver. But to think on an empty stomach—it's poisonous. Poisonous! **1916** 'TAFFRAIL' *Pincher Martin* xii. 225, I thought the weather was absolutely poisonous. **1929** P. GIBBS *Hidden City* xxxix. 189 It's something to do with that poisonous little beast Benito..the boy she dances with.

†**b.** With *of*: Having the quality of poisoning or destroying; destructive *of*. *Obs.*

1607 SHAKS. *Cor.* V. iii. 135 You might condemne vs As poysonous of your Honour.

3. *Comb.*

1611 SHAKS. *Cymb.* III. ii. 5 What false Italian, (As poysonous tongu'd, as handed)?

Hence **ˈpoisonously** *adv.* (in quot. 1646 = by poison); **ˈpoisonousness**.

1646 SIR T. BROWNE *Pseud. Ep.* 175 The Antipathy between a Toad and a Spider, and that they poisonously destroy each other, is very famous. **1727** BAILEY vol. II, *Poisonousness*, poisonous Quality. **1871** NAPHEYS *Prev. & Cure Dis.* I. viii. 245 Foul air which acts poisonously upon the system.

†**'poisonsome**, *a. Obs.* [f. POISON *sb.* + -SOME.] Charged or tainted with poison, poisonous.

c **1595** CAPT. WYATT *R. Dudley's Voy. W. Ind.* (Hakl. Soc.) 19 This ilande beinge soe poisensome a place .. might breed some contagious infection amonge our men. **1630** *R. Johnson's Kingd. & Commw.* 425 Most huge Dragons and poisonsome. **1650** S. CLARKE *Eccl. Hist., Calvin* (1654) 638 The poysonsom Doctrines of the Libertines and Carpocratians. **1688** R. HOLME *Armoury* II. 123/1 Poisonsom Smokes .. are .. in their Kinds and Degrees hurtful.

Hence †**'poisonsomeness.** *Obs.*

1645 USSHER *Body Div.* (1647) 143 Because there are principles of hurtfulnesse and poysonsomnes in them.

'poison-tree.

1. Name for various trees with poisonous properties.

†**a.** Some West Indian tree (? of the N.O. *Euphorbiaceæ*). *Obs.* **b.** The poison-sumac, *Rhus venenata*, and other poisonous species of *Rhus*. **c.** The upas-tree, *Antiaris toxicaria*. **d.** *Acacia varians* of Australia. **e.** *Croton Verreauxii* of Queensland.

1693 *Phil. Trans.* XVII. 622 There is an Arborescent sort with a very large Leaf, no less venomous than the *Mancinello*, .. by those of Barbados called the Poyson-tree. **1721** SHERARD *ibid.* XXXI. 147 The Poyson-Tree grows to the bigness of Elder. **1811** J. J. STOCKDALE (*title*) Civil and Military Sketches of the Island of Java, .. comprising .. authentic particulars of the Celebrated Poison-Tree. **1857** HENFREY *Elem. Bot.* §459 *Acacia varians*, of Australia, has been called the Poison-tree. **1884** MILLER *Plant-n.*, Poison-tree, .. Queensland, *Croton Verreauxii*. **1893** SPON *Mechanic's Own Bk.* (ed. 4) 163 Excoecaria Agallocha (Poison Tree) .. wood is hard, and fine-grained.

2. *gen.* Any tree of poisonous or deleterious nature. Also *fig.* (Cf. *upas-tree*.)

a **1835** MRS. HEMANS in H. F. Chorley *Mem.* (1837) I. 273 From such agonizing strife the mind will often seek refuge —though it be the shelter of a poison-tree. **1849** tr. *Fouqué's Sir Elidoc* 70, I feel myself like a poison-tree in the dukedom.

'poisonwood. **a.** Name for certain poisonous species of *Rhus*, as *R. venenata*, the Poison-sumac of N. America, and *R. Metopium* of the West Indies. **b.** *Sebastiania lucida* (N.O. *Euphorbiaceæ*), of the West Indies. Also *attrib.*

1721 DUDLEY in *Phil. Trans.* XXXI. 145 The Poyson-Wood-Tree grows only in Swamps, or low wet Grounds, and .. is by some called the *Swamp Sumach*. *Ibid.* 146 The Poyson-Wood .. has this effect only on some particular Persons and Constitutions. **1730** MORTIMER *ibid.* XXXVI. 430 *Toxicodendron, foliis alatis*, .. the Poison Wood. This Tree distills a Liquid, black like Ink, which the Inhabitants say is Poison. **1884** MILLER *Plant-n.*, Poisonwood, W. Indian, *Sebastiania lucida*. **1930** R. MACAULAY *Staying with Relations* ix. 127 There .. was .. the nettle that one chews when one has inadvertently been spattered by the milky juice of the poison-wood tree. **1965** F. KNEBEL *Night of Camp David* xv. 248 A crescent moon perched above the thicket of gumbo limbo and poisonwood trees.

†**'poisony**, *a. Obs. rare.* [f. POISON *sb.* + -Y.] Containing or of the nature of poison; poisonous.

1591 SYLVESTER *Du Bartas* I. iii. 709 The poysonie Serpents that unpeople quite Cyrenian desarts. *Ibid.* 1072 Pale Envies poysonie heads. **1746** BREINTAL in *Phil. Trans.* XLIV. 145 (149), I .. cupp'd it, and drew out a Quart or more of ugly poisony slimy Stuff.

‖**poissarde** (pwasard). [F., a low foul-mouthed woman, a market-woman, fem. of obs. *poissard* pickpocket, rogue, f. *poix* pitch + -ARD, because things 'stick to his fingers'; also a fishwife (by association with *poisson* fish).] A French-woman of the lowest class, *esp.* one of the Parisian market-women, who led riots during the first revolution.

1790 H. WALPOLE *Let. to Miss Berry* 3 July, The poissardes huzzaed them. **1797** CANNING, etc. in *Anti-Jacobin* No. 4 (1799) 137 While her sportive Poissardes with light footsteps are seen To dance in a ring round the gay Guillotine. **1833** HT. MARTINEAU *Fr. Wines & Pol.* vii. 109 The shrill voiced poissardes were broiling their rations, or heating their strong liquors. **1848** A. FONBLANQUE in *Life & Labours* ii. (1874) 223 The women .., animated with the spirit of the poissardes of '93.

b. A French fishwife.

1818 *Sporting Mag.* II. 161 The bathing women, the poissardes of the coast, in their blue flannel dresses. **1860** RUSKIN *Mod. Paint.* V. IX. ix. 294 A friendly turn of mind towards herring fishing, whaling, Calais poissardes and many other of our choicest subjects in after life.

Poisson (pwasɔ̃). *Math.* [The name of S. D. *Poisson* (1781–1840), French mathematician and physicist.] **1.** Used, chiefly *attrib.*, with reference to a discrete frequency distribution defined by $e^{-m}m^x/x!$, which gives the probability of x events occurring, m being its only parameter; it has mean m and variance m^2, and is appropriate if the events occur independently and there is no upper limit to their number, so that the distribution is the limit of the binomial distribution as the number of trials increases, the probability of success at each decreases, and the average number of successes tends to m; so ***Poisson('s) approximation, distribution, form, law***, etc.; ***Poisson-distributed*** adj. Also passing into adj. (= POISSONIAN) and used predicatively. [Described in Poisson's *Recherches sur la Probabilité des Jugements* (1837).]

1911 *Ark. för Matem., Astr. och Fysik* VII. XVII. 8, I shall generally understand with Poisson's theorem the expressions .. giving the probability for obtaining in s trials with variable chances in all m white and n black balls (where $m + n = s$). **1914** *Biometrika* X. 36 (*heading*) On the Poisson law of small numbers. **1919** G. U. YULE *Theory Statistics* (ed. 5) 372 [This] may be termed Poisson's limit to the binomial. **1922** *Ann. Appl. Biol.* IX. 331 When the statistical examination of these data was commenced it was not anticipated that any clear relationship with the Poisson distribution would be obtained. *Ibid.* 334 The curves strongly suggest that the departures in these data from the Poisson samples were not .. systematic. **1928** [see NORMAL *a.* 2 e]. **1931** L. H. C. TIPPETT *Meth. Statistics* ii. 34 This is known as Poisson's Limit to the Binomial, the Poisson Series, or as the Law of Small Numbers. **1939** H. JEFFREYS *Theory of Probability* ii. 75 Put $x = r/n$ and let n tend to infinity; then the law tends to the Poisson form. **1948** H. E. FREEMAN et al. *Sampling Inspection* xvii. 185 For such small values of n the Poisson approximation is not adequate. **1950** W. FELLER *Introd. Probability Theory* I. vi. 119 A radioactive substance emits α-particles, and the number of particles reaching a given portion of space during time t is the best-known example of random events obeying the Poisson law. *Ibid.* xvii. 367 In the Poisson process the probability of a change during $(t, t + h)$ is independent of the number of changes during (O, t). **1954** [see ERLANG 1]. **1958** CONDON & ODISHAW *Handbk. Physics* I. xii. 155/2 The discrete distribution .. termed the Poisson exponential distribution, is (with the normal, and binomial distributions) one of the three principal distributions of probability theory. **1966** *McGraw-Hill Encycl. Sci. & Technol.* X. 631/2 If p is so small that the mean np is of the order of unity in any given application, Bernoulli's distribution is then approximated by Poisson's law. **1968** P. A. P. MORAN *Introd. Probability Theory* iii. 162 We suppose that customers arrive at a servicing counter in a Poisson process with mean λ, i.e. the number arriving in any interval of length T has a Poisson distribution with mean λT, and the numbers arriving in different intervals are independent. **1971** J. B. CARROLL et al. *Word Freq. Bk.* p. xxxvi, The remaining entries show that .. 9,436 [words] would be expected not to appear at all in the AHI Corpus, but that 3,826 would appear once, 776 would appear twice, 105 would appear 3 times, 10 would appear 4 times, and 1 would appear 5 times. (These numbers are predicted by the Poisson distribution.) **1976** E. J. DUDEWICZ *Introd. Statistics & Probability* iii. 56 Suppose that X is binomial with parameters n and p... Then X is approximately Poisson with $\lambda = np$. **1979** *Nature* 15 Feb. 533/1, n_i, the number of abberations in the i-th culture, is Poisson-distributed.

b. *ellipt.* for *Poisson distribution*.

1962 S. R. CALABRO *Reliability Princ. & Pract.* vi. 65 If the expected number of failures .. is substituted in the Poisson, then it is possible to calculate the probability of 0, 1, 2, 3, etc., failures. **1975** R. M. BETHEA et al. *Statistical Methods for Scientists & Engineers* iii. 57 We can estimate the probability of getting less than two adverse reactions using the Poisson as follows.

2. Special Comb.: **Poisson bracket**, a function $[u, v]$ of two dynamical variables $u(p_1, p_2, \ldots p_n, q_1, q_2, \ldots q_n)$ and $v(p_1, p_2, \ldots p_n, q_1, q_2, \ldots q_n)$ equal to $\sum_{r=1}^{n}\left(\frac{\partial u}{\partial q_r}\frac{\partial v}{\partial p_r} - \frac{\partial u}{\partial p_r}\frac{\partial v}{\partial q_r}\right)$; **Poisson's equation** [discussed by Poisson in *Nouveau Bull. des Sci. par la Soc. philomath. de Paris* (1813) III. 390], the generalization of Laplace's equation produced by replacing the zero of the right hand side by a constant, or, more generally, by a specified function of position; **Poisson's ratio** [discussed by Poisson in *Ann. de Chim. et de Physique* (1827) XXXVI. 385], the ratio of the proportional decrease in a lateral measurement to the proportional increase in length in a sample of material that is elastically stretched.

1904 E. T. WHITTAKER *Treat. Analytical Dynamics* xi. 309 If ϕ and ψ are two integrals of the system, the Poisson-bracket (ϕ, ψ) is constant throughout the motion. **1960** DICKE & WITTKE *Introd. Quantum Mech.* v. 86 The Poisson bracket provides a powerful tool in formulating quantum theory. **1976** MATHEWS & VENKATESAN *Textbk. Quantum Mech.* 351 Canonically conjugate co-ordinate-momentum pairs are .. characterized by a unit value for the Poisson bracket. [**1872** *Trans. R. Soc. Edin.* XXVI. 71 If P be the potential at ρ, and if r be the density of the attracting matter, &c., at ρ, $\nabla\sigma = \nabla^2P = 4\pi r$ by Poisson's extension of Laplace's equation.] **1873** J. C. MAXWELL *Treat. Electr. & Magn.* I. I. ii. 80 This equation, in the case in which the density is zero, is called Laplace's Equation. In its more general form it was first given by Poisson... We may express Poisson's equation in words by saying that the electric density multiplied by 4π is the concentration of the potential. **1916** F. B. PIDDUCK *Treat. Electr.* iii. 61 This becomes .. $\Delta V = -4\pi\rho$, which is known as Poisson's equation. **1971** C. R. CHESTER *Techniques in Partial Differential Equations* iii. 87 The nonhomogeneous potential equation, $\nabla^2 u = F(x, y, z)$ is called Poisson's equation. **1886** J. D. EVERETT *Units & Physical Constants* (ed. 2) v. 62 The following values of Poisson's ratio have been found. **1930** *Engineering* 11 Apr. 465/1 The modern theory of the elasticity of isotropic materials makes use of a number of physical constants, all of which are definitely related to Young's Modulus E and Poisson's ratio $\eta = 1/m$ the latter of which is sometimes known as the 'stretch-squeeze' ratio. **1966** C. R. TOTTLE *Sci. Engin. Materials* vii. 153 An orthorhombic crystal can thus be defined by nine independent constants, three elastic moduli, three moduli of rigidity, and three values of Poisson's ratio.

Poissonian (pwa'səʊnɪən), *a.* [f. prec. + -IAN.] Of, pertaining to, or being the Poisson distribution.

1914 *Ark. för Matem., Astr. och Fysik* IX. xxv. 16 Repeating the experiment r times we obtain respectively $m_1, m_2, m_3, \ldots, m_r$ white balls in these r sets. These numbers form what is called a Poissonian series. **1951** *Jrnl. R. Statistical Soc.* B. XIII. 168 If they call for service in a random manner the input-process (while q customers are waiting or being served) will be Poissonian, but will depend on the value of q. **1972** *Science* 2 June 1034/1 The Poissonian probability times the efficiency of plating gave an actual distribution of ≤ 0.3 cell per well. **1976** *Physics Bull.* Mar. 111/1 If T was short compared with the inverse spectral linewidth of a random source, a geometric distribution was obtained while if T was long the photon counting distribution became Poissonian due to averaging of the photon arrivals.

poist, obs. Sc. form of POST.

†**poister**, *v. Obs.* [app. a variant of PESTER *v.*[1]; cf. OF. *enpaistrier* (12th c. in Hatz.-Darm.).] *trans.* To hopple, fetter, entangle, encumber.

In quot. 1523 (which is earlier than any instance of *pester*, *empester*, or *impester*), the sense is not very clear.

1523 LD. BERNERS *Froiss.* I. Pref. 2 [History] depresseth, poystereth, and thrusteth downe such as ben wicked, yuell, and reprouable. **1567** J. SANFORD *Epictetus* 6 When his foote is poistered and shakled, the bodie is also cumbred.

†**'poisure.** *Obs. rare.* [f. POISE *v.* + -URE. Cf. OF. *poisure* weight, what serves to weigh.] Poise, balance.

a **1619** FLETCHER *Wit without M.* I. i, Nor is this forc'd, but the meer quality and poisure of goodness. **1643** HERLE *Answ. Ferne* 33 The priority of the Peeres gives order and poysure .. to the whole body. **1669** W. SIMPSON *Hydrol. Chym.* 313 The pressure of ayr within and .. without the glass are brought to an .. equal poysure.

†**poisy**, *a. Obs. rare.* [f. POISE *sb.*[1] + -Y.] Heavy or bulky of body: cf. PEISY.

1538 ELYOT, *Crassus*, fatte, fleshy, thycke, grosse, poysye.

poite, obs. form of POET.

Poitevin ('pwætɪvɪn, ‖pwatəvɛ̃), *sb.* and *a.* Also 7 Poictevin. [Fr.] **A.** *sb.* **a.** A native or inhabitant of Poitou, an ancient province of west central France roughly corresponding to the modern *départements* of Vienne, Deux-Sèvres, and Vendée, or of its capital Poitiers, now capital of Vienne. **b.** The French dialect of Poitou or Poitiers. **B.** *adj.* Of, pertaining to, or characteristic of Poitou or Poitiers or the dialect spoken there.

1642 J. HOWELL *Instructions for Forreine Travell* x. 127 The law Norman useth to contract many words .. and the Poictevin will mince the word. **1653** [see BRETON *sb.* and *a.*]. **1866** C. M. YONGE *Prince & Page* i. 7 A Poitevin, a falconer at Kenilworth. **1880** —— *One Will & Three Ways* iii, in *Bye-words* 65 Stories .. of Poitevin castles won by escalade. **1934** M. K. POPE *From Latin to Mod. French* ii. 18 This sound was not, however, diphthongised, cf. Poitevin *amar*. *Ibid.* xvii. 211 The southern border dialects (e.g. Poitevin). **1957** A. DUGGAN *Devil's Brood* vi. 68 Geoffrey had been born .. in .. 1158... He grew up to be another fair handsome northerner, obviously more Norman than Poitevin. **1968** F. WHITE *Ways of Aquitaine* iv. 52 These delicate Poitevin carvings must be regarded primarily as adornment of the churches. **1974** P. RICKARD *Hist. French Lang.* ii. 33 Poitevin, which shows close affinity with Occitan up to and including the tenth century, can by the twelfth century be considered essentially a dialect of the *langue d'oïl*. *Ibid.* vii. 127 Non-standard constructions, too, may be used; for instance .. the Poitevin *les enfants sont après jouer* (= *en train de jouer*). **1976** *Sat. Rev.* (U.S.) 30 Oct. 25 The population [of St. Barthélemy] is 90 per cent Caucasian, descendants of Normans, Bretons, Poitevins, and the Swedes owners of St. Barts for a century.

poitrel ('pɔɪtrəl). Now *Hist.* and *arch.* Forms: 5–6 **poytrell**, 6 **poiterell**, 6–8 **poitrell**, 7 **-il**, **poictrel(l**, **poytrel**, 6–9 **poitrel**, 7–9 **-al**, 9 **-ail**. [a. OF. *poitral*, orig. *peitral*, now with change of suffix *poitrail*:—L. *pectorāle* breast-plate, PECTORAL. *Poitral* is the Central or Parisian Fr. form, introduced into Eng. app. by Caxton, the earlier form from Norman Fr. being PEITREL, q.v.]

a. A piece of armour to protect the breast of a horse: often richly gilt and ornamented, and retained for ornament after its defensive use had ceased.

c **1489** CAXTON *Sonnes of Aymon* viii. 197 The horses gyrthe nor the poytrell myghte not helpe. **1552** ELYOT, *Cucumis*, .. a bullion of copper, set on bridels or poitrels of horses, for an ornament. **1592** R. D. *Hypnerotomachia* 14 b, To the fore gyrth on eyther side was buckled a riche and gorgeous poiterell. *c* **1611** CHAPMAN *Iliad* XIX. 370 Alcymus put poitrils on, and cast upon their jaws their bridles. **1678** WANLEY *Wond. Lit. World* IV. xxvi. §6. 408/1 The horse had .. a pendant Jewel of Precious Stones at his Poictrel. **1714** STEELE *Poet. Misc., Ninth Thebais* 270 Below his Breast .. a bending Poitral hung. **1745** S. MADDEN *Boulter's Mon.* 67 Her beauteous Breast a golden Poitrell grac'd. **1805** C. JAMES *Mil. Dict.* (ed. 2) *Poitrel*, armour for the breast of a horse. It is generally written *poitrail*. **1817** MOORE *Lalla R.*

(1824) 86 Steeds.. Their chains and poitrels glittering in the sun. **1824** S. R. MEYRICK *Critical Inquiry into Antient Armour* III. Gloss. s.v. Pectorale, The poitrail, a steel plate for the protection of a horse's chest. **1830** J. SKELTON *Engraved Illustrations Antient Arms & Armour* Pl. LIV (fig. 2), The fleur-de-lis is seen on the horse furniture, twice on the croupière-base, and as an armorial bearing on that of the poitral. **1866** CONINGTON *Æneid* VII. 228 Golden poitrels grace their necks. **1918** E. S. FARROW *Dict. Mil. Terms* 459 *Poitrail*, that portion of the horse armor which covers the breast, fitted either with hinges or like a flounce. **1920** G. F. LAKING *Rec. European Armour & Arms* III. xxii. 178 For the head there was.. the chanfron, for the neck the crinet, for the chest the poitrel.

b. *transf.* A breast-plate; a stiff stomacher.

1607 R. C[AREW] tr. *Estienne's World of Wonders* 156, I haue.. heard of certaine gentlewomen.. who made no bones to weare poytrels or stiffe stomachers, endangering thereby the life of their child. **1717** BULLOCK *Wom. a Riddle* II. 24 Your own puissant eyes against which no Poitrel is able to defend the heart of man.

poitrell, error for POINTEL I.

‖**poitrinaire** (pwatrinɛr). [F., f. *poitrine* chest + *-aire*:—L. *-ārius*: see -ARY[1].] A person suffering from chest or lung disease.

1856 *Sat. Rev.* 25 Oct. 578/2 As a *poitrinaire*, he was the most devoted, extravagant, sentimental of lovers and husbands. **1882** *Standard* 22 Dec. 5/1 Comparatively youthful invalids,.. described graphically, if not gracefully, by the foreign name of *poitrinaires*. **1884** *Pall Mall Gaz.* 24 Sept. 2/1 The soft, warm air so dear and necessary to the poitrinaire. **1969** *Sunday Tel.* 12 Jan. 15/8 Although she cannot help suggesting a *poitrinaire* in the most comfortable health, deft make-up and still more a skilful modification of the voice suggested the growing physical weariness.

poitrinal (ˈpɔɪtrɪnəl). Now *Hist.* or *arch.* [ad. Fr. *poitrinal*: see PETRONEL.] **1.** = POITREL.

1786 [see PECTORAL *sb.* 1 c]. **1869** J. R. PLANCHÉ *Catal. Meyrick Coll. exhibited at S. Kensington Museum* p. x, The barding of the horse is also very fine, consisting of chamfron, crevette, and poitrinal, all fluted and in fine condition. **1918** E. S. FARROW *Dict. Mil. Terms* 459 *Poitrinal*, in ancient armor, the horse's breastplate, formed of metal plates, riveted together, as a covering for the breast and shoulders.

2. = PETRONEL.

1824 [see PETRONEL]. **1829** *Archæologia* XXII. 86 The President Fauchet.. introduces to our notice a piece called a Petronel or Poitrinal, because it was rested on the poitrine or chest.. and thence fired.

‖**poivrade** (pwavrad). Also 7–8 **poiverade**. [F. (1505 in Hatz.-Darm.), f. *poivre* pepper: see -ADE.] Pepper-sauce. Also *attrib.*

1699 EVELYN *Acetaria* App. O j b, How a Poiverade is made. **1792** CHARLOTTE SMITH *Desmond* I. 85 There was neither game gravy, nor poiverade, nor even bread sauce. **1806** A. HUNTER *Culina* (ed. 3) 215 When cold, and cut into slices, it eats well with poivrade sauce. **1902** *Daily Chron.* 11 Jan. 8/4 To make the poivrade sauce.

'**pokable**, *a.* [f. POKE *v.*[1] + -ABLE.] Capable of being poked.

1882 C. W. SIEMENS in *Nature* XXVI. 396/1 The advantages.. claimed for the open fireplace are, that it is cheerful, 'pokable', and conducive to ventilation.

‖**pokal** (poˈkaːl). [G., ad. L. *poculum*, a drinking-cup.] A large German glass tankard, often with a lid. Also *transf.*

1868 C. G. LELAND *Hans Breitmann's Party* 11 How stately rode der Breitmann oop!—how lordly he kit down? How glorious from de great *pokal* he drink de bier so prown! **1869** G. A. SALA in *More Yankee Drolleries* 25 'Pokal', drinking-cup: in this case the large glass pint beer-mug used in America. **1950** *Chambers's Encycl.* VI. 421/1 The great tankards and pokals were intended for display; their size was so great that they were too heavy to drink from. **1969** *Canadian Antiques Collector* Oct. 5/1 Two ceremonial cups or pokals, late 17th century, silver gilt. **1974** *Encycl. Brit. Micropædia* VI. 891/2 (*caption*) Milk glass pokal, German, 17th century.

pok-a-tok: var. POK-TA-POK.

poke (pəʊk), *sb.*[1] Now chiefly *dial.* Forms: *α.* (3) 4– poke; also 5–7 pooke, 6–7 (9 *dial.*) poake, 7– poak; *Sc.* 5 poyke, 5–6 poik, 6 polk. *β. Sc.* and *north. dial.* 5 pok, 5–6 pokke, 7 pocke, 8–9 pock. (9 *dial.* puok, puock, pooak, pwok(e, pwoak; also pook, pouk, powk: *Eng. Dial. Dict.*) [Not in OE.: ME. *poke* from 14th c., represented 1276 by Anglo-L. *poka* (*unam pokam lanę*), agrees in form with ONF. *poque* (12th c.), *poke* (14th c. in Godef.) = F. *poche*; also Icel. *poki* (13th c.), early mod.Flem. *poke* (Kilian); also Ir. *poc*, Gael. *poca* bag; the affinities of which are uncertain, as is the question of their relationship to OE. *pohha*, ME. *powhe*, *pouhȝ*, POUGH, bag (for which Lindisf. Gl. has also *pocca*). The later Eng. spellings *pook*, *poak* imply lengthened *o*, as do also the Sc. *poik*, *polk*. A form with short *o* (*pok*(*k*, *pock*) is found in Sc. and north. Eng. from 15th c., but this is not (ɒ), but (o), a vowel which, like that of Sc. *puock* and north. Eng. *pwoke*, *pwooak*, represents ME. *ō* from *o* in an open syllable. The mod.Sc. *pouk*, north. Eng. *pook*, with (u, uː), may correspond to NF. dial. *pouque* beside *poque*. The phonology offers difficulties both in Eng. and Fr.: cf. POUCH.]

1. a. A bag; a small sack: applied to a bag of any material or description, but usually smaller than a *sack*. Now *dial.* exc. in ***to buy a pig in a poke*** (PIG *sb.*[1]), in Sc. ***a cat in a poke***, F. *chat en poche*.

In Sc. applied to the bags or wallets in which a gaberlunzie or beggar carried provisions and portable property.

α. **1276** *Rot. Hundred.* (1812) I. 398/2 Quidam judei Lincolnie.. furebantur unam pokam lane. *c* **1300** *Havelok* 780 Hise pokes fulle of mele an korn. *c* **1380** WYCLIF *Serm.* Sel. Wks. II. 358 Þan shulde pees be in þe chirche wiþouten strif of doggis in a poke. *c* **1386** CHAUCER *Reeve's T.* 358 They walwe as doon two pigges in a poke. **1411** *Nottingham Rec.* II. 86, j. poke cum salt, vd. *c* **1440** *Promp. Parv.* 407/1 Pooke (or poket, or walette), *sacculus*. **1488** *Inv. R. Wardr.* (1815) 12 In a canves poik within the said box tuelf hundreth & sevin angel nobilis. **1508** DUNBAR *Flyting* 147 ȝe gang With polkis to mylne, and beggis baith meill and schilling. *c* **1530–1860** [see PIG *sb.*[1] 11 a, b]. **1558** in *Lanc. Wills* (1884) 20 Two secks and two lesse pookes. **1615** W. LAWSON *Country Housew. Gard.* (1626) 51 A gathering Apron like a Poake. **1648–60** HEXHAM, *Koren-sack*, a Corne-sack, or a corne-pooke. **1723** SWIFT *New Year's Gift* 17 A pair of leathern pokes [*rime* folks]. **1824** SCOTT *Redgauntlet* Let. xiii, The hare-brained goose saw the pokes. **1875** *Brighton Daily News* 10 Mar. 2/5 Bringing a poke of bran down a step-ladder. **1883** G. C. DAVIES *Norfolk Broads* xix. (1884) 141 The eel-net is set across the dyke to catch them in its long 'poke'. **1883** J. Y. STRATTON *Hops & Hop-pickers* 34 From the bin the hops are carried in 'pokes' to the 'oast-house'. **1902** *Berea* (Kentucky) *Quarterly* Nov. 17 It usually comes in two-pound paper packages, or 'pokes'. **1910** R. SERVICE *Trail of '98* 347 The girl will pry him loose from his poke. **1922** G. PRINGLE *Tillicums of Trail* 250 It wasn't safe to come out by way of Skagway with your gold,.. you were likely to be relieved of your 'poke' by desperados. **1935** A. J. CRONIN *Stars look Down* I. ix. 68 He had pie, too, in his poke. **1948** C. W. HOLLIDAY *Valley of Youth* 144 A miner might come into a store for provisions with no money, but a little poke of gold dust. **1966** *Indians, Eskimos, & Aleuts of Alaska* (U.S. Bureau of Indian Affairs) 12 (*caption*) These villagers are carrying a sealskin 'poke' filled with seal oil. **1976** *Islander* (Victoria, B.C.) 15 Aug. 12/2 Nearby lay an empty buckskin 'poke' such as early miners favored for their gold dust. **1978** *Guardian* 14 Aug. 7/2 You may also find yourself at a temporary disadvantage if, after buying several items from a shop, the young lady assistant asks if you would 'like a poke'.

β. **1447** in *Dundee Charters* (1880) 24 b, And of al vthir thinges pok, pak, and barel proporcionablie. *c* **1470** HENRYSON *Mor. Fab.* II. (*Town & C. Mouse*) xv, Pokkis [*v.r.* sekkis] full of grots. **1599** *Acc. Bk. W. Wray* in *Antiquary* XXXII. 243 Item iij sakes, iij pokkes. **1625** *Vestry Bks.* (Surtees) 296 Given for a pocke of coles, 2d. **1733** in *Ramsay's Tea-t. Misc.* I. 29 Ye shall hae twa good pocks. **1824** SCOTT *Redgauntlet* Let. xi, The pock of siller.

b. A bag holding a definite quantity, varying according to the nature of the commodity, as wool, coal, meal, hops; used as a measure of capacity.

(It is not clear whether the early quots. belong here.)

1347–8 *Rolls of Parlt.* II. 215/2, xi pokes de madder. **15..** *Aberdeen Regr.* XVI. (Jam.), Polk of wool. **1855** MORTON *Cycl. Agric.* II. 1125/3 *Poke*, of wool, 20 cwts.

c. A pocket worn on the person. *Obs.* or *arch.*

1600 SHAKS. *A.Y.L.* II. vii. 20 Then he drew a diall from his poake. **1675** COCKER *Morals* 6 All are but Smoke To him that has no mony in his Poke. **1700** T. BROWN *Amusem. Ser. & Com.* iii. (1709) 16 With his Pockes as empty as his Brains. **1880** WEBB *Goethe's Faust* III. x. 183 Apart from this I've nothing in my poke.

d. A purse or wallet; a pocketbook. *N. Amer. slang.*

1859 G. W. MATSELL *Vocabulum* 68 *Poke*, a pocket; a purse. **1883** *Echo* 25 Jan. 2/3 The poke, which a pick-pocket glories in having appropriated, is the Saxon bag or purse. **1908** J. M. SULLIVAN *Criminal Slang* 18 *Poke of leather*, a pocketbook. **1931** 'D. STIFF' *Milk & Honey Route* 211 *Poke*, a leather wallet. **1939** J. O'HARA *Pal Joey* 50 There I was with only about $85 in my poke. **1953** 'W. BURROUGHS' *Junkie* iv. 48 He took a crumpled mass of bills from his pocket and counted out eight dollars.. 'Had it in his pants pocket. I couldn't find a poke.' **1976** 'TREVANIAN' *Main* (1977) vi. 123, I notice his wallet's half out of his pocket.. it comes to me that I might as well lift his poke... So I reach over and pull it out.

e. A roll of bank-notes; money. *slang.*

1926 J. BLACK *You can't Win* xiv. 190 My hand was on the big fat 'poke'. **1933** E. SEAGO *Circus Company* 295 *Poke*, money. **1965** L. J. CUNLIFFE *Having it Away* iv. 38 It's a very satisfying feeling knowing you can put your finger on a bit of poke. (Which is more slang for money: get it, poke, loot, poppy—any of them will do!) **1974** *Evening News* (Edinburgh) 8 Oct. 3/2 Colgan asked him: 'Have you got your poke?' obviously referring to the money.

2. A bag or bladder filled with air, used by fishermen as a buoy. *U.S.*

1887 *Fisheries U.S.* Sect. v. II. 270 When the 'pokes' are used, the officer gives the order to 'Blow up! Blow up!' and a man with sound lungs grasps one of these membranous pouches and inflates it... It is then attached to the whale.

†**3.** A long wide or full sleeve. *Obs.*

1402 *Pol. Poems* (Rolls) II. 69 The pokes of purchace hangen to the erthe. **1432–50** tr. *Higden*, *Harl. Contin.* (Rolls) VIII. 514 Grete insolence of vesture.. gownes with longe pokus, made in the maner of a bagpype. [**1706** PHILLIPS s.v., Pokes were also a sort of long-sleev'd Gowns, which Fashion grew so affected and extravagant, that the wearing of them was forbidden.]

†**4.** A kind of net, a bag-net. *Obs.*

1579 *Sc. Acts Jas. VI* (1814) III. 147/1 That destroyis the smoltis and fry of salmond.. be polkis, creillis, trammel-nettis, and hery watteris.

5. A morbid bag-like swelling on the neck. †**a.** In man, The goitre, also called ***Bavarian poke***.

1621 BURTON *Anat. Mel.* I. ii. II. i. (1676) 42/2 Aubanus Bohemus referrs that *Struma*, or Poke of the Bavarians and Styrians to the nature of their waters. **1673** RAY *Journ. Low C.* 143 We saw.. many men and women with large swellings under their chins.. called.. by some in English, Bavarian Pokes.

b. In sheep, A bag growing under the jaws, symptomatic of the rot; hence, the disease itself.

1798 *Statist. Acc. Scot.* XX. 469 Seldom subject to that disease called by sheep-farmers the poke, (a swelling under the jaw), or to the scab... The poke, particularly, often proves fatal. **1878** *Cumberland Gloss.* 76/1 Sheep tainted with rot often exhibit the symptom of a poke or bag under the jaws.

6. The stomach of a fish. *colloq.* or *dial.* Also, the sound or air-bladder of a fish (*Cent. Dict.*).

1773 BARRINGTON in *Phil. Trans.* LXIV. 117 Mr. Hunter opened a charr.. and found the poke, as our fishmongers call it, very different. **1897** W. KINGSTON in *Daily News* 10 Sept. 2/1, I once saw a gold ring taken out of a cod's poke.

7. *attrib.* and *Comb.*: **poke-bag** (*dial.*), the Long-tailed Titmouse (*Acredula rosea*); **poke-boy** (see quot.); **poke-cheeked** *a.*, having baggy cheeks; **poke-hooked** *a.* (see quots.); **poke-horse**, a pack-horse carrying loads in two pokes or bags; **poke- (pock-) net** (see quot. 1805); **poke- (pock-) nook**, one of the corners at the bottom of a bag or sack; ***one's own poke-nook***, one's own means, one's private resources; **poke- (pock-) shakings**, the last portions of meal, etc., shaken out of a sack; *fig.* the smallest of a litter of pigs; the youngest child in a family; †**poke-sleeve**, a deep and broad sleeve: see sense 3. Also POKE-PUDDING.

1885 SWAINSON *Prov. Names Birds* 32 The penduline form of the nest, and the feathers which compose the lining, have obtained for the bird the names of.. Poke pudding or *Poke bag,.. Feather poke. **1805** R. W. DICKSON *Pract. Agric.* II. 753 (*Hops*) Another person will be requisite in the hop-plantation, in order to pick up the scattered branches of the binds, and convey the produce to the kiln. A boy is in general employed in this business, who, from the nature of his work, is commonly called the *poke boy. **1843** CARLYLE in Froude *Life in Lond.* (1884) 320 A long, soft, *poke-cheeked face, with busy, anxious black eyes. **1883** *Century Mag.* XXV. 902/1 Many.. fish.. are caught, not by the hook entering the jaws of the fish, but because it is fastened in their stomach,.. a fish so captured is called '*poke-hooked'. **1897** KIPLING *Captains Courageous* iii, Help us here, Harve. It's a big un. Poke-hooked, too... He had taken the bait right into his stomach. **1669** in *Northumbld. Gloss.* s.v., Bring all the *Poke-horses that trespasse upon the ffell into the comon pinefold. **1805** FORSYTH *Beauties Scotl.* (1806) III. 389 Drag-nets, or *pock-nets, that is, nets in form of a bag, are often used. **1845** *Statist. Acc. Scotl.* XIV. 165 Catching fresh water fish with a kind of pock-net. **1583** *Leg. Bp. St. Androis* 661 Bot menstrallis, serving man, and maid, Gat Mitchell in ane auld *pocke nucke. **1821** GALT *Ann. Parish* xiv. (1850) 57 It was thought that it [the cost] would have to come out of their own pock-nook. **1844** BALLANTINE *Miller of Deanhaugh* i. 18 Your mouter fills mony a pock nook. **1808** JAMIESON, **Pock-shakings*.., a vulgar term, used to denote the youngest child of a family... It often implies the idea of something puny in appearance. **1844** STEPHENS *Bk. Farm* II. 700 The small weak pigs are usually nicknamed *wrigs*, or *pock shakings*. **1592** STOW *Ann.* 519 Gownes with deepe and broade sleeues, commonly called *poke sleeues. **1714** *Spectator* No. 619 ¶9 My learned Correspondent who writes against Master's Gowns and Poke Sleeves.

poke, *sb.*[2] [app. either an application of prec. (from its shape or appearance), or (as more generally held) from POKE *v.*[1] (from its poking out or projecting). Actual evidence is wanting.]

1. A projecting brim or front of a woman's bonnet or hat.

(The meaning in quot. 1770 is not clear: cf. 1815 in sense 2.)

1770 LADY MARY COKE *Jrnl.* 28 Dec., The headdress.. must be black, that is to say the poke and the lappits, but upon the head you are permitted to wear the ribbon of the colour of your robe. **1813** LADY BURGHERSH *Lett.* (1893) 61 An immense quilling of lace or ribbon round the poke. **1859** GEO. ELIOT *A. Bede* l, The close poke of her little black bonnet hid her face from him.

b. Applied to a 'sun-shade' or 'ugly', i.e. a detachable brim affixed to a bonnet to shade the wearer's face.

1859 SALA *Gaslight & D.* xxix. 341 Ladies.. with blue pokes to their bonnets.

2. Short for POKE-BONNET. (In quot. 1815, perh. a woman's muslin cap, formerly worn.)

1815 LADY GRANVILLE *Let.* 5 Sept., Miss Smith in a little crushed muslin poke. *a* **1845** HOOD *Literary & Literal* xi, They came—each 'Pig-faced Lady', in that bonnet We call a poke. **1876** GEO. ELIOT *Dan. Der.* III. xxiv, A grey frieze livery and a straw poke, such as my aunt's charity children wear. **1896** GEORGIANA M. STISTED *Life Sir R. F. Burton* xi. 269 [In Gt. Salt Lake City] A poke-bonnet was universally worn—why is the Poke a symbol of piety, Quakers, Salvationists, Mormons, Sisters of Mercy retiring alike inside its ungraceful shape?

3. *attrib.* and *Comb.*: **poke-brim**, a projecting brim of a bonnet or hat; hence **poke-brimmed** *a.*; †**poke fly-cap**, app. a fly-cap (FLY *sb.*[1] 11) provided with a poke.

1892 *Pall Mall G.* 19 May 1/3 The 'Mentone' is a smart hat for the races. It is of fawn straw, with a *poke brim of moderate size lined with apple-green velvet, and a crescent-shaped back. **1899** *Daily News* 3 June 8/3 The *poke-brimmed hat, reminiscent of the thirties, is in cream-coloured straw trimmed with tulle. **1810** *Splendid Follies* II.

106 Her hair was.. adorned with a *poke-fly cap, and long lace lappets.

poke, *sb.*[3] [f. POKE *v.*[1]]

1. a. An act of poking; a thrust, push, nudge. In *slang*, A blow with the fist, esp. in phr. ***to take a poke at.*** Also colloq. phr. ***better than a poke in the eye*** (and variants), used of something minimally desirable. Also *fig.*

1796 *Grose's Dict. Vulg. T.* (ed. 3), *Poke*, a blow with the fist; I'll lend you a poke. **1831** *Society* I. 155 With a poke at the fire to make it blaze the brighter. **1848** DICKENS *Dombey* vi, Giving her such jerks and pokes from time to time. *Ibid.* xvii, The Captain making a poke at the door with the knobby stick to assure himself that it was shut. **1849** LYTTON *Caxtons* XVII. i, With a sly look.. giving me a poke in the ribs. **1852** GEO. ELIOT *Let.* 4 Dec. (1954) II. 71 'Then,' he said .. 'Here are those "Letters from Ireland" which I hope will be something better than a *poke in the eye*.' **1936** J. STEINBECK *In Dubious Battle* viii. 120 'They got those cops here quick,' said Burke. 'I'd like to take a poke at a few of 'em.' **1941** BAKER *Dict. Austral. Slang* 55 *Poke*, to hit a person. Also, 'a poke': a blow with the fist. **1944** J. CARY *Horse's Mouth* xvi. 81 Anarchists who love God always fall for Spinoza because he tells them that God doesn't love them. This is just what they need. A poke in the eye. To a real anarchist, a poke in the eye is better than a bunch of flowers. It makes him see stars. **1956** B. HOLIDAY *Lady sings Blues* (1973) ii. 24 She tried to get at me. I took a poke at her, and down the stairs she went. **1969** *Listener* 10 Apr. 478/1 What sort of salute, I wondered, amounted to a poke in the eye? On this occasion compromise *was* reached: it was agreed that the occasion should be marked by a second broadcast of my *Salute to Stalingrad.* **1974** *Bulletin* (Sydney) 6 July 44 An Australian way of expressing ecstasy is to say: 'It's better than a poke in the eye with a burnt stick.' **1976** *N.Y. Times Mag.* 10 Oct. 111/4 Better than a poke in the eye with a sharp stick.

b. with advbs., as **poke-out**, (*a*) an act of poking out; (*b*) *slang*, a bag of food handed to a beggar; a lunch; (*c*) *slang* (see quot. 1960); **poke-round**, a going round and poking into places; **poke-up**, an act of poking or stirring up.

1874 RUSKIN *Hortus Inclusus* (1887) 3 We go into the Sacristy and have a reverent little poke out of relics. **1894** 'J. FLYNT' in *Century Mag.* Mar. 713/2 He returned with a 'poke-out' (food given at the door). **1901** L. MALET *Sir R. Calmady* VI. vii, We could ride over that.. land and have a poke round for sites. **1905** *Westm. Gaz.* 18 Aug. 3/1 All the birds sit so close that 'good dog Ponto' almost has to give them a poke-up with his.. nose to induce them to rise at all. **1907** J. LONDON *Road* 12, I could 'throw my feet' with the next one when it came to 'slamming a gate' for a 'poke-out' or a 'set-down'. **1918** H. A. VACHELL *Some Happenings* i. 4 [He] finished what was left of a 'poke out' (cold food) handed to him by a good Samaritan. **1936** *New Republic* 15 July 289/1 Sympathetic women will often cook a meal for tramps, .. and 'lumps' or 'poke-outs' are possible at any time during the day. **1960** WENTWORTH & FLEXNER *Dict. Amer. Slang* 399/2 *Poke-out*,.. 2 An outdoor dinner cooked over wood or charcoal; a gathering for the purpose of preparing and eating such a meal; any long hike or camping trip which includes such meals. **1964** J. L. KORNBLUH *Rebel Voices* 407/2 *Pokeout*, handout.

c. *Cricket.* A batting-stroke made by jabbing at the ball.

1853 F. GALE *Public School Matches* 54 Sticker gets his runs by quiet little pokes one at a time. **1896** W. J. FORD in *Badminton Mag.* Sept. 278 Besides.. 'the draw', there was another weapon forged for the armoury of him for whom leg-hitting was not—viz. the 'Cambridge Poke', so called, I believe, in contemptuous irony. **1960** J. FINGLETON *Four Chukkas to Australia* xvi. 133 He was confusing the cut with the 'poke', a disastrous nibbling by so many Englishmen.

d. An act of sexual intercourse; also, a woman with whom one has sexual intercourse, a 'lay'; = FUCK *sb.* 1. *slang.*

1902 FARMER & HENLEY *Slang* V. 242 *Poke*,.. an act of coition. **1958** N. LEVINE *Canada made Me* ii. 82 When I met her I only want a poke. Then she tell me a baby made. **1968** H. C. RAE *Few Small Bones* II. i. 77 'Caroline', said Derek .. 'wouldn't make a good poke for a blind hunchback.' **1970** L. MEYNELL *Curious Crime* xii. 160 Landladies can nearly always be paid in kind. Services in lieu of rent. A poke a night. **1977** *Listener* 11 Aug. 184/4 Turning a series of squalid pokes into a series of honourable combats.

e. *fig.* Power, horsepower. *slang.*

1965 R. T. BICKERS *Hellions* vi. 69 With all that extra poke under the bonnet. **1977** *Drive* Mar.–Apr. 54/2 The Scirocco gives a worst figure of 28 mpg, using all the poke its free-revving engine will deliver. **1979** *Sunday Mail Mag.* (Brisbane) 1 July 3/5, I expect you'd prefer something with a bit more poke. A Ferrari say, or an Aston Martin.

f. *Computing.* (Usu. written POKE.) A statement or function in BASIC for altering the contents of a memory location, having as arguments the memory address concerned and the value to be placed there. Cf. POKE *v.*[1] 8 and PEEK *sb.*[1] 2.

1978, etc. [see PEEK *sb.*[1] 2]. **1982** J. S. COAN *Basic Apple BASIC* ii. 42 We can use POKE to change the width of the display screen. **1984** J. CAMPBELL *Programming Tips & Techniques for Apple II & IIe* iii. 40 Another way that you may control the positioning of the cursor is to use the POKE instruction... There are six of these pokes available that either control the positioning of the cursor or the size of the text window.

2. a. A contrivance fastened upon cattle, pigs, etc., to prevent them from breaking through fences: see quots.

(Supposed to refer to its action in poking the animal.)

1809 E. A. KENDALL *Travels through Northern Parts of U.S.* II. 198 A hog.. by some mischance had turned his poke, so that his throat was squeezed into one of the acuter angles. **1828** WEBSTER, *Poke*, in New England, a machine to prevent unruly beasts from leaping fences, consisting of a yoke with a pole inserted, pointing forward. **1859** HOLLAND *Gold F.* iv. 43 We put a poke upon a vicious cow. **1875** KNIGHT *Dict. Mech.*, *Poke*, a device.. to prevent its [an animal's] jumping over, crawling through, or breaking down fences... They vary with the kind of stock to which they are attached,—horses, cattle, hogs, or geese. **1949** R. J. SIM *Pages from Past* 105 Such a rig is known as a 'poke'. It is put on the neck of a critter with fence-jumping inclinations. **1956** W. R. BIRD *Off-Trail in Nova Scotia* viii. 220 And here were some sheep, too, with pokes. **1969** K. M. WELLS *Owl Pen Reader* I. 67 A poke is supposed.. to make it impossible for any living thing to get through even an ordinary wire fence.

b. *transf.* A collar. *slang.*

1908 'O. HENRY' *Man Higher Up* in *Gentle Grafter* 147 With only feetwear and a dozen 15$\frac{1}{2}$ English pokes in his shopping bag. **1924** *Truth* (Sydney) 27 Apr. 6 *Poke*, a collar.

3. (See quots.)

1860 BARTLETT *Dict. Amer.*, *Poke*, a lazy person, a dawdle; as 'what a slow poke you are!' A woman's word. **1864** WEBSTER, *Poke*,.. a lazy person; a dawdler; also, a stupid or uninteresting person.

4. *attrib.* and *Comb.*, as **poke-check** *Ice hockey*, a defensive play made by poking the puck off an opposing player's stick; hence as *v. intr.*; **poke-checking** *vbl. sb.*

1945 R. FONTAINE *Happy Time* 45 Frank Nighbor, Canada's immortal poke-check genius. **1964** *Maclean's Mag.* 2 May 46/1 To me some of the most fascinating moves in hockey.. are poke-checks, or well timed interceptions, or expeditions of forechecking. **1966** *Hockey News* (Montreal) 1 Jan. 13/2 He poke-checks and sweep-checks like the oldtimers. **1963** A. O'BRIEN *Headline Hockey* 60 At that point the defenceman will likely resort to poke-checking.

poke, *sb.*[4] Also 7 poak(e, pooke. [Of N. American Indian origin; in sense 1, app. the same as the Virginian word cited by early travellers as *uppowoc*, *apooke*, smoke, in Narraganset *puck* smoke; in sense 2, app. shortened from POCAN.]

†**1.** Some plant smoked by the North American Indians, hence called Indian tobacco. *Obs.*

It has been variously conjectured to be *Nicotiana rustica* (see quot. 1865); *Antennaria plantaginifolia* (in Britton & Brown *Flora Northern U.S.* III. Index, called 'Indian tobacco', 'Ladies' tobacco'); *A. margaritifera* (see quot. 1865); and *Lobelia inflata*, very commonly referred to as 'Indian tobacco'.

[**1599** T. HERIOT in Hakluyt *Voy.* III. 271 There is an herbe.. called by the inhabitants uppowoc.. the Spanyards call it tabacco. **1615** W. STRACHEY *Hist. Trav. Virginia* 121 There is here great store of tobacco which the salvages call apooke.] **1634** *Relat. Ld. Baltimore's Plantation* (Maryland) (1865) 20 After this, was brought.. a great Bagg, filled with a large Tobacco-pipe and Poake, which is the word they vse for our Tobacco. **1651** R. CHILD in *Hartlib's Legacy* (1655) 155, I.. have far greater hopes of the flourishing of this wild plant, than of Tobacco (either of that which in New England is called Poak, much differing from the Virginian, or of that other commonly used and sown in Virginia). **1672** JOSSELYN *New Eng. Rarities* 54 Tobacco,.. the Indians make use of a small kind with short round leaves called Pooke. **1792** BELKNAP *Hist. New Hampsh.* III. 126 A running vine, bearing a small berry, and a round leaf, which Josselyn (who wrote in 1672) says, the fishermen called poke; it is known to the hunters by the name of Indian tobacco. **1865** TUCKERMAN *Josselyn's N. Eng. Rarities* 85 (note to quot. 1672, above) The weak tobacco, cultivated.. by the Indians .. was not.. colt's-foot, but *Nicotiana rustica* L., well known to have been long in cultivation among the American savages... The name *poke*, or *pooke*,—if it be, as is supposable, the same with *puck* 'smoke' of the Narraganset vocabulary of R. Williams.. was perhaps always indefinite. *Ibid.* 87 The species intended by Josselyn [referred to by him as 'Live-for-ever, a kind of cud-weed'] is our everlasting... The dried herb [was] used by the fishermen instead of tobacco, and no doubt called by them poke.

2. a. A name for American species of *Phytolacca*, esp. *P. americana*, Virginian poke, poke-berry, poke-weed. **b. Indian poke**, the green hellebore or poke-root, *Veratrum viride.*

1731 CATESBY *Carolina* I. 24 They feed much on the berries of Poke, i.e. *Blitum Virginianum.* **1733** MILLER *Gard. Dict.*, *Phytolacca*;.. American Nightshade,.. commonly call'd Virginian Poke or Porke Physick. **1760** J. LEE *Introd. Bot.* App. 323 Virginian Poke, *Phytolacca.* **1770** J. R. FORSTER tr. *Kalm's Trav. N. Amer.* (1772) I. 153. **1866** *Treas. Bot.* 885/2 The Pocan, or Virginian Poke or Poke-weed, is a branching herbaceous plant, with a smooth green or sometimes purplish stem.. with large green or purplish leaves. **1874** GARROD & BAXTER *Mat. Med.* (1880) 382 Green Hellebore Root. The dried rhizome of Veratrum viride; American or Green Hellebore; called also Swamp Hellebore and Indian Poke. **1876** BARTHOLOW *Mat. Med.* (1879) 455 Poke has been proposed as an emetic, but.. the great depression of the powers of life which it causes.. will ever prevent its employment. **1945** *Chicago Tribune* 13 May VII. 1/3 Opal had found the first tightly curled leaves of poke, the best known of all Ozark greens. **1977** LEWIS & ELVIN-LEWIS *Med. Bot.* iv. 90/1 Poke.. has long been a favorite spring potherb in the southern United States.

3. Comb.: **poke-berry**, the dark purple berry of *Phytolacca americana*, or the plant itself; also *attrib.*; **poke-greens**, the young leaves of poke-weed used as a vegetable; **poke-milkweed** (see quot.); **poke-root**, (*a*) the white hellebore of N. America, *Veratrum viride* (2 b), also its root; (*b*) the root of poke-weed; **poke-salad, -salat, -sallet**, the young leaves of poke-weed used as a salad; **poke-weed**, *Phytolacca* (2 a).

1774 P. V. FITHIAN *Jrnl.* 15 Oct. (1900) 269 To Day Harry boil'd up a Compound of *Poke-Berries, Vinegar, Sugar &c to make a red Ink or Liquid. **1834** W. A. CARRUTHERS *Kentuckian in N.Y.* II. 215 His face looks like it was boiled in poke-berry juice and indigo. **1858** MAYNE *Expos. Lex.*, Poke-berries, Poke-root. **1869** LOWELL *Lett.* (1894) II. 50 Pokeberry juice, whereof we used to make a delusive red ink when we were boys. **1899** *Academy* 11 Feb. 184/1 Woollen cloth was dyed crimson in the juice of the poke-berry. **1911** G. S. PORTER *Harvester* xiii. 252 Pokeberry!.. Roots bring five cents a pound. Good blood purifier. *Ibid.* xv. 334 A few pokeberry plants for the colour. **1974** A. DILLARD *Pilgrim at Tinker Creek* xiv. 249 A skin-colored sandstone ledge beside me was stained with pokeberry juice. **1848** *Knickerbocker* XXXI. 222 The southern negro will dance after eating his *poke-greens and bacon. **1938** M. K. RAWLINGS *Yearling* i. 12 There were poke-greens with bits of white bacon buried in them. **1895** *Syd. Soc. Lex.*, *Poke-milkweed, the *Asclepias phytolaccoides*, which is not unlike Poke-weed. **1687** J. CLAYTON in *Phil. Trans.* XLI. 150 When they design to give a Purge, they make use of.. *Poke-root, i.e. *Solanum bacciferum.* **1698** G. THOMAS *Pennsylvania* (1848) 19 There grows also in great Plenty the Black Snake-Root,.. Rattle-Snake-Root, Poke-Root, called in England Jallop. **1807** *Med. Jrnl.* XVII. 295 Proofs of the efficacy of the poke-root. **1881** J. C. HARRIS *Uncle Remus* 197, I got mustard, en *poke salid, en lam's quarter in dat baskit. **1892** Poke salad [see CALLALLOO]. **1913** H. KEPHART *Our Southern Highlanders* xiii. 282 This poke salat eats good. **1947** *Sun* (Baltimore) 20 May 18/3, I was introduced to poke, as poke-salat, by a Southern Maryland family. **1751** *Gentl. Mag.* July 306/2 Tho' the Phytolacca be known to almost every one in America, by the name of *pokeweed,.. yet I think it proper .. to give a description of it. **1756** P. BROWNE *Jamaica* 232 Poke-weed. This plant is.. commonly found in all the cooler hills. **1880** *New Virginians* I. 53 They had stained it pink with poke-weed berries. This poke-weed is the Phytolacca—a tall, handsome plant which grows in fence corners. **1886** M. ARNOLD *Let.* 29 July (1895) II. 341 The pokeweed (*Phytolacca*) is, I think, American too. **1945** *New England Homestead* 13 Oct. 6/4 Pokeweed, huckle and blueberries, wild roses, bittersweet and hazelnut bushes are also appreciated. **1976** *National Observer* (U.S.) 3 July 15/2 A beautiful black woman.. supplied some delectable recipes (several ways to serve pokeweed, for instance).

poke, *sb.*[5] The small green heron of U.S.

1794 MORSE *Amer. Geog.* I. 165 Green Bittern. Poke. Skouk. *Ardea virescens.*

poke (pəʊk), *v.*[1] Forms: 3– poke; (4 pok), 5 pooke, 6–7 poak. *β.* 5 pouke, pukke, pucke. [ME. *pōken* = late MDu., Du., MLG., LG. *pōken* to poke, thrust; whence also OF. *poquer*, *pocher* to poke, thrust out (e.g. an eye) (Godef.). Cf. MDu. *poke*, Du. *pook*, MLG. *pōk*, LG. *poke*, a dagger, Sw. *påk*, a stick. These words seem to imply an OTeut. stem **puk-*, **pūk-*, preserved only in the LG. branch. But the history of the *β* forms is obscure. (Gael. *puc* push, jostle, Ir. *poc* a blow, kick, Corn. *poc* shove, push, are app. from Eng.)]

1. a. *trans.* To thrust or push (anything) with one's hand or arm, the point of a stick, or the like, usually so as to move or stir it.

c **1386** CHAUCER *Reeve's T.* 249 Aleyn the clerk.. He poked John and seyde slepestow. **1426** LYDG. *De Guil. Pilgr.* 13849 An Aungel Pookede hym and made hym ryse. **1811** *Sporting Mag.* XXXVIII. 92 The bellows is used at once to blow and to poke the fire. **1828** WEBSTER, *Poke*,.. to thrust at with the horns, as an ox; a popular use of the word in New England. **1889** HURST *Horsham, Sussex Gloss.*, Doant goo into that field, may be you'll be pooked [by a bull or cow] if you do. *Mod. colloq.* He poked me in the ribs.

β. **1377** LANGL. *P. Pl.* B. v. 620 Wrathþe.. pukketh [*v. rr.* puckeþ, poukeþ, pokeþ; A. VI. 100 puiteþ; C. VIII. 263 pokeþ] forþ pruyde to prayse þi-seluen. *Ibid.* 643 'Ȝus', quod Pieres þe plowman and pukked hem alle to gode. *c* **1450** *Merlin* 367 Bohors.. come to hym.. and putte the poynte of his swerde on his shelde and be-gan to pouke hym, and cleped 'Rise vp'.

b. Hence, to thrust or push (a thing) *away, out, in, up, down*; *from, into* (a place); etc.; *to poke through*, to thrust through (*with* a weapon).

c **1380** WYCLIF *Serm.* Sel. Wks. I. 12 And þan maist þou poke beter þe mot fro þi broþir. **1675** J. SMITH *Chr. Relig. Appeal* I. 20 To poak out Leviathan, from under that shelf of prejudice. **1700** S. L. tr. *Fryke's Voy. E. Ind.* 327 We found them [Pagods] ruin'd.. and poked again in the dark hole. **1781** MME. D'ARBLAY *Diary* May, I poked the three guineas in his hand, and told him I would come again another time. **1864** BURTON *Scot. Abr.* I. iv. 171 When Montgomery poked out the eye of Henry II in the tilt-yard. **1865** KINGSLEY *Herew.* ix, I cannot have you poked through with a Zeeland pike.

c. To shut *up* or confine in a poky place. *colloq.*

1860 MISS YONGE *Hopes* II. x, Poking himself up in such a horrid place. **1864** MRS. RIDDELL *G. Geith* I. xiv. 266 It would break her heart,.. to be poked up in a town. **1881** MISS YONGE *Lads & Lasses of Langley* iii. 124, I suppose she is not much of a lady, living poked up there.

d. To make, find *out*, produce, stir *up*, by poking.

1646 SIR T. BROWNE *Pseud. Ep.* III. xx. 155 If also these black extremities, or presumed eyes be clipped off, they [snails] will notwithstanding make use of their protrusions or hornes, and poke out their way as before. **1823** *Examiner* 337/2 Like children who poke a hole in a drum to see what it is. **1884** *Spectator* 12 July 201/2 To poke up a great conflagration in the country.

e. *Cricket.* To hit (the ball) with a jabbing stroke.

1836 *New Sporting Mag.* Oct. 360 He was very successful in poking leg stump balls for one run. **1862** J. PYCROFT *Cricket Tutor* 45 See, he is longing to poke the ball to the on-side. **1872** *Baily's Mag.* Aug. 166 The Eton men hit with freedom.. the same bowling that the day before.. they only poked or played with tameness and hesitation.

f. To have sexual intercourse with (a woman). *slang.*

1868 *Index Expurgatorius of Martial* 27 Saufeia,..though she was willing to be poked, would not enter the bath with the poet for decency's sake. *c* **1888–94** [see GET *v.* 42 h]. **1962** J. BRAINE *Life at Top* ix. 129, I wanted to poke Lucy so I poked her. **1967** L. MEYNELL *Mauve Front Door* ii. 24 Your uncle was..as randy as a goat... He poked them everywhere. **1971** R. FALKIRK *Chill Factor* xiv. 149 Are you out of your mind poking an Icelandic girl while you're on this sort of mission? **1975** N. LUARD *Robespierre Serial* xvi. 144 They're far from sure she's the one this GI poked.

g. To hit, strike (someone). *colloq.*

1906 *Dialect Notes* III. 122, I *poked* him on the nose. **1959** S. J. BAKER *Drum* 136 *Poke*, v., to hit a person with the fist.

h. *Baseball.* To hit.

1908 *Atlantic Monthly* Aug. 229/1 Sharky poked a bingle. **1951** in Wentworth & Flexner *Dict. Amer. Slang* (1960) 399/2 Jackie Robinson poked a pitch out of the park.

2. *fig.* To urge, incite, stir up, excite, irritate. Now *rare* or *Obs.*

13.. *Cursor M.* 11818 (Cott.) Þe parlesi has his a side þat dos him fast to pok [*v. r.* poke] his pride. **1393** LANGL. *P. Pl.* C. II. 129 Lucifer..For prude þat hym pokede hus peyne hath no ende. **1601** B. JONSON *Poetaster* II. i, You must still bee poking mee, against my will, to things. **1825** BROCKETT *N.C. Gloss.*, *Poked*, offended, piqued. 'Aw've poked him, sare'. **1851** *Lit. Gaz.* 7 June 388/3 A little too fond of poking up the prejudices and peculiarities of priests and bishops.

†3. To crimp, form the folds in (a ruff) with a poking-stick. Also *absol. Obs.*

1592 *Nobody & Someb.* in Simpson *Sch. Shaks.* (1878) I. 318, I shall turne Laundresse now, and learne to starch And set, and poke. **1614** J. COOKE *Tu Quoque* in Dodsley *O. Pl.* (1780) VII. 19 For pride, the woman that had her ruff poak'd by the devil, is but a puritan to her. **1636** DAVENANT *Platonic Lovers* Wks. (1673) 298 And then for push o' Pike, practise to poke a Ruff.

4. a. *intr.* or *absol.* To do the action of thrusting; to make a thrust or thrusts with a stick, the nose, etc.

1608 ARMIN *Nest Ninn.* (1880) 50 Now our Philosophical Poker pokte on, and poynted to a strange shew. **1643** DAVENANT *Unfortunate Lovers* v. i, Swords they have all.. they'll serve To poke. **1784** MME. D'ARBLAY *Diary* 15 Jan., I was really obliged to go and poke at the fire with all my might. **1828** WEBSTER s.v., *To poke at*, is to thrust the horns at. **1866** G. MACDONALD *Ann. Q. Neighb.* vi, I saw them.. poking with a long stick in the pond. **1867** TROLLOPE *Chron. Barset* II. lvii. 136 He raised his umbrella and poked angrily at the..notice. **1901** MAURICE HEWLETT *New Canterb. T., Dan Costard's T.* 79 It [a babe]..poked for the nipple and found it not.

b. *Cricket.* To make pokes at the ball (see POKE *sb.*[3] 1 c). Also const. *about.*

1851 J. PYCROFT *Cricket Field* vii. 114 Mere stopping balls and poking about in the blockhole is not cricket. **1899** E. V. LUCAS *Open Road* 146 (The Cricket Ball Sings) Perish the muff and the little tin Shrewsbury, Meanly contented to potter and poke. **1906** A. E. KNIGHT *Compl. Cricketer* viii. 268 His drive is a clean honest lift straight from the shoulders; he never pokes, 'puddling about his crease'. **1927** M. A. NOBLE *Those 'Ashes'* 193 His usual aggression was missing and he poked about, mistiming and apparently being unable to make a clean stroke.

c. Of a man: to have sexual intercourse with a woman. *slang.*

1973 *Nation Rev.* (Melbourne) 24–30 Aug. 1417/2 Working class morality where the male never 'pokes' after marriage but lusts away in obscenity and dirty jokes.

5. a. *trans.* To thrust forward (the finger, head, nose, etc.); *esp.* to thrust obtrusively.

1700 T. BROWN *Amusem. Ser. & Com.* 97 One of them would have been poking a Cranes Bill down his Throat. **1783** MME. D'ARBLAY *Diary* 4 Jan., He pokes his nose more into one's face than ever. **1812** H. & J. SMITH *Rej. Addr., Baby's Debut* ii, He pokes her head between the bars, And melts off half her nose! **1826** LADY GRANVILLE *Lett.* 15 Feb., Everybody poking in their little efforts at the expiration of the Carnaval. **1874** SYMONDS *Sk. Italy & Greece* (1898) I. xi. 217 A fig-tree poking ripe fruit against a bedroom window. **1884** A. LANG in *Century Mag.* Jan. 324/1 The poles..are everywhere to be seen poked out of windows.

b. *to poke fun* (*at*), to assail with jest, banter, or ridicule, esp. in a sly or indirect manner.

1840 HOOD *Up the Rhine* 157 The American..in a dry way began to poke his fun at the unfortunate traveller. **1844** THACKERAY *B. Lyndon* i, She was always 'poking her fun', as the Irish phrase it. **1861** HUGHES *Tom Brown of Oxf.* xiv, The first thing you do is to poke fun at me out of your wretched classics. **1880** DIXON *Windsor* IV. xxxiii. 320 London wits poke fun at him.

6. *intr.* **a.** To poke one's nose, go prying into corners or looking about one; *fig.* to make curious investigation.

1715 PRIOR *Down-Hall* 11 Hang Homer and Virgil; their meaning to seek, A man must have pok'd into Latin and Greek. **1809** W. IRVING *Knickerb., Acc. Author* (1849) 14 He was a very inquisitive body, and when not in his room was continually poking about town. **1819** SHELLEY *Peter Bell* VI. iv, No longer imitating Pope, In that barbarian Shakespeare poking. **1850** T. A. TROLLOPE *Impress. Wanderer* xvi. 255 In vain I poked among its obscure lanes. **1888** J. PAYN *Myst. Mirbridge* xx, Having a lawyer to poke and pry into his accounts. **1898** *Eliz. & Germ. Gard.* (1899) 38 She is off..to poke into every corner..and box, if necessary, any careless dairy-maid's ear.

b. To potter; to move *about* or work in a desultory, ineffective, or dawdling way.

1796 JANE AUSTEN *Sense & Sens.* II. iii, Lord bless me! how do you think I can live poking by myself? **1839** E. FITZGERALD *Lett.* (1889) I. 49, I dare say you think it very absurd that [I] should poke about here in the country, when I might be in London seeing my friends. **1877** MAR. M. GRANT *Sun-Maid* viii, I should enjoy poking about a bit on Dinah's back.

7. a. *trans. to poke the head*, and absol. *to poke*; to carry the head thrust inelegantly forward; to stoop.

1811 L. M. HAWKINS *C'tess & Gertr.* I. 185 'A quarter's dancing' would be well bestowed on the young lady, as she certainly poked most terribly. **1825** BROCKETT *N.C. Gloss.*, *Poke*, to stoop. 'To poke the head'. **18..** MISS H. SHELLEY in Symonds *Shelley* ii. (1878) 45 It was not worn as a punishment, but because I poked. **1847** [see POKING *ppl. a.* 1]. **1900** EL. GLYN *Visits Elizabeth* (1906) 3 They both poke their heads, and Jane turns in her toes.

b. *colloq.* To project obtrusively, to stick *out.*

1828 *Craven Gloss.* (ed. 2), *Poke*, to project, to lean forward, to bag out.

8. *Computing.* (Usu. written **POKE**, inflected **POKEing**, etc.) *intr.* To use POKE to store a new value in a memory location (const. *into*). Also *trans.*, to put (a value) *into* or *in* a memory location; to alter (a memory location) in this way. Cf. POKE *sb.*[3] 1 f and PEEK *v.*[1] 2.

1978 WAITE & PARDEE *BASIC Primer* v. 164 This program will pulse the speaker 100 times by POKEing into location 102. *Ibid.* 166 This code POKEs the character C into memory location specified by X and Y. **1981** R. NORMAN *Learning BASIC with your Sinclair ZX80* xxiv. 94 POKEing into the wrong places can upset the ZX80, so that you have to switch off to clear the RAM. **1981** D. INMAN et al. *More TRS-80 BASIC* ii. 22 It is often desirable to PEEK at the value in a memory location *before* you POKE in a new value. **1983** [see PEEK *v.*[1] 2]. **1984** J. HILTON *Choosing & using your Home Computer* 261/1 Having to POKE locations with numbers to produce graphics is a laborious process.

poke, *v.*[2] *Sc.* Also 6 polk. [f. POKE *sb.*[1]]

†1. *trans.* To catch fish with a poke-net (see POKE *sb.*[1] 4). *Obs.*

1574 *Reg. Privy Council Scot.* II. 399 Slauchter of blak fische, polking and polting or ony uther crymes.

2. To put in a poke or bag; to bag; *to poke up*, to put up in a bag or pocket.

1596 HARINGTON *Metam. Ajax* 49 Perhaps thou hast a minde to poke vp thy dish when you likest thy meate well. *a* **1758** RAMSAY *Eagle & Robin* 49 Poke up your pypes.

poke, *v.*[3] *U.S.* [f. POKE *sb.*[3] 2.] *trans.* To put a poke on.

1828 WEBSTER s.v., To poke an ox.

'poke-'bonnet. [f. POKE *sb.* or *v.*[1]: see POKE *sb.*[2]] Colloquial name for a bonnet with a projecting brim; *spec.* one of this shape worn in the early part of the 19th c. Also *attrib.*

1820 *Hermit in London* xcii. V. 35 Another street nuisance is your poke-bonnet ladies, who sometimes put out your eyes with these pent-house projections. **1833** T. HOOK *Love & Pride, Widow* viii, For young women as likes to look about 'em, them poke bonnets is old nick. **1837** LYTTON *E. Maltrav.* IV. vi, A few ladies of middle age..wear..straw poke bonnets. **1858** R. S. SURTEES *Ask Mamma* ix, [A] lady ..painted in one of the old poke bonnets of former days. **1884** *Century Mag.* XXVIII. 14 Eight or nine ladies, gentlemen, and children, in the poke-bonnets and high-collared coats of the year 1839.

b. Applied to the form of bonnet worn by Quakeresses, and later to that of Salvation Army women, etc.; hence, to the wearers of such.

1848 BARTLETT *Dict. Amer.*, *Poke-bonnet*, a long, straight bonnet, much worn by Quakers and Methodists. **1862** H. MARRYAT *Year in Sweden* II. lvi. 264 We dined at a farmhouse.., the property of Anabaptists, a sect most numerous in Götland. There's no mistaking the women by their downcast looks and black poke-bonnets. **1877** *Sat. Rev.* 12 May 577/2 At Croydon, Dorking, and other favourite haunts of Friends, the..broad-brimmed hats for the men, and close poke-bonnets for the women, may still be seen. **1899** *St. James' Gaz.* 17 Aug. 11/2 Never reached by the Church,..or any other spiritual organisations, except possibly the 'poke bonnets' at the corners of the streets. **1902** ELIZ. L. BANKS *Newspaper Girl* 107 The poke bonnet and dark blue dress, which I thought I would not get until I had spent a few days investigating what was the best way to join the Army.

Hence **poke-'bonneted** *a.*, wearing a poke-bonnet.

1877 *Sat. Rev.* 23 June 755/1 Marching in.., hatted or poke-bonneted, and silent, which it [a religious observance] is Quaker. **1901** *Daily Chron.* 16 Nov. 3/2 The poke-bonnetted young ladies who resided in the charming suburb of Paddington-green.

poked (pəʊkt), *a.* [f. POKE *sb.*[1], [2] + -ED[2].]

1. Furnished with a bag or poke; dilated.

1611 MARKHAM *Countr. Content.* I. xix. (1668) 83 She must be of large body, well poked behind for large Eggs. **1828** *Craven Gloss.* (ed. 2), *Poked*, having a bag or poke under the jaw, which is generally the case with consumptive or rotten sheep.

2. Of a bonnet or cap: Furnished with a poke.

1866 GEO. ELIOT *F. Holt* x, He..in a poked cap and without a cravat made a figure at which his mother cried every Sunday. **1871** MISS MULOCK *Fair France* iv. 125 Those frightful white poked caps or bonnets, which often hide such sweet, saintly, and even beautiful faces.

poked, *ppl. a.* [f. POKE *v.*[1] + -ED[1].]

1. Thrust, pushed, stirred, etc.: see the vb.

1898 *Westm. Gaz.* 21 Apr. 3/1 These..may be found in the poked-away forgotten trays of our jewellers' shops.

†2. Of a ruff: Crimped with a poking-stick. *Obs.*

1593 *Pass. Morrice* (1876) 74 The delight of their curious poked ruffes would be set aside. **1640** GLAPTHORNE *Hollander* III. Wks. 1874 I. 113 They shall weare Beaver Hats, Poak'd Ruffes, Grogram Gownes, or..wrought Taffata.

pokeful ('pəʊkfʊl). [f. POKE *sb.*[1] + -FUL.] A bagful, a small sackful.

1377 LANGL. *P. Pl.* B. VII. 191 A poke ful [**1393** C. x. 342 poke-ful; A. VIII. 178 *v.r.* pokeful] of pardoun þere, ne prouinciales lettres. **1575** G. HARVEY *Letter-bk.* (Camden) 91 Ifte bee not worth a pokefull of pence. **1581** J. BELL *Haddon's Answ. Osor.* 125 b, As farre dissentyng from the purpose of this Prophecie, as if he were demaunded the way to Canterbury, he might aunswere, a poake full of Plummes.

‖poke-'loken, poke'logan. *U.S.* [a. Odjibwa *pokenogun.*] (See quots.)

1848 THOREAU *Maine W.* (1894) 68 Now and then we passed what McCauslin called a pokelogan, an Indian term for what the drivers might have reason to call a poke-logs-in, an inlet that leads nowhere. *Ibid.* 132. **1855** HALIBURTON *Nat. & Hum. Nat.* II. 404 A poke-loken is a marshy place or stagnant pool connected with a river. **1872** DE VERE *Americanisms* 20 The term pokeloken, an Indian term, signifying 'marsh',..is still largely used by the lumbermen in Maine, and..in the Northwest.

pokemantie, variant of POCKMANTEAU.

'poke-,pudding. Also (*Sc.*) 9 pock-pudding, *contr.* 8–9 pock-pud. [f. POKE *sb.*[1] + PUDDING.]

1. A pudding made in a poke or bag, a bag-pudding. Now *Sc.* and *dial.*

1552 HULOET, Poke puddynge, *maza, farrata.* **1802** SIBBALD *Chron. Sc. Poetry* Gloss., *Pok-puds*, bag-puddings, dumplings. **1825** JAMIESON, Pock-pudding.

2. *Sc.* Applied contemptuously to a corpulent or gluttonous person; an opprobrious designation in Scotland for an Englishman. Now *humorous.*

c **1730** BURT *Lett. N. Scotl.* (1754) I. vi. 138 My Country-men..all over Scotland, are dignified with the Title of Poke Pudding, which, according to the Sense of the Word among the Natives, signifies a Glutton. *a* **1776** in Herd *Sc. Songs* I. 118 They'll fright the fuds of the Pockpuds, For mony a buttock bare's coming. **1816** SCOTT *Old Mort.* xx, 'We maun gar wheat-flour serve us for a blink', said Niel,..'the Englishers live amaist upon't; but, to be sure, the pock-puddings ken nae better'. **1827** —— *Diary* 20 Dec., Anent the copyrights—the pockpuds were not frightened by our high price. **1870** RAMSAY *Remin.* vi. (ed. 18) 228 A set o' ignorant pock-puddings. **1885** MORRIS in Mackail *Life* (1899) II. 143 Whether pock-pudding prejudice or not, I can't bring myself to love that country [Scotland].

3. A local name of the Long-tailed Titmouse.

1856 *Eng. Cycl. Nat. Hist.* IV. 203 This is the Poke Pudding, Huckmuck, and Mum-Ruffin of the English. **1885** SWAINSON *Prov. Names Birds* 32 (British Long-tailed Titmouse) Poke pudding or Poke bag (Gloucestershire; Salop). Pudding bag (Norfolk).

poker ('pəʊkə(r)), *sb.*[1] [f. POKE *v.*[1] + -ER[1].]

1. a. An instrument for poking or stirring a fire, consisting of a stiff metal rod, one end of which is fitted with or formed into a handle. *Jew's poker*: see quot. 1899.

1534 in W. H. Turner *Select. Rec. Oxford* (1880) 126 He ..came downe with a poker in his hande. **1714** ADDISON *Spect.* No. 608 ¶13 By her good Will she never would suffer the Poker out of her Hand. **1800** MRS. HERVEY *Mourtray Fam.* I. 70 The men say she is as stiff as a poker; and the women are afraid of her, she is so proud and prudish. **1829** LYTTON *Disowned* xviii, The ancient domestic..came, poker in hand, to his assistance. **1844** LD. BROUGHAM *A. Lunel* III. vi. 176 Of a stiffness so perfect that part of his toilette seemed to be swallowing a poker. **1899** R. WHITEING *No. 5 John St.* xix, A Jew's Poker is a Christian person who attends to Jewish fires on the Sabbath day.

b. *fig.* (in allusion to its proverbial stiffness): A person with a rigid stiff carriage or manner.

1812 MISS MITFORD in L'Estrange *Life* (1870) I. 184, I dare say our new cousin is just such a poker as Lord Selkirk, with an iron head and an iron heart. **1838** LADY GRANVILLE *Lett.* 14 July, He..would be very handsome if he would not stoop..Liz is a poker in comparison.

†2. = *poking-stick*: see POKING *vbl. sb.* 2. *Obs.*

1604 DEKKER *Honest Wh.* Wks. 1873 II. 25 Where's my ruffe and poker, you block-head? **1606** HEYWOOD *2nd Pt. If you know not me* I. Wks. 1874 I. 258 Now, your Puritans poker is not so huge, but somewhat longer; a long slender poking-sticke is the all in all with your Suffolke Puritane.

3. In various transferred uses. **a.** (See quot.)

1823 CRABB *Technol. Dict.*, *Poker*..or *driver*, an iron instrument, of various lengths and sizes, used for driving hoops on masts. It has a flat foot at one end, and a round knob at the other.

b. *humorous.* The staff or rod of office carried by a verger, bedell, etc.

1844 [implied in *poker-bearer*: see 9]. **1905** H. S. HOLLAND *Personal Stud.* ix. *Westcott* 130 Under the haughty contempt of the solitary verger [in Peterborough Cathedral], who had been forced to lend the authority of his 'poker' to those undignified and newfangled efforts.

c. *University slang.* One of the university bedells at Oxford and Cambridge, who carry staves or maces ('pokers') before the Vice-Chancellor.

1841 *Rime of New-Made Baccalere* (Farmer), Heads of Houses in a row, And Deans and College Dons below, With a Poker or two behind. **1867** *London Society* XII. 347 We attended duly at St. Mary's to see the vice-chancellor, doctors, proctors, 'pokers', &c. in their robes of state. **1897** *Jowett's Life & Lett.* II. viii. 226 There was a great procession, the Chancellor in black and gold, Doctors in scarlet gowns, the Vice-Chancellor with pokers.

4. *red-hot poker*, a popular name of species of *Tritoma* (or *Kniphofia*), South African liliaceous plants, bearing elongated spikes of scarlet or yellow flowers; called also *flame-flower* (FLAME *sb.* 10).

1884 MILLER *Plant-n.*, Red-hot-poker-plant. **1899** *Pall Mall G.* 11 Oct. 2/2 The clustered sunflowers and 'red-hot pokers', most gorgeous of September's old-fashioned blooms. **1902** CORNISH *Naturalist Thames* 179 Scarlet tritomas (red-hot pokers) look splendid among the deep greens of the summer grass.

5. The implement with which poker-work is done; hence, short for POKER-WORK. Also *attrib.*

1827 *Seaham Par. Reg.*, A drawing in poker, by him, of the Salvator Mundi, after Carlo Dolci. **1854** [see *poker-picture* in 9]. *c* **1900** W. D. THOMPSON *Poker Work* 10 The pokers were anything, from a knitting needle to an iron rod ⅜ in. thick, and were bound with yarn or other material to protect the hands from being burnt, and to enable the worker to obtain a firmer grip of the implement. *Ibid.* 17 The 'Pyro'.. is another development in Poker machines which.. does away with the spirit-lamp. *Ibid.* 24 Poker artists will find it convenient to be in possession of the principal manufacturer's list of Poker materials. *c* **1900** —— *Instruct. 'Pyro' Poker Machine*, Before starting any piece of work it is wise to become familiar with the lighting and working of the poker.

6. a. A person who pokes; *esp.* one who pokes or pries into things.

1608 ARMIN *Nest Ninn.* (1880) 50 Now our Philosophical Poker pokte on, and poynted to a strange shew. **1741** RICHARDSON *Pamela* (1824) I. xxxix. 359 Such thoughtful *futurity pokers* as I am!

b. = FUCKER. *slang.*

1879–80 *Pearl* (1970) 214 I've been told by jokers That the ladies they do all agree that he's the prince of pokers.

c. *Cricket.* A batsman who 'pokes' (POKE *v.*[1] 4 b).

1888 A. G. STEEL in Steel & Lyttelton *Cricket* iii. 143 But to the poker, the man who refuses to do anything but stick his bat in front of the wicket.. the high-dropping full-pitch is an excellent ball.

7. Phrase. ***by the holy poker.*** A humorous asseveration, of Irish origin and uncertain meaning.

1804 MAR. EDGEWORTH *Limerick Gloves* ii, 'By the holy poker', said he to himself, 'the old fellow now is out there'. **1828** *Lancet* 23 Feb. 773/2 He swears by the 'holy poker' and 'St. Patrick', that he will never again go to St. Bartholomew's. **1890** 'R. BOLDREWOOD' *Col. Reformer* (1891) 134 By the holy poker, sir,.. you've just hit it there.

8. = POKE *sb.*[3] 2. *rare.*

1805 T. B. HAZARD *Nailer Tom's Diary* (1930) 260/2 Put Poker on one of my oxen.

9. *attrib.* and *Comb.*, as ***poker-arm***; ***poker-backed***, ***poker-like***, ***-stiff***, ***-straight*** adjs.; **poker back**, (*a*) a perfectly straight back; (*b*) *Path.* (see quot. 1973); **poker-bearer**, a mace-bearer, a University bedell; **poker-drawing**, **poker-painting** = POKER-WORK; **poker-picture**, a picture made by poker-work; **poker spine** *Path.* = *poker back* (*b*) above; **poker-style**, the style of poker-work. (See also sense 5.)

1890 *Scots Observer* 25 Jan. 267/2 Mannerisms noticed thirty years ago on St. Andrews Links.. Alexander Hill's tip-toe eccentricities, and Mill's *poker-arm, imbecile, pushing motion! **1931** M. ALLINGHAM *Look to Lady* xxvi. 276 A single slim aristocratic figure, with the unmistakable *poker back of the old regime. **1960** H. EDWARDS *Spirit Healing* x. 87 The healing of certain troubles, as with poker-back spines. **1973** TAYLOR & COTTON *Short Textbk. Surg.* (ed. 2) xl. 539 [In ankylosing spondylitis] the normal spine curvatures become replaced by a single kyphosis, occasionally so acutely angled that the patient's back becomes horizontal (poker back). **1885** *Fortnight in Waggonette* 6 To assume his usual *poker-backed style of seat. **1898** *Pall Mall G.* 9 Mar. 2/2 The journal.. assumes its most poker-backed 'we-told-you-so' attitude. **1844** J. T. HEWLETT *Parsons & W.* ix, From vice-chancellor down to vice-chancellor's *poker-bearer. **1895** *Westm. Gaz.* 13 Aug. 3/3 'Black Rod',.. carrying a three-cornered hat in one hand, and a short gilt-headed *poker-like stick gracefully poised in the other. **1895** CLARA H. STEVENS in *Proc. 14th Conv. Amer. Instr. Deaf* 365 The art of *poker-painting has had more attention in England than elsewhere. **1854** FAIRHOLT *Dict. Terms Arts*, **Poker-pictures*, imitations of pictures or rather of bister-washed drawings executed by singeing the surface of white wood with a heated poker, such as used in Italian irons. **1917** *Brit. Med. Jrnl.* 30 June 860/1 Dr. John Drummond (Liverpool) asks for suggestions as to treatment in a case of *poker spine in a man 30 years of age. .. The back is now immobile. **1960** S. PLATH *Colossus* (1967) 27 Rigged *poker-stiff on her back. **1962** 'K. ORVIS' *Damned & Destroyed* xi. 77 Frankie's back was poker-stiff. **1966** J. S. COX *Illustr. Dict. Hairdressing* 119/1 **Poker straight*, without a vestige of curl. **1979** N. FREELING *Widow* ii. 3 The hair was poker-straight. **1887** MORRIS in Mackail *Life* (1899) II. 183 Some decoration that she was doing in the *poker-style, burning the pattern in.

ˈpoker, *sb.*[2] Now *U.S. colloq.* Also 7 pocar. [perh. from Norse; corr. to Da. *pokker*, Swed. *pocker* the devil. Cf. also PUCK, POOK.] A hobgoblin, bugbear, demon. ***Old Poker***, the devil.

[**1598**: see HODGE-POKER.] **1601** DENT *Pathw. Heaven* 109 Euen as a mother, when her childe is wayward,.. scareth it with some pocar, or bull-begger, to make it cling more vnto her and be quiet. **1784** H. WALPOLE *Let. to Hon. H. S. Conway* 5 May, The very leaves on the horse-chesnuts.. cling to the bough as if old poker was coming to take them away. **1828** WEBSTER, *Poker*, any frightful object, especially in the dark; a bugbear; a word in common popular use in America.

†**ˈpoker**, *sb.*[3] *dial. Obs.* [f. POKE *sb.*[1] sack + -ER[1].] (See quot.)

a **1700** B. E. *Dict. Cant. Crew*, *Poker*, one that conveys Coals (at Newcastle) in Sacks, on Horseback.

ˈpoker, *sb.*[4] Chiefly *U.S.* [Origin uncertain. Cf. Ger. *poch*, also *poche*, *pochen*, *pochspiel*, a similar bluffing card-game of considerable age, f. *pochen* to boast, brag, lit. to knock, rap.] **a.** A card game, popular in America, a variety of BRAG, played by two or more persons, each of whom, if not bluffed into declaring his hand, bets on the value of it, the player who holds the highest combination of cards as recognized in the game winning the pool. Also *fig.*

1836 J. HILDRETH *Campaigns Rocky Mts.* I. xv. 128 The M— lost some cool hundreds last night at poker. **1842** *Knickerbocker* XX. 305 Squeezing a great deal of boisterous amusement out of a game of 'poker'. [**1855** GEO. ELIOT in Cross *Life* (1885) I. 356 One night we attempted 'Brag' or 'Pocher'.] **1856** MRS. S. T. L. ROBINSON *Kansas* 156 Jones and others came in at night and 'played poker at twenty-five cents ante'. **1856** G. D. BREWERTON *War in Kansas* 354 He could cheat his companion at a 'friendly game of poker', and shoot him afterwards.. with as little remorse. **1869** O. W. HOLMES *Old Vol. of Life, Cinders from Ashes* (1891) 255 Do the theological professors take a hand at all-fours or poker on week-days? **1894** S. FISKE *Holiday Stories* (1900) 169 Poker, they call it ashore; but, as gambling is not allowed on government vessels, it becomes whist at sea. **1978** *Time* 3 July 42/3 The Justice Department was in no mood to be bluffed, even by troubled steelmakers, and talks dragged on and on in a months-long game of high-stakes political poker.

b. *attrib.* and *Comb.*, as ***poker-deck***, ***-game***, ***hand***, ***-player***, ***table***; **poker chip**, a chip [CHIP *sb.*[1] 2 d] used as a stake in poker; **poker dice**, (*a*) dice with the representation of a playing card on at least two of their faces; (*b*) a dice game, played with either poker or regular dice, in which the thrower aims for combinations which would constitute a winning hand in poker; **poker face**, an inscrutable face appropriate to a poker-player; a face in which a person's thoughts or feelings are not revealed; also, a person with such a face; hence as *v. trans.* (*rare*$^{-1}$) to regard with a poker-face; **poker-faced** *a.* (cf. PO-FACED *a.*); **poker machine** *Austral.*, a type of 'one-armed bandit' bearing card symbols; **poker patience**, a form of competitive patience the object of which is to form winning poker combinations in each row and column; **poker school**, a group of people meeting to play poker.

1879 *News & Press* (Cimarron, New Mexico) 20 Nov. 4/3 The toughest thing we have heard about any candidate in this section is that he got his *poker chips cashed after he 'experienced religion'. **1929** WODEHOUSE *Mr. Mulliner Speaking* iv. 122 At the end of five minutes, Osbert was mildly surprised to find himself in possession of a smoking-cap, three boxes of poker-chips, some polo sticks, [etc.]. **1973** E. PACE *Any War* (1974) III. 189 He heard.. no laughter, no rattle of poker chips. **1844** J. COWELL *Thirty Years among Players* 94 He was, apparently, quietly shuffling and cutting the *poker-deck for his own amusement. **1874** *Poker dice [see DIE *sb.*[1] 1 a]. **1901** *Game of Poker Dice* 1 The only Implements required are Sets of The Poker Dice and Cups, according to the number of players. **1926** E. HEMINGWAY *Sun also Rises* I. vi. 43 Harvey had won two hundred francs from me shaking poker dice. **1975** D. BLOODWORTH *Clients of Omega* x. 87 Poker dice, of course, man.. *Strip* poker. **1885** *Encycl. Brit.* XIX. 283/2 A good **poker face* is essential; the countenance should not betray the nature of the hand. **1919** G. A. MILLER *Prowling about Panama* xiii. 198 (*caption*) San Blas Indians have 'poker faces'. **1926** H. C. WITWER *Roughly Speaking* 243 His teeth clicked and he gave me a long, thoughtful look, but I poker-faced him and he went on plugging my [switch-]board. **1934** E. O'NEILL *Days without End* I. 20 His features automatically assume the meaninglessly affable expression which is the American business man's welcoming poker face. **1950** G. B. SHAW *Buoyant Billions* III. 28 Sunday clothes and poker faces. No peace, no joy. **1974** 'J. MELVILLE' *Nun's Castle* i. 21, I.. kept a poker-face. Inside, however, I was deeply distressed. **1976** P. DICKINSON *King & Joker* vii. 104, I hardly need say it to you, because you're such an old poker-face anyway, but.. you have to.. behave as though you are the only person who knows. **1923** *Nation* (N.Y.) 18 July 61 The picture of that *poker-faced gentleman placidly smoking a Pittsburg stogie. **1949** *Time* 12 Sept. 20/1 The poker-faced fellow was putting up a terrific fight. **1973** D. WESTHEIMER *Going Public* ix. 134 'We'd send them a letter, see,' said Margo poker-faced. 'Telling them how to commit suicide.' **1932** T. S. ELIOT *Sweeney Agonistes* 18 What about that *poker game? eh what Sam? What about that poker game in Bordeaux? **1957** *Times Lit. Suppl.* 13 Dec. 753/2 Ward politics, big poker-games, prostitution and murder. **1977** H. FAST *Immigrants* II. 97 He remembered such faces from poker games. **1935** *Encycl. Sports* 467/1 The object of the game [*sc.* poker patience] is so to place the cards as they are played that finally each row and each column will form a *poker hand. **1963** G. F. HERVEY *Handbk. Card Games* 231 There are nine possible poker hands at which to aim. **1974** *Encycl. Brit. Macropædia* XIV. 623/1 A poker hand consists of five cards. **1964** A. WYKES *Gambling* 330 Gamblers also managed to spend about $1,500,000 on '*poker machines' (a kind of slot machine that bears card symbols). **1973** *Sunday Mail* (Brisbane) 29 July 5/3 Canberra soon may be the first city in Australia to have poker machines in its hotels. **1976** *Daily Mirror* (Sydney) 14 Oct., Young poker-machine players should be given a warning about how much they could lose. **1912** 'SAKI' *Stampeding of Lady Bastable* in *Chronicles of Clovis* 55 He particularly wanted to teach the MacGregor boys.. *poker-patience. **1932** R. FRASER *Marriage in Heaven* III. ii. 292 The whole party joined in a game of poker-patience. **1972** A. CHRISTIE *Elephants can Remember* v. 78 They played picquet, and poker patience with each other. **1844** J. COWELL *Thirty Years passed among Players in England & Amer.* 94 The cabin was entirely cleared.. with the exception of one of the *poker players. **1912** M. NICHOLSON *Hoosier Chron.* 137 He had the reputation of being a poor poker player, but 'a good loser'. **1963** G. F. HERVEY *Handbk. Card Games* 237 Experienced poker players often say that what counts is not so much what they win as what the other players lose. **1882** *N. York Times* 11 Mar., *Poker-playing was carried to England in the old packet-ships. **1872** C. KING *Mountain. Sierra Nev.* xiv. 285 They shoved the jury into a commodious *poker-room, where were seats grouped about neat, green tables. **1949** J. R. COLE *It was so Late* 91 Men from the camp.. make up a *poker school. **1968** E. MCGIRR *Lead-Lined Coffin* iii. 129 Pope joined one of the large poker schools. **1977** A. C. H. SMITH *Jericho Gun* xi. 139 'Sorry to bust up the poker school.'.. 'I don't mind... I was two pounds ahead.' *a* **1861** T. WINTHROP *John Brent* (1862) 295 He sot his white head down to the *poker-table, and stuck thar. **1930** J. DOS PASSOS *42nd Parallel* VII. 94 Pokertables piled with new silver dollars. **1977** *Times* 29 Aug. 6/2 Batesy was an old hand at marshalling her clients, bringing together seven to make up a full poker table.

poker, *sb.*[5], a kind of duck: see POCHARD.

ˈpoker, *v.* [f. POKER *sb.*[1]]

1. *trans.* **a.** To use a poker to; to poke, stir, or strike with a poker. **b.** ***poker up***: To stiffen up, or make as stiff as a poker. *nonce-uses.*

1787 MME. D'ARBLAY *Diary* 19 June, I thought you had been too good-natured.. to poker the people in the King's-house! **1806–7** J. BERESFORD *Miseries Hum. Life* (1826) xx. xxv. 254 Portraits.. of your host's family all pinched and pokered up in the incredible costumes of their several centuries.

2. To draw in or adorn with poker-work.

1897 *Daily News* 2 June 5/2 The Duchess.. had executed several kid sachets in pokerwork, and her daughter, Princess Alice of Albany, had pokered a wooden stand. *c* **1900** W. D. THOMPSON *Poker Work* 12 Illustration of various articles which have been pokered by accomplished designers and artists.

3. *trans.* Of a verger, etc.: to escort (a church dignitary) ceremoniously. Cf. POKER *sb.*[1] 3 b.

1924 C. LANG *Let.* in R. C. D. Jasper *G. Bell, Bishop of Chichester* (1967) iii. 36, I shall feel more free to laugh when I see you clothed in apron and gaiters and being pokered at Canterbury. **1975** *Theology* LXXV. 260 Hamling was also verger, and did all the old establishment things like pokering the preacher to the pulpit, and generally gave the services tone.

Hence **ˈpokering** *vbl. sb.* (also *attrib.*).

1880 LOMAS *Alkali Trade* 21 In.. the 'front' plate, are placed.. the working door, pokering door, and means for getting at the grates.

ˈpokerish, *a.*[1] [f. POKER *sb.*[1] + -ISH[1].] Inclined to be 'stiff as a poker', esp. in manner. Hence **ˈpokerishly** *adv.*, **ˈpokerishness**.

1848 HAWTHORNE in *Life Longfellow* (1891) II. i. 36 A man of thought and originality, with a certain iron-pokerishness, an uncompromising stiffness in his mental character. **1867** MISS BROUGHTON *Cometh Up as Flower* xxxvi, 'I am afraid I'm interrupting a pleasant tête-à-tête!' says the old lady, pokerishly. **1880** *Argosy* XXIX. 230, 'I regret to have lost it', I said, stiff to pokerishness. **1888** *Century Mag.* May 35/1 Ella called her 'stiff and pokerish'.

ˈpokerish, *a.*[2] *U.S. colloq.* [f. POKER *sb.*[2] + -ISH[1].] Fraught with a kind of mysterious dread; ghostly, uncanny.

1827 *Massachusetts Spy* 21 Nov. (Th.), A patriarchal ram, who would fight anything but a pokerish looking ducking gun. **1833** H. BARNARD in *Maryland Hist. Mag.* (1918) XIII. 352, I feel quite pokerish in this region. **1835** WILLIS *Pencillings* II. xli. 28 A pokerish-looking dwarf. **1853** LOWELL *Moosehead Jrnl.* Prose Wks. 1890 I. 36 There is something pokerish about a deserted dwelling, even in broad daylight. **1871** MRS. STOWE *My Wife & I* viii, It was a lonesome and pokerish operation to dismantle the room that had long been my home. **1874** B. TAYLOR *Prophet* IV. vi, A pokerish place! There's something in the air Breeds thoughts of murder.

ˈpoker-work. [f. POKER *sb.*[1] + WORK *sb.*] Artistic work done by burning a design on the surface of white wood with a heated pointed implement. Also *fig.* Hence **poker-worked** *a.* (in example applied to a design resembling poker-work).

Originally, a pointed poker was used, later the 'heater' of an Italian iron (see quot. for *poker-picture* s.v. POKER[1] 9), etc.; now done with a special apparatus the essential feature of which is a platinum point or pointer kept continuously hot for the purpose.

1813 J. FORSYTH *Remarks Excursion Italy* 91 *note*, The process called cestrotum was, in my opinion, nothing but poker-work. **1892** EL. ROWE *Chip-carving* (1895) 37 Ready-made objects, such as are sold for painting or poker work. **1894** *Daily News* 2 May 8/4 There is a cedar-lined escritoire in deep poker work, a really beautiful piece of furniture. **1914** [see GEORGIANISM]. **1929** E. BOWEN *Last September* ix. 104 Cushions.. with poker-worked kittens. **1942** C. BARRETT *On Wallaby* x. 193 He.. does poker-work with red-hot wire, finishing off with tiny colour sketches. **1958** L. DURRELL *Balthazar* v. 104 He has had an immense and vivid firescreen made for the flat.. in poker-work. **1966** *Listener* 29 Dec. 959/2 The play relapses into what it looked as if it was going to satirize. By the end we are left with a stuffy, inhibiting piece of Victorian poker-work as a message. **1973** *Times* 31 July 14/8 She remembered well the famous Breton school of artists at Pont-Aven which included Gauguin. He made her a pair of 'sabots' in poker work. **1977** *Listener* 11 Aug. 171/3 An element of family creativity here, not too dissimilar to the Victorian samplers and poker-work.

pokey[1] ('pəʊkɪ). *slang* (chiefly *U.S.*). Also **poky**. [Alteration of POGEY, prob. infl. by POKY *a.*[1]] Prison, gaol.

1919 C. H. DARLING *Jargon Book* 26 *Pokey*, a jail. **1929** D. RUNYON in *Hearst's International* Aug. 73/2 He hears riding rum is illegal and may land a guy in the pokey. **1947** *Daily Progress* (Charlottesville, Virginia) 24 June 6/2 They gave the police a list of the phone numbers to call if it became necessary to turn any of the old grads in the direction of the pokey. **1955** 'S. RANSOME' *Deadly Bedfellows* viii. 70 Instead of thanking him, you've threatened to throw us both into the pokey. **1957** M. MILLAR *Soft Talkers* 151 This isn't the Royal York Hotel, but it's better than a cell in the local pokey. **1965** 'D. SHANNON' *Death-Bringers* (1966) iv. 50, I find that our star sleuth.. has.. carted him off to the pokey. **1974** *Maclean's* (Toronto) Dec. 30/2 A number of revered figures sat out the Depression in the poky, because they fiddled with other people's money. **1976** *National Observer* (U.S.) 29 May 18/4 Were it possible to prosecute an actor for stealing scenes, *The Missouri Breaks* (United Artists) would land Marlon Brando in the pokey for life.

pokey[2], **pokie**. *Austral.* [Familiar corruption of POKER *sb.*[4]] = *poker machine* s.v. POKER *sb.*[4] b.

1967 D. HORNE *Southern Exposure* 44 In the clubs of Sydney the poker machines ('the pokies') stand up in dozens and more beer flows than in a hotel. **1968** *TV Times* (Brisbane) 27 Nov. 6/2 In his unmarried days Henderson was surefire meat for bandits (the one-armed type). 'Never play the pokies now,' he says. **1969** *Telegraph* (Brisbane) 4 Jan. 6/2 He bought a beer and walked over to the nearest 'pokey' with the change from a £5 ($10) note. He put this through the machine and tripled his money. **1969** *Australian* 24 May 40/3 He painted a glowing picture of Melbournites banking their money or investing it in homes while the degenerate New South Welshmen frittered away their cash on the pokeys. **1976** *Sydney Morning Herald* 23 Sept. (Advt.), Entertainment... There are pokies, casino, disco, movies.

poking ('pəʊkɪŋ), *vbl. sb.* [f. POKE *v.*[1] + -ING[1].]

1. a. The action of the vb. POKE: thrusting, pushing; projecting forward.

1582 STANYHURST *Æneis* II. (Arb.) 60 With the push and poaking of launce hee perceth his entrayls. **1811** L. M. HAWKINS *C'tess & Gertr.* (1812) I. 189 The poking, and a bad inclination of her left foot, he cared not for. **1902** H. S. MERRIMAN *Vultures* i, Mr. Mangles.. who carried his head in the manner.. known at a girls' school as 'poking'.

attrib. **1599** PORTER *Angry Wom. Abingd.* vii. (1903) 232 This poking fight of rapier and dagger will come up then. **1821** SCOTT *Kenilw.* xi, I helped Pinniewinks to sharpen his pincers and his poking-awl. **1855** CARLYLE *Misc.* IV. 345 Madam, I drilled him soundly with my poking-pole.

b. Sexual intercourse. *slang.*

1968 J. SANGSTER *Foreign Exchange* i. 16 'There's no law against poking,' I said. 'There is when you poke a fifteen-year-old,' he said. **1978** J. I. M. STEWART *Full Term* xvi. 181 He was petting her future mother in the heather long before she was born. And later.. another young hopeful went from petting to poking. **1979** L. MEYNELL *Hooky & Villainous Chauffeur* xiv. 187 Lover-boy is going to be busy (pounds before poking any day).

2. 'poking-stick (-iron). A rod used for stiffening the plaits of ruffs; originally of wood or bone, afterwards of steel so as to be applied hot. *Hist.*

1592 NASHE *P. Penilesse* Wks. (Grosart) II. 44 That sin-washing Poet that made the Ballet of Blue starch and poaking stick. **1602** MIDDLETON *Blurt, Master-Constable* III. iii. 106 Your ruff must stand in print; and for that purpose, get poking-sticks with fair long handles. ? **1606** ROWLANDS *Terrible Battell* (Hunter. Cl.) 12 The poking yron is too hot. **1611** SHAKS. *Wint. T.* IV. iv. 228 Pins, and poaking-stickes of steele. **1664** COTTON *Scarron.* I. 4 Her Needles, Poking-sticks, and Bodkins. **1869** MRS. PALLISER *Lace* xxii. 268 When the use of starch and poking-sticks had rendered the arrangement of a ruff easy, the size began rapidly to increase.

poking ('pəʊkɪŋ), *ppl. a.* [f. POKE *v.*[1] + -ING[2].]

1. Projecting; thrust forward: esp. of the head.

1799 *Hull Advertiser* 22 June 3/3 A repulsive kind of hat, which may be called the poking hat; it has a long projection, like the beak of a snipe. **1847** L. HUNT *Men, Women & B.* I. iv. 70 [The giraffes'] necks.. make a feeble-looking, obtuse angle, completely answering to the word 'poking'.

2. a. Of a person or his work: That pokes or potters; pottering, peddling; hence petty, mean. Of a place: Petty, in size or accommodation; confined, mean, shabby, insignificant. = POKY *a.*[1] 1 a, b.

1769 GRAY *Let. to Wharton* 22 June, I am never so angry, as when I hear my acquaintance wishing they had been bred to some poking profession, or employed in some office of drudgery. **1814** JANE AUSTEN *Mansf. Park* xii, That poking old woman, who knows no more of whist than of algebra. **1850** KINGSLEY *Alt. Locke* xxiv, I shall be shoved down into some poking little country-curacy. **1864** M. EYRE *Lady's Walks in S. France* viii. (1865) 94 A chapel, which we reached.. through a poking little room.

b. *Cricket.* With a batting style characterized by 'pokes' (POKE *sb.*[3] 1 c).

1836 *New Sporting Mag.* Oct. 360 A remarkably bad poking back player, with no hit in him at all. **1898** J. A. GIBBS *Cotswold Village* xi. 241 If only something could be done to.. rid us of that awful nuisance the poking, time-wasting batsman, there would be little improvement possible.

‖**pok-ta-pok** ('pɒkta'pɒk). Also **pok-a-tok**. [Maya.] The Maya name of the sacred ball game of Middle America, called TLACHTLI by the Aztecs, which was played on a court as a religious ritual. The object of the game was to knock a rubber ball through a stone ring, using only the hips, knees, and elbows.

1959 *Times* 27 Apr. (Rubber Industry Suppl.) p. v/1 The Mayan game of Pok ta Pok. *Ibid.* 8 June (Latin America Suppl.) p. iv/5 It is recorded that the early Spaniards found the Indians of Guatemala playing a curious game with a ball called *pok-ta-pok*, but in which the players used not their feet, head, or hands, but their posteriors. **1962** V. W. VON HAGEN *Ancient Sun Kingdoms of Americas* ix. 161 The passion of the Maya, and one that they shared with most Central American Indians, was the game of *pok-a-tok*, it was not unlike the modern basket-ball. **1963** C. GALLENKAMP *Maya* ii. 32 Every city had a ball court consisting of a playing-field enclosed by viewing platforms where spectators could watch a game called *tlaxtli* or *pok-ta-pok*. **1973** *Times* 27 Oct. 14/4 Maya life is illustrated by dozens of pottery figurines showing the killing of a deer, musicians, animals and the helmeted men of Lubaantun who are thought to be participants in the sacred ball-game *pok-ta-pok*.

poky ('pəʊkɪ), *a.*[1] Also **pokey**. [f. POKE *v.*[1] + -Y.]

1. a. Of a person, or his life or work: Pottering, peddling; taken up with petty matters or narrow interests: = POKING *ppl. a.* 2.

1853 LADY LYTTELTON *Let.* 20 Aug. in *Corr. Sarah Spencer* (1912) xvi. 413 All *I* want is to love *more*, and to smile *more*, and to be *more* amused and *more* merry, and less poky and morose and dry and grave! **1854** E. TWISLETON *Let.* 29 June (1928) xi. 213 A dreadfully stiff and pokey set of people. **1856** MRS. STOWE *Dred* iv, If religion is going to make me so poky, I shall put it off as long as I can. **1888** 'R. BOLDREWOOD' *Robbery under Arms* iii, I laughed at myself for being so soft as to choose a hard-working pokey kind of life. *Ibid.* xlvii, The people.. had lived a pokey life.. for many a year.

b. Of a place: Petty in size or accommodation; affording scanty room to stir; confined, mean, shabby: = POKING *ppl. a.* 2.

1849 ALB. SMITH *Pottleton Leg.* xx. 174 In a little poky cottage under the hill. **1860** J. WOLFF *Trav. & Adv.* I. iv. 87 Sent to a poky lodging-house in High Holborn. **1876** F. E. TROLLOPE *Charming Fellow* II. v. 74 It is monstrous to think of burying his talents in a poky little hole. **1894** JESSOPP *Random Roaming* i. 18 Chichester seemed to me.. a poky place. **1930** J. B. PRIESTLEY *Angel Pavement* v. 209 All this for less than it would cost to live in some dingy and dismal boarding-house or the pokiest of pokey flats. **1971** *Daily Tel.* 28 Sept. 2/5 A pokey, little, highly rented flat.

c. Of dress, etc.: Shabby, dowdy.

c **1854** THACKERAY *Wolves & Lamb* I, Why do you dress yourself in this odd poky way? **1855** —— *Newcomes* lvii, The ladies were in their pokiest old head-gear and most dingy gowns.

2. *Cricket.* Inclined to 'poke' when batting.

1888 A. G. STEEL in Steel & Lyttelton *Cricket* iii. 142 To the pokey, nervous style of batsman it [*sc.* the high-dropping full-pitch] is fraught with considerable uneasiness. **1891** W. G. GRACE *Cricket* 263 Against a poky batsman, on a sticky wicket, he has often as many opportunities as point of bringing off a smart catch.

Hence **'pokiness**.

1886 *Chicago Advance* 14 Jan. 18 He detected the pokiness of the entire household this morning.

poky, *a.*[2] and *sb. rare.* [f. POKE *sb.*[2] + -Y.] In *poky bonnet*, also *poky* sb. = POKE-BONNET.

1861 MRS. BROWNING *Lett., to Isa Blagden* (1897) II. 430 The nearest approach to a poky bonnet possible in this sinful generation. **1880** *Daily News* 2 July 5 A pleasing contrast to those oppressive times when inexorable custom compelled all to wear spoon-bills or pokeys or Leghorns.

‖**pol**[1]. *Obs. rare.* [L. *pol*, contracted from *Pollux*.] A form of asseveration. Cf. EDIPOL.

1596 NASHE *Saffron Walden* Ep. Ded., Wks. (Grosart) III. 8 By Poll and Aedipoll I protest. **1600** DEKKER *Shoemaker's Holiday* i. (1862) 9 Your pols and your edipols. **1609** *Ev. Woman in Hum.* v. i. in Bullen *O. Pl.* IV. 378 Hee has his pols, and his ædypols, his times and his tricks.

pol[2] (pɒl). *N. Amer.* Colloq. abbrev. of POLITICIAN.

1942 BERREY & VAN DEN BARK *Amer. Thes. Slang* §854/1 *Politician*,.. pol, polly, poly. **1965** F. KNEBEL *Night of Camp David* ii. 54 The clutter of pols and stale whisky glasses in the hotel suites. **1966** *Economist* 18 June 1315/2 Gossip has it that the 'pols', as the state's professional politicians (particularly Democrats) are called, felt guilty about the shabby treatment delivered to Mr Peabody when he was Governor [of Massachusetts]. **1972** *Time* 17 July 15/3 The young pols beat them at their own game. **1976** *Toronto Star* 14 Feb. B1/2 Can a bunch of battle-scarred old pols—including a couple of Liberal party retreads—gang up to stop a brash young lawyer named Brian Mulroney? **1978** J. CARROLL *Mortal Friends* II. ii. 139 What had he become? A two-bit pol, flashing about other people's corridors, waiting for his break?

pol, obs. form of POLL, POOL *sb.*[1]

POL: see P II.

Polab ('pəʊlɑːb). Also **Polabe**. [Slav., cf. Pol. *po* on, *Labe* Elbe.] **a.** A member of a Slavonic people once inhabiting the region around the lower Elbe. **b.** The West Slavonic language of this people, now extinct. Also *attrib.*

1882 *Encycl. Brit.* XIV. 347/2 The earlier inhabitants of Lauenburg were a Slavic tribe known by the name of Polabes. **1895** *Funk's Stand. Dict.*, *Polabian*,.. one of an ancient Slavic people dwelling on the lower Elbe, now wholly Germanized... *Polab*. **1911** *Encycl. Brit.* XXI. 902/1 *Polabs*,.. the Slavs.. who dwelt upon the Elbe and eastwards to the Oder. **1911** [see LECH, LEKH *sb.*[5] and *a.*]. **1934** [see LECHITIC *sb.* and *a.*]. **1974** *Encycl. Brit. Micropædia* VIII. 72/3 By the early 9th century the Polabs were organized into two confederations or principalities.

Polabian (pəʊ'leɪbɪən), *sb.* and *a.* [f. as prec. + -IAN.] **A.** *sb.* = prec. **B.** *adj.* Of or pertaining to the Polabs or their language.

1866 *Chambers's Encycl.* VIII. 767/1 The Polabians never attained any distinct political footing. **1888** [see LECHISH *sb.* and *a.*]. **1891** M. MÜLLER *Sci. Lang.* I. vii. 270 The Polabian dialect became gradually extinct at the beginning of the last century. **1911** *Encycl. Brit.* XXI. 902/1 Polabian agrees mostly with Polish and Kašube with its nasalized vowels and highly palatalized consonants. **1925** P. RADIN tr. *Vendryès's Language* 287 Polabian has been absorbed into German, as Cornish into English. **1929** [see LECH, LEKH *sb.*[5] and *a.*]. **1934** O. JESPERSEN *Language* vi. 117 The now extinct Polabian language. **1939–40**, **1950** [see LECHITIC *sb.* and *a.*]. **1955** R. JAKOBSON *Slavic Lang.* (ed. 2) 2 The last remnant of Polabian on the left bank of the lower Elbe.. died out toward the middle of the eighteenth century, but is known through a few vocabulary lists and short texts recorded about 1700. **1972** W. B. LOCKWOOD *Panorama Indo-European Lang.* 157 A diminutive islet of Elbe Slavonic or Polabian (*po* 'on', *Laba* 'Elbe') lingered on into the first decades of the eighteenth century. It was situated just west of the Elbe in the Lüneburg Wendland north of Salzwedel.

Polabish (pəʊ'lɑːbɪʃ), *sb.* Also **Polabisch**. [ad. G. *polabisch*.] = POLAB b.

1877 A. H. KEANE tr. *Hovelacque's Sci. of Lang.* 280 We may conclude this notice by mentioning the old dialects of the Elbe Slavonians, known by the name of *Polabish*, idioms now extinct, and whose scanty records, greatly affected by German influence, date from the seventeenth and beginning of the eighteenth century. **1890** W. R. MORFILL *Ess. on Importance of Study of Slavonic Lang.* 15 The extinct Polabish, a language once spoken on the Elbe.., was restored from some fragments by Schleicher. **1908** T. G. TUCKER *Introd. Nat. Hist. Lang.* 226 *Polabish*, once spoken by Slavs on the lower Elbe, is now extinct. **1955** *Trans. Philol. Soc.* 1954 87 Cornish and polabisch exist in a modern period but, for the present purpose, they naturally cannot rank as 'modern' since they are no longer spoken.

‖**polacca**[1] (pəʊ'lækə, ‖po'lakka). [It., orig. adj. fem. of *polacco* Polish, ad. Ger. *Polack*, a. Pol. *Polak* a Pole, a native of Poland.] A Polish dance, a polonaise; also the music for it. Also applied more widely to other music of a (supposed) Polish character. Also *attrib.* and in phr. ***alla polacca***.

1806 T. BUSBY *Dict. Mus.* (ed. 2) *Polacca*, a Polish movement of three crochets in a bar, chiefly characterised by its emphasis being laid on the fifth quaver of the bar. *c* **1807** W. CROTCH *Specimens Various Styles Music* I. 10 Some modern composers have given the title Polacca to movements which would sound very foreign to the ear of a Polander. **1812** J. M. WILLIAMS *Dramatic Censor* 41 Master Byrne and Miss Smith executed a *pas de deux* (a polacca) in the second act. **1813** *Sk. Character* (ed. 2) I. 222 Maria had brought home some new music, and was in the middle of a favorite Polacca, when Gifford entered. **1862** E. PAUER *Programme* 8 Mar., Polacca, Polonaise. A Polish dance in $\frac{3}{4}$ time; its character is strictly solemn and dignified, and must express chivalrous firmness, combined with grace. **1898** STAINER & BARRETT *Dict. Mus. Terms* s.v., In No. 3 of Handel's twelve grand concertos is a polonaise or polacca. **1954** *Grove's Dict. Mus.* (ed. 5) VI. 836/1 Polaccas may be defined as polonaises treated in a denationalized manner, but still retaining much of the rhythm characteristic of their Polish origin. *Ibid.* 836/2 Instrumental movements with the tempo indication *alla polacca* also occur. **1970** W. APEL *Harvard Dict. Mus.* 683/2 The 'Polacca' in Bach's Brandenburg Concerto no. 1 shows hardly any affinity to the polonaise. **1975** *Gramophone* July 174/2 In the finale with its polacca rhythms, and particularly in the obviously Slavonic episodes.., the Broadwood does increasingly suggest a Hungarian cymbalom.

polacca[2]: see POLACRE.

Polack ('pəʊlək, 'pəʊlæk, 'pəʊlɑːk), *sb.* (*a.*) Also 6–7 **Polake**, 7 **Polaque**, **-eak**, **-ach**, (9 **-ak**) 9 **Pollack**, **Pullack** and with lower-case initial. [a. Pol. *Polak* a Pole; Ger. *Polack*, F. *Polaque*.]

A. *sb.* **1.** A native or inhabitant of Poland; a Pole; in quot. 1609, the king of Poland. So †**'Polaker** *Obs. rare.*

1574 SIDNEY *Let.* 27 Nov. in *Wks.* (1968) III. 99 The Polakes hartily repente their so fur fetcht election. **1599** SANDYS *Europæ Spec.* (1632) 192 Then for his Catholikes the Polakers, they clearly slip collar. **1601** R. JOHNSON *Kingd. & Commw.* 127 The last of these fower vertues the Polacks want, that is, celeritie. **1602** SHAKS. *Ham.* II. ii. 63. **1609** MIDDLETON *Sir R. Shirley* Wks. (Bullen) VIII. 307 He was received with great magnificence.. both of the Polack himself and of his people. **1657** *North's Plutarch, Add. Lives* (1676) 80 *margin*, The Moscovites discomfited by the Polacks in the battle of Orsa. **1895** *Funk's Stand. Dict.*, *Polack*, same as *Pole*. **1922** M. F. LIDDELL in *Contemp. Rev.* Dec. 770 Danzig fears and hates the 'Polacks' and still more the French. **1933** S. K. PADOVER *Let Day Perish* 140 You cowardly little sneak! It's craven pups like you that make the Polacks trample on us! If we Jews would learn to.. kill.. like they do, the—Polacks would grovel at our feet—!

2. A Jew from Poland.

1834 *Manch. Old Hebrew Congregation Acct. Bk.* in B. Williams *Making of Manchester Jewry* (1976) iii. 71 Given him the Polack for leaving Town 8/6. **1892** [see LITVAK]. **1909** *Cent. Dict.* (Suppl.) *Polack*, a name given to the Jews of the Polish provinces, by their Lithuanian co-religionists. **1971** M. A. SHULVASS *From East to West* i. 23 It is hard to arrive at any accurate estimate of the numbers of Jews who emigrated westward in this period... The strongest indication that they came in considerable numbers is the fact that the nickname Pollack was current both in the Germanies and in the Hapsburg monarchy. *Ibid.* iv. 111 Following the great influx of *Betteljuden* from Poland to the

West, the nickname Pollack assumed a more derogatory connotation than ever before.

3. *N. Amer.* A (usu. disparaging) term for a Polish immigrant or person of Polish descent.

1898 F. P. Dunne *Mr. Dooley in Peace & War* 234 'Well,' said Mr. Dooley, 'ye'er thoughts on this subject is inthrestin', but not conclusive, as Dorsey said to th' Pollack, that thought he cud lick him.' **1900** *Congress. Rec.* 7 Feb. 1625/2, I have some Polacks in my district, and..the blood of Pulaski, the brave Pole who fell at Savannah in the defense of American liberty, has never been avenged. **1905** [see cold *a.* 1 c]. **1922** E. E. Cummings *Enormous Room* iv. 61 Get out of the way you damn Polak! **1935** W. Saroyan *Daring Young Man* 108 All that mattered was this moment, Wolinsky in love, alive, walking down Ventura Avenue, in America, Wolinsky of the universe, the crazy Polak with the broken nose. **1944** *Sun* (Baltimore) 2 Aug. 2/3 'You know, I sure did hate to shoot him,' said the sergeant, 'Because he might have been a Polack, but he wouldn't stop.' **1952** F. L. Allen *Big Change* iii. 53 They were scornfully known as Dagoes, Polacks, Hunkies, Kikes. **1965** P. De Vries *Let me count Ways* vii. 101, I now recognized him as a blond Polak I had seen around town. **1971** [see hunk *sb.*[3]]. **1976** *National Observer* (U.S.) 26 June 1/3 The Crusher's a clean-living Polack from Milwaukee who don't truck with no drugs or bad women.

B. *adj.* Polish. Also, of Polish origin or descent.

1602 Shakes. *Hamlet* v. ii. 388 You from the Polake warres, and you from England Are heere arriued. **1831** Carlyle *Sart. Res.* iii. xii, Any soldier, were he but a Polack Scytheman, shall be welcome. **1928** [see fly *v.*[1] 5 a]. **1930** [see bohunk]. **1966** E. V. Cunningham *Helen* iv. 45 You're some cheap Polack hooker that was tossed out of a parochial school fer diddling little boys. **1974** L. Deighton *Spy Story* xix. 199 Any sign of that goddamn Polack sub?

polacre (pəʊˈlɑːkə(r)), **polacca**[2] (pəʊˈlækə). Forms: α. 7, 9 pollacre, 9 poleacre, 8– polacre. β. 7 polacra, 8 polacco, 8– polacca. γ. 7 polach, pollacke, 7–8 polaque. [In α and γ forms a. F. *polacre, polaque* = It. *polac(c)ra, polacca*, whence directly the β forms. So Sp. *polacra*, Pg. *polacra, -aca, polharca*; Du. *polaak*, Ger. *polack(e, -er*. Origin uncertain; F. *polacre, polaque*, It. *polacca*, Ger. *polacke*, mean also Polish, Pole; but it is difficult to understand how a Levantine or Mediterranean vessel should be so described.]

A three-masted merchant vessel of the Mediterranean. See quot. 1769–76 in α.

α. **1625** Purchas *Pilgrims* II. vi. 885 Here our Admirall had hyred a Pollacre about the burden of one hundred and twentie tunne. **1755** *Acts Gen. Assemb. Georgia* (1881) 53 All Masters of Vessells..shall pay into the Public Treasury..for every Snow Brig Polacre or Sactia Twenty Two shillings and Six pence. **1764** Smollett *Trav.* (1766) I. 222 The harbour..is generally full of tartanes, polacres, and other small vessels, that come from Sardinia, Ivica, Italy, and Spain, loaded with salt, wine, and other commodities. **1769–76** Falconer *Dict. Marine, Polacre*, a ship with three masts, usually navigated in the Levant, and other parts of the Mediterranean..generally furnished with square sails upon the main-mast, and *lateen* sails upon the fore-mast and mizen-mast. Some of them however carry square sails upon all the three masts, particularly those of Provence in France. Each [mast] is commonly formed of one piece, so that they have neither top-mast nor top-gallant-mast. **1820** J. W. Croker in *C. Papers* 1 Sept., She had two lieutenants of the English Navy with her in the polacre. **1889** Clark Russell *Marooned* (1890) 223 The high sterned pollacre..is riding within musket-shot of the beach.

β. **1628** Digby *Voy. Medit.* (1868) 36 Wee descryed a vessell (which wee made for a polacra) plying vp to windeward. **1794** Nelson 6 Feb. in Nicolas *Disp.* (1845) I. 350 Burned four polaccas loaded with wine for the French Ships at Fiorenzo. **1817** Byron *Beppo* xcv, He hired a vessel come from Spain, Bound for Corfu; she was a fine polacca, Mann'd with twelve hands and laden with tobacco.

γ. **1668** *Lond. Gaz.* No. 316/1 At his departure from Alexandria, there entred a French Polach. **1675** *Ibid.* No. 1024/1 All their Men of War are in Port, save a Pollacke, which is got out, and gone *in Corso*. **1687** A. Lovell tr. *Thevenot's Trav.* i. 228 On Wednesday..a Polaque fell in among us,..running foul of our Sanbiquer.

b. *attrib.* and *Comb.*

1745 *Gentl. Mag.* 695 A Spanish polacco ship. **1780** Capt. Knowles in *Naval Chron.* II. 518 They were two..Xebec ships, polacre rigged. **1801** *Ibid.* VI. 412 The Neapolitan polacre brig *Madona de Laure*. **1846** Raikes *Life of Brenton* 301 We gave chase to a polacre ship.

polaile, variant of pullaile *Obs.*, poultry.

†**polaine.** *Obs.* Also 6 pulleyne. See quots.

1582 in *Archæol. Æliana* XVI. 209 Foure threave of hempe and pulleyne iiijs. **1631** *New Hampshire Prov. Papers* (1867) I. 63, 4 pieces of polaines ffor sailes ffor shallops, at 25s per piece,..1 quoile of cordage.

polaly, variant of pullayly *Obs.*, poultry.

†**Polan.** *Obs.* [a. OF. *poul(a)in* Polish, a Pole.] A Pole, a native of Poland.

1502 in Ellis *Orig. Lett.* Ser. i. I. 50 The Hungaries, Boyams, and the Polans. **1604** T. Wright *Passions* i. x. 44, I might discourse over..Italians, Polans, Germanes.

polan, var. polayn *Obs.*, knee-armour.

†**poˈlancre.** *Naut. Obs.* Also pollankre. [Related to F. *palanc* (16th c. in Littré), now *palan*, a combination of two pulleys connected by a rope: cf. *palanquer* to hoist with tackle; also It. *palanga* a hoisting or raising apparatus, a lever, a roller, L. *p(h)alanga* a carrying pole, a roller on which a heavy body is rolled, Gr. φάλαγξ a round piece of wood, a trunk, block, log, pole.

(Fr. has also *palancre, palangre*, of the same origin, in the sense of a stout buoyed fishing-rope to which a series of lines are attached bearing the hooks.)]

A kind of pulley or tackle for hoisting heavy articles.

1485 *Naval Acc. Hen. VII* (1896) 47 Swyftyng takles..xj, pollankres..vj. *Ibid.* 75. **1485** *State Papers, Chapter Ho. Bk.* VII, Polancres with shivers of brasse. **1514** *Inv. Stores Henry Grace à Dieu*, Poleancres with shivers of wood, poleancres with shivers of brasse.

Poland[1] (ˈpəʊlənd). Also 6–7 **Poleland.** [f. Pole *sb.*[4] + land *sb.*[1] (or perh. ad. Ger. *Polen*, MHG. *Polân*, with ending assimilated to *land*).] A country of E. Europe; hence short for *Poland oats* or *wheat*, *Poland fowl*.

1564 *Brief Exam.* D iv, O woulde to God the state of the Churches of..Poleland were brought to this poynte. **1605** Camden *Rem.* (1637) 17 The Bridges of Poleland. **1812** *Examiner* 4 May 282/1 Oats 53s...57s. od. Polands 58s., 59s. od. **1849** D. J. Browne *Amer. Poultry Yd.* (1858) 56 The newly-hatched chicks are grey, much resembling those of the silver Polands.

b. *attrib.* and *Comb.*, as ***Poland breed, oat***; **Poland fowl**, one of a breed of domestic fowls, having black plumage and a white topknot; **Poland manna**: see manna[1] 6; **Poland wheat**, white cone wheat (*Triticum polonicum*).

1840 *Penny Cycl.* XVIII. 476/2 The *Poland breed, which is black-feathered, with white topknots, lays well. **1830** 'B. Moubray' *Dom. Poultry* (ed. 6) 15 The *Poland fowls, as they are generally called, were chiefly imported from Holland. **1764** *Museum Rust.* III. xxxv. 155 Most of my neighbours prefer the white *Poland oat. **1686** Plot *Staffordsh.* 342 White-Lammas, or *Poland-wheat.

Hence ˈ**Polander**, a native of Poland, a Pole (*obs.*); also a Poland fowl.

1601 R. Johnson *Kingd. & Commw.* 133 He [was]..inforced to leaue the whole possession of Liuonia to the Polander. **1796** H. Hunter tr. *St.-Pierre's Stud. Nat.* (1799) III. 450 You will not see..regiments formed of Russians, of Polanders, or of Venetians. **1830** 'B. Moubray' *Dom. Poultry* (ed. 6) 16 The Polanders..are one of the most useful varieties.

Poland[2]. The name of a town in Maine, U.S., used *attrib.* and *absol.* to designate the variety of mineral water obtained from springs there.

1881 J. G. Blaine *Let.* 6 Sept. in H. Ricker *Poland Mineral Spring Water* (1883) 37 Send two more cases Poland to the President [*sc.* Garfield]... The President will drink no other water. **1883** H. Ricker *Poland Spring, Maine* 18 The well-known effects following the use of Poland water were not discovered in a day. **1893** G. H. Haynes *State of Maine* 41 All parties are requested to examine the fine display of Poland Water..at this Columbian Exposition. **1917** H. Ricker *Poland Spring* Poland water can be obtained in dining-cars, transatlantic steamships and in the leading cities throughout Europe. **1937** *Maine: Guide 'Down East'* iii. 362 Poland Water is one of the few bottled waters that has continued to maintain a popularity. **1967** H. Johnson in C. Ray *Compleat Imbiber* IX. 148 Poland water is America's Perrier. It is not so fizzy but just as smart. **1968** J. Leasor *Passport for Pilgrim* x. 181 He had a bottle of Poland water and a glass... He never drank anything but Poland water. He had a weak stomach, and it was comforting to him. **1977** *Times Lit. Suppl.* 4 Feb. 120/1 The American billionaire, Howard Hughes... All he drank was Poland water (whatever that may be).

polar (ˈpəʊlə(r)), *a.* (*sb.*) [ad. med.L. *polār-is*, f. L. *pol-us* pole *sb.*[2]: see -ar[1]. Cf. It. *polare* (*c* 1300 in Dante), Sp. *polar*, F. *polaire* (1556 in Hatz.-Darm.).]

A. *adj.* **1.** *Astron.* and *Geog.* Of or pertaining to the poles of the celestial sphere or of the earth; situated near or connected with either pole. Also, of or pertaining to the poles of another heavenly body.

1551 Recorde *Cast. Knowl.* (1556) 41 Recken from one of the poles..23 degrees and an halfe,..draw a circle of that circuit about eche Pole... These circles maye well bee called Pole circles, or Polar circles. **1594** J. Davis *Seaman's Secr.* ii. (1607) 6 The Artick Polar circle is one of the lesser circles, deuiding the Sphere into two vnequall partes. **1667** Milton *P.L.* x. 289 As when two Polar Winds..together drive Mountains of Ice. **1669** Sturmy *Mariner's Mag.* vii. ii. 5, [I] call it a Polar Plane, because the Poles thereof are in the Poles of the World. *a* **1711** Ken *Hymnotheo* Poet. Wks. 1721 III. 120 Devotion cold as Polar Ice was grown. **1815** J. Smith *Panorama Sc. & Art* I. 277 The polar diameter of the earth. **1856** Kane *Arct. Expl.* I. xxiii. 302 Well known to the Polar traveller. **1878** Huxley *Physiogr.* 178 The cold polar waters sink by their density. **1894** [see *polar cap* in 1 b below]. **1922** H. S. Jones *Gen. Astron.* v. 134 The structure of the corona is very complex; it has no definite boundary and is generally symmetrical with respect neither to the centre of the Sun nor to the Sun's polar axis. **1973** [see *polar wandering* in 1 b below].

b. In specific combinations with sbs.: ***polar anæmia***, anæmia due to residence in the polar regions during the sunless winter. ***polar bear***, the white bear of Arctic regions, *Ursus* (or *Thalarctos*) *maritimus*, or its fur; also *attrib.*, *comb.*, and *fig.* ***polar cap***, a large region of ice or other frozen matter surrounding a pole of a planet. ***polar circle***, each of the circles parallel to the equator at the distance of 23° 28′ from either pole, bounding the Arctic and Antarctic zones. ***polar dial***, a dial having its gnomon in the plane of the earth's axis. ***polar distance***, the angular distance of any point on a sphere from the nearer pole; the complement of declination or latitude. ***polar flattening***, the extent to which the polar diameter of a planet is shorter than the mean equatorial diameter. ***polar front*** (Meteorol.), a front between polar and equatorial air masses. ***polar hare***, the white hare, *Lepus arcticus*; also called the Arctic hare. ***polar lights***, the aurora borealis or australis. ***polar orbit***, an orbit that passes over polar regions. *spec.* one whose plane contains the polar axis; so ***polar-orbiting*** adj. ***polar plant***, a name for *Silphium laciniatum*, from the fact of its leaves pointing due North and South (*Syd. Soc. Lex.*). ***polar projection***: see projection. ***polar star*** (mod.L. *stella polaris siue Polus*, in *Alphonsine Tables*, Venice 1518), the pole-star; also *fig.* = guiding star, guide, cynosure. ***polar wandering***, the slow, erratic movement of the earth's poles relative to the continents which is thought to have occurred throughout geological time and is ascribed largely to continental drift; also extended to corresponding movement on other planets.

1781 T. Pennant *Hist. Quadrupeds* II. 290 The *Polar bear might have been one [*sc.* an animal natural to a rigorous climate]. **1829** [see sea-bear 3]. **1834** Dickens *Sk. Boz* (1836) 1st Ser. I. 210 In their shaggy white coats they look just like Polar bears. **1847** T. Arnold *Let.* 23 Oct. in *N.Z. Lett.* (1966) 10 In Prince Edward's Island, the winter..is enough to deter anyone but a polar bear. **1910** E. T. Seton *Life-Histories Northern Animals* II. 1034 It [*sc.* the grizzly bear] is easily distinguished..from the Polar-bear by the latter's white colour. **1917** R. Fry *Let.* 2 Mar. (1972) II. 404 Lady Scott, the widow of the Antarctic man came in yesterday with Peter Scott, the most wonderful little monster of a polar bear cub. **1959** G. D. Painter *Proust* I. ix. 126 Montesquiou..had a room decorated as a snow-scene, with a polar-bear rug. **1968** A. Diment *Bang Bang Birds* iii. 37 The living room, with its nylon polar bearskin rug. **1974** P. Dickinson *Poison Oracle* i. 17 The polar bear was swimming, huge in its tiny pool. **1976** H. L. Gunderson *Mammalogy* xvi. 375 The female and sometimes the male polar bears..become dormant throughout the winter. **1894** *Astron. & Astrophysics* XIII. 542 So much for the terrestrial conditions under which the observations were made. The Martian ones were such as to make the *polar cap and its accompanying phenomena the centre of interest upon the planet. **1932** [see *fast ice* s.v. fast *a.* 11]. **1967** K. Lassen in B. M. McCormac *Aurora & Airglow* v. 453 We define the Polar Cap as the area with corrected geomagnetic latitude..greater than some 70°. **1968** S. Glasstone *Bk. of Mars* vi. 107 Even if the polar caps are largely carbon dioxide, it does not mean that they do not also contain some solidified water. **1551–94** *Polar circle [see 1]. **1704** J. Harris *Lex. Techn.* I, **Polar Dyals*, are those whose Planes are parallel to some Great Circle that passes thro' the Poles, or parallel to some one of the Hours. **1816** Playfair *Nat. Phil.* II. 35 From the azimuth, the *polar distance and the complement of latitude, compute the altitude. **1868** Lockyer *Elem. Astron.* §329. 146 Sometimes the distance from the north celestial pole is given instead of that from the celestial equator. This is called north-polar distance. **1895** *Astrophysical Jrnl.* II. 136 Micrometric measures of the diameters of Mars..give as the most probable value for the equatorial diameter of the planet at distance unity: 9″ ·40 ± ·007; for the polar one: 9″ ·35 ± ·005; and for the *polar flattening $\frac{1}{190}$ of the equatorial diameter. **1899** G. W. Myers tr. *Lommel's Exper. Physics* i. 85 From the values of the acceleration resulting from pendulum experiments and the magnitude of the centrifugal force, the polar flattening may be computed. **1966** *McGraw-Hill Encycl. Sci. & Technol.* XIII. 516/2 Clairaut's formula for polar flattening... $\alpha = \frac{5}{2}m - \beta$ in which m is the ratio of centrifugal force to gravity at the equator..and β is the coefficient of the principal latitude term. **1920** V. Bjerknes in *Nature* 24 June 524/1 This line shows how far the cold air has succeeded in penetrating; it is a kind of *polar front line. *Ibid.* 524/2 All meteorological events of the temperate zone..are derived from the general atmospheric circulation..as we know it from the polar front. **1935** C. F. Brooks et al. *Why the Weather?* (ed. 2) v. 50 The polar front is the forward edge of a moving mass of cold dry air, usually coming more or less directly from polar or sub-polar regions. **1973** R. G. & A. H. Perry *Synoptic Climatol.* iii. 184 The classical view of tropical and polar air, separated by the polar front, does not accord well with modern knowledge of the general circulation. **1823** J. Franklin *Narr. Journey to Shores of Polar Sea* 664 The *Polar hare appears to vary much in size, and consequently in weight. **1866** W. R. King *Sportsman & Naturalist in Canada* 26 In this respect it differs from the Polar-hare, the finer and softer fur of which is in winter pure white to the roots. **1895** [see *blue hare* (blue *a.* 12 a)]. **1911** E. T. Seton *Arctic Prairies* 231 It was only a Polar Hare, the second we had seen. **1961** *Times Rev. Industry* Feb. 26/3 There are a number of possible satellite systems using *polar, inclined and equatorial orbits. **1966** *McGraw-Hill Yearbk. Sci. & Technol.* 171/1 NASA is presently planning six or seven observatories to be launched alternately into the highly eccentric equatorial orbits..and the low polar orbits. **1978** *Times* 28 July 16/1 Europe's first lunar mission..would put a satellite in polar orbit round the moon. **1964** *Yearbk. Astron. 1965* 141 Transmissions from the United States were being sent by conventional means to Jodrell Bank for reflection to Gorky via the *polar-orbiting balloon-satellite. **1968** *New Scientist* 24 Oct. 175/3 It should now be possible, by means of a polar-orbiting satellite, to reap..data on..cloud heights. **1851** Mayne Reid *Scalp Hunt.* xxxv, We were traversing the region of the '*polar plant', the planes of whose leaves, at almost every step, pointed out our meridian. **1885** *Girl's Own Paper* Jan. 171/1 The Compass plant—variously known, also, as the pilot weed, polar plant, and turpentine weed. **1727–41** Chambers *Cycl.*, Pole Star, or *Polar Star. **1768–74** TUCKER *Lt. Nat.* (1834) II. 366 If we lose sight of our polar star, we shall quickly wander into inextricable difficulties. **1797** MRS. RADCLIFFE *Italian* i, Guided over the deep waters only by the polar star. **1854** MOSELEY *Astron.* iii. 14. **1860** READE *Cloister & H.* lxv, His pure and unrivalled love for Margaret had been his polar star. **1924** J. G. A. SKERL tr. *A. Wegener's Origin Continents & Oceans* viii. 123 Extensive, even if slow, *polar wanderings are then able to take place. **1969** *Times* 23 Apr. 7/4 Some of the more strange implications of the early studies of magnetism in ancient rocks—polar wandering, continental drift and the like. **1973** *Science* 9 Mar. 997 Polar wandering during the past 10^8 years may be recorded by unique quasi-circular structures in the polar regions of Mars.

2. *Magn.* Disposing itself in the direction of the poles of the earth; having polarity; of or pertaining to a magnetic pole or poles (see POLE *sb.*^{2} 5); magnetic.

1692 SIR T. P. BLOUNT *Ess.* 88 The Polar Vertue of the Loadstone was unknown to the Ancients. *a* **1696** SCARBURGH *Euclid* (1705) 2 In Loadstones it is commonly known that there are Polar Points, called North and South. **1849** NOAD *Electricity* (ed. 3) 296 The pole *N*, of the magnet ..acts favourably in inducing south polar magnetism in *n*, and north polar at *S*. **1860** TYNDALL *Glaciers* I. xx. 142, I examined the stones..and found them strongly polar. **1872** SIR W. THOMSON *Reprint Papers* 421 A polar magnet, as I shall henceforth call anything magnetized after the manner of a loadstone or a steel magnet. **1891** S. P. THOMPSON *Electro-magnet* 39 The pole or polar region of a magnet is simply that part of the surface of a magnet whence the internal magnetic lines emerge into the air.

3. a. *Electr.* Pertaining to the poles of a voltaic battery; having positive and negative electricity.

1836–41 BRANDE *Chem.* (ed. 5) 320 The decomposition was perfectly polar, and decidedly dependent upon a current of electricity passing from the zinc through the acid to the platinum in the vessel *c*, and back from the platinum through the iodic solution to the zinc at the paper *x*. **1850** DAUBENY *Atom. The.* x. (ed. 2) 352 Rendering the substances..positive and negative, or, to adopt the explanation of Faraday, causing a polar state in their particles. **1893** SLOANE *Stand. Electr. Dict.* 454 *Polar Region.* In electro-therapeutics the area or region of the body near the therapeutic electrode.

b. *Chem.* Applied variously in cases where bonding electrons are unequally shared between atoms in a molecule, so that there is some separation of electric charge: (i) applied *spec.* to electrovalent or ionic bonds, and to substances (usu. solids) in which bonding of this type predominates; (ii) applied to covalent bonds in which electrons are unequally shared between the atoms, to molecules or groups which contain such bonds, esp. those which possess a resulting electric dipole moment, and to substances (usu. liquids) which consist of such molecules.

1913 *Jrnl. Amer. Chem. Soc.* XXXV. 1443 In the preceding paragraphs we have suggested that there are two distinct types of union between atoms: polar, in which an electron has passed from one atom to the other, and non-polar, in which there is no motion of an electron. **1924** O. MAASS in H. S. Taylor *Treat. Physical Chem.* I. iv. 130 A polar molecule, one in which the molecular force of attraction is more concentrated in one particular part, so that if these molecules [of propionic acid] are oblong in shape, the field of force around one end, the –COOH end, will be more pronounced. **1927** N. V. SIDGWICK *Electronic Theory Valency* iv. 52 Polar or ionizable linkages between the oppositely charged ions of a salt. **1950** S. GLASSTONE *Elem. Physical Chem.* iii. 69 Compounds containing the groups –OH, –CN, –COOH and – NO_2, which are examples of polar groups, are generally highly polar in character, unless they happen to be completely symmetrical. *Ibid.*, Polar liquids have relatively high boiling points. **1950** W. J. MOORE *Physical Chem.* xi. 289 The polar compounds, of which NaCl was a prime example, could be adequately explained as being composed of positive and negative ions held together by coulombic attraction. **1951** I. L. FINAR *Org. Chem.* ii. 14 A symmetrical molecule is non-polar, although it may contain polar bonds. **1962** CORSON & LORRAIN *Introd. Electromagn. Fields* iii. 82 A water molecule ..possesses just such a permanent dipole moment and is thus called a polar molecule. **1966** GUCKER & SEIFERT *Physical Chem.* (1967) xi. 276 Both the Trouton and Hildebrand constants are abnormally high for many liquids like water and ammonia, which are known to be polar. **1970** S. W. BENSON *Atoms, Molecules, & Chem. Reactions* iv. 109 An extreme example of polar bonds occurs in the case of the alkali metal halides. **1974** J. S. BLAKEMORE *Solid State Physics* (ed. 2) iv. 338 Optical phonon scattering..is especially important for a solid with a polar (partially or completely ionic) lattice. **1975** HUGHES & POOLEY *Real Solids & Radiation* ii. 15 Crystalline solids which are held together by electrostatic forces between oppositely charged ions are known as ionic or polar crystals.

4. *Physics.* **a.** Of forces: Acting in two opposite directions. (Also in figurative applications.)

1809–10 COLERIDGE *Friend* (1865) 55 There is, strictly speaking, no proper opposition but between the two polar forces of one and the same power. **1862** GROVE *Corr. Phys. Forces* (ed. 4) 38 Cases where a dual or polar character of force is manifested. **1863** E. V. NEALE *Anal. Th. & Nat.* 45 The thought of centres of force becomes that of polar force, where the most entire union is produced by the most complete opposition.

b. Of molecules: Regularly or symmetrically arranged in a definite direction (as though under the action of a magnetic force, e.g. like iron filings under the influence of a magnet).

1850 GROVE *Corr. Phys. Forces* (ed. 2) 36 At the point of maximum density the molecules of these bodies assume a polar or crystalline condition. **1862** *Ibid.* (ed. 4) 39 In the rupture of crystals, we are dealing with substances having a polar arrangement of particles—the surfaces of the fragments cannot be assumed to be molecularly identical. **1870** H. SPENCER *Princ. Psychol.* (ed. 2) I. v. ii. 517 Adjacent molecules will be unsymmetrically placed..they will not stand in polar order.

5. *Biol.* Of or pertaining to the poles of a nerve-cell, an ovum, etc. See POLE *sb.*^{2} 7. ***polar body***, one of the small cells which bud off from an oocyte at the two meiotic divisions and do not develop into ova; = POLOCYTE. Cf. OOCYTE, OOTID.

1878 BELL *Gegenbaur's Comp. Anat.* 111 The polar areas, which are surrounded by short fringe-like processes. **1882** VINES *Sachs' Bot.* 581 In some instances the two polar nuclei meet, not in the centre, but towards the upper end of the embryo-sac. **1888** ROLLESTON & JACKSON *Anim. Life* Introd. 22 *note*, A clear spot, the polar spot or corpuscle, may appear at each pole of the spindle. *Ibid.* 23 As soon as the ovum has attained its definitive size, it very generally..gives origin to two polar bodies, or globules, or directive vesicles. **1898** J. HUTCHINSON in *Arch. Surg.* IX. No. 36. 356 Opacities in the vitreous and posterior polar cataract had made their appearance. **1908** [see OOTID]. **1927** HALDANE & HUXLEY *Animal Biol.* ii. 60 In order to retain the large size of the egg, three of every four gametes produced are minute and non-functional, and are called polar bodies, while only one becomes a functional ovum. **1945**, **1946** [see OOCYTE]. **1964** [see OOTID]. **1974** *Sci. Amer.* Sept. 54/3 The remaining 23 [human chromosomes] replicate once more, and it is only after a sperm makes contact with the surface of the egg that a second polar body is expelled.

6. *Geom.* Relating or referred to a pole (see POLE *sb.*^{2} 8); *spec.* Reciprocal to a pole; of the nature of a polar (see B.). ***polar co-ordinates***: see CO-ORDINATE B. 2. ***polar curve*** with respect to a line, the locus in tangential co-ordinates corresponding to the polar curve with respect to a point in polar co-ordinates. ***polar diagram***, a diagram in which the length of the radius joining a fixed point to any point of a curve represents the magnitude of something (as the sensitivity of an aerial or the brightness of a lamp) measured in the direction of the radius. ***polar equation***, an equation in polar co-ordinates. ***polar surface***, in geometry of three dimensions, a locus analogous in all respects to a polar curve in plane geometry. ***polar vector*** (see VECTOR).

1816 tr. *Lacroix's Diff. & Int. Calculus* 129 The variables in this equation are what Geometers have called polar co-ordinates. **1831** HIND *Diff. Calc.* 262 If r be the radius vector of a polar curve, and θ be the angle which it makes with a fixed axis. **1848** G. SALMON *Conic Sect.* (1855) i. §44 To find the polar equation of a right line. **1879** THOMSON & TAIT *Nat. Phil.* I. I. §134 The polar figure to any continuous curve on a spherical surface is the locus of the ultimate intersections of great circles equatorial to points taken infinitely near each other along it. **1895** *Electrician* 10 May 43/1 (*heading*) Representation of periodic currents by polar diagrams. **1923** GLAZEBROOK *Dict. Applied Physics* IV. 429/2 These diagrams are what are generally termed 'polar diagrams of light distribution'. In these curves the length of the radius vector at any angle gives the candle-power at that angle. **1943** *Electronic Engin.* XVI. 241/1 The field strength relations and polar diagrams of several aerials..were discussed. **1962** A. NISBETT *Technique Sound Studio* i. 20 (*caption*) In a polar diagram such as this the curve indicates the out-put of the microphone for a given sound arriving from any angle.

7. *fig.* **a.** Analogous to the pole of the earth, or to the pole-star; of or pertaining to a central or directive principle.

1799 *Chron.* in *Ann. Reg.* 156/1 Universal Emancipation, with Representative Legislature, was the polar principle which guided the Society of United Irishmen. **1858** CARLYLE *Fredk. Gt.* I. i. (1872) I. 4 A king over men; whose movements were polar, and carried..those of the world along with them. **1899** A. BLACK in *Expositor* Jan. 51 Both the Church and the world depend in crisis on the man of insight:..the polar primary man.

b. Directly opposite in character, action, or tendency. (See also 4 a.)

1832 J. WILSON in *Blackw. Mag.* XXXI. 998 Rusticity and Urbanity are polar opposites. **1840** CARLYLE *Heroes* iii. (1872) 90 Dante felt Good and Evil to be the two polar elements of this Creation, on which it all turns. **1953** T. PARSONS et al. *Working Papers in Theory of Action* 208 The instrumental and the system-integrative norms, which very closely characterize what..have been thought of as polar types of institutional structure. **1959** MCKINNEY & LOOMIS in J. S. Roucek *Contemp. Sociol.* 557 The polar extremes in point are clearly ideal or constructed types. *Ibid.* 558 The polar type formulations..have firmly established the point that the *continuum* is a vital notion in the comparative analysis of social phenomena. **1964** E. A. NIDA *Toward Sci. Transl.* ii. 24 The differences between literal and free translating are, however, no mere positive-negative dichotomy, but rather a polar distinction with many grades between them. **1965** *Language* XLI. 275 Only the conjunction of 'polar' adjectives in contexts of this kind seems odd. **1972** *Sci. Amer.* Jan. 35/1 Although sex-role ideologies form a continuum, we grouped the respondents into two polar categories, which we labeled 'traditional' and 'contemporary'. **1975** *Language* LI. 1 Polar interrogative sentences ('yes/no questions') are different from the corresponding declarative sentences not only pragmatically ..but also semantically.

B. *sb.* *Geom.* A curve related in a particular way to a given curve and a fixed point called the pole; in conic sections, the straight line joining the points at which tangents from the fixed point touch the curve.

1848 G. SALMON *Conic Sect.* (1855) vi. §86 Whether the tangents from $x'\,y'$ be real or imaginary, the line joining their points of contact will be the real line $xx' + yy' = r^2$ which we shall call the polar of $x'\,y'$ with regard to the circle. *Ibid.* xv. §302 The relation between the curves is reciprocal, that is..the curve S might be generated from s in precisely the same manner that s was generated from S; hence the name 'reciprocal polars'. **1885** LEUDESDORF *Cremona's Proj. Geom.* 201 The straight line s determined in this manner by the point S is called the polar of S with respect to the conic; and, reciprocally, the point S is said to be the pole of the straight line s.

†**ˈpolarchy**, obs. erron. form for POLYARCHY, government by many, or by a number of persons. So †**ˈpolarch**, one of the persons so governing; †**poˈlarchical** *a.*, pertaining to or of the nature of a 'polarchy'; †**ˈpolarchist**, an advocate of 'polarchy'.

1647 M. HUDSON *Div. Right Govt.* I. viii. 63 The Erection or institution of any Polarchicall Government. *Ibid.* II. iv. 95 A Polarchy in its own nature is inconsistent with Peace and Unity. *Ibid.* 99 The vocation and profession of Polarchs is cursed, unlawful and unwarrantable. *Ibid.* v. 102 In all which sorts of Polarchy, both Polarchs and Polarchists are obliged in conscience to endeavour the reducement of that Government to a Monarchie by all lawful meanes. **1648** PRYNNE *Plea for Lords* 4 Popular Polarchy and Tyranny. **1660** BOND *Scut. Reg.* 183, I appeal to the whole World, and even to the Consciences of our wicked Polarchical upstarts.

polard(e, obs. forms of POLLARD.

polari- (pəʊˈlærɪ), combining form of med.L. *polāris* polar; as in **polari-(bi)locular**, of a lichen spore (see quots. 1921^1 and 1967); **polari-guttulate** *a.*, having polar guttules (see GUTTULATE); **polari-nucleate** *a.*, having polar nuclei.

1871 W. LEIGHTON *Lichen Flora Gt. Brit.* 175 Spores 8, colourless, ellipsoid, polari-bilocular. **1887** W. PHILLIPS *Brit. Discomycetes* 276 Sporidia 8, linear-oblong, straight or curved, polari-nucleate. *Ibid.* 361 Sporidia 8, elliptic or slightly turbinate, polari-guttulate. **1921** A. L. SMITH *Handbk. Brit. Lichens* 9 In the family, Physciaceæ, the cross wall of the septate spore is so thickened that the lumen of each cell is reduced to a small area at the ends; hence the term polari-bilocular. **1921** —— *Lichens* 422 In such a phylum as the Physciaceæ (with colourless polarilocular spores) there is a clear example of a closely connected series. **1967** M. E. HALE *Biol. Lichens* ii. 37 Polarilocular spores: two-celled spores with a thick median wall and a thin isthmus, or conversely a single-celled spore with a median constriction.

poˈlaric, *a.* [f. POLAR + -IC.] = POLAR *a.* 4.

1863 *Atlantic Monthly* Oct. 499 The currents of that polaric opposition. **1864** in WEBSTER.

†**ˈpolarily**, *adv. Obs. rare.* [f. POLARY *a.* + -LY^2.] In a polar manner: see POLAR *a.* 2.

1646 SIR T. BROWNE *Pseud. Ep.* II. ii. 61 Iron..already informed by the Loadstone and polarily determined by its preaction.

polarimeter (pəʊləˈrɪmɪtə(r)). [f. med.L. *polāri-s* POLAR (with reference to POLARIZATION) + -METER.] A form of polariscope for measuring the amount of rotation of the plane of polarization, or the amount of polarized light in a beam.

1864 in WEBSTER. **1869** *Eng. Mech.* 24 Dec. 357/3 The detection..may be effected with the polarimeter, as pure glycerine has no action upon polarised light. **1897** *Allbutt's Syst. Med.* III. 214 Grape-sugar deflects polarised light to the right, and upon this is based a method of estimation by means of a somewhat expensive instrument called a polarimeter. **1899** CAGNEY tr. *Jaksch's Clin. Diagn.* v. (ed. 4) 162 The rotatory power of each of the four fluids is ascertained by means of the polarimeter.

Hence **polarimetric** (pəʊlærɪˈmɛtrɪk) *a.*, of or pertaining to a polarimeter or polarimetry; **polariˈmetrically** *adv.*; **polaˈrimetry**, the art or process of measuring or analysing the polarization of light or other electromagnetic radiation.

1864 WEBSTER, *Polarimetry.* **1899** CAGNEY tr. *Jaksch's Clin. Diagn.* i. (ed. 4) 88 The polarimetric test may be applied. *Ibid.* v. 163 This method..requires a very accurate polarimeter, light polarimetric examinations, and a highly-complicated calculation. **1930** [see FOUCAULT]. **1937** *Jrnl. Org. Chem.* II. 431 The mutarotation of glucose was measured polarimetrically, in 200 mm. tubes. **1973** *Jrnl. Biol. Chem.* CCXLVIII. 4165/1 Each solution was then diluted to 12 ml..and the further progress of the reaction followed polarimetrically. **1975** *Nature* 14 Aug. 537/1 In the past, the best-known argument for X-ray polarimetry has been that it is often symptomatic of non-thermal synchrotron-type emission.

Polaris (pəʊˈlɑːrɪs). [a. med.L. *polāris* polar.] The name of a type of guided missile developed for the U.S. Navy, having a nuclear warhead and designed to be carried by submarines and launched under water. Freq. *attrib.* and *Comb.*, as ***Polaris missile***, ***submarine***; ***Polaris-carrying*** adj.

1957 *N.Y. Times* 1 Jan. 1/3 The Navy is developing a ballistic missile to be fired from submerged submarines at targets hundreds of miles away, it was disclosed today. The missile is named the Polaris. **1957** *Life* 21 Jan. 121/2 Although Polaris can be launched from surface ships it will find its greatest strategic value with fast new nuclear-powered submarines. **1958** *Observer* 10 Aug. 3/4 Submarines of the Nautilus type equipped with 'Polaris' guided missiles could clearly use the Arctic Ocean as a base from which to threaten, with virtual impunity, the northern coasts of Russia. **1958** *New Statesman* 16 Aug. 181/1 They will be equipped with the deadly Polaris missile. **1960** *Daily Tel.* 22 Apr. 1/3 Britain has sounded the United States Defence Department on the possibility of having her own Polaris-carrying submarines, it was learned to-day. **1965** *New Statesman* 14 May 752/1 Last October, *The Times* felt able to predict with confidence that all Labour would do with Polaris would be to assign it irrevocably to Nato. **1965** H. KAHN *On Escalation* ii. 48 One can conceive of a slow-motion counterforce war lasting for weeks or months during which Polaris submarines are hunted down. **1973** D. KYLE *Raft of Swords* (1974) iii. 18 The Americans developed their Polaris programme very quickly... The Polaris rocket went from design to deployment in one and a half years.

polariscope (pəʊˈlærɪskəʊp). [f. med.L. *polāris* POLAR (cf. POLARIMETER) + -SCOPE. Cf. F. *polariscope*.] An instrument for showing the polarization of light, or viewing objects in polarized light; consisting essentially of two plates or prisms, a *polarizer* and an *analyser*; made in various forms, simple or complex, according to the special use. Also *attrib.*

1829 *Amer. Jrnl. Sci.* XV. 369 (*heading*) Description of the polariscope, an instrument for observing some of the most interesting phenomena of polarised light. **1842** G. FRANCIS *Dict. Arts* etc., *Polarising Apparatus, Polariscope*, any instrument which is capable of showing the phenomena of polarised light. **1854** *Pereira's Polarized Light* (ed. 2) 228 The plates of topaz sold in the opticians' shops, for polariscope purposes, have been obtained by cutting the crystal perpendicularly to one of the optic axes. *c* **1865** J. WYLDE in *Circ. Sc.* I. 81/1 In every polariscope there are two essential parts; namely, the *polariser* and the *analyser*; the former receives and polarises the incident rays of light, and the latter presents to the eye the polarised ray either by reflection or by refraction. **1866** BRANDE & COX *Dict. Sc.*, etc. II. 951/1 The polariscope proposed by Arago is formed of a tube closed at one extremity by a plate of rock crystal cut perpendicularly to the optical axis, and about five millimetres.. in thickness, and having at the other end, where the eye is applied, a prism possessing the property of double refraction placed transversely to the axis of the tube.

Hence **poˈlariscopist**, one skilled in the use of a polariscope; **polariscopy** (pəʊˈlærɪskəpɪ), the art of using a polariscope.

1872 PROCTOR *Ess. Astron.* xviii. 212 More likely to supply a correct answer.. than either spectroscopy, polariscopy, or photography. **1890** *Cent. Dict.*, Polariscopist.

polariscopic (pəʊlærɪˈskɒpɪk), *a.* [f. as prec. + -IC.] Of or pertaining to, made, obtained, or viewed by, a polariscope.

1865 *Intell. Observ.* No. 44. 112 Admirable polariscopic objects. **1872** PROCTOR *Ess. Astron.* xiii. 193 The spectroscopic and polariscopic analysis of the corona. **1887** *Athenæum* 1 Oct. 442/3 The gaseous molecules and the dust particles which polariscopic observations show are present in the corona.

polaˈristic, *a. rare*—°. [erron. f. POLARIZE: see -ISTIC.] = POLARIC.

1864 WEBSTER, *Polaristic*, pertaining to or exhibiting poles; having a polar arrangement or disposition; arising from, or dependent upon, the possession of poles or polar characteristics; as polaristic antagonism.

poˌlaristroˈbometer. [mod. f. med.L. *polāris* POLAR + Gr. στρόβος a whirling round + -METER; devised 1865 by Prof. H. Wild of Zurich.

(He objected to the term *polarimeter* for an instrument that measures, not the amount of polarization, but the angle of rotation of the plane of polarization.)]

A form of saccharimeter, giving a very delicate means for measuring the rotation of the plane of polarization produced by the sugar solution.

1870 *Chemical News* 21 Jan. 35 Newest shape of M. Wild's Polaristrobometer (Saccharimeter, Diabetometer). **1882** ROBB & VELEY *Landolt's Handbk. Polariscope* 98 The so-called polaristrobometers, what in England are known as polariscopes, which indicate the amount of rotation in angular measure.

polarite (ˈpəʊləraɪt). [f. POLAR *a.* + -ITE[1].] Trade name for an insoluble porous mineral substance, containing about fifty-three per cent. of magnetic oxide of iron, with silica, lime, magnesia, carbon, etc., and having the power of absorbing and giving off oxygen. Used in conjunction with 'Ferrozone' in the so-called 'International' process of sewage treatment. Also *attrib.*

1889 *Patent Specif.* No. 8088 The filtering medium.. is that now known as 'Polarite'. **1891–2** *Proc. Assoc. Munic. & County Engineers* XVIII. 318 A magnetic oxide of iron (to which the trade name of 'Polarite' has been given). **1898** *Engineer. Mag.* XVI. 157/1 The Purification of Sewage by the Ferrozone Polarite System.

polariton (pəʊˈlærɪtɒn). *Physics.* [f. POLAR(IZATION and related words + *-iton*, prob. after EXCITON.] A quasiparticle in an ionic crystal consisting of a photon strongly coupled to a quasiparticle such as a phonon or exciton.

1958 J. J. HOPFIELD in *Physical Rev.* CXII. 1558/2 The polarization field 'particles' analogous to photons will be called 'polaritons'. (Excitons will be shown to be one kind of polariton... Optical phonons are another example of polaritons.) **1963** R. S. KNOX *Theory of Excitons* iii. 133 An external photon excites a crystal to a state described by a polariton packet... If this new particle of excitation fails to interact with any energy sinks, it re-excites an external photon on the other side of the crystal. However, by virtue of its exciton component, it can decay into states which do not couple as easily to external photons (i.e., 'nonradiative' states). **1971** J. I. PANKOVE *Optical Processes in Semiconductors* i. 16 A polariton is the complex resulting from the polarizing interaction between an electromagnetic wave and an oscillator resonant at the same frequency... Although polaritons initially have designated the interaction between excitons and photons, they can also represent the interaction between photons and optical phonons and between photons and plasmons. *Ibid.* 17 The polariton is not to be confused with the polaron of ionic crystals, which results from an interaction between the electron and the lattice. **1972** *Physics Bull.* Aug. 490/1 Two chapters.. cover .. light scattering by polaritons.

polarity (pəʊˈlærɪtɪ). [f. POLAR *a.* + -ITY: cf. F. *polarité* (1806 in Hatz.-Darm., 1835 in *Dict. Acad.*) A form tried earlier was POLITY[2].]

1. *Magnetism.* The quality or property possessed by certain bodies, as a lodestone or magnetized bar, of turning (when free to move) so as to point with their two extremities to the two (magnetic) poles of the earth; the quality of being polar, or possessing magnetic poles.

1646 SIR T. BROWNE *Pseud. Ep.* II. ii. 59 This polarity from refrigeration upon extremity and in defect of a Loadstone might serve to invigorate and touch a needle anywhere. **1664** POWER *Exp. Philos.* III. 157 You may change the Polarity of many feeble Stones, by a long Position, in a contrary posture to that which it naturally affects. *a* **1691** BOYLE *Hist. Air* (1692) 64 One of their compasses which had quite changed the polarity, from north to south, is still extant in that country. **1751** FRANKLIN in *Phil. Trans.* XLVII. 289 By electricity we have here frequently given polarity to needles. **1815** J. SMITH *Panorama Sc. & Art* II. 176 If the bar be inverted, the polarity will be instantly reversed; so that in all cases the lower extremity is, in this hemisphere, the north pole: but on the south side of the equator, the lower extremity is always the south pole. **1823** J. BADCOCK *Dom. Amusem.* 166 An invention.. securing a more accurate polarity to the mariner's compass. *c* **1865** J. WYLDE in *Circ. Sc.* I. 81/1 Magnetic polarity, or that power by which a magnetised needle arranges itself in reference to the magnetic poles of the earth.

2. Hence in generalized sense: A property of matter or force, analogous or compared to that of a magnet or magnetism. **a.** The having of an axis with reference to which certain physical properties are determined; the disposition of a body or an elementary molecule to place its mathematical axis in a particular direction.

1674 PETTY *Disc. Dupl. Proportion* 128 All Atoms by their Motion of Verticity or Polarity, would draw themselves, like Magnets, into a streight Line, by setting all their Axes in *directum* to each other. **1827** ARNOTT *Physics* 33 When atoms are allowed to cohere according to their natural tendencies, they always assume a certain regular arrangement and form, which we call crystalline. Because in this circumstance they seem to resemble magnets, which attract each other only by their poles; the fact has been called the polarity of atoms. **1854** *Pereira's Polarized Light* (ed. 2) 184 In crystals it is necessary to admit, besides ordinary attraction and repulsion, a third molecular force called polarity. *Ibid.*, A molecule endowed with unequal attractive forces in different directions may be said to be possessed of polarity.

b. The quality of exhibiting opposite or contrasted properties or powers in opposite or contrasted directions; the possession of two points called poles having contrary qualities or tendencies.

1818 COLERIDGE *Method* in *Encycl. Metrop.* (1845) I. Introd. 12 Contemplating in all Electrical phenomena the operation of a Law which reigns through all Nature, viz. the law of polarity, or the manifestation of one power by opposite forces. **1840** WHEWELL *Philos. Induct. Sc.* I. v. i. 337 The general notion of polarity—opposite properties in opposite directions. **1841–4** EMERSON *Ess.* Ser. I. iii. (1876) 81 Polarity, or action and reaction, we meet in every part of nature. **1866** DK. ARGYLL *Reign Law* v. (ed. 4) 257 One of whose essential properties is Polarity,—that is, equal and similar action in opposite directions. **1870** TYNDALL *Lect. Electr.* 7 Two opposite kinds of magnetism may be supposed to be concentrated at the two ends. In this doubleness of the magnetic force consists what is called magnetic polarity.

c. Tendency to develop in two opposite directions in space, time, serial arrangement, etc.

1848 LINDLEY *Introd. Bot.* (ed. 4) I. 165 This disposition to develope in two diametrically opposite directions, sometimes called polarity, is found in all embryos. **1853** E. FORBES *Addr. Geol. Soc.* in Wilson & Geikie *Mem.* xv. (1861) 544 We speak of two [organic] groups [e.g. animals and vegetables] being in the relation of polarity to each other when the rudimentary forms of each are proximate, and their completer manifestations far apart. **1856** WOODWARD *Mollusca* III. 418 This group shows a tendency to 'polarity', or excessive development at the ends of the series.

d. ***uterine polarity***: see quot.

1881 *Trans. Obstetric Soc. Lond.* XXII. 47 The conditions of 'uterine polarity' enunciated by Reil at the beginning of this century. This 'uterine polarity' is exemplified by the antagonism which exists between the two poles of the uterus, contraction of one being accompanied by dilatation of the other. **1895** *Syd. Soc. Lex., Polarity*.. applied metaphorically, *e.g.* to the uterus, in reference to the fact that as the fundus contracts the cervix tends to relax and *vice versâ*.

e. *Biol.* The tendency of living matter to assume a specific form; the property observed in animals from which parts have been severed, and in severed parts of animals and plants, of regenerating the missing parts.

1864 G. J. ALLMAN in *Rep. Brit. Assoc. Adv. Sci. 1863* 392 The lower segment, on the other hand, instead of pushing forth from the cut extremity a simple continuation of the coenosarc, developes from this extremity a polypite. There is thus manifested in the formative force of the Tubularia-stem a well-marked polarity, which is rendered very apparent if a segment be cut out from the centre of the stem. **1864** H. SPENCER *Princ. Biol.* I. II. iv. 181 The vitalized molecules composing the tissues, show their proclivity towards a particular arrangement... For this property there is no fit term. If we accept the word polarity, as a name for the force by which inorganic units are aggregated into a form peculiar to them; we may apply this word to the analogous force displayed by organic units. **1895** *Jrnl. Morphol.* X. 322 If we assume the polarity of the egg to be pre-determined from the beginning, we must admit that the polarity determines the position of the segmentation-nucleus. **1924** E. G. CONKLIN in E. V. Cowdry *Gen. Cytol.* ix. 558 The polarity of the egg is the earliest recognizable and most fundamental differentiation of morphogenesis. **1926** J. S. HUXLEY *Ess. Pop. Sci.* xviii. 251 When small pieces of a planarian regenerate, they exhibit what we may call polarity; for (with a few special exceptions) the new head is formed from that region of the piece which was nearest to the old head, the new tail from that region which was nearest to the old tail. **1975** R. L. PETERSON in Torrey & Clarkson *Devel. & Function of Roots* vii. 146 The inherent polarity in most root segments, which manifests itself by the regeneration of buds at the proximal end and roots at the distal end, may be due to the polar distribution of more than one endogenous hormone.

3. *Electr.* The relation of a body to the poles or electrodes of an electric circuit; the electrical condition of a body as positive or negative.

1849 NOAD *Electricity* (ed. 3) 353 That side of the spiral which is towards the north, acts as the north pole; and the south side has an opposite polarity. Each side powerfully attracts iron filings. **1872** C. B. FOX *Ozone* 10 One of the Peroxides is in an opposite condition of polarity to that in the other. **1879** DU MONCEL *Telephone* 16 The adjacent poles of the two rods are of opposite polarity. **1887** GUMMING *Electr. treated Experimentally* 289 Its change of polarity at each half rotation keeps up a constant rotation.

4. *Optics.* The quality of light which admits of its polarization; hence, the condition of being polarized. (An inaccurate use.)

[**1812** SIR H. DAVY *Chem. Philos.* 53 The important discoveries.. of a property analogous to polarity in light.] **1861** HERSCHEL in G. F. Chambers *Astron.* (1876) 319 The light reflected from which [cloud].. exhibits no signs of polarity. [**1866** —— *Fam. Lect. Sci. Subj.* viii. 347 It would seem almost as if light consisted of particles having polarity, like magnets.]

5. *fig.* **a.** (from 1.) Direction (of thought, feeling, or inclination) towards a single point; tendency or trend in a particular direction; 'magnetic attraction' towards a particular object.

1767 CHESTERF. *Lett.* (1792) IV. 249, I find you are in motion and with a Polarity to Dresden. **1800** *Hist. Eur.* in *Ann Reg.* 61/2 Launching forth on the ocean of possibility.. conducted, not merely by shores and landmarks, but chiefly by the polarity of reasons. **1834** H. ROGERS in *J. Edwards' Wks.* I. p. lii, This polarity of mind, this intellectual magnetism towards universal truth, has always been a characteristic of the greatest minds. **1862** STANLEY *Jew. Ch.* (1877) I. xii. 226 One great change.. affected the polarity of the whole political and geographical organisation of the country. **1878** EMERSON *Sov. Ethics* Wks. (Bohn) III. 381 Now men fall abroad—want polarity—suffer in character and intellect.

b. (from 2 b.) Possession or exhibition of two opposite or contrasted aspects, principles, or tendencies.

1862 *Q. Rev.* Apr. 442 The whole system of the Church of England.. has, like all Truth, two faces: one silver, the other gold. Every part of it has a double polarity. **1870** EMERSON *Soc. & Solit.* iv. 80 Wherever the polarities meet, wherever .. the instinct of freedom and duty come[s] in direct opposition to fossil conservatism and the thirst of gain. **1888** R. BURN *Rom. Lit. & Art* 43 The Roman women, with that curious polarity which often sets the fashion in exactly the opposite direction to what would be expected, held that a narrow forehead with the hair drawn down over it was pretty and attractive. **1934** C. HARTSHORNE *Philos. & Psychol. of Sensation* iv. 134 Feeling involves an 'opposition' of positive and negative, liking and disliking. Does sensation exhibit a similar polarity?.. It is, as we have seen, precisely in terms of polarities that the facts of sensation are to be described. **1945** *Downside Rev.* 131 Be it remarked in passing that the relation between God and the world is not here conceived as one of polarity. **1950** D. RIESMAN *Lonely Crowd* (1952) i. 20 To what extent, in establishing America's polarity from Europe, he [*sc.* de Tocqueville] tendentiously noticed those things that were different rather than those that were the same. **1957** *New Statesman* 2 Nov. 555/3 We must ask ourselves what we can do to break this polarity [between the U.S. and Russia]. **1963** *Times Lit. Suppl.* 26 Apr. 306/5 Polarity, or the use of contrast as an artistic means. **1970** B. M. H. STRANG *Hist. Eng.* 134 The polarity *mental/physical*. *Ibid.* 237 It [*sc.* Northern English] thus heightened the polarity of tense-contrast, which in strong verbs was far less clear-cut in the south. **1972** *Encycl. Psychol.* III. 19/2 *Polarity*, a relationship between features or traits which are antithetical pairs. **1972** R. PLANT in Cox & Dyson *20th-Cent. Mind* III. iii. 69 The wholly necessary or the wholly contingent, the two polarities of empiricist epistemology.

c. (from 3.) Condition of consciousness as subjective or objective.

1846 TRENCH *Mirac.* v. (1862) 174 That quick shifting, so to speak, of the polarity, so that at one moment the human consciousness became the positive, at another the negative pole.

polarizable (ˈpəʊlərɑɪzəb(ə)l), *a.* [f. POLARIZE + -ABLE.] Capable of being polarized. Hence **polariza'bility**, *spec.* the degree to which an atom or molecule can be polarized, expressed in terms of the electric dipole moment induced by unit electric field.

1846 WORCESTER, *Polarizable*, that may be polarized. *Phil. Mag.* **1878** *Smithsonian Rep.* 364 Albumen electrodes (*i.e.*, non-polarizable electrodes). **1900** ILES *Flame, Electr. & Camera* 252 The conductivity, polarisability and other electrical properties of matter. **1930** PAULING & GOUDSMIT *Structure Line Spectra* iii. 45 The electric moment of the induced dipole is αF, in which α is called the 'polarizability' of the atom or ion. **1947** SLATER & FRANK *Electromagnetism* iv. 44 We thus have means for finding the dielectric constant of a material, if we know the polarizability of its molecules. **1964** PHILLIPS & WILLIAMS *Inorg. Chem.* I. iv. 132 The simplest theoretical treatment of the London effect leads to an energy between identical atoms or molecules given by $-\frac{3}{4}\frac{h\nu\alpha^3}{r^6}$. α, the polarizability of the atom or molecule, may be determined from its molecular refraction. **1974** *Nature* 23 Aug. 686/3 The fourth chapter..is an excellent account of the determination of dipole moments and polarisabilities of molecules in excited electronic states.

polarization (pəʊlərɑɪˈzeɪʃən). [In sense 1, a. F. *polarisation*, n. of action f. *polariser* (both introduced by Malus, 11 March 1811): see POLARIZE. In later uses, n. of action from the vb. in corresp. senses.] The condition or fact of being polarized; the action of polarizing.

I. 1. a. A modification of the condition of light or radiant heat, whereby the ray exhibits different properties on different sides, so that opposite sides are alike, while the maximum difference is between two sides at right angles to each other; the production of this condition, the action of polarizing. Also used of other kinds of wave. See POLARIZE *v.* 1.

angle of polarization = *polarizing angle*: see POLARIZING *vbl. sb.* ***circular, elliptic, plane polarization***: see POLARIZE 1. ***plane of polarization***: the plane which contains the incident ray and the reflected or refracted ray which is polarized.

1812 *Nicholson's Jrnl.* XXXIII. 345 By giving to these sides [of the ray] the names of poles, Malus has given the name of Polarisation to that modification which imparts properties to light which are relative to these poles. **1813** (23 Dec.) BREWSTER in *Phil. Trans.* (1814) 188 A ray of light transmitted through a plate of agate cut by planes perpendicular to the laminæ of which it is composed suffers polarisation like one of the pencils formed by double refraction. **1814** *Ibid.* 219 (*title*) On the Polarisation of Light by oblique transmission through all Bodies, whether crystallized or uncrystallized. **1831** —— *Optics* xxvii. 225 A new species of polarisation, which I have called elliptical polarisation, and which unites the two classes of phenomena which constitute circular and rectilineal polarisation. **1839** G. BIRD *Nat. Philos.* 354 When light suffers double refraction through a crystal with a positive axis.., as quartz, the plane of polarization of the ordinary ray..is horizontal, and that of the extraordinary ray vertical. In negative crystals, as Iceland spar, the direction of these rays is reversed. *Ibid.* 362 The angle of complete polarization for any substance, may be readily determined by the fact, discovered by Sir D. Brewster, that:—The index of refraction is the tangent of the angle of polarization. **1842** BRANDE *Dict. Sc.*, etc. s.v., Analogous phenomena to those of the polarization of light have been found to belong also to radiant heat. **1879** ROOD *Chromatics* iv. 50 A long-lived soap bubble displays every colour which can be produced by polarization. **1906** *Harmsworth Encycl.* 4811/3 The doubly refracted rays have what Newton called 'sides'; and it is this sidedness, or laterality, which is known as polarization. **1923** H. L. BROSE tr. *Sommerfeld's Atomic Structure & Spectral Lines* i. 23 Polarisation signifies that a ray favours a certain plane passing through it more than the one perpendicular to this plane. In the case of longitudinal vibrations..there is a symmetry about the ray and no such preference can be imagined. Longitudinal radiation must therefore be unpolarised. In the case of transversal vibrations..a favoured plane..is determined by the direction of vibration and the direction of the ray. **1929** *Physical Rev.* XXXIII. 760 (*heading*) A test for polarization of electron waves by reflection. **1936** *Wireless World* 16 Oct. 396/3 Although one would expect a slight departure from vertical polarisation of the received waves in this location, a vertical aerial was found to be 6 to 10 db. better than a horizontal. **1976** *IEEE Trans. Antennas & Propagation* XXIV. 5/1 In microwave communication links above 10 GHz the employment of frequency reuse in orthogonal polarizations is limited by cross polarization.

fig. **1851** SIR F. PALGRAVE *Norm. & Eng.* I. 172 In whom a moral polarization of light has taken place. **1900** F. H. STODDARD *Evol. Eng. Novel* 108 It is not history; it is rather the romantic polarization of history.

b. = *optical activity* s.v. OPTICAL *a.* 6. Now used chiefly with reference to sugar solutions.

1845 *Mem. & Proc. Chem. Soc.* II. 29, I shall explain.. what is meant by the deviation or rotation of the rays of polarized light when transmitted through fluids said to possess circular polarization. **1862** *Jrnl. Chem. Soc.* XV. 308 An experiment made..while examining the circular polarization of camphoric acid. **1912** C. A. BROWNE *Handbk. Sugar Anal.* ix. 236 The reading multiplied by 1·3 gives the polarization (degrees Ventzke) of the sugar cane. **1935** *Economist* 20 Apr. 906/2 Raw sugar of 97° polarisation ..pays a duty of 8s. 4$\frac{3}{10}$d. per cwt. **1963** D. BECKER in P. Honig *Princ. Sugar Technol.* III. ix. 455 In contrast to raw cane sugars, raw beet sugars for refining cannot be definitely characterized and graded by stating the polarization alone.

c. Measurement of the optical activity of a sugar solution. Cf. POLARIZE *v.* 1 c.

1905 G. W. ROLFE *Polariscope* 96 Polarizations made at average room temperature by the standard commercial methods give with requisite accuracy the per cent of sucrose in the sample. **1945** A. L. & K. B. WINTON *Anal. of Foods* 640/1 Addition of solid sodium carbonate to slight alkaline reaction after the immediate polarization..destroys the mutarotation without changing the dilution. **1973** SNELL & ETTRE *Encycl. Industr. Chem. Anal.* XVIII. 345 Direct polarization of the sugar solution or polarization before and after hydrolysis are commonly used assay methods.

2. *Physics.* A partial or complete alignment of the spin axes of particles; the degree to which this exists.

1928 *Proc. R. Soc.* A. CXVIII. 675 It will..suffice to treat of only one type of polarisation and we shall take that corresponding to *z*. **1929** *Ibid.* CXXIV. 427 This polarisation could be detected by letting the scattered beam fall on a second target. **1956** *Rev. Mod. Physics* XXVIII. 279/1 We shall speak of transverse polarization of an electron beam if the direction of the spin is perpendicular to the momentum, of longitudinal polarization if the spin is parallel or antiparallel to the momentum. **1963** K. NISHIJIMA *Fundamental Particles* vii. 380 Hyperon polarization is transverse rather than longitudinal unless parity is violated in production. **1979** *Sci. Amer.* May 64/3 The polarization is defined as the difference between the number of spin-up particles and the number of spin-down ones, divided by the total number of protons.

II. 3. *Electr.* and *Magn.* **a.** See POLARIZE *v.* 3. *spec.* the partial separation of positive and negative electric charge produced in a dielectric by an electric field, and expressed by a vector quantity equal to the electric dipole moment per unit volume of the dielectric; also, a similar state in an individual atom or molecule.

1866 R. M. FERGUSON *Electr.* (1870) 53 The pail was thus subjected to polarisation. **1885** WATSON & BURBURY *Math. Th. Electr. & Magn.* I. 254 All electrical phenomena within *S*, which in the ordinary theory are due to the action of E_2, are on the polarisation hypothesis deducible from the given polarisation. **1916** F. B. PIDDUCK *Treat. Electricity* iii. 93 The total electric moment of an element of volume $d\tau$ of a dielectric near the point (x, y, z) has components $P_x d\tau$, $P_y d\tau$, $P_z d\tau$, where the vector $P(P_x, P_y, P_z)$ is called the polarization at the point. **1933** N. V. SIDGWICK *Physical Properties of Covalent Link* v. 129 The polarization of the molecules in an electric field can take place in three ways: (1) The arrangement of the electrons will be displaced with respect to the nuclei... (2)..The nuclei themselves will be to some extent displaced with respect to one another... (3)..If the molecule has a permanent dipole moment of its own—if it is polar—the field will tend to orient it along the direction of the lines of force. **1935** J. DOUGALL tr. *Born's Atomic Physics* viii. 230 The polarization **P** is connected with Maxwell's displacement vector **D** by the relation $\mathbf{D} = \mathbf{E} + 4\pi\mathbf{P}$; on the other hand, by definition, $\mathbf{D} = \epsilon\mathbf{E}$, where ε is the dielectric constant. **1966** *McGraw-Hill Encycl. Sci. & Technol.* IV. 111/2 The dielectric constant of a material depends on its polarization in an applied field or, microscopically, on the relative displacements, in the field direction, of the electrons and nuclei comprising the molecules of the dielectric. **1973** P. C. CLEMMOW *Introd. Electromagn. Theory* vi. 232 **P** and **M** ..represent, respectively, electric and magnetic dipole moment densities. **P** is called the (electric) polarization, and **M** the magnetization or magnetic polarization.

b. In voltaic electricity, The production of an electromotive force at the electrodes, due to the presence of the products of electrolytic decomposition of the fluid between them, and acting in an opposite direction to the original current, thus producing an apparent increase of the resistance.

1839 GROVE *Contrib. Sc.* in *Corr. Phys. Forces* (1874) 237 It occurred to me that the inaction of amalgamated zinc was the effect of polarization. [*Note.* I know of no other word to express the effect here alluded to; the word is used in this sense by most French writers, but, from its numerous applications, is sadly inaccurate.] **1873** MAXWELL *Electr. & Magn.* I. 318 When an electric current is passed through an electrolyte bounded by metal electrodes, the accumulation of the ions at the electrodes produces the phenomenon called Polarization.

4. The arrangement of molecules, etc., in a definite direction.

1846 GROVE *Corr. Phys. Forces* 21 Exceptions..explicable by other interfering dynamic causes, such, possibly, as crystalline polarization, leaving interstitial spaces.

5. *fig.* **a.** See quot. and cf. POLARIZE 4 a.

1871 H. B. FORMAN *Living Poets* 6 The process of 'translating to our purposes' words already current, by giving them a new and special shade of meaning—a process best characterised as the polarisation of language.

b. The accentuation of a difference between two things or groups; the process of division into two groups representing the extremes of opinion, wealth, or the like.

1945 KOESTLER *Yogi & Commissar* II. v. 117 False polarizations and national splits which merely reflect latent conflicts. **1947** *Sun* (Baltimore) 15 Aug. 12/6 The same polarization of thought which is going on in the rest of the world is seen in Korea in extreme form. **1951** Y. MALKIEL in *Language* XXVII. 485 Lexical polarization is used in this paper as a convenient label for the influence exerted by one word on its semantic opposite. **1957** *Atlantic Monthly* Aug. 8/1 Any outside disturbance of the evolving polarization between moderate and extreme Arab nationalists may well bring disaster to the whole region. **1960** *Daily Tel.* 8 Nov. 12/2 But this does not alter the fact that every tendency towards polarisation of trade in separate camps in Europe, necessary and inevitable while the division stands, is in the long run a disaster for all. **1964** T. BOTTOMORE *Elites & Society* ii. 19 The development of capitalism brings about a more radical polarization of classes than has existed in any other type of society. **1970** *Daily Tel.* 7 Oct. 5/2 There were already signs in the central districts [of London] of 'social polarisation', areas peopled only by the richest and the poorest. **1972** M. L. SAMUELS *Ling. Evolution* iii. 39 Further phonetic divergence ('polarisation' of the existing difference) to /k/ and /tʃ/. **1975** *Chinese Econ. Studies* VIII. iv. 90 (*heading*) The polarization between the rich and the poor is a general law of capitalist accumulation.

III. 6. *attrib.* and *Comb.*, as ***polarization force***; **polarization charge**, the charge that appears on the surface of a dielectric when it is polarized in a direction not parallel to the surface; **polarization-microscope**, an instrument combining the functions of a polariscope and microscope.

1881 S. P. THOMPSON in *Design & Work* 24 Dec. 454 The degree to which a counter-electromotive force or polarisation force is set up depends very greatly on the quantity of current per unit of surface of the electrodes employed. **1895** *Syd. Soc. Lex.*, *P[olarisation]-microscope*, an instrument in which a polariscope and a microscope are combined; used particularly in petrography. **1947** SLATER & FRANK *Electromagnetism* iv. 45 We have the result that the normal component of *P*, pointing out of the dielectric, equals the surface polarization charge that appears on the surface as a result of the polarization. **1975** GRANT & PHILLIPS *Electromagnetism* ii. 53 Polarization charges induced on the surface of a dielectric material make a contribution to the macroscopic electric field inside the material... The sign of the induced charge always ensures that the field just inside the dielectric surface is less than the field just outside.

polarize (ˈpəʊlərɑɪz), *v.* [In sense 1, a. F. *polariser* (Malus, 11 March 1811), in form f. mod.L. *polāris* POLAR + *-iser*, -IZE, but referred by its author directly to F. *pôle* POLE *sb.*[2] In other senses, f. POLAR + -IZE.

See Malus in *Nouveau Bulletin des Sciences* No. 42, March 1811, p. 252 *Lumière polarisée.* Also *ibid.* No. 45, June 1811, p. 292 (*transl.*) 'In giving to these sides [of the vertical ray] the name of *poles*, he calls the modification which imparts to light properties relative to these poles, *polarization*... This new expression..signifies simply the modification that light has undergone in acquiring new properties, relative not to the direction of the ray, but solely to its *sides*, considered at a right angle, and in a plane perpendicular to its direction'. But this unfortunately assumed a sense of *pole* quite different from its use in astronomy, geography, and magnetism, with the consequence that *polarization* as applied to light and radiant heat has nothing in common with magnetic or electric polarization.]

I. 1. *Optics.* **a.** (*trans.*) To cause the vibrations of light (radiant heat, etc.) to be modified in a particular way, so that the ray exhibits different properties on different sides, opposite sides being alike, and those at right angles to each other showing the maximum of difference.

A ray of polarized light is reflected in different degrees in different positions of the reflecting body, and transmitted by certain crystals in different degrees in different positions of the crystal, and (in each case) completely quenched in one particular position. This is accounted for by supposing the etherial vibrations to be restricted to one plane (*plane polarization*), instead of being, as in ordinary light, performed in all directions perpendicular to that of the ray. Light is also said to be *circularly* or *elliptically polarized*, or to undergo *circular* or *elliptic polarization*, when it exhibits (in a polariscope) certain colour-phenomena, or modifications of the phenomena of plane polarization, which are accounted for by supposing the etherial particles to move in circles or ellipses. Polarization is produced (variously in the case of different media) by reflection, or by ordinary or double refraction.

1811 *Nicholson's Jrnl.* XXX. 192, tr. *Let. fr. Paris* 17 July, Mr. Malus is still pursuing with success his inquiries concerning *polarised light.* **1812** (Dec.) *Ibid.* XXXIII. 347 Transparent bodies totally transmit the light which they polarise in one direction or manner, and reflect that which is polarised in a contrary manner. **1813** (23 Dec.) BREWSTER in *Phil. Trans.* (1814) 192 That kind of crystallisation which polarises the incident light by separating it into two pencils. **1819** *Edin. Rev.* XXXII. 177 All diaphanous bodies polarise light at certain angles. **1854** *Orr's Circ. Sc., Chem.* 104 Bérard and Professor Forbes..succeeded in polarizing heat (non-luminous) by the agency of reflection. **1855** GROVE *Corr. Phys. Forces* (ed. 3) 114 A ray of light once polarized in a certain plane continues so affected throughout its whole subsequent course. **1873** MAXWELL *Electr. & Magn.* II. 7 *note*, A ray of light is said to be polarized when it has properties relating to its sides, which are identical on opposite sides of the ray. **1939** *Wireless World* 26 Jan. 83/1 Considerable attention has been paid to the question of whether the waves of the Alexandra Palace television transmitter should be vertically or horizontally polarised. **1966** *McGraw-Hill Encycl. Sci. & Technol.* X. 448/1 Electromagnetic radiation is difficult to polarize in certain spectral regions.

b. *absol.* or *intr.* To polarize the incident light; to exhibit the phenomena of polarization. Also, to rotate the plane of polarization of plane-polarized light by (a specified amount) under standard conditions.

1854 SCOFFERN in *Orr's Circ. Sc., Chem.* 82 The latter polarizes towards the left. **1879** RUTLEY *Stud. Rocks* x. 113 The whole crystal passes into zeolitic matter which polarises in variegated colours. **1900** *Bull. Div. of Chem., U.S. Dept. Agric.* No. 59. 52 The wine is fermented... [If] it polarizes −3° after fermentation. It contains only levorotatory sugar. **1945** A. L. & K. B. WINTON *Anal. of Foods* 616/1 Wash by decantation until the washings polarize zero in a 200-mm. tube.

c. *trans.* To measure the optical activity of (a solution) in order to determine the concentration of sugar in it. Also *ellipt.*

1905 G. W. ROLFE *Polariscope* 87 The sample which the chemist polarizes must be strictly representative of the total lot of sugar. **1945** A. L. & K. B. WINTON *Anal. of Foods* 615/1 Invert Polarization... Cool to about 20°, fill exactly to the mark, mix, and polarize at 20° in a 200-mm. tube. **1963** TRIEBOLD & AURAND *Food Composition & Qual.* iii. 60

According to their standard, a solution containing 26·000 grams of sucrose (normal weight) in 100 ml of solution at 20°C., and polarized in a 200-mm tube at 20°C., should give a reading of 100° on the saccharimeter. **1973** Snell & Ettre *Encycl. Industr. Chem. Anal.* XVIII. 348 Dilute the solution to 100 ml at 20°C. Mix well and polarize in a 200-mm tube.

2. *Physics.* To produce a partial or complete alignment of the spins of (particles).

1932 *Proc. R. Soc.* A. CXXXV. 431 The theoretical existence of these methods provides some evidence that electron beams can be polarised. **1953** *Progr. Nuclear Physics* III. 72 In order to polarize elementary particles, there must be some sort of coupling of the particle spin with a fixed spatial direction. **1974** Frauenfelder & Henley *Subatomic Physics* ix. 206 In a radioactive source at room temperature, the nuclear spins are randomly oriented. It is necessary to polarize the nuclei so that all spins J point in the same direction. **1979** *Sci. Amer.* May 64/2 The next stage polarizes the protons and depolarizes the electrons.

II. 3. *Magn.* and *Electr.* **a.** To give polarity to; to give opposite magnetic properties to opposite ends of (a bar, coil, etc. of iron or other substance). *spec.* to induce an electric dipole moment in (a substance, or an atom or molecule). Also *intr.* To acquire polarity.

1838 Faraday *Exp. Res.* (1839) I. 542 It is not the particles of oxygen and lead which polarize separately under the act of induction, but the molecules of oxide of lead which exhibit this effect. *Ibid.*, The reproduction of compound particles, which can again polarize as wholes. **1866** R. M. Ferguson *Electr.* (1870) 5 It is this double manifestation of force which constitutes the *polarity* of the magnet, and a bar of iron which is made to assume these poles is said to be polarised. **1873** Maxwell *Electr. & Magn.* II. 7 A conducting particle through which there is a current of electricity may be said to be polarized, because if it were turned round, and if the current continued to flow in the same direction as regards the particle, its direction in space would be reversed. **1887** W. Larden *Electr.* x. 161 Lines along which the molecules of the dielectrics are 'polarised' by a separation of + and − charges in them. **1945** A. F. Wells *Structural Inorg. Chem.* ii. 52 An atom is polarized when placed in an electric field. **1962** Corson & Lorrain *Introd. Electromagn. Fields* iii. 126 Consider a large block of dielectric polarized uniformly with a dipole moment per unit volume **P**. **1977** *Sci. Amer.* Feb. 91/3 The separation is accomplished by passing the atomic beam through an inhomogeneous electric or magnetic field, which deflects those atoms that are more readily polarized or have a larger magnetic moment.

b. In voltaic electricity: see polarization 3 b. Also *intr.* (of a cell), to exhibit polarization and consequently suffer a decrease in e.m.f.

1856 Walker tr. *De la Rive's Treat. Electr.* II. 671 When the zinc *z* is plunged into water..its molecules polarize each of the molecules of water that touch it; these polarize the following; and so on. **1864–72** Watts *Dict. Chem.* II. 429 Plates of platinum become polarised in a similar manner, when immersed in water either pure or acidulated, and connected with the poles of a battery, the effect, in this case, being due to the films of hydrogen and oxygen which collect on the negative and positive plates respectively. **1903** *Electr. World & Engin.* 24 Jan. 150/2 There is yet not a battery of this class known that will not polarize in a short time, which means that it has temporarily exhausted itself and must rest for awhile before it is as efficient as it was. **1969** J. J. DeFrance *Electr. Fundamentals* xi. 124 The prevention is not complete, and with age a cell does polarize.

c. In generalized sense: see quot. *rare.*

1873 Maxwell *Electr. & Magn.* I. 60 An elementary portion of a body may be said to be polarized when it acquires equal and opposite properties on two opposite sides. *Ibid.* II. 7.

III. 4. *fig.* **a.** To give an arbitrary direction, or a special meaning or application, to.

1860 O. W. Holmes *Prof. Breakf.-t.* i, The word, and consequently the idea it represents, is *polarized*. **1886** W. C. Wilkinson in *Homiletic Rev.* (U.S.) Mar. 252 That word [self-denial] also has been polarized somewhat—that is, twisted out of its right original meaning.

b. To give unity of direction to.

1868 Bushnell *Serm. Living Subj.* 171 It is not enough to rally their inventiveness, doing nothing to polarize their aim. **1892** *Pall Mall G.* 16 Mar. 2/2 A coherence of policy ..cannot be secured until the atoms of the Council, now facing every way, are polarised by party discipline.

c. *trans.* To accentuate a division within (a group, system, etc.); to separate into two (or occas. several) opposing groups, extremes of opinion, or the like. Also *intr.*, to undergo or exhibit such a process.

1949 Koestler *Promise & Fulfilment* I. xi. 125 The controversy about Zionism would have become as 'polarized' between pro- and anti-Russians as, say, the controversy about Poland. **1957** R. N. Carew Hunt *Guide to Communist Jargon* xxvii. 96 There could be no place for neutrality, and indeed such an attitude is explicitly excluded by the Marxist-Leninist dialectic which polarizes every issue and denies the possibility of intermediate solutions. *Ibid.* xxxvi. 122 As a result of the Industrial Revolution, society had polarized into two hostile classes, the bourgeoisie and the proletariat. **1957** *New Statesman* 2 Nov. 555/2 If we walked out of the nuclear arms race then the world would be 'polarised' between America and the Soviet Union. **1969** *N.Y. Rev. Books* 2 Jan. 41/1 New York was racially polarized as never before; hundreds of thousands of public school children were not being taught. **1972** *Nature* 3 Mar. 39/2 The problems are polarized into three areas... Only the first of these is really meteorological in character. **1972** M. L. Samuels *Ling. Evolution* vi. 132 Changes gather momentum when the upper classes polarise differences to maintain their value as prestige-markers. **1973** *Sci. Amer.* Apr. 86/3 Yet Henri labored..to avoid the utter disintegration of a France polarized and torn by civil war. **1977** *Time* 19 Dec. 8/2 From the first, Soares had insisted on governing without political alliances. Any compromise, he feared, would further polarize the country's politics.

polarized ('pəʊləraɪzd), *ppl. a.* [f. polarize *v.* + -ed[1].] Subjected to polarization.

1. a. Of light or other kinds of wave, or radiant heat. (See prec. 1.)

1811 July [see polarize *v.* 1]. **1813** (23 Dec.) Brewster in *Phil. Trans.* (1814) 199 The coloured image is..alike produced by polarised or depolarised light. **1831** —— *Optics* xviii. 158 These two beams..are therefore said to be polarised, or to be beams of polarised light, because they have sides or poles of different properties. **1845** Kelland *Young's Lect. Nat. Phil.* 371 Light which consists of vibrations in one direction only is termed polarized light. **1894** Turpin *Org. Chem.* 103 Three isomeric forms of malic acid which differ chiefly in their action upon polarized light. **1923** H. L. Brose tr. *Sommerfeld's Atomic Structure & Spectral Lines* i. 23 Barkla discovered that primary X-rays are partially polarised, secondary X-rays are wholly polarised in certain directions. **1946** *Wireless World* Aug. 251/1 If the receiving aerial is horizontal it will receive nothing from a vertically polarized wave. **1966** *McGraw-Hill Encycl. Sci. & Technol.* VIII. 418/1 A circular wave guide is particularly useful in transforming plane-polarized electric intensity into circularly polarized electric intensity.

b. *Physics.* Of a particle or beam of particles: exhibiting an alignment of the spins.

1929 *Proc. R. Soc.* A. CXXIV. 426 Our only hope of observing the moment of a free electron is to obtain a 'polarised' beam, in which all the spin axes are pointing in the same direction, or at any rate more in one direction than another. **1953** *Progr. Nuclear Physics* III. 75 It may be possible to produce polarized protons by using polarized thermal neutrons..as projectiles in an (n, p) reaction. **1975** *Nature* 5 June 514/1 These treatments will be of increasing value as polarised beams of deuterons and other ions become available.

c. Of a substance or device: causing the polarization of light passing through it; = polarizing *ppl. a.* 1.

1936 *Discovery* Oct. 302/1 Polarised glass has for some time been used..in certain scientific instruments. **1955** *Ann. Reg. 1954* 403 More than one critic referred to 1954 as the year of the decline of 3D on account of the general discomfort of polarized spectacles. **1977** *Sci. Amer.* Dec. 172/2 If a motorist wants to eliminate the glare from a road surface, he can wear polarized sunglasses.

†**2.** *Path.* **a.** Having a particular centre or axis, or a definite direction. **b.** Of a convex body: Having a pole or centre of convexity. *Obs.*

1822–34 *Good's Study Med.* (ed. 4) II. 36 In one or two examples..there was neither a polarized pain nor fluctuation. *Ibid.* 351 The centre [of the vaccine vesicle] dips, instead of being polarized, and is less elevated than the circumference. *Ibid.* III. 152 In the former [disease, i.e. presbyopia] the cornea is in all cases too much flattened, in the present it is too convex or polarized.

3. *Magn.* and *Electr.* **a.** (See prec. 3.)

1849 Noad *Electricity* (ed. 3) 39 He considers the first effect of an excited body upon neighbouring matter, to be the production of a polarized state of their particles, which constitutes induction... If the particles can maintain this polarized state, then insulation is the consequence; and the higher the polarized condition, the better the insulation. **1885** Watson & Burbury *Math. Th. Electr. & Magn.* I. 251 Such a system of polarised molecules as we are supposing gives rise to localised distributions with solid and superficial densities of determinate values throughout given regions and having the same potential at every point of the field as would result from such localised distributions.

b. See quot. 1886.

1878 Culley *Handbk. Pract. Telegraphy* (ed. 7) 277 In the polarized relay the force of the spring is replaced by magnetic attraction. **1879** G. Prescott *Sp. Telephone* p. ii, In 1830 he set up an electro-magnetic telegraph in Albany, ..using a polarized relay. *Ibid.* 26 Polarized magnets..so named on account of their armatures being permanent magnets. **1886** S. P. Thompson *Electromagnet* 291 It is usual to refer to those [electromagnetic] devices in which a permanent magnet comes into use as *polarized* mechanisms, while the ordinary electromagnets are *non-polarized*.

4. *fig.* **a.** Specialized in meaning or application.

1860 O. W. Holmes *Prof. Breakf.-t.* i, The religious currency of mankind,..consists entirely of polarized words.

b. Characterized by division into opposing groups or principles. Cf. polarize *v.* 4 c.

1957 *New Statesman* 2 Nov. 555/3 This gives the world something quite different from the polarised powers. **1962** E. Cleaver in A. Dundes *Mother Wit* (1973) 19/1 What we term *The Polarized Western Mind* derives from the symbolism attached to the two colors, black and white, in the mind of Western man. *Ibid.* 20/1 An obvious and striking example of polarized thinking.

polarizer ('pəʊləraɪzə(r)). [f. as prec. + -er[1].] One who or that which polarizes; *spec.* That plate or prism in a polariscope which polarizes the incident ray of light (opp. to *analyser*).

1854 Pereira *Polarized Light* (ed. 2) 50 There is no essential difference between the two parts,..and either part ..may be used as polarizer or analyzer; but whichever we use as the polarizer, the other then becomes the analyser. *Ibid.* 132 On rotating the film (the analyzer and polarizer remaining still), a brilliant colour is perceived at every quadrant of a circle, but in intermediate positions it vanishes altogether..so that when the film alone is revolved one colour only is seen, but when the analyzer alone is revolved, two colours are seen. **1863** [see analyser 3]. **1879** Rutley *Stud. Rocks* vii. 48 The polariser should revolve with perfect freedom.

'**polarizing**, *vbl. sb.* [f. as prec. + -ing[1].] The action of the vb. polarize, in various senses. Also *attrib.* as in ***polarizing angle*** (Optics), that angle of incidence (differing for different substances) at which the maximum polarization of the incident light takes place.

1812 (19 Dec.) Brewster in *Phil. Trans.* (1813) 105 The explanation which has now been given of the polarising power of the agate should be confirmed. **1829** *Nat. Philos.* I. *Polaris. Light* ii. 9 (U.K.S.) Placed at an angle of 52° 45′, the polarising angle for water. **1837** Brewster *Magnet.* 193 Mr. Barlow concludes that every place has its particular polarizing axis.

fig. **1901** *Dundee Advertiser* 16 Jan. 4 The newspaper.. renders possible the polarising of millions of men with one great idea.

'**polarizing**, *ppl. a.* [f. as prec. + -ing[2].] That polarizes or produces polarization.

1. *Optics.* (See polarize 1.)

1813 (23 Dec.) Brewster in *Phil. Trans.* (1814) 207 When we examine the transmitted light, either with the naked eye or with polarising crystals, no coloured fringes are visible. **1816** —— in *Edin. Phil. Trans.* VIII. 353 On the Laws which regulate the Distribution of the Polarising Force in Plates, Tubes, and Cylinders of Glass, that have received the Polarising Structure. **1869** Phipson tr. *Guillemin's Sun* (1870) 89 Polarising helioscopes have been manufactured.. and have realised the ideas of the illustrious English astronomer. **1890** *Athenæum* 29 Mar. 407/3 The method of evaluating the absorption of different thicknesses by comparison with a polarizing photometer.

2. *Magn.* and *Electr.* (See polarize 3.)

1866 R. M. Ferguson *Electr.* (1870) 131 Instead of one polarizing force there are several, all acting in the same direction. **1879** G. Prescott *Sp. Telephone* 32 One of these —the polarizing helix—is somewhat longer than the other.

polarly ('pəʊləlɪ), *adv.* [f. polar *a.* + -ly[2].] In a polar direction, manner, or degree; after the manner of or with reference to poles.

1830 J. Wilson in *Blackw. Mag.* XXVIII. 415 The miserable confusion of ideas polarly opposite. **1834** R. Mudie *Feathered Tribes Brit. Isl.* (1841) I. 15 Birds which migrate polarly, or for the purpose of breeding. **1849** Noad *Electricity* (ed. 3) 47 [The particles] being, as wholes, conductors, they can readily be charged either bodily or polarly. **1866** R. M. Ferguson *Electr.* (1870) 274 We have thus only one section polarly identified.

polarogram (pəʊ'lɑːrəʊ-, 'pəʊlərəʊgræm). *Chem.* [f. as next + -gram.] A graphical record of current against voltage produced by a polarograph (see next).

1925 Heyrovský & Shikata in *Recueil Travaux Chimiques Pays-Bas* XLIV. 496 The authors have set up a photographic auto-registering machine, which..records the polarisation curves, giving such 'polarograms' in less than 20 minutes. **1946** *Nature* 20 July 96/1 If several elements can be isolated simultaneously, there is the possibility of estimating them in a single polarogram. **1968** Pecsok & Shields *Mod. Methods Chem. Analysis* xiv. 339 The steps in the polarogram are called 'polarographic waves'. **1974** S. E. Allen *Chem. Analysis Ecological Materials* 398 If poor quality polarograms are produced even after passing nitrogen further bubbling may improve the display.

polarograph (pəʊ'lɑːrəʊ-, 'pəʊlərəʊgrɑːf, -græf). *Chem.* [f. polar(ization + -o + -graph.] An apparatus for automatic chemical analysis in which a sample solution is electrolysed using a steadily increasing voltage, and a graph, known as a polarogram, of current against voltage is produced; this usu. shows a series of steps each of which occurs at a voltage characteristic of a particular component and has a height proportional to the concentration of that component.

Polarograph is a proprietary term in the U.S.A.

1925 Heyrovský & Shikata in *Recueil Travaux Chimiques Pays-Bas* XLIV. 496 (*heading*) The polarograph. **1933** *Official Gaz.* (U.S. Patent Office) 15 Aug. 527/1 Polarograph Laboratories of America, Berkeley, Calif. Filed June 5, 1933. Polarograph. For Electrical Analyzing Apparatus... Claims use since Feb. 1, 1927. **1937** *Jrnl. Iron & Steel Inst.* CXXXVI. 109a From the current-potential curve the deposition potential for a given level on the curve can be determined, so that the polarograph can be used as a qualitative test. **1946** *Nature* 13 July 59/1 Iron can be determined satisfactorily on the polarograph if the solution contains triethanolamine. **1953** *Electronic Engin.* XXV. 314/1 One such instrument is the polarograph, which is used to determine the concentration of reducible ions in a solution, by measurement of the current that flows when the ions are electrolytically reduced. **1974** S. E. Allen *Chem. Analysis Ecol. Materials* 400 Oxygen is the only dissolved gas of interest to biologists which can be readily determined on the polarograph.

Hence **polaro'graphic** *a.*, of, pertaining to, or used in a polarograph or polarography; **polaro'graphically** *adv.*; **pola'rography**, the technique of using the polarograph.

1926 *Brit. Chem. Abstr.* A. 1184/1 (*heading*) Polarographic methods in biology. **1930** *Chem. News* 19 Dec. 388/2 Current-voltage curves obtained polarographically..reveal the presence of proteins in solutions. **1936** *Nature* 30 May 889/2 The last section, on polarography by Prof. J. Heyrovský, gives a comprehensive survey of the researches with the dropping mercury cathode. **1952** Kolthoff & Lingane *Polarography* (ed. 2) xviii. 397 This reaction may be utilized to remove dissolved oxygen from polarographic solutions. **1959** *Times* 30 Jan. 3/7 This involves supervision of staff engaged on a variety of analytical work, including.. infra-red spectroscopy and polarography. **1966** *McGraw-Hill Encycl. Sci. & Technol.* X. 455/1 The most widely used polarographic indicator electrode is the dropping-mercury electrode. **1970** C. N. Graymore *Biochem. Eye* x. 651 Noell ..measured oxygen tension polarographically. **1973** *Nature* 10 Aug. 370/2 Characteristic polarographic half-wave potential..values for proteins were attributed..to exposed, reactive sulphydryl..groups. **1975** M. R. Jenkins in Williams & Wilson *Biologist's Guide to Princ. & Techniques Pract. Biochem.* vii. 200 The main use of polarography in biochemistry is not, however, the measurement of oxidation-reduction potentials, but rather the qualitative and quantitative analysis of various compounds.

Polaroid (ˈpəʊlərɔɪd). Also **polaroid.** [Proprietary name.] **A.** *sb.* **1. a.** A material which in the form of thin sheets produces a high degree of plane polarization in light passing through it.

1936 *Official Gaz.* (U.S. Patent Office) 26 May 760/1 Sheet Polarizer Company, Inc., Union City, N.J... *Polaroid* for composite material comprising suspensions of crystalline particles in a light-transmitting medium adapted to be used in connection with optical devices such as microscope eye-pieces, glare eliminators,..gem testers, and the like. Claims use since Nov. 19, 1935. **1936** *Nature* 22 Aug. 312/2 Another [firm] manufactures ophthalmic instruments employing Polaroid. **1937** *Ann. Reg. 1936* II. 65 Land (*Nature*, Aug. 22) developed a new device for producing plane polarised light. Available commercially under the name Polaroid it consisted of a layer of ultramicroscopic needle-shaped crystals of herapathite.. oriented with their axes parallel on a cellulose film. **1940** *Trade Marks Jrnl.* 5 June 562/2 *Polaroid*... Materials specially prepared for use in the polarization of light. Polaroid Corporation.., Dover, State of Delaware, United States of America; manufacturers. **1942** *Chem. Abstr.* XXXVI. 2183 By use of film polarizers, e.g., polaroid, the expense is small. **1946** F. Schneider *Qualitative Organic Microanalysis* iv. 119 The sections of Polaroid are cut so that their planes of polarization include an angle of approximately 5° when the segments are mounted in place with a slight overlap. **1949** H. C. Weston *Sight, Light & Efficiency* iv. 133 If they are placed between two thin plates of polaroid, or between crossed Nicol prisms, so that the light passing through them is polarised, the presence of strain is shown by the formation of a coloured pattern due to double refraction by the strained glass. **1956** *Nature* 3 Mar. 434/1 A cylindrical unit..is formed by cementing a calcite crystal between two pieces of 'Polaroid'. **1976** *Nature* 19 Aug. 709/2 All stimuli were plane polarised by a 60-cm diameter rotatable disk of polaroid positioned between the screen and the eye.

b. A piece of 'Polaroid'.

1955 *Physical Rev.* XCIX. 1694/1 The action on polarized light of the rotating λ/2 plate followed by a polaroid is to produce an interruption of the light at four times the rotation frequency. **1967** H. von Klüber in J. N. Xanthakis *Solar Physics* ix. 261 For nearly all analysers used in the detection of such inverse Zeeman effects—such as polaroids, double-splitting crystals, quarter- or half-wave plates, etc.—the result..is just the same as in the emission case. **1976** *Nature* 11 Mar. 155/1 The relative intensities of the red and green components could then be varied by rotating a Polaroid interposed in the common beam.

2. *pl.* Sunglasses containing 'Polaroid'.

[**1942** *Official Gaz.* (U.S. Patent Office) 20 Oct. 463/1 Polaroid Corporation, Cambridge, Mass... *Polaroid*..for viewing devices—namely, filters, lenses, eyeglasses, and goggles. Claims use..on eyeglasses since July, 1936; and on goggles since December, 1937.] **1959** C. MacInnes *Absolute Beginners* 163 The water sparkling so that I had on my Polaroids. **1959** *New Statesman* 19 Sept. 354/2 The light.. beat back from the limestone with a spectral, otherworldly intensity that polaroids only served to accentuate. **1967** H. Hunter *Case for Punishment* i. 17 Cummings..was sporting a pair of heavy, black-rimmed spectacles. Inspector Shade had acquired a pair of green-tinted Polaroids. **1972** *Country Life* 23 Mar. 697/3 That afternoon my wife, wearing Polaroids, stationed herself opposite their lie and watched to see their reactions.

3. a. A kind of camera which develops the negative and produces a positive print within a short time of the exposure's being made.

1961 A. Gordon *Cipher* (1962) iv. 58 How about a nice picture, sir?.. I use a Polaroid... I'll have a print for you in a minute. **1966** H. B. Taylor *Triumvirate* xxxi. 168, I took a couple of pictures with my Polaroid, chatted a little. **1968** [see Long Tom 5]. **1977** *N.Y. Rev. Bks.* 23 June 25/4 From the first Kodak, when it took weeks before a developed roll of film was returned to the amateur photographer, to the Polaroid, which ejects the image in a few seconds.

b. A photograph produced by such a camera.

1972 D. Marlowe *Do You remember England?* iv. 57 All I got out of it were two Polaroids of her. **1975** *New Yorker* 19 May 12/3 (Advt.), Large toned prints of an abstract character. Manipulated color Polaroids of bizarre activities. **1977** *Rolling Stone* 13 Jan. 22/2 Grace snapped a couple of Polaroids for the wedding album.

B. *attrib.* **1.** Applied to the polarizing material (see A. 1) and articles in which it is employed.

1936 *Nature* 22 Aug. 312/2 It is by some such means described by Land that the Polaroid Corporation of Boston, U.S.A., has succeeded in manufacturing the 'Polaroid' sheets of polarizing material now on the market. *Ibid.*, One firm supplies Polaroid analysers and polarizers for the microscope. *Ibid.* 313/2 The details of reflecting objects can be seen more clearly through Polaroid films. **1951** *Electronic Engin.* XXIII. 10/2 The images.., plane polarized in mutually perpendicular directions by polaroid film, are superposed by a semi-reflecting mirror and are viewed through polaroid spectacles. **1954** *Ann. Reg. 1953* 365 Stereoscopic films viewed through polaroid spectacles were no novelty. **1958** *Woman* 9 Aug. 14/2 Polaroid sun-shield. **1961** E. N. Cameron *Ore Microsc.* ii. 20 The polarizer is a polaroid plate or a calcite prism. **1962** L. S. Sasieni *Optical Dispensing* xiii. 326 And Polaroid lenses are used as plano protective lenses (sun-glasses), or as sighted lenses to prescription. **1965** *Wireless World* July 340/2 Many of the digital instruments..incorporate polaroid filters to reduce reflected light.

2. Applied to a type of camera and photographs taken with it (see A. 3).

1963 L. Deighton *Horse under Water* xxxv. 136 Two armed policemen..photographed me with a Polaroid camera and filed the photo. **1965** H. C. Shands in J. H. Masserman *Sci. & Psychoanalysis* VIII. 135 The final 'discovery' in science is more like a cooperative collage than it is like a two-second Polaroid snapshot. **1973** C. Sagan *Cosmic Connection* (1975) xv. 109 Page 100 shows a Polaroid photo of the video-monitor image of Phobos. **1976** *Early Music* IV. 451/1 Polaroid cameras produce a result very fast, but only the most sophisticated models provide a negative so that duplicate prints and enlargements are usually unobtainable. **1976** A. Grey *Bulgarian Exclusive* iv. 30 Two polaroid colour photographs of a dark-haired man.

polaron (ˈpəʊlərɒn). *Physics.* [f. polar(ization and related words + -on[1]; orig. formed as Russ. *polyarón* (S. Pekar 1946, in *Zh. eksper. i teoret. Fiziki* XVI. 344).] A quasi-particle consisting of a free electron in an ionic crystal and the associated distortion of the crystal lattice.

1946 S. Pekar in *Jrnl. Physics* (Moscow) X. 343/2 Such local self-consistent quantum states of the electron in a crystal we shall briefly call polarons. **1955** *Physical Rev.* XCVII. 660/1 An electron moving with its accompanying distortion of the lattice has sometimes been called a polaron. **1969** *Nature* 15 Nov. 641/2 The interaction between an electron and its strain field in a polar solid gives rise to the excitation known as a polaron, the presence of which can be detected by irregularities in the shape of the conduction band. **1971** Mott & Davis *Electronic Processes in Non-Crystalline Materials* iv. 115 At low temperatures a polaron, whether large or small,..will behave exactly like a heavy particle, being scattered by impurities or lattice vibrations; moreover a high density of polarons can form a degenerate gas.

Hence **pola'ronic** *a.*

1978 *Nature* 16 Feb. 647/1 There will..be some stored energy involved in the system due to the polaronic nature of the moving charge carrier.

†**po'lartike**, *Obs.*, i.e. *pole arctic*, the north pole or pole-star: see pole *sb.*[2] 1, Arctic.

c **1391**, **1513** [see pole *sb.*[2] 1]. **1552** Lyndesay *Monarche* 6321, I se Polartike in the North appeir. **1596** Dalrymple tr. *Leslie's Hist. Scot.* viii. 90 Was..seine, betueine Pol artik and the Pleiades..a maruellous gret Comet.

'polarward, *adv.* (*a.*) [f. polar *a.* + -ward.] Towards the polar regions.

1832 *Fraser's Mag.* VI. 28 In the polarward parts of Thalabaw. **1860** Maury *Phys. Geog. Sea* (Low) x. §488 The water..goes polar-ward, dispensing warmth and moisture as it goes. **1890** *Nature* 16 Oct. 603/1 Polarward winds blow across the 45th degree of north latitude.

†**'polary**, *a. Obs.* Also 7 -arie. [ad. med.L. *polāris*, f. L. *polus* pole *sb.*[2]: see -ary[2]: cf. F. *polaire* (1556 in Hatz.-Darm.).]

1. Of or pertaining to a pole or the poles of the heaven or earth; = polar *a.* 1.

1559 W. Cunningham *Cosmogr. Glasse* 64 Vnder the two polary circles in the Heauen. **1623** tr. *Favine's Theat. Hon.* vii. viii. 243 The Polarie and Septentrionall Nations. **1658** Sir T. Browne *Gard. Cyrus* iv. 181 The poor inhabitants of the Moone have but polary life.

2. Of magnetic polarity; = polar *a.* 2.

1646 Sir T. Browne *Pseud. Ep.* ii. ii. 60 All which acquire a magneticall and polary condition, and being suspended, convert their lower extremes unto the North. **1665** Sir T. Herbert *Trav.* (1677) 351 That the Polary Direction was altogether unknown unto the Ancients, is agreed by most.

‖**polatouche** (pɒləˈtuːtʃ). *Zool.* [F. *polatouche*, ad. Russ. *poletuchiĭ* flying; cf. *letuchaya bêlka* flying squirrel.] The small flying squirrel of Europe and N. Asia, *Sciuropterus volans*.

1827 Griffith *Cuvier's Anim. K.* III. 84 Their molars.. are the same as those of the squirrels and polatouches. **1861** Wood *Nat. Hist.* I. 594 The polatouche of Siberia. **1896** *Cassell's Nat. Hist.* III. 89.

polax, pol-ax, obs. forms of pole-axe.

polayl, -aylle, var. of pullaile *Obs.*, poultry.

†**polayn, poleyn.** *Obs.* Forms: 4 poleyn, -e, 4–5 polayne, 5 polan, polayn, *Sc.* pu(l)lane. [ME. *poleyn*, *polayne*, a. OF. *po(u)lain*. Origin unknown.] A piece of defensive armour covering the knee.

c **1330** R. Brunne *Chron. Wace* (Rolls) 10027 Doublet & quysseux, wiþ poleyns ful riche. **13..** *Gaw. & Gr. Knt.* 576 His legez lapped in stel with luflych greuez, With polaynez piched þer-to. *c* **1400** *Sowdone Bab.* 176 Hawberke, spere, ner poleyne, ner pole. *c* **1470** Henry *Wallace* viii. 1203 His leg harnes he clappyt on so clene: Pullane greis he braissit on full fast. *c* **1475** *Rauf Coilȝear* 468 His Pulanis full prest of that ilk peir.

polayn(e, variant of poulaine, pullen *Obs.*

pold, obs. spelling of polled.

poldavy (pɒlˈdeɪvɪ), **poldavis** (pɒlˈdeɪvɪs). Now *rare.* Forms: 5– poldavy; also 6–7 pole-, 7 pool-, poole-, powle-, 7–8 poll-, poul-; 6 -dawy, 7 -daui, -davye, -davie, 9 -davey; poldway. *β.* 5–8 -davys, 6–7 -daves, 6–8 -davies, 7 -davyes, -dauice, 6– -davis. [app. f. *Poldavide*, a place on the south side of Douarnenez Bay, on the coast of Brittany. About 1548 a warrant for £70 11*s.* was issued to teach men here the art of making poldavies (Oppenheim *Royal Navy* 98, 103). The forms *poldavies*, *-davys*, *-davis*, etc. appear to have been the collective plural (cf. *silks*, *sheetings*, etc.), but were very often used as singular.]

A coarse canvas or sacking, originally woven in Brittany, and formerly much used for sailcloth.

1481–90 *Howard Househ. Bks.* (Roxb.) 37 Item, for trusing..a piece poldavy of xx. yerdes iij. quarters. **1562** *Reg. Privy Council Scot.* I. 225 He coft five ballis of poldavy and uther claith. **1613** Markham *Eng. Husbandman* i. ii. xix. (1635) 225 A Canvasse of the best Poldavie. **1622** Peacham *Compl. Gent.* vi. (1634) 54 If they have any wit at all, they set it like Velvet before, though the backe (like a bankerupts doublet) be but of poldavy or buckram. **1795** J. Aikin *Manchester* 302 The manufacture of sail-cloth or poldavy was introduced. **1860** Weale *Dict. Terms*, *Poldway*, coarse sacking for coal-sacks, etc. **1882** Jago *Cornish Gloss.*, *Poldavy*, a very coarsely woven linen cloth.

β. **1482** in I. S. Leadam *Star Chamb. Cases* 9, x. boltes of canuas callid poldavys. **1515** in Oppenheim *Royal Navy* 98 Canvas: Olron..Vitery..Poldavys. **1552** T. Barnabe in Strype *Eccl. Mem.* (1721) II. ii. App. E. 152 Whether yt were poldavis for saylis, or any other thing. **1604** *Act 1 Jas. I*, c. 24 (*heading*) An Acte againste the deceiptfull and false makinge of Mildernix, and Powle Davies, whereof Saile Clothes for the Navie..are made. **1614** 'Tobias Gentleman' *Eng. Way to Wealth* 22 Ipswich..is a principall place..for spinning of yarne, for the making of pouldauice. *a* **1642** Sir W. Monson *Naval Tracts* vi. (1704) 523/2 As also Pole-Davies for Sails. **1714** *Fr. Bk. of Rates* 190 The Linens called Poliseaux, or Poldavies shall be made Half Ell one Twelfth..broad. **1867** Smyth *Sailor's Word-bk.*, *Poldavis* or *Poldavy*, a canvas from Dantzic, formerly much used in our navy.

b. *attrib.* and *Comb.*

1558 in *Verney Papers* (Camden) 91 Francis Owdrey, of Abendon, in the countie of Berk, poldavis weaver. *Ibid.* 92 Fraunc̄is Owdreyne, of the towne of Ippiswitche, poldavyes maker. **1572** *Records of Elgin* (New Spald. Cl.) I. 134 Fyve quarters poledawy canves. *c* **1645** Howell *Lett.* ii. x, You must be content with homely Polldaui ware from me.

polder[1] (ˈpəʊldə(r)). Also 7 polther. [a. Du. *polder*, MDu. *polre*, *polder*; so EFris. *polder*, *poller*.] A piece of low-lying land reclaimed from the sea, a lake, or a river, from which it is protected by dikes: so called in the Netherlands; rarely used of similar land in other countries.

1604 E. Grimstone *Hist. Siege Ostend* 3 The *Polder* (so they call a..field wonne from the sea or riuer). **1632** *Contn. Weekly Newes* 25 July 8 (Stanf.) They did cut the dikes and drowned the enemies polther..and put all vnder water. *a* **1669** Somner *Rom. Ports & Forts Kent* (1693) 65 The soil is moorish, boggy and fenny, such as our Ancestors have usually called *Polder*:..i.e. a marish fenn, a meadow by the shore side, a field drain'd or gain'd from a river or the sea, and inclosed with banks. **1762** tr. *Busching's Syst. Geog.* III. 484 Several of them [lakes] have been drained and dyked under the name of *Polders*. **1839** W. Chambers *Tour Holland* 39/1 When the superincumbent mass has been entirely removed, the cleared space becomes a fertile polder. **1861** Smiles *Engineers* I. i. iv. 66. **1894** *Westm. Gaz.* 31 Mar. 8/1 Much of the asparagus eaten in London is grown in the polders reclaimed from the sea near Mont St. Michel.

b. *attrib.* and *Comb.*, as ***polder-land***; **polder-boy, polder-man**, a labourer employed in making polders. (All in reference to Holland.)

1873 W. K. Sullivan *O'Curry's Anc. Irish* I. Introd. 212 The privileges of the Abbey of St. Pierre of Ghent of about the year 830 mention the existence of a partnership..for the working of some polder-land. **1884** G. H. Boughton in *Harper's Mag.* Aug. 338/1 Little scattered hamlets of the fisher people and the polder-men. **1895** *Westm. Gaz.* 13 Apr. 6/1 This particular form of labour requires skilled navvies (polderboys we call them).

†**polder**[2]. *Obs.* or *dial.* [Corruption of *poller*, variant of pollard.] A pollard tree.

1704 *Dict. Rust.*, *Pollders*, are old Trees usually lopped, of which see *Shrowding of Trees*. **1736** Ainsworth *Lat. Dict.* i, Polders (old trees lopped), *arbores cædua*. **1902** *Westm. Gaz.* 7 Aug. 1/3 A canal fringed with polders.

polder, -dyr, obs. ff. powder.

polderne, -drand, -dren, -dron(e, var. pouldron *Obs.*

pold-gate. ? *Obs.* See quot.

1703 T. N. *City & C. Purchaser* 147 Pold Gates..are such as are set in Fences for to shut up the Passages into Fields, and..are of 2 sorts, either of sawed, or cleft Timber.

pole (pəʊl), *sb.*[1] Forms: 1 pál, 4 pool, 4– pole; also 4–6 poole, 5 poll (pulle, *Sc.* poille), 6 polle, poule, poale, 6–7 powle, 9 (*dial.*) powl. [OE. *pál* = OLG. **pâl* (OFris. *pâl*, MDu. *pael*, Du. *paal*, MLG., LG. *pāl*), OHG. *phâl* (MHG. *phâl*, *pfâl*, Ger. *pfahl*), ON. *páll* (Norw. *paale*, Sw. *påle*); ad. L. *pāl-us* stake, prop. OE. *pál* gave regularly ME. *pǭl*, mod.Eng. *pole*; the phonology of 15th c. *pulle*, 16th c. *poule*, and mod. dial. *powl*, *pow*, is obscure.]

1. a. In early use, A stake, without reference to length or thickness; now, a long, slender, and more or less cylindrical and tapering piece of wood (*rarely* metal), as the straight stem of a slender tree stripped of its branches; used as a support for a tent, hops or other climbing plants, telegraph or telephone wires, etc., for scaffolding, and for other purposes. (See also 2.)

The modern sense becomes clear first *c* 1440.

c **1050** *Voc.* in Wr.-Wülcker 334/2 *Palus*, pal. **1340** *Ayenb.* 203 þe eddre of bres arered ine þe pole. **1377** Langl. *P. Pl.* B. xviii. 52 Poysoun on a pole þei put vp to his lippes. **1387**

TREVISA *Higden* (Rolls) I. 369 Ȝif a pole [HIGD. *palus ligneus*, *Harl. MS.* a staffe or a thynge of a tree] is i-piȝt þerynne, þat partie of þe pole [CAXTON shaft or pool, *Harl. MS.* that tre] þat is in þe erthe schal turne in to iren. *c* **1440** *Promp. Parv.* 407/2 Pole, longe rodde, *contus, pertica.* *c* **1445** LYDG. *Nightingale* 309 This was the poole and the hygh[e] tree, Whilom sette vp by Moyses of entent. **1457** *Nottingham Rec.* II. 365 For c. allor polls vs. viiijd. *c* **1470** HENRY *Wallace* II. 33 He bar a sasteing in a boustous poille. **1484** CAXTON *Fables of Æsop* v. xiii. 91 b, I shalle haue alle the rote the pulle [*radices cum tota columna*] or maste and alle the braunches. **1541** *Nottingham Rec.* III. 383 For iij. powlez to make reylez in Cow Lane. *a* **1548** HALL *Chron., Hen. VI* 160 The Capitayne.. caused his head to be cut of, and pitched it on a highe poole. *Ibid., Hen. VIII* 139 b, The kyng.. lept ouer a diche beside Hychyn, with a polle and the polle brake. **1553** T. WILSON *Rhet.* (1580) 15 Some saie a long poule. **1559** *Mirr. Mag., Jack Cade* xv, On a poale. **1568** BIBLE (Bishops') *Num.* xxi. 8 Make thee a fyerie serpent, and set it vppon a pole [*Vulg.* pro signo, 1382 WYCL. for a tokne; 1388 for a signe; 1535 COV. for a token; 1539 (*Great*) for a sygne (so 1560 *Genev.*)]. **1607** in Stonehouse *Axholme* (1839) 404 [The boundary] towards the north, as the powles and stoupes were set [in the moors] by the said order, to Briscoe Dyke north east. **1616** SIR C. MOUNTAGU in *Buccleuch MSS.* (Hist. MSS. Comm.) I. 250 Lest a man be like a hop without a pole. **1717** PRIOR *Alma* II. 12 If, after some distinguish'd leap, He drops his pole, and seems to slip. **1869** E. A. PARKES *Pract. Hygiene* (ed. 3) 323 A conical tent, with a single pole. **1876** PREECE & SIVEWRIGHT *Telegraphy* (1905) 286 On the earliest telegraph lines square poles.. were employed. *Ibid.* 295 In countries where wood is extremely perishable.. iron poles are very extensively used.

b. Colloq. phr. ***up the*** (or ***a***) ***pole***: in trouble or difficulty; in confusion, in error; drunk; mad, crazy; pregnant but unmarried.

1886–96 A. R. MARSHALL in Farmer & Henley *Slang* (1902) V. II. 245/1 But, one cruel day, behind two slops he chanced to take a stroll, And.. he heard himself alluded to as being up the pole. **1896** *Daily News* 1 Apr. 7/6 She remonstrated with the latter, and told him he was 'up a pole'—i.e. in the wrong. **1897** *Daily Tel.* 11 Dec. 10/4 Plaintiff: .. but your little girl was frequently saying that you were 'up the poll [*sic*]'... The Judge: Up the what?.. The High Bailiff explained that the term was a slang one for being intoxicated. **1899** *Daily Mail* 29 Mar. 5/1 When there are nineteen Frenchmen to four Englishmen they were slightly up the pole. **1904** *Westm. Gaz.* 19 Mar. 7/2 Plaintiff's definition of the phrase 'up the pole' differed from that of her cousin.. who said it meant being drunk. Mrs. Frasier said that it.. meant being crazy. **1905** *Daily Chron.* 14 Dec. 6/4 Alec went to football smoker. Came home up the pole at one a.m... 'Up the pole,' Mrs. Norman said, was one of her husband's slang terms for a person under the influence of drink. **1906** E. DYSON *Fact'ry 'Ands* xiv. 188 Then, as a bright afterthought, she added, 'Yer fair up the pole!' **1915** C. J. DENNIS *Songs of Sentimental Bloke* 49 The dreams I dreamed, the dilly thoughts I thunk Is up the pole, an' joy 'as done a bunk. **1916** E. V. LUCAS *Vermillion Box* 165 It must require an awful lot of pluck... Either pluck or so much panic that one was practically up the pole with it. **1917** [see BLOTTO *a.*]. **1922** JOYCE *Ulysses* 23 That red Carlisle girl, Lily... Spooning with him last night on the pier. The father is rotto with money.—Is she up the pole?—Better ask Seymour that. **1922** *Daily Mail* 20 Dec. 3 Keith came to her, saying he was 'up the pole and in a frightful mess'. **1932** D. L. SAYERS *Have his Carcase* xxii. 295, I think we may take it for granted that our friend Weldon is a bit up the pole financially. **1950** J. CLEARY *Just let me Be* xi. 108 If I go and see 'em now, tell 'em what I done and why I done it, I'd be well and truly up the pole. **1961** 'F. O'BRIEN' *Hard Life* v. 37 To say nothing of a lot of crooked Popes with their armies and their papal states, putting duchesses and nuns up the pole, and having all Italy littered with their bastards. **1965** W. DICK *Bunch of Ratbags* vi. 92 'Right,' said Curly, agreeing with Ronnie's logic for once. He generally thought Ronnie was all up the pole when giving advice to someone. **1970** R. BEILBY *No Medals for Aphrodite* vi. 244 We'd 'a' been up the pole without him, that's why we didn't send him on his way. **1974** G. MOFFAT *Corpse Road* x. 142 'Do you really suspect that Pilgrim—*Pilgrim!*—killed the girl?..' 'You're up the pole,' Mrs Kent said to Page.

c. Colloq. phr. ***I wouldn't touch him*** (***it***) ***with a forty-foot*** (or ***ten-foot***) ***pole*** (and varr.): I refuse to have anything to do with him (it). Cf. BARGE-POLE.

1903 'T. COLLINS' *Such is Life* 22 The young feller he used to come sometimes an' just shake hands with her, but otherways he wouldn't touch her with a forty-foot pole. **1909** *Dialect Notes* III. 383, I wouldn't touch it with a ten-foot pole. **1941** *Coast to Coast* 167 'Me take the harness off him!' my mother said, surprised. 'Why, I wouldn't touch that mad thing with a forty-foot pole.' **1958** E. O. SCHLUNKE *Village Hampden* 26 Attracting a lot of business of the more or less shady sort that our reputable men wouldn't touch with a forty-foot pole. **1974** P. ERDMAN *Silver Bears* I. 11 No respectable bank.. would touch our business with a ten-foot pole.

2. In specific applications: **a.** A long tapering wooden shaft fitted to the fore-carriage of a vehicle and attached to the yokes or collars of the draught-animals, serving to guide and control the vehicle, and sometimes also bearing the whiffle-trees.

The application in quot. 1390 is uncertain.

[**1390** *Earl Derby's Exp.* (Camden) 7 Cum emptione poles, girthes, sursengles et aliis necessariis.] **1619** [implied in *pole-piece* in 5 c]. **1647** [implied in POLELESS]. **1683** WOOD *Life* 9 Nov. (O.H.S.) III. 79 The pole of a coach hit against his brest. **1699** S. SEWALL *Diary* 27 Sept., Pole of the Calash broken by the Horses frighted with a Pistol. **1813** *Sk. Charac.* I. 114 The pole of our carriage ran against the splendid chariot of the Marchioness of Arrangford.

b. Used as a tradesman's sign. Cf. ALE-POLE, *barber's pole* s.v. BARBER 3.

1566 *Ann. Barber-Surg. Lond.* (1890) 181 No Barber shall .. put out any bason or basons.. upon his poule on Sundays or Holy days. **1641** TATHAM *Distracted State* IV. i. (1651) 22/2 *Scotch Apothecary*.. I ha not ben a Poles-Screamer this twenty years far naught. **1797** LD. THURLOW in Hone *Every-day Bk.* (1825) I. 1269 By a statute still in force, the barbers and surgeons were each to use a pole. **1887** T. HARDY *Woodlanders* i, A master-barber that's left off his pole because 'tis not genteel.

c. *Naut.* A ship's mast: in phr. ***with*** or ***under*** (***bare***) ***poles***: with no sail set, with furled sails. Also, The upper end of a mast, rising above the rigging.

1669 STURMY *Mariner's Mag.* I. ii. 17 We may have.. to spoon before the Sea with our Powles. **1697** DAMPIER *Voy.* (1699) 415 We scudded.. before the Wind very swift, tho' only with our bare Poles. **1799** *Hull Advertiser* 20 July 2/4 The brig is painted black, with.. no pole to her fore top gallant-mast. **1816** 'QUIZ' *Grand Master* II. 22 The vessel rolls, At ocean's mercy under poles.

d. The long handle of a scythe or the like. *dial.*

1828 *Craven Gloss.* (ed. 2), *Pow*, a pole, a scythe pow, the long handle of a scythe. **1903** *Eng. Dial. Dict.*, (*S. Lancs.*) Scythe pow, stang pow.

e. (*a*) *Racing*, the inside fence surrounding a racecourse; the starting position closest to the inside fence; (*b*) *Motor racing*, esp. in phr. ***pole position***, the grid position which is on the front row and on the inside of the first bend; also *fig.*, any advantageous position.

1851 *Fraser's Mag.* XLIII. 657/1 The distance round is calculated at a mile,.. For a saddle horse that has the pole, it comes practically to a little less... A horse 'has the pole', means that he has drawn the place nearest the inside boundary-fence of the track. *Ibid.* 659/1 'What a beauty she is!' says Harry. 'And she has the pole too.' **1868** H. WOODRUFF *Trotting Horse* xxiv. 206, I had the pole with Kemble Jackson, and soon took the lead. **1902** A. D. MCFAUL *Ike Glidden* xxii. 198 This stroke apparently gave the friends of the colt more confidence in the result, as drawing the pole was a position in favor of the colt. **1953** *Motor* 22 July 857/3 The newest B.R.M.. had to be worked on all night and brought back to the course only just in time to come to the pole position on the starting line. **1963** *Times* 27 Apr. 3/3 J. Clark set a new unofficial lap record in his fuel injected Lotus 25.. which gives him pole position on the starting grid. **1966** *Telegraph* (Brisbane) 14 May 17/3 Australian Jack Brabham,.. former world champion racing driver, snatched pole position for tomorrow's international formula one race. **1968** *Globe & Mail* (Toronto) 3 Feb. 36/2 Two Ford GT40s broke a course record and grabbed the pole positions for this weekend's 24 Hours of Daytona at Daytona Beach, Fla. **1969** *Australian* 24 May 34/4 Won Mobile 12½f event here four starts back. Place claims from the 'pole'. **1971** *Sunday Times* 12 Sept. 50/3 The German company retained a pole position in hormone research which led to the Pill. **1976** *Milton Keynes Express* 11 June 42/7 Colin Hawker's Cosworth Grand Prix-engined VW was on pole. **1976** *Listener* 8 July 7/3 Brazil's foreign investment needs.. would double its foreign borrowing, and take Brazil to pole position in the big league of world debtors. **1977** *News of World* 17 Apr. 24/7 Ipswich relinquished their hold on the pole position to champions Liverpool.

3. a. A pole (in sense 1) of definite length used as a measure; hence, name of a lineal measure, esp. for land: in Statutory Measure, equal to 5½ yards or 16½ feet, but varying locally; a PERCH, a ROD.

1502 ARNOLDE *Chron.* (1811) 173 In dyuers odur placis.. they mete ground by pollis gaddis and roddis some be of xviij foote some of xx fote and som xvi fote in length. **1579** J. STUBBES *Gaping Gulf* F iij, Thold English liberall measure of syxtene foote and a halfe to the pole. **1603** OWEN *Pembrokeshire* (1892) 133 In some place the pole is but ix foote, and in some place xij foote. **1706** PHILLIPS, *Pole*, a long Stick: In measuring, it is the same with Pearch or Rod, or as some call it Lugg: By Stat. 35 Eliz. this Measure is a length of 16 Foot and a half, but in some Countries it consists of 18 Foot and is called Woodland-Measure; in some Places of 21 Foot termed Church-Measure; and in others of 24 Foot under the Name of Forest-Measure. **1725** BRADLEY *Fam. Dict.* s.v. *Mile*, Every Furlong forty Lugs or Poles.. every Pole sixteen Foot and a Half. **1813** T. DAVIS *Agric. Wilts* App. 268 A rod, pole, or perch.. is of three lengths in this county: 15, 18, and 16½ feet.

b. As a measure of area: A square rod or perch; 30¼ square yards.

1637 in *N. Riding Rec.* IV. 77 To be rated by acree and powle. **1660** SHARROCK *Vegetables* 19 A rod or pole of ground, which is the square of sixteen feet and a half. *Mod.* The land is let in ten-pole allotments at sixpence a pole.

4. In sporting phraseology: The tail of certain beasts and birds, as the otter, pheasant, etc.

1863 ATKINSON *Stanton Grange* (1864) 202 His hand missed the otter's hind-quarters, but closed upon its pole (or tail). **1900** *Shooting Times* 15 Dec. 15/2 *Pole*, the tail of an otter. *Ibid.*, *Pole*, the tail of a pheasant. **1904** *Westmld. Gaz.* 2 July 5/5 Captain T. presented the pole to Miss L., the pads to the Misses C.,.. and the mask most deservedly to.. the huntsman.

5. *attrib.* and *Comb.* **a.** Simple attrib.: Pertaining to, consisting or made of a pole or poles, as ***pole barn***, ***-bridge***, ***corral***, ***-end***, ***-fence***, ***-futchel***, ***-head*** (cf. *pole-mast* in c.), ***plantation***, ***-topmast***, ***-wood***. **b.** Objective and obj. genitive, instrumental, etc., as ***pole-balancing***, ***-bearer***, ***-jump***, ***-jumper***, ***-jumping***, ***leap***, ***-leaper***, ***-leaping***, ***-setter***, ***-setting***; ***pole-armed***, ***-shaped*** adjs.

1950 *Pole barn [see *pole corral*]. **1960** *Farmer & Stockbreeder* (Suppl.) 19 Jan. 41/1 In winter they are in pens of 45 in pole-barns. **1969** *Times* 24 Feb. 12/1 They [*sc.* bullocks].. were present by the score,.. making their systematic way to adjacent pole barn silos. **1972** *N.Y. Law Jrnl.* 22 Aug. 13/8 (Advt.), Five bedrooms, 14 room modern home.. on 12½ acres,.. pole barn suitable for horses, riding trails nearby, would make ideal ski lodge. **1800** *Sporting Mag.* XV. 28 The *pole-bearers were followed by a large ship. **1900** G. C. BRODRICK *Mem. & Impress.* ii. 38 In the early summer of 1844 I took part as a 'pole-bearer' in the last Montem. [See POLEMAN b, quots. 1844, 1898.] **1793** J. LINDLEY in *Michigan Pioneer & Hist. Coll.* (1892) XVII. 574 *Pole bridges.. made the tour very disagreeable. *a* **1817** T. DWIGHT *Trav. New Eng.*, etc. (1821) II. 131 Mr. L's horse, crossing a pole bridge, fell through, and threw his rider. **1850** *Congress. Globe* 29 Jan. 240/1 Now, his colleague must start by the most direct route the 23rd of November, making provision for.. contingencies of travel over corduroy roads, pole bridges, mud turnpikes, etc. **1974** D. SEARS *Lark in Clear Air* ii. 34 We crossed a pole bridge over the Perch. **1950** *Amer. Speech* XXV. 85 No longer heard is *old land*, though *pole barn* and **pole corral* still describe forms of construction. **1962** J. ONSLOW *Bowler-Hatted Cowboy* v. 51 Two saddle horses which we turned into a small pole-corral. **1973** *Whig-Standard* (Kingston, Ont.) 11 Aug. 7/4 His.. sheep.. didn't want to bunch in the pole corral for the night. **1788** G. WASHINGTON *Diaries* (1925) III. 346 All hands were.. finishing the *Pole fence round the Barley and Pease in field No. 1. **1835–40** HALIBURTON *Clockm.* (1862) 229 Who should I see but Bobbin in his waggon ag'in the pole fence. **1959** W. R. BIRD *These are Maritimes* x. 278 We saw.. many ancient pole fences crossing the fields. **1973** L. RUSSELL *Everyday Life Colonial Canada* ii. 32 Probably the pole fence was the kind most frequently constructed at this stage [of land clearing]. In this, the trunks of moderate-sized trees were used, cut in lengths of 12 to 15 feet. **1875** KNIGHT *Dict. Mech.*, **Pole-futchel*, the jaws between which the hinder end of a carriage-tongue is inserted. **1794** *Rigging & Seamanship* I. 16 *Top-gallant-masts*.. have commonly *pole-heads, either stump, common, or long. **1886** *Year's Sport* 21 The other winners .. were.. *pole jump, T. Ray; and wide jump, J. Purcell. **1898** *Daily News* 22 Feb. 3/4 A party of his pupils are exercising at the pole-jump, across a ditch. **1887** M. SHEARMAN *Athletics & Football* v. 163 Ulverston.. has produced many fine *pole-jumpers. **1908** *Westm. Gaz.* 1 July 8/4 Quite recently, Szathmary, the pole-jumper, broke the Hungarian record. **1912**, **1920** Pole jump [see DECATHLON]. **1868** H. F. WILKINSON *Mod. Athletics* viii. 88 *Pole jumping. The leaping pole should be made of fir or ash. **1912** [see *field events* s.v. FIELD *sb.* 21]. **1931** E. LINKLATER *Juan in America* I. vi. 59 He could not help being tickled by the thought of an American university; pole-jumping and cheer-leaders. **1868** *Kendal Times* 5 Sept. 2/5 (*heading*) Grasmere annual sports... High *pole leap for £1. **1869** *Ibid.* 18 Sept. 4/3 The high *pole leaping.. was gone through in capital style. **1885** F. GALE *Mod. Eng. Sports* vi. 67 Running, jumping, and pole-leaping were often the outcome of a very old-fashioned sport, 'Follow my leader'. **1888** T. BRIGHT *Pole Plantations & Underwoods* i. 1 A *pole plantation is an assemblage of young trees, the produce of plants that have been inserted in the soil at regular distances, or of the stems formed from such plants after their having been cut for poles. **1892** A. E. LEE *Hist. Columbus* (Ohio) I. 363 After the *polesetters had done their work the wires were quickly strung. **1887** *Pall Mall G.* 10 Sept. 7/1 An elderly man.. fights with a *pole-shaped stick against a constable. **1769** FALCONER *Dict. Marine* (1789), *Maté en caravelle*, fitted with *pole topmasts. **1742** *MS. Agreement* (co. Derby), [Lessee] to fall or cut all the large or *pole wood grounds.

c. Special Combs: **pole-bean**, any climbing bean (Webster, 1890); **pole-board**, a board or placard carried on poles like a banner; **pole-boat** now chiefly *Hist.*, a river-boat propelled by means of a pole or poles; so **pole-boating** *vbl. sb.*; **pole-bracket**, a bracket on a telegraph pole for supporting the wires; **pole-bullock**, a bullock that is harnessed alongside the pole of a wagon; **pole-burn**, a disease affecting tobacco during the curing process, due to overheating when hung too closely on poles (*Funk's Stand. Dict.* 1895); so **pole-burn** *v. intr.*, (of tobacco) to be discoloured and lose flavour by overheating (*Cent. Dict.* 1890); **pole-cap**, the insulating cap of a telegraph pole; **pole-carriage** (Knight *Dict. Mech.* 1875), **pole-cart**, a vehicle furnished with or drawn by means of a pole; **pole-chain**, (*a*) a measuring chain = CHAIN *sb.* 9; (*b*) the chain by which the end of a carriage-pole is connected with the collar; †**pole-clipt** *a.*, hedged in by poles; **pole-crab**, a double metal loop affixed to the end of a carriage-pole to receive the breast-straps of the harness (Knight); **pole-cure** *v.*, to cure (tobacco) by hanging it on poles; **pole-dray**, a dray furnished with or drawn by means of a pole; **pole-ground**, ground or river-bottom suitable for poling a barge, etc.; †**pole-hammer**, properly **poll-hammer**, the war-hammer or martel-de-fer; †**pole-hatchet**, ? = POLE-AXE; an opprobrious appellation (cf. HATCHET-FACE); **pole-hedge** = ESPALIER 1; **pole-hook**, (*a*) the hook on the end of a carriage-pole; (*b*) a boat-hook (Knight); **pole-horse**, a horse harnessed alongside of the pole, a wheeler as distinguished from a leader; **pole-lathe**, a lathe in which the work is turned by a cord passing round it, and fastened at one end to the end of an elastic pole, and at the other to a treadle; **pole-mast**, a mast formed of a single spar; so **pole-masted** *a.*; **pole-mule**, a mule harnessed alongside the pole of a wagon; **pole-net**, a net for catching fish, etc., fastened on a pole or poles; **pole-pad**, a stuffed leather pad fastened on the point of the pole of a gun-carriage, to prevent injury to the horses; **pole-piece**, (*a*) a heavy strap which attaches the end of the pole to the horse's collar; (*b*) in roof-construction, a ridge-pole; †**pole-pike**, ? a pike fixed in the end of a pole, a pike-staff; **pole-plate** (see quots.); **pole-prop**, a bar for supporting the end of the pole (esp. of an artillery carriage) when the horses are unhitched (Knight); **pole-puller**, one who is employed in drawing the poles in a hop-garden; so **pole-pulling**; **pole-rack**, a rack on which drying-poles are supported in dyeing, tanning, and other trades; **pole-railroad**, **-railway**, a temporary track constructed of two parallel lines of barked poles, serving as rails for the removal of the logs of a district to the sawmill; **pole-reed** (also *pool-reed*), *Phragmites communis*; **pole-road** = *pole-railroad*; **pole-rose** = *pillar rose* s.v. PILLAR *sb.* 12; **pole-rush** (also *pool-rush*), the Bulrush, *Scirpus lacustris*; **pole-screen**, a fire-screen mounted on an upright pole or rod, on which it may be fixed at any point; **pole-shank** = *pole-staff*; **pole-sling**, a kind of palanquin or travelling seat suspended from a pole or poles carried by bearers; †**pole-square**, a square pole; **pole-staff**, a net-pole (*Cent. Dict.*); **pole-strap** = *pole-piece* (*a*) (Knight); **pole-tip**, a metal cap covering the point of the pole of a carriage; **pole-tool**: see quot.; **pole-torpedo**, a torpedo carried on the end of a pole projecting from the bows of a vessel; a spar-torpedo; **pole-trailer** (see quot. 1971); **pole-trap**, a circular steel trap set on the top of a post; a bird-catching device which consists of a trap fixed to the top of a pole; **pole-trawl**, a trawl-net of which the mouth is kept open with a pole; so **pole-trawling**; **pole vault**, a jump over a horizontal bar which is achieved by means of a pole; = *pole jump*; also *attrib.*; hence as *v. trans.* and *intr.*; so **pole-vaulter**; also *fig.*; **pole-vaulting** *vbl. sb.*; **pole-wagon**, a wagon furnished with or drawn by means of a pole; **pole-wedge** (also **poll-**), in a plough: see quots.; **pole-wound** *rare*, a wound that has been inflicted with a pole.

c **1770** 'J. H. St. J. de Crèvecœur' *Sk. 18th-Cent. Amer.* (1925) 120, I had once some hops and *pole-beans, about twenty feet high. **1857** *Trans. Ill. Agric. Soc.* (1859) III. 503 There are many varieties of pole beans. **1865** [see Lima b]. **1871** Mrs. Stowe *Oldtown Fireside Stories* 246 There was thick pole-beans quite up to the buttery-door. **1941** J. Stuart *Men of Mountains* 192 We drove down past Shelton's polebean patch. **1976** *Washington Post* 19 Apr. A10/7 (Advt.), Fresh Florida pole beans. 4 lbs. $1. **1909** *Westm. Gaz.* 29 Dec. 6/4 Others, again, carrying *pole-boards setting forth all deceased's honours and titles. **1827** A. Sherwood *Gaz. Georgia* (1939) 22/1 Cargoes..are thrown into *pole boats. **1835** W. G. Simms *Partisan* II. ii. 12 At this point the river ceased to be navigable even for the common poleboats of the country. **1841** —— *Kinsmen* I. xiv. 163 Wherever a pole-boat had made its way, there had the name of Jack Bannister found repeated echoes. **1968** R. F. Adams *Western Words* 232/1 *Pole boat*, a river boat; so called because of the means by which it was propelled upstream. **1837** A. Sherwood *Gaz. Georgia* (ed. 3) 193 A revolution in the mode and manner of transshipping goods must take place. The slow, tedious and expensive process of *pole-boating will be exploded. **1876** Preece & Sivewright *Telegraphy* 211 *Pole-brackets..are of a tubular form..and made of malleable iron. **1930** L. G. D. Acland *Early Canterbury Runs* 1st Ser. vii. 150 In 1868 Strawberry, one of the *pole-bullocks, died after working ten years and seven months on the station. **1933** *Press* (Christchurch, N.Z.) 18 Nov. 15/7 *Pole-bullocks*, the two bullocks which work on the *p*[*ole*] of a dray or waggon. **1884** *Health Exhib. Catal.* 78/1 Insulators. *Pole Cap. **1833** *Wauldby Farm Rep.* 102 in *Libr. Usef. Knowl., Husb.* III, The wain or *pole-cart dragged by oxen is unknown here. **1725** Bradley *Fam. Dict.* s.v. *Surveying*, The surveyor..furnish'd..with a well divided *pole chain or off set rod. **1827** *Sporting Mag.* XXI. 102 The accidental breakings of reins, pole-chains, hame-straps. **1610** Shaks. *Temp.* iv. i. 68 Thy *pole-clipt vineyard, And thy Sea-marge stirrile, and rockey-hard. **1899** *Rep. U.S. Dept. Agric.* No. 62. 30 The present method of manipulating these tobaccos after they are *pole-cured is quite different from what it was years ago. **1848** H. W. Haygarth *Bush Life Australia* v. 49 In some districts..shaft-drays are used; but *pole-drays are found to be more suitable to the nature of the country. **1773** in Crisp *Richmond* (1866) 316 From the depth of water, the want of *Pole ground would render it difficult..to work the Craft. **1873** Sullivan *O'Curry's Anc. Irish* I. Introd. 459 In the fourteenth century the war hammer was in general use... The foot soldiers had it fixed on a long pole, whence the name *Pole-hammer. [This is an error, founded on false etymology; the *poll-hammer* (M.Du. *pol-hamer*) had its name from *poll* head, like *poll-ax*, POLE-AXE.] *a* **1529** Skelton *My darlyng dere*, etc. 28, I wys, *powle hachet, she bleryd thyne I. **1826** Hor. Smith *Tor Hill* (1838) II. 98 You pennyless pole-hatchet. **1665** Rea *Flora* (ed. 2) 6 Pallisados (or as we usually call them, *Pole-hedges) are much in fashion in France. **1706** London & Wise *Retir'd Gard.* I. 91 The Cultivation of Vines in Vineyards, on Pole-Hedges. **1889** *Harper's Mag.* June 160/2 The leaders sprang upward and onward.., the *pole-horses simultaneously crashing backward and downward. **1815** J. Smith *Panorama Sc. & Art* I. 66 The *pole lathe..made of the cheapest materials, and in the simplest manner. **1859** Pole-lathe [see BACK-REST 1]. **1881** Young *Ev. Man his own Mechanic* §539 The pole lathe and the 'dead-centre' lathe are ..the most simple forms of this useful contrivance. **1932** G. M. Boumphrey *Story of Wheel* 38 When the lathe came here, it was altered into what is called the pole-lathe. **1968** J. Arnold *Shell Book of Country Crafts* xv. 200 Whether a turner uses a pole-lathe or the treadle type seems a matter for individual inclination... The extremely primitive pole-lathe came firstly with a primitive society, but its retention appears largely due to its simplicity and easy portability. **1730** in *Patents Specific., Masts*, &c. (1874) 1 A *pole mast vessell for the better..catching..of all sorts of fish. **1824** *Ibid.* 19 Double pole masts. **1769** Falconer *Dict. Marine* (1789) B b ij b, A mast..is either formed of one single piece, which is called a *pole mast*, or composed of several pieces joined together. **1894** *Daily News* 22 Feb. 2/1 The Britannic is rigged as a *pole-masted schooner. **1915** *Yachting Monthly* XIX. 366/1 This necessitated a change of rig, and a pole-masted ketch was decided on. **1970** *Mariner's Mirror* LXVI. 165 Evidence for the pole-masted brigantine rig was found at the Dubrovnik museum. **1862** O. W. Norton *Army Lett.* (1903) 106 A driver riding the near *pole mule and guiding his team with one line. **1858** Simmonds *Dict. Trade*, **Pole-net*, a net attached to a pole for illegal fishing in rivers. **1885** Bompas *Life F. Buckland* 163 Imagine an old fashioned, bag-shaped night-cap, with a stick fastened on each side of it, and you have a pole net. **1619** in *Naworth Househ. Bks.* (Surtees) 108 For a paer of duble cotch rains and 2 *poolpeseis. **1794** W. Felton *Carriages* (1801) I. 212 *Pole-pieces* are the straps which couple the horses to the pole, and are regulated by the size and weight of the carriage. **1901** *J. Black's Illustr. Carp. & Build., Home Handicr.* 22 Deal rafters..the lower ends of which rest on the wall plates, ..and the upper extremities..abut on the 'ridge' or 'pole piece'. **1451–2** *Durham Acc. Rolls* (Surtees) 147 Pro j *polepike et quinque Sholyrnez, ijs. ijd. **1823** P. Nicholson *Pract. Build.* 128 A *pole-plate is a beam over each opposite wall, supported upon the ends of the tie-beam. **1889** *Cath. Household* 30 Nov. 4 Bold king-post principals and traceried windbraces to the purlins and pole plates. **1805** R. W. Dickson *Pract. Agric.* II. 753 The *pole-puller and pickers ..in the hop plantation. **1878** *Lumberman's Gaz.* 6 Apr., They use on these *pole railroads trucks with iron wheels. **1578** Lyte *Dodoens* iv. liv. 514 This plante is called in.. English, Common *Pole Reede, Spier, or Cane Reede. **1597** Gerarde *Herbal* i. xxiv. §6. 34 *Arundo Cypria*..in English, Pole reede, or Cane, or Canes. **1879** Prior *Names Brit. Plants* (ed. 3) 187 *Pole-reed*,..in our western counties, Pool-reed. **1879** *Lumberman's Gaz.* 16 July 6 The *pole road, ordinarily, is constructed of poles 4 or 5 inches in diameter, of pine or hard wood. **1893** *Scribner's Mag.* June 708/2 'Pole-roads'..where cars with wheels with concave faces run on poles instead of rails. **1848** W. Paul *Rose Garden* 67 Pillar or *Pole Roses. **1578** Lyte *Dodoens* iv. lii. 511 The fourth [kind of Rush] is called..in English, the *pole Rushe, or bull Rushe, or Mat Rushe. **1870** Mrs. Oliphant *Autobiogr. & Lett.* (1899) 225, I have just finished the most enchanting *pole-screen. **1937** *Burlington Mag.* Apr. p. xxiv/1 A mahogany Polescreen on a beautifully carved tripod stand. **1960** B. Snook *English Historical Embroidery* 98 Pole screens were not unconnected with vanity. Created in the 18th century to protect the make-up worn by elegant women from the heat of large open fires, they were very practical little pieces of furniture. **1976** *Northumberland Gaz.* 26 Nov. 18/4 (Advt.), Pair Regency mahogany pole screens. **1888** Goode *Amer. Fishes* 250 In this is inserted the end of the *pole-shank. **1707** Mortimer *Husb.* (1721) I. 86 Allowing a Bushel to a *Pole-square, or a hundred and sixty Bushels to an Acre. **1881** Raymond *Mining Gloss.*, **Pole-tools*, the tools used in drilling with rods. **1878** *N. Amer. Rev.* CXXVII. 386 The *pole-torpedo could not..avail. **1969** *Pole trailer [see EXPANDABLE *a.*]. **1971** M. Tak *Truck Talk* 120 *Pole trailer*, a trailer composed of a single telescopic pole, a tandem rear-wheel unit and a coupling device used to join the trailer to a tractor. **1892** *Daily News* 6 Jan. 5/7 Most cruel of all the instruments of destruction used by gamekeepers..is the '*pole trap'. **1909** *Westm. Gaz.* 17 Feb. 5/1 The catching of birds with hooks in Cornwall has been stopped by an Act passed last year, and efforts have been made to abolish entirely the illegal pole-trap. **1972** *Guardian* 3 May 7/2 The illegal and viciously cruel pole trap ..a spring trap fixed by a short chain to the top of a pole which kills the captured bird in an extremely slow and painful way—was made illegal in 1904... It appears to be still in common use. **1975** *Country Life* 2 Oct. 849/2 Even in Britain..prosecutions are still being brought for the illegal use of pole-traps. **1836** *First Rep. Irish Fisheries* 166 The *pole-trawl, used in shoal water, is the only one known here. **1774** Walsh in *Phil. Trans.* LXIV. 471 Small vessels, with which they practise *pole-trawling. **1893** *Outing* (U.S.) XXII. 154/2 He has..held the world's record in the *pole vault for distance. **1935** *Encycl. Sports* 467/1 In front of the pole-vault bar is a slideway, in which the base of the pole is placed when jumping. *Ibid.* 467/2 The world's record pole vault is 14 ft. 4$\frac{3}{4}$ in., made by W. Graber..in 1932. **1951** *Time* 29 Jan. 85 Did, or did not, the Rev. Robert Richards become the second man in history to pole-vault 15 feet? **1973** *Times* 2 May 11/2 She..will train regularly with Michael Bull, who holds the British pole vault record and who is preparing for the decathlon in the Christchurch Commonwealth Games next January. **1977** *Western Morning News* 30 Aug. 12/7 Brian Hooper edged a little closer to the magical 18-foot pole vault as another landslide of wins carried Britain to overwhelming victory against West Germany. **1978** *Times* 18 July 2/8 Ape pole-vaults over park moat... A chimpanzee..escaped from an island by pole-vaulting across a moat using an 8 ft. pole. **1888** A. Randall-Diehl *2000 Words* 165 **Pole Vaulter*, one who practices leaping by aid of a pole. **1891** W. M'Combie Smith *Athletes & Athletic Sports of Scotland* viii. 88 From the moment he takes hold of the pole as he commences his run till he lets it go as he crosses the bar the pole-vaulter never shifts his hands. **1893** *Outing* (U.S.) XXII. 154/2 Harding..began training as a pole-vaulter in 1891. **1956** *Sun* (Baltimore) 13 Oct. (B ed.) 12/2 The United States Air Force unit responsible for making these jaunts across the roof of the world a daily routing is the 58th Weather Reconnaissance Squadron—more colloquially known as 'the pole vaulters'. **1976** *Milton Keynes Express* 30 July 43/2 Saturday's performance was helped by the presence of two new pole vaulters. **1877** *N.Y. Times* 5 Apr. 8/4 The following programme was adopted: one-mile walk, two-mile walk, one-mile run,..*pole-vaulting. **1891** W. M'Combie Smith *Athletes & Athletic Sports of Scotland* viii. 88 Pole-vaulting is comparatively a recent introduction at Scottish sports. **1932** Webster & Heys *Exercises for Athletes* viii. 161 Now let us consider which are the muscles principally involved in the feat of pole-vaulting. **1968** M. Watman *Hist. Brit. Athletics* x. 168 Pole vaulting for height, as distinct from distance, was pioneered in the mid-nineteenth century by members of the Ulverston (Lancashire) Cricket and Football Club. **1908** S. Ford *Side-Stepping with Shorty* vi. 90 The *pole waggon brings up the rear. **1910** G. B. McCutcheon *Rose in Ring* i. i. 6 Here and there, in the gloomy background, stood the canvas and pole wagons. **1968** J. Arnold *Shell Book of Country Crafts* v. 76 The pole-wagon, which was the fore-runner of the present-day motor-hauled trolley, had iron stanchions at its four corners of two transverse beams, each above its respective axle. **1733** Tull *Horse-Hoeing Husb.* xxi. 308 The Coulter, which is wedged tight up to it [the Coulter-hole] by the *Poll-Wedge. *Ibid.* 309 Three Wedges at least will be necessary to hold the Coulter; the Pole-Wedge before it,..another Wedge on the left Side of it above, and a third on the right Side underneath. **1908** Hardy *Dynasts* III. iv. vi. 417 Who knows but that we should have been kings too, but for my crooked legs and your running *pole-wound?

pole, *sb.*^{2} Forms: 4– **pole**; also 4 **pool**, 4–6 **pol**, 5–6 **poole**, 6 **powle**, *Sc.* **poill**. [ad. L. *pol-us* the end of an axis, a pole ((Astron.) Plin.), the sky (Virg.), a. Gr. πόλος a pivot, axis, in Astron. the axis of the sphere (Plato), the sky (Æsch.). In OF. *pole* (1372 in Hatz.-Darm.), mod.F. *pôle*; so It., Sp., Pg. *polo*, Ger. *pol*, Du. *pool*, all from L.]

1. Each of the two points in the celestial sphere (***north pole*** and ***south pole***) about which as fixed points the stars appear to revolve; being the points at which the earth's axis produced meets the celestial sphere. Sometimes also = POLE-STAR.

c **1391** Chaucer *Astrol.* ii. §22 The heyhte of owre pool Artik fro owre north Orisonte. **1398** Trevisa *Barth. De P.R.* viii. xxii. (Bodl. MS.), Polus is a fulle litel sterre... And twei Polus [ed. 1495 Polis] there bene, þat one hatte Articus..þe oþer pole hiȝt antarticus. **1412–20** Lydg. *Chron. Troy* i. iii. (1555), To enhaunce thyne honour to the heauen Aboue the poole and the sterres seuen. **1432–50** tr. *Higden* (Rolls) V. 261 Alle the grownde that lyethe over the occean..vnder the northe pole. **1513** Douglas *Æneis* vi. i. 34 Dedalus, the wrycht,..To aventur hym self heich in the sky,..Towart the frosty poil artik he flaw. **1527** R. Thorne in Hakluyt *Voy.* (1589) 253 The altitude of the Poles, that is the North and South starres. **1602** H. Brigges (*title*) A Table to find the height of the Pole; the Magnetical Declination being given. **1604** Shaks. *Oth.* ii. i. 15 To cast water on the burning Beare, And quench the Guards of th' euer-fixed Pole. **1726–46** Thomson *Winter* 741 All one cope Of starry glitter, glows from pole to pole. **1868** Lockyer *Elem. Astron.* §328. 145 The points where the terrestrial poles would pierce this sphere, if they were long enough, we shall call the celestial poles.

fig. **1606** Shaks. *Ant. & Cl.* iv. xv. 65 The Souldiers pole is falne: young Boyes and Gyrles Are leuell now with men. **1916** K. J. Saunders *Adventures Christian Soul* 68 When God's will is thy heart's pole, Then is Christ thy very soul.

2. a. Each of the extremities (North and South) of the axis of the earth; also of any rotating spherical or spheroidal body (***pole of revolution***).

1551 Recorde *Pathw. Knowl.* i. Defin., The two poyntes that suche a lyne maketh in the vtter bounde or platte of the globe, are named polis, wch you may call aptly in englysh, tourne pointes. **1622** R. Hawkins *Voy. S. Sea* (1847) 228 Those found neere the pooles are not perfect, but are of a thick colour; whereas such as are found neere the line, are most orient and transparent. **1725** De Foe *Voy. round World* (1840) 19 They entertained a notion that I was going..to search for the South pole. **1798** Coleridge *Anc. Mar.* v. i, Oh sleep! it is a gentle thing, Beloved from pole to pole! **1820** W. Scoresby *Acc. Arctic Reg.* I. 46 The opinion of an open sea round the Pole is altogether chimerical. **1827** *Gentl. Mag.* XCVII. i. 159 Resolved..that another Expedition to the North-Pole shall be undertaken. **1834** *Nat. Philos.* III. *Astron.* iii. 83/1 (U.K. Soc.), The points *M* and *m* are called ..the poles of the moon. **1880** G. Meredith *Tragic Com.* (1881) 111 As for matters of the heart between us, we're as far apart as the Poles.

fig. **1509** Hawes *Past. Pleas.* v. (1555) Dj, The lady Gramer..To whose doctrine, I dyd me aduertise For to attayne, in her artyke poole, Her gylted dewe, for to oppresse my doole.

†**b.** Each extremity of the axis of a lens. *Obs.*

1704 J. Harris *Lex. Techn.* I, *Pole of a Glass* (in Opticks) is the thickest part of a Convex, but the thinnest of a Concave Glass..sometimes called, The Vertex of the Glass.

†**c.** Each of the two ends of any axle; a peg on which anything turns. *Obs. rare.*

1670 G. H. *Hist. Cardinals* ii. i. 124 The Poles upon which the Wheel of Cardinalism ought to turn. **1730** A. Gordon *Maffei's Amphith.* 303 These Doors have a round Hole in the Threshold, and another above, into which the Poles of the Impost entered.

d. colloq. phr. ***poles apart*** (or, less commonly, ***removed***), completely opposite to or different from (someone or something).

1917 A. Huxley *Let.* 30 Sept. (1969) 134 They are deeply engaged in something very far removed from the sordid present, poles apart from any clap trap I may be talking about English literature. **1922** Joyce *Ulysses* 618 On this knotty point, however, the views of the pair, poles apart as they were, both in schooling and everything else,..clashed. **1935** *Discovery* Feb. 52/2 Mr Dunne is poles apart from the dry-as-dusts who care not whether or no what they write is read. **1957** J. S. Huxley *Relig. without Revelation* iv. 95 Bringing together whole realms of fact.., which had hitherto seemed poles apart. **1966** *Listener* 13 Jan. 75/2 The world which his symphony inhabits is poles apart from that of Bruckner's symphonic 'confession'. **1971** *Scope* (S. Afr.) 19 Mar. 32/3 He is poles removed from men like Carel de Wet on the one side and Douglas Mitchell on the other.

3. *Geom.* ***pole of a circle of the sphere***: Each of the two points on the surface of the sphere, in which the axis of that circle cuts the surface; as the poles of the ecliptic on the celestial sphere. The poles of any great circle of a sphere are also the poles of every small circle parallel to it.

c **1391** CHAUCER *Astrol.* I. §18 This senyth is the verrey pool of the orisonte in euery regioun. **1559** W. CUNNINGHAM *Cosmogr. Glasse* 33 If I make B.D. the poles of th' equinoctiall.. then can thei not be the poles of the zodiack. **1594** BLUNDEVIL *Exerc.* III. I. xvi. (1636) 311 In this Colure there are set downe the two Poles of the Ecliptique line, being distant from the Poles of the world three and twenty degrees and 30′. **1669** STURMY *Mariner's Mag.* VII. ii. 3 Every Dial Plane hath his Axis, which is a straight Line passing through the Center of the Plane, and making Right Angles with it; and at the end of the Axis be the two Poles of the Plane, whereof that above our Horizon is called the Pole Zenith, and the other the Pole Nadir of the Dial. **1795** HUTTON *Math. Dict.* II. 255/1 The Pole of a great circle is a point upon the sphere equally distant from every part of the circumference of the great circle. **1816** PLAYFAIR *Nat. Phil.* II. 2 They all describe circles having the same point for their Pole.

b. Hence in *Cryst.*, the point at which a straight line perpendicular to a face or plane of a crystal meets the (ideal) sphere of projection.

1878 GURNEY *Crystallogr.* 31 The points in which the perpendiculars.. meet the surface of the sphere are called the poles of the respective faces. **1895** STORY-MASKELYNE *Crystallogr.* 27 A pole may therefore also be defined as the point of contact of the sphere and a tangent-plane parallel to a plane of the system on the same side of the origin with the plane.

4. *poet.*, after ancient Greek and Latin usage; also *pl.* The sky, heavens. *arch.* or *Obs.*

1572 *Satir. Poems Reform.* xxx. 134 The storme approches quhen ye Poills are fairest. **1649** G. DANIEL *Trinarch., Hen. IV*, cclxxiii, Hee,.. Ambitious of the Pole, has got moe Eyes But wᵗʰ less ease. **1715–20** POPE *Iliad* VIII. 692 Stars unnumber'd gild the glowing pole. **1770** W. HODSON *Ded. Temple Sol.* 2 Mingled Thunders shake the lab'ring Pole. **1794** BLAKE *Songs Exper., Poison-Tree* 14 When the night had veil'd the pole.

5. *Magn.* **a.** Each of the two opposite points or regions on the surface of a magnet (when of elongated form, usually at its ends) at which the magnetic forces are manifested.

So called originally by analogy with the poles of the earth or the celestial sphere, when it was discovered that a lodestone tends to dispose itself with one extremity towards the north, and the other towards the south.

1574 EDEN *Prof. Bk. Navigation* (1579), For lyke as in heauen are two poynts immoueable.. vpon the which the whole frame of heauen is turned.. euen so the stone Magnes reduced into a globous or rounde forme, laying thereon a needle turneth and resteth, thereby is shewed the place of the poles. **1625** N. CARPENTER *Geog. Del.* I. iii. (1635) 57 Let the two poles both North and South bee marked out in the Loadstone. **1646** SIR T. BROWNE *Pseud. Ep.* 60 A Loadstone .. wherein only inverting the extremes as it came out of the fire, wee altered the poles or faces thereof at pleasure. **1738** J. EAMES in *Phil. Trans.* Abridgm. VIII. 246 Concerning Magnets having more than two Poles. **1831** BREWSTER *Optics* x. 93 A steel wire.. became magnetic by exposure to the white light of the sun; a north pole appearing at each polished part, and a south pole at each unpolished part. **1866** R. M. FERGUSON *Electr.* (1870) 37 Gilbert considered the north pole of the magnet to be a south pole, as he took the north pole of the earth as his standard north pole. **1870** AIRY *Treat. Magnetism* 12 This suggests the idea that the whole of the magnetism peculiar to that end of the magnet is collected into that one point: and that point is called a 'pole'. **1873** MAXWELL *Electr. & Magn.* II. 3 The ends of a long thin magnet are commonly called its poles.

Comb. **1884** S. P. THOMPSON *Dynamo-electr. Mach.* 124 By substituting a four-pole field for the original two-pole field.. they could get exactly double. **1900** *Engineering Mag.* XIX. 748/2 There being two generating sets, with two-pole dynamos. *Ibid.* 754/2 A twelve-pole machine, the connections of whose winding can be altered so as to furnish pressures from 385 to 4,000 volts.

b. ***magnetic pole***: each of the two points in the polar regions of the earth where the dipping needle takes a vertical position.

1701 GREW *Cosm. Sacra* I. ii. 9 The Magnetick Poles are also a great Secret; especially now they are found to be distinct from the Poles of the Earth. **1797** *Encycl. Brit.* (ed. 3) X. 435/2 The magnetic poles of the earth may be considered as the centres of the polarities of all the particular aggregates of magnetic substances. **1815** J. SMITH *Panorama Sc. & Art* II. 178 It is found, that the magnetical poles of the earth change their situation, and this singular circumstance has opened a wide field for speculation.

6. *Electr.* Each of the two terminal points (positive and negative) of an electric cell, battery, or machine.

1802 *Med. Jrnl.* VIII. 319 It is particularly through the medium of the organs of sight and taste, that we find some difference in the respective action of the two poles. **1834** FARADAY *Exp. Res.* (1855) I. 196 The poles, as they are usually called, are only the doors or ways by which the electric current passes in or out. **1836–41** BRANDE *Chem.* (ed. 5) 290 The termination of the conductors or wires, connected with the opposite ends of the voltaic battery, are commonly termed its positive and negative poles. **1881** S. P. THOMPSON *Elem. Less. Electr. & Magn.* 127 The copper strip, whence the current starts on its journey through the external circuit, is called the *positive pole*, and the zinc strip is called the *negative pole.* **1905** PREECE & SIVEWRIGHT *Telegraphy* 15 *note*, The connection at the negative plate is the positive pole and that at the positive plate the negative pole.

7. *Biol.* Each extremity of the main axis of any organ of more or less spherical or oval form.

1834 MᶜMURTRIE *Cuvier's Anim. Kingd.* 462 Their parts are arranged round an axis and on one or several radii, or on one or several lines extending from one pole to the other. **1888** ROLLESTON & JACKSON *Anim. Life* Introd. 22 It is rare for the chromatin to be grouped in two masses on the equator [of the spindle] and the split of the nucleus to take place through its poles. **1893** TUCKEY tr. *Hatschek's Amphioxus* 39 The upper pole of the egg. **1897** *Allbutt's Syst. Med.* IV. 338 The upper pole of the right kidney is 5 cm. external to the tip of the eleventh thoracic spine.

8. *Geom.* **a.** A fixed point to which other points, lines, etc., are referred: as, the origin of polar co-ordinates; the point of which a curve is a polar. **b.** The point from which a pencil of lines diverges.

1849 CAYLEY *Wks.* I. 425 A fixed point *Q* (which may be termed the harmonic pole of the point *P* with respect to the system of surfaces). **1863** R. TOWNSEND *Mod. Geom.* I. x. 216 The inverse of the foot of the perpendicular from the centre of a circle upon any line is termed the pole of the line with respect to the circle. **1873** WILLIAMSON *Diff. Calculus* (ed. 2) xii. §175 The position of any point in a plane is determined when its distance from a fixed point called a pole, and the angle which that distance makes with a fixed line, are known; these are called the polar co-ordinates of the point. **1885** A. G. GREENHILL *Diff. Calculus* (1886) 241 The locus of *Y*, the foot of the perpendicular on the tangent of a curve drawn from the origin *O*, is called the pedal of the curve with respect to *O*, and *O* is called the pole of the pedal.

9. *fig.* Each of two opposed or complementary principles to which the parts of a system or group of phenomena, ideas, etc., are referable.

1471 RIPLEY *Comp. Alch.* IV. xv. in Ashm. *Theat. Chem. Brit.* (1652) 147 Losyng and knyttyng therefore be Princypalls two Of thys hard Scyence, and Poles most pryncypall. **1830** COLERIDGE *Table-t.* 30 Apr., The.. Nominalists and Realists.. each maintained opposite poles of the same truth. **1843** R. J. GRAVES *Syst. Clin. Med.* xxvii. 350 To develope itself [i.e. syphilitic poison] according to certain antitheses (poles or metastases). **1861** E. GARBETT *Bible & Critics* 245 Reverting.. to the very opposite pole of religious thought and practice. **1898** G. B. SHAW *Plays Pleasant* p. xi, These are the opposite poles of our system, represented in practice by our first rate managements at the one end, and the syndicates which exploit pornographic musical farces at the other. **1935** B. MALINOWSKI in M. Black *Importance of Lang.* (1962) 77 These two poles of linguistic effectiveness, the magical and the pragmatic. **1965** *New Statesman* 30 Apr. 690/2 At the opposite pole to Tchaikovsky's introversion stands Verdi.

10. *Math.* A point *c* in whose neighbourhood the magnitude of a function $f(z)$ becomes infinite, but in such a way that, were the function multiplied by an appropriate power of $(z-c)$, it would remain finite.

1879 *Encycl. Brit.* IX. 819/2 A rational (non-integral) function has a certain number of infinities, or poles, each of them of a given multiplicity. **1893** HARKNESS & MORLEY *Treat. Theory of Functions* iii. 112 If $f(z)$ be infinite at *c*, while $(z-c)^m f(z)$ is regular at *c*, *m* being a finite positive integer, *c* is said to be a pole of the function, and *m* is said to be the order of multiplicity, or simply the order, of the pole. **1935** E. T. COPSON *Introd. Theory of Functions of Complex Variable* iv. 79 If $f(z)$ has a pole at *a*, $|f(z)|$ tends to infinity as *z* tends to *a* in any manner. Moreover, if $f(z)$ has a pole of order *m* at *a*, $1/f(z)$ is regular and has a zero of order *m* there. **1968** P. A. P. MORAN *Introd. Probability Theory* vii. 299 $\phi_1(z)$ is therefore an analytic function with no zeros or poles. **1973** L. J. TASSIE *Physics Elem. Particles* xii. 162 $F(l, k)$ is an analytic function of *l* except for poles above or on the real axis. These poles in the complex angular momentum plane are called Regge poles. The positions of the poles are analytic functions of the energy.

11. *attrib.* and *Comb.*, as **pole-cell** [tr. G. *polzelle* (A. Weisman 1863, in *Zeitschr. f. wissensch. Zool.* XIII. 111)] any of the cells which move to the posterior end of the embryo in certain invertebrate species, and subsequently give rise to the germ line; **pole-changer**, a switch or key for reversing the direction of an electric current; †**pole-dial** = POLAR *dial*; **pole figure** *Metallurgy* [tr. G. *polfigur* (F. Wever 1924, in *Zeitschr. f. Physik* XXVIII. 72)], a circular diagram that is a stereographic projection of a sphere showing the positions of the poles of one or more lattice planes of a crystal or crystalline substance, the intensity of any spot in the diagram being proportional to the number of planes having the corresponding orientation; **pole-finding paper**, impregnated paper which can be used to identify the sign of an electric terminal or the like by the change of colour it undergoes when brought into contact with it; **pole-hunting** *vbl. sb.*, the act of going on an expedition to either the North or South Poles; **pole-piece**, a mass of iron forming the end of an electromagnet, through which the lines of magnetic force are concentrated and directed; **pole-shoe** *Electr.*, a detachable extension of a pole-piece.

1893 TUCKEY tr. *Hatschek's Amphioxus* 173 The *pole-cell of the mesoblast still distinguishable. **1941** JOHANNSEN & BUTT *Embryol. Insects & Myriapods* ii. 10 This mass of cells are [*sic*] the germ cells.., also called 'polar globules' or 'pole cells' by earlier writers. **1969** R. F. CHAPMAN *Insects* xviii. 365 In the Nematocera all the pole cells migrate in to form the germ cells in the gonads. **1839** Pole changer [see ALTERNATING *ppl. a.* d]. **1884** KNIGHT *Mech. Dict.* Suppl., *Pole-changer. **1905** PREECE & SIVEWRIGHT *Telegraphy* 209 Introducing the pole-changer and compound relay. **1669** STURMY *Mariner's Mag.* VII. A aaij, A Globe with two *Pole-Dials, and one Shadow-Dial. [**1938** *Mem. Geol. Soc. Amer.* VI. 101 These oriented textures have been.. recorded in the pole-diagram of metallography.] **1943** *Proc. Amer. Soc. Testing Materials* XLIII. 785/1 The only feasible method for studying two-dimensional preferment such as this is to make a *pole figure for the specimen. Such a pole figure is a summarization by stereographic projection of data obtained for one set of crystal planes from a series of X-ray photographs taken at different angles to the sheet. **1962** R. E. SMALLMAN *Mod. Physical Metallurgy* vi. 205 The scatter about the ideal orientation can only be represented by means of a pole-figure which shows the spread of orientation about the ideal for a particular set of (*hkl*) poles. **1902** J. E. HUTTON in A. C. Harmsworth *Motors* viii. 145 '*Pole-finding' paper may also be used for this purpose. **1963** G. M. B. DOBSON *Explor. Atmos.* v. 84 These instruments recorded on 'pole-finding' paper the sign of the electric current flowing through a long wire hanging from the balloon. **1907** *Daily Chron.* 30 July 4/6 The Nimrod.. sails from the East India Dock today to pick up Lieutenant Shackleton.. and convey him towards the South Pole... But the point is not merely that the Nimrod is to go *Pole-hunting. **1920** *Glasgow Herald* Aug. 4/2 Such an expedition [to the Antarctic], undertaken not for Pole-hunting but for observation and collection in all possible branches of science, accumulates abundant material. **1883** *Daily News* 10 Sept. 2/1 The *pole-pieces of the field magnets. **1884** HIGGS *Magn. & Dyn. Electr. Machines* 171 The distribution of the electromotive force in the various sections of the coils on the armature depends very greatly on the shape of the pole-pieces. **1962** M. G. SAY *Conc. Encycl. Electr. Engin.* 337/1 The magnets.. consist of a circular yoke of cast iron to which inwardly projecting laminated main pole pieces are bolted. **1892** S. P. THOMPSON *Dynamo-Electr. Machinery* (ed. 4) xxiii. 657 Field-magnet cores, 8½ inches long, 4½ inches diameter; *pole-shoes, 8 inches by 3½ inches. **1901** SHELDON & MASON *Dynamo Electr. Machinery* iv. 75 Pole shoes are put on the ends of the pole pieces to distribute this flux over a wider area where it has to pass through the air. **1957** *Encycl. Brit.* VIII. 148/2 The enlarged portions of the poles near the armature are the pole shoes.

pole (pəʊl), *sb.*³ *rare.* [a. F. *pole* 'the Sole-fish called a Dogs-tongue' (Cotgr.).] **1.** A marine flat-fish, *Glyptocephalus cynoglossus*, of the family Pleuronectidæ, found in north-west European waters and on the North American side of the Atlantic; = WITCH *sb.*⁴

1668 WILKINS *Real Char.* II. v. §3. 141 Plain or flat fish.. having the mouth on the left side of the eyes, having bigger scales. Pole. **1836** W. YARRELL *Hist. Brit. Fishes* II. 227 (*heading*) The Pole, or Craig Fluke. **1864** J. COUCH *Hist. Fishes Brit. Islands* III. 190 The Pole is a fish of the Arctic Sea.

2. *Comb.* **pole-dab, -flounder** = prec. sense.

1838 *Mem. Wernerian Soc.* VII. 370 The Pole Dab is distinguished from the plaise [*sic*] in having no tubercles on the head. **1896** J. T. CUNNINGHAM *Marketable Marine Fishes* 233 The witch.. has been called the pole dab, pole flounder, and long flounder by English naturalists. **1925** J. T. JENKINS *Fishes Brit. Isles* 184 The Witch, or Pole Dab, may be recognised by the fact that the eyes are on the right side of the head. **1969** A. WHEELER *Fishes Brit. Isles & N.-W. Europe* 542 (*heading*) Witch (Pole Dab). **1888** GOODE *Amer. Fishes* 260 In Greenland they are said to feed upon the pole-flounder. *Ibid.* 331. **1890** WEBSTER, *Pole-flounder*.. native of the northern coasts of Europe and America.. called also *craig flounder*, and *pole-fluke*. **1896** [see *pole-dab* above].

Pole, *sb.*⁴ Also 6 Poyle, Poole. [a. Ger. *Pole*, sing. of *Polen*, in MHG. *Polân*, pl. *Polâne*, a. Polish *Poljane* lit. field-dwellers, f. *pole* field.]

†**1.** Poland. *Obs.*

1533 ELYOT *Cast. Helthe* (1541) 34 In any other countrey than England, Scotland, Ireland, & Poyle. **1565** JEWEL *Def. Apol.* (1611) 368 Ireland, Poole, Denmarke, Sueden, and Hungarie. **1671** FRASER *Polichronicon* (S.H.S.) 491 After the peace he went up to Pole with other Scotsshmen.

2. A native of Poland.

Earlier names were (*pl.*) *Polones* [from L.] (1555 EDEN *Decades* 278, 280), POLACK, POLANDER.

1656 B. HARRIS *Parival's Iron Age* (1659) 308 After many hot charges,.. the Poles confusedly fled. *a* **1715** BURNET *Own Time* VI. ann. 1697 (1734) II. 196 To distribute Eight Millions of Florins among the Poles. **1840** *Penny Cycl.* XVIII. 324/1 The emperor Nicholas.. exercised the utmost severity against the Poles.

b. A Poland fowl.

1885 *Bazaar* 30 Mar. 1268/3 Polands. Golden spangled Poles, perfect birds.

Hence **ˈpoless**, a female Pole, Polish woman.

1828 CARLYLE *Werner* Misc. Ess. 1872 I. 102 A young Poless of the highest personal attractions.

pole, *v.*¹ Also 7–9 poll (8 pool). [f. POLE *sb.*¹]

1. *trans.* †**a.** To set on a pole. *Obs.*

1606 WARNER *Alb. Eng.* XIV. xc. (1612) 365 From whom.. they hewd his better-worthie head, And pold it on their Citie walls.

b. To convey (hay, reeds, etc.) on poles. *local.*

1828 WEBSTER, *Pole*,.. to bear or convey on poles; as, to pole hay into a barn. **1892** P. H. EMERSON *Son of Fens* xvii. 173 We began to pole it inter the boat. **1903** *Eng. Dial. Dict.*, *Pole*, to heap or move grass or reeds, etc., on long poles.

2. To furnish with poles. (Cf. *to stake.*)

1573 [see POLING *vbl. sb.*¹ 1]. **1594** PLAT *Jewell-h.* I. 48 *margin*, New manner of poling of hops. **1707** MORTIMER *Husb.* 135 Disperse your Poles between the Hills before you begin to pole, and begin not to pole till your Hops appear above the Ground. **1893** KATE SANBORN *Truthf. Wom. in S. California* 134 Beans do not need to be 'poled' here, but just lie lazily along the ground. **1898** *Daily News* 24 Aug. 5/2 The military telegraph wire is poled to this place.

3. To attach (a horse) to the carriage-pole.

1861 WHYTE MELVILLE *Mkt. Harb.* xxi, Crasher.. was.. revolving in his own mind.. whether he wouldn't pole up Marathon a little shorter going home.

4. a. To push, poke, or strike with a pole; to stir *up*, push *off*, with a pole.

1753 CHAMBERS *Cycl. Supp.*, *Polling*, in gardening, the operation of dispersing the worm-casts all over the walks, with long ash-poles. **1870** KEIM *Sheridan's Troopers* 270 While one was poling up the unknown occupants within, the others stood around the entrance with pistols..ready to greet the first appearance of the denizens. **1897** M. KINGSLEY *W. Africa* 381 The only thing was to pole the logs off.

b. To strike or pierce with a carriage-pole.
1728 VANBR. & CIB. *Prov. Husb.* II. i, If we had a mind to stand in his way, he wou'd pool us over and over again. **1824** *New Monthly Mag.* XI. 450 Yon heedless hack Has poled a deaf old woman's back. **1865** DICKENS *Mut. Fr.* I. ix, With a footman up behind, with a bar across, to keep his legs from being poled.

c. *Baseball.* To hit (the ball, a shot) hard. Also with *out*.
1905 C. DRYDEN *Champion Athletics* 40 At a tight spot in the game Hoffman poled out a vicious liner. **1943** *Amer. Speech* XVIII. 104 A batter who hits a line drive..is said..to *pole one out*. **1976** *Webster's Sports Dict.* 326/1 *Pole*, to hit the ball hard.

†**5.** *intr.* (?) To use a pole as a weapon; to fight or fence with a pole. *Obs.*
a **1601** ? MARSTON *Pasquil & Kath.* I. 6, I am as perfect in my Pipe, as Officers in poling, Courtiers in flatterie, or Wenches in falling. *c* **1645** T. TULLY *Siege Carlisle* (1840) 35 One Watson, poleing with a Skott, was shot by his Comraid. Scisson to revenge his death cut 2 of the Scotts.

6. a. *trans.* To propel (a boat or raft) with a pole.
1774 D. JONES *Jrnl.* (1865) 47 The canoe was poled up the stream. **1799** J. SMITH *Acc. Remark. Occurr.* (1870) 43 Sometimes paddling and sometimes polling his canoe along. **1893** F. F. MOORE *Gray Eye or so* II. 57 The boat..was being poled along in semi-darkness.
b. *intr.* or *absol.*
1831 R. COX *Adv. Columbia River* II. 193 After pushing off we poled away with might and main. **1895** H. NORMAN *Peoples & Pol. of Far East* xxxii. 537 We poled and paddled up the river.

7. To stir (molten metal or glass) with a pole of green wood, with the object of reducing the proportion of oxygen in the mass.
1842 [see POLING *vbl. sb.*^{1} 1]. **1869** ROSCOE *Elem. Chem.* (1871) 265 In order to get rid of the last traces of oxide, the molten copper is 'poled' or stirred up with a piece of green wood. **1884** *Chamb. Jrnl.* 1 Dec. 766/1 The tin is first melted and 'polled'—that is, stirred up with a stick of green wood.

8. To take advantage of someone; to impose or sponge *on*. *Austral. colloq.*
1906 E. DYSON *Fact'ry 'Ands* vi. 66 'What rot, girls; why don't yer get er shift on?' cried Feathers virtuously... ''Taint ther mealy pertater, polin' on the firm like this.' **1919** W. H. DOWNING *Digger Dialects* 38 *Poll*, to take advantage of another's good nature. **1938** X. HERBERT *Capricornia* (1939) xxxii. 486 Call me a wastrel, would ya? You—why, you're poling on Jesus Christ! **1945** BAKER *Austral. Lang.* v. 107 The N.S.W. Libraries Advisory Committee (1939).. said that inter-library loans had been summed up as 'poling instead of pooling'. **1946** K. TENNANT *Lost Haven* (1947) xiv. 214 Only his own obstinacy kept him working, but Launce was as independent as any other man in Lost Haven. He wasn't going to pole on Alec. **1947** V. PALMER *Hail Tomorrow* I. 10, I asked him why he should come up north and pole on men who were trying to win decent conditions for themselves, but he said he wanted a holiday. **1953** 'CADDIE' *Sydney Barmaid* xxxviii. 220 'And while there's anything in the Sutton cupboard, Caddie,' he assured me when I said I couldn't stay and pole on them, 'it's yours.' **1957** 'N. CULOTTA' *They're Weird Mob* (1958) xiii. 203 It [*sc.* bludger] means that you..'pole on yer mates'.

pole (pəʊl), *v.*^{2} *Physics.* [f. POLE *sb.*^{2}, or a back-formation from POLING *vbl. sb.*^{2}] *trans.* To render (a ferroelectric material) electrically polar by the temporary application of a strong electric field.
1961 *Proc. IRE* XLIX. 1162/1 Certain polycrystalline ferroelectric substances..can be given lasting polar properties, including pyroelectric and piezoelectric effects, by treatment with high electric fields for a short time. The term 'to pole' is recommended for this treatment. **1963** *IEEE Trans. Ultrasonic Engin.* X. 38/2 The shell is poled in the radial direction. **1976** *Ibid.* XXIII. 394/1 The bar is poled perpendicular to the length direction.
So 'poling *ppl. a.*
1956 *IRE Trans. Ultrasonic Engin.* IV. 55 The stress is applied along the axis of the poling field. **1961** *Proc. IRE* XLIX. 1166/2 The shear deformation..occurs in the plane containing both the poling and signal fields.

pole, obs. form of PAUL, POLL, POOL, PULLEY.

-pole, combining element from Gr. -πώλης a seller, dealer (as in οἰνοπώλης wine-seller), f. πωλεῖν to sell, used rarely to designate a merchant, as in BIBLIOPOLE, PHARMACOPOLE.

pole-axe, -ax, poleaxe ('pəʊlæks), *sb.* Forms: (4 poleax), 4–7 pollax, polax, 5 polle axe, polex, pollex (pol hax), 5–7 pollaxe, 6 polaxe, pol-ax (pulaxe), 7 poll-ax, 7– pole-ax, (6) 7– pole-axe, 6– poleaxe. *β. Sc.* 6 pow ax, 7 pow-aix. [ME. *pollax*, *polax*, Sc. *powax* = MDu. *polaex*, *pollaex*, MLG. and LG. *polexe*, *pollexe* (whence MSw. 15th c. *polyxe*, *pulyxe*, MDa. *poløxe*), f. *pol*, POLL *sb.*^{1}, Sc. *pow*, MDu., MLG. *polle*, *pol* head + AXE: cf. MDu. *polhamer* = poll-hammer, also a weapon of war. It does not appear whether the combination denoted an axe with a special kind of head, or one for cutting off or splitting the head of an enemy. In the 16th c. the word began to be written by some *pole-axe* (which after 1625 became the usual spelling), as if an axe upon a *pole* or long handle. This may have been connected with the rise of sense 2. Similarly, mod.Sw. *pålyxa* and Westphalian dial. *pålexe* have their first element = pole. Sense 3 may be a substitute for the earlier *bole-axe*, which was applied to a butcher's axe.]

1. A kind of axe formerly used as a weapon of war, a battle-axe; also, a form of this retained till the end of the eighteenth century in naval warfare for boarding, resisting boarders, cutting ropes, etc.
It probably varied in form at different times, but originally (and in naval use to the end) it was a short-handled weapon, which could be hung at the saddle-bow or held under the shield, and used in close fighting: in the quot. from Chaucer it is one of the short weapons specially forbidden at the combat. Its use to render L. *bipennis* two-edged axe, in the Promptorium and Catholicon, and by Sandys, suggests that it had usually a cutting edge or point also on the side opposite the broad face.
13.. *Coer de L.* (W.) 6870 If the dogge wyl come to me, My pollax schal hys bane be. *Ibid.* 6972 [cf. 5053 Hys ax on his fore arsoun hyng]. *c* **1386** CHAUCER *Knt.'s T.* 1686 No man ther fore vp peyne of los of lyf No maner shot polax [*v.r.* pollax] ne shorte knyf In to the lystes sende ne thider brynge Ne short swerd for to stoke with poynt bitynge. **1399** LANGL. *Rich. Redeles* III. 328 They..pletid wth pollaxis and poyntis of swerdis. **1422–61** in *Cal. Proc. Chanc. Q. Eliz.* (1827) I. Introd. 20 [He] woulde haf slayne me with ane polle axe. *c* **1440** *Promp. Parv.* 407/2 Polax, *bipennis*. **1465** MARG. PASTON in *P. Lett.* II. 215 Sum of hem havyng rusty polexis and byllys. **1483** *Cath. Angl.* 286/1 A Pollaxe, *bipennis*. **1513** DOUGLAS *Æneis* XI. xiii. 105 Hyr braid pollax, rasit sa on hie [*validam..securim, altior exsurgens*]. **1530** PALSGR. 179 *Bec de faulcon*, a poll-ax. *a* **1548** HALL *Chron., Hen. IV* 14 b, Sir Piers..with a strooke of his Pollax felled hym to the ground. **1551** ROBINSON *More's Utopia* II. (1895) 262 At hande strokes they vse not swordes but pollaxes. **1561** *Burgh Rec. Prestwick* (Maitl. Cl.) 66 Ane slot staf, or ane pow ax. **1567** *Lanc. Wills* (1857) II. 86 My pulaxe..ij bills or pulaxes. **1604** in Pitcairn *Crim. Trials* II. II. 432 With hagbuttis, pistolettis,..pow-aixes. **1621** G. SANDYS *Ovid's Met.* VIII. (1626) 160 Behold, Ancæus with a polax [*bipennifer Arcas*]. *Ibid.*, In both his hands Aduanc't his polax [*Ancipitemque manu tollens utraque securim*]. **1625** K. LONG tr. *Barclay's Argenis* IV. xxii. 320 Snatching their Pole axes which hung by their saddle-bowes, they fell afresh to the combat. **1644** VICARS *God in Mount* 164 They presently fell to it pell mell with their Swords and Pole-axes. **1688** R. HOLME *Armoury* III. 291/2 Their Cutting Knife..many would rather take to be a Poll-ax. **1715–20** POPE *Iliad* XIII. 766 His right [arm], beneath, the cover'd pole-ax held. **1769–76** FALCONER *Dict. Marine*, *Pole-axe*, a sort of hatchet ..having an handle about 15 inches in length, and being furnished with a sharp point, or claw, bending downwards from the back of it's head... It is principally employed to cut away..the rigging of any adversary who endeavours to board. **1819** W. TENNANT *Papistry Storm'd* (1827) 45 His henchman..Wi' ane pow-axe intill his hand. **1850** PRESCOTT *Peru* II. 211 To deal furious blows with their pole-axes and war-clubs.

†**b.** (?) Applied to an industrial implement. *Obs.*
Mentioned along with an iron hammer and 3 quarry wedges.
1356–7 *Durham Acc. Rolls* (Surtees) 557 *Marescalcia.* In uno malleo ferreo et I poleax, 3 Wharelwegges faciendis de proprio ferro.

2. A halbert or similar long-handled weapon carried by the body-guard of a king or great personage. (In quot. 1585 applied (as shown by the accompanying plate) to a small axe-blade on a long lance.)
The original *pollax* of the body-guard may have been the same weapon as in sense 1, mounted on a long staff or pole; but it became mainly an ornamental weapon, often gilt and of various fanciful shapes.
a **1562** G. CAVENDISH *Wolsey* (1893) 31, iiij footmen with gylt pollaxes in ther hands. **1585** T. WASHINGTON tr. *Nicholay's Voy.* IV. xiii. 126 b, His right hand bare a long launce, the poleaxe at the point being well steeled. **1598** FLORIO, *Mazzière*,..a halbardier or poleaxe man, such as the Queene of Englands gentlemen pencioners are. ? *a* **1600** *Bk. Precedence* in *Q. Eliz. Acad.*, etc. 22 (MS. 1604) Then the Pentioners with ther poleaxes on each side of her maiestie. [**1611** COTGR., *Bec de faulcon*, a fashion of Pollax borne by the Peeres of France, and by the French kings Pensioners.] **1849** MACAULAY *Hist. Eng.* iii. I. 326 His [Wolsey's] palaces..and body guards with gilded pole axes.

3. An axe with a hammer at the back, used to fell or stun animals; a butcher's axe.
1719 DE FOE *Crusoe* (1840) II. iii. 53 An ox is felled with a pole-axe. **1837** M. DONOVAN *Dom. Econ.* II. 7 The ox is first stunned by a violent blow on the head with a pole-axe.
Hence '**poleaxe** *v. trans.*, to fell with a pole-axe; also *fig.*; whence '**poleaxed** *ppl. a.*; '**pole,axer**, one who uses a pole-axe; '**pole,axing** *vbl. sb.*
1882 *Pall Mall G.* 15 Nov. 5/1 By the Christian mode of poleaxing, sensibility was almost instantaneously destroyed. **1898** *Daily News* 27 July 8/6 She ought to be poleaxed. **1904** *Daily Chron.* 30 Aug. 3/3 Your valiant poleaxer has returned to the fray. **1906** *Blackw. Mag.* May 701/1 The slaughterer pole-axes an ox.

polecat, pole-cat ('pəʊlkæt). Forms: α. 4–7 polcat, 5 -kat, 6 -catte, 6–7 pol-cat, 7 polcate, -catt, poll-cat, 8 poll cat, 9 pole cat, 6– pole-cat, 7– polecat. *β.* 5 pulcatt, -kat; 6 poulcatte, 6–8 -cat, powl(-)cat, poul-cat, 9 poulecat; dial. pow-cat. [ME. *polcat*, *pulcatt*, the second element being CAT *sb.*^{1}
The element *pole*, *pol-* (as already pointed out by Prof. Skeat) may have been OF. *pole*, *-poule*, chicken, fowl (cf. *sparrow-hawk*, *gos-hawk*, *honey-bear*); this is favoured by the forms in *pul-*, *poul-*, *powl-*; but *pow-cat* offers difficulty.]

1. A small dark-brown coloured carnivorous quadruped, *Putorius fœtidus*, of the *Mustelidæ* or Weasel family, a native of Europe; called also *fitchet*, *fitchew*, *foumart*.
1320 *Acc. Roll* No. 27205 *Westminster Deanery* 13–14th Edw. II (Surrey) Anceres..item in deuoracione per Polcat vj. *c* **1386** CHAUCER *Pard. T.* 527 And eek ther was a pol-cat in his hawe That as he seyde hise capons hadde yslawe. *c* **1440** *Promp. Parv.* 407/2 Pulkat, idem quod *fulmere*. **1545** ASCHAM *Toxoph.* (Arb.) 52 Nyghtecrowes and poul-cattes, foxes and foumerdes, with all other vermine. **1598** SHAKS. *Merry W.* IV. i. 29 Powlcats? There are fairer things then Powlcats, sure. **1601** HOLLAND *Pliny* I. 218 Grayes, Polcats and Brocks. **1714** GAY *What d'ye call it* I. i, How should he then Who killed but Poulcats, learn to murder Men? **1774** GOLDSM. *Nat. Hist.* (1776) III. 363 The Polecat is larger than the weasel, the ermine, or the ferret, being one foot five inches long. **1828** *Craven Gloss.* (ed. 2), *Pow-cat*, the pole cat. **1876** SMILES *Sc. Natur.* vii. 111 The bite..of a polecat ..is anything but agreeable.
b. Applied to other species of the genus *Putorius*, e.g. *P. nigripes*, the American polecat, *P. eversmanni*, the Siberian p., *P. sarmaticus*, the Mottled p., of Eastern Europe and Western Asia; also to other *Mustelidæ*, esp. in *U.S.* the skunks.
1688 J. CLAYTON in *Phil. Trans.* XVIII. 124 There are [in Virginia] several sorts of Wild Cats, and Poll-Cats. **1781** S. PETERS *Hist. Connecticut* 252 The Skunk is..very different from the Pole-Cat, which he is sometimes called. **1860** WARTER *Sea-board* II. 210 During the long winter, it [the *Mustela Vison* of N. America] leaves the frozen waters, and preys like other polecats on mice and land animals. **1864** WEBSTER, *Zorilla*..called also *mariput*, *Cape polecat*, and *African polecat*.
2. *fig.* Applied contemptuously to a vile person; a courtesan, a prostitute.
1598 SHAKS. *Merry W.* IV. ii. 195 Out of my doore, you Witch, you Ragge, you Baggage, you Poulcat, you Runnion, out, out. **1607** DEKKER & WEBSTER *Northw. Hoe* I. D.'s Wks. 1873 III. 4 To take their leaues of their London Polecats, (their wenches I meane Sir). *a* **1640** DAY *Parl. Bees* x. (1641) G j b, Hee's a male powl-cat; a meere heart-blood soaker. **1717** L'ESTRANGE & OZELL tr. *Sovorcano* (*title*) The Spanish Pole-Cat, or the Adventures of Seniora Rufina. **1790** WOLCOTT (P. Pindar) *Advice to Fut. Laureat* II. vi, Brudenell, thou stinkest; weazel, polecat, fly!
3. *attrib.* and *Comb.*, as ***polecat head***, ***perfume***, etc.; **polecat ferret**, a brown variety of the ferret; **polecat weed**, in *U.S.*, the skunk cabbage, *Symplocarpus fœtidus*; **wild polecat weed**, *Convolvulus panduratus* (Miller *Plant-n.*, 1884).
1596 NASHE *Saffron Walden* 59 With one Pol-cat perfume or another hee will poyson thee. **1631** P. FLETCHER *Sicelides* I ij, That same Foolishes had a pole-cat head. **1844** DUNGLISON *Med. Lex.*, Polecat weed, *Dracontium fœtidum*. **1869** G. ROOPER *Flood, Field & Forest* (1874) 178 The young ferret came but once a year. I refer to the pole-cat ferret. **1893** J. WATSON *Confess. Poacher* 123 In the north we have two varieties of ferret,—one a brown colour, the polecat-ferret; the other the common white.

Pol. Econ., colloq. abbrev. of *Political Economy*. See ECONOMY 3.
1893 W. K. POST *Harvard Stories* 12, I have not been tutoring you in Pol. Econ. **1900** *Dialect Notes* II. 16 Some tendencies in student English..are worth a passing remark. Most significant..is the tendency to use abbreviations... The subjects he studies..are all clipped... Thus he studies ..*pol-econ* (political economy).

poled (pəʊld), *a.*^{1} [f. POLE *sb.*^{1} or *v.*] **1.** Provided with or supported by a pole or poles.
1864 E. A. PARKES *Man. Pract. Hygiene* I. ix. 287 This is a two-poled tent, with a connecting ridge-pole. *Ibid.* 288 The first is a single poled pyramidal tent, with a second pole to sustain the entrance flap. **1894** *Westm. Gaz.* 1 Jan. 2/1 But it is pointed out that the proportion of 'poled' steamers, and of sailing ships with masts that can be readily lowered, is always increasing.
2. = POLEAXED *ppl. a.*
1920 *Outward Bound* Nov. 20/2 It caught him fairly above the ear so that he fell like a poled ox.

poled (pəʊld), *a.*^{2} *Physics.* [f. POLE *sb.*^{2}, POLE *v.*^{2} + -ED^1, -ED^2.] Of a ferroelectric material: rendered electrically polar (see POLE *v.*^{2}).
1961 *Proc. IRE* XLIX. 1162/1 Poled ferroelectric ceramics have become an important component in electromechanical devices. **1975** D. G. FINK *Electronics Engineers' Handbk.* VII. 58 Poled ferroelectric devices are capable of doing electric work when driven mechanically, or mechanical work when driven electrically.

poledavy: see POLDAVY.

pole-evil, obs. f. POLL-EVIL.

pole-footed, error for POLT-FOOTED.

'**polehead, powhead.** Now only *Sc.* and *north. dial.* Forms: 3 polheuede, 6 poled, polet, 6–7 pole-head; *Sc.* 8– pow-head (9 powet). [ME. *polheuede*, the second element being *head*; the first is uncertain, though perh. the same as in *tadpole*; the Sc. form *pow-* suggests that it is

POLL *sb.*[1], and that the etymological spelling would be *poll-head*.] A tadpole. Also *fig.*

c **1250** *Gen. & Ex.* 2977 Polheuedes, and froskes, and podes swile, Bond harde egipte folc in sile. **1530** PALSGR. 256/2 Poled a yonge tode... Polet the blacke thynge that a tode cometh of, *cauesot*. **1607** MARSTON *What you will* II. i. Cj, Why thou Pole-head, thou Ianus, thou poultron,..thou Eare-wig that wrigglest into mens braines. **1611** COTGR., *Cavesot*, a Pole-head, or Bull-head; the little black vermine whereof toads, and frogs do come. **1789** DAVIDSON *Seasons* 12 Powheads spartle in the oosy slosh. **1822** GALT *Sir A. Wylie* xliii, I would as soon meet wi' a pow-head in my porridge. **1876** SMILES *Sc. Natur.* i. 8 No end of horse-leeches, powets.., frogs, and other creatures that abound in ..muddy water.

poleine, variant of POULAINE *Obs.*, a shoe.

poleis, obs. Sc. form of POLISH *v.*

poleless ('pəʊllɪs), *a.* [f. POLE *sb.*[1] + -LESS.] Having no pole.

1647 R. STAPYLTON *Juvenal* x. 182 Horses that draw a pole-lesse chariot. **1854** *Tait's Mag.* XXI. 141 A pal, or small poleless tent, such as is customary for the wives of travelling natives.

polell, variant of PULLAILE, *Obs.*, poultry.

poleman ('pəʊlmən). [f. POLE *sb.*[1] + MAN.] A man who uses, carries, or fights with a pole.

1838 W. HERBERT *Attila* 321 A good horseman, a good archer and poleman. **1859** F. A. GRIFFITHS *Artil. Man.* (1862) 35 The pole-men lower the pole [of a tent]. **1889** *Pall Mall G.* 6 Feb. 3/2 Others [blocks of ice] are detached with ice chisels, and guided by the polemen to the bank. **1904** *Daily News* 11 Aug. 9 A poleman in the employ of a tramway company.

b. At Eton: see quots.

1844 DISRAELI *Coningsby* I. xi. (Montem at Eton), And all the Oppidans of the fifth form..class as 'Corporals'; and are severally followed by one or more lower boys, who are denominated 'Polemen', but who appear in their ordinary dress. **1898** A. D. COLERIDGE *Eton. Forties* 332 The lower boys carried long white poles, from which they derived the name of polemen.

polemarch ('pɒlɪmɑːk). *Anc. Hist.* Also 7 -**mark**. [ad. Gr. πολέμαρχ-ος, f. πόλεμ-ος war + -αρχος ruling, ruler. So F. *polémarque*.] The title of an officer in ancient Greece, originally, as the name implies, a military commander-in-chief, but having also civil functions varying according to date and locality.

In Athens, the third archon, originally the titular military commander-in-chief; afterwards a civil magistrate having under his care the children of parents who had lost their lives in the service of their country, and the resident aliens.

[**1579–80** NORTH *Plutarch* (1676) 747 Demetrius..made him [Pisis] Polemarchus (to wit, Camp-master).] **1656** BLOUNT *Glossogr.*, *Polemark*, a Lord Marshal of the field, a chief Officer of War. **1734** tr. *Rollin's Anc. Hist.* XII. 157 Polemarchs, that is, generals of the army and supreme magistrates of Thebes. **1807** ROBINSON *Archæol. Græca* II. vii. 155. **1822** T. MITCHELL *Aristoph.* II. 274 The polemarch had more particularly the strangers and sojourners of Athens under his care. **1859** RAWLINSON tr. *Herodotus* VI. iii. III. 500 [At Marathon] Callimachus the polemarch led the right wing, for it was at that time a rule with the Athenians to give the right wing to the polemarch. **1868** *Smith's Dict. Gr. & Rom. Antiq.* (ed. 7) 301/1 The polemarchs of Sparta appear to have ranked next to the king.

transf. **1656** J. HARRINGTON *Oceana* 56 Troops and Companies that were held in perpetuall discipline under the Command of a Magistrate called the Polemarche.

polemic (pəʊ'lɛmɪk), *a.* and *sb.* [ad. Gr. πολεμικός, f. πόλεμος war. So F. *polémique* (*a* 1630).]

A. *adj.* Of or pertaining to controversy; controversial, disputatious.

1641 R. BROOKE *Eng. Episc.* I. iii. 10 All truthes, Polemicke, positive,..are of neere consanguinity. **1642** SIR E. DERING *Sp. on Relig.* xvi. 86 Wee may bee alway sure in all Polemicke learning, to have some men of valour. **1654** H. L'ESTRANGE *Chas. I* (1655) 182 The master peece of Polemique Divinity of all extant. **1715** M. DAVIES *Athen. Brit.* I. 129 On several such like Polemick occasions. **1866** FELTON *Anc. & Mod. Gr.* II. II. vi. 373 To wrangle upon senseless questions of polemic theology. **1872** LYELL *Princ. Geol.* I. 33 They displayed far less polemic bitterness.

B. *sb.*

1. A controversial argument or discussion; argumentation against some opinion, doctrine, etc.; aggressive controversy; in *pl.* the practice of this, esp. as a method of conducting theological controversy: opposed to *irenics*.

1638 DRUMM. OF HAWTH. *Irene* Wks. (1711) 172 Unhappy we, amidst our many and diverse contentions, furious polemicks, endless variances,..debates and quarrels! **1706** PHILLIPS, *Polemicks*, Disputations, Treatises, or Discourses about controversial Points. *c* **1800** H. K. WHITE *Lett.* (1837) 201 Religious polemics..have seldom formed a part of my studies. **1847** HAMILTON *Let. to De Morgan* 40 My confessed dislike of the polemic. **1879** FARRAR *St. Paul* II. 247 In his most impassioned polemic he always unites a perfect conciliatoriness of tone with an absolute rigidity of statement. **1892** MONTEFIORE *Hibbert Lect.* iii. 128 A direct polemic against idols starts from the prophets of the eighth century, and more especially from Hosea.

†**b.** (See quot.) *Obs. rare*$^{-0}$.

1656 BLOUNT *Glossogr.*, *Polemicks*, verses treating of war, or treatises of war, or strifes; disputations.

2. One who writes or argues in opposition to another; a controversialist; esp. in theology.

a **1680** BUTLER *Rem.* (1759) I. 217 They did..like Polemics of the Post pronounce The same thing to be true and false at once. **1716** M. DAVIES *Athen. Brit.* III. *Diss. Drama* 22 He dy'd a real Polemick, if not a Martyr for the Church. **1825** THIRLWALL *Crit. Ess.* p. cxxxvii. *note*, An orthodox polemic in Tertullian's time. **1886** *Athenæum* 21 Aug. 239/1 The divines of James I.'s court were all casuists and polemics.

po'lemical, *a.* (*sb.*) [f. as prec. + -AL[1].]

†**1.** Of or pertaining to war; warlike, military.

1649 ROBERTS *Clavis Bibl.* 164 Davids Polemicall or warre-like Acts and Atchievements. **1656** BLOUNT *Glossogr.*, *Polemical*, pertaining to War, warlike, military. **1659** *Quæries Proposalls of Officers of Armie to Parlt.* 2 The third and fourth proposalls of these Polemicall gentlemen, (now plunged in politicks).

2. = POLEMIC *a.*

1640 BP. HALL *Chr. Moder.* II. i. 4 Those Polemicall discourses, which have beene so learnedly written of the severall points of difference. **1650** BULWER *Anthropomet.* Ep. Ded., Not..to engage you to a Polemical Defence of it. **1704** J. HARRIS *Lex. Techn.* I, *Polemical*, is a Word used in Reference to that part of Theology which relates to Controversie; which..is called *Polemical Divinity*. **1713** BERKELEY *Guardian* No. 55 ¶1 It is usual with polemical writers to object ill designs to their adversaries. **1878** GLADSTONE *Glean.* V. i. 81 *note*, This paper may be termed polemical, but I republish it..because it is also and yet more properly historical.

B. as *sb.* A polemical discussion, a controversy: cf. prec. B. 1. *rare.*

1808 KNOX & JEBB *Corr.* I. 423 Few things could be more truly delightful, than to see fierce polemicals thus charmed away, by the bland and kindly influences of affection and good will. **1844** B. BARTON *Select.* (1849) 63, I am not over-fond of polemicals; they are almost as bad as galenicals.

Hence **po'lemically** *adv.*, in the manner of a polemic; controversially, disputatively.

1702 C. MATHER *Magn. Chr.* III. I. i. (1852) 281 He was also sometimes put upon writing yet more polemically. **1886** *Manch. Exam.* 27 Jan. 3/2 A second article..which is able, sound, and polemically effective.

po'lemicist (-sɪst). [f. POLEMIC *sb.* + -IST.] A writer of polemics; = POLEMIST.

1864 in WEBSTER. **1884** A. M. FAIRBAIRN in *Brit. Q. Rev.* Apr. 384 The Church has had..able ecclesiastics, effective polemicists and apologists.

polemicize (pəʊ'lɛmɪsaɪz), *v.* [f. POLEMIC *a.* and *sb.* + -IZE.] *intr.* = POLEMIZE *v.* Hence **po'lemicizing** *vbl. sb.*

1953 *Encounter* Nov. 49/2 But Vigolo's edition arrived just in time to save Roman literary honour, and..to polemicise against her American view of the poet. **1968** *Listener* 6 June 728/3 You might want to polemicise and say: 'Hang on a minute! What about the swallowing up of small farms? What about the fact that British agriculture as a whole is subsidised by the taxpayer to the tune of something like three million pounds a year?' The trouble is that there isn't anyone to polemicise with. **1969** A. WALICKI in Ionescu & Gellner *Populism* 69 He sharply polemicized with Chernyshevsky and Dobroliubov, defending the spiritual heritage of the 'superfluous men' from the gentry. **1970** R. J. HOLLINGDALE tr. *Schopenhauer's Essays* 215 The polemicizing against the assumption of a life force which is now becoming fashionable.

polemist ('pɒlɪmɪst). [ad. Gr. πολεμιστής a warrior, f. πολεμίζειν to wage war; see POLEMIZE. So F. *polémiste*.] One versed in polemics; a controversialist; = POLEMIC *sb.* 2.

1825 *Gentl. Mag.* XCV. II. 228 Cardinal of St. Sabin and polemist. **1888** J. KER *Lect. Hist. Preaching* iv. 62 He was a critic, a polemist, an apologist.

polemize ('pɒlɪmaɪz), *v.* [ad. Gr. πολεμίζειν to wage war, f. πόλεμος war.] *intr.* To argue or write polemically; to carry on a controversy.

1828 PUSEY *Hist. Enq.* I. 150 Substituting common-place moral notions for its energetic doctrines..or polemizing against them under the title of the oriental idioms of the New Testament. **1898** DRIVER *Introd. Lit. O.T.* (ed. 7) 3 Prof. Sayce..polemizes much against the 'higher critics'.

polemology (pɒlɪ'mɒlədʒɪ). [f. Gr. πόλεμο- combining form of πόλεμος war + Gr. -λογία, -LOGY.] The science or study of war. Hence **polemological** *a.*; **pole'mologist**.

1938 *Nature* 23 Apr. 728/1 Last of all, perhaps, has been a lively call to solve the problems of polemology (*sit venia verbo*). **1968** *Sunday Times* 4 Feb. 53/3 Students of polemology will not find anything startlingly original in what he has to say. **1968** *N.Y. Times* 26 Aug. 35 There is a French Institute of Polemology in Paris and a Polemological Institute at Groningen in the Netherlands. **1970** H. ARENDT *On Violence* 59 A brand-new science, called 'polemology', has emerged. *Ibid.* 64 This..is precisely what the psychiatrists and polemologists concerned with human aggressiveness recommend. **1970** *Harper's* Dec. 28 Professor Gaston Bouthoul of the *Ecole des Hautes Etudes Sociales* in Paris..the founder of Polemology (a word he coined), or the study of war. **1976** *Times Lit. Suppl.* 2 Apr. 363/2 *Urban Guerrilla* contains the papers read at a conference in 1974 organized by the Polemological Centre of the Free University of Brussels.

,polemo'mania. *nonce-wd.* [f. Gr. πόλεμος war + MANIA.] Rage for war.

1874 L. TOLLEMACHE in *Fortn. Rev.* Feb. 243 At the thought of the 'giant liar', the poet is seized with a sort of polemomania.

polemoniaceous (pɒlɪməʊnɪ'eɪʃəs), *a. Bot.* [f. mod. Bot. L. *Polemōniāceæ* (f. *Polemōnium*, a. Gr. πολεμώνιον the Greek Valerian, f. proper name Πολέμων, or, according to Pliny, from πόλεμος war): see -ACEOUS.] Of or belonging to the *Polemoniaceæ*, a family of herbaceous plants, chiefly natives of temperate countries, the typical genus of which, *Polemonium*, contains the Jacob's ladder or Greek Valerian, *P. cæruleum*.

1858 in MAYNE *Expos. Lex.* **1890** in *Cent. Dict.*

polemonium (pɒlɪ'məʊnɪəm). [mod.L. (J. P. de Tournefort *Institutiones Rei Herbariæ* (1700) I. 146), a. Gk. πολεμώνιον: see POLEMONIACEOUS *a.*] An annual or perennial herb of the genus so called, belonging to the family Polemoniaceæ, native to America, Asia, or Europe, and bearing single or clustered bell-shaped flowers. Cf. JACOB'S LADDER 1.

1900 J. M. ABBOTT in W. D. Drury *Bk. Gardening* viii. 279 Polemoniums are free-flowering plants. **1931** *Times Educ. Suppl.* 25 July (Home & Classroom Sect.) p. iv/2 We fairly waded through flowers, including pale blue borage, mauve polemonium,..and blue primula. **1957** *Dict. Gardening* (R. Hort. Soc.) III. 1620/1 The Polemoniums are hardy and several good for the rock-garden, the larger ones for the border. **1968** J. BERRISFORD *Very Small Garden* viii. 95 Polemoniums, with their 'Jacob's ladder' leaves, and the taller geranium species are good.

polemoscope (pəʊ'lɛməskəʊp, 'pɒlɪməʊ-). [ad. mod.L. *polemoscopium* (Hevelius *a* 1668), f. Gr. πόλεμο-ς war: see -SCOPE. So F. *polémoscope*.] A telescope or perspective glass fitted with a mirror set at an angle to the line of vision, for viewing objects not directly before the eye. (So called from its proposed use in war.)

1668 *Phil. Trans.* III. 729 Some years ago I was framing one of Hevelius's Polemoscopes. **1727–41** CHAMBERS *Cycl.* s.v., Any telescope will be a polemoscope, if the tube be but crooked, like a rectangular syphon..and between the object glass..and first eye-glass..be placed a plain mirror. **1842** BRANDE *Dict. Sc.*, etc., s.v., Hevelius chose the name of polemoscope, because he thought the instrument might be applied, in time of war, to discover what was going on in the camp of the enemy, while the spectator remained concealed behind a wall or other defence.

b. (See quot.)

1884 KNIGHT *Dict. Mech.* Suppl., *Polemoscope*, a reflecting apparatus consisting of two plane mirrors so inclined as to enable the spectator, by glancing into one of them, to see the images of objects separated from direct view by intervening obstacles.

†**'polemy.** *Obs. rare*$^{-1}$. [f. Gr. πόλεμ-ος war + -Y: cf. Gr. (τὰ) πολέμια (Thuc.) matters of war, neut. pl. of πολέμιος adj.] Warfare, strife; controversial or polemical writing.

1642 SIR E. DERING *Sp. on Relig.* xvi. 85 You will maintaine the Pen as well as the Pulpit, Polemie as well as persuasive learning. *Ibid.* 86 For perfect Polemy in letters, you may guesse what our Universities can yeeld.

Polenske (pə'lɛnskə). [Name of E. *Polenske* (fl. 1904), German public health chemist.] ***Polenske number*** or ***value***: a number expressing the proportion of volatile, water-insoluble fatty acids in a fat (see quot. 1973).

1906 *Analyst* XXXI. 259 When a low Reichert-Wollny figure was associated with fluid insoluble volatile acids, and especially when the Polenske number exceeded 2, the proof of the presence of cocoanut oil [in the butter] was fairly definite. *Ibid.* 260 He knew nothing about the Polenske value under these conditions. **1928** [see KIRSCHNER]. **1936** *Analyst* LXVI. 407 (*heading*) Polenske (or insoluble volatile acid) value. **1973** D. PEARSON *Lab. Techniques Food Anal.* vi. 153 The proportion of butter fat present is frequently assessed from the Reichert and Polenske values... The Reichert value is the volume of 0·1 N alkali in millilitres required to neutralise the water-soluble volatile fatty acids distilled from 5 g of fat under specified conditions. From the same distillation, the Polenske value is the volume of 0·1 N alkali in millilitres required to neutralise the water-insoluble volatile fatty acids.

†**po'lent.** *Obs. rare*$^{-1}$. = next.

1609 BIBLE (Douay) *Josh.* v. 11 They did eate of the corne of the Land the next day, azyme loaves and polent of the same yeare [*Vulg.* azymos panes et polentam ejusdem anni].

‖**polenta** (pəʊ'lɛntə). Also poll-. [L. *polenta* peeled or pearl barley; in later use, repr. It. *polenta* 'a meate vsed in Italie made of barlie or chesnut flowre soked in water, and then fride in oyle or butter' (Florio 1598); now made also of maize flour.]

†**a.** Pearl-barley. *Obs.* †**b.** A kind of barley meal. *Obs.* **c.** Porridge made from steeped and parched barley or, later, of meal of chestnuts, maize flour, or other substances: now largely used in Italy.

c **1000** ÆLFRIC *Josh.* v. 11 Hiȝ..æton..polentan. **1398** TREVISA *Barth. De P.R.* XVII. lxvii. (Bodl. MS.), Som men meneþ þat polenta is a manere potage made of moste pure & dere floure. *Ibid.*, Pollenta is corne isode ipeled & holed & ischeled with frotinge of handes. **1562** TURNER *Herbal* II. 16 b, Polenta..is made of fried or perched barley. **1590** BARROUGH *Meth. Physick* III. viii. (1639) 111 Polenta is barly steeped in water one night, then fried, and then ground. **1601** HOLLAND *Pliny* I. 561 The ordinarie drie grout or meale also Polenta, which the Greeks so highly commend, was made of nothing els but of barley. **1764** SMOLLETT *Trav.* (1766) I. xx. 319 The nourishment of these poor creatures consists of..a kind of meal called polenta, made of Indian corn, which is very nourishing and agreeable. **1768** Jos. Baretti *Mann. & Cust. Italy* II. 192 As to the generality of our peasants and lower sort of people, they breakfast on polenta. **1866** Howells *Venet. Life* vi, Golden mountains of polenta (a thicker kind of mush or hasty-pudding made of Indian meal and universally eaten in Italy).

attrib. **1884** *Pall Mall Budget* 22 Aug. 14/2 The shepherd youths..eat their polenta cakes. **1888** *Pall Mall G.* 23 Aug. 5/2 The polenta pot..simmering over the glowing logs.

†**polen wax.** *Obs.* Also 5 pulleyn, poleyn. [Meaning and origin of *polen* uncertain; perh. a. OF. *poul(a)in* Polish.] A kind or quality of wax, used for wax candles before the Reformation.

[**1450** cited in Rogers *Agric. & Pr.* III. 299/4.] **1464** *Maldon, Essex, Court-Rolls* (Bundle 41, No. 8), C de pulleyn wax et quarter de lussheban wax. *c* **1470** Harding *Chron.* ccvii. v, Wynes swete, and mykell poleyn waxe. **1490–1** in Swayne *Sarum Churchw. Acc.* (1896) 38, iiij pounde & di. of polen wex for makynge of the Pascall. [**1898** *Athenæum* 27 Aug., 'Polen wex' is believed to have been a product of Livonia and other districts east of the Elbe.]

pole-pad to **pole-pulling**: see pole *sb.*^{1,2}.

poler ('pəʊlə(r)). [f. pole *sb.*^{1} or *v.*^{1} + -er^1.]

†**1.** A stirring pole: see quot. 1688. *Obs.*

1688 R. Holme *Armoury* iii. 350/2 A Tanners Pooler, or Poler..is..to stir up the Ouse, or Bark and Water. **1704** *Dict. Rust.*, *Pooler*, or *Poler*. **1730–6** Bailey (folio), *Pooler, Poler*. **1775** Ash, *Pooler*. So in mod. Dicts.

2. One who sets up or fixes hop-poles.

1848 *Jrnl. R. Agric. Soc.* IX. ii. 552 That the polers may place the poles to suit the apparent wants of the hills. *Ibid.* 554 If new poles require to be carried..the poler is paid extra.

3. The horse or other draught-beast harnessed alongside the pole; a wheeler. *Austral.* and *N.Z.*

1863 S. Butler *First Year in Canterbury Settlement* vii. 105 The leaders..slewed sharply round, and tied themselves into an inextricable knot with the polars. **1878** E. S. Elwell *Boy Colonists* 234 The polers, that is, the bullocks attached to the pole of the dray, and accustomed to bear the weight of the dray-load on their necks, are always the quietest. **1881** A. C. Grant *Bush Life Queensland* I. iv. 40 The intelligence displayed by the leaders and polers [bullocks] was very great. **1888** 'R. Boldrewood' *Robbery under Arms* (1890) 45 To..work like an old nearside poler. **1929** W. S. Smyth *Bonzer Jones* 97 The 'polers' pulled back. **1936** I. L. Idriess *Cattle King* viii. 68 They call the two polers the pin bullocks, because they swing the turntable of the wagon! **1941** —— *Great Boomerang* vi. 48 The leaders had reared right back on the polers, the team in terrified confusion. **1959** H. P. Tritton *Time means Tucker* ii. 36 A bullock-team is made up in four parts: polers, pin, body and leaders... The polers..have the job of steadying the dray or wagon while the pin-bullocks take the pull. **1972** *Sunday Mail Mag.* (Brisbane) 21 May 2/2 The team was made up as follows: Polers on the wagon pole were usually low set and chunky.

4. a. One who propels a barge, boat, or canoe by means of a pole.

1895 *Outing* (U.S.) XXVII. 71/1 A pole is attached to the bow of the lighter; the other end is held by a bare-footed negro... There are generally two polers to each lighter. **1896** *Daily Chron.* 15 Aug. 9/3 The poler, standing in the stern, can always push the stern out and so bring the bow into the bank. *Ibid.*, It is possible with one poler to keep a perfectly straight course, but it is not easy.

b. A boat propelled with a pole or poles.

1925 *Chambers's Jrnl.* Apr. 253/1, I was travelling by 'poler' because no steamer was available.

5. *Austral. slang.* A cadger, sponger; one who shirks work. Cf. pole *v.*^{1} 8.

1938 X. Herbert *Capricornia* (1939) xxxii. 486 'You long-jawed poler,' Norman roared. 'Living on the fat of the land, while your poor damn flock feeds on soup and coconuts and what they can root out of the bush.' **1945** [see hummer *sb.*^{2} 2]. **1947** I. Douglas *Opportunity in Australia* 89 *Poler*, one who does not pull his weight. **1952** A. G. Mitchell in *Chambers's Shorter Eng. Dict.* Suppl., *Poler*, one who sponges on another, or avoids his fair share of work... (The polers in a bullock team are yoked to the pole and often leave most of the pulling to the leading bullocks.)

poler, var. poller.

polerde, polesh(e, obs. ff. pollard *sb.*^{2}, polish *v.*

†**pole-'rivet.** *Obs.* [f. *pole* (?) + rivet *sb.*^{2}, bearded wheat: the meaning of the first element is obscure.] Bearded wheat.

1707 Mortimer *Husb.* 98 'Tis much sown in Essex upon their Hazelly Brick-earths or Loams, as the Red-wheat and the Pole-rivet or Bearded-wheat is there.

poless: see Pole *sb.*^{4}

pole-star ('pəʊlstɑː(r)). [f. pole *sb.*^{2} + star *sb.*]

1. The star α *Ursæ Minoris*, now within 1° of the northern pole of the heavens; also called *Polar star*, and *Polaris*.

1555 Eden *Decades* 32 The starre which we caule the pole starre or northe starre..is not the very poynte of the pole Artyke. **1634** Sir T. Herbert *Trav.* 94 The Pole-starre..in the tip of the little Beares taile. **1815** J. Smith *Panorama Sc. & Art* I. 515 We find, that the remarkable star called the pole-star is more or less elevated, according to the different parts of the earth from which we take our view. **1946** Dylan Thomas *Deaths & Entrances* 24 Your pole-star neighbour, sun of another street, Will dive up to his tears. **1955** *Sci. News Let.* 27 Aug. 138/1 This group [*sc.* Ursa Minor] contains the little dipper, with Polaris, the pole star, at the end of the handle. **1979** R. Laidlaw *Lion is Rampant* xiii. 108 As long as I could see The Plough I could get a fix on the Pole Star and check my direction.

2. *fig.* That which serves as a guide or director, a lodestar, a governing principle; a centre of attraction; a cynosure.

1604 T. Wright *Passions* iv. ii. §3. 147 Pleasure is the pole-stare of all inordinat passions. **1732** Berkeley *Alciphr.* vi. §19 Common-sense alone is the pole-star by which mankind ought to steer. **1834** *Tait's Mag.* I. 387/2 His moral pole-star was duty. **1890** Hall Caine *Bondman* ii. xiii, The pole-star of my life is gone out.

polet, obs. f. pole-head.

polete, -ette, obs. ff. pullet.

poletyk, obs. f. politic.

poleward ('pəʊlwəd), *adv.* and *a.* [f. pole *sb.*^{2} + -ward.]

A. *adv.* Towards or in the direction of the (north or south) pole.

1875 Croll *Climate & T.* viii. 139 To produce a general flow of the upper portion of the ocean poleward. **1895** J. W. Powell *Physiogr. Proc.* 2 The air about the equator rises, and flows poleward in both directions.

B. *adj.* Directed or tending towards the pole.

1881 W. C. Ley in *Nature* XXIV. 8/2 The pole-ward, and ..eastward movements of the atmosphere. **1901** *Dundee Advert.* 14 Jan. 5 Plans for the Poleward journey in the *Fram.*

polewards ('pəʊlwədz), *adv.* [f. as prec. + -wards.] = prec. A. Also in sense 7 of pole *sb.*^{2}

[**1644** Digby *Nat. Bodies* xx. §1. 176 The ayre which cometh from the polewardes, is heauyer then the ayre of the torride zone.] *a* **1866** Whewell (Ogilvie), The regions further polewards. **1895** *Anat. Anzeiger* XI. 74 The divergent limbs which travel polewards along the spindle are in reality the original halves of a chromosome, which has become doubled, or bent, upon itself. **1896** J. C. Irons *Autobiog. Sk. J. Croll* 229 A general movement of the ocean polewards. **1925** *Jrnl. Genetics* XV. 252 The constituent chromosomes of the bivalents are pulled polewards into loops.

polewig ('pəʊlwɪg). *local.* [See polliwog.]

1. A tadpole: see polliwog.

1882 in Ogilvie.

2. The name given by the Thames fishermen to a small fish, the Spotted or Freckled Goby.

1880–4 F. Day *Fishes Gt. Brit.* I. 166 *Gobius minutus*... Freckled or spotted goby. Polewig or pollybait, Thames local name.

polex, pol hax, obs. forms of pole-axe.

poley, polley ('pəʊlɪ), *a.* and *sb.* *Eng. dial.*, *Austral.*, *N.Z.*, and *U.S.* Also polly. [f. poll *sb.*^{5} + -y.] **A.** *adj.* Hornless, polled. Also *fig.*

1844 *Port Phillip Patriot* 4 July 1/5 Impounded..one mouse-coloured poley cow. **1859** H. Kingsley *G. Hamlyn* xxix, If it had been any other beast which knocked me down but that poley heifer, I should have been hurt! **1872** C. H. Eden *My Wife & I in Queensland* 83 A polley cow. Hornless cattle are so called. **1876** *Surrey Gloss.*, *Poly-cow*, a cow without horns. **1901** M. Franklin *My Brilliant Career* xxviii. 233 A couple of dirty knives and forks, a pair of cracked plates, two poley cups and chipped saucers. *Ibid.* 234 A cup was broken, and another, also a poley, was put in its stead. **1922** Joyce *Ulysses* 289 Angus heifers and polly bullocks of immaculate pedigree. **1930** L. G. D. Acland *Early Canterbury Runs* 1st Ser. vii. 173 A new-chum had a theory that if you turned your back on a beast and stooped down, and looked at him through your legs he wouldn't charge, and how a noted poley bullock completely exploded his theory. **1954** *Coast to Coast 1953–54* 14 Home made cartridges? There they go again! No. Poley chokes on their guns. That American idea for greater range.

B. *sb.* A type of saddle (see quots. 1958, 1966).

1958 *Amer. Speech* XXXIII. 167 *Poley*, a saddle without a pommel. **1966** Baker *Austral. Lang.* (ed. 2) iii. 67 Another type of saddle is the *poley*. This is a saddle without kneepads —'like a poley bull without horns, but generally considered to be derived from polo saddle'. **1975** *Sunday Mail Mag.* (Brisbane) 26 Jan. 15/1 My own poley had had its day... Good second-hand saddles were not easy to come by.

poley, obs. form of pulley.

poley, poley-mountain: see poly^1.

†**poleyn.** *Obs. rare*$^{-1}$. [a. OF. *po(u)lain* a colt, young animal: see pullen.] *attrib.* or as *adj.* Young male (horse).

[**1314–15** *Rolls of Parlt.* I. 302/2 Mesmes celes aveynes pristent pur los Poleyns. **1347** *Ibid.* II. 169/1 Les Chivalx le Roi, la Roigne, & le Prince pullains & autres.] *c* **1443** Lydg. in *Pol. Poems* (Rolls) II. 213 With a sharp swerd he sauh ridyng oon, Ffers and proudly, upon a poleyn steede.

poleyn, variant of polayn, polen (see polen wax), poulaine, puleyne, pullen.

polhode ('pɒlhəʊd). *Geom.* [mod. f. Gr. πόλος pole + ὁδός way, path (Poinsot 1852).] The non-plane curve traced on the surface of an ellipsoid with fixed centre by its point of contact with a fixed plane on which it rolls, as in the revolution of a top. Cf. herpolhode.

1868 E. J. Routh *Rigid Dynamics* 329 The point of contact of the ellipsoid with the plane on which it rolls traces out two curves, one on the surface of the ellipsoid, and one on the plane. The first of these..is called the polhode. **1882** Campbell & Garnett *Life J. C. Maxwell* 500 The curve which the extremity of the axis of rotation describes on the invariable plane is called a herpolhode, while that which it describes on the surface of the ellipsoid is called a polhode.

poliad ('pɒlɪəd). *nonce-wd.* [f. Gr. πόλις city + -ad 1 b, after oread, etc.] A city nymph.

1818 Shelley *Let. to Peacock* 16 Aug., Pray, are you yet cured of your Nympholepsy? 'Tis a sweet disease: but one as obstinate and dangerous as any—even when the Nymph is a Poliad. **1887** Dowden *Life Shelley* II. v. 188 *note*, This poem [in Leigh Hunt's 'Foliage'], with its Oreads, Napeads, Limniads, Nepheliads, probably suggested to Shelley the word 'Poliad', a city nymph.

poliadic (pɒlɪ'ædɪk), *a. rare.* [f. Gr. Πολιάς, -αδ- (female) guardian of the city, epithet of Athene as tutelary goddess of Athens (f. πόλις city) + -ic.] Of the nature of a tutelary deity of a city or state.

1886 E. B. Bax *Relig. Socialism* App. vii. 174 The poliadic or state divinity Yahveh being erected into the super-natural god of the universe.

Polian ('pəʊlɪən), *a. Zool.* [f. proper name *Poli*: see below + -an.] Of, pertaining to, or named after J. X. Poli, a Neapolitan naturalist (1746–1825), as in ***Polian vesicle***, one of the cæcal canals or sacs, generally five, connected with the circular vessel of an Echinoid or Holothurioid.

1841–71 T. R. Jones *Anim. Kingd.* (ed. 4) 229 The Polian vesicle (*b*) is largely increased in size. **1877** Huxley *Anat. Inv. Anim.* ix. 547 The circular vessel of the ambulacral system not only gives origin to polian vesicles, madreporic canals and tentacular vessels, but five canals proceed from it.

polianite ('pəʊlɪənaɪt). *Min.* [ad. G. *polianit* (A. Breithaupt 1844, in *Ann. der Physik* LXI. 191), f. Gr. πολιά greyness (in allusion to its colour): see -ite^1.] A variety of pyrolusite that occurs as large well-formed crystals.

1849 J. Nicol *Man. Mineral.* 420 Polianite..acts like pure hyperoxide of manganese. **1937** *Mineral. Mag.* XXIV. 521 (*heading*) X-ray studies on pyrolusite (including polianite) and psilomelane. *Ibid.*, The present study had for its main objective an attempt to settle..the uncertainty existing as to the relationship between polianite and pyrolusite. **1969** *Mineral. Abstr.* XX. 289/1 The Mn oxides ..have a microrhythmic structure..; in the veins they include polianite.

†**'polible**, *a. Obs. rare*$^{-1}$. [f. L. *polī-re* to polish: see -ible.] Capable of being polished.

1477 Norton *Ord. Alch.* v. in Ashm. *Theat. Chem. Brit.* (1652) 66 Soe that it be polible withall.

police (pə'liːs, pəʊ-), *sb.* Also 6 polyce, -yse, pollice. Also in reduced forms polie (*Sc.*), p'leece, etc. See also polis^2. [a. F. *police* (1477 in Godef.), organized government, civil administration, police, ad. med.L. *polītia* for earlier *polītīa*: see polity, policy, and -ice^1. In early use commonly pronounced ('pɒlɪs), as still often in Scotland and Ireland.]

I. †**1.** = policy *sb.*^{1} 3, 4, 4 b. ***public police*** = public policy. *Obs.*

c **1540** *Surr. Northampton Priory* in France *Addit. Narr. Pop. Plot* 36 Steryng them with all perswasions, ingynes, and Polyce to dedd Images and Counterfeit Relicts. **1547** Boorde *Introd. Knowl.* iv. (1870) 137 My scyences and other polyces dyd kepe me in fauour. *Ibid.* xxv. 186, I werke by polyse, subtylyte, and craught. **1632** Brome *North. Lasse* v. v, The plot smells of your Ladiships police. **1640** Nabbes *Bride* i. iii, What more police Could I be guilty of? **1766** Entick *London* IV. 208 Assisted by the police and interests of the Roman see. *a* **1768** Erskine *Inst. Laws of Scotl.* (1773) I. 152 If..the public police shall require that a highway be carried through the property of a private person.

II. †**2.** Civil organization; civilization. *Obs.*

1530 Palsgr. 167 *Police*, polyce. **1536** *Act 27 Hen. VIII* c. 42 §1 The knowlege of suche other good letters as in christoned Realmes be expedyent to be lerned for the conservacion of their good pollices. **1549** *Compl. Scot.* xvii. 145 Nature prouokit them to begyn sum litil police, for sum of them began to plant treis, sum to dant beystis, sum gadthrid the frutis. **1791** Burke *Let. Memb. Nat. Ass.* Wks. VI. 22 A barbarous nation [the Turks], with a barbarous neglect of police, fatal to the human race. **1820** J. R. Johnson tr. *Huber on Ants* 2 These insects, whose faculties, police, and sagacity have been, by some authors, as much overrated, as by others not duly appreciated. **1845** Disraeli *Sybil* ii. iii, These hovels were in many instances not provided with the commonest conveniences of the rudest police; contiguous to every door might be observed the dung-heap.

3. a. The regulation, discipline, and control of a community; civil administration; enforcement of law; public order.

The early quotations refer to France, and other foreign countries, and to Scotland, where *Commissioners of Police*, for the general internal administration of the country, consisting of six noblemen and four gentlemen, were appointed by Queen Anne, 13 Dec. 1714. This was app. the first official use of the word in Great Britain. In England, it was still viewed with disfavour after 1760. A writer in the *British Magazine*, April 1763, p. 542, opines that 'from an aversion to the French..and something under the name of *police* being already established in Scotland, English prejudice will not soon be reconciled to it'. (The name *Commissioners of Police*, or *Police Commission*, was in the 19th c. given to the local bodies having control of the Police force in Burghs and Police Burghs in Scotland.)

1716 *Lond. Gaz.* No. 5449/3 Charles Cockburn, Esq. to be one of the Commissioners of Police in North Britain. **1732** Swift *Exam. Abuses Dublin* Wks. 1761 III. 219 Nothing is held more commendable in all great cities . . than what the French call the *police*; by which word is meant the government thereof. **1733** P. LINDESAY (*title*) The interest of Scotland considered, with regard to its Police, in imploying of the Poor, its Agriculture, its Trade [etc.]. **1737** J. CHAMBERLAYNE *St. Gt. Brit.* III. 60 [Scotland] A List of the Lords and Others, Commissioners of Police. **1751** CORBYN MORRIS *Pres. State of London* (title-p.), Observations [etc.] . . to which are added, some Proposals for the better Regulation of the Police of this Metropolis. **1756** CHESTERF. in *World* No. 189 ¶ 1 We are accused by the French . . of having no word in our language, which answers to their word *police*, which therefore we have been obliged to adopt, not having, as they say, the thing. **1756–7** tr. *Keysler's Trav.* (1760) I. 502 (*Lucca*) Their police is very commendable, and great attention is shewn in suppressing luxury, superfluous magnificence, and . . dissipations. **1757** LD. KAMES *Statute Law Scotl.* 269 Police [Heading of a section of regulations as to prevention of fires, closing of taverns, etc.]. **1761** *Brit. Mag.* II. 556 The right hon. lord Napier is appointed one of the lords of police in Scotland, in the room of the earl of Hopetoun. *a* **1768** ERSKINE *Inst. Laws of Scotl.* (1773) II. 714 Offences against the laws enacted for the police or good government of a country, are truly crimes against the state. **1769** BLACKSTONE *Comm.* IV. xiii. 162 By the public police and economy, I mean the due regulation and domestic order of the Kingdom. **1795** J. AIKIN *Manchester* 263 The police of the town is managed by two constables. **1800** COLQUHOUN *Comm. Thames* iii. 156 Preventive Police may be considered as a New Science, yet in its infancy, and only beginning to be understood. **1817** H. A. MEREWETHER (*title*) A New system of Police; with Reference to the Evidences given before the Police Committee of the House of Commons. **1826** KENT *Comm.* 43 The consular convention between France and this country in 1778 allowed consuls to exercise police over all vessels of their respective nation. **1844** LD. BROUGHAM *Brit. Const.* xix. §3 (1862) 324 By police is properly meant the care of preventing infractions of the law, detecting offenders, bringing them to justice. **1850** MERIVALE *Rom. Emp.* (1865) II. xvii. 249 The police of the seas was imperfectly kept. **1871** FREEMAN *Norm. Conq.* IV. xvii. §2. 30 The strict police of his [William I's] reign began already; robbers, murderers, . . were kept in check. **1877** MORLEY *Crit. Misc.* Ser. II. 39 Such legislation was part of the general police of the realm.

†**b.** In commercial legislation, Public regulation or control of a trade; an economic policy. *Obs.*

1776 ADAM SMITH *W.N.* I. xi. III. (1869) I. 191 The elegant author of the essay on the Police of Grain. **1792** A. YOUNG *Trav. France* 141 Of such consequence it is to a country, and indeed to every country, to have a good police of corn; a police that shall, by securing a high price to the farmer, encourage his culture enough to secure the people at the same time from famine. [**1866** ROGERS *Agric. & Prices* I. viii. 146 The importance of the trade is proved by the strict police exercised upon the importation.]

c. The cleansing or keeping clean of a camp or garrison; the condition of a camp or garrison in respect of cleanliness. *U.S.*

1834 J. KEMPER in *Wisconsin Hist. Coll.* (1898) XIV. 412 The towels, basins &c here are not what they ought to be. The police of the boat is bad. **1893** *Outing* (U.S.) May 158/1 The police of the camp was found to be excellent. **1894** *Ibid.* July 312/2 The camp was at all times in good police.

4. The department of government which is concerned with the maintenance of public order and safety, and the enforcement of the law: the extent of its functions varying greatly in different countries and at different periods.

c **1730** BURT *Lett. N. Scotl.* (1818) I. 140 By the way, this police is still a great office in Scotland, . . it is grown into disuetude, though the salaries remain. **1739** CIBBER *Apol.* (1756) I. 232 Since we are so happy as not to have a certain power among us which in another country is call'd the Police, let us rather bear this insult than buy its remedy at too dear a rate. **1774** PENNANT *Tour Scot. in 1772*, 128 The police of Glasgow consists of three bodies; the magistrates with the town council, the merchants house, and the trades house. **1781** C. JOHNSTON *Hist. J. Juniper* I. 110 An insinuation so injurious to the honour of my country; which is governed by so supremely vigilant and wise a police. **1825** in Hone *Every-day Bk.* I. 441 Stepney, Hampstead, Westend, and Peckham fairs have been crushed by the police, that 'stern, rugged nurse' of national morality. **1863** H. COX *Instit.* III. vi. 667 The police of the country, by which is meant that department of government which has for its object the maintenance of the internal peace and prevention of crimes, the protection of public order and public health.

5. a. The civil force to which is entrusted the duty of maintaining public order, enforcing regulations for the prevention and punishment of breaches of the law, and detecting crime; construed as *pl.*, the members of a police force; the constabulary of a locality.

Marine Police, the name given to the force instituted *c* 1798 (orig. by private enterprise) to protect the merchant shipping on the Thames in the Port of London. (The earliest use in this sense.) ***New Police*** (quots. 1830, 1831, 1884): the name by which the police force established for London in 1829 (Act 10 Geo. IV, c. 44) was for some time known.

1800 COLQUHOUN *Comm. Thames* 165 The vigilance of the Marine Police detected one of the Boats conveying it on shore. *Ibid.* 219 To place their Vessels . . under the protection of the Police. **1826** SCOTT *Mal. Malagr.* ii. 41 A strong and well-ordered police would prevent the fatal agitations of a mob. **1830** WELLINGTON *Let. to Peel* 3 Nov., I congratulate you on the entire success of the Police in London. It is impossible to see anything more respectable than they are. **1830** JEKYLL *Corr.* 13 Nov., It is incredible with what spirit and firmness the new police has defeated the canaille. **1831** *Blackw. Mag.* Jan. 87/1 The alleged incompetency and misconduct of watchmen formed the great pretext for establishing the Police. *Ibid.* 104/1 The establishment of the New Police will . . be pronounced a sufficient reason for retaining it. **1867** TROLLOPE *Chron. Barset* I. viii. 60 Later in the day, he declared that the police should fetch him. **1884** E. YATES *Recollect. & Exper.* I. 45 In those days [1836–47] the 'new Police', as they were still called . . were very different in appearance from our present guardians. **1922** JOYCE *Ulysses* 162 Squads of police marching out, back. **1970** *Daily Tel.* 27 June 1/4 One hundred police and 200 civilians yesterday searched lonely country around Stephen's home. **1973** *Ibid.* 21 Mar. 10 The factory-gate clash between 400 pickets and 232 police . . foreshadows a new style of strike demonstration. **1976** *Daily Record* (Glasgow) 4 Dec. 32/2 The police then gave evidence, after being told they need not answer questions.

b. *transf.* Any body of men, officially instituted or employed to keep order, enforce regulations, or maintain a political or ecclesiastical system.

1837 *Civil Eng. & Arch. Jrnl.* I. 13/2 Flags of different colours hoisted to various heights, and worked by the railway police, to notify any . . stoppages or accidents. **1840** MACAULAY *Ess.*, *Ranke* (1851) II. 132 The new spiritual police was every where. **1855** PRESCOTT *Philip II*, II. vi. (1857) 259 To maintain the troops in the Netherlands, as an armed police on which he could rely to enforce the execution of his orders. **1859** MILL *Liberty* 52/1 They employ a moral police, which occasionally becomes a physical one, to deter skilful workmen from receiving, and employers from giving, a larger remuneration for a more useful service. **1880** *Contemp. Rev.* XXXVII. 477 He believed in a . . kind of watchful police of spirits and local heroes dead and gone before. **1884** *Pall Mall G.* 13 Nov. 5/1 The vexed question whether the police of the seas should be armoured or unarmoured.

c. (As a count noun.) A policeman. Chiefly *Sc.* and *U.S. colloq.*

1839 *Chicago American* 5 Sept., There is a police in attendance . . in the theatre. **1856** 'MARK TWAIN' *Adv. Thomas Jefferson Snodgrass* (1928) 8 He was a police. **1890** J. KERR *Reminisc.* I. 98 Then for a while the loon to jail Was taken by a polie, O. **1904**, etc. [see POLIS[2]]. **1951** M. MCLUHAN *Mechanical Bride* 107/2 Joyce's famous remark that, 'though he might have been more humble, there's no police like Holmes,' contains a world of insight. **1960** *Huntly Express* 19 Aug. 7 It was all over the market that 'the unco man wis a p'leece wi' plain claes'. **1964** J. H. CLARKE *Harlem* 277 He crawled out of th' door hollerin' for a police to save him. **1975** *Caribbean Contact* Feb. 14/1 His father was a police and his mother, familiarly known as 'Sister Lu', a laundry worker.

6. *attrib.* and *Comb.* (chiefly in senses 4 and 5), as ***police act***, ***agent***, ***ball***, ***barge***, ***boat***, ***cadet***, ***camp***, ***car***, ***cell***, ***charge-sheet***, ***chief***, ***college***, ***colonel***, ***commissioner***, ***constable***, ***control***, ***cordon***, ***courtroom***, ***department***, ***district***, ***doctor***, ***duty***, ***establishment***, ***force***, ***gazette***, ***headquarters***, ***horse***, ***house***, ***inspector***, ***jeep***, ***laboratory***, ***launch***, ***lieutenant***, ***medal***, ***patrol***, ***photograph***, ***photographer***, ***post***, ***power***, ***procedure***, ***protection***, ***radio***, ***raid***, ***rate***, ***regulation***, ***report***, ***sergeant***, ***-ship***, ***spy***, ***spying***, ***surgeon***, ***system***, ***-tax***, ***van***, ***-woman***, ***work***; also ***police-aided***, ***-controlled***, ***-guarded***, ***-harassed***, ***-protected***, ***-ridden*** adjs.; **police action**, (*a*) the deeds or activity of the police; (*b*) military intervention without a formal declaration of war when a nation or group within a nation is considered to be violating international law and peace; **police bail** (see quot. 1976); **police blotter**: see BLOTTER 4; **police board**, 'in several of the United States, a board constituted by the justices of the county for the control of county police, public buildings, roads, bridges . . etc.' (Murfree, *Justices' Practice*); **police box**, (*a*) a box or kiosk containing a telephone specially for the use of police or of members of the public wishing to contact the police; (*b*) a reinforced shelter on London streets during the 1939–45 war for the protection of policemen on duty during an air raid; **police boy**, in European colonies or former European territories, a 'native' police assistant or security officer; **police burgh**: see quot.; **police captain**, a subordinate officer in the police force in New York and other large cities of U.S., and Ireland; **police cruiser** *N. Amer.*, a police patrol car; **police dispatcher** *U.S.*, a member of the staff of a police station who receives information about crimes and transmits it to police patrols; **police dog**, (*a*) a dog employed by the police to track and capture criminals, to find lost persons, etc.; (*b*) = ALSATIAN *sb.* B. 2; **police grip** *rare*, a grip or hold used by policemen; **police informer**, a criminal who gives information about crime to the police; **police judge** (*Sc.*), a stipendiary police magistrate; also *U.S.*; **police jury**, the name in Louisiana of the local authority in each parish invested with the exercise of police powers; **police lock**, (see quot. 1975); **police magistrate**, a stipendiary magistrate who presides in a police court; **police-manure**, (*Scotl.*) manure collected in the streets, street-sweepings; **police-master**, a superintendent or chief of police in Russia; hence **police-mastership**; **police matron**, a policewoman who takes charge of women or juveniles at a police station or in court; **police message** (see quot. 1941); **police-monger**, *nonce-wd.*, one who busies himself about a police system; **police novel**, a detective novel in which police procedures in detecting crime form the central interest; **police officer**, †an official charged with the maintenance of public order (*obs.*); a member of a police force, a constable; **police orphanage**, a home for the orphans of policemen; **police positive**, a type of Colt's pistol; **police procedural** *a.*, of or pertaining to police procedure, applied *spec.* to a type of crime detection story; also as *sb.*, = *police novel*; **police record**, a dossier kept by the police on all persons convicted of crime; hence, a past which includes some conviction for crime; **police reporter**, a newspaper reporter who concentrates on stories concerning crime and police activity; †**police-runner**, a police officer of the lowest rank: cf. RUNNER; **police science**, the science dealing with the investigation of crime; so **police scientist**; **police siren**, the siren on a police vehicle; **police special**, a type of revolver; **police trap**, an arrangement made by police for detecting motorists who exceed the speed limit, or for apprehending criminals or other wanted persons; also *fig.*; so **police-trapped** *a.*; **police whistle**, a special type of loud whistle used by the police; **police-witness**, a witness whose testimony supports a police prosecution. See also POLICE COURT, etc.

1758 SIR J. FIELDING (*title*) An Account of the Origin and Effects of a *Police Act, set on foot by his Grace the Duke of Newcastle, in the year 1753. **1885** *Encycl. Brit.* XIX. 334/1 *Police action in relation to the serious matters constituting crime is familiar knowledge. **1933** *Week-end Rev.* 1 July 17/1 Blurring the distinction between war the duel and 'police action'. **1959** *Chambers's Encycl.* VII. 512/2 The Dutch started the first 'police action' and occupied large parts of the republic. After United Nations intervention a truce agreement was signed. **1968** *Listener* 19 Dec. 821/3 What's the difference . . between police action and war, if the soldiers of the two sides are killing each other? **1978** G. VIDAL *Kalki* iii. 51 He would have been able to avoid the Vietnam war—or 'police action', to properly designate that valiant attempt to save Southeast Asia for the free world. **1852** E. E. HALE *If, Yes, & Perhaps* (1868) 44, I had told the *police agent he might send it to the St. Nicholas. **1930** G. B. SHAW *Apple Cart* p. xvi, Proletariats are never revolutionary, and . . their direct action, when it is controlled at all, is usually controlled by police agents. **1910** *Times* 21 Mar. 13/1 Mr. Winston Churchill will visit Brighton on April 2 to make himself acquainted with the Brighton *police aided scheme for clothing poor children, in which the King recently showed an interest. **1922** JOYCE *Ulysses* 670 Embroidery, darning or knitting for the policeaided clothing society. **1976** *Daily Tel.* 6 Feb. 2/8 Where the police are unable to complete their inquiries immediately, they also have power under the Magistrates' Courts Act 1952 to grant what is known as '*police bail'. The person in custody is required to enter into a recognizance, with or without sureties, to appear again at a police station at a certain time for further questioning. **1977** *Gay News* 24 Mar. 1/3 All the customers were released on police bail. **1969** C. WATSON *Bump in Night* ii. 26 Don't forget it's the *police ball on the 14th. **1973** *Guardian* 12 Mar. 1/8 Saturday night's killings occurred while most of Bermuda's unarmed police force were at the semi-annual police ball. **1838** MISS PARDOE *River & Desert* II. 111 The gaily-painted and clean-looking *police-barge. **1800** COLQUHOUN *Comm. Thames* 207 The constant perambulation of the *Police Boats, both by night and by day. **1873** G. LENING *Dark Side of N.Y. Life* 155 The six police-boats cannot be usefully employed on the rivers in the interest of commerce. **1890** A. CONAN DOYLE *Sign of Four* ix. 182, I shall want a fast police-boat—a steam-launch—to be at the Westminster Stairs at seven o'clock. **1943** *Sun* (Baltimore) 13 Dec. 5/1 The children and guarding against sabotage now present the greatest number of police-boat problems. **1975** 'A. HALL' *Mandarin Cypher* vii. 105 A police boat had put to sea at full speed. **1932** *Daily Tel.* 23 May 12/2 A policeman was cut off in a *police-box by 10ft of water and had to be rescued. **1940** R. MORRISH *Police & Crime-Detection* iii. 36 Many police districts now possess their police-box system, by means of which officers performing duty in outlying districts are able to communicate with their stations. **1941** *Newsweek* 13 Oct. 29 One of many air-raid precautions taken in the British capital for the expected winter Luftwaffe attacks is the building of 'police boxes' at street intersections. The reinforced brick shelters will protect London Bobbies on duty during Nazi air raids. **1971** R. AMBERLEY *Ordinary Accident* xiii. 116 Someone, evidently ringing from the police box on the Banbury road. **1946** C. B. JEPPE *Gold Mining on Witwatersrand* II. xvi. 1758 On all the mines of the Witwatersrand (1943) there were 142 Europeans and 1,887 native '*police boys' in the police organisation (underground and surface). **1961** *Quest* Oct./Dec. 33/2 Motu prevailed over the candidates firstly because it was based on the speech of the police-boys who formed the larger part of the total mobilized section of the population, and secondly because these police-boys were much more accessible to the ordinary people than the English-speaking rulers. **1971** *Sunday Times* (Johannesburg) 28 Mar. 16/5 This clause shall not apply to . . labourers and watch men or police boys. **1889** *Act 52 & 53 Vict.* c. 50 §105 The expression '*police burgh' means a populous place, the boundaries whereof have been fixed and ascertained under the provisions of the General Police and Improvement (Scotland) Act, 1862, or of the Act first therein recited, or under the provisions of any local Act. **1959** M. GILBERT *Blood & Judgement* xii. 131 A *police cadet motor-cyclist was propping his machine up. **1976** *Southern Even. Echo* (Southampton) 12 Nov. 15/6 He wanted to become a police cadet—and had even been to the police station to find out details of what was involved in following this career. 1888 'R. Boldrewood' Robbery under Arms, xlix, All accounts.. may be sent to the *Police Camp. 1834 M. Edgeworth Let. in Tour in Connemara & Martins of Ballinahinch (1950) 93 The cottage at the end of the walk to Swinnerton, in which I believe a *police-captain Henderson lived in your time. 1902 Chambers's Jrnl. Oct. 674/1 The next grade above is that of sergeant. Above this comes the police captain. 1976 H. Nielsen Brink of Murder xxi. 187 He's smart. He knew the odds against nailing a police captain. 1924 A. Christie Poirot Investigates viii. 221 A large *police car was waiting for us, with some plain-clothes men. 1931 E. S. Gardner Candy Kid in Case of Crying Swallow (1972) 92 The two men in the police car glimpsed boxes of candy in the rear of the sedan. 1971 B. Patten Irrelevant Song 62 The sirens wailing on police-cars. 1898 McClure's Mag. X. 547/2 He was still in the infirmary attached to the *police-cells. 1965 D. Francis For Kicks xix. 240 Four nights and three days in a police cell. 1977 J. Wainwright Do Nothin' xiii. 220 They are already on their way to some all-mod-con police cell. 1922 Joyce Ulysses 180 *Police chargesheets crammed with cases get their percentage manufacturing crime. 1961 Copp & Peck Betrayal at UN iv. xxi. 208 Colonel Frank Begley, former *Police Chief of Farmington, Conn., and now head of U.N. special police. 1974 E. Ambler Dr Frigo ii. 104 How does he reward him? Make him police chief or head of intelligence? 1977 H. Fast Immigrants i. 65 He could have Mayor McCarthy and Police Chief Martin as guests in his house. 1936 N. Marsh Death in Ecstasy ix. 109 Have you been through the *Police College? 1958 S. Hyland Who goes Hang? i. v. 24 The senior lecturer in forensic studies at any of your admirable police colleges. 1976 Daily Mail (Hull) 16 Dec., He was chosen as the first member of that rank to go to the Police College at Ryton on Dunsmore. 1869 Harper's Mag. Oct. 754/1 The system of relief that has now become the perplexity of the *Police Commissioners. 1911 Daily Colonist (Victoria, B.C.) 11 Apr. 7/1 A meeting of the police commissioners will be held this afternoon.. when the department's estimates for the year will be considered. 1977 Hongkong Standard 12 Apr. 8/3 The courageous, determined and almost unique efforts of former Police Commissioner C.S. to root out internal graft backfired. 1800 Colquhoun Comm. Thames 206 A 'Caution against Pillage and Plunder' which the *Police Constables were instructed to read aloud as soon as the Lumpers and Coopers were assembled. 1855 London as it is 366 During two months out of every three, each police constable is on night duty. 1838 Encycl. Brit. (ed. 7) XVIII. 252/1 Expediency of placing discharged criminals under *police control. 1939 H. Hodge Cab, Sir? 236 A *police-controlled cross-roads. 1961 Times 6 Dec. 15/5 Let him [sc. the Minister of Transport] give us more police-controlled and light-controlled crossings. 1970 'D. Halliday' Dolly & Cookie Bird xii. 193 I'd put a *police cordon round the house with orders not to let anyone through. 1979 J. Gardner Nostradamus Traitor xvi. 59 He carried ID which would get him through any police cordon. 1866 'Mark Twain' Lett. from Hawaii (1967) 28 The old *police courtroom in San Francisco. 1937 C. Himes Black on Black (1973) 143 He broke away.. before the *police cruiser got there. 1958 'Castle' & 'Hailey' Flight into Danger viii. 107 At the turn-off from the main highway.. a police cruiser stood.. its roof-light blinking a constant warning. 1974 Globe & Mail (Toronto) 16 Jan. 8/5 With the red light flashing, the police cruiser tails the motorist down the street and flags him over to the curb. 1976 Billings (Montana) Gaz. 2 July 8-B/4 In Louisville, police began a slowdown and 41 police cruisers notified headquarters they had been disabled by flat tires. 1810 Rec. Early Hist. Boston (1904) XXXIII. 495 In the estimate of expences for the.. year, a sum was named for the *police department. 1931 E. S. Gardner Vanishing Corpse in Case of Crying Swallow (1972) 107 [He] was on terms of intimacy with most of the police department heads. 1963 'E. McBain' Ten Plus One (1964) 24 The police department is a vast organization, and a detective is only an organization man. 1977 H. Fast Immigrants ii. 110 In the annals of the San Francisco Police Department, a dead Chinese was statistically different from a dead Caucasian. 1973 Tucson (Arizona) Daily Citizen 22 Aug. 11/1 *Police dispatcher Bill Pyles called an aid car, then began telling Mrs. Sweet how to keep little Jeremy from dying. 1976 Billings (Montana) Gaz. 2 July 1-A/2 Heagerty was about to be fined when a police dispatcher intervened and told the judge of Heagerty's plans. 1838 Encycl. Brit. (ed. 7) XVIII. 249/2 The metropolitan *police district, according to that act [of 1829], consists of about ninety parishes, and ultra-parochial places, in and surrounding the metropolis. 1906 Harmsworth Encycl. 4814/3 At the present time the Metropolitan Police district is nearly 700 square miles in extent. 1934 M. Allingham Death of Ghost vii. 86 The altruistic murderer is rare, and of course I couldn't say what the chances of your being one were until we have the evidence of the *police doctor. 1972 K. Royce Miniatures Frame viii. 103 If I knew anything of police doctors the fuzz would ring around for hours until one reluctantly agreed to come. 1908 Daily Chron. 28 Aug. 7/2 Most of the principal German towns possess *police dogs. 1911 Chambers's Jrnl. Feb. 136/1 What is needed as an ideal police-dog is an animal that can not only track well, but that can attack the criminal. 1925 F. Scott Fitzgerald Great Gatsby ii. 32 I'd like to get one of those police dogs; I don't suppose you got that kind? 1974 Encycl. Brit. Macropædia XIV. 672/1 Police dogs. The training of dogs for police work was originally developed in Ghent, Belgium, about 1900 and was soon copied elsewhere. 1798 Dk. Portland Let. 16 May in Colquhoun Comm. Thames (1800) 160 note, The expence of the Marine *Police Establishment, which appeared to me ought to be borne by Government. 1838 Dickens in Bentley's Misc. Sept. 222 Professor Nogo wished to be informed what amount of automaton *police force it was proposed to raise. 1840 Penny Cycl. XVIII. 334 The establishment of a new police force for the metropolis, in 1829, has done more towards exhibiting the advantages of employing a trained body of men for all the purposes for which the old constabulary was appointed, than any other circumstance. 1883 Anna K. Green Hand & Ring iii, He is a member of the police force. 1956 H. Nicolson Diary 2 Nov. (1968) 314 There is a suggestion.. that UNO should police the area, but it will take a long time before the police-force can be assembled. 1968 Listener 21 Nov. 667/1 As I saw it, the UN must move quickly to set up some kind of international police force. 1976 Daily Record (Glasgow) 4 Dec. 2/5 More than 1000 officers from every prison, police force, and state mental institution in the country turned up for the funeral service at Carnwath village in Lanarkshire. 1838 Encycl. Brit. (ed. 7) XVIII. 251/1 An official newspaper, called the Hue and Cry or *Police Gazette, is also circulated amongst the authorities, throughout the kingdom. 1910 *Police grip [see ju-jitsu]. 1875 M. D. Landon E. Perkins 237 The first thing you must do after the child is lost is to go to the *Police Headquarters. 1952 Auden Nones 37 Between the burnt-out Law Courts and Police Headquarters. 1971 W. J. Burley Guilt Edged i. 9 The new police headquarters on the outskirts of the city. 1935 N. Mitchison We have been Warned iv. 453 She was knocked down.. almost under the nose of a *police horse. 1973 R. Busby Pattern of Violence x. 157 A troop of police horses from the mounted branch held the crowd back. 1969 J. Wainwright Big Tickle 52 To live in his own house and not a '*police house' gave Cohen a freedom denied most police officers. 1974 L. Lamb Man in Mist viii. 51 Its [sic] P. C. Marchant, sir, who has the police house at Buntingbury. 1965 N. Freeling Criminal Conversation ii. xx. 191 [He] looked like a gentleman... Janus had never imagined he might be a *police informer. 1969 G. Greene Travels with my Aunt i. vii. 60 He suspected me to be some unsavoury police informer. 1977 M. Kenyon Rapist vi. 73 Is it police informer I'm to be now, Sergeant? 1855 Mrs. Gaskell North & S. xxxiv, 'It's nothing, miss', said Dixon.. 'Only a *police-inspector. He wants to see you, miss.' 1899 Allbutt's Syst. Med. VIII. 289 If the police inspector pooh-poohed his appeal and turned him out of the police station. 1972 E. Hargreaves Fair Green Weed vii. 89 A sergeant, a corporal and a young police doctor arrived in the *police jeep. [1823: cf. Judge of Police in Police Court.] 1862 Act 25 & 26 Vict. c. 35 §25 If adjudged by any magistrate or *police judge of any royal or parliamentary burgh. 1956 B. Holiday Lady sings Blues (1973) ii. 23 It was Magistrate Jean Hortense Norris, the first woman police judge in New York, a tough hard-faced old dame. 1976 Pioneer (Big Timber, Montana) 30 June 12/2 He served in the Armed Forces during World War II, was a Montana Highway Patrolman and a police judge for the City of Billings. 1937 D. & H. Teilhet Feather Cloak Murders v. 85 The Chinese gentleman in the *police laboratory removed the wicked little steel dart from under the Zeiss microscope. 1974 'R. Tate' Birds of Blooded Feather iii. 53 He's a policeman... Something to do with the police laboratories. 1940 R. Morrish Police & Crime-Detection iii. 39 Some of the *police-launches on the river Thames are also fitted with radio. 1972 Police Rev. 1 Dec. 1565/2 Section Officer Marshall swept the pale blue and white Police launch across the lake surface. 1975 J. Aiken Voices in Empty House 15 The apartment was further defended by a *police lock, a rod which fastened into place on the back of the door and hooked into the floor, so that the door would not open beyond a certain point. 1976 New Yorker 1 Mar. 33/2 She slammed the door and I heard the police lock snap into place, then silence. 1800 Colquhoun Comm. Thames 199 Any *Police Magistrate.. may assist the Magistrates in their judicial Functions. 1838 Encycl. Brit. (ed. 7) XVIII. 250/1 When a complaint is made to a police magistrate he issues his warrant as he sees occasion, to a constable.. or to one of the metropolitan force. 1883 J. Shields in Trans. Highl. Soc. Agric. XV. 38 The whole was manured with *police manure—about 30 tons per acre. 1863 Mrs. Atkinson Tartar Steppes 224 We drove to the house of the *police-master, who courteously invited us to be his guests. 1883 Reade in Harper's Mag. Jan. 258/1 Vladimir got the promise of a *police mastership. 1934 Webster, *Police matron. 1942 A. Christie Body in Library xiv. 133 In the corner of Superintendent Harper's office sat an elderly lady... She was certainly no police matron. 1972 R. Bloch Night-World (1974) xvii. 113 You'd have a police matron assigned to you, but they wouldn't put you in a cell. 1955 M. Allingham Beckoning Lady ii. 72 Divisional Detective Chief Inspector Charles Luke.. had emerged from hospital with.. a recommendation for the coveted *Police Medal. 1977 'A. York' Tallant for Trouble ii. 13 He had proved.. a good policeman.. his courage during one of Guyana's mini-revolutions had earned him a Queen's Police Medal. 1938 N. Marsh Artists in Crime xv. 219 The B.B.C. had instructions to send out a *police message. 1941 B.B.C. Gloss. Broadcasting Terms 23 Police Message, message broadcast at the request of the police authorities. 1968 T. Stoppard Real Inspector Hound 13 We interrupt our programme for a special police message. 1808 W. Taylor in Monthly Mag. XXVI. 111 For the sake of pretending to be useful, these new *police-mongers will pry into every peculiarity, and meddle with every amusement of the people. 1896 G. B. Shaw Our Theatres in Nineties (1932) II. 223 As a novel, I can pass my idle hour with it, just as Bismarck used to pass his with the *police novels of Du Boisgobey. 1908 G. K. Chesterton All Things Considered 116 The police novel.. permits privacy only to explode and smash privacy. 1972 J. Symons Bloody Murder xiv. 197 The police novel, or the police-procedural as it has recently been called, concentrates upon the detailed investigation of a crime from the point of view of the police. 1800 Colquhoun Comm. Thames 206 A gang of Lumpers.. quitted their employment instantly on the appearance of the *Police Officers. 1806 A. Duncan Nelson's Fun. 26 Special, petty, and other constables, and all the police officers of every description.. were on duty. 1844 J. T. Hewlett Parsons & W. vi, He returned with a police-officer. 1976 M. Underwood Menaces xii. 114 Having been a police officer, she was much better equipped than most to be the wife of one. 1938 M. Allingham Fashion in Shrouds xx. 360 [He] made the suggestion as if he were announcing a rich gift to the *Police Orphanage. 1972 M. Gilbert Body of Girl xxiii. 199 Any unclaimed money goes to the Police Orphanage. 1899 Somerville & 'Ross' Some Experiences Irish R.M. iii. 63 Flurry espied the *police patrol on the road. 1936 'N. Blake' Thou Shell of Death xiv. 258 On the main road he'd have to go straight for a bit, and the police patrols would be out. 1947 Sun (Baltimore) 7 May 7/3 At first, the jail visitors balked at riding to the prison in a police patrol wagon. 1969 M. Pugh Last Place Left xxix. 209, I suppose you'll recognize a police patrol car? 1974 Times 4 Oct. 3/3 She was given the task of observing the strength of police patrols. 1943 G. Greene Ministry of Fear iii. i. 163 A *police photograph is like a passport photograph... We protest: This isn't me. 1965 E. S. Gardner Case of Beautiful Beggar (1972) 7 He took us into the police laboratory and museum, and started explaining the cases on which he had worked.. all.. illustrated by police photographs. 1978 'A. Garve' Counterstroke i. 38 There were two police photographs, full face and profile. 1931 M. Allingham Police at Funeral xv. 206 Mr. Bowditch and a *police photographer had completed their work on the footprint. 1970 W. J. Burley To kill a Cat i. 21 The police photographers.. had already taken pictures of the undisturbed room. 1907 Yesterday's Shopping (1969) 642/1 Colt's new *police positive revolver. 1931 'G. Trevor' Murder at School xii. 244 This is what is called a Colt Point 22 Police Positive. Not a nice thing to be plugged with. 1975 J. Gores Hammett (1976) xxxii. 221 He took out the long-barreled police positive... He thumbed back the hammer. 1827 U.S. Supreme Court Rep. XXV. 442 The power to direct the removal of gun-powder is a branch of the *police power which unquestionably remains.. with the states. 1932 N. M. Butler Looking Forward xi. 168 'Police power'—which in American law means the principle that the public interest often requires the extension of government authority in repression.. of individual activity or habit. 1964 Gould & Kolb Dict. Social Sciences 508/2 Police power may be defined as the broad and elastic power of government especially of one of the states of the United States, to restrict, control, regulate, and restrain individuals and groups in the use of their liberty and property in order to protect and promote the health, safety, morals, convenience, peace, order, and general welfare of other individuals and the public generally. 1967 Punch 16 Aug. 256/1 *Police-procedural thrillers must be original to compete, yet, of their nature, ordinarily plausible. 1972 'L. Egan' Paper Chase (1973) iii. 40 She'd always read mysteries, but mostly.. what they call the police-procedural ones. 1972 [see police novel above]. 1977 Time 27 June 56/2 Laidlaw is also the first police procedural by Scottish Author William McIlvanney. 1885 Encycl. Brit. XIX. 337/1 If they [sc. orders having the approval of the secretary of state for the government of the metropolitan police] are carefully considered and prepared, their issue must produce a uniform code of *police procedure for the force. 1974 Publishers Weekly 5 Aug. 51/2 European police procedure buffs might enjoy this, but the author makes it hard for the reader to grapple with the evidence. 1976 'J. Charlton' Remington Set iii. 18, I wish I had a book somewhere I could look up police procedure in. 1901 Sketch 17 July 518/2 Herr Kubelik.. will have to be *police-protected against the patrons of Señor Sarasate. 1908 London Mag. Oct. 240, I would demand *police protection. 1942 E. Paul Narrow St. xvi. 125 Mariette.. footed the bills of the establishment,.. arranged police protection and gave the place its personality and reputation for fair play. 1972 C. Drummond Death at Bar i. 40 Hundreds of people in this wicked city would relish the idea of police protection. 1958 A. Budrys in Venture Sci. Fict. Mar. 14/2 He'd used a *police radio often enough. 1975 Listener 2 Jan. 26/1 The loudspeakers.. crackled with voices from a police radio in the streets. 1919 G. B. Shaw Heartbreak House p. xx, The ordinary law was superseded by Acts under which newspapers were seized and their printing machinery destroyed by simple *police raids à la Russe. 1933 J. Buchan Prince of Captivity iii. i. 277 That cheerful party broke up in confusion... Yes, a police raid. 1975 Country Life 16 Jan. 155/1 A recent police raid led to the arrest of a well-organized gang. 1863 Alcock Capit. Tycoon I. 28 They pay road and *police-rates. a1911 D. G. Phillips Susan Lenox (1917) II. xi. 277 Once in the pariah class, once with a '*police record'. 1950 T. Walsh Nightmare in Manhattan iv. 106 Calhoun was examining his police record, which was long and bad. 1972 J. Wainwright Night is Time to Die 92 He has no police record. No previous convictions. 1802 C. Wilmot Diary in Irish Peer on Continent (1920) 61 It is a good display of the *Police regulations, for such order, method, and tranquillity I cou'd not have imagined. 1853 E. Twisleton Let. 23 May (1928) v. 85 Owing to the recent revolts, all the police-regulations were doubled in stringency. 1938 R. G. Collingwood Princ. Art xi. 255 Philosophical controversies are not to be settled by a kind of police-regulation governing people's choice of words. 1978 N. Freeling Night Lords i. 7 It was forbidden to park on the bridge. A lot Castang cared for municipal police regulations —. 1837 H. Martineau Society in America I. i. iii. 77 The disgustingly jocose tone of their [sc. British] *police reports, where crimes are treated as entertainments. 1882 C. M. Yonge Three Brides xix. 265 Such disgraces to England as I see in your police reports—brutal mechanics beating their wives. 1915 F. M. Hueffer Good Soldier i. iii. 31, I used.. to inspect the little police reports that each guest was expected to sign upon taking a room. 1976 J. Lee Ninth Man 257 Most of our leads so far have come from police reports. 1834 Sun (N.Y.) 23 July 2/3 Your *police reporter be one dam liar. 1959 [see corn belt s.v. corn sb.[1] 11]. 1977 L. Meyer Capitol Crime i. 9 The story.. was Sid Jacobson's, our police reporter. 1885 Globe 20 Apr. 1/4 The comparatively rare complaint of being too much *police-ridden. 1887 Times (weekly ed.) 23 Sept. 3/4 The patience of this police-ridden nation. 1818 Cobbett Pol. Reg. XXXIII. 520 *Police-runners had never been thought of as protectors of the lives of the Members of the two Houses. 1961 Webster, *Police science. 1971 Publishers' Weekly 6 Dec. 22/3 The Glencoe Press.. is doing very well with curricula in such new areas as fire science and police science. 1979 Internat. Jrnl. Sociol. of Law Feb. 112 Solomon's Soviet criminologists seem to be very similar to American 'police science' experts and to government scientific officers anywhere in the West. 1957 Encycl. Brit. XII. 562/2 A *police scientist does not have to be an expert in every branch of chemical analysis to use these instruments effectively. 1976 Billings (Montana) Gaz. 16 June 3-B/2 Ticks enclosed in an envelope received in the mail.. were being studied by police scientists Tuesday to see if they were .. infected with numerous diseases. 1852 Mrs. Carlyle Lett. II. 204 In the kitchen stood two *police-sergeants. 1827 Hone Every-day Bk. II. 329 He went on board the *police-ship stationed on the Thames. 1937 'M. Innes' Hamlet, Revenge! ii. i. 98 Billups would not have thought to requisition a fire-engine, the Prime Minister had. Its bell, he explained, gained more respect than did a *police siren. 1956 B. Holiday Lady sings Blues (1973) viii. 77 When the bus pulled out, you could hear the old sheriff's police siren coming after us. 1974 M. Birmingham You can help Me v. 132 The police sirens wailed up the street. 1959 I. Jefferies Thirteen Days viii. 100 The Legion officers had thirty-eight *police specials, the peak of revolver achievement. 1970 'J. Morris' Candywine Development xxiv. 263 That guy; he's holding something heavy. Police Special, maybe, or a ·44 magnum. 1849 J. S. Mill in Westm. Rev. LI. 4 Chenu.. is now admitted to have been.. a *police spy. *c* **1874** D. BOUCICAULT in M. R. Booth *Eng. Plays of 19th Cent.* (1969) II. 193 The police spy—Harvey Duff—the man that denounced me. **1897** MRS. E. L. VOYNICH *Gadfly* (1904) 114/1 'I am a minister of religion', he said, 'not a police-spy.' **1922** J. HERGESHEIMER *Bright Shawl* (1923) 66 Probably we are all ruined... The police spies will be waiting for us at home. **1973** G. SIMS *Hunters Point* xviii. 165 You police spies don't seem to be a very efficient bunch, letting an old man be drowned while you are supposed to be keeping a watch on him. *Ibid.* 166 It's just more *police spying activity. **1868** *N.Y. Herald* 2 July 8/3 Dr. Waterman, *police surgeon, was called and dressed the wounds. **1928** D. L. SAYERS *Unpleasantness at Bellona Club* xxi. 274 'Nervous shock with well-marked delusions,' said the police surgeon. **1978** N. FREELING *Night Lords* v. 23 I'll have the Parquet and the police surgeon standing by. Autopsy and lab report. **1885** *Encycl. Brit.* XIX. 336/2 The *police system of necessity involves the existence in a district of police stations or lock-ups, for the temporary detention of prisoners. *a* **1963** C. S. LEWIS *Discarded Image* (1964) v. 94 On the imaginative and emotional level it makes a great difference whether, with the medievals, we project upon the universe our strivings and desires, or with the moderns, our police-system and our traffic regulations. **1884** *Chr. World* 20 Mar. 206/1 He has advised the farmers.. to refuse to pay the *police-tax. **1903** *World's Work* July 123/2 To set *police traps for a man going thirteen miles an hour on an open road is sheer idiocy. **1914** BEERBOHM *James Pethel* in *English Rev.* Dec. 18 In France he always rather missed the British police-traps. **1966** M. R. D. FOOT *SOE in France* vii. 173 The others fell successively into a Vichy police trap.. at the Villa des Bois. **1974** J. WAINWRIGHT *Evidence* iv. 23 Motorways.. were.. police traps: box canyons into which a man on the run could be flushed and cornered. **1902** *Pall Mall Mag.* XXVIII. 410/2 Every police-constable on the much-*police-trapped Ripley Road. **1859** G. A. SALA *Twice round Clock* 201 Then.. troublesome bodies.. are securely shackled and straight-waistcoated up, and carted away in *police-vans. **1976** DEAKIN & WILLIS *Johnny go Home* ii. 49 She was in a police van on her way to Holloway. **1884** SWEET & KNOX *Through Texas* iv. 50 He began blowing a *police-whistle. **1922** JOYCE *Ulysses* 160 Police whistle in my ears still. **1967** O. WYND *Walk Softly* x. 163, I.. blew a long blast on a police whistle. **1979** J. SCOTT *Clutch of Vipers* x. 175 A whistle blew. A good old-fashioned police whistle such as is rarely heard nowadays. **1932** 'SOLICITOR' *Eng. Justice* iii. 94 On his version, supported by witnesses, he was clearly innocent. He seemed surprised when I said he was to plead 'Not guilty', and said, 'But there's a *police witness.'.. He got off. **1979** *Internat. Jrnl. Sociol. of Law* Feb. 71 The average Nigerian.. believes that to be a police witness is almost as bad as being the criminal offender. **1853** HICKIE tr. *Aristoph.* (1872) II. 398 You say well. Where is the *policewoman? **1894** *Westm. Gaz.* 13 June 3/3 A plea for policewomen. *a* **1930** D. H. LAWRENCE *Apocalypse* (1931) xvi. 233 Ah woman, you have known many bitter experiences. But never, never before have you been condemned by the old dragon to be a policewoman. **1955** W. GADDIS *Recognitions* II. vi. 560 A policewoman handed that nomadic laundress over to the stronger arm of the law. **1976** *Birmingham Post* 16 Dec. 3/5 Policewoman Susan Oliver, who was the first police officer on the scene, said lights on the side of the lorry's trailer were illuminated at the time of the accident. **1937** 'M. INNES' *Hamlet, Revenge!* II. ii. 112 In plain *police-work you could usually go straight for the truth. **1960** 'E. MCBAIN' *Give Boys Great Big Hand* (1962) iii. 20 Police work is not for you.. if you.. believe that corpses 'look just like they're sleeping'. **1977** L. MEYNELL *Hooky gets Wooden Spoon* xiii. 152 The basic rule of police work—get it down on paper.

Hence **po'liceful** *a.*, *nonce-word* full of policemen; **po'liceless** *a.*, without police; **policeocracy**, *nonce-word* the rule of the police.

1903 *Speaker* 9 May 133/1 To substitute a peaceful for a *policeful Ireland. **1882** E. W. HAMILTON *Diary* 2 Sept. (1972) I. 331 It was determined yesterday to dismiss summarily those insubordinate men; and the act of their dismissal was followed by the resignation of the force *en masse*. Accordingly Dublin is *police-less. **1898** *Westm. Gaz.* 30 June 1/3 Chevaliers of industry migrating to a policeless Alsatia. **1900** H. G. GRAHAM *Soc. Life Scot. in 18th C.* VII. i. (1901) 230 When a rare opportunity happened in policeless, jailless districts they [statutes] were carried out with rigour. **1887** *Pall Mall G.* 14 July 1 A Protest against *Policeocracy.

police (pə'liːs, pəʊ-), *v.* Also 7 pollice. [In senses 1, 2, a. F. *policer* (formerly *politier*, *policier*) (1461 in Godef.), f. *policie*, *police*; in senses 3, 4, f. POLICE *sb.*]

†**1.** *intr.* or *absol.* ? To enclose and improve land; to make policies. *Sc. Obs.* (Cf. POLICY *sb.*[1] II.)

1535 STEWART *Cron. Scot.* II. 106 The nobillis als of thame tha had sic want, But thame micht nother police nor ȝit plant. *Ibid.* 144 And gaif thame landis as tha lest, To plant and police quhair thame lykit best.

†**2. a.** *trans.* To keep in (civil) order, organize, regulate (a state or country). Chiefly in *passive*. *Obs.*

1589, 1605 [see POLICING *vbl. sb.* a]. *a* **1614** DONNE *Βιαθανατος* (1644) 78 Humane lawes, by which Kingdomes are policed. **1670** *Tryal R. Moor*, etc. in *Phenix* (1721) I. 406 Complaining of Julius Cæsar's Violation of that course of Law whereby the State was polliced. **1689–90** TEMPLE *Ess. Heroic Virt.* Wks. 1731 I. 205 By such Methods and Orders, the Kingdom of China seems to be framed and policed with the utmost Force and Reach of Human Wisdom, Reason and Contrivance. **1791** W. MAXWELL in Boswell *Johnson* an. 1770 (1831) I. 389 That country must be ill policed, and wretchedly governed.

b. To make or keep clean or orderly; to clean up (a camp): cf. POLICE *sb.* 3 c. Also const. *up*, as of an area: cf. CLEAN *v.* 6 c. *U.S.*

1851 *Colburn's United Service Mag.* LXVII. 57 All hands were then distributed in separate parties.. to 'police' or clean round the garrison. **1862** TROLLOPE *N. Amer.* II. vii. 192 Of the camps.. 44 per cent. [were] fairly clean and well policed. **1930** *Amer. Speech* V. 380 Nearly all our old army expressions were taken to France with the A.E.F. *Bunk fatigue*,.. *police up*, and *salvage* are some of these. **1956** *Ibid.* XXXI. 108 *Police up* (clean up an area). **1968** *Listener* 9 May 594/2 'Last night we *policed up* two sampans, killing six enemy,' said an Airborne major in modest triumph. **1977** M. HERR *Dispatches* i. 26 Some troops.. were pissing on the ground... The men finished.. and walked away laughing, leaving the captain alone shouting orders to police up the filth, thousands of empty and half-eaten ration cans, soggy clots of *Stars and Stripes*, and M-16 that someone had just left lying there and, worse, evidence of a carelessness unimaginable to the captain, it stank even in the cold rain, but it would police itself in an hour or two if the rain kept up.

3. a. To control, regulate, or keep in order by means of the police, or some similar force.

1841 R. OASTLER *Fleet Papers* I. No. 22. 176 Englishmen are too fond of Royalty to submit to be commissioned, and centralized, and policed, and bastiled. **1855** BROWNING *Bp. Blougram* 469 A vague idea of setting things to rights, Policing people efficaciously. **1891** *Review of Rev.* 14 Mar. 214/2 The maintenance of the navy which polices the seas. **1899** S. R. GARDINER *Cromwell* 183 The plan of policing the country by a militia of Major-Generals had broken down financially.

b. To furnish, provide, or guard with a police force, or some force having similar functions.

1858 *Times* 4 Nov. 6/5 Even the mouth of the Canton River may perhaps be well policed. **1868** M. E. G. DUFF *Pol. Surv.* 84 They are building gunboats to police their coasts. **1882** *Spectator* 11 Mar. 315/1 Why should not dangerous districts be decently policed?

c. *fig.* To keep in order, administer, control.

1885 F. W. MAITLAND *Justice & Police* x. 112 The Cornish St. Ives, without a commission of the peace, polices, or lately policed, itself. **1886** SYMONDS *Renaiss. It., Cath. React.* (1898) I. ii. 89 He.. left that institution [the Inquisition].. to pursue its function of policing the ecclesiastical realm. **1893** K. GRAHAME *Pagan Papers* (1894) 104 Policing the valleys with barbed wires. **1928** R. STRANGER *Wireless* xii. 150 Being policed by the aerial potentials the filament electrons will pass through in varying numbers. **1943** *Sun* (Baltimore) 13 Dec. 18/1 Lucien E. D. Gaudreau, area rent director, said yesterday that the agency definitely will not 'police' rent regulations. **1946** *R.A.F. Jrnl.* May 176 The future work of B.A.F.O. is to police the Reich in the sky. **1946** *Rep. Internat. Control Atomic Energy* (U.S. Dept. of State) II. iii. 15 While suppression is not possible where we are dealing with the quest for knowledge, this thirst to know (that cannot be 'policed' out of existence) *can* be used. **1970** T. LUPTON *Managem. & Social Sci.* (ed. 2) ii. 52 The organization cannot effectively police every individual item of behaviour. **1974** *Socialist Worker* 26 Oct. 14/5 It seems now that the social contract is to be policed by trade union leaders. **1977** *Time* 15 Aug. 37/2 He believes that fund members will approve some new articles that will enable him to police currency exchange rates.

4. To do *out of*, do *away*, or bring *into* a state or place by police administration.

1839 *Morning Herald* 17 June, That work of destruction by which the British nation is to be policed out of its immemorial liberties and franchises. **1876** BIRCH *Rede Lect. Egypt* 40 Internal administration and microscopic regulations had policed away the spirit of the people.

police, obs. form of POLICY *sb.*[2], POLISH *v.*

policeable (pə'liːsəb(ə)l), *a.* [f. POLICE *v.* + -ABLE.] That can be policed.

1926 H. W. FOWLER *Mod. Eng. Usage* 443/1 *Police*, vb., makes *-ceable*. **1976** *Listener* 23 Dec. 802/2 When those frontiers sucked forces too far inland for their logistical support, disasters like Kabul or Majuba compelled London to fall back on more policeable limits. **1979** *Guardian* 15 Jan. 12/2 There was no question at the moment of any action against secondary picketing.. 'One has to find out if it is illegal. And if you make it illegal, is it policeable?'

police court. A court of summary jurisdiction for the trial or investigation of charges preferred by the police. (At first called POLICE OFFICE.) Also *attrib.*

1823 STARK *Picture of Edinb.* (ed. 3) 152 An application was made to Parliament, in 1805, for a police bill for the city.. and a police court [was] opened in Edinburgh, on 15 July 1805.. under the superintendence of a Judge of Police. **1839** *Act 2 & 3 Vict.* c. 71 §1 The several police courts now established under the names of the public office in Bow Street and the police offices in the parishes of.. [seven named].. shall be continued. **1882** SERJT. BALLANTINE *Exper.* ii. 24 Police-courts were called offices [in the early part of this century]. **1898** *Westm. Gaz.* 29 Oct. 2/3 So far the latter have escaped police-court proceedings. **1930** D. H. LAWRENCE *Nettles* 19 And Mr. Mead.. said: 'Gross! coarse! hideous!'—and I, like a silly Thought he meant the faces of the police-court officials. **1964** [see FORM *sb.* 16 c]. **1965** [see MAGISTRATE *sb.* 3]. **1979** S. WEINTRAUB *London Yankees* iv. 113 English readers discovered Frederic in the newspaper transcripts from Croydon Police Court in 1898.

policed (-'iːst), *ppl. a.* [f. POLICE *v.* or *sb.* + -ED. Orig. ('pɒlɪst).]

1. Politically organized, regulated, or ordered; governed, disciplined. (In quot. 1735 ('pɒlɪst).)

1591 LAMBARDE *Archeion* (1635) 65 The necessitie of an Officer of this sort is inevitable in every well-polliced Kingdome. **1603** FLORIO *Montaigne* (1634) 189 Amongst the best policed and formalest nations. **1735** THOMSON *Liberty* IV. 734 As when, with Alfred, from the wilds she came To polic'd cities and protected plains. **1770** *Antiq.* in *Ann. Reg.* 104/2 Such a dispersion was little promotive of trade, which loves large and policed communities. **1858** M. PATTISON *Ess.* (1889) II. 39 To this policed society the old 'social contract' theory strictly applied.

2. Provided with or guarded by a police force.

1897 *All About Diamond Jubilee* (ed. Newnes) 58/1 London will be probably the best policed city in the world on June 22nd.

policedom (pəʊ'liːsdəm, pə-). [f. POLICE *sb.* + -DOM.] The police system as represented by its personnel.

1866 *Chambers's Jrnl.* 22 Sept. 608/1 Of Antoine the imperturbable, when he returned home,.. policedom could make nothing. **1889** *Chamb. Jrnl.* 2 Nov. 691/1 The hue and cry of the ten thousand hounds of policedom. **1892** *Argosy* May 380 He is one of the sleuth hounds of policedom.

policeman (pəʊ'liːsmən, pə-). **1. a.** A member of the police force; a paid constable. *New Policeman*, a constable of the New Police of 1829.

1801 R. MUSGRAVE *Mem. Different Rebellions in Ireland* I. 227 They boasted that they had killed the police-men at Dunboyne. **1824** J. S. MILL in *Westm. Rev.* II. 22 Thus they went on.. till November 1822, when,.. in rushed the sheriff with a number of police men. **1829** J. W. CROKER in *C. Papers* 28 Sept., I find a general opinion prevailing that your policemen are not paid sufficiently. **1830** *Morn. Chron.* 18 Aug. *heading*, Murder of a New Policeman by a Gang of Burglars. **1867** TROLLOPE *Chron. Barset* I. viii. 60 He would not go before the magistrates.. unless the policemen came and fetched him.

fig. **1887** RIDER HAGGARD *Allan Quaterm.* 20 The stern policeman Fate moves us and them on.

b. A soldier-ant.

1877 PASCOE *Zool. Classification* (1880) 149 *Heterogyna*.—Males, females and neuters,.. workers and soldiers... The soldiers (or 'policemen') have very large heads.

c. A police informer. *slang.*

[**1874** HOTTEN *Slang Dict.* 257 *Policeman*,.. among the dangerous classes, a man who is unworthy of confidence, a sneak or mean fellow.] **1923** E. WALLACE *Missing Million* xv. 128 Being an amateur, he left his finger-prints, and it's no job of mine to let 'em stay. 'Live and let live' is one of my mottoes, and 'Thou shalt not be a policeman' is another. *Ibid.* xvi. 134 Casey is a born 'policeman', and would sell his own mother if you paid him the right kind of money. **1924** [see COPPER *v.*[2] 2].

d. *Naut.* (See quots.)

1933 P. A. EADDY *Hull Down* 179 One of the boys, who was acting as 'policeman' (one of the watch who is told off to rouse the rest, should the Mate suddenly want them), came banging on the lamp-locker door. **1962** A. G. COURSE *Dict. Nautical Terms* 151 *Policeman*, a name used in sailing ships for the member of the watch on deck who kept awake to hear the officer's orders and call his shipmates.

e. *fig.* A person or object regarded as a deterrent or obstacle. In phr. ***sleeping policeman***: a ramp in the road intended to jolt a moving motor vehicle, thereby encouraging motorists to reduce their speed.

1951 E. COXHEAD *One Green Bottle* iii. 79 The climb above the crux was even more delightful; a knife-edge.. then a stone policeman barring the way. **1969** G. E. EVANS *Farm & Village* viii. 80 After the farm-workers had cleared a field of the crop they left one sheaf standing on it. This last sheaf was called the *Policeman*, and it was understood that no gleaner could enter the field while the Policeman was on guard. **1969** L. THOMPSON in R. Blythe *Akenfield* i. 35 The policeman was the name given to the last trave or stook which the farmers would leave standing in the middle of the field so they could have time to rake-up all the loose corn they could before the gleaners arrived. There was one farmer who made a habit of keeping the gleaners waiting and one night a young man stole the 'policeman'. **1973** *Guardian* 27 Feb. 1/4 Labour intends to.. build 'sleeping policemen' (ridges) into residential and shopping streets to slow traffic down. **1974** *Times* 24 July 4/7 The government would proceed with experiments in the use of 'sleeping policemen'—road humps to slow motorists.

2. *Chem.* A glass rod or tube with a short piece of rubber tubing on one end (see also quot. 1963).

1916 F. A. GOOCH *Representative Procedures in Quantitative Chem. Analysis* iii. 64 The precipitate, transferred from the container to the filter.. with the aid of a rubber-tipped glass rod (the 'policeman'). **1930** W. T. HALL *Textbk. Quantitative Analysis* xi. 149 This so-called policeman may be made by sticking together the end of a piece of rubber tubing that fits the rod tightly. **1963** N. L. PARR *Lab. Handbk.* vii. 103 Other means of separation [of solids] are sometimes adopted. Among them are dialysis, and the 'policeman' for dealing with solids in microchemistry, which is a small snipe feather mounted in a short length of glass tubing. **1974** *Nature* 6 Dec. 498/2 Attempts to passage stage 2 cells.. by scraping with a rubber policeman, resulted in a rapid degeneration of the cells in a new flask.

3. *attrib.* and *Comb.*, as **policeman fly** *Austral.*, a small wasp belonging to the family Nyssonidæ, Arpactidæ, or Stizidæ, which preys on flies; **policeman's helmet**, the Himalayan balsam, *Impatiens glandulifera*, a purple-flowered annual plant belonging to the family Balsaminaceæ.

1907 W. W. FROGGATT *Austral. Insects* 108 Several of these [small wasps] are known in the bush as policemen flies. **1926** R. J. TILLYARD *Insects Australia & N.Z.* xxii. 299 These wasps [*sc.* Arpactidæ] and the members of the following family [*sc.* Nyssonidæ] are known as 'Policeman Flies' in Australia. **1933** *Bulletin* (Sydney) 26 July 21/3 The robber fly, known [erroneously] in the back country as the policeman fly. **1969** *Courier-Mail* (Brisbane) 11 Jan. 6/8 Mr. Barrand found a fly which chases away other flies. He hopes to install tape-recorded sounds of the policeman fly in a transistorized unit. **1950** J. HUTCHINSON *Uncommon Wild Flowers* 226 Jumping Jack, Policeman's Helmet... A tall, sometimes very strong growing herb up to 6ft. or more. **1958** P. LEWIS *Brit. Wild Flowers* 125 Policeman's Helmet, a Himalayan plant grown in cottage gardens, has become naturalized along river-banks and in waste places. **1961** E. SALISBURY *Weeds & Aliens* iii. 65 The Policeman's Helmet is now to be met with in semi-wild stations in nearly half the British counties. **1971** *Country Life* 18 Feb. 384/2 An incongruous coloniser from the Himalayas, that Impatiens so appropriately known as policeman's helmet, attracting bumble-bees until the frosts come.

Hence **po'licemanish** *a.*, suggestive of a policeman; **po'licemanism**, the methods or conduct of policemen; **po'licemanlike** *a.*; **po'licemanly** *a.*, appropriate to or characteristic of a policeman; **po'licemanship**, the function, office, or action of a policeman.

1874 R. TYRWHITT *Sketch. Club* 142 That policemanlike faculty of coming round a corner. **1887** WALLACE in *Pall Mall G.* 2 Feb. 6/1 [In determining to restore order and neglecting to do justice, the Government..was exhibiting] policemanship, not statesmanship. **1891** *Star* 31 Oct. 4/3 Instances of policemanism crop up daily. **1897** A. HERBERT in *Daily News* 30 Aug. 5/7 One thing we have to resist is the growth of that ugliest of all ugly things, which goes by the name of 'policemanship'. **1908** *Daily Chron.* 30 Mar. 3/3 (*heading*) Policemanism. The Prince..went on to denounce a Government influenced by 'men with the education of a policeman, and with the convictions of a pogromshchik (official of massacre)'. **1916** A. BENNETT *Lion's Share* iii. 27 The heavy policemanish step of Mr. Cowl was heard on the landing. **1936** 'M. INNES' *Death at President's Lodging* ix. 171 The policemanly demand at last. **1973** —— *Appleby's Answer* xx. 172 The day had passed when she judged it amusing to join her husband in policemanly scampers. **1975** W. MARSHALL *Yellowthread Street* 64 He had been..firm and policeman-ish. **1977** 'E. CRISPIN' *Glimpses of Moon* x. 194 Policemanly instincts..reasserted themselves. Single-handed, he would make an arrest.

Police Motu (pə'liːs 'məʊtuː). [f. POLICE *sb.* + MOTU *sb.*] A Papuan pidgin, based on Motu.

1950 P. CHATTERTON (*title*) A primer of Police Motu. **1962** R. BRETT et al. (*title*) A dictionary of Police Motu. **1965** B. A. HOOLEY in *Language* XLI. 168 Police Motu, almost as important as a lingua franca in Papua as Neomelanesian is in ..New Guinea. *Ibid.* 169 Police Motu is derived from Motu, a member of the Malayo-Polynesian family. **1974** L. TODD *Pidgins & Creoles* i. 7 In the Pacific, in PNG [*sc.* Papua New Guinea], Police Motu arose from the contact between speakers of Motu and other Papuan vernaculars. It has recently expanded its vocabulary by adopting words from Neo-Melanesian. **1977** C. F. & F. M. VOEGELIN *Classification & Index of World's Languages* 47 Police Motu, a pidgin widely used as a lingua franca in Papua, is based on Motu.

police office. The head-quarters of the police force in a city or town, as of the Metropolitan and the City police in London, at which the police business is transacted.

These formerly included a court-room in which offenders were tried, as well as a place of detention in which they were confined till trial; hence the name was formerly regularly applied to what is now called a POLICE COURT, and is still in many places applied to a POLICE STATION, when this has a place of detention. The earliest name was PUBLIC OFFICE (in Act of 1792). *Police office* appears to have been first applied to the Marine or Thames Police Office at Wapping. (See POLICE *sb.* 5, *Marine Police.*)

1798 *Resolution* in Colquhoun *Comm. Thames* (1800) 224 Under the Regulation of the Marine Police Office No. 259, Wapping New Stairs. **1800** *Ibid.* 161 His indefatigable attention [as resident magistrate] to the public interest, since he has presided at the Marine Police Office. **1816** *Gentl. Mag.* LXXXVI. I. 32/1 The account of a transaction which took place in May last, at the Police-office in Hatton-Garden. **1817** COBBETT *Wks.* XXXII. 120 What, then, do the Pig-tail gentry, assembled at the 'Police Office, Manchester', object to this? **1826** J. WILSON *Noct. Ambr.* Wks. 1855 I. 113 Ye might hae been lugged awa to the Poleesh Office wi' a watchman aneath each oxter. **1836** DICKENS *Sk. Boz, Prisoners' Van*, We were passing the corner of Bow Street..when a crowd assembled round the door of the police-office attracted our attention [referred to below as 'Public Office, Bow Street']. *Ibid.*, Turn to the prisons and police-offices of London. **1838** *Encycl. Brit.* (ed. 7) XVIII. 249/2 The public office in Bow Street was for some time the only place in the metropolis where a police magistrate sat regularly, without the jurisdiction of the city of London. Seven additional police offices were established in 1792, by the act 32d Geo. III. cap. 53, and the Thames police-office in 1798. **1855** *London as it is to-day* 366 The City of London... There are two police offices, one in the Mansion House, where the lord mayor presides; and the other at Guildhall, where the aldermen sit in rotation. **1862** *Act 25 & 26 Vict.* c. 35 §19 (Scotland) And may be taken into custody..and detained in any police office or station house, or other convenient place. **1875** MCILWRAITH *Guide Wigtownshire* 95 On the ground-floor is also the police-office. **1882** OGILVIE (Annandale), *Police office, police station.* (So 1890 in *Cent. Dict.*) **1903** *Whitaker's Alm.* 183 Metropolitan Police Office, New Scotland Yard, S.W... City Police Office, 26 Old Jewry, E.C.

police state. A state regulated by means of a national police force having secret supervision and control of the activities of citizens. Also *attrib.*

1865 *Times* 6 Sept. 10/3 Austria was long known on the Continent as the 'police State', and..M. von Weiss will again obtain for her that unenviable title. **1896** B. RUSSELL *German Social Democracy* iv. 114 This infamous Law, the crowning endeavour of the enlightened police state. **1938** *New Statesman* 15 Jan. 74/1 Meanwhile, the atmosphere of the 'police state' is already with us. **1939** *War Illustr.* 28 Oct. 217/1 Spies are everywhere; indeed, Germany is the modern exemplification of the 'police state' in action. **1947** *Life* 7 June 37/1 They have failed in France and Italy because the peoples have had a chance to show their preference for Western democracy over a police state. **1950** G. B. SHAW *Farfetched Fables* 79 In the imagination of our amateur politician England is a Utopia in which everything and everybody is 'free' and all other countries 'police States'. I, being Irish, know better. **1959** *Listener* 8 Oct. 573/2 The Devlin Commission reported that Nyasaland has been turned into a 'police state'. **1967** COULTHARD & SMITH in Wills & Yearsley *Handbk. Management Technol.* 197 Short of introducing a police-state, in which people are directed to jobs and change them only with State approval, we must accept a degree of labour turnover as necessary and desirable. **1973** *Times* 12 Apr. 19/4 That Rhodesia is a police state, where the rights of individuals, the rule of law and the right to speak or report the truth count for nothing, is a fact for which there has long been ample evidence. **1975** *Times* 11 Jan. 12/6 A campaign to spot the terrorists before they act ..requires measures which smack of the police state.

police station. The office or head-quarters of a local police force, or of a police district. Also *attrib.*

1846 DICKENS *Pictures from Italy* 53 The hall..is as dirty as a police-station in London. **1858** SIMMONDS *Dict. Trade, Police-station*, the receiving-house where offenders are taken by the police; the place where the police assemble for orders, and to march out on duty. **1865** DICKENS *Mut. Fr.* I. iii, A little winding through some muddy alleys,..brought them to the wicket-gate and bright lamp of a Police-station. **1897** *Westm. Gaz.* 27 Sept. 2/1 This police-station confession proved (unlike most of such self-accusations) to be true. *a* **1930** D. H. LAWRENCE *Last Poems* (1932) 175 He has.. stepped down To the police-station cell.

polich, obs. form of POLISH *v.*

Polichinelle, -i, -o, obs. ff. PUNCHINELLO.

policial (pəʊ'lɪʃəl), *a. rare.* [f. POLICE *sb.* + -AL[1], after *office*, *official*.] Of or belonging to the police.

1843 POE *Purloined Let.* Wks. 1864 I. 273 When the case is of importance—or, what amounts to the same thing in the policial eyes, when the reward is of magnitude. *Ibid.* 276 The invariable principle of policial action in searches for articles concealed.

polician, variant of POLITIAN *Obs.*

†**po'liciar.** *Sc. Obs.* [f. POLICY *sb.*[1] + -AR[2].] The improver of a 'policy' or estate.

1562 WINȜET *Last Blast* Wks. (S.T.S.) I. 45 Quha.. trampis down the heuinlie incres and all decent policie of the samyn winȝarde, drest and deckit be the former workmen, vnfenȝeit policiaris of the samin.

policed, *ppl. a.*, **policier**: see POLICY *v.*[1], [2].

‖**policier** (pɔlisje). [a. F. *policier* detective novel.] A film based on a police novel. Cf. *roman policier* s.v. ROMAN *sb.*[4]

1975 *Listener* 21 Aug. 249/3 A *policier* of rare complexity. .. The plot threads of the film must..be followed down some labyrinthine byways. **1977** *Time* 18 Apr. 23/1 Not so in *Man on the Roof*, the Swedish-made *policier* based on one of the Martin Beck novels.

po'licing, *vbl. sb.* [f. POLICE *v.* + -ING[1].]

†**a.** The ordering or regulation of a state. *Obs.*

1589 PUTTENHAM *Eng. Poesie* I. viii. (Arb.) 36 The right pollicing of their states. **1605** BACON *Adv. Learn.* I. vii. §6. 34 b, For..pollicing of Cities, and Commonalties, with new ordinances and constitutions.

b. The action of keeping in order and cleaning up a camp. *U.S.*

1893 LELAND *Mem.* II. 60 There was no drill now..no special care of us, and no 'policing', or keeping clean.

c. The action of furnishing with a police force or the like for the maintenance of law and order.

1884 *Pall Mall G.* 22 Feb. 11/2 Holding him responsible ..for the policeing of the frontier. **1887** *Ibid.* 18 Mar. 5/1 They deal with the 'policing' of the whole river from Teddington Lock to Cricklade. **1890** *Daily News* 9 Sept. 6/2 A lively agitation..against the continued policing of the borough by the county constabulary.

d. The fact of being or acting as a policeman.

1899 *Tablet* 15 Apr. 570 Tired of policing, a wearisome life for an educated man.

policitation, obs. form of POLLICITATION.

†**'policize**, *v.*[1] *Obs.* [f. POLICY *sb.*[1] + -IZE.] *intr.* To use policy; to scheme, manœuvre. Hence †**policizing** *vbl. sb.* and *ppl. a.*, scheming; †**'policizer**, one who practises policy, a schemer.

1809 MAR. EDGEWORTH *Tales Fash. Life* III. *Manœuvring* 4 *note*, (Irish labourer) 'I'd call her a policīzer—I would say she was fond of policīzing'. *Ibid.* 85 For a week it might be practicable to keep them asunder by policising, but this could never be effected if he were to settle..in the country. **1820** C. C. COLTON *Lacon* ii. (1833) 16 As a policiser, the marquis reasoned badly. **1825** *New Monthly Mag.* XIV. 85 The indignities which spring up in the crooked paths of policizing favouritism.

'policize, *v.*[2] *rare.* [f. POLICE + -IZE.] *trans.* To organize, administer, discipline, reduce to law and order. Hence **'policized** *ppl. a.*

1840 *Tait's Mag.* VII. 392 The woman, as lady Morgan would say, of a more 'policized society'.

policlinic (pɒlɪ'klɪnɪk), *a.* Also *erron.* poly-. [ad. Ger. *poliklinik*, f. Gr. πόλι-ς city + *klinik* medical teaching at the bed-side of the patient (= CLINIC *sb.*[2]), hence a hospital by which this is provided, ad. Gr. κλινική the clinic art or practice.] *orig.* 'A clinic held in private houses in the town, as opposed to one held in a hospital' (*Syd. Soc. Lex.* 1895). Subsequently often extended to a dispensary, or that department of a hospital, at which out-patients are treated. Cf. POLYCLINIC.

The orig. system continued (*c* 1900) at smaller places in Germany while in larger cities the latter had become standard. Cf. Brockhaus *Konvers.-Lex.* (1846) s.v. *Klinik*: '*Poliklinik* [as distinguished from the *stationäre klinik* or hospital treatment of in-patients, and *ambulatorische klinik* or hospital treatment of out-patients] consists in the fact that the patients are treated in their own dwellings by the advanced medical students, while the professor, to whom these regularly report and who supervises the whole treatment of the patients, himself but seldom visits them'.

1827 *Lancet* 17 Nov. 256/2 [In Germany] Those students who have duly attended the clinics, are admitted to the policlinics. In these, poor patients are treated by students, under the superintendence of an experienced..physician. **1882–3** *Schaff's Encycl. Relig. Knowl.* III. 2284, 1,805 indoor-patients, and 73,432 outdoor-patients in polyclinique. **1886** GAIRDNER in *Life of Sir R. Christison* II. vii. 121 His was a true 'poliklinik', though in full operation here before the term was invented in Germany. **1897** *Allbutt's Syst. Med.* IV. 341 One woman out of every five or six in the polyclinic of the Augusta hospital, Berlin.

policy ('pɒlɪsɪ), *sb.*[1] Forms: 4–7 policie, 5 -ecye, 5–6 -icye, -ycie, -ycy(e, -ecy, -esy, 6 -ecie, -esie, -esye, -izy (*Sc.* -acie), 5– policy; (also 5 polleci, -isye, 5–6 -ecy, 5–7 -icie, 6 -icye, -yci, -ycy, 6–7 -icy, 7 -ecie). [In Branch I, ME. *policie*, a. OF. *policie* (14th c. in Oresme) civil administration, government, ad. L. *polītia* (Cic.), a. Gr. πολιτεία citizenship, government, constitution, polity, f. πολίτης citizen, f. πόλις city, state. See POLICE *sb.* Branch II appears to be due to the association of this Græco-L. word with L. *polītus* polished, refined, pa. pple. of *polīre* to polish, adorn, refine, cultivate, and late L. *polītiēs*, *polīciēs* polish, elegancy (Quicherat *Addenda*), Romanic type **polītia*, whence It. *pulizia* cleanness, neatness: cf. Sp., Pg. *policia* police, politeness, neatness.]

I. 1. a. An organized and established system or form of government or administration (of a state or city); a constitution, polity. Now *rare* or *Obs.*

1387–8 T. USK *Test. Love* II. ii. (Skeat) l. 78 To sene smale and lowe governe the hye and bodies above. Certes, that policye is naught. **1488–9** *Act 4 Hen. VII*, c. 19 To the subvercion of the polecy and gode rule of this lond. **1551** ROBINSON tr. *More's Utop.* I. (1895) 33 Suche peoples as do lyue to gethere in a cyuyle pollycye and good ordre. **1568** GRAFTON *Chron.* II. 433 He furnished his realme both with good learnyng, and Ciuile pollicie. **1602** WARNER *Alb. Eng.* x. lvii. (1612) 251 French Pollicie consists of Three Estates, The Princes, Nobles, Commons. *a* **1651** CALDERWOOD *Hist. Kirk* (1843) II. 41 Consultatioun was had how a good and godlie policie might be established in the church. **1759** ROBERTSON *Hist. Scot.* VI. Wks. 1813 I. 461 The forming of a system of discipline, or ecclesiastical policy. **1836** J. GILBERT *Chr. Atonem.* v. (1852) 136 In well constituted policies provision is always made for the exercise of clemency.

†**b.** An organized state, a commonwealth. *Obs.*

1390 GOWER *Conf.* III. 141 With the wyndes whiche he bloweth, Ful ofte sythe he overthroweth The Cites and the policie. **1447** BOKENHAM *Seyntys* (Roxb.) 28 Hym that was be tyrannye That tyme prynce of ther polycye. *a* **1533** LD. BERNERS *Gold. Bk. M. Aurel.* (1546) B viij, The diminyshing of the auncient Polycie of Rome. **1558** C. GOODMAN *Obed. Superior Powers* Pref., Most discreet governors of commonwealths and policies.

†**2. a.** Government, administration, the conduct of public affairs; political science. *Obs.*

c **1386** CHAUCER *Pard. T.* 272 If that a Prynce vseth hasardrye In alle gouernance and policye He is..Yholde the lasse in reputacion. *c* **1460** FORTESCUE *Abs. & Lim. Mon.* xv. (1885) 148 Thies counsellors mowe..delibre vppon..þe materes off þe pollycye off þe reaume. **1599** SHAKS. *Hen. V*, I. i. 45 Turne him to any Cause of Pollicy The Gordian Knot of it he will vnloose. **1641** MILTON *Reform.* II. Wks. 1851 III. 33 There..is no art that hath bin more canker'd in her principles, more soyl'd and slubber'd with aphorisming pedantry then the art of policie. *a* **1651** CALDERWOOD *Hist. Kirk* (1843) II. 514 We are now left as a flocke without a pastor, in civill policie. **1796** H. HUNTER tr. *St.-Pierre's Stud. Nat.* (1799) III. 625 By policy I mean not the modern art of deceiving mankind,..but..the antique art of governing them, which is a great virtue.

b. *Court of Policy*: the Legislative Council in British Guiana (which already existed when that country was a Dutch colony).

1769 E. BANCROFT *Guiana* 353 The lands are granted *gratis*, by the Governor and Court of Policy. **1824** MACKINTOSH *Sp. Ho. Comm.* 1 June, Wks. 1846 III. 432 They resolved, that the King and Parliament of Great Britain had no right to change their laws without the consent of their Court of Policy. **1903** *Whitaker's Almanack* 528 British Guiana... The Government consists of a Governor and a Court of Policy of 15 other members.

3. Political sagacity; prudence, skill, or consideration of expediency in the conduct of public affairs; statecraft, diplomacy; in bad sense, political cunning.

c **1420** LYDG. *Assembly of Gods* 304 Of worldly wysdom, sate the forteresse Callyd Othea, chyef grounde of polycy. *c* **1470** G. ASHBY *Active Policy* 643 But to youre richesse make neuer man liche, If ye wol stande in peas and be set by. So wol god and polleci sykerly. **1555** EDEN *Decades* Pref. (Arb.) 56 By the pollicie and wisedome of the Frankes, it came so to passe. **1596** SHAKS. *1 Hen. IV*, I. iii. 108 Neuer did base and rotten Policy Colour her working with such deadly wounds. **1715** SOUTH *Serm.*, *1 Kings xiii.* 33. 126

Jeroboam being thus advanced, and thinking Policy the best Piety. **1728** ELIZA HEYWOOD *Mme. de Gomez's Belle A.* (1732) II. 220 He had the Policy to discharge his new Subjects from the Impositions which their former Masters had laid on them. **1814** SCOTT *Ld. of Isles* VI. vii, King Robert's eye Might have some glance of policy. **1867** FREEMAN *Norm. Conq.* I. v. 435 In this..he was actuated by policy rather than by sentiment.

4. a. In reference to conduct or action generally: Prudent, expedient, or advantageous procedure; prudent or politic course of action; also, as a quality of the agent: sagacity, shrewdness, artfulness; in bad sense, cunning, craftiness, dissimulation.

c **1430** LYDG. in *Pol., Rel. & L. Poems* 15, I Counselle,.. Off polycye, forsight, and prudence. **1477** SIR J. PASTON in *P. Lett.* III. 187 It weer not polesy for me to sett that maner in suche case for alle maner of happis. **1533** MORE *Debell. Salem* v. Wks. 941/2, I wyl peradventure..here after..vse the same circumspeccion & polycye that I learne of his ensample here. **1587** *Mirr. Mag., Malin* x, Secretly by pollecy and sleight Hee slewe mee with his swoord, before I wist. **1599** SANDYS *Europæ Spec.* (1632) 102 Our grosse conceipts, who think honestie the best policie. **1604** DRAYTON *Owle* 419 In this base Bird I might well descry, The prosperous fruit of thriving Policy. **1752** FIELDING *Amelia* IX. ix, Tom, Tom, thou hast no policy in thee. **1791** BURKE *Corr.* (1844) III. 255 Have they no way of convincing this..illustrious person,..that her only policy is silence, patience, and refusal? **1868** HELPS *Realmah* iv. (1876) 56 If this is policy, then are the ways of children politic. **1883** *Law Times* 20 Oct. 409/2 The policy of allowing this sweeping right of appeal was doubted by many.

†**b.** A device, expedient, contrivance; a crafty device, stratagem, trick. *Obs.*

1406 HOCCLEVE *La male regle* 252 Whan þat Vlixes saillid to and fro By meermaides this was his policie, Alle eres of men of his compaignie With wex he stoppe leet. **1489** CAXTON *Faytes of A.* II. xxxv. 152 The besegers haue commonly one manere of a polycye. **1548** UDALL, etc. *Erasm. Par. Acts* xxvii. 87 They used other policies to preserue the shyp. **1640** YORKE *Union Hon., Battells* 18 By policy of these Iron stakes against the English horse, King Edward's battell was discomfited. **1678** WORLIDGE *Bees* (1691) 23 A swarm [of bees] drawn from one place to another by stales, baits, calls, or such like policies. **1849** HARE *Par. Serm.* II. 194 When a man is sharpening his policies he will grind them away to nothing.

5. A course of action adopted and pursued by a government, party, ruler, statesman, etc.; any course of action adopted as advantageous or expedient. (The chief living sense.)

c **1430** LYDG. *Min. Poems* (Percy Soc.) 82 Wherfor late soverayns use this policye, What ever they do late it in mesure be. **1544** *Supplic. to Hen. VIII* in *Four Supplic.* (1871) 35 Thys was the crafty polycye of the clergye. **1599** THYNNE *Animadv.* (1875) 1 Eche one..did, in the begynnynge of the monthe of Januarye..presente somme gyfte unto his frende..a pollicye gretlye to be regarded. *a* **1687** PETTY *Pol. Arith.* (1690) 23, I now come to the first Policy of the Dutch, viz. Liberty of Conscience. **1751** EARL ORRERY *Remarks Swift* (1752) 64 France, by her policy, has done the same. By policy, I mean the encouragement of arts and sciences. **1840** THIRLWALL *Greece* lv. VII. 75 The project attributed..to Alexander, is not the less in perfect harmony with his general policy. **1861** M. PATTISON *Ess.* (1889) I. 41 Edward's foreign policy led him to draw closer the ties which connected our country with Germany.

II. Scotch senses influenced by L. *polītus* polished, late L. *polītiēs, polīciēs* elegancy. (Cf. POLICE *v.* 1.)

6. †**a.** The improvement or embellishment of an estate, building, town, etc. *Obs.*

1475 *St. Giles' Charters* (1859) p. lxviii, For reparacioun, beilding and polesy to be maid in honour of..sanct Johan. **1535** *Sc. Acts Jas. V* (1814) II. 343/1 Item for polecy to be had wᵗin þe Realme In planting of woddis making of Edgeis orchartis ȝardis and sawing of browme. **1536** BELLENDEN *Cron. Scot.* XI. x. (1541) 163/2 Scho knew the mynd of kenneth geuyn to magnificent bygyng & polesy [BOECE, *Magnifica ædium structura atque ornatus delectaret*]. **1555** *Sc. Acts Mary* (1814) II. 491/2 It salbe lesum for policie and eschewing of deformitie of the towne.

†**b.** The improvements and embellishments so made; the buildings, plantations, etc. with which an estate is improved or adorned; property created by human skill and labour. *Obs.*

1535 *Sc. Acts Jas. V* (1814) II. 349/1 All oʳ souerane lordis burrowis are..waistit and distroyit in þeir gudis and policy and almaist Ruynous. **1536** BELLENDEN *Cron. Scot.* VII. vi. (1541) 84 b/2, The Pychtis spred fast in Athole, & maid syndry strenthis and polecyis in it [*arcibus, munitionibus castellisque plurimum ornantes*]. **1562** WINȜET *Last Blast* Wks. (S.T.S.) I. 45 Quha..trampis down the heuinlie incres and all decent policie of the samyn winȝarde. **1563** —— *Four Scoir Thre Quest.* lxxx. ibid. 128 Quhy hef ȝe wappit doun the monasteriis, and principal policeis of this realme? **1564** *Reg. Privy Council Scot.* I. 279 Apperandlie the haill polecie in that part is lyke to pereis, without sum substantious ordour and remedie be prouydit. [*Note.* A declaration that the woods are decaying through cutting and bark peeling.] **1594** *Sc. Acts Jas. VI* (1816) IV. 71 Oure souerane lord..apprevis the actis and statutis maid..for the..reparatioun of the decayed policie wᵗin burgh;..and gif the samyn be found auld, decayed and rwinous in ruif, sklattis, durris..to decerne that the coniunct fear.. sall repair the saidis landis and tenementis.

c. The (enclosed, planted, and partly embellished) park or demesne land lying around a country seat or gentleman's house.

1775 G. WHITE *Selborne* I. xlii, Lord Breadalbane's seat and beautiful policy are too curious and extraordinary to be omitted. **1775** JOHNSON *Journ. West. Isl., Aberbrothic,* A small plantation, which in Scotch is called a policy. **1791** NEWTE *Tour Eng. & Scot.* 207 The policies about the Noblemen and Gentlemen's houses..are but thinly scattered. **1842** J. WILSON *Chr. North* (1857) I. 242 The gravel-walks of our policy. **1875** JAS. GRANT *One of the 600* iii, The demesne (Scotice 'policy') around this picturesque old house, was amply studded with glorious old timber. **1883** *Pall Mall G.* 15 Nov. 9/1 The Prince of Wales went out yesterday with Lord Fife and party, and enjoyed some splendid shooting in the policies.

†**7. a.** The polishing or refining of manners. **b.** Polish, refinement, elegancy; culture, civilization. (Cf. the Latin words rendered.) *Obs.*

a. **1596** DALRYMPLE tr. *Leslie's Hist. Scot.* I. 160 Plutarchie sa artificiouslie quha could illustir histories, and was sa notable in the policie, dekking, and outset of maneris and honestie [L. *historiæ illustrandæ, morumque excolendorum insignis artifex*].

b. **1596** DALRYMPLE tr. *Leslie's Hist. Scot.* 9 In this north parte [of Scotland] ar sum prouinces sa plentifull and of gretter Ingines, that throuch thair policie [L. *politia*] thay ar athir to mony in the South compair, or than thay excel mony in the South. *Ibid.* 131 His people..allutterlie rude, and wᵗout all policie and ornat maneris [L. *rudes, nullaque morum elegantia politos*].

III. 8. *attrib.* and *Comb.*, as (sense 5) ***policy decision, document, -maker, -making, statement***; ***policy-making*** adj.; **policy science** (see quot. 1951); hence **policy scientist**.

1960 I. JEFFERIES *Dignity & Purity* iv. 66 Their purpose is the application of scientific method to policy decisions. **1964** GOULD & KOLB *Dict. Soc. Sci.* 510/1 Current interest centres on such questions as the nature of policy decisions. .. Policy decisions are contrasted, for instance, with judicial decisions by reference to the relatively greater freedom of choice in the former. **1974** S. GULLIVER *Vulcan Bulletins* 11 A policy decision had meant more careful buying. **1976** *Burnham-on-Sea Gaz.* 20 Apr., Mr Shore..can hardly have had time to read the policy documents before he was expected to stand up and defend them in the House. **1948** J. TOWSTER *Political Power in U.S.S.R.* III. xiii. 314 High-income executants, not policy-makers. **1975** *Times* 19 Feb. 14/6 American energy policy-makers find their own outlooks discouraging. **1978** *Dædalus* Fall 50 As citizens and policymakers, we can make explicit the potential personal and societal consequences of legislation. **1943** J. S. HUXLEY *TVA* xix. 137 The Board was always a policy-making body. **1946** *Nature* 9 Nov. 646/1 Authoritative information which those..at the policy-making or executive level might be expected to need. **1950** *N.Y. Times* 20 Apr. 1/3 The cataloging of persons eligible for policy-making positions would be..done without regard to their party affiliations. **1968** E. A. POWDRILL *Vocab. Land Planning* ii. 5 Policy-making and technique are a symbiosis, but it must be supported by wise and sound administration. **1976** *Times* 21 May 4/1 Mr. Len Murray..told the policy-making conference of the Society of Graphical and Allied Trades that the T.U.C. would expect the Government to take action. **1951** H. D. LASSWELL in Lerner & Lasswell *Policy Sciences* i. 4/1 We may use the term 'policy sciences' for the purpose of designating the content of the policy orientation during any given period. The policy sciences includes (1) the methods by which the policy process is investigated, (2) the results of the study of policy, and (3) the findings of the disciplines making the most important contributions to the intelligence needs of the time. **1964** I. L. HOROWITZ *New Sociology* 30 Sociology cannot be a 'policy science' until and unless there is a sociology of ethics. **1977** *Dædalus* Summer 59 It should move away from the contemporary, toward the past;..away from the impossible quest for stability; from the glide into policy science. **1970** *Nature* 19 Sept. 1189/2 There will have to be changes in the ways in which 'prime television time' is allocated so that the policy scientists can have their say..when people are most likely to be glued to their television sets. **1979** *Bull. Amer. Acad. Arts & Sci.* Mar. 28 International consultants and policy scientists serve as the conveyors and preservers of these untested staff papers until their ideas, approaches, and methodologies develop a life of their own. **1960** *Times* 1 Feb. 11/2 Mr. Macleod's speech..will be the most important policy statement that has been made on East Africa for many a long year. **1966** N. NICOLSON *Diaries & Lett. H. Nicolson 1930–1939* 258 He wrote the main policy-statement of the National Labour Party.

policy ('pɒlɪsɪ), *sb.*[2] Also 6 police, 7 -cie, -zy. [ad. F. *police* (1371) bill of lading, contract of insurance, etc., according to Hatz.-Darm. ad. Pr. *polissa*, also *polissia* (1428 in Diez), *podiza*, Cat. *police*, = Sp. *póliza*, Pg. *apólice*, OIt. *póliza, pólisa*, also *polizia*, It. *polizza*, 'schedule, bill, note, writing, remembrance, bond, inuentorie, obligation, ticket' (Florio), also in 16th c. 'bill of lading'; according to G. Paris *Romania* X. 620:—med.L. *apódissa, apódixa*, 'a receipt or security for money paid', altered from L. *apódīxis*, a. Gr. ἀπόδειξις a making known, demonstration, evidence, proof. The word appears to have had in Italian a very general sense, being applicable to a writing setting forth or serving as evidence of any kind of transaction.

The form-development *apódissa, pódissa, pólissa*, is supported by Pg. *apólice*:—L. *apódixem*, and the Prov. form *podiza*. The Eng. final *-ie, -y*, either represents the variants *apodixia, polissia*, or perhaps merely followed POLICY *sb.*[1] as a representative of F. *police*. Earlier suggestions of a derivation from L. *polyptichum* rent-roll, register, schedule, pl. *polyptycha* (5th c. Vegetius), registers, account-books, or from *pollex* thumb (as the supposed means of sealing a document), or from *pollicērī* to promise, are all untenable.]

1. a. More fully, ***policy of assurance*** or ***insurance policy***: A document containing an undertaking, in consideration of a sum or sums paid down at the time, or to be paid from time to time, called a ***premium*** or ***premiums***, to pay a specified amount or part thereof in the event of a specified contingency, such as the loss of property at sea, or its destruction by fire, or, in the case of a life insurance, on the death of the person named in the policy.

Also called *bill of assurance* in Lumbard Strete in 1562 (Marsden *Sel. Pl. Crt. Admir.* II. 52). ***floating policy, open policy***: see quots. ***wager*** or ***wagering policy***, a policy of insurance taken out where the insured has no real interest in the thing insured: declared illegal by various statutes as a species of gambling.

[**1523** in Pardessus *Collect. Lois Marit.* (1837) IV. 609/1 Non..essere tenuto a mostrare alcuna polizza di caricamento.] **1565** in R. G. Marsden *Sel. Pl. Crt. Admir.* (Selden) II. 56 [transl. of French document] Any order made..agaynst the tenor of this present Police of Assuraunce. **1601** *Act 43 Eliz.* c. 12 By meanes of which Policies of Assurance it commeth to passe, vpon the losse or perishing of any ship, there [etc.]. **1641** *Termes de la Ley* 219 Policy of Assurance is a course taken by Merchants for the assuring of their adventures upon the sea. **1681** *Lond. Gaz.* No. 1668/4 That all Persons that Insure their Houses shall have liberty till the First of January 1682, to bring back their Policies, and the Insurers will oblige Themselves and their Security by Indenture on their Policies, to accept of a Surrender, and repay their Premium. **1710** *Tatler* No. 241 ¶2 In all the Offices where Policies are drawn upon Lives. **1828–32** WEBSTER s.v. *Policy*, Wagering policies, which insure sums of money, interest or no interest, are illegal. **1848** ARNOULD *Mar. Insurance* I. I. ii. 17–19 A wager policy is one which shows on the face of it, that the contract it embodies is not really an insurance, but a wager... An open policy is one in which the value of the subject insured..is left to be estimated in case of loss... A time policy is one in which the limits of the risk are designated only by certain fixed periods of time. **1901** *Ibid.* (ed. 7) I. 11 A floating policy is one in which there is no limitation of the risk to a particular ship, as where goods 'on ship or ships' are insured for the same voyage. **1902** R. G. MARSDEN in *Trans. Roy. Hist. Soc.* XVI. 83 A policy of 1545 is the earliest known example of a policy entered into in England. It is a remarkable document, the body of it being in Italian, and the subscriptions in English.

b. A conditional promissory note, depending on the result of a wager.

1709–10 STEELE *Tatler* No. 124 ¶1 If any Plumb in the City will lay me an Hundred and Fifty Thousand Pounds to Twenty Shillings..that I am not this fortunate Man, I will take the Wager..having given Orders to Mr. Morphew to subscribe such a Policy in my Behalf, if any Person accepts of the Offer. **1832** J. TAYLOR *Rec. My Life* I. 338 Policies were opened to ascertain his sex, while he appeared in male and female attire.

c. A form of gambling in which bets are made on numbers to be drawn by lottery: cf. *policy-shop* in 3. Freq. in phr. ***to write policy***. *U.S.*

1830 [see *policy certificate*]. **1879** *Rep. N.Y. State Court of Appeals* LXXIV. 64 He testified that he paid to the defendant, at different times, sums amounting to $3,601.08 for tickets in a Kentucky lottery and in 'playing policy', as it is called. **1890** WEBSTER s.v., To play policy. **1890** J. A. RIIS *How Other Half Lives* (1891) xiii. 155 The game of policy is a kind of unlawful penny lottery. **1944** *Crisis* June 189/2 He even tried writing policy, but the players didn't like him. He couldn't shop the proper degree of sympathy when someone played 341 and 342 came out. **1949** *Amer. Speech* XXIV. 190 The oldest of the games, and very likely the parent of most contemporary forms, is policy, which is believed to have been in existence in England as early as the first half of the eighteenth century. **1968** P. OLIVER *Screening Blues* 133 During the Depression..many impoverished Negroes wrote policy in the hopes of winning sufficient to feed their families. **1972** *Times* 23 Nov. 9/8 Its most spectacular proposal is that gambling, prostitution and 'policy'—an illegal betting game—should all be legalized.

†**2.** = It. *polizza*, ticket; voting-paper; voucher, warrant. *Obs.*

1670 G. H. *Hist. Cardinals* III. II. 261 In this Scrutiny, all the Cardinals put in their Polizys open. *Ibid.* 285 Each of the Cardinals orders his Conclavist to bring him a Polizy, or Ticket of the vote he desires to give in the morning. **1675** tr. *Machiavelli's Prince* (Rtldg.) 285 Having received a new policy from three months to three months, the pensioners.. go then to the receivers.

¶ Johnson, as his only recognition of this word, has (1755) 'a warrant for money in the publick funds' (ed. 1785 adds 'a ticket'); and this is repeated in mod. Dicts. as a distinct sense; Mason (1801) drew attention to its incorrectness: 'Neither of these definitions extend to the most usual meaning of this word "*policy of insurance*". The interpretation should have been A warrant for some peculiar kinds of claim'.

3. *attrib.* and *Comb.*, as (sense 1 a) ***policy-book, business, -holder***; (sense 1 c) ***policy certificate, game, player, -playing, racket***; ***policy play*** vb. trans.; **policy blues** *U.S.*, a blues melody concerning the game of policy; **policy king** *U.S.*, one who has profited greatly from running policy games; **policy office** *U.S.*, = *policy-shop*; **policy-shop**, in *U.S.* a place for gambling by betting on the drawing of certain numbers in a lottery; **policy-slip**, in *U.S.* 'the ticket given on a stake of money at a policy-shop' (*Cent. Dict.*); **policy wheel** *U.S.*, a revolving drum used in the selection of winning numbers at policy; **policy writer** *U.S.*, one who collects bets from those playing policy.

1928 J. JACKSON (*song-title*) *Policy Blues. **1968** P. OLIVER *Screening Blues* iv. 134 Reflecting the popularity of the numbers game were innumerable policy blues. **1858** SIMMONDS *Dict. Trade*, **Policy-book*, a book kept in an insurance office for making entries of policies granted. **1844** G. WILKES *Mysteries of Tombs* 52/2 He is an old offender in the *policy business. **1883** 'MARK TWAIN' *Life on Miss.* xliii. 437 Dull policy-business till next fire. **1830** *Baltimore Amer.* 26 Aug. 3/2 To Adventurers and the Public, Policy Certificates, in the greatest variety. **1885** *Rep. Massachusetts Supreme Judicial Court* CXXXVII. 250 The defendant has been convicted of setting up and promoting a certain lottery for money; and the only question raised by his exceptions is whether the jury were warranted in finding that a game popularly known as the *policy or envelope game is a lottery within the Pub. Sts. *c.* 209, § 1. **1934** *Sun* (Baltimore) 30 Apr. 6/5 Skilled investigators have revealed that the slot machines and the policy games take $2,000,000 out of Richmond each year. **1964** A. WYKES *Gambling* 344 In 1957, nearly 12,000 people were convicted on policy-game charges. **1851** C. CIST *Cincinnati* 98 Penn Mutual Life Insurance Co... All the profits divided among the *policy holders every year. **1858** SIMMONDS *Dict. Trade, Policy-holders*, the persons insured in an office. **1906** *Times* (weekly ed.) 31 Aug. 549/4 Three leading American insurance companies will discontinue granting rebates on the annual premium to British policy-holders on account of British income-tax. **1915** [see CHINCHY *a.*] **1970** J. HANSEN *Fadeout* i. 4 My company—every insurance company—sends out investigators in cases like this... Where the policyholder's body can't be found. **1949** *Collier's* 15 Jan. 21/1 Thousands of other suckers.. are not only making millionaires out of a few dozen *policy kings, they also pay for the corruption of many police officials. **1968** P. OLIVER *Screening Blues* iv. 133 Policy kings made occasional magnanimous gestures with large donations to charities or churches and a mystique developed in which they were viewed as benefactors rather than as parasites. **1843** J. H. GREENE *Exposure of Arts & Miseries of Gambling* 283 These swindling shops are numerous, and are sometimes called **policy offices.* **1693** LUTTRELL *Brief Rel.* (1857) III. 17 Grand jury of London.. presented the *policy officers about wagers. **1926** C. JACKSON in P. Oliver *Screening Blues* (1968) iv. 130, I looked in my purse t'see if I had a little dough, So I could *policy play 4-11-44. **1847** C. WHITE (*title*) The *policy players. An Ethiopian sketch. **1901** E. HARRIGAN *Mulligans* 65 A policy player's chances are a hundred to one against him. **1972** *Sci. Amer.* Oct. 112/3 Thousands of Manhattan policy players bet on 932 and won. **1887** *Gen. Statutes Connecticut* cliv. 563 The court of common council of any city.. shall have power to make, alter, and repeal ordinances or by-laws to suppress and punish all kinds of gambling and gaming, pool selling, *policy playing, [etc.]. **1949** *Amer. Speech* XXIV. 190 In the early days policy playing was associated with the regular number lotteries, being a device whereby people unable to afford a regular lottery ticket could wager small amounts on the outcome of the drawing. **1938** *Sun* (Baltimore) 1 Sept. 1/4 Davis, the broken mouthpiece of the once-powerful Dutch Schultz *policy racket, swore.. that James J. Hines .. was paid thousands of dollars by the mob. **1968** P. OLIVER *Screening Blues* iv. 133 The policy racket had a folk-lore of its own. **1858** 'Q. K. P. DOESTICKS' *Witches of N.Y.* 54 The propinquity of the 'lottery agency' and the 'policy-shop', just round the corner. **1879** WEBSTER *Suppl., Policy-shop*, an office opened for gambling in connection with lotteries. **1903** *Daily Chron.* 3 Nov. 5/3 He.. has closed every gambling-den, pool-room, disorderly house and policy-shop that the extreme of vigilance could discover. **1934** *Sun* (Baltimore) 30 Apr. 6/5 The second fact can be done away with by making it a criminal offense to sell *policy slips to minors. **1972** 'T. COE' *Don't lie to Me* xi. 103, I knew.. he could make it stick. Find heroin in my car. Shake me down and find policy slips. **1906** *Southwestern Reporter* XCI. 785/1 Evidence that accused was seen.. in the house where people were betting at a lottery, and that he at one time turned the *policy wheel. **1968** *Sunday Tel.* 1 Sept. 13/6 An excursion into the cabalistic number symbolism employed by bettors on the 'policy wheels'—those intricate gambling devices surreptitiously played by millions of Americans. **1949** *Collier's* 15 Jan. 21/2 In Detroit, one auto-plant *policy writer explained to me, 'I been in this racket for twenny years.' **1968** P. OLIVER *Screening Blues* iv. 142 Within the lower class the policy writer was considered a parasite who lived off his fellows.

† **'policy**, *v.*[1] *Obs.* [a. obs. F. *policier* (1540 in Godef.) to administer, f. obs. F. *policie*; see POLICY *sb.*[1], POLICE *v.*] *trans.* To organize and regulate the internal order of, to order; = POLICE *v.* 2. Hence † **'policied** *ppl. a.*, civilly organized.

1565 SMITH in Froude *Hist. Eng.* (1863) VIII. viii. 165 There is no realm in Christendom better governed, better policied. **1646** SIR T. BROWNE *Pseud. Ep.* VI. vi. 302 Canaan and Ægypt;.. which he found well peopled and policied into Kingdomes. **1647–8** COTTERELL *Davila's Hist. Fr.* (1678) 2 Well policied Government. **1788** PRIESTLEY *Lect. Hist.* v. xliv. 324 We are not.. to consider all countries as barbarous that are not policied as ours. **1824** LANDOR *Imag. Conv., Pericles & Soph.* Wks. 1853 I. 147/1 A wide and rather waste kingdom should be interposed between the policied states and Persia.

† **'policy**, *v.*[2] *Obs.* In 5 poll-. [f. POLICY *sb.*[2] or F. *police*, in its early sense.] *trans.* To furnish with a certificate; to examine and certify to the purity or quality of. Hence † **policier** (in 5 poll-), the officer who performed this function.

c **1450** *Oath* in *Cal. Let. Bk. D Lond.* (1902) 196 The Office of Garbeler and pollicier of wex within the Citee of London. .. And after that ye have garbeled any bale or merchandises ye shall mark and signe the same bale by you garbeled and wex by you pollicied w[t] a mark to thentent that the common weyer may have knowledge thereof &c.

'policy, *v.*[3] *U.S. slang.* [f. POLICY *sb.*[2] 1 c.]

1889 FARMER *Dict. Amer.* 429/2 *To Policy*, to gamble with the numbers of lottery tickets.

polie: see POLICE *sb.*

poliencephalitis: see POLIOENCEPHALITIS.

† **po'lifugal**, *a. Obs. rare.* [f. L. *polus* POLE *sb.*[2], after CENTRIFUGAL.] Tending away from the pole.

1740 STACK in *Phil. Trans.* XLI. 421 By the Assistance of the polifugal Force.

poligamous, -gamy, obs. ff. POLYGAMOUS, -GAMY.

poligar ('pɒlɪgɑː(r)). Also 8–9 **polygar**. [ad. Marāthī *pālegār*, or Telugu *paḷegāḍu* (cerebral *d*), ad. Tamil *pāḷaiyakkāran* the holder of a *pāḷaiyam*, POLLAM.] In S. India, The holder of a pollam or feudal estate; a subordinate feudal chief.

1681 in J. T. Wheeler *Madras* (1861) I. 118 They pulled down the Poligar's house. **1761** *Char.* in *Ann. Reg.* 6/2 There are.. among the.. mountainous parts.. several petty princes, or heads of clans, distinguished by the name of Polygars. **1783** BURKE *Sp. Fox's India Bill* Wks. IV. 25 To .. Mahomet Ali they sold at least twelve sovereign princes called the Polygars. **1868** J. H. NELSON *Madura* III. 157 Some of the Poligars were placed in authority over others.

b. *transf.* One of the predatory followers of such a chief; the race descended from these.

1776 PIGOU in *Gentl. Mag.* (1792) 14/2 A people called Polygars, who inhabit [the woods] and attack, rob, and murder passengers. **1869** SIR W. ELLIOT in *Jrnl. Ethn. Soc.* I. 112 There is a third well-defined race mixed with the general population... I mean the predatory classes. In the South they are called Poligars, and consist of the tribes of Marawars [etc.].

c. *attrib.* and *Comb.*: **poligar-dog**: a variety of dog from the poligar country.

1800 DK. WELLINGTON in Arbuthnot *Mem. Munro* (1881) I. p. xcii, His operations were seldom impeded by poligár wars. **1830** MARRYAT *King's Own* xlviii, It's a Polygar dog from the East Indies. **1885** G. S. FORBES *Wild Life in Canara* 45 A poligar dog that was with me started off in pursuit.

Hence **'poligarship**, the office of a poligar.

a **1881** in Arbuthnot *Mem. Munro* I. p. xcii, The Mysore system, which removed all poligárships [and] expelled their turbulent chiefs.

polihistor, obs. f. POLYHISTOR.

polimechany, polimite, var. POLYMECHANY, POLYMITE, *Obs.*

† **polinc'd**, *pa. pple. Obs. rare*[−0]. [For *pollinct*, ad. L. *pollinct-us*, pa. pple. of *pollingĕre* to wash and prepare (a corpse) for the funeral pile.]

1623 COCKERAM II, *Embalmed*, Polinc'd.

poling ('pəʊlɪŋ), *vbl. sb.*[1] [f. POLE *v.*[1] + -ING[1].]

1. The action of the verb POLE[1] in various senses; furnishing or supplying with poles; the propelling of boats or canoes with poles; the stirring of a bath of copper, tin, or lead with a pole of green wood, to cause ebullition and deoxidation; etc.

1573 TUSSER *Husb.* (1878) 83 To arbor begun, and quick setted about, No poling nor wadling till set be far out. *a* **1601** [see POLE *v.*[1] 5]. **1753** [see POLE *v.*[1] 4]. **1816** BRACKENRIDGE *Jrnl. Voy. Missouri* in *Views Louisiana* 205 The water is generally too deep to admit of poling. **1842** *Civil Eng. & Arch. Jrnl.* V. 169/2 The process of 'polling',.. carried on by stirring.. the copper while in a fluid state with poles of green wood. **1864** WATTS *Dict. Chem.* II. 29 If.. the poling has been continued too long, the copper again becomes brittle, .. in this state it is said to be overpoled.

2. *concr.* Poles collectively, as used for poling hops, or for lining the sides of a tunnel.

1842 FRANCIS *Dict. Arts* etc., *Poling*, the small boards supporting the earth during the formation of a tunnel. **1881** RAYMOND *Mining Gloss.*, *Polings*, poles used instead of planks for lagging.

3. *attrib.* and *Comb.*, as **poling-board**, one of the boards used to support the sides in the excavation of a tunnel; **poling boat** *N. Amer.*, = *pole boat* s.v. POLE *sb.*[1] 5 c; **poling-ground**, shallow water where poling or punting is possible.

1839 *Civil Eng. & Arch. Jrnl.* II. 146/2 They frequently push the *poling boards before them. *Ibid.* 326/2 Each division.. has boards in front.. (known by the technical name of poling boards). **1900** J. LONDON *Son of Wolf* 163 Madelaine shook the dust of the Lower River from her moccasins, and with her husband, in a *poling-boat, went to live on the Upper River. **1973** D. ANDERSEN *Ways Harsh & Wild* ii. 70 We whipsawed lumber from birch logs and put together two large poling boats. **1901** J. G. MILLAIS in *Daily News* 8 Feb. 6/4 No puntsman should ever venture off *poling ground in Scotland when the wind is in the south.

poling ('pəʊlɪŋ), *vbl. sb.*[2] *Physics.* [f. POLE *sb.*[2] + -ING[1].] The process of polarizing a ferroelectric material (see POLE *v.*[2]).

1954 *Jrnl. Appl. Physics* XXV. 1166/2 The crystals.. were grown in our laboratory and the *c* axis was made to be perpendicular to the face of the crystals by means of a high-field poling technique. **1965** *IEEE Trans. Sonics & Ultrasonics* XII. 7/1 During the initial poling both 109°/71° and 180° domain switching occurs. **1976** *Ibid.* XXIII. 393/2 The common practice.. is to analyse the immittance behavior of a resonator with a certain geometry and poling axis.

polio ('pəʊlɪəʊ). *colloq.* [Abbrev. of POLIOMYELITIS.] **1.** Poliomyelitis, esp. the paralytic form. Freq. *attrib.*

1931 *Survey* 15 Oct. 93/1 (*heading*) Panic and polio. **1934** *Ladies' Home Jrnl.* Feb. 10/1 How did the polio fighter.. come to catch it? **1940** *Time* 2 Sept. 37/2 (*heading*) Polio scare. **1949** *New Harmony* (Indiana) *Times* 5 Aug. 1/5 New Harmony was doused.. by a spraying plane.. as a precautionary measure against polio. **1955** G. GREENE *Quiet American* IV. ii. 241 My son's got polio. He's bad. **1955** *Sci. News Let.* 23 July 51/1 Children are the principal carriers of polio, and if enough children are immunized, it would probably not be necessary to vaccinate the adults in order to stamp out the disease. **1962** *Observer* 11 Mar. 8/4 Last year I had a play.. out on tour... There was a polio scare in Hull, and the star didn't want to play. **1977** *Daily Tel.* 9 Mar. 8/4 Doctors have cleared two girl polio suspects in Greater Manchester.

2. A person who has, or has had, polio. *rare.*

1934 *Ladies' Home Jrnl.* Feb. 107/1 Health departments of cities and states poured out money to buy serum from recovered polios to try to cure already sick babies. **1962** *Guardian* 26 Sept. 8/5 'Polio',.. a person who has been paralysed by polio.

‖ **,polioencepha'litis.** *Path.* Also **poliencephalitis.** [mod.L., f. Gr. πολιός grey + ἐγκέφαλος brain + -ITIS; first formed in Ger. (C. Wernicke *Lehrb. d. Gehirnkrankheiten* (1881) II. ii. 229).

The form *poliencephalitis* is more correctly formed, but has been superseded in modern use by *polio-*.]

Inflammation of the grey matter of the brain.

1885 *London Med. Rec.* 16 Feb. 44/1 (*heading*) Strümpell on acute infantile polio-encephalitis (cerebral paralysis of children). **1885** J. ROSS *Handbk. Dis. of Nervous Syst.* 621 (*heading*) Poliencephalitis acuta infantum. **1890** BILLINGS *Med. Dict.*, *Poliencephalitis*, acute localized encephalitis, affecting chiefly the motor region of the cortex. **1905** *Brit. Med. Jrnl.* 27 May 1145 Strümpell has suggested that the disease is acute polioencephalitis. **1911** A. BRUCE tr. *H. Oppenheimer's Text-bk. Nervous Dis.* II. 837 The diagnosis of poliencephalitis.. should be made only with great reserve. **1923** J. H. PARSONS *Diseases of Eye* (ed. 4) xxix. 554 Acute polio-encephalitis accounts for not infrequent cases of paralytic squint following a febrile attack in young children. **1934** *Times Educ. Suppl.* 22 Sept. 341/1 Of polioencephalitis there were 88 notifications. **1971** *Jrnl. Neurol. Sci.* XII. 414 This disorder is a polioencephalitis of viral origin.

‖ **poliomyelitis** (,pɒlɪəʊmaɪə'laɪtɪs, 'pəʊlɪəʊ-). *Path.* [mod.L., f. Gr. πολιό-ς grey + μυελός marrow + -ITIS.] A disease caused by a neurotropic virus (infection with which usu. produces no symptoms) which may give rise to a temporary meningitis, with fever and delirium, or, esp. in older patients, a permanent and sometimes fatal localized paralysis as a result of the infection and death of groups of nerve cells in the spinal cord or brain stem. Also *attrib.*

1878 *Amer. Jrnl. Med. Sci.* LXXV. 411 The case was.. one of acute polio-myelitis. **1880** A. FLINT *Princ. Med.* 747 Anterior poliomyelitis, signifying inflammation of the anterior gray substance. **1899** *Allbutt's Syst. Med.* VI. 798 The facial nucleus was affected by acute poliomyelitis. **1934** R. W. FAIRBROTHER *Handbk. Filterable Dis.* vi. 95 The poliomyelitis virus only produces spontaneous disease in man. **1955** [see *infantile paralysis* s.v. INFANTILE *a.* 3]. **1966** WRIGHT & SYMMERS *Systemic Path.* II. xxxiv. 1192/2 The non-paralytic form of poliomyelitis—the main symptoms of which are those of catarrhal inflammation of the upper parts of the respiratory and alimentary tracts—is the commonest manifestation of the infection during epidemics. **1972** B. A. CURTIS et al. *Introd. Neurosci.* viii. 186/1 The majority of patients with poliomyelitis virus infection make a complete or significant recovery. *Ibid.* xxii. 590/1 With the development of effective vaccines.. poliomyelitis has become a preventable disease.

Hence **,poliomye'litic** *a.*, of or affected with poliomyelitis. Also **poliomye'lopathy**, *Path.* [-PATHY], any disease of the grey matter of the spinal cord.

1911 *Jrnl. Exper. Med.* XIV. 117 Flexner and Clark showed that the *poliomyelitic virus would survive for a period of days in the subcutaneous tissues of the rabbit. **1940** *Ann. Reg. 1939* 376 Evidence suggested that poliomyelitic virus may occur in urban sewage. **1958** *Jrnl. Bone & Joint Surg.* XL. A. 513 In a few convalescent poliomyelitic patients.. the Milwaukee brace has aided in reducing the curve and holding it in check until muscle balance has been re-established. **1971** *Biol. Abstr.* LII. 10390/1 (*heading*) Study of the circulation of poliomyelitic and other enteric viruses in waste water. **1890** in BILLINGS *Med. Dict.*, *Poliomyelopathy. **1899** *Allbutt's Syst. Med.* VI. 495 The so-called system diseases; such as ascending and descending lateral sclerosis.. the poliomyelopathies. *Ibid.* 502 Nuclear lesions or poliomyelopathies.. are often the starting points of such secondary degenerations.

poliorcetic (pɒlɪɔː'sɛtɪk), *a.* [ad. Gr. πολιορκητικ-ός, f. πολιορκητής besieger, f. πολιορκεῖν to besiege a city, f. πόλι-ς city + ἕρκ-ος fence, enclosure. So F. *poliorcétique.*] Of or pertaining to the besieging of cities or fortresses.

a **1859** DE QUINCEY *Posth. Wks.* (1891) I. 98 The 'arietes', or battering-rams.. were amongst the poliorcetic engines of the ancients. **1898** *Athenæum* 24 Sept. 423/2 The poliorcetic principles displayed at Château Gaillard. **1936** H. A. L. FISHER *Hist. Europe* I. xv. 187 To the marine skill of the Scandinavians they [*sc.* the Normans] added all that was then known of cavalry warfare and the poliorcetic art. **1975** C. J. BISHKO in K. M. Setton *Hist. Crusades* III. xii. 410 Its [*sc.* Lisbon's] stubborn defense..against the combined Portuguese and crusader resources, including the northerners' heavy siege machines and poliorcetic skills.

polior'cetics, *sb. pl.* [ad. Gr. (*τὰ*) *πολιορκητικά* things or matters pertaining to sieges, neut. pl. of *πολιορκητικός*: see prec.] The art of conducting and resisting sieges; siegecraft.

1569 J. SANFORD tr. *Agrippa's Van. Artes* 33 b, Poliorceticke s, fitte as well for the warres, as buildinges, & other vses. *a* **1859** DE QUINCEY *War* Wks. 1862 IV. 284 Into castrametation, into poliorcetics. **1893** T. A. ARCHER in *Contemp. Rev.* Mar. 341 *note*, The whole science of mediaeval poliorcetics was based on the principle of.. outworks. **1936** H. A. L. FISHER *Hist. Europe* II. xvii. 628 The sieges of Hertogenbosch, of Maestricht, and of Breda showed that in the art of poliorcetics the Dutch had lost none of their ancient cunning. **1958** M. ROBERTS *Gustavus Adolphus* II. iii. 185 Maurice [of Orange] was a great innovator in siege warfare. His massive barrages against a strictly limited objective enabled him greatly to quicken the pace of siege operations, and marked an epoch in poliorcetics.

poliosis (pɒlɪˈəʊsɪs). *Med.* [mod.L., f. Gr. *πολι-ός* grey + -OSIS.] Partial or general greyness or whiteness of the hair, esp. if premature.

1813 T. YOUNG *Introd. Med. Lit.* lxiv. 370 *Spilosis*, discolorations of the skin, or of the cuticular substances, without constitutional disease... *S. poliósis*, grey hairs. **1817** J. M. GOOD *Physiol. Syst. Nosology* 501 *Poliósis*, hairs prematurely grey or hoary. *Poliosis*, auct. var. **1868** *Jrnl. Cutaneous Med.* I. 277 Poliosis, or canities, was present in 9 cases in the two thousand... The white hairs were pretty uniformly dispersed through the rest of the hair, giving rise to incipient greyness. **1940** BECKER & OBERMAYER *Mod. Dermatol. & Syphilol.* xxx. 531/1 Poliosis is definitely hereditary, and..is due to complete lack of pigment function. **1968** EBLING & ROOK in A. Rook et al. *Textbk. Dermatol.* II. xlvi. 1414/2 Poliosis results from absence or deficiency of melanin in a group of neighbouring hair follicles. Clinically it presents as a strand or mesh of white hairs.

poliovirus (ˈpəʊlɪəʊvaɪərəs). *Med.* Also **polio virus.** [f. POLIO + VIRUS.] Any of a group of enteroviruses that includes those that cause the various forms of poliomyelitis. Also *attrib.*

[**1954** *Nature* 3 Apr. 621/1 Proposed 'non-Linnæan' binomials for some animal viruses... *Poliovirus hominis* (human poliomyelitis). *Poliovirus muris* (mouse encephalomyelitis, *TO* type).] **1955** *Virology* I. 186 (*heading*) The poliovirus group. **1958** *Economist* 26 July 283 To achieve that we must apparently wait for the successful development of vaccines made from live attenuated polioviruses. **1961, 1965** [see ECHO VIRUS]. **1968** RHODES & VAN ROOYEN *Textbk. Virol.* (ed. 5) v. iii. 541 The feature distinguishing polioviruses from other members of the enterovirus group is their capacity to produce poliomyelitis in man and other primates. **1970** PASSMORE & ROBSON *Compan. Med. Stud.* II. xviii. 113/2 At the beginning of the century, infection with poliovirus was widespread among children under 5 years of age, but only an occasional patient developed the typical infantile paralysis. **1973** R. G. KRUEGER et al. *Introd. Microbiol.* xix. 528/1 Polio virus will adsorb to certain cells of certain organs of primates but not to nonprimate cells.

Hence **'polioviral** *a.*

1977 *Lancet* 19 Feb. 434/1 Polioviral antigen has been detected in 3 patients.

polip(e, -ippe, polipus, obs. ff. POLYP, -US.

poliphant, obs. corrupt form of POLYPHONE.

poliphant: see POLYPHONE

polipode, -pragmatick, -pragmon: see POLYPODE, etc.

‖**polis** (ˈpɒlɪs), *sb.*[1] *Hist.* [Gr.] A Greek city-state; *spec.* such a state considered in its ideal form. Also *transf.*

1894 A. HOLM *Hist. Greece* I. xx. 252 In Greece state and city are one, and both are designated by the word 'Polis'. **1929** N. MALLINSON tr. *Glotz's Greek City* 2 From the association of many villages, the complete State was created, the perfect community, the *polis.* **1941** AUDEN *New Year Letter* III. 51 We can at least serve other ends, Can love the polis of our friends. **1941** H. G. WELLS *You can't be too Careful* IV. i. 222 Homo Tewler does not behave as a political animal should do, participating with the utmost fullness in the collective life of his *polis. Ibid.* 223 The *polis* of Aristotle. **1958** *N. & Q.* CCIII. 507/2 She appears an irreverent seductress pursuing Merlin in order to destroy the Arthurian polis. **1959** *Listener* 12 Feb. 292/1 The fully developed, classical *polis* was a new and original institution. **1968** *Ibid.* 5 Sept. 313/1 The epic and tragic were becoming increasingly hard to realise; an art that had emerged from the social organisation of the Greek *polis* no longer applied to the mysterious forces of capitalism. **1972** A. P. HINCHLIFFE in Cox & Dyson *20th-Cent. Mind* III. xiv. 416 The idea that no man can prosper unless his *polis* prospers. **1978** A. SANDERS *Victorian Historical Novel* viii. 172 The Florence of the novel [sc. *Romola*] is the Renaissance *polis.*

polis (ˈpɒlɪs, ˈpɔːlɪs), *sb.*[2] Chiefly *Ir.* and *Sc.* Also **poliss, pollis.** [Repr. regional pronunc. of POLICE *sb.* (see etym. note).] = POLICE *sb.* 5 a; a member or (construed as *pl.*) members of a police force. Also **'polisman.**

c **1874** D. BOUCICAULT *Shaughraun* (1884) I. iii. 7/2 The polis were in my cabin today about ye. **1892** KIPLING *Barrack-Room Ballads* 43 They sent the Polis there, The English were too drunk to know, the Irish didn't care. **1900** E. H. STRAIN *Elmslie's Drag-Net* 115 The poliss is no far awa. **1904** 'H. FOULIS' *Erchie* 124 Her niece Sarah, and Macrae the nicht polis. **1907** J. M. SYNGE *Playboy* I. 10 Is it yourself is fearing the polis? You're wanting, maybe? **1919** J. BUCHAN *Mr Standfast* iv. 84 Ye'll get a good turn-out at your meeting..but they're sayin' that the polis will interfere. **1922** JOYCE *Ulysses* 434 Don't be all night before the polis in plain clothes sees us. **1928** J. BUCHAN *Runagates Club* ii. 73 The pollisman..says they're looking for a man that personated an inmate. *a* **1930** N. MUNRO *Para Handy Tales* (1955) 109 'There's no a polisman in the island of Barra,' said Para Handy. 'If there wass any need for polismen they would have to send to Lochmaddy.' **1931** D. L. SAYERS *Five Red Herrings* ii. 20 Juist tummled intae the burn..an' drooned himself... The pollis'll be up there now. **1967** H. CALVIN *Nice Friendly Town* viii. 104 'But I'll have to get on to the police,' I protested, and Jumbo..pointed to Eddie Bone and said: 'He's a polis. Get on to him.' **1973** J. PATRICK *Glasgow Gang Observed* iii. 34 Tim bragged: 'We've chibbed aboot seven polis.' **1979** *Listener* 31 May 749/4 The odd *poliss* and such like..could be confusing to English ears.

-polis, repr. Gr. *πόλις* city, as in METROPOLIS, NECROPOLIS; sometimes used (in the form *-opolis*) to form names or nicknames of cities or towns, e.g. COTTONOPOLIS, *Leatheropolis, Porkopolis.*

1868 W. M. PUNSHON in Macdonald *Life* (1887) 305 Cincinnati, the 'Porkopolis' of the Union. **1881** *Chicago Times* 16 Apr., She [Chicago] has reached the position of the porkopolis of the world. **1901** *Westm. Gaz.* 2 Oct. 8/1 The first time the great annual gathering of Churchmen has taken place in Leatheropolis [Northampton].

Polisario (pɒlɪˈsɑːrɪəʊ). [f. the initial letters of Sp. *Frente Popular para la Liberacion de Sagnia el-Hamra y Rio de Oro* Popular Front for the Liberation of Sagnia el-Hamra and Río de Oro.] An independence movement in Western Sahara, formed in May, 1973. Also *attrib.*

1975 *Guardian* 17 Oct. 4/6 The Front for Liberation and Unity..has vowed to break up separatist movements such as the Algerian-backed Polisario Front, which is campaigning for independence for the territory. **1977** *Time* 3 Jan. 49/1 Polisario is fighting to gain independence for a new 'Saharan Arab Democratic Republic' and the 100,000 people, most Reguibet tribesmen, it would represent. **1977** *Kuwait Times* 23 Oct. 4/7 Spain ceded sovereignty of the Western Sahara to Morocco and Mauritania nearly two years ago but Algeria disputes the agreement and supports guerrillas of the Polisario Front fighting for independence for the territory.

polish (ˈpɒlɪʃ), *sb.*[1] [f. POLISH *v.*]

1. The act of polishing or condition of being polished; smoothness and (usually) glossiness of surface produced by friction.

1704 NEWTON *Optics* (1721) 24 Another Prism of clearer Glass and better Polish. **1705** ADDISON *Italy* 352 Consider the great Difficulty of hewing it.., and of giving it the due Turn, Proportion and Polish. **1777** MUDGE in *Phil. Trans.* LXVII. 325 In the beginning of the polish,..I worked round and round. **1806** *Gazetteer Scotl.* (ed. 2) 247/2 Some of the stones..take a very high polish. **1838** DICKENS *Nich. Nick.* viii, You must be content with giving yourself a dry polish till we break the ice in the well.

2. *fig.* Refinement: see POLISH *v.* 2.

1597 J. PAYNE *Royal Exch.* 19 This poore pamphlett,.. without fynenes of methode, or pullishe of art. **1713** ADDISON *Cato* I, What are these wond'rous civilizing arts, This Roman polish, and this smooth behaviour? **1778** MISS BURNEY *Evelina* xxvi, Where my education and manners might receive their last polish. **1841** ELPHINSTONE *Hist. Ind.* I. 425 What polish they have seems borrowed from the Mussulmans. **1902** F. W. H. MYERS *Wordsw.* 105 Poetry depends on emotion and not on polish.

3. a. A substance used to produce or to assist in producing smoothness or glossiness on any surface. See also FRENCH POLISH, FURNITURE-*polish*, SHOE-*polish*, STOVE-*polish*, VARNISH-*polish*, etc.

1819–1874 [see FRENCH POLISH]. **1881** YOUNG *Ev. Man his own Mech.* §1624 The method of applying these polishes is the same for all. A flannel rubber is..dipped in the polish.

b. Short for *nail polish* s.v. NAIL *sb.* 13 a.

1917 *Harrods Gen. Catal.* 410 (*heading*) Manicure preparations and sundries... Majestic Polish..1/6. **1924** M. A. BURBRIDGE *Road to Beauty* 115 Finish by using a bit more of the tinted polish and rub up with the buffer. **1937** H. RUBENSTEIN *This Way to Beauty* viii. 119 A very white hand is flattered by a very dark polish. **1957** N. WILLIAMS *Powder & Paint* v. 144 Until 1930..more 'colourless' polish was sold than of the three shades of pink that made up the manicurist's palette. **1976** 'M. ALBRAND' *Taste of Terror* x. 61 The salesgirls never look at a customer. They're always staring at their nails to see if the polish is chipped.

4. *Comb.*, as ***polish-brush***, ***-powder***, ***-stone***; **polish remover,** a preparation used for removing nail varnish.

1799 G. SMITH *Laboratory* I. 143 With a polish-stone and the whiten, polish your foils. **1858** SIMMONDS *Dict. Trade, Polish-powder*, a preparation of plumbago for stoves and iron articles. **1861** *Eng. Wom. Dom. Mag.* III. 48 No blacking-brush is needed, nor polish-brush either. **1935** D. COCKS *Help Yourself to Beauty* xii. 249 Moisten a small pad of absorbent cotton with polish remover. **1973** M. MACKINTOSH *King & Two Queens* iv. 58 He played absently with the small bottle of polish remover..running the tiny brush over a thumb-nail.

Polish (ˈpəʊlɪʃ), *a.* and *sb.*[2] [f. POLE *sb.*[4] + -ISH[1].]

A. *adj.* **a.** Of or pertaining to Poland or its inhabitants.

1674 R. SOUTH *Acct. of Travels into Poland in 1674* in *Posthumous Wks.* (1717) 26 The Queen is now about 33 Years of Age..and speaks the Polish Language full as well as her own natural Tongue. *a* **1704** T. BROWN *Lett. to Gent. & Ladies* Wks. 1709 III. II. 96 The unkinging of his Polish Majesty. **1795** S. JONES *Hist. Poland* I. xix. 24 The Paternoster in the Polish language is of the following tenor. **1831** SIR J. SINCLAIR *Corr.* II. 292 There is hardly any resemblance between the Polish Diet and the English Parliament, at least at present. **1842** *Penny Cycl.* XXII. 115/1 The Polish language is considered to be more flexible and euphonic than the other Slavonic dialects. **1884** W. R. MORFILL *Simplified Gram. Polish Lang.* i. 3 The sounds of the Polish language may be grouped as *hard* and *soft.* **1944** S. GRABSKI *Poland* III. xiv. 107 The magnificent song of the Knights..to the glory of the Virgin Mary, the first literary monument in the Polish language. **1975** *Language* LI. 407 These languages..differ from the Polish dialects discussed above in not permitting alternatives with singular and plural.

b. In the names of things of actual or attributed Polish origin; as **Polish disease, plait**: see PLAIT *sb.* 2 c; **Polish draughts,** a variety of the game of draughts played on a board of 100 squares with 20 men a side; called in French *le jeu de dames à la polonaise* (Manoury, 1750), in Poland itself *French draughts*; **Polish fowl** = POLAND[1] *fowl*; **Polish manna**: see MANNA[1] 6; **Polish wheat** = POLAND[1] *wheat.*

1849 D. J. BROWNE *Amer. Poultry Yd.* (1855) 60 The *plica polonica*, or *Polish disease, in which the hair in the human subject grows into an immense matted mass. **1733** R. in *Craftsman* No. 376. 156 The game of *Polish Draughts, where you will see the whole Board engaged in the important business of making Kings. **1768** BARETTI *Mann. & Cust. Italy* xxxiii. 217 As chess is superior to polish-drafts. **1816** KEATINGE *Trav.* (1817) I. 308 They play at what we call Polish drafts. **1960** R. C. BELL *Board & Table Games* ii. 75 Modifications in the rules have been made and as now played, Polish draughts must rank as one of the great board games of the world. **1971** *Country Life* 25 Nov. 1429/1 The board on this games table is arranged for Polish draughts..popular in England throughout the 18th century, the boards having 100 squares and each player 20 men. **1849** D. J. BROWNE *Amer. Poultry Yd.* (1855) 12 *Cirrus* is the Latin word..adopted by Aldrovandi to express the topknot of *Polish fowls. **1864** *Chambers' Encycl.* VI. 308/1 Known in shops as *Polish Manna, Manna Seeds, and Manna Croup. **1832** *Veg. Subst. Food* 34 *Polish Wheat —*Triticum polonicum*..is now to be found here only in botanic gardens. **1843** Polish wheat [see *hard wheat* s.v. HARD *a.* (*sb.*) 22 a]. **1908** Polish wheat [see DURUM].

c. Applied to logical theories, methods, or systems developed esp. in Lwow, Breslau, and Warsaw before the war of 1939–45, and to the related symbolism, as **Polish notation,** a bracketless and unpunctuated system of formula notation now freq. used in computing science to represent the order in which arithmetical operations are performed in many computers and calculators, often with operators following their operands (***reverse Polish***) instead of preceding them.

1940 *Jrnl. Symbolic Logic* V. 77 The second section is devoted to various present currents of thought: Hilbert formalism, German exact thought.., Polish logic.., the unity of science movement. **1954** I. M. COPI *Symbolic Logic* 254 The Polish notation has the obvious advantage of dispensing with all special punctuation marks. **1965** N. KRETZMANN *Elements of Formal Logic* p. vi, We use Łukasiewicz's so-called Polish notation for..the logic of statements. **1966** Y. BAR-HILLEL in *Automatic Transl. of Lang.* (NATO Summer School, Venice 1962) 15 In Polish notation calculi you cannot introduce syntactic ambiguity.. by omitting symbols, since there are no special scoping symbols to omit. **1968** *Jrnl. Assoc. Computing Machinery* XV. 466 The following is a simple Polish transduction grammar. **1975** D. G. FINK *Electronics Engineers' Handbk.* XXIII. 85 One possible Polish string would be AB + C + E =. In this string, the system would find A and B and, as determined by the plus sign *following* the two operands, add them. The result is then combined with C under addition called for by the second plus sign. The E = symbols indicate that the result is to be stored in E. **1975** *Physics Bull.* May 227/1 The Oxford 300 scientific calculator with either floating point or scientific notation and algebraic logic (as opposed to the reverse Polish logic used on the more familiar Sinclair Scientific).

B. *absol.* or as *sb.*[2]

†**1.** *absol.* Short for *Polish draughts. Obs. rare.*

1760–72 H. BROOKE *Fool of Qual.* (1792) III. xv. 67 Can you play at draughts, polish, or chess?

2. The Polish language.

1784 W. COXE *Travels into Poland, Russia, Sweden, & Denmark* I. II. iii. 176 The king informed me, that they had no good history of their country in Polish. **1807** G. BURNETT *Present State of Poland* xvi. 277 Within thirty or forty, or perhaps fifty miles of Dantzic, I found that the people knew scarcely a word of Polish. **1861** MAX MÜLLER *Lect. Sci. of Lang.* 1st Ser. v. 187 The oldest specimen of Polish belongs to the fourteenth century: the Psalter of Margarite. **1925** P. DE SOISSONS *Polish Self-Taught* 1 This work is issued as a practical introduction to Polish, a language spoken by about thirty millions of people. **1943** S. SEGAL *Nazi Rule in Poland* iv. 70 Only a few shows in Polish are at present permitted in Warsaw and Krakow. **1968** B. NEWMAN *New Poland* ii. 31 If a Lithuanian youth wanted an education, he had to learn Polish to get it. **1975** *Language* LI. 363 The passive construction is the same for both aspects in Polish and Bulgarian.

Hence **'Polishness,** the quality or state of being Polish or of displaying Polish characteristics.

1958 *Listener* 2 Oct. 499/2 They [*sc.* the Poles] need to reaffirm their past, their Polishness. **1964** E. HUXLEY *Back Street New Worlds* iii. 35 Few of their children attend Saturday schools or sustain their Polishness.

polish ('pɒlɪʃ), *v.* Forms: see below. [ME. *polis-, -iss-, -issh-*, a. F. *poliss-*, lengthened stem of *polir*:—L. *polīre* to polish, smooth, refine: see -ISH².]

A. Illustration of Forms.

α. 3–4 polis-, 4–5 polys(e, -yce, 4–6 police, 5–6 polise, *Sc.* poleis.

a **1300** *Cursor M.* 9975 (Cott.) þat roche þat es polist sa slight. **13..** *E.E. Allit. P.* B. 1131 He may polyce him.. Wel bryȝter þen þe beryl oþer browden perles. *Ibid.* 1134 Polysed als playn as parchmen schauen. **1390** GOWER *Conf.* I. 127 And was policed ek so clene. *c* **1480** HENRYSON *Test. Cres.* 347 Ane poleist glas.

β. 4 polich, 4–5 polisch(e, -issch(e, 4–6 -issh(e, 5 -esh(e, -ysh, -ysch, pollishe, 5–6 polys(s)h(e, -ishe, 6–8 pollish, 5– polish.

c **1340** *Cursor M.* 9975 (Gött.) þe Roche þat es polichit [*a* **1425** polisshid] so slight. **1362** [see B. 1]. *a* **1400–50** *Alexander* 3223 Polyshyd all of pure gold. *Ibid.* 5129 With pellicans & pape-ioyes polischt & grauen. *c* **1420** *Pallad. on Husb.* I. 406 Polish al vp thy werk. *c* **1430** LYDG. *Min. Poems* (Percy Soc.) 36 Thou thynkest hir pollisshed whan she is ful of rust. **1526** *Pilgr. Perf.* (W. de W. 1531) 138 The more it is polysshed or rubbed. **1552** HULOET, Polyshe paper or parchment smothe.

γ. 5 pulisshe, -isch(e, -ich(e, 5–6 pullysshe, -ysh(e, 5–7 pullish(e. (Cf. It. *pulire, pulito.*)

c **1400** MAUNDEV. (Roxb.) xvii. 80 þai myȝt noȝt be pulischt. **1483** *Cath. Angl.* 293/1 To Pulische (*A.* Puliche). **1555** EDEN *Decades* 194 As fayre and nette as though it were pullyshed. **1605** BACON *Adv. Learn.* II. xvii. §13 The rules will helpe, if they be laboured and pullished by practise.

δ. 4–5 pul(s)che, 5 pul(s)she, polshe.

c **1394** *P. Pl. Crede* 121 Portreid and paynt & pulched full clene. *c* **1400** *Chaucer's Merch. T.* 338 (Petw.) A myrour polshed bright. *c* **1400** *Beryn* 1734, I-pulsshid, & I-pikid. *c* **1407** LYDG. *Reson & Sens.* 5766 The cristal pulshede was so clene. *c* **1440** *Promp. Parv.* 416/1 Pulchon, *polio.*

B. Signification.

1. a. *trans.* To make smooth and (usually) glossy by friction. Also *absol.* or *intr.*

a **1300** *Cursor M.* 9887 (Cott.) Dunward þan es [þis castel] polist slight. **1362** LANGL. *P. Pl.* A. v. 257 þat Penitencia is pike he schulde polissche newe [*v. rr.* polisch, pulsshe]. *c* **1400** MAUNDEV. (Roxb.) xvii. 79 þai er so hard þat þare may na metell pulisch þam. *a* **1548** HALL *Chron., Hen. VIII* 156 b, These candelstickes wer polished lyke Aumbre. **1610** HOLLAND *Camden's Brit.* (1637) 719 Before it be polished, it is of a reddish and rusty colour. **1703** MOXON *Mech. Exerc.* 213 Hard Wood they polish with Bees-wax... But Ivory they polish with Chalk and Water. **1803** T. SHERATON *Cabinet Dict.* 289 At other times they polish with soft wax. **1828** WEBSTER, *Polisher, n.*, the person or instrument that polishes. **1855** MACAULAY *Hist. Eng.* xii. III. 201 For the purpose of being polished and shaped into a column. **1878** W. S. GILBERT *H.M.S. Pinafore* I, I polished up the handle of the big front door. **1902** *Daily Chron.* 9 June 7/2 A negro whose boots he had declined to polish. **1902** D. C. PEEL *How to Keep House* xii. 205 Dip a small piece of flannel lightly in colza oil and then into the bath-brick, and rub all the bright part well, wipe off with a soft cloth and polish with a leather. **1919** L. R. BALDERSTON *Housewifery* vi. 133 Rottenstone is a fine gray powder... Like any gritty substance, it works best with a lubricator like oil. In this way it cleans and polishes. **1957** M. DODD *America's Homemaking Bk.* xxiii. 189 There are commercial scratch removers that can be applied like a polish..or mix with varnish an oil paint to match the wood... Let it dry and then polish. **1961** *Modern Maturity* IV. VI. 19/2 Some women get a real thrill out of housework. They love to dust, scrub, polish, wax floors, move the furniture around from place to place, [etc.]. **1962** *Home Managem.* (Homecraft Series) 34/1 It can be sprayed straight on to a dusty surface and enables you to dust and polish in one operation.

b. *intr.* for *passive.* †(*a*) To become bright. *Obs. rare.* (*b*) To become smooth, take a smooth and (usually) glossy surface.

c **1400** *Destr. Troy* 4589 Zeforus with softe wyndes soberly blew, Planettes in the pure aire pullishet full clene. **1626** BACON *Sylva* §849 A kind of steel..which would polish almost as white and bright as silver. **1728** YOUNG *Love Fame* III. 224 'Tis solid bodies only polish well. **1898** J. HUTCHINSON in *Arch. Surg.* IX. 314 None of these patches ..shewed the least tendency to polish.

c. To wipe or scrape up and eat every morsel of food on (one's plate, bowl, etc.).

1908 A. J. DAWSON *Finn* xix. 289 Finn polish the tin dish clean and bright. **1962** M. DUFFY *That's how it Was* x. 85 The little Reeses polished their plates after every meal. **1972** M. BABSON *Murder on Show* vii. 79 Pandora ate her dinner ..and began polishing her bowl.

2. *fig.* **a.** *trans.* To free from roughness, rudeness, or coarseness; to imbue with culture or refinement; to make more elegant or cultured; to refine. (In quot. 13.., To cleanse, purify.) Also *absol.*

a **1340** HAMPOLE *Psalter* cxxxix. 3 þai polyst þe wordis of þaire felony as neddirs. **13..** *Gaw. & Gr. Knt.* 2393, I halde þe polysed of þat plyȝt, & pured as clene. *a* **1400–50** *Alexander* 4427 Bot he can practise & paynt & polisch his wordis. *c* **1570** *Pride & Lowl.* (1841) 3 Thou maiest finde Some matters (though not pullished with art,) To make thee laugh. **1667** MILTON *P.L.* XI. 610 Arts that polish Life. **1773** JOHNSON *Let. to Mrs. Thrale* 14 Sept., The eldest [daughter] is the beauty of this part of the world, and has been polished at Edinburgh. **1818** MACAULAY in Trevelyan *Life & Lett.* (1876) I. ii. 90 Books of amusement tend to polish the mind. **1946** K. TENNANT *Lost Haven* (1947) xv. 235 Mrs. Ayre was thrown back for employment on a series of maids, and was always to be found hard at work 'polishing' some raw girl. **1961** *Vogue* (N.Y.) July 100/3 They discovered any number of ways in which they wanted to polish their own interview techniques. **1961** E. STREETER *Chairman of Bored* xxiii. 221 Did men become perfectionists as they grew older, polishing, polishing, reluctant to let go? **1961** *PMLA* LXXVI. I. 310 The poet in a written tradition who generally never blots a line may once in a while pause and polish without incurring blame.

†**b.** To smooth or gloss over. *Obs. rare.*

a **1450** *Knt. de la Tour* (1868) 61 By hem.. that confessithe hem to the preest..that in shryfte excusithe hem and polysshithe her synne.

c. With adv. or advb. phr.: To do *away*, put *out*, bring *into* some state by polishing.

1712 STEELE *Spect.* No. 370 ¶2 Such elegant Entertainments as these, would polish the Town into Judgment in their Gratifications. **1718** *Free-thinker* No. 39. 281 An over-judicious Authour..polishes away the Strength and Energy of his Thoughts. **1858** HAWTHORNE *Fr. & It. Note-Bks.* II. 148 The wholesome coarseness.. which no education..can polish out of the genuine Englishman.

d. *intr.* for *passive.* To become refined.

1727 SWIFT *Let. on Eng. Tongue* Wks. 1755 II. I. 185 The French [language] for these last fifty years hath been polishing as much as it will bear. **1776** FOOTE *Capuchin* I. Wks. 1799 II. 384 She insists upon his polishing a little.

3. *trans.* To bring to a finished or complete state; to deck out, adorn. Const. *out, up.*

1581 MULCASTER *Positions* xxi. (1887) 89 To polishe out this point with those effectuall reasons. **1592** GREENE *Upst. Courtier* C iv, Other..there be..that pinche their bellies to polish their backs. **1885** DUNCKLEY in *Manch. Exam.* 15 June 6/2 To dot his i's and cross his t's and polish up his manuscript.

4. *to polish off*: to finish off quickly or out of hand; to do for or get rid of summarily. *colloq.* (orig. *Pugilistic slang*).

1829 *Sporting Mag.* XXIII. 247 Ned having polished off his sturdy opponent in thirty rounds. **1837** DICKENS *Pickw.* xxv, Mayn't I polish that ere Job off, in the front garden? **1850** SMEDLEY *F. Fairlegh* (1894) 53 He can polish off a boy half a head taller than himself. **1872** *Punch* 10 Aug. 66/1 We nearly polished off the Licensing Bill in the Commons. **1873** LELAND *Egypt. Sketch-Bk.* 282 The two between them could polish off a bottle of sherry in less time.

polishable ('pɒlɪʃəb(ə)l), *a.* [f. POLISH *v.* + -ABLE.] Capable of being polished.

1611 COTGR., *Polissable*, polishable, burnishable, furbishable. **1662** H. MORE *Philos. Writ.* Pref. Gen. (1712) 10, I do not look upon that Subject as any thing polishable by my hand. **1845** STOCQUELER *Handbk. Brit. India* (1854) 107 The lighter-coloured, but polishable and well-grained teak.

Polish-American, *sb.* and *a.* [f. POLISH *a.* + AMERICAN *a.* and *sb.*] **A.** *sb.* An American of Polish origin.

1898 F. BARINGER in *Memorial of Polish-American Organizations in U.S.* 29 The Polish-Americans in this city are very industrious. **1938** W. SEABROOK *These Foreigners* v. 258 The late Congressman Zionchek who went berserk on the White House lawn was a Polish American. **1943** *Who's Who in Polish America* (ed. 3) 9 This..is the outgrowth of a project begun modestly in 1939, with the publication of a brochure containing brief biographies of 100 leading Polish-Americans. **1945** *Polonia* 83 The New Poland that came out of the War proved disappointing to many Polish Americans. **1974** D. MACKENZIE *Zaleski's Percentage* ii. 40 A handful of Polish-Americans made the pilgrimage. **1977** B. GARFIELD *Recoil* i. 18 'She's married to a Polack.' 'Polish-American, Charlie.'

B. *adj.* Of or pertaining to Americans of Polish origin.

1911 *Cath. Encycl.* XII. 207/2 The most typical of the Polish American laymen to achieve distinction was Peter Kiolbassa. **1936** MENCKEN *Amer. Lang.* (ed. 4) 673 The Polish-American journalists are rather more careful than most. **1949** *Dziennik Zwiazkowy* (Chicago, Ill.) 19 Nov. 6/1 A banquet in honour of the Polish American public official. **1961** 'E. LATHEN' *Banking on Death* x. 80 The Buffalo Polish-American Democratic Club. **1976** *National Observer* (U.S.) 1 May B6/4 Television cameras invaded a Polish-American working-class home on the south side of Milwaukee.

polished ('pɒlɪʃt), *ppl. a.* [f. POLISH *v.* + -ED¹.]

1. a. Made smooth and (usually) glossy by friction.

c **1375** *Sc. Leg. Saints* l. (*Katerine*) 107 Schenand thru gold & polist stanys. *c* **1400** *Sege Jerusalem* 472 A plate of pulsched gold. *c* **1470** *Gol. & Gaw.* 708 Throw platis of polist steil. **1597** SHAKS. *2 Hen. IV*, IV. v. 23 O pollish'd Perturbation! Golden Care! **1736** GRAY *Statius* I. 41 In dust the polish'd ball he roll'd. **1860** TYNDALL *Glaciers* I. xv. 100 The road..lay right over the polished rocks.

b. Having naturally a smooth glossy surface.

1833 *Penny Cycl.* I. 76/2 *Acer lævigatum*, the polished maple.

c. Of rice: having the outer layers of the grain removed.

1922 W. G. R. FRANCILLON *Good Cookery* (ed. 2) xii. 236 Unpolished rice is cheaper and more nutritious than polished rice. **1948** *Good Housek. Cookery Bk.* II. 400 The natural rice has rather more flavour and food value than polished rice. **1979** P. B. MEDAWAR *Advice to Young Scientist* vi. 32 Scientists..demonstrated that..unpolished rice is much better for us than polished white rice.

2. *fig.* Refined, cultured, elegant: see POLISH *v.* 2.

c **1412** HOCCLEVE *De Reg. Princ.* 2939 Weyuë fauel with his polysshid speche. **1523** SKELTON *Garl. Laurel* 1093 Noble Chaucer, whos pullisshyd eloquence Oure englysshe rude so fresshely hath set out. **1639** *Hamilton Papers* (Camden) 100 Grace them with your more perfect and polished expressions. **1763** JOHNSON 16 May in *Boswell*, In more polished times there are people to do every thing for money. **1796** JANE AUSTEN *Pride & Prej.* vi, I consider it as one of the first refinements of polished societies. **1894** LD. WOLSELEY *Life Marlborough* I. 239 Charles..liked his polished manners.

Hence **'polishedly** *adv.*, **'polishedness.**

1594 CAREW *Huarte's Exam. Wits* ix. (1596) 121 He could not..deliuer his mind in them polishedly. *Ibid.* 123 Essay.. had ornament and polishednesse of speech. **1737** COVENTRY *Phil. to Hyd.* II. 9 A general Polishedness of Manners, and inward Character. **1889** GUNTER *That Frenchman!* ix, Polishedly polite to his equals.

polisher ('pɒlɪʃə(r)). [f. as prec. + -ER¹.]

1. One who polishes or produces a smooth and (usually) glossy surface on anything. Often in comb., as *brass-, shoe-, silver-, stone-polisher.*

1552 HULOET, Polisher of old wares to seme salable or new, *interpolator.* **1685** BOYLE *Effects of Mot.* Suppl. 144 A Polisher of Gems. **1723** *Lond. Gaz.* No. 6187/4 James Whitelegge,.. Looking-Glass Polisher. **1813** J. THOMSON *Lect. Inflam.* 607 The thick varnish which polishers or sword-cutlers use. **1899** *Allbutt's Syst. Med.* VII. 5 A polisher of parquet-flooring.

2. A tool or appliance for polishing anything.

1598 FLORIO, *Frucatore*, an iron furbishing toole, a rubber, a polisher. **1777** MUDGE in *Phil. Trans.* LX. 318 The ..polisher is..made by covering the tool with sarcenet. **1884** F. J. BRITTEN *Watch & Clockm.* 201 Polishers for steel are..of soft steel, iron, bell-metal, tin, zinc, lead or boxwood.

3. *fig.* One who refines: see POLISH *v.* 2.

1610 HEALEY *St. Aug. Citie of God* 355 You are the neate Polishers of the rude antient Latine and Greeke. **1749** FIELDING *Tom Jones* IX. v, Those great polishers of our manners..dancing-masters. **1801** HAN. MORE *Wks.* I. 26 Conversation, heav'nly fair..Soft polisher of rugged man!

polishing ('pɒlɪʃɪŋ), *vbl. sb.* [f. as prec. + -ING¹.] The action of the verb POLISH.

1. a. The action of making the surface of anything smooth or glossy; the fact of being polished.

1530 PALSGR. 256/2 Polysshing makyng smothe of a thynge, *polissure.* **1611** BIBLE *Lam.* iv. 7 They were more ruddy in body than rubies, their polishing was of sapphire. **1725** RAMSAY *Gentle Sheph.* III. iv, Till artful polishing has made it shine. **1894** *Athenæum* 4 Aug. 149/3 Some of the gems he has extracted need no polishing.

b. *pl.* The particles removed by any polishing process, *esp.* the dust produced in polishing articles of precious metal, or in cutting precious stones. (Cf. *filings.*) Also, the outer layers of rice grain usually removed during the milling process.

1890 in *Cent. Dict.* **1912** *Chambers's Jrnl.* Apr. 237/2 If the birds were fed on the milled rice mixed with the outer husks or 'polishings' which had been removed, the disease did not manifest itself. **1937** *Discovery* Nov. 348/2 Rice, or rather that part of it known as 'polishings', is the source of a vitamin product... Rice polishings are the external layers of the rice grain, usually removed by milling or 'polishing' in preparing the cereal for the market.

2. *fig.* **a.** The action of refining: see POLISH *v.* 2.

1617 BRATHWAIT *Smoaking Age* O iij b, Yea, he dislikes this polishing of Art, Which may refine the Core, but spoiles the heart. **1667** SPRAT *Hist. R. Soc.* 41 The English language ..has been hitherto a little too carelessly handled; and I think, has had less labor spent about its polishing, then it deserves. **1766** GOLDSM. *Vic. W.* ix, My wife..adding, that there was nothing she more ardently wished than to give her girls a single winter's polishing.

†**b.** The action of glossing *over.* *Obs. rare.*

1646 JENKYN *Remora* 21 This impure polishing over of Sin.

c. The filtration of the last traces of suspended solids from a liquid at the final stage in a process, *spec.* in the brewing of beer, and in the purification of effluent.

1938 *Jrnl. Inst. Brewing* XLIV. 466/2 One type of sheet filter composed of 160 sheets, 80 on each side, one side for 'roughing' and the other for 'polishing'. **1956** L. B. ESCRITT *Sewerage & Sewage Disposal* xviii. 361 The waterworks process of sand filtration has also been found satisfactory for effluent polishing. **1957** K. BARTON-WRIGHT tr. *J. de Clerck's Textbk. Brewing* I. xxii. 465 These sheet filters hold back yeast much better, and polishing is frequently omitted, whereas the metal mesh grids invariably let yeast pass through and a polishing filtration must always be carried out. **1958** *New Biol.* XXV. 88 Similar oxidation ponds are used in this country, e.g. in Bradford, for the final 'polishing' of a treated effluent, where the low flow in the receiving water demands this. **1971** R. L. & G. L. CULP *Adv. Wastewater Treatment* iii. 49 Effluent chlorination can provide more efficient disinfection of the effluent, which negates the only remaining virtue of the polishing pond for larger plants.

3. *attrib.* in names of tools, appliances, etc., used in producing a polish (in some of which *polishing* may be the ppl. adj.); as ***polishing-block, -brush, -disk, -file, -hammer, -iron, -jack, -machine, -paste, -powder, -room, -stick, -stone, -tool, -wheel***; **polishing-bed**, a machine in which the surface of stone is rubbed smooth (*Cent. Dict.* 1890); **polishing-cask** (*a*) a barrel in which articles are rolled and polished by friction with each other or with some polishing-powder; (*b*) a barrel in which grained gunpowder is placed with graphite to glaze it (Knight *Dict. Mech.* 1875); **polishing-mill**, a lap of metal or other material used by lapidaries in polishing gems (Knight); **polishing-slate**, (*a*) a grey or yellow slate found in the coal measures of

Bohemia, etc., used for polishing; (*b*) a kind of whetstone; **polishing-snake**, a kind of serpentine used formerly for polishing lithographic stones (Simmonds *Dict. Trade* 1858); **polishing-tin** (*Bookbinding*), a thin plate of tinned iron placed between the covers and the first and last leaves of a book, to keep the linings smooth and protect the leaves from the dampness of the cover (Simmonds).

1875 KNIGHT *Dict. Mech.*, **Polishing-block*, *a.* a block between the jaws of a vise on which an object is laid to polish it... *b.* A block shod with polishing material and moved over the face of the object to be polished. **1858** SIMMONDS *Dict. Trade*, **Polishing-brush*, a hand brush for shining stoves or grates with black lead. **1884** KNIGHT *Dict. Mech.* Suppl., **Polishing disk*,.. small instruments.. placed in a drill-stock, to polish the surfaces of dentures, teeth, or fillings. **1706** PHILLIPS, *Polisher*,.. a *Polishing-Iron. **1858** SIMMONDS *Dict. Trade*, *Polishing-iron*, a smoothing iron. **1884** KNIGHT *Dict. Mech.* Suppl., **Polishing Jack*,.. a machine.. for polishing leather when considerable pressure is required. **1853** BYRNE *Artisan's Handbk.* 205 Thus we have.. the smoothing-mill, and the *polishing-mill, all generally of metal. **1884** F. J. BRITTEN *Watch & Clockm.* 88 Polishing mills are usually of ivory or tortoise-shell. **1858** SIMMONDS *Dict. Trade*, **Polishing-paste*, a kind of blacking or paste for harness and leather;.. [or] for giving a polish to articles of household furniture. **1916** 'TAFFRAIL' *Pincher Martin* vi. 86 A convenient receptacle for dirty cotton-waste, polishing-paste, bath-brick, and emery-paper. **1969** *Gloss. Terms Dentistry (B.S.I.)* 64 *Polishing paste*, a blend of fine abrasive particles with bonding agents and flavouring. It is used for cleaning and polishing surfaces of teeth, restorations and appliances. **1849** C. BRONTË *Shirley* III. xiv. 299 The cup and platter he burnished up with the best *polishing-powder. **1854–67** C. A. HARRIS *Dict. Med. Terminol.* 542/2 A polishing powder, made by dissolving copperas in water [etc.]. **1895** [see BLUEING, BLUING *vbl. sb.* 2]. **1969** *Gloss. Terms Dentistry (B.S.I.)* 64 *Polishing powder*, a material containing fine abrasive particles for polishing teeth. **1890** W. J. GORDON *Foundry* 131 The smooth plate then finds its way to the *polishing-room, where the tables travel under a double series of rubbers. **1849** CRAIG, **Polishing-slate*, the Tripoli, or Polierschiefer of geologists, a substance used in polishing, and entirely composed of the silicious shields of microscopic Infusoria. **1858** SIMMONDS *Dict. Trade*, *Polishing-slates*, a name for hone-slates or whet-stones. **1875** SIR T. SEATON *Fret Cutting* 29, I generally use a *polishing-stick, a contrivance of my own. **1591** PERCIVALL *Sp. Dict.*, *Polidero*, a *polishing toole, *politorium*. **1867** C. A. HARRIS *Dict. Med. Terminol.* (ed. 3), **Polishing wheel*, a small wheel with the peripheral surface covered with buck-skin or other soft leather, and made to revolve on the mandrel of a lathe.

'polishing, *ppl. a.* [-ING².] That polishes.

1825 *Eng. Life* II. 92 She would send them to the most polishing boarding-schools.

† **'polishment.** *Obs.* [f. as prec. + -MENT.] The action of polishing; the fact of being polished.

1594 CAREW *Huarte's Exam. Wits* (1616) 124 The practise of languages, and the ornament and polishment of speech may verie well be ioyned with positiue diuinitie. **1633** WOTTON in *Reliq.* (1672) 465 It is strange to see what a polishment so base a stuffe doth take. **1694** PHILLIPS *Milton's Lett. St.* p. xxxii, The person that took the pains to prepare it for his Examination and Polishment.

† **'polishure.** *Obs. rare.* Also polissure. [a. F. *polissure* vbl. sb.: see POLISH *v.* and -URE.] The fact or condition of being polished.

1611 COTGR., *Polissure*, polissure, burnishment, smoothnesse. **1652** J. HALL *Height of Eloquence* p. lxiii, His elegancie and polishure in all these.. is inimitable.

‖ **polissoir** (pɔliswar). [F., a polishing instrument; f. *poliss-*, lengthened stem of *polir* to polish + *-oir*:—L. *-orium*.] A polishing instrument; = POLISHER 2. *spec.* **a.** in *Glass-manuf.*, A smooth block of wood with a long iron handle, used for flattening glass cylinders newly opened out; **b.** *Toilet.* An implement for burnishing the finger-nails (*Funk's Stand. Dict.* 1895).

18.. *Glass-making* 129 (Cent. Dict.), The flattener now applies another instrument, a *polissoir*, or rod of iron furnished at the end with a block of wood. **1897** *Archæol. Jrnl.* Dec. 367 The desirability of trimming them [flint implements] to the shape which could most easily be ground down afterwards on a polissoir.

‖ **polisson** (pɔlisɔ̃). [Fr.] An urchin or scamp; an ill-bred and uncouth person. Also *attrib.*

1866 G. J. WHYTE-MELVILLE *Cerise* II. x. 148 He was discovered as a coxcomb, an intruder and a *polisson*. **1897** G. DU MAURIER *Martian* 15 The polisson picked up his pocket-handkerchief and went. **1905** W. JAMES *Let.* 8 Feb. in R. B. Perry *Tht. & Char. W. James* (1935) II. 398 When will either you or I, to whom Locke's mind was that of a street *polisson* in point of subtlety and 'truth', have statuettes? **1915** M. F. SANDARS *Life & Times of Queen Adelaide* vii. 111 Instead of the polisson manner for which he used to be celebrated, he is now quiet and well-behaved, like anybody else.

politarch ('pɒlɪtɑːk). *Anc. Hist.* [ad. Gr. πολιτάρχης (Acts xvii. 6), f. πολίτης a citizen + -αρχης ruler, governor.] A governor of citizens; the title of civic magistrates in some Oriental cities, as Thessalonica, under the Romans.

1852 CONYBEARE & HOWSON *St. Paul* (1862) I. ix. 308 At Thessalonica we find an assembly of people and supreme magistrates, who are called politarchs. **1879** FARRAR *St. Paul* I. 513 They seized Jason and one or two others.. and dragged them before the Politarchs. **1884** *United Presb. Mag.* Apr. 178/1 The seven politarchs who ruled the city when the arch was built.

Politbureau, -buro ('pɒlɪt,bjʊərəʊ). Also politbureau, -buro. [a. Russ. *politbyuró*, f. *polit(icheskoe* political + *byuró* bureau.] The highest policy-making committee of the U.S.S.R., or of some other Communist country or party (in quot. 1930, a district committee). Also *attrib.*, *transf.*, and *fig.*

[**1926** *Encycl. Brit.* III. 428/1 This 'plenum' elects the Political Bureau of nine members with five deputies.] **1927** *Daily Express* 19 July 3/4 Stalin has packed the Politburo, which.. is practically the Cabinet, with his friends. **1930** *Morning Post* 13 Aug. 13 The factory Soviet asked the local politbureau for lecturers to explain the causes of the shortage. **1937** E. SNOW *Red Star over China* IV. v. 165, I [*sc.* Mao Tse-tung] was dismissed from the Politbureau, and also from the Party Front Committee. **1949** *Ann. Reg. 1948* 285 The names of the *Politburo* of the [Yugoslav Communist] party were.. made public. **1949** G. B. SHAW *Sixteen Self Sketches* xi. 67 For some years the leaders in the Politbureau or Thinking Cabinet of the Fabian policy were Webb, Olivier, Wallas, Shaw. **1952** [see BOLSHEVIK *a.*]. **1953** *Encounter* Oct. 67/1 Malenkov.. had.. a role more prominent than all other living Politburo members. **1962** *Listener* 6 Sept. 354/2 Mr Ben Bella's Politburo.. ordered nationalist troops to advance on Algiers. **1967** I. GREY *First Fifty Years* xxviii. 479 The congress [of 1966] revived the name 'Politburo', which had been changed to 'presidium' by the sixteenth congress in 1952. **1974** J. WHITE tr. *Poulantzas's Fascism & Dictatorship* IV. ii. 171 Insurrection was then decided on by the Comintern and the majority of the Russian politburo for October 1923. **1977** 'S. LEYS' *Chinese Shadows* (1978) v. 119 The keenness and energy with which.. old men cling to their seats on the Politburo. **1978** *Whitaker's Almanack 1979* 959/1 The real power of the Party is vested, however, in the *Politbureau*, the *Secretariat* and the permanent Departments of the Central Committee.

polite (pə(ʊ)'laɪt), *a.* Also 5 polyt, pollyte, 6 polyte. [ad. L. *polīt-us* polished, accomplished, refined, cultivated, polite, prop. pa. pple. of *polīre* to smooth, polish. Cf. It. *polito* (Florio), F. *poli* (12th c. in Littré), etc.]

† **1.** *lit.* Smoothed, polished, burnished. *Obs.*

c **1450** *Mirour Saluacioun* 1485 The Arche withinne & without was hiled with golde polyt. *c* **1470** HENRY *Wallace* IX. 1082 Throu polyt platis with poyntis persyt thair. **1601** B. JONSON *Poetaster* III. i, I am enamour'd of this street now.. tis so polite, and terse. **1675** EVELYN *Terra* (1729) 8 Potters-Earth.. became like Sand.. exceeding polite and smooth. **1678** CUDWORTH *Intell. Syst.* I. v. 731 Polite Bodies, as Looking-Glasses. **1737** WHISTON *Josephus, Antiq.* XV. ix. §6 Edifices.. made of the politest stone.

† **b.** Cleansed, furbished, trim, neat, orderly. *Obs.*

1497 BP. ALCOCK *Mons Perfect.* E j, Theyr monestery in every corner therof is all pollyte & clene. **1673** RAY *Journ. Low C.*, *Glaris* 427 At Suitz.. the people.. keep their houses neat and cleanly, and withal very polite and in good repair. **1703** MAUNDRELL *Journ. Jerus.* (1721) 77 To preserve these Chambers of the dead polite and clean.

2. *transf.* **a.** Of the arts, or any intellectual pursuits, esp. literature: Polished, refined, elegant; correct, scholarly, exhibiting a refined taste. (Now only in certain collocations.)

1501 DOUGLAS *Pal. Hon.* II. viii, Ȝone is.. the court rethoricall, Of polit termis. **1531** ELYOT *Gov.* I. v, That they speke none englisshe but that which is cleane, polite, perfectly and articulately pronounced. **1612** SELDEN *Illustr. Drayton's Poly-olb.* vi. 98 That polite Poem (in whose composition Apollo seemes to haue giuen personall aide). **1699** BENTLEY *Phal.* Pref. 49 All the Lovers of Polite Learning.. give me thanks. **1726** C. D'ANVERS *Craftsm.* i. (1727) 4 My natural inclination to the politer arts. **1786–7** BONNYCASTLE *Astron.* i. 12 One of the most useful branches of a polite education. **1824** L. MURRAY *Eng. Gram.* (ed. 5) I. 174 Every polite tongue has its own rules. **1891** *Speaker* 2 May 532/1 In it meta-physics have again condescended to speak the language of polite letters.

b. Of persons (*a*) in respect of some art or scholarship, (*b*) in respect of general culture: Polished, refined, civilized, cultivated, cultured, well-bred, modish.

1629 WADSWORTH *Pilgr.* viii. 91 One of the politest wits in the Kingdome for the Law. *a* **1664** KATH. PHILIPS *To Abp. of Canterb.* Poems (1667) 166 Majestick sweetness, temper'd and refin'd, In a Polite, and comprehensive Mind. **1711** ADDISON *Spect.* No. 39 ⁋2 In all the polite Nations of the World, this part of the Drama has met with publick Encouragement. **1759** JOHNSON *Idler* No. 47 ⁋14 Since his acquaintance with polite life. **1777** SIR W. JONES *Ess. Poetry E. Nat.* Poems, etc. 187 A very polite scholar, who has lately translated sixteen Odes of Hafez. **1840** MACAULAY *Ess.*, *Ranke* (1851) II. 142 Whatever the polite and learned may think.

c. Of refined manners; *esp.* showing courteous consideration for others; courteous, mannerly, urbane. (The chief current use.)

1762 GOLDSM. *Cit. W.* xxxix, [He] perceives that the wise are polite all the world over, but that fools are polite only at home. **1772** MACKENZIE *Man World* II. xx. (1823) 492 The French are the politest enemies in the world. **1781** GIBBON *Decl. & F.* xix. II. 151 Narses.. was endowed with the most polite and amiable manners. **1807** CRABBE *Par. Reg.* III. 841 To them, to all, he was polite and free. **1831** SIR J. SINCLAIR *Corr.* II. 426 He sent me the following polite acknowledgment of his having received the work. **1856** 'Doing the polite' [see DO *v.* 11 j]. **1883** *Manch. Guard.* 22 Oct. 5/5 Lord Dufferin obtains.. polite promises, but is not in a position to grant anything more.

3. *absol.* or as *sb.* In colloq. phr, *to do the polite*: to perform a polite action (freq. with *thing* understood); to behave politely.

1856 [see DO *v.* 11 j]. **1933** D. L. SAYERS *Murder must Advertise* vi. 95, I saw you doing the polite to Miss Rossiter. **1935** G. GREENE *England made Me* IV. 199 They are leaving at the end of the week. I've got to do the polite. **1939** 'M. INNES' *Stop Press* I. vi. 136 Some chaps over there. Must do the polite.

† **polite**, *v. Obs. rare.* [f. L. *polīt-*, ppl. stem of *polīre* to polish.] *trans.* To polish, refine; to clear up.

a **1676** HALE *De Successionibus* (1735) 50 There was some incertainty in the business of Descents, or Hereditary Successions, though it was much better polited than formerly. **1704** RAY *Creation* I. (ed. 3) 112 Exercises.. which polite Men's Spirits.

po'liteful, *a. rare.* [f. POLITE *a.* + -FUL.] Full of politeness.

1849 *Blackw. Mag.* LXVI. 436 The angrier.. for being *done* by a frog-eating bloody-politeful set of Frenchmen. **1896** *Daily News* 27 June 8/4 They were not politeful these footpads.

po'litely, *adv.* [f. POLITE *a.* + -LY².] In a polite manner. † **a.** Smoothly. *Obs.*

1597 A. M. tr. *Guillemeau's Fr. Chirurg.* lf. xiv b/2 A soundinge.. iron, the end wherof is rounde, and politely polishede. **1641** MILTON *Ch. Govt.* vii. Wks. 1851 III. 133 No marble statue can be politely carv'd, no fair edifice built without almost as much rubbish and sweeping. **1730** A. GORDON *Maffei's Amphith.* 288 The rustick Work.. is executed more politely.

† **b.** In a polished elegant manner; elegantly.

1698 FRYER *Acc. E. India & P.* 265 In the middle is a neat Bridge, built more politely than the other. **1731** *Gentl. Mag.* I. 21 Thy comedies.. shine, And read politely well. **1732** LAW *Serious C.* xiii. (ed. 2) 214 A Niece, whom he has politely educated in expensive finery.

c. Courteously; with refinement of manners.

1748 in Lady Chatterton *Mem. Ld. Gambier* (1861) I. ii. 18 We were very politely entertained with tea, &c. *c* **1775** WARTON (Mason), With the use of which I have been politely favoured. **1847** L. HUNT *Jar Honey* (1848) 191 He received us politely, but with a good deal of state.

politeness (pə(ʊ)'laɪtnɪs). [f. as prec. + -NESS.] The quality of being polite.

† **1.** *lit.* Polish, smoothness of surface. *Obs.*

1627 tr. *Bacon's Life & Death* (1651) 5 Smoothnesse, and Politenesse, of Bodies. **1669** GALE *Crt. Gentiles* I. III. iii. 47 Glasse is clear from its politenesse.

2. Mental or intellectual culture; polish, refinement, elegance, good taste (of writings, authors, etc.). Now *rare.*

1641 EVELYN *Diary* 28 Aug., The politeness of the character and editions of what he has publish'd. **1725** COTES tr. *Dupin's Eccl. Hist. 17th C.* I. v. 215 The Elegance and Politeness of the Stile of it. **1768** HUME *Ess.*, *Civil Liberty* xi. 51 Dresden, not Hamburgh, is the centre of politeness in Germany. **1837–9** HALLAM *Hist. Lit.* I. I. i. §86. 78 In politeness of Latin style.. we find an astonishing and permanent decline both in France and England.

3. Polished manners, courtesy. Also as a mock title for people of polite manners.

1702 *Eng. Theophrast.* 108 Politeness may be defined a dextrous management of our Words and Actions whereby we make other people have better Opinion of us and themselves. **1735** J. THOMSON *Let.* 20 Oct. (in *Sotheby's Catal.* 19–22 Feb. (1896) 87) The gallant French this year have made war upon the Germans (I beg their Politeness's Pardon) like vermin—eat them up. **1757** SMOLLETT *Reprisal* I. i, The French will treat us with their usual politeness. **1802** MAR. EDGEWORTH *Moral T.* (1816) I. vii. 45 Real politeness only teaches us to save others from unnecessary pain. **1856** EMERSON *Eng. Traits*, *Aristocr.* Wks. (Bohn) II. 83 Politeness is the ritual of society, as prayers are of the church. **1875** JOWETT *Plato* (ed. 2) I. 207 If politeness would allow me I should say, Perish yourselves.

‖ **politesse** (pɔlitɛs). [F. *politesse* (1611 in Cotgr.), ad. It. *politezza* (Florio 1598), f. *polito* polite.] Politeness; in mod. usage generally with depreciatory connotation.

1717 GAY *To W. Pulteney* 152 Pardon me, Sir; we know the Paris mode, And gather *Politesse* from Courts abroad. **1777** MME. D'ARBLAY *Early Diary* (1889) II. 200 He.. reserves his *politesses* pretty much for his favourites. *a* **1839** PRAED *Poems* (1864) II. 28 Sir Paul is skilled in all the tricks Of politesse and politics. **1863** COWDEN CLARKE *Shaks. Char.* ix. 228 Think, too, of the Tuileries etiquette;.. the powdered and embroidered politesse of the guests.

† **politian** (pəʊ'lɪʃən). *Obs.* Also 6 politien, 6–7 pollitian, 8 polician. [a. obs. F. *policien* (Godef.) a citizen, a politician, f. *police* (POLICE *sb.*) + *-ien* (see -IAN).] One who studies or is expert in polity; a politician.

1584 LYLY *Sappho* I. iii, We pages are Politians. **1589** PUTTENHAM *Eng. Poesie* III. iv. (Arb.) 159 Politien is rather a surueyour of ciuilitie than ciuil, and a publique minister or Counseller in the state. **1649** W. G. *Surv. Newcastle upon Tine* A iij b, Mechanicks will presume to Step into Moses Chaire, and become Politians to contradict and controle whatsoever is acted and done. **1788** *Trifler* No. 3. 34 A polician.. frequently effects such great revolutions in empires and kingdoms, as to a superficial observer would appear beyond the bounds of possibility.

politic ('pɒlɪtɪk), *a.* and *sb.* Forms: 5 poli-, poletyk, 5–6 politik, polytyk, -e, 6 poli-, polyticque, -tick, -tik, -tyke, -tycke, 6–7 politicke, -tike, -tique, 6–9 politick, 7 pol'tick, 6– politic. Also 5 polly-, 5–6 polle-, 5–7 polli-, -tick(e, -tique, etc. [a. F. *politique* (14th c. as adj. in Godef.) political, ad. L. *politicus*, a. Gr. πολῑτικός pertaining to citizens, civic, civil, political, f. πολίτης citizen (f. πόλις city, state): see -IC.]

A. *adj.* †**1. a.** = POLITICAL *a.* 1 (by which it is now superseded).

†*politic translation*, the translation of a Jewish feast on grounds of public expediency. †*politic year* = CIVIL year.

c **1420** LYDG. *Assembly of Gods* 1742 They polytyk philosophyrs & poetes were. **1426** —— *De Guil. Pilgr.* 11791, I am callyd 'vertu moral Polytyk & general'. **1556** BP. PONET (*title*) A Shorte Treatise of politike Pouuer, and of the true Obedience which Subjectes owe to..ciuile Gouernours. **1585** T. WASHINGTON tr. *Nicholay's Voy.* IV. xxii. 136b, The politique estate of the Ragusins, is Aristocratie. **1611** SPEED *Hist. Gt. Brit.* IX. xxi. (1623) 999 His ripe knowledge in politicke affaires. **1625** T. GODWIN *Moses & Aaron* III. (1641) 124 The reason of Politick translation, was, that two Sabbaths or feast dayes might not immediately follow each other. **1701** SWIFT *Contests Nobles & Com. Athens & Rome* Wks. 1755 II. I. 50 Those, who in a late reign began the distinction between the personal and politick capacity. **1709–29** V. MANDEY *Syst. Math., Astron.* III. II. ii. 411 A Politick or Civil Year, is a certain number of whole Days, collected either from other causes or reasons, or from the Sun or Moon, or from the Periods of both Motions; ..these being instituted by the People of any Nation, they are received. **1756** BURKE *Subl. & B.* IV. xxiv, Their superiours in politick and military virtues.

b. Pertaining or relating to a constitutional state, as distinct from a despotism; constitutional. *rare.*

c **1449** PECOCK *Repr.* I. xviii. 105 Gouernauncis..suche that ben politik (that is to seie, suche wherbi..ouerers gouerne othere men vndir hem bi..worldli policie). **1585** T. WASHINGTON tr. *Nicholay's Voy.* IV. xxxvi. 160 Græcia..In the end from honest common wealthes, and politike government, the inhabitants were brought under tiranny. **1878** STUBBS *Const. Hist.* III. xviii. 243 The politic royalty of England, distinguished from the government of absolute kingdoms by the fact that it is rooted in the desire and institution of the nation.

†**c.** *politic body = body politic*: see BODY *sb.* 14.

1604 JAS. I *Counterbl.* (Arb.) 97 It is the Kings part (as the proper Phisician of his Politicke-body) to purge it of all those diseases, by Medicines meete for the same. **1625** BACON *Ess., Boldness* (Arb.) 519 As there are Mountebanques for the Naturall Body: So are there Mountebanques for the Politique Body. **1631** MASSINGER *Emperor East* III. ii, I being the stomach To the politic body of the state.

2. Characterized by policy; of persons, Apt at pursuing a policy; sagacious, prudent, shrewd; of actions or things, Judicious, expedient, skilfully contrived. **a.** In political or public affairs.

c **1430** LYDG. *Min. Poems* (Percy Soc.) 163 Set a myrour of hihe discrecioun To-fore youre face by polityk governaunce. **1474** CAXTON *Chesse* 139 Good, trewe, and polletique councellours. **1558** KNOX *First Blast* Pref. (Arb.) 8 The wise, politike, and quiet spirites of this worlde. **1594** SHAKS. *Rich. III*, II. iii. 20 Then this Land was famously enrich'd With politike graue Counsell. **1686** tr. *Chardin's Trav. Persia* 348 He being a prudent and Politick Captain, ..resolv'd to make a desert of all the Country. **1790** BURKE *Fr. Rev.* Wks. V. 249 Henry of Navarre was a resolute, active, and politick prince. **1877** TENNYSON *Harold* III. ii, If this be politic, And well for thee and England..Care not for me who love thee.

b. In non-political or general sense.

c **1450** *Mankind* (Brandl 1898) 356 ȝyt well ȝe se, he ys polytyke. **1523** FITZHERB. *Surv.* viii. (1539) 13 More polytike in wysedome to improue their tenementes. **1542** BOORDE *Dyetary* xvi. (1870) 273 Conseruynge theyr polytycke wyt and lerenyng in Physycke. **1688** PRIOR *Ode on Exod.* iii. 12 The helm let politic Experience guide. **1758** JOHNSON *Idler* No. 8 ¶5 To learn of an enemy has always been accounted politick. **1858** FROUDE *Hist. E.* III. xvii. 473 Irritation is a passion which it is seldom politic to excite.

†**c.** Of an appliance: Ingeniously contrived; well adapted to its purpose. *Obs. rare.*

1549 *Compl. Scot.* vii. 69 Schips, marchantdreis, ande mony politic verkmanlumis for mecanyc craftis.

d. In a sinister sense: Scheming, crafty, cunning; diplomatic, artfully contriving or contrived.

1580 LYLY *Euphues* (Arb.) 225 For greater daunger is ther to ariue in a straunge countrey where the inhabitants be pollitique. **1609** DEKKER *Foure Birdes Noah's Arke, Pelican* Wks. (Grosart) V. 79 Breake (O my God) all the snares which daily and howerly this politick hunter [Satan] pitcheth to intrap me. **1667** PRIMATT *City & C. Builder* 12 These being the craftiest and politiquest sort of knaves. **1710** NORRIS *Chr. Prud.* ii. 95 The very notion we have of a Politic or Cunning Man,..one that knows how to compass his End. **1792** BURKE *Corr.* (1844) IV. 27 They are not so weak as to..imagine that you or I are playing any politic game with regard to them. **1879** DIXON *Windsor* II. xvi. 169 The one great fact of which her politic suitor took account.

¶**3.** Polished, refined, cultured. *Sc. Obs.*

Erron. rendering of L. *politus*.

1596 DALRYMPLE tr. *Leslie's Hist. Scot.* I. 85 The Ingles men, evin as the mair politick [L. *politiores*] Scottis, vses that ald Saxone toung. *Ibid.* 96 Vthiris of the mair politick sorte amang vs [L. *politiores*]. *Ibid.* III. 178 Thir verses albeit nocht verie politik [L. *politi*], ȝit throuch commendatione of ancient antiquitie maist probable.

B. *sb.* [With 1, cf. Gr. πολιτικός a politician; with 2 (OF. *politique*, 13th c. in Godef.), Gr. ἡ πολιτική (τέχνη) the art of government; with 3, Gr. τὰ πολιτικά affairs of state, politics.]

†**1. a.** A politician. *Obs.*

1559 AYLMER *Harborowe* C j, I doubte not, they had these consideracions that our polytikes haue. **1598** BACON *Sacr. Medit., Atheisme* Ess. (Arb.) 125 Amongst states men and politikes. **1611** W. SCLATER *Key* (1629) 274, I could wish all Christian politiques to consider, that righteousnes is the best vpholder of states, and transgression in the issue proues their ouerthrow. **1738** WARBURTON *Div. Legat.* I. Ded. 24 Now again, they are a Cabal of mere Politiques.

†**b.** An indifferentist in matters of religion, a temporizer, a worldly-wise man: orig. with reference to the *politiques* of France: see POLITIQUE.

1589 NASHE *Pasquil & Marfor.* 8 Secretarie Machiauell, a pollitick not much affected to any Religion. **1600** O. E. *Repl. Libel* I. v. 106 A carnall fellow, and a meere politicke. **1625** BACON *Ess., Unity in Relig.* (Arb.) 425 Worldlings, and Depraued Politickes, who are apt to contemne Holy Things. **1633** EARL MANCH. *Al Mondo* (1636) 127 Play not the hypocrite, nor the politicke, who cares not what Religion bee, so some be.

†**2.** Policy; politics. *Obs.*

1588 SIR W. STANLEY *Dr. Allen's Seditious Drifts* 88 *margin*, Certeine ouersights in policie escaped this great politicien in this Pamphlet, which is mere politike. **1639** N. N. tr. *Du Bosq's Compl. Woman* I. 10 Those lewd bookes, which..may very justly be termed the politick of the vicious and the Libertines. *a* **1649** DRUMM. OF HAWTH. *Skiamachia* Wks. (1711) 190 The politick they pitch'd upon was this: some noblemen, barons, and burgesses..met at Edinburgh. **1715** BENTLEY *Serm.* x. 361 This did not suit with Popish Politic.

3. *pl.* **politics. a.** The science and art of government; the science dealing with the form, organization, and administration of a state or part of one, and with the regulation of its relations with other states (hence, ***imperial, national, domestic, municipal, communal, parochial, foreign politics***, etc.). Also †***the politics***, public or social ethics, that branch of moral philosophy dealing with the state or social organism as a whole (*obs.*).

a **1529** SKELTON *Col. Clout* 625 But noble men borne To lerne they haue scorne,..Set nothyng by polytykes. **1565** COOPER *Thesaurus* s.v. *Ciuilis, Scientia ciuilis*, morall philosophie, the politikes. *a* **1619** FOTHERBY *Atheom.* II. xiv. §2 (1622) 356 Morall Philosophie..hath three parts: Ecclesiastickes, Oeconomickes, and Politickes. **1644** MILTON *Educ.* Wks. (1847) 100/2 The next removall must be to the study of politics; to know the beginning, end, and reasons of political societies. **1739** HUME *Hum. Nat.* (1874) I. Introd. 307 Politics consider men as united in society, and dependent on each other. **1789** GOUV. MORRIS in Sparks *Life & Writ.* (1832) II. 94, I mean politics in the great sense, or that sublime science which embraces for its object the happiness of mankind. **1791–1823** D'ISRAELI *Cur. Lit.* (1866) 339 'The art of governing mankind by deceiving them', as politics, ill understood, have been defined. [Cf. POLICY *sb.*[1] 2, quot. 1796.] **1883** J. A. SYMONDS in *Encycl. Brit.* XV. 150/1 Machiavelli..founded the science of politics for the modern world, by concentrating thought upon its fundamental principles. **1900** E. JENKS *Hist. Politics* 1 By *Politics* we mean the business of Government, that is to say, the control and management of people living together in a society.

b. ***the Politics***: name of the treatise on political science, τὰ πολιτικά, by Aristotle.

1651 HOBBES *Govt. & Soc.* iii. §13. 46 Aristotle in his first book of Politiques affirmes as a foundation of the whole politicall science, that some men by nature are made worthy to command, others only to serve. *a* **1656** USSHER *Power Princes* II. (1683) 134 As is observed..by Aristotle in his Politicks. **1831** *Encycl. Brit.* (ed. 7) III. 529/1 His [Aristotle's] two treatises of the *Nicomachean Ethics* and the *Politics*, are together a refutation of the erroneous doctrines in moral and political philosophy contained in Plato's political speculations.

c. Political actions or practice; policy. Freq. in unfavourable sense. Phr. ***to play politics***: see PLAY *v.* 16d.

1644 [H. PARKER] *Jus Pop.* 23 O that our Courtiers at Oxford would admit of such politicks, and blush to publish any directly contrary. *a* **1706** EVELYN *Mem.* (1819) II. 137, I looke upon our neglect of severely punishing them as an high defect in our politiques. **1711** POPE *Temp. Fame* 411 Calm, thinking villains, whom no faith could fix, Of crooked counsels and dark politicks. *c* **1740** CAREY *God save the King* ii, Confound their politicks, Frustrate their knavish tricks. **1741** MIDDLETON *Cicero* II. ix. 259 What strange politics do we pursue? **1930** N. W. STEPHENSON *Nelson W. Aldrich* xx. 327 Northern enemies were quick to draw a conclusion; the expulsion of the Brownsville soldiers was mere politics, a play to the gallery to make sure the hold of the administration on the Southern Republican machine. **1952** *Manch. Guardian Weekly* 11 Dec. 13 The 'politics' involved ..in key posts are not the private appetites of machine politicians or rarely that.

d. Political affairs or business; political life.

1693 *Humours Town* 42 The Coffee-house Politicks are but Fewel to Factions. **1710–11** SWIFT *Lett.* (1767) III. 141, I was an hour with him [Harley] this morning deep in politicks, where I told him the objections of the October Club. **1714** MRS. MANLEY *Adv. Rivella* 117 She now agrees with me, that Politicks is not the Business of a Woman. **1826** DISRAELI *Viv. Grey* IV. i, There is no act of treachery, or meanness of which a political party is not capable; for in politics there is no honour. **1879** GLADSTONE *Sp. at Dalkeith* 26 Nov., I said myself in 1865, and I believed, that it was out of the range of practical politics, that is to say the politics of the coming election. **1891** *Law Times* XCII. 124/1 Sugden ..re-entered politics, and sat in the House of Commons.

e. The political principles, convictions, opinions, or sympathies *of* a person or party.

1769 *Junius Lett.* iv. (1772) I. 35 Most men's politics sit much too loosely about them. **1842** MIALL in *Nonconf.* II. 656 Whig politics..appear to exert a peculiarly unhappy influence upon character. **1856** EMERSON *Eng. Traits, Aristocr.* Wks. (Bohn) II. 77 Too pleasing a vision to be shattered by..the politics of shoemakers and costermongers. **1897** RHOSCOMYL *White Rose Arno* 74 Oh what are all your politics to women? A woman's politics are the man she loves.

f. *fig.* Conduct of private affairs; politic management, scheming, planning.

1693 *Humours Town* 135 Thou art as much out in thy Politicks, as a Niggardly Father is. **1749** FIELDING *Tom Jones* XVI. vii, Mrs. Western was reading a lecture on prudence, and matrimonial politics to her niece. **1855** SMEDLEY *H. Coverdale* iii, The governor's letter contains a budget of family politics. **1902** *Westm. Gaz.* 21 Aug. 3/2 The fall of a skirt is a point second to none in importance in the politics of a costume.

g. Used as a singular noun.

1906 *Daily Chron.* 7 Dec. 6/4 She [*sc.* Australia] has a politics of her own, and Europe is all the poorer for being out of touch with it. **1931** M. DE LA BEDOYÈRE *Drift of Democracy* ii. 16 This politics is the vaguest of disciplines. **1970** I. L. HOROWITZ *Masses in Lat. Amer.* i. 23 If the United States model is to succeed in Latin America..a pluralistic politics of competitive, numerous, but autonomous groups must emerge.

h. *Comb.*, as ***politics-conscious, -free, -infested, -mad, -ridden*** adjs.

1957 H. READ *Tenth Muse* xxxv. 303 Futurism was more conscious of its environment, machine-conscious, politics-conscious. **1977** *New Yorker* 4 July 85/1 Considering the period it covers, the 'Memoir' is politics-free to an amazing degree. **1949** KOESTLER *Promise & Fulfilment* v. 270 The good, clean academic atmosphere acted like a disinfectant on our politics-infested minds. **1937** W. B. YEATS *Let.* 8 Feb. (1954) 880 He says that in England the educated classes are politics-mad. **1946** R. BLESH *Shining Trumpets* (1949) xiii. 299 The politics-ridden, local relief of Depression days.

politic (ˈpɒlɪtɪk), *v.* Also **politick.** [f. POLITIC *sb.* or (esp. in later use) a back-formation f. POLITICKING *vbl. sb.*] *intr.* To engage in political activity, esp. in order to strike political bargains or to seek votes (for oneself or another). Also *trans.* (rare).

1917 O. DOUGLAS *Setons* xiv. 225 He has been politic-ing down in Ayrshire. **1967** [see DROP *v.* 28a and b]. **1974** *Observer* (Colour Suppl.) 3 Nov. 31/2 Within the same square mile..Richard of Gloucester politicked. **1977** R. L. DUNCAN *Temple Dogs* (1978) II. i. 164 He was having to politic the old man to keep him from swerving away from his beliefs.

political (pəʊˈlɪtɪkəl, pə-), *a.* (*sb.*) [f. L. *politic-us*, a. Gr. πολιτικ-ός (see POLITIC *a.* and *sb.*) + -AL[1].]

A. *adj.* **1. a.** Of, belonging, or pertaining to the state or body of citizens, its government and policy, esp. in civil and secular affairs; public, civil; of or pertaining to the science or art of politics.

1551 T. WILSON *Logike* (1580) 15b, The pollliticall lawe doeth cause an outward discipline to bee obserued, euen of the wicked. **1637** R. HUMPHREY tr. *St. Ambrose* II. Pref., We must discerne betweene..political order..and..the vices incident thereunto. **1646** S. BOLTON *Arraignm. Err.* 317 In the execution of them, the King performs his part in a politicall way, the officers of the Church in an ecclesiasticall way. **1788** PRIESTLEY *Lect. Hist.* v. xxxix. 282 The share that he may have in directing the affairs of the society may be called his political liberty. **1825** J. S. MILL in *Westm. Rev.* Apr. 291 The subjects on which it is the interest of rulers that the people *should* be misled; the political religion of the country, its political institutions, [etc.]. **1846** —— in *Edin. Rev.* LXXXIV. 344 They [*sc.* the Greeks] were..the originators of political freedom. **1869** LECKY *Europ. Mor.* I. ii. 310 The distinct nationalities that composed the empire [Rome]..had lost all care for political freedom. **1878** GLADSTONE *Prim. Homer* vii. 100 What they [the Achaians] seem to have brought with them was the true political spirit; the faculty of nation-making. **1882** G. A. SALA *Amer. Revisited* I. xi. 161 For some mysterious reason..the Consumers' Ice Company figured as a political organisation in this astounding Parade. **1907** L. H. MORGAN *Anc. Society* II. xiii. 335 City wards and country townships..would have become the basis of the new political system. **1934** T. S. ELIOT *Rock* i. 15 Political religion is like invalid port: you calls it a medicine but it's soon just a 'abit. *a* **1942** B. MALINOWSKI *Scientific Theory of Culture* (1944) v. 50 The Chinese civilization differs from ours..in the economic and political organization of the country. **1949** M. MEAD in M. Fortes *Social Structure* 20 We have blocked out conceptually a large number of such areas as: the relationship between the representations of family structure and political structure in the psychology of the individual. **1957** P. WORSLEY *Trumpet shall Sound* 227 They occur.. among people living in..societies..which lack centralized political institutions. **1962** P. DIESING *Reason in Society* v. 170 The political structure of a group is the organization of forces which determines how its decisions are made. **1976** *Times* 21 May 2/5 The United Unionist M.P.s who provide most of Northern Ireland's political representation at Westminster.

b. Of persons: Engaged in civil administration; civil, as distinct from military; *spec.* in India, having, as a government official, the function of advising the ruler of a Native State on political matters, as ***political agent, resident***, etc. (now *Hist*).

1849 E. B. EASTWICK *Dry Leaves* 212 The junior political officers who served under the Envoy, or the Political Agent in Upper Sindh. **1861** W. H. RUSSELL in *Times* 29 July, The civilian Generals, or 'political' chiefs, are obnoxious to the regulars. **1880** GEN. ADYE in *19th Cent.* Apr. 699 The first class comprises political residents, commissioners of provinces, magistrates, officers of police and public works. **1903** *Whitaker's Almanack* 495/2 States of India..governed by their native Princes, Ministers, or Councils, with the help and under the advice of a political officer of the Supreme Government.

2. Having an organized government or polity. †Said also of animals such as bees and ants (*obs.*).

1657 S. Purchas (*title*) Theatre of Politicall Flying-Insects. **1658** Rowland *Moufet's Theat. Ins.* 921 The Philosopher doth rightly reckon them in the number of the Civil or Political sort of Insects. **1690** Locke *Govt.* II. vii. §89 There only is a Political or Civil Society. **1875** Maine *Hist. Inst.* xii. 358 Every independent political community, that is, .. every independent community neither in a state of nature .. nor in a state of anarchy.

3. Relating to, concerned or dealing with politics or the science of government.

1646 Sir T. Browne *Pseud. Ep.* 65 Beside his politicall wisdome; his knowledge in Philosophie was very large. **1758** Johnson *Idler* No. 5 ¶3 Men of a more political understanding are persuaded that we shall now see .. the ambassadors of France supplicating for pity. **1830** *Declar.* 25 Jan. in C. M. Wakefield *Life T. Attwood* x. (1885) 134 We propose to form in Birmingham a General Political Union of the Industrious Classes, for the Protection of Public Rights. **1885** *Spectator* 16 May, The ladder which leads to the highest positions in political life.

4. Belonging to or taking a side in politics or in connexion with the party system of government; in a bad sense, partisan, factious. Also (freq. in derogatory use), serving the ends of (party) politics; having regard or consideration for the interests of politics rather than questions of principle.

1749 [see machine *sb.* 4 *fig.*] **1769** *Junius Lett.* iii. (1772) 27 It has all been owing to the malice of political writers, who will not suffer the best and brightest of characters .. to take a single right step for the honour or interest of the nation. **1846** Wright *Ess. Mid. Ages* II. xix. 259 The oldest English political song preserved relates to the battle of Lewes in 1264. *a* **1859** Macaulay *Hist. Eng.* xxv. V. 241 He tried to make what is, in the jargon of our time, called political capital out of the desolation of his house and the blood of his first born. **1861** J. S. Mill *Repr. Govt.* i. 4 Political machinery does not act of itself. **1890** *Cent. Dict.* s.v. *Assessment*, Political assessments, in the United States, contributions of money levied by political committees upon .. office-holders .. in order to defray the expenses of a political canvass. **1900** *Daily News* 5 Nov. 7/1 Another feature of an American Presidential campaign is the lavish display of political 'buttons'. **1909** C. F. G. Masterman *Condition of England* iii. 83 They appear as the mainstay of the political machine in suburban districts. **1912** *Out West* (Los Angeles) June 401 Are you interested .. in the way people are defrauded, and bunkoed, and swindled, and played with by the political bosses? **1934** L. Mumford in W. Frank et al. *Amer. & Alfred Stieglitz* I. ii. 34 The political boss and his underlings. **1974** G. Woodbridge in H. van Thal *Prime Ministers* I. 349 He [*sc.* Lord Grey] concluded with a highly political and very clever speech, suggesting that all that was at stake was the acceptance of the principle that there should be some reform, leaving the exact details .. to be settled in the committee stage. **1977** *Times* 27 Jan. 5/1 If the Government chose the path of ill-considered and largely political legislation aimed at achieving a union takeover of private industry, it would have dealt a damaging blow. **1978** *Times* 3 Jan. 1/3 The union's vice-president .. told a rally of 1000 striking firemen that the employers were playing 'a political game'.

†**5.** = politic A. 2. *Obs.*

1614 B. Jonson *Barth. Fair* III. i, I cannot beget a project with all my political brain yet. **1654** tr. *Martini's Conq. China* 106 And sometimes suggested dangerous, but political Counsels to the Tartars. **1759** Sterne *Tr. Shandy* II. x, 'Twas natural and very political too in him, to have taken a ride to Shandy-Hall. **1778** [W. Marshall] *Minutes Agric., Digest* 19 From two to three hundred acres .. is the most political Farm. *a* **1817** in Jas. Mill *Brit. India* II. v. i. 334 Whether it would be political to interfere, or whether .. it would be expedient, must continue a doubt with us.

6. Phrases. ***political animal*** [tr. Gr. *πολιτικὸν ζῷον* (Aristotle *Politics* I. ii. §9) an animal intended to live in a city, a social animal] man, as acting in concert with others; a person who is interested in, or who participates in, politics; ***political anthropology***, the study of the origins, forms, and exercise of community authority as it has evolved in aboriginal or isolated societies; †***political arithmetic***, statistics of the population, trade, revenue, expenditure, etc. of a state; ***political asylum***, the condition of being, or permission to remain in a country as, a political refugee; ***political commissar***, in China, a representative appointed to a military unit to be responsible for political education and organization; ***political day*** = *civil day* (day 6); ***political economy***, ***economist***: see economy 3, economist 4; ***political football***, a subject of contentious political debate; ***political geography***, that part of geography which deals with the boundaries, divisions, and possessions of states; ***political hostess***, a hostess at a party or gathering attended by politicians; ***political morality***, public ethics; ***political novel***, a fictitious political narrative, a novel about imaginary politicians; ***political philosophy***, that department of philosophy which treats of politics or public ethics; hence ***political philosopher***; ***political police***, a police force concerned with offences against the state; ***political prisoner***, a person imprisoned for a political offence; ***political refugee***, a refugee from an oppressive government; ***political science***, the study of the factors involved in politics (see politic *sb.* 3) or the scientific analysis of political activity and behaviour; hence ***political scientist***; ***political sociology*** (see quot. 1968); hence ***political sociologist***; ***political theory***, theory that is concerned with philosophical ideas of political power and with the history, forms, and activity of the state; hence ***political theorist***; ***political trial***, a trial of a defendant charged with a political offence, or a trial conducted for political reasons; ***political verse***, in Byzantine and mod. Gr. literature (Gr. *πολιτικός* popular), verse composed by accent, not quantity, with an accent on the last syllable but one, esp. an iambic verse of this kind of fifteen syllables; ***political warfare***, propaganda against another state, calculated to weaken it.

1776 W. Ellis tr. *Aristotle's Treat. Govt.* I. ii. 6 Hence it is evident, that a city is a natural production, and that man is naturally a *political animal. **1892** I. Zangwill *Childr. Ghetto* II. 113 The East End Jew is only slowly becoming a political animal. **1960** *Victorian Studies* June 348 Characters who necessarily act and feel as isolated individuals as well as political animals. **1968** L. Durrell *Tunc* II. 89 If we get in again it will be to try and prove .. that the key to the political animal is magnanimity. **1975** *Times* 17 July 19/1 Lady Young is .. very much a political animal. **1970** A. M. S. Smith tr. *Balandier's Polit. Anthrop.* p. vii, This book is also intended to show how *political anthropology is contributing to a clearer definition and a better knowledge of the political field. **1975** in Beattie & Lienhardt *Stud. in Soc. Anthrop.* xiv. 336 What Evans-Pritchard treated as no more than one sub-system among others .. now seems .. to have become a specialization on its own, a 'political anthropology'. **1682** Petty *Tracts rel. Ireland* (1769) 90 (*title*) Essay in *Political Arithmetick, concerning the Growth of the City of London. **1710** J. Harris *Lex. Techn.* II, *Political Arithmetick*, is the Application of Arithmetical Calculations to the Extent and Value of Lands, Number of People, Publick Revenues, Taxes, Commerce, Manufactures, or whatever relates to the Power, Strength, Riches, &c. of any Nation or Common-wealth. **1735–7** Berkeley *Querist* §530 Whether a little reflection and a little political arithmetic may not shew us our mistake? **1954** *Times* 14 Dec. 9/3 A steady consensus of judicial interpretation sustains the tradition of *political asylum. **1962** *Weekly Law Reports* III. 1016 *Per* Viscount Radcliffe. In my opinion the idea that lies behind the phrase 'offence of a political character' is .. the analogy of .. 'political refugee', 'political asylum' or 'political prisoner'. It does indicate .. that the requesting State is after him for reasons other than the enforcement of criminal law. **1973** *Ann. Reg. 1972* I. iii. 25 Two officers of the Royal Moroccan Air Force .. arrived in Gibraltar and sought political asylum. **1937** E. Snow *Red Star over China* VIII. vi. 299 The discussion continued for over an hour. Occasionally the commander or *political commissar interrupted to summarize what had been said. **1956** F. F. Liu *Milit. Hist. Mod. China* ii. 19 The Kuomintang .. adopted a plan of gathering armed forces .. and then inserting trained political commissars at the various levels of the newly absorbed groups. **1965** J. Ch'ên *Mao & Chinese Revolution* (1967) I. viii. 175 At Iyang there was the 10th Red Army under Fang Chih-min with Shao Shih-p'ing as the political commissar. **1978** H. McLeave *Borderline Case* (1979) xiii. 134 Yao was a political commissar and was running a military setup. **1706** Phillips s.v. *Day*, The Parts of a *Political or Civil Day. [**1615** Antoine de Montchrestien (*title*) Traicte de l'Œconomie Politique.] **1740** Ld. Westmoreland in Johnson *Debates* (1787) I. 109 As in private life, so in *political œconomy, the demands of necessity are easily supplied. **1767–** [see economy 3]. **1971** *Financial Mail* (Johannesburg) 26 Feb. 673/3 The whole question of new negotiations seems to have become a *political football and little more. **1975** *Australasian Express* 27 Mar. 7/1 In a strong attack, Mr Perkins claimed Aborigines were a 'political football' in Australia. **1977** *New Scientist* 17 Mar. 641/2 Recombinant DNA research is rapidly assuming the shape of a political football. **1883** E. W. Hamilton *Diary* 18 Mar. (1972) II. 411 Lady Hayter has played the part of *political hostess this year excellently well. **1944** C. Dilke in *Wine & Food* Spring 24 The house of a well-known political hostess. **1977** J. Aiken *Last Movement* v. 92 Her .. husband had suddenly ditched her in favour of a fat blonde political hostess. **1827** J. S. Mill in *Arch. f. Sozialwissensch.* (1929) 450 There always ought to be .. a certain difference of opinion in every ministry. Let any one consider what the effect would be if the contrary maxim were received as a rule of *political morality. **1861** —— *Repr. Govt.* x. 193 Undoubtedly neither this nor any other maxim of political morality is absolutely inviolable. **1866** *Times* 26 June 6/3 *Felix Holt, the Radical*, is not .. a *political novel, though it necessarily touches on politics. **1976** *Hiroshima Stud. Eng. Lang. & Lit.* XXI. 69 It [*sc.* Nostromo] is regarded as a 'political novel', a 'historical novel' or a 'philosophical novel'. **1833** Lytton *England & English* II. 338 It is necessary .. to distinguish between Mr. Bentham's practical conclusions .. and his systematic views as a *political philosopher. **1924** V. L. O. Chittick *T. C. Haliburton* xiii. 326 It was unquestionably not Sam Slick the political philosopher .. that gave to his 'Sayings and Doings' the surprising vogue they formerly enjoyed. **1961** Kaplan & Katzenbach *Pol. Foundation of Internat. Law* I. iii. 64 Political philosophers will recognize its origins in the rejected doctrines of Hobbes. **1785** W. Paley (*title*) The principles of moral and *political philosophy. **1825** J. S. Mill in *Westm. Rev.* Apr. 286 The general question, to what extent restraints upon the freedom of the press can be considered as warranted by sound principles of political philosophy. **1958** A. R. Radcliffe-Brown *Method in Social Anthropology* II. i. 139 There is an abundant literature on the subjects of social philosophy, political philosophy, .. and the philosophy of art. **1976** *Listener* 3 June 705/1 There has been a real revival in political philosophy .. particularly .. in the U.S.A. **1910** R. Anderson *Lighter Side of my Official Life* xv. 246 Before coming to England as Ambassador, Count Schouvaloff was head of the *Political Police at St. Petersburg. **1953** *Encounter* Oct. 67/1 Never during the Stalin era was the political police charged with illegal extortion of evidence. **1974** J. White tr. *Poulantzas's Fascism & Dictatorship* VII. v. 341 None of this reorganization of the State apparatus can be understood without taking into account the growing and dominant role of the political police. **1860** Dickens in *All Yr. Round* 13 Oct. 14/2 All the town knew about the Englishman and his *political prisoner. **1927** B. Russell *Outl. Philos.* iii. 44 Perhaps in time the State will perform these experiments with the children of political prisoners. **1972** *Guardian* 8 May 1/2 The loyalists have already sent a letter to Mr Whitelaw demanding political prisoner status. **1941** Koestler *Scum of Earth* 137 Paragraph 19 of the Armistice Treaty, providing for the extradition of *political refugees. **1974** N. Freeling *Dressing of Diamond* 48 Marrying a political refugee .. hadn't done him any good. **1779** Hume *Dial. Nat. Relig.* I. 16 This is their practice in all natural, mathematical, moral, and *political science. **1794** A. Ferguson *Princ. Moral & Polit. Sci.* II. II. vi. 411 *Salus populi, suprema lex esto*, is the fundamental principle of political science. **1836** J. S. Mill *Ess. Pol. Econ.* (1844) v. 146 This we can seldom do in ethical, and scarcely ever in political science. We cannot try forces of government and systems of national policy on a diminutive scale in our laboratories. **1898** G. B. Shaw *Let.* 18 Oct. (1972) II. 66 You and I have been confronted often enough with the follies of current political science. **1958** A. R. Radcliffe-Brown *Method in Social Anthropology* I. iv. 102 Political systems, economic systems, and systems of law are studied in social anthropology and also in economics, political science and jurisprudence. **1974** A. Barbrook *Patterns Polit. Behav.* i. 3 We have been left with a considerable range of behavioural theory, some of which has been completely accepted into the methodology of political science. **1902** *Amer. Jrnl. Sociol.* Jan. 564 There is not a political evolution through steps a, b, c, d, etc., which the *political scientist can account for. **1974** *Listener* 24 Oct. 578/1 Professor Richard Rose .. is the most productive political scientist in Britain. **1972** Dowse & Hughes *Political Sociol.* i. 7 As a matter of fact *political sociologists do tend to concentrate on seeing in what ways society affects the state. **1957** *Current Sociol.* VI. 79 *Political sociology is one of these recent additions. The label is perhaps more novel than the field. **1968** *Encycl. Soc. Sci.* XII. 298/2 Broadly conceived, political sociology is concerned with the social basis of power in all institutional sectors of society. In this tradition, political sociology deals with patterns of social stratification and their consequences in organized politics... By contrast, in narrower terms, political sociology focuses on the organizational analysis of political groups and .. leadership. **1977** W. J. Goode *Princ. Sociol.* xiii. 399/2 Political sociology and political science as special fields have overlapped comfortably for several decades. **1951** D. Easton in Gould & Thursby *Contemp. Polit. Thought* (1969) xvii. 309 Speculations of the best *political theorists have always been founded on acute observations of the contemporary political scene and a knowledge of human history. **1896** J. N. Figgis *Divine Right of Kings* x. 256 It is a far cry from the conception expressed in the Holy Roman Empire, that theology is the source of *political theory. **1974** H. M. Drucker *Pol. Uses of Ideology* iv. 37 When a political theory points out that one kind of political system has such an advantage over another, we prefer the former. **1973** *Listener* 14 June 793/1 Every *political trial has a long hidden history of what went on behind the scenes. **1974** J. Banning *How I fooled World* xi. 52 There were the political trials in Czechoslovakia. **1780** Harris *Philol. Inq.* II. ii. Wks. (1841) 410 There are *political verses of the same barbarous character by Constantinus Manasses, John Tzetzes, and others of that period. **1788** Gibbon *Decl. & F.* liii. (1828) VII. 132 [Byzantine poets] confound all measure of feet and syllables in the impotent strains which have received the name of political or city verses. **1950** *Chambers's Encycl.* XI. 254/2 In 1941 .. Eden, .. Bracken, the minister of information, and Dalton, who supervised propaganda to the enemy, constituted a *Political Warfare Executive. **1977** E. Ambler *Send no more Roses* iv. 70 The only higher-ups who took any real interest in our findings were the political warfare people.

7. In *Comb.*, prefixed to an adj. to denote: **a.** 'politically, as applied to politics', as ***political-ethical***, ***-moral***, ***-strategic***; **b.** 'political and ...', as ***political-bureaucratic***, ***-cultural***, ***-economic***, ***-juridical***, ***-military***, ***-religious***, ***-social***.

1970 C. Furtado in I. L. Horowitz *Masses in Lat. Amer.* ii. 31 The political-bureaucratic structure exterted [*sic*] a strong influence within the society. **1959** C. W. Mills in —— *New Sociology* (1964) 85 [The] joint political-cultural struggle must be waged in intellectual and moral ways. **1937** *Science & Society* I. 153 There are abundant instances of the relation between 'standard' speech and the political-economic character of the ruling class. **1970** J. Cotler in I. L. Horowitz *Masses in Lat. Amer.* xii. 437 Due to the political-economic limitations in Mancha India, social opportunities for the Cholo are somewhat limited. **1936** L. Wirth in K. Mannheim *Ideology & Utopia* p. xviii, Political-ethical norms not only cannot be derived from the direct contemplation of the facts, but themselves exert a moulding influence upon the very modes of perceiving the facts. **1971** R. apRoberts *Trollope* iv. 78 The political-ethical dilemmas of that novel [sc. *Ralph the Heir*]. **1919** J. T. Garvin *Econ. Foundations of Peace* x. 231 The means .. will not be provided by the political-juridical part of the coming Constitution of the League. **1965** H. Kahn *On Escalation* vi. 125 Its possible worth in fulfilling European political-military objectives. **1970** H. Trevelyan *Middle East in Revolution* p. x, The withdrawal from Aden was a political-military operation conducted jointly by Headquarters, Middle East and the High Commission. **1953** S. Spender *Creative Element* 9 In the 1930's .. I wrote of a 'political-moral' theme in modern literature. **1970** R. Stavenhagen in I. L. Horowitz *Masses in Lat. Amer.* vii. 259 Individual economic pre-eminence .. arises, individually, through positions held in the political-religious structure. **1965** *English Studies* XLVI. 395 Melville is working in cosmic-religious, rather than political-social, terms. **1965** H. Kahn *On Escalation* vi. 122 It is not an improbable international political-strategic order for the future.

B. *sb.* (elliptical use of the adj.)

1. A political person; in various senses: **a.** = Political agent, officer, resident: see above, 1 b.
1848 SIR H. B. EDWARDES in Lady Edwardes *Mem.* (1888) I. 152 Another of your Lordship's 'young politicals' joined me in the middle of all this fighting, Edward Lake. **1856** J. W. COLE *Mem. Brit. Gen. Penin. War* I. ii. 71 He was superseded..by a 'political', who..involved him in a carte and tierce correspondence with the Madras officials. **1898** GEO. SMITH *12 Indian Statesm.* ii. 27 A man of action, whether as a soldier, a 'political' in the Anglo-Indian sense, or an administrator. **1926** [see FIDDLY *a.*]. **1939** *Times* 1 Aug. 13/3 Sir John Maffey..was an Indian political. **1958** L. DURRELL *Mountolive* iv. 91 Pursewarden as political feels that the Embassy has also in a way inherited Maskelyne's department. **1979** C. ALLEN *Tales from Dark Continent* viii. 110 Most administrators—other than the Sudan politicals—regarded themselves as badly paid.

b. A politician; a political writer. *rare*$^{-1}$.
1857 GEN. P. THOMPSON *Audi Alt.* II. App. 97 If there is a heaven for politicals, you and I, Sir, will ask for a corner of the Tory bench.

c. = *political prisoner*: see above, 6.
1888 *Century Mag.* XXXV. 402 Politicals suffering from nervous affections,..are often put in the same ward with insane criminals. **1895** *Westm. Gaz.* 16 Mar. 2/3 The flogging of politicals, and their degradation to the general treatment of thieves and murderers. **1938** *New Statesman* 19 Feb. 273/2 There are only 15 'politicals' still in gaol in the United Provinces and only 26 in Bihar. **1968** *Guardian* 22 Nov. 9/4 We started off being D Group prisoners, the lowest grade which only applies to politicals.

†**2.** *pl.* Political matters, politics. *Obs.*
1621 BP. MOUNTAGU *Diatribæ* 521 Alway in Naturalls: sometime in Politicalls. *a* **1734** NORTH *Lives* (1826) III. 308 He held a due respect to superiors, especially in politicals.

Hence **po'liticalism**, political activity or partisanship; **po'liticalize** *v.* (*a*) *trans.* to make or render political; (*b*) *intr.* to practise or discourse on politics; **po,liticali'zation**, the action of making political.
1846 WORCESTER, *Politicalism*..(*Ch. Ob.*). **1869** *Contemp. Rev.* X. 11 If you continue to allow him to politicalize in your paper. **1902** *19th Cent. & after* Nov. 733 In America the politicalisation can do more harm than elsewhere. **1935** *Sun* (Baltimore) 19 Dec. 12/1 The current strong tendency toward politicalization of the intellectuals. **1947** *Partisan Rev.* XIV. 485 The ever-growing politicalization of intellectual life makes more and more difficult a disinterested theoretical approach. **1959** *Times Lit. Suppl.* 5 June 330/4 This is what Professor Marcuse calls the 'externalization' or the 'politicalization' of ethics. **1974** *Nature* 1 Mar. 1/1 A move toward what NIH scientists refer to as 'politicalisation of research'.

politicalized, *ppl. a.* [f. POLITICALIZE *v.*] Made political in character.
1926 *Public Opinion* 13 Aug. 147/3 We are to have a politicalised Civil Service in this country. **1949** *Sun* (Baltimore) 19 Nov. 6/1 Does Congress wish to encourage big credit-seekers to turn..to a kind of politicalized or socialized banking setup?

po'litically, *adv.* [f. POLITICAL *a.* (*sb.*) + -LY^2.]
†**1.** In a politic manner; = POLITICLY. *Obs.*
1588 *Exhort. Her Majesty's Faithf. Subj.* in *Harl. Misc.* (Malh.) II. 95 The general musters, and training up of men, most prudently and politically commanded. **1764** GOLDSM. *Hist. Eng. in Lett.* (1772) I. 226 Henry politically pretended the utmost submission to the pope's decrees. **1796** BURNEY *Mem. Metastasio* II. 348 The protest..was only made politically, in order to deprecate my vengeance.

2. a. In a political manner; in respect of politics; from a political point of view.
a **1638** MEDE *Daniels Weeks* xxvii. Wks. (1672) 707 They should serve them not religiously, but politically, inasmuch as they were to become Slaves and Vassals to Idolatrous Nations. **1750** CHESTERF. *Let. to Son* 19 Mar., Never lose view of..the political affairs of Europe. Follow them politically, chronologically, and geographically, through the newspapers. **1841** MIALL in *Nonconf.* I. 1 A national establishment of religion is essentially vicious in its constitution—philosophically, politically and religiously. **1868** FREEMAN *Norm. Conq.* II. vii. 91 That part of the old Danish realm..which is now politically part of Sweden.

†**b.** As an organized state. *Obs.*
1779–81 JOHNSON *L.P., Pope* Wks. IV. 73 Society, politically regulated, is a state contra-distinguished from a state of nature.

3. *Comb.*, as ***politically-active***, ***-inclined***, ***-minded***, ***-motivated*** adjs.
1974 *Disturbances Univ. of Essex: Rep. Annan Enquiry* 17 Students protested that politically active ringleaders were singled out. **1969** J. MANDER *Static Soc.* iii. 95 Enough for the politically-inclined tourist. **1907** *Westm. Gaz.* 11 Dec. 2/1 The politically-minded stay-at-home citizen. **1973** W. J. BURLEY *Death in Salubrious Place* iv. 73 The suave, politically-minded Bellings. **1972** *Listener* 21 Dec. 854/2 A rising level of politically-motivated violence. **1975** *Ibid.* 21 Aug. 233/2 We are not dealing with..an irresponsible, politically-motivated organisation in trade unions.

So **po'liticalness**. *rare.*
1678 CUDWORTH *Intell. Syst.* I. v. 890 Not so much as any the least *seeds*, either of Politicalness, or Ethicalness at all in it. **1727** BAILEY vol. II, *Politicalness*, political quality. **1935** *Discovery* May 128/2 Notwithstanding all his politicalness and his zest for the letters and society..it is in the campaigns and battles that Mr Trevelyan is happiest.

politicaster (pəʊlɪtɪ'kæstə(r)). *rare.* [ad. It. (or Sp.) *politicastro*: see POLITIC B. and -ASTER.] A petty, feeble, or contemptible politician.
1641 MILTON *Reform.* II. Wks. 1851 III. 56 Though all the Tribe of Aphorismers, and Politicasters would perswade us there be..reasons against it. **1805** W. TAYLOR in *Ann. Rev.* III. 200 But those politicasters who to Spain are not just, will to Germany not be generous. **1892** *Pall Mall G.* 25 Nov. 2/2 The country is very sick of the parliamentary squabbles of politicasters.

politician (pɒlɪ'tɪʃən). Forms: 6 **politicien, -itien,** 7 **-isian, -ition, poll-,** 7– **politician,** (7–8 **-itian**). [f. as POLITIC + -IAN. So F. *politicien*.]
†**1.** A politic person; chiefly in a sinister sense, a shrewd schemer; a crafty plotter or intriguer. *Obs.*
1588 SIR W. STANLEY *Dr. Allen's Seditious Drifts* 89 Some ouersights euen in pollicie, escaped this great politicien. **1592** NASHE *P. Penilesse* A ij b, The Diuel..was..so famous a Politician in purchasing, that Hel, which at the beginning was but an obscure Village, is now become a huge citie. **1596** SHAKS. *1 Hen. IV*, I. iii. 241, I am whipt and scourg'd with rods, Netled, and stung with Pismires, when I heare Of this vile Politician Bullingbrooke. **1613** CHAPMAN *Rev. B. D'Ambois* I. i. Plays 1873 II. 119 This was a sleight well maskt. O what is man Vnlesse he be a Politician. **1749** FIELDING *Tom Jones* VI. ii, The squire..was, however, in many points, a perfect politician. **1764** FOOTE *Patron* III. Wks. 1799 I. 352 Ah, Bever, Bever! you are a miserable politician. Do you know, now, that this is the luckiest incident that ever occurr'd?

2. One versed in the theory or science of government and the art of governing; one skilled in politics; one practically engaged in conducting the business of the state; a statesman.
1589 PUTTENHAM *Eng. Poesie* I. iii. (Arb.) 23 Poets..were the first lawmakers to the people, and the first polititiens, deuising all expedient meanes for th'establishment of Common wealth. **1634** W. TIRWHYT tr. *Balzac's Lett.* (vol. I.) 33 That felicity Politisians search after, as being the end of civil life. **1696** PHILLIPS (ed. 5), *Politician*, one that understands the Art of Governing, or judges of it according to the Parts he has acquired. **1765** BLACKSTONE *Comm.* I. Introd. 96 Sir Edward Coke, and the politicians of that time, conceived great difficulties in carrying on the projected union. **1886** M. ARNOLD in *Times* 22 May 15/6 Lord Salisbury's bad and arbitrary temper (I mean, of course, as a politician,..) is as great a misfortune to the country as Lord Randolph Churchill's intriguing.

b. One keenly interested in politics; one who engages in party politics, or in political strife, or who makes politics his profession or business; also (esp. in *U.S.*), in a sinister sense, one who lives by politics as a trade.
1628 FORD *Lover's Mel.* IV. ii, So politicians thrive, That with their crabbed faces, and sly tricks,..do wriggle in Their heads first, like a fox, to rooms of state. **1632** HEYWOOD *2nd Pt. Iron Age* Wks. 1874 IV. 364, I am a pollitician, oathes with me Are but the tooles I worke with, I may breake An oath by my profession. **1646** BUCK *Rich. III*, I. 17 Lewis..was meerly a Politician, and studied only his owne ends. *a* **1732** GAY *Fables* II. ix. 14 Politicians you suggest, Should drive the nail that goes the best. **1776** ADAM SMITH *W. Nat.* IV. ii. (1869) II. 41 That insidious and crafty animal, vulgarly called a statesman or politician, whose councils are directed by the momentary fluctuations of affairs. **1828** MACAULAY *Hallam* Ess. (1887) 96 A politician, where factions run high, is interested not for the whole people, but for his own section of it. **1879** SIR G. CAMPBELL *White & Black* 68 The word 'politician' is used in a bad sense in America, as applied to people who make politics a profession, and are skilled in the art of 'wire pulling' and such practices.

†**3.** = POLITIQUE, POLITIC B. 1 b. *Obs.*
1656 M. CASAUBON *Enthus.* iii. 171 The use of this Theologie, doth most properly belong unto Jesuits,..and Jesuited Politicians, whether they call themselves Lutherans, or Calvinists, or otherwise. **1672** [H. STUBBE] *Rosemary & Bayes* 7 The Ecclesiastical Polititian writ in England. **1681** BAXTER *Acc. Sherlocke* iv. 189 Their minuter differences have made some called Lutherans,..some Independents, and some Politicians or Erastians.

4. (See quot.)
1868 WOOD *Homes without H.* xiii. 247 The White-Eyed Flycatcher (*Muscicapa cantrix*)..uses so much newspaper in the construction of its home, that it has gone by the name of Politician.

5. *attrib.*
1638 R. BAKER tr. *Balzac's Lett.* (vol. III.) 43 This is one of your politician subtleties, to make Angoulesme passe for a Frontier Towne. **1671** MILTON *Samson* 1195 Your ill-meaning Politician Lords,..Appointed to await me thirty spies. **1885** A. FORBES *Souvenirs Continents* 247 A turbulent ..sea of political or rather politician quasi-social life.

Hence (*nonce-wds.*) **poli'ticianess**, a female politician; **poli'ticianism**, practice characteristic of a politician; **poli'ticianize** *v. trans.*, to involve in party politics.
1887 *Sat. Rev.* 11 June 833/1 Mr. Lawson, and the other Radical politicians and *politicianesses who went out for to see what was to be seen at Bodyke. **1843** R. PAUL *Let.* 15 Aug. in *Mem.* xiii. (1872) 168 Lord Aberdeen has got his bill passed. It is a mere piece of *politicianism. **1893** *Resolution* in *Voice* (N.Y.) 26 Oct., The corrupt ring that has bound this city hand and foot,..*politicianizing the public schools and perpetrating bold, gigantic robberies upon the taxpayers.

†**poli'ticious,** *a. Obs.* Also 9 **-itious.** [irreg. f. *politic* or *politici-an* + -OUS.] Politic; political.
1638 SIR T. HERBERT *Trav.* (ed. 2) 171, I could..perceive that Mahomitan Princes are terrible crafty or mysteriously politicious. **1818** SCOTT *Hrt. Midl.* xii, One of the public and polititious warldly-wise men that stude up to prevent ane general owning of the cause in the day of power.

po'liticist (-sɪst). *rare.* [f. POLITIC + -IST.] A student of political science: see quot.
1885 SEELEY *Pol. Sc.* (1896) i. 26 The historian,..according to me, is distinct. He is not an anthropologist or an ethnologist, but if I may coin a word, he is a politicist. The political group or organism—the state—is his study.

politicization (pəʊ,lɪtɪsaɪ'zeɪʃən, pə-). [f. POLITICIZE *v.*] The action or process of rendering political or of establishing upon a political basis; the fact of being politicized.
1934 *Times Lit. Suppl.* 25 Oct. 724/2 The attempted politicization of the German Protestant Church. **1938** *Downside Rev.* LVI. 384 The totalitarian supremacy of the State is the outcome of that 'total politicization' of man and his activities which was of the essence of Marxist theory. **1962** *Times Lit. Suppl.* 4 May 308/1 The politicization of private life. **1968** *Internat. Encycl. Soc. Sci.* X. 284 The major political process of recent years [in 'Middle America'] has been referred to as 'politicization', the recognition of the State as the ultimate authority and the recognition of legitimacy of certain governmental processes. **1976** F. ZWEIG *New Acquisitive Society* I. v. 57 The rapidly growing 'pressure group' movement..definitely leads to politicization of economic life. **1978** *Listener* 2 Nov. 564/2 Politicisation does not mean mere organised political activity... Politicisation of religion means the internal transformation of the faith itself, so that..it becomes..concerned with social morality rather than with the ethereal qualities of immortality.

politicize (pəʊ'lɪtɪsaɪz, pə-), *v.* [f. as POLITIC + -IZE.]
1. *intr.* To act the politician; to discourse on or engage in politics.
1758 H. WALPOLE *Let. to Mann* 11 June, But while I am politicising, I forget to tell you half the purport of my letter. **1759** *Ibid.* 13 Sept., Not to politicize too much, I believe the world will come to be fought for somewhere between the North of Germany and the back of Canada. **1840** CARLYLE *Heroes* v. (1872) 177 Burns..could have governed, debated in National Assemblies; politicised, as few could. **1892** *Pall Mall G.* 3 Dec. 2/2 We talk and squabble and politicize about education as a vote-catching agency.

2. *trans.* To render political, give a political character to.
1846 GROTE *Greece* I. xi. I. 285 It was the tendency of the enlightened men of Athens, from the days of Solôn downwards, to refine and politicise the character of Thêseus. *Ibid.* xiv. 351 Conôn..historicises and politicises the whole legend. **1887** *Hour Glass* I. 60 The opinion of a literature-taster..whose intellectual palate is so 'politicised' that he detects a smack of the hustings where there is none. **1962** S. E. FINER *Man on Horseback* xii. 236 Such parties..seek to dominate and politicize all politically important voluntary bodies outside their ranks. **1970** *Guardian* 5 June 11/7 The skinheads who Mr Powell has managed to politicise. **1978** *Time* 3 July 38/1 We're not out to politicize the White House..but we've got to use the political resources we have better than before.

Hence **po'liticized** *ppl. a.*, interested or involved in politics, politically motivated; **po'liticizing** *ppl. a.* and *vbl. sb.*, talking politics, the action or process of rendering political.
1848 *Blackw. Mag.* LXIII. 578 Besides the politicising and haranguing crowds..your course is hemmed by countless others. **1887** *Contemp. Rev.* Nov. 711 Politicizing sophists threaten to be a perfect curse to India. **1887** [see POLITICIZE *v.* 2]. **1971** *Daily Tel.* 17 Aug. 10 Any danger in this arises from the majority of viewers being..unaware of the bias as they watch it because most people are manifestly less politicised. **1975** R. BUTT in Cox & Boyson *Black Paper 1975* 43/1 In this single statement, the politicizing of education in an entirely new sense—namely that it is now the vehicle used by those who, in varying degrees, wish to change the cultural basis of society—is explicit. **1977** *N.Y. Rev. Bks.* 12 May 50/4 (Advt.), I am a politicized, socialist, would-be scholar deeply isolated from academic radicalism.

politicking ('pɒlɪtɪkɪŋ), *vbl. sb.* [f. POLITIC *v.* or POLITIC *a.* and *sb.* + -ING^1.] The action or fact of engaging in (esp. partisan) political activity.
1928 M. H. WESEEN *Crowell's Dict. Eng. Gram.* 481 *Politicking*, a coined word that has no recognized standing. **1934** *Sun* (Baltimore) 10 July 1/3 Mr. Farley..confided to 'the boys' that he expects to do considerable 'politicking' along the way. **1943** *Sat. Even. Post* 30 Jan. 90/2 The politicking had started the minute his back was turned. **1957** *Economist* 5 Oct. 15/2 To dangle before the tenants..the idea that a Labour government will 'promptly' redress their grievances..might politely be described as politicking. **1975** F. HEER *Charlemagne & his World* x. 149 This is the elevated ideal that lay behind all the politicking and manoeuvering for position that took place in Rome in 800.

†'**politicless,** *a. Obs. rare*$^{-1}$. [f. POLITIC *a.* or *sb.* + -LESS.] Void of policy; impolitic.
1556 J. HEYWOOD *Spider & F.* lxix. 34 Betwene his politikelesse pittie (erst saide) And his pitteles polisie, (here erst laide).

politicly ('pɒlɪtɪklɪ), *adv.* [f. POLITIC *a.* + -LY^2.] In a politic manner; with policy or skilful management; shrewdly; artfully, craftily.
1477 SIR J. PASTON in *P. Lett.* III. 188, I thynke notte a mater..weell handelyd, nor poletykly dalte with. **1536** *Act 28 Hen. VIII*, c. 7 §9 Your maiestie most victoriousely prudently politikely and indifferently hath..ruled this realme. *a* **1548** HALL *Chron., Edw. IV* 230 The allegacions were well proued by the Englishmen, and pollitiquely defended by the Frenche men. **1603** KNOLLES *Hist. Turks* 255 The death of Mahomet had been politiquely concealed one and fortie daies. **1701** DE FOE *True-born Eng.* 5 They rule so politickly and so well. **1808** E. S. BARRETT *Miss-led General* 147 As if he had purposely and politicly selected them as a foil to himself. **1868** HOLME LEE *B. Godfrey* l, He had politicly relaxed a little towards her.

‖**politico** (po'litiko, pə'lɪtɪkəʊ). Pl. **politicoes, politicos.** [It. or Sp. *politico* politic, a politician.] A politician: chiefly with bad connotation.

Also, a political agent; a person holding strong political views.

1630 *R. Johnson's Kingd. & Commw.* A ij b, The nimblest Politico's of these active times. 1659 GAUDEN *Tears Ch.* II. xxxii. 256 He is counted cunning, a meere politico, a time-server, an hypocrite. 1692 *Vindication* Pref. A ij, Methinks I hear now our cautious Politico's asking, What ayls this Person? 1893 F. ADAMS *New Egypt* 129 Academic London politicos. 1929 *Times* 14 Aug. 11/4 The old 'politicos' and the members of the more progressive parties, may be recommended to remember the object-lesson of the fate of the Aventine Opposition in Italy. 1941 E. WILSON *Wound & Bow* v. 215 Going back over Hemingway's books to-day, we can see clearly what an error of the politicos it was to accuse him of an indifference to society. 1951 I. ASIMOV *Foundation* v. xiii. 218 You're an old dog of a politico. 1955 J. CARY *Not Honour More* 42 It's a lot deeper than politics. And I wish you'd get all these politicos out of my house. 1956 W. LEWIS *Red Priest* xxvii. 229 'The Mahatma was a very unusual man.' Father Makepeace replied. 'I referred to ordinary politicos.' 'There are no ordinary politicos in India,' said the elderly interrupter. 1958 *Listener* 18 Sept. 436/1 On Channel One..it was colour-bar week, with the Jamaican politico, Norman Manley, given a starring role. 1960 *Guardian* 8 Mar. 1/5 The press is here..and surprisingly important politicoes in ineffective disguises. 1967 *Observer* 26 Mar. 9 Hippies are sympathetic, but they are not politicos. 1973 *Black Panther* 11 Aug. 8/2 While publicly apologizing for Nixon, Colson managed to privately leak that the politicos Haldeman and Ehrlichman were guilty along with Mitchell and Dean. 1975 D. LODGE *Changing Places* iv. 145 Politicoes, frat rats, sallys and jocks and mommas for peace are..touching each other's hearts.

politico-, combining form of Gr. πολιτικό-ς civil, political, prefixed to an adj. to denote **a.** 'politically, as applied to politics', as ***politico-aesthetic***, ***-arithmetical***, ***-artistic***, ***ethical***, ***-geographical***, ***-moral***, ***-mythic***, ***-orthodox***, ***-Philistine***, ***-racial***; **b.** 'political and...', as ***politico-bureaucratic***, ***-commercial***, ***-criminal***, ***-diplomatic***, ***ecclesiastical***, ***-judicial***, ***-legal***, ***-literary***, ***-military***, ***-peripatetic***, ***-philosophical***, ***-physiographical***, ***-religious***, ***-sacerdotal***, ***-scientific***, ***-social***, ***-theological***; also used to form sbs., as ***politico'mania***, a mania for politics; ***politico'phobia***, a horror of politics.

In sense a used in the formation of adjectives from phrases containing *political*: e.g. from *political arithmetic*, *politico-arithmetical*; from *political economy*, *politico-economical*.

1974 *Times* 8 Jan. 14/6 Almost immediately he started giving long and fiery *politico-aesthetic lectures to adoring left-wing students. 1815 J. LAWRENCE in *Monthly Mag.* XXXVIII. 21 Of.. greater weight in the *politico-arithmetical scale. 1961 *Times* 31 Oct. 14/3 *Accatone* [*sc.* a film]..has become the subject of one of those *politico-artistic controversies. 1964 P. WORSLEY in I. C. Horowitz *New Sociology* 377 *Politico-bureaucratic machines are in the saddle from the beginning, and there is no 'heroic' period of Cuban-type mass participation in government. 1881 *Nature* XXIII. 420/2 The construction of the *politico-commercial road from Darjiling to the Jyalap Pass. 1955 D. W. MAURER in *Publ. Amer. Dial. Soc.* XXIV. 26 Very good connections with the *politico-criminal liaison,.. which extends like a network across the country. 1856 DICKENS *Little Dorrit* (1857) I. x. 84 He fully understood the Department to be a *politico diplomatico hocus pocus piece of machinery. 1973 P. A. ALLUM *Politics & Society in Post-War Naples* vii. 219 Their electoral and personal politico-diplomatic activities cannot be justified in straight *Gesellschaft* normative language. 1811 I. MILNER in *Life* xxiii. (1842) 467 Ecclesiastical and *politico-ecclesiastical questions of great magnitude. 1884 H. SPENCER in *Contemp. Rev.* July 45 Study of men's *politico-ethical ideas and sentiments. 1805 *Edin. Rev.* VI. 468 Mr. Cockburn's *politico-geographical sketch. 1825 BENTHAM *Offic. Apt. Maximized, Indic.* (1830) 76 One *politico-judicial virtue his lordship has. 1926 GALSWORTHY *Silver Spoon* I. ii. 9 Lady Alison's *politico-legal coterie no longer counted. 1970 B. BREWSTER tr. *Althusser & Balibar's Reading Capital* II. v. 133 In fact, this is to attribute to the concept 'superstructure' a breadth Marx never allowed, for he only ranged within it: (1) the politico-legal superstructure, and (2) the ideological superstructure. 1924 GALSWORTHY *White Monkey* 73 She..picked out the biggest 'bug', *politico-literary, and waited to pin him. 1978 D. DAICHES *Edinburgh* x. 182 There was some pretty savage politico-literary fighting, especially in the Tory *Blackwood's*. 1785 *Eng. Rev.* VI. 349 The *Politico-mania, and passion for news, our author alledges are unfavourable to literature. 1853 TH. ROSS *Humboldt's Trav.* III. xxxi. 230 In all the Spanish possessions in America, we must distinguish between the ecclesiastic, *politico-military, and financial divisions. 1931 *Times Lit. Suppl.* 29 Oct. 827/1 One of the objects of the Prussian campaign, a masterpiece of politico-military strategy, was to separate Prussia and Saxony. 1975 *Times* 1 Dec. 10/5 The then politico-military concepts of revolutionary war. 1875 H. C. WOOD *Therap.* (1879) 128 The question..is at present a very serious one, involving.. many moral and *politico-moral issues. 1920 B. RUSSELL *Pract. & Theory Bolshevism* I. ii. 30 The sincere Communists..are not unlike the Puritan soldiers in their stern politico-moral purpose. 1965 *Mod. Law Rev.* XXVIII. v. 536 There would seem to be much more force in Professor H. L. A. Hart's argument that the judges do not know or at least cannot evaluate what the 'politico-moral' principles behind their decisions are. 1974 *Publishers Weekly* 4 Nov. 62/1 This *politico-mythic tale..expresses wishes rather than facts. 1802 SYD. SMITH *Wks.* (1850) 7 This *politico-orthodox rage in the mouth of a preacher may be profitable as well as sincere. 1749 FIELDING *Tom Jones* VI. ii, Those wise tenets,..so well inculcated in that *Politico-Peripatetic school of Exchange-alley. 1960 *Times* 3 Oct. 13/3 They [*sc.* universities] may save themselves from the *politico-Philistine interference they fear. 1936 *New Yorker* 14 Mar. 24/1 Proletarianism..superimposed on some remarkably interesting *politico-philosophical formulae. 1973 *Nation Rev.* (Melbourne) 31 Aug. 1455/2 These uncertainties..are the ruination of most politico-philosophical series. 1830 HAY & BELFRAGE *Mem. A. Waugh* iii. (1839) 225 Many others displayed unmanly fears and the horrors of a *politicophobia. 1935 *Univ. Mich. Publ. Lang. & Lit.* XIII. 43 South of this point it coincides with the strong *politico-physiographical frontier already indicated. 1959 *Times Lit. Suppl.* 22 May 303/3 Lynchings and murders and other forms of *politico-racial violence have significantly diminished since the war. 1908 *Daily Chron.* 19 June 4/6 The Great Powers..should recall some of their agents and those *politico-religious missionaries, who, instead of putting out the fire, secretly throw fuel into the flames. 1937, 1953 [see CAODAISM]. 1978 D. MURPHY *Place Apart* xi. 235 In the midst of all the politico-religious dissension [in Ulster], one tends to overlook the general social problems. 1824 G. S. FABER *Diffic. Infidelity* (1833) 83 The code of religion, whice he [Moses] delivered.., was not a *politico-sacerdotal fraud. 1778 ABIGAIL ADAMS in *Fam. Lett.* (1876) 338 The *politico-scientific ladies of France. 1856 MORRIS in Mackail *Life* (1899) I. 107, I can't enter into *politico-social subjects with any interest.., things are in a muddle. 1950 M. CROSLAND tr. *Rovan's Germany* 99 The D.G.B...remains the richest and most powerful union confederation in Europe, constituting a genuine politico-social power. 1958 Politico-social [see MILTONIZING *ppl. a.* and *vbl. sb.*]. 1752 WARBURTON *Letter to Hurd* (1809) 108 *Politico-theological dissertations on Calvinism, Jansenism, Quietism, &c. 1890 LOWELL *Milton's Areop.* Latest Lit. Ess. (1891) 95 Williams..lived long enough to learn that there were politico-theological bores in Rhode Island.

c. prefixed to a noun, forming a quasi-*adj.*, as ***politico-crime***, ***politico-travel***.

1952 TURKUS & FEDER *Murder, Inc.* vi. 100 In November of 1950, an investigation of politico-crime tie-ups was launched in New York. *Ibid.* xiii. 291 The investigation shocked the public into a new consciousness of the politico-crime danger. 1970 *Daily Tel.* 14 May 6/2 A politico-travel diary, the book is useful background to the present crisis and conflict.

po'litico-eco'nomic, *a.* [POLITICO-.] = POLITICO-ECONOMICAL *a.*

1839 CARLYLE *Chartism* x. 97 Paralytic Radicalism.. which..sounds with Philosophic Politico-Economic plummet the deep dark sea of troubles. *a* 1854 MILL *Draft Autobiogr.* (1961) 82 The Benthamic & politico-economic form of Liberalism. 1910 J. W. WELSFORD (*title*) The strength of England: a politico-economic history of England from Saxon times to the reign of Charles I. 1933 E. E. EVANS-PRITCHARD in *Africa* VI. 372 Exchange of blood in such situations sacralizes and endows with sanctions a politico-economic transaction. 1955 *Bull. Atomic Sci.* June 205/2 A complete understanding of political and sociologic conditions will have to be used to decide what politico-economic incentives and assurances may be brought to bear. 1974 P. GORE-BOOTH *With Great Truth & Respect* 380 Such are the problems of politico-economic diplomacy.

po'litico-eco'nomical, *a.* [See POLITICO-.] Pertaining or relating to political economy.

1837 *Democratic Review* I. 113 In spite of the plain principles of politico-economical truth. 1857 RUSKIN *Pol. Econ. Art* i. (1868) 69 The real politico-economical signification of every one of those beautiful toilettes. 1858 [see ECONOMICAL *a.* 3 b]. 1873 H. SPENCER *Stud. Sociol.* (1882) 44 Certain classes of sociological facts (as the politico-economical).

Hence **politico-economist**, a student of, or writer on, political economics (cf. ECONOMIST 4 b).

1885 W. HARRIS *Hist. Radical Party* vii. 141 It is worth noticing that Ricardo, the politico-economist, was in the minority.

‖**politicone** (-'kone). *Obs. rare.* [It. f. POLITICO + *-one*: see -OON.] A politician: with hostile or contemptuous connotation.

a 1734 NORTH *Exam.* (1740) 118 He was certainly a true Matchiavellian Politicone, and his Skill lay in the English State. —— *Life Ld. Guilford* (1808) I. 155 (D.) Formal visitants and politicones often found him out at his chambers.

po'litico-re'ligious, *a.* [See POLITICO-.] *prop.* Pertaining to religion as influenced by politics; but commonly used as = Pertaining to politics as influenced by or dependent on religion; at once political and religious.

1754 O. in *Connoisseur* No. 47. ¶1 We were inspired with a detestation of the pope and pretender by the *Nonjuror*, the *Jesuit Caught*..and such other politico-religious dramas. 1804 C. B. BROWN tr. *Volney's View Soil U.S.* p. xiii, A power raised upon a politico-religious foundation, like that claimed by the Stuarts of England. 1841 TRENCH *Parables* iii. (1877) 46 The parables of Jesus have not primarily a moral, but a politico-religious, or theocratic purpose. 1878 STUBBS *Const. Hist.* III. xviii. 80 The politico-religious schemes of the Lollards.

So **po'litico-re'ligionist**, one whose religion is of a political character, or a matter of politics.

1835 *Brit. Mag.* VII. 596 Candour..is a quality well nigh banished from the morale of the politico-religionist.

politied ('pɒlɪtɪd), *a. rare.* [f. POLITY[1] + -ED[2].] Having or provided with a polity.

1816 G. S. FABER *Orig. Pagan Idol.* III. 625 A powerful and regularly politied people. 1827 —— *Sacr. Calend. Prophecy* (1844) III. 63 A distinct and regularly politied Church. 1838 —— *Inquiry* 571 Communions, which God himself has declared to be Churches, however they originated, and however they were politied.

†**po'lition.** *Obs.* $rare^{-0}$. [ad. L. *polītiōn-em* polishing.]

1623 COCKERAM, *Polition*, a diligent trimming.

‖**politique** (pɔlitik). [F., prop. adj. 'political': see POLITIC.] **1.** One of an opportunist and moderate party, which arose in France *c* 1573, during the Huguenot wars, and regarded peace and political reform as more urgent than the decision by arms of the religious quarrel; also, a sympathizer with this party elsewhere, and, opprobriously, an indifferentist, a temporizer: = POLITIC B. 1 b.

1609 BIBLE (Douay) *Exod.* x. Comm., Because Gods servants may not temporize in religion, politiques unjustly charge them to have bad intentions. 1644 BULWER *Chirol.* A ij b, Interpreters henceforth grow out of date, While Politiques usurpe the Sultans state. 1879 SAINTSBURY in *Encycl. Brit.* IX. 564/1 The middle party, the Politiques of Europe,—the English, that is, and the Germans,—sent help to Henry. 1888 *Q. Review* CLXVII. 21 At Court three great parties were contending for power in the King's name—the Guises, the Reformers, and the Politiques. 1958 *Times Lit. Suppl.* 11 July 390/4 It certainly attracted a number of outstanding political leaders to it. Dr. Zeldin introduces us to many of these latter-day politiques. 1959 *Encounter* July 45/2 Some presenting him [*sc.* Odysseus] as an enlightened statesman, others as a machiavellian *politique*. 1972 K. B. MCFARLANE *Lancastrian Kings & Lollard Knights* I. ii. 24, I would maintain that in politics Henry [IV] was not a man of constitutional principle at all but an opportunist and a *politique*.

2. A political concept or doctrine; an expression of political ideas.

1958 A. DRU tr. *Péguy's Temporal & Eternal* 27 A country, a *régime* does not need you, it does not need mystics, a *mystique*, or its *mystique*... It needs a sound *politique*, which means a good government policy. 1958 *Times Lit. Suppl.* 27 June 366/2 Péguy used the witness of the few independent supporters of Dreyfus to illustrate that radical distinction between *mystique* and *politique* which is the essential clue to all his thought... For him the Revolution and the Christian religion were in origin and in essence both *mystiques* that were profoundly true... But they had become *politiques*: 'It is one and the same movement which makes people no longer believe in the Republic and no longer believe in God.' *Ibid.* 366/3 The withering criticism of the clergy is always in terms of their compromising with the *mystique* which alone makes Christianity valid: the Church has devoted its energies instead to propagating a *politique*. 1959 *Listener* 4 June 999/1 His analysis of Communist politique had a tension which lent itself to radio dramatization. 1977 A. ECCLESTONE *Staircase for Silence* v. 88 *Politique*..set in as a process of dislocation,..a choosing to go it alone. It became an end in itself, ever seeking an aggrandisement of its own power, suspicious of and ready to suppress whatever challenged its own authority.

politique, -ly, obs. forms of POLITIC, -LY.

'politist. *rare.* [f. POLITY[1] + -IST.] A student of or writer on polity.

1869 *Contemp. Rev.* XI. 132 The pleasant society of Politists and Legists like Hooker, Taylor, &c.

polititian, -ious: see POLITICIAN, -IOUS.

'politize, *v. rare.* [f. POLITY[1] + -IZE.]

†**1. a.** *trans.* To deal with or treat (a matter) politicly, diplomatically, or craftily. **b.** *intr.* To deal politicly or diplomatically. *Obs.*

1598 TOFTE *Alba* (1880) 65 Matters of state we vse to politize, Procrastinating for aduantage great. 1641 MILTON *Reform.* II. Wks. 1851 III. 66 Let us not..stand hankering and politizing, when God..points us out the way.

2. *intr.* †**a.** To have political relations. *Obs.* **b.** To deal in politics. *rare.*

1623 LISLE *Ælfric on O. & N. Test.* To Rdr. 12 The Hebrew it selfe..temporizing with Ægypt, politizing with Chaldea, merchandizing with Syria,..&c. grew so out of knowledge among the people, that they vnderstood not our Sauiours *Eli, Eli.* 1900 *Blackw. Mag.* Feb. 182/1 To politise in advance is foreign to our nature.

3. *trans.* To make into citizens.

1884 J. RAE *Contemp. Socialism* iii. 123 Its [the state's] inhabitants must be politized, for they, all of them, constitute the *polis*.

†**'politure.** *Obs.* [a. obs. F. *politure* (Godef.) = It. *politura*, L. *polītūra* polishing, smoothing, f. *polīt-*, ppl. stem of *polīre* to polish: see -URE.] Polishing; polish, smoothness.

1592 R. D. *Hypnerotomachia* 21 Arch..of a rare and subtile devise, and exquisite polyture. 1625 N. CARPENTER *Geog. Del.* I. vii. (1635) 183 The roundnesse and politure, wherein Art should shew as much exactnesse as shee can. 1668 WILKINS *Real Char.* II. iii. §2. 62 Stones..either of a Shining Politure, or capable of it. 1776 DA COSTA *Conchol.* 59 The beauty, politure, and hardness of shells, render them very fit for luxurious uses.

b. *fig.* Elegance of form; polish of style, manners, or habits; refinement.

1593 NASHE *Christ's T.* Wks. (Grosart) IV. 232 If you should lende it (from the beginning to the ending,) but sutable descriptionate politure. 1607 TOPSELL *Four-f. Beasts* Ep. Ded., The neatness and politure of the Cat and Peacock. 1656 *Artif. Handsom.* 69 To reduce them [men] from the politure and improvement of after times..to their first caves and cottages. 1720 J. JOHNSON *Canons Eng. Ch.* Pref. to Rdr. 64 Men who wanted the Politure and Fineness of this Age.

polity[1] ('pɒlɪtɪ). Also 7 pollity. [a. obs. F. *politie* (1419), ad. L. *polītīa*: see POLICY *sb.*[1]]

1. Civil organization (as a condition); civil order.

1538 STARKEY *England* I. ii. 51 Pepul, rude, wythout polyty, can not vse that same [riches] to theyr owne commodyte. **1594** HOOKER *Eccl. Pol.* III. ii. §1 The necessitie of Politie, and Regiment in all Churches may bee held, without holding any one certayne forme to bee necessary in them all. Nor is it possible that any form of politie, much less politie ecclesiasticall should be good, vnlesse God himselfe bee authour of it. **1763** J. BROWN *Poetry & Mus.* iv. 40 In the Course of Time, and the Progress of Polity and Arts, a Separation of the several Parts..would naturally arise. **1868** GLADSTONE *Juv. Mundi* vi. 171 At a period antecedent to the formation of anything like polity in Greece.

b. Administration of a state, civil government (as a process or course of action).

1715 ATTERBURY *Serm., On Matt.* xxvii. 25 (1734) I. 127 They..were permitted..to retain some Shadow of their Domestick Polity and Government. **1774** JEFFERSON *Autobiog.* App., Wks. 1859 I. 144 The original constitution of the American colonies possessing their assemblies with the sole right of directing their internal policy. **1884** W. C. SMITH *Kildrostan* 60 To..help the growth Of civil polity, and self-control.

2. a. A particular form of political organization, a form of government.

1597 HOOKER *Eccl. Pol.* v. lxxix. §3 We preferre..the Spartan before the Athenian Politie. **1652–62** HEYLIN *Cosmogr.* Introd. (1674) 4/2 Of this kind also are the several Polities, and forms of Government. **1766** *Compl. Farmer* s.v. *Queen bee*, Some authors who have written of the polity of bees. **1876** GRANT *Burgh Sch. Scotl.* I. i. 3 *note*, The polity of Scotland remained as yet Celtic, though it very soon afterwards became feudal.

b. An organized society or community of men; a state. Also *fig.*

1650 TRAPP *Comm. Exod.* xx. 17 Moses his politie could not consist of true worshippers and professed Idolaters. **1828** CARLYLE *Misc.* (1857) I. 152 The polity of Literature is called a Republic. **1840** J. H. NEWMAN *Par. Serm.* (1842) V. xv. 244 The soul of man is intended to be a well-ordered polity. **1894** HUXLEY *Evol. & Ethics* 23 Those who should be kept, as certain to be serviceable members of the polity.

†**3.** Mode of administering or managing public or private affairs; *esp.* skilful, prudent, or crafty management; statecraft; = POLICY *sb.*[1] 2–4. *Obs.*

1562 PILKINGTON *Expos. Abdyas* Pref. 9 It is wonderfull to consider the foolishnes of the wicked, which in politie wold seme so wise. **1599** B. JONSON *Cynthia's Rev.* I. i, Tis your best politie to be ignorant. **1697** EVELYN *Numism.* vii. 229 The false Polity of Raising and Sinking. **1828** D'ISRAELI *Chas. I*, II. xii. 310 The age of heroism..was now settling into the age of polity. **1843** LYTTON *Last Bar.* III. iii, I know little of stratagem and polity, wars and kings.

†**4.** A political principle. *nonce use. Obs.*

1642 J. M[ARSH] *Argt. conc. Militia* 27 This is the reason of that pollity of Law, that the King is body politick.

†**polity**[2]. *Obs.* [erron. f. POLE *sb.*[2] + -ITY.] = POLARITY I.

1613 M. RIDLEY *Magn. Bodies* vi. 23 This alteration of polity is to be obserued likewise in Magneticall needles. *Ibid.* xvii. 64 From those paralels and parts, neere adioyning to the pole, the greatest vigour of politie Magneticall doth proceed. *Ibid.* xx. 72 That contrary nature of pollity that was in the weake Load-stone.

politzerize (pəʊˈlɪtsəraɪz), *v.* [f. name of Adam Politzer, a physician of Vienna, who introduced the method: see -IZE.] *trans.* To inflate the tympanic cavity of (a patient) through the Eustachian tube. Hence **po'litzerizing** *vbl. sb.*; also **po,litzeri'zation**.

1879 *St. George's Hosp. Rep.* IX. 786 Politzerising is now performed carefully several times, when a perforation sound is heard. *Ibid.* 791 The Eustachian tube..was found to be pervious, as ascertained by auscultation during Politzerisation. **1897** *Allbutt's Syst. Med.* II. 116 Politzerization.

poliue, obs. form ofø PULLEY.

polje (ˈpɒljə). *Physical Geogr.* Also **polye**. Pl. poljes, ‖polja, (after Ger.) poljen. [Serbo-Croat *polje* field.] An enclosed plain in a karstic region, esp. Yugoslavia, that is larger than a uvala and usu. has steep enclosing walls and a covering of alluvium.

1894 *Geogr. Jrnl.* III. 323 The *poljen* occur at low levels, and therefore receive an enormous supply of 'ground water', especially at the times of the autumn or winter rains, which the underground outlet cannot carry it [*sic*] off fast enough. **1902** *Ibid.* XX. 428 In spring..the floors of the polyes are flooded. **1918** D. W. JOHNSON *Topogr. & Strategy in War* xiv. 169 In the rear of the Serbian armies..runs the straight subsidiary trench formed by the Lepenatz valley, Kosovo Polye, and the Ibar valley. **1926** *Geogr. Jrnl.* LXVII. 197 Lakes in the high calcareous Alps of Switzerland occupy dolines or polyes, the bottom of which have been more or less filled by deposits of impervious material derived from the ground moraines of the ancient glaciers. **1934** *Discovery* Sept. 247/1 Some of these *polja* are periodic lakes. **1954** W. D. THORNBURY *Princ. Geomorphol.* xiii. 324 The largest polje in the Western Balkans, the Livno polje, is 40 miles long and 3 to 7 miles wide. **1958** *Geogr. Jrnl.* CXXIV. 41 Some of the largest polja are found among the Dinaric Alps in the hinterland of Split. **1960** B. W. SPARKS *Geomorphol.* vii. 155 The largest depressions of Yugoslavia, the poljes, are probably not solution forms at all but tectonic depressions modified by solution of the limestone preserved in them. **1972** *Science* 12 May 664/3 The perennial flooding of the farmlands in the poljes of Yugoslavia.

polk (pəʊlk), *v.* [ad. F. *polker* (Littré), f. *polka* POLKA *sb.*[1]] *intr.* To dance the polka. Hence **'polking** *vbl. sb.*

1845 M. J. HIGGINS *Ess.* (1875) 219 He waltzes smoothly, and gallops rapidly, and polks intricately. **1848** E. GRAY *Let.* in M. Lutyens *Ruskins & Grays* (1972) x. 95, I got introduced to good partners and got some good polking. **1852** *Fraser's Mag.* XLVI. 704 He..waltzed and polked with their daughters. **1853** J. R. PLANCHÉ *Mr. Buckstone's Ascent of Mount Parnassus* 30 Each night to some Casino.. Where I am pulled by fast young men about And with eternal polking quite worn out. **1876** GEO. ELIOT *Dan. Der.* II. xi, I shall not waltz or polk with any one.

polk, obs. Sc. spelling of POKE; var. PULK [1], [2].

polk, -e, obs. and dial. var. PULK, pool.

polka (ˈpəʊlkə), *sb.*[1] [= Fr. and Ger. *polka*: of uncertain origin. The dance being of Bohemian origin (orig. called *Nimra*), it has been suggested that *polka* was a corruption of Czech *pulka* half, 'a characteristic feature being its short half steps'. Another suggestion is that the actual form, whether or not altered from *pulka*, is due to the Polish *Polka*, fem. of *Polak* a Pole: cf. *polonaise* (also a dance), and *mazurka*.]

1. A lively dance of Bohemian origin, the music for which is in duple time.

Danced at Prague in 1835, at Vienna 1839, Paris 1840, London in the spring of 1842: see *Memoirs of Anna M. W. Pickering* (1903) xvi. ***polka-mazurka***, a modification of the mazurka dance to the movement of a polka; ***polka-time***.

1844 *Illustr. Lond. News* 23 Mar. 184 The Polka is an original Bohemian Peasant Dance, and was first introduced into the fashionable saloons of Berlin and St. Petersburg, about eight years since. **1844** LADY EASTLAKE *Jrnls. & Corr.* I. 153 A polka danced, only fit for children, because so evidently taught by a dancing-master. **1846** SMART Suppl., *Polka*, an Hungarian dance lately fashionable in France and England. **1852** MISS YONGE *Two Guard.* xiii. (1861) 237 'Thank you, I don't dance the Polka', she replied. **1881** *Academy* 15 Oct. 293 Prof. Helmar has the credit of being the inventor of the polka. **1884** *St. James' Gaz.* 28 Apr. 5/1 It was Taglioni who introduced into England the polka. **1898** STAINER & BARRETT *Dict. Mus. Terms* 372/1 The polka was so popular that it absorbed every other dance for a time. Articles of food, of clothing and of ornament, were named after it.

attrib. **1844** *Illustr. Lond. News* 11 May 301/1 You perform the galop waltz, substituting the Polka step just described. **1861** H. RHYS *Theatrical Trip for Wager!* xiii. 120 They advanced in line, in polka time, then right-about-turned. **1928** A. M. M. DOUTON *Bk. with Seven Seals* I. 112 The course of calisthenics..terminated with lessons in the ..polka-mazurka. **1957** G. B. L. WILSON *Dict. Ballet* 219 *Polka-mazurka*, dance derived from the polka, from which it differs in that it is in 3/4 time, and from the mazurka, by which it is distinguished by having an accent on the 3rd instead of the 2nd beat. **1967** CHUJOY & MANCHESTER *Dance Encycl.* (rev. ed.) 738/2 *Polka-Mazurka*, a Polish variation of the polka, in 3/4 time, danced as a ballroom dance in countries of Eastern Europe.

2. A piece of music for such a dance, or in its time or rhythm.

1844 *Illustr. Lond. News* 27 Apr. 280 The fourth polka by Jullien. Composed on National Bohemian and Hungarian Melodies. **1848** THACKERAY *Bk. Snobs* xxv, You recognise those polkas? They were played at Devonshire House..the day of the grand fête. **1867** MISS BRADDON *R. Godwin* I. i. 16 The guard's horn playing a joyous polka made itself heard among the trees.

3. On account of the popularity of the dance, *polka* was prefixed as a trade name to articles of all kinds (cf. quot. 1898 in 1); e.g. the ***polka curtain-band*** (for looping up curtains), ***polka-gauze***, ***polka hat***; **polka-dot**, a pattern consisting of dots of uniform size and arrangement; also *fig.*, *attrib.* or as *adj.*, and as *v. trans.*; hence ***polka-dotted*** adj.

1846 W. S. COTTERELL (*title*) Polka Song Book and Old Friends Olio, containing Comic and Sentimental Songs, Duets, Glees, etc. **1851** MAYHEW *Lond. Labour* I. 367/1 We won't give a farden for the polka hats with the low crowns. **1883** *Century Mag.* July 378/1 To the end of which [line] he looped,..what is known, technically, as the 'polka', with scarlet body, red hackle, brown and white tail, and wings of the spotted feathers of the guinea-fowl. **1884** J. G. BOURKE *Snake Dance Moquis* xi. 119 Covered with white spots which ..resolved themselves into white arrow-heads and polka-dots, the latter arranged longitudinally, two and two. **1894** ELIZ. L. BANKS *Camp. Curiosity* 160, I bought a black and white polka-dot blouse and apron for work in the laundry. **1895** *Montgomery Ward Catal.* Spring & Summer 9/3 Polka Dot Chambray, linen finish. **1906** 'O. HENRY' *Four Million* 136 The next day a person with red hands and a blue polka-dot necktie..called. **1908** W. G. DAVENPORT *Butte & Montana beneath X-Ray* 9 Miss P—— received her guests in a lovely polka dotted frock. **1924** W. M. RAINE *Troubled Waters* xxi. 224 He took off his big white hat and rubbed a polka-dot handkerchief over his bald head. **1928** F. N. HART *Bellamy Trial* i. 3 He wore a shabby tweed suit, a polka-dotted tie. **1956** *Daily Mail* 19 July 6/1 Camping sites are scattered like polka dots all over the Riviera. **1957** V. NABOKOV *Pnin* vi. 138 Amber-brown Monarch butterflies flapped.., their incompletely retracted black legs hanging rather low beneath their polka-dotted bodies. **1964** D. VARADAY *Gara-Yaka* ii. 23 Polka dots were becoming clearly defined on her tawny, golden hide. **1966** MRS. L. B. JOHNSON *White House Diary* 3 Apr. (1970) 382 A young newspaper-woman in a black-and-white polka-dot bikini, with a figure to suit it. **1969** *Better Homes & Gardens* (U.S.) Apr. 83 Tiny bright red fruits that polka-dot the long branches. **1970** *New Yorker* 16 May 18/1 (Advt.), Men often are remembered for odd reasons. Like our 11th President. Little did he dream when he designed the polka dot that one day it would become the epitome of fashion. **1972** *Daily Tel.* 16 Aug. 1/1 A blonde girl wearing a green polka dot bikini was found dead in the sea..yesterday. **1972** *Suttons Seeds* 16 Polka Dot mixed. These bushy Cornflowers stand up to weather well, with a good range of colours. **1978** J. WAINWRIGHT *Jury People* xxxvi. 111 Kids are out. Because the world ain't yet ready for polka-dot kids. Black is only beautiful in places. **1979** C. WOOD *James Bond & Moonraker* xi. 112 She had big puffed sleeves..and a petticoat effect of over-lapping polka-dotted skirts.

Hence (*nonce-wds.*) **'polka** *v. intr.*, to dance the polka; **pol'kaic** *a.*, of the character of a polka; **polka'mania**, a mania for dancing the polka; **'polkery**, an assembly for polka dancing; **'polkist, -iste**, one who dances the polka.

1846 DICKENS *Let.* 5 July (1977) IV. 580 The common people waltzed and *polka'd without cessation, to the music of a band. **1859** SALA *Tw. round Clock* (1861) 299 It does my heart good..to see the..children in our crowded London courts and alleys waltzing and polkaing to the Italian organ-grinder's music. **1873** MISS BROUGHTON *Nancy* II. 174 We have at length..left them to polka and schottische their fill until the morning. **1884** G. MOORE *Mummer's Wife* xii, He thought Offenbach too *polkaic. **1845** *Punch* VIII. 86 The *Polkamania is said to have originated in Bohemia. **1883** W. B. SQUIRE in Grove *Dict. Mus.* III. 8/1 Vienna, Paris, and London were successively attacked by this curious 'polkamania'; clothes, hats, and streets were named after the dance. **1845** M. J. HIGGINS *Ess.* (1875) 218 Morning *polkeries in Grosvenor Square. **1846** G. WARBURTON *Hochelaga* I. 93 Some of them are the best waltzers and *polkistes I have ever seen. **1851** (*title*) The Lorgnette or Studies of the Town,..contains Notices of Lodgings in Town, Fashionable Man,..the Polka and Polkists, Watering Places, [etc.].

polka (ˈpəʊlkə), *sb.*[2] [f. prec. sb., perh. with reference to Polish *Polka* a Polish woman: cf. *polonaise*.] A woman's tight-fitting jacket, usually knitted: more fully ***polka-jacket***.

1844 THACKERAY *Contrib. to Punch* Wks. 1898 VI. 89 Ladies with the most flaming polkas, and flounces all the way up. **1849** *Mechanic's Mag.* 17 Nov. 479 The Lady's Winter Polka Jacket. **1851** *Voy. to Mauritius* vi. 224 A sort of polka-jacket of dark cloth with many buttons. **1859** SALA *Tw. round Clock* (1861) 185 Stalls, laden with pretty gimcracks,..wax flowers and Berlin and crochet work, prints, and polkas, and women's ware of all sorts.

poll (pəʊl), *sb.*[1] Forms: 3–7 polle, 4–7 pol, 5–7 powle, 6 poulle, poolle, poil (*Sc.*), 6–7 powl (9 *north. dial.*), poul(e, pool(e, 6–9 pole, 5– poll; *β.* 5– *Sc.* and *north. dial.* pow. [ME. *polle* = obs. Du. *polle* 'le sommet de la teste' (Plantin), *polle*, *pol* 'caput', 'cacumen, fastigium' (Kilian), LG. *polle* head (Brem. Wb.); cf. Sw. dial. *pull* (Rietz), Da. *puld* crown of the head.]

I. The head of man or beast.

1. a. The human head. (Not now in serious literary use, but common dialectally everywhere.)

c **1290** *S. Eng. Leg.* I. 309/325 þe deuel..wolde fain henten heom bi þe polle. **13..** *E.E. Allit. P.* B. 1265 Pulden prestes by þe polle & plat of her hedes. *c* **1400** *Laud Troy Bk.* 5530 Thei stroke to-gedir with so gret myght, That bothe vpon here pol lyght. *c* **1440** *Promp. Parv.* 407/2 Pol, or heed, *caput*. **1584** HUDSON *Du Bartas' Judith* VI. in *Sylvester's Wks.* (1621) 750 From his shoulders flew his powle. **1597** SHAKS. *2 Hen. IV*, II. iv. 282 Looke, if the wither'd Elder hath not his Poll claw'd like a Parrot. **1639** T. DE GRAY *Compl. Horsem.* 71 Keeping his poule warm. **1820** L. HUNT *Indicator* No. 22 (1822) I. 172 Receiving the full summer showers with an uncovered poll. **1828** *Craven Gloss.* (ed. 2), *Powl*, the head. **1876** BROWNING *Pacchiarotto* ix, From silk shoe on heel to laced poll's-hood.

β. a **1500** P. JOHNSTON *Thre deid Powis*, Behold our heidis thre Oure holkit eine, oure peilit powis bair. **1596** DALRYMPLE tr. *Leslie's Hist. Scot.* VIII. 122 Andro Bartayne ..slew sa mony piratis, that mony puncheounis full of thair powis he sent to Scotland, in gifte, to the king. **1818** SCOTT *Hrt. Midl.* xliii, The..veteran soldier that has..heard the bullets whistle as aften as he has hairs left on his auld pow. **1871** C. GIBBON *Lack of Gold* xx, How is she ever to get married wi' a shaven pow? **1876** F. K. ROBINSON *Gloss. Whitby* 146/2 *Pow*, the poll; the human head. **1901** G. B. SHAW *Devil's Disciple* III. 79 The Devil's Disciple here will start presently as the Reverend Richard Dudgeon, and wag his pow in my old pulpit. **1919** *Kelso Chron.* 4 Apr. 3 My blood's not chill, though near the night, And grey-haired is my pow. **1940** E. POUND *Cantos* lxxi. 186 His daughter told me he had burnt all his papers In melancholia May be from that swat on the pow. **1947** E. A. MCCOURT *Flaming Hour* ix. 54 'Weren't ye lyin' locked up in yon shed no later than yesterday mornin' with a bump on your pow that should have kept ye still for a fortnight?' he demanded ferociously. **1963** G. THOMSON *Crocus & Meadowlark Country* xi. 75 Ethel added a drawing she made of Jim one cold day when he made his way there with Chaddy's red tam-o'-shanter pulled down on his red pow. **1965** *Buchan Observer* 12 Jan. 2 Ye'll hum an' hae an' claw your pow. **1973** *People's Jrnl.* (Inverness & Northern Counties ed.) 1 Dec. 4/5 I'd got no further than filling my pow with rollers and covering my head with a woollen head square.

†**b.** The figure or representation of a head.

1377 LANGL. *P. Pl.* B. XIII. 246 A pardoun with a peys of led and two pollis amydde.

†**c.** A skull. *Obs. rare.*

1721 RAMSAY *Elegy on Patie Birnie* viii, He..strak sounds fast and clear Out o' the pow [a mare's skull]. **1725** —— *Gentle Sheph.* II. ii, Boils up their livers in a warlock's pow.

2. *spec.* **a.** The part of the head on which the hair grows; the head as characterized by the colour or state of the hair.

1602 SHAKS. *Ham.* IV. v. 196 His Beard as white as Snow, All Flaxen was his Pole. **1713** C'TESS WINCHELSEA *Misc. Poems* 105 With wadling Steps, and frowzy Poles. **1790** BURNS *John Anderson my Jo* i, Blessings on your frosty pow, John Anderson, my jo. **1791** COWPER *Odyss.* XIX. 308 His back was bunch'd, his visage swarthy, curl'd His poll. **1855** THACKERAY *Newcomes* vi, His bald head might be seen alongside of Mr. Quilter's confidential grey poll.

b. The crown or top of the head; the vertex.

1382 WYCLIF *Dan.* xiv. 35 The angel of the Lord toke hym in the poll of hym [1388 top, *Vulg.* in vertice], and bare hym in an her of his hed, and putte hym in to Babyloyne. **1387** TREVISA *Higden* (Rolls) IV. 217 He wolde bende his heer from þe pol toward þe foreheed [L. *a. vertice ad frontem*]. **1603** OWEN *Pembrokeshire* (1892) 127 A great round hole in the pole of his head. **1607** TOPSELL *Four-f. Beasts* 359 Of diseases incident to the eares, and poll of the head. **1622** WALTER *Diary* (Camden) 62 The said fish [a Caaing whale] had no gills, but put out his water at his pole.

c. The nape of the neck.

1671 BLAGRAVE *Astrol. Physic* 120, I did.. apply raw-fresh meat to the powl or Neck to help.. divert the humour from the Eyes. **1675** HOBBES *Odyssey* (1677) 260 The arrow pierc'd his neck from throat to poll. **1711** STEELE *Spect.* No. 259 ⁋1 You shall sometimes see a Man begin the Offer of a Salutation, and.. stop short in the Pole of his Neck. **1816** *Sporting Mag.* XLVII. 302 An old hare.. having a wire round its neck so tight as to have sunk beneath the skin in its pole. **1833** *Regul. Instr. Cavalry* I. 48 The bend should be from the poll of the neck.

†3. *spec.* The head and shoulders of the ling (as a dish). Cf. JOWL *sb.*[3] 2. *Obs.*

1599 B. JONSON *Ev. Man out of Hum.* IV. iii, Hee lookes like a shield of brawne,.. or a drie Poule of Ling vpon Easter-eue, that has furnisht the table all Lent. **1671** CROWNE *Juliana* III, I was to go buy a pole o' Ling for the womens dinner.

†4. a. As the prominent or visible part in a crowd, put for: A person or individual in a number or list (= HEAD *sb.*[1] 7 b); esp. in phrases, e.g. ***by (the) poll***, by counting of heads; ***poll by poll***, one by one; ***per poll***, for each person. *Obs.* (exc. in legal phr. CHALLENGE *to the polls.*)

c **1325** *Pol. Songs* (Camden) 237 Of gedelynges, gromes,.. Harlotes, hors-knaves, Bi pate and by polle. **1387** TREVISA *Higden* (Rolls) IV. 33 Payde to here lordes for euery pol twenty schillynge. **1495** *Act 11 Hen. VII*, c. 21 §2 None of the said petite Jury.. shall.. have any Chalenge to tharray or to any persone or poll therin being ympanelled. *c* **1515** *Cocke Lorell's B.* 4 Ye shall here the names poll by poll. **1568** GRAFTON *Chron.* II. 329 The people greatly murmured for the payment of foure pence the polle. **1598** GRENEWEY *Tacitus' Ann.* XIII. vii. (1622) 188 There was bestowed a gift of forty sesterces by powle to the people. **1602** FULBECKE *2nd Pt. Parall.* 20, I agree to pay for the carriage of euerie poll or person of them a certaine summe of money. **1624** CAPT. SMITH *Virginia* 167 Some small tax.. as a Penny vpon euery Poll, called a head-penny. **1641** *Termes de la Ley* 51 Challenge to or by the Poll, is where exception is taken to any one, or more, as not indifferent. **1648** PRYNNE *Plea for Lords* 27 Take them poll by poll. **1678** WOOD *Life* 20 Mar. (O.H.S.) II. 401 An act for raising money by the poll. **1796** H. HUNTER tr. *St.-Pierre's Stud. Nat.* (1799) III. 516 Voting by poll.. and by orders.

†b. A unit in numbering domestic animals, chattels, etc. (Plural after a numeral also *poll.*) Cf. HEAD *sb.*[1] 7 c. *Obs.*

1494 in *Somerset Medieval Wills* (1901) 322 A dosyn pollys of pewter vessell. **1534** in Weaver *Wells Wills* (1890) 30, iij powles of peauter vessell. **1544** R. BROKER *Will* (B.M. Addit. MS. 24925 lf. 21 b), Twenty poule of pultrey. **1601** SHAKS. *All's Well* IV. iii. 190 The muster file, rotten and sound,.. amounts not to fifteene thousand pole.

5. Short for POLL-TAX. *Obs.* or *Hist.*

1684 *Col. Rec. Pennsylv.* I. 99 Ordered That a pole Proportionably Layd, be debated ye first thing tomorrow. **1689** *Lond. Gaz.* No. 2449/4 An Act for Raising Money by a Poll, and otherwise, towards the Reducing of Ireland. **1692** WASHINGTON tr. *Milton's Def. Pop.* M.'s Wks. 1851 VIII. 71 The Jews, even the poorest of them in the time of their Commonwealth, paid a Poll. **1884** S. DOWELL *Taxes Eng.* III. 6 When.. in 1379 an immediate sum of money was required.. recourse was again had to a poll.

II. From I. 4, app. influenced by POLL *v.*

†6. a. Number of persons as ascertained by counting heads; muster. *Obs.*

1607 SHAKS. *Cor.* III. i. 134 We are the greater pole, and in true feare They gaue vs our demands. *a* **1613** OVERBURY *Trav.* 6 The List and the Poll are neuer far disagreeing.

†b. Counting of heads or persons; census. *Obs.*

1659 J. HARRINGTON *Lawgiving* II. ii, As appears by the Pole made of Israel in the Wilderness of Sinai. **1674** HICKMAN *Hist. Quinquart.* (ed. 2) 137 He is.. afraid to come either to the pole or to the scale; either to weigh, or to number authorities with us. **1697** POTTER *Antiq. Greece* I. ii. (1715) 8 He instituted a Poll causing every one of the Men to cast a Stone into a place appointed.., and.. found them to be in number Twenty-Thousand.

7. a. The counting of voters; the entering of votes, in order to their being counted: esp. at the election of parliamentary or other representatives.

1625 SIR G. MOORE in *Commons Debates* (Camden) 36 Sir John Savill had sufficiently proved the pole demanded. **1653** *Relat. Proc. late Parlt.* 10 The Question being put, the No's, .. had they been prosecuted to the pole, had hazarded the passing of it. **1706** PHILLIPS s.v. *Poll* vb., To take a Poll, to set down the Names and reckon up the Number of Persons concern'd in an Election. **1765** BLACKSTONE *Comm.* I. ii. 178 All soldiers quartered in the place are to remove.. and not to return till one day after the poll is ended. **1857** MAURICE *Ep. St. John* xiii. 204 It is not a question to be decided by a poll. **1863** H. COX *Instit.* I. viii. 113 If.. a poll be demanded on behalf of any candidate rejected on the show of hands, the returning officer is bound to grant the poll.

b. The voting at an election; the action, or time and place, of voting.

1832 *Act 2 Will. IV*, c. 45 §67 The Poll shall on no Account be kept open later than Four o'Clock in the afternoon of such Second Day. **1860** EMERSON *Cond. Life, Fate* Wks. (Bohn) II. 321 What pious men in the parlour will vote for what reprobates at the polls! **1866** BRIGHT *Sp., Reform* 16 Oct. (1876) 379 Come to the poll and give their vote for the election of a new Parliament. **1877** BLACK *Green Past.* xxv, The recent reverses at the poll were only the result of a temporary irritation. **1883** *Women's Suffrage Jrnl.* Nov. 198/1 The exclusion of women from the poll was, in his opinion, nothing short of an injustice.

c. The numerical result of the voting; the total number of votes recorded, as ***a heavy*** or ***light poll.***

1853 LYTTON *My Novel* XII. xxxii, He stood at the head of the poll by a majority of ten. **1885** *Manch. Exam.* 10 July 5/3 At Wednesday's election there was a lighter poll. **1906** *Daily News* 16 Aug. 7/5 After the declaration of the poll Mr.—— thanked his constituents for their splendid victory.

d. A poll taken to estimate public opinion on a specified issue by questioning a sample intended to be representative of the whole people (see GALLUP); *spec.*, (*a*) = ***popularity poll*** s.v. POPULARITY 8; (*b*) a poll intended to forecast the result of a presidential, parliamentary, or other election (see ***opinion poll*** s.v. OPINION *sb.* 1 b). Also *attrib.*

1902 F. CLARKE tr. *Ostrogorski's Democracy and Organization of Political Parties* II. v. iv. 306 The poll taken in each locality is of general import for the whole Union, as well as of special significance for each political subdivision in the States. **1940** GALLUP & RAE *Pulse of Democracy* iii. 35 In this poll [of July 1824] Andrew Jackson received 335 votes; John Quincy Adams, 169; Henry Clay, 19, and William H. Crawford, 9. **1944** *Times* 9 June 5/5 The recent British Medical Association poll of members' opinions with regard to medical interests caused considerable controversy. **1950** *Times* 8 Feb. 7/6 Public opinion polls and investigations carried out by the Japanese Press show that the Yoshida Cabinet no longer enjoys as much support as it did at the time of the General Election in January, 1949. **1964** GOULD & KOLB *Dict. Social Sci.* 517/1 Poll denotes.. the canvas of opinions, prior to an election, by simple or complex interviewing. **1973** *Melody Maker* 31 Mar. 18 It's time to vote in the Melody Maker Jazz Poll. This.. is your opportunity to register your appreciation of the musicians, bands, and singers whom you think have made the finest contributions to jazz over the last year. **1974** *Times* 11 Feb. 15 The poll firms showed their anxiety by conducting their own inquest into their failure... Poll findings are being presented as *predictions* of the result. **1977** *New Yorker* 9 May 136/2 Polls conducted in April show that Carter currently has the approval of about two-thirds of the public. *Ibid.* 24 Oct. 42/3 Fetching coffee in paper cups for the poll watchers.

III. Transferred uses.

8. a. The top or crown of a hat or cap.

1704 J. PITTS *Acc. Mohammetans* vii. (1738) 99 Some what like the Poll of a Man's Hat-case covered with Broad-cloth. **1819** *Chron.* in *Ann. Reg.* 7/2 Surmounted by the poll of an old hat without a brim. **1875** R. F. BURTON *Gorilla L.* (1876) II. 116 From the poll of his night-cap protruded a dozen bristles of elephant's tail hair.

b. The flat or blunt end of the head of a miner's pick or similar tool.

1603 OWEN *Pembrokeshire* (1892) 91 Pickaxes with a rounde poll. **1839** URE *Dict. Arts* 835 The pick... One side used as a hammer is called the poll, and is employed to drive in the gads. **1881** RAYMOND *Mining Gloss.*, *Poll* (Cornw.), the head or striking part of a miner's hammer.

¶9. The chub or chevin. (? an error: cf. POLLARD *sb.*[3])

1755 in JOHNSON. **1773** *Ainsworth's Lat. Dict.*, A poll (club fish), *capito* [edd. 1736–61 Pollard, or chub fish, *capito*].

IV. 10. *attrib.* and *Comb.*, as (sense 7) ***poll-list, -room***; (sense 1) ***poll-clawed*** adj.; **poll-adze**, an adze with a poll or striking face opposite the cutting edge (Knight *Dict. Mech.* 1875); **poll-book**, an official register, previous to the Ballot Act, of the votes given; now, of those qualified to vote; **†poll-booth**, the booth or temporary structure at which the poll was formerly taken at a parliamentary election, a polling-booth; **poll-card**, an official notification informing voters of the place and date of voting; **poll-clerk**, a clerk who records the votes polled; a clerk officially connected with an election; **†poll-gatherer**, the collector of a poll-tax; **poll-hill**, *humorous*, a 'bump' on the head; **†poll-mad** *a.*, wrong in the head, mad-brained (cf. BILWISE); **poll-pick**, a miner's pick with a poll: see quot. 1865; **poll-rating**, the popularity of a person (usu. a political leader) as indicated by a poll; **poll-shorn** *a.*, having the head or crown shorn; *esp.* tonsured; **poll-sickness** = POLL-EVIL; **†poll-silver** = POLL-TAX; **poll-suffrage**, universal suffrage (*Cent. Dict.* 1890); **poll-taker**, usu. in *pl.*, a newspaper or other organization which conducts an opinion poll, = POLLSTER; hence **poll-taking** *vbl. sb.*; **pollwinner**, a successful candidate in a poll; so **poll-winning** *ppl. a.* Also POLL-BILL, etc.

1681 T. FLATMAN *Heraclitus Ridens* No. 51 (1713) II. 70 A Man in Authority promises to examine a *Poll-book by the Poors-book,.. if he put off the Performance of it till the Poll being declared, it cannot answer any End. **1832** *Act 2 Will. IV*, c. 45 §68 The Poll Clerks at the Close of each Day's Poll shall enclose and seal their several Poll Books, and shall publicly deliver them.. to the Returning Officer or his Deputy. **1853** LYTTON *My Novel* XII. xxvii, Convinced by his poll-books that he is not able to return both himself and his impertinent nephew. **1810** W. TAYLOR in *Monthly Mag.* XXIX. 51 It [Parliament] is becoming a *poll-booth of faction, a place for giving public suffrages on those questions of opinion, which divide the metropolitan public. **1817** BENTHAM *Parl. Reform* Introd. 280 Divide it into four practically equal districts, and, in a central spot of each, place the Poll-booth. **1908** *Westm. Gaz.* 4 May 2/2 Mr. Amery's final appeal.. is going with the *poll-card to every elector. **1975** *Times* 27 Feb. 4/3 Poll cards.. remind the elector of his right to vote and they tell him his voting number and where his polling station is. **1855** BROWNING *Old Pict. Florence* xxviii, You bald old saturnine *poll-clawed parrot. **1832** *Poll Clerk [see *poll-book*]. **1853** LYTTON *My Novel* XII. xxxii, Even the poll-clerks sprang from the booth. **1646** G. DANIEL *Poems* Wks. (Grosart) I. 99, I'de nothing Glorie, if I had ben made *Poll-gatherer of the Groats. *a* **1845** HOOD *Craniol.* i, Scratching o'er those little *pole-hills. **1889** GRETTON *Memory's Harkb.* 244, I saw by the *poll-list that he voted for the Prince. **1577** STANYHURST *Descr. Irel.* in *Holinshed* (1808) VI. 6 Cicero.. perceiving his countrimen to become changelings, in being bilwise and *polmad, and to sucke with the Greeke the conditions of the Grecians. **1865** BAUERMAN *Geol. Models* 22 **Poll pick*, single-armed pick with a short bluff point, used for hard veins and working into rock where the slitter is too slight. **1874** J. H. COLLINS *Metal Mining* (1875) 60 In the.. West of England the picks are usually of the form.. called the 'poll-pick', having its head or 'pane' steeled as well as its point... It serves as a hammer as well as a pick. **1967** *Guardian* 16 Oct. 6/1 Mr. Heath's *poll-ratings were unsatisfactory. **1859** SMILES *Self-Help* 30 A sum sufficient to have him put in a state fit to appear in the *poll-room. **1556** OLDE *Antichrist* 144 Lecherous *polleshorne masse monging priestes. **1630** J. TAYLOR (Water P.) *Sculler* xxviii. Wks. III. 21/2 All the poleshorne crew of Antichrists. **1899** RIDER HAGGARD in *Longm. Mag.* Oct. 529 *Poll-sickness.. is a kind of sore or abscess which horses get from knocking their heads against low door-ways and is commonly supposed to be incurable. **1610** HOLLAND *Camden's Brit.* (1637) 100 The Tribute Capitatio [*margin* *Pol-silver], which was personall and imposed upon the poll or person of every one. **1848** WHARTON *Law Lex.*, *Poll-money, Poll-silver, Poll-tax*, a capitation-tax.. formerly assessed by the head on every subject according to rank. **1959** *Spectator* 4 Sept. 288/2 When *poll-takers put the question directly to the citizenry, it seems that vast numbers think it good. **1964** *Economist* 12 Sept. 1021/1 A victory for Mr Goldwater would be the greatest upset for the poll-takers since the *Literary Digest* predicted a landslide for Mr Landon, the Republican who was crushed by President Roosevelt in 1936. **1976** *National Observer* (U.S.) 11 Dec. 5/3 Poll-taker Teeter told the governors that 'our Presidential elections have become nonpartisan media events'. **1964** I. L. HOROWITZ *New Sociology* 31 Problems of this kind can be multiplied a hundredfold—in every sphere of sociology, from *poll-taking to theory-making. **1966** *Melody Maker* 7 May 4 *Pollwinner Tubby Hayes heads a five-man British contingent which will join Austrian composer Friedrich Gulda's all-star international band on its tour of the continent this summer. **1958** P. GAMMOND *Decca Bk. of Jazz* xviii. 218 Jackson in particular was the equivalent of the *poll-winning trumpet men of today. **1962** *Melody Maker* 7 July 8 Pollwinning bandleader Chris Barber has firm views on the subject.

Poll (pɒl), *sb.*[2] [An alteration of *Moll*, a familiar equivalent of *Mary*: cf. *Peg* = *Meg*, Margaret.] A familiar equivalent of the name *Mary* (see also POLLY[1]), used as the conventional proper name of any parrot; hence, = parrot. So **Poll-'parrot**, also used *fig.*, and *attrib.*, with reference to the parrot's unintelligent repetition of words.

[**1630** J. TAYLOR (Water P.) *Epigrams* xxxi. Wks. II. 265 A Rope for Parrat.. O, pretty Pall, take heed, beware the Cat.] **1709** STEELE *Tatler* No. 27 ⁋6 Among the Favourites to the Fair One, he found her Parrat not to be in the last Degree: He saw Poll had her Ear, when his Sighs were neglected. **1719** DE FOE *Crusoe* (1840) I. viii. 141, I.. learnt him [a parrot] to know his own name;.. Pol. *Ibid.* xiii. 214, I had taught my Poll. *a* **1800** COWPER *Parrot* iii, Sweet Poll! his doating mistress cries, Sweet Poll! the mimic bird replies. *a* **1845** HOOD *Batchelor's Dream* iv, The mother brought a pretty Poll. **1851** D. JERROLD *St. Giles* iv. 30 You've no more manners than a poll-parrot. **1861** SALA *Dutch Pict.* xv. 235 This one poll-parrot cry had been taught him. **1886** *Sat. Rev.* 6 Mar. 347/1 Their mania for seeing spies in poll-parrots.

Hence **Poll-'parrot** *v. trans.* and *intr.* = PARROT *v.*; **Poll-'parroty** *a.*, of or proper to a parrot.

a **1845** HOOD *Hymeneal Retrospect.* I. iv, A sort of Poll-Parroty bill! **1865** DICKENS *Mut. Fr.* II. xii, Ain't you got nothing to do but.. stand a Poll Parroting all night? *Ibid.*, I am willing to be silent for the purpose of hearing. But don't Poll Parrot me.

poll (pɒl), *sb.*[3] *Camb. Univ. slang.* Also pol. [Traditionally explained as ad. Gr. *οἱ πολλοί* the many, the multitude.] ***the Poll***: those students who read for or obtain a 'pass' degree; the passmen. ***to go out in the Poll***: to come out in the list of those who take a pass degree. † ***Captain of the Poll***: formerly, the highest amongst those who passed without honours.

[**1791** in Bp. Wordsw. *Scholæ Acad.* (1877) 323 Poor Quiz Carver is one of the *οἱ πολλοί*.] **1831** DARWIN in *Life & Lett.* (1887) I. 183 You will see what a good place I have got in the Poll. **1834** *Oxf. Univ. Mag.* I. 289 Those who do not aspire to honours and in the vernacular of Cambridge are styled the Poll (*οἱ πολλοί*). **1852** BRISTED *Eng. Univ.* 342 There are also many men every year contending for the Captaincy of the Poll, some for the honor, such as it is, others because it will help them to get Poll pupils afterwards. **1889** W. A. WRIGHT *FitzGerald's Lett.*, etc. I. 2 FitzGerald.. modestly went out in the Poll in January 1830, after a period of suspense during which he was apprehensive of not passing at all.

b. Short for *poll degree, poll examination.*

1884 PAYN in *Cornh. Mag.* Apr. 370, I took my degree, however—a first-class 'Poll'; which my good folks at home believed to be an honourable distinction.

c. *attrib.* and *Comb.*, as ***poll coach, degree, -man.***

1837 B. D. WALSH *Hist. Acc. Univ. Cambr.* (ed. 2) 88 In the examination for an ordinary, or Pol degree.., the subjects are very limited. **1848** '*New Triposes*' in C. Whibley *Cap & Gown* 228 Go, Pollmen! nay, ye needs must go; for so the Heads determine. **1865** L. STEPHEN *Sketches Cambridge* 99 Next above schoolmasters in the scale of misery, I should place what we call a 'poll coach'. **1888** BRYCE *Amer. Commw.* III. VI. cii. 446 Separation..between pass or poll men and honour men. *Ibid.* 448 The poll or pass degrees of Cambridge or Oxford.

†**poll, polle,** *sb.*[4] *Obs.* exc. *Hist.* [Origin unascertained.] A measure of land in Ireland, of 50 or 60 acres.

1607 DAVIES *Lett. Earl Salisb.* i. Tracts (1787) 223 They reserved unto him a chief rent of ten shillings out of every poll (being a portion containing three score acres or thereabouts) in lieu of all Irish cuttings and exactions. **1689** R. COX *Hist. Irel.* I. Expl. Index, *Polle* of Land is fifty Acres.

poll (pəʊl), *a.* and *sb.*[5] Also 6–8 **pole**, 5–7 **pol-**. [Short for *pold*, POLLED *ppl. a.*]

A. *adj.* **1.** Polled or cut even at the edge (see POLL *v.* 3): applied to a legal writing or deed executed by a single party, and therefore not indented, as in DEED POLL, POLL DEED (q.v.), ***writing pole.***

1523– [see POLL DEED]. **1588–** [see DEED POLL]. **1596** BACON *Max. & Use Com. Law* I. (1635) 43 Such a lease [a lease for years] may be made by writing Pole.

2. in *Comb.* **a.** in names of animals without horns, as ***poll sheep.***

1773 G. WHITE *Selborne, Let. to D. Barrington* 9 Dec., As soon as you..mount Beeding-hill, all the flocks..become hornless, or, as they call them, poll-sheep.

†**b.** (Usually *pol-*). In names of beardless varieties of cereals, as ***polbarley, polbere, polwheat.***

c **1440** *Promp. Parv.* 407/2 Polbere, corne, idem quod hastybere, *trimensis.* **1574** in *Proc. Soc. Antiq.* XIV. 234 All manner of croppe ȝerelie..viz. wheet, rie,..barley, ottes, bigge, polbarley. **1601** HOLLAND *Pliny* I. 559 Pol-wheat both red and white, yea and Barley also, is threshed and driuen out of the husk vpon a floore.

B. *sb.* Short for *poll-beast, -ox, -cow* (see A. 2 a); *esp.* one of a breed of hornless oxen.

1789 *Trans. Soc. Arts* VII. 73 The cattle are..hardier than the Galloway Poles, or the short-horned breed. **1876** *Daily News* 6 Dec. 2/2 [They] gather in admiring groups behind Tillyfour's big poll. **1880** *Ibid.* 7 Dec. 2/3 The first prize in one of the classes for Scotch Polls.

poll (pəʊl), *v.* Forms: 4–5 **pollen**, 4–6 **polle**, 5– **poll**; also 5–7 **powle**, 6 **pol**, 6–7 **powl, poul(e, poulle, poole**, 6 **pol**, 7–8 **pole**. *Pa. pple.* (see POLLED *ppl. a.*). [A number of disconnected derivatives of POLL *sb.*[1] in its various senses. Branch I is the most difficult to account for, since the expected primary sense would be to take, not the hair, but the poll or head off: cf. HEAD *v.* I. No corresponding vb. is recorded in the cognate langs. which have the sb.]

I. 1. *trans.* To cut short the hair of (a person or animal); to crop, clip, shear; also **b.** with the head, hair, etc. as object. *Obs.* or *arch.*

1388 WYCLIF *Gen.* xli. 14 Anoon at the comaundement of the kyng thei polliden Joseph [1382 doddiden, L. *totonderunt*] led out of prisoun. *c* **1460** *Towneley Myst.* xii. 155 Many shepe can she polle, bot oone had she ay. **1540** *Rutland MSS.* (1905) IV. 302 To Edmond Gresbroke, barbar, for pollying my Lord Talbot.., xxd. **1592** GREENE *Upst. Courtier* D iij b, I come plain to be polde, and to haue my beard cut. **1603** KNOLLES *Hist. Turks* (1621) 174 Polling and shaving him. **1650** BULWER *Anthropomet.* 56 He..who being singular is Poled and closely Cut among those who wear a Bush. **1688** R. HOLME *Armoury* III. 128/2 Pole me, is cut my hair.

b. 13.. [see POLLED *ppl. a.* I]. *c* **1440** *Jacob's Well* 101 Sche pollyd here hevyd priuely,..& in an Abbey, ferre thens, sche was made a munke. **1557** NORTH *Gueuara's Diall Pr.* (1619) ***iij 2 The Romaines were in Rome 454 yeares without eyther powling or shaving the haires off the bearde of anie man. **1572** R. H. tr. *Lauaterus' Ghostes* (1596) 59 Putting knives unto his head, and therewith polling off his haires. **1609** HOLLAND *Amm. Marcell.* 192 Being commaunded to come and pole the Emperours head. **1737** WHISTON *Josephus' Antiq.* VII. xi. §3 David..was in such grief that he had not polled his head. **1841** D'ISRAELI *Amen. Lit.* (1867) 62 They polled their crowns.

II. 2. To cut off the top of (a tree or plant); *esp.* to top or head (a tree) at a few feet from the ground that it may throw out branches; to pollard; also, to lop the branches of.

1577 B. GOOGE *Heresbach's Husb.* II. (1586) 105 Some trees there are, which if you cutte and poule often, will fade and die. **1597** GERARDE *Herbal* I. lxxxvii. §2. 139 Ciues are ..cut and polled often, as is the unset Leeke. **1768–74** TUCKER *Lt. Nat.* (1834) II. 91 We prune, and poll, and cut our trees into unnatural shapes. **1818** KEATS *Endym.* I. 486 Again I'll poll The fair-grown yew tree, for a chosen bow. **1889** MORRIS in Mackail *Life* (1899) II. 221 There were some beautiful willows, and now the idiot Parson has polled them into wretched stumps.

b. *transf.* and *fig.*

1594 GREENE & LODGE *Looking Glasse* G.'s Wks. (Rtldg.) 139/2 When ministers powl the pride of common-weal. **1598** SYLVESTER *Du Bartas* II. ii. II. *Babylon* 159 Powle the broad Plains of their branchy glades. **1607** SHAKS. *Cor.* IV. v. 215 He will mowe all downe..And leaue his passage poul'd.

†**c.** To cut off the head of an animal or thing; to behead: cf. HEAD *v.* I. *Obs.*

1602 CAREW *Cornwall* 35 Some [pilchards] are polled (that is beheaded), gutted, splitted, powdred and dried in the Sunne. *c* **1611** CHAPMAN *Iliad* XVI. 112 Twas Ioues deed: Who, as he pold off his darts heads; so, sure he had decreed, That all the counsels of their warre, he would polle off like it, And giue the Troians victorie. *a* **1661** FULLER *Worthies, Cornwall* I. (1662) 194.

3. To cut even the edge of (a sheet, as in a deed executed by one person). Cf. POLL *a.* I.

1628 COKE *On Litt.* 229 A Deed poll is that which is plaine without any indenting, so called, because it is cut euen, or polled. **1766** BLACKSTONE *Comm.* II. xx. 296 A deed made by one party only is not indented, but polled or shaved quite even. **1844** WILLIAMS *Real Prop.* (1875) 151.

4. To cut off the horns of (cattle). See POLLED *ppl. a.* 2.

III. 5. *fig.* To plunder by or as by excessive taxation; to pillage, rob, fleece, strip; to despoil (a person or place) *of* (anything). *arch.*

c **1489** CAXTON *Blanchardyn* xxxii. 119 Whiche were wythin their enmyes tentes & pauyllions, whiche they powlyd & brought doune. **1529** S. FISH *Supplic. Beggers* 3 Subiectes..that be after this facion yerely polled. **1551** ROBINSON tr. *More's Utop.* I. (1895) 46 Their tenauntes.. whom they polle and shaue to the quycke by reysing their rentes. **1565** *K. Daryus* (Brandl) 775 He doth poule poore men and lyueth by theyr sweat. **1634** CANNE *Necess. Separ.* (1849) 158 Daily new devices to poll the poor priests of their money. **1670** LASSELS *Voy. Italy* I. 134 The people here mow their hay three times a yeare, and I am affrayd they are powled [*ed.* **1698** polled] as often with taxes. **1681** WHARTON *Mutations*, etc. *Empires* Wks. (1683) 139 When the Prince doth too much Poll his Subjects with heavy Tributes and Exactions. [**1874** DIXON *Two Queens* IV. XXI. i. 123 Men whom he had tolled and polled..assailed him in the public streets.]

†**b.** *absol.* or *intr.* To practise extortion, commit depredations. *Obs.*

1521–2 *Cardnall Wolse* 61 in Furniv. *Ballads fr. MSS.* I. 335 All prowde knavys full of dysdayne, And þat Can bothe polle & shave. **1566** DRANT *Horace* iii. B v, He, for to lend to moe, Doth sheare, and shave and powle, and presse. **1613** *Answ. Uncasing of Machivils Instr.* E iv, But if too nerely thou dost pinch or poule, It may be burdensome vnto thy soule.

†**c.** Phr. ***to poll and pill***: see PILL *v.*[1] 9. *Obs.*

1545, etc. [see PILL *v.*[1] 9]. **1575–85** ABP. SANDYS *Serm.* (Parker Soc.) 287 Not to poll and pill, to extort and wring out of the people what he could. **1650** CROMWELL *Lett. & Sp., Declar.* Jan., Whom you have fleeced and polled and peeled hitherto.

†**d.** *trans.* To get by extortion or pillage. *Obs.*

1559 *Mirr. Mag., Mowbray's Banishm.* xxii, Myghty summes whiche I had from hym polde.

IV. †**6.** To pay as poll-tax. *Obs. rare*$^{-1}$.

1693 DRYDEN *Juvenal* III. (1697) 57 The Man that poll'd but Twelve-pence for his Head.

V. †**7.** To count heads; to enumerate (persons, etc.). *Obs.*

1649 MILTON *Eikon.* 160 To little purpose is it that we should stand powling the reformed Churches, whether they equalize in number those of his three kingdoms. **1703** MAUNDRELL *Journ. Jerus.* (1732) 65 So prodigious a number ..as are said to have been poll'd in the Twelve Tribes at one time. **1711** SHAFTESB. *Charact.* (1737) I. 148 If they can poll an indifferent number out of a mob..to attest a story of a witch upon a broomstick,..they triumph in the solid proof of their new prodigy.

8. To take the votes of, register the suffrages of; in *pass.* to have one's vote taken, to record a vote.

1625 [see POLLING *vbl. sb.* 5]. **1679** WOOD *Life* 27 Feb. (O.H.S.) II. 443 We were poled by two writers, without swearing, in the Divinity School. **1679** *Essex's Excell.* 7 There were about 500 came to the Town on purpose to be Polled for Collonel Mildmay and Honeywood. **1723** DK. WHARTON *True Briton* No. 9 I. 79 Whether some Hundreds of Persons were not polled for Hopkins and Feast. **1858** BRIGHT *Sp., Reform* 10 Dec. (1876) 297 Would it be tolerated by the people of this country, if they were fairly polled? **1867** *Ibid.* 20 June 403 That more excellent way of polling by the Ballot. *a* **1888** W. PHILLIPS *Speeches*, etc. 379 (Cent.), I believe you might have polled the North, and had a response, three to one: 'Let the Union go to pieces, rather than yield one inch'.

b. Of a candidate for election: To bring to the poll as voters; to receive (so many votes).

1846 in WORCESTER. **1864** in WEBSTER. **1871** M. COLLINS *Mrq. & Merch.* II. iii. 71 Don't poll your men. **1885** *Daily Tel.* 26 Nov. (Cassell), His Liberal opponent polled two thousand four hundred and eighty-six votes. **1892** GOLDW. SMITH *W. L. Garrison* viii. 102 Birney polled just enough votes to defeat Clay and throw the government directly into the hands of Slavery.

9. *intr.* To vote at a poll; to give one's vote.

1678 SIDNEY in *S. Papers* (1746) I. 153 Many refused to pole, and others would give no Voice. **1679** *Essex's Excell.* 8 Those that Polled against the Collonel. **1709** STEELE *Tatler* No. 73 ¶ 15 All such that shall Poll for Sir Arthur de Bradly, shall have one Chaldron of good Coals gratis. **1885** *Act 48 Vict.* c. 17 §9 (3) So that..an equal number of electors may ..poll in each district.

b. *trans.* To give or record (a vote).

1717 TICKELL *Lady to Gentl. at Avignon* Poems (1790) 189 Shall he..pole for points of faith his trusty vote? **1858** GLADSTONE *Homer* III. 117 Votes were not polled in the Olympus of Homer.

10. *Comb.* **'poll-groat**, *a.*, that polls groats, extortionate.

1888 MORRIS *Dream J. Ball* 15 The valiant tiler had smitten a poll-groat bailiff to death with his lath-rending axe.

Hence **'pollable** *a.*, that can be polled; having the right to have one's vote recorded.

1844 (*title*) List of Pollable Persons within the Shire of Aberdeen, 1696. **1868** *Contemp. Rev.* IX. 83 Supposing all votes to be pollable.

poll, obs. erroneous f. POLE; obs. f. POOL *sb.*[1]; var. POL *Obs.*

pollack, pollock ('pɒlək). Forms: (6 *Sc.* **podlok**), 7– **pollock, pollack**. See also PODLER, PODLEY. [Origin obscure: Gael. *pollag*, Ir. *pollóg, pullóg*, seem to agree in form, but are applied to fresh-water fishes, entirely different from this (see POLLAN, POWAN); Ger. and Du. *pollack* are from Eng. The 16th c. Sc. was *podlok* (whence later *podlo'*, PODLEY, etc.). It does not appear which of the two forms *podlok* and *pollock* was the original.]

A sea-fish of genus *Pollachius*, allied to the cod, but having the lower jaw protruding; comprising several species used for food in Europe and America, *esp.* the true or whiting pollack, *P. pollachius*, of European seas, also called *greenfish, lythe*, etc.; and the green pollack or COAL-FISH, *P. virens* or *carbonarius*, of the North Atlantic generally.

[**1502** *Acc. Ld. High Treas. Scot.* II. 148 Item, to the men that brocht podlokis to the King in the schip,..xij d. **1525** in *Exc. e Libris Dom. Jac. V* (Bann. Cl.) 7 Grenbans, podlokis, ..crunans.] **1602** CAREW *Cornwall* 32 Brets, Turbets, Dories,..Pollock, Mackrell, &c. *a* **1672** Rawlin Pollack [see RAWLIN]. **1769** PENNANT *Zool.* III. 154 The Pollack... During summer they are seen in great shoals frolicking on the surface of the water. **1836** YARRELL *Brit. Fishes* II. 172 The Pollack is much less abundant on some parts of our coasts than the Coalfish. **1864** COUCH *Brit. Fishes* III. 80. **1885** *American* X. 78 The pollack is a large fish, often running up to twenty pounds or more. **1888** GOODE *Amer. Fishes* 354 The liver of the Pollock yields a great quantity of oil.

†**b.** Applied to the Powan of Loch Lomond. *Obs.*

1827 AIKMAN tr. *Buchanan's Hist. Scot.* I. 28 One [fish] of a peculiar species and very delicious flavour, which they call the pollack [*orig.* I. xxiii. pollacas vocant].

†**c.** See quots. *Obs.*

1774 PENNANT *Tour Scot. in 1772*, 271 (*Hebrides*) See several small whales, called here Pollacks. *Ibid.* 323 Whales, pollacks, and porpesses.

d. as *Comb.*

1901 *Blackw. Mag.* Sept. 331/1 A couple of hours pollock-fishing.

Hence **'pollacking** *vbl. sb.*, fishing for pollacks.

1821 *Blackw. Mag.* IX. 370 Going out pollocking with some of the wild youngsters of the west. **1886** *Globe* 22 July 3/1 Equipped for an evening or morning's pollacking.

Pollack, var. POLACK *sb.* (*a.*)

†**'pollage.** *Obs.* Also 6 **pollag.** [app. f. POLL *v.* + -AGE, after *pillage*, etc.; but often associated with the exaction of *poll-money*.] **a.** Extortion or legalized robbery. **b.** Exaction of a poll-tax.

1538 BALE *Brefe Comedy* in *Harl. Misc.* (Malh.) I. 206 A publicane I am, and moch do lyve by pollage. **1545** BRINKLOW *Compl.* xxiii. (1874) 55 Some wil say yes, his tributys, and other pollagys, be taken from him. **1583** STUBBES *Anat. Abus.* II. (1882) 32 As though these pollages and pillages were not ill enough. **1894** *Pop. Sc. Monthly* XLIV. 299 In Switzerland this pollage is still levied.

pollakanthic (pɒlə'kænθɪk), *a. Bot.* [f. Gr. πολλάκ-ις many times + ἄνθ-ος flower + -IC I.] = POLYCARPIC *a.* a. Also **polla'kanthous** *a.* in the same sense.

1909 GROOM & BALFOUR tr. *Warming's Oecol. Plants* ii. 6 In recent times these Candollean terms have been suppressed often in favour of..Kjellman's 'pollakanthic'. **1965** BELL & COOMBE tr. *Strasburger's Textbk. Bot.* 355 The production of vegetative members by the growing points changes over to that of flowers, fruits and seeds,.. periodically, as in pollakanthous plants. **1973** MCLEAN & IVIMEY-COOK *Textbk. Theoret. Bot.* IV. xlii. 3353 Polycarpic (pollakanthic) plants..flower and fruit repeatedly.

‖**pollam** ('pɒləm). *East Ind.* [ad. Telugu *pāḷemu*, Tamil *pālaiyam*: cf. POLIGAR.] A feudal estate or territory held by a poligar.

1783 BURKE *Sp. Fox's E. India Bill* Wks. IV. 79 There was no pollam, or castle, which in the happy days of the Carnatick was without some hoard of treasure. **1795** WYNCH in J. H. Nelson *Madura* IV. (1868) 15 Having submitted the general remarks on the Pollams I shall..observe that in general the conduct of the Poligars is much better than could be expected. **1798** WELLINGTON *Suppl. Desp.* (1858) I. 148 The polygars of the neighbouring pollams.

pollan ('pɒlən). Also 8 **pullein**, 8–9 **pollen.** [Cf. Gael. *pollag*, Ir. *pollóg, pullóg*, ? f. Ir. *poll* inland lake + *-óg (-ag), -an*, Celt. deriv. formatives.] A species of fresh-water fish, *Coregonus pollan*, found in the inland loughs of Ireland (L. Neagh, Earne, Derg, Corrib, etc.). It belongs to the same genus as the Powan or Gwyniad, and the Vendace (with both of which it has been mistakenly identified, as by Pennant and R. C. Hoare).

1713 NEVILL *Lough-Neagh* in *Phil. Trans.* XXVIII. 262 The English call them fresh Water Herrings, for want of another Name; for Pollan is an Irish Name. **1796** MORSE *Amer. Geog.* II. 177 (*Ireland*) The Pullein, or, as some call it, the fresh-water herring. **1807** SIR R. C. HOARE *Tour Irel.* 224 The pollen, which is the same as the *ferra* of the lake of Geneva. **1864** J. G. BERTRAM in *Vac. Tour* 65 The powan of Loch Lomond and the pollan of Lough Neagh are not the same fish, but both belong to the Corregoni; the powan is long and slender, while the pollan is an altogether stouter fish. **1898** *Daily News* 15 Mar. 9/4 Notice that it is illegal to buy, sell, or expose for sale,.. any fresh water fish other than pollan, trout, char, and eels, between the 15th day of March and the 15th day of June, both inclusive.

†**pollange.** *Obs. rare.* [? a. OF. *palange* (14th c. in Godef.) a lever for launching boats (in 13th c. *palanche, palangue* a pole or yoke for carrying buckets) = It. *palanga*, L. *p(h)alanga* carrying pole, roller: see POLANCRE.] ? Some appliance for lifting.

1373 in Riley *Lond. Mem.* (1868) 369, 2 upties, 2 pollanges ..20 poleynes, 2 wyndyng poleys, 2 skeynes of poletwyne.

pollankan, obs. form of PALANKEEN.

†'**pollantine.** *Obs. rare*⁻¹. [Origin unknown. Cf. POLLACK c.] ? A porpoise.

1557–8 PHAER *Æneid* v. O iv, Onweldy whales..And pollantines, and armies broade of seales, and dolphins blewe.

pollarchy ('pɒlɑːkɪ). *rare.* [f. Gr. πολλ-οί in phr. οἱ πολλοί the many, the multitude, after *monarchy, oligarchy*, etc.: cf. POLYARCHY.] The rule of the multitude; government by the mob.

1862 RUSSELL *Diary North & South* II. 340 A contest.. between those representing the oligarchical principle and the pollarchy. **1881** E. PEACOCK in *Academy* 15 Oct. 287 Pollarchy..if used with circumspection would raise any rural person.

†'**pollard**, *sb.*¹ *Obs.* exc. *Hist.* [app. f. POLL *sb.*¹ + -ARD (in reference to its device, a head: cf. the names *crocard, rosary, leonine, eagle*, etc. given to other foreign coins).] One of various base coins of foreign origin, current in England in the end of the 13th c., as an equivalent of the penny; in 1299 declared illegal.

1299 in *Liber Custumarum* (Rolls) I. 187 Ordene est par nous e nostre Counsaill,..qe la mauveise moneie, qe hom apele 'crocard' e 'pollard', e autre tele male moneie, ne courge en nostre dit reiaume, auxi com ad fait cea en ariere. **1308–9** *Rolls of Parlt.* I. 273/2 A ly furent disaloue sur sun ascunt LIV li del polards, del temps qe ele pollard corust pur une Esterlyng. *a* **1363** HIGDEN *Polychronicon* (Rolls) VIII. 288 Rex Edwardus damnavit subito monetam surreptitiam et illegitimam quam pollardas, crocardos, rosarios nominabant, qui paulatim et latenter loco sterlingorum irrepserant. **1387** TREVISA *transl.*, Kyng Edward dampned sodeynliche fals money þat was slyliche i-brouȝt up: Men cleped þe money pollardes, crocardes and rosaries, and were putte forþ litel and litel and priveliche in stede of sterlynges. First þey made oon of hem worþ an half peny, and þan he fordede hem all out. **1568** GRAFTON *Chron.* II. 182. **1601–2** FULBECKE *1st Pt. Parall.* 41 If..the obligee refuseth the money when it is tendered in pollardes, which afterward are embased. **1605** CAMDEN *Rem.* (1636) 186 The same King likewise called in certaine counterfeit pieces coyned by the French called Pollards. **1716** M. DAVIES *Athen. Brit.* III. 78 Forreign Coyns and Counterfeit-Money, cry'd down, or considerably loar'd by Edw. I by the Name of Pollards, Crocards, Staldings, Eagles, Leonines, Rosaries, and Steepings. **1866** ROGERS *Agric. & Prices* I. ii. 178 A considerable circulation of Flemish coins, apparently of low purity... Pollards, Crockards, Scaldings, Brabants, Eagles, Leonines [etc.].

pollard ('pɒləd), *sb.*² (*a.*) Also 6 polerde, 6–8 -ard, 7 -ord. [In senses 1–3, prob. also in 4, f. POLL *v.* + -ARD.]

I. 1. An animal of a kind naturally horned, as an ox or stag, which has cast or lost its horns; also, an ox, sheep, or goat of a hornless variety.

1546 *Plumpton Corr.* (Camden) 251 Ye shall se a polard or tow, both rid & falow, & se all our good coxs fight. **1611** BEAUM. & FL. *Philaster* v. iv, 2 *Cit.* He has no horns, sir, has he? *Cap.* No, sir, he's a pollard. **1623** COCKERAM, *Pollard*, is a Stagge, or any other male Deere, hauing cast his head. **1658** in PHILLIPS. **1736** BAILEY *Househ. Dict.* 304 The sort of goat without horns or such as are call'd pollards, are much commended.

2. A tree which has been polled or cut back, at some height above the ground, so as to produce at that point a thick close growth of young branches, forming a rounded head or mass.

1611 *MS. Acc. St. John's Hosp., Canterb.*, For sa[w]ing and cleving owt of polords vj. **1662** PETTY *Taxes* 44 The same ill husbandry, as to make fuel of young saplings, instead of dotards and pollards. **1796** *Campaigns* 1793–4 I. II. ii. 103 Impenetrable hedge rows, composed of sturdy pollards. **1816** SOUTHEY *Poet's Pilgr. Waterloo* I. xx, The pollard that the Flemish painter loves. **1859** W. S. COLEMAN *Woodlands* (1866) 89 Even the stunted pollard..is not without its pictorial value.

Comb. **1885** G. ALLEN *Babylon* xxix, Long straight pollard-lined roads.

†**3.** Short for *pollard wheat*: see B. 1. *Obs.*

1573 TUSSER *Husb.* (1878) 49 White pollard or red, that so richly is set, for land that is heauie is best ye can get. **1616** SURFL. & MARKH. *Country Farme* 543 The next is small Pollard, which loues an indifferent earth. **1688** R. HOLME *Armoury* III. 268/2.

II. 4. Bran sifted from flour; *techn.* a finer grade of bran containing some flour; also, flour or meal containing the finer bran. Cf. TOPPINGS.

1577 HARRISON *England* II. vi. (1877) I. 154 The coursest of the bran (vsuallie called gurgeons or pollard). **1601** in *Househ. Ord.* (1790) 291 The Serjeants of the pastry..to have for their fees all the pollard which comes of the meale. **1763** *Museum Rust.* I. lxxi. 309, I feed my horse with the chaff, and add but one eighth part of pollard. **1817–18** COBBETT *Resid. U.S.* (1822) 160 Will it be believed, in another century, that the law-givers of a great nation actually passed a law to compel people to eat pollard in their bread,..for the purpose of..adding to the quantity of bread in a time of scarcity? **1846** J. BAXTER *Libr. Pract. Agric.* (ed. 4) II. 405 A bushel of wheat..will yield, on being ground, —Of bread flour 47, fine pollard 4¼, coarse pollard 4, bran 2⅝, Loss of weight..2; = 60 lbs.

B. *attrib.* or as *adj.*

†**1.** Of wheat: Beardless, awnless. *Obs.*

1523 FITZHERB. *Husb.* §34 Polerde wheate hath noo anis. **1577** B. GOOGE *Heresbach's Husb.* (1586) 26 b, We call it pold or pollard, that hath no aanes upon the eares. *a* **1661** FULLER *Worthies, Middlesex* 189 The Mildew..which sticketh on notted or pollard Wheat. **1765** [see POLLED *ppl. a.* 4].

2. That is a pollard (tree); polled, lopped.

1669 WORLIDGE *Syst. Agric.* (1681) 108 These Pollard or Shrowded Trees need no Fence to be maintained about them. **1776** PENNANT *Zool.* (1812) I. 264 Grubbing up an old pollard ash. **1815** M. BIRKBECK *Journ. France* 48 The olive is a miserable looking tree, most like a pollard willow. **1831** LYTTON *Godolphin* xii, Grassy banks, over-grown with the willow and pollard oak. **1880** SHORTHOUSE *J. Inglesant* xxxiv. 487 The pollard firs upon the ramparts stood out distinctly in fantastic forms.

b. *transf.* or *fig.* Bald-headed.

1855 DICKENS *Dorrit* xxxi, Flecks of light in his flat vista of pollard old men.

†'**pollard**, *sb.*³ *Obs.* [f. POLL *sb.*¹ + -ARD: from its large head, whence also the names *testard, chevin, capito*, etc.] A fish: the chub or chevin.

1585 HIGINS *Junius' Nomencl.* 65/2 *Capito,..cephalus fluuialis.* Munier,..vilain,..testard, a capitis magnitudine. A Polard. **1611** COTGR., *Munier*, a miller..; also, a Pollard, or Cheuin (fish). **1706** in PHILLIPS. **1721** BAILEY, *Pollard*, a Chevin or Chub-fish. **1736–61** in AINSWORTH *Lat. Dict.*

pollard ('pɒləd), *v.* [f. POLLARD *sb.*²] *trans.* To cut off the branches of (a tree), leaving only the main trunk; to make a pollard of.

1670 EVELYN *Sylva* xviii. §1 (ed. 2) 80 The Black Poplar is frequently pollar'd when as big as ones arm, eight or nine foot from the ground. **1707** MORTIMER *Husb.* (1721) II. 39 Those that are pollarded grow the most knotty and full of Burs. **1887** MOLONEY *Forestry W. Afr.* 420 In order to obtain as large a yield of juice as possible the natives pollard the trees when at a height of ten to twelve feet.

fig. **1836** HARE *Guesses* Ser. II. (1874) 75, I hate to see trees pollarded—or nations. **1858** W. JOHNSON *Ionica* 62 They are pollarded by cares And give themselves religious airs And grow not. **1859** G. MEREDITH *R. Feverel* II. x. 185 Richard having been, as it were, pollarded by Destiny, was now to grow up straight.

Hence '**pollarded** *ppl. a.* (also *fig.*); '**pollarding** *vbl. sb.* (also *attrib.* as ***pollarding-knife***).

1821 CRAIG *Lect. Drawing* v. 286 Lopping and pollarding also produce wonderful changes on the aspect of trees. **1827** STEUART *Planter's G.* (1828) 519 A few pollarded, or at least mutilated Trees. **1830** COLERIDGE *Table-t.* 15 June, The pollarded man, the man with every faculty except the reason. **1868** FREEMAN *Norm. Conq.* II. viii. 287 A tree whose branches are cut off by the pollarding-knife.

'**pollardy**, *a.* [f. POLLARD *sb.*² 4 + -Y.] Of the nature of pollard or fine bran.

1872 J. G. FENNELL in Taunt *Map Thames* 15/1 The bran we get from the mill is either too coarse or too pollardy.

†**pollart.** *Obs. rare*⁻¹. [perh. the same word as POLLARD, f. POLL, head.] One of the fanciful names given in ME. to the hare.

a **1325** *Names of Hare* in *Rel. Ant.* I. 134 The fnattart, the pollart, His hei nome is srewart.

pollax, -axe, obs. forms of POLE-AXE.

pollayne, variant of PULLEN *Obs.*, poultry.

poll-bill. [f. POLL(-MONEY), or POLL *sb.*¹ + BILL *sb.*³ 3.] A bill for levying a poll-tax.

1641 in Rushw. *Hist. Coll.* III. (1692) I. 304 Sir Simon d'Ewes his Speech concerning the Assessing of the Peers in the Poll-Bill. **1666** MARVELL *Corr.* Wks. (Grosart) II. 191 Forain excise, home excise, a poll-bill.., have been all more or lesse disputed. **1761–2** HUME *Hist. Eng.* (1806) IV. lxiii. 680 Sums..levied..by a poll-bill and new assessments.

poll-cat, obs. f. POLECAT.

polldavy, obs. f. POLDAVY.

'**poll deed.** Now *rare.* [f. POLL *a.* + DEED.] = DEED POLL.

1523 FITZHERB. *Surv.* 20 Estates made of free lande by polle dede or dede indented. **1597** in *Cal. Proc. Chanc. Q. Eliz.* (1827) I. Introd. 146 As by the said pole deede, and the chirographe of the said fine..yt doth and maye appeare. **1627** HAKEWILL *Apol.* I. v. 47 The Pole-deede of their evidence, is this. **1854** W. PEIRCE *Princ. & Polity Wesleyan Methodists* Index, Poll Deed [i.e. 'The Deed of Declaration of the Reverend John Wesley']. **1899** *Daily News* 19 July 3/5 The President thought he would prepare to some extent for the duties, so read the Poll Deed.

pollderon, obs. f. POULDRON.

polle, obs. form of POLE, POLL, PULL.

polled (pəʊld), *a.* [f. POLL *sb.*¹ + -ED².] (In comb.) Having a poll or head of a specified form or appearance, as ***curly-polled***.

1795 *Fate of Sedley* I. 59, I would as soon marry a curly-poled nymph from Otaheite.

polled (pəʊld), *ppl. a.* Also 4 pollid, 6 poulde, 6–7 pold(e, 7 powled, poled. [f. POLL *v.* + -ED¹.]

†**1.** Having the hair cut short; shorn, shaven; also of the hair: cut off, clipped. *Obs.*

13.. *K. Alis.* 216 Neptanabus in theo way stod, With pollid hed, and of his hod. **1388** WYCLIF *Job* i. 20 Thanne Ioob roos, and to-rente hise clothis, and with pollid heed [1382 hed shauen: *Vulg.* tonso capite] he felde doun on the erthe. **1555** EDEN *Decades* 299 Men of meane stature, with roughe and thyck beardes and poulde heade. *a* **1586** SIDNEY *Arcadia* II. (1622) 187 These polled lockes of mine. **1650** BULWER *Anthropomet.* viii. (1653) 144 In the Province Cusco,..are those Auriti or great Ear'd Men,..who alwaies goe poled.

2. Hornless; having shed or been deprived of horns; of a hornless breed.

1607 TOPSELL *Four-f. Beasts* (1658) 490 The horned Beast ..is apter to fight then the pold Sheep, and also more luxurious among the Ewes. **1758** R. BROWN *Compl. Farmer* (1759) 32 The polled sheep (that is sheep without horns) are reckoned the best breeders. **1835** KIRBY *Hab. & Inst. Anim.* I. ii. 59 Some varieties of the common ox are polled. **1842** [see ANGUS]. **1867** W. MCCOMBIE *Cattle* iv. 138 Mr. Lyell.. has a very good herd of polled Angus cattle. **1891** R. WALLACE *Rural Econ. Austral. & N.Z.* xxxii. 415 Polled Angus cattle have come very rapidly into favour during the last few years. **1902** *Times* 13 Mar. 6/1 A herd of Red Polled cattle. **1909** J. WILSON *Evolution of Brit. Cattle* v. 57 The Sutherland polled cattle are long extinct. **1940** J. HAMMOND *Farm Animals* viii. 149 If we mate a polled red Aberdeen Angus bull to a Shorthorn cow we shall obtain polled calves. **1976** *Cumberland & Westmorland Herald* 4 Dec. 16/2 (Advt.), Fortnightly sale of Friesian, Hereford cross, Charolais' cross and polled bullocks and heifers of all ages.

3. Of trees: Pollarded.

1611 COTGR. s.v. *Fustée, Bois de fustée*, branchlesse wood; naked, or powled trees. **1882** *Mrs. Raven's Tempt.* I. 213 Standing behind a row of polled trees.

†**4.** Of wheat: Awnless, not bearded. *Obs. dial.*

1765 *Museum Rust.* IV. lxiii. 285, I wish I had it in my power to satisfy E. S. concerning the pollard wheat he mentions; but I can learn nothing of it, unless it is a bearded great wheat, which, in Suffolk, they formerly let stand in the field till the awns dropped off, and then they called it poll'd wheat.

†**5.** Plundered, pillaged. *Obs.*

1538 ELYOT, *Compilati*, polled by extorcion. **1552** HULOET, Polled or brybed, *compilatus, exactus.*

†**6.** ***polled deed*** = POLL DEED. *Obs.*

1706 PHILLIPS, *Polled Deed.* See Deed-poll.

7. *Comb.*, as ***polled-headed*** adj.

1583 FOXE *A. & M.* 1268/1 A man of talle stature, polled headed, and on the same a rounde Frenche cappe of the best.

pollee (pəʊ'liː). [f. POLL *sb.*¹ + -EE¹.] One who is questioned in a poll (sense 7 d).

1940 *Propaganda Analysis* IV. 4/2 The question, 'For whom will you vote for President of the United States?' illustrates Objectivism. It gives to the pollee full liberty to name any candidate. **1941** *Amer. Speech* XVI. 306 *Pollee*, one polled by a public-opinion 'institute'. **1945** *Richmond* (Va.) *Times-Dispatch* 25 Oct. 10/6 Mr. Gallup..should consult his little band of pollees and come up with their prophecy as to which of our service teams will go home with the goal posts. **1962** *Guardian* 3 Aug. 14/6 The 54 pollees who had voted last time had come within one percentage of splitting their 1960 votes.

pollen ('pɒlɪn), *sb.* [a. L. *pollen, -inem* fine flour, fine dust, in sense from mod.L. (Linn.).]

†**1.** Fine flour or meal; fine powder. *Obs.*

1523 LD. BERNERS *Froiss.* I. xvi. 18 As well of pollen, as of other vitailes. **1601** HOLLAND *Pliny* XVIII. x. I. 564 Wheat flower called Pollen. **1620** VENNER *Via Recta* i. 17 *Pollen* is the purest part of the meale, that is, the finest part of the flower. **1730–6** BAILEY (folio), *Pollen*,..a sort of fine bran.

2. *Bot.* The fine granular or powdery substance, produced by and discharged from the anther of a flower, constituting the male element destined for the fertilization of the ovules.

[**1751** LINNÆUS *Philos. Bot.* 56 Pollen est pulvis vegetabilium appropriato liquore madefactus.] **1760** J. LEE *Introd. Bot.* I. iv. (1765) 10 The Pollen, Meal, contained within the Antheræ, is a fine Dust secreted therein. **1792** J. E. SMITH *Eng. Bot.* 43 *Papaver hybridum*..flowers..deep crimson, or purplish, pollen bright blue. **1828** STARK *Elem. Nat. Hist.* II. 355 Furnished with a tuft of hairs proper for collecting the pollen of flowers. **1881** LUBBOCK in *Nature* XXIV. 404/2 He proved that flowers fertilised with pollen from the other form yield more seed than if fertilised with pollen of the same form.

3. *Comb.*, as ***pollen-content(s)***, ***-zone***; ***pollen-bearing***, ***-covered***, ***-dated***, ***-devouring***, ***-dusted***, ***-eating***, ***-free***, ***-like*** adjs.; **pollen analysis** = PALYNOLOGY; hence **pollen analyst**, a scientist who uses the techniques of pollen analysis; **pollen-analytic(al)** *adjs.*; **pollen-analytically** *adv.*; **pollen-basket**, a hollow structure on the leg of a bee, adapted for carrying pollen; = BASKET 7, CORBICULA (*Syd. Soc. Lex.* 1895); **pollen-brush**, a set of hairs forming a fringe on the *pollen-basket*; **pollen-catarrh** = *pollen-fever* (*Syd. Soc. Lex.*); **pollen-cell**, (*a*) a cell which develops into a pollen-grain, or forms part of one; (*b*) = *pollen-sac*; (*c*) a cell in a honeycomb in which pollen is stored; **pollen-chamber**, the cavity in which the pollen is deposited at the tip of the ovule in Gymnosperms; **pollen count**, an index of the quantity of pollen in the air, obtained by counting the grains collected on a given area of a coated glass plate exposed for twenty-four hours, and published as a warning to those allergic to it; also, an indication of the frequency of pollen in an archæological site; also *fig.*; **pollen diagram**, a sequence of pollen spectra from one site, showing changes in the frequencies of various types of pollen; **pollen-fever** = HAY-FEVER; **pollen-grain**, each of the grains of which pollen consists (usually a single cell, sometimes two or more united, of varying form and size in different plants, and having two coats, the *intine* and *extine*); **pollen-granule**, each of the ultimate granules contained in a pollen-grain; also = *pollen-grain*; **pollen graph** = *pollen diagram*; **pollen index** = *pollen count*; **pollen-mass** = POLLINIUM; **pollen mother cell**, a cell in a seed plant which undergoes meiosis to yield four pollen grains; **pollen parent**, the plant from which pollen is taken to fertilize another plant in an attempt to produce a hybrid; **pollen-paste**, a substance consisting of pollen mixed with a little honey, made by bees for feeding their larvæ (*Syd. Soc. Lex.*); **pollen-plate**, a flat or hollow surface fringed with hairs, occurring on the legs or body of bees, used for carrying pollen (cf. *pollen-basket*); **pollen profile** = *pollen diagram*; **pollen-sac**, each of the (usually four) cavities or loculi of an anther, in which the pollen is contained; **pollen spectrum**, the relative frequencies of the various types of pollen in a single sample; **pollen-sporangium**, a name for the antheridium in club-mosses, which contains the pollen-spores; **pollen-spore**, a name for the microspores in club-mosses, as analogous to pollen-grains; **pollen-tube**, a tube formed by protrusion of the intine of a pollen-grain when deposited upon the stigma, which penetrates the style so as to convey the fertilizing substance to the ovule.

1924 G. ERDTMAN in *Jrnl. Linn. Soc.: Bot.* XLVI. 450 The study of micro-fossils (and especially of fossil pollen-grains), upon which von Post's method of *pollen-analysis is based. **1935** *Discovery* Apr. 100/1 The methods of pollen-analysis . . enable one to know of the afforestation and in consequence of the climate of the period during which any particular stratum in a peat deposit was laid down. **1944**, **1958** [see PALYNOLOGY]. **1973** *Microscopy* XXXII. 321 Erdtman prepared and presented the first doctoral thesis ever to be based on pollen analysis. **1943** G. ERDTMAN *Introd. Pollen Analysis* i. 1 Still more remarkable appear the performances accomplished by the *pollen analyst today. **1973** *Microscopy* XXXII. 320 Gustav Lagerheim (1860–1926) was one of the earliest pollen analysts. **1949** *Bull. Geol. Soc. Amer.* LX. 1359/2 Events . . may have been contemporaneous in the astronomic as well as the *pollen-analytic sense. **1946** F. E. ZEUNER *Dating Past* iii. 59 Further important remarks on the principles and system of *pollen-analytical datings are included in a great many papers. **1976** *Nature* 24 June 628/1 Some new information . . has been gleaned . . as a result of a pollen analytical study of upper Miocene lignites. **1936** *Proc. Prehistoric Soc.* II. 146 One may quote an instance from the Baltic . . *pollen-analytically dated to Boreal times. **1946** F. E. ZEUNER *Dating Past* iv. 78 A good many localities have been studied pollen-analytically. **1860** *Chambers' Encycl.* I. 799/1 (*Bee*) Neither males nor queens have wax-pockets, nor have they *pollen-baskets. **1946** F. E. ZEUNER *Dating Past* iv. 80 Nilsson has studied the connexion of *pollen-bearing deposits with raised beaches. **1900** CUNNINGHAM *Sexual Dimorphism* v. 261 In the hive bee the *pollen-brush on the legs is wanting in the queen, but present in the worker. **1857** HENFREY *Elem. Bot.* §928 Compound pollen-grains, consisting of a number of *pollen-cells permanently coherent. **1875** BENNETT & DYER *Sachs' Bot.* 440 The four young pollen-cells are now freed by the rapid absorption of the cell-wall which surrounds and separates them. **1888** *Chambers' Encycl.* II. 22/2 A pollen-cell is (frequently at least) sealed with honey, and over this a thin cream-like pellicle is formed, which can be pushed aside for the deposition of more honey. **1887** tr. *Strasburger's Bot.* 304 The nucellar apex is hollowed out in order to receive the pollen-grains, giving rise to the so-called *pollen-chamber. **1898** *Ibid.* II. ii. 438 [The ovules of Cycas] are atropous, and provided . . with a cavity, the pollen-chamber, in which the pollen-grains . . accumulate preparatory to fertilisation. **1946** F. E. ZEUNER *Dating Past* iii. 57 The *pollen-contents of a peat are more or less characteristic of the tree-associations that grew in the neighbourhood of the spot under investigation. **1954** S. PIGGOTT *Neolithic Cultures* i. 3 The evidence for the natural conditions of vegetation in Atlantic and Sub-Boreal times is based most reliably on the pollen-content of stratified peats. [**1873** C. J. BLACKLEY *Experimental Researches on Catarrhus Æstivus* iv. 122 After being exposed for twenty-four hours, each slip was placed under the microscope, and any deposit it contained was carefully examined, and the number of pollen grains counted.] **1926** KOESSLER & DURHAM in *Jrnl. Amer. Med. Assoc.* LXXXVI. 1205/1 For the air study . . differential *pollen counts were made daily. **1944** URBACH & GOTTLIEB *Allergy* xix. 607 In order to become acquainted with the local flora, the physician should undertake pollen counts himself. **1965** *Punch* 15 Sept. 375/2 Throughout the summer, New York newspapers forecast daily . . a 'pollen count' for hay-fever victims. **1975** G. W. DIMBLEBY in R. Bruce-Mitford *Sutton Hoo Ship-Burial* I. i. 68 (*heading*) Soil under ship-barrow pollen counts. **1978** *Times* 7 July 2/8 The pollen count issued in London yesterday by the Asthma Research Council was one, very low. **1936** *Proc. Prehistoric Soc.* II. 239 The forest culture of S.E. Britain, best known from the *pollen-dated site of Lower Halstow, had diverged very markedly. **1859** DARWIN *Orig. Spec.* iv. (1860) 92 Carried . . by the *pollen-devouring insects from flower to flower. **1924** G. ERDTMAN in *Jrnl. Linn. Soc.: Bot.* XLVI. 453 By means of the percentage numbers a *pollen-diagram is constructed. **1954** S. PIGGOTT *Neolithic Cultures* i. 4 The pollen diagrams constructed from stratified peats in many parts of the British Isles show a consistent evolution of forest assemblages. **1973** PROCTOR & YEO *Pollination of Flowers* viii. 276 The pollen diagrams from different sites show striking correspondences in the course of events. **1883** G. ALLEN in *Knowledge* 8 June 336/2 *Pollen-eating flies, weevils, and caterpillars. **1887** SIR A. CLARK in *Lancet* 11 June 1169/1 The epithets of 'hay fever', 'hay asthma', '*pollen fever', 'rose cold', and 'peach cold'. **1963** *New Yorker* 15 June 117 Heated swimming pool. . . *Pollen-free air. **1975** G. W. DIMBLEBY in R. Bruce-Mitford *Sutton Hoo Ship-Burial* I. i. 55 This pollen profile appears to have developed in a pollen-free sand deposit. This would accord with the suggestion that at some time during or since the Anglo-Saxon period the soil was truncated down to the pollen-free subsoil. **1835** HENSLOW *Princ. Bot.* §262 The inner membrane of the *pollen grain. **1872** OLIVER *Elem. Bot.* I. i. 8 The fine powder is the pollen, and each of its globular cells is a pollen-grain. **1835** HENSLOW *Princ. Bot.* §262 A sort of rude sack, termed a 'pollen tube', . . contains a liquid, the 'fovilla', in which are dispersed a number of very minute '*pollen granules'. **1959** J. D. CLARK *Prehist. Southern Afr.* vi. 160 The grasslands of our Central Plateau Region which, the *pollen-graphs from Florisbad tell us, must have still been open country even at the height of the pluvial. **1973** 'D. JORDAN' *Nile Green* ii. 12 Most of us have hay fever and the *pollen index was high. **1863** GROSART *Small Sins* 83, I brushed off the fine *pollen-like powder of its wings. **1847** W. E. STEELE *Field Bot.* 166 Glands of the stalks of the *pollen-masses naked. **1884** *Jrnl. R. Microsc. Soc.* 714 We should have a case similar to that seen in the *pollen-mother-cells of *Fritillaria persica*. **1889** *Bot. Gaz.* XIV. 109 If any person has experienced difficulty in obtaining pollen mother-cells in excellent condition for study, their attention is called to the young anthers of *Negundo aceroides* Moench. **1926** *Ibid.* LXXXI. 154 In a given loculus of an anther the pollen mother cells of the apple show little variation in stage of development. **1976** BELL & COOMBE tr. *Strasburger's Textbk. Bot.* 39 (*caption*) Prophase of the first meiotic divisions of a pollen mother cell. **1910** *Nat. Rose Society's Rose Ann.* 50 Place the top of the finger upon the anthers of the variety it is proposed to use as the *pollen parent. **1933** *Lily Year-bk.* 173 The plant showed no trace of the pollen parent and was discarded. **1976** *Lilies* 36 The plant with narrow leaves had a long chromosome . . of a type found in the pollen parent. **1899** *Cambr. Nat. Hist.* VI. 12 In the species with *pollen plates, the pollen is made into a mass of a clay-like consistence. **1967** M. J. COE *Ecology Alpine Zone Mt. Kenya* 52 If the *pollen profile is correlated with a time scale . . it has been possible . . to demonstrate an interesting sequence of vegetation zone depression. **1972** *Computers & Humanities* VII. 40 Pollen analysis is now being aided by the computer, either to compile and print the pollen profiles . . or to perform statistical analysis of pollen data. **1875** BENNETT & DYER *Sachs' Bot.* 426 The surrounding layers of tissue become developed into the wall of the *pollen-sac. *Ibid.* 433. **1924** G. ERDTMAN in *Jrnl. Linn. Soc.: Bot.* XLVI. 453 The relative frequency-numbers . . constitute the *pollen-spectrum of the sample. **1946** F. E. ZEUNER *Dating Past* iii. 59 A circle with sectors giving the frequency of the most important species in the pollen-spectrum can be inserted on a map. **1977** *New Phytologist* LXXVIII. 711 The sequence of four pollen spectra from the Coralline Crag shows no great variation from one level to the next. **1861** BENTLEY *Man. Bot.* I. v. 375 The antheridia or *pollen-sporangia are somewhat reniform, two-valved cases . . containing a large number of small spores (microspores), in which spermatozoids are ultimately produced. *Ibid.* 372 The antheridia contain a number of small cells. . . These . . are sometimes called *pollen-spores or small spores, while the large germinating spore is called the ovulary-spore or large spore. **1835** *Pollen-tube [see *pollen-granule*]. **1875** HUXLEY & MARTIN *Elem. Biol.* (1883) 71 A pollen grain deposited on the stigma, sends out a hypha-like prolongation, the pollen tube, which elongates, passes down the style, and eventually reaches the micropyle of an ovule. **1946** F. E. ZEUNER *Dating Past* 389, 23 finds . . dated according to *pollen zones. **1973** P. A. COLINVAUX *Introd. Ecol.* vii. 100 A nine or ten pollen-zone sequence . . named in Roman numerals.

Hence ˈ**pollen** *v. trans.*, to convey pollen to, to pollinate; to cover or sprinkle with pollen; ˈ**pollened** (-ɪnd) *a.*, containing pollen.

1877 LANIER *Bee* 42 He beareth starry stuff about his wings To pollen thee and sting thee fertile. **1880** TENNYSON *Voy. Maeldune* v, And we wallow'd in beds of lilies . . Till each like a golden image was pollen'd from head to feet. **1895** A. AUSTIN in *Blackw. Mag.* Apr. 517 She made The gold of the pollened palm to float On her budding bosom.

pollen, variant of POLLAN, PULLEN.

pollenarious, pollenation, erron. ff. POLLIN-.

pollency (ˈpɒlənsɪ). *rare.* [ad. L. *pollēntia* strength: see POLLENT.] Power, strength.

1623 COCKERAM, *Pollencie*, power. **1665–6** *Phil. Trans.* I. 238 To determine readily what Pollency the Buble hath.

pollenger (ˈpɒlɪndʒə(r)). *dial.* [? f. POLLING *vbl. sb.* + -ER[1], or for earlier **pollager*, f. POLLAGE + -ER[1].] A pollard tree.

1573 TUSSER *Husb.* (1878) 78 Now lop for thy fewell old pollenger growen [*ed.* 1557 the powlinges well growen]. **1610** in *Coke's Rep.* (1738) XIII. 67 Consuevit ad ejus libitum amputare ramos omnimodarum arborum, called pollengers, or husbords. **1738** *transl.* A custom . . to cut down and take at their pleasure all manner of trees called pollengers or husbords.

polleniferous, erron. form of POLLINIFEROUS.

ˈ**pollenin.** *Chem.* [ad. F. *pollénine*, f. POLLEN: see -IN[1].] A supposed peculiar substance obtained from pollen, and from the spores of *Lycopodium*: see quots. Cf. SPOROPOLLENIN.

Quot. 1931 does not represent a new sense.

1816 *Thomson's Ann. Philos.* VII. 49 The pollen, he [Professor John] finds, always contains a peculiar substance, which has hitherto been considered as albumen; but to which he has given the name of pollenin. **1819** J. G. CHILDREN *Chem. Anal.* 293 Pollenin is obtained from the pollen of the pinus sylvestris; it is yellow, and has neither taste nor smell. **1895** *Syd. Soc. Lex.*, *Pollenin*, name incorrectly given to the combustible substance which forms the residue after treatment of Lycopodium powder with dilute alcoholic solution of potash. Lycopodium powder is formed of spores, and is not composed of pollen. **1931** *Chem. Abstr.* XXV. 2455 Qual[itative] tests on many pollens showed that their hulls or membranes are similar chemically to lycopodium-sporenin [*sic*], and the name *pollenin* is proposed for such compds. **1964** [see SPORONIN]. **1971** CHALONER & ORBELL in J. Brooks et al. *Sporopollenin* 274 In terms of modern usage, both John and Braconnot were using the word pollenin not only for the exine, but also for the underlying intine of cellulose—in fact the whole of the sporoderm or spore coat. **1974** STANLEY & LINSKENS *Pollen* ix. 138 Early studies . . reported pollen to contain about 40% pollenin.

pollenize, etc.: see POLLINIZE, etc.

pollenizer (ˈpɒlɪnaɪzə(r)). [f. POLLENIZE *v.* + -ER[1].] = POLLINATOR.

1897 *Bull. Central Exper. Farm Dept. Agric.* (Canada) No. 27. 18 This [variety of strawberry] is valuable as a pollenizer.

ˈ**pollenless,** *a.* [f. POLLEN + -LESS.] Destitute of pollen.

1882 H. MÜLLER in *Nature* XXV. 241/2 The anthers being pollenless. **1888** HENSLOW *Orig. Floral Struct.* xxv. 241 Their anthers become brownish and pollenless.

pollent (ˈpɒlənt), *a. rare.* [ad. L. *pollēntem*, pr. pple. of *pollēre* to be strong: cf. *equipollent*.] Powerful, strong.

1869 BROWNING *Ring & Bk.* VIII. 1193 An unimportant sword and blunderbuss, Against a foe pollent in potency.

poller (ˈpəʊlə(r)). [f. POLL *v.* + -ER[1].]

†**1.** A barber or hair-cutter. *Obs.*

1578 WHETSTONE *Promos & Cassandra* V. iv, *R.* I know him not, is he a deaft barber? *G.* O yea, why he is Mistris Lamias powler. **1608** H. CLAPHAM *Errour Right Hand* 78 Bald pated all, like to an holy Friar, That lately had been in the Pollers hands. **1688** R. HOLME *Armoury* III. 128/2 *Poler*, an ancient term used for the cutter of hair.

b. One who polls trees (Webster, 1828).

†**2.** A plunderer, spoiler, extortioner, despoiler.

1513 BRADSHAW *St. Werburge* I. 2401 True men myght lyue without vexacyon; Pollers, promoters, had no domynacyon. **1514** BARCLAY *Cyt. & Uplondyshm.* (Percy Soc.) p. liv, Porters & poulers, & specially false takers On these . . spare must thou none expence. **1607** HIERON *Wks.* I. 246 It was not enough for Zacheus, that . . hee was no poller or robber of the poore. **1640** SIR J. CULPEPER in Rushw. *Hist. Coll.* III. (1692) I. 33 A Nest of Wasps, or Swarm of Vermin, . . the Monopolers and Polers of the People. **1674** [see PILLER 1 β].

3. a. One who votes at an election; a voter. **b.** One who registers voters (Webster, 1828).

1776 *Chron.* in *Ann. Reg.* 121/1 The total number of pollers at this election. **1807** in *Spirit Pub. Jrnls.* XI. 58 Who'll come forward and now be my poller?

pollerone, obs. form of POULDRON.

†**pollet, -ette.** *Obs.* [app. aphetic form of F. *épaulette* (16th c. *espaulette*): see EPAULET.]

1. A small pouldron: = EPAULET 3.

a **1548** HALL *Chron., Hen. IV* 12 One sorte had the vambrases the pacegardes the grandgardes, the poldren the pollettes parted with golde and azure. **1846–60** FAIRHOLT *Costume* Gloss. (ed. 2), *Pollets* or *Epaullettes*, were small overlapping protections of plate for the shoulders.

†**2.** ? (Something pertaining to chimes.) *Obs.*

1633–4 in Swayne *Sarum Churchw. Acc.* (1896) 317 A pollett for y[e] Chimes, 2d. 3 clackes and 3 pollettes for the bigger bells, 1s.

polleti(c)ke, -tique, obs. forms of POLITIC.

ˈ**poll-ˌevil.** Also 7–8 **pole-evil.** [f. POLL *sb.*[1] + EVIL *sb.* 7a.] An inflamed or ulcerous sore between the ligament of the neck of a horse and the atlas or first bone of the neck. Also †*fig.*, an obsession with elections.

1607 TOPSELL *Four-f. Beasts* (1658) 280 The Poll evill . . is a disease like a Fistula growing betwixt the ears [of a horse] and the poll or nape of the neck. **1683** *Lond. Gaz.* No. 1883/4 She hath the Pole-Evil, and there are white Spots in the place. **1741** *Compl. Fam.-Piece* III. 451 To cure the Poll-Evil, and swell'd Neck from bleeding. **1755** *Pennsylvania Gaz.* 14 Aug. 3/2 They took with them a large bay horse, that has the pole-evil. **1794** J. BYNG *Torrington Diaries* (1938) IV. 76 Sir G. at present is plagued by the pollevil—reverting to the past election with all the possibilities of a future one. **1831** YOUATT *Horse* 153 Now comes the whole art of treating the poll-evil. **1873** J. H. BEADLE *Undevel. West* xxvi. 565, I . . reined up my horse suddenly and again butted him in the back of the head, at the imminent risk of giving us both the poll-evil. **1970** MILLER & WEST *Black's Vet. Dict.* (ed. 9) 730/2 'Poll evil' is an old, colloquial name sometimes incorrectly applied to any swelling in the poll region.

‖**pollex** ('pɒlɛks). *Anat.* Pl. pollices (-ɪsiːz). [Lat., = thumb, also great toe.]

1. The innermost digit of the fore limb in air-breathing vertebrates; in man, etc., the thumb. Sometimes used to include the corresponding digit of the hind limb (the great toe), distinctively called HALLUX.

1835–6 *Todd's Cycl. Anat.* I. 571/2 The pollex in the great whale has two bones. **1854** OWEN *Skel. & Teeth* in *Orr's Circ. Sc.* I. *Org. Nat.* 231 The pollex, or the first digit, exceeds the third..in length. **1872** MIVART *Elem. Anat.* iv. (1873) 174 When a digit is wanting it is generally the pollex, as in spider monkeys. **1897** PARKER & HASWELL *Text-bk. Zool.* II. xiii. 77 The first digit of the fore-limb is distinguished as the pollex or thumb. **1909** W. BATESON *Mendel's Princ. Heredity* xii. 213 The case is more probably to be regarded as a homoeotic variation of the digits into the likeness of the hallux and pollex. **1959** [see ALULA 1]. **1971** A. BURGESS *MF* xv. 169 She clutched her bag between index and pollex. **1975** *Nature* 17 Jan. 192/1 *Proteles* differs from *Hyaena* principally in having a dentition much reduced in size, and in retaining the pollex (a digit lost in both *Hyaena* and *Crocuta*).

2. *Zool.* The movable part of the forceps in some crustaceans.

1895 F. H. HERRICK *Amer. Lobster* ix. 147 The pollux [*sic*] is depressed, so that when the claw is closed it falls almost exactly midway between the normal and first superadded digit. **1904** *Biol. Bull.* VI. 75 The added structure [of an aberrant limb of a crayfish] is..a movable piece with two immobile prongs that otherwise resemble the index and pollex of a forceps.

polley, obs. form of PULLEY.

pollical ('pɒlɪkəl), *a. Anat.* [f. L. *pollex, pollic-em* (see POLLEX) + -AL¹.] Of or pertaining to the pollex or thumb, as ***pollical muscles.***

1890 in *Cent. Dict.*

'pollicar, *a.* [ad. L. *pollicāris*, f. *pollex* thumb.] †**1.** (See quot.) *Obs. rare*⁻⁰.

1656 BLOUNT *Glossogr.*, *Pollicar*, of or belonging to a thumb or toe; of an inch in length or breadth.

2. *Anat.* = POLLICAL.

[**1656**: see 1.] **1895** *Syd. Soc. Lex.*, *P[ollicar] artery*, a syn. for the *Arteria princeps pollicis.*

pollicate ('pɒlɪkət), *a. Zool.* [f. L. *pollex, pollic-em* (see POLLEX) + -ATE².] Having thumbs; belonging to the obsolete order *Pollicata*, including the Quadrumana and most Marsupials, with an opposable digit or thumb on each limb.

1890 in *Cent. Dict.* **1895** *Syd. Soc. Lex.*, *Pollicate*, possessing *Pollices*.

pollicate, dial. variant of PULLICATE.

pollice, pollicie, -cy, obs. ff. POLICE, POLICY.

†**po'llicitate**, *v. Obs. rare*⁻¹. [f. L. *pollicitāt-*, ppl. stem of *pollicitārī*, freq. of *pollicērī* to promise: see -ATE³.] *trans.* To promise.

1657 TOMLINSON *Renou's Disp.* 294 It evacuates blood and pollicitates many more commodities. [**1657** *Physical Dict.*, *Pollicitates*, promises, assures, warrants.]

pollicitation (pəlɪsɪ'teɪʃən). [ad. L. *pollicitātiō-nem*, vbl. sb. of *pollicitārī* to promise: see prec. and -ATION. So F. *pollicitation* (15th c. in Godefroy).] The action of promising; a promise; a document conveying a promise; *spec.* in *Civil Law*, a promise not yet formally accepted, and therefore in certain cases revocable.

1528 GARDINER in Pocock *Rec. Ref.* I. li. 133 As yet the pope's holiness hath not required the king's pollicitation. *c* **1555** HARPSFIELD *Divorce Hen. VIII* (Camden) 182 His promise and pollicitation passed upon the same. **1602** F. HERING *Anat.* 14 Vaunting Pollicitations of binding Beares, and mooving Mountaines. **1715** BURNET *Hist. Ref.* III. II. 41 These are in the Promise, or Pollicitation, which I do now publish. **1726** FIDDES *Wolsey* I. 433 His Holiness..signed a Pollicitation, whereby he obliged himself to confirm the sentence. **1875** POSTE *Gaius* III. Comm. (ed. 2) 360 Pollicitation is the offer of the one party before it is accepted by the other. **1894** MRS. HOPE *1st Divorce Hen. VIII* 121 They were to try to get a 'policitation', or promise, from the Pope that he would not remove the cause to Rome.

pollinar ('pɒlɪnə(r)), *a. rare*⁻⁰. [ad. L. *pollināris* of or belonging to fine flour: see POLLEN.] = POLLINOSE.

1858 MAYNE *Expos. Lex.*, *Pollinaris*, applied to a surface.. covered with a very fine dust resembling pollen: pollinar.

†**polli'narious**, *a. Obs. rare*⁻⁰. In 19th c. Dicts. erron. pollen-. [f. L. *pollinārius* of or belonging to fine flour (see POLLEN) + -OUS.]

1656 BLOUNT *Glossogr.*, *Pollinarious*.., pertaining to fine flower or meal. **1830** MAUNDER *Dict.*, *Pollenarious*, consisting of meal.

‖**pollinarium** (pɒlɪ'nɛərɪəm). *Bot.* Pl. **-ia.** [mod.L., f. as next, after *ovarium* ovary, etc.]

a. In phanerogams, = POLLINIUM. **b.** In cryptogams, = CYSTIDIUM 2.

1881 BENTHAM in *Jrnl. Linn. Soc.* XVIII. 301 His representation of the pollinarium of *Monomeria*. **1895** *Syd. Soc. Lex.*, *Pollinarium*, one of the organs of which several are present on the *hymenium* of certain Fungi, and which some observers consider to be male organs.

pollinary ('pɒlɪnərɪ), *a. Bot.* [f. L. *pollen, pollin-*, in mod. Bot. L. = POLLEN 2 + -ARY¹.] Of or pertaining to pollen; concerned in the production of pollen.

1881 BENTHAM in *Jrnl. Linn. Soc.* XVIII. 285 The confusion occasioned by the term [*caudicle*] having been applied to three very different parts of the pollinary system.

pollinate ('pɒlɪneɪt), *v. Bot.* [f. as prec. + -ATE³.] *trans.* To besprinkle with pollen or shed pollen upon (the stigma, or the nucleus of the ovule in Gymnosperms) in order to fertilization. Also *absol.*

1875 BENNETT & DYER *Sachs' Bot.* 813 In protogynous flowers..the stigma has already been pollinated by foreign pollen or has even withered up and fallen off. *Ibid.*, While the insect is moving about.., its back laden with pollen comes into contact with the stigmatic surface and pollinates it. **1919** J. N. MARTIN *Bot. for Agric. Students* iv. 49 These plants are not successfully pollinated when they are wet. **1935** C. ZIRKLE *Beginnings of Plant Hybridization* i. 6 It is not stated specifically in the description of this building [*sc.* Solomon's Temple] that the cherubim were engaged in pollinating the flowers of the palms. **1942** HAYES & IMMER *Methods of Plant Breeding* iv. 63 With wheat it is equally satisfactory to pollinate during the day. **1973** PROCTOR & YEO *Pollination of Flowers* i. 19 The role of insects in pollinating flowers is a commonplace. **1974** A. HUXLEY *Plant & Planet* xiii. 132 There is just a little nectar in each flower, so that the insects..pollinate more actively.

pollinating ('pɒlɪneɪtɪŋ), *ppl. a.* [f. POLLINATE *v.* + -ING².] That pollinates or facilitates pollination.

1911 F. O. BOWER *Plant-Life on Land* 69 The very genesis of the forms of flowers, their tints, and scents is in strict accordance with their efficiency as pollinating mechanisms.

pollination (pɒlɪ'neɪʃən). *Bot.* [f. as POLLINATE *v.* + -ATION.] The action of pollinating; deposition of pollen in order to fertilization. Also *attrib.* and *fig.*

1875 BENNETT & DYER *Sachs' Bot.* 429 A considerable time, occasionally even months, often elapses between pollination and fertilisation; but commonly only a few days or hours. **1882** *Nature* XXVI. 307/1 The insects which visit particular species and assist in their pollination. **1924** HOLMAN & ROBBINS *Textbk. Gen. Bot.* vii. 283 The transfer of pollen from the anther to the stigma is called pollination. **1941** D. C. PEATTIE *Road of Naturalist* i. 19 The paper-bag bush, too, had gone to pod, just a few of its purple mint flowers left, where I had seen the humming-birds at pollination. **1971** E. MAVOR *Ladies of Llangollen* v. 90 Romantic pollinations..were taking place between an ever growing number of cultivated women. **1974** A. HUXLEY *Plant & Planet* xiii. 131 The second classic pollination symbiosis is that of the American Yuccas with certain moths.

pollinator ('pɒlɪneɪtə(r)). [f. POLLINATE *v.* + -OR.] Any insect or other agent that pollinates plants.

1903 *Amer. Naturalist* XXXVII. 368 The small concealed flowers of Gaultheria..do not want for pollinators. **1924** *Chambers's Jrnl.* Aug. 501/2 The value of bees as pollinators is appreciated by progressive fruit growers. **1955** *Sci. Amer.* Aug. 52/1 It would be more appropriate to think of them [*sc.* bees] first of all as the great pollinators. **1977** M. ALLAN *Darwin & his Flowers* xi. 202 The pollinator is not known for any *Cryptophoranthus*.

po'llinctor. [a. L. *pollinctor*, agent-n. from *pollingĕre* to wash (a corpse) and prepare it for the funeral pile.] One who prepares a dead body for cremation or embalming, by washing, anointing, etc.

In quot. 1969, one employed by a funeral director to do this (*U.S. Blacks*).

1646 SIR T. BROWNE *Pseud. Ep.* VII. xix. 384 What is delivered by Herodotus concerning the Ægyptian Pollinctors, or such as annointed the dead. **1664** EVELYN *Sylva* (1776) 315 One of the greatest secrets used by our pollinctors and mountebanks who pretend to this embalming mystery. **1705** *Phil. Trans.* XXV. 2107 An Embalmer or Surgeon; a Pollinctor or Apothecary. **1969** *Liberator* Dec. 13/2, I left the funeral home along with the body and the pollinctor.

So †**po'llincture** *Obs.* [ad. L. *pollinctūra*], the washing, anointing, etc. of a dead body, in preparation for burning or burial. (In first quot. *fig.*)

16.. *Inscription on brass in Tredington Churchyard*, Praises on tombs are but a pollincture. **1656** in BLOUNT *Glossogr.* **1695** J. EDWARDS *Perfect. Script.* 188 [He] had skill to dissect bodies in order to their pollincture.

polling ('pəʊlɪŋ), *vbl. sb.* [f. POLL *v.* + -ING¹.] The action of the verb POLL, in various senses.

I. †**1.** The cutting of hair; shearing, clipping, cropping. *Obs.*

1439 *Litt. Red Bk. Bristol* (1900) 153 That no Craftesman ..do not ocupye his seid Crafte in schavyng nor polling..in non Sonday. **1585** ABP. SANDYS *Serm.* (Parker Soc.) 325 It cost him [Samson] a polling..wherein stood his strength. *a* **1653** GOUGE *Comm. Heb.* xi. 32 Had not man sinned, his hair would have had no need of polling.

2. The cutting off of the top of a tree.

1626 BACON *Sylva* §58 The oft cutting, or Polling of Hedges, Trees, and Herbs, doth conduce much to their Lasting. *Ibid.* §424 The Powling and Cutting of the Top, maketh them grow spread and bushy.

†**3.** Plundering, extortion, spoliation, pillage, robbery; an instance of this. ***polling and pilling***: see PILLING *vbl. sb.* 1 b. *Obs.*

1513 BRADSHAW *St. Werburge* II. 159 Extorcion, pollynge opteyned no grace. **1544** WRIOTHESLEY *Chron.* (Camden) I. 150 For misusinge of the Kinges commission and powelinge of his subjectes. **1547–1661** [see PILLING *vbl. sb.* 1 b]. **1581** J. BELL *Haddon's Answ. Osor.* 402 b, To prevent this peltyng powlyng of the Proctours. **1583** STUBBES *Anat. Abus.* II. (1882) 31 Polling, pilling and shauing of his poore tenants. **1651** WELDON *Crt. Jas. I*, etc. 205 The High-Commission Court..in which all Pollings and tyrannizings over our Estates and Consciences were practised. **1665** MANLEY *Grotius' Low C. Warres* 302 The unexpected Charges of the War, though oftentimes under that pretence, are hidden all manner of Deceit and Polling.

†**4.** *concr. pl.* The results or proceeds of polling (in various senses): see quots. *Obs.*

1557 TUSSER *100 Points Husb.* lxvi, Then lop for thy fewel, the powlinges well growen. **1585** HIGINS *Junius' Nomenclator* 167/1 A Barbars towell,..for the cuttings or pollings of the haire to fall vpon. **1675** tr. *Camden's Hist. Eliz.* IV. (1688) 440 Crammed with the Spoils and Pollings of the poorer sort. **1835** C. W. STOCKER *Juvenal* 57 *note*, The wealthier Romans, on arriving at manhood, dedicated the first shavings of their beard and pollings of their hair to some deity.

II. 5. a. The registering or casting of votes.

1625 in *Commons Debates* (Camden) 45 The pollinge would last three days. **1697** DAMPIER *Voy. round World* Introd. (1699) 5 Which Party soever should upon Polling appear to have the Majority, they should keep the Ship. **1756** TOLDERVY *Hist. 2 Orphans* I. 67 By keeping the estate in his hands, tho' mortgaged.., he preserved his right of poling at an election for the county. **1839** MCCULLOCH *Acc. Brit. Empire* II. 100 Such polling is to continue for two days only, being successive days, for seven hours on the first day, and eight hours on the second day of polling. **1883** *Manch. Exam.* 24 Oct. 4/6 The polling in the election of nine members of the..School Board.

b. The action or process of conducting an opinion poll.

1937 *Public Opinion Q.* Jan. 38 Scientific polling on individual issues fills a great gap in the democratic form of government. **1939** G. GALLUP *Public Opinion in Democracy* 13 The research man who..devises an accurate and efficient method of polling 'ballot cattle' is obviously not contributing much to better government. **1944** —— *Guide to Public Opinion Polls* 12 Although the layman doesn't recognize it as polling, he is himself daily conducting his own private poll of public opinion. **1951** 'A. GARVE' *Murder in Moscow* vii. 83 You go into the streets and do a little polling on the subject... You'll get a hundred per cent 'Yes' —not a single 'Don't know'. **1968** W. SAFIRE *New Lang. of Politics* 108/2 The power of polling, both on nose counts and in depth, was never more vividly demonstrated than in the 1968 New Hampshire primary campaign. **1974** *Encycl. Brit. Macropædia* XV. 214/1 Polling can..reveal something about the intensity with which opinions are held. *Ibid.*, Polling.. is unlikely to provide very much information about the elites who may have played an important part in developing the opinion.

III. 6. *attrib.* and *Comb.* †**a.** in sense 3; **b.** in sense 5, as ***polling-agent, -book, -booth, -clerk, -day, -district, -place, -station.***

a. 1557 STAFFORD *Proclam.* in Strype *Eccl. Mem.* (1721) III. App. lxxi. 262 This whole realme of Englande shall..be delyvered from all suche powling paymentes, as the quene dothe daylye geve to Spanyardes. **1581** J. BELL *Haddon's Answ. Osor.* 404 Peradventure these fellowes are to much ashamed of theyr powlyng pranckes, and..can render no reasonable excuse for their bribery and pilladge. **1613** WITHER *Abuses Stript* I. viii, What Rascall poling sutes doe they devise, To adde new Summes unto their Treasuries.

b. 1832 *Act 2 Will. IV*, c. 45 §70 In case the Proceedings shall be so interrupted or obstructed at any particular Polling Place or Places. **1852** DICKENS *Bleak Ho.* xl, Away to hustings and polling-booths. **1863** H. COX *Instit.* I. viii. 113 The vote is given *vivâ voce*, and entered in a polling-book by the polling-clerk. *Ibid.*, Not more than a limited number of voters may be polled at each polling-place. **1865** K. AMBERLEY *Diary* 13 July in B. & P. Russell *Amberley Papers* (1937) I. viii. 399 Polling Day—cloudy & windy. **1882** OGILVIE (Annandale), *Polling-sheriff*, in Scotland, the presiding officer at a polling-station. **1895** C. PORRETT in *Elections* (Yorks. Union of Conservative Assocs.) 12 An agent..should keep a list of gentlemen willing to lend conveyances to the various polling district committees. **1974** *Times* 6 Sept 1/4 He hinted heavily several times that polling day was only a matter of weeks away. **1976** *Western Mail* (Cardiff) 27 Nov. (Advt.), Before you can trace your name in the lists you must know in which Polling District you live. **1977** *Grimsby Even. Tel.* 5 May 1/2 Unfortunately not enough publicity was given by the parties to the fact that the polling stations close at 9 instead of 10.

polling ('pəʊlɪŋ), *ppl. a.* [f. POLL *v.* + -ING².] That polls; †that plunders; extortionate, exacting; cheating (*obs.*). See also PILLING ***ppl. a.***

1540 *St. Papers Hen. VIII*, VIII. 234 This [Valenciens] ys waxed the derest and pollyngst town of the worlde. **1562** J. HEYWOOD *Prov. & Epigr.* (1867) 147 Would thale wife [the ale-wife] play the poulyng queane: Yet measure will not lie. **1612** BACON *Ess.*, *Judicature*, Amongst the briers and brambles of catching and poling Clearkes and Ministers.

†**polling-penny, -pence**, *pl. Obs.* [f. POLLING *vbl. sb.* + PENNY, PENCE.] Money paid or exacted as poll-tax; hence, esp. in *pl.*, a poll-tax.

1555 BRADFORD *Supplic. Q. Eliz.* F ij, Wil englishmen.. suffer to be poled and pilled moste miserably, in payeng continually suche polingpence, and intollerable tollages? **1591** *Troub. Raigne K. John* (1611) 42 Neuer an Italian priest of them all, shall eyther haue tythe, tole, or polling penny out of England. **1592** GREENE *Upst. Courtier* C j b, Yea rather than thy brauery should faile begge powling pence for the verye smoke that coms out of poore mens chimnies. **1607** MARKHAM *Caval.* III. (1617) 35 To get vnhonest polling pence to their owne purses.

pollinic (pə'lɪnɪk), *a. Bot.* [f. L. *pollen, -in-em* + -IC.] Pertaining to, consisting of, or containing pollen. ***pollinic chamber*** = pollen-chamber; ***pollinic mass*** = pollen-mass: see POLLEN 3. Also **po'llinical** *a.*

1856 MAYNE *Expos. Lex.*, *Pollinicus*.. L. C. Richard terms *pollinic masses* the heap of compact pollen that fills each partial cavity of the anther in the *Orchideæ* and *Asclepiadeæ*. **1882** *Pop. Sc. Monthly* XX. 780 Designate the cavity as the pollinical chamber. **1885** GOODALE *Physiol. Bot.* (1892) 438 A sort of depression at the summit of the endosperm, which has been called the pollinic chamber.

polliniferous (pɒlɪ'nɪfərəs), *a.* Also erron. pollen-. [f. as. prec. + -(I)FEROUS.]

1. *Bot.* Bearing or producing pollen.

1830 LINDLEY *Nat. Syst. Bot.* 249 The male flowers consist of a peltate scale, around which are arranged several polliniferous cavities. **1881** *Gard. Chron.* XVI. 727 The polliniferous portion of the anther consists of a single sac.

¶**2.** *Entom.* = next. (*erron.*)

1866 W. E. SHUCKARD *Brit. Bees* 20 A bee without polliniferous organs cannot collect pollen.

pollinigerous (-'ɪdʒərəs), *a. Entom.* [f. as prec. + -(I)GEROUS.] Carrying, or adapted for carrying, pollen.

1819 G. SAMOUELLE *Entomol. Compend.* 272 Hinder feet not pollinigerous. **1866** W. E. SHUCKARD *Brit. Bees* 103 Pollinigerous and honey-collecting organs. **1895** E. SAUNDERS *Brit. Hymenoptera Aculeata* 303 Pollinigerous hairs either on the tibiae..or on the ventral surface of the abdomen.

‖**pollinium** (pə'lɪnɪəm). *Bot.* Pl. **-ia.** [mod.L., f. *pollen, pollin-*, POLLEN 2 + *-ium* as in *antheridium, archegonium*, etc.] A coherent mass of pollen-grains in each cavity of the anther, characteristic of the *Orchidaceæ* and *Asclepiadaceæ*.

1862 DARWIN *Orchids* Introd. 5 The pollen-masses, with their caudicles and other appendages, are called the Pollinia. **1863** —— in *Life & Lett.* (1887) III. 264 He has actually seen crowds of bees flying round Catasetum, with the pollinia sticking to their backs. **1875** BENNETT & DYER *Sachs' Bot.* 488 Contrivances by means of which insects.. extract from the pollen-sac the pollinia or the masses of pollen which are glued together.

polli'nivorous, *a.* (erron. pollen-.) [f. as prec. + L. *-vor-us* devouring + -OUS.] Devouring or feeding on pollen.

1836-9 *Todd's Cycl. Anat.* II. 897/2 In some of the pollenivorous..genera..the clypeus posterior seems to have become entirely obliterated.

'pollinize, pollenize, *v.* [f. L. *pollen, pollin-* (or directly f. POLLEN) + -IZE.] *trans.* = POLLINATE. So **pollini'zation (-en-)** = POLLINATION.

18.. *Nature* (O.), No flower gave a fruit without having its stigmata pollenized by crossing. **1878** T. MEEHAN *Flowers & Ferns U.S.* I. 59 The pistil has been fully developed and is ready for pollenization. **1896** HENSLOW *Wild Flowers* 167 A very similar method of pollinization will be seen in the enchanter's nightshade.

‖**pollinodium** (pɒlɪ'nəʊdɪəm). *Bot.* [mod.L., f. as prec. + *-ōdium*; see -ODE[1].] The antheridium or male reproductive organ in ascomycetous fungi, which grows close to the ascogonium or female organ of the same plant, and in fertilization unites with it directly or by an outgrowth. Hence **polli'nodial** *a.*, pertaining to or of the nature of a pollinodium.

1875 BENNETT & DYER *Sachs' Bot.* 258 From the lowest coil of the ascogonium two slender branches now shoot out ..; one of these developes more quickly... This branch is the Antheridium (Pollinodium of De Bary). **1882** VINES *Sachs' Bot.* 311 The carpogonia and pollinodia are developed together at the points at which the mycelial filaments cross one another... They are both small lateral branches. **1886** —— in *Encycl. Brit.* XX. 428/2 In some plants..which have pollinodial antheridia, self-fertilization alone is possible.

pollinoid ('pɒlɪnɔɪd). *Bot.* [f. as prec. + -OID.] Each of the (non-motile) male fertilizing cells of certain Cryptograms, as the red seaweeds, and the ascomycetous fungi.

1892 *Chambers' Encycl.* IX. 289/1 (*Seaweeds*) The male organs [of Dictyotaceæ] produce non-motile fertilising cells resembling the pollinoids of the Rhodophyceæ.

pollinose ('pɒlɪnəʊs), *a. Entom.* [ad. mod.L. *pollinōs-us*, f. as prec.: see -OSE.] (See quot.)

1826 KIRBY & SP. *Entomol.* IV. xlvi. 275 Pollinose.. Covered with a loose mealy and often yellow powder resembling the pollen of flowers.

pollipode, obs. f. POLYPOD.

pollish(e, obs. ff. POLISH *v.*

pollitick(e, etc., obs. ff. POLITIC.

pollity, obs. f. POLITY[1]; var. POLITY[2] *Obs.*

polliwog, pollywog ('pɒlɪwɒg). *dial.* and *U.S.* Forms: α. 5 polwygle, 7 porwig(g)le, 9 porriwiggle, purwiggy, pollywiggle, pollywoggle. β. 6 polwigge, 7 polewigge, po(o)lwig, 9 polliwig, polly-wig, polliwog, pollywog. [ME. *polwygle*, f. POLL *sb.*[1] + WIGGLE *v.* The forms *polwig*, etc., are either shortened from *polwygle*, or formed with the dial. *wig* vb. to wag.] **a.** A tadpole.

α. *c* **1440** *Promp. Parv.* 408/1 Polwygle, wyrme. **1646** SIR T. BROWNE *Pseud. Ep.* 329 The spawne is white, contracting by degrees a blacknesse, answerable..unto the porwigle or Tadpole, that is, that animall which first proceedeth from it. **1823** E. MOOR *Suffolk Words & Phrases* 288 *Pollywiggle*, the tad-pole—in Norfolk called *potladle*. *a* **1825** FORBY *Voc. E. Anglia*, *Purwiggy*, a tadpole. **1855** ROBINSON *Whitby Gloss.*, *Porriwiggles*, tadpoles and other tortuous animalcula in water. **1881** S. EVANS *Evans's Leicestershire Words* (new ed.) 216 *Pollywig*, or *pollywiggle*,..a tadpole. 'Poddywig' is, I think, the commoner form. **1933** H. G. WELLS *Bulpington of Blup* ii. 45 These things you call pollywiggles and pollywoggles. **1965** *East Anglian* May 242/1 Tadpoles were ..*pollywiggles*.

β. **1592** NASHE *4 Lett. Confut.* (1593) 63 Thou hast a prety polwigge sparrows taile peake. **1601** HOLLAND *Pliny* I. 265 Some little mites of blackish flesh, which they call Tadpoles or Polwigs. *a* **1825** FORBY *Voc. E. Anglia*, *Polliwigs*. **1835-40** HALIBURTON *Clockm.* (1862) 321 Little ponds..nothing but pollywogs, tadpoles, and minims in them. **1862** LOWELL *Biglow P.* Ser. II. 80 'Lord knows', protest the polliwogs, 'We're anxious to be grown-up frogs'. **1892** *Working Men's Coll. Jrnl.* Oct. 124 In this pond dwells the pollywog, loggerhead, or tadpole.

b. *U.S.* As a political nickname.

1854 L. OLIPHANT *Episodes* (1887) 47 Filibusters, pollywogs, and a host of other nicknames. **1864** SALA in *Daily Tel.* 27 Sept., 'The slimy machinations of the pollywog politicians have usurped the government of our city', said Poer.

†**poll-money** ('pəʊl,mʌnɪ). *Obs.* [f. POLL *sb.*[1] + MONEY *sb.*] Money levied, exacted, or paid, at a fixed rate per head for every person, or (quot. *a* 1618) for every head of cattle; capitation; poll-tax.

1526 TINDALE *Matt.* xvii. 24 They that were wont to gadre poll money, cam to Peter. *Ibid.* 25 Of whome do the kynges off the erth take tribute or poll money? *a* **1618** RALEIGH *Prerog. Parl.* (1665) 54 By reason of the trouble-some gathering of the polemony upon sheep,..this act of subsidy was repealed. **1638** DRUMM. OF HAWTH. *Irene* Wks. (1711) 169 To be slaves to your fellow-subjects, pay them intolerable taxes, loans, pole-monies, and odious excises. **1662** PETTY *Taxes* vii. Tracts (1769) 50 Poll money is a tax upon the persons of men, either upon all simply and indifferently, or else according to some known title or mark of distinction upon each. *Ibid.*, The poll-monies which have been levied of late, have been wonderfully confused. **1667** PEPYS *Diary* 5 Apr., This morning come to me the Collectors for my Poll-money... I paid for my title as Esquire and place of Clerk of Acts, and my head and wife's, and servants' and their wages, £40 17s. **1692** WOOD *Life* (O.H.S.) III. 386 Apr. 8 [Paid] pol-money 1*li.* 1*s.*, to carry on a vigorous war against the French king... April 13..paid 21*s.* for a gent. and my pole..whereas the fellowes of houses ..pay but their pole 1*s.*—a very heavy and unjust tax. **1727-41** CHAMBERS *Cycl.*, *Poll-money*, or *capitation*, a tax imposed..either on all indifferently, or according to some known mark of distinction, as quality, calling, etc... Thus, by the statute 18 Car. II every subject..was assessed.. according to his degree; every duke 100l. marquis 80l. baronet 30l. knight 20l. esquire 10l. etc. and every single private person 12d. **1796** MORSE *Amer. Geog.* II. 28 Paper, corporations, land, houses, and poll-money, also raise a considerable sum.

pollock: see POLLACK.

polloi (pɒ'lɔɪ). *slang.* [ad. Gr. πολλοί many: see HOI POLLOI.] *pl.* (const. as *sing.*). A crowd, a rabble (see also quot. 1940).

1940 M. MARPLES *Public School Slang* 90 *Polloi* (Cheltenham)..., the lowest football set. **1948** E. E. CUMMINGS *Let.* 27 Aug. (1969) 185 A very refreshingly authentic polloi, & some good lively winds.

pollone: var. PALONE.

pollster ('pəʊlstə(r)). orig. *U.S.* [f. POLL *sb.*[1] 7 d + -STER.] One who conducts an opinion poll; an analyst of such polls, or of voting patterns generally.

1939 *Time* 9 Oct. 11/3 Gallup pollsters reported that 43% of the voters want Mr. Roosevelt to run again. **1941** *Time* 6 Jan. 11 According to Pollster Gallup's figures 60 per cent of U.S. voters now want to aid Britain even at the risk of war. **1951** M. MCLUHAN *Mech. Bride* (1967) 46/2 On November 3, 1948..the pollsters were proved wrong in forecasting a Dewey victory over Truman. **1959** *Times Lit. Suppl.* 2 Oct. 556/3 This is not a swing towards Communism (as the pollsters would say), but an impulsive reaction to success. **1968** [see MOTIVATION 3]. **1972** M. WILLIAMS *Inside Number 10* xiii. 343 Possibly there was a reaction against the pollsters, a desire to prove the computers wrong. **1977** *Time* 21 Nov. 63/2 The pollsters asked people to make judgments on a series of actions, deciding whether such actions were morally wrong or not a moral issue.

poll-tax ('pəʊltæks). [f. POLL *sb.*[1] + TAX *sb.*] A tax levied on every person; a capitation or head-tax. A later name for POLL-MONEY.

1694 MOLESWORTH *Account of Denmark* 111 Here is commonly one Poll-tax at least every year. **1726** SHELVOCKE *Voy. round World* 462 The Dutch..exact from all the men a Poll-Tax of a dollar a month. **1794** SOUTHEY *Wat Tyler* II. iii, Why is this ruinous poll-tax imposed, But to support your court's extravagance? **1825** JEFFERSON *Autobiog. & Writ.* Wks. 1859 I. 29 The practice of the Southern colonies has always been to make every farmer pay poll taxes upon all his laborers, whether they be black or white. **1866** ROGERS *Agric. & Prices* I. iv. 84 The limit of age in the first poll-tax was sixteen, in the second fifteen, years.

†**po'llucible,** *a. Obs. rare*—[0]. [ad. L. *pollūcibilis* sumptuous, f. *pollūcēre* to offer as a sacrifice.]

1623 COCKERAM, *Pollucible*, gay, sumptuous.

'pollucite. *Min.* [orig. named *Pollux* (Breithaupt, 1846), being associated with *Castor* or CASTORITE.] Silicate of aluminium and cæsium, found in brilliant transparent colourless crystals.

[**1847** *Amer. Jrnl. Sc.* Ser. II. III. 430 Pollux resembles castor in crystallographic and physical characteristics.] **1868** DANA *Min.* (ed. 5) 249 Pollucite. **1896** *Amer. Jrnl. Sc.* Ser. IV. I. 458 Pollucite is not very abundant.

pollutant (pə'l(j)uːtənt). [f. POLLUTE *v.* + -ANT[1].] A polluting agent or medium.

1892 *Pall Mall G.* 22 Dec. 6/2 Waste acid as a pollutant. **1936** *Nature* 29 Feb. 353/2 The presence of pollutants in the atmosphere is proof of wastage of fuel. **1958** *Times* 13 Nov. 9/1 The even more harmful gaseous pollutants present a problem which will tax the resources of all engaged in the present campaign. **1966** *Listener* 3 Nov. 656/2 Fluoride.. can be used for the improvement of human welfare. Out of place it is a more serious pollutant than chlorinated hydrocarbons, in that it is indestructible. **1970** *Daily Tel.* 30 Dec. 3/1 Mercury is now the most dangerous environmental pollutant. **1977** *Guernsey Weekly Press* 21 July 3/1 Petrol could become a pollutant of the past if the device fitted to a local car is marketed worldwide.

pollute (pə'l(j)uːt), *ppl. a. Obs.* exc. *poet.* [ad. L. *pollūt-us* defiled, pa. pple. of *polluĕre* (see next).] = POLLUTED *ppl. a.* (Originally as pa. pple.)

c **1374** CHAUCER *Boeth.* I. pr. iv. 12 (Camb. MS.) þat I hadde polut and defowled my conscience with sacrilege. *c* **1380** WYCLIF *Serm.* Sel. Wks. II. 181 Tyme in his owne kynde may neþer be holy ne pollut. *c* **1425** WYNTOUN *Cron.* V. ix. 1663 A woman þan of pollute fayme, þat callit Melancia was be nayme. **1513** BRADSHAW *St. Werburge* I. 3473 Lest the..wiked myscreauntes With pollute handes.. Shulde touche her body. **1629** MILTON *Nativity* 41 And on her naked shame, Pollute with sinfull blame, The Saintly Vail of Maiden white to throw. **1830** W. PHILLIPS *Mt. Sinai* III. 327 With moral leprosy pollute of heart, And dead to righteousness. *Ibid.* IV. 150 The people..drank The wave pollute.

pollute (pə'l(j)uːt), *v.* Also 4-7 polute, 5 polewt. [f. L. *pollūt-*, ppl. stem of *polluĕre* to soil, defile, f. **por* (= *pro*) forth + *luĕre* to wash.]

1. *trans.* To render ceremonially or morally impure; to impair, violate, or destroy the purity or sanctity of; to profane, desecrate; to sully, corrupt.

[*c* **1374**: see POLLUTE *ppl. a.*] **1382** WYCLIF *Lev.* xxi. 6 Holi thei shulen be to her God, and thei shulen not polute [1388 defoule, Vulg. *polluent*] his name. *c* **1400** *Apol. Loll.* 36 Wiþ swilk cursidnes þei polewt þe hous. **1582** STANYHURST *Æneis* II. (Arb.) 66, I may not, I dare not pollute Gods heaunlye, with handling. **1633** PRYNNE *Histrio-M.* I. III. iii. 92 Grosse abominations..the very relation of which is sufficient to pollute the eares that heare them, the common aire that receives them. **1788** GIBBON *Decl. & F.* xl. (1869) II. 466 Churches and altars were polluted by atrocious murders. **1857** BUCKLE *Civiliz.* I. viii. 526 The clergy..urging him to exterminate the heretics, whose presence they thought polluted France.

2. a. To make physically impure, foul, or filthy; to dirty, stain, taint, befoul. *spec.* To contaminate (the environment, atmosphere, etc.) with harmful or objectionable substances. Also *absol.*

a **1548** HALL *Chron.*, *Edw. IV* 223 Thei..with their proper bloud, embrued and polluted their awne handes. **1585** T. WASHINGTON tr. *Nicholay's Voy.* IV. ii. 115 No drop of the bloud should fall into the water, least the same shuld therby be polluted. **1656** EARL MONM. tr. *Boccalini's Advts. fr. Parnass.* I. xxxv. (1674) 42 Cicero's divine and painfull labours..were polluted by flies and moths in every Book-binders shop. **1719** POPE *Iliad* XIX. 30 Shall flies and worms obscene pollute the dead? **1860-1** FLOR. NIGHTINGALE *Nursing* 20 Within the last few years, a large part of London was in the daily habit of using water polluted by the drainage of its sewers and water-closets. **1954** *Thorpe's Dict. Appl. Chem.* (ed. 4) XI. 885/1 Poisons like arsenic, etc., are rarely present in natural waters unless polluted by trade wastes or agricultural washes. **1966** *Petroleum Handbk.* (Shell Internat. Petroleum Co.) (ed. 5) 144/1 The absence of sulphur ensures that the products of combustion are non-corrosive..and do not pollute the atmosphere. **1973** *New Earth Catal.* 59/3 Plant—don't pollute.

†**b.** *pa. pple.* Marked as if stained. *Obs. rare.*

1658 ROWLAND *Moufet's Theat. Ins.* 972 The wings are long and blackish, and polluted with little black spots.

Hence **po'lluting** *vbl. sb.* and *ppl. a.*

1580 H. GIFFORD *Epist. Claudius Ptholomæus* Wks. (1875) 35 Euery one holdes her [poverty] in contempt, filling her with..most spitefull pollutinges. **1599** MARSTON *Sco. Villanie* I. iii. 183 Factors for lewdnes, Brokers for the deuill, Infect our soules with all polluting euill. **1609** DOWNAM *Chr. Liberty* 31 The contrarie to sanctifying, is polluting. **1819** SHELLEY *Prometh. Unb.* I. 160 Her pining sons uplifted Their prostrate brows from the polluting dust. **1897** MARY KINGSLEY *W. Africa* 475 It saved the polluting of a long stretch of market road.

polluted (pə'l(j)uːtɪd), *ppl. a.* [f. prec. + -ED[1].]

a. Defiled, rendered impure or unclean.

c **1400** *Apol. Loll.* 53 Wen þe body and blod of Crist is tretid wiþ foul hands, and polutid conciens. **1535** COVERDALE *Jer.* xxiii. 11 The prophetes and the prestes them selues are poluted Ypocrytes. **1667** MILTON *P.L.* XII. 110 Resolving from thenceforth To leave them to thir own polluted wayes. **1777** LOGAN in *Scott. Paraphr.* VIII. iii, Can troubled and polluted springs a hallow'd stream afford? **1888** MISS BRADDON *Fatal Three* I. v, She has been using that polluted water for the last three weeks—and poisoning a whole village.

b. *slang* (orig. *U.S.*). Intoxicated, drunk; under the influence of drugs, 'high'.

1912 *Dialect Notes* III. 585 *Polluted*,..very drunk. The same as *pickled* and *plastered*. **1914** 'HIGH JINKS, JR.' *Choice Slang* 16 *Polluted*, intoxicated, drunk, 'piffficated', 'soused'. **1927** *New Republic* 9 Mar. 71/2 The following is a partial list of words denoting drunkenness now in common use in the United States..polluted. **1938** *Amer. Speech* XIII. 185/2 High..usually infers that the addict is noticeably under the influence of drugs... The same is true of the following equivalents:..lit, polluted, shot up. **1974** WODEHOUSE *Aunts aren't Gentlemen* iii. 20, I was helping a pal to celebrate the happy conclusion of love's young dream, and it may be that I became a mite polluted.

Hence **po'llutedly** *adv.*, in a polluted condition, with pollution; **po'llutedness**, polluted state.

1617 HIERON *Wks.* II. 344 There is naturally a kinde of pollutednesse in the lips of man, whereof Isaiah complayned. **1635** HEYWOOD *Hierarch.* I. 28 Pollutedly into the world I came; Sad and perplext I liv'd.

polluter (pəˈl(j)uːtə(r)). [f. as prec. + -ER[1].]

a. One who pollutes; a defiler; one who profanes. *spec.* a person or organization that causes pollution of the environment.

1550 BALE *Eng. Votaries* II. 65 A defyler of relygyon and polluter of their holye ceremonyes. *a* **1665** J. GOODWIN *Filled w. the Spirit* (1867) 232 Purged and rid of such polluters and profaners of their dignity. **1823** *Examiner* 706/2 The polluter, not the purifier, of his fellow creatures. **1970** *New Society* 5 Feb. 209/2 The polluters often have a strong commercial lobby on their side, while the anti-polluters must rely on voluntary effort. **1970** *Toronto Daily Star* 24 Sept. 22/2 The federal government is in a much stronger position to deal with big industrial polluters than most provincial administrations are likely to be. **1974** *Times* 15 Mar. 6 (*heading*) Making Europe's polluters foot the bill. **1977** 'E. CRISPIN' *Glimpses of Moon* xi. 215 'Polluters,' said the hunt saboteuse.

b. A pollutant.

1975 *Physics Bull.* Mar. 100/3 Noise is now acknowledged as a major polluter of the environment.

pollution (pəˈl(j)uːʃən). Forms: 4 pollusyone, 4–5 pol(l)ucio(u)n, 5 polucyon, 7 pollusion, 6– pollution. [ad. L. *pollūtiōn-em* defilement, noun of action from *polluĕre* to POLLUTE. So F. *pollution* (12th c. in Hatz.-Darm.).]

1. a. The action of polluting, or condition of being polluted; defilement; uncleanness or impurity caused by contamination (physical or moral). *spec.* The presence in the environment, or the introduction into it, of products of human activity which have harmful or objectionable effects.

c **1420** LYDG. *Assembly of Gods* 1301 Safe I wold desyre yow spare Pollucion. *c* **1485** *Digby Myst.* (1882) III. 1988 Hys pryde owt of my love xall have polucyon. **1594** NASHE *Unfort. Trav.* 13 His purse was..I think verily a puritane, for it kept it selfe from any pollution of crosses. *a* **1684** LEIGHTON *Wks.* (1835) I. 114 The soul and body of all mankind are stained by the pollution of sin. **1792** *Anecd. W. Pitt* III. xliv. 195 Such a mode of warfare was a contamination, a pollution of our national character. **1876** MISS BRADDON *J. Haggard's Dau.* II. 16 It seemed to him that there was pollution in such contact. **1877** ROSCOE & SCHORLEMMER *Treat. Chem.* I. 255 The running water seldom reaches the sea in its natural or pure state, but is largely contaminated with the sewage of towns, or the refuse from manufactures or mines. So serious..is this state of things becoming that some steps are about to be taken to prevent the further pollution of the rivers. **1894** *Daily News* 25 Apr. 2/2 One of the principal difficulties of freeing the river from pollution was that certain persons had prescriptive rights to pass their sewage into the Thames at Staines and some other places. **1934**, **1947** [see ATMOSPHERIC *a.* 2]. **1955** *Sci. Amer.* May 63/3 As our economy uses more and more organic chemicals, air pollution by volatile organic compounds becomes more and more of a problem. **1969** *Financial Times* 9 Jan. 4/6 The danger of 'thermal pollution' is greatest where electric and other power plants return to rivers and streams water that has been heated by between six and 16 degrees Centigrade. This often proves deadly to fish. **1970** *New Society* 5 Feb. 209/3 At American universities, pollution has been a student rallying cry for some months now. **1970**, etc. [see *noise pollution* s.v. NOISE *sb.* 8]. **1975** *Physics Bull.* June 256/1 Noise pollution from aircraft and motorways and the design of speech and music reinforcement of St. Paul's cathedral are two of the varied aspects of noise and sound which have occupied Mr Allen.

b. *concr.* Anything polluted.

1605 BACON *Adv. Learn.* II. fol. 9 The Sunne..passeth through pollutions, and it selfe remaines as pure as before. **1870** BRYANT *Iliad* I. I. 17 The warriors purified the camp, And, casting the pollutions to the waves, They burned to Phœbus sound hecatombs.

2. Ceremonial impurity or defilement; profanation of that which is sacred.

1382 WYCLIF *Judith* iv. 10 Lest weren ȝyuen ther childer in to prei,..and the holi thingus of hem in to pollucioun. *c* **1645** HOWELL *Lett.* (1650) II. lv. 72 They will make a precedent prayer to their soules to depart from their bodies in the interim, for fear she partake of the same pollution. **1667** MILTON *P.L.* XII. 355 Thir strife pollution brings Upon the Temple. **1726** AYLIFFE *Parergon* 194 The contrary to Consecration is Pollution, which is said to happen in Churches by Homicide.

3. Seminal emission apart from coition; self-pollution.

c **1340** HAMPOLE *Prose Tr.* 11 Alswa here es forbodene all maner of wilfull pollusyone procurede..agaynes kyndly oys. *c* **1440** *Alphabet of Tales* 238 He had a pollucion of his sede. **1693** tr. *Blancard's Phys. Dict.* (ed. 2), *Pollutio nocturna*, an involuntary Pollution in the Night, caused by lecherous Dreams. **1878** tr. *von Ziemssen's Cycl. Med.* VIII. 828 This kind of loss is called a pollution.

4. *attrib.* and *Comb.*, as *pollution control*; *pollution-free* adj.

1961 *San Francisco Chron.* 27 Mar. 32 Stronger water pollution control programs. **1969** *New Scientist* 9 Oct. 90/1 Pollution-control measures are only an extra charge on the expenses of a company and have little direct return. **1978** *N.Y. Times* 30 Mar. D14/4 A $150 million pollution-control program in that state. **1974** *Spartanburg* (S. Carolina) *Herald* 25 Apr. C2/3 Engineers for Japan's Honda and Mazda car makers have developed some of the world's most pollution-free auto engines which are getting wide attention in the United States.

Hence †**po'llutionate** *a.* [cf. *affectionate*, *compassionate*, etc.], charged with pollution, foul; whence †**po'llutionately** *adv.*, foully.

1593 NASHE *Christ's T.* (1613) 57 No Hog-sty is now so pollutionate as the earth of Palestine. *Ibid.* 146 Their transplendent iuyce so pollutionately employd.

pollutional (pəˈl(j)uːʃənəl), *a.* [f. POLLUTION + -AL.] Causing or constituting pollution.

1921 *Bull. Nat. Hist. Survey Illinois* XIV. 40 Usually tolerant or pollutional species that have come into Peoria Lake since 1915 seem to be several in number. **1941** *Sewage Works Jrnl.* XIII. 270 (*heading*) The natural purification of river muds and pollutional sediments.

pollutive (pəˈl(j)uːtɪv), *a.* [f. L. *pollūt-* (see POLLUTE *v.*) + -IVE.] Causing environmental pollution.

1970 *New Scientist* 2 July 12/2 The diesel engine..is a naturally less pollutive engine than the spark ignition one. **1972** WARD & DUBOS *Only One Earth* xi. 247 Developing countries are hard put to it to raise the capital even for existing cheaper, though more pollutive, technologies and energy systems.

†**po'lluve**, *v. Sc. Obs.* [perh. for *polluue*, *pollue*, a. F. *polluer*, L. *polluĕre*: see POLLUTE *v.*] *trans.* = POLLUTE *v.*

1533 BELLENDEN *Livy* III. vii. (S.T.S.) I. 271 Herdonius..duelling proudlie in þe tempil of Jupiter, polluving [*v.r.* polloving] and defouling euery thing in It?

Pollux (ˈpɒləks). [a. L. *Pollux*, in earlier form *Pollūcēs*, ad. Gr. Πολυδεύκης.]

1. *Gr. Myth.* Name of one of the twin sons of Tyndarus and Leda; hence in *Astron.* the second star in the constellation Gemini: see CASTOR[3].

1526, **1647** [see CASTOR[3] 1]. **1868** LOCKYER *Guillemin's Heavens* (ed. 3) 324 Above Procyon, and towards the Zenith, Castor and Pollux point out the Twins.

2. *Min.* = POLLUCITE: see quot. 1847.

Polly[1] (ˈpɒlɪ). Dim. of POLL *sb.*[2] (cf. *Patty*, *Peggy*); as female name, and name for a parrot.

[**1616** B. JONSON *Epigr.* I. ci, And we will have no Poolye or Parrot by.] **1827** HONE *Every-day Bk.* II. 311 One of these 'images' was a 'Polly'.

b. *weeping Polly* (Australia): see quot.

1886 *Encycl. Brit.* XX. 174/1 The native [Queensland] grasses are nearly a hundred in number..the weeping Polly is *Poa cæspitosa*.

Polly[2] (ˈpɒlɪ). *slang*. Also 'polly. Abbrev. of APOLLINARIS; a bottle or glass of Apollinaris water. Also *attrib.*

1852 DICKENS *Bleak Ho.* (1853) xx. 200 Four small rums is eight and three, and three Pollys is eight and six. **1878** [see APOLLINARIS]. **1899** *Westm. Gaz.* 10 June 6/1 The dividend on Polly shares was announced too late to be public property in business hours yesterday. **1905** *Daily Chron.* 6 Sept. 4/7 'Johnny and Polly' is a common order in Piccadilly. **1907** *Westm. Gaz.* 17 Aug. 3/2 'Wagner and 'polly', or 'Tchaikowsky and soda'..would be both less stimulating and less harmful than some of the more popular intoxicants. **1954** J. BETJEMAN *Few Late Chrysanthemums* 43 And a host of little spiders Ran a race across the ciders To a box of baby 'pollies by the beer. **1969** S. HYLAND *Top Bloody Secret* ii. 165 Do not call it Appollinaris [*sic*] water... Nobody else..calls it that. They all say 'Polly water'. **1973** D. KYLE *Raft of Swords* (1974) viii. 77 'Soda? Apollinaris?' 'Whisky and Polly... I haven't had one in years.' 'It becomes increasingly difficult to come by.'

polly[3] (ˈpɒlɪ). *U.S.* and *Austral. slang*. Abbrev. of POLITICIAN.

1942 BERREY & VAN DER BARK *Amer. Thes. Slang* §854/1 *Politician*,..polly. **1955** *Publ. Amer. Dial. Soc.* XXIV. 151 Perhaps some *polly* (politician) can be interested sufficiently to intervene with the judge. **1969** *Courier-Mail* (Brisbane) 18 Oct. 13/7 The pollies..have been using television as an electronic soap box. **1974** *Bulletin* (Sydney) 12 Oct. 12 Pollies peel off the tax perks. **1978** *Sunday Sun* (Brisbane) 4 June 5/1 The eight pollies are members of an all-Party Parliamentary delegation led by Industry Minister Norm Lee.

polly, obs. f. PULLEY.

Pollyanna (ˌpɒlɪˈænə). Also **Polyanna** and with lower-case initial. The name of the heroine of stories written by Eleanor Hodgman Porter (1868–1920), American children's author, used with allusion to her skill at the 'glad game' of finding cause for happiness in the most disastrous situations; one who is unduly optimistic or achieves happiness through self-delusion. Also *attrib.*, *Comb.*, and as *adj.*

[**1913** E. H. PORTER *Pollyanna* xv. 148 'Her name is Pollyanna Whittier.'..'And what are the special ingredients of this wonder-working—tonic of hers?'..'As near as I can find out it is an overwhelming, unquenchable gladness... Her quaint speeches are constantly being repeated to me, and, as near as I can make out, 'just being glad' is the tenor of most of them.'] **1921** *Collier's* 11 June 11/1, I should not like to hold stock in a company with Pollyanna as president. **1925** WODEHOUSE *Carry On, Jeeves* ix. 214 Uncle Thomas, when his gastric juices have been giving him the elbow, can make Schopenhauer look like Pollyanna. **1926** B. BARTON *Bk. Nobody Knows* ii. 42 Job's crops are destroyed, his barns burned, his children taken sick, and he himself breaks out all over with horrid boils. In this condition he is visited by a group of three friends—professional moralists and Pollyannas. **1931** E. POUND *Let.* 27 Dec. (1971) 238 With Possum Eliot apptd. to Hawvud, he won't bring the glad polyanna yawp, but the ignorance of the Stork—Auslander—Mabie—Canby period can't continue. **1937** M. HILLIS *Orchids on your Budget* i. 14 The Pollyanna-like theory that you can have just as much fun with very little money as you can with a lot of it. **1939** WODEHOUSE *Uncle Fred* xv. 218 The Ovens home-brewed is a liquid Pollyanna, for ever pointing out the bright side and indicating silver linings. **1940** O. NASH *Face is Familiar* 203 Some people are just naturally Pollyanna, While others call for sugar and cream and strawberries on their manna. **1944** T. RATTIGAN *While Sun Shines* I. 32 You're not fooling anyone, Babe, but yourself with this Polyanna stuff. I want another drink, you want another drink, so we both have another little drink. **1953** *Amer. Scholar* XXIII. I. 22 As intellectuals, we the 'Pollyannas' inevitably..ask ourselves if we can be right, when the country..is with us. **1959** A. HUXLEY *Let.* 13 Feb. (1969) 866 A short section..devoted to what may be called negative quotations—utterances of pure nonsense, pollyanna uplift, anti-intelligence and anti-liberty. **1962** A. H. MASLOW *Summer Notes on Social Psychology* 3 Talk, talk, talk, not very effective, more optimistic and Pollyanna rather than realistic. **1963** 'E. LATHEN' *Place for Murder* ii. 20 Thatcher decided that a Pollyanna tone was necessary... 'I am looking forward to tomorrow night,' he said firmly. **1964** B. HARDY *Appropriate Form* iii. 57 Robinson Crusoe is a prototype Pollyanna, comparing what is bad with what might have been much worse. **1971** 'D. SHANNON' *Ringer* ix. 155 You're not exactly a Pollyanna today, Luis. **1977** *Time* 12 Sept. 60/2 Authors who try generally find themselves accused of going soft, of frivolously aping the Pollyanna fadeouts of popular schlock.

Hence **Polly'ann(a)ish** *a.*, naïvely cheerful or optimistic; **Polly'annaism**, a statement characteristic of (a) Pollyanna.

1922 E. E. CUMMINGS *Let.* 26 Feb. (1969) 83 Three Soldiers having, in his absence, been rendered Polyannish..by the highly moral Doran. **1923** *Grey Towers* 277, I wrote a paper for English 198 and the reader put on the outside, 'All right but Polly-Annaish.' **1946** G. STIMPSON *Bk. about Thousand Things* 33 We hear now not only of pollyannas and pollyannaisms, but of pollyanna statements, pollyanna propaganda. **1948** *Time* 6 Dec. 90/2 Mildly Saroyanesque throughout and a trifle Pollyannaish at the end, in its best scenes *The Silver Whistle* is genuinely funny. **1967** R. A. EPSTEIN *Theory of Gambling & Statistical Logic* xi. 411 Efforts to develop a complete and rigorous axiomatic treatment for psychological probability theory are sanguine, if not pollyannish. **1975** *Times* 18 June 7/5 The special brand of United Nations Pollyannaism. **1976** H. H. HUMPHREY *Educ. Public Man* ii. 25, I sound Pollyanna-ish when I speak of my childhood, my family, and Doland, but I think it is real and not simply nostalgia.

pollygony, pollymite, pollypod, obs. ff. POLYGONY, etc.

pollytick, pollywog: see: POLITIC, POLLIWOG.

polment, var. PULMENT *Obs.*, pottage.

polo[1] (ˈpəʊləʊ). [a. Baltī *polo*: cf. Tibetan *pulu*.]

1. A game of Eastern origin resembling hockey, played on horseback with long-handled clubs and a wooden ball.

An ancient game of the East; still played in the upper Indus valley, and in Manipur. Introduced first at Calcutta and a little later (*c* 1864) in Punjab. Played in England in July 1871. (Yule.)

[**1842** VIGNE *Trav. Kashmir* II. 289 At Shighur I first saw the game of the Chaughán... It is in fact hockey on horseback... The ball, which is larger than a cricket ball, is only a globe made of a knot of willow wood, and is called in Tibeti *Pulu*.] **1872** *Daily News* 20 July, The ball of contention once cast into the open field, Polo was entered upon in real earnest. **1875** BROWNING *Inn Album* I. 333 Polo, Tent-pegging, Hurlingham, the Rink, I leave all these delights. **1886** *Athenæum* 18 Sept. 367/3 The first historical event recorded in this volume is the death at polo of the Sultan Aikbar.

2. Also applied to various similar games derived from this, as WATER POLO, *rink polo* (see quots.).

1883 *Boston Daily Globe* 18 Nov. 6/2 (*heading*) The Winslow Rules Governing Polo on Skates. *Ibid.* 6/3 The American Roller..[is] to be published in the interests of roller skating, polo, and other popular sports. **1884** *Graphic* 30 Aug. 219/1 Polo proper may be defined as hockey on horseback, or rather pony-back, and..water polo is hockey on the water. **1885** *Providence* (Rhode Island) *Jrnl.* 29 Oct. 3/3 The game of polo at the Skating Academy last evening ..was an active game. **1890** in WEBSTER. **1895** in *Funk's Stand. Dict.* **1906** H. P. BURCHELL *Official Roller Skating Guide* 108 (Advt.), The Spalding 'Rink Polo' stick is made of the best..material.

3. Short for *polo hat*, *polo-neck*, etc.

1905 *Daily Chron.* 30 Jan. 8/1 Among the Victorian revivals..are various items of dress from the sixties... The small round hat that the French milliners call the 'polo' and we in this country term the pork-pie, is a detail in point. **1967** *Harper's Bazaar* Sept. 45 The neck..high everywhere

—emphasized by polos, wrapped, petal or stand-up collars. **1975** *Country Life* 29 May 1424/1 For summer, we are now diving into silky polos. **1976** *Woman's Weekly* 6 Nov. 36/2 (Advt.), Worn here over classic Polo in black, red, antrim, green, or cassis.

4. *attrib.* and *Comb.*, as ***polo-ball, boot, club, -ground, -match, -player, -playing, -pony, -stick***; also designating garments with a polo-neck, as ***polo jersey, -jumper, sweater*** (hence ***-sweatered*** adj.); **polo cloth**, a soft, loosely-woven camel's-hair cloth; **polo coat**, a type of camel's-hair coat; **polo collar**, (*a*) (see quot. 1960); (*b*) = *polo neck* (*a*); hence ***polo-collared*** adj.; **polo hat**, a small round hat worn esp. in the latter part of the nineteenth century; **polo-neck**, (*a*) a high, close-fitting roll collar; also *attrib.*; (*b*) a jersey with such a collar; hence ***polo-necked*** adj; **polo shirt**, (*a*) a shirt of the kind worn by polo-players; (*b*) a shirt having a polo-neck.

1895 *Outing* (U.S.) XXVI. 478/1 The regulation *polo-ball is of bass-wood, three inches in diameter, and painted white. Lightness and toughness are necessary. **1894** *Country Gentlemen's Catal.* 154 Hunting top-boots & butcher boots. *Polo boots. **1963** E. H. Edwards *Saddlery* xx. 149 Should the animal require greater protection..any of the heavier polo boots..may be more suitable. **1910** *Dry Goods Reporter* 22 Oct. 21 (Advt.), The *polo coat, 55 inches long, made in a complete line of mixtures..as well as the regular polo cloth. **1919** *Official Gaz.* (U.S. Patent Office) 23 Dec. 689/2 Polo cloth. Worumbo Mfg. Co., Bath, Me. Claims use since Jan. 10, 1910. Woolen goods in the piece. **1926** *Daily Colonist* (Victoria, B.C.) 13 Jan. 7/6 (Advt.), Plush and Polo Cloth Hats for Boys. Smart little shapes in black plush and light lovat polo cloth. **1879** *Scribner's Monthly* June 309/2 Three summers ago, some young men in New York formed the *Polo Club, and built a sumptuous house at Fordham, with grounds especially laid out for the game. **1885** *Providence* (Rhode Island) *Jrnl.* 1 Nov. 8/4 (*heading*) The Roller Skating Season... The members of the Chelsea Polo Club..have been engaged to form a Providence team. **1892** *Edin. Rev.* Jan. 40 In 1872 the Monmouthshire Polo Club was established. **1935** *Encycl. Sports* 468/1 The first polo club in London was at Lillie Bridge. **1975** *Oxf. Compan. Sports & Games* 788/2 British officers..began to establish polo clubs in India. **1910** *Polo coat [see *polo cloth*]. **1953** M. McCarthy *Groves of Academe* iii. 45 She jumped up..and seized her polo coat from the coat-rack. **1913** C. Mackenzie *Sinister Street* I. ii. v. 209 In his blue serge suit, wearing what the shops called a *Polo or Shakespeare collar, Michael felt more at ease. **1937** A. Thirkell *Summer Half* ix. 253 They take off their detachable polo collars and look just like us, only nastier. **1960** C. W. Cunnington et al. *Dict. English Costume* 169/1 Polo collar. C. 1899. A starched white stand-fall collar, the fronts sloping apart. **1955** J. Cannan *Long Shadows* vi. 102 I've corduroys..and a *polo-collared jersey. **1968** *Guardian* 22 Aug. 7/4 The current fashion for men to wear polo-collared shirts even with formal wear. **1895** Kipling in *Cosmopolitan* July 303 The hard, dusty Umballa *polo-ground was lined with thousands of soldiers. **1897** *Daily Tel.* 8 Oct. 7/1 Lieutenant Rattray galloped in from the Khar polo-ground to take command of the post. **1971** *Shankar's Weekly* (Delhi) 18 Apr. 19/3 A vaguely green building on the other side of the polo-ground. **1905** *Daily Chron.* 30 Jan. 8/4 (Advt.), A three-quarters redingote..and the revived *polo hat. **1897** *Outing* (U.S.) XXX. 479/2 The long coat and linen dusters which every *polo-hitter affects. **1929** D. L. Moore *Pandora's Letter Box* v. 92 *Polo jerseys were abandoned by normal men..because they were seen on many who were known to be unmanly. **1960** *Woman* 23 Apr. 73/4 What gave him most joy was a yellow polo jersey that Frances knitted for him. **1937** A. Christie *Death on Nile* vi. 77 He was wearing..a high-necked *polo jumper. **1949** 'M. Innes' *Journeying Boy* viii. 94 Two undergraduates in demodé polo-jumpers. **1944** 'N. Shute' *Pastoral* i. 5 A grey jumper with a *polo neck. **1951** 'A. Garve' *Murder in Moscow* ix. 96, I changed it for a polo-neck sweater. **1968** J. Ironside *Fashion Alphabet* 48 One [woman] may look very chic in a polo neck and another may look as if she were a kennel-maid manqué. **1971** *Vogue* 15 Oct. 73 Black poloneck, sleeves and back of thin black stripes. **1973** M. Amis *Rachel Papers* 128 He was wearing a fashionable black polo-neck jersey (fashionable, that is, among the weasly middle-aged). **1973** 'D. Halliday' *Dolly & Starry Bird* iv. 55 Wife and bambinos in suede jackets and knitted jackets and..enough polo necks to outfit the entire British Raj. **1955** M. Hastings *Cork & Serpent* vi. 79 She had changed into a pair of black ski trousers and a *polo-necked sweater. **1974** A. Price *Other Paths to Glory* ii. i. 111 An equally pink polo-necked sweater. **1885** Lady Brassey *The Trades* 221 Two or three good nags, which are used as chargers and *polo-ponies. **1920** F. Scott Fitzgerald *This Side of Paradise* (1921) i. ii. 44 The faces indistinct above the *polo shirts. **1938** 'E. Queen' *Four of Hearts* (1939) i. i. 11 You left out this wine-coloured polo shirt. **1974** R. B. Parker *God save Child* (1975) ii. 16 Six polo shirts of different colors with the sleeves neatly folded under. **1979** R. Gillespie *Crossword Mystery* iv. 100 He threw on a polo shirt and slacks. **1895** Kipling *Day's Work* (1898) 241 (*Maltese Cat*) The native officers held bundles of *polo-sticks, long cane-handled mallets. **1950** A. Koestler in *God that Failed* i. 58 A member of the intelligentsia could never become a real proletarian, but his duty was to become as nearly one as he could. Some tried to achieve this by forsaking neckties, by wearing *polo sweaters and black fingernails. **1955** N. Fitzgerald *House is Falling* ix. 156, I always wear..flannel bags, a polo sweater. **1963** Polo-sweater [see Chelsea 4]. **1950** A. Wilson *Such Darling Dodos* 136 The *polo-sweatered organist.

Hence **'poloist**, a player of polo.

1891 *Blackw. Mag.* May 651 The veteran poloist. **1898** *Westm. Gaz.* 9 Dec. 5/2 As a horseman and poloist he had not many rivals.

polo[2] ('pəʊləʊ). [Sp.] An Andalusian folk-dance, or the music which accompanies this dance.

1883 Grove *Dict. Mus.* III. 9/2 *Polo*, a Spanish dance accompanied by singing, which took its origin in Andalusia. **1902** *Encycl. Brit.* XXVII. 374/2 Other provincial dances now in existence are..the *Palotéa*, the *Polo*, the *Gallegada*, [etc.]. **1926** D. C. Parker *Georges Bizet* iv. 233 Gaudier..asserts that Bizet has..made use of a *polo*, sung by a serenading student. **1934** W. Starkie *Spanish Raggle-Taggle* vii. 76 She began to play a medley of Spanish airs—*polos, boleros, tangos, malagueñas.* **1967** 'La Meri' *Spanish Dancing* (ed. 2) vi. 81 The Polo dates back to the ancient and unaccompanied Andalucian songs.

polocrosse ('pəʊləʊ'krɒs). Also polo crosse. [Blend of polo and lacrosse.] A team game played on horseback with a rubber ball and a stick with a head like that of a lacrosse-stick.

1952 J. B. Pick *Phoenix Dict. Games* 105 The ground required by polo crosse is smaller than a polo field. **1965** *Newsweek* 19 Apr. 94 For a battering, breath-taking roughhouse on horseback, have a go at polocrosse in New South Wales. **1974** *Courier-Mail* (Brisbane) 16 Aug. 19 Polocrosse was far from being a poor cousin of the better known millionaire sport of polo. **1975** *Oxf. Compan. Sports & Games* 792/1 There were at least ten polo crosse clubs in Britain soon after the second world war, most of them in the West Country, but there is little evidence of the game in Britain now.

polocyte ('pəʊləsaɪt). *Biol.* [f. pol(e *sb.*[2] + -o + -cyte.] = *polar body* s.v. polar *a.* 5.

1915 C. W. Prentiss *Lab. Manual & Text-bk. Embryol.* i. 28 The cleavage is unequal and, instead of four cells of equal size resulting, there are formed one large ripe ovum or oöcyte and three rudimentary or abortive ova known as polar bodies or polocytes. **1927** [see ootid]. **1931** J. E. Frazer *Man. Embryol.* i. 6 Among the lower animals it seems to be usual for maturation not to be completed (*i.e.*, the second polocyte not to be cast off) before conjugation with the male cell is effected. **1969** F. D. Allan *Essentials Human Embryol.* (ed. 2) i. 14 Polocytes consist of a nuclear mass and a delicate cytoplasmic sheath and have no known function in addition to the passive role they play in meiosis, i.e., reduction or elimination of excess chromosomal material.

†**poloe**, obs. f. pilau [after Urdū *pulao*].

1741 *Compl. Fam.-Piece* i. ii. 134 To make a Poloe.

poloid ('pəʊlɔɪd), *sb. Geom.* [f. Gr. πόλος axle, pole *sb.*[2] + -oid.] = polhode (which is now the usual term). Also *attrib.* or *adj.* in ***poloid curve***.

1862 Cayley *Coll. Math. Papers* IV. 571 The 'Extrait'..establishes also the notions of the Poloid and Serpoloid curves. *Ibid.* 572 The pole of the instantaneous axis describes on the ellipsoid a certain curve, the 'Poloid', which is the locus of all the points for which the perpendicular on the tangent plane has a given constant value.

poloidal (pə'lɔɪdəl), *a.* [f. pol(ar *a.* (*sb.*) + tor)oidal *a.*] Being or representing a magnetic field of the form associated with a circular current loop, in which each line of force is confined to a radial or meridian plane.

1946 W. M. Elsasser in *Physical Rev.* LXIX. 108/1 We shall now introduce names for these three types of vectors. They will be designated as scaloidal (U), toroidal (T), and poloidal (S) vector fields. The electric field and vector potential pertaining to a poloidal magnetic field are toroidal, and *vice versa.* **1967** *McGraw-Hill Yearbk. Sci. & Technol.* 225 The magnetic field at the Earth's surface has a radial component and is thus of the poloidal type. **1972** *Sci. Amer.* July 67/3 A toroidal electric field maintains a toroidal current that flows inside the plasma, and this current in turn generates a magnetic-field component that is poloidal... The combination of the poloidal field with the toroidal field produces helical magnetic-field lines that lie on closed magnetic surfaces (nested toroids of circular cross section). **1973** *Nature* 20 Apr. 516/2 There are on the Moon weak, local, fairly randomly oriented magnetic fields but no overall poloidal field.

polology (pəʊ'lɒlədʒɪ). *Nuclear Physics.* [f. pol(e *sb.*[2] + -ology.] The theory of Regge poles.

1961 *Nuovo Cimento* XXII. 214 (*heading*) Polology and ND^{-1} solutions in the multiple-channel problems. **1964** S. DeBenedetti *Nucl. Interactions* vii. 471 This simple argument forms the basis of much of the present-day thinking about strong forces: perturbation methods may not be justified in general, but they are expected to give correct results near the predicted 'resonances' or 'poles'. The theory developed along these lines has received the informal name of 'polology'. **1966** D. Park *Introd. Strong Interactions* vii. 134 (*heading*) Polology and the determination of g.

polonaise (pɒlə'neɪz, pəʊl-), *sb.* Also 8 polonoise. [a. F. *polonaise*, prop. adj. fem. of *polonais* Polish; lit. a Polish *robe* or *redingote.*]

1. A name applied, at various periods from *c* 1770 onward, to an article of female dress originally suggested by that of Polish women, being a dress or over-dress, consisting of a bodice, with a skirt open from the waist downwards; variously modified at different times.

1773 Mrs. Harris in *Priv. Lett. Ld. Malmesbury* (1870) I. 266 The four ladies were to be dressed in white polonaises. **1790** *Guthrie's Geog. Gram., Poland* (ed. 12) II. 542 The habit of the women comes very near to that of the men, a simple Polonaise, or long robe edged with fur. **1820** Lady Granville *Lett.* (1894) I. 153 An added *or moulu* border to the Polonaise. **1835** *World of Fashion* Feb. 35/1 The Polonaise, is a very becoming carriage dress. The form resembles a short pelisse. **1883** *Truth* 31 May 768/2 Tabs are universal. They appear on tunics, polonaises, bodices, and sleeves. **1899** *Daily News* 15 Apr. 8/5 There is one point of difference between the modern polonaise and its ancestor... The former is rigidly tight, and plain about the hips.

†**b.** A similar garment worn by young boys: = Polony[1] A. 2. *Obs.*

1819 Scott *Leg. Montrose* xvii, This dress.. bore some resemblance to that called polonaise, still worn by children in Scotland of the lower rank.

c. A kind of overcoat for men, usually short and edged with fur.

1890 in *Cent. Dict.*

d. A cloth of a silk and cotton mixture. Cf. polonese *sb.* 1.

1894 J. E. Davis *Elem. Mod. Dressmaking* v. 93 Polonaise, a mixture of silk and cotton, which has the appearance of a soft dull silk with a distinct serge-like twill, is very much used as a skirt-lining for rich materials. **1923** *Daily Mail* 13 Aug. 4 (Advt.), The lining of the coat is silk Polonaise. **1932** G. Heyer *Devil's Cub* x. 152 Lady Fanny..in a négligée of Irish polonaise, with a gauze apron.

2. A slow dance of Polish origin, consisting chiefly of an intricate march, procession, or promenade of the dancers in couples; also, the music which accompanies this dance, or any music written in its peculiar triple rhythm.

1797 *Monthly Mag.* III. 466 The thirteenth [movement], a Polonoise, is characterised by much sweetness and novelty. **1813** Lady Burghersh *Lett.* (1893) 93 The ball began with polonaises, which are in fact only walking in time. **1861** *Daily Tel.* 22 Oct., The ball, as is usual..in Germany, commenced with a sort of general perambulation in couples. It is not dancing,..it is simply walking to the music. This solemn promenade is known as a Polonaise.

3. *Cookery.* Applied *absol.*, *attrib.*, or as *adj.* to dishes supposedly cooked in a Polish style. Also ***à la Polonaise***.

1889 J. Whitehead *Steward's Handbk.* iv. 405/2 Polonaise (*a la*), in Polish style. **1950** E. Brunet tr. *Saulnier's Répertoire de la Cuisine* 199 (*heading*) *Asparagus ..Polonaise.*—Dished in rows, sprinkle with hard boiled eggs and parsley chopped, pour over some bread crumbs tossed in butter nicely browned. *Ibid.* 203 (*heading*) *Cauliflowers..Polonaise.*—Dressed cauliflower on buttered dish, sprinkle with chopped parsley and hard boiled eggs, and bread crumbs, [etc.]. **1965** *House & Garden* Dec. 84/2 *Polonaise*, lightly fried breadcrumbs used in among other ingredients and not just as a topping or garnish. **1969** G. Payton *Proper Names* 355/1 *Polonaise* (Cooking), with beetroot and sour cream.

4. Used *attrib.* or as *adj.* to designate a type of rug woven in Iran during the sixteenth and seventeenth centuries using silver and gold warp threads. Also *absol.* as *sb.*

1911 G. G. Lewis *Pract. Bk. Oriental Rugs* xxi. 322 According to Dr. Valentiner the so-called Polanaise [*sic*] and Ispahan rugs belong to the 17th century. **1913** W. A. Hawley *Oriental Rugs* vii. 88 It was doubtless after..Shah Abbas I had begun to embellish his capital at Ispahan, that were made the famous 'Polish' silk or 'Polonaise' carpets about which there has been so much controversy. **1931** A. U. Dilley *Oriental Rugs & Carpets* ii. 44 Many of the king's rugs—the ones containing gold and silver, now called Polonaise—were woven at Kashan. **1962** C. W. Jacobsen *Oriental Rugs* 272 All Polonaise rugs belong to the 17th century, particularly the first half. The name Polonaise dates from the Paris exposition in 1878, when several rugs of this type were exhibited by Prince Czartorski of Warsaw. **1973** M. S. Dimand *Oriental Rugs in Metropolitan Museum of Art* v. 65/1 Because some of the rugs bear Polish coats of arms, they, too, have been called 'Polish' or 'Polonaise'. **1976** *Times* 15 Apr. 16/3 Christie's sale of Eastern rugs. A sixteenth-century Polonaise was unsold at £16,500.

Hence **polo'naise** *v. intr.*, to dance a polonaise; to move in a slow and stately manner; **polo'naise-wise** *adv.*, in the manner of a polonaise.

1828 De Quincey *Rhet.* Wks. 1860 XI. 363 Milton..polonaises with a grand Castilian air, in paces too sequacious and processional. **1858** Lady G. Bloomfield *Remin.* (1883) II. xiv. 64 After the presentations..Her Royal Highness polonaised with twenty-two Princes. **1888** *Times* (weekly ed.) 10 Feb. 1/3 The ball is opened by their Majesties and their Court parading round the house in polonaise-wise. **1898** *Westm. Gaz.* 5 May 3/2 A cherry red *voile* set in deep tucks placed polonaise-wise on the skirt.

polone, var. palone.

†**polo'nese**, *sb.* and *a. Obs.* Also 8 **poloneze**. [ad. F. *polonais* Polish, It. *Polonese*, f. med.L. *Polonia* Poland: see -ese.]

A. *sb.* **1.** = polonaise 1. Also apparently applied to the material for this.

1755 *Connoisseur* No. 52 I. 312 Some squire's aukward daughter, who never yet heard of a Poloneze. **1771** Mrs. Griffith *Hist. Lady Barton* I. 199 Her gown was a white silk polonese. **1774** *Lady's Mag.* July 379/1 Lady T—nell..chiefly wears a white Persian gown and coat, made of Irish polenese... The Irish polenese is made very becoming—it buttons down half the arm—no ruffles, [etc.].

2. A native of Poland, a Pole. (Sing. and pl.)

1810 E. D. Clarke *Trav. Russia* (1839) 47/1 Their features are those of the Polonese.

b. The Polish language.

1828 Webster cites *Encyc.*

B. *adj.* = Polish *a.* ***Polonese coat*** = polonaise 1 c.

1774 *Westm. Mag.* II. 288 It is not possible..to fix a standard for the dress of Gentlemen:—The Polonese Coats, with a silk edging, still prevail.

Polong (pəʊ'lɒŋ). [Mal.] A Malayan spirit or imp (see quots.).
1839 T. J. NEWBOLD *Straits of Malacca* II. xii. 191 The Polong is a small sprite which can be domesticated. **1900** W. W. SKEAT *Malay Magic* vi. 320 The Polong.. is described as a diminutive but malicious species of bottle-imp. **1972** *Daily Tel.* (Colour Suppl.) 12 May 58/3 Finally there is the Polong, a vampiristic imp who, in association with the demoniac house-cricket, the Pelasit, enters the victim's body at will.

†**Polonia** (pəʊ'ləʊnɪə). *Obs.* [med.L. *Polōnia* Poland.] The country Poland. *attrib.* † ***Polonia heel***: cf. POLONY[1] B.
1611 ROWLANDS *More Knaves yet* (Percy Soc.) 83 Bootes and stockins to our legs doth finde Garters, polonia heeles, and rose shooe-strings. **1653** MILTON *Hirelings* 144 Austria, Polonia and other places.

Polonial (pəʊ'ləʊnɪəl), *a. rare.* [f. POLONIA + -AL.] = POLISH *a.*
1922 *Blackw. Mag.* June 801/2 A very intelligent-looking secretary to the Polonial Embassy to the Vatican assured me [etc.].

Polonian (pəʊ'ləʊnɪən), *a.* and *sb.* [f. POLONIA + -AN.]
A. *adj.* Of Poland; = POLISH *a. Obs.* or *arch.*
1585 T. WASHINGTON tr. *Nicholay's Voy.* IV. xiii. 126 b, A long cappe after the Polonian or Georgian fashion. **1655** OWEN *Vind. Evangelicæ* Wks. 1853 XII. 18 This Captain-general of the Polonian forces. **1776** MICKLE tr. *Camoens' Lusiad* Introd. 55 He was a Polonian Jew by birth.
B. *sb.* **1.** A native of Poland, a Pole. *arch.*
1599 SANDYS *Europæ Spec.* (1632) 210 Which is the case of the Polonians and Venetians at this present. **1704** J. TRAPP *Abra-Mulé* I. i. 70 The rough insolence of stern Polonians. **1864** BURTON *Scot Abr.* II. ii. 179 Scottish colonels that served.. against the Tartar, and the Polonian.
†**2.** A (woman's) polonaise. *Sc. Obs.*
c **1817** HOGG *Tales & Sk.* IV. 216 Ladies,.. their number quite countless—dressed in green pollonians, and grass-green bonnets on their heads. **1818** —— *Brownie of B.* II. 183 The bogles will.. hae to pit on their pollonians o' the pale colour o' the fair day-light.
So †**Po'lonic**, †**Po'lonish** *adjs.* = POLISH; **'Polonism**, a Polish characteristic or peculiarity; **Poloni'zation**, the process of making Polish; **Polonize** ('pəʊlənaɪz) *v.*, to make Polish.
1612 BREREWOOD *Lang. & Relig.* Pref. 22 The Belgick, *Polonick, Argentine, Augustane, Saxonick,.. Bohemick or Waldensian Confession. **1599** SANDYS *Europæ Spec.* (1632) 121 Reported by the *Polonish Ambassadour. **1649** S. CLARKE *Lives Fathers, Luther* (1654) 253 A certain Polonish Jew. **1901** *Speaker* 9 Mar. 637/1 To discount.. the *Polonisms of Chopin.. and the Gallicisms of Berlioz. **1883** *Pall Mall G.* 17 Oct. 4/1 Demanding.. the *Polonisation of the Galician railways. **1886** *Contemp. Rev.* Feb. 286 That their residence there tends to *Polonize the districts in which they live. **1902** *Speaker* 6 Sept. 594/2 Instead of the Prussians Germanising the Poles, the Poles are Polonising the Germans.

polonium (pəʊ'ləʊnɪəm). *Chem.* [mod.L. and F. *polonium*, f. med.L. *Polōnia* Poland + -IUM: see quot. 1900.] A highly radio-active metallic element, discovered in 1898 by Prof. and Mme. Curie in pitchblende; atomic number 84, symbol Po.
1898 SIR W. CROOKES *Addr. Brit. Assoc.* 24 A new constituent of the uranium mineral pitchblende,.. The radiant activity of the new body, to which the discoverers have given the name of Polonium, needs neither the excitation of light nor the stimulus of electricity. **1900** *Nature* 14 June 151/2 That [substance] associated with bismuth being named polonium, a name derived from the Polish nationality of Mme. Curie. **1906** *Athenæum* 20 Jan. 82/1 In six days it becomes radium F, which Prof. Rutherford identifies with the polonium of Madame Curie and the radio-tellurium of Prof. Marckwald.

†**Polony**[1], *sb.* and *a. Obs.* [ad. med.L. *Polōnia* Poland, F. *Pologne*.]
A. *sb.* **1.** Poland.
1634 E. KNOTT *Charity Maintained* I. iv. §16 In Polony, Hungary, and Transilvania.
2. A kind of long coat or gown for young boys, having a close-fitting body with loose skirt; = POLONAISE I b.
1818 SCOTT *Hrt. Midl.* v, The blue polonie that Effie made for him.. was the first decent dress the bairn ever had on. **1825** —— *Lett.* II. 257 A sort of dress worn by children in Scotland, and called a polony.. which is just a jacket and a petticoat all in one.
B. *attrib.* or *adj.* Polish: in names of various articles of apparel, etc.
1610 ROWLANDS *Martin Marke-all* (Hunter. Cl.) 23 It is a Polony Shoe with a Bel. **1656** *Artif. Handsom.* 77 We wear Polony heels; or it may be Chopines. *c* **1660** *Gd. Counsel agst. Cold Weather* 14 Beloved, your Polony heel is good, your Wooden heeles better, but those of Corke the best of all. **1688** R. HOLME *Armoury* III. 129/1 The Caster [hat] is made of Coney Wool, mixt with Polony Wooll.

po'lony[2]. Also 8 **pullony**. [Origin uncertain: perh. the same as prec.; perh. corruption of BOLOGNA, q.v.] In ***Polony sausage***, a sausage made of partly cooked pork.
1764 ELIZ. MOXON *Eng. Housew.* (ed. 9) 75 To make Pullony Sausages. *a* **1845** HOOD *Sausage Maker's Ghost* ii, Preferr'd to all polonies, saveloys, And other foreign toys. **1878** GILBERT *H.M.S. Pinafore* I, I've chickens and conies, and pretty polonies, And excellent peppermint drops.

polony: var. PALONE.

‖**polos** ('pɒlɒs). [a. Gr. πόλος axis, sphere, vault of heaven; in late Gr. (Pausanias) a head-dress.] A head-dress of cylindrical form, seen in some representations of Greek and Oriental goddesses.
1850 LEITCH tr. *C. O. Müller's Anc. Art* (ed. 2) §363 Artemis Lusia is also perhaps to be recognised in the idol with the polos and torch and bow on the vase-painting at Berlin. **1887** B. V. HEAD *Hist. Numorum* 394 Europa sometimes.. wears upon her head a polos, showing that she was regarded at Gortyna in the light of a powerful goddess.

Polovtsy (pəʊ'lɒvtsɪ), *collect. pl.* Also **Polovtsi, Polovtzi, Polovzi.** [Russ.] A union of the nomad tribes belonging to the Kipchak Turks, which inhabited the steppes between the Danube and the Volga in the 11th–13th centuries. So **Polo'vetsian, Po'lovtsian** *a.*, of or pertaining to these people or their language; also as *sb.*
1799 W. TOOKE *View Russ. Empire* III. XI. ii. 581 The trade of the Krimea was heretofore uncommonly gainful and extensive; for, in the eleventh century, when a part of this peninsula fell under the dominion of the Polovtzi, better known from the byzantine history under the appellation of the Romanians, they granted the Genoese.. the permission to erect warehouses. **1803** H. CARD *Hist. Revolutions of Russia* 64 The Polovtsi took the imprudent resolution of observing a strict neutrality. *Ibid.* 66 One of the Polovtsian princes.. demanded and received the sacrament of baptism. **1878** *Encycl. Brit.* VIII. Pl. XII. opp. p. 715, Cumanians or Polovzians. **1885** *Ibid.* XIX. 286/1 He entered Kieff with the Polovtzi as his auxiliaries. *Ibid.* 410/2 As early as 988 the Russians erected several towns on the Sula and Trubezh for their protection against the Petchenegs and Polovtsy, who held the south-eastern steppes. **1938** *Oxf. Compan. Mus.* 750/2 Igor may go free if he will not make war on the Polovtsy again. **1954** *Grove's Dict. Mus.* (ed. 5) I. 821/1 Toward the end of 1874 Borodin's interest in 'Igor' was revived; the 'Polovtsian March' was composed, and in the following summer the famous dances. **1965** N. POPPE *Introd. Altaic Linguistics* 72 Kuman (Polovetsian, called so after the Russian name for Kumans) is also a Middle Turkic language. It was spoken in the XII–XVI centuries by Turkic nomads in Southern Russia, including the Crimea, and parts of Central Asia, and also by turkicized Armenians in the XV–XVIII centuries... There are no speakers of Kuman at the present time. **1968** M. GUYBON tr. *Solzhenitsyn's First Circle* I. 308 Half Polovtsian by blood, Prince Igor was for years an ally of the Polovtsians. **1973** R. C. HOWES *Tale of Campaign of Igor* 2 The Polovetsians (called Polovtsy, Cumans, or Kipchak Turks) had been moving into the steppes north of the Black Sea since the 1050s. *Ibid.* 3 The organization of two Polovetsian political units in the steppes.. also boded ill for Kiev. **1974** T. SZAMUELY *Russian Tradition* I. ii. 13 The Kievan state had been engaged in perpetual warfare since its foundation. Khazars, Pechenegs, Polovtsy—one wave followed the other.

polpody, polron(d, obs. ff. POLYPODY, POULDRON.

Pol Roger (pɔl rɔʒe). The proprietary name of a champagne produced in Épernay.
1889 *Trade Marks Jrnl.* 25 Sept. 916/2 *Pol Roger*... Champagne. Pol Roger, Albert Roger, and Veuve Julie Roger, trading as Pol Roger & Co., Epernay, France..; Champagne shippers. **1891** [see KRUG[2]]. **1912** C. MACKENZIE *Carnival* xx. 209 Maurice.. in a quandary of taste between Pol Roger and Perrier Jouet. **1925** H. ACTON in *Oxf. Poetry* 8 For after belching Pol-Roger the bile Will wreak revenge. **1957** L. DURRELL *Justine* III. 185, I was of course drunk by this time and exhausted—drunk as much on Justine as upon the thin-paper-bodied *Pol Roget* [sic]. **1968** E. HYAMS *Mischief Makers* x. 184 A steak and chips and a pint of Pol Roger will meet this case. **1979** P. ALEXANDER *Show me Hero* xv. 166 A maid had entered with a refreshment trolley. On it were two bottles of Pol Roger in ice-buckets.

‖**polroz** ('pɒlrəʊz). *Cornwall.* [a. Corn. *pulros*, f. *pul*, Welsh *pwll* pit + *ros*, Welsh *rhod*:—L. *rota* wheel.] The pit under a water-wheel.
1855 LEIFCHILD *Cornwall Mines* 278 These.. terms appear strange to the English language. I might add the words 'bryle', 'chats', 'terluing', 'dzhu','polroz', 'zyghyr', and others. **1881** RAYMOND *Mining Gloss.*, *Polroz* pronounced *Polrose*, Corn[wall], the pit underneath a water-wheel.

polrumptious (pɒl'rʌmpʃəs), *a. dial.* and *slang.* ? *Obs.* Also **pollrumptious.** [Perh. f. POLL *sb.*[1] + RUMPTI(ON + -OUS.] (See quots. 1787 and 1902.)
1787 F. GROSE *Provincial Gloss* s.v. *Pollrumptious*, restive, unruly. **1818** SCOTT *Heart Midl.* in *Tales my Landlord* 2nd Ser. III. vii. 170, I think thou doest not look so polrumptious as thy play-fellow yonder. **1888** 'Q.' *Troy Town* xvii. 213 I'll get the loan o' the Dearloves' blunderbust in case they gets polrumptious. **1902** FARMER & HENLEY *Slang* V. II. 247/1 *Pollrumptious*,.. restive: unruly; foolishly confident.

‖**pol sambol** (pɒl 'sæmbəl). [Sinhalese.] A spicy Indonesian dish: see SAMBAL.
1962 *Housewife* (Ceylon) Feb. 28 Learn to make a pol sambol. **1971** *Ceylon Daily Mirror* (Colombo) 4 Oct. 8/4 Miss Munasinghe had consumed a meal consisting of.. Pol sambol with maldive fish.

polshe, obs. form of POLISH *v.*

†**polshred**, *v. Obs. rare*[—1]. [prop. *poll shred*, f. POLL *sb.*[1] + SHRED *v.*] *trans.* = POLLARD *v.*
1530 PALSGR. 614/1, I loppe a tree, I croppe, I polshred.

polska ('pɒlskə). [Sw., f. *Polsk* Polish.] A Swedish folk dance of Polish origin in ¾ time; the music which accompanies such a dance.
1883 GROVE *Dict. Mus.* III. 11/2 Polskas are usually written in minor keys. **1910** C. WAERN *Mediæval Sicily* p. xiv, In Old Sweden the gaily decked Maypole is, or was, set up on Midsummer Eve, and people dance round it.. the brisk national 'polska' or the characteristic 'ring dance'. **1925** [see HAMBO]. **1947** A. EINSTEIN *Mus. in Romantic Era* xvii. 319 Here too the Romanitc movement began with the collecting and publishing of the old national treasures of folk song—full of feeling and dancelike, the folk songs of sentiment being often modal, the dancelike ones (polskas) being related to the mazurka.

polt (pəʊlt), *sb. Obs.* exc. *dial.* [Origin obscure: in sense 1 it may be a variant of PALT *sb.*; but cannot easily be connected with *pelt*. It is not certain that sense 2 is the same word.]
1. A blow, a hard rap or knock. Now *dial.*
c **1610** *MS. Bodl.* 30 lf. 24 b, I tooke him a polt of the pate. *a* **1700** B. E. *Dict. Cant. Crew*, *Polt on the Pate*, a good Rap there. **1700** J. ASGILL *Argument* 103 If any one hath spite enough to give me a polt,.. I only desire them first to qualify themselves for my Executioners. *a* **1739** JARVIS *Quix.* II. x. (1749) 162 One of those who stood close by him.. lifted up a pole he had in his hand, and gave him such a polt with it as brought Sancho Pança to the ground. **1782** MISS BURNEY *Cecilia* II. ix, He'd go nigh to give me a good polt of the head. *a* **1825** FORBY *Voc. E. Anglia*, *Polt*, a hard driving blow. **1849** *Blackw. Mag.* LXVI. 702 [It] fetched me an awful polt in the right side.
†**2.** A pestle or club (cf. POLT-FOOT). *Obs.*
1612 CAPT. SMITH *Map Virginia* 17 Their corne they rost in the eare greene, and bruising it in a morter with a Polt, lappe it in rowles in the leaues of their corne.
†**b.** The club-shaped stem and bulb of a leek.
1635 MARKHAM *Eng. Husb.* II. I. ii. 9 You shall cut the blades [of leeks] to the polt.

polt, *v.* Now *dial.* [f. prec. sb.] *trans.* To knock, thrash, beat, bang.
1649 BLITHE *Eng. Improv. Impr.* (1653) 179 Then polt it, or faulter it as some call it, that is, beat it over again in the husk. **1669** WORLIDGE *Syst. Agric.* (1681) 329 To *Polt*, to beat or thrash. **1706** PHILLIPS, To *Polt* (Country-Word), to beat, bang, or thrash. **1831** LOWER *T. Cladpole* cxxxviii, I aim'd ma swish an levell'd well, To polt un on de head.
Hence **polting-lug** (*dial.*): see quot.
1853 *Jrnl. R. Agric. Soc.* XIV. II. 441 In Herefordshire the ordinary mode of gathering the fruit is by sending men to beat the trees with long slender poles or rods,.. these poles are provincially termed 'polting lugs'.

polt, obs. form of POULT.

Poltalloch (pɒl'tæləx). The name of an estate in Argyll, Scotland, used *absol.* or *attrib.* to designate a small, stocky, rough-coated, white terrier belonging to a breed developed there by the Malcolm family, esp. Colonel E. D. Malcolm (1837–1930), and now usually called the West Highland White terrier.
1887 D. J. THOMSON GRAY *Dogs of Scotland* (1891) iii. 51 A white variety of the Scottish terrier existed at one time (and stray specimens may still exist) under the cognomen of Poltalloch terriers. **1920** R. MACAULAY *Potterism* II. i. 63 'We have two Pekingese, a King Charles, and a pug...' I answered with some inanity about my mother's Poltalloch. **1922** [see HIGHLAND *a.* 2 a]. **1932** E. WEEKLEY *Words & Names* ix. 129 We have the new class-names which come into existence, as new breeds of terriers are evolved to suit changing fashions, e.g... the poltalloch, first bred by Colonel Malcolm, of Poltalloch (Argyll). **1950** A. C. SMITH *Dogs since 1900* xi. 187 West Highland White Terriers.. were at first known as Poltalloch Terriers. **1968** C. G. E. WIMHURST *Bk. Terriers* xxvii. 189 These [*sc.* the Duke of Argyll's terriers] were not related to the Poltalloch terriers.

†**polte**, var. *pulte*, pa. t. of PILT *v. Obs.*
c **1380** *Sir Ferumb.* 2976 þe hardieste þat were of al þe trome polte hem to þe fliȝt.

poltergeist ('pɒltəgaɪst). [Ger. f. *polter* noise, uproar + *geist* ghost.] A spirit which makes its presence known by noises; a noisy spirit. Also *attrib.* and *fig.*
1848 C. CROWE *Night Side of Nature* II. vi. 238 (*heading*) The poltergeist of the Germans, and possession. *Ibid.* 239 The annoyances appear rather like the tricks of a mischievous imp. I refer to what the Germans call the *Poltergeist*, or racketing spectre. **1863** *Q. Rev.* July 193 It seems a suspicious circumstance that the old-fashioned visible ghost has in these modern *séances* been almost entirely superseded by the *Poltergeist* or noise-making spirit. **1871** TYLOR *Prim. Cult.* II. 176 Vampires appear in the character of the poltergeist or knocker. **1898** *Month* Sept. 229 If there be nothing in hallucinations, apparitions, scrying, second-sight, poltergeists, and the rest. **1902** F. PODMORE *Mod. Spiritualism* I. I. ii. 25. **1903** *Edin. Rev.* Oct. 308 Most poltergeists are not content with mere noises. **1927** J. S. HUXLEY *Relig. without Revelation* vi. 187 Exorcism is magic: the Rumanian poltergeist medium, Eleonore Zugun, whose case was recently investigated in London, was the subject of exorcist rites by Rumanian priests. **1940** [see DOPPELGANGER]. **1979** M. BABSON *So soon done For* i. 8 A disturbed adolescent in an area of intense poltergeist activity.
Hence **'poltergeistic** *a.*, of, pertaining to, or suggestive of a poltergeist; **'poltergeistism**, the manifestation or activity of poltergeists.
1952 R. F. JONES in 'E. Crispin' *Best SF Five* (1963) 44 Reports on poltergeistism at Leander Castle near London. **1973** L. M. BOSTON *Memory in House* v. 61 The house.. from time to time sent feelers out from its darkest corners,

such as slight poltergeistic displacements, footsteps up the wooden stairs,..etc.

'polt-foot, *arch.* Also 6 powlt-, 6–7 poult-, 7 polte-. [app. f. POLT *sb.* sense 2 + FOOT *sb.*]

1. A club-foot.

1579 LYLY *Euphues* (Arb.) 97 Venus was content to take the blake Smith with his powlt foote. **1604** DEKKER *Honest Wh.* Wks. 1873 II. 81 My eldest son had a polt foot, crooked legs. **1638** SIR T. HERBERT *Trav.* (ed. 2) 338 The women are commonly modest,..shewing nothing but their polt-feet which from their infancy are straitned. **1659** *Lady Alimony* v. in Hazl. *Dodsley* XIV. 308 Vulcan's poult foot or his smutted look. **1840** BROWNING *Sordello* v. 266 'Polt-foot', sang they, 'was in a pitfall now'.

2. *attrib.* (often poltfoot) = *polt-footed*.

c **1589** NASHE *Almond for Parrat* B iv b, My Bedlam brother Wig. and poltfoote Pag. with the rest of those patches. **1601** B. JONSON *Poetaster* IV. vii, What's become of ..the poult-foot stinkard, her husband? **1880** SWINBURNE *Stud. Shaks.* 185 The rough construction and the poltfoot metre, lame sense and limping verse.

Hence **'polt-footed** *a.*, club-footed.

1589 GREENE *Menaphon* (Arb.) 39 Though he [Vulcan] was polt-footed, yet he was a God. *c* **1619** B. JONSON *Merc. Vind.* Wks. (Rtldg.) 595/1 This polt-footed philosopher, old Smug here of Lemnos.

polther, poltice, obs. f. POLDER, POULTICE.

polthogue (pɒl'təʊg, -'əʊx). *Ir. colloq.* Also **palthogue**. [f. Ir. *palltóg*.] A blow with the fist; a thump or punch.

1830 W. CARLETON *Traits & Stories Irish Peasantry* II. 59 John Grimes hot him a *palthoge* on the sconce wid the but-end of a gun. *c* **1874** D. BOUCICAULT in M. R. Booth *Eng. Plays of 19th Cent.* (1969) II. 181 Be jabers, I'd have liked to see in your face when you got that polthogue in the gob. **1898** J. D. BRAYSHAW *Slum Silhouettes* 25 Faix, there's a polthogue will knock sinse into yez. **1899** S. MACMANUS *In Chimney Corners* 164 He draws the flail one polthogue at the lad in the door and just barely missed him.

polt-net: see POUT-NET.

poltre, obs. form of POULTRY.

poltroon (pɒl'tru:n). Forms: 6 **pultrowne, pultron, 6–7 pultrone, 6–8 poultron, 6–9 poltron, 7 poultroone, pultroon, pultran, -oun, 7–9 paltroon, 7– poltroon.** [a. F. *poltron* (also in 16th c. *poultron*) 'a knaue, rascall..; dastard, coward; sluggard, lazie-backe, base idle fellow' (Cotgr.), ad. It. *poltrone* 'a poltron, an idle fellow, a base coward, a lazie, lither or slothfull sluggard, a lout' (Florio 1611), whence also med.L. *pultro, -onem* (S. Francis *c* 1220, Du Cange), Sp. *poltron*, Pg. *poltrão*; f. It. *poltro* 'sluggard, idle, lazie, slothfull' (Florio) + *-one*: see -OON. The 16th c. spelling may have been influenced by med.L. Originally stressed *'pultron*; *pol'troon* (after Fr.) appears in 1664.

It. *poltro* adj. was app. from †*poltro* couch, bed (Florio): cf. Milanese *polter*, Romagn. *pultar* resting-place, Venet. *poltrona* couch, Pg. *poltrona* large arm-chair, and It. †*poltrare, poltrire*, beside *poltronare, poltroneggiare* 'to play the poltron,..to loll and wallow in sloth and idlenesse, to lye lazilie in bed as a sluggard' (Florio). *Poltro, polter, pultar*, are referred by Diez to OHG. *polstar* pillow, bolster. The fantastic conjecture of the derivation of *poltron* from L. *pollice truncus*, 'maimed or mutilated in the thumb' (*scil.* in order to shirk military service), was offered by Salmasius, and long passed current as an 'etymology'; it prob. gave rise in the 18th c. to the use in Falconry (sense 2).]

1. A spiritless coward; a mean-spirited, worthless wretch; a craven.

a **1529** SKELTON *Howe the douty Dk. of Albany* 170 Suche a proude pultrowne. *a* **1572** KNOX *Hist. Ref.* Wks. 1846 I. 235 That pultron and vyle knave Davie was justlie punished. *a* **1584** MONTGOMERIE *Cherrie & Slae* 374 Fortune helps the hardie ay, And pultrones plaine repellis. *a* **1592** GREENE *Jas. IV*, III. ii, Poltron, speak me one parola against my *bon gentilhomme*, I shall [etc.]. **1593** SHAKS. *3 Hen. VI*, I. i. 62 Patience is for Poultroones, such as he: He durst not sit there, had your Father liu'd. **1632** LITHGOW *Trav.* I. Table 509 A French Pultrone, playing the Palliard. **1664** BUTLER *Hud.* II. I. 232 They that..think one beating may for once Suffice, are Cowards, and Pultroons. **1678** *Ibid.* III. I. 346 And held my Drubbing of his Bones Too great an Honour for Pultrones. **1700** DRYDEN *Fables, Iliad* I. 413 For who but a poltron, possess'd with fear, Such haughty insolence can safely bear? **1748** SMOLLETT *Rod. Rand.* (1812) I. 66 As arrant a poltroon as ever was drummed out of a regiment. **1809** W. IRVING *Knickerb.* (1861) 214 As did Homer make that fine fellow Hector scamper like a poltroon round the walls of Troy.

attrib. **1645** HAMMOND *Serm. Acts* xxiv. 25, Wks. 1683 IV. 521 Our hellish oaths and imprecations, (that pultroon sin, that second part of Ægyptian plague of frogs and lice, and locusts). **1682** SIR T. BROWNE *Chr. Mor.* I. §36 He is like to be mistaken, who..relieth upon the Reed of narrow and poltron Friendship.

2. *Falconry.* (See quot.)

1727–41 CHAMBERS *Cycl.*, *Poltroon*, in falconry, is a name given to a bird of prey, when the nails and talons of his hind-toes are cut off, wherein his chief force and armour lay; in order to intimidate him, and prevent his flying at great game.

Hence **pol'troonish** *a.*; **pol'troonism**; **poltroonize** *v. intr.*, to play the poltroon.

1611 COTGR., *Poltroniser*, to pultronize it; to play the knave, scowndrell, coward. **1644** S. KEM *Messengers Preparation* Ded. 2 It would conclude me guilty of Poultranisme, to feare the *Sciopii* and *Pacientii* heere, when not the *Zosimi* at Oxford. **1837** MISS SEDGWICK *Live & let L.* (1876) 205 Patience may be very Christian in you, but it is very poltronish in me. **1906** *Q. Rev.* Apr. 363 Collinson—a weak, almost poltroonish creature.

poltroonery (pɒl'tru:nəri). [ad. F. *poltronnerie* (1573 in Hatz.-Darm.), = It. *poltroneria*: see POLTROON and -ERY.] The behaviour of a poltroon; †laziness; pusillanimity, cowardice.

1590 R. HICHCOCK *Quintess. Wit* 35 b, Firste they are industrious, suppliant, modest; and after, with pultronerie and in pride doo lead their age. **1632** B. JONSON *Magn. Lady* III. iv, There's no cowardize, No poultrounerie, like urging why? wherefore? **1677** *Govt. Venice* 125 That 'tis laziness and poltronery to retire from the Government to spend our age in ease. **1770** LANGHORNE *Plutarch* (1879) II. 608/2 His poltroonery and mean submission..deserve the greatest reproach. **1897** GLADSTONE *East. Crisis* 11 Counsels that had hitherto resulted in a concert of miserable poltroonery.

polulogy, polumath, etc.: see POLYLOGY, etc.

polut(e, obs. forms of POLLUTE.

†**'polverine.** *Obs.* [ad. It. *polverino*, f. *polvere*:—L. *pulverem* dust, powder + *-ino*, -INE[4]] The calcined ashes of a plant, probably *Salsola Soda*, brought from the Levant and Syria, of the nature of pot- or pearl-ash, and used in glass-making; glass-makers' ashes.

1662 MERRETT tr. *Neri's Art of Glass* i. 1 *Polverine*, or *Rochetta*, which comes from the Levant.., is the ashes of a ..herb. **1712** tr. *Pomet's Hist. Drugs* I. 104 Crystal Fritt, made with Polverine, or Pot-Ashes, and Salt of Tartar. **1753** CHAMBERS *Cycl. Supp.* s.v. *Crystal*, Mix this powder with the pure salts of polverine. **1823** CRABB *Technol. Dict.*, *Polverine*. **1828** WEBSTER, Polverin, polverine.

polvil, obs. form of PULVIL.

pol-wheat: see POLL *a.* 2 b.

polwig(ge, polwygle, obs. var. POLLIWOG.

†**poly, poley** ('pəʊli), *sb.*[1] *Obs.* [ad. L. *polium*, *polion* (Plin.), a. Gr. πόλιον (Theophr.) an aromatic herb, perh. f. πολιός hoary.] A species of Germander, *Teucrium Polium*, an aromatic herb of Southern Europe; also extended to other species of *Teucrium*, as Golden P. (*T. aureum*), Yellow P. (*T. flavescens*).

In quot. 1527 erroneously for PULIOL.

1527 ANDREW *Brunswyke's Distyll. Waters* C iv, Water of poley. Pulegium in latyn. The best tyme of hys dystylacyon is all the herbe chopped whan it bereth floures, and so dystylled. **1578** LYTE *Dodoens* II. lxvi. 233 Poley..is of two sortes, whereof one may be named..Poley of the Mountaine: and the other..small Poley. **1608** TOPSELL *Serpents* (1658) 618 The herb called Poley, Fern, and all other things that have a strong or vehement ill savour. **1866** *Treas. Bot.*, Poly, *Teucrium Polium*.

b. *grass poly*: see GRASS *sb.*[1] 14.

c. poly-mountain, also **poly of the mountain, mountain poly** [ad. L. *polium montanum*], name of an aromatic herb: identified in *Treas. Bot.* with *Bartsia alpina*; by Britten and Holland with *Calamintha Acinos*; by earlier writers app. also with *Teucrium Polium* (= POLY). See also PELLAMOUNTAIN, *pulimountain* in PULIOL.

1578 LYTE *Dodoens* II. lxvi. 233 Poley of the Mountayne is a little, small, tender, base, and sweete smelling herbe, having small stemmes, and slender branches. *Ibid.*, It is called..in English Poley and Poley mountayne. **1633** JOHNSON *Gerarde's Herbal* 676, I haue sometimes seene it [*Calamintha Acinos*] brought to Cheapside market, where the herbe women called it Poley mountaine, some it may bee that haue taken it for *Polium montanum* [*Teucrium Polium*, L.] mis-informing them. **1698** FRYER *Acc. E. India & P.* 244 Where..grew the Mountain-Poly, which struck our Scent. **1712** tr. *Pomet's Hist. Drugs* I. 82 Poley Mountain..is a Plant of the Height of half a Foot; having small, thick indented Leaves. **1866** *Treas. Bot.* 913/1 Poly mountain, *Bartsia alpina*. **1886** BRITTEN & HOLLAND *Plant-n.* 385 Poley Mountain, *Calamintha Acinos*.

poly ('pɒli), *sb.*[2], colloq. abbrev. of POLYTECHNIC *sb.* 2.

1858 M. TUCKETT *Diary* 30 Sept. (*c* 1975) 9 We came into Falmouth..and then went with Aunt to the Poly. **1882** Q. HOGG *Let.* Sept. in E. M. Hogg *Quintin Hogg* (1904) vi. 145 Our Poly. boys came to speak their word in the matter. **1892** *Scribner's Mag.* Feb. 170/1 The Young Men's Polytechnic Institute, which is universally known among young people in London as the 'Poly'. **1932** E. M. WOOD *Polytechnic & its Founder Quintin Hogg* (rev. ed.) 16, I have just tried to keep out of the light and let the Poly tell its own history. **1967** *Times Rev. Industry* May 115/2 The new polys will come into being largely as regroupings of existing colleges. **1970** *Guardian* 19 Aug. 9/2 Fowler..is taking the poly job and saying a regretful 'no thanks' to LSE. **1978** I. MURDOCH *Sea* 226 When he left school he went into the poly, you know, the polytechnic... He had a student grant. **1979** *Jrnl. R. Soc. Arts* July 489/1 So what we should like is for those institutions such as polys throughout the Commonwealth that are already running business management courses to devote part of them to the skills of publishing.

poly ('pɒli), *sb.*[3], colloq. abbrev. of POLYTHENE and POLYETHYLENE **b.** Chiefly *attrib.* and *Comb.*, as ***poly bag (polybag), poly-wrapped*** adj.

1965 *Supermarket & Self-Service* (Johannesburg) June/July 13/3 Quick-frozen polywrapped broilers. **1968** *Punch* 12 June 858/1 Little poly-wrapped trays in the frozen food counter. **1971** C. BONINGTON *Annapurna South Face* ix. 103 Tom and I finished packing our rucksacks, leaving a proportion of our gear in polybags outside the boxes to reduce our loads. **1976** *Canad. Forces Sentinel* (Ottawa) XII. III. 6/3 One three-pound polybag of the stuff served as a week-long protein supplement for..six. **1976** *Southern Even. Echo* (Southampton) 11 Nov. (Advt. Suppl.) 7/1 Fresh meat from the farm for your freezer:..All poly wrapped and cut to your requirements. **1977** *Undercurrents* June–July 34/3 Find an old boiler suit,..a small shovel, and a big thick poly bag or a cut away poly jerry can. **1978** *Detroit Free Press* 5 Mar. (Spring Fashion Suppl.) 14/1 (Advt.), Sleek soft sandals..latest styles, Spring colors, and the newest poly bottoms.

po'ly, poly ('pɔ:li), *a.* Repr. a U.S. dial. pronunc. POORLY *adv.* and *a.*

1890 *Dialect Notes* I. 69 'How d'you do?' 'I am po'ly to-day.' **1893** H. A. SHANDS *Some Peculiarities of Speech in Mississippi* 50 A negro, when asked about his health, if not well, will answer, 'Poly, poly, bress God!' **1929** W. FAULKNER *Sartoris* I. 26 'How is you?' 'Po'ly, ladies; po'ly.' **1935** Z. N. HURSTON *Mules & Men* (1970) I. vi. 140 My wife is po'ly.

poly, obs. form of PULLEY.

poly- (pɒli), repr. Gr. πολυ-, combining form of πολύς, πολύ, much, in pl., πολλοί, -αί, ά many, forming the first element in a large number of words, mostly scientific or technical.

The second element of such compounds is properly of Greek origin, but in recent formations is often of Latin; occasionally (chiefly in nonce-wds.) *poly-* is prefixed to an English word. The more important compounds will be found in their alphabetical places; those of less importance follow here.

1. General words.

polyabolo (pɒli'æbələʊ) [f. DI)ABOLO by deliberately false analogy (see quot.); cf. PENTOMINO], any planar shape formed by joining a number of identical right-angled isosceles triangles by their edges. **polyacanthous** (-ə'kænθəs) *a. Bot.* [Gr. ἄκανθα spine, thorn], having many thorns (Mayne *Expos. Lex.* 1858). †**polya'coustic** *a.* and *sb.* [see ACOUSTIC]: see quots. **poly'acron** (pl. **-ons** or **-a**), *Geom.* [Gr. ἄκρον summit], a solid having many vertices or solid angles; a polyhedron (classed according to the number of its vertices). **'polyact** (-ækt), **polyactinal** (-'æktɪnəl) *adjs.* [Gr. ἀκτίς, ἀκτῖν- ray], having numerous rays, as a sponge-spicule; multiradiate. **poly'actine**, a sponge spicule having numerous rays. **polyadamite** (-'ædəmaɪt) *a.* (*nonce-wd.*), asserting a plurality of 'Adams' or first parents of mankind. **polyadenopathy** (-ædɪ'nɒpəθɪ), *Path.* [Gr. ἀδήν gland: see -PATHY], 'simultaneous disease of several lymphatic glands' (*Syd. Soc. Lex.*). **polyadenous** (-'ædɪnəs) *a. Bot.* [see prec.], having many glands (Mayne). ‖**polyæsthesia** (-ɪs'θi:sɪə), *Path.* [Gr. αἴσθησις sensation]: see quot.; hence **polyæsthetic** (-ɪs'θetɪk) *a.* (*Syd. Soc. Lex.* 1895). **poly-a'ffectioned** *a.* (*nonce-wd.*), having a multiplicity of affections. **,polyallo'morphic** *a. Philol.*, having several allomorphs (ALLOMORPH[2]). **,polyalpha'betic** *a. Cryptography*, employing more than one alphabet, so that each letter of the alphabet may be represented in a code by any of two or more letters or other characters. †**'polyangle**, a figure having many angles, a polygon; so **poly'angular** *a.*, having many angles, polygonal. **poly'anion** *Chem.*, a negatively charged polyion (see below); hence **,polyani'onic** *a.* **polyarthritic** (-'ɪtɪk) *a.*, pertaining to or affected with polyarthritis. ‖**polyarthritis** (-ɑ:'θraɪtɪs), *Path.* [see ARTHRITIS], 'inflammation of several joints at once' (Billings); **,polyarte'ritis** *Path.* [mod.L., coined in Ger. as *polyarteritis acuta nodosa* (E. Ferrari 1903, in *Beiträge zur path. Anat. und zur allgem. Path.* XXXIV. 383) to replace *periarteritis*] = *periarteritis* s.v. PERI- 1 c. **polyarthrous** (-'ɑ:θrəs) *a.* [Gr. ἄρθρον joint], 'having many joints' (*Syd. Soc. Lex.*). **polyar'ticular** [L. *articulus* joint], = prec.; also (*Path.*) affecting many joints. **poly'axial** *a.*, having several axes (see AXIS). **poly'axon** [Gr. ἄξων axis], *a.* = prec.; *spec.* of a sponge-spicule, having more than six axes of growth; *sb.* a polyaxon sponge-spicule. **polybathic** (-'bæθɪk) *a.* [Gr. βάθος depth], living at great depths in the sea. **poly'bigamy** (*nonce-wd.*), repeated bigamy or re-marriage during the life of the first wife or husband. **'polyblast** (-blæst), *Biol.* [-BLAST], (*a*) a mass of many cells, as that formed by the segmentation of the ovum (also called *morula*); (*b*) *Histology* [a. G. *polyblast* (A. Maximow 1902, in *Beiträge zur path. Anat.*: *Suppl.* V. 43)], a wandering macrophage; hence **poly'blastic** *a.*, pertaining to or of the nature of a polyblast. **'polybranch** (-bræŋk), *Zool.*, *a.* having many branchiæ or gills, as a mollusc or crustacean; *sb.* a polybranch mollusc or crustacean; so

poly'branchian, *a.* and *sb.*; **poly'branchiate**, *a.* **poly'buttoned** *a.* (*nonce-wd.*), wearing many buttons. **poly'cation** *Chem.*, a positively charged polyion (see below); hence **,polycati'onic** *a.* **poly'cellular** *a.*, composed of many cells, multicellular. †**polycharacte'ristic** *a. Obs.*, having the characteristics of many (deities); ‖**polycholia** (-'kəʊlɪə), *Path.* [mod.L., f. Gr. χολή bile; in F. *polycholie*], excessive secretion of bile. **poly'choral** *a. Mus.*, in which the choral ensemble is divided into groups who sing alternately (and, properly, jointly also). ‖**polychorion** (-'kɔərɪɒn), *Bot.* [see CHORION]: see quot.; hence (irreg.) **polychori'onic** *a.*, pertaining to or of the nature of a polychorion. ‖**polychromia** (-'krəʊmɪə), *Path.* [mod.L., f. Gr. χρῶμα colour (cf. Gr. πολύχρωμ-ος many-coloured)], excessive formation of colouring matter, e.g. of bile-pigments. **poly'churchism**, the doctrine or system of a multiplicity of churches; so **'polychurch** *a.*, of or belonging to such a system; **poly'churchist**, an adherent of such a system (*nonce-wds.*). **polyci'stronic** *a. Genetics*, comprising or derived from more than one cistron and so containing the information for more than one gene product; hence **polyci'stronically** *adv.* **poly'clonal** *a. Biol.* and *Med.*, (of a population of organisms) comprising many clones; (of a population of cells) comprising several cell lines of separate origins; of or pertaining to the products of such cell lines; hence **polyclo'nality**. **poly'clonally** *adv.* **'polyclone** *Biol.* and *Med.* [CLONE *sb.*], a group of cells all descended from one or other of an initial small group of cells. **polycoccous** (-'kɒkəs) *a. Bot.* [Gr. κόκκος berry], composed of several separate carpels or *cocci*, as a fruit. **polycœlian** (-'siːlɪən) *a. Zool.* [Gr. κοιλία hollow, cavity], belonging to the *Polycœlia*, a synonym of CRANIATA, as having the brain-cavity divided into several chambers or ventricles. **poly'cormic** *a. Bot.* [Gr. κορμός trunk of a tree], having lateral stems equal to or co-ordinate with the main stem, as certain coniferous trees (opp. to *monocormic*). **polycracy** (pə'lɪkrəsɪ) [-CRACY], government by many rulers: = POLYARCHY 1 (Smart 1836). **po'lycratism** = *polycracy*. **'polycross** *Bot.* and *Agric.*, a cross made by planting two or more mutually fertile varieties together and allowing free natural pollination; freq. *attrib.*. **polycrotic** (-'krɒtɪk) *a. Physiol.* [after DICROTIC], (of the pulse) exhibiting more than two beats or waves for each beat of the heart. ‖**polycythæmia** (-saɪ'θiːmɪə), *Path.* [ad. G. *polycythaemie* (J. Vogel 1854, in R. Virchow *Handb. der speciellen Path. und Therapie* I. iv. 377), mod.L., f. Gr. κύτος (see -CYTE) + αἷμα blood], excess of red blood-corpuscles; hence **polycy'thæmic** *a.* of, involving, or suffering from polycythæmia. **poly'dentate** *a. Chem.* [L. *dentātus*: see DENTATE *a.*], (of a ligand) forming two or more separate bonds (usu. but not necessarily with the same central atom); (of a molecule or complex) formed by such a ligand. **polydia'bolical** *a.*, relating to a plurality of devils; in quot. as *sb.* = *polydiabolist*; so **polydi'abolism**, belief in many devils; **polydi'abolist**, one who believes in many devils (*nonce-wds.*). **poly'digital** *a. Zool.*, having several (separate) digits. **polydi'mensional** *a.* (*nonce-wd.*), having, or relating to, more than three dimensions of space. **poly'doggery** (*nonce-wd.*), the keeping of a number of dogs. **polyeidism** (-'aɪdɪz(ə)m), *Biol.* [Gr. εἶδος appearance, form], metamorphosis in which an organism passes through several different forms in different stages. **polyelec'tronic** *a. Chem.*, containing or consisting of more than one electron. **poly'endocrine** *Path.*, characterized by the involvement of several endocrine glands. **,polyendocri'nopathy** *Path.*, a polyendocrine disorder. **poly'energid** *a. Biol.* [ENERGID], having many complete sets of chromosomes; multinucleate or polyploid. **polyenzymatic** (-ɛnzaɪ'mætɪk) *a.* [*enzyme*, f. Gr. ἐν in + ζυμή leaven], producing several different ferments. **polyepic** (-'ɛpɪk) *a.* (*nonce-wd.*) [Gr. ἔπος word], consisting of several words. **polyergic** (-'ɜːdʒɪk) *a.* [Gr. ἔργον work: cf. πολύεργος hard-working], acting in many ways, having various functions. **poly'ethism** *Ent.* [Gr. ἦθος character], the display of different patterns of behaviour by particular individuals within a social group. **polyethnic** (-'ɛθnɪk) *a.* [Gr. ἔθνος nation], belonging to or containing many nations or races. **polyfe'nestral** *a.* (*nonce-wd.*) [L. *fenestra* window], having many windows. **'polyfoil** *a.* and *sb. Arch.* = MULTIFOIL. **poly'functional** *a. Chem.*, having two or more different functional groups in the molecule; orig. also applied to reactions involving two or more such compounds; hence **,polyfunctio'nality**. **poly-'glacial** *a.*, involving (a belief in) more than one ice age; hence **poly'glacialism**, the polyglacial theory. **poly'glacialist** *a.* and *sb.*, (of or pertaining to) a supporter of this theory. **'poly'grammar** (*nonce-wd.*), a grammar of several different languages. **'poly-groove** *a.*, having many, i.e. more than three, grooves, as a rifle; also *ellipt.* as *sb.* a poly-groove rifle; so **'poly-grooved** *a.* **polygyral** (-'dʒaɪərəl) *a.* [Gr. γῦρος circle, ring], having many whorls, as a shell. **poly'haploid** *Bot.* [HAPLOID *a.* (and *sb.*)], a plant descended from polyploids that has half of the set of chromosomes that would normally be expected from its ancestry. **polyhedroid** *Math.* [POLYHEDR(ON + -OID] = *polytope*. **polyhex** ('pɒlɪhɛks) [f. HEX(AGON], any planar shape formed by joining a number of identical regular hexagons by their edges. **polyiamond** (pɒlɪ'aɪəmənd) [f. D)IAMOND by deliberately false analogy; cf. PENTOMINO], any planar shape formed by joining a number of identical equilateral triangles by their edges. **polyi'deism**, the presence of many ideas or images at once. **polyion** ('pɒlɪ,aɪən) *Chem.*, an ion which consists of or contains a number of atoms of its parent element, or a large ion derived from a polyelectrolyte; so **polyi'onic** *a.* **poly'karyocyte** *Biol.* [KARYO- + -CYTE], an osteoclast, esp. a large osteoclast with many nuclei; hence **,polykaryo'cytic** *a.* **poly-'laminated** *a.*, having many laminæ or layers. **poly'lectal** *a. Linguistics* [-LECT], having or recognizing many regional or social varieties (within a language). **poly'lemma**, *Logic*, a complex syllogism resembling a dilemma but involving several alternatives. **polylepidous** (-'lɛpɪdəs) *a.* [Gr. λεπίς scale], having many scales (*Treas. Bot.* 1866). **poly'lingual** *a.* = MULTILINGUAL *a.* **poly'lingualism** = MULTILINGUALISM. **poly'linguist** *nonce-wd.* [see LINGUIST], a person learned in many languages. **polylithic** (-'lɪθɪk) *a.* [Gr. λίθος stone], made of several stones; also, containing several kinds of stone or rock; also *fig.* (cf. MONOLITHIC *a.* 4): opp. to *monolithic*. **poly'lithionite** *Min.* [ad. G. *polylithionit* (J. Lorenzen 1884, in *Zeitschr. f. Krist. und Min.* IX. 253), f. *lithion* lithia], a variety of lepidolite. **polylobular** (-'lɒbjʊlə(r)) *a.*, having many lobules. †**po'lyloquent** *a. Obs. rare*$^{-0}$ [L. *loquent-em* speaking], 'that speaketh much' (Blount *Glossogr.* 1656). **polylychnous** (-'lɪknəs) *a.* (*nonce-wd.*) [Gr. λύχνος lamp], having many lamps or lights. **poly'magnet**, an instrument consisting of two or more electromagnets so arranged as to admit of considerable variation in the field of magnetic force. ‖**poly'mania**, *Path.*, mania affecting several mental faculties: opp. to *monomania*. **poly'mastigate, poly'mastigous** *adjs. Zool.* [Gr. μάστιξ, μαστίγ- whip], having many flagella, as an infusorian; pluriflagellate. **polyme'tallic** *a.*, containing (ores of) several metals. **poly'metallism** (*nonce-wd.*) [after *bimetallism*], the use of several different metals for money. **poly,meta'meric** *a. Anat.*, pertaining to or connected with several metameres, as a muscle supplied with nerves from several portions of the spinal cord. ‖**polymetochia** (-mɪ'təʊkɪə), *Philol.* [Gr. μετοχή a participle: cf. POLYSYNDETON], the frequent use of participles or participial constructions; so **polymetochic** (-mɪ'tɒkɪk) *a.*, characterized by polymetochia. **poly'micrian** *a.* [Gr. μικρός little], containing much within a small space. **poly'microscope**, a microscope in which various objects are mounted on plates attached to a revolvable band, so that they can be brought successively into the field of observation. **'polymineral** *a. Petrol.*, composed of or containing more than one mineral. **polymor'phemic** *a. Linguistics*, consisting of two or more morphemes. **polymy'algia rheu'matica** *Path.* [MYALGIA] (see quot. 1957). ‖**polymyositis** (-maɪəʊ'saɪtɪs), *Path.* [see MYOSITIS]: see quot. 1890. **polyneu'ritic** *a.*, of, pertaining to, or suffering from polyneuritis. ‖**polyneuritis** (-njʊ'raɪtɪs), *Path.*, see quot. 1886. **polyneu'ropathy** *Path.*, a general degeneration of peripheral nerves that starts distally and spreads proximally. **polyodic** (-'ɒdɪk) *a. Mus.* (*rare*) [Gr. ᾠδή song] = POLYPHONIC. **polyœstrous** (-'iːstrəs) *a. Zool.* [see ŒSTRUM]: (see quot.) also, in mod. use, ovulating more than once each year. **polyomino** (pɒlɪ'ɒmɪnəʊ) [f. D)OMINO by deliberately false analogy; cf. PENTOMINO], any planar shape formed by joining a number of identical squares by their edges. **polyommatous** (-'ɒmətəs) *a.* [Gr. ὄμμα, ὀμματ- eye], having many eyes. **polyo'rama** [after PANORAMA], an optical apparatus presenting many views, or a view of many objects (Worcester 1846). **polyor'ganic** *a. Biol.*, having many different organs. †**poly'otical** *a. Obs.* (*nonce-wd.*) [Gr. οὖς, ὠτ- ear], having many ears. **'polypage** (-peɪdʒ) *a.* (*Printing*), comprising several pages, as a ***polypage*** (stereotype-) ***plate***. **poly'pantograph**, a form of pantograph producing several identical designs simultaneously from one pattern (Knight *Dict. Mech.*). **po'lyparous** *a.* [see -PAROUS], 'bringing forth many' (Webster 1864); multiparous. **polyped** ('pɒlɪpɛd) [after *quadruped*], *sb.* an animal having many feet; *adj.* many-footed. ‖**polyphobia** (-'fəʊbɪə), *Path.* [-PHOBIA], morbid fear of many things. **polyphotal** (-'fəʊtəl), **'polyphote** (-fəʊt) *adjs.* [Gr. φῶς, φωτ- light], applied to an electric arc-lamp so constructed that several may be used on the same circuit. †**poly'piety** (*nonce-wd.*), piety of many forms. **'polyplacid** (-,plæsɪd) *a. Zool.* [irreg. f. Gr. πλακοῦς flat cake], having more than one madreporic plate, as a starfish; opp. to *monoplacid*. **polyplastic** (-'plæstɪk) *a.* [PLASTIC], having or assuming many forms (Dunglison, 1844). **poly'pneustic** [Gr. πνευστ-ιάω to pant] *a. Ent.*, bearing many respiratory spiracles. ‖**polypnœa** (-'pniːə), *Path.* [Gr. πνοή (Dor. πνοά, πνοιά) breathing (cf. πολύπνοια a violent wind); in F. *polypnée*], 'very rapid respiration' (*Syd. Soc. Lex.*); also **polypnea**; hence **poly'pnœic** *a.* **polyponous** (-'ɪpənəs) *a.* (*nonce-wd.*) [Gr. πολύπονος much-labouring], occupied with many labours. **polyposist** (-'ɪpəʊsɪst), *nonce-wd.* [cf. Gr. πολυποσία hard drinking, πολυπότης a hard drinker], one who drinks much, a hard drinker. **'polyprism, polypris'matic** *a. Cryst.*: see quots. **'polyprotein** *Biochem.*, a protein which is composed of a number of smaller proteins. **polyprothesy** (-'prɒθɪsɪ), *Gram.* [Gr. πρόθεσις preposition: cf. POLYSYNDETON], the frequent use of prepositions; so **polyprothetic** (-prəʊ'θɛtɪk) *a.*, characterized by polyprothesy. **polypseudonymous** (pɒlɪsjuː'dɒnɪməs) *a.*, having many pseudonyms or aliases. †**'polypyrene** (-paɪəriːn), †**polypy'renous** (-paɪ'riːnəs) *adjs.* [Gr. πυρήν stone or hard seed of fruits], having two or more stones or kernels, as a fruit. **polyrhizal** (-'raɪzəl), **poly'rhizous** *adjs.* [Gr. ῥίζα root: cf. F. *polyrrhize* adj.], having many roots. **poly'ribosome** *Biol.* = POLYSOME; hence **,polyribo'somal** *a.* **,polysa'probic** *a. Ecol.* [(ad. G. *polysaprob* (Kolkwitz & Marsson 1902, in *Mittheilungen aus der K. Prüfungsanstalt f. Wasserversorgung und Abwässerbeseitigung* I. 46): see SAPROBE], of, being, or inhabiting an aquatic environment having in solution much reducing decayed organic matter and little or no oxygen. **polysemant** (-'siːmænt) [ad. late Gr. πολυσήμαντος adj., having many significations], a word having various senses; so **polyse'mantic** *a.*, having various senses; = POLYSEMIC, POLYSEMOUS *adjs.* **,polyseman'ticity, poly-se'mantism** = POLYSEMY. **poly'sensuous** *a.* [f. L. *sensu-s* sense + -OUS] = *polysemous*; hence **poly'sensuousness**. **,polysero'sitis** *Path.*, inflammation of serous membranes. **'poly-sided** *a.*, many-sided. **polysiphonic** (-saɪ'fɒnɪk), **polysiphonous** (-'saɪfənəs) *adjs.*, *Nat. Hist.*, having or consisting of several siphons or tubes. **'polysoap**, a detergent whose molecules are polymeric chains to which soap molecules are attached. **'polysoil** *a.*, containing various kinds of soil. **polyso'matic** *a.* [Gr. σῶμα body], applied to a grain of sandstone or the like which consists of an aggregation of smaller grains. **polysomatous** (-'səʊmətəs) *a.* [as prec.], applied to a monster having two or more bodies combined. **polysomitic** (-səʊ'mɪtɪk) *a. Zool.*, composed of a number of somites or body-segments. **'polyspike** [SPIKE *sb.*[2]] (see quot. 1950). **'polyspire**, a form of sponge-spicule: see quot. **polystachyous** (-'stækɪəs) *a. Bot.* [Gr. στάχυς ear of corn: cf. πολύσταχυς rich in ears of corn (Theocr.)], having many ears or spikes, as a grass (Mayne). **polystemonous** (-ˈstiːmənəs) *a. Bot.* [Gr. στήμων, taken as = stamen: cf. F. *polystémone* adj.], having the number of stamens more than double that of the petals or sepals. **polystethoscope** (-ˈstɛθəskəʊp): see quot. **polystichous** (-ˈɪstɪkəs) *a. Nat. Hist.* [Gr. στίχος row: cf. DISTICHOUS], arranged in numerous rows (*Cent. Dict.* 1890). **ˈpolystigm** (-stɪm), *Geom.* [Gr. στιγμή point], a figure made up of a number of points. **polystigmatic** (-stɪgˈmætɪk) *a.* (*humorous nonce-wd.*) [Gr. στίγμα mark, spot], relating to numerous spots. **polystigmous** (-ˈstɪgməs) *a. Bot.*, having many stigmas, as a flower (*Cent. Dict.*). **polystylar** (-ˈstaɪlə(r)), **ˈpolystyle** *adjs. Arch.* [Gr. στῦλος column], having or characterized by many columns. **polystylous** (-ˈstaɪləs) *a. Bot.*, having many styles, as the ovary of a flower (Mayne 1858). **polyˈsyllogism** (*Logic*), a combination or series of related syllogisms; so **polysylloˈgistic** *a.* [F. *polysyllogistique*], pertaining to or consisting of a polysyllogism. **ˌpolysymptoˈmatic** *a. Med.*, involving or exhibiting many symptoms. **ˈpolyˌtasted** *a.* (*nonce-wd.*), having many tastes or flavours. **polythelemism** (-θɪˈliːmɪz(ə)m), *nonce-wd.* [Gr. θέλημα will]: see quot. **polyˈthelia, polyˈthelism, ˈpolythely** *Med.* [ad. F. *polythélie*, f. Gr. θηλή nipple], the condition of having one or more supernumerary nipples. **ˈpolytone** [cf. F. *polytone* adj. (Voltaire)], varied tone, as in ordinary speaking: opposed to *monotone*. **ˈpolytope**, *Geom.* [ad. G. *polytop* (R. Hoppe 1882, in *Arch. der Math. und Physik* LXVIII. 30), Gr. τόπος place], a form, in geometry of more than three dimensions, corresponding to a polygon in plane, or a polyhedron in solid geometry; hence **polyˈtopal** *a.* † **polyˈtopian** (*nonce-wd.*) [as prec.], one who visits many places. **polyˈtopic** *a. Biol.* [Gr. τόπος place], of or pertaining to (the independent origin of a species in) several places. **polyˈtopical** *a.*, dealing with many subjects. † **polyˈtragic** *a.*, containing many tragedies. **polytrichous** (-ˈɪtrɪkəs) *a. Nat. Hist.* [Gr. θρίξ, τριχ- hair], very hairy; thickly covered with hair (Mayne 1858). ‖ **polyuresis** (-jʊˈriːsɪs), ‖ **polyuria** (-ˈjʊərɪə), *Path.* [Gr. οὔρησις urination, οὖρον urine], excessive excretion of urine; hence **polyuric** (-ˈjʊərɪk) *a.*, pertaining to or affected with polyuria. **polyˈvoltine** [Ital. *volta* turn, time], a silkworm of a breed which yields several broods of cocoons in a year. **polyˈxenic** *a. Biol.* [Gr. ξένος stranger], applied to a culture, or the cultivation, of an organism in the presence of more than one other species.

1967 *Sci. Amer.* June 129/1 The pieces had been suggested to him by S. J. Collins of Bristol, England, who gave the name 'tetraboloes' to the order-4 set because the Diabolo, a juggling toy, has two isosceles right triangles in its cross section. This implies the generic name '*polyaboloes'. **1683** in *Phil. Trans.* XIV. 483 By a Polyphone or *Poly-acoustick well ordered one sound may be heard as many. **1704** J. HARRIS *Lex. Techn.* I, *Polyacousticks*, are Instruments contrived to Multiply Sounds, as Multiplying glasses or Polyscopes do Images of Objects. **1755** JOHNSON, *Polyacoustick, adj.*, that multiplies or magnifies sounds. **1862** CAYLEY *Coll. Math. Papers* V. 38 A method of the derivation of the Δ faced *polyacrons of a given number of summits from those of the next inferior number of summits. **1886** LENDENFELD *Sponges* in *Proc. Zool. Soc.* 560, I. *Anaxonia.* Without definite axes and with numerous rays—*polyact. **1902** *Encycl. Brit.* XXXII. 813/1 Fig. 5 A, typical *polyactine. **1832** *Philol. Museum* I. 312 If any advocate of the *polyadamite doctrine, as it has been called. **1888** *Buck's Handbk. Med. Sc.* VI. 396/2 *Polyæsthesia, is a rare disturbance of sensation.. in which the point of a pin, when applied to the skin, is felt as two or more points. **1893** *Nation* (N.Y.) 5 Jan. 15/3 Any such hackneyed creation as an Osric of the emotions, without depth, or a *poly-affectioned Lothario. **1949** E. A. NIDA *Morphol.* (ed. 2) iv. 98 The suffix *-al* is *polyallomorphic /əl/ and /æl/. **1972** *Archivum Linguisticum* III. 40 In order to simplify their analysis one of the allomorphs of polyallomorphic morphemes is designated as the basic one, and the changes are described on that basis. **1927** *Daily Express* 24 Nov. 13 The '*polyalphabetic' codes.. are much more difficult to decipher, as a letter is often represented in a cryptogram by a dozen different signs, letters or numerals. **1939** H. F. GAINES *Elem. Cryptanalysis* (1940) viii. 68 Multiple-alphabet substitution (also called double-key substitution, polyalphabetic substitution, etc.) makes use of several different cipher alphabets. **1962** MOORE & WALLER *Cloak & Cipher* xv. 138 Edgar Allan Poe.. seems to have had a blind faith in polyalphabetic ciphers. **1612** STURTEVANT *Metallica* ix. 70 If the wheeles should haue beene made square, trencher wise, or in any other *polyangle, forty horses would not so easily draw them beeing laden, as two doth now with both speed and ease. **1690** LEYBOURN *Curs. Math.* 438 Of divers Figures or Faces, of a *Polyangular shape. **1797** *Monthly Mag.* III. 221 These hollow spandrils may be cylindrical, triangular, quadrangular, or polyangular. **1931** *Chem. Abstr.* XXV. 3261 The submicrons detected by the ultra-microscope are negatively charged and consist of aggregates of the *polyanions $[Pb_9]^{4-}$ or $[Sn_9]^{4-}$. **1948** *Jrnl. Polymer Sci.* III. 261 In the presence of excess electrolyte, the polyanion would be completely associated and behave approximately like an uncharged macromolecule. **1965** [see *polycation* below]. **1972** COTTON & WILKINSON *Adv. Inorg. Chem.* (ed. 3) xxv. 823 The decavanadate ion is only one example of the type of polyanion generally called isopolyanions. **1930** *Chem. Abstr.* XXIV. 2077 [Such] elements.. will combine in liquid NH_3 with Na to give polysulfide-like compds.,.. to which the name '*polyanionic' salts is given. **1974** *Amer. Jrnl. Anat.* CXXXIX. 404/1 Staining with ruthenium red.. reveals that a polyanionic surface coat, probably mucopolysaccharide in nature, covers all the microvilli.. on all cell types found in the nasal cavities. **1907** *Jrnl. Path. & Bacteriol.* XII. 54 *Polyarteritis acuta nodosa.—Characterised by the formation upon the smaller and medium-sized arteries of small localised nodules. **1951** E. N. CHAMBERLAIN *Text-bk. Med.* vi. 448 Sometimes known as polyarteritis nodosa, this is a rare disease generally affecting persons before mid-life. **1974** PASSMORE & ROBSON *Compan. Med. Stud.* III. xxv. 29/1 The term polyarteritis includes a number of uncommon disorders in which the changes are focal, segmental inflammation and necrosis of arteries, arterioles or capillaries... Besides the classical form, also known as polyarteritis nodosa.., there are five recognized variants. **1901** *Lancet* 16 Mar. 776/1 In addition to such *polyarthritic forms there is yet a fourth group of cases in which only one or two joints are involved. **1898** *Allbutt's Syst. Med.* V. 863 Rheumatic fever, or acute *polyarthritis. **1874** VAN BUREN *Dis. Genit. Org.* 86 Associated with the *poly-articular variety of gonorrhœal rheumatism. **1898** *Allbutt's Syst. Med.* V. 1026 There were no rheumatic phenomena for thirteen months when polyarticular rheumatism appeared. **1887** SOLLAS in *Encycl. Brit.* XXII. 416/2 Desma of an anomocladine Lithistid (*polyaxon). **1940** L. H. HYMAN *Invertebrates* I. vi. 299 Polyaxons.. are spicules in which several equal rays radiate from a central point. **1898** *Nature* 27 Jan. 310/2 A fauna capable of living and developing at depths of over 2000 metres, to which the name *polybathic is given. **1882** SALA *Amer. Revis.* (1885) 37 *note*, A great *polybigamy case. **1873** E. R. LANKESTER in *Ann. & Mag. Nat. Hist.* Feb. 86 The first step in development, after the formation by cleavage of the mass of embryo-cells or '*polyblast'. **1904** *Brit. Med. Jrnl.* 10 Sept. 586 The clasmocytes of Rauvier and Marchand, some of the polyblast of Maximow.. all belong to this category of cells. **1959** F. M. BURNET *Clonal Selection Theory* vii. 115 Macrophages.. include fixed macrophages, wandering tissue macrophages or polyblasts and the blood monocytes. **1967** *Biol. Abstr.* XLVIII. 9803/2 By the 6th day, a barrier of connective tissue, formed mainly from polyblasts and hist[i]ocytes, was beginning to be formed. **1904** *Brit. Med. Jrnl.* 10 Sept. 596 This last stage of the development of the *polyblastic cell. **1839** *Penny Cycl.* XIV. 322/1 Gastropods, are divided into.. I. Nudibranchians (Anthrobranchians and *Polybranchians). **1858** MAYNE *Expos. Lex.*, *Polybranchiatus, Zoöl.* applied.. to an Order (*Polybranchiata*).. *polybranchiate. **1846** R. CHAMBERS *Tradit. Edinburgh* 300 The little *polybuttoned personages. **1948** *Jrnl. Polymer Sci.* III. 259 Due to the high concentration of charge in the *polycation, which is itself quite large, electrostatic forces can be transferred over much greater distances than in solutions of ordinary electrolytes. **1965** PHILLIPS & WILLIAMS *Inorg. Chem.* I. xii. 465 The formation of polyanions is quite common among the heavier non-metals (e.g. polysulphides and selenides), although the formation of polycations from uncomplexed metals appears to be limited to Hg_2^{2+}. **1949** *Science* 25 Nov. 553/1 When excess acrylate is added, more polyanions attach themselves to the *polycationic exterior of the precipitate particles. **1970** R. W. MCGILVERY *Biochem.* xix. 451 They [sc. spermine and spermidine] appear to occur in association with nucleic acids, as might be expected from their polycationic character. **1705** *Phil. Trans.* XXV. 2107 Prophylactic and *Polycharacteristick Statues. **1842** DUNGLISON *Med. Lex.*, *Polycholia. **1880** J. W. LEGG *Bile* 396 Vulpian believes that jaundice from emotion may be caused by a catarrh of the ducts, by an abundant polycholia. **1898** P. MANSON *Trop. Diseases* iii. 78 Polycholia is a constant and often urgent feature in most malarial fevers. **1944** W. APEL *Harvard Dict. Mus.* 593/1 Early adumbrations of *polychoral treatment occur in the works of Josquin des Près who frequently interrupts the full-voiced writing in four parts.. by 'antiphonal' passages in which two half-choruses.. perform a short phrase twice, in an echo-like manner. **1963** *Times* 9 May 16/5 'Jauchzet dem Herren',.. a big polychoral 'concerto' from the *Psalmen Davids* of 1619, was a casualty, its elaborate antiphonies of voices and instruments blurred by the cathedral's hopelessly over-resonant sound. **1975** *Gramophone* Nov. 869/3 In 1628, Salzburg Cathedral was re-opened... Its inaugural Mass was a grand polychoral affair. **1978** *Early Music* Apr. 170 Venice and the grand manner of the polychoral motet seem so inseparable that it is hard to consider them apart. **1866** *Treas. Bot.* 913 **Polychorion*, a polycarpous fruit like that of Ranunculus. **1890** *Cent. Dict.*, **Polychorionic*. **1897** *Allbutt's Syst. Med.* IV. 21 It is not a polycholia.. but a *polychromia. *Ibid.* 61 The hæmoglobin liberated leads to an increased formation and excretion of bile pigments (polychromia). **1883** H. T. EDWARDS in *Ch. Times* XXII. 10/1 When a chapel is in debt, the *Polychurch hierarchy furiously rage against the Church. *Ibid.* XXI. 971/1 The large sums which they [the Welsh] spend upon '*Polychurchism'. **1891** BP. JAYNE in *Daily News* 21 Nov. 5/3 [He finds in the circular he has received a strong flavour of] what has been aptly termed the theory of Polychurchism. **1963** OHTAKA & SPIEGELMAN in *Science* 25 Oct. 493/2 An RNA molecule which can be translated into two or more proteins may be referred to as a '*polycistronic' message. **1968** H. HARRIS *Nucleus & Cytoplasm* ii. 23 The idea of a 'polycistronic' template, that is, one which can specify the amino acid sequences of a group of related proteins, now enjoys considerable popularity. **1974** *Nature* 1 Nov. 75/2 Kennel *et al.* concluded that each cistron in these polycistronic RNAs has a unique site that is vulnerable to attack. *Ibid.*, There is.. an indication that some tRNAs are made *polycistronically. **1978** *Nature* 25 May 304/2 The *polyclonality of B cell responses to LPS has excluded the participation of immunoglobulin combining sites in the process of triggering. **1977** *Lancet* 5 Nov. 958/2 We suggest that immunosuppression in this syndrome is the result of the collective immunosuppressive effects of trypanosome-derived immune-modulating free fatty acids, *polyclonally stimulating B-cell mitogen, and complement-activating factors. **1975** CRICK & LAWRENCE in *Science* 1 Aug. 341/3 The progeny of a cell marked at about the time of the drawing of boundary lines never fills a compartment completely, but often occupies an appreciable proportion of it. A compartment is thus made by the descendants of a small group of cells. We propose to call the cells in the compartment a *polyclone. Just as a clone is a group of cells which are all, without exception, the descendants of a single cell, so a polyclone is a group of cells that are descended from a certain (small) group of cells—the founder cells—which were present in the embryo at an earlier time. **1979** *Sci. Amer.* July 93/1 Each compartment is made by a set of complete clones, which we call a polyclone, that develops from a few founder cells. **1914** W. E. AGAR in *Phil. Trans. R. Soc.* B. CCV. 422 When a population.. is composed of a number of clones each descended from an original ancestor not asexually connected with the original ancestors of the other clones, the population may be called *polyclonal. **1961** *Harvey Lect. 1960–61* LVI. 221 He had a broad-banded, polyclonal γ-globulin with a rich serological picture. **1973** *Sci. Amer.* Aug. 44/2 If plaques were a simple response to an injury of some kind, as has been proposed, their cells should be polyclonal, the Benditts point out. **1899** *Nature* 9 Nov. 28/1 *Polycormic forms are met with in cypresses and junipers, in which the lateral branches are not all reduced to subordinate and graduated positions. **1921** *19th Cent.* July 148 The maximalists, of course, are for *polycratism, provincial rule, insubordination and importation of foreign ideas. **1948** TYSDAL & CRANDALL in *Jrnl. Amer. Soc. Agronomy* XL. 294 The present paper deals with methods for determining the combining ability of the components of a hybrid or variety. For convenience, the method is referred to as the '*polycross method'. *Ibid.*, The single crosses and polycrosses exhibited even greater superiority over the checks. *Ibid.* 297 Polycross seed is the seed produced on selected clones interpollinated at random in isolation. **1977** *Crop Sci.* XVII. 909/2 Twenty-one clones whose polycross progenies ranked high for rate of seedling emergence under field conditions or had high forage yield.. were selected for this study. Polycross seed from these clones was produced in isolated blocks. **1857** DUNGLISON *Dict. Med. Sci.* (rev. ed.) 741/2 **Polycythæmia*, a condition of the blood in which there is an increase of the red corpuscles. **1866** A. FLINT *Princ. Med.* (1880) 60 An increase.. in the number of the red blood-corpuscles beyond the healthy limit.. constitutes.. polycythaemia. **1906** *Lancet* 7 July 20/2 The following case is published as a contribution to the study of the *polycythæmic condition. **1935** [see *hypovolæmia* s.v. HYPO- II]. **1962** *Lancet* 26 May 1098/2 The patient was polycythæmic until 1958, when a leukæmic picture first appeared. **1937** *Chem. Rev.* XXI. 39 The simple variation of acidic and coördinating groups in the *polydentate molecules has escaped investigation. **1961** G. R. CHOPPIN *Exper. Nucl. Chem.* ix. 147 Complexes with a high degree of covalent character are formed by the interaction of metal ions with polydentate organic ions. **1972** *Nature* 21 Jan. 181/1 Recently his expertise in coordination chemistry was extended to the complexes formed by the alkali metals and alkaline earth elements with a variety of polydentate ligands. **1876** *Tinsley's Mag.* XVIII. 150 Whether we cast in our lot with Bishop Butler or the *Polydiabolicals. *Ibid.* 149 Why has no interesting heretic gone in for *Polydiabolism? *Ibid.* 150 The *poly-diabolists would put it in the plural, and say evil spirits. **1894** *Brit. Jrnl. Photogr.* XLI. 28 The evolution of the horse's leg from a *polydigital extremity to its present form. **1884** *Nature* 1 May 24/2 L. Martin, on the *poly-dimensional argument. **1875** MISS COBBE *False Beasts & True* 190 *Polydoggery is a thing against which all proper feeling revolts. **1874** LUBBOCK *Orig. & Met. Ins.* iv. 80 Those cases in which animals or plants pass through a succession of different forms might be distinguished by the name of dieidism or *polyeidism. **1909** *Cent. Dict.* Suppl., *Polyelectronic. **1939** L. PAULING *Nature Chem. Bond* i. 29 The electron distribution function for a poly-electronic atom or ion shows the presence of electron shells as regions of maximum electron density. **1947** *Amer. Scientist* XXXV. 185 Just as little tested in the laboratory is the conclusion that positrons, like protons.. can form short lived polyelectronic entities of the type e^+e^-, $e^+(e^-)_2$, [etc.]. **1964** J. W. LINNETT *Electronic Struct. Molecules* i. 9 The most important factor governing the electronic structures of the ground states of polyelectronic atoms is the effect summarized in the Pauli Principle. **1965** *Amer. Surgeon* XXXI. 695 (*heading*) *Polyendocrine adenomatosis with Zollinger-Ellison syndrome. **1967** S. L. ROBBINS *Path.* (ed. 3) xxix. 1243/2 (*heading*) Multiple endocrine adenomatosis (polyendocrine adenomas). **1976** *Lancet* 11 Dec. 1273/1 Antibodies reacting with normal human pancreatic islet cells have been described in patients with diabetes associated with autoimmune polyendocrine disease. **1964** *Medicine* XLIII. 176/1 It is suggested that Schmidt's syndrome with diabetes mellitus may be a *polyendocrinopathy. **1973** *Acta Endocrinol.* LXXII. 411 As for the theoretical implications of poly-endocrinopathies, the possibility of common aetiological factors lies near at hand. **1920** W. E. AGAR *Cytol.* vii. 209 Examples of such *polyenergid nuclei (Hartmann, 1909) are afforded by the great nuclei of the Radiolaria. **1939** *Nature* 14 Jan. 47/2 Schussnig.. reaffirms.. his view that the Conjugales are derived from a polyenergid ancestry, and a similar origin is suggested for the Red Algæ. **1961** MACKINNON & HAWES *Introd. Study Protozoa* 66 The gigantic nucleus [of *Aulacantha*] is remarkable for the number of its chromosomes, of which there are some 1,500... This remarkable structure, according to Grell, is really polyenergid. **1976** BELL & COOMBE tr. *Strasburger's Textbk. Bot.* (rev. ed.) 44 Free nuclear divisions, that is, divisions not accompanied by cell division, occur in those Thallophyta showing the polyenergid condition. **1892** THOMSON *Outl. Zool.* xiii. 239 It is a *poly-enzymatic gland, that is, one which produces diverse digestive ferments. **1811–31** BENTHAM *Language* Wks. 1843 VIII. 333/1 This proposition will consist of one word only, or of divers words, —will be either monoepic or *polyepic. **1889** BURDON SANDERSON *Address to Biological Section British Assoc.* in *Nature* 26 Sept. 524/1 Plant protoplasm, though it may be structurally homogeneous, is dynamically *polyergic—it has many endowments. **1967** J. H. SUDD *Introd. Behaviour Ants* viii. 154 Animals which show these variations in behaviour from one to another can be said to show *polyethism—a word formed by analogy with polymorphism. **1973** J. P. SPRADBURY *Wasps* vi. 155 There may occur several forms of polyethism, namely those based on age, physiological condition, and size. **1888** *Daily News* 22 Sept. 1/2 For purposes of communication and for interchange of ideas the polyglott, *poly-ethnic Indian continent has become one country. **1838** *Civil Eng. & Arch. Jrnl.* I. 311/2 There is no proportion observed between the *polyfenestral building itself, and the range of columns stuck up against it. **1842** Francis *Dict. Arts*, etc., **Polyfoile*, an ornament, like a leaf, of many round lobes. **1929** W. H. Carothers in *Jrnl. Amer. Chem. Soc.* LI. 2550 (*heading*) *Polyfunctional compounds. *Ibid.*, All these may be classed together as polyfunctional reactions. **1962** J. T. Marsh *Self-Smoothing Fabrics* v. 45 The finishing process.. consists of impregnating the fabrics with the appropriate polyfunctional compound and a catalyst, drying, heating and washing. **1963** J. Osborne *Dental Mech.* (ed. 5) i. 23 The basic ingredient is a polyfunctional mercaptan with.. the average formula $HS(R-S-S)_{23}-R-SH$. **1964** N. G. Clark *Mod. Org. Chem.* xv. 301 By employing polyfunctional halides in place of alkyl halides depicted above, more complex ketones are obtained. **1936** *Trans. Faraday Soc.* XXXII. 39 (*heading*) Polymers & *polyfunctionality. **1961** Sorenson & Campbell *Prep. Methods Polymer Chem.* iii. 59 The qualitative aspects of condensation polymerization, including.. effect of polyfunctionality on branching and gelation, have been thoroughly treated. **1927** Peake & Fleure *Apes & Men* 69 This *polyglacial, or preferably multiglacial, view was not well received, and considerable opposition was offered to it. **1937** *Geogr. Jrnl.* XC. 180 Formerly James Geikie, almost alone, insistently voiced the case for the polyglacial view and perhaps he strained it by over-statement. **1972** Sparks & West *Ice Age in Brit.* v. 123 The limits of the successive glaciations of this polyglacial sequence, imperfectly known at present, are shown. *Ibid.*, The evidence for *polyglacialism lay not so much in evidence for different end-moraines of successive ice advances.. but in the finding of non-glacial sediments between glacial deposits. **1946, 1968** *Polyglacialist [see *monoglacialist* sb. and adj. s.v. mono- 1]. **1972** Sparks & West *Ice Age in Brit.* v. 123 The supporters of the monoglacial theory.. were eclipsed by polyglacialists, though some survived till a few years ago. **1812** Southey in *Q. Rev.* VIII. 97 The title of this *poly-grammar must not be admitted as a proof that he was qualified for the task which he undertook. **1868** *Rep. to Govt. U.S. Munitions War* 88 These guns are rifled on the *polygroove system, and use lead-coated projectiles. **1886** *Field* 9 Jan. 54/3 Greatly improved the shooting of the old muzzle-loading polygroove. **1858** Greener *Gunnery* 403 They will shoot as well as *poly-grooved rifles. **18..** W. G. Binney (Cent. D.), *Polygyral. **1935** Y. Katayama in *Jap. Jrnl. Bot.* VII. 374 The writer has classified (though provisionally) the haploid plants as follows... If the haploid has occurred from allopolyploids, it is classified under the name of *polyhaploid. **1955** *Nature* 12 Mar. 469/1 This plant had the chromosome number $2n = 24$, suggesting that it might be a polyhaploid of S[*olanum*] *polytrichon*, having arisen by haploid parthenogenesis. **1975** *Ibid.* 17 Apr. 596/1 In wheat and oats, the polyhaploids show very little chiasmate pairing because genetic control is effective in the hemizygous state. **1880** W. I. Stringham in *Amer. Jrnl. Math.* III. 2 It will be convenient to designate as an *n*-fold *polyhedroid the *n*-dimensional figure which is bounded by $(n - 1)$-fold flat (not curved) figures. **1914** H. P. Manning *Geom. Four Dimensions* viii. 289 A regular polyhedroid.. consists of equal regular polyhedrons together with their interiors, the polyhedrons being joined by their faces so as to enclose a portion of hyperspace, and the hyperplane angles formed at the faces by the half-hyperplanes of adjacent polyhedrons being all equal to one another. **1972** C. S. Ogilvy *Tomorrow's Math* (ed. 2) iv. 79 A polytope is an *n*-dimensional polyhedroid. **1967** *Sci. Amer.* June 124/3 Other names have been proposed, but it seems to me that the best is '*polyhexes', the name adopted by David Klomer, who was one of the first to investigate them. **1975** *Ibid.* July 114/3 Combinatorial geometers have given special attention in recent years to tiling with polyominoes and their cousins the polyiamonds and polyhexes. **1967** *Ibid.* June 124/2 By joining equilateral triangles along their edges one obtains another well-explored family of shapes known as *polyiamonds. **1975** [see *polyhex* above]. **1903** F. W. H. Myers *Hum. Personality* I. 47 In one word, hypnosis is a state of *poly-ideism, not of mono-ideism. **1938** A. I. Oparin *Origin of Life* vi. 138 Regarding every living cell as a 'single chemical particle or, more correctly, as a colossal poly-ion'. **1947** *Jrnl. Polymer Sci.* II. 12 Both negative and positive polyions may be made; the former as polycarboxylic or sulfonic acids and their salts and the latter, for example, as onium salts of polymers such as vinylpyridine. **1959** *Acta Crystallogr.* XII. 165/2 The crystal structure of inyoite contains isolated polyions, $[B_3O_3(OH)_5]^{-2}$. **1963** *New Scientist* 11 Apr. 103/3 The chemistry of polyions, such as proteins, mucopolysaccharides, [etc.].. is very relevant to understanding the behaviour of the cell surface. **1972** Cotton & Wilkinson *Adv. Inorg. Chem.* (ed. 3) xvi. 486 There is slight evidence in the bromine system for Br_5^-, but the series of polyions I_5^-, I_7^- and I_9^- is well-established for iodine. **1907** *Publ. Carnegie Inst.* No. 63. xii. 352 A fuller experimental investigation of the properties of dissolved salts, especially of those of *polyionic types. **1970** Fox & Fried tr. *Staudinger's From Org. Chem. to Macromolecules* B. vii. 134 These anomalous phenomena in solutions of polyelectrolytes were termed 'polyionic viscosity phenomena'. **1890** W. H. Howell in *Jrnl. Morphol.* IV. 118 The first class might be named *polykaryocytes, or multinucleated giant cells. **1946** *Blood* I. 29 Morone sharply differentiated the polykaryocytes from osteoclasts, but in this he was disputed by Lambin and Lamers. **1968** E. Kelemen *Physiopath. & Therapy Human Blood Dis.* (1969) i. 36 Even larger cells, resembling megakaryocytes, are the osteoclasts or polykaryocytes. These two cells have to do with bone formation and are more often seen in a trephine biopsy. **1947** *Jrnl. Lab. & Clin. Med.* XXXII. 664 The concept of a *polykaryocytic origin of the megakaryocyte has not received general acceptance. **1964** *Biol. Abstr.* XLV. 3106/2 Injection of confluent polykaryocytic cultures into chicks resulted in the appearance of sarcomas which contained transformed cells and polykaryocytes. **1876** tr. *Wagner's Gen. Pathol.* (ed. 6) 333 Single or *poly-laminated cylindrical, and ciliated epithelia. **1972** B. Bickerton in *Georgetown Univ. Ser. Lang. & Linguistics* (1973) xxv. 34 The demonstration of similarities between Black English and Guyanese Creole.. was simply a by-product of the attempt to write a polylectal grammar of the latter. **1972** C.-J. N. Bailey in Stockwell & Macaulay *Linguistic Change & Generative Theory* 24 Rule changes of the sort being described could never occur in a homogeneous grammar... Without the retention of the older forms in a different style or in a different class lect known to a speaker long enough for a rule change to be generalized, such a generalization could not occur. Only a polylectal grammar is adequate for historical linguistics. **1977** *Word 1972* XXVIII. 166 The subject matter of dialectology may be viewed.. 1. As a complex of shared and differentiated items which function within a single diasystem (a pan-dialectal or polylectal system). **1978** *Archivum Linguisticum* IX. 37 That implicational (polylectal) patterning obtains in Table 1(b) is clear: some speakers are invariable users of the feature S, others are invariable users of the feature P, while a third group of speakers alternate S and P. **1867** Atwater *Logic* 151 The names Trilemma, Tetralemma, *Polylemma have been sometimes given to this sort of Syllogism according to the number of members or horns. **1933** 'E. Cambridge' *Hostages to Fortune* iii. vi. 184 Foreign students, slow south Germans, French boys from Rennes, *polylingual Swedes. **1958** *Times* 5 Dec. 16/3 Polytextual, polylingual wrestlings with canti fermi. **1978** *Amer. N. & Q.* XVI. 146/2 A few other bilingual and polylingual glossaries. **1956** J. Whatmough *Language* 241 Correlation methods may be used to show how much.. the *polylingualism of an interlingua may safely draw from different languages. **1977** *Word 1972* XXVIII. 193 Borrowing, especially when related to bilingualism or polylingualism, increases the number of opportunities for metanalytical processes to take place, both at the time of borrowing and subsequently. **1873** M. Collins *Squire Silchester* II. xix. 232 An old friend.. famous as *polylinguist, philologist, archæologist. **1839** *Civil Eng. & Arch. Jrnl.* II. 368/1 *Polylithic statues, or those composed of several stones. **1908** *Sci. Amer. Suppl.* 25 Jan. 61/1 These crevices and fissures are filled with a polylithic mass of brown and white 'calcic spar'. **1961** *Economist* 11 Nov. 538/2 Somewhere in the essentially 'polylithic' variety of the sisterhood there must be an answer. **1886** *Jrnl. Chem. Soc.* L. 677 Minerals from Kangerdluarsuk, in Greenland... *Polylithionite (lithium mica). **1927** *Amer. Mineralogist* XII. 275 Polylithionite is of doubtful stability, but mica of approximately this composition has been described from Greenland. **1962** *Geochemistry* xi. 1197 In lithium micas (polylithionites) the geochemical similarity of lithium and magnesium does not play an important part and lithium occupies an independent position in the structure of the mica lattice. **1896** *Allbutt's Syst. Med.* I. 117 Small round cells with *polylobular and fragmented nuclei. **1839** *Fraser's Mag.* XX. 709 Freely dispensing light from the huge *polylychnous gas-burners to a whole neighbourhood. **1828** *Lancet* 19 Apr. 73/2 Dr. Epps enumerated monomania; that is, when one faculty is affected: *polymania where more than one faculty is deranged. **1892** *Dental Rec.* XII. 488 Amalgams consist of the combination of either one or several metals with mercury,.. the bulk of a *polymetallic amalgam usually consisting of Tin and Silver. **1956** *Mineral. Abstr.* XIII. 38 Nests and lenses of plumbojarosite are found in the oxidized zone of polymetallic ore deposits. **1968** Bethell & Burg tr. *Solzhenitsyn's Cancer Ward* i. xv. 236 My theory is that you can discover deposits of polymetallic ore by looking for radioactive water. **1974** *Nature* 16 Aug. 545/1 The polymetallic province is particularly enriched in silver north of boundary 1. **1893** *Chicago Advance* 10 Aug., *Polymetallism is historical, and iron, copper, shells and wampum have all been used as money. **1888** *Nature* 13 Dec. 151/2 Most muscles, Fuerbringer argues, are *polymetameric, *i.e.* they receive nervous fibres from two or more spinal roots. **1900** H. W. Smyth *Grk. Melic Poets* p. lvii, The periods [in the dithyramb] were disjointed.. and *polymetochic: the heaping of participles added pomp and rapidity. **1829** W. Greenfield (*title*) *Polymician lexicon to the New Testament. **1838** *Bagster's Catal.* 22 Polymician series of New Testaments, Concordances, Lexicons, and Psalters, Small Pocket Volumes. **1899** W. I. Knapp *Life Borrow* I. 70 A small 4to volume.. in his polymician handwriting. **1938** *Mem. Geol. Soc. Amer.* VI. 134 Except for a few monomineral fabrics, such as those of pure quartzite.., most rock fabrics are *polymineral. **1975** *Nature* 25 Dec. 690/1 This suite of rather unusual minerals has received wide attention because the minerals have been identified in light-coloured, millimetre-sized polymineral inclusions present in carbonaceous chondrites. **1949** E. A. Nida *Morphol.* (ed. 2) iv. 97 Simple structures consist of a single morpheme, free or bound. Complex structures consist of more than one morpheme. Simple structures may be called 'monomorphemic' and complex structures '*polymorphemic'. **1962** H. C. Conklin in J. A. Fishman *Readings Sociol. of Lang.* (1968) 416 Single morphemes are necessarily lexemes, but for polymorphemic constructions the decision depends on meaning and use. **1964** R. H. Robins *Gen. Linguistics* 206 Polymorphemic words may consist wholly of free morphemes. **1957** H. S. Barber in *Ann. Rheumatic Dis.* XVI. 237/2, (1) A condition characterized by widespread muscular pains without arthritis but accompanied by a high erythrocyte sedimentation rate and occasional pyrexia is described. (2) The relationship to rheumatoid disease is discussed and it is concluded that this is probably a clinical entity within the rheumatic group of diseases. (3) It is proposed to term the syndrome '*polymyalgia rheumatica'. **1971** Boyle & Buchanan *Clin. Rheumatol.* xvi. 434/2 Polymyalgia rheumatica.. affects subjects in the later years of life, the average age of onset being the late sixties. **1878** D. F. Lincoln tr. A. Eulenburg in *Ziemssen's Cycl. Pract. Med.* XIV. 133 According to these, the disease consists in an essentially inflammatory process, a '*polymyositis chronica progressiva'. **1890** Billings *Med. Dict.*, **Polymyositis*, inflammation of a number of muscles, simultaneous or successive. **1899** *Allbutt's Syst. Med.* VI. 461 Primary affections of the muscle. (a) Acute polymyositis. **1895** *Jrnl. Nervous & Mental Dis.* XXII. 316 (*heading*) *Polyneuritic psychoses. **1932** *Times Lit. Suppl.* 7 Jan. 14/3 His results.. show that brain tissue from polyneuritic pigeons.. has *in vitro* a lower power of oxygen uptake. **1968** M. Pyke *Food & Society* ii. 17 The remarkable effects of a few milligrams of thiamine on a polyneuritic pigeon. **1886** W. R. Gowers *Man. Dis. Nerv. Syst.* I. 91 The term 'multiple neuritis' or '*polyneuritis' is applied to the condition in which many nerves are inflamed simultaneously or in rapid succession. **1899** *Allbutt's Syst. Med.* VI. 496 Certain mineral poisons.. induce paralysis by the establishment of polyneuritis. **1938** I. S. Wechsler in *Jrnl. Amer. Med. Assoc.* 4 June 1913/2 It is suggested that the term multiple neuropathy, *polyneuropathy or peripheral neuropathy be substituted for multiple neuritis in those cases in which both the cause and the pathologic changes point to a degenerative process. **1954** *Jrnl. Neuropath. & Exper. Neurol.* XIII. 168 Severe polyneuropathy with massive involvement of the large nerve trunks may not only appear in association with the more chronic forms of diffuse connective tissue disease,.. but may even dominate the clinical picture so as to obscure the diagnosis of the underlying disease. **1974** Passmore & Robson *Compan. Med. Stud.* III. xxxiv. 36/2 Polyneuropathy arises from dietary deficiencies, chemical poisoning and may be a manifestation of numerous diseases. **1818** Busby *Gram. Mus.* 99 *note*, The first of these styles of melody they term monodic, the second *polyodic. But this polyodic style of composition, after all, is nothing more than a compounding of harmony with melody. **1900** Heape in *Q. Jrnl. Microsc. Sc.* Nov. 16 There are two forms of sexual season evident in female mammals; the monœstrous, in which there is only a single œstrus at one or more particular times of the year (bitch), and the *polyœstrous, in which there are two or more concurrent diœstrous cycles at a particular time of the year (mare). **1919** *Amer. Jrnl. Anat.* XXVI. 131 The females of the wild swine of Europe are monoestrous, according to Kaeppeli ('08), having but one period of heat in the year; but under domestication the sow becomes polyoestrous, coming in heat at intervals of two to four weeks. **1975** *Sci. Amer.* July 77/1 The particular response of each species to light seems to depend on whether the species is monestrous or polyestrous, that is, on whether it normally ovulates once a year (in the spring or fall) or at regular intervals throughout the year. **1954** S. W. Golomb in *Amer. Math. Monthly* LXI. 675 We shall generalize the 'domino' to the '*polyomino'... We *define* an *n*-omino as a simply-connected set of *n* squares of the checker-board which are 'rook-wise connected'; that is, a rook placed at any square of the *n*-omino must be able to get to any other square, in a finite number of moves. **1965** —— *Polyominoes* 13 Ever since I 'invented' polyominoes in 1953 in a talk to the Harvard Mathematics Club, I have found myself irrevocably committed to their care and feeding. **1972** W. F. Lunnon in R. C. Read *Graph Theory & Computing* 108 Free polyominoes whose symmetry groups contain no improper elements.. are enantiomorphic. **1974** *Sci. Amer.* Feb. 106 Solomon W. Golomb's polyomino-placing game.. has finally reached the marketplace. **1864** Webster, **Polyommatous*, having many eyes. **1884** *Ch. Times* 8 Feb. 101 Like the mysterious Beings in the Apocalypse, polyommatous—full of eyes. **1887** *Science* 3 June 534/2 In the natural world some beings are monorganic, others are *polyorganic. **1613** Jackson *Creed* ii. xxvii. §3 As vsually is found in any *polyωticall Argus-eyed tyrannie. **1822** J. Wilson in *Blackw. Mag.* XII. 87 It is all right and fitting that a quadruped, or *polyped, like Jack-with-the-many-legs, should go on foot. **1829** Southey *Sir T. More* II. 193 Though it cannot be thrown down by a tempest, it may be shattered by it, and its polyped unity destroyed. **1647** Ward *Simp. Cobler* (1843) 5 *Poly-piety is the greatest impiety in the world. **1918** R. Newstead in *Ann. Trop. Med. & Parasitol.* XII. 93 The main pair of stigmata.. lie in the deep cup-shaped cavity or pit between the *polypneustic lobes. *Ibid.* 95 The low-convex anal lobes or callosities were distinctly polypneustic in character. **1925** A. D. Imms *Gen. Textbk. Entomol.* 110 In *Glossina* there are about 500 of these pores to a side which form the sculpturing on a pair of polypneustic lobes. **1962** Gordon & Lavoipierre *Entomol. for Students of Med.* xxix. 182 The larva contracts considerably to form a barrel-shaped object varying between 5 and 8 mm. in length, with the prominent polypneustic lobes of the larva still clearly visible. **1890** *Cent. Dict.*, **Polypnœa*. **1897** *Allbutt's Syst. Med.* II. 485 A probable compensatory polypnœa or attack of dyspnœa. **1921** *Physiol. Rev.* I. 296 Marsupials are the lowest mammals capable of 'heat polypnea'. **1966** *Amer. Jrnl. Physiol.* CCX. 1270/1 Free-breathing cats demonstrated a thermal polypnea similar to that reported for dogs, cattle, and monkeys. **1975** J. J. Groen in L. Levi *Society, Stress & Dis.* II. xxxiv. 350/2 The child may substitute in situations of frustration another form of respiratory behaviour such as apnoea, polypnoea, or a peculiar kind of pressing with the abdominal muscles during expiration which.. produces an expiratory wheeze. **1909** *Cent. Dict.* Suppl., *Polypnœic, polypneic. **1934** *Amer. Jrnl. Physiol.* CIX. 528 Any type of panting (the polypneic or the hyperpneic) that occurs after decortication is dependent on a rise in blood temperature. **1975** *Biol. Abstr.* LIX. 1795/1 (*heading*) Induction of polypneic threshold by heating during cat sleep cycle. **1853** *Fraser's Mag.* XLVII. 179 We have never had such a *polyponous individual as the Rector of Lyndon. **1821** *Sporting Mag.* IX. 53 The ancients boasted the power of their *Polyposists. **1873** Ganot *Physics* (ed. 6) vii. iii. §502 That the angle of deviation increases with the refractive index may be shown by means of the *polyprism. This name is given to a prism formed of several prisms of the same angle connected at their bases. **1849** Craig, **Polyprismatic*, presenting numerous prisms. **1864** Webster, *Polyprismatic*, having many lateral secondary planes, with or without the primary planes; said of a prismatic crystal. **1974** *Jrnl. Virol.* XIV. 261 (*heading*) Cleavage of mengovirus *polyproteins in vivo. **1975** *Sci. Amer.* May 27/3 This huge protein, really a polyprotein, is then systematically cleaved by proteolytic enzymes. **1896** J. Donovan in *Classical Rev.* Feb. 62/1 The gradual development from extreme oligoprothesy to considerable *polyprothesy, in the Tragic writers, is especially dwelt on. *Ibid.*, The enquiry leads to the general law that prose is *polyprothetic and poetry oligoprothetic. **1876** *World* V. No. 105. 9 If it is.. intolerable for one gentleman to call another a *polypseudonymous writer. **1902** Swinburne in *Q. Rev.* July 30 The polypseudonymous ruffian who uses and wears out as many stolen names as ever did even the most cowardly and virulent of literary poisoners. **1693** *Phil. Trans.* XVII. 928 The Pomiferous Trees and Shrubs,.. these are all *Polypyrene. **1706** Phillips, **Polypyrenous Fruit*,.. such Fruit of Trees, Herbs, etc. as contain two or more Kernels or Seeds within it. **1858** in Mayne *Expos. Lex.* **1890** *Cent. Dict.*, **Polyrhizal*. **1858** Mayne *Expos. Lex.*, *Polyrhizus*,.. having many roots, ..*polyrhizous. **1962** *Science* 28 Dec. 1401/2 An intrinsic property of the *polyribosomal unit. **1970** *Sci. Jrnl.* Apr. 36 In the unaltered cytoplasm surrounding these areas ribosomes were gathered into polyribosomal aggregates, indicating very active synthesis of protein. **1962** *Polyribosome [see polysome]. **1973** *Sci. Amer.* Apr. 41/1

As the synthesis of the messenger RNA proceeds, giving rise to a longer strand of RNA, more ribosomes attach themselves to the strand. They form a string called a polyribosome, which continues the translation of the elongating messenger RNA. **1925** *Bull. Illinois Nat. Hist. Survey* XV. 440 The septic or grossly polluted portions of a stream... The organisms of this zone are those which have been termed by Kolkwitz and Marsson..*polysaprobic and by Forbes and Richardson..septic or saprobic. **1932** *Trans. Brit. Mycol. Soc.* XVII. 112 The association of polysaprobic organisms occurs in waters rich in decaying organic matter. **1933** [see *oligosaprobic* adj. s.v. OLIGO-]. **1946** *Jrnl. Ecol.* XXXIII. 274 Judging from data obtained from other rivers the amounts of algal growth appear to fall into four groups, ..in the polysaprobic waters (e.g. the river Tame) the numbers..are low. **1950** *Folia Limnologica Scandinavica* V. 76 The polysaprobic zone is defined in a chemical respect as the zone in which reduction of the polluting substances takes place. **1973** M. A. SLEIGH *Biol. Protozoa* xi. 265 The largest numbers of protozoan organisms occur in polysaprobic conditions. **1873** F. HALL *Mod. Eng.* 170 Multivocals..are of three sorts. I. *Polysemants, where there is identity of form in the symbols of primary significations and their derivatives; as (*a*) *burst, cast, cost, cut, hit,* presents, preterites, and participles; as (*b*) *love,* substantive and verb, or *ill,* adjective, adverb, and substantive; and as (*c*) *post, stage,* the substantives. II. Homographs, identical to the eye;..III. Homophones, identical to the ear only. **1862** —— *Hindu Philos. Syst.* 75 *note,* This is not the Sánkhya 'nature', *prakṛiti,* but our own *polysemantic 'nature'. **1939** L. H. GRAY *Foundations of Lang.* 255 Words are very frequently polysemantic. **1960** E. DELAVENAY *Introd. Machine Transl.* vi. 81 In recent concise dictionaries the vocabulary of the English language comprises some 60,000 word entries: this number may run four times as high if each meaning of each polysemantic word is entered separately. **1961** *Amer. Speech* XXXVI. 5 (*heading*) Polysemantic extensions of 'dog' and allied terms. **1966** S. CECCATO in *Automatic Transl. of Lang.* (NATO Summer School, Venice, 1962) 75 First of all there is the problem of the *polysemanticity of the individual words. **1939** L. H. GRAY *Foundations of Lang.* ix. 258 The principle of analogy or metaphor in *polysemantism..appears when the name of a well known historical..figure is extended to persons supposed to resemble that character. **1946** *Word* II. 124 *Synchronic* semasiology..deals with..problems like homonyms, homophones, synonyms, polysemantism. **1904** GARDNER *Dante's Ten Heavens* 11 We are told in the Letter to Can Grande that the poem is *polysensuous.* **1899** *Dublin Rev.* Jan. 211 We do not think that Mr. Paget Toynbee quite realises in the Dictionary..the *poly-sensuousness of Beatrice. **1900** *Brit. Med. Jrnl.* 15 Dec. 1693/2 Italian physicians..have given a name or names to this multiple inflammation of the serous cavities... The names are *polyserositis and polyorromenitis. **1915** *Amer. Jrnl. Med. Sci.* CL. 518 (*heading*) Chronic lead-poisoning in guinea-pigs: with special reference to nephritis, cirrhosis, and polyserositis. **1966** WRIGHT & SYMMERS *Systemic Path.* I. i. 5/1 Occasionally, as a result of the compression of the inferior vena cava by the coarse fibrous tissue, a syndrome known as 'polyserositis' or Concato's disease develops in which fluid gradually collects in the pleural and peritoneal cavities. **1862** H. W. BELLEW *Jrnl. Pol. Mission Afghanistan* 216 The only clean..building is a *polysided domed mosque..that stands on an eminence overlooking the village. **1898** SEDGWICK *Textbk. Zool.* I. 125 *note,* The coenosark or hydrocaulus is said to be fascicled or *polysiphonic when it is composed of several adherent tubes. **1857** BERKELEY *Cryptog. Bot.* §133 Of those green Algae which are masked by calcareous matter, there are two series distinguished by their monosiphonous or *polysiphonous stems. **1951** STRAUSS & JACKSON in *Jrnl. Polymer Sci.* VI. *Polysoaps are defined as polymers to whose chain soap molecules are attached. **1976** *Nature* 5 Aug. 519/2 Some enzymes may be converted into surface-active amphipathic conjugates by covalent coupling to certain types of polymeric detergents (polysoaps). **1778** [W. MARSHALL] *Minutes Agric., Digest* 18 A Unisoil Farm requires fewer Implements than a *Polysoil Farm. **1904** *Brit. Med. Jrnl.* 17 Dec. 1643/2 The subject of *polysomatous terata. **1877** HUXLEY *Anat. Inv. Anim.* vi. 251 Groups of *polysomitic segments, which..receive the name of thorax and abdomen. **1950** H. GASTAUT in *Electroencephalogr. & Clin. Neurophysiol.* II. 250/1 In the EEG is a burst of very large amplitude rhythmic spikes of a frequency equal to that of the flashes; these are bilateral and synchronized, and appear predominantly in the precentral and frontal regions where they can in fact be localized... These spikes are sometimes quite pure and thus constitute the complex for which we have proposed the name '*polyspike'. **1975** S. ARIETI *Amer. Handbk. Psychiatry* (ed. 2) IV. xiii. 320/2 The state is associated with prolonged EEG discharge of the 3-Hz. spike-wave type as well as..slower and faster components with polyspikes. **1887** SOLLAS in *Encycl. Brit.* XXII. 417/2 (*Sponge*) A continued spiral growth through several revolutions gives the *poly-spire. **1888** —— in *Challenger Rep.* XXV. p. lxii, *Polyspire...* A spire of two or more revolutions. **1849** BALFOUR *Man. Bot.* §392 If the stamens are double the sepals or petals..the flower is *diplostemonous..;* if more than double, **polystemonous.* **1861** BENTLEY *Man. Bot.* 254 *Polystemenous* [sic],..as in the Rose. **1889** HANDERSON tr. *Baas' Outl. Hist. Med.* 1016 The stethoscope of Landouzy (*polystethoscope) with several tubes at one end, so that several persons can listen to the same murmur at once. **1863** R. TOWNSEND *Mod. Geom.* I. 144 A complete figure which..may be termed a *polystigm in the former case, and a polygram in the latter. **1881** BLACKMORE *Christowell* x. I. 152 As the *polystigmatic view deepened, her name accrusted finally to the positive form of 'Spotty'. **1843** *Civil Eng. & Arch. Jrnl.* VI. 195/1 A picturesque piece of *poly-stylar composition. *Ibid.* 263/2 Such apertures must prove..at variance with its columnar and *polystyle character. **1837–8** SIR W. HAMILTON *Logic* xix. (1866) I. 363 A series of correlative syllogisms, following each other in the reciprocal relation of antecedent and consequent is called a *Poly-syllogism. **1952** *New Biol.* XII. 28 The only method at present available for diagnosing monozygosity involves comparison of as many morphological and physiological characters as possible—the so called '*polysymptomatic similarity' method which is that normally used for determining the zygotic nature of twins in man. **1962** A. BOURNE *Doctor's Creed* vi. 117 The unhappy woman is the victim of constant physical troubles which present a polysymptomatic picture which is quite incurable by the ordinary methods of clinical medicine. **1977** *Lancet* 24/31 Dec. 1340/1 What do you do with a polysymptomatic patient in whom the only positive finding is an enlarged liver? **1709–10** HENLEY in *Swift's Wks.* (1841) II. 452/2 When the *polytasted wine excited jovial thoughts and banished serious reflections. **1905** *Faith of Christian* (ed. 2) 12/1 We have simply substituted what may be called *poly-thelemism, or the doctrine of many wills, for the doctrine of polytheism. **1894** W. R. WILLIAMS *Dis. Breast* iv. 56 In other cases one or more supernumerary nipples, each with its own areola, have been met with, in various positions, on a single breast (intramammary *polythelia). **1928** [see POLYMASTIA]. **1970** H. P. LEIS *Diagnosis & Treatm. Breast Lesions* iv. 60 Polythelia or accessory nipples may occur along the 'milk line' from the axilla to the symphysis pubis or anywhere over a given breast. **1886** *Polythelism [see POLYMASTISM]. **1928** F. Z. SNOOP *From Monotremes to Madonna* 23 *Polythely. This last form is commoner in men than women. **1852** *Ecclesiologist* XIII. 63 They are read,—we mean read in *polytone,—by the Priest. **1866** J. B. DYKES in P. Freeman *Rites & Ritual* 106 The use of the monotone dropped and gave place to our modern careless unecclesiastical polytone. **1974** *Tetrahedron* XXX. 1596/1 The concept of shape is presented in terms of a dihedral angle relationship between adjacent *polytopal faces. This procedure was first employed..to map out structural form in the relatively complicated 8-atom family. **1908** *Proc. Sect. Sci. Koninkl. Akad. van Wetensch. Amsterdam* X. 689 This leads us gradually to the question, whether it is not possible to point out one or more *polytopes—if not quite regular ones—which with C_5 fill the fourdimensional space. **1929** D. M. Y. SOMMERVILLE *Introd. Geom. N Dimensions* x. 190 In a plane there are an unlimited number of regular polygons and 3 regular networks, in space of three dimensions there are 5 regular polyhedra and one regular honeycomb, in S_4 there are 6 regular polytopes and three regular honeycombs, in space of more than four dimensions there are just three regular polytopes and one regular honeycomb. **1974** H. S. M. COXETER *Regular Complex Polytopes* xiii. 141 The regular polytopes and honeycombs so far considered are the only ones that can exist in unitary spaces. **1611** B. JONSON in Coryat *Crudities, Charac. Authour,* The character of yᵉ famous Odcombian or rather *Polytopian Thomas the Coryate. **1904** *Science* 10 June 885/1 The idea that a species may originate in more than one place..did not originate with Briquet, but he resuscitated it and christened it the *polytopic theory. **1939** *Geogr. Jrnl.* XCIII. 271 We are forced to fall back on the theory of polyphyletic and polytopic evolution. **1970** *Watsonia* VIII. 143 The distribution of the hexaploids in Britain does not show any obvious pattern.., and this agrees with Rousi's suggestion that hexaploids have had a polytopic origin from the tetraploids. **1876** C. A. CUTTER *Rules for Printed Dict. Catal.* 14 It will be well to have both words,—polygraphic denoting (as now) collections of several works by one or many authors, *polytopical denoting works on many subjects. **1961** T. LANDAU *Encycl. Librarianship* (ed. 2) 282/1 Polytopical. Descriptive of a book treating of several subjects. **1605** EARL STIRLING *Alexandræan* Argt., Which multitude of murthers gave..to me the subject of this *Polytragicke Tragedie. **1858** MAYNE *Expos. Lex.,* Polyuresia, **Polyuresis.* **1842** DUNGLISON *Dict. Med. Sci.* (ed. 3) 562/1 **Polyuria,* diabetes. **1870** J. R. CORMACK tr. *Trousseau's Lect. Clin. Med.* III. lxv. 533 Polyuria, saccharine diabetes, and also sometimes albuminuria, may, in succession, attack the same individual. **1876** tr. *Wagner's Gen. Pathol.* (ed. 6) 584 Polyuria is absent, but there exists a frequent desire for micturition. **1890** *Lancet* 1 Nov. 938/1 Reducing the polyuria and the thirst. **1870** J. R. CORMACK tr. *Trousseau's Lect. Clin. Med.* III. lxv. 536, I have..had the pain to see nearly all the *polyuric patients whom I had to treat, waste away rapidly. **1885** W. ROBERTS *Urinary & Renal Dis.* II. i. (ed. 4) 245 In poly-uric subjects the contractile power of the renal vessels is apparently paralysed. **1890** *Pop. Sc. Monthly* Feb. 500 For the protection of the mulberry-trees, the raising of *poly-voltines, or worms that hatch several broods a year, is forbidden in many countries. **1953** *Parasitology* XLII. 260 (*table*) *Polyxenic. [Number of associated organisms] Several. [Source of term] New. **1976** *Ann. Rev. Microbiol.* XXX. 128 Laboratory stocks of many protozoa are maintained on mono- to polyxenic substrates. In an attempt to establish axenic cultures of *Entamoeba histolytica,* spontaneous and sporadic lysis in these amoeba developed.

2. In *Chemistry,* a prefixed element indicating generally the higher members of a series of *mono-, di-, tri-,* etc. compounds; sometimes including all except the primary or *mono-*member.

a. Prefixed to sbs., forming sbs. used as the names of compounds formed by the combination of two or more atoms, molecules, or radicals (sometimes with elimination of hydrogen atoms, water molecules, etc.), as POLYETHYLENE; ***poly'glycerin:*** see quot. 1877; ***poly'oxide,*** a binary compound containing several oxygen atoms, as a pentoxide; so *poly'sulphide, poly'terebene, poly'terpene,* etc.

1854 J. SCOFFERN in *Orr's Circ. Sc., Chem.* 353 The designation of polysulphurets has been applied. **1866** WATTS *Dict. Chem.* IV. 687 *Polyterebenes,* hydrocarbons polymeric with oil of turpentine. **1877** WATTS *Fownes' Chem.* (ed. 12) II. 185 *Polyglycerins.* Two, three, or more molecules of glycerin can unite into a single molecule, with elimination of a number of water-molecules less by one than the number of glycerin molecules which combine together.

b. Prefixed to adjs. or sbs., forming adjs., meaning 'containing or derived from two or more molecules of the substance expressed by the second element': e.g. *polycarbic, polyethenic, polyoxygen, polysulphuretted.* See also POLYACID, POLYATOMIC, POLYBASIC, POLYTHIONIC.

1854 J. SCOFFERN in *Orr's Circ. Sc., Chem.* 353 These polysulphuretted combinations are decomposed. **1866** ODLING *Anim. Chem.* 113 We cannot doubt that corresponding acids with three and four atoms of oxygen are also formed, as in other modes of oxidation;..such poly-oxygen acids being much less volatile. **1873** WATTS *Fownes' Chem.* (ed. 11) 621 Polyethenic alcohols..contain the elements of two or more molecules of ethene oxide combined with one molecule of water.

c. Now used esp. to form the names of polymers and other types of compound which have a number of identical groups in their structure. The second element is in some cases a suffix. Usage of the prefix is restricted by some authors to cases where the number of constituent groups is large (in contrast to OLIGO-), but there is no uniformity in this respect. The prefix is now very abundant in *Chem.,* and only the more widely occurring formations are included below.

poly-A, poly A, etc. = *polyadenylic acid* below; **poly'acetal,** any of a class of polymers containing the repeating group –O·CH(R)–, which are prepared by addition polymerization of aldehydes and are typically strong thermoplastics used as moulding materials; **polya'cetylene,** any organic compound containing two or more carbon-carbon triple bonds; hence **,polyacety'lenic** *a.*; **polya'crylamide** (or *,polyacry'lamide*) [ACRYL + AMIDE], any of the polymers of acrylamide, $CH_2=CH·CONH_2$, or its substituted derivatives, which are water-soluble polymers widely used to form or stabilize gels and as thickening, suspending, or clarifying agents, etc.; **polya'crylic** *a.* (and *sb.*), designating compounds which are polymers of acrylic acid or its esters, or thermoplastic materials consisting of or made from such polymers; hence **poly'acrylate,** an ester or salt of polyacrylic acid; a polymer of an acrylic ester or, *loosely,* of acrylic acid; **,polyacrylo'nitrile,** any of the polymers of acrylonitrile, many of which are used commercially, esp. as man-made fibres; **,polyade'nylic acid** *Biochem.* [ADENYL], a polynucleotide formed from adenosine monophosphate by the action of polynucleotide polymerase, and isolated as fibres; abbrev. *poly-A*; **poly'alcohol,** a polyhydric alcohol; **poly'allomer** [f. ALLOMERISM after *polymer*], any of a class of crystalline thermoplastics which are copolymers of two or more different alkenes, esp. ethylene and propylene; **poly'amine,** any organic compound which contains two or more amine groups; **polyan'hydride,** any of a class of polymers in which the units are linked through the anhydride group, –CO·O·CO–, and which includes many resins used commercially, esp. as fibres; **polyanion, -anionic** *a.* (see sense 1 above); **poly'brominated** *a.,* applied to compounds in which two or more hydrogen atoms have been replaced by bromine atoms; **,polybuta'diene,** any of the polymers of 1,3-butadiene or its derivatives; also, any of the class of synthetic rubbers consisting of or made from such polymers; **,polycarbo'xylic** *a.,* having more than one carboxyl group in the molecule; **polycation, -cationic** *a.* (see sense 1 above); **poly'chloroprene,** any of the polymers of chloroprene; also, any of the class of synthetic rubbers (esp. neoprene) consisting of or made from such polymers; **poly'diene** *Chem.,* any polymer of a conjugated diene, esp. any of those forming a number of types of synthetic rubber; **polyene** ('pɒlii:n) [-ENE], any organic compound containing two or more carbon-carbon double bonds; hence **poly'enic, polye'noic** *adjs.*; **poly'ethenoid** *a.* = *polyenic* adj.; also as *sb.*; **poly'formal, -for'maldehyde** = *polyoxy-methylene* below; **polyglu'tamic acid** *Biochem.,* a synthetic polypeptide consisting of glutamic acid residues; **poly'glycine** *Biochem.,* any oligopeptide or polypeptide composed of glycine residues; *spec.* a synthetic crystalline long-chain polypeptide having this structure; **poly'glycol** = *polyethylene glycol* s.v. POLYETHYLENE a; **polygly'colic acid,** a polyester fibre which is made by polymerizing glycolic acid, $CH_2OH·COOH$, and is used in surgery for ligatures, as it is slowly and harmlessly absorbed by the body; **polyhydroxy(-),** *prefix* used to designate compounds or groups containing more than one hydroxyl group; also (without hyphen, as an independent word) as quasi-*adj.*; **polyhy'droxyl** = prec. (quasi-*adj.* use); **,polyiso'butylene,** any polymer of isobutylene; also, any of the large class of synthetic rubbers consisting of or made from such polymers; **poly'lysine** *Biochem.,* a synthetic polypeptide consisting of lysine residues; **,polymetha'crylic**

acid, any polymer of methacrylic acid; hence **polyme'thacrylate**, a salt or ester of polymethacrylic acid; also, any of the synthetic resins made by polymerizing esters of methacrylic acid; **polyol** ('pɒlɪɒl) (*a*) [OL], an ol complex which contains more than one bridging hydroxyl ligand; now *rare*; (*b*) [-OL], a polyhydric alcohol; **poly'olefin(e**, any polymer of an olefin, esp. any of the commercially important synthetic resins of this type; also = *polyene* above; **,polyoxy'ethylene**, designating, or used in the names of, compounds containing the polymeric group $-(CH_2{\cdot}CH_2{\cdot}O)_n-$; **,polyoxy'methylene**, any of a number of white, crystalline polymers which are prepared from formaldehyde and in which the repeating unit is $-CH_2{\cdot}O-$; *esp.* any of the tough, strong thermoplastics of this type which are used as moulding materials; **poly'phenol**, any compound which contains more than one phenolic hydroxyl group; hence **poly'phenolic** *a.*; **polyphenol oxidase**, **,polypheno'loxidase** *Biochem.* [ad. G. *polyphenoloxydase* (Battelli & Stern 1912, in *Ergebnisse d. Physiol.* XII. 96): see OXIDASE], any of the phenolases which oxidize polyphenols; *loosely*, any phenolase; **poly'phenylene**, any polymer in which the repeating unit is or contains the *para*-phenylene group; ***polyphenylene oxide***, a thermoplastic having the structure $-(p\text{-}C_6H_4O)_n-$, which is used as a moulding material; **,polypho'sphoric acid**, any oxyacid of pentavalent phosphorus which contains two or more phosphorus atoms, spec. a mixture of polymers of orthophosphoric acid which is used in organic chemistry esp. as a mild dehydrating agent; hence **poly'phosphate**, a salt, anion, or ester of any such acid; **polysi'loxane** [SILOXANE], any polymer which is based upon a chain of alternating silicon and oxygen atoms; *esp.* a silicone; **poly'styrol** = POLYSTYRENE; **poly'sulphide**, (*a*) a salt or other compound which contains two or more sulphur atoms bonded together, as an anion or group; also, such an anion or group; (*b*) any polymer in which the units are linked through polysulphide groups, esp. any of a class of synthetic rubbers with this structure; freq. *attrib.*; **poly'sulphone**, any polymer in which the units contain the sulphone linkage, $-SO_2-$, esp. a type of thermosetting synthetic resin which has this structure and is used as a moulding material, esp. in electrical and electronic applications; **poly'terpene** [ad. G. *polyterpen* (O. Wallach 1885, in *Ann. d. Chem.* CCXXVII. 302)], any of the higher members of the terpene series, $(C_5H_8)_n$; a polymer of a terpene; **poly'terpenoid** = prec.; **poly'uronide** [URONIC *a.* + -IDE], any polysaccharide which consists of uronic acid residues, usu. in combination with simple monosaccharides.

1957 *Jrnl. Amer. Chem. Soc.* LXXIX. 2023/2 Experiments were carried out with poly-A and poly-U prepared..with polyribonucleotide phosphorylase from *E.coli.* **1968** W. MÜLLER in E. Harbers et al. *Introd. Nucleic Acids* iii. 51 Below pH 6, polyA yields fibers with high negative birefringence. **1975** Poly(A) [see *polyadenylic acid* below]. **1931** *Chem. Rev.* VIII. 371 The reaction between glycols and acetaldehyde (or acetylene) presents the possibility of forming cyclic acetals..or polyacetals. **1967** *Times Rev. Industry* June 72/3 There are in hand expansion programmes covering polyvinyl chloride, polyethylene, polystyrene, butadiene, polyacetals, and polyesters. **1973** *Materials & Technol.* VI. viii. 578 Polyacetal is largely crystalline and not transparent. It resists weathering well and..shows little cold flow. **1885** *Jrnl. Chem. Soc.* XLVIII. 759 (*heading*) Polyacetylene compounds. **1952** *Jrnl. Amer. Chem. Soc.* LXXIV. 1588/2 From these spectra, Dr. Sörensen identified our compounds as polyacetylenes. **1967** *New Scientist* 13 Apr. 95/2 In recent years the widespread occurrence in fungi and plants..of straight-chain 'polyacetylenes'..has been recognized. **1978** *Sci. Amer.* Dec. 66/1 It is conceivable that a polyacetylene film could replace ordinary metal conductors in some special circumstances, such as where weight or resistance to corrosion is important. **1952** *Jrnl. Amer. Chem. Soc.* LXXIV. 1588/2 The isolation of polyacetylenic compounds from several genera of *Compositae.* **1961** *Chem. Nat. Products* (I.U.P.A.C.) I. 570 The *cis*-lachnophyllum ester.. is also most unusual in being a polyacetylenic compound which has been used in industry. **1944** *Jrnl. Org. Chem.* IX. 501 Another possible source of polyvinylamine would be the hypobromite degradation of polyacrylamide. **1962** H. BLOEMENDAL et al. in A. Pirie *Lens Metabolism Rel. Cataract* 300 The large size of α-crystallin is responsible for its electrophoretic behaviour..in polyacrylamide gel. **1976** *Nature* 18 Nov. 264/1 Polypeptides were identified by polyacrylamide slab gel electrophoresis and autoradiography. **1932** *Chem. Abstr.* XXVI. 1249 With the polyacrylate salts,..the process is approx. reversible. **1946** [see *polymethacrylate* below]. **1974** P. L. MOORE et al. *Drilling Practices Manual* v. 117 Polymers of the colloidal type..do not aggregate solids, as do the polyacrylates. **1930** *Chem. Abstr.* XXIV. 1563 Colloid mols. may be homeopolar (polystyrols, rubber), or heteropolar (polyacrylic acid salts, albuminoids). **1939** *Jrnl. R. Aeronaut. Soc.* XLIII. 241 The article deals with the mechanical and physical properties of four representative transparent plastic resins: Cellulose nitrate, cellulose acetate, polymer mixtures and polyacrylic esters. **1943** *Ibid.* XLVII. 140 The polyacrylic resins are thermoplastic, and articles can be made of them by moulding or extrusion. **1959** *Times Rev. Industry* Sept. 4/1 The last 20 years have seen the development of non-cellulosic fibres such as..polyacrylics (Courtelle, Orlon, Acrilan). **1973** *Materials & Technol.* VI. viii. 560 The chemical composition of polyacrylic acid, as the basic polymer of the whole class of acrylics, permits the production of many derivatives. **1935** C. ELLIS *Chem. Synthetic Resins* II. 1072 Hydrolysis of polyacrylonitrile in the presence of water also gives an aqueous solution of the polymerized acid. **1963** A. J. HALL *Textile Sci.* ii. 89 Great difficulty has attended the devising of a satisfactory process for spinning Orlon from polyacrylonitrile. **1969** *Nature* 25 Jan. 357/2 Cellulose and polyacrylonitrile..have been found to produce carbon fibre of good strength and modulus. **1956** *Jrnl. Amer. Chem. Soc.* LXXVIII. 3548/2 While studying the X-ray diffraction patterns of synthetic nucleotide polymers, we mixed together the sodium salts of polyadenylic acid and polyuridylic acid. **1961** *Jrnl. Molecular Biol.* III. 78 The helical molecule of polyadenylic acid consists of two polynucleotide chains organized about a twofold rotation axis. **1975** *Nature* 27 Nov. 357/1 Polyadenylic acid (poly(A)) is present at the 3' terminus of most classes of cytoplasmic messenger RNAs..in all eukaryotic organisms reported so far. **1900** E. F. SMITH tr. *V. von Richter's Org. Chem.* (ed. 3) II. 247 Of the aromatic polyalcohols, having the hydroxyl groups attached to different carbon atoms of the same side-chain, it is only the glycols and their oxidation products which have been studied in any sense completely. **1974** *Nature* 19 Apr. 668/1 The donor and acceptor groups were aliphatic hydroxyl groups in polyalcohols, saccharides and related compounds. **1962** *New Scientist* 22 Mar. 697/2 They are described as stereoregular crystalline plastics and have been given the name polyallomers because their highly crystalline structure differs in chemical composition from other crystalline plastics. **1962** H. J. HAGEMEYER in *Mod. Plastics* June 157/2 The term polyallomer was coined [by the writer] to identify this new class of polymers and to distinguish them from previous known homopolymers and copolymers... These new polymers are examples of allomerism in polymer chemistry. **1975** C. A. HARPER *Handbk. Plastics & Elastomers* i. 91 Polyallomers are superior to polyethylene in flow characteristics, moldability, softening point, hardness, stress-crack resistance, and mold shrinkage. **1975** *Nature* 18 Dec. 638/2 CsCl powder (5·4g) was added to the solution in a siliconised polyallomer tube. **1861** *Proc. R. Soc.* XI. 281 (*heading*) Monacid polyamines. **1875** *Chem. News* 2 July 1/1 (*heading*) The mono character of ethylen and other polyamines. **1910** N. V. SIDGWICK *Org. Chem. Nitrogen* iii. 72 This looseness of attachment of the nitrogen is characteristic of these poly-amines. **1965** *New Scientist* 25 Mar. 795/2 Polyamines such as spermine and putrescine have been found in vegetable embryos and the seeds of various plants. **1931** *Chem. Rev.* VIII. 371 (*heading*) Polyanhydrides. **1932** *Jrnl. Amer. Chem. Soc.* LIV. 1584 Polyanhydrides derived from dibasic acids of the series $HOOC(CH_2)_xCOOH$ are especially easy to obtain in the superpolymeric state. **1972** *Encycl. Polymer Sci. & Technol.* X. 649 The best fiber-forming properties are found.. in the series of polyanhydrides prepared from di(*p*-carboxyphenoxy)-α,ω-alkanes. **1940** *U.S. Patent* 2,199,397 4/2 A process for producing new surface active products which comprises reacting trimethylamine with a polybrominated palmitic acid. **1977** *Time* 4 Apr. 56/3 Michigan farmers..last year lost thousands of cattle to poisoning when a fire retardant called polybrominated biphenyl (PBB) was accidentally mixed with feed. **1977** *Lancet* 9 Apr. 790/2 When, in the U.S.A., flame resistance in children's sleeping clothes became mandatory, industry responded promptly, using those polychlorinated or polybrominated compounds which were to hand. **1935** *Chem. Abstr.* XXIX. 3976 Polyethylene sulfone.. and polypropylene sulfone..decompose..above 300°, polybutadiene sulfone, polyisoprene sulfone,..at 200–20°. **1946** F. MARCHIONNA *Butalastic Polymers* vii. 209 In this method there are obtained 1-ethenyl-3-cyclohexene and low molecular weight polybutadiene. **1960** *Times* 28 Sept. 21/6 When the Shell Chemical Company announced that they would be making polybutadiene and poly-isoprene in the United Kingdom it marked another important step in the production of synthetic rubbers in Britain. **1975** *Sci. Amer.* Dec. 101/1 Polymers that exhibit rubbery behaviour at room temperature include polyisoprene (natural rubber) and polybutadiene (a synthetic rubber). **1898** *Proc. Chem. Soc.* XIV. 179 The preparation of a number of salts of polycarboxylic acids..is described. **1947** [see *polyion* s.v. POLY- 1]. **1970** *Jrnl. Polymer Sci.* A. VIII. 1483 The polycarboxylic resins act in a manner similar to some monomeric polycarboxylic acids. **1931** W. H. CAROTHERS et al. in *Jrnl. Amer. Chem. Soc.* LIII. 4206 We will call this product μ-polychloroprene to distinguish it from other chloroprene polymers that will be described later in this paper. **1951** *Engineering* 7 Sept. 289/3 The insulation employed includes..vulcanised rubber with sheaths of lead alloy or polychloroprene compound. **1970** *Cabinet Maker & Retail Furnisher* 30 Oct. 208/3 Adhesives based on neoprene or more generally polychloroprene have been used for many years for bonding decorative laminates to various core materials. **1946** *Nature* 17 Aug. 224/1 Quite a number of vinyl polymers, poly-esters, polyamides, and polydienes give well-defined patterns indicative of a high degree of internal order, provided they are stretched as in rubber or are drawn into fibres as in polyamides. **1960** *Times Rev. Industry* May 53/3 Also at the end of March came the announcement from Shell Chemicals that it is to build a plant..for the manufacture of polydiene rubbers, polybutadiene and polyisoprene. **1960** *Economist* 28 May 896/2 The main increase will be in butyl rubber..and in the new polydienes—polyisoprene and polybutadiene rubber —which the makers hope will prove suitable for heavy-duty tyres. **1928** *Chem. Abstr.* XXII. 1768 (*heading*) Addition of hydrogen and bromine to the poly-enes. **1934** *Science* 25 May 489/1 The names which have been given to almost all the known polyene pigments have had a taxonomic origin in either botany or zoology. **1970** *New Scientist* 5 Nov. 260/1 The polyene macrolides are an important group of antibiotics. **1961** WEBSTER, Polyenic. **1972** *Nature* 21 Jan. 132/1 A quite different kind of molecule..is the polyenic visual pigment constituent, retinal. **1976** *Chem. Physics Lett.* XLIII. 270 The Raman spectra show..large shifts of vibrational frequencies relative to other polyenic polymers and oligomers. **1949** *Arch. Biochem.* XX. 333 Table II shows the composition of the various tissue fatty acids with respect to dienoic, trienoic, and polyenoic fatty acids. **1964** *Oceanogr. & Marine Biol.* II. 181 Gas-liquid chromatography revealed so little polyenoic C_{18} acids that the mean unsaturation could generally only be expressed as monethenoid. **1935** *Biochem. Jrnl.* XXIX. 1553 (*heading*) Polyethenoid acids. **1951** H. J. DEUEL *Lipids* I. ii. 20 From a quantitative standpoint, linoleic acid is the most important of the polyethenoid acids found in vegetable oils. **1957** *Lancet* 13 Apr. 787/1 The poly-ethenoids in fish oils are so different from those in the other food fats. **1964** *Oceanogr. & Marine Biol.* II. 177 The polyethenoid alcohols never seem to amount to more than traces [in the depot lipids of fish]. *Ibid.* 179 There are some suggestive findings to indicate that polyethenoids and long-chain homologues may ..be greatly reduced in amount [in the castor-oil fish, *Ruvettus pretiosus*]. **1935** HILL & CAROTHERS in *Jrnl. Amer. Chem. Soc.* LVII. 925/2 Compared with the polyesters derived from carbonic acid, the rate of distillation was quite slow; in this respect, the polyformals resembled the.. polyesters derived from the higher dibasic acids such as sebacic. **1962** J. T. MARSH *Self-Smoothing Fabrics* vii. 91 When fabrics are treated with the polyformal they have a softer handle and better resistance to abrasion than when treated with formaldehyde alone. **1959** *Trans. Faraday Soc.* LV. 1484 The polarized spectra of oriented films of Delrin, a commercial polyformaldehyde resin have been investigated. **1965** HASLAM & WILLIS *Identif. & Anal. Plastics* viii. 248 Polyformaldehyde is inherently an unstable polymer and if unmodified decomposes rapidly on heating. **1973** E. H. IMMERGUT tr. *Vollmert's Polymer Chem.* ii. 253 Polyformaldehyde..can be transformed to transparent and hard plastics with high mechanical strength. **1945** H. FRAENKEL-CONRAT et al. in *Jrnl. Amer. Chem. Soc.* LXVII. 317/1 Polyglutamic acid was prepared..from a bacterial culture medium. **1970** A. L. LEHNINGER *Biochem.* vi. 113 Polyglutamic acid is a random coil at pH 7·0 because its R groups at that pH are all negatively charged. However, at pH 2·0, its R groups have no charge, and it readily forms an α-helix. **1906** *Jrnl. Chem. Soc.* XC. I. 403 (*heading*) Action of nitrous acid on polyglycine esters. **1956** *Nature* 18 Feb. 326/1 The two crystallographic forms of polyglycine..have recently been reinvestigated. **1968** E. J. DUPRAW *Cell & Molecular Biol.* xii. 290 (*caption*) A molecule of polyglycine, the simplest possible polypeptide chain. **1889** G. M'GOWAN tr. *Bernthsen's Text-bk. Org. Chem.* 193 Ethylene glycol combines with glycol to form the so-called Polyglycols, e.g. Di-ethylene glycol, $C_2H_4(OH)-O-C_2H_4(OH)$. **1959** *Times* 3 Mar. 7/6 Shell chemicals are already extensively used..in hydraulic brake fluids (glycols, glycol ethers and polyglycols). **1961** H. R. SIMONDS *Source Bk. New Plastics* II. iv. 49 The polyglycols are receiving increased attention as intermediates in plastics compounds. **1956** *Chem. Abstr.* L. 11349 $HOCH_2CO_2H$..(7·6 g.) standing with 100 cc. dioxane-Et_2O (1:3) satd. with HCl at room temp. gave 0·8 g. of a polyglycolic acid $H(OCH_2CO)_nOH$.., m. 126–8°. **1969** *Brit. Med. Jrnl.* 3 May 308/1 A synthetic absorbable suture material made of polyglycolic acid (P.G.A.) has recently been developed. **1977** *Lancet* 28 May 1128/1 The results of using interrupted nylon skin sutures or subcuticular polyglycolic acid (P.G.A.) sutures after appendicectomy were compared in a prospective controlled trial in 127 patients. **1895** THOMSON & BLOXAM *Bloxam's Chem.* (ed. 8) 587 (*heading*) Polyhydroxy-monobasic acids. **1913** *Jrnl. Chem. Soc.* CIV. I. 1147 (*heading*) The spatial arrangement of the hydroxyl groups of polyhydroxy-compounds. **1945** [see POLYISOCYANATE]. **1965** PHILLIPS & WILLIAMS *Inorg. Chem.* I. xiv. 545 A number of elements and compounds have the ability to form glasses. Examples include..most polymeric materials such as polystyrene, and many polyhydroxy compounds, e.g. water, glycol and glycerol. **1967** *New Scientist* 4 May 270/3 The darkening in afrormosia, another African hardwood, is due to certain polyhydroxystilbenes. **1951** L. H. LONG tr. *Hückel's Struct. Chem. Inorg. Compounds* II. xi. 916 A further example is the intensification of the acidity of the very weak boric acid by complex-formation with organic polyhydroxyl compounds. **1957** B. A. DOMBROW *Polyurethanes* i. 2 If we take the urethane group, and, instead of..a simple alcohol,..utilize a polyhydroxyl material like glycol, etc., a point of growth is produced. **1957** G. E. HUTCHINSON *Treat. Limnol.* I. xi. 710 Various organic substances, either colloids, such as gum arabic, or crystalloids, such as ascorbic acid and other polyhydroxyl compounds.., stabilize ferric hydroxide sols. **1931** *Jrnl. Physical Chem.* XXXV. 1893 (*table*) Polyisobutylene. **1935** C. ELLIS *Chem. Synthetic Resins* I. ix. 166 Staudinger and Brunner have examined isobutylene polymerized in the presence of floridin... They separated the resulting mixture..into tri-isobutylene, pentaisobutylene, and a polyisobutylene. **1942** *Industr. & Engin. Chem.* Oct. 1192/1 The high degree of chemical stability and excellent dielectric properties of polyisobutylene have led to its widespread commercial use. **1966** *Economist* 1 Oct. 84/3 Later the two companies may co-operate in making polyisobutylene, plastic foam and other products. **1947** E. KATCHALSKI et al. in *Jrnl. Amer. Chem. Soc.* LXIX. 2564/2 On extending experiments concerning polymerization of amino acids to basic amino acids, we succeeded in preparing poly-lysine. **1964** G. H. HAGGIS et al. *Introd. Molecular Biol.* iii. 55 In acid solution,.. polylysine forms a flexible chain, the repulsion between the side chains preventing helix formation. **1973** *Nature* 6 Apr. 361/1 He [*sc.* E. Katchalsky] was the first to synthesize polylysine, a molecule that is much used in immunological research. **1935** C. ELLIS *Chem. Synthetic Resins* II. liii. 1078 The metallic..polymethacrylates are said to possess useful thermoplastic and film-forming properties. **1946** *Nature* 17 Aug. 224/1 The most notable exceptions are polyacrylates and polymethacrylates, and polyvinyl acetate. The X-ray diffraction patterns produced by these amorphous polymers yield practically no information regarding their constitution. **1973** *Sci. Amer.* Aug. 111/3 Lenses, mirrors and fiber optics of plastics, usually polymethacrylate and polystyrene, are often made by glass-working techniques. **1897** *Jrnl. Chem. Soc.* LXXII. I. 399 (*heading*) Polymethacrylic acid. **1935** C. ELLIS *Chem. Synthetic Resins* II. liii. 1080 Polymethacrylic acid begins to decompose at 200°C. **1973** *Materials & Technol.* VI. viii. 559 In polyacrylic acid, polymethacrylic acid and the amide derivatives..the polymers decompose on heating as the softening point is reached. **1931** *Jrnl. Physical Chem.* XXXIV. 44 To account for lack of mobility in the shift of equilibrium, we can picture the aluminum oxychloride sol as resembling the polyol basic chromic salts reported by Bjerrum. **1948** W. Pigman *Chem. Carbohydrates* vi. 232 The designation 'polyols' introduced here is synonymous with the longer, customary term, polyhydric alcohols. **1962** R. van Heyningen in A. Pirie *Lens Metabolism Rel. Cataract* 396 A comprehensive review on the biochemistry of acyclic polyols has just been published. **1975** *Nature* 17 Jan. 194/1 Since glycerol causes cell fusion, other polyols have been investigated for fusogenic properties. **1930** *Industr. & Engin. Chem.* June 591/1 Polymerization (A polymers). Examples: Olefins and poly-olefins, unsaturated hydrocarbons, azo-compounds. **1936** *Trans. Faraday Soc.* XXXII. 5 Dimerisation is observed with the olefines and it is possible that the polyolefines may be built up in this way. **1959** *Economist* 7 Mar. 895/2 By 1961, with these new plants, British capacity in 'polyolefin' plastics will be over 150,000 tons a year. **1962** *B.S.I. News* Dec. 19/2 The viscosity number of polyolefines. **1969** L. S. Mounts in W. R. R. Park *Plastics Film Technol.* v. 122 Low density polyethylene films..constitute the largest segment of the polyolefin film market. **1939** *Jrnl. Amer. Chem. Soc.* LXI. 1905/2 This method..was used in the present work to synthesize the 6-, 18- and 42-membered polyoxyethylene glycols. **1952** *Martindale's Extra Pharmacopœia* (ed. 23) I. 574 The polyoxyethylene derivatives are mostly soluble or dispersible in water. **1960** A. E. Bender *Dict. Nutrition* 100/1 Monoglycerides are soluble in fat, but by reacting with ethylene oxide the resulting polyoxyethylene derivatives become water-soluble to whatever degree is required. **1972** *Materials & Technol.* V. ix. 265 Polyoxyethylene dioleate and polyoxyethylene lauryl ether are viscous liquids and act as non-ionic emulsifiers. *Ibid.* x. 309 The polyoxyethylene alcohol surfactants range in solubility from completely oil-soluble to completely water-soluble, depending on the number of moles of ethylene oxide added. **1908** *Jrnl. Chem. Soc.* XCIV. i. 131 When heated in the open, these three poly-oxymethylenes volatilise without first melting. **1930** *Chem. News* 24 Oct. 264/2 The ends of the long chains might be saturated by groups such as hydroxyl, methoxyl, or acid residues, as in the case with poly-oxymethylenes. **1952** *New Biol.* XII. 109 The clouds in the atmosphere of Venus..are said by some to be dust and by others to be polyoxymethylene. **1959** *Jrnl. Appl. Physics* XXX. 1516/1 (*caption*) Single crystals of an acetal resin, polyoxymethylene. **1975** *Sci. Amer.* Dec. 104/2 Examples of drawable semicrystalline polymers are polyethylene, polypropylene, polyoxymethylene, and nylon. **1894** *Jrnl. Chem. Soc.* LXVI. i. 415 It is noteworthy that all polyphenols derived from pyrogallol yield blue compounds. **1947** *Sci. News* V. 90 Many substances to be found in soil will reduce manganese dioxide, for example, polyphenols and sulphydryl compounds. **1973** *Sci. Amer.* Dec. 62/1 The abundance in the leaves of plants of distasteful and toxic compounds such as alkaloids and polyphenols. **1928** *Chem. Abstr.* XXII. 411 (*heading*) Complexes of uranyl with polyphenolic acids. **1958** *Times* 22 Dec. 1/5 (Advt.), Synthesis and testing of natural polyphenolic compounds as anti-oxidants. **1913** *Chem. Abstr.* VII. 796 They [*sc.* Battelli and Stern]..defend the use of the term polyphenoloxidase used to designate the enzyme which oxidizes chiefly the polyphenols and polyamines. **1956** *New Biol.* XX. 96 Browning [of tomatoes] may be associated with phenolic substances..and their subsequent polymerization to melanins by the action of polyphenoloxidases present in the host cells. **1973** F. B. Abeles *Ethylene in Plant Biol.* viii. 205 Polyphenol oxidase is a copper-containing enzyme which catalyzes the oxidation of phenols such as tyrosine and is responsible for the blackening of cut raw potatoes on exposure to air. **1974** R. G. S. Bidwell *Plant Physiol.* vi. 119 Several enzymes that oxidize phenols to quinones are known. Two of the most important are monophenol oxidase (tyrosinase) and polyphenol oxidase (catechol oxidase). **1931** *Chem. Rev.* VIII. 375 In a similar way the oxidation of phenols may lead to the formation of polyphenylene ethers. **1965** *Jrnl. Appl. Polymer Sci.* IX. 513 Polyphenylenes tend to be brittle and intractable. **1965** *Mod. Plastics Encycl. 1966* 303/1 Polyphenylene oxide (PPO) is a new high performance engineering thermoplastic, with a unique combination of properties. **1971** *New Scientist* 24 June 761/1 Printed circuitry utilises..polyphenylene oxide parts. **1975** J. A. Brydson *Plastics Materials* (ed. 3) xxi. 470 Several substituted linear polyphenylenes have also been prepared but none appear to have the resistance to thermal decomposition shown by the simple poly-*p*-phenylene. **1908** *Jrnl. Chem. Soc.* XCIV. ii. 838 The various supposed polyphosphates can be considered theoretically as formed by the union of pyrophosphate and metaphosphate in various proportions. **1960** A. E. Bender *Dict. Nutrition* 100/2 *Polyphosphates*, complex phosphates added to foods, in particular to meat products... Include pyrophosphate ($Na_4P_2O_7$), tripolyphosphate ($Na_5P_3O_{10}$), longer phosphate chains of 100 phosphate units, polyphosphate glasses prepared by rapid quenching of $Na_2O-P_2O_5$ melts. **1962** Cotton & Wilkinson *Adv. Inorg. Chem.* xx. 397 Linear polyphosphates..are salts of anions of general formula $[P_nO_{3n+1}]^{(n+2)-}$. *Ibid.* 398 Cyclic polyphosphates..are salts of anions of general formula $[P_nO_{3n}]^{n-}$. **1895** *Jrnl. Chem. Soc.* LXVIII. ii. 445 (*heading*) New polyphosphoric acid, $H_5P_3O_{10}$, and its salts. **1950** *Jrnl. Amer. Chem. Soc.* LXXII. 2962/2 In order to test this hypothesis the reaction was carried out in polyphosphoric acid, a commercially available mixture of the 'strong phosphoric acids'. **1967** I. L. Finar *Org. Chem.* (ed. 5) I. ix. 229 Snyder *et al.* (1954) have shown that the hydrolysis of cyanides with polyphosphoric acid gives very good yields of amide. **1944** *Mod. Plastics* Nov. 124/1 (*caption*) The formation of silicones... Condensation to siloxanes... A polysiloxane. **1946** *Industr. & Engin. Chem.* Nov. 1117/1 Industrial attention has been directed to the liquid polysiloxanes since the announcement in 1944 that silicones were in commercial production. **1955** Brown & Dey *India's Mineral Wealth* (ed. 3) 391 The resultant organosilicon chlorides are hydrolysed to silanols which condense into the polysiloxanes or silicones. **1959** B. S. Garvey in M. Morton *Introd. Rubber Technol.* i. 33 The silicone rubbers are polysiloxanes. **1932** *Nature* 19 Nov. 756/1 He [*sc.* H. Staudinger] has prepared a polystyrol $(C_8H_8)_{6000}$, with about 100,000 atoms in the molecule and a molecular weight of 600,000. **1940** 'Plastes' *Plastics in Industry* vi. 73 Polystyrol..is mechanically somewhat weaker than cellulose acetate. **1966** *Economist* 16 July 263/1 (Advt.), Technical synthesis of styrol for polystyrol and Buna synthesis. **1849** H. Watts tr. *Gmelin's Handbk. Chem.* III. ii. 98 The aqueous solution of the polysulphide of sodium is yellow. **1871** Roscoe *Elem. Chem.* 215 From the formation of polysulphides of ammonium and water. **1882** *Rep. to Ho. Repr. Prec. Met. U.S.* 615 Some sulphurets from Nevada County were digested in a solution of sodium polysulphide, with the addition of free sulphur. **1935** C. Ellis *Chem. Synthetic Resins* II. lviii. 1170 As some of the commercial sulphur resins are polysulphides, Thomas and Riding's work on the alkyl polysulphides should be considered. **1959** B. S. Garvey in M. Morton *Introd. Rubber Technol.* i. 33 The Thiokols are polysulfides of organic dihalides. **1959** J. S. Jorczak in *Ibid.* xv. 363 Polysulfide polymers were first introduced in 1930. **1963** C. R. Cowell et al. *Inlays, Crowns, & Bridges* v. 50 One brand of polysulphide rubber is supplied in two viscosities, a more fluid grade for use with a syringe and injection into the cavity, and a more viscous grade for use in an impression tray. **1965** Phillips & Williams *Inorg. Chem.* I. xvi. 578 The sulphides redissolving in excess sulphide mostly give rise to polysulphide anions, e.g. $[SnS_3]^{2-}$. **1934** *Jrnl. Amer. Chem. Soc.* LVI. 1815/2 Seyer and King have suggested a polysulfone structure..for the addition product of cyclohexene and sulfur dioxide. **1967** *Times Rev. Industry* June 68/1 In the main these are specialist materials offering advances in thermal, mechanical or electrical properties, and include the phenoxy polymers, the polysulphones, methyl pentene polymers, to mention a few. **1971** *New Scientist* 24 June 761/1 Polysulphone moulded components perform satisfactorily in various aircraft parts. **1885** *Jrnl. Chem. Soc.* XLVIII. i. 551 The author [*sc.* O. Wallach] proposes to classify the terpenes as follows:..C *Polyterpenes.* 1. Tripentenes, $C_{15}H_{24}$.. 2. Tetrapentenes, $C_{20}H_{32}$.. 3. Polyterpenes, $(C_{10}H_{16})_x$, such as caoutchouc, &c. **1956** I. L. Finar *Org. Chem.* II. viii. 250 Rubber is the most important polyterpene. **1970** *Encycl. Polymer Sci. & Technol.* XIII. 577 Serious attempts are being made by the resin manufacturers to develop a substitute for polyterpenes from petroleum distillates. *Ibid.* 591 Polyterpene and terpene-urethan resins are used as additives in the preparation of hot-melt coating mixtures. **1936** L. F. Fieser *Chem. Nat. Products related to Phenanthrene* 358 Previously polyterpenoid compounds had been known to occur only in plants. **1964** *New Scientist* 22 Oct. 220/1 A feature of polyterpenoids which had already been noted by chemists was that the carbon skeletons of their molecules could usually be dissected into five-carbon units with branched chains. **1971** G. P. Moss in K. H. Overton *Terpenoids & Steroids* I. v. 198 Although the best-known polyterpenoid is rubber, recent work has demonstrated a range of polyprenols and related compounds such as vitamins E and K. **1930** *Jrnl. Amer. Chem. Soc.* LII. 2474 Conjugated uronic acids, the so-called polyuronides found in pectins, gums, alginic acids, the specific polysaccharide substances of certain micro-organisms, and other plant materials also yield carbon dioxide when heated with 12·0‰ hydrochloric acid. **1957** G. E. Hutchinson *Treat. Limnol.* I. xvii. 889 The main part of the humus of acid peat is not a lignin derivative but apparently consists of hemicelluloses or polyuronides. **1975** *Nature* 11 Dec. 483/2 The natural soil 'cements' include polysaccharides and polyuronides.

3. Words in which poly- represents or is derived from another Eng. word beginning with the element, as ***poly-cotton*** [f. poly(ester]; **'polyreaction** *Chem.*, any reaction that yields a polymer; **'polyrod** *Radio* [see quot. 1950], an antenna consisting of a rod of dielectric material (usu. tapered) projecting from a waveguide. Cf. poly[3].

1978 *Country Life* 28 Dec. 2237/1 The basic Burberry trenchcoat..now costs around £99, made in poly-cotton. **1979** *Times* 1 Dec. 10/1 (Advt.), Dreamy Nightwear... The skirts of both garments are polycotton; 65% polyester and 35% cotton. **1941** Mark & Raff *High Polymeric Reactions* 3 To avoid the lengthy expressions, polymerization reactions and polycondensation reactions,..we shall designate both as polyreactions. **1959** *New Scientist* 2 July 34/2 The remaining lectures were divided into two groups with the general titles 'Physics and Physical Chemistry of Macromolecules' and 'Polyreactions'. **1945** *Electronic Industries* Sept. 222 *Polyrod antenna*, an antenna in which the radiating element is a rod of polystyrene. **1947** *Bell Syst. Technical Jrnl.* XXVI. 844 The principal defect of the uniform polyrod is the strong minor lobes. **1950** H. P. Williams *Antenna Theory & Design* II. iv. 190 This form of dielectric antenna is commonly called a 'polyrod' antenna, since the dielectric material is often polystyrol. **1967** E. L. Gruenberg *Handbk. Telemetry & Remote Control* iv. 130 Plastics, foams, and ceramics can be used for the radiating element. The most common type is called a polyrod and the usual construction contains a dielectric that is linearly tapered over slightly more than half its length.

poly-A to **polyacetylenic**: see poly-.

polyacid (pɒlɪˈæsɪd), *a.* and *sb.* *Chem.* Also poly-acid. [f. poly- + acid.] †**A.** *adj.* Applied to a base which requires more than one equivalent of acid for neutralization, and to a salt of such a base; of an alcohol, polyhydric. *Obs.*

1858 *Proc. R. Soc.* IX. 152 It became extremely probable that the action of ammonia upon poly-acid alcohols would give rise to poly-ammonium bases. **1880** Cleminshaw *Wurtz' Atom. Th.* 198 Some time afterwards, when the existence of polyacid bases was admitted,..Graham discovered polybasic acids. **1904** *Jrnl. Chem. Soc.* LXXXVI. i. 698 (*heading*) The polyacid salts of rosaniline. **1912** E. Feilmann tr. *Molinari's Treat. Inorg. Chem.* 423 When the salt is formed by the action of an acid on a base which has more than one hydroxyl (OH) group, that is, in the case of polyacid bases, such as $Bi(OH)_3$, $Pb(OH)_2$,.. various types of salts may be formed. **1920** [see B]. **1926** N. H. Furman *Kolthoff's Indicators* iv. 117 When all of the dissociation constants of polybasic acids, or polyacid bases are large, they behave like strong monobasic or acid compounds upon neutralization.

B. *sb.* A compound which has more than one acidic group; *esp.* an acid containing polymeric anions. Occas. also *attrib.* or as *adj.*

1911 *Jrnl. Chem. Soc.* C. i. 265 The extension of Werner's co-ordination theory to poly-acids..facilitates the correct formulation of these acids. **1920** T. H. Pope tr. *Molinari's Treat. Inorg. Chem.* (ed. 2) 274 Several molecules of a polybasic acid are able to condense and form polyacids, such as pyroantimonic, pyrophosphoric, and pyrosilicic acid, etc., and in the same way it is known that the polyacid bases, also called polyhydric bases, condense to form polybases or polyhydroxides. **1939** L. Pauling *Nature Chem. Bond* vii. 226 The pyro, meta, and other polyacids of the second-row atoms contain MO_4 tetrahedra condensed by sharing oxygen atoms. **1950** N. V. Sidgwick *Chem. Elements* II. 999 The molybdates and tungstates go much further, forming the highly condensed polyacids and hetero-poly-acids. **1964** *Biophysical Jrnl.* IV. i. Suppl. 11 The polyelectrolyte nature of some polyacid and polybase polypeptides endows them with inhibitory activity in enzymatic reactions. **1974** D. M. Adams *Inorg. Solids* vii. 239 The main features of polyacid chemistry have been recognized for a long time, but not understood.

polyacoustic to **polyactine**: see poly-.

polyad (ˈpɒlɪæd). [f. poly-, after *dyad*, *triad*, etc.]

1. *Chem.* A polyatomic element or radical.

1879 Rossiter *Dict. Sci. Terms* 270/2 *Polyads* = Poly-atomic elements: triads, tetrads, hexads, &c.

2. *Philos.* A relative containing more than two elements.

a **1914** C. S. Peirce *Coll. Papers* (1931) I. 146 A thorough study of the logic of relatives..shows that logical terms are either monads, dyads, or polyads, and that these last do not introduce any radically different elements from..triads. *Ibid.* (1933) IV. 301 If the number of blanks exceeds two, I term it a Polyad, or Plural Relative.

polyadamite: see poly-.

polyaddition (pɒlɪəˈdɪʃən). *Chem.* [a. G. *polyaddition* (O. Bayer 1947, in *Angewandte Chem.* A. LIX. 263/2), f. *poly-* poly- + *addition* addition.] An addition reaction between two compounds which yields a polymeric product.

1948 *Chem. Abstr.* XLII. 6160 (*heading*) The diisocyanate polyaddition process. **1970** E. L. McCaffery *Lab. Prep. for Macromolecular Chem.* 58 Condensation polymerization.. may take place either by a polycondensation reaction, whereby low molecular-weight by-product is formed along with the polymer,..or by a polyaddition reaction in which the total reactants are incorporated in the polymer chain, as is typified by polyurethane formation. **1973** K. J. Saunders *Org. Polymer Chem.* i. 23 Some authors..apply the term rearrangement polymerization (or, sometimes, polyaddition) to polymerization which proceeds through the interaction of functional groups without elimination of a small molecule.

‖**Polyadelphia** (ˌpɒlɪəˈdɛlfɪə). *Bot.* [mod.L. (Linnæus, 1735), f. Gr. πολυ-, poly- + ἀδελφός brother + -ia[1].] The eighteenth class in the Linnæan Sexual System, comprising plants whose flowers have the stamens united in three or more bundles. Hence **'polyadelph** (*rare*[−0]), a plant of this class; **polya'delphian** (*rare*[−0]), **polya'delphous** *adjs.*, belonging to this class; having the stamens so united; also said of such stamens.

1828 Webster, **Polyadelph.* **1753** Chambers *Cycl. Supp.*, **Polyadelphia*,..a class of plants, whose stamina are formed into three or more separate bodies. **1770** Ellis in *Phil. Trans.* LX. 521 In the class of Polyadelphia. **1835** Henslow *Princ. Bot.* §138. 149 The class Polyadelphia is exceedingly small (the genus Hypericum forming its most prominent feature). **1828** Webster, **Polyadelphian.* **1807** J. E. Smith *Phys. Bot.* 450 Nor does it appear to be *polyadelphous at all. **1860** Oliver *Less. Bot.* (1873) 145 Hypericum is the only British genus with polyadelphous stamens. **1878** Masters *Henfrey's Bot.* 224.

polyadelphite (ˌpɒlɪəˈdɛlfaɪt). *Min.* [f. as prec. + -ite[1]: so named as consisting of five different silicates united.] A massive brownish-yellow variety of iron garnet, found in New Jersey.

1836 T. Thomson *Min.* I. 154 Polyadelphite..was sent me by Mr. Nuttall. **1892** Dana *Min.* (ed. 6) 443.

polyadenopathy to **polyadenylic acid**: see poly-.

polyadic (pɒlɪˈædɪk), *a.* [f. polyad + -ic.] Involving many (usu., three or more) quantities or elements. Hence **poly'adically** *adv.*; **polya'dicity**, the state or quality of being polyadic.

1906 C. S. Peirce in *Monist* XVI. 512 A Predicate is either non-relative, or a monad..as is 'black'; or it is a dyadic relative, or dyad, such as 'kills', or it is a polyadic relative, such as 'gives'. **1919** A. N. Whitehead *Enquiry Princ. Nat. Knowl.* vii. 84 A percipient event in the polyadic relation of a sense-object to nature is the percipient event of an awareness which includes this recognition of that sense-object. **1933** C. D. Broad *Exam. McTaggart's Philos.* I. iv. xv. 282 We must distinguish extent of application, which belongs to *all* characteristics, from 'polyadicity', which belongs only to relations. **1950** W. V. Quine *Methods of Logic* (1952) iii. 135 We *also* have occasion to speak of monadic and polyadic schemata, referring thereby rather to the absence or presence of polyadically occurring predicate letters. **1964** E. A. NIDA *Toward Sci. Transl.* v. 111 For the most part these differences are binary or dyadic, but they may be singular or multiple (or polyadic). **1972** W. V. QUINE *Methods of Logic* (ed. 3) III. xxv. 141 The polyadic ingredients—'*Hxy*' and its suite—are what are new.

polyæmia: see POLYHÆMIA.

polyæsthesia to **polyalphabetic**: see POLY-.

polyamide (pɒlɪˈeɪmaɪd). [f. POLY- + AMIDE.] Any of a large class of polymers in which the units are linked by an amide group, −CO·NH−, and which includes many synthetic resins used commercially, notably fibres of the nylon group. Also *attrib.*

1929 *Jrnl. Amer. Chem. Soc.* LI. 2550 Polyintermolecular condensation requires as starting materials compounds in which at least two functional groups are present in the same molecule (*e.g.*, hydroxy acids..might lead to poly-esters,.. amino-acids, to poly-amides..). **1942** *Endeavour* Apr. 72/2 *Nylon*, the new and truly synthetic fibre (a polyamide) that is now rivalling natural silk. **1963** H. R. CLAUSER *Encycl. Engin. Materials* 501 The presence of the polyamide resin brings about the gelation and provides thixotropy to the paint. **1969** L. S. MOUNTS in W. R. R. Park *Plastics Film Technol.* v. 136 Polyamide films are produced from two types of nylon polymer. **1971** *Daily Tel.* (Colour Suppl.) 30 Apr. 8/3 The fabric..is an industrial nylon polyamide, tightly woven with a glistening surface and faintly translucent. **1972** *Sci. Amer.* Dec. 48/3 Some 10 different basic types of nylon are now produced, and the worldwide consumption of these polyamide fibres exceeds four billion pounds per year.

Hence ˌ**polyamiˈdation**, a reaction or process which yields a polyamide.

1946 *Chem. Rev.* XXXIX. 146 The polyamidation reaction parallels closely the rate, temperature coefficient, and reaction order of monoamidations. **1961** SORENSON & CAMPBELL *Prep. Methods Polymer Chem.* iii. 63 An alternative method for carrying out polyamidations from a nylon salt is to use a pipe autoclave.

polyamine: see POLY-.

polyander (pɒlɪˈændə(r)). [In sense 1, ad. med.L. *polyandrum*, for earlier POLYANDRIUM. In sense 2, ad. F. *polyandre* adj., ad. mod.L. *polyandrus* POLYANDROUS. Cf. DIANDER.]

†**1.** = POLYANDRIUM. *Obs. rare.*

1631 WEEVER *Anc. Fun. Mon.* 241 Ethelbert lieth here closde in this Polyander. *a* **1683** STAVELEY *Hist. Ch. Eng.* xv. (1712) 255 Famous King Ethelbert lies here, Clos'd in this Poliander.

2. *Bot.* A plant of the class *Polyandria. rare*⁻⁰.

1828 in WEBSTER.

polyandria (pɒlɪˈændrɪə). [mod.L., a. Gr. πολυανδρία, n. of state from πολύανδρος having many men or husbands (f. πολυ-, POLY- + ἀνδρ-man, male), employed by Linnæus (1735) in the sense 'having many stamens or male organs'.]

1. *Bot.* The thirteenth class in the Linnæan Sexual System, comprising plants having twenty or more stamens inserted on the receptacle (cf. ICOSANDRIA). Also the name of one of the orders in certain classes, as *Monadelphia*, *Gynandria*, *Monœcia*, in which the number of stamens is used to subdivide them into orders.

1753 CHAMBERS *Cycl. Supp.*, *Polyandria*,..a class of plants with hermaphrodite flowers, and a large number of stamina, or male parts, in each. **1835** HENSLOW *Princ. Bot.* §138. 148 In Icosandria they [the stamens] adhere to the calyx..whilst in Polyandria they are free from the calyx, or are hypogynous.

2. *Zool.* and *Anthrop.* = POLYANDRY.

1876 *Beneden's Anim. Parasites* 56 It is a case of polyandria which we see realized in the Scalpellum. **1879** KEANE *Lefèvre's Philos.* i. 28 A long period of polyandria in which the mother was the centre and only bond of the family.

polyandria, pl. of POLYANDRIUM.

polyˈandrian, *a. rare.* [f. prec. + -AN.]

1. *Bot.* = POLYANDROUS 1.

a **1794** SIR W. JONES *Tales* (1807) 170 Taught..To class by pistil and by stamen, Produce from nature's rich dominion Flow'rs polyandrian monogynian.

2. = POLYANDROUS 2.

1809 SOUTHEY in *Q. Rev.* II. 115 In Malabar the polyandrian system of polygamy prevails. **1891** G. W. COOKE *Browning Guide-Bk.* 385 Of this polyandrian lady, no further mention occurs.

Hence **polyˈandrianism** = POLYANDRY.

1820 SOUTHEY *Lett.* (1856) III. 200. **1829** —— *Sir T. More* (1831) II. 199 The regulated polyandrianism which Cæsar found established in the south of Britain.

polyˈandric, *a. rare.* [f. Gr. πολύανδρ-ος (see POLYANDROUS) + -IC. So F. *polyandrique*.] = POLYANDROUS 2. (Corresp. to POLYGYNIC.)

1868 *Westm. Rev.* Apr. 410 The tradition of their polyandric marriage. **1875** A. WILSON *Abode of Snow* xxiv. 234, I never knew of a case where a polyandric wife was left without the society of one at least of her husbands.

polyandrion: see POLYANDRIUM.

polyandrious, *a. Bot. rare*⁻⁰. [f. POLYANDRI-A + -OUS.] = POLYANDROUS 1.

1858 in Mayne *Expos. Lex.*

polyˈandrism. *rare.* [f. Gr. πολύανδρ-ος (see POLYANDROUS) + -ISM.] = POLYANDRY.

1800 *Chron.* in *Ann. Reg.* 473 Here polyandrism prevails.

polyandrist (pɒlɪˈændrɪst). [f. as prec. + -IST.] One who practises polyandry; a woman who has several husbands at the same time. In quot. 1887 *euphem.* for 'prostitute'. Also *attrib.* (= POLYANDROUS 2). (Corresp. to POLYGYNIST.)

1833 *Blackw. Mag.* XXXIII. 143 Her elder sister, Imagination, once so prolific in her loveliness, a Polyandrist with all her Passions of old. **1878** C. S. WAKE *Evol. Morality* II. 241 From the legend of the Pendavas,..it would seem that they [the Kshatriyas] were actually polyandrists. **1887** *Pall Mall G.* 14 July 2/1 Attempts to make the regulation of the movements of female polyandrists a police function.

‖**polyandrium** (pɒlɪˈændrɪəm), -**ion** (-ɪən). Pl. -**ia**. [Late L. *polyandrium*, *-ion*, a. Gr. πολυάνδριον, as below, prop. neut. sing. of πολυάνδριος adj., of or relating to many men.] In *Gr. Antiq.* A burial-place for a number of men, esp. those who had fallen in battle. Hence allusively.

a **1661** FULLER *Worthies*, *Warwick.* (1662) III. 121 Then each Church yard was indeed a Polyandr[i]um, so that the Dead might seem to justle one another for room therein. **1820** T. S. HUGHES *Trav. Sicily* I. xi. 335 That polyandrium which covered the remains of those brave Thebans who fell in defence of Grecian liberty. **1846** C. MAITLAND *Ch. Catacombs* 55 Tombs..mentioned by antiquarians under the name of *Polyandria*.

polyandrous (pɒlɪˈændrəs), *a.* [f. Gr. πολύανδρος (see POLYANDRIA) + -OUS.]

1. *Bot.* Having numerous stamens; *spec.* belonging to the class *Polyandria*.

1830 LINDLEY *Nat. Syst. Bot.* 259 In this order..there are polyandrous species: a remarkable anomaly in monocotyledons, which rarely exceed the number 6 in their stamens. **1870** HOOKER *Stud. Flora* 367 Flowers 1-sexual, polyandrous... Sagittaria.

2. Having more than one, or several, husbands; practising, pertaining to, or involving polyandry. (Corresp. to POLYGYNOUS 2.)

1865 MCLENNAN *Prim. Marriage* viii. 171 The polyandrous arrangement. **1870** LUBBOCK *Orig. Civiliz* iii. (1875) 134 The passage..in Tacitus does not appear to me to justify us in regarding the Germans as having been polyandrous. **1882** *Athenæum* 22 Apr. 501/3 The existence of the ancient, uncivilized, and polyandrous forms of the family.

b. *Zool.* Characterized by polyandry, as a species.

1885 C. TROTTER in *Academy* 6 June 395/3 He also records a polyandrous species among the birds. **1904** *Contemp. Rev.* Oct. 495 Cuckoos are probably polyandrous.

polyandry (ˈpɒlɪændrɪ). [ad. Gr. πολυανδρία: see POLYANDRIA. So F. *polyandrie*.] That form of polygamy in which one woman has two or more husbands at the same time; plurality of husbands. (Corresp. to POLYGYNY.)

1780 M. MADAN *Thelyphthora* (1781) I. 279 This surely affords a strong proof that polyandry (as it is called) is contrary to nature. **1816** SOUTHEY *Lett.* (1856) III. 18, I can account for the system of Polyandry, as he calls it, only in one way;..that it originated in necessity. **1885** CRODD *Myths & Dr.* I. vi. 104 The custom of female infanticide.. rendering women scarce, led at once to polyandry.

b. *Zool.* The fact of a female animal having more than one male mate.

1871 DARWIN *Desc. Man* I. viii. 269 Three starlings not rarely frequent the same nest; but whether this is a case of polygamy or polyandry has not been ascertained.

polyangle to **polyanion(ic**: see POLY-.

Polyanna, var. POLLYANNA.

polyanth (ˈpɒlɪænθ). *rare.* Anglicized form of POLYANTHUS.

1828 WEBSTER, *Polyanth*, *Polyanthos*. **1856** DELAMER *Fl. Gard.* (1861) 41 Polianth narcissuses are annually imported from Holland, with tulips, and other Dutch bulbs.

polyantha (pɒlɪˈænθə). [f. POLY- + Gr. ἄνθος flower.] A small shrub rose or a climbing rose belonging to a group of hybrids of *Rosa chinensis* and *R. multiflora* and bearing flowers in clusters. Freq. *attrib.*

1889 *Jrnl. R. Hort. Soc.* XI. p. cv, The pretty and interesting Polyantha Roses comprised such sorts as Mignonette, Golden Fairy, [etc.]. **1894** A. FOSTER-MELLIAR *Bk. of Rose* ii. 26 Turner's Crimson Rambler..is a very strong-climbing perpetual Polyantha from Japan. **1931** E. S. ROHDE *Scented Garden* v. 134 The double flowered white and pink multiflora or polyantha roses were introduced as cultivated plants from Chinese gardens more than a hundred years ago. **1934** *Times Educ. Suppl.* 24 Nov. (Home & Classroom Sect.) p. iv/1 A new group of hybrid *polyantha* varieties has been created. **1945** G. GRAVES *Trees, Shrubs, & Vines for Northeastern U.S.* 175 The polyanthas have the ruggedness and the ability to thrive under conditions that would discourage the more tender hybrid teas. **1955** G. S. THOMAS *Old Shrub Roses* ix. 92 'Floribunda' is now accepted as a group name for these large-flowered 'polyanthas'. **1962** R. PAGE *Educ. Gardener* iv. 129 Roses, particularly the polyantha or floribunda kinds, are good plants for these small formal gardens. **1976** *Hortus Third* (L. H. Bailey Hortorium) 980/2 The Floribundas..owe their origin to crosses between Polyanthas, Hybrid Teas, and other classes.

†**polyanthea** (pɒlɪænˈθiːə). *Obs.* [a. med. L. *polyanthēa*, f. Gr. type *πολυάνθεια, f. πολυανθής much blooming (f. ἄνθος flower).] A collection of the 'flowers' of poetry or other literature, i.e. of choice literary extracts; an anthology.

Appears in 1503 as title of a work by Domenico Nani Mirabelli, *Polyanthea, idest Florum multitudo* (Savona 1603); subseq. in titles of many similar works, as the *Polyanthea Nova* of J. Lange (Geneva 1600).

1618 SELDEN *Hist. Tithes* Pref., What were patcht up out of Postils, Polyantheas, common place books. **1641** 'SMECTYMNUUS' *Vind. Answ.* Pref. a ij b, As destitute of all learning, as if our reading had never gone beyond a *Polyanthea*. [**1730–6** BAILEY (folio), *Polyanthéa*, a famous collection of common places, in alphabetical order, made first by *Domini Nanni de Mirabella*, of great service to orators, preachers, &c. of the lower class.]

Hence †**polyanˈthean** *a. Obs.*, pertaining to, of the nature of, or using a 'polyanthea'; also as *sb.* one who uses a 'polyanthea'.

1621 BURTON *Anat. Mel.* I. ii. III. xv, [One] that by..some trivially polyanthean helps, steals and gleans a few notes from other men's harvests. **1621** BP. MOUNTAGU *Diatribæ* 38 My selfe, a poore Postillating Polyanthean Clergy-man. *Ibid.* 434 As we poore Breuiarists and Polyantheans of the Clergie vse to do.

polyanthous (pɒlɪˈænθəs), *a. rare*⁻⁰. [f. as next + -OUS.] Bearing many flowers, or many blooms in one flower.

1858 MAYNE *Expos. Lex.*, *Polyanthus*, *Bot.* applied to a plant which bears many flowers,..as in the *Narcissus polyanthus*. Applied by Wachendorff to plants the flowers of which are compound or aggregate: polyanthous.

polyanthus (pɒlɪˈænθəs). Also 7–8 -**os**. [a. mod.L. *polyanthus*, f. Gr. πολυ-, POLY- + ἄνθος flower: cf. Gr. πολύανθος much blooming.]

1. A favourite ornamental cultivated form of *Primula* (supposed to have originated from the cowslip, *P. veris*, or a cross between that and the primrose, *P. vulgaris*), having flowers of various shades, chiefly brown or crimson with yellow eye and border, in an umbel on a common peduncle.

[Cf. **1583** DODONÆUS *Stirp. Hist. Pempt. sea* 146 Primularum Veris una maior et polyanthemos. **1625** TABERNÆMONTANUS *Neu u. volkom. Krauterbuch* II. 33 Primula veris multiflora. **1629** PARKINSON *Paradisus* xxxv. 242 *Primula veris & Paralysis*, Primroses and Cowslips. *Ibid.* 244. 9. *Paralysis altera odorata flore pallido polyanthos*, the Primrose Cowslip.]

1727 BRADLEY *Fam. Dict.* s.v. *Flower*, You are now also to transplant your Seedling Polyanthos upon a shady Border, and divide the old Roots. **1728–46** THOMSON *Spring* 531 The daisy, primrose, violet darkly blue, And polyanthus of unnumbered dyes. **1748** LADY LUXBOROUGH *Lett. to Shenstone* 16 Oct., [We] have now primroses and polyanthuses growing. **1779** SHERIDAN *Critic* II. ii, The vulgar wallflower, and smart gillyflower, The polyanthus mean, the dapper daisy. **1840** E. ELLIOTT *Withered Wild Flowers* 1, Thy gemm'd auricula, a growing flame, Or polyanthus, edged with golden wire, The poor man's flower. **1863** KINGSLEY *Water-Bab.* ii, As smart as a gardener's dog with a polyanthus in his mouth.

2. *attrib.* or *adj.* ***polyanthus narcissus***: any one of a group of species of Narcissus, as *N. Tazetta*, which have the flowers in an umbellate cluster on a common peduncle. So ***polyanthus primrose***, = sense 1.

[**1856**: see POLYANTH.] **1866** *Treas. Bot.* 776 The numerous species of Narcissus..have been thrown into several groups or subgenera,..*Ajax*: the Daffodils... *Ganymedes*: the Rush Daffodils... *Hermione*: the Polyanthus Narcissus, distinguished by the slender cylindrical tube and shallow cup, the filaments unequally adnate near the mouth, and the style slender, as in *N. Tazetta*. **1882** *Garden* 18 Feb. 119/2 The centre bed is filled with..pale-coloured Polyanthus Narcissus, and Lily of the Valley. *Ibid.* 13 May 323/1 The Polyanthus Primrose sent is an undoubtedly novel form of the ancient Jack-in-the-Green.

polyarch (ˈpɒlɪɑːk), *a. Bot.* [f. Gr. πολυ-, POLY- + ἀρχή beginning, origin.] Proceeding from many points of origin: said of the primary xylem or woody tissue of a stem or root.

1884 BOWER & SCOTT *De Bary's Phaner.* 351 The xylem is according to the particular case diarch or polyarch, and its starting-points..all lie at equal distances from one another. **1914** [see *hexarch* adj. s.v. HEXA-]. **1964** H. J. DITTMER *Phylogeny & Form in Plant Kingdom* xxiii. 563 The xylem may be termed diarch when only two points are present, triarch with three, tetrarch with four, or polyarch with many.

polyˈarchal, *a. rare*⁻¹. [f. as POLYARCHY + -AL¹.] Having many rulers. So **polyˈarchical** *a.* (*rare*), of the nature of or pertaining to a polyarchy (opp. to *monarchical*); ˈ**polyarchist** (*rare*), one who advocates or believes in a polyarchy.

1896 BOSCAWEN *Bible & Monuments* v. 112 The Deluge formed the rubicon between the mythic period and the heroic and *polyarchal age. **1660** R. SHERINGHAM *King's Supremacy Asserted* viii. (1682) 84 The state of a Commonwealth is either Monarchical, or *Polyarchical. **1673** H. STUBBE *Further Vind. Dutch War* To Rdr. 13 It was a maxime transmitted unto them from the first Pr. William that this Polyarchical Government could not subsist without a State-holder, who was to reconcile all emergent difficulties betwixt the Towns and Provinces. **1678** CUDWORTH *Intell. Syst.* I. iv. 403 Yet is it undeniably evident, that he [Plato] was no *Polyarchist, but a Monarchist, an assertor of One Supreme God.

polyarchic (pɒlɪˈɑːkɪk), *a.* [f. POLYARCH(Y + -IC.] Of, pertaining to, or having the characteristics of a polyarchy.

1892 G. GISSING *Born in Exile* II. IV. i. 164 He could admit that such men as Runcorn and Kenyon—the one with his polyarchic commercialism, the other with his demagogic violence—had possibly a useful part to play. **1970** R. A. H. ROBINSON *Origins of Franco's Spain* 22 Society was 'polyarchic', being composed of a series of 'intermediate republics' (guild, municipality, region) between the 'monarchies' of the State and family. **1974** *Govt. & Opposition* IX. 29 During the 1950s, the polyarchic formula, which took for granted the unconditional adherence of individuals and groups to majority rule insofar as it assumed that there was no permanent majority or minority on any particular question, seemed to be about to take root in a great many liberal democracies.

polyarchism (ˈpɒlɪɑːkɪz(ə)m). [f. POLYARCH(Y + -ISM.] The principles or practice of polyarchy.

1915 E. BARKER in *Political Q.* Feb. 120 This may seem anarchism. Really it is polyarchism. And as for the problem of polyarchism—why..it is likely to be settled by the needs of mere ordered life. **1917** H. J. LASKI *Let.* 20 Nov. in *Holmes-Laski Lett.* (1953) I. 110, I shall preach anarchism or rather polyarchism in the guise of political theory.

polyarchy (ˈpɒlɪɑːkɪ). Also 7-8 erron. **polygarchy**. [ad. Gr. πολυαρχία rule by many, f. πολυ-, POLY- + -αρχία rule. The *β* form polygarchy, after med.L. *polygarchia*, obs. F. *poligarchie*, Sp. *poligarquia*, Pg. *polygarchia*, It. *poligarchia*, arising (in med.L. or the Romanic langs.) from assimilation to *oligarchia*, OLIGARCHY, was the usual one in 17-18th c.]

1. The government of a state or city by many: contrasted with *monarchy*.

1609 C. BUTLER *Fem. Mon.* (1634) 5 The Bees abhor as well Polyarchy as Anarchy. **1686** J. SCOTT *Chr. Life* (1696) 56 Any Government..whether it be Monarchy or Polyarchy. **1823** SOUTHEY *Hist. Penins. War* I. 615 The inevitable ruin which a polyarchy of independent Juntas would bring on. **1890** J. H. STIRLING *Gifford Lect.* viii. 153 Polyarchy is anarchy.

β. [**1611** COTGR., *Poligarchie*, a monarchie diuided into sundrie parts; or such a diuision.] **1643** HERLE *Answ. Ferne* 32 The extreames of these three kinds of..Government are tyrannie, oligarchie, polygarchie (i.e.) of one, of many, and of all, when arbitrary and unbounded in their governments. **1656** BLOUNT *Glossogr.*, *Polygarchy*. **1706** PHILLIPS, *Polygarchy*, the Government of a Commonwealth in the Hands of many. **1721-90** BAILEY, *Polygarchy*. **1804** *Ann. Reg.* 682 It was thought that an infallible remedy had been discovered for popular convulsions in a polygarchy.

¶ **b.** (erron. use, after *heptarchy*.) A group of many kingdoms.

1826 SOUTHEY *Vind. Eccl. Angl.* 68 Wessex, one of the most flourishing kingdoms of the Anglo-Saxon polyarchy. **1832-4** DE QUINCEY *Cæsars* Wks. 1862 IX. 200 A polyarchy (such as the Saxons established in England).

2. *Bot.* [f. POLYARCH; cf. *dichogamy*, *heterostyly*, etc.] The condition of being polyarch.

1884 BOWER & SCOTT *De Bary's Phaner.* 357 The thick roots of Iris, Asparagus, Smilax (Sarsaparilla), Palms, &c., are examples of a high degree of polyarchy.

polyargite (pɒlɪˈɑːdʒaɪt). *Min.* [ad. Swed. *polyargit* (L. F. Svanberg 1840), f. Gr. πολυ-, POLY- + ἀργός shining, sparkling: see -ITE[1].] A rose-coloured lamellar variety of PINITE.

1844 DANA *Min.* 303 Polyargite..occurs in larger grains than Rosite.

polyargyrite (pɒlɪˈɑːdʒɪraɪt). *Min.* [ad. Ger. *polyargyrit* (F. v. Sandberger 1869), f. Gr. πολυ-, POLY- + ἄργυρος silver: see -ITE[1].] Sulphantimonide of silver containing a very high percentage of the latter metal.

1872 DANA *Min.* App. I. 12 Polyargyrite... Lustre metallic Color iron-black to dark blackish-gray... The mineral is between argentite and pyrargyrite. **1893** CHAPMAN *Blowpipe Pract.* 115 Polyargyrite is closely related [to polybasite].

polyarsenite (pɒlɪˈɑːsənaɪt). *Min.* [mod. (L. J. Igelström 1885) f. POLY- + ARSENITE.] A synonym of SARKINITE.

polyarteritis to **polyarticular**: see POLY-.

polyatomic (pɒlɪəˈtɒmɪk), *a. Chem.* [f. POLY- + ATOMIC. So F. *polyatomique*.] Containing or consisting of many atoms of some substance; *esp.* having many replaceable hydrogen atoms; also = multivalent. See DIATOMIC, TRIATOMIC, TETRATOMIC, HEXATOMIC. In mod. use, (composed of molecules) containing many atoms (usu., three or more). Also as *sb.*, such a molecule.

1857 MILLER *Elem. Chem.* III. 431 Another class..which may be termed polybasic or polyatomic alcohols. **1866** ROSCOE *Elem. Chem.* 242 Amongst the carbon compounds some radicals exist in which more than one combining power remains unsaturated, and which therefore act as polyatomic radicals. **1880** CLEMINSHAW *Wurtz' Atom. The.* 89 Other facts..introduced into science..the clearly defined notion of polyatomic compounds. **1937** L. S. STEBBING *Philos. & Physicists* ix. 215 Human beings are polyatomic. **1958** *Oxf. Univ. Gaz.* 23 Apr. 880 Vibration-rotational bands of polyatomic molecules. **1961** G. R. CHOPPIN *Exper. Nucl. Chem.* iii. 37 Counting gases are usually one of the noble gases mixed with a small amount of a polyatomic gas. **1971** *Nature* 3 Dec. 277/1 There are chapters on diatomic radicals, linear polyatomic ones, non-linear polyatomics and a discussion of dissociation.

polyautography (ˌpɒlɪɔːˈtɒgrəfɪ). [f. POLY- + AUTOGRAPH, after words in -GRAPHY.] Early name for LITHOGRAPHY, as applied to the production of numerous copies of autographs or original drawings, etc.

1806 (*title*) Specimens of Polyautography consisting of impressions taken from original drawings made on stone purposely for this work. **1819** *Gentl. Mag.* LXXXIX. I. 350 This useful invention [lithography] introduced into this country a few years since, and then called Polyautography. **1898** *Daily News* 11 May 9/7 Mr. Pennell prefers the term 'polyautography', the word lithography being 'a seed-bed of misconceptions'.

polyaxon: see POLY-.

polybag: POLY[3].

polybase (ˈpɒlɪbeɪs). *Chem.* [f. POLY- 2 + BASE *sb.*[1]] A compound which contains more than one basic group. Cf. POLYBASIC *a.*

1920 [see POLYACID *sb.*]. **1956** *Nature* 24 Mar. 586/1 This polybase, $-[-CH_2-CH_2-NH_2-]_n-$, has the advantage of being stained by naphthalene black 12*B* as well as by sudan black. **1966** G. M. FLECK *Equilibria in Solution* v. 83 Ion-exchange resins are familiar examples of polyacids and polybases.

polybasic (pɒlɪˈbeɪsɪk), *a. Chem.* [f. POLY- + BASIC. So F. *polybasique*.] Requiring more than one equivalent of base for neutralization; containing two or more atoms of hydrogen capable of replacement by a base. Formerly also applied to salts derived from polybasic acids by replacement of more than one hydrogen atom.

1842 PARNELL *Chem. Anal.* (1845) 68 By a polybasic acid is meant an acid, one equivalent of which requires more than one equivalent of a base to form a neutral salt. **1851** H. WATTS tr. *Gmelin's Hand-bk. Chem.* V. 225 Phosphate of ferric oxide, or ferric phosphate... Polybasic. **1880** CLEMINSHAW *Wurtz' Atom. The.* 76 The discovery of polybasic acids proved a serious difficulty to the theory of equivalence. **1889** G. M'GOWAN tr. *Bernthsen's Text-bk. Org. Chem.* 206 The tri- and polybasic alcohols are capable of yielding the most various products upon oxidation. **1926** H. G. RULE tr. *J. Schmidt's Textbk. Org. Chem.* 59 These differences are so considerable that they may be used to distinguish between mono- and polybasic acids. **1972** NORMAN & WADDINGTON *Mod. Org. Chem.* xxi. 321 Polyester fibres are formed by condensation of polyhydric alcohols and polybasic acids.

Hence **polybasicity** (-beɪˈsɪsɪtɪ), the property of being polybasic.

1890 in *Cent. Dict.* **1912** E. FEILMANN tr. *Molinari's Treat. Inorg. Chem.* 46 In 1835 Graham demonstrated the polybasicity of phosphoric acid. **1931** *Jrnl. Physical Chem.* XXXV. 2226 (*heading*) The polybasicity of several common sugars.

polybasite (pəʊˈlɪbəsaɪt). *Min.* [ad. Ger. *polybasit* (H. Rosé 1829), f. Gr. πολυ-, POLY- + βάσις, in sense of BASE *sb.*[1] 13: see -ITE[1].

According to Chester, alluding to the large amount of the base, sulphide of silver, in proportion to the acids, sulphides of arsenic and antimony.]

A sulpharseno-antimonite of silver and copper, of an iron-black colour, and metallic lustre, occurring in short tabular hexagonal prisms, also massive and disseminated.

1830 *Edin. Phil. Jrnl.* VIII. 148 A new species of mineral named polybasite. **1868** DANA *Min.* (ed. 5) 107 Stephanite and pyrite occur as pseudomorphs alter polybasite. **1879** RAYMOND *Statist. Mines & Mining* 319 Rich silver-ores, such as ruby silver, stephanite, polybasite and tetrahedrite.

polybathic to **polyblastic**: see POLY-.

polyborine (pəˈlɪbəraɪn), *a. Ornith.* [ad. mod.L. *Polyborīnæ*, f. *Polyborus*, name of the typical genus.] Belonging to the subfamily *Polyborinæ* of *Falconidæ*, comprising the Caracaras or American Vulture-hawks.

1884 *Ibis* 360 A specimen of the very singular Polyborine form, *Polyboroides typicus*, from West Africa.

polybranch to **polybutadiene**: see POLY-.

polycarbonate (pɒlɪˈkɑːbəneɪt). *Chem.* [f. POLY- + CARBONATE *sb.*] †**1.** A carbonate containing several equivalents of the acid radical. *Obs.*

1886 T. S. HUNT *Mineral Physiol. & Physiogr.* viii. 289 It was further declared that the carbon-spars must be represented as polycarbonates, having not less than from 'twelve to eighteen equivalents of base replaceable so as to give rise to a great number of species'. **1891** *Chem. News* 23 Oct. 212/2 (*heading*) Contamination of alkaline polycarbonates by heavy metals.

2. Any of a class of polymers in which the units are linked by the carbonate group, $-O\cdot CO\cdot O-$, many of which are thermo-plastic resins widely used esp. as moulding materials and films. Also *attrib.*

1930 *Jrnl. Amer. Chem. Soc.* LII. 315 It seems quite certain, therefore, that these polycarbonates are also open chains. **1959** *Mod. Plastics* XXXVI. 39 Farben fabriken-Bayer..has been manufacturing polycarbonates on a commercial scale in Germany for nearly a year. **1965** *Wireless World* Aug. 409/2 In the manufacture of an optical filter gold has been sputtered onto a polycarbonate substrate. **1969** L. S. MOUNTS in W. R. R. Park *Plastics Film Technol.* v. 138 Due to good forming characteristics, heat resistance, and toughness, polycarbonate film and sheet are used in skin and blister packaging. **1976** *Sci. Amer.* Feb. 19/2 (Advt.), The instrument is housed in a tough, high-impact polycarbonate case. **1978** *Skatcat's Quiz Bk.* (R. Soc. Prevention of Accidents) 2/1 Also O.K. are polycarbonate laminates of glass or carbon-fibre reinforced resins with plywood cores.

polycarboxylic: see POLY-.

polycarpellary (ˌpɒlɪˈkɑːpɛlərɪ), *a. Bot.* [f. POLY- + CARPEL, as CARPELLARY.] Having or consisting of several carpels.

1860 OLIVER *Less. Bot.* I. iv. (1872) 31 Bramble... Pistil superior, apocarpous, polycarpellary. **1875** BENNETT & DYER *Sachs' Bot.* 492 A polycarpellary ovary is always the result of the union of all the carpels of a flower, the number being usually two, three, four, or five, arranged in one whorl, and the floral axis terminating in the midst of them.

polyˈcarpic, *a. Bot.* [f. as next + -IC.] **a.** = POLYCARPOUS *a.* a. †**b.** = POLYCARPOUS *a.* b. *Obs. rare.*

1849 BALFOUR *Man. Bot.* §634 *Polycarpic*,..those which flower and fruit several times before the entire plant dies. **1858** MAYNE *Expos. Lex.*, *Polycarpicus*,..applied by de Candolle to plants that bear fruit many times during their existence. Applied by Bartling to a Class..in which the ovaries are often in indefinite number: polycarpic. **1909** GROOM & BALFOUR tr. *Warming's Oecol. Plants* ii. 6 These plants are divided into monocarpic and polycarpic: the former produce flower and fruit (or spores) once, and then die; the latter may produce fruit repeatedly before death claims them. **1951** MCLEAN & IVIMEY-COOK *Textbk. Theoret. Bot.* I. xxi. 834 The common factor in all perennials is that they are polycarpic, that is to say, they flower and fruit repeatedly.

polycarpous (pɒlɪˈkɑːpəs), *a. Bot.* [f. Gr. πολύκαρπος rich in fruit (f. πολυ-, POLY- + καρπός fruit) + -OUS.] †**a.** Bearing fruit many times, as a perennial plant; sychnocarpous. **b.** (More properly) = POLYCARPELLARY.

1832 LINDLEY *Introd. Bot.* 401 *Polycarpous* (better sychnocarpous), having the power of bearing fruit many times without perishing. **1866** *Treas. Bot.* 913 *Polycarpous*, ..more properly, bearing many distinct fruits or carpels in each flower. **1882** VINES *Sachs' Bot.* 560 When the gynæceum of a flower consists of a single ovary only one fruit is formed, and the flower is said to be monocarpous.., in contradistinction to the polycarpous flowers, the gynæceum of which consists of several isolated ovaries from which the same or a smaller number of fruits are developed.

polycation(ic to **polycellular**: see POLY-.

polycentric (pɒlɪˈsɛntrɪk), *a.* [f. POLY- 1 + -CENTRIC.] = *multicentric* adj. s.v. MULTI- 1 a; in *Politics*, characterized by polycentrism. Also as *sb.*, a polycentric chromosome or chromatid.

1887 H. M. WARD in *Nature* 27 Jan. 301/2 As soon as the sapvacuoles appear, in many cases making the cell not monocentric but polycentric. **1909** *Q. Rev.* Apr. 499 The Messina earthquake belongs to the class known in Italy as that of 'polycentric' earthquakes. **1945** M. J. D. WHITE *Animal Cytol. & Evol.* iv. 57 The example of *Ascaris megalocephala* shows us that in some other organisms polycentric chromosomes can exist in nature. **1953** *Heredity* VI. Suppl. 73 The occurrence of high polycentrics such as C_3, C_4, C_5 and rarely even C_6..with a high frequency after treatment at meiosis shows..that reunion is not low. **1956** tr. *Togliatti's Probl. Devel. Socialist Democracy* 12/2 The advance towards socialism is an objective for which there is a concentration of forces from different movements... The whole system is becoming polycentric, and even in the Communist movement we cannot speak of a single guide. **1965** *N.Y. Times* 18 Jan. 34 After the success of Tito's revolt against Moscow Togliatti conceived of 'polycentric' Communism. This means adjusting party methods in each country to national traditions and requirements. **1965** *Economist* 3 Apr. 43/2 The reality of an increasingly 'polycentric' world, marked by the growing self-assertion of the middle and smaller states. **1967** G. STEINER *Lang. & Silence* 80 African English, Australian English..represent a complicated, polycentric field of linguistic force. **1968** R. RIEGER et al. *Gloss. Genetics & Cytogenetics* 351 Polycentrics are in most cases the result of chromosome mutations. **1971** *Physics Bull.* Jan. 16/2 There are several nuclei so that orbitals are not monocentric but polycentric. **1976** T. EAGLETON *Crit. & Ideology* v. 164 Literature is multiple and polycentric, saturating the very textures of our social life.

Hence ˌ**polycenˈtricity**, the fact of being polycentric.

1959 [see HOLOGENESIS]. **1973** *Times Lit. Suppl.* 3 Aug. 897/2 The year 1963 was also one in which polycentricity became a conspicuous feature of international relations.

polycentrism (pɒlɪˈsɛntrɪz(ə)m). [f. POLY- + CENTR(E + -ISM.] In Communist political theory, the idea first promulgated by P. Togliatti (1892-1964) in 1956 that each separate Communist party has the right of full national autonomy and that the Soviet model need not be binding for all Communist parties. Also in extended use. Hence **polyˈcentrist** *a.* and *sb.*

1961 *Economist* 2 Dec. 918 He [*sc.* Gomulka] rejected the Italian idea of 'polycentrism'. **1963** *Ann. Reg. 1962* 199 'Polycentrist' tendencies within the world Communist movement. **1963** *Spectator* 28 June 829 Pelung is in effect returning to the position of support for East European polycentrism against Moscow. **1966** *Times* 7 July 7 Many more responsible non-communists were becoming polycentrists, including General de Gaulle. **1968** *Economist* 24 Feb. 36/1 The monolithic structure of the international communist movement has collapsed under the combined pressure of the Sino-Soviet conflict, and the bid for greater freedom of the ex-satellites in Eastern Europe. The result is the rise of 'polycentrism'. **1969** P. ALLUM in Henig & Pinder *European Political Parties* 206 Khrushchev's denunciation of Stalinist errors..permitted Togliatti to formulate explicitly the doctrines of 'polycentrism' and the 'Italian way to Socialism'. **1971** W. LAQUEUR *Dict. Politics* 568 The final break with China as well as Albania came at the second Moscow Conference of Communist parties in Nov. 1960... After the 1960 Conference, polycentrism..became a fact. **1974** *Times* 19 Feb. (European Defence Suppl.) p. i/1 Long before the Middle East war it had become commonplace to contrast the bipolarity of the past decade with the new pattern of polycentrism as developing forces in Europe, China and Japan impinged upon the distribution of world power.

polycephalic (ˌpɒlɪsɪˈfælɪk), *a. rare.* [f. Gr. πολυκέφαλος many-headed + -IC.] Having many heads; many-headed. So **polycephalist** (-ˈsɛfəlɪst), one who has or acknowledges many heads or rulers; **polyˈcephalous** *a.*, many-headed.

1850 MURE *Lit. Greece* III. 36 One of those [*sc.* nomes] to Apollo was called, from its compass and variety of parts, the *Polycephalic, or many-headed, Nome. **1659** GAUDEN *Tears Ch.* IV. xix. 541 Both which methods must have left the.. Churches of Christ either Acephalists, confused without any head, or *Polycephalists, burdened with many heads. **1824** MᶜCULLOCH *Highl. Scotl.* IV. 138 The *polycephalous monster. **1845–50** MRS. LINCOLN *Lect. Bot.* xv. 90 They [capsules] are monocephalous, as in the lily, or polycephalous, as in Nigella. **1875** JOWETT *Plato* (ed. 2) III. 484 The form of a multitudinous, polycephalous beast, having a ring of heads of all manner of beasts.

polychæte, -chete (ˈpɒlɪkiːt), *a.* and *sb. Zool.* [ad. mod.L. *Polychæta*, f. Gr. πολυχαίτης having much hair, f. πολυ- much + χαίτη mane (here taken in sense 'bristle': cf. OLIGOCHÆTE).]

a. *adj.* Belonging to the *Polychæta*, one of the two divisions of the *Chætopoda*, a class of worms (see CHÆTOPOD), characterized by numerous bristles on the foot-stumps or parapodia. **b.** *sb.* A worm of this order or division.

1886 *Athenæum* 3 July 19/1 The entire twelfth volume.. is devoted to Prof. W. C. MᶜIntosh's monograph on the polychæte annelids. **1896** *Cambr. Nat. Hist.* II. 243 The worm itself [Dinophilus] is more like a larval Polychaete than a full-grown worm.

So **polychætan** (pɒlɪˈkiːtən), **polyˈchætous** *adjs.*

1877 *Amer. Naturalist* XXI. 581 The spines of the polychætous worms. **1877** HUXLEY *Anat. Inv. Anim.* iv. 184 Among the polychætous Annelida. **1888** ROLLESTON & JACKSON *Anim. Life* 582 Larval or provisional nephridia.. occur in many Polychætan Trochospheres.

polycharacteristic: see POLY-.

polychlorinated (pɒlɪˈklɔərɪneɪtɪd), *a. Chem.* [f. POLY- 2 + CHLORINATED *ppl. a.*] Applied to compounds in which two or more hydrogen atoms have been replaced by chlorine atoms; esp. in ***polychlorinated biphenyl*** [*biphenyl* = *diphenyl*], any of a class of such compounds derived from biphenyl, $(C_6H_5)_2$, or its derivatives, which have a wide variety of industrial applications and are persistent environmental pollutants; abbrev. *PCB* (s.v. P II d).

1935 C. ELLIS *Chem. Synthetic Resins* II. lviii. 1178 Amino and hydroxy compounds are formed when polychlorinated paraffins are heated with solutions of ammonia or caustic alkali, respectively. **1951** H. H. SHEPHARD *Chem. & Action Insecticides* xi. 271 The higher polychlorinated naphthalenes are utilized as noninflammable waxes in electric insulation. **1962** *Chem. Abstr.* LVII. 8498 (*heading*) Polychlorinated biphenyl derivatives. **1968** *Times* 17 Dec. 10/5 The chemicals, called polychlorinated biphenyls, are in some ways similar to chlorine containing pesticides such as DDT and..can poison the liver even in minute amounts. **1971** P. GRESSWELL *Environment* 201 Polychlorinated biphenyls were found in high concentration in birds which died in 1969 in the Irish Sea.

polychloroprene: see POLY-.

polychœrany: see POLYCŒRANY.

polycholia, -choral: see POLY-.

polychord (ˈpɒlɪkɔːd), *a.* and *sb.* Also 7 -cord. [ad. Gr. πολυχόρδ-ος many-stringed, f. πολυ-, POLY- + χορδή CHORD.]

A. *adj.* Having many strings, as a musical instrument.

1674 PLAYFORD *Skill Mus.* I. 60 He with his Harp, or Polycord Lyra, expressed such effectual melody. **1728** NORTH *Mem. Music* (1846) 43 It was plainely revealed by the polychord instruments. **1899** A. LAYARD *Mus. Bogeys* 36 The Poly-chord Bogey performs on three strings.

B. *sb.* **1.** An instrument having ten gut strings, resembling a double-bass without a neck, played with a bow or with the fingers; invented by F. Hillmer of Leipzig in 1799, but never generally used.

1838 *Encycl. Brit.* (ed. 7) XVIII. 311/1.

2. Trade-name for a kind of octave-coupler.

1858 SIMMONDS *Dict. Trade, Polychord*,..an apparatus which couples two octave notes, and can be affixed to any piano-forte or similar instrument with keys.

polychoric (pɒlɪˈkɔərɪk), *a. Statistics.* [f. POLY- + χώρ-ισις separation (f. χωρίζειν to separate) + -IC; cf. TETRACHORIC *a.*] Used to describe a table in which data are divided into three or more classes by each of two criteria; of or pertaining to such a table; applied *esp.* to an estimate of the product-moment coefficient derived from such a table, and to concepts used in obtaining such an estimate.

1918 *Biometrika* XII. 93 (*heading*) The correlation coefficient of a polychoric table. **1922** *Ibid.* XIV. 149 What we actually desire is to compare the observations and the regression lines as given by the present polychoric method with those obtained by product-moment methods. **1964** *Psychometrika* XXIX. 386 In what follows, the tetrachoric series method is generalized to produce a new polychoric estimate of ρ.

polychotomous (pɒlɪˈkɒtəməs), *a.* [Erroneously formed by substituting POLY- for *di-* in *dicho-tomous*, DICHOTOMOUS.] Divided, or involving division, into many (or more than two) parts, sections, groups, or branches: = POLYTOMOUS. So **polyˈchotomy**, division into more than two parts or groups, as in classification: = POLYTOMY.

1858 MAYNE *Expos. Lex.*, *Polychotomus*, applied to a body that is divided into numerous articulations..: polychotomous. **1887** *Amer. Naturalist* Oct. 915 Polychotomy is probably never more than provisional, and all classification will eventually be dichotomous.

polychrest (ˈpɒlɪkrɛst). ? *Obs.* Also 7 in Gr.-L. forms **polychrestum, -on.** [a. med.L. *polychrēstus*, a. Gr. πολύχρηστος useful for many purposes, f. πολυ-, POLY- + χρηστός useful. So F. *polychreste* (1690).] Something adapted to several different uses; *esp.* a drug or medicine serving to cure various diseases.

[**1620** BACON *Instauratio Magna, De Augm. Scient.* III. v, Inventorium opum humanarum, et catalogus polychrestorum.] **1656** BLOUNT *Glossogr.*, *Polychrests*, things of much use, fit for many uses, or divers ways profitable. *Bac.* **1685** J. COOKE *Marrow Chirurg.* VII. i. (ed. 4) 263 Many Physicians have studied out Polychrestons. **1729** *Evelyn's Sylva* IV. i. 313 There is nothing necessary for life..which these Polychrests afford not. **1802–12** BENTHAM *Ration. Judic. Evid.* (1827) IV. 382 Of admirable use: like most other articles in the catalogue, a polychrest.

†**b.** *attrib.* ***polychrest salt*** (also ***salt polychrest***): 'an old name for neutral sulphate of potassium; and for sodio-potassic tartrate' (Watts *Dict. Chem.*).

1727–41 CHAMBERS *Cycl.* s.v., *Sal Polychrest* is a compound salt, made of equal parts of salt-petre and sulphur. **1750** MRS. DELANY in *Life & Corr.* (1861) II. 550, I have taken Salt Polychrest and Cheltenham waters. **1799** M. UNDERWOOD *Diseases Children* (ed. 4) I. 91, I have usually directed..the polychrest salt and rhubarb occasionally in the course of the day.

So **polyˈchrestic** *adj.*, serving for various uses; *sb.* = *polychrest*; †**polyˈchrestical** *adj. Obs.* = prec.; **ˈpolychresty**, adaptation to various uses, capability of being used in several ways.

1657 TOMLINSON *Renou's Disp.* 124 Other medicaments, called polychrestical, which consist of contrary medicaments. **1694** WESTMACOTT *Script. Herb.* 213 These names shew it was a great Polychrestick. **1889** *Buck's Handbk. Med. Sc.* VIII. 518/1 The same word may do duty in many different connections... Such words, useful in many ways, may be called *polychrestic*, although this adjective is commonly applied to drugs of various utility. *Ibid.*, In a greater or less degree polychresty is predicable of many other words, e.g., frontal, dorsal, etc.

polychroic (pɒlɪˈkrəʊɪk), *a. Cryst.* [a. F. *polychroïque*, f. Gr. πολύχροος many-coloured (f. πολυ-, POLY- + χρόα colour) + -IC.] Showing different colours when viewed in different directions; more properly called PLEOCHROIC. So **ˈpolychroism** = PLEOCHROISM.

1858 MAYNE *Expos. Lex.*, Polychroism. **1861** L. L. NOBLE *Icebergs* 125 Nature..is no monochromist, but polychroic. **1890** *Nature* 2 Jan. 215/1 Optical properties of the polychroic aureolas present in certain minerals.

polychroite (ˈpɒlɪkrəʊaɪt). *Chem.* [a. F. *polychroïte* (*Ann. Chim.* 1806), f. Gr. πολύχρο-ος (see POLYCHROIC): see -ITE¹.] Name for the colouring matter of saffron (also called SAFRANIN), which exhibits various colours under various reagents.

1815 W. HENRY *Elem. Chem.* (ed. 7) II. 254 *Polychroite.* This name has been given, by Bouillon La Grange and Vogel, to the extract of saffron prepared with alcohol. **1831** J. DAVIES *Manual Mat. Med.* 245 The substance.. denominated Polychroite, is but a compound of colouring matter and volatile oil. **1874** GARROD & BAXTER *Mat. Med* (1880) 373 Saffron..yields to water and alcohol an orange-red colouring matter called polychroite, changed into blue by oil of vitriol.

polychromasia (ˌpɒlɪkrəʊˈmeɪzɪə). *Med.* [mod.L., back-formation from POLYCHROMATIC *a.* (see -IA¹).] = POLYCHROMATOPHILIA.

1909 R. J. M. BUCHANAN *Blood in Health & Dis.* xi. 196 Polychromasia is common; with stains containing methyl blue and eosin such cells may be a light violet or even a distinct blue, with methylene blue and iodine the erythrocytes in this disease exhibit a green colour not usually met with in other forms of anæmia. **1935** WHITBY & BRITTON *Disorders of Blood* iii. 64 For many years polychromasia was considered to be a degeneration until Hawes (1909) showed that the number of polychromatic cells was always approximately parallel to the number of reticulocytes. **1956** [see *anisocytosis* s.v. ANISO-]. **1973** WOODLIFF & HERRMANN *Conc. Haematol.* i. 18 In many cells polychromasia of the cytoplasm remains after loss of the nucleus. **1977** *Proc. R. Soc. Med.* LXX. 284/2 Film was leukoerythroblastic and showed polychromasia, anisopoikilocytosis, occasional erythroblasts..and tear-drop cells.

Hence **ˌpolychroˈmasic** *a.* = POLYCHROMATOPHIL *a.*; cf. POLYCHROMATIC *a.* 2.

1911 *Jrnl. Path. & Bacteriol.* XV. 9 Degenerate forms with vacuolated or irregularly stained and polychromasic cytoplasm are often seen. **1933** [see POLYCHROMATOPHILIA]. **1942** M. M. WINTROBE *Clin. Hematol.* ii. 56 A close parallelism between the numbers of polychromasic and reticulated cells in various samples of blood has been found, although the proportion of reticulocytes is always higher.

polychromatic (ˌpɒlɪkrəʊˈmætɪk), *a.* [f. POLY- + CHROMATIC: see below. Cf. Gr. πολυχρώματ-ος many-coloured.]

1. a. Having or characterized by various colours; many-coloured.

polychromatic acid (Chem.): = POLYCHROMIC *acid*, q.v.

1849 FREEMAN *Archit.* I. i. 40 The polychromatic effect.. was sought after in these early times. **1884** T. WALDEN in *Harper's Mag.* Aug. 434/2 The glory of polychromatic decoration. **1895** *Contemp. Rev.* Oct. 479 A 'polychromatic edition of the Old Testament' is being published in America.

b. Of radiation: containing a number of wavelengths, not monochromatic.

1935 H. HARRIS *Metallic Arc Welding* iii. 13 Asterism is caused by the diffraction of a polychromatic X-ray beam by a deformed crystal. **1976** *Nature* 12 Aug. 541/2 A parallel beam of white (polychromatic) radiation falls on an oriented sample.

2. *Med.* = POLYCHROMATOPHIL *a.*; *esp.* as ***polychromatic normoblast***, an immature erythrocyte. Cf. POLYCHROMASIC *a.*

1899 *Jrnl. R. Microsc. Soc.* 379 Polychromatic normoblasts which become violet in eosin and methylen-blue and red in triacid. **1935** [see POLYCHROMASIA]. **1938** W. MAGNER *Textbk. Hematol.* i. 4 Normoblasts showing this mixture of red and blue in their cytoplasm are known as polychromatic normoblasts. **1958** G. C. DE GRUCHY *Clin. Haematol.* ii. 43 Polychromatic cells are young red cells which have not yet completely lost their ribose nucleic acid; they are normally present in only small numbers in the peripheral blood (0·2–2·0 per cent). **1973** B. A. BROWN *Hematol.* ii. 28/1 The production of heme and globin takes place independently of each other, beginning in the polychromatic normoblast, and ending in the reticulocyte stage.

So **polychromatist** (-ˈkrəʊmətɪst), one who uses, or favours the use of, many colours (in painting or decoration); **polyˈchromatize** *v. trans.*, to paint or adorn with many colours; **polyˈchromatous** *a.*, many-coloured.

1849 *Ecclesiologist* IX. 160 It is slightly polychromatized. **1854** *Blackw. Mag.* LXXVI. 319 The new professors, polychromatists, must bring out..new editions of all our classics. **1889** *Daily News* 22 Jan. 3/7 Paris is now the most polychromatous city in the world... General Boulanger.. changes the colour of his posters. He has had every shade of green, of yellow, of orange, of grey, and red from pink to magenta.

polychromatism (pɒlɪˈkrəʊmətɪz(ə)m). [f. as POLYCHROMATIC *a.*: see -ISM.] The property of having or responding to many colours.

1950 *Sci. News* XV. 26 There may be, as it were, polychromatism of the retinal sense organs but trichromatism of the brain, and therefore of the organ of vision as a whole. **1965** B. E. FREEMAN tr. *Vandel's Biospeleol.* xxv. 408 Populations of *Asellus aquaticus cavernicolus*..show extreme polychromatism.

polychromatophil (pɒlɪˈkrəʊmətəʊfɪl), *a. Med.* Also -phile (-faɪl). [a. G. *polychromatophil* (G. Gabritschewsky 1890, in *Arch. f. exper. Path. und Pharmakol.* XXVIII. 86), f. Gr. πολυχρώματ-ος many-coloured: see -PHIL, -PHILE.] Of an erythrocyte: having an affinity for basic as well as for acidic stains, and so recognizable by its appearance when a mixed stain is used. Of or pertaining to such erythrocytes. Also **ˌpolychromatoˈphilic** *a.*, in the same sense. So **ˌpolychromatoˈphilia**, polychromatophil condition.

1897 R. C. CABOT *Guide Clin. Exam. Blood* 77 The typical megaloblast is an abnormally large cell.., frequently showing marks of degeneration (polychromatophilia) in its protoplasm, which is therefore brownish or purplish with the Ehrlich-Biondi stain. *Ibid.* 124 More common than in any other form of anæmia are the polychromatophilic red corpuscles (see Plate IV.). **1898** A. C. COLES *Blood* Pl. I (*caption*) Polychromatophile corpuscles. **1908** *Practitioner* Aug. 324 In polychromatophil degeneration, the stained cell may vary in colour from lilac to quite deep blue (when Jenner's stain has been used). **1933** A. PINEY tr. *Morawitz's*

Blood Dis. in Clin. Pract. ii. 12 Among the non-nucleated red corpuscles Jenner's stain often shows elements which are not purely red, but violet: this is polychromatophilia.. More rarely erythrocytes with blue stippling are found: these have the same significance as the polychromasic ones. **1947** *Jrnl. Lab. & Clin. Med.* XXXII. 765 The polychromatophile normoblasts likewise were identified by their nuclei..and not by the cytoplasm which was basophilic rather than polychromatophilic. **1956** E. PONDER tr. *Bessis's Cytol. Blood* ix. 246 In the normal state, the circulating blood contains an extremely small number of polychromatophil red cells... In pathological conditions.. polychromatophil red cells can appear in the blood in large numbers and their basophil material can take the form of little structures. **1973** B. A. BROWN *Hematol.* ii. 34/2 Polychromatophilia..indicates red blood cells containing RNA. They will stain a pinkish-gray to pinkish-blue color. **1974** *Exper. Parasitol.* XXXVI. 6 Early in the course of the developing anemia, many polychromatophilic erythrocytes and occasional normoblasts were found in the blood.

polychrome (ˈpɒlɪkrəʊm), *a.* and *sb.* Also 9 (as *sb.*) polychrom. [a. F. *polychrome*, ad. Gr. πολύχρωμος many-coloured, f. πολυ-, POLY- + χρῶμα colour.]

A. *adj.* **1.** Many-coloured, polychromatic; *esp.* painted, decorated, or printed in many colours. Also *fig.*

1837 *Civil Eng & Arch. Jrnl.* I. 72/2, I have already had occasion to construct a great polychrome edifice, a post-office. **1850** LEITCH tr. *C. O. Müller's Anc. Art* §414 (ed. 2) 576 The probably Lucanian vase, found in Magna Grecia, is polychrome. **1884** *Harper's Mag.* May 834/2 Old pieces of faïence and polychrome ornaments. **1898** (*title*) The Polychrome Bible. Edited by Paul Haupt. **1898** *Westm. Gaz.* 20 July 8/1 A Chantilly lace shawl,..wrought of polychrome threads like Venetian embroidery instead of being in one colour only. **1959** [see DEBUSSYAN *a.* and *sb.*]. **1962** I. MURDOCH *Unofficial Rose* vii. 75 Her polychrome being fell into an authoritative pattern which proclaimed her free.

2. *Biol.* Of a stain or dye: containing quantities of a number of derivatives which differ in colours from the parent compound; esp. in ***polychrome methylene blue***.

1895 G. W. CALE tr. P. G. Unna in *St. Louis Med. & Surg. Jrnl.* July 30 All that is necessary is to decolorize with a concentrated tannin solution the sections overstained with my polychrome-methyl-blue solution. **1896** *Ibid.* Feb. 83 This secondary effect of the polychrome methylene blue solution proves its value because it made the differential diagnosis of mast-cells (red) and plasma cells (blue) a very easy matter. **1909** *Boston Med. & Surg. Jrnl.* 7 Oct. 494/1 Widal, Abrami and Brulé recommend the use of polychrome blue of Unna 1:10. **1925** H. J. CONN *Biol. Stains* v. 47 The polychrome properties just mentioned are likely to develop in a methylene blue solution upon standing. Anyone who has had much experience with the stain is familiar with the occasional green tones from methylene green, the reddish shades of methylene azure.. and methylene violet. Such a solution is known as 'polychrome methylene blue'. **1960** E. GURR *Encycl. Microsc. Stains* 415 Wright's stain..is prepared by neutralising polychrome methylene blue with eosin. **1960** JACOBS & GERSTEIN *Handbk. Microbiol.* 248/2 *Jenner's Stain*, a polychrome stain prepared by mixing 0·5 per cent eosin in methyl alcohol with 0·5 per cent methylene blue in methyl alcohol in the ratio 5:4.

B. *sb.* **1.** A work of art executed or decorated in several colours; *spec.* a coloured statue.

1801 FUSELI in *Lect. Paint.* i. (1848) 351 The superinduction of different colours, or the invention of the polychrom. **1803** *Edin. Rev.* II. 462 We should be glad to hear no more of..polychroms. **1959** [see BICHROME *a.* and *sb.*[2]]. **1972** *Trans. Oriental Ceramics Soc.* XXXVIII. 41 It was difficult, apart from the fine Ch'êng-hua *tou-ts'ai*, to discover really good pieces of the more usual polychromes.

2. A collection or association of many colours; varied colouring. Also *fig.*

1870 C. SCHREIBER *Jrnl.* (1911) I. 101 He had procured for us..a dish with house in blue,..and a larger one with pastoral subjects in polychrome. **1882** *Macm. Mag.* Feb. 326 Having abandoned ourselves to the perfume, the polychrome,..the penetrative music of his art. **1889** GLADSTONE in *19th Cent.* XXV. 155 A side of human nature that..was also necessary for the completion of the rich polychrome exhibited by a man in whom exacting business and overwhelming care never arrested..the lively..play of the affections.

3. *Chem.* A name for ÆSCULIN, from the fluorescence of its solution and infusion.

1838 T. THOMSON *Chem. Org. Bodies* 96 [Raab's] name of *schillerstoff*..was by Martius of Erlangen translated into *bicolorin*, and by Kastner into *polychrome.* **1857** MILLER *Elem. Chem.* III. 513.

4. *Med.* A polychromatophil erythrocyte or normoblast.

1909 *Boston Med. & Surg. Jrnl.* 7 Oct. 495/1 The blood showed 6% of reticulated forms, with ·4% of polychromes. **1933** *Lancet* 3 June 1173/1 Hawes..hazarded the suggestion that the stippled cell was merely a variant of the polychrome.

polychrome (ˈpɒlɪkrəʊm), *v. Biol.* [f. prec.] To convert (a stain or dye) to a polychrome form (sense A. 2). Hence **ˈpolychroming** *vbl. sb.*

1925 H. J. CONN et al. *Biol. Stains* v. 48 Methylene blue should be partly polychromed in order to have its best staining powers. **1958** J. R. BAKER *Princ. Biol. Microtechnique* xiv. 268 It was his [*sc.* G. Giemsa's] purpose to avoid methylene blue that had been polychromed at random, and to use instead known quantities of known dyes. *Ibid.* 271 No dye that does not arise spontaneously in the polychroming of methylene blue has any special virtue in Romanowsky dyeing. **1963** M. J. LYNCH et al. *Med. Lab. Technol.* xiii. 256/1 The methylene blue is polychromed by heating with sodium bicarbonate. *Ibid.* xxxv. 630/2 The polychroming involves the oxidation of the methylene blue so that methyl groups are lost and formaldehyde gas is given off.

polychromed (ˈpɒlɪkrəʊmd), *ppl. a.* [f. prec. + -ED[1].] Rendered polychrome: chiefly *Biol.*, of stains and dyes.

1924 *Jrnl. Bacteriol.* IX. 405 The method involves pipetting about one cc. of a well polychromed, Loeffler's methylene blue over the agar slant culture and tilting the tube so that the stain comes in contact with the bacterial film. *Ibid.* 407 A polychrome methylene blue divised [*sic*] by Novy has given results surpassing in clearness those obtained by the ordinary polychromed methylene blue. **1958** J. R. BAKER *Princ. Biol. Microtechnique* xiv. 268 It is necessary to know what substances besides methylene blue itself are present in the polychromed dye. **1978** K. BONFIGLIOLI *All Tea in China* iv. 44 An incomparable saucer, polychromed, yet from the very earliest part of the Ming Dynasty.

polychromed (ˈpɒlɪkrəʊmd), *a.* [f. POLYCHROME *a.* and *sb.* + -ED[2].] = POLYCHROME *a.* 1.

1922 *19th Cent.* May 804 The polychromed wooden statue of St. Paul recalls a work in stone from the hand of Vecchietta. **1936** *Burlington Mag.* July 48/2 The low relief polychromed stucco ornament. **1947** J. C. RICH *Materials & Methods Sculpture* x. 308 The Chinese and Japanese produced a large amount of polychromed wood sculpture. **1972** K. BONFIGLIOLI *Don't point that Thing at Me* xiii. 101 A great polychromed Mexican carving of an agonized Madonna.

polychromia: see POLY-.

polychromic (pɒlɪˈkrəʊmɪk), *a.* [f. as POLYCHROME + -IC.]

1. = POLYCHROMATIC, POLYCHROME *a.*

1839 *Civil Eng. & Arch. Jrnl.* II. 367/2 Thence originated polychromic sculpture. **1859** GULLICK & TIMBS *Paint.* 310 Polychromic decoration was added to many parts of the architectural details. **1891** *Anthony's Photogr. Bull.* IV. 420 It would be impossible to so easily obtain with fat ink polychromic prints at one operation.

2. *Chem.* ***polychromic acid***: a name for aloetic acid, from the various colours it exhibits in powder, in solution, and in combination.

1863–72 WATTS *Dict. Chem.* I. 148 *Aloetic Acid... Polychromic Acid...* Produced by the action of nitric acid upon aloes, chrysammic acid being formed at the same time. .. The acid is obtained in the form of an orange-yellow powder... It..dissolves..in boiling water, forming a solution of a splendid purple colour. **1866–8** *Ibid.* IV. 687 *Polychromic* or *Polychromatic Acid*, syn. with *Aloetic Acid.*

So **ˈpolyˌchromist** (*nonce-wd.*), one who holds a theory of polychromy; one who holds that statues ought to be painted in the natural colours; **ˈpolychromize** *v. trans.*, to render polychromic, to execute in or decorate with several colours; **ˈpolyˌchromous** *a.* = POLYCHROME *a.*

1861 *Jrnl. Soc. Arts* IX. 424/1 Is the addition of coloring to statues..an advance in art, or a retrogression? The *polychromist will..hold it to be the former. **1864** *Sat. Rev.* 21 May, The unquestioning assumption of the polychromists that 'circumlitio' in this passage means 'painting'. **1881** *Eng. Mechanic* No. 874. 373/2 Any metallic piece, *polychromised by his process, is covered at once with a layer of pure copper, of fine red colour, when treated with nascent hydrogen. **1882** *Nature* 30 Nov. 119/2 He presented pieces of gold and silver jewellery, polychromised industrially with oxides of copper, by his processes. **1880** *Academy* 2 Oct. 245 Have reproduced this MS. in facsimile by their *polychromous phototype or light-printing in many colours. **1894** DU MAURIER in *Harper's Mag.* Feb. 337 A polychromous decoration not unpleasing.

polychromism (pɒlɪˈkrəʊmɪz(ə)m). [f. as POLYCHROMIC *a.*: see -ISM.]

= POLYCHROMATISM.

1903 *Amer. Naturalist* XXXVII. 295 (*heading*) Albinism, partial albinism and polychromism in hag-fishes. **1933** THORPE & LINSTEAD *Synthetic Dyestuffs* (ed. 7) viii. 72 Polychromism..is the name assigned to the phenomenon of colour variation in salts.

polychromy (ˈpɒlɪˌkrəʊmɪ). [ad. F. *polychromie*, f. as POLYCHROME: see -Y.] The art of painting or decorating in several colours, esp. as anciently used in pottery, architecture, etc.

1859 GULLICK & TIMBS *Paint.* 38 In polychromy several colours are, of course, employed. **1861** WRIGHT *Ess. Archæol.* I. ix. 193 Polychromy is observable in all the architectural subjects throughout the [Anglo-Saxon] manuscript. **1879** ROOD *Chromatics* 311 In the best polychromy great use is made of outlines or contours. **1883** *Athenæum* 30 June 834/3 An Egyptian bas-relief in red granite, with traces of polychromy.

‖**polyˈchronicon.** *Obs.* [med.L., f. Gr. πολυ-, POLY- + χρονικόν (neut. sing. of χρονικός adj. concerning time), in pl. (sc. βιβλία books) annals, chronicles.] A chronicle of many events or periods.

[*a* **1363** HIGDEN (*title*) Polychronicon.] **1570** FOXE *A. & M.* (ed. 2) 124/2 In whyche persecution our stories and Polichronicon do recorde, that all Christianitie almost in the whole Ilelande was destroyed. **1815** W. H. IRELAND (*title*) Scribbleomania; or, the printer's devil's polichronicon.

polycie, obs. form of POLICY.

polycistronic(ally: see POLY-.

polyclad (ˈpɒlɪklæd), *a.* and *sb. Zool.* [ad. mod.L. name of suborder *Polycladidea* (A. Lang 1884, in *Fauna und Flora des Golfes von Neapel* XI. 1), f. POLY- + Gr. κλάδος branch.] **a.** *adj.* Belonging to the division *Polycladida* of turbellarian worms, having a main intestine with more than four branches. **b.** *sb.* A worm of this division. (Distinguished from TRICLAD.).

1888 ROLLESTON & JACKSON *Anim. Life* 578 A more or less apparent radial symmetry is observable in some Polyclad *Turbellaria*. *Ibid.* 672 Two curious Polyclads have..been described with certain Ctenophore-like characters. **1896** F. W. GAMBLE in *Cambr. Nat. Hist.* II. i. 16 The Polyclads were so called by Lang on account of the numerous primary branches of their intestine. They are free-living, purely marine Platyhelminthes. **1918** *Proc. Nat. Acad. Sci.* IV. 381 Muscular creeping operations are probably general among polyclads. **1941** J. STEINBECK *Sea of Cortez* xi. 111 Beautiful purple polyclad worms crawled over lawns of purple tunicates. **1975** *Nature* 28 Aug. 737/1 Polyclads have limited powers of regeneration. *Ibid.* 11 Dec. 518/1 We..found them [*sc.* reddish-brown streaks in the sea] to consist of high densities of the dinoflagellate *Noctiluca* and of a polyclad turbellarian.

polycladose (ˈpɒlɪklədəʊs), *a.* [f. as next + -OSE.] Many-branched: said of a sponge spicule.

1887 SOLLAS in *Encycl. Brit.* XXII. 417/1 *Candelabra* (a polycladose microcalthrops).

polycladous (pəˈlɪklədəs), *a. Bot.* [f. Gr. πολύκλαδος having many branches + -OUS.] Having many, or more than the normal number of, branches; much or excessively branched. So **polyclady** (pəˈlɪklədɪ), the formation of an abnormal number of branches.

[**1866** *Treas. Bot.* 913 *Polycladia*, the same as *Plica*.] **1886** *Cassell's Encycl. Dict.*, Polyclady. **1890** *Cent. Dict.*, Polycladous.

polyclimax (pɒlɪˈklaɪmæks). *Ecol.* [f. POLY- + CLIMAX *sb.*] The presence of several distinct stable communities of plants within a given region. Usu. *attrib.*

1934 *Empire Forestry Jrnl.* XIII. 21 An appreciation of some, at least, of these truths, has led many ecologists to adopt a poly-climax theory as a working hypothesis. **1953** *Ecol. Monogr.* XXIII. 43/1 A significant difference in climax interpretation has..been described in the monoclimax and polyclimax theories. **1960** N. POLUNIN *Introd. Plant Geogr.* xi. 331 It seems best to admit the likelihood, in any one region, of several different climax communities as representing what may then be termed a 'polyclimax'. **1973** P. A. COLINVAUX *Introd. Ecol.* xl. 551 Whether you believed in the monoclimax required by dogmatic interpretations of Clements' writings, or whether you took the pragmatic view that there could be many local climaxes in any clima[c]tic region (so-called polyclimax theory) you tacitly assumed that succession was a process of social organization; that it led to an organized entity which you called a society.

polyclinic (pɒlɪˈklɪnɪk). [app. an alteration of the earlier word *policlinic*, in which it is referred to the Greek πολυ- (see POLY-), and used in a different sense.]

1. a. 'A general clinic devoted to the treatment of various diseases' (*Syd. Soc. Lex.*); (*a*) 'an institution furnishing clinical instruction in all kinds of diseases'; (*b*) 'a hospital in which all forms of disease are treated'. **b.** In mod. use, a clinic not attached to a hospital where specialists in various branches of medicine are available to outpatients.

1890 *Cent. Dict.*, *Policlinic*..sometimes written *polyclinic*. A general city hospital or dispensary. **1963** *Spectator* 11 Oct. 446 Other nations whose medical services are based primarily on the hospital or the polyclinic are beginning to see the virtues of a personal doctor. **1967** *Guardian* 15 July 10/3 These doctors [in the U.S.S.R.] work from *polyclinics* which are a combination of general practice, as we know it, and hospital out-patient departments. **1973** *Times Lit. Suppl.* 3 Aug. 896/2 The Soviet Union..has based its system on the use of the polyclinic, with its specialist staff. Here there is no 'physician of primary contact' or general practitioner service as we know it. **1975** J. DE BRES tr. *Mandel's Late Capitalism* xii. 385 [In the age of late capitalism] the independent general medical practitioner is replaced by a polyclinic with affiliated specialists. **1976** *Times Lit. Suppl.* 7 May 555/2 Cuba is perhaps nearest to ordinary Western experience... Much is made of the rate of increase of district hospitals, polyclinics and local health centres.

2. (See quot. 1900.)

1898 *Times* 16 Dec. 9/5 Mr. Hutchinson's 'Polyclinic', a title which, whatever it has 'come to denote', seems an odd one to apply to an institution which will have 'no beds of its own'. **1900** J. HUTCHINSON in *Westm. Gaz.* 3 Feb. 3/2 The 'Medical Graduates College and Polyclinic' is an association for giving gratuitous consultations to patients, and at the same time affording opportunities to medical men for obtaining advanced knowledge. The word *Polyclinic* implies that we have made arrangements to include many (or all) branches of practical medicine and surgery. **1903** *Daily Chron.* 16 May 7/2 A distinguished professional company assembled at the Polyclinic yesterday to hear Mr. Jonathan Hutchinson's account of his tour in India and Ceylon.

polyclonal(ity to **polycœlian**: see POLY-.

†**polyˈcœrany, -chœrany.** *Obs. rare.* Also 7 -coyranie, -coiranie. [ad. Gr. (Ionic) πολυκοιρανίη,

f. πολυ-, POLY- + κοίρανος ruler, prince.] A government by many rulers or princes.
1640 BP. HALL *Episc.* III. vi. 34 What doe you think of this lawlesse Polycoyranie? **1678** CUDWORTH *Intell. Syst.* I. iv. 411 The Government of the World would be a Polychœrany or Aristocracy of Gods.

ˌpolycondenˈsation. *Chem.* Also poly-condensation. [ad. G. *polykondensation* (H. Staudinger *Hochmolekularen Verbindungen* (1932) II. 255): see POLY- and CONDENSATION.] A condensation reaction between molecules each having at least two functional groups which yields a polymer, or a process based on such a reaction. Freq. *attrib.*
1936 *Trans. Faraday Soc.* XXXII. 52 The formation of high polymeric products can also take place by a polycondensation process in which numerous reactive molecules condense. **1949** *Jrnl. Textile Inst.* XL. A307 Polycondensation products, such as phenolic plastics, phenolacetylene resins, urea-formaldehyde resins, linear and branched polyesters, and super polyamides. **1962** *Times* 26 Feb. (Canada Suppl.) p. vii/2 (Advt.), Complete chemical plant and equipment including plant for thermosetting and thermoplastic polymers and synthetic fibres from polymers and polycondensation products. **1963** A. J. HALL *Textile Sci.* ii. 79 It [*sc.* nylon] is made by the melt-spinning of polyhexamethylene adipamide which in its turn is produced by the polycondensation of equimolecular proportions of adipic acid.. and hexamethylene diamine. **1971** *Jrnl. Oil & Colour Chemists' Assoc.* LIV. 888 The volatile components (solvents, monomers and low molecular weight poly condensation products) evaporate almost completely from the liquid paint during the process of film formation. **1978** *Nature* 29 June 738/2 Polymers of related structures have long been known, however, prepared by polycondensation of alkali metal polysulphides and *α, ω*-dihaloalkanes.
Hence (as back-formations) **polyconˈdense** *v. trans.*, to cause to undergo polycondensation; **polyconˈdensed** *ppl. a.* Also **polyˈcondensate** [after *filtrate*, *precipitate*, etc.], a product or preparation resulting from polycondensation.
1942 *Jrnl. Amer. Chem. Soc.* LXIV. 2269/2 The results.. show that the poly-condensates are built up quantitatively from alanine units linked by –CONH– bonds. **1967** *Immunochem.* IV. 77 (*heading*) Sensitization of erythrocytes by polycondensed proteins of immune serum and their use for determining antigen content. **1968** J. CHAMBION in H. F. Mark et al. *Chem. Man-Made Fibers* II. 448 For higher homologs of polyamide 6, the corresponding monomer amino acid can be polycondensed. **1971** B. BUCK tr. *Ludewig's Polyester Fibres* iv. 90 The whole process from dissolution to extrusion can be carried out in one single apparatus in which the dimethyl terephthalate is dissolved in glycol, transesterified, and polycondensed. *Ibid.* 125 Moisture promotes degradation of the polyester melt in the further processing of the polycondensate. **1976** *Nature* 6 May 76/3 Structures.. much more easily oxidisable than polycondensed aromatics.

polyconic (pɒlɪˈkɒnɪk), *a.* [f. POLY- + CONIC.] Involving or based upon a number of cones; applied to a system of map-projection in which each parallel of latitude is represented by the development of a cone touching the earth's surface along that parallel. Also *sb.* a polyconic projection.
1864 in WEBSTER. **1879** A. R. CLARKE in *Encycl. Brit.* X. 209/1 Polyconic Development. [See description.] **1901** C. F. CLOSE *Map Projections* 31 Simple polyconic projection... The employment of polyconics saves much tabulation, and they are well suited for a topographical series. They are not so well adapted for single maps of large areas. *Ibid.* 32 Rectangular polyconic projection, sometimes called the *rectangular tangential*.

polycormic, poly-cotton: see POLY-.

polycotyledon (ˌpɒlɪkɒtɪˈliːdən). *Bot.* [f. mod.L. *Polycotylēdonēs* (pl.): cf. DICOTYLEDON.] A plant of which the seed contains more than two cotyledons. So **ˌpolycotyˈledonary, ˌpolycotyˈledonous** *adjs.*, having more than two cotyledons in the seed, as many Gymnosperms; **ˌpolycotyˈledony**, the condition of being polycotyledonous.
[**1760** J. LEE *Introd. Bot.* III. xi. (1765) 199 *Polycotyledones*, with many Cotyledones.] **1813** SIR H. DAVY *Agric. Chem.* iii. (1814) 70 These plants are called polycotyledonous. **1828** WEBSTER, *Polycotyledon*. **1880** GRAY *Struct. Bot.* ii. (ed. 6) 23 The Polycotyledonous Embryo is one having a whorl of more than two seed-leaves.

polycracy: see POLY-.

polycrase (ˈpɒlɪkreɪs). *Min.* [ad. G. *polykras*; named by Scheerer, 1844, f. Gr. πολυ-, POLY- + κρᾶσις mixture, from its many constituents.] A shining black mineral, consisting of columbate and titanate of uranium, zirconium, yttrium, and other bases.
1845 *Amer. Jrnl. Sc.* XLIX. 394 Polycrase is near polymignite. **1892** DANA *Min.* (ed. 6) 745 Scandium is prominent in the sprectrum of the American polycrase.

polycratism to **polycrotic:** see POLY-.

polycrystal (ˈpɒlɪkrɪstəl). [f. POLY- + CRYSTAL *sb.* and *a.*] A polycrystalline body. Also *attrib.*, = next.
1925 *Physical Rev.* XXV. 248 The crystal was then hammered and swaged to change it into polycrystal copper. **1932** *Proc. R. Soc.* A. CXXXVIII. 358 The complete change [in density] from single crystal to polycrystal.. is.. of the order of 1 in 3000 for, *e.g.*, iron, nickel and aluminium. **1966** C. R. TOTTLE *Sci. Engin. Materials* iv. 93 More than one nucleus inevitably gives rise to a polycrystal, where several points of growth lead to crystallites of different crystallographic orientation. *Ibid.* vi. 136 A polycrystal of iron is not always magnetized.

polycrystalline (pɒlɪˈkrɪstəlaɪn), *a.* [f. POLY- + CRYSTALLINE *a.* and *sb.*] Composed of many crystals or crystallites; having a crystalline structure in which there is a random variation in the orientation of different parts.
1925 *Proc. R. Soc.* A. CIX. 144 The figures for single crystals are higher than for the polycrystalline test piece. **1932** *Ibid.* CXXXVIII. 364 A polycrystalline wire can be considered as an assemblage of crystallites in which the axes of crystal symmetry are oriented at random. **1950** *Sci. News* XV. 61 Distorted lattice planes will not slide over one another easily and hence polycrystalline metals are often hard. **1959** *Times Rev. Industry* Mar. 32/3 Fine grinding stone.. consisting of a sintered polycrystalline ruby material. **1970** *Sci. Jrnl.* Feb. 46/1 Bulk metals are polycrystalline and the grains are randomly oriented.
Hence **ˌpolycrystaˈllinity**, polycrystalline condition or structure.
1955 *Rep. Progress Physics* XVIII. 233 Research on these materials has been impeded by the anomalous effects of polycrystallinity. **1978** *Nature* 19 Oct. 634/1 There was evidence of polycrystallinity with definite, but usually very weak, X-ray lines assignable to diamond.

polyculture (ˈpɒlɪkʌltjʊə(r)). [irreg. f. POLY- + CULTURE *sb.* Cf. MONOCULTURE.] **a.** The simultaneous cultivation or exploitation of several crops or animals. **b.** An area in which this is practised. Opp. MONOCULTURE. Hence **polyˈcultural** *a.*
1915 C. R. ENOCK *Tropics* xl. 439 It is not to 'monoculture' but to 'polyculture'—that is, to varied production as contrasted with single products—that any community must look for its economic and social security. The peculiar conditions of the tropics must always of necessity call for a considerable exercise of monoculture.. but it must be balanced by equitable regard for the native producer and the exercise to the utmost possible extent of polycultural principles, whereby a supply of all products and all articles necessary for life are producible locally. **1967** *Geo. Abstr.* D. 15 Much of the area has a polyculture of nuts, fruits and vines. **1973** *Country Life* 21 June 1818/3 The polycultural tradition in Italy may be seen from the fact that Frescobaldi [*sc.* a wine producer] have considerable tree plantations and 70,000 olive trees. **1974** *Oryx* XII. 358 A polyculture of wild ungulates can be likened to a sophisticated system of crop rotation at a secondary level.

polycyclic (pɒlɪˈsaɪklɪk), *a.* [f. POLY- + CYCLIC *a.*] †**1.** *Math.* (See quots.) *Obs.*
1869 W. THOMSON in *Trans. R. Soc. Edin.* XXV. 253 When the function is cyclic with reference to several different mutually irreconcilable circuits, it is called polycyclic. *Ibid.*, Irrotational motion may be either acyclic or cyclic. If cyclic it is monocyclic if there is only one distinct circuit, or polycyclic if there are several distinct circuits, in which there is circulation. **1888** A. B. BASSET *Treat. Hydrodynamics* I. iv. 74 If ϕ be a polycyclic velocity potential, the circulation round any closed curve, which does not cut any of the barriers is.. zero. *Ibid.* 75 Every polycyclic function may be expressed as the sum of.. monocyclic functions.
2. [Gr. κύκλος circle.] Having or consisting of many rounds, turns, or whorls.
1890 *Cent. Dict.*, *Polycyclic*. **1899** *Allbutt's Syst. Med.* VIII. 553 A curved figure, having a polycyclic outline.
3. *Chem.* Having more than one ring of atoms in the molecule. Also as *sb.*, a polycyclic compound.
1903 *Chem. News* 13 Mar. 130/2 (*heading*) A method for the synthesis of polycyclic hydrocarbides. **1909** C. A. KEANE *Mod. Org. Chem.* xv. 414 The most important of these polycyclic substances are built up of benzene rings. **1943** *Endeavour* Jan. 32/2 Carcinogenic potency is by no means confined to polycyclic compounds. **1968** I. L. FINAR *Org. Chem.* (ed. 4) II. xi. 462 This is only possible if rings B and C are fused together in a *trans* manner (*cf.* polycyclics, §11 d. IV). **1971** *Daily Tel.* (Colour Suppl.) 28 May 27/2 Other potential dangers in exhaust fumes are polycyclic hydrocarbons—which can cause cancer in laboratory animals. **1976** *Nature* 9 Sept. 93/1 Binding of carcinogenic polycyclics to DNA.. has been well established.
4. *Electr. Engin.* Involving the simultaneous transmission along a conductor of currents of different frequencies and voltages.
1903 *Jrnl. Inst. Electr. Engin.* XXXII. 751 The advantages of low frequency for power work and of high frequency for lighting are combined in this polycyclic system. **1906** A. RUSSELL *Treat. Theory Alternating Currents* II. xvii. 478 (*heading*) Three phase polycyclic system of distribution. **1913** S. P. SMITH tr. *La Cour & Bragstad's Theory & Calculation Electr. Currents* xvi. 289 The object of the polycyclic system.. is to simultaneously transmit electrical energy by means of currents at different pressures and frequencies through one and the same conductor, and to distribute the same without their affecting one another.
5. *Geol.* [ad. F. *polycyclique* (E. Argand 1922, in *Compt. Rend. XIII Session, Congrès Géol. Internat.* (1924) I. 365).] Produced by or having undergone many cycles, esp. of erosion and deposition. Cf. *multicyclic* adj. s.v. MULTI- 1 a.
1935 H. BAULIG *Changing Sea Level* ii. 13 (*caption*) Block-diagram of a polycyclic valley. **1947** *Trans. R. Geol. Soc. Cornwall* XVII. 341 Polycyclic forms in the valleys still witness the later Pliocene stillstands despite intense peri-glacial solifluction. **1958** [see MORPHOMETRY]. **1968** R. W. FAIRBRIDGE *Encycl. Geomorphol.* 554/2 A lateritic crust.. reflects a polycyclic regime, usually as a result of repeated alternation of hot, humid conditions.. with dry, evaporating conditions. **1975** *Nature* 13 Feb. 502/3 Such sediments may incorporate.. duplicated or polycyclic layers.
6. *Biol.* Producing several generations during a year by sexual reproduction.
1957 *New Biol.* XXIII. 58 These polycyclic populations are found in complex environments like ponds where there are successive outbursts of different planktonic algae which cause fluctuations in the amount of food available. **1965** J. JOHNSTON tr. *Danilevskii's Photoperiodism & Seasonal Devel. Insects* vii. 194 They are all potentially polycyclic, and in southern provinces may have several generations a year. **1970** *Amer. Naturalist* CIV. 398 In most polycyclic insects of the temperate zone, long days cause continuous development, while short days cause diapause.

polycystic (pɒlɪˈsɪstɪk), *a.* *Path.* [f. POLY- + CYSTIC.] Having or consisting of several cysts, as a tumour.
1872 PEASLEE *Ovar. Tumors* 30 The tendency to become monocystic or to remain polycystic. **1872** T. G. THOMAS *Dis. Women* (ed. 3) 665 The monocyst.. develops the power of cysto-genesis and becomes polycystic.

polycystid (pɒlɪˈsɪstɪd). *Zool.* [f. mod.L. *Polycystid-ea* (neut. pl.), as POLYCYSTINE: see -ID.] A member of the order *Polycystidea* of Gregarines, having the body divided into three (rarely two) segments.
1888 ROLLESTON & JACKSON *Anim. Life* 858 A Polycystid possessing all three segments is known as a Cephalin or Cephalont. *Ibid.* 859 The Polycystids lose the epimerite wholly or in part.

polyˈcystidan, *a.* (*sb.*) *Zool.* [f. as prec., or (in b.) from mod.L. *Polycystida* + -AN.]
a. Belonging to the *Polycystidea*; as *sb.* one of these: see prec. **b.** Belonging to the *Polycystida*, a family of *Polycystina*; as *sb.* one of these: see next.

polycystine (pɒlɪˈsɪstaɪn), *a.* and *sb.* *Zool.* [f. mod.L., *Polycystina* (neut. pl.), f. Gr. πολυ-, POLY- + κύστις bladder, CYST: see -INE[2].] **a.** *adj.* Belonging to the *Polycystina*, a group of Radiolarians (also called *Nassellaria*), characterized by a fenestrated siliceous shell or skeleton divided into several chambers. **b.** *sb.* A radiolarian of this group.
1862 WALLICH *N. Atlantic Sea-bed* 127 The Barbadoes and other Polycystine earths have a calcareous basis derived from the same source.. as the pure calcareous deposits of the deep-sea bed. **1862** MRS. BURY (*title*) Figures of Remarkable Forms of Polycystins, or allied Organisms, in the Barbados Chalk Deposit. **1883** H. DRUMMOND *Nat. Law in Spir. W.* (ed. 2) 371 If the Polycystine urn be broken, no inorganic agency can build it up again.

polycythæmia, -ic: see POLY-.

polycyttarian (ˌpɒlɪsɪˈtɛərɪən), *a.* and *sb.* *Zool.* [f. mod.L. *Polycyttari-a* neut. pl. (f. Gr. πολυ-, POLY- + κύτταρος cell) + -AN.] **a.** *adj.* Belonging to the group *Polycyttaria* of Radiolarians, comprising compound or 'colonial' forms with several central capsules; pluricapsular. **b.** *sb.* A member of this group.

polydactyl (pɒlɪˈdæktɪl), *a.* (*sb.*) Also -yle. [a. F. *polydactyle*, ad. Gr. πολυδάκτυλος many-toed; see POLY- and DACTYL.] Having more than the normal number of fingers or toes. **b.** *sb.* A polydactyl animal. So **polyˈdactylism** [so F. *-isme*], **polyˈdactyly**, the condition of being polydactyl; **polyˈdactylous** *a.* = *polydactyl* adj.
1894 BATESON *Variation* 324 Some normal cats belonging to this family gave birth to *polydactyle kittens. **1865** *Pall Mall G.* 19 Aug. 9/2 You will entail on your grand-children sterility, *polydactylism, and all sorts of physical and moral imperfections. **1868** DARWIN *Anim. & Pl.* II. xii. 12 Polydactylism graduates by multifarious steps from a mere cutaneous appendage, to a double band. **1858** MAYNE *Exp. Lex.*, *Polydactylous. **1899** *Q. Rev.* Oct. 412 Cæsar's favourite horse was polydactylous, and so was Alexander's Bucephalus. **1886** J. B. SUTTON in *Proc. Zool. Soc.* 552 The majority of cases of *polydactyly occurring in Horses.

polydæmonism, -demonism (pɒlɪˈdiːmən ɪz(ə)m). [f. Gr. πολυ-, POLY- + δαίμον divinity, demon + -ISM, after *polytheism*.] A belief in many divinities (i.e. simply, supernatural powers, or *spec.* evil spirits: see DEMON[1] 1, 2). So **polydæmoˈnistic (-de-)** *a.*, pertaining to or characterized by polydemonism.
1711 SHAFTESB. *Charac.* (1737) II. 13 All these sorts both of dæmonism, polytheism, atheism, and theism, may be mix'd..; which opinion may be call'd polydæmonism. **1877** J. E. CARPENTER tr. *Tiele's Hist. Relig.* 5 The polydæmonistic magic tribal religions of the present day. *Ibid.* 10 An unorganized polydæmonism, which does not, how-ever, exclude the belief in a supreme Spirit. **1881** MONIER WILLIAMS in *19th Cent.* Mar. 505 Hindūism

developed into an all-comprehensive corrupt system which may be described as a loose conglomerate of pantheism, dualism, polytheism, and polydemonism held in cohesion by an alleged monotheism. *Ibid.*, A combination of dualism with polytheistic and polydemonistic ideas.

polydentate: see POLY-.

polyde(s)oxyribo-: see s.v. POLYRIBO-.

polydiabolical to **polydimensional:** see POLY-.

‖**polydipsia** (pɒlɪˈdɪpsɪə). *Path.* (In 7 anglicized as poludipsie.) [a. Gr. type *πολυδιψία: cf. πολυδίψιος very thirsty, πολύδιψος causing excessive thirst. So F. *polydipsie.*] Morbidly or abnormally excessive thirst. In quot. 1660 *fig.*

1660 HICKERINGILL *Jamaica* (1661) 40 Such is some mens prophane Bouhmy and insatiable Poludipsie after Gold. **1795** *Gentl. Mag.* LXV. II. 926/1 About the time this case was first published a case of Polydipsia occurred in this country. **1846** G. E. DAY tr. *Simon's Anim. Chem.* II. 305 Hydruria, which is also known as diuresis, polyuresis, and polydipsia, seems to be capable of continuing sometimes for several years without.. any other morbid symptoms than a frequent desire to micturate, and an insatiable thirst.

polydisperse (pɒlɪdɪˈspɜːs), *a.* [ad. G. *polydispers* (W. O. Ostwald *Grundriss d. Kolloidchem.* (ed. 2, 1911) i. 39), f. *poly-* POLY- + *dispers* disperse (cf. DISPERSE *v.* 9).] Existing in the form of or containing colloidal particles (which may be macromolecules) having a range of sizes; applied esp. to macromolecular substances in which there is a simple distribution of particle size (or occas. some other specified physical property) with one peak; also applied to such a property or its distribution. Also **polydiˈspersed** *a.* Cf. POLYMOLECULAR *a.* d.

1915 M. H. FISCHER tr. *Ostwald's Handbk. Colloid-Chem.* i. 35 These systems in which the disperse phase is composed of particles having different degrees of dispersion may be called polydisperse systems. **1938** *Nature* 4 June 1001/2 The specific polysaccharide of type I pneumococcus is polydisperse with an average weight of approximately 225,000. **1941** *Jrnl. Franklin Inst.* CCXXXI. 1 Fine powders and colloidally dispersed material are also typically polydispersed. **1948** *Chem. Abstr.* XLII. 1787 (*heading*) Birefringence of flow in polydispersed mixtures. **1962** H. BLOEMENDAL et al. in A. Pirie *Lens Metabolism Rel. Cataract* 303 Prolonged dialysis of 7 M urea-treated α-crystallin against 1·25 M urea results in the appearance of a polydisperse peak with sedimentation coefficient of 10 S. **1963** *Nature* 16 Nov. 665/2 A preparation may be monodisperse with respect to one parameter, polydisperse with respect to a second and heterogeneous with respect to a third; the foregoing terms are only meaningful if the parameter measured is.. specified. **1968** H. HARRIS *Nucleus & Cytoplasm* iii. 56 Preparations of the total RNA in the cell cytoplasm.. did not show any fraction which had either the kinetic characteristics or the polydisperse sedimentation of the rapidly labelled nuclear RNA. **1973** *Sci. Amer.* June 112/1 With a calibrated grid in the viewing field of the microscope one can measure the relative sizes of the particles in a polydisperse suspension (a suspension containing particles of widely varying size).

Hence **polydiˈspersity**, the condition or property of being polydisperse.

1927 H. S. VAN KLOOSTER tr. *Kruyt's Colloids* x. 154 Viewed in the ultramicroscope, this sol presents a very colorful picture which reveals the poly-dispersity very plainly. **1936** *Trans. Faraday Soc.* XXXII. 49 It appears that determinations of polydispersity by measurement of sedimentation velocity can only be effected in extremely dilute solutions. **1963** *Nature* 16 Nov. 665/2 Some degree of random variability in secondary or tertiary structure may confer polydispersity with respect to frictional coefficient on some proteins. **1967** MARGERISON & EAST *Introd. Polymer Chem.* ii. 47 The value of the parameter $\bar{M}_w/\bar{M}_n$ in a practical case thus gives a measure of the range of molecular weights in the sample;.. a value of two or greater indicates considerable polydispersity. **1976** [see POLYMOLECULARITY].

polydromic (pɒlɪˈdrɒmɪk), *a. Math.* [f. POLY- + Gr. δρόμος course + -IC: cf. δρομικός good at the course.] = POLYTROPIC 2. (Opp. to *monodromic.*)

1890 in *Cent. Dict.*

polydymite (pəˈlɪdɪmaɪt). *Min.* [Contr. for **polydidymite*; named by Laspeyres, 1876, f. Gr. πολυ-, POLY- + δίδυμος twin.] Sulphide of nickel, of a light grey colour, with metallic lustre, occurring in polysynthetic twin crystals.

1878 *Min. Mag.* II. 98 Polydymite.. occurs in macled octahedrons. **1892** DANA *Min.* (ed. 6) 75 A nickel ore from Sudbury.. corresponds to.. the general formula of polydymite.

polydynamic (ˌpɒlɪdaɪˈnæmɪk, -dɪn-), *a.* [f. POLY- + Gr. δύναμις power + -IC: cf. *dynamic.*] Relating to or possessing many forces or powers.

1828 E. HENDERSON in *Congregational Mag.* Jan. 31/2 The Cocceian, or polydunamic hypothesis, according to which, the Hebrew words are to be interpreted in every way consistent with their etymological import, or, as it has been expressed, in every sense of which they are capable. **1872** THUDICHUM *Chem. Phys.* 18 It is a polydynamic alcohol capable of forming ethers analogous to fats.

polye, obs. form of PULLEY.

polyedral, etc.: see POLYHEDRAL, etc.

polyeidism: see POLY-.

polyelectrolyte (pɒlɪɪˈlɛktrəlaɪt). *Chem.* [f. POLY- + ELECTROLYTE.] A substance which consists of large, usu. polymeric molecules containing several ionizable groups.

1947 *Jrnl. Polymer Sci.* II. 12 By using salts of quaternary nitrogen compounds, polyelectrolytes can be made which are soluble in organic solvents. **1959** *Times* 3 Dec. 9/4 There are water softeners using poly-electrolyte membranes with an output of 50 cubic feet an hour. **1964** *Biophysical Jrnl.* IV. 1. Suppl. 10 Many important plant products such as the pectic acids of fruit jellies and alginic acid of seaweed are typical polyelectrolytes. **1968** *New Scientist* 26 Dec. 703/3 Pure poly-electrolytes also promise to be valuable additives in many foodstuffs and beverages. **1973** *Nature* 2 Nov. 34/1 Polyelectrolytes are increasingly being used as flocculants for electrostatically stabilised dispersions of colloidal particles.

Hence ˌ**polyelectroˈlytic** *a.*

1948 *Science* 19 Nov. 548/2 We are thus led to the assumption that the high viscosity of polyelectrolytic solutions and its concentration dependence are due to the presence of the high charge density at the polyions. **1958** *New Scientist* 29 May 75/1 Some of the defence mechanisms of the living body are polyelectrolytic in nature.

polyembryonate (pɒlɪˈɛmbrɪənət), *a. Bot.* [f. POLY- + EMBRYON + -ATE¹.] Containing more than one embryo, as a seed. So **polyembryˈonic** *a.* = prec.; also, pertaining to polyembryony. **polyˈembryony**, the formation or presence of more than one embryo in a seed; also *Zool.*, the development of more than one embryo from a single egg.

1849 BALFOUR *Man. Bot.* §509 Cases of polyembryony in Coniferæ, Cycadaceæ, Mistletoe, Onion, &c. *Ibid.* §586 In Coniferæ, Cycadaceæ, Mistleto, &c., there are frequently several embryos, giving rise to what is called polyembryony. **1864** WEBSTER, *Polyembryonate.. Polyembryonic.* **1906** *Science* 21 Dec. 813/2 Polyembryony [in *Encyrtus* eggs] reaches its greatest intensity.. when the young larvæ of the *Hyponomeuta* leave their winter shelter. **1912** *Anatomischer Anzeiger* XLI. 369 (*heading*) The demonstration of polyembryonic development in the armadillo. **1925** A. D. IMMS *Gen. Textbk. Entomol.* I. 154 Polyembryony is met with among insects in certain parasitic families of Hymenoptera. **1947** *Arch. Path.* XLIV. 501 There has been much speculation concerning the cause of polyembryony (monozygotic multiple birth) as it occurs regularly in the armadillo. **1956** *Nature* 28 Jan. 191/1 An examination of the seeds of different species of *Cassia*.. has shown the occurrence of polyembryony to be geographically widespread. **1969** R. F. CHAPMAN *Insects* xix. 377 The effect of polyembryony is to increase the reproductive potential of the insect, but the net effect is not always much greater than in related monoembryonic species because polyembryonic forms tend to lay fewer eggs.

polyendocrine to **polyergic:** see POLY-.

Polyergus (pɒlɪˈɜːgəs). *Ent.* Also **polyergus.** [mod.L. (P. A. Latreille 1804, in *Nouveau Dict. Hist. Nat.* XXIV. 179), f. Gr. πολύεργος hard-working.] A slave-making ant of the genus so called, found in Europe and North America; = AMAZON-ANT.

1882 J. LUBBOCK *Ants, Bees, & Wasps* vii. 180, I presented a slave of *Polyergus* with a dead fly pinned down. **1908** *Westm. Gaz.* 21 Jan. 2/1 The polyergus seems to lose even the faculty of making a nest. **1924** J. A. THOMSON *Sci. Old & New* xiii. 72 Slave-keeping is much more marked among the Amazon Ants, of which the European Polyergus is a good representative. **1945** C. P. HASKINS *Of Ants & Men* ix. 175 Not only is *Polyergus* little interested in its nesting site, but it is compelled to abandon it and to move about at frequent intervals. **1954** BORROR & DELONG *Introd. Study Insects* 729 The *Polyergus* ants are often called amazons.

polyester (pɒlɪˈɛstə(r)). [f. POLY- + ESTER.] Any polymer in which the units are joined by the ester linkage, $-CO{\cdot}O-$; also (*a*) (more fully *polyester fibre*), a man-made fibre consisting of a polyester; (*b*) (more fully *polyester resin*), any of numerous synthetic resins or plastics consisting of or made from a polyester, different kinds of which are used as fibres or films, in paint, and as moulding materials or reinforced plastics. Freq. *attrib.*

1929 [see POLYAMIDE]. **1935** C. ELLIS *Chem. Synthetic Resins* II. l. 1002 Strong, oriented fibers were obtained from polyesters of molecular weights greater than 9330. **1952** *Jrnl. R. Aeronaut. Soc.* LVI. 707 Working with glass fibres, the Americans have used the polyester or 'contact resins' almost exclusively. **1955** *Times* 4 May 21/3 Production items based on polyester resins and glass fibres.. include panels and bodies for the transport and aircraft industries, mouldings for boat hulls, [etc.]. **1958** *Times Rev. Industry* Feb. 77/1 The advent of resins of the polyester and epoxide types.. meant that laminates could be produced without the application of high pressures. **1958** *Engineering* 7 Mar. 311/1 Cellulose-acetate and, more recently, polyester are used at present for data-recording tape bases. **1958** *Manch. Guardian* 25 Sept. 1/3 Polyester fibre was discovered in 1941 by Mr. J. R. Whinfield and Dr. J. T. Dickson in the laboratories of the Calico Printers' Association. **1964** *Which?* Aug. 253/3 Fabrics made from polyester tend to attract dirt but can be easily washed. **1968** J. IRONSIDE *Fashion Alphabet* 210 Polyester fibres have very similar properties to the polyamides but they are perhaps even more durable. **1969** L. S. MOUNTS in W. R. R. Park *Plastics Film Technol.* v. 135 Polyester films have great strength and good aging characteristics. **1973** *Materials & Technol.* VI. viii. 568 The polyesters are usually marketed dissolved in the cross-linking monomer in the form of a syrup, to which inhibitors are added. **1975** *Guardian* 27 Jan. 16/3 Today the accent is on.. blends of a polyester fibre with cotton or polynosic rayon. **1977** *R.A.F. News* 22 June–5 July 2 (Advt.), 'Tootal' Polyester/Cotton Wedgwood Blue Shirts.

Hence ˌ**polyesteˈramide**, any polymer which contains both ester and amide linkages, esp. any of various rubbery materials of this type which are usu. made by mixed condensation reactions and can be drawn into fibres; ˌ**polyesterifiˈcation**, a reaction or process which yields a polyester.

1932 *Jrnl. Amer. Chem. Soc.* LIV. 1560 The polyesterification thus consists in a series of intermolecular couplings resulting in the formation of progressively longer chains. **1943** H. FOSTER *U.S. Pat. 2,333,922* 1/1 The above objects are accomplished through the production of electrically insulated conductors in which the insulation is a polyester-amide which has been treated with polyisocyanate. **1950** *Thorpe's Dict. Appl. Chem.* (ed. 4) X. 45/2 Among the second class of amide interpolymers are the polyesteramides. These are made by condensing together di-reactive amide-forming and ester-forming components, or more specifically by condensing di-reactive components containing carboxy groups in proportions equivalent to the sum of the amine and hydroxyl groups. **1958** *Technology* Mar. 12/3 Not long after Carothers' pioneering work, J. R. Whinfield took up the study of similar polyesterification processes, the main idea being to use starting materials which might give some sense of rigidity to the high-polymer substances made by these reactions. **1974** K. F. HEINISCH *Dict. Rubber* 508/2 The production of the polyesteramide is performed without a deficiency of dicarboxylic acid, as for Vulcolan. **1976** *Nature* 24 June 658/2 This demonstrated that ester interchange reactions were slow compared with polyesterification in the conditions used to make commercial alkyd resins.

polyethenoid: see POLY-.

polyether (pɒlɪˈiːθə(r)). [f. POLY- + ETHER.] Any of a variety of polymers in which the repeating unit contains an ether linkage, $C-O-C$, many of which are used commercially, esp. as plastic foams and epoxy resins. So ***polyether foam.***

1922 *Chem. Abstr.* XVI. 1741 (*heading*) Polyethers of trimethyleneglycol. **1962** *Listener* 8 Mar. 451/1 The less expensive polyether foam is edging its way in. **1966** [see EPOXY]. **1968** *Times* 28 Mar. 9 All three versions are available in either Burma teak, or prime beech and are fitted with specially composed polyether foam cushions. **1972** *Physics Bull.* Oct. 582/3 A fluorocarbon polyether, recently used as a rotary pump lubricant.., has allowed pump operation at above 100° C. **1975** P. BROWNE *Bodywork Maintenance* vi. 80/1 Polyether is mainly used as stuffing in cheap upholstery.

polyethism, polyethnic: see POLY-.

polyethylene (pɒlɪˈɛθɪliːn). [Back-formation from POLYETHYLENIC *a.* Cf. F. *polyéthylène* (Berthelot 1867, in *Jrnl. de Pharm. et de Chim.* VI. 28).] **a.** *Chem.* Used *attrib.* in the names of polymeric substances prepared from derivatives of ethylene, as †**polyethylene alcohol** = next; **polyethylene glycol**, any polymer of ethylene glycol; *esp.* any of a series of water-soluble oligomers and polymers which have the structure $H-(OCH_2CH_2)_n-OH$, of which the lower members are used as solvents and the higher esp. as waxes; **polyethylene oxide**, any polymer having the structure $-(OCH_2CH_2)_n-$; *esp.* any of the thermoplastics of high molecular weight made from ethylene oxide or ethylene glycol (usu. by copolymerization of both) and used esp. as water-soluble films; **polyethylene terephthalate**, a thermoplastic condensation polymer of ethylene glycol and terephthalic acid which is widely used to make polyester fibres.

1862 MILLER *Elem. Chem.* (ed. 2) III. 251 *note*, These bodies [Glycol, Diethylene alcohol and Triethylene alcohol].. are termed *polyethylene alcohols* by Wurtz. **1884** ROSCOE & SCHORLEMMER *Treat. Chem.* III. II. 37 Ethylene glycol,.. in its turn, combines with the free ethylene oxide to form polyethylene alcohols. **1886** E. F. SMITH tr. *V. von Richter's Org. Chem.* 258 (*heading*) Polyethylene glycols or alcohols. **1947** R. L. WAKEMAN *Chem. Commercial Plastics* xxvi. 779 Polyethylene glycols are.. soluble in both water and aromatic hydrocarbons. **1971** P. TOOLEY *High Polymers* ii. 43 Polyethylene glycols.. vary from oily liquids to waxy solids according to their degree of polymerization. **1930** *Chem. Abstr.* XXIV. 3003 On cooling the fused polyethylene oxides they crystallize like paraffin. **1935** C. ELLIS *Chem. Synthetic Resins* II. l. 991 All the polyethylene oxides were shown by X-ray diagrams to be crystalline and viscosity measurements indicated a meandering structure for the molecule. **1969** L. S. MOUNTS in W. R. R. Park *Plastics Film Technol.* v. 140 The solubility of PVA and polyethylene oxide films increases with increasing water temperature. **1946** ASTBURY & BROWN in *Nature* 14 Dec. 871 Polyethylene terephthalate (terylene) gives a well-oriented x-ray fibre diagram. **1967** E. CHAMBERS *Photolitho-Offset* ix. 118 The more recent introduction of the thermoplastic material polyethylene terephthalate.. as a support for photographic emulsions has increased considerably the dimensional stability of films. **1967** *Times Rev. Industry* June 70/3 Polysulphones, polyphenylene oxide and polyethylene terephthalate.. are claimed to have improved creep resistance and temperature stability.

b. Chiefly *N. Amer.* = POLYTHENE. Also *attrib.* and *Comb.*

1939 *Plastics* III. 289/1 Compounding polyethylenes with polyisobutylenes has yielded some very useful compounds. **1942** *Electronic Engin.* Mar. 668/2 Polyethylene and polyisobutylene..are finding extensive use as flexible coatings for wires intended for low-loss work. **1956** *Nature* 25 Feb. 393/1 The reaction was also measured in a polyethylene flask. *Ibid.* 3 Mar. 440/1 A polyethylene-covered magnetic stirring bar. **1966** T. PYNCHON *Crying of Lot 49* iii. 56 Suddenly, a dozen boats away, a form, covered with a blue polyethylene tarp, rose up. **1967** *Economist* 30 Sept. 1225/1 Heavy over-capacity seems to be on the way in Europe in the production of high-density polyethylene (polythene). **1968** J. UPDIKE in *Transatlantic Rev.* XXVIII. 6 The hydra's swollen coelenteron..veiled the preceding meals like polyethylene film protecting a rack of dry-cleaned suits. **1969** L. S. MOUNTS in W. R. R. Park *Plastics Film Technol.* v. 122 Polyethylene films also are used in many nonpackaging applications. **1969** *Daily Colonist* (Victoria, B.C.) 7 Dec. 26/5 A new television antenna designed for boats... An entire signal receiving system anchored in polyethylene foam. **1976** *Country Life* 22 Jan. 211/1 A fabric of the future... Spun, bonded polyethylene, a synthetic material made from bonded, random fibres.

polyethylenic (ˌpɒlɪeθɪˈliːnɪk), *a. Chem.* [ad. F. *polyéthylénique* (A. Wurtz 1860, in *Compt. Rend.* L. 1195), f. *poly-* POLY- + *éthylène* ETHYLENE + *-ique* -IC.] †**1.** Used to designate polymeric compounds prepared from derivatives of ethylene. Cf. POLYETHYLENE a. *Obs.*

1860 A. WURTZ in *Chem. News* 25 Aug. 121/1 Glycolic, lactic, and oxalic acids..are acids of very simple constitution; but such is not the case with those obtained by oxidising the complex glycols, which I have called polyethylenic alcohols. **1878** C. M. TIDY *Handbk. Mod. Chem.* xxiii. 574 By heating glycol with ethylenic oxide in sealed tubes, a series of compounds called polyethylenic glycols (or alcohols) are formed. **1895** *Jrnl. Chem. Soc.* LXVIII. I. 320 Ethylenic oxide and sodium ethoxide..give a product which boils at 110–120°..; this..must therefore be regarded as a complex ethylic polyethylenic oxide.

2. Polyunsaturated; of the nature of polyunsaturation.

1928 *Proc. R. Soc.* A. CXXII. 564 Two polyethylenic acids.., namely, linoleic acid of soya bean or cotton-seed oil ..linolenic acid of linseed oil. **1958** *Jrnl. Sci. of Food & Agric.* IX. 777 The polyethylenic C_{20} and C_{22} acids, so characteristic of the animal glycerophosphatides. **1964** *Oceanogr. & Marine Biol.* II. 176 The pattern of polyethylenic unsaturation in the fatty acids of marine invertebrates is probably the same as that in fish lipids. **1965** E. F. JANSEN in Bonner & Varner *Plant Biochem.* xxv. 655 The hexahydromatricaria ester is included to illustrate the occurrence of homologous polyethylenic compounds.

polyfenestral: see POLY-.

polyff, obs. variant of PULLEY.

polyfoil, polyformal(dehyde: see POLY-.

Polyfoto (ˈpɒlɪfəʊtəʊ). Also **-photo.** [f. POLY- + *foto*, alteration of PHOTO.] A proprietary name for a kiosk in which a person can sit and have a number of photographs taken of himself in quick succession (now usu. automatically). Also *transf.* and as *vb. trans.*

1938 *Trade Marks Jrnl.* 2 Feb. 131/1 Polyfoto... Photographs. Polyfoto (International) Limited,..London, ..merchants. **1945** 'A. GILBERT' *Don't open Door* xiii. 105 'Have you got a photograph of the girl?' 'She was polyfotoed the other day to please me.' **1962** —— *No Dust in Attic* v. 63 They ran against Miss Malpas coming out of the Polyfoto kiosk... Out of forty-eight positions there must be one that would reproduce satisfactorily. **1964** G. SIMS *Terrible Door* xxv. 132 My husband was one of the first photographers to make strips of little films, rather like Polyphotos nowadays. **1965** E. J. HOWARD *After Julius* xviii. 277 He got himself polyphotoed..for his passport. **1976** 'A. HALL' *Kobra Manifesto* iv. 44 Worn Polyphoto of current girl friend.

polyfunctional(ity: see POLY-.

polygala (pəˈlɪgələ). [mod.L., f. Gr. πολύ much + γάλα milk.] An annual or perennial herb or a shrub belonging to the large genus so called, which is a member of the family Polygalaceæ and is widely distributed in most regions of the world; = MILKWORT 1 (in quot. *a* 1661 = SAINFOIN).

1578 [see MILKWORT 1]. *a* **1661** FULLER *Worthies* (1662) Kent 57 Saint-Foine or Holy-hay..otherwise called *Polygala*, which I may English *much Milk*, as causing the cattle to give abundance thereof. **1671** [see MILKWORT 1]. **1823** *Curtis's Bot. Mag.* L. 2437 The common Polygala is so very variable a plant. **1840** [see IVY-BERRY b]. **1870** W. ROBINSON *Wild Garden* I. 9 The small sapphire buds of the alpine Polygala. **1936** *Discovery* Feb. 48/2 Large anchusas were beginning to flower.., huge polygala, and I don't know what else. **1977** S. DEALLER *Wild Flowers for Garden* iv. 67, I think of the Polygalas as generally trouble free, non-aggressive, slightly vulnerable plants.

polygalaceous (pəlɪgəˈleɪʃəs), *a. Bot.* [f. mod.L. *Polygalace-æ* (f. *Polygala* (pəˈlɪgələ), name of the typical genus, f. Gr. πολύ much + γάλα milk) + -OUS: see -ACEOUS.] Belonging to the natural order *Polygalaceæ* or milkwort family.

Mod. The species of the polygalaceous genus *Securidaca* are mostly natives of tropical America.

polygalin (pəˈlɪgəlɪn). *Chem.* [f. mod.L. *Polygala* (see prec.) + -IN[1].] A substance obtained from the root of *Polygala Senega*; also called SENEGIN, and **poly'galic** *acid.* Hence **po'lygalate**, a salt of polygalic acid.

1830 LINDLEY *Nat. Syst. Bot.* 146 M. Reschier is also said to have procured a principle called Polygaline from the same plant [Polygala Senega]. **1838** T. THOMSON *Chem. Org. Bodies* 164 The alkaline polygalates are obtained by saturating the aqueous solution of polygalic acid with the respective bases. **1876** HARLEY *Mat. Med.* (ed. 6) 716 Senegin or polygalin is contained in the cortical part, which has a short fracture.

‖**Polygamia** (pɒlɪˈgeɪmɪə). *Bot.* [mod. L. (Linnæus).] The twenty-third class in the Linnæan Sexual System, comprising species which bear both hermaphrodite and unisexual (male or female) flowers, on the same or different plants. Hence **'polygam**, a plant of this class; **poly'gamian** *a.*, belonging to the class *Polygamia*; *sb.* = *polygam*.

1753 CHAMBERS *Cycl. Supp.*, *Polygamia*..a class of plants, which have a diversity of combinations of the male and female parts of their flowers, and many ways of fructification in the same species. **1785** MARTYN *Rousseau's Bot.* ix. (1794) 96 It is entitled *polygamia*, from this variety in the flowers. **1828** WEBSTER, *Polygam*, *Polygamian*. **1835** HENSLOW *Princ. Bot.* §139 In Polygamia..we have three kinds of flowers, which may all, or some only, be placed on the same plant.

polygamic (pɒlɪˈgæmɪk), *a.* [f. late Gr. πολύγαμος often married, polygamous + -IC. So F. *polygamique.*] Of or pertaining to polygamy; (less correctly) practising polygamy, polygamous.

1819 SHELLEY *P. Bell* Prol. 36 He was an evil Cotter, And a polygamic Potter. **1882** *Athenæum* 23 Sept. 393/1 Umpengula's account of the [Zulu] law of heritage in polygamic households. **1884** J. W. BARCLAY in *19th Cent.* Jan. 183 Governor Murray lays comparatively little stress on the polygamic difficulty.

So **poly'gamical** *a.*; **poly'gamically** *adv.*, in the way of polygamy.

1819 *Metropolis* II. 156 With every polygamical inclination, neither of his present wives seem to claim him. **1863** DICKENS *Uncomm. Trav.* xx, To suppose the family groups of whom the majority of emigrants were composed, polygamically possessed, would be to suppose an absurdity. **1914** CHESTERTON *Flying Inn* 69 Why should you shrink then, ladies, from this great polygamical experiment?

poly'gamious, *a. Bot.* [f. POLYGAMIA + -OUS.] Belonging to the Linnæan class *Polygamia.*

1761 STILES in *Phil. Trans.* LV. 259 Not only in the Diœcious plants, but in the Monœcious and Polygamious also.

polygamist (pəˈlɪgəmɪst). [f. late Gr. πολύγαμος (see POLYGAMIC) + -IST.] One who practises or favours polygamy; usually, a man who has several wives: cf. POLYGAMOUS 1.

1637 G. DANIEL *Genius this Isle* 245 A Profane, Profuse, Proud Polygamist. **1662** HIBBERT *Body Div.* I. 271 The first author of polygamy..was Lamech..as was also Esau another polygamist. **1861** *Times* 21 Aug., In order to distinguish the wives of a polygamist from each other, the Christian name of each is prefixed to the husband's name; as, for instance, Mrs. Anna Young, Mrs. Mary Young, &c. **1886** P. S. ROBINSON *Valley Teet Trees* 84 The sparrow is accused as being 'a bird of bad habits and of infamous character..a communist and a polygamist'.

b. *attrib.* Practising polygamy, polygamous.

1875 JOWETT *Plato* (ed. 2) III. 163 Polygamist peoples either import and adopt children from other countries, or dwindle in numbers. **1886** *Pall Mall G.* 5 Oct. 3/2 That it was a greater evil to dissolve *bonâ fide* marriages..than to refuse baptism to polygamist husbands and their wives.

Hence **polyga'mistic** *a.*, of or pertaining to polygamists or polygamy; favouring polygamy.

1875 POSTE *Gaius* IV. Comm. (ed. 2) 545 A monogamist forum will not enforce polygamistic laws. **1885** *Chicago Advance* 12 Feb., What reply do the polygamistic Mormons make to the non-polygamistic Josephites?

po'lygamize, *v. rare* [f. late Gr. πολύγαμος (see above) + -IZE.] *intr.* To practise polygamy.

1598 SYLVESTER *Du Bartas* II. i. IV. *Handie-crafts* 693 Did it not suffize (O lustfull Soule!) first to polygamize? **1830** COLERIDGE *Table-t.* 20 May, Things which David and Solomon actually did,..making a treaty with Egypt, laying up treasure, and polygamising.

polygamous (pəˈlɪgəməs), *a.* Also 7 **poli-**. [f. late Gr. πολύγαμος (see POLYGAMIC) + -OUS.]

1. Practising or addicted to polygamy; of, pertaining to, or involving polygamy. Usually said of, or in reference to, a husband having several wives (distinctively expressed by *polygynous*), but including also the case of a wife having several husbands (*polyandrous*).

1613 PURCHAS *Pilgrimage* (1614) 266 His daughter Fatima (the onely issue of this libidinous poligamous Prophet) married to Hali. [Not in BAILEY, JOHNSON, ASH.] **1828** in WEBSTER. **1835** SIR J. ROSS *Narr. 2nd Voy.* xxvi. 373 This strange polygamous family. **1885** SIR J. W. CHITTY in *Law Times Rep.* LIII. 712/2 The marriage was a Mahommedan and by consequence a polygamous marriage. **1894** H. DRUMMOND *Ascent of Man* 387 Even in a polygamous community it is usually only a minority who have more wives than one.

2. *Zool.* Having more than one, or several, mates of the opposite sex, as an animal; characterized by polygamy, as a species. Usually used as = *polygynous*: cf. 1.

1834 R. MUDIE *Feathered Tribes Brit. Isl.* (1841) I. 24 Other [*Gallinidæ*] are polygamous; or have a number of females united with one male. **1859** DARWIN *Orig Spec.* iv. (1860) 88 The war is, perhaps, severest between the males of polygamous animals.

3. *Bot.* Bearing some flowers with stamens only, others with pistils only, and others with both, on the same or on different plants; belonging to the Linnæan class *Polygamia.*

1760 J. LEE *Introd. Bot.* I. xx. (1765) 64 *Polygamous*, such as either on the same, or on different Roots bear Hermaphrodite Flowers; and Flowers of either or of both Sexes. **1830** LINDLEY *Nat. Syst. Bot.* 138 Flowers [of *Pittosporeæ*] terminal or axillary, sometimes polygamous. **1872** OLIVER *Elem. Bot.* II. 206 The flowers of Common Ash are termed polygamous, because they are either staminate, pistillate, or hermaphrodite, and the different kinds of flowers may be upon the same or different trees.

Hence **po'lygamously** *adv.*

1874 T. G. BOWLES *Flotsam & Jetsam* iv. (1882) 24 Their [women's] ideas are always married to themselves—and sometimes polygamously to somebody else besides. **1886** *Princeton Rev.* July 47 The polygamously disposed party.

polygamy (pəˈlɪgəmɪ). Also 6–8 **poli-**. [ad. F. *polygamie* (*a* 1564 Calvin in Godef.), ad. eccl. Gr. πολυγαμία, f. πολύγαμος often married, polygamous; f. πολυ-, POLY- + γάμος marriage.]

1. Marriage with several, or more than one, at once; plurality of spouses; the practice or custom according to which one man has several wives (distinctively called *polygyny*), or one woman several husbands (*polyandry*), at the same time. Most commonly used of the former.

a **1591** R. GREENHAM *Wks.* (1599) 29 Poligamie was not very hurtfull, so long as it was within Lamech his house. **1617** MORYSON *Itin.* III. 41 Though Poligamy be permitted among them, (I meane the hauing of many wiues for one man). **1768** BLACKSTONE *Comm.* IV. xiii. 163 Polygamy can never be endured under any rational civil establishment. **1857** GLADSTONE *Glean.* VI. l. 79 Among the Greeks of Homer we find no trace of polygamy. **1906** N. W. THOMAS *Kinship Organisation* 108 This state is constituted by the union of several men with several women. It may be distinguished as before, into primary and secondary polygamy.

b. *fig.*: esp. applied to plurality of benefices.

1638 R. BAKER tr. *Balzac's Lett.* (vol. III.) 63 Monsier.. shall send you word, whether he persist in his pernicious design, to bring Polygamie into France... I meane whether he have a good word from those nine Sisters to all whom he hath offered his Services. **1710** BURNET *Autobiog.* II. (1902) 501 For the heaping up of benefice upon benefice that were well endowed,..I openly declared against such as I found possessed of them as..living in a spirituall poligamy. **1873** HAMERTON *Intell. Life* IV. v. (1876) 165 A sort of polygamy to have different pursuits.

2. *Zool.* The habit of mating with more than one, or several, of the opposite sex; usually, one male with several females (*polygyny*), as in gallinaceous birds.

1890 in *Cent. Dict.*

†**3.** *Bot.* The condition of being polygamous; see POLYGAMOUS 3. *Obs. rare.*

1793 MARTYN *Lang. Bot.* s.v. *Polygamia*, This term Polygamia or Polygamy, as applied to a compound flower,.. signifies that several distinct flowers (called Florets) are included in one common calyx.

polygar, variant of POLIGAR.

polygarchy, obs. form of POLYARCHY.

polygastric (pɒlɪˈgæstrɪk), *a.* (*sb.*) [ad. F. *polygastrique*: see POLY- and GASTRIC.] Having many stomachs or digestive cavities; belonging to certain infusorians formerly called *Polygastrica*, in the belief that their food-vacuoles were separate digestive organs. **b.** as *sb.* A 'polygastric' animalcule. Also **poly'gastrian** *a.* and *sb.*

1845 WHEWELL *Indic. Creator* 39 The lowest kind of animal developement, which has been termed polygastric monads. **1846** DANA *Zooph.* vii. §106 (1848) 107 The Lernæoid division appears to reach the Polygastrics in the Acephalocist. **1864** WEBSTER, *Polygastrian, Polygastric*... An animal having, or supposed to have, many stomachs. **1865** *Intell. Observ.* No. 47. 389 Ehrenberg's polygastric theory.

polygene (ˈpɒlɪdʒiːn). *Genetics.* [Back-formation from POLYGENIC *a.* 3; cf. GENE [1].] A gene whose individual effect on the phenotype of a single organism is too small to be observed, but which can act together with other, non-allelic polygenes to produce observable phenotypic variation in a quantitative character.

1941 *Jrnl. Genetics* XLI. 163 The inbreeding this line had undergone had in fact made it homozygous for the hair-number polygenes. **1949** [see POLYGENIC *a.* 3]. **1961** *Lancet* 9 Sept. 601/2 One might envisage a system of pleiotropic masculinising polygenes located more or less randomly along the whole of the Y chromosome. **1973** *Nature* 21/28 Dec. 498/2 Techniques for the location of polygenes, developed in *Drosophila* but also very successful in mice and wheat, have not been applied to human material.

poly'geneous, *a. rare.* [f. POLY-, after *heterogeneous.*] Of many kinds; heterogeneous.

1818 *Blackw. Mag.* III. 305 A patched, pyebald, and polygeneous affair. *Ibid.* IV. 356 As motley and polygeneous an array, as ever found the elements of ruin in disunion.

polygenesis (pɒlɪˈdʒɛnɪsɪs). [f. POLY- + GENESIS.] **a.** *Biol.* (Theoretical) origination of a race or species from several independent ancestors or germs: in reference to man usually called POLYGENY. Hence **polygeˈnesic** (-dʒɪˈnɛsɪk) *a.* = POLYGENETIC 1; **polyˈgenesist** = POLYGENIST.

1862 *Temple Bar Mag.* V. 214 The ethnological polygenesists assert that, during the whole historic period, there have existed the same differences in the human races that are seen at the present time. **1864** *Reader* No. 94. 476/3 System of polygenesic doctrine. **1882** OGILVIE, *Polygenesis.*

b. *Linguistics.* The theory that there is a plurality of independent sources for languages. Opp. MONOGENESIS 3.

1936, 1949 [see MONOGENESIS 3]. **1979** *Amer. Speech 1978* LIII. 247 My gut feeling is that radical polygenesis is impossible. It would require either a biologically unrealistic degree of parallelism, or else that languages be much more varied in their groundplans than in fact they are.

c. *gen.*

1962 G. KUBLER *Art & Archit. Anc. Amer.* i. 11 (*heading*) Diffusion or polygenesis?

polygenetic (ˌpɒlɪdʒɪˈnɛtɪk), *a.* [f. prec., after GENETIC.]

1. *Biol.* Of or pertaining to polygenesis.

1861 MAX MÜLLER *Sc. Lang.* (1862) 348 Professor Pott, the most distinguished advocate of the polygenetic dogma, has pleaded the necessity of admitting more than one beginning for the human race and for language.

2. *Geol.* **a.** Having more than one origin; formed in several different ways.

1873 *Amer. Jrnl. Sc.* Ser. III. V. 429 A composite or polygenetic range or chain, made up of two or more monogenetic ranges combined. **1889** *Amer. Jrnl. Sci.* XXXVII. 431 The present topography .. is an uncompleted advance in a second cycle of development, with recent complications by glacial action and slight changes of level. Like mountains of repeated growth, this topography may be called 'polygenetic'. **1943** *Ibid.* CCXLI. 486 Polygenetic complex soils and Late Quaternary alluvial bodies may preserve duplicate records of climatic changes for a given region. **1969** BENNISON & WRIGHT *Geol. Hist. Brit. Isles* ix. 201 In the thrust block of Roman Fell, the Roman Fell Beds .. rest on the Polygenetic Conglomerate of unknown age but with pebbles including andesites probably derived from the Old Red Sandstone. **1975** *Nature* 27 Mar. 369/2 Coasts and mountains are treated separately as polygenetic landscapes, the former being the zone of contact between two distinct environments and the latter the areas within which internal uplift conflicts markedly with external erosion.

b. (See quot. 1959.) [After G. *polygen* in this sense (A. Stübel *Die Vulkanberge von Ecuador* (1897) III. 352).]

[**1903** A. GEIKIE *Text-bk. Geol.* (ed. 4) I. 322 A volcano formed in this way he terms monogene; while where it has been built up by the gradual accumulations of successive eruptions he calls it polygene.] **1959** A. A. G. SCHIEFERDECKER *Geol. Nomencl.* 239 *Polygenetic volcano*, formed by several volcanic outbursts. **1962** E. A. VINCENT tr. *Rittmann's Volcanoes* iii. 114 In the case of the great polygenetic volcanoes, the old topography is completely buried. **1976** *New Scientist* 9 Sept. 527/1 Those which erupt many times are called polygenetic volcanoes.

c. *Linguistics.* Deriving historically from a number of sources; having more than one antecedent.

1952 *Archivum Linguisticum* IV. 93 The outstanding trait in the history of -*(i)ego* .. is its polygenetic character.

Hence **polygeˈnetically** *adv.*, by, or in the way of, polygenesis.

1900 E. R. LANKESTER *Treat. Zool.* III. 158 *Eucladocrinus* .. was evolved polygenetically by modification of the arms.

polygenic (pɒlɪˈdʒɛnɪk), *a.* [f. Gr. πολυ-, POLY- + γενικός, f. γένος kind, or (in sense 2) from -GEN 1 + -IC.]

1. *Geol.* = POLYGENOUS 1.

1858 MAYNE *Expos. Lex.*, *Polygenicus*, .. applied to a rock which owes its origin to fragments of different rocks united by calcareous cement ..; or to divers fragments of homogeneous rocks being united by a variable cement: polygenic.

2. *Chem.* Forming more than one compound with hydrogen or other monovalent element.

1873 WATTS *Fownes' Chem.* (ed. 11) 231 All other elements are polygenic, uniting with the Monogens. **1877** *Ibid.* (ed. 12) I. 261 It seems most probable that the true quantivalence or atomicity of a polygenic element is that which corresponds with the maximum number of monad atoms with which it can combine.

3. *Genetics.* [ad. G. *polygen* (L. Plate *Vererbungslehre mit besonderer Berücksichtigung des Menschen* (1913) ii. 75).] Of, pertaining to, or determined by polygenes.

[**1927** *Zeitschr. für Induktive Abstammungs- und Vererbungslehre* XLIII. 331 The discovery of polygenous characters, especially the phenomenon of polymeria discovered by Nilsson Ehle, made it necessary to recognize, that at least a great many characters are determined not by one but by several and even many genes.] **1941** *Jrnl. Genetics* XLI. 160 Qualitative variation is usually monogenic or digenic in inheritance. Cases of trigenic and tetragenic inheritance are known, but are relatively rare. In contrast with these, quantitative variation may be said to be polygenic, and this term will be adopted. **1949** DARLINGTON & MATHER *Elem. Genetics* iii. 66 These genes are inherited in the mendelian way, but their differences have effects which are small in relation to those of non-heritable agencies (or at least in relation to the total variation), similar to one another and supplementary to one another... Such a set of genes constitutes a polygenic system, and its individual members may be conveniently termed polygenes. **1954** *Antiquity* XXVIII. 197 A genetic analysis of such polygenic characters as bone size and shape. **1961** *Brit. Med. Bull.* XVII. 241 All polygenic inheritance is polymeric, but not all polymeric inheritance is polygenic. **1971** *Heythrop Jrnl.* Apr. 171 The analysis of complex (polygenic) hereditary determination is most commonly conducted by means of twin studies. **1978** *Dædalus* Spring 215 Much more complex choices will confront us when we think we know enough to tackle polygenic traits which may have important expression in emotional behavior or intellectual capacity.

Hence **polyˈgenically** *adv.*, by means of or with regard to polygenes.

1943 *Biol. Rev.* XVIII. 61 Polygenically controlled differences are quantitative rather than qualitative and do not lead to the sharp segregation shown by the more familiar genetical differences. **1957** *Heredity* XI. 392 Such an approximately even distribution .. might even be anticipated given that any sizeable block of heterochromatin near the centromere is, mitotic length for length, about as polygenically active as the euchromatin of more distal regions. **1976** *Nature* 23 Sept. 317/1 A common feature of many selection experiments, when polygenically determined traits are involved, is a reduction in the reproductive fitness of the selected strains.

polygenism (pəˈlɪdʒɪnɪz(ə)m). [f. as next + -ISM. So F. *polygénisme*.] The doctrine of polygeny; the theory that mankind are descended from several independent pairs of ancestors, or that the human race consists of several independent species.

1878 *N. Amer. Rev.* CXXVI. 554 Belief in the authenticity of the Mosaic records, which no sophistry on the part of the advocates of polygenism has been able to shake. **1880** A. H. KEANE in *Nature* XXIII. 199/1 More rational and philosophic than any conceivable form of polygenism.

polygenist (pəˈlɪdʒɪnɪst). [app. f. POLYGENY + -IST: cf. *botany, botanist*, etc. So F. *polygéniste*.] An adherent of the theory of polygeny.

1861 *Sat. Rev.* 23 Nov. 544 Among the polygenists (or upholders of a plurality of species) there are many sincere, if not very logical, Christians. **1881** A. H. KEANE in *Nature* XXIII. 251/1 All polygenists .. have regarded the Malays as one of their human species.

attrib. **1865** HUXLEY *Critiques & Addr.* (1873) 163 The granting of the Polygenist premises does not, in the slightest degree, necessitate the Polygenist conclusion. **1878** BARTLEY tr. *Topinard's Anthrop.* Introd. 15 The opposite, a polygenist school .. maintained the plurality of races.

Hence **polygeˈnistic** *a.*, of or pertaining to polygenists or polygenism.

1879 tr. *De Quatrefages' Hum. Species* 47 We shall have undermined the foundation of the whole polygenistic doctrine.

polygenous (pəˈlɪdʒɪnəs), *a.* [irreg. f. Gr. πολυγεν-ής of many kinds (f. πολυ-, POLY- + γένος kind) + -OUS: perh. associated with words from L. such as *indigenous*, *calcigenous*, etc.]

1. Composed of constituents of different kinds; *spec.* in *Geol.* composed of various kinds of rocks.

1799 KIRWAN *Geol. Ess.* 164 Some are unigenous, consisting for the greater part, at least, of one species of stone or aggregate; some polygenous, consisting of various species, alternating with, or passing into, or mixed with each other. *Ibid.* 226 Secondary mountains are either formed of one species of stone, or of strata of different species, .. the former I call unigenous, the latter polygenous: these are commonly stratified, the former often not.

2. *Chem.* = POLYGENIC 2.

1870 F. HURTER in *Eng. Mech.* 11 Feb. 524/1 Chlorine forms only one compound with hydrogen, whilst oxygen and carbon form several compounds with that element. Chlorine may, for this reason, be called a monogenous element: the others .. polygenous elements.

3. Of, pertaining to, or involving polygeny.

1860 *Reader* 15 Sept. 796 Thus domestic pigeons may be said to be 'monogenous' as to their origin from one wild species, 'polygenous' as to the individual ancestor of each variety.

polygeny (pəˈlɪdʒɪnɪ). [f. POLY- + Gr. -γενεια birth.] The (theoretical) origination of mankind (or of any species) from several independent pairs of ancestors; *loosely*, the theory of such origination, polygenism.

1865 *Reader* 14 Oct. 433/3 An anthropological paper entitled 'Monogeny and Polygeny'. **1879** *Athenæum* 30 Aug. 276/1 Nowadays both slavery and polygeny have so dropped out of sight that a single paragraph is enough to record their unholy alliance. **1893** S. LAING *Hum. Origins* 405 Polygeny, or plural origins, would at first sight seem to be the most plausible theory to account for the great diversities of human races.

polyglacial(ism, -ist: see POLY-.

polyglot (ˈpɒlɪglɒt), *a.* and *sb.* Also -glott. [ad. Gr. πολύγλωττ-ος many-tongued, speaking many languages, f. πολυ-, POLY- + γλῶττα tongue. So F. *polyglotte* (1639 in Hatz.-Darm.).]

A. *adj.* **1.** Of a person: That speaks or writes many or several languages.

1656 BLOUNT *Glossogr.*, *Polyglot*, that speaks many Languages, a Linguist. **1854** *L'pool Albion* Nov., Always remarkable for plain speaking in his mother-tongue, though a polyglot linguist. **1873** HAMERTON *Intell. Life* III. ix. (1875) 124 That there should be polyglot waiters who can tell us when the train starts in four or five languages.

2. a. Of or relating to many languages; *esp.* of a book or writing: In many or several languages.

1673 *Ess. Educ. Gentlewom.* 11 The Authors of the Polyglot-Bible. **1706** PHILLIPS, *Polyglott*, that is of many Languages, as, The Polyglott Bible, a Polyglott Dictionary. **1881** *Nature* XXV. 208/1 A French meteorological balloon sent up .. with a polyglot request that it be forwarded by the finder to the address given.

b. Characterized by the use of a plurality of languages, or of elements derived from a plurality of languages.

1952 W. D. JACOBS *William Barnes* i. 12 Dorset gave Barnes the material by which to judge the polyglot English of our day. **1957** *Thought* XXXII. 240 In his early polyglot days .. he [*sc.* T. S. Eliot] wrote often with odd patches and tags of French, German—and even Sanskrit—as well as Latin and Greek. **1965** *Economist* 3 Apr. 44/2 The use in, say, Cyprus of a polyglot (or mixed-manned) force. **1972** W. B. LOCKWOOD *Panorama Indo-European Lang.* 214 Here some 900,000 of them compete with the Gujaratis for the position of second largest linguistic group in that remarkably polyglot city [*sc.* Bombay].

B. *sb.* **1. a.** One who speaks or writes several languages.

c **1645** HOWELL *Lett.* III. viii. (1650) 16 A polyglot or good linguist may be also term'd a usefull learned man, 'specially if vers'd in School-languages. *a* **1840** [see POLYMATH]. **1842** MRS. BROWNING *Grk. Chr. Poets* (1863) 151 As learned a polyglott as ever had been. **1867** BAKER *Nile Tribut.* i, The interpreter was nearly ignorant of English, although a professed polyglot.

†**b.** A bird that imitates the notes of other birds.

[**1706** PHILLIPS, *Polyglotta*, the American Mock-bird, so call'd because it imitates the Notes of all Birds. **1753** CHAMBERS *Cycl. Supp.*, *Polyglotta avis* .. the name of a bird described by Nieremberg.] **1770** G. WHITE *Selborne* 15 Jan., The [sedge-bird] has a surprising variety of notes resembling the song of several other birds... It is .. a delicate polyglot. **1776** PENNANT *Zool.* (ed. 4) I. 322 It [sedge warbler] is a most entertaining polyglot, or mocking bird.

2. a. A book or writing (*esp.* a Bible) in several languages.

1666 PEPYS *Diary* 5 Oct., Among others, the Polyglottes and new Bible. **1725** HENLEY tr. *Montfaucon's Antiq. Italy* (ed. 2) 9 A Polyglot of the Acts of the Apostles, .. in Armenian, Arabic, Coptic, Ethiopic. **1840** [see COMPLUTENSIAN]. **1892** C. A. BRIGGS *Bible, Ch. & Reason* iv. 96 The great Polyglotts had settled that.

b. A mixture of several languages. *rare.*

1715 tr. *Pancirollus' Rerum Mem.* I. Pref. 6, I wish I had a Polyglot into which I might render it. **1830** CUNNINGHAM *Brit. Paint.* II. 311 His wrath aired itself in a polyglott. **1862** MISS JEWSBURY *Mem. Lady Morgan* II. 457 The style is not so much disfigured by a polyglott of languages.

C. *Comb.*, as **polyglot-wise** *adv.*, in a polyglot manner, or like a polyglot; in several languages.

1875 JAS. GRANT *One of the 600*, vii. 53 We shall have .. talked polyglot-wise with fellows of all nations.

So **polyˈglottal**, **polyˈglottic**, **ˈpolyglottish** (*nonce-wd.*), **polyˈglottous** *adjs.* = *polyglot* A.; **polyˈglottally** *adv.*; **ˈpolyglotted** *ppl. a.*, furnished with or speaking several languages; **ˈpolyglotter** (*nonce-wd.*), a polyglot person; **polyˈglottery** = POLYGLOTTISM; **polyˈglottically** *adv.* = POLYGLOTTALLY *adv.*; **ˈpolyglottism**, polyglot character, use of or acquaintance with many languages; **ˈpolyglottist** = *polyglot* B. 1; **ˈpolygloˌttize** *v. trans.*, to render polyglot; †**ˌpolygloˈttology** [see -LOGY], a speaking in many languages (*obs.*).

1837 *Fraser's Mag.* XVI. 670 Panurge the *Polyglottal. **1892** *Athenæum* 16 July 90/1 A profuse display of easy polyglottal information. **1839** *Fraser's Mag.* XIX. 680 Most *polyglot[t]ally rendered in our own pages by Father Prout. **1897** *Daily News* 30 Jan. 6/3 A *polyglotted giant bows you into a luxurious chair, and there you sit, waiting for your host. **1898** *Westm. Gaz.* 22 Feb. 2/1 'The meat, m'sieu', —though polyglotted, he is a Frenchman, I believe. **1912** 'R. DEHAN' *Between Two Thieves* 616 That white haired *Polyglotter in the shabby togs .. is a queer kind of chap. **1915** *Singapore Free Press* 14 Jan., If its *polyglottery were all that was wrong with it [*sc.* Austria-Hungary], it still might be possible to jog along in a sort of mutual unintelligibility. **1931** *Time & Tide* 8 Aug. 943 (*heading*) Polyglottery [*review of W. Gerhardi's* Memoirs of a Polyglot]. **1962** *Times Lit. Suppl.* 14 Sept. 685/3 Rebuses abound, as do polyglottery (classical and modern), Finnegans wakefulness, and enormous catalogues *à la* Rabelais. **1801** W. TAYLOR in *Monthly Mag.* XII. 583 The author is *polyglottic as the hydra. **1903** *Daily Chron.* 11 July 5/1 Pope Gregory the Sixteenth .. was correcting the proof-sheets of a polyglottic book that Wiseman was bringing out. **1910** W. J. LOCKE *Simon* vi. 71 Mr. Papadopoulos *polyglottically acknowledged the honour I had conferred upon him. **1878** E. JENKINS *Haverholme* 206 Screeching their raven-voiced praises in *polyglottish discord. **1882** *Century Mag.* XXIV. 106 The *polyglottism implies so close a familiarity with many literatures. **1889** LOWELL *Latest Lit. Ess.*, *Stud. Mod. Lang.* (1891) 139, I will not say .. with Lord Burleigh that such polyglottism is but 'to have one meat served in divers dishes'. **1890** *Spectator* 29 Mar., The great *polyglottist, Mr. Thomas Watts, who probably surpassed the more famous Mezzofanti, gives his testimony to the linguistic importance of the work in a notable letter. **1871** MISS MULOCK *Fair France* i. 37 Plain English (which we found ourselves rapidly forgetting, and becoming *polyglottized). **1658** ROWLAND *Moufet's Theat. Ins.* 907 At the first Honey had but one name, called in the Hebrew *Dabesch*; but since that strange and confused *Polyglottology, or speaking with divers tongues it was called of the inhabitants of Arabia, *Hel, Han*; of the French, *Miel*; of the English, *Honey* [etc.]. **1861** MAX MÜLLER *Sc. Lang.* iv. 130 While working as a missionary among the *polyglottous tribes of America. **1885** GRESWELL in *Sat. Rev.* 26 Dec. 845 [The temptation to talk of a Kaffir policeman as] a polyglottous individual.

polyglutamic to **polyglycol(ic**: see POLY-.

polygon ('pɒlɪgən), *sb.* and *a.* Also 7 **polygone.** [ad. L. *polygōnum*, a. Gr. πολύγωνον, prop. neut. of πολύγωνος adj. polygonal, f. πολυ-, POLY- + -γωνος, from stem of γωνία angle. Cf. F. *polygone*, †*poligone* (Cotgr. 1611). Used at first in Latin forms *poly'gōnum, poly'gōnium*.]

A. *sb.* **1.** *Geom.* **a.** A figure (usually, a plane rectilineal figure) having many, i.e. (usually) more than four, angles (and sides); a many-sided figure.

complete polygon, a polygon in which lines are drawn connecting each angular vertex with every one of the others. ***stellated polygon***, a polygon which wraps its interior more than once, the continuous joining of alternate or more remote angles, producing a stellate or starlike figure, as in the PENTAGRAM (q.v.) which is a stellated pentagon wrapping its interior twice. So with similar figures of 7, 8, 9, 10, etc. points, in which the variety of form increases with the number of different points that can be continuously joined.

1571 DIGGES *Pantom.* I. Elem. B iij b, Polygona are such Figures as haue moe than foure sides. *Ibid.* II. xx. O iv, To diuide the superficies of any irregular Pollygonium. **1656** BLOUNT *Glossogr.*, *Polygon*, a Geometrical figure, that hath many corners. **1753** HOGARTH *Anal. Beauty* iv. 22 Instead of ..circular bases, polygons of different but even numbers of sides, have been substituted. **1881** ROUTLEDGE *Science* ii. 37 The circle is..said to be the limit of the inscribed polygon.

b. ***polygon of forces***: a polygonal figure illustrating a theorem relating to a number of forces acting at one point, each of which is represented in magnitude and direction by one of the sides of the figure, analogous to the *parallelogram of forces*; hence, the theorem itself. So ***polygon of velocities***, etc.

1842 BRANDE *Dict. Sc.*, etc., *Polygon of forces*,..a theorem, the discovery of which is attributed to Leibnitz. **1879** THOMSON & TAIT *Nat. Phil.* I. I. §256. **1882** MINCHIN *Unipl. Kinemat.* 1 Linear velocities follow the same laws of composition and resolution as Forces in Statics; and with these (such as the parallelogram and polygon of velocities) the student is assumed to be already familiar.

c. *Arith.* A polygonal number: see POLYGONAL 2. Hence extended to higher orders of figurate numbers, as the PYRAMIDAL numbers, etc. *rare.* (Cf. *square*, *cube*.)

1842 BRANDE *Dict. Sc.*, etc. s.v. *Figurate Numbers*, First sums, or polygons of the first order. Tri. 1, 3, 6, 10. Sq. 1, 4, 9, 16. Pent. 1, 5, 12, 22. Hex. 1, 6, 15, 28. Second sums, or polygons of the second order. 1, 4, 10, 20. 1, 5, 14, 30. 1, 6, 18, 40. 1, 7, 22, 50.

2. a. A material object of the form of a polygon. ***funicular polygon***: see FUNICULAR 2.

1669 STAYNRED *Fortification* 1 The Semidiameter of the Outward Polygon. **1706** PHILLIPS, *Polygon*... Also a spot of Ground of that Figure, which is, or may be fortify'd according to the Rules of Art. **1796** KIRWAN *Elem. Min.* (ed. 2) I. 318 Very seldom in pellucid needles, tables, or polygons. **1853** STOCQUELER *Milit. Encycl.*, *Polygon*, the name applied to the many-angled forms in which the outer walls of all fortified places are built. **1899** *Allbutt's Syst. Med.* VII. 608 Four large vessels which here form the remarkable anastomosis known as the circle, or polygon, of Willis.

b. *Physical Geogr.* One of the approximately polygonal figures characteristic of patterned ground (cf. PATTERNED *ppl. a.* b).

1913 *Amer. Jrnl. Sci.* CLXXXVI. 459 The shale surfaces are flat, the polygons not being concave upward as is commonly the case in the Mauch Chunk and Newark shales. **1914** T. THORODDSEN in Rosenvinge & Warming *Bot. Iceland* I. I. 258 The surface is divided into squares or less regularly formed polygons, by bands of small stones or gravel, while the clay of the interior of the squares or polygons is destitute of stones. **1921** *Geogr. Jrnl.* LVIII. 308 The snow falls, and when it melts, the spare gravel that remains on the clay substratum has taken upon itself the same system of polygons..which we see in Polar lands. **1950** [see PATTERNED *ppl. a.* b]. **1960** B. W. SPARKS *Geomorphol.* xiv. 318 Boulders weighing..over one hundredweight.. have been observed in some Greenland polygons. **1974** *Environmental Conservation* I. 58/1 He found no serious thermokarst conditions along the trails, except where ice-wedges of polygons were crossed.

†**B.** *adj.* Having many angles; polygonal. ? *Obs.*

1570 BILLINGSLEY *Euclid* IV. xvi. 125 A Poligonon figure is a figure consisting of many sides. **1681** CHETHAM *Angler's Vade-m.* vii. §7 (1689) 77 The best Rivers to angle in, are.. such as have many Polygone windings, and turnings. **1761** DA COSTA in *Phil. Trans.* LII. 103 The rocks..rise into polygon pillars. **1796** MORSE *Amer. Geog.* II. 182 The surface of the causeway exhibiting to view a regular and compact pavement of polygon stones.

polygonaceous (pəˌlɪgəʊ'neɪʃəs), *a.* *Bot.* [f. mod.L. *Polygonāceæ* (f. POLYGONUM) + -OUS: see -ACEOUS.] Belonging to the natural order *Polygonaceæ*, of which the typical genus is POLYGONUM.

1874 COOKE *Fungi* 41 The species attack the flowers and anthers of composite and polygonaceous plants.

polygonal (pə'lɪgənəl), *a.* (*sb.*) [f. L. *polygōn-um* POLYGON + -AL[1]. So F. *polygonal*.]

1. a. Having the form of a polygon; having many, i.e. (usually) more than four, angles (and sides); many-sided. As applied to a solid body, denoting a prismatic or similar form whose base or section is a polygon.

1727–41 CHAMBERS *Cycl.*, *Polygonal column.* **1756** *Phil. Trans.* XLIX. 513 Its whole surface is covered with small shallow polygonal cells. **1857** HENFREY *Bot.* §652 The mutual pressure of cells..converts the spheroidal into polygonal forms. *a* **1878** SIR G. G. SCOTT *Lect. Archit.* I. 195 The polygonal chapter-house is an equally English feature.

Comb. **1847–9** *Todd's Cycl. Anat.* IV. 516/1 Polygonal-celled serous membranes.

b. Containing or forming polygonal features.

1924 *Geogr. Jrnl.* LXIII. 213 One is apt to mistake this polygonal system of ice-wedges for a continuous sheet of ground-ice. **1930** *Ibid.* LXXVI. 417 Polygonal shrinkage fissures in clay are widespread. **1960** B. W. SPARKS *Geomorphol.* iii. 33 Basalt..often displays a very well defined, polygonal, vertical joint pattern. **1974** T. L. PÉWÉ in Smiley & Zumberge *Polar Deserts & Mod. Man* iii. 42/1 One of the most widespread geomorphic features associated with permafrost in the polar deserts is the microrelief pattern of the ground generally called polygonal ground or tundra polygons.

2. a. *Arith.* Applied to the several series of numbers, each beginning with unity, and obtained by continued summation of the successive terms of an arithmetical progression whose common difference is a whole number. So called because each of these numbers, represented (e.g.) by dots, can be arranged according to a certain rule in the form of the corresponding regular *polygon* (the term being here extended to a figure of any number of sides).

Thus the A. P. 1, 2, 3, 4, 5, 6...(comm. diff. 1) gives, by summation of successive terms (1, 1 + 2, 1 + 2 + 3, etc.), the series of *triangular* numbers 1, 3, 6, 10, 15, 21... Similarly, with comm. diff. 2, 3, 4, etc., are obtained the series of *square*, *pentagonal*, *hexagonal*, etc., numbers. The polygonal numbers constitute the first order of figurate numbers: see FIGURATE *ppl. a.* 3 b.

1704 J. HARRIS *Lex. Techn.* I, *Polygonal Numbers*, are such as are the Sums or Aggregates of Series of Numbers in Arithmetical Progression, beginning with Unity; and so placed, that they represent the Form of a Polygon. **1727–41** CHAMBERS *Cycl.* s.v. **1842** BRANDE *Dict. Sc.*, etc. s.v., A very general and remarkable property of polygonal numbers was discovered by Fermat:—Every number whatever is the sum of one, two, or three triangular numbers; the sum of one, two, three, or four squares; the sum of one, two, three, four, or five pentagonal numbers; and so on.

b. as *sb.* A polygonal number. *rare.*

1795 HUTTON *Math. Dict.*, *Polygonal Numbers*,..are called Polygonals, because the number of points in them may be arranged in the form of the several Polygonal figures in geometry.

Hence **po'lygonally** *adv.*

1870 ROLLESTON *Anim. Life* 254 A polygonally-shagreened capsule. **1884** BOWER & SCOTT *De Bary's Phaner.* 374 The outermost layer, which..consists of polygonally prismatic cells in uninterrupted connection.

po'lygonar, *a.* *rare*[−1]. [f. L. type **polygōnār-is*: see prec. and -AR[1].] = prec. 1.

1836 CDL. WISEMAN *Sc. & Relig.* I. ii. 102 The polygonar structures of the ancients.

polygonate (pə'lɪgənət), *a.* *Nat. Hist.* *rare*[−0]. [f. Gr. πολυ-, POLY- + γόνυ knee + -ATE[2].] Having many joints.

1856 THOMAS *Med. Dict.* (1864) 436 *Polygonate*, applied to certain plants and animals.

polygonboden ('pɒlɪgənˌbəʊdən). *Physical Geogr.* Const. as *pl.* [a. G. *polygonboden*, lit. 'polygon ground', tr. Sw. *rutmark* chequered ground (F. R. Kjellman 1879, in *Öfversigt af K. Vetenskaps-Akad. Förhandl.* XXXVI. IX. 11).] Polygons (sense A. 2 b).

1924 *Geogr. Jrnl.* LXIII. 226 Schimper..saw well-developed 'polygonboden' and arrangement of vegetation with respect to the polygons, in the high plateaux of the Pamirs. **1933** *Bull. Geol. Soc. Amer.* XLIV. 949 Numerous minor forms, including polygonboden, increase the contrasts between alpine surfaces and those of lower elevations. **1947** *Geogr. Rev.* XXXVII. 640 Plainly visible.. are the polygenboden, a phenomenon of frozen ground. **1970** MACDONALD & ABBOTT *Volcanoes in Sea* viii. 150/1 The fragments..are arranged in stripes of varying coarseness, or in polygonal patterns ('Polygonboden'), that ..are the result of frost action.

polygoneutic (ˌpɒlɪgəʊ'njuːtɪk), *a.* *Zool.* [f. POLY- + Gr. γονεύ-ειν to beget: cf. πολυγονεῖσθαι to produce much offspring.] Producing several broods in a year. So **polygo'neutism**, polygoneutic character or condition.

1890 in *Cent. Dict.* **1895** *Syd. Soc. Lex.*, *Polygoneutic*, having several broods or litters every year. *Polygoneutism*, the state of being *Polygoneutic*.

†**poly'gonial**, *a.* (*sb.*) *Obs.* [f. L. *polygōni-us* polygonal + -AL[1].]

a. *adj.* = POLYGONAL *a.* **b.** *sb.* = POLYGON.

1703 T. N. *City & C. Purchaser* 238 Polygonial Turrets. **1766** *Compl. Farmer* s.v. *Surveying*, To find the content of a regular polygonial, or multangular figure. *Ibid.*, [How] to divide triangles, parallelograms, and regular polygonials, in an artifical way.

polygonic (pɒlɪ'gɒnɪk), *a.*[1] *rare.* [f. Gr. πολύγων-ον (see POLYGON) + -IC.] = POLYGONAL *a.* Hence **poly'gonically** *adv.*

1842 *Civil Eng. & Arch. Jrnl.* V. 151/1 The earliest buildings were circular, octagonal, or polygonic. **1852** T. WRIGHT *Celt, Roman, & Saxon* (1861) 183 Flag-stones cut square or polygonically.

poly'gonic, *a.*[2] [f. POLYGON-UM + -IC.] Pertaining to the botanical genus *Polygonum*; ***polygonic acid***, an acrid crystallizable acid, found by Rademacher 1871, in *Polygonum Hydropiper.*

1890 in BILLINGS *Med. Dict.* **1895** in *Syd. Soc. Lex.*

polygonization (ˌpɒlɪgənaɪ'zeɪʃən). *Metallurgy.* [f. POLYGON + -IZATION.] The formation of smaller grains within the grains of a metal as a result of the migration of dislocations following deformation and annealing.

1948 R. W. CAHN in *Rep. Conf. Strength of Solids, 1947* 137 The x-ray and microscopical results together lead to an interpretation as follows: the deformation leads to elastic bending of glide lamellae; when the crystal is annealed, the lamellae undergo 'polygonization'. **1949** —— in *Jrnl. Inst. Metals* LXXVI. 136 It is suggested that the process be named polygonization, to distinguish it from other forms of recrystallization. The name derives from the fact that the crystallographic direction which coincides with the wire axis, while bent along an arc before annealing, becomes part of a polygon afterwards. **1950** *Engineering* 5 May 499/3 Polygonisation could be obtained in hexagonal metals only after plastic bending and not after deformation in tension. **1957** D. MCLEAN *Grain Boundaries in Metals* vii. 204 The word 'polygonization' has lost its original geometrical significance and now refers to the process of dislocations gathering into stable arrays. **1976** COTTERILL & MOULD *Recrystallization & Grain Growth in Metals* iv. 74 The basic differences between the formation of a substructure by polygonization, during annealing, and the formation of subgrains, directly, during cold-work have been summarized by Byrne.

polygonize ('pɒlɪgənaɪz), *v.* *Metallurgy.* [Back-formation from prec.] *intr.* To undergo or give rise to polygonization.

1949 *Jrnl. Inst. Metals* LXXVI. 138 Zinc crystals bent at −180° C. would not polygonize on subsequent annealing. **1967** A. H. COTTRELL *Introd. Metall.* xxi. 402 Dislocations of opposite signs come together and annihilate each other. Those of the same sign polygonize into well-defined cell walls.

Hence **'polygonized** *ppl. a.*

1950 *Progress Metal Physics* II. 188 The grains..were in a polygonized condition. **1954** A. R. BAILEY *Text-bk. Metall.* v. 110 (*caption*) Polygonised structure in super-purity aluminium, developed by creep at 200° C. **1976** COTTERILL & MOULD *Recrystallization & Grain Growth in Metals* iv. 74 Although the energy per dislocation is reduced, the total energy of the boundary is increased, and that of the regions away from the boundary is decreased, by the conversion from the deformed structure to the polygonized one.

polygonometry (ˌpɒlɪgəʊ'nɒmɛtrɪ). *Math. rare.* [f. as POLYGON + -METRY. So F. *polygonométrie*.] A branch of mathematics dealing with the measurement and properties of polygons, as trigonometry with those of triangles. Hence **polygonometric** (pəˌlɪgəʊnəʊ'mɛtrɪk) *a.*, pertaining to polygonometry.

1811 HUTTON *Course Math.* III. 148 The theorems and problems in Polygonometry bear an intimate connection and close analogy to those in plane trigonometry. **1890** *Cent. Dict.*, *Polygonometric.*

polygonoscope (pə'lɪgənəskəʊp). [f. as POLYGON + Gr. -σκοπος, -ον viewing, he or that which views.] An instrument on the principle of the kaleidoscope, consisting of two mirrors connected by a hinge, and capable of being set at any required angle, so as to produce an indefinite variety of patterns, which may be copied or photographed for artistic purposes.

1884 in KNIGHT *Dict. Mech.* Suppl.

polygonous (pə'lɪgənəs), *a.* Now *rare* or *Obs.* [f. L. *polygōn-um* + -OUS.] = POLYGONAL *a.*

1660 BARROW *Euclid* XII. i. 296 Like polygonous figures.. described in circles..are one to another, as the squares described of the diameters of circles. **1727–41** CHAMBERS *Cycl.* s.v. *Column*, Polygonous Column has several sides, or faces: the most regular of these have eight faces. **1789** J. KEIR *Dict. Chem.* 172/1 This ammoniacal salt shoots into polygonous crystals. **1842** *Blackw. Mag.* LI. 726 Harmony of design seems entirely wanting in this vast polygonous building.

‖**Polygonum** (pə'lɪgənəm). *Bot.* [mod.L. *polygonum* (*polygonos*, *-us*, *-on* Plin.), a. Gr. πολύγονον knotgrass, etc., f. πολυ-, POLY- + γόνυ knee, joint.] A large and widely distributed genus of plants, type of the N.O. *Polygonaceæ*, consisting of herbs (rarely undershrubs), with swollen stem-joints sheathed by the stipules, and small apetalous flowers, usually with red or white perianth.

It includes knotgrass (*P. aviculare*), snakeweed (*P. Bistorta*), black bindweed (*P. Convolvulus*), water-pepper (*P. Hydropiper*), persicaria (*P. Persicaria*), buckwheat (*P. Fagopyrum* or *Fagopyrum esculentum*), etc. The *polygonum* of Sturt (1833) is a *Muehlenbeckia*, N.O. *Polygonaceæ*.

1706 PHILLIPS, *Polygonum*, Polygony or Knot-grass, an Herb chiefly us'd for stopping all sorts of Fluxes, Wounds [etc.]. **1833** C. H. STURT *Two Exp. Interior S. Austral.* I. 146 Its [the creek's] bed was choaked up with bulrushes or the polygonum. **1838** T. THOMSON *Chem. Org. Bodies* 974 The *bidens*..in general did not vegetate so long as the polygonum. **1887** *Amer. Naturalist* XXI. 580 We also find that the ants rear the young, before the ground is planted, upon the roots of *Setaria* and *Polygonum*.

b. *attrib.* as ***polygonum creek, flat*** (i.e. covered with a growth of *Polygonum* or *Muehlenbeckia*).

1890 'R. BOLDREWOOD' *Col. Reformer* xvi. 190 He had shot more than one polygonum creek, straight and true as an Indian. **1898** —— *Rom. Canvass Town* 126 They drew back by degrees into the polygonum flat which at that point bordered the river.

†**po'lygony.** *Obs.* [ad. L. *polygoni-um* (Scribonius) f. Gr. *πολύγονον*.] A plant of the genus *Polygonum*; esp. snakeweed, *P. Bistorta*, the astringent root of which was formerly used in medicine.

1450-80 tr. *Secreta Secret.* 30 Take wormode,..and lete it boyle with the Rote þat is callid Pollygony,..and wasshe welle þi mouth therwith. **1590** SPENSER *F.Q.* III. v. 32 There, whether yt divine Tobacco were, Or Panachæa, or Polygony, Shee fownd, and brought it to her patient deare. **1706** [see POLYGONUM].

polygram ('pɒlɪgræm). [f. POLY- + Gr. *γράμμη* line; (cf. Gr. *πολύγραμμος* many-lined, Arist.).]

1. A figure or design consisting of many lines. (In quot. 1903 in imitation of *monogram*.)

1696 PHILLIPS (ed. 5), *Polygram*, a Geometrical Figure that has many Lines. **1863** R. TOWNSEND *Mod. Geom.* I. 144 A complete figure which in the absence of any as yet generally recognized nomenclature may be termed a polystigm in the former case, and a polygram in the latter. **1903** G. F. ABBOTT *Tour Macedonia* 43 A mystic design which..in reality was the imperial polygram. The document, polygram and all, cost me five shillings.

2. A recording made with a polygraph (sense 3).

1923 W. D. REID *Heart in Mod. Pract.* iii. 60 It is frequently not possible to determine from the polygram whether the tachycardia originates in the auricle or in the ventricle unless the tracing shows the onset or cessation of the paroxysm. **1966** R. J. FERGUSON *Polygraph & Private Industry* vii. 299 Extreme caution must be used in interpreting polygrams.

Hence **polygra'mmatic** *a.*, pertaining or relating to a polygram.

1890 in *Cent. Dict.*

polygraph ('pɒlɪgrɑːf, -æ-), *sb.* [ad. Gr. *πολυγράφ-ος, -ον* adj. writing much; cf. F. *polygraphe* (1536 in Hatz.-Darm.), It. *poligrapho* (Florio) in sense 4. In senses 1-3, app. directly f. the Greek elements.]

I. 1. a. An apparatus, on the principle of the pantograph, for producing two or more identical drawings or writings simultaneously. **b.** An apparatus for taking a number of copies of a writing; *esp.* a gelatine copying-pad.

[Cf. **1763** *Hist. Acad. des Sci.* 147 Un instrument, inventé et présenté par M. de Cotteneude auquel il donne le nom de *polygraphe* ou *Copiste habile*.]

1805 JEFFERSON *Writ.* (1830) IV. 33, I have laid aside the copying press, for a twelvemonth past, and write always with the polygraph. **1807** YOUNG *Lect. Nat. Phil.* II. 100 An ingenious instrument..by means of which copies may be multiplied with great facility; it is called the polygraph. **1819** REES *Cycl.* s.v. *Copying*, Fig. 4 represents one of Hawkins' patent polygraphs [Patent dated 1803 No. 2735]. **1829** MACKENZIE *Five Thous. Receipts* 394 To frame a polygraph, or instrument for writing two letters at once. **1884** KNIGHT *Dict. Mech.* Supp., *Polygraph*, one of the names given to the gelatine copying pad.

†**2.** *fig.* (in allusion to POLYGRAPHIC 2). A person who imitates, or is a copy of, another; an imitator or imitation. *Obs.*

1794 COLERIDGE *Lett.* (1895) 117 The move of bepraising a man by enumerating the beauties of his polygraph is at least an original one. **1797** MRS. M. ROBINSON *Walsingham* IV. 10 A polygraph is a fellow that apes one's dress and manners.

3. An instrument for obtaining tracings of movements in various parts of the body; a myograph. Also, one used to obtain tracings of other physiological characteristics (such as rates of pulse and respiration, or the electrical conductivity of the skin), and made to serve as a lie-detector.

1871 *Lancet* 25 Nov. 739/1 The most direct method for recording the heart's motion is that which we owe to Chauveau and Marey. These ingenious experimenters have supplied us with many instruments adapted for the registration of movements, but none more generally useful than the following, which has been well named the 'polygraph'. **1876** A. RANSOME *Stethometry* vi. 126 A tube, placed in the trachea of a recently killed dog, is made to communicate with the drum of a polygraph. **1890** in BILLINGS *Med. Dict.* **1895** *Syd. Soc. Lex.*, *Polygraph*, a syn. for *Myograph*. **1905** H. D. ROLLESTON *Dis. Liver* 93 J. Mackenzie has made an exhaustive study of hepatic pulsation by means of the polygraph, a modification of the cardiograph. **1923** J. A. LARSON in *Jrnl. Exper. Psychol.* VI. 424 A deception test based upon the correlation between the physiological and emotional activities... The technique consists of securing a continuous blood pressure curve (secured by an Erlanger sphygmomanometer or more preferably by a modification of the McKenzie or the Jacquet polygraphs) taken synchronously with a respiratory and a timing curve. **1942** F. E. INBAU *Lie Detection* i. 5 Until 1939 the Keeler Polygraph consisted only of the blood pressure-pulse-respiration units; since then it has been obtainable either with or without a galvanometer unit for recording electrodermal responses. **1959** M. DOLINSKY *There is no Silence* iii. 47 Anxiety causes subtle and involuntary increases in the heartbeat, respiration,..and blood pressure which the polygraph records. **1971** *Nature* 9 July 124/2 Instantaneous blood flows to the two hindlimbs..were displayed on a 'Grass P7' polygraph together with the instantaneous and mean (integrated) blood pressure. **1973** *N.Y. Law Jrnl.* 20 Mar., The court then explained that there is no scientific proof that lying heightens anxiety, and that a subject's emotional responses as measured by the polygraph are no proof either of truthfulness or lying. **1976** *Time* 27 Dec. 41/2 Patients spend the night hooked up to a polygraph, a lie-detector-like machine that monitors sleep-related physiological functions (breathing, muscle twitching, rapid eye movement). **1977** *New Yorker* 30 May 29/1 A lot of firms..now routinely give standard polygraph tests to prospective employees.

II. 4. A writer of many or various works; a voluminous author. [Cf. F. *polygraphe* one who writes on many subjects (1536).]

1854 A. G. HENDERSON tr. *Cousin's Philos. of Kant* i. 8 Leibnitz..was led away by a passion for universal knowledge... Wolf endeavoured to bring all the scattered views of the great polygraph to a common centre. **1883** *Century Mag.* VI. 251 M. Jules Claretie, most prolific of polygraphs, has..added another novel to his already long list. **1891** *Sat. Rev.* 8 Aug. 152/1 M. Auguste Vitu was..what his own countrymen call a 'polygraph'.

5. A collection of many or various writings. *rare*$^{-0}$.

1882 in OGILVIE (Annandale).

III. 6. *Cryptography.* A group of two or more letters; also, in *Phonetics*, a group of three or more letters expressing a simple sound of speech.

1943 L. D. SMITH *Cryptogr.* iv. 82 A method that represents a distinct departure from Vignère's..is found in polygraph substitution—that is, the substitution of cipher digraphs or trigraphs for the plain-text digraphs or trigraphs. **1959** *Brno Studies in English* I. 18 The following stage..replaced the cumbersome digraphs (and polygraphs) by simple but diacriticized graphemes. **1974** *Encycl. Brit. Macropædia* V. 332/1 In substitution ciphers, the characteristic relative frequencies of single letters, digraphs, and longer polygraphs serve as a basis for the assignment of plaintext equivalents to cipher values.

polygraph ('pɒlɪgrɑːf, -æ-), *v.* [f. prec. sb.] **a.** *intr.* To perform (satisfactorily, etc.) when examined with a polygraph. **b.** *trans.* To examine with a polygraph, esp. for truthfulness. Hence **'polygraphing** *vbl. sb.*

1969 H. H. COOPER *Cave with Two Exits* I. 68 The checks on him were being completed. He polygraphed okay, for what that's worth. **1978** 'W. WINGATE' *Bloodbath* ii. 15 He was..a mystery, and this despite all his debriefings..and polygraphings. *Ibid.* 16 In the two years since his defection, Yazov had been repeatedly polygraphed. **1979** P. FRIEDMAN *Termination Order* (1980) i. 14 Your superiors..will want to polygraph me. *Ibid.* iv. 57 All this nonsense—calling people back for polygraphing, or debriefing or whatever.

po'lygrapher. Also 6 poli-. [f. Gr. *πολυγράφος* (see POLYGRAPH *sb.*) + -ER[1].]

1. A writer of POLYGRAPHY (sense 1). *rare.*

1588 J. HARVEY *Disc. Probl.* 29 Whose mightie and wonderfull proceedings no Poligrapher can expresse, or Steganographer decipher. **1871** L. B. PHILLIPS *Dict. Biogr. Ref.* 298 Cunaeus, Peter (*Van der Kun*), Dutch savant and polygrapher; 1586-1638.

†**2.** = POLYGRAPH *sb.* 2. *Obs.*

1810 *Splendid Follies* II. 7, [I] wear my hat in half a dozen positions, so that I defy the mimickry of a polygrapher.

3. A user of a polygraph (sense 3).

1954 *Reporter* (N.Y.) 8 June 14/3 (*heading*) Eminent polygraphers. **1962** *Harvard Business Rev.* Nov.-Dec. 128/2 The National Board of Polygraph Examiners, an organization of polygraphers..set forth minimum standards for polygraphs. **1973** *Biomed. Engin.* VIII. 155/3 Regarding the opposing views on the skin-resistance channel; many practising polygraphers consider it to be too sensitive an indicator of emotional responses. **1978** 'W. WINGATE' *Bloodbath* ii. 25 Kruger watched the polygrapher flop into the easy chair.

polygraphic (pɒlɪ'græfɪk), *a.* (*sb.*) [f. Gr. *πολυγράφ-ος* POLYGRAPH *sb.*, or f. POLYGRAPHY, + -IC. So F. *polygraphique*.]

1. a. Writing much; voluminous or copious, as an author; treating of many subjects, as a book. *rare.*

1735 (*title*) Dictionarium Polygraphicum: Or, The Whole Body of Arts Regularly Digested. (*heading of text*) The Polygraphick Dictionary. **1807** T. HORNE tr. *Goede's Trav.* II. 131 The polygraphic Nicolls has contrived to swell his work into 20 volumes.

†**b.** Pertaining to POLYGRAPHY (sense 1). *Obs.*

1791-1823 D'ISRAELI *Cur. Lit.* (1867) 481/2 This ingenious abbot's [Trithemius] polygraphic attempts at secret writing.

2. Applied to a method of mechanically copying pictures: see POLYGRAPHY 3 a.

1788 J. BOOTH (*title*) An Address to the Public on the Polygraphic Art; or the copying or multiplying Pictures, in Oil Colours, by a Chemical and Mechanical Process. **1800** in *Spirit Pub. Jrnls.* IV. 161 These, by means of the polygraphic art, may be multiplied. **1828** LANDOR *Imag. Conv.* Wks. 1853 I. 290/2 Polygraphic transparencies..to be had for next to nothing. **1864** BOULTON *Rem. conc. Photogr. supposed of early date* 8 There can..be little doubt that these pictures are specimens of the 'polygraphic' process.

†**3.** *fig.* **a.** (in allusion to 2, or to POLYGRAPH *sb.* 2). That is an exact copy or imitation of another. *Obs.*

1797-1805 S. & HT. LEE *Canterb. T.* V. 400 A sort of polygraphic copy of a man, that might be seen in some corner of almost every collection in London. **1824** SCOTT *St. Roman's* v, He began to doubt whether the Lady Penelope and her maidens..were not..actually polygraphic copies of the same individuals.

†**b.** as *sb.* = POLYGRAPH *sb.* 2. *Obs. rare*$^{-1}$.

1797 MRS. M. ROBINSON *Walsingham* II. 100, 'I shall leave Bath to-morrow', cried the polygraphic of Narcissus.

4. Of or pertaining to a polygraph (POLYGRAPH *sb.* 1 a, 1 b); used for multiplying copies of a drawing or writing; produced, as a copy, by a polygraph.

1828 WEBSTER, *Polygraphic, Polygraphical*... 2. Done with a polygraph; as, a polygraphic copy or writing. **1883** R. HALDANE *Workshop Receipts* Ser. II. 189/2 Place a sheet of damped polygraphic paper on each page.

5. Of, pertaining to, or involving a polygraph (sense 3).

1871 *Lancet* 25 Nov. 741/2 When the capsule is pressed firmly upon the skin, the interior of the instrument is converted into a closed chamber, and every shock of the heart expels air out of the chamber into the polygraphic tambour. **1927** *Welfare Mag.* May 667/1 The exact value of this deception technique can only be determined by..the study of all possible types of pathology associated with polygraphic reactions. **1954** *Reporter* (N.Y.) 8 June 13/2 The fear of being found out and/or conscious efforts to deceive are the main causes of significant reactions in polygraphic tests of deception. **1972** *Science* 29 Sept. 1205/3 Polygraphic sleep data were scored according to standardized criteria.

6. Applied to a cipher in which the letters of the plain text are enciphered or deciphered two or more at a time.

1929 L. S. HILL in *Amer. Math. Monthly* XXXVI. 312 If polygraphic ciphers based upon normal transformations (linear ciphers) prove to be of real interest, we shall indicate a surprising way in which these ciphers may be manipulated easily and quickly. **1967** D. KAHN *Codebreakers* xiii. 406 Such a system is genuinely polygraphic, and its cryptographic security is substantial. *Ibid.* 407 A polygraphic encipherment of this magnitude is possible only with a Hill transformation. **1968** A. SINKOV *Elem. Cryptanal.* iv. 113 A system of cryptography in which a group of *n* plain text letters is replaced as a unit by a group of *n* cipher letters is called a polygraphic system.

So **poly'graphical** *a.* (in quot. = sense 1 b above: cf. POLYGRAPHER 1); **poly'graphically** *adv.*, by means of a polygraph.

1588 J. HARVEY *Disc. Probl.* 65 A booteles labor, to make a special Analysis, either of their Abcedary and Alphabeticall Spels, or of their Characteristicall, and Polygraphical suttelties. **1828** [see 4 above]. **1911** T. LEWIS *Mechanism of Heart Beat* v. 45 (*caption*) An irregularity due to premature contractions arising in the ventricle (the actual events were determined polygraphically). **1970** *Psychophysiol.* VII. 323/1 Plasma samples were obtained from 4 infants during four behavioral states..monitored polygraphically.

polygraphist. [f. POLYGRAPH + -IST.] = POLYGRAPHER 3.

1954 *Reporter* (N.Y.) 8 June 13/2 Only thirty-six percent of the psychologists (as against seventy-five percent of the polygraphists) agreed with this statement.

polygraphy (pə'lɪgrəfɪ). [ad. Gr. *πολυγραφία* a writing much; see POLYGRAPHIC *a.* (*sb.*) So F. *polygraphie* (1561 in Hatz.-Darm.) in sense 1.]

I. †**1.** A kind of cipher or secret writing (? a combination of various ciphers, or ? an abbreviated cipher resembling shorthand, i.e. containing much in little space): **a.** orig. An arbitrary name by Trithemius 1518 for his system of secret writing. **b.** Applied by Aulay Macaulay to his system of shorthand. *Obs.*

[**1518** J. TRITHEMIUS (*title*) Poligraphiæ libri VI, cum clave seu enucleatorio.] **1593** R. HARVEY *Philad.* 56 The Histories were written in some strange kind of polygraphy and steganography. **1621** BURTON *Anat. Mel.* III. ii. III. v. (1651) 498 Such occult notes,..Polygraphy,..or magnetical telling of their minds. **1727-41** CHAMBERS *Cycl.*, *Polygraphy*,..the art of writing in various unusual manners or cyphers; as also of decyphering the same... The word is usually confounded with steganography and cryptography. **1747** A. MACAULAY (*title*) Polygraphy; or Short-Hand made easy..Being an universal character fitted to all Languages. **1855** *Chamb. Jrnl.* IV. 134/2 These decipherers gave the high-sounding names of Cryptography, Cryptology, Polygraphy, and Steganography, to their art.

II. 2. Much writing; copious or various literary work.

a **1661** FULLER *Worthies, Cambr.* (1662) I. 162 One, considering his Polygraphy, said merrily, 'that he must write whilst he slept, it being unpossible he should do so much when waking'. **1831** *Fraser's Mag.* III. 715 Even Sir Walter Scott, with all his multifarious polygraphy—what is he beside the goodly *Summa Theologiæ* of Thomas Aquinas? **1890** *Sat. Rev.* 22 Nov. 602/2 It has been too much the fashion to dismiss his wonderful 'polygraphy', his miscellaneous journalism.., with a sort of allowance as merely wonderful of its kind.

III. 3. a. A method of producing copies of paintings, invented by Joseph Booth *c* 1788: see POLYGRAPHIC 2.

1788 J. BOOTH *Addr. Polygraphic Art* 13 Having thus considered the invention of Polygraphy.

b. The use of a polygraph (POLYGRAPH *sb.* 1 a).

1828 WEBSTER, *Polygraphic, Polygraphical*, pertaining to polygraphy, as a polygraphic instrument. **1886** *Cassell's Encycl. Dict., Polygraphy*... 3. The art of making a number of drawings or writings simultaneously. **1895** *Funk's Stand. Dict., Polygraphy*. 1. The use of a polygraph.

c. The use of a polygraph (sense 3).

1923 W. D. REID *Heart in Mod. Pract.* iii. 63 Polygraph tracings are also taken from the apex of the heart, the carotid artery, and over the liver, but their importance does not warrant description in this limited presentation of polygraphy. **1954** *Reporter* (N.Y.) 22 June 22/2 The most acute current problem in polygraphy.. is how to set and maintain professional standards. **1973** *Biomed. Engin.* VIII. 155/3 To readers outside of the field of polygraphy, it will perhaps seem remarkable that electronic recording is not used for all three channels and that other physiological events are not recorded routinely.

poly-groove, -grooved: see POLY-.

polygyn (ˈpɒlɪdʒɪn). *Bot.* [ad. mod.L. *polygyn-us*: see POLYGYNIA.] (See quot.)

1828 WEBSTER, *Polygyn*, a plant having many pistils.

polygynæcial, -œcial (ˌpɒlɪdʒɪˈniːsɪəl), *a. Bot. rare*⁻⁰. [f. POLY- + *gynœcium*, GYNÆCEUM + -AL¹.] Applied to a multiple fruit formed by union of the pistils of several flowers.

1876 BALFOUR in *Encycl. Brit.* IV. 150/2 Multiple fruits are called polygynœcial, as being formed by many gynœcia.

polygyˈnaiky. *rare*⁻¹. [f. POLY- + Gr. γυναικ-, stem of γυνή woman, wife + -Y.] = POLYGYNY.

1880 T. E. HOLLAND *Jurisprudence* (1882) 131 Polygamy, i.e. polygynaiky or polyandry, has been and is recognised as marriage in many parts of the world.

‖**Polygynia** (pɒlɪˈdʒɪnɪə). [f. mod.L. *polygyn-us*, f. Gr. πολυ-, POLY- + γυνή woman, wife (taken by Linnæus in sense 'pistil').]

1. *Bot.* An order in some classes of the Linnæan Sexual System, comprising plants having flowers with more than 12 styles or stigmas.

[**1748** LINNÆUS *Hortus Upsal.* 154 Polygynia.] **1760** J. LEE *Introd. Bot.* II. viii, *Polyginia*, comprehending such Plants as have many Styles. **1770** ELLIS in *Phil. Trans.* LX. 528 Dr. Linnæus.. places it among the Dodecandria Polygynia.

2. = POLYGYNY. *rare.*

1865 MᶜLENNAN *Prim. Marr.* viii. 181 In certain cantons of Media, according to Strabo, polygunia was authorised by express law which ordained every inhabitant to maintain at least seven wives.

polyˈgynian, *a. Bot. rare*⁻⁰. [f. prec. 1 + -AN.] = POLYGYNOUS 1.

1828 WEBSTER, *Polygynian*, having many pistils.

polygynic (pɒlɪˈdʒɪnɪk), *a. rare.* [f. as POLYGYNY + -IC.] = POLYGYNOUS 2.

1876 H. SPENCER *Princ. Sociol.* (1885) I. III. ix. 675 Among the Esquimaux,.. we see, along with monogamic unions, others that are polyandric and polygynic.

polyˈgynious, *a. Bot. rare*⁻⁰. [f. mod.L. POLYGYNI-A + -OUS.] = POLYGYNOUS 1.

1858 MAYNE *Expos. Lex., Polygynius*,.. applied to an order.. of plants.. polygynious.

polygynist (pəˈlɪdʒɪnɪst). [f. as POLYGYNY + -IST.] One who practises (or favours) polygyny.

1876 H. SPENCER *Princ. Sociol.* I. III. iv. §285 The Fuegians.. are polygynists. *Ibid.* ix. §315 The Merovingian kings were polygynists.

polygynous (pəˈlɪdʒɪnəs), *a.* [f. mod.L. *polygyn-us* (see POLYGYNIA) + -OUS.]

1. *Bot.* Having many pistils, styles, or stigmas; *spec.* belonging to the order *Polygynia*.

1846 WORCESTER, *Polygynous*, having many styles. *Loudon.* **1880** GRAY *Struct. Bot.* (ed. 6) 261 Less general.. terms are such as.. *Polygynous* (of many pistils).

2. Having more than one, or several, wives (or concubines); practising, pertaining to, or involving polygyny. (Corresp. to POLYANDROUS 2.)

1874 SIDGWICK *Meth. Ethics* xi. 337 A legal polygynous connexion. **1876** FOX BOURNE *Locke* I. viii. 429 The frivolous, corrupted, polygynous and polyandrous society by which he was surrounded. **1891** E. WESTERMARCK *Hist. Hum. Marr.* (1894) 439 Even in Africa, the chief centre of polygynous habits, polygyny is an exception.

b. *Zool.* Of a male animal: Having several female mates; characterized by polygyny, as a species. (Corresp. to POLYANDROUS 2 b.)

polygyny (pəˈlɪdʒɪnɪ). [f. POLY- + Gr. γυνή woman, wife; corresp. to a Gr. type *πολυγυνία, f. πολυ- many + γυνή woman, wife. So mod.F. *polygynie*.] That form of polygamy in which one man has several wives at the same time; plurality of wives (or concubines). (Corresp. to POLYANDRY.)

1780 M. MADAN *Thelyphthora* II. 91 There is not a nation under heaven, where polygyny is more openly practised, than in this Christian country. **1861** *Times* 21 Aug. 10/2 It is doubtless this teaching that polygyny is a divine institution which has such an effect in repressing the rebellious instincts of the women. **1876** H. SPENCER *Princ. Sociol.* (1877) I. 646 Where wife-stealing is now practised, it is commonly associated with polygyny. **1892** *Nation* (N.Y.) 24 Nov. 398/3 The license, not of polygamy but of polygyny, was completely established in the case of kings.

b. *Zool.* Of a male animal: The having more than one female mate.

polygyral: see POLY-.

‖**polyhæmia** (pɒlɪˈhiːmɪə). *Path.* Also polyemia, -æmia, -hemia. [mod.L., a. Gr. πολυαιμία, f. πολυ-, POLY- + αἷμα blood.] Fullness or excess of blood; plethora.

1858 MAYNE *Expos. Lex., Polyæmia*, abundance of blood; an old term for true Plethora. **1866** A. FLINT *Princ. Med.* (1880) 61 Recent experiments on animals render improbable the existence of a permanent polyæmia. **1876** tr. *Wagner's Gen. Pathol.* (ed. 6) 543 Polyhæmia, and polycythæmia as well, are in most cases only transitory states.

polyhalite (pɒlɪˈhælaɪt). *Min.* [ad. Ger. *polyhalit* (Stromeyer, 1818), f. Gr. πολυ-, POLY- + ἅλς salt: see -ITE¹.] Hydrous sulphate of calcium, potassium, and magnesium, usually occurring in fibrous masses of a red or yellowish colour.

1818 *Q. Jrnl. Sc.* VI. 170 It.. has now received the name of polyhalite. **1852** *Phillips' Introd. Min.* 538 Polyhalite.. is found with rock salt. **1876** PAGE *Adv. Text-bk. Geol.* xvi. 305 These deposits consist of a series of saliferous strata—carnallite.. polyhalite, etc.

polyhaploid: see POLY-.

polyhedra, pl. of POLYHEDRON.

polyhedral (pɒlɪˈhiːdrəl, -ˈhɛdrəl), *a.* Also polyedral. [f. Gr. πολύεδρος (Plut.) (f. πολυ-, POLY- + ἕδρα base, side of a solid figure) + -AL¹.]

1. Of the form of a polyhedron; having many faces or sides, as a solid figure or body.

1811 PINKERTON *Petralogy* I. 324 A granular serpentine, .. which.. splits in small polyhedral fragments. **1845** TODD & BOWMAN *Phys. Anat.* I. 81 The fat vesicles.. assume a polyhedral figure more or less regular. **1885** GOODALE *Physiol. Bot.* (1892) 47 Starch.. occurs as minute.. polyhedral granules.

2. Pertaining or relating to a polyhedron; in *Higher Algebra* applied to a class of functions.

1880 CAYLEY *Coll. Math. Papers* XI. 183 The functions so transformable into themselves must be Polyhedral functions .. the linear transformations.. corresponding to the rotations whereby the spherical polyhedron can be brought into coincidence with its own original position.

3. Of an angle: Formed by three or more planes meeting at a point. (Usually called a *solid angle.*) Cf. DIHEDRAL.

1864 in WEBSTER.

4. *polyhedral disease* = POLYHEDROSIS.

1913 *Jrnl. Econ. Entomol.* VI. 482 In Europe there is a tendency to group all the caterpillar diseases which are characterized by the formation of polyhedral bodies under the name of 'polyederkrankheit' or polyhedral diseases. **1971** *Indian Jrnl. Entomol.* XXXIII. 111 (*heading*) Investigations on the nuclear polyhedrosis of *Prodenia litura* Fabricius: 1. Nature of the polyhedral disease.

polyhedric (pɒlɪˈhɛdrɪk), *a.* Also polyedric. [f. as prec. + -IC.] = prec. 1. Also *fig.* 'many-sided'.

1819 SHELLEY *P. Bell the Third* Ded., Peter is a polyhedric Peter, or a Peter with many sides... He is a Proteus of a Peter. **1853** KANE *Grinnell Exp.* xliii. (1856) 400 The ice, broken into polyhedric masses, gave at a few hundred yards no indications to the eye of the lines of separation. **1893** *Sat. Rev.* 28 Jan. 88/1 Most questions are polyhedric.

So **polyˈhedrical** *a. rare.*

1663 BOYLE *Exp. Hist. Colours* I. iii. §6 The protuberant particles may be of very great variety of figures, spherical, elliptical, polyedrical, and some very irregular. **1664** POWER *Exp. Philos.* I. 42 They all seem like Fragments of Crystal.. of irregular polyhedrical figures. *c* **1817** HOGG *Tales & Sk.* II. 199 Which body must be spherical or polyedrical.

polyhedroid: see POLY-.

polyhedrometry (-ˈɒmɛtrɪ). [f. POLYHEDRON + -METRY, after *geometry* or *trigonometry*.] That part of solid geometry which deals with the numbers of faces, edges, and angles of polyhedra. Hence **polyhedrometric** (-əʊˈmɛtrɪk) *a.*, pertaining to polyhedrometry.

1890 in *Cent. Dict.*

polyhedron (pɒlɪˈhiːdrən, -ˈhɛdrən). Also polyedron. Pl. -a (rarely -ons). [a. Gr. πολύεδρον a polyhedron, prop. neut. of πολύεδρος adj.: see POLYHEDRAL.] *Geom.* A solid figure contained by many (i.e., usually, more than six) plane faces; a many-sided solid. Hence, a material body having such a form.

1570 BILLINGSLEY *Euclid* XII. xvii. 377 A solide of many sides (which is called a Polyhedron). **1690** LEYBOURN *Curs. Math.* 289 In the Sphere *EDF* inscribe a Polyedron. **1727-41** CHAMBERS *Cycl.* s.v., *Gnomonic Polyhedron*, is a stone with several faces, whereon are projected various kinds of dials. **1762** H. WALPOLE *Vertue's Anecd. Paint.* (1765) I. vii. 181 Holding a pair of compasses, and by his side a Polyedron, composed of twelve pentagons. **1871** TYNDALL *Fragm. Sc.* (1879) I. xii. 368 The little polyhedra become converted into laminæ.

fig. **1851** J. HAMILTON *Royal Preacher* xiv. (1854) 180 They are the polyhedrons of the Church, each punctilio of their own forming a several face.

b. *spec.* A lens having many facets, multiplying the image of an object; a multiplying-glass.

1727-41 CHAMBERS *Cycl.* s.v., The eye, through a polyhedron, sees the object repeated as many times as there are sides. **1764** REID *Inquiry* VI. xii. (1801) 272 Instances wherein the same object may appear double, triple, or quadruple to one eye, without the help of a polyhedron or multiplying glass.

polyhedrosis (pɒlɪhiːˈdrəʊsɪs, -hɛˈdrəʊsɪs). *Ent.* Pl. -oses (-ˈəʊsiːz). [f. POLYHEDR(AL *a.* + -OSIS.] A fatal disease of caterpillars, characterized by the presence of polyhedral virus particles.

1947 *Science* 3 Oct. 323/2 The fragility of the integument and the marked internal liquefaction of tissues, so characteristic of polyhedroses, is absent. **1967** K. M. SMITH *Insect Virology* ii. 8 The polyhedroses are subdivided into nuclear and cytoplasmic diseases. **1973** *Nature* 2 Nov. 5/3 The outbreak tends to end abruptly in the spring of the third year, because of the explosive spread of a nuclear polyhedrosis virus which kills off some of the caterpillars at the end of their first moult (instar).

polyˈhedrous, *a.* Also polyedrous. [f. as POLYHEDRAL + -OUS.] = POLYHEDRAL.

1678 CUDWORTH *Intell. Syst.* I. iv. 531 The same Object beheld through a Polyedrous Glass.. is thereby rendred Manifold to the Spectator. **1769** RASPE in *Phil. Trans.* LXI. 582 Many of these are formed in polyedrous pillars. **1807** W. TAYLOR in *Ann. Rev.* V. 586 He not only sees double, but through the polyedrous eyes of a dragon-fly.

polyhex: see POLY-.

polyhistor (pɒlɪˈhɪstə(r)). Also 6 polihistor. [a. Gr. πολυΐστωρ very learned, f. πολυ-, POLY- + ἵστωρ (see HISTORY).] A man of much or varied learning; a great scholar.

[**1573-80** G. HARVEY *Letter-bk.* (Camden) 166 He hath bene countid heer.. a πολυΐστωρ, and in deed is so commonly termid amongst us.] **1588** J. HARVEY *Disc. Probl.* 63 In poets, philosophers, polihistors, antiquaries, philologers, schoolemen, and other learned discoursers. **1621** BP. MOUNTAGU *Diatribæ* 453 So great a polyhistor as Ioseph Scaliger. **1885** MASSON *Carlyle* ii. 63 Himself a polyhistor or accomplished universal scholar.

So **polyhiˈstorian** = *polyhistor*; **polyhiˈstoric** *a.*, of or pertaining to a polyhistor, widely erudite; **polyˈhistory**, the character or quality of a polyhistor, wide or varied learning.

1669 GALE *Crt. Gentiles* I. I. iii. 20 Alexander the *Polyhistorian cites this. **1693** *Phil. Trans.* XVII. 808 He regrets the loss also of many Polyhistorians, as, Theopompus, Phavorinus, and Alexander Polyhistor. **1881** MASSON *De Quincey* xi. 137 Much of that *polyhistoric character, that multifariousness of out-of-the-way learning. **1819** J. RICHARDSON *Kant's Logic* 61 Mere *polyhistory is, so to say, learning which is cyclopic, or wants an eye—that of philosophy. **1869** A. W. WARD tr. *Curtius' Hist. Greece* II. III. iii. 509 Sophistry.. thus necessarily led to a vain and superficial polyhistory, such as was most fully represented in the person of Hippias of Elis.

polyhybrid (pɒlɪˈhaɪbrɪd), *sb.* and *a. Biol.* [f. POLY- + HYBRID *sb.* and *a.*]

A. *sb.* A hybrid that is heterozygous at several genetic loci. B. *adj.* Of, pertaining to, or characteristic of such a hybrid, or a cross resulting in one.

1911 FARMER & DARBISHIRE tr. *H. De Vries's Mutation Theory* II. 586 The di-polyhybrids are mongrels whose parents differ from one another in respect of two or more elementary characters. *Ibid.* 681/1 (Index), Polyhybrids, 586. **1922** *Hereditas* III. 233 The segregation is evidently polyhybrid showing transgression in one direction. **1965** BELL & COOMBE tr. *Strasburger's Textbk. Bot.* 334 The genetic consequences of crossing both dihybrids and polyhybrids are directly dependent upon the manner in which the chromosomes are distributed at the reductional division.

polyhydramnios (ˌpɒlɪhaɪˈdræmnɪəs). *Obstetrics.* [f. POLY- + HYDR(O- + AMNIOS.] = HYDRAMNIOS.

1889 R. R. RENTOUL *Causes & Treatm. Abortion* iv. 114 Delore holds that polyhydramnios exists when the quantity exceeds four and two-tenths of a pint. *Ibid.* 115 In a few rare cases of twins, polyhydramnios was found with one child, while oligohydramnios accompanied the other. **1923** E. P. DAVIS *Complications of Pregnancy* xxi. 256 At the stage of fetal development, very often polyhydramnios may be mistaken for ascites as well as ovarian cyst. **1976** *Lancet* 30 Oct. 960/2 She was admitted to hospital with significant polyhydramnios.

polyhydric (pɒlɪˈhaɪdrɪk), *a. Chem.* [f. POLY- + HYDRIC *a.*] Containing more than one hydroxyl group in the molecule.

1879 *Jrnl. Chem. Soc.* XXXVI. 1033 The action of sulphuric monochloride on monhydric alcohols gives rise to ethereal sulphates.., and a similar reaction takes place with polyhydric alcohols. **1937** *Discovery* Sept. 284/1 On this type of polyhydric phenol resin.. a further.. discovery has been made. **1946** *Nature* 3 Aug. 155/2 Manganese dioxide is reduced with great ease to form divalent manganese ion by .. polyhydric phenols such as quinol, catechol, gallic acid, etc. **1951** I. L. FINAR *Org. Chem.* I. xi. 208 The polyhydric alcohols chemically resemble glycerol in many ways. **1972** *Materials & Technol.* V. ix. 266 The epoxy resins differ from most of the other polyhydric alcohols in that they are polymeric.

polyhydroxy(l, -iamond: see POLY-.

polyimide (pɒlɪ'ɪmaɪd). [f. POLY- + IMIDE.] Any polymer in which the units contain imide groups, usu. in the form

$$-CO-\overset{|}{N}-CO-;$$

esp. any of a class of thermosetting resins widely used for heat-resistant films and coatings.

1945 *Brit. Pat. 570,858*, The products are referred to as polyamide-imides. When a tetracarboxylic acid of the above mentioned kind is used each pair of carboxyl groups reacts with an amino group of the diprimary diamine through imide-formation so that the polymer is a polyimide rather than a polyamide-imide. **1955** *U.S. Pat. 2,710,853* 1 This invention relates to a novel group of linear polymeric polyimides,..said polyimides differing from previously known polyimides in properties which are important in injection molding applications. **1965** *New Scientist* 19 Aug. 443/1 Du Pont's polyimide known as H-film, or Kapton, a plastic film that finds its chief use as a high-temperature electrical insulation. **1975** WEN-HSUAN CHANG et al. in M. Lewin et al. *Flame-Retardant Polymeric Materials* x. 442 Decorative coatings for cookware are possible with polyimide coatings because of their ability to withstand direct contact with flame.

polyion(ic, -isobutylene: see POLY-.

polyisocyanate (,pɒlɪaɪsəʊ'saɪəneɪt). [f. POLY- + *isocyanate* s.v. ISO- b.] Any organic compound containing two or more isocyanate groups; also applied to polymers prepared from such compounds, esp. polyurethanes.

1943 [see POLYESTERAMIDE]. **1945** *Chem. & Engin. News* 25 Sept. 1615/2 The polyurethanes..are produced by the reaction of polyisocyanates with polyhydroxy compounds such as polyesters. **1958** *Times Rev. Industry* June 37/3 An I.C.I. special product known as Suprasec K is a 50 per cent. solution in ethyl acetate of a newly developed polyisocyanate designed for use in high-quality lacquers for wood, rubber, and other materials. **1959** *Times* 27 Apr. (Rubber Industry Suppl.) p. vi/7 Natural rubber, neoprene and polyisocyanates play the same part in ships as in hotels—for luxury upholstery, non-slipping table covering, fire-resisting foam bedding, floor covering, &c. **1968** E. R. WELLS in C. R. Martens *Technol. Paints, Varnishes & Lacquers* xiii. 205 Urethane is now the accepted description for a group of polymers that are sometimes called polyurethanes, isocyanates or polyisocyanates.

polyisoprene (pɒlɪ'aɪsəʊpriːn). [f. POLY- + ISOPRENE.] Any of the polymers of isoprene, which include the major constituent of natural rubber and some synthetic rubbers very similar to it.

1935 [see *polybutadiene* s.v. POLY- 2]. **1946** F. MARCHIONNA *Butalastic Polymers* xvi. 483 The sodium butadiene rubber can be admixed with 50 per cent of a polyisoprene or purified natural rubber. **1959** *Economist* 21 Mar. 1101/1 Shell Chemical Corporation has announced that it will shortly begin commercial production of polyisoprene. **1963** H. R. CLAUSER *Encycl. Engin. Materials* 580/1 New 'synthetic natural rubber', *cis*-polyisoprene is said to have performance characteristics virtually identical with those of natural rubber. **1975** *Sci. Amer.* Dec. 101/1 Polymers that exhibit rubbery behaviour at room temperature include polyisoprene (natural rubber) and polybutadiene (a synthetic rubber).

polykaryocyte(-cytic), poly-laminated: see POLY-.

polyle, variant of PULLAILE *Obs.*, poultry.

polylectal to **polylobular:** see POLY-.

polylogue ('pɒlɪlɒg). [f. POLY- + -LOGUE.] A discussion between more than two persons.

1941 *Horizon* 15 Mar. 207 English people..tend to think of America..as a polylogue of cigars. **1961** *Lancet* 29 July 251/1 The polylogue here reported is not word-perfect, but the stenographer has tried to catch the to-and-fro of animated discussion. **1964** *Amer. Speech* XXXIX. 206 It is important as another voice in what has..become a 'polylogue' on a matter having wide interest. **1969** P. L. BERGER *Rumor of Angels* iv. 100 The ecumenical movement ..has tried to bring Eastern Christianity more and more into the 'polylogue' (if the term will be permitted). **1977** *N.Y. Rev. Bks.* 23 June 30/2 For us there are dispersed, interchangeable 'points of view'; photography is a polylogue.

polylogy (pə'lɪlədʒɪ). *rare.* Also 7 polu-. [ad. Gr. πολυλογία, f. πολυλόγος loquacious: see POLY- and -LOGY.] Much speaking, loquacity. So **po'lylogize** *v. intr.* (*nonce-wd.*), to talk much.

1602 R. T. *Five Godlie Serm.* 287 Vsing Polulogies and Battologies that is vaine repetitions, and much babblings. **1621** T. GRANGER *On Eccles.* 115 Many words, (batologie or polylogie)..are signes of a foole. **1845** S. JUDD *Margaret* II. ii, I have 'polylogized' quite long enough. **1890** *My Curates* 19 Mr. Slimmer's vigorous energy in polylogy (if I may coin a word).

polyloquent to **polymania:** see POLY-.

polymastia (pɒlɪ'mæstɪə). *Med.* Also anglicized as **-masty.** [mod.L., ad. G. *polymastie*, f. Gr. πολυ- POLY- + μαστός breast.] The condition of having more than two breasts (the supernumerary ones being generally very small). Cf. POLYMASTISM.

1878 *Glasgow Med. Jrnl.* X. 70 Polymastia is not extremely rare in the female sex, but is so in the male. **1904** G. S. HALL *Adolescence* (1908) I. vi. 421 Polymasty or supernumerary breasts occurs about once in five hundred persons. **1928** M. SUMMERS *Discovery of Witches* 40 A large number of cases may be explained by polymastia and polythelia, anatomical divagations which are far commoner than is generally supposed. **1970** H. P. LEIS *Diagnosis & Treatm. Breast Lesions* i. 15 Polymastia, presenting as more than one breast on one or both sides, is due to the persistence of part of the milk ridge and these supernumerary breasts can occur anywhere along the milk line.

Hence **poly'mastic** *a.* and *sb.*, (a person or animal) having more than two breasts; **poly'mastoid** *a.* (*rare*).

1879 *Jrnl. Anat. & Physiol.* XIII. 434 In the dog, which is the only polymastoid animal readily available, the position of the nipples seems to be irregular and unsymetrical [*sic*]. **1891** *Ibid.* XXV. 228 The additional mammary structures do not develop just anywhere; but they appear only in certain definite positions, which almost invariably correspond with those occupied normally by the glands of polymastic animals. **1918** DEAVER & MCFARLAND *Breast* iii. 54 Robert..points out that the mother of his famous case of supernumerary mammae on the outer side of the thigh, was a polymastic. **1934** *Jrnl. R. Anthrop. Inst.* LXIV. 93 The best known examples of the first form are the paleolithic figures at Laussel and the polymastic Diana of the Ephesians. **1943** C. F. GESCHICKTER *Dis. Breast* i. 12 Most authors have found the majority of the accessory mammae below the normally situated pair... Iwai, however, in 511 Japanese polymastics, found 88 per cent of the supernumerary breasts above the normal ones.

polymastigate, -mastigous: see POLY-.

poly'mastism. *Med.* [f. as prec. + -ISM.] = POLYMASTIA.

1886 W. N. PARKER tr. *Wiedersheim's Elem. Compar. Anat. Vertebr.* A. 28 The occasional existence in men of supernumerary teats, and in women of supernumerary mammæ and teats (polymastism and polythelism) is very remarkable. **1903** *Lancet* 28 Feb. 613/2 It may be concluded ..that human polymastism is a reversion to a primitive condition in which many glands were developed and many young were brought forth at a birth. **1936** NEAL & RAND *Compar. Anat.* IV. 181 (*caption*) The presence of supernumerary teats (polymastism) in man supports the theory of the animal origin of the human body.

polymastodont (pɒlɪ'mæstədɒnt), *a.* and *sb. Palæont.* [f. mod.L. *Polymastodon, -ont-*, f. Gr. πολυ-, POLY- + μαστός breast, nipple + ὀδούς tooth: cf. MASTODON.] **a.** *adj.* Belonging to the genus *Polymastodon* or family *Polymastodontidæ* of small extinct N. American marsupials, having numerous tubercles on the molar teeth. **b.** *sb.* A marsupial of this genus or family.

polymath ('pɒlɪmæθ), *sb.* (*a.*) Also 7 **polumathe.** [ad. Gr. πολυμαθής having learnt much, f. πολυ- much + μαθ-, stem of μανθάνειν to learn. So F. *polymathe.*] **a.** A person of much or varied learning; one acquainted with various subjects of study.

1621 BURTON *Anat. Mel.* Democr. to Rdr. (1676) 4/2 To be thought and held Polumathes and Polyhistors. *a* **1840** MOORE *Devil among Schol.* 7 The Polymaths and Polyhistors, Polyglots and all their sisters. **1855** M. PATTISON *Ess.* I. 290 He belongs to the class which German writers..have denominated 'Polymaths'. **1897** O. SMEATON *Smollett* ii. 30 One of the last of the mighty Scots polymaths.

b. *attrib.* or *adj.* Very learned. as *adj.*

1881 *Athenæum* 31 Sept. 300/3 [His] literary criticism..is generally judicious and free from 'polymath terminology'. **1893** *Jrnl. Educ.* 1 Dec. 657/1 A polymath headmaster. **1919** T. S. ELIOT *Poems*, The masters of the subtle schools are controversial, polymath. **1959** *New Scientist* 15 Oct. 712/2 Polymath historians, who command the language and literature and science of the period. **1976** *Nature* 16 Sept. 261/3 The book is polymath, up-to-date and non-mathematical.

So **poly'mathic** *a.*, pertaining to a polymath, characterized by varied learning; † **po'lymathist** = *polymath*; **po'lymathy** [ad. Gr. πολυμαθία], much or varied learning, acquaintance with many branches of knowledge.

1828 WEBSTER, *Polymathic, pertaining to polymathy. **1849** OTTÉ tr. *Humboldt's Cosmos* II. 541 Necessity for a certain amount of polymathic learning. **1976** *Publishers Weekly* 16 Feb. 82/2 Crichton's polymathic talent has settled on another exotic site for a fanciful story. **1976** S. HYNES *Auden Generation* viii. 259 A synthesizing, diagnostic, polymathic mind, given to schematizing knowledge and history in elaborate diagrams. **1621** BP. MOUNTAGU *Diatribæ* 322 An Atlas of Learning, the only *Polymathist of the World. *c* **1645** HOWELL *Lett.* (1650) III. viii. 13 Polymathists, that stand poring..upon a moth-eaten Author. **1642** HARTLIB *Ref. Schools* 53 That high, and excellent learning, which men, for the large extent of it, call *Polymathie. **1865** GROTE *Plato* I. ii. 88 Aristotle..exhibits ..much of that polymathy which he transmitted to the Peripatetics generally. **1895** BENEKE *Comparetti's Vergil in Mid. Ages* 224 The tendency..of the scholars of the time,.. was entirely towards polymathy.

polymatype ('pɒlɪmətaɪp). *Printing.* [a. F. *polymatype*, arbitrary f. POLY- + TYPE *sb.*] A method, now disused, of casting a large number of types at one operation. Also *attrib.*

1890 in *Cent. Dict.* **1896** T. L. DE VINNE *Moxon's Mech. Exerc., Printing* 416 Didot's polymatype mould, made to cast fifty types at one operation.

† **poly'mechany.** *Obs. rare.* Also poli-. [ad. Gr. πολυμηχανία fullness of resources, inventiveness, f. πολυμήχανος adj., f. πολυ-, POLY- + μηχανή contrivance, MACHINE.] Multifarious contrivance or invention.

1592 G. HARVEY *Four Lett.* iv. Wks. (Grosart) I. 230 In actuall Experimentes, and polymechany, nothing too-profound.

polymely (pə'lɪmɪlɪ). *Anat.* [ad. mod.L. *polymelia*, f. Gr. πολυ-, POLY- + μέλος limb.] The occurrence of supernumerary or redundant limbs or members, as a monstrosity. So **poly'melian** *a.*, exhibiting polymely.

1890 *Cent. Dict.*, *Polymelian*..*Polymely.* **1895** in *Syd. Soc. Lex.* **1899** *Proc. Zool. Soc.* 857 *note* (Cassell *Suppl.*), New growths comparable to the bifid or trifid regenerated tails of Lizards, and to the polydactyly and even polymely arising from mutilations in Batrachians.

polyme'niscous, *a.* [f. POLY- + MENISCUS + -OUS.] Composed of many lenses, as the eye of an insect.

1888 ROLLESTON & JACKSON *Anim. Life* 492 (*Arthropoda*) A polymeniscous eye. **1899** J. A. THOMSON *Outl. Zool.* xiv. 304 They have only one lense (monomeniscous), whereas the compound forms have many lenses (polymeniscous).

polymenorrhœa (,pɒlɪmɛnɒ'riːə). *Path.* Also -rrhea. [f. POLY- + MENORRHŒA.] Excessively frequent or unduly profuse menstrual bleeding.

1931 *Endocrinol.* XV. 180 The problem of polymenorrhea, too profuse and too frequent menses,..is a very vital one to the gynecologist. **1956** C. F. FLUHMANN *Managem. Menstrual Disorders* xvii. 196 Polymenorrhea may supervene as the result of an endocrine disorder such as hypothyroidism. **1964** L. MARTIN *Clin. Endocrinol.* (ed. 4) viii. 247 (*heading*) Polymenorrhoea and postponement of menstruation. **1968** VORYS & NERI in J. J. Gold *Textbk. Gynecol. Endocrinol.* xi. 253 Polymenorrhea may also be seen frequently as a premenopausal symptom.

Hence **polymeno'rrhœal, -'rrhœic** *adjs.*

1963 *Jrnl. Jap. Obstetr. & Gynecol. Soc.* X. 40/2 Frequency of corpus luteum insufficiency..differed according to difference in the length of the cycle, being higher in polymenorrheal cycle of 15-24 days and in oligomenorrheal cycle of 39-43 days. **1968** VORYS & NERI in J. J. Gold *Textbk. Gynecol. Endocrinol.* xi. 261 Polymenorrheic cycles of less than 20 days.

polymer ('pɒlɪmə(r)). *Chem.* [mod. (Berzelius, 1830) f. Gr. πολυμερ-ής having many parts, manifold, f. πολυ-, POLY- + μέρος part, share; so mod.F. *polymère* adj. See ISOMER.] **1.** A substance polymeric with another; any one of a series of polymeric compounds. In mod. use, any substance which has a molecular structure built up largely or completely from a number (freq. very large) of similar polyatomic units bonded together.

The repeating units are often molecules of a single compound, but polymers may also result from combination of two or more different constituents; in either case linking of units may be accompanied by elimination of small molecules, and the formula and molecular weight of the polymer are not necessarily exact multiples of those of any component monomer. Also, esp. in contexts of Applied Chemistry, the use of the term is sometimes restricted to cases where the number of units in the structure is large.

1866 ROSCOE *Elem. Chem.* 314 Cyanuric Acid... This polymer of cyanic acid is a solid crystalline substance formed on heating urea. **1889** CROLL *Stellar Evol.* 95 The bodies thus formed are known as polymers. **1929** W. H. CAROTHERS in *Jrnl. Amer. Chem. Soc.* LI. 2548 Whatever the term polymer may mean now, it does not mean precisely what Berzelius intended, and the conditions which he set up are not sufficient to define it. *Ibid.* 2549 Two types of polymers may be distinguished... (1) Addition or A polymers. The molecular formula of the monomer is identical with that of the structural unit... (2) Condensation or C polymers: the molecular formula of the monomer differs from that of the structural unit. **1935** C. ELLIS *Chem. Synthetic Resins* I. iv. 53 In a condensation reaction, the polymer is no longer a multiple of the monomer as in the case of the addition polymer. **1958** *Times* 21 Nov. 5/6 All of them are formed by the joining together of simpler molecules; they are therefore polymers, as are plastics and synthetic fibres. **1967** MARGERISON & EAST *Introd. Polymer Chem.* iii. 131 As the conversion of the monomers into polymer proceeds, the number of possible ways in which the monomers may add on to the growing polymer increases rapidly. **1969** *Times* 3 July 7/7 The substance is a polymer of ordinary water molecules linked together by an unusual kind of chemical bond. **1973** *Nature* 6 Apr. 420/1 Natural rubber is still the preferred polymer for many high performance applications. **1974** *Sci. Amer.* Mar. 66/3 Glass is an inorganic polymer made up of rings and chains of repeating silicate units. **1974** D. M. ADAMS *Inorg. Solids* vii. 239 The most stable polymers for other metals are $M_6O^{8-}{}_{19}$ (M = Nb, Ta), $Mo_7O^{6-}{}_{24}$, $Mo_8O^{4-}{}_{26}$ and $HW_6O^{5-}{}_{21}$. **1978** *Prospects for Polymers* (Shell Internat. Petroleum Co.) 1 Not all polymers are man-made: wool, rubber, cotton and silk are examples of natural polymers.

2. *attrib.* and *Comb.*, as ***polymer chemistry***, that branch of chemistry concerned with the preparation and properties of polymers; so ***polymer chemist.***

1929 *Industr. & Engin. Chem.* Feb. 131/1 Beyond certain degrees of polymerization x-ray methods do not longer enable estimations of polymer length. **1933** *Ibid.* Feb. 132/1 Development of the best binder—be it resin or another member of the polymer family—is the next step. **1948** *Science* 19 Nov. 545/2 In recent years polymer chemists have shown how it is possible to synthesize compounds of high molecular weight..from known compounds (monomers) of low molecular weight. **1950** *Nature* 22 Apr. 634/1 (*heading*) Polymer chemistry as applied to plastics. **1953** *Endeavour* Apr. 92/1 In terms of polymer-chemistry concepts, the molecular shape is changed by the electrostatic field. **1966** C. R. TOTTLE *Sci. Engin. Materials* p. vi, An enormous quantity of synthetic polymer materials has replaced much of the metal in the domestic kitchen, leather, wool, and cotton in furnishings, and natural rubber, wood, and metal in vehicles, prime movers. **1967** MARGERISON & EAST *Introd. Polymer Chem.* i. 16 However, in the case of a real polymer chain, the finite size of the backbone carbon atoms and the substituents cannot be neglected. *Ibid.* 22 Polymer molecules in the pure liquid state can easily be pictured in the terms used to describe concentrated solutions. **1975** *Nature* 31 July 443/3 For those wishing to get a feel for what is going on in a selection of other areas of polymer science this volume will provide much of interest.

polymerase (ˈpɒlɪməreɪz, pəˈlɪməreɪz). *Biochem.* [f. POLYMER + -ASE.] Any enzyme which catalyses the formation of a polymer, esp. a polynucleotide.

1958 I. R. LEHMAN et al. in *Jrnl. Biol. Chem.* CCXXXIII. 163/2 In order to facilitate reference in this report, the enzyme responsible for deoxyribonucleotide incorporation is designated as 'polymerase'. **1964** *New Scientist* 23 Jan. 211/1 DNA has been bio-synthesised from its four basic building blocks put together with the enzyme polymerase and some natural DNA to act as a template. **1973** B. J. WILLIAMS *Evolution & Human Origins* vi. 89/1 RNA polymerase is active when the cell is carrying on its normal metabolic functions.

polymeria, var. POLYMERY.

polymeric (pɒlɪˈmɛrɪk), *a. Chem.* [f. as POLYMER + -IC, after Ger. *polymerisch* (Berzelius, 1830).] **1.** Of two or more compounds, or of one compound in relation to another (const. *with*): Composed of the same elements in the same proportions, but so that the numbers of atoms of the several elements in the molecule in one substance are some multiple of those in another, and thus the molecular weight of the one is the same multiple of that of the other. (Distinguished from ISOMERIC.) In mod. use, of the nature of or characteristic of a polymer; consisting of a polymer or polymers. Of a reaction: giving rise to a polymer. Cf. POLYMER.

1833 *Rep. Brit. Assoc. Adv. Sci. 1831–32* 435 To designate compounds approaching in atomic constitution very nearly to those properly called Isomeric, Berzelius has proposed the introduction of two new terms, polymeric and metameric. **1845** W. GREGORY *Outl. Chem.* II. 394 Hydrated lactic acid is a syrupy liquid... It is..polymeric with dry grape sugar and with gum. **1847** TURNER *Elem. Chem.* (ed. 8) 175 The second case of isomerism is that of bodies in which, while the relative proportion of the elements are the same, the absolute number of atoms of each element, and consequently the equivalent or atomic weights of the compounds, differ... Such compounds are called polymeric. **1850** DAUBENY *Atom. The.* viii. (ed. 2) 265 Olefiant gas and cetene are polymeric bodies. **1880** J. W. LEGG *Bile* 233 Asserted to be polymeric with bilirubin. **1935** C. ELLIS *Chem. Synthetic Resins* I. ix. 169 Natural rubber is supposed to consist of a mixture of polymeric hydrocarbons. **1941** MARK & RAFF (*title*) High polymeric reactions. **1951** UVAROV & CHAPMAN *Dict. Sci.* (ed. 2) 171 Many important products, such as plastics and textile fibres, consist of polymeric substances, either natural (e.g. cellulose..) or synthetic (e.g. nylon). **1967** MARGERISON & EAST *Introd. Polymer Chem.* iii. 137 At the early stages of the reaction, the mixture consists mainly of low molecular weight species, dimers, trimers, etc., with only a few molecules of polymeric size. **1974** *Environmental Conservation* I. 63/1 The term resin is usually applied to the long chains of repeating units in the polymeric material.

2. *Genetics.* Of, pertaining to, or displaying polymery.

1949 DARLINGTON & MATHER *Elem. Genetics* iii. 68 Genes such as those with which Nilsson-Ehle was concerned have two of the properties of polygenes. They are of similar and supplementary action. But they cannot be described as polygenes because their effects are so large as to cause a sharp discontinuity in the variation, a discontinuity which permits the analysis of the system by the mendelian method. Genes like these are often termed polymeric genes. All polygenes are therefore polymeric, but not all polymeric genes are polygenes. **1961** [see POLYGENIC *a.* 3]. **1970** *Genetika* VI. x. 124 It is established that complementary maltose factors MA_{1-p} and MA_{2-g} are recessive alleles of polymeric genes, MA_1 and MA_2, respectively.

†**polymeride** (pəˈlɪməraɪd). *Chem. Obs.* [f. as POLYMER + -IDE.] = POLYMER.

1857 MILLER *Elem. Chem.* III. i. 5 The formation of isomerides, metamerides, and polymerides..can only be accounted for by supposing that differences of chemical arrangement occur in these different cases. **1864** H. SPENCER *Biol.* I. 10 Essential oil of turpentine being converted into a mixture of several of these polymerides, by simple exposure to a heat of 460°. **1906** *Nature* 21 June 190/2 A semi-solid brown substance..formed when acetylene is subjected to discharges... It is apparently a polymeride of acetylene. **1943** R. HILL in R. S. Morrell et al. *Synthetic Resins* (ed. 2) v. 194 A defect of polystyrene is a tendency for mouldings and castings to develop fine cracks... It is said that this is due to the evaporation of low molecular weight polymerides.

†**polymerism** (pəˈlɪmərɪz(ə)m). *Obs.* [f. as POLYMER + -ISM; cf. F. *polymérisme.*]

1. *Chem.* The condition of being polymeric.

1833 *Rep. Brit. Assoc. Adv. Sci. 1831–32* 435 (*heading*) Polymerism and metamerism. **1847** TURNER *Elem. Chem.* (ed. 8) 679 It is by the assumption of compound radicals, that we are enabled to explain the numerous cases of isomerism and polymerism which occur in organic chemistry. **1850** DAUBENY *Atom. The.* viii. (ed. 2) 265 The former case Berzelius has distinguished by the term polymerism; the latter, by that of metamerism. **1882** STALLO *Concepts Mod. Physics* 302 This rule applies..likewise to cases of allotropy and polymerism.

2. *Biol.* The condition of being polymerous.

1849 CRAIG, *Polymerism*, the state of monstrosity in which an animal or plant is characterized by the presence of a multiplicity of parts. **1871** ALLMAN *Monogr. Gymnoblastic Hydroids* I. p. xiv, Polymerism... Simple multiplicity of the component zooids of the colony.

polymerizable (ˈpɒlɪməraɪzəb(ə)l), *a. Chem.* [f. POLYMERIZ(E *v.* + -ABLE.] Capable of being polymerized. Hence ˌ**polymerizaˈbility**.

1884 *Jrnl. Chem. Soc.* XLV. 419 Just as the pentine is polymerisable by heat or by the action of sulphuric acid into a dipentine, so the heptine may be converted into a diheptine. **1928** *Proc. & Trans. R. Soc. Canada* XXII. III. 39 The influence of methyl substitution on the polymerizability of butadiene. *Ibid.*, Both the α- and the β-methyl butadienes are polymerizable to caoutchoucs. **1939** *Brit. Plastics* XI. 320/1 Methacrylic acid amide copolymerized with other polymerizable compounds. **1948** C. E. H. BAWN *Chem. High Polymers* i. 15 The polymerizability of diolefins is determined by the relative positions of the double bonds. **1963** A. J. HALL *Textile Sci.* ii. 88 It [*sc.* acrylonitrile] very readily undergoes polymerisation by itself (homopolymerisation) and with other polymerisable compounds (copolymerisation). **1978** (*title*) Solventless polymerizable resinous compounds used for electrical insulation. (Brit. Standards Inst.)

polymerizate (ˈpɒlɪməraɪzeɪt). [f. next + *-ate*, after *filtrate, precipitate*, etc.] A product or mixture of products obtained from a polymerization reaction or process.

1931 *Brit. Chem. Abstr.* B. 264/1 By polymerising a mixture of an aliphatic conjugated diolefine such as butadiene..with styrene..an intimately mixed polymerisate is obtained. **1959** *Times Rev. Industry* Feb. 57/1 The later Ziegler developments in the higher olefin field relate only to a process which yields polymerisates of practically no commercial interest. **1973** *Materials & Technol.* VI. viii. 558 The polymerizates of acrylic acid,.. methacrylic acid,..and their derivatives such as acrylonitrile,..are known collectively as acrylics.

polymerize (ˈpɒlɪməraɪz), *v.* [f. as POLYMER + -IZE.]

1. *Chem.* **a.** *trans.* To render polymeric; to form a polymer of. Cf. POLYMER. **b.** *intr.* To become polymeric; to be converted into a polymer.

1865 MANSFIELD *Salts* 247 That..two molecules of the same body, when formed side by side, shall become polymerized or dimerized into a compound of double equivalent weight. **1867** *Proc. R. Soc.* XVI. 158 If we remember the facility with which the aldehydes are polimerized [*sic*], the question presents itself, whether the aldehyde formed by the slow combustion of methylic alcohol is represented by the formula CH_2O, or a multiple thereof. **1883** *Athenæum* 7 Apr. 447/3 M. Berthelot..is led to suspect that..the various kinds of carbon which occur in nature are in reality polymerized products of the true element carbon. **1893** [see AFTERGLOW b]. **1910** *Encycl. Brit.* X. 667/2 It is not possible to obtain the aldehyde in a pure condition, since it readily polymerizes. **1930** H. F. LEWIS *Fund. Org. Chem.* viii. 95 Three molecules of acetaldehyde polymerize under the influence of a small amount of concentrated sulfuric acid. **1936** H. W. ROWELL *Technol. Plastics* ix. 57 The primary ester may be polymerized by heating in the presence of a peroxide catalyst. **1957** *Times* 10 Sept. 11/1 The effect was to produce reactive groups which could be used to polymerize a different material with the result that mixed polymers of very varied properties could be produced. **1971** *Brit. Printer* Jan. 64/2 The use of ultra-violet radiation for polymerising polyester wood lacquers has been known for some time. **1972** *Nature* 18 Feb. 404/3 This leads into a subsidiary argument: which were the first to polymerize, amino-acids or polynucleotides?

2. *Biol.* (*trans.*) To render polymerous.

1879 W. DITTMAR in *Encycl. Brit.* IX. 98/1 *note*, The vibriones are seemingly nothing more than polymerized bacteria, with intensified powers of locomotion. With regard to their position in the world of life, present evidence leaves it uncertain whether they are plants or animals.

Hence **poˌlymeriˈzation**, the action or process of polymerizing; formation of polymers; also, the state of being polymeric; hence also ˈ**polymerized** *ppl. a.*, ˈ**polymerizing** *vbl. sb.* and *ppl. a.*; ˈ**polymerizer**, an apparatus or installation in which polymerization occurs.

1867 BLOXAM *Chem.* 665/2 (Index), Polymerising by sulphuric acid. **1872** *Jrnl. Chem. Soc.* XXV. 433 Besides the olefines which are derived from compounds having the general formula $C_nH_{2n+1}R$ (R representing a monad radical), by the abstraction of HR, there exists another group, formed by the polymerisation of the members of the first group. **1879** *Ibid.* XXXV. 743 We purposely avoided distilling the polymerised product until entirely freed from substances volatile in a current of steam. **1880** *Nature* XXIII. 193/2 This one fundamental form yields our ordinary elements and many others by ordinary polymerisation. **1900** *Nation* (N.Y.) 10 May 366/2 That the same matter exists everywhere throughout the stellar system in a few different grades of evolution—that is, of polymerization and combinations of polymers—depending upon the temperature to which it is subjected. **1923** B. D. W. LUFF *Chem. of Rubber* vii. 74 In the meantime it had been observed that not only isoprene but many other unsaturated hydrocarbons were capable of polymerising. **1929** *Jrnl. Amer. Chem. Soc.* LI. 2549 Polymerization then is the chemical union of many similar molecules either..without or..with the elimination of simpler molecules. **1930** *Chem. Abstr.* XXIV. 612 $SnCl_4$ was employed as the polymerizing agent. **1933** *Industr. & Engin. Chem.* Feb. 126/2 The length and shape of the chain must be considered when comparing two different resins or the same resin in different degrees of polymerization. **1940** A. N. SACHANEN *Conversion of Petroleum* i. 64 The absorption of olefins by sulphuric acid and the polymerization take place in the reactor. No special polymerizer is necessary. **1945** A. T. BIRKBY *Phenolic Plastics* ii. 16 The larger or polymerised molecule possesses different physical properties from the constituent smaller molecules. **1946** J. GRANT in *Mod. Petroleum Technol.* (Inst. Petroleum) 165 In the separator the acid phase settles to the bottom and is withdrawn to the polymerizer. **1950** *Thorpe's Dict. Appl. Chem.* (ed. 4) X. 21/1 A polymerising unit of such polyfunctionality that gelation will ensue through the cross-linking which accompanies the oxidation. **1956** *Atlantic Monthly* Sept. 24/3 It is a polymerized ethylene glycol that differs from what you pour into your radiator only in being solid at room temperature. **1965** P. W. MORGAN *Condensation Polymers* iii. 107 Many continuous polymerizers are comprised of a cascade system of reactors or a reacting chamber provided with high-speed stirring followed by a larger holding reservoir with lower speed agitation. **1967** MARGERISON & EAST *Introd. Polymer Chem.* iii. 146 When 50% of the original carboxylic acid groups have reacted, the average degree of polymerization has only doubled. **1971** *Brit. Printer* Jan. 65/1 These highly reactive molecular units can then react with unsaturation in resin molecules to cause polymerisation and hence drying. **1974** E. AMBLER *Dr. Frigo* II. 112 Polymerisation is..a change of state, a molecular rearrangement. Raw rubber becomes vulcanized rubber, say... The second is a polymer of the first. **1977** *Lancet* 19 Nov. 1070/2 How much of a toxic gas such as vinyl chloride will escape from the polymeriser pots where it is turned into P.V.C.?

ˈ**polymerone.** *Chem. rare.* [a. F. *polymérone* (Laurent), f. as POLYMER + -ONE a.] An organic compound constituted of two or more aplones or simple groups of molecules, as salicin, = $C_6H_{12}O_6 + C_7H_2O_2 - H_2O$. Also *attrib.*

1866 ODLING *Anim. Chem.* 30 We regard highly complex or polymerone bodies as compounds formed by the union of less complex or aplone bodies with one another. *Ibid.* 83 Capable of entering into combination with one another..to form still more numerous and complicated polymerone bodies.

polymerosomatous (pəˌlɪmərəʊˈsəʊmətəs), *a. Zool.* [f. mod.L. *polymerosōmătus* (f. Gr. πολυμερής having many parts + σῶμα (σωματ-) body) + -OUS.] Having the body composed of many segments, as in the order of *Arachnida* containing the scorpions and allied animals.

1858 MAYNE *Expos. Lex.*, *Polymerosomatus*, applied by Leach to an Order (*Polymerosomata*) of the *Arachnides Cephalotomata*, having the body formed of a long series of rings: polymerosomatous.

polymerous (pəˈlɪmərəs), *a.* [f. as POLYMER + -OUS.]

1. *Nat. Hist.* Composed of many parts, members, or segments.

1858 MAYNE *Expos. Lex.*, *Polymerus*,..applied by Blainville to the *Chetopoda*, which have numerous articulations: polymerous. **1866** *Treas. Bot.* 915 *Polymerous*, consisting of many parts. **1869** *Student* II. 12 Polymerous leaves are those in which the bundles anastomose once or more between their two extremities. **1896** *Allbutt's Syst. Med.* I. 71 In these regions the leucocytes were mainly polymerous or multinuclear.

2. *Chem.* = POLYMERIC. *rare*$^{-0}$.

1864 in WEBSTER.

polymery (pəˈlɪmərɪ). *Genetics.* Also as mod.L. polyˈmeria. [ad. G. *polymerie* (A. Lang 1911, in *Zeitschr. für induktive Abstammungs- und Vererbungslehre* V. 113), ad. Gk. πολυμέρεια a consisting of many parts: see -IA[1], -Y[3].] The phenomenon whereby a number of non-allelic genes can act together to produce a single effect.

1914 *Zeitschr. für induktive Abstammungs- und Vererbungslehre* XII. 118 The phenomenon of plurality of genes having a similar function, i.e., independently producing the same character, is called by Lang (1911) 'polymery'... Johannsen (1913) suggests that..[this term] be retained..for the phenomenon in general. **1927** [see POLYGENIC *a.* 3]. **1929** [see ISOLATION 3].

polymetallic to **polymetameric**: see POLY-.

polymeter (pəˈlɪmɪtə(r)). [mod. f. POLY- + -METER: in F. *polymètre.*] A technical or trade name given to various measuring devices.

Among these are: **a.** 'An instrument for measuring angles' (Knight *Dict. Mech.* 1875). **b.** An apparatus for testing the distance between railway rails, and detecting inequalities of elevation [= F. *polymètre*, of Couturier 1879]. **c.** A form of hygrometer with thermometer and tables of dew-points, etc., attached (Funk's *Stand. Dict.*).

polymeter var. POLYMETRE.

polymethacrylate, -acrylic: see POLY-.

polymethyl (pɒlɪˈmɛθɪl, -miːθaɪl). [f. POLY- + METHYL.] **a.** *polymethyl acrylate* (also as one word): a resinous material obtained by polymerizing the methyl ester of acrylic acid.

1936 *Industr. & Engin. Chem.* Oct. 269/2 Polymethyl acrylate is a colorless, transparent substance. **1950** *Thorpe's Dict. Appl. Chem.* (ed. 4) X. 107/1 Polymethyl acrylate is a tough, transparent, and colourless material, highly extensible, and to a limited degree rubber-like. **1973** *Materials & Technol.* VI. viii. 559 The softening point of polymethylmethacrylate lies accordingly about 90 degrees higher than that of polymethylacrylate.

b. ***polymethyl methacrylate*** (also as one word): = *methyl methacrylate* (*b*) s.v. METHYL.

1936 *Industr. & Engin. Chem.* Oct. 270/1 Polymethyl methacrylate is a very hard, tough mass which can be sawed, carved, or worked on a lathe with ease. **1942** *Endeavour* I. 111/2 Cellulose acetate and polymethyl-methacrylate are fabricated into cockpit covers.. for aircraft by this process. **1960** *Times* 2 Sept. 14/1 They could be eating sandwiches from polyethylene packs with polymethylmethacrylate dentures. **1965** ZIGROSSER & GAEHDE *Guide to Collecting Orig. Prints* vii. 111 The most durable are the acrylic sheets, particularly Plexiglas (polymethyl methacrylate), which is produced in thicknesses from 1·5 to 25·0 mm. **1973** [see sense a above]. **1975** *Sci. Amer.* Dec. 96/2 Familiar thermoplastic polymers include polyethylene,.. polymethyl methacrylate,.. and nylon.

polymethylene (pɒlɪˈmɛθɪliːn). *Chem.* [f. POLY- + METHYLENE.] A compound, group, or polymeric structure which consists of or contains a chain of methylene groups, $-(CH_2)_n-$; *orig. spec.* any of the series of saturated cyclic hydrocarbons of formula $(CH_2)_n$. Freq. *attrib.*

1892 *Jrnl. Chem. Soc.* LXII. 1310 In this paper the author discusses the question of the identity of the naphthenes from Caucasus petroleum and the polymethylenes. *Ibid.*, The naphthenes in general may also include derivatives of other polymethylene rings. **1910** N. V. SIDGWICK *Org. Chem. Nitrogen* ii. 21 In the polymethylene derivatives the ring is often affected. **1930** *Jrnl. Amer. Chem. Soc.* LII. 317 Those poly-esters in which the structural units contain polymethylene chains $(CH_2)_x$, in which *x* is greater than 3–5, show great solubility in benzene. **1953** R. J. W. REYNOLDS in R. Hill *Fibres from Synthetic Polymers* v. 98 Other addition reactions which can give rise to linear polymers are those involving the polymerisation of.. diazomethane or diazoalkanes to give polymethylenes or their alkyl substituted products. **1967** MARGERISON & EAST *Introd. Polymer Chem.* i. 17 Taking a portion of the polymethylene chain as the simplest case, the configuration.. in which the CH_2 groups on adjacent carbon atoms are staggered relative to one another is more frequently assumed.. than any other.

polymetochia, -metochic: see POLY-.

polymetre (ˈpɒlɪmiːtə(r)). *Mus.* Also (*U.S.*) -meter. [f. POLY- + METRE *sb.*[1]] **a.** The succession of different metrical patterns in sixteenth-century vocal music. **b.** Music using two or more different time-signatures simultaneously. So **polyˈmetric, -ˈmetrical** *adjs.*; also **ˈpolymetered** *a.*

1922 S. GREW in *Contemp. Rev.* Aug. 226 The first voice of the above has a 'metre' of four pulses, the second has a 'metre' of three; on the authority of the musical terms *polyphonic* and *polytonic*, I have ventured to coin and use the word *polymetrical*. Students of polymetre do not appear to have sufficiently considered the fact that in certain words Elizabethan accent was different from ours. **1944** W. APEL *Harvard Dict. Mus.* 594/1 Twice in the history of music have polymetric designs played a prominent role: around 1400, and in present-day music. **1946** R. BLESH *Shining Trumpets* (1949) 344 The second type of rhythmic peculiarity, technically known as a polymetric, is the cross-rhythm or overrhythm. **1947** W. RUSSELL in R. de Toledano *Frontiers of Jazz* 60 The ability of Lux to create great swing and rhythmic effect from apparently so simple a polymetrical device. **1966** C. KEIL in T. Kochman *Rappin' & Stylin' Out* (1972) 90 It is a subjective pulse that Richard Waterman is speaking of when he uses the concept 'metronome sense' as the ordering principle in the polymetered rhythms of West African ensembles. In jazz groups polymeter or even a sense of polymeter may or may not exist, but the subjective pulse or metronomic sense remains. **1970** P. OLIVER *Savannah Syncopators* 15 These [*sc.* characteristics of African music] included: dominance of percussion; polymeter; off-beat phrasing of melodic accents [etc.].

polymicrian, polymicroscope: see POLY-.

polymict (ˈpɒlɪmɪkt), *a. Petrol.* [f. POLY- + Gr. μικτ-ός mixed, perh. after G. *polymikt* (H. Rosenbusch *Elemente der Gesteinlehre* (1898) 17).] = POLYMICTIC *a.* 1.

[**1931** A. JOHANNSEN *Descr. Petrogr. Igneous Rocks* I. i. 7 Rocks may be composed of a single mineral only.. or they may be composed of aggregates of several minerals. The former are called monomineral rocks by Vogt and monomikt by Rosenbusch, and the latter polymikt by Rosenbusch.] **1952** W. WAHL in *Geochim. et Cosmochim. Acta* II. 91 It is proposed to call.. breccias in which the enclosed fragments are of a foreign material as compared with the surrounding principal mass of stone.. 'polymict breccias'. **1958** *Proc. Geologists' Assoc.* LXIX. 85 Two kinds of conglomerate are worth distinguishing, first the oligomict.. and, second, the polymict, with a variety of pebbles of unstable rocks undergoing decay and most likely formed by rapid deposition of material worn quickly from high mountains. **1973** *Phil. Trans. R. Soc.* A. CCLXXIII. 392 The conglomerates are characterized by the extreme polymict nature of the boulders, cobbles and pebbles. **1975** TINDALL & THORNHILL *Rock & Mineral Guide* III. 167 A rock with grains of various materials is polymict.

polymictic (pɒlɪˈmɪktɪk), *a.* [f. as prec. + -IC.] **1.** *Petrol.* [ad. Russ. *polimiktovȳĭ* (M. S. Shvetsov *Petrografiya Osadochnȳkh Porod* (1934) viii. 155).] (See quot. 1935.)

1935, 1949 [see OLIGOMICTIC *a.* 1]. **1959** W. W. MOORHOUSE *Study of Rocks in Thin Section* xix. 337 The polymictic conglomerate.. comprises a great variety of pebbles, including granite, schist, sediments such as shale, slate, sandstone, and even limestone. **1969** S. H. HAUGHTON *Geol. Hist. Southern Afr.* iv. 89 At various horizons above the Intermediate Reefs bands of polymictic conglomerates occur.

2. *Limnology.* Applied to a lake that has no stable thermal stratification but exhibits perennial circulation.

1956 [see OLIGOMICTIC *a.* 2]. **1966** *McGraw-Hill Encycl. Sci. & Technol.* V. 523/2 In addition there are.. low-altitude tropical oligomictic lakes with irregular circulation, and high-altitude tropical polymictic lakes with continuous circulation.

polymignite (pɒlɪˈmɪgnaɪt). *Min.* [Named by Berzelius, 1824, f. Gr. πολυ-, POLY- + μιγνύναι to mix + -ITE[1].] A rare mineral, containing the oxides of titanium, zirconium, yttrium, iron, cerium, calcium, manganese, and other metals; occurring in thin slender black crystals with submetallic lustre.

1826 *Thomson's Ann.* XI. 23, I have named it Polymignite, from the multiplicity of its elements. **1892** DANA *Min.* (ed. 6) 743 The axial ratios of polymignite and æschynite are closely similar.

polymineral: see POLY-.

†**ˈpolymite, polimite**, *a. Obs.* [a. OF. *poli-*, *polymite*, ad. late L. *poly-*, *polimitus* of many colours (Vulg. *Gen.* xxxvii. 3, tr. Gr. ποικίλος in LXX), a. Gr. πολύμιτος composed of many threads.] Woven of many different, or different-coloured, threads; many-coloured, as a garment.

c **1410** LYDG. *Life Our Lady* MS. Soc. Antiq. 134 lf. 13 (Halliw.) Of ȝonge Josephe the cote polimite [= Vulg. *tunicam polymitam*] Wrouȝte by the power of alle the Trinite. **1412–20** —— *Chron. Troy* III. xxii. (1555), Though my wede be not pollymyte As of coloures forth I wyll endyte. [**1876** ROCK *Text. Fabr.* i. 3 So as to work the cloths called polymita.]

polymitosis (pɒlɪmaɪˈtəʊsɪs). *Biol.* [f. POLY- + MITOSIS.] The occurrence of multiple mitotic cell divisions, esp. following meiosis in microsporogenesis; one of these divisions. So **polymiˈtotic** *a.*, pertaining to, affected by, or being such cell divisions.

1931 G. W. BEADLE *Mem. Cornell Agric. Exper. Station* No. 135. 3 This genetic factor.. has been given the name *polymitotic* for which the genetic symbol *po* is used. *Ibid.*, On first thought, the term *polymitotic* may seem to be inappropriate on the grounds that normal maize plants have many mitoses. It may be pointed out that the polymitotic character is expressed only in the gametophytic generation in which there are normally but two mitotic divisions in maize. **1932** C. D. DARLINGTON *Recent Adv. Cytol.* xiii. 367 This property of having 'polymitosis' is inherited as a mendelian recessive character. **1937** *Ibid.* (ed. 2) ix. 399 The spermatids are originally tetraploid through double non-reduction and by three polymitotic divisions become 32*x*. **1948** *Nature* 5 June 874/1 Plants heterozygous for this gene must produce two genetically different kinds of pollen, one of which will be like the lethal polymitotic pollen borne on the homozygous plant. But none of this pollen shows polymitotic behaviour. Thus polymitosis is like incompatibility in heterostyled plants. **1973** *Cytologia* XXXVIII. 515 A gene responsible for supernumerary cell division following meiosis which Beadle.. termed the polymitotic division gene (po). *Ibid.* 518 Postmeiotic polymitoses were observed in reciprocal interspecific hybrids between two diploid *Clarkia* species... The genetic system responsible for these polymitoses is most likely not a simple recessive gene as is the case in maize but rather genic disharmony between the two parental sets of chromosomes.

†**ˈpolymix**, *a. Obs. rare*[−1]. [ad. F. *polymixe* (Rabelais), ad. L. *polymyxos* (Martial), f. Gr. πολυ-, POLY- + μύξα lamp-nozzle.] Having many wicks.

1694 MOTTEUX *Rabelais* v. xxxiii, Martial's Polymix Lantern made a very good Figure there. [**1832** GELL *Pompeiana* I. vi. 94 Names expressive of the number of burners, as.. polymixi.]

polymixin, var. POLYMYXIN.

polymodal (pɒlɪˈməʊdəl), *a.* [f. POLY- + MOD(E *sb.* + -AL[1].] **1.** *Mus.* Of, pertaining to, or designating music using two or more modes.

1929 W. W. COBBETT *Cycl. Survey Chamber Music* I. 44/1 Since we are polymodal as well as polytonal, each of these combinations may take the following four different forms according as one or the other triad is major or minor. **1938** *Scrutiny* VII. 174 It becomes quite obvious that his [*sc.* Roussel's] polymodal melodic thinking must condition his scheme of harmony. **1957** W. MELLERS *Romanticism & 20th Cent.* II. v. 157 Roussel in his later work has more self-consciously to recover a tradition: which may explain the more strenuous quality of his (often polymodal) melodic power.

2. = MULTIMODAL *a.* a.

1934 *Jrnl. Sedimentary Petrol.* IV. 73/1 Curve *C* represents a glacial till, in which more than one mode occurs, and is an example of a polymodal frequency curve. **1975** *Nature* 28 Aug. 723/1 In general it seems that cells of different sizes, whether they follow a normal or a polymodal distribution, are randomly distributed throughout the tissue.

Hence **polymoˈdality** = MULTIMODALITY; **polyˈmodally** *adv.*

1929 W. W. COBBETT *Cycl. Survey Chamber Music* I. 38/2 It is at this point that polymodality commences to impinge upon polytonality. *Ibid.* 45/2 A total of five major and five minor keys, representing polymodally six tonalities. **1934** C. LAMBERT *Music Ho!* v. 289 The slow destruction of the key system that we find in Milhaud's polytonality or Vaughan Williams' polymodality. **1952** R. STEVENSON *Music in Mexico* i. 7 For those whose ears have become conditioned by long familiarity with the European diatonic system, the 'polymodality' of indigenous music inevitably sounds as if it were 'polytonality'. **1962** *Lancet* 26 May 1092/2 Hoobler's remarks, together with the recent discussions about polymodality in frequency distributions of blood-pressure, prompted me to examine some experimental data on 'pressor responses'. **1975** *Nature* 28 Aug. 724/1 Techniques based on sorting cells after digestion of the tissue would certainly reveal polymodality.

polymolecular (pɒlɪməˈlɛkjʊlə(r)), *a. Chem.* [ad. G. *polymolekular* (Van 't Hoff & Cohen *Studien zu chem. Dynamik* (1896) 4): see MOLECULAR *a.*] **a.** In chemical kinetics: having or pertaining to an order or a molecularity of more than one.

1896 T. EWAN tr. *Van 't Hoff & Cohen's Stud. Chem. Dynamics* 4 We will call a change in which the interaction of several molecules is required, polymolecular. **1896** *Jrnl. Chem. Soc.* LXX. II. 158 (*heading*) The velocity law of polymolecular reactions. **1937** *Jrnl. Amer. Chem. Soc.* LIX. 2539/2 The polymolecular nature of the solvolysis is strongly evidenced by the fact that it occurs only with a high concentration of hydroxylic molecules.

b. Consisting of or built up from more than one molecule.

1930 *Jrnl. Amer. Chem. Soc.* LII. 4110 The direct preparation of this anhydride by the removal of water from the acid should give a polymolecular product. **1936** *Trans. Faraday Soc.* XXXII. 116 Oleic acid is bimolecular in apolar solvents, and forms polymolecular micelles in aqueous alkaline solution.

c. With reference to a film or layer: being more than one molecule in thickness. Of adsorption: characterized by the formation of such a layer.

1931 *Jrnl. Physical Chem.* XXXV. 869 There was no evidence that the layer of adsorbed molecules was of polymolecular thickness. **1931** J. W. MCBAIN *Sorption of Gases & Vapours by Solids* x. 325 Such built-up polymolecular layers differ in principle from the third conception,.. that all the molecules coming within a certain range of the solid are directly attracted. **1972** M. M. DUBININ in F. Ricca *Adsorption-Desorption Phenomena* 4 On the surface of intermediate pores there occurs monomolecular and polymolecular adsorption of vapours.

d. Consisting of macromolecules which have similar polymeric structures but differing molecular weights. Cf. POLYDISPERSE *a.*

1940 *Chem. Abstr.* XXXIV. 1228 Such compds. of high mol. wt. are also polymolecular and yield polydisperse solns. Since compds. whose mols. are identical with respect to structure and mol. wt... may form in soln. colloidal particles of varying size, polydispersivity is a condition or state whereas polymer homogeneity and polymolecularity are properties of mols. **1943** H. M SPURLIN in E. Ott *Cellulose* V. ix. 930 The expression 'polymolecular' is preferable to 'polydisperse' as a term to describe systems composed of molecules all having substantially the same chemical composition and mode of linkage but differing in chain length. **1970** FOCK & FRIED tr. *Staudinger's From Org. Chem. to Macromolecules* 116 In order to characterize a polymolecular macromolecular material with accuracy, it is necessary to know its distribution and to determine how many low and high molecular parts it contains. **1976** H.-G. ELIAS in K. Solc *Order in Polymer Solutions* 218 Most synthetic polymers are polymolecular, *i.e.*, the unimers possess a distribution of degrees of polymerization.

Hence **polymolecuˈlarity**, the condition or property of being polymolecular (esp. in sense d); as a back-formation **polyˈmolecule**, a polymeric molecule.

1938 *Chem. Abstr.* XXXII. 2810 A distinction is made between the terms polydispersion and polymolecularity. **1940** [see sense d above]. **1943** H. M. SPURLIN in E. Ott *Cellulose* V. ix. 930 The quantitative relationships between such physical properties as viscosity in solution, physical strength, and flexibility of films may differ as the degree of polymolecularity is changed. **1951** *Jrnl. Polymer Sci.* VII. 400 Let us take a momentary picture of an assembly of equal polymolecules of polymerization degree *P* each carrying *ν* charged groups. **1964** *Biophysical Jrnl.* IV. I. Suppl. 11 As a first demonstration of the joint operation of polymeric and electrical properties within polyelectrolyte molecules, we shall consider the shape dynamics of charged polymolecules. **1976** H. -G. ELIAS in K. Solc *Order in Polymer Solutions* 218 The problem on [*sic*] how the polymolecularity of the unimers influences the polydispersity of the multimers has been solved recently for end-to-end and segment-to-segment associations.

polymorph (ˈpɒlɪmɔːf). [mod. f. Gr. πολύμορφ-ος of many forms, f. πολυ-, POLY- + μορφή form. Cf. F. *polymorphe* adj. multiform.]

1. *Nat. Hist.* A polymorphous organism, or an individual of a polymorphous species. Also *attrib.*

1828 WEBSTER, *Polymorph*, a name given by Soldani to a numerous tribe or series of shells, which are very small, irregular and singular in form, and which cannot be referred to any known genus. *Dict. Nat. Hist.* **1890** in *Cent. Dict.* **1895** *Syd. Soc. Lex.*, *Polymorph*, one of a series the members of which are characterised by *Polymorphism*. **1950** *Evolution* IV. 298/1 There is an interesting correlation between habitat differences and shifts in polymorph frequencies. **1958** *Proc. Zool. Soc.* CXXXI. 87 Comparisons are often made between different polymorphs in the same population. **1975** *Zool. Jrnl.* CLXXVII. 334 This species [*sc. Charaxes zoolina*] is a simple dual polymorph with respect to wing shape.

2. *Chem.* and *Min.* A substance that crystallizes in two or more different forms: see

POLYMORPHOUS 3. In mod. use, each of the different forms of such a substance.

1890 in *Cent. Dict.* **1902** *Jrnl. Chem. Soc.* LXXXII. II. 448 With polymorphs..a quite different behaviour is observed. The melting point of the stable form is scarcely altered by the addition of the unstable modification. **1944** [see EDISONITE]. **1957** G. E. HUTCHINSON *Treat. Limnol.* I. x. 660 $CaCO_3$ exists under ordinary conditions in nature in two crystalline polymorphs, calcite and aragonite. **1973** *Nature* 23 Mar. 241/1 Anhydrite, $CaSO_4$, is the higher temperature polymorph of calcium sulphate.

3. *Biol.* A polymorpho-nuclear leucocyte.

1904 *Brit. Med. Jrnl.* 10 Sept. 583 The polymorpho-nuclear neutrophiles, or as I shall call them for the sake of brevity, polymorphs... There is no relation between the transitionals and the polymorphs. *Ibid.* 584 They [transitionals] are not increased in number in the blood in a polymorph leucocytosis. **1970** *Nature* 5 Sept. 1052/1 Red cells, monocytes and the majority of polymorphs had grain densities within the range of control preparations. **1977** *Lancet* 29 Jan. 225/1 Evidence indicates that steroids prevent the accumulation of macrophages and polymorphs in inflammatory areas.

polymorphean, *a. rare.* [irreg. f. as POLYMORPH, after words in *-ean.*]

= POLYMORPHOUS *a.* 1.

1656 BLOUNT *Glossogr., Polymorphean*, of many forms or fashions. **1658** in PHILLIPS. **1874** tr. *Lange's Comm. Zeph.* 30 The polymorphean practics of error.

polymorphemic: see POLY-.

polymorphic (pɒlɪˈmɔːfɪk), *a.* [f. as POLYMORPH + -IC.]

1. Multiform; = POLYMORPHOUS *a.* 1.

1816 G. S. FABER *Orig. Pagan Idol.* I. 49 Every animal was a symbol or form of the great polymorphic deity. *Ibid.* III. 642 The polymorphic images of the principal hero-god. **1885** *Pall Mall G.* 17 Apr. 5/1 Other varieties of independent fancy, in which word-twisting scholars have chosen to discover but the one polymorphic and elusive sun-god.

2. *Nat. Hist.*, etc. = POLYMORPHOUS *a.* 2.

1859 DARWIN *Orig. Spec.* ii. (1860) 46 Genera which have been called 'protean' or 'polymorphic', in which the species present an inordinate amount of variation. **1881** *Gard. Chron.* XVI. 621 Polymorphic states of a Phoma. **1898** *Allbutt's Syst. Med.* V. 416 The shape of the nucleus is constantly undergoing variation, for which reason it is generally described as polymorphic. **1925** A. D. IMMS *Gen. Textbk. Entomol.* III. 257 Termites live together in large communities composed of polymorphic individuals. **1940** E. B. FORD in J. S. Huxley *New Systematics* 503 Though polymorphic forms are to be distinguished from geographical variation, they may be a function of it. **1976** R. A. GOLDSBY *Basic Biol.* xx. 330/1 (*caption*) Polymorphic variation in one species of snail, *Helicella virgata*: different banded and unbanded forms on one plant.

3. *Chem.* and *Min.* = POLYMORPHOUS *a.* 3.

Now the more usual adj. in this sense.

1895 C. S. PALMER tr. *Nernst's Theoret. Chem.* I. iii. 86 The different polymorphic modifications may exist together ..if they are not easily convertible into each other, as diamond and graphite. **1924** A. E. HILL in H. S. Taylor *Treat. Physical Chem.* I. ix. 380 At high pressures there exist several polymorphic forms of ice, differing from the common variety in density, heat of formation, crystalline structure and other physical properties. **1974** K. FRYE *Mod. Mineral.* ii. 83 Quartz, tridymite, and cristobalite have high- and low-temperature polymorphs... The high-low polymorphic inversion is rapid and nonquenchable, since it involves no rupture of Si-O bonds.

polymorphism (pɒlɪˈmɔːfɪz(ə)m). [f. as POLYMORPH + -ISM; so F. *polymorphisme.*] The condition or character of being polymorphous; the occurrence of something in several different forms.

1. *gen.*: cf. POLYMORPHOUS *a.* 1.

1839 *Fraser's Mag.* XX. 699 The various portraits of her majesty astonish by their perplexing poly- or heteromorphism. **1871** H. MACMILLAN *True Vine* iii. (1872) 112 This polymorphism of the Christian character..secures the charm and the contrast of an endless variety.

2. *Nat. Hist.*, etc.: cf. POLYMORPHOUS *a.* 2.

1857 DARWIN in *Life & Lett.* (1887) II. 101 The perplexing subject of polymorphism. **1874** COOKE *Fungi* 4 What is now known of the polymorphism of fungi. **1899** CAGNEY tr. *Jaksch's Clin. Diagn.* i. (ed. 4) 56 The plague bacillus exhibits an unusual degree of polymorphism. **1913** *Phil. Trans. R. Soc.* B. CCIV. 227 The following paper gives an account of a series of breeding experiments..in the course of one and a half years' research on insect polymorphism. **1940** E. B. FORD in J. S. Huxley *New Systematics* 505 It is important to distinguish true polymorphism..from the existence of multiple phases attained at different stages of development. **1976** R. A. GOLDSBY *Biol.* xxiii. 552/2 Recent analysis of enzymes and other proteins has..revealed a previously unsuspected number of genetic polymorphisms in protein chains.

3. *Chem.* and *Min.*: cf. POLYMORPHOUS *a.* 3.

1848 *Mem. & Proc. Chem. Soc.* III. 93 (*heading*) Dimorphism and polymorphism. **1858** BUCKLE *Civiliz.* (1869) II. vii. 400 *note*, The difficulties introduced into the study of minerals by the discovery of isomorphism and polymorphism. **1878** GURNEY *Crystallogr.* 83 Dimorphism and trimorphism are particular cases of polymorphism. **1966** PHILLIPS & WILLIAMS *Inorg. Chem.* II. xix. 7 Polymorphism is commonly found among metals, and for one metal there is in general very little difference in energy between one structure and another. **1971** I. G. GASS et al. *Understanding Earth* iii. 60/2 This property, polymorphism, occurs in the minerals of the mantle.

polymorˈphistic, *a. rare.* [f. as prec. + -ISTIC.] Of or relating to polymorphism.

1897 *Nat. Science* Aug. 107 We find in Kützing the belief that lower algae transform themselves into higher forms, even into moss-protonema. Hitherto these polymorphistic ideas..have not succeeded in establishing themselves.

polymorpho-, combining form repr. Gr. πολύμορφος multiform (cf. POLYMORPHIC, POLYMORPHOUS): in **polymorpho-ˈcellular** *a.*, 'composed of cells of various shapes' (*Syd. Soc. Lex.* 1895); **polymorpho-ˈnuclear, -ˈnucleate** *adjs.*, having several nuclei of various shapes; (usu. written as one word), also used esp. to designate a class of leucocyte (see quot. 1968); also *ellipt.* as *sb.*

1897 R. C. CABOT *Clin. Exam. Blood* I. v. 49 Next in age come the cells usually known as 'polynuclear' but more properly called *polymorphonuclear neutrophiles*. These cells constitute the vast majority of those found in ordinary pus. **1901** *Lancet* 23 Mar. 848/1 A leucocytic count now gave: large mononuclear, 24 per cent.; small mononuclear, 10 per cent.; and polymorphonuclear, 66 per cent. **1901** *Brit. Med. Jrnl.* 29 June 1606 The polymorphonuclear leucocytes are essentially derived from the bone marrow. **1903** *Amer. Jrnl. Med. Sci.* CXXVI. 190 A differential count of the leucocytes shows a slight increase in the polymorphonuclears and a diminution in the small mononuclears since the previous record. **1904** *Brit. Med. Jrnl.* 10 Sept. 560 The polymorpho-nucleate cell. **1950** *Brain* LXXIII. 144 An early puncture gave 10 polymorphonuclears and 3 lymphocytes per c.mm. **1961** R. D. BAKER *Essent. Path.* ii. 12 The inflammatory lesion is rich first in polymorphonuclear cells and later in macrophages. **1968** PASSMORE & ROBSON *Compan. Med. Stud.* I. xxvi. 2/1 There are three varieties of white cell, the polymorphonuclear leucocyte or polymorph, the lymphocyte and the monocyte.

polymorphous (pɒlɪˈmɔːfəs), *a.* [f. Gr. πολύμορφ-ος (f. πολυ-, POLY- + μορφή shape) multiform + -OUS.] Having, assuming, or occurring in, many or various forms; multiform.

1. *gen.*

1823 DE QUINCEY *Herder* Wks. 1863 XII. 116, I still find it difficult to form any judgment of an author so 'many-sided' (to borrow a German expression)—so polymorphous as Herder. **1888** M. THOMPSON in *Literature* (N.Y.) 22 Sept. 330 Hayne..did not take kindly to that flexible, elastic, polymorphous vehicle through which..our later poets deliver their imaginings. **1894** ABP. BENSON in *Westm. Gaz.* 22 Sept. 1898, 1/3 These terrors of a polymorphous religion in which a child is being taught in one standard by a Baptist, and in the next by a Congregationalist, and in the next by a Roman Catholic, and in the next by an agnostic, do not exist.

2. *Nat. Hist., Biol., Path.* **a.** Having or occurring in several different forms in different individuals, or in different conditions of growth; having many varieties: as a species of animal or plant, the zooids of a compound organism, an eruptive disease, etc. **b.** Assuming various forms successively; of changing form: as an amœba, infusorian, etc. **c.** Passing through several markedly different forms in successive stages of development; having several definitely marked metamorphoses.

1785 MARTYN *Rousseau's Bot.* xxv. (1794) 368 There is a species of Medicago called polymorphous or many-form. **1828** STARK *Elem. Nat. Hist.* II. 447 Infusoria. Microscopic animals, gelatinous, transparent, polymorphous, and contractile. **1856** W. CLARK *Van der Hoeven's Zool.* I. 56 Stentor... Body conical, from its contractility polymorphous. **1876** DUHRING *Dis. Skin* 55 The polymorphous erythemata. **1899** *Allbutt's Syst. Med.* VIII. 636 A polymorphous eruption accompanied by itching. **1928** C. K. OGDEN tr. *Forel's Social World of Ants* II. v. 337 The formicary is a society of females and their polymorphous derivative forms.

3. *Chem.* and *Min.* Crystallizing in two or more forms, esp. in forms belonging to different systems; dimorphous or trimorphous. Also, of or pertaining to polymorphism (sense 3).

1848 *Mem. & Proc. Chem. Soc.* III. 57 (*heading*) On the relation in volumes between simple bodies, their oxides and sulphurets, and on the differences exhibited by polymorphous and allotropic substances. **1866** WATTS *Dict. Chem.* IV. 687 *Polymorphism.* A body is said to be polymorphous when it crystallises in two or more forms not derivable one from the other. **1895** C. S. PALMER tr. *Nernst's Theoret. Chem.* I. iii. 86 The different kinds of crystals of a polymorphous substance, are to be regarded as different modifications analogous to the different states of aggregation. **1906** J. P. IDDINGS *Rock Minerals* I. i. 19 Silica (SiO_2) is certainly dimorphous and possibly polymorphous. **1964** J. SINKANKAS *Mineral. for Amateurs* vi. 170 Another polymorphous pair also shows marked though less striking differences in hardness: calcite (H $2\frac{1}{2}$ – 3) and aragonite (H $3\frac{1}{2}$ – 4).

4. *Mus.* Applied to contrapuntal compositions in which the subjects are treated in various ways, as by inversion, augmentation, diminution, etc.

1890 in *Cent. Dict.* **1898** in STAINER & BARRETT *Dict.*

5. *Psychol.* Phr. ***polymorphous-perverse***, polymorphously perverse (see next); so ***polymorphous perversity***.

1909 A. A. BRILL tr. *Freud's Sel. Papers on Hysteria* ix. 191 The constitutional sexual predisposition of the child is more irregularly multifarious than one would expect, that it deserves to be called 'polymorphous-perverse', and that from this predisposition the so-called normal behavior of the sexual functions results through a repression of certain components. **1910** —— tr. *Freud's Three Contrib. to Sexual Theory* II. 49 Under the influence of seduction the child may become polymorphous-perverse. *Ibid.*, The child does not behave differently from the average uncivilized woman in whom the same polymorphous-perverse disposition exists. **1954** W. MAYER-GROSS et al. *Clin. Psychiatry* iv. 179 The active male and the passive female [homosexual]..adopt their homosexual behaviour as a *pis aller*, or, as frequently occurs, out of an abundance of sexual urge and interest and as part of a polymorphous perversity. **1954** D. RIESMAN *Individualism Reconsidered* (1955) VI. xxii. 355 He [*sc.* Freud] makes the famous charge that children are 'polymorphous-perverse'—that is, that their sexual life is not confined to the genital zone. **1963** AUDEN *Dyer's Hand* 411 Three kinds of erotic life are possible... The polymorphous-perverse promiscuous sexuality of childhood, courting couples whose relation is potential, .. and the chastity of natural celibates who are without desire. **1974** *Encycl. Brit. Macropædia* XVI. 610/1 Most people with a polymorphous-perverse personality are either nearly or wholly psychotic persons or nonpsychotic persons who, in sexual and nonsexual areas of living, are unable to develop lasting, affectionate relations with others.

polymorphously (pɒlɪˈmɔːfəslɪ), *adv.* [f. prec. + -LY².] ***polymorphously perverse*** (Psychol.): characterized by a diffuse sexuality that can be excited and gratified in many ways and is normal in young children but regarded as perverted in adults. Also *transf.*

1949 J. STRACHEY tr. *Freud's Three Ess. Theory of Sexuality* II. 69 Under the influence of seduction children can become polymorphously perverse, and can be led into all possible kinds of sexual irregularities... In this respect children behave in the same kind of way as an average uncultivated woman in whom the same polymorphously perverse disposition persists. **1957** *Ann. N.Y. Acad. Sci.* LXVI. 429 Is not a child infinitely potential rather than polymorphously perverse? **1980** *Church Times* 22 Feb. 11/3 Traditional Christianity..offers us encouragement about living with..shame and dependence, which, in the polymorphously perverse landscape of chaos, need some careful (and painful) thought.

polymorphy (ˈpɒlɪmɔːfɪ). [ad. Gr. πολυμορφία multiformity: see POLYMORPHOUS and -Y; so F. *polymorphie.*] = POLYMORPHISM.

1846 WORCESTER, *Polymorphy*, state of having many forms. *Ec. Rev.* **1874** COOKE *Fungi* 185 Two distinct kinds of phenomena have been grouped under the term 'polymorphy'. **1902** D. H. CAMPBELL *Univ. Text-bk. Bot.* vi. 176 Rusts are characterized by the production of several quite different forms [of spores]. This polymorphy is complicated in some species by heterœcism.

poly-mountain: see POLY¹ c.

polymyalgia: see POLY-.

polymyarian (ˈpɒlɪmaɪˈɛərɪən), *a.* and *sb. Zool.* [f. mod.L. *Polymȳārii-* pl. (Schneider) (f. Gr. πολυ-, μῦς, μῡ- muscle + *-ari-us*: see -ARY¹) + -AN.]

a. *adj.* Belonging to the section *Polymyarii* of Nematode worms, having many muscle-cells in each quadrant of the body. **b.** *sb.* A worm of this section.

polymyodian (ˌpəʊlɪmaɪˈəʊdɪən), *a. Ornith.* [f. mod.L. *Polymȳōdī* pl. (Müller 1847) (irreg. f. Gr. πολυ-, POLY- + μῦς muscle + ᾠδή song) + -AN: cf. MESOMYODIAN] Belonging to the division *Polymyodi* of passerine birds, having numerous muscles of the syrinx or 'song-muscles': corresponding to OSCINES 2. Also (erron.) **polyˈmyoid** *a.*

1867 *Proc. Zool. Soc.* 471 In no one of them does the structure of the skull differ so much from that of a typical polymyodian Coracomorph (e.g. one of the Corvidæ) as does that of the also polymyodian Coccothraustes.

polymyositis: see POLY-.

polymythy (ˈpɒlɪmɪθɪ). [ad. mod.L. *polymȳthia*, f. Gr. πολυ-, POLY- + μῦθος fable, story + *-ia*, -Y: cf. Gr. πολύμυθος wordy, full of story.] Combination of a number of stories in one narrative or dramatic work.

[**1725** POPE *Odyssey* I. *View Epic Poem* iv. p. xii, This Multiplication cannot be call'd a vicious and irregular *Polymythia*.] **1727–41** CHAMBERS *Cycl.*, *Polymythy*,..a multiplicity of fables in an epic or dramatic poem. **1879** *N. Shaks. Soc. Trans.* 46* Polymythy..in Shakespeare's Dramatic Poems.

polymyxin (pɒlɪˈmɪksɪn). *Pharm.* Also **polymixin.** [f. mod.L. *polymyxa*, specific epithet (f. POLY- + Gr. μύξα mucus, slime) + -IN¹.] Any of a class of antibiotics (*polymyxin A, B*, etc.) which are polypeptides obtained from strains of the soil bacterium *Bacillus polymyxa* and are used against Gram-negative bacteria in infections of the urinary tract and the skin.

1947 P. G. STANSLY et al. in *Bull. Johns Hopkins Hosp.* LXXXI. 43 The antibiotic-producing organism has been identified as *Bacillus polymyxa* and the antibiotic substance accordingly designated 'Polymyxin'. **1950** *Lancet* 17 June 1139/2 Polymyxin D in doses of 40 mg. per kg. for ten days produced definite injury in canine kidneys. **1956** *New Biol.* XXI. 18 Various methods for purifying pitching yeast have been in vogue for some years... The latest approach to this problem is the suggested use of antibiotics such as polymixin. **1974** M. C. GERALD *Pharmacol.* xxvii. 473 Polymyxin attaches to the cell membrane of bacteria, disrupting its function and causing the loss of essential intracellular materials.

polyneme (ˈpɒlɪniːm). [ad. mod.L. *Polynēm-us* (Gronovius 1754), f. Gr. πολυ-, POLY- + νῆμα thread.] A fish of the genus *Polynemus* or family *Polynemidæ*, found in tropical seas, and characterized by having the lower part of each pectoral fin divided into a number of slender rays. So **polyˈnemiform** *a.*, having the form or structure of a polyneme; **polyˈnemoid** *a.*, resembling a polyneme; *sb.* a polynemoid fish.

1828 WEBSTER, *Polyneme... Pennant.*

Polynesia (pɒlɪˈniːʃ(ɪ)ə, -sɪə, -ʒ(ɪ)ə, -zɪə). [mod.L. form of F. *Polynésie* (De Brosses 1756), f. Gr. πολυ-, POLY- + νῆσος island.

(It has been asserted that the name had been used by certain authors two centuries before De Brosses. This is an error, app. founded on the circumstance that De Brosses in the *Table des Articles* of his *Histoire*, arranges the voyages under his three heads of *Magellanie, Australie*, and *Polynésie*, and also uses these designations in the headings which he prefixes to the narratives themselves, in the originals of which no such terms occur. These headings are retained by Callander in his *Terra Australis*, 1766 (an unacknowledged transl. of De Brosses).)

Collective name for the numerous small islands in the Pacific Ocean, east of Australia and the Malay archipelago (or, in restricted sense, for those east of Melanesia and Micronesia). Hence allusively.

[1756 DE BROSSES *Hist. Navig. aux Terres Australes* Pref. 2 La division de la terre australe y étoit faite [i.e. in a memoir previously read by De Brosses to a private literary society, which formed the germ of his *Histoire*], relativement à ces trois mers, en Magellanique, Polynésie et Australasie. *Ibid.* vi, Surtout dans la Polynésie.] 1766 J. CALLANDER *Terra Australis Cognita* I. 49 We [i.e. De Brosses] call the third division *polynesia*, being composed of all those islands, which are found dispersed in the vast Pacific Ocean. *Ibid.* 73 (*Heading*) Ferdinand Magellan to Magellanica and Polynesia [DE BROSSES I. 121 Ferdinand Magellan en Magellanique & en Polynésie]. 1815 TUCKEY *Maritime Geog.* IV. 1842 M. RUSSELL *Polynesia* i. 22 The name Polynesia was first applied to this interesting portion of the globe by the learned President de Brosses, in his *History of Navigation.*

fig. 1889 *Cornh. Mag.* July 69 On the floor a polynesia of spittoons in a sea of sawdust.

Polynesian (pɒlɪˈniːʃ(ɪ)ən, -ʒ(ɪ)ən, -sɪən, -zɪən), *a.* and *sb.* [f. POLYNESIA + -AN; cf. F. *polynésien.*]

a. *adj.* Belonging to Polynesia.

1812 W. MARSDEN *Gram. Malayan Lang.* p. xxii, The Polynesian or general East-insular language.. does not include those spoken by the description of people termed *Papūa* and *Samang*. 1820 J. CRAWFURD *Hist. Indian Archipelago* II. v. v. 93 The Sanskrit language exists indeed embodied in writing, while the Polynesian language can be traced only as it is scattered over a thousand living dialects. 1828 WEBSTER, *Polynesian*, pertaining to Polynesia. 1863 J. C. PATTESON *Let.* 8 Aug. in C. M. Yonge *Life J. C. Patteson* (1874) II. ix. 69 One might almost get together all the *disjecta membra*, and reconstruct the original Polynesian tongue. 1874 TROLLOPE *Harry Heathcote* iv. 89 A gang of Polynesian labourers.. from the South Sea Islands. 1876 BANCROFT *Hist. U.S.* II. xxxviii. 458 The possibility of an early communication between South America and the Polynesian world. 1899 ELLA in *Jrnl. Anthrop. Inst.* XXIX. 158 Tongues of mixed Polynesian and Melanesian origin. 1901 *Chambers's Jrnl.* May 343/1 With me was a young Polynesian half-caste named Alan, about twenty-two years of age. 1931 R. CAMPBELL *Georgiad* III. 52 The huge jaws of Polynesian clams. 1960 T. & L. DAVIS *Makutu* I. i. 13 It had to be a Polynesian island. 1978 B. PRIESTLEY *Island Emperor* iii. 26 'My great-grandfather used to eat men...' He seemed rather ashamed.. talking about the darker side of the Polynesian past.

b. *sb.* A native or inhabitant of Polynesia, a South Sea islander. Also, the language of Polynesia.

1812 W. MARSDEN *Gram. Malayan Lang.* p. xviii, This language.. may be conveniently termed the Polynesian, and distinguished.. into the *Hither* (frequently termed the *East insular* language) and the *Further* Polynesian. 1820 J. CRAWFURD *Hist. Indian Archipelago* II. v. v. 84 All agree in borrowing from the same source—from the great Polynesian. 1842 M. RUSSELL *Polynesia* i. 33 The Indo-Americans and Polynesians are one people. 1874 TROLLOPE *Harry Heathcote* iv. 91 Picky was one of the Polynesians, who at once started on his errand. 1901 *Chambers's Jrnl.* Dec. 799/2 His eyesight, like that of all Polynesians, was better than that of any white man. 1923 A. L. KROEBER *Anthropol.* v. 121 Articles.. recur in Semitic, in Polynesian, and in several groups of American languages. 1960 T. & L. DAVIS *Makutu* I. iii. 43 Family relationships are important among the Polynesians and families are large. 1962 [see MORIORI]. 1976 'M. DELVING' *China Expert* I. 16 He had several times been mistaken for a Japanese or a Polynesian.

polynesic (pɒlɪˈniːsɪk), *a. Path.* [f. as POLYNESIA + -IC.] Occurring in insulated patches.

1899 *Allbutt's Syst. Med.* VII. 50 Multilocular sclerosis, Polynesic sclerosis.

polyneuritic to **polyneuropathy**: see POLY-.

polynoid (ˈpɒlɪnəʊɪd), *a.* and *sb. Zool.* [f. mod.L. *Polynoidæ*, pl. f. generic name *Polynoë* (Savigny *Système des Annélides*, 1809), f. Gr. Πολυνόη, name of one of the Nereids or sea-nymphs of Greek mythology: cf. πολύνοος much thinking, thoughtful. See -ID.]

a. *adj.* Belonging or allied to the genus *Polynoë* (pəʊˈlɪnəʊiː) of polychæte worms, having a flat body covered with a series of plates or elytra. **b.** *sb.* A polynoid worm.

1896 *Camb. Nat. Hist.* II. 262 Probably the typical number [of tentacles] is three.. as in Polynoids, Syllidæ, and some Eunicidæ.

polynome (ˈpɒlɪnəʊm), *sb.* and *a. rare.* Also -nom. [Back formation f. next.]

A. *sb.* = POLYNOMIAL B. 1.

1828 WEBSTER, *Polynome*, in *Algebra*, a quantity consisting of many terms. 1868 SANDEMAN *Pelicotetics* 113 A polynome is said to be homogeneous of which all the terms are homogeneous.

B. *adj.* Having many names.

1830 *Fraser's Mag.* I. 130 His father was as well known as polynom Wellesley.

polynomial (pɒlɪˈnəʊmɪəl), *a.* and *sb.* [Hybrid f. POLY- after BINOMIAL (irreg. f. L. *nōmen* name).]

A. *adj.* **1.** *Alg.* Consisting of many terms; multinomial. ***polynomial theorem*** (also called *multinomial theorem*): an extension of the binomial theorem, for the expansion of any power of a polynomial expression.

1704 J. HARRIS *Lex. Techn.* I, *Polynomial*, or *Multinomial Roots*, in Mathematicks, are such as are composed of many Nomes, Parts or Members; as, $a + b + d + c$. 1706 in PHILLIPS.

2. Consisting of, or characterized by, many names or terms: as the old scientific nomenclature in which species were denoted by names of more than two terms, or any modern nomenclature in which the genus, species, sub-species, variety, etc. are indicated by a number of terms (instead of only the genus and species by two terms: see BINOMIAL A. 2).

1828 WEBSTER, *Polynomial*, containing many names or terms. 1964 *Huntia* I. 34 He makes the essential distinction between the old Aristotelian polynomial phrase-names and the new trivial names.

B. *sb.* **1.** *Alg.* An expression consisting of many terms; a multinomial. The terms are usually taken to be multiples of powers, finitely many in number.

1674 JEAKE *Arith.* (1696) 273 Those knit together by both Signs are called.. by some Multinomials, or Polynomials, that is, many named. 1753 CHAMBERS *Cycl. Suppl.* s.v., To raise a polynomial to any given power, may be done by Sir Isaac Newton's binomial theorem. *c*1865 in *Circ. Sc.* I. 481/1 We conclude that the polynomial is not a square. 1906 *Athenæum* 19 May 613/3 The Expansion of Polynomials in Series of Functions. 1941, 1966 [see FACTOR *v.* 2].

2. A scientific name consisting of many terms (see A. 2).

1885 *Nature* XXXI. 413/1 Trinomials—that is the usage of three names, of which the last is that of the sub-species —are in great favour... Quadrinomials and Polynomials must necessarily follow. 1951 G. H. M. LAWRENCE *Taxon. Vascular Plants* ix. 194 Before the middle of the eighteenth century the names of plants commonly were polynomials. 1971 W. T. STEARN in W. Blunt *Compleat Naturalist* 248/1 Such a polynomial determines the application of the binomial.

Hence **polyˈnomialism**, a system of polynomial nomenclature; **polyˈnomialist**, one who uses or favours polynomial nomenclature.

polynomic (pɒlɪˈnɒmɪk), *a. rare.* [f. POLYNOME + -IC.] = POLYNOMIAL A. 1, 2.

1868 SANDEMAN *Pelicotetics* 112 The symbolized result of .. a Polynomic Expression or Polynome in *x*. 1898 *Nature* 1 Dec. 114/2 To make a polynomic terminology of members run parallel with a polyphyletic development.

Polynosic (pɒlɪˈnəʊzɪk), *a.* and *sb.* Also polynosic. [ad. F. *polynosique*, contraction of *polymère d'un glucose* + *-ique* -IC (see N. Drisch 1959, in *Reyon, Zellwolle u. andere Chemiefasern* IX. 436).] **A.** *adj.* A proprietary term applied to fibres of a type made from regenerated cellulose and resembling cotton in such properties as a high wet modulus, alkali-resistance, and a crystalline multi-fibrillar structure. **B.** *sb.* A fibre of this type.

A number of erroneous accounts of the etymology occur in the literature.

1959 *Chem. & Engin. News* 24 Aug. 23/1 Hartford Fibres, a division of Bigelow-Sanford Carpet, takes the wraps off a new 'polynosic' fiber. 1959 *Skinner's Silk & Rayon Rec.* Nov. 1084/1 Recent reports from the Continent about a new class of cellulosic fibres, the polynosics,.. have aroused interest in the British trade. 1963 *Trade Marks Jrnl.* 16 Jan. 82/1 *Polynosic*... Threads made of synthetic or natural textile materials. Association Internationale Polynosic.., Geneva, Switzerland; merchants. 1964 *Financial Times* 3 Mar. 15/4 Courtauld's polynosic fibre is Vincel, which has already passed from the pilot plant stage to commercial production. 1964 *Economist* 7 Mar. 913/3 The two companies will collaborate on the research, development and production of viscose rayon; particularly important will be their joint work on the 'polynosics', modified viscose fibres with properties similar to cotton. 1967 *Encycl. Polymer Sci. & Technol.* VI. 547 Within the last few years, regenerated cellulosic fibers having higher moduli values than the standard rayon fibers have been developed... These fibers have been given the generic name of polynosics. 1970 *Which?* Oct. 311/2 *Vincel* and *Zaryl* are polynosic rayons, as strong as cotton and with many of its wet strength properties.

polynuclear (-ˈnjuːklɪə(r)), *a.* [POLY- 1]

a. *Biol.* Having several nuclei, multinucleate. Also, applied *spec.* to polymorphonuclear leucocytes. Also as *sb.*

1876 tr. *Wagner's Gen. Pathol.* (ed. 6) 273 In atrophic increase of fat, in polynuclear bone-cells. 1891 [see MYELOCYTE 2]. 1894 *Jrnl. Physiol.* XVII. 85 The other term which was applied to the finely granular oxyphile cells by Metschnikoff and others, namely, 'polynuclear leucocyte' is not satisfactory, seeing that.. the different nuclear masses.. are, in point of fact, joined by threads or bars of nuclear substance so that the cell is really mononuclear with a very much branched nucleus. 1897 [see POLYMORPHO-NUCLEAR *a.*]. 1901 W. OSLER *Princ. & Pract. Med.* I. 19 Acute diseases, in which the polynuclear neutrophiles are increased. 1907 *Med. Rev.* X. 364/1 Centrifugalisation showed 68 per cent. of polynuclears, 14 per cent. of large mononuclears, and 18 per cent. of lymphocytes. 1935 *Trans. R. Soc. Trop. Med. & Hygiene* XXVIII. 477 The polynuclear count can also be used in the study of populations in which some pathological element exists. 1936 *Ibid.* XXX. 173 Infection provides a strong stimulus in modifying the percentage of neutrophiles with a segmented nucleus (polynuclear cells). 1967 *Jrnl. Reticuloendothelial Soc.* IV. 168 (*heading*) Influence of serum on intracellular digestion of *Staphylococcus aureus* by polynuclear neutrophils from the guinea pig.

b. *Chem.* Of a complex: containing more than one metal atom. Of a compound: having more than one nucleus (NUCLEUS *sb.* 8).

1908 *Chem. Abstr.* II. 1101 (*heading*) Polynuclear metalammonias. 1924 W. THOMAS *Complex Salts* v. 54 This latter compound is an example of what may be termed a polynuclear complex, since the complex contains more than one central atom. 1933 *Jrnl. Soc. Chem. Industry* 8 Dec. 422T/2 Any polynuclear compound from, say, phenol possesses free positions in internal rings at which further condensation with formaldehyde.. is possible. 1951 I. L. FINAR *Org. Chem.* I. xxix. 571 Polynuclear hydrocarbons may be divided into two groups, those in which the rings are isolated,.. and those in which two or more rings are fused together in the *o*-positions. 1971 *Nature* 20 Aug. 539/1 Studies of a synthetic and structural nature of polynuclear metal complexes containing hydrogen and organic groups as ligands may eventually allow a better understanding of heterogeneous reactions.

polyˈnucleated, *a.* [POLY- 1] **a.** Also **polynucleate.** = POLYNUCLEAR *a.* a

1878 T. BRYANT *Pract. Surg.* I. 138 In some examples there are large polynucleated cells. 1895 *Syd. Soc. Lex.*, *Polynucleate*, multinucleate. 1898 P. MANSON *Trop. Diseases* i. 26 Poly-nucleated leucocytes.

b. Designating an urban area planned in the form of a number of smaller, self-contained communities.

1938 [see MONONUCLEATED *a.*]. 1965 *Listener* 27 May 774/2 The Clyde Valley plan proposals were for a polynucleated urban system designed on a tight pattern and set in a green background.

polynucleotide (pɒlɪˈnjuːklɪətaɪd). *Biochem.* [ad. G. *polynucleotid* (Levene & Mandel 1908, in *Ber. d. Deut. Chem. Ges.* XLI. 1906): see POLY- and NUCLEOTIDE.] A polymeric compound whose molecules are composed of a number (usu. large) of nucleotides.

1911 *Jrnl. Biol. Chem.* IX. 394 Yeast nucleic acid is a polynucleotide. 1916 [see HEXOSE]. 1953 S. E. LURIA *Gen. Virol.* v. 100 Watson and Crick.. have proposed for DNA a structure consisting of two helical polynucleotide chains coiled around the same axis and held together by bonds between the purine and pyrimidine bases. 1964 G. H. HAGGIS et al. *Introd. Molecular Biol.* ix. 225 Nucleic acids formed by *in vitro* synthesis with restricted base composition are termed polynucleotides. *Ibid.* 226 Synthetic polynucleotides form a variety of double and triple helices. 1970 R. W. MCGILVERY *Biochem.* iii. 23 A particular arrangement of three nucleotide units in the DNA polynucleotide specifies a particular amino acid. 1971 *Sci. Amer.* July 28/2 Antibody responses in animals were enhanced by certain synthetic polynucleotides. These are analogues of the nucleic acids DNA or RNA that are made in the laboratory by combining nucleotides (the subunits of nucleic acids) in arbitrary ways.

‖**polynya** (pəʊˈlɪnjə). Formerly also polynia. Pl. polynyas (rarely ‖polynyi.). [Russ. *polúinya* a rotten place in the ice, an open place amidst ice, f. root of *pole, polyana* field.] A space of open water in the midst of ice, esp. in the arctic seas.

1853 KANE *Grinnell Exp.* (1856) 544 It is an annulus, a ring surrounding an area of open water—the Polynya, or Iceless Sea. 1856 —— *Arct. Expl.* I. xx. 244 The stream-holes (stromhols) of the Greenland coast, the polynia of the Russians. 1870 J. K. LAUGHTON *Phys. Geog.* iv. 235 Adm. Von Wrangell found open water—or what is now often called a 'Polynia', an open sea. 1894 CAPT. F. G. JACKSON *Thous. Days in Arctic* (1899) I. 39 Lay all day in a 'polynia'. 1957 *Sat. Even. Post* 8 Dec. 7 From the deck of the A-sub, here surfaced in a 'polynya'—a hole in the ice-pack—crewmen took a close look at the perpetually frozen Arctic Ocean. 1963 G. L. PICKARD *Descriptive Physical Oceanogr.* vii. 154 Some of this cap ice melts in the summer... Open water spaces, 'polynyas', may form. 1963 *Sunday Tel.* 22 Sept. 15 Learning to find holes, or *polynias*, was one of the primary tasks of the two British submarines Porpoise and Grampus. 1971 *Nature* 1 Jan. 37/2 The present study was undertaken to measure the actual distribution of CO_2 between the atmosphere and the sea over open leads and polynyi in the ice-covered Bering Sea. 1974 L. DEIGHTON *Spy Story* xix. 206 We found a suitably large polynya—

which is the proper name for a lagoon in the ice—and.. the Captain began surfacing procedures.

polyodic: see POLY-.

polyodont (ˈpɒlɪədɒnt), *a.* and *sb. Zool.* [ad. mod.L. *Polyodon*, *-ont-* (Lacépède 1798), generic name, ad. Gr. πολύοδους, -οδοντ- having many teeth, f. πολυ-, POLY- + ὀδοντ- stem of ὀδούς tooth; so F. *polyodonte*.] **a.** *adj.* Having many teeth; *spec.* belonging to the genus *Polyodon* or family *Polyodontidæ* of fishes, which in the young state have numerous crowded teeth. **b.** *sb.* A fish of this genus or family.

polyœstrous to **polyolefin(e**: see POLY-.

polyoma (pɒlɪˈəʊmə). *Microbiol.* [f. POLY- + -OMA.] In full ***polyoma virus***. A papovavirus that is endemic in mice without producing tumours but which can produce many kinds of tumour in young rodents.

1958 B. E. EDDY et al. in *Proc. Soc. Exper. Biol. & Med.* XCVIII. 848/1 A virus, which we shall refer to as SE polyoma virus, was recovered from tissue cultures inoculated with tumor material from mice and was shown to induce multiple tumors in mice.. and hamsters. **1962** [see PAPOVAVIRUS]. **1962** *Times* 27 July 21/6 In many fully formed growths induced by the polyoma virus, no sign of the virus can be found under the electron microscope. **1967** AMBROSE & EASTY in E. J. Ambrose et al. *Cancer Cell in Vitro* v. 41 Several viruses will produce malignant transformations *in vitro* when grown on cells of animal origin, for example, polyoma virus, Rous sarcoma virus, and SV 40 virus. The polyoma transformation is the one most extensively studied. **1969** A. M. CAMPBELL *Episomes* xiv. 169 Mammalian DNA viruses such as polyoma and SV 40 cause the formation of tumors. **1973** R. G. KRUEGER et al. *Introd. Microbiol.* xxviii. 699/1 All of the tumors induced by polyoma virus in various different mouse strains and hamsters have a common antigen. **1975** MELIEF & SCHWARTZ in F. F. Becker *Cancer* I. v. 123 The polyoma virus, which commonly infects both wild and laboratory mice.., does not produce tumors under natural conditions even though it is potentially very oncogenic.

polyomino, polyommatous: see POLY-.

polyonym (ˈpɒlɪənɪm). *rare.* [ad. Gr. πολυώνυμ-ος: see POLYONYMOUS.]

1. Each of a number of different words having the same meaning; = SYNONYM. *rare* or *Obs.*

1858 *Sat. Rev.* 6 Mar. 241/1 The Stoics wished to substitute the term polyonyms for that of synonyms, and no reader of Plato will need to be reminded of the banter with which Prodicus is more than once assailed on account of his lectures on synonyms.

2. Proposed by Coues for: A scientific name (of a species, etc.) consisting of more than three terms.

1884 COUES in *Auk* Oct. 321, I would therefore suggest and recommend as follows:—..*Polyonym*. An onym consisting of more than three terms.

3. Used by Buck for a technical term consisting of two or more words, as *pia mater*, *ascending vena cava*.

1889 *Buck's Handbk. Med. Sc.* VIII. 518/1 There are two methods of securing mononyms from pre-existing polyonyms: A. By the omission of unessential words... B. By the compounding of two or more of the separate words. *Ibid.* 524/1 In reducing polyonyms to mononyms the retained word should be as distinctive as possible.

So **polyˈonymal**, *a.* = POLYNOMIAL A. 2; **polyˈonymist** = POLYNOMIALIST.

polyonymic (ˌpɒlɪəʊˈnɪmɪk), *a.* [f. as prec. + -IC.] Of the nature of a polyonym or name consisting of several words.

1889 *Buck's Handbk. Med. Sc.* VIII. 516/2 The conversion of the polyonymic, simile name into one which is mononymic and metaphorical, may commonly be effected by omitting the common noun and reducing the adjective to the substantive from which it was derived.

polyonymosity (ˌpɒlɪɒnɪˈmɒsɪtɪ). *rare*$^{-1}$. [f. as POLYONYMOUS *a.* + -ITY.] The availability of different names for the same person or thing.

1923 W. DE LA MARE in *Times Lit. Suppl.* 3 May 293/4 But how happy is the country polyonymosity that hails it [*sc. Oxalis acetosella*] also as sheep-sorrel, cuckoo-spice, hallelujah, [etc.].

polyonymous (pɒlɪˈɒnɪməs), *a.* Also 9 *erron.* **-onomous**. [f. Gr. πολυώνυμος having many names (f. πολυ-, POLY- + ὄνομα, Æol. ὄνυμα name) + -OUS: cf. *anonymous*.] Having many names or titles; called or known by several different names.

1678 CUDWORTH *Intell. Syst.* I. iv. 477 The supreme God amongst the Pagans was polyonymous, and worshipped under several personal names. **1754** FIELDING *Voy. Lisbon* Wks. 1882 VII. 97 That polyonymous officer aforesaid. *a* **1843** SOUTHEY *Doctor* ccix. (1848) 565/2 The polyonomous Arabian philosopher Zechariah Ben Mohammed Ben Mahmud Al Camuni Al Cazvini. **1890** E. JOHNSON *Rise Christendom* 469 Their mysterious and polyonymous ancestry.

b. Applied to the various names given to the same thing. (Usually *synonymous*.) *rare*$^{-1}$.

'Συνώνυμα were called πολυώνυμα by the Peripatetics' (Liddell & Scott s.v. πολυώνυμος). **1856** MAX MÜLLER *Chips* (1880) II. xvi. 52 The large proportion of.. polyonymous terms by which every ancient language is characterized.

polyonymy (pɒlɪˈɒnɪmɪ). Also 9 *erron.* **-onomy**. [ad. Gr. πολυωνυμία a multitude of names, f. πολυώνυμ-ος: see prec. and -Y.]

1. The use of several different names for the same person or thing; variety of names or titles (esp. in ancient mythology).

1678 CUDWORTH *Intell. Syst.* Pref., The Many Pagan, Poetical and Political Gods,.. prove them Really to have been, but the Polyonymy of one God. **1803** G. S. FABER *Cabiri* I. 177 Remarks on the polyonymy of the solar Noah. **1895** *Q. Rev.* Jan. 227 The Normans.. had.. a system of polyonomy which led to much confusion.

2. The use of a designation consisting of several names; the use of scientific names consisting of more than two terms or words, to denote species, varieties, etc., of animals or plants; polynomial nomenclature.

‖**polyopia** (pɒlɪˈəʊpɪə). *Path.* Also in anglicized form ˈpolyopy. [mod.L., f. Gr. πολυ-, POLY- + ὤψ, ὠπ- eye: cf. *amblyopia*, *diplopia*, *myopia*.] An affection of the eyes in which one object is seen as two or more; multiple vision.

1853 DUNGLISON *Med. Lex.*, Polyopy. **1879** P. SMITH *Glaucoma* 75 The effect upon the refraction was such as to produce polyopia. **1899** *Allbutt's Syst. Med.* VIII. 107 Monocular diplopia, that is the seeing of two or even of more (polyopia) images with one eye.

So ‖**polyˈopsia** [Gr. -οψία, from ὄψις sight] = POLYOPIA.

1842 DUNGLISON *Med. Lex.*, *Polyopsia*,.. vision is so called, when multiple. **1896** BALDWIN tr. *Binet's Alt. Personality* 67 On the left the field of vision is normal. Further, there is achromatopsia and monocular polyopsia.

‖**polyoptron** (pɒlɪˈɒptrən), **-um** (-əm). [mod.L., f. Gr. πολυ-, POLY- + -οπτρον, naming instruments of sight: see DIOPTER.] An optical instrument through which objects appear multiplied; a multiplying-glass (see quot. 1842). Cf. POLYSCOPE 1.

1727-41 CHAMBERS *Cycl.*, *Polyoptrum*,.. a glass through which objects appear multiplied, but diminished. **1842** BRANDE *Dict. Sc.*, etc., *Polyoptron*, in Optics, a glass through which objects appear multiplied, but diminished. It consists of a lens one side of which is plane, but in the other are ground several spherical concavities.

polyorama, polyorganic: see POLY-.

polyose (ˈpɒlɪəʊs). *Chem.* [f. POLY- + -OSE².] A general term for those carbohydrates in which the complex molecule contains several groups of sugar-molecules.

1900 *Nature* 15 Mar. 462/1 The complex polyoses, such as starch and cellulose.

polyotical: see POLY-.

Polyox (ˈpɒlɪɒks). A proprietary name for polyethylene oxide resin.

1957 *Official Gaz.* (U.S. Patent Office) 6 Aug. TM4/2 Union Carbide Corporation, New York.. Polyox. For water soluble resins. First use on or about Mar. 4, 1957. **1958** *Industr. & Engin. Chem.* Jan. 9 (*caption*) A little Polyox resin goes a long way in thickening water. **1973** *Trade Marks Jrnl.* 6 June 1072/2 Polyox... Synthetic water-soluble resins. Union Carbide Corporation.., New York,.. United States of America; manufacturers and merchants. **1976** *Nature* 1 July 47/1 We have reported that polyethyleneoxide (Polyox) in solution reduced the damping of free oscillations in a semicircular manometer.

polyoxyethylene, -methylene: see POLY-.

polyp, polype (ˈpɒlɪp). Forms: 5 polippe, 6 polipe, 7 polip, 7- polype, polyp. See also POULP. [a. F. *polype* (*polipe*, v.r. *polpe* in Brun. Lat. 13th c.), ad. L. *polyp-us*: see POLYPUS.]

†**1.** *Zool.* Properly, an animal having many feet or foot-like processes: but in use restricted to certain organisms, not all answering to this description. †**a.** *orig.* A cephalopod having eight or ten arms or tentacles, as an octopus or a cuttle-fish; = POULP (F. *poulpe*). *Obs.*

1583 GREENE *Mamillia* II. Wks. (Grosart) II. 257 The Polipe chaunge themselues into the likenesse of euerie obiect. **1590** LODGE *Euphues' Gold. Leg.* (Hunter. Cl.) 12 Their passions are as momentarie as the colours of a Polipe, which changeth at the sight of euerie obiect. **1602** F. HERING *Anat.* 10 Beeing himselfe more variable then the Polyp. **1616** BULLOKAR *Eng. Expos.* s.v., Inconstant persons are sometimes said to be Polypes. *a* **1693** *Urquhart's Rabelais* III. xiii. 108 The Preak (by some called the Polyp). **1752** WATSON in *Phil. Trans.* XLVII. 462 The great sea polype (which is eaten in Lent in the Mediterranean).

b. In later use, widely applied to various animals of low organization; chiefly to cœlenterates of different classes, esp. a hydra or other hydrozoan, a 'coral-insect' or other anthozoan; also to the polyzoa, to certain echinoderms, and loosely to rotifers, infusorians, etc. **c.** Many of the above being compound or 'colonial' organisms, the term is hence used *spec.* for a single individual, 'person', or zooid of the colony (also POLYPIDE, POLYPITE).

1742 H. BAKER *Microsc.* II. v. 97 A Creature called Polype found adhering to the Lens Palustris. **1743** —— in *Phil. Trans.* XLII. 616, I chuse a Polype to my Mind, and put it in a small convex Lens with a Drop of Water. **1752** WATSON *ibid.* XLVII. 467 There are some species of the polype of the madrepora, which are produced singly, others in clusters. **1754** BRANDER *ibid.* XLVIII. 806 The polyp is an animal of the vermicular kind. **1788** SMITH *ibid.* LXXVIII. 163 But their animated flowers or polypes, in which the essence of their being resides, are endued with both these properties in an high degree. **1855** KINGSLEY *Glaucus* (1878) App. 232 The simplest form of polype is that of a fleshy bag open at one end, surmounted by a circle of contractile threads or fingers called tentacles. **1872** MIVART *Elem. Anat.* 8 A 6th primary group.. Cœlenterata, contains all sea-anemones, jelly-fishes, Portuguese men-of-war, and all polyps. **1875** HUXLEY & MARTIN *Elem. Biol.* (1883) 98 These are Polypes, the brown ones belonging to the species termed *Hydra fusca*, the green to that called *H. viridis*. **1878** HUXLEY *Physiogr.* xv. 256 The growth of the coral polypes. **1879** tr. *De Quatrefages' Hum. Spec.* I Polyps were long regarded as plants. **1888** ROLLESTON & JACKSON *Anim. Life* 726 The zooids are sometimes dimorphic and then are known as autozooids (= polypes).

fig. **1829** GEN. P. THOMPSON *Exerc.* (1842) I. 41 The polype of human happiness, though cut in pieces and turned inside out, still lives, and applies itself to multiply and grow.

2. *Path.* = POLYPUS 2.

c **1400** *Lanfranc's Cirurg.* 19 In doynge awey polippis [*v.r.* polippes] þat is fleisch þat growiþ wiþinne þe nose. **1579** LANGHAM *Gard. Health* (1633) 35 The iuice healeth the polip in the nose. **1897** *Allbutt's Syst. Med.* III. 823 When a polyp exists at the apex of the intussusceptum, it forms.. a very definite impediment to reduction. **1955** *Sci. News Let.* 1 Oct. 217/1 Polyps are small growths which may be non-cancerous but which are believed capable of developing into cancers. **1961** [see POLYPUS 2]. **1966** *Economist* 12 Nov. 654/3 Power can corrupt—the Far Eastern tour apparently made both Mr Johnson's incisional hernia and the polyp in his throat worse. **1974** PASSMORE & ROBSON *Compan. Med. Stud.* III. xxviii. 43/1 Endometrial polyps are frequently asymptomatic and discovered in the course of a curettage... Recurring polyps associated with adenomatous hyperplasia in the postmenopausal patient should be regarded as premalignant and treated by hysterectomy.

3. *attrib.* and *Comb.* (in sense 1), as ***polyp-bearer***, ***-cell***, ***-colony***, ***-cup***, †***-fish*** (= 1 a), ***-mass***; **polypstem**, **-stock**, the stem, stock, or common support of a compound polyp; = POLYPARY, POLYPIDOM; †**polyp-stone**, app. some precious stone supposed to change colour like the 'polyp' (see 1 a); **polyp-tree** = ***polyp-stem***.

1846 DANA *Zooph.* ii. (1848) 15 *note*, Polypifer, polypary, and polypidom, signifying *polyp-bearer, or a hive or house of polpys. **1846** PATTERSON *Zool.* 22 The stem is covered with one continuous living membrane, in which are the *polype-cells. **1846** DANA *Zooph.* (1848) 182 Nine to twelve lamellæ meet at each *polyp-centre. **1854** MURCHISON *Siluria* x. 214 The parent *polype-cup. *a* **1618** DAVIES *Wittes Pilgr.* G j, The *Polipp Fishe sitts all the Winter longe Stock-still, through Slouthe. **1846** PATTERSON *Zool.* 20 A community, forming altogether a *polype-mass, variable in form, and strengthened in different ways. **1884** *Stand. Nat. Hist.* (1888) I. 99 In larger specimens the length of the nectostem is about one-third that of the *polystem. **1583** GREENE *Mamillia* Wks. (Grosart) II. 77 Comparing them to the *Polipe stone, that chaungeth colours euery houre. **1915** E. R. LANKESTER *Diversions of Naturalist* xi. 97 The little jelly-fish are the ripe individuals of the polyps, and produce eggs and sperm which grow to be *polyp-trees.

polypage to **polyparous**: see POLY-.

polypary (ˈpɒlɪpərɪ). Also 9 in Lat. form **polyparium** (pɒlɪˈpɛərɪəm), pl. **-ia**; erron. sing. **polyparia**, pl. **-iæ**. [ad. mod.L. *polypārium*, f. *polypus* POLYP + -ARIUM.] The common stem, stock, or supporting structure of a colony of polyps (see POLYP 1 c), to which the individual zooids are attached, usually each in a cell or cavity of its own; also called POLYPIDOM.

1750 *Phil. Trans.* XLVII. 107 The size and shape of this polypary is sufficiently seen in Fig. A. **1835** KIRBY *Hab. & Inst. Anim.* I. v. 166 A fixed calcareous house or polypary as it is called consisting often of innumerable cells. **1861** J. R. GREENE *Man. Anim. Kingd.*, *Cœlent.* 85 The firm horny layer, or polypary, which the cœnosarc excretes in *Tubularia* and its allies. **1872** DANA *Corals* i. 17 Science is hardly yet rid of such terms as polypary, polypidom, which imply that each coral is the constructed hive or house of a swarm of polyps. **1875** HUXLEY in *Encycl. Brit.* I. 131/1 The superficial portion of the polyparium. **1880** H. S. COOPER *Coral Lands* I. iii. 24 Polyparia are composed of two separate parts.

Hence **polyparian** (pɒlɪˈpɛərɪən) *a.*, of or pertaining to a polypary.

poˈlypean, *a. rare.* [f. L. *polyp-us* POLYP + *-ean*, after L. adjs. in *-eus*: see -AN.] Pertaining to, or resembling that of, a polyp.

1822 *New Monthly Mag.* V. 110 Dividing their discourses into heads—Cerberean, Polypean, and Hydraform. **1825** *Ibid.* XIII. 212 His polypean power was in his faculty of reproduction.

polypectomy (pɒlɪˈpɛktəmɪ). *Surg.* [f. POLYP + -ECTOMY.] Excision of a polyp.

1950 *Surg. Clinics N. Amer.* XXX. 661 For nasal polypectomy.. anesthesia is accomplished by painting the polyp and its area of attachment or pedicle with a saturated solution of cocaine. **1974** PASSMORE & ROBSON *Compan. Med. Stud.* III. xxviii. 43/1 The diagnosis is established by exploration of the uterus with polypectomy forceps during diagnostic curettage.

polyped: see POLY-.

polypeptide (pɒlɪˈpɛptaɪd). *Biochem.* [ad. G. *polypeptid* (E. Fischer 1903, in *Sitzungsber. d. k. preuss. Akad. d. Wissensch.* 389, after *di-*, *tripeptid*, etc. (Fischer 1902: see PEPTIDE)).] Any peptide in which the number of amino-acid residues that go to make up the molecule is not small (cf. *oligopeptide* s.v. OLIGO-), but is not so large that it can be regarded as a protein; **polypeptide chain** = *peptide chain* s.v. PEPTIDE 2.

1903 *Jrnl. Chem. Soc.* LXXXIV. I. 466 These acid chlorides combine easily with glycylglycine esters and similar compounds to form chains of amino-acids joined together by an anhydride linking. Such are termed polypeptides. **1935** R. H. A. PLIMMER in Harrow & Sherwin *Textbk. Biochem.* v. 177 Fischer held the view that the polypeptide chain was not long enough for attack by pepsin. **1949** H. W. FLOREY et al. *Antibiotics* I. i. 38 The active preparation made from this organism.. contains two antibiotics, gramicidin and tyrocidine, both crystalline polypeptides. **1951** *New Biol.* XI. 99 Larger molecules that show biological activity when applied to living organisms are exemplified by polypeptides, such as A.C.T.H. (the pituitary hormone which controls the secretion of cortisone). **1959** *Times* 2 Jan. 11/3 Further evidence suggested that this particular polypeptide was a precursor of the cell wall of the staphylococcus. **1961** *Ann. Reg. 1960* 401 The polypeptide chain, the backbone of the protein molecule, was found to be coiled in a helix-like spiral spring with only a space inside. **1978** *Sci. Amer.* Dec. 68/2 A hemoglobin molecule is made up of four polypeptide chains, two alpha chains of 141 amino acid residues each and two beta chains of 146 residues each.

Hence **polyˈpeptidase** [-ASE], any enzyme which hydrolyses polypeptides.

1922 *Chem. Abstr.* XVI. 3491 (*heading*) Influence of materials obtained from yeast cells and organs on the rate of hydrolysis of substrates by polypeptidases, carbohydratases and esterases. **1929** R. P. WALTON tr. *Waldschmidt-Leitz's Enzyme Actions* 159 The yeast polypeptidases are totally inactive against dipeptides. **1940, 1961** [see EREPSIN].

ˈpolypetal, *a.* and *sb. Bot. rare.* [ad. F. *polypétale* (1732), or ad. mod.L. *polypetal-us* (fem. pl. *-petalæ*, Tournefort 1694), f. Gr. πολυ-, POLY- + πέταλ-ον leaf, PETAL*sb.*.] **a.** *adj.* = POLYPETALOUS. **b.** *sb.* A polypetalous plant.

[**1760** J. LEE *Introd. Bot.* II. iii. (1765) 79 Polypetala is expressive of such Plants as have many Petals.] **1802** *Ann. Reg.* 761/2 It is of the genus of the polypetal plants. **1882** G. ALLEN *Colours Flowers* iii. 63 They [Geraniaceæ] are on the whole a comparatively high family of polypetals.

polypetalous (pɒlɪˈpɛtələs), *a.* [f. mod.L. *polypetal-us* (see prec.) + -OUS.]

1. *Bot.* Literally, having many petals; but commonly used for: having the petals distinct or separate, not coherent or united. Also *apopetalous*, *choripetalous*, *dialypetalous*, *eleutheropetalous*. Opp. to *monopetalous* or *gamopetalous*.

1704 J. HARRIS *Lex. Techn.* I, *Polypetalous Flower*, is the Term in Botany for the Flower of a Plant which consists of more than six distinct Flower-leaves set round to form it; and which fall off singly. **1767** ELLIS in *Phil. Trans.* LVII. 427 Pedunculated flowers, or fruit, with their polypetalous cups. **1881** GRIFFITHS in *Science Gossip* No. 203. 248 The calyx is polysepalous and inferior; the corolla is polypetalous and hypogynous.

2. *nonce-use.* Having many leaves, as a book.

1803 W. TAYLOR in *Ann. Rev.* I. 431 The polypetalous tomes of an encyclopædia.

‖**polyphagia** (pɒlɪˈfeɪdʒɪə). Also in anglicized form **polyphagy** (pəˈlɪfədʒɪ). [mod.L., a. Gr. πολυφαγία, f. πολυφάγος: see POLYPHAGOUS. So F. *polyphagie*.]

1. *Phys.* and *Path.* Excessive eating, or desire for eating: voracious or ravenous appetite, esp. as a morbid symptom.

1693 tr. *Blancard's Phys. Dict.* (ed. 2), *Polyphagia*, the taking much Aliment. **1802** *Med. Jrnl.* VIII. 285 Cit. Percy ..concludes from the numerous examples of Polyphagy which he has collected, that the unhappy subjects of it most frequently find the end of their miseries in death before the age of forty years. **1866** A. FLINT *Princ. Med.* (1880) 474 The polyphagia which attends diabetes thus becomes a cause of dilatation. **1946** *Nature* 28 Sept. 454/1 Such animals [*sc.* diabetic rabbits]..exhibited classical symptoms of diabetes mellitus—hyperglycæmia, glycosuria, polyuria, polyphagia.

2. *Zool.* The habit of feeding on various kinds of food; polyphagous character.

1890 in *Cent. Dict.* **1907** W. R. FISHER *Schlich's Man. Forestry* (ed. 2) IV. iv. 158 Observations are not yet complete regarding the monophagy, or polyphagy of certain insects. **1950** *New Biol.* VIII. 64 Predaceous insects, spiders, birds and so on, exhibiting various degrees of polyphagy (i.e. eating more than one kind of food) usually come into the picture. **1965** B. E. FREEMAN tr. *Vandel's Biospeleol.* xix. 337 The categories which have been recognised must remain fluid because of the marked tendency of cavernicoles towards polyphagia. **1970** K. R. NORRIS in *Insects of Australia* (Commonwealth Sci. & Industr. Res. Org., Australia) v. 114/2 An example of polyphagy is afforded by the scale insect *Ceroplastes rubens* feeding on hundreds of different host plants.

So **ˈpolyphage** [cf. F. *polyphage*], one who eats much or to excess; **polyˈphagian** *a.*, eating much; *sb.* = *polyphage*; **polyphagic** (-ˈfædʒɪk) *a.* = POLYPHAGOUS; **poˈlyphagist**, one who eats much, or who eats many kinds of food.

1623 COCKERAM, *Poliphage, an extraordinarie eater. **1924** *Scribner's Mag.* Aug. 156/2 The flimsy telegraph copy of a presidential message fluttered out of the window and was lost... 'Oh, say that the office cat ate it.'.. The animal immediately became popular as a polyphage in hundreds of other newspaper-offices. **1965** B. E. FREEMAN tr. *Vandel's Biospeleol.* xxx. 472 Only the polyphages..have a chance of subsisting underground. **1658** PHILLIPS, **Polyphagian*,.. one that eats much, a great feeder. **1825** *New Monthly Mag.* XIII. 481 Without possessing his polyphagian powers. **1890** *Cent. Dict.*, **Polyphagic*. **1895** in *Syd. Soc. Lex.* **1819** *Sporting Mag.* V. 15 All the *polyphagists, or general devourers,..are superseded by the famous Tarrare.

polyphagous (pəˈlɪfəgəs), *a.* [f. L. *polyphag-us* (a. Gr. πολυφάγος (Hippocrates) eating to excess, f. πολυ-, POLY- + -φάγος eating) + -OUS: see -PHAGOUS.] Eating much, voracious; *Zool.* feeding upon various kinds of food.

1815 KIRBY & SP. *Entomol.* ii. (1818) I. 30 Some larvæ are polyphagous, or feed upon a variety of plants. **1838** J. G. MILLINGEN *Curios. Med. Exper.* (1839) 196 Dr. Boehmen.. witnessed the performance of one of these polyphagous individuals, who commenced his repast by eating a raw sheep. **1879** tr. *Semper's Anim. Life* 51 Polyphagous creatures, which eat a variety of food or even anything that comes in their way.

polyphagy: see POLYPHAGIA.

Polyphant (ˈpɒlɪfənt). Properly **Pollaphant**, name of a place between Bodmin and Launceston, whence ***polyphant stone***, a kind of Cornish potstone, in colour between greenish and iron-grey.

[**1830** H. BOASE in *Trans. Geol. Soc. Cornwall* (1832) IV. 224 Greenstones, both compact and schistose, prevail between Trewint and Pollaphant. **1839** DE LA BECHE *Rep. Geol. Cornwall*, etc. 59 Near Pollaphant there is a kind of pot-stone which has been noticed by Dr. Boase, who states that not long before he wrote..several vessels formed of this stone had been discovered under the rubbish of an old quarry about a quarter of a mile distant.] **1899** BARING-GOULD *Bk. of West* II. 88 In the porch under the stone bench, a hare hunt is carved on polyphant stone.

polyphant: see POLYPHONE.

polypharmaceutical (ˌpɒlɪfɑːməˈsjuːtɪkəl), *sb.* and *a. Med.* [f. POLY- + PHARMACEUTICAL.]

A. *sb.* A medicinal preparation containing several drugs. **B.** *adj.* Of or pertaining to polypharmacy.

Usu. disparaging; cf. next.

1961 *Lancet* 16 Sept. 658/2 The [pharmaceuticals] industry, say some doctors, makes excessive profits;.. indulges in excessive and irrelevant promotion of its products;..goes in for dubious polypharmaceuticals. **1974** M. C. GERALD *Pharmacol.* i. 6 A very simple preparation was Paracelsus' laudanum, which contained opium, gold, and pearls. (Note that even Paracelsus retained vestiges of polypharmaceutical formulation.)

polypharmacy (pɒlɪˈfɑːməsɪ). *Med.* [= F. *polypharmacie*: see POLY- and PHARMACY; cf. Gr. πολυφάρμακ-ος knowing or characterized by many drugs or poisons.] The use of many drugs or medicines in the treatment of disease. Freq. with the suggestion of indiscriminate, unscientific, or excessive prescription.

1762 *Gentl. Mag.* 214 Polypharmacy was never carried to a greater excess. **1832** SIR W. HAMILTON *Discuss.* (1852) 253 The murderous polypharmacy of the Solidists. **1904** J. F. PAYNE *Eng. Med. Anglo-Sax. T.* 148 The profuse polypharmacy of the old Anglo-Saxon leechdoms. **1906** H. SAINSBURY *Principia Therapeutica* vi. 109 The purist.. whilst limiting himself scrupulously to the use of one drug at a time, will seldom hesitate to prescribe the crude drugs, —opium, digitalis, bark, [etc.]..entirely oblivious of the fact that in so doing he is guilty of the most flagrant polypharmacy. **1928** SOLIS-COHEN & GITHENS *Pharmacotherapeutics* v. 379 There is a tendency at the present time to decry the association of remedies as 'polypharmacy', and to advocate the use of 'single medicines'. **1953** J. L. SIMONSEN *Plant Products & Utilisation* (Univ. Nottingham: Sir Jesse Boot Found. Lect.) 4 There is less polypharmacy now than formerly, but I am satisfied that there is less good prescribing now than in my student days. **1977** *Lancet* 26 Mar. 685/2 Therapeutic misadventures..are more likely in the elderly because of inappropriate dosage,..erratic pill-taking, and polypharmacy for multiple diseases.

So **polyˈpharmacal** *a.*, 'that hath many medicines' (Blount *Glossogr.* 1656); **polyˈpharmacist** (-sɪst), one who practises polypharmacy.

1886 W. T. GAIRDNER in *Life Sir R. Christison* II. vii. 134 Dr. Graham, a strong and unhesitating therapeutist, and also not a little of a polypharmacist. **1927** C. H. LA WALL *4,000 Yrs. Pharmacy* iii. 93 The Arabians perpetuated the polypharmacal combinations which had come down from the Egyptians. **1966** G. WATSON *Theriac & Mithridatium* iii. 114 Texts of ancient medical writers with polypharmacal formulae had become available.

polyphase (ˈpɒlɪfeɪz), *a.* (*sb.*) *Electr.* [f. POLY- + PHASE *sb.* 3.] **a.** *lit.* Of many phases: applied to systems of alternating electric currents (magnets, transformers, etc.) in which are employed two, three, or more such currents of identical frequency but differing from one another in phase, that is, which recur one after the other with regular successions of phase; also called *multiphase*.

1891 *Electrician* XXVII. 376 Three articles on the polyphase alternate current system. **1895** S. P. THOMPSON *Polyphase Electric Currents* 53 By the adoption of polyphase systems, as compared with single-phase systems, there is effected a saving. **1900** *Engineering Mag.* XIX. 754/1 In other fields the rotary or polyphase current has of late made marked advance.

(*b*) as *sb.* **1901** *Daily Chron.* 7 Nov. 7/3 The witness..came to discover that the polyphase was capable of being stopped within a remarkably short space.

b. Consisting of or occurring in a number of separate stages.

1936 *Proc. Prehist. Soc.* II. 155 In 1932..I attempted an analysis of the evidence for a polyphase Ice Age. **1938** *Mem. Geol. Soc. Amer.* VI. 84 Heteroaxial symmetry means, therefore, a sideward drag in the course of tectonic flow, or a polyphase deformation. **1958** R. S. WOODWORTH *Dynamics of Behavior* ii. 39 The child's developing purposiveness spreads in the opposite direction. It is visible first in the little two-phase and polyphase acts, their time span being only a few seconds. **1969** BENNISON & WRIGHT *Geol. Hist. Brit. Isles* iv. 85 The Manx Slates have been affected by polyphase folding and low-grade metamorphism.

c. Consisting of or involving a number of different phases of matter.

1940 *Jrnl. R. Aeronaut. Soc.* XLIV. 538 Precipitation hardening leads generally to the formation of polyphase systems, and a solution hardened metal shows distinct advantages. **1950** *Proc. Amer. Acad. Arts & Sci.* LXXVIII. 167 Poly-phase, poly-component chemical systems. **1975** *Physics Bull.* May 225/1 The last chapter deals with microstructural and polyphase effects.

polyphasic (pɒlɪˈfeɪzɪk), *a. Physiol.* [f. POLY- + PHAS(E + -IC.] Having several successive peaks.

1922 *Amer. Jrnl. Physiol.* LIX. 278 The fall of temperature..ought to occupy about the same place in the diphasic as it does in the polyphasic thermocardiograms. **1936** *Brit. Jrnl. Psychol.* XXVII. 71 We observed three types of voluntary movements: The 'motor impulse effect', the polyphasic movement and the amorphous movement. **1968** *Brit. Med. Bull.* XXIV. 257/2 An example..is the so-called 'polyphasic' potentials occurring following partial denervation, in which a normal spike with a duration of several msec. is replaced by a repetitive series of much shorter spikes.

Polypheme (ˈpɒlɪfiːm). Also 7 **Polyphem.** [a. F. *Polyphème*, ad. L. POLYPHEMUS.] Name of a Cyclops or one-eyed giant in Homer's *Odyssey*; hence used allusively.

1641 MILTON *Animadv.* Wks. 1851 III. 215 Goe therefore ..to heave and hale your mighty Polyphem of Antiquity to the delusion of Novices, and unexperienc't Christians. **1656** BLOUNT *Glossogr.*, *Polypheme*, generally taken for a Gyant, or any big, over-grown, disproportionate fellow. **1814** MRS. J. WEST *Alicia de Lacy* II. 311 Such prodigality as will suffice to gorge a race of Polyphemes. **1878** GEO. ELIOT *Coll. Breakf. P.* 637 His Handel-strain As of some angry Polypheme.

So **Polyˈphemian, Polyˈphemic, Polyˈphemous** *adjs.*, belonging or relating to, resembling, or having the character of, Polyphemus.

1601 ? MARSTON *Pasquil & Kath.* I. 124 Nor doe I enuie *Polyphemian puffes, Swizars slopt greatnesse. **1610** *Chester's Tri.* (Chetham Soc.) Chester's last Speech 3 That can escape the Poliphemian eye of Envie, that for ever lookes awry. **1796** BURNEY *Mem. Metastasio* II. 49 There comes an order from Court for a little *Polyphemic Cantata. **1837** *New Monthly Mag.* LI. 236 With my agonized gaze still fixed on the Polyphemic orb of my loathsome neighbour. **1890** *Cent. Dict.*, **Polyphemous*, one-eyed, monoculous, cyclopean.

‖**Polyphemus** (pɒlɪˈfiːməs). [L., ad. Gr. Πολύφημος (lit. many-voiced, also much spoken of) name of a Cyclops in *Odyssey* IX.]

1. = POLYPHEME; a Cyclops, a one-eyed giant.

1829 J. L. KNAPP *Jrnl. Naturalist* 317 It riots the polyphemus of the pool. **1845** R. W. HAMILTON *Pop. Educ.* v. (ed. 2) 99 When the eyes of the many open, their Polyphemus will cease to be famous for his cyclopean vision.

2. *Zool.* **a.** A (naturally or abnormally) one-eyed animal. **b.** The common name for a very large American silkworm-moth, *Telea polyphemus*. (*Cent. Dict.*)

polyphenol(ic, -phenylene: see POLY-.

ˌpolyphiloproˈgenitive, *a.* [f. POLY- + PHILOPROGENITIVE *a.*] Very prolific, *spec.* of a person's talent, imagination, inventive powers, etc.

Quot. 1919 is perhaps influenced also by PHILOPROGENITIVE *a.* 2.

1919 T. S. ELIOT *Poems*, Polyphiloprogenitive The sapient sutlers of the Lord Drift across the window-panes. **1947** [see NATTER *sb.*]. **1953** G. WILLIAMSON *Reader's Guide to Eliot* iv. 93 The first line, 'Polyphiloprogenitive', is not merely a *tour de force*, but a learned word which derides the quality that unites the modern Church functionary with the caterpillar world. **1963** *Punch* 4 Sept. 358/3 There remains his polyphiloprogenitive invention, which occasionally pushes a story across the starting line if you can bear the writing. **1966** *Ibid.* 31 Aug. 339/2, I find Heinlein too sentimental and full of cracker-barrel drollery for my taste; but he certainly has a polyphiloprogenitive talent.

polyphloisbic (pɒlɪˈflɔɪzbɪk), *a. rare*⁻¹. [f. as POLYPHLOISBOIAN *a.* + -IC.]
= POLYPHLOISBOIAN *a.*
1915 R. BROOKE *Lett.* (1968) 662 Will the sea be polyphloisbic and wine dark and unvintageable (you, of course, know if it is)?

polyphloisboian (ˌpɒlɪflɔɪsˈbɔɪən), *a.* Also **poluphloisboian, polyphlœsbœan, -phloisbean.** [Humorously f. Gr. πολυφλοίσβοιο (θαλάσσης) ‘of the loud-roaring (sea)’, echoic phrase often used by Homer; Epic gen. of πολύφλοισβος, f. πολύς much + φλοῖσβος roaring, din. The Roman spelling is *polyphlœsbœ-*, whence various intermediate adaptations.] Loud-roaring, boisterous.
1824 *Blackw. Mag.* XV. 675 We leave that.. to critics of a more polyphloisboian note. **1858** O. W. HOLMES *Aut. Breakf.-t.* iv, Two men are walking by the polyphlœsbœan ocean. **1881** T. DAVIDSON in *Fortn. Rev.* No. 179. 560 The unreliable, erratic, polyphloisbean Loewenbruk also put in an appearance.
So **poly-, poluphlois'boiic, -phloisboi'otic, -phloisboiota'totic** [as if f. Gr. superlat. suffix -οτατος], **poluphlois'boisterous** [with allusion to BOISTEROUS] *adjs.*; all humorous nonce-words. Also **polyphlois'boioism, -boism**, noisy bombast.
1823 *Blackw. Mag.* XIV. 157 What hammering of epithets!.. what helpless polyphloisboioism! **1843** THACKERAY *Irish Sk. Bk.* xxix, The line of shore washed by the poluphloisboiotic, nay, the poluphloisboiotatotic sea. **1863** E. FITZGERALD *Lett.* (1889) I. 294 How is it the Islandic.. was not more Poluphloisboi-ic? **18..** in A. Godley *Verses to Order* (1892) 25 Poluphloisboisterous Homer of old Threw all his augments into the sea. **1892** *Blackw. Mag.* Sept. 395 An ororotundity, a polyphloisboism that is delicious.

polyphobia: see POLY-.

polyphonal (pɒˈlɪfənəl), *a. Mus.* [f. as POLYPHONE + -AL, after ANTIPHONAL *a.* and *sb.*] = POLYPHONIC *a.* 1. Hence **po'lyphonally** *adv.*
1946 R. BLESH *Shining Trumpets* (1949) i. 8 The ultra-modern polyphonal and dissonantal school of today. *Ibid.* iii. 68 A woman's chorus.. that sings, part antiphonally, part polyphonally, in undulating lines of chain-fourths.

polyphone (ˈpɒlɪfəʊn). Also 7 poli-, 7– -phon; β. 7–8 (corruptly, but usually in sense 1 a) **poliphant, polyphant.** [mod. ad. Gr. πολύφων-ος having many tones, manifold in expression, f. πολυ-, POLY- + φωνή voice, sound; cf. F. *polyphone* adj. polyphonic. In sense 1 c, generally spelt *polyphon*, Ger. *polyphon*.]
1. †**a.** A musical instrument formerly in use, somewhat resembling a lute, but having a large number of wire strings. *Obs.* except *Hist.*
1655 F. PRUJEANE in *12th Rep. Hist. MSS. Comm.* App. v. 5 The polyphon is an instrument of so different a stringing and tuning that its impossible to play what is sett to it on any other hand instrument.
β. **1674** PLAYFORD *Skill Mus.* Pref. 8 Queen Elizabeth.. did often recreate herself on an excellent Instrument called the Poliphant, not much unlike a Lute, but strung with Wire. **1789** BURNEY *Hist. Mus.* (ed. 2) III. i. 15. **1954** *Grove's Dict. Mus.* (ed. 5) VI. 838/2 Queen Elizabeth was particularly partial to the poliphant. **1968** *New Oxf. Hist. Music* IV. xiii. 727 The drawing of the polyphant in Randle Holmes's *Academy of Armory* suggests a flat bandora-body surmounted by a harp-like frame. **1977** D. GILL *Wire-Strung Plucked Instruments contemp. with Lute* 19 Two other contemporary wire instruments have to be mentioned. One is the ‘polyphant’ or ‘polyphone’. *Ibid.* 20 The 1671 inventory of Belvoir Castle does not list a polyphant.
†**b.** Some instrument or apparatus for producing a variety of sounds or notes. *Obs.*
1683 *Phil. Trans.* XIV. 483 By a Polyphone or Polyacoustick well ordered one sound may be heard as many.
c. A large kind of musical box, driven by clockwork or by hand, and capable of playing any tune when the corresponding perforated disk is inserted.
1902 *Daily Chron.* 7 Apr. 8/5 Polyphon for Sale, including stand; cost £14. **1954** *Grove's Dict. Mus.* (ed. 5) VI. 848/1 In the 1880s the Polyphon was invented, in which projections punched up on a steel disc were used.. to pluck the teeth of the comb. **1973** A. W. J. G. ORD-HUME *Clockwork Music* 108 Probably the best known of the musical box dealers and wholesalers was Henry Klein... His main business was in Polyphons and amusement machines. **1975** *Country Life* 11 Dec. 1715/2 (Advt.), Antique clocks, musical boxes, polyphones.
d. *fig.*
1875 LANIER *Symphony* 106 Life's strident polyphone.
2. *Philol.* A written character having more than one phonetic value; a letter or other symbol which stands for different sounds.
1872 SAYCE *Assyr. Gram.* Pref. 7 Polyphones—that is, characters with more than one value.. actually exist in Japanese for the same reason that they existed in Assyrian. **1880** R. N. CUST *Linguistic & Oriental Ess.* 350 It was all very well to tolerate Ideographs and Polyphones in documents.. relating to the future world. **1896** BOSCAWEN *Bible & Mon.* i. 18 Its elaborate syllabary, the use of polyphones.. all tend to show clearly that this writing was not the invention of the Semites. **1937** *Antiquity* XI. 273 Many of the Sumerian word-signs were polyphons.

†**poly'phonian**, *a. Obs. rare*⁻¹. [f. Gr. πολύφων-ος (POLYPHONE) + -IAN.] Many-voiced.
1635 QUARLES *Embl.* v. vi, I love the air;.. Her shrill-mouth'd choir sustain me with their flesh, And with their polyphonian notes delight me.

polyphonic (pɒlɪˈfɒnɪk), *a.* [f. as prec. + -IC.]
1. *Mus.* **a.** Composed or arranged for several voices or parts, each having a melody of its own; consisting of a number of melodies combined; contrapuntal; of or pertaining to polyphonic music.
1782 BURNEY *Hist. Mus.* (1789) II. ii. 88 He asserts that he not only invented polyphonic music, or counterpoint, but the polyplectrum or spinet. **1876** tr. *Blaserna's Sound* vii. 121 In the tenth and eleventh centuries an attempt was begun.. at polyphonic music. **1884** *Athenæum* 13 Sept. 346/1 The choruses.. are marvellous specimens of the composer's polyphonic skill.
b. Applied to an instrument capable of producing more than one note at a time, as a keyboard instrument, a harp, etc.
1890 in *Cent. Dict.*
2. a. Producing many sounds; many-voiced. Also *fig.*
1864 WEBSTER, *Polyphonic*, having, or consisting of, many voices or sounds. **1868** *Sat. Rev.* 11 Apr. 496/2 The barking crow [of British Columbia] possesses the most remarkable polyphonic powers. It can shriek, laugh, yell, shout, whistle, scream, and bark. **1890** *Daily News* 28 Mar. 5/4 A grand organ.. called a polyphonic organ... The chief characteristic of this organ is the perfect imitation which it can produce of almost the whole orchestra, especially of the strings and the wood wind. **1920** H. CRANE *Let.* 15 Jan. (1965) 31 Your aristocrat is much more vital and admirable than the polyphonic God, chosen to symbolize the artist.
b. Of prose: written to sound pleasant and melodious.
1916 J. G. FLETCHER in *Poetry* Apr. 35 It seems fitting that a new name should be given to these poems of hers [*sc.* Amy Lowell's], which, printed as prose, or as prose and verse interspersed, display all the colors of the chromatic palette. The title that fits them best is that of Polyphonic Prose. **1917** A. LOWELL in *N. Amer. Rev.* Jan. 115 Metre, cadence, and rhyme are some of the many ‘voices’ employed in ‘polyphonic prose’. Others are assonance, alliteration, and return. **1920** H. CRANE *Let.* 18 Aug. (1965) 41 Conrad's *Nigger of the Narcissus* seems to me all polyphonic prose. **1925** I. A. RICHARDS *Princ. Lit. Crit.* 135 Even the most highly organised lyrical or ‘polyphonic’ prose raises as it advances only a very ambiguous expectation. **1940** C. STRATTON *Handbk. Eng.* 249/2 *Polyphonic prose*, prose very carefully written to make the sounds pleasant and harmonious... The sound is obtained by attention to combinations and sequences of letters and syllables. **1977** *Amer. N. & Q.* XVI. 39/2 It is not improbable that the master of polyphonic prose was conscious of some metempsychosis which had taken place.
3. *Philol.* Of a letter or other written character: Having more than one phonetic value (as *c*, *g*, *s*, and the vowels in many European languages).
1891 tr. *De La Saussaye's Hist. Sc. of Relig.* liii. 463 They are often polyphonic, that is the same sign represents various sounds. **1901** *Speaker* 1 June 244/2 His feeling for the colours of vowels and the polyphonic properties of consonants was impeccable.
So **poly'phonical** *a.*; also **poly'phonically** *adv.*, as regards polyphony, in a polyphonic manner.
1864 A. MCKAY *Hist. Kilmarnock* 259 The greatest success has attended his polyphonical and gastriloquial displays. **1936** *Jrnl. Theol. Stud.* XXXVII. 168 This is exactly the point needed to explain the presence of a set of polyphonical Sequelae in our MS. **1936** *Scrutiny* V. 268 The increasing tendency in Beethoven's music to think of harmony.. vertically and dramatically instead of horizontally and polyphonically. **1942** Polyphonically [see MONOPHONICALLY *adv.* a]. **1946** R. BLESH *Shining Trumpets* (1949) iv. 87 The response lines begin to lose their strictly harmonic division into set chords and separate into independent melodic lines woven together polyphonically. **1959** *Listener* 8 Jan. 80/1 The polyphonically derived harmony intensifies the seventeenth-century partiality for modal variety and false relation.

polyphonism (ˈpɒlɪfəʊnɪz(ə)m). *rare.* [f. as POLYPHONE + -ISM.]
1. Multiplication of sound, as by an echo.
1713 DERHAM *Phys.-Theol.* IV. iii. 133 The magnifying the Sound by the Polyphonisms, or Repercussions of the Rocks, Caverns, and other phonocamptick Objects.. in the Mount.
2. *Mus.* The use of polyphony; polyphonic style or composition.
1864 WEBSTER, *Polyphonism*.. composition in parts; contrapuntal composition.

polyphonist (ˈpɒlɪfəʊnɪst). [f. as prec. + -IST.]
1. One who produces a variety of vocal sounds; a ventriloquist. *rare.*
1829 W. E. LOVE in *Dict. Nat. Biog.* XXXIV. 161 The Peregrinations of a Polyphonist. **1846** WORCESTER, *Polyphonist*, one producing many sounds. *Black.*
2. *Mus.* One versed in polyphony; a polyphonic composer or theorist; a contrapuntist.
1864 WEBSTER, *Polyphonist*... a master of the art of polyphony; a contrapuntist. **1944** *Scrutiny* XII. 205 They [*sc.* Gesualdo's phrases] are related not so much to the great polyphonists as to the new technique of Monteverdi. **1954** *Grove's Dict. Mus.* (ed. 5) VI. 863/2 His [*sc.* Tallis's] music .. has that expressive power characteristic of the later English polyphonists in its feeling for tonality and harmonic progression. **1968** *New Oxf. Hist. Mus.* IV. vii. 375 The Spanish polyphonists of this century [*sc.* the 16th] express a religious devotion and mystic fervour parallel to that of the painters and religious poets and prose-writers of the same epoch.

polyphonous (pəˈlɪfənəs), *a.* [f. Gr. πολύφων-ος (see POLYPHONE) + -OUS.]
1. = POLYPHONIC 2.
1677 PLOT *Oxfordsh.* 13 Tautological Polyphonous Echo's, such as return a word or more, often repeated from divers objects by simple reflection. **1846** WORCESTER, *Polyphonous*, having many sounds. *Dr. Black.* **1875** JOWETT *Plato* (ed. 2) III. 36 One of these polyphonous pantomimic gentlemen offers to exhibit himself.
2. *Mus.* = POLYPHONIC 1.
1872 F. HÜFFER in *Fortn. Rev.* Mar. 277 Hence the prodigious skill in the polyphonous texture of Bach's and Handel's Counterpoint. **1876** *Macm. Mag.* XXXIV. 193 The rich harmony of polyphonous church music.
3. *Philol.* = POLYPHONIC 3.
1880 SAYCE in *Nature* 19 Feb. 380/1 [We] cling so tenaciously to our own polyphonous alphabet. **1905** W. T. PILTER tr. *König's Bible & Babylon* Notes 121 The majority of signs were polyphonous.. they had more than one syllable value. **1956** *Jrnl. Theol. Stud.* VII. 87 Transliterations would have been a great help to a Babylonian in enabling him to read ideograms and to determine the value of polyphonous signs.

polyphony (pəˈlɪfənɪ, ˈpɒlɪfəʊnɪ). [ad. Gr. πολυφωνία variety of tones or of speech, f. πολύφωνος: see POLYPHONE. So F. *polyphonie*.]
1. Multiplicity of sounds: = POLYPHONISM 1.
1828 WEBSTER, *Polyphonism, Polyphony.*
2. *Mus.* The simultaneous combination of a number of parts, each forming an individual melody, and harmonizing with each other; the style of composition in which the parts are so combined; polyphonic composition; counterpoint. Also *transf.* and *fig.*
1864 [see POLYPHONIST 2]. **1867** MACFARREN *Harmony* i. 20 Let me not arrogate.. that the origination of polyphony belongs to this country. **1898** *Dict. Nat. Biog.* LIV. 232/2 The tendency to a harmonized melody, to homophony rather than polyphony. **1965** *New Statesman* 10 Dec. 939/1 A polyphony of death, art and ‘incorporeal love’ was perhaps the most exalted solution for a girl who would have disliked fulfilment. **1968** COATES & ABRAHAM in *New Oxf. Hist. Mus.* IV. vi. 329 The movement gradually expands into a suave polyphony.. and reaches a fine climax at ‘Gloria in excelsis’. **1973** C. D. GARRATT *Masterpieces in Steam* 133 The Austerity created a steady, even blast whilst the ancient lady in front wheezed and rasped away in a totally different rhythmic pattern, so creating a marvellous polyphony of sound. **1977** A. SHERIDAN tr. *Lacan's Écrits* ii. 17 This formal fixation.. is the very condition that extends indefinitely his world and his power, by giving his objects their instrumental polyvalence and symbolic polyphony.
3. *Philol.* The symbolization of different vocal sounds by the same letter or character; the fact or quality of being polyphonic.
1880 SAYCE in *Nature* 19 Feb. 380/2 The whole cumbrous hieroglyphic system with its ideographs, its syllabic values, and its polyphony. **1882–3** *Schaff's Encycl. Relig. Knowl.* I. 583 The difficulty of reading which this polyphony involved.

polyphore (ˈpɒlɪfɔə(r)). *Bot. rare.* [a. F. *polyphore* (Richard *c* 1810), ad. Gr. πολυφόρος bearing many.] Term for a receptacle bearing a number of ovaries, as in the buttercup, strawberry, etc.
1835 LINDLEY *Introd. Bot.* 176 Richard calls it *Polyphore.* **1858** in MAYNE *Expos. Lex.* **1866** *Treas. Bot.* 915.

polyphorous (pəˈlɪfərəs), *a. rare.* [f. Gr. πολυφόρος (see prec.) + -OUS.] †**a.** Of wine: That will bear much water, strong. *Obs.* **b.** Bearing or producing much, fruitful.
1657 TOMLINSON *Renou's Disp.* 220 Wines differenced.. from their virtue, vinous, aquous, polyphorous.. and oligophorous. **1858** MAYNE *Expos. Lex.*, *Polyphorus*, bearing or yielding much; fruitful; polyphorous.

polyphosphate to **polyphote**: see POLY-.

Polyphoto: see POLYFOTO.

polyphylesis (ˌpɒlɪfaɪˈliːsɪs). *Biol.* [Back-formation f. POLYPHYLETIC *a.*, after GENESIS.] The polyphyletic development of a species or other taxon. Also **poly'phyletism.**
1897 *Amer. Naturalist* XXXI. 281 Reinke.. labors constantly under the delusion that those who contend for the distribution of the lichens, deny their polyphylesis. **1905** F. E. CLEMENTS *Res. Methods Ecol.* iv. 232 All have ignored the fact that the polyphylesis of genera carries with it the admission of such origin for species. **1926** *Jrnl. Bot.* LXIV. 119 The difficulties which arise from polyphylesis complicate the problem. **1951** G. H. M. LAWRENCE *Taxon. Vascular Plants* vii. 164 Polyphylesis is the situation represented by a polyphyletic origin. **1969** *Biol. Rev.* XLIV. 576 The appearance of bifid and trifid lobed forms [of ammonoids].. with the shell sculpture were seen as evidence of polyphyletism. **1978** *BioSystems* X. 82/1 This paradox may be due to polyphyletism within the chytrids.

polyphyletic (ˌpɒlɪfaɪˈlɛtɪk), *a.* [f. POLY- + Gr. φυλετικ-ός PHYLETIC, after G. *polyphyletisch*.] Belonging to several tribes or families; originating, as a species, from several independent ancestors or sources; relating to such origination; polygenetic.
1875 tr. *Schmidt's Desc. & Darw.* 325 The hypothesis of descent from many families (*polyphyletic*) possesses more

probability. **1879** tr. *Haeckel's Evol. Man* II. xix. 182 Comparative Philology has recently shown that the present human language is polyphyletic in origin. **1881** WETTERHAN in *Nature* 17 Mar. 458/1 The question of monophyletic or polyphyletic evolution of species.

Hence **polyphy'letically** *adv.*

1887 *Amer. Naturalist* XXI. 429 The epibolic gastrula of *Polyxenia leucostyla* might arise polyphyletically from totally different methods of forming the endoderm.

polyphyllous (pɒlɪ'fɪləs), *a. Bot.* [f. Gr. πολύφυλλ-ος many-leaved + -OUS.] Properly, Having or consisting of many leaves; usually, Having the (perianth-) leaves separate, not united. Also *apophyllous, dialyphyllous, eleutherophyllous.* (Cf. POLYPETALOUS, POLYSEPALOUS.) Opp. to *monophyllous* or *gamophyllous.*

1785 MARTYN *Rousseau's Bot.* xv. (1794) 160 The two genera.. agree in having the common calyx polyphyllous, or consisting of many leaves. **1857** HENFREY *Bot.* §189 We have a regular polyphyllous perianth in the Tulip and Lily.

So **poly'phylline** *a.* = prec.; **'polyphylly**, the condition of having the number of (foliage or floral) leaves in a whorl in excess of the normal.

1890 in *Cent. Dict.* **1895** in *Syd. Soc. Lex.*

polyphyly ('pɒlɪˌfaɪlɪ). *Biol.* [f. POLY- + Gr. φυλή tribe.] = POLYPHYLESIS.

1927 *Q. Jrnl. Geol. Soc.* LXXXII. p. ci, The whole of our System..is riddled through and through with polyphyly and convergence. **1961** G. G. SIMPSON *Princ. Animal Taxon.* iv. 124 The level of polyphyly is specified by the category of the highest ranking taxa two or more of which were immediately ancestral to the taxon in question. **1963** DAVIS & HEYWOOD *Princ. Angiosperm Taxon.* ii. 47 Proved or suspected polyphyly may lead us to see if there is a way of reclassifying the group into monophyletic units. **1978** *BioSystems* X. 110/1 Later modifications..considerably reduce this polyphyly, but at the expense of making the Protista even more of a rag bag.

polyphyodont (pə'lɪfɪəʊdɒnt), *a. Zool.* [f. Gr. πολυφυ-ής manifold (f. πολυ-, POLY- + φυή growth) + ὀδούς, ὀδοντ- tooth, after DIPHYODONT.] Having several successive growths or sets of teeth.

1878 BELL tr. *Gegenbaur's Comp. Anat.* 552 The change of teeth in the Mammalia may be regarded as a process which has been developed from a polyphyodont condition.

polypi, plural of POLYPUS.

po'lypian, *a. nonce-wd.* [f. L. *polyp-us* POLYP + -IAN.]

Belonging to a polyp.

1859 G. MEREDITH *R. Feverel* xxii, It is something for the animal to have had such mere fleshly polypian experiences.

polypiarian (ˌpɒlɪpɪ'ɛərɪən), *a.* and *sb. Zool.* [f. mod.L. *Polypiaria*, neut. pl., f. *polypus* POLYP.]

a. *adj.* Belonging to the *Polypiaria*, a division in some classifications nearly conterminous with the modern *Cœlenterata*. **b.** *sb.* An animal belonging to this division, a polyp (see POLYP 1 b).

1849 CRAIG, *Polyparous, Polypiarian.*

polypide ('pɒlɪpaɪd). *Zool.* [f. POLYP + *-ide*; cf. -ID[3].] An individual or zooid of a compound polyzoan. (Cf. POLYP 1 c, POLYPITE.)

1850 ALLMAN in *Brit. Assoc. Rep.* (1851) 307 For the term Polype, therefore, originally applied not only to the Anthozoal radiata, to which its use ought to be confined, but also to the retractile portion of the Polyzoa, I have substituted in the following Report that of Polypide. **1877** HUXLEY *Anat. Inv. Anim.* viii. 453 Each zooid which buds from the common stock is a polypide.

polypidom (pə'lɪpɪdəm, 'pɒlɪpɪdəm). *Zool.* [f. L. *polyp-us* POLYP + *domus*, Gr. δόμος house.] The common supporting structure of a colony of polyps, regarded as the dwelling-place of the individual zooids: = POLYPARY.

1824 tr. *Lamouroux* (*title*) Corallina; a Classical Arrangement of Flexible Coralline Polypidoms. **1838** G. JOHNSTON *Brit. Zooph.* 31 *note, Polypidom.* I borrow this term from the translator of Lamouroux's work on Corallines... Kirby.. uses the word *Polypary* to express the same thing. Both of them are translations of *Polypier*, a word invented by Reaumur, and now in general use among the French naturalists. **1846** PATTERSON *Zool.* 18 Their common habitat or 'polypidom' assumes a tree-like aspect. **1855** KINGSLEY *Glaucus* (1878) App. 233. **1876** PAGE *Adv. Text-bk. Geol.* iii. 67 The coral animalcule rears its polypidom.

polypier ('pɒlɪpɪə(r)). *Zool.* [a. F. *polypier* (pɔlipje) (Réaumur *a* 1757), f. *polype* POLYP + *-ier*, as in *poirier, pommier*, etc.] = POLYPARY; sometimes applied to a distinct part of this to which an individual zooid is attached. Also *fig.*

1828 WEBSTER, *Polypier*, the name given to the habitations of polypes, or to the common part of those compound animals called polypes. *Dict. Nat. Hist.* **1856** MILNE-EDWARDS *Man. Zool.* §619. 486 Sometimes each polyp has a distinct *polypier*, but in general it is the common portion of a mass of aggregated polypi which presents the characters peculiar to these bodies. **1868** WRIGHT *Ocean World* vi. 121 Their polypier is often formed of spiculæ. **1904** A. L. TEIXEIRA DE MATTOS tr. *Maeterlinck's Double Garden* 85 All nations have the natural right to pass through this phase of the political evolution of the human polypier.

polypifer (pə'lɪpɪfə(r)). *Zool.* [f. L. *polypus* POLYP + *-fer* bearing; after mod.L. *Polypifera*: see next.] A polyp-stock, polypary, or polypidom; also, the whole compound organism; usually in pl. as an English equivalent of *Polypifera.*

1832 DE LA BECHE *Geol. Man.* (ed. 2) 149 Large masses, supposed to be the work of myriads of polypifers. **1875** LYELL *Princ. Geol.* II. III. xlix. 613 The stone-making polypifers grow most luxuriantly on the outer edge of the island.

polypiferous (pɒlɪ'pɪfərəs), *a. Zool.* [f. mod.L. *polypifer*, f. *polypus* + *-fer* bearing (in *Polypifera*, a former division of Invertebrates) + -OUS.] Bearing polyps, as a polyp-stock or polypary.

1775 ELLIS in *Phil. Trans.* LXVI. 6 He thinks that there is a communication of juices from the polypiferous pores on the cortical part to the inside or horny part. **1828** STARK *Elem. Nat. Hist.* II. 422 For a long period these polypiferous masses were conceived to be marine plants. **1875** C. C. BLAKE *Zool.* 334 In Cristatella the polypary is free, disciform, and polypiferous on the margin.

polypiform ('pɒlɪpɪfɔːm), *a. Zool.* [f. L. *polypus* + -FORM.] Having the form of a polyp.

1847-9 *Todd's Cycl. Anat.* IV. 20/2 Animals polypiform. **1849-52** *Ibid.* 850/2 The quondam polypiform being.

polypigerous (pɒlɪ'pɪdʒərəs), *a. Zool. rare*[−0]. [f. as prec. + -GEROUS.] = POLYPIFEROUS.

1890 in *Cent. Dict.*

polypine ('pɒlɪpaɪn), *a. Zool.* [f. as prec. + -INE[1].] Of the nature of or belonging to polyps.

1836-9 *Todd's Cycl. Anat.* II. 433 The best known examples of this kind of generation occur in the polypine.. animals. **1859** *Ibid.* V. 41/2 The free polypine stock is first developed from the fecundated ovum.

polypiparous (pɒlɪ'pɪpərəs), *a. Zool. rare*[−0]. [f. as prec. + -PAROUS.] Producing polyps; polypiferous.

1864 in WEBSTER.

polypite ('pɒlɪpaɪt). [f. L. *polyp-us* POLYP + -ITE[1].]

1. *Palæont.* A fossil polyp. (Webster 1828.)

2. *Zool.* An individual or zooid of a compound polyp, esp. of a cœlenterate. (Cf. POLYP 1 c, POLYPIDE.) Also sometimes applied to a free polyp, as a *Hydra.*

1867 MURCHISON *Siluria* App. (ed. 4) 539 Common cœnosarc continuous with the polypites. **1875** C. C. BLAKE *Zool.* 372 Hydrozoa.. A branched, composite hydrosoma, carrying many polypites. **1877** HUXLEY *Anat. Inv. Anim.* iii. 133 A hydranth or polypite attached to the centre of a gelatinous contractile swimming disk.

polyplacid: see POLY-.

polyplacophoran (ˌpɒlɪplə'kɒfərən), *a.* and *sb. Zool.* [f. mod.L. *Polyplacophora*, neut. pl. (J. E. Gray, 1821), f. Gr. πολυ-, POLY- + πλάξ, πλακο- tablet, plate, etc. + -φορος bearing.] **a.** *adj.* Belonging to the division *Polyplacophora* of isopleurous gastropod molluscs, having a dorsal shell composed of a series of eight plates, as the CHITONS. **b.** *sb.* A mollusc of this division. So **polyplacophore** (-'plækəʊfɔə(r)) *a.* and *sb.*; **ˌpolypla'cophorous** *a.*

[**1839** *Penny Cycl.* XIV. 322/1 Cyclobranchians (Chismobranchians and Polyplaxiphores).] **1858** MAYNE *Expos. Lex.*, Polyplacophorous. **1890** *Cent. Dict.*, Polyplacophoran.. Polyplacophore. **1962** D. NICHOLS *Echinoderms* xii. 163 It is only fair to mention that other animal groups, such as the polyplacophoran molluscs,.. have claimed them. **1973** P. TASCH *Paleobiol. Invertebr.* viii. 329/1 The polyplacophoran shell is composed of aragonite. **1976** *Nature* 2 Sept. 50/1 (*caption*) A polyplacophoran (*Chiton*) has removed sediment cover.

polyplastic: see POLY-.

poly'plastid, -ide, *sb. Biol.* [f. POLY- + PLASTID.] An organism consisting of many plastids or cells: opposed to *monoplastid*(*e*. Also *attrib.* or as *adj.*

1895 MOORE in *Sci. Progress* June 323 There are many monoplastid forms with affinities among the polyplastids.

polyploid ('pɒlɪplɔɪd), *a.* (*sb.*) *Biol.* [a. G. *polyploid* (H. Winkler 1916, in *Zeitschr. f. Bot.* VIII. 422): see POLY- and -PLOID.] Having more than two homologous sets of chromosomes (in each cell nucleus). Also as *sb.*, a polyploid organism.

1920 W. E. AGAR *Cytol.* vii. 209 In the Protista..it appears that the nucleus may be polyploid, containing, not one or two, but a great number of series of elements. **1924** *Hereditas* V. 168 The chromosome number of a polyploid species must necessarily contain a certain number of complete haploid chromosome sets and it must have arisen through addition of such sets. **1928** [see ALLOPOLYPLOIDY]. **1936** *Discovery* May 162/1 An account of the breeding behaviour of polyploid plants would be of almost universal interest since this class includes important crops such as wheat, oats, and tobacco. **1949** A. G. SANDERS in H. W. Florey et al. *Antibiotics* II. xvi. 683 In the field of agriculture polyploid forms of plants produced by chemical means have been of great importance as they are larger and often more vigorous than the normal plant. **1956** [see EUPLOID *a.*]. **1963** E. MAYR *Animal Species & Evolution* xv. 439 Two types of polyploids are distinguished that have a rather different significance in evolution: autopolyploids and allopolyploids. **1975** J. B. JENKINS *Genetics* iv. 135 Although some animal tissues are commonly polyploid (the liver, for example), polyploid animals are rare. Most animal polyploids reproduce either hermaphroditically..or parthenogenetically.

Hence **'polyploidy** [cf. G. *polyploidie* (E. Strasburger 1910, in *Flora* C. 406)], the condition of being polyploid.

1922 *Genetics* VII. 545 The value of polyploidy may have certain limitations. **1942, 1943** [see *endomitosis* s.v. ENDO-]. **1973** *Nature* 11 May 87/2 Polyploidy may increase the flexibility of a species.

polyploidize ('pɒlɪplɔɪdaɪz), *v. Biol.* [f. prec. + -IZE.] *trans.* To render polyploid. Chiefly as **'polyploidizing** *ppl. a.* Hence **ˌpolyploidi'zation.**

1941 *Amer. Naturalist* LXXV. 128 It is often assumed that treatment with colchicine or other polyploidizing agents, if effective, will induce an exact doubling of each chromosome so that a balanced $4n$ condition, for example, will result throughout the part of the plant affected. This is very far from what actually happens. **1945** *Bot. Rev.* XI. 162 Schmuck found that wheat and barley seeds were polyploidized by acenaphthene, acenaphthylene, [etc.]. **1968** G. B. WILSON *Elem. Cytogenetics* v. 58 Many species of plants have been polyploidized by man through the use of conditions which disrupt mitosis and meiosis by preventing anaphase separation. **1974** *Oncology* XXIX. 520 Besides the loss and acquisition of chromosomes and polyploidization, these tumours were mainly characterized by the occurrence of multiple more or less complex translocations. **1975** *Nature* 31 Jan. 361/2 Cells treated with any one of the polyploidising agents gave rise to colonies, 13 of which were isolated and developed into established lines.

polyploidogenic (ˌpɒlɪplɔɪdə'dʒenɪk), *a. Cytology.* [f. as prec. + -O + -GENIC.] Tending to produce polyploidy.

1944 [see DIBENZANTHRACENE]. **1974** *Biol. Abstr.* LVII. 3982/2 In the sprouts there appear morphological changes (tumor-like thickenings in some parts) similar to those evoked by polyploidogenic substances.

polypneustic to **polypnœic**: see POLY-.

polypod ('pɒlɪpɒd), *sb.*[1] Now *rare.* Also 5 **pollypod**, 7 **poli-, polli-, polypode.** [a. OF. *polipode* (13th c. in Hatz.-Darm., mod.F. *polypode*), ad. L. POLYPODIUM.] = POLYPODY.

[*c* **1265** *Voc. Names Plants* in Wr.-Wülcker 556/4 *Felix arboratica, i.* pollipode, *i.* eueruern.] **14..** *Nominale* ibid. 711/37 *Hoc polipodicum*, a pollypod. **1612** DRAYTON *Polyolb.* xiii. 217 Heere findes he on an Oake Rheum-purging Polipode. **1664** EVELYN *Sylva* (1679) 27 Nor may we here omit to mention the Galls, Missletoe, Polypod, Agaric.. Fungus's..and many other useful Excrescencies [of the oak]. **1845** S. JUDD *Margaret* I. xvi, The bright green polypods and maiden's-hair waved in silent feathery harmony.

'polypod, *a.* and *sb.*[2] *Zool.* Also **polypode.** [a. F. *polypode* adj., f. Gr. πολυποδ-, stem of πολύπους many-footed: see POLYP.]

A. *adj.* Having many feet or foot-like organs; *spec.* belonging to the *Polypoda*, a name for various groups of animals in different classifications, as (*a*) a former division of insects, corresponding to the modern class *Myriapoda* or millepeds; (*b*) a division of worms; (*c*) of cephalopod molluscs, having more than eight arms or tentacles; (*d*) of crustaceans, having more than ten feet; (*e*) [tr. It. *polipodo* (A. Berlese 1913, in *Redia* IX. 127)], esp., of a phase in the development of certain insect larvæ, having a segmented abdomen with rudimentary or functional appendages.

1826 KIRBY & SP. *Entomol.* IV. 344 Polypod... Having more than eight legs but under fifty. **1925** A. D. IMMS *Gen. Textbk. Entomol.* 179 In the polypod phase the abdomen has acquired its complete segmentation and full number of appendages. **1969** R. F. CHAPMAN *Insects* xx. 400 A second basic form is the polypod larva... The larvae of Lepidoptera, Mecoptera and Tenthredinidae are of the polypod type.

B. *sb.* An animal having many feet; a member of the *Polypoda* in any sense (see A.).

1753 CHAMBERS *Cycl. Suppl.*, *Polypodes*, a word used by some as a name for the millepedes. **1828** WEBSTER, *Polypode*, an animal having many feet; the milleped or wood-louse. **1860** WRAXALL *Life in Sea* i. 11 The cachalot lives principally on cuttle-fish and polypods. **1880** BLACKMORE *Mary Anerley* lvi, Like a polypod awash, or a basking turtle.

polypodiaceous (ˌpɒlɪpəʊdɪ'eɪʃəs), *a. Bot.* [f. mod.L. *Polypodiācе-æ*, f. POLYPODIUM: see -ACEOUS.] Belonging to the natural order (or sub-order) *Polypodiaceæ*, comprising the large majority of ferns.

1852 TH. ROSS *Humboldt's Trav.* I. viii. 282 A beautiful fern,..a new genus of the order of polypodiaceous plants. **1858** in MAYNE *Expos. Lex.*

‖**Polypodium** (pɒlɪ'pəʊdɪəm). *Bot.* Also 6 **polipodium.** [L. (Pliny), a. Gr. πολυπόδιον (Theophr.) a kind of fern, f. πολυ- many + πούς, ποδ- foot, with dim. suffix -ιον: from the numerous branches of the root-stock.] A large and widely distributed genus of ferns, of various forms.

1525 *Herball* G j, Polipodium. This is called Pollypody. **1527** ANDREW *Brunswyke's Distyll. Waters* X iij b/1 This figure of polipodium. ? **1540** tr. *Vigo's Lytell Practyce* D j b, Take Polipodium of the oke. **1616** BULLOKAR *Eng. Expos.*, *Polypodium*, Okeferne: a kind of hearbe like Ferne, growing much about the roots of oakes. **1776** WITHERING *Brit. Plants* (1796) I. 352 The disposition of its fructification accords with the Polypodium's.

polypody (ˈpɒlɪpɒdɪ). Forms: 4-5 **polypodye**, 5 **pollipodie, polipodi**, 5-6 **polipodie**, 5-7 **-pody**, 6 **pollypody, polypodie**, 7 **-podi**, 6- **polypody**. [ad. L. *polypodium* (Plin.): see prec.] A fern of the genus *Polypodium*; esp. *P. vulgare*, the Common Polypody, a widely distributed species, growing on moist rocks, old walls, and trees (hence formerly known as ***polypody of the oak*** or ***of the wall***).

14.. *Stockh. Med. MS.* I. 455 in *Anglia* XVIII. 306 The rotys of polypodye, þat is wylde brake. *c* **1440** *Promp. Parv.* 408/1 Polypodye, herbe, *polipodia*. **1486** *Bk. St. Albans* C v, Take smale flambe rotis and polipodi. **1562** TURNER *Herbal* II. 4 Polypody drieth and lesseth or thinneth the body. **1597** GERARDE *Herbal* II. ccccli. 972 Wall Ferne, or Polypodie of the wall. **1653** WALTON *Angler* vi. 140 Take the stinking oil drawn out of Polypody of the Oak, by a retort mixt with Turpentine. **1785** MARTYN *Rousseau's Bot.* xxxii. (1794) 490 Common Polypody has pinnatifid fronds. **1863** ATKINSON *Stanton Grange* (1864) 157 All three of the commoner polypodies.

polypoid (ˈpɒlɪpɔɪd), *a.* [f. L. *polyp-us* POLYP, POLYPUS + -OID.]

1. *Zool.* Resembling or of the nature of a polyp.

1850 ALLMAN in *Brit. Assoc. Rep.* (1851) 305 Those polypoid molluscous animals. **1871** —— *Gymnobl. Hydroids* 17 The polypoid phases of the *Hydroida*. **1877** LE CONTE *Elem. Geol.* (1879) 294 The larval form of most if not all Medusae is a compound polypoid animal.

2. *Path.* Resembling or of the nature of a polypus.

1842 in DUNGLISON *Med. Lex.* **1843** R. J. GRAVES *Syst. Clin. Med.* xxvi. 334 Polypoid condylomata. These were fleshy, roundish, soft. **1884** M. MACKENZIE *Dis. Throat & Nose* II. 365 Polypus and polypoid thickening of the mucous membrane of the nose.

So **polyˈpoidal** *a.*

1890 in *Cent. Dict.* **1897** *Allbutt's Syst. Med.* IV. 693 The growth has been somewhat soft and of a polypoidal appearance.

polypomedusan (ˌpɒlɪpəʊmɪˈdjuːsən), *a.* and *sb. Zool.* [f. mod. Zool. L. *Polypomedusæ* pl. (f. *polypo-*, comb. form of *polypus* POLYP + MEDUSA) + -AN.]

a. *adj.* Belonging to the *Polypomedusæ*, a group of *Cœlenterata* comprising the *Hydrozoa* and *Actinozoa*. **b.** *sb.* A cœlenterate belonging to this group.

1890 in *Cent. Dict.*

polypomorphic (ˌpɒlɪpəʊˈmɔːfɪk), *a. Zool.* [f. Gr. πολυπο-, f. πολύπους POLYP + μορφή form + -IC.] Having the form of a polyp, polypiform, polypoid; *spec.* Belonging to the *Polypomorpha*, a synonym of *Hydrozoa*.

1890 in *Cent. Dict.*

polyponous: see POLY-.

polypore (ˈpɒlɪpɔə(r)). [f. mod.L. *Polyporus* (P. A. Micheli *Nova Plantarum Genera* (1729) 129), f. POLY- + Gr. πόρος pore.] A bracket-fungus belonging to the genus *Polyporus* or the family Polyporaceæ.

1902 *Science* 12 Dec. 954/1 A correspondent.. sent me a fine specimen of a polypore which he found on the trunk of a tall tree. **1923** F. DICKSON in L. H. Bailey *Cultivated Evergreens* iv. 150 Most of the fungi causing these wood-rots are of one general type commonly known as 'bracket-fungi' or 'polypores'. **1946** *Nature* 7 Sept. 325/1 The paper contains an extensive key to the principal white resupinate polypores in culture. **1971** P. H. B. TALBOT *Princ. Fungal Taxon.* xii. 201 The polypores and hydnums are typically woody, corky or membranous in texture. **1976** G. C. AINSWORTH *Introd. Hist. Mycol.* iii. 35 Greek and Roman writers certainly distinguished between agarics, polypores, and truffles.

polyporic (pɒˈlɪpɒrɪk), *a. Biochem.* [tr. G. *polyporsäure* polyporic acid (C. Stahlschmidt 1877, in *Ann. d. Chem. u. Pharm.* CLXXXVII. 180), f. mod.L. *polypor-us* (see prec.) + -IC.] ***polyporic acid***: a bronze-coloured crystalline solid, 3, 6-dihydroxy-2, 5-diphenyl-*p*-benzoquinone, $C_{18}H_{12}O_4$, which is a colouring matter found in certain fungi and lichens, and was first isolated from a fungus of the genus *Polyporus*.

1877 *Jrnl. Chem. Soc.* XXXII. II. 620 The fungus.. seems to be closely allied to Polyporus purpurascens... When brought into contact with dilute ammonia, its colour changes to a fine deep violet, and it yields a solution from which hydrochloric acid throws down a yellow precipitate of the new acid—polyporic acid. **1931** *Jrnl. Amer. Chem. Soc.* LIII. 2373 Two of the important coloring matters found in fungi are polyporic acid.. obtained from *Polyporous* [sic] *nidulans* and atromentin.. from *Paxillus atrotomentosus*. **1957** R. H. THOMSON *Naturally occurring Quinones* ii. 26 Polyporic acid also occurs in the fungus *Peniophora filamentosa*.. and.. has been found in two lichens. **1967** M. E. HALE *Biol. Lichens* viii. 106 Polyporic acid is known from *Sticta coronata* and *Polyporus nidulans*.

polyporite (pəˈlɪpəraɪt). *Palæont.* [f. *Polypor-us* (see next) + -ITE[1] 2 a.] A fossil resembling a species of *Polyporus* (see next), found in the Welsh coal-measures.

1846 SMART Suppl., *Polyporite*, a many-pored fossil plant.

polyporoid (pəˈlɪpərɔɪd), *a. Bot.* [f. mod.L. *Polyporus* (Fries 1836-8) (a. Gr. πολύπορος: see next) + -OID.] Resembling or belonging to *Polyporus*, a large widely distributed genus of hymenomycetous fungi, growing in the form of projecting shelves or brackets on dead or decaying trees.

1890 in *Cent. Dict.*

polyporous (pəˈlɪpərəs), *a. Nat. Hist.* [f. Gr. πολύπορος having many passages (see PORE *sb.*) + -OUS.] Having many pores.

1858 in MAYNE.

polyporus (pəˈlɪpərəs). [mod.L.: see POLYPORE.] **a.** = POLYPORE.

1887 W. PHILLIPS *Brit. Discomycetes* 334 Nylander and Karsten find it on poplar and elder, also on dead polyporus. **1907** T. R. SIM *Forests & Forest Flora Cape Good Hope* iii. 31 The attack of a Polyporus.. softens and disintegrates the living heartwood.

b. A slice of a dried fungus of the genus *Polyporus*, esp. *P. betulinus*, used as a mount for particularly delicate insects. Also *attrib.*

1900 *Instructions for Collecting Insects* (Brit. Mus. (Nat. Hist.)) 6 A very useful material for staging is a fungus called *Polyporus*, which is cut into strips sold for the purpose by dealers. **1940** J. SMART *Instructions for Collectors, No. 4A: Insects* (Brit. Mus. (Nat. Hist.)) iv. 153 The smaller forms should be pinned on fine stainless steel points which are stuck into small strips of polyporus. **1951** COLYER & HAMMOND *Flies Brit. Isles* 334 If it is desired to pin medium-sized or small flies with short pins, they can be subsequently 'staged' on polyporus or slips of celluloid. **1962** GORDON & LAVOIPIERRE *Entomol. for Students of Med.* l. 303 Other forms of very useful.. specialised equipment are entomological forceps and polyporus strips.

polypose (ˈpɒlɪpəʊs), *a.* [ad. L. *polypōsus* (Martial) in sense 2: see POLYPUS, POLYP, -OSE.]

1. *Zool.* = POLYPOUS 1.

1748 HARTLEY *Observ. Man* I. i. 32 One may question whether in animals of the serpentine Form, and in all those of the polypose Kind, the Sensorium be not equally diffused over the whole medullary Substance.

2. *Path.* = POLYPOUS 2.

1731 ARBUTHNOT *Aliments* vi. (1735) 162 It will produce Polypose Concretions in the Ventricles of the Heart. **1761** PULTENEY in *Phil. Trans.* LII. 346 To suppose an aneurism, rather than polypose affections. **1822-34** *Good's Study Med.* (ed. 4) IV. 350 Polypose Strangury.

polyposis (pɒlɪˈpəʊsɪs). *Path.* [f. POLYP + -OSIS.] A condition characterized by the presence of numerous internal polyps, *esp.* a hereditary disease in which the large intestine is so affected and which becomes malignant if untreated.

1914 *Surg., Gynecol. & Obstetr.* XIX. 31/2 The symptoms of intestinal polyposis vary within wide limits. **1952** *Ann. Eugenics* XVII. 1 Polyposis is caused by an excessive proliferation of the glandular epithelium in the mucous membrane of the colon and rectum. **1961** [see POLYPUS 2]. **1974** PASSMORE & ROBSON *Compan. Med. Stud.* III. xix. 112/2 Isolated cases of colonic polyposis without a family history are attributed to gene mutation.

polypostyle (ˈpɒlɪpəʊˌstaɪl). *Zool.* [f. *polypo-*, Gr. πολυπο-, from πολύπους POLYP + στῦλος pillar.] An imperfect zooid in certain Hydrozoa: = DACTYLOZOOID. Hence **polypoˈstylar** *a.*, pertaining to or of the nature of a polypostyle.

1890 in *Cent. Dict.*

polypotome (ˈpɒlɪpəʊˌtəʊm). *Surg.* [f. as prec. (see POLYPUS 2) + Gr. -τομος cutting.] (See quot. 1857.)

1857 DUNGLISON *Med. Dict.*, *Polypotome*.. an instrument for the removal of polypus by excision. **1872** T. G. THOMAS *Dis. Women* (ed. 3) 516 Should the pedicle be within reach of knife or scissors, it may be divided; or if higher.. the polypotome may be employed.

polypous (ˈpɒlɪpəs), *a.* [f. L. *polypus* POLYP, POLYPUS + -OUS; so F. *polypeux* (1552 in sense 2).]

1. *Zool.* Pertaining to, or of the nature of, a polyp; also *fig.* like that of a polyp (esp. in reference to its reproduction by budding, as in *Hydra*).

1748 B. MARTIN *Eng. Dict.* Introd § 111 Little aware.. that it [*sc.* the distinction of sex] was deficient in any sort of animals, as we are assured it is (by late discoveries) in all the Polypous kinds. **1862** RUSKIN *Unto this Last* iv. 146 If that ploughshare did nothing but beget other ploughshares, in a polypous manner,.. it would have lost its function of capital. **1866** SIR J. E. TENNENT in Felton *Anc. & Mod. Gr.* II. II. vii. 396 Extortion.. insinuated itself with polypous fertility into every relation and ordinance of society.

2. *Path.* Pertaining to, or of the nature of, a polypus; characterized by polypi.

1758 WRIGHT in *Phil. Trans.* L. 597 Polypous concretions in the larger vessels. **1809** *Med. Jrnl.* XXI. 455 In one of these the ventricles of the heart had polypous concretions. **1862** *N. Syd. Soc. Year-bk. Med.* 211 An early stage of the same polypous formation.

polypragmatic (ˌpɒlɪprægˈmætɪk), *a.* (*sb.*) [f. Gr. πολυπράγματ-ος busy about many things, over-busy (f. πολυ-, POLY- + πρᾶγμα(τ-) thing done) + -IC.] Busying oneself about many affairs (that are not one's own); meddlesome, officious.

1616 JAS. I. *Sp. in Starre-Chamb.* 20 June 48 For those Polypragmaticke Papists, I would you would studie out some seuere punishment for them. **1638** DRUMM. OF HAWTH. *Lines on Bishops* Poems (1856) 340 Like to polypragmatic Machiavel. **1656** in BLOUNT *Glossogr.* **1885** *Sat. Rev.* 22 Aug. 248/2 Troublesome and polypragmatic operosity.

†**B.** *sb.* A meddlesome person, a busybody. *Obs.*

1636 H. BURTON *Apology* Ep. to Nobility 20 Shall we see Religion overturned.. by a Faction of Iesuited Polypragmatiques? **1684** T. GODDARD *Plato's Demon* 23 Do you not think it a little arrogance in our Polypragmatick.. to assume the Title even of Plato himself?

So †**polypragˈmatical** *a.*; **polyˈpragmatism**, officious or over-busy conduct; **polyˈpragmatist**, †**polyˈpragmist**, a busybody; **polyˈpragmaty**, 'the state of being over-engaged with business or matters' (Webster 1864).

1597 in G. Harvey *Trimming Nashe* Wks. (Grosart) III. 13 To the *polypragmaticall.. Puppie, Thomas Nashe. **1657** PURCHAS *Pol. Flying Ins.* 329 This idle Gamster with a blind bone out of his jugling box, with the activity of a polypragmaticall finger, can.. undoe many an hopefull heire. **1890** *Sat. Rev.* 24 May 622/2 The Council's elder brother in extravagance and *polypragmatism, the School Board. **1631** HEYWOOD *Eng. Eliz.* Pref. (1641) 7 And such *Polypragmatists this age is full of. **1613** SIR E. HOBY *Countersnarle* 4 This *Polypragmist, forsooth, to shew his inuincible courage.. hath vndertaken the Combat.

†**polyˈpragmon.** *obs.* [a. Gr. πολυπράγμων: see prec.] A meddlesome person; a busybody.

[**1573** G. HARVEY *Letter-bk.* (Camden) 28 At the motion of two or thre πολυπράγμονες, home he knew ful wel to be mi ennemies.] **1600** W. WATSON *Decacordon* (1602) 282 This most Atheall Polypragmon father Parsons. **1679** PRANCE *Addit. Narr. Pop. Plot* 40 The Jesuites, who are the great Polypragmons, or Busie-bodies amongst them all.

Hence †**polypragmoˈnetic** (irreg.), **polypragˈmonic** *adjs.*, of the nature of a 'polypragmon' (= POLYPRAGMATIC); †**polyˈpragmonist** = *polypragmon*; †**polyˈpragmony**, the character or practice of a 'polypragmon' (= next).

a **1693** *Urquhart's Rabelais* III. xx, What is it that this *Polypragmonetick Ardelione to all the Fiends of Hell doth aim at? **1866** BLACKMORE *C. Nowell* xiv, [He] admitted the *polypragmonic doctor. **1609** DEKKER *Gvlls Horne-bk.* Proem. (1812) 18 Good dry-brained *polypragmonists. **1602** F. HERING *Anat.* 20 *Polypragmony is the Companion of Ignorance, and common Pest of Mankinde.

†**polypragˈmosyny.** *Obs. rare*[−1]. [ad. Gr. πολυπραγμοσύνη (f. πολυπράγμων), with the termination assimilated to that of words in -Y.] Meddlesomeness. So **polypragmoˈsynic** *a.* (*rare*[−1]), officious, meddlesome.

1607 J. CARPENTER *Plaine Mans Plough* 219 Seditionaries, who in their polypragmosynie, minister vehement causes. **1886** BP. STUBBS *Visit. Charges* (1907) 53 The excitable, the idle, and the polypragmosynic among the laity.

polyprism, -prismatic: see POLY-.

polypropylene (pɒlɪˈprəʊpɪliːn). [f. POLY- + PROPYLENE. Cf. F. *polypropylène* (Berthelot 1867, in *Jrnl. de Pharm. et de Chim.* VI. 31).] Any of the polymers of propylene, which include a number of thermoplastic materials widely used as films, fibres, or moulding materials.

1935 [see *polybutadiene* s.v. POLY- 2]. **1957** *Times* 17 July 7/3 As dense polythene advances in commercial use another type of plastic—the polypropylenes—appears to be established at the laboratory stage. **1964** *Which?* Aug. 253/3 Fabrics made from polypropylene can be easily washed and boiled. **1973** *Materials & Technol.* VI. viii. 528 Polypropylene is an eminently suitable material from which to prepare thin films. **1976** E. SCARROW *N.Z. Vegetable Gardening Guide* 14 Many modern spades have steel handles, with a polypropylene 'D' grip fitted to the handle.

polyprotein to **polyprothetic**: see POLY-.

polyprotic (pɒlɪˈprəʊtɪk), *a. Chem.* [f. POLY- + PROTON 2 + -IC.] Of an acid: capable of donating more than one proton to a base; polybasic; occas. also used of bases which can accept more than one proton.

1944 J. A. TIMM *Gen. Chem.* xxxii. 343 Acids whose molecules may donate more than one proton are called polyprotic acids. **1968** J. G. MORRIS *Biologist's Physical Chem.* v. 114 In biological media we frequently encounter polyprotic, weak acids (e.g. carbonic, phosphoric, citric acids), whose complete neutralization requires the addition of two or more equivalents of sodium hydroxide. **1969** H. T. EVANS tr. *Hägg's Gen. & Inorg. Chem.* xii. 316 Acids and bases that can give up or take up more than one proton are called polyvalent..or polyprotic.

polyprotodont (pɒlɪˈprəʊtəʊdɒnt), *a.* and *sb. Zool.* [f. Gr. πολυ-, POLY- + πρῶτο-ς first + ὀδούς, ὀδοντ- tooth; cf. DIPROTODONT.] **a.** *adj.* Having more than two front or incisor teeth in the lower jaw, as the carnivorous and insectivorous marsupials. **b.** *sb.* A polyprotodont marsupial. (Opp. to DIPROTODONT.) Hence **polyprotoˈdontid** *a.*, of or belonging to the polyprotodonts.

1889 NICHOLSON & LYDEKKER *Palæont.* (ed. 3) II. 1273 A feature occurring in many recent Polyprotodonts. **1892** *Athenæum* 14 May 636/2 He came to the conclusion that this anomalous form [*Notoryctes typhlops*, a newly discovered mammal of Central Australia] should stand as a distinct family of polyprotodont marsupials. **1900** B. SPENCER in *Proc. Zool. Soc.* 794 The ancestors of the recent Diprotodontia were beginning to diverge from the original Polyprotodontid stock.

polypseudonymous: see POLY-.

polypsychical (pɒlɪˈpsaɪkɪkəl), *a. nonce-wd.* [f. Gr. πολυ-, POLY- + ψυχή soul: cf. *psychical.*] Having many souls, many-souled. So **polyˈpsychic** *a.* = prec.; **polypsychism** (-ˈpsaɪkɪz(ə)m), (*a*) the belief in a multiplicity of souls in one person; (*b*) the belief in a multiplicity of spiritual beings as the causes of natural phenomena.

1842 MRS. BROWNING *Grk. Chr. Poets* 206 The master [Wordsworth], indeed, was a prophet of humanity;..a poet of one large sufficient soul, but not polypsychical like a dramatist. **1856** W. A. BUTLER *Hist. Anc. Philos.* I. 237 Even in the human frame itself there is found among savage nations the belief of a multiplicity of souls; the process leading to polypsychism being exactly the same as that which multiplies the directors or animators of the universe. **1903** MYERS *Hum. Personality* I. 34, I regard each man as at once profoundly unitary and almost infinitely composite.., polyzoic and perhaps polypsychic in an extreme degree. *Ibid.* I. Gloss. s.v. *Polyzoism*, Polypsychism is sometimes used to express the psychical aspect of polyzoism.

polypterid (pəˈlɪptərɪd). *Ichthyol.* [f. mod.L. *Polypterus* (Geoffroy 1802), generic name, a. Gr. πολύπτερος many-winged (f. πολυ-, POLY- + πτερόν feather, wing) + -ID[3].] A fish of the family *Polypteridæ* of crossopterygian ganoids, having the dorsal fin replaced by a series of spines with finlets attached; now represented only by the genus **Poˈlypterus** of tropical African rivers. So **poˈlypteroid** *a.*, akin in form to *Polypterus*, belonging to the sub-order *Polypteroidei*; *sb.* a polypteroid fish.

1849 CRAIG, *Polypterus*, a genus of fishes. **1880** RAMSAY in *Times* 26 Aug. 5/3 The nearest analogies of the fish are, according to Huxley, the polypterus of African rivers [etc.]. **1890** *Cent. Dict.*, *Fin-pike*, a fish of the family *Polypteridæ* and genus *Polypterus*; a polypterid. **1899** *Daily News* 29 Nov. 7/2 Two examples of a most ancient African fish have just been deposited in the new Tortoise House at the Zoological Gardens... The name of this fish is Polypterus, and it belongs to a group which has mostly become extinct.

polyptote (ˈpɒlɪptəʊt), *a.* and *sb. rare*[—0]. [ad. Gr. πολύπτωτ-ος, f. πολυ-, POLY- + πτωτός falling, cognate with πτῶσις case, f. πίπτ-ειν (stem πετ-) to fall. So F. *polyptote.*] **a.** *adj. Gram.* Having many cases, as a noun. **b.** *sb.* (*a*) *Gram.* A noun having many cases. (*b*) *Rhet.* = next.

1656 BLOUNT *Glossogr.*, *Polyptote*, (*polyptoton*) that hath many cases. **1678** PHILLIPS (ed. 4), *Polyptote*, in Rhetorick Polyptoton.

‖**polyptoton** (pɒlɪpˈtəʊtɒn). *Rhet.* [L., a. Gr. πολύπτωτον adj. neut.: see prec.] A rhetorical figure consisting in the repetition of a word in different cases or inflexions in the same sentence.

1586 A. DAY *Eng. Secretary* II. (1625) 86 *Polyptoton* or *Traductio*, when one word is often repeated by variety of cases. **1588** FRAUNCE *Lawiers Log.* 50 b. **1654** TRAPP *Comm. Hosea* x. 1 A dainty agnomination, and a double polyptôton. *a* **1679** HOBBES *Rhet.* IV. vi. (1681) 151 [Repetition of sounds] unlike:..a small changing of the end or case, as Polyptoton.

polyptych (ˈpɒlɪptɪk). [ad. late L. *polyptycha*, neut. pl. account-books, registers, ad. Gr. πολύπτυχος having many folds, f. πολυ-, POLY- + πτυχή fold. Cf. mod.F. *polyptyque* (1732 in Hatz.-Darm.).] Anything consisting of more than three leaves or panels folded or hinged together, as a picture or an altar-piece. (Cf. DIPTYCH, TRIPTYCH.)

1859 GULLICK & TIMBS *Paint.* 307 The great altar-piece of the Van Eycks at Ghent is a polyptych. **1862** *Sat. Rev.* XIII. 711/1 There are triptychs, and polyptychs, and statuettes, and pastoral staves, of the thirteenth and fourteenth centuries. **1897** *Edin. Rev.* Apr. 345 They carried off a vast but not altogether first-rate polyptych, 'The Virgin and Child with Saints'.

polypus (ˈpɒlɪpəs). Forms: 5–8 polipus, 6 polippus, polipos, 6– polypus. Pl polypi (-paɪ); also (7 polypodes, polipusses), 8 polypuses (-pusses). [a. L. *pol-*, *pōlypus*, *-pi* cuttle-fish, etc., also polypus in the nose, a. Doric or Æolic Gr. πωλύπος, gen. -που = Ionic πουλύπους (acc. -οδα and -ουν), Attic πολύπους a cuttle-fish, etc., also polypus in the nose, f. πολυ- many + πούς foot.]

1. a. A cuttle-fish, an octopus; = POLYP 1 a. *Obs.* (exc. in allusion to Lat. or Gr.).

c **1520** ANDREW *Noble Lyfe* lxvii, Polippus hath gret strength in his fete, what he therin cacheth, he holdeth it fast. **1603** SIR C. HEYDON *Jud. Astrol.* v. 153 This Polypus can change himselfe into all colours. **1635** SWAN *Spec. M.* VIII. i. (1643) 378 These Polypodes suddenly prey upon them [fish] and devoure them. **1694** MOTTEUX *Rabelais* IV. ii. (1737) 9 The Sea-pulp, or Polypus. **1839** T. BEALE *Nat. Hist. Sperm Whale* 57 The octopus..was the animal denominated polypus by Aristotle. **1877** BRYANT *Odyssey* v. 518 To the claws of polypus, Plucked from its bed, the pebbles thickly cling.

b. = POLYP 1 b, c. Now *rare* or *Obs.*

[**1693** tr. *Blancard's Phys. Dict.* (ed. 2), *Polypodes*, Sows, Hog-lice.] **1742** *Phil. Trans.* XLII. 219 A small Insect called a Polypus, which is found sticking to the common Duckweed. *a* **1759** SIR C. H. WILLIAMS *Isabella* Odes (1780) 7 It's call'd a Polypus..And 'tis a reptile of so strange a sort, That if 'tis cut in two, it is not dead; Its head shoots out a tail, its tail a head. **1768–74** TUCKER *Lt. Nat.* (1834) II. 160 Those who have changed their opinion..upon the sexes of blossoms, or upon the hatching of polypuses. **1828** STARK *Elem. Nat. Hist.* II. 417 The class of Polypi or Zoophytes is one of the largest and most singular of the Animal Kingdom. **1845** DARWIN *Voy. Nat.* i. (1852) 99 Each polypus, though closely united to its brethren, has a distinct mouth, body and tentacula.

2. *Path.* A general term for tumours of various kinds, arising from a mucous or serous surface, usually pedunculated, and having ramifications like the tentacles of a polyp. Also formerly applied to a fibrinous blood-clot occurring in the heart or blood-vessels. Cf. POLYP, POLYPE 2.

1398 TREVISA *Barth. De P.R.* VII. xxii. (Bodl. MS.), Polipus is a superfluite of flessch growing of þe nostrelles. **1578** LYTE *Dodoens* II. cxii. 305 Being layd to with Copperous..it taketh away..the Polypus growing in the Nosthrilles. **1707** FLOYER *Physic. Pulse-Watch* 118 In a Polypus the Pulse intermits, and vibrates, and is obscure. **1732** ARBUTHNOT *Rules of Diet* in *Aliments*, etc. 265 Being mix'd with the Blood in the Veins would produce Polypus's in the Heart, and Death. **1797** M. BAILLIE *Morb. Anat.* (1807) 367 By a polypus is meant a diseased mass, which adheres to some part of the cavity of the uterus, by a sort of neck or narrower portion. **1878** T. BRYANT *Pract. Surg.* I. 110 Forms of softer polypi and cutaneous pendulous tumours. **1961** R. D. BAKER *Essent. Path.* xvi. 390 Adenomatous polyps and gastric polyposis are quite like their counterparts in the large bowel. The polypi are pedunculated or sessile and are composed of mucosa like that of the gastric wall. **1974** PASSMORE & ROBSON *Compan. Med. Stud.* III. xix. 52/2 A subtotal gastrectomy is recommended if the polypi occur in the mid and lower stomach.

3. *attrib.* and *Comb.*, as (in sense 1 a) ***polypus-arms*** sb. pl., ***-fish***; (in sense 1 b) ***polypus-like***, ***-wise*** advs.; (in sense 2) ***polypus-growth***.

1607 TOPSELL *Four-f. Beasts* (1658) 121 Whom Oppianus compareth to the Polypus fish. **1789** MRS. PIOZZI *Journ. France*, etc. II. 60 The polypus fish, who..extend their arms for prey. **1809** COLERIDGE *Lett.*, *to T. Poole* (1895) 552, I will divide them polypus-wise, so that the first half should get itself a new tail of its own, and the latter a new head. **1815** SIMOND *Tour Gt. Brit.* II. 199 London extends its great polypus-arms over the country around. **1865** PUSEY in Liddon, etc. *Life* (1897) IV. iii. 80 We cannot divide Holy Scripture or Christianity, polypus-like, so that one part might be cut off, and the rest remain in the same life as before. **1897** *Allbutt's Syst. Med.* IV. 689 Every characteristic of ordinary polypus growth.

polypyrene to **polyrhizous**: see POLY-.

polyrhythm (ˈpɒlɪrɪð(ə)m). *Mus.* [f. POLY- + RHYTHM *sb.*] The use of two or more different rhythms simultaneously; music using such rhythms.

1929 P. ROSENFELD *Hour with Amer. Mus.* i. 12 Its alternation of bars of three and four and five units, the so-called jazz polyrhythm, is sheer willful contrast and change. **1942** *Scrutiny* XI. 12 The thirteenth century composer may teach the composer of the twentieth century how polytonalities and polyrhythms..may be reconciled with..the natural resources of the art of sound. **1949** *Funk's Stand. Dict. Folklore* I. 151/1 Musically, the blues are distinguished by..syncopation and polyrhythm characteristic of Negro music. **1956** W. MELLERS in A. Pryce-Jones *New Outl. Mod. Knowl.* III. 363 Messiaen has created some fascinating noises out of the complex scales and polyrhythms of Indian music. **1973** *Black World* Sept. 37 The polyrhythms of 'bop' jazz are..in the contrasted regular rhythms of the first stanza and the irregularly punctuated rhythms of the second stanza. **1979** *Daily Tel.* 1 Nov. 15/6 In its simultaneous use of conflicting time signatures, of extremely intricate syncopations and polyrhythms, the late 14th century produced music of a complexity that has hardly been equalled until our own time.

polyrhythmic (pɒlɪˈrɪðmɪk), *a.* Chiefly *Mus.* [f. POLY- + RHYTHMIC *a.* and *sb.*] Involving or using two or more different rhythms, esp. at the same time. Also **polyˈrhythmical** *a.*

1893 J. S. SHEDLOCK tr. *Riemann's Dict. Mus.* 609/2 *Polyrhythmical*, i.e. containing a mixture of various rhythms. **1917** E. C. FARNSWORTH *Ideals & Tendencies Mod. Art* 69 That ultra phase of poetry *vers libre*, or, as some prefer, 'unrhymed cadence' or, what is more impressive, 'polyrhythmical poetry'. **1932** L. SAMINSKY *Music of our Day* I. 40 Jazz has shown that synthetic rhythm embraces not only straight polyrhythmic structures. **1942** *Scrutiny* XI. 15 A tonal structure based, however..polyrhythmic the music may grow, on the absolute and perfect consonances rather than on the diatonic triad. **1944** W. APEL *Harvard Dict. Mus.* 593/2 Properly speaking, all truly contrapuntal or polyphonic music is polyrhythmic, since rhythmic variety in simultaneous parts more than anything else contributes to giving the voice-parts that quality of individuality which is essential to polyphonic style. **1958** P. GAMMOND *Decca Bk. Jazz* xv. 178 He maintains an incredibly difficult polyrhythmical contrivance, playing in 3/4 time in the bass against the normal 4/4 in the treble. **1958** *Times* 9 Sept. 5/4 The relevant departments of the London Philharmonic proved inadequate to Bartok's polyrhythmic counterpoint. **1970** P. OLIVER *Savannah Syncopators* 6 It was possible to agree on generalities concerning..the polyrhythmic texture of piano, guitar, bass and drums.

Hence **polyˈrhythmically** *adv.*

1946 R. BLESH *Shining Trumpets* (1949) xiii. 314 The ragtime left hand..is beyond the ability of the classically trained executant, let alone its combination polyrhythmically with the right. **1963** *Listener* 14 Mar. 457/1 African drumming relies on the interweaving of different strands of rhythm each of fixed beats, conflicting polyrhythmically with each other.

polyribo- (pɒlɪraɪbəʊ). *Biochem.* [f. POLY- + RIBO-.] Formative element used in the names of polymers of ribonucleotides, as ***poly,riboadeˈnylic***, ***-cytiˈdylic***, ***-inoˈsinic***, etc., ***acid***; also ***ˌpolyriboˈnucleotide***. Cf. *polyribosome* s.v. POLY- 1.

1956 *Nature* 11 Feb. 271/1 Some 10–20 per cent of the total polyribonucleotide content of the bacteria was extracted by this procedure. **1959** *Times* 10 Nov. (Guinness Suppl.) p. ii/6 An important series of papers on the synthesis of polyribonucleotides which have an important function in cellular metabolism. **1961** STEINER & BEERS *Polynucleotides* i. 6 The equimolar complexes formed by polyriboadenylic acid with polyribouridylic acid and with polyriboinosinic acid appear to have doubly stranded helical structures. *Ibid.* viii. 263 Even less is known of the detailed fine structure of polyribocytidylic acid... All that can be said is that some helical structure is present. **1964** G. H. HAGGIS et al. *Introd. Molecular Biol.* ix. 228 (*caption*) T = polyribothymidylic acid (a polyribonucleotide containing only the base thymine found in natural DNA but not in natural RNA). **1970** *New Scientist* 15 Jan. 96/2 Poly I:C—a combination of polyriboinosinic and polyribocytidylic acids—would stimulate interferon production both in cell cultures and in animals. **1976** *Nature* 15 Jan. 141/2 Antibodies to native DNA, double-stranded RNA, and various synthetic polyribonucleotides occur with great frequency in patients with systemic lupus erythematosus (SLE).

So also **polyde(s)oxyribo-** (see DEOXY-), in names of polymers of deoxyribonucleotides, as ***ˌpolyde(s)oxyriboˈnucleotide***.

1956 *Federation Proc.* XV. 291/2 To define the chemical events in the development of a bacterial virus, we have explored the pathways of polydesoxyribonucleotide synthesis in normal and infected cells. **1961** STEINER & BEERS *Polynucleotides* i. 5 The primary structures of polydeoxyribonucleotides and polyribonucleotides are identical except for the absence of the hydroxyl group on $C_{2'}$ of deoxyribose. **1976** W. GUSCHLBAUER *Nucleic Acid Struct.* vi. 86 Single-stranded polydeoxyribonucleotides are, as a rule, less stacked and structured than their ribo counterparts.

polys, obs. form of POLISH *v.*

polysaccharide (pɒlɪˈsækəraɪd). *Chem.* Formerly also -id. [ad. G. *polysaccharid* (B. Tollens *Kurzes Handbuch d. Kohlenhydrate* (1888) 16), f. POLY- + *saccharid* SACCHARIDE.] Any carbohydrate whose molecules consist of a number of monosaccharide residues (or their simple derivatives) bonded together, usu. in a chain structure, and esp. one of high molecular weight; also applied to such a structure which forms part of a larger molecule.

1892 E. F. SMITH tr. *V. von Richter's Org. Chem.* (ed. 2) 512 It is very probable that the polysaccharides having the empirical formula $C_6H_{10}O_5$, really possess a much higher molecular weight, $(C_6H_{10}O_5)_n$. **1895** *Jrnl. Chem. Soc.* LXVIII. II. 322 It appears probable that the fermentation of the polysaccharides by saccharomycetes is preceded by their conversion into monosaccharides through the agency of enzymes. **1902** *Encycl. Brit.* XXXI. 723/2 By further polymerization and loss of water the group of polysaccharids ..is produced. **1947** *Endeavour* VI. 89/2 Other substances of high molecular weight, such as the polysaccharides, consist mostly of molecules of continuously varying size. **1951** *Sci. News* XXI. 72 Any carbohydrate, such as glucose, cellulose, cane-sugar, or starch, can be represented by the formula $C_n(H_2O)_m$ where *m* is equal, or very nearly equal, to *n*... For polysaccharides such as starch or cellulose, *n* and *m* may run up to hundreds. **1960** *New Biol.* XXXI. 72 The virulent and avirulent types [of pneumococcus] can be quickly and easily distinguished because the virulent cells are enclosed in a polysaccharide capsule that can be seen under the microscope. **1968** A. WHITE et al. *Princ. Biochem.* (ed. 4) xli. 910 (*caption*) Two units from neighboring polysaccharide chains can be bridged by a peptide. **1969** *New Scientist* 7 Aug. 270/1 Some natural polysaccharides show startlingly similar conformational behaviour to proteins and nucleic acids. **1973** R. G. KRUEGER et al. *Introd. Microbiol.* xxiv. 590/2 The major antigenic components of bacteria and their products are polysaccharides of one sort or another.

†**polyˈsaccharose.** *Chem. Obs.* [f. POLY- + SACCHAROSE.] = prec.

1894 PERKIN & KIPPING *Org. Chem.* I. xv. 275 The polysaccharoses do not ferment with yeast, and do not reduce Fehling's solution. **1931** E. C. MILLER *Plant Physiol.* viii. 411 The polysaccharoses have the general formula $(C_6H_{10}O_5)_n$ or $(C_5H_8O_4)_n$ depending on whether they yield hexoses or pentoses on hydrolysis.

polysaprobic: see POLY-.

‖**polysarcia** (pɒlɪˈsɑːsɪə). [late L. (Cæl. Aurel., 6th c.), a. Gr. πολυσαρκία fleshiness, f. πολύσαρκος very fleshy, f. πολυ- POLY- + σάρξ, σαρκ- flesh.]

1. *Path.* Excessive growth of flesh (or, loosely, of fat); corpulence, obesity.

1693 tr. *Blancard's Phys. Dict.* (ed. 2), *Polysarcia*, Corpulency. **1706** PHILLIPS, *Polysarcia*, bigness, or grossness of Body. **1845** TODD & BOWMAN *Phys. Anat.* I. 84 A disease, which has been not very correctly called polysarcia. **1875** R. F. BURTON *Gorilla L.* (1876) I. 64 Both sexes, even when running to polysarcia, have delicate limbs and extremities.

2. *Bot.* (See quot.)

1866 *Treas. Bot.* 916 *Polysarcia*, an excess of sap, giving rise to unnatural growth, &c.

So **polysarcous** (-ˈsɑːkəs) *a.*, affected with polysarcia, corpulent.

1890 in *Cent. Dict.* **1895** in *Syd. Soc. Lex.*

polyschematist (pɒlɪˈskiːmətɪst), *a.* *Pros.* [ad. Gr. πολυσχημάτιστος 'multiform; of verses, composed of various metres'.] Having many forms: said of ancient metres in which feet not metrically equivalent to the normal ones may be substituted for them. Also **polyscheˈmatic** *a.*

1846 WORCESTER, *Polyschematist, a.*, having many forms. **1890** *Cent. Dict.*, *Polyschematic.*

polyscope (ˈpɒlɪskəʊp). [f. POLY- + -SCOPE; so F. *polyscope.* Cf. Gr. πολύσκοπος far-seeing.]

1. An optical instrument through which objects appear multiplied; a multiplying-glass: *spec.* (see quot. 1842). Cf. POLYOPTRON.

1704 J. HARRIS *Lex. Techn.* I, *Polyscopes*, or *Multiplying Glasses*, are such as represent to the Eye one Object as many. **1842** BRANDE *Dict. Sc.*, etc., *Polyscope*, .. a lens plane on one side .. of which the convex side is formed of several plane surfaces, or facettes, so that an object seen through it appears multiplied.

2. (See quots.)

1881 *Eng. Mechanic* 18 Feb. 562/1 M. Trouvé described his polyscope, an apparatus for examining cavities of the body with the aid of incandescent platinum. **1895** *Syd. Soc. Lex.*, *Polyscope*, an apparatus invented by Trouvé, consisting of a combination of the instruments for visual examination of the eye, ear, larynx, urethra, etc., and fitted up with an electric light.

polyse, obs. form of POLICE, POLISH *v.*

polysemant to **polysemantism**: see POLY-.

polysemous (pɒlɪˈsiːməs), *a.* [Orig. f. med.L. *polysēm-us* (Dante), a. Gr. πολύσημ-ος of many senses, f. πολυ-, POLY- + σῆμα sign, σημαίνειν to signify; in modern linguistic use, prob. reformed on POLYSEMY + -OUS.] Having many meanings; *spec.* in *Linguistics*, = POLYSEMIC *a.*

1884 *Athenæum* 17 May 628/2 What Dante himself, in his dedication to Can Grande, calls the 'polysemous' character of the poem. [DANTE *Epist.* x. §7 Istius operis non est simplex sensus, immo dici potest polysemum, hoc est plurium sensuum.] **1931** G. STERN *Meaning & Change of Meaning* iii. 32 Different meanings can be expressed by the same word, as instanced by *crown* or any other polysemous word. **1957** N. FRYE *Anat. Crit.* 72 The principle of manifold or 'polysemous' meaning, as Dante calls it, is not a theory any more .. but an established fact. **1973** *Times Lit. Suppl.* 8 June 640/2 The book begins with an essay .. which makes the point that a work of thought is polysemous, that its meaning is not a message but rather the effect which it has on its readers.

polysemy (ˈpɒlɪsiːmɪ). *Linguistics.* Also in mod.L. form **polyˈsemia**. [ad. F. *polysémie* (M. Bréal *Essai de Sémantique* (1897) xiv. 155), f. med.L. *polysēmus* (see POLYSEMOUS *a.*): see -Y[3], -IA[1].] The fact of having several meanings; the possession of multiple meanings.

1900 N. CUST tr. *Bréal's Semantics* xiv. 140 The new meaning of a word, whatever it may be, does not make an end of the old. They exist alongside of one another... In proportion as a new signification is given to a word, it appears to multiply and produce fresh examples, similar in form, but differing in value. We shall call this phenomenon of multiplication *Polysemia*. All the languages of civilised nations have their part in it. **1928** O. JESPERSEN *Monosyllabism in Eng.* 26 We now see the reason why polysemy is found so often in small words to an extent which would not be tolerable in longer words. **1931** G. STERN *Meaning & Change of Meaning* iv. 74 *I wish you luck*... This polysemy is quite different from the polysemy .. of *Hund*, signifying either 'dog', or 'kind of cart used in mines'. **1937** J. ORR tr. *Iordan's Introd. Romance Linguistics* 192 In Gilliéron's view, sound-change, with all its consequences, homonymy polysemia, and the like, are causes of disease in words. **1950** S. POTTER *Our Language* 110 If we assume that the central meaning of *place* is still 'square' and that these other diverse uses *radiate* from that centre, we might equally well put it into our third semantic category: radiation, polysemia, or multiplication. **1951** S. ULLMANN *Princ. Semantics* ii. 115 Should one describe 'a straight line' and 'shipping line, air line' as radical shifts in application or as mild cases of polysemy? *Ibid.* 117 Polysemy is the pivot of semantic analysis. **1960** W. F. TWADDELL *Eng. Verb Auxiliaries* 3 We can acknowledge the existence of meaningful lexical verbs in our syntax, and gracefully recognize a linguistically reasonable polysemia of our grammatical signals within different lexical contexts. **1972** M. L. SAMUELS *Linguistic Evol.* v. 75 The effect of polysemy is in principle the same as that of homonymy—the representation of two or more meanings by a single form. **1975** *Times Lit. Suppl.* 16 May 531/1 Matters are complicated by the polysemy of the noun *linguist*, both 'polyglot' and 'scientific student of language'. **1977** *Dædalus* Summer 77 Thus symbol is distinguished from sign both by the multiplicity (multivocality, polysemy) of its signifieds, and by the nature of its signification.

So **ˈpolyseme**, a word having several or multiple meanings; **polyˈsemic**, *a.*, of or pertaining to polysemy; having several meanings, exhibiting polysemy.

1930 *S.P.E. Tract* xxxiv. 463 Even the names of concrete things are nearly always polysemic, though this may not be perceptible until we compare them with corresponding words in other languages. The word *leg*, for instance, may be applied to the supports of a table or chair, and the legs of an insect in English, but not in French. **1953** *Trans. Philol. Soc.* 60 Identifications of this type are .. most convincing when parallel translation-pairs are found as homonyms within a single language, which one would then wish to consider as polysemes. **1954** *Eng. Stud.* XXXV. 170 The cropping up of new senses may lead to polysemic conflicts, causing older senses to disappear. **1969** *Times Lit. Suppl.* 18 Dec. 1445 The earnest digging goes on, and we are .. grateful for the unearthing of new polysemes [in *Finnegans Wake*]. **1974** *Amer. Speech 1971* XLVI. 125 Polysemes, or terms that exhibit more than one denotation each, even though their connotations are synonymous in their negativism. **1976** G. STEINER in D. Villiers *Next Year in Jerusalem* 67 The elaborate investigations of the Kabbalists into the polysemic nature of the written word.

polysensuous, etc.: see POLY-.

polysepalous (pɒlɪˈsɛpələs), *a.* *Bot.* [f. POLY- + mod.L. *sepal-um* SEPAL + -OUS: cf. POLYPETALOUS. In F. *polysépale.*] Properly, Having numerous sepals; but used for: Having the sepals distinct or separate, not coherent or united. Also *aposepalous*, *chorisepalous*, *dialysepalous*, *eleutherosepalous*. Opp. to *gamosepalous* or *monosepalous*.

1829 CLINTON tr. *Richard's Elem. Bot.* 269 The polysepalous calyx is generally caducous. **1861** BENTLEY *Man. Bot.* 425 Both floral envelopes present, the outer being monosepalous or polysepalous, free or united to the ovary.

polyserositis to **polysoil**: see POLY-.

polysomatic (ˌpɒlɪsəʊˈmætɪk), *a.* [f. Gr. πολυσώματ-ος with many bodies: see -IC.]

1. *Petrol.* [ad. G. *polysomatisch* (G. Tschermak *Die mikrosk. Beschaffenheit der Meteoriten* (1885) i. 12).] Consisting of more than one grain or more than one mineral.

1888 *Amer. Geologist* I. 201 The boundaries between the different members of these 'polysomatic' masses of augite are traceable only with difficulty. **1910** *Mineral. Mag.* XV. 356 The commonest are polysomatic olivine chondrules with either granular or porphyritic structure. **1920** *Proc. Nat. Acad. Sci.* VI. 455 The porphyritic forms [of chondrule] .. pass gradually into those which are almost or quite holocrystalline and polysomatic. **1973** G. J. H. MCCALL *Meteorites & their Origins* xv. 191 Polysomatic chondrules may consist of numerous grains of a single mineral .. or of more than one mineral species.

2. *Biol.* [ad. G. *polysomatisch* (O. F. I. Langlet 1927, in *Svensk Bot. Tidskr.* XXI. 3).] Of, pertaining to, or exhibiting polysomaty.

1937 *Cytologia* VIII. 270 Although the possibility exists that polysomatic cells may arise in a number of different ways, there is evidence, if we can consider as significant the paired condition of polysomatic metaphase chromosomes, that the process involving two successive cleavages of the chromosomes is more widespread in plants than heretofore supposed. **1948** *Nature* 17 Jan. 80/2 These first studies .. indicated that a very large proportion of differentiated cells behind the meristematic region are polysomatic. **1969** BROWN & BERTKE *Textbk. Cytol.* xxiii. 538/1 Examples of the second category, replication, are differentiating cells that produce polytene and/or polysomatic nuclei .. [etc.].

polysomaty (pɒlɪˈsəʊmətɪ). *Biol.* [f. as prec.: see -Y[3].] The occurrence of polyploid cells together with diploid cells in the same somatic tissue.

1937 *Cytologia* VIII. 247 In *Kochia scoparia* L. .. the large periblem cells of the root were found to exhibit the same phenomenon of polysomaty as those of *Spinacia*. **1962** *Lancet* 12 May 1005/1 Very possibly, spindle formation is upset in the divisions preceding the formation of orthochromatic erythroblasts, thus giving rise to polysomaty. **1969** BROWN & BERTKE *Textbk. Cytol.* xix. 424/2 In numerous species such as spinach, *Cannabis*, potato, onion, beet, etc., polysomaty occurs typically in root tips and in many species in shoot tips and leaves.

polysome (ˈpɒlɪsəʊm). *Biol.* [f. POLY- + RIBO)SOME.] A cluster of ribosomes, held together by a strand of messenger RNA which each is translating; = *polyribosome* s.v. POLY- 1.

1962 J. R. WARNER et al. in *Science* 28 Dec. 1399/2 We have been able to show that the site of hemoglobin synthesis in vivo is not the single ribosome but rather a cluster of ribosomal particles, which we have called a 'polyribosome' or simply a polysome. **1970** *New Scientist* 15 Oct. 113/1 This reticulum is a series of intracellular membranes which carry on them the polysomes (messenger RNA and ribosomes) thought to be responsible for the biosynthesis of proteins destined for export from the cell. **1971**, **1972** [see MONOSOME 2]. **1973** R. G. KRUEGER et al. *Introd. Microbiol.* xi. 336/2 Each ribosome in the polysome has a growing polypeptide attached to it, and the ribosomes near the 3′ terminus of the mRNA molecule will have the most nearly complete polypeptide chains attached to them.

Hence **polyˈsomal** *a.*, of or pertaining to a polysome.

1962 *Science* 28 Dec. 1402/1 Dialysis followed by spraying causes considerable degradation of the polysomal structure. **1972** *Nature* 31 Mar. 237/2 The ratio of cytoplasmic to chloroplast polysomal RNA is increased two to three times 24h after inoculation.

polysomic (pɒlɪˈsəʊmɪk), *sb.* and *a.* *Cytology.* [f. POLY- + -SOME[4] + -IC.] **A.** *adj.* Having one or a few normal chromosomes in excess of the usual diploid or polyploid complement; being such a chromosome. **B.** *sb.* A polysomic organism.

1932 C. D. DARLINGTON *Rec. Adv. Cytol.* iii. 66 Polysomic forms arise in a diploid through two daughter chromosomes passing to the same pole at mitosis, or at meiosis. **1937** T. DOBZHANSKY *Genetics & Origin of Species* iv. 80 Spontaneous polysomics, monosomics, polyploids, haploids, and translocations were observed in *Datura stramonium* by Blakeslee (1922). **1939** *Jrnl. Genetics* XXXVIII. 409 All five asynaptic polysomics possessed three extra chromosomes. **1949** R. A. FISHER *Theory of Inbreeding* iv. 78 Polysomic organisms differ from disomic in having more than two chromosomes mutually homologous and capable of pairing, and of interchange of segments. **1949** K. MATHER *Biometrical Genetics* x. 305 A general treatment of polysomic inheritance has not been attempted because of its inherent complexity. **1966** J. A. SERRA *Mod. Genetics* II. xii. 35 Cases in which one chromosome of the set becomes polysomic (above the normal number) are known in which the chromosome remains euchromatic and other cases in which it is heterochromatinized. Genetic imbalance and diminished viability or more or less marked lethality accompany, as a rule, the cases of polysomy when the chromosome remains euchromatic, while heterochromatic supernumeraries do not, in general, produce such effects and, probably, are of use to the cell.

polysomitic: see POLY-.

polysomy (ˈpɒlɪsəʊmɪ). *Cytology.* [f. as prec. + -Y[3].] The state of being polysomic.

1932 C. D. DARLINGTON *Rec. Adv. Cytol.* iii. 59 Reduplication of some of the chromosomes of a set beyond the normal diploid number is called polysomy. **1946** *Nature* 17 Aug. 239/2 It is not impossible that polysomy and failure of pairing may be jointly responsible for the abnormal numbers [of chromosomes] observed. **1966** [see prec.]. **1973** *Cytogenetics & Cell Genetics* XII. 87 The first recorded observation of XYY polysomy in man was made by Sandberg et al. in 1961.

†**ˈpolyspast**. *Obs. rare*$^{-0}$. [ad. Gr. πολύσπαστον a compound pulley, neut. of πολύσπαστος drawn by many cords.] (See quots.)

[**1693** tr. *Blancard's Phys. Dict.* (ed. 2), *Polyspaston*, a Machine for reducing Joynts. **1706** PHILLIPS, *Polyspaston.*] **1730–6** BAILEY (folio), *Polyspast*, a windlass having many pullies or truckles. *Polyspast* (in *Surgery*), a machine for the reduction of dislocated joints.

polysperm (ˈpɒlɪspɜːm), *a.* *Bot. rare.* [ad. Gr. πολύσπερμος abounding in seed, f. πολυ-, POLY- + σπέρμα seed.] Having, containing, or producing numerous seeds; many-seeded. Also **polyˈspermal**, **polyˈspermatous**, **polyˈspermous** *a.*

1686 *Phil. Trans.* XVI. 287 Those Herbs .. being Polyspermous. **1719–26** QUINCY *Med. Dict.*, *Polyspermous*, .. those Plants are thus called which have more than four Seeds succeeding each Flower, and this without any certain Order. **1729** *Evelyn's Sylva* II. iii. 118 Easily rais'd of the Kernels and Nuts, which may be gotten out of their Polysperm and Turbinate Cones. **1845** LINDLEY *Sch. Bot.* iv. 26 Ovary polyspermous, many-celled. **1882** OGILVIE, *Polyspermal*, *Polyspermous*. **1895** *Syd. Soc. Lex.*, *Polyspermatous.*

[*Polysperm*, as *sb.*, in various Dicts., an error due to misquotation of Evelyn, quot. 1729 above.]

polyspermic (pɒlɪˈspɜːmɪk), *a.* *Physiol.* [f. POLYSPERM(Y + -IC.] Involving or exhibiting polyspermy.

1890 BILLINGS *Med. Dict.* II. 368/2 *Polyspermic*, requiring more than one spermatozoon to fructify the egg. **1894** *Anatomischer Anzeiger* IX. 146 Stained preparations of these eggs show them to be, previous to division, polyspermic. **1953** *Austral. Jrnl. Biol. Sci.* VI. 674 In the polyspermic rat egg, the chromosome complements from the female pronucleus and the male pronuclei all take part in the formation of the first cleavage spindle. **1975** *Nature* 8 May 112/1 Since silkworms are polyspermic the opportunity then arises for two different male pronuclei to fuse and form a diploid zygote nucleus.

polyspermy (ˈpɒlɪspɜːmɪ). *Phys.* [mod. ad. Gr. πολυσπερμία abundance of seed, f. πολύσπερμ-ος: see POLYSPERM *a.* Cf. F. *polyspermie.*] Impregnation of an ovum by more than one spermatozoon.

1889 GEDDES & THOMSON *Evol. Sex* 34 It has, however, been shown .. that 'polyspermy', or the entrance of more than one sperm, is extremely rare. **1904** *Brit. Med. Jrnl.* 17 Dec. 1643 The phenomenon of polyspermy or the fertilization of the ovum by more than one spermatozoon, the cause, according to modern ideas, of double monsters.

polyspike, polyspire: see POLY-.

‖**polysporangium** (ˌpɒlɪspɒˈrændʒɪəm). *Bot.* [mod.L., f. POLY- + SPORANGIUM.] A sporangium containing numerous spores.

1890 in *Cent. Dict.* **1895** in *Syd. Soc. Lex.*

polyspore (ˈpɒlɪspɔə(r)). *Bot.* [f. POLY- + SPORE; cf. Gr. πολύσπορος bearing much fruit. So F. *polyspore.*] **a.** A spore-case containing numerous spores. **b.** A compound spore, as in certain algæ.

1859 *Todd's Cycl. Anat.* V. 221/1 The term *Polyspore* is usually applied..[to] a gelatinous..pericarp or conceptacle. **1867** J. HOGG *Microsc.* II. i. 272 The first form to which the term *polyspore* has been applied, is that of a gelatinous or membranous pericarp or conceptacle in which an indefinite number of sporidia are contained.

polysporean (pɒlɪˈspɔəriːən), *a.* and *sb.* [f. mod. Zool. L. *Polysporea*, neut. pl. of *polysporeus* (f. Gr. πολύσπορ-ος + *-eus*) + -AN.] **a.** *adj.* Of or belonging to the *Polysporea*, a group of Protozoa of the class *Sporozoa* and family *Coccidiidæ*, which produce numerous spores (distinguished from *Monosporea* and *Oligosporea*). **b.** *sb.* A sporozoan of this order.

polyspored (-spɔəd), *a.* [f. POLY- + *spored*, f. SPORE.] = next. Also **polysporic** (-ˈspɒrɪk) *a.*

1882 J. M. CROMBIE in *Encycl. Brit.* XIV. 555/1 In some species..they [the spores in each theca] are 20–100, when the thecæ are said to be polyspored.

polysporous (pəˈlɪspərəs, pɒlɪˈspɔərəs), *a. Bot.* and *Zool.* [f. Gr. πολύσπορ-ος (see POLYSPORE) + -OUS.] Having or producing numerous spores, as certain cryptogamous plants and protozoans.

1858 MAYNE *Expos. Lex.*, Polysporous. **1861** BENTLEY *Man. Bot.* (1870) 375 In rare cases the asci have a large number of spores, and are hence said to be polysporous.

polyspory (ˈpɒlɪspɔərɪ). *Bot.* [f. POLY- + SPOR(E + -Y³.] The production of unusually many spores.

1929 *Genetics* XIV. 213 Giant spores, dyads, quartets and polyspory with and without extra, small nuclei or chromatin masses were repeatedly observed. **1959** *Canad. Jrnl. Plant Sci.* XXXIX. 272 A case of polyspory in a *Triticum-Agropyron* hybrid line..proved to be due to spindle misfunction. **1970** *Indian Jrnl. Exper. Biol.* VIII. 128/2 The chromosome fragmentation and lack of active polar movement result in laggards which persist as micronuclei and consequently lead to polyspory.

polystachyous: see POLY-.

polystelic (pɒlɪˈstiːlɪk), *a. Bot.* [a. F. *polystélique* (P. van Tieghem & H. Douliot 1886, in *Ann. Sci. Nat. Bot.* 7 ser. III. 276), f. POLY- + STELE 2 + -IC.] Of a stem or root: having more than one internal vascular cylinder or stele. So **ˈpolystele** (see quot. 1965); **ˈpolystely**, polystelic condition.

1891 *Ann. Bot.* V. 515 In the Cryptogams above cited..the original cylinder branches and the stem becomes polystelic. *Ibid.* 516 The two Dicotyledonous genera, in which alone, so far as we know, polystely prevails, belong to families remote from each other. **1896** CORMACK in *Trans. Linn. Soc., Bot.* Ser. II. V. 275 His description of the polystelic condition of stems of *Pteridophyta*. *Ibid.*, With polystelic roots must be classed certain abnormal Palm-roots. **1902** *Phil. Trans. R. Soc.* B. CXCV. 128 In *Anemia phyllitidis* the adult stem is characterised by the presence of so-called polystelic structure. **1902** *Encycl. Brit.* XXV. 413/2 This is the condition of astely, entirely parallel with polystely except that the separate strands are usually all or mostly leaf-traces. **1908** BOODLE & FRITSCH tr. *Solereder's Systematic Anat. Dicotyledons* II. vi. 1156 When the axis shows several steles in a transverse section, it is said to be polystelic. **1925** EAMES & MACDANIELS *Introd. Plant Anat.* v. 133 In contrast with the monostele was the 'polystele', a type of stele in which the vascular tissues are in the form of strands. **1938** *Current Sci.* VI. 383 Polystely occurs in the cortical region of the stolons. *Ibid.* 384 The polystelic condition observed in these plants might be regarded as the anatomical expression of the renewed adoption of the terrestrial habit. **1965** BELL & COOMBE tr. *Strasburger's Textbk. Bot.* 136 We come..to the polystele, consisting of a system of individual vascular bundles, distributed over the whole of the transverse section. **1969** F. E. ROUND *Introd. Lower Plants* x. 125 (*caption*) Stellar arrangements in the vascular cryptogams... N_1 polystele.

polystemonous to **polystigmous**: see POLY-.

polystomatous (pɒlɪˈstɒmətəs), *a. Zool.* [f. POLY- + Gr. στόμα, στοματ- mouth + -OUS: cf. next.] Having many or several mouths or suckers: *spec.* belonging to the *Polystomata*, a name for the Sponges, and also for the acinetiform Infusoria.

1877 HUXLEY *Anat. Inv. Anim.* iii. 137 The polystomatous condition..brought about.

polystome (ˈpɒlɪstəʊm), *a.* and *sb.* [a. F. *polystome* (1813 in Littré), ad. Gr. πολύστομ-ος many-mouthed, f. πολυ-, POLY- + στόμα mouth.] **a.** *adj.* Having many mouths. **b.** *sb.* An animal having many mouths or suckers, as a sponge, an acinetiform infusorian, or a parasitic trematode worm or fluke of the genus *Polystomum* or suborder *Polystomea* (polystome-fluke). So **poˈlystomous** *a.* [f. Gr. as above + -OUS], many-mouthed, polystomatous; ‖**polyˈstomium** (pl. **-ia**) [mod.L.], each of the fine pores which represent the original mouth in certain medusæ.

1859 J. R. GREENE *Man. Anim. Kingd., Protozoa* 77 'Acineta Forms'..rather constitute a distinct group of *Infusoria*, to which the term '*polystome' might, without objection, be perhaps applied. For each of the radiating filaments..with which the *Acinetæ* are provided is, in truth, a retractile tube, susceptible of elongation to a remarkable extent, and furnished at its extremity with an adherent disk. **1848** E. FORBES *Naked-eyed Medusæ* 79 Included in the *Polystomous section. **1878** BELL *Gegenbauer's Comp. Anat.* 116 Branched canals, which open at the ends of the ramifications of the arms by numerous fine pores (*polystomia).

polystylar to **polysulphuretted**: see POLY-.

polystyrene (pɒlɪˈstaɪəriːn). [f. POLY- + STYRENE.] Any polymer of styrene, esp. a hard, colourless thermoplastic resin; also, any of various plastics made from or containing this, which are widely used as moulding materials, films, and rigid foams. Also *attrib.*

1927 G. S. WHITBY in *India-Rubber Jrnl.* 16 Apr. 16/2 Poly-styrene becomes markedly elastic when warmed or swollen. *Ibid.*, Unstretched poly-styrene gave only an 'amorphous ring' when subjected to X-ray examination. **1939** *Nature* 13 May 787/2 The vinyl and polystyrene resins have valuable properties some of which are not possessed by the other resinoids. **1945** *Electronic Engin.* XVII. 698/1 Polystyrene..has long been considered to be the lightest in weight of all plastics. **1959** *Economist* 7 Mar. 895/2 The present output of polystyrene is about 28,000 tons a year, divided between Shell, Distillers and Monsanto. **1961** *Wall St. Jrnl.* 9 June 20/3 Koppers Co. is displaying a complete 12-foot sailboat made of polystyrene foam. **1970** N. SAUNDERS *Alternative London* 18 Sack chairs..consist of a chair-shaped bag three-quarters full of expanded polystyrene granules. **1973** *Materials & Technol.* VI. viii. 530 Polystyrene is readily polymerized exothermally to the straight polystyrene (homopolymer). *Ibid.* 533 Polystyrenes are manufactured in two stages. In the first stage the monomer styrene, possibly together with other monomers, is converted into the polymer... In the second stage the polymer is granulated, other substances frequently being added at the same time; rubbers,..oxidizers, pigments and the like, are such additions.

polystyrol, -sulphide, -sulphone: see POLY-.

†**polysyllabe.** *Obs.* [a. F. *polysyllabe* (1464 in Godef. *Compl.*), ad. med.L. *polysyllabus*, a. Gr. πολυσύλλαβος polysyllabic, f. πολυ-, POLY- + συλλαβή syllable.] = POLYSYLLABLE *sb.*

[**1580** G. HARVEY *Let. to Spenser* Wks. (Grosart) I. 105 You shal as well..heare *fayer*, as *faire*,..with an infinyte companye of the same sorte: sometime *Monosyllaba*, sometime *Polysyllaba*.] **1585** JAS. I. *Ess. Poesie* (Arb.) 59 Gif zour Sectioun be nocht..a monosyllabe,..bot the first syllabe of a polysyllabe.

polysyllabic (ˌpɒlɪsɪˈlæbɪk), *a.* [f. med.L. *polysyllab-us*, Gr. πολυσύλλαβ-ος (see prec.) + -IC. So F. *polysyllabique* (1550 in Hatz.-Darm.).] **a.** Of a word: Consisting of many (i.e., usually, more than three) syllables. **b.** Of language, etc.: Characterized by polysyllables.

1782 WARTON *Rowley Enq.* 42 He would rather have acquiesced in this laxity of the polysyllabic termination. **1817** COLERIDGE *Biog. Lit.* II. xx. 113 In the 'Excursion' the number of polysyllabic..words is more than usually great. **1875** WHITNEY *Life Lang.* xii. 244 Their greatly varying dialects are polysyllabic and agglutinative. **1906** *The King's English* iii. (ed. 2) 171 Polysyllabic humour.

So **polysyˈllabical** *a.*, in same senses. Hence **polysyˈllabically** *adv.*, in a polysyllabic manner, in polysyllables; **polysyˈllabicism** (-sɪz(ə)m), *nonce-wd.*, polysyllabic style; **polysyllabicity** (-ˈɪsɪtɪ), *nonce-wd.*, the condition of being polysyllabic.

1656 BLOUNT *Glossogr.*, *Polysyllabical, that hath many syllables. **1677** PLOT *Oxfordsh.* 7 As for Polysyllabical articulate Echo's, the strongest and best..is in the Park at Woodstock. **1868** J. H. NEWMAN *Verses Var. Occasions* 25 Terms strange and solemn That figure in polysyllabical row In a treatise. **1893** *Star* 18 May 1/6 The temptation to talk *polysyllabically to a popular audience. **1807** W. TAYLOR in *Ann. Rev.* V. 274 Having the *polysyllabicism without the precision of Johnson. **1871** EARLE *Philol. Eng. Tongue* §14 Inflections..are there [in Gothic] seen standing forth in all their archaic rigidity and *polysyllabicity.

polysyllabilingual (pɒlɪˌsɪləbɪˈlɪŋgwəl), *a. nonce-wd.* [f. as POLYSYLLABE + LINGUAL.] Relating to polysyllabic languages.

1824 *Crit. Res. in Philol. & Geog.* 172 The practice of the Chinese, and other monosyllabic tongues, absolutely stultifies the polysyllabilingual theorist.

polysyllabism (pɒlɪˈsɪləbɪz(ə)m). [f. as POLYSYLLABE + -ISM.] The use of polysyllables (as a stage in the development of language).

1860 FARRAR *Orig. Lang.* 181 The progress to polysyllabism from a state originally monosyllabic. **1875** WHITNEY *Life Lang.* x. 211 A primitive period of polysyllabism.

polysyllable (pɒlɪˈsɪləb(ə)l), *sb.* and *a.* Also 6 polli-, poli-, -sillable. [f. med.L. *polysyllaba*, fem. (sc. *vox* word) of *polysyllabus* (see POLYSYLLABE), after SYLLABLE.] **A.** *sb.* A word of many (i.e., usually, more than three) syllables.

1570 LEVINS *Manip.* Pref., In the Pollisillables, by diuersitie of pronunciation,..one worde maye haue diuers significations. **1589** PUTTENHAM *Eng. Poesie* II. xii. (Arb.) 126 Our vulgar Saxon English standing most vpon wordes monosillable, and little vpon polysillables. **1755** JOHNSON *Dict., Eng. Gram.*, Polysyllables..are seldom compared otherwise than by *more* and *most*, as *deplorable, more deplorable, most deplorable.* **1871** G. MEREDITH *H. Richmond* li, My father was losing his remarkably moderated tone, and threatening polysyllables.

B. *adj.* = POLYSYLLABIC. Now *rare.*

1589 PUTTENHAM *Eng. Poesie* II. xii. (Arb.) 131 The ill shapen sound of many of his wordes polisillable. **1591** HARINGTON *Orl. Fur.* Pref. (1634) ¶ viij b, For them that find fault with polysyllable meeter. **1669** HOLDER *Elem. Speech* 101 In a Poly-syllable word. **1817** COLERIDGE *Satyrane's Lett.* iii. in *Biog. Lit.* (1882) 268 *note*, The German, not less than the Greek, is a polysyllable language.

polysyllogism, -syllogistic: see POLY-.

polysymmetrical (ˌpɒlɪsɪˈmɛtrɪkəl), *a.* [f. POLY- + SYMMETRICAL.] Symmetrical about several planes of division; chiefly *Bot.*, divisible into exactly similar halves by two or more different planes, as a regular flower; actinomorphous. Hence **polysyˈmmetrically** *adv.*; **polyˈsymmetry**, the condition of being polysymmetrical.

1875 BENNETT & DYER *Sachs' Bot.* 183 So-called 'regular' flowers, stems with alternating whorls, and most roots, are polysymmetrical. *Ibid.* 533 If..the parts are all arranged in whorls, they are usually distributed monosymmetrically or polysymmetrically on the receptacle. *Ibid.* 184 The same relationship occurs between polysymmetry and multilateral arrangement as between monosymmetry and bilateral arrangement; polysymmetry must also be considered only as a particular case of the multilateral structure.

polysymptomatic: see POLY-.

‖**polysyndeton** (pɒlɪˈsɪndɪtən). *Rhet.* Also 6 **polisindeton.** [mod.L., a. Gr. *τὸ πολυσύνδετον, prop. neut. adj. (cf. ASYNDETON), f. πολυ-, POLY- + σύνδετος, verbal adj. f. συν-δέ-ειν to bind together.] A figure consisting in the use of several conjunctions in close succession; usually, the repetition of the same conjunction (as *and*, *or*, *nor*) to connect a number of co-ordinate words or clauses. Opp. to ASYNDETON.

1589 PUTTENHAM *Eng. Poesie* III. xvi. (Arb.) 186 Ye haue another maner of construction which they called *Polisindeton* we may call him the *couple clause* for that euery clause is knit and coupled together with a coniunctiue. *a***1637** B. JONSON *Eng. Gram.* II. viii, The two general exceptions are termed, Asyndeton and Polysyndeton. **1657** J. SMITH *Myst. Rhet.* 184 Polysyndeton,..a figure signifying superfluity of conjunctions. **1883** MARSH *Anglo-Sax. Gram.* 141 There may be too many conjunctions (polysyndeton).

polysynthesis (pɒlɪˈsɪnθɪsɪs). [f. POLY- + SYNTHESIS.] Synthesis or composition of many elements; complex or multiple synthesis; *spec.* in *Philol.* the combination of several words of a sentence in one word: = INCORPORATION 1 b, ENCAPSULATION.

1869 FARRAR *Fam. Speech* iv. (1873) 130 Polysynthesis is the synthesis of many words into one.

Hence **polyˈsynthesism** = POLYSYNTHETISM.

1881 R. BROWN *Language* 21 Others see in polysynthesism a survival of the universal early state of languages.

polysynthetic (ˌpɒlɪsɪnˈθɛtɪk), *a.* [f. Gr. πολυσύνθετος much compounded; of clauses, united by many particles: see POLY- and SYNTHETIC.] Of the nature of or characterized by polysynthesis; combining numerous elements; complex. *spec.*

1. *Cryst.* Applied to a compound crystal consisting of a series of twin crystals united so as to form a laminated structure. Also applied to twinning of this kind.

1805–17 R. JAMESON *Char. Min.* (ed. 3) 207 When the form is very complicated, as in the polysynthetic tourmaline. **1879** RUTLEY *Stud. Rocks* x. 109 In such polysynthetic crystals the twinning planes lie in four directions. **1944** *Amer. Mineralogist* XXIX. 199 Under the microscope, hydrotungstite is seen to occur as tiny green plate-like crystals which show polysynthetic twinning.

2. *Philol.* Characterized by combining several words of a sentence (as a verb and its object or complement) into one word: = INCORPORATING *ppl. a.* c, ENCAPSULATING *ppl. a.*

1816 P. S. DUPONCEAU *Let.* 30 Aug. in *Trans. Hist. & Lit. Comm. Amer. Philos. Soc.* (1819) I. 430 Crantz and Egede prove in the most incontrovertible manner that the language of Greenland is formed on the same *syntactic* or *polysynthetic* model. **1821** SOUTHEY *Lett.* (1856) III. 271 The polysynthetic, to which the various languages of the American tribes belong. **1869** FARRAR *Fam. Speech* iv. (1873) 132 Its structure is polysynthetic. **1889** MIVART *Orig. Hum. Reason* 231 Mr. Romanes describes..the Isolating, Polysynthetic, Agglutinative, Inflectional and Analytic forms of language. **1977** *Language* LIII. 10 Particularly interesting would be a polysynthetic language with many layers of morphology built into a single word.

Hence **polysynˈthetical** *a.* (*rare*$^{-0}$) in same sense; **polysynˈthetically** *adv.*; **polysynˈtheticism** (-sɪz(ə)m), **polyˈsynthetism**, polysynthetic character or condition; **polyˈsynthetize** *v. intr.*, to use polysynthesis, exhibit a polysynthetic character.

1846 WORCESTER, *Polysynthetic*, **Polysynthetical*, forming a manifold compound or composition. **1880** *Athenæum* 9 Oct. 459/2, 'I strike him with a sword to kill him' is another thought. Must all this be expressed *polysynthetically? **1903** *Amer. Geologist* XXXII. 67 Within it are small, triclinic, polysynthetically twinned feldspars which are rather vaguely crystallized. **1968** I. KOSTOV *Mineral.* 394 The crystals are almost invariably polysynthetically twinned. **1862** R. G. LATHAM *Elem. Compar. Philol.* lxv. 520 There is *polysyntheticism to a certain degree—though much of it is of the grammarian's making. **1860** FARRAR *Orig. Lang.* 172 Agglutination or *Polysynthetism is the name which has been invented for the complex condition of early language, when words follow each other in a sort of idyllic and *laissez-aller* carelessness, and the whole sentence, or even the whole discourse, is conjugated or declined as though it were a single word, every subordinate clause being inserted in the main one by a species of incapsulation. **1875** WHITNEY *Life Lang.* xii. 262 All sign of polysynthetism has been denied to the great Tupi-Guarani stock. **1874** SAYCE *Compar. Philol.* ii. 93 The *polysynthetising languages of North America, where the idea of time or mode is altogether absent from the verb.

polysystemic (ˌpɒlɪsɪˈstiːmɪk), *a. Linguistics.* [f. POLY- + SYSTEMIC *a.*] Composed of, characterized by, or recognizing many systems; used esp. with ref. to prosodic analysis.

1949 J. R. FIRTH in *Trans. Philol. Soc. 1948* 151 The monosystemic analysis based on a paradigmatic technique of oppositions and phonemes with allophones has reached, even overstepped, its limits! The time has come to try fresh hypotheses of a polysystemic character... The phonological structure of the sentence and the words which comprise it are to be expressed as a plurality of systems of interrelated phonematic and prosodic categories. **1957** *Year's Work Eng. Stud. 1955* 28/2 It remains a matter for regret that Firth's polysystemic approach to language has not yet been fully and explicitly formulated, for it is clear..that it has much to offer us. **1964** *Language* XL. 315 Firth..indicated that it is a property of language itself to be irreducibly multistructural and polysystemic. **1970** B. M. H. STRANG *Hist. English* 11 Language..is not mono- but polysystemic. **1973** *Archivum Linguisticum* IV. 21 Such a three-choice system is inherent in all polysystemic approaches to linguistic structure.

So **polysyˈstemically** *adv.*, in a polysystemic manner; **ˌpolysysteˈmicity**, **polyˈsystemy**, the fact or condition of being polysystemic.

1964 *Archivum Linguisticum* XVI. 72 Martinet's recognition of the polysystemicity of language (instanced by the different vowel contrast systems in French final open and closed syllables..) puts him in some agreement on this point..with the Firthian position in linguistic analysis. **1964** *Language* XL. 315 There is at least one instance..in which the appeal to linguistic polysystemy has the consequence of preventing the analyst from making an adequate descriptive statement. **1966** T. HILL in C. E. Bazell *In Memory of J. R. Firth* 218 The examples will also illustrate the principle of polysystemicity as applied to different grammatical categories. **1973** *Archivum Linguisticum* IV. 21 The choice of tone at each place in the structure can be considered polysystemically.

polyte, obs. form of POLITE.

Polytec, -tech (pɒlɪˈtɛk), colloq. abbrev. of POLYTECHNIC *sb.* 2; = POLY².

1911 O. ONIONS *Widdershins* x. 192, I don't think I shall go to the Polytec. to-night. **1974** 'E. LATHEN' *Sweet & Low* xix. 182 Why shouldn't I speak English well? I went to Rensselaer Polytech. **1977** *N.Z. Woman's Weekly* 10 Jan. 16/3 The weaving course at the Polytec has generated a great interest in looms. **1977** *Belfast Tel.* 14 Feb. 22/3 Now they have given the Polytech's first big romance a fairy tale ending by getting engaged.

polytechnic (pɒlɪˈtɛknɪk), *a.* and *sb.* [ad. F. *polytechnique* (*école polytechnique*, 1795), f. Gr. πολύτεχνος skilled in many arts + *-ique*, -IC: see POLY- and TECHNIC.]

A. *adj.* Pertaining to, dealing with, or devoted to, various arts; esp. in *polytechnic school*, an educational institution for giving instruction in various technical subjects.

Orig. applied to that established in Paris in 1794 by the National Convention, under the name of *École des Travaux publics*, changed in 1795 to *École Polytechnique*, and more particularly devoted to the instruction of recruits for the corps of civil and military engineers. ***Polytechnic Institution***: name of an institution in London, opened in 1838, for the exhibition of objects connected with the industrial arts, and providing a laboratory and theatre or lecture-room; closed in 1881, and subsequently re-opened as a technical and recreative school.

1805 W. TAYLOR in *Ann. Rev.* III. 258 The polytechnic school has long been distributing among select pupils, all the military sciences, through the best teachers. **1807** *Ibid.* V. 579 The Tractate of Education is a singular plan for a polytechnic school. **1837** *Penny Mechanic* II. 92/2 A Sample School, to be called the Polytechnic University, No. 1 for 2000 students. **1838** [Royal Polytechnic Institution, 309 Regent St., London, opened, Aug. 6]. **1845** R. W. HAMILTON *Pop. Educ.* ii. (ed. 2) 29 Polytechnic science may invent the instruments which shall dive as his substitute into the bowels of the earth. **1881** ROSCOE in *Nature* XXIII. 217 The scientific training they had received at their universities and polytechnic schools. **1888** *Resolution at Meeting Mansion H. London* 8 June, That this meeting being convinced of the urgent need in this country of technical and commercial education approves of the scheme for the establishment in South London of Polytechnic institutes to be endowed by public subscription with the aid of the Charity Commissioners. **1921** BEERBOHM *Lett. to R. Turner* (1964) 258 The incredible job [*sc.* H. G. Wells's *History of the World*], done so neatly..in a very awful cheap sciolistic polytechnic way. **1965** *Economist* 11 Sept. 1000/1 In the eyes of authority, naval history has remained a soft option in a polytechnic world.

B. *sb.* †**1.** (app.) Collective industrial action. *Obs. nonce-use.*

1835 URE *Philos. Manuf.* 278 It has, however, been the fate of this *polytechnic*, as of the best philanthropic dispensation ever made to man, to be misrepresented and reviled.

2. Short for *Polytechnic Institution* (rarely for *polytechnic school*): see A. Hence used as the name for several similar technical schools in different parts of London, etc. In mod. use, a kind of institution of higher education offering courses mainly in technical and vocational subjects (see quot. 1973).

1836 C. FOX *Jrnl.* 31 Aug. (1972) 31 Dr. Buckland..came on to the Polytechnic and stayed with us. **1841** M. EDGEWORTH *Let.* 25 May (1971) 593 Lestock..took Honora and Captain Beaufort and me to the Polytechnic and we all had our likenesses taken. **1850** W. HOWITT *Yr.-Bk. Country* iv. 111 Such places as Saint Paul's and Westminster Abbey should stand wide open; the Colosseum and the Polytechnic be accessible at the smallest price. **1857** C. KINGSLEY *Two Yrs. Ago* I. vii. 171 He would thrust his head into lectures at the Polytechnic and the British Institution. **1881** in *Daily News* 12 Sept. 2/4 Mr. Buckland..concluded his entertainment with the following address, which was cheered to the echo:—This very night the Polytechnic dies, Dies as a good Knight should, in martial guise. **1888** *Pall Mall G.* 27 Sept. 2/2 An excursion made by some sixty boys from the Young Men's Christian Institute at the Polytechnic to Belgium, Germany, and Switzerland. **1903** *Whitaker's Alm.* 267/2 The passing of the City of London Parochial Charities Act in 1883..provided for the establishment of polytechnics in various parts of London on the model of Mr. Quintin Hogg's original institution at Regent Street. **1934** G. B. SHAW *On Rocks* II. 237 Jafna's grandsons will go to Eton. Mine will go to a Polytechnic. **1967** *Listener* 6 July 5/1 Mr. Crosland and his advisers envisage rather an eternal separation between the universities and an entirely new race of animals they have created called the polytechnics. **1973** *Times* 4 Oct. 4/4 Polytechnics differ from universities in that they are not centrally financed, teach courses for degrees of the Council for National Academic Awards (CNAA), have a substantial proportion of students on courses below degree level, do much less research, and have, in theory, a greater commitment to the vocational aspect of higher education. **1975** *Physics Bull.* Jan. 6/2 It is natural to think of the polytechnics as being primarily concerned with science and technology but this is not so. Only one third of the work of the average polytechnic lies in these fields. **1975** *Guardian* 27 Jan. 5/1 The higher education building programme.. will contain a bias in favour of the polytechnics.

3. *pl.* 'The science of the mechanical arts' (Ogilvie, 1882). *rare*⁻⁰.

4. *attrib.*

1839 C. FOX *Jrnl.* 8 Oct. (1972) 58 The Bucklands dined with us, after a Polytechnic morning. **1911** O. ONIONS *Widdershins* 184 It was of Polytechnic classes that he spoke. *Ibid.* 189 The young Polytechnic student. **1972** R. K. KELSALL et al. *Graduates* i. 53 Parents of..university students..find university education more acceptable than do parents of..Polytechnic students. **1972** *Accountant* 19 Oct. 483/2 Polytechnic lecturers on a secondment period of six weeks for updating in auditing techniques. **1973** *Times Higher Educ. Suppl.* 20 July 12/1 With the formal inauguration of the Association of Polytechnic Teachers.. yet another teachers' organization has emerged. **1979** V. S. NAIPAUL *Bend in River* x. 170 The polytechnic term was over.

Hence **polyˈtechnical** *a.* = A. (in quot. 1880, practising many arts); **polyˈtechnican** (*nonce-wd.*), a member of the or a Polytechnic; **polytechnician** (-tɛkˈnɪʃən), [F. *-nicien*] a student of a (French) polytechnic school; **ˌpolytechniˈzation**, the action or process of making (some activity) polytechnic; *spec.* in Communist countries, the process of educating children in technical and industrial subjects considered essential for the proper running of the State.

1846 WORCESTER, **Polytechnical*, same as *polytechnic. Clarke.* **1880** BIRDWOOD *Indian Arts* I. 138 The trade guilds of the great polytechnical cities of India. **1892** K. GOULD tr. *von Kobell's Convers. Dr. Döllinger* iv. 75 Professor of Mathematics at the Gymnasium and Polytechnical School. **1894** *Daily News* 12 Mar. 5/4 M. Carnot, who, with his brother, graduated at the Polytechnique, and was so permeated with its spirit as only to be able to enjoy the company of 'Pipos', or old-boy *Polytechnicans. **1904** *Dundee Advertiser* 10 June 10 A number of *Polytechnicians were so dealt with quite recently by General André. **1932** *Times Lit. Suppl.* 17 Mar. 204/2 It would have been of advantage to provide a fuller and more detailed account..of the system of '*polytechnization' in the primary schools [of the U.S.S.R.]. **1933** *Times Educ. Suppl.* 25 Feb. 57/4 Polytechnization 'aims at producing a nation of socialistically thinking technical specialists'. **1949** K. DAVIS *Human Society* viii. 229 Economically, through 'polytechnization', the school is geared with productive life. **1974** *Encycl. Brit. Macropædia* VI. 375/2 From the 1950s onward, much attention has been paid [in Communist education] to the ideal of 'polytechnization'.

polytene (ˈpɒlɪtiːn), *a. Cytology.* [POLY- + -TENE.] Applied to giant chromosomes found in certain interphase nuclei, esp. in dipterous insects, and composed of many parallel copies of the genetic material, in which the active regions may be identifiable microscopically.

1935 P. C. KOLLER in *Proc. R. Soc.* B. CXVIII. 372 We can regard these chromosomes as corresponding with paired pachytene chromosomes at meiosis in which the intercalary parts between chromosomes have been stretched and separated into smaller units, and in which, instead of two threads lying side by side, we have 16 or even more. Hence they are 'polytene' rather than pachytene; I do not, however, propose to use this term; I shall refer to them as 'multiple threads'. **1959** C. M. M. BEGG *Introd. Genetics* iii. 27 The specificity of this pairing [of homologous chromosomes] is shown very strikingly in the case of the exceptional polytene threads of the much enlarged salivary gland nuclei of Diptera. **1971** *Nature* 21 May 184/2 Individuals of the species which breeds in freshwater can only be identified with certainty by the banding patterns of their polytene chromosomes. **1976** BELL & COOMBE tr. *Strasburger's Textbk. Bot.* (rev. ed.) 31 (*caption*) Giant chromosome, polytene and consisting of about 2048 strands, from the suspensor of the embryo of *Phaseolus vulgaris*.

Hence **polytenic** (-ˈtiːnɪk) *a.*, in the same sense; **ˈpolyteny**, the state of being polytene; also **ˌpolyteniˈzation**, the production of polyteny; **polyˈtenized** *ppl. a.* (of a chromosomal constituent) reduplicated owing to the polyteny of the chromosome.

1942 *Proc. R. Soc. Edin.* B. LXI. 318 The degree of polyteny found in the tissues of a dipteran larva varies with the species. **1953** W. HOVANITZ *Text-bk. Genetics* vii. 100 The terms salivary chromosomes and polytenic chromosomes have been applied to them [*sc.* giant chromosomes]. **1958** Polyteny [see MIXOPLOIDY]. **1966** *Proc. R. Soc.* B. CLXIV. 280 After many steps of polytenization (12 or 14 consecutive replications) such a labelled chromosome thread may still extend as a single linear unit from the one end of the giant chromosome to the other end. **1968** H. HARRIS *Nucleus & Cytoplasm* iv. 77 The chromosomes in these [salivary] glands are extraordinary for two reasons. The first is that they are grossly polytenic. Each chromosome contains thousands of identical parallel copies of the basic diploid genetic structure. The extent of polyteny may vary in different species, but for *Chironomus tentans* it has been estimated that each chromosome contains about 16000 times the normal diploid amount of DNA. **1974** *Nature* 29 Mar. 446/1 Mutational data also rule out simple polyteny and polyploidy, where every single gene on every chromosome is polytenised or where every chromosome is present in two or more copies. **1976** *Ibid.* 17 June 614/2 Ciliata and Diptera..show a high tendency for endopolyploidisation and polytenisation. **1976** BELL & COOMBE tr. *Strasburger's Textbk. Bot.* (rev. ed.) 31 In rare cases repeated multiplication of chromonemata leads to multistranded (polytenic), cable-like, giant chromosomes.

polyterebene to **polyterpenoid**: see POLY-.

ˌpolytetraˌfluoroˈethylene. *Chem.* Also **-fluorethylene.** [f. POLY- + TETRAFLUOROETHYLENE.] A highly crystalline resinous polymer of tetrafluoroethylene having the structure $-(CF_2CF_2)_n-$, which is tough, resistant to chemicals, stable over a wide range of temperature, and widely used as a moulding material, esp. under the trade name *Teflon*; abbr. *P.T.F.E.* (s.v. P II. d).

1946 *Industr. & Engin. Chem.* Sept. 877/1 Although pure polytetrafluoroethylene is white in color, frequently commercially fabricated articles are somewhat gray and speckled, apparently as a result of minute traces of contamination. **1951** *Electronic Engin.* XXIII. 370 In order to obtain a smooth bearing, use has been made of polytetrafluoroethylene for the bearing surface. **1959** *Times Rev. Industry* June 22/1 Gaskets of polytetrafluorethylene or Fluon have proved invaluable in difficult services, since this material is resistant to all 'searching' chemical reagents except molten sodium and gaseous fluorine. **1961** *Lancet* 19 Aug. 410/1 Polytetrafluoroethylene (P.T.F.E., 'Fluon', 'Teflon') is at present the most suitable material for permanent cannulation. **1962** *Which?* Aug. 255/1 There are two kinds of non-stick frying pans—those with a silicone finish and those with a plastic called polytetrafluoroethylene, or PTFE. **1975** *Sci. Amer.* July 63/1 Non-metals such as..polytetrafluoroethylene and carbon-graphites are successful bearing materials because of their excellent resistance to scoring and corrosion. **1978** J. SHERWOOD *Limericks of Lachasse* i. 8 The plant..made polytetrafluorethylene, a polymer with three times the density of polypropylene and enormously strong.

polythalamous (pɒlɪˈθæləməs), *a. Nat. Hist.* [f. Gr. πολυ-, POLY- + θάλαμος bed-chamber (see THALAMUS) + -OUS.] Having or consisting of several chambers or cells; many-chambered, multilocular.

1816 KIRBY & SP. *Entomol.* xiv. (1828) I. 451 Some galls are polythalamous or consisting of several chambers. **1835-6** *Todd's Cycl. Anat.* I. 517/2 A..series of minute polythalamous shells. **1876** PAGE *Text-bk. Geol.* xx. 428 Calcareous ooze and marls, rich in polythalamous.. foraminifera.

So **polythalamaceous** (-ˈeɪʃəs) *a.*, belonging to the *Polythalamācea*, an order of cephalopods with many-chambered shells, as the nautilus (synonymous with *Tetrabranchiāta*) (Mayne *Expos. Lex.* 1858); **polythalamian** (-θəˈleɪmɪən) *a.*, belonging to the *Polythalamia*, a division of Protozoa, having a many-chambered test; **polythalamic** (-θəˈlæmɪk) *a.* = *polythalamous.*

[**1860** MAURY *Phys. Geog. Sea* (Low) xiv. §616 *note*, Polythalamia are abundant in the Arctic Seas. **1867** J. HOGG *Microsc.* II. ii. 376 The Polythalamia or Multilocular Rhizopods, in their earliest state are unilocular.] **1863** LYELL *Antiq. Man* App. (ed. 3) 529 Mr. Chydenius obtained ..*polythalamian shells. **1890** *Cent. Dict.*, **Polythalamic.*

‖**polythecium** (pɒlɪˈθiːʃɪəm, -ˈθiːsɪəm). *Zool.* Pl. -ia. [mod.L., f. Gr. πολυ-, POLY- + θηκίον, dim. of θήκη box, case.] Name for a colony or zoothecium of certain infusorians, in which the loricæ are united by their stalks. Hence **poly'thecial** *a.*, pertaining to a polythecium.

1880 W. S. KENT *Infusoria* I. 360 Forming by the serial conjunction of their respective loricæ a more or less extensive branching colony-stock or polythecium.

polytheism ('pɒlɪθiːɪz(ə)m). Also 7 poli-, polu-, (polythisme). [ad. F. *polythéisme* (16th c.), f. Gr. πολύθεος of or belonging to many gods (f. πολυ-, POLY- + θέος god): see -ISM.] Belief in, or worship of, many gods (or more than one God).

1613 PURCHAS *Pilgrimage* (1614) 49 An exchanged Polytheisme in worshipping of Saints, Images, and the Host. **1638** SIR T. HERBERT *Trav.* (ed. 2) 315 Some Temples..furnisht with wooden gods for politheisme. **1658** BP. REYNOLDS *Van. Creature* Wks. (1679) 8 There is yet a bitter root of Atheisme, and of Polutheisme in the minds of Men by nature. **1782** PRIESTLEY *Corrupt. Chr.* I. I. 101 Celsus..justifies the polytheism of the heathens. **1835** THIRLWALL *Greece* I. vi. 183 It has sometimes been made a question whether polytheism or monotheism is the more ancient form of natural religion.

polytheist ('pɒlɪθiːɪst), *sb.* (*a.*) [f. as prec. + -IST. Cf. F. *polythéiste* (1762 in Hatz.-Darm.).] One who believes in or worships many gods (or more than one); an adherent of polytheism.

a **1619** FOTHERBY *Atheom.* I. vi. §3 (1622) 45 They were of all other the most palpable Polytheists. **1711** SHAFTESB. *Charac.* (1737) I. 11 To believe no one Supreme designing Principle or Mind, but rather two, three, or more..is to be a Polytheist. **1877** CARPENTER tr. *Tiele's Hist. Relig.* 109 The Aryans like the Indo-Germans, were polytheists.

b. *attrib.* or *adj.* = next.

1875 MERIVALE *Gen. Hist. Rome* lxxi. (1877) 583 For the first time the two principles of faith, the monotheist and the polytheist, met in combat.

polytheistic (,pɒlɪθiː'ɪstɪk), *a.* [f. prec. + -IC: see -ISTIC.] Of, pertaining to, holding, or characterized by polytheism.

? *a* **1770** ADAM SMITH *Hist. Astron.* iii. Ess. (1795) 25 All Polytheistic religions. **1773** BURKE *Sp. Ho. Comm.* Wks. 1869 VI. 108 Was it ever heard that polytheism tolerated a dissent from a polytheistick establishment? **1878** GLADSTONE *Prim. Homer* vi. 92 Zeus..appears to be..a representative of an old monotheism which merges into supremacy in a polytheistic system.

polythe'istical, *a.* [f. as prec. + -AL[1]: see -ICAL.] †**a.** = prec. *Obs.* **b.** In distinctive sense: Having a polytheistic character or quality.

1678 CUDWORTH *Intell. Syst.* I. iv. 298 That Orpheus, the Orphick Doctrine, and Poems, were Polytheistical, is a thing acknowledged by all. **1748** HARTLEY *Observ. Man* II. ii. 191 Remarks upon the Polytheistical Religions of the Antient World. **1847** LEWES *Hist. Philos.* (1867) I. 47 He was a monotheist in contradistinction to his polytheistical contemporaries. **1870** DISRAELI *Lothair* xxx.

Hence **polythe'istically** *adv.*

1846 WORCESTER cites DR. ALLEN. **1909** W. JAMES *Pluralistic Universe* viii. 310 It [*sc.* the superhuman consciousness] may be polytheistically or it may be monotheistically conceived of.

polytheize ('pɒlɪθiːaɪz), *v.* *rare.* [f. as POLYTHEISM + -IZE: so F. *polythéiser.*] *intr.* To act the polytheist; to profess or practise polytheism.

1864 in WEBSTER. **1882** OGILVIE cites MILMAN.

polythelia, -ism, -y: see POLY-.

polythene ('pɒlɪθiːn). [Contraction of POLYETHYLENE.] A tough, light, translucent thermoplastic made by polymerizing ethylene and used esp. for moulded and extruded articles, as film for packaging, and as a coating. Freq. *attrib.* and in *Comb.*

1939 *Plastics* III. 231/2 Polythene, the new polymerized ethylenic resin. *Ibid.* 289/1 Polymerized ethylenes manufactured..under the trade name of Polythene by I.C.I. have excellent electrical properties... These new compounds are now being carefully considered by well-known cable companies. **1943** *Brit. Plastics* XV. 417 Polythene is a general term for a range of solid polymers of ethylene, first discovered and prepared in I.C.I. Research Laboratories by subjecting ethylene to extremely high pressures under carefully controlled conditions. These products are sold under the registered name 'Alkathene'. **1945** *Times* 25 May 8/6 An outstanding I.C.I. achievement in the field of plastics was the discovery and development of polythene or polymerised ethylene. Polythene was seen to be a most valuable insulating material for high-frequency radio and television. **1951** *Catal. of Exhibits, South Bank Exhib., Festival of Britain* 109/1 Polythene ice cube mould. **1957** E. BONE *Seven Years' Solitary* xiv. 211, I had never heard of polythene bags. **1958** *Economist* 29 Mar. 1138/1 Sealed polythene bags offering protection and convenience in handling, have become commonplace for many small consumer products which used to be sold unpackaged. **1959** *Spectator* 25 Sept. 409/1 Polythene-wrapped food may be staler than it looks. **1960** *Farmer & Stockbreeder* 8 Mar. 105/2 There is a water trough supplied by the polythene pipe laid up one grass verge of the road. **1973** R. FIENNES *Headless Valley* vii. 129 We camped above the river beneath a thin sheet of polythene and slept. **1973** *Materials & Technol.* VI. viii. 524 Polythene has the simplest chemical structure of all plastics, consisting only of carbon and hydrogen in a straight chain. *Ibid.* 525 There are now many manufacturers of polythene, which is marketed under trade names such as Alkathene (UK), Bakelite, Alathon (USA), Lupolen (Germany) and so on. **1973** J. ROSSITER *Manipulators* xxii. 213 She put on a glistening white polythene raincoat.

†**polytheous,** *a.* *Obs. rare*[−1]. [f. Gr. πολύθεος (see POLYTHEISM) + -OUS.] Relating to many gods; polytheistic.

1648 J. BEAUMONT *Psyche* XXI. lviii, Heav'n most abhor'd Polytheous Piety.

polythetic (pɒlɪ'θɛtɪk), *a.* [f. POLY- + Gr. θετ-ός placed, arranged + -IC I.] Sharing a number of common characteristics, without any one of these being essential for membership of the group or class in question. So **poly'thetically** *adv.*

1962 P. H. A. SNEATH in Ainsworth & Sneath *Microbial Classification* 291 Such groups, in which several sets of characters occur, are called 'polytypic' by Beckner, but are better called polythetic. Phenetic taxa are always in theory polythetic. **1963** SOKAL & SNEATH *Princ. Numerical Taxon.* ii. 15 Polythetic groups can..be arranged polythetically to give higher polythetic groups, as is done in building a hierarchy in the natural system. **1969** E. MAYR *Princ. Systematic Zool.* iv. 83 No single feature is essential for membership in a polythetically defined taxon. **1972** S. THEMERSON *Special Branch* 75 Let it take a polythetic way of classifying: let it consider the largest possible number of characteristics for each fact or object. **1972** C. RENFREW *Emergence of Civilisation* 11 It is now possible to make a statement about civilisations which does not seek to define them in terms of a single principal culture trait, or even polythetically, in terms of, for example, two out of three traits. **1976** *Brit. Jrnl. Psychol.* LXVII. 379 Most human concepts are polythetic..which means that no particular attribute or combination of attributes need necessarily be present (or absent) for an object to belong to a given category.

polythionic (pɒlɪθaɪ'ɒnɪk), *a.* *Chem.* [f. POLY- + *-thionic*, f. Gr. θεῖον sulphur: see DITHIONIC.] Containing several atoms of sulphur in combination with H_2O_6 (distinguished from *sulphuric*, in which S is combined with H_2O_4); in ***polythionic acids***, a general name for the acids of this constitution, e.g. *pentathionic acid*, $H_2S_5O_6$.

1849 D. CAMPBELL *Inorg. Chem.* 57 Besides the oxides of sulphur already described, three new acids have lately been added. These are known as the polythionic acids,—a name given them by Berzelius. **1868** WATTS *Dict. Chem.* V. 540 A remarkable series..called polythionic acids, containing six atoms of oxygen and two or more atoms of sulphur.

†**polythore.** *Obs. rare*[−1]. App. an error for *polyphone*: see POLYPHONE I a, quot. 1655.

1661 EVELYN *Diary* 9 Aug., He plaid to me likewise on the *polythore*, an instrument having something of the harp, lute, theorbo, &c.

polytick, -tik(e, etc., obs. forms of POLITIC.

polytocous (pə'lɪtəkəs), *a.* Also -tokous. [f. Gr. πολυτόκος producing numerous offspring, prolific + -OUS.]

a. *Zool.* Producing several young at a birth; multiparous. **b.** *Bot.* Bearing fruit many times: a term proposed instead of POLYCARPOUS. So †**po'lytoky** *Obs. rare* [Gr. πολυτοκία], production of numerous offspring, fecundity.

1702 C. MATHER *Magn. Chr.* III. xxix. 165/1 Altho' New England has no Instances of such a Polytokie, yet it has had Instances of what has been remarkable: one Woman has had not less than Twenty two Children. **1715** THORESBY *Ducatus Leodiensis* App. 608 Dorothy..Wife of Mr. Joseph Cowper of this Parish, died in childbed of her twenty-fifth or twenty-sixth Birth, which is the greatest Instance of such a Polytokie in these Parts. **1880** GRAY *Struct. Bot.* (ed. 6) 33 *note*, Polytocous (bearing many times) would be more appropriate [than polycarpic]. **1932** *Proc. 6th Internat. Congr. Genetics* I. 188 In polytokous mammals we may expect that genes favoring rapid embryonic growth will spread, as slower growing embryos are at a disadvantage. **1936** *Nature* 12 Sept. 451/2 This..process [*sc.* fœtalization] has been essential for the evolution of man:..it could not have occurred in a polytocous form, where slowing of early growth would be prevented by intra-uterine selection. **1956** *Ibid.* 11 Feb. 288/2 Many observers have stressed the importance of a change in the nutrition of polytocous ewes during late pregnancy in the etiology of the disease. **1971** *Ibid.* 8 Oct. 379/1 In the polytocous species such as the small mammals and even the pig, it is not normally necessary to induce superovulation in order to provide the requisite number of eggs.

polytomous (pə'lɪtəməs), *a.* [f. Gr. type *πολύτομ-ος (f. πολυ- much + -τομος cut) + -OUS.] Divided, or involving division, into many parts.

1. *Bot.* **a.** *spec.* Applied to a leaf having several divisions, but not articulated with the midrib so as to form leaflets (e.g., a pinnatifid or pinnatipartite leaf). **b.** Applied to branching in which the axis divides into more than two secondary axes at the same point.

1858 MAYNE *Expos. Lex.*, *Polytomus, Bot.*, applied by L. C. Richard to leaves the median nervure of which, not the foliaceous part, is combined with the common petiole, but without articulation, which distinguishes them from compound leaves: polytomous. **1866** *Treas. Bot.* 917 *Polytomous*, pinnate, but without having the divisions articulated with the common petiole.

2. *Logic.* Involving polytomy: see next, 2. Distinguished from DICHOTOMOUS and TRICHOTOMOUS.

polytomy (pə'lɪtəmɪ). [f. Gr. πολυ-, POLY- + -τομια, f. -τομος cut. Cf. F. *polytomie.*] The condition or character of being polytomous. (Distinguished from DICHOTOMY and TRICHOTOMY.)

1. *Bot.* Division into several (more than two) branches at the same point.

1875 BENNETT & DYER *Sachs' Bot.* 148 Dichotomy (rarely Polytomy)..is caused by the cessation of the previous increase in length of a member at the apex, and by two (or more) new apices arising at the apical surface close to one another, which..develope in diverging directions.

2. *Logic.* Division into several (usually, more than three) members.

a **1856** W. HAMILTON *Lect. Metaphysics & Logic* (1860) IV. xxv. 23 If a division has only two members, it is called a dichotomy..; if three, a trichotomy..; if four, a tetrachotomy; if many, a polytomy, &c. **1864** BOWEN *Logic* iv. 101 Division into many members may be called a polytomy. **1867** ATWATER *Logic* 71 A division in three members is called a Trichotomy: into many members, a Polytomy.

polytonality (,pɒlɪtəʊ'nælɪtɪ). *Mus.* [f. POLY- + TONALITY.] The simultaneous use of two or more keys in a musical composition.

1923 [see ATONAL *a.*]. **1934** S. R. NELSON *All about Jazz* i. 12 Polytonality, dissonance, and the more lurid forms of Expressionism are the shibboleths of Schönberg, Stravinsky, Bartók and the moderns. **1946** G. ABRAHAM in A. L. Bacharach *Brit. Music* iii. 61 The experiment is in polytonality—the flute plays in A, the oboe in A flat, and the viola in C. **1955** L. FEATHER *Encycl. Jazz* 32 Many young jazzmen were experimenting with atonality and polytonality. **1969** *Daily Tel.* 8 Nov. 9/3 Cold admiration seems to have been the response to his consciously manufactured rhythms, systematic polytonality and pattern building. **1977** J. CROSBY *Company of Friends* xxxiv. 220 'Roger found out, did he?' asked Sascha idly, playing simultaneous D-minor and C-sharp triads. Polytonality—while naked. Very sexual.

So **poly'tonal** *a.*, containing or pertaining to polytonality; **poly'tonalist**, one who writes or advocates polytonal music.

1924 P. A. SCHOLES *Crotchets* 164 The device of 'canon' sometimes pointed to a polytonal future for music. **1934** C. LAMBERT *Music Ho!* II. 68 The polytonal choral writing of Milhaud. **1938** *Oxf. Compan. Mus.* 406/1 The polytonalists appear to claim that the value of their work lies in the significance of the horizontal lines. **1949** *Penguin Music Mag.* July 24 The polytonal writing, in which different parts in the polyphony may have, not only their individual harmonization, but also each their own tonality, is chiefly a tentative realization of a stage that music is steadily approaching. **1952** B. ULANOV *Hist. Jazz in Amer.* (1958) xxiii. 332 All of the trio and octet scorings and performances partake..of the controlled but not stifling disciplines of a music which is polytonal, polyrhythmic at times, and spontaneous too. *Ibid.*, Dave..is another polytonalist. **1976** *New Yorker* 15 Nov. 194/2 Rich in feeling, sometimes polytonal (or, at any rate, of indefinite tonality), the piece is not without interest.

polytone: see POLY-.

polytonic (pɒlɪ'tɒnɪk), *a.* [f. POLY- + TONIC *a.* and *sb.*] Using or having several (musical or vocal) tones.

1948 D. DIRINGER *Alphabet* I. vi. 99 So characteristic are the tones in the Tibeto-Chinese languages, that some scholars have suggested to term them 'polytonic'. **1955** *Sci. News Let.* 13 Aug. 102/1 A new signaling system for telephone dialing..has been developed... The device, called a polytonic coder, sends out digits just about as fast as they can theoretically be packed into a line. *Ibid.* 102/2 The tests showed the polytonic signal could be used on all except a few telephone connections in this country. **1961** J. BLADES in A. Baines *Mus. Instruments* 342 The ingenious steel drums recently introduced in Trinidad are polytonic gongs. .. Each sector is tuned to a different note.

polytopal to **polytopical:** see POLY-.

†**polytrich** ('pɒlɪtrɪk). *Obs. rare.* (Erron. politrich.) [ad. L. *polytrichon*, Gr. πολύτριχον, name of two ferns = MAIDENHAIR I a, b; f. πολύς much + θρίξ, τριχ- hair.] A rendering of L. *Polytrichon*, under which the herbalists (e.g. Dodoens and Lyte) included the ferns *Adiantum Capillusveneris* and *Asplenium Trichomanes*, both called Maidenhair, and the moss *Polytrichum commune* (Golden Maidenhair).

[**1578** LYTE *Dodoens* III. lxviii. 409 The first kinde is called ..in Latine *Adiantum, Polytrichum* [etc.]. *Ibid.* lxix. 410 This herbe is called..in Latine..*Trichomanes*; in the Shoppes *Polytrichon. Ibid.* lxxi. 412 [Mosse] 3. Goldylockes, *Polytrichon*, or Golden Maydenheare. The third kind which some call Golden Polytrichon, hath very small slender stalkes.] **1725** BRADLEY *Fam. Dict.* s.v., The Virtues of Politrich are to dry, dissolve, and digest.

polytrichous: see POLY-.

polytrochal (pə'lɪtrəkəl), *a.* *Zool.* [f. mod.L. *polytrochus* (Ehrenberg) (f. Gr. πολυ-, POLY- + τροχός wheel: see below) + -AL[1].] **a.** Having several circlets of cilia, as the larva of a polychæte worm. **b.** Belonging to the division *Polytrocha* of rotifers, in which the trochal disk or 'wheel' has several lobes. So **polytroch**

('pɒlɪtrɒk), a polytrochal animal; **po'lytrochous** *a.* = *polytrochal*.

1858 MAYNE *Expos. Lex.*, *Polytrochus*, applied by G. C. Ehrenberg to two Families..of the *Infusoria Rotifera*, having many crowns of hairs: polytrochous. **1878** BELL *Gegenbaur's Comp. Anat.* 137 The larvæ of the Chætopoda are divided into mesotrochal, telotrochal, and polytrochal forms. **1890** *Cent. Dict.*, *Polytroch.*

polytrope ('pɒlɪtrəʊp). *Physics* and *Astr.* [Back-formation from POLYTROPIC *a.*, or a. G. *polytrope* in the same sense (R. Emden *Gaskugeln* (1907) I. i. 13).] A polytropic body of gas (see POLYTROPIC *a.* 4).

1926 A. S. EDDINGTON *Internal Constitution of Stars* iv. 86 The polytrope $n = 3$, which is believed to correspond nearly to the actual conditions of the stars. **1939** S. CHANDRASEKHAR *Introd. Study Stellar Struct.* iv. 170 So far we have considered only complete polytropes. We shall now proceed to a consideration of composite polytropes, i.e., configurations which consist of different zones each characterized by a different value of the index *n*. **1975** *Nature* 27 Mar. 295/1 The energy required to break up a star of mass *m* and radius *R* is..$\frac{3}{7}(Gm^2/R)$ for a polytrope of index $n = 3\frac{1}{2}$.

polytrophic (pɒlɪ'trɒfɪk), *a.* [In sense a, f. Gr. πολυτρόφος giving much nourishment (f. πολυ-, POLY- + τρέφειν to feed) + -IC; with sense b, cf. Gr. πολύτροφος (f. as above) highly nourished.]

†**a.** ? Affording much nourishment; highly nutritive. *Obs.* **b.** Of a parasitic organism: Infesting more than one host. So **po'lytrophy**, abundant or excessive nutrition (? *obs.*).

1661 LOVELL *Hist. Anim. & Min.* 16 Hoggs flesh..is of easie concoction,..polytrophick, and of a thick and viscous juyce. **1667** DENHAM *Direct. Paint.* IV. viii, Themselves must share in this Polutrophy. **1858** MAYNE *Expos. Lex.*, *Polytrophia*, term for excessive nutrition: polytrophy. **1900** *Nature* 13 Sept. 465/1 Sometimes parasitic (facultative parasites), monotrophic or polytrophic [bacteria].

polytropic (pɒlɪ'trɒpɪk), *a.* [f. Gr. πολύτροπος turning many ways, versatile, etc., also much-travelled (epithet of Ulysses in the *Odyssey*), f. πολυ-, POLY- + τρόπος turn.]

1. Capable of turning to various courses or expedients; versatile.

1838 *Fraser's Mag.* XVII. 506 In the Odyssey..his polytrophic powers are brought into full play. **1862** *Temple Bar Mag.* VI. 243 We may encounter men in that city who are as polytropic as Ulysses.

2. *Math.* Turning several times round a pole; also applied to a function which has several different values for one of the variable (opp. to *monotropic*).

3. [ad. G. *polytrope* (E. Loew 1884, in *Jahrbuch K. Bot. Gartens Berlin*).] Of a bee: collecting nectar from many kinds of flower.

1899 C. ROBERTSON in *Bot. Gaz.* XXVIII. 29 If a bee has a long flight it must be regarded as polytropic. **1919** J. H. LOVELL *Flower & Bee* 120 There are also on the wing at the same time 6 species which are polytropic.

4. *Physics* and *Astr.* [ad. G. *polytropisch* (G. Zeuner *Technische Thermodynamik* (ed. 3, 1887) I. xxix. 143).] Pertaining to or designating a body of gas or a process in which pressure and volume change in such a way that a specific heat remains constant. Also as *sb.*, a graph showing such a variation of pressure and volume.

1907 J. F. KLEIN tr. *Zeuner's Technical Thermodynamics* I. xxix. 152 If the initial condition is given by p_1 and v_1, we accordingly have $pv^n = p_1v_1^n$..as the equation of the sought pressure curve, which we will hereafter call the polytropic curve. **1926** A. S. EDDINGTON *Internal Constitution of Stars* iv. 94 A class of problems arises in which the polytropic condition..applies only to part of the star. **1933** *Monthly Notices R. Astron. Soc.* XCIII. 390 Emden's well-known researches on the equilibrium of polytropic gas spheres has been of fundamental importance in its repercussions on the modern theories of stellar structure. **1939** S. CHANDRASEKHAR *Introd. Study Stellar Struct.* ii. 40 An adiabatic..is a polytropic of zero specific heat, and an isothermal a polytropic of infinite heat capacity. **1952** W. M. DEANS tr. *Prandtl's Essent. Fluid Dynamics* v. 391 If we assume a polytropic law for the variation of density with height, $p/p_g = (\rho/\rho_g)^n$, where the suffix *g* refers to the ground. **1968** COX & GIULI *Princ. Stellar Struct.* II. xxiii. 703 A polytropic star is one which obeys an equation of the form $P = K\rho^{(n+1)/n}$, where *n*, the polytropic index..and *K* are constants throughout the star. **1976** *Nature* 17 June 561/1 The moment of inertia of a spherical star can be written $I = km_pNR^2$ where for stable polytropic stars $0{\cdot}04 \leq k \leq 0{\cdot}132$.

polytyke, obs. form of POLITIC.

polytype ('pɒlɪtaɪp). [a. mod.F. *polytype*: see POLY- and TYPE.]

1. A cast, or form of stereotype, made from an intaglio matrix obtained by pressing a woodcut or other plate into semi-fluid metal; also, a copy of an engraving, of printed matter, etc. made from such a cast. Also *attrib.* So **'polytypage** [F. *polytypage*], the art of making polytypes; **'polytype** *v. trans.* [F. *polytyper*], to produce by polytypage.

1802 *Paris as it was* II. lxxxiv. 534 *note*, The learned Camus, in his 'Historical Sketch of Polytypage and Stereotypage'. **1839** T. C. HANSARD in *Encycl. Brit.* (ed. 7) XVIII. 567/1 (*heading*) Of Polytypage. *Ibid.* 567/2 Guillot ..reported that from one engraving, for the 400 livres assignats, he had struck or polytyped 897 mother-punches and 1487 daughters. *Ibid.*, Didot..issued proposals for printing polytyped editions of the classics. *Ibid.* 568/1 Professor Wilson of Glasgow..thought it possible to make polytypes of glass from engraved copperplates. **1864** WEBSTER, *Polytype, a.*,..as, a polytype plate. **1888** *Pall Mall G.* 28 Nov. 6/1 A handsome quarto volume with portraits, twenty phototypes, and three polytypes.

2. *Cryst.* A polytypic form of a substance.

In quot. 1916 rendering G. *polytypie* polytypism.

1916 *Chem. Abstr.* X. 872 (*heading*) The various modifications of carborundum and the occurrence of polytypes. **1922** *Mineral. Abstr.* I. 318 Three modifications or polytypes of carborundum crystals are distinguished as types I, II, and III. **1951** *Phil. Mag.* XLII. 1019 Unstable structures will not grow if the supersaturation is small: but probably most of the observed polytypes of carborundum differ in thermodynamic potential by an amount negligible compared with the supersaturation actually occurring. **1972** *Physics Bull.* Dec. 712/1 The difficult areas of x ray crystallography, such as in the study of martensitically transformed materials, mixed polytypes of a mineral or certain nonstoichiometric oxides, can be opened up by an electron microscope technique. **1974** *Nature* 22 Feb. 537/2 The basic structural unit of tin sulphide polytypes consists of two layers of hexagonal close-packed sulphide ions with smaller tin ions nested between them.

polytypic (pɒlɪ'tɪpɪk), *a.* [f. Gr. πολυ-, POLY- + τυπικ-ός, f. τύπος TYPE.] **1.** Having several variant forms; esp., of a species, including several subspecies or other lower taxa. Also **poly'typical** *a.*

1888 J. T. GULICK in *Linn. Soc. Jrnl., Zool.* XX. 201 Polytypic evolution or Divergent Evolution is any transformation of a species in which different types appear in different sections. **1890** *Amer. Jrnl. Sc.* Ser. III. XXXIX. 22 'A new species' may be one that has been formed by monotypic transformation, the old form disappearing with the production of the new, or it may be one that has arisen through polytypic transformation. **1945** *Bull. Amer. Mus. Nat. Hist.* LXXXV. 16/2 This morphological scope may be almost entirely filled or exploited by known species if the genus has many (is polytypic). **1953** [see ALLOPATRIC *a.*]. **1959** *New Biol.* XXVIII. 81 This process [*sc.* the variation of isolated populations] might produce simply what the systematist calls a polytypic species, consisting of a sequence of subspecies each occupying a distinct geographical region and each somewhat different in ecology. **1970** *Nature* 5 Sept. 1065/1 It is now recognized that *Papio* is a single polytypic species with morphologically different subspecies interbreeding wherever they meet. **1975** *Trans. R. Entomol. Soc.* CXXVI. 613 We will discuss the data for this polytypic species under the four form names.

2. *Cryst.* Exhibiting polytypism (sense 1); of the nature of a polytype.

1944 [see POLYTYPISM 1]. **1974** VERMA & TRIGUNDAYAT in C. N. R. Rao *Solid State Chem.* ii. 52 The list of polytypic substances includes minerals, layer silicates, chalcogenides, and several other inorganic and organic compounds.

3. = POLYTHETIC *a.*

1959 M. BECKNER *Biol. Way of Thought* ii. 25 Polytypic concepts are found in many branches of biological theory, but the clearest instances are afforded by taxonomy. **1961** G. G. SIMPSON *Princ. Animal Taxon.* ii. 43 The defining attributes do not appear in all individuals... The principle (which he calls 'polytypic') has been elucidated at greater length and in ultramodern terms by Beckner.

polytypism (pɒlɪ'taɪpɪz(ə)m). [f. POLYTYP(IC *a.* + -ISM.] **1.** [After G. *polytypie* (H. Baumhauer 1915, in *Zeitschr. f. Krist. u. Min.* LV. 252).] A kind of polymorphism in which a substance occurs in a number of crystalline modifications (polytypes) which differ only in one of the dimensions of the unit cell.

1944 N. W. THIBAULT in *Amer. Mineralogist* XXIX. 266 Following Baumhauer, the phenomenon is called 'polytypism' the adjective being 'polytypic' and each one of the different modifications a 'type'. **1951** *Phil. Mag.* XLII. 1016 It has long been recognized that the relationship between the various forms of carborundum is so close as to deserve a special name 'polytypism'. **1973** L. SUCHOW in P. F. Weller *Solid State Chem. & Physics* I. ii. 130 All compounds exhibiting polytypism are..of the layer-structure type. **1974** VERMA & TRIGUNDAYAT in C. N. R. Rao *Solid State Chem.* ii. 52 The modifications, called polytypes or simply types, differ only in the arrangement of packing of the close-packed planes of the solids... In this sense the polytypism may be termed one-dimensional polymorphism, although its origin seems to be distinctly different from the latter.

2. *Biol.* The occurrence of several variant forms within a single species. Also **'polytypy** in the same sense.

1949 W. F. ALBRIGHT *Archaeol. of Palestine* iii. 57 The polytypism now known to be characteristic of early man is equally characteristic of dogs, whose classification as a single species is not disputed by zoologists. **1961** G. G. SIMPSON *Princ. Animal Taxon.* iv. 135 In cases of extreme polytypy, first consideration should be given to making the taxon less unwieldy by use of intermediate lower taxa or subgroups.

polyue, obs. form of PULLEY.

polyunsaturated (ˌpɒlɪʌn'sætjʊəreɪtɪd), *a. Chem.* Also **poly-unsaturated.** [f. POLY- + UNSATURATED *ppl. a.*] Containing more than one multiple bond between carbon atoms at which addition can normally occur; applied esp. to fatty acids in which the hydrocarbon chain has more than one multiple bond, which occur esp. in some vegetable oils.

1932 *Biochem. Jrnl.* XXVI. 1978 The marine flora contains poly-unsaturated fatty acids of high molecular weight similar to those found in the fat of fishes, although in very small amounts. **1958** *Jrnl. Sci. Food & Agric.* IX. 779 In animal tissues the glycerophosphatides are outstanding in their high content of long-chain polyunsaturated acids. **1960** *Farmer & Stockbreeder* 22 Mar. 133/1 Polyunsaturated fats for peak condition, healthy skin and coat, more efficient metabolism. **1961** *Sunday Times* 7 May 36/3 American housewives,..concerned about their husbands' health, are shopping for 'poly-unsaturated fats'. The rush is on because medical research has established a connection between arterial diseases and the level of cholesterol in the blood—and cholesterol seems to be formed chiefly from the intake of the 'saturated fats', particularly animal and dairy fats. **1970** *New Scientist* 19 Feb. 356/2 It might also be possible to increase the proportion of poly-unsaturated acids in ruminant tissue fats. **1973** *Which?* Feb. 54 Butter generally has 2 per cent polyunsaturated fatty acids. **1977** B. PYM *Quartet in Autumn* xiii. 115 A tub of polyunsaturated margarine. **1979** *Times* 7 Dec. 10/3 'Polyunsaturated' has become a totem word... The idea that heart attacks can be avoided by replacing saturated fats in the diet with polyunsaturated fats has been promoted with great skill and large budgets.

So **polyun'saturate** *sb.*, a polyunsaturated fatty acid; also as *adj.*

1950 *Arch. Biochem.* XXV. 6 Polyunsaturates were also concentrated in high amounts in the liver fatty acids. **1962** *Seattle Sunday Times* (Sunday Pictorial) 25 Mar. 18/2 (Advt.), It's a face cream that contains essential polyunsaturates. That's right—polyunsaturates, the natural elements you've been reading so much about that are so important to your health. **1962** *Chicago Sun-Times* 20 July 28/3 Maybe, so current thinking goes, we would be better off in the long run to reduce our costly animal fats and substitute the vegetable (polyunsaturate) fats and oils. **1974** *Observer* (Colour Suppl.) 17 Mar. 15/1 There are doubts.. about the side-effects of the various polyunsaturate oils used. *Ibid.*, Only a few vegetable oils are high in polyunsaturates.

polyuresis: see POLY-.

polyurethane (pɒlɪ'jʊrəθeɪn). Formerly also **-an.** [f. POLY- + URETHANE.] Any of a large class of synthetic resins and plastics consisting of or made from polymers with the units linked by the group −NH·CO·O−, which are made esp. by the reaction of polyisocyanates with polyhydroxy compounds and are important commercially as plastic foams, as fibres, and in paints, adhesives, synthetic rubbers, films, etc. Also *attrib.* and *Comb.*, esp. ***polyurethane foam.***

1944 *Chem. Abstr.* XXXVIII. 381 (*heading*) Polyurethans and polyureas. **1945** *Chem. & Engin. News* 25 Sept. 1615/1 Among the new or less well-known polymers which they [*sc.* the Germans] have been manufacturing are polyvinyl ethers ..and polyurethanes. **1945** *Mod. Plastics* Oct. 152F/2 Polyurethane resin was used on a small scale as an adhesive in aircraft construction. **1957** B. A. DOMBROW *Polyurethanes* i. 8 In the latter part of 1947..Lockheed Aircraft Corporation began independently to develop polyurethane foam systems for use in radome construction and in filling aircraft components. **1958** *Engineering* 7 Feb. 167/2 A lightweight portable shelter suitable for aircraft, vehicles or stored goods, consisting of a tubular light-alloy framework covered with polyurethane-proofed nylon. **1964** *Which?* Aug. 254/1 Polyurethane has become known in the form of plastic foam for sponges among other things, but is now finding its way into the textile field. **1968** W. WARWICK *Surfriding in N.Z.* 16/3 At present surfboards are being constructed from the material polyurethane. **1969** *Sears Catal.* Spring/Summer 9 Exclusive 3-inch thick cushions.. softly padded with shredded Serofoam polyurethane. **1971** *New Scientist* 10 June 630/2 Polyurethane-coated fabrics are still at an early stage of development. **1974** *Nature* 16 Aug. 526/3 Polyurethane foam is sprayed on to the inside of a lightweight aluminium mould.

Hence as *v. trans.*, to coat or protect with polyurethane.

1977 B. RANDALL *Fan* 22 Don't go in the dining room, I polyurethaned the floor. **1978** J. UPDIKE *Coup* (1979) iii. 109 I've seen blueprints, concrete wings supported by polyurethaned nylon cables. **1979** M. PAGE *Pilate Plot* ix. 137 Washed Chinese carpets on the sanded and polyurethaned floorboards.

polyuria to **polyuronide**: see POLY-.

polyvalent (pə'lɪvələnt), *a.* [Hybrid f. POLY- + VALENT.]

1. a. *Chem.* = MULTIVALENT. Now usu. with pronunc. (pɒlɪ'veɪlənt).

1881 WILLIAMSON in *Nature* 1 Sept. 417/1 Polyvalent atoms can combine partly with one element, partly with another, and also..like atoms can combine with one another. **1950** N. V. SIDGWICK *Chem. Elements* I. 177 The polyvalent state of gold..is much more stable than the monovalent. **1964** N. G. CLARK *Mod. Org. Chem.* xxiv. 510 With all other polyvalent species of atom accounted for, the side chain..must consist of three linked carbon atoms. **1975** *Nature* 6 Nov. 19/1 The formation of a ring structure by a protein factor or possibly polyvalent ions, the use of the ring as a nucleating centre, [etc.]..were discussed.

b. *Med.* = MULTIVALENT *a.* b.

1912 *Amer. Jrnl. Med. Sci.* CXLIV. 815 The complement fixation test (using a polyvalent antigen) for gonococcus antibodies should prove an addition to our methods of diagnosticating between..gonococcus infection and..other causes. **1951** WHITBY & HYNES *Med. Bacteriol.* (ed. 5) vi. 72 When an antigen in colloidal solution is mixed with antibody under suitable conditions a precipitate of antigen-antibody complex appears. Most of the precipitate consists of antibody, since antibody molecules in general are larger than those of antigens, whilst antigens are polyvalent and each molecule combines with two or more molecules of antibody. **1975** *Nature* 11 Sept. 103/1 Interaction of divalent or polyvalent ligands (for example, antibodies, lectins) with cell surface structures on lymphocytes and many other cell types induces redistribution of the largely diffuse binding sites into clusters and into highly polarised single aggregates or 'caps'.

2. *Med.* Having the property of counteracting various poisons or affording immunity against various species of micro-organism.

1904 *Brit. Med. Jrnl.* 10 Sept. 574 One can easily obtain polyvalent antivenenes. **1905** H. D. ROLLESTON *Dis. Liver* 155 The hypodermic injection of a bactericidal serum which is polyvalent. **1929** [see BOTULIN]. **1965** C. ANDREWES *Common Cold* xix. 168 'Polyvalent' vaccines—those effective against many bacteria or viruses—are very fine in theory. **1966** *Jrnl. Immunol.* XCVII. 517/2 A third antigen preparation consisted of a single polyvalent antigen prepared by combining equal amounts of the 12 flexner stock antigens and a stock *Shigella sonnei* antigen.

3. = MULTIVALENT *a.* 3.

1957 S. ULLMANN *Style in French Novel* 20 Stylistic elements, it will be remembered, are 'polyvalent'; the same device may produce several effects, and conversely, the same effect may be obtained from several devices. **1960** E. DELAVENAY *Introd. Machine Transl.* iii. 36 The grammatical value of polyvalent words. **1966** *New Statesman* 25 Feb. 266/2 The colour-symbolism in [Tarsis'] *Red and Black* is pervasive and bafflingly polyvalent. **1975** J. DE BRES tr. *Mandel's Late Capitalism* viii. 268 Full automation reduces the number of semi-skilled workers and gives rise to a new and highly skilled polyvalent work force. **1977** *Word 1972* XXVIII. 294 The analyst will be tempted to ignore the systems based on very general concepts yielding the simplest description for all languages in favor of a very specific system adapted to the specific language of the texts to be recorded: the kind of simplicity he will look for is of the monovalent rather than of the polyvalent type.

Hence **po'lyvalence**, the character of being polyvalent; multivalence; also stressed *poly'valence*.

1902 *Brit. Med. Jrnl.* 12 Apr. 918 The polyvalence of the amboceptor would be more difficult to understand [etc.]. **1971** *Archivum Linguisticum* II. 104 Now he writes..about the polyvalence of the injunctive—including *s*, *ā* and *ē* stems. In spite of this polyvalence he thinks that there is a common core in the subjunctive and preterite use of these stems.

polyvinyl (pɒlɪˈvaɪnɪl, -ˈvaɪnaɪl). [f. POLY- + VINYL.] **a.** Used *attrib.* in the names of polymeric substances derived from vinyl compounds, as **polyvinyl acetal**, any of a class of synthetic resins prepared by condensing polyvinyl alcohol with an aldehyde (sometimes *spec.* acetaldehyde), and mainly used, esp. polyvinyl butyral (see below), in safety glass and in lacquers and paints; **polyvinyl acetate**, a fairly soft plastic having the structure $-[CH_2-CH(O{\cdot}CO{\cdot}CH_3)]_n-$, which is made by polymerizing vinyl acetate and is used chiefly in paints and adhesives; abbrev. *PVA* (s.v. P II. d); **polyvinyl alcohol**, any of a series of polymers consisting wholly or largely of the repeating unit $-[CH_2-CHOH]-$ which are prepared by hydrolysis of polyvinyl esters and have a wide range of uses, e.g. as emulsifiers, adhesives, coatings, films, and fibres; abbrev. *PVA* (s.v. P II. d); **polyvinyl butyral**, the most widely used of the polyvinyl acetals (see above), which is prepared from butyraldehyde; **polyvinyl chloride**, any of various thermoplastics consisting of or made from a polymer having the structure $-[CH_2-CHCl]_n-$ and made by polymerizing vinyl chloride, which are produced in a wide variety of rigid and plasticized forms and are characterized esp. by their toughness, chemical inertness, and electrical resistivity; abbrev. *PVC* (s.v. P II. d); **polyvinyl pyrrolidone**, a water-soluble polymer of vinyl pyrrolidone which is physiologically harmless and has a great variety of applications, esp. in solution, e.g. as a synthetic blood plasma substitute, as a thickening, suspending, or binding agent in the cosmetic, drug, and food processing industries, and in fibres and films; abbrev. *PVP* (s.v. P II. d).

All these often occur as single words.

1933 *Industr. & Engin. Chem.* Feb. 129/1 The structure of polyvinyl acetal. **1944** [see PHENOLIC *a.* b]. **1973** *Materials & Technol.* VI. viii. 552 The use of polyvinyl butyral for making safety glass was patented in 1938 and this has since become one of the most important applications, certainly in America. The next important consumer of polyvinyl acetals is the lacquer and paint industry (for wash-primers). **1927** *Brit. Chem. Abstr.* A. 1051/2 Hydrolysis of polyvinyl acetate yields polyvinyl alcohol which resembles starch in its insolubility in organic media. **1958** W. M. SMITH *Vinyl Resins* i. 19 Polyvinyl acetate emulsions as a replacement for conventional grain starch are stated to withstand as many as 15 launderings. **1967** W. GAUNT *Compan. Painting* ii. 85 Some modern artists have..found congenial qualities in such synthetic paints as ripolin and polyvinyl acetate. **1972** *Homes & Gardens* Mar. 106/2 In their infancy, emulsion paints were regarded with some suspicion, partly because early ones, based on a polyvinylacetate (pva) medium, tended to become brittle and flake off. **1927** Polyvinyl alcohol [see *polyvinyl acetate* above]. **1962** J. T. MARSH *Self-Smoothing Fabrics* x. 133 There are occasions where a slightly stiff finish is required and polyvinyl alcohol is a popular choice of additive in this connection. **1971** D. POTTER *Brit. Eliz. Stamps* vi. 68 A synthetic adhesive was invented. Completely non-toxic, colourless, odourless and tasteless, it is known as Polyvinyl Alcohol, and familiarly named PVA by philatelists. **1973** *Materials & Technol.* VI. viii. 548 The usual method of preparing polyvinyl alcohol is by the hydrolysis of a polyvinyl ester, generally polyvinyl acetate. **1943** *Industr. & Engin. Chem.* Feb. 175/2 In polyvinyl butyral resin..certain fillers appear to have reinforcing action. **1955** *Sci. News Let.* 16 Apr. 247/1 Adhesives for bonding two pieces of glass together are best made of polyvinyl-butyral resin mixed with modified phenol. **1973** Polyvinyl butyral [see *polyvinyl acetal* above]. **1933** *Industr. & Engin. Chem.* Feb. 129/1 Co-polymerization of vinyl chloride and vinyl acetate gives a better resin than the mere admixture of polyvinyl chloride and polyvinyl acetate. **1937** *Chem. Abstr.* XXXI. 6434 A mixt. of water with polyvinyl-chloride..is used for coating glass plates and is dried upon them, and then the coated plates are united by the action of heat and pressure. **1945** *Electronic Engin.* XVI. 499/3 Plastic sleeving of the polyvinylchloride type is the real answer to all these problems. **1958** *Engineering* 7 Mar. 294/2 The folding top is in leather-cloth, coated with polyvinyl chloride. **1976** *Nature* 3 June 409/1 Each trough held 50 oysters on a false bottom consisting of polyethylene grids resting on polyvinylchloride pipe. **1945** *Chem. Abstr.* XXXIX. 5408 Such solns. [i.e. blood plasma substitutes] are prepared by adding polyvinylpyrrolidone..to a physiol. salt soln. **1957** *Financial Times Ann. Rev. Brit. Industry* 86/3 Experiments have shown that polyvinyl pyrrolidone..used as a blood thickener can be readily broken down..to..the most useful molecular size for medical use. **1974** M. C. GERALD *Pharmacol.* ix. 164 The plasma substitutes, dextran and polyvinylpyrrolidone (PVP), are also histamine releasers.

b. Any of the plastics or synthetic resins made by polymerizing a compound containing the vinyl group, $CH_2=CH-$; applied *esp.* to those derived from a compound usu. designated as vinyl (see prec. sense), but sometimes extended to include polyvinylidenes, polystyrene, etc. Freq. *attrib.*

1933 *Industr. & Engin. Chem.* Feb. 129/1 To render the normal polyvinyl resin more water-resistant, it is converted partly or wholly to the acetal by reaction with an aldehyde, usually formaldehyde or acetaldehyde. **1937** *Brit. Plastics* IX. 172/1 Vinyl esters of both inorganic and organic acids are well known..raw materials for conversion to polyvinyls. **1940** 'PLASTES' *Plastics in Industry* ii. 15 More recently polyvinyl plastics have been employed as floorcloth, long-playing phonograph records, [etc.]. *Ibid.*, An interesting series of thermo-plastics which resemble the polyvinyls closely. **1946** *Nature* 16 Nov. 689/2 The use of methacrylate esters and the various polyvinyls is increasing in these fields [*sc.* arts and crafts]. **1963** [see POLYVINYLIDENE b]. **1966** *Punch* 26 Jan. 116/3 Palpitations on finding sleek strangers at the front door in answer to my inquiry about polyvinyl tiling. **1969** R. MAYER *Dict. Art Terms & Techniques* 422/2 Few of the vinyl products are practicable for use in artists' materials... One exception is a polyvinyl isolating varnish containing isopropyl alcohol that thins with alcohol.

polyvinylidene (ˌpɒlɪvaɪˈnɪlɪdiːn, -vaɪˈnaɪlɪdiːn). *Chem.* [f. POLY- + VINYLIDENE.] **a.** Used *attrib.* in the names of substances which are polymers of vinylidene compounds, esp. ***polyvinylidene chloride***, any of a class of resinous polymers of vinylidene chloride which have the structure $-[CH_2-CCl_2]_n-$, and have a wide range of applications, esp. as impact- and chemical-resistant films and fibres.

1940 *Chem. Rev.* XXVI. 163 Natta and Rigamonti.. found..polyvinylidene chloride to be quite highly crystalline. **1942** *Industr. & Engin. Chem.* Mar. 327/2 These polyvinylidene chloride plastics are known by the trade name, 'Saran'. **1964** *Discovery* Oct. 17/1 The lamination consists of an aluminum foil and three plastic films—one of polythene, another of polyvinylidene chloride and a third of polyester. **1966** *McGraw-Hill Encycl. Sci. & Technol.* X. 496/2 Films of polyvinylidene chloride, and especially the copolymer containing about 15% of vinyl chloride, are resistant to moisture and gases. **1973** *Materials & Technol.* VI. viii. 547 Because of its resistance to chemicals, polyvinylidene fluoride is used for tubes, valves, and pumps in the chemical industry. **1975** P. BROWNE *Bodywork Maintenance* vi. 79/2 Cloths such as Tygan, woven from polyvinylidene chloride filaments, need an interlayer..to prevent a chemical reaction between the Tygan and the rubber.

b. Any of the synthetic resins prepared from vinylidene compounds. Freq. *attrib.*

1941 *Plastics* V. 249/2 (*caption*) Flow sheet showing production of polyvinylidene polymers from petroleum and brine. **1960** *Times Rev. Industry* Sept. 65/3 The tendency seems to be for polythene yarns to replace some of the earlier types such as polyvinylidene. **1963** A. J. HALL *Textile Sci.* ii. 18 (*table*) Polyvinyls and polyvinylidenes. **1972** *Homes & Gardens* Mar. 107 One firm has now introduced a full gloss emulsion paint based on a polyvinyledene [*sic*] medium.

polyvoltine: see POLY-.

polywater (ˈpɒlɪwɔːtə(r)). [f. POLY- + WATER *sb.*] A supposed polymeric form of water having properties markedly different from those of ordinary water and reported to have been found in fine capillary tubes.

1969 E. R. LIPPINCOTT et al. in *Science* 27 June 1482/3 The properties, therefore, are no longer anomalous but rather, those of a newly found substance—polymeric water or polywater. **1969** *Daily Tel.* 13 Sept. 22/3 American scientists have confirmed the existence of a new kind of water which freezes at 40deg C and boils at 500deg C... The new water, known as 'polywater' has a density of about 40 per cent. greater than ordinary water. **1972** *Britannica Yearbk. Sci. & Future 1971* 216 Anomalous water (or polywater), which has attracted much attention in recent months, was shown to be not an unusual form of water but ordinary water containing ionic impurities. **1972** F. FRANKS *Water* I. i. 13 During 1969 the 'polywater' bandwagon began to roll. *Ibid.*, A climax was provided by a warning to scientists against experimenting with polywater as this might affect the oceans, turning them solid. **1975** J. CLIFFORD in *Ibid.* V. ii. 119 Defenders of the water polymer idea have suggested that polywater could be a weakly bonded complex that disintegrates under electron impact and does not appear in the mass spectrum.

polyxenic: see POLY-.

‖**Polyzoa** (pɒlɪˈzəʊə), *sb. pl. Zool.* Sing. **polyzoon** (-ˈzəʊɒn). [mod.L., f. Gr. πολυ-, POLY- + ζῷον an animal.] A class of compound or 'colonial' aquatic (chiefly marine) invertebrate animals (sometimes reckoned as a group of *Mollusca*), of small size and various forms, often plant-like; popularly called *moss-animalcules*, *sea-mosses*, *sea-mats*, etc. Also called BRYOZOA.

[**1830** J. V. THOMPSON *Zool. Res. & Illustr.* v. 89 (*heading*) On Polyzoa, a new animal discovered as an inhabitant of some zoophites. *Ibid.* 92 The Polyzoa will probably be found in many dissimilar Genera of the Zoophytes.] **1842** BRANDE *Dict. Sc.*, etc., *Polyzoons, Polyzoa*, a class of compound animals, resembling in their organs of support the Sertularians, but in their internal organization approaching nearly to the compound Ascidians. **1847** G. JOHNSTON *Brit. Zooph.* (ed. 2) I. 256 The Polyzoa or ascidian polypes the Creator has cast in the mould not of the Radiata, but of the Mollusca. **1877** HUXLEY *Anat. Inv. Anim.* viii. 468 The resemblance of the larval Brachiopod to a Polyzoon, and especially to Loxosoma, is striking. **1901** *Cambr. Nat. Hist.* II. 475 The name Polyzoa being employed by the majority of English writers..while Bryozoa is employed by practically all the Continental writers.

b. A name for the colonial radiolarians, also called *Polycyttaria*: see POLYCYTTARIAN.

Hence **poly'zoal** *a.* = next, a.

1856 G. J. ALLMAN *Monogr. Fresh-Water Polyzoa* 3 The investigations of Trembley and Baker..clearly demonstrated..all the essential characters of polyzoal structure.

polyzoan (pɒlɪˈzəʊən), *a.* and *sb. Zool.* [f. POLYZOA + -AN.] **a.** *adj.* Belonging to or having the character of the *Polyzoa*; = BRYOZOAN *a.* and *sb.* **b.** *sb.* A polyzoan animal, a polyzoon; an individual polyp or zooid of a polyzoan colony.

1856 P. H. GOSSE *Man. Marine Zool. Brit. Isles* II. 5 A tiny Annelid or other animal, caught by the bird's-head of a Polyzoan and tightly held, would presently die. **1864** WEBSTER, *Polyzoan*, one of a compound group among the *Bryozoa*... *Dana*. **1880** T. HINCKS *Hist. Brit. Marine Polyzoa* I. p. xvii, The tentacular sheath is an important element..of the ordinary Polyzoan type. **1924** S. J. HICKSON *Introd. Study Recent Corals* viii. 159 Zooecia.. build up the various kinds of branching, net-like, or encrusting structures of the Polyzoan corals. **1959** *Jrnl. Exper. Biol.* XXXVI. 613 (*heading*) Experiments on the selection of algal substrates by polyzoan larvae.

polyzoary (pɒlɪˈzəʊərɪ). *Zool.* Also in Lat. form **polyzoarium** (ˌpɒlɪzəʊˈɛərɪəm), pl. **-ia.** [ad. mod.L. *polyzoārium*, f. POLYZOA + *-arium*, -ARY[1].] The polypary or polypidom of a colony of *Polyzoa*, or the colony as a whole.

1856 GOSSE *Man. Marine Zool.* II. 5 The entire assemblage of cells springing from one root-thread, or originating from a single cell, is called the *polyzoary*. **1872** DARWIN *Orig. Spec.* vii. (ed. 6) 192 [Avicularia] Their movement caused the whole polyzoary to tremble. **1874** WOOD *Nat. Hist.* 663 The general shape of the whole group, or 'polyzoary',..is very shrub-like, standing bodily erect, and giving out branches by two and two. **1877** HUXLEY *Anat. Inv. Anim.* viii. 459 The polyzoarium of Cristatella is free and creeps about as a whole.

Hence **polyzoarial** (-zəʊˈɛərɪəl) *a.*, pertaining or relating to a polyzoary.

1885 E. R. LANKESTER in *Encycl. Brit.* XIX. 431/2 'Ectocyst' and 'endocyst'..form part of a special 'polyzoarial' nomenclature, but do not appear to be any longer needful.

polyzoic (pɒlɪˈzəʊɪk), *a.* [f. POLYZOA + -IC. So F. *polyzoique*.]

1. *Zool.* Pertaining to or of the nature of the Polyzoa; composed of a number of individual zooids constituting a 'colony', compound, colonial.

1855 *Eng. Cycl., Nat. Hist.* III. 858/2 The Polyzoic type [of Mollusca] itself presents five subordinate modifications in the five principal orders of the group. **1861** HULME tr. *Moquin-Tandon* II. ii. 60 Duvernoy believed in the polyzoic nature of the Tænias and similar animals. **1903** [see POLYPSYCHIC].

b. In *Sporozoa*, Applied to a spore which produces many germs or sporozoites.

1901 G. N. CALKINS *Protozoa* 153 The archispores..form a definite number of sporozoites, varying from one (monozoic) or two (dizoic) to many (polyzoic).

2. *Anthropol.* Characterized by a belief in many imaginary living beings.

1886 *Encycl. Brit.* XX. 367/2 Perhaps the best name for this first stage of religious development might be the 'polyzoic' stage.

So **polyzoism** (-ˈzəʊɪz(ə)m), the character of being polyzoic (sense 1).

1890 W. JAMES *Princ. Psychol.* I. vi. 179 It may be called the theory of polyzoism or multiple monadism. **1903** MYERS *Hum. Personality* I. Gloss., *Polyzoism*, the property, in a complex organism, of being composed of minor and quasi-independent organisms (like the *polyzoa* or 'sea-mats').

polyzome ('pɒlɪzəʊm). *Geom.* [f. POLY- + Gr. ζῶμα girdle.] (See quot.) Hence **poly'zomal** *a.*

1867 CAYLEY *Coll. Math. Papers* VI. 470 If *U*, *V*, &c., are rational and integral functions.., all of the same degree *r*, in regard to the coordinates (*x*,*y*,*z*), then $\sqrt{U} + \sqrt{V}$ + &c. is a polyzome, and the curve $\sqrt{U} + \sqrt{V}$ + &c. = *O* a polyzomal curve.

polyzonal (pɒlɪ'zəʊnəl), *a.* [f. POLY- + ZONAL.] Applied to a form of lens invented by Brewster, composed of a number of annular segments or zones; chiefly used in lighthouses.

1831 BREWSTER *Optics* xxxviii. 323 Those compound lenses, to which I have given the name of *polyzonal* lenses. **1863** TYNDALL *Heat* xvii. 504 With a large polyzonal lens, Melloni converged an image of the moon upon his pile. *c* **1865** J. WYLDE in *Circ. Sc.* I. 258/2 A polyzonal lens, such as was employed..at the South Foreland lighthouse.

polyzooid (pɒlɪ'zəʊɔɪd), *a. Zool.* [f. POLYZOA + -OID.] Resembling or of the nature of the Polyzoa; polyzoan, polyzoic.

1884 tr. *Claus's Zool.* 210 The polyzooid nature of these [sponge-stocks] is made apparent by the presence of many oscula.

polyzoon, sing. of POLYZOA, q.v.

polyzoonite (pɒlɪ'zəʊənaɪt). *Zool. rare.* [irreg. f. POLYZOON + -ITE[1]: cf. POLYPITE.] An individual zooid of a polyzoon.

1871 T. R. JONES *Anim. Kingd.* (ed. 4) 504 When the Polyzoonite retires into its abode, the setæ and soft termination of the cell are gradually folded inwards, in the manner exhibited in the annexed figures..representing the various stages of the process.

Pom[1] (pɒm). Also **pom.** Colloq. abbrev. of POMERANIAN *sb.*

1904 *Outing* Feb. 484/2 Collies and 'poms' in America have hardly maintained their status because of this coat trouble. **1910** *Bazaar, Exchange & Mart* 10 June 1523/2 *(heading)* Coming shows... Dogs... Manchester (Poms). **1911** F. T. BARTON *My Bk. Little Dogs* iii. 33 The Pekinese and the Pom are the most popular toy dogs at the present time. **1923** R. MACAULAY *Told by Idiot* II. xxi. 138 Rome.. drove elegantly in hansoms, often with an enormous wolf-hound or a couple of poms. **1939** T. S. ELIOT *Old Possum's Pract. Cats* 27 And the Pugs and the Poms..will now and again join in to the fray. **1956** E. BERCKMAN *Beckoning Dream* vi. 46 Lydia..bred miniature Poms. In the vast living-room..twenty little dogs disported themselves. **1973** R. HILL *Ruling Passion* II. i. 85 'Not much of a guard-dog,' he said. 'It's a pom,' Pascoe said patiently.

Pom[2] (pɒm). *Austral.* and *N.Z. colloq.* Also **pom.** Abbrev. of POMMY *sb.* (*a.*)

1919 W. H. DOWNING *Digger Dial.* 38 *Pommy*, an English soldier. *Pom*, see *Pommy*. **1941** BAKER *Dict. Austral. Slang* 56 *Pom*, an Englishman. **1946** F. SARGESON *That Summer* 92 He was a big matelot, though not a Pom, it was easy to tell he was a Pig Islander. **1957** *Economist* 9 Nov. 510/2 New British migrants are more readily assimilated than continental Europeans. Australians do not consider the 'Poms' as foreigners. **1963** A. LUBBOCK *Austral. Roundabout* 83 'Be seein' yer soon in England... Good on yer, Pom.' **1975** D. BLOODWORTH *Clients of Omega* ix. 84 You a Pom or something, sister?.. You've got a swine of a Pom accent. **1977** *Bulletin* (Sydney) 22 Jan. 20/1 And there's New Zealand to come; and then the Centenary Test against the Poms.

Pom[3] (pɒm). Also **pom.** The proprietary name of a brand of dried and powdered cooked potato.

1947 *Trade Marks Jrnl.* 23 Apr. 234/1 Pom... Cooked potatoes and potato preparations..M.P.P. (Products) Limited,..Norwich; Manufacturers. **1955** G. BAND *Road to Rakaposhi* xii. 136 The menu was..complicated..stewed steak and pom, fruit cake and tea. **1968** *Economist* 15 June 64/3 Oddly enough, the greatest potential market for dried food is those old wartime standbys—dried milk and dried potatoes. Dehydrated potato, indistinguishable from the 'pom' of the 1940s,..now has a market worth £2 million a year. **1970** *Times* 26 Nov. 17/4 The late André Simon compiled his Dictionary of Gastronomy during the War years, presumably to cheer himself up among the snoek and pom.

‖**poma**[1] ('pəʊmə) *Anat.* [a. Gr. πῶμα, -ατ- lid.] The occipital operculum of the brain of a monkey.

1889 *Buck's Handbk. Med. Sc.* VIII. 162/1 Since the dorsal termination of the occipital fissure is covered by the poma, there results an apparent continuity of the pomatic and occipital fissures. **1895** in *Syd. Soc. Lex.*

Poma[2] ('pəʊmə). *N. Amer.* Also **poma.** [f. the name of J. *Pomagalski*, its inventor.] The proprietary name of a type of ski-lift having detachable hangers; so ***Poma lift, Pomalift.***

1954 *Amer. Ski Ann. & Skiing Jrnl.* Jan. 55/1 The POMA lift at Arapahoe Basin, once the wooden towers were in place, was erected in sixteen days in the worst possible weather. **1955** *Ski Mag.* Oct. 51/2 (Advt.), Big news at Big Bromley..a new 2,190 ft. Poma lift has been installed. **1957** T. KESTING *Outdoor Encycl.* 403/2 On the Pomalift—a kind of platter-pull—the hangers are stored at the bottom and clamped onto the cable as needed. **1963** *Amer. Speech* XXXVIII. 206 Skiers usually do not differentiate between *platter pull* and *poma*; the latter seems to have become the universally accepted term for both types working with disks. **1968** *Globe & Mail* (Toronto) 13 Jan. 35/3 Other Muskoka resorts offering modern accommodation as well as T-bar or pomalift include Muskoka Sands, [etc.]. **1970** *Official Gaz.* (U.S. Patent Office) 14 Apr. TM 80/2 Jean Pomagalski S.A., Fontaine-Grenoble, France... *Poma* for cable transport or towing apparatus and installations—namely, cable cars, gondola-lifts, chair-lifts, ski-lifts. **1973** P. A. WHITNEY *Snowfire* vi. 105 A chair lift, with T-bar, J-bar and poma lift off to our right. **1977** *Forest Sci.* XXIII. 168 Area 1..is only affected by skiing activity (ski runs, poma lifts).

pomace ('pʌməs). Forms: 6 **pomes, pomois,** 7– **pomace**; also 7 **pumis,** 8–9 **pom(m)ice, pummice, pummace.** See also POMMEY. [A derivative of L. *pōmum* or F. *pomme* apple: the form *pomace*, if original, appears to correspond to med.L. *pōmācium, pōmātium* cider (? for L. **pōmāceum*); but the sense makes a difficulty, as do also the variant forms.

Cf. also OF. *pomat* (Godef.), in mod. patois of Yères (near Havre) *poma* 'la masse de pommes, après que le pressoir a exprimé le jus': thus exactly = Eng. *pomace*.]

1. The mass of crushed apples in the process of making cider: **a.** after the juice is pressed out; **b.** before the juice is pressed out.

a. 1572 MASCALL *Plant. & Graff.* 6 Though the Pepins be sowen of the pomes of Peares and good Apples. **1664** EVELYN *Kal. Hort.* Dec. (1729) 225 Sow, as yet, Pomace of Cider-Pressings to raise Nurseries. **1676** WORLIDGE *Cyder* (1691) 133 Scalding water wherein you may boyl apple-pumis. **1693** EVELYN *De la Quint. Compl. Gard.* Dict., *Pomace*, is the mash which remains of pressed Apples, after the Sider is made, used for producing of Seedling Stocks in Nursery-Gardens. **1707** MORTIMER *Husb.* (1721) I. 5 If you sow Apple or Crab Kernels, sow the Pummace with them, which will come up the first Year. **1884** T. HARDY *Wessex Tales, Interlopers at Knap* (1889) 157 Where the..dunghills smell of pomace instead of stable-refuse. **1897** *Evesham Jrnl.* 16 Jan., The pomice or must after cider abstraction.

b. 1764 CROKER, etc. *Dict. Arts*, etc. s.v. *Cyder*, The apples are then ground, and the pummice is received in a large open-mouthed vessel. *a* **1825** FORBY *Voc. E. Anglia*, *Pummace*, the mass of apples mashed under a stone roller before they are placed between layers of straw or the cyder-press. **1886** [see POMMEY].

2. *transf.* **a.** Anything crushed or pounded to a pulp. **b.** Any solid refuse whence oil has been expressed or extracted; e.g. the refuse of the menhaden and other fish after the oil has been extracted, formerly known as ***fish-guano, fish-cake, pogy-chum***; also (more fully ***castor pomace***), the cake left after expressing castor oil from the beans; both used as fertilizers.

a. 1555 W. WATREMAN *Fardle Facions* I. vi. 101 Then put they the fisshe into the hollowes of the rocques, and beate it to pomois. **1705** HICKERINGILL *Priest-cr.* II. i. 13 Thus we poor frail Mortals (like Corn between two great contrary Mill-stones) are bruised to Pommice. **1766** *Compl. Farmer* s.v. *Madder*, These roots are cut..and pounded in mortars ..till they are reduced into a kind of pummice.

b. 1861 *Agric. Maine* VI. 44 The residuum left after expressing the oil, that is the cake, pumice, or as commonly called, the *chum*, which contains nearly the whole fertilizing portions of the fish. **1864** *Ibid.* IX. 43 Fish pomace, or the residuum of herring after the oil is pressed out, is greedily eaten by sheep, swine and fowl. **1898** *U.S. Comm. Fish & Fisheries* XXII. 479 The 'fish cuttings' and refuse fish which accumulate at the canneries are made into pomace and sold for fertilizer.

1877 *Rep. Connecticut Board of Agric.* (1878) 395 In some [fertilizers], castor pomace, leather scraps, and other cheaper materials are used. **1878** *Ann. Rep. Connecticut Agric. Exper. Station* (1879) 38 Castor Pomace,..the crushed seeds of the castor-oil plant after the extraction of the oil—is a long-known and well-tested fertilizer. **1895** *Yearbk. U.S. Depmt. Agric.* (1896) 192 Castor-oil plants... The pomace is considered valuable for fertilizing purposes.

†**3.** The head, heart, lights, liver, and windpipe of a sheep or lamb. *Obs.*

1688 R. HOLME *Armoury* III. iii. 83/2 Pomass of a sheep, is all the Intrals. *Ibid.* 88/1 Sheep Pummices is the Head, Heart, Lights, Liver, and Wind-Pipe of a Sheep all hanging together. **1750** E. SMITH *Compl. Housew.* (ed. 14) 66 To hash a Lamb's Pumice.

4. *Comb.*, as **pomace-fly** = DROSOPHILA; **pomace-shovel**, a shovel used for pomace (in sense 1).

1886 T. HARDY *Woodlanders* xxviii, The blades of the pomace-shovels, which had been converted to steel mirrors by the action of the malic acid. **1897** J. H. COMSTOCK *Insect Life* 185 As these insects are often abundant about pomace in cider-mills and wineries, they have been termed pomace-flies. **1924** J. A. THOMSON *Sci. Old & New* xxvii. 152 When the pomace-fly, Drosophila, is feeding on fermenting fruit, it must have yeasts to help it. **1946** C. T. BRUES *Insect Dietary* v. 194 The pomace fly, *Drosophila*, so successfully used by geneticists to elucidate the processes of inheritance, has likewise served..to demonstrate some of the food relations of microphagous insects.

pomacentroid (pəʊmə'sɛntrɔɪd), *a.* and *sb.* [f. mod.L. *Pōmacentrus* (Lacépède 1802), generic name (f. Gr. πῶμα lid, cover + κέντρον centre) + -OID.] **a.** *adj.* Of, pertaining to, or resembling the *Pomacentridæ*, a family of tropical fishes, of which *Pomacentrus* is the typical genus. **b.** *sb.* A fish of this family.

1890 in *Cent. Dict.*

pomaceous (pəʊ'meɪʃəs), *a.*[1] [f. mod.L. *pōmāce-us* (f. L. *pōmum* apple) + -OUS: see -ACEOUS.]

1. Of, pertaining to, or consisting of apples.

1706 BAYNARD in Sir J. Floyer *Hot & Cold Bath.* II. (1706) 128 Apples and pomaceous Juices, are the greatest Pectorals. **1708** J. PHILIPS *Cyder* II. 58 English Plains Blush with pomaceous Harvests, breathing Sweets. **1757** DYER *Fleece* I. 61 Lawns, and purple groves Pomaceous.

fig. **1861** *Temple Bar Mag.* I. 486 An extra feast of pomaceous trash, in the shape haply of..*Clarissa Harlowe.*

2. *Bot.* Of the nature of a pome or apple; of or pertaining to the *Pomeæ*, a division of rosaceous trees bearing pomes or pome-like fruits.

1858 MAYNE *Expos. Lex.*, *Pomaceus, Bot.*..pomaceous.

po'maceous, *a.*[2] *rare*$^{-0}$. [f. POMACE + -EOUS.] Resembling or consisting of pomace.

1828 in WEBSTER. **1882** in OGILVIE.

†**po'mada, po'mado.** *Obs.* Also 7 **pommada, -ado, pom(m)ade.** [a. It. *pomada, -ata* (Florio), f. *pomo* pommel of a saddle: see -ADA. In form *pomm-*, after F. *pommade*; see also -ADO.] An exercise of vaulting upon or over a horse by placing one hand on the pommel of the saddle.

1596 NASHE *Saffron Walden* 28 Mercury..to inspire my pen with some of his nimblest Pomados and Sommersets. **1599** B. JONSON *Cynthia's Rev.* II. i, How oft he hath done the whole or the halfe pommado in a seuen-night before. *a* **1697** AUBREY *Brief Lives* (1898) I. 418 He was..very.. active. He did the pomado in the saddle of the third horse in his armour. **1706** PHILLIPS, *Pomada.* **1727–41** CHAMBERS *Cycl.*, *Pomada*, an exercise of vaulting the wooden horse, by laying one hand over the pommel of the saddle.

†**po'made,** *sb.*[1] *Obs. rare*$^{-1}$. [= med.L. *pōmāta* (Du Cange), obs. F. *pommade* (1514 in Godef., from Gascony or Bearn), Pr. *pomada* cider: see POME *sb.*[1], -ADE 1.] A drink made of apples; cider.

1393 LANGL. *P. Pl.* C. XXI. 412 May no pyement ne pomade ne presiouse drynkes Moyste me to þe fulle ne my þurst slake.

pomade (pəʊ'meɪd, ‖pɔmad), *sb.*[2] Also 6–7 **pomado,** 7 **pomada, -ata, pommade.** [a. F. *pommade* (in this sense) = Sp. *pomada*, It. *pomata*. See POMATUM, and cf. prec.] A scented ointment (in which apples are said to have been originally an ingredient) for application to the skin; now used esp. for the skin of the head and for dressing the hair.

pomade divine, name of a healing salve.

1562 WARDE tr. *Alexis' Secr.* II. 11 To make a sweete Suet called in Frenche and Italian Pommade in latine pomatum. **1598** FLORIO, *Pomada, Pomata*, a pomado to supple ones lips, lip-salue. **1599** A. M. tr. *Gabelhouer's Bk. Physicke* 264/2 [Recipe for] an excellent spanishe Pomado. **1611** COTGR., *Pommade*, Pomatum, or Pomata (an oyntment). **1655** tr. *Com. Hist. Francion* x. 28, I have a Pomada to make fair the skin. **1657** *Physical Dict.*, *Pomada*, or *pomata*, a sweet smelling salve made of apples. **1756** FOOTE *Eng. fr. Paris* II. Wks. 1799 I. 122 Your washes, paints, pomades. **1799** M. UNDERWOOD *Dis. Children* (ed. 4) III. 107 A cold ..usually requires nothing more than a little pomade divine ..to be put to the nostrils. **1874** BURNAND *My time* vi. 48 He was partial to sweet-smelling pomade.

Hence **po'made** *v. trans.* [cf. F. *pommader* (18th c. in Godef.)], to anoint or dress with pomade: whence **po'maded** *ppl. a.*

1889 MRS. OLIPHANT *Poor Gentlem.* xliv, A powdered and pomaded woman like Mrs. Sam. Crockford. **1893** VIZETELLY *Glances Back* I. xxi. 411 The bachelors.. pomaded their hair with great liberality.

pomage, obs. form of POMMAGE.

pomaise, pomall, obs. ff. PUMICE, POMMEL.

Pomak ('pəʊmæk). [Bulg.] A Muslim Bulgarian.

1887 *Encycl. Brit.* XXII. 149/2 Those Bulgarians who have embraced Islam are called Pomaks,—a word of which no satisfactory derivation has been given. **1897** E. A. BARTLETT *Battlefields Thessaly* iii. 49 The local militia were mostly Pomaks, or Mussulman Bulgarians. **1900** 'ODYSSEUS' *Turkey in Europe* viii. 363 The country between Seres and Philippopoli is inhabited by people called Pomaks, who are commonly described as Mohammedan Bulgarians. **1921** *Contemp. Rev.* May 587 It is not unusual to find that in any computation made by the Greeks,..the Pomaks—*i.e.*, Bulgarians who have embraced the Mohammedan faith, are reckoned with the Turks. **1972** D. DAKIN *Unification of Greece* 269 The Slav minority, which included 16,000 Pomaks, was about 80,000.

pomander ('pəʊ-, 'pɒməndə(r), pəʊ'mɑːndə(r), -æ-). Also 6 **pomaunder, pommaundre, pomemaunder, pom(e)amber,** 6–7 **pommander.** [Early mod.E. *pom(e)amber* (whence by dissimilation *pomander*), a. OF. **pome ambre*, *pomme d'embre* (13th c.), f. *pome* apple (see POME) + *ambre* AMBER; in med.L. *pōmum ambrę* (13th c.).

Stressed *poman'der* by Skelton, J. Heywood, Wither, and so given by Bailey, Ash, Walker, Smart, Worcester; *pom'mander* or *po'mander* in *Dr. Dodypoll* (1600), Drayton, G. Herbert, Herrick, and so given by Johnson, Webster 1828, Ogilvie, Cassell.

c **1280** *Roman de la Rose* 21008 Plus olant que pomme d'embre. **13..** *MS. Harl.* 2378 in Henslow *Med. Wks. 14th C.* 122 *Pomum ambre.*]

1. a. orig. A mixture of aromatic substances, usually made into a ball, and carried in a small box or bag (see 2) in the hand or pocket, or suspended by a chain from the neck or waist, esp. as a preservative against infection. Now, a piece of fruit, esp. an orange, stuck with cloves and usu. tied with ribbon, which is hung or placed in a wardrobe.

1492 *Privy Purse Exp. Hen. VII* in Bentley *Excerpta Hist.* (1831) 90 To one that brought the King a box with pomandre 10s. **1509** Hawes *Past. Pleas.* xxvii. 125 The rofe was.. Knotted with pomaunders right swetely, Encencing out the yll odours misty. **1523** Skelton *Garl. Laurel* 1027 Colyaunder, Swete pomaunder, Good cassaunder. **1542** Boorde *Dyetary* xxvii. (1870) 290 Make a pomemaunder vnder this maner. **1562** Bulleyn *Bulwark, Bk. Simples* 59 b, A precious Pomamber to be worne against foule stinkyng aire. **1564–78** —— *Dial. agst. Pest.* (1888) 49 Be not without a good Pomeamber made of Storax, Calamite [etc.]. **1628** Wither *Brit. Rememb.* ii. 9 Or like Pomanders of a curious Sent. **1633** G. Herbert *Temple, Odour* iv, Then should the Pomander, which was before A speaking sweet, mend by reflection. **1648** Herrick *Hesper., Pomander Bracelet,* The beads I kist, but most lov'd her That did perfume the pomander. **1661** Lovell *Hist. Anim. & Min.* 55 Balls are therefore called vulgarly *poma ambræ,* or Pomanders. **1683** *Lond. Gaz.* No. 1804/4 A little Gold Box, with a sweet Pomander in it. **1710** Steele *Tatler* No. 245 ¶2 Bracelets of braided Hair, Pomander, and Seed-Pearl. **1852** Thackeray *Esmond* ii. xi, The courtier.. bowed out of the room, leaving an odour of pomander behind him. **1864** Hawthorne *Dolliver Rom.* (1879) 23 Pomanders, and pomades, the scented memory of which lingered about their toilet tables. **1931** E. S. Rohde *Scented Garden* viii. 219 *Pomanders, Etc.* .. The orange.. will scent a drawer deliciously for well over a year. **1946** J. De Both *Mod. Househ. Encycl.* 237/1 Pomanders may be made from apples, oranges, or lemons. —*to make,* select firm fruit and stick whole cloves into entire surface; hang in clothes closet or place in dresser drawers. **1963** *Good Housek. Home Encycl.* (rev. ed.) 367/2 The pomander... looks prettier if tied round with ribbon or tinsel, with a loop for hanging it up. **1974** Westland & Critchley *Art of Dried & Pressed Flowers* ix. 80 Hang the pomander in a wardrobe, on a coat hanger or over your dressing table.

b. *transf.* and *fig.* Something scented, or having a sweet odour.

1599 B. Jonson *Ev. Man out of Hum.* v. vii, [said to a fop] Away, good pomander, goe. *a* **1625** Fletcher *Woman's Prize* v. i, Oh what a stinking thief is this?.. Tames street to him Is a meere Pomander. **1629** R. Hill *Pathw. Piety* II. 185 [We] God's Pomander, smell better by rubbing.

2. a. orig. The case in which this perfume was carried, usually a hollow ball of gold, silver, ivory, etc., often in the shape of an apple or orange. Now, a small perforated ceramic container filled with pot-pourri or other aromatic substances, for hanging in a wardrobe, placing on a dressing-table, etc.

1518 *Privy Purse Exp. Princess Mary* 1 Jan. (1831) p. xxii, To the frenche quenes seruant that brought a pomander of gold. **1601** Holland *Pliny* II. 605 A ball or pomander of crystall held opposit between the member and the Sun beams. **1668** R. L'Estrange *Vis. Quev.* (1708) 108 Abundance of Hair Bracelets, Lockets, Pomanders, Knots of Ribbands. **1880** Shorthouse *J. Inglesant* (1882) II. 272 He himself carried a pomander of silver in the shape of an apple, stuffed with spices. **1973** *Woman's Jrnl.* Dec. 108 (Advt.), Colognes, bath essences, soaps, pot-pourri and pomanders from.. J. Floris Ltd. **1975** *Lady* 6 Nov. p. vii/2 (Advt.), Bone china pomander, traditional long-lasting perfume. **1976** *S. Wales Echo* 25 Nov. 8/2 (Advt.), There are pots of French herbs.., jams laced with whisky, silk scarves and pomanders.

b. *fig.* Applied to a book containing a collection of prayers; also of secrets, etc.

1558 Becon (*title*) The Pomander of Prayer, wherein is contained many godly Prayers, whereunto are added certayne Meditations, called S. Augustin's. *Ibid.* Ded., I thought it good.. to geue vnto you this mi Pommander of praier, wher in ar breifli contained such godli praiers as ar most mete in this our age to be vsed of al degres & estates. **1650** (*title*) The Divine Pymander of Hermes Mercurius Trismegistus,.. Translated.. into English By.. Doctor Everard. **1895** E. Nesbit (*title*) A pomander of verse.

3. *attrib.*, as ***pomander box, bracelet, chain.***

1599 B. Jonson *Ev. Man out of Hum.* ii. i, Walkes all day hang'd in pomander chains. **1610** —— *Alch.* i. iv, Offring citizens-wiues pomander-bracelets, As his preseruatiue, made of the elixir. **1759** Robertson *Hist. Scot.* vii. Wks. 1813 I. 527 An *Agnus Dei* hung by a pomander chain at her neck. **1906** *Athenæum* 3 Feb. 133/1 We see the clouded cane and pomander box of Sir Plume.

‖**Pomard, Pommard** (pɔmar). Also with small initial. [From Pomard, Pommard, the name of a village in the department of Côte d'Or, France.] A red Burgundy wine.

1833 C. Redding *Mod. Wines* v. (1836) 100 Pomard, of somewhat more body than Volnay. **1875** [see Beaune]. **1883** *Chamb. Jrnl.* 15 Dec. 787/1 A dozen of oysters.. and a bottle of pomard. **1889** [see Corton]. **1905** *Wine Merchant's Price List, Burgundies*... Pommard, a fine full-flavoured wine. **1920** G. Saintsbury *Notes on Cellar-Bk.* iv. 56 Less distinguished representatives of the Slope of Gow [*sc.* Côte d'Or].. Pommard, Santenay, Chenas and others. **1962** R. Jeffries *Exhibit No. 13* v. 48 He.. picked up a bottle of Pommard. **1979** I. S. Black *Journey to Safe Place* ix. 95 We'll have another bottle of this Pommard.

pomarine ('pɒmərain), *a.* *Ornith.* [ad. F. *pomarin,* arbitrary repr. of mod.L. *pōmatorhīnus.*] = pomatorhine; applied to a species of Skua.

1838 *Encycl. Brit.* (ed. 7) XVI. 633/1 The skua.. the pomarine jager.. and Richardson's jager. **1863** *Spring Lapl.* 359, I could never detect the pomarine skua.. breeding in this district. **1885** Seebohm *Brit. Birds* III. 349 *note,* The Pomarine Skua does not differ from the other Skuas in the structure of its nostrils.

†**po'marious,** *a.* *Obs. rare*$^{-0}$. [f. L. *pōmāri-us* of or relating to fruit (f. *pōmum* fruit, *pōmus* fruit-tree) + -ous.]

1656 Blount *Glossogr., Pomarious,*.. of or belonging to an Orchard or to fruit in general, but most commonly Apples. **1658** Phillips, *Pomarious,* (lat.) belonging to a Pomary, i. an Orchard, or place set with Apple-trees. **1775** in Ash.

†**'pomarist.** *Obs. rare*$^{-1}$. [f. L. *pōmārium* (see next) + -ist.] The keeper or proprietor of an orchard.

1688 R. Holme *Armoury* ii. 86/1 Pomarists or Lovers and Keepers of Orchards.

†**'pomary.** *Obs.* In 4 pomeri, 5 **-arie.** [ad. L. *pōmārium* an orchard, prop. neut. of *pōmārius* adj., f. *pōmum* fruit.] A fruit-garden; an orchard.

a **1380** *Pistill of Susan* 63 Euery day bi day In þe Pomeri þei play. *Ibid.* 209 þorw-out þe pomeri we passed us to play. ? *a* **1400** *Morte Arth.* 3364 Was no pomarie so pighte of pryncez in Erthe. [**1656** Blount *Glossogr., Pomary,* a place set with Fruit trees, an Orchard; also an Apple Loft.]

pomate ('pəʊmət), *sb.* *rare. Obs.* exc. *dial.* Also 8 *Sc.* pomet. [ad. mod.L. *pōmātum*: see -ate¹.]

a. = pomace 2 a. **b.** = pomatum 1.

1699 Evelyn *Acetaria* (1729) 175 There is made a Mash or Pomate of this Root. **1773** Fergusson *Auld Reikie* Poems (1785) 206 The pomet slaister'd up his hair. **1903** in *Eng. Dial. Dict.*

pomate (pəʊ'meɪt), *v.* *rare. Obs.* exc. *dial.* [f. pomatum: cf. -ate³.] *trans.* **a.** To reduce to a pomatum or paste. **b.** To dress (the hair) with pomatum.

1684 tr. *Bonet's Merc. Compit.* xix. 743 Tincture of Steel pomated. **1823** Galt *R. Gilhaize* xlii, His hair.. was as if it had been pomated.

pomatic (pəʊ'mætɪk), *a.* [f. Gr. πῶμα, πωμ ατ- lid, cover (see poma) + -ic.] Of or pertaining to the poma; arising from the overlapping of the poma, as a fissure in a monkey's brain.

1889 *Buck's Handbk. Med. Sc.* VIII. 162/1 A lateral between the pomatic margin and the ectal surface of the temporal gyre. *Ibid.* [see poma].

pomatioid (pəʊ'mætɪɔɪd), *a.* *Zool.* [f. mod.L. *Pōmātias,* generic name, a. Gr. πωματίας a snail with an operculum (πῶμα).] Resembling or pertaining to the genus *Pomatias,* or the family *Pomatiidæ,* of operculated terrestrial snails.

1895 in *Funk's Stand. Dict.*

pomato (pəʊ'mɑːtəʊ, -'eɪtəʊ). [f. p(otato + t)omato.] A name used by Luther Burbank (1849–1926), American horticulturist, for the fruit of a hybrid potato, which resembled a tomato; later used to designate the result of attempts to hybridize the potato and the tomato, by grafting or other methods. Also *attrib.*

1905 *Century Mag.* Mar. 668/1 The 'pomato', one of the most wonderful creations, now under way. This may be called a tomato growing upon a potato. It produces in abundance a white, fragrant, succulent, delicious fruit upon potato tops. **1914** L. Burbank in J. Whitson et al. *L. Burbank: his Methods & Discoveries* II. ix. 283 As the fruit grew on a hybrid potato vine, and in itself had much the appearance of a tomato, it was christened the 'Pomato'. The name.. led to the unauthorized assumption that the fruit was really a cross between the tomato and the potato. In point of fact, I have never been able to cross these two plants. *Ibid.* 284 The pomato plant produced fruit abundantly, but very few tubers. **1971** *New Scientist* 27 Apr. 263 (*caption*) Protoplasts of potato and tomato are fused... These cells are then cultured, and from them are grown embryoids and eventually whole 'pomatoes'. At the moment, research has got as far as the protoplast-fusion stage. **1976** *Nat. Geographic* Sept. 388/1 'Pomatoes'—hypothetical vegetables with the fruit-bearing foliage of a tomato and the tuberous roots of a potato. To some botanists, it is just a matter of time until almost any type of plant can be hybridized with another. **1980** *Garden* CV. 46/2 Am I the only person who doesn't grow pomatoes?

pomatorhine ('pəʊmətəʊraɪn), *a.* *Ornith.* [ad. mod.L. *pōmatorhīnus* adj., f. Gr. πῶμα, -ατ- lid, cover + ῥίς, ῥιν- nose.] Having the nostrils partly covered with a scale. Applied ineptly to a single species of *Stercorarius* or Skua, all the genus being really 'pomatorhine': cf. pomarine.

1884 Yarrell *Brit. Birds* (ed. 4) III. 671 The Pomatorhine Skua is said.. to deposit two eggs in a mere depression of the moss on the tundras of the Taimyr. **1896** *List Anim. Zool. Soc.* 530 *Stercorarius pomatorhinus* (Temm.), Pomatorhine Skua.

pomatum (pəʊ'meɪtəm), *sb.* [a. mod.L. *pōmātum,* f. *pōmum* apple + *-ātum,* -ate¹.]

1. = pomade *sb.*²

1562 Warde tr. *Alexis' Secr.* ii. 42 b, This Pomatum wil be as whyte as snowe. **1597** Gerarde *Herbal* iii. xcv. 1276 There is likewise made an ointment with the pulpe of Apples and Swines grease and Rose water, which is vsed to beautifie the face.. called in shops *Pomatum,* of the Apples whereof it is made. **1657** W. Coles *Adam in Eden* clxviii. 258 Pomatum, which is of much use to soften and supple the roughnesse of the skin. **1712–14** Pope *Rape Lock* ii. 129 Gums and Pomatums shall his flight restrain. **1783** *Phil. Trans.* LXXIII. 240 Its essence is mixed with pomatums for the face and hands. **1855** Thackeray *Newcomes* ii, Their.. hair.. disguised with powder and pomatum.

attrib. **1629** Davenant *Albovine* v. i, They say it is your custom to sleep in Pomatum Masques. **1683** *Lond. Gaz.* No. 1808/4 One Silver Pomatum-Pot. **1885** T. A. Guthrie *Tinted Venus* x. 121 Your bottles and pomatum-pots.

†**2.** = cider. *Obs. rare*$^{-0}$.

1657 *Physical Dict., Pomatum,* a drink made of apples.

Hence **po'matum** *v. trans.,* = pomade *v.*; **po'matumed** (-əmd) *ppl. a.,* anointed with pomatum; **po'matumy** (-əmɪ) *a.,* sticky with pomatum.

1786 *Pogonologia* 80 His whiskers.. combed, and pomatumed by his mistress. **1821–30** Ld. Cockburn *Mem.* i. 29 Powdered and pomatumed hair. **1857** Ld. Campbell *Lives Chief Justices* III. lii. 250 The wigs that had been properly frizzed and pomatumed. **1894** Mrs. Ritchie *Chapters fr. Mem.* i. 10 Features, ornamented with little pomatumy wisps of hair.

pomayse, obs. form of pumice.

‖**pombe** ('pɒmbeɪ). [Swahili *pombe.*] An intoxicating drink made by fermentation from many kinds of grain and some fruits in Central and East Africa. Also *attrib.* and *Comb.*

1857 R. F. Burton *Centr. Afr.* (1860) I. iii. 95 Grain is so abundant that the inhabitants [of Zungomero] exist almost entirely upon the intoxicating pombe, or holcus-beer. **1866** Livingstone *Last Jrnls.* v. (1873) I. 117 The chief brought a huge basket of *pombe.* **1878** H. M. Stanley *Dark Cont.* I. vii. 151 The great jar of froth-topped pombé is then brought up. **1935** H. Thurnwald in R. C. Thurnwald *Black & White in E. Afr.* iv. 158 The brewing of beer (pombe) is not done by women everywhere. It is a complicated process requiring time and performed especially for feasts. **1952** *Chambers's Jrnl.* May 278/1 The local fermented beverage will be flowing freely—be it coconut pombe, or barley talla, or honey tej, depending on where in Africa the ceremony is taking place. **1966** C. Sweeney *Scurrying Bush* v. 67 The local beer, called *pombe,* and made, in this case, from sorghum grain. **1969** *Tanzania Notes & Rec.* July 26 In 1947 women pombe sellers.. brought their case before Kimalando... He saw no justification for mounting a patrol in the African pombe markets. **1977** D. Beaty *Excellency* iv. 54 A big black policeman with breath that smelled strongly of banana pombe. **1978** J. Updike *Coup* (1979) v. 213 An entire American boom town, with..*pombe*-dispensing saloons.

pombgranade, obs. form of pomegranate.

pombil: see pomely *a.*

pome (pəʊm), *sb.*¹ (Also in comb. 5 **powm(e,** 6 poum, 6–7 pom.) [a. OF. *pome* (F. *pomme*):—late L. or Romanic **pōma* apple, orig. pl. of L. *pōmum* 'fruit', later, 'apple'.]

1. A fruit of the apple kind or resembling an apple; now only *poet.* an apple. † ***Punical pome,*** pomegranate: = Apple Punic (apple *sb.* 3).

c **1420** *Pallad. on Husb.* iii. 742 Ox dong aboute her roote if that me trete, The pomes sadde & braune wil hit gete. *c* **1430** Lydg. *Ballad Commend. our Lady* 121 O punical pome ayens al pestilence. **1589** Fleming *Virg. Georg.* ii. 22 A taste.. of wholsome cytron pome. **1729** *Evelyn's Sylva* ii. v. 154 They have sometimes produced a pretty small Pome. **1839** Bailey *Festus* xxvii. (1851) 466 Like her of old, ere dropped the golden pome.

b. *Bot.* A succulent inferior fruit, consisting of a firm fleshy body formed of the enlarged calyx, inclosing two or more few-seeded carpels (rarely only one) of cartilaginous or bony texture, forming the core: as an apple, pear, quince, haw, etc.

1816 Keith *Phys. Bot.* II. 160 In the pear the pome tapers down gradually to the point of insertion. **1853** in *Pharmac. Jrnl.* XIII. 14 The fruit is a small black pome.

†**2.** The heart or head of a cabbage, cauliflower, or broccoli. (F. *pomme.*) *Obs.*

1658 Evelyn *Fr. Gard.* (1675) 178 When their heads, and pomes are formed, if you perceive any of them ready to run to seed, draw the plant half out of the ground. **1664** —— *Kal. Hort.* Aug. (1729) 213 Cauly-flowers over-speeding to pome and head.

3. *transf.* A ball or globe, especially of metal; the royal globe or ball of dominion = *golden apple* (apple *sb.* 6); see also quot. 1866.

? *a* **1400** *Morte Arth.* 3355 And syne profres me a pome pighte fulle of faire stonys.. In sygne þat I sothely was soueravne in erthe. **1579** *Inv. R. Wardr.* (1815) 293 A belt with.. ane pome garnissit with perll. **1814** Southey *Roderick* xviii. 131 Where was the rubied crown, the sceptre where, And where the golden pome. **1866** *Direct. Angl.* (ed. 3) 257 *Pome,* a round ball of silver or other metal; which is filled with hot water, and is placed on the altar in winter months to prevent danger or accident with the chalice, from the hands of the priest becoming numb with cold.

†**4.** *Fortif.* The rounded projecting shoulder of a bastion. *Obs.*

1598 Barret *Theor. Warres* v. i. 125 The parts of a Bulwarke are.. the Orecchion or Pome, or gard, or shoulder. **1598** Florio, *Orecchione,* that part of a bulwarke which is called by some the pome, guard, or shoulder.

†**5.** = pomander 1. *rare.*

1513 Douglas *Æneis* xii. Prol. 146 Precyus invnctment, salve, or fragrant pome.

6. *Comb.,* as ***pome-bearing, -shaped*** adjs.; †**pome-adam** [in F. *pomme d'Adam* = mod.L. *pomum Adami*] = Adam's apple 1, lime-fruit; †**pome-paradise** [cf. F. *pomme de paradis* (Cotgr. 1611)], a sweet kind of apple, = paradise apple a, honey-apple b; †**pome-quince,** ? an apple-shaped variety of quince;

†**pome-warden**, ? = POME-PEAR. See also POME-CITRON, etc.

1600 SURFLET *Countrie Farme* III. xxvi. 482 As for *pome-adams [*Fr. orig.* pommes d'Adam] they are round, twise or thrise as great, as orenges. **1901** *G. Nicholson's Dict. Gard., Cent. Suppl.* 645/2 *R[osa] pomifera* (*pome-bearing). Great Apple Rose. **1601** HOLLAND *Pliny* II. 164 The *Pome-Paradise, or hony Apples called Melimela. **1611** COTGR., *Passe-pomme*, the Pome-paradice, Honny-apple, or Honny-meale; (an apple thats quickly ripe, and quickly rotten). **1658** PHILLIPS, *Pome-paradice*, a fruit called a John-apple. **1601** HOLLAND *Pliny* II. 105 A liniment of it and *Pome-quinces or Peare-quinces, easeth the head-ach. **1895** *Syd. Soc. Lex.*, *Pomiform*, *pome-shaped. **1494** FABYAN *Chron.* VII. 605 Other more comon fruytes: as costardes, wardens, *pomewardons, richardons, damysyns, and plummes.

pome (pəʊm), *sb.*[2] A jocular alteration of 'poem'.

1861 G. MEREDITH *Let.* 16 Aug. (1970) I. 100 Did you get the Pome I sent? **1897** A. R. MARSHALL *(title)* Pomes from the Pink 'un. **1927** JOYCE *(title)* Pomes Penyeach. **1959** *News Chron.* 12 Aug. 4/5 My next pome,..is dedicated to a very fine poet. **1975** A. COREN *Further Bull. Pres. Idi Amin* 7 Come on out, John Milton!..wot about dis year's jumbo pome you lazy bum?

†**pome**, *v. Obs.* [ad. F. *pommer*, f. *pomme*: see POME *sb.*[1]] *intr.* To form a close compact head or heart, as a cabbage, lettuce, etc.; to head, to heart.

1658 EVELYN *Fr. Gard.* (1675) 175 There is another sort of cabbage..they seem to me the most natural of all the rest; for they pome, close to the ground. **1699** —— *Acetaria* (1729) 150 Lettuce ty'd close up, Pome and Blanch of themselves. **1727** S. SWITZER *Pract. Gard.* III. xxiii. 130 The time of sowing the chief of the *Brassica's*, especially those that pome or cabbage.

pomeamber, obs. form of POMANDER.

†**pome-apis.** *Obs.* Also 7 **pome-appease**, 8 **pomme d'Api, -d'Apis.** [ad. F. *pomme d'api*: cf. L. *malus appiana* (Pliny), f. the name of one *Appius*, who is said to have grafted the apple on a quince-stock.] A variety of apple.

[**1577** B. GOOGE *Heresbach's Husb.* (1586) 87 In the olde time the cheefest Apples were..Claudians, Matians, and Appians, so called of their first founders. **1611** COTGR. s.v. *Pomme, Pomme Appie, ou d'Appie*, an Apple thats like a Quince, both in smell, and bignesse.] **1664** EVELYN *Kal. Hort.* (1729) 232/1 Fruit Trees..for a moderate Plantation. Apples..Passe-pome: Pome Apis: Cour-pendue. **1669** WORLIDGE *Cyder* (1691) 211 There is a curious apple newly propagated, called Pome-appease... I suppose this is that which is called the Ladies Longing. **1741** *Compl. Fam.-Piece* II. iii. 361 Pomme d'Api,..and some Apples of less Account. **1767** J. ABERCROMBIE *Ev. Man his own Gard.* (1803) 671 Apples... Aromatic russet, Pomme d'Apis, Newtown pippin.

†**pome-'cedre.** *Obs.* [f. POME + F. *cèdre*, It. *cedro* citron.] = next.

c **1430** LYDG. *Min. Poems* (Percy Soc.) 15 The pome-cedre corageos to recomfort. **1481** BOTONER *Tulle on Old Age* (Caxton) F iv, Pomegarnades, orenges, figges, dates, almandes, pomecedres.

†**pome-'citron.** *Obs.* [f. POME + CITRON. Cf. L. *mālum citreum*.] = CITRON 1.

1555 EDEN *Decades* 81 A great frute as bygge as pome citrons. **1577** B. GOOGE *Heresbach's Husb.* II. (1586) 92 If they [citrons] be very great and rounde like Pompeons, they call them Pomcidrons. **1601** HOLLAND *Pliny* I. 359 The Pomecitron is not so good to be chewed and eaten of it selfe. **1625** PURCHAS *Pilgrimage* IV. 1173 The Iland yeeldeth Figs, Pomegranates, Muske-millions, Pome-Citrons very faire. **1709** DAMPIER *Voy.* III. II. 56 Pine-Apples, Pome-citrons, Pomegranates, and other sorts of Fruits. **1802** JAMIESON *Use Sacr. Hist.* I. II. 439 The pome-citron is said to bear fruit at all times.

b. *Comb.*, as ***pome-citron pill, tree, wood.***

1624 DARCIE *Birth of Heresies* xvi. 66 In stead of incense they vsed Cedar or Pomecytron wood for perfume. **1641** G. SANDYS *Paraphr. Song Sol.* VIII. iii, From under the Pomecitron tree. **1675** H. WOOLLEY *Gentlew. Comp.* 177 The Pomo-citron-pills preserve and help digestion.

†**pome-dorry.** *Obs.* Also 5 **-dorreng, -de Oringe.** [f. POME + DORY *a.* 2, F. *doré* gilded.] In *Old Cookery*, A meat ball or rissole coated with yolk of egg, etc.: cf. ENDORE *v.*

c **1381** *Anc. Cookery* §42 (1780) 106 For to make Pomme-dorry. Take Buff and hewe yt smal al raw..rost yt and endorre yt wyth ȝolkys of eyryn. *c* **1420** *Liber Cocorum* (1862) 37 For powme dorrys..Endore hit with ȝolkes of egges. *c* **1430** *Two Cookery-bks.* 58 Pome dorreng. *c* **1440** *Anc. Cookery* in *Househ. Ord.* (1790) 442 Frasure to make Pome de Oringe. Take the lyvre of porke, and bray hit all rawe right smal [etc.]..do therto a lytel floure, and endore hom therwith in the rostynge.

pomege, obs. form of PUMICE.

pomegranate (pɒm-, pʌm'grænɪt, 'pɒm-, 'pʌmgrænɪt, now usu. 'pɒmɪˌgrænɪt). Forms: 4 **pomme-, poom-, powmbe-,** 4–5 **poum(e-, pum-,** 4–6 **powm-,** 4–8 **pom-,** 6 **pomb-,** 4–8 **pome-;** *α.* 4–6 **-garnade, -garnard(e, -garnat(e, -garnet(t(e,** (4 **-gernett,** 5 **-garned);** *β.* (5 **-grenet),** 5–7 **-granad(e, -granat,** 5 **-granarde,** 6–8 **-granet;** 6– **pomegranate.** *γ.* 4 **pown-, poun-garnette,** 4–6 **-garnard,** 4–7 **-garnet,** (5 **-karnet);** 5 **pon-,** 6 **poyngarnette, ponegarnarde, pound garnette.** *δ.* 5 **bamegarnade,** 6 **palm-garnete.** [ME. a. OF. *pome (pomme, pume) grenate, -ade, -et(t)e, garn-, gharn-, guarn-, guern-, gern-ate, -ade, -et(t)e*, f. *pomme* apple + *grenate*, in mod.F. *grenade* = It. *granata*, Sp. *granada*:—pop.L. or Com. Romanic *grānāta* for cl. L. *grānātum* (= *mālum grānātum*, in med.L. *pōmum grānātum*), a pomegranate, lit. (an apple) having many grains or seeds. The stem-part *gren-* became in OF. by metathesis *gern-, garn-*, whence the Eng. forms in *-garn-* from 14th to 16th c.; the OF. ending *-ate* became in Eng. *-at(e, -ette, -et(t*, the F. *-ade* of southern origin (see -ADE) gave Eng. *-ade* and *-ard*. (Cf. GARNADE[1], GARNET[2], GRANATE[2], GRENADE[1].) The first element (in Norman F. *pume, poume*) became in ME. variously *pomme, poom, pome, pom, pomb*, and *poum, pum, powmb*, corrupted to *poun, pown, pon, poyn*, and *pound*. Stressed by the poets generally from 17th to 19th c., and by Bailey, Johnson, Walker, Smart, *pome'granate*; from late nineteenth century *'pomegranate*.]

1. a. The fruit of the tree *Punica Granatum*, N.O. *Myrtaceæ*, a large roundish many-celled berry, with many seeds, each enveloped in a pleasantly acid juicy reddish pulp, enclosed in a tough leathery rind of a golden or orange colour tinged with red.

α. **1320–30** *Horn Ch.* 374 A poumgarnet þer sche brak. **13..** *E.E. Allit. P.* B. 1466 As þay prudly hade piked of pomgarnades. **1382** WYCLIF *Num.* xiii. 24 [23] Of the powmgarnettis [**1388** of pumgarnadis] forsothe..thei token. **1398** TREVISA *Barth. De P.R.* XVII. xcix. (Bodl. MS.), Malus granata is a tre þat bereth pommegarnettes. *c* **1400** tr. *Secreta Secret., Gov. Lordsh.* 84 Take þe iowse of þe poume garnet. *c* **1430** LYDG. *Min. Poems* (Percy Soc.) 15 Orengis, almondis, and the pome garnade [*rime* glade]. *c* **1460** *Play Sacram.* 186 Pumgarnetis & many other spycis. **1530** PALSGR. 256/2 Pome garnet, *pomme de granade*. **1541** R. COPLAND *Guydon's Quest. Chirurg.* N j b, Ye must gyue hym some of a pomgarnade to eate. **1547** BOORDE *Brev. Health* cxlii. 53 The juyce of pome Garnardes. **1613** R. CAWDREY *Table Alph.* (ed. 3), *Pomegarnet*, or *pomegranet*, a kind of fruit.

β. **1422** tr. *Secreta Secret., Priv. Priv.* 244 Gourdes and Poumgrene[t]s. **1432–50** tr. *Higden* (Rolls) I. 108 Bawmes, oliues, pomegranardes. **1533** ELYOT *Cast. Helthe* II. vii. (1541) 21 b, Pomegranates be of good iuyce, and profitable to the stomacke. **1553** EDEN *Treat. Newe Ind.* (Arb.) 35 The tree, that beareth the pomgranate. **1590** WEBBE *Trav.* (Arb.) 33 Al manner of fruites whatsoeuer,..Pombgranades, Orenges, Limons. **1591** DRAYTON *Harmonie of Ch.* (Percy Soc.) 27 Pleasant liquor that distils from the pomgranet fine. *c* **1620** ROBINSON *Mary Magd.* 1095 Her temples, peices of Pomegranates seeme. **1655** E. TERRY *Voy. E. Ind.* 96 Here are..store of Pome-granats, Pome-citrons. **1725** POPE *Odyss.* VII. 149 With deeper red the full pomegranate glows. **1727–46** THOMSON *Summer* 681 Nor, on its slender twigs Low-bending, be the full pomegranate scorn'd. **1866** ROGERS *Agric. & Prices* I. 632 Pomegranates are quoted in 1284 at a shilling each.

γ. **1382** Poungarnet [see b]. **1398** TREVISA *Barth. De P.R.* XVII. i. (MS. Bodl.), Almaundes and poungarnardes leueþ here malice bi crafte of tileinge. *c* **1425** *Voc.* in Wr.-Wülcker 647/37 *Hoc malum granatum*, poun-karnet. **1466** *Mann. & Househ. Exp.* (Roxb.) 330 Item, for xvj. pongarnettes, the same day, ij.s. vj.d. **1502** *Privy Purse Exp. Eliz. of York* (1830) 74 A present of poyn-garnettes and apulles. **1545** *Rates of Customs* c ij b, Pound garnettes the M. vis. iiiid. **1545** *Nottingham Rec.* III. 224 Unum pomum granatum vocatum 'a pound gayner' [? *error for* garnet]. **1547** BOORDE *Introd. Knowl.* xxxix. (1870) 218 Olyues, ponegarnardes,.. Figges and Raysins, and all other fruites. **1577** FRAMPTON *Joyfull Newes* III. (1596) 97 Granadas, which wee call Poungarnardes. **1604** E. G[RIMSTONE] *D'Acosta's Hist. Indies* IV. xxvi. 281 Like vnto the graines of a Poungarnet. **1660** R. MAY *Accomplisht Cook* 2 Almonds, Poungarnet and Lemons.

δ. **1480** Bamegarnade [see 5]. **1599** DALLAM *Trav.* (Hakl. Soc.) 85 Heare dothe grow good store of..palm garnetes.

fig. *a* **1529** SKELTON *Sp. Parrot* 39 With Kateryne incomparable,..That pereles pomegarnet. *a* **1658** CLEVELAND *Times* 80 Those precious Spirits that can deal The Pome-granates of Grace at every Meal.

b. The tree (*Punica Granatum*) which bears this fruit, a native of northern Africa and western Asia, now naturalized in the warmer regions of the globe generally; a POMEGRANATE-TREE.

1382 WYCLIF *Song Sol.* vi. 10 [11] Beholde, if..the poungarnetis [1388 Pumgranate trees] hadden buriouned. **1644** EVELYN *Diary* 9 Feb., A labyrinth of cypresse, noble hedges of pomegranates. **1741** *Compl. Fam.-Piece* II. iii. 380 There are several other Trees and Shrubs..now in Flower, as.. Pomegranates with double and single Flowers. **1813** BYRON *Giaour* 493 The young pomegranate's blossoms strew Their bloom in blushes ever new. **1856** BRYANT *Momero* ii, I see thy fig-trees bask, with the fair pomegranate near. **1856** DELAMER *Flower Gard.* (1861) 127 The Double-flowered Pomegranate will thrive out-doors, in England, against a wall.

c. The flower of the pomegranate; usually scarlet, rarely white or yellowish.

1873 'OUIDA' *Pascarèl* II. 122 A woman goes by with a knot of pomegranate in her dark hair. **1886** SHELDON tr. *Flaubert's Salammbô* 14 As rosy as a half-opened pomegranate.

d. A colour resembling that of the pomegranate. Usu. *attrib.* or as *adj.*

a **1855** C. BRONTË *Emma* in *Cornh. Mag.* (1860) I. 495 Miss Wilcox..in her blue merino dress and pomegranate ribbon. **1881** C. C. HARRISON *Woman's Handiwork* I. 47 Pomegranate, Bokhara red, Damascus blue..are some of the colours to be had in plushes. **1906** W. J. LOCKE *Beloved Vagabond* vii. 83 A beautiful gipsy, holding fascinating allurements in lustrous eyes and pomegranate lips. **1927** [see ASH *sb.*[2] 1 d]. **1955** E. BOWEN *World of Love* v. 94 Mamie's pomegranate toenails. **1958** J. CANNAN *And be a Villain* iv. 100 A high-waisted pomegranate satin with gold lace sleeves. **1972** *Guardian* 17 Oct. 13/4 The walls are pomegranate with pomegranate velvet lighting in the recesses.

2. A carved or embroidered representation of a pomegranate as an ornament or decoration.

1382 WYCLIF *Exod.* xxviii. 34 In the myddil litel belles menged, so that the litel belle be gold, and a powm garnet [1388 pyn appil]. *Ibid.* xxxix. 23 Litil bellis of moost puyr gold, the whiche thei puttiden bitwix the powmbe garnettis [1388 pum garnadis], in the nether more party of the coote bi enuyroun. **1542** *Test. Ebor.* (Surtees) VI. 168 Tapstre warke with pounde garnettes. **1834** LYTTON *Pompeii* I. iv, Those walls were ornamented with the pomegranate consecrated to Isis. **1875** W. McILWRAITH *Guide Wigtownshire* 33 For finial, it [the Old Cross of Wigtown] has a pome-granate cut in stone.

3. Applied, with defining words, to other trees in some way resembling the pomegranate; as the Native P. (*Capparis nobilis*), and Small Native P. (*Capparis mitchelli*) of Australia.

1889 J. H. MAIDEN *Usef. Native Plants* 12 'Small Native Pomegranate', 'Native Orange'. **1894** *Melbourne Museum Catal., Economic Woods* 10 (Morris) Native Caper Tree or Wild Pomegranate. Found in the Mallee Scrub.

†**4.** *transf.* A rissole. *Obs.*

c **1430** *Two Cookery-bks.* I. 38 Pome-Garnez.—Take lene Raw Porke..& hew it smal..þanne make þer-of pelettys, as it were Applys, be-twene þin hondys.

5. *attrib.* and *Comb.*, as ***pomegranate apple, bark, colour*** (hence ***pomegranate-coloured*** adj.), ***kernel, root; pomegranate-like, -red,*** adjs.; **pomegranate-water**, a drink made from pomegranates.

1480 CAXTON *Ovid's Met.* x. iv, Trees beryng Bamegarnade apples. **1589** GREENE *Menaphon* (Arb.) 77 Her cheekes like..faire pomegranade kernels washt in milke. **1754** J. BARTLET *Farriery* 22 Take pomegranate bark, or oak bark, two ounces. **1822–34** *Good's Study Med.* (ed. 4) I. 692 The tongue..is now dry, livid, black or of a pomegranate colour. **1825** *Greenhouse Comp.* I. 130 (*Dahlia superflua*), the purple..brick-red, dark red, pomegranate-coloured, dark purple. **1836** J. M. GULLY *Magendie's Formul.* (ed. 2) 177, Grenadia, and bark of the pomegranate root. **1876** 'OUIDA' *Winter City* viii, That small pomegranate-like mouth. **1879** MRS. A. E. JAMES *Ind. Househ. Managem.* 87 Pomegranate-water..an agreeably cooling drink.

pomegranate-tree. = prec. 1 b.

1382 WYCLIF *1 Sam.* xiv. 2 Saul dwellide..vndur a poomgarnet tree. **1483** *Cath. Angl.* 286/1 A Pomgarnett tree, *malogrenatus*. **1577** FRAMPTON *Joyfull Newes* I. (1596) 7 The Balsamo..is made of a tree greater then a Powngarnet Tree. **1680** OTWAY *Caius Marius* IV. i, Nightly on yon Pomegranate tree she sings. **1811** A. T. THOMSON *Lond. Disp.* (1818) 325 The pomegranate tree is a native of the south of Europe, Asia, and Barbary.

pomeis: see POMEYS.

pomel, -ele, -ell, -elle, obs. ff. POMMEL, -ELLE.

†**'pomeled,** *a. Obs.* [f. OF. *pomelé*: see POMELY.] Dappled; = POMELY *a.*

c **1410** *Master of Game* (MS. Digby 182) v, þer kyddes ben kydded with pomeled here, as þe hynde calfes. **14..** *Voc.* in Wr.-Wülcker 587/28 *Guttatus*, pomeled *ut equus*.

pomelion, variant of POMMELION.

pomellated ('pɒməˌleɪtɪd), *a.* *rare*$^{-1}$. [Presumably ad. Fr. *pommelé* 'dappled'.] ? Dappled, mottled.

1922 JOYCE *Ulysses* 289 Thither the extremely large wains bring foison of the fields, flaskets of cauliflowers..and red green yellow brown russet sweet big bitter ripe pomellated apples.

pomelo ('pɒmələʊ, 'pʌmələʊ). Also **pomello, pum(m)elo, pomolo, pommelo.** [Of uncertain formation and history; app. related to *pomum, pomo, pome* apple.] **a.** In the East Indies, a synonym of the POMPELMOOSE or SHADDOCK (*Citrus grandis*). **b.** In America, applied to the variety or sub-species of *Citrus*, also called 'grapefruit' and (in the English market) 'forbidden fruit'. Also = GRAPEFRUIT. Also *attrib.*

1858 SIMMONDS *Dict. Trade, Pomelloes*, a name under which forbidden fruit is sometimes sold in this country by fruiterers. **1859** *All Year Round* No. I. 17, I cannot agree.. that the Amoy pomelo is the finest fruit in the world. **1884** *Q. Rev.* Apr. 332 Mangosteen, pomolo, banano. **1885** LADY BRASSEY *The Trades* 139 The orange, lemon, shaddock, pomelo,..were weighed down by their own golden fruit. **1885** *Macm. Mag.* Nov. 77/1 Water-melons, jack-fruit, pummeloes, and plantains. **1886** *Guide Mus. Econ. Bot., Kew Gardens* No. I. 29 Pumpelmousse or Shaddock, fruit of *Citrus decumana*... The Pumelo is a smaller fruited variety. **1905** SIR J. K. LAUGHTON in *Let.* 19 Mar., I gather that now the name *pummelow* has been partially adopted in the West Indies, and has come thence to England; but..45 or 50 years ago this name was special to China; the Amoy pummelow, with a pink rose flesh, was specially noted. **1908** R. W. CHAMBERS *Firing Line* v. 54 Is that the pomelo grove? **1943** WEBBER & BATCHELOR *Citrus Industry* I. v. 568 The grapefruits and the pummelos, or shaddocks, are very closely related. **1968** J. W. PURSEGLOVE *Trop. Crops: Dicotyledons* II. 502 C[*itrus*] *grandis* is highly esteemed in the East as a dessert fruit, where it is known as the Pomelo. **1971** 'A. Burgess' *MF* vi. 68 A papier-mâché cornucopia spilling bananas, pomelos . . and jackfruit.

†**'pomely**, *a. Obs.* Forms: 5 **pomely, pomly, pomelee** (also *Sc.* **pommill, pombil, pompyll, poumle**), 7 **pomele**. [ad. OF. *pomelé* (mod.F. *pommelé*) marked with round spots, dappled, f. OF. *pomel* little apple: see POMMEL, and cf. DAPPLED.] Marked with rounded spots, dappled.

c **1386** Chaucer *Prol.* 616 This Reue sat vp on a ful good stot That was al pomely grey. *c* **1400** Maundev. (1839) xxviii. 288 In Arabye þei ben clept Gerfauntz, þat is, a best pomelee or spotted. *c* **1420** *Pallad. on Husb.* iv. 829 The pomly gray for hym y vndirtake. *c* **1425** Wyntoun *Cron.* iv. iii. 217 Apone a coursere pommill [*v. rr.* pombil, poumle, pomely, pompyll] gray Adressaly he sat. **1460** *Lybeaus Disc.* 844 Upon a pomely palfray. [**1658** Phillips, *Pomele-gryse*, (old word) dapple-gray.]

pomemaunder, obs. form of POMANDER.

†**pome-pear.** *Obs.* Forms: 5 **powmpere**, 6 **poumper**, 7 **pom-poire, pome-peare**, 7–8 **pompire**. [f. POME + PEAR *sb.*, after F. *pomme poire*, 'a peare apple' (Cotgr.), or med.L. *pomum pirum.*] See quot. 1640.

c **1440** *Promp. Parv.* 411/2 Powmpere, frute, *pomum pirum.* **1530** Palsgr. 257/2 Poumper, frute. **1601** Holland *Pliny* I. 438 The Melapia: for their resemblance and participation of apples and peares together, as a man would say, Peare-apples, or pom-poires. **1617** Rider *Dict.*, A Pompire, or Pearemaine. **1640** Parkinson *Theat. Bot.* xvi. lxxii. 1501 The Pome-peare, or Apple-peare, which is a small Peare, but round at both ends like an Apple, yet the tree is a Peare tree.

pome-pirk, abbrev. form of POMPERKIN.

Pomeranchon (pɒmə'ræntʃɒn). *Nuclear Physics.* [f. next + -ON[1].] = POMERON.

1967 *Physical Rev. Lett.* XIX. 1061/1 The observed nonshrinkage of diffraction peaks has indicated that the Pomeranchon has an anomalously small slope, so that at present it is the only trajectory generally accepted by Regge phenomenologists which has no particles assigned to it. **1973** *Physical Rev.* D. VII. 1496 Pomeranchon exchange is assumed to be mediated by an isoscalar scalar σ meson.

Pomeranchuk (pɒmə'ræntʃʊk). *Physics.* [Name of Isaak Yakovlevich *Pomeranchuk* (1913–66), Russian physicist.] **a.** Used *attrib.* with reference to the cooling that a mixture of liquid and solid helium 3 undergoes when it is solidified by compression. [Described by Pomeranchuk in *Zh. éksper. i teoret. Fiziki* (1950) XX. 919.]

1958 *Chem. Abstr.* LII. 17841 (*heading*) Theory of the Pomeranchuk effect in helium-3. **1971** *McGraw-Hill Yearbk. Sci. & Technol.* 86/2 First proposed in 1950, the Pomeranchuk method is based on the unusual thermodynamic properties of a solid-liquid mixture of He^3 at low temperatures. **1974** *Nature* 6 Dec. 441/3 Compressional solidification of ^3He, known as Pomeranchuk cooling, . . restricts experiments to the solidification pressure of 34 atmospheres. **1976** *Ibid.* 23 Sept. 276/1 A pair of Pomeranchuk cells was used both for cooling the ^3He into the superfluid A-phase and also for inducing a flow of liquid through the narrow tube which connected them together.

b. Used, chiefly *attrib.*, to designate certain concepts relating to the scattering of sub-atomic particles at high energies, as **Pomeranchuk pole**, a special Regge pole with $\alpha(0) = 1$ and even signature, and with zero isospin, charge, hypercharge, and baryon number (α being the trajectory function); **Pomeranchuk('s) theorem**, a theorem according to which the reaction cross-sections for a particle and for its anti-particle incident on the same target particle should approach the same constant value as the energy of the incident particle is increased; (proposed by Pomeranchuk in *Zh. éksper. i teoret. Fiziki* (1958) XXXIV. 725); **Pomeranchuk trajectory**, the trajectory traced by a Pomeranchuk pole as α increases.

1961 *Physical Rev.* CXXIV. 2049/2 We shall present . . a rigorous generalization of Pomeranchuk's theorem. **1962** *Nuovo Cimento* XXV. 735 We are assuming *either* that the coupling constant of the ρ Regge pole is much smaller than that of the Pomeranchuk (vacuum) pole, *or* that their trajectories lie close together. **1963** *Physical Rev.* CXXIX. 1456/1 Further insight into the behavior of two Pomeranchuk trajectories can be achieved by evaluating the two leading terms in the high-energy behavior of the total elastic cross section. **1973** *Physics Bull.* Mar. 183/2 There is some doubt about the validity of the Pomeranchuk theorem on the constancy of cross sections for K^+, K^- production. **1973** M. Leon *Particle Physics* xii. 244 Elastic scattering . . is supposed to be dominated by the Pomeranchuk pole. **1976** N. W. Dean *Introd. Strong Interactions* xvi. 303 If all total cross sections are to become asymptotically constant, the Pomeranchuk trajectory must be present in all elastic scattering amplitudes. *Ibid.*, The f (1270) and the f′ (1514) mesons have the correct quantum numbers, but there is considerable question whether either of them actually belongs to the Pomeranchuk trajectory.

Pomeranchukon (pɒmə'ræntʃʊkɒn). *Nuclear Physics.* [f. prec. + -ON[1].] = POMERON.

1968 *Physical Rev. Lett.* XX. 236/2 Assuming the continuum contribution to the FESR for the amplitude *B* to be confined to the Pomeranchukon, one could subtract the Pomeranchuk contribution on the right-hand side and the continuum contribution on the left-hand side of the FESR. **1973** *Physical Rev.* D. VIII. 3050 The *S* matrix for the Pomeranchukon enters here because we must include the possibility of Regge-pole exchange without any diffractive interaction between the incoming or outgoing particles.

Pomeranian (pɒmə'reɪnɪən), *a.* and *sb.*) Also **Pomoranian.** [f. *Pomerania*, name of the province, a. med.L. *Pomerānia*, f. *Pomerānī* a Slavonic tribe. (Ger. *Pommern.*).

The form *Pomoranian*, reflecting Pol. *Pomorze* 'Pomerania' (f. *po* 'on', *morze* 'sea') is used chiefly in linguistic writings.]

A. *adj.* Of or pertaining to Pomerania, a district on the south coast of the Baltic Sea in Germany and Poland (formerly a province of Prussia).

P. bream, a variety of bream (*Abramis buggenhagii*) supposed to be a hybrid between the Bream and the Roach. ***P. dog***, a small dog of a variety characterized by a pointed muzzle, pricked ears, full eyes, and long thick silky hair, either black, white, or cream-coloured.

1760 Mrs. Delany in *Life & Corr.* (1861) III. 604 A droll Pomeranian puppy. **1787** Hunter in *Phil. Trans.* LXXVII. 265 The shepherd's Dog in Germany, called Pomeranian. **1865** Couch *Fishes Brit. Isl.* IV. 42 Pomeranian Bream. **1880** E. W. Hamilton *Diary* 23 June (1972) I. 21 It seems that Bismarck, though unwilling to 'sacrifice a single Pomeranian soldier' in the cause of Greece, will give Germany's moral support, at any rate, to a demonstration. **1884** Day *Fishes* II. 194 Pomeranian bream... This gregarious fish, which is of a hardy nature, is found in many sluggish rivers, canals, ponds, broads, and lakes in this country. **1919** G. B. Shaw *Augustus does his Bit* in *Heartbreak House* 235 The Colonel of the Pomeranian regiment which captured me. **1934** Priebsch & Collinson *German Lang.* I. i. 11 The Western group [of the Slavonic languages] . . includes . . the Cassubian and almost extinct Slovinzian (brought by Lorentz under the collective name of Pomoranian) along the Baltic coast of Pomerania. **1935** F. Lorentz in F. Lorentz et al. *Cassubian Civilization* 6 The whole Pomeranian language is divided into seventy-six dialects, which are, in many cases, very different from one another. **1955** R. Jakobson *Slavic Lang.* (ed. 2) 2 These are the remnants of the Pomoranian group. **1957** [see Kashube]. **1965** G. Y. Shevelov *Prehist. of Slavic* 1 Pomoranian or Baltic Sl[avic] dialects of such Sl[avic] tribes as Vilci-Veletians, Obodrites, etc. **1972** [see Kashube]. **1974** *Encycl. Brit. Macropædia* XVI. 867/1 Kashubian dialects (including Slovincian) are considered to be the remnants of a Pomeranian subgroup that belonged to the Lekhitic group.

B. *sb.* **a.** A native or inhabitant of Pomerania.

1870 W. B. Ullathorne in C. Butler *Vatican Council* (1930) I. xii. 237 Then there was a Pomeranian, who gave . . an interesting and pathetic account of the difficulties of religion in his country. **1919** [see Kashube]. **1939** [see Lech, Lekh *sb.*[5] and *a.*].

b. *sb.* Short for *Pomeranian dog.*

1882 Edna Lyall *Donovan* v, The handsome Pomeranian . . his tail bristling with wrath.

c. The West Slavonic dialect of Pomerania, a subgroup of Lechitic, now represented only by Kashube (cf. LECHITIC *sb.* and *a.*, KASHUBE).

1934 [see kashube]. **1935** F. Lorentz in F. Lorentz et al. *Cassubian Civilization* 5 Popular speech . . is nowhere uniform... A classic instance of this is furnished by Cassubian, or, as it is more scientifically termed, Pomeranian. This language is divided into Northern Pomeranian and Southern Pomeranian. **1935** T. Lehr-Splawinski in *Ibid.* iii. i. 347 The dialects spoken in the Middle Ages . . by the ancestors of the modern Cassubians constituted an intermediate belt between the dialects of Pomeranian properly speaking and those of Polish.

pomeri, variant of POMARY.

pomeridian (pəʊmə'rɪdɪən), *a.* [ad. L. *pōmerīdiānus* postmeridian, f. *post* after + *merīdiānus* MERIDIAN.] †**a.** = POSTMERIDIAN *a. Obs.*

1560 Rolland *Crt. Venus* ii. 485 About the third hour Pomeridiane. **1653** R. G. tr. *Bacon's Hist. Winds* 40 The West windes are attendants of the Pomeridian or afternoon houres.

b. *Entom.* Flying in the afternoon, as some lepidopterous insects. **c.** *Bot.* Opening or closing in the afternoon, as a flower.

1866 *Treas. Bot.*, *Pomeridian*, occurring in the afternoon.

pomerium, obs. form of POMŒRIUM.

Pomerol ('pɒmərɒl). The name of a commune in the department of Gironde in SW. France, used *attrib.* or *absol.* to designate the red wine produced there.

[**1833** C. Redding *Hist. Mod. Wines* v. 141 With this quality of wines also may be ranked those grown on the level grounds where the soil is sand and gravel. The most in repute are those of Pommerol and of the environs of Libourne.] **1951** R. Postgate *Plain Man's Guide to Wine* iv. 75 As there is no classification of Pomerols, I am reduced to making a personal list. **1959** W. James *Word-bk. Wine* 146 All are agreed on one point—Pomerol wines taste of truffles. **1969** J. Wainwright *Take-Over Men* vi. 92 He swirled the wine in his glass, . . moistened his lips with it, . . then said: 'Graves, I think.' . . 'No. I rather think Pomerol.' **1971** P. Purser *Holy Father's Navy* viii. 43 The meal was indifferent but Father Freeloader's choice of wine impeccable, even if they had brought him the '64 Pomerol and not the '62. **1974** *Times* 29 Oct. 1/5 The alleged fraud consisted in transforming ordinary table wines of the Languedoc into nobler Pomerols or Medocs.

pomeron ('pɒmərɒn). *Nuclear Physics.* Also **Pomeron.** [f. POMER(ANCHUK + -ON[1].] The Pomeranchuk pole or trajectory, or a virtual particle regarded as exchanged in the type of scattering they represent.

1967 R. J. Eden *High Energy Collisions* ix. 234 If total cross-sections are asymptotically constant, there must be a Regge pole of *even* signature . . having, $l = a_1{}^+(0) = 1$... The corresponding trajectory is called the Pomeranchuk trajectory. The object exchanged at $t = 0$ is called the 'Pomeron'. It is not a physical particle. **1971** *Physics Bull.* Sept. 517/2 With a linear trajectory this required that the pomeron has a slope of 0·64 GeV^{-2}. Several factors however have led to the abandoning of the association of the pomeron with the f^0. **1973** B. H. Bransden et al. *Fund. Particles* ix. 181 At present it does not seem that the Pomeron corresponds to a physical particle and it probably should be thought of as a device to bring diffraction scattering into the same exchange framework as other reactions. **1974** M. L. Perl *High Energy Hadron Physics* xvii. 408 It also became common to speak of the Pomeranchuk trajectory as representing the exchange of a virtual particle called the pomeron.

†**pomeroy.** *Obs.* Also 7 **pome-roie, pomroy.** [app. f. F. *pomme* (OF. *pome*) apple + *roi* king.] An old variety of apple; perh. = king-apple.

1600 Breton *Strange Fort. Two Princes* (Grosart) 19/2 Plucking off an apple called a Pome-roie. **1606** *Sir G. Goosecappe* v. i. in Bullen *O. Pl.* III. 92 Thou Pomroy or thou apple of mine eye. **1622** Peacham *Compl. Gent.* i. 2. **1664** Evelyn *Kal. Hort.* Jan. (1729) 191 Apples . . Pome-water, Pomeroy. **1823** Crabb *Technol. Dict.*, *Pomeroy*, a good-tasted apple, not very juicy, but of a pulpy substance.

†**pome'royal.** *Obs.* Also 6 **pome riall.** [app. f. F. *pomme* (OF. *pome*) apple + *royal* royal.] Some kind of apple, ? the same as POMEROY.

1534 T. Goldwell in Ellis *Orig. Lett.* Ser. iii. II. 288 We have one frute growing here with us in Kent, the which is called a Pome riall. He is called a very goode apull, and goode to drynke wyne withall. **1577** B. Googe *Heresbach's Husb.* (1586) 87 The Pippen, the Romet, the Pomeroyal. **1617** Rider *Dict.*, A Pomeroiall, *Malum apionium.*

†**'pomery.** *Rom. Antiq. Obs.* Forms: 6–7 **pomerie**, 7 **pomœrie**, 7–8 **pomery.** [Anglicized form of L. *pōmērium.*] = POMŒRIUM.

1533 Bellenden *Livy* i. x. (S.T.S.) I. 61 Than sall his hede be coverit, his body skurgit, owthir vtouth or Inwith þe pomerie, and eftir all hingit on ane vnhappy tre. *Ibid.* xvii. 97 Pomerie is callit ane certaine boundis passand round about ony toun nixt þe wallis þareof. **1600** Holland *Livy* i. xxvi. 19 Having whipped and scourged him . . either within the Pomœrie or without. **1656** Blount *Glossogr.*, *Pomery.* [**1766** Entick *London* IV. 83 A . . church, . . known by the name of St. Martin in the Pomery.]

†**'pomet.** *Obs.* (?)

1583 *Rates of Customs* D vj b, Passemin lace, look pomet lace. *Ibid.* D viij, Pomet lace of silk the groce viii *s.*

†**pomet**, in *pomet touris*, error for *pount*: see PONT[1].

pometée, -etie, -ettie, obs. ff. POMMETTY.

'pome,water. *Obs.* exc. *dial.* Also 6–7 **pom-**. [app. f. POME + WATER *sb.*] A large juicy kind of apple.

c **1430** Lydg. *Min. Poems* (Percy Soc.) 15 The pomewatyr, and the gentylle ricardons. **1588** Shaks. *L.L.L.* iv. ii. 4 Ripe as a Pomwater. **1600** Dekker *Old Fortunatus* I j, Tis de sweetest apple in de world, tis better den de Pomewater, or apple John. **1657** R. Ligon *Barbadoes* 72 The fruit when 'tis ripe, as big as the largest Pomewater. **1706** Phillips, *Pome-water*, a large sort of Apple full of a very sweet Juice. **1832** L. Hunt *Sir R. Esher* (1850) 116 The pomewater . . far surpasses the queening. **1883** *Hampsh. Gloss.*, *Pomewater*, a large apple, tempting to the sight, but excessively sour.

b. *fig.* (Cf. *apple of his eye.*)

1607 W. S[mith] *Puritan* C j b, The Captaine louing you so deerely, I, like the Pomwater of his eye, and you to be so vncomfortable, fie, fie.

pomeys, pomeis ('pəʊmɪs), *sb. pl. Her.* Also *sing.* (in Dicts.) 8 **pomey**, 8–9 **pomme.** [Of uncertain form, app. only in plural, which may possibly be an antiquated spelling of *pommes*; cf. later quots.] The name given to roundels when of a green colour.

1562 Leigh *Armorie* 150 He beareth Argent iii. pomeis in pale, which is as much to be vnderstand as iii. grene Appels. **1610** Guillim *Heraldry* iv. xix. (1660) 352 Pomeis are taken for Apples without their Stalkes. **1706** Phillips, *Pomey*, (in Heraldry) the figure of an Apple or Ball, which is always drawn of a green Colour. **1766–87** Porny *Her.* Dict., *Pommes*, green roundelets used in Coats-of-arms. **1882** Cussans *Her.* (ed. 3) 73 Roundles... The Pomme . . *vert.*

pomeys, obs. form of PUMICE.

pomfret ('pɒmfrɪt). Also **pamflet, pomphlet.** [App. derived from Pg. *pampo*, F. *pample*, said to be applied to the same fish. A dim. **pamplet* may have become *pamphlet, pomphlet*, and *pomfret.*] A fish of the genus *Stomateoides*, inhabiting the Indian and Pacific Oceans, much esteemed for food, particularly the two species *S. niger*, the ***black pomfret***, and *S. sinensis*, the ***white pomfret***, which when young is known as

silver pomfret, and when old is the ***grey pomfret***.

1727 A. HAMILTON *New Acc. E. Ind.* I. 393 A very delicious Fish called the Pamplee, comes in Sholes. **1812** in Mar. Graham *Jrnl. India* App. ii. 201 Another face look'd broad and bland, Like pamflet floundering on the sand. **1813** J. FORBES *Oriental Mem.* I. 52–3 The pomfret is not unlike a small turbot,.. epicures esteem the black pomfret a great dainty. **1886** YULE *Hobson-Jobson* 545 The French of Pondicherry call the fish *pample.* **1891** *19th Cent.* Jan. 98, I have enjoyed..pomphlet at Bombay, and blue-fish at Boston.

b. A species of sea-bream, *Brama Rayi*, found near Bermuda.

1890 in *Cent. Dict.*, and in later Amer. Dicts.

pomfret-cake (ˈpɒmfrɪt keɪk). [f. *Pomfret* (AN. and ME. *Pontfret*, now spelt *Pontefract*), a town in Yorkshire.] A liquorice cake made at Pontefract.

1838 *Encycl. Brit.* (ed. 7) XVIII. 347/2 The soil around it [Pontefract]..produces..liquorice-roots, from the juice of which the medicine called pomfret-cakes is made. **1866** MRS. GASKELL *Wives & Dau.* v, He'll have the run of the pomfret cakes. **1893** *Westm. Gaz.* 14 Feb. 7/1 The Pontefract (or Pomfret) cake is a dainty little circular confection, into the composition of which liquorice enters largely.

pomgarnade, -garnat(e, -granat(e, etc., obs. ff. POMEGRANATE.

pomice, obs. form of POMACE, PUMICE.

pomiculture (ˈpəʊmɪˌkʌltjʊə(r)). [f. L. *pōm-um* a fruit + CULTURE.] The art or practice of fruit-growing. Hence **pomiˈculturist**.

1876 A. J. EVANS *Thro' Bosnia* vi. 250 The Bosniacs show themselves absolutely incapable of pomiculture. **1894** *Tablet* 27 Oct. 648 Valuable directions..with reference to pomiculture. **1895** *N.B. Daily Mail* 27 Sept. 4 We pay.. upwards of seven hundred thousand pounds annually..to Transatlantic pomiculturists.

†**pomier.** *Obs. rare*$^{-1}$. [a. OF. *pomier*, F. *pommier* an apple-tree:—L. *pomārius.*] A pome-bearing tree; an apple or pear tree.

1480 CAXTON *Ovid's Met.* XIV. xii, She lovyd nothynge savyng trees and gardyns, as pomiers or apple and pere trees.

pomiferous (pəʊˈmɪfərəs), *a.* [f. L. *pōmifer* (f. *pōmum* apple, fruit + *-fer* bearing) + -OUS.]

1. Producing fruit, or specifically apples; *spec.* in *Bot.*, applied to trees and plants bearing pomes or pome-like fruits (formerly including cucumbers, melons, and the like), as distinguished from bacciferous or berry-bearing plants.

1656 BLOUNT *Glossogr.*, *Pomiferous*, that beareth fruit. **1664** H. POWER *Exp. Philos.* I. 48 The Seeds of all pomiferous Plants. **1691** RAY *Creation* I. (1692) 101 All Pomiferous Herbs, Pumpions, Melons, Gourds, Cucumbers. **1704** J. HARRIS *Lex. Techn.* I, *Pomiferous Trees*, ..are such as have their Flower on the top of the Fruit, and their Fruit in the Form of an Apple or Pear. **1750** G. HUGHES *Barbadoes* 121 By pomiferous fruits I would be understood to mean all of the Apple kind, such as have thick fleshy substance inclosing many seeds. **1851** GOSSE *Nat. in Jamaica* 145 Sunny, spicy, pomiferous groves. **1893** *Cornh. Mag.* July 60 The sunny sloping pomiferous town of Hexham.

2. Carrying an apple. *nonce-use.*

1757 STUKELEY *Medallic Hist. Carausius* 29 A coin represents Adam pomiferous in this manner.

pomiform (ˈpəʊmɪfɔːm), *a.* [f. L. type **pōmiformis*, f. *pōmum* fruit, apple: see -FORM.] Having the shape of a pome or apple.

1858 MAYNE *Expos. Lex.*, *Pomiformis*,..having the round form of an apple..pomiform. **1892** *Tablet* 16 Apr. 633 It would not surprise us if pomiform galls were some day found on the willow.

pomiglion, obs. form of POMMELION.

pomis(e, pomised, obs. ff. PUMICE, PUMICED.

pomivorous (pəʊˈmɪvərəs), *a. nonce-wd.* [f. L. *pōmum* fruit + -VOROUS.] That devours apples.

1855 BAGEHOT *Lit. Stud.* (1879) I. 262 The common boy. The small and pomivorous animal which we so call.

pomly, variant of POMELY *Obs.*

pommada, -do, var. POMADO *Obs.*

pommade, pommander, pommaundre, obs. ff. POMADE, POMANDER.

pommage (ˈpɒmɪdʒ). Also 6–8 **pomage.** [Cf. F. *pommage* cider harvest or production, f. F. *pomme* apple + -AGE. In sense 2 perh. a variant of POMACE.]

†**1.** Cider. *Obs. rare.*

1570–6 LAMBARDE *Peramb. Kent* (1826) 4 In the wealdish, or woody places,..of late daies they used muche pomage, or cider for want of barley. **1577** HARRISON *England* II. vi. (1877) I. 161 In some places of England, there is a kind of drinke made of apples, which they call cider or pomage.

2. = POMACE 1.

1789 W. MARSHALL *Glocestershire* (1796) II. 304 In common practice, the pomage is pressed, immediately as it is ground. **1825** J. NICHOLSON *Operat. Mechanic* 291 The bridge or cross-piece which acts on the pommage. **1884** THUDICHUM *Alcoholic Drinks* 32 The ground apples are termed pommage. A man grinds, with one horse, between two and three hogsheads of pommage a day.

pommard, pomme: see POMARD, POMEYS.

‖**pomme** (pɒm). *Gastron.* [Shortened form of next.] A potato. Chiefly *pl.*, esp. in ***pommes allumettes***, 'potato matchsticks', i.e. matchstick-thin chips; ***pommes frites***, 'fried potatoes', i.e. chips.

1910 A. MARIO *Easy French Cookery* 140 *French Fried Potatoes* (Pommes frites). Cut some potatoes in strips.., and cook as for Straw Potatoes. **1931** A. DE CROZE *What to eat & drink in France* xxix. 260 Pommes frites à la Gasconne (diced potatoes fried with goose dripping or lard). **1952** G. MAUROIS *Cooking with French Touch* vii. 118 There are forty different ways of preparing potatoes known to the French cuisine. *Pommes frites* is probably the best known of all. **1962** L. DEIGHTON *Ipcress File* xix. 127 The steak was.. served with asparagus tips and *pommes allumettes.* **1966** *Vogue* Nov. 148/2 *Pommes frites* (they are thinner than chips half fried). **1975** P. ORGAN *House on Cheyne Walk* xv. 126 The smell of the beach and *pommes allumettes.*

‖**pommé, -ee** (pɔme), *a. Her.* [F. *pommé*, pa. pple. of *pommer* to come to a round head, f. *pomme* apple: see POME.] = POMMETTY.

1725 COATS *Dict. Her.* s.v. *Pommettée*, A Cross Pommettée is certainly the same above call'd Pommee and Pommelee. **1727–41** CHAMBERS *Cycl.*, A *cross-pommé*, or *pommetté*, called also *trophee*, is a cross with a ball or knob, like an apple, at each end. **1882** [see POMMELLÉ].

‖**pomme de terre** (pɒm də tɛːr). *Gastron.* Pl. **pommes de terre.** [Fr.] A potato.

1823 [see GROUND-PEA]. **1846** A. SOYER *Gastronomic Regenerator* 470 (*heading*) Pommes de terre sautées au beurre. **1877** [see LYONNAIS B *adj.* b]. **1963** R. CARRIER *Great Dishes of World* 211/2 *Pommes de terre Anna* sets overlapping layers of sliced raw potatoes in a small buttered baking dish or round mould, each layer dotted with butter and the whole then baked. **1977** *Zigzag* Mar. 8/1 We ate mashed pommes de terre.

pommel (ˈpʌməl, ˈpɒməl), *sb.* Forms: α. 4–7 (9) **pomel, -elle,** 5 **poomel,** 5–6 **pomele,** 5–7 **pommell,** 6– **pommel,** (6 **pomall, poemell, pomeaw**). β. 5 **pumelle,** 6 **-ill,** 6–7 **-el, -ell, pummell, -ill,** 6–9 **pummel.** [ME. a. OF. *pomel* (12th c. in Hatz.-Darm., mod.F. *pommeau*) rounded knob, pommel of a sword or of a saddle, = Pr. *pomel*, It. *pomello*:—late L. type **pōmellum* (med.L. *pōmellus* in Du Cange), dim. of *pōmum* apple (see POME).]

I. †**1.** A globular body or prominence; a ball; a round boss, knob, or button. *Obs.*

1388 WYCLIF *Prov.* xxv. 11 A goldun pomel in beddis of siluer is he, that spekith a word in his time. **1426** LYDG. *De Guil. Pilgr.* 6717 Lower doun ek ther was set A-nother poomel, wych off makyng Was lasse & Round, (to my seemyng). **1481** CAXTON *Myrr.* II. xxxi. 125 In the mone is a body polysshyd and fair lyke a pommell right wel burnysshed. **1541** COPLAND *Guydon's Quest. Chirurg.* Fj, Makynge a party of the orbytall or emynent pomall that is rounde bryght. **1688** R. HOLME *Armoury* III. 325/1 He beareth..a Rowel of six points, at each a pomell or Button.

†**2.** A ball or spherical ornament placed on the summit of a tower, dome, gable, or pillar, at the corners of an altar, etc.; the ornamental top of the pole of a tent, a flag-staff, or the like; a finial. *Obs.*

c **1330** *Florice & Bl.* (1857) 249 The pomel aboue the led Is iwrout with so moche red. *c* **1394** *P. Pl. Crede* 562 þouȝ a man in her mynster a masse wolde heren, His siȝt schal so [be] set on sundrye werkes, þe penounes & þe pomels & poyntes of scheldes Wiþ-drawen his deuocion. *c* **1400** MAUNDEV. (Roxb.) xxx. 136 Abouen þe principall toure er twa pomelles of gold. *c* **1500** *Melusine* 357 Euery yere vpon the last day of August was sene a grete hand that toke the pommel of the said toure & pullyd it fro the toure. **1720** STRYPE *Stow's Surv.* (1754) I. III. viii. 639/2 A new Cross, with a Pomel well gilt, [was] set on the Top thereof [the Spire]. [**1842–76** GWILT *Archit.* Gloss., *Pomel*, a globular protuberance terminating a pinnacle, etc.]

3. A rounded knob; an ornamental knob generally. **a.** The knob terminating the hilt of a sword, dagger, or the like.

α. *c* **1330** R. BRUNNE *Chron. Wace* (Rolls) 10037 Ffro þe hilte vnto þe pomel Was twenti vnche large. **1470–85** MALORY *Arthur* II. xix. 99 Merlyn toke his swerd and toke of the pomel and set on an other pomel. **1584** LYLY *Sappho* II. iii, Hee that can..weare his dagger pomel lower then the point. **1617** MORYSON *Itin.* III. 167 The Gentlemen..that haue priuiledge to weare Swords, as the Doctors of Ciuill Law, haue plaine pommels to them, neuer guilded. **1864** BOUTELL *Her. Hist. & Pop.* xvii. 256 It is also charged upon a small shield upon the pommel of his sword-hilt.

β. **1483** *Cath. Angl.* 293/2 A Pumelle (*A.* Pomel), *tolus.* **1583** FLEETWOOD in Ellis *Orig. Lett.* Ser. I. II. 291 His man haithe stricken the carrman with the pumell of his sword. **1588** SHAKS. *L.L.L.* v. ii. 618 The pummell of Cæsars Faulchion. **1685** *Lond. Gaz.* No. 2050/4 A Rapier Sword, the Hilt of which was made with a whole Shell, and a long Bar from the Shell to the Pumel. **1715** tr. *Pancirollus' Rerum Mem.* I. III. iv. 136 The two Pummels or Ends of this Staff, which jutted out.

†**b.** The knob on the breech of a muzzle-loading cannon; = CASCABEL 1: cf. POMMELION. *Obs.*

1639 R. WARD *Animadv. Warre* 129 The Center of the pummell or Caskable of the Peece. **1672** W. P. *Compl. Gunner* iv. 5 The Pumel or Button at her Coyl or Britch-end is called the Casacabel. **1692** in *Capt. Smith's Seaman's Gram.* II. vi. 94 The Cascabel or Pummel.

†**c.** An ornamental knob on a chair, the cover of a cup, etc. *Obs.*

1424 in *E.E. Wills* (1882) 57 My flat couered pece [of plate] whith a sqware pomell. ? *c* **1475** *Sqr. lowe Degre* 745 Ye shall..ryde, my doughter, in a chare,..Your pomelles shalbe ended with gold. **1526** *Inv. Goods Dk. Richmond* in *Camden Misc.* (1855) 19 A Chaire of clothe of golde, frynged with redde silk and gold, with iiij. pomelles of silver and gild. **1608** BEAUM. & FL. *Four Plays in One* Induct., To touch the pomel of the king's chair..is better security..than three of the best merchants.

†**d.** The pole-star (? the knob of the sky). *Obs.*

1503 *Kalender of Sheph.* L j b, The stern that we cal the pomeaw of hewyns & ryght vnder yt ys the sown at the howr of mydnyght. **1570** LEVINS *Manip.* 56/45 A Pomel, *polus, i.*

†**4.** A rounded or semi-globular projecting part. *Obs.* **a.** The rounded top of the head; the crown.

c **1386** CHAUCER *Knt.'s T.* 1831 He pighte hym on the pomel of his heed.

b. A woman's breast. *poet.*

1413 HOCCLEVE *Compl. Soul* 199 Wks. (E.E.T.S.) III. p. lvii, Of this pomel will I my selfe rest... That is, thi selfe, moder, maide and wiffe, The sustenaunce and solace of my liffe. *a* **1586** *Bankis of Helicon* 63 in *Montgomerie's Poems* (S.T.S.) 275 With yvoire nek, and pomellis round, And comlie intervall.

c. The lower side of the closed fist.

1644 BULWER *Chirol.* 75 The nether part of this Hand in this posture Chiromancers call the pomell or percussion of the Hand.

d. A bastion.

1687 A. LOVELL tr. *Thevenot's Trav.* I. 18 A square Castle, with a Tower, joined to it by a Pomel of a Wall.

5. a. The upward projecting front part of a saddle; the saddle-bow.

α. *c* **1450** *Merlin* xiii. 191 Their swerdes hangynge at the pomell of theire sadeles be-fore. **1591** FLORIO *2nd Fruites* 41 Now hold me that stirop. Get vp, and hold fast by the pomell. **1711** STEELE *Spect.* No. 109 ¶3 Taking him.. before him on the Pommel of his Saddle. **1809** *Med. Jrnl.* XXI. 367 The rider..was forcibly thrown forward on the pommel of the saddle.

β. **1620** SHELTON *Quix.* II. xiii. 79 This bottle hanging at the pummel of my saddle. **1677** *Lond. Gaz.* No. 1242/4 A large Scar under the pummel of the Saddle. **1720** W. GIBSON *Diet. Horses* viii. (1731) 126 A Saddle broad under the Pummel is always very uneasy.

b. Either of a pair of removable curved handgrips fitted to a vaulting horse.

1887 A. ALEXANDER *Mod. Gymnastic Exercises* 137 The Vaulting Horse..contains a set of pommels, which are removable if required. **1895** W. MACLAREN *A. Maclaren's Physical Educ.* (new ed.) 103 For vaulting with one hand, circling, feint exercises &c..., it is customary to have pommels fitted on the horse. **1908** *Man. Physical Training* (H.M.S.O.) viii. 184 Bend the knees and spring quickly from the ground up to the 'First position', with the hands gripping the pommels. **1920** NAYLOR & TEMPLE *Mod. Physical Educ.* 125 The starting position is taken by grasping the pommels with 'inward-grip'. **1932** T. MCDOWELL *Vaulting* vii. 28 This vault may also be performed with one hand on a pommel and the other on the horse proper. **1971** L. KOPPETT *N.Y. Times Guide Spectator Sports* 242 The gymnast balances himself on the pommels..and performs various maneuvers with leg movements, handstands, and so forth. **1972** B. TAYLOR et al. *Olympic Gymnastics for Men & Women* viii. 181/2 The left arm pushes off the left pommel enabling the gymnast to gain the necessary height.

II. [? f. POMMEL *v.*, PUMMEL *v.*]

6. *techn.* **a.** (In form *pummel.*) A square-faced tool used by stonemasons as a punch. **b.** An oblong wooden block with a convex ribbed face for making leather supple and graining it.

1793 SMEATON *Edystone L.* §36 The three holes were broke into one, by square-faced Pummels. **1852** MORFIT *Tanning & Currying* (1853) 465 All leather should be submitted to the action of the pommel. **1875** KNIGHT *Dict. Mech.*, *Pommel*,..a block of hard wood used by curriers in pressing and working skins to render them supple. It is flat above and rounded below.

7. The bat used in the game of 'knur and spell'.

1845 [C. ROGERS] *Tom Treddlehoyle's Thowts*, etc. 39 (E.D.D.) Burd-caiges, pumils, waukin-sticks, an' knurs. **1870** *Routledge's Ev. Boy's Ann.* Jan. 48 The bats, or sticks, known as pommels. **1893** 'SILPHEO' *Random Rhymes* 8 (E.D.D.) Those who the 'pummel' well can wield With 'spell and bullet' take the field.

8. *Comb.* ***pommel vault***; **pommel-foot, pummel-foot**, club-foot; **pommel horse**, a vaulting horse having pommels; also **pommelled horse.**

1861 W. BARNES in *Macm. Mag.* June 127 Man may be marred..by perverse fashions—as in the pummel feet of Chinese women. **1895** *Syd. Soc. Lex.*, *Pommelfoot*, a syn. for *Clubfoot.* **1908** *Man. Physical Training* (H.M.S.O.) viii. 185 Progression should be obtained by gradually raising the height of the pommel horse till it is somewhat higher than the average troop horse. **1932** T. MCDOWELL *Vaulting* p. v, Where the teacher has a 'box horse' and not a 'pommelled horse', it will be found that many of the vaults are adjustable to the apparatus available. *Ibid.* p. vi, Then comes the 'pommel horse' with pad. *Ibid.* vii. 30 *Pommel Vault.* Take off from both feet as the hands grasp the pommels. **1957** *Encycl. Brit.* XI. 20/2 The 'Olympic six' for men comprise floor exercises, work on the horizontal bar, parallel bars and rings, pommelled horse and vaulting. **1962** [see HORSE 6 c]. **1964** D. M. KUNZLE in G. C. Kunzle *Parallel Bars* 13 All sorts of climbing instruments—ropes, bars, beams and the pommelled horse. **1971** *Sportsweek* (Bombay) 21 Feb. 9/1 Jim Prestidge recalls..the basic pommel horse exercises developed by German Ludwig Jahn, the father of the sport, in the last century. **1972** B. TAYLOR et al. *Olympic*

Gymnastics for Men & Women viii. 180/1 Place the pommel horse under the parallel bars.

pommel (ˈpʌməl), *v.* Also 6 pomel(l: see also PUMMEL. [f. POMMEL *sb.* 3 a, *lit.* to strike with the pommel of a sword instead of its edge or point.] *trans.* To beat or strike repeatedly with or as with a pommel; to beat or pound with the fists; to bruise.

1530 PALSGR. 662/1, I pomell, I beate one aboute the eares, *je torche*. *a* **1548** HALL *Chron., Hen. VIII* 49 b, Yͤ duke..tooke hym..and pomeled so aboute the hed that the bloud yssued out of hys nose. **1768–74** TUCKER *Lt. Nat.* (1834) I. 645 Calling in his imps to hold their arms while he pommels them. **1821** LAMB *Elia* Ser. I. *Old Benchers I. T.*, He..pommelled him severely with the hilt of it [a sword]. **1863** 'OUIDA' *Held in Bondage* (1870) 70 There is a degree of absurdity in two mortals setting solemnly to work to pommel one another.

Hence **ˈpommelling, -eling** *vbl. sb.*; also **ˈpommeller, -eler**, one who pommels.

1824 W. IRVING *T. Trav.* I. 334 The old man's ire was somewhat appeased by the pommeling of my head. **1874** BURNAND *My Time* xvii. 146 A contention in which your pommellings are active. **1890** *Cent. Dict.*, Pommeler.

†**poˈmmelion.** *Obs.* Forms: 8 pomiglion, pummelion, 9 pommillion, pomelion, pommelion. [An unexplained extension of POMMEL in sense 3 b; said to be originally a sailors' word.] A cascabel: = POMMEL *sb.* 3 b.

1769 FALCONER *Dict. Marine* (1789) H j, The..cascabel of the gun..sailors call the pomiglion, or pummelion. **1823** CRABB *Technol. Dict.*, *Pomelion*, the cascabel, or hindmost knob of a cannon. **1837** MACDOUGALL tr. *Graah's E. Coast Greenland* 74 The entire length of the gun, from muzzle to pommillion, was sixtyfive inches and a half. **1867** SMYTH *Sailor's Word-bk.*, Pommelion.

‖**pommellé, -elé** (ˈpɒməleɪ), *a. Her.* Also -elly. [F. *pommelé*, pa. pple. of *pommeler* (in obs. sense) to assume a rounded or knobbed form, f. OF. *pommel*: see POMMEL.] = POMMETTY *a.*

1562 LEIGH *Armorie* 61 b, A crosse pomelle, Sable. This is so termed for the roundness thereof at the endes. **1725** COATS *Dict. Her.*, *Pommee*, a *Cross pommillee*. **1823** CRABB *Technol. Dict.*, Pomelled (*Her.*) or Pommelly. **1882** CUSSANS *Her.* (ed. 3) 62 A Cross, the limbs of which are terminated by a single ball, is termed a Cross Pommé, or Pommellé.

pommelled, pomelled (ˈpʌməld), *a. Her.* [f. POMMEL *sb.* + -ED².] Of a sword: Having the pommel of a specified tincture.

1766–87 PORNY *Her.* (ed. 4) 182 Three Swords in Pile.. Pearl, pomeled and hilted Topaz. **1864** BOUTELL *Her. Hist. & Pop.* xxi. §10 (ed. 3) 317 A sword erect gu., hilted and pomelled or.

b. = POMMELLÉ.

1823 [see prec.].

pommer (ˈpɒmə(r)). *Mus.* [G., altered form of BOMBARD *sb.*] A type of shawm; = BOMBARD *sb.* 4.

1878 [see BOMBARD *sb.* 4]. **1884** *Encycl. Brit.* XVII. 706/2 The little schalmey and tenor pommer seem to have disappeared in the 17th century. **1911** E. F. COOK *Dict. Mus. Terms* 202 *Pommer*, an ancient wooden wind reed instrument of various sizes. **1950** *Oxf. Jun. Encycl.* IX. 487/1 The lower ones were called 'pommers' and 'bombards'. In the 17th and 18th centuries hautboys.. developed from shawms, and 18th-century bassoons from the pommers. **1967** *Daily Tel.* 10 Feb. 19/4 The strength of the group lies..in the diversity and precision of its wind instruments, which include such rarities as the shawm, pommer, crumhorn and cornet. **1976** D. MUNROW *Instruments Middle Ages & Renaissance* vi. 40 Praetorius says that shawms are designated by the term *bombarde* or *Pommer* irrespective of their size. **1977** *Early Music* July 347/1 A collection of different pirouettes may be useful. I have five (made from corks) for my soprano pommer.

Pommery (ˈpɒmərɪ). Also **Pommery and Greno.** The proprietary name of a brand of champagne produced by the firm of Pommery & Greno, founded in Rheims in 1836.

1882 *Official Gaz.* (U.S. Patent Office) 7 Nov. 1540/2 Champagne-Wine.—Veuve Pommery & Fils, Reims, France... The designation 'Pommery & Greno'. **1887** *Trade Marks Jrnl.* 27 July 867 A. Pommery. Wines... Pommery & Cie. Reims. **1891** [see PERRIER JOUËT]. **1892** A. W. PINERO *Magistrate* II. 55 *Cis*:..You'll look better after a glass or two of Pommery, Guv. *Mr. Posket*: No, no, Cis —now, no champagne. **1896** *Westm. Gaz.* 8 Dec. 2/1 'It is so awful to think of the suffering among the masses and to feel that one can do so little to alleviate it,' he said as he sipped his Dry Pommery. **1907** [see MUMM]. **1918** G. FRANKAU *One of Them* xix. 144 Crimson, the orchids flaunted; gold, the chalice Bubbled with Pommery's unstinted measure. **1920** [see HEIDSIECK]. **1951** R. SENHOUSE tr. *Colette's Chéri* 86 'What d'you drink, now you're married?'.. 'Pommery,' Chéri said. **1966** M. BREWER *Man against Fear* vii. 70 And a bottle of the Pommery. Properly iced, please. **1975** *Woman's Jrnl.* Sept. 73/2 They drank Pommery & Greno 1889.

pommes, obs. form of PUMICE.

pommetty (ˈpɒmətɪ), *a. Her.* Also 7 -etie, 8 -etée. [a. F. *pommetté*, f. *pommette*, dim. of *pomme* apple.] Terminating in a knob or knobs, as the arms of a cross. So †**ˈpommeture**, *Obs.* [a. obs. F. *pommeture*], the condition of being pommetty.

1611 COTGR., *Pommetté, ée*, pommetie;..*Pommeture*, pommeture; or the being Pommetie. **1709** HEARNE *Collect.* 6 Nov. (O.H.S.) II. 302 Three Crosses pometées. **1766–87** PORNY *Her.* (ed. 4) Dict., *Pommetty*, this is said of a cross, whose extremities terminate with a button or knob at each end, like an apple.

pommey (ˈpʌmɪ). *dial.* Also **pommy, pummy.** [app. a. obs. F. *pom(m)ee, pomeye* cider, also apple sauce (Godef.):—L. type **pōmāta*; see POMADE. But it may be a popular corruption of POMACE (*pommis, pommice*), or in some other way related to that word.] = POMACE 1.

1843 FALKNER in *Jrnl. R. Agric. Soc.* IV. II. 383 The pommey (that is, the pulp after it has been pressed) will generally contain a large number of entire seeds. **1874** T. HARDY *Madding Crowd* II. 275 Saying 'ware o' the pommy ma'am; 'twill spoil yer gown'. **1886** ELWORTHY *W. Somerset Word-bk.*, *Pummy*, ground apples, in process of cider making. Always so called before the juice is expressed; and the same word is applied to the refuse when pressed dry; this latter is, however, sometimes called cider-muck.

pommice, -is, obs. ff. POMACE, PUMICE.

pommill: see POMELY *a.*, dappled.

pommillion, variant of POMMELION *Obs.*

†**pomming-stone.** *Obs.* = PUMICE-STONE.

1615 SWETNAM *Arraignm. Wom.* (1880) p. xv, In their loue a woman is compared to a pomming-stone, for which way soeuer you turne a pomming stone it is full of holes.

Pommy (ˈpɒmɪ), *sb.* (*a.*) *Austral.* and *N.Z. colloq.* Also **Pommie** and with lower-case initial. [Origin obscure.]

A. *sb.* A derogatory term for an immigrant from the United Kingdom; an Englishman or Englishwoman, a Briton. **B.** *attrib.* or as *adj.* Of or pertaining to a Pommy; British, English, *spec.* (often as a term of affectionate abuse) in ***Pommy bastard***. Cf. POM².

The most widely held derivation of this term, for which, however, there is no firm evidence, is that which connects it with *pomegranate* (see quots. 1923, 1963). A discussion of this and of other theories may be found in W. S. Ramson *Australian English* (1966) 63.

1915 in B. Gammage *Broken Years* (1974) 86 We call the Regulars—Indians and Australians—'British'—but Pommies are nondescript. **1916** in *Ibid.* 240 They're only a b—— lot of Pommie Jackeroos and just as hopeless. **1916** *Anzac Bk.* 31 A Pommy can't go wrong out there if he isn't too lazy to work. **1920** D. O'REILLY in Murdoch & Drake-Brockman *Austral. Short Stories* (1951) 144 The 'Pommy' parson made good, as a good man always will. **1923** D. H. LAWRENCE *Kangaroo* vii. 162 Pommy is supposed to be short for pomegranate. Pomegranate, pronounced invariably pommygranate, is a near enough rhyme to immigrant, in a naturally rhyming country. Furthermore, immigrants are known in their first months, before their blood 'thins down', by their round and ruddy cheeks. So we are told. *Ibid.* 164 In this way Mr Somers had to take himself to task, for his Pommy stupidity. **1926** GALSWORTHY *Silver Spoon* II. iv. 137 They call us Pommies and treat us as if we'd took a liberty in coming to their blooming country. **1933** 'P. CADEY' *Broken Pattern* xii. 130 'You should have heard the English accent!' 'Pommy gab, eh?' commented his mate. **1938** N. MARSH *Artists in Crime* ix. 128 She was always shooting off her mouth about the way the Aussies don't know a good thing when they see it. These pommies! She gave me the jitters. **1946** B. JAMES in *Coast to Coast 1945* 63 He was an Englishman, not a 'pommy', mind you. It seemed he hadn't even reached to that dignity. **1947** B. MASON in D. M. Davin *N.Z. Short Stories* (1953) 333 What time we had left was spent on fruitless errands for the Pommie matelots. **1949** F. SARGESON *I saw in my Dream* II. xiii. 118 Look at Wally's ma—she got over her Pommy ways. **1951** D. STIVENS *Jimmy Brockett* 214 Like most of these pommy bastards, he had funny ways but he wasn't a bad old bloke at heart. **1957** *New Scientist* 23 May 13/3 There is..an elusive background of strangeness, imbued with an element of timelessness, which comes home to the sensitive 'new chum', or 'pommy', only after he has lived for a while in this new-old southern continent. **1962** J. FRAME *Edge of Alphabet* vii. 47 Look at the foreigners flooding the country on every immigrant ship, la-di-da Pommies and all. **1963** X. HERBERT *Disturbing Element* vi. 91 He still wore the heavy clumsy British type of clothing of the day [before 1914]. When we kids saw people on the street dressed like that we would yell at them: 'Jimmygrants, Pommygranates, Pommies!' **1966** R. D. EAGLESON in *Southerly* XXVI. 200 Lest British readers should be misled, *pommy* is frequently pejorative. **1974** P. MCCUTCHAN *Call for Simon Shard* iv. 36 I'm Australian born and bred, not a pommie immigrant... Now, grand-dad, 'e *was* a pommie bastard! **1975** *Times* 27 Aug 10/8 Colin Shaw..has just sent Ernest Whitehouse an explanation of how God came to be described in the television programme *Beneath the News* as a 'Pommy bastard'... Shaw adds that 'Pommy bastard' is an 'affectionate colloquialism' in Australia. **1979** *Guardian* 31 Oct. 3/2 British Leyland reacted angrily..to antipodean 'pommy-bashing' about the quality of buses.

Hence **ˈPommyland**, Britain, England.

1957 R. STOW *Bystander* 21 I'm a Pommy. And going back to Pommy-land, after twenty-four years. **1967** F. HARDY *Billy Borker yarns Again* 61 Sir Robert himself wanted to be a whiskey-taster at the Melbourne show, but ended up as some kind of wharfie over in Pommy Land. **1973** *Times* 12 Oct. 15/7 An adaptation of Barry Humphries's cult strip cartoon about the life of darkest Pommie-land seen through the eyes of an antipodean innocent. **1979** M. KAUFMAN *Container* iii. 31, I suppose you'll head off back to Pommyland now?

pommy, var. POMMEY; obs. form of PUMICE.

Pomo (ˈpəʊməʊ), *sb.* and *a.* [See quot. 1978.]

A. *sb.* **a.** An Indian people of Northern California; a member of this people. **b.** Any of the languages of this people. **B.** *adj.* Of, pertaining to, or designating this people or their languages. Hence **Poˈmoan**, the group of Pomo languages. Also as *adj.*

[**1852** G. GIBBS *Jrnl.* 2 Feb. in H. R. Schoolcraft *Hist. & Stat. Information Indian Tribes* (1853) III. 112 Four bands consented to enter into a treaty, viz., the Sah-nel, Yukai, Pomo, and Masu-ta-kaya; numbering in all, as was supposed, 1042 souls.] **1872** *Overland Monthly* Apr. 328/1 The great family of Pomos on Russian River..have many dialects, and a name for each—as Ballo Ki Pomos, Cahto Pomos, etc. **1875** H. H. BANCROFT *Native Races Pacific States* I. 362 The *Pomos*, which name signifies 'people', and is the collective appellation of a number of tribes living in Potter Valley... Each tribe of the nation takes a distinguishing prefix to the name of Pomo, as, the *Castel Pomos* and *Ki Pomos*. **1881** [see KLAMATH]. **1910** F. W. HODGE *Handbk. Amer. Indians* II. 277/1 The Pomo were the most southerly stock on the coast not brought under the mission influence of the Franciscans. **1913** [see HOKAN]. **1933** M. R. HARRINGTON *Gypsum Cave, Nevada* 87 The Pomo 'tee-weave' is somewhat similar. **1936** G. A. REICHARD *Navajo Shepherd & Weaver* 149 To demonstrate his skill..a Pomo Indian basket-maker fashions a basket so small it must be kept in a tiny bottle. **1959** E. TUNIS *Indians* 113/2 One tribe, the Pomos, made baskets that were possibly the finest ever made in the world. **1965** *Language* XLI. 304 Well-known families such as Pomoan, Chumashan, and Yuman. *Ibid.* 305 Pomo..shows no initial vowel in any of the languages. **1973** A. H. WHITEFORD *N. Amer. Indian Arts* 39 One-rod coiling was done by the Pomo and Paiute. **1977** *Language* LIII. 260/2 This work..is the first descriptive account ever published of the phonology and grammar of Southeastern Pomo, one of seven distinct languages comprising the Pomoan family within the Hokan stock. **1978** *Handbk. N. Amer. Indians* VIII. 277/1 The word Pomo originated in two Northern Pomo forms that are quite distinct in the native language but that became confused in early writings. The earliest known recordings..give Pomo as the name of an Indian group on the east fork of the Russian River. For a village in southern Potter Valley, on the east fork of that river, Vihman..provides the full phonemic form: *pʰóˑmoˑ* 'at red earth hole'... A second source..is based on Northern Pomo *pʰóʔmaʔ*.., which is added to place-names to designate those that live at that place.

‖**poˈmœrium.** *Rom. Antiq.* Also 7 pomerium. [L. *pōmœrium, -mērium*, f. *post* behind + *mœrus, mūrus* wall.] The open space running inside and outside the walls of a city, which was consecrated by the pontifex and ordained to be left free from buildings; = POMERY. Hence *transf.*

1598 R. GRENEWEY *Tacitus' Ann.* XII. vi. (1622) 162 After that, the circuit or pomœrium was augmented, according to the fortune and riches of the Kings. **1618** BACON *Let. to King* 2 Jan. in *Cabala* (1654) I. 9 The City grown from wood to brick, your Sea-walls or *Pomerium* of your Island surveyed. **1814** *Regent's Park* 25 It reserves a great pomœrium for the public health and recreation. **1852** CONYBEARE & HOWSON *St. Paul* (1862) II. xxiv. 382 The ancient wall, with its once sacred pomœrium, was rather an object for antiquarian interest..than any protection against the enemies.

pomois, obs. f. POMACE.

pomolio: see PUMILO.

pomolo, variant of POMELO.

pomology (pəʊˈmɒlədʒɪ). [ad. mod.L. *pōmologia*, f. *pōm-um*: see POME and -LOGY. So F. *pomologie* (Littré).] The science and practice of fruit-culture; also, a treatise on fruit-culture.

1818 *Gentl. Mag.* LXXXVIII. I. 160/1 Repeated experiments..which I made for the promotion of Pomology. **1839** *Pomological Mag.* I. 106 Diel, in his Pomology..suggests its having been derived from a kind of Spanish gold coin called a real. **1851** R. HOGG (*title*) British Pomology—The Apple. **1880** *Sat. Rev.* 8 May 613/1 No intelligent pomologist, whether grower or amateur, should neglect to furnish his shelves with so thorough a directory.. to our more familiar branch of pomology, apple and pear fruits.

Hence **pomoˈlogical** (ˌpəʊməʊ-) *a.*, **pomoˈlogically** *adv.*; **poˈmologist.**

1833 *Chambers's Edin. Jrnl.* II. 96/1 It is..the chief object of the modern pomologist to obtain..new varieties. **1839** (*title*) The Pomological Magazine; or, Figures and Descriptions of the most important varieties of fruit cultivated in Great Britain. *Ibid.* 14 The Summer Bonchretien Pear... By some Pomologists it is supposed to be the Regalia of Valerius Cordus. **1856** EMERSON *Eng. Traits* i. 14 Our pomologists..select the three or the six best pears 'for a small orchard'. **1863** D. G. MITCHELL *My Farm of Edgewood* 153, I once had the hardihood, in a little group of pomological gentlemen, to express a modest opinion in praise of the flavor of the Bartlett pear. **1920** R. FROST *Let.* 14 May (1964) 105 Their report was that pomologically it was all right, but poetically not. **1976** *Jrnl. R. Soc. Arts* CXXIV. 577/1 Pomologists are now busy 'taking the fruit tree back to the drawing board', seeking better ways of intercepting light. **1976** *Nature* 12 Aug. 574/1 Pomological literature contains two reports of the influence of grafted scions on the size, colour and ripening season of apples borne on the stock portions of topworked trees.

Pomona (pəʊˈməʊnə). *Rom. Mythol.* [L. *Pōmōna.*] The goddess of fruits and fruit-trees; hence, the fruit-trees of a country, or a treatise on them (cf. *flora*). ***Pomona green***: see quot. 1842.

1584 PEELE *Arraignm. Paris* I. i, To them that do this honour to our fields Her mellow apples poor Pomona yields. **1706** PHILLIPS, *Pomona*, a Nymph of Latium reckon'd to be the Goddess of Orchards and Fruits; whence the Word is taken for a Title to several Treatises of Fruit-trees. **1727–46** THOMSON *Summer* 663 Bear me, Pomona, to thy citron groves. **1833** T. HOOK *Love & Pride, Widow* ii, The pleasing viridity..of her mother's pomona pelisse. **1842** D. R. HAY *Nomencl. Colours* (1846) 44 *Pomona green* is the popular name of all full-toned greens in which yellow predominates. **1873** E. SPON *Workshop Receipts* Ser. I. 48/1 The rose colour, cornelian red, and pomona green require a less degree of heat.

pomonal (pəʊˈməʊnəl), *a. rare.* [f. POMONA + -AL.] Of or pertaining to fruit-trees; pomonic.

1859 *Trans. Illinois Agric. Soc.* III. 354 We may proudly claim this land..as the favorite seat of horticultural and pomonal progress.

pomonic (pəʊˈmɒnɪk), *a.* [f. POMONA + -IC.] Consisting of or pertaining to fruits.

1864 in WEBSTER. **1890** TALMAGE *Pathw. Life, Jesus* 332 (Funk) What floral and pomonic richness!

Pomoranian, var. POMERANIAN *a.* (*sb.*).

† **po'moun.** *Obs. rare.* [a. F. *poumon* lung.] The lungs.

13.. *K. Alis.* 4374 (Bodl. MS.), He carf his herte & his Pomoun [*v.r.* pomon] And þrew hym ouere his arsoun.

pomp (pɒmp), *sb.* Also 4–7 **pompe**, 5 **pumpe**. [a. F. *pompe* (13th c. in Du Cange):—L. *pompa*, ad. Gr. πομπή a sending, a solemn procession, a train, parade, display, pomp, f. πέμπειν to send.]

1. Splendid display or celebration, magnificent show; splendour, magnificence.

c **1315** SHOREHAM iv. 260 Who hys hit þat neuer yþouȝt Of pompe þat he seȝ? **1340** HAMPOLE *Pr. Consc.* 7077 Þus salle alle þair pomp oway pas, And be als thyng þat never was. **1483** CAXTON *Gold. Leg.* 317 b/2 For the pompe of my clothynge men calle me Margaryte. **1535** COVERDALE *Wisd.* v. 8 What profit hath the pompe of riches brought vs? *a* **1548** HALL *Chron., Hen. VII* 54 Thys mariage of prince Arthur was kept at London with great pompe and solempnitie. **1604** SHAKS. *Oth.* III. iii. 354 Farewell..The Royall Banner, and all Qualitie, Pride, Pompe, and Circumstance of glorious Warre. **1633** BP. HALL *Hard Texts, Nahum* ii, Thine enemy..shall come fiercely upon thee, with great pompe of terror. **1697** DRYDEN *Virg. Georg.* IV. 559 High o'er the Main in wat'ry Pomp he rides. **1750** GRAY *Elegy* ix, The boast of heraldry, the pomp of pow'r. **1888** BRYCE *Amer. Commw.* II. lxiii. 453 He generally avoids publicity, preferring the substance to the pomp of power.

b. with *a.* and *pl.*

1651 JER. TAYLOR *Holy Dying* v. §8 (1727) 250 In the grave of her husband, in the Pomps of mourning. **1847** EMERSON *Repr. Men, Shaks.* Wks. (Bohn) I. 352 The church has reared him amidst rites and pomps.

c. *fig.* Said of the splendours of nature.

c **1750** SHENSTONE *Elegies* i. 39 Where the turf diffus'd its pomp of flow'rs. **1825** LONGF. *Sea-Diver* vii, I saw the pomp of day depart. **1868** HAWTHORNE *Amer. Note-Bks.* (1879) II. 48 The whole landscape is now covered with this indescribable pomp.

† **2.** A triumphal or ceremonial procession or train; a pageant; a splendid show or display along a line of march. *Obs.*

1482 *Monk of Evesham* (Arb.) 43 By the vyctoryse pompys of her enmyes. **1530** PALSGR. 256/2 Pompe tryumphe, *triumphe*. **1576** GASCOIGNE *Steele Gl.* (Arb.) 58 In olden dayes, good kings..Contented were, with pompes of little pryce. **1583** FULKE *Defence* xxi. (Parker Soc.) 564 As for the Greek word πομπεύειν, it signifieth to go in a solemn pomp, such as your processions are. *c* **1618** MORYSON *Itin.* IV. IV. i. (1903) 334 In the Pompe the wemen goe first and of them the best and the neerest frendes next to the herse. **1667** MILTON *P.L.* VII. 564 The Planets in thir stations list'ning stood, While the bright Pomp ascended jubilant. **1770** GOLDSM. *Des. Vill.* 317 Here, while the proud their long-drawn pomps display. **1807** ROBINSON *Archæol. Græca* I. i. 7 Those pomps or processions of young men and damsels..who.. displayed themselves at the festivals.

† **b.** *fig.* (Cf. *train.*)

1667 MILTON *P.L.* VIII. 61 With Goddess-like demeanour forth she went; Not unattended, for on her as Queen A pomp of winning Graces waited still.

† **c.** *fig.* Said of any great natural movement.

1595 DANIEL *Civ. Wars* II. vii, How Thames, inricht with many a Flood..Glides on, with pompe of Waters. **1712** ADDISON *Spect.* No. 420 ¶3 Worlds..sliding round their Axles in such an amazing Pomp and Solemnity.

† **3.** Ostentatious display; parade; specious or boastful show; vain glory; esp. in phr. ***pomp and pride***. *Obs.*

c **1325** *Spec. Gy Warw.* 158 Gret los of pompe and pride. *a* **1340** HAMPOLE *Psalter* xxxi. 12 þaire pompe in speche, fordo it, that neghis noght til the in meknes. *c* **1400** *Destr. Troy* 3785 Þe pompe and proude wordis ay þe prinse hated. **1525** LD. BERNERS *Froiss.* II. CCXXV. [ccxxi.] 704 Bycause they suffred the prelates of the churche to medell so moche; therfore some sayde, it was tyme to abate their pompes, and to bringe them to reason. **1563** B. GOOGE *Eglogs*, etc. (Arb.) 98 For all the pompe and Pryde, the Bodie tournes to dust. **1653** MILTON *Hirelings* (1659) 49 After a long pomp and tedious preparation out of heathen authors. **1705** STANHOPE *Paraphr.* III. 376 Deceiving the World with a Pretence and Pomp of Godliness. **1772** PRIESTLEY *Inst. Relig.* (1782) II. 390 A mere piece of pomp and parade.

b. *pl.*

In the baptismal formula, repr. L. *pompa* or *pompæ diaboli* (2nd c., Tertull.), orig. the processions, public shows, spectacles of the circus, etc., associated with or sanctioned by the pagan worship (see sense 2 above); then, more vaguely, any 'shows' held to be under the patronage of the devil; finally (from 17th c.) tacitly transferred to those of 'the world', and associated with its 'vanities'.

1303 R. BRUNNE *Handl. Synne* 4665 Y forsake þe, here, Satan, And alle þy pompes, and all thy werkys. **1526** *Pilgr. Perf.* (W. de W. 1531) 169 b, Whether thou renounce & forsake yᵉ deuyll & all his pompes. **1548–9** (Mar.) *Bk. Comm. Prayer, Catechism*, That I should forsake the deuil and all his workes and pompes, the vanities of the wicked worlde. [1603 the deuill and all his workes, the pomps and vanities of the wicked world.] **1746** EARL OF KILMARNOCK in A. McKay *Hist. Kilmarnock* (1880) 89 The pomps and gaudy shows of the world. **1835** MRS. SHERWOOD *Stories Ch. Catech.* (1873) 401 *Q.* What are pomps and vanities? *A.* All kinds of fine things which we use, or wear, to gratify our pride or vanity. **1845** G. A. POOLE *Churches* vii. 73 His armorial bearings (the very essential hieroglyphic of the pomps of this world which we renounce at Baptism). **1858** MISS SEWELL *Amy Herbert* x. 128 The pomps and vanities of the world are different to different people. If Susan Reynolds..were anxious to..wear a silk dress like yours, she would be longing for pomps and vanities, because she would be coveting something beyond her station.

† **4.** *concr.* Something to make a brave show.

1632 BROME *North. Lasse* I. ii, Here's five peeces to buy pomps against my Sisters Wedding.

5. Phrases. † ***magistrate of the pomps***: a sumptuary officer in Venice. † ***to save one's pomp***: see quot. 1801.

1705 ADDISON *Italy* 78 The Magistrate of the Pomps is oblig'd by his Office to see that no Body wears the Cloth of another Country. **1801** *Sporting Mag.* XVIII. 101 To save one's pomp at whist, is to score five before the adversaries are up, or win the game.

6. *Comb.*, as ***pomp-fed, -like, -loving*** adjs.

1711 HICKES *Chr. Priesth.* (1847) II. 107 The highest pomp-like celebrity of words. **1813** SHELLEY *Q. Mab* IV. 245 A pomp-fed king. **1903** BRANDES *Poland* I. iii. 24 An enthusiastic and unpractical people..pomp-loving and volatile.

pomp, *v.*[1] Now chiefly *poet.* [f. prec. sb. Cf. late L. *pompāre* to do (a thing) with pomp (Sedul.); obs. F. *pomper* to celebrate with pomp, act splendidly, etc.] *intr.* To exhibit pomp or splendour; to conduct oneself pompously. Also ***pomp it***. So **pomped** (pɒmpt) *a.*, honoured with pomp, celebrated; **'pomping** *a.*, † (*a*) in ***pomping pride***, prob. a corruption of ***pomp and pride***: see prec. 3; (*b*) *dial.*, involved in acting.

c **1500** *Sir Beues* (Pynson) 172 He pryked forth before the oste For pompynge pryde to make great boste. **1555** BRADFORD *Supplic.* B ij b, For example, take their pompynge pryde. *c* **1632** B. JONSON *Expost. w. Inigo Jones* 29 What is the cause you pomp it so, I ask? **1919** W. DE LA MARE *Flora*, Mount to the porch the pomped grandees In lonely state, by twos, and threes. **1922** HARDY *Late Lyrics* 48 And once or twice she has cast me As she pomped along the street Court-clad,..A glance from her chariot-seat. **1937** G. FRANKAU *More of Us* xiv. 153 And all that day, despising fun and frolic With Janes or Joans, he pomped about the ship. **1969** G. MACBETH *War Quartet* 26 So few yards Beyond this dust-whirl, those pomped victors. **1976** *Birmingham Post* 16 Dec. 2/4 Rover, one of the pomping folk, thinks principally in Shakespearean tags. **1976** J. C. TREWIN in D. V. Baker *Cornish Short Stories* 134 It [sc. the rain] hammered against the side of the tent where the pomping folk had prepared hopelessly for the evening.

pomp, *v.*[2] Now *dial.* [A variant of *pamp*, radical of *pamper* vb. See PAMP *v.* (the existence of which it confirms).] *trans.* To feed (any one) luxuriously, feed up, pamper.

[? *a* **1400**: see PAMP *v.*] **1509** HAWES *Past. Pleas.* v. (1554), The pomped carkes wyth fode delicious They did not fede. *a* **1518** SKELTON *Magnyf.* 2012 Where that ye were pomped with what that ye wolde, Nowe must ye suffre bothe hunger and colde. **1884** LAWSON *Worc. Gloss., Pomp, v.*, to pamper or feed up; spoiled children are said to be pomped up; also horses and other animals for sale. **1896** OUTIS *Vig. Mon.* in *Berrow's Worc. Jrnl.* (E.D.D.), [The ladies] wuz hall pomped hoff and togged up.

pomp, pompe, obs. forms of PUMP.

pomp, erron. form of POP *v.*[2]

‖ **pompa.** Latin for POMP.

a **1704** T. BROWN tr. *Æneas Sylvius' Lett.* lxxxii Wks. 1709 III. II. 79 'Tis true, you put on Mourning..and all the *Pompa Rogi* in wonderful Decency and Order. **1850** LEITCH tr. *C. O. Müller's Anc. Art* §387 (ed. 2) 503 Pan..sitting.. over a grotto in which the great mother and the nymphs.. are likewise receiving a pompa.

pompadour (ˈpɒmpədʊə(r)), *sb.* Also 8 **pompedore**. After the Marquise de Pompadour, mistress of Louis XV (1721–64), used subst. and attrib. to designate fashions, a colour, etc.: either contemporary by way of compliment, or in later times with reference to the fashions of her time.

1. *gen.* Designating fashions of dress, hair-dressing, furniture, etc.: see quots.

1752 MRS. DELANY in *Life & Corr.* (1861) III. 110, I think there is a time of life..when very gaudy entertainments are as unbecoming, as pink colour and pompadours! **1755** *Ibid.* 321, I don't know what you mean by a *pompadour*, unless it is what we call in this part of the world a *pelisse*; which in plain English is a long cloak made of satin or velvet,..lined or trimmed with silk, satin, or fur,..with slits for the arms to come out and a head like a capuchin. **1756** *Univ. Mag.* XIX. 133/2 No decent coif—but just before Was grandly plac'd a pompedore. **1765** *Ibid.* XXXVII. 366/1 Much resembling the modern pompadour. **1849** *Sidonia Sorc.* I. Pref. 9 In her hand she [Sidonia] carries a sort of pompadour of brown leather, of the most elegant form and finish. **1889** 'J. S. WINTER' *Mrs. Bob* (1891) 77 She had a Pompadour stick with a big silver knob on top. **1885** A. EDWARDES *Girton Girl* I. xii. 238 It was not Louis Seize furniture, or Pompadour cabinets..that Marjorie missed. **1890** *Cent. Dict.*, *Pompadour parasol*, a form of parasol used by women about 1860, having a folding handle, and generally covered with moire antique, or other heavy silk. **1909** *Daily Chron.* 17 Sept. 5/3 Charged..with stealing..two silver pompadour boxes. **1925** O. SITWELL in E. Sitwell et al. *Poor Young People* 35 Through her pompadour-peruke. **1971** S. JEPSON *Let. to Dead Girl* xii. 143 She opened the skirt of a pompadour doll on a side table, pulled out a white telephone.

2. A shade of crimson or pink; also, a fabric of this colour. Also *attrib.*

1756 COWPER in *Connoisseur* No. 119 ¶9 His taylor.. having dressed him in a snuff-coloured coat, instead of a *pompadour*. **1762** SMOLLETT *L. Greaves* xxv. (1793) II. 272 Mr. Clarke was dressed in pompadour, with gold buttons. **1787** 'G. GAMBADO' *Acad. Horsemen* (1809) 31 He..ever recommended a coat of pompadour, or some conspicuous colour. **1840** HOOD *Up Rhine* 110 His coat was chocolate brown, with a pompadour velvet collar. **1896** *Daily News* 29 May, The stall-holders will be in the dress of Irish peasants —green petticoats, pompadour polonaises, and kerchiefs worn picturesquely over their heads. **1968** *N.Y. City* (Michelin Tire Corp.) 57 The most precious types of Sèvres porcelain, in the pink known as 'Pompadour'. **1976** N. ROBERTS *Face of France* x. 107 Balloons, scarlet, orange, blue and..Pompadour pink.

3. Designating a pattern consisting of sprigs of flowers in pink, blue, and sometimes gold, scattered on a white ground.

1807–8 W. IRVING *Salmag.* (1824) 146 My aunt..put on her pompadour taffeta gown, and sallied forth to lament the misfortune of her dear friend. **1835** *Court Mag.* VI. *Fashions* p. ix/2 Pompadour satins, a white ground embroidered in bouquets of different flowers in colours, are much in request. **1889** *Pall Mall G.* 9 Jan. 6/1 A very becoming loose cloak of some pompadour-looking material. **1902** *Westm. Gaz.* 7 July 3/2 Wearing a delicately Pompadour-patterned muslin frock.

4. A tropical S. American bird (*Xipholena pompadora*), characterized by the brilliant crimson-purple hue of its plumage. Also *attrib.*

1759 G. EDWARDS *Gleanings* III. 275–6 The Pompadour. .. Birds taken in a French prize... They were said to be for Madam Pompadour. It being a Bird of excessive beauty, I hope that Lady will forgive me for calling it by her name.. Mr. Brisson..calls it Cotinga Pourpre. **1871** W. H. G. KINGSTON *Banks of Amazon* (1876) 462 The delicate white wings and claret-coloured plumage of a lovely pompadour would glance from the foliage. **1893** NEWTON *Dict. Birds* 86 *Xipholena pompadora*—known as the Pompadour Chatterer, is of a hue scarcely to be seen in any other bird.

5. a. *U.S.* A fashion of dressing men's hair. Also *advb.*

1887 *Evening Sun* (N.Y.) 15 Apr. 3/4 A tall, slender young man, with a full blonde beard and pompadour hair. **1895** *Weekly Examiner* (San Francisco) 19 Sept. 1/7 Henry Jacob has a pompadour and a profile not unlike Durrant's. **1905** *News* (Malden, Mass.) in *Westm. Gaz.* 7 Nov. 12/1 Because Congressman Roberts has been so successful a campaigner and still had his hair cut pompadour, it does not follow that General Bartlett can win with his hair cut banged. **1920** S. LEWIS *Main St.* 76 The meek ambitiousness..clouded like an aura his pale face, flap ears, and sandy pompadour. **1955** W. GADDIS *Recognitions* I. vi. 208 His hair, a shiny black pompadour which he wore like a hat. **1976** *New Yorker* 24 May 107/1 Reagan looks good at the rostrum: a tall figure with ruddy cheeks, his reddish-brown hair swept back in a slight pompadour.

b. A style of arranging women's hair, in which it is turned back off the forehead in a roll, sometimes over a pad. Also *attrib.*

1899 *Westm. Gaz.* 11 May 4/2 The hairdresser..might.. cease to coax us to the conviction that a..pompadour puff of his manufacture were better. **1901** *Daily News* 23 Mar. 6/6 The hair dressed low in the neck and arranged in a Pompadour roll round the face. **1904** *Daily Chron.* 7 Oct. 8/5 It is absolutely impossible for a woman..to produce the strange erections known to-day as Pompadours, Regency curls, &c., naturally. **1975** J. DRUMMOND *Slowly the Poison* I. 97 Her hair..was not worn in the current high pompadour style, but cut short.

'pompadour, *v.* [f. POMPADOUR *sb.* 5.] *trans.* To dress (hair) in the pompadour style; to arrange (hair) in a pompadour. Chiefly as *pa. pple.* or *ppl. adj.*

1908 *London Opinion* 22 Aug. 362/2 She was large, plumply built, with grey hair artfully pompadoured and undulated. **1909** L. M. MONTGOMERY *Anne of Avonlea* xiv. 153 Gertie Pye swept in, pompadoured and frilled. *a* **1913** F. ROLFE *Desire & Pursuit of Whole* (1934) xvii. 178 Some pretentious pompadoured image trailing satin. **1957** V. J. KEHOE *Technique Film & Television Make-Up* ix. 111 Other tribes pompadoured the front of the hair and had two side partings. **1971** *Daily Tel.* (Colour Suppl.) 3 Sept. 42/4 They wore their hair very long, very high, pompadoured, swept up..and back. **1973** R. ROSENBLUM *Mushroom Cave* (1974) 18 The squat bully with greasy pompadoured black hair.

pompal (ˈpɒmpəl), *a. rare.* [ad. late L. *pompālis*: see POMP and -AL[1].] Of the nature of a 'pomp' or procession; splendid, showy.

1650 TRAPP *Comm. Num.* x. 7 The sound of Gods word, must not be broken or quavering; (Pompall, Tertullian calleth it). *a* **1784** *Fall Duch. Gloster* in Evans *Old Ball.* (1784) I. 318 In height of all his pompal majesty, From Cobham's house with speed he marry'd me. **1850** LEITCH tr. *C. O. Müller's Anc. Art* §336 (ed. 2) 397 In Dionysian pompal processions.

pompano (ˈpɒmpənəʊ). Also **pampano, pompono, pompinoe.** [a. Sp. *pámpano*, applied to a stromateoid fish, *Stromateus fiatola.*]

1. A North American or West Indian marine fish belonging to the genera *Trachinotus*, *Parona*, or *Zalocys*, of the family Carangidæ, esp. *Trachinotus carolinus*, the common pompano, found near south-eastern coasts of North America.

1778 tr. *J. Chappe d'Auteroche's Voy. California* 24 The pampano is very plenty in the southern part of the gulph of Mexico. **1840** *Picayune* (New Orleans) 1 Sept. 2/1 Pompanos were plentiful, and sparkling hock flew about. **1851** A. O. HALL *Manhattaner in New Orleans* 161 We forgot our military sighings in the discussion..of the momentous question whether it was orthodox to eat rum-omelette with 'pompano'-fish. **1863** RUSSELL *Diary North & South* I. 340 The best dish was, unquestionably, the pompinoe, an odd fish, something like an unusually ugly John Dory. **1883** 'MARK TWAIN' *Life on Mississippi* xliv. 445 We had dinner [in New Orleans]..—the chief dish the renowned fish called pompano, delicious as the less criminal forms of sin. **1885** *Pall Mall G.* 7 Mar. 5/1 Soft shell crabs, terrapin, canvas-back ducks, blue fish, and the pompono of New Orleans, are all wonderful delicacies. **1888** GOODE *Amer. Fishes* 198 The Pompano..is not an angler's fish. **1891** V. STUART *Adv. Forests S. Amer.* 138 Another excellent fish was the pompono, several of which jumped on board. **1892** STEVENSON & OSBOURNE *Wrecker* xix. 289 There we sat..eating pompino and drinking iced champagne. **1931** [see CARANGID *a.* and *sb.*]. **1965** A. J. MCCLANE *Standard Fishing Encycl.* 693/2 Pompano cookery is an art in Florida and Louisiana. **1971** P. CRAMPTON tr. *Heyerdahl's Ra Expeditions* ix. 198 A fat little pampano fish ..waggled its tail. *Ibid.* xi. 297 We had pampano among the pilot fish underneath us. **1973** *New Yorker* 17 Feb. 30/2 Hundreds of red snappers, Carolina mullets,..pompano, Palm Beach mackerels, and others,..lie in neat rows on a bed of shaved ice. **1977** *Time* 19 Dec. 42/2 Newly appreciated..are such home-grown marvels as Long Island duckling,..Chesapeake oysters, Gulf shrimp and pompano, [etc.].

2. pompano-shell. A bivalve shell of the genus *Donax*; a species of wedge-shell, found on the coast of Florida.

(Said to be so called because eaten by the pompano.)

1890 in *Cent. Dict.*

†**pompardy.** *Obs. rare.* Alleged name for a disease of horses.

1630 J. TAYLOR (Water P.) *Navy of Land Ships* Wks. I. 90/1 The Chinegall, the Nauelgall, Windgall, Spurgall,.. the Anticore, and the Pompardye.

†**pompatic** (pɒmˈpætɪk), *a. Obs.* [ad. late L. *pompāticus* showy, splendid (Tertull.), f. *pompātus*, prop. pa. pple. of *pompāre* to do (a thing) with pomp, f. *pompa* POMP *sb.*] Pompous, splendid, ostentatious. So †**pomˈpatical** *a. Obs.*

1535 JOHN AP RICE in Ellis *Orig. Lett.* Ser. III. II. 356 In his going he is too insolent and pompatique. **1610** BP. CARLETON *Jurisd.* 78 He deuiseth by the pride of this Pompaticall title to subdue to himselfe. *a* **1677** BARROW *Pope's Suprem.* (1687) 122 These pompatick, foolish, proud, perverse, wicked, profane words. [**1903** G. F. BROWNE *St. Aldhelm* 255 The genius of Aldhelm was on the whole too pompatic to be pleased with the lilt of pentameters.]

Pompeian (pɒmˈpiː(ɪ)ən, now usu. -ˈpeɪən), *a.*[1] and *sb.*[1] Also 9 **Pompeiian.** [ad. L. *Pompeiān-us*, f. *Pompeii*: see -AN.]

A. *adj.* Of or pertaining to Pompeii, an Italian town, buried by an eruption of Mount Vesuvius in the year 79 A.D., and since 1755 gradually laid bare by excavation. Also, characteristic or imitative of the architecture or painting of Pompeii, esp. frescoes. Hence ***Pompeian red***, a shade of red resembling that found on the walls of houses in Pompeii.

1834 LYTTON *Pompeii* I. iii, A tolerable notion of the Pompeian houses. **1869** D. G. ROSSETTI *Let.* 21 Aug. (1965) II. 716 She built..a Pompeian house for the schoolmaster. **1879** A. HOLT *Fancy Dresses* 60 *Pompeian lady.* White llama skirt, with Grecian border worked in purple. **1881** C. C. HARRISON *Woman's Handiwork* I. 20 Pompeian red velvet, for portières. **1882** J. HATTON in *Harper's Mag.* Dec. 21/2 The balustrades of the stairs, Pompeiian red. **1939** A. THIRKELL *Before Lunch* iv. 106 The ceiling..painted in what were called Pompeian colours. **1962** *Listener* 18 Oct. 632/2 The story of this horrifying episode was told in 'Hurricane!'.. The presentation..had a subtly Pompeian quality about it. *a* **1967** A. RANSOME *Autobiogr.* (1976) xxvii. 230 A well-designed preparation for life in this Pompeian society, Pompeian in the sense that all these people were living as it were on the slopes of a volcano. **1972** *Sci. Amer.* Sept. 86/1 The Pompeiian mosaic in the museum in Naples.

B. *sb.*[1] A native or inhabitant of Pompeii.

1823 LADY BLESSINGTON *Jrnl.* 12 Aug. in E. Clay *Lady Blessington at Naples* (1979) 62 The repairs speak little for the taste of the Pompeians. **1840** *Penny Cycl.* XVIII. 380/2 The emperor Nero..adjudged that the Pompeians should be deprived of all theatrical amusements for ten years. **1869** 'MARK TWAIN' *Innoc. Abr.* xxxi. 330 Those Pompeiians were very luxurious in their tastes and habits. **1974** *Encycl. Brit. Macropædia* XIV. 789/2 Pompeians and colonists seem to have adjusted with a minimum of friction. **1976** *Times* 23 Nov. 11/3 The faces of the Pompeians as they recorded themselves are reminiscent of those one can still see in Campania.

Pompeian (pɒmˈpeɪən, pɒmˈpiːən), *sb.*[2] and *a.*[2] [ad. L. *Pompēiān-us*, f. the name *Pompēius* Pompey.] **A.** *sb.* A follower of Gnaeus Pompeius Magnus (106–48 B.C.), Roman consul, or of his son. **B.** *adj.* Of or pertaining to Pompey or his party.

1845 J. H. NEWMAN in *Encycl. Metrop.* X. 281/2 Bent on retiring to the Pompeians in Sicily. *Ibid.* 282/1 The remains of the Pompeian party. **1908** W. W. FOWLER *Social Life at Rome in Age of Cicero* iii. 87 Some £17,500, all of which, while in deposit at Ephesus, was seized by the Pompeians in the Civil War. **1913** D. HANNAY *Navy & Sea Power* ii. 31 When Julius Caesar followed Pompey into Thrace he crossed the Adriatic under the very nose of a superior Pompeian fleet. **1949** L. R. TAYLOR *Party Politics in Age of Caesar* iii. 68 In the year 61, when Pompey was pouring out money to elect his man to the consulship, Cato charged in the senate that the money was being distributed from the house of the Pompeian consul in office. *Ibid.* viii. 171 Caesar also contributed by the policy he followed when..he came home from his victory over the Pompeians in Spain. **1974** E. S. GRUEN *Last Generation of Roman Republic* ii. 56 Bibulus and Domitius could be counted on by Cato for steady co-operation in reducing the influence of Cæsarians and Pompeians in Roman politics. *Ibid.* 62 It was a standard Pompeian practice to express his own ambitions in terms of the needs and desires of his soldiers.

†**pompelmoose, pampelmouse** (ˈpɒmp-, ˈpæmp(ə)lmuːs). Forms: 7–8 **pompelmoes,** 7 **pampelimouse,** 8 **pomplemose, pumplemus,** 8–9 **pompelmoose,** 9 **pompel-mos, pompelmousse, -mouse, -mous; pumple-, pamplemousse, pampelmouse;** also 7–9 **pumplenose,** 8 **pumble-, pummel-, pimple-nose.** [A name which arose in the Dutch Indies in 17th c., and is given by early writers as the Dutch name of the fruit. Du. *pompelmoes* is recorded from 1676; F. *pampelimouse* (now *pamplemousse*) from 1696.

There is no native name in Malaysia resembling *pompelmoes*; the Javanese name is *djeroek*, the Chinese *yu*. In the opinion of Dr. Kern of Leiden, who has given special attention to oriental words, this is a compound, of which the second element is prob. *limoes* (in Fr. orthography *limousse*), a name applied to this fruit in Old Javanese, Malay, and Lampung, borrowed from the Pg. *limoes* pl. of *limão*, lemon, citron, under which the Portuguese included the species of *Citrus* found by them in the East. In Malay, *limu* or *limau* is still used in this general sense. The first element may prob. represent the Du. *pompoen* pumpkin, in reference to the large size of *Citrus decumana*, so that *pompelimoes*, *pompelmoes* may have been compressed forms of *pompoenlimoes*, i.e. 'pumpkin-like citron', an apt descriptive designation. The name *pompone* was actually applied to the fruit by Tavernier, *Voyages aux Indes*, Paris 1676, Eng. translation, London 1677: see POMPION 2. The corrupt Tamil *bambolmas*, given by Littré and Hatz.-Darm. as source of the Fr., with the more correct Tamil *pampalimāsu*, and numerous variants cited by Watson, Yule, etc., are merely corruptions of the Du. or Fr. form. The fruit is not native to India, but was introduced from Java (app. in the 17th c.), in Ceylon under its Dutch name; in Bengal its source is indicated by the designation *Batavi-nimbū* or *nebū*, Batavian Citron.]

The large fruit of *Citrus decumana*, a native of Java and Malaysia, now established in many tropical countries, called also SHADDOCK; esp. the larger variety: cf POMELO. Also the plant itself.

[**1676** SCHOUTEN *Oost-Indische Voy.* II. 165 De vrucht by de Nederlanders *pompelmoes*, en by de Portuguesen *jamboa* genoemt, *i.e.* The fruit named by the Dutch *pompelmoes*, and by the Portuguese *jamboa*.] **1696** SLOANE *Catal. Plant. Jamaica* 212 Malus arantia, fructu rotundo maximo pallescente humanum caput excedente. Malus Arantia Indica, fructu omnium maximo, pumpelmus dicto medulla pallescente... *The Shaddock Tree.* In hortis & agris Insularum Jamaicæ & Barbados ubique provenit. **1696** PLUKENET *Almag.* 239 in Sloane *Voy. Jamaica* I. 41 Belgis orientalibus Pompelmus, Virginiensibus nostratibus (ab Inventoris nomine qui ex Ind. orient. ad oras Americanas primo transtulit) *Shaddocks* audiunt. **1697** *Phil. Trans.* XIX. 587 They have Limons, Citrons, Pampelimouses, Limes. **1699** DAMPIER *Voy.* II. I. vii. 125 The Pumple-nose is a large Fruit like a Citron, with a very thick tender uneven rind. *a* **1706** RUMPHIUS *Herbarium Amboin.* (1741) II. 96 Limo Decumanus, Pompelmoes, Lemon Cassomba quam ob ejus magnitudinem Decumanam cognovimus. **1711** C. LOCKYER *Trade in India* vi. 177 The Pumplemus is like a pale Orange, contains a Substance much like it, and is five times as big. **1737** tr. *Bruyn's Trav.* II. lxv. 92 Two large Pompelmoeses. **1770** *Cook's Voy.* Dec. in *Hawkesworth's Voy.* (1773) III. 734 Pumplemoeses, which in the West Indies are called Shaddocks. These were well flavoured, but not juicy. **1773** E. IVES *Voy. India* 468 Chaddock..the fruit ..grows as large as a man's head, and is round; it is a fine pleasant fruit,..there are plenty of them at Ceylon and other places, and they commonly are called pumple or pimple-noses. **1792** FORREST *Voy. Mergui Archip.* 32 In his garden we found limes, oranges and pummel noses. **1794** *Gentl. Mag.* LXIV. II. 811/2 The woods of Leuconia produce the *pomplemous*, a kind of orange near five inches in diameter... This is what our sailors commonly call the *pumblenose.* **1813** MARIA GRAHAM *Jrnl. India* 96 The fruits are..the pamplemousse or shaddock, the plantain and the orange. **1846** LINDLEY *Veg. Kingd.* 458 The Orange, Lemon, Lime, Shaddock, Pompelmoose, Forbidden Fruit, and Citron, Indian fruits.

pompeon, -eous, obs. ff. POMPION, POMPOUS.

†**pomperkin, pompirkin.** *Obs.* Also 8 pomepirk. [Origin uncertain: ? f. *pome* or *pomepear.*] A 'small drink' made from refuse pomace and water; ciderkin.

1637 J. TAYLOR (Water P.) *Drinke & Welcome* A iij b, The sixt sort of Brittish drinkes is Pomperkin..being nothing but the Apples bruised and beaten to mash, with water put to them. **1744–50** W. ELLIS *Mod. Husbandm.* IV. IV. 15 The Produce of Large Quantities of Cyder, and what we call Pompirkin, or Cyderkin. *Ibid.* V. I. 101 Pome-pirk, which they generally prefer to any of the best small Beer.

pompernickel, obs. form of PUMPERNICKEL.

†**ˈpompery.** *Obs. rare.* [ad. OF. *pomperie* pomp, display, f. *pompe* POMP *sb.*: see -ERY.] Pomp, splendour, magnificence.

c **1400** *Beryn* 2668 The vij sciencis, & eke lawe of Armys, Experimentis, & pompery, & al maner charmys. *c* **1440** *Gesta Rom.* xlii. 170 (Harl. MS.) þe whiche in tyme of baptime made homage to god, & forsoke the devill and alle his pomperis. **1491** CAXTON *Vitas Patr.* (W. de W. 1495) I. xli. 65/2 In her grete beaulte and pompery.

pompet, -ett, obs. variants of PUMPET.

Pompey (ˈpɒmpɪ). [Origin unknown.]

1. A nickname for: **a.** The town and dockyard of Portsmouth, in Hampshire. **b.** Portsmouth Football Club. Also *attrib.*

1899 *Evening News* 9 Dec. 3/6 Wilkie, amid tremendous cheering from the Pompey lads, won the toss, and played with the wind in their favour. **1916** 'TAFFRAIL' *Pincher Martin* iii. 40 The *Belligerent* was a 'Pompey' ship. **1930** *Daily Express* 6 Oct. 16/7 Despite their undeniable superiority Portsmouth could not penetrate the Derby defence... A brilliant Pompey could do everything except score. **1943** C. S. FORESTER *Ship* xviii. 109 The grim wife he had in Pompey. **1944** WILLIAMS & SAVAGE *Second Penguin Problems Bk.* 160 Shouting 'Good old Pompey,' Portsmouth supporters went home. **1959** *Observer* 22 Mar. 17/5 An old roadman..: 'There's been a lot of unemployment in Pompey and Southampton.' **1966** (*title*) Pompey chimes: the journal of the Portsmouth West Conservative Association. **1972** E. GRIERSON *Confessions of Country Magistrate* xv. 149 That Plymouth should possess a second-tier court and Portsmouth only a third-tier one will infuriate, and with reason, the good citizens of Pompey. **1976** *Oxf. Compan. Ships & Sea* 659/1 '*Pompey*', the sailors' slang name for Portsmouth... It is not known how or when the name came into being, one theory being that it owes its origin to the fact that the local fire brigade, known as the Pompiers, used to exercise on Southsea Common, adjacent to the town of Portsmouth. **1977** *Navy News* June 6/3 Is there any chance of recreating the Bluejacket Band at Pompey?

2. ***to dodge Pompey***: see DODGE *v.* 13.

Hence **ˈPompeyite,** a sailor from Portsmouth.

1916 'TAFFRAIL' *Pincher Martin* iv. 63 Down wi' the Pompeyites!

pompey (ˈpɒmpɪ), *v.* [Extended form of POMP *v.*[2]; a word of Dickens.] *trans.* To pamper.

1860 DICKENS *Gt. Expect.* vii, When I was old enough, I was to be apprenticed to Joe, and until I could assume that dignity I was not to be what Mrs. Joe [Gargery] called 'Pompeyed', or (as I render it) pampered. **1885** *Daily News* 13 Oct. 4/8 Now boys are 'pompeyed', in a Pumblechookian sense, to a degree which makes men envious. **1892** *Sat. Rev.* 20 Aug. 213/2 This kind of notoriety cannot but 'pompey' boys.

pompeyous, obs. form of POMPOUS.

pompholygous (pɒmˈfɒlɪgəs), *a.* [f. as next + -OUS.] Affected with pompholyx. Also *fig.* puffed up.

1855 TENNYSON in Ld. Tennyson *Mem.* I. xix. 410 That mighty man, that pompholygous, broad-blown Apollodorus, the gifted X. **1858** MAYNE *Expos. Lex.*, *Pompholygodes*,..pompholygous.

pompholyx (ˈpɒmfəlɪks). [a. Gr. πομφόλυξ (-λυγ-) a bubble, the slag of ore.]

†**1.** *Chem.* Crude zinc oxide, flowers of zinc.

1678 PHILLIPS (ed. 4), *Pompholix* [**1706** Pompholyx], a small and volatile spark, which whilest Brass is trying in the Furnace, flies upwards and adheres to the upper part of the Furnace. **1725** BRADLEY *Fam. Dict.* s.v. *Prick in foot*, The Ointment of Pompholix is also an excellent Remedy for Oxen that are prick'd in the Feet. **1836–41** BRANDE *Chem.* (ed. 5) 771 The whiter parts of such oxide used to be called pompholix, and the gray..portions, tutty. **1866** WATTS *Dict. Chem.* IV. 688 *Pompholyx*, an old name for impure zinc-oxide, sublimed in the roasting of zinc-ores.

2. *Path.* A vesicle on the skin; also, an eruption of vesicles, without inflammation or fever, appearing chiefly on the palms of the hands and the soles of the feet.

[**1706** PHILLIPS, *Pompholyx*, a Bubble of Water.] **1818–20** E. THOMPSON tr. *Cullen's Nosol. Method.* (ed. 3) 328 Pompholyx; Water Blebs. **1822–34** *Good's Study Med.* (ed. 4) II. 359 Certain peculiarities of erysipelas and pompholyx. **1899** *Allbutt's Syst. Med.* VIII. 751 In addition to the typical pompholyx vesicle, sudamina are often present.

pompian, obs. form of POMPION.

‖**pompier** (‖pɔ̃pje, ˈpɒmpɪə(r)). [F. *pompier* (pɔ̃pje), f. *pompe* PUMP *sb.*: see -IER.]

1. The French name for a fireman. Hence **pompier ladder**, a firemen's scaling ladder, having a central pole and crossbars for rungs, and a hook at the top to attach it to a building, etc.

[**1838** H. GREVILLE *Diary* (1883) 120 Last night the Italian Opera House was burnt to the ground, and poor Severini.. lost his life, as did several of the *pompiers*.] **1871** E. G. E. WARD *Jrnl.* 24 May in D. P. Carew *Many Years, Many Girls* (1967) I. 51 All the 'pompiers' from St. Germain are gone to Paris, but the fire is enormous. **1893** *Westm. Gaz.* 6 June 4/3 Their apparatus consisted of a water tower, a gun shot life line, a pompier ladder, and two horses. **1905** *Prot. Alliance Mag.* Aug. 89/1 Rescue was effected..by means of Pompier ladders. **1958** L. DURRELL *Balthazar* x. 203 The hall was full of fancy-dress figures of *pompiers* with hatchets and buckets.

2. *transf.* An artist who paints in an academic, imitative, vulgarly neo-classical style. Also *attrib.*

1924 A. Huxley *Let.* 9 Aug. (1969) 231 It may be mere folie de grandeur and pompier prejudice on my part. 1950 Wyndham Lewis *Let.* 22 Mar. (1963) 520 The greatest news of all is that you have taken to the brush and palette! Are you a *Douanier*, or a *pompier*? 1974 *Times* 23 Nov. 14/1 The names of the so-called Pompier artists—late nineteenth-century French academic painters—are on every lip... The term 'Pompier'..is thought to derive from the helmets worn by the Greek gods and heroes depicted in the canvases of the late Classical painters and their close similarity to that of the Paris firemen, or *pompiers*. *Ibid.* 14/4 The Pompiers are exotic and flamboyant. 1977 *Times* 30 Mar. 12/4 The art of the *Pompiers* as they have been contemptuously called... The exhibition of *French Nineteenth-century Paintings* at the Alpine Club Gallery..is ..welcome.

pompilid ('pɒmpɪlɪd), *sb.* and *a.* *Zool.* Also Pompilid. [ad. mod.L. family name *Pompilidæ*, f. the generic name *Pompilus* (J. C. Fabricius *Supplementum Entomologiæ Systematicæ* (1798) 212), f. Gr. πομπίλ-ος a fish which followed ships + -ID[3].] **A.** *sb.* A predatory fossorial wasp belonging to the family Pompilidæ. **B.** *adj.* Of or pertaining to this group of insects.

1909 *Cent. Dict.* Suppl., *Pompilid* n. & a. 1913 *Oxf. Univ. Gaz.* 4 June 952/1 The specimens show the resemblance of the black red-banded Hemipteron to a common pattern of the Pompilid group of Fossorial Hymenoptera. 1924 J. A. Thomson *Sci. Old & New* xxxv. 200 There are predatory wasps called Pompilids that hunt spiders. 1941 W. S. Bristowe *Comity of Spiders* II. vii. 354 Spiders are the sole prey of Pompilids. 1962 *Oxf. Univ. Gaz.* 19 Mar. 852/1 A Pompilid wasp and its spider prey from Trinidad. 1973 J. P. Spradbery *Wasps* xiv. 307 Among some pompilids at least, considerable powers of orientation have been evolved.

†**pom'pillion.** *Obs. rare*[−1]. [Cf. POMPION 2.] A term applied in contempt to a man.

*a*1625 Fletcher *Women Pleas'd* III. iv, He, hang him, poore Pompillion.

pompillion, erron. f. POPULEON, an ointment.

pompine: see next.

pompinoe, var. POMPANO.

pompion, pumpion ('pʌmpɪən). Now *rare*. Forms: 6–7 **pompon, -one**; (6 **pompine**), 6–7 **pompeon**, 6– **pompion, pumpion**, (7 **pom-, pumpian**). [Orig. a. obs. F. *pompon* 'a pumpion or melon' (Cotgr.), nasalized form of *popon, poupon*, also in 16th c. *pepon*, ad. L. *pepo, -onem*, a. Gr. πέπων, -ον-, large melon, pumpkin. From F. also MDu., Du. *pompoen*. In Eng. *pompon* has undergone two anomalous transformations, first to *pompeon, pompion, pumpion*, and finally to *pumkin*, PUMPKIN, q.v.]

1. The large fruit of a cucurbitaceous plant (*Cucurbita Pepo*); a pumpkin; also the plant itself.

α. 1545 Elyot *Dict.*, *Pepo*,..a kynde of Melones called Pompones. 1555 Eden *Decades* 127 Gourdes melones cucumers pompons citrons. 1587 Harrison *England* II. xiii. (1877) I. 259 An acre of ground..whereon to set cabbages.. pompons, or such like stuffe. 1601 Holland *Pliny* XIX. v. 14 Now when they exceed in greatnes, they be called Pepones, i. Melons or Pompons.

β. 1573 Tusser *Husb.* (1878) 95 Herbes and rootes to boile or to butter... Pompions in May. 1577 [see POMECITRON]. 1588 Parke tr. *Mendoza's Hist. China* 326 They haue great store of Maiz,..pompines and mellons. 1640 Brome *Sparagus Garden* III. viii, Pompeons are as good meat for such a hoggish thing as thou art. 1657 R. Ligon *Barbadoes* 33 Pompians of a rare kind, almost as sweet as Milions. 1828 W. Irving *Columbus* xii. (1848) I. 380 Melons, gourds, pompions, and cucumbers.

γ. 1599 R. Gardiner *Kitch. Gard.* 12 Pumpions, Cucumbers, Beanes and Radish seedes. 1626 Bacon *Sylva* §486 Take Cucumbers, or Pumpions, and set them (here and there) among Musk Melons. 1771 Lady Mary Coke *Jrnl.* 22 Nov., Yesterday I tasted some bread the half of which was made with pumpion. 1796 C. Marshall *Garden* xv, Pumpions are raised on a moderate hot-bed in April or May.

†**2.** Sometimes applied to the POMPELMOOSE. *Obs.*

1677 J. Phillips tr. *Tavernier's Voy., India* III. xxiii. 199 Coming to Bantam..We had also Mango's, and a certain large Fruit call'd Pompone [*orig.* gros fruit qu'ils nomment Pompone], red also within, the meat of it being soft and spungy, but of an excellent taste. 1704 tr. *Jan Nieuhof's East Indies* in *Churchill's Voy.* II. 326 The apples call'd pompions by the Dutch [*orig.* De vruchten of appelen, pompelmoesen by d'onzen..genoemt],..grow scarce anywhere else in the Indies but in the Isle of Great Java.

†**3.** Applied in contempt to a (big) man. *Obs.*

1598 Shaks. *Merry W.* III. iii. 43 We'l vse this vnwholsome humidity, this grosse-watry Pumpion. 1623 Fletcher *Rule a Wife* I. v, O here's another pumpion, the cramm'd son of a starv'd usurer. *a*1625 Fletcher & Massinger *Cust. Country* I. ii, What Should I call thee? Pompeon, Thou kisse my lady?

4. †**a.** *attrib. fig.* Swelling, big, magniloquent.

*a*1670 Hacket *Abp. Williams* I. (1692) 120 Without pumpian words and ruffling grandiloquence.

b. *Comb.* as *pompion-bottle, -twine*; **pompion berry**: see quot. 1872.

1672 tr. *Bernier's Mem. Gt. Mogul* III. 16 That..the servants may easily, with their Pompion-bottles, water them. 1840 Browning *Sordello* II. 775 Observe a pompion-twine afloat. 1872 Schele de Vere *Americanisms* 403 Hack berries or Pompion berries..are obtained from a shrub ..(*Celtis occidentalis*), and are sweet and edible.

pompious, obs. f. POMPOUS.

pompire, pompoire, var. POME-PEAR.

pompirk, -pirkin: see POMPERKIN.

pompkin, obs. f. PUMPKIN.

†**pomple, pumple.** *Obs.* [Etymology unascertained.] Some kind of fodder for oxen used in the north of England in the 14th century.

One suggestion is that it was vetches (*Lathyrus sativus*) still commonly sown with oats as green fodder; another that it was a mixture of pease and oats, which was even in the 19th c. a common fodder in the district. But the season of the year in the one case, and the association with hay (*cum feno*) in the other, make difficulties.

1347 *Durham Acc. Rolls* (Surtees) 42 [Feb.] In xliij travis straminis avenæ et xxiij travis de Pomple, emp. pro sustentacione Boum, xj s. viij d. [April] In xliij travis straminis avenæ et xxij travis de Pomple cum feno, xj s. iiij d. q[a]. 1348–9 *Ibid.* 43 [Feb.] In xlij travis straminis x travis de Pomple et feno emp. xv s. Extra Coq. In xxiij travis straminis et viij travis de Pomple cum feno empt. pro bobus pascendis. *c*1350 *Ibid.* 44 [December] In..iiij travis de Pumple. 1349 *Finchale Invent.* (Surtees) p. xxxiii, xviij qu. vj bus. avenæ et pumple. 1394 *Jarrow & Wearmouth Invent.* (Surtees) 183 In campis seminatæ sunt..xxxij. acræ frumenti,..lj. acræ cum fabis et pisis, x. acræ avenæ et pumpyl. [1900 *N. & Q.* 9th Ser. VI. 235 A field of six acres on..Bury (or Berry) Court Farm in Cliffe, near Rochester, Kent, was long known as 'Pompill Croft',..in a bill in Chancery..*temp.* James I,..'Pumple Croft'.]

pomplemose, variant of POMPELMOOSE.

pompless ('pɒmplɪs), *a.* [f. POMP *sb.* + -LESS.] Without pomp.

1792 R. Cumberland *Calvary* (1803) II. 7 The cold dust, in which I sleep Pompless and from a scornful world withdrawn. 1848 Lytton *K. Arthur* VII. lxii, With burghers in his pompless train.

pompoleon (pɒm'pəʊliːən). [a. F. *pompoléon* (Littré); cf. *Citrus Pompoleum*, the shaddock, in Buisson 1779; app. connected with *pompelmoose*.] A name in some places of the SHADDOCK or POMPELMOOSE (*Citrus decumana*).

1837 *Penny Cycl.* VII. 215/2 Shaddocks..when they arrive at their greatest size they are called Pompoleons, or Pomplemousses. 1848 D. W. Hoffmeister *Trav. Ceylon* 99 Tropical fruits new to me, pompoleons or shaddocks, jamboos, and mangoes.

pom-pom ('pɒmpɒm). [Echoic.]

1. The name given during the South African war, 1899–1902, to the Maxim automatic quick-firing gun: see MAXIM *sb.*[2] Also *fig.*, and *attrib.* as ***pom-pom gun, ammunition***. In later use: any of various heavier guns, esp. if multi-barrelled or one of a group.

1899 *Daily News* 6 Dec. 5/4 Automatic guns, nicknamed pom-poms. *Ibid.* 26 Dec. 2/3 An automatic gun, which Tommy Atkins, with his aptitude for expressive phrases, promptly christened 'Pom! Pom!' 1900 *Ibid.* 5 Mar. 2/3 Near where the 'pom-pom' gun was placed, is the overflowing supply store. *Ibid.* 25 June 3/3 We secured a Hotchkiss gun, 500 rounds of pom-pom ammunition. 1902 *Westm. Gaz.* 27 Jan. 1/2 The fact..has never influenced him ..towards a modification of his verbal pom-poms. 1916 'Boyd Cable' *Action Front* 131 The muzzles of the two pounder pom-poms moved slowly after their target. 1940 'N. Shute' *Landfall* vii. 175, I should think the multiple pom-poms would have got the machine. 1944 *R.A.F. Jrnl.* Aug. 272 (*caption*) Battleship..; carries forty pom-poms in multiple mountings. 1973 J. Quick *Dict. Weapons* 353/1 *Pom-pom.* 1. A rack of antiaircraft cannons, usually mounted in fours, as on the deck of a ship. 2. An automatic cannon.

2. A representation of a repetitive sound, e.g. the beat of a popular tune or poem. Also ***pom-pom-pom***, etc.

1909 Beerbohm *Lett. to R. Turner* (1964) 181 They have been re-printing *Yet Again*. Second impression ready within a few days. Pom-pom-pom. 1916 A. Huxley *Let.* 31 Mar. (1969) 95 Time percolates with a distressing rapidity through the coffee-machines of life... So you see, pom, pom, where are we?..as the old song says. 1945 W. Stevens *Let.* 26 Jan. (1967) 485 Many lines exist because I enjoy their clickety-clack in contrast with the more decorous pom-pom-pom that people expect. 1978 M. Kenyon *Deep Pocket* ix. 105 *Pom* pom pom *pom* pom, something sweet Willies.

Hence **'pom-pom** *v. intr.*, to fire a pom-pom; **pom-'pomming** *vbl. sb.*

1901 'Linesman' *Words by Eyewitness* vii. 147 Continuous sniping, pom-pomming, and occasional shelling. *Ibid.* ix. 191 Boers can fire shrapnel, Britons can pom-pom with the best.

pompon ('pɒmpɒn, ‖pɔ̃pɔ̃), **pom-pom** ('pɒmpɒm). Also 8 **pong pong, pomponne**, 8–9 **pom'poon**, 9 **pompom, ponpon, pompone**. [a. F. *pompon* (1725 in Hatz.-Darm.) a tuft, top-knot; of uncertain origin; possibly a colloq. deriv. of *pompe*, POMP.

OF. had *pompon*, POMPION, but this seems unconnected.]

1. A jewel or ornament attached to a long pin; a tuft or bunch of ribbon, velvet, flowers, threads of silk, etc., formerly worn in the hair, or on the cap or dress; now worn on women's and children's hats and shoes, and used to ornament the borders of mantles; also, the round tuft on a soldier's or sailor's cap, the front of a shako, etc. Also *attrib.*

1748 *Song* in *Charmer* (1751) II. 51 While you're placing a patch, or adjusting pong pong. 1748 *Lond. Mag.* (Fairholt), *Pong-pong*, an ornament worn by the ladies in the middle of the forepart of their head-dress. Their figures, size, and composition are various, such as butterflies, feathers, tinsel, coxcomb lace, etc. 1753 Chesterf. in *World* No. 18 ⁋11 'How do you like my *pompon*, papa?' continued my daughter..putting up her hand to her head, and showing me in the middle of her hair a complication of shreds and rags of velvets, feathers, and ribbands, stuck with false stones of a thousand colours. 1754 Mrs. Delany in *Life & Corr.* (1861) III. 300 Lady Betty is to have a very fine sprig of pearl diamonds and turquoises for her hair, by way of *pomponne*. 1782 Miss Burney *Cecilia* I. v, A milliner may have sent a wrong pompoon. 1826 *Hist. Pelham, Mass.* (1898) 191 Voted that the town will furnish the Money to purchase Pompons and feathers. 1840 Barham *Ingol. Leg.* Ser. I. *Leech Folkest.*, Pieces of black pointed wire with which, in the days of toupees and pompoons, our foremothers were wont to secure their fly-caps and head-gear. 1887 *Daily News* 6 Jan. 3/1 Black gauze dotted over with pompons of chenille of about the size of a shilling. 1897 S. Crane in *Westm. Gaz.* 3 May 2/2 The blue sailor bonnets with their red pom-poms. 1904 P. N. Hasluck *Upholstery* 19 Pom-poms are used for ornamenting upholsterers' work. To make a pom-pom lap a wool or cardboard washer with three or four thicknesses of fibres. 1924 D. H. Lawrence *Pansies* 148 My! the bloomin' pom-poms! Even as trimmings they're stale. 1927 [see EVZONE, EVZONE]. 1952 Granville *Dict. Theatr. Terms* 139 *Pom-pom dress*, the conventional Pierrot costume of white pantaloons, white jacket, decked with black pom-poms, or any other good combinations of colour. 1968 *Listener* 3 Oct. 445/3 The making of Bunny Girls' pom-poms for export. 1975 *Times* 9 Dec. 9/8 Mink jacket..has..mink pom-pom ties at the neck. 1977 *Time* 4 Apr. 42/2 He has rigged it with 100,000 steel darts, which, if detonated at just the right moment, can wipe out everybody in the stadium, down to the last pompon girl.

2. A variety of chrysanthemum, and of dahlia, bearing small globular flowers. Also *attrib.* Also, one of a group of dwarf varieties of *Rosa centifolia* with small double flowers. Also with capital initial.

1843 *Florist's Jrnl.* IV. 106 *R[osa] centifolia* (the Provence or Cabbage rose), with its varieties, including the 'mossy' and 'pompone' roses. 1861 *Morn. Post* 12 Nov., The pompons, or dwarf chrysanthemums. 1866 *Treas. Bot.* s.v. *Chrysanthemum*, Chrysanthemums are classed by growers into Large-flowered, Anemone-flowered, Pompons, and Anemone-flowered Pompons. *Ibid.* s.v. *Dahlia*, A race of pompons with remarkably small flower-heads has been obtained. 1869 [see MINIATURE *a.* a]. 1891 *Times* 15 Oct. 5/5 The four great divisions of show dahlias, cactus dahlias, decorative dahlias, and pompons. 1894 A. Foster-Melliar *Bk. of Rose* ii. 15 A sub-variety of the Provence is the Pompon Rose. 1908 E. J. Banfield *Confessions of Beachcomber* I. ix. 130 Stalkless mushrooms [of coral], gills uppermost,..blossom as pom-pom chrysanthemums. 1922 Mrs. C. H. Stout *Amateur's Bk. Dahlia* i. 7 At that time [*sc.* 1870] appeared a tiny ball-shaped blossom, originating probably with Hartweg of Karlsruhe, which he called 'pompon'. 1943 F. Thompson *Candleford Green* i. 20 Old-fashioned pompom dahlias in autumn. 1952 W. E. Shewell-Cooper *Chrysanthemum Growing* xv. 161 These chrysanthemums are said to have been quite popular in the Victorian era... They are called 'Pompoms' in some parts of the country, 'Pompons' in other districts, and even 'Pompones'. 1955 C. C. Hurst in G. S. Thomas *Old Shrub Roses* ix. 91 Both varieties were dwarf Pompons a few inches high. 1958 [see COLLARETTE c]. 1961 [see *Korean chrysanthemum*]. 1974 J. Berrisford *Window Box & Container Gardening* v. 48 The smaller-growing of the Pompoms [*sc.* chrysanthemums] are also useful.

Hence **'pomponed** *a.*, decked with pompons.

1753 *World* No. 22 ⁋7 Exhibiting themselves in public places,..patched, painted and pomponed. 1767 *Woman of Fashion* I. 109 The Head frizzled, egretted, pomponed, befeather'd, and beribbon'd all over.

pompon, -pone, a pumpkin: see POMPION.

pompoon, pompose: see POMPON, POMPOUS.

pomposity (pɒm'pɒsɪtɪ). In 5 **pomposite**. [ad. med.L. *pompōsitās*: see POMPOUS and -ITY.] The quality of being pompous.

†**1.** Pomp, solemnity. *Obs. rare*[−1].

1432–50 tr. *Higden* (Rolls) I. 41 Iulius Cesar ordeneide by the cownselle of the senate sette in pomposite alle the worlde to be dimencionate.

2. Display of dignity or importance in deportment or language; ostentatiousness. (In quot. 1620 as a mock-title.)

1620 Shelton *Quix.* (1746) IV. xi. 92 Let not your Pomposity forget to write to me. 1763 in Boswell *Johnson* 25 June, An affectation of pomposity, unworthy of a man of genius. 1841 D'Israeli *Amen. Lit.* (1867) 135 Furious Latinisms, bristling with polysyllabic pomposity. 1879 M. Arnold *Mixed Ess., French Critic on Goethe* 302 Some acute remarks on the pomposity of diction.

‖**pomposo** (pom'pozo), *adv.* (*adj.*) and *sb.* [It.]

A. *adv. Mus.* In a stately manner. Also as *adj.*, affected, pompous.

1801 Busby *Dict. Mus.*, *Pomposo*,..a word implying that the movement to which it is prefixed is to be performed in a grand and dignified style. 1847 Webster 845/2 *Pomposo*,.. grand and dignified. 1876 Stainer & Barrett *Dict. Mus. Terms* 364/1 *Pomposamente, pomposo*..pompously. 1959 *Collins Mus. Encycl.* 508/2 *Pomposo*, in a pompous manner. 1960 'A. Bridge' *Numbered Account* 220 Don't be so pomposo, Colin—really you bore me.

B. *sb.* **1.** An affected, self-important person.

1930 *New Statesman* 15 Nov. 176/1 Their satyrs, pomposos, and ninnies..became the delight of future generations. **1938** C. S. FORESTER *Ship of Line* ix. 116 'And now,' said Bolton, 'we must await in idleness the arrival of Sir Mucho Pomposo, Rear Admiral of the Red.'

2. *Mus.* A movement, musical passage, or the like to be played in a stately manner; a piece of music marked *pomposo*.

1966 E. R. REILLY tr. *Quantz's On Playing Flute* xvii. 231 A Maestoso, Pomposo, Affetuoso, or Adagio spiritoso must be played seriously, and with a rather heavy and sharp stroke.

pompous ('pɒmpəs), *a.* (*adv.*) Also 5 **pompyus**, *Sc.* **pomposs**, 5–6 **-ouse**, 5–8 **-ose**, 6 **-os**, *Sc.* **-us**, 6–7 **-eous**, 6–8 **-ious**. [= F. *pompeux* full of display (14th c. in Hatz.-Darm.), ad. late L. *pompōsus* pompous, stately, solemn, f. *pompa* POMP: see -OUS.]

1. Characterized by pomp or stately show; magnificent, splendid; †processional.

1430–40 LYDG. *Bochas* VIII. xxvi. (MS. Bodl. 263) 2 With a gret host, most Pompous in his glorie. **1528** ROY *Rede me* (title-p.), I will ascende makynge my state so hye That my pompous honoure shall never dye. **1561** T. NORTON *Calvin's Inst.* IV. xix. (1634) 724 They..goe in a long pompous shew to carrie a Pageant of holy oyle. **1638** JUNIUS *Paint. Ancients* 60 The Poets bring..upon a stage..all what is pompous, grave, and delightfull. **1720** WATERLAND *Eight Serm.* 175 Upon this Occasion,..it pleased God, in the most solemn and pompous Manner to proclaim the high Dignity of God the Son. **1738** BIRCH *Milton* M.'s Wks. 1738 I. 47 The pompous Edition of it [*Paradise Lost*] printed by Subscription in 1688. **1841** ELPHINSTONE *Hist. India* II. 342 There was a general fair and many processions and other pompous shows. **1896** T. F. TOUT *Edw. I*, iv. 82 At the head of a pompous embassy.

2. Characterized by an exaggerated display of self-importance or dignity; boastful, vainglorious, arrogant; consequential, pretentious, ceremonious; of language: inflated, turgid.

c **1386** CHAUCER *Monk's T.* 565 Was neuere Capitayn vnder a kyng..moore pompous in heigh presumpcioun Than Oloferne. *c* **1460** *Wisdom* 1125 in *Macro Plays*, Conforme yow not to þis pompyus glory, But reforme in gostly felynge. **1529** MORE *Dyaloge* III. Wks. 225/2 If they kepe few seruauntes we call them nyggardes. If they kepe many we cal them pompouse. **1631** WEEVER *Anc. Fun. Mon.* 785 Coming, after a pompous and bragging manner. **1749** CHESTERF. *Lett.* (1792) II. 311 In spite of all the pompous and specious epithets he may assume. **1804** *Med. Jrnl.* XII. 108 It has, however, often been dignified with pompous names. **1814** JANE AUSTEN *Mansf. Park* viii, Mrs. Rushworth, a well-meaning, civil, prosing, pompous woman, who thought nothing of consequence, but as it related to her own and her son's concerns. **1875** JOWETT *Plato* (ed. 2) I. 118 Those who spin pompous theories out of nothing.

comb. **1897** FLANDRAU *Harvard Episodes* 44 In one hand he carried a pompous looking bottle.

B. as *adv.* = POMPOUSLY.

1754 SHEBBEARE *Matrimony* (1766) II. 55 The Earl having talked extremely pompous of the Honour and Antiquity of his Family.

pompously ('pɒmpəslɪ), *adv.* [f. prec. + -LY².]

1. In a pompous manner; with magnificence or splendour; in pomp or state.

1513 DOUGLAS *Æneis* XI. ii. 53 And bad thai suld tak gud kepe and attend, To leid the pray per ordour pompusly. **1596** LODGE *Marg. Amer.* 125 Their horses, were all pompously garnished with golde and siluer. **1737** J. CHAMBERLAYNE *St. Gt. Brit.* I. III. (ed. 33) 275 The Benefactor's Body having been pompously buried before in Barbados, was yet..brought over.

2. With display or parade; with affected dignity; ostentatiously, vauntingly.

1718 HICKES & NELSON *J. Kettlewell* III. li. 318 Preferring Truth and Righteousness to all other Considerations how Pompiously soever set off. **1847** C. BRONTË *J. Eyre* viii, This charge which Mr. Brocklehurst has weakly and pompously repeated at second-hand.

pompousness ('pɒmpəsnɪs). [f. as prec. + -NESS.] The quality or condition of being pompous: see the adj.

1447 BOKENHAM *Seyntys* (Roxb.) 243 Quoth Agas I sey yt for no pompousnesse A jentyl wumman I am as bern wytnesse [etc.]. **1583** GOLDING *Calvin on Deut.* clx. 992 If wee haue wherewith to maintaine ourselues well, we fall to gluttonie, pompousnesse, whoredom, and other loosenesse. **1660** JER. TAYLOR *Duct. Dubit.* I. iv. Rule ii. ¶14 They [Christ's miracles] had nothing of pompousness and ostentation. **1793** GOUV. MORRIS in Sparks *Life & Writ.* (1832) II. 283 The pompousness of this Embassy could not but excite the attention of England. **1870** LOWELL *Among my Bks.* Ser. I. (1873) 76 In verse, he had a pomp, which, excellent in itself, became pompousness in his imitators.

pompyll: see POMELY *a.*

‖**pomum** ('pəʊməm). *Bot. Obs.* [L., = fruit of any kind; in med.L. an apple.] = POME 1 b.

1760 J. LEE *Introd. Bot.* I. vi. (1765) 14 *Pomum*, is a fleshy or pulpy Pericarpium without Valve, containing a Capsule. **1785** MARTYN *Rousseau's Bot.* xxviii. (1794) 451 They all agree in..a *pomum* for a fruit.

pomyce, pomys, obs. forms of PUMICE.

pon, obs. f. PAN *sb.*¹, PAWN *sb.*¹ (at Chess), POND, PONE³.

'pon, pon (pɒn), aphetic form of UPON *prep.*

1557 in *15th Rep. R. Comm. Hist. Manuscripts* App. III. 39 in *Parl. Papers 1897* (C. 8364) XLVIII. 71 Suche impositions as the lorde deputie for the tyme beinge shall taxe and set pon them. *c* **1560** [see MATTER *sb.*¹ 25 c]. **1796** F. BURNEY *Camilla* iv. 119 Much obliged to him, 'pon honour! **1821** M. EDGEWORTH *Let.* 5 Dec. (1971) 287 Fanny quite well p'on honor. **1850** F. E. SMEDLEY *Frank Fairleigh* v. 47, I didn't think you had it in you; 'pon my word, I didn't. **1901** M. FRANKLIN *My Brilliant Career* xiii. 78 'Pon my honour, Miss Melvyn, I had no idea it was you. **1914** 'BARTIMEUS' *Naval Occasions* xxiv. 244 Have you any rich aunts, Guns? 'Pon my word, I might get off this afternoon. **1924** D. MOORE *Fen's First Term* x. 108 'Pon my word, I can't say. **1973** 'M. INNES' *Appleby's Answer* ii. 18 A delightful-looking creature, madam, 'pon my soul.

ponade, -ado, obs. ff. PANADE², PANADA.

ponard, obs. form of PONIARD.

ponask ('pəʊnɑːsk, -æsk, 'puːnɑːsk, -æsk), *v.* *Canad.* Also **poonask**. [Algonquian.] *trans.* To cook (game or fish) by splitting it and roasting it on a spit or stick over an open fire. Hence **'ponasked** *ppl. a.*; **'ponasking** *vbl. sb.*

1922 *Beaver* Mar. 39/2 As we had no kettle..we were forced to 'ponask' the fish on a pointed stick before a bright fire. **1934** P. H. GODSELL *Arctic Trader* 46 She had, therefore, taken the heart, impaled it on a stick, and ponasked it as one would roast a duck. **1944** C. CLAY *Phantom Fur Thieves* 31 Thus were the two pieces of duck held up to the blaze and heat. 'That's called "ponasking", Dave,' said the old trapper. **1961** J. W. ANDERSON *Fur Trader's Story* viii. 66 With the addition of salt, the ponasked fish was a delightful repast. **1963** G. S. MCTAVISH *Behind Palisades* 90 While the kettles would be boiling their meat, they [*sc.* Indians] would be 'Poonasking' strips of meat and delicacies like leg-bones in front of the fire. *Ibid.*, 'Poonasking' is a method of cooking before a campfire by splitting meat or game, impaling on a pointed stick, where it is quickly roasted from the intense heat.

ponce (pɒns), *sb. slang.* [perh. from POUNCE *v.*]

a. One who lives off a prostitute's earnings; a prostitute's protector; a pimp.

[**1861** MAYHEW *Lond. Labour* III. 354/1 The 'pounceys', (the class I have alluded to as fancy-men, called 'pounceys' by my present informant).] **1872** *Clerkenwell News* 27 Jan., Prostitutes, or their 'ponces' or bullies. **1888** *Pall Mall G.* 13 Oct. 3/1 The ruffians who form the rank and file of the predatory gangs, are almost always the bullies or 'ponces' of prostitutes. **1914** C. MACKENZIE *Sinister St.* II. IV. ii. 868 You're nothing more than a dirty ponce. I've gone five years without keeping a fellow yet. **1916** W. S. MAUGHAM *Writer's Notebk.* (1949) 98 A raid was made, and fourteen ponces were arrested. **1957** C. MACINNES *City of Spades* II. iv. 127 These whores are always masters of their ponces. One word to the Law, and the lucky boy's inside. **1965** *New Statesman* 23 Apr. 642/2 If a girl has to get 10 clients for a male ponce, she will need 20 to satisfy the monetary demands of a woman ponce. From my observations at least one ponce in four in London is a lesbian. **1970** G. GREER *Female Eunuch* 131 The role of the ponce..is too established for us to suppose that prostitutes have found a self-regulating lifestyle. **1975** J. SYMONS *Three Pipe Problem* xviii. 182 What do you think I am, a tart trying to find a ponce?

b. A male homosexual; a lazy or effeminate man. Also as a vague term of abuse.

1932 AUDEN *Orators* III. 98 Dyers and bakers And boiler-tube makers, Poofs and ponces, All of them dunces. **1953** K. AMIS *Lucky Jim* xi. 119 As if I'd have said a word in front of that little ponce. **1969** N. COHN *A WopBopaLooBop* (1970) xix. 185 Mods thought that Rockers were yobs, Rockers thought that Mods were ponces. **1974** P. WRIGHT *Lang. Brit. Industry* xi. 95 An infuriated spectator may shout at a plump, sleek referee, 'You nasty little ponce!' **1978** in P. Marsh et al. *Rules of Disorder* ii. 46 Anybody that works in a lesson..that you know you're going to doss about in,..you get called 'ponce' and everything.

ponce (pɒns), *v. slang.* [f. the sb.] *intr.* To act as, or behave like, a ponce; to live *on* the earnings of a prostitute; *fig.* to sponge (on), take advantage (of). Usu. const. *on* or *off*. Also, ***to ponce about***, to act in an effeminate or languid manner; to fool or mess about; ***to ponce up***, to tart up, to make effeminate or effete. Hence **'poncing** *vbl. sb.* and *ppl. a.*; **ponced up** *ppl. a.*

1932 G. S. MONCRIEFF *Café Bar* IV. 35 Lou left her periodically, usually to live with some other tart, poncing. *Ibid.*, Now he was unemployed and they were saying to her that he was poncing on her. **1936** J. CURTIS *Gilt Kid* ii. 23, I didn't say no one was poncing on her. **1936** [see KITE *sb.* 4 c]. **1937** J. CURTIS *You're in Racket* i. 13 Why the hell don't you buy some for yourself instead of poncing on other people? **1938** G. KERSH *Night & City* iii. 42, I don't ponce it orf 'em. **1953** P. SCOTT *Alien Sky* I. ii. 18 Urdu's a man's language... Don't ponce it up with that bastard higher standard muck. **1954** Ponce about [see *brothel-creeper* (*shoe*)]. **1955** 'C. H. ROLPH' *Women of Streets* x. 114 He was arrested a third time for poncing on the girl and sent to prison. *Ibid.* 115 The man was sentenced to two years for his third poncing offence. **1957** C. MACINNES *City of Spades* II. ii. 120 Best of all..is poncing on some woman, but I haven't got the beauty enough for that. **1966** J. WAINWRIGHT *Evil Intent* 46 'Why the hell can't they stick to plain facts?' he snarled. 'Why must they ponce everything up to suit their own ends?' **1969** N. COHN *A WopBopaLooBop* (1970) vi. 57 No poncing about, no dressing up or one-shot gimmicking. **1970** G. LORD *Marshmallow Pie* v. 49 What do you think you look like, all ponced up like that? Fucking queer! **1971** *Guardian* 24 June 13/2 Let's face it, New Zealand has been poncing on us for years. **1972** D. LEES *Zodiac* 132 If my own mother had been murdered I wouldn't ponce about like you're doing. **1973** K. GILES *File on Death* vi. 150 Part-time poncing as well, but he thought bookmaking was more honest. **1974** J. GARDNER *Corner Men* vii. 54 Their Rolls is in the Dean Street car park and Chung Yin's sitting in it ponced up like the sweet and sour faggot he is. **1977** *Zigzag* Aug. 14/1, I mean the one before that was just like a stopgap when we was poncin' around, so much to do and nothing was being done for us. **1977** M. KENYON *Rapist* v. 52 Poncing rapist English..thinking they owned the place.

‖**ponceau** (pɔ̃so). [F. (OF. *pouncel* poppy, 12th c. in Hatz.-Darm.).] The bright red colour of the corn poppy. Also the name of a coal-tar dye of red colour.

1835 *Ladies' Cabinet* Feb. 135 Those [flowers] of cherry colour..are now superseded by ponceau, which has a much better effect by candle-light. **1861** J. BROWN *Horæ Subs.*, *Myst.* (1882) 131 A gown of rich ponceau satin. **1885** GOODALE *Physiol. Bot.* (1892) 19 [Name of the dye] Ponceau.

poncelet ('pɒnslɪt). [After J. V. Poncelet, a French mathematician, 1788–1867.] A unit for measuring the rate of expenditure of energy, equal to 100 kilogrammeters per second.

poncer, ponchion, obs. ff. POUNCER¹, PUNCHION.

poncey ('pɒnsɪ), *a. slang.* Also **poncy**. [f. PONCE + -Y¹.] Of, pertaining to, or resembling a ponce (sense b); effete, homosexual.

1964 J. HALE *Grudge Fight* xi. 179 'Come on, sissy boy,' says Brooks, 'come on you poncy bastard.' **1970** 'D. CRAIG' *Young Men may Die* xii. 118 Stephen read..from his notes in that poncy briefing voice he could put on. **1970** L. HENDERSON *Sitting Target* xii. 106 This smells like a poncey brothel. **1973** M. AMIS *Rachel Papers* 174 You haven't half got poncy mates. **1973** J. WAINWRIGHT *Pride of Pigs* 160 Wot yer bring this poncey gear for, anyway? **1977** *Listener* 6 Jan. 13/1 If you are an intellectual sort of chap, not well-versed in small-talk and tittle-tattle, you cannot make much headway with the dumb blonde. You will scare her off by being too poncey or too high-hat.

poncho ('pɒntʃəʊ, 'pɒnʃəʊ). Also 8 **puncho**, **pancho**, 9 **poncha**, **ponche**. [a. S. Amer.-Sp. *poncho*, a. Araucanian *poncho*, *pontho*. (See Febres *Dict. Araucanian* 1765, repr. 1883, Granada *Vocab. Rioplatense*, Montevideo 1890.)] **a.** A South American cloak, consisting of an oblong piece of cloth with a slit in the middle for the head; hence applied to similar garments worn elsewhere: see quot. 1849. Now in common use as a fashion garment.

1717 tr. *Frezier's Voy. to South-Sea* II. 71 The Spaniards have taken up the Use of the *Chony*, or *Poncho*..to ride in, because the Poncho keeps out the Rain. **1748** *Earthquake of Peru* iii. 287 The Men instead of the Poncho have a Surtout made like a sack. **1768** J. BYRON *Narr. Patagonia* 174 A puncho, which is a square piece of cloth, generally in stripes of different colours, with a slit in the middle of it wide enough to let their heads through. **1783** JUSTAMOND tr *Raynal's Hist. Indies* IV. 207 The savages supply it [Chili] chiefly with the Pancho. **1844** G. DODD *Textile Manuf.* iv. 137 The 'poncho', or South American cloak, of which specimens are to be seen in the smart shops of some of our London tailors. **1849** *Illustr. Lond. News* 5 May 296/2 One of the chief novelties of the season, suitable for promenading or for evening wear, is the Poncho, a description of shawl mantilla, somewhat resembling, in shape, the mantilla worn by the Spanish senoras. **1869** E. A. PARKES *Pract. Hygiene* (ed. 3) 323 The poncho is a piece of oilcloth with a slit in the centre, through which the head is put. **1885** C. M. YONGE *Two Sides of Shield* I. iv. 40 'Here are some overshoes and Poncho.'..Poncho..turned out to be a sort of cape. **1887** J. BALL *Nat. in S. Amer.* 179 A genuine poncho woven by the Indian women. **1907** *Yesterday's Shopping* (1969) 320 c The Mercedes motor cycling poncho. In fawn cashmere, fitted with rubber neck band and wrists, when worn with overalls, rendering the wearer absolutely proof against rain, dust, or wind. **1929** F. A. POTTLE *Stretchers* (1930) 40 We had now been issued ponchos... A poncho is simply a rectangular sheet of water proofed material, with a hole in the center to put one's head through. **1952** W. R. BURNETT *Vanity Row* (1953) i. 9 The little Italian newsboy, wearing a black rubber poncho and cursing the weather, was trying to make up his mind to go home and the hell with it! **1956** G. DURRELL *Drunken Forest* i. 18, I found him clad in pyjamas and a *poncho*, that useful Argentine garment that resembles a blanket with a hole in the middle through which you stick your head. **1967** *Observer* 26 Mar. 9 Girls..wear what men wear, though Inca ponchos have a strong appeal. **1969** I. KEMP *Brit. G.I. in Vietnam* iv. 84, I sat out in the open, wrapped miserably in my poncho. **1974** *Times* 4 Oct. 7/3 There will be no central heating in the Elysée until October 15... The staff has been allowed to sport..polo-necked pullovers and South American ponchos. **1976** T. SHARPE *Wilt* ii. 13, I was thinking of trying Felicity Fashions for a shantung poncho.

b. *attrib.*, as **poncho dress**, (*a*) a costume including a poncho; (*b*) a dress made like a poncho; **poncho liner**, a lining garment worn under a poncho; **poncho-'mattress**, a poncho adapted for use as a mattress.

1811 W. WALTON *Hist. & Descr. Acct. Peruvian Sheep* ii. 52 The Indian driver in this plate is also represented in his proper *poncho* dress. **1862** *Catal. Internat. Exhib.* II. XII. 26 Granulated cork poncho-mattress. **1968** *Vogue* 15 Apr. 28 Poncho dress..25 gns. **1969** I. KEMP *Brit. G.I. in Vietnam* iv. 76 Nights at this altitude were beautifully cool and we often slept under our padded poncho liners.

Hence **'ponchoed** *a.* [-ED²], wearing a poncho.

1901 SIR M. CONWAY *Bolivian Andes* xxv. 289 The sun shining on this field of ponchoed natives.

poncho(u)n, ponchong, obs. ff. PUNCHEON.

‖**poncif** (pɔ̃sif). [Fr.] Stereotyped or conventional literary ideas, plot, character, etc.

1923 J. M. MURRY *Pencillings* 136 The modern spirit, with its almost fanatical desire to get rid of the *poncif*, might make a fine thing of classical translation. **1940** *Scrutiny* IX. 258 He [*sc.* Verlaine] revived some of the oldest and loveliest verse-forms; and he managed, in his best work, to escape from the Romantic *poncif* and to go back to something more human.

poncy, var. PONCEY *a.*

pond (pɒnd), *sb.* Also 4-7 ponde, 4-5 poond(e, pounde, 5 poynde, 5-6 pownde, (7 pon); *dial.* 7-9 pownd, 9 pound. [ME. *ponde*, app. a variant of POUND *sb.*², which is commonly used in the same sense in Sc., and Eng. dialects.]

1. a. A small body of still water of artificial formation, its bed being either hollowed out of the soil or formed by embanking and damming up a natural hollow. Often described according to its use, etc., as a ***compensation-pond*** (for a canal, etc.), ***duck-pond, fish-pond, mill-pond, parish*** or ***village pond, skating-*** or ***curling-pond***, etc. Formerly often *spec.* = fish-pond.

a **1300** *K. Horn* 1173 (Laud. MS.) My net hys ney honde In a wel fayr ponde [*Harl. MS.* hende..pende; *Cambr. MS.* stronde]. **1387** TREVISA *Higden* (Rolls) I. 69 Wateres fallynge of þe hiȝest hill of Paradys makeþ a grete ponde [*aquae lacum efficiunt*]. **1388** WYCLIF *Ps.* cxiii[i]. 8 Which turnede a stoon in to pondis [*v.r.* a poond; 1382 poolis] of watris. **1398** TREVISA *Barth. De P.R.* XIII. xiv. (1495) 447 A ponde is water gaderyd to fedynge of fysshe, though ofte gaderynge of water wythout fysshe be callyd ponde by contrary meanynge. *c* **1425** *Voc.* in Wr.-Wülcker 652/35 *Hoc stagnum*, poynde. *c* **1450** *Pol. Poems* (Rolls) II. 228 Hit is a shrewde pole, pounde, or a welle, That drownythe the dowghty, and bryngethe hem abeere. **1483** *Cath. Angl.* 286/1 A Poonde,..*piscina, stagnum, viuarium.* **1552** HULOET, Ponde for fyshe, *lucana, piscina*... Ponde to washe shepe in, *probatica piscina.* **1622** DRAYTON *Poly-olb.* xxviii. 1197 Near to the foot..it makes a little pon, Which in a little space converteth wood to stone. **1622** CALLIS *Stat. Sewers* (1647) 60 A Pond is a standing Ditch cast by labor of mans hand in his private grounds for his private use,..but a Pool is a low plat of ground by nature, and is not cast by mans hand. **1676** LADY CHAWORTH in *12th Rep. Hist. MSS. Comm.* App. v. 34 Drownded by the breaking of ice upon a pond where he was sliding. **1684** G. MERITON *Praise Yorks. Ale* 132 Our awd meer is slidden into th' pownd. **1756-7** tr. *Keysler's Trav.* (1760) IV. 346 A large pond, or ditch, on the east side of the city wall being drained. **1879** MISS JACKSON *Shropsh. Word-bk.* s.v. *Pounded*, A mill-pound is the backwater which is held in reserve for the supply of the mill. **1880** MISS BRADDON *Just as I am* ii, The pond and the fountain were as old as the house.

b. Locally in England (esp. in Surrey), also in New England, etc., applied to a natural pool, tarn, mere, or small lake; in colonial use also to a pool in a river or stream.

1480 CAXTON *Descr. Brit.* 6 Ther is a grete ponde that conteyneth lx ilondes. **1693** H. KELSEY *Kelsey Papers* (1929) 3 This wood is poplo ridges with small ponds of water. There is beavour in abundance but no Otter. **1765** T. HUTCHINSON *Hist. Mass.* I. 459 The Nipnets..were seated upon some lesser rivers and lakes or large ponds, more within the continent. **1794** A. THOMAS *Newfoundland Jrnl.* (1968) 27 In this Island is a fresh water pond a full mile in length, and in it are large Eels and other Fish. **1801** J. QUINCY in *Proc. Mass. Hist. Soc.* (1889) 2nd Ser. IV. 132 Nantucket whale-fishers pursuing perch in a pond half a mile in circumference are objects ludicrous enough. **1809** KENDALL *Trav.* II. 39 Valleys and hollows that contain small streams, and lakes or pools, in New England always denominated *ponds.* **1831** J. J. AUDUBON *Ornith. Biogr.* I. 479 It searches for food..by the margins of such inland lakes as, on account of their small size, are called by us ponds. **1835** *Trans. Zool. Soc. Lond.* I. 234 A tranquil part of the river, such as the colonists call a 'pond'. **1900** G. C. BRODRICK *Mem. & Impress.* xiv. 304 The county of Surrey, with..its numerous heaths, its lonely tarns modestly called 'ponds', its hollow lanes. **1948** *Canad. Geogr. Jrnl.* Mar. 49/1 Everyone knows what a lake is and there are lakes of all sizes from coast to coast, but if you happen to reside in the Eastern Townships of Quebec you may find your *lake* is called a *pond.* **1969** H. HORWOOD *Newfoundland* 220 In Newfoundland almost all lakes, no matter how large, are called 'ponds'. **1974** *Maclean's Mag.* Dec. 83/2 The Syncrude pond will cover nine square miles.

c. *transf.* and *fig.*

1526 TINDALE *Rev.* xix. 20 These bothe were cast into a ponde off fyre burnynge with brymstone. **1555** R. SMITH in Foxe *A. & M.* (1583) 1697/1 That I may passe out of this ponde, Wherein I am opprest. **1792** A. YOUNG *Trav. France* 65 His pond of quicksilver is considerable, containing 250lb.

d. = LAGOON¹ 4.

1956 K. IMHOFF et al. *Disposal of Sewage* xii. 205 The area of pond required for waste purification may be computed by means of the oxygen balance. **1961** BOLTON & KLEIN *Sewage Treatm.* vi. 88. If properly operated, the ponds are reasonably free from bad smells, due possibly to the deodorizing effect of the chlorophyll in the algae. **1973** T. H. Y. TEBBUTT *Water Sci. & Technol.* ix. 138 In warm climates biological treatment is sometimes achieved in oxidation ponds. **1978** *Coal Option* (Shell Internat. Petroleum Co.) 8 Substantial research is also going into agglomeration processes to recover coal from potential waste material, such as the effluent streams from existing colliery washeries, and coal from existing slurry ponds and tips.

2. Applied *fig.* or humorously to the sea, esp. the Atlantic Ocean: cf. HERRING-POND.

1641 *Time's Alterations* in N. Wallington *Notices Chas. I* (1869) II. App. 306 It seems that you have taken flight over the great Pond, pray what newes in England? **1665** SIR T. HERBERT *Trav.* (1677) 374 Through this Womb of moisture the great pond of the World (as Bishop Hall terms the Ocean). **1780** *Royal Gaz.* (N.Y.) 22 Jan., Then Jack was sent across the Pond To take her in the rear, Sir. **1832** MOTLEY *Corr.* (1889) I. ii. 11, I should have been very sorry to have crossed the Atlantic (or the pond, as the sailors call it) without a single storm. **1864** THOREAU *Cape Cod* x. (1894) 329 It is but a step from the glassy surface of the Herring Ponds to the big Atlantic Pond where the waves never cease to break. **1902** *Outing* (U.S.) June 345/1 [They] have hardly sustained their reputation on either side of the big pond.

3. In a canal: = POUND *sb.*² q.v.

4. *attrib.* and *Comb.*, as ***pond-beetle, -carp, -dregs, -earth, -keeper, -maker, -mud, -mussel, -side, -water***; **pond-apple**, a small tree (*Anona laurifolia*) of the W. Indies and Gulf States, or its fruit (*Cent. Dict.* 1890); **pond-barrow** *Archæol.*: see quots.; **pond-bay**, a dam; † **pond-caster**, one who digs out ponds; **pond-culture**, the keeping of fish in ponds; hence **pond-cultured** *a.*; **pond-dogwood**, the Button-bush of N. America (*Cephalanthus occidentalis*); **pond-duck**, the wild duck; **pond-fish**, (*a*) a fish usually reared in a pond, as the carp; (*b*) *spec.* in U.S., a fish of the genus *Pomotis* or *Lepomis*, a sunfish or pond-perch; **pond-head**, a bank or dam which confines a pond; **pond-hunter**, a naturalist who investigates pond-life; **pond-land**, marsh, fen-land; **pond-life**, the animals, esp. the invertebrata, that live in ponds or stagnant water; **pond-perch** = *pond-fish* (*b*); **pond-pickerel** = PICKEREL¹ b; **pond-pine**, see PINE *sb.*² 2; **pond-shrimp**, a fairy shrimp (FAIRY C. 2); **pond-skater**, an aquatic insect belonging to the family Gerridæ, found on the surface of fresh or salt water; **pond-snail**, any freshwater snail inhabiting ponds; esp. one belonging to the genus *Limnæa*; **pond-spice**, a N. Amer. shrub (*Litsea* or *Tetranthera geniculata*) growing in sandy swamps (Miller *Plant-n.* 1884); **pond tortoise, -turtle** (*U.S.*), any freshwater tortoise of the family *Emydidæ*; a terrapin or mud-turtle; **pondwort, knight's p.**, Water-soldier (*Stratiotes*); † **pond-yard**, a yard containing a fish-pond or ponds.

1845 *Statist. Acc. Scotl.* XIV. *Ross-shire* 254 On the north-west side of Knock-farril is a circular enclosure or ring, formed of small stones, having the earth somewhat scooped out in the interior... They are not unlike the *pond-barrows of Wales... The common people call them fairyfolds. **1941** *Proc. Prehist. Soc.* VII. 89 The so-called pond-barrow consists of a slight depression,..the material from which has been placed round the circumference to form an embanked rim. **1963** *Field Archaeol.* (Ordnance Survey) (ed. 4) 47 The pond barrow appears as a regular circular shallow depression,..surrounded by a small bank. **1863** SMILES *Indust. Biog.* 32 Dams of earth, called '*pond-bays', were thrown across watercourses. **1602** *Burford Reg.* (Hist. MSS. Comm.) *Varr. Collect.* I. 166 [Wages for the day] For a *Bondcaster..iij. **1655** *Ibid.* 172 For a Pondcaster vᵈ. **1885** *Encycl. Brit.* XIX. 127/2 *Pond-culture ..has been practised for many centuries. **1977** *Undercurrents* June-July 30/3 The mirror carp is by far the best fish for pond culture in Britain. **1972** *Country Life* 7 Dec. 1565/1 There are no public-health worries about eating *pond-cultured fish. **1778** [W. MARSHALL] *Minutes Agric., Observ.* 22 *Pond-dregs laid on a clayey Meadow, in November, are of no obvious service. **1774** GOLDSM. *Nat. Hist.* VI. 129 *Pond-ducks..have a straight and narrow bill, a small hind toe, and a sharp pointed train. *a* **1677** HALE *Prim. Orig. Man.* II. ix. 208 Carps, Tench, and divers other *Pond-fish. **1567** in F. J. Baigent *Crondal Rec.* (1891) 166 Mylles, weares, myldammes, brydges, pondes, and *ponde heades within the same mannor. **1821** CLARE *Vill. Minstr.* II. 24 On the sloping pond-head. **1896** *Daily News* 12 Dec. 6/2 Kept in captivity..in the *pond-hunter's aquarium. **1779** G. WHITE *Let.* 7 May in *Selborne* (1789) I. 259 Five of those most rare birds..were shot upon the verge of Frinsham-pond... The *pond keeper says there were three brace in the flock. **1909** *Westm. Gaz.* 12 Jan. 5/2 The pondkeeper was unavoidably absent from his post. **1686** *1st Cent. Hist. Springfield* (1899) II 270 Twenty acres..of *Pond or Low Land by the Way to Hadley. **1886** E. A. BUTLER (*title*) *Pond Life. **1632-3** *Canterb. Marr. Licences* (MS.), William Cook of Hollingbourne, *pondmaker. **1707** MORTIMER *Husb.* (1721) II. 79 You must cool the Mould about the Roots with *Pond-mud and Cow-dung. **1855** KINGSLEY *Glaucus* (1878) 67 The Common *Pond-Mussel (Anodon Cygneus). **1621** LADY M. WROTH *Urania* 471 By a *Pond side, where the Stagge had taken soile. **1895** L. C. MIALL *Nat. Hist. Aquatic Insects* xiii. 382 The *Pond-skaters stand or run upon the surface of the water, which they dimple but do not break. **1923** E. A. BUTLER *Biol. Brit. Hemiptera-Heteroptera* 244 Popularly known as pond-skaters or water-measurers, they attract the attention of even the least observant by the free and easy way in which they dart along over the surface of the water. **1952** J. CLEGG *Freshwater Life* xiii. 198 The Pond Skaters feed largely on dead or dying insects that fall on the water. **1973** *Nature* 9 Mar. 132/1 The family Gerridae..includes the common pond-skaters or water-striders. **1855** C. KINGSLEY *Glaucus* 159 A few of the delicate *pond-snails (unless they devour your *Vallisneria* too rapidly). **1889** MARY E. BAMFORD *Up & Down Brooks* 50 Pond-snails..surrounded by dancing beetles. **1952** J. CLEGG *Freshwater Life* xvi. 261 The Pond Snails proper..belong mainly to the genus *Limnaea.* **1896** LYDEKKER *Roy. Nat. Hist.* V. 68 The *pond-tortoises differ by having the toes fully webbed, and also by the more elongated tail. **1896** *List Anim. Zool. Soc.* 556 *Emys orbicularis* (Linn.), European Pond-tortoise. **1633** T. JAMES *Voy.* 45 This *pond-water had a..lothsome smell. **1875** HUXLEY & MARTIN *Elem. Biol.* (1883) 47 Chara flourishes in pond-water under the influence of sunlight. **1578** LYTE *Dodoens* I. ci. 143 Knights *Pondeworte. **1485** in Willis & Clark *Cambridge* (1886) II. 235 Pro firma Piscarii vocat' le *pond-yarde per annum xvˢ. **1796** *Sporting Mag.* VII. 142 He..built Verulam House, close by the pond-yard.

pond (pɒnd), *v.* [f. POND *sb.* See also POUND *v.*]

1. a. *trans.* To hold *back* or dam *up* (a stream) into or as into a pond; to pound.

1673 [implied in PONDING *vbl. sb.* a]. **1694** *Ibid.* 283 [He] did desire..the stream of Pacowseek Brooke to set a Saw mil on, and the Low land for ponding. **1742** *De Foe's Tour Gt. Brit.* (ed. 3) I. 319 Another Flood-gate..ponds the whole River [Exe], so as to throw the waste Water, over a strong Stone Weir, into its natural Chanel. **1840** *Evid. Hull Docks Comm.* 139 The water was ponded above the North Bridge. **1865** GEIKIE *Scen. & Geol. Scot.* vii. 200 The mass of ice which choked up the mouth of Glen Spean, and ponded back the water. **1894** SIR C. MONCRIEFF in *Working Men's Coll. Jrnl.* Dec. 130 Drop-gates, to be kept down during low Nile so as to pond up the water.

fig. **1810** BP. COPLESTON *1st Repl. Edin. Rev.* Mem. (1851) 299 By so doing, we..pond back the wealth which ought to circulate through a thousand ducts and channels.

b. To produce (a lake) by forming or acting as a dam.

1949 *Bull. Geol. Soc. Amer.* LX. 1383/2 In southern Ohio it is claimed that certain coastal-plain plants..are still avoiding the deposits of the proglacial lakes that are supposed to have been ponded by the advancing Nebraskan ice in the upper drainage of the Teays River. **1971** *Nature* 8 Oct. 391/1 Potassium-argon determinations on trachyte lavas which possibly ponded the former Chemoigut lake gave results of 1·1 and 1·2 m.y.

2. *intr.* Of water, etc.: To form a pool or pond; to collect by being held back.

1857 [implied in PONDING *vbl. sb.* a]. **1893** H. M. WILSON in *Whitby Gaz.* 3 Nov. 3/7 So that no sewage can pond in the channels or escape from them.

†**3.** *trans.* **a.** To confine in a pond. **b.** To dip or submerge in a pond. *Obs. rare.*

1589 [implied in PONDED *ppl. a.* a]. **1657** J. WATTS *Dipper Sprinkled* 107 You ran out to the Anabaptist to be dipt and laver'd in a Pond, or to be ponded and plunged at Laver [in Essex].

pond, -e, obs. forms of POUND, weight, etc.

pondage ('pɒndɪdʒ). [f. POND *sb.* + -AGE. See also POUNDAGE.] Storage or ponding of water; the capacity of a pond or dam for holding water.

1877 J. T. FANNING *Water-Supply Engineering* iv. 68 Basins having limited pondage or available storage of rainfall. **1885** *Sanitary Engineer* 24 Dec. 80 1 The stream was surveyed, and the survey demonstrated the practicability of pondage far beyond the necessities of city supply.

pondage, obs. form of POUNDAGE.

ponded, *ppl. a.* [POND *v.*] **a.** In senses of the verb.

1589 WARNER *Alb. Eng.* v. xxvii. 120 The Citizens, like ponned Pykes, The lessers feede the greate. **1697** R. PEIRCE *Bath Mem.* II. i. 251 There is..some Ponded Water also in the little Ditches. **1838** MARY HOWITT *Birds & Fl., Heron* xxxv, Where mountain-torrents run and moan, Or ponded waters sleep. **1900** *Westm. Gaz.* 10 July 1/3 The cutting of a channel..set free at first an enormous quantity of ponded-up water.

b. Of a sewage filter: blocked; under a depth of liquid.

1940 IMHOFF & FAIR *Sewage Treatm.* vi. 106 *Psychode* prefers an open bed and *Achorutes* a ponded surface. **1967** *Jrnl. Inst. Public Health Engineers* LXVI. 170 This large accumulation of film did not affect the performance of the filters very markedly, even though at times the surfaces of both were quite badly ponded. **1971** T. H. Y. TEBBUTT *Princ. Water Quality Control* xii. 122 A ponded filter can be brought back into use by applying the partially stabilized effluent from another filter.

†'**ponder**, *sb.*¹ *Obs.* [f. PONDER *v.* to weigh, or ? immed. f. L. *pondus, ponder-* weight. (No corresponding sb. is recorded in F.)] Weight, heaviness; in quot. 1613, a heavy blow.

? **1477** NORTON *Ord. Alch.* v. in Ashm. *Theat. Chem. Brit.* (1652) 58 For God made all things, and set it sure, In Number, Ponder, and in Measure. **1613** HEYWOOD *Silver Age* III. i. Wks. 1874 III. 142 Il'e lay so huge a ponder on thy skull. **1621** G. SANDYS *Ovid's Met.* IX. (1626) 175 The rock ..By his owne ponder firmely fortifi'd. **1631** J. DONE *Polydoron* 201 To sustaine the bodies ponder and grossnesse.

ponder, *sb.*² *rare.* [f. PONDER *v.*] An act of pondering (or ? something to ponder on).

1788 MME. D'ARBLAY *Diary* 11 Jan., He..soon after took his leave, not without one little flight to give me for a ponder. **1970** [see COME *v.* 74 m]. **1976** T. MCCLURE *Rogue Eagle* iv. 66 The obese sunbather..went away to think about it. Buchanan had a bit of a ponder himself.

ponder, -dre, *sb.*³: see POUNDER¹.

ponder ('pɒndə(r)), *v.* Also 4 poundre, pundre, 4-6 pondre, 5 -yr, punder (also 9 *dial.*), 6 pondur. [ME. a. OF. *ponder-er* (14th c. in Hatz.-Darm.), F. *pondérer* to weigh, poise, ad. L. *ponderāre* to weigh, f. *pondus, ponder-* weight.]

†**1.** *trans.* To ascertain the weight of; to weigh. In quot. *c* 1470 *absol.* Also *fig. Obs.*

c **1470** HARDING *Chron.* CXVI. viii, Vnegally he pondred then and peysed. **1532** FRITH *Mirror* Wks. (1829) 263 If all men living were pondered in one balance. **1547** BOORDE *Brev. Health* Pref. 2 b, To ponder and way the dregges or porcions the whiche ought to be ministred. **1645** USSHER *Body Div.* 203 A Rule, Line, Square, Measure, and Ballance, whereby must be framed, ordered, measured, and pondered.

†**2.** Of a thing: To weigh (so much), to amount in weight to. *Obs.*

1524 in G. Oliver *Hist. Coll.* (1841) App. 17 On [chales]..all goolde, with the Patent of goolde ponderyng 15 oz. 10dwt. **1553** *Inv. Ch. Goods* (Surtees, No. 97) 89 Two bells, pondryng by estymacion seven hundreds. *Ibid.* 92 One chalise of sylver, pondring iiij unces.

†**3.** To estimate or judge the worth, value, or amount of; to estimate, appraise, value. *Obs.*

c **1330** R. BRUNNE *Chron.* (1810) 110 þe date of Ihesu pundred, þat men tellis bi, A þousand & a hundred & sex & þritti. **1387** TREVISA *Higden* (Rolls) VII. 155 Eche man dede aught to be poundred or demed after þe entencioun of hym þat doþ. *c* **1435** B. BURGH *Cato* in Herrig's *Archiv* (1906) CXV. 308 Peise nat the gifte, ne pondre nat the pris. *a* **1483** *Liber Niger* in *Househ. Ord.* (1790) 23 To pondyr the dayes of grete festes with the dayes of abstinence. **1566** PAINTER *Pal. Pleas.* I. 44 Vertues are not to be pondered by the sexe or kinde by whom they be done, but by the chaste and honest minde.

4. To weigh (a matter, words, etc.) mentally; to give due weight to and consider carefully; to think over, meditate upon.

c **1380** WYCLIF *Sel. Wks.* III. 433 ȝit þei pondren blasphemye in among þis apostasye. *c* **1420** LYDG. *Assembly of Gods* 134 Consydre thys mater and ponder my cause. **1511** in W. H. Turner *Select. Rec. Oxford* (1880) 4 Y..pray yow iiij arbitrors to pondre the seying. *a* **1662** HEYLIN *Laud* II. 244 The cause being heard, and all the Allegations on both sides exactly pondered, his Majesty..gave Sentence. **1697** DRYDEN *Æneid* I. 789 The modest queen..Ponder'd the speech, then briefly thus replies. **1832** HT. MARTINEAU *Demerara* i. 13 Alfred pondered the matter as he went home. **1900** MORLEY *Cromwell* v. iv. 418 He and the council had already pondered the list of members returned to the parliament.

b. with *obj. clause.*

c **1380** WYCLIF *Wks.* (1880) 456 þei ponderen wiþ þis suspending þat þey don it for riȝtwisenesse to teche curatis obedience. **1519** *Interl. Four Elements* in Hazl. *Dodsley* I. 7 Which in his mind hath ofttimes pondered, What number of books..be made and imprinted. **1587** TURBERV. *Trag. T.* (1837) 151 Pondring in his thought To howe extreme a poynt be wyle Of Rosmond he was brought. **1848** W. H. KELLY tr. *L. Blanc's Hist. Ten Y.* I. 119 [He] at that very instant, was pondering only how he might save that monarch's crown. **1855** PRESCOTT *Philip II*, I. I. viii. 116 The government should ponder well whether the prize would be worth the cost.

c. To find or make out by pondering. *rare.*

1816 H. KER *Trav.* 117 Expecting he should have to ponder his way through wilderness on foot.

5. *intr.* To consider, meditate, reflect; to think deeply or seriously *on*, muse *over*.

1605 SHAKS. *Lear* III. iv. 24 This tempest will not giue me leaue to ponder On things would hurt me more. **1697** DRYDEN *Æneid* I. 311 Pondering thus on human miseries. **1791** COWPER *Odyss.* xx. 30 So he from side to side roll'd, pondering deep. **1832** TENNYSON *Œnone* 165 Here she ceased, And Paris ponder'd, and I cried, 'O Paris, Give it to Pallas!' **1840** DICKENS *Barn. Rudge* xxxi, Pondering on his unhappy lot. **1881** BESANT & RICE *Chapl. of Fleet* I. 10 A message from the dead, to keep and ponder over?

†**6.** *trans.* To support the weight or severity of, to bear. *Obs. rare*$^{-1}$.

c **1485** *Digby Myst.* (1882) IV. 217 For our faithe & fidelitee, He ponderite the rigore Off his passion.

Hence ˈ**pondering** *vbl. sb.*

1535 COVERDALE *2 Macc.* xii. 43 He had some consideracion & pondringe of yᵉ life yᵗ is after this tyme. **1809** W. IRVING *Knickerb.* (title-p.) The unutterable ponderings of Walter the Doubter.

ponderable (ˈpɒndərəb(ə)l), *a.* (*sb.*) [ad. late L. *ponderābilis* that may be weighed: see PONDER *v.* and -ABLE. Cf. F. *pondérable* (15–16th c. in Hatz.-Darm.).] Capable of being weighed; having appreciable weight.

1646 SIR T. BROWNE *Pseud. Ep.* III. xxvii. 177 If the bite of an Aspe will kill within an houre, yet the impression scarce visible, and the poyson communicated not ponderable. **1794** G. ADAMS *Nat. & Exp. Philos.* I. xi. 448 Water constitutes the ponderable part of all aeriform fluids. **1860** MAURY *Phys. Geog. Sea* (Low) ii. §120 All substances, whether ponderable or imponderable. **1881** ARMSTRONG in *Nature* XXIV. 450/1 In the ponderable application of falling water in hydraulic machines.

b. *fig.* Capable of being mentally weighed; appreciable.

1813 W. TAYLOR in *Monthly Rev.* LXXI. 306 Still it is ponderable in the scales of criticism. **1884** SYMONDS *Shaks. Pred.* ix. 361 Any ponderable qualities of craftsmanship.

B. as *sb.* A substance or object having weight; *pl.* heavy articles.

1856 KANE *Arct. Expl.* I. viii. 85 Put out all our boats and filled them with ponderables alongside.

Hence **ponderaˈbility** [= F. *pondérabilité*], ˈ**ponderableness**, weight, heaviness.

1846 FARADAY *Exp. Res.* xlix. 368 Let us not be confused by the ponderability and gravitation of heavy matter. **1846** WORCESTER, Ponderableness. **1890** R. H. HUTTON *Newman* v. (1891) 61 The ponderability of the atmosphere.

ponderal (ˈpɒndərəl), *a.* [f. L. *pondus*, *ponder-* weight + -AL[1]: cf. L. *ponderāle* place where weights were kept, in origin neuter of an adj. **ponderālis*; also mod.F. *pondéral* relating to weight (a neologism in Littré).] Of or pertaining to weight; determined or estimated by weight.

1674 JEAKE *Arith.* (1696) 89 Whether by confounding the Attick and Roman Sextaries, or the Pounds Mensural or Ponderal,..I know not. **1705** ARBUTHNOT *On Coins* (1727) 20 Thus did the money Drachma in process of time decrease: but all the while we may suppose the ponderal Drachma to have continued the same. **1880** CLEMINSHAW *Wurtz' Atom. The.* 322 The atomic weights..only express ponderal relations.

ponderance (ˈpɒndərəns). [f. L. *ponder-āre* or F. *pondérer* (see PONDER *v.*) + -ANCE.] Weight; gravity, importance. So ˈ**ponderancy**, weight, weightiness; ˈ**ponderant** [= F. *pondérant* (15th c.)]: see quot.; ˈ**ponderary** *a.*, = PONDERAL.

1812 W. TAYLOR in *Monthly Rev.* LXVIII. 503 The ballanced *ponderance of opinion under Julian. **1881** DUFFIELD *Don Quix.* II. 468 Which of my exploits are of greater ponderance in this history? **1676** H. MORE *Remarks* 44 The virtue of this twelve pound perpendicular *ponderancy is felt entire still. **1768–74** TUCKER *Lt. Nat.* (1834) I. 122 He will distinguish the glare of tinsel from the ponderancy of gold. **1656** tr. *Hobbes' Elem. Philos.* (1839) 351 The body which presses is called the *ponderant. **1845** STOCQUELER *Handbk. Brit. India* (1854) 41 The unit of the British Indian *ponderary system is called the tola. It weighs 180 grains English troy weight.

†ˈ**ponderate**, *ppl. a. Obs.* [ad. L. *ponderātus*, pa. pple. of *ponderāre* to weigh: see PONDER *v.*] Weighed: = PONDERATED. (Const. as pa. pple.)

1432–50 tr. *Higden* (Rolls) VI. 347 Theire intencions be ponderate afore Allemyȝhty God. *Ibid.* VII. 155 Everyche operacion or dede of man awe to be ponderate [*librari*] after the intention of the doer.

ponderate (ˈpɒndəreɪt), *v.* [f. L. *ponderāt-*, ppl. stem of *ponderāre*: see prec. and -ATE[3].]

1. *intr.* **a.** To have weight or heaviness; to be heavy, to weigh. †**b.** To weigh down, press down, 'gravitate' (*obs.*).

1659 STANLEY *Hist. Philos.* XIII. (1701) 577/1 The Center, towards which, all things that ponderate are directed in a streight line. **1664** POWER *Exp. Philos.* II. 103 The Ayr..also ponderates, and is heavy, in its own Atmosphære. **1698** W. CHILCOT *Evil Thoughts* iii. (1851) 29 The soul..thereby..ponderates towards God. **1730** SAVERY in *Phil. Trans.* XXXVI. 331 This must make it apparently..to ponderate less, as is the Case of Stilliards. **1775** FALCK *Day's Diving Vessel* 14 The upper column of water ponderating downwards. **1789** T. TAYLOR *Proclus' Comm.* II. 3 We desire it may be granted..that things equally heavy, from equal lengths, will equally ponderate. **1864** CARLYLE *Fredk. Gt.* XVI. xiv. (1872) VI. 300 To ponderate or preponderate there.

†**2.** *trans.* To weigh down, press down; to influence, bias. *Obs.*

1670 BAXTER *Cure Ch.-Div.* 156 His opinion,..or secret affection, doth byas and ponderate his mind, more to one side than to the other. **1709** MRS. MANLEY *Secret Mem.* (1720) II. 232 Those persons..put Favour and Corruption in the Ballance, ponderating the Scale, not as they ought, but as they will.

†**3.** *trans.* To weigh in the mind, ponder. *Obs.*

1513 JAS. IV *Let. to Hen. VIII* in Hall *Chron.* (1548) 30 The greate wronges and vnkyndnes done before to vs and our lyeges we ponderate. **1560** ROLLAND *Crt. Venus* I. 760 Thay..Ponderat weill the falt superlatiue. **1626** JACKSON *Creed* VIII. xii. §8 If wee ponderate Sᵗ Luke's relation of his agony aright. **1752–3** A. MURPHY *Gray's-Inn Jrnl.* No. 18 They is to ponderate how far they agrees.

†**b.** *intr.* (with *on*, *upon*). *Obs.*

a **1652** J. SMITH *Sel. Disc.* ix. 483 They ordinarily ponderate and deliberate upon every thing more than how it becomes them to live.

4. *trans.* To estimate the importance or value of; to appraise. *rare.*

a **1649** DRUMM. OF HAWTH. *Answ. to Objections*, Wks. (1711) 214 The baseness of the deed would be ponderated. **1868** *Contemp. Rev.* IX. 39 Mr. Lowe 'ponderates' (as he says) education more by the value of the thing learnt than by the value of the process in learning. *Ibid.* 41 The attempt to 'ponderate' various kinds of learning.

Hence ˈ**ponderated**, ˈ**ponderating** *ppl. adjs.*

1892 *Harper's Mag.* Sept. 505/2 Sarcey's ponderated common-sense prose. **1890** *Cent. Dict.*, Ponderating sinker.

ˈ**ponderate**, *a. rare.* [f. L. *ponderāt-*, ppl. stem of *ponderāre* to weigh, consider.] Careful; deliberate.

1922 *Times* 7 Oct. 11/2 It is a time for calm and ponderate consideration of the issues involved. **1970** P. O'BRIAN *Master & Commander* x. 257 The mature, the ponderate mind does not embark itself upon a man-of-war—is not to be found wandering about the face of the ocean in quest of violence.

ponderation (pɒndəˈreɪʃən). [ad. L. *ponderātiōnem*, n. of action f. *ponderāre*: see PONDER *v.* So F. *pondération* (1519 in Hatz.-Darm.).]

1. Weighing; balancing; adjustment of weight. Also *fig.*

1646 SIR T. BROWNE *Pseud. Ep.* 196 Upon an immediate ponderation, we could discover no sensible difference in weight. **1658** —— *Hydriot.* ii. (1736) 26 The common Fraud of selling Ashes by Measure and not by Ponderation. **1706** *Art of Paint.* (1744) 28 In the Attitudes, the Ponderation and the Contrast are founded in nature. *a* **1735** ARBUTHNOT (J.), The quantity of perspired matter, found by ponderation. **1849** MACAULAY *Hist. Eng.* iii. I. 408 The ponderation of air, the fixation of mercury. **1849** *Fraser's Mag.* XL. 608 A juster ponderation of property would increase its value by promoting its stability. **1866** MILL in *Edin. Rev.* CXXIII. 303 After a comparison and ponderation of evidence. **1875** POSTE *Gaius* IV. Comm. (ed. 2) 538 The numeration, ponderation, or mensuration of the principal.

2. Mental weighing (of the importance of a matter); grave consideration or meditation; pondering. Now *rare* or *Obs.*

1556 J. HEYWOOD *Spider & F.* lvi. 43 Weing this thing in ponderashin, In hering of him what equaltie ye show. **1604** T. WRIGHT *Passions* VI. 346 Most of those meanes..require a certaine meditation and ponderation. **1683** E. HOOKER *Pref. Pordage's Mystic Div.* 12 The consideration and ponderation of which..maketh mee not so promptly to approve [etc.]. **1711** in *10th Rep. Hist. MSS. Comm.* App. v. 110 Your nicest ponderation ought to be imploy'd.

†**3.** Gravitation. *Obs. rare.*

1661 BOYLE *Examen* (1682) 95 Ponderation is an endeavour every way by right lines into the centre of the earth.

4. The fact of weighing more; preponderance.

1873 F. HALL *Mod. Eng.* 35 It is not the ponderation of personal evidence for or against a word that should accredit or discredit it.

†**5.** Something that adds weight. *Obs.*

1609 SIR E. HOBY *Let. to T. Higgins* 74 Who with a Catalogue of great names, with Ponderations, and Considerations thinke to beard the truth. **1620** BP. HALL *Hon. Mar. Clergy* III. xiii, Because his heart told him how light these proofes were, he layes in the scales with them certaine graue ponderations.

†ˈ**ponderative**, *a. Obs. rare.* [f. L. *ponderāt-*, ppl. stem of *ponder-āre* to weigh: see -ATIVE.] Given to weighing mentally or judicially.

1610 HEALEY tr. *Vives' Comm. St. Aug. Citie of God* (1620) 354 We haue the minde and the ponderatiue iudgment of reason.

ponderer (ˈpɒndərə(r)). [f. PONDER *v.* + -ER[1].] One who ponders.

1538 ELYOT *Dict.*, *Pensit[at]or*, a ponderer or wayer. *Verborum pensitatores subtilissimi*, the mooste subtyll ponderers of wordes. **1654** WHITLOCK *Zootomia* 149 The Ponderer and shaper of his Discourses. **1824** SCOTT *St. Ronan's* x, He made an attempt to attract the attention of the silent and sullen ponderer.

ˈ**pondering**, *ppl. a.* [f. PONDER *v.* + -ING[2].] That ponders; meditative, thoughtful.

1680 EVELYN *Diary* 18 Apr., He is a sober, wise, judicious, and pondering person. **1813** BYRON *Br. Abydos* I. ii, His pensive cheek and pondering brow Did more than he was wont avow.

Hence ˈ**ponderingly** *adv.*, in a pondering way.

1647 HAMMOND *Power of Keys* ii. 14 When he reades the Scripture more ponderingly. **1870** MORRIS *Earthly Par.* III. IV. 318 And going ponderingly She noted her grey shadow slim to see.

†**ponˈderity.** *Obs. rare*$^{-0}$. [ad. L. *ponderitās* (Attius) weight.] = PONDEROSITY.

1656 BLOUNT *Glossogr.*, *Ponderity*, weightiness, heaviness, ponderosity. **1775** in ASH.

†ˈ**ponderize**, *v. Obs. rare*$^{-1}$. [f. L. *pondus*, *ponder-* weight + -IZE.] *trans.* To weigh.

1634 SIR T. HERBERT *Trav.* 150 The sheepe are sweete, and fattest in the taile, whose weight oft ponderizes twenty pound, and many times their whole body [*ed.* 1665 and may well ballance the rest of the carcass]. [**1656** BLOUNT, *Ponderize*, to ponder, weigh, poise, or consider. (*Herb. Trav.*)]

ˈ**ponderling.** *nonce-wd.* [f. PONDER *v.* + -LING[1]: cf. *suckling*, *foundling*.] A child that is weighed.

1860 READE *Cloister & H.* xxxvi, The child was weighed, and yelled as if the scale had been the font... She hushed her ponderling against her bosom, and stood aloof watching, whilst another woman brought her child to scale.

ponderment (ˈpɒndəmənt). [f. PONDER *v.* + -MENT.] Pondering, cogitation, thought.

a **1763** BYROM *Robbery of Cambridge Coach* xii, In deep and serious Ponderment I watch'd the Motions of his next Intent. **1898** MÉNIE M. DOWIE *Crook of Bough* 20 Her lips folded too tight, her cheeks sucked to the hollows of indecision, ponderment, and perplexity.

ponderoˈmotive, *a. Physics.* [f. L. *pondus*, *ponder-* weight, after *electromotive*.] That tends to move a weight; weight-moving; usu. applied *spec.* to such forces exerted upon bodies by electric or magnetic fields.

1881 *Phil. Mag.* XII. 17 The force with which one quantity of electricity acts upon another quantity of electricity may be regarded either as an electromotive force or as a true ponderomotive force; for it tends to move electricity, and also to move matter, if matter be associated with the electricity. **1884** tr. Clausius in *Phil. Mag.* Jan. 59. **1884** HIGGS *Magn. Dyn. Electr. Mech.* 272 The other ponderomotive force which the rotating helix experiences from its magnetic iron core..further depends upon the magnetic moment of the iron core. **1934** I. M. FREEMAN tr. *Joos's Theoret. Physics* xv. 296 The current in the segment, the magnetic field, and the ponderomotive force must form a right-handed orthogonal system in this order (Fleming's left-hand rule). **1964** R. R. BIRSS *Electr. & Magnetic Forces* i. 1 Ponderomotive forces are also exerted on dielectric bodies in electric fields. **1964** S. K. RUNCORN in A. E. M. Nairn *Probl. Palaeoclimatol.* 192 The varying fields generated in the core..will also generate induced currents in the mantle, and the ponderomotive forces resulting from these will cause angular acceleration and deceleration of the mantle on time-scales of 100 years. **1978** *Nature* 23 Mar. 316/2 In this case, ponderomotive forces were used to overcome the power barrier.

ponderosa (ˌpɒndəˈrəʊzə, -sə). [a. the specific epithet of *Pinus ponderosa* (P. & C. Lawson *Agriculturist's Manual* (1836) 354), f. L. *ponderōsus* heavy.] In full, ***ponderosa pine***. A large conifer, *Pinus ponderosa* or western yellow pine, native to western North America and widely cultivated elsewhere; also, the timber of this tree. Also *attrib.*

1878 R. J. Hinton *Hand-bk. Arizona* 292 Ponderosa reaches a height of 70 feet; some firs are higher. **1937** *Range Plant Handbk.* (U.S. Dept. Agric. Forest Service) B-44 Deerbrush is most commonly found in the ponderosa pine and mixed confier belts. **1949** *Democrat* 2 June 3/1 Ponderosa wood is light in color, varying from creamy white to straw. **1951** V. Nabokov *Speak, Memory* vi. 96 Mariposa lilies bloomed under Ponderosa pines. **1957** *Handbk. Softwoods* (Forest Prod. Res. Lab.) 41 Canadian-grown ponderosa pine is about 20 per cent more resistant to splitting along the rings than Baltic redwood. **1966** Mrs. L. B. Johnson *White House Diary* 2 Apr. (1970) 379 He described the 'relic forest' of maple.. and ponderosa pine with huge trunks. **1971** *New Scientist* 10 June 628/3 The study considered growing douglas fir and ponderosa pine, but concluded that softwoods would not be economically feasible. **1976** *Billings* (Montana) *Gaz.* 20 June 9-A/1 (Advt.), Enjoy living in a beautiful natural setting, abundant with ponderosas, junipers, chokecherries, and wild roses. **1978** *Times* 11 Mar. 3/3 A finely balanced relationship has evolved between scale insects and ponderosa pine trees in the north-western United States.

†**'ponde,rose**, *a. Obs. rare.* [ad. L. *ponderōsus* heavy, weighty, f. *pondus, ponder-*: see -ose.] Weighty, ponderous, huge.

[*c* **1400**, *c* **1485**: see ponderous 1, 3.] *a* **1734** North *Exam.* i. iii. §98 (1740) 191 Bulky Sums paid, ponderose Armies raised. *Ibid.* iii. vi. §64. 470 A grand Alliance, with the Emperor and Spain, brought down a ponderose Army out of Germany.

ponderosity (pɒndəˈrɒsɪtɪ). [ad. med.L. *ponderōsitās* (Wyclif *c* 1381), f. L. *ponderōsus* heavy, weighty (see prec.) + -ity.]

1. The quality of being ponderous or weighty; heaviness, weightiness, weight.

c **1450** Lydg. & Burgh *Secrees* 1798 Whoo slepith wel be natural reson, Tyl wombe avoyde al pondorosite, Excludyng seknesse stant in liberte. **1519** *Interl. Four Elements* (1530) A vij, The yerth because of his ponderosyte Avoydyth equally the mouyngs great Of all extremytes and sperys that be. **1555** Eden *Decades* 328 Yow owght to consyder of what ponderositie of weyght they are. **1624** Wotton *Archit.* in *Reliq.* (1651) 240 Ponderosity is a naturall inclination to the Center of the World. **1727** Bradley *Fam. Dict.* s.v. *Baroscope*, The Tube by its Ponderosity presses downwards into the Vessel. **1874** Carpenter *Ment. Phys.* i. i. §10 (1879) 11 Those most general Properties of Matter, resistance and ponderosity.

2. *fig.* Weightiness, importance; profoundness, seriousness (*obs.*); heaviness, dullness. (Chiefly of literary productions or style.)

1589 Puttenham *Eng. Poesie* iii. xvi. (Arb.) 185 The most excellent makers of their time, more..respecting the fitnesse and ponderositie of their wordes then the true cadence or simphonie. **1637** Bastwick *Litany* ii. 2 With all the ponderosity of Arguments and solidest tractats. **1780** H. Walpole *Vertue's Anecd. Paint.* IV. Advert. 5 If, as refinement generally verges to extreme contrarieties, Kent's ponderosity does not degenerate into filligraine. **1787** *Minor* 107 Your late rare history has conferred so large a portion of ponderosity on your opinions. **1881** Shairp *Asp. Poetry* v. 139 He falls into ponderosity and pomposity.

ponderous (ˈpɒndərəs), *a.* Also 5-7 -owse, 6 -ouse, 7 pondrous. [ad. F. *pondéreux* (*c* 1410 in Godef.), ad. L. *ponderōsus*: see prec. and -ous.]

1. Having great weight; heavy, weighty; massive; clumsy, unwieldy.

c **1400** *Lanfranc's Cirurg.* 88 þe rotynes þat goiþ out þerof is greet in substaunce, ponderous [*Add. MS.* ponderose] & vneuene. **1486** *Bk. St. Albans* D iij b, An Egle, a Vawtere, a Melowne..theis be not enlured, ne reclaymed, by cause that thay be so ponderowse to the perch portatiff. **1555** Eden *Decades* 16 Clusters of grapes very ponderous. **1602** Shaks. *Ham.* i. iv. 50 Why the Sepulcher..Hath op'd his ponderous and Marble iawes, To cast thee vp againe? **1725** Pope *Odyssey* iv. 892 The pondrous engine raised to crush us all. **1805** Scott *Last Minstr.* Introd. ii, Whose ponderous grate, and massy bar, Had oft rolled back the tide of war. **1861** Thackeray *Four Georges* i. (1862) 38 The stout coachmen driving the ponderous gilt wagon.

b. *fig.* (Of things non-material.)

1605 Shaks. *Lear* i. i. 80, I am sure my loue's More ponderous then my tongue. **1804** J. Grahame *Sabbath* 771 Ponderous bequests of lands and goods. **1835** Browning *Paracelsus* iv. 157 To sink beneath such ponderous shame.

†**c.** Having some weight; = ponderable. *rare.*

1646 Sir T. Browne *Pseud. Ep.* 196 After a draught of wine a man may seem lighter in himself.., although he be heavier in the balance, from a corporall and ponderous addition.

†**d.** Tending by its weight *towards*. *Obs.*

1792 Sir W. Herschel in *Phil. Trans.* LXXXII. 16 If it be founded on such a construction of the figure of the secondaries, as makes them more ponderous towards their primary planets.

2. Of great weight in proportion to bulk; of high specific gravity; = heavy *a.* 2. ***ponderous earth, spar***: = heavy spar. ? *Obs.*

1531 Elyot *Gov.* i. i, The erthe, which is of substance grosse and ponderous. **1660** Boyle *New Exp. Phys. Mech.* xix. 143 A Liquor so much less ponderous then Quicksilver, as Water is. **1669** —— *Contn. New Exp.* i. (1682) 37 One of the ponderousest Liquors I have prepared. **1726** Swift *Gulliver* i. ii, Globes, or balls, of a most ponderous metal. **1800** tr. *Lagrange's Chem.* I. 187 It [barytes] was called Ponderous Earth, Ponderous Spar. **1800** Vince *Hydrostat.* vii. (1806) 80 The condensed and ponderous air from the neighbourhood of the pole.

†**3.** *fig.* Of grave import; weighty, serious, important, profound. *Obs.*

c **1485** *Digby Myst.* (1882) iv. 1328 The wordes of Andrewe beyn sadd & ponderose. **1602** Fulbecke *1st Pt. Parall.* 73 That words be ponderous and emphaticall, where the matter seemeth to bleed. **1649** Roberts *Clavis Bibl.* 179 Some of acute and ponderous Judgement. **1794** Paley *Evid.* ii. ii. (1817) 50, I know nothing which would have so great force as strong ponderous maxims, frequently urged and frequently brought back to the thoughts of the hearers.

†**4.** Given to weighing, considering, or pondering matters; grave, deliberate. *Obs.*

1641 Symonds *Serm. bef. Ho. Comm.* B j b, Take what I am saying into thy most ponderous thoughts. **1646** Crashaw *Steps to Temple* (1857) 35 Both he lays Together: in his pond'rous mind both weighs. **1647** Ward *Simp. Cobler* (1843) 3 The next perplexed Question with pious and ponderous men.

5. Of a literary or other task: Heavy, laborious. Of style: Laboured, lacking lightness of touch; gravely grandiloquent; dull, tedious.

a **1704** T. Brown *1st Sat. Persius Imit.* Wks. 1730 I. 53 More pond'rous guess with lighter banter meets. **1791** Boswell *Johnson* Introd., Sir John Hawkins's ponderous labours..exhibit a farrago. **1874** Mahaffy *Soc. Life Greece* i. 3 The ponderous minuteness and luxury of citation in the works of the former. **1885** J. Payn *Talk of Town* I. 20 'Your son has made a good choice of locality', said Mr. Dennis, in his rather ponderous manner.

'ponderously, *adv.* [f. prec. + -ly[2].] In a ponderous manner; heavily, weightily; gravely.

c **1420** Lydg. *Assembly of Gods* 9 Slepe me gan oppresse So ponderously, I cowde make noon obstacle. **1637** Bastwick *Answ. Inform. Sir J. Banks* 8 That they may more ponderously waigh the businesse in hand. **1859** Hawthorne *Fr. & It. Note-Bks.* II. 267 Old houses built ponderously of stone. **1884** *Nonconf. & Indep.* 16 May 471/1 Mr. C...was ponderously dull.

ponderousness (ˈpɒndərəsnɪs). [f. as prec. + -ness.] The quality of being ponderous; heaviness, weightiness, weight. **a.** Of things material.

1597 A. M. tr. *Guillemeau's Fr. Chirurg.* 5 b/1 Whether the bullet, throughe his ponderousnes, might be descended. **1672** *Phil. Trans.* VII. 4096 By finding out the Ponderousness of Crystal in reference to Water. **1853** Ruskin *Stones Ven.* II. vii. §10. 239 Thus the greater ponderousness of the traceries is only an indication of the greater lightness of the structure.

b. *fig.* Of a task, words, style, etc.

1547-64 Bauldwin *Mor. Philos.* (Palfr.) 28 Pacuuius..is commended of Quintilian for the grauity of his sentences, the ponderousnesse of his words. **1664** Flecknoe *Love's Kingd.* etc., *Disc. Eng. Stage* G vj, Shakespear excelled in a natural Vein, Fletcher in Wit, and Johnson in Gravity and ponderousness of Style. **1881** M. Arnold in *Macm. Mag.* XLIII. 370/2 The slovenliness and tunelessness of much of Byron's production, the pompousness and ponderousness of much of Wordsworth's.

pondfolde (a pound): see pinfold.

ponding, *vbl. sb.* [pond *v.*] **a.** In senses of the verb.

1673 *1st Cent. Hist. Springfield* (U.S.) (1899) II. 119 Provided it be not prejudiciall to the high way nor to any mans propriety by ponding up of water. **1830** Lyell *Princ. Geol.* I. 291 The ponding back..of this great body of fresh-water. **1857** Ruskin *Elem. Drawing* i. 35 The use of turning the paper upside down is to neutralise the increase of darkness towards the bottom of the squares, which would otherwise take place from the ponding of the colour.

b. Blockage *of* a sewage filter; the accumulation of liquid above a filter.

1939 L. B. Escritt *Sewerage Engin.* vii. 133 Excessive flows..are often the cause of 'ponding' of the filters. **1953** E. W. Steel *Water Supply & Sewerage* (ed. 3) xxiv. 488 Media of small size will furnish more surface, but unloading will be less complete and ponding on the surface [of the filters] is more likely. **1971** T. H. Y. Tebbutt *Princ. Water Quality Control* xii. 120 Film growths may result in blockage of the voids causing ponding of the filter and anaerobic conditions. *Ibid.* 122 When the first filter shows signs of ponding the direction of flow..is reversed.

pondlet (ˈpɒndlɪt). [f. pond *sb.* + -let.] A very small pond.

1880 Baring-Gould *Mehalah* I. xiv. 264 A thin film of ice was formed about the edges of these pondlets. **1890** I. D. Hardy *New Othello* I. iv. 75 Tiny shallow pondlets.

pond-lily. *orig. U.S.* Also **pond lily**. [f. pond *sb.* + (water-)lily.] A water-lily, esp. the common yellow spatterdock, *Nuphar advena.*

1748 J. Eliot *Ess. Field-Husbandry New Eng.* (1760) i. 5 A natural Pond..over grown with Pond Lillies. **1778** J. Carver *Trav. N. Amer.* 167 The lake is covered..with the large pond-lily. **1827** *Western Monthly Rev.* I. 251 The flowers are large, of a pure white, nearest resembling the northern pond-lily. **1845-50** Mrs. Lincoln *Lect. Bot.* 169 The white Pond lily..is a splendid..plant. **1846** *Knickerbocker* XXVII. 52 A little mill-pond..is covered all over with pond-lilies and rank grasses. **1873** T. B. Aldrich *Marjorie Daw* 14 All this splendor goes into that hammock, and sways there like a pond-lily. **1911** G. Stratton-Porter *Harvester* vii. 121 The pond lilies are just beginning to open. **1938** F. Perry *Water Gardening* vii. 82 The Yellow Pond Lily will flourish in shady positions. **1947** E. Paul *Linden on Saugus Branch* 367 On the Linden ponds, frogs' eggs, turtles, pond lilies with flat leaves, not shaped like plates. **1974** H. W. Rickett *Wild Flowers U.S.* VI. i. 130 The conspicuous part of the yellow pond-lilies is the calyx.

pond-lock, obs. variant of pound-lock.

Pondo (ˈpɒndəʊ). [Nguni.] **a.** A member of a Xhosa-speaking Nguni people in the eastern part of the Cape Province in South Africa. Cf. Amapondo. **b.** The language spoken by the Pondos, a dialect of Xhosa. Also *attrib.*

[**1835** A. Steedman *Wanderings Interior S. Afr.* (1966) I. p. iv, The third division are the Amapondo tribes,..whose territories extend from the Bashee to the River Umsikalia. **1876** *Encycl. Brit.* V. 42/2 The Amapondo country of Kaffraria. **1884** K. Johnston *Africa* (ed. 3) xxiv. 399 The remaining portions of Kafraria, including..that of the Amapondo extending across the St. John's River between the Umtata and the Umtamfuna, the boundary river of Natal.] **1919** H. H. Johnston *Compar. Study Bantu & Semi-Bantu Lang.* I. iii. 298 The [Kafir] dialects include Feñgu, Baca and Pondω words. *Ibid.* v. 797 The divergent dialects of ʔōsa, such as Isi-pondω, Isi-baca, Feñgu, &c. **1950** *Cape Argus* 18 Mar. (Mag. Section) 7/7 The area from Umtata down to the sea, and northwards to the borders of Natal, belongs to the Pondos—a tribe that would have been exterminated long ago by raiding bands of Zulus if the British Government had not intervened. **1973** *Times* 19 Feb. 12/1 The hillsides are dotted with clusters of neat.. round huts.., the homes of the local Africans who are a mixture of Zulu and Pondo tribes. **1979** A. McCoy *Insurrectionist* vi. 56 The grinning one is a Pondo. There is bad blood already between the Swazi and the Pondo.

pondok (ˈpɒndɒk). *S. Afr.* Also **pondokkie, pandokkie** (-ˈɒkɪ), **pandok, pondhock, pondhok, bond-hoek**. [Afrikaans, f. Malay.] A hut or shack made of oddments of wood, corrugated iron, etc.; a mean house or hovel, esp. one inhabited by non-whites. Also *attrib.*

1815 A. Plumptre tr. *Lichtenstein's Trav. S. Afr.* II. xli. 185 Near it stand six or eight *pandokken*, as they are called, a kind of huts made of reeds woven into a wooden frame, which are inhabited by the principal Bastard-Hottentots. **1818** C. I. Latrobe *Jrnl. Visit S. Afr.* 218 The present dwelling..is a hovel, not much better than a Hottentot's bondhoek. **1832** A. Smith in P. R. Kirby *Andrew Smith & Natal* (1955) 35 In the afternoon to the Komga River to the 'pondok' (straw hut) of a trader. **1843** J. C. Chase *Cape Good Hope* iii. 235 The Hottentots..planted themselves at the outskirts of the country villages in small pondhoks, or huts, partly covered with old rags, decayed hides, sugar bags, and occasionally a little thatch. **1899** *Eastern Province Herald* (S. Afr.) 4 Nov. (Pettman), The poor burghers are living in pandokkies. **1911** *State* (Cape Town) Dec. 612 In the morning we found that a dozen or more Hottentots had pitched their pondhocks close to the wagon. **1944** *Cape Argus* 23 June, The people who are living in overcrowded shanties and pondokkies. **1948** L. G. Green *To River's End* xiv. 161, I built myself a pondok in a lonely kloof and became tame. **1952** E. H. Burrows *Overberg Outspan* iv. 103 They were the original herdsmen. Each inhabited his own *pondok*, and each was master of his own field. **1960** D. Lessing *In Pursuit of English* 29 He painted..pondokkies. In other words, African huts, slums, broken-down villages. **1971** *Post* (S. Afr., Cape ed.) 9 May 4/6 Here we are..in our well ventilated pondok in the bundu. **1974** *Cape Times* 2 Aug. 3/6 He said that he had read reports about alleged 'pondok farming' published in the Cape Times recently.

pond pine. *U.S.* [f. pond *sb.* + pine *sb.*[2]] A conifer belonging to the species *Pinus serotina*, growing on wet or marshy ground in south-eastern parts of the United States.

1810 F. A. Michaux *Hist. Arbres Forestiers de l'Amérique Septentrionale* I. 17 Pond pine (Pin des mares). **1832** D. J. Browne *Sylva Amer.* 240 The Pond Pine frequently recurs in the maritime parts of the Southern States. **1858** J. A. Warder *Hedges & Evergreens* ii. 249 *Pinus serotina*, or Pond Pine, is thirty five or forty feet high. **1860** M. A. Curtis *Woody Plants N. Carolina* 21 Pond Pine..has considerable resemblance to the Pitch Pine. **1940** *Amer. Forests* Oct. 462/2 Pond pine bears such local names as marsh pine, bay pine, and pocoson pine. **1967** N. T. Mirov *Genus Pinus* iii. 187 *Pinus serotina*, or pond pine, grows in the Coastal Plain from south-eastern Virginia south to central and southeastern Alabama.

†**pondre**, *v. Obs. rare*$^{-1}$. [a. F. *pondre* to lay eggs:—L. *pōnĕre* to deposit.] *intr.* To lay eggs; to engender, breed.

c **1430** *Pilgr. Lyf Manhode* iii. xix. (1869) 145 She dooth bisinesse to sette bras and yren to brode, for to engender oother pondre [*v.rr.* poudre, powdre].

pondur, -dyr, obs. forms of ponder.

†**pondure.** *Obs.* app. = ponder *sb.*[1], weight.

1661 Feltham *Resolves* ii. xlix. 282 When Man shall be over-swayed by the pondure of his own corruptions.

‖**pondus** (ˈpɒndəs). *Obs.* [L. *pondus* weight: formerly often used in English context.] A weight; chiefly *fig.* power to influence or bias; moral force.

1677 Gale *Crt. Gentiles* II. iv. 20 By Love, as a Divine pondus, the Soul reduceth althings to its last end, namely God. *a* **1680** Charnock *Disc. John* i. 13 Wks. 1684 II. 175 Unless God give a *pondus* to his own motion. *a* **1711** Ken *Hymns Festiv.* Poet. Wks. 1721 I. 263 Devotion fervent he instills, And turns to God the Pondus of our Wills. **1719** F. Hauksbee *Phys. Mech. Exp.* v. 116 As reasonable, as that a greater Power should sustain a greater Pondus, or take off more of the Pressure of the same Pondus.

'pondweed. [f. pond *sb.* + weed.] An aquatic herb that grows in ponds and still waters: *spec.* in Great Britain, the species of *Potamogeton.* With distinguishing prefix applied to other aquatic plants; as ***American, Canadian***, or ***Choke P.***, *Elodea canadensis* (*Anacharis*

Alsinastrum); ***Cape P.***, *Aponogeton distachyon*; ***Horned*** or ***Triple-headed P.***, *Zannichellia palustris*; ***Tassel P.***, *Ruppia maritima* (*Treas. Bot.* 1866).

1578 LYTE *Dodoens* I. lxxi. 104 The first..of these kindes of floting herbes..is called water spyke, or most commonly Pondeweede. **1657** S. PURCHAS *Pol. Flying-Ins.* I. xv. 94 Pondweed with a flower like Patience. **1760** J. LEE *Introd. Bot.* App. 323 Pond-weed, *Potamogiton. Ibid.*, Pond-weed, Triple-headed, *Zannichellia.* **1789** J. PILKINGTON *View Derbysh.* I. 344 *Potamogeton natans.* Broad-leaved Pond-weed. **1855** KINGSLEY *Glaucus* (1878) 206 Some of the more delicate pond-weeds, such as Callitriche, Potamogeton pusillum. **1866** *Treas. Bot.*, *Zannichellia palustris*, the Horned Pondweed. **1897** *Westm. Gaz.* 22 Nov. 2/1 In the stream,..the creamy Cape pond weed sent out the delicious perfume from its quaint large flowers. **1901** *Ibid.* 26 Nov. 12/2 The career of the Canadian pondweed (*Anacharis alsinastrum*..) is interesting because of the extraordinary rapidity with which it spreads itself throughout the country. **1902** *Ibid.* 17 Oct. 10/1 The American pondweed seems to be playing havoc with angling in Loch Leven.

pondy ('pɒndɪ), *a. U.S.* [f. POND *sb.* + -Y.]

1. Abounding in ponds or pools; marshy, swampy.

1687 *1st Cent. Hist. Springfield* (1899) II. 266 Thirty or forty acres of wet Pondy Land at poor brooke. **1711** *Ibid.* 317 Two or three acres of Pondy Land at the South end of his medow neer the Ponds. **1796** MORSE *Amer. Geog.* I. 501 In swamps and pondy ground.

2. Belonging to or suggestive of a pond.

1922 *Chambers's Jrnl.* July 440/1 The peculiar 'pondy' smell of the bird [*sc.* moorhen] does not suggest that it would prove a great delicacy.

‖**pone**[1] ('pəʊnɪ). *Law. Obs.* [L. *pōne* 'place thou', sing. imper. of *pōnĕre* to place.] **a.** A writ by which a suit was removed from an inferior court to the Court of Common Pleas. **b.** A writ requiring the sheriff to secure the appearance of the defendant by attaching his goods or by causing him to find sureties for his appearance.

1292 BRITTON VI. iv. §3 Et puis tendra lu le *Pone* a remuer la parole jekes par devaunt nos Justices. [*tr.* After that, a Pone will lie to remove it before our Justices.] *Ibid.* x. §5 El plee de *Pone* [in the plea of Pone]. *a* **1500** *Natura Breuium* (1531) 2 b, Si le plee soit remoue par vn Pone hors del countie en le banke. **1544** *transl.*, Yf the ple be remoued by a Pone out of the counte in to the comon banke. **1607** COWELL *Interpr.*, *Pone*, is a writ, whereby a cause depending in the County court, is remoued to the common Banke... *Pone per vadium*, is a writ commaunding the Shyreeue to take suretie of one for his appearance at a day assigned. **1768** BLACKSTONE *Comm.* III. xix. 280 The next process is by writ of attachment or *pone.* **1876** DIGBY *Real Prop.* ii. §2. 73.

pone[2] ('pəʊniː). [Derivation as in prec.] In certain card games: see quots.

1890 *Cent. Dict.*, *Pone*, in the game of vingt-et-un, the player to the left of the dealer; the eldest hand. **1901** R. F. FOSTER *Bridge Manual* 5 The leader, or eldest hand, is on the dealer's left, and the pone, or leader's partner, is on the dealer's right.

pone[3] (pəʊn). [ad. Algonkin *pone* (see quot. 1683), *apone* (Strachey *Vocab. Virgin. c* 1615), *oppone* (Beverley), bread, perh. orig. a pa. pple. 'baked'.] **a.** *orig.* The bread of the N. Amer. Indians, made of maize flour in thin cakes, and cooked in hot ashes; now, in southern U.S., any bread made of maize, esp. that of a coarse or poor kind; also, very fine light bread, enriched with milk, eggs, and the like, and made in flat cakes. Also *attrib.*

[**1612** CAPT. SMITH *Map Virginia* 17 Eating the broth with the bread which they call Ponap.] **1634** *Relat. Ld. Baltimore's Plantat.* (1865) 17 Their ordinary diet is Poane and Omine, both made of Corne. **1683** PENN *Let. Descr. Pennsylvania* 5 Of words of Sweetness, *Anna*, is Mother ..*pone*, Bread, *metse*, eat. **1708** E. COOK *Sot-weed Factor* (1900) 14 While Pon and Milk, with Mush well stoar'd, In wooden Dishes grac'd the Board. *a* **1716** BEVERLEY *Virginia* IV. §72 (1722) 253 The Bread in Gentlemen's Houses, is generally made of Wheat, but some rather choose the Pone, which is the Bread made of Indian Meal,..so called..from the Indian Name *Oppone.* **1799** J. SMITH *Acc. Remark. Occur.* (1870) 160 We are not above borrowing language from them, such as homoni, tomahawk, pone, &c. **1861** LOWELL *Biglow P.* Poems 1890 II. 229 To see how he liked pork 'n' pone. **1901** MAX ADELER *Capt. Bluett* 108 Becky's surpassing power with pone muffins.

b. A cake or loaf of such bread.

1796 B. H. LATROBE *Jrnl.* (1905) 16 A few biscuits, and pones of Indian and wheat bread. **1887** *Boston* (Mass.) *Jrnl.* 31 Dec. 2/4 The meal consisted partly of half a dozen pones. **1894** *Outing* (U.S.) XXIV. 201/1 In a short time the pones were shaped and placed in the ashes.

c. *attrib.* as ***pone bread.***

c **1785** in *Maryland Hist. Mag.* (1907) II. 258, I procured some milk and excellent pone bread from a hut. **1833** J. NEAL *Down-Easters* I. 47, I should like to know..what upon irth he means by..hoe-cakes an pone bread. **1879** *Scribner's Monthly* June 223/1 Now that the wagons were up and 'pone' bread and beef stews had re-appeared in the menu, the Foot Cavalry, feeling its keep, waxed fat and kicked. **1935** Z. N. HURSTON *Mules & Men* (1970) I. viii. 175 Nobody..don't take de fork and turn over every fish in de dish in order to pick de best one. You does dat wid yo' eye whilst youse choosin' yo' pone bread. **1936** J. C. CHENAULT *Old Cane Springs* xviii. 78 Then pone bread, light bread, and biscuits were brought out.

pone, -garnarde, obs. ff. POON *sb.*[1], POMEGRANATE.

'**ponency.** *rare.* [f. L. *pōnent-em*, pr. pple. of *pōnĕre* to place, put: see -ENCY.] The action of positing or stating the existence of anything, as in ***self-ponency***, the positing of one's own existence.

1865 *Sat. Rev.* 9 Dec. 741 The Absolute Will in the act of self-ponency, which constitutes the personality of the Divine Nature, does not and cannot affirm Himself to be finite.

ponent ('pəʊnənt), *a.* (*sb.*) [ad. It. *ponente*, Sp. *poniente*, obs. F. *ponent*, *-ant*, med.L. (It. 13th c.) *ponens*, *-entem*, west, west wind, sunset, lit. setting, pr. pple. of L. *pōnĕre* to put, place, set, lay down; in Sp. also 'to set' as the sun or a star.]

†**1.** Situated in the west, western; occidental. Also as *sb.* The place or direction of the sunset; the west; the occident. *Obs.* or *arch.*

1538 ELYOT *Dict.*, *Occidens, tis*, the west, or ponent. **1561** EDEN *Arte Nauig.* II. xvi. 43 The true ponent or west. **1568** C. WATSON *Polyb.* 2 b, Nations which inhabite towardes the Ponent, or west parts. **1588** PARKE tr. *Mendoza's Hist. China* 2 His next neighbour towards the Ponent is the kingdome of Quachin china. **1667** MILTON *P.L.* x. 704 Forth rush the Levant and the Ponent Windes. **1819** H. BUSK *Vestriad* III. 655 The ponent wind in vain he plies.

2. *Geol.* Name (proposed by H. D. Rogers) for the twelfth of the fifteen subdivisions of the Palæozoic strata of the Appalachian chain.

1858 H. D. ROGERS *Geol. Pennsylv.* II. II. 749 These periods, applicable only to the American Palæozoic day, are the Primal, Auroral, Matinal, Levant,..Ponent, Vespertine, Umbral, and Seral,—signifying the periods, respectively, of the Dawn, Daybreak, Morning, Sunrise,..Sunset, Evening, Dusk, and Nightfall. *Ibid.* 756 Ponent series, or Catskill Group of New York. **1859** PAGE *Handbk. Geol. Terms*, *Ponent*,..the 'Sunset' of the North American palæozoics, and the equivalents of our Upper or true Old Red Sandstone.

3. *Logic.* The posits or affirms.

1837–8 SIR W. HAMILTON *Logic* xviii. (1866) I. 344 The Ponent or Constructive Syllogism:—If Socrates be virtuous, then he merits esteem; But Socrates is virtuous; Therefore, he merits esteem.

‖**ponente** (po'nente). [It.: see PONENT *a.* (*sb.*).] (See quot. 1959.) Also ***ponente wind.***

1906 W. MARRIOTT *Hints to Meteorol. Observers* (ed. 6) 67/2 *Ponente*, a Westerly wind in the Mediterranean. **1959** R. E. HUSCHKE *Gloss. Meteorol.* 433 *Ponente*, a west wind on the Côte d'Azur.., the northern Roussillon region, and Corsica. On the Côte d'Azur it is a weakened mistral and brings clear skies. In northern Roussillon it is the land breeze of early morning, changing to southeast during the day. **1974** *Country Life* 25 Apr. 996/3 On some days the drying mistral blows, on others the damp *ponente* wind. **1978** S. SHELDON *Bloodline* vii. 84 The winds blew... The mistral and the *ponente*, the tramontana and the *grecate* and the levanter.

ponerid (pəʊ'nɛrɪd), *a.* (*sb.*) *Zool.* [f. mod.L. *Ponēra* (Latreille 1804), generic name (a. Gr. πονηρά, fem. of πονηρός wicked) + -ID[3].] Of or pertaining to the *Ponēridæ*, a family of tropical ants. *sb.* An ant of this family. So **poneroid** (pəʊ'nɪərɔɪd) *a.*, related in form to the *Poneridæ*. Cf. next.

1895 J. H. & A. COMSTOCK *Man. Study Insects* xxii. 642 The Ponerids... The ants of this family resemble [the Formicidæ]..in that the peduncle of the abdomen consists of a single segment.

ponerine ('pɒnəraɪn, -iːn), *a.* and *sb. Ent.* Also Ponerine. [ad. mod.L. name of subfamily *Ponerinæ*, f. generic name *Ponera* (P. A. Latreille 1804, in *Nouveau Dict. Hist. Nat.* XXIV. 179), f. Gr. πονηρά, fem. of πονηρός wicked + -INE[1].] **A.** *adj.* Of, or pertaining to, or designating ants of the subfamily Ponerinæ, which includes mainly tropical species. **B.** *sb.* A ponerine ant.

1910 W. M. WHEELER *Ants* ii. 26 The base of the abdomen is more primitive and more like that of certain Ponerine ants. **1933** *Discovery* Sept. 286/1 Professor W. M. Wheeler..paid special attention to the colony-foundation among the primitive Ponerine ants. **1945** C. P. HASKINS *Of Ants & Men* xi. 207 Australia is pre-eminently the home of the Ponerines of today. **1966** C. SWEENEY *Scurrying Bush* vii. 101 *Platythrea cribinodis*, a common, large, dull-black ponerine ant. *Ibid.* 103 As with the giant solitary black ponerine,..the black stink ants were not attacked because of their strong odour. **1977** M. V. BRIAN *Ants* iii. 39 All ponerines have a constriction between the first and second segments of the gaster. *Ibid.*, The Myrmicinæ are thought to have evolved from ponerine ants.

ponerology (pɒnə'rɒlədʒɪ). *Theol.* [f. Gr. πονηρός evil, wicked + -LOGY.] The theory or doctrine of evil or of the evil one.

1890 in *Cent. Dict.* **1893** *Q. Rev. United Brethren* July 274 It ['evil' in the Lord's Prayer] may stand for both the abstract and concrete idea, and so comprehend the whole circle of moral evil, embracing the science of ponerology.

ponewe, poney, poneyard, obs. ff. PENNY, PONY, PONIARD.

ponfald, -folde: see PINFOLD.

pong (pɒŋ), *sb.*[1] [Echoic.] **a.** The sound of a ringing blow; a bang; taken as the name of such a blow, or of an explosion. Cf. PING.

1823 *New Monthly Mag.* VIII. 502 (Devon Dial.) To-day have I dealt thee a pong in the midriff. **1896** *Daily Chron.* 25 Aug. 3/5 The deafening 'pong' of the Hotchkiss strikes on the jaded ear.

b. Abbrev. PING-PONG *sb.* Also, an electronic game resembling ping-pong, played on a pinball machine or a television screen. Also *attrib.*

1968–70 *Current Slang* (Univ. S. Dakota) III–IV. 94 *Pong, n.* ping-pong. **1976** *Washington Post* 19 Apr. A15/2 (Advt.), Now the whole family can play the new & exciting pong on your home TV. **1976** *Billings* (Montana) *Gaz.* 16 June 11-c/6 (Advt.), The new amusement machine, Pachinco, is sweeping the country like the pong games did five years ago. **1978** *Chicago* June 36/1 Game room with pong and pinball machines used by neighborhood folks.

pong (pɒŋ), *sb.*[2] *colloq.* Also (*rare*) **ponk.** [Etym. obscure.] An unpleasant smell; a stink.

1919 W. H. DOWNING *Digger Dial.* 38 *Pong*,..stink. **1925** FRASER & GIBBONS *Soldier & Sailor Words* 226 *Pong*, a stink. **1936** F. CLUNE *Roaming round Darling* xxiv. 257 Avoid the smell of camel. They were complete with permanent, pyramid, and perfume, commonly called pong. **1941** BAKER *Dict. Austral. Slang* 56 *Ponk*, a stink. As verb, to stink. **1957** J. BRAINE *Room at Top* iv. 44 'What a pong,' he said. 'Don't know how you stand it.' **1960** H. PINTER *Dumb Waiter* 130 What, you mean it might be my pong? (He sniffs sheets.) Yes... It could be my pong I suppose. **1973** G. MOFFAT *Deviant Death* I. v. 64 She's burning the feathers... She only does it when the wind takes the smell away from us... The pong's not bothering us. **1974** J. GARDNER *Return of Moriarty* 292 There ain't half a pong down here.

Pong (pɒŋ), *sb.*[3] Chiefly *Austral. slang.* [Origin uncertain.] A derogatory name for a Chinese.

1931 V. PALMER *Separate Lives* 221 Blow into one of those Chow joints..and call for a dollar's worth of duck and fowl. Enough for two those pongs always give you. **1938** X. HERBERT *Capricornia* 339 Your grandmother was a lubra and your grandfather was a Pong. **1941** BAKER *Dict. Austral. Slang* 56 *Pong*, a Chinese. **1957** D. STIVENS *Scholarly Mouse* 65 He was too tall to be a Pong or an Eyetoe. **1962** J. FRANKLYN *Dict. Nicknames* 86/1 *Pong* is a nickname given to a Chinaman in Australia—punning the *ong* sound in some Chinese words, and *pong*, a bad smell. **1970** 'B. MATHER' *Break in Line* i. 11 I'm the only Pong I know who wouldn't say Charling Closs.

pong (pɒŋ), *v.*[1] *Theatrical slang.* Of an actor: To amplify the text of his part; = GAG *v.*[1] 5.

1893 J. PITT-HARDACRE in *Clarion* (Summer No.) 30 (Funk) Ponging is a lost art... Consisting as it did, of a kind of bold free-hand dramatic sketching, Ponging had no place in an age of 'photographic acting'. Hence we pong no more. **1894** *Even. News* 18 Oct. 2/6 If he expands the text he is said 'to pong'... Why will not 'gag' do instead of 'pong'?

pong (pɒŋ), *v.*[2] *colloq.* Also (*rare*) **ponk.** [f. PONG *sb.*[2]] *intr.* To stink. Also *fig.*

1927 [see HUM *v.*[3]]. **1939** R. CAMPBELL *Flowering Rifle* 21 What matters most to them is—'Does it Pong?' **1941** [see PONG *sb.*[2]] **1944** 'N. SHUTE' *Pastoral* ii. 17, I think it looks ugly as sin, and it's starting to ponk a bit. **1948** M. ALLINGHAM *More Work for Undertaker* xiii. 164 The old boy never bought a sausage that didn't pong. **1950** A. BARON *There's no Home* i. 16 'It don't 'alf pong,' he observed. **1960** [see DRAIN *sb.* 1 e] **1972** P. CLEIFE *Slick & Dead* ii. 22 This loving thing could be a cover story for any old racket?.. Pongs a bit, don't you think? **1979** R. RENDELL *Make Death love Me* ix. 85 The place..just pongs of dirty clothes.

ponga ('pʌŋə). Also **bunger, bungy, punga.** [Maori.] An evergreen New Zealand tree-fern, *Cyathea dealbata*, belonging to the family Cyatheaceæ; also *attrib.*

1832 G. BENNETT in *London Med. Gaz.* 22 Sept. 793/2 This fern..is named Ponga by the natives, who use the trunks as posts in the erection of their houses. **1855** R. TAYLOR *Te Ika a Maui* viii. 115 Some of the trees themselves..held down their heads, and have never been able to hold them up since; amongst these, were the *ponga* (a fern tree) and the *kareao* (supple jack), whose tender shoots are now always bent. **1874** J. WHITE *Te Rou* xi. 179 Round two sides and one end [of the hangis, or ovens] a ponga fence is put. **1892** E. S. BROOKES *Frontier Life* xv. 139 The Survey department graded a zigzag track up the side to the top, fixing in punga steps. **1898** MORRIS *Austral Eng.* 65/1 Bunga or Bungy,..a New Zealand settlers' corruption of the Maori word *punga.* **1905** W. B. *Where White Man Treads* 232 It irks to go back to ponga whare and earthen floors. **1926** *Trans. N.Z. Inst.* LVI. 670 In some instances the Maori name has been adopted but corrupted:..'bunger' (now fortunately seldom heard) for 'ponga'. **1933** *Press* (Christchurch, N.Z.) 23 Sept. 13/7 Bungy.—Tree fern. I [*sc.* L. G. D. Acland] have only heard this word used on the West Coast; it is just as often pronounced pungy. **1935** 'J. GUTHRIE' *Little Country* iii. 58 Tall punga ferns spread their proud fronds. **1949** F. SARGESON *I saw in my Dream* II. xiv. 172 On the ridge it was too dry for pungas. **1959** *Times* 10 June 12/6 We strained our eyes..to see the punga fern under which the first white child was born in New Zealand. **1963** B. PEARSON *Coal Flat* xxii. 376 Peter was urinating urgently against a ponga. **1966** *Encycl. N.Z.* I. 650/1 *C*[*yathea*] *dealbata* or ponga has distinctive whitish undersurfaces to the leaves. **1966** G. W. TURNER *Eng. Lang. Austral. & N.Z.* viii. 168 Other Maori words in changed form are cockabully from kokopu,..bunger (Maori ponga), a common name for the treefern [etc.]. **1968** *N.Z. Listener* 11 Apr. 10/1 He built himself a ten-foot-high punga fence and was snug. **1977** *N.Z. Herald* 5 Jan. 2-16/8 (Advt.), Genuine bush with pongas, totara and kauri surrounding this most impressive 4-brm contemporary home.

ponga, var. PANGA[1].

pongal ('pɒŋgəl). Also **pongol, pongul, ponkal.** [ad. Tamil *poṅkal*, 'boiling'.] The Tamil New Year festival at which new rice is cooked; hence, a dish of cooked rice.

1788 F. MAGNUS tr. *Sonnerat's Voy. East-Indies & China* I. v. 142 The second day the festival is called Maddou-Pongol, or Pongol of cows:—they paint the horns of these animals, cover them with flowers, make them run in the streets, and lastly make the Pongol at home for them. **1809** *Asiatic Ann. Reg. 1807* Misc. 141 (*heading*) An interesting account of the great Hindu festival Pongal, by Teroovercadoo Mootiah. *Ibid.* 144/1 The Hindoos visit and compliment each other, wishing a happy Pongal, or many returns of that Pongal, for the preservation of each other. **1855** H. H. WILSON *Gloss. Indian Terms* 421/1 *Pongal*.., a boiling or bubbling up, the boiling of rice, whence it becomes the name of the popular festival held by the Hindus in the Madras provinces. **1877** M. MONIER-WILLIAMS *Hinduism* xii. 182 In the South of India this festival is commonly called 'Pongal', and is the commencement of the Tamil year. **1897** H. K. BEAUCHAMP tr. *Dubois's Hindu Manners* II. III. iii. 580 The pongul, or Maha-sankranti, always takes place during the winter solstice, the period when the sun, having finished its course towards the southern hemisphere, turns to the north again and comes back to visit the people of India. **1906** W. CROOKE *Things Indian* 211 The opening of the agricultural year is marked.. by the *Pongol* of South India. **1913** *Encycl. Relig. & Ethics* VI. 44/1 The central rite of the great Pongol festival of S. India consists in cooking new rice, some of which is offered to Ganeśa, the remainder being eaten by the family. **1961** [see IDLI]. **1968** P. LAL *Indian Recipes* 58 Many delicacies are prepared for the Pongal feast... The six months following Pongal are considered auspicious for marriage. **1974** F. W. CLOTHEY tr. L. S. Ramamirtham in *New Writing in India* 97 No matter how poor a man is, it's only at Poṅkal that his rice boils in a new pot.

pongarnette, obs. form of POMEGRANATE.

pongee (pʌn'dʒiː). Also 8–9 **paunche**; cf. also BUNGEE. [perh. ad. North Chinese *pŭn-chï*, for Mandarin *pŭn-kï* own loom, or ad. *pŭn-chəh* own weaving, *quasi* 'home-made'. (Here *ŭ* means (ʌ).)]

A soft unbleached kind of Chinese silk, made from the cocoons of a wild silk-worm (*Bombyx Pernyi* or *Fantoni*) which feeds on oak-leaves; known in the East as Chefoo silk. Also *attrib.*

1711 C. LOCKYER *Acc. Trade India* 122 Wrought Silks are cheap and good, of innumerable Sorts.. Damasks, Sattins, Taffetas, Paunches. **1813** W. MILBURN *Oriental Comm.* II. 518 China wrought Silks.. paunches, plain blues, pinks and whites. **1883** MRS. ROLLINS *New Eng. Bygones* 102 The shawl she wears, of some printed pongee stuff, is a family heirloom. **1890** SARAH J. DUNCAN *Social Departure* 193 In garments of pongee silk and a pith helmet. **1893** C. KING *Foes in Ambush* 2 A broad-brimmed straw hat, a pongee shirt, loose trousers.

pongelo ('pɒŋgələʊ). *slang.* Also **pongelow.** [Etym. obscure.] Beer. Also *attrib.*

1864 HOTTEN *Slang Dict.* 204 *Pongelow*, beer, half-and-half. **1880** M. E. BRADDON *Just as I Am* I. ix. 130 'He stood sam for a pot o' pongelo,' continued Mr. Scaffers, 'and narchurly we got talkin'.' **1898** A. M. BINSTEAD *Pink 'Un & Pelican* viii. 185 Some well-known publican has given twenty thousand pounds for the local pongelo palace, with the plate-glass saloon bars. **1899** *Westm. Gaz.* 9 Jan. 5/2, I hope **** is quite well and keeping himself allright [*sic*] and not soaking to [*sic*] much pongelow. **1899** H. WYNDHAM *Soldiers of Queen* 256 One night I had a drop too much 'pongelow', and there was a bit of a row. **1905** *Daily Chron.* 2 Mar. 4/5 You said, 'What're you goin' to 'ave?' an' the pongelos flow'd free as advice. **1909** J. R. WARE *Passing Eng.* 199/1 *Pongelo*, (Anglo-Indian Army), pale ale—but relatively any beer.

pongid ('pɒŋgɪd), *sb.* and *a. Zool.* [f. mod.L. family name *Pongidæ*, f. generic name *Pongo* (B. G. E. de La V. Lacépède *Tableau des Mammifères* (1799) 4: see etym. of PONGO) + -ID³.] **a.** *sb.* An anthropoid ape belonging to the family Pongidæ, which includes the gorilla, the chimpanzee, and the orang-utan. **b.** *adj.* Of or pertaining to this group of apes.

1955 W. E. LE GROS CLARK *Fossil Evidence Human Evolution* iv. 141 The differential characters of the dentition.., on the basis of the comparative study of large numbers of hominids and pongids.., have been established. **1957** *Antiquity* XXXI. 191 Another tarsioid line produced the primitive apes (the pongid line). **1963** *New Scientist* 27 June 737/1 Dr Leakey revealed that there were true pongids (apes) living in East Africa during the Miocene period. **1968** *Nature* 9 Nov. 548/1 To split the African apes from the Pongidae and place them in the Hominidae would ignore the extraordinary change in the hominid line since it split off from the pongid line. **1973** B. J. WILLIAMS *Evolution & Human Origins* ix. 127/2 The genus *Dryopithecus* is ancestral to the present-day African pongids, the gorilla and chimpanzee. *Ibid.* 129/1 *Ramapithecus* is smaller than most species of the fossil pongid genus *Dryopithecus*. **1977** A. HALLAM *Planet Earth* 284 The hominids are a family containing Man and his close relatives, distinct from the family of apes, the pongids.

‖**pongo** ('pɒŋgəʊ). [Native name in a dialect of Angola or Loango; cf. also the forms *mpongo*, *mpongi* (Bentley *Dict. Congo Lang.* 1887), *impungu*.]

1. a. A name in early writers of a large anthropoid African ape: variously identified with the Chimpanzee, and the Gorilla.

1625 BATTEL in Purchas *Pilgrims* II. VII. iii. 982 Here are also two kinds of Monsters, which are common in these Woods [of Mayombe], and very dangerous. The greatest of these two Monsters is called, *Pongo*, in their Language: and the lesser is called, *Engeco*. This Pongo is.. more like a Giant in stature, then a man: for he is very tall, and hath a mans face, hollow-eyed, with long haire vpon his browes. [**1766** BUFFON *Hist. Nat.* (1837) III. 590 Pongo, nom de ce même animal à Lowango, province de Congo.] **1766** *Ann. Reg.* II. 104/2 The Pongo.. is of a very great size, sometimes eight feet in height. **1781–5** SMELLIE tr. *Buffon's Nat. Hist.* (1791) VIII. 77 In the East Indies this animal is called orang-outang; in Lowando, a province of Congo, pongo. **1861** DU CHAILLU *Equat. Afr.* xx. 361 The gorilla has been mentioned.. under the following names: *pongo*, by Battel, 1629; *ingena*, Bowditch, 1819. [**1876** R. F. BURTON *Gorilla L.* II. 5 The Gorilla and perhaps the more monstrous 'Impungu' ('Mpongo').]

b. Later transferred to the orang-utan, an anthropoid ape native to Borneo and Sumatra, and adopted as its generic name by Lacépède in 1799; see PONGID *sb.* and *a.*

1798 *Phil. Mag.* I. 238 The orang outang of the large kind, or the pongo of Buffon, is not common even in its native country Borneo. **1834** MᶜMURTRIE *Cuvier's Anim. Kingd.* 44 There is a monkey in Borneo, hitherto known only by his skeleton, called the *Pongo*, which so closely resembles the Ourang-Outang.. that we are tempted to consider him an adult—if not of the species of the Ourang-Outang, at least of one very nearly allied to it. **1861** DU CHAILLU *Equat. Afr.* xx. 342 In 1780 the skeleton of another large ape was sent from Batavia to Holland by Baron Wurmb, the resident governor, who called it the Pongo. It received from naturalists the name *Pongo Wurmbi*. **1913** D. G. ELLIOTT *Rev. Primates* I. [Errata] The premier genus of the Great Apes is Pongo. **1972** D. BLOODWORTH *Any Number can Play* xii. 104 An intelligent pongo digging a twig into a wasp's nest.

2. a. *Naut. slang.* A marine, a soldier. Also *attrib.*

1917 'B. COPPLESTONE' *Lost Naval Papers* vi. 85 You could pass as a naval officer more easily than you could as a Pongo. **1919** W. H. DOWNING *Digger Dial.* 38 *Pongo*, a soldier; one of the rank and file. **1923** F. H. VIZETELLY *Desk-Bk. Idioms* 328 *Pongo*, a marine: in playful British usage, from a native African name for an anthropoid ape. **1943** D. GLOVER in *Penguin New Writing* XVI. 15 What about that bloody pongo what's been loafing round since I come ashore last? **1946** J. IRVING *Royal Navalese* 137 *Pongo*, the matelot's name for a soldier. In the First World War it was his name for a Royal Marine. **1955** 'N. SHUTE' *Requiem for Wren* iii. 92 Each service at that time had its own slang; to her the army were all Pongoes. **1961** B. FERGUSSON *Watery Maze* i. 40 Captain (afterwards Admiral Sir Frederick) Dalrymple-Hamilton having an elder brother in the Army, and consequently, as he said, 'a soft spot for Pongoes'. **1964** J. HALE *Grudge Fight* ii. 33 Just before the admiral's car got to the pier the pongos blew a great hole in it. **1975** *Canad. Forces Sentinel* (Ottawa) XI. VI. 7/2 Cpl. Don Lyons won praise from naval techs who described him as the only 'pongo stoker' with the maintenance team. **1977** *Daily Mail* 17 Nov. 15/1 Fourteen youths.. went out looking for soldiers to beat up... Favourite expressions of the gang were 'squaddy bashing' and 'pongo bashing'.

b. *Austral.* and *N.Z. slang.* An Englishman. Also *attrib.*

1942 2 *N.Z.E.F. Times* 7 Sept. 5 A big bronzed Pongo came in. **1945** J. HENDERSON *Gunner Inglorious* 148 The successful applicant [for the position of Batman], an elderly, quiet-spoken Pongo, was a dinkum butler. **1947** D. M. DAVIN *For Rest of Our Lives* xxxii. 165 That pongo cobber of yours, the homo. **1947** —— *Gorse blooms Pale* 208 The poor old pongos are probably still indenting in triplicate for mine-detectors. **1949** *Here & Now* (N.Z.) Oct. 11/2 He long ago began featuring himself as a 'New Zealander born and bred', a sop to the vague public feeling against Pommies, Pongoes, Homies. **1964** *Courier-Mail* (Brisbane) 19 Nov. 12 Mr. Arthur Bryan.. dislikes what he calls the 'pongo' Englishman. 'This is the bloke who is so bound by tradition and the old establishment that he can think of nothing else,' he says. **1969** *Private Eye* 19 Dec. 5/2 The *pongos* are shooting through like streaks of *weasle piss*! **1972** G. W. TURNER *Eng. Lang. Austral. & N.Z.* (ed. 2) 109 Like Australians, New Zealanders call the English *pommies*, but also have a variant *pongo* which seems rather less tolerant in its tone.

c. *Mil. slang.* An army officer.

1943 B. J. HURREN *Eastern Med.* xii. 139 In the slang of the desert the word 'pongo' is used for all Army officers. **1943** C. H. WARD-JACKSON *Piece of Cake* 48 *Pongo*, an army officer. **1949** F. MACLEAN *Eastern Approaches* II. vii. 269 'Operation PONGO'.. was the code-name I had chosen for the abduction of the General. **1965** O. MANNING *Friends & Heroes* xxii. 237 What were you doing walking about holding on to that bloody little pongo?

d. *slang.* A Black, a Negro. Also *attrib.*

1968 L. DEIGHTON *Only when I Larf* vii. 99 You wouldn't want no breech block blowing back and crippling some poor pongo, no matter what country he's in. **1972** M. WOODHOUSE *Mama Doll* viii. 89 Our Pongo brothers in darkest Africa.

pongo, var. PANGA¹.

pongol, var. PONGAL.

Pongola (pɒn'gəʊlə). Also **Pangola**, and with lower-case initial. In full, ***Pongola*** or ***Pangola (finger-)grass.*** The name of a South African river used *absol.* and *attrib.* to designate a variety of the perennial grass *Digitaria decumbens*, originally native to regions near the river, but now widely cultivated in tropical areas.

1947 D. B. D. MEREDITH *Effect of Fertilisers on Grasses in S. Afr.* v. 115 The area selected had been planted.. to alternate rows of the Pongola Finger grass and *Digitaria Smutsii*. **1952** M. A. FLORES in *Proc. 6th Internat. Grassland Congr.* II. 1435 Pangola grass, introduced within recent years from Africa through Florida, U.S.A., is finding favor with livestock producers because of its resistance to drought. **1959** *Agronomy Jrnl.* LI. 111/1 Napier or elephant grass.. guineagrass.. and pangola-grass.. are among the most important of the forage grasses of the Tropics. **1966** A. M. M. REES in Davies & Skidmore *Trop. Pastures* xi. 171 Recorded grass outputs of over £50 per acre were obtained ..from milk and beef produced from Pangola pastures. **1972** E. HARGREAVES *Fair Green Weed* vii. 93 We're putting in pangola to make pastures of the old banana plantations. **1972** *Stand. Encycl. S. Afr.* V. 320/2 The quick-grasses.., Pongola finger-grass.. and Swaziland finger-grass.. are amongst those grasses that are commonly planted as lawns or on sports grounds. **1977** A. V. BOGDAN *Trop. Pasture & Fodder Plants* 113 The name Pangola grass has been derived from the Pongola River in the Piet Retief district of eastern Transvaal.. and some authors suggested the name Pongola grass, possibly with a view of avoiding confusion with any other forms of *Digitaria* which may come from the Pangola River area of western Transvaal. It has also been suggested that the name Pangola grass should be applied only to those clones which.. were originally brought to USA in 1935 and which are now widely grown in a number of countries.

pongul, var. PONGAL.

pongy ('pɒŋɪ), *a. colloq.* [f. PONG *sb.*² + -Y¹.] Malodorous; smelly.

1936 'TAFFRAIL' *Mystery at Milford Haven* xi. 153 'Kippers!' she groaned. 'They are a bit pongy sometimes,' Victor had to confess. **1960** *Times Lit. Suppl.* 4 Nov. 714/2 A cheap forty-eight-hour excursion in contemporary Gauguin-land complete with Papeete night-spots, pongy with frangipani. **1965** G. MCINNES *Road to Gundagai* xii. 215 Dad.. kept turning up.. with loot from the Prahran market: strings of saveloys and frankfurters, pongy cheeses, ..and huge Portuguese sardines. **1975** *Islander* (Victoria, B.C.) 3 Aug. 2/2 After lunch the pongy wharf became too much for us.

pongyi, var. POONGHIE, PHOONGYEE.

ponhaus ('pɒnhɔːs). *U.S. dial.* Also **pawnhaus, ponhaws, ponhoss.** [ad. Ger. *panhas*, f. *pfanne* frying pan + *hase* rabbit. Said to be used in a similar sense in Ger. dial.: see M. B. Lambert *Dict. Non-English Words of Pennsylvania-German Dial.* (1924) 117.] = SCRAPPLE *sb.*² Also *attrib.*

1869 *Atlantic Monthly* Oct. 483/1 Some make *pawn-haus* from the liquor in which the pudding was boiled; adding thereto corn-meal. **1882** P. H. GIBBONS *Pennsylvania Dutch* (ed. 3) 423 Mr. W. liked the fried *pawn-haus* although he found it rather rich. **1923** *Dialect Notes* V. 236 *Ponhaws*, scrapple. **1931** *Sun* (Baltimore) 11 Mar. 8/7 He's goin' to have one more grand ponhaus celebration this season. **1943** *Chicago Daily News* 8 Sept. 25 Originally, Ponhaws or scrapple was made from the head of the freshly killed porker, but good, fresh, lean pork of any cut may be used. **1944** *Sun* (Baltimore) 4 Dec. 8-0/3 The Pennsylvania Germans.. called it 'Pfännhaas', which.. was corrupted into.. 'Ponhaus',.. which simply means.. 'pan rabbit'. This is in line with the use of 'Welsh rabbit'. **1953** *Amer. Speech* XXVIII. 244 Certainly *ponhaus* and *smearcase*, standard food items from colonial days, are old words in the area [*sc.* Bedford, Pennsylvania].

poniard ('pɒnjəd), *sb.* Forms: 6– **poniard**; also 6 **poynyard**, 6–7 **poyniard, puniard**, 6–8 **poynard**, 7 **ponard, poneyard, poigniard, poinyard, pugniard, punyard, (poinred)**, 7–8 **ponyard**, 7–9 **poin-, poignard.** See also POIGNADO. [a. F. *poignard*, *poingnart*, *poyniard*, *pognard* (1519 in Hatz.-Darm.), f. *poing* fist: see -ARD.]

1. A short stabbing weapon; a dagger.

1588 SHAKS. *Tit. A.* II. iii. 120. *c* **1590** GREENE *Fr. Bacon* vi. 132 'Twere a long poniard, my lord, to reach between Oxford and Fressingfield. **1598** B. JONSON *Ev. Man in Hum.* I. iv, Let your poynard maintain your defence, thus. **1601** ? MARSTON *Pasquil & Kath.* II. 120 If his skinne be ponyard proofe. **1631** MASSINGER *Believe as You List* IV. ii, What have wee heere? A poinard and a halter! **1632** LITHGOW *Trav.* III. 89 He weareth.. a broad Ponard ouer-thwart his belly. *Ibid.* VIII. 350 A French Ponyard. *Ibid.* 351 My gold and my Poneyard. **1656** EARL MONM. tr. *Boccalini's Advts. fr. Parnass.* I. xviii. (1674) 20 Puniard, venom, or any other mischievous machination. *Ibid.* II. xcviii. 250 The twentieth blow that he hath received.. by Pugniard or Cudgel. **1666** PEPYS *Diary* 27 Oct., Ugly knives, like poignards. *c* **1680** *Jus Populi* 414 in G. Hickes *Spirit of Popery* 68 They need not fear either Dag, or Dagger, Pistol, or poisoned poinyard. **1725** POPE *Odyss.* XI. 120 Sheath thy ponyard. **1756–7** tr. *Keysler's Trav.* (1760) IV. 287 Here are several daggers or poignards. **1780** COWPER *Progr. Error* 305 Worse than a poinard in the basest hand. **1843** LYTTON *Last Bar.* I. iv, The stranger warded off the thrust of the poniard. **1869** BOUTELL *Arms & Arm.* ix. (1874) 179 A dagger, sometimes so short that it is really a poignard.

fig. **1599** SHAKS. *Much Ado* II. i. 255 Shee speakes poynyards, and euery word stabbes. **1641** EARL MONM. tr. *Biondi's Civil Warres* v. 104 Every motion made them give Allarum's, all which were punyards which wounded Philip. **1901** *N. Amer. Rev.* Feb. 220 Gibraltar is a poniard, always plunged into a wound that has never been healed.

2. *dial.* (See quot.)

1874 T. HARDY *Far fr. Madding Crowd* xxxvii, He had stuck his ricking-rod, groom, or poignard, as it was indifferently called—a long iron lance, sharp at the extremity and polished by handling—into the stack to support the sheaves.

poniard ('pɒnjəd), *v.* Forms: see the sb. [f. PONIARD *sb.* Cf. F. *poignarder* (16th c.).] *trans.* To stab or pierce with a poniard; *esp.* to stab to death by this means.

[**1593** NASHE *Christ's T.* Wks. (Grosart) IV. 123 He was all to be beponyarded in the Senate house.] **1601** W. T. *Ld. Remy's Civ. Consid.* 16 In continual feare to be poyniarded. **1718** LADY M. W. MONTAGU *Let. to C'tess of Mar* 10 Mar., She threw herself at the sultan's feet, and begged him to poniard her. **1781** COWPER *Charity* 508 Prepared to poignard whomsoe'er they meet. **1887** SAINTSBURY *Hist. Elizab. Lit.* iii. (1890) 76 He was poniarded in self-defence by..a serving-man.

†**b.** To furnish or fix up with long pins. *rare.*

1620 MIDDLETON& ROWLEY *World Tost at Tennis* 834 Those fair ladies..are neither trimmed, nor trussed, nor poniarded.

†**poni'bility.** *Obs. rare.* [f. **ponible* (f. L. *pōnĕre* to place) + -ITY.] Capability of being placed.

1734 tr. *Barrow's Math. Lect.* x. 176 Space is nothing else but the mere Power, Capacity, Ponibility, or (begging pardon for the Expression) Interponibility of Magnitude.

ponissement, obs. form of PUNISHMENT.

[**ponk** in Johnson, etc., mispr. for *pouke*, PUCK.]

ponk, var. PONG *sb.*[2] or *v.*[2]

ponkal, var. PONGAL.

ponne, obs. form of PAN *sb.*[1], PUN *v.*[1]

ponor ('pəʊnə(r)). *Physical Geogr.* [Serbo-Croat.] A steep natural shaft leading from the surface of the ground in a karstic region.

[**1921** *Geogr. Rev.* XI. 593 The article of Professor Cvijić marks a step forward in the science of physiography; but it is far from easy reading for the average geographer since many unfamiliar terms, such as 'bogaz' and 'ponor' are used without either definition or explanation by synonyms. *Ibid.* 600 The shaftlike aperture Cvijić called 'ponor'.] **1922** *Geol. Mag.* XIX. 406 The funnel-shaped hollows which are so frequently met with on the surface of the karst are termed ponors. **1937** WOOLDRIDGE & MORGAN *Physical Basis Geogr.* xix. 290 They [*sc.* limestone caves] commonly form part of a complex system of channels, widening locally into chambers, and fall broadly into two sets, viz. roughly horizontal galleries, and vertical or steeply inclined shafts, of which the higher members are the 'ponors' communicating with the surface. **1971** J. N. JENNINGS *Karst* vi. 139 In some poljes certain ponors change function for a period in the wet season and spew out water. **1976** S. T. TRUDGILL in E. Derbyshire *Geomorphol. & Climate* iii. 92 They observed in the Kuh-E-Parau limestone area of Iran how the overall form on a large scale is solutional in origin, with rounded hills, dolines and ponors.

‖**pons** (pɒnz). The Latin word for 'bridge': used in certain phrases.

1. pons asinorum (= bridge of asses): a humorous name for the fifth proposition of the first book of Euclid, from the difficulty which beginners or dull-witted persons find in 'getting over' or mastering it. Hence allusively.

1751 SMOLLETT *Per. Pic.* I. xviii. 130 Peregrine..began to read Euclid..but he had scarce advanced beyond the *Pons Asinorum*, when his ardor abated. **1845** FORD *Handbk. Spain* I. 217/2 This bridge was the *pons asinorum* of the French, which English never suffered them to cross. **1870** *Eng. Mech.* 4 Feb. 502/1 He knows the operation..to be the *pons asinorum* of incompetent workmen. **1877** BESANT & RICE *Harp & Cr.* xxvii.

2. pons Varolii (= bridge of Varolius or Varoli, an Italian anatomist of the 16th c.), also **pons cerebri** or **cerebelli**, and often simply pons (*Anat.*): a band of nerve-fibres in the brain, just above the medulla oblongata, consisting of transverse fibres connecting the two hemispheres of the cerebellum, and longitudinal fibres connecting the medulla with the cerebrum.

1693 tr. *Blancard's Phys. Dict.* (ed. 2), *Pons varolii*, certain globous Processes of the *Cerebellum.* **1704** J. HARRIS *Lex. Techn.* I, *Pons Cerebri*,..is a Congeries or Heap of innumerable Filaments divaricated out of the Solider Substance of the Brain. **1831** SIR W. HAMILTON *Metaph.* I. App. 420 The average of children under seven, exhibits the Pons, in proportion to the cerebellum, much smaller than in the average of adults. **1875** H. WALTON *Dis. Eye* 324 Disease of the pons is a very rare condition.

attrib. **1899** *Allbutt's Syst. Med.* VI. 807 In thirty cases of pons tumour..in five only was there defect of hearing.

pons, obs. f. *pence*, pl. of PENNY.

ponsion, ponsone, obs. ff. PUNCHEON.

Ponsonby rule ('pɒnsənbɪ ru:l). [Named after Arthur A. W. H. *Ponsonby* (1871–1946), 1st Lord Ponsonby, English politician.] A rule by which the Government may authorize an agreement without Parliamentary approval (see quot. 1976).

1957 *Erskine May's Law of Parl.* (ed. 16) xiii. 275 This practice, which is known as the 'Ponsonby rule', had its origin in a departmental minute dated 1 February 1924 and signed by Mr. Arthur Ponsonby, then Under-Secretary of State for Foreign Affairs. **1967** P. G. RICHARDS *Parliament & Foreign Affairs* iii. 43 These arrangements constituted the so-called Ponsonby Rule. **1976** H. WILSON *Governance of Britain* x. 185 Under the so-called Ponsonby rules specific parliamentary ratification is not required. The Government assumes authority in respect of any treaty or agreement it has negotiated if Parliament has not reacted within twenty-one days.

[**ponsondie**, mispr. for *pousoudie*, POWSOWDY.]

ponsway. Also **pauncesoy, ponsoy, ponsay.** Variants of PANCHWAY, E. Indian boat.

1737 in C. R. Wilson *Old Fort William* (1906) I. 147 Two Carts broke to pieces and four Ponsways. **1742** *Ibid.* 162 Pauncesoys. **1744** *Ibid.* 177 Ponsoys. **1756** *Ibid.* II. 58 His servant who stood in a Ponsay a little above the Gaut.

†**pont**[1]. *Obs.* Also 4–5 pount(e. [a. F. *pont*:—L. *pons, pont-em* bridge. So Welsh *pont.*] A bridge.

1470–85 MALORY *Arthur* XI. i. 571 Syr launcelot rode on his adventure tyl..he past ouer the pounte of Corbyn. **1639** *Glasgow Council Rec.* 11 Oct., Ordanit that ane dyke be built at Stockwall-heid, and ane Pont put therein. [**1875** W. MCILWRAITH *Guide Wigtownshire* 25 Strange thoughts present themselves anent the old pont.]

b. pont tournis. [OF. *pont torneïs*, f. *pont* bridge + *torneïs*, L. type **tornātīcius*, f. late L. *tornare* to turn.] A drawbridge.

13.. *Seuyn Sag.* (W.) 743 The leuedi stod, in pount tournis, For to bihelde the burdis. *a* **1400** *Lybeaus Disc.* (Kaluza) 1385 Boþe lordes and ladis Leyn out in pount tournis [*v.rr.* pomet tours, pount tornere, etc.] To se þat selly siȝt.

‖**c. pont-volant.** [F. (pɔ̃vɔlɑ̃), = flying-bridge.] (See quot.)

1727–41 CHAMBERS *Cycl.*, *Pont volant, flying bridge*, a kind of bridge used in sieges; made of two small bridges laid one over another, and so contrived by means of cords and pullies placed along the sides of the under-bridge, that the upper may be pushed forwards, till it join the place where it is designed to be fixed. **1861** in BUCHANAN *Dict. Arts.* **1864** in WEBSTER; and in mod. Dicts.

†**pont**[2]. *Obs.* [a. Du. *pont(e*: see next, and cf. PUNT *sb.*[1]] **a.** A large flat boat or transport; a float; = PONTOON 1. **b.** = CAISSON: see quots.

a. 1631 PORY *Let.* 22 Sept. in *Crt. & Times Chas. I* (1848) II. 133 King of Spain's forces by sea,..taken by the Prince of Orange..ten great pontes, in every one of which four-score men. **1776** G. SEMPLE *Building in Water* 99 You must also have..a Boatman to keep your Float or Pont steady. **1816** W. S. MASON *Statist. Acc. Irel.* II. 267 Two boats, called by the fishermen [on Lough Neagh] ponts, of 30 cwt. each, used principally in the carriage of turf.

b. 1721 PERRY *Daggenh. Breach* 31 Large Ponts or Chests ..he propos'd to sink at about twelve Foot space from each other, beginning from a Peer. **1840** *Civil Eng. & Arch. Jrnl.* III. 106/2 Mr. Boswell was first to make piers and then sink 6 ponts or chests 60 feet in length, 30 feet broad.

‖**pont**[3] (pɒnt). [Du. *pont* ferry-boat, pontoon:—MDu. *ponte* = MLG., LG. *punte*, ad. L. *ponto, -ōnem* a punt, a pontoon, a floating bridge, f. *pons* bridge.] Name in S. Africa for a large ferry-boat attached to an iron or steel cable.

1775 MASSON *Journ. to Cape* in *Phil. Trans.* LXVI. 279 We came to the pont or ferry. **1899** *Daily News* 11 Dec. 5/3 The Boers have seized the pont on the Orange River at Prieska, and cut the wire cable attached to it. **1900** *Ibid.* 13 Jan. 5/2 Pont is the name given in South Africa to the ferry boats plying on the large and more rapid rivers, and worked by steel cables.

pont, obs. form of PANT *v.*

pontac ('pɒntæk). Also 7 -aque, 7–8 -ack, 9 -ak, -acq. [a. F. *Pontac*, local name.] A sweet wine obtained from Pontac in the Basses Pyrénées, in the south of France. Also, a South African wine.

1674 BLOUNT *Glossogr.* To Rdr. (ed. 4) A ij b, The Vintner will furnish you with..Alicant,..Pontac, Tent. **1680** A. RATCLIFFE *Ovid Travestie* (1705) 18 Wine in abundance,—I drank none but Sack, But all you Men did ply it with Pontack. **1714** MANDEVILLE *Fab. Bees* (1733) I. 118 Those, that cannot purchase true hermitage or pontack, will be glad of more ordinary French claret. **1812** A. PLUMPTRE tr. *Lichtenstein's Trav. S. Afr.* I. 151 Du Toit gave us an excellent sort of wine, called here Pontac, a sweet deep-red wine. **1868** W. C. BALDWIN *Afr. Hunting* 365 An excellent omelette for breakfast, with a very fair amount of Pontac.

pontage ('pɒntɪdʒ). Now *Hist.* or *local.* [a. OF. *pontage* (1401 in Godef.):—med.L. *pontāticum* (Du Cange) a bridge-toll, f. L. *pons, pont-em* bridge + *-āticum*, -AGE.] A toll paid for the use of a bridge; a tax paid for the maintenance and repair of a bridge or bridges; bridge-toll.

[**1157** in *Chron. Stephen*, etc. (Rolls) IV. App. 337 Fecit liberas de omni consuetudine et theloneo et passagio et pontagio. **1292** BRITTON I. xx. §1 Lestage..ou murage, ou pontage, ou cheminage.] *c* **1450** *Godstow Reg.* 666 A Charter ..to the mynchons..for tol, passage, pountage, and all custome thurgh all Englond. *a* **1500** tr. *Charter Rich. II* in Arnolde *Chron.* (1811) 22 Y^t^ they..be quyt for euer of pauage pontage and murage by al our reame. **1597–8** *Act 39 Eliz.* c. 34 §6 Pontage shall be payde..at the sayde Brydge ..for every..Wayne, Carre, or Carte..two pence. **1735** J. PRICE *Stone-Br. Thames* 5 A House on each Head of the Bridge, erected to receive the Toll or Pontage. **1895** *Glasgow Weekly News* 19 Jan. 7/8 Subscriptions so as to have the Leven bridges free from the objectionable pontage.

†**b.** *free pontage*, freedom from bridge-toll.

1695 KENNETT *Par. Antiq.* ix. 201 All right and title to a new Mill,..with free pontage or passage over the River.

pontal ('pɒntəl), *a. rare.* [f. L. *pons, pont-em* + -AL[1].] Of or pertaining to a bridge, or (in *Anat.*) to the *pons Varolii*: = PONTIC *a.*[2]

1863 P. S. WORSLEY *Poems & Transl.* 11 A league above this pontal arc, Now seeming one with heaven. **1890** *Cent. Dict.*, *Pontal*, same as *pontile.* **1895** in *Syd. Soc. Lex.*

ponte, pontee, obs. forms of PUNTY.

Pontet-Canet (põte kane). The name of a château in the Pauillac commune of the Médoc, applied to a claret produced there.

1883 H. JAMES in *Atlantic Monthly* Oct. 458/1 There is a touch of French reason, French completeness, in a glass of Pontet-Canet. **1891** in C. Ray *Compleat Imbiber* (1967) IX. 122 *Claret*..St. Estèphe..St. Emilion..Pontet Canet. **1912** 'SAKI' *Chron. Clovis* 184 Waiter, a bottle of *Pontet Canet.* **1920** G. SAINTSBURY *Notes on Cellar-Bk.* iv. 64 Pontet Canet ..became..a 'literary' wine a good many years ago. **1966** H. YOXALL *Fashion of Life* xxv. 240 A Soho restaurant where.. they served a pre-war Ch. Pontet-Canet at 2*s.* 9*d.* a half-bottle. **1967** A. LICHINE *Encycl. Wines* 409/1 Classified a Fifth Growth..in 1855, and traditionally at the head of the Fifths, Pontet-Canet actually sells with the Seconds and Thirds. **1975** 'D. JORDAN' *Black Account* xiii. 65 The House had..lashed out on a Pontet-Canet..and a port which set out to impress the Minister.

Pontian ('pɒntɪən), *a. Geol.* [ad. Russ. *Ponticheskiĭ* (N. Barbot de Marny *Geol. ocherk' Khersonskoĭ Gubernii* (1869) xiv. 106), f. as PONTIC *a.*[1]: see -IAN.] Of, pertaining to, or designating the uppermost stage of the Miocene series in Europe (sometimes regarded as the lowest of the Pliocene series). Also *absol.*

1893 P. LAKE tr. *Kayser's Text Bk. Compar. Geol.* iv. 361 Congeria or Pontian series. **1895** J. D. DANA *Man. Geol.* (ed. 4) IV. iv. 927 Above the Tortonian, the stages Sarmatian and Pontian are recognized in Dauphiné, Austria and Italy. **1903** A. GEIKIE *Text-bk. Geol.* (ed. 4) II. 1291 The top of the Miocene series (Pontian stage). **1940** A. W. GRABAU *Rhythm of Ages* xxxviii. 466 The Pontian Hipparion clays, which were formerly considered in part Miocene, are here placed in the base of the Pliocene. **1971** *Nature* 30 Apr. 562/1 In 1929, Matthew..pointing to the occurrence of a relatively primitive *Hipparion* fauna in the lower part of the stratotype Pontian at Sebastopol,..argued that the first appearance of *Hipparion* could thus be used to define the base of the Pliocene in continental mammalian successions. In this way, 'early Pliocene' and 'Pontian' became equivalent terms in vertebrate biostratigraphy. **1973** *Ibid.* 15 June 391/1 Estimates by most vertebrate palaeontologists have ranged between 10–12 m.y. because of the supposed initial appearance of the three-toed *Hipparion* in the lower part of the stratotype Pontian of the eastern Mediterranean.

‖**pontianak**[1] (pɒntɪ'ɑ:næk). [a. Malay *pontianak*, f. *pati-anak* child-killer.] A type of vampire (see quots.). Cf. LANGSUIR, PENANGGALAN.

1839 T. J. NEWBOLD *Pol. & Statistical Acct. Straits of Malacca* II. xii. 191 Spirits..supposed to exert a baneful influence over them [*sc.* Malays] in this sublunary world. First, the Plissit and the Pontianak. **1900** W. W. SKEAT *Malay Magic* vi. 320 The Pontianak or Mati-anak..is also a night-owl, and is supposed to be a child of the Langsuir. **1965** C. SHUTTLEWORTH *Malayan Safari* vi. 86 Perhaps the most fearsome of all superstitions is that of the *pontianak* or vampire, widely prevalent throughout Malaya. **1966** D. FORBES *Heart of Malaya* xiii. 185 She had turned into what they call a *pontianak.* **1972** *Daily Tel.* (Colour Suppl.) 12 May 58/3 The Malayan vampire family includes..the Pontianak (the stillborn child of the Langsuir) which adopts the shape of a night owl.

pontianak[2] (pɒntɪ'ɑ:næk). Also Pont-, -ac. [The name of a city and formerly of a sultanate on the island of Borneo.] = *gutta-jelutong* s.v. GUTTA[2] 2 (orig. that from Borneo).

1911 *India Rubber World* XLIII. 130/2 Different qualities of jelutong are known in the trade, according to the districts from which they are derived, as Palembang (Sumatra), Pontianak (South Borneo), Sarawak, and so on. **1923** D. W. LUFF *Chem. of Rubber* iii. 35 An inferior rubber which in the days of high rubber prices became of importance industrially is that known variously as Jelutong, Gutta Jelutong, Pontianac, Bresk, or Dead Borneo, which is obtained from the *Dyera costulata*, a large tree growing in Borneo, Sumatra and Malaya. **1927** [see *gutta-jelutong*]. **1947** H. BARRON *Mod. Rubber Chem.* (ed. 2) iii. 27 Jelutong (or pontianak) comes chiefly from Sumatra.

Pontic ('pɒntɪk), *a.*[1] [ad. L. *Ponticus*, a. Gr. *Ποντικός*, f. *πόντος* sea, spec. the Black Sea, hence the country of Pontus.]

1. Of, belonging to, found in, or obtained from, the district of Pontus: esp. in names of plants and animals, e.g. ***Pontic nut***, the hazel nut; ***Pontic rhubarb***, *Rheum rhaponticum*; ***Pontic wormwood***, *Artemisia pontica.*

1551 TURNER *Herbal* I. A iv, Those ij. kindes of wormwode which diuerse take for pontyke wormwode, are none of pontike wormwood. **1597** GERARDE *Herbal* II. lxxix. §4. 317 The Ponticke Rubarbe is lesser and slenderer then that of Barbarie. **1620** VENNER *Via Recta* vii. 127 Those that haue their skins red, are the right Ponticke Nuts, and are.. the best Filberds. **1655** H. VAUGHAN *Silex Scint.*, *Providence* viii, Gladly will I, like Pontick sheep, Unto my wormwood-diet keep. **1726** SWIFT *Let.* 15 Oct. in Pope *Corr.* (1956) II. 407 They must have been pontic mice, which as Olavs Magnus assures us always devours whatever is green. **1887** A. T. DE VERE *Legends & Rec. Church & Empire* 208 Thou Pontic Paradise! **1895** W. ROBINSON *Eng. Flower Garden* (ed. 4) I. ix. 126 We too often see the common pontic kind [of rhododendron]. **1906** KIPLING *Puck of Pook's Hill* 167 I've tramped Britain and I've tramped Gaul, And the Pontic shore where the snow-flakes fall. **1935** *Discovery* July 199/1 There is, e.g., another orthopter which lives in the Pontic and west Mediterranean areas, and in some places in Central Europe as a 'Pontic relic'. **1956** R. MACAULAY *Towers of Trebizond* xv. 178, I lay in a swoon, pretending to be dead, because the barbarous Pontic natives, the Mossynoici, were all about.

b. *Pontic Sea*, the Black Sea.

1598 GRENEWEY *Tacitus, Germanie* i. (1622) 258 Danubius..falleth by six channels into the Ponticke sea. **1604** SHAKS. *Oth.* III. iii. 453. **1865** SWINBURNE *Atalanta* 2132 The thunder of Pontic seas.

c. Of or pertaining to the ancient kingdom of Pontus, its kings (see MITHRIDATIC *a.*), its people, or the dialect of Greek attributed to them. Also as *sb.*

1665 D. LLOYD tr. *Plutarch's Worthies* 372 According to the Pontick Kings dream of floating on the waters. **1816** BYRON *Dream* viii, in *Prisoner of Chillon* 44 Like to the Pontic monarch of old days, He fed on poisons, and they had no power. **1939** [see MEDIAN *sb.* 2]. **1972** W. B. LOCKWOOD *Panorama Indo-European Lang.* 267 It would not be surprising if the language known to the Greeks as Pontic were a descendant of Kaskian. **1974** *Encycl. Brit. Micropædia* VIII. 115/2 An independent Pontic kingdom with its capital at Amaseia was established at the end of the 4th century BC in the wake of Alexander's conquests. *Ibid. Macropædia* VIII. 396/2 The Asia Minor dialects [of Greek] also display archaic features (*e.g.*, Pontic *e* for ancient *ē* in certain word elements).

d. *Anthropol.* Designating a type of peoples identified in the Balkans and southern Russia (see quots.). Also as *sb.*

[**1932** V. BUNAK in *Zeitschr. für Morphologie u. Anthropologie* XXX. 471 Die zwei südlichen analogen Kombinationen—nordkaukasische und ostbalkanische—sind untereinander ähnlicher und stehen von den nordpontischen Varietät weiter ab. Sie bilden eine andere Rasse des östlichen mediterranen Zweigs, den ich vorläufig als pontische Rasse..bezeichnen werde.] **1939** C. S. COON *Races Europe* xii. 617 The Mediterranean racial divison which the Russian anthropologists call Pontic..is with little doubt of Neolithic date in southern Russia, Rumania, Bulgaria, and the Hellespont region, and probably in Greece and the Aegean. *Ibid.* 679 Pontic. A variety of Mediterranean or Atlanto-Mediterranean,..is concentrated in Bulgaria and in the Rumanian lowlands; it also is found in the Caucasus and Ukraine and westward sporadically as far as Germany, Poland, and Lithuania.

†**2.** Having a somewhat sour and astringent taste. [? like Pontic rhubarb, or Pontic wormwood.] *Obs.*

1477 NORTON *Ord. Alch.* v. in Ashm. *Theat. Chem. Brit.* (1652) 74 And so is Sowerish tast called Sapor Pontick, And lesse Sower allso called Sapor Stiptick. **1572** J. JONES *Bathes of Bath* III. 26 b, Spittle, not bitter, but pontique or harshe. **1576** NEWTON *Lemnie's Complex.* (1633) 218 Somewhat tart and sowrish, and as it is commonly tearmed, Ponticke: such a relish..as is in a Grape..being not as yet come to his perfect ripenesse and maturity. **1684** tr. *Bonet's Merc. Compit.* VIII. 272 Causticks..close and bind the Veins, by reason of their pontick, styptick parts.

'pontic, *a.*[2] and *sb. Anat.* and *Path.* [f. L. *pons, pont-em* bridge + -IC.]

A. *adj.* Pertaining to the *pons Varolii* (see PONS 2): = PONTAL, PONTILE, PONTINE.

1890 *Lancet* 5 Apr. 739/2 The only case over forty being one of pontic abscess.

B. *sb. Dentistry.* An artificial tooth that forms part of a dental bridge, being held in place by attachment to its neighbouring teeth, and not fixed directly to the jaw.

1916 J. H. PROTHERO *Prosthetic Dentistry* (ed. 2) xxix. 785 The term 'pontic' has been suggested as a substitute for 'dummy' in describing a bridge tooth replacement. The term seems scarcely appropriate, since practically all fixed bridges are of the rigid truss type. **1932** F. R. FELCHER *Art of Porcelain in Dentistry* xi. 133 Pontics should not be so built that they extend too far into the sockets, as a recession will usually result if this is done. **1956** J. N. ANDERSON *Appl. Dental Materials* xiii. 128 When making a bridge, the 'pontic' or bridging part is joined to the supports or 'retainers'. **1974** D. H. ROBERTS in Harty & Roberts *Restorative Procedures Practising Dentist* xxii. 327 Where metal-ceramic full crowns are used as retainers then the same material is normally employed for the pontic.

ponticello (pɒntɪ'tʃɛləʊ). *Mus.* [a. It. *ponticello* little bridge.] **a.** The bridge of a stringed instrument.

1740 J. GRASSINEAU *Mus. Dict.* 182 *Ponticella* [*sic*], a small bridge. **1849** *Hamilton's Celebrated Dict.* 92 *Ponticello*.., the bridge, in speaking of the violin, guitar, etc. **1961** A. BAINES *Mus. Instruments* 356 *Ponticello*,..the bridge of a violin, etc.

b. Phr. ***sul ponticello***: a direction in a musical score that bowing should be close to the bridge. Also *ellipt.* as *ponticello*. Also applied *attrib.* to the sound produced by such bowing.

1849 *Hamilton's Celebrated Dict.* 112 *Sul ponticello*, on or near the bridge. **1883** GROVE *Dict. Mus.* III. 15/2 *Ponticello* ..or *sul ponticello*, a term indicating that a passage on the violin, tenor, or violoncello, is to be played by crossing the strings with the bow close to the bridge. **1931** G. JACOB *Orchestral Technique* ii. 6 The ponticello tremolo in which a most eerie effect is produced by bowing the strings nearer to the bridge than the normal position. **1959** *Collins Mus. Encycl.* 509/1 *Sul ponticello* (or *ponticello* alone), on the bridge, *i.e.* play near the bridge, thus producing a glassy, brittle tone. **1967** *Listener* 8 June 769/2 The famous passage in the finale where the first violin skips aloft, high over a sinister progression of rapid *ponticello* chords on the lower strings. **1977** 'E. CRISPIN' *Glimpses of Moon* iii. 41 'And then *erk, skerk*,' he added, possibly attempting to convey ponticello strings.

†**pon'ticity.** *Obs.* [ad. OF. *ponticité*, ad. med.L. *ponticitās* (Constantinus Africus, 11th c., in Du Cange), f. *Ponticus*: see -ITY.] The quality of having a 'pontic' flavour (see PONTIC *a.*[1] 2).

c **1400** tr. *Secreta Secret., Gov. Lordsh.* 98 Egrenesse & vnsauournesse, ponticite, stipticite, & acuement. **1559** MORWYNG *Evonym.* 391 That Must or newe wyne..dothe get a certain ponticitie or tast lyke wormwood and bynding. **1669** W. SIMPSON *Hydrol. Chym.* 68 The over acidness or spurious ponticity of the stomachical ferment.

ponticum ('pɒntɪkəm). Also **Ponticum** [a. mod.L. specific epithet of *Rhododendron ponticum* (Linnæus *Species Plantarum* (ed. 2, 1762) II. 562): see PONTIC *a.*[1]] A mauve-flowered, evergreen shrub, ***Rhododendron ponticum***, of the family Ericaceæ, native to Spain, Portugal, and Asia Minor and naturalized in many other temperate regions. Also *attrib.*

1875 H. FRASER *Handy Bk. Ornamental Conifers* 185 The best and most commonly-used stocks for grafting are free-grown seedlings of the robust form of the common Ponticum. **1917** J. G. MILLAIS *Rhododendrons* I. viii. 227/2 Enormous numbers of young ponticums are annually used as stocks for the finer varieties. **1962** R. PAGE *Educ. Gardener* 27 We uprooted the ponticums and burned them. **1972** 'I. DRUMMOND' *Frog in Moonflower* 5 A heavy clump of Ponticum rhododendrons grew unexpectedly on top of the little cliff. **1976** J. LEES-MILNE *William Beckford* iv. 59 Today the lake, swathed in rampaging ponticum.., lies dark and almost unapproachable. **1977** *Evening Standard* 22 Apr. 19/2 Those ponticums..are not the ordinary purple ones, but very rare.

‖**pontifex** ('pɒntɪfɛks). Pl. **pontifices** (pɒn'tɪfɪsiːz). [L. *pontifex, -icem* a Roman high-priest: app. f. *pons, pont-em* bridge + *-fic-* from *facĕre* to make; but the first element was perh. Osc.-Umb. *puntis* propitiatory offering, assimilated to *pons, pont-em*.]

1. *Rom. Antiq.* A member of the principal college of priests in ancient Rome, the head of which was the ***Pontifex Maximus*** or chief priest. Also *transf.*

1579–80 NORTH *Plutarch* (1595) 73 The first and chiefest of these bishops, which they call the great Pontifex. **1647** R. STAPYLTON *Juvenal* 63 There was in Rome a colledge of pontifices, which were exempted from the authority of any lay-court of judicature. **1777** P. THICKNESSE *Year's Journey* II. xlii. 83 The consecration of the Roman Pontifex Maximus. **1794** SULLIVAN *View Nat.* I. 16 From the commencement to nearly the conclusion of the Roman empire, the king was always priest or pontifex. **1881** S. H. HODGSON *Outcast Ess.* 384 Long as the Pontifex and Silent Maid Shall go together up the Capitol. **1934** *New Statesman* 3 Nov. 614/2 Stalin has exiled Trotsky and become the Pontifex Maximus of the new Russo-Catholic Church of Communism. **1957** *Oxf. Dict. Chr. Ch.* 1089/2 *Pontifex Maximus*,..originally a pagan title of the chief priest at Rome, Tertullian used it satirically..of the Pope, and from the 5th cent. onwards it was a regular title of honour for the Popes, and occasionally used also of other bishops.

2. *Eccl.* A bishop; *spec.* the pope: = PONTIFF 2.

[**1377** LANGL. *P. Pl.* B. xv. 42 Bisshopes..bereth many names, *Presul* and *pontifex* and *metropolitanus*, And other names an hepe, *episcopus & pastor*.] **1651** HOBBES *Leviath.* IV. xlv. (1839) 661 The bishop of Constantinople.. pretended to be equal to the bishop of Rome; though at last, not without contention, the Pope carried it, and became the *Pontifex Maximus*. **1851** HUSSEY *Papal Power* v. 132 The Bishop of Rome, the Pontifex, is the spiritual sovereign of the world.

†**3.** = PONTIFF 3. *Obs. rare.*

1655 FULLER *Ch. Hist.* III. vi. §35 In their spiritual government they [the Jews in England] were all under one Pontifex, or High Priest.

4. With allusion to the reputed etymological meaning: = Bridge-maker.

1831 CARLYLE *Sart. Res.* I. xi, Never perhaps since our first Bridge-builders, Sin and Death, built that stupendous Arch from Hell-gate to the Earth, did any Pontifex, or Pontiff, undertake such a task. **1851** LONGF. *Gold. Leg.* v. 7 Well has the name of Pontifex been given Unto the Church's head, as the chief builder And architect of the invisible bridge That leads from earth to heaven.

pontiff ('pɒntɪf). Also 7 -ife, 7–8 -if. [a. F. *pontife* (*pontif* 1516), ad. L. *pontifex*: see PONTIFEX]

1. *Rom. Antiq.* = PONTIFEX 1.

1626 BACON *Sylva* §771 Livy doth relate, that there were found..two coffins..whereof the one contained the body of king Numa,..and the other, his books of sacred rites and ceremonies, and the discipline of the pontifs. **1706** PHILLIPS s.v. *Pontifex*, There were also *Pontifices Minores*, or Inferiour Pontiffs who were Assistants to the chief Pontiff. **1845** GRAVES *Rom. Law* in *Encycl. Metrop.* II. 755/1 It is probable that Papirius, who was himself a pontiff, directed his attention principally to religious ceremonies. **1868** *Smith's Dict. Grk. & Rom. Antiq.* 303/1 The Roman pontiffs formed the most illustrious among the great colleges of priests.

2. A bishop (of the mediæval Western church); *spec.* and usually, the bishop of Rome, the pope (in full, ***sovereign pontiff***).

a **1677** BARROW *Pope's Suprem.* (1680) B iv b, We.. pronounce it to be of necessity to Salvation..to be subject to the Roman Pontife. **1769** BLACKSTONE *Comm.* IV. viii. 105 The then reigning pontiff having favoured duke William in his projected invasion. **1841** W. SPALDING *Italy & It. Isl.* II. 275 By far the most remarkable among modern pontiffs, was Sixtus the Fifth, the son of a peasant in the March of Ancona. **1854** MILMAN *Lat. Chr.* VI. i. (1864) III. 369 The Bishop of Toul did not travel to Rome as a pontiff, but as a pilgrim. **1906** *Q. Rev.* July 267 M. Loubet had grievously offended the Sovereign Pontiff.

3. *gen.* A chief or high priest (of any religion). Also *fig.*

1610 HOLLAND *Camden's Brit.* (1637) 711 Coy-fi, who had beene a Pontife or Bishop of the heathen rites and ceremonies. **1727–41** CHAMBERS *Cycl.* s.v. *Pontifex*, The Jews too had their pontif or high-priest. **1878** G. SMITH *Life J. Wilson* xvii. (1879) 306 These pontiffs of Krishna waxed fat with organised adultery. **1895** *Westm. Gaz.* 9 Sept. 2/3 Which only shows that the Pontiffs of Science are no more infallible than other Infallibles.

4. *attrib.* **pontiff purple**, a shade of purple.

1742 YOUNG *Nt. Th.* III. 204 'Twas not the strife of malice, but of pride; The strife of pontiff pride, not pontiff gall. **1900** *Daily News* 13 Oct. 6/5 In all the new colours, brown, mauve, heliotrope, Pontiff purple.

pontific (pɒn'tɪfɪk), *a.* Now *rare* or *Obs.* [f. L. *pons, pont-em* bridge + *-ficus* making; but used in sense of *pontificius*: see PONTIFICIAL.]

1. *Rom. Antiq.* = PONTIFICAL *a.* 5.

1644 MILTON *Areop.* (Arb.) 37 What their twelve Tables, and the Pontifick College with their Augurs and Flamins taught them.

2. = PONTIFICAL *a.* 1–3.

1716 *Loyal Mourner* 64 For both Pontific, and Schismatick Chair; Nay, all the World of Errors stood in fear. *a* **1770** AKENSIDE *Poems* (1789) II. 45 [He] to eternal exile bore Pontific rage and vassal dread. *a* **1797** H. WALPOLE *Mem. Geo. II* (1847) I. 342 The Pontific power arrogated by the Head of the Law.

3. ? = PONTIFICAL *a.* 4.

1716 SWIFT *Pethox* 94, You o'er the high triumphal arch Pontifick made your glorious march.

¶**4.** *catachr.* Pertaining to a bridge. (Cf. PONTIFICAL *a.* 6.) *humorous nonce-use.*

1768 STERNE *Sent. Journ.* (1775) II. 125 To be driven forth out of my house by domestic winds, and despoiled of my castor by pontific ones.

†**pon'tificacy.** *Obs.* [irreg. f. med.L. *pontificātio*: see -ACY 3.] = PONTIFICATE *sb.*

1529 RASTELL *Pastyme* (1811) 53 Put downe from hys Pontyfycacy. **1579** FENTON *Guicciard.* 839 An evill prognostication of his Pontificacie. **1665** SIR T. HERBERT *Trav.* (1677) 267 Omar sat twelve years..in the Pontificacy. **1793** HELY tr. *O'Flaherty's Ogygia* II. 202 Lucius consulted pope Eleutherus at the beginning of his pontificacy.

pontifical (pɒn'tɪfɪkəl), *a.* and *sb.* [ad. L. *pontificālis* of or belonging to a PONTIFEX: see -AL[1]. So F. *pontifical* (1404 in Hatz.-Darm.).]

A. *adj.* **I.** Pertaining to a pontiff.

1. Pertaining or proper to a bishop or prelate; episcopal.

c **1440** *Alphabet of Tales* 74 A holie hermett..saw þis Basilius on a tyme walk in his pontificall abbett. **1530** PALSGR. 321/1 Pontyfycall, belongyng to a bysshop, *pontifical, episcopal*. **1641** MILTON *Ch. Govt.* vi. Wks. 1851 III. 126 The rending of your pontificall sleeves. **1688** R. HOLME *Armoury* III. 176/2 The Mitred Abbot..exerciseth Pontifical, or Episcopal Jurisdictions. **1890** *Durham & Northumb. Arch. Trans.* IV. 19 Mr. Bond..has omitted the Pontifical years of the Bishops of Durham altogether.

2. *spec.* **a.** Of or pertaining to the pope; papal.

1447 BOKENHAM *Seyntys* (Roxb.) 95 That he wold be so bestyal To forsakyn hys glorye pontifical. **1525** LD. BERNERS *Froiss.* II. clv. 426 She came to the popes palays in Auignon, and..went to se the pope, who sate in consystory in a chayre pontyficall. **1614** JACKSON *Creed* III. xxxi. §1 Thus did Innocent the third, and other Popes, write diuers books,.. as if they had proceeded from their Pontificall authority. **1765** BLACKSTONE *Comm.* I. Introd. iii. 82 Besides these pontifical collections, which, during the times of popery, were received as authentic in this island. **1864** BRYCE *Holy Rom. Emp.* xiii. (1875) 218 Leo III did not suppose..that it was by his sole pontifical authority that the crown was given to the Frank.

†**b.** Adhering to the pope or the papacy; popish, papistical. *Obs.*

1533 TINDALE *Supper of Lord* B vij b, Lorde how thys pontificall poet playeth hys parte.

3. *gen.* Of or pertaining to a chief or high priest; high-priestly.

c **1440** *York Myst.* xxx. 207 As I [Caiaphas] am pontificall prince of all prestis. **1578** T. N. tr. *Conq. W. India* 380 Then came the high priest cloathed in his pontificall vestmentes. **1635–56** COWLEY *Davideis* IV. Note 20 It will be therefore askt, Why I make him here perform the Office of the High-Priest, and dress him in the Pontifical Habits? **1708** OCKLEY *Saracens* (1848) 141 Omar was invested with the regal and the pontifical dignity, and saluted by universal consent 'the Caliph of the Apostle of God'. **1775** ADAIR *Amer. Ind.* 81 Their pontifical office descends by inheritance to the eldest.

4. a. Characterized by the pomp, state, dignity, authority, or dogmatic character of a pontiff.

1589 *Marprel. Epit.* F iij, As though he could not be as popelike and pontificall, as my Lorde of Canterburie. **1604** R. CAWDREY *Table Alph.*, *Pontificall*, lordly, stately, Bishoplike. **1632** MASSINGER *City Madam* IV. i, *Luke.* You know Mistress Shave'em? *Gettall.* The pontifical punk? **1672** MARVELL *Reh. Transp.* I. 32 The..leading party of the English Clergy..retained such a Pontifical stiffness towards the foreign Divines. **1892** MORLEY in *19th Cent.* Feb. 313 Littré..less provoked..by Comte's arrogance, his pontifical airs, and his hatred of liberty.

b. Applied to a shade of purple. (Cf. PONTIFF 4.)

1899 *Daily News* 27 Feb. 6/6 A new half-mourning dress ..in cloth of a pontifical purple tint.

II. 5. *Rom. Antiq.* Of or belonging to the *pontifices* of ancient Rome: see PONTIFEX 1.

1579–80 NORTH *Plutarch* (1595) 73 The great Pontifex.. hath the place, authoritie, and dignitie of the..maister of their pontificall lawe. **1865** TYLOR *Early Hist. Man.* vi. 124 This practice, Pliny adds, still remains in the pontifical discipline. **1897** A. DRUCKER tr. *von Ihering's Evol. Aryans* IV. v. 306 All the branches of the pontifical duties may be traced back to the original demands laid upon the technical bridge-makers of the migratory period.

III. 6. In reputed etymological sense: Bridge-making, bridge-building.

1667 MILTON *P.L.* x. 313 Now had they brought the work by wondrous Art Pontifical, a ridge of pendent Rock, Over the vext Abyss. **1887** RUSKIN *Præterita* II. xi. 402 The single-arched bridge..signed for sacred pontifical work by a cross high above the parapet.

B. *sb.*

†**1.** A papal document or edict. *Obs. rare.*

c **1380** WYCLIF *Wks.* (1880) 480 Alle þes pontificals ben byneþe hooly writ, so þat ȝif þey alle weren brent cristendom shulde stonde wel.

†**2. a.** *pl.* The offices or duties of a pontifex or a pontiff. **b.** The office of a pontiff, pontificate. **c.** An office celebrated with pontifical ceremony. *Obs.*

1432–50 tr. *Higden* (Rolls) IV. 405 To fullefille the ministery off pristes to the peple commenge to theyme, and notte the pontificalles [*non autem pontificalia*]. **1567** *Gude & Godlie B.* (S.T.S.) 178 Thocht thow be Paip or Cardinall, Sa heich in thy Pontificall. **1621** BP. MOUNTAGU *Diatribæ* 459 Hee was..skilfull in the Romane Histories, Religion, Pontificals, and Ceremonies. **1691** tr. *Emilianne's Frauds Rom. Monks* 217 The whole Ceremony is carried on at their own Charges, and the Feast they make is called a Pontifical. *Ibid.* (ed. 3) 223 She had been so extreamly satisfi'd with the Pontifical, which had been celebrated with so much Pomp and Majesty.

3. a. A bishop's or priest's robe; now always *pl.* the vestments and other insignia of a bishop (or of a priest): = PONTIFICALIA.

13.. *Leg. St. Erkenwald* 130 in Horstm. *Altengl. Leg.* (1881) 269 Þe prelate in pontificals was prestly atyride. *c* **1430** LYDG. *Min. Poems* (Percy Soc.) 19 Salisbury, Norwiche, and Ely, In pontificalle arrayed richely. **1559** in *Reg. Episc. Aberdonensis* (Spalding Cl.) I. App. 89 Item the pontificall, viz. a chesabill, 4 tunicks, 3 stols. **1660** JER. TAYLOR *Duct. Dubit.* II. ii, For a bishop to ride on hunting in his pontificals..is against public honesty. **1774** J. ADAMS in *Fam. Lett.* (1876) 37 Next morning he [an Episcopal clergyman] appeared with his clerk and in his pontificals, and read several prayers. **1851** D. WILSON *Preh. Ann.* (1863) I. II. vi. 463 The archpriest robed in his most stately pontificals.

†**b.** A bishop's ring; also ? a ring or some ornament in imitation of this. *Obs.*

1507 *Test. Ebor.* (Surtees) IV. 319 For a pontificall put upon my lordes fynger in tym of sering [= cering] xvj d. **1508** *Will of Joan Hampton* (Somerset Ho.), A peyre of owches otherwise callid pontificalles of siluer & gilt.

4. An office-book of the Western Church, containing the forms for sacraments and other rites and ceremonies to be performed by bishops.

1584 R. SCOT *Discov. Witchcr.* XV. xxvii. (1886) 375 Certaine conjurations taken out of the pontificall and out of the missall. **1624** BP. HALL *Impress of God* I. Wks. 445 If euer play-booke were more ridiculous, than their Pontificall, and booke of holy Ceremonies. **1844** LINGARD *Anglo-Sax. Ch.* (1858) I. vii. 296 The pontifical of Archbishop Egbert. **1905** C. E. OSBORNE *Life Father Dolling* xix. 168 The discovery of the Canons of Hippolytus, and of the Pontifical of Bishop Serapion.. has drawn attention to the primitive and Catholic character of this rite.

†**5.** A papal or episcopal court. *Obs.*

1628 GAULE *Pract. The.* (1629) 241 Though their owne Pontificall might Conuent and Accuse, yet must anothers Tribunall Condemne and Execute.

†**6. a.** A pontiff, a church dignitary. **b.** Alleged name for a company of prelates. **c.** An adherent of the pontiffs or prelates. *Obs.*

?*a* **1400** *Morte Arth.* 4336 Relygeous reveste in theire riche copes, Pontyficalles and prelates in precyouse wedys. *c* **1470** in *Hors, Shepe & G.* etc. (Caxton 1479, Roxb. repr.) 31 A pontifical of prelates, a state of princes, a dignite of chanons. [Cf. PONTIFICALITY 2.] **1590** GREENWOOD in L. Bacon *Genesis New Eng. Ch.* vii. (1874) 125 Hence arise these schisms and sects in the Church of England;..these are hereupon called Precisians, or 'Puritans', and now lately 'Martinists'. The other side are the 'Pontificals', that in all things hold and jump with the time, and are ready to justify whatever is or shall be by public authority.

7. Short for *pontifical mass.*

1923 R. SETON *Memories Many Yrs.* 291 The most interesting of my pontificals was in San Nicola *in carcere*.

‖**pontificalia** (pɒntɪfɪˈkeɪlɪə), *sb. pl.* [L., neut. pl. of *pontificālis* adj. pontifical. (In med.L., in Matthew Paris 1259.)] The vestments and other insignia of a bishop; pontificals (see prec. B. 3). Also *transf.* Official robes.

1577–87 HOLINSHED *Chron.* II. 31/2 In another prouince he may be in his pontificalibus, so that pontificalia differeth from the pall. **1691** WOOD *Ath. Oxon.* II. 114 He appeared in his *Pontificalia*. **1754** SHEBBEARE *Matrimony* (1766) I. 189 When we see a Doctor in Divinity dressed in his Pontificalia, we conclude that these Robes include a pious, learned, and humane Man.

‖**pontifiˈcalibus.** [Lat., abl. of *pontificālia* (see prec.), in phr. *in pontificālibus* in pontificals.] Used as = prec., almost always in phr. *in his* (or *their*) *pontificalibus*, in imitation of the L. phrase (see ‖IN 22). Hence (sometimes) improperly as if an ordinary Eng. noun (quots. 1620, 1772, and 1855 in b).

[**1306** in *Beverley Chapter Act Bk.* (Surtees) I. 120 Imago Episcopi stantis in pontificalibus induti.] **1387** TREVISA *Higden* (Rolls) VIII. 69 Þis Baldewyn had..songe in every cathedral chirche of Wales a masse in pontificalibus. *c* **1530** LD. BERNERS *Arth. Lyt. Bryt.* (1814) 402 The byshop of Pancopone, reuest in his *pontificalibus*. **1577–87** [see prec.]. **1591** G. FLETCHER *Russe Commw.* (Hakl. Soc.) 23 The patriarch, with metropolitanes, bishops, abbots, and priors, all richly clad in their *pontificalibus*. **1620** MELTON *Astrolog.* 64 Pope Syluester the second,..with such learning had attained to his *Pontificalibus*. **1728** FIELDING *Love in Sev. Masques* IV. vii, The parson is drest in his Pontificalibus. **1772** tr. *J.F. de Isla's Fr. Gerund* IV. iii. 70 It was an ornament as necessary as precious to the bravery of his pontificalibus.

b. *transf.* Official or ceremonial attire.

1693 RYMER *Short View Tragedy* 3 The Venetian Senate in their Pontificalibus. **1855** SMEDLEY, etc. *Occult Sc.* 189 The proper attire or 'pontificalibus' of a magician.

pontificality (pɒntɪfɪˈkælɪtɪ). [ad. obs. F. *pontificalité* (Godef.) pontifical dignity: see PONTIFICAL and -ITY.]

1. Pontifical office or dignity. **a.** The office, state, or dignity of a bishop, esp. of the pope.

1556 OLDE *Antichrist* 89 b, The 40 daye of his pontificalitie. **1581** HANMER *Answ. Jesuit's Challenge* 19 Places where the Pope dareth not once peepe, for all hys Pontificalitye at Rome. **1587** HARRISON *England* II. ii. (1877) I. 47 Cobham..during the time of his pontificalitie there [at Worcester], builded the vault of the north side of the bodie of the church. **1641** *Parallel betw. Wolsey & Laud* in *Harl. Misc.* (Malh.) IV. 465 By which he might make so vain-glorious a shew of his pontificality, or archiepiscopal dignity. *a* **1656** USSHER *Judgm. See of Rome* (1659) 20 When the Pontificality was first set up in Rome.

b. *transf.* or *gen.* Priesthood; high-priesthood.

1593 G. HARVEY *Pierce's Super.* 83 How the Principalitie, or Pontificalitie of a Minister according to the degenerate Sanedrim, should be sett-vpp. **1613** PURCHAS *Pilgrimage* VI. xii. 532 One Marvan seized on the Pontificality. **1651** *Raleigh's Ghost* 211 As if Moses and Aaron had ambitiously sought the Principality and Pontificality.

†**2.** Alleged name for a company of prelates. *Obs.*

1486 *Bk. St. Albans* F vij, A Pontificalite of prelatis. [Cf. PONTIFICAL B. 6 b.]

†**3.** (Usually in *pl.*) Pontifical robes, pontificals.

1601 DEACON & WALKER *Answ. to Darel* To Rdr. 2 Like a pettie new Pope among his owne Cardinals;..and that also in his pontificalities. **1611** CORYAT *Crudities* 28 He himselfe was that day in his sumptuous Pontificalities. *a* **1645** HABINGTON *Surv. Worc.* in *Worc. Hist. Soc. Proc.* I. 120 The Bishop of Chester is set out in his pontificality.

4. Pontifical air or demeanour; pomposity, stateliness of manner; dogmatic assumption.

1600 J. MELVILL *Diary* 245 Placing himselff besyde me with a grait pontificalitie and big countenance.

5. A pontifical rite, ceremony, or function.

1840 CARLYLE *Heroes* iii. (1858) 259 All cathedrals, pontificalities, brass and stone,..are brief in comparison to an unfathomable heart-song like this. **1858** —— *Fredk. Gt.* VI. vi. (1872) II. 204 A Public Mass, or some other so-called Pontificality.

pontifically (pɒnˈtɪfɪkəlɪ), *adv.* [f. PONTIFICAL + -LY[2].]

1. In a pontifical character; as a pontiff or bishop (in quot. *a* 1711, as a high priest).

c **1380** *Antecrist* in Todd *Three Treat. Wyclif* (1851) 143 Þei maken a grete lowe voice in blissynge & masse syngynge pontificaly. **1638** SIR T. HERBERT *Trav.* (ed. 2) 303 The Priest is pontifically attyred in pure fine Lawne. **1662** J. DAVIES tr. *Olearius' Voy. Ambass.* 19 The Patriarch, attended by almost 400 Priests, all Pontifically habited. *a* **1711** KEN *Psyche* Poet. Wks. 1721 IV. 256 Aaron when pontifically dress'd. **1865** *Pall Mall G.* 10 July 15/2 Dr. Manning preached his first sermon since his accession.., having previously assisted pontifically at high mass.

2. In a pontifical or stately manner; with the air of a pontiff; in grand style; dogmatically.

1590 MUNDAY *Eng. Rom. Life* in *Harl. Misc.* (Malh.) II. 185 He..liueth there among the Theatines very pontifically. **1661** EVELYN *Diary* 10 Feb., After sermon the Bishop..gave us the blessing very pontifically. **1906** *Athenæum* 10 Mar. 304/1 From this to giving them the right to decide pontifically on questions of science is a long step.

pontificate (pɒnˈtɪfɪkət), *sb.* [ad. L. *pontificātus* the office or dignity of a pontifex: see -ATE[1]. So F. *pontificat* (15th c. in Hatz.-Darm.).] The office or dignity of a pontiff; the period during which any person holds this office. **a.** The office of an ancient Roman *Pontifex*.

1581 MULCASTER *Positions* xxxix. (1887) 219 Cesar at his going furth from his house in his sute for the great pontificate. **1868** *Smith's Dict. Gr. & Rom. Antiq.* 304/2 Whatever..civil or military office..a pontifex maximus held beside his pontificate.

b. The office, or period of office, of a bishop; usually, of the pope; papacy; popedom.

1685 *Long. Gaz.* No. 2081/1 [The Pope] entred that day into the tenth year of his Pontificate. **1756–7** tr. *Keysler's Trav.* (1760) II. 119 Imperiali..having been in a fair way of obtaining the pontificate. **1849** MACAULAY *Hist. Eng.* vi. II. 54 In the sixteenth century the Pontificate, exposed to new dangers..was saved by a new religious order. **1860** HOOK *Lives Abps.* I. vi. 310 During Etheldred's pontificate.. Cameliac came to Canterbury to be consecrated.

c. *gen.* High-priesthood (of any religion).

1727–41 CHAMBERS *Cycl.* s.v. *Imam*, Some think it [the imamate] of divine right, and attached to a single family, as the pontificate of Aaron. **1833** CRUSE tr. *Eusebius* I. x. 39 With the pontificte of Annas. **1879** FARRAR *St. Paul* (1883) 677 The pontificate of these truckling Sadducees.

pontificate (pɒnˈtɪfɪkeɪt), *v.* [f. ppl. stem of med.L. *pontificāre* to perform pontifical functions, f. *pontific-em* PONTIFEX: see -ATE[3].]

1. a. *intr.* To perform the functions of a pontiff or bishop; to officiate as a bishop, esp. at mass.

1818 HOBHOUSE *Hist. Illustr.* (ed. 2) 262 When the Pope pontificates, the Senator stands amidst a seated assembly. **1898** BODLEY *France* I. I. iv. 220 Talleyrand..publicly pontificated as a bishop. **1928** G. B. SHAW *Intelligent Woman's Guide Socialism* 439 The Russian archbishop..is now presumably pontificating much more freely than the Archbishop of Canterbury.

b. *trans.* To celebrate (mass) as a bishop.

1889 *Cath. Househ.* 11 May 5/1 The Holy Sacrifice [was] pontificated by Cardinal Schiaffino.

2. a. *intr.* To act the pontiff, assume the airs of a pontiff; to behave or speak in a pompous or dogmatic manner. (Cf. PONTIFICAL *a.* 4.)

1825 [implied in PONTIFICATING *vbl. sb.* and *ppl a.*]. **1901** *Academy* 16 Nov. 459/1 Victor Hugo pontificating in his own salon. **1909** *Englishwoman* Apr. 296 The need of such a group as that which pontificates from Villa Wahnfried is past. **1921** R. HICHENS *Spirit of Time* v. 76 Why should I allow this young woman to pontificate about human nature. **1952** *Times Lit. Suppl.* 4 Jan. 1/4 Success made him pontificate more than ever. **1979** *Kansas City Times* 22 May 6A/1 They [*sc.* senators] must think they are pontificating on the moon or Mars or somewhere remote from Jefferson City.

b. *trans.* To say or utter (something) in a pontifical manner.

1922 A. S. M. HUTCHINSON *This Freedom* IV. i. 252 All modern teaching, if this new stuff that they pontificate may be called teaching, offers us [etc.]. **1973** *N.Y. Law Jrnl.* 24 July 4/5 The court pontificated, 'One cannot look at a rainbow with mud on his shoes'. **1976** *Verbatim* Dec. 15/1 He also pontificated, 'The Reds are favored to win, and, as we all know, everybody hates a favorite.'

So **ponˈtificating** *vbl. sb.* and *ppl. a.*; **ponˈtificator**.

1825 *New Monthly Mag.* XV. 164/1 A sample of his admirable faculty of pontificating. **1926** W. J. LOCKE *Stories Near & Far* 156 Pontifex—Pontifex something..a playful title given him by her mother, for his possible pontificating aims as a young man. **1930** *Radio Times* 17 Jan. 127/2 Nine out of ten people are fond of pontificating. **1934** B. DOBRÉE *Mod. Prose Style* IV. i. 221 If we examine the writings of the pontificators, people skilled in 'a way of saying things', we invariably find that their style is bad. **1972** *Daily Tel.* (Colour Suppl.) 10 Nov. 7/1 Highbrows—the pontificators about Television—are apt not merely to condone but to applaud: the gratuitous nastiness of allegedly 'serious' plays and aggressive documentaries. *Ibid.*, The pontificators make it so clear that they never watch television for pleasure and don't intend that other people should.

pontifiˈcation. [n. of action from med.L. *pontificāre* to perform pontifical functions.]

†**1.** = PONTIFICATE *sb.* b. *Obs. rare*$^{-1}$.

1521 LD. DACRE *Answ.* in *Archæologia* XVII. 206 The xiijth yere of the Pontificacion of the said lord Thomas [Wolsey].

2. The act or an instance of pontificating (PONTIFICATE *v.* 2).

1925 C. D. BROAD *Mind & its Place* viii. 389 It is a pity to create prejudice..by ignorant pontifications about 'the New Psychology'. **1959** *Spectator* 4 Sept. 307/1 They will resent his careless pontification ('Marxian materialism and Freudian psychology are excuses for laziness').

†**ˈpontifice**[1]. *Obs. rare.* [ad. L. *pontifex, -icem*: see PONTIFEX.] = PONTIFEX 1.

1603 HOLLAND *Plutarch's Mor.* 441 You shall have this day your sonne to be chiefe Pontifice and high priest, or else banished from the citie of Rome.

†**ˈpontifice**[2]. *Obs. rare.* [f. L. *pons, pont-*bridge, after *edifice*: cf. L. *pontificium* office of a *pontifex*.] The edifice of a bridge; a bridge. (Cf. PONTIFICAL *a.* 5.)

1667 MILTON *P.L.* x. 348 At the brink of Chaos, neer the foot Of this new wondrous Pontifice.

†**pontiˈficial**, *a.* and *sb. Obs.* [f. L. *pontificius* pertaining to a pontifex (f. *pontifex, -icem*) + -AL[1].]

A. *adj.* **I. 1.** = PONTIFICAL *a.* 1, 2. ***pontificial law***, canon law.

1591 HARINGTON *Orl. Fur.* 279 *note*, Giuen them by the Pope, who sent them the Pontificiall banner. **1651** G. W. tr. *Cowel's Inst.* 132 By the Rules of the Civill and Pontificiall Law. **1758** BLACKSTONE *Study of Law* in *Comm.* (1765) I. Introd. i. 15 The law of the land takes place of the law of Rome, whether antient or modern, imperial or pontificial. **1769** —— *Comm.* IV. viii. 109 This plan of pontificial power was so indefatigably pursued by the unwearied politics of the court of Rome.

2. = PONTIFICAL *a.* 2 b.

1621 BURTON *Anat. Mel.* II. i. i. i. 290 Our Pontificiall writers retaine many of these adiurations. **1641** SIR S. D'EWES in Rushw. *Hist. Coll.* III. (1692) I. 314 The other Pontificial Princes and Prelates, the sworn Enemies to the Protestant Religion. **1684** T. BURNET *The. Earth* I. 261 The protestant authors having lessen'd the authority of traditions, the pontificial doctors content themselves to insist only upon such as they thought useful or necessary.

3. = PONTIFICAL *a.* 4.

1613 PURCHAS *Pilgrimage* (1614) 280 The Caliph..setting aside all his Pontificall formalitie. **1682** SIR T. BROWNE *Chr. Mor.* II. § 1 (1716) *note*, Metellus his riotous pontificial supper. **1709** STRYPE *Ann. Ref.* I. vii. 106 Simple men without pontificial ornaments to set them out.

II. 4. = PONTIFICAL *a.* 5.

1609 HOLLAND *Amm. Marcell.* 89 The rites under the pontificiall priests and their Colledges.

B. *sb.* **1.** An adherent of the prelates, or of the pontiff.

1631 R. BYFIELD *Doctr. Sabb.* 128 The Pontificials pronounce that the Lords day, is onely a Canon law. **1838** G. S. FABER *Inquiry* 262 The people..inclined to maintain what the Pontificials were pleased to call heresy.

2. = PONTIFICAL *sb.* 4.

1660 J. LLOYD *Prim. Episc.* 63 The Form of Ordination, both in our Church, and in the Roman pontificial. **1920** *Trans. Scottish Ecclesiol. Soc.* VI. 79 We are enabled to do this, as the pontificial or book of offices used by him has been printed.

†**ponti'ficially,** *adv. Obs.* [f. prec. + -LY².] = PONTIFICALLY.

1599 SANDYS *Europæ Spec.* (1632) 188 The Pope himselfe, seated royally and pontificially in the midst. **1681** *Lond. Gaz.* No. 1667/2 To assist at the Mass of the Holy Ghost, which was said Pontificially by the Archbishop of Paris.

†**ponti'fician,** *a.* and *sb. Obs.* [f. L. *pontifici-us* (see PONTIFICIAL) + -AN.]

A. *adj.* **1.** = PONTIFICIAL *a.* 1.

1645 BP. HALL *Peacemaker* xii. 103 The Pontifician Lawes. **1664** H. MORE *Myst. Iniq.* 397 The Pontifician Power, which is a kinde of revived Image of the Pagan Imperial Power of Rome. *a* **1709** ATKYNS *Parl. & Pol. Tracts* (1734) 280 There was an Endeavour to bring in part of the Pontifician Law.

2. = PONTIFICIAL *a.* 2.

1625 BP. MOUNTAGU *App. Cæsar* 78 Moderate men, either of the Pontifician or Protestant side. **1664** H. MORE *Exp. 7 Epist.* vi. 84 The Albigenses, which were martyred in the Field by the Pontifician Forces. **1817** COLERIDGE *Biog. Lit.* ix. (1882) 67 The scholastic definition of the Supreme Being ..was received in the schools of Theology, both by the Pontifician and the Reformed divines.

3. = PONTIFICIAL *a.* 3.

1629 H. BURTON *Babel no Bethel* 100 Shee..is all for outward glory, Pontifician honour, splendour and magnificence.

B. *sb.* = PONTIFICIAL B. 1.

1614 T. ADAMS in Spurgeon *Treas. Dav.* Ps. i. 2 The pontificians beat off the common people..by objecting this supposed difficulty: Oh, the Scriptures are hard to be understood. **1691** WOOD *Ath. Oxon.* I. 513 He was..a severe enemy to the Pontificians.

†**ponti'ficious,** *a. Obs. rare.* [f. as prec. + -OUS.] Papal.

1624 *Gag for Pope* 36 The Maiesty of England hath written a discourse against this Pontificeous vsurpation. **1638** *Penit. Conf.* vii. (1657) 186 How defective this particular is in proofs, I appeal to all Pontificious Writers, and indifferent Readers.

pontify ('pɒntɪfaɪ), *v.* [ad. F. *pontifier*, ad. med.L. *pontificāre*: see PONTIFICATE *v.*] *intr.* To play the pontiff; to speak or behave 'pontifically', or with assumption of authority or infallibility.

1883 *Times* 19 Feb. 8 Wagner always seemed to pontify when he talked. **1892** *Sat. Rev.* 28 May 635/2 He is one of the few scientific men who do not 'pontify'. **1900** *Macm. Mag.* Jan. 185 Stevenson was always inclined to preach, to pontify, to be didactic.

pontil ('pɒntɪl). *Glass making.* [a. F. *pontil*, app. ad. It. *pontello*, *puntello*, dim. of *punto* point, etc.]

1. An iron rod used for handling, and especially for rapidly twirling the soft glass in the process of formation, esp. in the manufacture of crown-glass. Also called PUNTY.

1832 G. R. PORTER *Porcelain & Gl.* 171 At this stage another implement, called a punt, or pontil, is brought into use. *Ibid.* 214 The glass is then..separated from the pontil, and immediately removed to the hottest part of the annealing oven. **1918** [see GADGET 1 d]. **1961** E. M. ELVILLE *Collector's Dict. Glass* 190/1 In the eighteenth century.., the foot of a three-piece glass was attached to a 'pontil', for the finishing operation in the chair. The pontil is a solid rod of iron about the same length but not quite so thick as the blow-iron. **1977** *Lancashire Life* Feb. 35/1 (*caption*) At Cumbria Crystal,..the base of a stem having been formed, it is transferred to a 'pontil' for finishing.

2. *attrib.* and *Comb.*, as ***pontil mark***; **pontil rod**, a pontil.

1937 *Burlington Mag.* Nov. 221/1 Several of these have a round base with a mere trace of pontil mark. **1968** *Canad. Antiques Collector* Oct. 27/2 The long window of crown glass in one of the farm buildings where the pontil marks are evident in each pane. **1975** A. A. C. HEDGES *Bottles* 23/2 There is little chance of them being mistaken for free-blown bottles with all their 'blemishes',..pontil marks and kick-ups. **1955** G. STEVENS *In Canad. Attic* 60 The basic tools necessary to a glass blower are a blowpipe, a pontil rod. **1970** *Awake!* 8 Jan. 23/2 During the final forming the glass is attached to a long, solid 'pontil' rod that leaves a mark in the base.

pontile ('pɒntaɪl), *a. Anat. rare.* [ad. L. *pontīlis* pertaining to a bridge, f. *pons*, *pont-em* bridge: see -IL, -ILE.] Of or pertaining to the pons of the brain; = PONTINE.

1889 *Buck's Handbk. Med. Sc.* VIII. 524/1 Among the mononyms which may now be said to be in somewhat common use are *pons*, *thalamus* [etc.]. In some cases also the appropriate adjectives are employed, e.g. pial, dural.. pontile (sometimes, incorrectly, pontine or pontal).

pontinal ('pɒntɪnəl), *a.* (*sb.*) *Ichthyol.* [f. as next + -AL¹.] Name for a special bone in the skull of dactylopteroid fishes: see quot.

1888 GILL in *Amer. Nat.* XXII. 358 The third developed as a small special bone (pontinal) bridging the interval between the second suborbital and the antero-inferior angle of the preoperculum.

pontine ('pɒntaɪn), *a.*¹ *Anat.* and *Path.* [f. L. *pons*, *pont-* + -INE¹.] Pertaining to or occurring in the *pons Varolii*: = PONTAL, PONTIC *a.*², PONTILE.

1889 [see PONTILE]. **1897** *Allbutt's Syst. Med.* II. 849 In cerebral hæmorrhage and in pontine hæmorrhage, pinpoint pupils are usually present. **1899** *Ibid.* VI. 782 The sixth nucleus appears to be the pontine centre for conjugate movement.

Pontine ('pɒntaɪn, 'pɒntiːn), *a.*² [f. L. *Pontus*, Gr. *Πόντος*, the Black Sea + -INE¹.] = PONTIC *a.*¹

1920 *Q. Rev.* Jan. 244 It would be necessary to guarantee a local autonomy to the Greeks of the Pontine littoral. **1968** S. JOHNSON *Turkish Panorama* x. 96, I was now in the very foothills of the Pontine Mountains.

pontioune, obs. form of PUNCHEON.

'pontitecture. *nonce-wd.* [f. L. *pons*, *pont-em* bridge, after *architecture*.] Bridge-building.

1853 URE *Dict. Arts* I. 681 There is perhaps no other form of pontitecture which can compete with the wrought-iron girder when the clear space exceeds 70 feet.

‖**Pont l'Évêque** (pɔ̃ levɛk). The name of a town in Normandy, northern France, used *attrib.* and *absol.* to designate a type of sweet, soft cheese made there.

[**1881** J. P. SHELDON *Dairy Farming* xxxv. 515/1 *Fromage de Pont l'Évêque*, this cheese was made as long ago as the thirteenth century.] **1896** LONG & BENSON *Cheese* v. 57 Pont l'Évêque cheese is a variety with a great local reputation in the north..of France. **1910** [see GORGONZOLA]. **1932** R. FRASER *Marriage in Heaven* 1. xiv. 85 Taste this Pont L'Eveque... A friend brought it to me yesterday from Normandy. **1967** T. A. LAYTON *Wine & Food Soc. Guide Cheese & Cheese Cookery* 86 Pont l'Evêque requires from 15–24 days to reach maturity. **1979** N. & I. LYONS *Champagne Blues* 75 Is this a Pont-l'Evêque I see before me?

‖**pont-levis** (‖pɔ̃ləvi, pɒnt'lɛvɪs). Also 5 **pount.** [a. F. *pont-levis*, f. *pont* bridge + *levis*, OF. *leveïs*, adj. movable up and down = Pr. *levadis*:—L. type **levātīcius*, f. *levāre* to raise.]

1. A drawbridge.

1489 CAXTON *Faytes of A.* II. xxxv. K ij, Pount leveiz that be made faste therto whiche are called flyghyng bryggës. **1844** BROWNING *Sibrand. Schafnab.* iii, Yonder's a plum-tree with a crevice..A lap of moss like a fine pont-levis In a castle of the middle age, Joins to a lip of gum, pure amber.

2. *Horsemanship.* (See quot.)

1727 BAILEY vol. II, *Pontlevi's* (in Horsemanship) is a disorderly resisting Action of a Horse in Disobedience to his Rider, in which he rears up several Times running, and rises up so upon his hind Legs, that he is in Danger of coming over.

ponto (*Cards*, and *Glass-blowing*): see PUNTO.

Pontocaine ('pɒntəʊkeɪn). *Pharm.* Also **pontocaine.** Formerly also **-cain.** A proprietary name in the U.S. for PANTOCAIN.

1935 *Surg. Clinics N. Amer.* Dec. 1501 Anesthetists have recently turned to the longer-acting drugs pontocain and nupercaine. **1935** *Official Gaz.* (U.S. Patent Office) 10 Dec. 259/2 Winthrop Chemical Company, Inc., New York, ..*Pontocaine* for anesthetic. Claims use since Aug. 26, 1935. **1938** *New Eng. Jrnl. Med.* 27 Jan. 170/1 For the past four years at the Faulkner Hospital, pontocaine and novocain have been combined for spinal anesthesia. **1946** *Anesthesiology* VII. 500 Since 1943 we have employed ephedrine in combination with pontocaine hydrochloride for spinal anesthesia in over 2,500 cases. **1975** *Nature* 24 Apr. 710/2 Twelve Dorset and Western ewes at days 67–147 of gestation were starved for 48 h and then placed under pentobarbitol sedation (5 mg kg⁻¹) and spinal anaesthesia (6 mg pontocaine in hyperbaric glucose).

pontoneer, -ier (pɒntəʊ'nɪə(r)). *Mil.* Also **pontooneer, -ier.** [ad. F. *pontonnier* (12th c. in Hatz.-Darm.):—med.L. *pontōnārius* (855 in Du Cange) a ferryman, f. *ponto*, *-ōnem* PONTOON: see -EER¹.] One who has charge of pontoons, or of the construction of a pontoon-bridge.

1830 MAUNDER *Dict.*, *Pontonier*, a constructer of pontoons. **1853** SIR H. DOUGLAS *Milit. Bridges* (ed. 3) 130 With an expert corps of artificers and pontoneers, such boats might very soon be put together. **1864** CARLYLE *Fredk. Gt.* XVII. vii. (1872) VII. 71 We had with us..only Four Pontoneers, or trained Bridge-builders. **1884** *Century Mag.* XXIX. 280 The drilled engineers and pontoniers of the regular army.

pontoon (pɒn'tuːn), *sb.*¹ Forms: 7–9 **ponton**, 8– **pontoon.** [ad. F. *ponton* (14th c. in Littré) a flat-bottomed boat, a pontoon:—L. *ponto*, *-ōnem* a punt, floating bridge, pontoon, f. *pons*, *pont-em* bridge: see -OON.]

1. a. A flat-bottomed boat used as a lighter, ferry-boat, or the like (cf. PONT² and ³); *spec.* in *Mil. Engineering*, such a boat, or other floating vessel (as a hollow metal cylinder), of which a number are used to support a temporary bridge over a river. More widely, any structure designed to provide buoyancy in the water.

[**1591** BURGHLEY in *Unton's Corr.* (Roxb.) 266, 3,000 charrets laden with certeine peeces of wood, 'quilz appelent le ponton, pour faire les pontz'.] **1676** *Lond. Gaz.* No. 1087/4 One of the Batteries is raised upon Pontons on the Water. **1681** BLOUNT *Glossogr.* (ed. 5), *Ponton*, a Wherry, or Ferry-Boat. *Gazette.* **1690** LUTTRELL *Brief Rel.* (1857) II. 286 He layed a bridge of pontoons over the Shannon. **1702** *Lond. Gaz.* No. 3785/2 A great number of Pontons made of Leather, of a new Invention, very useful and light of Carriage. **1710** J. HARRIS *Lex. Techn.* II. s.v., The late Invented Ponton is a Boat of Tin or rather Latten, eight Yards long and two broad, having a large Ring at each Corner. **1723** *Pres. St. Russia* I. 9 It was proposed to the Czar to make a Bridge on Pontons over it. **1763** *Brit. Mag.* IV. 556 He was..pleased..to order the tin pontoons of the Marquis of Kildare's regiment of artillery to ply on the rivers, where the bridges have been broken down, till they can be repaired. **1811** WELLINGTON in Gurw. *Desp.* (1838) VII. 414 Tin pontoons are just as good as others..they will positively bear field pieces. **1823** J. BADCOCK *Dom. Amusem.* 206 The ponton..to be formed of oval plates (in pairs) each of these being hollow in the middle,..and two being laid together, the edges are to be soldered, or welded strongly, and the case or ponton is complete. **1941** *Sun* (Baltimore) 15 Sept. 13/1 Just before the regatta ended, he was driving Onwego, a hydroplane, out of the pits and ran his pontoon well over the side of one of the Coast Guard picket boats. **1975** *North Sea Background Notes* (Brit. Petroleum Co.) 11 The hull platform rests on a number of legs which have at their bases pontoons. During moves from one location to another, the entire vessel floats on the sea surface, but on reaching the new location the pontoons are then ballasted with water so that they sink. **1976** *Offshore Platforms & Pipelining* 121/1 Pipe leaves the barge via the curved ramp and a straight or curved pontoon and progresses to the sea floor.

†**b.** Sometimes applied to the floating bridge so formed. *Obs.*

1704 J. HARRIS *Lex. Techn.* I, *Ponton*, in Fortification, is a Bridge made of two Boats, at some Distance one from another, both covered with Planks; as also the Internal Space betwixt them. **1835** SIR J. ROSS *Narr. 2nd Voy.* xli. 546 They..had observed our pontoon without meddling with it.

2. *Naut.* A large flat-bottomed barge or lighter furnished with cranes, capstans, and tackle, used for careening ships, raising weights, etc.

1769–76 FALCONER *Dict. Marine*, *Pontoon*, a low flat vessel, nearly resembling a lighter, or barge of burthen, and furnished with cranes, capsterns, tackles, and other machinery, necessary for careening ships of all sizes. These are very common in the principal parts of the Mediterranean, but are rarely used in the northern parts of Europe. **1867** in SMYTH *Sailor's Word-bk.*

3. *Hydraulic Engineering.* = CAISSON 2 c, 2 d.

1875 KNIGHT *Dict. Mech.* 1764 *Ponton*..3. *a.* A water-tight structure..placed beneath a submerged vessel and then filled with air to assist in refloating the vessel. *b.* A water-tight structure which is sunk by filling with water, and raised by pumping it out, used to close a sluiceway or entrance to a dock. **1879** *Cassell's Techn. Educ.* IX. 162 The entrances to docks are sometimes closed by means of pontoons, which are large hollow vessels fitted with a kind of keel or projection round the sides and bottom.

4. *attrib.* and *Comb.*, as ***pontoon equipment***; **pontoon-bridge**, a bridge constructed upon pontoons; **pontoon-train**, a train of wagons carrying pontoons.

1796 *Compaigns* 1793–4, II. 68 On the 21st, a Pontoon Bridge was thrown over the Rhine. **1834–47** J. S. MACAULAY *Field Fortif.* (1851) 132 An army provided with a good pontoon train cannot be prevented effecting the passage of a river, if that army be skilfully commanded. **1838** *Civil Eng. & Arch. Jrnl.* I. 327/2 The pontoon equipment having been landed on the Marsh, a bridge consisting of 20 pontoons at open order,..was laid across the Medway.

pontoon (pɒn'tuːn), *sb.*² [Appar. corrupted from VINGT-ET-UN, VINGT-UN.] A popular name for the card game VINGT-ET-UN, VINGT-UN.

1917 A. G. EMPEY *Over Top* 304 *Pontoon*, a card game, in America known as 'Black Jack' or 'Twenty One'. The bank is the only winner. **1927** *Daily Express* 26 July 9/5 A ghostly platoon wouldn't frighten me!..perhaps they'd be playing pontoon. **1961** A. WYKES *Gambling* vii. 177 The three modern banking games—baccarat (or chemin-de-fer), *blackjack*, (or vingt-et-un or *pontoon*), and *seven-and-a-half* —are all complicated versions of European games of the 15th and 16th centuries. **1973** J. WOOD *North Beat* x. 134 The locker-room table..used for pontoon and brag sessions. **1976** J. BINGHAM *God's Defector* iii. 28 He was playing pontoon and drinking with four friends in a back room... Rob Flint had just laid two cards face up on the table, an ace and a king.

b. A prison sentence or term of twenty one months (occas. twenty one years). *slang* (chiefly *Criminals'*).

1950 C. FRANKLIN *She'll love you Dead* vii. 90 'They'll get me a pontoon for assault when Mr. Garfield tells 'is story,' said Al miserably. 'A pontoon?' 'Twenty-one months,' explained Garfield. **1958** F. NORMAN *Bang to Rights* 177 This geezer was doing a pontoon. **1962** *John o' London's* 25 Jan. 82/3, 21 months [imprisonment], *pontoon.* **1977** 'E. CRISPIN' *Glimpses of Moon* xii. 235 He had been put away three times..the third for a pontoon.

pon'toon, *v.* [f. PONTOON *sb.*¹: cf. *to bridge.*] *trans.* To cross (a river) by means of pontoons. Also *fig.*

1864 BLACKMORE *Clara V.* lxii, For this power..a great historian employs a happy expression not welcomed by our language; he calls it the power to 'pontoon the emergency'. **1870** *Daily News* 6 Dec., It is believed that they had pontooned the stream. **1890** *Spectator* 8 Mar., They would have pontooned the distance, agreeing to do the work over and over again when needful.

Hence **pon'tooning** *vbl. sb.*

1853 Sir H. Douglas *Milit. Bridges* (ed. 3) 142 Cultivating, practically and experimentally, the art of pontooning. **1878** W. S. Sherman in *N. Amer. Rev.* CXXVI. 206 A school of instruction in pontooning. **1893** Mrs. Swinton *Lady de Ros* 79 To..witness their pontooning operations.

pontooner (pɒn'tu:nə(r)). [f. pontoon + -er[1].] = pontoneer.

1799 *Hist.* in *Ann. Reg.* 283/1 The marquis having sent an officer of pontooners..to reconnoitre the banks of the river. **1832** Southey *Penins. War* III. 699 The Spaniards could not prevent the pontooners from completing their work.

pont-tournis, pont-volant: see pont[1].

ponty, variant of punty.

Pontypool ('pɒntɪpu:l). Also 8–9 **Ponty-pool, Pont-y-Pool, Pont y Pool.** The name of a town in Gwent, Wales, used *attrib.* and *absol.* to designate a type of Japanned metal ware originally produced there or items made from this Japanned metal.

[**1734** C. H. Williams *Let.* Dec. in L. T. Davies *Men of Monmouthshire* (1933) I. 72 Tom Allgood has found a new way of japanning which I think so beautiful that I'll send you a couple of pieces of it. **1763** *Gloucester Jrnl.* 4 July 2/1 (Advt.), By Allgood, Davies, and Edwards, all Sorts of the real and most durable Japan Ware is continued to be made and sold at the Manufactory at Pont-y-Pool.] **1764** in W. D. John *Pontypool & Usk Japanned Wares* (1953) iv. 36 (Advt.), Great Variety of Ponty-pool Goods Sold by Henry Johns, At his Ponty-pool Warehouse... Great variety of Snuff-Boxes, Japan'd Waiters, Bread Baskets, Tea Kitchens, Tea Kettles, and Lamps, Coffee Pots. **1781** J. Byng *Diary* 16 June in E. Burton *Georgians at Home* (1967) iv. 183, I bought a Pontypool snuff box, a beautiful and dear ware. **1801** W. Coxe *Hist. Tour Monmouthshire* II. xxv. 234 The town..is likewise remarkable for the japan manufacture, known by the name of Pont y Pool ware. **1872** *Art Jrnl.* XI. 24 (*caption*) The premises in which the Allgoods last manufactured Pontypool ware. *Ibid.* 24/1 'Now,' said Old Billy in the highest glee, 'now you shall see what real Pontypool Japan is!' **1928** *Daily Express* 6 Oct. 11/7 The secret formula for the production of the artistic lacquer work known as 'Pontypool japan', which had been missing since 1864, has been found. **1953** *Ann. Sci.* IX. 218 Several firms [in the Midlands] that paid special attention to the production of wares of high artistic merit were calling themselves 'Pontypool makers' in the early years of the nineteenth century, when the trade was in a flourishing condition. **1960** *House & Garden* May 56/4 Red and gold decorated Pontypool tray, £65. **1969** *Canad. Antiques Collector* Jan. 8/1 This japanned tinware was generally known by the name Pontypool (even when it was later manufactured at Wolverhampton and Birmingham). **1971** H. Huth *Lacquer of West* viii. 112 A color effect typical of Pontypool but later much imitated was a tortoiseshell ground made by placing irregular pieces of silver foil under brown lacquer, thus giving it the appearance of gold.

pony ('pəʊnɪ), *sb.* Forms: 7–9 *Sc.* **powny**, 8 *Sc.* **powney, -nie**, 8–9 **poney**, 8– **pony**. [Sc. *powney*, prob. (as suggested by Prof. Skeat, 1890):—**poulney*, ad. OF. *poulenet* a little foal (1444 in Godef.), dim. of *poulain, polain* a foal, colt:—late L. *pullānus*, f. L. *pullus* young animal, foal: see poleyn. (Examples of an earlier spelling in *poul-* or *pol-* are wanted to make the origin certain.)]

1. a. A horse of any small breed; *spec.* a horse not more than 13 or (in popular use) 14 hands high.

1659 *MS.* (Scot.) *Diary* in *N. & Q.* 6th Ser. VII. 163/1, I caused bring home the powny & stugged him. **1710** *Acc. Last Distemper T. Whigg* II. 19 Union Ponies, a Kind of Horses foaled upon the Borders, and occasionally owning either Country. **1730–6** Bailey (folio), *Pony*, a little Scotch horse. **1751** Holcroft *Mem.* (1816) I. 6 He had a beautiful poney (at least so he called, and so I thought it). *a* **1774** Fergusson *Rising of Session* Poems (1845) 28 The powney that in spring-time grazes Thrives a' the year. **1781** Cowper *Retirement* 467 To cross his ambling pony day by day, Seems at the best but dreaming life away. **1785** Burns *Epist. to J. Lapraik* 21 Apr. i, While..pownies reek in pleugh or braik. **1789** *Bath Jrnl.* 22 June Advt., Stolen or stray'd..A Black Poney, about thirteen hands high. **1841** *Penny Cycl.* XXI. 384/2 The 'Shetland pony' is now well known..These diminutive horses..are only from nine to eleven hands high. **1855** Thackeray *Newcomes* v, Clive..much preferred poneys to ride. **1902** *Badminton Mag.* XV. 699 A pony, I find it stated, is strictly applicable to an animal under 13 hands; above 13 and up to 13·3 the creature should be known as a galloway, and over 13·3 it becomes a horse. This, however, is not the modern interpretation... I should be inclined to say that in general parlance anything under 14 hands is a pony.

b. A race-horse. Usu. *pl. slang* (chiefly *U.S.*).

1907 J. London in *Cosmopolitan* May 17/2, I had been out to the race-track watching the ponies run. **1942** Berrey & Van den Bark *Amer. Thes. Slang* §731/1 *Race horse*.., pony. *a* **1953** E. O'Neill *Long Day's Journey into Night* (1956) I. 21 If it takes my snoring to make you remember Shakespeare instead of the dope sheet on the ponies, I hope I'll keep on with it. **1958** [see play *v.* 21 d]. **1961** *Dallas Morning News* 17 Feb. I. 5 Rep. Berry, an ex-gambler from San Antonio, got elected on his advocacy of betting on the ponies.

2. *slang.* The sum of twenty-five pounds sterling.

1797 Mrs. M. Robinson *Walsingham* II. 97 There is no touching her even for a poney. [*Note.* Half a rouleau or twenty-five guineas.] **1824** Scott *St. Ronan's* v, 'Done, for a poney,..', said the Squire. **1861** Hughes *Tom Brown at Oxf.* iii. (1889) 26 Well done, Jack,..you've saved your master a pony this fine morning. **1892** *Pall Mall Gaz.* 23 Mar. 6/3 Mr. Kisch said the bets were two ponies. The Master of the Rolls: What? Two what? Mr. Kisch said a pony was £25. **1928** D. Byrne *Destiny Bay* vii. 318 It would have to be done very carefully,..in ponies and fifties and hundreds. **1958** *Times* 18 Feb. 5/1 Heath said that for a 'pony' (£25) he would see what could be done. **1966** B. Naughton *Alfie* xxix. 188 'A pony is neither here nor there to me,' I said. 'It's just that I want to give somebody something.' **1976** J. O'Connor *Eleventh Commandment* xiv. 178 'Bet you the next three guys that come by do that,' he said. 'Make it a pony (£25),' said Charlie.

3. a. *U.S. slang.* A literal translation of a classical text, for the use of learners; a school or college 'crib': cf. horse *sb.* 13. Also *transf.* (see quot. 1977).

1827 *Harvard Reg.* Sept. 194 I'll tell you what I mean to do. Leave off my lazy habits..and stick to the law, Tom, without a *Poney*. **1832** *Tour through College* 30 (Farmer), Their lexicons, ponies, and text-books were strewed round their lamps on the table. **1893** W. W. Goodwin in *Classical Rev.* Apr. 162/1 A 'crib' or 'pony' to help them to learn their Greek lessons without the aid of dictionary and grammar. **1931** W. Faulkner *Sanctuary* xviii. 182 She kept the dates written down in her Latin 'pony'. **1952** G. Sarton *Hist. Sci.* I. iii. 89 The tablets were used not so much for study as for recapitulation and remembrance, like cribs or ponies. **1972** *Catholic Biblical Q.* Jan. 93 The Hebrew syntax is 'Akkadianized'... The result is that the book provides an excellent 'pony' for the student who is weak in Akkadian. **1977** *Sounds* 9 July 22/2 After leaving college his vaguely literary ambitions found him earning a living by turning out 'ponies', the Stateside word for those little revision booklets English (or US, in this case) Lit. students buy when they haven't read, say, 'Bleak House' and there's an exam tomorrow morning.

b. *U.S.* Used *attrib.* to designate an abridged news report or the service whereby such reports are supplied to particular news agencies.

The service has appar. been discontinued.

1877 *Harper's Mag.* Dec. 57/1 Condensed abstracts, known as 'pony' reports, are made and forwarded to smaller towns. **1909** *Census Bull.* (U.S.) No. 216. 67 Besides the full reports delivered to large papers are the 'pony' reports—condensations of the full reports, sold at a cheaper rate. **1915** G. M. Hyde *Newspaper Editing* vi. 199 Certain members, too small to be full members [of the Associated Press], receive a daily 'pony' service—a condensed version of the world's news to the extent of a few hundred or few thousand words—and pay proportionately. **1923** M. V. Atwood *Country Newspaper* 133 The writer wonders if it may not be that the country daily..furnishing a reasonably adequate service of telegraph news through a 'pony' service..may not become of increasing importance. **1931** C. E. Rogers *Journalistic Vocations* iii. 57 The United Press developed the use of the telephone for delivering abbreviated news reports—P.N.T. (public news transmission) or pony service. *Ibid.* 61 There are shorter leased wire reports, too, and pony reports. **1942** Radder & Stempel *Newspaper Editing, Make-up & Headlines* (ed. 2) vii. 125 Such reports, known as pony calls, usually amount to only 15 minutes of service (1,000 to 1,500 words) once or twice a day. The pony service still is used by a number of smaller newspapers, and some rely on a bulletin service or pony service by telegraph.

4. *slang.* **a.** A small glass or measure of liquor.

1849 G. G. Foster *N.Y. in Slices* 81 The game is kept up, mollified now and then by a choice swig at the 'poney'. **1884** *U.S. Newspaper*, A 'Pony'..in America a glass of beer. **1885** *New York Jrnl.* Aug. (Farmer), A pony of beer. **1896** *Omaha Daily Bee* (U.S.) 18 Feb. 4/7 A couple of ponies of brandy. **1896** *N.B. Daily Mail* 7 Apr. 2 The pony, another Glasgow beer measure, contained 9-10ths of an imperial gill of beer. **1943** *Harper's Mag.* Dec. 44/2 Dr. Stuker rapidly downed two ponies of brandy. **1959** G. Hamilton *Summer Glare* 155 Os pulled a beer each for me and Tommy, and a pony for himself. He always drank small beers. **1966** [see pot *sb.*[1] 3].

b. A small chorus girl or dancer.

1908 K. McGaffey *Sorrows of Show Girl* 118, I went into the pony ballet of a LaSalle Theatre show—can you see me as a pony? **1920** [see drag *sb.* 7 f]. **1930** *Daily Express* 23 May 10/5 We have what are known in stage parlance as 'ponies'—a troupe of girls, ages ranging from sixteen to twenty-three or four. **1948** *Sat. Even. Post* 3 July 63/2 In the chorus of ponies—the smallest sized dancers—there was a pert redhead named Gracie Barrett. **1950** Blesh & Janis *They all played Ragtime* (1958) ix. 180 The music that follows is a 'rush-on' of the period, so called because it was the cue for the high-stepping, brown-skinned 'ponies' to get out on the stage.

5. A name of *Tecoma serratifolia* (N.O. *Bignoniaceæ*), a small tree of the West Indies.

1866 in *Treas. Bot.* **1884** Miller *Plant-n.*, *Tecoma serratifolia*, 'Pony', Saw-leaved Trumpet-flower.

6. A dance originating in the U.S. and popular in the early 1960s.

1963 *N.Y. Times Mag.* 27 Oct. 104/2 That brings us to our own young and the Twist, the Pony, the Slop, the Mashed Potato. **1968** M. & J. Stearns *Jazz Dance* i. 5 The Pony employed bits of the Slow Drag. **1969** N. Cohn *AWopBopaLooBop* (1970) ix. 85 Dance crazes bossed pop right up until the Beatles broke. There was the Hully Gully, the Madison, the Fly, the Pony [etc.].

7. *attrib.* and *Comb.* **a.** General, as ***pony-back*** (cf. horseback), ***-boy, -carriage, -cart, -chair, -chaise, -girl, -horse, -man, -mare, -pack, -phaeton, race, ride, -sled, -track, -trap***; ***pony-buyer, -buying, -catcher, -catching, -hunter, -hunting, -penning, -racing, -rearer***; ***-rider, -riding, pony-mounted*** adj.; (in sense 2) ***pony point***; see also sense 3 b. **b.** Special combs. (often in names of things that are small of their kind): **pony club**, a club founded in 1929 and now run by the British Horse Society for young people with ponies; hence as *vb. trans.* (chiefly *pass.*) to enter (a pony) for a pony club competition; **pony clubber**, a member of a pony club; **pony clubbing**, participating in pony club activities; the pony club movement; **pony-engine**, a small locomotive for shunting; **pony express**, a postal agency using relays of ponies for the transmission of mails, etc.; also *attrib.*; **pony-glass**, a small glass holding a pony (sense 4); **pony post** = *pony express*; **pony-purse, pony-putter**, see quots.; **pony-skin**, the (dressed) hide of a pony; also *attrib.*; **pony-tail**, a hair-style in which the hair is gathered back through a band or other fastening to resemble the shape of the tail of a horse or pony (cf. horse-tail 1 c); also *attrib.*; hence ***pony-tailed*** adj.; **pony-trekking**, pony-riding for long distances across country, esp. as undertaken as a group holiday activity; hence ***pony-trekker***; **pony-truck**, a two-wheeled leading or trailing truck in some forms of locomotive; **pony-truss**, a truss so low that overhead bracing cannot be used (Webster 1890).

1813 *Examiner* 26 Apr. 265/1 A well-known quack..appeared on *poney-back. **1859** Lang *Wand. India* 401 We commenced the ascent on ponyback. **1909** *Daily Chron.* 16 Feb. 5/1 Murten..is employed as a *pony-boy in the Woolley Colliery, Barnsley. **1946** B. Naughton (*title*) Pony boy. **1831** M. Edgeworth *Let.* 11 Apr. (1971) 520 Dr. Fitton in the *pony carriage behind me was giving..another derivation to Fanny from the German. **1870** Geo. Eliot *Jrnl.* 26 May in *Geo. Eliot Lett.* (1956) V. 100 Mrs. Pattison took me a drive in her little pony carriage. **1905** 'P. Pennington' *Woman Rice Planter* (1913) iv. 150, I sent Chloe to Gregory in the pony carriage, and she brought back the money. **1823** *Blackw. Mag.* XIV. 510 Holborn and Snow Hill are crowded with *pony-carts. **1827** T. Hamilton *Youth & Manhood C. Thornton* I. xvi. 282 Mr Pynsent with some difficulty did so, pleading an engagement to drive Lady Amersham in her *pony-chair. **1880** Disraeli *Endym.* xi, The only things she cared for in the country were a hall and a pony-chair. **1831** Disraeli *Young Duke* I. II. x. 239 A *pony-chaise was Lady Faulconcourt's delight. **1852** Miss Mitford *Recoll.* I. 301 The place in the pony-chaise..was found vacant. **1900** El. Glyn *Visits Elizabeth* (1906) 81 One of those old-fashioned, very low pony-shays, with a seat up behind for the groom. **1929** *Horse* I. 60 The *Pony Club..has been inaugurated for the purpose of interesting young people in riding and sport. **1936** A. Thirkell *August Folly* ii. 50 Pony Clubs! No pony clubs when I was young. You got on and you fell off, and there you were. **1941** M. Treadgold *We couldn't leave Dinah* iii. 50 Pony club members and their guests were sedately walking their ponies round and round the lawn. **1972** J. McClure *Caterpillar Cop* i. 12 'You're strong,' he murmured. 'Riding,' she said, 'I'm in the pony club.' **1976** *Horse & Hound* 3 Dec. 63/1 (Advt.), Moonmaster... Very pretty strawberry roan gelding. 10 yrs. Leading rein, gymkhanaed, *Pony Clubbed. Good in traffic. **1977** *Ibid.* 14 Jan. 40/2 (Advt.), Gelding... He jumps well, has hunted, and been Pony Clubbed etc. **1970** J. Campbell *World of Ponies* 127 (*caption*) Australian *Pony Clubbers are always sure of good weather for their outdoor activities. **1977** *Horse & Hound* 14 Jan. 33/2 Always a keen 'pony clubber', Alison has competed in numerous inter-branch competitions. **1970** J. Campbell *World of Ponies* 125 It has been the ponies of all breeds, cross-breeds, shapes and sizes, that have made *Pony Clubbing. **1977** *Horse & Hound* 14 Jan. 46/3 (Advt.), Four children 3–9, 4 ponies, 1 horse. Pony Clubbing, showing etc. **1864** Webster, **Pony-engine*. **1847** *N.Y. Weekly Tribune* 18 Dec. 4/5 By our *Pony Express from the South, we have intelligence from New Orleans to the afternoon of the 2d. **1860** *San Francisco National* 19 Mar. 2/3 The Central Overland Pony Express Co. will start their Letter Express from San Francisco to New York and intermediate points, on Tuesday, the 3rd day of April next. **1861** *Illustr. Lond. News* 12 Oct. 386 The American Pony Express, en route from the Missouri River to San Francisco. **1886** *Kansas Hist. Coll.* III. 395, I was present when the first fleet horse of the pony express started. **1894** *Daily News* 1 Oct. 5/5 The pony express from Pekin brought the Viceroy many despatches. **1948** *Chicago Daily News* 26 Aug. 4/1 St. Joseph, Mo... The original Pony Express stable was put up for sale for $442.32 but no one bid on it. **1976** *Times* 23 July 11/6 Buffalo Bill Cody..had been in turn horse wrangler, pony express rider, unlucky prospector, [etc.]. **1889** T. A. Guthrie *Pariah* vi. i, I'm not a horsewoman yet. If I'm anything, I'm a *pony-girl. **1880** *Barman's Man.* 58 Fill the *pony-glass with Sasarac. **1900** *Geogr. Jrnl.* XV. 563 Group of Astor *pony-men at Lob jungle. **1968** *Economist* 10 Aug. 45/1 Four ponies need four pony-men which adds another £10 a day to the bill. **1971** *Daily Tel.* 10 June 9/3 The future livelihood of ghillies, stalkers, gamekeepers and ponymen is threatened by the 'punitive' proposed rating reassessments of estates with sporting facilities, the Scottish Landowners' Federation claims. **1932** *Sun* (Baltimore) 27 July 4/3 *Pony-penning has attracted thousands to the island. **1958** *Washington Post* 30 July A 24/1 The pony penning dates back to 1835 but the firemen took it over in 1924 as their fund raising project. **1799** Malthus *Diary* 1 July (1966) 109 Mr A had insisted on our taking his small *poney phaeton. **1838** Lytton *Alice* III. vii, Do..come..and look at my pony-phaeton. **1892** M. Williams *Round London* (1893) 202 He plays whist at his club for *pony (twenty-five pound) points. **1893** M. H. Cushing *Story of our Post Office* 420 Before railroads led to every part of the country the only communication was by *pony post. **1901** W. Churchill *Crisis* II. vii. 178 Three-weeks letters from San Francisco, come by the pony post to Lexington. **1860** Bartlett *Dict. Amer.*, **Pony-purse*, a subscription collected upon the spot, or from a few persons. **1883** Gresley *Coal Mining Gloss.*, **Pony-putter*, a boy who drives a pony in the workings. **1765** J. Woodforde *Diary* 27 May (1924) I. 47 After dinner Jack went to Wincanton to a *Pony Race. **1824** J. Decastro *Mem.* 155 The pony races were brought out, and they had a more than usual run for a whole season. **1949** *Sun* (Baltimore) 29 July 20/6 The spectators stayed on for the day-long program of pony sales..pony races..and band concerts. **1827** W. CLARKE *Every Night Bk.* 174 Furnishes a neat stud for *poney racing. **1943** *Sporting Life* 12 July 5 Pony racing will have an eager Turf Authority, a second-to-none race course at its disposal, and cash in the bank. **1969** *Pony* Sept. 57/2 Two centuries ago..Charles O'Neill.. established a pony-racing event on Broughshane race-course, near Ballymena. **1819** M. EDGEWORTH *Let.* 17 Apr. (1971) 200 She has just come in from her *poney ride. **1840** C. FOX *Jrnl.* 16 Feb. (1972) 67 They joined Mamma and Anna Maria in a pony ride. **1871** 'MARK TWAIN' *Lett. to Publishers* (1967) 62 Stretching our necks and watching for the *pony-rider. **1975** *Country Life* 13 Feb. 393/1 Pony riders will have to keep on to the country lanes. **1949** R. COLVILLE (*title*) *Pony riding. **1908** *Daily Chron.* 26 Dec. 3/4 Among the novelties are the *pony-skin suits. **1960** *Times* 26 Sept. 17/2 In Mongolian ponyskin..it [*sc.* a coat] is very hard-wearing. **1971** 'A. BURGESS' *MF* viii. 94 The upholstery was black-and-white ponyskin. **1976** 'J. ROSS' *I know what it's like to Die* xvi. 102 Your lady-friend with the ponyskin coat. **1872** TROLLOPE *Eustace Diamonds* (1873) II. xxxiv. 100 'How a man can like to kiss a face with a dirty horse's tail all whizzling about it...' 'I haven't even a *pony's tail,' said Lucy. **1952** *Sun* (Baltimore) 23 Feb. 2 The panel of high-school boys and girls discusses the latest teen-age fashions, including..the pony tail. **1954** J. TRENCH *Dishonoured Bones* iv. 150 She pulled her own hair back and fastened it into a pony-tail. **1957** *New Yorker* 16 Nov. 104/2 The young lady..was wearing a ponytail hairdo. **1971** M. SPARK *Not to Disturb* iii. 88 She loosens her hair which has been pulled back, pony-tail style. **1975** *New Yorker* 28 Apr. 31/2 She, too, had her hair in a ponytail, held by a rubber band. **1977** *Time* 30 May 40/3 The counter-culture ponytail is gone, sacrificed to the heat of arena lights and the sizzling sweat of the fast-break pace. **1956** *Time* 26 Mar. 72/2 *Pony-tailed Carol stood aside. **1958** S. ELLIN *Eighth Circle* II. i. 18 She bore the sallow-complexioned, nail-bitten, pony-tailed earmarks of adolescence. **1974** *Times* 14 Nov. 16/6 A bearded, pony-tailed, 42-year-old..is not everyone's idea of a nanny-raised child. **1872** JENKINSON *Guide Eng. Lakes* (1879) 149 To the left will be seen a *pony-track which winds over the hill to Watendlath. **1894** ASTLEY *50 Years Life* I. 85 To sit in my *pony-trap. **1972** *Guardian* 3 July 7/3 Pathways were being worn down by *pony-trekkers and others. **1959** *Sunday Times* 8 Mar. 20/1 Golf, Tennis, Fishing, Ballroom, *Pony-trekking, Dinghy sailing. *Ibid.* 29 Mar. 18/1 Guided pony-trekking is a fine way to explore wild country in the company of other adventure-seekers. **1962** *Times* 21 Apr. 11/3 Over the past few years..great has been the demand for pony-trekking holidays. **1971** *New Yorker* 27 Feb. 21/1 (Advt.), Come to Ireland. Go pony-trekking through Macgillycuddy's Reeks. **1884** KNIGHT *Dict. Mech.* Suppl., *Pony Truck, a truck with a single pair of wheels.

pony ('pəʊnɪ), *v. U.S. slang.* [f. prec. sb.]
1. *trans.* and *intr.* To pay *up*, settle *up*.
1824 *Atlantic Mag.* I. 343 Every man..vociferously swore that he had ponied up his 'quarter'. **1894** STEAD *If Christ came to Chicago* 367 'Pony up or we will run you in' is the formula. **1903** *Architect* Suppl. 24 Apr. 28/2 To-day a walking delegate told him he would have to pony up 10 dols. if he wanted to stay on the job.
2. a. *trans.* and *intr.* To prepare (lessons) by means of a pony or crib.
1852 *Yale Tomahawk* May (Bartlett), We learn that they do not pony their lessons. **1847** in W. G. Hammond *Remembrance of Amherst* (1946) 153 The others are ponying most unmercifully. *c* **1853** in Root & Lombard *Songs of Yale* 23 If you poney he will see.
b. *trans.* To give extra tuition to. *rare.*
1865 *Harper's Mag.* July 213/2 A classmate, whom..I had ponied through term after term, in Latin, Greek, and mathematics. **1908** W. G. DAVENPORT *Butte & Montana* 134 It were a hundred times better to teach the average boy how to build a fence..than to..'pony' his way through three or four years of Latin.

ponyard, ponysch, etc., obs. ff. PONIARD, PUNISH.

Ponzi scheme ('pɒnzɪ). *U.S.* [f. the name of Charles *Ponzi*, who perpetrated such a fraud 1919–20.] A form of fraud in which belief in the success of a fictive enterprise is fostered by payment of quick returns to first investors from money invested by others.
[**1957** *Encycl. Brit.* IX. 708/1 *The Ponzi Scheme*... Beginning in Dec. 1919 Ponzi..produced a scheme involving the purchase of International Postal Reply coupons in countries where the exchange was low, trading them in for postage stamps at their face value in a country where the rate was high, and then selling the stamps at a great profit... The slogan of the swindle was 40% in 90 days... Actually..Ponzi made no purchases whatever of International Postal Reply coupons.] **1973** *Guardian* 14 Apr. 2/4 The indictments..allege that Mackell's staff invested in what is called a Ponzi scheme, a confidence game named after a famous Italian. **1976** *Billings* (Montana) *Gaz.* 27 June 9-G/1 The Home-Stake scandal is a form of the 'Ponzi' scheme, named for a self-educated, slight but dapper Italian immigrant named Charles Ponzi whose intricate schemes in the 1920s were front-page stuff. **1976** *National Observer* (U.S.) 10 July 8/3 'He was operating a Ponzi scheme,' says Michael Mustokoff, chief of the unit. The first few investors were paid 'dividends' out of the money invested by people who came in later, and word spread that the club was raking in the bucks.

Ponzo ('pɒnzəʊ). [The name of Mario *Ponzo* (b. 1882), Italian psychologist.] ***Ponzo illusion***: an optical illusion in which two parallel straight lines of equal length appear to be of unequal length when seen side by side against a triangular background (such as a set of straight lines radiating from a single point and passing through the two parallel lines).
1942 *Jrnl. Exper. Psychol.* XXX. 84 (*heading*) Experimental evidence for the electrical character of visual fields derived from a quantitative analysis of the Ponzo illusion. **1968** *Science* 22 Mar. 1375/1 The Ponzo illusion increases in magnitude between childhood and adulthood. **1976** *Sci. Amer.* Apr. 50/1 In the Ponzo illusion, although both vertical lines are the same length, the effect of the subjective triangle is to make the line at the left appear to be longer.

poo, obs. f. POOH; Sc. and n. dial. f. PULL.

‖**pooah** ('puə). [Native name in Nepālese.] An urticaceous plant of North India, the fibre of which is used for cordage, sail-cloth, etc.
1866 *Treas. Bot.* 153/2 This plant [*Böhmeria Puya*] is called Pooah or Puya in Sikkim and Nepal.

pooay, var. PWE.

pooch (puːtʃ), *sb.* and *a. colloq.* (orig. *U.S.*). [Etym. obscure.] **A.** *sb.* A dog, esp. a mongrel. **B.** *adj.* Mongrel. *rare.*
1924 B. HECHT *Cutie* vi. 46 All you do is sink your teeth in my shoulder and make noises like a basket full of hungry pooches. **1927** *Collier's* 3 Dec. 32/4 Therefore, at home, the trick pooch got all the attention, eating at the table with the family. **1941** BAKER *N.Z. Slang* vii. 60 Hundreds of Australian terms are unused here...*pooch*.., for instance, ..a greyhound. **1951** C. ARMSTRONG *Black-Eyed Stranger* (1952) iii. 27 It wasn't even my dog... But..I'd more or less met the pooch. **1962** *Country Life* 19 Apr. 895/1 The training of dogs, whether pedigree or pooch, has assumed considerable importance during the last 80 years. **1963** O. BRELAND *Animal Life & Lore* I. 15 There is one very old claim of an ancient pooch of 34 years. **1971** *Sunday Australian* 8 Aug. 39/2 You've got some useful ammunition to aim at that noisy cherished little pooch next door. **1977** *Cornish Times* 19 Aug. 15/1, I tend to fury when children cannot play games on fields intended for their use without falling on some pooch's revolting mess. **1977** J. WAMBAUGH *Black Marble* (1978) v. 68, I got more invested in that pooch than you *made* in the last five years.

pooch, obs. and dial. form of POUCH.

‖**pood** (puːd). Forms: 6–7 pode, 7 poude, 7–8 poad(e, 8 (pœd), pudde, 8–9 pud, 9 poud, 7- pood. [Russ. *pud*ᵘ, ad. LG. or Norse *pund* POUND.] A Russian weight, equal to 40 lb. Russian, or slightly more than 36 lb. avoirdupois.
1554 J. HASSE in Hakluyt *Voy.* (1903) II. 274 The pode doth containe of the great weight, 40 pounds, and of the smal 80: there goe 10. podes to a shippond. **1630** *R. Johnson's Kingd. & Commw.* 474 Of Wax fiftie thousand poad; every poad contayning fortie pounds. **1662** in M. Blundell *Cavalier* (1933) vi. 103 Twenty Russe Pud of the tooth of Sea-Horse—each Pud is 40 pound weight. Ten thousand Pud of hemp. **1662** J. DAVIES tr. *Olearius' Voy. Ambass.* 111 Raising the Poude (that is 40. pound) of Salt, to thirty pence. **1723** *Pres. St. Russia* I. 76 At the Rate of four Rubels a Pudde. **1753** HANWAY *Trav.* (1762) I. II. xiii. 58 These waggons usually carry from twenty-five to thirty poods. **1814** tr. *Klaproth's Trav.* 297 Rock salt..in large..blocks, weighing five or six pud. **1884** *Pall Mall G.* 10 Sept. 5/2 The gold mines of Russia have yielded 31,627 poods. **1890** *Daily News* 27 Nov. 6/4 The Russian poud weighs as nearly as possible thirty-six English pounds,..there are nearly sixty-two pouds to the ton. **1901** A. M. B. MEAKIN *Ribbon of Iron* xvi. 226 From mines discovered in 1866..2,500 puds of gold were extracted during a period of twenty years. **1952** E. H. CARR *Bolshevik Revolution* II. xix. 285 Kalinin estimated the total of relief supplies up to December 1921 at 1,800,000 puds of grain and 600,000 puds of other foodstuffs from home stocks.

poodding, pooding, -ynge, obs. ff. PUDDING.

poodle ('puːd(ə)l), *sb.* [a. Ger. *pudel*, short for *pudelhund* (so LG., Swed., Da. *pudel*, Du. *poedel(-hond)*) a poodle, f. LG. *pud(d)eln* to splash in water, the poodle being a water-dog. Cf. Ger. *pudel* a pool, PUDDLE; *pudelnass* dripping wet.]
1. a. One of a breed of pet dogs, of which there are numerous varieties, with long curling hair, usually black or white, which is often clipped and shaved in a fantastic manner.
1825 LYTTON *Falkland* I. xi, Mrs. Dalton..asked very tenderly after your poodle and yourself. **1858** WHEWELL *Hist. Sci. Ideas* II. 133 The Poodle and the Greyhound are well marked varieties of the species dog. **1866** G. MACDONALD *Ann. Q. Neighb.* xxv, A fat asthmatic poodle lay at her feet upon the hearth-rug.
b. *fig.* A lackey or cat's-paw.
1907 LLOYD GEORGE in *Hansard Commons* 26 June 1429 The House of Lords consented. This is the defender of property! This is the leal and trusty mastiff which is to watch over our interests... A mastiff? It is the right hon. Gentleman's poodle. It fetches and carries for him. It barks for him. It bites anybody that he sets it on to. **1944** J. JONES *Man David* vii. 144 There were certain barriers to progress, the greatest being 'that Tory poodle', the House of Lords. **1954** R. JENKINS (*title*) Mr. Balfour's poodle. An account of the struggle between the House of Lords and the government of Mr. Asquith. **1967** *Daily Tel.* 10 Feb. 30/2 Labour MPs did not appear to find the speech objectionable. One comment was that Prince Philip had shown himself to be 'nobody's poodle'. **1968** *Guardian* 9 Aug. 16/1 Mr Curran..vigorously denied suggestions that he would be Lord Hill's 'poodle'. **1969** 'G. BLACK' *Cold Jungle* viii. 114 Bill would have been more likely to have a heart attack living as her tame poodle down on the Riviera. **1974** LD. ALDINGTON *Advising BBC* 13 The suspicious will say that such a close link between the advisors and the advised..ensures that at least the Chairman of GAC, if not all its members, become the poodle of the BBC. **1976** *Times* 12 Nov. 14/4 Mr Foot is happy to act as Mr Jones's poodle in introducing the Bill.
†**2.** A woolly sort of cloth; a garment of this cloth. *Obs.*
1827 *Sporting Mag.* XX. 167 A good drab surtout—if not a poodle. **1859** SALA *Gas-light & D.* xxii. 254 A short green cloak, adorned with a collar of the woolly texture, generally denominated poodle.
3. *attrib.* and *Comb.*, as ***poodle-barber, -clippers, -clipping, -coat, -dog, -head; poodle-fashion, -like*** adj.; ***poodle collar*** (in sense 2); **poodle cloth**, a woolly sort of cloth; also *attrib.*; cf. sense 2; **poodle-cut**, a hair-style in which the hair is cut short and curled all over.
1902 ELIZ. L. BANKS *Newspaper Girl* 169 Having purchased a pair of poodle clippers..I myself became his barber. **1957** M. B. PICKEN *Fashion Dict.* 261/2 *Poodle cloth*, a coating of knotted yarn or loopy bouclé. Woven in all fibers and also knitted. Originally was made only in wool. **1959** *Observer* 13 Dec. 14/6 For country-house wear a poodlecloth wool is in allied tones, such as violet and amethyst. **1977** *New Society* 30 June 665/3, I managed to purchase a square-cut, early sixties coat in a fabric we used to call poodle cloth. **1859** SALA *Gas-light & D.* x. 121 A short cloak, decorated with the almost obsolete poodle collar. **1952** *Sun* (Baltimore) 25 Mar. 3/2 (*caption*) In this recent picture, Mrs. Truman wears what is described as one variation of the 'poodle cut'. **1960** C. DALE *Spring of Love* I. i. 29 Gloria, with her cross little painted face and her yellow poodle cut. **1975** R. L. SIMON *Wild Turkey* (1976) x. 8 A well-dressed woman with a poodle cut. **1820** in *Amer. Speech* (1965) XL. 131 Called 'a Hog, a Poodle dog' all the sailors joking me. **1822** M. EDGEWORTH *Let.* 27 Jan. (1971) 336 A new poodle dog..milk white silken curls all over except the poor shorn half that is sacrificed to poodle-fashion. *a* **1839** PRAED *Belle of Ball-Room* x, Her poodle dog was quite adored. **1876** SMILES *Sc. Natur.* vii. (ed. 4) 109 The Fox may be known by his bark, which resembles that of a poodle dog.
Hence (*nonce-wds.*) **'poodledom, 'poodleish** *a.*, **'poodleship.**
1883 MRS. LYNN LINTON *Girl of Period* I. 263 Many a fine stalwart fellow..sinks into mere poodledom at home. **1888** H. W. PARKER *Spirit of Beauty* (1894) 118 His owner should have been able to tell fifty like anecdotes of his poodleship. **1890** B. L. GILDERSLEEVE *Ess. & Stud.* 260 His whole demeanor was poodleish in the extreme.

'poodle, *v.* [f. prec. sb.]
1. *trans.* To make into or treat as a poodle; to clip and shave the hair of. Also, to overdress, to dress *up*. Hence **'poodled** *ppl. a.*, **'poodling** *vbl. sb.*
1828 *Lancet* 16 Feb. 725/2 Simply twisting it up, without the present fashion of poodling the head. **1902** *Blackw. Mag.* July 45/2, I thought it as well to 'poodle' him [a dog] occasionally. **1905** *Ibid.* Dec. 816/1 The poodled Spitz, in Germany apparently a favourite animal, I avoid. **1962** N. STREATFEILD *Apple Bough* iii. 39 Why do they want to poodle the poor kid up?
2. *intr.* (Usu. with advbs.) To move or travel in a leisurely manner. *colloq.*
1938 F. D. SHARPE *Sharpe of Flying Squad* i. 10 The long, low cars poodle through the streets. *Ibid.* ii. 30 For the most part these sleek, unobtrusive-looking cars poodle about the Metropolis well under 30 m.p.h. **1960** M. CECIL *Something in Common* xii. 131 She tells the patrons which gangway and then they poodle off the opposite way. **1972** *Police Rev.* 8 Dec. 1598/1 What will happen to the chap who wants to quietly poodle along at 50 m.p.h. even when there is no fog? **1973** *Radio Times* 22 Mar. 36/2 (Advt.), A sports jacket should protect you from dawn till dusk on a Scottish moor. Not merely while you're poodling down to the local on Sunday morning. **1975** *New Society* 2 Oct. 26/3 One member of each two-man [bicycle racing] team doing the racing while the other poodles round high on the banking until it's his turn to take over the attack. **1976** J. O'CONNOR *Eleventh Commandment* i. 24, I went indoors, messed around, poodled about for quite a while.
Hence **'poodler** *slang*, a small motor vehicle.
1951 *Brit. Road Services Mag.* Dec. 94/2 *Poodler*, small vehicle. **1968** *Drive* Spring 113/1 A poodler [is] a small vehicle, a roller skate a small, light wagon, and Billy Bunter is a shunter.

'poodle-faker. *slang* (chiefly *Services*). [f. POODLE *sb.* 1 + FAKER.] A man who cultivates female society, esp. for the purpose of professional advancement; a ladies' man; a socialite; also, a young, newly commissioned officer. So **'poodle-faking** *vbl. sb.* and *ppl. a.*
1902 *T.C.D.* 22 Nov., The 'poodle-faker' is just as much a social necessity as tea-cakes. **1914** 'I. HAY' *Knight on Wheels* (ed. 2) III. xxiii. 228 And now my lad, you are going to put on your best duds and come poodle-faking with me! **1915** 'BARTIMEUS' *Tall Ship* iv. 75 Don't tell me the lad is going poodle-faking! **1918** A. H. CHUTE *Real Front* xiv. 240 He [*sc.* a big Australian private] encountered a pink-faced English youth, who had just got his commission, one of the Percival or Cuthbert type, whom we refer to in the army as 'poodle-fakers'. **1918** 'TAFFRAIL' *Watch Below* 57 The ladies' men or 'poodle-fakers', as we called them, had their tea-parties, dinner-parties, and dances more often than was good for them. **1925** F. C. BOWEN *King's Navy* 239 The tea party to which the other sex is invited from 'the beach' is a 'tea-fight' or 'bun-worry', while paying calls ashore is 'poodle-faking'. **1929** A. B. E. CATOR in *Hoghunters' Ann.* 52 Man is primævally a killer; by the word man I mean a real man, not the long haired poodle faking, over dressed idiot, all too common at home in these post-war days. **1938** C. L. MORGAN *Flashing Stream* I. i. 59 Brissing, you're the poodle-faker in this mess. **1939** A. POWELL *What's become of Waring?* vii. 200 But what did you live on?.. A bit of journalism here and there, a good deal of poodle-faking.

1949 H. Pakington *Young W. Washbourne* 38 John had said quite frankly that one didn't always want to be saddled with one's cousins, however charming, and William had retorted that he'd be damned if he'd go round poodle-faking all the time, and what was a flag-lieutenant for except to amuse the Admiral's guests. **1963** M. Malim *Pagoda Tree* 93 Women are not admitted to the main club premises except once a year at the ball. Traditionally, married members are confined to the club between 7.30 and 8.30 pm while poodle-fakers dally with their wives in their victorias outside on the fan. **1963** N. Marsh *Dead Water* (1964) vi. 134, I left my regiment. Took on this damned poodlefaking instead. **1967** D. Busk *Craft of Diplomacy* vii. 184 In Britain it is still widely assumed, perhaps largely because of ignorant or malevolent press comments, that the Service requires private means and anyhow is only poodlefaking. **1977** J. Porter *Who the Heck* xi. 97 There's some blooming Parisian couturier coming to see her... To hear her talk you'd think a bunch of corn slicers and foreign poodle-fakers was more important than solving the crime of the century. **1978** M. M. Kaye *Far Pavilions* xi. 175 He could go and shoot in Kashmir..which would do him a lot more good than poodle-faking at tea-parties.

poodler, dial. var. PODLER, young coal-fish.

poof (pʊf, puːf), *sb.*¹ *slang*. Also **pooff, pouf**, etc. [Prob. a corruption of *puff* (see PUFF *sb*. 8 d).] An effeminate man, a male homosexual; a man who acts or speaks in an affected manner. Also *attrib*. Similarly **poove** (puːv) *sb*.; also as *v. intr*., to act like a poof, to speak or behave in an effeminate or affected manner; **pooved-up** *ppl. a*.

Often considered offensive.

c **1850–60** in G. R. Taylor *Angel-Makers* (1958) iv. 80 These monsters in the shape of men, commonly designated Margeries, Pooffs, &c. **1932** Auden *Orators* III. 98 Poofs and ponces, All of them dunces. **1951** I. Shaw *Troubled Air* xvi. 272 Don't be a traitorous old poof. **1952** A. Wilson *Hemlock & After* ii. 37 'Bloody little pouff,' said Ron aloud. **1955** 'C. H. Rolph' *Women of Streets* x. 131 Although I never met any who lived with male homosexuals, several..girls.. referred to other prostitutes living with 'pouffs' who reciprocally kept them by their earnings when necessary. **1955** G. Greene *Quiet American* IV. ii. 241 He made a feeble attempt to mock my accent. 'You all talk like poufs. You're so damned superior.' **1959** C. MacInnes *Absolute Beginners* 51 The Hoplite has been in business with some of the city's top poof raves. **1962** *Private Eye* 30 Nov. 15/3, I may be a poove but I'm a terrific engineer. **1964** *New Statesman* 6 Mar. 374/1 We have a pooved-up tenor introducing a parade of Variety Girls. **1967** J. Rathbone *Diamonds Bid* xiii. 116 'Do you remember meeting Stephen Hamilton-Rose..?' 'A fat poove?' I asked. **1968** A. Diment *Gt. Spy Race* III. xi. 206 The woolly-headed pooves in the widely various Ministry of Defence networks are all completely mad with jealousy. **1968** *Listener* 19 Sept. 372/3 On the first occasion the loved object..was an able-bodied seaman,..who never manifested the slightest interest in girls but who nevertheless was totally remote from the world of pansies, pouffs and queans. **1971** F. Forsyth *Day of Jackal* xx. 336 You bloody pooves make me sick. **1971** *Melody Maker* 9 Oct. 11/1 He reckoned they pooved around a little, but commented that..their music wasn't all that rough after all. **1974** J. Betjeman *Nip in Air* 45 Touching the little children, better pooves Or murderers, they said. **1975** J. Symons *Three Pipe Problem* ix. 60 It's some poove who's been done, named Sonny Halliwell. **1976** A. Richards *Former Miss Merthyr Tydfil* 14 A young man..had been heard in the showers to refer to Elgar as 'a bit of a pouf'. **1977** W. McIlvanney *Laidlaw* xxviii. 128 Harry Rayburn's a poof. .. Whit's a poof doin' wi' a lassie? **1978** R. Rendell *Sleeping Life* xiii. 109 All you can do is get your picture in the papers like some poove of a film actor.

Hence ˈ**poofdom** *nonce*, the state or condition of being a homosexual.

1972 F. Raphael *April, June & Nov.* 466 He's a late convert to the joys of poofdom.

poof (pʊf), *int*. and *sb*.² Also **pouf, pouff**. [A natural utterance. Cf. F. *pouf*.] **A.** *int*. A sound imitating a short sharp puff of the breath as in blowing something from the mouth, or blowing out a candle; hence an expression of contemptuous rejection: cf. POOH *int*.

1824 J. Morier *Adventures Hajji Baba* II. i. 39 Putting up her five fingers to his face, she said, 'Poof! I spit on such a face.' **1829** G. Griffin *Collegians* I. viii. 159 Gi' me the hat, sir, an' I'll hang it up—poof, it's full of dust. **1857** W. Collins *Dead Secret* II. iii, Pouf! the very anticipation of them [clouds of dust] chokes me already. **1862** H. Marryat *Year in Sweden* II. 55 As for the others, poof! **1865** Dickens *Mut. Fr.* III. ii, Call that a quantity..Poof! What do you say to the rest of it? **1868** Yates *Rock Ahead* I. iv, 'She will go out like that—pouf!'..blowing out an imaginary candle in explanation. **1905** E. Glyn *Viciss. Evangeline* 62 'Pouff!' I said, and I pointed at him. **1921** H. Williamson *Beautiful Yrs.* 80 'Pouff, what a lot of rot,' scoffed Willie. **1935** M. de la Roche *Young Renny* x. 82 Pouf! You don't know anything. **1949** P. Hastings *Cases in Court* v. 281 He said the three shots were fired in rapid succession or, as he put it somewhat dramatically, 'pouf, pouf, pouf'. **1951** M. Kennedy *Lucy Carmichael* II. i. 88, I get quite interested.. for about 5 minutes and then—poof! I go flat like a burst balloon. **1968** C. M. Vines *Little Nut-Brown Man* xiii. 237 'Pouf!' he said when he had recovered from choking, 'supposing I had been dead before the water got here?' **1974** S. Coulter *Chateau* II. xii. 359 Oh, pouff! Bravado, Madame. Sheer bravado. **1979** J. Rathbone *Euro-Killers* v. 55 Poof! Rubbish! This is some ruse.

B. as *sb*. An utterance of 'poof'; a short sharp puff.

1908 *Westm. Gaz.* 25 May 5/2, I was riding on the back of the balloon..when suddenly I heard a 'pouff', as if someone had blown a blast from a bellows. **1915** D. H. Lawrence *Rainbow* vi. 148 She burst into a 'Pouf' of ridiculing laughter. **1951** Koestler *Age of Longing* II. iv. 242 Father Millet..gave a scornful poof. **1971** B. Malamud *Tenants* 68 [He] left so cleanly,..it seemed to Lesser as though he had willed his disappearance in a prestidigitated poof. **1973** J. McKelvey *Man against Tsetse* iii. 196 Refinements on the use of a dash of poison now go well beyond a squirt of spray or a poof of dust to the habitat of the fly.

poof (pʊf), *v. colloq*. Also **pouff**. [f. POOF *int*.] *intr*. **a.** To blow up, to peter *out*. Also *refl*.

1915 *N.Y. World Mag.* 9 May 14 *Pooff*, to blow up. **1923** Wodehouse *Inimitable Jeeves* xviii. 242 The fact is, I suppose, I'd seen so many of young Bingo's love affairs start off with a whoop and a rattle and poof themselves out halfway down the straight that I couldn't believe he had actually brought it off at last. **1934** —— *Right Ho, Jeeves* xxi. 231 Then the dialogue sort of poofed out once more, and we stood eating cheese straws and cold eggs respectively in silence.

b. To utter a 'poof'. *rare*.

1915 D. H. Lawrence *Rainbow* vi. 148 Again she poufed with mockery.

poofter (ˈpʊftə(r), ˈpuːftə(r)). *slang* (chiefly *Austral*.). Also **pooftah, poufter, pufter**. [Fanciful extension of POOF *sb*.¹] A homosexual; an effeminate man. Also used as a general term of abuse to a man. Also *attrib*. and *Comb*., as **poofter rorter** (see quot. 1945). So ˌ**poofteˈroo** [see -EROO].

Often considered offensive.

1910 O'Brien & Stephens *Material for Dict. Austral. Slang 1900–10* (typescript), *Pouf or poufter*, a sodomite or effeminate man. **1941** Baker *Dict. Austral. Slang* 56 *Poofter*, a homosexual. **1945** —— *Austral. Lang.* 123 A procurer for homosexuals is known as a *poofter rorter*. **1952** *Here & Now* (N.Z.) Jan. 19/1 The butcher's assistant was as likely to have a star bird dog or rabbit dog as the richest pooftah. **1953** T. A. G. Hungerford *Riverslake* iii. 49 He hawked disgustingly and spat on the floor between his feet. 'They want men in the unions, not poofters!' **1955** D. Niland *Shiralee* 207 They'd play around like poofters, with the kid gloves and the soft soap. **1961** P. White *Riders in Chariot* IV. xi. 392 They will tell you,' she said, 'that Norman is a pufter. .. Norm could not impress a woman even if he tried.' *Ibid.* 401 'You are a proper pufter rorter, Hannah!' Reen had to remark, because she was a cow. **1964** I. Fleming *You only live Twice* iv. 59 'You pommy poofter.'.. Bond said mildly, 'What's a poofter?' 'What you'd call a pansy.' **1966** *Punch* 9 Mar. 352/3 'It is illegal to ingratiate oneself with the Examiner.' Ingratiate oneself! Good heavens! It was slowly beginning to dawn on me that this man was a poofteroo. **1966** P. White *Solid Mandala* 18 You ought to move in with that pair of poofteroos across the road. **1969** W. Dick *Naked Prodigal* 12, I turned and exploded. 'You poofter bastard!' I yelled... 'I'll kill him. The bastard's a poofter. He touched me up.' **1973** A. Broinowski *Take One Ambassador* v. 53 The feller's a bloody poofter. Queer's a four pound note. **1974** R. Gadney *Something Worth Fighting For* xxi. 139 Looking at all them pooftahs. I was thinking what some people do for money. **1976** *Telegraph* (Brisbane) 21 Sept. 50/1 'Poofter-bashing' is a strong and blunt phrase, but the only way to describe the latest wave of discrimination against homosexual men and women in Brisbane. **1977** *Listener* (N.Z.) 15 Jan. 6/1 The white-legged Pommy poofter is an integral part of one view of the English. **1978** J. Barnett *Head of Force* ix. 82 He was..a poufter... He was having it off with somebody he called Soldier.

poofy (ˈpuːfɪ, ˈpʊfɪ), *a. slang*. Also **poovey, poovy, pouffy, poufy**. [f. POOF *sb*.¹ + -Y¹.] Of, pertaining to, or characteristic of a poof; effeminate or homosexual. Also *Comb*.

1964 J. Hale *Grudge Fight* v. 74 Being Windy the soap is scented, pink stuff sent to him by Momma in the last parcel. 'Very pouffy,' says Tug, sniffing it. **1967** *Observer* 1 Jan. 24/7 Wailed a poovy young author named Ned, 'I'd rather be dead than unread.' **1968** A. Diment *Gt. Spy Race* II. vii. 99 He was just what I wanted. Stupid, poor, poovey. **1969** J. Gardner *Founder Member* x. 160 'Get into those poufy drawers and..hurry.' Boysie pulled on the nylon briefs. **1970** *Guardian* 8 July 8/4 The material..makes fun of..old-fashioned 'pouffy' homosexuals. **1970** M. Tripp *Man without Friends* vi. 61 In our cockeyed civilisation it's regarded as poovey for a man to enjoy housework. **1972** D. Lees *Zodiac* 73 One hand raised..like a poofy traffic cop. **1976** J. O'Connor *Eleventh Commandment* i. 17 After being given the once over by a poofy-looking scout who gave me a pat on my arse, I was sworn in.

‖**poogye** (ˈpuːgiː). Also **-gyee, pungi**. [Hindī *pūṅgī* (*ūṅ* = nasalized *ū*).] The Hindū nose-flute.

1864 Engel *Music Ancient Nations* 59 One of the most curious double-pipes at present extant in Asia is the poogyee of the Hindoos.., the tubes of which are inserted into a gourd, and are blown with the nose instead of with the mouth. **1898** Stainer & Barrett *Dict. Mus. Terms*, *Poogye*, the nose-flute of the Hindoos.

pooh (puː, puːh), *int*. (*v*., *sb*.) Also 7 **puh, pue, pow**, 7–8 **pugh**, 8– **poo**: see POH, POOF. [A 'vocal gesture' expressing the action of puffing or blowing anything away. Prob. orig. (pux, puh), whence also the variants *pough*, *pogh*, *poh*, *po*; and cf. POOF.] **A.** *int*. An ejaculation expressing impatience, or contemptuous disdain or disregard for anything. Cf. PHEW, PHO, PHOO.

1602 Shaks. *Ham.* I. iii. 101 Affection, puh! You speake like a greene Girle. **1604** Marston & Webster *Malcontent* I. vi, Pugh!.. Thou speakest like a fool. **1607** Shaks. *Cor.* II. i. 157 *Virgil.* The Gods graunt them true. *Volum.* True? pow waw. *a* **1627** Middleton *Quiet Life* II. i, Pue wawe, this is nothing, till I know what he did. **1694** Congreve *Double-Dealer* I. ii, Pooh, ha, ha, ha, I know you envy me. **1749** Fielding *Tom Jones* XVII. ix, 'Pugh', says she, 'you have pinked a man in a duel, that's all'. **1768** Sterne *Sent. Journ.* (1778) II. 151 Poo! said they, we have no money. **1829** Lytton *Devereux* II. ii, 'Pooh, man', said Tarleton haughtily, 'none of your compliments'. **1880** 'Ouida' *Moths* II. 378 'Pooh', he said, as he read it, and tore it up.

B. as *sb*. **1.** An utterance of this.

1667 Pepys *Diary* 29 July, With that she made a slighting puh with her mouth. **1817** Byron *Beppo* vii, A thing which causes many 'poohs' and 'pishes'. **1861** Clayton *F. O'Donnell* 23 This puffy one always ended his subject with a long 'pooh'.

2. *slang*. Excrement, faeces. Also *transf*. and *fig*.; ***in the pooh*** = *in the shit* s.v. SHIT *sb*. 1 d.

1960 Wentworth & Flexner *Dict. Amer. Slang* 401/1 *Poo*.., feces. **1961** 'J. Danvers' *Living come First* x. 177 'You're rather in the pooh with the Adelaide police.' 'How much do I stink with them?' **1967** Partridge *Dict. Slang* Suppl. 1303/2 *Pooh*, anything smelly or disgusting, esp. *faeces*: Australian juvenile. **1970** R. Beilby *No Medals for Aphrodite* 229 If they catch you with her, then you're really in the pooh. **1975** X. Herbert *Poor Fellow my Country* 873 She'll put you in the poo if she writes anything 'bout you. **1976** J. McClure *Rogue Eagle* ii. 33 'But what..if someone ..gave him the money and support he needed?' 'We might be right in the poo.'

Hence **pooh** *v*., *intr*., to utter the exclamation 'pooh!'; *trans*., to say 'pooh!' to.

1630 J. Taylor (Water P.) *Apol. for Watermen* Epil., Wks. II. 267/2 The wrymouth'd Critick..That mewes, and puh's and shakes his brainlesse head. **1798** Charlotte Smith *Yng. Philos.* I. 44 The Doctor..pshaw'd and pooh'd for some time. **1858** Polson *Law & L.* 15 'Pooh! pooh!' re-echoed his mother, 'don't pooh me, John'.

Pooh Bah (puː bɑː). Also with small initials. [Name of a character in W. S. Gilbert's *Mikado*.] A person who holds a large number of offices at the same time. Also in extended use, a person or body with much influence or many functions; a self-important person. Also *attrib*. Hence **Pooh-ˈBahism**.

1888 L. D. Powles *Land of Pink Pearl* 77 To the first of these [vacancies] the Governor appointed an English jeweller, named Brown, to the second one of the local 'Pooh Bahs!' named Crawford. **1923** *Westm. Gaz.* 4 May 1/6 (*heading*) Pooh-Bah Role for Local Bodies. **1927** M. Terry *Through Land of Promise* 44 Although principally protectors of aboriginals, stock inspection, mining wardens' responsibilities and a host of other offices make them a collection of veritable 'Poo-Bahs'. **1949** F. Swinnerton *Doctor's Wife comes to Stay* 163, I do a bit of painting, myself; enough to take the boys in art. You see, we're so short-handed—' 'Good God! You must be the Pooh Bah of this school.' **1956** *Newsweek* 7 May 59/2 TV Pooh-Bahs expect this year's giveaway shows to reach a total handout of $8 million. **1962** S. E. Finer *Man on Horseback* xi. 187 In his Pooh-bah capacities as Prime Minister, Minister of War and Marine, Commander-in-Chief and Military Governor of Egypt, Neguib's power now rested on two pillars, the military and the civilian. **1964** C. Duffy *Wild Goose & Eagle* xii. 175 In a magnificent display of Pooh-Bahism Francis Stephen, as Emperor, supported strictness and vigilance, but in his capacity as Grand Duke of Tuscany protested against interference with vessels on their peaceful way from Tuscan ports to Genoa. **1972** W. A. Pantin *Oxford Life* v. 65 In the late eighteenth century a serious moral case..would now be dealt with by the Hebdomadal Board, that all-purpose, constitutional Pooh-Bah of the period. **1972** *Publishers' Weekly* 13 Nov. 16/1 His first book ..was a tough, illuminating picture of what happens in the surgical wards of a metropolitan hospital, and it did not exactly endear him to the pooh-bahs of medicine.

pooh pooh (ˈpuːˈpuː), *int*. (*sb*., *a*.) Reduplication of POOH *int*.

[**1679** Pough, Pough: see POH.] *a* **1814** *Woman's Will* III. i. in *New Brit. Theatre* IV. 90 Poo, poo, you know not what you say. **1844** Dickens *Mart. Chuz.* xii, Pooh, pooh!.. Never mind that. **1902** A. Lang in *Longm. Mag.* Sept. 146 The sceptic will say 'Pooh pooh!' (at least on paper—nobody ever *says* 'Pooh pooh!')

B. *sb*. (*pooh-pooh*). **a.** An utterance of the exclamation 'pooh pooh!' **b.** One who is addicted to using this exclamation.

1798 Charlotte Smith *Yng. Philos.* I. 6 Before the Doctor had vented his pshaws and pooh poohs. **1867** *Morn. Star* 6 Aug. 6/4 The Pooh-poohs think the rest of mankind was made for their pleasure and profit. **1875** O. W. Holmes *Old Vol. of Life, Crime & Automatism* (1891) 326 This is the tribe of the Pooh-Poohs, so called from the leading expression of their vocabulary. **1891** G. Meredith *One of our Conq.* III. ii. 29 Dartrey blew his pooh-pooh on feminine suspicions.

C. *attrib*. or *adj*. (ˈpuːpuː), as in ***pooh-pooh theory***, a humorous designation of the theory that language is a development of natural interjections. Cf. BOW-WOW *theory*.

1860 Thackeray *Round. Papers, Late Gt. Victories* (1876) 40 A Saturnine philosopher..has a pooh-pooh expression as the triumph passes. **1861** Max Müller *Sc. Lang.* ix. 352 These cries or interjections were represented as the natural and real beginnings of human speech... This is what I call the Interjectional, or Pooh-pooh, Theory.

pooh-pooh (puːˈpuː), *v*. [f. prec. int.] *trans*. To express contempt or disdain for; to make light of, dismiss as unworthy of notice.

1827 J. W. Croker *Diary* Feb. (1884) I. xii. 365 Peel pooh-poohed that difficulty. **1840** Barham *Ingol. Leg.* Ser. I. *Leech of Folkest.* (1877) 376 An old gentleman..was deservedly pooh-pooh'd down. **1850** Kingsley *Alt. Locke* xxxii, [They] pooh-poohed away every attempt at further enlargement of the suffrage. **1854** Huxley in *Life* (1900) I. viii. 119 A stipend..between £800 and £1200 a year is not to be pooh-poohed. **1893** *Times* 22 Apr., Mr. Gladstone cannot pooh-pooh difficulties in Committee. **1926** [see À LA *phr*. c]. **1957** *Observer* 29 Sept. 13/4 It is one thing to pooh-pooh the final scene as melodrama..and quite another thing to remain detached as Salome lies, on your own fireside, intoxicated with passion. **1962** *Hovering Craft & Hydrofoil* Nov. 20/2 A few years ago most of us would have pooh-poohed the idea of a modern version of Jules Verne's atom-powered 'Nautilus', which has since become a reality several times over. **1971** *Petticoat* 24 July 39/1 If he refuses, or pooh-poohs your concern, go to a new family doctor, and try again. **1977** *New Yorker* 27 June 30/3 My companion pooh-poohed the mishap and bade me choose an apéritif.

Hence **pooh-'pooher, pooh-'poohist; pooh-'poohing** *vbl. sb.* and *ppl. a.*; **pooh-'pooh-ingly** *adv.*, in a dismissive or contemptuous manner, **pooh-'poohy** *a.* (*nonce*), inclined to pooh-pooh.

1841 DICKENS *Let.* 2 Apr. (1969) II. 249 The pooh-poohers and Lord Burleighs have it hollow, all the world through. **1855** THACKERAY *Newcomes* xxv, Slatter..was..silenced by the unanimous pooh-poohing of the assembly. **1861** W. H. W[HITE] in *Rec. Astro-meteorol. Soc.* No. 1. 13, I mean the Pooh-poohists. These objectors..rear high their crests on the announcement of any novelty in practical science. **1862** FURNIVALL *Let. to Sub-editors N.E. Dict.* 4, I believe that more roots will prove to be *imsons* than is supposed by pooh-poohers of the bow-wow theory. **1876** H. PARRY *Diary* in C. L. Graves *Hubert Parry* (1926) I. 169 Before the performance I met Otto Goldschmidt, and he was rather pooh-poohy about it. **1898** W. JAMES *Coll. Ess. & Rev.* (1920) 423 Concerning this question, at any rate, the positivists and pooh-poohers of metaphysics are in the wrong. **1906** SLADEN *Lovers Japan* iv, I had not the courage to tell her pooh-poohing uncle so. **1911** G. B. SHAW *Doctor's Dilemma* p. lvii, The moment his practice is tracked down to its source in human passion there is a great and quite sincere poohpoohing..from the mass of the public. **1939** JOYCE *Finnegans Wake* III. 498 The poohpooher old bossloose, with his arthurious clayroses..busted to the wurld at large. **1956** Poohpooingly [see BORROVIAN *sb.* and *a.*]. **1959** *Economist* 7 Feb. 490/1 For all his pooh-poohing of 'sentimentalism', he admitted that he never heard 'God Save the Queen'..without feeling tears in his eyes.

Pooh-sticks, pooh-sticks ('puːstɪks). [f. the name of Winnie-the-*Pooh*, a character created by A. A. Milne + STICK *sb.*[1]] A game in which sticks are thrown over one side of a bridge into a stream and the first to emerge on the other side wins.

1928 A. A. MILNE *House at Pooh Corner* vi. 94 And that was the beginning of the game called Poohsticks, which Pooh invented, and which he and his friends used to play on the edge of the Forest. But they played with sticks instead of fir-cones, because they were easier to mark. **1972** *Times* 16 May 10/4 He spends most of his time playing pooh-sticks. **1974** C. MILNE *Enchanted Places* i. 15 The bridge where they had played Pooh-sticks was a real bridge, looking just like the drawing in the book. *Ibid.* viii. 58 We used to stand on Pooh-sticks Bridge throwing sticks into the water and watching them float away..until they re-emerged on the other side. **1979** *Guardian* 16 May 1/1 The horde of visitors who..chuck[ed] a twig or two into the sun-dappled stream in honour of the bear of very little brain who invented Poohsticks.

‖**poojah, puja** ('pudʒa). *E. Indies.* Also 7 **poujah, pudgiah,** 9- **pooja,** 20 **pujah.** [a. Skr. *pūjā* worship.] Rites performed in the worship of Hindū deities; any Hindū religious ceremony or rite; also *fig.* (in ridicule). Also **puja pantai** (pan'taɪ) [Malay *pantai*, = beach, seashore] (see quot. 1965).

1681 R. KNOX *Ceylon* III. iv. 80 In this Poujah or Sacrifice the King seems to take delight. *Ibid.* v. 85 They reckon the chief poynts of goodness to consist in giving to the Priests, in making Pudgiahs, sacrifices to their Gods, in forbearing shedding the blood of any creature. **1800** S. TURNER *Embassy Tibet* iv. 243 It was only the Gylongs at their *pooja*, or religious exercises. *c* **1806** MRS. SHERWOOD in *Life* xxi. (1847) 361 To this he made his daily poojah, or worship. **1826** HOCKLEY *Pandurang Hari* I. ii. 18 The person..now approached the sacred tree, and having performed *pūja* to a stone deity at its foot, proceeded [etc.]. **1863** TREVELYAN *Compet. Wallah* (1866) 295 The high festivals of our religion would be among the most popular Poojahs of the year. **1875** FREEMAN in Stephens *Life & Lett.* (1895) II. 95 My sin is that of not doing poojah to old Carlyle, who..took upon himself to write some nonsense about early kings of Norway. **1893** KIPLING *Day's Work* (1898) 10 In London I did poojah to the big temple by the river for the sake of the God within. **1909** M. DIVER *Candles in Wind* i. 14 Is it permitted that we kill a goat and make *poojah*? **1913** E. M. FORSTER *Let.* 6 Mar. in *Hill of Devi* (1953) 28 The Rajah is doing Pujah after his bath. **1936** J. NEHRU *Autobiogr.* 8 The women of the family indulged in various ceremonies and *pujas*. **1951** *Chambers's Jrnl.* Oct. 611/2 The main religious ceremonies or 'poojas'..take place in the temple sanctum, and..eventually terminate with the bath and the fire-walk. **1951** *Jrnl. Malayan Branch R. Asiatic Soc.* XXIV. III. 33 The *pelas negri* ceremony of Perak was, in Malaya, known by other names too:..in Kelantan, and in Province Wellesley, for fishermen, the ceremony is known as *puja pantai*. **1965** C. SHUTTLEWORTH *Malayan Safari* vi. 77 A rare and colourful ceremony known as the *Puja Pantai*, it is performed by Malay fishermen when they believe that the sea gods are angry with them and need to be propitiated. **1968** *Jrnl. Music Acad. Madras* XXXIX. 59 Every home has its family idol and the pujas are performed according to the ..16 types of ceremonies. **1969** *Cultural News from India* Nov. 20 The heavy and intermittent rains which, a few days ago, threatened to dampen the Puja spirit are now over. *Ibid.*, Calcutta, or for that matter, entire Bengal is in the grip of the Puja celebrations. **1971** *Northern India Patrika* 1 Feb. 1/1 Sub-inspector Makhan Lal Dutta..was attacked..near a Saraswat puja pandal. **1971** *Illustr. Weekly India* 18 Apr. 29/3 (*caption*) Gujarati women sway and swoon at a *puja*. **1972** M. SHEPPARD *Taman Indera* 197 The general name which incorporated all the ceremonies and offerings on such an occasion [*sc.* a Malay folk festival] was *Puja Pantai*. **1977** W. H. S. SMITH *Young Man's Country* ii. 36 The Puja holiday was the biggest Hindu festival in the Bengali year.

poojari, var. PUJARI.

pook (pʊk), *sb. local.* Also 9 **puck.** [Goes with next: derivation uncertain.]

1. A heap; *esp.* a roughly thrown up heap of hay, a cock; also, a heap of oats, barley, or other unsheafed produce, not more than 5 feet high, pitched together for carting to the rick.

1718 HEARNE *Rem.* II. 80 [The farmer and his men] went up into the common fields..to fetch home two loads of oats, and the land not being yet in cocks or pooks [etc.]. **1853** MISS YONGE *Heir of Redclyffe* vii, She saw Guy's ready greeting, and their comparison of the forks and rakes, the pooks and cocks of their countries. **1863** MORTON *Cycl. Agric.* Gloss. (E.D.S.), *Pucks* or *Pooks* (West Eng.), are large heaps, little ricks of hay, corn, &c. **1868** TREGELLAS *Cornish Tales* 20 O'er shoading-heaps and pooks of turves. **1905** *Westm. Gaz.* 8 July 3/1 The hay was dry and 'up in pook'.

2. A thin tall stack of corn in the sheaf, in shape a steep cone, 9 or 10 feet high, built up temporarily in the harvest-field in wet seasons, for drying the corn before it is carried to the main rick. So generally in s.w., but in central Dorset called more definitely a 'wind-mow'. (T. Hardy.)

a **1722** LISLE *Husb.* (1757) 211 In making the wheat-pooks in Wiltshire, the sheaves are set [etc.]. *Ibid.*, In a pook may be put a load or two. **1766** *Complete Farmer* s.v. *Harvest*, In their wheat-pooks..in Wiltshire, the sheaves are set in a circle, with their ears uppermost, and another circle of sheaves is placed upon that, and so on, contracting each round, till the pile ends in a point, upon which a sheaf opened, and turned with the ears downward, is placed, like the shackle of a hive... A load, or two loads, may be thus put into a pook, which is a very good way to secure corn against rain. **1829** KNAPP *Jrnl. Nat.* 28 Saving our crops in bad and catching seasons, by securing the hay in windcocks, and wheat in pooks.

pook (pʊk), *v.*[1] *local.* [Goes with prec.] *trans.* To heap up; *esp.* to put up (newly mown hay or unsheafed corn) in cocks or pooks (POOK *sb.* 1).

1587 *Mirr. Mag.*, *Bladud* xv, Beneath on earth pompe, pelfe and prayse they pooke. **1627** *MS. Acc. St. John's Hosp., Canterb.*, For gatherng of viij busshells of apples & for pookeing. **1718** HEARNE *Rem.* II. 81 The master and the other servant were pooking in part of the land. **1813** T. DAVIS *Agric. Wilts.* Gloss. s.v. *Cocked*, Barley and oats are always pooked or cocked, seldom carried from the swath... Hay is pooked, cocked, first in foot-cocks, and when dry in hay-cocks. **1901** *Times* 19 Aug. 11/1 Experience shows..that where barley is pooked, as it often is in the south, it takes less harm from heavy rain and dries much sooner than where it is sheafed.

b. To put up (corn) in pooks (POOK *sb.* 2).

a **1600** 'A Wiltshire Rent Roll, temp. Q. Eliz.' in *N. & Q.* 3rd Ser. VII. 277/1 The tenant to cut down, sheafe, pooke, and rake the said thirdes and tenths [of wheat and barley].

Hence **'pooking** *vbl. sb.*; also *attrib.* in *pooking-fork* (see quot. 1893); also **'pooker.**

1635 *Wilts. Rec.* (Hist. MSS. Comm.) *Varr. Collect.* (1901) I. 169 Men labourers in haymaking, pookeing, or gripping of Lent corne shall not take by the day..of wages above v[d]. **1794** T. DAVIS *Gen. View Agric. Wilts.* 90 The price is seldom higher than eighteen-pence per acre for mowing, and one shilling for pooking, etc. **1893** *Wilts. Gloss.*, *Pooker*, a woman employed in pooking. *Pooking-fork*, the large prong, with a cross handle, for pushing along in front of the pookers, to make up the hay into pooks. **1894** *Times* 14 Aug. 15/1 The relative merits of pooking and sheafing in the work of barley-harvesting are sure to present themselves for consideration... The barley lies strewn over the entire surface, to be occasionally turned with the pooking fork till the crop is ready for stacking.

pook (puːk), *v.*[2] *Sc.* Forms: (7 puik), 8-9 **pouk,** 9 **pook.** [Origin unascertained.] *trans.* To pluck, pull, pick, or pinch with the thumb and finger: e.g. in plucking a fowl, picking the stalks off fruit, and the like. Also *fig.*

1633 *Orkney Witch Trial* in *Abbotsford Club Misc.* 154 The said Catrein cam in to the said Barbarayis house to puik sum bair. **1785** BURNS *Death & Dr. Hornbook* xiv, The weans haud out their fingers laughin And pouk my hips. *a* **1810** in Cromek *Rem. Nithsdale Song* 74 I'll clip, ouo' she, yere lang gray wing, An' pouk yere rosie kame. *c* **1817** HOGG *Tales & Sk.* III. 205 Pook a craw with us. **1823** GALT *Entail* lii, Pooking and rooking me, his mother, o' my ain lawful jointure. **1894** CROCKETT *Raiders* 274 Your leddyship will hae to come and pook the chucky.

Hence **pooked** (puːkt), *Sc.* **pookit** ('puːkɪt) *ppl. a.*

1818 MISS FERRIER *Marriage* xxxiv, They hadnae thae pooket-like taps ye hae noo. **1824** —— *Inher.* lxxxiv, It [the name] 's rather short and pookit. **1894** HUNTER *J. Inwick* ii. 20 He's a puir, poukit-like cratur. **1895** CROCKETT *Men of Moss-Hags* lv, I had not the spirit of a pooked hen.

‖**pooka, phooka** ('puːkə, 'phuka). *Irish.* [Ir. *púca* (gen. and dat. with article *an phúca*), = OE. *púca*, ON. *púki*, ME. *pouke* (see PUCK), Welsh *pwca* goblin.] In Irish folk-lore, A hobgoblin, a malignant sprite.

1825 T. C. CROKER *Fairy Leg.* I. 316 Irish superstition makes the Phooka palpable to the touch. To its agency the peasantry usually ascribe accidental falls. **1847** LE FANU *T. O'Brien* 74 The Cavalier had heard of Phookas and other malignant sprites who..scare..the benighted traveller. **1888** W. B. YEATS *Fairy & Folk T.* 94 The Pooka..seems essentially an animal spirit;..[a] wild, staring phantom. **1894** *Q. Rev.* Oct. 331 The pranks of the Phooka..and the vision of the long-haired, long-robed Geilt.

‖**pookaun** (pu'kɔːn). *Irish.* Also **pookawn, pookhaun.** [Ir. *púcán.*] A small Irish fishing-boat, for rowing or sailing, in the latter case having a single mast with a kind of lateen sail.

1878-84 D. KEMP *Yacht Sailing* xxiv. 337 The Galway pookhaun is a smaller boat than the hooker, and used for both rowing and sailing. **1892** JANE BARLOW *Irish Idylls* v. 108 On board quaint little curraghs and pookawns. **1899** *Blackw. Mag.* Oct. 490/2 The pookaun, a small boat with a sort of lateen sail, pretty to look at, but dangerous.

pooke, obs. f. POKE; var. PUKE *Obs.* (colour).

pookoo, var. PUKU[1].

pool (puːl), *sb.*[1] Forms: 1-4 **pól,** (1 poll, 4 powl), 5-6 **pole,** 5-7 **poole,** 3, 5- **pool.** Also *β. Sc.* 5 **poll,** 5- **pule,** 6- **puil,** 8-9 (*n.e. dial.*) **peel.** [OE. *pól* masc. = OLG. **pōl*, MLG., MD. *pōl*, LG. *pōl*, *pohl*, *pūl*, Du. *poel*; WGer. stem **pôlo-*.

OE. had also *pull* and *pyll* (see PILL *sb.*[3]), ON. *pollr*, Sw., Da. *pól*, the relations of which to OE. *pól* are obscure, as are also those of the Celtic words: W. *pwll*, Corn. *pol*, Breton *poull* pool; Ir. *poll*, *pull*, Gael. *poll* hole, bog, pond, pit, mire, Manx *poyll* pool, puddle.]

1. a. A small body of standing or still water, permanent or temporary: chiefly, one of natural formation.

c **897** K. ÆLFRED *Gregory's Past. C.* xxxviii. 278 Salomon sæde ðætte swiðe deop pol wære ʒewered on ðæs wisan monnes mode. *Ibid.* xxxix. 282 Swelce mon deopne pol [*Hatton MS.* pool] ʒewerige. *c* **950** *Lindisf. Gosp.* John ix. 11 Gaa to ðæm pole [Siloam] & aðuah. *c* **1205** LAY. 21748 þer, if æluene ploʒe in atteliche pole. *c* **1275** *XI Pains of Hell* 81 in *O.E. Misc.* 149 Ifulled is þat fule pool þat euer is hot, and neuer cool. **1297** R. GLOUC. (Rolls) 2773 Let delue vnder þe foundement, & me ssal binеþe finde A water pol. **13..** *E.E. Allit. P.* C. 310 Alle þe gotez of þy guteres [*text* guferes], & groundelez powlez. *c* **1425** *Voc.* in Wr.-Wülcker 653/3 *Hec piscina*, pole. *c* **1440** *Promp. Parv.* 407/2 Pool, or ponde for fysche kepynge, *vivarium, stagnum.* **1482** *Rolls of Parlt.* VI. 202/1 Ryvers, Pooles [204/2 Poles], Milnes, Fisshing places. **1535** COVERDALE *2 Sam.* ii. 13 They met together by the pole [**1611** poole] at Gibeon, and these laye on the one syde of the pole, the other on the other syde. **1596** DALRYMPLE tr. *Leslie's Hist. Scot.* I. 7 Poles, stankes, and standeng Lochis. *a* **1618** SYLVESTER *Hymn of Alms* 135 His Fens with Fowl, his Pils and Poles with Fish; His Trees with Fruits, with Plenty every Dish. **1622** CALLIS *Stat. Sewers* (1647) 59 A Pool is a meer standing water, without any current at all, and hath seldom or never any issue to convey away the waters. **1770** GOLDSM. *Des. Vill.* 119 The noisy geese that gabbled o'er the pool. **1846** RUSKIN *Mod. Paint.* I. II. v. i. §4 There is hardly a road-side pond or pool which has not as much landscape in it as above it.

β. **1487** *Barbour's Bruce* XII. 395 In the kersse pollis [*MS. E.* pulis, *ed. Hart* puilles] ther war. **1508** KENNEDIE *Flyting w. Dunbar* 342 Thou come, Fule! in Marche or Februere, Thair till a pule, and drank the paddok rod. **1567** *Gude & Godlie B.* (S.T.S.) 185 Stinkand pulis of euerie rottin sink. **1789** ROSS *Helenore* 58 She..made nae stop for scrabs, or stanes, or peels [*ed.* 1768 pools]. *a* **1828** in P. Buchan *Ballads* I. 26 Then she became a duck..To puddle in a peel.

†**b.** Applied to a whirlpool. *Obs. rare*[−1].

1536 BELLENDEN *Cron. Scot.* IX. xxi. (1821) II. 108 Comparit justly to ane insaciabil pule.

c. A small shallow collection of standing water or other liquid; a small plash, a puddle.

1843 MACAULAY *Lays Anc. Rome, Horatius* lii, Where, wallowing in a pool of blood, The bravest Tuscans lay. **1860** TYNDALL *Glac.* I. xvii. 317 One of the little pools upon the surface of the glacier. **1867** H. MACMILLAN *Bible Teach.* xv. (1870) 291 Those little pools that are left behind among the rocks by the retiring tide. *Mod. Sc.* Keip oot o' the puils.

d. *transf.* and *fig.*

1587 FLEMING *Contn. Holinshed* III. 1352/2, [I] was forced to open the poole of my head, and to unstop the gate of my heart. **1870** MRS. RIDDELL *Austin Friars* i, A quiet pool apart from the human torrent. **1875** G. MACDONALD *Parables, Somnium Mystici* x, On the floor I saw..A little pool of sunlight. **1894** WEYMAN *My Lady Rotha* xxxi, The very gules and purpure that lay in pools on the floor. **1903** *Smart Set* IX. 114 Hid in the marsh of years, Lies the still pool of memory.

e. (See quot.)

1883 *Century Mag.* July 324/1 When once a new 'pool' or belt of [oil-] producing territory is found.

f. = *oil pool* s.v. OIL *sb.*[1] 6 e.

1902 *Bull. U.S. Geol. Survey* No. 198. 23 North and northeast of the Snyder pool six wells have been sunk. **1976** M. MACHLIN *Pipeline* ii. 32 It tests over two thousand barrels a day—and God knows how much gas. I don't know how big the pool is.

g. A swimming pool.

1921 A. HUXLEY *Crome Yellow* iv. 33 That part of the garden that sloped down from the foot of the terrace to the pool. **1941** B. SCHULBERG *What makes Sammy Run?* iv. 61 Collier was urging him to come early and try the pool. **1961** J. S. SALAK *Dict. Amer. Sports* 337 It is recommended that pools for championship meets should be at least 75 feet in length and 42 feet in width. **1974** R. THOMAS *Porkchoppers* v. 38 He..lived..in a house with a pool, two Russian wolfhounds, and his wife.

2. A deep and still place in a river or stream. *the Pool*: (*a*) the part of the Thames between London Bridge and Cuckold's Point; (*b*) Liverpool.

a **1000** in Birch *Cart. Sax.* I. 57 Of þane grete wiþ iʒ endlonge burne in þane pol buue Crocford. **1632** MASSINGER *City Madam* I. i, The ship is safe in the Pool, then? **1661** WALTON *Angler* I. xx. (ed. 3) 241 Such Pools as be large and have most gravel. **1722** DE FOE *Plague* (1840) 111 The river..between the houses which we call Ratcliff and Redriff, which they name the pool. **1806** *Gazetteer Scotl.* (ed. 2) 272 After passing the linn, it [R. Isla] forms a deep pool of water, called Corral. **1812** J. WILSON *Isle of Palms* II. 171 A stream comes dancing from a mount... Then, tamed into a quiet pool Is scarcely seen to glide. **1885**

Law Rep. 10 Appeal Cases 380 It is not a very big burn, but there are some very deep pools in it. **1963** *Austral. T.V. Times* 18 Apr. 10/2 *The pool*, the port of Liverpool. **1966** D. FRANCIS *Flying Finish* (1968) i. 11 A small.. wharf down in the Pool. **1969** R. BUSBY *Robbery Blue* xxii. 151 I'd reckon on Liverpool... I'd head for the 'Pool, get myself swallowed up in a big city. **1972** P. DRISCOLL *Wilby Conspiracy* (1973) ii. 29 His origins: a street of back-to-backs.. off the Scotland Road.. the toughest part of the Pool to grow up in. **1975** *Times Lit. Suppl.* 31 Jan. 100/1 (Advt.), A fifteen year old tearaway from the 'pool brilliantly portrayed in a talented first novel. **1976** *Observer* 8 Aug. 11 (Advt.), Ar Alf sez darrevry Scouse Big'ead's brood special fer d'Pool, like. **1978** K. BONFIGLIOLI *All Tea in China* ix. 88 We could drop down-river to the Pool.. without feeing a pilot.

3. *attrib.* and *Comb.*, as ***pool-bird, -ground, -side***; ***pool-clear, -haunting*** adjs.; **pool cathode** *Electronics*, a cathode consisting of a pool of mercury used in certain types of discharge tube; **pool house, poolhouse** chiefly *U.S.*, (*a*) a house by a swimming pool, for the use of bathers; (*b*) a building with a swimming pool in it; **pool-lily**, a water-lily; **pool-measure, pool-price**, the measure or price of coal at the Pool on the river in London; **pool party**, a party at which the guests bathe; **pool-pass**, a fish-way into or out of a pool (PASS *sb.*[1] 3 h); **pool-reed** (called also *pole-reed* and *pull-reed*), the common Reed (*Phragmites communis*); **pool room**, a room with a pool in it; **pool-root**, White Snakeroot, *Eupatorium ageratoides* (Billings *Med. Dict.* 1890); **pool-rush** (called by Lyte *pole-rush*), the Bulrush, *Scirpus lacustris*; sometimes erroneously, *Typha latifolia*; **pool-snipe**, †**-snite**, the Redshank, *Totanus calidris*; **pool-spear** = *pool-reed*; **poolwort**, a name given in U.S. to *Eupatorium aromaticum* (Billings).

1591 FRAUNCE *Heliodorus' Æthiopia*, Fit neast for a *poole-byrde. **1934** *Electrical Engineering* (N.Y.) Jan. 75/2 If a rectifier having a single anode and mercury *pool cathode within a separate small tank were to be built, no continuous back current could flow to the anode when it is negative. **1966** *McGraw-Hill Encycl. Sci. & Technol.* VIII. 236/2 Tubes with a pool cathode have a higher current capacity and longer life than the hot-cathode tubes because of the indestructible nature of the mercury-pool cathode. Pool-cathode mercury-arc tubes are widely used for medium and high-power applications in welding and rectifier service. **1924** E. SITWELL *Sleeping Beauty* xiv. 51 Pierced through the *pool-clear heart. **1847** EMERSON *Poems, Monadnoc*, Pasture of *pool-haunting herds. **1957** P. QUENTIN *Suspicious Circumstances* ii. 24 He was way off, down by the pool... They'd eaten at the *poolhouse. **1975** A. BERGMAN *Hollywood & the Vine* (1976) ix. 123 The poolhouse had showers, marked 'Fillies' and 'Stallions'. **1978** R. MOORE *Big Paddle* (1979) xxix. 269 'Seems to me I remember a pool house around here somewhere.' 'You're planning on taking a swim, sir?' **1902** *Contemp. Rev.* Oct. 576 Her heart sank like a *pool-lily at shadow. **1768** *Chron.* in *Ann. Reg.* 74/2 An action brought.. against two coal merchants.. for selling five chaldrons of coals for *pool-measure, without delivering the full quantity. **1973** *Ottawa Jrnl.* 16 July 27/5 Arch, if Veronica's having a *pool party, why don't I wear a bathing suit? **1883** *Fisheries Exhib. Catal.* (ed. 4) 125 Plan and Section of Fish Pass.. example of a *Pool Pass. **1832** *Examiner* 23/1 Upon each chaldron of coals brought to the market twelve shillings.. was added to the *pool or market price, which addition furnished the profits to the merchant. **1587** T. NEWTON *Lemnie's Bible Herbal* 150 Another kinde of Reede there is growing by the banks of standing waters, and on the shores of riuers, which hath a long, round and hollowe stalke or strawe, full of knottie ioints.. This kinde, is our common *Poole Reede, Spear or Cane reede. **1879** PRIOR *Names Brit. Plants* (ed. 3) 187 *Pole-reed*, properly.. called in our western counties, Pool-reed, from its place of growth, *Arundo Phragmites*. **1925** F. SCOTT FITZGERALD *Great Gatsby* (1926) v. 110 Through dressing-rooms and poolrooms, and bathrooms with sunken baths. **1968** J. SANGSTER *Touchfeather* xiv. 151 Where's the pool room? **1712** M. HENRY *Life P. Henry* i. Wks. 1853 II. 608/2 If we lay our children by the *pool-side, who knows but the Blessed Spirit may help them in, and heal them. **1921** W. DE LA MARE *Veil* 6 Wan glow-worms greened the pool-side grass. **1963** *New Yorker* 22 June 109 Poolside buffet luncheon daily. **1968** *Globe & Mail* (Toronto) 17 Feb. 31 Sitting by the poolside at the Trinidad Hilton. **1970** P. ZELVER *Honey Bunch* (1971) vii. 34 Trays of hot hors d'œuvres.. which she brought to the poolside. **1973** H. NIELSEN *Severed Key* iv. 39 Zachariah O'Hara.. sat at a poolside table. **1892** JEAN A. OWEN *Within an hour of London Town* (ed. 2) 256 The redshank, *pool-snipe, teuke or took..; all these names are given to him. **1661** LOVELL *Hist. Anim. & Min.* 182 *Poole-snite... They have a strong and unpleasant rellish, and live wholly upon fish.

pool, *sb.*[2] *local.* [Origin unascertained.] A measure of work in roofing and flooring: see quots.

1669 S. COLEPRESS in *Phil. Trans.* IV. 1010 Charges of Covering Houses with Slate... Every Poole of work is either 6 foot broad and 14 foot up, on both sides, or 168 foot in length and one in breadth. **1847–78** in HALLIWELL. **1886** ELWORTHY *W. Somerset Word-bk.* s.v., In building, it is usual to speak of 'a pool of joists'; meaning the number of joists sufficient for the space between the wall and a beam or girder, or between two beams... The word only applies where main beams or short joists between dwarf walls are used... Also used for a similar space on a roof, which is covered by a 'pool o' rafters'.

pool, *sb.*[3] [= F. *poule* in same sense (1676 in Mme. de Sévigné): see Note below.]

1. a. In certain card games, etc.: The collective amount of the stakes and fines of the players joining in the game.

[If, as appears to be the fact, sense 2 was derived from 1, this must have been in use before 1693.]

1711–12 SWIFT *Jrnl. to Stella* 26 Jan., I played at cards this evening at Lady Masham's, but I only played for her while she was waiting; and I won her a pool. **17..** *Reversis*, So that the great quinola pool will consist of 26 fish, and the little quinola pool of 13 fish. Each time that the stakes are drawn, or when there are fewer fish in the pool than the first original stake, the pool must be replenished as at first. **1766** [C. ANSTEY] *Bath Guide* viii 90 Industrious Creatures that make it a Rule To secure half the Fish, while they manage the Pool. **1772** *Town & Country Mag.* 29 Miss D——n.. was hopping away with the pool from the Coterie. **1776** MRS. HARRIS in *Priv. Lett. Ld. Malmesbury* (1870) I. 341 The ton here is the game of 'Commerce', which the fine people play immoderately high, sometimes 1000*l.* the pool, the lowest hand giving ten guineas each deal. **1887** BLACK *S. Zembra* 215 They continued the game.. with the addition of a half-a-crown pool to increase the attraction.

b. The receptacle containing the stakes; the pool-dish. (Quot. 1886 appears to be an error.)

1770 *Streets & Inhabitants of Birmingham* 87 Enamel Manufacturers. These ingenious Artists make Candlesticks, Snuff Boxes, Ink Stands,.. Quadrille Pooles, Smelling Bottles.. and all sort of small Trinkets for Ladies Watches, etc. **1816** SINGER *Hist. Cards* 262 (*Gleek*) If an odd number is given the eldest hand claims the largest half, or else the odd one is given to the pool [1680 COTTON *Gamester* 65, 1734 SEYMOUR *Compl. Gamester* 26, or else it is given to the box]. [**1886** F. G. S. in *N. & Q.* 7th Ser. I. 477/2 Quadrille pools are the fishes or other counters used in playing the old-fashioned game of quadrille.]

†**2.** A party in a card-game, as comet or quadrille, in which there is a pool; a 'game' or match. *to make* (*up*) *a pool*, to form or make up the party or requisite number of players for such a game. *Obs.*

1693 SOUTHERNE *Maid's last Prayer* III. iii, What say you to a Pooile at Comet, At my House? **1732** MRS. DELANY *Autobiogr. & Corr.* (1861) I. 346, I played two pools at commerce. **1796** JANE AUSTEN *Pride & Prej.* xiv, She.. had sent for him only the Saturday before, to make up her pool of quadrille in the evening. **1801** *Sporting Mag.* XVIII. 21 Our party was put off till the Monday, when we played six pools. **1859** THACKERAY *Virgin.* ix, I daresay the resolute lady sat down with her female friends to a pool of cards and a dish of coffee.

3. a. A game played on a billiard-table, in which each player has a ball of distinctive colour with which he tries to pocket the balls of the other players in a certain order, each player contributing an agreed sum, the whole of which at the end falls to the winner; also, a similar game in U.S. played with balls numbered 1 to 15, the number of each ball a player pockets being added to his score. *to shoot pool*: see SHOOT *v.*

1848 THACKERAY *Bk. Snobs* xxiii, He plays pool at the billiard-houses, and may be seen engaged at cards and dominoes of forenoons. **1851** FITZGERALD *Euphranor* (1904) 26 He was waiting till some men had finished a pool of billiards upstairs. **1873** BENNETT & 'CAVENDISH' *Billiards* 5 'French billiards' was essentially single pool. **1887** MISS BRADDON *Like & Unlike* x, They played billiards, pool, or pyramids with skill and success.

b. Colloq. phr. *to play* etc. *dirty pool*: to use unfair tactics; to be dishonest. *N. Amer.*

1951 H. WOUK *Caine Mutiny* xxxvii. 445, I played pretty dirty pool, you know, in court. **1973** *Maclean's Mag.* Feb. 85/2 'You use as much dirty pool as possible,' says an alumnus cheerfully. **1976** *Times Lit. Suppl.* 19 Mar. 326/4 It is, of course, a combination of petty carping and dirty pool to demand of the author of a scholarly work information that does not fall within the limits he has meticulously drawn up for his work.

4. a. *Rifle-shooting.* A contest in which each competitor pays a certain sum for every shot he fires, the proceeds being divided among the winners. Also *attrib.*

1861 *Sat. Rev.* 20 July 57 The attractions of the review and the temptations of pool targets have filled up the void left by the slackness of contributions. **1862** *Ibid.* 5 July 7 The sort of pot-hunting known at Wimbledon and elsewhere as Pool, where the value of a bull's-eye is much more considered than the credit of handling with success the Queen of weapons. **1869** *Daily News* 6 July, Pool and other breech-loading firing is made continuous instead of intermittent.

b. *Betting.* The collective stakes of a number of persons who each stake a sum of money on one of the competitors in some contest, the proceeds being divided among the backers of the winner. Also ***auction pool***, the total sum realized when the names of horses in a race, or likely winners in other contests, are sold by auction to those who wish to hold them; ***to scoop the pool***: see SCOOP *v.*[1] 5 a.

1868 *N.Y. Herald* 3 July 10/1 Let us take a glance at the pool stand before the races begin. **1874** 'MARK TWAIN' *Sk. New & Old* 310 No pools permitted on the run of the comet —no gambling of any kind. **1881** [see PARI MUTUEL]. **1913** A. BENNETT *Regent* II. x. 311 The *Lithuania* was lagging... Every day, in the auction-pool on the ship's run, it was the holder of the lower field that pocketed the money. **1928** *Daily Mail* 7 Aug. 12/5 Stewards are stationed at different points to give weary travellers a welcome lift and prevent them from getting off the beaten track and missing the auction pool. **1949** *Radio Times* 15 July 6/1 Wilfred acts as auctioneer on board the 'Queen Mary' during the pool on the ship's daily run. **1955** *Times* 30 Aug. 5/1 Under the Act, the balance-sheets, to be deposited with the local authority, must show the aggregate total stakes in all pools,.. or, at the option of the promoter, the percentage of the total stakes. **1973** *Irish Times* 2 Mar. 2/6 The unexpected victory of Game Sauce in the second division scuttled jackpot hunters and the pool of £1,027 goes forward to Naas tomorrow.

c. = *football pool*. Usu. *pl.*

1938 *Mass-Observation: First Year's Work 1937–38* iv. 39 The Pools provide an outlet for personal frustration, ambition and faith. **1947** [see BANKER[2] 5]. **1948** M. ALLINGHAM *More Work for Undertaker* xiv. 174, I wouldn't have had this happen, not for a thirty-thousand win in the pools. **1957** *London Mag.* May 48 They see themselves being eaten alive by this ignorant creature, with his telly and his pools, swallowing up all culture. **1958** *Listener* 28 Aug. 308/1 He is telling us about the important things about the working class, how they feel about pools and pubs as well as about socialism, trade unionism, and religion. **1966** A. E. LINDOP *I start Counting* xxi. 266 I'm saving up to buy her a big book on birds... We had a nuthatch last Friday, and you'd think she'd won the pools. **1974** A. FOWLES *Pastime* iv. 39 He sat at the main desk doing his pools... He'd never won a sausage. **1979** *Times* 20 Dec. 15/6 Nearly 60 per cent of people in the country as a whole replied to the question, 'How often do you do the pools?' with 'Never'.

5. a. A common fund into or from which all gains or losses of the contributors are paid; hence, a combination of capitalists for united speculative operation in a stock or commodity; a combine.

1872 W. R. TRAVERS in *N. York Herald* 25 Nov. 8/3, I find myself charged by Mr. Jay Gould.. with being interested in a put or pool in Northwestern common with Mr. Drew,.. and others. **1884** *Boston* (Mass.) *Jrnl.* 29 Jan. 4/4 Stamford rich men have formed a pool to pay the fines imposed upon them for fast driving. **1906** *Blackw. Mag.* Jan. 146/1 His little history of the fifty-million dollar pool in Union Pacific Preferred Stock showed that it was a 'blind pool', to run for five years.

b. A common reservoir of commodities, resources, etc. Cf. *gene pool* s.v. GENE[1] 2.

1917 'CONTACT' *Airman's Outings* 127 Before they join a squadron pilots fresh from their instruction in England gain experience on service machines belonging to the 'pool' at Saint Gregoire. **1940** *Times* (Weekly ed.) 7 June 15 A rice pool has been formed from August 1 through which all rice imported into Singapore must pass. The pool will be used as a means for turning over the emergency stocks of rice which the Government have now acquired. **1943** J. S. HUXLEY *Evolutionary Ethics* vi. 46 The more individuals there exist whose desirable potentialities are fully developed, the more health, vigour, knowledge, wisdom, happiness, beauty and the rest can go into the common pool, and the better that common pool will work. **1946** S. SPENDER *European Witness* i. 11 People like myself could draw on an alleged 'pool' of cars to take them on journeys. **1958** *Observer* 15 June 13/7 Each animal and plant population draws on a large pool of genes. **1963** *Higher Educ.: Rep. Comm. under Ld. Robbins 1961–3* 53 in *Parl. Papers 1962–3* (Cmnd. 2154) XI. 639 The increase has been almost as great among the children of professional parents, where the pool of ability might have been thought more nearly exhausted. **1967** E. SHORT *Embroidery & Fabric Collage* i. 28 A useful 'pool' of ideas will soon be built up to be referred to when needed.

c. A group of persons any one of whose abilities or services may be drawn upon or who share duties; spec. ***typing, typists'***, etc., ***pool***: a number of typists in an organization, department, etc., among whom work is distributed. Hence, also, the office or building where such typists work.

1928 I. CURTIS in *Schools of England* xvii. 333 The staff as a whole is organized as a 'pool' for various miscellaneous duties, such as examination work, the preparation of the tutorial courses. *Ibid.* 334 All the examination work which falls to the Education Board,.. is carried out by the pool as part of the regular work. **1937** V. BARTLETT *This is my Life* x. 150 The typists [of the League of Nations] were.. relegated to a 'pool' at the top of the building. **1942** N. BALCHIN *Darkness falls from Air* vi. 104 How many people are there in your typing pool? **1944** 'N. SHUTE' *Pastoral* iv. 75 Chap with a face like a burglar—came in with the last lot from the pool. **1949** *Manch. Guardian Weekly* 20 Jan. 3 A secretarial 'pool'. **1958** G. GREENE *Our Man in Havana* 58 The secretaries' pool should have been informed. *Ibid.* v. vi. 260 I'll try to stay in the typists' pool. **1959** *Times* 3 Sept. 14/1 A married woman, aged 23, who has settled down in the audio-typing pool after only a few years as a secretary, confessed that she hated it at first but soon changed her mind. **1960** *Guardian* 11 July 3/3 The Derby force opens a new typing pool where the reports.. will be typed. **1960** M. SPARK *Ballad of Peckham Rye* iii. 42 That Miss Coverdale in the pool.. is working Dixie to death. **1970** G. GREER *Female Eunuch* 126 She can command better money and have time off as well if she would only walk out of her typing pool. **1972** K. BENTON *Spy in Chancery* iv. 32 Diana's a competent girl, and she doesn't chatter about her work to the typists' pool.

d. = *pool petrol.*

1940 M. NICHOLSON *How Britain's Resources are Mobilized* 4 In war it [petrol] all goes round in grey tankers and is all called 'Pool'. **1944** *Amer. Speech* XIX. 294 The word 'pool', printed on a strip of paper pasted on a gasoline pump, announces that the pump contains an unidentified brand of gasoline from the nation's pooled supplies, instead of the brand advertised on the pump. **1952** *Economist* 6 Sept. 581 Early in the war all petrol was of uniform quality, the Pool.

e. In a sporting tournament, a group the members of which play against each other to decide which of the competitors or teams qualify for the next round; a minor league.

1955 *Times* 26 May 12/5 His many successes in the matches and 'pools' inaugurated at that time. **1972** *Sunday Tel.* 30 Apr. 34/7 The team flies to Groningen tomorrow, drawn in a tough pool with Poland, Spain and Hungary.

f. A register of free-lance dockworkers seeking employment.

1958 *Engineering* 14 Mar. 329/2 Members of the National Dock Labour Board's 'pool' at the.. group of docks decided to ban overtime in order to spread the work available among the registered workers. **1964** O. E. MIDDLETON in C. K. Stead *N.Z. Short Stories* (1966) 194 The usual round and the same stale answers on every ship: 'All hands are hired through the Pool. Are you established members of the Pool?' **1972** *Guardian* 17 Aug. 1/4, 2,000 [dockers] are going to be put out in Liverpool, and there are 1,200 in the Royal Group on the 'pool' (the temporary, unattached register which is to be abolished under the new proposals).

g. *Biochem.* A quantity of one or more metabolites in some definite part or tissue of the body which is continually being diminished and replenished by cellular activity.

1961 in WEBSTER. **1962** *Bacteriol. Rev.* XXVI. 292/1 Bacteria maintain internally synthesized small molecules at high internal concentrations and in addition have the capacity to concentrate many compounds from the environment. Since the majority of these compounds are intermediates in synthesis, they are collectively termed the pool of metabolic intermediates or, simply, the 'pool'. **1968** *Brit. Med. Bull.* XXIV. 249/2 Fowle, Matthews and Campbell (1964).. put forward a model which separated the body CO_2 into intracellular and extracellular pools. **1971** *Nature* 30 July 329/1 Thus shorter chain acids.. would have been produced by partial degradation of palmitic acid, with concomitant dilution of label by the cellular pool of palmitic acid.

h. A small number of reporters who have access to news sources and pass information to other journalists.

1967 R. J. SERLING *President's Plane is Missing* (1968) vi. 102 Call a press conference and lay it on the line. They can choose themselves between a permanent pool or a one-shot visit. **1973** *Washington Post* 13 Jan. C2/3 Instead of limiting coverage to a selected 'pool' of a few reporters, all accredited reporters and photographers—more than 100—were allowed to attend.

6. An arrangement between previously competing parties, by which rates or prices are fixed, and business or receipts divided, in order to do away with mutually injurious competition: see quot. 1882. Also *attrib.* Originally *U.S.*

1881 *Chicago Times* 1 June, The marine insurance men are still striving to form a pool, and expect soon to succeed. *Ibid.* 4 June, The company will now compete with the other pool lines leading eastward. *Ibid.* 17 June, The agreement for a reorganization of the south-western freight pool. **1882** BITHELL *Counting Ho. Dict.* (1893) 231 The object of a 'pool' is to put an end to the 'war of rates' which breaks out so frequently between two or more competing lines... Sometimes the proceeds of the traffic on competing lines are put into a common fund, and afterwards distributed according to conditions previously agreed on. This is called a 'Financial Pool'. In other cases, arrangements are made for a distribution of the traffic, each line agreeing to accept a specified proportion. This is called a 'Physical Pool'. **1887** *Pall Mall G.* 11 Oct. 12/1 Salt is the latest commodity placed under the control of a pool in the United States... The object of such a pool is 'to keep up the price of salt, and to be able to compete with the foreign manufacturers'.

7. *Fencing.* A contest between teams, in which each member of one side fights each member of the other.

1901 *Oxford Times* 9 Mar. 12/4 What is termed a Poule à l'epée was arranged between teams of six a side, each member of the one team fighting a duel with the six members of the other, in rotation. *Ibid.*, Came out head of the pool, receiving only one hit in his six engagements.

8. *Comb.*, as (in sense 1) ***pool-dish, -game***; (sense 3) ***pool-ball, hall, joint, parlour, -shooter, -shooting, -table***; (sense 4 b) ***pool box, -check, -seller, -selling, -ticket***; (sense 4 c) ***pool-betting, coupon, promoter***; (sense 5 b) ***pool currency, driver, product, service, transport***; (sense 5 c) ***pool typist***; (sense 5 f) ***pool office***; (sense 5 h) ***pool group, policy, reporter, representative***: see also 4 a and 6.

1858 SIMMONDS *Dict. Trade*, *Pool-balls, ivory balls, 9 or 12 to the set, about 2 inches in diameter, for playing a kind of billiards. **1955** T. H. PEAR *Eng. Social Differences* xiii. 293 It is easy to understand why the popularity of all-in wrestling and speedway racing has not spread 'upwards', while that of *pool-betting has. **1957** *Encycl. Brit.* IX. 998/2 In Great Britain the Pool Betting act of 1954 set certain requirements for the conduct of pool betting, including the registration of operators and inspection and publication of financial details. **1878** M. LONG *Life Mason Long* vi. 102 The field won, and after the race I drew six hundred and twenty-five dollars from the *pool-box. **1902** A. D. MCFAUL *Ike Glidden* 171 The vehement cheers of those about the pool box seemed more deafening as the race progressed. **1890** L. C. D'OYLE *Notches* 11, I walked up ter see wot the preacher had giv' him; boys, 'twas nothing but a brass *pool-check. **1951** 'M. INNES' *Operation Pax* II. iv. 63 A few brought *pool coupons from their pockets and studied them. **1955** *Times* 15 Aug. 6/4 The first Brazilian auction of '*pool' currency will be tendered for on Thursday, the statement continues, and the currency thereby made available,.. will be available for the three participating countries. **1878** H. H. GIBBS *Ombre* 19 The Dealer then setting the *pool-dish at his right hand, places in it five points. **1973** A. MANN *Tiara* x. 91 Four or five are in the motor pool for the use of Vatican people on official journeys, but they would have *pool drivers. **1865** *Compl. Domino-Player* 16 Domino *Pool Game.. is played by fitting the same numbers together, as in all the games with dominoes, except the matadore. **1970** *Globe & Mail* (Toronto) 26 Sept. 10/5 The patients spoke mostly in Arabic to an Arab journalist in a *pool group of reporters who were taken to the hospital by the Jordanian army. **1928** *Collier's* 29 Dec. 43/2 He entered a *pool-hall speak-easy. **1944** J. S. PENNELL *Hist. Rome Hanks* 63, I heard a young pool-hall lounger standing idly in Pawnee street refer to him as Old Man Beckham. **1951** [see *joke book*]. **1973** *Black World* May 77/1 Their penchant for open debate in the chop bars.. reappears in our barber shops and pool halls. **1975** *Listener* 18 Dec. 834/3 An endless succession of dreary bars, pool-halls and discos. **1930** H. ZINK *City Bosses in U.S.* 137 Money paid by saloons, gambling and *pool joints, and houses of the underworld. **1964** O. E. MIDDLETON in C. K. Stead *N.Z. Short Stories* (1966) 194 Why do they think we are tramping fifteen miles of dockside, when the other way, you have only to show your papers at the *Pool office, and wait for a ship? **1912** *Pool parlour [see CABARET[1] 2 b]. **1932** J. DOS PASSOS *1919* 413 Izzy had gotten to loafing in poolparlours. **1973** *Washington Post* 13 Jan. C2/3 The new '*pool' policies under which Washington Post reporter Dorothy McCardle was excluded from five previous social events involving President and Mrs. Nixon. **1939** *New Statesman* 18 Nov. 740 The only mystery about the Petroleum Board (the wartime name for the powerful trade committee which fixes distributors' quotas and agrees prices) is that it is unable to get permission from the Government to charge what prices it likes for the imports of '*pool' products. **1940** HARRISON & MADGE *War begins at Home* x. 279 Despite all the efforts of *Pool-promoters, postal facilities were denied, and the vast Pool vested interests were closed down. **1967** MRS. L. B. JOHNSON *White House Diary* 14 Mar. (1970) 496 There were John Gardner and Liz and I and a *pool reporter.. in the tiny room. **1972** *Guardian* 9 June 13/8 The pool reporter ..is the duty man who attends the senator in his intimate and most insignificant moments. Clearly five hundred pressmen.. cannot accompany the senator into a small shirt shop: the pool reporter is their eyes and ears. **1974** *Times* 17 Apr. 14/7 The briefing was open to all Israel newspapers.. but the Foreign Press Association was told it must choose one *pool representative. **1887** *Advance* (Chicago) 13 Oct. 6/1 No less than 15 *poolsellers were in the grand stand. **1888** *Outing* May 118/1 John Hatfield is a bookmaker and pool-seller in St. Louis. **1892** *Pall Mall G.* 4 May 5/1 The New York police have steadfastly resisted the efforts of enterprizing 'pool-sellers' to make betting on horse racing as easy for women as for men. **1869** J. H. BROWNE *Great Metropolis* 573 *Pool selling is managed in this way. **1872** *Alabamian & Times* (Tuscumbia, Alabama) 26 Sept. 4/2 Pool selling is lively and fine sport is anticipated. **1887** *Daily Tel.* 12 Mar. 5/1 Wagering, or, as it is called on the other side of the Atlantic, pool-selling. **1964** *B.E.A. Advance Timetable* (Summer), Pool Services from London: Flights to Denmark, Norway and Sweden are in co-operation with S.A.S... to Prague with C.S.A. and to Warsaw with LOT. **1961** *John o' London's* 2 Nov. 495/1 A professional *pool-shooter. **1974** *Greenville* (S. Carolina) *News-Piedmont* 20 Apr. 8/2 Rudolph Wanderone, known internationally as Minnesota Fats, king of the pool-shooting hustlers, was reported in serious condition Friday after undergoing emergency surgery. **1868** *Pool stand [see sense 4 b above]. **1860** HUGHES *Tom Brown at Oxf.* xxxiii, Tom's good eye and steady hand, and the practice he had had at the.. *pool-table, gave him considerable advantage. **1945** *News Chron.* 7 June 4/3 The bicycles which are being used in these country trips are needed to provide *pool transport for mine workers and farm labourers. **1942** N. BALCHIN *Darkness falls from Air* ix. 121 Pearce rang up with a long tale of woe about being very short of *pool typists. **1979** G. HAMMOND *Dead Game* x. 140 McLure got one of the pool typists put onto it.

b. Pl. (sense 4 c), as ***pools coupon, entry, investor, panel, win, winner***.

1951 A. BARON *Rosie Hogarth* v. iv. 337 Children will be educated.., not just to be office boys and fill in the pools coupon. **1978** J. GALWAY *Autobiogr.* ii. 20 The set.. became the whole focal point of his life every Saturday afternoon when it was time to check the football results for his pools coupon. **1972** A. DRAPER *Death Penalty* i. 5 The copy coupon of his pools entry. **1958** Pools investor [see BANKER[2] 5]. **1976** *Daily Record* (Glasgow) 4 Dec. 30/2 And with the arctic weather spreading south, the Pools Panel have been put on active stand-by. **1963** *Times* 14 Feb. 15/3 An innocent from academe, made footloose by a pools win, incautiously agrees to become guest dramatic critic to the *Evening Gazette*. **1977** J. WAINWRIGHT *Pool of Tears* 203 You know about the pools win. **1960** I. JEFFERIES *Dignity & Purity* xii. 187, I suddenly felt almost like a pools winner. **1973** *Guardian* 1 Mar. 28/5 The biggest pools winner in history.. came to London yesterday to receive his cheque for £542,252—won from a £1 stake.

c. Special Combs., as **pool butter**, the butter of uniform quality available in Britain during the war of 1939–45; **pool car**, (*a*) a freight wagon shared by a number of hirers; (*b*) a car available for the use of a number of drivers; **pool-drive** *v.*, to share vehicles and driving duties on a regular journey; **pool petrol**, the unbranded petrol which was the only grade available in Britain during and just after the 1939–45 war; **pool room**, (*a*) room with billiard tables where pool can be played, usu. for a fee; (*b*) a room where a betting pool is held; a betting shop; **pool shark** *U.S. colloq.*, an expert pool player; one who makes money by winning at pool; **pool train** *Canada*, a train run jointly by more than one railway company; also **pool passenger train**.

1940 Pool butter [see *pool petrol* below]. **1926** *Daily Colonist* (Victoria, B.C.) 18 July 3/5 Victoria Baggage Company. Furniture Moved, Crated and Shipped. Pool Cars for Prairies and All Points East. **1967** *Lebende Sprachen* XII. 186/1 Pool car.. = *Sammelwagen*. **1973** A. MANN *Tiara* xiii. 118 There are five pool cars. **1974** *Globe & Mail* (Toronto) 18 Mar. S6/1 Most go back and forth from Oshawa—working at General Motors is a way of life. They pool-drive. **1959** *Kingston* (Ontario) *Whig-Standard* 28 Sept. 1/5 His death was the fifth caused by the collision in which a CNR freight ripped open the side of a dining car on a pool passenger train being shunted in the yards. **1940** *Weekly Chron.* (Newcastle) 23 Mar., The war has given us special meanings of a number of words already in use—*pool* (for *pool-butter*, *-petrol* etc.). **1949** *Punch* 28 Sept. p. iv, When the days of 'Pool petrol only' are over. **1968** B. FOSTER *Changing Eng. Lang.* iii. 123 Wartime conditions frequently give a new twist to an existing term, e.g. 'austerity, pool (as in 'pool petrol', the unbranded petrol of wartime days), [etc.].' **1861** T. HUGHES *Tom Brown at Oxf.* II. iii. 51 He could go and smoke a cigar in the pool room. **1887** *Chicago Advance* 13 Oct. 6/1 The betting.. is now mostly done in pool-rooms. **1892** *Pall Mall G.* 4 May 5/1 Only one or two of the women came out of the pool-room with more money than when they entered it. **1931** D. RUNYON in *Collier's* 26 Sept. 57/2 We get the race results by phone off a pool room downtown as fast as they come off. **1944** AUDEN *For Time Being* (1945) 50 Back to the upland mill town.. with its grope-movie and its pool-room lit by gas. **1959** N. MAILER *Advts. for Myself* (1961) 74 The poolroom itself was down in the cellar. **1973** *Black World* June 79/1 This style.. emanates from the urban street world of pimps, prostitutes, poolroom sharks. **1978** *Detroit Free Press* 5 Mar. B1/1 My best friend Antoine.. and I were hanging around O'Quinn's poolroom. **1908** *Busy Man's Mag.* Mar. 128 The Pool Shark. Bide Dudley... Blue Book. **1944** W. RUSSELL in *Needle* July 21/2 On the Gulf Coast they'd call him a pool shark and gambler. **1971** J. H. GRAY *Red Lights on Prairies* i. 13 Sometimes they [*sc.* prostitutes] travelled from town to town with pool sharks. **1965** *Globe & Mail* (Toronto) 10 Nov. 19/8 At one time the pool trains ran over the CNR to Brockville and then by CPR tracks to Ottawa... As at the end of October, the pool trains ceased to exist and the two railways went on their separate ways.

[*Note.* In Eng. use this word has undoubtedly from the 18th c. been identified with POOL *sb.*[1]: see quots. 17.., 1766 in sense 1, with their references to the *fish* in the *pool*. But the French use of *poule* for the same thing, with the fact that the French is found earlier, makes it almost certain that the term was taken from Fr., and associated with the Eng. word *pool*. F. *poule* is held to be a sense of *poule* hen, chicken, being perh. at first slang for 'booty, spoil, plunder'. Mme. de Sévigné in a letter of 29 July 1676 uses *poule* exactly in the sense of Eng. *pool*; and in a letter of 30 June 1680 says 'Si Denjean est de ce jeu, il prendra toutes les poules: c'est un aigle', a play upon the sense 'hen'. The Dict. of the Académie, ed. 1, 1694, and that of Furetière, ed. 2, 1701, also explain *poule* almost in the words in which it stands in the Dict. Acad. ed. 7, 1878: 'Poule se dit, à certains jeux, de la quantité d'argent ou de jetons qui résulte de la mise de chacun des joueurs et qui appartient à celui qui gagne le coup. *La poule est grosse. Mettre à la poule. Gagner la poule*'. There is perh. a similar relation between F. *fiche* a fish at cards, and the Eng. 'fish' in the 'pool'.]

pool (puːl), *v.*[1] [f. POOL *sb.*[1]]

1. *intr.* Of land: To be or become marshy or full of pools. Of water: To form pools, to stand, stagnate. Also *transf.* (Not recorded in 18th and 19th c.)

c **1420** *Pallad. on Husb.* I. 89 Ne poole [*v.r.* pulle; L. *stagnet*] hit not, but goodly playn elonge. **1626** BACON *Sylva* §537 On the other side the Water must but Slide, and not stand or Poole. **1973** D. ANDERSEN *Ways Harsh & Wild* iv. 107 Behind our cabin there was a meadow that gradually pooled with water. **1977** *Rolling Stone* 13 Jan. 38/3 An afternoon sun pools warmly on the hardwood floor in the rambling frame house. **1978** C. TOMLINSON *Shaft* 20 The brook.. entered the garden, pooling.

2. *trans.* In quarrying granite: To sink or make (a hole) for the insertion of a wedge; hence ***pool-hole***, a hole made in this process. In coal-mining: To undermine (coal) so as to cause it to fall.

1793 SMEATON *Edystone L.* §91 Holes or notches, cut (or, as they term it, *pooled*) in the surface of the stone. *Ibid.*, These pool-holes are sunk with the point of a pick. **1816** J. A. PARIS *Guide Mounts Bay & Land's End* ii. 45 The method of splitting it [granite] is by applying several wedges to holes cut or (pooled) in the surface of the stone. **1839** URE *Dict. Arts* 979 The first set [of workmen] curves or pools the coal along the whole line of walls, laying in or pooling at least 3 feet. **1863** *N. Brit. Daily Mail* 5 May, [He] was working at the face of the seam, undermining or pooling the coal so as to bring it down.

3. *intr.* Of blood: to accumulate in parts of the venous system, e.g. as a result of the forces produced by continuous acceleration.

1933 *Jrnl. R. Aeronaut. Soc.* XXXVII. 398 Fig. 6 shows a sketch of a device which I suggest might serve to counteract the tendency of centrifugal force to make the blood leave the head and pool in the thin-walled abdominal vessels. **1945** [see ANTI-GRAVITY]. **1962** [see G-SUIT, G-SUIT]. **1962** F. I. ORDWAY et al. *Basic Astronautics* xii. 463 The blood.. increases in weight to the point where the heart can no longer pump it, and it pools in the extremities of the body. **1973** TOWLER & BUTLER-MANUEL *Mod. Obstetr.* xvii. 469 Here the blood 'pools' in the large muscles and is effectively lost to the circulation.

pool (puːl), *v.*[2] [f. POOL *sb.*[3]] **1.** *trans.* To throw into a common stock or fund to be distributed according to agreement; to combine (capital or interests) for the common benefit; *spec.* of competing railway companies, etc.: To share or divide (traffic or receipts). Also *transf.*

1879 *Daily Chron.* 30 Apr., A diminution in the volume of traffic passing over the line under the arrangements made with competing lines to 'pool', or, as in England would be said, to 'divide' the traffic carried. **1879** H. GEORGE *Progr. & Pov.* III. iii. (1881) 166 It is this general averaging, or as we may say, 'pooling' of advantages, which necessarily takes place. **1884** *Pall Mall G.* 2 Aug. 5/1 The arrangement for 'pooling' the Continental traffic of the two companies to Folkestone. **1895** *Westm. Gaz.* 25 Sept. 1/3 The endowed funds of the Church ought to be pooled, equalised, and redistributed according to the work done. **1921** G. B. SHAW *Back to Methuselah* p. lxxvii, What we should do, then, is to pool our legends and make a delightful stock of religious folk-lore on an honest basis for all mankind. **1926** *Amer. Mercury* Dec. 462/2 Sime countered by pooling his stories with the other fellow. **1927** E. THOMPSON *These Men, thy Friends* 245 Hart and Kenrick pooled friends. **1940** *Hutchinson's Pict. Hist. War* 14 Feb.–4 Sept. 68 Petrol was pooled, buildings were seized, children were sent to safety. **1955** *Times* 16 Aug. 9/3 The sterling, Deutschmarks, and guilders which the Brazilian exchange control authorities secure from the proceeds of Brazilian exports will be 'pooled', and when in future they are 'auctioned' importers who buy them will be free to use them for imports from any one of the three countries. **1978** S. BRILL *Teamsters* vi. 220 In a rare display of cooperation,..the IRS and FBI agreed to pool their efforts. **1979** *Canad. Jrnl. Linguistics* XXIV. i. 35 Unfortunately, Brown pooled the data, so that if any developmental trends were present, they were obscured in the analysis.

2. *Austral. slang.* To implicate; involve a person against his will; inform on.

1919 W. H. DOWNING *Digger Dial.* 39 *Pool*, to involve; cast blame or a burden on. **1928** A. WRIGHT *Good Recovery* 117 Leave the sheilas alone; they're sure to pool a man sooner or later. **1932** W. HATFIELD *Ginger Murdoch* 282 To rig that evidence against him—pool him. **1942** L. MANN *Go-Getter* 313, 'I got pooled into it,' he explained. **1967** K. TENNANT *Tell Morning This* 85 A man thought he'd do the decent thing and tide a girl over a patch of trouble, and she pools him every time. You can't prove it isn't your kid.

Hence **pooled** *ppl. a.*; **'pooling** *vbl. sb.*

1884 *American* VII. 229 A pooling combination to regulate prices. **1884** *Pall Mall G.* 30 Apr. 11/1, I don't think this pooling of the [railway] rates will stand. **1888** *Ibid.* 21 Jan. 2/2 Negotiations..with a view of extending the pooled area. **1892** *Nation* (N.Y.) 15 Dec. 446/1 The repeal of the section of the law prohibiting railway pooling. **1928** *Manch. Guardian Weekly* 10 Aug. 104/2 Washington, too, is shown by the dispatches to suspect something like an Anglo-French alliance or merger or pooling behind the text of the naval compromise. **1936** *Discovery* Aug. 232/1 It was to be hoped that such pooling of knowledge might become world-wide. **1943** J. S. HUXLEY *Evolutionary Ethics* 39 Part of the blind struggle for existence between separate individuals or groups is transposed into conflict in consciousness..within the tradition which is the vehicle of pooled social consciousness. *Ibid.* 45 The pooling of experience and co-operative action in a cumulative tradition. **1946** J. W. DAY *Harvest Adventure* xvi. 278 As to the waste of 'pooled' machinery, this is a sore point in many counties. **1951** *N.Y. Times* 21 Aug. 1/6 A pooled dispatch said the services had 'an almost carnival atmosphere'. **1955** *Bull. Atomic Sci.* Apr. 146/1 In science, only a pooling of all new ideas can lead to progress. **1967** *Oceanogr. & Marine Biol.* V. 162 When animals are small, biochemical study of a pooled sample from many specimens is imperative. **1971** *Jrnl. Gen. Psychol.* LXXXV. 111 The baseline performance of the pooled controls. **1975** *Language for Life* (Dept. Educ. & Sci.) iii. 40 It is an essential principle of the item pooling system that assessment can reflect changes in the use of language and stylistic differences over the years.

pool, dial. f. PULL *v.*

pool, poole, obs. ff. POLE, POLL.

Poole (pu:l). The name of a town in Dorset, used *attrib.* to designate a type of clay suitable for pottery found near there, or pottery manufactured there.

1878 *Encycl. Brit.* VIII. 229/2 Of importance next to it [*sc.* kaolin], as potter's material, is the 'Poole clay' of Dorsetshire. **1924** *Design in Mod. Industry: Year-Bk. of Design & Industries Assoc. 1923–24* 51 (*caption*) The painted dish in the upper illustration is a piece of Poole pottery, and shows how essentially decorative simple colour groupings may appear on surfaces uncomplicated by needless corrugations. **1938** *Decorative Art* p. x, Poole pottery... If there is a mantleshelf..it is a narrow one, but there are Poole Pots to meet the difficulty. **1957** [see DORSET]. **1971** R. RENDELL *No More Dying Then* i. 11 There were flowers..in the Poole pottery vases.

pooled (pu:ld), *a. rare.* [f. POOL *sb.*[1] + -ED[2].] Furnished with or placed in a pool. Also *fig.*

1947 DYLAN THOMAS *Let.* 20 May (1966) 307 The pooled ponded..garden. **1967** F. WARNER *Madrigals* 10 You stand Pooled in discarded clothes.

pooler, var. POLER (sense 1).

pool-hole: see POOL *v.*[1] 2.

pooly ('pu:lɪ), *a.* [f. POOL *sb.*[1] + -Y.] Resembling a pool; abounding in pools; swampy.

1821 JOANNA BAILLIE *Metr. Leg., Wallace* viii, As angler in the pooly wave. **1822** *Blackw. Mag.* XI. 181 The water struggled onwards through narrow gullets, boiling caldrons, and pooly whirls.

pooly ('pu:lɪ), *sb. rare.* [f. POOL *sb.*[1] + -Y[6].] A small pool, *spec.* of urine.

1922 JOYCE *Ulysses* 529 It's as limp as a boy of six's doing his pooly behind a cart.

pooly, obs. f. PULLEY.

poomel, obs. f. POMMEL.

poomgarnet, -gernett, obs. ff. POMEGRANATE.

poompe, obs. f. PUMP.

‖**poon** (pu:n), *sb.*[1] Also 7 pone, 9 puhn, puna, poona, -ay. [Singhalese *pūna*, Tamil *punnai*.] One of several large East Indian trees of the genus *Calophyllum*, esp. *C. Inophyllum*; also, the timber furnished by these trees, used for masts and spars, and for building purposes. Chiefly *attrib.*, as *poon-mast*, *-spar*, *-tree*, *-wood*; **poon-oil**, a dark-green thick oil, having a strong scent and bitter taste, expressed from the seeds of *C. Inophyllum* (**poon-seed**), used in medicine and for burning in lamps.

1699 DAMPIER *Voy.* II. I. 64 For Masting, the Fir and Pone Trees are the best. **1727** A. HAMILTON *New Acc. E. Ind.* I. xxii. 264 There is good Poon Masts, stronger, but heavier than Fir. **1840** *Encycl. Brit.* (ed. 7) XXI. 300/2 Poon is also of two kinds, the dark and the light. It is a wood that answers very well for masts... The Malacca red poon is that of which masts and yards are made. **1858** SIMMONDS *Dict. Trade*, *Poon-wood*, an Indian wood,..used for ship-building, for planks, and also for spars. **1880** C. R. MARKHAM *Peruv. Bark* 377 The poon trees..are chiefly found in Coorg.

poon (pu:n), *sb.*[2] *slang* (chiefly *Austral.*). [Origin obscure.] **a.** A simple or foolish person. **b.** A person living alone in the outback.

1940 M. MARPLES *Public School Slang* 60 Another considerable group of words in recent use has a definite trans-atlantic flavour, as, for example: boob..goof..mutt.. poon (Dulwich, 1930 +). **1941** BAKER *Dict. Austral. Slang* 56 *Poon*, a lonely, somewhat crazy dweller in the Outer Beyond... A simpleton or fool. **1945** —— *Austral. Lang.* v. 97 Another outback term for a person who lives alone is *poon*. **1972** G. MORLEY *Jockey rides Honest Race* 73 They don't look for the guts of a lecture; just the mistakes. Then they can get up and shoot their mouths off and everybody else nods wisely and tries to pick up the mistakes of the poon that's just said his piece. **1974** D. WILLIAMSON *Jugglers Three* in *Three Plays* 69 What possessed Keren to shack up with a poon like you?

poon, *sb.*[3] *slang.* Abbrev. of POONTANG *sb.*

1969 J. LEASOR *They don't make them like that any More* vi. 192 It's against my principles to pay for poon: if I can't get it for what is laughingly called love, then I'll do without. **1972** J. WAMBAUGH *Blue Knight* (1973) i. 16 Watching all that young poon.

poon (pu:n), *v. Austral. slang.* [Origin obscure.] To dress *up*; esp. to dress flashily. Also in pa. pple. *pooned up*.

1943 BAKER *Dict. Austral. Slang* (ed. 3) 61 *Poon up*, to dress up, especially in flashy fashion. **1945** —— *Austral. Lang.* 206 School slang...*poon up*, to dress up, especially with considerable care. **1951** D. STIVENS *Jimmy Brockett* 48 Some of 'em were young lairs, all pooned up to kill. **1972** A. CHIPPER *Aussie Swearer's Guide* 48 *Pooned up*, dressed to impress, often with sexual success in view.

Poona ('pu:nə). Also **Poonah**. Name of an Indian city in the Bombay Presidency (now in Maharashatra State); *attrib.* in **Poona painting**, an artistic process in imitation of oriental work, in which pictures of flowers, birds, etc. were produced on rice (or other thin) paper, by the application of thick body-colour, with little or no shading, and without background: fashionable in England in the early part of the 19th c. So **Poona brush**, a stumpy round-headed brush used for this; **Poona paper**, the paper on which it was done; **Poona-painted** *a.*; **Poona painter**. (See *N. & Q.* 10th s. VII. 107, 152.) Also as *adj.*, with allusion to the attitudes, way of life, etc., held to be characteristic of the Army officers stationed there during British rule.

1821 *Examiner* 272/2 The Poonah taught in a superior style. Ladies instructed in the above Elegant Art. **1822–3** *Pigot & Co.'s Directory*, Cheltenham..Stanton Mrs., Indian poonah painter, 21 Bath Street. **1829** *Yng. Lady's Bk.* 469 A piece of tracing-paper, of a peculiar manufacture, which is sold at the stationers' shops as Poonah-paper. **1840** THACKERAY *Paris Sk.-bk.* (1869) 153 What are called 'mezzotinto' pencil-drawings, 'poonah paintings', and what not. **1859** SALA *Tw. round Clock* (1861) 179 Two pairs of silver grape-scissors, a poonah-painted screen, a papier-mâche work-box. **1889** *Anthony's Photogr. Bull.* II. 48 It may be applied by using a strong hog hair or poonah brush charged with vermilion. **1939** G. TREAST in *Best One-Act Plays 1938* 63 Major Manners is discovered playing patience... He is an elderly, heavily jovial man, who, in spite of twenty years' Isolation, remains essentially pukka and Poona. **1944** 'N. SHUTE' *Pastoral* vi. 138 They're county people, all frightfully toffee-nosed and Poona. **1973** 'B. MATHER' *Snowline* iv. 49 Blimey! Class consciousness rearing its ugly head... How Poonah-Poonah can you get? **1975** A. CHRISTIE *Curtain* i. 7 One of your so British old Colonels—very 'old school tie' and 'Poona'.

‖**poonac** ('pu:næk). [Tamil *Punnakku*, Singhalese *Punakku*.] The oil-cake or mass left after the oil has been expressed from coco-nut pulp: used as fodder or manure.

1890 in WEBSTER. **1927** *Trop. Agriculturalist* LXVIII. 279 As regards Phosphorus, there are many food-stuffs, available in Ceylon, rich in this element. For example, the various poonacs and pollard.

poonahlite ('pu:nəlaɪt). *Min.* Also **poona-**, **punah-**. [f. *Poonah* (*Púna*) in India, where found + -LITE.] A variety of SCOLECITE from Poonah.

1831 H. J. BROOKE in *Philos. Mag.* Ser. II. X. 110 *Poonahlite*..a beautiful variety of apophyllite from Poonah, ..accompanied by some slender crystals, which I at first supposed were mesotype or needle-stone, but which differ from both substances in measurement; the *Poonahlite* being a rhombic prism of 92°20'. **1866** WATTS *Dict. Chem.* IV. 689 Poonahlite. *Ibid.* Index, *Punahlite*.

poonask, var. PONASK *v.*

poond, -e, obs. ff. POND, POUND (an enclosure).

‖**poonga-oil** ('pu:ŋgəɔɪl). [f. Tamil *punga* or Malayal(an) *pungam*, name of the plant.] A dark-yellow oil expressed from the seeds of the KURUNG, *Pongamia glabra*, and used in India as lamp-oil and as a remedy in skin-diseases; Kurung oil.

1866 *Treas. Bot.* 919/1 In India an oil, called Kurunj, or Poonga oil, is expressed from the seeds. **1890** BILLINGS *Med. Dict.* II. 370/2 Poonga oil is in high repute in India as an application for scabies and other skin diseases.

‖**poonghie, phoongyee, phungyi** ('pɒŋgi, 'pʌndʒɪ). Forms: 8 pongui, 9 phonghi, -gee, phoongee, -gye(e, poongee, -ghee, -ghie, -gy, -gyee, pongyi. [Burmese *hpōngyī*, f. *hpōn* glory, *kyī* great.] The name generally given in Burma to a Buddhist priest or monk. Also *attrib.*

1788 F. MAGNUS tr. *Sonnerat's Voy.* III. 17 Their Priests ..are called Ponguis, and are less informed than the Bramins. **1834** BP. BIGANDET in *Jrnl. Ind. Archip.* IV. 222–3 (Y.) The Talapoins are called by the Burmese Phonghis, which term means 'great glory'. **1879** F. POLLOK *Sport Brit. Burmah* II. 7 The poonghee houses or monasteries are splendid. **1897** LD. ROBERTS *41 Yrs. India* lxvi. (1898) 518, I still hear occasionally from one or other of my Poonghie friends. **1899** F. T. BULLEN *Log Sea-waif* 302 Yellow-garbed, close-shaven Phoongyees were squatting all over the pavement. **1929** F. T. JESSE *Lacquer Lady* I. v. 36 The King had allowed it [*sc.* the house] to be built with a triple roof, a thing usually only permitted to Princes and poongyis. *Ibid.* II. i. 118 After the litter came sixty-five poongyis..; they walked with downcast eyes, holding their fans up so that they should not by any chance catch sight of a woman. **1930** *Aberdeen Press & Jrnl.* 29 May 7/5 Last night a pongyi (Burmese priest) attempted to stab a military policeman. **1951** 'N. SHUTE' *Round Bend* 122 He has been a Buddhist monk, a pongyi we call them, for over thirty years. **1966** D. FORBES *Heart of Malaya* xi. 129 Miss Khan..took me across the lane to the Burmese *wat* and kowtowed to the *pongyi* in the temple hall.

poontang ('pu:ntæŋ), *sb. U.S. slang.* Also **poon tang** and with capital initial(s). [Prob. ad. Fr. *putain* prostitute.] Sexual intercourse, sex; women collectively, or a woman, regarded as a means of sexual gratification. Also *attrib.* Hence as *v. intr.*, to copulate.

1929 T. WOLFE *Look Homeward, Angel* 343 A fellow's got to have a little Poon Tang. **1947** C. WILLINGHAM *End as Man* II. vii. 78 Poley looked out the window and saw a pretty Negro girl on the sidewalk... 'Eye that poon tang there,' he said. **1959** R. CONDON *Manchurian Candidate* ii. 21 Every now and then I think about you coming all the way to Korea from New Jersey to get your first piece of poontang. **1966** C. HINES *Heat's On* xv. 122 That ain't our racket. We just sells poontang here. **1968** E. J. GAINES *Bloodline* 144 Yesterday this time I was poon-tanging like a dog. **1970** D. DODGE *Hatchetman* x. 127 'Is it true what they say about gook women?'..'I heah it changes youah luck, though. Like black poontang.' **1972** 'T. COE' *Don't lie to Me* iv. 44 May be you're some kind of poontang sex maniac. **1972** *Listener* 22 June 845/2 Massa gonna smack yo black ass, nigger. You can't go chasing white poontang all night long. **1976** *Honolulu Star-Bull.* 21 Dec. E-10/6 (Advt.), The other girls majored in home ec...but Debby majored in Poon-tang.

poop (pu:p), *sb.*[1] Forms: 5 pouppe, pope, poppe, 5–7 powpe, 6 pupe, pewpe, 6–7 poup(e, poope, puppe, pup, (7 pub), 7– poop. [ME. a. OF. *pupe*, *pope* (*c* 1400 in Godef. *Compl.*), F. *poupe* = It. *poppa*, Prov., Sp., Pg. *popa*:—late L. **puppa* for L. *puppis* poop, stern.]

1. a. The aftermost part of a ship; the stern; also, the aftermost and highest deck, often forming the roof of the cabin built in the stern.

1489 CAXTON *Faytes of A.* II. ii. 93 The pouppe whiche is the hindermost partye of the shippe. **1495** *Naval Acc. Hen. VII* (1896) 195 In the poppe of the seid shipp. **1496** *Ibid.* 176 The dekke ovyr the somercastell & the pope. **1497** *Ibid.* 227 The powpe abaft. **1555** EDEN *Decades* 203 The highest parte of the Castel of the poope. **1558** PHAER *Æneid* I. A ij b, There fell a sea that made the puppe to yelde. **1566** J. PARTRIDGE *Plasidas* 492 The lusty fish begin at paynted pupe to toy. **1573** TWYNE *Æneid* x. E e j, She with right hand pup did shoue. **1581** J. BELL *Haddon's Answ. Osor.* 452 The chief prore and pewpe (as the Proverbe is) and shooteanker of their whole Idolatrous Sacrifice. **1606** SHAKS. *Ant. & Cl.* II. ii. 197 The Poope was beaten Gold. **1643** PRYNNE *Sov. Power Parl.* App. 209 Those are equally safe who are in the fore part, as those who are in the puppe. **1674** tr. *Scheffer's Lapland* xxi. 101 Made in the fashion of half a boat having ..the poupe of one flat board. **1704** J. HARRIS *Lex. Techn.* I, *Poop of a Ship*, is the Floor or Deck over the Round-house or Master's Cabbin, being the highest part or uppermost part of her Hull astern. **1776** MICKLE tr. *Camoens' Lusiad* 53 High on the poop the skilful master stands. **1868** *Regul. & Ord. Army* §1305 When the prisoners are on deck, the detachment of Troops is to be on the poop.

†**b.** *at poop, in* (*the, one's*) *poop*, of the wind: Astern. Hence *fig. Obs.*

1567 GOLDING *Ovid* XII. 148 b, The thousand shippes had wynd at poope. **1588** HICKOCK tr. *Frederick's Voy.* 31 They goe to Pegu, with the winde in powpe. **1598** BARCKLEY *Felic. Man* (1631) 411 They continue with him so long as the wind bloweth in the poope. **1621** MOLLE *Camerar. Liv. Libr.* IV. ix. 255 When they saw the wind blew merrily in their poope. **1687** A. LOVELL tr. *Thevenot's Trav.* I. 16 We bore away to the starboard..with a Wind in Poop.

c. *transf.* A cabin built on the after part of the quarter-deck; a round-house. *rare.*

1551 *Acts Privy Counc.* (1891) III. 257 The covering of clothe of golde belonging to the captaines cabane or powpe of the Gallie.

†**2.** *transf.* The dickey or seat at the back of a coach; the hinder part of a man or animal, the posteriors, rump. *colloq.* or *vulgar. Obs.*

c **1614** FLETCHER, etc. *Wit at Sev. Weap.* IV. i, If you.. meet a footman by the way, in orange-tawny ribbands, running before an empty coach, with a buzzard [the bare-headed lackey] i' th' poop on't. *c* **1645** HOWELL *Lett.* (1650) II. 25 She took a mouthfull of claret, and spouted it into the poope of the hollow bird. **1706** E. WARD *Wooden World Diss.* (1708) 96 While he manages his Whip-staff with one Hand, he scratches his Poop with the other.

3. *attrib.* and *Comb.*, as ***poop-cabin, -deck, -end, -ladder, -rail, -staff***; **poop-break**, the front of the poop of a ship; **poop-lantern, -light**, a lantern or light carried at the stern to serve as a signal at night; **poop-ornament** *Naut. slang*, a ship's apprentice; **poop-royal**, the deck forming the roof of the poop-cabin; a top-gallant-poop.

1912 J. MASEFIELD in *Eng. Rev.* Oct. 353 Under the *poop break, sheltering from the rain. **1851** W. COLTON *Deck & Port* i. 16 Another order soon came for the construction of a *poop-cabin. **1840** R. H. DANA *Bef. Mast* xvii, A large, clumsy ship,..with her top-masts stayed forward, and high *poop-deck. **1839** MARRYAT *Phant. Ship* x, Philip remained on deck by the *poop-ladder. **1727–41** CHAMBERS *Cycl.* s.v. *Ship*, Plate, Hull..*Poop Lanthorns. **1769** FALCONER *Dict. Marine* (1789), *Aiguille de fanal*, an iron crank or brace, used to sustain the poop-lanthorn. **1836** E. HOWARD *R. Reefer* lvii, We carried..the customary *poop-light of the commodore. **1902** *Athenæum* 8 Feb. 177/1 He [*sc.* the apprentice in the merchant service] was and is emphatically the ship's loblolly-boy..miscalled 'a blarsted *poop ornament', the drudge even of ordinary seamen. **1934** J. MASEFIELD *Taking of Gry* 75, I looked at these fellows, and concluded that the lieutenant was a young poop-ornament and that the men were slacking. **1867** SMYTH *Sailor's Word-bk.*, **Poop-rails*, the stanchions and rail-work in front of the poop. **1769** FALCONER *Dict. Marine* (1789), *Dunette sur Dunette*, the *poop-royal. **1800** *Naval Chron.* III. 274 The poop royal, in our present first rates is omitted. **1847** GROTE *Greece* II. xxxvi. IV. 472 Kynegeirus..in laying hold on the *poop-staff of one of the vessels, had his hand cut off by an axe.

poop (puːp), *sb.*[2] Also 6 poope; (*S. Afr.*) ‖poep. [Echoic, or f. POOP *v.*[1] Cf. LG. *pup, pūp*, Du. *poep* crepitus ventris.] **1.** A short blast in a hollow tube, as a wind instrument; a toot; a gulping sound. Also, the report of a gun.

a **1553** UDALL *Royster D.* II. i. (Arb.) 32 Then to our recorder with toodleloodle poope As the howlet out of the yuie bushe should hoope. *c* **1580** JEFFERIE *Bugbears* v. vii. in *Archiv Stud. Neu. Spr.* (1897), I taught them thier lerrie, and thier poop to, for their knacking. **1674** RAY *N.C. Words* 37 *Poops*, Gulps in drinking. **1772** *Ann. Reg.* 99/1 When this captain [frog] gives the signal for stopping, you hear a note like *poop* coming from him. **1908** K. GRAHAME *Wind in Willows* vi. 128, I faithfully promise that the very first motor-car I see, poop-poop! off I go in it! **1919** W. DEEPING *Second Youth* xxviii. 240 The faint 'poop-poop' of distant anti-aircraft guns..brought Laverack sharply back to the immediate present.

2. *slang* (orig. children's). An act of breaking wind or of defecation; faeces. Also *fig.*

Quot. *c* 1744 is an *interj.*

c **1744** [see HOLE *sb.* 8]. **1937** PARTRIDGE *Dict. Slang* 648/2 *Poop*,..a breaking of wind. **1948** *Amer. Speech* XXIII. 264 We used the words *poop* and *poot* with their onomatopoeic significance in regard to bodily discharges. **1974** *Amer. Speech 1971* XLVI. 82 *Fart*,..poop. **1976** *Telegraph* (Brisbane) 7 June 9/2 A young woman claims a 'bird poop treatment' has cured her of a chronic dandruff... She's been free of dandruff since a mynah bird relieved himself on her head during lunch one day. **1977** J. MCCLURE *Sunday Hangman* x. 105 Ja, we scared the poop out of him that time. **1977** *Listener* 22–29 Dec. 842/3 That's just a set-up... He just says all that kind of poop about you in the beginning.

3. *attrib.* and *Comb.*, as **poop-butt** (see quot.); **poophead** *U.S.* (see quot.); **poop-hole** (in quot. *S. Afr.*), anus; **poop-pusher** (see quot.); **poop-scared** *a.* (in quot. *S. Afr.*), extremely frightened, = *shit-scared* adj.; **poop scoop** *joc.*, an implement used for clearing up faeces; so **pooper scooper**; **poop-stick**, a fool, ineffectual person (cf. POOP *sb.*[4]).

1973 C. & R. MILNER *Black Players* ii. 42 A *poop-butt* is a lazy person. **1977** *Amer. Speech 1975* L. 64 *Poophead*, person regarded as dull or stupid. **1969** A. FUGARD *Boesman & Lena* I. 26 That tickey deposit heart of his is tight like his *poephol* and his fist. **1966** 'L. LANE' *ABZ of Scouse* 83 *Poop-pusher*, a laxative, especially one of satisfactory violence. **1976** in J. Branford *Dict. S. Afr. Eng.* (1978) 188/1 OK so they give up at last, but..never been so poep-scared in my whole entire life before or since. **1976** *Maclean's Mag.* 12 Jan. 34/1 A man on a motor-cycle with a pooper-scooper would be dispatched to clean up. **1977** J. WAMBAUGH *Black Marble* (1978) viii. 112 Bring your pooper-scoopers, boys. The dogs are covering the red carpet in a sea of shit. **1978** *Daily Tel.* 24 July 13/6 It may soon be common to see people holding a dog lead in one hand and a 'poop scoop' in the other. **1978** *Daily Tel.* 17 Aug. 3/3 The 'pooper-scooper' law in New York requires dog-owners to pick up anything their dogs drop. **1930** 'HAY' & WODEHOUSE *Baa, Baa, Black Sheep* II. 55, I believe she really does care for that poop-stick... Fancy loving a man called Osbert Bassington-Bassington! **1932** P. MACDONALD *Rope to Spare* viii. 100 'You make me sick!' he said. 'Let a little poop-stick like that walk all over you!'

†**poop**, *sb.*[3] *Obs.* In 6 pope, 7 poope. [Origin unascertained.] Some part of the furniture of a church bell: 'perh. the "stay" by which the swing of a bell is regulated, moving against the "slider"' (*Gloss.* to work cited for quot. 1625).

1527–8 *Rec. St. Mary at Hill* 264 Item, payd for v bell popys for the bell Ropys xv d. **1625** *Churchw. Acc. St. Mary, Reading* (1893) 137 Paid for a board for the treble poope to save it 11 d. **1631** *Ibid.* 147 Paid to willis for poopes and strapes for the bell this yeire, 9s. 9d.

poop (puːp), *sb.*[4] *colloq.* [Perh. abbrev. of NINCOMPOOP.] A stupid or ineffectual person; a fool, a bore.

1915 V. WOOLF *Voyage Out* iii. 51 They talk about art, and think us such poops for dressing in the evening. **1924** 'SAPPER' *Third Round* vii. 189 The genuine Professor Scheidstrun appeared to be a harmless old poop, who was more sinned against than sinning. **1936** C. S. FORESTER *General* xv. 155 Every little poop of a temporary major-general. **1942** WODEHOUSE *Money in Bank* (1946) xx. 169 For God's sake, don't put your trust in that poop. **1952** S. KAUFFMANN *Philanderer* (1953) iii. 42 Yes, yell for your father. I'd like to get a look at the poop. I'd like to pick you up and throw you at him. **1966** H. MARRIOTT *Cariboo Cowboy* ix. 86 It seemed to me that a real snotty-nosed poop like him was a poor character to have in that sort of job. **1971** R. DENTRY *Encounter at Kharmel* xii. 211 Those stupid bloody Yankee poops blew the panic whistle and the whole shebang went sky-high. **1972** D. DELMAN *Sudden Death* iv. 95 'Honey, I do declare you've turned into nothing but an old poop,' she said.

poop (puːp), *sb.*[5] *slang* (orig. and chiefly *U.S.*). [Origin obscure.] Up-to-date or 'inside' information, 'low-down'. Freq. *attrib.* in **poop-sheet**, a written notice, bulletin, or report.

1941 *Amer. Speech* XVI. 167/2 *Poop sheet*, drill schedule or any written announcement. **1947** *Ibid.* XXII. 216 The word *poop*, which indicated the latest information, whether official or unofficial, was also incorporated into *poop sheet*, denoting the latest bulletin or directive. **1950** 'D. DIVINE' *King of Fassarai* ii. 14 Have you picked up any poop about where the ship's going..? *Ibid.* xxiv. 205 'Have you seen the poop sheet anywhere?..' 'Aw, hell... There ain't any news anyway.' **1961** B. MALAMUD *New Life* (1962) 300, I sent out a poop sheet this afternoon..with the names of the nominees. **1963** H. SLESAR *Bridge of Lions* (1964) v. 84 I've asked Sandy to send me a poop sheet on him, but may be you can add something. **1973** R. HAYES *Hungarian Game* xxi. 130 How did you get the poop on Kovács? **1974** 'M. ALLEN' *Super Tour* vii. 264 He sends in a report—straight facts, no frills, and a minimum use of adjectives. What he says is included in the mimeographed poop sheet the organization sends out every month. **1976** *Sounds* 11 Dec. 33 (*heading*) Hot poop on old punks.

poop (puːp), *v.*[1] Forms: 5 poupe, powpe, pope, 6– poop, (9 *dial.* pup). [ME. *poupen*, of echoic origin: cf. MLG., LG. *pūpen*, MDu., Du. *poepen*.] **1.** †**a.** *intr.* To make an abrupt sound as by blowing a horn; to blow, toot; to gulp in drinking.

c **1386** CHAUCER *Nun's Pr. T.* 579 Of bras they broghten bemes and of box Of horn of boon in whiche they blewe and powped [*v.rr.* poupid, pouped, poped]. *c* **1386** —— *Manciple's Prol.* 90 And whan he hadde pouped in this horn To the Manciple he took the gourde agayn. **1593** R. BARNES *Parthenophil & P.* Ode xi. in Arb. *Garner* V. 457 The Shepherds poopen in their pipe.

b. (See quots.) *dial.* and *vulgar.*

1721–36 BAILEY, *To Poop*, to break Wind backwards softly. **1903** *Eng. Dial. Dict.*, Poop, *v.*, *Cacare*, used of and by children. **1937** PARTRIDGE *Dict. Slang* 648/2 *Poop*,..to defecate..mostly of and by children. **1972** L. HANCOCK *There's a Seal in my Sleeping Bag* vii. 165 The joys of motherhood were considerably lessened when a baby murre pooped with regularity between my shirt and bare warm skin. **1974** *Cape Times* 1 Aug. 11/5 Five-year-old eyes grow round with wonder at the memory of the elephant 'pooping' on the carpet.

2. a. *trans.* To fire (a bullet, shell, or other missile); to discharge (a gun); to shoot (a person or animal). Freq. with *off*. Also *transf.* and *fig.*

1917 W. OWEN *Let.* 6 Dec. (1967) 514, I shall continue to poop off heavy stuff at you, till you get my range at Scarborough, and so silence me. **1929** [see HEAT *sb.* 12 b] **1937** P. B. HAWK *Off Racket* ii. 99 At any rate he pooped the ball into the [tennis] net. **1940** *Manch. Guardian Weekly* 5 Apr. 277 An old wildfowler..earns a precarious living by stealing down the estuaries with a home-made blunderbuss or duck-gun and pooping it off at..sea-fowl. **1940** 'N. SHUTE' *Landfall* 142 'Can't we fly it over a known ship and poop it off?' he said. 'Poop off half a dozen of them.' **1960** *Guardian* 9 Nov. 7/7 The emergency code word has just been flashed through... Is it all right by London if they poop off their Polarises? **1974** A. PRICE *Other Paths to Glory* II. vi. 187 There was this Jerry prisoner..and this Aussie comes up..and he poops him... Kills him—shoots him.

b. *intr.* Of a person: to fire a gun, to shoot; also in weakened sense: to go. Of a gun or similar device: to go off, to fire. Usu. with adv., as *away, off*, etc.

1919 *Chambers's Jrnl.* Jan. 43/1 As soon as the artillery opens up, poop off for all you're worth. Let 'em have a hurricane. **1928** BLUNDEN *Undertones of War* ii. 22 A field battery glaring brutally out would 'poop off'. **1930** R. PERTWEE *Pursuit* 59, I arrived about eight last night and the guns were pooping away like mad. **1931** N. COWARD *Post Mortem* i. 13 If it only stays quiet the way it has the last three nights, and that machine-gun from the sunken road doesn't start pooping at us—we'll get through it in a few hours. **1942** T. RATTIGAN *Flare Path* I. 112 What in hell was the idea of pooping off the Station like that? They told you this morning something still might come through. **1945** *Tee Emm* (Air Ministry) V. 40 It will not..poop off automatically. **1956** 'TAFFRAIL' *Arctic Convoy* xxiii. 237 See to it you don't open up on anything unless you've a damn good chance of hitting. No wild pooping off at targets out of range—understand? **1961** *Encounter* June 21/1 Take getting up in the morning. 'I arise,' he says..'and poop along..to the end of the passage..to get in the milk and the papers.'

†**poop**, *v.*[2] *Obs.* Forms: 6 powp(e, 6–7 poup(e, poop(e. [Of obscure derivation: cf. Du. *poep* a clown (Franck).] *trans.* To deceive, cheat, cozen, befool.

1575 *Gamm. Gurton* II. i, But there ich was powpte indeede. **1596** NASHE *Saffron Walden* 134 Wee shall.. trumpe and poope him well enough if..he will needes fall a comedizing it. **1608** SHAKS. *Per.* IV. ii. 25, I, shee quickly poupt him, she made him roast-meate for wormes. *a* **1650** MAY *Satyr. Puppy* (1657) 26 My two Gallants, (being poopt of what they enjoyed meerly to feel misery in the losse). **1663** DRYDEN *Wild Gallant* IV. ii, Hee's poopt too.

poop (puːp), *v.*[3] *Naut.* [f. POOP *sb.*[1]] **a.** *trans.* Of a wave: To break over the stern of (a vessel). Also *transf.*

1748 *Anson's Voy.* III. ii. 319 A large tumbling swell threatened to poop us. **1769** FALCONER *Dict. Marine* (1789) Llj b, The principal hazards incident to scudding are generally, a pooping sea; the difficulty of steering. **1836** MARRYAT *Midsh. Easy* xxvi, The frigate was pooped by a tremendous sea, which washed all those who did not hold on down into the waist. **1916** 'TAFFRAIL' *Pincher Martin* xi. 210 There is a grave risk of the craft being pooped by a heavy sea. **1955** *Times* 3 May 5/2 The worst seas they encountered in the whole great voyage, however, were between the Start and Portland Bill. They were pooped. **1972** *Daily Tel.* 22 Jan. 11/4 Returning home via a less dizzy gradient (it is only 1-in-4), we [*sc.* the writer and his dog] faced the same sort of spate that had tried to poop us while we were descending.

b. *transf.* Of a ship: To receive (a wave) over the stern; to ship (a sea) on the poop.

1894 *Westm. Gaz.* 7 Dec. 5/1 An enormous wave was pooped which demolished the hatchways and flooded the hold with several feet of water. **1898** F. T. BULLEN *Cruise Cachalot* xxviii, The supreme test..is the length of time she will scud before a gale without 'pooping' a sea.

poop (puːp), *v.*[4] *colloq.* (orig. *U.S.*). [Origin unknown.] **a.** *intr.* To break down, 'conk' out. **b.** *trans.* To tire, to exhaust. So **pooped** *ppl. a.*, exhausted, worn out. Freq. with adv., esp. *out*.

1931 *Technol. Rev.* Nov. 65/2 If his engine *poops* or *konks*, he will be *forced down*. **1932** *Amer. Speech* VII. 335 *Pooped*; *all pooped*, tired out; exhausted. **1934** J. T. FARRELL *Young Manhood* xii. 187 He was tired and pooped. *Ibid.* xxii. 377 Studs took a large rocker, and carried it slowly downstairs. .. When he set it down in the alley, he was breathless, and all pooped out. **1938** 'E. QUEEN' *Four of Hearts* (1939) iv. 57 He ain't had a drink in five days. That would poop up any guy. **1944** E. B. WHITE *Let.* 15 May (1976) 253 This would be a very bad time to pull our exhaustion on our readers, a lot of whom are pretty well pooped out themselves for one reason or another. **1949** R. CHANDLER *Little Sister* xxx. 222 'Tired?' he asked. 'Pooped.' **1955** M. DICKENS *Winds of Heaven* iv. 93 He'd better be..or he'll find his mother-in-law in the hospital with him. You've really pooped yourself, mother. **1957** D. KARP *Leave me Alone* xviii. 274, I don't think he understood me. The poor old guy is pooped out. **1959** N. MAILER *Advts. for Myself* (1961) 45 He remembered the old man sitting on the porch..all pooped out after work. **1960** *Sunday Express* 24 July 4/2 Bringing up eight kids..really has me pooped. **1966** *New Scientist* 22 Sept. 658/1 Lt Cdr Richard Gordon's space walk was cut short because..'he was blinded by sweat and felt pooped'. **1967** *Time* 2 June 33 Paley Park offers pooped passers-by a respite at little white tables and chairs in a setting of geraniums, honey locust trees, and a 20-ft. waterfall. **1971** B. MALAMUD *Tenants* 7 If it [*sc.* the heating system] pooped out, and it pooped often—the furnace had celebrated its fiftieth birthday—you called the complaint number of Rent and Housing Maintenance. *Ibid.* 183 His electric heater has pooped out and is being repaired. **1977** *Time* 18 Apr. 64/3 Pheidippides..was so pooped by his performance that he staggered into Athens.

poope, obs. f. POOP, POPE *sb.*[1]

pooped (puːpt), *a.* [f. POOP *sb.*[1] + -ED[2].] Having a poop: chiefly in comb. as ***high-pooped***.

1879 BEERBOHM *Patagonia* i. 7 Magellan dropped anchor there, with his quaint, high-pooped craft. **1897** *Westm. Gaz.* 30 Dec. 1/3 There were soldier sentries..ready to shoot from the pooped watch-tower [on a convict-ship].

poope-holy, variant of POPE-HOLY *Obs.*

poopet, obs. form of POPPET.

†**'poop-noddy.** *Obs.* [? f. POOP *v.*[2], to cheat, cozen + NODDY, fool, simpleton, as if = cozen-the-simpleton.] ? = CONY-CATCHER, CONY-CATCHING. Cf. NODDYPOOP.

1606 *Wily Beguiled* C j b, I am sure I saw them close together at Poop-noddie, in her Closet. **1616** J. DEACON *Tobacco Tortured* 57 Alas poore Tobacco..thou that hast bene hitherto accompted the Ale-knights armes, the Beere-brewers badge,..the Poope-noddies paramour, the Ruffians reflection.

poor (pʊə(r), pɔə(r)), *a.* (*sb.*) Forms: α. 3–5 pouere (povere), 3–6 pouer (pover), (4 poeuere, poeure, pouir), 4–5 poer, powere, 5 poyr, 5–6 power, (6 poware). β. 3–5 poure, 4– 6 powre, pour. γ. 3–7 (–9 *dial.*) pore, 4–7 poore, (6) 7– poor. δ. *Sc.* and *north. dial.* 4–6 pur, 4–8 pure, (4 puyre, 5 pwyr, poyr, 6 peur(e, pwir, puire), 6– puir (ü), (9 peer). [ME. *pov(e)re, pouere, poure*, a. OF. *povre, -ere, poure*, in mod.F. *pauvre*, dial. *paure, pouvre, poure* = Pr. *paubre, paure*, It. *povero*, Sp., Pg. *pobre*:—L. *pauper*, late L. also *pauper-us*, poor. The mod.Eng. *poor* and Sc.

puir represent the ME. *pōre*: with mod. vulgar *pore*, cf. *whore* and the pronunciation of *door*, *floor*.

On account of the ambiguity of the letter *u* and its variant *v* before 1600, it is uncertain whether ME. *pouere*, *poure*, *pouer*, meant *pou-* or *pov-*. The phonetic series *paupere(m*, *paupre*, *paubre*, *pobre*, *povre*, shows that *povre* preceded *poure*, which may have been reached in late OF., and is the form in various mod.F. dialects. But the 15th and early 16th c. literary Fr. form was *povre*, artificially spelt in 15th c. *pauvre*, after L. *pauper*, and ME. *pōre* (the source of mod.Eng. *poor*) seems to have been reduced from *povre* like *o'er* from *over*, *lord* from *loverd*. Cf. also POORTITH, PORAIL, POVERTY. But some Eng. dialects now have *pour* (paʊr), which prob. represents ME. *pour* (puːr).]

A. Illustration of Forms.

α. c 1205 LAY. 22715 Riche men and pouere. c 1300 *Cursor M.* 19775 (Edin.) Wiþ pouir [*v.r.* pouer] widus umbisette. c 1375 *Sc. Leg. Saints* vi. (*Thomas*) 453 Vith powere folk. c 1380 WYCLIF *Wks.* (1880) 69 Be þe peple neuere so poer. c 1380 —— *Sel. Wks.* III. 518 Poeure nedy men. c 1440 *York Myst.* xli. 48 And yf so be that she be power [*rime* honoure]. 1434 MISYN *Mending Life* iii. 110 Blissyd be þai þat ar poyr in spirytt. 1540 *Test. Ebor.* (Surtees) VI. 108 My power frendes and neghbors. 1554–9 in *Songs & Ball.* (1860) 11 Uppone the poware commens.

β. c 1200 *Trin. Coll. Hom.* 47 Gif hie was poure. 13.. *Cursor M.* 4375 (Cott.) Leuer es me be pour [*v.rr.* pouer, pore] and lele. c 1489 CAXTON *Sonnes of Aymon* iv. 117 The foure powre knyghtes. *Ibid.* xviii. 400 He lived like an heremyte a poure liffe. 1535 *Bury Wills* (Camden) 125 The helpe and socour of my pour soule.

γ. c 1275 LAY. 22715 Riche and pore. a 1400 *Prymer* (1891) 84 [Ps. xl. 17] Forsoþe y am a beggere and poore. 1475 *Bk. Noblesse* (Roxb.) 73 The pore comons. 1536 in *Lett. Suppress. Monasteries* (Camden) 132 Desyuryng you.. to be good and gracyus lord unto me synful and poor creatur. 1592 C'TESS SHREWSBURY in Ellis *Orig. Lett.* Ser. II. III. 165 Ageinst the pore chyld. 1611 BIBLE *Jas.* ii. 2 A poore man in vile raiment. 1629 SIR W. MURE *True Crucif.* 2587 In soule most pore [*rime* Ore]. 1650 Poor [see B. 1 c]. 1677 LADY CHAWORTH in *12th Rep. Hist. MSS. Comm.* App. v. 36 To honour my poore house.

δ. 1340 HAMPOLE *Pr. Consc.* 509 Naked we come hider, and bare And pure. c 1375 *Sc. Leg. Saints* vi. (*Thomas*) 365 Puyre and riche men elyke. c 1470 HENRY *Wallace* VIII. 467 Our rewme is pur, waistit be Sotheroun blud. 1483 *Cath. Angl.* 294/1 Pure (*A.* Pwyr). 1533 GAU *Richt Vay* 14 Thair pwir frendis. 1539 *Aberdeen Regr.* (1844) I. 165 Puyr boddeis. 1568 *Satir. Poems Reform.* xlvii. 82 Quhat cummer castis the formest stane.. At tha peure winschis. 1802 R. ANDERSON *Cumberld. Ball.* 43 She.. can always feel For peer fwok when distress.

B. Signification.

I. 1. a. Having few, or no, material possessions; wanting means to procure the comforts, or the necessaries, of life; needy, indigent, destitute; *spec.* (esp. in legal use) so destitute as to be dependent upon gifts or allowances for subsistence. In common use expressing various degrees, from absolute want to straitened circumstances or limited means relatively to station, as 'a poor gentleman', 'a poor professional man, clergyman, scholar, clerk', etc. The opposite of *rich*, or *wealthy*. ***poor people***, the poor as a class: often with connotation of humble rank or station.

c 1200 [see A. β]. a 1240 *Sawles Warde* in *Cott. Hom.* 261 Ich iseh þe apostles poure ant lah on eorðe. 13.. *Cursor M.* 13312 (Cott.) To petre þat he pouerest fand, Of all he mad him mast weldand. 1390 GOWER *Conf.* III. 155 He wiste wel his pours was povere. 1432–50 tr. *Higden* (Rolls) V. 7 The son of a pover wedowe. 1547–8 in E. Green *Somerset Chantries* (1888) 12 Ther is within the saide paryshe a house of poore people, callyd the spitle howse. 1605 SHAKS. *Lear* I. iv. 21 If thou be'st as poore for a subiect, as hee's for a King, thou art poore enough. 1665 BRATHWAIT *Comment Two Tales* 8 This *Poor* hath been an Epithete for Scholars in all Ages. a 1687 PETTY *Pol. Arith.* Pref., The whole Kingdom grows every day poorer and poorer. 1789 W. BUCHAN *Dom. Med.* (1790) 23 Mothers of the poorer sort. 1847 C. BRONTË *J. Eyre* iv, They are almost like poor people's children!

b. In proverbial comparisons: see CHURCH-MOUSE, JOB *sb.*[4] 1, RAT *sb.*[1] 2 c.

1390 GOWER *Conf.* II. 211 To ben for evere til I deie As povere as Job. 1533, etc. [see JOB *sb.*[4] 1]. 1782 MISS BURNEY *Cecilia* IX. iv, See, he's as poor as a rat. 1900 WEYMAN *Sophia* v, All as poor as rats, and no one better than the other.

c. Of, involving, or characterized by poverty.

13.. *Cursor M.* 13272 (Cott.) Mene men o pour lijf [*Fairf.* men of pouer fode]. c 1380 WYCLIF *Sel. Wks.* III. 518 Crist wiþ his apostlis lyvede most povere lif. 1650 FULLER *Pisgah* II. vi. 143 Here he [Christ].. had his poor and painfull education, working on his Fathers trade. a 1661 —— *Worthies* (1662) I. 57 Forced.. to take.. poor and painful Employments for their Livelyhood. 1816 SCOTT *Antiq.* xxvii, I'm sorry to see ye in sic a peer state, man.

d. *fig.* (or in generalized sense).

c 1325 *Spec. Gy Warw.* 164 Þouh man haue muche katel ..3it he may be pore of mod And low of herte. 1390 GOWER *Conf.* II. 128 So is he povere, and everemore Him lacketh that he hath ynowh. c 1400 MAUNDEV. (Roxb.) xi. 48 Blissed be þai þat er pouer in spirit. 1867 JEAN INGELOW *Regret* 12 They are poor That have lost nothing; they are poorer far Who, losing, have forgotten. 1876 C. D. WARNER *Wint. Nile* ii. 33 People are poor in proportion as their wants are not gratified.

e. Phr. ***poor but honest***.

1748 SMOLLETT *R. Random* I. xviii. 150, I am a poor, but honest cobler's son. 1824 KNAPP & BALDWIN *Newgate Calendar* I. 149/1 John Hawkins was born of poor but honest parents. 1869 'MARK TWAIN' *Innoc. Abr.* xxi. 211 'He was the son of——' 'Poor but honest parents—that is all right—never mind the particulars—go on with the legend.' 1922 W. J. LOCKE *Tale of Triona* viii. 90, I was born—I shan't tell you the year—of poor but honest parents. 1939 A. THIRKELL *Before Lunch* v. 126 'Do you mean to say you ride one of those things.' Daphne said she was poor but honest, and why not. 1972 C. WESTON *Poor, Poor Ophelia* (1973) iii. 18 'So he's a slave, too,' she commented. 'Right on for Poor-But-Honest headed for the top.'

2. a. Lacking, ill supplied; having a want or deficiency of some specified (or implied) possession or quality: const. †*of* (obs.), *in*.

1377 LANGL. *P. Pl.* B. XIII. 301 Pore of possessioun in purse and in coffre. 1393 *Ibid.* C. XVII. 161 He þat haþ londe and lordshep,.. Shal be pourest of power at hus partyng hennes. 14.. *Tundale's Vis.* 22 He hadde ynowȝ of all rychesse, But he was pore of all godenesse. 1581 MARBECK *Bk. of Notes* 717 So long as God is not poore of mercie, so long cannot I be poore of merite. 1638 BAKER tr. *Balzac's Lett.* (vol. II.) 30 They that are poore in reputation ought to presse up to the trenches. 1842 MACAULAY in Trevelyan *Life & Lett.* (1876) II. ix. 109 The English language is not so poor but [etc.]. 1863 E. V. NEALE *Anal. Th. & Nat.* 157 Stratified masses, rich in organic remains, though poor in mineral substances.

b. Of soil, ore, etc.: Yielding little, unproductive.

1592 NASHE *P. Penilesse* (Shaks. Soc.) 32 Onely poore England giues him bread for his cake. 1600 E. BLOUNT tr. *Conestaggio* 30 All other delights that poore Iland coulde yeelde. 1604 E. G[RIMSTONE] *D'Acosta's Hist. Indies* IV. v. 218 They cal that [ore] poore which yields least silver. 1765 A. DICKSON *Treat. Agric.* (ed. 2) 475 The poor clays require such manures as contain the greatest plenty of the vegetable food. 1813 SIR H. DAVY *Agric. Chem.* (1814) 192 Poor and hungry soils. 1877 RAYMOND *Statist. Mines & Mining* 385 The poor slag contains about 7 ounces of silver and a trace of gold. It is too poor to treat, and is thrown away.

3. a. In lean or feeble condition from ill feeding.

1539 BIBLE (Great) *Gen.* xli. 19 Seuen other kyne.. poore [COVERD. thynne] and very euell fauored and leane fleshed. 1600 HOLLAND *Livy* XXI. xl. 415 Their horses, no other than lame jades and poore hidebound hildings. 1697 DRYDEN *Virg. Georg.* III. 321 Before his Training, keep him poor and low. 1716 SWIFT *Progr. Poetry* Wks. 1755 III. II. 161 Cackling shews the goose is poor. 1778 *Maryland Jrnl.* 10 Feb. 4/2 [The sheep] are very poor, and appear to have been out all winter. 1878 J. H. BEADLE *Western Wilds* xvii. 276 They get poor as snakes on such food; but it does keep body and soul together for awhile. 1887 RIDER HAGGARD *Jess* xxxi, The horse perished, as 'poor' horses are apt to do.

†b. Out of health, unwell: = POORLY *a. Obs.*

1758 L. LYON in *Milit. Jrnls.* (1855) 15 Corperal Carpenter was taken poor. *Ibid.* 25 This day at night Leiut. Smith came back and very poor he was. 1758 S. THOMPSON *Diary* (1896) 12 Our men are very poor, and we scarce could get men for work or for guard.

4. a. Small in amount; less than is wanted or expected; scanty, insufficient, inadequate.

a 1255 *Ancr. R.* 114 Hwar was euer iȝiuen to eni blodletunge so poure pitaunce? 13.. *Cursor M.* 11307 (Cott.) Pouer gift can sco for him giue þat com in pouert for to liue. 1535 STEWART *Cron. Scot.* (Rolls) II. 239 Schir Modred, his power wes so puir, Into the feild no langar micht induir. 1585 T. WASHINGTON tr. *Nicholay's Voy.* I. xv. 16 b, By reason of the poore treasure of the religious ..[the place] coulde not haue bin fortified. 1652 NEEDHAM tr. *Selden's Mare Cl.* 493 Every man and maid servant, or Orphant, having any poor stock may venture the same in their Fishing-voiages. 1703 ROWE *Ulyss.* II. i. 850 Death is too poor a Name, for that means Rest. 1849 MACAULAY *Hist. Eng.* iii. I. 314 The crop of wheat would be thought poor if it did not exceed twelve millions of quarters.

b. Depreciatively, with a numeral, connoting the smallness of the number or sum.

1596 SHAKS. *1 Hen. IV*, III. iii. 180 One poore peny-worth of Sugar-candie. 1600 —— *A.Y.L.* I. i. 2 It was.. bequeathed me by will, but poore a thousand Crownes. 1712 ARBUTHNOT *John Bull* IV. ii, What are twenty-two poor years towards the finishing a Lawsuit? 1737 BRACKEN *Farriery Impr.* (1757) II. 11 All.. he had wagered was poor Thirteen-Pence. 1759 STERNE *Tr. Shandy* II. viii, It is but poor eight miles from Shandy-Hall. 1819 KEATS *Isabella* xxvi, A poor three hours' absence.

5. a. Deficient in the proper or desired quality; of little excellence or value; not worth much; of inferior quality, paltry, 'sorry'; mean, shabby (also ***poor-quality*** used *attrib.*). Usually of abstract things: in reference to material objects, often approaching 1 c.

a 1300 *Cursor M.* 14869 Þis folk.. O littel wijt, o pour resun. 1432–50 tr. *Higden* (Rolls) I. 71 After some men of pover and breve intellecte, and also of lytelle experience. 1551 T. WILSON *Logike* (1580) 62 b, Although it be a poore helpe. 1624 CAPT. SMITH *Virginia* 51 Such poore bridges, onely made of a few cratches thrust in the o[o]se, and three or four poles laid on them. 1714–15 HEARNE *Collect.* (O.H.S.) V. 37 'Twas a poor Discourse. 1719 DE FOE *Crusoe* (1840) II. xiii. 264 They made but poor work of it. 1777 BURKE *Corr.* (1844) II. 149 The House never made so poor a figure as in the debate on that bill. 1843 MRS. CARLYLE *Lett.* (1883) I. 252 Seditious cries will make a poor battle against cannon. 1888 BRYCE *Amer. Commw.* II. lii. 301 The poor paving of the streets and their lack of cleanliness. 1892 [see IGNORANT *a.* 1 b]. a 1908 *Mod.* It was poor consolation to me to know [etc.]. 1948 C. L. B. HUBBARD *Dogs in Brit.* 234 The English Setter appears to be in danger of deteriorating into a very pretty but poor-quality worker. 1960 *Farmer & Stockbreeder* 9 Feb. 57/3 When I was a boy we used to chaff poor-quality hay and mix it with molasses. 1966 G. GREENE *Comedians* I. i. 23 Cynicism is cheap.. it's built into all poor-quality goods.

b. Mentally or morally inferior; mean-spirited, sneaking; paltry, despicable, 'small'; wanting in courage, spiritless.

1425 *Paston Lett.* I. 19 So fals, and so pouere,—but he was nevere of my kyn. 1611 TOURNEUR *Ath. Trag.* II. v, A poore spirit is poorer than a poore purse. 1627 tr. *Bacon's Life & Death* (1651) 17 A Man of a poore Minde, and not valiant. 1685 EARL OF ROCHESTER *Valentinian* v. ii, Shall I grow then so poor as to repent? 1796 NELSON in Nicolas *Disp.* (1846) VII. p. lxxxviii, He is a poor creature and more of a Genoese than an Englishman. 1882 STEVENSON *New Arab. Nts.*, *Rajah's Diamond*, He seemed altogether a poor and debile being. 1884 *St. James' Gaz.* 12 Jan. 3/1 From the intellectual point of view, there could not be a poorer creature.

c. Slight, insignificant, of little consequence.

1603 KNOLLES *Hist. Turks* (1621) 1 The glorious Empire of the Turkes,.. hath.. nothing in it more wonderfull or strange, than the poore beginning of itself. 1721 STRYPE *Eccl. Mem.* III. iv. 38 Henry Earl of Surrey.. for.. the poor crime of assuming somewhat into his coat of arms, was actually beheaded. 1903 MYERS *Hum. Personality* 2 Each one of those great sciences was in its dim and poor beginning.

d. In modest or apologetic use, said depreciatively of oneself, one's performance, or something belonging to or offered by oneself: Of little worth or pretension; humble, lowly, insignificant.

1423 JAS. I. *Kingis Q.* xcix, Vnto ȝoure grace lat now ben acceptable My pure request. ? a 1500 *Chester Pl.* (E.E.T.S.) 250 Well is me that I may se thy face, here in my house, this poore place! 1585 T. WASHINGTON tr. *Nicholay's Voy.* Ep. Ded., To exclude olde men.. is (in my poore conceipt) palpable erronious. 1602 SHAKS. *Ham.* I. v. 131 For mine owne poore part, Looke you, Ile goe pray. 1605 CAMDEN *Rem.* Ded. 1 This silly pittiful, and poore Treatise. a 1745 SWIFT (J.), To be without power or distinction, is not, in my poor opinion, a very amiable situation to a person of title. 1814 WORDSW. *Excurs.* III. 118 If from my poor retirement ye had gone Leaving this nook unvisited.

e. Used with *little* in depreciatory (and freq. ironical) senses, esp. in the phrases ***poor little guy***, the ordinary individual, the 'man in the street'; ***poor little me*** (see LITTLE *a.* 13); ***poor little rich boy, girl***, used (sometimes ironically) of a person whose wealth has not brought happiness.

1925 N. COWARD *Poor Little Rich Girl* (song) 3 Poor little rich girl, You're a bewitched girl, Better beware! 1934 'G. ORWELL' *Burmese Days* v. 91 Unmanly whinings; poor-little-rich-girl stuff. 1940 GRAVES & HODGE *Long Week-End* xvii. 300 Spender wrote poor-little-rich-boy poems, full of genuine pity for the exploited poor, and for himself. 1958 [see MASS *sb.*[2] 4 a]. 1961 *Guardian* 28 Apr. 30/6 A disturbing flavour of the poor little rich boy, of the attitude which claims privilege for me just because I am me. 1967 *Boston Sunday Herald* 26 Mar. I. 9/7 Only the poor little guy is subject to the zoning code. 1973 *Times* 23 Mar. 17/6 A comedy-weepie about a poor little rich girl. 1974 J. MANN *Sticking Place* ii. 37 There was still something pathetic about her.. a poor little rich girl. 1977 *Daily Tel.* 4 Mar. 3/5 A Conservative M.P.'s daughter on a heroin charge was 'really just a poor little rich girl.. who has had an unhappy life' a magistrate said yesterday.

f. ***to take a poor view***, to have a low opinion (*of* something); to regard unfavourably.

1943 HUNT & PRINGLE *Service Slang* 52 If you do not agree with a statement or with your C.O.'s ruling.. or, in fact, with the world in general, you take a poor view. 1944 'N. SHUTE' *Pastoral* i. 4 The Wing Commander had taken a poor view of that. 1946 E. LINKLATER *Private Angelo* x. 115 The Germans are about to do something that we take a poor view of, and I'm going to see if I can put a stop to it. a 1966 'M. NA GOPALEEN' *Best of Myles* (1968) 41 The brother took a very poor view and said she'd be a sorry woman.

6. Such, or so circumstanced, as to excite one's compassion or pity; unfortunate, hapless. Now chiefly *colloq.*

In many parts of England regularly said of the dead whom one knew; = late, deceased.

c 1275 LAY. 15421 To ȝam saide þo þer þe pore king Vortiger. 1390 GOWER *Conf.* III. 296 This yonge lord.. Al naked in a povere plit. c 1400 *Destr. Troy* 9596 Then Deffibus.. Pletid vnto Paris with a pore voise. 1484 CAXTON *Fables of Æsop* I. iv, Thus was the poure sheep vaynquysshed. 1513 MORE *Rich. III* in Grafton *Chron.* (1568) II. 776 Going her waye, leaving the poore innocent childe weeping as fast as the mother. a 1568 ASCHAM *Scholem.* (Arb.) 113 If Osorius would leaue of.. his ouer rancke rayling against poore Luther. 1577 B. GOOGE *Heresbach's Husb.* II. (1586) 85 Betwixt the Oke and it [the Olive] there is great hatred.. though you cut downe the Oke, yet the very Rootes poysoneth and killeth the poore Oliue. 1691 J. WILSON *Belphegor* v. iii, Poor comfortless Woman; she's fall'n asleep at last. 1787 MME. D'ARBLAY *Diary* 26 Feb., Till his [Boswell's] book of poor Dr. Johnson's life is finished and published. 1834 MEDWIN *Angler in Wales* II. 347, I often think of poor Leyden's lines. 1857 MRS. CARLYLE *Lett.* (1883) II. 330 He looked dreadfully weak still, poor fellow! 1870 E. PEACOCK *Ralf Skirl.* III. 82 The poor thing had fallen asleep also. 1886 ELWORTHY *W. Somerset Word-bk.* s.v., People who are dead are always spoken of as *poor* so-and-so... 'You mind the poor old Farmer Follett, that's th' old Farmer George's father you know'. 1887 *How to Make a Saint* viii. 114–15 In common parlance the word 'poor' had by general consent been prefixed to the names of the dead in this country... [They] had been in the habit of speaking of their departed friends as 'poor So-and-so'. a 1907 *Oxford boatman.* 'When my poor dad was ferryman here'.

II. 7. *absol.* or as *sb.* (almost always in sense 1). a. *absol.* in *pl.* sense (usually with *the*): poor people as a class; those in necessitous or humble circumstances (often contrasted with *the rich*); *spec.* those dependent upon charitable or parochial relief; paupers. Freq. with a preceding epithet, as ***the aged poor***, ***the deserving poor***, ***the good poor***, ***the respectable***

poor, the sick poor, the undeserving poor. Also, ***the very poor.***

a 1225 *Leg. Kath.* 50 Poure ba & riche comen þer to-foren him. c 1230 *Hali Meid.* 9 Hwen þus is of þe riche, hwat wenes tu of þe poure? 13.. *Cursor M.* 4707 þe wrecche pouer [*Gött.* þe wrecched pore] moght find na fode. 1375 BARBOUR *Bruce* I. 276 Bath pur, and thai off hey parage. c 1475 *Litt. Red Bk. Bristol* (1900) I. 141 Aswell to the power as to the riche. 1526 TINDALE *Mark* xiv. 5 It myght have been soolde for more then two houndred pens, and bene geven vnto the povre. 1560 DAUS tr. *Sleidane's Comm.* 47 b, Colledges and such other places were fyrst founded for the pore. 1621 FLETCHER *Pilgrim* I. i, What poor attend my charity to-day, wench? c 1658 in F. J. Furnivall *Harrison's Descr. Eng.* (1908) IV. 207 Cures Colledge.. with maintenance for 16.. aged poore of the parish. a 1687 PETTY *Pol. Arith.* (1690) 80 The poor of France have generally less Wages than in England. 1750 GRAY *Elegy* viii, The short and simple annals of the poor. 1795 BURKE *Th. Scarcity* Wks. VII. 377 Nothing can be so base and so wicked as the political canting language, 'The labouring poor'. 1823 E. WEETON *Let.* 16 Apr. in *Jrnl. of Governess* (1969) II. 217 Going about.. to visit the sick poor as a Member of the Benevolent Society. 1845 E. SMITH *Jrnl.* 28 Oct. (1980) 81 Sick poor, destitute poor, idle, prejudiced poor, oppress me. 1852 DICKENS *Bleak Ho.* (1853) vi. 48 It is said that the children of the very poor are not brought up, but dragged up. 1864 TENNYSON *Northern Farmer, New Style* xii, Taäke my word for it, Sammy, the poor in a loomp is bad. 1907 G. B. SHAW *Major Barbara* Pref. 154 'The respectable poor', and such phrases are as intolerable and as immoral as 'drunken but amiable' [etc.]. a 1908 *Mod.* Money left to the poor of the parish. 1909 W. J. LOCKE *Septimus* i. 6 Cousin Jane held distinct views on the cut of under-clothes for the deserving poor. 1910 E. M. FORSTER *Howards End* vi. 53 We are not concerned with the very poor. They are unthinkable and only to be approached by the statistician or the poet. 1928 A. M. M. DOUTON *Bk. with Seven Seals* I. 14 In those days pews were only for those who could pay for them, and free benches.. were occupied by the respectable poor. 1937 The sick poor [see HOSPITALIZATION]. 1972 *Listener* 9 Mar. 317/1 The Tolpuddle Martyrs.. were.. the good poor—and little enough they got by it. 1972 J. MANN *Mrs. Knox's Profession* xiii. 102 The man was obviously one of the old-fashioned 'good poor'. 1973 *Guardian* 21 Mar. 10/4, I have no sympathy at all with the kind of people who.. do not believe in private property. There is a difference between the undeserving poor and the deserving. *Ibid.* 18 May 16/2 Many of those who want to be owner-occupiers could properly be described as the deserving poor. 1974 *Times* 11 Apr. 20 (*heading*) How can we decide who are the deserving poor? 1977 P. LASLETT *Family Life Earlier Generations* iv. 171 During the next 2 years of life, ages 4 and 5, infants remain very dependent, and even amongst the very poor in pre-industrial society were extremely unlikely to be sent out of the home. 1979 P. THEROUX *Old Patagonian Express* xv. 220 On the higher harder-to-reach slopes.. were the huts of the very poor.

†**b.** *sing.* = poor man, poor person. (In quot. 13.., in sense 5 d.) *Obs.*

13.. *E.E. Allit. P.* B. 615 Passe neuer fro þi pouere, ȝif I hit pray durst, Er þou haf biden with þi burne & vnder boȝe rested. c 1400 *Rom. Rose* 5601 But the povre that recchith nought, Save of his lyflode, in his thought. 1484 CAXTON *Fables of Alfonce* iii, I byleue not that this poure may be maculed ne gylty of the blame. c 1500 KENNEDY *Passion of Christ* 480 Thoucht now I stand dispitit as a pure. 1625 JACKSON *Creed* v. xvi. §6 He had given somewhat to every poore in the Parish.

†**c.** *sb. pl.* **poors.** *Obs.*

[1343 *Rolls of Parlt.* II. 136/2 La Lei eit owel Cours entre Poures & Riches.] 1483 CAXTON *G. de la Tour* I iv b, Who that receyueth the prophetes the predycatours and the poures he receyueth my owne self. 1556 LAUDER *Tractate* 336 Quhilk nother techis ryche nor puris. 15.. *Burgh Rec. Glasgow* I. 395 (Jam. *Suppl.*) Sua that the gude toun nor nane resortand thairto sall be trublit with thair puris.

d. possessive **poor's** (in sing. or pl. sense). Now *rare* exc. *dial.*

c 1412 HOCCLEVE *De Reg. Princ.* 4893 þat your hye dygnite .. No desdein haue of þe pores sentence. a 1425 *Cursor M.* 19766 (Trin.) To sewe þe pores cloþing. a 1656 HALES *Gold. Rem.* III. *Serm.*, etc. (1673) 16 It is the poors money, and the Talent of thy Lord which thou hidest under the ground. 1844 A. PAGE *Suppl. Kirby's Suffolk Trav.* 799 The poor's estate comprises a cottage.. and 13 A. 3 R. 7 P. of land. *Sc. dial.* She is now in the Poor's-house.

III. Combinations and Phrases.

8. Qualifying a sb. in special collocations: **poor boy (sandwich)** *Southern U.S.*, a large sandwich containing a wide variety of simple but substantial ingredients; **poor child**, a pupil at a charity school (CHILD *sb.* 4); **poor Clares**, an order of nuns (see CLARE); **poor debtor** (see DEBTOR 1 c); **poor do** *U.S.*, a dish made up of scraps of food; a hash; **poor mouth** *v. trans.* and *intr.*, (*a*) to claim to be poor; to make demands (on someone) alleging poverty; (*b*) to deprecate, make little of (something); so **poor-mouthing** *vbl. sb.*; ***to make*** (***put on***, etc.) ***a poor mouth***; see MOUTH *sb.* 3 m; ***to talk poor-mouth*** (U.S.), to plead poverty; **poor preachers, poor priests**, an order of itinerant preaching clergy founded by Wyclif; **poor relation**, a relative or kinsman in humble circumstances (also *transf.*); †**poor Robin** *sb.*, an almanack (from the title of *Poor Robin's Almanack*, first published in 1661 or 1662); *v. intr.* (with *it*), to play the part of 'poor Robin' (? in allusion to *Poor Robin's Jests*, c 1669, or one of various works with similar titles); **poor vicar** (see VICAR); **poor white** (see WHITE *sb.*). See also POOR JOHN, POOR MAN.

1952 *New Orleans Item* 28 Feb. 17/5 'Way back yonder when a *poorboy sandwich was just that—namely, a five-cent filling of bread, meat and mixed pickles for a poor boy. 1954 *Newsweek* 15 Mar. 99 In the South, a poor boy is a frankfurter in a long bun. 1962 E. WASON *Cooks, Gluttons & Gourmets* 271 Eventually they became known.. as 'poor boy' sandwiches, as they are called in New Orleans to this day. 1968 *Amer. Speech* 1967 XLII. 286 A term [for sandwich] which is used primarily in the South is *poor boy*. .. The usual interpretation of this term is that those who eat the sandwich are in the lower social and economic classes. 1976 *National Observer* (U.S.) 6 Nov., Exploring Greenwich Village, I found Poor Boys, salami and cheese and chili peppers on great hunks of Italian bread. 1706 *Poor children [see CHILD *sb.* 4]. 1714 J. WALKER *Suff. Clergy* II. 214/2 Educated at Queen's-College in Oxford; where he became successively Poor Child, Taberder, Fellow and Proctor. 1909 *Pioneer Days in Southwest 1850–1879* 253 When we had hogmeat we would fry a few pieces, take the grease and crumble corn bread in it, putting in water and salt, and we had a pot of soup called '*poor doo'. 1913 H. KEPHART *Our Southern Highlanders* 292 The old Germans taught their Scotch and English neighbors the merits of scrapple, but here it is known as poor-do. 1965 *Lebende Sprachen* X. 37/1, I am intrigued.. by the abundance of 'poor' edibles which we have in the States... *poor-do* is scrapple, etc. 1967 WEBSTER Add., *Poor mouth v. 1968 *New Yorker* 21 Sept. 169 [Eugene] McCarthy's advertising campaign, despite the McCarthy camp's constant poor-mouthing on the subject, wasn't exactly modest. 1970 *Globe & Mail* (Toronto) 26 Sept. 9/1 Six months ago, it was sacrilegious to poormouth the fight against air pollution. It was akin to being against motherhood. 1972 T. ARDIES *This Suitcase* xvi. 176 What prompted the Professor to start poor mouthing me? 1972 *Time* 17 Apr. 25/1 Some democrats.. are already poor-mouthing his victory. 1976 *Times Lit. Suppl.* 26 Mar. 339/2 The latter [book] came to be poormouthed by its author as 'a literary exercise'. 1941 in H. Wentworth *Amer. Dial. Dict.* (1944) 469/1 College professors are supposed to talk *po' mouth. 1961 *Newsweek* 14 Aug. 15/1 Because they are politicians, they like to talk as poor-mouth as the lowliest voter. 1965 *N.Y. Times* 29 July 16 It is hard to talk poor mouth just after the papers have written of your daughter's coming-out party for 2,000 guests. 1978 R. THOMAS *Chinaman's Chance* xv. 168 My teeth hurt whenever you start talking poormouth. 1968 *Guardian* 28 Jan. 16/8 *Poor-mouthing at home feeds the doubts of foreigners abroad.. and gloomy prognostications from abroad in turn further depress the spirits of the British. 1969 'R. MACDONALD' *Goodbye Look* xxviii. 163 She became a bit of a miser... Her poor-mouthing actually had me convinced. But of course she'd been quite wealthy all along. c 1380 in *Wyclif's Wks.* (1880) 245 (*title*) Whi *pore prestis han none benefice. *Ibid.* 248 ȝit þouȝ pore prestis myȝtten frely geten presentacion of lordis to haue benefices wiþ cure of soulis. 1880 F. D. MATTHEW *ibid.* Pref. 16 Wyclif's aim in instituting the poor priests was to supply the defects of the existing parsons, who too often, after collecting their tithes and dues,.. left their flock without preaching or spiritual instruction. 1720 DEFOE *Capt. Singleton* 338 Seeing.. he had some *poor Relations in England.. he would write to know.. what Condition they were in. 1748 SMOLLETT *R. Random* I. i. 1 My father.. fell in love with a poor relation.. whom he privately espoused. 1804 COLERIDGE *Lett.* II. 475 You sometimes see thirty or forty together of these our poor relations [monkeys]. 1823 LAMB *Elia* Ser. II. *Poor Relations*, A Poor Relation—is the most irrelevant thing in nature,—a piece of impertinent correspondency,—an odious approximation,—a haunting conscience,—a preposterous shadow, lengthening in the noontide of your prosperity. 1898 *Westm. Gaz.* 16 July 2/1 The discarded ones [clothes] .. were not sold. They were bestowed on the Poor Relation. 1906 J. M. SYNGE *Lett. to Molly* (1971) 13, I dont like hanging about their house as a poor relation. 1962 *Rep. Comm. Broadcasting 1960* 26 in *Parl. Papers 1961–2* (Cmnd. 1753) IX. 259 The suggestion or fear that sound radio was becoming the 'poor relation' of broadcasting. 1970 J. EARL *Tuners & Amplifiers* ii. 36 Most attention.. is usually focused on to the f.m. department where the quality potential truly exists, the a.m. department of a composite model then being very much a 'poor relation'. 1972 *Guardian* 14 Jan. 11/1 In many cases servicing and spare parts were the poor relations subsidised by sales. 1977 D. FRANCIS *Risk* viii. 100 Novice hurdles were customarily first or last.. the poor-relation races for the mediocre majority. 1978 J. SYMONS *Blackheath Poisonings* I. 28 He resented.. the mother who had inconsiderately died and left him a poor relation. 1682 T. FLATMAN *Heraclitus Ridens* No. 82 (1713) II. 251, I never *Poor-Robin'd it, I never fasten'd upon any notorious Servant of the City, the Name of Sir Thomas Creswel, upon the score of any private Immoralities. 1716 *Gentlem. Instructed* (ed. 6) 120, She discern'd.. a Feast from a Feria, without the Help of poor Robin.

9. General Combs. **a.** Attributive (from the absol. or sb. use), Of or for the poor, as ***poor-hour, -money, -relief, -school.*** **b.** Objective, as ***poor-bettering, -feeding*** adjs. **c.** Parasynthetic and adverbial, as ***poor-ass*** (*U.S.*), ***-blooded, -charactered, -clad, -looking, -minded, -sighted*** adjs.

1957 J. KEROUAC *On Road* (1958) 113 Find out just what he's *poor-ass pondering about this year's turnip greens. 1970 R. D. ABRAHAMS *Positively Black* iii. 72 Colored man went to the store and bought him one of them poor-ass damned roosters. 1973 E. BULLINS *Theme is Blackness* 163 I'm only a weak little old pore/ass black woman. 1818 BENTHAM *Ch. Eng.* 90 *note*, The objection, urged against that system.., in the name of the *Poor-bettering Society. 1889 W. F. RAE *Austrian Health Resorts* 71 *Poor-blooded patients may indulge in a little old red wine. 1654 GATAKER *Disc. Apol.* 80 He might produce.. a *poor Charactered man, to do something for them. a 1586 SIDNEY *Arcadia* (1622) 82 To heare The *poore-clad truth of loues wrong-ordred lot. 1902 *Westm. Gaz.* 6 Dec. 7/1 Shivering, starving, poor-clad men and boys. 1657 J. WATTS *Vind. Ch. Eng.* 265 Is it not to deal our bread unto the hungry, etc., *poor-feeding fasts? 1897 H. DRUMMOND *Ideal Life* 68 The soul-sick had to take their turn like the out-patients at the *poor-hour outside the infirmary. 1799 MALTHUS *Diary* 11 July (1966) 139 Saw some *poor-looking houses. 1847 E. SMITH *Jrnl.* 13 Jan. (1980) 116 Poor looking house with three rooms. 1622 DEKKER & MASSINGER *Virgin Martyr* II. i, To.. give your *poor-minded rascally servants the lie! 1796 J. BENSON in *Mem.* (1822) 295 The choice of stewards to manage the *poor-money. 1898 *Dublin Rev.* Jan. 131 Questions of property, capital, labour, and *poor-relief. 1857 G. OLIVER *Collect. Hist. Cath. Relig. in Cornwall*, etc. 427 He established a *poor-school on the premises. 1901 *Westm. Gaz.* 10 Dec. 3/2 In the poor-schools where the bairns get more warmth.. than anywhere else. 1898 J. D. REES in *19th Cent.* June 1023 These beasts [elephants] are very *poor sighted, though their noses are extremely good.

10. Special Combs.: †**poor and rich**, name of some game; **poor-basket**, a basket containing material from which clothes for the poor could be made; **poor-chest** = POOR-BOX; **poor-farm** (U.S.), 'a farm maintained at public expense for the housing and support of paupers' (*Cent. Dict.*); **poor-fellow** *v. trans.* (*nonce-wd.*), to address commiseratingly as 'poor fellow' (cf. 6); **poor-master** (*U.S.*), a parish or county officer who superintends the relief and maintenance of paupers; †**poor-tax** (also *poor's tax*), a tax for the relief of the poor, a poor-rate; **poor-thing** *v. trans.* (*nonce-wd.*), to speak of or address as 'poor thing' (cf. *poor-fellow*); **poor-work**, work done to provide clothes etc. for the poor. See also POOR-BOOK, -BOX, etc.

1621 J. TAYLOR (Water P.) *Motto* D iv, At Nouum, Mumchance, mischance,.. or at *Poore and rich. 1814 JANE AUSTEN *Mansf. Park* I. vii. 147 If you have no work of your own, I can supply you from the *poor-basket. 1612 W. PARKES *Curtaine-Dr.* (1876) 67 Hadst thou a gainefull hand a rich *poore-chest. 1852 J. W. GUNNISON *Hist. Mormons* 145 A *Poor Farm of forty acres is in the centre, controlled by the bishops. 1895 A. BROWN *Meadow-Grass* 168 The latter had actually taken to her bed.. announcing that 'she'd rather go to the poor-farm and done with it than resk her life there another night'. 1949 *Chicago Tribune* 2 Dec. 20/7 It used to be a disgrace to go to the 'poor farm' and be cared for by the rest of society. 1961 N. LOFTS *House at Old Vine* VI. vi. 380 I've thought about what I owed you... You'd have fared better at the Poor Farm! 1889 G. HUNTINGTON in *Chicago Advance* 31 Jan., Now don't *poor-fellow me, or imagine that I find life a bore. 1883 *American* VI. 40 When he spares both undertaker and *poor-master further trouble. 18.. *Amer. Mission.* XXXIX. 8 (Cent.) The Agent of the United States to the Sioux Indians was to act as a sort of national poor-master, and deal out rations. 1721 BERKELEY *Prev. Ruin Gt. Brit.* Wks. 1871 III. 198 If the *poor-tax.. was fixed at a medium in every parish. 1793 *Friendly Address to Poor* 3 The Poor's Tax is much increased in every part of the kingdom. 1860 *New Virginians* II. 9 In my inexperience I '*poor thinged' her from the bottom of my heart. 1854 C. M. YONGE *Castle Builders* v. 69 Each good lady had a great basket full of *poor-work. 1876 *Monthly Packet* Feb. App. 5 The Sisters at Kilburn are glad to have 'poor work' done for them, and.. will provide the material.

poor, *v.* Forms: see prec. adj. [f. POOR *a.* Cf. OF. *pouverir* to impoverish (Froissart).]

†**1.** *intr.* To become poor. *Obs. rare.*

c 1275 *Digby MS.* 86 lf. 126/1 Now þou art riche, and now þou pouerest [*rime* couerest].

†**2.** *trans.* To make poor, impoverish. *Obs.*

c 1380 WYCLIF *Sel. Wks.* I. 216 þus ben lordis and rewmes poorid. c 1450 in *3rd Rep. Hist. MSS. Comm.* (1872) 280/2 Thus is he riched, the kynge poured. c 1470 HENRY *Wallace* XI. 43 This land is purd off fud that suld ws beild. a 1500 *Priests of Peblis* in Pinkerton *Scot. Poems* (1792) I. 14 Your tennants.. ar puird: And, quhan that thay ar puird, than are ye pure.

3. To call 'poor' (POOR *a.* 6). *nonce-use.*

1865 DICKENS *Mut. Fr.* I. iv, Miss Lavinia.. put in that she didn't want to be 'poored by pa', or anybody else. 1868 HELPS *Realmah* viii. (1869) 227 Don't 'poor' me, Sir. Nobody ever 'poored' me before.

†**'poorable**, *a. Obs. rare*⁻¹. In 6 **pooreable**. [Anomalous f. POOR *a.* + -ABLE.] Able through poverty, poor enough.

1570 LEVINS *Manip.* Ep. Ded., His [Huloet's Dict.] is great & costly, this is little & of light price, his for greter students, & them yᵗ are richable to haue it, this is for beginners, & them that are pooreable to haue no better.

†**poo'rality.** *Obs. rare*⁻¹. [f. POOR *a.*, app. after *commonality*.] The poor (collectively).

1536 *Petit. Lincoln Rebels to Hen. VIII* (P.R.O.), Whereby.. the pooralitie of your Realme by vnreleuyd.

Pooranic, Pooraun: see PURANIC, PURANA.

poorblind, obs. form of PURBLIND.

†**'poor-book.** *Obs.* Also 7 **poor's-book.** A book containing a list of the poor in receipt of parish relief.

1681 [see *poll-book*, POLL *sb.*¹ 10]. 1682 LUTTRELL *Brief Rel.* (1857) I. 165 Such poor people who goe to conventicles, and not to their parish churches, shall be putt out of the poors book, and have no parish collections. 1819 *Sporting Mag.* IV. 274 It [a parish meeting] was called for the inspection of our poor-book.

'poor-box. Also 7–9 **poor's box.** A money-box (esp. in a church) for gifts towards the relief of the poor. Cf. *poor man's box*, POOR MAN 5.

1621 B. JONSON *Gipsies Metamorph.* Wks. (Rtldg.) 624/2 On Sundays you rob the poor's box with your tabor. 1662 PEPYS *Diary* 5 Mar., To the pewterer's, to buy a poor's box, to put my forfeits in, upon breach of my late vows. 1708 *Diss. on Drunkenness* 27 Overseers go to the Tavern and get drunk with the Poor's Box. 1738 POPE *First Epistle of First Bk. of Horace Imitated* 15 The rest, some farm the Poor-box, some the Pews. **1777** SHERIDAN *Sch. Scand.* II. ii, She draws her mouth till it..resembles the aperture of a poor's-box. **1851** MAYHEW *Lond. Labour* II. 76/2 The magistrates.. gave me 2*s*. out of the Poor's-box. **1852** HOOK *Ch. Dict.* (1871) 591 In Ireland the Poor Man's Box, or 'poor-box', as it is generally called, is still in use. It is an oval box, half-covered, of copper or wood, with a long handle.

poorche, obs. f. PORCH.

poor-cod ('puəkɒd, 'pɔə-). [f. POOR *a.* 5 + COD *sb.*[3]] A small marine fish, *Trisopterus minutus*, belonging to the cod family Gadidæ, and found in coastal waters of north-western Europe; = POWER *sb.*[2]

[**1828** J. FLEMING *Hist. Brit. Animals* 191 Morhua. Cod. .. *M. minuta.* Poor.—Nine punctures on each side of the jaws and gill-covers.] **1836** [see POWER *sb.*[2]]. **1925** J. T. JENKINS *Fishes Brit. Isles* 149 The Poor Cod ranges from Trondhjem to the Mediterranean. **1959** A. HARDY *Open Sea* II. xi. 227 The poor-cod..is the smallest of all our gadoid fish, rarely exceeding 8 inches in length. **1969** A. WHEELER *Fishes Brit. Isles & N.-W. Europe* 272/1 The poor-cod is caught mainly in trawls.

poore, obs. f. PORE, POUR, POWER; var. PORR *v. Obs.*

poore-blind, obs. f. PURBLIND.

poorety, obs. f. POVERTY.

†**'poorful**, *a. Obs.* In 4 porful. [irreg. f. POOR *a.* + -FUL. Cf. *direful*, *fierceful*.] Poor; thoroughly poor.

13.. *Pol. Rel. & L. Poems* 226 Iesu, swete son dere! On porful bed list þou here, And þat me greueþ sore.

poorge, obs. form of PURGE.

†**'poorhead.** *Obs.* In 4 poure-, pouerehede. [f. POOR *a.* + *hede*, -HEAD.] The condition of being poor; poverty.

1340 *Ayenb.* 130 Huanne þe man..onderstant and knauþ his pourehede, þe vilhede, þe brotelhede of his beringe. *Ibid.* 138 Þe guodes þet byeþ in guode pouerehede.

poorhouse ('puərhaʊs, 'pɔə-). A house in which poor people in receipt of public charity are lodged; a workhouse.

1782 *Phil. Trans.* LXXII. 376 Examination of the Poor-house at Heckingham. **1821** BYRON *Occas. Pieces, Irish Avatar* xix, And a palace bestow for a poor-house and prison! **1894** BARING-GOULD *Kitty Alone* II. 74 The parish officers would interfere, and carry her off to the poor-house.

'poorify, *v. nonce-wd.* [f. POOR *a.* + -(I)FY (with pun on *purify*).] *trans.* To make poor.

1711 *Countrey-Man's Let. to Curat* 6 That Prince seem'd calculat rather for Poorifying (pardon the Clench) than Purifying the Church.

poorish ('puərɪʃ, 'pɔərɪʃ), *a.* [f. as prec. + -ISH[1].] Somewhat poor, rather poor (in various senses).

1657 in R. Potts *Liber Cantabr.* (1855) 408 Born of poorish parents. **1766** J. BARTRAM *Jrnl.* 9 Jan. in W. Stork *Acc. E. Florida* 29 Generally poorish land. **1801** CHARLOTTE SMITH *Lett. Solit. Wand.* I. 34 His honour is living, though in a poorish state of health. **1884** H. COLLINGWOOD *Under Meteor Flag* 236 It's poorish weather for a fight, I'll allow.

†**Poor-Jack.** *Obs.* = next, 1. Cf. JACK[1] 31 d.

c **1682** J. COLLINS *Salt & Fishery* 93 The sort of Cod that is caught near the Shore, and on the Coast of Newfoundland and dryed, is called Poor-Jack. **1775** R. TWISS *Trav. Spain & Port.* 267 Salt bacallâo, which is like the fish called poor-jack.

Poor 'John, 'poor-john. [f. POOR *a.* + proper name JOHN: cf. prec.]

1. A name for hake (or ? other fish) salted and dried for food; often a type of poor fare. ? *Obs.* exc. *Hist.*

c **1585** T. CATES *Drake's Voy. W. Indies* in *Hakluyt's Voy.* (1905) X. 100 In this ship was great store of dry Newland fish, commonly called with us Poore John. **1592** SHAKS. *Rom. & Jul.* I. i. 37. *a* **1612** HARINGTON *Epigr.* II. l, Poore-Iohn, and Apple-pyes are all our fare. **1657** R. LIGON *Barbadoes* (1673) 113 Two barrels of salt Fish, and 500 poor-Johns, which we have from New England. **1695** CONGREVE *Love for L.* II. vii, I warrant nou he'd rather eat a Pheasant, than a Piece of poor John. **1769** PENNANT *Zool.* III. 157 When cured it [the hake] is known by the name of Poor John. **1841** *Mann. & Househ. Exp.* (Roxb.) p. xlii, Salted cod, and hake or Poor John, had been in long esteem as Lenten food.

†**b.** Applied to a person. *Obs.*

1589 *Pappe w. Hatchet* 29 It is your poore Johns, that with your painted consciences haue coloured the religion of diuers.

2. Name for some sea bird. ? *Obs.*

1775 DALRYMPLE in *Phil. Trans.* LXVIII. 399 A. M. saw a bird like a booby, but shorter winged and necked, called by sailors, poor John. **1778** *Ibid.* 404 Saw several poor Johns, some sheerwaters, and a young alcatrass.

poork, poork poynt, obs. ff. PORK, PORCUPINE.

poor-law ('puəlɔː, 'pɔə-). The law, or system of laws, relating to the support of paupers at the public expense.

1752 T. ALCOCK (*title*) Observations on the Defects of the Poor Laws. [**1758** J. MASSIE *Plan for Charity-Houses* (title-p.), Considerations relating to the Poor and the Poor's-Laws of England.] **1764** R. BURN (*title*) The History of the Poor Laws. **1818** COBBETT *Pol. Reg.* XXXIII. 165 In these documents..the calamities of the nation have..been traced back to the Poor-Laws. **1838** LYTTON *Alice* II. vii, The abuses of the old poor-laws were rife in his neighbourhood.

b. *attrib.*, as ***poor-law bill, officer, system***, etc.; **poor-law parish**: see PARISH *sb.* 2.

1835 MARRYAT *Olla Podr.* xi. How the new Poor Law Bill will work remains to be proved. **1857** KINGSLEY *Two Y. Ago* viii, In the present dependent condition of poor-law medical officers.

Hence **'poor-lawism** (*nonce-wd.*), the framing and practical application of poor-laws.

1858 S. G. OSBORNE in *Times* 12 Nov. 7/4 Something more was wanted than stringent poorlawism.

'poorless, *a. rare.* [See -LESS.] Free from poor people.

1778 *Eng. Gazetteer* (ed. 2) s.v. *Wimborn*, When Harley is hareless, Cranborn whoreless, and Wimborn poorless, the world will be at an end.

poorliness: see after POORLY *a.*

†**'poorling.** *Obs. rare.* [f. POOR *a.* + -LING[1] 1.] A child of poverty, one of the poor.

1581 MULCASTER *Positions* xxxvii. (1887) 147 Be there not as vntoward poorelinges, as there be wanton wealthlinges?

poorly ('puəlɪ, 'pɔəlɪ), *adv.* and *a.* [f. POOR *a.* + -LY[2].] In a poor manner or condition.

A. *adv.* **1.** In a state of poverty or indigence; indigently, necessitously. Now somewhat *rare.*

c **1386** CHAUCER *Clerk's T.* 157 Poureliche yfostred vp was she. **1483** CAXTON *Cato* D iij, Bycause that nature hath created the pourly & al naked. **1588** GREENE *Perimedes* 31 Poorely content is better then richlye couetous. **1698** FRYER *Acc. E. India & P.* 121 The Banyans that live poorly and meanly. **1876** S. C. J. INGHAM *White Cross* xxxvii, I will use all these ill-gotten gains in doing good, while I live poorly myself.

2. With deficiency of supply, or of some desirable quality; scantily, inadequately, insufficiently, imperfectly, defectively; in mean style, in lowly guise, humbly; in an inferior way, not well, rather badly, with no great success; not highly, with low estimation.

c **1300** *Havelok* 323 And ther-hinne dede hire fede Pourelike in feble wede. *c* **1386** CHAUCER *Knt.'s T.* 554 Oonly a Squier..Which was disgised pourely as he was. **1483** CAXTON *G. de la Tour* H ij b, The poure wymmen that lay pourely in theyr childbedde. **1552** LATIMER *Serm. Luke* ii. 6–7 Rem. (Parker Soc.) 98 His first coming is but very poorly, without any jollity or pomp. **1626** BACON *Sylva* §669 If you sow one ground still with..the same kind of grain, as wheat, barley, &c. it will prosper but poorly. *a* **1715** BURNET *Own Time* IV. an. 1686 (1823) III. 98 Their books were poorly but insolently writ. **1748** *Anson's Voy.* III. iii. 320 They knew how poorly she was manned and provided for struggling with so tempestuous a gale. **1823** SOUTHEY *Hist. Penins. War* I. 772 From the beginning Sir John Moore had thought..poorly of the Spaniards. **1883** MRS. F. MANN *Parish of Hilby* xviii. 219 Even now the wives and children came but poorly off.

b. Often with ppl. adj. (to which, when used *attrib.*, it is properly hyphened).

1840 DICKENS *Barn. Rudge* iii, Long lines of poorly-lighted streets. **1877** BLACK *Green Past.* v, A spacious, poorly-furnished chamber. **1894** SIR E. SULLIVAN *Woman* 19 Male births are more numerous than female births amongst the poorly-fed of the country. **1897** *Westm. Gaz.* 10 Dec. 4/3 The best modes of dealing with poorly-gifted children.

†**3.** In a way unworthy of one's position; unhandsomely, meanly, shabbily. *Obs.*

13.. *St. Gregory* (Vernon MS.) 579 Þe penaunt porliche he gret [*Cotton MS.* Gregori wiþ scorn he gret]. **1666** PEPYS *Diary* 6 Aug., They told me how poorly my Lord carried himself the other day to his kinswoman, Mrs. Howard, and was displeased because she called him uncle. **1676** DRYDEN *Aurengz.* v. i, The Gods have poorly robb'd my Virgin Bloom. **1680** OTWAY *Orphan* II. vii. 738 'Twas poorly done, unworthy of your self. **1723** STEELE *Consc. Lovers* II. i, A Man, who poorly left me, to marry an Estate.

4. Piteously, abjectly, humbly; despicably, contemptibly; mean-spiritedly, without courage.

1525 LD. BERNERS *Froiss.* II. cxiii. [cix.] 326 To put hymselfe poorely, without any reseruacyon into his obeysaunce and commaundement. **1535** STEWART *Cron. Scot.* (Rolls) I. 64 Out throw the thrang rycht puirlie he flaw. **1649** MILTON *Eikon.* xxviii, To set free the minds of Englishmen from longing to return poorly under that captivity of Kings. **1664** PEPYS *Diary* 24 Dec., He, instead of opposing..did poorly go on board himself, to ask what De Ruyter would have. *a* **1811** LEYDEN *Lord Soulis* Poet. Wks. (1875) 82 Young Branxholm peeped, and puirly spake, 'Oh, sic a death is no for me!'

B. *adj.* Chiefly *colloq.* [app. evolved from the *adv.*, through such a use as *to look poorly*: cf. *to look ill.*] In a poor state of health; somewhat ill; unwell, indisposed. (Always *predicative.*)

[**1573** TUSSER *Husb.* (1878) 79 Some cattle waxe faint, and looke poorely and thin.] **1750** B. LYNDE *Diary* (1880) 171 All summer I complaining and poorly, and my eyes troublesome. **1756** TOLDERVY *Hist. 2 Orphans* III. 201 This quotation caused even Mrs. Nightley to laugh, tho' she was but poorly. **1797** J. BENSON in *Mem.* (1822) 304, I have been rather poorly today. **1855** MACAULAY *Hist. Eng.* xx. IV. 530 His wife had..been poorly.

Hence **'poorliness**, the condition of being poorly; **'poorlyish** *a.*, somewhat poorly. Both *rare.*

1827 J. J. GURNEY in Braithwaite *Mem.* (1854) I. 323 Notwithstanding my poorliness. **1827** LAMB *Let. to Barton* 28 Aug., I am but poorlyish, and feel myself writing a dull letter.

poor man.

1. *lit.* A man who is poor (in any sense of the adj.); *esp.* a man who is indigent or needy, or who belongs to the class of the poor. Also *attrib.*

a **1225** *Ancr. R.* 86 Ase þe þe seið to þe knihte þet robbeð his poure men. *a* **1350** *Cursor M.* 10386 (Gött) To godd he gaue þe lambis to lottis, And to þe pore men þe bole stottis. *c* **1400** MAUNDEV. (Roxb.) xxii. 101 In þat land es na beggar, ne na pouer man. *c* **1450** in Parker *Dom. Archit.* III. 82 Be hit distributed & deportyd to poure men, beggers, syke folke & febull. **1677** YARRANTON *Eng. Improv.* 169 But the poor Man is forced many times to buy his Materials he makes his Commodity with, of some of his own Trade. **1831** J. BANIM *Smuggler* I. xi. 127 What have you to do with..my poor-man sneers at a viscount?

2. Applied in Banffsh., Aberdeensh., etc., with the local pronunciation *peerman* ('pirmən), to a rude device for holding a fir-candle (i.e. a splinter of resinous wood), formerly the ordinary source of artificial light in farm-houses, barns, and cottages.

In the times of licensed mendicancy, the duty of holding and attending to the fir-candle was usually imposed upon the 'bedesman' or vagrant 'poor man', who was granted a night's shelter; and it is generally believed that from him the name *peer-man* passed to the mechanical holder.

1866 GREGOR *Dialect of Banffsh.* 123 *Peer-man*, a candle-stick for candles made of bog-fir..with a cleft piece of iron into which the candle was fixed. **1870** —— *Echo of Olden Time* 20 Light was given either by pieces of bog-fir laid on the fire, or by *fir-can'les*, that is thin splinters of bog-fir, from one to two and a half or three feet long, fixed in a sort of candle-stick called the *peer-man* or *peer-page*. **1880–83** J. LINN in *Trans. Inverness Scientific Soc.* II. 342 It was from this [employment of a mendicant] that the stand on which the fir-candle..was fixed..got its name Peer-Man, Pure-Man, or Puir-Man, these being local pronunciations of Poor Man.

3. poor man of mutton (Sc. colloq.): name for the remains of a shoulder of mutton, consisting mainly of the blade bone, broiled.

1818 SCOTT *Br. Lamm.* xix, I should like well..to return to my sowens and my poor-man-of-mutton. *Ibid.* (note), I think, landlord..I could eat a morsel of a poor man.

4. Also **poorman.** = *poorman('s orange* (see sense 5 a below).

1912 *Jrnl. Dept. Agric. N.Z.* IV. 141 He has several varieties all doing well, amongst them Paramatta, Poor Man, Navel. **1956** F. T. BOWMAN *Citrus-Growing in Austral.* ii. 20 Poorman was mentioned in Shepherd's catalogue (1851) as having been recently introduced from Shanghai by a Captain Simpson.

5. a. Combs. with *poor man's* (or *poor men's*): **poor man's diggings** *U.S.*, *Austral.*, and *N.Z.* (see quot. 1941); †**poor man's (men's) box** = POOR-BOX (*obs.*); **poorman('s orange**, a variety of grapefruit, *Citrus paradisi*, once cultivated in New Zealand; **poor man's orchid**, an annual or biennial plant belonging to the genus *Schizanthus* of the family Solanaceæ, native to Chile and bearing flowers thought to resemble orchids; **poor man's remedy**, local name for wild valerian, *Valeriana officinalis*; **poor man's salve**, local name for *Scrophularia nodosa* and *S. aquatica* (Britten & Holl.); **poor man's sauce**: see quots.; **poor man's torment** *U.S.* (see quot.); **poor man's weather-glass**, the pimpernel, *Anagallis arvensis*, from its closing its flowers before rain; **poor man's** MUSTARD, PARMACETY, PEPPER, PLASTER, TREACLE (see these words).

1548–9 (Mar.) *Bk. Com. Prayer, Communion*, So many as are disposed, shall offer vnto the *poore mennes boxe. **1560** DAUS tr. *Sleidane's Comm.* 70 The rest to be geven to the poore mens boxe. **1875** *Chicago Tribune* 14 Oct. 7/3 If it did pay, it would be what is called *poor man's diggings, for it was no place where capital could be successfully employed. **1876** R. I. DODGE *Black Hills* 109 It has passed into a proverb that 'placer' mining is the poor man's diggings, while 'quartz' mining is only for the rich. **1941** BAKER *Dict. Austral. Slang* 56 *Poor man's diggings*, alluvial gold deposits, i.e., gold which a poor man can work, contrasting with reef-gold which requires capital to develop. **1884** G. E. ALDERTON *Treat. & Handbk. Orange-Culture in Auckland* 66 The *Poor Man's Orange is only good for preserving. **1929** *Jrnl. N.Z. Inst. Hort.* I. 65 The Poorman Orange is really a Pomelo. **1949** R. PARK (*title*) Poor man's orange. **1966** *Encycl. N.Z.* I. 758/2 The main kinds of citrus grown commercially in New Zealand include..so-called New Zealand grapefruit ('Poorman' orange, selected strains). **1959** *Listener* 20 Aug. 298/3 Now is the time to sow schizanthus—the '*poor man's orchid'—for next May. **1976** *Hortus Third* (L. H. Bailey Hortorium) 1018/1 Schizanthus. .. Butterfly Flower, Poorman's orchid. **1657** W. COLES *Adam in Eden* 220 Of Valerian.. They never make any pottage or broath for any one that is sick, but they put some of this Herb therein, be the disease what it will, and is called of them, *The *Poor Mans Remedy.* **1706** PHILLIPS, **Poor-man's Sauce* or *Carrier's Sauce*, Sauce made of a Shalot, cut very small, with Salt, white Pepper, Vinegar and Oil. **1723** J. NOTT *Cook's & Confectioner's Dict.* sig. Mm3 Poor Man's Sauce, *i.e.* a Shalot cut small, white Pepper, Vinegar, and Oil. **1899** W. STEVENS *Jrnl.* 17 July in *Lett.* (1967) 28 Snap-dragon, or as it is vulgarly known: the weed—'*poor man's torment' is a close-knit, yellow, tumbled sort of thing. **1847** *Nat. Cycl.* I. 661 The Pimpernel, or '*Poor Man's Weather-Glass', so called because its flowers..refuse to expand in rainy weather.

b. Now commonly used *fig.* in Combs. to denote a cheaper, usu. simpler or inferior version or imitation of something, or a less satisfactory substitute for something or someone.

1854 H. Melville in *Harper's Mag.* June 95/2 A cup of cold rain water..is called by housewives a 'Poor Man's Egg'. *Ibid.* 97/1 'It is only rice, milk, and salt boiled together.' 'Ah, what they call "Poor Man's Pudding", I suppose you mean.' **1891** *Tit-Bits* 8 Aug. 277/2 There are thousands of costers who earn a livelihood by the sale of.. mussels, which are regarded as the poor man's oyster. **1906** *Dialect Notes* III. 151 *Poor man's pudding*,..cottage pudding. **1924** R. Lardner in *Cosmopolitan* July 60/2 Another nickname for the town [*sc.* St. Petersburg, Florida, U.S.A.] is the Poor Man's Palm Beach. **1949** *Amer. Speech* XXIV. 94 The cheapness and abundance of rabbit pelts.. have made them the 'poor man's mink'. **1951** M. McLuhan *Mech. Bride* (1967) 63/1 Huck Finn, the poor man's Thoreau, is to be read there, too. **1959** *Observer* 9 Aug. 11/2 I.T.V.'s *This Week* has recently become not much better than a very poor man's 'Panorama'. **1962** A. Huxley *Island* v. 46 Chemical and biological weapons—Colonel Dipa calls them the poor man's H-bombs. **1963** *Guardian* 8 Feb. 9/3 The long, many-scened story..is superficially like a poor man's 'Peer Gynt'. **1963** 'R. Erskine' *Passion Flowers in Italy* iv. 42 The porter was heavy-set, with burning Latin eyes: a kind of poor man's Marlon Brando. **1971** *Jrnl. Chem. Documentation* X. 249/1 A general-purpose text-editing system can be a valuable 'poor man's' information-handling tool. **1973** *Times* 21 Apr. 12/1 'Good King Henry' or 'Poor Man's Spinage' must have been tried out for centuries before being used traditionally and regularly, in spring 'messes'.

poorness ('pʊənɪs). [f. poor *a.* + -ness.] The quality or condition of being poor; poverty.

†**1.** Want of wealth or possessions; indigence. *Obs.* (Now replaced by poverty.)

c **1275** *Sinners Beware* 113 in *O.E. Misc.* 75 Þe poure may wel mysse Bute he his pouernesse Mid mylde heorte þolye. **1382** Wyclif *1 Chron.* xxii. 14 Loo! I in my lytyl pornesse haue mad redy before the expenses of the hous of the Lord. *c* **1450** *Godstow Reg.* 71 For powrenesse of his vicariage. **1613** Chapman *Revenge Bussy D'Ambois* I. i, See how small cause..the most poore man [has] to be grieu'd with poorenesse. *a* **1661** Fuller *Worthies* (1662) III. 11 Which See,..for the poorness thereof, lay Bishopless for three years.

b. *fig.* (Cf. poor *a.* 1 d.)

1380 *Lay Folks Catech.* 1265 (Lamb. MS.) To schew hem meknesse and porenesse to stoppe pride. **1786** A. Maclean *Christ's Commission* iii. (1846) 129 [The Gospel] enjoins poorness of Spirit.

2. Deficiency in some good constituent; unproductiveness; leanness or want of vigour caused by ill feeding; thinness, scantiness, insufficiency.

1577 B. Googe *Heresbach's Husb.* III. (1586) 142 b, Lacke of good feeding, whereof proceedeth poorenesse, and of poorenesse, skabbes and manginesse. **1626** Bacon *Sylva* §665 The Poorenesse of the Herbs..shew the Poorenesse of the Earth. **1782** H. Watson in *Med. Commun.* (1784) I. 89 From the poorness of the blood contained in its vessels. **1883** *Contemp. Rev.* June 904 Exhausted from poorness of diet.

3. Deficiency in some desirable quality; smallness of worth; inferiority, paltriness, meanness. Also (with *pl.*) an instance of this, a paltry or inferior piece of work.

1628 Wither *Brit. Rememb.* v. 1493 Let none the poorenesse of my gifts deride. **1712** Addison *Spect.* No. 285 ¶4 Ovid and Lucan have many Poornesses of Expression upon this Account. **1884** *Law Times* 29 Nov. 73/2 The poorness of the accommodation provided for the judges.

b. Want of spirit or courage; paltriness or meanness of character or conduct.

1625 Bacon *Ess., Simulation* (Arb.) 507 A Habit of Dissimulation, is a Hinderance, and a Poorenesse. *a* **1716** South *Serm.* (1744) X. 226 Those indeed..would, no question, account all refusal of a duel poorness and pusillanimity. **1822** C. Wells *Stories after Nat.* 99 The duke unhorsed the lady, chiding Alfred for his poorness.

'poor-rate. Also 8–9 poor's rate. A rate or assessment, for the relief or support of the poor.

1601 *Acc. Bk. W. Wray* in *Antiquary* XXXII. 80, ixs. xd. ..for the pur rait mony. **1782** Miss Burney *Cecilia* IX. iv, I pay the poor's rate, and that's what I call charity enough for any man. **1797** *Monthly Mag.* III. 74 The exorbitant poor-rates with which the public there have been burthened for some time past. **1817** Byron *Beppo* xlix, Poor's rate, Reform, my own, the nation's debt. **1863** H. Cox *Instit.* III. ix. 730 Householders..paying poor-rates and borough-rates.

poorshouse ('pʊəzhaʊs, 'pɔə-). Also **poors house, poor's house.** Mainly *Sc.* var. of poorhouse.

1745 *Sessions Papers* (Donaldson v. Home) 3 July 2 Samuel Neilson, late Deacon of the Masons, Undertaker for building of the Poors House. **1756** *Bristol* (Virginia) *Vestry Bk.* (1898) 164 Ordered that Stephen Dewey..agree in settleing the Terms of the Poors House. **1820** J. Flint *Lett. from Amer.* (1822) 192 Some paupers in a poor's house at Cincinnati refused to carry water for their own use. **1870** J. Nicholson *The Puir's-Hoose Laddie* in *Idylls* 45, I was glad to become a wee Puir's-hoose laddie. **1899** E. F. Heddle *Marget* ii. 10 She..is to gang to the sale; but she's no' to gang to the puirs-hoose. **1907** [see poor *a.* 7 d]. **1923** T. Johnston *Hist. Working Classes in Scot.* 35 There were 30 hospitals or poorshouses from Turriff to the Lowlands.

'poor-,spirited, *a.* Having or showing a poor spirit (cf. quot. 1611 s.v. poor *a.* 5 b); †having a paltry spirit, low-minded (*obs.*); deficient in spirit or courage, cowardly.

1670 G. H. *Hist. Cardinals* II. II. 170 Certain pittifull and poor-spirited reasons. **1710** Norris *Chr. Prud.* viii. 363 That sottish and poor-spirited Vice, the Vice of Covetousness. **1749** Fielding *Tom Jones* III. v, Master Blifil was generally called a sneaking rascal, a poor-spirited wretch, with other epithets of the like kind. **1860** Geo. Eliot *Mill on Fl.* III. i, Mr. Tulliver would never have asked anything from so poor-spirited a fellow for himself.

Hence **,poor-'spiritedness.**

1662 Gurnall *Chr. in Arm.* verse 19. xiii. §2 (1669) 515/2 Ye that think it childish and poor-spiritedness to weep at a Sermon. **1898** R. F. Horton *Commandm. Jesus* iv. 50 He does not praise poverty as such, still less does He refer to what we mean by poor-spiritedness.

‖**poort** (pɔət). *S. Afr.* [Du. *poort* (poːrt) gate, port *sb.*², in S. Africa, a pass.] A mountain pass, *esp.* one cut by a stream or river.

1796 tr. *F. Le Vaillant's New Trav. Afr.* II. 194 We issued from the mountains through a sort of passage, or defile, which is called the *Poort*. **1801** J. Barrow *Acct. Trav. S. Afr.* I. ii. 109 The Poort may be considered as the entrance into Camdeboo. **1834** Pringle *Afr. Sk.* ii. 149 We entered the poort, or gorge of the mountains, through which the River of Baboons issues. **1850** R. G. Cumming *Hunter's Life S. Afr.* (ed. 2) I. 45 This poort, or mountain pass, the terror of waggon-drivers. **1894** B. Mitford *R. Fanning's Quest* xxii, A poort is a pass or defile as distinct from a kloof. **1932** C. Fuller *Louis Trigardt's Trek* vi. 68 Once through the poort, the junction of the spruit with the river is but a few hundred yards off. **1949** L. G. Green *In Land of Afternoon* i. 21 A poort is different from a pass, for it is a passage through the mountains along the bed of a stream.

poort, poort colyce, obs. ff. port, portcullis.

poortith ('pʊətɪθ). *Sc.* and *north. dial.* Forms: 6 **purteth, puirteith,** 6– **puirtith,** 8– **poortith.** [a. OF. *pouer-, poverteit* (12th c. in Littré), *povretet* (1329 in Godef. *Compl.*), *poevreteit* (1466 Ibid.), *povretez* (pl. of *-tet*, 15th c. Ibid.):—L. *paupertāt-em*, accus. of *paupertās* poverty. The examples cited show the OF. form in *-tet*, surviving almost to the date of the Sc. examples in *-teth*.] The condition of being poor; poverty.

1508 Dunbar *Flyting* 118 Bot now, in winter, for purteth thow art traikit. **1567** *Gude & Godlie B.* (S.T.S.) 73 Extreime puirteith, nor greit ryches, Thow gif me not. **1721** Ramsay *Prospect of Plenty* 199 Curs'd poortith! love and hymen's deadly fae. **1786** Burns *Twa Dogs* 104 They're no sae wretched's ane wad think, Tho' constantly on poortith's brink. *a* **1839** Praed *How Poetry is best paid for* i. Though sorrow reign within his heart, And poortith hold his purse. [In E.D.D. from Shetland to Northumbld. and Cumbld.]

poorty: see poverty.

'poor-will. [So named in imitation of its disyllabic note: cf. whip-poor-will.] A bird of the N. American genus *Phalænoptilus*, esp. *P. nuttalli*, common in the Western United States.

1888 Roosevelt in *Century Mag.* Mar. 664/2 At nightfall the poor-wills begin to utter their boding call from the wooded ravines back in the hills; not 'whip-poor-will', as in the East, but with two syllables only. *Ibid.*, A poor-will lit on the floor beside me.

poory, poose, poost, obs. ff. pory *a.*, pose, post.

pooste, var. poustie, power.

poot (pʊt), *sb.*¹ Now chiefly *north.* A dial. form of poult, applied not only to chickens and young game birds, but to the young of various other animals, e.g. a small haddock, a young trout.

(In the latter application some would refer it to OE. *púta* in *ǽle-púta* eel-pout.)

1512 *Will of J. Barlowe* (Somerset Ho.), Fur of fox pootes. **1616** Surfl. & Markh. *Country Farme* 679 Partridge, pheasant, quaile, raile, poots, and such like. **1688** R. Holme *Armoury* II. 311/1 A Cock [is called] first a Peep, then a Chicken, then a Poot. **1697** *Phil. Trans.* XIX. 573 Found them as big as Poot-Eggs. **1825** Jamieson, *Poot*, this seems to be the same with *Pout*, used to denote a small haddock, *Fife*. **1828** *Craven Gloss.* (ed. 2), *Poot*, a young growse or moor poot. **1890** J. Service *Thir Notandums* i. 5 The lambin' o' the yowes, the cleckin' o' the poots.

poot, *sb.*² *Obs.* [A variant of pote *sb.*¹: cf. *poot* pote *v.*] A stirring rod: see quot.

1683 Moxon *Mech. Exerc., Printing* xviii. ¶2 A long strong round Iron Stirring Poot; the Handle of which Stirring Poot is also about two Yards long or more, and the Poot it self almost twice the length of the depth of the Melting Pot.

poot, poote, var. pote *v.*; obs. or dial. f. put *v.*

†**pooter,** *sb.*¹ *Obs. rare.* [f. *poot*, pote *v.* + er¹.] = poting-stick, or poking-stick.

1602 Warner *Alb. Eng.* IX. xlvii. 218 Busks, Perrewigs, Maskes, Plumes of feathers fram'd, Supporters, Pooters, Fardingales aboue the Loynes to waire, That be she near so bomle-thin, yet she crosse-like seem's four-squaire.

pooter ('puːtə(r)), *sb.*² [f. the name of F. W. *Poos* (b. 1891), U.S. entomologist + -er¹.] A suction bottle for collecting insects, having one tube through which they are drawn into the bottle and another, protected by muslin or gauze, which is sucked.

1939 *Amateur Entomologist* Sept. 33 A coleopterist's sucking tube (a pooter) is useful when collecting large numbers. **1959** Southwood & Leston *Land & Water Bugs* 401 If the pooter is of standard size, say 3" × 1", then when an empty bottle is needed, tap the glass sharply—so that the bugs fall to the bottom—remove the rubber bung and replace it with a cork. **1968** M. Tweedie *Pleasure from Insects* 115 Not all kinds of ants can be collected by the convenient tin-and-slate method, and a more usual way is to use an aspirator or 'pooter', a piece of entomological apparatus designed for collecting all sorts of small insects. **1982** *Times* 21 Aug. 20/1 When they get a catch the net is thrown over the head so that the fly hunters can suck out the flies into a pooter, a glass container.

pooter ('puːtə(r)), *v.* [Etym. unknown.] *intr.* To depart in a hurry; to hasten away. Also with *off*.

1907 *Dialect Notes* III. 196 *Pooter*,..to depart speedily. 'I told him to git, and he just *pooter*, I can tell you.' **1966** *Punch* 6 July 32/3 The ex-bookseller, his fortune depleted, is left on the last page pootering off to his ex-girl-friend.

Pooterish ('puːtərɪʃ), *a.* [f. the name *Pooter* (see below) + -ish¹.] Resembling, characteristic of, or associated with Charles Pooter, an assistant in a mercantile firm, whose mundane domestic, social, and business troubles are the subject of the fictional *Diary of a Nobody* by George and Weedon Grossmith (1892).

1966 *New Statesman* 11 Mar. 349/3 Take a Pooterish Little Man with sexual and cultural ambitions outside his class, [etc.]. **1976** *Times Lit. Suppl.* 31 Dec. 1626/2 So many square miles of vapid and banal and Pooterish suburb. **1977** *Times* 14 May 10/4 George VI's deadpan account of Pooterish bishops blundering through his coronation. **1978** *Times Lit. Suppl.* 24 Feb. 229/3 The Pooterish touch in 'inexpensive' betrays a lack of awareness.

poother, obs. or dial. f. pother, powder.

pooty ('puːtɪ), *a.* (*sb.*) Affected or childish var. pretty *a.* (*sb.*)

1825 [see cross lots *advb. phr.*]. **1848** J. R. Lowell *The Courtin'* in *Biglow Papers* 1st Ser. 10 The wannut logs shot sparkles out Towards the pootiest, bless her! **1849** C. Brontë *Shirley* II. iv. 105 Purchase in his stead some sweetly pooty pug or poodle. **1850** Thackeray *Pendennis* II. xv. 147 She's a little money too..a pooty little bit of money. *a* **1854** [see *country jake* s.v. country 16]. **1906** Galsworthy *Man of Property* II. iii. 149 'You'll have room here,' he said, 'for six or seven hundred dozen—a very pooty little cellar!' **1932** Auden *Orators* III. 104 That piss-proud prophet, that pooty redeemer. **1961** Partridge *Dict. Slang* Suppl. 1229/1 Pooty is a favourite mid-Victorian adjective meaning 'pretty'—of which, via *purty*, it is a perversion. **1980** G. Nelson *Charity's Child* iii. 45 Do 'e remember.. the pooty shells I collected?

poove: see poof *sb.*¹

poovey, poovy, varr. poofy *a.*

pop (pɒp), *sb.*¹ Forms: see pop *v.*¹ [Onomatopœic: goes with pop *v.*¹]

1. An act of popping. **a.** A blow, knock, stroke, slap; now, a slight rap or tap. *Obs.* exc. *dial.*

c **1400** *Laud Troy Bk.* 4421 Philomene..ȝaff him certes suche a poppe, That he fel ouer his hors croppe. *Ibid.* 9300 He hadde lauȝt many a pop, For ther was many a strok ȝeuen. **1483** *Cath. Angl.* 286/2 A Poppe; vbi a strake. **1825** Jamieson, *Pap, pawp*, a blow, a thwack. *Aberd.* **1857** G. Outram *Lyrics* (1887) 137 Ilka pap wi' the shool on the tap o' the mool.

†**b.** A humorous remark, a joke; cf. crack *sb.* 5. *Obs. rare.*

a **1550** *Image Hypocr.* I. 518 in *Skelton's Wks.* (1843) II. 420 With your mery poppes: Thus youe make vs sottes, And play with vs boopepe.

c. In Baseball: a ball hit high into the air but close to the batter, thus providing an easy catch. Usu. *attrib.*, as *pop fly* [fly *sb.*² 2 b], etc. *N. Amer.*

1935 J. T. Farrell *Judgment Day* viii. 185 A line single was driven to left, the pitcher picked a pop out of the air. **1945** *Sun* (Baltimore) 12 Mar. 10-0/5 A pamphlet which knocked the Doubleday legend higher than one of Babe Ruth's pop fouls. **1961** *Rocky Mountain News* (Denver, Colorado) 2 May 50 The White Sox had taken a 5-4 lead in the top of the sixth on a pair of pop fly hits. **1969** *Sci. Amer.* Jan. 49/1 The outfielder is watching..a pop fly to the infield. **1972** *N.Y. Times* 4 June v. 2/5 Gentry retired the great man on a pop foul to Mays. **1975** *New Yorker* 14 Apr. 98/2 Jay Kleven, a young non-roster catcher, hit two pop flies to center. **1978** *Verbatim* Feb. 2/2 One of my favorites is the phrase for a towering pop fly that shoots straight up to the sky and comes down in the same area, usually caught by the catcher. The announcer says, 'He could have hit that ball in a silo.'

d. An injection of a narcotic drug. *slang.*

1935 A. J. Pollock *Underworld Speaks* 118/1 *Take a pop*, to take an injection of morphine. **1953** W. Burroughs *Junkie* Gloss. 14 *Pop, bang, shot, fix*... Injection of junk. **1956** R. Thorp *Viper* vi. 92 'Care for a pop now and again?' This was a kick I hadn't made, I told him. **1970** N. Marsh *When in Rome* v. 126 I'm not hooked. Just the odd pop. Only a fun thing.

2. a. A short abrupt sound of explosion.

1591 Percivall *Sp. Dict.*, *Buchete*, the cheeke and a pop with the mouth. **1634** T. Johnson tr. *Parey's Wks.* 629 By the only regresse of the extended muscles into themselves.. somewhiles with a noyse or pop. **1855** Chamier *My Travels* II. vi. 91 The common pops of the squibs and crackers. **1876** Geo. Eliot *Dan. Der.* xxxix, I cannot bear people to keep their minds bottled up for the sake of letting them off with a pop.

b. The moment occupied by a pop; *at a pop*, in one instant, suddenly [cf. F. *tout à coup, tout d'un coup*]; *on the pop of*, about to, on the point of. *dial. rare.*

1534 MORE *Comf. agst. Trib.* II. Wks. 1202/2 At a poppe, down they descende into hell. **1847–78** HALLIWELL, *Pop*, a short space. *Lanc.* **1903** in *Eng. Dial. Dict.* **1922** JOYCE *Ulysses* 66, I was on the pop of writing Blazes Boylan's.

c. A turn (at doing something); an attempt; a 'go'.

1868 'MARK TWAIN' *Let.* 20 Nov. (1917) I. ix. 156, I am simply lecturing for societies, at $100 a pop. **1904** W. N. HARBEN *Georgians* 2 Ef I don't whack it to you this pop, old hoss, I'll eat my hat. **1916** 'TAFFRAIL' *Pincher Martin* xv. 271 'Why doesn't we 'ave a pop at 'er?' ''Ave a pop at 'er! She's twenty mile orf, if she's a hinch, an' yer knows as well as I does that none o' our ships 'ere 'as got hanti-haircraft guns wot'll 'it 'er at that range.' **1928** WODEHOUSE *Money for Nothing* ii. 35 He decided to have a pop at it. **1946** F. SARGESON *That Summer* 66, I thought no, the going's good, I'll give it one more pop. **1954** WODEHOUSE *Jeeves & Feudal Spirit* i. 12 But why didn't Florence tell Percy to go and have a pop at Stilton Cheesewright? **1971** *Southerly* XXXI. 136 But I couldn't keep that game up for too long; at five cents a pop you can't afford to waste too many. **1976** R. BARNARD *Little Local Murder* x. 133, I don't suppose he makes much more than seventy-five pee a pop for them.

d. The rapid opening of a pop-valve.

1901 M. M. KIRKMAN *Locomotive Appliances* 122 Should the valve close with too much drop of boiler pressure, move the screw-ring (*C*) to the left..until sufficient change has been accomplished. To increase the pop, move ring (*C*) to the right. **1905** C. S. LAKE *World's Locomotives* vi. 112 The screw-down valve is set so that the limit of 'pop' action is 2 lbs. per sq.in. above the nominal boiler pressure, and the valves close when that pressure has been reduced to 2 lbs. per sq.in. less than the nominal boiler pressure. **1951** E. A. STEEL *Greenly's Model Steam Locomotives* (rev. ed.) xiii. 234 A 'pop' action (an accelerated discharge of the valve) can be obtained by making the head of the valve nearly fit a cylindrical recess in the seating.

3. a. A shot with a fire-arm. Also *fig.*

1657 W. MORICE *Coena quasi Κοινή* xxiv. 249 They have onely faced the enemy,..given a pop or two, and raised a smoak. **1829** W. T. MONCRIEFF *Giovanni in Lond.* II. i, You've quite made up your mind to have a pop at him? **1881** FREEMAN in Stephens *Life & Lett.* (1895) II. ix. 228 Prestige, you know, I always like to have a pop at.

b. *transf.* A pistol. *slang.*

1728 [DE FOE] *Street Robberies Consider'd* 33 Popps, Pistols. **1748** SMOLLETT *Rod. Rand.* viii, I gleaned a few things, such as a pair of pops, silver mounted. **1834** H. AINSWORTH *Rookwood* III. v, His pops in his pocket. **1896** *Harper's Mag.* XCII. 784/2 Pops all put away, so she won't be finding one and be killing herself.

4. In the names of two West Indian species of *Physalis* (Bladder-herb or Winter Cherry): the ***cow-pop*** or ***pops***, and ***horse pop*** or ***pop-vine***: see quots.

1750 G. HUGHES *Barbadoes* 161 Pops; *Lat.* Alkekengi Indicum majus. This Plant hath..thin bluish capsular Pods, which inclose a round..Fruit of about the Bigness of a small Cherry... There is another Plant, which bears the same kind of Fruit..being a creeping scandent Plant... This is called the Pop-Vine, and grows in most Parts of the Island. **1848** SCHOMBURG *Hist. Barbados* 610 *Physalis barbadensis*, Jacq. Pop Vine, *Hughes*. Horse Pop. *Physalis angulata*, Linn. Pops, *Hughes*. Cow Pop.

5. A name for any effervescing beverage, esp. ginger-beer or (later) champagne, from the sound made when the cork is drawn from the vessel containing it. *colloq.*

1812 SOUTHEY *Lett.* (1856) II. 284 A new manufactory of a nectar, between soda-water and ginger-beer, and called pop, because 'pop goes the cork' when it is drawn. **18..** J. WILSON *Laking* in *Casquet of Lit.* I. 39/2 With plenty of ginger-beer,..soda, and imperial pop. **1884** H. SMART *Post to Finish* II. xvi. 251 He don't warrant my calling for 'pop' [champagne]. **1894** H. DRUMMOND *Ascent Man* 214 [A man], when he calls champagne fizz, or a less aristocratic beverage pop, is following in the wake of the inventors of Language. **1926** *Scribner's Mag.* Aug. 116/2 Senior officers may for dignity's sake get off with light treatment and a fine of cigars or pop (it was beer in the good old days). **1931** W. S. MAUGHAM in *Hearst's International* Oct. 51/2 A bottle of pop tonight, my pet, and a slap-up dinner. **1969** L. KENNEDY *Very Lovely People* ii. 106 The waiter said, 'All I got is bottled pop. Take your choice.' **1976** A. HILL *Summer's End* i. 18 We sat in the stern drinking the pop, trying to count the bubbles as they rose behind our noses.

6. a. A mark made by a slight rapid touch; a dot; a spot, a speck. Also *fig.*

1718 MRS. BRADSHAW in *Lett. C'tess Suffolk* (1824) I. 28 You are a pop nearer being a countess than you was last week. *c***1840** J. D. HARDING in Collingwood *Life Ruskin* (1893) I. viii. 92 That marvellous pop of light across the foreground. **1886** C. SCOTT *Sheep-Farming* 138 The draft ewes..only receive a 'pop' or dot of the same tar from a round stick on the shoulder. **1894** R. S. FERGUSON *Westmorland* xviii. 290 Strokes and pops and letters marked with tar or ruddle.

b. ***pops and pairs***: app. a corruption of *post and pair* (see POST *sb.*[4]).

*c***1780** M. LONSDALE *Upshot* in S. Gilpin *Songs* (1866) 276 At pops an' pairs laikt long an' sair. **1804** R. ANDERSON *Cumberld. Ball.* 94 Pay me the tuppence I wan frae thee Ae neet at pops and pairs.

7. *slang.* The act of pawning. ***in pop***: in pawn or pledge: cf. POP *v.*[1] 7, POP-SHOP.

1866 *Routledge's Every Boy's Ann.* 292 'Great shame—put him in pop—gentleman's son'..I knew that her 'put him in pop' meant that I was pawned when a baby. **1886** J. K. JEROME *Idle Thoughts* (1896) 7 Yet what a piece of work a man makes of his first 'pop'... He hangs about outside the shop..he enters..he comes out of the shop [etc.].

pop (pɒp), *sb.*[2] [app. short for POPPET or POPLET. Cf. also obs. F. *popine*, *poupine* a pretty little woman (see POPPIN).] A term of endearment for a girl or woman; darling; also, a mistress, a kept woman.

1785 G. A. BELLAMY *Apology* II. 39 A few nights after my benefit, Lord Tyrawley came into the room smiling, and said,..'Pop, I have got you a husband!' **1825** T. CREEVEY *Papers*, etc. (1904) II. 87 When I look at these three young women, and at this brazen-faced Pop who is placed over them,..the marriage appears to me the wickedest thing I ever heard of. *Ibid.* 209, 268. **1898** *Tit-Bits* 11 June 201/1 Well, pop, since I'm your father, I'm going to give you a ticket to the circus.

pop, *sb.*[3] *dial.* [perh. from prec. sb.] A local name of the Redwing (*Turdus iliacus*).

1848 *Zoologist* VI. 2258 The redwing is a 'pop'.

pop (pɒp), *sb.*[4] A colloquial abbreviation of *popular concert*: see POPULAR 3 b.

1862 GEO. ELIOT in *Life* (1887) 355 We have been to a Monday Pop, to hear Beethoven's Septett. **1891** *Newcastle Even. Chron.* 14 Dec. 2/6 The Saturday Pops in Newcastle are in a bad way. **1898** *Westm. Gaz.* 19 Dec. 10/2 A Dohnanyi 'Pop'. In every respect Mr Ernest von Dohnanyi was the hero of Saturday's Popular Concert at St James's Hall. **1934** M. H. WESEEN *Dict. Amer. Slang* 381 Pop..a popular concert.

Hence **'poppite**, a performer at, or a frequenter of, the popular concerts.

1895 *Westm. Gaz.* 5 Nov. 3/2 The death of that old and famous 'Poppite', Sir Charles Hallé. **1902** *Ibid.* 13 May 1/3 The itinerant muffin-man who vexes the souls of devout 'Poppites' on Saturday afternoons.

Pop, *sb.*[5] [Said to be so called from L. *popina*, or Eng. *lollipop shop*, 'the rooms having been orig. in the house of Mrs. Hatton, who kept such a shop'.] At Eton College, The name of a social club and debating society, founded in 1811.

1865 *Etoniana* 207 (Farmer) The chief attraction of Pop lies in its being a sort of social club,..the members are strictly limited (originally twenty-two, since increased to twenty-eight). **1883** J. B. RICHARDS *Seven Years at Eton* xxxiii. 366 He [W. W. Wood] was one of the most fluent speakers at 'Pop'. **1889** MAXWELL LYTE *Hist. Eton College* 375 Pop has always had a great social power. **1902** G. W. E. RUSSELL in *Encycl. Brit.* XXVIII. 733/2 He [Gladstone at Eton] was seen to the greatest advantage..in the debates of the Eton Society, learnedly called 'The Literati' and vulgarly 'Pop'.

pop (pɒp), *sb.*[6] *colloq.* (chiefly *U.S.*).

a. Abbreviation of POPPA.

1838 in *Southwestern Hist. Q.* (1926) XXX. 147 Sent my packet..to pop in the post office at N Orleans. **1840** *Knickerbocker* XVI. 207 'Pop!' screamed a white-headed urchin from the house, 'Mam says supper's ready.' **1904** H. R. MARTIN *Tillie* iii. 33 Are you feelin' too mean to go help pop? **1911** [see MOM]. **1948** *Denison* (Texas) *Herald* 1 July 1/3 Butch..was vacationing with his pop at the popular National Park Service Lake Texoma resort. **1958** H. E. BATES *Darling Buds of May* i. 11 'Larkin, that's me,' Pop said... 'Larkin by name, Larkin by nature.' *Ibid.* ii. 39 'We're in the library,' Ma said. 'Pop, look at the library.' **1962**, etc. [see MOM]. **1973** P. DICKINSON *Gift* v. 77 'Oh yes, Pop' *please*,' said Sonia. **1979** R. RENDELL *Make Death love Me* i. 12 His father-in-law came in... Alan and Pam called him Pop, and Christopher and Jillian called him Grandpop.

b. Hence in extended use, an elderly man.

1844 in *Amer. Speech* (1965) XL. 131 And I'll go down to ole birginy, And marry pop Miller's sister. **1889** *Sporting Life* (Philadelphia) 29 May 2/6 'Pop' Chadwick is among those who are opposed to the wire. **1943** K. TENNANT *Ride on Stranger* (1968) vii. 78 You've just told us, pop,..that if the cops catch up on you, you'll be lining a cell. **1947** *Daily Oklahoman* (Oklahoma City) 28 Dec. 5/8 'Pop', as he is known in this area, will use the 'fancy' cane to help guide his sightless way during his strolls along Shamrock streets. **1980** P. GOSLING *Zero Trap* iii. 29 'Can somebody give me a hand with Pop, here? He still wants to stay sleepies for a while.

pop (pɒp), *sb.*[7] Abbrev. of POPPYCOCK.

1890 KIPLING *Barrack-Room Ballads* (1892) 11 All we ever got from such as they Was pop to what the Fuzzy made us swaller. **1924** GALSWORTHY *White Monkey* II. iv. 151 Nobody pitied her; why, then, should she pity them? Besides, pity was 'pop', as Amabel would say.

pop (pɒp), *a.* (*sb.*[8]) *colloq.* [Abbrev. of POPULAR *a.* (*sb.*): cf. POP *sb.*[4]] **1. a.** Designating music (esp. song) having or regarded as having a wide popular appeal (see POPULAR *a.* (*sb.*) 6 b). Freq. *absol.* as *sb.*, a popular song or piece of music; popular music collectively.

Quot. 1862 is an isolated nonce-use influenced by and alluding to POP *sb.*[4]

1862 GEO. ELIOT *Let.* 26 Nov. (1956) IV. 67 There is too much 'Pop' for the thorough enjoyment of the chamber music. **1926** *Amer. Mercury* Dec. 465/1 She coos a pop song. **1935** *Hot News* Aug. 19/1 Turn the record over and you have another winner—'Add a Little Wiggle'—a masterpiece made out of a song-and-dance 'pop'. **1945** S. HUGHES in C. Madge *Pilot Papers* 78 Cole Porter's 'Begin the Beguine'..has twice the regulation number of bars that a good 'pop' should have. **1947** A. J. MCCARTHY *Jazzbook 1947* 119 Jelly would play one of his new 'pop' songs, watching..for its effect. **1954** *Unicorn Bk. 1953* 320/1 A magazine..each December publishes a list of the year's top pop music and musicians. *Ibid.* (*heading*) Top pop tunes. **1954** *Billboard* 13 Nov. 38 It is interesting to note that the preponderance of local over national sponsorship of deejay programs varies according to the program category, with the weight of local sponsorship most evident in rhythm & blues then country & western and finally pop. **1957** D. HAGUE in S. Traill *Concerning Jazz* 129 The veteran Lizzie Miles from New Orleans has evoked nostalgia with her selections of blues and early 'pops'. **1959** J. BRAINE *Vodi* iv. 63 At this time there'd be some pop tunes... They could sometimes induce a vapid cheerfulness. **1959** D. COOKE *Lang. Mus.* ii. 62 The Irving Berlin tune..is a rare example of minor 'pop' music. **1962** D. LESSING *Golden Notebk.* I. 102, I remember the sharp feeling of dislocation it gave me to hear the pop-song in London, after Willi's sad nostalgic humming of what he told us was 'A song we used to sing when I was a child'. **1963** *Daily Tel.* 7 Dec. 9/7 A 'pop music' dispute between song writers and concert promoters is to go before the Performing Right Tribunal in London on Monday next. **1967** *Crescendo* Feb. 23/2 A pop that will only last a couple of weeks. **1970** *Observer* 20 Sept. 26/1 In the world of pop, the death of Jimi Hendrix on Friday from a suspected overdose of drugs will seem as if Tchaikovsky or Mozart had also been struck down at only 24. **1973** *Country Life* 13 Dec. 2015/1 Pop-song writers masquerading as composers in the grand manner. **1974** J. COOPER *Women & Super Women* 9 During the holidays they..play pop music too loudly for their parents' liking. **1975** *Gramophone* Jan. 1357/2 Incidentally the 'pop' purchaser may well be disconcerted that the battery and carillon at the end of '1812' are relatively restrained. **1976** H. NIELSEN *Brink of Murder* i. 12 An aged spinster..not only refused to sell to Pucci but insulted the dignity of his project by leasing the premises to a group of pop musicians. **1977** *Rolling Stone* 21 Apr. 91/1 He..makes a misguided stab at pop blues in 'Bluesman'.

b. Phr. ***top of the pops***, applied to the most popular or the best-selling gramophone record over a given period; also *transf.* and *fig.*, highly successful or popular.

1958 *Punch* 8 Oct. 483/1 'Wagon Train' stays top of the pops in ITV features on every channel. **1964** [see DOLLY *a.* c]. **1965** [see CHART *sb.* 3 c]. **1970** J. PORTER *Rather Common Sort of Crime* vi. 64 Your little friend Rodney was a dodo, a brontosaurus, last week's top of the pops..but dead, finished, a stale bun. **1978** G. GREENE *Human Factor* II. iii. 84 The top of the pops for any given year came as readily to Davis's memory as a Derby winner.

c. In various special collocations: attributive, as ***pop album***, ***ballad***, ***band***, ***concert***, ***disc***, ***fan***, ***festival***, ***group***, ***lyric***, ***number***, ***opera***, ***record***, ***single***, ***star***, ***world***; objective, as ***pop-singer***, ***-singing*** adj.; similative, as ***pop-style(d)*** adj.

Quot. 1880 for *pop-concert* is properly in the sense of POP *sb.*[4]

1949 *Billboard* 8 Oct. 26/2 (*heading*) Pop albums. **1955** L. FEATHER *Encycl. Jazz* 100 Basie also used a girl singer, usually for the pop ballads. **1964** *Punch* 28 Oct. 658/2 Those sentimental pop-ballads of the 'thirties. **1958** *Amer. Speech* XXXIII. 225 A *mickey* or *Mickey Mouse* band is..the kind of pop band that sounds as if it is playing background for an animated cartoon. **1967** *Listener* 16 Feb. 229/1 Some acoustical engineers in the United States believe that the sound produced by teenage pop bands is actually damaging to human ears. **1880** GEO. ELIOT *Jrnl.* in *Lett.* (1956) VII. 342 Went to our first Pop-Concert and heard Norman Neruda, Piatti, etc. **1963** 'D. SHANNON' *Death of Busybody* iv. 51, I went to the Hollywood Bowl... It was a pop-concert night, Gershwin. **1973** R. PARKES *Guardians* ii. 49 He imagined continental pop-concerts had something to do with the youth counter-culture. **1957** *Times* 19 Dec. 5/1 The most recent phenomenon in the world of the 'pop disc' has been the astonishing rise of the 'teen-age' singer. **1973** R. PARKES *Guardians* iii. 64 His income as a disc-jockey; his profits from the few pop-discs he cut; and..his chairman's salary. **1960** *Guardian* 13 Apr. 3/3 An out and out 'pop' fan. **1966** *B.B.C. Handbk.* 44 They have to cater for..the 'pop' fan. **1979** S. SMITH *Survivor* xvii. 176, I was obviously beyond the age group of the average hippy or pop fan. **1970** *Guardian* 31 July 9/5 Pop festivals..are big business. **1975** *Times* 8 Aug. 1/1 The Government has ordered an urgent review of public policies on pop festivals. **1965** M. BRADBURY *Stepping Westward* i. 65 A pop group, called the Haters, were tunelessly celebrating dim proletarian adolescent oestrus. **1967** *Listener* 18 May 644/1 Two of the Rolling Stones 'pop group' are sent for trial on drugs charges. **1977** 'E. CRISPIN' *Glimpses of Moon* viii. 147 Ten minutes alone inside the tent, with Miss Bale to keep intruders away, and that pop group to cover up any noise. **1960** *Guardian* 22 July 10/2 The committee have found that pop lyrics are drivel and often debasing. **1966** *Vogue* Oct. 177/1 Almost the only simple, open-hearted verse we now have are pop-lyrics. **1945** S. HUGHES in C. Madge *Pilot Papers* 76 The term Dance Music is used here to denote..the playing and singing of 'pop' numbers as opposed to the cult of 'Jazz'. **1958** P. GAMMOND *Decca Bk. Jazz* ii. 38 The popularity of jangle-piano, and of pop numbers performed in cool ragtime style. **1960** *News Chron.* 31 Mar. 4/4 Pop numbers..can be sung and understood outside the story's context. **1969** N. COHN *A Wop Bopa Loo Bop* (1970) xviii. 172 Townshend has finally written a full-scale pop opera. **1976** *Cumberland News* 3 Dec., 56 11-year-olds..were practising an ambitious production of 'Smike', a pop opera based on the Dickens novel, 'Nicholas Nickleby'. **1950** *Billboard* 7 Oct. II. 27/2 (*heading*) Top pop records of the year. **1961** H. E. BATES *Day of Tortoise* 60 She played pop records such as *What Do You Want If You Don't Want Money?* **1973** L. COOPER *Tea on Sunday* ii. 27 The..strident noise of pop records. **1948** *Billboard* 25 Dec. 38 At press time it was learned that Apollo had re-signed pop singer Mary Small for another year with options. **1955** L. FEATHER *Encycl. Jazz* 79 The Decca company began to record him..in duets with pop singers. **1958** J. TOWNSEND *Young Devils* 8 The sickly exhortations of 'pop' singers. **1973** J. WAINWRIGHT *Pride of Pigs* 30 The pop singer finished his protest song and there was a thin ripple of applause. **1955** L. FEATHER *Encycl. Jazz* 160 Grotesque distortions..valid more as entertainment than as jazz or pop singing. **1962** *Times* 28 Feb. 5/4 An atmosphere more suggestive of pop-singing..than great artistry. **1949** *Billboard* 8 Oct. 26/1 (*heading*) Best-selling pop singles. **1962** A. NISBETT *Technique Sound Studio* 252 Pop singles contain the same amount as a 10-inch 78, whereas e.p. records contain perhaps double. **1978** *Sunday Times* 29 Jan. 43/1 A record by two Jamaican girls is currently No. 2 in the BBC's top twenty pop singles. **1967** *Listener* 23 Feb. 271/2 We were taken, step by step, through the process of manufacturing a pop star. **1972** J. MCCLURE *Caterpillar Cop* v. 71 She was behaving as if Boetie had become a pop star, rather than a corpse. **1955** L. FEATHER *Encycl. Jazz* 159/2 Eddie [Heywood], Jr...formed own sextet late '43, made name through pop-style arr. of *Begin the Beguine*. **1963** *Times* 24 May 15/7 The pop-style hymn-settings of John Gardner. **1974** *Publishers Weekly* 26 Aug. 302/2 It's a pop-styled run-through of the big moments, great plays and subway series heroics. **1959** 'F. NEWTON' *Jazz Scene* i. 22 Jazz has made much of its way as part of the pop world. **1967** M. DRABBLE *Jerusalem the Golden* vii. 170 She had as resolutely and as puritanically scorned the pop world.. as her mother had done before her. **1973** *Melody Maker* 25 Aug. 27 In the pop world, the rule is that musicians are a special breed.

2. ***pop art***, art that uses themes drawn from popular culture, *spec.* an art form characterized by the depiction of commonplace subjects using strong colour and imagery, sharp features, and a photographic technique of representation (see also quot. 1967). Also *ellipt.*, as *pop*. Hence ***pop artist***, ***-painter***; ***pop-painting*** vbl. sb.

1957 *Listener* 26 Sept. 464/1 A sophisticated apologia for subtopia is to call it 'pop art' which the middle-aged are perverse to frustrate. *Ibid.* 470/1 Some people even defend Subtopia as a type of vigorous folk art—or 'pop art'—to be fostered. **1958** *Archit. Rev.* CXXIII. 208/1 Four chairs.. would not have been known to the designer of this room had they not been published in the popular magazine *Look*, which gave the *chaise-longue* version the full pop-art treatment. **1962** *Listener* 9 Aug. 217/3 All three of the painters are adherents of the new school of 'pop'. *Ibid.* 30 Aug. 324/1 Certain of the 'pop' painters can apparently be paired off with artists on the other side of the Atlantic. *Ibid.* 324/2 The tendency of 'pop' paintings, Hockney's for instance, to resort to the use of words in order to help out the images is in itself significant. *Ibid.* 27 Dec. 1087/1 The third wave of pop artists use their imagery to differentiate themselves from the regular audience for art. **1964**, etc. [see OP[4]]. **1966** 'H. MACDIARMID' *Company I've Kept* iii. 78 The pop artist does not address any audience, does not represent any point of view; he has staked everything on nothingness. **1967** L. ALLOWAY in L. R. Lippard *Pop Art* 27 The term 'Pop Art' is credited to me, but I don't know precisely when it was first used. (One writer has stated that 'Lawrence Alloway first coined the phrase "Pop Art" in 1954'; this is too early.) Furthermore, what I meant by it then is not what it means now. I used the term, and also 'Pop Culture', to refer to the products of the mass media, not to works of art that draw upon popular culture. In any case, sometime between the winter of 1954–55 and 1957 the phrase acquired currency in conversation, in connection with the shared work and discussion among members of the Independent group. **1968** *New Yorker* 24 Feb. 100 There were about a hundred and fifty paintings on view in the huge Main Hall ..and they ranged from Op and Pop to Picasso. **1971** 'A. BURGESS' *MF* xiii. 144 There was a big pop-art poster whose crude yellows and blues were an obscenity. **1972** E. LUCIE-SMITH in Cox & Dyson *20th-Cent. Mind* III. xvi. 470 The first example of Pop is now generally conceded to have been a small collage made by the English painter Richard Hamilton..in 1956. **1976** *New Yorker* 22 Mar. 107/1 Among the Pop artists shown, Claes Oldenburg is by far the most gifted as a draftsman. **1977** *Jrnl. R. Soc. Arts* CXXVI. 47/2 Out of Léger came aspects of Pop: in particular that aspect known as Roy Lichtenstein.

3. Appealing to or expected to appeal to popular taste generally (chiefly in the senses of POPULAR *a.* (*sb.*) 4a). Also *absol.* as *sb.* Spec. ***pop culture***, culture based on popular taste and disseminated widely and usu. on a commercialized basis; hence ***pop-cultural*** adj. Also, of a technical subject, etc.: popularized, presented in a popular form, as ***pop psychology*** (hence ***pop-psycher***, ***-psychologist***).

1958 *Spectator* 14 Feb. 197/2 The promoters of 'pop' fiction must ruthlessly wipe out any tragedy that remains unique and personal. **1958** *Observer* 23 Mar. 14/3 As a sop to pop, the gallants on the benches at the sides of the stage could be TV personalities. **1958** *Ibid.* 25 May 14/2 His admirable pop science *New Horizon* series. **1959** C. MACINNES *Absolute Beginners* 73 It's my aim..to bring quality culture material to the pop culture masses. **1962** *Observer* 20 May 12/7 Pop archaeology books sell like hot cakes. **1962** *Punch* 12 Sept. 390/2 A highly competent performer on these pop-science occasions. **1963** *Ibid.* 3 July 30/2 Pop religion is the dreariest mixture imaginable. **1963** *Dædalus* Winter 22 Available critiques of pop-cultural depravities (from *Playboy* to the *National Geographic*) and compilations of economic facts about massification..are, to be sure, of some help. **1964** *Punch* 5 Feb. 211/1 An almost naïvely sensational bit of pop-psychology sex. **1966** D. JENKINS *Educated Society* ii. 58 That commercialized 'pop culture' which is a form of anti-culture. **1967** *New Scientist* 25 May 473/1 Expo is dominated by technology, but it is a gay, often pop technology that you meet, technology that is confident enough to laugh at itself. **1968** *Punch* 27 Nov. 753/1 Pop-psychologists are saying that certain trigger phrases used by Enoch Powell expose a sub-conscious racial prejudice. **1969** *Listener* 17 July 92/2 If Pop means mass media and consumer goods, ads and comics, Coke bottles and plastic, what then can it have to do with Art? **1970** G. GREER *Female Eunuch* 171 The pop revolution..has replaced sentiment with lust. **1970** K. MILLETT *Sexual Politics* (1971) II. iv. 186 In such cases Freud and his school after him will do all in their power to convince her of the errors of her ways:..by the actual mental policing of 'pop psych'. **1971** *Time* 14 June 16/2 The fact that Ed [Cox] proposed so quickly after Tricia [Nixon] began her new life at the White House might suggest to pop-psychers that he was afraid of losing her. **1972** *Nature* 25 Aug. 471/2 The author has shrugged off..practically everything that animal ethologists have tried to contribute to our understanding ..—dismissing..[Desmond] Morris's books as 'pop ethology'. **1973** J. WAINWRIGHT *High-Class Kill* 41 Pop culture: garbage done up in poster-colours and caterwauling to badly played guitars. **1975** *Imperial Oil Rev.* IV. 30/2 How to make work more satisfying or, to use the word of pop sociology, how to 'humanize' it. **1975** *New Yorker* 21 Apr. 111/1 No one has yet piously complained of too much violence in the Ngorongoro Crater or tried to shroud a beehive in pop psychology. **1977** P. JOHNSON *Enemies of Society* xi. 160 At various levels, too, psychology and sociology have become the pop-science, or folk-science, of the western urban masses. **1977** *Time* 14 Mar. 43/1 Most of the Morgan message is standard to all the pop self-help books that publishers have been churning out ever since Dale Carnegie and Norman Vincent Peale reaped their first millions. **1978** *Encounter* July 96/1 On the debit side..are the evils of 'development' and the pap of pop culture.

pop (pɒp), *v.*[1] Also 5–7 poppe, 7–8 popp, 9 *dial.* pap, pawp. [Onomatopœic: goes with POP *sb.*[1], *int.*, *adv.*]

1. *trans.* To strike, rap, knock (? *obs.*). Also, to strike with a slight rap or tap. *dial.*

c **1386** [implied in POPPER *sb.* 1]. *c* **1442** *Chron. London* (1827) 130 Redy to a popped hym in the face with his dagger. **1483** *Cath. Angl.* 286/2 To Poppe; vbi to stryke. *c* **1817** HOGG *Tales & Sk.* I. 336 She popped her master on the forehead.

2. *intr.* To make a small quick explosive sound; to burst or explode with a pop.

1576 NEWTON *Lemnie's Complex.* 124 b, Popping or smacking with the mouthe. **1809** MALKIN *Gil Blas* x. iii. ¶9 The report of musketry, popping so near the head-quarters of our repose. **1855** DELAMER *Kitch. Gard.* (1861) 179 When you hear the first gun pop at the unhappy partridges. **1859** [see 3]. **1894** K. GRAHAME *Pagan P.* 159 When the chestnuts popped in the ashes.

b. Of the eye: To protrude (as if to burst *out*).

1680 J. AUBREY in *Lett. Eminent Persons* (1813) III. 565 Full eie, popping out and working. **1931** E. O'NEILL *Mourning becomes Electra* (1932) 217 Small comes tearing out and down the portico steps, his face chalky white and his eyes popping. **1940** W. FAULKNER *Hamlet* I. ii. 37 They looked exactly like two fellows that had done hung themselves in one of these here suicide pacts, with their heads snubbed up together and pointing straight up..and their eyes popping. **1951** M. KENNEDY *Lucy Carmichael* II. i. 73 Pray Bess, what was he like? Oh, says Bess, her eyes popping, he's *terrific*! **1961** N. MANERO *Cook-Out Barbecue Bk.* 16 You'll have the neighbor's eyes popping as well as their mouths watering! **1979** G. HAMMOND *Dead Game* xi. 143 He sold the Dickson Round Action [gun] there for a price that made Molly's eyes pop.

3. *trans.* To cause to make a sudden explosive report; to fire, let off, as an explosive or fire-arm (also *fig.*); to cause (anything) to burst with a pop. ***to pop corn***: see quot. 1859, and cf. POP-CORN.

1595 *Drake's Voy.* (Hakl. Soc.) 23 We popt away powder and shott to no purpose. *a* **1652** A. WILSON *Inconstant Ladie* II. i, Haue a speech readie to popp of in triumph. **1832** LYTTON *Eugene A.* I. ix, When a musket's half worn out, schoolboys buy it—pop it at sparrows. **1850** *Quincy* (Illinois) *Whig* 12 Nov. 4/1 One barrel of rice corn will make 32 barrels after popping. **1853** *Harper's Mag.* May 853/1 A little boy sat by the kitchen-fire, A-popping corn in the ashes. **1859** BARTLETT *Dict. Amer.* (ed. 3), *To Pop Corn*, to parch or roast Indian corn until it 'pops' open... 'A little boy sat by the kitchen fire A popping corn in the ashes.' **1873** 'S. COOLIDGE' *What Katy Did* x. 201 'I popped the corn!' cried Philly. **1883** O. W. HOLMES *Seasons* in *Pages fr. Old Vol. Life* 160 The ginger-beer carts rang their bells and popped their bottles. **1887** *Daily News* 17 June 5/1 There was popped corn. **1907** *St. Nicholas* May 614/1 Grandma lives on a farm and we used to have great fun popping corn whenever we went to see her. **1949** *Sat. Even. Post* 21 May 36/1 Last year American farmers grew some 300,000,000 pounds of pop-corn. This, when popped, is enough to fill 2,400,000,000 ten-cent bags. **1979** *Sunset* Apr. 129/2 (Advt.), The Popaire hot air popper pops 4 quarts of light, fluffy pop-corn in 5 minutes!

4. *intr.* To shoot, fire a gun. *colloq.*

1725 *New Cant. Dict.*, *To pop*, to fire a Pistol. **1776** EARL PERCY *Lett.* (1902) 74 They sent down..a number of their rangers to pop at our advanced posts and sentries. *a* **1845** BARHAM *Ingol. Leg.* Ser. III. *Ld. Thoulouse*, Popping at pheasants. **1877** A. B. EDWARDS *Up Nile* xix. 563 We heard our sportsman popping away..in the barley.

b. *trans.* To shoot *down*; to pick *off* with a shot.

1762 *Pennsylv. Archives* (1853) IV. 84 They knew the woods well, and would pop them down 3 for 1. **1813** SIR G. JACKSON *Diaries & Lett.* (1873) II. 280 Many unwary stragglers have been popped off in this way. **1861** DU CHAILLU *Equat. Afr.* ix. 106 Keeping our guns in readiness to pop down anything which should come in our way.

5. *trans.* To put promptly, suddenly, or unexpectedly (sometimes implying quiet or furtive action): usually with some extension, as *down*, *in*, *on*, *out*, *up*, *into* or *out of* (a place), etc.

a **1529** SKELTON *Replyc.* 122 Whan ye..porisshly forthe popped Your sysmaticate sawes Agaynst Goddes lawes. **1553** *Respublica* (Brandl) v. vii. 18 He vaire [= fair] popt me to silence. **1567** GOLDING *Ovid* VI. 73 b, Now diue they to the bottome downe, now vp their heades they pop. **1577** HANMER *Anc. Eccl. Hist.* (1619) 329 To put by him that poppeth in any other seeds. **1587** GREENE *Tritameron of Loue* Wks. (Grosart) III. 77 What moues you..to pop forth so sodainlie this darke probleme? **1596** NASHE *Saffron Walden* Wks. (Grosart) III. 174 You..popt out your Booke against me. **1662** R. MATHEW *Unl. Alch.* §82. 109 She.. popt it into her mouth, and swallowed it all at once. **1750** H. WALPOLE *Lett.* (1846) II. 355 Another fellow of Eton has popped out a sermon against the Doctor since his death. **1778** MISS BURNEY *Evelina* xxxiii, He takes and pops me into the ditch! **1834** LYTTON *Pompeii* I. vii, To..pop him slily into the reservoir. **1852** MRS. STOWE *Uncle Tom's C.* ix, Popping his head out of some window or door. **1858** *Punch* 20 Nov. 206 If you will pop on your hats..I'll take you and your friend out for a drive. **1860** THACKERAY *Round. Papers*, *Screens in Dining Rooms*, One dear little lady..popped her paper under the tablecloth. **1891** B. POTTER *Let.* in J. Mackenzie *Victorian Courtship* (1979) ix. 125, I popped on an old skirt and a mackintosh and trudged through the rain. **1977** B. PYM *Quartet in Autumn* ii. 22 'I should put the bacon in a cooler place if I were you,' said Letty. 'Yes, I'll pop it in one of the filing cabinets.' **1977** K. O'HARA *Ghost of T. Penry* viii. 67 Sit you down and I'll pop the kettle on.

b. *spec.* To put *out* (a light) suddenly; to jot *down* (words); †to put *off* (a person) *with* (something), put *off* or put aside (a thing).

1602 MARSTON *Antonio's Rev.* IV. iii, Ile conquer Rome, Pop out the light of bright religion. **1602** —— *Ant. & Mel.* I. Wks. 1856 I. 16 Swarthy darknesse popt out Phœbus eye. *a* **1625** FLETCHER *Noble Gent.* I. i, And do you pop me off with this slight answer? **1658–9** in *Burton's Diary* (1828) III. 149, I would have you not to pop off the question. **1774** MME. D'ARBLAY *Early Diary* (1889) I. 304 Popping down my thoughts from time to time upon paper. **1822** E. A. PORDEN in L'Estrange *Friendships Miss Mitford* (1882) I. v. 141, I..shall at once pop down what occurs to me. **1844** DICKENS *Mart. Chuz.* xxviii, Pop me down among your fashionable visitors. **1894** A. DOBSON *18th Cent. Vignettes* Ser. II. i. 3 He popped out the guttering candle.

6. To put (a question) abruptly, to 'come out with' (†also with *out*); spec. ***to pop the question*** (*slang* or *colloq.*), to propose marriage (also ellipt. *to pop*).

1725 BYROM *Rem.* (1854) I. I. 148 Dear Governor and Governess, the boy here having given me leave to ask you how you do, I have made bold to pop the question to you. **1754** RICHARDSON *Grandison* (1810) VI. xx. 101 Afraid he would now, and now, and now, pop out the question; which he had not the courage to put. **1809** MALKIN *Gil Blas* IV. i. ¶6 You..pop the question without making any bones of it. **1826** MISS MITFORD *Village* Ser. II. (1863) 432, I have reason to think the formidable interrogatory, which is emphatically called 'popping the question', is actually the only question which he has never popped. **1867** TROLLOPE *Chron. Barset* I. 58 'Is it settled?' she asked. 'Has he popped?' **1885** E. C. JOHNSON *Track of Crescent* xv. 190 When a young man wanted to 'pop' to the object of his affections, he called at the house. **1960** M. SHARP *Something Light* vii. 64, I haven't actually...popped, yet. **1972** *N.Y. Times* 3 Nov. 7/1 (Advt.), Now's the time to pop the question! 20% off diamond engagement rings. **1976** *Daily Mirror* 16 Mar. 9/3 The thought of popping the question to Princess Marie Therese de Bourbon Parma 'has never entered my head,' he added.

b. *intr.* ***to pop off***, to speak hastily, angrily, or wildly; to state one's opinions vociferously; to complain loudly. *U.S. colloq.*

1933 PARTRIDGE *Slang To-day & Yesterday* 455 *Pop off, to*, talk wildly, threateningly, argumentatively. C20. **1934** M. H. WESEEN *Dict. Amer. Slang* 381 *Pop off*, to lose one's temper; to give vent to anger. **1943** *Sun* (Baltimore) 20 Sept. 16/8 The dealer 'popped off without knowing what he was talking about'. **1951** R. S. PRATHER *Bodies in Bedlam* vi. 47, I popped off to Brane last night, but I didn't kill him. **1970** *Daily Tel.* 7 Feb. 16/2 Company chairmen have been popping-off about the iniquities of selective employment tax for four years. **1977** *Time* 7 Mar. 40/3 Most Plains residents dismissed Billy's charge. 'He was just poppin' off,' said one woman. **1977** J. WAMBAUGH *Black Marble* (1978) x. 241 He remembered what happened to him today in a phone booth when he popped off, so he bit his lip and kept quiet.

7. To put in pledge, to pawn. *slang.*

1731 FIELDING *Lett. Writer* II. ii, Ay,..he'll make us pop our unders for the reckoning; we'll not go with him. **1851** MAYHEW *Lond. Lab.* I. 474 [She] took one to pop..for an old 'oman what was on the spree. **1902** BARRIE *Little White Bird* vi, It was plain for what she had popped her watch.

8. *intr.* To pass, move, go or come promptly, suddenly, or unexpectedly (*up*, *down*, *in*, *out*, *about*, *between*, *over*, *off*, etc.). Also (*Austral. colloq.*) phr. ***how are you popping*** (***up***)?: how are you getting on?

1530 PALSGR. 662/1 He went so nere the banke that soudaynly he popped in to the water over heed and eares. **1589** NASHE *Anat. Absurd.* Wks. (Grosart) I. 25 The temperature of the wether will not permitte them to pop into the open ayre. **1602** SHAKS. *Ham.* v. ii. 65 He that hath.. Popt in betweene th' election and my hopes. **1660** FULLER *Mixt Contempl.* (1841) 200 Some presently popped up into the pulpit. **1706** E. WARD *Wooden World Diss.* (1708) 76 A hundred or more Cartesian Puppits pop up upon Deck. **1710** *Brit. Apollo* III. No. 67. 3/1 She might Pop in. **1770** J. BARETTI *Journ. Lond. to Genoa* IV. App. 266, I expected.. to see some beautiful damsel pop out suddenly. **1780** MME. D'ARBLAY *Diary* 6 Dec., In the evening..I just popped down to play one rubber with dear Mr. Thrale. **1829** SCOTT *Jrnl.* 27 Feb., Some [copies]..will be popping out one of these days in a contraband manner. **1834** *Tait's Mag.* 421/2 Just pop home for a bundle of prospectuses. **1860** F. NIGHTINGALE *Notes on Nursing* iv. 29 Many of the accidents which happen from feeble patients tumbling down stairs.. happen..from the nurse popping out of a door. **1899** F. T. BULLEN *Log Sea-waif* 151 He requested me to 'pop across the road' and get him a drop of rum. **1904** E. NESBIT *Phoenix & Carpet* xii. 224 If you'll excuse me, I'll just pop out and see what I can do. **1913** C. MACKENZIE *Sinister St.* I. i. iv. 54 Nurse..had acquired a habit..of popping out of the back-door on secret errands. **1919** WODEHOUSE *Damsel in Distress* xv. 186 'And now you get along,' said the man. 'You pop off.' **1934** C. LAMBERT *Music Ho!* III. 156 He [*sc.* Glinka] was more than a gifted amateur who happened to pop up at the right time. **1942** *Tee Emm* (Air Ministry) II. 88 A cunning safety switch..pops up when there is a short. **1960** *Guardian* 26 Feb. 5/4 Mrs Harris popped out to do some shopping. **1960** I. JEFFERIES *Dignity & Purity* ii. 28 Let's pop off for a drive. **1965** *Listener* 2 Dec. 934/2 'Afternoon Theatre', sometimes infinitely trivial, popped up with a winner in *The Aquarium on Platform Two*, by Peter Preston. **1968** 'N. BLAKE' *Private Wound* v. 79 Maire'll look after you till I get back. I just have to pop out and see a fella for a minute or two. **1977** B. PYM *Quartet in Autumn* vii. 63 'Goodbye, then,' she said. 'I'll pop in again some time.' **1978** J. THOMSON *Question of Identity* xiv. 146 Will you pop over to my tent and bring me my little box?

1894 H. LAWSON *Short Stories in Prose & Verse* 89 'How are yer?' 'Oh! I'm alright!' he says. 'How are ye poppin' up!' **1907** N. SPIELVOGEL *Cocky Farmer* 16 Whatto, Joe. How are you popping up? **1933** N. LINDSAY *Saturdee* 10 What-oh, Stinker, how you poppin' up? **1942** S. CAMPION *Bonanza* 207 Howya poppin', cobber?

b. To come *on* or *upon* abruptly, suddenly, unexpectedly, or by chance; to light *upon*, happen *upon*.

1741 Richardson *Pamela* (1824) I. 61, I was but talking to one of her maids just now,..and she popt upon us. **1759** Sterne *Tr. Shandy* I. xiv, I had the good fortune to pop upon the very thing I wanted. **1791** Mary Wollstonecr. *Rights Wom.* v. 131 We pop on the author when we only expected to meet the father. **1815** W. H. Ireland *Scribbleomania* 165 She pops, as perchance, upon kind Mistress Meeke.

c. ***to pop off*** (or ***off the hooks*** or ellipt. *to pop*): to die. *slang.* Also *trans.*, to kill, destroy.

1764 Foote *Patron* I. (1781) 17 If Lady Pepperpot should happen to pop off. **1778** Mme. D'Arblay *Lett.* 5 July, What a pity it would have been had I popped off in my last illness. *c* **1820** Keats *Let. to Haydon* Poet. Wks. (1886) 24, I am afraid I shall pop off just when my mind is able to run alone. **1824** J. Hogg *Private Mem. Justified Sinner* 253 Might we not..pop him off in private and quietness? **1887** G. R. Sims *Mary Jane's Mem.* 112 He'd said his mother would soon pop off the hooks, and he'd have all her money. **1922** E. Wallace *Flying Fifty-Five* x. 58 'If he'd only popped off in the war, Jacques.'.. 'You might have been 'popped off' yourself if you'd only got within range of a bullet.' **1928** D. L. Sayers *Unpleasantness at Bellona Club* ix. 110 Perhaps it's just as well he popped off when he did. He might have cut me off with a shilling. **1940** G. S. Gordon *Let.* 24 May (1943) 221, I have joined the Defence Volunteers, and hope to pop a parachutist before the business ends. **1945** J. B. Priestley *Three Men in New Suits* v. 65 He fancies he might pop off at any time. **1952** W. R. Burnett *Vanity Row* (1953) v. 45 She'd be worrying how to knock me off. Or trying to get me het up..so's I'd pop. **1975** J. Goulet *Oh's Profit* vi. 36 Oh popped a carpenter ant, chewed. **1975** *New Yorker* 26 May 32/2, I agreed not to say 'death', 'dying',..'go home feet first', 'pop off the hooks'. **1977** *Navy News* Sept. 21/5 It is possible for a Seacat or Seaslug missile to get close enough to topple the target off course and 'pop' the parachute recovery system.

d. ***to pop in and out***: to visit or come and go frequently or casually.

1858 Mrs. Gaskell *Let.* 19 Oct. (1966) 517 We have more people popping in & out than we expected. **1926** Wodehouse *Heart of Goof* iv. 126 He drew a picture of their little home, with Crispin for ever popping in and out. **1971** N. Freeling *Over High Side* I. 40 Martinez was not altogether unknown... He had often 'popped in and out'. **1974** 'S. Woods' *Done to Death* 14 He can't keep popping in and out... But if she had a companion—. **1979** 'M. Hebden' *Death set to Music* iii. 26 He spent most of his time off duty popping in and out of bed with any pretty woman he could find.

e. *Cricket.* Of the ball: to rise sharply off the pitch when bowled; to get up (get *v.* 80 h). Also ***to pop up***.

1871 'Thomsonby' *Cricketers in Council* 39 'Spin' is not twist, it is that which gives the ball a tendency to twist, break back, shoot, pop up, or, in fact, do something eccentric. **1888** Steel & Lyttelton *Cricket* iii. 153 The ball will twist a great deal on this class of wicket [hard and crumbled]... It is also inclined both to 'pop' and keep low. **1906** A. E. Knight *Compl. Cricketer* iii. 119 The ball, too, will rear up quickly, kick or 'pop up'. **1921** P. F. Warner *My Cricketing Life* vi. 126 On a sticky wicket he was capable of sending down a difficult off break, and of making the ball pop. **1926** J. B. Hobbs *Test Match Surprise* xxi. 211 Then the ball commenced to 'pop', in cricket parlance—to 'stop and look at them'—and Grimmell..had the two brilliant batsmen in difficulties. **1959** *Times* 29 May 4/2 Nicholls skied a catch.. aiming across the line at one that popped.

f. To pay (*for*). *slang.*

1959 R. Bloch *Big Kick* in *Blood runs Cold* (1961) 213 He popped for three jugs tonight, just to get in. Likes to make the scene. *Ibid.* 218 He didn't pop... I said we were leaving ..and all he did was smile. **1968** L. J. Braun *Cat who turned on & Off* (1969) xxi. 182 Hell. I didn't buy you anything, but I'll pop for lunch.

9. *trans.* In Baseball: to hit (a ball) high into the air but close to the batter, thus providing an easy catch. Also *intr.*, to get put out by hitting a high ball that is caught by an opponent. *N. Amer.*

1867 *Ball Players' Chron.* 6 June 2/3 On Hunniwell popping one up which fell into Sumner's hands, Smith had to retire, a double play putting both out. **1886** [see fan *v.* 8 b]. **1912** C. Mathewson *Pitching in a Pinch* 204 Then Doyle popped up a weak foul behind the catcher. **1931** *Kansas City* (Missouri) *Times* 19 Oct., Hallahan replaced Grimes on the mound for the Cardinals and then Bishop popped out to 'Pepper' Martin. **1947** *Los Angeles Times* 3 Oct. II. 1/7 Johnson swung and popped up to end the inning. **1948** *Chicago Tribune* 7 Mar. II. 1/4 Lupien popped to Johnson. **1974** *Los Angeles Times* 13 Oct. III. 10/2 Bando struck out. Messersmith grounded to the pitcher. Rudi popped to short.

10. *trans.* To inject (a narcotic drug). Also, to take (a narcotic drug). Also *intr. slang.*

1956 R. Thorp *Viper* vi. 92 Nearly everyone there seemed to be popping. There were so many needles working you might have thought it was a tailors shop. **1959** W. Burroughs *Naked Lunch* 29 Ever pop coke in the mainline? **1962** 'K. Orvis' *Damned & Destroyed* xii. 79 Was there ever a junkie..that was too pooped to pop? **1968** *N.Y. Times* 2 Aug. 46 Executives of finance and insurance companies are popping pills these days to tranquilize their nerves. **1968** M. Woodhouse *Rock Baby* ii. 109 For him the day..started when he swallowed the first pill or popped the first vein. **1972** *Sunday Sun* (Brisbane) 2 July 14/3 The addict..now bangs, pops, shoots and jabs his veins with the hypodermic needle. **1976** R. Rosenblum *Sweetheart Deal* iv. 46 The half-million ghetto kids who'll start popping junk this year. **1977** *Amer. Speech 1975* L. 64 *Pop*,..take an amphetamine in order to stay awake (to study). 'I popped for my history final.'

†**pop**, *v.*[2] *Obs. rare.* (Also 5 erron. **papphe.**) [Origin uncertain: cf. OF. *popiner* (later *poupiner*) to adorn (oneself), said of a woman (Godefr.), f. *po(u)pin* dressy, showy: see poppin.] *trans.* To paint or patch (the face) with a cosmetic.

? *a* **1366** Chaucer *Rom. Rose* 1019 No wyntred browis had she, Ne popped hir, for it neded nought To wyndre hir, or to peynte hir ought. *c* **1407** Lydg. *Reson & Sens.* 1368 It needed noght to papphe hir face, For she was..Ryght agreable of look and chere. **1430–40** —— *Bochas* I. xx. (MS. Bodl. 263) 81/1 To farce and poppe ther visage. *a* **1450** *Knt. de la Tour* 68 Whi popithe they, and pluckithe her uisage? **1483** *Quatuor Sermones* in *Festivall*, etc. a v b, Ne haue not your vysage poppyd, ne your here pullyd or crowlyd [*ed.* 1532 pomped].

Hence †'**popping** *vbl. sb.* Also **b.** *concr.* (?) materials used in painting the face.

1426 Lydg. *De Guil. Pilgr.* 13372 In ffrench ycallyd 'ffarderye' And in ynglyssh, off old wrytyng, Ys ynamyd ek 'poppyng'. *a* **1450** *Knt. de la Tour* 70 Doughtres, takithe here..ensaumple to leue all suche lewde folyes and counterfeting, poppinge, and peintinge.

b. 14.. *Voc.* in Wr.-Wülcker 562/1 *Acumen*, a popyn. **1483** *Cath. Angl.* 286/2 Poppynge, *acus, cerusa, stibium, venenum.*

pop (pɒp), *int.*, *adv.* [The same onomatopœic word as pop *sb.*[1], pop *v.*[1], used interjectionally and adverbially.] **1. a.** With (the action or sound of) a pop; instantaneously, abruptly; unexpectedly.

pop goes the weasel, name of a country dance very popular in the eighteen-fifties, in which these words were sung or exclaimed by the dancers while one of them darted under the arms of the others to his partner; also the name of the tune; hence as a vb. and in other humorous uses. See *N. & Q.* (1905) 10th Ser. III. 492, IV. 209.

1621 Fletcher *Pilgrim* III. ii, Into that bush Pop goes his pate, and all his face is comb'd over. **1672** Villiers (Dk. Buckhm.) *Rehearsal* I. (Arb.) 31 As soon as any one speaks, pop I slap it down, and make that, too, my own. **1801** G. Colman *Poor Gentlem.* I. ii, It fell out unexpected—pop, on a sudden; like the going off of a field-piece. *c* **1854** (*Music-seller's Advt.* in *Newspaper*), The new country dance 'Pop goes the weasel', introduced by her Majesty Queen Victoria. —— *Musical Bouquet* No. 409, *Pop goes the Weasel*; *La Tempête*; and *Le Grand Père*. These fashionable dances as performed at the Court balls. **1855** in *N. & Q.* 10th Ser. IV. 211/1 This dance is very popular, it is without deception, 'Pop goes the weasel' has been to Court, and met a good reception. **1855** Smedley *H. Coverdale* xxxiv, Dear old Punch, with his private band pop-going-the-weasel like an harmonious steam-engine. **1855** O. W. Holmes *Poems* 139 Pop cracked the guns! *Mod.* I heard it go 'pop'.

b. *spec.* in phr. ***to go off pop*** (N.Z. colloq.), to break into angry speech.

1933 'P. Cadey' *Broken Pattern* xii. 126 There's no need to go off pop like that. **1940** F. Sargeson *Man & Wife* (1944) 65 He'd do things wrong too, and every chance he got he'd pick on me and go off pop. And of course I'd tell him off back.

2. In repeated form, with (the action or sounds of) a series of pops. Also as *adj.* and *sb.*, the sound of such a series.

1928 V. Woolf *Writer's Diary* 22 Mar. (1953) 124 A rabbit that passes across a shooting gallery, and one's friends go pop-pop. **1951** J. Frame *Lagoon* 10 The pop-pop boats we used to whizz round in the bath on Christmas morning. **1957** —— *Owls do Cry* 29 Sometimes the coal makes a pop-pop.

pop-, in *Comb.* [Cf. pop *v.*[1], *sb.*[1]] Usually the verb in combination with a sb. or adv., meaning something that pops, or that which pops in some way; rarely the sb. or adv.: **pop-beer**, ginger-beer or some other aerated drink; **pop-bottle**, a bottle for an aerated drink; **pop-call** *U.S.*, a sudden or unexpected visit; **popcorked** *a.*, provided with a cork which pops when drawn; **pop-dock, pop-glove**, the Foxglove (*Digitalis purpurea*); **pop-eye**, an out-starting, bulging, prominent eye (cf. pop-eyed *a.*); **pop-hole**, a hole in a hedge, fence, etc., through which animals can pass; **pop-in**, a drink composed of beer into which a small proportion of whisky or brandy is 'popped'; †**pop-mouth**, a mouth able to utter an exclamation with a sharp outburst; **pop-off**, (*a*) the discharge of fire-arms; (*b*) used *attrib.* to designate a safety valve which operates with a pop; **pop-rivet**, a kind of tubular rivet used for fastenings where only one side of the work is accessible, and which is inserted into the hole and then clinched by the action of withdrawing a central mandrel; hence as *v. trans.*; **pop-riveting** *vbl. sb.*; **pop safety valve** = *pop-valve*; **pop-shooter** = popgunner; **pop-top** *U.S.* = *ring-opener* (ring *sb.*[1] 19); also *attrib.*; hence **pop-topping** *vbl. sb.*; **pop-valve**, a spring-loaded safety valve designed to open or close very rapidly at a predetermined pressure; **pop-weed**, a provincial name of the Bladderwort.

1887 C. D. Warner *Their Pilgrimage* (1888) ii. 40 Shooting-galleries, *pop-beer and cigar shops, restaurants, [etc.]. **1900** Ade *Fables in Slang* 28 More than once he had let drive with a pop bottle at the umpire. **1921** A. G. Empey *Madonna of Hills* 2 The occasional noise of an empty '*pop' bottle kicked over under the seats, indicated the audience was restless. **1946** C. Himes *Black on Black* (1973) 259, I looked around and saw cases of pop bottles stacked against the wall. **1971** *Country Life* 23 Dec. 1788/1 That cherished book, its olive green covers carefully clothed in brown paper as a safeguard against pop-bottle rings. **1941** W. C. Handy *Father of Blues* (1957) iii. 27 The *pop-calls of policemen dropping in to catch vagrants. **1974** *News & Reporter* (Chester, S. Carolina) 24 Apr. 4-B/8 Mr. and Mrs. Mark Winchester from Charlotte made 'pop calls' at the Fergusons, W. C. Gladdens, and Countermans. **1922** Joyce *Ulysses* 260 Pat paid for diner's *popcorked bottle: and over tumbler tray and popcorked bottle ere he went he whispered. **1878** Britten & Holland *Plant-n.*, *Pop Dock, *Digitalis purpurea*.—Cornw...from the habit of children to inflate and burst the flower. **1828** A. Royall *Black Bk.* II. 377 But the lawyer..is a shrimp in size, a sallow complexion, small face, and little blue *pop eyes. **1885** 'C. E. Craddock' *Prophet Gt. Smoky Mts.* ii. 45 He had wide pop-eyes, and long ears, and a rabbit-like aspect. **1887** *Pall Mall G.* 29 June 13/2 She has the 'pop eyes' of a voluble talker. **1847–78** Halliwell, **Pop-glove*, the fox-glove. *Cornw.* **1944** *Living off Land* ii. 30 Kangaroos, often hard to shoot, are fairly easy to snare in country where there are netting fences, as often their pads run alongside the fence to a spot where they either jump it or crawl through a '*pop-hole'. **1945** 'G. Orwell' *Animal Farm* i. 9 Mr Jones, of the Manor Farm, had locked the hen-houses for the night, but was too drunk to remember to shut the pop-holes. **1949** D. M. Davin *Roads from Home* 159 'One thing I will say for a pop-hole,' Paddy said, 'once you've found it you're pretty well set. They always make for it.' **1963** *Times* 14 Jan. 13/2 They [*sc.* pigs] get two-thirds of their food outside, having free access through a pop-hole, the rest they forage for in the litter. **1748** Smollett *Rod. Rand.* vi, A liquor called **pop-in*, composed by mixing a quartern of brandy with a quart of small beer. **1870** J. K. Hunter *Life Stud. Charac.* 273 A 'gang o' pap-in' was the order. **1594** Nashe *Terrors of Nt.* Wks. (Grosart) III. 270 Fellowes they were that had good big *pop mouths to crie Port a helme Saint George. **1843** Col. Hawker *Diary* (1893) II. 239 Not even the *pop-off of a Milford snob to be heard. **1944** H. Kerwin *Arc & Acetylene Welding* ii. 6 Keep all pop-off valves on the [carbide] generator in good working order. **1977** *Brit. Jrnl. Anaesthesia* XLIX. 71/1 There is a cooling coil and a safety pop-off valve, by which extra pressure is released and extra moisture in the circuit is expelled intermittently. **1932** *Air Ann. Brit. Empire 1932–33* 396 The most interesting type of rivet which has been specially developed is a tubular rivet known as the *pop-rivet. **1953** *Flight* 18 Sept. 410/2 A corrugated core is sandwiched between two skins, the outer skin being spot-welded and the inner skin pop-riveted to this core. **1967** J. Mills *Low-Cost Car Repairs* xii. 243 Pop-rivets are easily and quickly drilled out in a matter of seconds. **1973** P. Revere *Do Your Own Car Body Repairs* vii. 36 Any area to be pop riveted which is on a surface liable to to be seen, will have to be countersunk first. **1978** *Daily Tel.* 18 Nov. 14/6 His 1924 version was the first all-steel aircraft produced in Britain and necessitated the now universally-used pop-rivet. **1934** M. Langley *Metal Aircraft Construction* (ed. 2) ix. 309 Some very ingenious methods of tubular or '*pop' riveting have been devised by the A.T.S. Co., Ltd., which..combines the patented processes for metal construction of the Armstrong-Whitworth, Boulton & Paul, and Gloster firms. **1973** P. Revere *Do Your Own Car Body Repairs* vii. 37 The cost of a pop riveting gun is about a third the price of a new tyre. **1908** G. F. Gebhardt *Steam Power Plant Engin.* xv. 598 (*heading*) Consolidated *pop safety valve. **1961** F. A. S. Brown *N. Gresley* xvii. 123 One of the new 'B12s', No. 8579, was the subject of extensive rebuilding, and the opportunity was taken to mount a larger boiler..and a round-topped fire-box with pop safety valves. **1845** Col. Hawker *Diary* (1893) II. 258 To avoid the *popshooters. **1970** *Time* 21 Sept. 60/3 Insert finger, tug and quaff: in those few seconds, the aluminium ring atop a *pop-top can of beer or soda fulfills its function. **1972** *Washington Post* (Potomac Suppl.) 29 Oct. 15/3 Acres and acres of sweeping lawn without a styrofoam cup, a pop-top, [etc.]. **1977** C. McFadden *Serial* (1978) xxxiii. 72/2 Joan snapped the pop top on the last can of beer. **1975** *Publishers Weekly* 27 Jan. 42/3 (Advt.), *Pop-topping... New craft with pull-tabs from beverage cans. [**1881** *Engineering News* 10 Sept. 362/2 The great peculiarity of the 'Pop' nickel-seated safety valve ..is that by the use of a stricture the recoil action of the steam is made available to overcome the increased pressure of the spring on the valve-head as it rises.] **1884** Knight *Dict. Mech.* Suppl. 778/1 To do away with the din of the steam escaping from ordinary locomotive *pop valves. **1908** V. Pendred *Railway Locomotive* xxiv. 185 On some lines 'Pop' valves have been tried. They are so called, because instead of rising gradually as the pressure increases after they have begun to blow off, they lift suddenly with a 'pop' and blow off hard for a minute or so. **1927** E. L. Ahrons *Brit. Steam Railway Locomotive 1825–1925* xxiii. 364/2 Ramsbottom safety valves, though still used, are rapidly giving place to pop valves of the Ross pattern. **1968** J. H. White *Amer. Locomotives* viii. 148 The Richardson valve was said to open more than twice as far as an ordinary safety valve. Because of its quick opening it became popularly known as the 'pop' valve. **1869** Blackmore *Lorna D.* vii, I stuck awhile with my toe-balls on the slippery links of the *pop-weed.

‖**popadam** ('pɒpədəm). Also **papadam, papadom, papadum, papodam, papodum, poppadom, poppadum, puppadum, puppodum, -odam.** [Tamil *pappaḍam*, contr. from *paruppu aḍam* 'lentil cake' (Yule).] (See quots.)

1820 *Asiat. Res.* XIII. 315 Papadoms, (fine cakes, made of gram flour, and a fine species of alkali, which gives them an agreeable salt taste and serves the purpose of yeast). **1883** *Fisheries Exhib. Catal.* (ed. 4) 155 Poppadums, from Madras (cakes eaten with curries). **1904** *Daily Chron.* 19 Mar. 8/5 The Anglo-Indian may have with his curry toasted poppodams, water biscuits made from Indian dhall. **1906** *Mrs. Beeton's Bk. Househ. Managem.* lviii. 1601 Thin wafer-like cakes called Papodums. **1928** *Daily Express* 19 July 5/2 There are Bombay ducks and papodams. **1928** *Sunday Express* 12 Feb. 10 And then add the curry... The hot chutney of Madras is the best accompaniment, and with it you may take, if you will, poppadums, Bombay ducks, and a little powdered mint. **1931** *Punch* 13 May 506/3 A puppodum is a thin wafer-like cake made of lentil-flour or something like that. **1932** *Times Lit. Suppl.* 22 Dec. 978/1 *Papadums* are essential to a curry; but to make a *papadum* requires the accumulated experience of a few generations. **1936** *Times Lit. Suppl.* 3 Oct. 792/2 A reputable firm will supply..curry powder, puppadums, [etc.]. **1951** *Good Housek. Home Encycl.* 432/2 Chupatties and papadum are types of Indian breads often served with curries. **1959** *Good Food Guide* 316 Curried chicken Madras with poppadoms and Bombay duck. **1962** *Housewife* (Ceylon) Feb. 33 A meal devoid of appetizers, in the form of a salad, papadams or a blob of cream on the fruit salad, is, I feel, a miserable failure. **1969** *Guardian* 21 Mar. 11/3 A new play opens at the Arts Laboratory..'Chicken Curry and Poppadoms' by Richard Huggett. **1974** 'J. Le Carré' *Tinker, Tailor* xxviii. 243 Jerry Westerby with his enormous hands shattered a popadam on to the hottest curry on the menu.

†**'popal**, *a.* *Obs. rare*⁻¹. [f. POPE + -AL¹.] = PAPAL *a.* So **'popan** *a.* = PAPANE *a.*

1651 C. Cartwright *Cert. Relig.* I. 175 Neither the Vestall nor the Popall Virgins will find any great cause of boasting. **1839** J. Rogers *Antipopopr.* XIII. ii. 294 Quite above the range of popan and priestal philanthropy.

†**'popard.** *Obs. rare.* [Origin uncertain: cf. POPELER, POPPEL. The suffix as in CANARD, MALLARD, etc.] Some kind of fowl: ? = POPPEL.

1413 in *Exeter Reg., Stafford* (1886) 403 *note*, Dorsorium largum, avium volucribus vocatis popardys.

popatrye, obs. form of PUPPETRY.

'pop-corn. orig. *U.S.* [f. POP *v.*¹ 3 + CORN *sb.*¹ 5; in a orig. *popped corn*.] **a.** Maize or Indian corn parched till it bursts open and exposes the white inner part of the grain; 'popped' corn: see POP *v.*¹ 3. Also *transf.* and *fig.* **b.** A variety or sub-species of maize suitable for 'popping'. Also *attrib.*

1823 W. Faux *Memorable Days Amer.* 302, I crossed the Big Wabash..at La Valette's ferry, where is beautiful land, fine young orchards, and two lonely families of naked-legged French settlers, from whom I received two curious ears of poss [*sic*] corn. [**1848** Bartlett *Dict. Amer.*, *Popped corn*, parched Indian corn, so called from the noise it makes on bursting open. The variety usually prepared in this way is of a dark color, with a small grain.] **1850** *Quincy* (Illinois) *Whig* 12 Nov. 4/1 Pop corn is dependent for its peculiar powers..upon the quantity of oil which its whole contains. **1855** 'Q. K. P. Doesticks' *Doesticks, what he Says* xix. 257 [He] had just pawned his coat and a spare shirt to get money to set himself up in business again, as a pop-corn merchant. **1858** *N. York Tribune* 14 Jan. 2/3, I got on the cars..after..flattening out an apple-boy and pop-corn vender. **1875** Emerson *Lett. & Soc. Aims* iv. 119 The pop-corn and Christmas hemlock spurting in the fire. **1875** *Chicago Tribune* 21 Nov. 2/6 Each one had grown tired of jaw-breakers and popcorn balls. **1893** Kate Sanborn *Truthf. Wom. S. California* 129 A farmer raised one thousand bushels of popcorn and stored it in a barn. **1903** *Book of Corn* 327 Popcorn, known botanically as *Zea everta*, is a species group, characterized by the excessive proportion of the corneous endosperm and the small size of the kernels and ear.. Twenty-five varieties were catalogued by Sturtevant. **1922** 'R. Crompton' *Just—William* xi. 220 He purchased a large bag of pop-corn. **1947** *Downtown Shopping News* (Chicago) 2 Jan. 16/3 Pop corn balls are the delight of every child. **1949** F. Peto *Amer. Quilts & Coverlets* ii. 23 The loom-made tufted type used candlewicking for the warp of the foundation and..the characteristic 'popcorn' decoration. **1953** [see HUSTLER 1]. **1965** Mrs. L. B. Johnson *White House Diary* 20 Dec. (1970) 340 There were garlands of popcorn. **1968** *Guardian* 15 Nov. 1/6 Miss Plummer won through on dazzling good looks. As far as a popcorn poll went, they appeared to be a popular choice. **1972** *Country Life* 9 Mar. 591/1 Popcorn is an extremely hard form of maize whose corns expand and 'pop' on heating; it is used only in confectionery. **1973** C. & R. Milner *Black Players* ii. 41 *Popcorn* is a humorous insult which may be translated as 'light-weight'.

pope (pəʊp), *sb.*¹ Forms: α. 1–2 pápa, 2–6 pape, 4–7 *Sc.* paip(e; β. 3– pope, 5–6 poope, (7 *Sc.* pop). [OE. *pápa*, a. eccl. L. *pāpa* (in Juvenal *pāpas*), ad. late Gr. πάππας, παπᾶς, late var. of πάππας father (orig. a child's word; cf. PAPA). Thence also It., Sp., Pg. *papa*, F. *pape*.

In eccl. Gr. πάπας was applied to bishops (in Asia Minor), patriarchs, and popes; it was a recognized title of the Bp. of Alexandria, *a* 250. L. *pāpa*, used as a term of respect for ecclesiastics of high position, esp. bishops (cf. mod. 'Father'), occurs in Tertullian *a* 220, and was applied so late as 640 by St. Gall to Desiderius Bp. of Cahors. But from the time of Leo the Great (440–461) it was in the Western Church applied especially to, and from 1073 claimed exclusively by, the Bishop of Rome.]

I. 1. (With capital initial.) **a.** The Bishop of Rome, as head of the Roman Catholic Church.

Black, Red, White Pope: allusive designations: see quot. 1902.

α. *a* **900** tr. *Bæda's Hist.* IV. i. (1890) 252 Þa wæs in þa tid Uitalius papa þæs apostolican seðles aldorbiscop. *c* **1122** *O.E. Chron.* an. 1115 On þison ȝeare sænde se papa Paschalis Raulfe ærceb' on Cantwarabyriȝ pallium hider to lande. *c* **1154** *Ibid.* an. 1124 On þæs dæies..forðferde se pape on Rome Calistus wæs ȝehaten. *c* **1205** Lay. 29738 Þas þinges weoren idone þurh þene pape of Rome. *Ibid.* 29750 Of Gregorie þan pape [*c* 1275 þe pope]. *a* **1300** *Cursor M* 22596 Gregor þat was pape o rome. *c* **1375** *Sc. Leg. Saints* xxvii. (*Machor*) 1248 A paipe of Rome. **1405** *Lay Folks Mass Bk.* 64 For the pape of Rome and al his cardinals. **1483** *Cath. Angl.* 268/2 A Papes dygnite, *papatus*. **1549** *Compl. Scot* 165 Victht out the lecens of the pape. **1567** *Gude & Godlie B.* (S.T.S.) 204 The Paip, that Pagane full of pryde. **1609** Skene *Reg. Maj., Stat. Robt. III* 53 b, Induring the time of the schisme (quhilk was betwix paip Vrban the 6. and Clement the 6). **1627** H. Burton *Baiting Pope's Bull* 67 Pape and Ape differ but a letter; but their charitie to their Sonnes lesse.

β. *c* **1200** *Trin. Coll. Hom.* 163 Þe holie lorðewes, prophetes, apostles, popes, archebissopes, bissopes, prestes. *c* **1275** Lay. 10130 An holy man þar was pope. *c* **1290** *S. Eng. Leg.* I. 22/90 Þe pope and þe king Edgar. **1362** Langl. *P. Pl.* A. VIII. 8 Part in þat pardoun þe Pope haþ I-graunted. *c* **1440** *Promp. Parv.* 408/2 Poope, *papa*. **1503** Hawes *Examp. Virt.* XIII. iii, There was saynt peter the noble pope. **1526** *Pilgr. Perf.* (W. de W. 1531) 225 Christes vicar in erth, our holy father yᵉ pope. **1581** Mulcaster *Positions* xxxvii. (1887) 163 Make not all priestes that stand vpon the bridge as the Poope passeth. **1624** Bedell *Lett.* x. 138 Paulus V. *Vice-deus* takes too much vpon him, when hee will bee Pope-almightie. *a* **1651** Calderwood *Hist. Kirk* (1843) II. 187 By vertue of the Pop's Bulls. **1700** Farquhar *Constant Couple* I. i, I would rather kiss her hand than the Pope's toe. **1750** Gray *Long Story* iv, Tho' Pope and Spaniard could not trouble it. **1861** M. Pattison *Ess.* (1889) I. 33 England began to look in another quarter for support against France and the Pope. **1873** *Times* 30 May 8/1 The only practical result has been an almost unanimous vote by which the General of the Jesuits, Father Becks—the 'Black Pope' as he is called—will be instantly..turned out of the apartments. **1902** *Daily Chron.* 23 Dec. 5/1 Under this [crucifix] is enthroned Leo XIII, clad all in white—whence his name the White Pope—and receives the allegiance of the Red Pope (the Prefect of the Propaganda), the Black Pope (the General of the Jesuits). **1911** *Encycl. Brit.* XV. 339/2 It is said that the general of the Jesuits is independent of the pope; and his popular name, 'the black pope', has gone to confirm this idea. **1976** P. van Rjndt *Tetramachus Collection* (1977) i. 15 Political details gleaned by the ranks of the 'black pope',..head of the Society of Jesus.

b. An effigy of the pope burnt on the anniversary of the Gunpowder Plot (Nov. 5), on Queen Elizabeth's night, or at other times. *Obs.* or *dial.*

1673 Evelyn *Diary* 5 Nov., This night the youths of the Citty burnt the Pope in effigie, after thay had made procession with it. **1678** Dryden *Œdipus* Epil 34 We know not what you can desire or hope, To please you more, but burning of a Pope. **1732** Pope *Ep. Bathurst* 214 He..heads the bold Train-bands, and burns a Pope. **1828** *Craven Gloss.* (ed. 2), *Pope*, a long pole, to which an effigy of the Pope was attached and burnt on the 5th of Nov. **1849** Macaulay *Hist. Eng.* I. viii, II. xxv. **1887** *Kentish Gloss.*, *Popeing*, to go popeing is to go round with Guy Fawkes on the 5th of November. 'Please, sir, remember the old Pope!'

†**c.** Short for *pope-day celebration*. *Obs. rare.*

1766 J. Adams *Diary* 5 Nov., Wks. 1850 II. 201 Popes and bonfires this evening at Salem, and a swarm of tumultuous people attending them. **1769** *Boston Chron.* 6–9 Nov. 361/2 Description of the Pope, 1769.

2. a. *transf.* Applied to the spiritual head of a Muslim or other non-Christian religion.

c **1400** Maundev. (1839) xxxi. 307 In þat yle dwelleþ the Pope of hire lawe, þat þei clepen Lobassy. **1613** Purchas *Pilgrimage* (1614) 542 In this Citie dwelleth the chiefe Pope, or High Priest, of that Superstition. **1638** Sir T. Herbert *Trav.* (ed. 2) 51 (*Religion of Persees*) The *Distoore* or *Pope*.. has 13 [precepts]. **1836** *Pop. Encycl.* I. 813/2 Those who were henceforward caliphs,..these Mussulman *popes* had not by any means the power of the Christian. **1897** *Westm. Gaz.* 24 Aug. 8/1 A probability that his Majesty of Siam may soon become Pope as well as King—a Buddhist Pope.

b. *fig.* One who assumes, or is considered to have, a position or authority like that of the pope.

1589 *Hay any Work* 34 Leaue your Nonresidencie, and your other sinnes, sweete Popes now. **1689** *Andros Tracts* II. 106 We often say, that 'every man has a pope in his belly'. **1762–71** H. Walpole *Vertue's Anecd. Paint.* (1786) II. 67 This Coquerel, I find by another note, was Generalis monetarius, or Pope of the mint, into which the reformation was to be introduced. **1801** Strutt *Sports & Past.* IV. iii. (1876) 446 In the churches immediately dependent upon the papal see [there was elected] a pope of fools. *Ibid.* 447 The bishop, or the pope, of fools performed the divine service habited in the pontifical garments. **1854** Hawthorne in *H. & Wife* (1885) II. 40 The family are..followers of Dr. McMill, who is the present Low-Church pope of Liverpool. **1893** *Nation* (N.Y.) 19 Jan. 46/3 Burne-Jones..accepted him [Rossetti] as the infallible Pope of Art.

3. a. In early times, A bishop of the Christian Church; *spec.* in the Eastern Church, the title of the Bishop or Patriarch of Alexandria.

1563 *Homilies* II. *Idolatry* II. (1859) 185 *margin*, All notable Bishops were then called Popes. **1570** Foxe *A. & M.* (ed. 2) 11/1 Yᵉ name Pope.. may peraduenture seme more tolerable, as which hath ben vsed in the olde time emong bishops. **1636** Prynne *Unbish. Tim.* (1661) 148 From the time of Heraclas, the Patriarch of Alexandria was called Papa: that is, Pope, or Grandfather, (before the Bishop of Rome was so stiled). **1850** Neale *East. Ch.* I. 126 In correctness of speech,..the Patriarch of Antioch is the only Prelate who has a claim to that title: the proper appellation of the Bishops of Rome and Alexandria being *Pope*, of Constantinople and Jerusalem, *Archbishop*. **1902** *Encycl. Brit.* XXVII. 237/2 'The most holy Pope and patriarch of the great city of Alexandria and of all the land of Egypt, of Jerusalem the holy city, of Nubia, Abyssinia, and Pentapolis, and all the preaching of St. Mark', as he is still called. **1925** [see BEATITUDE 1 b]. **1976** *Daily Tel.* 24 Aug. 4/5 Pope Shenouda the Third, Patriarch of the Egyptian Coptic Church, said..that the deposition of Abuna Theophilos was 'illegal and inhuman'.

†**b.** *Pope John* = PRESTER JOHN. *Obs. rare.*

c **1511** *1st Eng. Bk. Amer.* (Arb.) Introd. 30/2 They of Indyen hath one prynce & that is pope Iohn. *Ibid.* 32/1 Pope Iohn..ye mooste myghtyste kynge.

II. Transferred uses.

4. A small thick-bodied freshwater fish of the Perch family; the Ruff. (So Ger. *papst*.)

1653 Walton *Angler* Table, Directions how and with what baits to fish for the Ruffe or Pope. **1740** R. Brookes *Art of Angling* I. xv. 44 The Ruff or Pope..seldom exceeds six inches [in length], and is cover'd with rough prickly Scales. **1836** F. S[ykes] *Scraps fr. Jrnl.* 21, I purchased a quantity of pope, which are much like perch. **1883** *Fisheries Exhib. Catal.* (ed. 4) 111 Dace [and] Pope from Thames.

†**5.** A weevil which infests malt or grain. *Obs.*

1658 Rowland *Moufet's Theat. Ins.* 1086 The English call the Wheat-worm Kis, Pope, Bowde, Weevil and Wibil. **1743** *Lond. & Country Brew.* IV. (ed. 2) 259 At Winchester they call this Insect [Weevil], Pope, Black-bob, or Creeper.

6. A local name for various birds, from their colouring or stout form: **a.** The Puffin (*Fratercula arctica*). **b.** The Bullfinch (cf. Ger. *dompfaff*). **c.** The Red-backed Shrike (*Lanius collurio*). **d.** The Painted Finch or Nonpareil (*Passerina ciris*).

1674 Ray *Collect., Water Fowl* 92 The Pope, called in some places Puffins. **1864** *N. & Q.* 3rd Ser. V. 124/2 Pope, Nope, Alp, Red-Hoop, and Tony-Hoop, are all provincial appellations of..the common Bullfinch. **1885** Swainson *Prov. Names Birds* 47 Red-backed shrike..Pope (Hants). **1894** Newton *Dict. Birds*, *Puffin*,..known as the Bottlenose, Coulterneb, Pope, Sea-Parrot.

7. A hot spiced drink of mull based on any of various wines. Cf. BISHOP *sb.* 8, CARDINAL *sb.* 5.

1920 G. Saintsbury *Notes on Cellar-bk.* xi. 162 'Pope', *i.e.* mulled burgundy, is Antichristian, from no mere Protestant point of view. **1965** O. A. Mendelsohn *Dict. Drink* 264 *Pope*, a spiced drink made from tokay.., ginger, honey and roasted orange. **1976** *Times* 15 Jan. 12/8 Many of these hot drinks have clerical names—Bishop being a type of mulled port, Cardinal using claret, and Pope Champagne. **1977** *Centuryan* (Office Cleaning Services) Christmas 8/2 A mull ..using Tokay, the famed Hungarian dessert wine, was known as 'The Pope'.

III. 8. *attrib.* and *Comb.* (all from 1), as ***pope-burning*** (1 b), ***-conjurer***, ***-trumpery***; ***pope-bulled***, ***-consecrated***, ***-given***, ***-pleasing***, ***-powdered***, ***-prompted***, ***-rid*** adjs.; **pope-catholic**, a Roman Catholic; **pope-day**, the anniversary of the Gunpowder Plot (Nov. 5); **pope-fly**, an insect which infests grain (cf. sense 7); †**pope-horn**, ? a conch-shell as used in celebrating pope-day; **pope-king**, the pope as a sovereign; **pope-night**, see *pope-day*; **pope-worshipper**, hostile term for a Roman Catholic.

1602 Warner *Alb. Eng.* IX. xlviii. 226 But Godhoode none in Indian Golde, and *pope-buld hopes shall mis. **1762** Hume *Hist. Eng.* lxviii. (1806) V. 126 One of the most innocent artifices..was the additional ceremony, pomp, and expense, with which a *pope-burning was celebrated in London. **1873** Christie *Dryden's Poems, Hind & P.* III. 10 *note*, The pope-burnings of Queen Elizabeth's night, which had occurred every year since the excitement of the Popish Plot. *c* **1554** G. Menewe (*title*) A Plaine subuersyon..of all the argumentes, that the *Popecatholykes can make for the maintenaunce of auricular confession. **1570** Foxe *A. & M.* (ed. 2) 1705/1 *margin*, The procedinges of the Popes catholickes in maintayning their Religion. **1679** C. Nesse *Antichrist* 228 The *pope-conjurers, necromancers, robbers, murderers. **1779** Sheridan *Critic* II. ii, Haughty Spain's *Pope-consecrated fleet. **1821** *Columbian Centinel* (Boston, U.S.) 10 Nov. 1/4 Monday last, Nov. 5th, being '*Pope Day'. **1903** A. Matthews in *Publ. Col. Soc. Mass.* VIII. 104 It is possible that he [Joyce Junior] continued to parade the streets of Boston on Pope Day. **1750** G. Hughes *Barbadoes* 84 The *Pope-fly. This insect is better known.. by the great destruction it causes in almost every kind of grain, than by its shape. **1772** *Boston Gaz.* (U.S.) 3 Feb. 3/2 The ingenuity of some of those nocturnal Sley-frolickers, had added the Drum and Conk-shell, or *Pope-horn, to their own natural, noisy, abilities. **1882** Mario *Garibaldi* in *Macm. Mag.* XLVI. 250 We will settle with the pontiff when we have dethroned the *Pope-king. **1773** J. Rowe *Lett. & Diary* 5 Nov. (1903) 254 Very quiet for a *Pope Night. **18** .. Whittier *Pr. Wks.* (1889) II. 390 Pope Night..was celebrated by the early settlers of New England. **1556** Olde *Antichrist* 82 b, Yon *pope pleasing slaues. *a* **1683** Oldham *Wks. & Rem.* (1686) 39 By Popes, and *Pope-rid Kings upheld, and lov'd. **1603** Harsnet *Pop. Impost.* xxi. 137 To enritch their purses by selling their *Pope-trumpery. **1579** J. Stubbes *Gaping Gulf* E iij, Who so marieth with any *pope-worshipper can not tell when to be sure of him.

b. Combinations with **pope's**: **Pope's hat**, applied to the head-dress of the Grenadier Guards (*Literary*); †**pope's knight**, a designation sometimes applied in Scotland to a priest of the Roman Church, who was commonly styled *Schir* (i.e. Sir) So and So, as a rendering of L. *Dominus*: see Jamieson, s.v., and cf. 'Sir Hugh Evans' in *Twelfth Night*; †**pope's-milk**, a jocular name for some kind of drink; **pope's nose** = *parson's nose*.

1886 R. L. Stevenson *Kidnapped* ii. 5/1 An old red-faced general on a grey horse at the one end, and at the other the company of Grenadiers with their *Pope's-hats. **1558** W. Mill in Spottiswood *Hist. Ch. Scot.* (1655) 95 They call me Walter, and not Sir Walter; I have been too long one of the *Popes Knights. **1795** Brydson *View Herald.* v. 175 A title [Sir] thus employed judicially, and disclaimed as characterising the pope's knights, appears to have had some other foundation, than mere courtesy. **1808** Jamieson s.v., The phrase, *Pope's Knights*, seems to have been used only in contempt. **1872** J. A. H. Murray *Compl. Scot.* Introd. 109 This Sir James Inglis, a 'Pope's Knight', was a churchman of considerable distinction at court in the reign of James V. **1635** Brereton *Trav.* (Chetham Soc.) 130 Burnt aquavitæ and *popes-milk. **1796** *Grose's Dict. Vulg. T.* (ed. 3), **Pope's Nose*, the rump of a turkey. **1854** Thackeray *Rose & Ring* vii, Giglio..picked the last bone of the chicken—drumsticks,..back, pope's nose, and all.

pope (pəʊp), *sb.*² [= F., Ger. *pope*, a. Russ. and OSlav. *popŭ*, app. ad. WGer. **papō* (whence OHG. *pfaffo*), ad. later Gr. παπᾶς priest; see

PAPA².] A parish priest of the Greek Church in Russia, Serbia, etc.

1662 J. DAVIES tr. *Olearius' Voy. Ambass.* 139 The other Ecclesiastical Orders are distinguish'd into Proto-popes, Popes, (or Priests) and Deacons. **1723** *Pres. St. Russia* I. 86 He was followed by a great number of Popes, or secular Priests, and a multitude of People. **1855** *Englishwoman in Russia* 119 Of course, you are aware that no pope can have a cure unless he be married. **1886** W. J. TUCKER *E. Europe* 26 The Roumanian pope, seated opposite us, practised, amongst other vices, those of a Bacchanalian tendency. **1889** *Morn. Post* 23 Jan. 2/3 The Church in Hungary, with its keen party fights and its 'popes', whose chief function seems to be to make their parishioners dependent on their help in all the ordinary concerns of life.

pope (pəʊp), *sb.*³ [Echoic: see quot.] A name given in New England to the Whip-poor-will (*Antrostomus vociferus*).

1781 S. PETERS *Hist. Connecticut* 257 The Whipperwill has so named itself by its nocturnal songs. It is also called the pope, by reason of its darting with great swiftness, from the clouds almost to the ground, and bawling out Pope!

pope, *v.* [f. POPE *sb.*¹]

1. *intr.* (Also *to pope it.*) To play the pope, to act as pope.

1537 CROMWELL in Merriman *Life & Lett.* (1902) II. 89 Paul popith Jolyly, that woll desire the worlde to pray for the kinges apeyrement. **1624** BP. MOUNTAGU *Gagg* 95 Urban the eight, that now Popeth it. **1646** BP. MAXWELL *Burd. Issach.* 6 There be..some few Patriarchs..who Lord it, and Pope it over the Lords inheritance. **1966** *Duckett's Reg.* Feb. 14/2 He [*sc.* Pope John XXIII] would pope it in his own way, God guiding him.

2. a. **'poping** *vbl. sb.*, going after the pope, embracing popery. (Cf. *to go a Maying.*) See also POPE *sb.*¹ 1 b, quot. 1887.

1608 H. CLAPHAM *Errour Left Hand* 8 Are you now ready to go a poping?.. I had thought there had bin many grounds that would have kept you from poping.

b. To be converted to Roman Catholicism; to become a Roman Catholic.

c **1916** in E. Waugh *Life R. Knox* (1959) II. i. 142 I'm *not* going to 'Pope' until after the war (if I'm alive). **1954** R. MACAULAY *Last Lett. to Friend* (1962) 163, I was..very sorry that your friend..has 'poped', as we call it here. **1961** *Spectator* 19 May 709 In another generation the Upper Chamber may be riddled with families who have poped. **1966** J. BETJEMAN *High & Low* 37 Kensit threatens and has Sam Gurney poped? **1977** *Observer* 27 Nov. 28/6 Wilfred [Knox], an Anglo-Catholic priest who never showed the least inclination to follow his younger brother into the Roman Church—or 'to Pope' as it was facetiously called among the undergraduates of Ronnie's generation.

Popean, Popeian varr. POPIAN *a.*

popedom ('pəʊpdəm). [Late OE. *pápdóm*, f. *pápa* POPE *sb.*¹ + *-dóm*, -DOM.]

1. The office, position, or dignity of pope (of Rome); the tenure of office of a pope; = PAPACY 1.

a **1123** *O.E. Chron.* an. 1118 Ðises geares eac forðferde se papa Paschalis. & feng Iohan of Gaitan to þam papdome. *a* **1154** *Ibid.* an. 1124 Honorius feng to pape dom. **1456** SIR G. HAYE *Law Arms* (S.T.S.) 74 Thai had na rycht to the pape dome. **1568** GRAFTON *Chron.* II. 103 Geuen at Laterane the tenth yere of our popedome. **1678** WANLEY *Wond. Lit. World* v. i. §74. 466/1 Leo..received the Popedom at the Emperours hands. **1741** LADY POMFRET *Lett.* (1805) III. 76 The riches acquired by the family in the long popedom of their uncle, Urban the Eighth. **1825** LD. COCKBURN *Mem.* 239 After as much plotting as if it had been for the Popedom he got in [to the town Council].

b. *transf.* and *fig.* Applied to a position of supreme authority in any religious system; also, satirically, in other capacities.

1588 *Marprel. Epist.* (Arb.) 22 Walde-graues profession ouerthroweth the popedome of Lambehith. **1589** *Hay any Work* 34 Good Iohn of Canterbury leaue thy Popedome. **1613** PURCHAS *Pilgrimage* (1614) 239 After this time was the Caliphate or Popedome diuided. **1836** *Pop. Encycl.* I. 814/1 He continued to be called caliph,..and bequeathed the Mohammedan popedom to his posterity. **1837** LOCKHART *Scott* xxxiv, Absurdities into which his reverence for the popedom of Paternoster-Row led him.

2. The papal government; esp. as a political state; = PAPACY 2.

1641 MILTON *Ch. Govt.* v. Wks. 1851 III. 116 What the Bishop hath laid together to make plea for Prelaty... Though indeed, if it may stand, it will inferre Popedome all as well. **1676** *Doctrine of Devils* 21 Yet now are many such broachars..within the Popedom. **1820** H. MATTHEWS *Diary of Invalid* 206 His Holiness claims feudal superiority over the kingdom, as a fief of the Popedom. **1880** SHORTHOUSE *J. Inglesant* xxiv, Bologna..delivered itself up to the Popedom upon a capitulation.

b. An ecclesiastical polity resembling the papacy.

1545 BRINKLOW *Compl.* xiv. (1874) 36 Lesse there shuld want anything to a perfyght pope dome, the bisshops caused a proclamacyon to be set out in the kyngs name, that from henseforth the ceremonyes of the church, that were of the popys makyng, shuld no more be taken for the popys ceremonys, but the kyngs. **1642** MILTON *Apol. Smect.* iv. Wks. 1851 III. 289 A Church-government, which wants almost no circumstance, but only a name to be a plaine Popedome. **1781** S. PETERS *Hist. Connecticut* 96 The lay-magistrates, who were further mortified to see Ministers among the Representatives..cried out, 'This is a presbyterial popedom'. **1882–3** *Schaff's Encycl. Relig. Knowl.* III. 2520/1 Flacius, with whom he labored at one time for the establishment of a Lutheran popedom.

Hence *erron.* †**'popedomship**. *Obs.*

1588 J. ASKE *Eliz. Triumphans* 6 His Popedomship with Myter, Crowns & Crosse, Are all bestow'd on Pius quintus grace.

†**'popehead.** *Obs.* [f. POPE *sb.*¹ + -HEAD.] = POPEHOOD.

1387 TREVISA *Higden* (Rolls) VII. 87 Iohn þe nyntenþe, pope, satte in þe popehede fyve ȝere. **1480** CAXTON *Chron. Eng.* IV. (1520) 37/2 This man lefte his popehead and wente to Agrippa. **1556** OLDE *Antichrist* 91 In the thrid moneth of hys popeheadde.

†**pope-holy**, *a.* (*sb.*) *Obs.* Forms: 4 papholy, 5 poope-, poppe-, (pomp-)holy, 5–6 pop holy, 5–7 pope-holy. [app. f. POPE *sb.*¹ + HOLY *a.*, but taken in some way to represent F. *papelard* hypocritical: see PAPELARD. In the first recorded instance translating OF. *papelardie* hypocrisy (Rom. Rose).] Pretending to great holiness; (of actions, words, etc.) characterized by a show or pretence of piety; sanctimonious, hypocritical.

1377 LANGL. *P. Pl.* B. XIII. 284 Was none suche as hymself, ne none so pope-holy [*v. rr.* pomp holy, poppe holy; C. VII. 37 pop, poppe, pope, pomp holy]. **1387** TREVISA *Higden* (Rolls) V. 165 þis Iulianus..bycam a monk, and made hym ful papholy [*v.r.* pop holy] under monkes wede [L. *Cui tunc sub monachatu magnam religionem simulanti*]. *c* **1440** *Jacob's Well* 74 Seynt gregorie seyth,..þat an ypocryte, a popholy man, is lyche an irane. *a* **1460** *Pol. Poems* (Rolls) II. 251 Ye poopeholy prestis fulle of presomcioun. *a* **1529** SKELTON *Replyc.* Wks. 1843 I. 209 Popholy and peuysshe presumpcion prouoked them [Lollards] to publysshe and to preche..howe it was idolatry to offre to ymages of our blessed lady. **1570** FOXE *A. & M.* (ed. 2) 205 b/2 To cast yᵉ dyrt of these Popeholy Monkes in their owne face. **1589** COOPER *Admon.* 223 Some hypocrites and Pope-holie persons.

¶**b.** *erron.* Popishly devout or holy.

1633 D. R[OGERS] *Treat. Sacram.* i. 5 Pope-holy persons, who are so leavened with superstition, that they thinke the Sacraments are holy things even by the work wrought.

B. *sb.* Hypocrisy. *to play the pope-holy*: to play the hypocrite.

?*a* **1366** CHAUCER *Rom. Rose* 415 Another thing was don there write, That semede lyk an ipocrite, And it was clepid Poope-holy [*Papelardie ert apelée*]. *c* **1430** LYDG. *Min. Poems* (Percy Soc.) 46 For popholy and vyce loke wel aboute. *a* **1518** SKELTON *Magnyf.* 467 Counterfet conscyence, peuysshe pope holy. *a* **1555** BP. GARDINER in Foxe *A. & M.* (1563) 746 Though some accompt me a papist, yet I cannot play the pope holy, as thold term was.

Hence †**pope-'holiness** *Obs.*, sanctimoniousness, hypocrisy.

1528 TINDALE *Obed. Chr. Man* 88 Twich the scabbe of ypocresye or popeholynes and goo aboute to vtter their false doctrine. **1535** *Goodly Primer, Passion* v, Such is the pope holiness & feigned righteousness of hypocrites. **1583** GOLDING *Calvin on Deut.* lx. 359 To their seeming it is a spice of moonkish hypocrisie or popeholinesse to thanke God.

popehood ('pəʊphʊd). [OE. *pápan-hád*, f. *pápa*, POPE *sb.*¹ + *-hád*, -HOOD.] The condition of being pope; the papal dignity.

c **1000** ÆLFRIC *Hom.* (Th.) II. 126 Hwæt ða Gregorius, siððan he papan-had underfeng. **1387** TREVISA *Higden* (Rolls) VII. 85 þe pope Iohn satte in his popehode sex monthes. *c* **1449** PECOCK *Repr.* (Rolls) 439 Popehode is of the wil of Crist to be had in sum persoon to be chose as the successour of Peter. **1838** LONGF. *Drift-Wood* Prose Wks. 1886 I. 376 As soon..as he undertook the popehood, the monks were sent to their beloved work.

popeism: see POPISM.

Pope Joan. [After the fabulous female pope Joan. (But cf. its Fr. name *nain jaune* yellow dwarf.)

1590 SPENSER *F.Q.* II. vi. 3 Sometimes she laught, as merry as Pope Jone. *c* **1597** HARINGTON *Nugæ Ant.* (1779) II. 195 Pope Julio..was a greate and wary player,..being a goode companyon, and as the phrase is, as mery as Pope Joane.]

A card-game played by three or more persons, with a pack from which the eight of diamonds has been removed, and a tray or board having eight compartments for holding the stakes, these being won by the players who play out certain cards; see quot. 1887. Also *attrib.*

1732 MRS. DELANY in *Life & Corr.* (1861) I. 373 After supper play at pope Joan or commerce till eleven. **1791** A. C. BOWER *Diaries & Corr.* (1903) 118 We had a great Rout last night, I lost ten shillings at Pope Joan. **1826** HONE *Every-day Bk.* I. 90 A juvenile party closely seated round a large table, with a Pope Joan board in the middle; each well supplied with mother-o'-pearl fish and counters..watching the turn-up, or peeping into the pool to see how rich it is. **1837** DICKENS *Pickw.* vi. **1887** *All Year Round* 5 Feb. 66 Pope Joan has survived to the present day in the modified form of 'Newmarket'.

popekin ('pəʊpkɪn). *contemptuous.* [See -KIN.] A little or petty pope.

1890 in *Cent. Dict.*

†**popel.** *Obs.* Also 4 popelle -ill, -ulle, 5 -ell, -il, -le. [ME. a. OF. *pople* (1355 in Godef.), *pouple* (Picard, Tournia), variant of *popre* (1316), *pop(p)e*, *poupe*, an inferior kind of fur; derivation unknown.] The name of a kind of fur: in quot. 1351 said to be that of the squirrel.

The French documents in which it is mentioned, cited by Godefroy, belong to Flanders and Picardy. In England, frequently mentioned in documents written in Latin and French; rarely in Eng. context.

1327 *Lett. Bk. E. Lond.* lf. 183 b, Forura de popell' de vij tiris sexaginta bestias; Forura de popell' de vj tiris Quinquaginta et duas bestias. [tr. in Riley *Mem. Lond.* (1868) 153 A fur of popelle of 7 tiers, 60 beasts; a fur of popelle of 6 tiers, 52 beasts.] **1342** in Rogers *Agric. & Prices* II. 539/3 (Merton Coll. Accts.) Furrura de popel. **1351** *Lett. Bk. F. Lond.* lf. 208 Furree de Pellure come de meneveyr, Gris, Purree Destranlyng, Popell' Desquirels [tr. in Riley 267 Popelle of squirrels], Bys des Conyns des levres. **1365** *Lett. Bk. G. Lond.* lf. 162 b, Qe nul entremelle Roskyn en popull'. [tr. in Riley 329 That no one shall mingle *roskyn* with *populle*.] **1380–1** *Durham Acc. Rolls* (Surtees) 590 In una furura de popill empt. pro d'no Priore, *xs.* **1421** *Will of Norton* (Somerset Ho.), Vnam de togis meis furratis cum popell. **1493** *Will of Mag. Thome Overey* 18 July, Unam togam talarem de scarlett penulatam cum popilfurr.

†**popelard, popilarde, poplart**, etc., var. PAPELARD, altered after POPE or POPE-HOLY.

?*a* **1500** *Chester Pl.* v. 233 What the Devilles! eyles the poplart. *Ibid.* 273 Popelard! thou preachest as a pie. *Ibid.* (E.E.T.S.) 447 This popelard pope here present, with Couetuousnes aye was fully bent.

†**'popeler.** *Obs.* Also 4 popler, 5 popelere. [Origin obscure: cf. POPPEL, OF. *popelle*; also f. med.L. *popia* spoon (Du Cange), POPARD.] A water-bird, the spoon-bill.

1400 in *Test. Ebor.* (Surtees) I. 276 Aulam meam cum poplers textam, et lectum meum integrum cum costeris de rubeo cum poplers et armis meis broudatum. *c* **1440** *Promp. Parv.* 408/2 Popelere, byrd (or schovelerd, infra), *populus*. **1459** in *Paston Lett.* I. 479, ij. clothis portrayed full of popelers. *Ibid.* 483 Item, j. hangyng clothe of popelers. [**1894** NEWTON *Dict. Birds*, *Popeler*, an old name for the Spoonbill, *Platalea leucorodia*. **1905** *Westm. Gaz.* 28 Oct. 3/2 The spoonbill, which still nests as near as Holland,.. used to breed in the Eastern Counties, where it was known as the popeler.]

popeless ('pəʊplɪs), *a.* [f. POPE *sb.*¹ + -LESS.] Without a pope.

1868 W. C. CARTWRIGHT *Papal Conclaves* 57 At present the peace of the Popeless city is left entirely to the care of Monsignor Governatore. **1902** A. LANG *Hist. Scot.* II. xix. 518 He might become a Catholic after the manner of Henry VIII, and enforce a popeless Catholicism.

popelican, -quan, obs. forms of PUBLICAN.

popelike ('pəʊplaɪk), *a.* (*adv.*) [f. POPE *sb.*¹ + -LIKE.] Like or resembling a pope.

1553 BECON *Reliques of Rome* (1563) 215 Their forefathers and Popelike predecessours. **1589** *Marprel. Epit.* (1843) 53 As popelike and pontificall, as my Lord of Canterburie. **1613** PURCHAS *Pilgrimage, India* (1864) 150 The Brama, or Popelike Bramene in these parts, who by his authority dispenseth with many of their Lawes, and dissolueth Marriages. **1808** MOORE *Corruption* iii, Nor..Could pope-like kings escape the levelling blow.

b. *adv.* In the manner of a pope.

1574 *Life 70th Abp. Canterb.* Pref C viij b, From Scotland he takes shipping, and popelike steppes over into Ireland.

popeling ('pəʊplɪŋ). [f. POPE *sb.*¹ + -LING¹ 1, 2. Perh. sometimes associated with F. *papalin*, It. *papalino*: cf. PAPALIN.]

†**1.** An adherent, follower, or minister of the pope; a papist; in 16th c. mostly, a popish ecclesiastic. *Obs.*

1561 DAUS tr. *Bullinger on Apoc.* (1573) 93 b, I can see that the old Popelynges haue all to berayde vs. **1570** FOXE *A. & M.* (ed. 2) 284/1 The sentence of the pope and his popelings. **1606** WARNER *Alb. Eng.* XIV. lxxxi. (1612) 340 Nor meruell we that Popelings her nor Puritanes should brook. **1643** PRYNNE *Popish R. Favourite* 73 Our English Nation too, now devoted as a prey to the barbarous Irish, and other forraigne Popelings. **1677** W. HUGHES *Man of Sin* I. vii. 31 Whatever wild Discourses, or Behaviours, Popes and Popelins have been guilty of. **1705** HICKERINGILL *Priest-cr.* I. 8 How can the Pope and all his Popelings, and General Councils..be infallible in their Faith?

2. A little or petty pope; one who acts as pope on a small scale. (*contemptuous.*)

1588 *Marprel. Epist.* (Arb.) 6 None but Antichristian popes and popelings euer claimed this authoritie vnto themselues. *c* **1629** LAYTON *Syons Plea* (ed. 2) 23 The Prelats..derive their Authority from the Pope; carry themselves as Popelings. **1654** GATAKER *Disc. Apol.* 75 Having given a Bill of divorce to one Pope, beyond the Seas, enstal and enthrone a goodlie number of Popelings..at home. **1799** W. TAYLOR in *Monthly Mag.* VII. 139 Still the pope bears sway; And would-be popelings, arm'd with Birmingham keys, Yet rouse us from the dead repose we seek. **1880** E. HERRIES *Mem. J. C. Herries* II. 284 An anti-Protestant Church,..over which, and over a prostrate laity, a legion of parochial popelings should reign supreme.

†**'popelote.** *Obs. rare*⁻¹. [perh. ad. OF. *poupelet* 'petit poupon' (Godef.), with changed suffix: cf. POPLET.] A pet, darling.

c **1386** CHAUCER *Miller's T.* 68 There nas no man so wys þat koude thenche So gay a popelote or swiche a wenche.

popely ('pəʊplɪ), *a.* In 6 *Sc.* paiplie. [f. POPE *sb.*¹ + -LY¹.] Of, pertaining to, or befitting a pope.

a **1600** *Lindesay's Chron. Scot.* (S.T.S.) I. 413 (MS. I.) His prelacie pomp nor paiplie [LYNDESAY *Test. Papyngo* 577 papale] gravitie..Availled him nocht. **1826** SOUTHEY *Vind. Eccl. Angl.* 308 Taking upon himself what may be called the Popely privilege of selling indulgences.

Popemobile ('pəʊpməbiːl). [f. POPE *sb.*¹ + -MOBILE.] A popular name for a specially-designed vehicle with a raised viewing platform surrounded by bullet-proof glass, used by the Pope when on an official visit to a foreign country.

This type of vehicle was introduced by Pope John Paul II. **1979** *Irish Times* 1 Oct. 10/1 The Pope drove through the crowds in the specially constructed 'Popemobile'. **1979** *Observer* 7 Oct. 12/4 In Madison Square Garden he [*sc.* the Pope] lifted a child from the audience and set her on the roof of his custom-built Jeep—known even to his entourage as 'The Popemobile'. **1982** G. PRIESTLAND *At Large* (1983) 174 The usual 'Popemobile' has been harshly renamed the SPT or 'Special Papal Transport'. **1986** *Catholic Leader* (Brisbane) 7 Dec. 11/1 The Pope..alighted from the popemobile and happily strode off down the road.

†**'popeness.** *Obs. nonce-wd.* [f. POPE *sb.*[1] + -NESS.] Quality or characteristic of a pope.

a **1684** LEIGHTON *Comm. 1 Pet.* (1817) I. iii. 8 There is naturally this Popeness in every man's mind,..a kind of fancied infallibility in themselves.

†**poper**[1]. *Obs.* prob. = POPARD.

c **1430** *Two Cookery-bks.* 63 A Ryal Fest... Le iij cours. Gely. Datys in comfyte. Fesaunt. Gullys. Poper [etc.].

†**poper**[2]. *Obs. rare*$^{-1}$. (?) (Hazlitt suggests 'a papist'.)

1575 GASCOIGNE *Pr. Pleas. Kenilw.* Poems 1870 II. 93 When her maiestie entred the gate, there stoode Hercules for Porter,..presenting the keyes..with these words:..My frends a Porter I, no Poper here am plast.

poper: see POPPER *v.*

†**'poperiche.** *Obs. rare.* [f. POPE *sb.*[1] + RICHE, after *kingrich*, *bishopric*, etc.] = POPEDOM.

1387 TREVISA *Higden* (Rolls) V. 231 In þe nynþe ȝere of his poperiche. *Ibid.* VI. 409 Þanne he hym self occupiede þe poperiche.

popery ('pəʊpərɪ). Also 6 **papry, popyrie,** 7 **poprie.** [f. POPE *sb.*[1] + -ERY.]

1. The doctrines, practices, and ceremonial associated with the pope as head of the Roman Catholic Church; the papal ecclesiastical system; the Roman Catholic religion, or adherence to it. (A hostile term.)

a **1534** TINDALE *Exp. Math. v–vii.* (*a* 1550) 64 To beleue the faininges of oure mooste holy father, al his superstityouse poperye and inuisible blessynges. *c* **1540** *Pilgr. T.* 277 in *Thynne's Animadv.*, etc. (1865) App. i. 85 Nothing but papry sprong owt of Antichrist, full of foxry. **1550** CRANMER *Wks.* (Parker Soc.) I. 6 But what availeth it to take away beads, pardons, pilgrimages, and such other like popery, so long as two chief roots remain unpulled up? **1594** HOOKER *Eccl. Pol.* IV. iv. §1 The name of Popery is more odious than very Paganisme amongst diuers of the more simple sort. **1638** *Hamilton Papers* (Camden) I. 32 All discipline and seramonies..to haue beine estimed and damned as poyntes of poprie. **1686** EVELYN *Diary* 5 May, All engines being now at work to bring in Popery. **1689** *Declar. Right Will. & Mary* c. 2 His highness the Prince of Orange (whom it hath pleased Almighty God to make the glorious Instrument of delivering this Kingdom from Popery and arbitrary Power). **17..** *Orange Toast* in Sir J. Barrington *Recoll.* (1827) *Aldermen of Skinners' Alley*, The glorious, pious, and immortal memory of the great and good King William—not forgetting Oliver Cromwell who assisted in redeeming us from Popery, Slavery, Arbitrary Power, Brass Money, and Wooden Shoes. **1779–81** JOHNSON *L.P.*, *Garth* Wks. III. 26 It is observed by Lowth, that..there is less distance than is thought between scepticism and popery: and that a mind wearied with perpetual doubt, willingly seeks repose in..an infallible church. **1840** CARLYLE *Heroes* iv. (1872) 126 The cry of 'No Popery' is foolish enough in these days.

2. *fig.* Assumption, or acceptance, of authority like that of the pope.

1721 AMHERST *Terræ Fil.* No. 21 (1754) 106, I would therefore humbly propose a reformation of learning from the philosophical popery, which prevails at present in our universities. **1735** BERKELEY *Def. Free-think. in Math.* §16 It is even introducing a kind of philosophic popery among a free people.

Hence **,popery'phobia**, dread or horror of popery.

1826 [H. BEST] *Four Years France* 18 My mother was perfectly free from popery-phobia. **1895** W. MASON in *Church Times* 2 Aug. 108/3 The old Poperyphobia which one had hoped had been long ago dead and buried.

Pope's eye. [Called in Ger. *pfaffensbisschen* priest's bit, prob. as being a tit-bit which the priest was supposed to claim; in F. *œil de Judas* Judas's eye; 'eye' referring app. to its rounded form.] The lymphatic gland surrounded with fat in the middle of a leg of mutton; regarded by some as a tit-bit.

1673 J. W. *Vinegar & Mustard* B iv, Husband, pray cut me the Popes Eye out of the Leg of Mutton, I'le try if I can eat a bit of it. **1682** T. GIBSON *Anat.* IV. (1697) App., A gland which we commonly call in sheep the Nut or Pope's eye. **1755** JOHNSON, *Popeseye*, the gland surrounded with fat in the middle of the thigh: why so called I know not. **1844** H. STEPHENS *Bk. Farm* II. 98 The piece of fat in it called the Pope's eye, is considered a delicate morceau by epicures.

pope's head. [From its appearance.]

1. A species of cactus, *Melocactus communis*, growing on barren sandy wastes in S. America and some of the W. Indian islands, and producing its flowers on a woolly cushion or head, beset with bristles and spines.

1699 L. WAFER *Voy.* (1729) 284 Fenced with hollow Bamboos, Popes-heads, and Prickle pears. **1866** *Treas. Bot.* 733 *M[elocactus] communis*, the Turk's-cap Cactus,.. sometimes called Englishman's Head, or Pope's Head.

2. A round brush or broom with a long handle, for sweeping ceilings, dusting pictures, etc.; also called *Turk's head*.

1824 SCOTT *Let. to Miss Baillie* 12 Feb. in Lockhart *Life*, What sweeping is required is most easily performed by a brush like what the housemaids call a Pope's head. **1825** MAR. EDGEWORTH *Love & Law* I. v, You're no witch, indeed, if you don't see a cobweb as long as my arm. Run, run, child, for the pope's head. **1890** LECKY *Eng. in 18th C.* VIII. xxix. 60 The long mops known as 'Popes' heads' were made use of as pike handles.

popeship ('pəʊpʃɪp). [f. POPE *sb.*[1] + -SHIP.]

1. The office of pope; popedom, popehood.

c **1440** *Alphabet of Tales* 402 He was asoylid, & restorid tó com agayn vnto Rome; and he tuke þe popeshup agayn on hand. **1597** BEARD *Theatre God's Judgem.* (1612) 358 So he passed the blessed time of his holie Popeship with this vertuous dame. **1640** SIR E. DERING *Sp. on Relig.* 23 Nov. iii. 8 Hee pleads Popeship under the name of a Patriarch. **1840** CARLYLE *Heroes* iv. (1872) 124 Popeship, spiritual Fatherhood of God's Church, is that a vain semblance, of cloth and parchment?

2. The personality of a pope: with possessive pronoun as a humorous appellation.

1640 SIR E. DERING in Rushw. *Hist. Coll.* III. (1692) I. 100 The Canon-Law, of more use unto his Popeship than both the other. **1705** HICKERINGILL *Priest-cr.* II. i. 11 And who dare..question what his Popeship would be at? **1826** W. E. ANDREWS *Crit. Rev. Foxe's Bk. Martyrs* II. 187 What necessity could there be for all this attention on the part of his royal popeship?

popess ('pəʊpɪs). [f. POPE *sb.*[1] + -ESS. Cf. PAPESS.] A supposed female pope.

1529 MORE *Dyaloge* III. Wks. 227/2 But were I Pope. By my soule quod he, I would ye wer, & my lady your wife Popesse too. **1677** W. HUGHES *Man of Sin* II. xii. 239 His Farewell to her was, Were you but Popess, I would willingly relinquish my Claim. **1830** W. TAYLOR *Hist. Surv. Germ. Poetry* I. 153 In another scene, the Virgin thus intercedes with her Son for the popess [Pope Joan] in purgatory.

popestant ('pəʊpɪstənt). Also 6 **popistant.** [f. POPE *sb.*[1] after PROTESTANT.] A nonce-word for PAPIST as opposed to *protestant*.

a **1550** *Pore Helpe* 270 in Hazl. *E.P.P.* III. 262, I feare me he be wext A popistant stout. **1551** MORRYSON in Froude *Hist. Eng.* V. xxviii. 339 *note*, Would God the French king were as like to become a right Protestant as our master is unlike to become a blundering Popistant. **1880** DIXON *Windsor* III. xiv. 132 Protestants and popestants were to him the same.

†**'popet.** *Obs.* A contemptuous diminutive of POPE *sb.*[1], perh. with allusion to POPPET, PUPPET.

1550 BALE *Eng. Votaries* II. 27 Moche a do had Berengarius Turonensis..with the foreseyd Popet Nycolas, for Christes naturall presence in the eucharisticall breade. **1641** PRYNNE *Antip.* 114 This Popet hath blasphemed, and betrayed all Protestants.

popet, obs. f. POPPET.

popetishe, popetly, popetry, obs. ff. PUPPETISH, PUPPETLY, etc.

pop-eyed, *a.* orig. *U.S.* [POP-.] Having bulging or prominent eyes; wide-eyed (with amazement, etc.).

1830 A. ROYALL *Lett. from Alabama* 176 The first countenance I caught, was Senator Foot of Connecticut—a handsome middle-sized black pop-eyed Yankee. **1860** BARTLETT *Dict. Amer.*, *Pop-eyed*, having prominent eyes. *Southern.* **1906** *Atlantic Monthly* Oct. 573 The class was open-mouthed, and the professor pop-eyed with wonder. **1923** R. D. PAINE *Comrades of Rolling Ocean* ix. 152 They are simply pop-eyed to hear all about the speedy apprentice. **1937** *John o' London's Weekly* 22 Jan. 682/1 The king [*sc.* George III] fumbled for a few years with makeshift ministries,..and then committed his affairs to Lord North, an amiable pop-eyed creature, rather like himself in appearance. **1947** V. NABOKOV *Bend Sinister* II. 12 Paying perhaps terrific fines, but stopping the train. Say, why did you do it? the popeyed conductor might ask. **1952** WODEHOUSE *Pigs have Wings* iv. 74 The landlord of the Emsworth Arms..and the half dozen Shropshire lads who were propping up the establishment's outer wall had stamped her with the seal of their popeyed approval. **1973** 'E. MCBAIN' *Let's here It* viii. 124 Her audience..watched her every move in pop-eyed fascination. **1978** A. PRICE *'44 Vintage* x. 131 He stared pop-eyed at Butler..then started to wave madly.

pop-gun, 'popgun, *sb.* [f. POP *sb.*[1] or *v.*[1] + GUN *sb.*; prob. suggested by POT-GUN in sense 2.]

1. A child's toy, consisting of a short straight tube from the mouth of which a tight-fitting pellet is expelled with a pop by compressing the air in the tube with a piston.

1622 HOBBES *Seven Philos. Prob.* iii. (1682) 18 Tis of the nature of a Pop gun which Children use. **1749** FIELDING *Tom Jones* X. vi, I value a pistol, or a blunderbuss, or any such thing, no more than a pop gun. **1801** STRUTT *Sports & Past.* IV. iv, The trunks were succeeded by pot-guns made with hollow pieces of elder, or of quills... These were also called pop-guns. **1847** ALB. SMITH *Chr. Tadpole* xv, Just as one pellet in a pop-gun drives out another. **1967** D. ABERCROMBIE *Elem. Gen. Phonetics* ii. 24 An air-stream mechanism can be compared to a fruit-spray, a Flit gun, a syringe, or a child's pop-gun.

fig. **1711** ADDISON *Spect.* No. 46 ¶6 She is a meer Sermon Popgun, repeating and discharging Texts, Proofs [etc.]. **1777** MRS. E. MONTAGU in Doran *Lady of last Cent.* viii. (1873) 215 The scriblers weekly let fly their pop-guns at the Duchess. **1883** HALL CAINE *Cobwebs of Crit.* iii. 54 Volleys from the popgun of criticism.

2. Contemptuously applied to a small, inefficient, or antiquated fire-arm. Also *transf.* (contextually an aeroplane).

1849 E. E. NAPIER *Excurs. S. Africa* II. 389, I instantly stepped into the next room, to get the old pop-gun there;.. my finger was in an instant on the trigger. **1864** in A. Bisset *Omitted Chapters Hist. Eng.* VI. 376 Cromwell's pop-guns, which I will engage did not kill twenty men during the action [of Dunbar]. **1919** M. BEER *Hist. Brit. Socialism* I. II. vii. 240 To equip men with pop-guns for a hunting expedition in the jungle. **1929** W. FAULKNER *Sartoris* I. 43, I tried to keep him from going up there on that goddam little popgun... I tried to keep him from going up there on that damn Camel.

3. *attrib.* and *Comb.*, as ***pop gun-pellet***, etc.

a **1704** T. BROWN *Walk round Lond., Presbyt. Meeting-Ho.* (1709) 17 His merry Posture and Pop-gun-way of Delivery. **1823** SCOTT *Fam. Lett.* 11 Jan., Bells rung on the true pop-gun principle by the action of air alone. **1826** MISS MITFORD *Village* Ser. II. (1863) 279 She had sitten out..by help of.. putting her fingers in her ears, two or three popgun lectures, on chemistry and mechanics. **1844** *Knickerbocker* XXIII. 182 To the United States in reference to the pop-gun shots of foreign tourists, might be addressed the warning which Peter Plymley thundered against Bonaparte. **1874** E. EGGLESTON *Circuit Rider* ix. 87 He had been flogged in boyhood for shooting pop-gun wads into the face of a portrait of the reigning monarch. **1895** *Montreal Med. Jrnl.* XXIII. 565 The physician without physiology and chemistry flounders along in an aimless fashion, never able to gain any accurate conception of disease, practising a sort of pop-gun pharmacy, hitting now the malady and again the patient, he himself not knowing which. **1963** *Times* 5 Jan. 12/3 A complicated regimen of treatment which Dr. Walton described as 'pop-gun polypharmacy'. **1968** *Wall St. Jrnl.* 29 Mar. 1 (*headings*) Centers in Slums Offer Legal, Employment Assistance; 'Outreachers' Make Rounds. A Popgun Effort, Critics Say.

Hence **'pop-gun** *v. trans.*, to discharge a pop-gun at; **'pop,gunner; ,pop'gunnery; 'pop,gunning** *ppl. a.*

1721 AMHERST *Terræ Fil.* No. 48 (1726) 269 Those abominable monsters..pop-gun with their huge trunks the poor constellations, and turn the milky way into a salt posset. **1831** COL. HAWKER *Diary* (1893) II. 25 The..tag-rag popgunners blazing away at the fieldfares. **1846** *Ibid.* 273 Loads of popgunning blackguards. *a* **1849** POE *Marginalia* Wks. 1864 III. 499 The lightness of the artillery should not degenerate into popgunnery.

pop-holy, variant of POPE-HOLY *Obs.*

popi, obs. form of POPPY.

Popian ('pəʊpɪən), *a.* (and *sb.*) Also **Po'pean, Po'peian.** [f. *Pope*, proper name + -IAN.] Of or pertaining to the poet Alexander Pope (or his poetry). ***Popian couplet***: a heroic couplet in the manner of Pope. Also as *sb.*, an imitator of Pope.

1802 ANNA SEWARD *Lett.* (1811) VI. 33 The ear may be contented to want the luxury of the Popean numbers. *a* **1849** H. COLERIDGE *Ess. & Marginalia* (1851) II. 121 Neither Rogers nor Campbell are Popeans. They belong to another school—the sentimental. **1865** *Sat. Rev.* 9 Dec. 738/1 Taken as a translator of the Popian school,..Mr. Worsley deserves to rank very high. **1892** LOUNSBURY *Stud. Chaucer* III. vii. 136 One of several evidences that the Popean couplet existed before Pope had produced anything which any one felt it desirable to imitate. **1895** W. D. HOWELLS *My Literary Passions* 55, I..hammered away at my blessed Popean heroics till nine, when I went regularly to bed, to rise again at five. **1914** J. A. ROY *Cowper & his Poetry* 54 He [*sc.* Johnson] failed to remark the absence of the Popeian inversions in the seemingly orthodox verse. **1953** R. FULLER *Second Curtain* v. 74 What nourishment could he give his Popean young poet? **1975** *Times Lit. Suppl.* 14 Mar. 275/1 There is no philistine repudiation of the achievements of Popeian scholarship.

†**'popify**, *v.* *Obs.* Also 8 **popefy.** [See -FY.] *trans.* To render popish.

a **1670** HACKET *Abp. Williams* I. (1692) 121 As if all were well, so they be not popified, though they have departed from the church in which they were baptized. **1746** W. HORSLEY *Fool* (1748) II. 67 Though he may not make them Traitors, yet he may Popefy, or Papisticate them.

†**'popil**, *a.* (or *sb. attrib.*) *Sc. Obs. rare*$^{-1}$. [app. f. L. *popul-us* people.] Of the people; plebeian.

1536 BELLENDEN *Cron. Scot.* IV. xiv. (1821) I. 146 Forfair; in quhilk sumtime was ane strang castel, within ane loch, quhare sindry kingis of Scottis maid residence..thocht it is now bot ane popil town.

popil(l, popille, obs. forms of POPPLE.

popilion, early form of POPULEON *Obs.*

popinac ('pɒpɪnæk). *U.S.* Also **popinack.** [f. OPOPANAX.] A tropical or subtropical leguminous shrub, *Acacia farnesiana*, whose fragrant yellow flowers yield an essential oil used in perfume; also called the opopanax tree.

1900 L. H. BAILEY *Cycl. Amer. Hort.* I. 8/2 Acacia... Farnesiana... Popinac, Opopanax, Cassie... Grown in S. France for perfumery. **1945** R. P. WODEHOUSE *Hayfever Plants* iii. 113 One of the best known [acacias] is the opopanax or huisache,..also called popinack and cassie. It is a small tree, 20 to 30 feet high, with spreading spiny branches bearing bright yellow flowers closely compacted in small globular heads. **1952** [see CASSIE[3]].

† **'popinal**, *a.* *Obs.* *rare*⁻⁰. [ad. L. *popīnālis*, f. *popīna* cook-shop.]
1656 BLOUNT *Glossogr.*, *Popinal*, of Cookery, or belonging to riot or places of riot, as Alehouses, Taverns, etc.

† **popi'nation.** *Obs.* *rare*⁻⁰. [n. of action f. L. *popīnārī* to frequent eating-houses, f. as prec.]
1623 COCKERAM, *Popination*, an outragious drinking. 1658 PHILLIPS, *Popination*, (lat.)..also a haunting Popinas, i. Taverns, or Victualing houses.

† **po'pinian.** *Obs. nonce-wd.* [f. POPE *sb.*¹ on analogy of *Socinian*.] A Papist.
1613 SIR E. HOBY *Countersnarle* 66, I was loath such rare creatures should be ouer gudgeoned by so foule Popinians.

popinjay ('pɒpɪndʒeɪ). Forms: see below. [In ME. earliest forms a. OF. (and mod.F.) *papegai* (12th c.), *papingay* (13th c. in Godef.), AF. also *papeiaye* (= *-jaye*) (1355 in *Royal Wills*), = Pr. *papagai*, Sp. *papagayo*, Pg. *papagaio*; also MHG. *papagey*, Ger. *papagei* MLG. *papegoie* Du. *papegaai*. OF. had also *papegau*, *papegau(l)t* (13th c.), mod.F. *papegaut* = Cat. *papagall*, It. *pap(p)agallo*, med.L. *pap(p)agallus* (14th c. in Du Cange), mod.Gr. παπαγάλλος. Other forms were med.Gr. παπαγάς, Arab. *babaghā*, *babbaghā*, Pers. also *bapghā*, med.L. *papagen*, MHG. *papegân*. Probably the med.Gr. and Arabic represent the earliest form, due to an imitation of the cry of the bird in some African or other non-European language. The form in *-gayo*, *-gaio*, *-gai*, appears to have arisen by assimilation to the name of the European chattering bird, the jay, med.L. *gaius*, Sp. *gayo*, Pr. and ONF. *gai*, central F. *geai* (= *jai*), whence the OF. and ME. *papegai* and *papejai*, subsequently changed (? after *pape*, *pope*) to *popegay* and *popejay*, and (like *nightingale*, *passenger*, etc.) to *papengay popinjay*. The forms in *-gallus*, *-gallo*, *-gall*, *-gau*, appear to have been assimilated to L. *gallus* cock; the OF. *papegau* gave the Sc. *papingaw*, *papingo*.]

1. An early name for a parrot. *Obs.* or *arch.* (In all the early forms *iay*, etc. = *jay*.)

α. 4 **papiaye, (papeiaie, -gai)**, 4–5 **papeiay**, 5 **papageye, papeiai, -ioy(e**, *Sc.* **pape-iay(e**, (7 **papgay)**.
[*a* 1310 Papeiai: see 4 a.] 13.. *E.E. Allit. P.* B. 1465 Pyes & papeiays purtrayed with-inne. *c* 1386 CHAUCER *Shipman's T.* 369 Hoom he gooth murie as a Papeiay [*Harl.* papiniay]. *c* 1400 MAUNDEV. (Roxb.) xxv. 117 Nyghtgales syngand, and papeiays spekand. 1423 JAS. I *Kingis Q.* cx, Vnlike the crow is to the pape-lay. 1483 *Cath. Angl.* 268/2 A Papeiay (*A.* A Papeioye). [1653 Papgay: see 3.]

β. 4–5 **popeiay**, 5 **popegaye, pope iaye.**
1393 LANGL. *P. Pl.* C. xv. 173 þe pokok and þe popeiay with here proude federes. *c* 1400 MAUNDEV. (1839) xxvii. 274 Manye Popegayes that thei clepen Psitakes in hire Langage.

γ. 4 **papengay**, 5 **-ioye, papyniay(e, -gaye, papiniay(e**, 6 **-geay(e**, *Sc.* **-gay.**
1387 TREVISA *Higden* (Rolls) IV. 307 Oon mette hym wiþ a papengay on his hond. 14.. *Pol. Rel. & L. Poems* 101/251 The pellycan and the papynjaye. 1508 DUNBAR *Twa Mariit Wemen* 382, I thoght my self a papingay.

δ. 4– **popin-**, 5–7 **popen-**, 5–6 **popyn-**, 6–8 **poppin-**; 4–7 **-gay**, 5 **-ȝay, -yay**, 5–6 **-iay, -iaye, -geay**, 6 **-gaye, -iae, -ioye, -gei, -giay, -gjoye**, 6–7 **-gaie, -iaie**, 6–8 **-gey**, 7 **-gie, -ia, -jaye, -gjay**; 7–9 **poppinjay**, 7– **popinjay.**
1392–3 *Earl Derby's Exp.* (Camden) 286 Pro j cage pro le popingay. *c* 1400 MAUNDEV. (1839) xxvii. 271 Of Popengayes, as gret plentee as men fynden here of Gees. 14.. *Chaucer's Merch. T.* 1878 (Camb. MS.) Syngith ful muriere than the popyniay [*v. rr.* -iaye, -gay, popeniay]. 14.. *Metr. Voc.* in Wr.-Wülcker 625/5 *Psitagus*, popynyay. 1481 CAXTON *Myrr.* II. viii. 84 Ther ben popengayes, whiche ben grene & shynyng lyke pecoks. 1540 ELYOT *Image Gov.* (1556) 7 b, With the tounges of Popingaies, Nightyngales, and other sweete singyng birdes. 1544 TURNER *Avium Præcip.* H vj, *Psitacus*, Anglicè a popiniay. 1553 EDEN *Treat. Newe Ind.* (Arb.) 19 There bee also grene popingeays. 1577 FRAMPTON *Joyfull Newes* III. (1596) 94 He had eaten much fleshe of Popingeies. 1580 BABINGTON *Exp. Lord's Prayer* (1596) 20 The Cardinals Popiniay that could pronounce distinctly all the Articles of the Creede. 1600 J. PORY tr. *Leo's Africa* IX. 349 Of the parrat or poppiniay. These parrats are commonly founde in the woods of Ethiopia. *a* 1649 DRUMM. OF HAWTH. *Fam. Ep.* Wks. (1711) 156 The artificial notes of the learned popingayes in the guilt cages. 1657 OWEN *Schism* Wks. 1852 XIII. 164 An empty insignificant word like the speech of parrots and popinjays. 1792 WOLCOTT (P. Pindar) *Ode Directors* i, Lo, lofty poets are no longer priz'd, That to an eagle turn'd a popinjay. 1816 SCOTT *Old Mort.* ii, The figure of a bird decked with party-coloured feathers, so as to resemble a popinjay or parrot.

ε. (*Sc.*) 6 **papinga, -gaw, -go**, 8 **popingoe.**
1530 LYNDESAY *Test. Papyngo* 63 The complaynt of ane woundit Papingo. *a* 1550 *Freiris of Berwik* 148 in *Dunbar's Poems* (S.T.S.) 290 Als prowd as ony papingo. 1570 *Satir. Poems Reform.* xv. 37 ȝe plesand Paun and Papingaw Cast of ȝour blyithlyke cullour. *a* 1583 A. ARBUTHNOT *Praises of Women* in Pinkerton *Anc. Scot. Poems* I. 142 The papingo in hew Excedis birdis all. [1794 Popingoe: see 3.]

2. A representation of a parrot. † **a.** As an ornament: chiefly in tapestry. *Obs.*
[1328 *Inv. Bp. Stapleton* (Hingeston-R.) 566 Tria tapecia crocei coloris pulverizata de papegais.] 13.. *Gaw. & Gr. Knt.* 611 Bryddez on semez, As papiayez paynted pernyng bitwene. *a* 1400–50 *Alexander* 5129 With pellicans & papeioyes polischt & grauen. *a* 1440 *Sir Degrev.* 1480 Perreye in ylke a plas, And papageyes of grene. ? *c* 1475 *Sqr. lowe Degre* 798 A cloth of golde abought your heade, With popinjayes pyght with pery reed. 1546 *Inv. Ch. Goods* (Surtees, No. 97) 140 One suyt of baldking with popingjoyes. 1578 T. N. tr. *Conq. W. India* 198 They will make a Parret or Popin Jay of mettall, that his tongue shall shake, and his heade move, and his wings flutter.

b. As a heraldic charge or bearing; also as the sign of an inn.
c 1420 LYDG. *Assembly of Gods* 817 A popyniay was hys crest; he was of gret dyffence. 1687 *Lond. Gaz.* No. 2306/4 And the Thursday after, at the Popinjay in Norwich. 1868 CUSSANS *Her.* (1882) 92 After the Eagle and the Falcon, the Birds of most frequent occurrence in Armory are the Swan, Game cock, Cornish Chough, Pelican, Heron, Popinjay (or Parrot). [1881 BURKE *Peerage & Baronetage* 7/1 (Sir R. J. Abercromby, Bart.) Three papingoes, vert, beaked and membered, gu.]

3. The figure of a parrot fixed on a pole as a mark to shoot at. *Obs.* exc. *Hist.*
a 1548 HALL *Chron.*, *Hen. VIII* 60, I sawe on a Sondaye this Lent .vi. C. straungiers shotyng at ye Popyngaye with Crosbowes. 1630 *R. Johnson's Kingd. & Commw.* 185 There is in each City a shooting with the Peece at a Popingay of wood, set upon some high Steeple. 1653 URQUHART *Rabelais* I. xxiii. 107 Gargantua..shot at but-marks, at the papgay [Fr. *papegay*] from below upwards, or to a height. 1794 *Statist. Acc. Scot.* XI. 173 One is a perpendicular mark, called a popingoe...cut out in wood, fixed in the end of a pole, and placed 120 feet high, on the steeple of the monastery. 1816 SCOTT *Old Mort.* ii, The chief [sport] was to shoot at the popinjay. 1825 C. M. WESTMACOTT *Eng. Spy* II. 8 We'll shoot at pride and poppinjays.

4. *fig.* † **a.** Formerly applied to a person in a eulogistic sense, in allusion to the beauty and rarity of the bird. *Obs. rare.*
a 1310 in Wright *Lyric P.* v. 26 He is papeiai in pyn that beteth me my bale, To trewe tortle in a Tour y telle the mi tale. *c* 1430 LYDG. *Commend. Our Lady* 81 O popiniay, plumed with al clennesse. *c* 1450 HOLLAND *Howlat* 125 The Pacoke of pryce That was Pape cald..He callit on his cubicular..That was the proper Pape Iaye, provde in his apparale.

b. More usually taken as a type of vanity or empty conceit, in allusion to the bird's gaudy plumage, or to its mechanical repetition of words and phrases, and thus applied contemptuously to a person: cf. PARROT 2.
1528 TINDALE *Obed. Chr. Man* 89 b, The prest ought to.. Christen them in the english tonge, and not to playe the popengay with Credo saye ye: volo saye ye and baptismum saye ye, for there ought to be no mummynge in soch a mater. 1596 SHAKS. *1 Hen. IV*, I. iii. 50, I then, all-smarting, with my wounds being cold, (To be so pestered with a Popingay). *a* 1618 RALEIGH *Invent. Shipping* 41 Popinjayes that value themselves by their out sides, and by their Players coats. 1678 OTWAY *Friendship in F.* v. i, Shall I draw my Cerebrus and cut you off, you gaudy Popinjays? 1819 SCOTT *Ivanhoe* xxxv, The fond fool was decked in a painted coat, and jangling as pert and as proud as any popinjay. 1881 BESANT & RICE *Chapl. of Fleet* II. 216, I think the players are better company than your priggish popinjays.

† **5.** The prevailing colour of the green parrot; a shade of green; also *attrib.* or as *adj.*, as ***popinjay blue, colour, green, yellow.*** *Obs.*
1547 RECORDE *Judic. Ur.* 16 b, There are also oyle coloures (that is popingey grene) of iii sortes. 1573 *Art of Limming* 8 If you mingle Azure and Masticot together, you shal haue thereof a perfite Popinjay greene. 1577 BRETON *Flourish Fancie* (Grosart) 14/2 The colours of her cloath are..red, blewe, greene, Cernation, Yelow and popyniay. 1578 LYTE *Dodoens* VI. lxix. 746 Couered with a barke of a light greene or Popingay colour. 1587 HARRISON *England* II. vii. (1877) I. 172, I might here name..hewes deuised for the nonce..as ..popingaie blue. 1622 PEACHAM *Compl. Gent.* 114 If more inclining to a Popingjay, adde more Pinke to your white Lead. 1688 R. HOLME *Armoury* III. xix. (Roxb.) 157/2 All mixt colours..as carnation, Oreng-tawny, Sky colour, Popengie, Russett, are bastard and dishonorable colours. 1719 D'URFEY *Pills* II. 19 Beck had a Coat of Popin-jay. 1865 *N. & Q.* 3rd Ser. VIII. 372/2 Popinjay-green, philomel-yellow, &c., no longer appear in the Army Lists.

† **b.** Name of a plant. *Obs. rare*⁻⁰ and *doubtful*.
1658 PHILLIPS, *Popingey*,...also an Herb, so called from being of the colour of that bird, being a kinde of greenish colour, this Herb is called in Latin Symphonia.

6. A local name of the green woodpecker.
[1612 PEACHAM *Gentl. Exerc.* 128 Terpsichore would bee expressed..vppon her head a coronet of..those greene feathers of the poppiniaie, in token of that victory, which the Muses got of..the daughters of Pierius,..who after were turned into poppiniaies or wood-peckers.] 1833 *G. Montagu's Ornith. Dict.* 385 Poppinjay, *Picus viridis*. 1894 NEWTON *Dict. Birds*, *Popinjay*..has in this country been transferred to the Green Woodpecker. 1902 T. HARDY *Mother Mourns* Poems 73 My popinjays fail from their tappings.

Hence **'popinjayess**, *nonce-wd.*
1890 W. A. WALLACE *Only a Sister?* 192 You sweet future popinjayess.

popish ('pəʊpɪʃ), *a.*¹ [f. POPE *sb.*¹ + -ISH¹.]
† **1.** Of or pertaining to the pope; papal. *Obs.*
a 1540 BARNES *Wks.* (1573) 324/2 By the authoritie of Councels, and by some certaine lawes, both Emperiall, and Popish. *a* 1548 HALL *Chron.*, *Hen. V* 34 b, From his foolishe usurped name and Popishe dignitee. 1567 *Gude & Godlie B.* (S.T.S.) 204 His Popische pryde, and thrinfald Crowne, Almaist hes loste thair mycht.

2. Of or pertaining to popery; of or belonging to the Church of Rome; papistical. (In hostile use.)
1528 ROY *Rede me* (Arb.) 116 Though popisshe curres here at do barcke. 1549 LATIMER *4th Serm. bef. Edw. VI* (Arb.) 104 He wyl kepe hys possession quyetly as he dyd in the popyshe dayes. 1553 BALE *Vocacyon* Pref. 6 b, Myne hoste Lambert..was delyuered from hys vayne beleue of purgatorye, and other Popysh peltryes. 1556 *Chron. Gr. Friars* (Camden) 62 The occasyone came by popysse presttes. *Ibid.* 64 He sayd that men wolde have up agayne ther popych masse. 1685 EVELYN *Diary* 9 Nov., The King ..required..indemnity and dispensation to Popish officers from the Test. 1689 *Declar. Rights Will. & Mary* c. 2 §9 That it is inconsistent with the Safety and Welfare of this Protestant Kingdom, to be governed by a Popish Prince. 1769 BLACKSTONE *Comm.* IV. iv. 57 A short summary of the laws against the papists, under their three several classes, of persons professing the popish religion, popish recusants convict, and popish priests. 1862 S. WILBERFORCE in *Life* (1882) III. ii. 71 It is quite sure to stir up a vast amount of prejudice from its singularly un-English and Popish tone.

3. *Comb.* **'popish-like** *a.*, that looks like popish.
1689 R. WARE *Foxes & Firebrands* III. 19 Neither would she Countenance any thing that would seem Popish-like. 1705 HICKERINGILL *Priest-cr.* II. vii. 70 This Popish-like Adoration (I do not say *Popish*, but *Popish-like* Adoration).

Popish ('pəʊpɪʃ), *a.*² Also **Popeish.** [f. *Pope*, proper name + -ISH¹.] = POPIAN *a.*
1825 *Gentl. Mag.* XCV. I. 334 In this *Popish* controversy, though Mr. Bowles may affix the term 'final' to his Appeal, we have some doubt whether he will be permitted to have the last word. 1882 MRS. OLIPHANT *Lit. Hist. Eng.* I. 76 The very words of the Popish era still lingered on Cowper's tongue. *c* 1885 —— in A. L. Coghill *Autobiogr. & Lett. Mrs. Oliphant* (1899) 13 She..was fond of quoting Pope, so that we used to call her Popish in after-days when I knew what Popish in this sense meant. 1944 *New Yorker* 9 Dec. 97/2 The *Times'* vigorous and somewhat Popeish effort included this stern couplet.

popishly ('pəʊpɪʃlɪ), *adv.* [f. POPISH *a.* + -LY².] In a popish way; in the direction of or in accordance with popish doctrine, practice, or ideas.
1538 LATIMER *Let. to Cromwell* Rem. (Parker Soc.) 403 Their school,..maintained..by a brotherhood,..not without some guile, popishly pardoning, and therefore now worthily decried. 1613 PURCHAS *Pilgrimage* (1614) 535 He affirmes that the conuerts of these parts are more popishly Christian, then in the midst of Rome or Spaine. 1678 WOOD *Life* 1 Dec. (O.H.S.) II. 424 All such..that are suspected to be popishly addicted. 1705 HICKERINGILL *Priest-cr.* II. vii. 69 In Popishly affected, or Popishly suspected Reigns. 1896 *Protestant Echo* XVII. 126/1 This popishly styled 'Prince of the Apostles'.

popishness ('pəʊpɪʃnɪs). Now *rare*. [f. POPISH + -NESS.] The quality or condition of being popish; popish doctrine or practice; popery.
1530 TINDALE *Answ. More* I. ii. Wks. (1572) 280/2 To wishe them in better case,..is fleshly mynded popishnes. 1538 BALE *Thre Lawes* 1966 The olde popyshnesse is past whych was dampnacyon. 1657 J. WATTS *Vind. Ch. Eng.* 232 As there is no popishnesse, so, I do not see what superstitiousnesse there can be in it.

popism ('pəʊpɪz(ə)m). *nonce-wd.* [f. POPE *sb.*¹ + -ISM.] The papal system or religion; = POPERY 1.
1840 CARLYLE *Heroes* iv. (1872) 123 Formulism, Pagan Popeism, and other Falsehood. *Ibid.* 126 To..say: See, Protestantism is dead; Popeism is more alive than it, will be alive after it!

popisme, popistant, varr. POPPISM, POPESTANT.

† **'popistry.** *Obs.* Var. PAPISTRY, after *pope*.
1545 BRINKLOW *Compl.* xvi. (1874) 38 That all the whole pope, with all popistry, may be vtterly denyed and banysshed.

† **po'pize**, *v.* *Obs.* [f. POPE *sb.*¹ + -IZE. Cf. PAPIZE.] *intr.* To play the pope; = PAPIZE. Hence † **popizing** *ppl. a.*
1611 SPEED *Hist. Gt. Brit.* IX. ix. 528/2 Some Popizing Bishops and ambitious Clerks.

'popjoy, *v.* ? To amuse oneself.
1853 G. H. KINGSLEY *Sport & Trav.* (1900) 472 His stream—in which he himself was wont to popjoy in a very aboriginal manner. 1857 HUGHES *Tom Brown* I. ii, And after a whole afternoon's popjoying, they caught three or four small coarse fish.

poplar ('pɒplə(r)). Forms: 4–5 **poplere**, 4–6 **popler**, 5 **poppeler, populer(e**, 6 **popelare, poplare, popeler**, 6–7 **popular**, 6– **poplar.** [ME. *popler*, a. OF. *poplier* (13th c. in Hatz.-Darm.), F. *peuplier*, f. L. *pōpul-us* poplar + *-ier* (:—L. *-ārius*) forming names of trees. Cf. POPPLE *sb.*¹]

1. a. A tree of the genus *Populus*, comprising large trees of rapid growth, natives of temperate regions, some species remarkable for tremulous leaves, and producing soft light timber of loose texture; also, the timber of this tree. The Black Poplar, White Poplar, Lombardy Poplar, and Trembling Poplar or Aspen are the familiar European species.
The name is not native, and was used to render L. *pōpulus* before it was identified with any native or introduced tree.

1382 WYCLIF *Hos.* iv. 13 Thei brenneden tymyame vnder ook, and poplere, and terebynt. **1387** TREVISA *Higden* (Rolls) II. 303 þerfore Iacob took grene ʒerdes of populers of almand trees and of platans, and pyled of þe rynde [cf. POPPLE *sb.*[1] b, quot. 1382]. *a* **1400** *Pistill of Susan* 70 þe palme and þe poplere, þe pirie, þe plone. *c* **1440** *Promp. Parv.* 408/2 Poplere, or popultre, *populus.* **1523** FITZHERB. *Husb.* §130 In many places..[they] set such wethyes and pepelers in marshe grounde to nourysshe wode. **1562** TURNER *Herbal* II. 98 Poplers grow by water sides and in moyst places. *c* **1630** DRUMM. OF HAWTH. *Poems* 8 The Poplar spreads her Branches to the Skye, And hides from sight that azure Canopy. *a* **1800** COWPER *Poplar Field* 1 The poplars are felled, farewell to the shade, And the whispering sound of the cool colonade. **1830** TENNYSON *Mariana* iv, Hard by a poplar shook alway, All silver-green with gnarled bark.

b. With word distinguishing the species, as **balsam poplar** (*P. balsamifera*) of N. America and Canada, with large resin-covered buds; **black poplar** (*P. nigra*), of wide branching habit; **Carolina** or **necklace poplar** (*P. monilifera*), the common Cottonwood of U.S., a tall tree, the light wood of which is valuable for making packing-cases, etc.; **grey poplar** (*P. canescens*), a variety of the white poplar; **Lombardy** or **Italian poplar** (*P. pyramidalis, fastigiata,* or *dilatata*), of tapering pyramidal habit and great height, also called **pine poplar** and **Po-poplar**; **soft** or **paper poplar** (*P. grandidentata*), of N. America, the soft wood of which is extensively used for paper-making; **trembling poplar** (*P. tremula*), the ASPEN; **white poplar** (*P. alba*), a large spreading tree, with deeply indented roundish leaves, which are downy and white beneath; the ABELE.

1884 MILLER *Plant-n.*, *Balsam Poplar, *Populus balsamifera.* **1887** *Nicholson's Dict. Gard.* s.v. *Populus*, *P[opulus] balsamifera*,..Balm of Gilead; Balsam Poplar; Tacamahac. **1579** LANGHAM *Gard. Health* (1633) 504 The leaues and yong buds of *black Poplar, stampt and applyed, swageth the paine of the gout in the hands or feet. **1859** W. S. COLEMAN *Woodlands* (1862) 76 Early in spring, when the branches of the Black Poplar are yet leafless, they are loaded with..a profusion of deep red catkins, or pendulous flower-spikes. *Ibid.* 72 There is a variety..very common in the country, and sometimes called the *Grey Poplar (*Populus alba, v. canescens*), which has leaves more heart-shaped, and less deeply indented. **1782** J. SCOTT *Poet. Wks.* 264 Hears the grey poplars whisper in the wind. **1766** *Museum Rust.* VI. 176 The *Italian, or *Lombardy poplar, is of very quick growth, easily multiplied. **1882** *Garden* 14 Jan. 26/1 This beautiful upright Cypress is among evergreen shrubs what the Lombardy Poplar is among timber trees. **1789** *Trans. Soc. Arts* I. 78 This tree is called by some the *Pine Poplar. **1795** *Gentl. Mag.* LXV. II. 628 On the older leaves of the *Po-poplar it [a fungus] is observable this season very frequent. **1837** *Spirit of Woods* 66 The Lombardy or Po poplar, a native..of Italy, where it grows very plentifully, especially on the banks of the Po. **1884** MILLER *Plant-n.*, *Populus grandidentata*, Large-toothed Aspen, *Soft or Paper Poplar. **1698** FRYER *Acc. E. India & P.* 248 Here is beheld the *Trembling Poplar. **1846** J. BAXTER *Libr. Pract. Agric.* (ed. 4) II. 205 The trembling poplar does not succeed so well on stiff clayey soils, but will thrive in almost any other. **1562** BULLEYN *Bulwark, Bk. Simples* 58 b, Pine trees, and *white Populars. **1859** W. S. COLEMAN *Woodlands* (1862) 72 The White Poplar often grows into a very large and lofty tree.

2. Applied to other trees resembling the poplar in some respect: the tulip-tree (also **tulip poplar**) of N. America (*Liriodendron tulipiferum*); an Australian tree with poplar-like leaves, *Carumbium populifolium* (*Omalanthus populifolius*), N.O. *Euphorbiaceæ*, also called **Queensland poplar**; a small Australian timber-tree, *Codonocarpus cotinifolius* = HORSE-RADISH *tree* (b), also called **native poplar**; **yellow poplar** = *tulip poplar* (*Treas. Bot.* 1866).

1766 *Compl. Farmer, Tulip-tree*,..a native of North America,..is generally known through all the English settlements by the title of poplar. **1852** MORFIT *Tanning & Currying* (1853) 93 The bark of the poplar (*Liriodendron tulipiferum*) also contains tannin. **1894** *Melbourne Museum Catal., Economic Woods* No. 61 (Morris), *Raddish-Tree*... The poplar of the Central Australian explorers. Whole tree strong-scented. **1896** SPENCER *Thro Larapinta Land* 47 A Codonocarpus, the 'native poplar' with light green leathery leaves. **1898** MORRIS *Austral Eng.* 365 *Poplar*, in Queensland, a timber-tree, *Carumbium populifolium.*

3. *attrib.* and *Comb.*, as ***poplar-block***, ***-board***, ***-branch***, ***grove***, ***-leaf***, ***log***, ***shade***, ***-timber***, ***-tree***, ***-twig***; ***poplar-covered***, ***-crowned***, ***-flanked***, ***-lined*** adjs.; **poplar aphis**, *Pemphigus bursarius* or *P. spirothecæ*, both of which form galls on the leaf-stalks of poplar-trees; **poplar beetle**, *Lina populi*, of the family *Chrysomelidæ*, feeding on the leaves of the poplar; **poplar birch**, (*U.S.*) the common birch, *Betula alba*; **poplar-borer** *U.S.*, the larva of a beetle, *Saperda calcarata*, which attacks the trunk and branches of poplar and certain other trees; **poplar dagger**, a moth, *Acronycta populi*, the larva of which feeds on poplar leaves; **poplar girdler**, a beetle, *Saperda concolor*, the larva of which girdles the trunks of poplar saplings; **poplar grey**, a British moth, *Acronycta megacephala*; **poplar hawk (moth)**, *Smerinthus populi*, a large species of the *Sphingidæ*; **poplar kitten**, a small British puss-moth, *Cerura* or *Dicranura bifida*; **poplar lutestring**, a rare British moth, *Ceropacha* or *Cymatophora or*; **poplar pine** = *Lombardy poplar*; **poplar-spinner**, a N. Amer. geometrid moth, *Biston ursaria*, the larva of which strips poplars of their leaves; **poplar-worm**, the caterpillar of a poplar moth.

1816 KIRBY & SP. *Entomol.* ii. (1818) I. 29 The *poplar and apple Aphis are distinct species. *Ibid.* xxi. II. 245 The grub of the *poplar-beetle..is remarkable for similar organs. **1870** MORRIS *Earthly Par.* II. III. 278 From off the *poplar-block white chips would fly. **1481–90** *Howard Househ. Bks.* (Roxb.) 517 Payd to Umfray, carpenter, for c.c. of *popler bord. **1884** *Rep. Comm. Agric.* (U.S. Dept. Agric.) 383 The *Poplar-Borer..has been destructive to poplar trees on the shore of Casco Bay. **1942** S. W. FROST *Gen. Entomol.* xix. 381 The poplar borer..and the carpenter worm..keep at least a portion of their burrows free from frass and other waste material. **1972** SWAN & PAPP *Common Insects N. Amer.* 455 Poplar Borer... The larvae work in the trunk and large limbs of felled and weakened poplar. **1590** SPENSER *F.Q.* II. ix. 39 What wight she was that *Poplar braunch did hold? **1798** LANDOR *Gebir* VI. 157 *Poplar-crown'd Sperchios. **1832** J. RENNIE *Conspectus Butterfl. & Moths* 78 *Acronycta*... The *Poplar Grey. **1591** PERCIVALL *Sp. Dict., Alameda*, a *popler groue, *Populetum.* **1832** J. RENNIE *Conspectus Butterfl. & Moths* 23 The *Poplar Hawk. **1887** *Nicholson's Dict. Gard.* III. 471/2 The Poplar Hawk Moth..lives on Poplars and Willows, and on Laurel and Laurustinus. *Ibid.* 254/2 The *Poplar Kitten..feeds on Aspen and other Poplars. **1561** HOLLYBUSH *Hom. Apoth.* 13 b, Make hym a playster of *Popular leaues. **1725** POPE *Odyss.* VII. 135 Their busy fingers move, Like poplar-leaves when Zephyr fans the grove. **1832** J. RENNIE *Conspectus Butterfl. & Moths* 82 The *Poplar Lutestring. **1770** H. WALPOLE *Let. to Hon. H. S. Conway* 25 Dec., If *poplar-pines ever grow, it must be in such a soaking season as this. **1497** *Naval Acc. Hen. VII* (1896) 235 Certeyn *poppeler-tymbre for making of cc pavysses. **14..** *Voc.* in Wr.-Wülcker 604/8 *Populus*, a *populertre. **1809** A. HENRY *Trav.* 128 Young wood of the birch, aspen, and poplar-tree. **1899** MACKAIL *Life Morris* I. 335 Ordering three hundredweight of *poplar-twigs for experiments in yellow dyeing. **1807–8** W. IRVING *Salmag.* (1824) 223 Last year the *poplar-worm made its appearance.

Hence **'poplared** *ppl. a.*, planted with poplars.

1886 MRS. CADDY *Footsteps Jeanne D'Arc* 85 The poplared levels of the southern bank. **1902** *Daily Chron.* 4 Sept. 7/4 The afternoon was lovely, by the poplared Loire.

Poplarism ('pɒplərɪz(ə)m). [f. *Poplar*, the name of a district, formerly a borough in the East End of London + -ISM.] The policy of giving out-relief on a generous or extravagant scale, practised by the Board of Guardians of Poplar about 1919 and later; any similar policy which lays a heavy burden on ratepayers. Hence **'Poplarist**, one who practises or advocates Poplarism; also *attrib.*; **,Poplari'zation**, the adoption or implementation of Poplarism; **'Poplarize** *v. trans.*, to make like Poplar; to subject to Poplarism.

1922 *Glasgow Herald* 3 Nov. 8 The hard-headed workers of Yorkshire..have learned the lesson of Poplarism. **1923** *Daily Mail* 31 July 5/3 'Poplarism' was a portent of the changing of the modern state. **1923** R. MACAULAY *Told by Idiot* I. 44 So Poplarised..did she become that she took to speaking of her parental home in Bloomsbury as being in the West End. **1923** *Glasgow Herald* 1 Oct. 8/6 A decision in the opposite sense would simply mean an indefinite continuance of the Highland variety of 'Poplarisation' in the Lewis. **1924** *Ibid.* 7 Apr. 12/4 Mr. Wheatley..had been accused of desiring to 'Poplarise' the British people. **1925** *Ibid.* 6 Mar. 9 Even the cautious prophets..foretell the announcement of a rebuff to the Poplarists tomorrow. **1928** *Daily Tel.* 6 Nov. 12/6 Those..will demand increased subsidies, allowances, and 'Poplarised' social services, to be paid for out of the proceeds of very high taxation. **1931** *Times* 20 Feb. 7/6 The chief issue of the election is whether or not the policy of 'Poplarism' advocated by the Labour-Socialist Party is to be applied to London government. **1962** B. KEITH-LUCAS in *Public Law* Spring 67 The central government was finding that the weapons available to it were inadequate for the purpose of defeating Poplarism. The Poplar Order was being defied week by week. **1973** G. W. JONES in *Ibid.* Spring 28 Morrison had been opposed to the three elements of 'Poplarism', the payment of excessive wages and excessive relief and the refusal to honour legal obligations. **1976** H. WILSON *Governance of Britain* ii. 29 It was all done by agreement, Snowden recording that, as George Lansbury had to be found a job, despite his 'Poplarist' reputation, it was he who suggested Lansbury for the Office of Works.

pople, obs. f. PEOPLE, POPPLE; var. POPEL *Obs.*

popler, obs. f. POPLAR; var. POPELER *Obs.*

† **'poplesy, 'poplexy.** *Obs.* Chiefly *Sc.* [Aphetic form of APOPLEXY. So obs. Du. *popelcye* (Plantin).] = APOPLEXY.

c **1386** CHAUCER *Nun's Pr. T.* 21 (Harl. MS.) The goute lette hir no þing for to daunce Ne poplexie schente not hir heed. **1490** CAXTON *Eneydos* xxviii. 110 The gowte or the poplesie. *c* **1500** *Rowlis Cursing* 43 in Laing *Anc. Poet. Scot.* 212 Pouertie, pestilence or poplecy. *a* **1585** MONTGOMERIE *Flyting* 322 The painfull poplesie and pest.

† **'poplet.** *Obs.* [app. ad. OF. **poupelette*, fem. of *poupelet* darling.] A female favourite; a light woman; a wench. So † **pop'lolly**, a mistress.

1577 STANYHURST *Descr. Irel.* in *Holinshed* (1808) VI. 32 The prettie poplet his wife began to be a fresh occupieing giglot at home. **1658** PHILLIPS, *Poplet*, a young wench. **1694** *Ladies Dict.* 377/1 *Popelet, lote*, a Puppet or young wench. **1825** CREEVEY in *C. Papers* (1904) II. 86 This house..presided over by a poplolly! a magnificent woman, dressed to perfection, without a vestige of her former habits.

† **'poplin**[1]. *Obs.* Also 8 poupelin. [a. obs. F. *poup(e)lin*, *popelin* (16th c. in Godef.), mod.F. dial. *poplin*, in same sense; of uncertain origin, possibly a fanciful application of obs. F. *popelin*, 'a little finicall darling' (Cotgr.).] A kind of cake: see quots.

1600 SURFLET *Countrie Farme* v. xxii. 723 Poplins are made of the same flower, knodden with milke, yolkes of egges, and fresh butter. **1725** BRADLEY *Fam. Dict.* s.v. *Poupelin*, You must plunge the nether crust first,..and afterwards do the same by the upper crust of the Poupelin.

poplin[2] ('pɒplɪn). [ad. F. *popeline*, for earlier *papeline* (1667 in Hatz.-Darm.), ad. It. *papalina*, fem. of *papalino* adj., papal (whence F. *papalin* adj., *a* 1646 in Hatz.-Darm.); applied to this material because manufactured at Avignon, until 1791 a papal town, which still has manufactures of silk goods.] A mixed woven fabric, consisting of a silk warp and worsted weft, and having a corded surface; now made chiefly in Ireland. Also applied to imitations of this (see next).

double poplin, a stiff poplin in which the silk warp and the worsted weft are both very heavy.

1710 *Lond. Gaz.* No. 4706/4 For Sale.., Poplins,..and other Stuffs. **1737** *N. Jersey Archives* XI. 517 The other lin'd with light colour'd Silk Poplin that is pretty well worn. **1796** MORSE *Amer. Geog.* II. 199 (*Ireland*) The mixed goods, or tabinets and poplins have been long celebrated. **1815** JANE AUSTEN *Emma* xxxv, I have some notion of putting such a trimming as this to my white and silver poplin. **1882** BECK *Draper's Dict.* s.v., Many poplins now made have not a particle of silk in their structure, but are composed of worsted and flax or worsted and cotton, to the great detriment of their appearance, wear, and reputation.

attrib. **1751** MRS. DELANY in *Life & Corr.* (1862) III. 34, I have bought for my mourning a dark grey Irish poplin sack. **1861** SALA *Ship-Chandler* iv. (1862) 78 Ladies, with fans, and topknots, and poplin gowns, and pearl necklaces.

poplinette (pɒplɪ'nɛt). [f. POPLIN[2] + -ETTE.] A woollen or linen fabric in imitation of poplin.

1861 *Englishwom. Dom. Mag.* III. 69/1 Mohairs still continue in vogue, as also poplinettes and chalés. **1889** *Pall Mall Gaz.* 3 Apr. 6/2 Favourite materials for children's dresses are poplinettes. **1904** *Daily Chron.* 16 May 8/3 Among the novelties..are the poplinettes—linen materials, so silky-looking and lustrous that they might almost be mistaken for rich silk poplins.

† **'poplite,** *a. Obs. rare*$^{-1}$. [irreg. ad. mod.L. *poplite-us*: see below.] = POPLITEAL.

1758 J. S. *Le Dran's Observ. Surg.* (1771) Dict., *Poplitæa Vena*, the Poplite Vein, formed by two Branches of the Crural Vein.

popliteal (pɒ'plɪtiːæd), *adv. Anat.* [f. POPLITE-US + *-ad*, towards: see DEXTRAD.] Towards the popliteal aspect.

1803 BARCLAY *New Anat. Nomencl.* 166 In the sacral extremities,..Popliteal will signify towards the popliteal aspect. **1808** —— *Muscular Motions* 444 The motion popliteal, which is called extension.

popliteal (pɒ'plɪtiːəl, *erron.* pɒplɪ'tiːəl), *a. Anat.* [f. mod.L. *poplite-us* (see next) + -AL[1].] Pertaining to, situated in, or connected with the ham, or hollow at the back of the knee; esp. in names of parts, as ***popliteal artery***, ***glands***, ***ligament***, ***nerve***, ***space***, ***tendons*** (= ham-strings), ***vein***.

1786 J. PEARSON in *Med. Commun.* II. 99, I began by dissecting the popliteal artery. **1808** BARCLAY *Muscular Motions* 335 The muscles on the rotular and popliteal aspects of the legs. **1831** J. F. SOUTH *Otto's Pathol. Anat.* 454 Morgagni..found, in a popliteal aneurysm, the nerve..almost completely destroyed. **1892** *Lancet* 2 July 59/2 Total extirpation of the popliteal aneurysm.

‖ **popliteus** (pɒ'plɪtiəs, *erron.* pɒplɪ'tiːəs). *Anat.* [mod.L. adj. (sc. *musculus*), f. *poples*, *poplit-em* ham, hough. Erroneously spelt *poplitæus*: the L. suffix is *-ĕus*, as in *corporeus*, *osseus*, *sanguineus*, etc.] More fully ***popliteus muscle***: a flat triangular muscle at the back of the knee-joint.

1704 J. HARRIS *Lex. Techn.* I, *Popliteus*, by some called *Subpopliteus*, is a Muscle of the Leg. **1840** E. WILSON *Anat. Vade M.* (1842) 80 Immediately beneath this is the groove which lodges the tendon of origin of the popliteus. **1872** MIVART *Elem. Anat.* 182 On its outer surface is a pit for the tendon of the popliteus muscle.

† **poplitic,** *a. Obs.* (erron. -et-). [f. L. *poples*, *poplit-em* ham, hough + -IC. So obs. F. *poplitique* (Cotgr.) the popliteal vein.] = POPLITEAL. So † **poplitical** (erron. -et-) *a. Obs.*

1541 R. COPLAND *Guydon's Quest. Chirurg.* K iv, Howe many and what veynes ben let blode commonly in the great fote? Answere... The scyatyke vnder the ancle outwarde and the popletyke that is vnder the kne. **1597** A. M. tr. *Guillemeau's Fr. Chirurg.* lf. xii b/2 The Hockes, where we open the Popleticalle Vayne. **1656** BLOUNT *Glossogr.* s.v. *Vein*, *Popletick vein*, the ham-veine. **1658** PHILLIPS, *Poplitick* (lat.) belonging to the ham, or leg.

poplolly: see POPLET.

‖ **popo, popoi**, variants of PAWPAW.

1750 G. HUGHES *Barbadoes* 181 As hollow as a popo. **1892** E. REEVES *Homeward Bound* 135 Bread-fruit, mango, popoi, and other tropical fruits.

popocracy[1] (pəʊ'pɒkrəsɪ). *U.S. Obs.* exc. *Hist.* Also with capital initial. [f. POP(ULIST + DEM)OCRACY 4.] The rule or policy of the Populists or People's Party in the United States.

So **'popocrat**[1] [DEM)OCRAT 2], a member or supporter of the People's Party; a Populist; **popo'cratic** *a.*, of or pertaining to the Popocrats. Also earlier **poplocracy** (pəʊ'plɒkrəsɪ); so **poplo'cratic** *a.*

1895 T. R. SMITH in *Voice* (N.Y.) 18 July 5/3 Our fight will be for poplocracy, popular rule... I think no more significant name could be found than the Poplocratic Party. **1896** *Chicago Tribune* 4 Aug. 1/1 The first returns are always in favor of the Popocrats. *Ibid.*, Incomplete returns.. indicate Popocratic gains. **1896** *Boston Jrnl.* 24 Oct. 7/3 *(heading)* He is ready to support Popocracy. *Ibid.* 31 Oct. 4/3 *(heading)* Popocratic claims about Iowa. **1896** *North Amer. Rev.* CLXIII. 744 The threats.. of the Popocrats to change .. our financial system. **1904** *Omaha Bee* 16 Aug. 4 If it is so important that the people of Nebraska move cautiously in the selection of their chief executive this year, why did not the popocratic conventions discover the fact before? **1972** *Time* 17 Apr. 32/1 Populists who joined the Democrats were known as 'popocrats'.

'popocrat[2]. *Temporary.* [f. POP *a.* (*sb.*[8]) 2 + ARIST)OCRAT.] A leading figure in fashionable pop culture or society. So **po'pocracy**[2].

1970 *Tailor & Cutter* 4 Dec. 1180/2 Mick Jagger has moved far away from his former scruffy image—in fact, he is one of our more elegant popocrats. **1973** *Observer* 7 Oct. 39/1 He is a Nobel prizewinner, dresses with the Byronic panache of the popocracy.

popoi, var. POIPOI.

†**popo'mastic**, *a. Obs. humorous nonce-wd.* [irreg. f. POPE *sb.*[1] + Gr. μάστιξ whip, scourge, after words in -IC.] Scourging the pope.

1630 J. TAYLOR (Water P.) *Sculler* Wks. III. 16/1 To you from faire and sweetly sliding Thames A popomasticke Sculler warre proclaimes.

Po-poplar, Lombardy Poplar: see POPLAR 1 b.

‖**po po po** (po po po), *int.* An exclamation used in Greece expressing surprise, astonishment, commiseration, etc.

1936 L. DURRELL *Spirit of Place* (1969) 45 I'm almost tempted to come back and join you. Only the English weather po po po as they say here, shaking their rueful heads. **1972** J. AIKEN *Butterfly Picnic* i. 16, I.. said, 'Po, po, po', which is the Greek equivalent of the French 'oh la la', or the English 'tut tut'. **1973** 'M. YORKE' *Grave Matters* I. i. 12 'The *Kiria* had no sons.' '*Po, po, po.*' The Greek tossed his head in sympathy. **1974** —— *Mortal Remains* III. vi. 83 Their talk was punctuated with cries of '*po, po, po*'.

‖**popote** (pɔpɔt). [Fr.] A French military kitchen or canteen.

1928 *Observer* 11 Mar. 17/7 By 1870 the young cook had become a chef, and he had charge of the kitchen of the Headquarters of the Army of the Rhine and later of MacMahon's Headquarters Mess, or 'popote', at Versailles during the Commune. **1934** A. WOOLLCOTT *While Rome Burns* 74 This, then, is the story.. as they tell it.. in the smoky *popotes* of the French army. **1966** J. DOS PASSOS *Best Times* (1968) ii. 43 The French cooks were getting dinner at the popote behind me.

pop-out ('pɒpaʊt). [POP-.] **1.** The act of popping out, as when a cork is drawn.

1836 T. HOOK *G. Gurney* III. 32 The creaking of a corkscrew, followed by the pop-out of a cork.

2. In surfing: a mass-produced surfboard.

1963 *Surfing Yearbk.* 42/2 *Popouts*, mass produced surfboards. **1965** *N.Z. Listener* 17 Dec. 5/1 Surflers will advise you to buy a custom-built board.. rather than the mass-produced 'pop-out'. **1969** *Observer* 3 Aug. 31/2 Mass-produced fibreglass surfboards, known as 'pop outs', were soon being produced in this country as well as special custom-built boards to meet more individual requirements. Pop outs today sell from about £27 and custom-built boards from £37. **1970** *Studies in English* (Univ. Cape Town) I. 28 The air of individuality surrounding a surfer extends to his board, and so *pop-out*, meaning a mass-produced surfboard 'popped out' of a mould, is usually a derogatory term.

3. *attrib.* or as *adj.* Designating that which pops out (in various senses); *spec.* of the windscreen of a motor vehicle: designed to 'pop out' on impact.

1963 *Lebende Sprachen* VIII. 167/1 Pop-out windshield. **1967** *Autocar* 5 Oct. 45 (Advt.), The same people who care about all-round disc brakes, 'pop-out' safety windscreen, rally-proved suspension and seats designed by an orthopaedic surgeon. **1968** *Listener* 21 Mar. 391/3 The new high-peformance laminated windscreens which since 1966 have cut injuries substantially in the States, or the 'pop-out' screens favoured by Mercedes-Benz and Volvo. **1968** A. DIMENT *Bang-Bang Birds* v. 72, I rejected.. pop-out piano wire.. and poison gas spray.

pop-over ('pɒpəʊvə(r)). Chiefly *U.S.* Also **popover, pop over.** [f. POP *v.*[1] + OVER *adv.*]

1. A very light cake made of flour, milk, eggs, and butter (? so called because it swells over the edge of the tin in which it is baked). Also *attrib.*

1876 M. N. HENDERSON *Pract. Cooking* 71 Breakfast Puffs, or Pop-overs... May be baked in roll-pans. **1887** A. A. HAYES *Jesuit's Ring* 120 Broiled chicken and pop-overs. **1892** KIPLING & BALESTIER *Naulahka* 70 The hot brown pop-overs, with their beguiling yellow interiors. **1902** *Fortn. Rev.* June 1008 The cook.. is expected to have ready for breakfast either fresh baked 'biscuits' (scones), 'muffins', or 'pop-overs'. **1906** *Mrs. Beeton's Bk. Househ. Managem.* lix. 1626 *Pop overs*.. white flour.. milk.. egg.. salt... Pop-over tins are similar to sheets of patty pans. **1932** J. DOS PASSOS *1919* 251 Then she set down the popovers and went out. **1935** M. DE LA ROCHE *Young Renny* xiv. 122 Two golden popovers wrapped in a snow-white napkin. **1945** B. MACDONALD *Egg & I* (1946) 66 Recipes for pop-overs, cup cakes and other hot oven delicacies. **1958** L. WHISHAW *As Far as You'll take Me* ii. 15 They gave me a meal of chicken and popovers. **1973** E. TAYLOR *Serpent under It* (1974) v. 73 Comforted by two cups of coffee, six popovers, and the promise of veal paprika for dinner. **1976** *Woman's Day* (N.Y.) Nov. 156/1 Serve pop-overs at once with lemon-honey butter.

2. A loose casual garment put on by slipping it over the head.

1945 *Sun* (Baltimore) 11 Jan. 7-0/3 Miss McCardell, author of the bareback sun dress, the wraparound 'pop-over' housedress, [etc.]. **1963** *Harper's Bazaar* Oct. 44/1 A well-shaped pop-over—superbly smart in warm wool. **1968** [see *boat neck (-line)*]. **1973** *New Yorker* 3 Dec. 68/1 (Advt.), Sunbound popover, to be paired with pants,.. loosely string-tied, and loosely kimono-sleeved. **1974** *Index-Jrnl.* (Greenwood, S. Carolina) 23 Apr. 3/2 (Advt.), Baby popover & pantie. **1976** *Times* 8 Apr. 7/4 Waterproof pop-overs fit over his blanket coats.

'poppa. *U.S. colloq.* **a.** = PAPA[1]. Also *transf.*

1897 G. B. SHAW *Our Theatres in Nineties* (1932) III. 20 We are permitted to take to our bosoms an American girl, because, to gratify her Poppa's love of a title without forfeiting her own self-respect, she has heroically refused a silly young Duke and married a venal old Earl. **1902** HOWELLS *Kentons* xii, Well, there's one thing; I won't call him *poppa* any more.. and I won't say papá and mammá. Everybody that knows anything says father and mother now. **1902** *Daily Chron.* 10 May 3/3 The decline of 'poppa' and 'momma' in Ohio may convince some Western politicians that England is still exercising her insidious and baleful influence. **1910** *Punch* 28 Sept. 227 Say, if that's poppa's notion of 'literary calm' I wish he'd never come home. **1956** [see *Father's Day* (FATHER *sb.* 12)]. **1959** *Listener* 10 Sept. 375/1 It is a strange feeling, unfamiliar I imagine to most other countries, which.. divide the rituals of the state and its political leadership between at least two dignitaries, so that Poppa is always at home. **1962** *Amer. Speech* XXXVII. 35 Another song which became popular sometime early in the century was entitled 'I Wonder Where My Sweet, Sweet Poppa's Gone'. The 'poppa' of this song is again a male lover. **1970** G. GREER *Female Eunuch* 158 Baby-talk, even to the extent of calling the husband.. 'poppa'. **1977** *N.Z. Herald* 5 Jan. 2-20/3 [Deaths] Lucich, Stipan Bartul... dear poppa of 19 grandchildren; in his 81st year.

b. *poppa stoppa* (U.S. Blacks' slang): see quots.

1944 D. BURLEY in A. Dundes *Mother Wit* (1973) 210 Elderly man—*Poppa Stoppa.* **1945** L. SHELLY *Jive Talk Dict.* 31/1 *Poppa stoppa*, smart old man. **1970** C. MAJOR *Dict. Afro-Amer. Slang* 92 *Poppa-stoppa*,.. any old man who is effective at what he does.

poppe, obs. form of POOP *sb.*[1]

po'ppean, *a. nonce-wd.* [irreg. f. POPPY + -AN.] Of or pertaining to poppy-juice; soporific.

1790 COLERIDGE *Poems, Inside the Coach* 15 In drizzly rains poppean dews O'er the tired inmates of the Coach diffuse.

popped (pɒpt), *ppl. a.* [f. POP *v.*[1] + -ED[1].]

a. Of eyes: bulging; protruding.

1927 *Scribner's Mag.* Apr. 383/2 Prentice's slightly popped blue eyes wandered to the colored folders.

b. *U.S. slang.* Arrested; apprehended by the police.

1960 R. G. REISNER *Jazz Titans* 163 *Popped*, caught (with drugs in one's possession). Example: I got popped. **1968–70** *Current Slang* (Univ. S. Dakota) III–IV. 94 *Popped*, arrested by the police.

popped corn: see POP-CORN.

poppe-holy, variant of POPE-HOLY *Obs.*

†**'poppel.** *Obs.* [a. OF. *popelle* (Neckham); cf. POPELER, POPARD.] (?) The Spoon-bill.

[*a* **1300** NECKHAM *De Utensilibus* Gloss. (MS. Bruges) (Godefroy), *Alunbes*, popelles [no gloss in MS. Cotton in Wright].] **1579** J. JONES *Preserv. Bodie & Soule* I. xiv. 26 Dottrel, Snipe, Godwipe, Dicken, Poppel, Bitter, Hearon.

poppell, obs. variant of PEBBLE.

popper ('pɒpə(r)), *sb.* [f. POP *v.*[1] + -ER[1].]

†**1.** A small dagger. *Obs.*

c **1386** CHAUCER *Reeve's T.* 11 A ioly poppere baar he in his pouche Ther was no man for peril dorste hym touche.

2. One who or a thing which makes a popping sound. **a.** A gun, fire-arm, or the like; *spec.* a pistol (*slang*). **b.** One who shoots; a gunner.

1750 COVENTRY *Pompey Litt.* I. xvi. (1785) 40/1, I.. bought a second-hand pair of poppers. **1826** COL. HAWKER *Diary* (1893) I. 291 Spoiled by some rascally shore popper. **1834** BUCKSTONE *Agnes de Vere* II. iii, I've an excellent case of poppers here that I always keep loaded. **1845** BROWNING *Englishm. in Italy* 280 On the plain will the trumpets join chorus And more poppers bang.

3. A utensil for popping 'corn' (maize). See also *corn popper* s.v. CORN *sb.*[1] 11. *U.S.*

1875 KNIGHT *Dict. Mech.*, *Popper*,.. usually a wire basket, which is held over the fire and shaken or revolved so as to keep the corn moving. **1893** W. D. HOWELLS *Coast of Bohemia* 207 She bought a popper and three ears of corn. **1911** S. E. WHITE *Bobby Orde* (1916) xviii. 201 The pan.. was replenished with popcorn, Bobby unhooked the long-handled wire popper from its nail.. and set to work over the open fire. **1949** *Sat. Even. Post* 21 May 36/2 It operates popcorn machines on a concession basis.. and turns out home poppers for the kitchen trade. **1957** HESELTINE & DOW *New Basic Cook Bk.* (rev. ed.) 592 Success in popping corn depends upon the quality of the popcorn and the equipment used as well as the skill of the person doing the popping. For popping over coals, a wire popper may be used; for cooking on a gas or electric range, a pressure saucepan or a heavy frying pan with a tightly fitting lid is more satisfactory. Electric corn poppers are convenient. **1972** F. VAN W. MASON *Roads to Liberty* 179 When she bent over to pop a popper of corn [etc.].

4. One who moves promptly and quietly.

1825 *New Monthly Mag.* XIV. 194 The popper over to France and peep-taker at Holland.

5. In Cricket, a ball that pops (POP *v.*[1] 8 e) when bowled.

1857 *Bell's Life in London* 19 July 7/5 Mortlock defended his wicket well against the 'breakers' and 'poppers', which had by that time commenced their work. **1870** *Baily's Monthly Mag.* July 295 Mr. Grace was caught at point off a 'popper' of Emmett's. **1921** G. R. C. HARRIS *Few Short Runs* ii. 38 In my first Eton *v.* Harrow Match I calculated the batsman had to stop something like three shooters every eight balls, and at the same time one had to look out for poppers.

6. (The snapper on) a whip-lash. *U.S.*

1870 *Great Trans-Continental Tourist's Guide* (rev. ed.) 27/1 How often the sharp ring of the 'popper' aroused the timid hare or graceful antelope? **1877** H. RUEDE *Sod-House Days* (1937) 80 The lash is about 1¼ inches thick at the handle, and tapers to the popper, and a good hand will make them crack like a pistol. **1934** *Amer. Ballads & Folk Songs* 375 And the stage-driver loves the popper of his whip. **1935** [see *bull-whip* (BULL *sb.*[1] 11)].

7. A press-fastener.

1959 *Woman* 9 May 46/4 Sandwich a length of plastic foam between two layers of canvas held together with poppers. **1970** *Guardian* 17 June 13/6 He would help me dress him in his night things, laboriously doing up every popper and zip. **1973** *Times* 15 May 20/2 *(caption)* Beach bloomers in striped lawn have big sleeves to save shoulders from burning and practical poppers between the legs. **1974** N. FREELING *Dressing of Diamond* 33 Bernard, stop it, you're bursting my poppers.

†**'popper**, *v. Obs. rare*[−1]. In 4 poper. [freq. of POP *v.*[1]: see -ER[5].] *intr.* To 'pop' to and fro; to 'pop about'; to trot.

1362 LANGL. *P. Pl.* A. XI. 210 Ac now is religioun a ridere & a rennere aboute,.. Poperiþ on a palfrey [B. x. 308 A priker on a palfray] to toune and to toune.

Popperian (pɒ'pɪərɪən), *sb.* and *a.* [The name of Sir Karl Raimund *Popper* (b. 1902), philosopher + -IAN.] **A.** *sb.* A person who advocates the theories or methods of Popper. **B.** *adj.* Of or pertaining to Popper's theories or methods, esp. the theory that scientific laws are justified only by their resistance to falsification, and his criticism of the philosophical basis of Marxism and other ideologies which entail limitations on freedom. So **'Popperism**, the theory or practice of Popper's philosophical ideas.

1962 T. S. KUHN in *Internat. Encycl. Unified Sci.* II. II. xii. 146 If only severe failure to fit justifies theory rejection, then the Popperians will require some criterion of 'improbability' or of 'degree of falsification'. **1963** R. M. HARE *Freedom & Reason* vi. 91 We must.. notice an analogy between it and the Popperian theory of scientific method. **1966** *Sci. & Society* XXX. I. 1 *(heading)* Popperism: the scarcity of reason. **1971** *Nature* 28 May 269/2 Feyerabend goes on to criticize the Popperians for not making good their claim to exhibit science as a rational enterprise. **1972** *Ibid.* 10 Nov. 110/1 The author then delineates in turn three theories of the logical structure of science—inductivism, Popperian falsificationism and positivism. **1973** B. MAGEE *Popper* iii. 41 [T. S.] Kuhn's theory.. about the working activity of scientists.. is not irreconcilable with Popperism. *Ibid.* vi. 85 The Popperian approach has this consequence..: instead of encouraging one to think about building Utopia it makes one seek out.. the specific social evils under which human beings are suffering. **1977** A. GIDDENS *Stud. in Social & Polit. Theory* i. 72 Lakatos's studies, although nominally directed at supporting main elements of the Popperian standpoint, show how wide the discrepancy is.

†**'poppering.** *Obs.* Forms: 6–7 poperin, 7 popring, -rin, popperin, poppring, 7–8 -ering. [f. Flem. *Poperinghe*, name of a town in W. Flanders.] A variety of pear. Also *poppering pear*.

[*a* **1529** SKELTON *Sp. Parrot* 72 In Popering grew peres, whan Parrot was an eg.]

1592 SHAKS. *Rom. & Jul.* II. i. 38 O Romeo that she were, O that she were An open, or thou a Poprin Peare. **1609** *Ev. Woman in Hum.* IV. i. in Bullen *O. Pl.* IV, No plums, nor no parsneps, no peares, nor no Popperins. **1611** TOURNEUR *Ath. Trag.* IV. i, The wanton Streame,.. still seeming to play and dally under the Poppring so long that it has almost wash'd away the earth from the roote. **1750** E. SMITH *Compl. Housewife* (ed. 14) 214 Take poppering pears, and thrust a picked stick into the head of them.

poppet ('pɒpɪt), *sb.* Forms: 4–6 popet, 5 poopet, 6 pop-, poppette, 6–8 poppit, 6– poppet. See also PUPPET. [ME. *popet*, *-ette*, agreeing in sense with F. *poupette* doll, known in 1583, in Cotgr. 1611 'a little babie, puppet, bable'; a dim. of a form **poupe*, not found in this sense in French; but cf. It. *pupa*, also *puppa* 'a babie or puppet like a girle; used also for a lasse or wench' (Florio):—Romanic **puppa* for L. *pūpa* a girl, damsel, lass; also, a doll, puppet. Cf. Rhæt. *popa*, also late MHG. and Ger. *puppe*, MLG. *poppe*, Du. *pop*, all from Romanic, meaning 'doll'; also F. *poupée* doll (13th c. in Littré). The absence from French of *poupe* in a corresponding sense, and of *poupette* before the 16th c., makes the immediate source of the ME. word uncertain. *Poppet* was the earlier form of

PUPPET, with which in the earlier senses it agrees, but in sense 1 it is not contemptuous; it does not occur in several senses of *puppet*, but in sense 6 it is the usual form.]

1. A small or dainty person; in quot. 1699, a dwarf, pygmy; usually, in later use, a term of endearment for a pretty child, girl, or young woman; darling, pet. (Cf. PUPPET *sb.* 1.)

c **1386** CHAUCER *Sir Thopas* Prol. 11 This were a popet in an Arm tenbrace For any womman smal and fair of face. **1426** LYDG. *De Guil. Pilgr.* 11635, I am a poopet, in sothnesse, Douhter to dame Ydelnesse. **1597** BEARD *Theatre God's Judgem.* II. xxix. (1612) 404 As one of the three chapmen was employed..abroad, so the pretty poppet his wife began to play the harlot at home. **1699** GARTH *Dispensary* VI. (1700) 79 So when the Pigmies..Wage puny War against th'invading Cranes; The Poppets to their Bodkin Spears repair. **1718** *Free-thinker* No. 57 ¶1, I have been always told that I was a very pretty Miss, and a sweet Poppet. **1830** MISS MITFORD *Village* Ser. IV. (1863) 253 The little girl as pretty a curly-headed, rosy-cheeked poppet, as ever was the pet and plaything of a large family. **1840** MRS. F. TROLLOPE *Widow Married* ii, So the darling poppet was not always prepared for company. **1849** DICKENS *Dav. Copp.* (1850) iv. 45 Davy, dear. If I ain't been azackly as intimate with you. Lately, as I used to be. It ain't becase I don't love you. Just as well and more, my pretty poppet. **1937** M. ALLINGHAM *Dancers in Mourning* ii. 26 'That how you see it, poppet?' he said. **1954** A. SETON *Katherine* xii. 201 'Whist, poppet!' Hawise stroked the girl's arm. **1959** E. H. CLEMENTS *High Tension* x. 163 Cheer up, poppet, it's going to be all right. **1973** 'M. UNDERWOOD' *Reward for Defector* i. 11 He cast a doting glance at his wife. 'Well, poppet, it's time we were off.' **1978** D. DEVINE *Sunk without Trace* iii. 33 'No, you don't eat the spoon, poppet.' She hoisted the child out of his chair and put him in the play-pen.

attrib. **1581** J. BELL *Haddon's Answ. Osor.* 38 Mainteine your untruth with pretie popet demaundes. **1719** D'URFEY *Pills* II. 339 Those Poppet Hours are wasted now, I'll sneak and cringe no more.

†**2. a.** A small figure in the form of a child or a human being; a doll; = PUPPET *sb.* 2. *Obs.*

1413 *Pilgr. Sowle* (Caxton 1483) IV. xxxvi. 84 Childeren maken popetis for to pleyen with whyle they ben yonge. **1530** PALSGR. 256/2 Popet for chyldre to play with, *povpee*. **1531** TINDALE *Exp. 1 John* v. (1537) 81 A chylde..yf he crye ..men styll wyth a poppet. **1693** DRYDEN *Persius* ii. Notes (1697) 434 Those Baby-Toys were little Babies, or Poppets, as we call them. **1729** MRS. DELANY in *Life & Corr.* (1861) I. 230 The little poppets are very well cut, but you must take more pains about the trees and shrubs, for no white paper must be left.

†**b.** A small human figure, used for purposes of sorcery or witchcraft. *Obs.*

13.. *K. Alis.* 77 Of wax made him popetis, And made heom fyghte with battes [*Bodley MS.* popatrices..latrices]. **1693** C. MATHER *Invis. World* vii. (1862) 35 When there can be found their [witches'] Pictures, Poppets, and other Hellish Compositions. *Ibid.* xii. 137 They did in holes of the said old Wall, find several Poppets, made up of Rags and Hogs bristles, with headless Pins in them, the Points being outward. **1693** in I. Mather *Tryals New-Eng. Witches* (1862) 213 Without any Poppits of Wax or otherwise.

†**c.** Contemptuously applied to an image used in worship; hence, any material thing worshipped; an idol, a maumet. *Obs.*

1550 BALE *Image Both Ch.* I. Pref. A vj b, Bablynges, brawlinges, processyons, popettes, and suche other mad masteries. **1553** BECON *Reliques of Rome* (1563) 88 He [Nicephorus] also destroied al her [Irene's] poppets, sufferyng no images to remayne in the temples. **1687** DRYDEN *Hind. & P.* III. 780 You..will endeavour in succeeding space, Those houshold Poppits on our hearths to place. [**1880** WEBB *Goethe's Faust* III. vii. 164 And knead and mould your poppet well As many a foreign tale will tell.]

†**3. a.** A human figure with jointed limbs, which can be moved by means of strings or wires; *esp.* one of the figures in a puppet-show; a marionette: see PUPPET *sb.* 3. Also *attrib. Obs.*

a **1586** SIDNEY *Arcadia* II. (1622) 160 As if they had beene poppets, whose motion stood only vpon her pleasure. *a* **1610** BABINGTON *Exp. Cath. Faith* v, On Easter day in the morning they raise vp a Poppet, and make him walk by wyers and strings. *a* **1694** TILLOTSON *Serm.* cxxv. (1743) VII. 2162 These are mere engines and poppets in religion, all the motions we see without proceed from an artificial contrivance. **1702** *Lond. Gaz.* No. 3823/4 No Permission shall be given for acting Plays,..or exposing any Poppets, or other things that may disturb the Fair. *a* **1745** SWIFT (L.), He writ, 'A Merry Farce for Poppet', Taught actors how to squeak and hop it.

†**b.** A person whose actions, while ostensibly his own, are really actuated and controlled by another; = PUPPET *sb.* 3 b. *Obs.*

1550 BALE *Eng. Votaries* II. 78 b, Beholde here what popettes these lecherouse luskes made of their kynges. **1624** BP. MOUNTAGU *Gagg* vii. 62 Therefore in conclusion your texts of Scripture are not to any purpose at all to prove Peter's primacy, but you a poppet.

4. A cylindrical case for pins and needles, pencils, etc.; = PUPPET *sb.* 6. Now *dial.*

1866 *Routledge's Ev. Boy's Ann.* 642 Driven into the 'pin-poppet', the old name by which these curious cases were best known. **1903** *Eng. Dial. Dict.* s.v., A smaller kind, called a pin-poppet, is used to hold pins and needles; a larger, called a pencil-poppet, is used by school-children for pens and pencils. 'I want a poppet to keep my needles in'.

5. a. One of the upright pieces in a turning-lathe, in which the centres are fixed on which the work turns; a lathe-head; = PUPPET *sb.* 7.

1665 [see POPPET-HEAD 1]. **1875** *Carpentry & Join.* 18 We have..designed the latter to take a circular saw as well, by adding the wooden poppets..with their centre screws. **1881** YOUNG *Ev. Man his own Mechanic* §526 From a strong frame called the lathe-bed rises a couple of uprights called heads or poppets.

b. An overhanging or projecting bracket supporting a pendulum or the like: cf. COCK *sb.*[1] 16.

1779 *Trans. Soc. Arts* (1783) I. 240 The aforesaid pendulum suspended from a brass or metal poppet, called a cock.

c. = POPPET-VALVE.

1875 KNIGHT *Dict. Mech.*, *Poppet* (*Steam-engine*), a valve having an axial stem and reciprocating vertically on its seat. See *Puppet-valve*.

attrib. **1902** LIEUT. DAWSON in *19th Cent.* Feb. 225 The inlet and exhaust valves are of the poppet type.

6. *Naut.* Applied to short pieces of wood, used for various purposes: *esp.* **a.** Stout vertical squared pieces placed beneath a ship's hull to support her in launching; **b.** Pieces on the gunwale of a boat, supporting the wash-strake, and forming the rowlocks; **c.** The bars with which the capstan is turned.

c **1850** *Rudim. Navig.* (Weale) 138 *Poppets*, those pieces (mostly fir) which are fixed perpendicularly between a ship's bottom and the bilgeways, at the fore and aftermost parts of a ship, to support her in launching. **1867** SMYTH *Sailor's Word-bk.* s.v., Also, poppets on the gunwale of a boat support the wash-strake, and form the rowlocks. **1886** J. M. CAULFEILD *Seamanship Notes* 1 Always see your poppets shipped and fenders in. **1890** W. J. GORDON *Foundry* 70 A series of struts or 'poppets' is raised on them [the sliding ways, to launch a ship].

7. *attrib.* and *Comb.*, as †*poppet deity* (sense 2 c), *poppet spindle* (sense 5); **poppet-holes**, the holes in the drumhead of the capstan in which the bars are inserted; **poppet-leg** (*Australia*), one of the upright pieces of timber at the mouth of the shaft of a mine, supporting the piece from which the cage is suspended: cf. POPPET-HEAD 2. (For *poppet-play*, *-show*, *-valve*, see PUPPET-PLAY, etc.)

a **1641** BP. MOUNTAGU *Acts & Mon.* iii. (1642) 184 To appease the fury, forsooth, of their angry *poppet Deities. **1886** J. M. CAULFEILD *Seamanship Notes* 3 Parts of the Capstan. Drum head,..*poppet holes. **1890** *Melbourne Argus* 26 May 7/8 Wanted, 4 *Poppet Legs, bluegum, separate prices, 65 ft., 70 ft., 75 ft. long, 12 in. to 15 in. small end. **1896** *Westm. Gaz.* 20 Apr. 8/1 The forests around will supply good straight timber, suitable for all mining purposes, inclusive of poppet legs. **1873** J. RICHARDS *Wood-working Factories* 85 For drilling, have a stem pad,..to go into the *poppet spindle.

Hence †**'poppet** *v. trans.*, to treat as a poppet, to carry like an image or effigy. *Obs.*

1748 RICHARDSON *Clarissa* (1810) V. ii. 15 These lines of Rowe have got into my head; and I shall repeat them very devoutly all the way the chairmen shall poppet me towards her by-and-by.

'poppet-,head. Also *rarely* **puppet-head**.

1. In a lathe: = POPPET *sb.* 5, PUPPET *sb.* 7.

1665 R. HOOKE in *Phil. Trans.* I. 61 There must be two Poppetheads, into which the Mandril must pass. **1725** W. HALFPENNY *Sound Building* 56 Two level Pieces on each side the Puppet-Head. **1875** KNIGHT *Dict. Mech.*, *Poppet-head* (*Turning*), the part of a lathe which holds the back-center and can be fixed to any part of the bed. *Ibid.*, *Puppet-head*. **1888** HASLUCK *Model Engin. Handybk.* (1900) 58 This will afford a bearing for the back poppet-head centre.

2. *Mining.* The frame at the top of a shaft, supporting the pulleys for the ropes used in hoisting; a pit-head frame: = HEAD-GEAR 3. (Often in *pl.* in same sense.)

1874 J. H. COLLINS *Metal Mining* (1875) 129 Describe the construction of poppet heads, and give sketches in illustration of your answer. What will be the cost of poppet heads for whim drawing? **1888** F. HUME *Mme. Midas* I. v, The wheels were spinning round in the poppet-heads as the mine slowly disgorged the men who had been working all night. **1900** *Daily News* 26 Nov. 2/1 Lofty poppet heads have been erected on this shaft, 115 ft. high, in order to raise the auriferous gravel in one operation to a considerable height above the surface of the ground.

'poppet-,valve. Also (earlier) **puppet-valve**. [f. POPPET *sb.* + VALVE; in allusion to its movement.] A disk valve which is opened by being bodily lifted from its seat, not by turning upon a hinge. Earlier called PUPPET-CLACK. Hence **poppet-valved** *a.*

1829 [see PUPPET-CLACK]. **1835** *Amer. Railroad Jrnl.* 25 Apr. 245/3 Let the valve be..of the kind called puppet valves. **1874** RAYMOND *Statist. Mines & Mining* 41 The engines are fitted with puppet-valves and 'cross variable cut-off', which is worked by the engineer. **1877** *Jrnl. Franklin Inst.* CIII. 13 These dimensions would have been reduced by the use of the poppet in place of the lantern valve. **1887** D. A. LOW *Machine Draw.* (1892) 108 Sketches showing the construction of a conical metal lift or puppet valve and seating. **1890** *Cent. Dict.*, *Poppet-valve*, same as *Puppet-valve*. **1912** *Motor Traction* 12 Oct. 328/2 The writer has in his possession a list of some 250 poppet-valved engines, together with such data as valve diameters, [etc.]. **1919** W. H. BERRY *New Motoring* xvi. 126 The poppet-valved engine, badly made and of unsuitable materials, can be an atrocious production. **1961** F. A. S. BROWN *Nigel Gresley* xvii. 122 With poppet valves there is less restriction of steam flow through the ports and consequently less throttling of the steam supply to the cylinders. **1970** *Railway World* Dec. 532 The poppet valves were actuated by a semi-internal form of Walschaerts valve gear.

poppied ('pɒpɪd), *a.* [f. POPPY *sb.* + -ED[2].]

1. Filled or adorned with poppies.

1818 KEATS *Endym.* I. 255 Their fairest-blossom'd beans and poppied corn. **1896** *Westm. Gaz.* 25 Sept. 8/1 Cornfields and woodlands coming right to the edge of the poppied cliffs. **1935** E. R. EDDISON *Mistress of Mistresses* viii. 143 The poppied frieze, the walls, the very floor of marble, seemed to waver. **1943** C. DAY LEWIS *Word over All* 15 Over the corn, over the poppied plains.

2. Having, or affected by, the sleep-inducing quality of the poppy; slumberous, drowsy, narcotic.

1805 T. HARRAL *Scenes of Life* III. 209 To admit the popied influence of Somnus. **1854** B. TAYLOR *Poems of Orient, Nubia*, A land of dreams and sleep, a poppied land! **1865** SWINBURNE *Ilicet* 6 The poppied sleep, the end of all. **1881** O. WILDE *Poems* 75 O for Medea with her poppied spell!

'poppin. Now only *dial.* Also 5 **popyn**, 6 **poppyn**. [Late ME. *popyn*, ad. OF. *popine* (later *poupine*) a doll, a pretty little woman (15th c.), also *Popin* (proper name, 1390), *poupin* baby, fop (16th c. in Godef. *Compl.*); f. Romanic type **puppa*: see POPPET.] A doll, a PUPPET.

c **1440** *Promp. Parv.* 409/1 Popyn, chylde of clowtys.., *pupa*. **1552** HULOET, Poppyn, *oscillum*... *Circulatorious*, perteynynge to poppyn players. **1570** LEVINS *Manip.* 134/14 A Poppin, *oscillum*. *a* **1825** FORBY *Voc. E. Anglia*, *Poppin-shew*, a puppet-shew.

popping ('pɒpɪŋ), *vbl. sb.*[1] [f. POP *v.*[1] + -ING[1].] The action of POP *v.*[1] in various senses.

1652 H. L.'ESTRANGE *Amer. no Jewes* 53 Wee finde no mention of any sound made of the kissing of the hand..or.. any such popping or smacking. **1710** C. SHADWELL *Fair Quaker of Deal* II. ii. 23 Upon the first popping of the Question. **1844** THACKERAY *Wand. Fat Contrib.* v, The popping of the soda-water corks. **1887** FENN *Dick o' the Fens* (1888) 124 A peculiar popping and crackling began to be heard, as the flames attacked the abundant ivy. **1929** J. MASEFIELD *Hawbucks* 80 'What do you think about popping?' 'You mean proposing?' 'Yes, popping.' **1957** C. MACINNES *City of Spades* I. ix. 65 'Charging is different from popping...' 'Popping?' 'With needles. White stuff —man, that's danger!' **1965** 'E. MCBAIN' *Doll* (1966) xii. 155 She has..been hopelessly hooked since she first began skin-popping. **1978** *Amat. Photographer* 29 Nov. 71/1 The fibre-optic Light Pipe gives efficient light mix and transmission at a low operating temperature, reducing the possibility of negative popping, and absorbing ultraviolet.

popping, *vbl. sb.*[2]: see after POP *v.*[2]

popping ('pɒpɪŋ), *ppl. a.* [f. POP *v.*[1] + -ING[2].] That pops, in various senses.

†**1.** Whose speech is mere popping; chattering.

a **1518** SKELTON *Magnyf.* 232 What, Syr, wolde ye make me a poppynge fole? *a* **1529** —— *Replyc.* 39 Lyke pratynge poppyng dawes. **1540** PALSGR. *Acolastus* M iv, For a suretie this [fellow] is a very popyng foole.

2. Of firing: Desultory, occasional, dropping.

1761 *Chron.* in *Ann. Reg.* 139/1 The enemy annoyed us with some popping musquetry from behind trees. **1779** *Gentl. Mag.* XLIX. 469 Many popping shots were fired at him by the rebel crew from the woods. **1836** F. SYKES *Scraps fr. Jrnl.* 149 The frequent popping noise of the sharpshooters.

†**3.** Of the sea: ? Tumbling, choppy. (Cf. POPPLE *v.* 1, *sb.*[3] 2, POPPLY.) *Obs.*

1628 DIGBY *Voy. Medit.* (1868) 35 Being a high popping sea some of my shippes had like to haue bin foule of one another.

4. Of the eyes: Protuberant. (Cf. *pop-eyed* in POP-.)

a **1696** AUBREY *Brief Lives* (1898) I. 411 His eie full and popping, and not quick; a grey eie.

'popping-crease. *Cricket.* [f. POPPING *vbl. sb.*, prob. in sense 'striking' + CREASE *sb.*[2] 2.] A line drawn four feet in front of and parallel to the wicket, within which the batsman must stand.

Probably the crease orig. marked the line which the ball, when bowled or trundled along the ground (see BOWL *v.* 4), must have passed before it might be 'popped' or struck.

1774 *Laws of Cricket* in Grace *Cricket* (1891) 13 Ye popping crease..must be exactly 3 foot 10 inches from ye Wicket. **1833** NYREN *Yng. Cricketer's Tutor* 28 In reaching in too, be especially careful that the right foot remain firmly in its place behind the popping-crease. *Ibid.* 35 The first player I remember to have broken through the old rule of standing firm at the popping crease for a length ball. **1897** RANJITSINHJI in *Daily Chron.* 23 Aug. 8/1 The rules state that a batsman is out unless his foot is within the popping-crease. A batsman often considers himself hardly treated when given out because his foot is on the line.

poppish ('pɒpɪʃ), *a.* [f. POP *sb.*[1] 5 + -ISH[1].] Of the nature of pop; effervescent.

1881 BLACKMORE *Christowell* (1882) III. xi. 164 The art of discharging a cork full bang, from a bottle of poppish fluid, without loss.

†**'poppism.** *Obs. rare.* Also 7 **popisme**. [a. F. *popisme*, 'the popping, or smacking sound wherewith Riders incourage, or cherish, their horses' (Cotgr.); ad. L. *poppysma*, *-ysmus*, a. Gr. πόππυσμα, ποππυσμός, sbs. f. ποππύζειν to smack the lips, make a clucking sound.] The making of a smacking sound with the lips.

1653 URQUHART *Rabelais* I. xxiii. 104 The prancing flourishes, and smacking popismes [F. *popismes*], for the better cherishing of the horse, commonly used in riding. **1753** CHAMBERS *Cycl. Supp.* s.v. *Adoration*, The method of adoring lightening,..was poppisms, or gentle clappings of the hands.

poppit (ˈpɒpɪt). Also poppet. [f. POP *v.*¹] A kind of bead (see quot. 1968).

1958 N. MARSH *Singing in Shrouds* (1959) v. 85 He started in on her rope of beads which, being poppets, broke. **1968** J. IRONSIDE *Fashion Alphabet* 178 Poppits were beads with a small bar which pushed into a hole in the next bead so that one could make necklaces or bracelets. **1969** *Observer* 23 Feb. 31/1 There was a time when everyone wore diamonds or poppit-beads. **1974** *Sci. Amer.* Oct. 48/3 They are strung together like Poppit beads in a row to form protofilaments.

poppite: see POP *sb.*⁴

popple (ˈpɒp(ə)l), *sb.*¹ Now *dial.* and *U.S.* Forms: (1 popul), 4–6 popil, 5 -ille, -ul(e, 5–6 -ill, -yl(l, 6–8 pople, (8 popel), 7– popple, (9 *dial.* poople). [Late OE. *popul-*, ME. *popul* ad. L. *pōpulus* poplar; with ME. *popil*, 16th c. *pople*, cf. obs. and dial. F. *pouple*, F. *peuple*. So MHG. *papel, popel*, Du., LG., Ger. *pappel*, Sw., Dan. *poppel*, all ultimately from L.]

a. = POPLAR.

[? *a* **1000** (MS. 12th c.) in Kemble *Ced. Dipl.* III. 219 Of ðam ellene to populfiniȝe; of populfiniȝe to Lambhyrste.] **1549** *Compl. Scot.* vi. 57 The oliue, the popil, & the oszer tree. **1617** MORYSON *Itin.* III. 110 The Cypresse, Pople, and Oake trees, grow in many places. **1699** *Providence* (R.I.) *Rec.* (1893) IV. 183 A small bush being an Aspe or Pople. *a* **1825** FORBY *Voc. E. Anglia, Popple*, a poplar tree. **1840** SPURDENS *Suppl. Voc. E. Anglia, Poople*, the poplar tree. **1879** A. S. PACKARD in *Hist. Bowdoin College* (1882) 91 Popple, or bass, or white maple.

b. *esp.* in *attrib.* use, as ***popple tree***, etc.

1382 WYCLIF *Gen.* xxx. 37 Jacob takynge green popil ȝerdis [**1388** ȝerdis of popeleris], and of almanders, and of planes. **1431–2** in Willis & Clark *Cambridge* (1886) II. 446 Pro popill bord pro coopertoriis studiorum xv^s. *c* **1440** *Promp. Parv.* 409/1 Popul tre, idem quod poplere. **1530** PALSGR. 256/2 Popyll tree, *pevplier*. **1563** T. GALE *Antidot.* II. 15 The Pople buddes must bee broused. **1740** *Dudley Rec. Mass.* (1893) I. 86 From thense..to a popel stump with a heap of stones about it. **1789** *Ibid.* (1894) II. 318 Thence by Browns Line on Whitfords Land to a Popple Tree. **1910** S. E. WHITE *Rules of Game* xii. 66 The remains of the forest, overgrown with scrub oak and popple thickets, pushed down to the right-of-way.

popple (ˈpəʊp(ə)l), *sb.*² Now *local.* Forms: 5 popil, -yl, -ylle, ulle, 6 pople, *Sc.* poppill, 7– popple, (9 *dial.* poppel, *Sc.* papple). [Late ME.; origin and etymology uncertain.

A mediæval Lat.-Gr. Vocabulary quoted by Du Cange has '*populia*, λύχνις'; but although cockle is now placed in the genus *Lychnis*, it is very doubtful whether this is connected with *popple*. *Cockle* (*cocle, kokkel*) and *popple* (*poppel*) have the appearance of parallel forms with exchange of consonants. On the other hand, this plant appears to have been sometimes included under the name *popy* (see POPPY 2), and conversely the name *popple* is now in some districts (esp. Cumbria and Yorkshire) applied to the corn poppy; so that the names may possibly have been originally related, *popil* being a derivative either of *popi, popy*, or of one of the Romanic representatives of *papaver*: see POPPY. But further evidence is wanted.]

1. = COCKLE *sb.*¹ 1, i.e. the wild plant *Lychnis* (or *Agrostemma*) *Githago*, a well-known field weed.

c **1425** *Voc.* in Wr.-Wülcker 664/30 *Hoc lollium*, populle. **1483** *Cath. Angl.* 286/2 Popylle, *gith* indeclinabile, *lollium, nigella*. **1538** TURNER *Libellus, Githago* siue *Nigellastrvm*,.. herba illa procera, que in tritico flauescente existit..uulgus appellat Coccle ant pople. **1853** *Jrnl. R. Agric. Soc.* XIV. II. 304 It was difficult to find a sample-bag of wheat without papple. **1868** ATKINSON *Cleveland Gloss., Popple*, the common Corn Cockle. **1877** *N.W. Linc. Gloss., Popple*, corn-cockle..the seeds of which are difficult to separate from or 'dress out' of the grain when thrashed.

b. Popple or cockle, being erroneously confounded by early herbalists with *Nigella*, and so with the *lolium* of Pliny and *zizania* of the Vulgate, was taken metaphorically for the darnel or 'tares' sown by the Evil One among the wheat: see COCKLE *sb.*¹ 2, DARNEL.

a **1532** *Will. of Thorpe's Exam.* in Foxe *A. & M.* (1563) 167/1 Thy deceit whiche thou hast learned of them that trauell to sowe popill among the wheate. *a* **1568** in *Bannatyne Poems* (Hunter. Cl.) 220 Thus weidit is the poppill fra the corne. **1644** MAXWELL *Prerog. Chr. Kings* 72 It sprang not up till..that malicious one did sow popple among the good Wheat of Christ's field.

2. Extended locally to other field weeds and their seeds; esp. the corn poppy, and charlock.

1855 ROBINSON *Whitby Gloss., Popple*, the wild red poppy of the corn fields. (So in *Eng. Dial. Dict.* Cumberland and Yorksh.) **1878** *Cumbld. Gloss.* Pref. 19 *Brassica*, the seeds of the tribe are called Popple. **1886** BRITTEN & H. *Plant-n., Popple*..(2) *Sinapis arvensis*, Cumb.

popple (ˈpɒp(ə)l), *sb.*³ Also 4 pople. [Goes with POPPLE *v.*]

†**1.** A bubble such as rises and breaks in boiling water. *Obs.*

a **1350** *St. Nicholas* 268 in Horstm. *Altengl. Leg.* (1881) 14 Hale and faire hir child scho fand, With þe water poples him playand. **1530** PALSGR. 256/2 Popple, suche as ryseth whan water or any lycour set[h]eth fast, *bovillon*.

†**b.** ? A swelling or bulge like, or caused by, a bubble. *Obs.*

1635 in *Earl of Stirling's Reg. Roy. Lett.* (1885) II. 819 He will mak a scheit of lead..more solide, less porie, and consequentlie more voyd of all cracks, holls, or popill.

2. An act or condition of 'poppling'; a rolling or tossing of water in short tumultuous waves; a strong ripple.

1875 BUCKLAND *Log-bk.* 80 If there is a bit of a popple at all, a big ship will lay rolling about in the sea just like a half-tide rock. **1881** CLARK RUSSELL *Ocean Free Lance* I. v. 252 As we neared the bay the popple grew ugly enough to demand the closest vigilance. **1897** *Daily News* 27 Aug. 3/1 There was a very nasty roll and popple on the sea.

b. The agitation on the surface of a boiling liquid; the sound of this.

1889 *Spectator* 7 Dec. 805/1 Cowper [after he heard] that popple from the urn which showed it to be..'on the boil'.

popple (ˈpɒp(ə)l), *v.* Also 4–6 (6– *Sc.*) pople, 5–6 *Sc.* popule, 6 poppell. [Has the form of a frequentative of POP *v.*¹, but in sense 1 prob. an independent onomatopœic formation, expressive of sound and action. Cf. MDu., Du. *popelen* to murmur, babble; to quiver, throb; med.L. *populāre* (Franck), *papellāre* (Kilian) to murmur; these refer mainly to the sound, while the Eng. word refers mainly to the action.]

1. *intr.* To roll or tumble about, to flow in a tumbling interrupted manner, as water flowing from a spring or over a pebbly surface, or boiling, or agitated by a strong wind; to bubble up, boil up; to ripple; to toss to and fro in short waves.

13.., *a* **1400–50** [see *poppling* below]. **1513** DOUGLAS *Æneis* III. ix. 69 Quhill brane, and ene, and blude all popillit out. *Ibid.* VI. v. 5 Popland and bullerand furth on athir hand. **1530** PALSGR. 662/2, I poppell up, as water dothe, or any other lycoure whan it boyleth faste on the fyre,..*je bouillonne*. **1675** COTTON *Scoffer Scoft* 103 His Brains came poppling out like water. **1725** RAMSAY *Gentle Sheph.* II. iii. Prol., A little fount, Where water poplin springs. **1818** SCOTT *Hrt. Midl.* xviii, The bits o' bonny waves that are poppling and plashing against the rocks. **1875** R. F. BURTON *Gorilla L.* II. 90 Small trembling waves poppled and frothed in mid-stream, where the fresh water met wind and tide. **1902** CORNISH *Naturalist Thames* 10 The sound of waters dropping, poppling, splashing, trickling.

b. To move to and fro, or up and down, when floating or immersed in rippling or boiling water.

1555 W. WATREMAN *Fardle Facions* xi. Q viij b, Rindles of Christalline watre. In whose botomes the grauelle, popleth like glisteryng golde. *a* **1825** FORBY *Voc. E. Anglia, Popple, v.* to tumble about with a quick motion, as dumplins,.. when the pot boils briskly. **1849** *Blackw. Mag.* LXVI. 562 We left them poppling up and down, like a cork, in the broken water. **1881** PHILLIPPS-WOLLEY *Sport in Crimea* 322 The birds are rattling and poppling down in the dark little forest pools.

2. [app. freq. of POP *v.*¹ 2.] To make a continuous popping or firing.

1898 G. W. STEEVENS *With Kitchener to Khartum* 81 The Maxims poppled away above them.

Hence ˈ**poppling** *vbl. sb.* and *ppl. a.*

13.. *E.E. Allit. P.* C. 319 þe pure poplande hourle playes on my heued. *a* **1400–50** *Alexander* 1154 The wawes of þe wilde see vpon þe walle betyn, The pure populand perle passyd it vmbe. *a* **1801** R. GALL *Poems* (1819) 9 Upon the ear The popling Leven wimples clear. **1826** HOR. SMITH *Tor Hill* (1838) I. 6 The calm guggling and poppling of the waves as they were parted by the piles. **1854** H. MILLER *Sch. & Schm.* xx. (1858) 440 A peculiar poppling noise, as if a thunder-shower was beating the surface with its multitudinous drops, rose around our boat. **1883** J. FERGUSON in *Blackw. Mag.* Aug. 248 The mother stirred the poppling porridge on the fire.

†ˈ**poppling.** *Obs. rare*⁻⁰. [f. POPPLE *sb.*¹ + -ING³.] = POPLAR.

1570 LEVINS *Manip.* 136/26 A Poppling, *populus*.

popply (ˈpɒplɪ), *a.* [f. POPPLE *sb.*³ + -Y.] In a 'poppling' condition; broken, choppy, ripply.

1889 P. H. EMERSON *Eng. Idylls* 113 The popply water all streaked with foam. **1895** *Times* 15 Mar. 8/2 As they passed the Duke's Head hostelry and Alexander's boatyard some popply water caused them to splash a little. **1904** *Daily News* 28 Mar. 12/2 Off the wall at Harrod's..the 'popply' water somewhat discomposed the Oxford crew.

poppy (ˈpɒpɪ), *sb.* Forms: α. 1 popaeȝ, popæȝ, popeȝ, popei, popiȝ, 1–4 popi, 4–7 popy, 5–6 popie, 6 poppi, 6–7 poppie, 5– poppy. β. 1 papoeȝ, papiȝ, 5 papy, 6 pappy. [Early OE. *popæȝ, papoeȝ*, app. repr. an earlier WGer. **papāg*, **popāg*, altered from **papāv, -au*, **popāv, -au*, ad. a. popular L. **papāv-um*, **papau-um* (whence OF. **pavau, pavo*), for L. *papāver*, neut. poppy. The alteration may have taken place, after the Teutonic change of stress, by assimilation to the suffix *-ag*. As with that suffix, the ending was subseq. weakened to *-iȝ* (cf. *éadiȝ, moniȝ* from *audag, monag*), giving the typical WSax. *popiȝ*, whence ME. *popi, popy*, mod. *poppy*, with doubled consonant expressing short vowel; cf. *peni, peny, penny*. (See Note below.)]

I. 1. a. A plant (or flower) of the genus *Papaver*, comprising herbs of temperate and subtropical regions, having milky juice with narcotic properties, showy flowers with petals (usually four in number) of delicate texture and various colours (often becoming 'double' in cultivation), and roundish capsules containing numerous small round seeds.

a **700** *Epinal Gloss.* (O.E.T.) 824 *Popaver*, popaeȝ. *c* **725** *Corpus Gloss.* 1516 *Papaver*, popei. *Ibid.* 1621 *Popaver*, popæȝ. *a* **800** *Erfurt Gloss.* 824 *Papaver*, papoeȝ. *c* **1000** *Ælfric's Vocab.* in Wr.-Wülcker 134/33 *Papauer*, popiȝ. *c* **1265** *Voc. Names Plants* in Wr.-Wülcker 558/30 *Astula regia, i.*, popi. **1390** GOWER *Conf.* II. 102 Popi, which berth the sed of slep. *c* **1475** *Pict. Voc.* in Wr.-Wülcker 787/11 *Hoc papaver*, a papy. **1578** LYTE *Dodoens* III. lxxxi. 431 There be three sortes of Poppie..the first kind is white, and of the garden, the two other are blacke and wilde. **1597** GERARDE *Herbal* II. lxviii. 296 Double blacke Poppie. Double white Poppie. **1697** DRYDEN *Virg. Georg.* I. 115 Sleepy Poppies harmful Harvests yield. **1718** PRIOR *Knowledge* 72 The blushing poppy with a crimson hue. **1813** SIR H. DAVY *Agric. Chem.* (1814) 94 Many other substances besides the juice of the poppy possess Narcotic properties. **1853** HUMPHREYS *Coin-Coll. Man.* 2 Poppies were sacred to Ceres.

b. Allusively, *spec.* as ***tall poppy***: in Australia, an especially well-paid, privileged, or distinguished person; also *transf.*

1641 MILTON *Ch. Govt.* v. Wks. 1851 III. 119 He little dreamt then that the weeding-hook of reformation would after two ages pluck up his glorious poppy from insulting over the good corne. *a* **1683** SIDNEY *Disc. Govt.* II. xxiv. (1704) 159 He..would certainly strike off the heads of the most eminent remaining Poppys. [Cf. POPPY-HEAD 1, 1650.] **1931** *New South Wales Parl. Debates* 30 July 4840 The Premier cannot truthfully say that a measure which deals with a certain section of the community which he refers to as the privileged class and as 'tall poppies' is in accord with the Melbourne agreement. **1963** *Times* 12 Mar. (Australia Suppl.) p. xviii/2 The youthfulness is explained by the fact that nearly all the buildings visible at this distance are new ones, the tall commercial poppies that now..compare with the cathedral spires. **1967** J. YEOMANS *Scarce Australians* viii. 85 If there is one place where the genuine eccentric is crushed, the tall poppy lopped and the penetrating discussion stifled, it is Australia. **1969** *Listener* 13 Nov. 660/1 They booed this great man, and he had to take it. It was part of the thing—no tall poppies. You've got to do well, but there's supposed not to be any sense of excellence making any difference to human equality. **1975** *Sydney Morning Herald* 8 Apr. 6 Labor is obsessed with the 'tall poppies', and seems determined to pull them down.

c. = ***Flanders poppy*** s.v. FLANDERS 2 b.

1921 *Times* 4 Nov. 9/3 Lord Haig..visited yesterday the headquarters of the British Legion, where the work of distributing poppies throughout the country for Poppy Day is being carried out. **1940** *Brit. Legion Poppy Ann.* 89/1 Nearly forty million poppies are sold each year on the anniversary of Armistice Day. **1972** *Guardian* 13 Nov. 12/4 Armistice Day passes round again... We cannot go on salving our consciences by buying a penny poppy once a year. **1976** *Wymondham & Attleborough Express* 10 Dec. 5/2 The sale of poppies in Occold raised £25.

d. Money. *slang.*

1943 *Police Jrnl.* XVI. 69 *Poppy*, money. **1959** A. WESKER *Roots* I. 29 How's poppy?.. Tight as ever. **1960** [see CABBAGE *sb.*¹ 1 e]. **1963** *Autocar* 6 Sept. 427/1 A good many British families which run their own cars must spend at least 13 per cent of the family poppy on that. **1972** L. HENDERSON *Cage until Tame* xvii. 148, I don't know why he's around without the gelt, because Tolly's not the boy to be parted from the poppy.

2. Rarely applied in ME. and *dial.* to the corn-cockle; also (with qualification) to the corn bluebottle (see *blue poppy* in 3); and [app. by association with POP *v.*¹, POP-] to plants whose corolla or calyx is inflated and 'popped' by children in sport, e.g. the bladder campion and foxglove (see *frothy poppy, spatling poppy, green poppy*, in 3). (Britten & Holland *Eng. Plant-n.*)

14.. *Stockh. Med. MS.* 200 Cokkyl or popy or wyldsanogre, *lolium*. *c* **1440** *Promp. Parv.* 409/1 Popy, weed, *papaver, codia,..nigella,..git*. **1886** BRITTEN & HOLLAND *Eng. Plant-names*, Poppy.. 3 *Lychnis Githago* (W. Cheshire).

3. With qualifying words, applied to various species of *Papaver* or other genera of *Papaveraceæ* (rarely to plants of other orders: cf. 2).

black poppy, a variety of the *opium poppy*, having purple flowers and dark seeds (cf. *white poppy*); **blue poppy**, (*a*) the corn bluebottle, *Centaurea Cyanus* (? obs.); (*b*) a blue-flowered species of *Meconopsis* (Miller *Plant-n.* 1884); **Californian poppy**, '*Platystemon californicus* and the genus *Eschscholtzia*' (Ibid.); **corn, field poppy**, the common wild poppy of cornfields, *Papaver Rhœas*, with bright scarlet flowers, or any other species growing in corn, as *P. dubium*; **frothy poppy**, the bladder campion, *Silene inflata*: see FROTHY 1 b; **garden poppy**, any species of *Papaver* cultivated in gardens, *esp.* the *Opium Poppy*; **green poppy**, local name of the foxglove, *Digitalis purpurea*; **horn-poppy, horned poppy**, any plant of the genus *Glaucium*, distinguished by its long horn-like capsules; esp. *G. luteum*, a sea-shore plant with yellow flowers; **Iceland poppy**, a variety of *Papaver nudicaule*: see ICELAND; **long-headed poppy**, *P. dubium*, a British species with long-shaped capsules; **Mexican poppy**, *Argemone mexicana* or other species; **opium poppy**, *Papaver somniferum*, a species with white or light purple flowers; from the juice of the unripe capsules opium is obtained; **oriental poppy**, *P. orientale*, a common garden species, with very large deep red flowers; **prickly poppy**, see PRICKLY *a.* 3; **red poppy**, the field poppy, *Papaver Rhœas*, or other species with red flowers; **sea** or **seaside poppy**, the common horned poppy, *Glaucium luteum*; **spatling poppy** = *frothy poppy*; **spring poppy** = *prickly poppy*; **tree poppy**, a Californian poppy, *Dendromecon rigidum*, with yellow flowers, remarkable for its shrubby growth; **Welsh** or **Cambrian poppy**, *Meconopsis cambrica*: see quot.; **white poppy**, a variety of the *opium poppy*, having white flowers and seeds (cf. *black poppy*); **wild poppy**, (*a*) the field poppy, *Papaver Rhœas*, or other wild species; †(*b*) *bastard wild poppy* = *prickly poppy*; **yellow poppy**, any species of *Papaver* or allied genus with yellow flowers; *spec.* the common horned poppy.

14.. *Synon. Herbarum* (MS. Harl. 3388 lf. 229), Anglice *bleu popi vel carlō vel langwort..crescit inter frumentum et alia blada et dicitur iacintus quia assimilatur cuidam lapidi qui sic vocatur. **1671** SALMON *Syn. Med.* III. xxii. 416 *Corn-Poppy, it is Narcotick, allays Pain, is used in Feavers. **1865** GOSSE *Land & Sea* (1874) 115 Except the corn poppy, this [the pimpernel] is said to be the only scarlet flower we have. **1863** HOGG & JOHNSON *Wild Fl. Gt. Brit.* II. Pl. 147 *Papaver Rhæas.* *Field Poppy. **1866** *Treas. Bot.* 842 The Field Poppy, *P[apaver] Rhœas*, one of the most brilliant of our wild plants. **1577** B. GOOGE *Heresbach's Husb.* (1586) 58 *Garden Poppy..is thought best to grow where olde stalkes haue been burnt. **1699** EVELYN *Acetaria* 74 To these add the Viola Matronalis,..nay the *Green Popy, by most accounted among the deadly Poysons. **1548** TURNER *Names of Herbs, Papauer corniculatum*..is called..in englishe *horned poppy or yealow poppy. **1731–3** MILLER *Gard. Dict.* s.v. *Glaucium*, Horned Poppy,..having Husks resembling Horns. **1870** MORRIS *Earthly Par.* III. IV. 215 The horned poppies' blossoms shone Upon a shingle-bank. **1863** *Sowerby's Eng. Bot.* I. 84 *Papaver somniferum* Sleepbearing Poppy, Garden Poppy, White Poppy, *Opium Poppy. *c* **1450** *Alphita* (Anecd. Oxon.) 134 Papauer rubeum ..gall. rougerole, angᵉ. *redpopy. **1578** LYTE *Dodoens* III. lxxxii. 433 There be two sortes of red Poppie, or Cornerose, the great and the small. **1876** HARLEY *Mat. Med.* (ed. 6) 738 The Red Poppy is found in cornfields and on roadsides throughout Europe. **1597** GERARDE *Herbal* II. lxviii. §4. 295 Called..in English *sea Poppie, and horned Poppie. *Ibid.* ccxiv. 551 *Behen album*,..of some..called *Ocymastrum*, and *Papauer spumeum*, which I have Englished *Spatling Poppie... In English Spatling Poppie, frothe Poppie, and white Ben. **1760** J. LEE *Introd. Bot.* App. 323 Poppy, Spatling, *Cucubalus.* **1866** *Treas. Bot.* 392 *Dendromecon*, literally *Tree Poppy, is a most appropriate name, the plant having all the aspect and character of the poppy tribe, combined with a woody stem and branches. *Ibid.* 727 *M[econopsis] cambrica*, the *Welsh Poppy, a native of Wales, Devonshire, North Britain, and the North of Ireland. *c* **1000** *Sax. Leechd.* I. 156 Popiȝ..ðat grecas moecorias & romane papauer album nemnað & engle *hwit popiȝ hatað. *c* **1450** *Alphita* (Anecd. Oxon.) 134 Papauer album..cuius semen coconidium appellatur angᵉ. whatpopy. **1876** HARLEY *Mat. Med.* (ed. 6) 739 White Poppy is now cultivated in the plains of India. *c* **1265** *Voc. Names Plants* in Wr.-Wülcker 559/11 *Alimonis, i.* *wilde popi. **14..** *Stockh. Med. MS.* 212 Wylde popy, *papauard.* **1548** *Yealow poppy [see *horned poppy* above]. **1871** R. ELLIS *Catullus* lxi. 200 White as parthenice, beyond Yellow poppy to gaze on.

4. a. Formerly, the plant or its extract used in pharmacy. Revived in *slang* use in the sense 'opium'.

1604 SHAKS. *Oth.* III. iii. 330 Not Poppy, nor Mandragora, Nor all the drowsie Syrrups of the world Shall euer medicine thee to that sweete sleepe. **1621–3** MIDDLETON & ROWLEY *Changeling* I. i. 150 A little poppy, sir, were good to cause you sleep. **1804** *Med. Jrnl.* XII. 41 He prepared the extract from a..quantity of poppy by decoction. **1935** A. J. POLLOCK *Underworld Speaks* 90/2 *Poppy*, opium. **1950** H. E. GOLDIN *Dict. Amer. Underworld Lingo* 162/2 *Poppy*, opium. **1977** H. OSBORNE *White Poppy* xv. 114 The village people would see nothing wrong in what the smugglers were doing —most of the other men still smoked the poppy.

b. A perfume derived from the poppy.

1905 *Smart Set* Sept. 113/1 Wistaria, oil of cloves,.. poppy and crab-apple. **1923** W. A. POUCHER *Perfumes & Cosmetics* I. 96 Oakmoss resin..is a liquid of characteristic odour... It is useful in oriental bouquets, particularly those of the 'poppy' type. **1954** A. J. KRAJKEMAN tr. *Jellinek's Pract. Mod. Perfumery* I. 72 (*heading*) Tables of Perfume Complexes... Peau D'Espagne... Poppy.

5. *fig.* or in allusive use, with reference to the narcotic or sleep-inducing qualities of the plant.

1591 SYLVESTER *Du Bartas* I. v. 248 The Cramp-Fish, knowing that she harboureth..A secret Poppy, and a sensless Winter, Be-numming all that dare too-neer her venter. **1637** CARTWRIGHT *Royall Slave* III. iv, E're night shed Poppy twice o're th' weary'd world. *a* **1790** WARTON *Ode to Sleep* i, On this my pensive pillow, gentle sleep! Descend,..And place thy crown of poppies on my breast. **1847** EMERSON *Repr. Men, Uses Gt. Men*, Nature.. wherever she mars her creature..lays her poppies plentifully on the bruise.

6. The bright scarlet colour of the common field poppy or other species.

1796 H. HUNTER tr. *St.-Pierre's Stud. Nat.* (1799) I. 523 The nearer you approach to this.., the more lively and gay are the colours. You will have in succession the poppy, the orange, the yellow, the lemon, the sulphur, the white. **1949** *Dict. Colours Interior Decoration* (Brit. Colour Council) III. 22/1 *Poppy*, a colour standardised by B.C.C. in 1934, matched to the flower. Similar to Gules. **1971** *Vogue* 15 Sept. 130/2 Dress..sizes: 36–42 in.; colours: green, cactus, poppy.

II. 7. = POPPY-HEAD 2. [It is uncertain whether this is the same word, but the forms are the same. Conjectures of its identity with F. *poupée*, 'babie, puppet, or bable' (Cotgr.), or derivation from Eng. *poppet*, *puppet*, appear to have no foundation.]

1429 *Rec. St. Mary at Hill* 71 Also payd to Serle for makyng of þe newe porche..xx marces. Also payd for a papye ..ij s. **1512–13** *Ibid.* 282 Paid for makyng of iij Mennys pewys, for the popeys & other stuff xx s. **1844** *Ecclesiologist* III. 153 In the Nave the seats terminate in square standards, but under the tower in poppies. **1875** PARKER *Gloss. Archit.*, *Poppie, Poppy, Poppy-head*,..an elevated ornament often used on the tops of the upright ends, or elbows, which terminate seats, &c., in churches.

III. 8. *attrib.* and *Comb.*, as *poppy-bed*, †*-boll* (BOLL *sb.*[1] 3), *family*, *-flower*, *-garland*, *-juice*, *-land*, *-leaf*, *-life*, *-plain*, *rain* (cf. 5), *-syrup*, *-wreath*; (sense 1 c) *poppy appeal*, *cross*, *organizer*, *seller*; instrumental, as *poppy-bordered*, *-crowned*, *-haunted*, *-hung*, *-laden*, *-sprinkled* adjs.; similative, as *poppy-crimson*, *-drowsy*, *-glossy*, *-pink*, *-red*, *-shallow*, *-sleepy* adjs. and sbs.; **poppy anemone**, *A. coronaria*, with poppy-like flowers of various colours; **poppy-bee**, a kind of upholsterer-bee (*Anthocopa papaveris*) which lines its cells with the petals of poppies; **poppy-colour**, a bright scarlet; so **poppy-coloured** *a.*; **Poppy Day**, a day (= *Remembrance Day*) on which those killed in the world wars of 1914–18 and 1939–45 are commemorated by the wearing of a Flanders poppy (see sense 1 c above and FLANDERS 2 b); also *attrib.*; †**poppy-grain**, a seed of the poppy; formerly used as a minute measure of length (= POPPY-SEED 2; cf. BARLEY-CORN 3); **poppy mallow**, the N. American malvaceous genus *Callirhoe*, having poppy-like flowers; **poppy oil**, an oil obtained from the seeds of the opium poppy; also, a similar oil from the seeds of other species; **poppy straw**, poppy plants, or a plant, from which the seeds have been removed; **poppy tea**, an imaginary liquor made by infusion of poppies; **poppy-tree** = *tree poppy* (see 3) (Miller *Plant-n.* 1884); **poppy-water**, a soporific drink made from poppies (also *fig.*). Also POPPY-HEAD, -SEED, -WORT.

1866 *Treas. Bot.* 65 The *Poppy Anemone, *A. coronaria*, ..has..large flowers,..very variable in colour. **1977** *Belfast Tel.* 14 Feb. 4/6 Area chairman Mr. G. A. R. Finlay thanked the people of Northern Ireland for their support to the Legion's *Poppy Appeal. **1896** *Westm. Gaz.* 1 July 1/1 The mass of vivid colour in the costumes reminded one of a *poppybed. **1688** R. HOLME *Armoury* II. 67/2 This Seed-Pod [of the Poppy] by all Florists is termed a *Poppy Bolle. **1815** J. SMITH *Panorama Sc. & Art* II. 542 The *poppy, cherry, rose, and flesh colours, are given to silk by means of carthamus. **1791** J. WOODFORDE *Diary* 24 Dec. (1927) III. 321 He brought with him..a pair of black Spanish Leather Shoes with black and *poppey coloured roses, very pretty. **1889** *Daily News* 12 Nov. 3/1 An accordion skirt of poppy-coloured silk. **1898** G. B. SHAW *Plays* II. *You never can tell* 308 The Columbine's petticoats are..golden orange and *poppy crimson. **1976** *Norwich Mercury* 19 Nov. 7/2 Mr. John Wiltshire, read the names of the fallen from Costessey as a *poppy cross for each one was laid on the memorial. **1881** O. WILDE *Poems* 212 That *poppy-crownèd God. **1903** *Blackw. Mag.* May 671 The poppy-crowned king of sleep. **1911** E. POUND *Canzoni* 1 Fairer than these the Poppy-crownèd One flees. **1921** *Daily Mail* 11 Nov. 9/4 To-day.. is *Poppy Day. Twenty million red Flanders poppy emblems will be on sale in the streets. **1971** *Guardian* 28 Oct. 7/3 The Royal British Legion..faces a continuing drop in the number of collectors on Poppy Day. **1976** *Cumberland News* 3 Dec. 12/4 Aspatria's Poppy Day collection for the Earl Haig Fund totalled £216.59, an increase of £42 on last year. **1894** O. WILDE *Sphinx*, The *poppy-drowsy queen. **1866** *Treas. Bot.* 1108 In the plants of the *poppy family. **1697** DRYDEN *Virg. Georg.* IV. 196 Some-times white Lillies did their Leaves afford, With wholsom *Poppy-flow'rs to mend his homely Board. **1717** FENTON *Florelio* Poems 27 Nor *Poppy-Garlands give the Nymph Repose. **1922** D. H. LAWRENCE *Birds, Beasts & Flowers* (1923) 141 Your sort of gorgeousness, Dark and lustrous And skinny repulsive And *poppy-glossy. **1656** W. D. tr. *Comenius' Gate Lat. Unl.* §524 The measures of distances are thus: four *poppy-graines make one barley-corn. **1889** W. B. YEATS *Wanderings of Oisin* I. 5 In the *poppy-hung house. **1853** KINGSLEY *Hypatia* xxvi, The same who made wine made *poppy-juice. **1878** O. WILDE *Ravenna* 6 Like Proserpine, with *poppy-laden head. **1910** *Westm. Gaz.* 11 Feb. 2/3 An' drowsy somethings whisper in the air, An' drunken breaths sweep from the *poppy-lands. **1958** *Times* 10 Nov. 19/1 A field yellow with charlock is a matter for comment, and 'poppyland' has long ceased to be an attraction to tourists. **1700** DRYDEN *Amaryllis* 64, I try'd th' infallible prophetick way A *poppy-leaf upon my palm to lay. **1949** BLUNDEN *After Bombing* 25 Yet these rebuild A distant world, a summer dead Millions of *poppy-lives ere ours. **1870** *Amer. Naturalist* III. 162 The *Poppy mallow..with its purple blossoms and dark green leaves, forms one of the most brilliant figures in the prairie carpet. **1939** *Nat. Geogr. Mag.* Aug. 220/1 Callirhoe..the musical Greek name of the poppy mallow.., is the same as that borne by a nymph of the sea. **1972** F. PERRY *Flowers of World* 185/2 *Callirhoe papaver* from the southern USA is the Poppy Mallow, a scrambling or sometimes erect herbaceous perennial with reddish-purple Poppy-like flowers on stems of 60 cms (2 ft) and delicate Mallow-like leaves. **1756** T. BARDWELL *Pract. Painting & Perspective* 7 This colour [*sc.* flake-white] should be ground with the finest *poppy oil that can be made. **1825** J. NICHOLSON *Operat. Mechanic* 735 To give a drying quality to Poppy Oil. **1859** GULLICK & TIMBS *Paint.* 206 Poppy oil..has the reputation of keeping its colour better than linseed. **1912** tr. *C. Moreau-Vauthier's Technique of Painting* 130 Nut oil is never used in France. French artists prefer the so-called *œillette*, or poppy oil. **1937** A. F. HILL *Econ. Bot.* ix. 215 Poppy Oil.—An important drying oil.. obtained from the seeds of the opium poppy. **1976** *Wymondham & Attleborough Express* 19 Nov., Reg Knight ..has been *poppy organiser for the area for 12 years now. **1896** *Daily News* 18 July 6/3 Deep *poppy-pink geraniums. **1844** MRS. BROWNING *Drama of Exile* 467 We call your thoughts home..To the *poppy-plains. **1708** OZELL tr. *Boileau's Lutrin* 35 Morpheus pours continual *Poppy Rain. **1831** BREWSTER *Optics* xxiv. 286 A very brilliant *poppy-red. **1976** *Norwich Mercury* 19 Nov. 3/4 Nearly 100 *poppy-sellers were out on the streets of Norwich on Saturday. **1957** L. DURRELL *Bitter Lemons* 214 Most of the *poppy-shallow cabaret girls had gone. *a* **1963** S. PLATH *Crossing Water* (1971) 21 The pills are worn-out and silly, like classical gods. Their *poppy-sleepy colours do him no good. **1950** *Chem. Abstr.* XLIV. 4245 Expts. are made with potato, tomato, and beet tops, tobacco stalks, and *poppy and mustard straws in 'handmade' board manuf. **1953** *Ibid.* XLVII. 6605 (*heading*) Production of morphine extracted from poppy straw grown in Poland. **1975** *Times* 10 Mar. 12/1 The United Nations intend to make sure the latex is not culled and that the crop becomes poppy straw for codeine. *a* **1845** HOOD *Serenade* iv, Is no *poppy-syrup nigh? **1922** JOYCE *Ulysses* 83 Paragoric poppysyrup bad for cough. **1709–10** STEELE *Tatler* No. 118 ¶4 Several warm Liquors made of the Waters of Lethe, with very good *Poppy Tea. **1682** N. O. *Boileau's Lutrin* II. 202 And Sleep drop't *Poppy-water on her Brows. **1765** GOLDSM. *New Simile* 36 No poppy-water half so good; For let folks only get a touch, Its soporific virtue's such,..That quickly they begin to snore.

[*Note.* Beside It. *papavero*, Pr. *papaver*, *paver*, Walloon *pavoir*, the Latin *papaver* has come down in various anomalous forms; viz. OF. *pavo* (12th c.), now *pavot*, in Berry dial. *papou*:—L. type **papāu-um*, **papāu-um*; Pg. *papoula*, Sardinian *pabaule*:—L. **papaula*, **papăvula*. OF. had also *popelure*, Milanese *pópola* (Lodi *pómpola*), Pavia *popolón*, Como *popolana* poppy, pointing to a L. type **papula*, **popula*.]

'poppy, *a. colloq.*

[f. POP *sb.*[1] or *v.*[1] + -Y.]

a. Characterized by popping or exploding. *rare.*

1894 KIPLING *Jungle Bk.* 195 Watch the little poppy shells drop down into the tree tops.

b. Of eyes: protuberant.

1907 *Westm. Gaz.* 11 Dec. 12/1 An American exclaiming before a family picture: 'My, what poppy eyes these Churchills have got!' **1915** *Pearson's Mag.* Jan. 106/1 Hair dark and curly; eyes poppy; lips, full. **1968** J. R. ACKERLEY *My Father & Myself* 29 A rich foreign nobleman with rather poppy eyes.

poppych, obs. form of POPISH.

'poppycock. *slang.* (orig. *U.S.*)

Nonsense, 'rubbish', 'humbug'.

1865 C. F. BROWNE *A. Ward: his Travels* I. iii. 35 You won't be able to find such another pack of poppycock gabblers as the present Congress of the United States. **1884** *Pall Mall G.* 17 July 4/1 All what you see about me bein' drunk was poppycock. **1892** *Nation* (N.Y.) 24 Nov. 386/1 Their wails were all what the boys call 'poppycock'. **1914** *New Age* 3 Sept. 410/2 The Headmaster of Eton became aware that he was talking poppycock for boys. **1924** M. KENNEDY *Constant Nymph* iii. 54 Sometimes, you know, you talk..poppycock. **1935** *Punch* 9 Jan. 30/1, I am not going to..ruin the perfect cadences of my English prose by pointing out to you in courteous and dignified language that your objections are all poppycock and my eye. **1955** *Times* 24 June 4/5 The peculiar capacity for pumping generals into jobs for which they were never suited continued the poppycock started by the Labour Government. **1973** *Nation Rev.* (Melbourne) 31 Aug. 1443/6 He was..a 'dangerous, raving, psychotic, stupid, vicious, sickening writer of poppycock'. **1977** *Punch* 31 Aug.–6 Sept. 335/3 If you still think that harmonisation is so much Brussels poppycock.. then draw comfort from this statistic.

'poppy-'head.

1. The capsule of the poppy. Also *attrib.*

1585 HIGINS *Junius' Nomencl.* 112/2 The seuerall places wherein the seedes doe lye, as may be seene in poppie heades. **1650** R. STAPYLTON *Strada's Low C. Warres* I. 14 He [Death] cropt the heads of Nations, as Tarquin struk off the Poppy-heads. **1822–34** *Good's Study Med.* (ed. 4) II, Poppy-head fomentations. **1896** *Allbutt's Syst. Med.* I. 435 Made with decoction of boiling poppy-heads.

2. *Arch.* An ornamental finial, often richly carved, at the top of the end of a seat in a church. Also *attrib.* [See remark in POPPY *sb.* 7.]

1839 *Hints Eccl. Antiq.* (Camb. Camden Soc.) 8 St. Andrew's, Histon..viii. Ornaments, &c...8. Poppy Heads. **1841** C. ANDERSON *Anc. Models* 129 These seats have the ends usually ornamented, sometimes with raised ends, which are called poppy-heads. **1875** J. C. COX *Ch. Derbysh.* I. 202 The poppy-head ends..carved in the fleur-de-lis pattern. **1904** T. H. LONGFIELD in *Athenæum* 9 Apr. 473/3 Many remains..of poppyhead bench-ends and benches.

'poppy-seed.

1. a. The, or a, seed of the poppy. Esp. the seed of cultivated varieties of *Papaver somniferum*, the opium poppy, used as a flavouring, filling, or garnish for cakes, bread, etc.

c **1420** *Pallad. on Husb.* III. 579 Now popy seed in grounde is good to throwe. **1712** tr. *Pomet's Hist. Drugs* I. 149 A cold oil is drawn from White-Poppy Seeds. **1899** *Allbutt's Syst. Med.* VI. 315 Swellings, varying in size from a poppy-seed to a pea. **1932** L. GOLDING *Magnolia St.* I. viii. 127 The special bread sprinkled with poppy-seed for the Sabbath repast. **1947** F. GREENBERG *Cookery Bk.* 382 Brush over with beaten egg, sprinkle with poppy seeds, and bake.. about 50 minutes. **1978** *Observer* (Colour Suppl.) 3 Dec. 81/2 For poppy seeds, you have to go to the delicatessen, and be prepared to grind them at home in an electric coffee mill.

b. *fig.* (Cf. POPPY *sb.* 5.)

1640 *Erotomania* 40 The eyes of his soule are brought asleep by the Poppy seed of Inconsideration and Carelesnesse.

†2. Formerly used as a measure of length, varying from $\frac{1}{12}$ to $\frac{1}{20}$ of an inch. (Cf. BARLEY-CORN 3.)

1688 R. HOLME *Armoury* III. iii. 136/2 Barly Corn, is the length of 4 Poppy seeds, and 3 Corns make an Inch. **1729** SHELVOCKE *Artillery* I. 76 The Barley-corn (the fourth part of an Inch) is subdivided into 5 Poppy Seeds.

3. *attrib.* and *Comb.*, as *poppy-seed cake*, *cookie*, *roll*; **poppy-seed oil** = *poppy oil* (POPPY *sb.* 8).

1943 A. L. SIMON *Conc. Encycl. Gastron.* IV. 100/1 (*heading*) Poppy-seed Cake. **1976** 'B. SHELBY' *Great Pebble Affair* 134 The religious group..supported themselves by ..baking poppy seed cakes. **1959** *Tamarack Rev.* Summer 7

Hey, poppyseed cookies! *Real* stuffed fish! **1897** *Allbutt's Syst. Med.* IV. 832 A peculiar small poppy-seed-like growth. **1893** G. Terry *Pigments, Paint, & Painting* xi. 305 Poppy-seed Oils.—Oil is yielded by the seeds of three kinds of poppy—the opium-poppy (*Papaver somniferum*), the spiny-poppy (*Argemone mexicana*), and the yellow-horn poppy (*Glaucium luteum*). **1942** Gettens & Stout *Painting Materials* 50 The cold-drawn oil is pale straw..in colour and is the 'white poppy-seed oil' of commerce. **1974** G. Usher *Dict. Plants used by Man* 438/1 The seeds [of the opium poppy]..have some 44–50 per cent oil (Poppy Seed Oil). **1973** *Listener* 20 Sept. 377/2 Tea was served by Auntie Golda.., smoked salmon on black bread, poppy-seed rolls coated with cream cheese.

poppy-show. *dial.* and *Sc.* Also puppie-show. [f. *poppy, puppy,* dial. varr. of puppet *sb.*: cf. poppy *sb.* 4 b.] A puppet-show; a peep-show. Also *transf.* and *fig.*

1798 D. Crawford *Poems* 88 You'd mak a noble poppey-show. **1828** D. M. Moir *Mansie Wauch* vii. 64 They..let me in with a grudge for twopence..to see a punch and puppie-show business. **1886** J. P. Reid *Facts & Fancies* 43 It was there we used to gather floo'ers to mak' a poppy-show. **1887** T. Darlington *Folk-Speech S. Cheshire* 298 A pin to see a poppy-show. **1917** N. Douglas *South Wind* xl. 459 When you watch some of these local marionette theatres the illusion is complete. Why is a poppy show more convincing than the Comédie Française? **1924** D. H. Lawrence *Let.* Aug. (1962) II. 803 In the next window-hole, a poppy-show of Indian women in coloured shawls. **1937** Partridge *Dict. Slang* 650/1 *Poppy-show*, a display, esp. if accidental, of underclothes. **1950** L. Bennett et al. *Anancy Stories & Dial. Verse* ii. 45 All de ballerina head dem, tie Wid ballerina bow, Ballerina glamour mix wid Ballerina pappy-show!

poppysmic (pɒˈpɪzmɪk), *a. rare*$^{-1}$. [f. L. *poppysma, -ysmus* (see poppism) + -ic.] Produced with smacking of the lips.

1922 Joyce *Ulysses* 552 Florry whispers to her. Whispering lovewords murmur liplapping loudly, poppysmic plopslop.

poppywort (ˈpɒpɪwɜːt). [f. poppy *sb.* + wort.] **a.** Lindley's name for plants of the N.O. *Papaveraceæ.* **b.** *satin poppywort*, a name for *Meconopsis Wallichiana* (Miller *Plant-names*).

1846 Lindley *Veg. Kingd.* 430 *Papaveraceæ*... Poppyworts. *Ibid.*, Bernhardi..denies that true Poppyworts are universally lactescent plants. **1882** *Garden* 15 July 39/1 This Poppywort may well be reckoned amongst the best of the hardy plants introduced of late years.

pops[1], a name in Barbados of *Physalis angulata*: see pop *sb.*[1] 4.

pops[2], var. pop *sb.*[6] [see -s[2].] Also used in Jazz slang as a form of address to a man.

1928 Barrie *Half an Hour* in *Plays* 616, I never heard how much you paid Pops for me? **1933** 'E. M. Delafield' *Gay Life* ii. 32 My Pops says I'm ever such a lucky girl to have such heaps of friends. **1944** C. Calloway *Hepsters Dict.*, *Pops*, salutation for all males. **1944** [see Fatso]. **1948** [see daddy 3]. **1961** *Metronome* Feb. 60 Jazz..is..an art in which a musician can become known as 'Pops' by the time he is 22 or even at 18. **1976** 'S. Harvester' *Siberian Road* ii. 30 Me a defenceless girl..without my Mom and Pops.

ˈpop-shop. *slang.* [f. pop *v.*[1] 7 + shop *sb.*] A pawnbroker's shop. Also *attrib.*

1772 *Town & C. Mag.* 73 The Pop-shop was ready for pledges, the gin-shop was ready for the money lent upon them. **1846** Lytton *Lucretia* ii. xvi, I might have been wicked enough to let it go with the rest to the pop-shop. **1898** Hume *Hagar* iii. 54 Rosa..might pawn it,..so I sent a printed slip to all the pop-shops in London. **1919** G. B. Shaw *O'Flaherty V.C.* in *Heartbreak House* 183 She hadnt half the jewelry of Mrs Sullivan that keeps the popshop in Drumpogue. **1942** Wodehouse *Money in Bank* (1946) iv. 36 This makes me feel like a pawnbroker... As if you had brought it in to the old pop shop and were asking me what I could spring on it. **1974** P. Wright *Lang. Brit. Industry* i. 22 For many families the *pop-shop* was a necessity.

popsicle (ˈpɒpsɪk(ə)l). orig. and chiefly *U.S.* Also popsickle and with capital initial. [Fanciful name.] An ice-lolly. Also *fig.* and *attrib.*

Popsicle is a proprietary name in the U.S.

1923 *Official Gaz.* (U.S. Patent Office) 25 Sept. 600/1 Trade-mark 'Popsicle'. Particular description of goods.—Lollypops. Claims use since May 28, 1923. **1932** H. H. Somner *Theory & Pract. Ice Cream Making* xxi. 502 Frozen Suckers, Popsicles, etc...patterned after candy suckers, or lollypops, are made by freezing ice mixes in suitable forms with wooden sticks inserted to serve as a handle. **1941** S. V. Benét in *Life* 7 July 90/1 The usual crowd..Kidding the local cop and eating popsicles. **1945** A. Kober *Parm Me* 177 Leon Blatt..had just consumed a Popsicle and was now busy scraping its stick with his tongue. **1952** E. B. White *Charlotte's Web* xvi. 123 In the hard-packed dirt of the midway..you will find a veritable treasure of..salted almonds, popsicles, partially gnawed ice cream cones, and the wooden sticks of lolly-pops. **1961** A. Sexton in *Poetry* (Chicago) Dec. 161 The maid As thin as a popsicle stick Holds dinner as usual. **1962** J. Ludwig in R. Weaver *Canad. Short Stories* (1968) 2nd Ser. 250 'I look like a big popsicle, eh Josef?' Mrs Goffman said to her chauffeur. **1963** E. B. White *Let.* 22 July (1976) 504, I am always astonished to discover that my haphazard literary popsicles have found takers in places like Helsinki. **1967** M. McCarthy in *Observer* 30 Apr. 11/7 All the children who had gathered round to buy popsicles..from the popsicle man. **1972** *Last Whole Earth Catalog* (Portola Inst.) 291/3 Every bookstore has a line of ocean popsicles for your refreshment now. **1973** *Nation Rev.* (Melbourne) 31 Aug. 1460/3 Perhaps you would prefer one of these nice laudanum popsicles? **1977** *Time* 2 May 42/3 All they have to show an employer is a Social Security card, which is about as hard to acquire as a Popsicle. *Ibid.* 18 July 47/2 The delectable nymphet Lolita has a cruel, popsicle heart.

ˈpopskull. *N. Amer. slang.* [f. pop *v.*[1] + skull[1].] A powerful or unwholesome (esp. home-made) liquor; inferior whisky. Also *attrib.*

1867 G. W. Harris *Sut Lovingood* 222 Well, Maje cum blowin mad intu the doggery, an seein nobody, he jis' grabbed a bottel, an' tuck hisself a buckload ove popskull. **1917** *Dialect Notes* IV. 415 *Pop-skull*, bad whiskey. **1932** V. Randolph in B. A. Botkin *Folk-Say* IV. 237 He died from drinking too much popskull whisky. **1946** *Amer. Speech* XXI. 195 Distillers never refer to a still coil as a 'worm', as did the bootleggers who manufactured popskull and rotgut during Prohibition. **1950** *Amer. Legion Mag.* Apr. 19/1 Although much of the 'panther sweat' or 'popskull scotch' brewed today is distributed to customers who know it's moonshine and don't care, thousands of gallons are sold..to unsuspecting customers. **1956** *Wall St. Jrnl.* 21 Sept. 1/1 About one out of every four gallons of hard liquor..was moon-shine—also known by devotees as corn squeezins, white lightning, popskull, bumblebee stew and mountain dew. **1973** B. Broadfoot *Ten Lost Years* xxiv. 286 Old pop skull, the kind we made by freezing a milk pail of cider and when the..alcohol had collected in the middle of the ice block, then we drained that off.

popster (ˈpɒpstə(r)). [f. pop *a.* (*sb.*[8]) + -ster.] A pop musician or artist; an enthusiast for pop music, pop art, or pop culture in general.

1963 *Meet the Beatles* 37 12.45 p.m. Popsters posing in the park. **1965** [see opster]. **1967** [see hippie, hippy *sb.* and *a.*]. **1967** *Listener* 1 June 727/1 There were quizzes,..teenage popsters (though in skirts down to the knee), professionally sincere teeth-gleamers—the lot. **1968** *Economist* 14 Dec. p. vii/2 The school-teachers of Monmouthshire, banning transistor radios from the play-ground for fear of the linguistic pollution of Anglo-Saxon popsters.

ˈpopsy. Also poppsie, popsie. [app. a kind of nursery extension of pop *sb.*[2], with dim. ending: cf. *Bet, Betsy, Nan, Nancy, Topsy.*] An endearing appellation for a girl; *gen.*, a woman or girl; a casual female acquaintance, girl-friend. Also *popsy-wopsy* and *attrib.*

1862 *Pippins & Pies* 9 This I'm bound to say: that four sweeter lovelier popsies, never blessed [etc.]. **1887** E. J. Goodman *Too Curious* ix, Now go along like a good little popsy-wopsy, and don't cry to sit up. **1896** *Idler* Mar. 278/1 All right, my popsy-wopsy. **1931** C. Lithgow *Simple Sailor* xv. 194 Chase me, you fast women; ginger yourselves up, you slow 'uns!..Lord, but I *like* a good popsy! **1943** J. Hillier in *Penguin New Writing* XVI. 26 He ached too much for her to be satisfied in regarding her as a short-term poppsie, and yet ops. really permitted only a poppsie outlook. **1944** M. Laski *Love on Supertax* viii. 82 American colonels with their popsies. **1953** *Chambers's Jrnl.* June 325/1, I usually line up a local popsy. **1959** 'J. Welcome' *Stop at Nothing* ix. 135 The blonde popsie. **1968** *Listener* 10 Oct. 475/2 The Christine of *Lucky Jim* is a somewhat conventionally pretty high-class popsy. **1973** Wodehouse *Bachelors Anonymous* xii. 155 The door was opened by a rather personable popsy, who proved to be a girl who lives with the Fitch. **1978** J. Krantz *Scruples* iii. 75 Meanwhile, he had his popsies and he had his friend, Valentine, whose cozy, crazy stage set of a Paris attic had become a special refuge for him.

†ˈpopulable, *a. Obs. rare*$^{-0}$. [ad. L. *populābilis*, f. *populārī*: see populate *v.*[1] and -able.]

1623 Cockeram, *Populable*, which may be destroyed.

populace (ˈpɒpjʊlɪs). [a. F. *populace* (16th c. in Hatz.-Darm.), ad. It. *popolaccio, popolazzo* 'the grosse, base, vile, common people, rifraffe people' (Florio), f. *popolo* (:—L. *populus* people) + pejorative suffix *-accio, -azzo*:—L. *-āceus.*] The mass of the people of a community, as distinguished from the titled, wealthy, or educated classes; the common people; *invidiously*, the mob, the rabble.

1572 Sir T. Smith in Ellis *Orig. Lett.* Ser. iii. III. 378 The unruly malice and sworde of the raging populace. **1601** Daniels *Civ. Wars* (1609) vii. lxxvii, T'accommodate, And calme the Peeres, and please the Populasse. *c* **1645** Howell *Lett.* (1688) III. 415 'Tis the Populass only, who see no further than the Rind of Things. **1723** *Pres. St. Russia* II. 141, I spit upon all the others. God bless the Populace. **1785** Burns *Cotter's Sat. Night* xx, A virtuous populace may rise the while, And stand a wall of fire around their much-lov'd Isle. **1792** Gouv. Morris in Sparks *Life & Writ.* (1832) II. 191 Thank God, we have no populace in America. **1821** Byron *Two Foscari* v. i. 259 The people!—There's no people, you well know it,..There is a populace, perhaps, whose looks May shame you. **1892** Ld. Lytton *King Poppy* viii, And, being but the Populace, presumes To call itself the People.

b. *poet.* A multitude, crowd, throng. *rare.*

1871 R. Ellis *Catullus* lxiii. 65 With a throng about the portal, with a populace in the gate.

c. *fig.*

1742 Young *Nt. Th.* iii. 124 Queen lilies! and ye painted populace! Who dwell in fields, and lead ambrosial lives. **1807–8** W. Irving *Salmag.* xx, The turtle-dove, the timid fawn, the soft-eyed gazelle, and all the rural populace who joy in the sequestered haunts of nature.

†populacy (ˈpɒpjʊləsɪ). *Obs.* [irreg. formation from populace: see -acy.]

1. The order of the common people; = populace.

1613 T. Godwin *Rom. Antiq.* (1625) 29 The third order, or degree in the Romane Common-wealth was *Populus*, the populacy, or Commone. **1644** [H. Parker] *Jus Pop.* 59 Disputes between the optimacy and populacy. **1700** Astry tr. *Saavedra-Faxardo* II. 356 In Peace, Nobility is distinguisht from Populacy. **1721** Strype *Eccl. Mem.* III. App. xx. 59 To obtain the favour of the populacy by feigned pretences of bloud. *a* **1834** Coleridge *Notes & Lect.* (1849) I. 305 The only predilection..shows itself in his contempt of mobs and the populacy.

fig. **1640** Gauden *Love of Truth* (1641) 11 The populacy of affections or passions are regular, and subject to the rule, and soveraignety of reason. **1667** *Decay Chr. Piety* vi. ¶7 Or ..let in the whole populacy of sin upon the soul.

2. = populousness.

1613–18 Daniel *Coll. Hist. Eng.* (1626) 8 The vicinage, and innumerous populacie of that Nation [the Saxons]. **1679** Penn *Addr. Prot.* ii. vi. 197 Increasing the Trade, Populacy and Wealth of this Kingdom. **1725** *Ways Inhab. Delaware to become Rich* 2 Means in pursuit whereof we may ..become rich..'Tis not Populacy only.

3. Popular government, or a popular government; also, a state so governed; democracy.

1632 H. Seile *Augustus* 22 They had naturally, and almost insensibly falne from a Monarchy, to a Populacy, or Democracy. **1679** Puller *Moder. Ch. Eng.* (1843) 193 Such democracy and populacy as is held in the Independent and Presbyterian party.

4. = popularity 4. *rare*$^{-1}$.

1687 in *Magd. Coll. & Jas. II* (O.H.S.) 189 Men, who are led by populacy, which is the Fool's Paradise, but the wise men's scorn.

popular (ˈpɒpjʊlə(r)), *a.* (*sb.*) Forms: 5–7 populer, 6 *Sc.* -air, 7 -are, 6– popular. [ad. L. *populār-is* adj. belonging to the people, f. *populus* people. So OF. *populeir, -ere*, F. *populaire.*]

A. *adj.* **1.** *Law.* Affecting, concerning, or open to all or any of the people; public; esp. in ***action popular.***

1490 *Act 4 Hen. VII*, c. 20 Accions populers in divers cases have ben ordeigned by many gode actes and statutes. **1579** *Expos. Termes Law, Accion populer*, is an accion which is geeuen vppon the breach of some Penal statute, which.. euery man that wyll may sue for him selfe, and the Queene, by information, or otherwise,..& because that this action is not geeuen to one man specyally but generally to the Queenes people that wyll sue, it is called an actyon populer. **1581** Lambarde *Eiren.* ii. ii. (1588) 132, I have knowen it doubted, whether the Suertie of the good abearing (commanded upon complaint) may be released by any speciall person or no: because it seemeth more popular, then the Suertie of the Peace. **1766** Blackstone *Comm.* II. xxix. 437. **1872** *Wharton's Law Lex.* (ed. 5), *Popular action*, brought by one of the public to recover some penalty given by statute to any one who chooses to sue for it.

2. a. Of, pertaining to, or consisting of the common people, or the people as a whole as distinguished from any particular class; constituted or carried on by the people.

1548 W. Thomas in Strype *Eccl. Mem.* II. App. S. 66 What popular estate can be read, that hath thirty years together eschewed sects, sedition and commotions? **1579–80** North *Plutarch* (1676) 230 Timoleon..did by this means stablish a free State and Popular Government. **1671** Milton *Samson* 16 Retiring from the popular noise, I seek This unfrequented place to find some ease. **1761** Hume *Hist. Eng.* III. liv. 170 Popular tumults were not disagreeable to them. **1833** Alison *Hist. Europe* (1847) II. vii. §1. 269 The Legislative Assembly affords the first example,..in modern Europe, of the effects of a completely popular election. **1888** Bryce *Amer. Commw.* II. lxix. 541 From 1824 till 1840, nominations irregularly made by State legislatures and popular meetings.

†b. Of lowly birth; belonging to the commonalty or populace; plebeian. *Obs.*

c **1555** Harpsfield *Divorce Hen. VIII* (Camden) 42 More ..than when it is granted to any popular or common person. **1600** E. Blount tr. *Conestaggio* 118 Him they sent being a popular man. **1640** T. Pierse in *Horti Carol., Rosa altera*, A drop of Royall blood is dearer farre Than a whole Ocean of the popular. **1691** Norris *Pract. Disc.* 87 This is..the Measure that all Popular Spirits do go by, and the Wisest can hardly refrain it.

†c. Having characteristics attributed to the common people; low, vulgar, plebeian. *Obs.*

1599 B. Jonson *Ev. Man out of Hum.* i. i, Such as flourish in the spring of the fashion, and are least popular. **1603** Florio *Montaigne* (1632) 624 It is a custome of popular or base men to call for minstrels or singers at feasts. *a* **1635** Naunton *Fragm. Reg.* (Arb.) 22 Had the House been freed of half a dozen of popular and discontented persons.

†3. Full of people; populous; crowded. *Obs.*

1588 Parke tr. *Mendoza's Hist. China* 13 These two prouinces, which are two of the mightiest, and most popularst of people. **1641** J. Jackson *True Evang. T.* iii. 184 How doth the popular City sit solitary? *a* **1699** Kirkton *Ch. Hist.* (1817) 215 The most popular part of Scotland. **1727** *Philip Quarll* 47 Oppression and Usury, and all the Evils that attend this popular World.

4. Intended for or suited to ordinary people. **a.** Adapted to the understanding or taste of ordinary people, 'understanded of the people'. *spec.* in ***popular (news)paper, press, romance,*** etc., designating literature and ephemeral publications intended for a general readership.

1573 G. Harvey *Letter-bk.* (Camden) 11 In philosophical disputations to give popular and plausible theams. **1759** Franklin *Ess.* Wks. 1840 III. 188 All he said was in popular language. **1817** Coleridge *Biog. Lit.* I. xii. 253 To an Esquimaux or New Zealander our most popular philosophy would be wholly unintelligible. **1835** J. S. Mill in *London Rev.* II. 273 Not only has it no leaders in Parliament, but it has none in the popular press. **1841** T. Wright (*title*) Popular treatises on science. *Ibid.* p. vii, They [*sc.* the treatises] are important documents of the history of popular science. **1849** Macaulay *Hist. Eng.* vi. II. 109 Every question..was debated, sometimes in a popular style which boys and women could comprehend. **1865** J. S. MILL *Auguste Comte* 48 The truths which popular philosophy calls by the misleading name of Contingent. **1872** (Aug.) *Longmans' List Works* 8 Miscellaneous Works and Popular Metaphysics. *Ibid.* 12 Natural History and Popular Science. **1876** W. JAMES *Let.* 21 Sept. (1920) I. 190 The free-thinking tendency which the 'Popular Science Monthly'.. represents. **1890** —— *Princ. Psychol.* I. iii. 81 The popular-science notions of cells and fibres are almost wholly wide of the truth. **1901** CHESTERTON *Defendant* 16 The coarse and thin texture of mere current popular romance. **1901** G. B. SHAW *Three Plays for Puritans* p. vii, They read a good deal, and are at home in the fool's paradise of popular romance. **1907** *Boston Med. & Surg. Jrnl.* 26 Dec. 847/2 A second means of dissemination of knowledge of the psychotherapeutic movement is through the medium of the popular press. **1937** W. S. CHURCHILL *Let.* 20 Sept. in *Second World War* (1948) I. I. xiv. 193, I was very glad to see that Neville [Chamberlain] has been backing you up, and not, as represented by the Popular Press, holding you back by the coat-tails. **1937** *Discovery* Sept. 292/2 A contribution to popular science. **1952** H. HERD *March of Journalism* xvii. 326 Many popular newspapers..aim to interest everyman without indulging in sensationalism... Most of the 'populars' come within this classification. **1957** R. HOGGART *Uses of Literacy* vi. 144 The leader-writers of the popular Press make great play with horizons, new dawns, broad highways, forward movements..and forward-lookers. *Ibid.* 149 The popular papers, always identifying themselves with 'the people', conduct polls on this matter and questionnaires on that matter among their readers, and so elevate the counting of heads into a substitute for judgment. **1960** K. AMIS *New Maps of Hell* (1961) ii. 53 A popular-science article on atomic physics. **1964** HALL & WHANNEL *Popular Arts* vii. 165 Popular romance..is full of variants on the Romeo-and-Juliet or Cinderella themes. **1972** S. HYNES *Edwardian Occasions* 178 Hewlett..had begun by working entirely within the established conventions of the popular romance. **1976** *Conservation News* Sept./Oct. 9/1 The wartime slogan 'Digging for Victory' has reappeared in the popular press. **1977** *New Yorker* 19 Sept. 133/1 Why is it that there is not more good popular-science writing?

b. Adapted to the means of ordinary people; low, moderate (in price). Also *attrib.*

1859 *Illustr. Lond. News* 2 July 11/2 The Monday Popular Concert..was the last of the series for this season. **1885** C. E. PASCOE *London of To-day* iv. 67 The multitude which invades the 'Zoo' on Monday, which is the 'popular-price' day, when a sixpence opens the gate to the neediest. **1890** *Lady's Pictorial* 15 Mar. 347/3 The book is to be produced at the popular price of one shilling. **1902** *Encycl. Brit.* XXIX. 751/2 After the foundation of the Popular Concerts in 1859..he [Joachim] played there regularly in the latter part of the season. *a* **1907** *Mod.* All seats at popular prices. A popular concert will be given. **1911** G. B. SHAW *Doctor's Dilemma* p. xxxvii, Yet people expect to find vaccines.. retailed at 'popular prices' in private enterprise shops just as they expect to find ounces of tobacco and papers of pins. **1916** *Variety* 27 Oct. 12/1 Sid Grauman's 'Night at the World's Fair' is drawing well at the Majestic, attendance doubtless being encouraged by popular prices. **1971** L. LAMB *Worse than Death* ii. 23 'Teas at popular prices?' 'Oh, the teas were cheap enough.'

c. ***popular capitalism***, a style of capitalism characterized by the extension to the populace at large of greater opportunity and encouragement to own shares, property, small businesses, etc.; the theory or practice of this.

1979 *Summary World Broadcasts: Eastern Europe* (B.B.C.) 31 Jan. B1 Hoxha analyses..theories used to justify the..capitalist revisionist order, such as..'popular capitalism'. **1983** *Financial Times* 25 Jan. 2/2 Transferring shares to employees as part of a genuine popular capitalism. **1987** *Sunday Tel.* 28 June 6/6 Free market and popular capitalism is proving to be the efficient engine of wealth creation, growth and enterprise many of us always knew it was.

†**5. a.** Studious of, or designed to gain, the favour of the common people. **b.** Attached or devoted to the cause of the people (as opposed to the nobility, etc.). *Obs.*

1579–80 NORTH *Plutarch* (1595) 874 Diuers were of opinion, that he [Caius Gracchus] was more popular, and desirous of the common peoples good will and fauour, then his brother had bene before him. **1622** BACON *Hen. VII*, 165 The lord Avdley..a Noble-man of an ancient Family, but vnquiet and popular,..came in to them [rebels]. **1701** SWIFT *Contests Nobles & Com. Athens & Rome* iii, The practices of popular and ambitious men. **1771** GOLDSM. *Hist. Eng.* I. 204 The first acts of an usurper are always popular.

6. a. Finding favour with or approved by the people; like, beloved, or admired by the people, or by people generally; favourite, acceptable, pleasing.

1608 CHAPMAN *Byron's Conspir.* II. i. Plays 1873 II. 205 He is a foole that keepes them with more care, Then they keepe him, safe, rich, and populare. **1623** COCKERAM, *Popular*, in great fauour with the common people. **1710** *Tatler* No. 190 ⁋4 This..will make me more popular among my Dependants. **1812** *Religionism* 24 The popular Preachers,—men of high renown. **1883** *Manch. Guard.* 22 Oct. 5/4 When the bashful bard had committed his verses to print they soon became popular.

b. Designating (aspects of) art and culture whose forms appeal to or are favoured by people generally; esp. in ***popular art, music, song***, etc. Also influenced by sense 4.

1841 S. BAMFORD *Passages in Life of Radical* (ed. 2) I. xxxiii. 200 A hundred or two of our handsomest girls.. danced to the music, or sung snatches of popular songs. **1855** W. CHAPPELL (*title*) Popular music of the olden time. **1866** C. ENGEL *Introd. Study National Mus.* v. 168 The peculiar character of the popular music of a nation appears to be in great measure determined by the climate of the country, by the occupation and habits of the people, and even by the food upon which they principally subsist. **1898** G. B. SHAW *Plays Pleasant & Unpleasant* I. p. v, I had no taste for what is called popular art, no respect for popular morality, [etc.]. **1911** H. G. HEWLETT *Chorley's National Mus. of World* (ed. 3) 201 The large share,..which popular, if not Church, music has taken and takes in mourning for the dead in Ireland, is a characteristic not to be overlooked. **1927** R. H. WILENSKI *Mod. Movement in Art* 28 The nineteenth century produced original and popular art of the romantic and descriptive kinds. **1934** A. HUXLEY *Beyond Mexique Bay* 267 Where popular art is vulgar, there the life of the people is also essentially vulgar in its emotional quality. **1935** *Vanity Fair* (N.Y.) Nov. 38/1 Our jazzmen have had no attention except for the exploitation of a few Tin-Pan Alley terms concerning the popular song industry. **1941** *Musical Q.* XXVII. 48 The prevalent false dichotomy of 'classical' and 'popular' based on a belief in the inferiority of the latter as music. **1947** *Sat. Rev. Lit.* (U.S.) 10 May 9/2 By popular art we mean creative work that measures success by the size of its audience and the profit it brings to its makers. **1956** B. NETTL *Mus. in Primitive Culture* ix. 121 American Negro material..has had its effect on folk music, on popular music in the form of jazz, and on a good deal of cultivated music. **1957** R. HOGGART *Uses of Literacy* I. v. 129 The finest period in English urban popular song seems to have been between 1880 and 1910, when each great music-hall star had errand boys and earls singing his or her characteristic songs. **1959** *News Chron.* 10 July 3/2 'Search your attics, turn out your cupboards,' exhorted the B.B.C., 'and join in a television treasure hunt.'.. This is a first-class idea for popular culture. **1962** A. NISBETT *Technique Sound Studio* iii. 65 This method is employed a great deal in the recording of popular music—but very rarely indeed for serious music. **1964** HALL & WHANNEL *Popular Arts* iii. 66 In the previous chapter we tried to show the continuity between folk art and popular art. Then, by following the line of continuity into the early cinema and Chaplin, we indicated the way in which this popular art emerged within the new media. **1966** D. JENKINS *Educated Society* ii. 58 Popular culture, which..is to be sharply distinguished from ..commercialized 'pop culture'..is the style of life of the majority of the members of a community. **1978** J. PASCALL *Illustr. Hist. Rock Music* 12 Popular music has never existed to be analysed. It has existed purely to give pleasure. Rock & roll, more than any other popular music, defies intellectual examination. **1979** *Jrnl. R. Soc. Arts* July 511/2 It is a catalogue of one of the largest collections of Indian popular painting outside India itself.

7. a. Prevalent or current among, or accepted by, the people generally; common, general; †(of sickness) epidemic (*obs.*).

1603 FLORIO *Montaigne* (1632) 432, I remember a popular sickenesse, which some yeares since, greatly troubled the townes about mee. **1616** B. JONSON *Devil is an Ass* I. iii, Sir, that's a popular error, deceiues many. **1651** JER. TAYLOR *Serm. for Year* II. xxvi. 329 Does not God plant remedies there where the diseases are most popular? **1727–41** CHAMBERS *Cycl.*, *Popular errors*, are such as people imbibe from one another, by custom, education, and tradition. **1803** *Med. Jrnl.* IX. 422 In all popular diseases prostration of strength forbids its repetition. **1875** JOWETT *Plato* (ed. 2) I. 241 A popular aphorism of modern times.

b. ***popular etymology*** [tr. G. *Volksetymologie*] = *folk etymology* (FOLK 6).

1880 A. H. SAYCE *Introd. Sci. of Lang.* II. ix. 246 Such myths are created by those popular etymologies—that *Volksetymologie* as the Germans call it—which play so large a part in local names. **1901** H. OERTEL *Lect. Study of Lang.* iii. 187 In all cases of so-called popular etymology it is necessary that the meaning of one of the two words should be unknown, that of the other familiar. **1926** FOWLER *Mod. Eng. Usage* 227/1 It is true..that *-yard* [in *halyard*] is no better than a popular-etymology corruption. **1933** L. BLOOMFIELD *Language* xxiii. 423 So-called popular etymologies are largely adaptive and contaminative. An irregular or semantically obscure form is replaced by a new form of more normal structure and some semantic content —though the latter is often far-fetched. **1934** S. ROBERTSON *Devel. Mod. Eng.* (1936) xi. 456 Words altered by popular etymology have often..displaced the original forms and become thoroughly accepted in standard speech. **1958** A. S. C. ROSS *Etym.* i. 68 There is..another subject to which the General Public applies the name *etymology*, a subject which philologists often call *Popular Etymology*. This subject is one quite without value but..it is one of the great breeders of popular fallacies.

8. *U.S. dial.* or *slang*. **a.** Conceited. **b.** Good.

1848 LOWELL *Biglow P.* Poems 1890 II. 43 He see a cruetin Sarjunt a struttin round as popler as a hen with 1 chicking. **1884** *Sat. Rev.* 8 Nov. 590/2 New York restaurant. .. 'I don't call this very popular pie'. They have come..to take popular quite gravely and sincerely as a synonym for good.

9. *Parasynth. comb.*, as ***popular-minded***, ***-priced***, ***-shaped***.

1837 J. S. MILL in *Westm. Rev.* XXXVII. 8 This want is most felt..by the most popular-minded public men. **1902** *Daily Chron.* 23 Dec. 2/7 The directors had resolved to produce popular-priced cycles. **1902** *Westm. Gaz.* 20 Mar. 3/2 The popular-shaped flounce. **1916** *Variety* 27 Oct. 12/1 'The Little Girl that God Forgot', the popular priced attraction at the Crescent opened Sunday. **1958** *Newnes Compl. Amat. Photogr.* xvi. 158 The more popular-priced cameras fitted with lenses of f/3·5 or f/4·5, will be fast enough for instantaneous exposures in artificial light.

B. *absol.* or as *sb.* (from sense 2).

†**a.** In collective sense (with *the* or other demonstr. adj.; cf. *the public*): The commonalty, the populace. *Obs.*

1552 LYNDESAY *Monarche* 4966 Ane holy exemplair Tyll ws, thy pure lawid commoun populair. *a* **1577** SIR T. SMITH *Commw. Eng.* (1633) 5 The rule or the usurping of the popular, or rascall or viler sort. *a* **1578** [see POPULARY]. **1633** J. DONE *Hist. Septuagint* 19 All the rest of the Populer..he instituted as Colonies.

†**b.** sb. pl. ***populars***, the common people, the commons. Sometimes rendering L. *populārēs*, the plebeians (as opp. to the *patricians*). *Obs.*

1579 FENTON *Guicciard.* (1618) 28 He confirmed with gifts,..the courage and intention of Iohn Lewis de Fiesguo ..and many other gentlemen and populars. **1600** W. WATSON *Decacordon* (1602) 319 Together with all the populars of euery Prince in Christendome. **1610** HEALEY *Vives' Comm. St. Aug. Citie of God* (1620) 77 The newes of his death stirred vp both Patricians and Populars to ioy and mirth.

c. Short for *popular concert*: cf. POP *sb.*[4]

1865 *Punch* 4 Mar. 92/1 Pity poor Lucy! Obliged to go to the Monday Popular with Cousin Bess (from the country). **1885** RUSKIN *Pleasures Eng.* 139. I suppose her presence at a Morning Popular is as little anticipated as desired. **1885** *Boston* (Mass.) *Jrnl.* 18 May 3/3 Music Hall Populars. **1894** [see BRAHMSIAN *a.* and *sb.*].

d. Short for *popular newspaper*: see sense 4 a above.

1952 [see sense 4 a above]. **1961** *Times* 11 Feb. 5/5 (Advt.), Choosing one's Sunday newspaper seems to have become a shade less straightforward in 1961. For forty years the alternative has had such a bonny simplicity about it: on the one hand the 'posh Sundays', on the other the populars. **1964** 'W. HAGGARD' *Antagonists* xviii. 169 The Press was besieging Nikola Mitrovic... He was hinting at women and money... The populars would run it hard. **1968** *Economist* 7 Sept. 67/2 If the decline of the populars continues, Fleet Street stands to lose a third of its present newspapers. **1976** T. HEALD *Let Sleeping Dogs Die* vi. 110 Bognor..picked up the paper. It was one of the populars.

Hence †**popular** *v. trans.*, to people, populate; **'popularish** *a.*

1588 PARKE tr. *Mendoza's Hist. China* 181 There was but a quarter of a league distant one towne from an other, and.. in all the Prouinces of the Kingdome, it is *populared in the same order. *Ibid.* 374 Yet are they populared with much people. **1824** J. WILSON in *Blackw. Mag.* XV. 721 *Butterbrodt*, as the Germans call it in their superb and now *popularish dialect.

Popular Front. Also with lower-case initials. [tr. Sp. *frente popular*, F. *front populaire* in the same sense: see FRONT *sb.* 5 g.] An international political alliance of Communist, radical, and Socialist elements formed in 1935 and gaining power in France (1936–38), Spain (1936), and Chile (1938–42), although in Europe it was largely ineffective after 1938. Also *transf.*, of other radical or popular movements.

1936, etc. [see FRONT *sb.* 5 g]. **1936** *Age* (Melbourne) 5 May 11/7 The crowds last week were predominantly hostile to the Popular Front. **1937** 'G. ORWELL' in *New English Weekly* 29 July 308/1 The worker and the bourgeois,..are fighting side by side. This uneasy alliance is known as the Popular Front. **1940** H. G. WELLS *Babes in Darkling Wood* IV. iii. 380 The idea seems to be to make it the working credo of one world-wide popular front. **1942** E. PAUL *Narrow St.* xxxi. 280 The Popular Front election, April 16 to 21, 1936, was the last held in France, as the Popular Front election in February of that same year was the last held in Spain. **1958** *Spectator* 6 June 721/1 A Popular Front drifting into Communism. **1960** C. DAY LEWIS *Buried Day* x. 219 The Spanish war began: the Popular Front was formed 'against fascism and war'. In Cheltenham the Party group sought to engage the local Labour Party in popular-front activities. **1963** *Listener* 14 Mar. 450/1 He [*sc.* Khrushchev] looks forward to the appearance of strong Popular Front movements, similar to those in the late nineteen-thirties. **1966** K. MARTIN *Father Figures* x. 205 Was it true that a Popular Front was the only hope of salvation? **1970** *Guardian* 25 Feb. 1/2 The 'hardline' guerrilla groups are led by the Popular Front for the Liberation of Palestine. **1971** I. DEUTSCHER *Marxism in our Time* (1972) 291 The Popular Front was Stalinism's reaction against its own ultraleft follies through which it had smoothed Hitler's road to power. **1976** S. HYNES *Auden Generation* vii. 210 At the Albert Hall in February 1937..Harry Pollitt..spoke in support of the Spanish Loyalists and the Popular Front.

Hence **Popular Fronter**, one who supports the Popular Front; **Popular Fronting**, activity associated with the Popular Front; **Popular Frontism**, the principles or policies maintained by the Popular Front.

1938 *Nation* (N.Y.) 14 May 555/1 He [*sc.* Philip F. La Follette] wants no more to be tied to trade unionism, as the British progressives are, than he wants to be tied to popular frontism, as the French progressives are. **1940** *Economist* 13 July 36/1 The Russians were liquidating Popular Frontism at home. **1941** 'G. ORWELL' in *Partisan Rev.* Mar.–Apr. 110 It was extremely amusing to watch the behaviour of orthodox Popular Front-ers, who were exclaiming dolefully 'It's going to be another Munich.' **1957** *New Republican* 7 Jan. 14/2 What kind of liberals will you find in the average large university? A handful of ADA people, most of them far from firebrands; *perhaps* one liberal of the sort who feels a nostalgic attachment to Popular Frontism. **1969** M. STEED in Henig & Pinder *European Pol. Parties* 157 There has been no suggestion that any formal links should be created between the FGDS and the Communist Party... Whilst the popular fronting of 1966–68 was happily accepted by both sides.., it broke up in May 1969, when rival presidential candidates were chosen.

'popularism. [f. POPULAR *a.* + -ISM]

a. A word or phrase in common use amongst the people; a colloquialism.

1888 *Sat. Rev.* 20 Oct. 466/2 The popularisms of 'pallis', 'linning', 'cushing',..heard in London streets as corruptions and vulgarisms.

b. = POPULISM a.

1961 *Sewanee Rev.* Autumn 519 French Egalitarianism had only nominal influence in this country before the days of Popularism. **1962** *Listener* 5 Apr. 584/1 For a clearer understanding of what is happening we should be ready to play down these uneasy notions of right and left, and, instead, study British political attitudes in terms of republicanism and popularism.

ˈpopularist. [f. POPULAR *a.* + -IST.]

a. A democrat. **b.** = POPULIST 2.

1895 *19th Cent.* Sept. 526 There she finds two sorts of women: if I am allowed to use two Russianisms, she finds the 'careerist', and the 'popularist'.

c. *attrib.* or as *adj.*, concerning or appealing to the people generally, popular; also, democratic.

1890 *Times* 22 Feb. 1/1 Even in Alsace-Lorraine one Socialist has been returned, while the Democrat or Popularist party has again been restored to life in the persons of two members. **1922** *New Witness* 25 Aug. 120/2 The P.P.I. must now be reckoned with as the most powerful political force in Italy... When one comes finally to examine the main points in the Popularist programme, one meets old friends often discussed in these pages. **1962** *Listener* 5 Apr. 585/2 The popularist fear of going into Europe is the fear of being swamped in another Holy Roman Empire. **1970** *New Yorker* 10 Oct. 150 What emerged was a popularist outlook (Hightower called it 'human') and the determination to dissolve painting and sculpture into broader aesthetic streams. **1970** *Guardian Weekly* 14 Nov. 3/4 There is no doubt that, after two years of passive and effacingly popularist administration, the President of All the People [*sc.* Nixon] tried to become President of Most of the People; a President who saw an opening to the.. right.

popularity (pɒpjʊˈlærɪtɪ). [ad. F. *popularité* (15th c. in Hatz.-Darm.) populace, popular bearing, popularity, ad. L. *populāritās* fellow-citizenship, popular bearing, in late L. popularity, f. *populāris* POPULAR: see -ITY.]

†**1.** Popular or democratic government. *Obs.*

1548 W. THOMAS in Strype *Eccl. Mem.* II. App. S. 65 The Swizzers, that destroyed their gentlemen in a day and that now glory most in their popularity. **1632** C. DOWNING *St. Eccles. Kingd.* (1634) 24 An Aristocracie cannot be immediately dissolved, either into a tyranny or a tumultuous popularity. **1701** SWIFT *Contests Nobles & Com. Athens & Rome* v, In a very few years we have made mighty leaps from prerogative heighths into the depths of popularity.

†**2.** The principle of popular or democratic government; democracy. *Obs.*

1574 WHITGIFT *Def. Aunsw.* To Rdr. a iv, Contempt of magistrates, popularitie, Anabaptistrie and sundrie other pernicious and pestilent errors. *a* **1648** LD. HERBERT *Hen. VIII* (1683) 166 He taught, All goods should be Common; and diuers other Articles tending to Popularity. **1689** D. GRANVILLE *Lett.* (Surtees, No. 37) 71 The contagion of the age, the spirit of popularity and republicanisme.

†**3. a.** The action or practice of courting, or trying to win, popular favour. *Obs.*

1597–8 BACON *Ess., Followers & Friends* (Arb.) 34 So it be without too much pompe or popularitie. **1690** NORRIS *Beatitudes* (1692) 240 A very laudable affectation of Popularity,.. to engage men's affections to our Persons. **1697** COLLIER *Ess. Mor. Subj.* II. (1703) 71 Popularity is a courting the favour of the people by undue practices. *a* **1715** BURNET *Own Time* an. 1664 (1823) I. 355 He said, there was such a remissness, and so much popularity appeared upon all occasions, that.. it would be impossible to preserve the church.

†**b.** *pl.* Popular arts or practices. *Obs. rare*$^{-1}$.

1597 BACON *Coulers Good & Evill* Ess. (Arb.) 138 It may be represented also by coulers, popularities and circumstances, which are of such force, as they sway the ordinarie iudgement.

4. The fact or condition of being approved, beloved, or admired by the people, or by many people; favour or acceptance with the people.

1601 HOLLAND *Pliny* II. 526 At the next election of Magistrates, his popularitie gained him a Consulship. **1673** *Essex Papers* (Camden) I. 77 They have no man of eminent popularitie to head them. **1780** BENTHAM *Princ. Legisl.* xvii. §22 By popularity is meant the property of being acceptable or rather not unacceptable to the bulk of the people. **1841** D'ISRAELI *Amen. Lit.* (1867) 540 Numerous editions of these poems confirm their popularity. **1882** A. W. WARD *Dickens* i. 17 He had found the way short from obscurity to the dazzling light of popularity.

†**5.** Vulgarity in speech. *rare*$^{-1}$.

1599 B. JONSON *Ev. Man out of Hum.* II. i, This gallant, labouring to avoid popularity, falls into a habit of affectation, ten thousand times hatefuller than the former.

†**6.** = POPULACE. *Obs.*

1632 C. DOWNING *St. Eccles. Kingd.* (1634) 18 That was approved and received by many of the popularity for a happie equality. **1715** M. DAVIES *Athen. Brit.* I. Pref. 65 To curry Favour with the vulgar Popularity. **1771** LUCKOMBE *Hist. Print.* 119 [He] incensed the popularity of London, as in a common cause.

†**7.** = POPULOUSNESS. *Obs. rare.*

1654 E. JOHNSON *Wonder wrkg. Provid.* (1867) 212 The last Church that compleated the number of 30. was gathered at Boston, by reason of the popularity thereof. **1720** BARHAM *Barrenness Enq.* i, Of the antediluvian world, and its popularity before the flood.

8. *Comb.*, as ***popularity-hunting, -monger***; **popularity contest**, a competition in which the popularity of the contenders is judged; freq. *transf.* and in allusive uses with reference (chiefly in negative contexts) to one's supposed popularity; **popularity poll** [POLL *sb.*^{1} 7 d], a poll taken from a section of a population in order to assess the popularity of a particular person or proposition in terms of the population as a whole; **popularity rating**, an assessment of popularity based on the findings of a *popularity poll*.

1941 B. SCHULBERG *What makes Sammy Run?* i. 15 I'm not running a popularity contest; I'm running a business office. **1952** *Manch. Guardian Weekly* 24 Apr. 8/4 This is a 'popularity contest' only; the results are not binding on the delegates of either party. **1959** R. CONDON *Manchurian Candidate* (1960) xvii. 211 Life isn't a popularity contest... I didn't ask them to like me. **1964** E. AMBLER *Kind of Anger* i. 16 You wouldn't win a popularity contest where he's concerned, and.. he can be a vindictive old bastard. **1973** 'E. MCBAIN' *Hail to Chief* i. 15 The decisions I make ain't always popular, but.. I'm not running no popularity contest. **1976** *National Observer* (U.S.) 1 May 4/5 Unless he can really blast a hole through this interest screen in the Democratic Party by winning handsomely in the primaries, not just in the popularity contests but in the delegate races as well, then I suspect he could be squeezed out at the convention. **1875** JAS. GRANT *One of the 600* i, The sly broad-brims and popularity-hunters of the Peace Society. **1843** THACKERAY *Irish Sk. Bk.* v, A courtly popularity-hunting air. **1946** W. S. CHURCHILL *Victory* 162 Sir, I trust there will be no popularity-hunting at the public expense. **1846** MRS. GORE *Eng. Char.* (1852) 10 One of the most accredited popularity-mongers of society. **1938** 'E. QUEEN' *Four of Hearts* ix. 127 Three outstanding stars (selected.. on the basis of the latest popularity poll conducted by Paula Paris for the newspaper syndicate). **1958** *Punch* 1 Jan. 50/1 Continuing to top the popularity poll for the masses was Princess Margaret. **1962** *Sunday Times* (Colour Suppl.) 10 June 3 A fact recognised in this year's *Melody Maker* popularity poll. **1972** *Country Life* 10 Feb. 347/3 Let us pray that they [*sc.* poodles] will never find themselves leading the popularity poll. **1979** J. WAINWRIGHT *Duty Elsewhere* lxiii. 176 Calling an assistant chief constable a flaming liar doesn't win popularity polls. *a* **1974** R. CROSSMAN *Diaries* (1977) III. 327 *The Times* has a poll showing a 20 per cent lead for the Tories, with a new popularity rating specially designed so that Ted Heath can be ahead of Harold Wilson. **1974** *Listener* 17 Jan. 70/1 The Japanese Prime Minister.. enjoys an even lower popularity-rating.. than President Nixon.

popularization (ˌpɒpjʊləraɪˈzeɪʃən). [f. POPULARIZE + -ATION. So F. *popularisation*.] The action of popularizing or fact of being popularized, in various senses: see the verb. *spec.* (in sense 2 c of the vb.), the adapting of ideas or theories to the level of an educated but non-specialist public; freq. with derogatory connotations, the over-simplification of a subject to suit popular taste (cf. POPULAR *a.* (*sb.*) 4 a). Also, the result or product of this process.

1797 W. TAYLOR in *Monthly Rev.* XXII. 546 The popularization of the measure. **1801** —— in *Monthly Mag.* XI. 301 The popularization of those.. doctrines. **1860** MARSH *Eng. Lang.* 449 The universality of literature, its general popularization by the press. **1866** *Sat. Rev.* 21 Apr. 457/2 An advance.. towards the popularization of the constituencies. **1887** SAINTSBURY *Hist. Elizab. Lit.* xii. (1890) 453 The popularisation of the pamphlet led the way to periodical writing. **1926** WYNDHAM LEWIS *Art of Being Ruled* XIII. iv. 423 It is plainly the popularization of science that is responsible for the fever and instability apparent on all sides. **1951** M. MCLUHAN *Mech. Bride* (1967) 28/1 The lethal psychological and social effects.. arise not from science but from its popularization. **1962** *Listener* 18 Jan. 119/1 Popularization is, then, a word with a moral identity. .. It implies.. that the cases it describes are those where the subject is misrepresented by this treatment; where the truth of the matter has been diluted, if not falsified. **1973** *Nature* 23 Mar. 280/1 This book is more than an extraordinarily successful popularization. **1974** B. PEARCE tr. *Amin's Accumulation on World Scale* II. 591 Mandel places alongside a popularization of *Capital* a diatribe against the Soviet bureaucracy. **1977** M. COHEN *Sensible Words* 157 John W. Yolton.. discusses Gildon's *Deist's Manual* (1705) as an important imitation and popularization of Locke's epistemology.

popularize (ˈpɒpjʊləraɪz), *v.* [f. POPULAR + -IZE. So F. *populariser* (1798 in *Dict. Acad.*).]

†**1.** *intr.* To act popularly; to court popular favour. *Obs. rare*$^{-1}$.

1593 G. HARVEY *Pierce's Super.* 111 Some Popes haue bene glad for their aduantage, to tyrannise Popularly, so he may chaunce be content for his aduauncement, to popularise tyrannically: and shall not be the first.. that hath cunningly done it with a comely grace.

2. *trans.* To make popular. **a.** To gain popular favour for; to cause to be generally known and accepted, liked, or admired.

1797 EARL MALMESBURY *Diaries & Corr.* III. 512 He depended a little on the word peace to popularize him in his own country. **1835** *Fraser's Mag.* XII. 37 To preserve their power they must popularise themselves. **1879** *Brit. & For. Evang. Rev.* XXVIII. 54 These godly ballads and sacred rhymes had done their work in popularising the truth.

b. To render democratic; to extend to the common people.

1831 *Blackw. Mag.* XXIX. 598 'Popularize the government', say they: 'reform the representation'. **1884** *Manch. Exam.* 26 June 5/1 Protestations of their willingness to popularise the suffrage.

c. To present (an abstruse or technical subject) in a form popularly intelligible or attractive. Also *absol.*

1833 J. S. MILL in *Monthly Repos.* VII. 266 The peculiar 'mission' of this age.. is to popularize among the many, the more immediately practical results of the thought and experience of the few. **1836** *Tait's Mag.* III. 80 He possesses .. the power of seizing upon and popularizing the finer parts of his subject. **1850** GROTE *Greece* II. lxvii. VIII. 451 A powerful instrument in popularising new combinations of thought with variety and elegance of expression. **1871** EARLE *Philol. Eng. Tongue* §654 Engaged in the diffusion of knowledge, in popularising history or science. **1916** G. B. SHAW *Pygmalion* 100 His [*sc.* Henry Sweet's] great ability as a phonetician.. would have entitled him to high official recognition, and perhaps enabled him to popularize his subject, but for his Satanic contempt for all academic dignitaries and persons in general who thought more of Greek than of phonetics. **1923** *Times Lit. Suppl.* 4 Jan. 10/3 True-blue musicians; they knew their facts and.. looked at them steadily in order to check their theories, and they did not popularize.

d. To make (a word) generally known, *spec.* to use or encourage the use of (technical vocabulary) in general contexts or in everyday language.

1921 G. B. SHAW *Back to Methuselah* p. xliii, Why did not Erasmus Darwin popularize the word Evolution as effectively as Charles? **1926** [implied in POPULARIZED *ppl. a.*]. **1965** E. GOWERS *Fowler's Mod. Eng. Usage* (ed. 2) 461/1 Our interest in our bodies has always made us prone to popularize medical terms.

Hence **ˈpopularized** *ppl. a.*, **ˈpopularizing** *vbl. sb.* Also **ˈpopularizer.**

1848 W. H. KELLY tr. *L. Blanc's Hist. Ten Y.* II. 523 One of the most successful popularizers of science. **1855** MILMAN *Lat. Chr.* XIV. iii. (1864) IX. 120 The popularising of religious teaching. *a* **1882** T. H. GREEN *Prol. to Ethics* Introd. (1883) 2 Inferences from popularised science. **1897** *Daily News* 23 Sept. 5/3 In these days of popularised photography. **1919** M. BEER *Hist. Brit. Socialism* I. I. vi. 80 Adam Smith and Abraham Tucker's populariser, Paley, either use and interpret natural law in a conservative sense or draw its social-revolutionary teeth. **1926** FOWLER *Mod. Eng. Usage* 444/2 A few examples of these popularized technicalities may be gathered together. **1934** H. G. WELLS *Exper. Autobiogr.* II. viii. 546 He.. began writing books for the general reader and essays in natural history. He was a successful popularizer. **1951** M. MCLUHAN *Mech. Bride* (1967) 48/1 Professor Kinsey's book is a *carte blanche* for maximal genital activity. As popularized science, that is its entire drift. **1974** *Nature* 30 Aug. 754/1 The populariser of science, as he functions today, cannot disseminate the subtle ideas of science. **1978** *Ibid.* 31 Aug. 930/3 Popularisers have a duty to be scrupulous in matters of fact and clarity of presentation.

ˈpopularly, *adv.* [f. POPULAR + -LY^2.] In a popular manner.

1. By or among the people at large, esp. the common people; generally, prevalently, commonly, ordinarily; by popular vote as opposed to nomination or election by one or a few.

1576 FLEMING *Panopl. Epist.* 55 Not meete to be so popularly praysed. **1594** T. BEDINGFIELD tr. *Machiavelli's Florentine Hist.* (1595) 205 Hee feared many times to haue bene popülerly slaine. **1612** WOODALL *Surg. Mate* Wks. (1653) 185 A Dysentery slaying popularly and killing many. **1807** G. CHALMERS *Caledonia* I. III. vii. 424 He had a son, who was popularly called the Boy of Egremont. **1849** MACAULAY *Hist. Eng.* iii. I. 291 The whole number.. was popularly estimated at a hundred and thirty thousand men. **1863** H. COX *Instit.* III. ix. 730 A Town Council popularly elected.

2. In the ordinary language or style of the people; so as to be generally intelligible.

1581 E. CAMPION in *Confer.* III. (1584) R iij b, Saint Augustine there speaketh popularly. **1589** PUTTENHAM *Eng. Poesie* I. xxxi. (Arb.) 77 They had not written so much nor so popularly. **1621** CADE *Serm.* 19 The nature of conscience, which I will describe as popularly as I can. **1680** BAXTER *Cath. Commun.* (1684) 20 You will say that the Scripture speaketh popularly, and after the manner of Men. **1861** GOSCHEN *For. Exch.* 138 The difficulty lies not in the apprehension of them, when they are plainly and popularly stated.

†**3.** In a way that wins popular favour. *Obs.*

1593 [see POPULARIZE *v.* 1]. **1681** DRYDEN *Abs. & Achit.* 336 Why then should I.. Turn rebel and run popularly mad? *Ibid.* 689 On each Side bowing popularly low. **1739** 'R. BULL' tr. *Dedekindus' Grobianus* 223 To twirl the Ringlets, which in Order grow, On each Side waving popularly low.

ˈpopularness. *rare.* [f. as prec. + -NESS.] The quality of being popular, popularity.

1727 BAILEY vol. II, *Popularness*, a being full of People; also an Affectedness of popular Applause. **1809–10** COLERIDGE *Friend* (1818) I. 32 That ensnaring meretricious popularness in Literature.

†**ˈpopulary.** *Obs. rare.* [ad. F. *populaire*: see POPULAR and -ARY^2.] The populace.

a **1578** LINDESAY (Pitscottie) *Chron. Scot.* (S.T.S.) I. 135 We doubt of the popularie [*v.r.* popular] quhilk appeirandlie .. fawouris the kingis partie. **1670** G. H. *Hist. Cardinals* III. I. 249 The Populary being in suspence, by reason of the variety of reports.

populass, -lasse, obs. forms of POPULACE.

†**ˈpopulate,** *ppl. a. Obs.* exc. *poet.* [ad. late L. or early med.L. *populāt-us*, pa. pple. of *populāre* (*a* 800) to inhabit (Du Cange).] Peopled; = POPULATED *ppl. a.*^{2} (Const. as pa. pple.)

1574 HELLOWES *Guenara's Fam. Ep.* (1577) 376 The countrie of Caldea.. the Region after the floud first inhabited and populate. **1634** SIR T. HERBERT *Trav.* 42 The kingdome is much populate. **1871** B. TAYLOR *Faust* (1875) II. I. iii. 47 In a place so populate.

†**ˈpopulate,** *v.*^{1} *Obs. rare.* [f. L. *populārī, -āre* to lay waste, ravage, plunder + -ATE^3.] *trans.* To lay waste, ravage, devastate, destroy. Hence †**ˈpopulated** *ppl. a.*^{1}

1552 HULOET, Populate or conquere. Loke in Conquere, waist. **1570** LEVINS *Manip.* 41/1 To Populate, *populari.* **1601** W. WATSON *Import. Consid.* (1831) 23 To bring in the Spaniard to populate, waste, and destroy this whole Isle. **1747** *Gentl. Mag.* XVII. 242/2 Nor pines it [the rose] languid to the Sirian blaze, With flaccid leaves, and populated breath.

populate ('pɒpjʊleɪt), *v.*[2] [f. L. *populāt-*, ppl. stem: see POPULATE *ppl. a.* and -ATE[3].]

1. *trans.* **a.** To people, inhabit, form the population of (a country, etc.). **b.** To furnish or supply (a country, etc.) with inhabitants; to people.

1578 FLORIO *1st Fruites* 7 b, Adorned with fayre women, populated of many people. **1615** G. SANDYS *Trav.* 20 They populated then The foote of fountfull Ide. **1798** in *Spirit Pub. Jrnls.* (1799) II. 167 And would gradually populate all the sub-marine portion of the globe. **1862** DANA *Man. Geol.* 559 Ox and deer—all of which then populated Britain. **1885** *Manch. Exam.* 14 Feb. 5/2 The great countries we have populated in North America and at the Antipodes.

2. *intr.* Of people: To increase, grow in numbers by propagation. *rare.*

1625 BACON *Ess., Viciss. Things* (Arb.) 574 When there be great Shoales of People, which goe on to populate, without foreseeing Meanes of Life and Sustentation. **1820** SYD. SMITH *Wks.* (1850) 285 As if..it would not set mankind populating faster than carpenters and bricklayers could cover in their children.

3. *intr.* (for *refl.*) To become peopled or populous. *U.S. rare.*

1796 MORSE *Amer. Geog.* I. 556 Its trade..must increase, in proportion as the surrounding country populates. **1822** *Niles' Reg.* 12 Oct. 96/2 This territory [Michigan] is rapidly populating.

Hence **'populated** *ppl. a.*[2]; **'populating** *vbl. sb.*

1652 H. L'ESTRANGE *Amer. no Jewes* 8 To the populating of America. **1884** BLACK *Jud. Shaks.* xvi, A populated place filled with a..number of his fellow-creatures.

†**popu'lation**[1]. *Obs.* [ad. L. *populātiōn-em* devastation, n. of action from *populārī*, *-āre*: see POPULATE *v.*[1]] Devastation, laying waste.

1552 HULOET, Foraging, population, or wastinge of a countrey, *populatio.* **1577–87** HOLINSHED *Chron.* (1807) II. 82 The effusion of innocent bloud, the population of countries, the ruinating of ample regions. **1600** W. WATSON *Decacordon* (1602) 75 Population, ruine, and destruction of their natiue country and commonwealth. **1656** BLOUNT *Glossogr.*, *Population* (*populatio*), a wasting, destroying, robbing, and spoiling of people. **1658** in PHILLIPS.

population[2] (pɒpjʊ'leɪʃən). [ad. late L. *populātiōn-em* (Sedulius *c* 470) population, multitude, having the form of a n. of action f. *populāre* to people (see POPULATE *v.*[2]). So F. *population* (1335 in Godef. *Compl.*) peopling, population.]

†**1.** *concr.* A peopled or inhabited place. *Obs.*

1578 T. N. tr. *Conq. W. India* 130 They received their advise that neere at hand were great populations, and soone after he came to Zimpanzinco. **1613** PURCHAS *Pilgrimage* (1614) 479 It hath in it, by estimation, threescore thousand Populations, or inhabited places.

2. a. 'The state of a country with respect to numbers of people' (J.); the degree in which a place is populated or inhabited; hence, the total number of persons inhabiting a country, town, or other area; the body of inhabitants.

1612 BACON *Ess., Greatness Kingd.* (Arb.) 476 Not the hundreth pole will be fit for a helmet, and so great population and little strength. **1625** *Ibid., Seditions & Troubles* 405 It is to be foreseene, that the Population of a Kingdome, (especially if it be not mowen downe by warrs) doe not exceed, the Stock of the Kingdome, which should maintaine them. **1770** GOLDSM. *Des. Vill.* 125 But now the sounds of population fail. **1798** MALTHUS *Popul.* I. i. 14 Population..increases in a geometrical ratio, subsistence in an arithmetical ratio. **1803** *Ibid.* I. vii. 100 The population of the tribe is measured by the population of its herds. **1809–10** COLERIDGE *Friend* (1865) 48 The formidable state ..in which the population should consist chiefly of soldiers and peasantry. **1849** MACAULAY *Hist. Eng.* iii. I. 281 The population of England in 1685 cannot be ascertained with perfect accuracy. **1868** ROGERS *Pol. Econ.* xii. (1876) 156 To make increased population the cause of improved agriculture, is to commit the absurd blunder of confounding cause and effect.

†**b.** (See quot.) *Obs.*

1817 COBBETT *Taking Leave* 7 We now frequently hear the working classes called 'the population', just as we call the animals upon a farm 'the stock'.

c. *transf.* Of animals, plants, and of other entities.

1803 [see 2]. **1885** J. BALL in *Jrnl. Linn. Soc.* XXI. 207 A gradual increase in the vegetable population would come about. **1897** MARY KINGSLEY *W. Africa* 76 Its resident population consists of sharks, whose annual toll of human life is said by some authorities to be fourteen. **1956** A. H. COMPTON *Atomic Quest* ii. 89 If the neutron population is increasing generation after generation, the reaction grows in intensity. **1968** *Brit. Med. Bull.* XXIV. 244/1 Much study has therefore gone into the effect of radiation on proliferating cell populations in various environments.

d. *Statistics.* A totality of objects or individuals under consideration, of which the statistical attributes may be estimated by the study of a sample or samples drawn from it.

1877 F. GALTON in *Nature* 12 Apr. 513/2 The number of pellets in each compartment represents the relative number in a *population* of seeds, whose weight deviates from the average, within the limits expressed by the distances of the sides of that compartment from the middle point. **1903** *Biometrika* II. 273 If the whole of a population were taken we should have certain values for its statistical constants, but in actual practice we are only able to take a sample, which should if possible be a random sample. **1922** *Phil. Trans. R. Soc.* A. CCXXII. 329 It is unfortunate that in this memoir no sufficient distinction is drawn between the *population* and the *sample.* **1939** D. D. PATERSON *Statistical Technique in Agric. Res.* i. 1 The sum total of all the units of any one kind is called, in statistical terminology, the population. **1970** *Jrnl. Gen. Psychol.* LXXXIII. 14 The experimenter notes that Ss used in this study had experienced only a brief period of hospitalization... Consequently, he cautions against the generalization of his findings to other neurotic and schizophrenic populations. **1977** *Accountants Weekly* 29 July 17/1 The tests built into the program ensured that sample data extracted for audit checks came from a complete population, a fundamental requirement in auditing.

e. *Genetics.* A breeding group of animals, plants, or humans; **population biology, genetics**, the branches of biology and genetics which treat such groups statistically. So ***population biologist, geneticist.***

1889 F. GALTON *Nat. Inheritance* iv. 35 The science of heredity is concerned with Fraternities and large Populations rather than with individuals, and must treat them as units. **1949** C. STERN *Princ. Human Genetics* x. 168 Both fields, population genetics and pedigree genetics, are significant and both rest on the Mendelian analysis of inheritance. *Ibid.* 594 The genic constitution of the later populations will obviously depend on the genotypes of their second-generation ancestors. **1960** *Biol. Abstr.* XXXV. 1729/1 (*heading*) Data on ecology and population biology of mosquitoes. **1966** MACARTHUR & CONNELL *Biol. of Populations* p. x, Experiments performed by population biologists indicate another difference between population biology and other branches of science. **1966** R. ARDREY *Territorial Imperative* iv. 138 A population, in biology, is a reproductive community. More sharply stated, it is any group of individuals who have a modest probability, within any generation, of meeting and mating. **1968** R. C. LEWONTIN *Population Biol. & Evolution* 2 It is a problem of population biology to discover under what circumstances a one-to-one sex ratio is evolved. **1972** *Sci. Amer.* Jan. 100/3 He maintained four populations of *Drosophila* in the laboratory over a 48-month period. **1973** *Listener* 28 June 850/2 He [*sc.* A. Jensen] now knows a good deal more about population genetics than he did..in 1968. **1977** *Nature* 6 Jan. 26/2 The basic interests of the population geneticist of course lie in the realm of population dynamics, and the knowledge of allele frequencies is an essential prerequisite to further work. **1979** *Ibid.* 9 Aug. 455 (*heading*) Population biology of infectious diseases.

f. *Physics.* The (number of) atoms or subatomic particles that occupy any particular energy state.

1931 *Physical Rev.* XXXVII. 143 (*caption*) Illustrating the relation between spectral intensity distribution in the Compton line (left) and population of electron speed states (right). **1938** R. W. LAWSON tr. *Hevesy & Paneth's Man. Radioactivity* (ed. 2) viii. 88 The resulting gap in the atom, due to the incomplete population of the *K*-shell, may now be filled by the transition of an electron from the *L*-level into the *K*-level. **1961** [see INVERSION 2 l]. **1971** *Sci. Amer.* June 22/1 By elevating more atoms to an upper energy level than exist at a lower level the absorption of excitation radiation produces an 'inverted' atomic population in the laser.

g. *Astr.* Either of the two groups into which stars can be approximately divided: those of ***population I*** are formed from the debris of other stars, those of ***population II*** are coeval with their galaxy.

[**1944** W. BAADE in *Astrophysical Jrnl.* C. 137 The stellar populations of the galaxies fall into two distinct groups, one represented by the..stars in our solar neighborhood (the slow-moving stars), the other by that of the globular clusters. Characteristic of the first group (type I) are highly luminous O- and B-type stars and open clusters; of the second (type II), short-period Cepheids and globular clusters.] **1951** *Astrophysical Jrnl.* CXIII. 413 Highly luminous stars of population I. **1952** C. PAYNE-GAPOSCHKIN *Stars in Making* iv. 74 The names 'Populations I and II' were originally given by Baade to the two groups of stars. As we shall see, they probably represent extremes rather than an absolute distinction. **1974** F. W. COLE *Fund. Astron.* xiii. 344/1 Two very different populations of stars can be recognized: population I consisting of the normal, metal-rich stars found in spiral arms of galaxies; and population II, the metal-poor stars found in globular clusters, as isolated stars in the galactic halo, and in the central galactic nucleus.

h. The general body of inmates in a prison, rehabilitation centre, etc. (see quot. 1950). Freq. in phr. ***in population.***

1950 H. E. GOLDIN *Dict. Amer. Underworld Lingo* 162/2 *Population*,..the general body of inmates as differentiated from convicts in trusty jobs, hospital patients, and occupants of punishment or psychopathic observation wings. **1953** W. BURROUGHS *Junkie* viii. 79 After eight days, you get a sendoff shot and go over in 'population'... You are allowed seven days to rest in population after medication stops. **1956** J. RESKO *Reprieve* (1959) III. xvi. 135 Our friends out in population took care of us. **1971** *Black Scholar* June 54/1 The officials told me that I would never be returned to the general population (Auburn) and advised me to put in for transfer to another institution. **1973** *Philadelphia Inquirer* (Today Suppl.) 7 Oct. 50/3 Sprague tried to block Soleni's move into general population. **1977** *New Yorker* 24 Oct. 68/2 Collectively, the inmates are referred to as 'population'.

3. The action or process of peopling a place or region; increase of people.

1776 *Declar. Indep. Amer.* in *Gentl. Mag.* XLVI. 361/2 He [the king] has endeavoured to prevent the population of these states. **1796** MORSE *Amer. Geog.* I. 563 The population of the province was extremely rapid. **1856** EMERSON *Eng. Traits, Wealth* Wks. (Bohn) II. 72 Population is stimulated, and cities rise. **1869** FREEMAN *Norm. Conq.* III. xii. 232 [Polygamy]..could..be hardly looked on as on the whole conducive to population.

4. *attrib.* and *Comb.* (chiefly from 2), as ***population basis, census, control, cycle, distribution, drift, growth, increase, -monger, planning, policy, pressure, question, return, survey, theory, trend***; **population biology**: see sense 2 e above; **population curve**, a graph showing the variation of population with time; **population explosion**, a rapid or sudden marked increase in the size of a population; hence ***population-explosive*** adj.; **population genetics**: see sense 2 e above; **population inversion**: see INVERSION 2 l; **population pyramid**, a roughly triangular figure on a level base, the width of which at any height is proportional to the numbers having an age proportional to that height.

1903 *Westm. Gaz.* 31 Oct. 10/2 Australia,..on a population basis, is undoubtedly one of the largest consumers of books in the world. **1968** *Internat. Encycl. Social Sci.* XII. 369/1 In most advanced countries illiteracy has been almost eliminated, and therefore questions on literacy are no longer included in population censuses. **1931** J. S. HUXLEY *What dare I Think?* v. 166 Might it not have been better to have left the death side of nature's population-control to itself until we have some future policy for dealing simultaneously with birth? **1959** *New Statesman* 21 Mar. 401/1 Countries like India and Japan have made population-control a central feature in national policy, because they know that without it they are headed for disaster. **1973** J. M. WHITE *Garden Game* 117 War is becoming a necessary instrument of population-control. **1889** F. GALTON *Nat. Inheritance* 245 The population curve will..be a straight line. **1935** *Proc. Prehist. Soc.* I. 11 Advances of critical importance to humanity should be followed by such a multiplication as to be conspicuously reflected in the population curve. **1968** *N.Y. City* (Michelin Tire Corp.) 139 Long Island... The population curve is constantly rising. **1969** N. W. PIRIE *Food Resources* ii. 70 A few plant and animal species..go through fairly regular population cycles. **1968** R. A. LYTTLETON *Mysteries Solar Syst.* vi. 185 The density of finds does show some relation to the population-distribution. **1974** *Encycl. Brit. Macropædia* XVII. 67/2 The pattern of population distribution and density closely follows that of the rainfall pattern. **1964** *Ann. Reg. 1963* 22 The Minister of Housing and Local Government..was wrestling with the problems of population drift, regional planning, and slum clearance. **1977** *Modern Railways* Dec. 480/1 Population drift from the London area to central and north-east Essex necessitated a fundamental restructure of Great Eastern line services. **1953** *Population Bull.* Oct. 65 (*heading*) Latin America: area of population explosion. **1953** [see EXPLOSION 4 b]. **1964** 'J. MELVILLE' *Murderers' Houses* vii. 116 Emily knew all about the Bomb and the Pill and could advocate one remedy for the declining Middle Classes and another for the Population Explosion. **1970** *Oxf. Univ. Gaz.* C. Suppl. VI. 5 A kind of documentary population-explosion, in fact. **1970** *Daily Tel.* 18 July 11/7 Population explosions in summer may result in up to 10 million aphides taking to the air each day from an acre. **1974** *Times* 21 Jan. 6 (*heading*) Leading the fight to head off the population explosion. **1967** *Punch* 3 May 637/3 This two-way flow, once started, would never stop; no government, much less any shipping company, could ever stop such a flow, population-explosive, travel-agency-prodded and democratic. **1927** J. S. HUXLEY *Relig. without Revelation* ix. 325 The study of heredity and population-growth. **1970** G. GERMANI in I. L. Horowitz *Masses in Lat. Amer.* viii. 295 With regard to the other Latin American states, it is clear that immigration made a crucial contribution to population growth. **1978** R. MITCHISON *Life in Scotland* vi. 108 Industrialization..was..the 'answer' to that population growth. **1931** J. S. HUXLEY *What dare I Think?* iv. 135 Population-increase cannot go on indefinitely. **1959** *New Statesman* 21 Mar. 401/1 In under-developed countries, excessive population-increase reduces the possibility of an economic break-through. **1826** in Cobbett *Rur. Rides* (1885) II. 239 The Scotch population-mongers, and Malthus and his crew. **1974** *Times* 21 Jan. 6/2 The idea of population planning antagonized many countries. **1944** J. S. HUXLEY *On living in Revolution* xii. 131 It is very important that there should be a well-thought-out population policy for backward areas. **1974** *Times* 21 Jan. 6/5 Opposition to..population policies is led by countries with..large natural resources. **1931** J. S. HUXLEY *What dare I Think?* v. 165 Causing more babies to live and so creating greater population-pressure. **1969** *Times* 26 June 14/7 The migrations..could be a means of relieving the population pressure in a particular area. **1950** *Chambers's Encycl.* XI. 93/2 The age distribution in populations of plaice and other fish has been examined; and attempts have been made to study honey-bee colonies and wireworm populations from this point of view. All show, under natural conditions, the expected 'population pyramid', formed by large numbers of young individuals and gradually decreasing numbers of individuals of the higher age-groups. **1976** *Nature* 1 July 19/1 As a result of their high crude birth rate..the population pyramid has a relatively broad base; 51·8% are less than 20 yr old and 28·7% are less than 10 yr old. **1885** *Encycl. Brit.* XIX. 517/2 We cannot here deal with what is known as the 'population question'... The 'population question' is a question of conduct. **1911** G. B. SHAW *Getting Married* 116 St. Paul's reluctant sanction of marriage;..his contemptuous 'better to marry than to burn' is only out of date in respect of his belief that the end of the world was at hand and that there was therefore no longer any population question. **1845** DISRAELI *Sybil* II. xvi, The Population Returns of this country are very instructive reading. **1953** Population survey [see ATTRACTANT]. **1966** *Economist* 17 Dec. 1253/3 Except in the matter of population theory, where he anticipated and influenced Malthus, Steuart had little or no effect on later economic thought in Britain. **1933** THOMPSON & WHELPTON (*title*) Population trends in the United States. **1950** THEIMER & CAMPBELL *Encycl. World Politics* 347/1 In the U.S.S.R., Eastern Europe and Latin America population trends are like those of the West in the later nineteenth century. **1976** J. S. MOORE *Goods & Chattels of our Forefathers* 9 The main population-trends can already be seen from a study of the data contained in the numerous ecclesiastical and private censuses taken in Gloucestershire in the early modern period.

Hence **popu'lational** *a.*, of, pertaining to, or based on population; **popu'lationist**, one who holds a theory about population, esp. a

Malthusian; also, one who considers the population to be a significant element in a state's power; **popu'lationless** *a.*, without population, uninhabited.

1893 *Nation* (N.Y.) 21 Sept. 213/3 Cities..ranged according to their populational rank. **1865–77** H. TAYLOR *Autobiog.* (1885) I. 92 It is not long since I heard a Populationist vehemently reproach a poor but very respectable married gentleman for the sin of having nine children. **1949** K. DAVIS *Human Society* 552 If the populationist stopped here, however, his work would have little to do with social science. **1968** *Internat. Encycl. Social Sci.* XII. 350/2 In Germany, Hermann Conring also attributed the power of states mainly to population. In England..another confirmed populationist was William Petty, who founded the science of 'political arithmetic', or demography. **1885** HARE *Stud. Russia* ii. 76 Endless are the open spaces..almost populationless.

'populator. [Agent-n. in L. form from POPULATE *v.*[2]] One who or that which populates or peoples.

1882 OGILVIE (Annandale), The populators of a country.

†**'popule,** *v. Obs. rare.* [f. late L. *populāre.*] *trans.* = PEOPLE *v.* 1.

1588 PARKE tr. *Mendoza's Hist. China* 142 The rest were separated in the discouering and populing of other Ilands. *Ibid.* 204 The greatest towne and most populed of all that prouince.

†**po'puleal,** *a. Obs. rare*$^{-1}$. [f. L. *pōpule-us* of poplar + -AL[1].]

1688 R. HOLME *Armoury* III. 7/2 The Crown Popler, or Populeal [*mispr.* -teal] Garland, is made of the Leaves of Poplar.

†**populeon.** *Obs.* Forms: 5 popylyon, 5–7 -ilion, 6–7 -uleon, (7 pompil(l)ion). [a. OF. *populeon* (15th c. in Godef. *Compl.*), ad. med.L. **pōpuleum*, f. *pōpulus* poplar. OF. had *popelion a* 1300 (P. Meyer).] An ointment made of the buds of the Black Poplar.

1398 TREVISA *Barth. De P.R.* XVII. cxx. (1495) 683 Ofte of the croppe of the populer is oynement made..amonge physicyens the oynement hyghte Popilion. **14..** *Stockh. Med. MS.* 90 An oynement þ at es callyd popylyon. *c* **1550** LLOYD *Treas. Health* C iv b, Distempre them wᵗ populeon. **1611** COTGR., *Populeon*, popilion, or pompillion; an ointment made of blacke Poplar buds. **1616** SURFL. & MARKH. *Country Farme* 41 Rub his browes and all his head ouer with oyle of Roses, Vineger, and Populeon. **1702** YOUNG in *Phil. Trans.* XXIII. 1280, I then anointed the passage with Populeum [*mispr.* Populkeum]. **1712** tr. *Pomet's Hist. Drugs* I. 79 The cooling Quality of the Ointment Populeon holds not above a Year.

populicide ('pɒpjʊlɪsaɪd). *rare.* [a. F. *populicide* adj. (18th c.), f. L. *popul-us* people + *-cide*, -CIDE 1.] The murder of a people or nation.

1824 BENTHAM *Mem. & Corr.* Wks. 1843 X. 544 Tyrannicide would be less flagitious than populicide. **1865** RUSKIN *Arrows of Chace* (1880) II. 78, I hate regicide as I do populicide—deeply, if phrenzied; more deeply, if deliberate.

†**popu'liferous,** *a. Obs. rare*$^{-0}$. [f. L. *pōpul-us* poplar + -FEROUS.]

1656 BLOUNT *Glossogr.*, *Populiferous*, that beareth Poplar-trees. **1658** in PHILLIPS.

populin ('pɒpjʊlɪn). *Chem.* [ad. F. *populine* (Braconnot 1831), f. L. *pōpul-us* poplar: see -IN[1].] A white crystalline substance, $C_{20}H_{22}O_8$, having a sweetish taste, obtained from the bark, leaves, and roots of the aspen (*Pōpulus tremula*).

1838 T. THOMSON *Chem. Org. Bodies* 766 Populin has a sweet taste, not unlike that of liquorice. **1873** WATTS *Fownes' Chem.* (ed. 11) 642 Populin is a substance resembling salicin in appearance.

Hence **'populinate** *v. trans.*, to impregnate with populin as an antiseptic.

18.. in *U.S. Dispensatory* 1489 (Cent. D.).

populism ('pɒpjʊlɪz(ə)m). [f. as next + -ISM.]

a. The political doctrine or principle of the Populists. Also *transf.*

1893 GOLDW. SMITH in *19th Cent.* July 139 The politicians have been compelled in some degree to pander to Populism. **1896** *Sat. Rev.* 9 May 468 Populism being, in fact, pretty much a resurrection of Greenbackism under another form and name. **1896** *Daily News* 3 Nov. 2/4 The central idea of Populism is a concentrated paternalism. **1960** *Encounter* July 13 Russian Populism is the name..of a widespread radical movement in Russia in the middle of the 19th century. **1969** [see POPULISTIC *a.*]. **1972** *Time* 17 Apr. 31/1 Populism is a label that covers disparate policies and passions: among many others, New Deal reforms, consumer rage against business, ethnic belligerence. Often it is merely a catch phrase. Yet it describes something real: the politics of the little guy against the big guy—the classic struggle of the haves against the have-nots or the have-not-enoughs. **1973** *Black Panther* 21 July 3/2 The result was the defeat of western Populism and the further entrenchment of racism. **1976** T. EAGLETON *Crit. & Ideology* v. 166 Populism and theoreticism, in aesthetics as in politics, are familiar deformations of Marxist-Leninism. **1977** *Time* 3 Jan. 7/1 His creed combines traditionally antithetical elements of help-the-deprived populism and deny-thyself fiscal conservatism.

b. The theories and practices of the populist movement in French literature.

[**1929** L. LEMONNIER in *Revue Mondiale* 1 Oct. 281 (*title*) Du naturalisme au populisme.] **1930** —— in *This Quarter* Mar. 440 (*title*) Populism. *Ibid.* 443 At last, we hit upon the word 'populism'. It clearly expressed the fact that we meant to depict the people; it was not altogether a new word in French, inasmuch as it had been used to translate the name of the German political party *Volkspartei*, but it had never as yet been applied to any artistic, political or literary movement specifically French. Having then dubbed ourselves populists, we decided to write a manifesto. **1931** *French Rev.* IV. 473 Since the opening of the twentieth century, only three schools have counted [in French literature], unanimism, between 1908 and 1911, surrealism, about 1924, and populism in 1929. **1932** *Ibid.* V. 389 Populism is the antonym of 'snobisme'. **1934** F. WALTER tr. *Lemonnier's Populisme* in *PMLA* Mar. 356 Populism is a reaction founded on the realistic tradition and directed against the literature of analysis. **1934** *N. & Q.* 26 May 361/1 The beginnings of Populism, adumbrated somewhat obscurely in 1924, came out into shape in 1929 under the initiative of M. André Thérive and M. Léon Lemonnier. *Ibid.* 361/2 In Thérive's 'Le Baiser de Satan,' Populism has attempted what Naturalism shied from the historical novel.

populist ('pɒpjʊlɪst). Also **Populist**, esp. in *spec.* senses. [f. L. *popul-us* people + -IST.] *lit.* 'A member of the People's party' (Funk).

1. An adherent of a political party formed in the U.S. in Feb. 1892, the chief objects of which were public control of railways, limitation of private ownership of land, extension of the currency by free coinage of silver and increased issue of paper-money, a graduated income-tax, etc. Also *attrib.*

1892 *Columbus* (Ohio) *Dispatch* 8 Oct., It is officially reported from Democratic headquarters in Cheyenne, Wyoming, that fusion with the populists has been perfected. The Democrats will support Weaver electors and the People's party the Democratic State Ticket. **1892** *Pall Mall G.* 14 Nov. 6/2 The United States Senate, after March 4, will be composed of forty-four Democrats, forty Republicans, and four Populists. **1893** GOLDW. SMITH in *19th Cent.* July 138 A peoples party,—Populists as by a barbarism they are called. **1901** *N. Amer. Rev.* Feb. 278 The organization of the Populists, trampling under foot the Constitution, in pursuit of objects over a greater part of which Congress has no jurisdiction.

2. A member of a Russian socio-political party advocating a form of collectivism.

1895 P. MILYOUKOV in *Athenæum* 6 July 25/1 The first [group] values primitive collectivism because it regards it as an inalienable trait in the character of the Russian people... [It] sticks to its old name of 'Populists'. **1905** *19th Cent.* Jan. 43 Nobody but a 'populist' who loves the people..will come and stay.

3. A member of a group of French novelists in the late 1920s and early 1930s who placed emphasis upon observation of and sympathy with ordinary people.

[**1929** L. LEMONNIER in *Revue Mondiale* 1 Oct. 285 Tous ces romanciers viennent de se grouper et de se donner un nom: ils veulent être les *romanciers populistes*. Ils entendent le mot dans un sens très large.] **1930** [see POPULISM b]. **1934** *PMLA* XLIX. 361 A sort of Tolstoyan sympathy is a cardinal virtue in the eyes of the Populists. **1934** *N. & Q.* 26 May 361/2 Eugène Dabit (a genuine proletarian), though a populist, begins somewhat to abandon the political and social neutrality.

4. One who seeks to represent the views of the mass of ordinary people.

1961 *Listener* 30 Nov. 897/2 They are not Populists or Poujadists. **1972** *New Society* 20 Jan. 131/1 LBJ was a true populist, as he recognised himself, remarking tartly (and justly enough) that it is 'the term some liberals reserve for Progressives who come from the southern and western parts of the nation'. **1977** *Time* 7 Mar. 7/1 Brogan questions whether Carter is a bona fide populist at all.

5. *attrib.* or as *adj.*

1893 *Nation* (N.Y.) 19 Jan. 43/2 The situation results from the rise of the Populist party. **1898** *Nation* (N.Y.) 7 July 6/2 The Populist Governor abused his power by appointing as commissioners only men of his own party. **1924** *Glasgow Herald* 4 July 7 He [*sc.* the Russian intellectual] has lost much of his former 'populist' idealism, of his old worship of the people. **1928** [see CENTRIST b]. **1931** *French Rev.* IV. 473 This paper will give an account of the rise and origins of the populist school. **1934** R. MICHAUD *Mod. Thought & Lit. in France* xi. 228 A so-called 'populist movement' was launched in 1929 by Léon Lemonnier and André Thérive, as a protest against the précieux and individualistic novel and as a return to the great naturalistic traditions of Zola. **1954** E. A. SHILS in Christie & Jahoda *Stud. Scope & Method of 'The Authoritarian Personality'* 45 A vein of xenophobia, populist, anti-urban and anti-plutocratic sentiment. **1955** H. PEYRE *Contemp. French Novel* ii. 47 Duhamel never made a speciality of the study of misery, as did the proletarian novelists and later a short-lived group of 'populist' novelists (Henri Poulaille, André Thérive, Eugène Dabit). **1961** *Listener* 7 Dec. 997/1 There is the ascending conception [of law and government], according to which the law-creating power may be ascribed to the community or people—the populist theory. **1968** W. SAFIRE *New Lang. Politics* 346/2 When the Populist candidate, General James B. Weaver, won 22 Electoral College and 1,029,846 popular votes in the 1892 election, many people..were fearful of impending revolution. **1969** R. BLACKBURN in Cockburn & Blackburn *Student Power* 190 A wholesale revision of classic liberal democratic theory to eliminate its dangerously populist tendencies and to accommodate the elitist features of contemporary capitalist society. **1974** M. B. BROWN *Econ. of Imperialism* xi. 275 Populist forms of government in the ex-colonial underdeveloped lands were overthrown mainly because they failed to develop their economies. **1976** *Survey* Summer-Autumn 15 There is little doubt that US policy.. will be dominated by self-consciously populist politicians. **1977** *Time* 21 Mar. 53/3 Ironically, the very success of Carter's populist appeal may cause him special backlash problems.

Hence **popu'listic** *a.*; **popu'listically** *adv.*

1894 *Chicago Advance* 4 Oct., It was Mr. Bryan and his populistic ideas which were the bone of contention. **1902** *Nation* (N.Y.) 19 June 490/2 The sentiment is populistic and the treatment of materials is eclectic. **1969** D. MACRAE in Ionescu & Gellner *Populism* 162 That Ireland did not produce a full-fledged populism—as distinct from populistic themes that continue through De Valera to the present—is a paradox of European history. **1971** S. CAVELL *World Viewed* 54 A film like *Mr. Smith Goes to Washington* ..suggests, populistically,..that they are curable by the individual or mass goodness of the little people. **1976** *Times Lit. Suppl.* 16 Apr. 457/2 A man with his own blend of simple, populistic dignity and even honesty.

†**popu'losity.** *Obs.* [f. L. *populōs-us* full of people, POPULOUS + -ITY. So F. *populosité* (Cotgr. 1611).] = POPULOUSNESS.

1614 RALEIGH *Hist. World* I. (1634) 98 That the Easterne people were most ancient in populositie. **1720** STRYPE *Stow's Surv.* I. 305/2 For Hugeness, Concourse, Navigation, Trade and Populosity, it very hardly gives way to any City in Europe. **1778** [W. MARSHALL] *Minutes Agric., Digest* 3 In the present state of Populosity,..the spontaneous growth would be found far short of his indispensable exigencies.

populous ('pɒpjʊləs), *a.* Forms: 5–7 populus, 6 -os, (peopulous, *Sc.* popelus, pepulus), 6–7 populouse, 6– populous. [ad. L. *populōs-us* (Appuleius *c* 160), f. *popul-us* people: see -OUS. Cf. F. *populeux* (1564 in Hatz.-Darm.).]

1. Full of people or inhabitants; having many inhabitants, absolutely or in proportion to area, etc.; thickly inhabited; fully occupied.

1449 J. METHAM *Amor & Cleopes* 302 This cuntre was gret & populus. **1538** STARKEY *England* I. iii. 75 The cuntrey hath byn more populos, then hyt ys now. **1549** *Compl. Scot.* i. 20 The maist pepulus toune abufe the eird. **1555** EDEN *Decades* 6 An other Ilande which the captyues sayde to bee verye peopulous. **1613** PURCHAS *Pilgrimage* (1614) 477 The whole space betweene is as a continuall populous Market. **1709** MRS. MANLEY *Secret Mem.* II. 2 How populous of Mortals must be the Court of Pluto? how solitary that of Jupiter? **1880** HAUGHTON *Phys. Geog.* iv. 190 The rivers on the west coast..running through more populous districts.

b. *transf.* and *fig.* Of animals or things.

1654 WHITLOCK *Zootomia* 321 As habitable a Part of the Microcosme or little World as any, for abilities or vertues, though not so Populous. **1836** W. IRVING *Astoria* II. 175 The river,..with many populous communities of the beaver along its banks. **18..** W. SAWYER *New Year Numbers* iv, The rain-drop glitters populous with life.

c. Of a time or season: Productive, prolific.

1789 GIBBON *Let.* 28 Mar. (in *Sotheby's Sale Catal.* 21 May (1900) 43), The Autumn was remarkably populous in such Englishmen as I am not ashamed to acknowledge in foreign countries. **1820** HAZLITT *Lect. Dram. Lit.* 12 There is no time more populous of intellect,..than the one we are speaking of.

†**2.** Of a body of people: Numerous, abundant.

1535 STEWART *Cron. Scot.* (Rolls) III. 157 And tuke thame baith,..With his power quhilk wes richt populos. *a* **1548** HALL *Chron., Hen. VII* 43 Furnished with a populous army. **1652–62** HEYLIN *Cosmogr.* II. (1682) 212 The over-throw of the populous Navy of Xerxes. **1662** HIBBERT *Body Div.* I. 276 A populous posterity is the blessing of God.

3. Of or pertaining to the populace: = POPULAR *a.*, in various senses. *Obs.* exc. *poet.*

1592 *Arden of Feversham* I. iii. B iv, It should have bene some fine confection,..This powder was to grosse and populos. **1638** *Penit. Conf.* vi. (1657) 102 Mine Author avoucheth it rather for a populous rumor. **1721** AMHERST *Terræ Fil.* No. 35 (1726) 190 A populous scandal was invented and reported about town. **1830** D'ISRAELI *Chas. I*, III. ix. 200 The courtly flattery and the populous shout died away together. **1851** MRS. BROWNING *Casa Guidi W.* II. 35 Between those populous rough hands Raised in the sun, Duke Leopold outleant, And took the patriot's oath.

Hence **'populously** *adv.*, in a populous manner or degree.

1630 *R. Johnson's Kingd. & Commw.* 562 Jewes,..in such infinite numbers, that scarce no Towne nor Village, but is very populously replenished with their families.

populousness ('pɒpjʊləsnɪs). [f. prec. + -NESS.] The state or condition of being populous; density of population.

1601 R. JOHNSON *Kingd. & Commw.* (1603) 47 Constantinople exceedeth all the cities in Europe in populousnes. **1761–2** HUME *Hist. Eng.* (1806) III. 803 England has probably, since that time [1583], increased in populousness. **1884** *Spectator* 4 Oct. 1289/2 A bare fact, as much outside discussion as..the populousness of London.

†**b.** Numerousness; multitudinousness. *Obs.*

1683 CAVE *Ecclesiastici, Ambrose* 361 The temperature of its Air, fertility of Soyl,..and populousness of its Inhabitants. **1759** B. MARTIN *Nat. Hist. Eng.* I. *Guernsey* 127 From the Populaceness of the Inhabitants several Families reside in a House.

c. Prolific quality, productiveness. *rare*$^{-1}$.

1881 JEFFERIES *Wood Magic* I. viii. 218 The wood-pigeons ..were continually being increased both by their own populousness and by the arrival of fresh bands.

pop-up ('pɒpʌp), *sb.* and *a.* [f. POP *v.*[1] + UP *adv.*[1]] **A.** *sb.* **1.** *Baseball.* A ball which is hit softly up into the air and is easily caught.

1906 *Spalding's Offic. Base Ball Guide* 126 A trapped ball play was made when runners were on bases, and a 'pop-up' fly ball was expected to be caught. **1926** *Amer. Speech* I. 369/1 A 'pop-up', for an infantile attempt to hit, is beautifully characteristic of the contempt prompting its use. **1950** *Sun* (Baltimore) 6 Oct. (B ed.) 19/6 He hoisted four infield pop-ups. **1974** *Evening Herald* (Rock Hill, S.

Carolina) 19 Apr. 7/1 Hager drew another intentional walk loading the bases but Holmes escaped the jam by getting Conner on a popup to third and Larry Hinson on a fly to right. **1978** *Time* 3 July 60/1 One of their catchers, Frank Mancuso, was a former lieutenant who had injured his back during parachute training; he could neither remain in the Army nor look skyward for a pop-up.

2. A pop-up toaster, trailer, etc.

1970 *New Yorker* 14 Nov. 49/3 Browned off like a piece of toast in a broken pop-up. **1976** *Times Lit. Suppl.* 6 Aug. 991 (Advt.), We manufacture jigsaw puzzles, pop-ups and other educational toys. **1978** *Sunday Sun-Times* (Chicago) 1 Jan. 122/1 Another popular RV type is the camping trailer, or 'pop-up'. **1978** *Detroit Free Press* 2 Apr. 17F/3, '75 Apache pop-up, slps 8, refrig, stove, heater, awning, exc cond.

B. *adj.* **a.** Designed to pop up or having a component that pops up. **b.** With a mechanism which causes something to pop up; esp. ***pop-up toaster***: an electric toaster in which the sliced bread pops up when it is ready.

1934 in WEBSTER. **1959** C. OGBURN *Marauders* (1960) ii. 65 We shot off quantities of ammunition, mostly at informal or pop-up targets. **1959** 'E. MCBAIN' *Pusher* v. 42 The precinct house.. did not boast chintz curtains or pop-up toasters. **1960** S. KAUFFMANN *If it be Love* I. vi. 90 An electric dishwasher and deep freeze and pop-up toaster. **1962** N. FREELING *Love in Amsterdam* I. 29 The pretty girl.. flipped a pop-up file like those for telephone numbers. **1962** *Which? Car Suppl.* Apr. 55/1 The Austin A60 was the only car which did not have pop-up knobs.. which show easily whether the doors are locked or not. **1963** S. MARSHALL *Exper. in Educ.* iv. 153 Every illustration is conceived and executed as a 'pop-up' scene. **1966** *Listener* 24 Nov. 755/1 This is a toaster of standard performance—the pop-up kind. **1972** *Times* 6 Dec. 22/6 A birthday card, with a pop-up centre. **1973** *Country Life* 19 July 151/3 For large lawns the most advanced system is the pop-up sprinkler.. small spray nozzles which only appear above turf level when the water is turned on. **1975** *Evening News* 26 Apr. 4/1 London motorists may soon face.. pop-up metal barriers.. to keep them off bus-only lanes. **1978** *Dumfries Courier* 20 Oct. 27/3 (Advt.), Hoover pop-up toaster in very good order, £8.50. **1978** *Times Lit. Suppl.* 1 Dec. 1400/3 Pop-up books are a different roaming ground for the imagination.

pop-valve: see POP-.

pop-vine: see POP *sb.*[1] 4.

'pop-'visit. [f. POP *v.*[1] + VISIT *sb.*] A short, hasty, or unannounced visit, in which one 'pops in'. Also ***pop-in visit***.

1767 STERNE *Tr. Shandy* IX. xxxiii, Obadiah had led his cow upon a pop-visit to him. **1822** W. IRVING *Braceb. Hall* (1823) II. 50, I have watched him, too, during one of his pop visits into the cottage. **1887** *Pall Mall G.* 30 June 6/1 Mr. Balfour.. is beginning to imitate the Leader of the House in the making of 'pop-in' visits.

pop-weed: see POP-.

popych, popysh(e, -ysse, obs. forms of POPISH.

popylyon, variant of POPULEON *Obs.*

poquauhock, obs. or var. form of QUAHAUG.

por, var. PORR, a poker, a thrust; obs. f. PURE *a.*

poraceous, obs. form of PORRACEOUS.

†porail, poveraille. *Obs.* Forms: α. 3 poueray1, 3-4 -ail(e, 4-5 -al(e, 4 pouraille, *Sc.* 5 poueralȝe, 5-6 -all, 6 puuerale. β. 4-5 poral, (purraile), 4-6 porail(e, -aill(e, -ayle, 5 -ayll(e, -eil, 6 -all, poorall, *Sc.* purale, -all, (7 *Sc.* -aill). [ME. *poveraile*, a. OF. *povraille, -alle* (a1236 in Godef.), collective sb. f. *povre* POOR + *-aille*:— L. *-ālia*, neut. pl. of *-ālis*, adjectival suffix.

The 16th c. Eng. and the Sc. point alike to an early ME. *pōrail*, syncopated from *poverail*, like *o'er* from *over*, *lōrd* from *hloverd*: cf. POOR *a.*]

1. Poor people as a class; the poor.

α. **1297** R. GLOUC. (Rolls) 5082 þe pouerail [*v.rr.* poueral, poraylle] ouer Seuerne fley þat þer was þo & bileuede vorþ in walis in sorwe & in wo. *a***1300** *Cursor M.* 12259 þat the poueral get sum bote. **1375** BARBOUR *Bruce* VIII. 368 The king, in set battalȝe, With a quheyn lik poueralȝe. **1514** *Aberdeen Regr.* (1844) I. 90 All vther persounis puuerale cumand within this burgh.

β. *c***1330** R. BRUNNE *Chron. Wace* (Rolls) 6664 How þat þe poraille [*v.r.* poueraile] Gracian slow. *c***1350** *Will. Palerne* 5123 Neuer þe pore porayle be piled for þi sake. *c***1475** *Pol. Poems* (Rolls) II. 285 A ordynaunce wolde be maad for the poore porayle, That in thyse dayes have but lytyll avayle. **1503-4** *Act 19 Hen. VII*, c. 32 The poraill of his Comens of this his land. **1549** *Aberdeen Regr.* (1844) I. 270 To eschait and daill the samin to the purale for thair contentioun. *a***1550** *Schole-ho. Women* 797 in Hazl. *E.P.P.* IV. 136 He gaue.. so liberall Parte of his goods to the porall. **1561** *Godly Q. Hester* (1873) 18 Almes to the poorall.

b. *pl.* Poor persons. *rare.*

*c***1380** WYCLIF *Wks.* (1880) 14 Bodily almes bi whiche þes poralis schulden be cloþid and kept fro deþ. **1388** —— *Prov.* xxx. 14 Nedi men of erthe, and the porails of men [1382 pore men].

2. The condition of the poor; poverty. *rare*[−1].

*c***1450** LYDG. *Secrees* 810 A kyng that.. them Relevith that be falle in porayle.

poral ('pɔərəl), *a.* [f. L. *por-us* PORE + -AL[1].] Of or pertaining to the pores of the body.

1879 G. MEREDITH *Egoist* xiv, As if it were.. by form of perspiration,.. unconscious poral bountifulness. **1926** *Jrnl. Bot.* LXIV. 144 The poral outline is much like that of *Pseudonavicella*. **1961** D. M. PILLSBURY et al. *Man. Cutaneous Med.* ii. 49 In acne the sebaceous gland may atrophy as a result of concomitant poral occlusion.

poran, obs. form of PURANA.

porbeagle ('pɔː,biːg(ə)l). [Of uncertain origin: orig. Cornish dialect. (Has been conjectured to be f. F. *porc* swine or *porpoise* (= *porcus piscis*) + BEAGLE, though no reason for such a name appears.)] A shark of the genus *Lamna*, esp. *L. cornubica*, sometimes attaining the length of 10 feet, and having a pointed snout; a mackerel-shark.

1758 BORLASE *Hist. Cornw.* 265 We have also another shark, which we call the Porbeagle, of which I give an icon. **1774** GOLDSM. *Nat. Hist.* (1862) II. II. i. 269 The Dog Fish, the Tope, the Porbeagle. **1863** C. A. JOHNS *Home Walks* 165 On two occasions I saw a shark lying on the beach. One was the species known as the Porbeagle, a malicious-looking monster about six feet long, with a mouth armed with three rows of very sharp triangular teeth. **1901** *Scotsman* 19 Sept. 5/1 The Natural History Museum at South Kensington has ..just received.. a porbeagle shark, caught.. off.. Skye.. 7 feet long, and weighed 350 lb.

porcapyne, pore de spyne, obs. forms of PORCUPINE.

porcate ('pɔːkət), *a. Zool.* [f. L. *porca* ridge + -ATE[2].] (See quot.) So **'porcated** *a.*

1826 KIRBY & SP. *Entomol.* IV. xlvi. 272 Porcate (*Porcata*). Having several parallel elevated longitudinal ridges. **1828** WEBSTER, *Porcated*, ridged, formed in ridges.

porcelain ('pɔəsɪlein, 'pɔəslən). Forms: α. (6 porcelana, 6-7 porcellana), 7- porcelain, (6-7 -cellan, -e, 6-9 -celaine, 7 -c'lane, 7-8 -celline, 8 -c'lain, 7-9 -celane; 6 (porseland) porslin, 7 porselan). β. 6-7 purcelan, 7 -ane, -ain, -aine, -ine, purcellan, pourcelain; 6-7 purslane, 6-8 -laine, 7 -lan; purselan, -lain. [a. F. *porcelaine* (also OF. 13th c. *pourcelaine*, still in Cotgr. 1611), a Venus shell, cowrie, or similar univalve; hence, the dense polished substance of these shells, and (from its resemblance to this) china-ware; ad. It. *porcellana* (13th c. in Marco Polo) in same senses, a deriv., of adjective form, of *porcella*, dim. of *porca*: cf. Florio 1611, '*Porcelle*, as *Porche*, the fine Cockle or Muscle shels which Painters put their colours in'; '*Porcellana*,.. Purcelane earth or dishes'. From It. also Sp., Pg. *porcelana*, and early 16th c. Eng. uses; also Ger. *porzellan*, Du. *porselein*, Da. *porcellæn*, Sw. *porslin*. In the Romanic langs., the name ran together with that of the herb PURSLANE, in It. *porcellana*, OF. *porcelaine, pourcelaine*.

The ulterior etymology of It. *porca, porcella* is unsettled; see Skeat, Mahn *Etymol. Untersuch.* (1855) 13 Körting *Lat. Rom. Wbch.* 7313.]

1. a. A fine kind of earthenware, having a translucent body and a transparent glaze; = CHINA[1] 3.

The name properly belongs to the hard paste or ***natural porcelain***, composed of KAOLIN combined in China with PETUNTSE, elsewhere with some siliceous material; but it is also applied to soft paste or ***artificial porcelain***, which is essentially a substance intermediate between glass and earthenware, and ***hybrid*** or ***mixed porcelain***, which contains a certain amount of kaolin.

α. *c***1530** in Ellis *Orig. Lett.* III. II. 242, iij. potts of Erthe payntid, callyd Porseland [? Porselana]. **1555** EDEN *Decades* 226 He had two vesselles made of the fine earth cauled *Porcellana*. **1582** LICHEFIELD tr. *Castanheda's Conq. E. Ind.* I. xlix. 106 Sixe great Tynages of fine Earth, which they doe call Porcelanas, and the same is verye costlye. **1596** HARINGTON *Apol. for Ajax* B b vj, Serued in as fine plate, and Porslin, as any is in the North. **1613** PURCHAS *Pilgrimage* (1614) 524 They vse much the powder of a certaine herb called Chia, of which they put as much as a Walnut-shell may containe, into a dish of Porcelane, and drinke it with hot water. **1644** EVELYN *Diary* 3 Feb., Here [in Paris] is a shop.., where are sold all curiosities naturall or artificial,.. as cabinets, shells, ivory, porselan. **1650** *Ibid.* 25 Apr., Of earth painted like Porcelain or China-ware. **1727** A. HAMILTON *New Acc. E. Ind.* II. li. 239 We have the same Sort of Clay in several Parts of Great Britain, that Porcelline is made of, but we want the warm Sun to prepare it. **1756** NUGENT *Gr. Tour, Germany* II. 260 Porcelane or Dresden china. **1825** BENTHAM *Ration. Rew.* 303 The potteries of Wedgwood and Bentley have excelled the porcelain of China. **1869** ROSCOE *Elem. Chem.* (1871) 246 Chromium Sesquioxide is employed as a green colour for painting on porcelain.

β. **1585** T. WASHINGTON tr. *Nicholay's Voy.* III. x. 90 The meat.. they lay into platters of purcelan. **1594** PLAT *Jewell-ho.* II. 35 In sawcers of glasse or purslaine. **1653** J. HALL *Paradoxes* 95 Purselain and Venice Glasses are the most apt to be broke. **1683** *Weekly Mem. Ingen.* 95 As for the pourcelain, 'tis not made of plaster or egg shells beaten fine, but of a certain earth. **1687** A. LOVELL tr. *Thevenot's Trav.* III. viii. 17 China also, as Purceline. **1703** *Lond. Gaz.* No. 3953/1 A Manufacture of Lame, Purslaine and Earthen Ware.

b. Used in *Dentistry*.

1845 C. A. HARRIS *Princ. & Pract. Dental Surg.* (ed. 2) VI. i. 541 A want of resemblance to the other teeth, in colour, transparency, and animation, was the great objection, that was urged against the porcelain. **1863** *Trans. Odontol. Soc.* III. 228 The universal use of porcelain as a material of which to construct artificial teeth. **1911** G. H. WILSON *Man. Dental Prosthetics* viii. 311 The materials entering into dental porcelain are feldspar, silica, kaolin or clay, alkalies, and pigments. **1956** J. N. ANDERSON *Appl. Dental Materials* xxiv. 324 Today, porcelain is finding a resurgence of life, particularly in its application to crowns. **1965** *Brit. Dental Jrnl.* CXIX. 251/1 One of the main criticisms levelled at dental porcelain is the liability to fracture under low impact stress.

c. *fig.* with allusion to the fineness, beauty, or fragility of this ware.

1640 BROME *Sparagus Gard.* v. viii, She is herself the purest piece of Purslane.. that e're had liquid sweet meats lick'd out of it. **1821** BYRON *Juan* IV. xi, Thrice fortunate! who, of that fragile mould, The precious porcelain of human clay, Break with the first fall. **1875** TENNYSON *Q. Mary* II. i, That fine porcelain Courtenay, Save that he fears he might be crack'd in using.. should be in Devon too.

†d. Applied in the 17th c. to the supposed natural plaster or paste then believed to congeal into porcelain. *Obs.*

1599 HAKLUYT *Voy.* II. II. 91 That earthen or pliable matter commonly called porcellan, which is pure white,.. wherof vessels of all kinds are very curiously framed. **1615** BACON *Argts. Law, Impeachm. Waste* Wks. 1859 VII. 528 If we had in England beds of porcelain, such as they have in China,—which porcelain is a kind of a plaster buried in the earth and by length of time congealed and glazed into that fine substance. **1658** PHILLIPS, *Porcelane*,.. also the cream, or flowring on the top of a certain chalky earth, in China steeped in water, of which they make China dishes.

2. An article or vessel made of porcelain; a piece of porcelain or china-ware. Usually in *pl.*

1604 E. G[RIMSTONE] *D' Acosta's Hist. Indies* IV. xvii. 259 They seethe it in purcelaines. **1660** F. BROOKE tr. *Le Blanc's Trav.* 47 Silks, purslanes, sendals,.. come from China. **1714** J. MACKY *Journ. thro' Eng.* (1724) I. iii. 58 In another Gallery.. [is] a good Collection of Porcelaines (China-ware) and other Curiosities. **1886** *Pall Mall G.* 19 Aug. 14/1 Windsor is full of these precious porcelains, and they adorn all her residences.

3. a. The COWRIE (*Cypræa moneta*). Hardly Eng., exc. in ***porcelain shell***.

1601 HOLLAND *Pliny* II. 88 The third [dye or colour] is ordinarily made of the purple & porcellane shel-fishes. **1601** R. JOHNSON *Kingd. & Commw.* 146 In the kingdomes of Caiacan and Carazan, certaine sea shels are currant, which some men terme Porcelline. **1677** PLOT *Oxfordsh.* 111 It must needs extravagantly exceed the biggest Nautilus or Porcellane-shell, both in latitude and number of turns. **1797** *Encycl. Brit.* (ed. 3) V. 129/1 In many places shells are current for coins; particularly a small white kind.. called in the Indies *cowries*, or *coris*, on the coast of Africa *bouges*, in America *porcelaines*. **1875** JEVONS *Money*, iv. 24 Cowry shells, which, under one name or another—chamgos, zimbis, bouges, porcelanes, &c.—have long been used.

b. A variety of pigeon, having dark brown and cream plumage.

1855 [see HYACINTH 3 b]. **1876** in R. Fulton *Illustr. Bk. Pigeons* xxv. 348 Porcelains.. are closely allied to Suabians. .. These birds are of a nice rich brown.., the under parts being of an ashen tint.

4. *attrib.* or as *adj.* **a.** *lit.* Of porcelain, made of porcelain or china.

1598 FLORIO, *Porcellana*,.. porcellan dishes. **1625** B. JONSON *Staple of N.* II. iv, In porc'lane dishes There were some hope. **1682** WHELER *Journ. Greece* III. 216 The Walls cased with Porcelane Tiles. **1759** JOHNSON *Rasselas* iv, A maid who had broken a porcelain cup. **1800** tr. *Lagrange's Chem.* II. 312 Bring the porcelain tube to a red heat. **1877** W. JONES *Finger-ring* 8 The porcelain finger-rings of ancient Egypt are extremely beautiful.

b. *fig.* Likened to porcelain in some respect: fine, delicate, fragile; superfine.

1638 W. CARTWRIGHT in *Jonsonus Virbius*, Though those thy thoughts, which the now queasy age Doth count but clods,.. Will come up porcelain-wit some hundreds hence. **1870** H. SMART *Race for Wife* i, The dispensary ball, at which the porcelain portion of the community danced. **1884** BIRRELL *Obiter Dicta* 183 China creeds and delicate porcelain opinions.

5. *attrib.* and *Comb.*, as ***porcelain-blue, earth, grain, -maker, -making, ware***; also ***porcelain-like, -tinted, -white*** adjs.; **porcelain cement**, a cement for mending china or glass; **porcelain colour**, a pigment employed for painting on porcelain; **porcelain-crab**, a crab of the genus *Porcellana*, so called from its smooth and polished shell; **porcelain enamel**, †(*a*) = GLAZE *sb.* 1; (*b*) = ENAMEL *sb.* 1 a; so **porcelain-enamelled** *a.*; hence **porcelain-enamel** *v. trans.*, **porcelain enamelling** *vbl. sb.*; **porcelain jasper** = PORCELLANITE: see JASPER *sb.*[1] 1; **porcelain-kiln** = *porcelain oven*; **porcelain lace**, porcelain in thin filaments made by soaking lace in the porcelain slip and then burning the threads and leaving the porcelain, used in the decorative work of Berlin porcelain; **porcelain oven**, the oven or kiln in which porcelain is baked; **porcelain-paper**, name of a kind of glazed French paper; **porcelain shell**: see sense 3; **porcelain spar**, a variety of ekebergite; **porcelain tooth**, a false tooth made of porcelain; **porcelain tower**, a famous tower at Nankin in China, covered with porcelain tiles.

1703 tr. *H. van Oosten's Dutch Gardener* II. xxxviii. 91 The Hyacinth that is handsom, must have a clear *Porcelin, or China Blew, or near white Colour. **1882** *Garden* 4 Nov. 396/1 Pretty porcelain-blue blossoms. **1600** J. PORY tr. *Leo's Africa* III. 209 They haue such abundance of *porcellan earth. *a***1774** HARTE *Confessor* 31 True fame, like porc'lain earth, for years must lay Bury'd, and mix'd with elemental clay. **1883** *Jrnl. Chem. Soc.* XLIV. 397 (*heading*) Composition of *porcelain enamels. **1924** E. G. BLAKE *Plumbing* II. iii. 40 Porcelain enamel is practically everlasting, does not chip with reasonable treatment, and can be kept perfectly clean with very little trouble. **1946** SIMONDS & BREGMAN *Finishing Metal Products* (ed. 2) xxxiii. 332 The compound word 'porcelain enamel' was made necessary by the wrong use of the word 'enamel' by manufacturers of paints. **1951** *Good Housek. Home Encycl.* 224/2 Porcelain enamel, being essentially a glass fused to a metal, has the properties of glass. **1955** INSLEY & FRÉCHETTE *Microsc. Ceramics & Cements* xi. 211 Porcelain enamel may be defined as an inorganic, glassy coating on a metal base, prepared by covering the preformed metal with a wet or dry powder coating of suitable composition and firing it for a few minutes to melt and smooth the surface. **1969** *Sears Catal.* Spring/Summer 13 Two porcelain-enamel shelves. **1921** *Chem. & Metall. Engin.* XXIV. 486/1 In 1860 the enameling of sheet iron was begun, and upon the advent of the drawing press and clay muffle in 1870 the process of *porcelain enameling steel as we know it today developed into the enameling industry. **1968** *Engineering* 26 July 171/3 Electron microbe examinations were made on a number of the magnesium-bearing alloys which had been porcelain enamelled without prior chromating treatments. **1896** J. J. LAWLER *Amer. Sanitary Plumbing* 229 (*heading*) The *porcelain-enamelled iron bathtub. **1935** H. R. SIMONDS *Finishing Metal Products* xxviii. 299 Some architects.. have been successful in making these buildings more attractive.. by giving them new faces made of porcelain-enameled steel. **1975** *Specification* (ed. 76) II. 109/2 Cast iron porcelain enamelled baths continue to maintain pre-eminence at the luxury end of the market. **1921** *Chem. & Metall. Engin.* XXIV. 486/2 A temperature difference of more than 400 deg. F. (204 deg. C.) between the flue temperature and muffle temperature is not justifiable in the light of the latest developments in *porcelain enameling ovens. **1968** *Engineering* 26 July 171/1 Since the end of the Second World War increasing attention has been given to the porcelain enamelling of aluminium, particularly in the fields of architecture and kitchen ware. **1796** KIRWAN *Elem. Min.* (ed. 2) I. 313 Porcellanite, *Porcelain Jasper, of Werner. **1876** PAGE *Adv. Text-bk. Geol.* xiv. 259 Shales converted into porcelain-jasper. **1893** E. A. BARBER *Pott. & Porc. U.S.* 258 It [*sc.* hard porcelain] is fired in biscuit at a low temperature, in the second story of the *porcelain-kiln. **1836–9** *Todd's Cycl. Anat.* II. 79/2 A smooth *porcelain-like deposit. **1908** *Westm. Gaz.* 29 June 2/4 Made of white, porcelain-like glass. **1964** S. DUKE-ELDER *Parsons' Dis. Eye* (ed. 14) xxvi. 378 In less severe cases a dense leucoma forms, porcelain-like in lime burns, and sight is lost. **1905** *Daily Chron.* 12 Aug. 3/1 The influence of Japanese decoration.. was predominant with the English *porcelain-makers of the eighteenth century. **1903** *Ibid.* 7 Jan. 3/2 The historian of an art, so many-sided in its efforts,.. as English *porcelain-making. **1914** E. A. DAWE *Paper* 129 **Porcelain paper*, thick transparent paper of the nature of celluloid, made of well-beaten pulp. Used for Christmas cards and similar work. **1962** F. T. DAY *Introd. to Paper* 119/1 *Porcelain papers*, bulky variety of glazed, imitation parchment, similar to celluloid. **1845** C. A. HARRIS *Princ. & Pract. Dental Surg.* (ed. 2) VI. i. 540 The manufacture of *porcelain teeth, did not for a long time promise to be of much advantage to dentistry. **1872** L. P. MEREDITH *Teeth* (1878) 227 Of late years these have been entirely superseded by porcelain teeth. **1976** R. M. BASKER et al. *Prosthetic Treatm. Edentulous Patient* vi. 56 If the patient's masticatory habits have been responsible for an excessive amount of wear in a short period of time, porcelain teeth must be used if the succeeding dentures are to be serviceable for an adequate period. **1881** *Scribner's Mag.* XXI. 76/1 A blonde beauty, of the delicate, *porcelain-tinted type. **1752** T. SALMON *Univ. Trav.* I. ii. 8/2 The grandest of all the Chinese Buildings is the *Porcelain Tower, which stands before one of the Gates of Nankin. **1638** SIR T. HERBERT *Trav.* (ed. 2) 37 The Bannians.. sell Callicoes, Chena-satten, *Purcellan ware. **1899** *Daily News* 29 June 6/7 A cameo.. wrought in a beautiful *porcelain-white upper stratum of a sardonyx.

Hence **'porcelainist**, a maker or decorator of porcelain; a connoisseur or collector of porcelains; **'porcelainite**, a trade-name for certain kinds of fine white stone-ware.

1890 in *Cent. Dict.* **1895** *Athenæum* 2 Mar. 287/3 Signatures of potters and European (not Asiatic) porcelainists.

'porcelain-clay. The clay used in the manufacture of porcelain; china-clay, kaolin. Also *fig.*

1690 DRYDEN *Don Sebastian* I. (1692) 7 This is the porcelain clay of humane kind. **1778** WOULFE in *Phil. Trans.* LXIX. 20 Such were the porcellane clay from Cornwall, the procellane clay from Saxony. **1837** CARLYLE *Fr. Rev.* II. I. i, Pity-struck for the porcelain-clay of humanity rather than for the tile-clay. **1838** LYELL *Elem. Geol.* ii. (1874) 12 The purest clay found in nature is 'porcelain' clay or Kaolin, which results from the decomposition of a rock composed of felspar and quartz.

porcelaine, -ane, -ayn, -ene, -eyne, etc., obs. ff. PURSLANE.

porcelainic (pɔəsə'leɪnɪk), *a.* [f. PORCELAIN + -IC.] = PORCELLANIC *a.*

1839 H. T. DE LA BECHE *Rep. Geol. Cornwall, Devon & W. Somerset* ix. 267 The fragments of them included in the greenstone of Kellan Head have a porcelainic appearance. **1971** *Materials & Technol.* II. v. 314 Ceramic ware of the porcelainic type was made in China from very early times.

porcelainize ('pɔəsɪlənaɪz), *v.* [f. PORCELAIN + -IZE.] *trans.* To convert into porcelain or a substance of the same nature.

1863 A. C. RAMSAY *Phys. Geog.* 14 It has been 'porcelainized', or baked like potter's clay. **1865** PAGE *Handbk. Geol. Terms* (ed. 2), *Porcelainised*,.. applied to clays, shales, and other stratified rocks that have been hardened and altered by igneous contact.

Hence **porcelaini'zation.**

1907 W. BURTON *Porcelain* (in *Athenæum* 16 Feb. 203/3) So that the porcelainisation of the body and the fusion of the glaze go side by side.

porcelainous ('pɔəslənəs), *a.* [f. as prec. + -OUS.] = PORCELLANEOUS.

1832 G. R. PORTER *Porcelain & Gl.* 318 Its toughness [etc.].. render this porcelainous glass well qualified for chemical vessels. **1852** DANA *Crust.* I. 108 Upper and under surface.. shining porcelainous.

†**'porcelet.** *Obs. rare.* Also 6 pour-. [a. F. *porcelet* (*de S. Antoine*) a woodlouse, *lit.* little pig (of St. Anthony), dim. of *porcel*, mod.F. *porceau* pig.] A woodlouse.

1578 LYTE *Dodoens* I. lxxvii. 115 Capraria brused with pourcelets.. and oyle of Roses, cureth the blind Hæmorrhoides. **1601** HOLLAND *Pliny* II. 323 Being ioined with hony, it healeth the sores occasioned by the biting of the Porcelets called Multipedæ.

porcellaneous (pɔəsə'leɪnɪəs), *a.* Also 9 -ela-. [f. It. *porcellana* PORCELAIN + -EOUS.] Of the nature of or resembling porcelain.

1799 HATCHETT in *Phil. Trans.* LXXXIX. 316 Of the porcellaneous shells, various species of Voluta, Cypræa, and others of a similar nature, were examined. **1800** *Ibid.* XC. 327 The porcellaneous shells resemble the enamel of teeth in the mode of formation. **1851** WOODWARD *Mollusca* I. 91 The shell of the ammonitidæ.. consists of an external porcellaneous layer.. and of an internal nacreous lining. **1880** *Archæologia* XLVI. 79 From the twenty-fifth century B.C. to the ninth century B.C., an opaque or porcellaneous glass.. was pretty extensively manufactured.

So **porcella'naceous**, *a.* in same sense (Ogilvie 1882); **porce'llanian**, of or pertaining to the porcelain crabs *Porcellana* (*Cent. Dict.* 1890).

porcellanic (pɔəsə'lænɪk), *a.* Also porcelanic. [f. as prec. + -IC. So mod.F. *porcelanique.*]

a. Like or having the texture of porcelain.

1829 *Glover's Hist. Derby* I. 85 Limestone.. of different texture and consistency, as compact, porcellanic, granular, crystalline. **1863** A. C. RAMSAY *Phys. Geog.* i. 21 Shales.. hardened or baked into a kind of porcellanic substance.

b. Characteristic or suggestive of porcelain.

1930 J. CANNAN *No Walls of Jasper* 29 His tooth brush dropped into its stand with the accustomed porcellanic chink.

porcellanite (pɔə'sɛlənaɪt). *Min.* Also -ela-. [a. Ger. *porzellanit* (J. T. A. Peithner 1794), f. *porzellan* PORCELAIN + *-it*, -ITE[1]. So F. *porcellanite.*] A hard naturally-baked clay, somewhat resembling jasper: also called *porcelain jasper*. Also, a synonym of *porcelain-spar* (Chester).

1796 KIRWAN *Elem. Min.* (ed. 2) I. 314 Porcelain Jasper, of Werner... Mr. Peithner called it porcellanite, which name should be continued. **1865** LIVINGSTONE *Zambesi* xi. 222 They [mountains] are generally of igneous or metamorphic rocks, clay-slate, or trap, with porcellanite and zeolite.

por'cellanize, *v.* [f. as next + IZE.] = PORCELAINIZE.

1882 J. GEIKIE in *Nature* XXVII. 45 The grits.. are hardened.. and the shales baked and porcellanised.

porcellanous (pɔə'sɛlənəs), *a.* [f. It. *porcellana* PORCELAIN + -OUS.] = PORCELLANEOUS.

1833 LYELL *Princ. Geol.* III. 368 The shale is converted into hard porcellanous jasper. **1851** WOODWARD *Mollusca* iv. 39 The most complex shell-structure is presented by the porcellanous gasteropoda. **1870** NICHOLSON *Man. Zool.* 47 The porcellanous shell is quite homogeneous in its composition.

porcellayn(e, -ine, -yne, obs. ff. PURSLANE.

porch (pɔətʃ). Also 3–7 **porche**, 5 **poorche**, 6 **portche**, 7 **portch**. [a. F. *porche*:—L. *portic-us* colonnade, gallery, porch. (OE. had *portic* = OHG. *pforzih*, directly from L. *porticus*.)]

1. a. An exterior structure forming a covered approach to the entrance of a building; sometimes applied to an interior space serving as a vestibule.

c **1290** *S. Eng. Leg.* I. 381/158 Est-ward þe dore and þe porche. *a* **1300** *E.E. Psalter* cxv. 18 In porches ofe lauerdes hous. **1340** *Ayenb.* 135 He is ase þe y-maymed ate porche of þe cherche. **1377** LANGL. *P. Pl.* B. XVI. 225 In a somer I hym seigh, as I satte in my porche. *c* **1430** LYDG. *Min. Poems* (Percy Soc.) 143 No stynkyng flesshe myht in the poorche abyde. **1530** PALSGR. 257/1 Portche of waynscot, *conterquayre*. **1590** SPENSER *F.Q.* II. ix. 24 Of hewen stone the porch was fayrely wrought. **1663** GERBIER *Counsel* 99 If a Portch be affected, let it then be a vaste Portuco. **1840** DICKENS *Old C. Shop* xvi, The church was old and grey, with ivy clinging to the walls, and round the porch. **1898** G. B. SHAW *Candida* I. 80 The parsonage is semi-detached, with a front garden and a porch. **1916** JOYCE *Portrait of Artist* (1969) 162 He pushed open the latchless door of the porch and passed through the naked hallway into the kitchen. **1919** G. B. SHAW *O'Flaherty V.C.* in *Heartbreak House* 167 The porch, painted white, projects into the drive. **1980** R. McCRUM *In Secret State* vii. 60 He returned to the porch, unlocked the front door and stepped inside.

b. *transf.* and *fig.*

1611 B. JONSON *Catiline* I. i, Not infants in the porch of life were free. **1692** WAGSTAFFE *Vind. Carol.* Introd. 12 But I stay too long in the Porch. **1866** B. TAYLOR *Passing the Sirens* 222 It penetrates The guarded porches of the brain.

c. A small platform outside the hatch of a spacecraft.

1969 *Daily Tel.* 14 July 16/5 Wearing their bulky suits and life-support packs, they will open the narrow hatch. Armstrong will squeeze himself out on to a small platform called the 'porch'. **1970** N. ARMSTRONG et al. *First on Moon* xi. 266 Armstrong: 'Yes. Got it... Okay, Houston, I'm on the porch.'

2. In the north of England applied to a transept or side chapel in a church.

1522 *Durham Wills* (Surtees) II. 105 My body to be buried in the Churche of Kellowe in my Porch of or Ladye. **1613** *Vestry Bks.* (Surtees) 167 Rec. of Mr Robert Hilyard for the halfe part of the porch in the North Allye, which part Mr Hilyard did new build of his owne cost.. ijs. **1794** W. HUTCHINSON *Hist. Durham* III. 151 On the north side is a porch, in which lie the tombs of Conyers. **1893** C. HODGES in *Reliquary* Jan. 5 The term porch is used for a transept or chapel in the north of England to the present day.

3. †**a.** A colonnade, portico, cloister, stoa; spec. in the East, such a place used as a hall of justice; hence, the tribunal held there. Cf. PORTE. *Obs.*

c **1420** LYDG. *Story Thebes* II. in *Chaucer's Wks.* (1561) 362/2 In a porche, bilte of square stones.. Where the domes, and ples of the toun Were executed, and lawes of the king. **1585** T. WASHINGTON tr. *Nicholay's Voy.* I. xxi. 26b, [A] square place enuironed with.. pillers in two ranks after the manner of a porch. **1599** HAKLUYT *Voy.* II. 295 Your Maiesties Embassadour resident in the blessed and glorious porch of his imperiall Highnesse. **1601** SHAKS. *Jul. C.* I. iii. 126 They stay for me In Pompeyes Porch: for now this fearefull Night, There is no stirre, or walking in the streetes. **1687** A. LOVELL tr. *Thevenot's Trav.* II. 31 A Gallery or very wide vaulted Porch, runs all round the Court.

b. A verandah. *N.Amer.*

1832 J. P. KENNEDY *Swallow Barn* II. 41 Hafen Blok was regaling his circle of auditors in the porch at Swallow Barn. **1840** MALCOM *Trav.* 43/1 About twenty or thirty patients, mostly Chinese, meet daily in his porch at four o'clock. **1867** D. G. MITCHELL *Rur. Stud.* 99 A country house without a porch is like a man without an eyebrow. **1901** S. E. WHITE *Westerners* 251 Then there was the gambler, the faro man, who sat on the hotel 'porch'. **1916** H. L. WILSON *Somewhere in Red Gap* v. 195 Wilbur Todd had once endeavoured to hold her hand out on the porch at a country-club dance. **1925** F. SCOTT FITZGERALD *Great Gatsby* (1926) i. 14 The two young women preceded us out onto a rosy-colored porch, open toward the sunset, where four candles flickered on the table in the diminished wind. **1932** *Atlantic Monthly* Feb. 193/2 Broad porches ran the length of the house on both sides. **1948** *Manch. Guardian Weekly* 30 Dec. 13/1 President Truman has left the neo-Roman slabs of Washington to go home to Independence in Missouri, where he can feel more comfortable sitting on the back porch of an old frame house. **1968** *Globe Mag.* (Toronto) 13 Jan. 13/1 Raymond Souster would be the amiable fellow on the porch reminiscing with complacent nostalgia for lost times. **1978** C. MACLEOD *Rest you Merry* ix. 60 The student .. had dumped the suitcases on the short walk in front of the brick house, and was studying the porch.

c. A small utility room attached to the back of a house. *N. Amer. dial.*

1916 *Dialect Notes* IV. 335 [Nantucket] *Porch*, an ell kitchen. **1929** *Amer. Speech* V. 124 'Piazzer' was the only term applied to a veranda [*sc.* in the dialect of Maine]. The 'porch' was a sort of extra shed-kitchen used as a laundry. **1969** in Halpert & Story *Christmas Mumming in Newfoundland* 211 The 'porch' is a small room at the rear of the house used for storing wood, hanging coats, cooking utensils, and so on. A door, which is always kept closed, leads from the porch into the kitchen.

4. spec. ***the Porch***, the Painted Porch (Gr. στοὰ ποικίλη), a public ambulatory in the agora of ancient Athens, to which Zeno the philosopher and his disciples resorted; hence (οἱ τῆς στοᾶς, those of the porch), the Stoic school, the Stoic philosophy.

[**14..** *Voc.* in Wr.-Wülcker 613/35 *Stoica*, a porche peyntyd.] **1670** *Moral State Eng.* 101 They commended the ingenuity of the ancient Schools and Porch. **1677** GALE *Crt. Gentiles* II. III. 132 Specially from Plato's Academie; some also from Zeno's porch. **1693** DRYDEN *Juvenal* (1697) p. lxxx, Ev'n there he forgets not the Precepts of the Porch. **1751** J. BROWN *Shaftesb. Charact.* 160 In the same high style of the Athenian porch, he passeth judgment on the hopes of the religious. **1871** BLACKIE *Four Phases* I. 51 The words of a great son of the porch.

5. *Coal-mining.* An arched excavation at the bottom of a shaft. *dial.*

1883 GRESLEY *Gloss. Coal Mining*, *Porch*, (Yorks.) the arching at the pit bottom inset. **1903** *Eng. Dial. Dict.* s.v., At the bottom of the shaft Dick and I made a porch for about 6 yards... From the end of the porch I cleared out and packed an old bord.

†**6.** *Billiards.* (See quot.) *Obs.*

a **1700** B. E. *Dict. Cant. Crew*, *Pass*,.. a Term of Billiards, when the Ball goes through the Court or Porch, it is said to pass.

7. *Television.* In a video signal, either of the two periods of line blanking immediately before and after the line-synchronizing pulse; known respectively as the ***front*** and ***back porch***.

1941 *Proc. IRE* XXIX. 307/1 The difference between 0·06*H* and 0·07*H*, namely 1 per cent of *H*, is the 'front porch' of the pedestal. **1953** AMOS & BIRKINSHAW *Television Engin.* I. ii. 32 The period of blanking level immediately following the line-sync signal.. is termed the back porch. *Ibid.*, There is a brief period of blanking level occurring immediately before each line-sync signal. This is known as the front porch. **1965** *Wireless World* Aug. 389/1 The phasing of the oscillator is determined by the duration of the front porch of the composite video wave-form, the flyback time of the line circuit and the tightness of lock. **1966** [see *line blanking* s.v. LINE *sb.*[2] 32].

8. *attrib.* and *Comb.*, as ***porch chair***, ***-door***, ***-gable***, ***-pillar***, ***rail***, ***roof***, ***-seat***, ***-tomb***, ***-tower***, ***-trellis***, ***-way***; **porch-climber** *N. Amer. slang*, a burglar; hence ***porch-climbing*** ppl. adj.; **porch-post support**, see quot. 1875.

1908 *Sears, Roebuck Catal.* 753/2 Folding porch chair, made of wood frame with denim body. **1911** *Daily Colonist* (Victoria, B.C.) 25 Apr. 6/7 (Advt.), Porch and Verandah Chairs. There are no chairs more suitable for the porch or verandah than Sea Grass or Rattan. **1948** *Democrat* 22 Apr. 1/7 Porch and Lawn Chairs, Swings, Gliders and Metal Tables. **1900** ADE *More Fables* 218 He had a Chinaman for a Servant, because the Chinaman did not know he was an Author, but supposed him to be a Retired Porch-Climber. **1901** 'J. FLYNT' *World of Graft* 27 The remaining third of Chicago's professional thieves are good, bad, and indifferent 'sneaks', 'porch-climbers', [etc.]. **1916** *Daily Colonist* (Victoria, B.C.) 27 July 6/3 Some well-intentioned citizens see a potential second-storey man or porch-climber in everyone who is not within doors after the stroke of midnight. **1927** *Scribner's Mag.* Feb. 180/1 The depredations of porch-climbers, safe-blowers,..and common thieves were a source of alarm. **1912** *Collier's* 28 Dec. 15/3 Beware of the beautiful ladies who have porch-climbing, safe-blowing pals. *c* **1440** *Alphabet of Tales* 349 þer was made abown þe porch-dure many ymagis of stone. **1855** *Ecclesiologist* XVI. 337 A part of this porch-gable was to be erected in 1854. **1875** KNIGHT *Dict. Mech.*, *Porch-post Support*, a casting placed between the foot of a post and the floor of a porch to prevent decay of the two at that point. **1929** *Oxf. Poetry* 53 Brown meadow grass and cat-tails My banisters and porch rails—All these belonged to me. **1948** E. POUND *Pisan Cantos* (1949) lxxvi. 43 As the cat walked the porch rail at Gardone. **1869** 'MARK TWAIN' *Innoc. Abr.* xliii. 448 The porch-roof is composed of tremendous slabs of stone. **1552** HULOET, Porche seate, *præstega*. **1880** *Archæol. Cant.* XIII. 377 This porch-tomb's canopy is handsomely carved. **1875** PARKER *Gloss. Archit.* s.v., They have sometimes rooms over them, and are carried up as many stories in height as the rest of the building, and this projection is called the porch-tower. **1884** in *Harper's Mag.* Oct. 703/2 There are..friendly porchways to get under.

Hence **porched** *a.* [-ED[2]], having a porch; **'porchless** *a.*, without a porch.

1859 F. FRANCIS *N. Dogvane* (1888) 236 The porched door-way of the hostelry. **1873** WHITNEY *Other Girls* xv, The pillars in the porched veranda. **1881** T. HARDY *Laodicean* III. ii, He reached the porchless door.

porchace, -as, -ase, -ass, obs. ff. PURCHASE.

porcine ('pɔːsaɪn), *a.* [a. F. *porcin, -e*, ad. L. *porcīnus* of or belonging to a hog, swinish.]

1. Of or consisting of swine; related to or resembling the swine. (In quot. *a* 1845 *humorously*, Made of swine's flesh; pork-.)

1656 BLOUNT *Glossogr.*, *Porcine*.., of or belonging to an Hog, hogish. **1782** A. MONRO *Compar. Anat.* (ed. 3) 5 Common to all quadrupeds, the porcine kind excepted. *a* **1845** HOOD *Sausage Maker's Ghost* i, He..drove a trade In porcine sausages. **1862** TROLLOPE *N. Amer.* II. 107 In this portion of the world the porcine genus are all hogs. One never hears of a pig.

2. Resembling or suggesting a hog, like that of a hog (in appearance, manners, or character); swinish, hoggish, piggish.

1660 GAUDEN *Life Bp. Brownrigg* 236 Their Physiognomy is canine, vulpine, caprine, porcine, lupine or leonine. **1811** L. M. HAWKINS *C'tess & Gertr.* I. 34 Do we hear of such a porcine exhibition of the philosophy of Epicurus as that of Cuzzoni? **1866** G. MACDONALD *Ann Q. Neighb.* xvii, The porcine head of the church-warden was not on his shoulders by accident. **1880** SWINBURNE *Stud. Shaks.* i. (ed. 2) 64 Three doggrel sonnets..noticeable only for their porcine quality of prurience.

Hence **porcinity** (pɔː'sɪnɪtɪ) *nonce-wd.*, porcine quality, piggishness; in quot. as a humorous title.

1859 SALA *Gas-light & D.* vi, Very few customers..at the bar of the Green Hog; yet does its verdant porcinity considerable business with Barclay Perkins [brewers].

porcion(e, -oun, -onel, obs. ff. PORTION, -AL.

porcipize, porcpisce, etc., obs. ff. PORPOISE *sb.*

porciunkle, var. form of PORTIUNCLE *Obs.*

porckespicke, obs. form of PORCUPINE.

† **porcu'lation.** *Obs. rare*[−0]. [ad.L. *porculātiōn-em*, agent-n. from **porculāre*, f. *porculus* pig, porkling, dim. of *porcus* swine.]

1623 COCKERAM, *Porculation*, a feeding of swine. **1656** in BLOUNT *Glossogr.* **1658–78** in PHILLIPS.

porcules, -ier, porcupice, obs. ff. PORTCULLIS, PORPOISE *sb.*

porcupine ('pɔːkjʊpaɪn), *sb.* Forms: see below. [ME. *porke despyne, porkepyn*, etc., a. OF. and Pr. *porc espin* (*c* 1220 in Godef.), also *porc d'espine* (*c* 1275) = Sp. *puerco espin*, Pg. *porco espinho*, It. *porcospino* (also *porco spinoso*), corresp. to a L. type **porcus spinus*; f. *porco, porc*:—L. *porcus* hog, pig + *spino, espin, épin*, deriv. of L. *spīna* thorn (cf. L. *spīnus*, Sp. *espin*, OF. *espin* a thorn-tree). The genesis of the compound is not very clear, unless it began as short for *porco spinoso*:—L. type **porcus spīnōsus* spiny or prickly pig. The *β*, *γ*, and *δ* forms appear to be English corruptions, due to imperfect apprehension of the foreign word, and to 'popular etymology' identifying the ending with *pen, point*, etc.; the type *portepyne* may have arisen out of F. *por(c) d'épin*, with *c* mute. The *ε* forms really represent a different compound, viz. F. *porc-épic*, in 16th c. *porc-espic*, OF. and Pr. *porc-espi* (13th c. in Littré), in which the second element is F. *épi*, OF. *espi*:—L. *spīcus, -um*, collateral forms of *spīca* spike. (This form, confined to Fr. and Pr., was prob. and alteration of *porc espin*.)]

1. a. A rodent quadruped of the genus *Hystrix* or family *Hystricidæ*, having the body and tail covered with defensive erectile spines or quills; formerly supposed to shoot or dart its spines at an enemy.

The Old-World porcupines (subfamily *Hystricinæ*) are terrestrial, and have long quills, variegated in colour, and often used for penholders; the New-World porcupines (subfamily *Sphingurinæ* or *Synetherinæ*) are more or less arboreal, and have short quills.

α. 5 **porke despyne, porc de spyne,** (5 *Sc.* **porpapyne**), 6 **porcapyne, porcupyne, porkepyn(e, porkpine,** 6–7 **porkepine,** 7 **porkespine, porcuspine, porcupin, porkpen,** 6– **porcupine.**

? *a* **1400** *Morte Arth.* 183 Pacokes and plouers in platers of golde, Pygges of porke despyne, þat pasturede neuer. *c* **1400** MAUNDEV. xxviii. [xxxi.], Wee clepen hem Porcz de Spyne [*F.* Porcz Spinous, *v.rr.* porcs espinoys; pors espis]. **1423** JAS. I. *Kingis Q.* clv, The nyce ape; the werely porpapyne. *c* **1470** HENRYSON *Mor. Fab.* v. (*Parl. Beasts*) xvi, Otter, and Aip, and Pennit Porcupyne [*Bann. MS.* porcapyne]. **1530** PALSGR. 256/2 Porkepyn a beest, *porc espin*. **1538** ELYOT, *Histrix, icis*, a beaste hauyng sharpe prickes on his backe, called a porkpine [**1545, 1548**, porkepyne]. **1601** HOLLAND *Pliny* I. 215 The Porkpen hath the longer sharp pointed quilles, and those, when he stretcheth his skin, he sendeth and shooteth from him. *Ibid.* II. 364 Whatsoever vertue we attribute unto hedgehogs, the same is more effectuall in the porkespine. **1607** TOPSELL *Four-f. Beasts* (1658) 457 Of the Porcuspine or Porcupine. **1613** PURCHAS *Pilgrimage* (1614) 831 Here are store of Deare, Hares, Conies, Hogs,.. Porkepines. **1676** *Phil. Trans.* XI. 714 That Porcupins kill Lions, by darting into their body their quills. **1795** SOUTHEY *Joan of Arc* VII. 179 Heavy, thick-bristled with the hostile shafts, Even like a porcupine. **1872** DARWIN *Emotions* iv. 93 Porcupines rattle their quills and vibrate their tails when angered.

β. 5 **portpen, portepyne,** 6 **porpyn, -in.**

1413 *Pilgr. Sowle* (Caxton 1483) III. viii. 55 These sowles ..were al ful of pryckes lyke to a portpen. *c* **1440** *Jacob's Well* 154 Lyche a beeste of Inde þat is clepyd a portepyn. **1552** HULOET, Porpyn beaste, hauinge prickes on his backe, *histrix*. **1570** LEVINS *Manip.* 134/13 A Porpin, *histrix*.

γ. 5 **poork poynt, porpoynt, perpoynt.**

c **1440** *Promp. Parv.* 409/2 Poork poynt,..(or perpoynt, ..*MS. S.* porpoynte).

δ. 6 **porpantine, -pentyn, -pintine, purpentine,** 6–7, 20 (*humorous*) **porpentine,** (6 **porcuntine**).

(*Porpentine* was the form known to Shaks. who uses it 7 times, in 4 of these as the sign of an inn.)

1530 in *Ancestor* XI. (1904) 180 Prestwich..beryth to his creest a porpantine in his kinde. **1545** ASCHAM *Toxoph.* I. (Arb.) 31 Nature gaue example of shotyng first, by the Porpentine, which shote his prickes. **1562** BULLEYN *Bulwark, Bk. Simples* 80b, What is the nature of a beast called the Porpintine? **1585** GREENE *Planetomachia* Wks. (Grosart) V. 97 The enuious Porcuntine, who coueting to strike others with her pennes leaueth her selfe void of any defence. **1589** PUTTENHAM *Eng. Poesie* II. xi. [xii.] (Arb.) 118 The Purpentines nature is, to such as stand aloofe, to dart her prickles from her. **1593** SHAKS. *2 Hen. VI*, III. i. 363 And fought so long, till that his thighes with Darts Were almost like a sharpe-quill'd Porpentine. **1602** —— *Ham.* I. v. 20 Each particular haire to stand an end, Like Quilles vpon the fretfull Porpentine. **1657** HOWELL *Londinop.* 24 Leopards, Linxes, and Porpentines. **1936** T. S. ELIOT *Coll. Poems 1909–1935* 147 How unpleasant to meet Mr. Eliot! With a bobtail cur In a coat of fur And a porpentine cat.

ε. 6 **porkenpick, pork(e)pik, porkspik, porcupike,** 6–7 **porkespick(e,** 7 **porke-espike, porcke-spicke,** 8 (*humorous*) **porcupig.**

1561 HOLLYBUSH *Hom. Apoth.* 13 They cluster together lyke porkenpickes. **1600** J. PORY tr. *Leo's Africa* II. 90 Their game were hare, deere, porcupikes. **1613** PURCHAS *Pilgrimage* (1614) 750 Pater nosters and chaines, enterlaced made of the haire of the Porkespicke died of diuers colours. *a* **1700** *Dragon of Wantley* 84 in Percy *Reliques* (1765) III. III. xi. 283 You would have thought him for to be, Some Egyptian porcupig.

b. A figure of this animal, esp. as a device. ***Order of the Porcupine*** (F. *ordre du Porc-épic*): see quot. 1725.

1578 *Inv. R. Wardr.* (1815) 248 Ane cannon of the fonte merkit with the porkspik. *Ibid.* 250 Ane uther cannon.. markit with the porkpik. **1589** PUTTENHAM *Eng. Poesie* II. xi. (Arb.) 118 He gaue for his deuice the Porkespick. **1725** COATS *Dict. Heraldry* 279 Lewis [XII] of France..in the year 1394..instituted this Order of the Porcupine, which he had before chosen for his Device.

† **c.** Old name of a certain fixed star. *Obs.*

1503 *Kalender of Sheph.* I. vij, Wnder the syng of lybra.. wnder ys xvii. degre so aleftys oon stern fyxyt, that oon that the sheppar[s] callys pork apyk [*ed.* **1506** porcarpyke].

d. ***English porcupine***: applied to the hedgehog.

1834 MARY HOWITT *Sk. Nat. Hist.* (1851) 111 Thou poor little English porcupine.

2. *fig.* **a.** Applied allusively to a person. **b.** In quot. 1861, a prickly multitude (of pens).

1594 ? GREENE *Selimus* Wks. (Grosart) XIV. 286 What are the vrchins crept out of their dens, Vnder the conduct of this porcupine? **1606** SHAKS. *Tr. & Cr.* II. i. 27 *Ther.* Thou art proclaim'd a foole... *Aia.* Do not Porpentine, do not; my fingers itch. **1861** FITZ-PATRICK *Life Doyle* (1880) II. 7 This letter to Lord Farnham drew forth a porcupine of pens.

† **3.** Name of a form in which meat was dressed.

1769 MRS. RAFFALD *Eng. Housekpr.* (1778) 89, To make a Porcupine of a Breast of Veal. *Ibid.* 299 To make a cold Porcupine of Beef.

4. Applied to machines or mechanical devices having numerous projecting spikes or teeth; *esp.* an apparatus for heckling flax, worsted, or cotton; a kind of masher used in brewing.

1869 W. MOLYNEUX *Burton-on-Trent* 243 *note*, At some of the breweries the porcupine is supplanted by an instrument known as Steele's Patent Mashing Machine. **1875** KNIGHT *Dict. Mech.*, *Porcupine*, a heckling apparatus for flax; or a cylindrical heckle for worsted yarn. **1891** R. MARSDEN *Cotton Spinning* (ed. 4) 87 This porcupine is another opener, whose chief difference from the willow [etc.].

5. a. A small Australian monotreme, the echidna or spiny ant-eater, *Tachyglossus aculeatus*. **b.** = *porcupine fish*: see 6.

1832 J. BISCHOFF *Sk. Hist. Van Diemen's Land* ii. 29 The native porcupine or echidna is not very common. **1843** J. BACKHOUSE *Narr. Visit Austral. Colonies* vii. 89 The Porcupine of this land..is a squat species of ant-eater, with short quills among its hair. **1875** *Melbourne Spectator* 4 Sept. 213/2 The echidna, or native porcupine. **1888** GOODE *Amer. Fishes* 205 In this limpid pool were..the angel-fish, the parrot fish,..the porcupine. **1924** *Truth* (Sydney) 27 Apr. 6 *Porcupine*, a rather large rodent with spiked quills, and which feeds chiefly upon bark, leaves and ants. **1944** *Living off Land* ii. 29 The spiny ant-eater (sometimes called porcupine) is a good food. **1970** W. D. L. RIDE *Guide Native Mammals Austral.* xii. 191 The most widespread Australian monotreme is the Echidna or Spiny-anteater which is called 'The Porcupine' by many country people.

6. *attrib.* and *Comb.*, as ***porcupine mustachio, quill, skin, tribe***; ***porcupine-backed, -like*** adjs.; **porcupine ant-eater** = sense 5 a; **porcupine crab**, a Japanese crab (*Lithodes hystrix*), having spiny carapace and limbs; **porcupine disease**, a malformation of the skin characterized by the growth of spine-like projections (Billings *Med. Dict.*); **porcupine fish**, a fish having the skin covered with spines, as *Diodon hystrix*; a sea-porcupine; **porcupine grass**, name for (*a*) *Triodia irritans* and other species, of Australia, with stiff sharp-pointed leaves; (*b*) *Stipa spartea*, of the western U.S., with long stiff awns; hence **porcupine-grass ant**, an Australian ant (*Hypoclinia flavipes*) which makes its nest round the root of a species of porcupine grass (*Triodia pungens*); **porcupine hair** (*Path.*) = HYSTRICIASIS; **porcupine man** (*Path.*), a man affected with *porcupine disease*; **porcupine roller**, a roller in a spinning-machine, set with projecting spikes (cf. 4); **porcupine skin disease**, = *porcupine disease*; † **porcupine stone**, a hard concretion alleged to be found in the head or body of a porcupine; **porcupine teeth**, the teeth of a contrivance for carding wool; **porcupine-wood**, the wood of the coco palm, which when cut across shows variegated markings like those of a porcupine-quill.

1847 *Porcupine ant-eater [see ECHIDNA]. **1860** G. BENNETT *Gatherings of Naturalist in Australasia* vii. 147 The Porcupine Ant-eater of Australia..and the Ornithorhynchus..form the only two genera of the order Monotremata. **1867** WOOD *Pop. Nat. Hist.* I. 247 Echidna or Porcupine Ant-eater.—*Echidna Hystrix.* **1899** *Daily News* 10 Apr. 8/2 The duck-billed platypus and the porcupine ant-eater, two of the chief objects of the expedition. **1598** E. GILPIN *Skial.* (1878) 52 Gulfe-brested is he, silent, and profound *Porpentine backed, for he lies on thornes. **1681** GREW *Musæum* I. v. ii. 106 A sort of *Porcupine-Fish. **1773** *Gentl. Mag.* XLIII. 220 From these I will proceed to the exotics,..the Porcupine Fish, the Porcupine Globe Fish, the Porcupine Bladder Fish. **1885** LADY BRASSEY *The Trades* 407 'Porcupine-fish' (*Chilomycterus reticulatus*), looking..very much more like hedgehogs swimming about than porcupines. **1830** P. J. HOLDSWORTH *Station-hunting on Warrego*, Rough tufts of bristly grass..stemmed like quills (and thence termed '*porcupine'). **1902** *Westm. Gaz.* 2 Apr. 10/2 The desert North of Lake Eyre, where the vegetation consists largely of porcupine grass—a serious obstacle to explorers and useless as fodder. **1822** GOOD *Study Med.* IV. 686 The hystriacis or *porcupine hair of Plenck. **1859** DARWIN *Orig. Spec.* vii. (1878) 201 Monstrosities, such as six-fingered men, *porcupine men. **1603** DEKKER *Wonderfull Yeare* B ij, The quills of his stiffe *Porcupine mustachio. **1664** POWER *Exp. Philos.* I. 5 Her body is..stuck all over with great black Bristles, like *Porcupine quills, set all in parallel order. **1836** W. IRVING *Astoria* II. 51 A spear or bow decorated with beads, porcupine quills and painted feathers. **1884** W. S. B. McLAREN *Spinning* (ed. 2) 107 A revolving brush, or star wheel, or *porcupine roller, is placed at H,..which guides the fibres forward. **1809** A. HENRY *Trav.* 146 The fat of our deer was melted down, and the oil filled six *porcupine-skins. **1899** *Allbutt's Syst. Med.* VIII. 670 *Porcupine skin disease. **1676** *Phil. Trans.* XI. 757 There is another Stone, highly esteem'd, called the *Porcupine stone, which is in the head of this Animal, though sometimes also in its belly. **1845** *Specif. Lister's Patent* No. 11004. 2 Card, or what are known in the trade as '*porcupine teeth' are caused to operate upon wool to comb the same. **1857** HENFREY *Bot.* §569 The wood of the Cocoa-nut Palms..(*Porcupine-wood). **1887** MOLONEY *Forestry W. Afr.* 441 The wood is commercially known as Porcupine wood, and is used in India for rafters and ridge poles, house-posts,..also for spear-handles, walking-sticks, and fancy work.

Hence **'porcupinal** *a.*, suggestive of a porcupine, prickly (in quot. *fig.*); **'porcupine** *v. trans.*, to make like a porcupine; to cause (the hair) to stand on end like a porcupine's quills; **'porcupinish, 'porcupiny** *adjs.*, resembling or suggesting a porcupine.

1716 M. DAVIES *Athen. Brit.* II. 139 'Tis not call'd Declamation or Invective, or Satyr, but a certain Mediastin Genius, porcupin'd all over with all the three. **1827** *Mirror* II. 37/2 Pull your gills and porcupine your hair. **1829** SOUTHEY *Sir T. More* I. 15, I had now..a distinct sense of that sort of porcupinish motion over the whole scalp which is so frequently described by the Latin poets. **1846** R. FORD *Gatherings from Spain* xii. 139 The nerves tighten up into the catgut of an overstrung fiddle, getting attuned to the porcupinal irritability of the tension of the mind. **1857** R. WILLIAMS *Rev. Bp. Ollivant's Charge* 60 You may goad any one, by three years of organised libelling,..into a porcupinish method of expressing himself. **1890** *Sat. Rev.* 2 Aug. 151/1 A rather porcupiny, and not wholly consistent bundle [of prejudices].

porcupisce, -pise, obs. forms of PORPOISE *sb.*

porcyon(e, -oun, obs. forms of PORTION.

pore (pɔə(r)), *sb.*[1] Forms: 4-6 poore, 6 powre, poure, 5- pore. [a. F. *pore* (*porre*, 1312 in Hatz.-Darm.) = Sp., It. *poro*, ad. L. *porus*, a. Gr. πόρος passage, pore.]

1. A minute opening, orifice, aperture, perforation, or hole (usually, one imperceptible to the unaided eye), through which fluids (rarely solid bodies) pass or may pass. **a.** In an animal body (or substance); esp. applied to those in the skin (the orifices of the ducts of the sweat-glands).

1387 TREVISA *Higden* (Rolls) I. 53 þe contrarie is of norþeren men, in þe whiche colde wiþ oute stoppeþ smale holes and poorus, and holdeþ þe hete wiþ ynne. **1422** tr. *Secreta Secret., Priv. Priv.* 239 Men wyche haue the complexcion hote and stronge, and haue throgh al the body the ouertures large, that clerkys callyth Pores. **1563** HYLL *Art Garden.* (1593) 145 A stopping both of the vaines & poures. **1582** HESTER *Secr. Phiorav.* I. xv. 15 Those..you shal washe with Aqua vitæ, because it openeth the powres. **1601** B. JONSON *Poetaster* Prol., A freezing sweate Flowes forth at all my pores. **1704** F. FULLER *Med. Gymn.* (1711) 5 A sudden Constriction of the Pores of the Skin. **1822-34** *Good's Study Med.* (ed. 4) I. 271 The articulations are long and narrow, with marginal pores by which it [tape-worm] attaches itself to the intestines. **1858** O. W. HOLMES *Aut. Breakf.-t.* xi, As a hide fills its pores lying seven years in a tan-pit.

b. *fig.* (and in *fig.* expressions), esp. in phrase ***at every pore***.

1632 J. HAYWARD tr. *Biondi's Eromena* 53 Their raies.. penetrating through the pores of the heart, made themselves knowen. *a* **1720** SHEFFIELD (Dk. Buckhm.) *Wks.* (1753) I. 13 Love's pow'r can penetrate the hardest hearts; And through the closest pores a passage find. **1847** EMERSON *Repr. Men, Goethe* Wks. (Bohn) I. 388 He sees at every pore. **1865** DICKENS *Mut. Fr.* III. x, I see him chafe and fret at every pore.

c. In a plant (or vegetable substance); as the stomata in the epidermis of leaves, etc., or the small openings in certain anthers and capsules when ripe, for the discharge of the pollen or seeds.

1398 TREVISA *Barth. De P.R.* XVII. i. (Tollem. MS.), Tren wiþ þinne substaunce and nouȝt harde, but ful of holes, and poores. **1634** HABINGTON *Castara* (Arb.) 20 The flowers adore The Deity of her sex, and through each pore Breath forth her glories. **1712** tr. *Pomet's Hist. Drugs* I. 96 A Bark that is adorn'd with Pores like Stars. **1776** WITHERING *Brit. Plants* (1796) III. 761 Leaves..transparent, with many minute pores. **1861** MISS PRATT *Flower. Pl.* IV. 88 Snapdragon..capsule..opening by pores at the top. **1873** E. SPON *Workshop Recip's* Ser. I. 16/1 This coat closes all the pores of the wood, and does not crack or scale off.

d. In inanimate bodies or substances; esp. applied to the minute interstices or spaces between the particles of matter.

1398 TREVISA *Barth. De P.R.* XIX. cxxx. (1495) nn iij/1 For shyrenesse of partyes in suche [*sc.* thynne matere] ben many poores. **1501** DOUGLAS *Pal. Hon.* I. xxvii, The eirth,..with poris seir Vp drinkis air that mouit is be sound. *c* **1645** HOWELL *Lett.* I. VI. xxxv, The Sun, whose all-searching Beams penetrating the Pores of the Earth, do heat the Waters. **1660** BOYLE *New Exp. Phys. Merch.* xxi. 154 In the Pores or invisible little recesses of Water it self there lie.. many parcels..of..Air. **1706** PHILLIPS, *Pores*..are small void Spaces between the Particles of Matter, of which all Bodies are made up. **1748** H. ELLIS *Hudson's Bay* 223 The Form or Essence of a Magnet..is supposed to consist in it's being perforated by an infinite Number of parallel Pores. **1830** HERSCHEL *Stud. Nat. Phil.* III. i. 235 Water was forced through the pores (as was said) of a golden ball.

†**e.** In abstract or collective sense. *Obs. rare.*

1756 P. BROWNE *Jamaica* 50 The substances..are seldom of a very strong texture, though frequently of a fine pore and smooth grain. **1773** HORSLEY in *Phil. Trans.* LXIV. 271 A large proportion of pore, or interspersed vacuity, is sufficient for all purposes.

†**2.** A passage, channel, canal, duct (esp. in an animal body). *Obs. rare.*

c **1400** *Destr. Troy* 8801 þen [the balm] sewit furth soberly, & sanke fro aboue,..Passond by poris into þe pure legges. **1541** R. COPLAND *Guydon's Quest. Chirurg.* N iv b, The wayes and poores wherby the vryne passeth from the reynes to the bladder. **1615** H. CROOKE *Body of Man* 138 But this pore of choler is inserted into the small guts, not at their beginning, least the Choler should flye vp into the stomack ..but into the end of the Duodenum.

3. A small point or dot resembling a pore.

1833 HERSCHEL *Astron.* v. 208 Its ground [sun's disk] is finely mottled with an appearance of minute, dark dots, or pores. **1869** PHIPSON tr. *Guillemin's Sun* (1870) 234 It explains neither the faculæ nor the pores nor the curious granulations known as 'willow-leaves'.

4. *attrib.* and *Comb.*, as ***pore-area, -canal, -facet, -size, -space***; ***pore-like*** adj.; **pore-capsule**: see quot.; **pore-coral, pore-stone**, a stone-coral having pores; **pore pressure**, the pressure of pore water; **pore-sieve**, name for some part of a sponge; **pore water**, water contained in pores in soil or rock.

1880 *Nature* XXI. 450/1 Hollow spines with peculiar *pore-areas at their bases. **1878** BELL *Gegenbaur's Comp. Anat.* 111 The number of these *pore-canals (dermo-gastric pores), which have consequently a dermal and gastric orifice, is generally very great. **1877** A. W. BENNETT tr. *Thomé's Bot.* (ed. 6) 149 Some capsules again dehisce by pores, as the poppy.., when they are termed *pore-capsules. **1880** *Nature* XXI. 450/2 The shell has a large opening, as well as scattered *pore-facets. **1887** *Amer. Nat.* XXI. 565 Lateral surfaces with irregular, shallow, *pore-like fossæ. **1947** D. P. KRYNINE *Soil Mech.* (ed. 2) iv. 112 (*caption*) Analogy between (*a*) *pore pressure in clay and (*b*) hydraulic uplift in a dam. **1969** C. R. SCOTT *Introd. Soil Mech. & Foundations* ix. 201 The stability of a retaining wall is adversely affected by large pore pressures in the soil behind it. **1977** A. HALLAM *Planet Earth* 64/3 Decreasing the pore pressure increases the resistance of the rock to fracturing. **1887** SOLLAS in *Encycl. Brit.* XXII. 415/2 Section through the cortex of *Cydonium eosaster*,..showing the *pore-sieve overlying the chone. **1947** *New Biol.* III. 175 If a series of filters of known *pore-size is used, the size of particles which just fail to pass a certain filter can be obtained. **1915** L. V. PIRSSON *Text-bk. Geol.* I. xvi. 388 The rocks are penetrated by cracks, crevices and jointing planes, and on a more minute scale there are the *pore spaces between rock grains. **1975** *Nature* 17 Apr. 585/2 Usually the pore-space in a porous medium is visualised as a more or less complicated assembly of isolated or interconnected capillaries, and such porespace models are used in describing transport phenomena in porous media. **1708** *Phil. Trans.* XXVI. 79 The *Pore Stone, or Pore Coral. **1936** *Proc. 1st Internat. Conf. Soil Mech.* III. 51 The ultimate deformations and conditions of failure of cohesive soils are governed mainly by the principal effective stresses, defined as the difference between the total principal stresses and the hydrostatic pressure of the *porewater. **1943** K. VON TERZAGHI *Theoret. Soil Mech.* i. 15 When dealing with clays, we are seldom in a position to compute the pressure which develops in the pore water while the point of failure is approached. **1972** L. ZEEVAERT *Foundation Engin. for Difficult Subsoil Conditions* viii. 337 Upon dissipation of the excess pore water pressures, the soil tends to resume its initial elevation. **1977** *Offshore Engineer* June 35/2 The engineers are looking for tell-tale signs of soil fluidisation by large increases in pore water pressure caused by water trapped within the steel skirts and forced out beneath the skirt.

†**pore**, *sb.*[2] *Physiol. Obs. rare.* [ad. Gr. πῶρος callus.] The callus, or matter exuded at the site of the fracture of a broken bone.

[*c* **1400** *Lanfranc's Cirurg.* 48 If þat ilk mater þat is restorid be nyȝ as hard as is þe boon, it is clepid porus sarcoides.] **1543** TRAHERON *Vigo's Chirurg.* (1586) 273 When the bone is hardened and somewhat bound together with the pore called Sarcoeides. [**1657** *Physical Dict.*, *Poros*, that matter which consolidateth the broken bones within.]

pore, *sb.*[3] *rare.* [f. PORE *v.*] An act of poring over something; a careful or close examination.

1871 *Daily News* 12 Aug., I brought the book..and Madge..and myself shall have many a good pore over it.

†**pore**, *sb.*[4] *Obs.* (Said to be a Huntsman's term: see quot.)

1630 J. TAYLOR (Water P.) *Navy Land Ships, Huntsm. Ship* Wks. I. 93/1 What Necromanticke spells are Rut, Vault, Slot, Pores, and Entryes, Abatures, and Foyles, Frayenstockes,..and a thousand more such Vtopian fragments of confused Gibberish.

pore (pɔə(r)), *v.* Forms: 4 pure, pouri, 4-5 poure, 5-7 powre, 6 poor, 6-8 poar, 5- pore. [ME. *pūren, pouren, pouri*, of obscure origin. There is no corresp. verb in OF. or OE., though the early ME. forms answer to an OE. **pūrian*. Sense 2 is strikingly identical with the main sense of PEER *v.*[2], PIRE *v.*, both also of obscure origin; but, although an OE. double form **pūrian*, **pȳran* would explain the forms, there is no trace of such a verb in OE. or the cognate languages. The phonology is abnormal; the ME. (puːr-) would normally have given mod. *pour* (paʊə(r)), whereas in the 15th c. the form began to be *pore, poar* (pɔə(r)).]

1. *intr.* **a.** To look intently or fixedly, to gaze (*in, on, upon, at, over*); to search *for* or *into* something by gazing. (Often, now always, with admixture of sense b.)

a **1300** *K. Horn* 1092 Aþulf was in þe ture [*v.r.* toure] Abute for to pure [*v.r.* poure] After his comynge. **13..** *K. Alis.* 5799 There he seighen a selcouth folk Al day pouren in the walken. **1340** *Ayenb.* 177 þe men þet doþ zuo grat payne ham to kembe and to pouri ine sseaweres. *c* **1384** CHAUCER *H. Fame* III. 31 And for to powren [*v.r.* poure] wonder low Yf I koude eny weyes know What maner stoon this roche was. **1553** T. WILSON *Rhet.* (1580) 224 Some pores vpon the grounde as though they sought for pinnes. **1621** QUARLES *Esther* Medit. v. E iv, All Creatures else pore downward to the ground, Man lookes to heauen. **1722** DE FOE *Plague* (1840) 24 No wonder if they who were poring continually at the clouds, saw shapes and figures, representations and appearances. **1834** HT. MARTINEAU *Farrers* iv, Down on his knees, poring over the pavement, to see which way the stones were laid. **1854** MACAULAY *Biog., Johnson* (1867) 82 He would stand poring on the town clock without being able to tell the hour.

b. To look at something (usu. a book) with fixed attention, in the way of study; to read or study earnestly or with steady application; to be absorbed in reading or study. (Const. *on, upon*, (now chiefly) *over*; rarely *in, into*, or absol.)

c **1386** CHAUCER *Prol.* 185 What sholde he studie and make hym seluen wood Vpon a book in Cloystre alwey to poure [*MS. Lansd.* powre]. *c* **1449** PECOCK *Repr.* I. xvi. 87 Thouȝ ȝe wolden labore, and powre, and dote alle the daies of ȝoure lijf in the Bible aloon. **1594** LYLY *Moth. Bomb.* I. iii, Instead of poaring on a booke, you shall holde the plough. **1610** HOLLAND *Camden's Brit.* Auth. to Rdr., I have pored upon many an old Rowle. **1718** *Free-thinker* No. 37. 271 He rises by Three in the Morning to pore over Mathematicks. **1768** BEATTIE *Minstr.* I. li, Where dark cold-hearted sceptics, creeping, pore Through microscope of metaphysic lore. **1874** L. STEPHEN *Hours in Library* (1892) II. iii. 90 He had pored over their pages till he knew them by heart.

c. To fix one's thoughts earnestly upon something; to meditate, muse, or think intently; to ponder. Const. *on, upon, over*; rarely with dependent clause (quot. 1856).

1423 JAS. I *Kingis Q.* lxxii, The longe day thus gan I prye and poure, Till phebus endit had his bemes bryght. *a* **1591** H. SMITH *Wks.* (1866) I. 173 So, while he pores and gapes upon it, by little and little the love of it grows more and more in his heart, until at last he hath mind on nothing else. *a* **1628** PRESTON *Saint's Daily Exerc.* (1629) 138 If a man be poring on his wants still. **1722** DE FOE *Moll Flanders* (1840) 64 When he has thought and pored on it. **1856** MRS. BROWNING *Aur. Leigh* I. 348 She had pored for years What sort of woman could be suitable To her sort of hate. **1882** PEBODY *Eng. Journalism* xviii. 137 Dickens..took himself off..to Geneva,..to pore over the story of 'Dombey and Son'.

†**2.** To look with the eyes half shut; to look closely, as a near-sighted person; to peer. *Obs.*

1699 WAFER in *Phil. Trans.* LV. 51 For they see not well in the sun, poring in the clearest day. **1706** PHILLIPS, To *Pore*, to look close, as they do that are short-sighted. **1709** STEELE *Tatler* No. 27 ¶5 Poring with her Eyes half shut at every one she passes by. **1774** FOOTE *Cozeners* I. Wks. 1799 II. 157 He doesn't pore, with his eyes close to the book, like a clerk that reads the first lesson. **1862** THOREAU *Excursions, Ch. Night* (1863) 310 Their eyes which are weak and poring.

3. *trans.* To bring or put into some state by poring; in phrase ***to pore one's eyes out***, to blind oneself or ruin one's sight by close reading or over-study; to tire (one's eyes) by close reading.

1593 NASHE *Christ's T.* 43 b, I that haue poor'd out myne eyes vpon bookes. **1698** *Phil. Trans.* XX. 455 Old, rusty, Moth eaten Books, upon which a Man may pore his Eyes out before he can read a Word or a Line. **1706** E. WARD *Wooden World Diss.* (1708) 37 He might have..por'd himself into Stupidity. **1712** SWIFT *Jrnl. to Stella* 7 Aug., I have been poring my eyes all the morning. *a* **1754** FIELDING *Fathers* v. v, Though I have hated books as I do the devil,..I'll pore my eyes out rather than lose her.

Hence **'poring** *vbl. sb.* and *ppl. a.* (whence **'poringly** *adv.*).

c **1374** CHAUCER *Troylus* III. 1411 (1460) Dispitous day.. Thi pouryng In wol no where late hem dwelle. *c* **1449** PECOCK *Repr.* I. xvi. 85 Bi her powring in the Bible aloon thei miȝten leerne. **1594** NASHE *Unfort. Trav.* Wks. (Grosart) V. 120 He that viewd them a farre off, and had not directly stood poaringly ouer them, would haue sworne they had liued. **1615** G. SANDYS *Trav.* 124 Many of the Pilgrims by poaring on hot bricks, do voluntarily perish their sights. **1728** POPE *Dunc.* III. 191 There, dim in clouds, the poreing Scholiasts mark. **1874** L. STEPHEN *Hours in Library* (1892) II. vii. 211 That disposition which..delights in poring over its own morbid emotions.

pore, obs. (and dial.) var. of POOR *a.*; obs. f. PORR, POUR, POWER.

pore(-)blind, obs. f. PURBLIND.

pored (pɔəd), *a.* [f. PORE *sb.*[1] + -ED[2].] In parasynthetic combs.: Having pores (of some kind).

1688 CLAYTON in *Phil. Trans.* XVII. 945 If a Gummous Plant or Tree, that grows low, and close pored, it abounds with acid Spirits,..if it grow tall, and be open pored, it abounds with a subtile volatile Spirit. **1930** *Engineering* 28 Nov. 670/2 A wall built with Fletton bricks and very finely pored mortar. **1963** *Agra Univ. Jrnl. Res.* (*Sci.*) XII. 63 (*heading*) A note on the double pored dilepidid tape worms of some of the Indian carnivores. **1973** B. SHELMIRE *Art of Looking Younger* (1974) iv. 45 This cellular buildup causes the whole layer to become thicker and, in turn, makes the skin look coarse, leathery, and large-pored.

poreger, obs. form of PORRINGER.

†**'porelet.** *Obs. nonce-wd.* [f. *pore*, POOR + -LET. (Rendering L. *pauperculus*, dim. of *pauper* POOR.)] A poor man.

1382 WYCLIF *Isa.* lxvi. 2 To my porelet [1388 a pore man] and contrit in spirit.

‖**porencephalus, -on** (pɔərɛn'sɛfələs, -ɒn). *Path.* [mod.L., f. Gr. πόρος PORE *sb.*[1] + ἐγκέφαλος brain.] A defect of the cerebral hemisphere consisting in the formation (congenital or caused by disease) of a depression or hollow, sometimes communicating with the lateral ventricle. So **poren'cephaly** [ad. mod.L. *porencephalia*] in same sense. Hence

porencephalic (pɒrɛnsɪˈfælɪk), **porencephalous** (-ˈsɛfələs) *adjs.*, pertaining to, of the nature of, or affected with porencephalus.

1890 BILLINGS *Med. Dict.*, *Porencephalus..Porencephaly.* **1890** *Cent. Dict.*, *Porencephalic..Porencephalous.* **1896** *Allbutt's Syst. Med.* I. 179 Atrophy of the fillet and the posterior column nuclei has resulted from porencephalon of the central convolution of the cortex cerebri. **1899** *Ibid.* VI. 534 Diseases..which give rise to a porencephalic condition. *Ibid.* VII. 292 Cases of porencephaly.

porer (ˈpɔərə(r)). [f. PORE *v.* + -ER[1].] One who pores *upon* or *over* something, as a book.

1670 H. STUBBE *Plus Ultra* 69 The Disputative followers of Hippocrates, Aristotle, Galen, those superstitious Porers upon the Writings of the Ancients. **1797** W. TAYLOR in *Monthly Rev.* XXII. 345 The multitudinous porers in black literature. **1892** *Pall Mall G.* 16 Aug. 2/1 The wielder of the spade has outrun the porer over manuscripts.

poret(e, -ett(e, variants of PORRET *Obs.*

† **porˈfend**, *v. Obs. rare*[−1]. [a. OF. *po(u)rfendre* to cleave completely (*c* 1145 in Godef.), f. *pour* (:—L. *prō* forth), with intensive force + *fendre*:—L. *findĕre* to cleave.] *trans.* To cleave or split through.

c **1489** CAXTON *Blanchardyn* vii. 28 The goode swerde entred in to the brayne porfended, and cloue his hed vnto the chynne.

‖ **ˈporfido.** *Obs.* [It.] = PORPHYRY.

1611 SPEED *Hist. Gt. Brit.* IX. xxi. §134 The pauement.. shall be of Orientall stones; That is to say, of Alabaster, Porfido, Serpentines, and other stones of diuers colours.

porfil, -e, porfyl, obs. ff. PROFILE, PURFLE.

porful: see POORFUL.

porge, obs. f. PURGE.

porge (pɔədʒ), *v. Jewish Ritual.* [ad. Judæo-Spanish *porgar*, Sp. *purgar* to cleanse, f. L. *purgāre* PURGE *v.*[1]] *trans.* To make (a slaughtered beast) ceremonially clean by drawing out and removing the sinews and veins (esp. from the hinder quarters: cf. Gen. xxxii. 32). Also *absol.* Hence **ˈporger**, a man whose business is to do this.

1773 J. R. MOREIRA *Kehilath Jahacob* 110/2 Porger of meat.—Purgadór. **1864** *Times* 4 Aug. Advt., I. I. M... Butcher..Walworth begs to inform the Jewish Public that he has succeeded in obtaining a qualified killer and porger for himself. **1871** [see KOSHER *v.*]. **1908** (*Notice* in *Jewish Newspr.*). The licence of Mr. A. B. has been revoked for having sold (to Jewish customers) meat which has not been porged. **1932** C. ROTH *Hist. Marranos* vii. 179 The children of Israel did not eat the sinew of the thigh; and it was customary..to 'porge' the leg before preparing it for food. **1973** *Jewish Chron.* 18 May 39/4 (Advt.), Shomer. Able to porge and knowledge of kashrus requirements for butchers and poulterers.

porgo, pargo. [a. Sp. and Pg. *pargo*, app.:—L. *pagrus* a kind of fish.] A fish; the sea bream.

1557 W. TOWRSON in Hakluyt *Voy.* (1589) 113 We found there certain Caruels fishing for Pargoes. **1616** CAPT. SMITH *Descr. New Eng.* 12, 40 or 50 Saile yearely to Cape-blank, to hooke for Porgos, Mullet, and [to] make Puttardo. **1624** —— *Virginia* 227 The Duke of Medina receiueth yeerely tribute of the Fishers, for Tunny, Mullit, and Porgos, more then ten thousand pounds. [*a* **1642** SIR W. MONSON *Naval Tracts* VI. (1704) 532/1 Porgus, somewhat like to an over-grown Sea-Bream, but much bigger.] **1688** R. HOLME *Armoury* III. xv. (Roxb.) 40/1 Fish hookes for Porgos, Bonettos or dorados. **1902** JORDAN & EVERMANN *Amer. Food & Game Fishes* 405 The Snappers, or Pargos, genus *Lutjanus*..species very numerous, Asiatic, American, or African.

porgy (ˈpɔːgɪ). Also 8 pargie, porgie, 9 porgee, -ghee. See also PAUGIE. [Of obscure and app. various origin; in part = PORGO, PARGO; in part = PAUGIE, q.v.; also corruptly for POGY, q.v. Much vagueness appears to prevail in the use of the name.] **1.** A name in U.S. applied, with or without distinctive adjuncts, to various sea-fishes, chiefly N. American species of *Sparidæ* or sea breams, but also locally to fishes of other families.

Among the Sparoid fish, applied to **a.** the braise, *Sparus pagrus* (*Pagrus vulgaris*), of the Mediterranean and N. Atlantic; **b.** *Stenotomus chrysops*, the scuppaug, scup, or paugie, and *S. aculeatus*, the fair maid, found along the Atlantic coast of U.S., to the north and south respectively; **c.** *Lagodon rhomboides*, also called sailor's choice and pin-fish; **d.** various species of *Calamus* found at Bermuda and near Florida; **e.** one or more species of *Lutjanus*, called also snapper and grunt. Among those of other families: **f.** in southern U.S. an ephippioid fish, *Chætodipterus faber*, also known as moon-fish, spade-fish, or angel-fish; **g.** in Florida, the toad-fish, *Chilomycterus geometricus*; **h.** in California, one of various viviparous perches, as *Ditrema jacksoni* or *Damalichthys argyrosomus.* ¶**i.** Erron. for POGY, the menhaden.

1725 SLOANE *Jamaica* II. 286 The Pargie. It was taken at Old Harbour, and reckoned very good food. **1734** MORTIMER in *Phil. Trans.* XXXVIII. 317, 16. *Aurata Bahamensis.* The Porgy. It is a good eating Fish. **1848** SCHOMBURGK *Hist. Barbados* 668 *Haemulon heterodon*, porghee grunt..the peculiar noise which they emit when caught, has given rise to the vernacular name. **1849** H. W. HERBERT *Fish & Fishing U.S.* 280 The colour of the Porgee is a deep brownish black on the head and back. **1883** *Fisheries Exhib. Catal.* (ed. 4) 170 The principal salt-water fishes are:—The Calipeva..Hog-fish..Porgee, Grouper, Sun-fish, Grunts, Croakers, and Drummers. **1883** GOODE *Fish. Industries U.S.* 70 Saint Jerome's Creek, Point Lookout, Maryland. A station for the artificial propagation of..the bandy porgy (*Chætodipterus faber*). **1884** *Ibid.* Sect. I. Plates. Pl. 137 The Margate Fish, Bastard Snapper, or Charleston 'Porgy', *Sparus pagrus.* **1885** C. F. HOLDER *Marvels Anim. Life* 68 I've tossed a dead porgy to one [sword-fish] and seen him knock it up and down. **1888** GOODE *Amer. Fishes* 43 In the North the Sea-Bass occupies the feeding grounds in company with the scuppaug or porgy. *Ibid.* 80 The Red-mouth Grunt, *Diabasis aurolineatus*, is probably the Flannel-mouthed Porgy familiar to Florida fishermen. *Ibid.* 92 About New York, the second syllable of the abbreviated Indian name (*mishcuppauog*) has been lengthened into 'Paugy' or 'Porgy'. *Ibid.* 99 *Lagodon rhomboides*..in the St. John's River,..the 'Sailor's Choice' and 'Porgy'. *Ibid.* 100 There are other species known by the name of Porgy..found in this region, such as *Calamus bajonado* common also at Charleston, where it is called the 'White-boned Porgy', the 'Jolthead Porgy' of Key West, *C. megacephalus*, *C. arctifrons*, the 'Shad Porgy' or 'Grass Porgy' of Key West, and *C. macrops. Ibid.* 146 The Moonfish or Spadefish, *Chætodipterus faber*..at Beaufort N.C. where it is called the Porgee or Porgy... Three-tail Sheepshead and Three-tailed Porgee are names said to have been formerly in use among the New York fishermen. **1897** H. G. CARLETON in *Outing* (U.S.) XXIX. 329/2 Dibbling with a light rod for little porgies and whiting.

2. *attrib.*, as ***porgy boat, fleet, steamer***; ***porgy-hunting*** vbl. sb. (see quot. 1904).

1906 *N.Y. Even. Post* 18 Aug. (Saturday Suppl.) 1/2 The 'porgy' boats, dirty, snub-nosed..are far..removed in standing from their fellows. **1960** J. J. ROWLANDS *Spindrift* 211 The porgy boats are built and operated for just one purpose—fishing. **1914** W. D. STEELE *Storm* 191 For the first time that season the porgie fleet moved in around Long Point. **1904** *Scribner's Mag.* May 548 When we cruise about, hooking on to any job we can catch, and at any price we can get for it, that's porgy hunting. **1880** Porgy steamer [see MACKERELING *vbl. sb.*]. **1914** *Oysterman & Fisherman* Jan. 7/3 The porgie steamer Long Island which..has been undergoing repairs.

‖ **Porifera** (pɒˈrɪfərə), *sb. pl. Zool.* [mod.L., neut. pl. of *porifer*, f. L. *porus* (a. Gr. πόρος) PORE *sb.*[1] + *-fer* bearing.] The sponges, reckoned as a class or main division of *Cœlenterata*, characterized by having the body-wall perforated by numerous inhalant pores. Hence **porifer** (ˈpɔərɪfə(r)), a member of the *Porifera*, a sponge; **poˈriferal** *a.* = next; **poˈriferan**, *a.* belonging or relating to the *Porifera*; *sb.* = *porifer.*

1843 CARPENTER *Anim. Phys.* ii. 113 Satisfactory reasons for placing the class of *Porifera*, or the Sponge tribe, in the animal kingdom. **1864** WEBSTER, *Poriferan*, an animal of the group comprising the sponges. **1867** J. HOGG *Microsc.* II. ii. 385 The term *Porifera*..was applied by Professor Grant to designate the remarkable class of organized beings known as sponges. **1877** HUXLEY *Anat. Inv. Anim.* iii. 113 The fundamental type of Poriferal organisation is to be sought among the Calcispongiæ. *Ibid.* xii. 678 Comparable to Physemarian or Poriferan embryos. **1888** ROLLESTON & JACKSON *Anim. Life* 716 The irregular and continuous growth of a Poriferan. **1890** *Cent. Dict.*, *Poriferan theory*, that theory which considers the tracheæ or tubes of some animals as having a common origin with the incurrent tubes of the *Porifera* or sponges.

poriferous (pɒˈrɪfərəs), *a.* [f. L. *por-us* PORE *sb.*[1] + -FEROUS: in mod.L. *porifer.*] Bearing or having pores.

1862 DANA *Man. Geol.* iii. 313 The poriferous side of the same. **1870** NICHOLSON *Man. Zool.* 124 The other five double rows of plates alternate regularly with the former, and are termed the 'ambulacral areas' or poriferous zones.

poriform (ˈpɔərɪfɔːm), *a.* [f. as prec. + -FORM.] Having the form of, or resembling, a pore.

1846 DANA *Zooph.* (1848) 706 Minute, poriform cells. **1858** MAYNE *Expos. Lex.*, *Poriformis*,..having the form of simple pores, as the cellules of certain *polypi*..: poriform.

poriger, obs. form of PORRINGER.

† **ˈporime.** *Obs. rare*[−0]. [ad. Gr. πόριμ-ος able to be passed, practicable, f. πόρος passage.] See quot. and APORIME.

1704 J. HARRIS *Lex. Techn.* I, *Porime*,..in Geometry, is a Theorem or Proposition so easie to be demonstrated, that 'tis almost self-evident; as, *That a Chord is all of it within the Circle.* Hence **1706** in PHILLIPS. **1727-41** in CHAMBERS *Cycl.* **1730-6** in BAILEY (folio). **1823** in CRABB *Technol. Dict.*; and in mod. Dicts.

porina (pɒˈraɪnə). *N.Z.* [mod.L. (F. Walker *List Specimens Lepidopterous Insects in Brit. Mus.* (1856) VII. 1572).] The larva of a moth formerly belonging to the genus *Porina*, now usually included in the genus *Oxycanus*, which damages grassland. Freq. *attrib.*

1929 W. MARTIN *N.Z. Nature Bk.* I. xvi. 153 The Porinas, Swifts, or Bull Moths... The subterranean larvae thus attacked [by fungi] have long been known as Vegetable Caterpillars. **1940** *N.Z. Jrnl. Agric.* Apr. 245/1 The Porina moth makes its first appearance in early October... It is the caterpillar..which causes the damage during the winter. *Ibid.* 246/1 Porina larvae feed almost entirely on surface leafage. **1950** *Ibid.* Apr. 357/1 Porina..and grass-grub are a serious hindrance. **1966** *Encycl. N.Z.* I. 319/1 The larval stages of the moths commonly called porina moths..are important pasture pests in New Zealand. They live in tunnels in the soil during the day and feed at night at the surface of the soil on grass foliage. **1969** [see *grass grub* s.v. GRASS *sb.*[1] 14]. **1973** A. D. LOWE in G. R. Williams *Nat. Hist. N.Z.* viii. 198/2 The practice of closing paddocks for hay and seed crops frequently appears to have accentuated the porina problem.

† **ˈporiness.** *Obs.* [f. PORY + -NESS.] The condition of being 'pory' or porous; porosity; also *concr.* a porous part.

1653 WALTON *Angler* iii. 86 It is reported, there is a fish that hath not any mouth, but lives by taking breath by the poriness of her gils. **1662** J. CHANDLER *Van Helmont's Oriat.* 57 Vapours may be contained in the porinesses or hollow places of the Air. **1676** WISEMAN *Chirurg. Treat.* V. ix. 392, I took off the Dressings, and set the Trepan above the fractured Bone,..considering withall the Poriness of the Bone below.

poring, poringly: see under PORE *v.*

porion (ˈpɔərɪɒn). *Anat.* Pl. poria. [f. Gr. πόρ-ος way through, passageway + -ION[2].] (See quot. 1937.)

1909 in *Cent. Dict.* Suppl. **1920** H. H. WILDER *Lab. Man. Anthropometry* 47 *Porion*, the uppermost point in the margin of the auditory meatus. **1933** *Jrnl. R. Anthrop. Inst.* LXIII. 417 The poria [are] widely separated. **1937** *Amer. Jrnl. Physical Anthrop.* XXII. 485 *Porion*, a point on the upper margin of the external auditory meatus which according to Martin is vertically over the middle of the meatus, and according to Wilder is simply the uppermost point. **1970** *Monogr. Soc. Res. Child Devel.* XXXV. III. 48 As a rule, the two poria are instrumentally determined by contact of the upper margin of the rounded ear rods of the headspanner as they are inserted into the *S*'s external auditory meatus.

† **ˈporish**, *a.*[1] *Obs. rare*[−0]. [f. PORE *v.* + -ISH[1].] Having the character of 'poring' or looking with the eyes half shut (see PORE *v.* 2). Hence † **ˈporishly** *adv. Obs.*

1523 SKELTON *Garl. Laurel* 626 Sum were made peuysshe, porisshly pynk iyde, That euer more after by it they were aspyide. **1530** PALSGR. 840/2 *Porisshly*, as one loketh that can nat se well, *louchement.*

† **ˈporish**, *a.*[2] *Obs.* [f. PORE *sb.*[1] + -ISH[1].] Porous. Hence † **ˈporishness** *Obs.*, porosity.

1652 GAULE *Magastrom.* 119 That the stars are made of an earthy porish matter, much like to that of a pumice stone. **1670** CAPT. J. SMITH *Eng. Improv. Reviv'd* 16 All barren sands are loose and light,..by reason of their porishness or hollowness.

porism (ˈpɔərɪz(ə)m, ˈpɒr-). *Math.* [ad. L. *porisma*, a. Gr. πόρισμα a deduction from a previous demonstration, a corollary, also a problem, f. πορίζειν to carry, deduce, f. πόρος way. So F. *porisme.*] With the ancient Greek mathematicians, a kind of geometrical proposition, the nature of which has been much disputed; app. one arising during the investigation of some other proposition, either by immediate deduction from it (= COROLLARY *sb.* 1), or by consideration of some special case in which it becomes indeterminate.

The sense indicated by Playfair's definition (quot. 1792) is that now most generally accepted and used; but other widely different definitions have been given.

c **1374** CHAUCER *Boeth.* III. pr. x. 71 (Camb. MS.) Ryht as thyse geometryens whan they han shewyd hyr proposicions ben wont to bryngen in thinges þat they clepyn porysmes or declaracions of forseyde thinges. Ryht so wole I yeue the heere as a corolarye or a mede of coroune. [*c* **1645** *Enquiry*, etc. in *Harl. Misc.* (Malh.) V. 499 It may be proposed a problem, or porisma, to be considered, whether the souls of brutes are not more than rarefied, or inflamed matter.] **1704** J. HARRIS *Lex. Techn.* I, *Porisme.* Proclus and Pappus define this Geometrical Term to signifie a kind of Theorem, in the form of a Corollary, which is dependant upon, or deduced from some other Theorem already demonstrated. And 'tis commonly used to signifie some General Theorem, which is discovered from finding out some Geometrical Place. **1792** PLAYFAIR in *Trans. Roy. Soc. Edinb.* III. II. 156 There was another subject, that of Porisms, the most intricate and enigmatical of any thing in the ancient geometry. *Ibid.* 170 From this account of the origin of Porisms, it follows, that a Porism may be defined, A proposition affirming the possibility of finding such conditions as will render a certain problem indeterminate, or capable of innumerable solutions. **1795** HUTTON *Math. Dict.* s.v., Pappus says, a Porism is that in which something was proposed to be investigated. **1798** H. BROUGHAM in *Phil. Trans.* LXXXVIII. 383 This is a case of a most general enunciation, which gives rise to an infinite variety of the most curious porisms. **1853** CAYLEY *Coll. Math. Papers* II. 56 Researches on the Porism of the in- and circumscribed triangle. **1855** J. MARTINEAU *Ess.* (1890) I. 434 An epic or song..may have a human power greater than the Porisms or the Principia. **1887** H. DELEVINGNE in *N. & Q.* 7th Ser. IV. 424/2 Between i. 15 and 16 occurs the first porism or corollary, to the effect that the angles formed by two straight lines at their point of intersection are together equal to four right angles.

porismatic (pɔərɪzˈmætɪk, pɒr-), *a.* [f. Gr. πόρισμα, -ατ- PORISM + -IC.] Pertaining to or of the nature of a porism. So † **porisˈmatical** *a. Obs.* (in quot.) following immediately as a corollary; whence **porisˈmatically** *adv.* (in quot.) as a corollary, by direct inference.

1646 J. HALL *Horæ Vac.* 119 It will Porismatically follow. **1649** J. H. *Motion to Parl. Adv. Learn.* 11 If they be not guided by forcible demonstrations and porismaticall inferences. **1792** PLAYFAIR in *Trans. Roy. Soc. Edinb.* III. II. 190 Another species of impossibility may frequently arise from the porismatic case of a problem. **1886** FARRAR *Hist.*

Interpr. vii. 361 The porismatic method consisted in the abstraction of dogmatic results.

poristic (pɒ'rɪstɪk), *a. Math.* [ad. Gr. ποριστικός able to procure, f. πορίζειν: see PORISM.] Relating to a porism, porismatic; having the quality of rendering a determinate problem indeterminate.

1704 J. HARRIS *Lex. Techn.* I, *Poristick Method*, in Mathematicks, is that which determines when, by what way, and how many different ways, a Problem may be resolved. **1890** *Cent. Dict.* s.v., *Poristic points*, a set of points of the number which usually suffice to determine a curve of a given order, but so situated that an indefinite number of such curves can be drawn through them.

So **po'ristical** *a. rare*$^{-0}$.

1828 WEBSTER, *Poristic, Poristical.* Hence in later Dicts.

porite ('pɔəraɪt). *Zool.* [ad. mod.L. generic name *Porītēs* (Lamarck); f. Gr. πορός passage, pore, or ? πῶρ-ος calcareous stone, stalactite: see MADREPORE and -ITE¹.] A coral of the genus *Porites* or family *Poritidæ* of perforate sclerodermatous corals.

1828 WEBSTER, *Porite*, a petrified madrepore. *Dict. Nat. Hist.* **1846** DANA *Zooph.* vii. (1848) 110 The Porites.. graduate into the Astræsporæ, and thence to the Astroites.

pork¹ (pɔək). Forms: 3 **porc**, 5 **poork, -e**, 5–7 **porke**, 6 **porcke**, 8 **porck**, 4– **pork**. [a. F. *porc* = Pr. *porc*, It. *porco*, Sp. *puerco*:—L. *porc-us* swine, hog.]

†**1. a.** A swine, a hog, a pig. Sometimes distinguished from a pig or young swine. *Obs.* or *Hist.*

?*a* **1400** *Morte Arth.* 3122 Poveralle and pastorelles passede one aftyre, With porkes to pasture at the price ȝates. *c* **1400** *Destr. Troy* 3837 Polidarius was pluccid as a porke fat. **1528** PAYNEL *Salerne's Regim.* F j, Porkes of a yere or .ij. olde are better than yonge pygges. **1533** BELLENDEN *Livy* I. ix. (S.T.S.) I. 55 He slew þe pork with ane hevy stane. **1598** STOW *Surv.* (1842) 145/1 There were brought to the slaughter-house.. 34 porks, 3*s.* 8*d.* the piece; 91 pigs, 6*d.* the piece. **1682** J. COLLINS *Salt & Fishery* 83 Very large like Calves,.. and as fat as Porks. [**1799** SOUTHEY *Pig* 24 Woe to the young posterity of Pork! Their enemy is at hand. **1887** ROGERS *Agric. & Prices* V. 343 Hogs and porks, the word appearing to be used indifferently, are occasionally found.]

†**b.** Applied opprobriously to an uncultured person. *Obs.*

1645 MILTON *Colast.* Wks. 1851 IV. 358, I mean not to dispute Philosophy with this Pork, who never read any.

2. a. The flesh of swine used as food; *spec.* the fresh flesh.

c **1290** *S. Eng. Leg.* I. 472/343 Huy nomen with heom into heore schip.. porc, motoun and beof. **1398** TREVISA *Barth. De P.R.* XVIII. vii. (Bodl. MS.) lf. 246 b/1 Boores flesche is more hard and drye.. þan tame porke. *c* **1440** *Promp. Parv.* 409/2 Poork, flesche, *suilla.* **1486** *Bk. St. Albans* C vij, Take a quantyte of poorke and ony [= honey] and butter. **1533** ELYOT *Cast. Helthe* (1539) 27 b, Aboue all kyndes of fleshe in nouryshyng the body, Galene most commendeth porke. **1598** W. PHILLIP *Linschoten* I. iv. 9/1 Porke is there a very costly dish. **1748** E. DARWIN *Let.* in *Life* (1879) 9 We affirm Porck not only to be flesh but a devillish Sort of flesh. **1848** THACKERAY *Bk. Snobs* xxv, Roast ribs of pork.

b. *U.S. slang.* Federal funds obtained for particular areas or individuals on the basis of political patronage. Cf. PORK BARREL.

[**1862** in D. W. Mitchell *Ten Yrs. in U.S.* xv. 271 To put myself in a position in which every wretch entitled to a vote would feel himself privileged to hold me under special obligations, would be giving rather too much pork for a shilling.] **1879** *Congress Rec.* 28 Feb. 2131/1 St. Louis is going to have some of the 'pork' indirectly; but it will not do any good. **1916** *N.Y. Even. Post* 12 May 8/2 'Pork' has hitherto stood for just one process, the parcelling out of Federal moneys for court houses, post offices, and waterways, not by States, but by Congressional districts. **1949** *Marshfield* (Wisconsin) *News-Herald* 19 July 4/3 That difference of more than $54,000,000 includes a lot of pork for individual senators. **1962** *Economist* 20 Oct. 252/1 Pork is the generic name for the tasty morsels of federal spending ..which a member of congress likes to bring back to his constituents. **1964** D. M. BERMAN *In Congress Assembled* xii. 323 One of the first facts of congressional life is that it does not pay to antagonize the committee to which one will someday have to appeal for funds to support a local project. Such projects are commonly referred to as 'pork'.

c. Phr. ***pork and beans*** (Mil. slang), a name given to Portuguese soldiers serving in the war of 1914–18.

1919 *Athenæum* 8 Aug. 727/2 He [*sc.* the soldier] gave nicknames to the Overseas troops, as.. 'Chinks' for Chinese labourers.. and 'Pork and Beans' for Portuguese. **1919** W. H. DOWNING *Digger Dial.* 39 *Pork-and-beans*, Portuguese soldiers. **1925** FRASER & GIBBONS *Soldier & Sailor Words* 228 *Pork and beans*, a nickname for the Portuguese troops serving on the Western Front.

3. *attrib.* and *Comb.*: simple attrib., as ***pork-blubber, -fat, -griskin, -sausage, -shop, steak, trade***; obj. and obj. gen., as ***pork-curer, -dealer, -eater, -packer*** (PACKER¹ 2 b), ***-packing, -pickling, raiser, raising***; **porkburger**, a kind of hamburger made from pork; **pork-butcher**, (*a*) one who slaughters pigs for sale (BUTCHER *sb.* 1); (*b*) a shop-keeper who specializes in pork; so **pork-butchering** *vbl. sb.*, **-butchery**; **pork-eater** *Canad.*, a canoeman engaged on the run between Montreal and Grand Portage; also, by extension, any canoeman, esp. a new recruit; *obs.* exc. *hist.*; **pork-fish**, a local name of various American fishes: see quots.; †**pork-hog** = PORKER 1; **pork house**, a business house trading in pork; **pork king**, a magnate in the pork trade; **pork-knocker, porknocker**, in Guyana (formerly British Guiana), an independent or casual prospector for gold or diamonds; hence **pork-knocking** *vbl. sb.*, the activity of a pork-knocker; **pork-pit**, that part of a produce exchange where pork is dealt in. Also PORK-FLESH, etc.,

1804 A. WILSON in *Poems & Lit. Prose* (1876) I. 114 We ate some *pork-blubber and bread. **1939** *Amer. Speech* XIV. 154/2 **Porkburger*, ground pork, in other words, sausage! **1969** R. & D. DE SOLA *Dict. Cooking* 180/1 *Porkburger*, pork patty fried and eaten like a hamburger. **1807** SOUTHEY *Lett. from Eng.* III. lxiii. 182 The *pork-butchers are commonly Jews. **1836–48** B. D. WALSH *Aristoph., Knights* I. iii, We'll observe pork-butcher's laws. **1922** JOYCE *Ulysses* 59 The porkbutcher snapped two sheets from the pile, wrapped up her prime sausages and made a red grimace. **1925** W. DE LA MARE *Two Tales* 40 Yet to judge from some poets' faces, you might be easily justified in supposing they would have flourished better in the *pork-butchering line. **1935** *Times Lit. Suppl.* 24 Oct. 673/1 [They] set a rabbinical winkle-seller on the road to fortune which leads to *pork-butchery. **1844** H. STEPHENS *Bk. Farm* II. 232 *Pork-curers buy from farmers and dealers in the carcass. **1596** SHAKS. *Merch. V.* III. v. 27 If wee grow all to be *porke-eaters, wee shall not shortlie haue a rasher on the coales for money. **1705** (*title*) A Pill for Pork Eaters, or a Scots Lancet for an English Swelling. **1793** J. MACDONELL *Diary* 5 July in C. M. Gates *Five Fur Traders* (1933) 94 Between two and three hundred yards to the East of the N.W. Fort beyond the Pork eaters camp is the spot Messʳˢ David and Peter Grant have selected to build upon. **1801** A. MACKENZIE *Voy. from Montreal* p. xxvii, Of these, five clerks, eighteen guides, and three hundred and fifty canoe men, were employed for the summer season in going from Montreal to the Grande Portage, in canoes, part of whom proceeded from thence to Rainy Lake,.. and are called Pork-eaters, or Goers and Comers. **1823** J. FRANKLIN *Narr. Journey Shores Polar Sea* vii. 281 There is a pride amongst 'Old Voyagers', which makes them consider the state of being frost-bitten as effeminate, and only excusable in a 'Pork-eater', or one newly come into the country. **1829** J. MCLOUGHLIN *Let.* 8 Dec. (1948) 69 By this opportunity I send you all you requested.. and four Pork eaters. **1859** P. KANE *Wanderings of Artist* 34 The men who usually work this brigade of [Hudson Bay Company] canoes are hired at Lachine, and are called by the uncouth names of mangeurs du lard, or pork-eaters. **1953** *Beaver* Dec. 50 The provisions for the Crew were Pork & Biscuits; from which circumstance the young recruits were called 'Pork Eaters' to distinguish them from the old Winterers, who feed chiefly on 'Pemican'. **1969** E. W. MORSE *Fur Trade Canoe Routes* I. ii. 23 The voyageurs plying the run between Montreal and Lake Superior were known derisively among the tougher breed wintering in the North West as 'pork eaters', *mangeurs de lard.* **1856** KANE *Arct. Expl.* II. xix. 193 Hung a dripping slab of *pork-fat over their lamp-wick. **1734** MORTIMER in *Phil. Trans.* XXXVIII. 315 The *Pork-Fish. The Bahamians esteem this a good Fish. **1888** GOODE *Amer. Fishes* 81 The Norfolk Hog-fish, *Pomodasys fulvomaculatus*,.. is the.. 'Pork-fish' and 'Whiting' at Key West. **1902** WEBSTER Suppl., *Pork-fish*,.. a sparoid fish (*Anisotremus Virginicus*). **1727** *Pork grisking [see GRISKIN]. **1755** J. SHEBBEARE *Lydia* (1769) II. 284 Attending a pork-griskin which the parson had also ordered for their suppers. **1470–85** MALORY *Arthur* VII. i. 214 As fatte.. as a *porke hog. **1837** W. JENKINS *Ohio Gazetteer* 171 Eaton contains.. four *pork houses. **1848** *Rep. Comm. Patents 1847* (U.S.) 527 The hogs are taken into the pork house from the wagons and piled up in rows. **1890** W. D. HOWELLS *Boy's Town* 36 Cooper-shops where the barrels were made, alternated with the pork-houses. **1893** M. ELLIOTT *Honor* 155 Gwendoline O'Shaunessey, the daughter of old O'Shaunessey the Western *pork-king. **1930** R. MACAULAY *Staying with Relations* xv. 222, I should like to go off with a president,.. or a film or pork king. **1910** M. B. & C. W. BEEBE *Our Search for Wilderness* vi. 187 The universal Guianian name for this type of independent miner is '*pork-knocker', the explanation being that by knocking the rocks to pieces, they find just enough gold to procure the pork upon which they live. **1930** *Times* 14 Mar. 5/3 The pork-knockers make a night of it before they go up into the bush. **1949** P. HASTINGS *Cases in Court* iii. 130 These gentlemen employed a number of natives who enjoyed the somewhat peculiar title of 'Pork knockers'. **1957** [see INBOARD *a.*]. **1972** *Guardian* 1 Dec. 14/1 The famous gold and diamond prospectors of the interior (the so-called 'porknockers' whose name derives from their salt pork rations). **1974** H. MACINNES *Climb to Lost World* iii. 42 A couple of prospectors, or 'porknockers', were staying in the Park Hotel... They are called pork-nockers because salted pork was their staple diet; when they had a run of bad luck, they used to borrow, or 'knock' pork from their more prosperous friends. **1965** 'LAUCHMONEN' *Old Thom's Harvest* vii. 95 Winston, man, you better had go back to your *pork-knocking. **1974** H. MACINNES *Climb to Lost World* xii. 221 We had some Brazilian natives with us... They.. had come over for the diamond prospecting but, since the water had been too high for porknocking, they had agreed to work for us instead. **1838** *N.Y. Advertiser & Express* 7 Feb. 3/3 It is due to that enterprising class of citizens, the *pork packers, that the error should be corrected. **1884** SIR L. GRIFFIN in *Fortn. Rev.* Jan. 55 Annually, a flight of pork-packers and successful tradesmen cross the Atlantic. **1905** *Athenæum* 5 Aug. 174/2 In a few days fashionable people, from the peer to the pork-packer, will be rushing to the Highlands. **1949** *Boston Sunday Globe* 26 June (Fiction Mag.) 2/1 These corporations were principally distillers, manufacturers of tobacco, and, especially, beef and pork packers. **1851** C. CIST *Sk. Cincinnati in 1851* 228 *Pork and Beef Packing. **1870** *Trans. Illinois Agric. Soc. 1867–68* VII. 475 The only reliable statement of the pork-packing of the West we have any knowledge of. **1892** A. CRAIB *America* 66 Pork-packing is one of the chief sources of wealth in Illinois, Ohio, and Kentucky. **1890** *Pall Mall G.* 8 May 3/2 A *pork-pickling establishment.. has lately been opened there. **1839** *Jrnl. Indiana Ho. Representatives* 8 Jan. 231 The scarcity.. is likely to prove so mischievous to the interests of our *pork raisers and dealers. **1872** *Trans. Illinois Dept. Agric. 1871* IX. 390 Dark, cold, damp Piggeries are a nuisance to any farmer or pork raiser. **1880** G. T. INGHAM *Digging Gold* 203 Is this the *honor* of Western pork-raisers? **1872** *Trans. Illinois Dept. Agric. 1871* IX. 354 He had said that *pork raising stood pre-eminent as a branch of stock raising in our State. **1829** MARRYAT *F. Mildmay* xvi, That fellow is only fit for fly-flapper at a *pork shop! **1783** J. WOODFORDE *Diary* 8 Apr. (1926) II. 68 We had for Dinner.. Mutton Stakes, *Pork Stakes, Peas Soup. **1922** JOYCE *Ulysses* 230 Master Patrick Aloysius Dignam came out of Mangan's.. carrying a pound and a half of porksteaks. *Ibid.* 251 Master Patrick Aloysius Dignam.. raised also his new black cap with fingers greased by porksteak paper. **1957** *Encycl. Brit.* XVIII. 245/2 Pork chops or steaks are usually browned in a hot skillet. **1851** A. O. HALL *Manhattaner* 13 Here, too, is modest beauty from Ohio (papa in the *pork trade).

†**pork**². *Obs.* [Echoic.] An imitative name for the hoarse croak of the raven: cf. MOREPORK. So †**pork** *v. intr.*, to croak; hence †'**porking** *vbl. sb.*; and (with reduplication expressing repetition) **pork-porking** *ppl. a.*

1606 SYLVESTER *Du Bartas* II. iv. III. *Schism* 285 From the Mountains nigh The Rav'ns begin with their pork-porking cry. **1640** BROME *Sparagus Gard.* IV. iv, Harke, the Ravens cry porke for him and yet he dyes not. **1655** MOUFET & BENNET *Health's Impr.* 5 They foresee by porking of raven ..when it will raine.

pork barrel. orig. and chiefly *U.S.* [PORK¹ 3.]

1. A barrel in which pork is kept. Also *fig.*, a supply of money; the source of one's livelihood.

1801 *Farmer's Almanack 1802* (Boston) sig. C2 *Better spare at the brim, than at the bottom*, is an old proverb, and should teach us to mind our pork and cider barrels. **1842** *Joliet* (Illinois) *Courier* 2 Feb. 3/1 Farmers can be accommodated with a very good Pork Barrel in exchange for Oats Butter or Wheat. **1861** *Harper's Mag.* Oct. 643/1, I came very near tumbling over a pork-barrel, and made a remark concerning obstructions in the street which was more forcible than chaste. **1863** *Frank Leslie's Illustr. Newspaper* 24 Jan. 277/3 We find that those who work honestly, and only seek a man's fair average of life, or a woman's, get that average... And thus we find that when an extraordinary contingency arises in life.. we have only to go to our pork-barrel and the fish rises to our hook or spear. **1909** *Chambers's Jrnl.* Mar. 178/2 We had bought ten empty pork-barrels. **1946** S. NEWTON *Paul Bunyan* xxvii. 158 It was as big around as a pork barrel. **1978** M. PUZO *Fools Die* xi. 106 The Army Reserve of the United States was a great pork barrel. By just coming to a meeting for two hours a week you got a full day's pay.

2. *fig.* The state's financial resources regarded as a source of distribution to meet regional expenditure; the provision of funds (in U.S., Federal funds) for a particular area achieved through political representation or influence. Freq. *attrib.* or as *adj.*

1909 *Westm. Gaz.* 1 June 2/1 The Democratic Party.. has periodically inveighed against the extravagance of the administration, but its representatives in the Legislature have exercised no critical surveillance over the appropriations. They have preferred to take for their own constituencies whatever could be got out of the Congressional 'pork barrel'. **1913** R. M. LA FOLLETTE *Autobiogr.* 60 It was on the so-called 'pork-barrel' bill for river and harbor appropriations. **1916** *N.Y. Even. Post* 12 May 8/2 The River and Harbor bill is the pork barrel par excellence, and the rivers and harbors are manipulated by Federal machinery and not by State machinery. **1926** R. LUCE *Congress* 82 Undoubtedly there was once a 'pork-barrel', a metaphorical barrel from which legislators pulled out 'pork' to satisfy the ravenous appetites of greedy constituents. **1950** *Reader's Digest* Jan. 96/2 The Army Civil Functions appropriation bill—once known as the Rivers and Harbors bill and still called the 'pork barrel' bill—this year provided for 275 projects. **1950** *Sun* (Baltimore) 24 Aug. 4/3 The section of the bill is sometimes called the 'pork-barrel', and as it contains funds for projects in virtually every state, it is one that is the hardest to cut item by item. **1953** *Manch. Guardian Weekly* 11 June 10/4 We are shown.. the way in which members of Congress.. deal with the problem of public works (coarsely called the pork barrel). **1960** *Economist* 15 Oct. 266/2 It [*sc.* the Macmillan Government] has treated some nationalised industries almost as if they were its positive enemies, while a quite considerable pork-barrel has been opened up for a growing number of private firms. **1961** D. L. MUNBY *God & Rich Society* vi. 122 'Pork-barrel' politics, by which governments step in to help particular economic groups in the community. **1973** *Sat. Rev. Sci.* (U.S.) Mar. 29/3 Present fire allocations.. have reached pork-barrel dimensions. **1976** H. WILSON *Governance of Britain* x. 172 In Westminster, the Government has complete control over expenditure... Thus, in Britain, 'pork-barrel' expenditure is ruled out.

Hence **pork-barrelling** *vbl. sb.*, the process of providing regional funds by these means.

1967 *Economist* 14 Oct. 133/3 The one piece of regional pork-barrelling at last week's Labour party conference was the Prime Minister's promise that two aluminium smelters, using subsidised electricity, would be built, probably in development areas. **1974** *Camden* (S. Carolina) *Chron.* 22 Apr. 2/1 The commission needs stronger authority than it has in that field if legislative pork-barreling on higher education is to be kept to a minimum. **1976** *Guardian Weekly* 12 Sept. 7/5 Pork barrelling—the way Congressmen with political influence can obtain Federal funds for local projects. **1977** *N.Y. Rev. Bks.* 26 May 36/3 Such reallocation would sorely affect agricultural usage of the land and stimulate the construction of various water aqueducts, dams, and other projects currently denounced as mere congressional pork-barreling.

pork chop. [PORK^1.] **1.** A slice of pork (CHOP *sb.*^{1} 2 b).

1858 SIMMONDS *Dict. Trade, Pork-chop*, a slice from the rib of a pig. **1872** *Punch* 3 Feb. 46/2 The *menu* consisted of sausages.. and pork-chops.

2. An American black who accepts an inferior position in relation to whites. Chiefly *attrib. U.S. slang.*

1970 *Rep. 20th Ann. Round Table Meeting Lang. & Ling. Stud., Georgetown Univ.* 9 *CR*: Who can make magic? *Greg*: The son of po'—... I'm saying' the po'k chop God! He only a po'k chop God! *Ibid.* 36 A *pork chop* is a Negro who has not lost traditional subservient ideology of the South.. and the *pork chop God* would be the traditional God of the Southern Baptists. **1977** *N.Y. Rev. Bks.* 4 Aug. 35/1 This is the year of the Bionic Black, and porkchop nationalists have lost prestige.

Hence **,pork-'chopper** *U.S. slang*, a full-time union official (see quots.).

1946 *N.Y. Times* 11 Aug. IV. 7/7 In the UAW, the rank and file call those who live by income derived from the union 'pork-choppers'. **1953** BERREY & VAN DEN BARK *Amer. Thes. Slang* (1954) §527/2 *Pork-chopper*, an official who is in the union for self-interested reasons. **1960** WENTWORTH & FLEXNER *Dict. Amer. Slang* 403/1 *Pork-chopper*, a political appointee, union official, or relative or friend of a politician, union officer, or the like, who receives payment for little or no work; one who is put on a payroll as a favor or as a return for past services. **1968** *Economist* 2 Nov. 30/2 They feel mostly contempt for the 'pork-chopper'—the former factory workers who have become full-time members of the union staff. **1977** *Time* 17 Jan. 32/3 Rank-and-filers have never considered him a 'pork-chopper', their term for a high-hat leader.

porke despyne, etc., early f. PORCUPINE.

porkepes, obs. form of PORPOISE *sb.*

porker ('pɔəkə(r)). [f. PORK^1 + -ER^1 1.]

1. a. A young hog fattened for pork; also, any swine or pig raised for food.

1657 HEYLIN *Ecclesia Vind.* 181 They sacrificed a swine or porker, with this solemn form. **1670** CAPT. J. SMITH *Eng. Improv. Reviv'd* 195 Beech-mast is very good feeding for Swine to make them Porkers, and for Bacon. **1726** POPE *Odyss.* XVII. 201 Then sheep and goats and bristly porkers bled. **1828** SCOTT *F.M. Perth* ii, As round and full as a six-weeks' porker. **1880** MISS BRADDON *Just as I am* ii, Even the pigs were the aristocracy of the porker tribe. **1884** *St. James' Gaz.* 11 Dec. 12/1 The stock.. consisted of.. bacon hogs and porkers.

b. *fig.* A fat or porcine person.

1892 [see BALZACIAN *a.*]. **1959** I. & P. OPIE *Lore & Lang. Schoolch.* ix. 168 The unfortunate fat boy.., is known as: back end of a bus.. porker, [etc.]. **1959** *Good Food Guide* 42 So many restaurants in the Thames Valley have been ruined by the expense-account porkers, who neither care what they pay nor know what they eat.

†**2.** A sword. *Obs. slang.* (Cf. *pigsticker*, a long-bladed pocket-knife, or sword.)

1688 SHADWELL *Sqr. Alsatia* I. i, The Captain whipt his porker out. *Ibid.* II. *a* **1700** B. E. *Dict. Cant. Crew, Porker*, a Sword. **1725** in *New Cant. Dict.*

porkery ('pɔəkərı). [f. PORK^1 + -ERY. Cf. ONF. *porkerie*, OF. *porcherie* herd of swine, med. (Anglo-) L. *porcaria, porcheria* a piggery.]

1. Swine collectively, stock of swine.

1829 LANDOR *Imag. Conv., Emp. China & Tsing-Ti* Wks. 1853 II. 146/1, I have killed rats as good meat as your Excellencies, and where your Excellencies (pest on such porkery!) dared not come.

2. Stock of pork, bacon, ham, and the like; pork department.

1890 *Balance Sheet of Co-op. Store*, Balance to Profit and Loss Account Bakery.. Porkery.. General.

porkespine, -pick, etc., obs. ff. PORCUPINE.

porket ('pɔəkıt). [a. ONF. *porket, porquet*, OF. *porchet*, dim. of *porc* PORK^1.] A small or young pig or hog; in mod. dial. use = PORKER 1.

[**1312** *Bolton Priory Comp.* 244 b, Preter, vj. bacones de dono Petri de Mytone. Et .ix. porchettos de dono Eue de Landa.] **1554** BRADFORD in Strype *Eccl. Mem.* (1721) III. App. xxix. 82 Nor any liberty or power upon a poor porket have al the devils in hel. **1563–87** FOXE *A. & M.* (1684) III. 277 We are now become Gergesites, that would rather lose Christs than our Porkets. **1697** DRYDEN *Æneid* XII. 257 [He] off'rings to the flaming altars bears—A porket, and a lamb that never suffer'd shears. **1837** WHEELWRIGHT tr. *Aristophanes* II. 139 Bring.. figs to my porkets. **1900** *Oxford Times* 1 Dec. 2 Prizes.. for bacon hogs and porkets.

pork-flesh. Now *rare.* The flesh of the hog or pig; = PORK^1 2.

1477 EARL RIVERS (Caxton) *Dictes* 10 He commaunded that porke flesshe and camelys sholde be eten. **1563–87** FOXE *A. & M.* (1596) 1417/1 He delighted greatlie in Porke fleshe and Peacockes. **1643** TRAPP *Comm. Gen.* iv. 24 Bring me my pork-flesh. **1904** *Daily Chron.* 4 Aug. 3/3, I almost taste the pork-flesh of Brother Wainwright.

†**'porkin.** *Obs.* [f. PORK^1 + -KIN.] = PORKLING.

1570 LEVINS *Manip.* 134/12 A Porkin, *porcellus.* **1575** TURBERV. *Venerie* 206 They will roundely carie a sheepe or gote or a good porkine in their mouths.

†**'porkish**, *a. Obs.* [f. PORK^1 + -ISH^1.] Piglike, swinish.

1554 BALE *Declar. Bonner's Art.* 66 See.. how arrogaunt this porkishe papist is here. **1570** B. GOOGE *Pop. Kingd.* (1880) 10 And rounde about his porkish necke, his Pall of passing price, He casteth on.

porkling ('pɔəklıŋ). Also 6–7 porklin. [f. PORK^1 + -LING^1.] A little or young pig.

1570 LEVINS *Manip.* 137/31 These be diminutiues, and may be expounded by this signe little, as gosling, or little goose, porkling or little porke. **1577** B. GOOGE *Heresbach's Husb.* III. (1586) 148 b, Twelve hogsties, everie stie conteyning fiftie Porklinges. **1598** FLORIO, *Maranello*, a young pig, or a porklin. **1684** tr. *Agrippa's Van. Arts* lxxxix. 309 The other.. devoured a whole Boar, a hundred Loaves, a Weather, and a Porkling. **1843** *P. Parley's Ann.* IV. 267 The little porkling might have squeezed his way through the palings. **1898** *Blackw. Mag.* Feb. 231/2 A mottled porkling crashed through a little rug of branches.

b. Contemptuously or derisively applied to a person. Also *attrib.*

1542 BECON *Potation for Lent* K viij, The fat Pharise.. the porkelynge Justiciarie, whiche trust in theyr owne righteousnes, are no fytte Gestes for this mooste delicious table. **1550** BALE *Image Both Ch.* II. 92 b, The gloryouse glottons, and franke fedde porkelynges of that gredye gulfe ..whose God ye their bellye. **1602** *Contention Betw. Liberality & Prodigal.* v. i. in Hazl. *Dodsley* VIII. 369 Come, porkling, come on.

'porkman. [f. PORK^1 + MAN *sb.*^{1}] A man who sells pork, a dealer in pork.

1764 *Low Life* (ed. 3) 31 Pork-Men busy in their Shops and Cellars. **1859** DICKENS *T. Two Cities* I. v, The butcher and the porkman painted up only the leanest scrags of meat.

†**'porknell.** *Obs. rare.* [Arbitrary derivative of PORK^1: cf. *cracknel.*]

1. One as fat as a pig.

c **1400** *Destr. Troy* 6368 Polidarius, the porknell, and his pere Machaon, Suet with the xvij [batell].

2. Some part of the offal of a sheep.

1596 NASHE *Saffron Walden* 111 No more doth he feed on anie thing when he is at Saffron Walden, but trotters, sheepes porknells, and buttered rootes.

porkpen, obs. form of PORCUPINE.

†**pork physic**, for *poke physic*, old name of Virginian poke, POKE *sb.*^{4} 2 a.

1733 [see POKE *sb.*^{4} 2 a]. **1753** CHAMBERS *Cycl. Supp.* App., *Poke, or Pork Physic*, the name by which the *Phytolacca* of botanists is sometimes called. **1760** J. LEE *Introd. Bot.* App. 323. **1858** in MAYNE *Expos. Lex.*

pork-'pie. [f. PORK^1 + PIE *sb.*^{2}]

1. A pie of pastry enclosing minced pork.

1732 FIELDING *Miser* III. iii, Let there be.. some dainty fat pork-pye or pasty. **1859** *Eng. Cookery Bk.* 202 A Plain Crust for Pork Pies. **1896** *Cassell's Dict. Cooking* 610 Pork pies are generally made of the trimmings taken from a hog when it is cut up.

2. (In full *pork-pie hat.*) Popularly applied to a hat with a flat crown and a brim turned up all round, worn by women *c* 1855–65, recalling the shape of a deep circular pie; also applied loosely to similar hats worn by men. Also *pork-pie cap.*

1860 G. A. SPOTTISWOODE in *Vac. Tour.* 98 Pork-pie hats with streaming ribbons. **1863** MRS. H. WOOD *Shadow Ashlydyat* (1878) 329 Charlotte rose.. and carried the pork-pie to the chimney-glass, to settle it on. **1883** LD. R. GOWER *My Remin.* I. x. 173 He [Garibaldi] wore a sort of large pork-pie hat. **1888** C. M. YONGE *Beechcroft at Rockstone* II. xv. 41 There certainly was a figure in somewhat close proximity, the ulster and pork-pie hat being such as to make the gender doubtful. **1891** *Spectator* 26 Dec. 924/1 The bull-fighter's hat known in England as the 'pork-pie'. **1910** *Blackw. Mag.* Jan. 113/1 In the dreadful mustard-coloured uniform and pork-pie cap which the Government has ordained for these unusually fat servants. **1937** *Evening News* 12 Feb. 8/3, I seem to remember that porters at the entrances of big hotels once wore greatcoats reaching almost to their ankles and that each had a pork-pie cap with a peak and a little round button on top. **1940** GRAVES & HODGE *Long Week-End* xxi. 376 Low-crowned pork-pie hats were in fashion again. **1943** R. CHANDLER *Lady in Lake* xxi. 118 His blue pork-pie hat was set very square on his head. **1948** M. ALLINGHAM *More Work for Undertaker* xvii. 199 The inevitable green demob pork-pie sat a little too far back from his lined forehead. **1955** *Times* 16 Aug. 8/7 The men had white handkerchiefs on their faces, and wore raincoats and 'pork-pie' hats. **1968** R. CLAPPERTON *No News on Monday* vi. 60, I.. limped down the hot pavement with a straw pork pie tipped forward over my eyes. **1977** *New Yorker* 25 July 61/2 Lawford, the arrant individualist, sometimes showed up on the court wearing a pork-pie hat, a striped jersey, tight knickers, and long stockings.

porkpik, porkpin, obs. ff. PORCUPINE.

porkpisce, obs. form of PORPOISE *sb.*

†**'porkrel.** *Obs. rare*$^{-1}$. [dim. of PORK^1: see -REL.] A young swine; a pig.

1688 CLAYTON in *Phil. Trans.* XVIII. 122 Shoats, or Porkrels are their general Food.

'porkwood. [f. PORK^1 + WOOD *sb.*] The name of certain trees or shrubs. **a.** A bush or small tree (*Kigellaria capensis*) found in the warmer parts of Africa. **b.** *Pisonia obtusata*, the Pigeon-wood, Beef-wood, or Corkwood of the West Indies and Florida.

1880 *S. Africa* (ed. 3) 127 In these kloofs grow.. the Spechout or Porkwood.

porky ('pɔəkı), *a. colloq.* [f. PORK^1 + -Y.] Of, pertaining to, or resembling pork; fleshy, obese.

1852 R. S. SURTEES *Sponge's Sp. Tour* li, Mr. Sponge was a good deal more put out by the incident.. than his porky host. **1866** MRS. RIDDELL *Race for Wealth* xxix, A fat, light-haired, snub-nosed, porky kind of a child. **1890** *Cent. Dict.* s.v., A porky odor permeated the whole place.

porky ('pɔəkı), *sb.* Also porcy. Abbrev. of PORCUPINE *sb.*

1902 W. D. HULBERT *Forest Neighbors* 146 We found the Porky asleep in the sunshine. **1921** *Chambers's Jrnl.* May 290/2 An encounter in which 'Porcy' had the best of it. **1936** D. MCCOWAN *Animals Canad. Rockies* xxvii. 235 A pair of shoes left carelessly outside a tent forms a tasty meal for a prowling Porky. **1956** W. R. BIRD *Off-Trail in Nova Scotia* x. 267 They heard the familiar complainings of a 'porky' on the move.

porle, obs. form of PURL.

Porlock ('pɔːlɔːk). The name of a town in Somerset, used allusively (see quot. 1816) in phr. ***a person*** etc. ***from Porlock***, a person who interrupts at an inconvenient moment.

[**1816** COLERIDGE *Kubla Khan* in *Christabel* 53 At this moment he [*sc.* Coleridge] was unfortunately called out by a person on business from Porlock, and detained by him above an hour.] **1959** *Listener* 1 Jan. 37/3 All the incidental distractions—the telephone-bell, the Christmas carollers at the door, the gentleman or lady 'from Porlock'—to which one is subject.

pormanton, obs. corrupt f. PORTMANTEAU.

porn (pɔːn), **porno** ('pɔːnəʊ), *a.* and *sb. colloq.*

A. *adj.* Abbrevs. of PORNOGRAPHIC *a.*

1952 N. MAILER *Man who studied Yoga* in *Advts. for Myself* (1961) 175, It is dirty, downright porno dirty, it is a lewd slop-brush slapped through the middle of domestic exasperations and breakfast eggs. **1963** 'D. CORY' *Hammerhead* ii. 21 Judging from the script.. it might be just the *tiniest* bit porno. **1964** N. FREELING *Double-Barrel* v. i. 148 Looking at Miss Burger through binoculars was porno ..anything porno is so hatefully sad. **1970** *Time* 16 Nov. 92 So busy are the makers of porn films in San Francisco that they have depressed the market for imported sex movies. **1972** J. BROWN *Chancer* xv. 208 First, take the evidence. The joints, the photos, the porno magazines. **1972** *Screw* 12 June 19/1 This week I am reviewing the very best porn film ever made, so superior to others that it defies comparison. **1972** *New Yorker* 2 Dec. 164/2 They use their porno fantasies as part of the case they make for the slaughter of the whites. **1973** 'D. HALLIDAY' *Dolly & Starry Bird* iii. 36 Jacko had put away his porn pictures. **1974** *Publishers Weekly* 18 Nov. 45/2 A teenage girl who had been trying to make the big time by performing at Beverly Hills orgies and doing porno films. **1976** *Daily Tel.* 13 Feb. 13/5 If only he would feed her, or take her to a porno movie—or even for a walk! **1978** S. SHELDON *Bloodline* xxii. 249 It's a porno film.

B. *sb.* **1.** Abbrevs. of PORNOGRAPHER. *rare.*

1958 L. DURRELL *Balthazar* vi. 144 'The old Porn himself!' (He had coined this nickname from the word 'pornographer'.) **1969** *Time* 5 Sept. 27 The right-wing National Democratic Party derides [Gunther] Grass as a 'porno', because his works are peppered with four-letter words.

2. Abbrevs. of PORNOGRAPHY. Also *attrib.* and qualified by *hard* or *soft* (cf. PORNOGRAPHY 2 a).

1962 *John o' London's* 10 May 456/2 The central character and narrator, the Captain, is a seedy but not at all unsympathetic individual who makes a precarious living by writing 'porn'. **1964** *New Society* 13 Feb. 5/3 The stuff men pass round in barrack rooms as 'a nice bit of porn'. *Ibid.* 6/2 'There's nothing odd about our customers,' the porn shop assistant said. **1967** L. DEIGHTON *London Dossier* 192 Books ..divided into two main sections, straight 'porn' and sadism. **1968** *Punch* 31 July 144/1 Gavin, the Old Etonian ex-monk who is now one of London's most around publishers ('Not porno, love, the word's *engagé*, ha-ha-ha!'). **1969** R. AIRTH *Snatch!* ii. 21 Cognac, cigarettes, porn—small-time, Harry, small-time. **1970** *Guardian* 17 Jan. 10/1 However thin and tippling the Lennon lithographs.. they were not pure tosh or porn. *Ibid.* 26 Nov. 4/4 The porno and sex wave crashes relentlessly on. **1972** *Daily Mirror* 12 Oct. 1 An all-out attack is to be mounted against the porn-pushers in Britain's High Streets. **1973** L. MEYNELL *Thirteen Trumpeters* i. 8 A large and flourishing porn shop. **1974** *Publishers Weekly* 4 Mar. 67/3 The condition of the cinema today (lousy stories, no real stars, too much porno). **1975** D. LODGE *Changing Places* ii. 96 Standing amid the alien porn of Soho. **1976** T. HEALD *Let Sleeping Dogs Die* viii. 154 An elderly woman.. looked up from the nudie magazine... More soft porn lay around her. **1977** E. J. TRIMMER et al. *Visual Dict. Sex* (1978) xxiv. 274 Perhaps the institution of an Oscar for the best hard porn movie of the year might give the producers an incentive to quit conning their public. **1978** M. PUZO *Fools Die* xii. 130, I could write the soft-porn love stories for the top-of-the-line magazine. **1980** G. GREENE *Dr. Fischer* xv. 108, I.. sat for an hour before a soft porn film.

pornerastic (pɔːnə'ræstık), *a.* [f. Gr. πόρνη harlot + ἐραστ-ής lover + -IC.] Addicted to harlotry; whoremongering.

1870 F. HARRISON *Choice Bks.* (1886) 151 We hear nothing of.. those pornerastic habits in high places,.. which are too often thrust before our eyes in fiction.

[**pornial** (in *Cent. Dict.* and Funk's *Standard Dict.*), a spurious word, due to a misreading or misprint of *primal.*]

pornie ('pɔːnı). *slang.* [f. PORN *a.* and *sb.* + -IE.] A pornographic film.

1966 R. H. RIMMER *Harrad Experiment* (1967) 157 'What the devil are pornies?' Beth demanded. Jack grinned. 'Flickers a little on the pornographic side.' **1967** I. HAMILTON *Man with Brown Paper Face* ii. 27 We're planning a pornie for the blue movie racket. **1975** *Publishers Weekly* 17 Feb. 80/3 A nice California kid until she was conned into filming pornies to pay off her lover's addict brother's connection.

porno-, comb. form of PORNOGRAPHY or PORNOGRAPHIC *a.*, prefixed to sbs. and adjs., as ***porno-biography, -film, -movie, -photographer; porno-chic, -gothic*** adjs. (also as sb.); **'pornogram**, a pornographic short poem; **porno'mania**, a mania for pornography; **'pornophile** a lover of pornography; **porno-'phobic** *a.*, having a horror of pornography (in quot. *absol.*); **'Pornosec**, a name given to a department of the Ministry of Truth by George Orwell in his novel 'Nineteen Eighty-Four'; **porno'topia**, an ideal setting for the activities described in pornographic literature.

1970 *Sat. Rev.* (U.S.) 17 Oct. 32 The mildly lascivious may be grateful that he gives the longest plot summary of *Glenarvon* I know of, and prints the entire text of *Don Leon*, a not very titillating piece of pornobiography. **1971** *New Yorker* 11 Dec. 24 The Music Lovers—Ken Russell seems to have invented a new genre of pornobiography. In this film, Tchaikovsky is the chief victim of Russell's baroque vulgarity. **1973** *Times* 17 Feb. 12/8, I went to see *Deep Throat*, which is the big porno-chic movie of all time. **1969** *Truth* (Melbourne) 12 July 13/2 In these two countries [*sc.* America and England], there are something like 350 theatres and cinema clubs which feature and openly advertise movies under the name of pornofilms. **1968** *Tribune* 16 Feb. 11/1 So one must, I think acquit James Saunders of all but the technical responsibilities of adapting 'The Italian Girl', a pornogothick novel by Iris Murdoch, for the stage. **1975** *New Yorker* 19 May 23/1 *The Night Porter*—A porno gothic, set in Vienna in 1957 and veneered with redeeming social values. **1936** C. S. LEWIS *Allegory of Love* vi. 251 He [*sc.* Dunbar] practises every form from satiric pornogram to devotional lyric. **1979** K. BONFIGLIONI *After you with Pistol* xvi. 119 Death..lays on others the chore of hiding the pornograms, the illegal firearms, the incriminating letters. **1969** *Daily Tel.* 25 Apr. 20/3 Haven't we got a steadily increasing amount of violence, bigotry and gang warfare (to say nothing of..nihilism and pornomania)? **1969** *Truth* (Melbourne) 12 July 13/5 Pornomovies which are being shown in theatres in America, England and Western Europe known as sex houses. **1976** *Publishers Weekly* 16 Feb. 80/2 He comes in contact with porno movies and a girl who makes them. **1977** M. DRABBLE *Ice Age* I. 61 He'd been had up for offering bribes to council employees: the whole story had been ridiculous, tales of..call girls and twenty-pound notes, of tax evasion and porno-movies. **1960** *20th Cent.* May 434 The great social surveys..are no diet for the pornophile. *a* **1966** E. WAUGH in D. Pryce-Jones *Evelyn Waugh* (1973) xiv. 226 Will not this bit in the *Sunday Times* excite your pornophiles to fancy prices? **1973** *Austral. Humanist* XXVI. 4/2 Mary Whitehouse could provide fresh impetus for the pornophobic. **1965** *Listener* 3 June 837/1 A sequence of Gaby..untrussing for Pierre Louys in a room full of Oriental knick-knacks, then being somewhat primly caressed by the great pornophotographer. **1949** 'G. ORWELL' *Nineteen Eighty-Four* I. 46 There was even a whole sub-section [*sc.* of the Ministry of Truth]—*Pornosec*, it was called in Newspeak—engaged in producing the lowest kind of pornography. *Ibid.* II. 132 Pornosec, the sub-section of the Fiction Department which turned out cheap pornography for distribution among the proles. **1966** S. MARCUS *Other Victorians* v. 216 The results..are to turn the novel in the direction of pornotopia—that vision which regards all of human experience as a series of exclusively sexual events or conveniences.

pornocracy (pɔː'nɒkrəsɪ). [f. Gr. πόρνη harlot + -CRACY.] Dominating influence of harlots or prostitutes: *spec.* the government of Rome during the first half of the tenth century.

1860 EDERSHEIM tr. *Kurtz's Ch. Hist.* II. §126. 379 For half a century Theodora..and her equally infamous daughters, ..filled the See of Peter with their paramours, their sons, and grandsons,..(the so-called Pornocracy). **1874** DEUTSCH *Remains* 245. **1882–3** *Schaff's Encycl. Relig. Knowl.* I. 484 A century of shameless intrigue and fighting—the period of the Pornocracy.

So **'pornocrat**, a member of a pornocracy.

1894 *Contemp. Rev.* Aug. 286 The most licentious and shameless of the Pornocrats.

pornograph ('pɔːnəgrɑːf, -græf-), *sb.* (*a.*) [In sense 1 of the *sb.*, a. F. *pornographe* pornographer, ad. Gr. πορνογράφ-ος: see next; for sense 2 cf. -GRAPH.]

A. *sb.* †**1.** = PORNOGRAPHER. *Obs.*

1877 *Contemp. Rev.* Mar. 562 He would recognize..the difference between Pheidias and the pornographs.

2. An obscene writing or pictorial illustration.

1890 in *Century Dict.* **1955** M. ALLINGHAM *Beckoning Lady* vii. 109 Through the window, a line of bladders, now a trifle flabby, were..visible. 'Listen.' Tonker seized the mouthgrip... Mr. Campion pulled himself together. 'It's horrible,' he said. 'A pornograph, Tonker.' **1967** *Spectator* 1 Dec. 683/1 A pornograph can be either verbal or visual, but the visual stimulus is generally more intense than the verbal one.

B. as *adj.* = PORNOGRAPHIC.

1893 SALTUS *Madam Sapphira* 165 Here the reporter can be as pornograph as the Marquess of Sade, if he knows how.

pornographer (pɔː'nɒgrəfə(r)). [f. Gr. πορνογράφ-ος writing of harlots (f. πόρνη harlot + -γράφος writing, writer) + -ER[1].] One who writes of prostitutes or obscene matters; a portrayer of obscene subjects.

1850 LEITCH tr. *C. O. Müller's Anc. Art* §429 (ed. 2) 619 The pornographers of the later times. **1886** *Lit. World* (U.S.) 1 May 152/1 They call themselves 'naturalists',..but they are in fact only pornographers, and immature, inexperienced, conceited, love-mad youngsters. **1890** *Harper's Mag.* Nov. 904/2 Parisian artistic pornographers.

pornographic (pɔːnə'græfɪk), *a.* [f. as prec. + -IC. So F. *pornographique.*] Of, pertaining to, or of the nature of pornography; dealing in the obscene.

1880 *Guardian* 27 Oct. 1450 The excesses of the [French] press designated as 'pornographic'..have..become such as to compel the authorities to adopt strong measures against them. **1881** SYMONDS *Ital. Renaiss., Ital. Lit.* II. xiv. 365 Pornographic Pamphleteers and Poets. **1894** STEAD *If Christ Came to Chicago* 117 Two booksellers..whose windows still contain a large and varied collection of pornographic literature.

Hence **porno'graphica**, pornographic literature or art; **porno'graphical** *a.* (in quot. *fig.*); **porno'graphically** *adv.*; **pornographico-** *comb. form*, as ***porno'graphico-de'votional*** adj.; **porno-graphize** *v. trans.*, to make pornographic in character.

1917 J. B. CABELL *Cream of Jest* II. v. 65 The latest masterpiece of a pornographically gifted genius. **1921** *Times Lit. Suppl.* 10 Feb. 90/4 She introduced him to a coward, an alienist who was himself mad, a pornographically minded professor. **1939** A. TOYNBEE *Study of Hist.* V. 531 Apuleius's pornographico-devotional romance [*sc. Metamorphoses*]. **1966** *New Statesman* 16 Dec. 912/3 Within half a mile of Great Marlborough Street, shops with red neon signs offering 'Books' go on selling printed pornographica at eight quid a time. **1968** *Economist* 7 Dec. 79/3 Facing the exchange rate problem, he maintained, does not mean that 'pornographical financial thoughts are being harboured'. **1971** S. CAVELL *World Viewed* xiii. 95 Godard perceives..that our tastes and convictions in love have become pornographized. **1973** J. MONEY in Zubin & Money *Contemp. Sexual Behavior* 414 *True Confessions* and *True Love* magazine stories are, in fact, the genuine pornography of women. So women have been allowed to enjoy themselves pornographically as much as they desire. **1978** D. MURRAY *Place Apart* ix. 199, I stood in the middle of the road being pornographically insulted.

pornography (pɔː'nɒgrəfɪ). [f. as prec. + -Y. So F. *pornographie.*]

1. (See quot.)

1857 DUNGLISON *Med. Dict.*, *Pornography*, a description of prostitutes or of prostitution, as a matter of public hygiene. **1858** in MAYNE *Expos. Lex.* **1895** in *Syd. Soc. Lex.*

2. a. Description of the life, manners, etc., of prostitutes and their patrons; hence, the expression or suggestion of obscene or unchaste subjects in literature or art; pornographic literature or art. Also qualified by *hard* or *soft*, with reference to *hard core* (b) s.v. HARD *a.* 23 b, *soft core* s.v. SOFT *a.* 29, to denote pornography of a more, or less, obscene kind. Also *transf.*

1864 WEBSTER, *Pornography*, licentious painting employed to decorate the walls of rooms sacred to bacchanalian orgies, examples of which exist in Pompeii. **1882** *Daily Tel.* No. 8313. 5/4 Pictorial and glyptic 'pornography'..grew, flourished, declined, and fell with the Second Empire. **1896** MACKAIL *Lat. Lit.* 18 The Casina and the Truculentus [of Plautus] are studies in pornography which only the unflagging animal spirits of the poet can redeem from being disgusting. **1930** W. S. MAUGHAM *Gent. in Parlour* xii. 64 Pornography rather than brevity is the soul of wit. **1968** *Sat. Rev.* (U.S.) 19 Oct. 23 In recent years the movies and television have developed a pornography of violence far more demoralizing than the pornography of sex, which still seizes the primary attention of the guardians of civic virtue. **1972** *Times Lit. Suppl.* 7 Jan. 12/2 Of course pornography should never be treated as if only its sexual aspects mattered—that is, as if no other kind of stimulus offered by the written word could be as socially or ethically significant. **1976** *Time* (Canada ed.) 5 Apr. 36/1 What pornography is can endlessly be debated. One rough definition: explicit books, films and other materials (including, by extension, performances) designed chiefly for sexual arousal. **1977** *Broadcast* 30 May 3/3 [Italian] 'pirate' TV stations which flourish on..'soft pornography'. **1977** *Lancet* 11 June 1241/2 A distinction could be drawn between erotic art (or soft pornography)..and hard pornography, which by connecting sex with violence, hatred, pain, and humiliation, stimulated gratification of sexual desire in deviant ways.

b. In *transf.* and extended uses.

1968 [see above]. **1977** *Listener* 17 Nov. 655/4 Turgid moralising..is the real English vice, the pornography of our day.

So **por'nographist**, a writer on pornography.

1893 *Nation* (N.Y.) 3 Aug. 79/2 The 'grossness of the naturalists and the subtleties of the pornographists', to use the words of M. Lavisse, cannot have any other result.

porny ('pɔːnɪ), *a. slang.* [f. PORN *sb* + -Y[1].] Of, pertaining to, or characteristic of pornography; pornographic.

1961 S. PRICE *Just for Record* viii. 65 He had a real porny article... Not just dirty, mind you, but Art. **1967** [see KINKY *a.* B]. **1973** J. WILSON *Truth or Dare* i. 12 You make it sound like one of those porny books—'His hand caressed her silken knee' and all that rubbish. **1974** *Daily Tel.* 18 Oct. 16 A reduction in repeats, inane quizzes and cheap porny [television] programmes could do nothing but good. **1977** L. MEYNELL *Hooky gets Wooden Spoon* xiii. 157 Once he starts looking at those porny photos of his he can't think of anything else.

Poro ('pɒrəʊ). Also poro, Porro, purra, Purrow. [W. Afr.] The name of a secret tribal cult for men, based on circumcision and a school of initiation, which is widespread amongst tribes in Sierra Leone and Liberia, and is socially powerful; the head of such a tribal group; also *attrib.* Cf. SANDE.

1788 J. NEWTON *Thoughts upon Afr. Slave Trade* 15 The Purrow has both the legislative and executive authority. *Ibid.*, Everything belonging to the Purrow is mysterious and severe. **1803** T. WINTERBOTTOM *Acct. Native Africans Sierra Leone* I. viii. 135 They [*sc.* the Bulloms] have a superior, or head purra man, assisted by a grand council. **1925** T. N. GODDARD *Handbk. Sierra Leone* iii. 57 Initiation into the Porro society takes place in youth. While boys remain in the Porro bush they are taught the arts and crafts of their tribe. **1930** R. P. STRONG *Afr. Republ. Liberia* I. v. 83 The *poro* or presiding official of the society also uses signs to indicate the entrance to the bush school. **1954** E. WARNER *Trial by Sasswood* (1955) ix. 161 The Loma have the most vigorous of Poro cults and are credited with having introduced the Poro into Liberia. **1962** C. FYFE *Hist. Sierra Leone* xx. 571 Those who planned the rising had used the Poro as a cover to ensure secrecy. **1968** HARRIS & SAWYERR *Springs of Mende Belief* i. 1 The principal tribal cults, *poro* and *sande*... Poro..is made manifest by a series of rites and ceremonies depicting death to the early stages of life, and re-birth through resurrection to adulthood.

porocyte ('pɒrəʊsaɪt). *Zool.* [f. Gr. πόρο-ς PORE *sb.*[1] + -CYTE.] In sponges, a cell containing a pore.

1898 E. A. MINCHIN in *Q. Jrnl. Microsc. Sci.* XL. 485 The especial functions and consequent peculiar form of the pore-cells, or porocytes, as they may be termed generally,..enable us to regard the pore-cells as constituting a distinct class of cell-elements. **1932** BORRADAILE & POTTS *Invertebrata* iii. 111 Other cells, known as porocytes, of a conical shape, extend through the jelly, having their base in the covering layer. **1940** G. S. CARTER *Gen. Zool. Invertebrates* xix. 384 These pores pass through the substance of cells which surround them—the porocytes. **1966** *McGraw-Hill Encycl. Sci. & Technol.* II. 393/1 Cells called porocytes..pierce the walls [of calcareous sponges] at intervals and allow water to enter the central cavity.

porodinic ('pɒrəʊ-, pɔərəʊ'dɪnɪk), *a. Zool.* [f. Gr. πόρος PORE *sb.*[1] + ὠδίς, ὠδῖν- travail, birth + -IC.] Discharging the genital products by means of a pore: opp. to SCHIZODINIC.

1883 E. R. LANKESTER in *Encycl. Brit.* XVI. 682/1 *note*, Cœlomate animals are, according to this nomenclature, either Schizodinic or Porodinic. The Porodinic group is divisible into Nephrodinic and Idiodinic, in the former the nephridium serving as a pore, in the latter a special (ἴδιος) pore being developed.

po'rodinous, *a. Geol. rare.* [Improperly f. Ger. *porodine* (Breithaupt 1832) (f. Gr. πωρώδης having the form of stalactite (f. πῶρος hardened stone, stalactite): see -INE[2]) + -OUS. A better form would be *porodine*, like *crystalline*, *hyaline*.] See quot.

1876 A. H. GREEN *Phys. Geology* ii. §4. 45 *Porodinous* [rocks], or those which have solidified from a gelatinous state. Certain minerals, such as Opal,..have in all likelihood been formed in this way.

porogamic (pɒrəʊ-, pɔərəʊ'gæmɪk), *a. Bot.* [mod. f. Gr. πόρος PORE *sb.*[1] + γάμ-ος marriage + -IC. (Treub, *Ann. Jardin Bot. de Buitenzorg*, (1891.)] Applied to fertilization in which the pollen-tube enters the ovule by the micropyle, as in most plants: opposed to *chalazogamic*. (Also said of the plant.) So **'porogam**, a plant characterized by this mode of fertilization.

1894 *Times* 11 Aug. 11/3 Professor Balfour hesitated to adopt Treub's division into chalazogams and porogams until the limits of the former group were better defined. **1895** OLIVER tr. *Kerner's Nat. Hist. Plants* II. 412 This type of fertilization has been termed chalazogamic in contradistinction to the more usual micropylar or porogamic method.

porogamous (pɒ'rɒgəməs), *a. Bot.* [f. as POROGAMIC *a.* + -OUS.] = POROGAMIC *a.* So **po'rogamy**, fertilization of this kind.

1902 *Encycl. Brit.* XXV. 436/1 The pollen-tube normally reaches the apex of the embryo-sac through the micropyle (acrogamy or porogamy). **1905** I. B. BALFOUR tr. *C. E. von Goebel's Organogr. Plants* II. 615 The micropyle in all porogamous plants evidently conducts the pollen-tube. **1950** P. MAHESHWARI *Introd. Embryol. Angiosperms* vi. 183 The tube may enter the ovule either through the micropyle or by some other route. The former is the usual condition and is known as porogamy. *Ibid.* 184 Even in plants classed as porogamous, there are several modifications. **1965** BELL & COOMBE tr. *Strasburger's Textbk. Bot.* 631 The pollen tube may reach the micropyle and hence the embryo sac by traversing the cavity of the ovule at a point where it is commonly filled with mucilage (porogamy, Fig. 757).

porokeratosis (ˌpɒrəʊ-, ˌpɔərəʊkɛrə'təʊsɪs). *Path.* [mod.L., ad. It. *porocheratosi* (V. Mibelli 1893, in *Giorn. Ital. delle Malattie Veneree* XXVIII. 340), f. Gr. πόρο-ς PORE *sb.*[1]: see *keratosis* s.v. KERATO-.] A skin disease in which the lesions are annular horny ridges enclosing an atrophic area and (in the rare classic form of the disease) usu. occur early in life on the hands and feet.

1893 tr. V. Mibelli in P. G. Unna et al. *Internationaler Atlas Seltener Hautkrankenheiten* xxvii. (1) 10/2 As regards the microscopic examination the case presents itself as a pathological fact *sui generis*, inasmuch as the principal alteration consists in hyperkeratosis of the sudoriferous ducts; and it is on this account that it deserves to be considered apart under the designation of 'Porokeratosis' which I propose provisionally as it has the merit of indicating clearly the anatomo-pathological significance of the alteration itself. **1899** *Allbutt's Syst. Med.* VIII. 478 In connection with these ringed nodules of the hands the peculiar disease known as Porokeratosis should be mentioned. **1943** *Arch. Dermatol. & Syphilol.* XLVII. 2 The extension of a lesion of porokeratosis is usually centrifugal, slow and insidious in onset, leaving a somewhat atrophic area in the center free of hair and glandular structures. **1960** J. MARSHALL *Dis. Skin* xxix. 777 Porokeratosis is a misnomer as the lesions are not, as Mibelli believed, related to sweat pores. **1967** *Arch. Dermatol.* XCVI. 611/1 This study of 31 patients presents disseminated superficial actinic porokeratosis (DSAP) as a distinctive and recognizable entity characterized by many uniformly small, minimal, annular, anhidrotic, keratotic lesions developing during the third or fourth decade of life on sun-exposed areas of skin. **1973** *Internat. Jrnl. Dermatol.* XII. 152/1 Our recent studies indicate that disseminated superficial actinic porokeratosis (DSAP) is a distinct entity which differs in many aspects from classic porokeratosis described by Mibelli and by Respighi.

Hence ˌ**porokera'totic** *a.*

1943 *Arch. Dermatol. & Syphilol.* XLVII. 14 This consideration excludes the necessity of calling the lesion a nevus, in spite of the strong tendency of porokeratotic lesions to arrange themselves in linear and systematized configuration. **1972** *Brit. Jrnl. Plastic Surg.* XXV. 325 The tumours in both our cases were multifocal, and appeared to have arisen in the atrophic zone of the Porokeratotic lesion.

†**po'rology.** *Obs. nonce-wd.* [f. Gr. πόρος PORE *sb.*[1] + -LOGY.] A scientific treatise on, or investigation of, pores or minute openings.

1684 BOYLE *Porousn. Anim. & Solid Bod.* i. 2 If such little things had not escaped the sight of our illustrious Verulam, he would have afforded a good Porology..among his *Desiderata*.

poromeric (pɔərəʊ'mɛrɪk), *a.* and *sb.* [f. PORO(US *a.* + POLY)MERIC *a.*] **A.** *adj.* Applied to synthetic leather-like materials that are permeable to water vapour. **B.** *sb.* A poromeric material.

1963 *Boot & Shoe Recorder* 1 Oct. 117/3 Du Pont has coined a generic term for it [*sc.* 'Corfam']: 'poromeric', which means a 'microporous and permeable coriaceous sheet material'. **1964** *Times Rev. Industry* Mar. 23/2 Another new Du Pont development is Corfam, a 'poromeric' material which has brought a breakthrough in the manufacture of shoe uppers, since it 'breathes' like leather. **1966** *Chem. & Engin. News* 19 Dec. 13/1 Farbwerke Hoechst's subsidiary, Kalle, A.G., has a poromeric at the development stage. **1967** *Economist* 4 Nov. 544/3 Both Du Pont's and ICI's products are porous, or poromeric, as the trade chooses to say,..but Courtaulds' Quox is not, and is therefore only suitable for sandals. **1971** *New Scientist* 12 Aug. 370/2 The collagenous poromerics currently under development..are mostly in the form of a fibrous mat composed of intermingled collagen and synthetic fibres agglomerated by a polymeric bonding agent. **1978** *Times* 26 Apr. 12/2 The high quality poromeric synthetic materials.. launched in the 1960s never fulfilled..expectations. *Ibid.* 12/4 The breakthrough..came with the poromerics.. which, the makers claimed breathe like leather.

porometer (pɒ'rɒmɪtə(r)). [f. Gr. πόρο-ς PORE *sb.*[1] + -METER.] An instrument for measuring the degree of porosity; *spec.* one for estimating the sizes of the stomata of leaves by measuring the rate at which air can be passed through them.

1911 DARWIN & PERTZ in *Proc. R. Soc.* B. LXXXIV. 137 We believe that a much more intimate knowledge of the *living* stoma and its movements would be necessary to prove his contention..that 'the regulatory function is almost *nil*'. With a view to testing the question we have designed an instrument which we propose to call a porometer. The idea is to estimate changes in the stomata by recording the change in the velocity of a current of air drawn through them in the living leaf. **1939** *Geogr. Jrnl.* XCIV. 124 The effect of the continuous illumination of the arctic summer in the stomatal mechanism of leaves was studied by porometers. **1970** *Nature* 25 July 377/2 The stomatal activity of fully hydrated..broad bean plants..was investigated using a recording porometer attached to the second mature leaves from the apex. **1975** G. ANDERSON *Coring* iv. 77 The basic instruments [for core analysis] are the porometer for porosity measurements, the permeameter for permeability measurements, and the saturation retorts for saturation measurements.

porophyllous (pɒrəʊ-, pɔərəʊ'fɪləs), *a. Bot. rare*$^{-0}$. [f. mod.L. *porphyllus* (f. Gr. πόρος PORE *sb.*[1] + φύλλον leaf) + -OUS.] (See quot.)

1858 MAYNE *Expos. Lex.*, *Porophyllus, Bot.*, having leaves sprinkled with transparent points like pores..: porophyllous.

poroplastic (pɒrəʊ-, pɔərəʊ'plæstɪk), *a.* [f. Gr. πόρος PORE *sb.*[1] + PLASTIC.] Both porous and plastic: applied to a kind of porous felt, plastic when heated, becoming stiff when cold, used for splints and other surgical appliances.

1879 *St. George's Hosp. Rep.* IX. 615 Severer cases..have had the plaster of-Paris or 'poro-plastic' jacket applied. **1898** *Westm. Gaz.* 19 July 5/1 An elastic kneecap costs half a crown, a moleskin one five shillings, a leather one five to twenty, and a poroplastic any sum.

poroporo ('pɒrəʊpɒrəʊ). [Maori name.]

A shrub, *Solanum aviculare*, belonging to the family Solanaceæ, native to Australia and New Zealand, and bearing violet-blue flowers followed by large orange berries; also called bullibulli or kangaroo apple.

1853 J. D. HOOKER *Bot. Antarctic Voy.*: *Flora Novæ-Zelandiæ* I. 182 Nat[ive] name [of *Solanum aviculare*], 'Poroporo' in the northern, and 'Kohoho' in the southern parts of the Islands. **1857** C. HURSTHOUSE *N. Zealand* I. 136 The Poroporo..is a sodden strawberry flavoured with apple peel. **1872** A. DOMETT *Ranolf* XVIII. vi. 312 Potato-apples of the poroporo tall. **1882** W. D. HAY *Brighter Britain!* II. 152 Among indigenous vegetable productions came..the berries of poroporo..and other trees. **1921** H. GUTHRIE-SMITH *Tutira* xxii. 216 At other times of the year kowhai and hill-flax..will provide nectar,..poroporo..and other native plants, seeds and berries. **1965** [see GUNYANG]. **1970** M. E. FISHER et al. *Gardening with N.Z. Plants* 112 The poroporo is a leafy shrub.

porose (pɒ'rəʊs), *a.* [ad. L. type *porōs-us (in mod.L.); in It. and Sp. *poroso.*] Containing or abounding in pores; porous; now rare exc. in *Zool.*, said of corals of the division *Perforata*, as opposed to the *Aporosa*, and of the sculpture of insects dotted or pitted as if with minute holes.

[*c* **1400**: see POROUS.] **1656** BLOUNT *Glossogr.*, *Porose* or *Porous* (*porosus*), full of pores or little holes. *Bacon.* **1697** A. DE LA PRYME *Diary* (Surtees) 147 There is a most delicate fine freestone,..but so porose..that, troughs being made of it, it will let the water run out for a year or two. **1715** CHEYNE *Philos. Princ. Relig.* I. (1716) 15 These Porose Bodies must be equally heavy with the most compact ones. **1826** KIRBY & SP. *Entomol.* IV. 270 Porose, beset with many pores. Ex. *Elytra* of most *Apions*.

Hence **po'roseness** = POROSITY.

1746 ARDERON in *Phil. Trans.* XLIV. 282 *note*, The Nature of these Horns seems..changed into that of Chalk; only retaining their outward Form, and the Poroseness of their inward Parts.

‖**porosis** (pɒ'rəʊsɪs). *Physiol.* [mod.L., a. Gr. πώρωσις in same sense, f. πωροῦν to form a callus, f. πῶρος PORE *sb.*[2]] The formation of a callus, as in a fractured bone.

1693 tr. *Blancard's Phys. Dict.* (ed. 2), *Porosis*, the breeding of callous Matter. **1706** in PHILLIPS. **1858** in MAYNE *Expos. Lex.*

porosity (pɒ'rɒsɪtɪ). [ad. med.L. *porōsitās* (Albertus Magnus *a* 1250), f. L. type *porōs-us POROUS: see -ITY. Cf. F. *porosité*.] **a.** The quality or fact of being porous; porous consistence. Also, the degree to which a substance is porous (see quots.).

1398 TREVISA *Barth. De P.R.* IV. ii. (1495) e v b/1 The porosytee of the tree drawyth þe fumosyte from the rynde. **1615** CROOKE *Body of Man* 385 This porosite also makes their vpper face smooth, and bedewed with a kind of slimy moisture. **1796** KIRWAN *Elem. Min.* (ed. 2) I. 231 It is the porosity of this stone that renders it so light. **1871** TYNDALL *Fragm. Sc.* (1879) I. v. 183 In virtue of its extreme porosity, a similar power is possessed by charcoal. **1939** *U.S. Dept. Agric. Yearbk. 1938* 1174 *Porosity, soil*, degree to which the soil mass is permeated with pores or cavities. **1971** *Gloss. Soil Sci. Terms* (Soil Sci. Soc. Amer.) 13/2 *Porosity*, the volume percentage of the total bulk not occupied by solid particles. **1975** G. ANDERSON *Coring* i. 2 Porosity is a measure of the space in a rock not occupied by the solid structure or framework of the rock. It is defined as the fraction of the total bulk volume of the rock not occupied by solids. *Ibid.*, A commercial oil-bearing sandstone can have varying porosities... The formation should contain at least 8–10% porosity before it can be considered commercially interesting.

b. *concr.* A porous part or structure; an interstice or pore. (Usually in *pl.*)

1597 A. M. tr. *Guillemeau's Fr. Chirurg.* 9 b/2 The Diploe, that is, the porositye which is betweene them bothe [tables of skull]. **1669** W. SIMPSON *Hydrol. Chym.* 284 Sudden floods filling the porosities and chanels of the superficies of the earth. **1831** R. KNOX *Cloquet's Anat.* 15 Found in the interstices of the laminæ of the compact tissue, and the porosities with which they seem perforated.

po'roso-, combining form of mod.L. *porōsus* POROSE, as in **poˌroso-'punctate** *a.*, minutely punctate as if with pores.

1846 DANA *Zooph.* (1848) 416 Interstices smooth, porosopunctate.

porostomatous (pɒrəʊ-, pɔərəʊ'stɒmətəs), *a. Zool.* [f. mod.L. *Porostomata* (f. Gr. πόρο-ς pore + στόμα(τ-) mouth) + -OUS.] Belonging to or having the characters of the *Porostomata*, a group of nudibranchiate gastropods in which the mouth is pore-shaped.

porotic (pɒ'rɒtɪk), *a.* and *sb. Med.* ? *Obs. rare*$^{-0}$. [ad. mod.L. *pōrōtic-us*, f. Gr. πωρόειν to form a callus, f. πῶρος PORE *sb.*[2]: see -IC.] (See quots.)

1696 PHILLIPS (ed. 5), *Porotick Medicines*, Medicines which by drying, thickning and astringent Qualities turn part of the Nourishment into brawny or callous Matter. **1753** CHAMBERS *Cycl. Supp.*, *Poroticks*, a term used by the antients for such medicines as would consume callus. **1842** DUNGLISON *Med. Lex.*, *Porotic*, a remedy believed to be capable of assisting the formation of callus. **1895** *Syd. Soc. Lex.*

porotype ('pɒrəʊ-, 'pɔərətaɪp). [mod. f. Gr. πόρος PORE *sb.*[1] + TYPE.] A print made upon prepared paper by exposing an engraving or writing to some gas which penetrates those parts not rendered impervious by the ink, and bleaches or discolours the paper so as to produce a copy of the original, in the same way as light produces a copy from a photographic negative.

1884 KNIGHT *Dict. Mech.* Suppl., *Porotype*, a method of copying engravings. It depends upon the fact that the portion of the face of the print occupied by ink is non-porous.

porous ('pɔərəs), *a.* [= F. *poreux* (14th c. in Hatz.-Darm.), It., Sp. *poroso*, ad. L. type *porōs-us (in mod.L.), f. *porus* PORE *sb.*[1]: see -OUS.] Full of or abounding in pores; having minute interstices through which water, air, light, etc. may pass.

porous plaster, a plaster having numerous small holes pierced through it so as to enable it to lie smoothly (*Syd. Soc. Lex.*).

c **1400** *Lanfranc's Cirurg.* 107 It schulde ben more rare & more porous [*v.r.* porose], þat is to seie, more ful of hoolis. **1567** MAPLET *Gr. Forest* 33 It is nothing solide or massie, but much porouse. **1625** N. CARPENTER *Geog. Del.* II. ix. (1635) 153 The Porous and spongy nature of the Earth is apt to drinke in the water of the sea. **1692** BENTLEY *Boyle Lect.* 207 If gold it self be admitted, as it must be, for a porous concrete. **1794** SULLIVAN *View Nat.* I. 359 Light, in its passage, penetrates the porous vacuities. **1879** RUTLEY *Stud. Rocks* i. 5 Questions of water supply hinge mainly on the porous or impervious character of rocks.

b. *fig.*

1642 H. MORE *Song of Soul* III. Pref., Many [arguments]..go through their more porous and spongy minds without any sensible impression. **1795** COLERIDGE *Plot Discovered* 19 But our minister's..style is infinitely porous. **1864** CARLYLE *Fredk. Gt.* XVI. vii. (1872) VI. 207 Men are very porous; weighty secrets oozing out of them, like quicksilver through clay jars.

c. Acting or performed by means of pores.

1861 BENTLEY *Man. Bot.* (1870) 302 Porous dehiscence is an irregular kind of dehiscence.

'**porously**, *adv.* [f. prec. + -LY[2].] In a porous manner; with porousness; by means of pores.

1847 in WEBSTER; and in later Dicts.

'**porousness.** [f. as prec. + -NESS.] The quality or condition of being porous; porosity.

1668 WILKINS *Real Char.* II. vii. §6. 186 Porousness, Spunginess, fungous, sinking, hollow. **1670** CAPT. J. SMITH *Eng. Improv. Reviv'd* 16 Marle..by its glutinous substance being incorporated with the sand, closes the hollows and porousness thereof. **1775** STRANGE in *Phil. Trans.* LXV. 419 This porousness I also remember to have once before observed. *Mod.* There is a constant evaporation from the surface of the jar, on account of the porousness of the material.

fig. **1904** *Daily News* 6 June 3 Not less striking was the evident porousness of this over seventy-year-old man to fresh conceptions of truth.

b. *concr.* Porous substance or part. *rare.*

1644 DIGBY *Nat. Bodies* iv. §4. 28 They will forcibly gett into the porousnesse of it, and passe with violence betweene part and part.

porpaise, -pas(s(e, -pes(s(e, obs. ff. PORPOISE *sb.*

porpan-, porpentine, etc.: see PORCUPINE.

porpere, obs. form of *purpure*: see PURPLE.

porphere, -erie, -ier, -ir(e, -iry, -ure, -yr, obs. forms of PORPHYRY.

porphin ('pɔːfɪn). *Chem.* Also **-ine**. [a. G. *porphin* (Fischer & Halbig 1926, in *Ann. der Chem.* CDXLVIII. 194), f. *porph(yr)in* PORPHYRIN.] A synthetic, purple, crystalline solid, $C_{20}H_{14}N_4$, which has a macrocyclic aromatic molecule consisting of four pyrrole residues linked by −CH= groups, and from which the porphyrins are formally derived; now also = PORPHYRIN.

1926 *Brit. Chem. Abstr.* A. 963/1 The name 'porphin' is suggested for the parent substance of (II), containing no β-substituents. **1939** *Nature* 10 June 967/1 The chlorophyll molecule may be likened to a signet, or rubber stamp, the disk representing a so-called porphine ring. **1939** *Thorpe's Dict. Appl. Chem.* (ed. 4) III. 82/2 Porphin and the porphyrins..possess a characteristic type of absorption spectrum, and the power to form stable derivatives with metals, in which the two imino-hydrogen atoms are substituted, *e.g.* by a divalent metal atom. **1954** A. WHITE et al. *Princ. Biochem.* x. 201 Porphin was first synthesized by Hans Fischer and Gleim in 1935; the compound is not known to occur in nature. **1966** *Q. Rev. Chem. Soc.* XX. 211 When each of the four pyrrole rings of a porphin bears two different substituents A and B in the β-positions, then four isomers exist. **1968** I. L. FINAR *Org. Chem.* (ed. 4) II. xix. 797 Fleischer *et al.* (1965) have also examined porphin by X-ray analysis, and found the molecule is nearly planar, the observed small deviations from planarity not being large enough to be significant. *Ibid.*, Substituted porphins are known as porphyrins. **1973** *Jrnl. Amer. Chem. Soc.* XCV. 8506/2 The porphine used in this study was prepared by the acid-catalyzed condensation of pyrrole-2-carbinol in 10% acetic acid-xylene solution.

porphobilin (pɔːfəʊ'baɪlɪn). *Biochem.* [a. G. *porphobilin* (Waldenström & Vahlquist 1939, in *Zeitschr. f. physiol. Chem.* CCLX. 191), f. *porphyrie* PORPHYRIA + -O + L. *bīl-is* BILE: see -IN[1].] Any of a group of red-brown pigments derived from porphobilinogen.

1939 *Chem. Abstr.* XXXIII. 8777/1 Boiling in acid destroys I by conversion to a red porphobilin (II) with a mol. wt. of 750 to 800. **1952** *Science* 2 May 496/2 Solutions of porphobilinogen obtained by the above method, after having been acidified to pH 4·0 and boiled for 30 min, gave rise only to porphobilin, a dark-brown pigment without characteristic absorption spectrum or any porphyrin characteristics. **1964** A. WHITE et al. *Princ. Biochem.* (ed. 3) xlii. 793 The urine darkens markedly on standing, because of the conversion of abnormal quantities of porphyrinogens and other heme precursors into porphyrins, porphobilins, and other unidentified pigments.

porphobilinogen (ˌpɔːfəʊbaɪˈlɪnədʒən). *Biochem.* [a. G. *porphobilinogen* (Waldenström & Vahlquist 1939, in *Zeitschr. f. physiol. Chem.* CCLX. 191), f. prec.: see -OGEN.] A colourless, crystalline, substituted pyrrole, $C_{10}H_{14}N_2O_4$ (see quot. 1972), which in animals is a precursor of porphyrins and is excreted in the commoner forms of porphyria.

1939 *Chem. Abstr.* XXXIII. 8777/1 In acute porphyria the urine contains a colorless substance (porphobilinogen) .. which is a pyrrole deriv. and is converted to uroporphyrin on standing. **1961** *Lancet* 22 July 175/2 The clinical signs disappeared quickly, but the patient continued to excrete rather a lot of porphobilinogen and uroporphyrin in the urine. **1964** A. WHITE et al. *Princ. Biochem.* (ed. 3) xlii. 790 Enzymic preparations utilizing porphobilinogen for porphyrin synthesis have been isolated from plant, bacterial, and animal sources. **1970** R. W. MCGILVERY *Biochem.* xxi. 496 The parent indole ring is made in the next step by the condensation of two molecules of 5-aminolevulinate to form porphobilinogen. **1972** *Stedman's Med. Dict.* (ed. 22) 1004/2 *Porphobilinogen*, .. 2-aminomethyl-4-(2ʹ-casboxyethyl)-3-carboxy-methylpyrrole.

Hence ˌ**porphobiˌlinogeˈnuria**, the presence of porphobilinogen in the urine.

1961 *Ann. Rev. Med.* XII. 265 The probable relationship between this syndrome [*sc.* toxic porphyria] and the consumption of seed wheat treated with hexachlorobenzene-containing fungicides is supported by the production of massive uroporphyrinuria and porphobilinogenuria in rats by mixing hexachlorobenzene with the food. **1970** PASSMORE & ROBSON *Compan. Med. Stud.* II. xxxi. 4/1 In hepatic porphyria of Swedish type, new methods of measuring aminolaevulinic acid and porphobilinogen enable subclinical cases to be detected. Such cases are said to have a low degree of expressivity by comparison with their relatives who have obvious clinical manifestations and readily detectable porphobilinogenuria.

porphyr-, porphyro-, repr. Gr. πορφυρ(ο-, comb. stem of πόρφυρο-ς purple, and its derivatives; in Eng. (and other mod. langs.) a formative element, in senses 'purple' and 'porphyry', as in *porphyr-aceous, porphyr-ite, porphyr-ize, porphyro-genetic*, etc. ˌ**porphyroˈblastic** *a. Petrol.* [ad. G. *porphyroblastisch* (F. Becke 1903, in *Compt. Rend. IX Sess. Congr. Géol. Internat.* (1904) II. 570): see -BLAST], applied to (the texture of) rock (usu. metamorphic) in which larger grains formed by recrystallization occur in a finer groundmass; so ˈ**porphyroblast**, one of these larger crystals; ˌ**porphyroˈclastic** *a. Petrol.* [ad. G. *porphyroklastisch* (F. Becke 1903, in *Compt. Rend. IX Sess Congr. Géol. Internat.* (1904) II. 570): see CLASTIC *a.*], applied to (the texture of) rock which has undergone dynamic metamorphism and in which larger grains remain in a finer groundmass; hence ˈ**porphyroclast**, one of these larger crystals; **porphyˈropsin** *Biochem.* [RHOD)OPSIN], any of a class of light-sensitive pigments found in the retinas of freshwater vertebrates, differing from rhodopsin in containing the aldehyde of vitamin A_2 rather than that of A_1 and in having a maximum absorption at a slightly longer wavelength.

1920 A. HOLMES *Nomencl. Petrol.* 188 *Porphyroblast*,.. a term given to the pseudo-porphyritic crystals of rocks produced by thermodynamic metamorphism. The corresponding texture is called *porphyroblastic*. **1926** G. W. TYRRELL *Princ. Petrol.* xvi. 270 When idioblasts form large crystals embedded in a fine-grained groundmass, like the phenocrysts of a porphyritic igneous rock, the term *porphyroblastic* is used to describe the texture. *Ibid.* 272 Maculose structure is that in which porphyroblasts of strong minerals such as andalusite, cordierite,..etc., are well developed. **1966** *McGraw-Hill Encycl. Sci. & Technol.* VII. 11/2 The large crystals of some plutonic rocks are probably more properly classed as porphyroblasts. They may have formed essentially in solid rock by recrystallization aided by residual fluids from the solidifying magma. **1975** G. ANDERSON *Coring* ii. 31 Mottled dolomite is the result of incomplete dolomitization and exhibits itself as porphyroblasts in an altered calcareous matrix or as scattered patches of dolomite. **1920** A. HOLMES *Nomencl. Petrol.* 188 Porphyroclastic structure. **1926** G. W. TYRRELL *Princ. Petrol.* xvi. 272 The more resistant minerals.. or rock fragments.. may be less crushed, and may stand out in a pseudo-porphyritic manner from the finer material produced by the crushing of the softer constituents. This structure is called porphyroclastic. **1954** R. L. PARKER tr. *Niggli's Rocks & Min. Deposits* vi. 239 Porphyroclastic, with porphyroclasts. **1975** *Nature* 20 Feb. 598/2 Rocks of the anorthosite association *per se* are separated from an amphibolite facies gneiss complex.. by clearly marked zones of blastomylonite and porphyroclastic gneiss. *Ibid.* 10 Apr. 489/2 Xenoliths with variable microscopic fabric patterns containing porphyroclasts seem to have suffered increasingly intense shearing stresses through progressive deformation. **1937** G. WALD in *Ibid.* 12 June 1017/1 The visual purple of freshwater fishes possesses different spectral properties. I shall refer to it as porphyropsin. **1962** K. F. LAGLER et al. *Ichthyol.* xi. 376 The retinas of fishes yield two kinds of light-sensitive pigments, rhodopsin and porphyropsin. **1975** *Compar. Biochem. & Physiol.* A. LII. 720/2 While terrestriality appears to act as a selective force for the predominance of rhodopsin, the function of the porphyropsin and mixed porphyropsin-rhodopsin systems remains obscure.

‖**Porphyra** (ˈpɔːfɪrə). *Bot.* [mod.L. (Agardh), a. Gr. πορφύρα purple.] A small genus of Algæ or Seaweeds, type of the sub-order *Porphyreæ*, with fronds varying in colour from a clear rose to a livid purple. The chief species are *P. laciniata* and *P. vulgaris*, known as Purple Laver.

1849 CRAIG, *Porphyra*, a genus of Algæ: Order, Confervaceæ. **1857** WOOD *Com. Objects Sea-shore* 69 The ulva and porphyra, if intended to be eaten, must be gathered in the winter... The purple laver is said to be much superior to its green companion.

porphyraceous (pɔːfɪˈreɪʃəs), *a.* ? *Obs. rare.* [f. PORPHYR- + -ACEOUS.] Of the nature of or allied to porphyry; porphyritic.

1799 KIRWAN *Geol. Ess.* 207 Charpentier mentions a sort of stone which he calls porphyraceous, though he does not ascribe felspar to it. Hence **1828** in WEBSTER; and in mod. Dicts.

†ˈ**porphyrat**, *a. Obs. rare*⁻¹. [f. as prec.: see -ATE².] = PORPHYRITIC.

1611 SPEED *Theat. Gt. Brit.* I. xl. 78/1 His ashes bestowed in a little golden potte or vessell of the Porphyrat stone, were carried to Rome.

porphyrate (ˈpɔːfɪrət). *Chem.* [f. as PORPHYRIC + -ATE¹.] A salt of porphyric acid.

1866 WATTS *Dict. Chem.* IV. 690 The porphyrates explode when heated.

†**porphyre.** *Obs.* [a. F. *porphyre* (Cotgr. 1611), ad. med.L. *porphyrius*, f. Gr. πορφύρεος purple.] Name applied to a kind of serpent.

[**1584** GREENE *Anat. Fort.* Wks. (Grosart) III. 220 He resembleth the serpent *Porphirius*, who is full of poison, but being toothlesse hurteth none but him selfe.] **1608** TOPSELL *Serpents* (1658) 745 Of the Porphyre. There is among the Indians a Serpent about the bignesse of a span or more, which in outward aspect is like to the most beautiful and well coloured Purple. *Ibid.*, Unto this Porphyre I may add the Palmer Serpent.

porphyre, -ie, obs. forms of PORPHYRY.

porphyria (pɔːˈfɪrɪə). *Path.* [mod.L., f. PORPHYR(IN + -IA¹.] Any of various metabolic disorders characterized by the excretion of abnormally large quantities of porphyrins.

1923 A. E. GARROD *Inborn Errors of Metabolism* (ed. 2) viii. 144 Pigmentation of the enamel is a rare phenomenon. .. Even in congenital porphyria it is evidently an exceptional sign. **1945** *Jrnl. Biol. Chem.* CLVII. 330 A complex mixture of pigments occurs in porphyria urine. **1969** MACALPINE & HUNTER *George III & Mad-Business* xii. 197 The galaxy of patients assembled in these pages is due to our method of selection and must not create the impression that porphyria is commoner among the great than the not so great. **1970** PASSMORE & ROBSON *Compan. Med. Stud.* II. xxxi. 10/2 The Swedish type of hepatic porphyria.. may appear clinically only after administration of certain drugs, particularly barbiturates. **1975** *Victoria* (B.C.) *Times* 29 Apr. 14/3 Dermatologists.. had been treating the man who lived in a soldiers' home for.. porphyria.

Hence **porˈphyric** *a.*, of, pertaining to, or affected with porphyria; also as *sb.*, a person so affected.

1934 *Acta Med. Scand.* LXXXIII. 286 Hans Fischer.. has found a violet substance in the gallstones of the famous porphyric Petry. **1944** *Ibid.* CXVII. 8 A latent porphyric may suffer from another acute abdominal malady than a porphyric colic. **1974** *Nature* 9 Aug. 504/1 We noticed that skin lesions were provoked in porphyric rats, whose coats were shaved.

†**porˈphyrian**, *a.*¹ *Obs.* [f. med.L. *porphyri-us* (see PORPHYRY) + -AN.] Of, or composed of, porphyry.

1638 SIR T. HERBERT *Trav.* (ed. 2) 62 Foure hundred porphirian pillars. **1687** A. LOVELL tr. *Thevenot's Trav.* I. 124 Many lovely Pillars of Porphyrian Marble.

Porphyrian (pɔːˈfɪrɪən), *a.*² (*sb.*) [ad. L. type **Porphyriānus*, f. *Porphyri-us* (a. Gr. Πορφύριος), proper name (f. πόρφυρ-ος purple) + *-ānus*, -AN.] Of or pertaining to Porphyrius or Porphyry, the Neo-Platonic philosopher and antagonist of Christianity (A.D. 233-*c* 306), or to his doctrines.

Porphyrian scale or *tree*, a definition of *man*, in the form of a kind of genealogical table or tree displaying the series of subaltern genera to which he may be assigned below the summum genus *substance*, and the differentiæ by which each subaltern genus is distinguished within the genus next above it. The 'tree' is frequently used as an example of dichotomy. Its origin is to be found in Porphyry's *Isagoge in Aristotelis Categorias* 2a 13 seqq. (ed. Brandis).

1593 NASHE *Christ's Teares* Wks. (Grosart) IV. 194 Prosecute with all your authority, these Porphirian deriders. **1656** COWLEY *Misc. Tree of Knowledge* i, That right Porphyrian Tree which did true Logick shew, Each Leaf did learned Notions give, And th' Apples were Demonstrative. **1678** CUDWORTH *Intell. Syst.* 589 Even according to the Porphyrian Theology it self.. the Three Hypostases in the Platonick Trinity, are ὁμοούσιοι, Co-Essential. **1678** NORRIS *Coll. Misc.* (1699) 59 You err, if you think this is he, Tho' seated on the top of the Porphyrian Tree. **1802-12** BENTHAM *Ration. Judic. Evid.* (1827) I. 286 Every step it takes in the region of particulars, whether downwards in the Porphyrian scale, or sideways all round in the field of circumstances affords an additional security.

B. *sb.* A disciple or follower of Porphyry; also called **Porˈphyrianist.** [F. *Porphyrien*]

1678 CUDWORTH *Intell. Syst.* I. iv. 594 The Arians (as Socrates recordeth) were by Constantine called Porphyrianists,.. because Arius and Porphyrius did both of them alike, though upon different grounds, make their Trinity a foundation for creature-worship and idolatry. **1701** tr. *Le Clerc's Prim. Fathers* (1702) 125 In another Letter.. he [Constantine] enjoins the Name of Porphyrus to be given to Arius, and his Followers to be called Porphyrians. **1882-3** *Schaff's Encycl. Relig. Knowl.* I. 640 [Diodorus] combated Platonists and Porphyrians, Manichaeans and Apollinarists.

porphyric (pɔːˈfɪrɪk), *a.*¹ *Geol. rare.* [f. PORPHYR- + -IC: in mod.F. *porphyrique.*] = PORPHYRITIC.

1824 J. HODGSON in J. Raine *Mem.* (1858) II. 43 The bold red seared line of porphyric hills lying east and west.

porphyric (pɔːˈfɪrɪk), *a.*² *Chem.* [f. Gr. πόρφυρ-ος purple + -IC.] In *porphyric acid* ($C_{10}H_4N_2O_7$), obtained, as a yellow crystalline powder, or in minute crystals, by the action of nitric acid on euxanthone, and producing a blood-red colour with ammonium carbonate.

1866 WATTS *Dict. Chem.* IV. 690 Porphyric acid is slightly soluble, with red colour, in pure water; very slightly soluble in cold, more soluble in boiling alcohol.

porphyrin (ˈpɔːfɪrɪn). *Chem.* [a. G. *porphyrin* (Willstätter & Fritzsche 1909, in *Ann. d. Chem.* CCCLXXI. 33), f. *haemato-porphyrin* hæmatoporphyrin (s.v. HÆMATO-), f. Gr. πόρφυρ-ος purple + *-in* -IN¹.] Any of a large class of deeply-coloured red or purple fluorescent crystalline pigments that are substituted derivatives of porphin, many of which occur widely in nature, both in the free state and as complexes with metals (as in the hæms).

1910 *Jrnl. Chem. Soc.* XCVIII. I. 127 The phyllins are converted by acids into the corresponding porphyrins, compounds which do not contain magnesium. **1939** [see PORPHIN]. **1949** *Endeavour* VIII. 83/1 In both [*sc.* adult and fœtal haemoglobin], the prosthetic group (to which the oxygen becomes attached) is the same iron porphyrin compound. **1950** *Sci. News* XV. 95 Porphyrin is the coloured part of hæmoglobin minus the iron. Porphyrin is easily detected because it shows an intense red fluorescence when held before an ultra-violet lamp. **1961** *Lancet* 22 July 175/1 A deficiency in purine synthesis could result, during porphyria, from the increased formation of porphyrins. **1970** AMBROSE & EASTY *Cell Biol.* vii. 228 The biologically important compounds chlorophyll, haemoglobin, and the cytochromes all contain a common cyclic structure, called a porphyrin, which consists of four pyrrole rings linked by methine bridges (–CH=). **1974** *Sci. Amer.* Dec. 73/1 In chlorophyll the central cavity of the ring is occupied by a magnesium atom... Porphyrin rings in the blood protein hemoglobin and in the cytochromes contain an atom of iron instead.

Hence ˌ**porphyriˈnopathy** (see quot. 1950).

1950 *Thorpe's Dict. Appl. Chem.* (ed. 4) X. 132/2 Porphyrinopathies, or diseases accompanied by abnormal porphyrin production or excretion. **1961** *Ann. Rev. Med.* XII. 258 In this review, the main porphyrinopathies will be listed using Waldenström's classification.

porphyrine¹ (ˈpɔːfɪraɪn). Also 6 **porphurine**, 9 **porphyrin.** [f. as PORPHYRIC *a.*¹ + -INE⁴.]

†**1.** = PORPHYRY. *Obs. rare.*

1588 GREENE *Perimedes* Wks. (Grosart) VII. 57 Houses stuffed within with plate and outwardly decked and adorned with such curious worke of porphurine, as nature in them seemeth to be ouerlaboured with arte.

2. *Geol.* A porphyritic rock: see quots.

1811 PINKERTON *Petralogy* I. 88 The Swedish porphyry, already mentioned, approaches nearer to a porphyrin,.. forming the passage from basaltin to porphyry. **1862** DANA *Man. Geol.* 79 Porphyrine. Opaque or nearly so... Consists of feldspar; sometimes quartzose.

ˈ**porphyrine**². *Chem.* [f. Gr. πόρφυρ-ος purple + -INE⁵.] An amorphous alkaloid obtained from the bark of an Australian species of *Alstonia* (N.O. *Apocynaceæ*), which exhibits a characteristic red colour with nitric acid.

1872 WATTS *Dict. Chem.* VI. 955 On evaporating the ether, the porphyrine remains in the form of a varnish soluble in water and in alcohol. **1890** BILLINGS *Med. Dict.*, *Porphyrine*, $C_{21}H_{25}N_3O_2$, an amorphous alkaloid.

porphyrinogen (pɔːfɪˈrɪnədʒən). *Biochem.* [a. G. *porphyrinogen* (Fischer & Bartholomäus 1913, in *Ber. d. Deut. Chem. Ges.* XLVI. 512), f. *porphyrin* PORPHYRIN: see -OGEN.] Any of the colourless, reduced derivatives of porphyrins in which the four pyrrole nuclei are linked by methylene groups, $-CH_2-$.

In quot. 1913 applied *spec.* to the first such compound to be prepared.

1913 *Jrnl. Chem. Soc.* CIV. I. 409 A colourless, crystalline reduction product, $C_{33}H_{42}O_4N_4$, of high molecular weight is obtained. This is termed porphyrinogen in view of its ready conversion into a red product having the spectroscopic properties of porphyrin. **1938** *Chem. Soc.*

Ann. Rep. XXXIV. 384 Until this work was carried out, only three crystalline leuco-compounds of porphyrins, or porphyrinogens, were known, and none of these was derived from chlorophyll. **1955** *Endeavour* XIV. 135/1 It is possible that the porphyrins are not on the direct line of biosynthesis but are produced by reversible side reactions from closely related precursors, possibly the more highly reduced porphyrinogens. **1968** PASSMORE & ROBSON *Compan. Med. Stud.* I. xxvi. 7/2 Porphyrinogens are similar [to porphyrins] but in these compounds the pyrrole rings are linked by methylene ($-CH_2-$) bridges.

porphyrinuria (ˌpɔːfɪrɪˈnjʊərɪə). *Path.* [mod.L., f. PORPHYRIN + -URIA.] The presence of excessive or abnormal porphyrins in the urine.

1916 *Chem. Abstr.* X. 1671 The term porphyrinuria is used in place of hematoporphyrinuria because the subtance isolated from the urine is not identical with hematoporphyrin. **1944** *Jrnl. Amer. Med. Assoc.* 29 Jan. 287/1 The term porphyrinuria should be reserved to indicate those instances in which the porphyrins occurring naturally in the urine are present in amounts above the normal range, a condition which exists in a great variety of diseases. **1967** *Amer. Jrnl. Med.* XLII. 476/2 Marked porphyrinuria was an additional feature in this case, and the urine also consistently contained another brown pigment.

‖**porphyrio** (pɔːˈfɪrɪəʊ). *Ornith.* Also 7–8 **porphir-, -phyrion.** [L. *porphyrio* (Plin.), ad. Gr. πορφυρίων the purple coot. In F. *porphyrion.*] A name given by the ancients to the purple coot, sultana, or water-hen (see quot. 1894); taken by Brisson, 1760, as name of the genus of *Rallidæ* including this, distinguished by their deep-blue plumage and scarlet bill and legs, widely distributed in warm and tropical regions.

1609 BIBLE (Douay) *Lev.* xi. 18 The storke, and the swanne, and the onocratal, and the porphirion [*Vulg.* porphyrionem, 1611 gier eagle, 1885 vulture]. **1678** RAY *Willughby's Ornith.* 318 There is such a Porphyrio as they picture, akin to the Coots or Water-hens. **1753** CHAMBERS *Cycl. Supp., Porphyrio,* in zoology, the name of a bird figured and described by all natural historians from one another... It appears to be of the gallinula or moor-hen kind. **1872** A. DOMETT *Ranolf.* XIII. iv. 213 The crimson-billed porphyrio, that jerking struts among the cool thick rushes. **1890** *Victorian Stat., Game Act* Sched. iii, [Close Season] Land-rail, all other members of the Rail family, Porphyrio, Coots, &c... From the First day of August to the Twentieth day of December. **1894** NEWTON *Dict. Birds* 591 Of the larger species [of the genus *Porphyrio*], *P. cæruleus* seems to be the 'Porphyrio' of the ancients, and inhabits certain localities on both sides of the Mediterranean.

Hence **porˈphyrionine** *a. Ornith.*, belonging to the subfamily *Porphyrioninæ* of the *Rallidæ*, of which the genus *Porphyrio* is the type; *sb.*, a bird of this subfamily.

1890 in *Cent. Dict.* **1895** in *Funk's Stand. Dict.*

porphyrism (ˈpɔːfɪrɪz(ə)m). *Path.* [ad. G. *porphyrismus* (H. Günther 1920, in *Deutsch. Arch. f. klin. Med.* CXXXIV. 257): see -ISM.] = PORPHYRIA.

1923 A. E. GARROD *Inborn Errors of Metabolism* (ed. 2) viii. 139 In a more recent paper the same author puts forward the view that a constitutional anomaly, which he styles 'porphyrism', underlies acute and chronic cases alike. **1934** *Acta Med. Scand.* LXXXIII. 298 No signs of porphyrism in the family.

porphyrite (ˈpɔːfɪraɪt), *sb.*[1] Also 6 **-phirite,** 7 **-phyrit, -pherite.** [ad. L. *porphyrītēs* a purple-coloured precious stone in Egypt (Pliny), ad. Gr. πορφυρίτης adj. like purple, π. λίθος stone of this colour, porphyry, f. πόρφυρ-ος purple: see PORPHYR- and -ITE[1] b. So mod.F. *porphyrite,* in sense 2.]

†**1.** = PORPHYRY 1. *Obs.*

1589 PUTTENHAM *Eng. Poesie* III. xx. (Arb.) 254 Polishers of marble or porphirite. **1601** HOLLAND *Pliny* II. 579 A number of columnes and statues there be, all of porphyrit or red marble. **1658** W. BURTON *Itin. Anton.* 67 It was of Porphyrite, or Red Marble Stone.

attrib. **1577** HARRISON *England* II. xiii. (1877) I. 253 Some were of porphyrite stone. **1601** HOLLAND *Pliny* II. 573 The Porphyrite marble, which also commeth out of Ægypt, is of a red colour. **1736** DRAKE *Eboracum* I. ii. 14 His Ashes were collected, and..put into a Porphyrite Urn.

2. *Min.* A rock of porphyritic structure; a mass principally felsitic, containing also crystals of oligoclase (or sometimes orthoclase) felspar, and occasionally other minerals; = PORPHYRY 3.

1796 KIRWAN *Elem. Min.* (ed. 2) I. 358 That [porphyry] described by Herman..and which he calls a *porphyrite.* It consists of small sparks of felspar, grains of quartz, splinters of hornblende, and fragments of shorl cemented together by a scarcely discernible jaspidean cement. **1878** LAWRENCE tr. *Cotta's Rocks Class.* 162 The porphyritye of the Pentland Hills, near Edinburgh, with crystals of oligoclase, and specular-iron, sparkling in a reddish-brown matrix. **1879** RUTLEY *Stud. Rocks* xii. 238 The porphyrites are..divided into diorite and diabase-porphyrites.

†**porphyrite,** *a.* (*sb.*[2]) *Obs. rare.* [ad. L. *porphyrīt-is* purple-coloured, a. Gr. πορφυρῖτις.] Purple-coloured. Also *ellipt.* as *sb.*: see quot.

1601 HOLLAND *Pliny* I. 442 The Porphyrite Figs first shew upon the tree, and ordinarily be longest tailed. The smallest Figs..come next after and beare the Porphyrites companie. [**1706** PHILLIPS, *Porphyritis,* a Fig of a purple Colour.]

porphyritic (pɔːfɪˈrɪtɪk), *a.* Also 7 **-etick.** [ad. med.L. *porphyrīticus,* f. L. *porphyrītēs* PORPHYRITE; so F. *porphyritique.* The classical L. was *porphyreticus.*] Of or pertaining to the porphyry of the ancients; of the nature or structure of the porphyry of modern mineralogists; *spec.* containing distinct crystals or crystalline particles embedded in a compact ground-mass.

[**1387** TREVISA *Higden* (Rolls) V. 131 þe emperour..made þerynne a fount stoon of a maner stoon þat hatte porphiriticus.] **1432–50** tr. *Higden* ibid., He made a fonte or baptistery of a ston porphiritike. **1656** BLOUNT *Glossogr., Porphyretick,* belonging to red Marble, or purple. **1658** PHILLIPS, *Porphyretick,* (lat.) belonging to *Porphyrie,* i. a fine reddish marble, streaked with diverse colours. **1799** KIRWAN *Geol. Ess.* 303 It reposes on indurated clay, as this does on a porphyritic rock. **1862** ANSTED *Channel Isl.* 6 Pinnacles of granitic and porphyritic rock would be seen to rise out of large rounded masses of similar rock. **1878** LAWRENCE tr. *Cotta's Rocks Class.* 80 The texture of a rock is termed Porphyritic when distinct crystals or crystalline particles are distributed through an otherwise compact principal mass or matrix. **1884** DAWSON in *Leisure Ho.* June 356/2 Two sphinxes in the porphyritic diorite of Assouan.

So **porphyˈritical** *a.* (Worcester 1846); hence **porphyˈritically** *adv.*

1879 RUTLEY *Stud. Rocks* xi. 198 The crystals which occur porphyritically in the different varieties afford us a very imperfect clue to these relations. **1882** GEIKIE in *Nature* 7 Dec. 121/2 Mica-schists, in which crystalline aggregates of mica have been porphyritically developed.

porphyrize (ˈpɔːfɪraɪz), *v.* [f. PORPHYR- + -IZE. So, in sense 1, F. *porphyriser* (Dict. Trévoux).]

1. *trans.* To pound or triturate on a slab of porphyry or the like.

1747 tr. *Astruc's Fevers* 151 The iron is reduced to an impalpable powder, which must be porphyrized, and ordered as occasion requires.

2. To cause to resemble porphyry.

1828 in WEBSTER.

Hence **porphyriˈzation** (so F. *porphyrisation*).

1831 J. DAVIES *Manual Mat. Med.* 32 Porphyrization or levigation is an operation by means of which very hard substances..are reduced to an impalpable powder. **1842–57** in DUNGLISON *Med. Lex.* **1895** in *Syd. Soc. Lex.*

porphyroˈgene, *a. rare.* [See PORPHYROGENITE.] Born in the purple.

a **1849** POE *Haunted Palace* iii, Round about a throne where, sitting (Porphyrogene!)..The ruler of the realm was seen.

porphyrogenetic (ˌpɔːfɪrəʊdʒɪˈnɛtɪk), *a.* [f. PORPHYR-, PORPHYRO- + GENETIC.] Producing or generating porphyry.

1882 in OGILVIE (Annandale).

†**porphyˈrogenite.** *Obs.* exc. in L. form **porphyroˈgenitus,** fem. **-a.** Also 7 **-genete.** [ad. med.L. *porphyrogenitus,* ad. late Gr. πορφυρογέννητος, f. Gr. πορφυρο-, comb. form of πόρφυρος purple + γεννητός born. So F. *porphyrogénète* (Balzac 1635).] Originally, one born of the imperial family at Constantinople, and (as is said) in a chamber called the *Porphyra* (πορφύρα). Hence, a child born after his father's accession to the throne; and in more general or vague sense, = One 'born in the purple': see PURPLE *sb.*

The actual origin of the name *Porphyra* is disputed.

1614 SELDEN *Titles Hon.* 82 There he found Irene the Empresse,..in a house anciently appointed for the Empresses childbirth... They call that house, *Porphyra,* whence the name of the *Porphyrogeniti* came into the world. **1619** PURCHAS *Microcosmus* lxxxi. 788 Not in a Palace prepared, (as the *Porphyrogeniti* had in Constantinople).. but in an Inne! *a* **1662** HEYLIN *Laud* (1668) 145 Purple is the Imperial and Regal colour, so proper therefore unto Kings and Emperours, that many of the Constantinopolitan Emperours were called *Porphyrogenites,* because at their first coming into the world they were wrapt in Purple. **1727–41** CHAMBERS *Cycl., Porphyrogenitus,* in antiquity, an appellation given to the children of the eastern emperors... Cedrenus will have the word to signify, *born in the purple palace,* or the *palace of porphyry,* a palace so called in Constantinople; wherein the empresses used to lie in. Others derive the appellation hence, that the imperial children, as soon as born, were wrapped in purple; others.., that the chamber wherein they were born was hung with purple hangings. **1788** GIBBON *Decl. & F.* (1790) IX. xlviii. 57 In the Greek language *purple* and *porphyry* are the same word:..an apartment of the Byzantine palace was lined with porphyry: it was reserved for the use of the pregnant empresses: and the royal birth of their children was expressed by the appellation of *porphyrogenite,* or born in the purple... This peculiar surname was first applied to Constantine the seventh. **1831** SCOTT *Ct. Robt.* iii, Anna Comnena..an imperial Princess, porphyrogenita, or born in the sacred purple chamber. **1857** SIR F. PALGRAVE *Norm. & Eng.* II. iii. 210 Henry, the Porphyrogenitus, though a younger son relatively to Otho, was the eldest son of royal blood, first born after the accession of Duke Henry to the Throne of Charlemagne. **1893** *Athenæum* 11 Feb. 184/2 The kind of fun which is to be got out of bringing the porphyrogenitus of the English aristocracy face to face with all that is most modern in the American democracy.

Hence **porphyroˈgenitism,** the doctrine of succession in a royal family which prefers a son born after his father's accession to one born before that event; **porphyroˈgeniture,** the condition of being born 'in the purple' (see above).

1857 SIR F. PALGRAVE *Norm. & Eng.* II. 210 The doctrine of Porphyrogenitism, congenial to popular sentiment and not without some foundation in principle, prevailed influentially and widely in many countries and through many ages. *a* **1859** DE QUINCEY *Posth. Wks.* (1891) I. 59 This brought him within the description of porphyrogeniture, or royal birth.

porphyroid (ˈpɔːfɪrɔɪd), *sb.* (*a.*) *Geol.* and *Min.* [f. PORPHYR(O)- + -OID. So F. *porphyroïde.*]

A. *sb.* A rock resembling porphyry or of porphyritic structure.

1796 KIRWAN *Elem. Min.* (ed. 2) I. 369 Many aggregates ..cannot be arranged under any general denomination now in use. Hence I would propose to call them..*Porphyroids.* **1811** PINKERTON *Petralogy* I. 88 Porphyroid. This denomination includes such substances as approach the porphyritic structure. In a strict derivation of the term porphyry,..the black and green kinds could only be termed porphyroids. *Ibid.* 211 Granitic porphyroids are so abundant in all primitive mountains, that it is scarcely necessary to select examples. **1885** GEIKIE *Text-bk. Geol.* 131 Porphyroid occurs among the schistose rocks of Saxony, in the palæozic area of the Ardennes, as well as in Westphalia and other parts of Europe.

B. *adj.* Resembling or akin to porphyry.

1798 GREVILLE in *Phil. Trans.* LXXXVIII. 428 Like the crystals of feldspar which we meet with in the porphyroid granites. **1852** TH. ROSS *Humboldt's Trav.* I. ii. 96 Porphyroid masses having bases of compact feldspar. **1862** DANA *Man. Geol.* §85. 79 These are porphyries, or porphyroid rocks.

porphyrous (ˈpɔːfɪrəs), *a. poet. rare.* [f. Gr. πόρφυρ-ος purple + -OUS.] Purple.

1884 R. BRIDGES *Prometh. Firegiver* 1272 Her porphyrous heart-veins boil.

porphyroxin (pɔːfɪˈrɒksɪn), *sb. Chem.* [a. F. *porphyroxine* (Merck 1837), f. Gr. πόρφυρ-ος purple + *-ox-,* f. OXYGEN: see -IN[1].] 'Name for a neutral crystallisable substance, composed of a mixture of alkaloids (laudanin, meconidin, etc.), obtained from opium' (*Syd. Soc. Lex.* 1895).

1838 R. D. THOMSON in *Brit. Annual* 332 Porphyroxin. **1854–67** C. A. HARRIS *Dict. Med. Terminol., Porphyroxin,* an alkaloid, supposed to exist in Bengal opium. **1872** WATTS *Dict. Chem.* VI. 956 Porphyroxine.

porphyry (ˈpɔːfɪrɪ). Forms: α. 5 porˈfurie, -ˈfurye, -ˈforie, -ˈphurye, -ˈphiri(e, -ˈfirie. β. 5 ˈpurfire, 7 -fere, -fure; 6 -phure, ˈporphier, -phuer, 6–7 -phir, -e, 6–9 -phyre, 7 -phere, ˈpurphire, 7–8 ˈporphyr. γ. 6 ˈporpherie, -phury, 7 -phyrie, prophyry, purphorie, 8 porphiry, 6– porphyry. [The ultimate source of the word in all its forms is Gr. πόρφυρος adj. purple, πορφύρα sb. the purple-whelk, and its dye; but the stone was called in Gr. πορφυρίτης, L. *porphyrītēs,* whence PORPHYRITE. The Romanic names of the stone point however to late L. forms **porphyrius,* **porphyrus* (sc. *lapis*), purple (stone), or **porphyrium,* **porphyrum*: cf. Romaic πόρφυρον. (*Porphyrius,* Πορφύριος existed as a proper name: see PORPHYRIAN[2].) For the stone, English shows three types: α. (in Chaucer, in sense 2) *porˈfurie, -ˈfirie,* etc., a. AF. **porˈfiriĕ* = OF. *porˈfire,* mod.F. *porˈphyre,* ad. late L. type **porˈphyrius, -um.* β. *ˈporphir, -phyr,* earlier *ˈporfire, ˈporphyre,* app. (with shifted stress) for *purˈfire, porˈphyre,* a. OF. *porˈfire.* γ. *ˈporphyrie, -phyry,* 16th c. ad. late L. type **porphyrius, -um.*

For the relation of AF. *porˈfiriĕ* to F. *porˈfire,* cf. AF. *naˈvirie,* OF. *naˈvire,* AF *ˈglorie,* OF. *ˈgloire.* From F. come also Du. *porˈfier, -ˈphier,* Ger. *porˈphyr,* Da., Sw. *porfyr.* From the late L. **ˈporphyrus, -um,* also *ˈporfidum* (Dante) came It. *ˈporfiro, ˈporfido,* Sp., Pg. *pórfido.*]

1. a. The word used to render L. *porphyrītēs,* Gr. πορφυρίτης, the name given to a beautiful and very hard rock anciently quarried in Egypt, composed of crystals of white or red plagioclase felspar embedded in a fine red ground-mass consisting of hornblende, plagioclase, apatite, thulite, and withamite, the last two being bright red in colour. By modern poets often used vaguely, in the sense of a beautiful and valuable purple stone taking a high polish, including red granite and marble.

The site of the ancient quarries, after being long lost, was discovered by Burton and Wilkinson at Gebel Dokhān, near the Red Sea, in lat. 27° 20′ N.

In It., *porfido nero, porfido verde,* were applied to black and green rocks of porphyritic structure obtained from Sardinia, Greece, and elsewhere, and these have been englished as *black* and *green porphyry.*

β. *a* **1400–50** *Alexander* 5275 þe pilars ware of purfire polischt & hewen. **1560** BIBLE (Genev.) *Esther* i. 6 *margin,* The beds were of gold and of siluer vpon a pauement of porphyre. **1562** LEIGH *Armorie* (1597) A vj b, The third is a piller of Porphier in a golden field. **1589** LODGE *Scillaes Metam.* (Hunter. Cl.) 41 Where purphure, Ebonie, white, and red, al colours stained bee. **1590** GREENE *Mourn. Garm.* (1616) 31 The Saphir [is] highlier esteemed for the hue, then the Porphuer for his hugenesse. **1596** DANETT tr. *Comines* (1614) 278 Beautified with many great peeces of Porphire and Sarpentine. **1615** G. SANDYS *Trav.* 10 Cerigo..once called *Porphyris* of his excellent Porphyr. **1634** W. TIRWHYT tr. *Balzac's Lett.* (vol. I) 77 Precious as Marble and Purphire. **1648** *Bury Wills* (Camden) 217 My great grinding-stonne of purfure with the muller to it, and the little grinding-stonne of purfere with the muller to it. **1690** LOCKE *Hum. Und.* II. viii. §19 Let us consider the red and white Colours in Porphyre. *a* **1693** *Urquhart's Rabelais* III. xxviii. 227 The most durable Marbre or Porphyr.

γ. **1540–1** ELYOT *Image Gov.* (1556) 66 Pillers of Porpherie, whiche is a stone of purple colour. **1602** WARNER *Alb. Eng.* XII. lxxiii. (1612) 301 The Statures huge, of Porphyrie and costlier matters made. **1644** EVELYN *Diary* 17 Oct., Red-plaster flores which are made so hard and kept so polished, that..one would take them for whole pieces of porphyrie. **1645** *Ibid.* June, The floore [of St. Mark's] is all inlayed with achats,..jaspers, porphyries and other rich marbles. **1750** JOHNSON *Rambler* No. 82 ¶9, I have two pieces of porphyry found among the ruins of Ephesus. **1818** BYRON *Ch. Har.* IV. lx, Her pyramid of precious stones, Of porphyry, jasper, agate, and all hues Of gem and marble. **1861** C. W. KING *Ant. Gems* (1866) 64 Porphyry..is easily recognised by its deep red colour, thickly dotted with small white spots. **1871** ROSSETTI *Burden of Nineveh* xiii, Made proud with pillars of basalt, With sardonyx and porphyry.

†**b.** *transf. Obs.*

1589 GREENE *Tullie's Loue* Wks. (Grosart) VII. 115 Tempering the porphury of hir face with a vermilion blush, looking like Diana when shee basht at Acteons presence.

†**2.** With *a* and *pl.* A slab or block of porphyry, esp. a slab used for grinding and triturating drugs and the like upon. *Obs.*

α. *c* **1386** CHAUCER *Can. Yeom. Prol.* & *T.* 222 Oure grounden litarge eek in the Porfurie [*v.rr.* porphirie, -phurye, -forie; *rime* mercu·rie].

γ. **1634** PEACHAM *Gentl. Exerc.* I. xx. 65, I like best the porphyry, white or greene marble, with a mullar or upper stone of the same. **1644** EVELYN *Mem.* 29 Nov., The laver or basin is of one vast, intire, antiq porphyrie. **1694** SALMON *Bate's Dispens.* (1713) 341/2 The dried Mass to be ground each time upon a Porphyry.

3. *Geol.* and *Min.* **a.** A rock consisting of a compact base of felspathic or other unstratified rock containing scattered crystals of felspar of contemporary age.

1796 KIRWAN *Elem. Min.* (ed. 2) I. 349 Any stone which in a siliceous or argillaceous ground, or basis, contains scattered specks, grains, or dots of felspar,..is at present denominated a *porphyry*. **1813** SIR H. DAVY *Agric. Chem.* iv. (1814) 193 Porphyry..consists of crystals of feldspar. **1833** LYELL *Princ. Geol.* III. Gloss. 77 *Porphyry*..is hence applied to every species of unstratified rock, in which detached crystals of felspar are diffused through a base of other mineral composition. **1839** URE *Dict. Arts*, *Porphyry*, is a compound mineral or rock, composed essentially of a base of hornstone, interspersed with crystals of felspar. **1869** BRISTOW tr. *Figuier's World bef. Deluge* ii. 33 True porphyry presents a paste essentially composed of compact felspar. **1876** PAGE *Adv. Text-bk. Geol.* vii. 134 The porphyry of the mineralogist consists of a reddish felspar basis with disseminated crystals.

b. In more general sense: Any unstratified or igneous rock having a homogeneous base in which crystals of one or more minerals are disseminated.

Variously specified as ***felspar porphyry*** (= a), ***basaltic, claystone, granitic, greenstone, hornstone, mica, pitchstone, trachytic porphyry***, etc. ***quartz porphyry*** has as ground-mass an intimate mixture of orthoclase and quartz, containing distinct crystals or large grains of quartz.

The name is sometimes applied even to rocks in which the porphyritic crystals are absent. Many limitations or definitions of the term have been proposed by modern mineralogists, continental and British, but without any general agreement as to the basis of definition: see, in English, Sir A. Geikie *Text-bk. Geol.* (ed. 1885) 149, Prof. Bonny in *Prof. Geol. Soc.* (1886) XLI. 72, Harper *Petrology for Students* (ed. 1902) 126, etc.

1813 BAKEWELL *Introd. Geol.* (1815) 119 The term porphyry is very vague, being applied to all rocks that have a compact base or ground in which crystals of any kind are imbedded and distinctly visible. **1838** LYELL *Elem. Geol.* xxviii. (1874) 506 When distinct crystals of one or more minerals are scattered through a compact base the rock is termed a 'porphyry'. **1838** *Murray's Handbk. N. Germ.* 455 High and romantic cliffs, chiefly of porphyry or amygdaloid, abounding in agates, amethysts, &c. of great beauty and variety. **1858** GEIKIE *Hist. Boulder* xii. 240 When a trap displays distinct disseminated crystals..it becomes a porphyry. **1872** R. B. SMYTH *Mining Statist.* 32 Quartz porphyries and felspar porphyries—massive, and dykes of diorite and diabase, occur in many parts. **1878** LAWRENCE tr. *Cotta's Rocks Class.* 88 Porphyry is the general designation for all porphyritic rocks with compact main mass or matrix. **1883** *Chambers' Encycl.* VII. 690 Crystals of felspar, quartz, or calcareous spar, disseminated through a base of greenstone, form a greenstone porphyry. In the same way, there are pitchstone porphyry, basaltic porphyry, claystone porphyry, etc.

4. A collector's name for various moths (so called from the colour or markings of their wings).

1819 SAMOUELLE *Entomol. Compend.* 427 The Porphyry (*Botys cespitalis*). Chalky places. **1832** RENNIE *Conspect. Butterfl.* & *Moths* 74 The Porphyry (*Scotophila porphyrea*) appears the end of July. Wings..; first pair dusky red, with a purplish tinge, with several white streaks and spots. *Ibid.* 149 The Porphyry (*Pyrausta porphyrialis*). Wings.. purplish, with a large golden red or white spot among many very minute ones.

5. *attrib.* and *Comb.*, as ***porphyry column, grot, house, hue, mortar, slab***; ***porphyry-red, -smooth*** adjs.; **b. porphyry-born** *a.*, born in the purple (see PURPLE *sb.* 2 d); **porphyry-chair**, a chair used in the installation of a pope; **porphyry chamber**, name of a room in the palace of the Emperors at Byzantium (cf. quot. 1727–41 s.v. PORPHYROGENITE); **porphyry knot-horn**, a moth: see quot.; **porphyry-shell**, a shell of the genus *Murex*, esp. that from which the purple dye was obtained; **porphyry-stone** = senses 1 and 2.

1605 TIMME *Quersit.* II. v. 125 Beaten into pouder in a purphorie morter of smal bignesse. **1633** P. FLETCHER *Purple Isl.* III. viii, His porphyre house glitters in purple die; In purple clad himself. *Ibid.* II. x, With luke-warm waters di'd in porphyr hue. *c* **1645** HOWELL *Lett.* (1650) II. 103 Your Eccho deserves to dwell in som marble or porphyry grot. **1827** FARADAY *Chem. Manip.* v. 150 Excellent porphyry mortars are brought to this country from Sweden. **1870** MORRIS *Earthly Par.* III. IV. 180 Porphyry cliffs as red as blood. **1930** E. POUND *XXX Cantos* xvii. 78 And the cave salt-white, and glare-purple, cool, porphyry smooth. **1963** A. LUBBOCK *Austral. Roundabout* 194 The range thrust its porphyry-red battlements into the forested valley.

b. 1964 AUDEN in *Listener* 1 Oct. 525/1 Neither of our Dads, like Horace's, Wiped his nose on his forearm, Neither was *porphyry-born. **1656** BLOUNT *Glossogr.*, **Porphyry Chair*, a Chair of Porphyry Marble in the Cloister of St. John Lateran at Rome, called Sedes Stercoraria. **1854** MILMAN *Lat. Chr.* IV. viii. (1864) II. 397 Constantine was seized..conducted to the *porphyry chamber in which Irene had borne him—her firstborn son. **1832** RENNIE *Conspect. Butterfl.* & *Moths* 214 The *Porphyry Knot-horn (*P*[*hycita*] *Porphyrea*, Curtis). **1753** CHAMBERS *Cycl. Supp.*, **Porphyry-shell*, a name given by authors to a species of sea-shell of the purpura kind, with a short clavicle and beak. **1460** CAPGRAVE *Chron.* (Rolls) 129 The Pope gave him a ryng and a superaltarie of *porphiri ston, whech he had hallowid and blessid. **1644** DIGBY *Nat. Bodies* xv. (1658) 165 A subtile pouder..much like what filing..of leaf gold upon a porphyre stone, may reduce it into. **1715** LEONI *Palladio's Archit.* (1742) II. 86 It was adorn'd with white Marble, Porphyr-stone,..and..Statues.

porpice, -piece, -pisce, obs. ff. PORPOISE *sb.*

porpin, -pintine: see PORCUPINE β, δ.

‖**Porpita** (ˈpɔːpɪtə). *Zool.* [mod.L., f. Gr. πόρπη buckle-pin, brooch.] Name of a genus of *Siphonophora*: see quots. So **porˈpitid**, an animal of the family *Porpitidæ*; **ˈporpitoid** *a.*, resembling this genus or family.

1842 BRANDE *Dict. Sc.* etc., *Porpita*, the name of a genus of sea-nettles.., characterized by an internal circular flattened disk of a calcareous and horny texture. **1878** BELL *Gegenbaur's Comp. Anat.* 98 In Porpita, the disc remains flat and circular. **1883** C. F. HOLDER in *Harper's Mag.* Dec. 107/1 Delicate shapes of ianthina, vellela, and porpita.

porpoise (ˈpɔːpəs, -pɔɪs), *sb.* Forms: see below. [ME. *porpays, -peys, -poys*, a. OF. *porpeis* (12–13th c. in Godef.), *porpais, -pois* (Norman dial. of Guernsey *pourpeis*) = L. type **porcus piscis*, lit. hog-fish or fish-hog: cf. OIt. *pesce porco*, Pg. *peixe porco* = L. type **piscis porcus*. In cl. L. *porcus marīnus* (Pliny) = sea-hog, whence It. *porco marino*, Sp. *puerco marino*; cf. also Ger. *meerschwein* 'sea-swine', whence mod.F. *marsouin*. In Eng. the first element varied in 14–16th c. with *pur-* (Caxton *pour-*); the second element had many variations. In 17th c. there was an attempt to Latinize both elements as *porc-* or *porcu-pisce*, pl. *-pisces*; in the 18th c. *porpus* was prevalent; Johnson has *porpoise*, *porpus*; in the 19th c. usually written *porpoise* and pronounced *porpus*.]

1. a. A small cetaceous mammal (*Phocæna communis*) about five feet in length, of a blackish colour above and paler beneath, having a blunt rounded snout not produced into a 'beak' as the dolphin's. Hence extended to other species of the genus *Phocæna*, and to various small cetaceans of the family *Delphinidæ*. (Formerly also as collective pl.)

bay porpoise or ***skunk porpoise***, a larger North American porpoise of the genus *Lagenorhynchus*, distinguished by wide bands of yellow and white along its sides.

α. 4 **porpayse**, 4–5 **-pays, -poys**, 4–6 **-pas**, 5 **-peys, -e, -pys**, 5–6 **-pes**, 6 **-passe, -pose, -pyse, -pyshe**, 6–9 **-pesse**, 7 **-paise -piece, -pois, -poce, -puis, -puise, -pisce**, 7–8 **-pess, -pos, -pice**, 9 **-pass**; 6–9 **porpus**, 6– **porpoise**.

1309–10 *Durham Acc. Rolls* (Surtees) 7, j porpas. **1324–5** *Ibid.* 14, j porpayse et cc Haddoks. **1329** *Acc. Chamberl. Scotl.* (1771) 7 In emptione unius porpoys, 5 s. ?*c* **1390** *Form of Cury* §108 Porpeys in broth. **1530** PALSGR. 256/2 Porpas a fysshe, *mersovyn*. *c* **1532** DU WES *Introd. Fr.* in *Palsgr.* 913 Porpasse, *daulphin*. **1533** ELYOT *Cast. Helthe* (1539) 69 b, Greatte fyshes of the see, as thurle-pole, porpyse and sturgeon. **1541** *Act 33 Hen. VIII*, c. 2 Sturgeon porpose or seale. **1542** BOORDE *Dyetary* xiii. (1870) 268 A young porpesse, the whiche kynde of fysshe is nother praysed in the olde testament nor in physycke. **1552** HULOET, Porpyshe fyshe. **1590** GREENE *Never too late* (1600) 63 Neither flesh nor fish as the Porpus. **1601** HOLLAND *Pliny* I. 241 The Porpuisses..are made like the Dolphins. **1612** DRAYTON *Poly-olb.* v. 80 Wallowing Porpice sport and lord it in the flood. **1628** DIGBY *Voy. Mediterran.* (1868) 9, I neuer yet saw store of porposes playing, but soone a storme ensewed. **1634** SIR T. HERBERT *Trav.* 213 Porpiece. **1657** R. LIGON *Barbadoes* 28 Fishes..over-grown with fat, as you have seen Porpisces. **1661** LOVELL *Hist. Anim.* & *Min.* 217 Porpaise. .. Tursions or Sea Hoggs are fatter than Dolphins. **1687** A. LOVELL tr. *Thevenot's Trav.* II. 6 A Porpess..taken with a Fish-gig above Malta. **1698** TYSON in *Phil. Trans.* XX. 128 The Dolphin and Porpois. **1700** W. KING *Transactioneer* 48 He had the Misfortune to be Scratched by the Tooth of a Porpos. **1709** T. ROBINSON *Vind. Mosaick Syst.* 45 Porpices ..which delight in sporting and playing upon the waves. **1727** *Philip Quarll* 59 A great number of Porpuses. **1774** GOLDSM. *Nat. Hist.* (1776) VI. 329 There the porpess and the shark continue their depredations. **1802** BINGLEY *Anim. Biog.* (1813) II. 16 The Porpesse is well known in all the European seas. **1835** J. NEAL *Bro. Jonathan* III. 416 Throwing up the water, like a porpass, in a gale o' wind. **1834** MCMURTRIE *Cuvier's Anim. Kingd.* 111 The Porpoise has no rostrum, but a short and uniformly convex muzzle. **1837** M. DONOVAN *Dom. Econ.* II. 193 The grand shoal..of which the arrival is announced by the number of its greedy attendants, the gannet, the gull, the shark, and the porpus.

β. 4–5 **purpays**, 5 **-peys, -paysse, -poys, pourpays**, 5–6 **purpose**.

1400–1 *Durham Acc. Rolls* (Surtees) 603 Famulo.. portanti j purpays. *c* **1440** *Anc. Cookery* in *Househ. Ord.* (1790) 427 Make the nombuls of purpoys. *c* **1440** *Promp. Parv.* 417/1 Purpeys, fysche. *c* **1460** J. RUSSELL *Bk. Nurture* 724 Purpose rosted on coles. *c* **1483** CAXTON *Dialogues* 12/2 Fro the see to you come Whales, pourpays [F. Balainnes, porc de mer]. **1586** BRIGHT *Melanch.* vi. 27 The Monsters of the sea..are ceals purposes and such like.

γ. 6 **pork pisce, porkepes**, 6–7 **porcpisce**, 7 **porcpis, porkpisce, porcupisce, -pice, -pise, porcipize, porcˈpisce**.

1565 GOLDING *Ovid's Met.* I. (1593) 10 The ugly seales and pork pisces now to and fro did flote. **1595** SPENSER *Colin Clout* 251 His heard Of stinking Seales and Porcpisces. **1613** PURCHAS *Pilgrimage* VIII. iii. 739 A great dead fish, round like a Porcpis. **1654** GAYTON *Pleas. Notes* III. 67 A Sturgeon, a Sea-Calfe, a Porcipize. **1661** FELTHAM *Low Countries* in *Resolves*, etc. 60 The people that thrive and grow rich by war, like the Porcpisce, that playes in the storm. **1678** DRYDEN *All for Love* IV. i, Her Eunuch there! That Porcˈpisce bodes ill Weather. **1684** O'FLAHERTY *W. Connaught* (Irish Arch. Soc.) 105 Eighteen porcupices.. were taken near Tombeola.

b. *attrib.* and *Comb.*, as ***porpoise beef, diving*** (hence ***-dive*** *v. intr.*), ***hide, lace, oil, skin***; ***porpoise-like*** *adj.* and *adv.*

a **1533** LD. BERNERS *Gold. Bk. M. Aurel.* (1546) N vj, His shooes of a porkepes skynne. **1555** EDEN *Decades* 351 This cape may be easely knowen, by reason the rysynge of it is lyke a porpose hedde. **1618** BRETON *Courtier* & *Country-Man* (Grosart) 14/1 A great man..sent him for a great dainty a Porpose Pye or two cold. **1651** DAVENANT *Gondibert* I. xxxi, The Prince, could Porpoise-like in Tempests play. **1833** W. F. TOLMIE *Jrnl.* 21 Jan. (1963) 97 Ate some porpoise beef at breakfast. **1884** C. G. W. LOCK *Workshop Receipts* Ser. III. 376/1 Some find porpoise-oil to give most uniform satisfaction [for lubricating a watch]. **1894** *Outing* (U.S.) XXIV. 123/1 The oild porpoise-hide thigh-boots. **1898** F. T. BULLEN *Cruise Cachalot* 19 Porpoise beef improves vastly by keeping. **1905** *Westm. Gaz.* 26 Aug. 9/2 The 'Plunger' was put through her paces at porpoise diving, ascending repeatedly to the surface, long enough to get her bearings, and immediately disappearing again. **1973** V. CANNING *Flight of Grey Goose* vii. 138 He..took a deep breath, and porpoise-dived down, swimming strongly.

2. (See quots.)

1929 F. C. BOWEN *Sea Slang* 105 *Porpoise, doing a*, said when a submarine dives down nose first at a sharp angle. **1931** *Times* 21 Aug. 7/1 It [*sc.* a seaplane] dropped back on to the water and then porpoised again, double the height of the first porpoise. **1961** F. H. BURGESS *Dict. Sailing* 74 *Doing a porpoise*, said of a submarine taking a sharp dive. **1963** *Amer. Speech* XXXVIII. 119 *Porpoise*, an undesired landing in which the airplane bobs up and down like a porpoise playing in the waves, caused by landing on the nose gear first.

porpoise (ˈpɔːpəs), *v.* [f. the sb.] *intr.* To move like a porpoise; *spec.* **a.** Of an aircraft, esp. a seaplane: to touch the water or the ground and rise again. **b.** To move through the water like a porpoise, alternately rising above it and submerging.

1909 H. G. WELLS *Tono-Bungay* I. iii. 110 'Just as though an old Porpoise like him would ever make money,' she said. .. 'He'll just porpoise about.' **1919** *Rep.* & *Mem. Advisory Comm. Aeronaut.* No. 437. 6 The author has seen a machine ..porpoise very badly in waves of only one to two feet high. **1930** P. WHITE *How to fly Airplane* xiv. 216 Sometimes, students fail to level off at all. This is an error which is bound to result either in a crash, or in a 'wheel' landing from which the plane will bounce or 'porpoise' quite high. **1931** [see PORPOISE *sb.* 2]. **1939** G. H. JONES *No less Renowned* 46 The Coxswain and the Second Coxswain had their work cut out to prevent the vessel [*sc.* a submarine] from 'porpoising'. **1944** *Richmond* (Virginia) *Times-Dispatch* 21 Sept. 6/6 The Liberator [bomber]..touched the water at a speed of approximately 100 miles per hour, porpoised (bounced) once, and struck again tail-first. **1968** F. W. HOLIDAY *Great Orm of Loch Ness* v. 39 These objects were moving south-west... They were 'porpoising'—rolling under the surface and then reappearing. **1969** D. BAGLEY *Spoilers* vii. 206 I've set her [*sc.* a torpedo] to run at twelve feet. Any less than that an' she's likely to porpoise—jump in an' out o' the water. **1976** *Province* (Vancouver) 8 Mar. 1/3 From 500 feet there appeared an island full of seals and an ocean full of an enormous whale porpoising through his domain before diving out of sight. **1977** *Modern Boating* (Austral.) Jan. 34/2 With the trim..right out the boat begins to porpoise badly.

So **ˈporpoising** *vbl. sb.*

1915 G. C. LOENING *Military Aeroplanes* xi. 134 The latter condition, causing sudden changes in the angle of the bottom and its planing pressure,..gives rise to the disagreeable effect of 'porpoising'—a fore and aft rocking and jumping. **1920** L. BAIRSTOW *Appl. Aerodynamics* ii. 55 Such phenomena as the depression of the bow due to switching on the engine and 'porpoising' are reproduced in the model with sufficient accuracy for the phenomena to be kept under control in the design stages of a flying boat. **1933** [see HYDROFOIL 1]. **1974** P. LOVESEY *Invitation to Dynamite Party* xii. 152 We have to steer by coming to the surface at intervals. It's a process known as 'porpoising'.

porporate ('pɔːpərət), *a. rare.* [ad. It. *porporato*, epithet of a Cardinal:—L. *purpurātus* clad in purple, PURPURATE, f. *purpura* purple: see -ATE².] Clad or robed in purple.

1868 BROWNING *Ring & Bk.* v. 227 Paul shall be porporate, and Girolamo step Red-stockinged in the presence when you choose.

porpore, -pre, -pur(e, obs. ff. *purpure*, PURPLE.

porpos, -e, obs. forms of PORPOISE *sb.*, PURPOSE.

porpoynte, -pyn: see PORCUPINE *β, γ*.

porprise, variant of POURPRISE *Obs.*, precinct.

porpuis(e, -pus, -pys(he, obs. ff. PORPOISE *sb.*

porr, purr (pɔː(r), pɜː(r)), *sb.* Now *dial.* Also 4–5, 9 por, 6 porh(e, 9 pore, pur. [f. PORR *v.*]

1. A fire poker.

1357–8 *Durham Acc. Rolls* (Surtees) 124, j porr pro camino, ix d. **1387–8** *Ibid.* 266 In emendacione unius por de ferro. **1407–9** in *Eng. Hist. Rev.* (1897) XII. 518 In iii porres alias naundirens. **1564** *Wills & Inv. N.C.* (Surtees) I. 223 One Iron chimney, one porr, one payre of toynges. **1629** in *Naworth Househ. Bks.* (Surtees) 265 For mendinge the kitchinge fire porre. *a* **1700** B. E. *Dict. Cant. Crew, Poker*, a pointed Porr to raise the Fire. **1825** BROCKETT *N.C. Gloss., Por, Pore*, a poker for stirring the fire. **1855** ROBINSON *Whitby Gloss., Porr*, the fire-poker.

2. A thrust, a poke; a kick.

1589 J. MELVILL *Diary* (Wodrow Soc.) 273 Missing his ward, he gettes a porh at the left pape, wharof he dies. *Ibid.* 275 A porhe of a rapper. **1844** JAMIE *Muse of Mearns* 155 (E.D.D.) A simple pur wi' a bodie's fit Maks 't rin a most prodigious bit. **1888** *Sheffield Gloss.* s.v., He gave him a pur in the side with his thumb.

3. *fig.* A state of agitation or trouble.

1842 H. J. DANIEL *Bride of Scio* 175 In sich a pore. **1865** TREGELLAS *Cornish Tales* (1868) 84 Nothing but pors will be this night.

porr, purr (pɔː(r), pɜː(r)), *v.* Now only *dial.* Forms: 4–6 porre, 6 poore, 6– por(r, pore, 9 pur(r. [ME. *porre* = MDu. *porren* (*purren*), Du. *porren*, MLG., LG. (whence Ger.) *purren* (LG. also *puren*), MHG. *phurren*, Ger. dial. *pfurren*, Dan. (from LG.) *purre*, to poke, prod, thrust, stir up, instigate. Cf. Gael., Ir. *purr* to thrust, drive, jerk; app. from English.

This verb has the appearance of being of onomatopœic origin, *pŭrr* being a natural expression of thrusting. But its common use in ME., MDu., and MLG., indicates a common origin in WGer., and it is remarkable that no trace of it is found in any of the langs. before the 14th c.]

1. *trans.* To thrust, prod, poke, push (anything), as with a spear or stick. In mod. dial. esp. used of poking the fire: cf. PORR *sb.* 1.

a **1400–50** *Alexander* 5560 Þai sett in a sadd sowme & sailid his kniȝ its, Porris doun of his princes & persys þar schildis. **1532** MORE *Confut. Tindale* Wks. 432/2 He..gyrneth as a dogge dooeth, when one porreth hym in the teeth with a stycke. **1570** LEVINS *Manip.* 155/38 To Podde or porre, *pungere.* **1903** *Eng. Dial. Dict., Purr*, to stir, poke, esp...the fire [or] the embers of a brick oven. (Cited from Lancashire, Lincoln, East Anglia.)

b. To thrust, push, poke (anything) *in*, etc.; *refl.* to intrude.

1573–80 BARET *Alv.* P 579 To porre in. **1870** AXON *Black Knt.* 43 (Lancs.) If he were to pur his ugly face through th' dur hoyle. **1879** MISS JACKSON *Shropshire Work-bk.* s.v., 'Er hanna invited me, so I shanna pore myself.

2. *intr.* To make a poke or thrust.

1560 BECON *New Catech.* Wks. I. 519 Let them not bite their lippes, nor scratte their heade, nor rubbe theyr elbowes, nor pore in theyr eares. *c* **1566** *Merie Tales of Skelton* in *S.'s Wks.* (1843) I. p. lx, Then with her distaff she would poore in at hym.

3. *trans.* To stuff, stop, cram, fill (a receptacle or space) with anything.

1398 TREVISA *Barth. De P.R.* XVII. clx[i]. (Bodl. MS.), Hurden..is clensinge of offal of hempe oþer of flaxe and men in olde tyme cleped it stipa as it were stoppinge oþer porringe for þerwiþ chynes and cliftes of schippes beene porred and stoppid. **1538** ELYOT *Dict., Confercio*, to stuffe, or porre. **1777** *Horæ Subsecivæ* 335 (E.D.D.) You quite pore me.

4. To thrust or push with the foot; to kick, 'esp. to kick with thick boots or clogs' (*E.D. Dict.* cited from Lancash., Chesh., Derby).

1812, 1827 [implied in *purring, purrer* below]. *c* **1860** STATON *Rays fro' th' Loomenary* (Bolton) 37 Hoo up wi har foot an purred th' book reet into th' lone. **1867** *Wigan Observer* 23 Feb., But Shaw would not give over, and 'purred' me behind the ear as I was picking my money up. **1886** B. BRIERLEY *Cast upon World* xxiii. 279 Folk thinkin' if they con purr a clod i' pieces..they're fit for a farmin' job.

Hence **'porring, 'purring** *vbl. sb.* (also *attrib.*); **'porrer, 'purrer**, a heavy boot or clog to kick with.

15.. in *Retrospective Rev.* Feb. (1853) 208 Lyke as the fissher wolle take on hym to selle An ele in Themmys by porrynge with his spere. **1519** HORMAN *Vulg.* 182 Yf the cattell..be nat kepte fro the leese: they wyll be in parel of brastynge, for porrynge. **1717** *Closeburn Inv.* (Nithsdale) (Jam.), A chimney tongues, and shovel, a porring iron, and hearth besome. **1812** *Sporting Mag.* XL. 249 Carter..sent forth from the purring part of Lancashire. **1827** *Blackw. Mag.* Oct. 453/1 One smashed his os frontis with the nailed heel of a two-pound wooden clog, a Preston Purrer. **1855** MRS. GASKELL *North & S.* xxv, He and I will have an up and down fight, purring an' a'. **1899** *Birmingham Weekly Post* 21 Jan. 12/4 You put your purring clogs on, and you insisted on having a purring match with Grey.

porraceous (pɒ'reɪʃəs), *a.* Also 7–9 erron. -acious. [f. L. *porrāceus* of or like leeks, leek-green, f. *porrum* leek: see -ACEOUS. So F. *porracé.*] Of the nature or colour of the leek; leek-green.

1616 SURFL. & MARKH. *Country Farme* 198 Hard tumours, whether scirrous or porracious. **1676** WISEMAN *Chirurg. Treat.* VI. vii. 432 If the lesser Intestines be wounded, he will be troubled with poraceous Vomiting. **1730** STUART in *Phil. Trans.* XXXVI. 347 The Vomiting of porraceous Bile. **1847** E. J. SEYMOUR *Severe Dis.* I. 48 It is known..as 'porracious vomiting', or leek-green sickness, from its colour. **1891** MISS DOWIE *Girl in Karp.* x, The queerly-formed porraceous glass bottle.

porray, porrey. Now *Sc.* Forms: α. 5 porre, -y, -ay, -ey, (poyra, 8 poiree, porree). β. 5 pur(r)e, 8– *Sc.* purry. γ. 4–5 perre, 5 -ey(e, -y(e, pereye, 6 perrie. [ME. a. OF. *porée*:—late and med.L. *porrāta*, f. *porrum* leek + *-ata*: see -ADE. The mod.F. *poirée* goes with *poireau*, OF. *porrel, porreau* leek. The history of the γ. forms is obscure; they may have another origin.

The word was possibly associated in sense with F. *purée* thick soup: cf. 'porry of pese' with F. *purée de pois.*]

A soup or broth made of vegetables (as leeks, peas, or cabbage) or fish, boiled and passed through a sieve, and added to soup-stock or almond-milk, with various flavourings.

In *Sc.*, *purry* is pottage made of chopped kale and oatmeal. ? *c* **1390** *Form of Cury* §70 (1780) 39 Perrey of Peson. *Ibid.* §73. 40 Take and seeþ white peson and take oute þᵉ perrey. *c* **1420** *Liber Cocorum* (1862) 42 Þen þoroughe þe wyntur his curse schal holde, Neghe lentone seson þat porray be bolde. *Ibid.* 44 For blaunchyd porray. Take thykke mylke of almondes..heke [? leke] hedes. *Ibid.*, Porry of white pese. *Ibid.* 47 Porray of mustuls [mussels]. *c* **1430** *Two Cookery-bks.* 14 Blawnche Perrye. Take þe Whyte of the lekys.. Almaunde Mylke, an a lytil of Rys [etc.]. *c* **1440** *Promp. Parv.* 409/2 Porre, or purre, potage (*S.* pese potage), *piseum.* *c* **1450** *Two Cookery-bks.* 90 Blanche porrey. Take blanche almondes, And grinde hem, and drawe hem with sugur water thorgh a streynour;..þe white of lekes [etc.]. **1483** *Cath. Angl.* 286/2 Porray, *porreta, porrata.* **1578** LYTE *Dodoens* III. xliii. 377 The broth of a chicken, or..Perrie made of Pease, or some other lyke liquor. **1780** FORBES *Dominie Depos'd* 9 Tartan-purry, meal an' bree, Or butt'ry brose. *a* **1800** in R. Jamieson *Pop. Ball.* (1806) I. 312 Put on the pat wi' the purry.

porrect (pə'rɛkt), *a. Zool.* [ad. L. *porrectus* stretched out, extended: see next.] Stretched out or forth; extended, esp. forward.

1819 G. SAMOUELLE *Entomol. Compend.* 233 Palpi filiform ..scarcely longer than the head, porrect. **1826** KIRBY & SP. *Entomol.* IV. 317 Antennæ...Porrect.., when they are placed parallel with each other, and in the same line with the body. **1866** E. C. RYE *Brit. Beetles* 87 Porrect mandibles, one of which—the left—is toothed on the lower side.

porrect (pə'rɛkt), *v.* [f. L. *porrect-*, ppl. stem of *porrigĕre* to stretch out in front of oneself, put forth, extend, offer, f. *por-* = *pro-* forth + *regĕre* to stretch, direct. The pa. pple., the first part to be used, was orig. *porrect* (ad. L. *porrectus*: cf. prec.).]

1. *trans.* To stretch out, extend (usually, a part of the body). Now only in *Nat. Hist.*

1412–20 LYDG. *Chron. Troy* III. xxviii. (MS. Digby 230) lf. 134/1 To eche partie and extremyte Of his body lyneally porrecte Thoruȝ nerfe and synewe driven & directe. **1432–50** tr. *Higden* (Rolls) VI. 17 The Romane empyre, that was porrecte from the occean of Briteyne unto the costes of Persida. **1826** HOR. SMITH *Tor Hill* (1838) II. 94 The Doctor again porrecting his forefingers. **1874** WESTWOOD *Thesaur Entom. Oxon.* 24 The prosternum is porrected in front of the anterior coxæ, forming a sharp, compressed, curved and setose point.

b. To hold (a thing) out *to* some one for his acceptance: cf. PORRECTION 2. ? *Obs. rare.*

1432–50 tr. *Higden* (Rolls) VI. 181 Supposynge hym to have porrecte the chesable after to [*sic*] masse to oon of his ministres.

†**2.** To direct or present (a prayer or petition).

c **1425** *Found. St. Bartholomew's* 18 And he..felle downe a-forne the Awter, porrectynge his meke prayers to heuyn. **1460** CAPGRAVE *Chron.* (Rolls) 266 The praiere of certeyn peticiones which were porrect in the Parlement. **1483** in *Lett. Rich. III & Hen. VII* (Rolls) I. 12 A bill of peticion which the lordes..and the commons..solemplye porrected unto the kinges highnes.

3. To put forward, tender (a document, etc.); to produce or submit for examination or correction. *Obs.* exc. in eccl. law.

1774 BP. HALLIFAX *Anal. Rom. Law* (1795) 96 By the new Law, an Actor gave caution to contest the Suit, within two Months after porrecting his Libel. **1848** in *State Trials* VI. 413, I porrect a schedule, which I pray to be read. **1872** *Wharton's Law Lex.* (ed. 5), *Porrecting*, producing for examination or taxation, as porrecting a bill of costs, by a proctor. **1880** *Times* 22 Dec., It is part of the old practice that the promoter of the suit should draw up the sentence, and 'porrect' it, as it is called, to the Judge for his adoption, subject to any alterations that he may make.

b. *humorously.* To tender, deal out.

1746 FIELDING *True Patriot* No. 13 Which I no sooner perceived than I porrected him a remembrance over the face.

Hence **po'rrected** *ppl. a.*, extended forward.

1653 R. SANDERS *Physiogn.* 277 Consider the porrected form of the nose. **1848** HARDY in *Proc. Berw. Nat. Club* II. No. 6. 337 The antennæ are distant, porrected.

So **po'rrectate** *a.*

1890 in *Cent. Dict.*

porrection (pə'rɛkʃən). [ad. L. *porrectiōn-em*, n. of action f. *porrigĕre*: see prec. So F. *porrection.*]

†**1.** Stretching out; extension. *Obs. rare.*

1649 BULWER *Pathomyot.* II. iv. 154 The Broad Muscle.. by its porrection..may serve to open the Eye.

2. The action of holding out for acceptance; proffering; offer; presentation. Now only *Eccl.*

1715 M. DAVIES *Athen. Brit.* I. 322 With Porrections or Surrenders of the Submissive Herba (*porrigere herbam*) or of the more Victorious Palm or Laurel. **1890** *Guardian* 25 June 1030/2 This decree declared the porrection of the cup and paten to be the matter essential to validity in the ordination of priests. **1897** *Tablet* 8 May 726 How are we to account for their retaining the porrection or delivery of the Gospel Book?

porret ('pɒrɪt). Now only *dial.* Forms: 4 porete, (porrecte), 4–6 poret, porett(e, 5 porrete, -ette, 5–7 (9 *dial.*) porret, 9 *dial.* pouret(t, purrit. [ME. *poret, porette*, a. OF. *poret* leek (also *porette* small kind of onion), f. L. *porrum* leek + dim. suffix *-et* (*-ette*), -ET¹.] A young leek or onion; a scallion.

[*c* **1265** *Voc. Names Plants* in Wr.-Wülcker 555/7 *Porius*, i. poret, i. lek.] **1362** LANGL. *P. Pl.* A. VII. 273, I haue porettes and percyl and moni Colplontes. *a* **1400** *Pistill of Susan* 107 Þe persel, þe passenep, poretes to preue. **1483** CAXTON *Gold. Leg.* 267/2 Thou etar of porrette wene thou to take me out of myn hows. **1530** PALSGR. 256/2 Porret yong lekes, *porette.* **1573** TUSSER *Husb.* xxxix. (1878) 94 Seedes and herbes for the Kitchen..31 Poret. **1646** SIR T. BROWNE *Pseud. Ep.* 323 Why Garlick, Molyes, and Porrets have white roots, deep green leaves, and blacke seeds? **1858** MAYNE *Expos. Lex., Porret*, the common name of the plant *Allium porrum.*

porrey: see PORRAY.

porridge ('pɒrɪdʒ), *sb.* Forms: 6 porage, porradge, 6–7 -edge, 6–8 -ige, 6–8 (9 *dial.*) -age, 7 -idg, *Sc.* (9 *dial.*) -itch, 7– porridge. β. 6 parage, 8 *dial.* parrage, 9 *Sc.* parridge, -itch. [Altered form of POTTAGE, PODDISH (cf. PORRINGER). In sense 1, possibly influenced by PORRAY. In Sc. and Eng. dial., usually construed as collective plural.]

†**1. a.** Pottage or soup made by stewing vegetables, herbs, or meat, often thickened with pot-barley or other farinaceous addition. Cf. GRUEL *sb.* 3. *Obs.*

c **1532** DU WES *Introd. Fr.* in *Palsgr.* 1070 Ye have alredy eaten your porage. **1538** BALE *Thre Lawes* 1566 They loue no pese porrege nor yet reade hearynges in lent. **1550** LEVER *Serm.* (Arb.) 122 Hauyng a fewe porage made of the brothe of the same byefe, wyth salte and otemell. **1561** HOLLYBUSH *Hom. Apoth.* 18 b, Take a dishe full of Hempe sede..Braye it well and strayne it wyth warme water so that it become as a thyn parage. **1573** *Tindale's Obed. Chr. Man* Wks. 166 If the porage [1528 podech] be burned..or the meate ouer rosted, we say The bishop hath put his foote in the potte. **1577** B. GOOGE *Heresbach's Husb.* II. (1586) 56 This sort [of Colworts]..is sod with Baken and vsed in Porredge. **1601** B. JONSON *Poetaster* III. iv, He will eate a legge of mutton, while I am in my porridge. **1660–1** PEPYS *Diary* 25 Feb., There we did eat some nettle porrige, which was made on purpose to day,..and was very good. **1748** SUSANNA DARWIN in *E. Darwin's Life* (1879) 8 Till one, Pease Porrage, Pottatoes and Apple Pye. **1755** JOHNSON, *Porridge* .., food made by boiling meat in water; broth. **1805** *Med. Jrnl.* XIV. 427 Some persons have been rendered delirious by eating porridge, wherein it [Fool's parsley] had been used instead of parsley.

b. See PLUM-PORRIDGE.

2. A soft food made by stirring oatmeal (or occas. some other meal or cereal) into boiling water (or milk); in cooling, it becomes more or less congealed. Often with distinguishing word, as ***oatmeal p., wheatmeal p., rice p.***

a **1643** W. CARTWRIGHT *Bill of Fare* Comedies, etc. (1651) 228 *Imprimis* some Rice Porredge, sweet, and hot. *a* **1674** CLARENDON *Hist. Reb.* XIII. §86 Here he had such Meat and Porridge as such People use to have. **1705** WALL *Hist. Inf. Bapt.* (1844) I. xix. 355 Having his belly filled, and his head bedulled, with Scotch porridge. *a* **1776** in Herd *Collect. Scot. Songs* II. 182 Ye's get a panfu' of plumpin parrage; And butter in them. **1816** SCOTT *Old Mort.* vi, They're gude parritch eneugh. **1856** KANE *Arct. Expl.* II. xix. 193 Cooked them a porridge of meat-biscuits and pea-soup. **1859** JEPHSON *Brittany* ix. 139 Oatmeal porridge formed a considerable part of the people's food.

3. *fig.* **a.** A conglomeration, a hotchpotch; unsubstantial stuff.

1642 G. CALSINE (*title*) A Messe of Pottage, very well seasoned and crumbd, with Bread of Life,..against the contumelious slanderers of the Divine Service, terming it Porrage. **1662** PEPYS *Diary* 24 Aug., Young people..crying out 'Porridge' often and seditiously in the Church, and they took the Common Prayer Book, they say, away. **1705** HICKERINGILL *Priest-cr.* II. ii. 22 All other Devotion in the Church is but Porridge, as they prophanely word it; give us Sermons, Sermons, Long-winded Sermons. **1790** BURKE *Fr. Rev.* Wks. V. 41 A..sermon, in which there are some good moral and religious sentiments,..mixed up in a sort of porridge of various political opinions and reflexions. **1852** *P. Parley's Ann.* 81 Peter Parley's literary porridge for the month of March. **1972** *Listener* 18 May 662/2 Sometimes the programme has been a radio porridge, sometimes a shapely..necklace of sound, but never anything really remarkable. **1976** *Brit. Jrnl. Sociol.* XXVII. 36 On the other side of the great divide are the empiricists who..correlate vaguely-worded, interchangeable scales with each other and call the subsequent statistical porridge, alienation.

b. *transf.* Something of the consistency of thick soup or porridge.

1700 S. Sewall *Diary* 5 Dec., Because of the Porrige of snow, Bearers..rid to the Grave. **1870** *Scribner's Monthly* I. 154 While the engineers were floundering in the porridge at the west end, they wisely resolved to..sink a shaft to grade. **1966** H. Sheppard *Dict. Railway Slang* (ed. 2) 9 *Porridge*, sludge removed from drains.

c. A prison sentence; a term of imprisonment. *slang*.

1954 *Britannica Bk. of Year* 637/1 Several examples of underworld slang, probably of a date earlier than 1953, appeared in the newspapers. Thus, the reader learned that *Porridge* meant a term of imprisonment. **1955** D. Webb *Deadline for Crime* i. 16 He did his porridge quietly, peacefully, earned full remission and came out. **1958** F. Norman *Bang to Rights* III. 171 Week excuses that's all you get, when you go away to do a bit of porridge. **1968** J. Wainwright *Edge of Extinction* 92 D'you think I'd forget the frigging jack 'ut sent me down for two years' porridge? **1972** J. Brown *Chancer* xiii. 169 You think I'm not sick of doing porridge too? **1977** 'E. Crispin' *Glimpses of Moon* xii. 236 His emotions at the prospect..of yet another dose of porridge were such that he was..incapable of thinking clearly.

4. In proverbial phrases; e.g. ***a mess of porridge***: see mess *sb.* 2; ***not to earn salt to one's porridge***, i.e. to earn practically nothing; ***to keep one's breath to cool one's*** (***own***) ***porridge***, to reserve one's advice, etc. for one's own use (cf. pottage 4). ***to make a porridge***, to blunder, to make a mess *of* something.

1596 Nashe *Saffron Walden* 75 He carries the poake for a messe of porredge in Christs Colledge. **1678** Dryden *Limberham* iv. i, That is a chip in porridge; it is just nothing. **1694** Motteux *Rabelais* v. xxviii. (1737) 129 Spare your Breath to cool your Porridge. **1764** Foote *Patron.* i. Wks. 1799 I. 335, I never got salt to my porridge till I mounted at the Royal Exchange. **1816** Scott *Old Mort.* xxxvi, Hold your peace, sir,..and keep your ain breath to cool your ain porridge. **1836** *Magopico* 35 (E.D.D.), It's as plain as parridge that he was both a Roman and Socinian. **1883** R. Cleland *Inchbracken* xii. 92 If our young Captain has wance ta'en the notion, they may save their breath to cool their parritch, that would gainsay him. **1924** G. B. Shaw *Saint Joan* ii. 29 If you are going to say 'Son of St Louis: gird on the sword of your ancestors, and lead us to the victory' you may spare your breath to cool your porridge. **1930** E. Pound *XXX Cantos* xxii. 99 He said He would save his breath to cool his own porridge. **1969** D. Clark *Nobody's Perfect* iii. 79 'Three months sounds like generous notice.' Hunt said soberly, 'For a man who has made a porridge, perhaps.' **1971** 'H. Calvin' *Poison Chasers* ii. 26 These boffins have made a porridge of this place. **1976** A. White *Long Silence* xi. 101, I knew I would make a porridge of explaining it.

5. *attrib.* and *Comb.*, as ***porridge basin, bowl, dish, pan, saucepan, seasoner, -supping***; ***porridge-coloured, -faced, -fed, -like*** adjs.; †**porridge-belly**: see quots.; **porridge-ice**, broken ice forced into a continuous mass, pack-ice; **porridge-pot**, the pot in which porridge is cooked; **porridge-stick**, a stick used for stirring porridge; **porridge-time** (*Sc.* and *dial.*), breakfast-time (or supper-time).

1580 Hollyband *Treas. Fr. Tong, Grand potager*, or *mangeur de potage*, a *porrige belly. **1681** W. Robertson *Phraseol. Gen.* (1693) 446 A huge, great,..porridge-belly Friar. **1902** Farmer & Henley *Slang* V. 258/2 **Porridge-bowl*.., the stomach. **1925** *Heal & Son Catal.: Table Wares*, Porridge Bowl..1/-. **1936** J. Buchan *Island of Sheep* ii. 25 Archie Roylance..looked up sympathetically from his porridge bowl. **1974** P. Lovesey *Invitation to Dynamite Party* ix. 110 A tin porridge-bowl..and a mug. **1977** 'J. Fraser' *Hearts Ease* xv. 166 You can go to that orphanage.. stand in line and hold out your porridge bowl at breakfast time. **1949** E. Coxhead *Wind in West* i. 11 Grimy *porridge-coloured upholstery. **1979** *Homes & Gardens* June 57/3 The village ground, with a guaranteed vicar in porridge-coloured flannels and a blacksmith in belted greys. **1830** Scott *Demonol.* i. 45 In the case of the *porridge-fed lunatic. **1880** *Scribner's Mag.* Jan. 331/2 The water was full of *porridge-ice. **1589** R. Harvey *Pl. Perc.* Ded. 2 A large P. with a wide mouth like a *porradge pott. **1843** Lytton *Last Bar.* i. vi, Love and raw pease are two ill things in the porridge-pot. **1926–7** *Army & Navy Stores Catal.* 150/1 Double milk or *porridge saucepan..4 pt. 9/-. **1975** C. Fremlin *Long Shadow* iii. 24 A porridge saucepan soaking in the sink. **1895** Doyle *Stark Munroe Lett.* iii. (1902) 53 Always a lady, whether she was [etc.]..or stirring the porridge, which I can see her doing with the *porridge-stick in one hand. **1816** Scott *Old Mort.* xiv, This morning about *parritch-time.

Hence **'porridge** *v.*, (*a*) *intr.* to form porridge; (*b*) *trans.* to supply with porridge (*Cent. Dict.* 1890); (*c*) to send to prison (*slang*) (cf. porridge *sb.* 3 c). **'porridgy** *a.*, resembling porridge.

1629 Winthrop *Let.* in *New Eng.* (1853) I. 435 Let my son Henry provide such peas as will porridge well, or else none. **1859** Atkinson *Walks & Talks* (1892) 356 Their damp cloud seats and porridgy mists. **1897** *Allbutt's Syst. Med.* III. 791 Becoming gradually thicker, till in the second week a porridgy consistency may be attained. **1965** B. Knox *Taste of Proof* i. 27 Jean reckoned you blokes had porridged the wrong fella when you pulled in Frank for the Glen Ault job.

porriginous (pə'rɪdʒɪnəs), *a.* [ad. L. *porrīginōsus* full of scurf, f. *porrīgo, -inem* scurf, dandruff: see -ous.] Of, pertaining to, or affected with porrigo.

1828 *Glasgow Med. Jrnl.* 1 Feb., Porriginous ophthalmia is a disease of early life. **1842** T. H. Burgess *Man. Dis. Skin* 164 They have described six varieties..under the title of porriginous eruptions.

‖**porrigo** (pə'raɪgəʊ). *Path.* [L. *porrīgo* scurf, dandruff.] A name for several diseases of the scalp characterized by scaly eruptions.

1706 Phillips, *Porrigo*,..Scurf or Scales on the Head, Eye-brows, or Beard. *a* **1801** W. Heberden *Comm.* xxiii. (1806) 127 The porrigo, or scald head, begins with little spots of a branny scurf. **1899** *Allbutt's Syst. Med.* VIII. 526 Recognised as a distinct disease under the name of 'Contagious porrigo'.

porringer ('pɒrɪndʒə(r)). Forms: α. 6 por(r)eger, porrager. β. 6 porrynger, 6–7 poringer, 7 porrenger, 7– porringer. [An alteration of the earlier *potager, poddinger*, going with *porridge* from *potage, poddige*. For the *n* cf. *passenger, messenger*.] A small basin or similar vessel of metal, earthenware, or wood, from which soup, broth, porridge, children's food, etc., is eaten: variously specialized in different localities: see *Eng. Dial. Dict.*

1522 in *Bury Wills* (Camden) 115, iiij sawcers of pewter, iij poregers of pewter. **1538** *Ibid.* 135, vj pewter porryngers. **1578** in *Gentl. Mag.* July (1861) 36, vi. porragers of pwter, xiid. **1579** Langham *Gard. Health* (1633) 239 Put the iuyce into a Tinne Poringer. **1594** Nashe *Unfort. Trav.* Wks. (Grosart) V. 145 From Spaine, what bringeth our Traueller? A scull crownd hat of the fashion of an olde deepe porringer. **1596** Shaks. *Tam. Shr.* iv. iii. 64. **1661** Pepys *Diary* 29 May, Rose early, and put six spoons and a porringer of silver in my pocket to give away to-day. **1784** Franklin *Autobiog.* Wks. 1840 I. 102, I ate it out of a two-penny earthen porringer. **1798** Wordsw. *We are Seven* 47 And often after sunset, Sir, When it is light and fair, I take my little porringer, And eat my supper there. **1840** Dickens *Old C. Shop* lxi, A tin porringer containing his breakfast. **1855** Robinson *Whitby Gloss., Porringer*.., a coarse earthen pipkin, with a loop handle at the side. **1871** G. H. Napheys *Prev. & Cure Dis.* ii. ii. 431 A porringer, graduated so as to mark the quantity of its contents, is useful.

b. A hat or cap resembling a porringer: cf. quot. 1594 in prec. *humorous*.

1613 Shaks. *Hen. VIII*, v. iv. 50 A Habberdashers Wife.. rail'd vpon me till her pinck'd porrenger fell off her head. **1820** W. Irving *Sketch-bk., Little Brit.* §16 There is the little man with a velvet porringer on his head.

c. *attrib.* and *Comb.*

1860 Motley *Netherl.* (1868) I. ii. 39 Their little velvet porringer-caps stuck on the sides of their heads. **1901** *Athenæum* 27 July 132/1 Anothe of these porringer-shaped cups with two handles.

Hence **'porringerful.**

1904 *Brit. Med. Jrnl.* 3 Dec. 1517/1 Half a porringerful of foul fluid making its escape.

porriwiggle, variant of polliwog.

Porro, var. Poro.

‖**porron** (po'rron). Pl. **porrones, porrons.** [Sp.] In Spain, a wine-flask with a long spout from which the contents are drunk directly.

1845 R. Ford *Hand-bk. for Travellers Spain* I. vi. 479/1 They are..drinking out of *Porrones*. **1936** *Burlington Mag.* June 301/1 An interesting fourteenth or fifteenth-century ancestor of the *porron* which is still used in Soho. **1968** K. Bird *Smash Glass Image* iv. 50 Francisco tilted the teapot-shaped *porrón* and ejected a stream of wine from the spout. It curved through the air..into his open mouth. **1972** 'D. Craig' *Double Take* x. 133 Porrón, that's what those wine bottles were called. Really, it should be a skin, in the true Spain. **1976** *Scotsman* 24 Dec. (Weekend Suppl.) 2/5 We.. drink our modest bottle of vino corriente while the crowd below swill porrons and pigskins of the stuff which makes them very vocal indeed.

'porry. *Silk Weaving.* [?] The portion of the warp lying between the warp-roll or beam and the back of the heddles or harness through which the threads pass.

1790 *Trans. Soc. Arts* VIII. 166 A power of shortening the porry occasionally. *Ibid.* 169 The porry may be made of any length. **1831** G. R. Porter *Silk Manuf.* 274 Removing all roughnesses and inequalities in the warp threads, or, as the weavers call it, picking the porry.

porry: see porray.

pors, -e, obs. f. purse.

porselan, -seland. -slin, obs. ff. porcelain.

porselane, -sulaigne, obs. ff. purslane.

porsewe, -sue, obs. ff. pursue.

Porson ('pɔːsən). The name of Richard *Porson* (1759–1808), English classical scholar, used (*a*) in the possessive to designate a metrical law formulated by him and governing Greek tragic trimeters (see quots.); (*b*) *attrib.* and *absol.* to designate certain founts of Greek type influenced by his handwriting.

(*a*) **1894** W. W. Goodwin *Greek Gram.* (ed. 2) v. 358 When the *tragic* trimeter ends in a word forming a cretic (–∪–), this is regularly preceded by a short syllable or by a monosyllable... This is known as 'Porson's rule'. **1949** *Oxf. Classical Dict.* 565/2 The comic trimeter..is not bound by Porson's Law. **1962** H. Lloyd-Jones tr. *Maas's Greek Metre* 35 The rule..is known in this connexion as 'Maas's Law', as it is known as 'Porson's Law' with respect to the tragic trimeter and as 'Havet's Law' with respect to the tetrameter. **1973** A. H. Sommerstein *Sound Pattern Anc. Greek* 136 The iambic trimeter..is governed in tragedy by, among other constraints, a rule known as Porson's Law. **1976** R. Pfeiffer *Hist. Classical Scholarship 1300–1850* xii. 160 Bentley had led the way in the scholarly treatment of Greek and Latin metre, and Porson was the first to make a further substantial advance; we may say that his claim to immortality is based above all on the rule called 'Porson's Law': that no word may end after a long *anceps* in the last iambus of the tragic iambic trimeter.

(*b*) **1894** *Amer. Dict. Printing & Bookmaking* 240/2 Greek type is cast by one foundry in New York... Some kinds now in use in the United States have been imported from England and from Germany... A heavy face, generally known as a Porson, is in use for headings and emphasis. **1927** D. H. Stevens et al. *Man. Style* (ed. 9) 269 Monotype Porson Greek. **1960** *Penrose Ann.* LIV. 38/2 Austin cut the Porson greek type in London.

Hence **Por'sonian** (-əʊn-) *a.*, pertaining to or characteristic of Porson, his work, or the fount of Greek type named after him. Also *absol.* as *sb.*

1840 *Penny Cycl.* XVIII. 420/2 Porson's great reputation during his lifetime converted all the promising young scholars of the time into servile imitators of the great critic, and the 'Porsonian school of critics', as they have been termed, threw many impediments in the way of sound and comprehensive scholarship. **1896** *Dict. Nat. Biogr.* XLVI. 163/2 There was a reaction..against the Porsonian school. **1929** *N. & Q.* 13 Apr. 267/2 A stronger and more dignified type than the common current Porsonian. **1976** R. Pfeiffer *Hist. Classical Scholarship 1300–1850* xv. 179 In his editions of Greek tragedies he [*sc.* Hermann] may be said to rival Porson and the Porsonians or even surpass them.

porsyllogism, var. of prosyllogism.

port (pɔət), *sb.*[1] Also 4–6 porte, 5 poort. [OE. *port* haven, harbour, ad. L. *port-us* haven, harbour. In ME. reinforced by F. *port* (= Pr. *port*, Sp. *puerto*, Pg., It. *porto*) of same origin. Sense 5 directly from OF.]

I. 1. a. A place by the shore where ships may run in for shelter from storms, or to load and unload; a harbour, a haven.

c **893** K. Ælfred *Oros.* i. i. §20 þonne is an port on suðeweardum þæm lande, þone man hæt Sciringes heal. *Ibid.* §21, He seȝlode on fif daȝan to þæm porte þe mon hæt æt Hæþum. *c* **1330** R. Brunne *Chron.* (1810) 31 At a hauen of Sandwich, in þe portis mouth. **1390** Gower *Conf.* III. 288 He arryveth: Sauf in the port of Antioche. **1432–50** tr. *Higden* (Rolls) II. 163 Hauenge also more plesaunte portes [L. *portus accommodatiores*, 1387 more profitable hauenes]. **1455–6** *Cal. Anc. Rec. Dublin* (1889) I. 290 Al maner schyppys that cumyth withyn the portys of the cittie of Dyvelyng. **1585** T. Washington tr. *Nicholay's Voy.* i. iii. 3 The yles Baleares..haue good ports. *Ibid.* xi. 13 We arryued at the porte of Bone. **1687** A. Lovell tr. *Thevenot's Trav.* i. 8 Being Master of that Isle, they could break the Chain that secured the Port, which was stretched from the Castle St. Angelo to the Spur of the said Isle. **1726** Swift *Gulliver* ii. viii, To set me safe ashore in the first port where we arrived. **1887** Stevenson *Underwoods* xxviii. 61 I must arise..and to port Some lost complaining seaman pilot home.

b. *fig.* A place, position, or condition which one takes refuge in, or endeavours to arrive at.

1426 Lydg. *De Guil. Pilgr.* 16987 To aryven vp at so holsom a Port, and at so notable an havene, to ffynde Reffuyt and Refuge, O blyssed lady, in the. *c* **1430** —— *Min. Poems* (Percy Soc.) 238 Thoruhe helpe of Jhesu, at gracious poort t'aryve, Ther to have mercy kneelyng on our kne. **1555** Hooper in Coverdale *Lett. Mart.* (1564) 152 He by praier humbly resorted vnto god as the onely porte of consolation. **1865** Dickens *Mut. Fr.* i. vii, 'Harmon's, up Battle Bridge way'. Mr. Wegg admits that he is bound for that port. **1879** *Echo* No. 3273. 2 Doubt was expressed..as to the possibility of the measure reaching port this year.

c. Phr. ***port in a*** (or ***the***) ***storm***, a refuge in difficulties or troubled circumstances (also in weakened senses); *spec.* in proverbial phr. ***any port in a storm***, any refuge or escape (is welcomed) in adverse circumstances.

1749 J. Cleland *Mem. Woman of Pleasure* II. 133, I feeling pretty sensibly that it was going by the right door, and knocking desperately at the wrong one, I told him of it: 'Pooh, says he my dear, any port in a storm.' **1787** J. Cobb *First Floor* ii. ii. 51 Here is a door open, i' faith—any port in a storm, they say. **1821** Scott *Pirate* I. iv. 60 As this Scotsman's howf lies right under your lee, why, take any port in a storm. **1897** R. L. Stevenson *St. Ives* xxv. 188 'Any port in a storm' was the principle on which I was prepared to act. **1936** B. Adams *Ships & Women* x. 229 'How do you like Maggie Cuddeford?' she asked. I replied, 'Any port in a storm. I like you heaps better.' **1965** J. Porter *Dover Three* ii. 19 It was not quite the sort of company with which Dover would mix from choice but, as the jolly sailors say, any port in a storm. **1970** *Guardian* 7 Apr. 18/1 Midnight cries of scorn and indignation rang round the Commons, which was celebrating its return to work with a row over the Ports Bill... Well, any port in a storm these days. **1977** A. Morice *Murder in Mimicry* i. viii. 67 Henry and I moved on to our next port in the storm, which was a bar round the corner.

2. a. A town or place possessing a harbour to which vessels resort to load or unload, from which they start or at which they finish their voyages; *spec.* a place where customs officers are stationed to supervise the entry of goods.

Often as a part of the proper name of towns, etc., which are also harbours, e.g. Port Arthur, Port Chalmers, Port Elizabeth, Port Erin, Port Glasgow, Port Patrick, Port Royal, Port Said, Port Victoria; also in composition as Bridport, Devonport, Maryport, etc.

a **900** tr. *Bæda's Hist.* iv. i. §3 (1890) 256, & hine ȝelædde to þam porte, þe is nemned Cwæntwic [Etaples]. [**1340** *Act 14 Edw. III*, Stat. ii. c. 4 Les Custumers des portz ou les leynes se chargeront [etc.].] *c* **1400** Maundev. (Roxb.) viii. 29 Men may passe by see to þe porte Iaffe. **1432** *Rolls of*

Parlt. IV. 417/2 Other Havenes under the Port of Chichester. **1486** C'TESS OF OXFORD in *Four C. Eng. Lett.* (1880) 7 That such wetche..be used and hadde in the poorts, and creks. **1487** *Act 3 Hen. VII*, c. 7 Every merchaunt..which shall bryng..eny maner of goodez into any porte within this realme. *Ibid.*, The custumers of the seid porte. **1535** COVERDALE *Ezek.* xxvii. 1 Tyre, which is a porte off the see yͭ occupieth with moch people. *a* **1548** HALL *Chron., Hen. VIII* 260 The Frenche kyng wrote to the Emperor..that his armie had gotten the isle of Wight, the Portes of Hampton and Portesmouth, & diuerse other places. **1610** HOLLAND *Camden's Brit.* (1637) 211 The priviledges of a port or haven town. **1759** B. MARTIN *Nat. Hist. Eng.* II. *Norfolk* 75 This is the greatest Port for Importation. **1766** BLACKSTONE *Comm.* I. vii. 264 These legal ports were undoubtedly at first assigned by the crown; since to each of them a court of portmote is incident, the jurisdiction of which must flow from the royal authority. **1849** MACAULAY *Hist. Eng.* iii. I. 302 The profit of conveying bullion and other valuable commodities from port to port.

b. *close port, free port*: see quots.

1567 *Sc. Acts Jas. VI* (1814) III. 42/1 It salbe lesum to na strangear..To lois or laið bot at fre portis alanerly vnder þe pane of confiscatioun. **1727–41** CHAMBERS *Cycl.* s.v., *Close Ports*, are those within the body of a city; as those of Rhodes, of Venice [etc.]. *Free Port*,..a port open and free for merchants of all nations to load and unload their vessels in. ..Marseilles was declared a free port by an edict of Louis XIV. bearing date 5th March 1669. *Free Port* is also used for a total exemption and franchise, which any set of merchants enjoy, for goods imported into a state, or those of the growth of the country exported. **1867** SMYTH *Sailor's Word-bk.*, *Close ports*, those which lie up rivers; a term in contradistinction to *out ports*.

c. *port of entry*: a port by which people and goods may enter a country. Cf. PORT *sb.*³ 4 b.

1840 *Niles' Reg.* 23 May 188/1 Mr. King..reported a bill for the establishment of ports of entry in the states of Missouri and Arkansas. **1936** *Phytopathology* XXVI. 476 The suggested system of field inspection and certification.. will..relieve the port-of-entry inspection services of the sole responsibility of passing materials offered for import. **1977** *Arab Times* 13 Nov. 4/7 Ercan is not an internationally recognised port of entry into Cyprus. Only the Turkish state airline THY and the tiny Turkish Cypriot airline, KTHY use it.

d. *port of call*: a port visited by a vessel in the course of a voyage. Also *transf.*

1884 [see CALL *sb.* 5 a]. **1919** W. T. GRENFELL *Labrador Doctor* (1920) viii. 168 We..put down our helm..to avoid the wash... The last port of call was Henley, or Château, where formerly the British had placed a fort. **1980** J. B. HILTON *Anathema Stone* ix. 93 Waiting for me to be out of earshot..so that I would not know what was to be her next port of call.

†**3.** *the five ports*: = CINQUE PORTS. Also the barons of the Cinque Ports. *Obs.*

1297 R. GLOUC. (Rolls) 1169 Þe vif tounes of þe vif pors [*v.rr.* ports, -es] he let walli aboute. *c* **1330** R. BRUNNE *Chron.* (1810) 252 Þe fiue portes þorgh powere þe se had so conquerd. *c* **1400** *Brut* 235 Þe V Portes token to kepe hem [sea coasts], and also the see. **1429** *Pol. Poems* (Rolls) II. 146 Six erles in their estate shewid them alle; And the v. poortis beryng up the palle. *c* **1460** FORTESCUE *Abs. & Lim. Mon.* xvii. (1885) 151 Chambirlayns off Countreis, þe warden off þe portes, and such oþer. **1631** [see FIVE *a.* 1].

†**4.** The mouth of a river. *Obs. rare.*

[Rendering L. *portus*, sometimes used in this sense.]

1555 EDEN *Decades* 165 This riuer fauleth into the furthest corner of the goulfe of Vraba by seuen portes or mowthes.

II. †**5.** (?) A recess in the mountains; a defile, a mountain pass: applied esp. to those of the Pyrenees, in OF. (pl.) *porz d'Espagne*, med.L. *Hispani portūs, Pyrenæi portūs* (Du Cange).

[a. OF. (and local Fr.) *port*, pl. *porz, pors* (11th c. in *Chans. Roland, ports* = Sp. *puertos*, med.L. *portūs* 'fauces, claustra montium' (Du Cange, citing *Pseudo-Turpin c* 1125), the same word as L. *portus* haven, and app. an ancient local application of that word, perh. originally in sense 'recesses of the mountains'; cf. COVE *sb.*¹ 3, 4, 'a recess in the coast, or amid mountains', also locally in U.S. a gap, a pass.]

c **1205** LAY. 24415 Nes na cniht ne na swein..from þa porz of Spaine to þan tune of Alemaine, þat þider icomen nere, ʒif he iboden weore, al for Arðures æie.

III. 6. *attrib.* and *Comb.* **a.** General combs., as (in senses 1, 2) *port-bell, clearance* (CLEARANCE 8), *-fog, -gauger* (GAUGER 1), *guardship, haven, -master, -officer, -order, -trade*; *port-seizing* adj.

1608 H. CLAPHAM *Errour Right Hand* 51 The *Port-bell ringes, it is now about the eleuenth hower. **1815** *Gen. Hist.* in *Ann. Reg.* 136/2 Several English vessels provided with *port-clearances were fired at. **1891** KIPLING *Barrack-Room Ballads* (1892) 206 O the mutter overside, when the *port-fog holds us tied. **1923** —— *Land & Sea Tales* 173 When the port-fog holds us Moored and helpless, a mile from the pier. **1737** J. CHAMBERLAYNE *St. Gt. Brit.* III. xxviii. (ed. 33) II. 85 *Port-Guagers, each 66l. per annum. **1899** *Westm. Gaz.* 1 July 5/1 The *port guardship of l'Orient, the *Caudan.* **1662** OWEN *Animadv. on Fiat Lux* Wks. 1851 XIV. 60 This is the *port-haven of Protestants, whatever real darkness may be about them. **1590** MARLOWE *Edw. II*, IV. iii, Our *portmasters Are not so careless of their King's command. **1901** *Chambers's Jrnl.* Aug. 522/2 The *port-officer, and one or two Eurasian residents, came to the office..to interview us. **1796** NELSON in Nicolas *Disp.* (1846) VII. p. cxxiv, *Port-orders. **1897** *Westm. Gaz.* 30 Dec. 2/2 The *port-seizing Power for the day is France, and the port seized is Hainan.

b. Special combs.: **port-admiral**, an admiral in command of a naval port; **port-bar**, (*a*) a shoal or bank across the entrance to a port; = BAR *sb.*¹ 15; (*b*) = BOOM *sb.*² 3 (Webster 1864); **port-bound** *a.*, detained in port by contrary winds, foul weather, etc.; **port-charge**, harbour-due (see HARBOUR *sb.*¹ 5); **port-duty** = prec.; **port-head**, the most landward part of a harbour (HEAD *sb.*¹ 15); †**port-pass**, authorization to leave or land at a port: see PASSPORT; **port-pay**, wages due for time during which one's ship is detained in port.

1829 MARRYAT *F. Mildmay* iv, The junior *port-admiral had a spite against our captain. **1833** —— *P. Simple* x, The captain applied to the port-admiral, and obtained permission to send parties on shore to impress seamen. **1695** CONGREVE *Love for L.* III. vi, I love to roam about from Port to Port..; I could never abide to be *Port-bound, as we [sailors] call it. **1822** SCOTT *Pirate* vii, Does she get rich by selling favourable winds to those who are port-bound? **1652** *Suffolk Deeds* I. 234 By their third part of 942Rs. *port chardges at St. Lucar. **1776** ADAM SMITH *W.N.* v. i. III. (1869) II. 307 A moderate *port-duty upon the tonnage of the shipping. **1776** G. SEMPLE *Building in Water* 154 The *Port-head at the Custom-house Quay. **1678** in Marvell *Growth Popery* 63 Having a Pass from the Lords of the Admiralty, and a *Port-Pass from Dover. **1758** J. BLAKE *Plan Mar. Syst.* 11 He will have eight months wages remaining due to him, besides his *port-pay.

† **port**, *sb.*² *Obs.* exc. *Hist.* or in *Comb.* [OE. *port* m. = MFl., MDu. *port* fem., town, burgh, city. In origin, the same word either as the prec. or as the following; its proper place being somewhat doubtful, it is here provisionally separated, and placed between the two. See *Note* below.]

A town: perhaps *spec.*, a walled town, or a market-town; but identified with *burh* as a rendering of L. *cīvitās*, and, like 'town', contrasted with *uppelond* 'country'.

(The Netherlandish *port* was identified with *borch*, and, generally, with *stat* 'city'; but was app. also applicable to places inferior in rank or privileges to a city.)

901–924 *Laws Eadw. I*, I. c. 1 Ic wille þæt..nan man ne ceapiʒe butan porte [*extra portum*], ac hæbbe þæs portʒerefan ʒewitnesse oððe oðera unʒeliʒenra manna. *c* **950** *Lindisf. Gosp., Capitula Lectionum Matt.* XXXI. (ed. Skeat 18), In ciuitate sua, *gloss* in buruʒ *vel* in port his. *Ibid.* xxxx, Increpat ciuitates, *gl.* burʒas *vel* portas. *Ibid.* Mark vi. 6 Et circumibat castella, *gl.* ymb-eode ða portas. **10..** *O.E. Chron.* an. 1010 Ða com se here to Hamtune, and þone port sona forbærndon. *a* **1100** *Ibid.* (an. 1052 MS. D, Worc.), þa ferdon his men dyslice æfter inne, & sumne man ofsloʒon of þam porte [i.e. Dover], & oðer man of þam porte heora ʒeferan. *a* **1122** *Ibid.* an. 1087 (Laud MS.) Se cyng..bead ꝥ ælc man..sceolde cuman to him, Frencisce & Englisce, of porte & of uppe lande. **11..** *Voc.* in Wr.-Wülcker 550/7 *Castellum*, wic *uel* lutel port. [**1876** FREEMAN *Norm. Conq.* V. xxv. 516 *Port*, in the sense of town, is now known only in a few compound words, like *Port-reeve* and *Port-meadow*.]

b. *attrib.* and *Comb.* as †*port-dog*, †*-hound*; †**port-highway**, †**port-street** (only in OE. port-stræte) = PORT-WAY. See also PORTMAN, PORT-MOTE, PORT-REEVE, PORT-SALE, etc.

c **1290** *S. Eng. Leg.* I. 307/267 He [devil] fierde ase doth a *port-doggue I-norischet in port-toun: For he geth ofte in prece of Men a-mong heom op and doun. *Ibid.* 274 None more þane þe *port-hound, þat neiȝ men geth I-nouȝ. **1601** HOLLAND *Pliny* I. 140 At this town [Petra] meet both the *port high waies, to wit, the one which passengers trauell to Palmyra in Syria, and the other, wherein they go from Gaza. ? *a* **1000** in Kemble *Cod. Dipl.* III. 36 In ðære *portstræt; and swa æfter ðære stræte.

[*Note.* The extension of the sense 'haven' or 'harbour-town' to an inland town presents difficulties, though an explanation has been sought in the definition of L. *portus*, in the *Digest* L. xvi. (*De verb. signif.*) 59 'Portus appellatus est conclusus locus, quo importantur merces et inde exportantur; eaque nihilo minus statio est conclusa atque munita'. The transference of sense from 'gate' to 'walled town with gates' is also unlikely. Inasmuch as PORT¹ and PORT³, though representing respectively L. *portus* and *porta*, were both masc. in OE., the fact that this *port* was also masc. affords no evidence either way. The MFl. words are in a similar position: there *port* 'haven' and *porte* (later *poort*) 'gate' are both fem., and, *port* 'town' being also fem., the gender gives no indication. But the oldest and prevalent form of the word was *port* or *poort*, *porte* being unusual and late, and prob. due to confusion with *porte* 'gate'; Verwijs and Verdam take it therefore as certain that *port* 'town' represented L. *portus*; and if this was so in Flemish, it was doubtless so also in OE. The Netherlandish word was extensively used down to *c* 1500, and had numerous derivatives (of which *poorter* citizen, *poort-* or *poorterregt* burgess-ship, citizenship, are still in use). Cf. also PORTERY.]

port (pɔət), *sb.*³ Also 3–8 porte, 5 poort(e. [ME. *porte, port*, a. F. *porte*:—L. *porta* door, gate. The cognate langs. had in this sense words directly adopted from L., viz. OS. *porta*, OFris., MLG. *porte*, MDu. *porte, poort(e*, Du. *poort*, OHG. *pforta*, MHG., Ger. *pforte*, all fem. OE. had irregularly *port* m. (in form identical with PORT *sb.*¹), in several instances also rendering L. *porticus* porch, whence also OE. *portic*, OHG. *pforzih*. ON. had also *port*, perhaps from OE. If the OE. *port* survived into ME. (which is doubtful), it was then merged in the Fr. word, which became in Sc. the ordinary word for the gate of a town or city.]

1. a. A gate or gateway: from 14th c., usually that of a city or walled town. Now chiefly *Sc.*

c **950** *Lindisf. Gosp.* Matt. vii. 13 Innʒeonges ðerh nearuo port *vel* dure *vel* ʒæt forðon ðiu wide ʒeat [etc.] *c* **975** *Rushw. Gosp.* John x. 23, & eode ðe hælend in tempel in ðone port salamonnes [L. *in portico Salomonis*]. *c* **1000** *Ags. Ps.* (Th.) lxviii. 12 Me wiðerwearde wæron ealle, þa him sæton sundor on portum [L. *in porta*]. *a* **1300** *Cursor M.* 14612 At þe port o salamon Cum vr lauerd in-to þe tun. **1387** TREVISA *Higden* (Rolls) I. 221 A wal i-made of brent tile and strecchep dounward oute of þe hiȝe hulles by þe ȝate port Asinaria. **14..** *Customs of Malton* in *Surtees Misc.* (1888) 58 Thay schall haffe iiij portes, that is to say iiij ȝattes. **1490** CAXTON *Eneydos* xiv. 49 The brydges, poortes and passages ben lefte wythoute warde. **1500–20** DUNBAR *Poems* lxxvii. 17 Ane fair processioun mett her at the Port. *c* **1520** M. NISBET *Acts* iii. 10 He it was that sat at almouse at the fair port of the tempile. **1535** COVERDALE *Judith* xiii. 10 So these two.. came thorow the valley vnto the porte of the cite. **1537** BIBLE (Matthew) *Ps.* ix. 14 *note*, The portes or gates of the daughter of Syon are the companies of the good and faythfull. **1607** SHAKS. *Cor.* v. vi. 6 Him I accuse: The City Ports by this hath enter'd. **1667** MILTON *P.L.* IV. 778 And from thir Ivorie Port the Cherubim Forth issuing..stood armd. **1672** DRYDEN *Def. Epilogue* Ess. (ed. Ker) I. 169 He [Jonson] perpetually uses ports for gates; Which is an affected error in him, to introduce Latin by the loss of the English idiom. **1712–30** *Gideon Guthrie* (1900) 21 He was passing the port of Templebar. **1802** HOME *Hist. Reb.* iii, The Scots call the gate of a town the Port. **1828** SCOTT *F.M. Perth* vii, Let us meet at the East Port. **1904** C. S. DOUGALL *Burns Country* i. 7 Travellers setting out through the Kyle port, the eastern exit of the 'ancient borough'.

b. *transf.* and *fig.* (Cf. GATE *sb.*¹ 3– 5.)

1535 *Goodly Primer* (1834) 238 From the ports of hell.. Lord, deliver our souls. **1545** RAYNOLD *Byrth Mankynde* (1564) 10 The entraunce of the matrix or wombe, is named the womb port or mother port. **1601** B. JONSON *Forest* xi, Th'eye and eare (the ports vnto the minde). **1603** KNOLLES *Hist. Turks* (1621) 3 This people..by the Caspian ports passing thorow the Georgian country. *a* **1677** HALE *Prim. Orig. Man.* I. i. 1 These five ports or gates,..the five exterior Senses. **1742** YOUNG *Nt. Th.* IV. 292 Then first Humanity Triumphant, past the Crystal Ports of Light.

†**c.** *Sc.* An open space near the gate of a town, at which labourers were hired in open market; hence, a hiring-market or fair there held. Hence *port-day. port-wages*: the rate of pay fixed at the 'port'. *Obs.*

1786 *Har'st Rig* (1801) 39 Masters far and near hae been At port, they say. *Ibid.* 41 To Dun-eudain they hie with haste The next port-day. *Ibid.* 38 The West-port of Edinburgh, or rather the Grass market adjoining, is the place where reapers are hired every day during harvest.. particularly on Mondays. **1883** J. MARTIN *Remin. Old Haddington* 346 Linton..had from an early date a weekly established 'Port', every Monday morning during the harvest season for hiring shearers and fixing the wages. **1903** J. LUMSDEN *Toorli*, etc. 8 Port wages and the halesome harvest fare.

2. *Naut.* **a.** An opening in the side of a ship for entrance and exit, and for the loading and discharge of cargo. **b.** Each of the apertures in a ship of war through which cannon were pointed; now, an aperture for the admission of light and air; a PORT-HOLE.

1390 GOWER *Conf.* I. 197 This knyht..cam to Schipe.. To the porte anon he ferde:..And sodeinliche he was out throwe And dreynt. **1495** *Naval Acc. Hen. VII* (1896) 164 Calkyng the porte of the seid Ship. *a* **1548** HALL *Chron., Hen. VIII* 259 b, The *Mary Rose*..was laden wyth muche ordinaunce, and the portes left open, whiche where very lowe,..when the ship should turne, the water entered, and sodainly she sanke. *c* **1595** CAPT. WYATT *R. Dudley's Voy. W. Ind.* (Hakl. Soc.) 58 A verie fine snugg long shipp, havinge on each side vi. portes open, beside her chace and her sterne peeces. **1627** CAPT. SMITH *Seaman's Gram.* ii. 5 All the Ports may be of such equall height, so that euery peece may serue any Port. **1727–41** CHAMBERS *Cycl.* s.v. *Ship*, Plate, Fig. 2. 66 The Lower Tyre Ports. 67 The Middle Tyre of Ports. 68 The Entring Ports. **1836** *Lett. fr. Madras* (1843) 11 We came up with a French brig... I put my head out of the port to admire her. **1840** R. H. DANA *Bef. Mast* xxiii. 72 We were so near as to count the ports on her side. **1867** SMYTH *Sailor's Word-bk.*, *Entering-ports*, ports cut down on the middle gun-deck of three-deckers, to serve as door-ways for persons going in and out of the ship. **1890** *Cent. Dict.* s.v. *Lumber-port*, Vessel Unloading Lumber through Lumber-port.

c. The cover or shutter of a port-hole; a port-lid. *half-port*: see quot. 1823.

c **1627** [see *port-rope* in 6]. **1669** STURMY *Mariner's Mag.* I. ii. 19 The Ports, all knockt open..to run out our Guns. **1759** *Hist.* in *Ann. Reg.* 120/2 We..hauled our ports up and run our weather guns out. **1793** SMEATON *Edystone L.* §290 To make the holes preparatory for hanging the Ports for the windows;..got the ports hung so as to keep the sea from coming in at the windows [in lighthouse]. **1823** CRABB *Technol. Dict.* s.v. *Ports, Half-ports*, a kind of shutters with circular holes in their centre large enough to go over the muzzles of the guns. *c* **1860** [see *port-lid* in 6].

d. *transf.* = PORT-HOLE 2 a.

1882 CUSSANS *Her.* (ed. 3) 112 When the tincture of the Field is to be seen through the windows or ports, they are said to be *Voided of the Field*.

e. *U.S.* An aperture in the body of an aircraft (see quots.).

1946 *Aeroplane Spotter* 21 Sept. 226/1 (*caption*) This photograph shows well the fabric covering the three machine gun ports in each wing. **1954** D. M. DESOUTTER *All about Aircraft* 415/2 Details of the armament and interior arrangements are sparse, but two large gun ports are visible in pictures. **1958** *N.Y. Times Mag.* 6 Apr. 68/4 The bombardier tightens the canvas over his ports. **1959** F. D. ADAMS *Aeronaut. Dict.* 128/1 *Port*, a circular window in the side of an aircraft fuselage, hull, or cabin, or a side aperture for a gun, a camera, etc.

3. In various games, a passage through which a ball or the like must pass.

†**a.** *Billiards.* See quots. *Obs.* exc. *Hist.*

1688 R. HOLME *Armoury* III. 262/2 Billiards..the Port is the Arch of Ivory, standing at a little distance from the other end of the Table. **1873** BENNETT & 'CAVENDISH' *Billiards* 4 The peculiarity of the game at this time consisted in the use of a small arch of ivory called the 'port'.

b. *Curling* or *Bowls*. A passage remaining open between two stones or bowls: see quot. 1898.

1789 D. DAVIDSON *Thoughts on Seasons* 169 They closed fast on every side—A *port* could scarce be found. **1811** J. RAMSAY *Acct. Game of Curling* 10 Whether they will have to draw, strike, wick, or *enter a port*, they will seldom deviate an inch from their aim. [Note] To *enter a port*, is to make a stone pass through an opening made by two others lying opposite to one another. **1817** *Lintoun Green* III. xiii, To draw, guard, strike, or wick, he tries, Or through a port to steer. **1820** *Blackw. Mag.* VI. 572 Anon a Port is to be taken. **1898** *R. Caledon. Curling Club Ann.* 26 d, *diagram*, Drawing through a Port... If the played Stone pass between these two Stones without touching either. **1937** T. HENDERSON *Lockerbie* ix. 60 If ye mak' yersel' sma' ye'll can squeeze through the port. Here's the tee; noo canny. **1975** SCOTSMAN 17 Mar. (Curling Suppl.) p. v/7 The whys and wherefores of shots made and lost, the backring take-outs, in-wicks, out-wicks and draws through narrow ports were all double Dutch.

4. a. *Mech.* An aperture for the passage of steam, gas, or water; *esp.* in a steam-engine, for the passage of steam into or out of the cylinder, a ***steam-port***. Also, an aperture by which the mixture enters the cylinder or combustion chamber of an internal-combustion engine, or by which the exhaust gases leave it.

1839 R. S. ROBINSON *Naut. Steam Eng.* 101 To shut the steam port before the eduction port, leaving the expansive power of the steam, already in the cylinder, to finish the remainder of the stroke. **1848** Exhaust port [see EXHAUST *sb.* 3]. **1859** RANKINE *Steam Engine* (1861) 487 The seat of a steam engine slide valve consists usually of a very accurate plane surface, in which are oblong openings or ports.. at least two in number. **1875** KNIGHT *Dict. Mech.* 1767/1 The entering port for live steam is the inlet or induction port; the port of departure is the outlet, eduction, or exhaust port. **1886** D. CLERK *Gas Engine* vii. 168 An exhaust valve, leading into the space by a port, is also actuated at suitable times from the secondary shaft. **1895** *Model Steam Engine* 39 When both the ports are equally uncovered, the length of the eccentric-rod is correct. **1913** *Autocar Handbk.* (ed. 5) ii. 33 During the compression and firing strokes all four ports are out of line, so that the cylinder is completely closed. **1956** F. PRESTON *Pract. Car-Owner* i. 19/1 The upward stroke not only drives out burnt gas through an exhaust port in the cylinder wall but also draws in fresh mixture.. through an inlet port. **1966** B. D. POWER *High Vacuum Pumping Equipment*. xi. 387 Conditions remote from the pumping port are being considered. **1967** L. HOLMES *Odhams New Motor Man.* i. 34/1 Valves and a camshaft are not required, as there are ports in the cylinder walls which are uncovered by the moving pistons to let fuel mixture into and exhaust gas out of the cylinders. **1978** L. PRYOR *Viper* (1979) ii. 25 Around the perimeter there are two ports. The fuel comes in one port, explodes between ports, then is expelled through the other port.

b. *Med.* = PORTAL *sb.*[1] 1 f. Also ***port of entry*** (cf. PORT *sb.*[1] 2 c).

1908 [see CRYPTOGENETIC *a.*]. **1928** B. J. LEGGETT *Theory & Pract. Radiol.* II. vii. 220 Risk [of injury to surrounding tissues] becomes smaller the greater the number of fields or ports of entry. **1928** *Amer. Jrnl. Roentgenol.* XX. 135/2 It is not really necessary to have two separate ports for the useful radiation. **1936** B. J. M. HARRISON *Textbk. Roentgenol.* iii. 50 Considering the physical conditions of the technique adopted, the milliamperage, the kilovoltage.. and the size of the area treated (port of entry). **1962** ROSS & MOORE in *Surg. Pract. Lahey Clinic* (ed. 3) 369 If successive biopsies are desired, the biopsy port is reopened by strong negative pressure applied on 'H' syringe for 5 seconds. **1977** *Radiologia Clinica* XLVI. 225 In order to obtain greater homogeneity of biological effects within the treatment volume, all prescribed ports should be used at each treatment session.

c. An aperture in any kind of container or vessel for the entry or egress of fluid.

1944 *Plastics* Jan. 18/2 In transfer moulding the material is placed in a heated pot from which it is forced through a narrow port into the actual mould. **1962** V. GRISSOM in *Into Orbit* 131 In the rush to get out before I sank I had not closed the air inlet port in the belly of my suit, where the oxygen tube fits inside the capsule. **1971** *Sci. Amer.* Sept. 222/3 A filter should be inserted between the inlet port of the compressor and the gas outlet of the laser.

d. An aperture in a loudspeaker enclosure.

1949 FRAYNE & WOLFE *Elem. Sound Recording* xxx. 627 Ports are provided at the front of the enclosure in order to utilize some of the back-radiated energy to reinforce the energy from the horn at the lower frequencies. **1975** G. J. KING *Audio Handbk.* vi. 143 The box has two main apertures, one to accommodate the driver unit and the other, called the vent or port, which allows air to move in and out of the enclosure in sympathy with the air pressure changes inside.

e. (i) *Electr.* A pair of terminals where a signal enters or leaves a network or device, the current flowing into one terminal at any instant being equal to that flowing out of the other. Freq. *ellipt.* with preceding numeral adj.

1953 WHEELER & DETTINGER in *Wheeler Monogr.* IX. 7 After considering many alternatives, the writer has adopted the term 'portal' or simply 'port' as the general designation of an entrance or exit of a network. A self-impedance becomes a 'one-port'. The usual transducer becomes a 'two-port' with one 'in-port' and one 'out-port'. The general network is designated a 'multi-port'. **1958** N. BALABANIAN *Network Synthesis* i. 9 The simplest network.. is the one-terminal pair, or one-port. **1966** L. A. MANNING *Electr. Circuits* xii. 256 A two-port network may be driven by either a voltage or a current source of input, and either voltage or current may be measured at the output. **1973** *Nature* 3 Aug. 264/1 The switching element was a four-port ferrite switch driven at 1 kHz. **1975** D. G. FINK *Electronics Engineers' Handbk.* III. 43 A transistor is a two-port network, although it has three terminals. Connecting an extra wire to one of the terminals provides the extra terminal without violating any network laws.

(ii) A place where signals enter or leave a data-transmission system or a device in such a system.

1970 C. S. CARR et al. in *Proc. AFIPS Conf.* XXXVI. 592/2 We assume here that a process has several input-output paths which we will call ports. Each port may be connected to a sequential I/O device, and while connected, transmits information in only one direction. **1972** *Proc. IEEE* LX. 1409/1 The combiner may have a fixed number of input ports to which the terminals are either always connected, or to which they may be connected, if not already occupied. *Ibid.* 1412/1 Each remote TYMSAT is capable of accommodating up to 31 simultaneous users... In addition, each CPU has 60 input ports, each corresponding to a different user. **1976** *U.S. Agric. Outlook 1977* (Nat. Agric. Outlook Conf., U.S.) 366 The University user can lease either a 10-character per second or a 30-character per second port. The monthly rate varies.. depending on the speed. **1976** *Rep. Computer Board of Managem., 1975–76* (University Coll., London, Computer Centre) I. 4 For several years we have had a single dial-up line, operating at only 1200 bands. This single port was heavily used.

5. The curved mouthpiece of some bridle-bits.

1587 TURBERV. *Trag. T.* (1837) 94 A pleasant porte doth rule a raging horse, When harder brakes doe breake the mouth too much. **1607** MARKHAM *Caval.* II. (1617) 62 Many ..haue added in stead of the plights which fold the two partes of the bytte together, another peece in fashion of a round hoope, or a half moone, which they call a Port, and sometimes this Port must consist of one peece, and then it is called a whole Port, sometimes of two peeces, and then it is called a broken Port. **1875** 'STONEHENGE' *Brit. Sports* II. III. i. §3. 523 The ordinary curb with a port on the mouthpiece. **1884** E. L. ANDERSON *Mod. Horsemanhsip* I. v. 17 The mouth-piece should have a liberty for the tongue, so that the bit may take effect upon the bars of the mouth. The size of this liberty, or port as it is called, should depend upon the size of the tongue of the horse.

6. *attrib.* and *Comb.*, as (in sense 2) ***port-bar, -flange, -hook, -lid, -nail, -sail, -sash, -shackle, -sill, -tackle***: see quots.; †**port-base**, a small piece of ordnance, formerly in naval use; **port-bit** (sense 5), a bridle-bit of which the mouthpiece is curved into an arch; **port-face**, in a steam-engine, the flat surface in the steam-chest containing the ports or steam-passages; **port-light** (see quot. 1927); **port-mouth** = *port bit*; also *attrib.*; **port-mouthed** *a.*, having a port mouthpiece, as a bit; also *transf.*; **port-pendant** = *port-rope*; **port-piece**, an obsolete kind of ship's gun; **port-rope**, a rope for raising and lowering a port-lid; **port-stopper**, a revolving shutter for closing a port in a turret-ship; **port-way** = sense 4.

1864 WEBSTER, **Port-bar*. **1867** SMYTH *Sailor's Word-bk.*, *Port-bars*, strong pieces of oak, furnished with two laniards, by which the ports are secured from flying open in a gale of wind, the bars resting against the inside of the ship; the port is first tightly closed by its hooks and ring-bolts. **1600** in Hakluyt *Voy.* (1811) IV. 47 The barke..*Content* had but one Minion, one Falcon, one Saker, and 2 *port-bases. **1662** SIR A. MERVYN *Speech on Irish Affairs* 31 If they will not mannage with a Snaffle, perchance their Heads may be brought into a Rane with a *Port-bit. **1585** *Records of Elgin* (New Spald. Cl.) I. 177 Na maner of persone..within the kirkȝaird..to play at kylis, *portbowlis, or ony uther pastime. **1867** SMYTH *Sailor's Work-bk.*, **Port-flange*, in ship-carpentry, is a batten of wood fixed on the ship's side over a port, to prevent water or dirt going into the port. **1823** CRABB *Technol. Dict.*, **Port-Hooks*,..for the purpose of hooking the hinges that are fastened to the port-lids. *Ibid.*, **Port-Lids*, a sort of hanging doors that shut in the ports at sea. *c* **1860** H. STUART *Seaman's Catech.* 71 What are the port-lids, or ports for? For closing the ports. **1926** *Chambers's Jrnl.* July 478/2 *Portlights as fitted to deck cabins have some drawbacks. **1927** G. BRADFORD *Gloss. Sea Terms* 132/2 The usual round openings closed with glass for light and air are called ports. The glass is set in a hinged brass frame called the port light. **1589** *Pappe w. Hatchet* D iv, Thou shalt be broken..with a muzroule, *portmouth, and a martingall. **1908** *Animal Managem.* 140 Swimming mounted, requires a capable horseman, who should be a good swimmer himself. Before riding in, it is well to remove the portmouth bit if one is worn. **1965** C. E. G. HOPE *Riding* v. 62 The best known variety of the Pelham must be the British military bit, the *port-mouth universal, reversible*. **1739** *N. Eng. Hist. & Gen. Reg.* (1850) IV. 260 A *port mouthed Bitt. **1848** ELIZA COOK *Curls & Couplets* xvi, The port-mouthed parapet. **1710** J. HARRIS *Lex. Techn.* II. **Port-nails*, are such Nails as are used to fasten the Hinges to the Ports of Ships. *c* **1850** *Rudim. Navig.* (Weale) 134 *Port nails* ..are similar to clamp nails, and used for fastening iron-work. **1527** in *Archæologia* XLVII. 332 For a bumbardell, ij *portpeces with iiij. chambers of one sorte, xxxvij. barrelles saltpetre..c. li. **1884** *Encycl. Brit.* XVII. 282/2 There were ..in the first period of naval history basilisks, port pieces, stock-fowlers, sakers, and bombards. **1627** CAPT. SMITH *Seaman's Gram.* vi. 27 The *Port ropes hale vp the Ports of the Ordnances. **1867** in SMYTH *Sailor's Word-bk.* **1769** FALCONER *Dict. Marine* (1789), *Violes à Lest*, *port-sails, or pieces of canvas, depending from the port-hole of the ship, into which the ballast is thrown, to the side of the ballast-lighter. **1823** CRABB *Technol. Dict.*, **Port-Sashes*, glass frames that are put into the cabin-ports and other rooms at sea. **1769** FALCONER *Dict. Marine* (1789), *Sole*, a name sometimes given to the lower side of a gun-port, which however is more properly called the *port-sill. **1869** SIR E. J. REED *Shipbuilding* viii. 149 To obtain a good height of the port-sill above the water-level. **1823** CRABB *Technol. Dict.*, **Port-Tackles*, those which serve to haul up the Port-lids.

port (pɔət), *sb.*[4] Also 4–8 porte, 5 poort. [a. F. *port* a carrying, bearing, manners, gait, etc., vbl. sb. f. *porter*: see PORT *v.*[1] So It. *porto*, Sp., Pg. *porte*.]

I. 1. a. The manner in which one bears oneself; external deportment; carriage, bearing, mien.

c **1369** CHAUCER *Dethe Blaunche* 834 She had so stedfast countenaunce, So noble porte and mayntenaunce. *c* **1386** —— *Prol.* 69 And of his port as meeke as is a mayde. **1387–8** T. USK *Test. Love* I. v. (Skeat) l. 73 Let thy port ben lowe in every wightes presence. *c* **1430** LYDG. *Min. Poems* (Percy Soc.) 143 [He] sauhe by ther poort that they stood in dreede. *c* **1440** *Promp. Parv.* 409/2 Poort, of cowntenawnce, *gestus*. **1514** BARCLAY *Cyt. & Uplondyshm.* (Percy Soc.) 21 Thus with proude porte to cloke theyr poverte. **1667** MILTON *P.L.* IV. 869 With them comes a third of Regal port, But faded splendor wan. **1704** ADDISON *Poems, Campaign* 417 Such easie greatness, such a graceful port. **1805** WORDSW. *Prelude* IX. 146 His port, Which once had been erect and open, now Was stooping and contracted. **1874** SYMONDS *Sk. Italy & Greece* (1898) I. viii. 155 She has the proud port of a princess.

b. *fig.* Bearing, purport (of a matter).

1568 GRAFTON *Chron.* II. 721 The English Herault had shewed him playnely how to enter into the port of the treatie. **1841** EMERSON *Lect. Times* Wks. (Bohn) II. 249, I wish to consider well this affirmative side, which has a loftier port, and reason than heretofore. **1876** LOWELL *Among my Bks.* Ser. II. 285 Phrases of towering port, in which every member dilated stands like Teneriffe or Atlas.

†**c.** Behaviour, conduct. *Obs. rare*[−1].

1588 LAMBARDE *Eiren.* IV. xiv. 563 A Writ of allowance, testifying that he hath found suerties for his good port, according to the Statute.

d. Dignified carriage; stately bearing. *rare.*

1633 BP. HALL *Hard Texts, Prov.* xxx. 29 Which carry.. a kind of port, and pleasure in their motion. **1873** HOLLAND *A. Bonnic.* i. 9 The growing port of later years, and the ampler vestments are laid aside.

e. *transf.* Habit or mode of growth (of a plant). *rare.*

1721 BRADLEY *Philos. Acc. Wks. Nat.* 27 They have given the Feminine Character to some Plants for the sake of their beautiful Flowers, or from the Port or Appearance of the whole plant. **1882** *Garden* 10 June 402/2 It [the Umbrella Tree] is somewhat straggling in growth, but this does not detract from its handsome port.

2. a. Style of living; *esp.* a grand or expensive style; state; hence *transf.* social position, station. Now *rare* or *Obs.*

1523 LD. BERNERS *Froiss.* I. xxviii. 42 Eche of them kept a great estate and port, and spared nothynge. **1530** PALSGR. 431/2 He is nat worth two pens all men payed, and yet he kepeth a porte lyke a lorde. **1570** ABP. PARKER *Corr.* (Parker Soc.) 360 For that Mr Bickley is master of a house and keepeth thereby a port of worship, I think he would well serve the turn. **1657** R. LIGON *Barbadoes* (1673) 9 By his port and house he kept he was more like a Hermite, than a Governour. *a* **1713** ELLWOOD *Autobiog.* (1765) 5 My Father ..having accepted the Office of a Justice of the Peace..put himself into a Port and Course of Living agreeable thereunto. **1806** SCOTT *Fam. Lett.* 23 Nov., It became more and more difficult..to keep the name and port of gentlemen. **1839** KEIGHTLEY *Hist. Eng.* I. 431 If they were spenders, they must needs have, because it was seen in their port and manner of living.

†**b.** *transf.* A train of attendants (as indicating a splendid style of living); a retinue. Also *fig.*

1545 ASCHAM *Toxoph.* Ded. (Arb.) 13 What tyme..your highnes..tooke that your moost honorable and victorious iourney into Fraunce, accompanied with such a porte of the Nobilitie and yeomanrie of Englande. **1577** R. S. (*title*) The Covrt of ciuill Courtesie. Fitlie furnished with a pleasant port of stately phrases and pithy precepts. **1621** FLETCHER *Pilgrim* I. ii, Well, madam, ye've e'en as pretty a port of pentioners——. Vain-glory would seek more and handsomer.

II. †**3.** Means of carriage, conveyance. *Obs.*

c **1500** *Chaucer's Dreme* 29 That some gode spirit, that eve, By mene of some curious port, Bar me, wher I saw peyne and sport.

†**4.** The action of carrying; the fee or price for carrying; postage, carriage. *Obs.*

1615 *Lett. E. India Co.* (1899) III. 194 You are to pay the bringer 5 mas port; he hath promised me to make haste. **1622** MABBE tr. *Aleman's Guzman d' Alf.* II. 24 He bethought himselfe of feigning a packet of Letters, and to put there-vpon two Ducats Port. **1635** in *Secret Committee on Post-Office* (1844) 56 The further the lettres shall goe, the port thereof is to be advanced. **1692** *N. York Stat.* in *Laws & Acts N.Y.* (1694) 74 For the port of every single letter from Boston to New York..nine pence.

†**5.** Weight that has to be carried or borne. *rare.*

1660 SHARROCK *Vegetables* 38 It has root to grow, body to bear the port of the plant. **1682** N. O. *Boileau's Lutrin* I. 108 And his Fat comely Corps, so thick and short Made the Soft Pillows groan under his Port.

6. Something that is used to carry, a carrier: †**a.** A socket attached to the saddle or stirrup in which the butt of the lance rested when carried upright. **b.** Some part of the handle of a sword, ? the hilt or grip. *Obs.*

a **1548** HALL *Chron., Hen. IV* 12 One company had the plackard, the rest, the port, the burley, the tasses, the lamboys,..all gylte. **1679** *Lond. Gaz.* No. 1404/4 Lost..a large agget handle Sword, with a Silver Hilt Cross and Port, ..the Hilt gilt in Ports.

c. A frame for carrying; *spec.* in candle-making: see quots.

1839 URE *Dict. Arts* 247 A frame, or port, as the work-men call it..containing 6 rods, on each of which are hung 18 wicks. *c* **1865** LETHEBY in *Circ. Sc.* I. 93/2 The wicks are cut into proper lengths by a machine, according to the sort of candle to be made, and then suspended from a rod or frame, called a port.

†**7.** *Venery.* (See quots.) *Obs.*

1688 R. HOLME *Armoury* II. 132/2 An Harts..Footing is called, slot, or portes. *Ibid.* 188/1 Ports, or Slot, is the print or tread of a Deers foot.

†**8.** *Mus.* (See quot.) *Obs. rare.*

1727–41 CHAMBERS *Cycl.*, *Port of the voice*, in music, the faculty and habit of makeing the shakes, passages, and diminutions.

9. [fr. Mil. phr. *Port arms.*] The position required by the order '*Port arms*': see PORT *v.*[1] 2, esp. in phr. ***at the high port***; also *transf.* and *fig.* Cf. CARRY *sb.* 3.

1833 *Regul. Instr. Cavalry* I. 30 The whole..drop their carbines smartly to the port. **1887** *Times* (weekly ed.) 28 Oct. 18/4, I..brought the rifle from the 'slope' to the 'port'. [**1918** E. S. FARROW *Dict. Mil. Terms* 294 *High port*, a position in bayonet training.] **1937** PARTRIDGE *Dict. Slang* 19/2 *At the high port*, at once; vigorously; unhesitatingly; very much: military; from ca. 1925. I.e. in fine style. **1956** D. M. DAVIN *Sullen Bell* II. vi. 148 'You seem very much at the high port,' Hugh said. 'I haven't seen you so bright since the evening you flung the smoke bomb into the Yank mess at Caserta.' **1970** *Daily Tel.* 28 Apr. 2/5 He began to climb the stairs with the gun at the 'high port' position. **1971** S. MAYS *No More Soldiering for Me* xv. 153 He spun round with fists at the high port.

†**port**, *sb.*[5] *Obs.* [Aphetic f. ME. *aport*, APPORT *sb.*[2], a. OF. *aport*. F. *apport*, f. *apporter* to bring; in med.L. *apportum* (Du Cange).] That which anything 'brings in', yields, or contributes; a customary or legal contribution, a payment in kind or money, by way of rent, rent-charge, tribute, etc.; in early use, the tribute rendered by a daughter religious house to the mother-house. Also *attrib.*, as ***port-corn***, ***port-tithe***.

1450 *Rolls of Parlt.* V. 198/1 Fermez, Pensions, Portions yeerly, Portes, Annuitees, Feefermes, Knyghtes Fees, Advowsons. **1473** *Ibid.* VI. 93/1 A Graunte by us to hym made.., of a port [= *aport*] C s. by yere, to be taken by the handes of the Priour and Covent of Wenlok. **1536** CROMWELL in Merriman *Life & Lett.* (1902) II. 8 Ye haue aledgyd that I haue letten to Ferme the port tythe. **1541–2** in Bolton *Stat. Irel.* (1621) 227 Which were not..let to ferme for money, but only for porte of corne or marts, or for porte of corne and money. **1715** *Lond. Gaz.* No. 5394/3 Port Corn issuing yearly out of the Vicar's Part of Killrumper Tythes.

port (pɔət), *sb.*[6] (*a.*) *Naut.* [Derivation obscure: see Note below.]

1. The left-hand side of a ship looking forward: = LARBOARD *sb.* Opposed to STARBOARD. (Often in phr. *to port*, A-PORT.)

In recent times generally substituted for the older *larboard* to obviate misunderstandings arising from the similarity in sound of *starboard* and *larboard*. By international convention, ships, esp. steamers, carry a red light on the port side.

1543–4 (Jan. 11) *Adm. Ct. Exam.* 92 (Rypper's Depos.) The sayd [ship] mighte have layed his helme a porte. **1625–44** MANWAYRING *Sea-mans Dict.*, *To Port.* Is a word used in Conding the Ship,..they will use the word steddy a-Port, or Steddy a Star-boord, the Ship heeles to Port: bring things neere to port, or the like. **1633** T. STAFFORD *Pac. Hib.* III. viii. (1821) 562 With two takles hee might steere the Hoy either to Starboard or to Port. **1748** *Anson's Voy.* I. x. 104 The ship heeled..two streaks to port. **1813** SOUTHEY *Nelson* I. iii. 124 They..put the helm a-port, and stood after her again. **1844** *Admlty. Order* 22 Nov., The word 'Port' is frequently..substituted..for the word 'Larboard', and as ..the distinction between 'Starboard' and 'Port' is so much more marked than that between 'Starboard' and 'Larboard', it is their Lordships direction that the word 'Larboard' shall no longer be used. **1846** *U.S. Navy Department Notice* 18 Feb., It having been repeatedly represented to the Department that confusion arises from the use of the words 'larboard' and 'starboard' in consequence of their similarity of sound, the word 'port' is hereafter to be substituted for 'larboard'. **1875** BEDFORD *Sailor's Pocket Bk.* iii. (ed. 2) 61 If two sailing ships are meeting end-on,..so as to involve risk of collision, the helms of both shall be put to port, so that each may pass on the port side of the other. **1884** *Pall Mall G.* 25 Aug. 8/2 The..port bow of the *Camden* struck the port of the *Dione* between her rigging.

2. a. *attrib.* or as *adj.* Situated on, or turned towards the left side of a ship (or aircraft): = LARBOARD B.

1857 R. TOMES *Amer. in Japan* vii. 149 It was thought better to stand off on the port tack, in order to get well clear of the land. **1857** DUFFERIN *Lett. High Lat.* (ed. 3) 226 A promising opening was reported..a mile or so away on the port-bow. **1875** BEDFORD *Sailor's Pocket Bk.* i. (ed. 2) 21 The Port Wing Ship of a Column is the ship on its extreme left. **1883** *Law Times Rep.* XLIX. 332/1 The *Clan Sinclair* ..was about to round Blackwall Point under a port helm. *Mod.* A green light seen on your port bow shows that a vessel is approaching on your left front on a transverse course (the green light being shown from the starboard side of that vessel). **1917** R. B. MATTHEWS *Aviation Pocket-bk.* vi. 164 The leading edges of the port and starboard top wing should be in a straight line. **1939** [see *flight engineer* s.v. FLIGHT *sb.*[1] 15]. **1948** [see ASSEMBLY 1 c]. **1971** R. DENTRY *Encounter at Kharmel* ii. 25 He had landed at Peshawar..because the port motor was running too roughly to warrant continuing the flight. **1976** J. MCCLURE *Rogue Eagle* iv. 69 The landscape sliding away beneath the port wing. **1977** *R.A.F. News* 27 Apr.–10 May 8/2 Then the port engine burst into flames.

[Note. This use of *port* may have arisen either from PORT *sb.*[1], senses 1, 2, or from PORT *sb.*[3], sense 2. When the steering apparatus was on the right side of the vessel (the *steereboord* or *starboard*), it would be convenient, in order to leave this free, to have the *port* (entering port) on the opposite side (the *lade board* or *larboard*). For the same reason, the vessel when in port, would naturally be placed so as to lie with her larboard alongside or facing the shore or port. For either reason, the larboard would be the port side. *Port* for *larboard* was in recorded use more than two centuries before it became official; the existence of PORT *v.*[2] indicates a still earlier colloquial use.]

b. ***port-watch***: see quot. 1883.

1867 [see LARBOARD *sb.* (*a.*) B]. **1883** *Man. Seamanship for Boys' Training Ships R. Navy* (Admiralty) (1886) 5 The starboard watch work the starboard side of the deck, and the port watch the port side of the deck. **1953** C. S. FORESTER *Hornblower & Atropos* xvi. 228 Port watch wins!.. Starboard watch provides the entertainment tomorrow night!

port (pɔət), *sb.*[7] [Shortened form of *O Porto* (*wine*), f. *Oporto* (Pg. *O Porto*, lit. 'the Port') name of a city of Portugal, the chief port of shipment for the wines of the country, formerly also called in Eng. *Port O Port*(*o*. So F. (*vin de*) *Porto*.] **a.** A well-known strong dark-red wine of Portugal, having a sweet and slightly astringent taste. Also called ***Oporto*** (***wine***), † ***Port O Port wine***, † ***Porto***, and PORT-WINE. Hence, a drink of port; a glass used for port.

Formerly also called ***red port***, as opposed to ***white port***, a white wine of Portugal (now little imported).

1691 LUTTRELL *Brief Rel.* (1857) II. 314 English ships that went to Bourdeaux and took in wine, and after sailed to port O Porto, and then came home, pretending it to be port. **1693** *Bacchanalian Sessions* 21 But we've the best Red Port— What's that you call Red Port?—a Wine Sir comes from Portugal. *c* **1717** PRIOR *Epitaph* 29 Their beer was strong; their wine was port. **1739** 'R. BULL' tr. *Dedekindus' Grobianus* 263 Wines of ev'ry Sort, From potent Cyprus down to humble Port. **1784** R. BAGE *Barham Downs* I. 23 It was his constant custom to smoak tobacco, drink red-port. **1837** MARRYAT *Dog-fiend* xxx, I mean to take my share of a bottle of Oporto. **1880** BROWNING *Clive* 77 Let alone that filthy sleep-stuff, swallow bold this wholesome Port! **1889** *N.-W. Linc. Gloss.* (ed. 2) s.v. *Red Port*, The generation which is passing away, and their predecessors, always spoke of port wine as red port. **1907** *Yesterday's Shopping* (1969) 937 Table glass services... 12 Sherries... 12 Ports... 12 Clarets [etc.]. **1925** [see LIQUEUR *sb.* 2]. **1938** G. GREENE *Brighton Rock* III. i. 98 Give me another port. **1974** *Times* 5 Apr. 12/3 The goblet is £4.25... A claret is £3.15 and a sherry/port £2.95.

b. *attrib.* and *Comb.*, as ***port club***, ***-drinking*** (sb. and adj.), ***-negus***; ***port-bibbing***, ***-complexioned*** adjs.

1751 SMOLLETT *Per. Pic.* IV. xcviii, [One] who had shone at almost all the Port-clubs in that end of the town. **1771** FOOTE *Maid of B.* I. Wks. 1799 II. 204 A few port-drinking people, that dine every day in the Lion. **1865** DICKENS *Mut. Fr.* I. vi, Miss Potterson [took] only half her usual tumbler of hot port negus. **1900** *Daily News* 24 Oct. 10/2 The old days of port-complexioned dons.

port (pɔət), *sb.*[8] *Sc.* Also 8 porte. [a. Gael. *port* tune, = Ir. *port* tune, jig (O'Reilly).] A lively tune, a catch, an air.

1721 KELLY *Scott. Prov.* 397 What the English call a Catch, the Scottish call a Port; as Carnagies Port, Port Arlington, Port Athol, &c. **17..** in Scott *Pirate* xv. *note*, You, minstrel man, play me a porte. **1805** SCOTT *Last Minstr.* v. xiv, The pipe's shrill port aroused each clan. **1896** N. MUNRO *Lost Pibroch* (1902) 16 You played a port that makes poor enough all ports ever one listened to.

port, *sb.*[9], obs. form of (Sublime) PORTE.

port (pɔət), *sb.*[10] *Austral.* colloq. abbrev. of PORTMANTEAU *sb.*

1908 E. G. MURPHY *Jarrahland Jingles* 82 Silently they packed their 'ports' and flitted to the West. **1915** J. P. BOURKE *Off Bluebush* 122 They see a young chap with a 'port' on his back. **1928** J. DEVANNY *Dawn Beloved* ix. 107 'Get my working togs out of my port, will you?'.. Dawn.. opened his old portmanteau and took out the things. **1934** T. WOOD *Cobbers* xviii. 236 A dignitary festooned in silver lace opened the door and asked me if I had any more ports. in the brake. **1946** D. STIVENS *Courtship Uncle Henry* 53 You take your port up and come back to the car. **1954** G. DUTTON in *Coast to Coast 1953–54* 149 Well grab your ports, and I'll take you out to the huts. **1967** *Sunday Truth* (Brisbane) 17 Sept. 16/3 She went back to her hut and happily unpacked her ports. **1972** R. MAGOFFIN *Chops & Gravy* 46 Roly grabbed his port..charged towards the bus.

port (pɔət), *v.*[1] Also 7 porte. [a. F. *port-er*:—L. *portāre* to bear, carry.]

1. *trans.* To carry, bear, convey, bring.

1566 J. PITS *Poor Man's Benev.*, *Ps. c*, He did vs make, and port And guyde vs all our dayes. **1608** *Act of Kirk Session Aberdeen* in *Caled. Merc.* 24 Aug. 1816 (Jam.) It becumis the people..to leave their sinnes quhilk porte on Gods judgmentis aganes us. *a* **1637** B. JONSON *Underwoods, Epithal.* vii, The virgins..Porting the ensigns of united two Both crowns and kingdoms, in their either hand. *a* **1661** FULLER *Worthies, Shropsh.* (1662) II. 1 They [coals] are easily ported by Boat into other Shires. **1706** PHILLIPS, To *Port*, to carry, as To port Books about to sell. **1711** in *10th Rep. Hist. MSS. Comm.* App. v. 178 They had ported arms without license. **1973** W. H. HALLAHAN *Ross Forgery* iv. 53 The skids..had been ported into the press rooms. **1979** 'E. PETERS' *One Corpse too Many* vii. 113 The boat..was of the light, withy-and-hide type that could be ported easily overland.

2. *Mil.* To carry or hold (a pike or the like) with both hands; *spec.* to carry (a rifle or other weapon) diagonally across and close to the body, so that the barrel or blade is opposite the middle of the left shoulder; esp. in the command ***Port arms!*** Also ***port arms***, the position adopted at this command.

1625 MARKHAM *Souldier's Accid.* 23 [In] charging [with Pikes]..Port over-hand. Port vnder-hand. **1677** R. BOYLE *Treat. Art of War* 191 And have caused my Pike-men to trail their Pikes, that they might not have been seen by the Enemy; which if shoulder'd, or ported, they would be. **1688** R. HOLME *Armoury* III. xix. (Roxb.) 147/2 Port your pike, is in three motions to take it by the But end, with your right hand, and beare the point forward aloft. **1803** *Compl. Drill Serjeant* 18 In some regiments it is called porting arms or preparing for the charge. **1820** SCOTT *Abbot* iii, To mimic the motions of the warder as he alternately shouldered, or ported, or sloped pike. **1833** *Regul. Instr. Cavalry* I. 36 Officers recover swords.., and 'Port' them. **1877** *Field Exerc. Infantry* 374 On the approach of any person, the sentry will port Arms, and call out Halt, who comes there? **1918** E. S. FARROW *Dict. Mil. Terms* 462 *Port arms*, a position in the Manual of Arms. **1973** D. BARNES *See the Woman* (1974) I. 38 The..white-helmeted officers..stood with batons in a port-arms position, facing the crowd. *Ibid.* 81 Johnson held the shotgun at port-arms. **1974** D. E. WESTLAKE *Help* (1975) xix. 128 The sentry..was still at port arms as though frozen in that position.

port (pɔət), *v.*[2] *Naut.* [f. PORT *sb.*[6]: cf. STARBOARD *sb.* and *v.*]

1. *trans.* In *to port the helm*, to put or turn it to the left side of the ship; also ellipt. *to port*.

1580 H. SMITH in *Hakluyt's Voy.* (1809) I. 505 The *William* had her sterne post broken, that the rudder did hang clean besides the sterne, so that she could in no wise port her helme. **1594** [See *pop-mouth* s.v. POP-]. **1627** CAPT. SMITH *Seaman's Gram.* ix. 37 Port, that is, to put the Helme to Larboord, and the Ship will goe to the Starboord. **1630** J. TAYLOR (Water P.) *Praise of Hempseed* Wks. 65/2 Cleere your maine brace, let goe the bolein there, Port, Port the helme hard. **1704** J. HARRIS *Lex. Techn.* I. s.v., They never say *Larboard the Helm*, but always *Port it*; tho' they say *Starboard the Helm*, when it is to be put to the Right side of the Ship. **1829** MARRYAT *F. Mildmay* xx, 'Port the helm'... 'Port it is, sir', said the man at the helm. **1875** BEDFORD *Sailor's Pocket Bk.* iii. (ed. 2) 59 Seamen are to be found who port at every light seen ahead, or nearly ahead.

2. *intr.* Of a ship: To turn or go to her port or left side.

1890 in *Cent. Dict.* **1905** *Westm. Gaz.* 10 Aug. 9/2 She was an unwieldy oil-tank in ballast, and for a moment her huge bulk, slowly porting, was bow on.

port, *v.*[3] [f. PORT *sb.*[1]] *trans.* **a.** To bring to port. **b.** To land at, reach (a port). **c.** *nonce-use.* To furnish with ports or harbours.

1612 *Two Noble K.* v. i, So hoyst we The sayles, that must these vessells port [*v.r.* part] even where The heauenly lymiter pleases. **1632** LITHGOW *Trav.* VIII. 350 Coasting the ..shoar.., I ported Ligorne, the great Dukes Sea-Haven. **1635** QUARLES *Embl.* III. viii. 155 The way to Heav'n is through the Sea of Teares: Earth is an Island ported round with Feares. **1648** EARL OF WESTMORELAND *Otia Sacra* (1879) 18 A fresh-Mackerell Gale, whose blast May Port them in true happiness at last.

port, *v.*[4] [f. PORT *sb.*[3]]

†**1.** *trans.* To furnish or shut in with a gate. Hence '**ported** *ppl. a. Obs.*

a **1548** HALL *Chron.*, *Hen. V* 65 b, The Englishmen had their parte only barred and ported. **1616** B. JONSON *Masques, Hymenæi, Barriers*, Designing power to ope the ported skyes.

2. *Curling.* (See quot. and PORT *sb.*[3] 3 b.)

1831 *Blackw. Mag.* XXX. 971 *Porting*, is to come up, *inter Scyllam et Charybdim*, i.e. to draw a shot through a strait formed by the stones upon the rink.

port, *v.*[5] *nonce-wd.* [f. PORT *sb.*[7]] *intr.* To drink port (cf. *to wine*). Also *to port it*.

1825 *Sporting Mag.* XV. 323, I have ported and clareted it 'many a time and oft' with Sir John.

‖**porta** ('pɔətə). *Anat.* [L., a gate; also applied to a part of the liver (Cic.). See PORT *sb.*[3]] **a.** The transverse fissure of the liver, at which the portal vein, hepatic artery, etc. enter it: the portal fissure. Also applied to a similar part in other organs. **b.** The *vena portæ* or portal vein: see PORTAL *a.* 2.

1398 TREVISA *Barth De P.R.* v. xxxix. (Bodl. MS.) lf. 21 b/1 Oute of þe brode holownes of þe lyuour comeþ a veyne, þat phisicians clepen porta. *c* **1400** *Lanfranc's Cirurg.* 26 Smale veynes þat comen out of þe veyne þat is clepid porta. **1704** J. HARRIS *Lex. Techn.* I, *Porta*, the same with *Vena Portæ.* **1895** *Syd. Soc. Lex.*, *Porta*..term applied by anatomists to that fissure in the liver (the *transverse* or *portal* fissure) by which the vessels enter... Sometimes also extended to other organs... *P. omentorum*..a name for the foramen of Winslow..*P. renum*, the hilum of the kidney.

‖**port-a-beul** ('pɔrʃtə'bial). *Sc.* Pl. (also used erron. as sing.) **puirt-a-beul.** [Gael., lit. 'music from mouth'.] 'A quick tune, gen. a reel-tune or the like, of Lowland Sc. orig. to which Gael. words of a quick repetitive nature have been added to make it easier to sing, now occasionally used as an accompaniment to dancing in the absence of instrumental music' (*Sc. Nat. Dict.*). Also *transf.* and *attrib.*

1901 K. N. MACDONALD *Puirt-a-beul* 3 Puirt-a-beul, 'mouth-tunes', or 'tunes for dancing'. **1938** [see *mouth music* s.v. MOUTH *sb.* 21]. **1945** B. FERGUSSON *Lowland Soldier* 12 The burn's making ever its own port-a-beul. **1952** N. MITCHISON *Lobsters on Agenda* viii. 94 The three from the Glen, Janet, Sheila and young Mrs. Macrae, were trying over a port a beul, very lightly, a living breath of humming. **1957** *Scottish Stud.* I. 133 The *Puirt-a-beul* are popularly supposed to have originated as a result of the religious opposition to musical instruments such as the bagpipes and the fiddle, which was at its strongest in the middle of the nineteenth century. **1964** *Listener* 15 Oct. 595/2, I shall never forget.., in a Roman street, a childish jet of water dancing, like MacDiarmid's duck, to its own *port a beul.* *c* **1970** A. MacPhee *Story of Highland Bagpipe* (An Comunn Gaidhealach) 8 All Gaelic music and pipe tunes are not sad and plaintive. Merely listen to a good 'puirt-a-beul' (mouth-music) singer. **1974** *People's Jrnl.* (Inverness & Northern Counties ed.) 5 Jan. 13/2 Other lively numbers are 'Ta-Ra-Ra Bhoom Di-Ay', written in Gaelic when that rhythm was the fashion and 'Tha na Cailean Mealldа', a swinging puirt-a-beul.

portability (pɔətəˈbɪlɪtɪ). [f. late L. *portābilis* PORTABLE + -ITY.] The quality or state of being portable; fitness for being carried or moved from place to place, esp. with ease; portableness. Also *transf.* and *fig.*

1667 Waterhouse *Fire Lond.* 23 The River of Thames, and the portability of that which it brings up to the Keyes of London. **1669** Sturmy *Mariner's Mag.* II. vi. 68 This Quadrant..I hold to be as necessary an Instrument as Seamen can use, in respect of its plainness..and portability. **1794** G. Adams *Nat. & Exp. Philos.* II. xxii. 476 *note,* Of a form the most convenient for portability and readiness in management. **1875** Jevons *Money* v. 35 The portability of money is an important quality. **1955** *Sci. News Let.* 5 Mar. 160/1 Portable rink for outdoor ice skating makes this winter sport possible in some areas from April to November. Installed or dismantled in six days, the portability is achieved by more than eight and one-half miles of plastic piping. **1969** *Courier-Mail* (Brisbane) 19 May 11/4 Advocates of portability of superannuation benefits overlook the fact that private schemes have always been voluntary. **1970** A. Cameron et al. *Computers & Old Eng. Concordances* 24 Commenting on portability, I'm as great a sinner as anyone. **1972** *Sci. Amer.* Nov. 100/2 Nine-ounce portability and advanced computational capability. **1975** *Times* 14 Oct. 19/3 To make computer applications more independent of the manufacturer by developing 'software portability' (the ability to carry programmes, in effect, from one maker's machine to another). **1977** *Daily News* (Perth, Austral.) 19 Jan. 2/3 Seek long service leave after 10 years' continuous service, with 'portability' in the building industry and in the government.

portable (ˈpɔətəb(ə)l), *a.* and *sb.* [a. F. *portable,* ad. late L. *portābilis* that may be carried, f. *portāre* to bear, carry: see PORT *v.*[1] and -ABLE.]

A. *adj.* **1. a.** Capable of being carried by hand or on the person; capable of being moved from place to place; easily carried or conveyed. Also used to distinguish mechanical devices or electrical apparatus manufactured in forms smaller and lighter than normal, to enable them to be easily carried about.

Often used to distinguish modified movable forms of machines or structures which as a rule are constructed as immovable fixtures, as *portable derrick, dial, fence, furnace, railway, steam engine,* etc.

c **1400** tr. *Secreta Secret., Gov. Lordsh.* 91 Þat portable kynde... he þanne, þat yn his name racys hit, and berys it with hym clanly, he shal purchace reuerence and honour. **1594** Plat *Jewell-ho.* III. 36 A portable ynke to be caried in the forme of a powder in any paper, leather purse or boxe. **1597** A. M. tr. *Guillemeau's Fr. Chirurg.* lf. xvi b/1 The Instrumentes of a little portable case. *a* **1653** W. Gouge *Comm. Heb.* II. (1655) 300 The [tabernacle] was a kind of portable Temple. **1669** Sturmy *Mariner's Mag.* v. xii. 49 Very portable and fit for his Pocket. **1706** Phillips, *Portable Barometer.* **1730** A. Gordon *Maffei's Amphith.* 337 Portable Forms or Benches. **1821** J. Q. Adams in C. Davies *Metr. Syst.* III. (1871) 200 The pound weight should be a specific gravity easily portable about the person. **1831** Brewster *Optics* xl. §192. 330 A very convenient portable camera obscura. **1837** W. Irving *Capt. Bonneville* II. 192 He..put up a small stock of necessaries in the most portable form. **1872** Yeats *Growth Comm.* 50 Holding property not in lands but portable goods. **1913** *Wireless World* Apr. p. xxxiv/2 The hon. secretary showed some model Marconi apparatus and a portable set. **1926** *Scribner's Mag.* Aug. 76/2 (Advt.), Portable receiving sets..now make it possible to carry this fine radio entertainment to summer camps and cottages. **1929** *Radio Times* 8 Nov. 444/1 What fun you can have with a portable gramophone. **1932** A. Christie *Peril at End House* ii. 31 There was a gramophone and..a portable wireless. **1937** E. Wharton *Ghosts* 22 In the middle of the carefully scoured table stood a portable wireless. **1951** *Catal. of Exhibits, South Bank Exhib., Festival of Britain* 128/2 Portable radio..mains or battery. **1961** *Lebende Sprachen* VI. 70/1 Portable typewriter. **1976** H. Nielsen *Brink of Murder* i. 11 The sportscast on the portable TV was in progress. **1977** *Wandsworth Borough News* 16 Sept. 17/4 To permit portable radios and accept the inevitability of dog mess, whilst stridently prohibiting children from cycling seems to reflect odd standards.

b. Said of liquid substances congealed, and of gaseous substances liquefied, so as to be more conveniently carried or transported.

1758 J. Blake *Plan Mar. Syst.* 53 Portable soop was recommended. **1836** W. Irving *Astoria* II. 192 Five pounds of portable soup, and a sufficient quantity of dried meat to allow each man a pittance of five pounds and a quarter. **1836–41** Brande *Chem.* (ed. 5) 546 Large quantities of this liquid were obtained at the Portable Gas-works, by subjecting the gas produced by the decomposition of whale oil, to a pressure of 30 atmospheres. **1849** *Punch* XVII. 91/2 We have all heard of 'Portable Soup'... Now we have 'Portable Milk'. A small jar of this solidified material, we are told, contains the equivalent of six gallons of fluid milk.

c. *fig.* Easy to carry in the memory, to carry out in practice, etc.

1655 Fuller *Ch. Hist.* VII. i. §31 These Psalms were therefore translated, to make them more portable in peoples memories. **1711** Steele *Spect.* No. 100 ¶4 This portable Quality of Good-humour seasons all the Parts and Occurrences we meet with.

d. Of a building or the like: not of a permanent construction; capable of being dismantled and re-erected elsewhere.

1860 *Players* I. v. 39 (Advt.), Portable Theatres with scenery, Gas Fittings, &c. fitted up in town or country. **1955** [see PORTABILITY]. **1968** *Globe & Mail* (Toronto) 3 Feb. 50/1 All have temporary lodging, two in portable halls and one in Woodbine Junior High School. **1972** [see MODULAR *a.* 1 b].

e. *fig.* Of rights, privileges, information, etc.: capable of being transferred or adapted in changed circumstances.

1965 *Economist* 13 Feb. 671 Pension rights..should not be lost when an employee is sacked or moves to another firm; ideally they should be 'portable'. **1967** *Wall St. Jrnl.* 5 Jan. 2/3 (*heading*) Hoffa to seek portable pensions for teamsters moving into new jobs. **1970** A. Cameron et al. *Computers & Old Eng. Concordances* 22 The proposal never says..what care he's going to take to make sure that his work is portable, that his work really can be used by people at other institutions.

†**2.** *fig.* Supportable; bearable; endurable; that can be borne or tolerated. *Obs.*

c **1500** *Melusine* 209 To putte me to raisounable raunson & payement portable to me. **1589–90** *Reg. Privy Council Scot.* IV. 452 Fra all watcheing,..stent or contributioun, or beiring or sustening of ony uther portable chargeis. **1605** Shaks. *Lear* III. vi. 115 How light and portable my pain seems now. *a* **1653** Binning *Serm.* (1845) 585 The soul puts upon Him that unsupportable yoke of Transgressions, and takes from Him the portable yoke of His commandments.

†**3.** Capable of carrying ships or boats; navigable.

1600 Hakluyt *Voy.* III. 46 If you find great plentie of tymber on the shore side or vpon any portable riuer. **1645–52** Boate *Irel. Nat. Hist.* (1860) 21 The Nuric-water ..is not portable but of very little barkes and boats, and that only when the tide is in. **1685** Wood *Life* 23 Mar. III. 136 A drie winter: no flood: waters very low, not portable.

†**4.** Portly. *Obs. rare.*

1769 R. Cumberland *Brothers* (1808) 29 He..is a little peaking, puling thing; I am a jolly portable man, as you see.

B. *sb.* That which is portable; *spec.* a piece of machinery that is portable (in sense 1 a above); usu. ellipt. for ***portable camera, computer, gramophone, radio, typewriter,*** etc.

1883 J. Hay in *Century Mag.* Dec. 281/2, I don't doubt.. but what we could pay ourselves well for the job,—spoil the 'Gyptians, you know,—forage on the enemy. Plenty of portables in them houses, eh! **1918** C. Stone *Let.* 3 Apr. in C. Mackenzie *My Life & Times* (1966) V. 132 The gramophone (a Decca portable) is going again this evening after a fortnight's silence. **1926** *Wireless World* 26 May 16/1 (Advt.), For sale... Portables. **1930** T. E. Lawrence *Let.* 8 Jan. (1938) 677 An Italian bad-hat dashed me one of those electric gramophones... All the same that portable was good at Miranshah. **1931** B. Brown *Talking Pictures* v. 132 The Western Electric portable for sound-on-film. **1933** *Hearst's International* Mar. 101/2, I doubt if Mrs. Norris could type out a really good chapter on her rickety portable. **1952** M. Laski *Village* vi. 103 We've got an old portable we used to use for the farm correspondence... But she can't do touch-typing. **1957** *Practical Wireless* XXXIII. 530/2 Next comes the portable. It is probably here that it [*sc.* the transistor] finds its greatest application. **1960** *Life* 5 Dec. 8 (Advt.), This is the new Motorola portable—forerunner of all TV to come and gift idea of a lifetime. **1966** Auden *About House* 18 The Olivetti portable, The dictionaries (the very Best money can buy). **1973** *Times* 30 Oct. 32/9 (Advt.), Colour T.V. portables. **1976** J. Lee *Ninth Man* II. 201 He would steal some of these carbons. Sarah had a little portable at his apartment. He would retype them. **1983** *Observer* 19 June 21/1 Although perception of portability differs radically, three categories can be discerned... These are the handhelds, the true portables, and the transportables. **1984** *Computer News* 6 Dec. 11 It's the only portable that can give you the benefits of integrated office automation. **1986** *Guardian* 14 Apr. 22/5 Portables should run for at least a few hours on batteries and be small enough to fit into a briefcase.

Hence ˈ**portableness,** portability.

1727 Bailey vol. II, *Portableness,* capableness of being carried.

portacabin, var. PORTAKABIN.

portacaval (pɔətəˈkeɪvəl), *a. Surg.* Also **portocaval,** and with hyphen. [f. PORTAL *a.* (+ -O) + CAV(A + -AL.] Applied to an anastomosis between the portal vein and one of the venæ cavæ, esp. an artificial one made so that blood in the former bypasses the liver.

1945 *Ann. Surg.* CXXII. 488 Every one of the ten cases of portacaval shunts..went through a successful postoperative convalescence. **1958** A. H. Hunt *Contrib. Study Portal Hypertension* xii. 99 The history of the modern operative treatment of portal hypertension begins with Ecle who suggested in 1877 that his portacaval anastomosis applied to human beings would provide the correct treatment for portal stasis. **1961** *Lancet* 19 Aug. 389/2 Portocaval anastomosis sometimes offers a way out of this quandary. **1968** Passmore & Robson *Compan. Med. Stud.* I. xxx. 47/1 The tributaries of the portal vein anastomose in certain sites with adjacent caval veins which return blood to the heart through either the superior or the inferior vena cava. Little blood passes through these porto-caval anastomoses in health. **1974** Marin & Ostrow in F. P. Brooks *Gastrointestinal Pathophysiol.* vi. 205 Surgeons have expended much time and effort in attempts to reduce portal hypertension by bypassing the hepatic sinusoidal bed, especially with portocaval shunts.

portage (ˈpɔətɪdʒ), *sb.*[1] Also 7 portaidg, -e. [a. F. *portage* the action of carrying, in OF. a tax paid on entering a town, etc. = med.L. *portāticum* 'idem quod valvarum theloneum' (Du Cange), also *portāgium,* It. *portaggio,* etc., f. L. *portāre* to carry: see PORT *v.*[1] and -AGE.]

I. 1. The action or work of carrying or transporting; carriage.

[**1252** in *Rep. Secret Comm. P.-O.* 29 Pro portagio cere quam quesierit ibidem..j d.] *c* **1440** *Promp. Parv.* 410/1 Portage, of berynge, *portagium.* **1463** *Rolls of Parlt.* V. 497/2 Their diligence and labour of gaderyng, portage and payment of the seid somes. **1487** *Naval Acc. Hen. VII* (1896) 32 Paid..for the portage of the same ropes to the water side..v^s. **1577–87** Holinshed *Chron.* III. 1205/1 Vessels..that should be appointed for the portage and conueieng awaie of the said things. **1626** C. Potter tr. *Sarpi's Hist. Quarrels* 138 They dispended yearely aboue an hundred crownes in the portage of Letters. **1630** M. Godwyn tr. *Bp. Hereford's Ann. Eng.* (1675) 92 Two chests ..each of them required eight strong men for the portage. **1710** *G.P.O. Notice* in *Lond. Gaz.* No. 4734/4 The Rates for the Portage of Letters..are as follow. **1820** Jekyll *Corr.* (1894) 91 Cleopatra's Needle is not to come from Egypt to Waterloo Place, as the portage would cost £10,000. [**1879** Stevenson *Trav. Cevennes* (1886) 23, I must..take the following items for my own share of the portage: a cane, a quart flask, a pilot-jacket. ? b.]

†**b.** That which is carried or transported; cargo; freight; baggage. *Obs.*

1454 *Cal. Anc. Rec. Dublin* (1889) I. 283 Salte, ire, pych, rosyne, collys ne no portage that commyth within the fraunches of the saide cite in no shippis. **1513** Douglas *Æneis* III. ii. 6 Ȝe mycht haue sene the costis and the strandis Fillit with portage and peple thairon standis. **1632** *Docum. St. Paul's* (Camden) 133 That no man..profane the church by the cariage of burthens, or baskets, or any portage whatsoeuer. **1667** Waterhouse *Fire Lond.* 46 Fishermen, Passengers, and other Boats and Portages.

†**c.** Weight, as regards transport. *Obs. rare.*

1612 Woodall *Surg. Mate* Wks. (1653) 237 Such medicines as are small of dose, and light of portage. **1760–72** H. Brooke *Fool of Qual.* (1809) IV. 152 Jewels of high value but light portage.

2. The cost or price of carriage; porterage; freight-charges; †also, a due levied in connexion with the transport of goods. *Obs.* exc. *Hist.*

1472–3 *Rolls of Parlt.* VI. 58/2 Almaner of Freghtes, Cariage, Portage, Batellage, and other expenses. **1588** Parke tr. *Mendoza's Hist. China* 61 Customes, dueties, portages and other rents. **1600** Holland *Livy* II. ix. 50 The Commons..were freed of portage, tollage, and tribute. *a* **1631** Donne *Lett.* (1651) 161 Your last hath been the cheapest Letter, that ever I paid Portage for. **1763** Smollett *Trav.* (1766) I. 12 He..saved about fifteen shillings portage. **1860** J. White *Hist. France* (ed. 2) 51 The needy baron was obliged to sign away..his portage and tax on entrance within the walls.

†**3.** *Naut.* Burden of a vessel; tonnage. *Obs.*

[**1378** in Selden *Mare Cl.* (1635) 192 Primerement, pur prendre de chescun Nief & Craier, de quel portage q'il soit.] **1436** *Rolls of Parlt.* IV. 500/2 Shippes, every of iiii^{xx} Tonne portage, or lesse. **1531–2** *Act 23 Hen. VIII,* c. 8 §1 All maner of shippes being vnder the portage of .viii.C. tonnes.. might at the lowe water easely enter into the same. **1591** *Art. conc. Admiralty* 21 July §34 Any Ship of the portage and burthen of fifty tunnes and vpwardes. **1710** *N. Eng. Hist. & Gen. Reg.* (1876) XXX. 200 The Good Ship ——, of the Portage or Burthen of thirty five tuns or thereabouts.

4. In full, ***mariner('s portage***: A mariner's venture, in the form of freight or cargo, which he was entitled to put on board, if he took part in the common adventure and did not receive wages, or which formed part of his wages; the space allowed to a mariner for his own venture or to be let by him for freight payable to him in lieu of wages; hence, in late use, a mariner's wages (in recent works, erroneously explained as his wages *while in port*). (Also corruptly PORTLEDGE.) *Obsolescent.*

[*a* **1300** *Laws of Oleron* c. 28 in *Blk. Bk. Admlty.* (Rolls) I. 122 Est estably pour coustume de la mer que se les mariners dune nef soient a portage chascun deulx aura ung tonnel franc de frett. **1375** *Inq. Queenborow* c. 5 ibid. 139 Entre Londres,..et la Rochelle en vendange prendra ung mariner huit souez de loyer et le portage dung tonnel.] **1500** in J. Latimer *Merch. Venturers of Bristol* (1903) 33 The verry value of the Portage that the said maister, quarter maister, or maryner shall hold for his wages in the said ship in the same viage. **1522–3** *Ordinance of Waterford* in Gross *Gild Merch.* (1890) I. 136 All manere marchandis..and mariner portages commyng in any shippe. **1579** *Reg. Privy Council Scot.* III. 247 They..have been in use and consuetude, past memorie of man, of portage as ane part of thair fie and hyir for the said navigatioun. **1588** Hickock tr. *Frederick's Voy.* 18 b, Neither doo they carrye anye particular mans goods, sauing the portage of the Marriners and Soldiers. **1622** Malynes *Anc. Law-Merch.* (1636) 104 A mariner may keepe either his portage in his owne hands, or put forth the same for fraight, and yet the Ship shall not stay vpon her lading of his portage. **1648** *Doc. Hist. St. Maine* III. 376 For ⅓ part of this Years Portage £20. **1705** A. Justice *Gen. Treat. Dominion Sea* 349 The Seamen shall not lade any Goods upon their own Account, under Pretence of Portage, nor otherwise, without paying the Fraight, except it be mentioned in their Agreements. [**1809** R. Langford *Introd. Trade* 134 *Portage,* sailors wages while in port, also the amount of a sailor's wages for a voyage. So in **1858** Simmonds *Dict. Trade.*] **1847** Sir N. H. Nicolas *Hist. Royal Navy* II. 206 Of masters and mariners who take extravagant wages or portage, contrary to ancient usage.

fig. **1608** Shaks. *Per.* III. i. 35 Thy losse is more then can Thy portage quit, with all thou canst find heere.

b. Comb. ***portage-bill***: the register or account of the names and claims for wages, allowances, etc., of the crew of a ship.

[**1679**: see PORTLEDGE.] **1743** in W. B. Weeden *Econ. & Soc. Hist. N. Eng.* (1890) II. 469 *note,* A Portage bill of mens Names and Wages due on board the Snow Jolly Bachelor.

1776 *Rhode Island Col. Rec.* (1862) VII. 553 To amount of cargo, outfits and portage bill, of the schooner Eagle, by Joseph Stanton, supposed..303 00 00. **1795** *Ship-Master's Assist.* (ed. 6) 7 Ship Favourite Nancy's Portage-Bill on a Voyage to St. Petersburgh. **1890** W. B. WEEDEN *Econ. & Soc. Hist. N. Eng.* II. 469 Gridley curiously enough rejected the 'Portage bill' of officers' and men's wages, £102 17*s*. 4*d*., from Sierra Leone to Newport.

II. 5. The carrying or transporting of boats and goods from one navigable water to another, as between two lakes or rivers, or past a rapid or cataract on a river. (Originally American.)

1698 tr. *Hennepin's New Discov. Amer.* xviii. 74 We.. brought up our Bark to the great Rock of Niagara,..where we were oblig'd to make our Portage; that is, to carry overland our Canow's and Provisions, and other Things, above the great Fall of the River, which interrupts the Navigation. **1755** L. EVANS *Mid. Brit. Colonies* 16 They are obliged to make one or two very long Portages. **1856** KANE *Arct. Expl.* I. ix. 96 We had a portage of about three miles, the sledge being unladen and the baggage carried on our backs. **1857** LIVINGSTONE *Trav.* xv. 264 Five or six rapids with cataracts, one of which could not be passed at any time without portage. **1879** J. W. BODDAM-WHETHAM *Roraima & Brit. Guiana* 144 We had to unload the boats and make a portage of about two hundred yards.

b. A place or track at or over which such portage is necessary; a break in a chain of water-communication over which boats, goods, etc. must be carried; = CARRY *sb.* 5, CARRYING-*place*.

1698 tr. *Hennepin's New Discov. Amer.* xviii. 75 The Portage was two Leagues long. **1756** W. SHIRLEY in *N. Hampshire Prov. Papers* VI. 462 The portage or carrying place at the fall of the Wood Creek is not above 300 yds. **1807** P. GASS *Jrnl.* 104 Captain Clarke measured the length of this portage accurately and found it to be 18 miles. **1889** STEVENSON *Master of B.* iii, As we were carrying the canoe upon a rocky portage, she fell, and was entirely bilged.

III. 6. *attrib.* and *Comb.*, as ***portage beer, -duty, -money, -path, -station, strap, track***: see also 4 b.

1552 in Strype *Eccl. Mem.* (1721) II. II. xii. 345 Whether the receiuers of the kings monies and such like officers had portage-money allowed them. **1622** MALYNES *Anc. Law-Merch.* 353, I take the perill vpon mee of the carriage of a great masse of money; I may lawfully take portage money for my paines. **1640** in Entick *London* (1766) II. 182 All other goods..shall pay portage duties. **1720** STRYPE *Stow's Surv.* II. 204/2 Concerning the transporting of Beer beyond Sea, which they called Portage Beer. **1871** HUYSHE *Red River Exp.* vii. 106 Indians and experienced voyageurs use a long strap called a 'portage strap'. **1894** J. WINSOR *Cartier to Frontenac* 258 The party began to carry the material..along the portage track for twelve miles.

† **'portage**, *sb.*[2] *Obs. rare*[−1]. [f. PORT *sb.*[3] + -AGE.] Provision of ports or port-holes.

1599 SHAKS. *Hen. V*, III. i. 10 Lend the Eye a terrible aspect: Let it pry through the portage of the Head, Like the Brasse Cannon.

'portage, *v.* [f. PORTAGE *sb.*[1]] *trans.* To carry or transport (boats, goods, etc.) over land between navigable waters; to convey over a PORTAGE (*sb.*[1] 5 b). Also with the place (rapids, cataract, etc.) as obj.; also *absol.* Hence **'portaging** *vbl. sb.*

1864 A. GORDON *N. Brunswick* in *Vac. Tour.* 508 Some falls where we were compelled to portage the canoes. **1871** HUYSHE *Red River Exp.* vii. 105 The labour of 'portaging' was very severe. **1882** G. BRYCE *Manitoba* 24 Portaging around rapids too fierce to be faced. **1900** A. G. BRADLEY *Fight w. France for N. Amer.* iv. 109 There were numerous rapids too, and shallows to be portaged.

Portagee, var. PORTUGUEE.

† **portague, -igue.** *Obs.* Forms: 6 portygewe, -ingue, -ugue, 6–7 -ague, -egue, -igue. [App. a false singular deduced from *porta-, porteguse* (PORTUGUESE B. 3), taken as a plural, as if *portagues*.] A Portuguese gold coin, the great 'crusado', current in the 16th century; its value ranged, according to time and circumstances, between £3. 5*s*. and £4. 10*s*.: = PORTUGAL 4.

Often kept as an heirloom or keepsake: see quots.

1532 in Strype *Eccl. Mem.* (1721) I. xviii. 138 By Hasilwood of the receipt iiij portagues 10. 00. 00. **1535** *Bury Wills* (Camden) 127 To my nece Harvy my portygewe of gold. **1577** HARRISON *England* II. xxv. (1877) I. 364 The portigue, a peece verie solemnelie kept of diuerse. **1579** J. JONES *Preserv. Bodie & Soule* I. xxviii. 54 Our Coyne, be they as little as Pence, or as great as Portigues. **1610** B. JONSON *Alch.* I. iii, No gold about thee? *Dru.* Yes, I haue a portague I ha' kept this halfe yeere. **1658** PHILLIPS, *Portegue*, a certain Coyn in Gold, valuing three pound ten shillings.

portail ('pɔətel). *Arch.* Also 5 -ayl, 6 -aile. [a. F. *portail* façade of a church, containing the principal door, also †city-gate:—Latin type **portāculum*, dim. of L. *porta* gate, door. See PORTAL *sb.*[1], with which this has been confused in Fr. and Eng.] = PORTAL *sb.*[1] I.

1483 CAXTON *G. de la Tour* F vj, She wente vp vnto a hyhe portayl or gate. **1600** HOLLAND *Livy* x. 368 They caused to be made a brasen portaile in the Capitoll. **1723** CHAMBERS tr. *Le Clerc's Treat. Archit.* I. 129 The Portail or Frontispiece of a Church, Palace, or any other great Building, shou'd always have a Rise of some Steps. **1749** RHYS *Tour Spain & Port.* (1760) 61 It..has a noble Portail, in which are Three Gates. **1823** P. NICHOLSON *Pract. Build.* 590 *Portail*, the face of a church, on the side in which the great door is formed.

Portakabin ('pɔːtəˌkæbɪn). Also portacabin [f. PORTA(BLE *a.* + *kabin* altered f. CABIN *sb.*] The proprietary name of a make of portable building. Cf. PORTABLE *a.* 1 d.

1963 *Trade Marks Jrnl.* 4 Dec. 1742/1 *Portakabin* B 851, 268. Buildings (not being fixed metal structures) and parts thereof included in Class 19. Portasilo Limited, Blue Bridge Lane, York..; Manufacturers. **1975** *Times* 23 Sept. 6/1 The Portakabin which served as his drawing office. **1977** 'R. ROSTAND' *Killing in Rome* xiii. 69 A large Portakabin, set on concrete blocks at the edge of the apron..the head office of Essex Air Ltd. **1979** *Jrnl. R. Soc. Arts* July 500/1 We created an artists' village—a collection of portacabins used in arctic oil exploration.

portal ('pɔətəl), *sb.*[1] Also 4 -ale, 5–7 -all, 6 -alle; (6 porthal, 6–7 port(-)hall). [ME. a. obs. F. *portal* gate, ad. med.L. *portāle* city-gate, porch (Du Cange), orig. neut. of *portālis* adj., f. L. *porta* gate: see PORT *sb.*[3] and -AL[1]. Cf. PORTAIL.]

1. a. A door, gate, doorway, or gateway, of stately or elaborate construction; the entrance, with the immediately surrounding parts, of an edifice, esp. of a large or magnificent building, when emphasized in architectural treatment. Hence often a poetical or rhetorical synonym for 'door' or 'gate'.

13.. *E.E. Allit. P.* A. 1035 Þe portalez pyked of rych platez. **1484** CAXTON *Fables of Alfonce* i, That man whiche lay dede before the portall or gate of the temple. *a* **1533** LD. BERNERS *Gold. Bk. M. Aurel.* II. vii. (1536) 119 b, I haue sene his..portall and gates ful of knightes, & not marchauntis. **1600** HOLLAND *Livy* XXX. xxi. 754 The monie they laid downe in the very port-hall or entrie of the Senate house. **1667** MILTON *P.L.* VII. 575 Through Heav'n, That open'd wide her blazing Portals. **1711** ADDISON *Spect.* No. 59 ¶5 Erected over two of the Portals of Blenheim House. **1756** tr. *Keysler's Trav.* I. xxxvi. 323 The gates of the portal are by tradition said to be the same which St. Ambrose shut against the emperor Theodosius, till he had done penance. **1813** SCOTT *Trierm.* I. v, Not a foot has thy portal cross'd. **1862** *Rickman's Goth. Archit.* 424 The portals of Abbeville,..are some of the finest specimens of this style. **1871** R. ELLIS *Catullus* lxi. 76 Fling the portal apart. The bride Waits.

b. *transf.* A valve of the heart; a natural entrance, as of a cave.

1666 J. SMITH *Old Age* 231 The great vein..hath at its entrance into the heart, certain portals, from their form called *valvulæ tricuspides*. **1809–10** COLERIDGE *Friend* (1865) 2, I was reposing in the vast cavern, out of which, from its northern portal, issues the river that winds through our vale. **1863** BARING-GOULD *Iceland* 230 A river wending towards a portal of black rock.

c. *fig.*

c **1590** GREENE *Fr. Bacon* ii. 64 The brazen walls fram'd by Semiramis, Carv'd out like to the portal of the sun. **1592** SHAKS. *Ven. & Ad.* 451 Once more the ruby-colour'd portal open'd, Which to his speech did honey passage yield. **1593** —— *Rich. II*, III. iii. 64 As doth the blushing discontented Sunne, From out the fierie Portall of the East. **1727–46** THOMSON *Summer* 640 Issuing from out the portals of the morn. **1846** TRENCH *Mirac.* x. (1862) 216 Death, which by the portal of disobedience had found entrance into natures made for immortality.

d. *Engin.* A rigid structural frame consisting essentially of two uprights connected at the top by a third member; orig. such a frame forming the end of a truss bridge.

1876 *Trans. Amer. Soc. Civil Engineers* V. 178 This bill of materials is calculated: chords, latticing, joint and reinforcing plates..85,912 pounds... Struts and portals.. 6,000 [pounds]. **1882** *Min. Proc. Inst. Civil Engineers* LXIX. 101 The Author [C. B. Bender]..believes it to be conducive to greater stiffness to put the material needed for knees and gussets into two effective end-portals and into the lateral top and bottom bracings. **1908** A. TOLHAUSEN tr. *Böttcher's Cranes* VI. 245 The portal is to cover double railway lines of normal gauge. **1937** *Sunday Express* 14 Feb. 11/1 A series of vast concrete underground bridges, 'portals' they were called technically, were built. There were sixty in all, and each one bridged a railway tunnel under the earth and made a platform on which the building could be built. **1950** *Engineering* 31 Mar. 366/1 A simple portal structure built from broad-flanged beams may be used for spans up to about 40 ft. **1971** *Timber Trades Jrnl.* 21 Aug. 23/3 After the gale had been blowing for a whole week, the temporary bracing finally gave way and two portals were destroyed.

e. (The structural frame forming) the entrance to a tunnel.

1881 *Engineering* 25 Mar. 296/3 The geologist of the St. Gothard Tunnel..has been giving careful attention to the variations in the air currents between the two portals at Goeschenen and Airolo. **1909** J. W. ORROCK *Railroad Struct.* iv. 85 The end portals for the tunnel consist of 12″ × 12″ posts..for a distance of 8 feet from the ends, with 12″ × 12″ timbers built over and across the end posts, to form retaining wall on top. **1941** RICHARDSON & MAYO *Pract. Tunnel Driving* xxi. 364 Some kind of parapet over the portal is necessary to catch loose rocks rolling into the cut. **1971** K. G. MESSENGER *Flora of Rutland* 109/1 At the southern portal, the cutting is wider and deeper and it is obvious that it offered serious drainage problems to the engineers.

f. *Med.* Usu. ***portal of entry*** or ***entrance*** (or ***entrance portal***), ***portal of exit*** (or ***exit portal***). (*a*) The place where a micro-organism or drug enters or leaves the system. (*b*) The area of the body where a beam of radiation enters or leaves it; = PORT *sb.*[3] 4 b.

1910 *Jrnl. Amer. Med. Assoc.* 24 Sept. 1109/2 We have been led..to view the nasopharynx as the location in the body to be regarded with special suspicion as being the portal of entry of the virus. **1919** *Jrnl. Exper. Med.* XXIX. 380 Other portals of experimental infection were.. disclosed, such as the large nerves, subcutis, subarachnoid space, nasal mucosa, eye, and..the general blood. **1930** J. S. FRIEDENWALD *Path. of Eye* xi. 227 An occasional individual contracting the infection in spite of having taken every conceivable precaution to protect against infection through all other known portals. **1931** *Jrnl. Amer. Med. Assoc.* 23 May 1756/1 If the portal is of limited area, the lateral scatter [of X-rays] is small. **1960** A. L. SMITH *Carter's Microbiol. & Path.* (ed. 7) xii. 135/1 Pathogenic agents..have rather definite routes of discharge from the body, known as portals of exit, which, to a great extent, depend on the part of the body that is the site of disease. **1963** S. E. WEDBERG *Paramedical Microbiol.* xix. 410 Portal requirements limit the number of opportunities provided for pathogens to cause damage to tissues. **1966** A. A. DE LORIMIER in *Radiol. in World War II* (U.S. Army) iv. 86 Except for the portal of exit of the primary beam, the roentgen tube housing is impregnated with material possessing a protective equivalence of no less than 1·5 mm. of lead. **1973** FLETCHER & TAPLEY in G. H. Fletcher *Textbk. Radiotherapy* (ed. 2) i. 65/1 With a 22 Mev beam and a single homolateral portal, the skin reaction is minimal on the entrance side and is moderate on the opposite side. **1977** *Lancet* 8 Jan. 78/1 Disposable devices are now becoming available for prolonged controlled delivery of appropriate drugs at other portals of entry such as the eye and uterus.

g. *U.S. Theatr.* (See quots. 1947, 1959.)

1947 *Gloss. Technical Theatr. Terms* (Strand Electr. & Engin. Co.) 23 *Portal*, German and American terms for pros[cenium] opening. **1959** W. C. LOUNSBURY *Backstage from A to Z* 94 *Portal*, a gate, door, or entrance, usually downstage on either side of the stage. Portals may be scenery constructed for the play, or they may be a permanent part of the proscenium. In many theatres of newer design, portals are built to accommodate spot-lights for sidelighting. **1978** *English Jrnl.* Dec. 44/1 'Gel the lights in the upstage right portal' are heard shouted across the auditorium.

†**2.** A space within the door of a room, partitioned off, and containing an inner door; also, such a partition itself (sometimes made as a moveable piece of furniture). *Obs.*

1516 in Willis & Clark *Cambridge* (1886) II. 244 Wyth 2 Portalls, wherof one shall be at the parlour doore and the other at the great Chamber doore wythin the said College. **1569** *Bury Wills* (Camden) 155, I will that theas implements,..the benche in the hall, the portall, and the skryne..shall remayne in and withe the howse. **1598** [see 4]. **1703** T. N. *City & C. Purchaser* 229 *Portal*..was us'd to signifie a little square corner of a Room, shifted off from the rest of the Room by the Wainscot.

3. (See quots.)

1706 PHILLIPS, *Portal*, a lesser Gate, where there are two of a different Bigness. **1842–76** GWILT *Archit.* Gloss., *Portal*, the arch over a door or gate; the framework of the gate; the lesser gate, when there are two of different dimensions at one entrance. **1873** HALE *In His Name* viii. 70 A little side portal, which gave entrance to a vestry.

4. a. *attrib.* and *Comb.*, as ***portal arch, capital, door, gate, post, seat, way***. **portal bracing** = sense 1 d above; also, the technique of using such a frame; **portal crane**, a crane mounted on a portal frame, so as to allow the passage of vehicles underneath; **portal frame** = sense 1 d above; **portal strut**, a horizontal member rigidly joining the tops of two uprights, esp. in a portal frame.

1813 SCOTT *Trierm.* III. xviii, But full between the Warrior's way And the main portal-arch, there lay An inner moat. **1881** *Trans. Amer. Soc. Civil Engineers* X. 164 Strong top lateral and portal bracing would greatly increase the strength and durability of the bridge. **1908** M. S. KETCHUM *Design of Highway Bridges* vii. 112 Portal bracing is placed at the ends of through bridges in the planes of the end-posts to transfer the wind loads from the upper lateral system to the abutments. **1928** W. A. MITCHELL *Civil Engineering* xvi. 479 The sway bracing at the entrance of the span..is called portal bracing. **1974** *Sci. Amer.* Feb. 95/1 The Crystal Palace was..the first [building] in which a light frame was made rigid against wind loads by the technique that came to be known as portal bracing. **1895** A. NUTT in *K. Meyer's Voy. Bran* I. 205 The arched doorway..with its wide valves and portal-capitals of burnished gold. **1908** A. TOLHAUSEN tr. *Böttcher's Cranes* VI. 245 (*heading*) Hydraulic portal crane. **1958** *Times Rev. Industry* Oct. 20/3 No. 21 Quay at Alexandra Dock has been opened this year after being re-equipped with five 6/3 ton electric portal cranes. **1592** GREENE *Cony-Catching* III. Wks. (Grosart) X. 183 Lifting vp the latch of the hall portall doore [he] saw nobody neere to trouble him. **1598** in Willis & Clark *Cambridge* (1886) III. 325 Item a portall Dore to the vpper studdye. **1908** A. TOLHAUSEN tr. *Böttcher's Cranes* VI. 245 The portal or gantry frame..shall be of built-up plates, and shall carry the platform on its top side. **1949** *Archit. Rev.* CVI. 287 The mullions in front of the portal frames are bright ultramarine. **1971** *Timber Trades Jrnl.* 21 Aug. 23/3 Each portal frame is constructed using 50mm (2in) nominal timber throughout. **1894** W. H. WARREN *Engineering Construction* xix. 294 The perpendicular distance between the end strut of the top lateral system and the intermediate portal strut. **1938** C. T. BISHOP *Structural Design* x. 194 Portal struts are used at the ends of through bridges to transmit top-lateral stresses to the abutments through the end posts acting as girders. **1795** SOUTHEY *Joan of Arc* VII. 292 Narrow was the portal way, To one alone fit passage.

b. portal-to-portal *attrib.*, *spec.* of workers' pay: pertaining to the time spent on the premises of one's place of work, for example in travelling to and from the entrance, changing, or washing, as distinguished from the time spent working. *U.S.*

1943 *Time* 25 Oct. 21/3 He emerged with proposed Contract No. 3: an intricate formula which cagily skirts any mention of increased hourly wages or 'portal-to-portal' pay. **1944** *Birmingham* (Alabama) *News* 27 Mar. 1/5 The Supreme Court ruled Monday that underground iron ore miners are entitled to 'portal-to-portal' pay for the time spent traveling between the mouth of the mine and the place where the ore is actually mined. **1948** *Ann. Reg. 1947* 231 Long-pending retrospective claims for portal-to-portal pay (*i.e.* pay for time spent inside factory gates but not actually on the job) were unequivocally disallowed. **1965** *McGraw-Hill Dict. Mod. Econ.* 385 Proponents of portal-to-portal pay insist that the worker should be paid for the time involved in necessary activities before or after actual on-the-job time on the ground that otherwise the work could not be done.

Hence '**portalage**, the construction of portals.

1903 *Architect* 24 Apr. 269/1 Some sketches in connection with portalage.

‖**portal** (pɔː'tɑːl), *sb.*[2] Also **portale, portales.** [ad. Sp. *portal*, pl. *portales*, porch, portico, piazza.] In S. America and the southwestern U.S., a veranda, portico, or arcade.

1844 J. GREGG *Commerce of Prairies* I. 144 The only attempt at anything like architectural compactness and precision, consists in..buildings, whose fronts are shaded with a fringe of *portales* or *corredores*. **1892** C. F. LUMMIS *Tramp across Continent* 153 Outside, in the long *portal*, was enough blue, and red, and white corn to feed an army of horses. **1910** [see MAJOR-DOMO c]. **1927** W. CATHER *Death comes for Archbishop* II. i. 51 Under this *portale* the adobe wall was hung with bridles, saddles [etc.]. **1927** *South Amer.* Nov.-Dec. 181/1 Our hall not being large enough, the *portales*—a large corridor with arches running down one side —was swept and tastefully decorated. **1948** *Southwest Rev.* Summer 245/2 What are now empty mule stalls then used to be the *portales* of a convent. **1973** D. HAMILTON *Intriguers* ix. 59, 'I..crawled to where I could watch the long porch outside the living room.'.. I said, 'Around these parts [*sc.* Arizona], that porch is known as a portal, ma'am. Accent on the last syllable.'

Portal ('pɔətəl), *sb.*[3] Name of Lord *Portal* (1885–1949), Minister of Works and Planning and First Commissioner of Works and Public Buildings 1942–4: **Portal house,** a steel-framed type of prefabricated house proposed in 1944. Also *ellipt.*

1944 *Archit. Rev.* Sept. p. lii/1 It is not clear whether the 250,000 [houses] will all be of the Portal ('Churchill') design which..is far from perfect of its kind. **1945** *Ann. Reg. 1944* 66 The Government had chosen the so-called Portal house of steel... The model Portal house..had been seen by about 30,000 persons. **1945** *Punch* 16 May 425/1 But my aunt was good for me when I was a child, and will possibly offer me accommodation if I cannot secure a Portal when I go home, so I suppose I must oblige her. **1948** A. M. TAYLOR *Lang. World War II* (rev. ed.) 158 *Portal houses*, proposed prefabricated houses for England, so called after Lord Portal, whose ministry was in charge of housing. Punch played up the name in jokes about 'crossing one's portal'.

portal ('pɔətəl), *a. Anat.* [ad. med.L. *portālis* of or belonging to a gate (see PORTAL *sb.*[1]).]

†**1.** Of, pertaining to, or of the nature of a door or gate: in quot. applied to the valves of the heart.

1615 CROOKE *Body of Man* 375 Not farre from the beginning [it] is diuided or slitte into three small but strong portall membranes or values.

2. Pertaining to the *porta* or transverse fissure of the liver. ***portal vein***: the *vena porta*, or great vein formed by the union of the veins from the stomach, intestine, and spleen, conveying blood to the liver, where it divides again into branches; also (***renal portal*** or ***reni-portal vein***), a vein similarly passing to the kidney and dividing into branches there, in many of the lower vertebrates.

Hence applied to structures, etc. connected with the portal vein, as ***portal canals***, the tubular passages in the liver, each containing a branch of the portal vein, hepatic artery, and biliary duct; ***portal circulation***, the circulation of blood through the portal system; ***portal fissure***, the transverse fissure of the liver, at which the portal vein enters it, the PORTA; ***portal system***, the system of vessels consisting of the portal vein with its tributaries and branches; also, any other system of blood vessels which runs directly from one system of smaller vessels to another.

1845 BUDD *Dis. Liver* 11 The ducts..accompany the arteries in the portal canals. Each portal vein, however small, has an artery and a duct running along it. **1851** CARPENTER *Man. Phys.* (ed. 2) 333 This is termed the portal system of vessels. **1872** HUXLEY *Phys.* ii. 50 The flow of the blood from the abdominal viscera, through the liver, to the hepatic vein, is called the portal circulation. **1875** HUXLEY & MARTIN *Elem. Biol.* 227 The renal portal vein: running from the bifurcation of the pelvic vein to enter the lower-outer border of the kidney. **1881** MIVART *Cat* 187 One set of canals diverge from the portal fissure, and these are called hepatic veins. **1888** ROLLESTON & JACKSON *Anim. Life* 353 A renal-portal circulation or supply of venous blood to the kidneys exists in all *Amphibia*. **1930** *Jrnl. Anat.* LXV. 88 These vessels of the portal system lose their heavy neuroglial wrapping and open out into a network of very fine channels. **1974** M. HILDEBRAND *Analysis Vertebr. Struct.* xii. 262 In several places in the body (digestive organs, kidneys, hypophysis) blood that has passed a capillary bed elsewhere enters a second capillary bed before reaching the heart. The veins between two capillary networks constitute a portal system. **1974** D. & M. WEBSTER *Compar. Vertebr. Morphol.* xvi. 416 This is renal portal system, filtering blood from the tail through a kidney capillary system before sending it to the [piscine] heart.

Hence '**portal-'venous** *a.*, of or pertaining to the portal vein.

1845 BUDD *Dis. Liver* 45 Mr. Kiernan has applied to this ..the term portal-venous congestion.

†**portal,** obs. erron. form of PORTAS.

1660 R. COKE *Power & Subj.* 255 Popish Catechisms, Missals, Breviaries, Portals, Legends and Lives of Saints. **1686** EVELYN *Diary* 12 Mar., The printing Missalls, Offices, Lives of Saints, Portals, Primers, &c.

portalled, portaled ('pɔətəld), *a.* [f. PORTAL *sb.*[1] + -ED[2].] Furnished with or having a portal.

1635 HEYWOOD *Hierarch.* v. 325 [Nature] hath afforded Man but one Tongue and that portall'd with lips and percullis'd with teeth. **1905** HOLMAN HUNT *Pre-Raphaelitism* i. 8 New surprises through narrow lanes and portalled walls.

‖**porta'mento.** *Mus.* [It., lit. a bearing, carrying.] A gliding or passing continuously from one pitch to another, in singing, or in playing a violin or similar instrument. Also *attrib.*

1771 C. BURNEY *Present State of Mus. France & Italy* 18 The French voice never comes further than from the throat; there is no *voce di petto*, no true *portamento* or direction of the voice, on any of the stages. **1774** J. COLLIER *Mus. Trav.* 33 Her shake was good, and her *portamento* admirably free from the nose, mouth, or throat. **1789** BURNEY *Hist. Mus.* IV. 40 Trills, graces, and a good *portamento*, or direction of voice. **1889** *Athenæum* 14 Sept. 361/2 Madame Albani.. marred her efforts by excessive indulgence in the *portamento* style. **1926** *Amer. Speech* I. 500/2 Two Italian words, *glissando* and *portamento* are similar in meaning to the word 'smear', the principal difference being that the last-named is used [in trombone-playing] for a comic effect while the others are used for carrying the voice or sliding the fingers on the violin from one stop to the next. **1931** *Times Lit. Suppl.* 11 June 461/1 The notation of the tunes [in Bartok's *Hungarian Folk Music*] includes a number of signs to signify graces, quarter-tones, *portamento* and other of the fok-singer's idiosyncracies. **1961** C. BUNTING in A. Baines *Mus. Instruments* vi. iii. 142 The cellists were trying to..achieve the eloquence and directness of the human voice... There was felt a need to 'carry' the music (*portamento*) through the intervals without a break. **1971** *Guardian* 26 Aug. 10/1 Imrat..is a master of fluid portamento effects and of creating an illusion of sustained legato—obtained by pulling a sitar-string sideways across the frets. **1975** *New Yorker* 20 Jan. 86/3 She oscillated in portamento between the A on the staff and the C sharp above it, swinging pendulum-true. **1976** *Gramophone* Aug. 337/2 The sheer certainty of the vocal delivery is remarkable, with the singer's famous portamento much in evidence.

portance ('pɔətəns). *arch.* Also 6 **-aunce.** [a. obs. F. *portance* action of carrying, support, favour, importance, etc., vbl. sb. f. *porter* to carry, PORT *v.*[1]: see -ANCE.] Carriage, bearing, demeanour (= PORT *sb.*[4] 1); conduct, behaviour.

1590 SPENSER *F.Q.* II. iii. 5 In court gay portaunce he perceiv'd. *Ibid.* 21 A goodly Ladie..That seemd to be a woman of great worth, And by her stately portance borne of heavenly birth. **1607** SHAKS. *Cor.* II. iii. 232 Your Loues, Thinking vpon his Seruices, tooke from you Th'apprehension of his present portance. **1881** DUFFIELD *Don Quix.* II. 504 A good knight errant..with a gentle portance and intrepid heart.

portant ('pɔətənt), *a. Her.* [a. F. *portant*, pr. pple. of *porter* to carry, PORT *v.*[1]: see -ANT.]

1. Carrying. (Const. as a pple. with direct obj.)

1572 BOSSEWELL *Armorie* II. 51, I. beareth Azure, an Elephante d'Argente, portant a turret d'Or.

¶**2.** = PORTATE. (? an error.)

c **1828** BERRY *Encycl. Herald.* I. Gloss., *Portate*, or *Portant*, a cross portate is so called, because it..lies sloping, ..as if it were carried on a man's shoulder. **1889** ELVIN *Dict. Her.*, Portante.

‖**portantina** (portan'tina). [It.] = SEDAN CHAIR.

1758 M. W. MONTAGU *Let.* May (1967) III. 149 He hopes you took nothing ill, tho' you refused the Portantina. **1937** *Tablet* 11 Dec. 800/1 Carried in the *portantina*—the Sedan chair which he now invariably uses in the palace—the Pope passed through the *Salone Sistino* into the Sacred Museum.

portapak ('pɔətəpæk). [f. PORTA(BLE *a.* + PA(C)K *sb.*[1]] A portable system comprising a small television camera and a video tape recorder.

1974 *Cablevision* (Rediffusion) 10 Since October 1973 Jessica Stanley Clarke..has spent most of her time in Knowle West with one of the station's portapaks. *Ibid.* 12 The Youth Department had purchased a Sony portapak. **1974** *New Society* 26 Dec. 805/1, I showed them how to set up and operate the portapak. **1975** *Listener* 9 Jan. 40/1 The miniature and monochrome amateurism of the 'portapak' suitcase studio.

portary: see PORTERY, *Obs.*

portas, -eous, -es, -ess, -hos. Now only *Hist.* Forms: (3–4 portehors), 4–5 porthors, -hous, -os, 4–9 -ous, -hos, -oos, 5 -oce, -oes, -ose, -ues, -eux (?), poortos, *Sc.* porteus, -owis, -wis, 5–6 -as, -es, -us, *Sc.* -uus, -eouss, 5–9 -uous, 6 -ais, -eise, -eyse, -ew(a)s, -is, -oues, -uos, -uess, -uys, -yes, 6–7 -ass(e, -ess(e, -oose, -uouse, -use, 6–7 -house, 6–8 -uass, -uis, 6–9 *Sc.* -eous, 7 -ise, -ius, -uise. *β. erron.* 5 portor, *pl.* -eres. [ME. (*portehors*) *porthors*, a. OF. *portehors*, 13th c. (= med.L. *portiforium*, 13th c. in Du Cange) a portable breviary, f. *porte*, imperative of *porter* to carry (see PORT *v.*[1]) + *hors*:—L. *foris* out of doors, abroad.]

1. A portable breviary in the mediæval church.

[**1249–52** in *Camden Misc.* (1895) IX. 23 Item liber portehors, qui est Vicarij. *c* **1250** *Newminster Cartul.* (1878) 273 Unum portehors.] **1377** LANGL. *P. Pl.* B. xv. 122 A portous þat shulde be his plow, *placebo* to segge. *c* **1380** WYCLIF *Wks.* (1880) 194 Newe costy portos, antifeners, graielis, & alle oþere bokis. *c* **1386** CHAUCER *Shipman's T.* 135 By god and by this Porthors [*v.rr.* portoos, portos] I yow swere. **14..** *Voc.* in Wr.-Wülcker 604/19 *Portoforium*, a Porthos. **14..** *Nom.* ibid. 719/31 *Hoc portiferium*, a portas. **1426** in *E.E. Wills* (1882) 76 My masseboke, my portus. *c* **1440** *Promp. Parv.* 410/1 Poortos, booke, *portiforium, breviarium.* **1459** *Test. Ebor.* (Surtees) II. 227 A Graile, a Manuell, a litel Portose, the which the saide Sir Thomas toke w[t] him alway when he rode. **1460** EDW. (IV) as EARL OF MARCH in Ellis *Orig. Lett.* Ser. I. I. 10 Beseching your good lordeschip to remembre our porteux. *c* **1475** *Pict. Voc.* in Wr.-Wülcker 755/19 *Hoc portiforium*, a portes. **1483** CAXTON *Gold. Leg.* 427/1 [He] bare euer with hym the byble & his breuyary or portoes. **1507** *Pilton Churchw. Acc.* (Som. Rec. Soc.) 52 A grett portuos of prynte. **1519** in *5th Rep. Hist. MSS. Comm.* 555/2 A lytelle Portewas, called our Lady Portewas. **1528** TINDALE *Obed. Chr. Man* 71 b, That know no moare scripture then is written in their portoues. **1530** PALSGR. 257/1 Portyes, a preestes boke, *breuiayre*. **1533** *Lanc. Wills* (1857) II. 13 My ij portews. **1533** MORE *Apol.* iii. Wks. 848/1 In stede of a long portuous, a shorte primer shall serue them. **1534** —— *Comf. agst. Trib.* I. xv. (1573) 31 b, No such praiers are put in the Priestes Portesse, as far as I can heare. **1549** *Act 3 & 4 Edw. VI*, c. 10 §1 All Bookes called.. Manuelles Legends Pyes Portuyses Prymars..shalbe.. abollished. *a* **1550** *Pore Helpe* 102 in Hazl. *E.P.P.* III. 256 And also the Paraphrasies, Moche dyfferyng from your portaises, They wolde haue dayly vsed. **1550** BALE *Image Both Ch.* I. Pref. A viij, Their babling praiers their portases, bedes, temples [etc.]. **1570** T. WILSON *Demosthenes* Ded. 3 There was never Olde Priest more perfite in his Porteise. **1583** STUBBES *Anat. Abus.* II. (1882) 77 As the doting papists did their blasphemous masses out of their portesses. *a* **1604** HANMER *Chron. Irel.* (1633) 130 Laurence the Archbishop (whom it had beseemed better to have beene at home with his porthouse). **1611** BIBLE *Transl. Pref.* 9 Their Seruice bookes, Portesses, and Breuiaries. **1641** 'SMECTYMNUUS' *Vind. Answ.* v. 66 The Liturgie is never the worse, because the words of it are taken out of the Roman Portuise. **1711** HEARNE *Collect.* (O.H.S.) III. 175 Breviarie or portuass for the Quire. **1817** SCOTT *Border Antiq.* II. Introd. 82 A monk from Melrose, called, from the porteous or breviary which he wore in his breast, a *book-a-bosom*. **1846** MASKELL *Mon. Rit.* I. p. lxxxvii, The Portiforium, with its various English names of..Portuis, Portuasse, Porthoos, and Portfory. **1890** ST. JOHN HOPE in *Archæologia* LII. 706 A subject derived from the York porthos.

β. **1465** *Mann. & Househ. Exp.* (Roxb.) 284 A portor [?-os] of Salusbury use. **1500** in *Gentl. Mag.* Dec. (1837) 571/2, ij porteres, off the gefte off Syr Ryc. Long.

b. *transf.* A manual (*of* some subject).

1508 *Twelve Virtues of ane Nobleman* ad fin. (Jam.), Heir ends the Porteous of Noblenes. **1621** BURTON *Anat. Mel.* III. ii. IV. i. (1651) 539 Their whole books are a Synopsis or breviary of Love, the portuous of Love, Legends of Lovers lives and deaths.

c. *attrib.*

1458 *Yatton Churchw. Acc.* (Som. Rec. Soc.) 100 For byndyng ij portose bokys. **1549** CHALONER tr. *Erasm. on Folly* P iij b, As long as they mumble ouer theyr portes seruice. **1550** BALE *Eng. Votaries* II. L iij, The order of portasse men.

2. *Sc. Law.* (In later use ***porteous roll.***) 'A roll of the names of offenders, which, by the old practice of the Justiciary Court, was prepared by the Justice-Clerk from the informations of crimes furnished..by the local authorities' (W. Bell *Dict. Law Scotl.*).

1436 *Sc. Acts Jas. I* (1814) II. 23/2 It is..ordanit, þat al crownaris sal arrest..all þaim þat salbe gevin hym in portuis be þe Justice clerk, & nane vthir. *c* **1470** HENRYSON *Tale of Dog* 128 Quhilk hes ane porteouss of the indytement. **1582** *Reg. Privy Council Scot.* III. 491 The porteous and rollis of the last justice air..wes deliverit..to be execute. **1708** *Royal Proclam.* 11 July in *Lond. Gaz.* No. 4456/1 That Porteous Rolls be orderly and in due time taken up, conform to the Law and Custom in such cases. **1752** J. LOUTHIAN *Form of Process* 230 Form of the Porteous Rolls. Names of the Criminals and their Designations... Names and Designations of the Witnesses... Indictment. **1872** C. INNES *Lect. Scott. Legal Antiq.* 301 The Raven is like a false crowner who has a porteous of the indictment. **1883** OMOND *Ld. Advocates Scot.* I. 287.

Hence †'**portas, portess,** *v.* (*Obs. nonce-wd.*), *trans.* to include among the saints named in the breviary; to canonize.

1570 FOXE *A. & M.* (ed. 2) 1217/1 After an hundreth yeares expired, they shal also be shryned and portessed, dying as they did in that quarell of the Church of Rome.

†**port-assiet.** *Obs. rare.* [ad. F. *porte-assiette*, f. PORTE- + *assiette* plate.] A disk of metal, wood, etc., placed under a plate or dish.

1663 *Rutland MSS.* (1905) IV. 541 For 8 balls of box, with hinges and hesps, for the feet of the 2 sylver portassiets, 2*s*.

portasystemic, var. PORTOSYSTEMIC *a.*

portate ('pɔətət), *a. Her.* [ad. L. *portātus* carried, borne, pa. pple. of *portāre* to carry.] In ***cross portate***, a cross represented in a sloping position (*in bend*), as if carried on the shoulder.

1562 LEIGH *Armorie* 54 b, Wherefore call you the same portate? For on this fashion it laye on Christes showlder, who bare the same to the mounte of Calvary. **1572** BOSSEWELL *Armorie* II. 99 b, A Crosse portate in his propre coloure. **1725** COATS *Dict. Her.* s.v., A *Cross-Portate*,..lies athwart the Escutcheon in Bend, as if it were carry'd on a Man's Shoulder. c **1828** [see PORTANT 2].

portatile ('pɔətətɪl, -taɪl), *a.* Now *rare.* [ad. med.L. *portātil-is* (obs. F. *portatil*) that may be carried, f. L. *portāre* to carry: see -ATILE.]

†**1.** *Her.* = prec. *Obs.*

1587 FLEMING *Contn. Holinshed* III. 1355/2 A crosse portatile gold, to the lower end whereof this distichon is fairelie fixed.

2. Adapted for carrying; = PORTABLE, PORTATIVE *a.* 1: esp. (in later use only) of an altar.

1657 TOMLINSON *Renou's Disp.* 486 Some [furnaces] are portatile and rotund. *a* **1660** *Contemp. Hist. Irel.* (Ir. Archæol. Soc.) III. 143, £3000 sterling was giuen the Leutenant in readie coine, all his portatill armes [etc.]. **1710** tr. *Dupin's Eccl. Hist. 16th C.* I. II. xxxii. 198 That Bishops shall not..consecrate portatile altars without necessity. **1845** *Ecclesiologist* IV. 86 We think the Bishop ought..to have carried a portatile altar.

†**por'tation.** *Obs. rare*$^{-1}$. [ad. L. *portātiōn-em* carrying, n. of action from *portāre* to carry.] The action of carrying; carriage.

1654 FLECKNOE *Ten Years Trav.* 67 For the commodity of Traffique, and portation of Merchandise.

portative ('pɔətətɪv), *a.* and *sb.* Also 5 -if(f, 4-6 -yf, 5-6 -yue, 6 -yff(e, (portetyve). [ME. *portatif*, a. F. *portatif*, *-ive* adj. that may be carried, f. L. *portātus*, pa. pple. of *portāre* to carry + *-if*, -IVE.]

A. *adj.*

1. Adapted for carrying from place to place; portable; *spec.* applied to a kind of small organ (cf. POSITIVE *a.* 14): see B. 1. Now chiefly *Hist.*

1377 LANGL. *P. Pl.* B. I. 155 Portatyf and persant as þe poynt of a nedle. *c* **1391** CHAUCER *Astrol.* Prol. 3 As ferforth and as narwe as may be shewed in so smal an instrument portatif. **1432-50** tr. *Higden* (Rolls) V. 133 Syngenge masse in secrete places on awters portative. **1518-19** *Will of Issley* (Somerset Ho.), To the said church my portatyf organes. **1568** GRAFTON *Chron.* I. 8 Portatiue tents or lodgings,..vsed by the Shepeheardes. **1656** *French Pastry Cook* 22 Others have portative Ovens. **1849** J. WHITESIDE *Italy* xlii. (1860) 439 The Pope is carried in his portative throne to the front window. **1905** *Ch. Times* 30 June 842/3 The portative organ, which could be carried in procession and played by the same person.

†**b.** Of a bishop (repr. L. *portātilis*: see PORTATILE): Not having a fixed diocese. *Obs.*

1550 J. COKE *Eng. & Fr. Heralds* §196 (1877) 114 The bysshop of Rome maketh bysshoppes portatyves.

2. Having the function of carrying or supporting.

1881 FITCH *Lect. Teaching* v. 124 Some study..of the wise and practical distinction..between what he calls respectively the 'portative', the 'analytical', the 'assimilative', and the 'index' memory would be of great value. **1887** GUMMING *Electricity* 37 So [to] determine its portative power [i.e. of a horse-shoe magnet]. **1892** *Amer. Ann. Deaf* Apr. 86 It is far from my purpose to lend encouragement..to any practice of making the memory a portative faculty.

B. *sb.* **1.** (usually *pl.*) A portative organ: see A. 1. *Obs.* exc. *Hist.*

c **1450** HOLLAND *Howlat* 765 Claryonis lowde knellis, Portatiuis, and bellis. **1526-7** *Rec. St. Mary at Hill* 341 Rec' of the Orgon Maker for þe olde portatyffis in þe quere xxvj s viij d. **1533** in Weaver *Wells Wills* (1890) 94 To my church of Norton a payre of portetyves that stand in the chauncell ther. **1552** *Inv. Ch. Goods* (Surtees, No. 97) 97 One peyre of portatyves. **1633** J. CLARKE *Two-fold Praxis* 25 Harpers, luters,..such as goe with..portatives, bagpipes, recorders. **1885** A. J. HIPKINS in Grove *Dict. Mus.* IV. 303/2 The organ and portative end at g'' instead of d'''.

†**2.** A portable breviary: = PORTAS 1. *Obs.*

1454 *Test. Ebor.* (Surtees) II. 175 My Portatyue which I say opon my selfe, and my rede Salter.

†**3.** ? A tray or other carrying utensil. *Obs.*

a **1483** *Liber Niger* in *Househ. Ord.* (1790) 75 Ewers, lavours, and cupboarde-clothes, cuppe-clothes, hangers, ferrers, and portatives. *Ibid.* 76 One page..to helpe to wasshe barrelles, portatives, tubbes, pottes, or cuppes.

†**portator.** *Obs. rare* Forms: 5 -ur, 6 -our, 7 -or. [a. AF. *portatour* = obs. F. *portateur* (1540 in Godef.), ad. L. **portātōr-em*, agent-n. f. *portāre* to carry.] A bearer, carrier, supporter.

c **1485** *Digby Myst.* (1882) III. 306 Also I am þe prymatt portatur next heueyn, yf þe trewth be sowth, & that I Iugge me to skryptur. **1529** *St. Papers Hen. VIII*, IV. 562, I haue send this present portatour to the Kingis Hienes.., amply instructit with my mynd, as he will informe ȝow. *a* **1660** *Contemp. Hist. Irel.* (Ir. Archæol. Soc.) I. 158 Some of the ministers, portators of this money. *Ibid.* III. 68 Tellinge..that he was portator of both his parents curse.

portature, obs. erron. form of PORTRAITURE.

port-bar, port-bit: see PORT *sb.*[1] 6 b, *sb.*[3] 6.

†**port-'canon, -'cannon.** *Obs.* [f. PORT *sb.*[4] (?) + *canon*, CANION.] An ornamental roll around the legs of breeches: = CANION.

1663 BUTLER *Hud.* I. iii. 926 The French..Now give us Laws for Pantaloons..Port-cannons, Perriwigs, and Feathers. **1677** [see CANION]. *a* **1680** BUTLER *Rem.* (1759) II. 83 He walks in his Portcannons like one that stalks in long Grass.

portch, -e, obs. forms of PORCH.

portclose, -cluse, obs. var. PORTCULLIS.

port-crayon (pɔət'kreɪɒn), ‖**porte-crayon** (pɔrtkrɛjɔ̃). [ad. F. *porte-crayon*: see PORTE- and CRAYON.] An instrument used to hold a crayon for drawing; usually a metal tube split at the end and held by a sliding ring so as to grasp the crayon.

1720 T. PAGE *Art Paint.* 4 Black Lead in the Lump..used in an Instrument..called a Porto-Crion. **1769** SIR J. REYNOLDS *Disc.* ii. (1876) 324 That the port-crayon ought to be for ever in your hands. **1859** *Athenæum* 6 Aug. 182/2 [They] desire us to say that the testimonial is not a 'pencil-case', but a 'port-crayon'. **1887** RUSKIN *Præterita* II. ix. 304 He painted a charming water-colour of me..with a magnificent port-crayon in my hand.

portcullis (pɔət'kʌlɪs), *sb.* (Formerly often written as two words or hyphened.) Forms: 4 **portecules, portcoles, port colice,** 4-5 **portecolys,** 5 **porte-colis, portecoles, -koles, portcolys, -isse, (-culer), porte colisse, porte colyse, poortcolys, -colyce, portculis,** *Sc.* **-culys,** 5-6 *Sc.* **portculȝeis, -cules,** 5-7 **portcullise,** 6 **portcolyse, -ece, -ice, -is, porte coullys, -colice, portcullesse, -ize, port collice, port-cullies, (portculiouse);** 6- **portcullis,** (6-8 **-cullice,** 7 **-culleis**). *β.* 4 **porcules,** (5 **-culier**), 6 **purcoloys, -cholis, -ious, percollice, -ois, -cullyze,** 6-7 **percullis, -ice,** 7 **purculleis, -ess, perculless, par-cullis, porculace.** *γ.* 6-7 **portclose,** 6-8 **portcluse.** [ME. a. OF. *porte coleïce* (*c* 1200 in Godef.) lit. sliding door or gate, f. *porte* door, gate + *col(e)ïce*, *couleïce* (mod.F. *coulisse*), fem. of *couleïs* adj. flowing, gliding, sliding:—L. type **cōlāticius*, f. L. *cōlāt-us*, pa. pple. of *cōlāre* to strain, filter, in Romanic (F. *couler*), to flow; see COULISSE. The *γ* forms simulate F. *close*, fem. pa. pple., closed, shut. The forms *portculeres*, etc. (in sense 2) are app. erroneous with *r* for *s*. (The plural was in early use the same as the sing.)]

1. A strong and heavy frame or grating, formed of vertical and horizontal bars of wood or iron (the vertical ones being pointed at the lower end), suspended by chains, and made to slide up and down in vertical grooves at the sides of the gateway of a fortress or fortified town, so as to be capable of being quickly let down as a defence against assault.

c **1330** *Arth. & Merl.* 8320 Alle the gates thai schetten fast. And lete falle port colice on hast. *a* **1400** *Sir Beues* (E.E.T.S.) 67 *note* (MS. S.), With brugges and portecules. *Ibid.* 210 þe portcoles weren draw. *c* **1400** *Ywaine & Gaw.* 674 At aither entre was, i-wys, Straytly wroght, a port-culis, Shod wele with yren and stele. *c* **1440** *Promp. Parv.* 410/1 Poort colyce, *antephalarica*. *c* **1450** *Merlin* 254 At eche entre two porte colyses and stronge yates covered with Iren nailed. *c* **1470** HENRY *Wallace* IX. 506 A cruell portar gat apon the wall, Powit out a pyn, the portculys leit fall. *c* **1489** CAXTON *Sonnes of Aymon* xxiv. 518 He sholde put it vnder the porte colisse that it sholde not be shet lightly agen. **1535** STEWART *Cron. Scot.* (Rolls) II. 13 Drew draw briggis, and lute portculȝeis fall. *a* **1552** LELAND *Itin.* I. 107 The which Ward in the Entering is exceding stronge with Toures and Portcoleces. **1563** GOLDING *Cæsar* (1565) 132 b, Towres were plaunchered, and battlements and portcolyses of timber set vp. **1600** HEYWOOD *1st Pt. Edw. IV*, Wks. 1874 I. 15 And tear in pieces your port-cullises. **1600** HOLLAND *Livy* XXVII. xxviii. 650 The rope was let goe, at which the port-cullies hung, and it fell downe with a mightie noise. **1667** MILTON *P.L.* II. 874 And towards the Gate rouling her bestial train, Forthwith the huge Portcullis high up drew. **1808** SCOTT *Marm.* VI. xiv, Up drawbridge, grooms—what, Warder, ho! Let the portcullis fall. **1843** LYTTON *Last Bar.* II. i, Under the portal as he entered, hung the grate of the portcullis.

β. **13..** *Coer de L.* 1929 Porcules and gates up he won, And let come in every man. *a* **1533** LD. BERNERS *Huon* ci. 335 For hast they cut a sonder the corde that helde vp the purcoloys. **1560** WHITEHORNE *Arte Warre* (1573) 96 b, Also they fortifie the gate with a Perculis. **1599** HAKLUYT *Voy.* II. I. 125 A Portall, with a Percollois annexed to it, the which Percollois by the cutting of a small cord, was a present defence to the gate. **1607** TOPSELL *Four-f. Beasts* (1658) 160 In those trees they hang up a great par-cullis gate. *a* **1634** CHAPMAN *Alphonsus* III. Plays 1873 III. 249 Some speedily let the Purculless down. **1688** R. HOLME *Armoury* IV. ix. (Roxb.) 399/1 The Earle of Worcester..used for his badge a paire of stocks, or close Porculace.

γ. **1585** HIGINS *Junius' Nomencl.* 395/2 *Cataracta*, a portcluse or percullice. **1598** STOW *Surv.* vii. (1603) 29 There hath beene two Portcloses. **1640** SOMNER *Antiq. Canterb.* 14 The Waterlocke, through which in Arches, with a Portclose, the Riuer now passeth. **1773** *Gentl. Mag.* XLIII. 536 The gate-house is still standing which is fortified with a portcluse or port-cullis.

b. *fig.*

c **1430** LYDG. *Min. Poems* (Percy Soc.) 237 For upon Jhesu al parfitnesse is foundid,..Our poortcolys, our bolewerk, and our wal. *c* **1510** MORE *Picus* Wks. 8/2 A sure portculiouse against wicked spirites. **1609** HOLLAND *Amm. Marcell.* XXV. viii. 277 That the Emperour..would in the same state keepe this citie, the strongest port-cluse and key of all the East. **1635** QUARLES *Embl.* II. ix. 97 Ah, where's that pearle Percullis [i.e. teeth], that adorn'd Those dainty two-leav'd Ruby gates [i.e. lips]?

2. A figure of a portcullis, as an ornament or a heraldic charge. In *Her.* also applied to a design formed of a number of vertical and horizontal strips crossing each other over the field; also *lattice.*

The portcullis was the badge of the Beauforts, and hence of their descendants the Tudor sovereigns.

[*c* **1449** in *Pol. Poems* (Rolls) II. 221 The castelle is wonne where care begowne, The Portecolys [= Edmund Beaufort] is leyde adowne.] **1485** in *Mat. illustr. Reign Hen. VII* (Rolls) II. 16 To Mathew Hoberd, Goldsmythe, for making of cv. porculiers of siluer and gilte. *Ibid.* 18 For setting of a trappour of purpulle veluet wt cii. portculeres therein. **1513** in Willis & Clark *Cambridge* (1886) II. 347 All the Wyndowes..also with Rosez and purcholious. **1563-4** *Ibid.* 571 A greate Rose A flowerdelice and a purcholis..in the weste wyndowe. **1523** *Act 14 & 15 Hen. VIII*, c. 12 All suche farthinges.. shall haue vppon the one side thereof the printe of the port collice. **1565** *Act 8 Eliz.* c. 12 §2 The Queenes Highnes Seale of Leade, having the Porteculllies crowned, ingraved on the one syde thereof. **1697** EVELYN *Numism.* iii. 87 A pensile *Cataracta* or Portcluse and Coronet between the Chains. **1711** HICKES *Two Treat. Chr. Priesth.* (1847) II. 361 The rose, portcluse, fleur-de-lis, and harp, are crowned. **1864** BOUTELL *Her. Hist. & Pop.* ix. 50 In Heraldry, a Portcullis is always represented as having rings at its uppermost angles.

3. †**a.** A popular name for the silver halfpenny of Queen Elizabeth (the smallest silver coin issued by her), which bore on the obverse a portcullis and a mint-mark. *Obs.* **b.** *portcullis coins, money*, a name given by numismatists to the coins (crown, half-crown, shilling, and sixpence) struck by Queen Elizabeth in 1600-2 for the East India Company, having the figure of a portcullis on the reverse. (Cf. quot. 1523 in sense 2.)

[Cf. **1597** BACON *Ess.* Ded., The late new halfe-pence, which though the Siluer were good, yet the peeces were small.]

1599 B. JONSON *Ev. Man out of Hum.* III. vi, I had not so much as the least Portcullice of Coyn before. **1600** ROWLANDS *Lett. Humours Blood* xix. 25 Then doth he diue into his sloppes profound, Where not a poore port-cullice can be found. **1784** PINKERTON *Ess. Medals* 168 The Portcullis coins of Elizabeth, coined in rivalship of the Spanish king..of different sizes from the crown downwards. **1898** G. B. RAWLINGS *Story Brit. Coinage* 196 They [coins for use of the E.I.C.] are called the 'portcullis-money' from their reverse type.

4. Title of one of the Pursuivants of the English College of Arms, from his badge.

1616 BULLOKAR *Eng. Expos.*, *Percullis*, the name of an office of one of the Pursiuants at armes. **1631** WEEVER *Anc. Fun. Mon.* 682 Segar being Portcullis Pursuiuant of Armes in the yeare 1586. **1656** BLOUNT *Glossogr.* s.v. *Harold*, There be four others called Marshals or Pursuivants at Arms,..those are Blew-mantle, Rouge-cross, Rouge-dragon, and Percullis. **1722** *Lond. Gaz.* No. 6084/5 Port-cullis, Pursuivant of Arms. **1905** *Whitaker's Alm.* 157/1 Arms, College of, or Heralds' College... Four Pursuivants... Portcullis, Thomas Morgan Joseph-Watkin.

†**5.** (?) Name of some room in an inn. *Obs.*

1631 HEYWOOD *Fair Maid of West* I. Wks. 1874 II. 268 Besse, you must fill some wine into the Portcullis, the Gentlemen there will drink none but your drawing. *Ibid.* III. 293 *Enter the Kitchin-maid. Maid.* I pray forsooth, what shall I reckon for the Iolle of Ling in the Port-cullis?

port'cullis, *v.* In 7 **portcullice, perculis, purcullise.** [f. prec. sb.] *trans.* To furnish with a portcullis; to close with or as with a portcullis.

1593 SHAKS. *Rich. II*, I. iii. 167 Within my mouth you haue engaol'd my tongue, Doubly percullist with my teeth and lippes. **1611** FLORIO, *Rastellare*..to purcullise. *a* **1640** DAY *Parl. Bees* (1881) 25 *note*, Portcullice up the gates; hees poore and base.

portcullised (pɔət'kʌlɪst), *a.* Also 6 **portcolized, -culliz'd;** *β.* 6. **purculleised,** 7 **perculliz'd, percullist,** ? 9 **perculaced.** [f. prec. sb. or vb. + -ED.]

1. Furnished with or having a portcullis; closed or barred with or as with a portcullis.

1572 N. ROSCARROCK in Bossewell *Armorie* Prelim. Verses, A hugie building olde, Portcolized and bard with bolts. **1598** DRAYTON *Heroic. Ep.*, *Mortimer to Q. Isabel* 125 And all those Townes..Within their strong port-culliz'd Ports shall lie. **1598** FLORIO, *Cataratto*, purculleised or cataracted. **1611** HEYWOOD *Gold. Age* IV. i. Wks. 1874 III. 58 The rest keep watchfull eye On your percullist entrance. *a* **1763** SHENSTONE *Progr. Taste* II. 118 The stately fort, the turrets tall, Portcullis'd gate, and battled wall. **1861** M. PATTISON *Ess.* (1889) I. 45 A lofty massive front with three fortified and portcullised gateways.

2. *Her.* (See quot.) Cf. PORTCULLIS *sb.* 2.

1828 BERRY *Encycl. Herald.* I. Gloss., *Portcullised*, barred upright and across, after the form of a portcullis, termed also *latticed.* **1882** OGILVIE, *Perculaced*, in *her.* latticed.

‖**port de bras** (pɔr də bra). *Ballet.* Pl. **ports de bras.** [Fr., lit. 'carriage of the arms'.] The act or manner of moving and poising the arms; also, one of a series of exercises designed to develop the graceful movement and poising of the arms.

1912 *Dancing Times* Aug. 449/2 Arms... The Port de Bras, and exercises thereon. **1920** *Ibid.* Dec. 181 In operatic dancing..certain exercises have been evolved..known as the side and centre practice, the ports de bras and the adage. **1922** BEAUMONT & IDZIKOWSKI *Man. Classical Theatr. Dancing* II. ii. 56 *Port de Bras* deals with the positions and movements of the arms. **1940** C. W. BEAUMONT *Diaghilev Ballet in London* ix. 203 The attention paid to such details..makes the dance a work of art and not a mere combination of steps and *port de bras* rendered by a woman in ballet costume. **1948** *Ballet Ann.* II. 68 The eight *ports de bras*, or exercises to develop the graceful movement and co-ordination of the arms. **1952** [see ÉPAULEMENT]. **1958** *Times* 22 Aug. 6/3 So gracious and erect was her head held on her shoulders, so beautifully poised her *ports de bras.* **1963** *Times* 9 May 16/7 Her footwork proved exemplary... Her *ports de bras* were a little inelegant, sometimes giving a slightly gauche appearance to her line. **1975** *New Yorker* 18 Aug. 77/3 The grandeur of her carriage makes even a simple rhythmic port de bras, such as the one she does standing in a cluster of Wilis, an exciting dance experience.

‖**port de voix** (pɔr də vwa). *Mus.* [Fr., lit. 'carrying of the voice'.] A kind of appoggiatura (see quot. 1944).

1740 J. GRASSINEAU *Mus. Dict.* 182 *Port de voix*, a French term, which signifies the faculty and habitude of making shakes, passages, and diminutions, wherein the beauty of a song or piece of music greatly consists. **1876** STAINER & BARRETT *Dict. Mus. Terms* 364/2 *Port de voix* (Fr.), a kind of appogiatura combined with the Pincé. **1944** W. APEL *Harvard Dict. Mus.* 595/1 *Port de voix*,..one of the most important French *agréments* of the 17th and 18th centuries. Essentially it is an upward-resolved suspension or appoggiatura... Usually..both appoggiatura and resolution are repeated, so that the ornament consists of four notes, the last three forming a *pincé*. **1978** *Early Music* Oct. 518/2 The *port de voix*, being firstly a connecting note and secondly a fluctuation of pitch, usually upwards, but also downwards, can be viewed as the most rudimentary form of decoration. **1979** *Ibid.* Jan. 22/1 When the *Port de voix* was shown as a rising grace note it could often be followed by a *pincé* without the need for a separate sign.

Port du Salut, var. *Port Salut* s.v. PORT SALUT 2.

porte (pɔət). Also 6–8 port. [a. F. *porte*, in full *la Sublime Porte* = It. *la Porta Sublima*, transl. Turkish (Arabic) *bāb i-ɛāliy*, lit. 'the sublime, high, or lofty gate', the official title of the central office of the Ottoman government, comprising the office of the Grand Vezir, of the Minister of Foreign Affairs, and of the Council of State (Redhouse, *Turkish Lex.* 1890). 'Gate' is supposed to refer to the ancient place of audience, etc., at the gate of the tent, or the king's gate; the attribute 'high' or 'lofty' is not literal, but the honorific attribute of the Turkish government. According to Zenker, the Western application of 'Sublime Porte' to the Turkish government or Ottoman state answers rather to the Turkish *dawlet-i-ɛāliye*, 'the sublime empire or state.'

In the 17th and 18th c., often erroneously taken as referring to the position of Constantinople as a sea-port.]

(In full, ***the Sublime*** or ***Ottoman Porte***.) The Ottoman court at Constantinople; hence *transf.* the Turkish government.

1600 R. C. *Fumée's Hist. Hungary* 248 [Sultan speaks] Send your Ambassadours, as well towards our royall Port, as also to him. **1615** G. SANDYS *Trav.* I. 48 Some Vizers of the Port. *c* **1645** HOWELL *Lett.* (1650) II. 44 He that had bin Ambassadour at the Port to the greatest Monark upon earth. [**1671** *Charente's Let. Customs Mauritania* 48 The King of Morocco usually gives audience at the Gate of this Palace, and here, as well as at Constantinople, La Porta signifies the Court or Kings Palace.] **1676** *Lond. Gaz.* No. 1145/1 Articles of Peace concluded between the King of Poland and the Ottoman Port. **1706** PHILLIPS, The *Port*, the Court of the Grand Seignior..at Constantinople. **1721** *Lond. Gaz.* No. 5983/1 Before the Port has had any Account of it. **1747** *Gentl. Mag.* Nov. 350/2 Report of which being made to the sublime Porte, the sultan advanced him to the post of Cadi. **1772** *Hist.* in *Ann. Reg.* 78/2 That haughty capital, which had been named the Porte by way of eminence, from its incomparable naval and commercial situation. **1847** MRS. A. KERR tr. *Ranke's Hist. Servia* 210 A better understanding was in consequence soon established between him [Napoleon] and the Porte. **1886** *Queen's Speech in opening Parlt.*, Under a convention..concluded with the Ottoman Porte, Commissioners have been appointed, on behalf of England and Turkey, to confer with His Highness the Khedive. **1891** *Blackw. Mag.* Oct. 470 The Sublime Porte is a time-honoured institution.

‖**porte-** (pɔrt), Fr. imperative of *porter* to bear, carry; used in combination with a sb. as obj. in numerous compound words in Fr., several of which are more or less used in Eng.; the first element is occasionally anglicized as *port-*; and other words have been formed after these with the second element English (PORT-ELECTRIC, PORT-FIRE, etc.). From French: **porte-acide** (-asid), an instrument for the application of an acid to a part of the body. **porte-aiguille** (-egɥij) [F. *aiguille* needle], a fine forceps for holding a surgical needle; a needle-holder. **porte-bonheur** (-bɔnœr) [F. *bonheur* good luck], an amulet, or a trinket worn like an amulet. **porte-bouquet** (-buke), a bouquet-holder. **porte-caustique** (-kostik), also anglicized ***port-caustic***, an instrument for applying a caustic. **porte-feu** (-fø) (*port-feu*) [F. *feu* fire] = PORT-FIRE. **porte-lumière** (-lymjɛr) [F. *lumière* light], an apparatus consisting of a mirror so arranged as to reflect light in any desired direction; used as a substitute for the heliostat. **porte-parole** (-parɔl) [F. *parole* word], a spokesman, a mouthpiece. See also PORTEFEUILLE, etc.

1890 BILLINGS *Med. Dict.*, **Porte-acid*, a glass tube through which a platinum wire passes carrying a tuft saturated with the acid to be applied. **1857** DUNGLISON *Dict. Med.*, **Porte-aiguille*, an instrument for accurately laying hold of a needle, and giving it greater length. **1895** in *Syd. Soc. Lex.* **1884** G. MOORE *Mummer's Wife* (1887) 206 She had..a little gold **porte-bonheur*..she had bought that morning. **1839** C. SCHREIBER *Jrnl.* (1950) 93 The Ex-Chancellor..took the nosegay in his hand, extricated it from the *porte-bouquet..and instead of giving the flowers into Mr. Pamther's expectant hands, he smelt them himself. **1900** *Daily News* 6 Nov. 6/1 Some of them [prizes] were cut chrysanthemums in artistically-carved porte-bouquets. **1846** BRITTAN tr. *Malgaigne's Man. Oper. Surg.* 274 Preference should always be given to a *porte-caustique like that of Ducamp for the urethra. **1884** M. MACKENZIE *Dis. Throat & Nose* II. 252 An ingenious porte-caustique has been invented by Dr. Fauvel. **1802** JAMES *Milit. Dict.* s.v. *Entonnoir*, the tin-case or *port-feu which is used to convey the priming powder into the touch-hole of a cannon. **1656** BLOUNT *Glossogr.*, **Porte-guidon*, an Ensign-bearer to a troop of men at Arms. **1884** *Century Mag.* XXIX. 238/2 This apparatus consisted of a long photometer-box with a **porte lumière* at one end. **1946** J. FLANNER in *New Yorker* 23 Mar. 74/2 Milch gave the appearance of being Göring's **porte-parole*. **1966** T. REESE *Story of Accusation* xi. 158 He is a lawyer. He is only a *porte-parole*.

‖**porte-cochère** (pɔrtkɔʃɛr). Also 7–8 (anglicized) **port-cocher**. [F., f. *porte* PORT *sb.*^{3} + *cochère*, fem. adj. f. *coche* COACH *sb.*] A gateway for carriages, leading into a court-yard; a carriage-entrance.

1698 W. KING tr. *Sorbière's Journ. Lond.* 3 Divers of the Citizens Houses have Port-cochers [*mispr.* -ezs] to drive in a Coach, or a cart either, and Consequently have Courts within. **1699** M. LISTER *Journ. Paris* 8 All the Houses of Persons of Distinction are built with Port-cochers, that is, wide Gates to drive in a Coach. **1769** *De Foe's Tour Gt. Brit.* (ed. 7) II. 170 Kensington cannot be named without mentioning the King's Palace there:..there are two great Wings built..and a large Port-cocher at the Entrance, with a Postern. **1804** *Edin. Rev.* Apr. 95 The darkness of their court-yards and *portes cocheres*. **1848** THACKERAY *Van. Fair* lxiv, Their carriage stood in the *porte-cochère* of the hotel. **1882** *Century Mag.* XXIV. 843/1 The *porte-cochères*..afford glimpses of..court-yards.

porte-colis, -cules, etc., obs. ff. PORTCULLIS.

porte-crayon: see PORT-CRAYON.

ˈ**ported**, *a.*^{1} [f. PORT *sb.*^{3} + -ED^{2}.] **1.** Having 'ports' or gates: in comb. *rare.*

c **1611** CHAPMAN *Iliad* IV. 433 We tooke the seuen-fold ported Thebes, when yet we had not there So great helpe as our fathers had.

2. Having one or more ports or apertures; freq. in comb. with preceding numeral or adj.

1850 J. BOURNE *Catechism of Steam Engine* 67 Of the slide valve there are many varieties; but the kinds most in use are the D valve..and the three ported valve. **1884** *Engineering* 19 Dec. 566/2 The face on the cylinder is double ported. **1897** C. HURST *Valves* II. i. 98 The exhaust valves may assume the double-ported form. This type permits a considerable reduction of travel compared with the single-ported valve. **1952** H. F. OLSON *Musical Engin.* ix. 319 (*heading*) Phase inverter or ported cabinet. **1975** G. J. KING *Audio Handbk.* vi. 143 Because an aperture is an important part of the enclosure, the terms 'vented-box', 'ported' and 'tunnelled' are sometimes used to describe the system.

ˈ**ported**, *a.*^{2} [f. PORT *sb.*^{7} + -ED^{2}.] Supplied with port-wine.

1929 J. MASEFIELD *Hawbucks* 27 We're all dined and ported, thanks.

ported (ˈpɔətɪd), *ppl. a.* [f. PORT *v.*^{1} + -ED^{1}.] Of arms: Held in the position of the port: see PORT *sb.*^{4} 9 and *v.*^{1} 2.

1650 T. BAYLY *Herba Parietis* 51 His own hair, standing stiffe an end, like ported feathers of some porcupine. **1667** MILTON *P.L.* IV. 978 Th' Angelic Squadron bright..began to hemm him round With ported Spears. **1844** *Regul. & Ord. Army* 265 The man or men going on the Post, who, with ported Arms, approach the Sentinels to be relieved.

portée (ˈpɔəteɪ, ‖pɔrte). Also **portee**. [a. Fr. *portée* (in various senses), f. *porter* to bear, carry.] **1.** The importance or weight (of a theory, an argument, etc.); the (far-reaching) consequences (of an action or an event).

1894 A. LANG *Cock Lane* 9 It is with this majority, if they choose to find time, and can muster inclination for the task of prolonged and patient experiment, that the ultimate decision as to the *portée* and significance of the facts must rest. **1899** W. JAMES *Let.* 28 Jan. in R. B. Perry *Tht. & Char. W. James* (1935) II. 136 You seem to take my intention in the lecture to have had a wider *portée* than I ever thought of. **1904** H. JAMES *Golden Bowl* II. xxv. 10 She called it [*sc.* her action] names, the invidious, the grotesque attitude, holding it up to her own ridicule, reducing so far as she could the *portée* of what had followed it.

2. In hand-loom weaving, a specified number of threads grouped together to form the warp. Also *attrib.*, as ***portee cross***.

1910 L. HOOPER *Hand-Loom Weaving* I. ii. 37 It only remains to take the group of eight threads *below* and *over* peg A in order to finish the first *portee*, as such a collection of threads warped in one round is called. *Ibid.* iv. 57 An excellent way of keeping account of the portees as they are warped is shown at fig. 27. *Ibid.* The fifty threads, taken all together, will pass above the first peg W, below the last one, then round it, and under the first, which completes the portee cross. **1954** H. J. BROWN *Hand-Weaving* v. 76 This second leash is called the portee cross. **1954** M. E. PRITCHARD *Short Dict. Weaving* 67 One portee makes two warp 'ends'. The word..dates back to the days of the Huguenot weavers in England, deriving from the French *portee*, meaning 'carried'. **1958** A. HINDSON *Designer's Drawloom* vi. 55 The portee, or grouped, crosses must not be split when they are spaced in the raddle. **1965** J. TOVEY *Technique of Weaving* II. 30/1 For convenience in keeping count of the number of threads warped, the ends of a strong yarn of a contrasting colour are crossed between groups of portées.

3. *Mil.* A self-propelled vehicle on which an anti-tank gun can be mounted. Also *attrib.* and in phr. ‖***en portée*** (ɑ̃) [Fr. *en* in].

1942 *Times* 22 Apr. 4/6 Finally, only two guns remained in action... Immediately afterwards one of these was destroyed and the portee of another was set on fire. **1944** *Return to Attack* (Army Board, N.Z.) 22 (*caption*) Anti-tank gun on portee at night. *Ibid.* 28/2 Portee anti-tank guns. **1948** R. FARRAN *Winged Dagger* viii. 141 It was a large command for a subaltern—ten armoured cars of mixed varieties, eight Bofors guns, a two-pounder portee and a tank. **1948** E. H. SMITH *Guns against Tanks* (N.Z. Dept. Internal Affairs) 3 The two-pounders were carried on the decks of specially constructed lorries, termed *portées*, which were fitted with ramps and winches to enable the guns to be quickly hoisted into place. Special fittings..enabled the trail and spade to be clamped firmly to the deck so that the gun, pointing over the rear of the *portée*, was ready for immediate action. *Ibid.*, Great attention should be paid to training the gun crews in fighting the two-pounders from the decks of the *portées*: that is, *en portée*. **1952** *Times* 30 Aug. 5/6 Through it the light vehicles of 7th Armoured Division, portees, carriers, and light tanks, began to pass across our front as they skilfully drew on the enemy. **1958** M. K. JOSEPH *I'll soldier no More* viii. 151 It was eight o'clock before they piled into the portee-waggon.

‖**portefeuille** (pɔrtfœj). [F., f. PORTE- + *feuille* leaf, sheet; cf. PORTFOLIO.]

1. = PORTFOLIO 1.

1699 M. LISTER *Journ. Paris* 92 He shewed his *Portefeuilles* in Folio, of Red Spanish Leather finely adorned. **1768** in *N. & Q.* 10th Ser. VI. 466/1 Ninety-five capital drawings..in two Russia portefeuilles. **1815** MME. D'ARBLAY *Diary* (1846) VII. 227 Neither..were of any avail, till he condescended to search his portefeuille for a passport.

2. = PORTFOLIO 2.

1792 *Amer. St. Papers, Foreign* (1832) I. 390 (Stanf.) The portefeuille was given to Monsieur Delessart. **1836** LADY H. STANHOPE *Mem.* (1845) I. x. 369 It was not Napoleon that he was so much attached to; it was to him who had the *portefeuille*.

portegue, var. PORTAGUE *Obs.*

portekoles, obs. form of PORTCULLIS.

ˌ**port-eˈlectric**, *a.* [See PORTE-.] Carrying by electricity: applied to a proposed system of electric traction for transmission of parcels, etc.

1890 *Globe* 14 Nov. 3/1 The *Portelectric* car is an air cylinder 10 inches in diameter, 12 feet long, and 350lb. in weight. It runs on two wheels, one above, the other below, along an elevated railroad which supports the..hollow coils.

portemantue, obs. form of PORTMANTEAU.

‖**porte-monnaie** (pɔrtmɔnɛ). Also (in vulgar use) anglicized as **port-money**. [F., f. PORTE- + *monnaie* MONEY.] A flat leathern purse or pocket-book.

1855 THACKERAY *Newcomes* lxxix, Mrs. Mackenzie briskly shut her porte-monnaie. **1878** B. HARTE *Man on Beach* 78, I left my portmoney at home. **1885** C. F. WOOLSON in *Harper's Mag.* Apr. 785/1 A battered porte-monnaie.

‖**Porteño** (porˈteɲo). Also **porteño**. Fem. **Porteña**. [Sp.] A native or inhabitant of Buenos Aires, the capital of Argentina and (until 1884) of the province of Buenos Aires. Also *attrib.* or as *adj.*

1884 R. G. WATSON *Spanish & Portuguese S. Amer.* II. xviii. 274 The great majority of the people of *Buenos Ayres* were not..passive spectators... The colonial society opened its *salons* to the English officers, and the *Porteña* beauties were not displeased to number them amongst their admirers. **1904** C. E. AKERS *Hist. S. Amer.* ii. 37 The provincial representatives, whilst entertaining most vindictive feelings towards Rosas, had no real sympathy with the Porteños. *Ibid.* 39 He was to check *porteño* influence that the majority of the provinces joined hands against Mitre. **1910** *Encycl. Brit.* II. 472/1 The national army..assaulted the *porteños* posted before Buenos Aires. **1959** *Chambers's Encycl.* I. 580/2 The relatively wealthy and cultivated oligarchy of merchants and professional men, the *porteños*, who dominated Buenos Aires (which then meant both the present city and the present province of that name). *Ibid.* 581/2 Rosas was by birth a member of the *porteño* oligarchy. *Ibid.* 582/1 The *porteño* army under Bartolomé Mitre..was defeated and Buenos Aires was incorporated in the Confederation in 1859. **1973** G. M. D. HOWAT *Dict. World Hist.* 1212/1 *Porteño* municipal loyalty was clearly manifested in 1806–7, when..local leaders organized the defeat of the British expeditions. *Ibid.*, *Porteños* demanded free trade and free movement of European capital, technology, immigrants, and ideas. **1978** *Times* 4 Feb. 5/3 Rats..can be spotted worrying refuse bags in the streets... For the *Porteños*..have waited to the last moment to start installing the [refuse] compactors now required in large buildings.

portenans, -aunce, varr. PURTENANCE *Obs.*

portend (pɔːˈtɛnd), *v.*^{1} Also 5 **portende**, 6 **pourtende**. [ME. ad. L. *portendĕre* to foretell, presage, archaic form of *protendĕre* to stretch forth, specialized in ritual sense, f. *por-* = *pro-* forth + *tendĕre* to stretch; see PROTEND.]

1. *trans.* To presage as an omen; to foreshow, foreshadow.

1432–50 tr. *Higden* (Rolls) VII. 33 A blasynge sterre was seene in the firmamente, whiche is wonte to portende other a pestilence of provinces other the chaungenge of a realme.

1560 DAUS tr. *Sleidane's Comm.* 285 [They] judged that it did pourtende and signifie some great trouble. **1654** BRAMHALL *Just Vind.* vi. (1661) 146 Like as that single meteor Castor appearing without Pollux portends an unfortunate voyage. **1868** FARRAR *Seekers* II. iv. (1875) 225 The croak of the raven can portend no harm to such a man.

b. By extension: To point to or indicate beforehand; to give warning of, by natural means.

1592 KYD *Sp. Trag.* I. ii, What portends thy cheerful countenance? **1685** EVELYN *Diary* 5 Nov., Bonfires were forbidden on this day; what does this portend! **1756** FRANKLIN in *Phil. Trans.* LV. 188 Small black clouds thus appearing in a clear sky..portend storms, and warn seamen to hand their sails. **1878** BOSW. SMITH *Carthage* 160 Everything portended an early renewal of the conflict.

2. Of a person: To foretell, predict, forecast, prognosticate, as by interpreting an omen. *rare.*

1611 HEYWOOD *Gold. Age* III. i. Wks. 1874 III. 48 What portend you in these hostile sounds Of clamorous warre? **1731** SWIFT *On his Death* 119 Some great misfortune to portend, No enemy can match a friend. **1851** GLADSTONE *Glean.* VI. iii. 2 A fact plain enough to those..who in the moral hemisphere can portend foul weather when 'the sky is red and lowering'.

†**3.** To signify, symbolize, mean, indicate. *Obs.*

1586 A. DAY *Eng. Secretary* II. (1625) 87 *Antanaclasis*, when we produce a word in a contrary signification to that it commonly portendeth. **1601** SHAKS. *Twel. N.* II. v. 130 What should that Alphabeticall position portend..? Softly, M.O.A.I. **1726** POPE *Odyss.* XIX. 645 The geese (a glutton race) by thee deplored, Portend the suitors fated to my sword. **1782** HAN. MORE *Belshazzar* II. 76 What do the mystic characters portend?

4. *intr.* To utter or give portents. *rare.*

1887 BOWEN *Virg. Eclogue* I. 18 Oft from the holm-oak's hole on the left did a raven portend.

Hence **por'tending** *vbl. sb.* and *ppl. a.*; also †**por'tendance**, †**por'tendment**, the quality or fact of portending; presage, omen, signification; **por'tender**, one who or that which portends.

1644 J. GOODWIN *Fighting agst. God* 22 It is a thing of the saddest consideration under heaven, and of more grievous *portendance unto us. **1657** —— *Triers Tried* 5 [It] must needs be of a sad abode and portendance unto the people. **1635** SWAN *Spec. M.* v. §2 (1643) 125 They have appeared as the *portenders of change in states and kingdomes. **1675** TEONGE *Diary* (1825) 26 An absolute portendor of a prosperous voyage. **1590** WATSON *Eclogue Sir F. Walsingham* 419 For they portending stormie windes surcease, but by *portending cause the hearts content. **1632** LITHGOW *Trav.* x. 459 The portending heauinesse of my presaging soule. **1626** BP. HALL *Contempl., O.T.* xx. ii, Like comets who were never seene without the *portendement of a mischeife. **1634** JACKSON *Creed* VII. vii. §2 It only argues some deeper insight in ominous forewarnings or portendments.

portend (pɔː'tɛnd), *v.*[2] [ME. a. OF. *portend-re* to stretch forth, extend, to drape, cover, etc.:—L. *protendĕre* to stretch forth, with pop. L. *por-* for *pro-* forth. See prec. and PROTEND.]

†**1.** *trans.* To put forward, as authority or excuse; to pretend. *Obs. rare.*

1432-50 tr. *Higden* (Rolls) VIII. 93 William bischop of Hely..oppressede moche the clergy, portendynge the power of the kynge [L. *regis prætendens potestatem*].

2. To stretch forth, to extend, hold out (something). Now *rare* or *Obs.*

1657 TOMLINSON *Renou's Disp.* 678 The Alembick sometimes..portends out of its head..a Pipe. **1782** MICKLE *Q. Emma* III. 298 Spear to spear was now portended, And the yew-bows half were drawn. **1803** *Edwin* I. xii. 192 The fury that marked my brow as I portended my sword over the senseless bodies of my wife and child.

portent ('pɔətənt). Also 7 **portend**, and in L. form **portentum**. [ad. L. *portent-um* a portent, sign, omen, monster, marvellous tale (whence also It., Sp., Pg. *portento*, obs. F. *portente*), f. L. *portendĕre* to PORTEND. Orig. stressed *por'tent*, which came down to 19th c.; but *'portent* is found also in 1711. Pope has both.]

1. That which portends or foretells something momentous about to happen, esp. of a calamitous nature; an omen, significant sign or token.

1563-87 FOXE *A. & M.* (1596) 762 (R.) A strange portent and prodigious token from heauen, in the yeare of our Lord 1505. **1596** SHAKS. *1 Hen. IV*, II. iii. 65 O what portents are these? *c* **1611** CHAPMAN *Iliad* II. 268 And there appear'd a huge portent, A Dragon with a bloody skale, horride to sight, and sent To light by great Olympius. **1671** MILTON *P.R.* IV. 491 As false portents, not sent from God, but thee. **1697** DRYDEN *Virg. Past.* I. 22 My Loss by dire Portents the Gods foretold. **1711** POPE *Temp. Fame* 452 Of prodigies and portents seen in air. **1736** S. WESLEY *Hymn*, From whence these dire Portents around, That Earth and Heaven amaze? **1814** SCOTT *Ld. of Isles* VI. xxx, Portents and miracles impeach Our sloth. **1821** BYRON *Sardan.* II. i, Let us think Of what is to be done to justify Thy planets and their portents. **1845** HIRST *Poems* 73 Such portents shook the soul of Rome. **1871** FROUDE in *Devon. Assoc. Trans.* IV. 20 The early records of all nations are full of portents and marvels.

b. The fact or quality of portending; in phr. *of dire* (etc.) *portent.*

1715-20 POPE *Iliad* II. 372 A mighty dragon shot, of dire portent; From Jove himself the dreadful sign was sent. **1865** PARKMAN *Huguenots* iii. (1875) 28 A cloud of black and deadly portent was thickening over France.

c. In weakened sense: A sign of coming weather or other natural phenomena.

1868 HAWTHORNE *Amer. Note-Bks.* (1879) II. 37 Lowering with portents of rain. **1882** 'OUIDA' *Maremma* viii, She was not so familiar with the portents of the land.

2. Something considered portentous; a prodigy, wonder, marvel.

1741 MIDDLETON *Cicero* II. x. 422 L. Antony, the portent and disgrace of his species. **1842** MACAULAY *Ess., Fredk. Gt.* (1877) 671 Frederic was not one of these brilliant portents. **1863** GEO. ELIOT *Romola* i, If you talk of portents, what portent can be greater than a pious notary? **1881** M. G. WATKINS in *Academy* 19 Mar. 202 That portent the 'general reader' will find this book entertaining.

3. *Comb.*, as ***portent-like*** adj. and adv.

1744 HANMER *Shaks. Wks., L.L.L.* v. ii. 67 Portent-like [Hanmer's emendation of *pertaunt-*, *perttaunt-like* of the Quartos and Folios]. **1747** WARBURTON in *Shaks. Wks.* II. 256 Portent-like, i.e. I would be his fate or destiny, and like a portent hang over, and influence his fortunes.

Hence †**por'tentful** *a. Obs.*, portentous.

1633 T. ADAMS *Exp. 2 Peter* iii. 5 There are bred those portentful comets and exhalations, out of which fantastical heads pick fanatical meanings.

†**porten'tifical**, *a. Obs. rare*$^{-0}$. [f. L. *portentificus* (f. *portentum* PORTENT: see -FIC) + -AL[1].]

1656 BLOUNT *Glossogr.*, *Portentifical*, which worketh wonders, or whereby monstrous and strange things are done.

†**por'tention.** *Obs. rare.* In 7 **portension.** [ad. med.L. *portentiō-nem* a portent, f. *portendĕre* to PORTEND.] The action of portending; a portent.

1658 SIR T. BROWNE *Pseud. Ep.* VI. xiv. 417 Why although the Red Comets do carry the portensions of Mars, the brightly-white should not be of the Influence of Jupiter or Venus,..is not absurd to doubt.

portentious (pɔː'tɛnʃəs), *a.* [Corruption of PORTENTOUS *a.*, infl. by PRETENTIOUS *a.*] Pretentious, pompous; portentous. Hence **por'tentiously** *adv.*

1863 K. STONE *Jrnl.* 16 July in *Brokenburn* (1955) 227 The earth, the air, the sky, all are a dull dead grey. The sun seems to emit neither heat nor light, gleaming with a red glare like a blood-red moon... Some think it porteneous, a sign of great victories or defeats. **1937** in PARTRIDGE *Dict. Slang.* **1949** *Sun* (Baltimore) 21 Jan. 3/1 A portentious feature of this first telecast of a presidential inauguration was the use made of it in schools. **1956** *Ibid.* 20 Feb. (B ed.) 8/3 If you were lucky enough to have seen them, you witnessed a portentious enlargement of mankind's field of knowledge. **1958** *Times* 29 Oct. 3/1 A poem..was hammered home as a portentious statement containing the whole truth about the meaning, or meaninglessness, of life. **1962** *John o'London's* 15 Feb. 163/4 An Italian send-up of the portentious I.Q. flummery. **1975** *Publishers Weekly* 3 Mar. 64/2 Loving Ty whom she sees as somehow portentiously East Coast.

†**por'tentive**, *a. Obs. rare.* [f. L. *portent-*, ppl. stem of *portendĕre* to PORTEND + -IVE.] Having the quality of portending; = PORTENTOUS 1.

1594 NASHE *Terrors Night* Wks. (Grosart) III. 245 Commonly that [dream] which is portentiue in a King is but a friuolous fancie in a beggar. **1659** FULLER *App. Inj. Innoc.* I. 51* The Portentive Idolls of their Country. **1773** J. ROSS *Fratricide* IV. 9 (MS.) The Heavens Portentive roll'd their thunders o'er his head.

portentous (pɔː'tɛntəs), *a.* Also 6 **portentius**, 7–9 **-uous**, 7 **-eous**. [ad. L. *portentōsus*, *-uōsus* (whence also obs. F. *portenteux*, It. *portentoso*), f. *portentum* PORTENT: see -OUS and -UOUS.]

1. Of the nature of a portent; foreboding some extraordinary and (usually) calamitous event; ominous, threatening, warning.

c **1540** tr. *Pol. Verg. Eng. Hist.* (Camden) I. 140 With these portentius thinges albeit he was feared,..yeat, fearinge noe deceite..went forward on his waye. **1573** L. LLOYD *Marrow of Hist.* (1653) 153 Such portentuous miracles then seen in Rome. **1603** HOLLAND *Plutarch's Mor.* 1332 Many portenteous signes were given by terrible tempests. **1611** B. JONSON *Catiline* IV. ii, Stop that portentous mouth. **1641** MILTON *Reform.* II. Wks. 1851 III. 45 Let the Astrologer be dismay'd at the portentous blaze of comets. **1708** *Brit. Apollo* No. 14. 2/1 Actual Bleeding must needs be more Portentuous than a meer Dream. **1727** DE FOE *Syst. Magic* I. iv. (1840) 106 Having foretold the portentous events of the late meteor. **1829** LYTTON *Devereux* I. iii, There is something portentous in this sudden change. **1878** STEWART & TAIT *Unseen Univ.* ii. §66. 81 The event loses from thenceforth much of its portentous significance.

2. Applied, without any connected sense of augury, to an object exciting wonder, awe, or amazement; marvellous, monstrous, prodigious; hence as an intensive (sometimes *humorous*) = extraordinary.

1553 EDEN *Treat. Newe Ind.* (Arb.) 36 A foure foted beast of monstrous shape..hauinge..beneath his comon belye, an other belye lyke vnto a purse or bagge, in which he kepeth his yonge whelpes... This portentous beast with her three whelpes was broughte to Cimle in Spaine. **1555** —— *Decades* 159 A towne of such portentous byggenes. **1607** BP. J. KING *Serm. 5 Nov.* 23 So nefarious, flagitious, portentuous a wickednesse, as this was. **1639** FULLER *Holy War* V. xix. (1840) 275 By such portentous and extravagant numbers. **1695** WOODWARD *Nat. Hist. Earth* III. ii. (1723) 175 Such a Deluge..would require a portentous Quantity of Water. **1790** BURKE *Fr. Rev.* 252 See whether we can discover in their schemes the portentous ability, which may justify these bold undertakers. **1821** CRAIG *Lect. Drawing* i. 4 Since that portentuous period, the wealth of our happy country has..increased. **1823** LOCKHART *Reg. Dalton* II. i, A portentous apple-dumpling. **1877** GLADSTONE *Glean.* IV. xvii. 352 Russia will have to make..a portentous effort, when she is to leap from Constantinople to Calcutta.

por'tentously, *adv.* [f. prec. + -LY[2].] In a portentous manner; in a way that portends or foreshadows something unusual; hence (loosely) prodigiously, extraordinarily, astonishingly.

1656 TRAPP *Comm. 2 Thess.* ii. 3 That breathing devil, so portentously, so peerlessly vicious. **1755** WARBURTON *Div. Legat.* (ed. 4) I. II. iv. 246 Creatures, which by a reciprocal translation of the parts to one another, became all portentously deformed. **1816** SCOTT *Antiq.* vii, The distant sea..lay almost portentously still. **1858** BUCKLE *Civiliz.* (1869) II. viii. 468 The decline was portentously rapid. **1872** MORLEY *Voltaire* i. (1886) 9 Portentously significant silence. **1882** HAWTHORNE *Fort. Fool* I. xviii, He would be portentously severe against very trifling shortcomings.

porteous: see PORTAS. (Common in Sc. legal use.)

portepyne, obs. form of PORCUPINE.

porter ('pɔətə(r)), *sb.*[1] Forms: 3– **porter**; 3–5 **-ere**, 4 **-or**, (6 *Sc.*) **-ar**, 4–5 **-are**, **-our**, 5 **-eour**, **-iere**, 6 *Sc.* **-eir**. [ME. and AF. *porter* = OF. *portier* (12th c. in Godef.):—late L. *portārius* door-keeper, f. L. *porta* door: see -ER[2].]

1. a. One who has charge of a door or gate, esp. at the entrance of a fortified town or of a castle or other large building, a public institution, etc.; a gate-keeper, door-keeper, janitor.

c **1290** *S. Eng. Leg.* I. 382/210 þat ich moste here porter beo. *a* **1300** *Cursor M.* 10013 At ȝates four er four porters [*v.rr.* -eris, -eres] þat nathing mai cum in þat ders. **1382** WYCLIF *John* x. 3 To this the porter openeth, and the scheep heeren his vois. *c* **1400** *Apol. Loll.* 35 þei schal be in my sanctuari huschers, & portars. **1413** *Pilgr. Sowle* (Caxton) I. x. (1859) 7 Peter is porter of heuen and lyeutenant of the souerayn lord in erthe. **1433** *Rolls of Parlt.* IV. 475/2 By the hondis of his Portour of the said Castell. **1530** PALSGR. 257/1 Porter, a kepar of a gate, *portier*. *a* **1631** DONNE *Lett.* (1651) 32 Like a porter in a great house, ever nearest the door, but seldomest abroad. *c* **1720** PRIOR *Wandering Pilgrim* 46 Let him in thy hall but stand, And wear a porter's gown. **1800** *Med. Jrnl.* III. 178 There shall be a resident Apothecary,..a Secretary, a Collector, a Porter, and such other Officers as shall be found necessary. **1885** MORLEY *Crit. Misc., Pattison's Mem.* III. 151 Accomplishments..more fitted for the porter of a workhouse than for the head of a college. *fig.* **1377** LANGL. *P. Pl.* B. xx. 296 And made pees porter [*C.* portor, -our] to pynne þe ȝates. *c* **1400** tr. *Secreta Secret., Gov. Lordsh.* 97 þes v. portours byfore-sayd er þe v. wyttes, þat dwellys yn þe eighen, yn þe eryn, yn þe nese, yn þe tonge, and yn þe hondes. **1423** JAS. I *Kingis Q.* cxxv, I fand, full redy at the ȝate, The maister portare, callit pacience. **1610** T. COLLINS *Mercy* in Farr *S.P. Jas. I* (1848) 357 Mercy's the porter of heauen's pretious dores. **1614** PURCHAS *Pilgrimage* 531 Two mightie Colosses or statues of Lions, were set as porters at the doore. **1668** BP. HOPKINS *Serm.*, *Vanity* (1685) 72 God hath set that grim porter, Death, at the gate.

b. Applied to a watch-dog. **c.** (See quot. 1846.)

c **1420** LYDG. *Assembly of Gods* 37 Cerberus, the porter of hell, with hys cheyne. *a* **1661** FULLER *Worthies*, *Somerset* (1662) III. 18 [Mastiffs] are not (like Apes) the fooles and jesters, but the useful Servants in a Family, viz. the Porters thereof. **1846** *P. Parley's Ann.* VII. 325 Gamekeepers give various names to rabbits: with them they are warreners, porters, sweethearts, and hedgehogs... The porter's favourite haunt is in gentlemen's pleasure grounds.

†**2.** *Anat.* (tr. Gr. πυλωρός): The pyloric orifice of the stomach, where it opens into the small intestine. *Obs.*

1594 T. B. *La Primaud. Fr. Acad.* II. 349 It beginneth at the porter of the stomach, and is so seated beside the liuer. **1615** CROOKE *Body of Man* 119 It is called πυλωρός or the Porter, commonly the neather orifice.

3. *attrib.* and *Comb.*: **porter's chair** (see quot. 1969); **porter's lodge** (†**porter-lodge**), a lodge for the porter at the gate of the castle, park, etc. (formerly a place of corporal punishment for servants and dependants); †**porter-vein**, the *vena portæ* or portal vein (see PORTAL *a.* 2).

1939 A. CHRISTIE *Ten Little Niggers* viii. 109 On the main terrace, Mr. Justice Wargrave sat huddled in a *porter's chair. **1953** J. CARY *Except the Lord* xxxv. 152, I was able to assist her own efforts enough to get her into her usual armchair, one of those great leather chairs with a high domed back, which were called porter's chairs and were valued in farmhouses for their power of keeping out draughts. **1969** J. GLOAG *Short Dict. Furnit.* (rev. ed.) 532 *Porter's chair*, a high-backed armchair with wings raised to an arched hood, upholstered in leather, and placed in the hall of a town or country house, so that the porter or page boy on door duty could sit protected from draughts. Such chairs were introduced in the 16th century, and during the Georgian period were found in the entrance hall to every well-furnished house. **1972** N. MARSH *Tied up in Tinsel* viii. 195 He..sat down in one of two great porter's chairs that flanked the fireplace. **1471-2** *Durham Acc. Rolls* (Surtees) 644 Factura muri infra le *Porterloge. **1500-20** DUNBAR *Poems* xlii. 76 Strangenes, quhair that he did ly, Wes brint in to the porter luge. *a* **1592** GREENE *Newes fr. Heaven & Hell* (1593) Bj, Wee be not farre from Heauen gates, and if S. Peter should understand of your abuse, I knowe he would commit you both to the Porters Lodge. **1623** MASSINGER *Dk. Milan* III. ii, Fit company only for pages and for footboys That have perused the porter's lodge. **1822** W. IRVING *Sketch Bk.*, *Christmas Eve*, Close adjoining was the porter's lodge. **1899** CROCKETT *Kit Kennedy* 106 Gang doon to the porter-lodge, and wait till I come till ye. **1625** HART *Anat. Ur.* II. viii. 105 But what if such creatures were conueyed..through the mesaraicke veines into the great *porter veine? **1686** A. Snape *Anat. Horse* I. ix. 17 A small Vein..called *pylorica* or Porter-vein.

Hence **'porter** *v.*[1] *intr.*, to be or act as a porter.

1605 [see DEVIL *sb.* 23 a]. **1627** P. Fletcher *Locusts* IV. xxviii, Wee'l hold their heart, wee'l porter at their eare.

porter ('pɔətə(r)), *sb.*[2] Also 4 portour, 5 -oure, -owre. [ME. *portour*, a. OF. *porteour* (12th c. in Godef.) (mod.F. *-eur*):—L. *portātōr-em*, agent-noun f. L. *portāre* to carry, PORT *v.*[1] The ending *-our* was changed in 16th c. to *-er*: see -ER[2] 3.]

1. a. A person whose employment is to carry burdens; now *esp.* a servant of a railway company employed to carry luggage at a station (in full, ***railway porter***).

† ***porter's ale, beer***: see PORTER *sb.*[3] ***porter's knot***: see KNOT *sb.*[1] 5.

1382 Wyclif *1 Chron.* xvi. 42 The sonis forsothe of Ydithym he made to ben porters. **1393** Langl. *P. Pl.* C. VII. 370 A dosen harlotes Of portours and of pykeporses and pylede toþ-drawers. **1469** *Cal. Anc. Rec. Dublin* (1889) I. 336 If any of the portoures goo owt with cariage into the contry. **1530** Palsgr. 257/1 Porter of burdens, *crochetevr*. **1650** Bulwer *Anthropomet.* 114, I saw a Porter..drink up a Flagon of Beer. **1683** Moxon *Mech. Exerc., Printing* xxi. ¶2 About an hundred Pounds weight, viz. a Porters Burthen. **1809** R. Langford *Introd. Trade* 134 Porters,..employed to carry goods or parcels, also persons duly authorised, who attend wharfs for employment in various capacities respecting shipping. **1878** F. S. Williams *Midl. Railw.* 621 Porters for the passenger department are not accepted if they are less than 5 ft. 8 in. high. **1890** *Daily News* 17 Nov. 5/4 The Fellowship Porters—who must not be confounded with their humbler brethren the 'Ticket Porters' and the 'Tackle Porters'—are an association with a standing that entitles them to a hearing. **1898** *Westm. Gaz.* 15 July 4/2 The porter's rest, which stood so long on the north side of St. Paul's, disappeared at Jubilee time last year. **1901** *Census Schedule, Instruct.*, Porters..should specify the nature of their employment—as Railway Porter. The term Porter should never be used alone.

b. *gen.* and *fig.* One who or that which carries or conveys; a bearer, carrier.

1581 Marbeck *Bk. of Notes* 700 There is no need of porter, of a mediatour or minister, say onely, Lord haue mercie vpon me. **1634** Bp. Hall *Contempl., N.T.* IV. xxxii, Simon of Cyrene is forced to be the porter of Thy cross. **1659** T. Pecke *Parnassi Puerp.* 67 The Grecian Tongue, Porter of Wit, and Art. **1817** *Sporting Mag.* L. 231 It enables him [the spaniel] to be a good roader, as it is styled in the south; in the north it is termed a good porter. **1896** *Allbutt's Syst. Med.* I. 868 Ships..are not such good porters of cholera as caravans, armies, hordes of pilgrims and unsanitary travellers.

c. (See quot.)

1607 Cowell *Interpr.*, Porter in the circuit of Iustices, is an officer that carieth a verge or white rodde before the Iustices in Eyre, so called, *a portando virgam, an. 13 Ed. I cap.* 24. **1772** *Jacob's Law Dict.* s.v., There is also a porter bearing a verge before the justices of either bench.

d. In full, ***hospital porter***: a person employed by a hospital to convey patients and to carry out other general duties.

1950 G. B. Shaw *Farfetched Fables* III. 109 They offered me a job as hospital porter because I'm physically strong. **1964** D. Francis *Nerve* vi. 64 The nurse came back with a stretcher trolley and two khaki-overalled porters... We waited outside in the hall, and saw them trundle Pip off towards the open lift. **1975** *Oxford Times* 7 Nov. 4/8 An Oxford hospital porter with a grudge against his employers used cheques he had stolen and forged..to obtain over £700 from banks in the city.

2. An appliance for lifting, carrying, or supporting.

†**a.** A lever. *Obs.*

1538 Elyot *Dict.*, *Palange*, leauers or porters, wherewith they left and beare tymbre, and suche like thynges of greatte weight. *Palango*.., to beare on leyuars or porters. **1566** Withals *Dict.* 32/1.

†**b.** A supporting structure of timber or stone. (Cf. BEARER 9.) *Obs.*

1591 Lodge *Diogenes* (Hunter. Cl.) 19 He..swore that he would ouerthrowe the porters and bearers, which he practising to doo, the timber fell sodainly in the midst of his sawing.

c. An iron bar attached to a heavy body to be forged, by which it may, when suspended from a crane, be guided beneath the hammer or into the furnace; a porter-rod. Also, a bar from the end of which something (e.g. a knife-blade) is forged. (Knight *Dict. Mech.*)

1794 *Rigging & Seamanship* I. 78 (*Anchor*), *Porter*, a straight bar of iron, about 2 inches square, confined at one end to the end of the shank. **1839** Ure *Dict. Arts* 44 The lower part [of an anchor] is left disunited, but has carrier iron bars, or *porters*, as these prolongation rods are commonly called, welded to the extremity of each portion. *Ibid.* 704 The *bloom* or rough ball, from the puddle furnace, is laid and turned about upon it, by means of a rod of iron welded to each of them, called a *porter*. **1875** Knight *Dict. Mech.* s.v., A cross lever fixed to the porter is the means of rotating the forging beneath the hammer.

d. A light carriage with two or three wheels, to hold up from the ground the chain or rope of a steam plough.

1864 *Jrnl. R. Agric. Soc.* XXV. II. 416 The Travelling-porters are intended to carry the implement rope, the outer rope being best carried by the ordinary three-wheel porters.

3. *Weaving.* (*Sc.*) = BEER *sb.*[3]

1814 A. Peddie *Manuf., Weaver & Warp. Assist.* (1818) 152 What the Scotch weavers term a Porter, the English term a beer. **1846** G. White *Treat. Weaving* 277 The hundred splits in all kinds of reeds is nominally divided into five equal portions for the sake of calculation, called porters in Scotland and beers in England. **1867** Black *Hist. Brechin* xii. 271 A thirty porter or 600 reed is divided into 600 openings in the breadth of 37 inches: 20 of these openings are called a porter. **1894** *Dundee Advertiser* 5 July 4 The new duty of 20 per cent. would also apply to tarpauling up to 11 or 12 porters.

4. *attrib.* and *Comb.*, as ***porter-beer*** (see PORTER *sb.*[3]), ***-clerk***, ***-crab*** (see quot.), ***-guard***, ***-riot***, ***-rod*** (= sense 2 c).

1906 *Daily Chron.* 25 Jan. 6/7 A youth of seventeen, engaged there as *porter-clerk. **1904** *Ibid.* 11 Jan. 3/3 At Patami was obtained the '*porter' crab, which lies in the mud clasping a sea anemone to its back by means of modified legs. **1851** Gallenga *Italy* 181 Student-plots at Pisa, *porter-riots at Leghorn, and demonstrations at Florence. **1839** Ure *Dict. Arts* 44 (*Anchor*) To one end a *porter rod is fastened, by which the palm is carried and turned round in the fire during the progress of the fabrication.

Hence **'porter** *v.*[2] *trans.*, to carry as a porter (sense 1), or by means of a porter or porters (sense 2 d); also, (of any person) to carry from one place to another; = PORTAGE *v.*; **'portering**, the work or occupation of a porter; also as *ppl. a.*

1609 *Ev. Woman in Hum.* II. i. in Bullen *O. Pl.* IV, At night he shall be portered to our chamber. **1864** *Jrnl. R. Agric. Soc.* XXV. II. 395 It would have been interesting..to have tested the draft of this rope dragging on the surface, against the wire rope properly 'portered'. **1904** *Daily Chron.* 4 July 6/7 Nominally he is a licensed porter,..but he does not do much portering. **1927** *Glasgow Herald* 13 Aug. 8 This impressionable passenger thinks that it must be a rule of the railway portering brotherhood to make each footfall 'tell' to its uttermost. **1966** D. Varaday *Gara-Yaka's Domain* xiii. 147 Tau decided to camp there..and..strengthen Cwgki and save himself the unwelcome bother of portering his riches. **1967** D. Cooper *Psychiatry & Anti-Psychiatry* v. 99 A member of the portering staff who witnessed the incident called a nurse who took her back to her ward. **1971** C. Bonington *Annapurna South Face* iv. 46 The Sherpas, who hold a monopoly in high-altitude portering, come from Sola Khumbu just opposite Everest. **1974** *Daily Tel.* 13 Dec. 14 We portered all the rapids. We did this because it would have been foolhardy for two relatively inexperienced canoeists to attempt them. **1977** J. I. M. Stewart *Madonna of Astrolabe* iii. 60 I've just been talking to a couple of young men who have been doing some portering for you. **1978** *Morecambe Guardian* 14 Mar. 29/7 (Advt.), Applicants should be fit and active as the work entails some portering and assisting the physiotherapists with the walking of elderly patients.

porter ('pɔətə(r)), *sb.*[3] [Short for ***porter's ale***, ***porter's beer***, or ***porter beer*** (PORTER *sb.*[2]), app. because orig. made for or chiefly drunk by porters and the lower class of labourers: cf. the early quots.

There is no direct contemporary evidence as to the origin of the name. Statements going back to *c* 1750 attribute the first brewing of the liquor to Ralph Harwood 'at the place afterwards called Doctor's Brewhouse, on the east side of High Street, Shoreditch'; but these statements concern the origin not of the appellations *porter's ale*, *porter's beer*, but of the term *entire*. The probability is that *porter's ale* or *beer* arose as a popular descriptive appellation.]

a. A kind of beer, of a dark brown colour and bitterish taste, brewed from malt partly charred or browned by drying at a high temperature.

α. **1727** Swift *Further Acc. E. Curll* Wks. 1755 III. I. 161 Nursed up on grey peas, bullocks liver, and porters ale. **1734** Swift in *Mrs. Delaney's Life & Corr.* (1861) I. 502, I cannot make shifts..by starving in scanty lodgings,..as I used to do in London, with port-wine, or perhaps Porter's ale, to save charges! **1745** Mortimer in *Phil. Trans.* XLIII. 552 Their Urine..as high-coloured as Porter's Beer. **1770** Massie *Reas. agst. Tax on Malt* 5 So that every Person.., must pay more than Three Halfpence for a Pint of Porter-Beer in London.

β. **1739** 'R. Bull' tr. *Dedekindus' Grobianus* 139 The Fumes of Porter, Stout, or Home-brew'd Ale. **1743** *Lond. & Country Brew.* III. (ed. 2) 221 Of Brewing Butt-Beer, called Porter. *c* **1750** J. Gutteridge (of Shoreditch) in *Gentl. Mag.* May (1819) 394/2 Harwood, my townsman, he invented first Porter to rival wine, and quench the thirst. Porter,..Whose reputation rises more and more. **1772** *Town & Country Mag.* 117 Hard working people delight in a kind of strong beer called porter, brown, clear, bitter and wholesome. **1781** in Hone *Every-day Bk.* (1827) II. 836 My electors shall have porter at threepence a pot. **1839** Ure *Dict. Arts* s.v., At first the essential distinction of porter arose from its wort being made with highly-kilned brown malt. **1846** McCulloch *Acc. Brit. Empire* (1854) I. 757 Breweries... The latter principally produce porter, the favourite beverage of the Londoners. **1903** Somerville & 'Ross' *All on Irish Shore* 73 Mrs Brennan added another spoonful of brown sugar to the porter that she was mulling in a saucepan on the range. **1919** G. B. Shaw *O'Flaherty V.C.* in *Heartbreak House* 179 And look at your fine new uniform stained already with..the porter youve been drinking. **1922** E. O'Neill *Anna Christie* (1923) I. 6 Johnny draws the lager and porter and sets the big, foaming schooners before them. **1939** Joyce *Finnegans Wake* (1964) III. 511 I've a big suggestion it was about the pint of porter. **1973** [see PORTER-HOUSE 2].

b. *attrib.* and *Comb.*, as ***porter bar***, ***-bottle***, ***-brewer***, ***-brewery***, ***-malt***, ***-pot***, ***-pump***, ***-shop***, ***-yeast***; ***porter-coloured***, ***-drinking***, ***-hued*** adjs.; **porter-cup**, a mixed beverage containing porter (see quot.) See also PORTER-HOUSE.

1935 Dylan Thomas *Let.* July (1966) 157 One day a week I shall walk the miles to Glendormatie where there is a shop and *porter bar. **1922** Joyce *Ulysses* 42 A *porterbottle stood up, stogged to its waist, in the cakey sand dough. **1818** Calvert in *Parl. Deb.* 1012 It had been proved by those *porter brewers who had been examined before the police committee. **1776** Adam Smith *W.N.* v. ii. (1869) II. 486 In the *porter brewery of London, a quarter of malt is commonly brewed into more than two barrels and a half, sometimes into three barrels of porter. **1898** Kipling in *Morn. Post* 9 Nov. 5/2 Clumps of gorse and heather and the *porter-coloured pools of bog water. **1880** *Barman's Manual* 51 *Porter Cup. Mix, in a tankard, a bottle of porter and an equal quantity of table ale; pour in a glass of brandy and a dessert-spoonful of syrup of ginger; add 3 or 4 lumps of sugar and a nutmeg grated [etc.]. **1851** G. Blyth *Remin. Mission. Life* II. 121 His *porter-drinking propensities. **1863** *Royal Exchange Assurance* Art. ii, Maltsters (who make no high-dried or *porter malt). **1807** Southey *Lett. from Eng.* I. viii. 90 A transparency..which represented a loaf of bread saying to a pot of porter, I am coming down; to which the *porter-pot made answer, So am I. **1824** —— in *Life* (1849) I. 137 He used to..fling the porter-pot or the poker at me. **1838** Dickens *O. Twist* xxvii, A porter-pot and a wine-bottle. **1804** Larwood *No Gun Boats* 15 The Caffés of France, and the *Porter Shops of England. *c* **1796** Sir J. Dalrymple *Observ. Yeast-cake* 2 London *porter-yeast..is preferred..by the distillers.

porter *v.*[1], [2]: see PORTER *sb.*[1], [2].

porter, variant of PORTURE *v. Obs.*

porterage ('pɔətərɪdʒ), *sb.*[1] [f. PORTER *sb.*[2] + -AGE.]

1. The action or work of a porter; carriage or transportation of goods, parcels, etc.; also, the charge for this, or the manpower available for hire as porters.

1437–8 in *5th Rep. Hist. MSS. Comm.* 541/1, 5*s.* 8*d.* received from the Porters in the Strande, for the porterage of fish this year. **1611** *Lett. E. India Co.* (1896) I. 141 Item for porterage of particulars above to the barque, 03. 13. **1671** L. Roberts *Merch. Map Commerce* (ed. 2) 54 Other charges are Boat-hire, Wharfage, Porterage and Ware-house room. **1761** *Chron.* in *Ann. Reg.* 123/2 The carrier had no right to stop the goose for the porterage. **1809** R. Langford *Introd. Trade* 134 *Porterage*, the hire of porters. **1869** Tozer *Highl. Turkey* I. 241 Female porterage is the custom of the country. **1880** *Post Office Guide* 235 When the addressee resides beyond the free delivery, porterage is charged. **1884** *G.W.R. Time Tables* July 83 No charge for porterage..at Holyhead. **1925** E. F. Norton *Fight for Everest: 1924* 122 He went down with Bruce and Irvine that same day to Camp III, intent on investigating afresh with Bruce's aid the question of available porterage.

†**2.** Something to be carried, a burden. *Obs. rare.*

1666 J. Smith *Old Age* (1676) 179 These Porters do now become a porterage themselves, and those parts that were wont to bear the greatest burdens, are now so great a burden.

3. *attrib.* as ***porterage fee***, ***work***.

1774 *Acts Gen. Assembly Georgia* (1881) 418 For any Porterage Work from the several parts of the Town..to any of the Wharves the like rates. **1895** *Westm. Gaz.* 18 Apr. 7/1 Even the British Commissioner when he journeys to and from Uganda has to employ slave labour for porterage purposes. **1906** *Daily Chron.* 12 Nov. 5/4 A tariff regulating porterage fees. **1957** M. Banton *W. Afr. City* ii. 31 Members of this tribe had started coming to Freetown to pick up a living by doing porterage work in the streets.

'porterage, *sb.*[2] [f. PORTER *sb.*[1] + -AGE.] The duty or occupation of a porter or door-keeper. Also, the availability of the services of a porter or caretaker.

1763 Churchill *Duellist* II. 161 In rules of Porterage untaught. **1975** *Country Life* 22 May (Suppl.) 48/1 Luxury flats..24 hour porterage. **1980** *Sunday Times* 20 Jan. 49/1 Purpose-built studio flat..CH, CHW, porterage.

porteress: see PORTRESS.

'porter-house. Chiefly *U.S.* [f. PORTER *sb.*[3] + HOUSE *sb.* Cf. *ale-house*.] **1. a.** A house at which porter and other malt liquors are retailed; also, one where steaks, chops, etc. are served, a chop-house.

c **1758** S. Foote *Diversions of Morning* in T. Wilkinson *Wandering Patentee* (1795) IV. 239, I heard a goodish-looking well-dress'd man, that sat in the next box at the porter-house, affirm, that to his knowledge, if you proceeded to exhibit, you and your pupils would be all sent to Bridewell. **1786** *N.Y. Directory* 41 Norris Rich. porter-house, 3, Broad-street. **1800** Cobbett in Polwhele *Trad. & Recoll.* (1826) II. 531 They adjourned from the porter-houses and gin-shops to the cheese-mongers and bakers. **1807–8** W. Irving *Salmag.* (1824) 286 Those temples of politics, popularity, and smoke, the ward porter-houses. **1858** *N.Y. Tribune* 16 Mar. 3/3 This morning, an altercation took place in the porter-house of Michael Byrne,..between Joseph Kelly..and others. **1939** Joyce *Finnegans Wake* 405 He was immense, topping swell for he was after having a great time of it..in a porterhouse..if you want to know, Saint Lawzenge of Toole's, the Wheel of Fortune.

b. *attrib.*, as ***porter-house boy***; **porter-house steak** (*U.S.*), 'a beefsteak consisting of a choice cut of the beef between the sirloin and the tenderloin..: supposed to derive its name from a well-known porter-house in New York' (*Cent. Dict.*).

1807 Southey *Espriella's Lett.* (1808) I. 67 Then came the porter-house boy for the pewter-pots. **1842** C. Mathews *Career of Puffer Hopkins* xiii. 90 But I guess I'll take a small porter-house steak, without the bone. **1864** Sala in *Daily Tel.* 27 Sept., The 'tenderloin', the 'porterhouse' steak of America, are infinitely superior to our much-vaunted rump steak. **1883** *Harper's Mag.* Aug. 462/2 A porter-house steak learned to expect him on the noon of every day. **1902** *Westm. Gaz.* 11 Apr. 6/3 Porterhouse steaks sold for 15 *c.* and now sell for 24 *c.* **1904** *Nation* (N.Y.) 31 Mar. 245 The picture was drawn of the country stepping up to the butchers' block and demanding porterhouse and sirloin steaks in abundance. **1959** [see CHATEAUBRIAND]. **1979** W. H.

CANAWAY *Solid Gold Buddha* xxiii. 148 Two porterhouse steaks..washed down with three bottles of Rhône wine.

2. *ellipt.* A porter-house steak. Also *attrib.*

1854 *Harper's Mag.* Jan. 269/2 Will you have it rare or well-done? Shall it be a porter-house? **1908** G. H. LORIMER *Jack Spurlock* iv. 63 That [dream] in which the waiter is just taking the covers off a double porter-house, medium, with fresh mushrooms on top. **1911** [see RARE *a.*² b]. **1958** V. P. JOHNS *Servant's Probl.* ii. 17 This is a juicy porterhouse neighborhood. **1973** G. BEARE *Snake on Grave* vii. 38 He would never pass up a pint of porter for a pound of Porterhouse.

'porterless, *a.* [f. PORTER *sb.*² + -LESS.] Lacking a porter or porters.

1885 [see GARE *sb.*⁵]. **1973** *Daily Tel.* 30 June 12/6 Here is my timetable: Arrive Weymouth Town Station shortly before midnight..; hump baggage up long, dark, porterless platform and hurl it bodily into waiting pantechnicon.

'porterlike, *a.* [f. PORTER *sb.*² + LIKE *a.*] Like a porter: = PORTERLY *a.*²

1598 FLORIO, *Facchinarie*, base, filthie, rascally, porter-like-tricks.

† **'porterly,** *a.*¹ *Obs. rare*⁻¹. [f. PORTER *sb.*¹ + LY¹.] Proper to a porter or door-keeper.

1581 J. BELL *Haddon's Answ. Osor.* 397 b, Wherein he promised full remission..in the fullnesse of his Porterly power [= power of the keys].

† **'porterly,** *a.*² and *adv. Obs.* [f. PORTER *sb.*²]

A. *adj.* Pertaining to, or characteristic of, a porter (PORTER *sb.*²); hence, Rude, vulgar, low.

1603 FLORIO *Montaigne* (1634) 140 Off the stage,..they are base rascals, vagabond abjects, and porterly hirelings. **1673** KIRKMAN *Unlucky Citizen* 108 That Porterly Game of Nine-pins. **1709** *Brit. Apollo* II. No. 48. 2/2 Silly and Porterly Reflections on you. **1765** WESLEY *Jrnl.* 4 Sept., His language was as..foul, and porterly, as ever was heard at Billingsgate.

B. *adv.* In a 'porterly' manner; vulgarly.

1659 TORRIANO, *Facchinésco*, basely, or porterly. **1663** DRYDEN *Wild Gallant* I. i, I was porterly drunk, and that I hate of all things in nature.

portership¹ ('pɔətəʃɪp). [f. PORTER *sb.*¹ + -SHIP.] The office of porter or door-keeper; also with possessive, as a humorous title.

1450 *Rolls of Parlt.* V. 197/2 Th' office of the Portership of the Castell of Rutland. **1503** *Act 19 Hen. VII*, c. 10 §7 The office of Porter or Portershipp of the same Castell. **1592** NASHE *P. Penilesse* Wks. (Grosart) II. 95, I commend them ..to the protection of your Portership. **1610** T. COCKS *Diary* (1901) 98 Yf Short and he got not through for the patent of the portershipp. **1886** LOWELL *Lett.* (1894) II. 349 Content with a portership in the House of the Lord.

'portership². [f. PORTER *sb.*² + -SHIP.] The office of a porter or carrier of burdens.

1521 *Maldon, Essex, Liber B.* 57 The tyme yew shall contynewe in the office of portershipp of this towne.

† **portery, portary.** *Sc. Obs.* [a. MFl. *porterie, -erije*, f. *porter* citizen, burgher, f. *port* town, city: see PORT *sb.*²] Citizenship or burghership in a Flemish or Dutch city; the body of citizens collectively; the rights or privileges of a citizen or burgher (in the Netherlands).

(In the quotation referring to Scottish merchants or factors residing in Flanders.)

1565 *Reg. Privy Council Scot.* I. 333 All factouris that ar Scottismen..sall answer to the Conservatour, and nocht allege fra him to thair portary; and gif thai will abyde at thair portary, and nocht obey to the said Conservatour, the Quenis majestie..charges the said Conservatour that he discharge..hir liegis.

portes(s, porteur, var. PORTAS, PORTURE *sb.*¹

‖ **porteur** (pɔrtœr). *Ballet.* [Fr., lit. 'one who carries'.] (see quot. 1957.)

1936 A. HASKELL in 'C. Brahms' *Footnotes to Ballet* 5 Taglioni (1821) was frail and ethereal, and..she shone so brightly that the male was soon degraded to the rôle of *porteur* from which Nijinsky finally rescued it. **1949** *Ballet Ann.* III. 93 With the advent of the Italian ballerina..ballet became even more a vehicle for the virtuosity of the female dancer backed by rows of pretty girls in the *corps de ballet*. The male dancer was..relegated to the position of *porteur*. **1957** G. B. L. WILSON *Dict. Ballet* 220 *Porteur*, Fr. lit. one who carries, a porter. A male dancer whose sole function is to lift the ballerina in supported leaps and similar movements. **1961** *Ibid.* (rev. ed.) 235 The male dancer in Western Europe was relegated to the rôle of a porteur during the half century preceding the coming of the Diaghileff Ballet and male dancing rôles were taken by the danseuse travestie.

portfire ('pɔətfaɪə(r)). [After F. *porte-feu*, in same sense: see PORTE-.] A device used formerly for firing artillery, and now for firing rockets and other fireworks, and for igniting an explosive in mining, etc.; = FUSE, MATCH *sb.*² 2.

1647 NYE *Gunnery* ix. 77 For the priming thereof, make a Potfire [*sic*], or Fuse. **1669** STURMY *Mariner's Mag.* v. xiii. 90 Leaving a small hole or a Port-Fire. **1710** J. HARRIS *Lex. Techn.* II, *Portfire*, is a Composition of Meal, Powder, Sulphur and Salt-Peter drove into a Case of Paper, but not very hard; 'tis about 9 or 10 Inches long, and is used to fire Guns and Mortars instead of Match. **1798** CAPT. BERRY in Nicolas *Disp. Nelson* (1845) III. 52 A port fire from L'Orient fell into the main royal of the Alexander. **1859** F. A. GRIFFITHS *Artil. Man.* (1862) 95 Portfires are of four different natures—viz., Common portfires, Percussion portfires, Miners' portfires, and Slow portfires. **1875** KNIGHT *Dict. Mech.* s.v., The *common port-fire* is sixteen inches long, and is packed with a composition which burns at the rate of about one inch per minute. The *slow port-fire* consists of paper impregnated with saltpeter and rolled into a solid cylinder about sixteen inches long. It will burn three or four hours.

attrib. **1814** LEWIS & CLARK *Exp. Missouri* (1893) III. 922 Taking a port-fire match from his pocket. **1828** J. M. SPEARMAN *Brit. Gunner* (ed. 2) 331 Portfires... Papers for forming portfire cases. **1875** KNIGHT *Dict. Mech.*, *Port-fire Clipper*, a nippers for cutting off the ends of port-fires.

† **'port-flask.** *Obs. rare.* [See PORTE-.] A belt or attachment for carrying a drinking-flask.

1598 R. BARRET *Theor. Warres* III. i. 34 With his flaske at his girdle, or hanging by a Port-flask, or Flask-leather vpon the right thigh.

portfolio (pɔət'fəʊlɪəʊ). Also 8 porto folio, portefolio, port folio, 8–9 port-folio. [In 18th c. *porto folio*, ad. It. *portafogli*, f. *porta*, imper. of *portare* to carry + *fogli*, leaves, sheets of paper, pl. of *foglio*:—L. *folium* leaf. First element altered after F. *portefeuille*: see PORTE-.]

1. a. A receptacle or case for keeping loose sheets of paper, prints, drawings, maps, music, or the like; usually in the form of a large book-cover, and sometimes having sheets of paper fixed in it, between which specimens are placed. Also *fig.*

1722 J. RICHARDSON *Statues, etc. Italy* 13 Another Porto Folio, all of Raffaele. **1764** *Chron.* in *Ann. Reg.* 85/1 A porto folio of choice original designs. **1768** FORSTER in *Phil. Trans.* LVIII. 215 More than 3000 MSS. maps and drawings were kept in their portefolios. **1796** *Mod. Gulliver* 53, I tied up my port folio. **1806–7** J. BERESFORD *Miseries Hum. Life* (1826) XII. vii, An huge portfolio of Miss' or Master's early school drawings. **1812** COMBE *Picturesque* XIV. (1813) 113 The Doctor forward stepp'd to shew The wealth of his port-folio. **1838** LYTTON *Alice* I. ix, His servant..placed his portfolios and letter-boxes on the table. **1858** C. W. GOODWIN in *Cambr. Ess.* 246 The compilers did not always confine themselves to the stores of their own portfolios.

b. The collection of securities held by an investing institution or individual; also, a list of such securities.

1930 *Economist* 4 Jan. 2/1 This fall is partly due to the banks' failure to secure any of last week's Treasury Bills, which is forcing them to replenish their portfolios in the market. *Ibid.* 11 Jan. 83/2 The more notable changes in the portfolio comprise an increase in the number of Chartered shares. **1948** *Ibid.* 3 Jan. 29/2 The banks last year took a hard knock on their gilt-edged portfolios. *Ibid.* 32/1 These examples demonstrate how important it is for the discount houses to keep their portfolios short. **1955** *Times* 3 June 10/3 The investment policy of the Company is under the constant review of the board and the portfolio periodically examined by a special committee of directors. **1967** [see *investment trust* s.v. INVESTMENT 5 b]. **1967** *Listener* 5 Oct. 423 (Advt.), M & G General Trust Fund is a very big Fund (over £26m.) with a portfolio largely of British 'blue chips', plus a number of overseas stocks. **1969** J. ARGENTI *Managem. Techniques* 199 Just as an investor tries to select a portfolio of shares to give him a good return without too much risk, so the Board of a company tries to do the same thing when choosing a 'portfolio' of subsidiary companies. **1972** *Accountant* 17 Aug. 206/1 A valuation of the entire portfolio, the result to be incorporated in the current year's accounts. **1973** C. WILLIAMS *Man of Leash* (1974) 63 He was ..buying more stock all the time. His portfolio was worth a million or a little over. **1978** *N.Y. Times* 30 Mar. D 1/2 Analysts said that institutions stepped up their stock purchases yesterday to dress up their portfolios before the end of the first quarter.

2. *spec.* Such a receptacle containing the official documents of a state department; hence *fig.* the office of a minister of state. Orig. said in reference to France and other foreign countries. Also in phr. ***without portfolio***, (of a government minister), not being in charge of a specific department of state. Cf. *Minister without Portfolio* s.v. MINISTER *sb.* 3 c.

1835 ALISON *Hist. Europe* (1849–50) V. xxxii. §8. 405 The portfolio of the war office was put into the hands of Carnot. **1845** M. PATTISON *Ess.* (1889) I. 2 As the subs of office quit their desks when premiers deliver up their portfolios. **1860** FREEMAN *Hist. Ess.* I. ii. 46 On the other side of the Channel, the Minister bears his portfolio, here the Secretary bears his seal. **1891** W. FRASER *Disraeli & his Day* 370 At the time when Lord John Russell held office under Lord Aberdeen 'without portfolio', Disraeli made a very happy hit. **1898** *Westm. Gaz.* 10 May 2/2 It seems hard that Lord Salisbury may do with impunity..what would cost Lord Rosebery not merely his windows but his portfolio.

3. *attrib.* and *Comb.*, as ***portfolio capital, form, -hunter*** (cf. *place-hunter*), ***manager, official, policy, security, selection***; **portfolio investment**, the purchase of stocks and shares in a variety of companies; **portfolio-stand**, a piece of furniture for holding portfolios, drawings, music, etc.

1964 *Economist* 30 May 1015/1 Flows of *portfolio capital. **1902** *Daily Chron.* 1 Oct. 3/4 The present monograph will be in *portfolio form, with many illustrations. **1899** *Westm. Gaz.* 13 June 1/2 Falls of Cabinets have become a custom and startle only *Portfolio-hunters. **1955** *Times* 29 July 5/2 It was a very complicated question because United States investment might be direct or it might be *portfolio investment. **1965** *Guardian* 8 Jan. 1 (Advt.), Possibilities of portfolio investment in Australia. **1972** *Accountant* 23 Mar. 386/2 Last month Kingside negotiated a $4 million, seven-year, multi-currency loan facility with Lloyds and Bolsa International Bank primarily for the purpose of portfolio investment in the United States and Europe. **1969** *Times* 5 May (Wall St. Suppl.) p. vi/3 'Mutual funds are being bought as equity equivalents..and I'm frankly very worried about it,' said a *portfolio manager for one of these funds. **1973** *N.Y. Law Jrnl.* 2 Aug. 3/3 Another bull market similar to the one that occurred following Thanksgiving 1971, says Kenneth Herlihy, portfolio manager of Philadelphia-based Decatur Income Fund. **1940** H. G. WELLS *Babes in Darkling Wood* IV. i. 322 They [*sc.* the Bolsheviks] only half-did the job, they cleaned up the site and then they jerry-built some unattractive sheds... A sort of mushroom growth of nasty little *portfolio officials may have sprung up on the clearing. **1969** *Times* 5 May (Wall St. Suppl.) p. iii/3 Credit demanders and institutional investors may not yet be convinced that there are downside risks in the aggressive implementation of economic plans and *portfolio policies. **1959** *Listener* 12 Feb. 272/1 American *portfolio securities. **1965** H. I. ANSOFF *Corporate Strategy* (1968) ii. 30 While CIT [*sc.* capital investment theory] deals with selection of physical assets for the firm, *portfolio selection concerns selecting securities, either for an individual investor or for an investment firm. **1969** J. ARGENTI *Managem. Techniques* 199 Portfolio Selection methods are very advanced mathematically. They are similar to Linear Programming.. but include a means of balancing risks and returns. **1887** RUSKIN *Præterita* II. 20 In his *portfolio-stands..were the entire series of the illustrations to Scott, to Byron.

Hence **port'folioed** *a.*, furnished with a portfolio.

1848 *Blackw. Mag.* Aug. 185 All portfolioed, all hand-booked..without compassion or conscience. **1892** *Review of Rev.* Jan. 6/2 Bewailing the consequences of portfolioed incapacity.

† **'port-glaive.** *Obs.* [ad. F. *porte-glaive*: see PORTE- and GLAIVE.] A sword-bearer; a member of the military and religious Order of the Knights Sword-bearers founded 1201 in Livonia.

1656 BLOUNT *Glossogr.*, *Portglaive*, a Sword-bearer. **1725** COATS *Dict. Her.* s.v., Knights of the Order of the Port-glaive, or Sword-Bearers in Poland, in Latin called *Ensiferi*. **1755** JOHNSON, *Portglave*, a sword bearer.

port-grave: see PORT-REEVE.

porth (pɔəθ). *Cornw. dial.* [Corn. and W. *porth*, ad. L. *portus* PORT¹.] A small bay or cove.

1860 *Biog. & Crit. fr. 'The Times'* 245 Romantic coves provincially called Porths. **1880** CHARL. M. MASON *Forty Shires* 301 One of the little lovely inlets, or porths, as they are called, which break every part of the Cornish coast.

port-hole ('pɔəthəʊl). Also porthole. [f. PORT *sb.*³ + HOLE *sb.*]

1. a. *Naut.* An aperture in a ship's side; *spec.* formerly one of those through which cannon were pointed; now, one of the apertures for the admission of light and air; = PORT *sb.*³ 2 b.

1591 PERCIVALL *Sp. Dict.*, *Portañola*, a port-hole, *porta*. *a* **1618** RALEIGH *Royal Navy* 26 Wont to plant great red Port-holes in their broad sides, where they carried no Ordnance at all. **1691** T. H[ALE] *Acc. New Invent.* p. x, So contrived the Port Holes therein, that most of her Guns might point to one Center. **1707** *Lond. Gaz.* No. 4329/5 [They] went through the Port-holes into the Long-boat. **1759** FALCONER *90-Gun Ship* 41 Full ninety brazen guns her port-holes fill. **1802** *Naval Chron.* VIII. 481 The contrivance of port-holes..is attributed to Descharges, a French ship-builder at Brest, in the reign of Louis the Twelfth. **1892** CLARK RUSSELL *Marriage at Sea* iii, A black steam-boat,..her portholes glittering as though the whole length of her was studded with brilliants.

fig. **1602** MARSTON *Antonio's Rev.* II. ii, The port holes Of sheathed spirit are nere corb'd up.

b. A small glazed window, often round, in the side of an aircraft or spacecraft.

1956 W. A. HEFLIN *U.S. Air Force Dict.* 395/1 *Porthole*, a naval term sometimes applied to a circular window in an aircraft. **1962** W. SCHIRRA in *Into Orbit* 33 They..pointed out that they had already stuck on a periscope and a couple of small port-holes, but we all felt strongly that a pilot ought to have a clear, visual reference to his surroundings. **1968** *Listener* 27 June 827/1 Departure by air could involve hazards quite separate from the lurking fears..of being sucked, à la James Bond, out of a porthole. **1970** T. HUGHES *Crow* 13 It was cosy in the rocket, he could not see much But he peered out through the portholes at Creation. **1970** W. SMITH *Gold Mine* xxxii. 79 The Boeing began to roll forward. Manfred twisted his head against the neck rest and peered through the Perspex porthole.

2. *transf.* **a.** An aperture in a wall for shooting through, etc.; an embrasure; **b.** a similar aperture in other structures, e.g. in the door of a furnace.

1644–5 N. DRAKE *Siege Pontefr.* (Surtees) 37 One of our men was looking out of a porthole on the round tower. **1703** MAUNDRELL *Journ. Jerus.* (1721) 19 It has the face of a Castle, being built with portholes for Artillery, instead of Windows. **1753** HANWAY *Trav.* (1762) I. III. xxxiv. 157 This city is inclosed within a wall above a mile in each square, with a great number of regular turrets and port-holes for arrows. **1870** J. ROSKELL in *Eng. Mech.* 18 Feb. 547/2 The 'port holes' are left open.

c. *Austral.* and *N.Z.* An aperture in the wall of a shearing shed through which each shearer passes the sheep when shorn into his indivdual counting-out pen.

1882 ARMSTRONG & CAMPBELL *Austral. Sheep. Husbandry* xv. 175 Upon the opposite side of the shearing board, 'port-holes', or small doorways, are made (one for each shearer), through which the sheep are turned when shorn. **1933** L. G. D. ACLAND in *Press* (Christchurch, N.Z.) 30 Sept. 15/7 *Counting out pens.* Each shearer has his own and passes his sheep through a *porthole* into his, so that each man's tally may be counted. **1956** G. BOWEN *Wool Away!* (ed. 2) iii. 43 A lot of time and effort can be wasted in switching off and kicking sheep out the porthole. **1965** [see CHUTE *sb.*¹ 3 b].

d. *Archæol.* A hole in a slab or two adjacent slabs of stone, large enough to allow the passage of a body into a chambered tomb.

1940 *Proc. Prehist. Soc.* VI. 133 Problems associated with the nature and origin of portholes in megalithic tombs in Europe. **1954** S. PIGGOTT *Neolithic Cultures Brit. Isles* v. 136 The chamber entrance was formed by a 'porthole' made by hollowing the edges of two adjacent slabs to form an oval hole through which it is just possible to gain access to the burial chamber. **1958** G. DANIEL *Megalith Builders W. Europe* ii. 44 Port-holes occur in southern Iberia and in a small number of tombs in France and Britain, as well as in the Gallery Graves of southern Sweden. **1963** *Field Archaeol.* (Ordnance Survey) (ed. 4) 30 Space does not permit a description of all the variations of entrances true and false, forecourts, passages, portholes, different forms of chamber, horn features, revetments, etc.

3. A steam port (PORT *sb.*³ 4).

1875 in KNIGHT *Dict. Mech.* **1888** HASLUCK *Model Engin. Handybk.* 27 On turning the fly-wheel the crank draws the piston-rod out and inclines the cylinder sideways, bringing the port-hole to the left. *Ibid.* 37 Fig. 29, where the size and position of each port-hole may be seen.

4. *attrib.* and *Comb.*, as ***port-hole shutter, window***; (sense 2 d) ***porthole cist, slab, stone***.

1766 ENTICK *London* IV. 88 The roof is..enlightened by four port-hole windows. **1892** E. REEVES *Homeward Bound* 95 We now find the advantage of the port-hole shutters. **1939** V. G. CHILDE *Dawn European Civilization* (ed. 3) ix. 168 Forssander seems inclined to explain Pontic elements in Central Europe by a migration from the Caucasus of the makers of Globular Amphoræ who would also have brought the idea of the porthole cist and the pit-cave tombs. *Ibid.* xii. 206 A porthole stone often enhances the resemblance of a built tomb's doorway to the entry into a natural or artificial cave. The desire to emphasize the similarity has in fact been suggested as an explanation for the porthole stone's origin. **1970** BRAY & TRUMP *Dict. Archaeol.* 185 *Port-hole slab*, a stone slab with a circular hole, often, though not exclusively, forming the entrance to a chamber tomb. Sometimes the hole is square, or the entrance is made from two slabs set side by side with notches cut from their adjoining edges.

Hence **'port-holed** *a.*, provided with a port-hole or port-holes.

1938 *Antiquity* XII. 302 Some of these (e.g. Züschen, Fritzlar) have a portholed septal slab. **1940** *Proc. Prehist. Soc.* VI. 155 These figures should give the lie to the frequent assertion..that Britain is peculiarly rich in portholed tombs. **1969** *Daily Tel.* (Colour Suppl.) 11 Apr. 40/2 The port-holed headquarters of the National Maritime Union.

porthors, -hos, early forms of PORTAS.

portia¹ ('pɔəʃə). [f. Tamil *puarassu* flower-king.] In full, ***portia tree***. An Indian name for *Thespesia populnea*, a tropical evergreen tree belonging to the family Malvaceæ and bearing yellow flowers.

1861 H. CLEGHORN *Forests & Gardens S. India* 197 It is usual to plant large branches of the portia..and banyan.. trees in such a slovenly manner, that there is little probability of the trees thriving or being ornamental. **1881** J. S. GAMBLE *Man. Indian Timbers* 43 *T[hespesia] populnea* Corr...the Portia or Tulip Tree... A moderate-sized evergreen tree. **1921** R. S. TROUP *Silvicult. Indian Trees* I. 150 Tulip tree, portia tree... A small or moderate-sized evergreen tree of the coast forests of India and Burma. **1969** T. H. EVERETT *Living Trees of World* 237/1 The most important of this genus [sc. *Thespesia*]..is the Portia tree... Common along the coasts of tropical Asia and the Pacific Islands, this evergreen attains a height of 60 feet.

Portia² ('pɔəʃə). The name of the heroine of Shakespeare's *Merchant of Venice* used as the type of a female advocate or barrister. Hence **'Portian** *a.*, pertaining to or resembling Portia.

1901 *Westm. Gaz.* 22 Jan. 12/2 The Paris Portia's First Success... Mdlle. Chauvan, the young lady barrister, made her first appearance yesterday in the Paris courts. **1909** *Ibid.* 17 Aug. 2/1 China..then took refuge in an interpretation of the letter of the Treaty which was quite Portian in its meticulousness. **1923** *Brewer's Dict. Phr. & Fable* (new ed.) 868/1 *Portia*, a rich heiress and 'lady barrister' in Shakespeare's *Merchant of Venice*... Her name is often used allusively for a female advocate. **1932** E. WEEKLEY *Words & Names* 33 *Portia*, which is good journalese for a lady barrister. **1977** J. MITCHELL *Half-Life* II. 39 Good Christ, they've brought back the people's Portia.

†**portic.** *Obs. rare.* Also 7 portick. [OE. ad. L. *porticus*: see next; cf. OHG. *pforzih*, etc. Not in ME., where F. *porche* PORCH took its place; re-introduced in 17th c.] A portico, a porch.

a **900** tr. *Bæda's Hist.* II. iii. (1890) 106 Forðon in þone forecwedenan portic ma ne meahte beon [L. *eo quod praedicta porticus plura capere nequiuit*]. *c* **950** *Lindisf. Gosp.* John x. 23 And ȝe-eade se hælend in temple in portic salamones. *c* **1000** *Ags. Gosp.* John v. 2 Se mere hæfð fif porticas.

1682 WHELER *Journ. Greece* I. 18 It hath on the outside a Portic round it... Each side of the Portick is of Fourteen foot long. *Ibid.* 76 A fine Mosque; whose Portick is supported by Red Marble Pillars.

b. A philosopher of the Porch; a Stoic philosopher. *nonce-use.*

a **1644** QUARLES *Funeral Elegies* Poems (1717) 417 Thou dry-brain'd Portick, whose Ahenean brest Transcending passion, never was opprest With grief.

portico ('pɔətɪkəʊ). Pl. -oes, -os (also 7 -o's). [a. It. (also Sp., Pg.) *portico*:—L. *porticus* colonnade, arcade, porch, f. *porta* door, gate, PORT *sb.*³]

1. *Arch.* **a.** A covered ambulatory consisting of a roof supported by columns placed at regular intervals, usually attached as a porch to a building, but sometimes forming a separate structure; a colonnade; †a pergola in a garden (*obs.*).

1605 B. JONSON *Volpone* II. i, I..wont to fix my bank in face of the public Piazza, near the shelter of the Portico to the Procuratia. **1649** EVELYN *Diary* 30 May, His Majesty's statues thrown down at St. Paule's Portico and the Exchange. *a* **1662** HEYLIN *Laud* I. 210 He caused a stately Portico to be erected at the West end of the Church. **1686** BURNET *Trav.* iv. (1750) 233 The Beauty of their Temples, and of the Porticos before them, is amazing. **1706** *Lond. Gaz.* No. 4249/3 Making all sorts of Parterres, Porticoes, Arbours. **1758** JOHNSON *Idler* No. 33 ¶27 The porticos where Socrates sat. **1870** BRYANT *Iliad* I. VI. 194 Priam's noble hall, A palace built with graceful porticos. **1886** RUSKIN *Præterita* I. 325 Porticoes should not be carried on the top of arches.

b. *spec.* The Painted Porch at Athens: see PORCH 4; hence *fig.* the Stoic philosophy. Also *allusively*.

1788 GIBBON *Decl. & F.* xliv. IV. 352 From the portico, the Roman civilians learned to live, to reason, and to die. **1825** LAMB *Elia* Ser. II. *Barbara S*——, Poor men's smoky cabins are not always porticoes of moral philosophy. **1837** MACAULAY *Ess., Bacon* (1877) 403 Suppose that Justinian.. had called on the last few sages who still haunted the Portico.

2. *transf.* and *fig.*

1720 OZELL *Vertot's Rom. Rep.* I. IV. 228 Two Javelins were fixed in the Earth, and a third fastened across upon the Points of those. All the Æqui..passed under this military Portico. **1727-46** THOMSON *Summer* 1393 Now to the verdant portico of woods..they walk. **1831** CARLYLE in Froude *Life* (1882) II. 226 Now it seems to me as if this life were but the inconsiderable portico of man's existence.

3. *attrib.* as ***portico area***; **portico thief** = *cat-burglar* (s.v. CAT *sb.*¹ 18 and 19).

1977 *N.Z. Herald* 5 Jan. 2-16/8 (Advt.), Portico area for outdoor entertainment. **1934** P. SAVAGE *Savage of Scotland Yard* xxiv. 260 Suspicion fell on half a dozen or more cat burglars—or portico thieves as they were officially called. **1938** F. D. SHARPE *Sharpe of Flying Squad* xxv. 254 Cat-burglars have existed since there have been houses to climb, but until comparatively recently they were always known by the more prosaic title of Portico Thieves.

Hence **'porticoed** *a.*, furnished with a portico.

1665 J. WEBB *Stone-Heng* (1725) 103 the Temples..were circumalated, or either singly or doubly porticoed about. **1856** MISS MULOCK *J. Halifax* i, The High Street, with the mayor's house..porticoed and grand.

‖**'porticus.** Pl. porticus, porticuses. [L.; see prec.] **1.** = prec.

1624 B. JONSON *Masque, Neptune's Triumph* Wks. (Rtldg.) 640/2 Till the whole tree become a porticus, Or arched arbour. *a* **1661** HOLYDAY *Juvenal* 146 Their baths..were of a less extent then their porticus or arch'd walks. **1682** SIR T. BROWNE *Chr. Mor.* III. §21 Sleep not in the Dogma's of the Peripatus, Academy, or Porticus: be a moralist of the mount. **1685** H. MORE *Paralip. Prophet.* xxxii. 289 Porticus's likewise ran through the whole Ground-plot of the Temple. **1850** J. H. PARKER *Gloss. Terms Grecian, Roman, Italian, & Gothic Archit.* (ed. 5) I. 371 In the middle ages the word *porticus* was used for the *entrance porch* of a church, and for the *apses*... The structure over a tomb was termed *porticulus* and *porticus*. But *porticus* also retained its original sense of a long ambulatory... This porticus [by Cuthbert Tunstall at Durham] is a long gallery still in existence.

2. *spec.* in *Anglo-Saxon Archit.*, an aisle or transept on the north or south side of a church, containing a chapel.

1888 C. C. HODGES *Abbey of St. Andrew, Hexham* iii. 16 We may assume the word *porticus* to mean side chapels at the east and west ends of the aisles, as at Brixworth, on transepts, as at Norton, Stow, Sompting, and the church in Dover Castle. **1911** A. H. THOMPSON *Ground Plan Eng. Parish Ch.* ii. 35 A feature of the early cathedral and of St Pancras at Canterbury, was the projection of *porticus*, porches or side chapels, from the nave. These were entered by archways pierced in the centre of the lateral walls. **1936** A. W. CLAPHAM *Romanesque Archit.* i. 8 Early Anglo-Saxon building... The southern group of churches..are distinguished by a simple aisle-less plan with an apsidal chancel and a series of annexes called 'porticus' adjoining or surrounding the nave. **1959** H. M. TAYLOR in P. Clemoes *Anglo-Saxons* 142 From the earliest days the Saxon builders showed a fondness for separate chapels, or *porticus*, opening from the naves or chancels of their churches through comparatively small doorways. **1968** J. W. PARKER *Great Ch. of St. Mary, Stow in Lindsey* 11 What, we may ask, is the reason for the Saxon doorway into the transept? Did it lead to a porticus or chapel? **1971** D. M. WILSON *Anglo-Saxons* (rev. ed.) ii. 49 Various ancillary elements were added to this basic pattern—porches, porticuses, crypts, towers, western galleries and even, in the latest period, transepts. **1975** *Archaeologia Aeliana* III. 123 The church [of St. Peter, Bywell, Northumberland] formerly had *porticus* over-lapping the junction of nave and chancel on the north and south. The roof-raggle of the north *porticus* is still visible. **1977** R. MORRIS in Binney & Burman *Change & Decay* 135/2 The digging of a trench around the base of a church to combat rising damp may destroy the remains of an Anglo-Saxon *porticus*.

‖**portière** (pɔrtjɛr). [Fr.:—med.L. *portāria*, prop. fem. sing. of adj. *portārius* belonging to a door or gate; see PORTER *sb.*¹] A curtain hung over a door or doorway, to prevent draught, to serve as a screen, or for ornament. Also *fig.*

1843 *Ainsworth's Mag.* IV. 111 Her ladyship's cozy house refurnished with *portières* to all the doors. **1855** THACKERAY *Newcomes* lxiii, What frightful Boucher and Lancret shepherds and shepherdesses leered over the portières! **1881** *Cornh. Mag.* July 50 He drew aside the portière that concealed the door. **1905** *Spectator* 7 Jan. 11/2 The waters go chasing down the cliffs in deep descending channels hung with curtains and *portières* of moss. **1909** *Chambers's Jrnl.* Oct. 664/2 The Cashmere dyes are fitted only for shawls and portières and tapestries for walls. **1927** F. B. YOUNG *Portrait of Clare* v. 524 A chair went over with a crash, the portière was ripped from its hanging. **1944** S. BELLOW *Dangling Man* 184, I sat down at a desk in a corner, near one of the portieres. **1975** *New Yorker* 11 Aug. 71/1 At the gala it was done against a black backcloth that opened into portières.

attrib. **1893** SALTUS *Madam Sapphira* 83 There was a jostle of portière rings. **1897** *Daily News* 9 Nov. 6/5 A pair of portière curtains, old appliquée embroidery on crimson silk velvet ground.

Hence **porti'èred** *a.*, furnished with a *portière*.

1923 F. L. PACKARD *Four Stragglers* v. 184 She turned her head a little, facing the portièred window beside the fireplace of the living-room in which they stood.

†**porti'folium, portyfolyom.** *Obs. rare.* Corruption of med.L. *portiforium*, a PORTAS.

1546 BALE *1st Exam. A. Askew* 34 b, Their popish porty-folyoms and maskynge bokes. **1550** —— *Image Both Ch.* I. 141 Though they neuer haue Beades, Latine Primers, porti-folyomes, nor other signes of hipocrisie.

portiforium (pɔətɪ'fɔərɪəm). Pl. portiforia. [a. med.L. *portiforium* portable breviary.] = PORTAS 1, PORTUARY.

1880, 1884 [see PORTUARY]. **1916** H. M. BANNISTER in C. H. Turner *Early Worcester MSS.* p. lx, The traditional title *Portiforium S. Oswaldi*..is clearly wrong, as that Saint's name appears by the first hand in its kalendar; it might justly be called the *Portiforium S. Wulfstani*. **1929** *Jrnl. Theol. Stud.* XXX. 174 In the library of Corpus Christi College.. is preserved a book..known until recently as the *Portiforium* (or *Breviarium*) *Oswaldi*. *Ibid.* 175 The book..is a stout vellum volume... It is in fact almost a Breviary, or *Portiforium*. **1931** A. ESDAILE *Student's Man. Bibliogr.* vi. 200 On small breviaries, intended to be carried about and hence named 'portiforia', the chemise was at the head. **1956** *In Great Tradition* (Benedictines of Stanbrook) ix. 176 She [*sc.* Dame Laurentia McLachlan] had contributed..an article on the so-called *Portiforium Oswaldi*, an eleventh-century volume. **1974** *Bodl. Libr. Rec.* Dec. Dr. Emden's Register provides the information that John Neele, master of Holy Trinity College, Arundel, from 1484 until his death in 1498, bequeathed all his books at Arundel, with the exception of his bible and portiforium, to Magdalen College.

'portify, *v. nonce-wd.* [f. PORT *sb.*⁷] To convert (claret) into port; in quot. *fig.*

1861 THACKERAY *Round. Papers* xiv, I grant you..that this claret is loaded, as it were; but your desire to *portify* yourself is amiable, is pardonable, is perhaps honourable.

portigue, -ingue, var. PORTAGUE *Obs.*, gold coin.

portinance, variant of PURTENANCE *Obs.*

porting ('pɔətɪŋ), *vbl. sb.* [f. PORT *sb.*³ + -ING¹.] The arrangement, size, etc., of the ports in an internal-combustion engine.

1960 C. F. TAYLOR *Internal-Combustion Engine* I. vii. 238 (*caption*) Two-stroke engine porting. **1972** *Proc. Inst. Mech. Engin.* CLXXXVI. 746/2 The only cycle for which the porting requirements have compromised the rotor shape is the compressor-expander.

Portingale, -gall, etc., obs. ff. PORTUGAL.

portion ('pɔəʃən), *sb.* Forms: 4 porciun, 4-6 -ion, -ioun (etc.); 4-5, 7 portioun, 7- ione, 5- portion. [ME. *porciun, portion*, a. OF. *porcion, portion* (12th c. in Hatz.-Darm.), ad. L. *portiō-nem* share, part, proportion (whence also Prov., Sp. *porcion*, It. *porzione*, Pg. *porção*).]

I. 1. a. The part (of anything) allotted or belonging to one person; a share. Also *fig.*

a **1300** *Cursor M.* 4746 (Cott.) He salde ilk man his porcion [*v.rr.* -ciun, -cioun]. *c* **1325** *Chron. Eng.* 352 (Ritson) The kyng of Esex wes riche mon, He hade to ys portion Wylteschire, Barkschyre. **1382** WYCLIF *Luke* xv. 12 Fadir, ȝyue to me the porcioun of substaunce, ethir catel, that by-fallith to me. *c* **1400** *Ywaine & Gaw.* 3585 Gif the yonger damysele The half, or els sum porciowne, That sho mai have to warisowne. **1535** COVERDALE *1 Esdras* v. 8 Euery man sought his porcion agayne in Iewry. **1591** SHAKS. *1 Hen. VI*, v. iii. 125, I vnworthy am To woe so faire a Dame to be his wife, And haue no portion in the choice my selfe. **1696** PHILLIPS (ed. 5), *Portion*, a Lot, or Share of any thing that is to be parcell'd out or divided. **1772** *Junius Lett.* lxviii. (1820) 338 The study of the law requires but a moderate portion of abilities. **1847** MRS. A. KERR tr. *Ranke's Hist. Servia* 25 He honourably performed his portion of the compact.

b. A quantity or allowance of food allotted to, or enough for, one person.

1484 CAXTON *Fables of Poge* ii, She dyd brynge to hym [a poor man] his porcion as she was custommed for to doo. **1525** LD. BERNERS *Froiss.* II. ccxxii. [ccxviii.] 691 To close you vp in a castell, and there to be holden vnder subiection, and to lyue by porcion. **1611** BIBLE *Esther* ix. 22 Daies of feasting and ioy, and of sending portions one to another. **1629** WADSWORTH *Pilgr.* iii. 16 Each man hath..brought him..halfe a pound of beefe which they call their portion. *c* **1880** *Newspaper*, The demand, in London alone, for soles [fish] of the size to make one 'portion'.

2. The part or share of an estate given or passing by law to an heir, or to be distributed to him in the settlement of the estate. Also *fig.*

a **1340** HAMPOLE *Psalter* xv. 5 He is porcioun & mede of myn heritage. *c* **1440** *Jacob's Well* 21 In defraude of here wyves & chylderyn, to lettyn hem fro þe porcyoun þat longyth to hem, be ryȝt. **1538** STARKEY *England* I. iv. 113 Inheritarys to a grete porcyon of intaylyd land. **1590** SPENSER *F.Q.* II. ii. 2 Full little weenest thou what sorrows are Left thee for porcion of thy livelyhed. **1642** FULLER *Holy*

& Prof. St. v. xix. 437 On whom the earth as their common mother bestowed a grave for a childs portion. **1818** CRUISE *Digest* (ed. 2) II. 21 Sir Joseph Jekyll decreed, that the plaintiffs were entitled to their original portions, as well as to the additional portions given by the will. **1855** MACAULAY *Hist. Eng.* xii. III. 210 On what security..could any man invest his money or give a portion to his children, if he could not rely on positive laws and on the uninterrupted possession of many years?

3. Dowry; a marriage portion. Also *portion-money*. (In quot. 1511 = DOWER 1.)

1511 FABYAN *Will* in *Chron.* (1811) Pref. 7 Also I will that my chalice, wt my ij crewetts and pax of siluer,..whiche before daies I gave to my wif, remayn styll to her, in augmentyng of hir porcion. **1602** WARNER *Alb. Eng.* IX. xlvii. 221 Who loues not for the Person but the Portion loues no whit. **1625** BOSWELL in Ellis *Orig. Lett.* Ser. I. III. 195 Her portion money..is already paying here. **1647** N. BACON *Disc. Govt. Eng.* I. xli. (1739) 64 This custom..[was] from the Latins, who used to give Dower with the man, and receive Portion with the woman. **1726** SWIFT *Gulliver* I. i, I married Mrs. Mary Burton..with whom I received four hundred pounds for a portion. **1861** M. PATTISON *Ess.* (1889) I. 35 Edward, on his side, is to give the moderate portion of 10,000 marks with his daughter.

4. That which is allotted to a person by providence; lot, destiny, fate. †*to lay one's portion with*, to cast in one's lot with (LOT *sb.* 1 e).

a **1325** *Prose Psalter* xlix. [l.] 19 þou..laid þy porcioun wyþ spouse-breches. *c* **1400** *Apol. Loll.* 51 If ani presume aȝen þis, know he him to haue porcoun wiþ Giezi. **1535** COVERDALE *Job* xx. 29 This is the porcion that ye wicked shal haue of God, and the heretage that he maye loke for of the Lorde. —— *Ecclus.* xxv. 19 Ye porcion of the vngodly shal fall vpon her. **1667** MILTON *P.L.* I. 70 Eternal Justice..here their Prison ordain'd In utter darkness, and their portion set. **1709** STEELE *Tatler* No. 54 ¶1 When Labour was pronounced to be the Portion of Man. **1851** NEALE *Hymn*, Brief life is here our portion.

II. 5. a. A part of any whole: = PART *sb.* 1.

1340 HAMPOLE *Pr. Consc.* 8118–20 A day here may be a porcyon Of ane hundreth yhere, als men may se, Alle-if þat porcyon fulle lytylle be. **1387** TREVISA *Higden* (Rolls) I. 99 þe norþ est portioun of Arabia hatte Saba. **1480** CAXTON *Chron. Eng.* ccxvii. 204, xxx thousand pounde of syluer to be payed within iii yere..euery yere x thousand pound by euyn porcyons. **1633** *Sc. Acts Chas. I.* (1817) V. 103/1 That..portioun of the lordshipe of Dumbar boundit meithit and merchit as eftir-followes. **1715** tr. *Gregory's Astron.* (1726) I. 416 Such a Portion of the Ecliptic, as the Sun describes in the mean while by its Annual Motion towards the East. **1831** MACAULAY *Ess., J. Hampden* (1887) 205 Almost every part of this virtuous and blameless life..is a precious and splendid portion of our national history. **1860** TYNDALL *Glac.* I. vii. 48 A portion of the pressure was transmitted laterally.

b. *Judaism.* The section of the Pentateuch or of the Prophets appointed to be read on a particular Sabbath or Festival.

1892 I. ZANGWILL *Childr. Ghetto* II. 87 Reb Shemuel was already poring over a Pentateuch in his Friday night duty of reading the portion twice in Hebrew and once in Chaldaic. **1901** M. GASTER *Bk. of Prayer* I. 47 The Minister then reads the first section of the Parashá (Portion of the Law for the ensuing Sabbath). **1932** L. GOLDING *Magnolia St.* I. ii. 17 She should have kept Sam in..to say the week's portion out of the Pentateuch, to do his soul good. **1978** H. KEMELMAN *Thursday the Rabbi walked Out.* x. 57 After the portion is read, you say another blessing..normally the Bar Mitzvah boy chants the portion from the Prophets, too. **1980** *Jewish Chron.* 15 Feb. 22/1 In next week's portion of the law, 'Terumah' (Exodus 25). *Ibid.* 39/4 Saturday, February 16 (Shevat 29). Portions of the Law (Torah)..*Parashat Shekalim*... Portion of Prophets (Haftara) [etc.].

6. A part of the whole existing stock (of anything); a (limited) quantity or amount; some.

13.. *Coer de L.* 5413 The Sarezynes..cryede, trewes!..To the false Kyng off Fraunse; And he hem grauntyd..For a porcioun off golde. *c* **1386** CHAUCER *Shipman's T.* 56 Toward the toun of Brugges for to fare To byen there a porcion of ware. **1426** in *Surtees Misc.* (1888) 6 He boght of John Lyllyng a porcion of alom. **1526** *Pilgr. Perf.* (W. de W. 1531) 12 b, But grace, ye the leest porcyon of grace,..is sufficyent. **1817** JAS. MILL *Brit. India* III. VI. i. 8 Nujeef Khan, whose talents had..given a portion of stability to the imperial throne. **1838** T. THOMSON *Chem. Org. Bodies* 965 It would not be surprising if a portion of water, so far from being decomposed, were actually formed by the union of its constituents previously existing in the grain.

†7. The action of dividing; division, partition, distribution. *Obs. rare.*

c **1450** *Life St. Cuthbert* (Surtees) 4796 And parted in to twa knyghts hande, Be euen porcioune. **1494** FABYAN *Chron.* VI. cxlix. 136 After ye which porcion, Charlmayne, herynge of the dyuycion & stryfe among the Almayns..sped hym thyther. **1635** SWAN *Spec. M.* (1670) 174 That proportion is quite taken away which God the Creator hath observed in all other things: making them all in number, weight and measure, in an excellent portion and harmony.

portion ('pɔəʃən), *v.* [ad. obs. F. *portionner*, *porcionner* (1339 in Godef.) to apportion, divide into shares (= med.L. *portiōnāre*, 1374 in Du Cange), f. F. *portion* PORTION; see APPORTION.]

1. *trans.* To divide into portions or shares; to assign or distribute in shares, to share *out*; = APPORTION *v.* 2.

c **1330** R. BRUNNE *Chron.* (1810) 51 þe barons portiond þe lond euen þam bituene. **1725** POPE *Odyss.* VIII. 514 Now each partakes the feast, the wine prepares, Portions the food, and each his portion shares. *a* **1763** SHENSTONE *A Vision* Wks. 1765 II. 87 The journey seemed to be portioned into four distinct stages. **1859** JEPHSON *Brittany* xvi. 254 The petty chiefs among whom the country was portioned out. **1887** BOWEN *Æneid* v. 362 After the races are ended, the prizes portioned as due.

b. To allot or assign to any one as his portion or share; = APPORTION *v.* 1.

1871 BROWNING *Balaustion* 2326 No: it was praise, I portioned thee, Of being good true husband to thy wife! **1904** LD. BURGHCLERE *Virg. Georg.* I. 43 Not that the gods Have portioned them some special gift [L. *quia sit divinitus illis Ingenium*], or fate Bestowed a deeper sense of things to be.

2. To give a portion or dowry to; to dower, endow.

1712 M. HENRY *Commun. w. God* (1822) 365 The Psalmist having given preference to God's favour,..and portioned himself in that, here expresseth his great complacency in the choice he had made. **1838** *Murray's Handbk. N. Germ.* 449 Louis of Arnstein, having no son, married and portioned off his seven daughters, dividing among them a part of his estates. **1855** M. ARNOLD *Balder Dead* 114 That one, long portion'd with his doom of death, Should change his lot, and fill another's life. **1865** DICKENS *Mut. Fr.* III. iv, When I marry with their consent they will portion me most handsomely.

3. To mix in due proportion; = APPORTION *v.* 3.

1811 *Self Instructor* 514 Roman oker..when properly portioned with gum-water.

Hence **'portioned** *ppl. a.*, **'portioning** *vbl. sb.*

1732 POPE *Ep. Bathurst* 267 Him portion'd maids, apprentic'd orphans blest. **1845** S. AUSTIN *Ranke's Hist. Ref.* III. 521 Revenues..consecrated to the portioning of noble young ladies in marriage. **1850** BLACKIE *Æschylus* II. 22 We all must bear our portioned lot.

'portionable, *a.* [f. PORTION *sb.* + -ABLE: cf. *proportionable*.] **†1.** Proportional. *Obs. rare.*

c **1374** CHAUCER *Boeth.* III. met. ix. 68 (Camb. MS.) Thow byndest the elementus by nowmbyres porcionables, þat the colde thinges mowen acorden with the hote thinges.

2. Designating a woman endowed with a marriage portion or dowry.

1875 PALEY & SANDYS *Select Private Orations of Demosthenes* II. 162 'Orphan-sons or heiresses', meaning by the latter 'orphan-daughters' 'portionable-sisters'. **1910** *Blackw. Mag.* Aug. 200/1 Prût had carried off a portionable lady of the island on whom Sidd also had cast his eye.

portional ('pɔəʃənəl), *a. rare.* [ad. late L. *portiōnālis* partial; see PORTION *sb.* and -AL[1].]

1. Pertaining to or of the nature of a portion or part; partial.

1382 WYCLIF *1 Esdras* viii. 31 These ben the prouostis, after ther kuntres, and porciounelis [*v.r.* porciounel, **1388** porcionel] princehodis [*Vulg.* porcionales principatus] of hem, that with me steyeden vp fro Babiloine. **1662** GUNNING *Lent Fast* 30 Why apply we the 4th, and 6th day of the week to stations? (or meetings for prayer, portional-fasting, and Sacrament). *a* **1670** HACKET *Cent. Serm.* (1675) 247 The Christians should punctually observe a portional abstinence, according to the time of forty days.

2. Of the nature of a portion or dowry.

1683 EVELYN *Mem.* 16 Mar., He [Sir J. Child] lately married his daughter to the eldest son of the Duke of Beaufort,..with £50,000 portional present, and various expectations.

Hence **'portionally** *adv.*, by way of a portion or part; partly, in part. *rare.*

1617 COLLINS *Def. Bp. Ely* I. i. 29 Peter receiued, and receiued for himselfe,..but μερικῶς, not ὁλικῶς, portionally and particularly, not wholly and entirely. **1865** ELIZA METEYARD *J. Wedgwood* I. 330 The 'Brick House and Works' stood on what now forms portionally the site of the Wedgwood Institute.

'portionary. *Obs.* exc. *Hist.* [ad. med.L. *portiōnārius* a canon's deputy in a cathedral, receiving half a prebend (*c* 1200 in Du Cange) (so OF. *porcionaire* 1442 in Godef.): see PORTION *sb.* and -ARY[1].] = PORTIONIST 2.

1548 *Act 2 & 3 Edw. VI*, c. 13 §3 That all and everie person..shall paye their tythes for thincrease of the saide cattell so goinge in the saide waste or common, to the parson vicar proprietorie porcyonarie owner or other their fermors. **1620** BRENT tr. *Sarpi's Counc. Trent* VIII. (1676) 734 That in Cathedral Churches, all the Canons and Portionaries shall be Priests, Deacons, or Sub-deacons. **1778** *Eng. Gazetteer* (ed. 2) s.v. *Wolverhampton*, In this parish K. Edgar founded a chapel of 8 portionaries, the chief of whom he made patron to them all.

†'portionate, *a. Obs. rare*[−0]. [ad. med.L. *portiōnātus* provided with a portion.] = PROPORTIONATE. Hence **†'portionately** *adv. Obs. rare*[−1], in equal shares, proportionately.

1548 UDALL, etc. *Erasm. Par. John* 115 b, They so deuided the resydue of his garmentes saue his coate..that euery manne had hys parte porcionately.

portioner ('pɔəʃənə(r)). [f. PORTION *sb.* or *v.* + -ER[1, 2]. Cf. med.L. *portiōnārius*.]

I. 1. *Scots Law.* The proprietor of a small piece of land forming a portion of an original forty-merk land, which has been subdivided among co-heirs or otherwise broken up; a small laird.

1552 *Reg. Privy Council Scot.* I. 130 Quhair happinis to be sindrie portioneris of landis within the Schyir, the Scheref sall adjown the samyn togidder, quhill he mak the fouretie mark land of auld extent. **1569** *Ibid.* 676 Alexander Chalmer portioner of Petty. **1674** in Wodrow *Hist. Suff. Ch. Scot.* (1721) I. 367 Robert Schaw Portioner in Auchmouty [fined] in 49 Pounds. **1791** *Statist. Acc. Scot.* I. 9 There are sixteen greater, and a considerable number (about a hundred) of smaller proprietors, called here Portioners, from their having a small portion of land belonging to them. **1833** *Fraser's Mag.* Oct. 396 My father belonged to that respectable class of landowners termed portioners.

b. *heir-* or *heiress-portioner*: One of two or more heirs female who succeed to equal portions of a heritage in default of heirs male; or the son or other male representative of such a joint-heiress.

1576 *Reg. Privy Council Scot.* II. 571 Alisoun Dunbar ane of the airis portionaris of the lordschip of Loch and Kilconquhair. **1655** in Z. Boyd *Zion's Flowers* (1855) App. 29 2 We Marion Boyd and Zacharias McCallum aires portionairis to umquhill Mr. Zacharias Boyd. **1765** *Act 5 Geo. III*, c. 26 *Preamble*, The eldest heir female always succeeding without division and excluding heirs portioners. **1886** *Act 49 & 50 Vict.* c. 29 §19 The eldest of such heirs portioners shall succeed to the tenancy without division.

†2. *Eccl.* = PORTIONIST 2. *Obs.*

1670 BLOUNT *Law Dict.*, *Portioner* (..*Portionarius*),..where a Parsonage is served by two or sometimes three Ministers alternately..the Ministers are called Portioners, because they have but their Portion or Proportion of the Tythes or Profits of the Living. **1848** WHARTON *Law Lex.*, *Portioner*, a minister, who, together with others, serves a benefice, because he has only a portion of the tithes or profits of the living.

3. *Eng. Law.* One of several persons among whom a settled fund is appointable; a sharer. (Cf. PORTION *sb.* 2.) *rare.*

1884 SIR E. E. RAY in *Law Times Rep.* L. 261/1 In none of the decisions or dicta has the prior right of the portioners to receive their portions out of the estate been questioned.

4. *techn.* One of a number of artificers who each contribute a certain part of the complete article.

1879 *Globe* 11 Oct. 1/4 Each of the several contributors—technically called *portioners*.

II. 5. One who divides (anything) into portions or shares. *rare*[−0].

1775 in ASH; and in later dicts.

'portionist. [ad. med.L. *portiōnista* (1499 in Du Cange), f. *portiōn-em* PORTION: see -IST.]

1. A student in a college, receiving or entitled to a defined portion or allowance of food (whether as a boarder or as recipient of a benefaction).

†a. At St. Andrews, A student who boarded with the principal of the college, and was entitled to his 'commons'. *Obs.*

1563–7 BUCHANAN *Reform. St. Andros* Wks. (S.T.S.) 7 The steuart to be payit be the principal off the profet of the portionistis.

b. In reference to Merton College, Oxford: A rendering of the Latin term *portionista*, applied to the class of poor scholars usually called *post-masters*.

The official terms are, in Latin documents, *portionista*, in English, *postmaster*; *portionist* appears to be merely a 17th c. literary rendering of the former by Wood, Hearne, and others after them.

a **1672** WOOD *Life* 1 Aug. an. 1635 (O.H.S.) I. 45 The old stone-house, wherein his son A. Wood was borne (called antiently Portionists or Postmasters hall). *Ibid.* 52 The second brother of A. Wood, named Edward, became one of the portionists or postmasters of Merton Coll. [in 1642]. **1710** HEARNE *Collect.* (O.H.S.) III. 54 He..was enter'd at 15 Years of Age, as one of the Portionists or Post-Masters of Merton Coll. **1826** SOUTHEY in *Q. Rev.* XXXIV. 343 Parkhurst (afterwards Bishop of Norwich) whose portionist and pupil he was at Merton College. **1895** RASHDALL *Universities* II. 488 The body of Portionists (now corrupted to Postmasters) was engrafted..about the year 1300.

2. *Eccl.* One of two or more incumbents who share the duties and revenues of a benefice.

1743 *Act. 16 Geo. II*, c. 28 §35 All..Easter offerings, and other dues..that have been usually paid to the said rector or vicar, or portionists of the parish church of Stepney. **1794** W. COMBE *Boydell's Thames* I. 59 Its parochial tithes are divided between three portionists, who are all presented by the church of Exeter. **1888** *Dict. Nat. Biog.* XIII. 247/2 He was also canon resident and portionist at Hereford.

'portionize, *v. rare*[−1]. [f. PORTION *sb.* + -IZE.] *trans.* To express or describe only in part.

1594 *Zepheria* ii. 14 Then though my pencil glance here on thine eyes; Sweet! think thy Fair it doth but portionise!

portionless ('pɔəʃənlɪs), *a.* [f. PORTION *sb.* + -LESS.] Without a portion; dowerless.

1782 MISS BURNEY *Cecilia* VIII. ii, Were this excellent young creature portionless, I would not hesitate in giving my consent. **1859** THACKERAY *Virgin.* iv, Harry, Harry! I wish I had put by the money for thee, my poor portionless child. **1863** MISS BRADDON *Eleanor's Vict.* iii, The daughters found themselves left portionless.

†'portitor. *Obs. rare.* [a. med.L. *portitor*, irreg. f. *porta* door, gate.] A door-keeper, a janitor.

1480 *Wardr. Acc. Edw. IV* (1830) 128 To the portitour at iiij d. by the day. *Ibid.* 170 Thomas Stanes Portitour of the same grete Warderobe. **1737** CHAMBERLAYNE *St. Gt. Brit.* Lists 213/2 Portitor and Taylor to the great Wardrobe, Mr John Mills.

portiture, obs. form of PORTRAITURE.

†portiuncle. *Sc. Obs.* In 5 porciunkle. [a. F. *portioncule*, †-*uncule*, ad. L. *portiuncula*, dim. of *portiōn-em* PORTION: see -UNCLE.] A small portion (of land); a pendicle.

1470 *Burgh Recs. Prestwick* 7 May (Maitl. Cl.) 2 Efftir þe lyntht of þe said porciunkle of lande. *Ibid.* 4 A porciunkle of commoun land, paiand ȝerli at sanct Nicholas dai ijd to sainct Nicholas lycht in þe said kirk.

Port Jackson (pɔət ˈdʒæksən). The name of the harbour of Sydney, Australia, used *attrib.* and *absol.* in the names of plants and animals native to the region, esp. **Port Jackson fig**, a small tree, *Ficus rubiginosa*, of the family Moraceæ; **Port Jackson (shark)**, a small bullhead shark belonging to the genus *Heterodontus*, esp. *H. portusjacksoni*, which is light brown with black markings; **Port Jackson (willow)** *S. Afr.*, a large shrub, *Acacia cyanophylla*, of the family Leguminosæ, which was introduced to South Africa from Australia and has become naturalized there.

1889 J. H. MAIDEN *Useful Native Plants Austral.* iv. 225 *Ficus rubiginosa*... 'Port Jackson Fig'... This fig, like other figs, exudes a juice when the bark is wounded. **1904** [see ILLAWARRA]. **1954** *Coast to Coast 1953–54* 133 Today Ellen planted the Port Jackson Fig. **1965** Port Jackson fig [see ILLAWARRA]. **1880** A. C. L. G. GÜNTHER *Introd. Study of Fishes* 716/3 (Index), Port Jackson Shark. **1932** *Nat. Geogr. Mag.* Sept. 369/2 There were sharks there in abundance —all sorts and sizes—..'gummies', 'angels', and 'Port Jacksons'. **1974** D. & M. WEBSTER *Compar. Vertebr. Morphol.* iv. 63 (*caption*) The jaws of a chondrichthyean, the Port Jackson shark, and of a teleost, the sheepshead. **1902** *Trans. S. Afr. Philos. Soc.* XI. 61 The value of Port Jackson bark on trees still standing.. is worth 6s. per acre. **1950** *Cape Times* 12 Dec. 9/7 Great masses of *rooikrantz* and Port Jackson willow grow to within a few feet of the houses. **1959** *Ibid.* 27 Mar. 1/7 A man was shot dead at Durbanville last night after a 400-yard police chase at dusk through thick Port Jackson bush. **1973** PALMER & PITMAN *Trees S. Afr.* II. 731 Some Australian species, such as the aggressive and fast-spreading Port Jackson willow, *Acacia cyanophylla* Lindl., are cultivated in South Africa.

Portland[1] (ˈpɔətlənd). A peninsula or 'island' on the coast of Dorsetshire; *attrib.* in names of natural and artificial products of Portland Island, or of objects connected with it; as **Portland arrowroot, Portland beds**: see quots.; **Portland cement**, a cement resembling *P. stone* in colour: see CEMENT *sb.* 1 *note*; also *attrib.*, as *P. cement maker, mill*, etc.; **Portland oolite**, a limestone of the Upper Oolite formation, especially developed in the Isle of Portland; **Portland powder**: see quot. 1858; **Portland sago** = *P. arrowroot*; also called *Portland Island sago*; **Portland sand, Portland screw**: see quots.; **Portland spurge**, *Euphorbia Portlandica*; **Portland stone**, a valuable building stone quarried in the Isle of Portland; also *ellipt.*; also, applied to the colour of Portland stone.

1854–67 C. A. HARRIS *Dict. Med. Terminol.*, *Portland Sago*, *Portland arrow-root, a fecula prepared from *Arum maculatum* in the Isle of Portland. **1866** *Treas. Bot.* 97/1 From the tubers of this plant [*Arum maculatum*]..a starch called Portland Arrowroot was formerly..prepared. **1849** CRAIG, **Portland beds*, or *Portland limestone*, a series of calcareous strata belonging to the upper part of the Oolite formation, found chiefly..in the Isle of Portland. **1824** *Specif. J. Aspdin's Patent* No. 5022 An improvement in.. artificial stone..which I call *Portland cement. **1858** SIMMONDS *Dict. Trade*, *Portland-cement Maker*, a manufacturer of cement for builders. **1885** *Times*, *Engineering Suppl.* 12 Apr. 60/1 'Portland' cement..was patented in 1824 by Joseph Aspdin, a bricklayer, of Leeds, who fancied that it bore some resemblance to the oolitic limestone of Portland Island. **1900** *Westm. Gaz.* 17 July 6/3 The neighbourhood of these two rivers [Thames and Medway], from being the cradle of the Portland Cement industry, has now become the chief seat of the manufacture. **1833** J. PHILLIPS *Geol.* in *Encycl. Metrop.* (1845) VI. 533 Names of Strata on Mr. Smith's Map and Sections [1815].. 9 Portland rock... Present Names [1833]..*Portland oolite. **1801** *Med. Jrnl.* V. 417 A Printed paper...recommending a revival of the old remedy for the Gout, known by the name of the *Portland Powder. From [this] we should be led to believe that this remedy was purchased and dispersed by the present Duke of Portland; whereas, it was by his father, many years ago. **1858** MAYNE *Expos. Lex.*, *Portland Powder*, a name of a formerly celebrated gout remedy, consisting of equal parts of birthwort, gentian, germander tops and leaves, ground pine and lesser centaury, dried, powdered, and sifted. **1849** CRAIG, **Portland sago*. **1859** PAGE *Handbk. Geol. Terms*, *Portland Stone* and **Portland Sand*, a well-known group of the upper oolite... It consists of shelly freestones of variable texture underlaid by thick beds of sand. **1885** LYELL *Elem. Geol.* (ed. 4) 294 The cast of a spiral univalve called by the quarrymen the '*Portland Screw'..is common. **1861** MISS PRATT *Flower. Pl.* V. 11 Order Euphorbiaceæ... *Euphorbia Portlandica* (*Portland Spurge). **1673** J. RAY *Observations Journey Low-Countries* 120 These figured Bodies were of very different Substances as to hardness..some soft Stone..others as hard as *Portland Stone. **a 1706** EVELYN *Diary* an. 1666 (1955) III. 459 All the ornaments, Columns, freezes, Capitels & projectures of massie Portland stone flew off. **1711** J. THORNHILL *Jrnl.* 21 May in *Proc. Suffolk Inst. Archæol. & Nat. Hist.* (1907) XIII. 1. 35 Mr. Martin having cap'd his peers with Keitan stone & made Pedestalls of Portland, ye paving is genly Newcastle stone. **a 1720** SHEFFIELD (Dk. Buckhm.) *Wks.* (1729) II. 258 Each step of one entire Portland-stone. **1851** BORROW *Lavengro* xciv, Lunatic-looking erections, in what the simpletons call the modern Gothic taste, of Portland-stone. **1869** *Bradshaw's Railway Manual* XXI. p. xxiv. (Advt.), Anitcorrosion paint. White. Light Stone. Bath do. Cream Colour. Light Portland Stone. Drab or Portland do. **1963** *Times* 17 May 15/7 Viewed with a shaft of sunlight on it, the Portland stone is startlingly white.

Hence **Portˈlandian** *a. Geol.*, the specific designation of a subdivision of the Upper Oolite, developed in the Isle of Portland.

1885 GEIKIE *Text-bk. Geol.* (ed. 2) 798 The Upper or Portland Oolites..are divisible into three groups: (1) Kimmeridgian, at the base; (2) Portlandian... This group, resting directly on the Kimmeridge clay, consists of two divisions, the Portland Sand and Portland Stone. *Ibid.* 799 Among Portlandian fossils a single species of coral (*Isastræa oblonga*) occurs.

portland[2]: see PORT-LAST.

portlandite (ˈpɔətləndaɪt). *Min.* [f. PORTLAND[1] (see quot. 1933) + -ITE[1].] A form of calcium hydroxide that occurs naturally as minute hexagonal colourless plates and is a common product of the hydration of Portland cement.

1933 C. E. TILLEY in *Mineral. Mag.* XXIII. 420 The occurrence of $Ca(OH)_2$ as a well-defined species is the contact-zone of Scawt Hill [Co. Antrim] merits a new mineral name, and in view of its occurrence as a common product of hydration of Portland cement, and furthermore as crystals from this source have provided the first reliable physical and optical data on crystalline $Ca(OH)_2$, it is fitting that the mineral name should bear record of these facts. The name Portlandite is accordingly proposed. **1968** I. KOSTOV *Mineral.* 221 Periclase group... The calcium members are rare minerals: portlandite occurs in metasomatic deposits in limestones. **1977** *Sci. Amer.* Aug. 84 In a hardened cement this gel..occupies about 70 percent by volume of the hydrated material... The major part of the other crystalline products consists of calcium hydroxide (portlandite).

Portland Place (ˈpɔətlənd pleɪs). The name of a street in London, applied allusively to the B.B.C., whose headquarters are there. Also *attrib.*

1937 D. L. SAYERS *Busman's Honeymoon* xvi. 324 Now, my little minstrels of Portland Place! Strike, you myrtle-crownéd boys! **1939** 'N. BLAKE' *Smiler with Knife* ii. 29 Bursting out..into Somerset folk-songs in perfect harmony and Portland Place accents. **1941** C. KING *Diary* 17 July in *With Malice toward None* (1970) 135 Walker had been spending the morning with the B.B.C... These birds from Portland Place..took his criticisms with a very bad grace. **1967** *Guardian* 16 Oct. 5/3 The most popular disc jockey.. might almost have been born in Portland Place. **1974** C. HILL *Behind Screen* xxxi. 266 If it is interventionist to work for a more powerful..Board of Governors, then an interventionist chairman I was at Portland Place. **1977** T. JACKSON in *Rep. Comm. Future of Broadcasting* III. xiv. 227 Without the local stations Portland Place will be like a severed head.

ˈport-last. *Naut.* ? *Obs.* Also 7 **portlasse, -lesse**, 8–9 (*erron.*) **portland**. [Original form and derivation obscure: cf. PORTLOF.] Of uncertain meaning: explained, from 1704, as the gunwale of a ship. Chiefly in phrase (***down***) ***a portlast***: said of a yard.

1633 T. JAMES *Voy.* 11 The Portlesse of the Fore-Castell was in the water. *Ibid.* 113 The Portlasse. **1699** DAMPIER *Voy.* II. III. 64 Our Main-yard and Fore-yard were lowered down a Port last, as we call it, that is down pretty nigh the Deck. **1704** J. HARRIS *Lex. Techn.* I, *Port-last*, the same as the Gun-wale of a Ship; therefore they say a Yard is down a Port-last, when it lies down on the Deck. **1726** SHELVOCKE *Voy. round World* 3 By 11 of the clock we were under bare poles, with our yards a portland. **1769** FALCONER *Dict. Marine* (1789), *Hutter*, to lower the lower yards down a port-last. **1815** *Sporting Mag.* XLVI. 164 A ship lying to, with her yards a portland. **1867** SMYTH *Sailor's Word-bk.*, *Port-last*, or *Portoise*, synonymous with *gunwale*.

†**ˈportledge.** *Naut. Amer. Obs.* Forms: 7 **portlige, porledge**, 7–8 **portledge, -lidge**, 8 **-lege, -ledg, -lage**. [Corruption of PORTAGE *sb.*[1] in sense 4, perh. through confusion with the sometimes synonymous *privilege*.] = PORTAGE *sb.*[1] 4; usually *attrib.*, as ***portledge bill, money***.

1636 *Doc. Hist. St. Maine* III. 95, I think we shall make little lesse then £11 share for the last yeares worke, which was £6 portledge, and £1 3s. 3d. for the fish deliuered Mr. Winter, and £3 you promised me for my Charge in Bringinge ouer the shippe. **1639** *Ibid.* 185 Eduard Trebie.. Creditor for his ½ share for his portledge monye 2 5 0. *Ibid.* 190 Markes Gaude..Creditor..for his porledge Money 2 Moneths. **1679** *Rec. Crt. Assistants, Mass.* (1901) II. 131 For Refusing to pay..his wages after the Rate of three pounds tenn shillings per moneth as by the Portlidge bill may Appeare. **1775** *Mass. Archives* CCVI. 94 To amount of Mens wages as per Portledg Bill 56. 17. 11½.

portless, *a.* [f. PORT *sb.*[1] + -LESS.] Without a port.

1807 J. BARLOW *Columb.* x. 199 Her plains, long portless, now no more complain Of useless rills and fountains nursed in vain.

portlet (ˈpɔətlɪt). [f. PORT *sb.*[1] + -LET.] A small or tiny port; a creek.

1587 HARRISON *England* I. xii. in *Holinshed* I. 60/2 Being past these portlets [mouths of the Erme and Yealm] then next of all we come to Plimmouth hauen. **1603** OWEN *Pembrokeshire* (1892) 99 Where it maketh a portlett for smale shippinge. **1775** R. CHANDLER *Trav. Asia M.* (1825) I. 178 The artificial islands and portlets which he made by the seaside, are all now equally invisible. **1888** W. DENTON *Eng. in 15th C.* 89 Attacks on the ports and portlets along the south coast of England.

†**portlike,** *a. Obs. rare.* [f. PORT *sb.*[4] + -LIKE.] = PORTLY.

1603 FLORIO *Montaigne* (1632) Pref. Poem, When first this portlike Frontispeece was wrought. **1748** *Drayton's Wks., Poly-olb.* v. 262/2 Where once the portlike [*edd.* 1612, 1622 portly] oak and large-limb'd poplar stood.

ˈportlily, *adv. rare*—[0]. [f. as next + -LY[2].] In a portly manner.

1727 BAILEY vol. II, *Portlily*, statelily, gracefully.

portliness (ˈpɔətlɪnɪs). [f. PORTLY *a.* + -NESS.] The quality or condition of being portly.

a. Stateliness, dignity of bearing, appearance, and manner. **b.** Fullness of body, bulkiness, corpulence.

1530 PALSGR. 257/1 Portlynesse, *magnificence*. **1548** UDALL *Erasm. Par. Luke* i. 8 b, A tendre young virgin, not set furth to the worlde..by famousnesse of name, not with portlynesse of life, ne with the other thynges whiche this world vseth to haue in high regarde. **1580** BLUNDEVIL *Horsemanship* 4 b, His portlinesse in his gate. **1658** ROWLAND *Moufet's Theat. Ins.* 892 As he doth excell all the rest in portliness and feature of body.

†**portlof.** *Naut. Obs.* [a. F. *porte-lof*, f. *porte-*, PORTE- + *lof* LUFF.] ? = BUMKIN.

1397 *Foreign Acc.* No. 31 G (P.R.O.), In ij tabulis grossis de ferre emptis et expensis super le portloves dicte navis iij s. iiij d.

portly (ˈpɔətlɪ), *a.* (*adv.*) Also 6 **portely**. [f. PORT *sb.*[4] + -LY[1], [2].]

Characterized by stateliness or dignity of bearing, appearance, and manner; stately, dignified, handsome, majestic; imposing.

a 1529 SKELTON *Sp. Parrot* 453 So myche portlye pride, with pursys penyles. **a 1536** *Calisto & Melibæa* in Hazl. *Dodsley* I. 61 Her resplendent virtue, her portly courage. **a 1553** UDALL *Royster D.* III. iii. (Arb.) 47 Ye must haue a portely bragge after your estate. **1586** MARLOWE *1st Pt. Tamburl.* I. ii. 186 To be my queen and portly emperess. **1602** WARNER *Alb. Eng.* x. lix. (1612) 257 So gracious, portly, fresh and faire..had Nature her compact. **1687** DRYDEN *Hind & P.* III. 1141 A portly prince, and goodly to the sight. **1706** PHILLIPS, *Portly*, that bears a good Port or Meen, stately, comely. **1882** SERJT. BALLANTINE *Exper.* i. 7 He was a man of portly presence, a good scholar, I believe, and much respected.

b. Now usually connoting 'Large and bulky in person; stout, corpulent'.

[Cf. **1596** SHAKS. *1 Hen. IV*, II. iv. 464 A goodly portly man yfaith, and a corpulent.] **1598** SHAKS. *Merry W.* I. iii. 69 Sometimes the beame of her view guilded my foote: sometimes my portly belly. **1727** BAILEY vol. II, *Portly*, bulky, majestical. **1755** JOHNSON, *Portly*..2. Bulky, swelling. **1832** LYTTON *Eugene A.* II. vii, Whatever might have been the maladies entailed upon the portly frame of Mr. Courtland.., a want of appetite was not among the number. **1855** MACAULAY *Hist. Eng.* xiv. III. 403 He dwindled in a few weeks from a portly and even corpulent man to a skeleton. **1871** *Punch* 23 Sept. 127/2 He's got so round and portly.

c. Of things: Stately, magnificent, grand, fine; in quot. *a* 1845 with pun, and allusion to b.

1548 UDALL *Erasm. Par. Luke* xix. 148 Jesus..viewyng and beholdyng the same citie [Jerusalem] portely and gorgeous of buildynges. **1577** HANMER *Anc. Eccl. Hist.* (1619) 437 The portly gates of the pallace. **1639** MASSINGER *Unnat. Combat* III. i, Portly and curious viands are prepared. **1656** HEYLIN *Surv. France* 91 Adorned with portly and antick imagery. **1812** L. HUNT in *Examiner* 7 Dec. 771/1 Comely sentences and portly veracities. **a 1845** HOOD *Turtles* vi, With sherry, brown or golden, Or port, so olden, Bereft of body 'tis no longer portly.

†**B.** as *adv.* In a stately or dignified manner. *Obs.*

1607 MIDDLETON *Your Five Gallants* IV. viii. 250 One so fortunate..Shall bear himself more portly, live regarded, Keep house.

ˈportman. Now *local.* [f. PORT *sb.*[1], [2] + MAN *sb.*[1] Cf. MDu. *porter* townsman, burgher.]

1. In OE. use, a citizen of a town, a burgess or burgher; *spec.* (after the Conquest) = *capital* or *head portman*, one of a select number of citizens, chosen to administer the affairs of a borough.

c **1000** ÆLFRIC *Saints' Lives* xxxiii. 749 Se port-ȝerefa and þa yldostan port-men. **10..** *Voc.* in Wr.-Wülcker 333/11 *Ciuis*, ceasterȝewara, oððe portman. *c* **1122** *O.E. Chron.* an. 1068 (Laud MS.) Eadgar æðeling com þa..to Eofer wic & þa port men [*Cotton MS.* burh menn] wiþ hine griðedon. [**1200** *Charter* (Ipswich) in Gross *Gild Merch.* (1890) II. 118 Quum cito predicti xii. Capitales Portmenni fuerant iurati. **1254** *Charter* (Reading) ibid. 202 Quod predicti burgenses habeant gildhallam suam..in uilla de rading'..cum prato quod uocatur portmanebroc.] **1346** *Litt. Red Bk. Bristol* (1900) II. 26 Est ordinee qe nul portman del dit mestier soit receu en portmanrie por vendre ne achater des estraunges nul manere nouel drap. (*Mod. transl.* It is ordained that no portman of the said craft be received in the portmanry to sell to or buy any kind of new cloth from strangers.) **1527** in Fiddes *Wolsey* II. (1726) 103, 24 gentilmen of the countrey, besides the bayliffs, portemen of the towne. **1681** *Lond. Gaz.* No. 1633/3 The Bayliffs, Portmen, and Common-Council of Your Town and Burrough of Ipswich. **1704** *Ibid.* No. 4076/3 The Mayor, Recorder, Portmen, Chief Burgesses, and Freemen, of the Corporation of Orford in the County of Suffolk. **1880** *Rep. Commiss. Munic. Corpor.* I. 88 The Corporation [of Orford] consists, as heretofore, of a mayor, eight portmen, and twelve capital burgesses. *Ibid.*, One of the portmen is coroner. **1890** GROSS *Gild Merch.* I. v. 62 The twelve portmen (i.e. the two bailiffs, four coroners, and six others) were elected and sworn 'to take charge of, and to govern' the town [Ipswich], to maintain its franchises, and to administer justice.

2. A citizen or inhabitant of the Cinque Ports. (In med.L. *portensis*.)

1658 PHILLIPS, *Portmen*, a name commonly given to the inhabitants of the Cinque Ports. **1875** STUBBS *Const. Hist.*

II. xv. 288 He [Edw. I] appointed William Leyburne captain of all the portmen and mariners of the king's dominions. [**1294** B. DE COTTON *Hist. Anglic.* (Rolls) 234 Capitaneus omnium portensium et omnium aliorum marinariorum].

†'**portman-'mote.** *Obs.* exc. *Hist.* [f. prec. + ME. *imote*, MOOT *sb.*: corresp. to an OE. **portmanna ȝemót*, not found.] *lit.* The assembly of the portmen; the borough-mote; the court or common council of the portmen of a borough or town.

a **1189** *Charter* in *Calr. Charter Rolls* (1903) I. 25 Sciatis me concessisse .. Sancto Salvatori de Beremundseia .. terras suas .. quietas .. a placitis et querelis et hustingis et portmanmot et tunscipmot. **1198** *Chron. Jocel. de Brakelonda* (Camden) 74 Et curia celerarii veniret ad portmanne-mot. **1277** *Indent. Edmund Crouchback's Ordinances* in *8th Rep. Hist. MSS. Comm.* App. I. 409/1 Les delays de la curt de portemannemot de Leycestre. **1706** PHILLIPS, *Portmannimote*, (in ancient Deeds) the Portmote or Port-men's Court, held in any City, Town, or Community. **1881** *8th Rep. Hist. MSS. Comm.* App. I. 409/1 The long-lost Charter of Edmund (Crouchback) Earl of Leicester: reforming the laws and processes of the Leicester portmanemote, and confirming all the franchises of the burgh, not affected by the charter.

†'**portmanry.** [f. as prec. + -RY: cf. ALDERMANRY] The position or rank of a portman.

1346 [see PORTMAN 1].

portmanteau (pɔət'mæntəʊ), *sb.* Forms: see below. [ad. F. *portemanteau* (1547 in Godef. *Compl.*) an officer who carries a prince's mantle, a valise, a clothes-rack, f. PORTE- + *manteau* (OF. *mantel*) MANTLE; see also MANTEAU, MANTUA, POCKMANTEAU.]

1. a. A case or bag for carrying clothing and other necessaries when travelling; originally of a form suitable for carrying on horseback; now applied to an oblong stiff leather case, which opens like a book, with hinges in the middle of the back.

α. 6 **portmanteo, -mantieu, -manteaw(e, porte-manteau,** 7 **portmantau, -to, -toe, -tue, -tu, -tew;** also **porte-;** 6– **portmanteau,** *pl.* **-eaus** (9 also **-eaux).**

1584 W. FLEETWOOD in Wright *Q. Eliz. & her Times* (1838) II. 243 One of Mr. Docwraye's sonnes .. was arrained for stealing of a portmanteo, with 84*l.* in the same, taken out of an inne in Bardey. **1585** HIGINS *Junius' Nomencl.* 171/2 *Ascopera*, a bag; a wallet; a portmanteau. **1586** J. HOOKER *Hist. Irel.* II. 163/2 A note found in the port-mantieu of doctor Allen. **1598** FLORIO, *Balice*, a cloke-bag, a male, a port-manteawe. **1611** COTGR., *Ferriere*, .. a great case, or powch of leather (closed, as a Portemantue, with chaine, and locke). **1617** MORYSON *Itin.* I. 107 A souldier came out .. and demaunded of euery man fiue baocci, .. though it were onely due from them, who had port-manteaues with locks. **1624** HEYWOOD *Captives* II. i. in Bullen *O. Pl.* IV, A budget or portmantau which includes All the bawdes wealth. **1635** J. HAYWARD tr. *Biondi's Banish'd Virg.* 124 Taking .. from off his saddle-bow a portmanteau, and out of it some victuals. **1650** B. *Discolliminium* 25, I would wish the world to chaine up its breeches to its doublet as they doe Portmantu's. **1652** *Season. Exp. Netherl.* 5 Besides what .. they carryed home in their Port-mantos. **1689** D. GRANVILLE *Lett.* (Surtees, No. 37) 76 They search'd my portmantoe and plundered me of a bagg of mony. **1751** SMOLLETT *Per. Pic.* (1779) II. xxxv. 8 Their trunks and portmanteaus must be carried to the Custom-house. **1866** GEO. ELIOT *F. Holt* i, Feeling in his pockets for the keys of his portmanteaus. **1879** MISS BRADDON *Vixen* III. 265 Violet's portmanteaux were packed.

β. 6–8 (9 *Sc.* and *north. dial.*) **portmantle,** 7–8 (9 *Sc.* and *arch.*) **portmantel,** (9 **portmantillo).**

1602 Portmantle [see b]. **1612** *North's Plutarch* 977 The flesh and the portmantle [*ed.* 1595 -mantew] it was wrapt in. **1651** *Lanc. Tracts* (Chetham Soc.) 310, 600 Arms and many Portmantels and good Booty. **1654** GAYTON *Pleas. Notes* IV. ii. 181 The spoiles of Cardenio's Port-Mantle. **1702** FARQUHAR *Twin-Rivals* III. ii, What makes you sit upon the portmantle, Teague? **1821** SCOTT *Kenilw.* viii, The small portmantle which contained his necessaries. **1883** E. PENNELL-ELMHIRST *Cream Leicestersh.* 189 The portmantillos that in these days .. fill up the small of each belted second horseman's back. **1888** *Times* (weekly ed.) 2 Nov. 21/2 A saddle-horse, which also carried the Judge's port-mantle.

γ. 7–8 **port-mantua, portmantua.**

1601–2 *Archpriest Controv.* (Camden) II. 41 They sent theyr portmantuas to St. Paules monastery. **1765** H. TIMBERLAKE *Mem.* 9 One of them .. actually fell, letting my port-mantua into the water.

δ. 7 **port-mantick, -manque, portmante,** 7–9 **-manty.**

a **1613** Port-manque [see b]. *a* **1670** HACKET *Abp. Williams* I. (1692) 160 Till the Messenger with the Port-mantick came from Rome. **1680** in *12th Rep. Hist. MSS. Comm.* App. VII. 394 Paid for a new large portmante 16*s.* **1686** *Lond. Gaz.* No. 2100/4 [They] had with them a Leathern Port-manty. **1897** C. M. CAMPBELL *Deilie Jock* 259 We .. got oor portmantys and booked to Worcester.

ε. 7 **portmantuan, -ium, -eam, -en.**

a **1632** T. TAYLOR *God's Judgem.* II. v. (1642) 73 Feeling what weight the portmantuan had. **1682** *Providence Rec.* (1894) VI. 80 In ye out Celler, i. Portmantium .. In ye Portmanteam, 3 Cases of leather. **1698** [R. FERGUSON] *View Eccles.* Pref., He .. is degraded to come behind with the Portmanten.

b. *fig.* (See also 4 b.)

1602 *Narcissus* (1893) 283 O thou whose breast .. is .. prudences portmantle. *a* **1613** OVERBURY *A Wife* (1638) 263 That the soules of Women and Lovers, are wrapt in the port-manque of their senses. **1641** R. BROOKE *Eng. Episc.* I. IV. 11 As sure to finde the Spirit in a *conge d'eslire*, as others not long since, in the Tridentine Port-mantile. **1900** *Westm. Gaz.* 28 Apr. 3/1 The demand for the franchise was .. a kind of portmanteau into which all our grievances could be stuffed and dispatched to Pretoria.

‖**2.** An officer of the king of France: 'The Kings Cloake-bag-bearer' (Cotgr.) [Fr.].

1597 G. GILPIN *Let.* 12 Feb. in *N. & Q.* 9th Ser. IV. 537/1 Here is arrived from the King of France a porte-manteau, who brought the ratification under the great seal of the agreements and treaty.

‖**3.** A clothes-rack, an arrangement of pegs to hang clothes on. [Fr.]

1727–41 CHAMBERS *Cycl.*, *Port-manteau*, a piece of joiners work, fastened to the wall, in a wardrobe, armory, &c., proper for the hanging on of cloaks, hats, &c. **1847** C. BRONTË *J. Eyre* xxv, Not to me appertained that suit of wedding raiment: .. the vapoury veil pendent from the usurped portmanteau. *Ibid.*, It took the light, held it aloft, and surveyed the garments pendent from the portmanteau.

4. *attrib.* and *Comb.*, as ***portmanteau robbery, thief***; ***portmanteau gelding, horse*** (a baggage horse); ***portmanteau-maker, manufacturer***, †***-trunk***; **portmanteau saddle**: see quot. 1688.

1681 *Lond. Gaz.* No. 1583/4 A coloured leather Port-mantle Saddle, Blew fring in the seat. **1683** *Verulam MSS.* (Hist. MSS. Comm. 1906) 210 For a portmantue trunk, 0. 11. 0. **1688** R. HOLME *Armoury* III. 345/1 A Portmantle Saddle hath a Cantle behind the seat to keep the Portmantle .. off the Riders back. **1694** *Lond. Gaz.* No. 2996/4 A bright bay Portmantua-Gelding, about 8l. price. **1772** NUGENT tr. *Hist. Fr. Gerund* I. 438 Mounted on a raw-boned, .. hollow-eyed, pyballed portmanteau-horse. **1819** M. EDGEWORTH *Let.* 2 June (1971) 210 The boxes and small portmanteau trunk .. have not arrived. **1885** *List of Subscribers, Classified* (United Telephone Co.) (ed. 6) 213 (*heading*) Trunk and Portmanteau Manufacturers. **1899** *Daily News* 19 June 6 A portmanteau maker. **1900** *Westm. Gaz.* 22 Aug. 5/3 A series of portmanteau robberies from the roofs of four-wheeled cabs.

b. In the sense of 'that into which things are packed together'; originally applied by 'L. Carroll' to a factitious word made up of the blended sounds of two distinct words and combining the meanings of both; hence used *attrib.*, and subseq. extended to things that are or suggest a combination of two different things of the same kind.

[**1872** 'L. CARROLL' *Through Looking-Gl.* vi. 127 Well, 'slithy' means 'lithe and slimy'... You see it's like a portmanteau—there are two meanings packed up into one word. *Ibid.* 129 'Mimsy' is 'flimsy and miserable' (there's another portmanteau for you).] **1882** *Cornh. Mag.* July 25 They admirably illustrate the portmanteau word 'slithy' in the Jabberwocky poem. **1896** [see BRUNCH]. **1902** *Westm. Gaz.* 10 June 2/2 As a fact Lord Rosebery was guilty of what we may call a 'portmanteau' quotation, in that he combined into one what Lord Salisbury said about Ireland and South Africa. **1905** *Ibid.* 15 Aug. 4/2 It is a wise bird that will not foul its own nest, if this portmanteau proverb may be allowed. **1972** *Amer. Speech 1968* XLIII. 201 He was particularly concerned with .. *portmanteau forms* of the sort illustrated by *motel* for 'motor hotel'. **1973** *Sci. Amer.* Dec. 116/2 A more interesting blend, called a portmanteau word by Lewis Carroll, combines two words with similar meanings into one: 'instantaneous' and 'momentary' into 'momentaneous', 'splinters' and 'blisters' into 'splisters', 'shifting' and 'switching' into 'swifting' and 'edited' and 'annotated' into 'editated'. **1978** *Dædalus* Fall 93 But such names are more often nothing more than the portmanteau terms describing a group of contemporaries who come together for a few years and then go their own ways.

c. Applied *attrib.* to a general description or category, or to a word or expression which has a general or generalized meaning.

1909 *Daily Chron.* 18 Feb. 4/7 You may notice the same 'portmanteau' descriptions of persons wanted by the police. They would fit a dozen men in every hundred yards of London. **1949** [see BAROQUE *a.* (*sb.*)]. **1955** *Times* 12 May 7/3 The phrase *Britanniarum omnium*, which had appeared on the coinage since 1902, was discontinued from the beginning of 1954. The words were a portmanteau expression designed as a free rendering in Latin of 'The British Dominions beyond the seas'. **1957** *Listener* 18 July 86/2 The Act of 1897 .. is one of those portmanteau measures under which a person can be charged with any action. **1960** [see CASSEROLE 1]. **1960** *Times* 14 Oct. 15/6 Such portmanteau terms as 'sprays', 'seed dressings', and 'insecticides' have been used uncritically. **1962** *Listener* 19 Apr. 674/1 The concept, or rather the concepts, of 'culture'. This portmanteau word has been indispensable to intellectuals for 100 years at least.

d. portmanteau morph *Linguistics*, a morph which represents two morphemes simultaneously; also ellipt. ***portmanteau***.

1947 [see BIMORPHEMIC *a.*]. **1950** *Language* XXVI. 84 If we find it more convenient to regard these forms as single morphs, we must at least take them to be portmanteaus, and not completely arbitrary ones. **1953** C. E. BAZELL *Linguistic Form* 54 Furthermore this terminology renders superfluous the family of subtractive morphs, zero-morphs, and portmanteau-morphs. **1972** HARTMANN & STORK *Dict. Lang. & Linguistics* 180/1 *Portmanteau morph*, a single morph which stands for two morphemes. The best known example is French *au* |o| 'to the' which represents *à* + *le*.

portmanteau (pɔət'mæntəʊ), *v.* [f. PORTMANTEAU *sb.* 4 b.] *trans.* To combine. Also *intr.* for *pass.*

1902 *Westm. Gaz.* 28 May 2/2 We are amused at the attempt to portmanteau into one (as Lewis Carroll would say) the Education Bill and the Bread Tax. **1906** *Daily Chron.* 22 Mar. 6/7 Hotten's Slang Dictionary .. has only two [words] for threepence—'thrums' and 'thrups'—neither of which will portmanteau with 'telegram' comfortably. **1967** G. F. FIENNES *I tried to run a Railway* v. 58 Chingford, Enfield, Hertford and Bishops Stortford (portmanteaud as the 'Chenford').

portman'tologism. [f. PORTMANTEAU *sb.* 4 b + -OLOG(Y + -ISM.] = PORTMANTEAU *sb.* 4 b. Hence **portman'tologist**, one who utters or studies portmanteau words.

1887 *Spectator* 9 Apr. 492/2 An allusion to the 'Torrible Zone' which is one of the most beautiful of portmantologisms. **1920** T. NICKLIN *Sounds of Stand. Eng.* 85 Sometimes we may surmise that these constructions are what may be called 'portmantologisms'. **1934** *Times* 16 Mar. 15/5, I wonder how many 'portmantologists' realize that the Russian language as spoken in the U.S.S.R. is resorting more and more to the invention of portmantologisms.

portment ('pɔətmənt). *rare.* [a. F. *portement* a carrying, bearing, †behaviour, f. *porter* to carry.]

†**1.** Bearing; ***portement of arms***, bearing of arms, achievement in arms. *Obs. rare*⁻¹.

1485 CAXTON *Chas. Gt.* 81 It is not redde .. that euer ony man .. bare hym so wel and dyd so grete portemente of armes.

2. Deportment. *nonce-use.*

1850 BLACKIE *Æschylus* II. 141 But be your portment such As breeds no shame to us.

†'**portmote.** *Obs.* exc. *Hist.* Forms: 3 **portimote,** 4 **portemot,** (6 **portemounte),** 7 **portmoote,** 6– **portmote; portmoot.** [f. PORT *sb.*¹, ² + ME. *imote*, MOOT *sb.* = OE. type **port-ȝemót*: cf. *burh-ȝemót*.]

1. The court of a borough; a borough-mote. (Esp. used of cities and boroughs in the County Palatine of Chester.)

[**1267** *Charter Hen. III* in Rymer *Fœdera* (1816) I. 471 Prohibeo et precipio ne ullo modo respondeant, nisi illorum proprio portimoto. *a* **1377** *Abingdon Rolls* (Camden) 34 De portemot', pede pulverizato, et assisa fracta.] **1574** *Acts Privy Council* (1894) VIII. 228 The same to be openly redde at the next Portemounte [at Chester] after the receipt hereof. **1601** *Act 43 Eliz.* c. 15 §1 Any originall Writ or Writs of Covenant .. retornable before the Mayor of the saide Citie for the tyme beinge, in the Portmoote Courte to be holden within the saide Citie [of Chester]. **1727–41** CHAMBERS *Cycl.* s.v., Portmotes are also held in some inland towns, as at Knolst in Cheshire. **1765** *Act 5 Geo. III*, c. 26 *Preamble*, Courts Baron, Courts of Admiralty, Courts of Portmote, and Leets. **1890** GROSS *Gild Merch.* I. 64 The general laws of the burghal community emanated from the burghmotes or assemblies (Court Leet, Burghmote, Portmote, &c.). **1902** (*title*) The Portmote or Court Leet Records of the Borough or Town and Royal Manor of Salford. **1951** D. M. STENTON *Eng. Society Early Middle Ages* 177 The ancient borough court, the portmoot, was presided over by the reeve.

2. The court of a (legal) sea-port town.

(Perhaps orig. an error of the Law Dicts.)

1598 MANWOOD *Lawes Forest* xxiii. §1 (1615) 217/2 Portmote is euer in a Hauen towne, for it is the Court of the Port or Hauen. **1607** COWELL *Interpr.*, *Portemote*, .. signifieth a Court kept in hauen townes... It is sometime called the Portmote Court, an. 43 Eliz. cap. 15 [cf. quot. 1601 in 1]. **1765** BLACKSTONE *Comm.* I. vii. 264 These legal ports were undoubtedly at first assigned by the crown; since to each of them a court of portmote is incident, the jurisdiction of which must flow from the royal authority.

‖**porto** ('pɔətəʊ). [a. Pg. *pôrto* port wine.]

a. = PORT *sb.*⁷ **b.** In full ***porto français***: an aperitif made from port; also *attrib.*

1847 DISRAELI *Tancred* I. i. 9 A capon in every platter, with some fountains of ale and good Porto. **1857** DICKENS *Dorrit* II. xxviii. 564 Bring Port wine! I'll drink nothing but Porto-Porto. **1926** R. FIRBANK *Concerning Eccentricities Cardinal Pirelli* vi. 65 All this Porto and stuff to keep awake make a woman liverish. **1935** SCHOONMAKER & MARVEL *Compl. Wine Bk.* iii. 88 The dark red Priorato of Catalonia, which was formerly sold as 'Tarragona Port', .. is annually shipped to France, where it forms the base of several well-known commercial *apéritifs*, and is liberally used in the manufacture of '*Porto français*'. **1951** R. POSTGATE *Plain Man's Guide to Wine* iii. 61 If he is with a Frenchman he can offer him 'un porto' which is like a cold and thin port, or 'un malaga français'... But he should not drink them himself. **1961** N. FROUD et al. tr. *Montagné's Larousse Gastronomique* 761/1 *Port, Porto*, Portuguese wine... Sweet and soft, and in France it is sometimes drunk as an aperitif. It is used in preparing sauces. **1970** N. FREELING *Kitchen Bk.* ii. 16 Porto, the invariable bourgeois apéritif. **1972** A. L. SIMON *Gazetteer of Wines* 194/2 Port, Porto or Vinho do Porto can only be produced in this area [*sc.* Douro]. **1974** S. COULTER *Château* I. xxii. 172 It was foie gras with porto jelly.

†**portobello** (pɔətəʊ'bɛləʊ). *Obs.* [The capture of Portobello in South America in 1739 prob. gave rise to the name of the game.] ? A kind of game resembling billiards.

1777 HOWARD *Prisons Eng.* 26 Gaming in various forms is very frequent: cards, dice, skittles, Missisippi and Portobello tables, billiards, fives, tennis, &c. *Ibid.* 198 One can scarcely ever enter the walls [of the King's Bench Prison] without seeing parties at skittles, missisippi, portobello, tennis, fives, &c.

portocaval, var. PORTACAVAL *a.*

†**portoir.** *Obs. rare.* [a. F. *portoir* (16th c. in Godef.), *le portoir des vignes*, 'the braunch that beares the grapes'.] A bearing branch (of a vine).

1601 HOLLAND *Pliny* XVII. xxi. 527 Braunches..which were portoirs and bare grapes the yeare before. *Ibid.* XVIII. xxxi. 605 The..greene braunches called the Portoirs.

†**'portoise.** *Naut. Obs.* [Origin uncertain.] = PORT-LAST.

1710 J. HARRIS *Lex. Techn.* II. s.v., For a Ship to ride a Portoise, is to ride with her Yards a Portlast, or struck down on the Deck. **1794** *Rigging & Seamanship* II. 255* *Portoise,* the same as *Port-last.* **1867** [see PORT-LAST].

portolan ('pɔətəʊlən). Also **portolano, portulan.** [ad. It. *portolano,* f. *porto* PORT *sb.*¹: cf. L. *hortulānus,* It. *ortolano* gardener, f. *hortus* garden; thence F. *portulan.*] A book of sailing directions, describing harbours, sea-coasts, etc., and illustrated with charts. Also *attrib.* and *Comb.*

1858 SIMMONDS *Dict. Trade, Portulan* (French), a ship-master's guide; a book containing the situation and description of sea-ports, etc., with instructions for navigation. **1878** *Nature* XVIII. 151/1 Among these old maps and portulans..are:—1. The Medicean Portulan (1351). 2. The Catalan Atlas. **1891** J. WINSOR *Columbus* App. 530 About the beginning of the fourteenth century Italy and the western Mediterranean islands began to produce those atlases of sea-charts, which have come down to us under the name of 'portolanos'. **1894** —— *Cartier to Frontenac* 7 It seems to be evident from a Portuguese portolano of 1504..that at this time they had not developed the entrances to this gulf north and west of Newfoundland. **1897** F. A. BATHER tr. *Nordenskiöld's Periplus* 18 The portolan-manufacturer or draughtsman used by preference gaudy and bright colours. **1898** *Geogr. Jrnl.* XII. 374 We then have..a Series of World-maps and Mediterranean portolans. **1935** *Ibid.* LXXXV. 105, 430 portolans dating from the fourteenth to the sixteenth centuries. **1941** *Antiquity* XV. 186 Portolan charts were intended for the use of mariners. **1972** *Daily Tel.* 12 Dec. 14/6 Dolphin Book Company, of Oxford, paid £7,000 for a complete Mediterranean portolan atlas signed Joannes Oliva and dated Messina 1582. **1978** *Nature* 1 June 409/1 For many the intriguing question remains: whether the keenly observant craftsmen-sailors of Northern Europe did not have a recorded lore of their own—effective but, like the portolan charts, tardily acknowledged by the churchmen?

porto-pyæmic (ˌpɔətəʊpaɪ'iːmɪk), *a. Path.* [f. *porto-*, taken as comb. form of L. *porta* in *vena portæ.*] Pertaining to pyæmia of the portal vein.

1897 *Allbutt's Syst. Med.* IV. 127 Porto-pyæmic liver abscess—Pylephlebitis.

Porto Rican: see PUERTO RICAN *sb.* and *a.*

portos, portoos, portous, obs. ff. PORTAS.

portosystemic (ˌpɔətəʊsɪ'stɛmɪk, -'iːmɪk), *a. Surg.* Also **porta-,** and with hyphen. [f. as PORTO-PYÆMIC *a.* + SYSTEMIC *a.*] Applied to an anastomosis between the portal vein and a systemic vein.

1962 *Lancet* 22 Dec. 1289/2 These studies have shown abnormalities of serum-I.L.A..in patients with portal hypertension and its associated portosystemic bypass. **1974** PASSMORE & ROBSON *Compan. Med. Stud.* III. xx. 21/2 Another site for porta-systemic anastomosis is in the territory of the junction of the inferior mesenteric and the inferior rectal veins. **1976** *Lancet* 11 Dec. 1268/2 An exploration was attempted..but was quickly abandoned because of massive blood-loss due to extensive portosystemic shunts and bleeding tendency.

portour, portoure, obs. ff. PORTER, PORTURE.

†**port-pain.** *Obs.* Also 5–6 **-payne,** 7 **-pane.** [a. obs. F. **porte-pain,* lit. carry-bread: see PORTE- and PAIN *sb.*²] A cloth in which to carry bread to the table without touching it with the hands.

*c*1460 J. RUSSELL *Bk. Nurture* 262 To þe port-payne forthe ye passe, & þere viij. loues ye leese. **1519** HORMAN *Vulg.* 164 Put thy loues in a portpayne. **1566** WITHALS *Dict.* 44 A porte payne to beare bread fro the pantree to the table with, *lintheum panarium.* **1658** PHILLIPS, *Port-pain* (French), a kinde of Towel used at Court, wherein they carry their bread to serve for the Table.

portpen, obs. form of PORCUPINE.

portrait, [F. *portrait*], obs. pa. pple. of PORTRAY *v.*, q.v.

portrait ('pɔətrət), *sb.* Forms: α. 6 **purtrait, -e, -trayt, -e,** 6–7 **purtraict.** β. 6 **portrayt,** 6–7 **portrate, -traite, -tract,** 6–8 **portraict,** 6– **portrait.** γ. 6 **pourtreict, -tracte,** 6–7 **-traite, -trayt(e, -tract,** 6–8 **-traict, pourtrait.** [a. F. *portrait,* OF. also *portret* (13th c. in Hatz.-Darm.), obs. *pourtrait, po(u)rtraict* sb., from *portrait* pa. pple. of *portraire* obs. to portray: cf. med.L. *protractus* plan, image, portrait, f. *protractus,* pa. pple. of L. *protrahĕre*: see PORTRAY.]

1. A figure drawn, painted, or carved upon a surface to represent some object. **a.** A drawing, painting, or other delineation of any object; a picture, design (in general). Now *rare* or *Obs.*

1570 BUCHANAN *Chamæleon* Wks. (1892) 43 Mony that hes nowther sene yᵉ said beist, nor na perfyte portraict of it. **1589** PUTTENHAM *Eng. Poesie* II. xi. (Arb.) 110 By this noble pourtrayt..Is plainely exprest..The sounde Pillar. **1606** HOLLAND *Sueton.* 24 The full pourtraict and proportion of which horse, he dedicated..before the Temple of Venus Genitrix. **1610** —— *Camden's Brit.* (1637) 97 The Britans Coines, the portracts whereof I have here shewed. *c*1620 *Mary Magd.* 1271 Yᵉ pourtract of this outward frame. **1756–7** tr. *Keysler's Trav.* (1760) II. 279 The portrait of Eve is much admired by all connoisseurs. **1821** CRAIG *Lect. Drawing* vi. 333 The back-grounds of your portraits.

b. *spec.* (now almost always) A representation or delineation of a person, esp. of the face, made from life, by drawing, painting, photography, engraving, etc.; a likeness.

1585 T. WASHINGTON tr. *Nicholay's Voy.* III. xiv. 97 The pourtractes and figures of the principallest amongst them. **1596** SHAKS. *Merch. V.* II. ix. 54 What's here, the portrait of a blinking idiot. *a*1649 DRUMM. OF HAWTH. *Poems* 12 Draw thousand Pourtraits of her on your face. **1649** *Sc. Acts Chas. II* (1819) VI. 363/1 Ordains His Royall Name, Portract and Seal to be used in the publick writings. **1710** STEELE *Tatler* No. 118 ¶6, I would rather see you work upon History-Pieces, than on single Portraicts. **1858** LYTTON *What will he do* I. vi, The gentleman who wanted to take your portrait.

†**c.** A solid image, statue, effigy. *Obs.*

1585 T. WASHINGTON tr. *Nicholay's Voy.* IV. xxix. 151 Prometheus..inuented the natural pourtractes with the fatte earth. **1600** FAIRFAX *Tasso* XII. xciv, Her tombe was..built of polisht stone, and thereon laid The liuely shape and purtrait of the maid. **1638** SIR T. HERBERT *Trav.* (ed. 2) 144 On one side the gate stands a..great Elephant, on the other a Rhinoceros;..the portraicts are out of the shining Marble.

2. *abstr.* The action or art of making a portrait (in quot. 1846 in *spec.* sense: see 1 b); portraiture.

1589 PUTTENHAM *Eng. Poesie* III. i. (Arb.) 150 Th' excellent painter bestoweth the rich Orient coulours vpon his table of pourtraite. **1846** RUSKIN *Mod. Paint.* II. III. I. xiv. §14 That habit of the old and great painters of introducing portrait into all their highest works.

3. *fig.* **a.** Something that represents, typifies, or resembles something else; an image, representation, type; likeness, similitude. (In quot. 1623 *absol.* A striking or impressive sight, a scene.)

1577 NORTHBROOKE *Dicing* (1843) 39 Poetes terme sleepe an image, or pourtraite of death. **1590** SPENSER *F.Q.* II. xii. 23 Dreadfull pourtraicts of deformitee. *c*1614 SIR W. MURE *Dido & Æneas* II. 158 Then ȝoung Ascanius..His parents portrate perfectly presenting. **1623** T. GOAD *Dolef. Euen-Song* 16 If any man could looke in at those gates,..he would report such a pourtrait as was this spectacle. **1866** LIDDON *Bampt. Lect.* iv. (1875) 192 Jesus reveals a moral portrait.

b. A verbal picture or representation; a graphic or vivid description.

1596 BELL *Surv. Popery* Ded., The liuely purtraite of the foure monarchies. **1738** WARBURTON *Div. Legat.* I. 126 An exact Pourtrait of natural Religion. **1837** CARLYLE *Misc. Ess., Mirabeau* (1875) V. 242 Her portrait, by the seconding Marquis himself, is not very captivating.

c. *Typogr.* A format in which the height of an illustration or page is greater than the width; cf. UPRIGHT *a.* 5 c. Often used as quasi-*adj.* or quasi-*adv.*

1932 [see LANDSCAPE *sb.* 1 c]. **1956** H. WILLIAMSON *Methods Bk. Design* iii. 16 The book is in fact taller than it is wide, and by analogy with the painter's method these proportions are sometimes called portrait. **1975** J. BUTCHER *Copy-Editing* 304 *Portrait,* (1) the shape of a book or illustration is referred to as 'portrait' when its height is greater than its width; (2) if a table is 'set portrait' it is set upright on the page and not turned to read up the page.

4. *attrib.* and *Comb.,* as *portrait-collector, -group, -head, -photographer, -photography, -sculpture, -sketch, -study, -work; portrait-like* adj.; **portrait-bust,** a bust giving an exact (i.e. not idealized) likeness; **portrait-gallery,** a gallery containing a collection of portraits, or the collection itself (also *fig.*); **portrait-lathe,** a lathe adapted for turning copies of busts or medallions; **portrait-lens,** a compound photographic lens adapted for taking portraits; **portrait-painter,** a painter of portraits; so **portrait-painting** *vbl. sb.* (also *fig.*) and *ppl. a.*; **portrait-ring,** a ring with a miniature portrait set in it; **portrait-statue** (cf. *portrait-bust*); **portrait-stone,** a lasque or flat diamond used to cover a miniature portrait.

1887 *Boston* (Mass.) *Jrnl.* 22 Sept. 4/1 Governor Ames has given the sculptor..an order for a *portrait-bust. **1814** W. H. IRELAND (*title*) Chalcographimania; or, the *Portrait-Collector and Printseller's Chronicle. **1841** EMERSON *Lect. Times* Misc. (1855) 215 Why not draw for these times a *portrait-gallery? **1905** J. FITZMAURICE-KELLY *Cervantes in Eng.* 4 To find place in Cervantes's rich portrait-gallery. **1911** *Encycl. Brit.* XXII. 129/1 The magnificent *portrait groups at Haarlem by Hals..must also be mentioned. **1937** *Burlington Mag.* Jan. 47/2 Concerning Cotes's portrait-group (represented by a colour plate), one may suspend judgment. **1970** *Oxf. Compan. Art* 452/1 He [*sc.* Gainsborough] also painted some small portrait groups in landscape settings. **1899** MACKAIL *Life Morris* I. 277 A *portrait-head of the author. **1884** KNIGHT *Dict. Mech.* Suppl., **Portrait Lathe,* a lathe adapted to copying busts. **1905** *Westm. Gaz.* 27 June 1/3 He was engaged in the Paris Mint, and while there invented a portrait lathe by which medallion dies of any size might be engraved in steel. **1862** *Catal. Internat. Exhib.* II. XIII. 9 A pair of quick-acting *portrait Lenses. **1789** T. TWINING *Aristotle's Treat. Poetry* (1812) II. 378 With too close and *portrait-like delineation of general nature. **1758** *N.Y. Gaz.* 21 Aug. 3/3 Thomas Milworth, *Portrait Painter, Has removed to the House of Mr. Samuel Deall in Broadstreet. **1780** J. WEDGWOOD *Let.* 21 Oct. (1965) 260 Methinks I would not be a portrait painter upon any condition whatever. **1797** TWEDDELL *Rem.* xxvii. (1815) 155 Mad. Le Brun is most decidedly the best portrait-painter in Europe. **1856** MRS. CARLYLE *Lett.* II. 277, I have a friend, who has constituted herself a portrait-painter. **1959** *Observer* 29 Mar. 7/2 You have no idea what portrait painters suffer from the vanity of their sitters. **1765** T. H. CROKER et al. *Compl. Dict. Arts & Sci.* II. s.v. *Portrait,* We use the term *portrait-painting, in contradistinction to history painting. **1791** BOSWELL *Johnson* 18 Apr. an. 1775, He thought portrait-painting an improper employment for a woman. **1821** H. C. ROBINSON *Diary* 2 Dec. (1967) 71, I have finished *Waverley*... Its merit lies in portrait and scene painting. **1840** CARLYLE *Heroes* iii. (1872) 96 It is in what I called Portrait-painting, ..that Shakspeare is great. **1842** DICKENS *Let.* 2 Apr. (1974) III. 179 My portrait-painting friend told me. **1875** tr. *Vogel's Chem. Light* xiv. 150 *Portrait-photography makes greater demands than any other branch on the good taste of the photographer. **1898** *Daily News* 8 Aug. 5/6 The above *portrait-pictures must include some 5,000 faces, to say nothing of busts, half, quarter lengths, and full figures. **1877** W. JONES *Finger-ring* 496, I have mentioned several *portrait-rings of remarkable interest. **1877** A. B. EDWARDS *Up Nile* xxii. 709 *Portrait-statues of private individuals. **1904** *Daily Chron.* 15 Apr. 3/4 A very excellent *portrait-study, a tender and loving reminiscence of the high-spirited, ..noble-hearted woman.

†**'portrait,** *v. Obs.* or *rare.* Forms: see PORTRAIT *sb.* [Represented first in pa. pple. *portraited* (found earlier than *portrait* sb.), being app. an extended form of the ME. (orig. French) pa. pple. *portrait* (see PORTRAY *v.*); this implied a vb. *portrait,* which appears after 1550.]

1. *trans.* To make a portrait, picture, or image of: = PORTRAY *v.* 1. (Also with *forth, out.*)

*a*1548 HALL *Chron., Hen. VIII* 84 b, In it was the whole spere [= sphere] portrated. **1581** SAVILE *Tacitus' Hist.* II. ii. (1591) 54 She [Venus] is not elswhere purtraited so. **1596** SPENSER *F.Q.* IV. v. 12 To pourtraict beauties Queene. **1596** R. L[INCHE] *Diella* (1877) 73 To..portraite forth thy Angel-hued beautie. **1610** GUILLIM *Heraldry* III. xxiv. 243, I am far from their opinion who damne it for superstition to portract that Glorious Virgin or her Babe. **1689** tr. *Buchanan's De Jure Regni* 32 The perfect Image of the true Helena, pourtracted with her lively Colours. **1864** DK. MANCHESTER *Court & Soc.* I. xi. 216 To sit to a limner to be 'portraited', as the phrase ran. **1908** *Daily Chron.* 3 Apr. 4/4 We are not puffed and paragraphed and portraited in the papers.

2. *fig.* To represent or describe graphically, to set forth: = PORTRAY *v.* 3 b, 4. (Also with *forth, out.*)

*a*1581 N. WOODS *Conflict of Consc.* I. i. A iij, I will therefore in breefe purtraict and paint him out. **1593** BILSON *Govt. Christ's Ch.* 25 That Christ did portrait out for the regiment of his Church. **1611** SPEED *Hist. Gt. Brit.* IX. xv. §6 Our learned Knight Eliot setting his pen to portrait a perfect Gouernour. **1655** FULLER *Ch. Hist.* I. ii. §13 The Authour..doth pourtraict and describe the Bounty and Church-buildings of that King.

3. a. *transf.* To draw or make (a picture, figure, or image): = PORTRAY *v.* 1 b.

1552 HULOET, Portraytynge of ymages in mettall or stone, *sculptura.* **1594** T. B. *La Primaud. Fr. Acad.* II. 47 No image or picture, howe well soeuer it bee painted and purtrayted, is to be compared with the forme and figure of mans bodie. **1635** J. HAYWARD tr. *Biondi's Banish'd Virg.* 107, I caused to be pourtrayted on my shield the Impresa of the Swan. **1669** STURMY *Mariner's Mag.* VII. v. 9 To pourtraict this on a.. Plane, first draw the Horizontal Line.

b. *fig.* (cf. 2).

1576 NEWTON *Lemnie's Complex.* (1633) 52, I will pourtrait and set before your eyes, a patterne and image thereof, first conceived in minde or imagination. **1613** DRUMM. OF HAWTH. *Cypress Grove* Wks. (1711) 125 As those images were pourtraicted in my mind.

Hence †**'portraiting** *vbl. sb.*

1552 [see 3]. **1608** WILLET *Hexapla Exod.* 455 Such delineation and portraiting of Christ.

'portraitist. [f. PORTRAIT *sb.* + -IST: so F. *portraitiste.*] One whose occupation it is to take portraits (by painting or photography); *esp.* a portrait-painter. (In quot. 1899 applied to a sculptor.) Also *fig.*

1866 *Standard* 12 Sept. 2/3 After the sitter has, by movement or contortion, baffled the portraitist. **1875** tr. *Vogel's Chem. Light* 149 Most persons conceive under the term photographer only a portraitist. **1881** *Times* 5 Jan. 4/3 Gainsborough we have seen as portraitist and as landscapist. **1899** *Daily News* 24 July 7/3 Houdon was the great portraitist in marble of the eighteenth century. **1976** *Amer. N. & Q.* XIV. 151/2 JEB [*sc.* James E. Buttersworth] was becoming an authentic ship portraitist, in response to demands from the owners of the shipping lines. **1977** V. S. PRITCHETT *Gentle Barbarian* viii. 119 Turgenev..is a portraitist who gives the surface of people.

†**portraitour.** *Obs. rare.* [prob. AF. = OF. **portraiteur,* f. as PORTRAITURE + *-our*: see -OUR: cf. OF. *portraitierre* (*a* 1200 in Godef.).] = PORTRAYER.

*c*1386, *c*1425 [see PORTRAYER].

‖**portrait parlé** (pɔrtrɛ parle). Pl. **portraits parlés.** [Fr., = spoken portrait.] A detailed description of a person's physical characteristics in mainly anthropometric terms, esp. one of a type used in the identification of criminals and developed by Alphonse Bertillon (see BERTILLONAGE). Also *transf.*

1913 A. B. REEVE *Poisoned Pen* v. 141 Neither the 'portrait parlé' nor the ordinary photography nor any other system will suffice alone against the arch-criminal. **1940** N. MARSH *Surfeit of Lampreys* (1941) xiv. 205 Is this the B-b-Bertillion [*sic*] system?.. P-portrait parlé? **1956** H. T. F. RHODES *Alphonse Bertillon* xiv. 105 The *portrait parlé* is a derivative of the anthropometric system. **1963** T. TULLETT *Inside Interpol* iii. 35 One system is unique in police work and based on the Portrait Parle method of facial identification and the famous Bertillon system of measurement of certain key parts of the human frame. **1972** R. Cobb *Reactions to French Revolution* iii. 67 *Portraits parlés* tell us perhaps more about the police.. than about those to whom these visible passports were so painstakingly fixed. **1973** *Daily Tel.* 20 Dec. 7/3 He left an enormous volume of papers. Martin Gilbert has made of them not so much a biography as a *portrait parlé.* **1974** *Encycl. Brit. Macropædia* XIV. 671/2 Long before the birth of Christ, Egyptians used detailed word descriptions of individuals, a concept known today as 'portrait parle'.

portraiture (ˈpɔətrətjʊə(r)). Forms: α. 4-5 **purtreyture, -treiture,** 5 **-treture, -trayture, -tretur, -tatur,** 5-6 **-trat(o)ure,** 6-7 **-traiture.** β. 4-5 **portreiture, -treyt(o)ure;** *Sc.* **-tratore, -owre,** 4-6 **-treture,** 5-6 *Sc.* **-tratour(e;** 5-7 **-trature, -trayture,** 6-7 **-tracture,** *Sc.* **-traitour,** (6 **-turature, -terature, -tature, -titure,** *Sc.* **protatour),** 6-7 **portracture,** *Sc.* **-traitour,** 7-8 **-traicture,** 5- **portraiture.** γ. 5 **pourtreture,** 5-7 **-trature,** 5-8 **-traiture,** 6-8 **-traicture,** 7 **-tracture.** [ME. a. OF. *pur-, pour-, portraiture* (12-13th c. in Hatz.-Darm.), f. *pourtrait* pa. pple. and sb., PORTRAIT + -URE.]

1. The action or art of portraying; representation of an object by painting, drawing, etc.; delineation. Also in concrete or collective sense; esp. in phr. ***in portraiture*** = portrayed, delineated.

c **1375** *Sc. Leg. Saints* xi. (*Symon & Judas*) 68 A paynteore, þat rycht sle wes in portratore. *c* **1384** Chaucer *H. Fame* I. 131 In portreytoure I sawgh anoon ryght hir figure Naked fletynge in a see. *c* **1386** —— *Knt.'s T.* 1110 The portreiture [*v.rr* purtreyture, pourtrature, purtratoure, etc.] that was vp on the wal. **1390** Gower *Conf.* II. 83 Zeuzis fond ferst the pourtreture. **1461** *Liber Pluscardensis* xi. viii, With plesand propirnes of purtratoure. **1546** Langley *Pol. Verg. De Invent.* II. xvi. 62 Porturature Gykes a Lidiun as Plinie thinketh did first inuent & deuyse it in Egipte. *a* **1568** Ascham *Scholem.* (Arb.) 137 As in portracture and paintyng. **1711** Steele *Spect.* No. 4 ¶7 The Portraitures of insignificant People by ordinary Painters. **1718** *Free-thinker* No. 63. 56 How lovely sacred Pourtraiture appears! **1846** Ruskin *Mod. Paint.* II. III. I. xiv. §14 We find the custom of portraiture constant with them. **1874** *Edin. Rev.* July 172 Portraiture rose to its highest excellence as the nobler characteristics of sculpture faded.

2. *concr.* A figure or delineation of a person or thing; a picture, drawing, etc.: = PORTRAIT 1, 1 b.

(In quot. *c* 1440, A diagram, figure.)

? *a* **1366** Chaucer *Rom. Rose* 141 With many riche portraitures. *c* **1440** Capgrave *Life St. Kath.* I. 387 In euclidis bokys wyth his portraturys. *c* **1449** Pecock *Repr.* I. xix. 114 Picturis and purtraturis or graued werk. **1542** Udall *Erasm. Apoph.* 88 Images and porteratures of menne. **1555** Eden *Decades* 105 Portitures of herbes floures and knottes. **1563** Man *Musculus' Commonpl.* 48 To be worshipped in images and portatures. **1631** Weever *Anc. Fun. Mon.* 257 His pourtraiture engrauen thereupon. **1652-62** Heylin *Cosmogr.* I. (1682) 210 There is a Portraicture representing Rome. **1677** R. J. Thoroton *Antiq. Nottingham* (title-p.), Beautified with Maps, Prospects, and Pourtraictures. **1873** Longf. *Chaucer*, The chamber walls depicted all around With portraitures of huntsman, hawk, and hound.

†**b.** A solid image, a statue: = PORTRAIT *sb.* 1 c.

1548 Udall *Erasm. Par. Luke* xvi. 137 To embrace in his armes the countrefaicte porterature of a man. **1594** Constable *Diana* VI. iii, A Carver.. Hewed out the portrature of Venus sonne In Marble rocke. **1628** Coke *On Litt.* Pref., A fair tomb of marble with his statue or portraiture upon it. **1720** Hearne *Collect.* (O.H.S.) VII. 122 A large Grave-stone, whereon is the portraicture of a Man, seemingly in a warlike habit.

3. *gen.* and *fig.* An image, representation, figure; a mental image, idea; †a type, exemplar (*obs.*). (Cf. PORTRAIT *sb.* 3.)

c **1420** *Chron. Vilod.* 1785 þis purtatur he bare euer in here clene hert Of goddus Passion.. & of his wo. *a* **1548** Hall *Chron., Hen. VII* 53 The wyse deuises, the prudent speches, the costly woorkes, the conninge portratures practised and set foorth in .vii. goodly beutiful pageauntes. **1625** Jackson *Creed* v. iii. §4 Him.., whose portraiture their first parents had blurred. **1650** S. Clarke *Eccl. Hist.* I. (1654) 30 A plain Image and Portracture of that effectual Doctrine which I was thought worthy to hear. **1713** Berkeley *Guardian* No. 62. ¶7 The more enlarged views and gay portraitures of a lively imagination. **1867** Freeman *Norm. Conq.* I. v. 288 We can recover a distinct portraiture of many of the actors in these scenes.

4. The action or art of portraying in words; verbal 'picturing', graphic description.

c **1430** Lydg. *Min. Poems* (Percy Soc.) 211 Ploughmen, carterys,.. Dichers, delverys,.. The staatis alle set here in portrature. **1855** Brimley *Ess., Tennyson* 86 The poet, too, should attempt to rise above the portraiture of individual life. **1878** Seeley *Stein* II. 358 A tempting subject for literary portraiture.

b. A verbal representation or 'picture'; a vivid description: = PORTRAIT *sb.* 3 b.

1610 North *Plutarch, Seneca* 1223 In his portraiture of this wise man, he imagineth in this life a thing that is not to be found. **1648** (*title*) Eikon Basilike. The Povrtraictvre of His Sacred Majestie in his solitudes and sufferings. **1774** Warton *Hist. Eng. Poetry* II. 97 A striking portraiture of antient manners. **1818** Scott *Hrt. Midl.* To Rdr., The pleasing pourtraictures of Peter Pattieson, now given unto thee. **1863** Cowden Clarke *Shaks. Char.* xv. 374 Shakespeare's portraiture of John of Gaunt.

5. Figure, form, likeness, appearance (as an attribute of a thing). Now *rare* or *Obs.*

1500-20 Dunbar *Poems* lxxvii. 35 The Bruce.. Richt awfull, strang, and large of portratour, As nobill, dreidfull, michtie campioun. **1567** *Satir. Poems Reform.* iii. 40 Not hir fyrst spous, for all his greit puissance, In portratour and game mycht be his peir. **1632** Lithgow *Trav.* I. 30 That resplending Image thou seest, was made.. for eternizing the memory of my portraiture, as I was aliue. **1797** Mrs. Radcliffe *Italian* xxiii, Every abbess.. came to her imagination in the portraiture of an inexorable jailer.

†**b.** *concr.* A material form, shape, or figure. *Obs.*

a **1578** Lindesay (Pitscottie) *Chron. Scot.* (S.T.S.) I. 233 Frome the waist wpe was tuo fair persouns witht all memberis and protratouris perteinand to tua bodyis. *a* **1680** Charnock *Attrib. God* (1834) II. 48 God.. draws.. from this indisposed chaos many excellent portraitures.

ˈ**portraiture,** *v.* Now *rare* or *Obs.* [f. prec. sb.] *trans.* To make a portraiture or portrait of, to portray (*lit.* and *fig.*).

1577-87 Holinshed *Chron.* (1807-8) IV. 164 Upon the top.. stood the armes of England, roiallie purtraitured with the proper beasts to uphold the same. **1601** Deacon & Walker *Answ. Darel* 22 Intending.. to portraiture in the person of Iob, an absolute patterne of perfect patience. **1651** C. Cartwright *Cert. Relig.* I. 14 That the child be not pourtractured greater then the Nurse. **1711** Shaftesb. *Charac.* (1737) I. 225 We.. shall be contented to see him portraitur'd by the artist who serves to illustrate prodigys in fairs, and adorn heroick sign-posts. **1903** G. R. Hall *Hum. Evol.* vii. 165 Men who were striving to portraiture a Christ who had not condemned wealth and the power of riches.

ˈ**portray,** *sb. rare.* Also 7 **por-, pourtrai,** 7-9 **pourtray.** [f. PORTRAY *v.*] The act of portraying; portrayal; a portrait, picture (*lit.* and *fig.*).

1611 Speed *Hist. Gt. Brit.* Proeme, Hauing thus farre trauelled in the portrai, and description of this famous Empire. **1622** Peacham *Compl. Gentl.* vii. (1634) 61 Pourtraies of their Kings and Queenes, in their severall Countrey habits. **1630** Lennard tr. *Charron's Wisd.* II. iii. §6 (1670) 242 The edicts and ordinances of Princes are no other but piety and particular pourtraies thereof. **1877** *Fraser's Mag.* XV. 103 We have here.. a most striking pourtray.. of the wondrous living guise of the Unknowable.

portray (pɔːˈtreɪ), *v.* Forms: α. 4 **purtreie, -treye,** 4-5 **-traye, -traie,** 5 **-trey,** 5-7 **-tray.** β. 4 **portreie, -traye,** 4-5 **-treye, -trai(e,** (5 **portrewe,** *Sc.* **-tra, -tura,** 6 **-try);** 5- **portray.** γ. 5-7 **pourtraie,** 6 **-trahe,** 7 **-trey,** 6-9 **pourtray.** Pa. pple. **portrayed;** also, in ME. [from OF.] **purtrait, -treit, portrait.** [ME. a. OF. *pourtrai-, pourtray-*, stem of *pourtraire* (12th c. in Hatz.-Darm.) to portray, fashion, represent:—L. *protrahĕre* to draw forth, reveal, extend, prolong, in med.L. also to draw, portray, paint, f. *pro-* forth + *trahĕre* to draw.]

1. *trans.* To represent (an object) by a drawing, painting, carving, etc. (in early use also by a solid image or statue); to make a picture or image of; to delineate, picture, depict.

c **1330** R. Brunne *Chron.* (1810) 51 At Westmynstere he ligges in a toumbe purtrait. —— *Chron. Wace* (Rolls) 15088 þer-on purtraied a crucyfix. **13..** *K. Alis.* 1520 (Bodl. MS.) Sonne & mone & sterren seuene, Was þereinne purtraied, & heuene. **1375** Barbour *Bruce* x. 743 Scho in hir chapell Gert weill be portrait ane castell. *c* **1375** *Sc. Leg. Saints* xi. (*Symon & Judas*) 78 To portra it he had na silcht. *Ibid.* xxiii. (*vii Sleperis*) 473 Bot [þ e emperoure] gert portura þare þe story. *c* **1430** Lydg. *Min. Poems* (Percy Soc.) 26 The fyve rosis portraid in the shelde. **1490** Caxton *Eneydos* xxxvi. 124 Withyn hys halle, where as were purtrayed fulle rychely alle the kynges of his lynage, connyngly made. **1587** Golding *De Mornay* ii. (1592) 19 One man portrayeth out the whole world in a little peece of Paper, painting out all the Images. **1590** Spenser *F.Q.* II. ix. 33 In which was nothing pourtrahed nor wrought; Not wrought nor pourtrahed, but easie to be thought. **1613** Purchas *Pilgrimage* VI. xi. 521 That Knightly Order of Saint Iames, who haue in their habite purtraied a purple sword, in token of bloud. **1675** Ogilby *Brit.* 50 A Chapel.. in the Roof of which was lively Portraid His Apostles and Disciples. ? **1800** W. B. Rhodes *Bomb. Fur.* iii. (1830) 18 Painters no other face pourtray. **1852** Mrs. Jamieson *Leg. Madonna* (1857) 204 It was considered little less than heretical to portray Mary reclining on a couch.

†**b.** *transf.* To make (a picture, image, or figure); to draw, paint, or carve; to trace. *Obs.*

13.. *E.E. Allit. P.* B. 1536 A fust faylaynde þe wryst, Pared on þe parget, purtrayed lettres. **1450-80** tr. *Secreta Secret.* 38 The disciplis of ypocras portreweden the liknes of her maystir. **1483** Caxton *Gold. Leg.* 431 b/1 They ne shold.. pourtraye nor pycte the forme or fygure of the crosse. **1557** in *Tottell's Misc.* (Arb.) 169 Behold my picture here well portrayed for the nones. **1601** Holland *Pliny* II. 497 Two other statues or images portraied in clokes or mantles, were his handiwork. *a* **1604** Hanmer *Chron. Irel.* (1633) 174 One stone, whereupon the picture of a Knight is portraied.

†**c.** *absol.* To make drawings, pictures, or statues; to draw, paint, mould, or carve. *Obs.*

c **1369** Chaucer *Dethe Blaunche* 783 A white walle.. hit ys redy to cachche and take Al þat men wil theryn make Whethir so men wil portrey or peynt. *c* **1386** —— *Prol.* 96 He koude.. weel purtreye and write. *c* **1420** *Chron. Vilod.* 1158 Wryte he couthe & purtrey also. *a* **1533** Ld. Berners *Gold. Bk. M. Aurel.* xxiii. (1535) L ij b, Other coude graue images and portry in wood or erthe.

†**2.** *transf.* To paint or adorn (a surface) *with* a picture or figure. *Obs.*

13.. *Guy Warw.* (A.) st. 250 A targe listed wiþ gold, Portreyd wiþ þre kinges corn, þat present god when he was born. ? *a* **1366** Chaucer *Rom. Rose* 897 His garnement was everydel Y-portreyd and y-wrought with floures. *c* **1430** *Syr Gener.* (Roxb.) 5682 The champe of the feld was goules.. with a broode bourdure Purtraied with sable and with asure. *c* **1475** *Partenay* 1003 Into a pauilon made she a retrair... Portreid it was with briddes freshly. **1667** Milton *P.L.* VI. 84 Shields.. with boastful Argument portraid.

3. *fig.* †**a.** To form a mental image of; to picture to oneself; to imagine, fancy; in first quot., to conceive, devise, invent. *Obs.* **b.** To represent (e.g. dramatically).

13.. *E.E. Allit. P.* B. 700 þe play of paramorez I portrayed my seluen. *c* **1350** *Will. Palerne* 619 Him so propirli haue i peinted & portreide in herte. **1390** Gower *Conf.* III. 255 So as him thoghte in his corage, Where he pourtreieth hire ymage. **1791** Cowper *Odyss.* I. 143 Telemachus.. sad amid them all he sat. Pourtraying in deep thought contemplative His noble Sire. **1798** Mrs. Inchbald *Lovers' Vows* Introd., The actor.. forms his notion of the passion he is to pourtray.. from the following lines.

4. *esp.* To represent or depict in words; to describe vividly or graphically; to set forth.

c **1366** Chaucer *A.B.C.* 81 Ladi þi sorwe kan j not portreye. **1387** Trevisa *Higden* (Rolls) I. 27 In þe firste book of þis werk.. mappa mundi is purtrayed and i-peynt [L. *describitur*]. **1586** Marlowe *1st Pt. Tamburl.* II. i, Well hast thou pourtray'd in thy terms of life The face and personage of a wondrous man. *a* **1662** Heylin *Laud* II. 237 He that desires to pourtray England in her full structure of external glory. **1796** Morse *Amer. Geog.* I. 315 *note*, It remains for future ages to pourtray the virtues and exploits of this truly great man. **1846** Trench *Mirac.* Introd. (1862) 51 We having in the Gospels the lively representation of our Lord portrayed for us.

†**5.** To form, fashion. *Obs.*

1375 Barbour *Bruce* x. 281 (Cambr. MS.) He wes of mesurabill stature, And portrait weill at all mesure [cf. Porturat]. **1481** Caxton *Myrr.* I. xiv. 48 To deuyse the facion of the world how it is by nature made and pourtrayed of god.

Hence **porˈtrayed** *ppl. a.*, **porˈtraying** *vbl. sb.*; also **porˈtrayable** *a.*, capable of being portrayed.

1340 Hampole *Pr. Consc.* 6619 þe fire þat es brinnand here, Es hatter and of mare powere, þan a purtrayd fire on a waghe. **1632** Lithgow *Trav.* I. 17, I espied the portrayed image of S. Peter erected of pure Brasse. **1638** Junius *Paint. Ancients* 62 A speedy pourtraying of the conceit. **1864** Carlyle *Fredk. Gt.* XVII. i, He is not portrayable at present.

portrayal (pɔːˈtreɪəl). [f. PORTRAY *v.* + -AL[1] 5.] The action of portraying (or its product); delineation, picturing; a picture, portrait.

a. *lit.* Pictorial representation.

1847 Webster, *Portrayal*, the act of portraying. **1872** 'Ouida' *Crayon Head* (ed. Tauchn.) 82 It is a bad portrayal of [her] face. **1881** *Times* 4 Jan. 3/5 One of the most marvellous feats, however, of photography is the portrayal of the motion of trotting, cantering, and galloping horses by Mr. Muybridge in America.

b. *fig.* Representation in general (e.g. mental, dramatic); *esp.* verbal picturing, graphic description.

1859 C. Barker *Assoc. Princ.* iii. 62 The reproduction and pourtrayal of manners and of scenes which pertain to an age.. passed away. **1875** McClellan *New Test., Harmony* 374 An essential unity in the several portrayals of his Work and Person. **1884** *Times* (weekly ed.) 26 Sept. 6/2 Feeling genuine contempt for the pourtrayal of meanness, treachery, &c.

porˈtrayer. Also 4-5 **our.** [f. PORTRAY *v.* + -ER[1] 2, for earlier -OUR. So obs. F. *po(u)rtrayeur* (16th c.).] One who portrays; a painter or drawer of pictures or portraits; a delineator (*lit.* and *fig.*).

c **1386** Chaucer *Knt.'s T.* 1041 (Harl. MS.) Ne purtreyour [*v.rr.* purtreiour, -traiour, -treoure; *Ellesm.* portreitour] ne keruer of ymages. **1412-20** Lydg. *Chron. Troy* II. xi. (MS. Digby 232) lf. 31/2 He sent also For euery ymagour Bothe in entaylle & euery portreyour [*MS. Digby* 230 (*c* 1425) portratoure]. **1479** J. Paston in *P. Lett.* III. 268 The man at Sent Bridis is no klenly portrayer. **1621** Brathwait *Nat. Embassie* (1877) 89 Portrayers of thy wit and learning too. **1828** in Webster. **1874** Carpenter *Ment. Phys.* I. vi. §2 (1879) 269 To bear in mind the essential difference.. between the characters of the 'subject' and his pourtrayer.

portrayist (pɔːˈtreɪɪst). *rare.* [f. PORTRAY *v.* + -IST.] = PORTRAYER.

1924 *Glasgow Herald* 25 Sept. 4 His considerable skill as portrayist and his narrative genius.

porˈtrayment. *rare.* [f. as PORTRAYER + -MENT: cf. OF. *po(u)rtraiement.*] = PORTRAYAL.

1802 Mrs. Radcliffe *Gaston de Blondeville* Posth. Wks. 1826 II. 11, I hold it not meet to speak here, with greater pourtrayment, of the more solemn ceremonies in the chapel itself. **1891** *Spectator* 18 Apr., From this most graphic portrayment of the state of national feeling at the time.

portred, *pa. pple.*: see PORTURE *v. Obs.*

portreeve (ˈpɔətriːv). Forms: 1 **portȝerefa, -irefa,** 3 **-yreue,** 3-5 **-ereve,** 3-8 **-reve,** 6 **-rief, porte ryve, port reeue,** 7 **portriefe, -reive, -riff, port riffe,** 8 **portrieve,** 7- **port-reeve,** 9 **portreeve.** β. 5-7 **portgreve,** 6-8 **-grave.** [OE. *port-ȝeréfa* (whence ON. *port-greifi*), f. PORT *sb.*[2] town + *ȝerǽfa, ȝeréfa,* REEVE *sb.*[1]; as to the forms *portgreve, -grave,* see 1 β.]

1. *orig.* The ruler or chief officer of a town or borough (= BOROUGH-REEVE a); after the Norman Conquest often identified with the Mayor or holding an equivalent position, as still in some boroughs; in later times, sometimes an officer, or one of two or more officers, inferior to the Mayor; a bailiff.

901-924 *Laws of Edward I*, c. i, Ic wille ðæt..nan man ne ceapiȝe butan porte, ac hæbbe þæs portȝerefan ȝewitnesse oððe oþera..manna, ðe man ȝelyfan mæȝe. *c* **1000** ÆLFRIC *Gram.* xiv. (Z.) 88 *Hic prefectus urbis*, ðes portȝerefa oððe burhealdor. *c* **1000** —— *Gloss.* in Wr.-Wülcker 111/6 *Municeps*, portȝerefa *uel* burhwita. **1066-75** WILL. I *Charter to London* (Stubbs *Select Ch.* 79), Willelm kyng gret Willelm bisceop and Gosfregð portirefan, and ealle þa burhwaru binnan Londone, Frencisce and Englisce, freondlice. **12..** *transcr.* of *Charter of Brihtmær* (1053) in Kemble *Cod. Dipl.* IV. 133 Hyerto byeð ywiðnesse Lyefstan portyreue and biscop, and Eylwyne stikehare, and manie oðre. **1297** R. GLOUC. (Rolls) 11205 Willam þe spicer & geffray of hencsei þat þo were Portreuen & nicole of kingestone þat was mere [of Oxford] Nome of þis clerkes & in prison caste. *Ibid.* 11223 Suþþe þe portereues house hii sette afure anon. *a* **1300** *St. Gregory* 601 in Herrig's *Archiv* LVII. 65 He toke an In as a knyȝt ful large at þe portreues hous. **1449** *Rolls of Parlt.* V. 155/2 The Maire, Baillifs, Porterevys, Customers..and Sarcheours. **1541** in P. H. Hore *Hist. Wexford* (1900) I. 242 [Not to sell] any franke tenement..to any forrener, without speciall license of the Soverayne and Portriefs. **1599** in Harington *Nugæ Ant.* 35 Mr. Hammon..who is this year Port Reeue of Trim, as much in effect as Mayor. **1603** OWEN *Pembrokeshire* ii. (1892) 22 And licenced them to chose yeerelye amonge them selues two portriefes for theire gouernement. **1660** in J. Simon *Ess. Irish Coins* (1749) 127 All mayors, sheriffs, portriffs, baylifs, and other chief officers of corporations. **1702** *Lond. Gaz.* No. 3809/5 An humble Address of the Portrieves, Burgesses, and Freemen, of the ancient Borough of Tulske, in the County of Roscomon. **1824** HITCHINS & DREW *Cornwall* I. xvii. §17. 650 Formerly the government [of Tregony] was vested in a portreeve or mayor. **1883** *Standard* 28 Sept. 3 The Drake Memorial was unveiled yesterday at Tavistock by the Portreeve. **1894** *Northumbld. Gloss.*, *Reeve*, the chief officer in the ancient borough of Warkworth. He is to this day usually styled the 'borough-reeve' or 'port-reeve' at that town. **1898** *Daily News* 19 Apr. 3 Hungerford is..electing to-day, in place of Mayor and Corporation, a constable, a portreeve, a keeper of the coffers, a hayward, two aletasters and a bellman.

β. In the forms 5-8 **portgreue**, (6 **-gereue**), 6-7 **-graue**, **-grave**, partly scribal modifications of the OE. form, partly after MDu. *portgrave* (in Kilian *poortgrave*) and the synonymous *greyve*, *grave*: see GRIEVE, *sb.*, GRAVE *sb.*[3]

1494 FABYAN *Chron.* VII. 293 At the comynge of Wyllyam Conquerour into this londe..the rulers of the sayd citezens [were] named portgreuis, whiche worde is deriuat or made of .ii. Saxon wordis,..*port* is to mean a towne, and *greue* is meant for a gardyen or ruler. **1568** GRAFTON *Chron.* II. 83 The same before tyme was gouerned by persones graue and wyse, and were named Portgreues, or rather Portgraues, the which is deriued of..Greue, or rather Graue, for so are the rulers of the townes in Duchelande called at this day. **1598** STOW *Surv.* (1842) 185/2 In the time of King Henry II., Peter Fitzwalter was portgrave [of London]. **1631** WEEVER *Anc. Fun. Mon.* 378 Portgraue and principall Magistrate..of this Citie. **1772** *Jacob's Law Dict.* s.v., Instead of the portgreve [of London], Richard the first ordained two bailiffs, but presently after him King John granted them a mayor for their yearly magistrate.

2. Erroneously referred (by later compilers) to PORT *sb.*[1] 2, as if the reeve of a sea-port town.

1607 COWELL *Interpr.*, *Portgreue*..signifieth with vs the chiefe magistrate in certaine coast townes. **1616** BULLOKAR *Eng. Expos.*, *Portgreue*, a chiefe officer in certaine Port tounes. **1622** CALLIS *Stat. Sewers* (1647) 34 That Officer called Portgreve, which signifieth the Governor of the Port. **1727-41** CHAMBERS *Cycl.*, *Portgreve*, or *Portgrave*, was anciently the principal magistrate in ports and other maritime towns. **1851** DIXON *W. Penn* i. (1872) 6 When the country wanted fleets,..she had only to send for the port-reeves and masters of companies.

Hence **'portreeveship**, the office of portreeve.

1467-8 *Rolls of Parlt.* V. 593/2 Th' Office of Portreveship of Prestende. **1487** *Ibid.* VI. 406/2 The Portreveshipp of Llanvayr in Buelld.

portress[1] ('pɔətrɪs), **porteress** ('pɔːtərɪs). Forms: α. 5-6 **porteresse**, 6 *Sc.* **-aress**, 6- **-eress**. β. 5-7 **portresse**, 6 **-res**, 7- **portress**. [f. PORTER *sb.*[1] + -ESS.] A female porter; a woman who acts as porter or door-keeper, esp. in a nunnery.

c **1407** LYDG. *Reson & Sens.* 2615 Of the gardyn and the close She is the chiefe porteresse, Of the entre lady and maistresse. **1509** HAWES *Past. Pleas.* iv. (Percy Soc.) 16, I came to ryall gate, Where I sawe stondynge the goodly portres. **1548** Q. CATHERINE in Ellis *Orig. Lett.* Ser. I. II. 152 That yowr porteresse may wayte at the gate..for yow. **1613-31** *Primer our Lady* 264 The wench..that was portresse sayth to Peter, art not thou also of this mans disciples? **1797** MRS. RADCLIFFE *Italian* xiii, The porteress appeared immediately upon the ringing of the bell. **1862** 'SHIRLEY' *Nugæ Crit.* viii. 364 The old porteress, with her rusty keys, will admit you within the deserted church. **1895** F. M. CRAWFORD *Casa Braccio* iv, The portress and another nun came to let him in.

b. *fig.*, or in personification.

1426 LYDG. *De Guil. Pilgr.* 4577, I am my-sylff the porteresse, (Maad off verray Ryghtwysnesse,) Off the releff that ye sen her. **1521** R. COPLAND in Barclay *Introd. to wryte French*, In eschewynge of ydlenesse the portresse of vyces. **1607** WALKINGTON *Opt. Glass* 48 The Goddesse of eloquence and perswasion was the portresse of his mouth. **1792** S. ROGERS *Pleas. Mem.* II. 8 Sweet Memory..Thee, in whose hands the keys of Science dwell, The pensive portress of her holy cell.

†**'portress**[2]. *Obs. rare*[−1]. [? corruption of obs. F. *portice* (16th c. in Godef.):—L. (*porta*) *postica* a postern. (The ending perh. influenced by *fortress*.)] The gate of a fortification.

1638 SIR T. HERBERT *Trav.* (ed. 2) 158 The wall..has a dozen Portresses [*ed.* 1665 *adds* or Gates], of which, foure are shut up.

Port-Royal (pɔət'rɔɪəl). The name of a convent near Versailles (*Port-Royal des Champs*) which in the 17th c. became the home of a lay community celebrated for its connexion with Jansenism and its educational work.

1692 NORRIS *Curs. Refl. Ess. Hum. Und.* 65 A sort of men whose Talent was never known to lie much towards Philosophy, will needs turn a Conventicle into a Port Royal. **1714** ADDISON *Spect.* No. 562 ¶3 The Gentlemen of Port-Royal,..were more eminent for their Learning and their Humility than any other in France. **1727-41** CHAMBERS *Cycl. s.v.*, We say..the Greek and Latin methods of Port-royal, which are grammars of that language. **1864** BOWEN *Logic* ii. 39 The excellent 'Art of Thinking', which commonly passes under the name of the 'Port-Royal Logic'. **1883** *Chambers' Encycl.* VII. 693/1 The establishment of a school, for which they prepared the well-known educational books known under the name of Port Royal, the Greek and Latin Grammars, General Grammar, Geometry, etc.

Hence **Port-'Royalist**, a member or adherent of the community of Port-Royal des Champs.

1727-41 CHAMBERS *Cycl.* s.v. *Port-royal*, All that adhered to that party, took the name of Port-royalists. **1844** EMERSON *Ess.* Ser. II. viii. (1876) 194 Why so impatient to baptize them Essenes, or Port-Royalists, or Shakers, or by any other known and effete name? **1864** BOWEN *Logic* xiii. 450 'We employ reason', said the Port-Royalist logician, 'as an instrument for acquiring the sciences, whereas we ought to use the sciences as a means of perfecting our reason.

†**'port-'sale.** *Obs.* Also 5-6 **porte-**, 6-7 **-sail(e.** [f. PORT *sb.*[2] or *sb.*[3] (cf. sense 1 c) + SALE.]

1. Public sale to the highest bidder; sale by auction.

1494 FABYAN *Chron.* VII. 594 That all marchaunt straungers shuld be set to an Englisshe hoost, within .xv. dayes of theyr commynge to their porte sale. **1542** UDALL *Erasm. Apoph.* 169 Philippus sate at the portesale his garment or robe short tucked vp about hym. **1543-4** *Act 35 Hen. VIII*, c. 7 § 1 That the saide Marchauntis doggers and fishermen at their commynge home..can [not] have porte sale nor redy utterance for their Fishe. **1573-80** BARET *Alv.* S 206 To sell publikely, or by portsaile, as they sell by the crier, when ones goods are forfeited for lacke of paiement. **1600** HOLLAND *Livy* XLI. 1103 Five thousand sixe hundred and two and thirtie persons were sold out-right in port-sale under the guirland [*sub corona veniere*]. *a* **1653** GOUGE *Comm. Heb.* xiii. 4 They who commit uncleannesse for gain, are said to sell their body; or to set it, as we speak, to port-sail. *a* **1670** HACKET *Abp. Williams* II. (1692) 168 Like the last bidding for a thing at the port-sale.

¶ Erroneously referred to PORT[1] 2: see quots.

1607 COWELL *Interpr.*, *Portsale*,..sale of fish presently vpon returne in the hauen. Whence **1616** in BULLOKAR *Eng. Expos.*, **1706** in PHILLIPS, **1848** in WHARTON *Law Lex.*

(Fish are commonly sold on the strand by *port-sale* or auction: whence the error.)

2. *Comb.* †**portsale-maker**, an auctioneer.

1552 HULOET, Portsale maker, *auctionarius*.

port sa'lut. Forms: 5 **port salut**, **-salow**, **-salue**, 6 **-salu.** [app. a. OF. *port salut*, in mod.F. *port de salut* = L. **portus salūtis* port or haven of safety.]

†**1.** 'Haven of safety'; the port or goal one is making for. *Obs. rare.*

c **1407** HOCCLEVE *Balade to Somer* 22 Whethir our taille Shal soone make vs with our shippes saille To port salut. **1472-5** *Rolls of Parlt.* VI. 156/1 Such Citees or Tounes.., where any such Caryk, Galee or Shipp, shall happen here-after to make his Port salow. **1481** BOTONER *Tulle Old Age* (Caxton) G v b, When men be vpon the riuer in to the hauen warde and to haue takyn their porte salue. **1523** SKELTON *Garl. Laurel* 541 When at the port salu Ye fyrste aryuyd.

2. Port Salut (pɔr saly). [f. the name of a Trappist monastery, *Port du Salut* (also used), in Mayenne, N.W. France, where it was first produced.] A kind of soft pressed cheese.

1881 J. P. SHELDON *Dairy Farming* xxxv. 512 Cooked, heated, and pressed cheese.... Gruyères français, Port du Salut, Rangiport. **1896** LONG & BENSON *Cheese* ii. 15 Camembert, Brie, Bondon, Neufchâtel, and Port du Salut, all..hail from France. **1902** *Encycl. Brit.* XXVII. 355/2 In France the pressed varieties of cheese with hard rinds include Gruyère..and Port Salut. **1935** [see BEL PAESE]. **1942** E. PAUL *Narrow St.* iii. 22 Cheese was forthcoming (a Port Salut that increased my respect for the fat cook who did the daily marketing). **1951** [see MAKE *v.*[1] 91 c (*b*)]. **1960** *Sunday Times* 17 Jan. 9/1 A full moon, the colour of Port Salut. **1966** P. V. PRICE *France* 283 There are..two sorts of cheese involved: *Port du Salut* is that made by the Trappist monks at Entrammes, near Laval... Other Trappists, however, and other cheese makers..are able to make and market a cheese under the name of *Port Salut*, which, unlike Port du Salut, is not a trademark. **1972** *Sat. Rev.* (U.S.) 24 June 77/3 French Trappist monks in northern Touraine have been making Port Salut cheese for 150 years.

port-'sider. *N. Amer. colloq.* [f. PORT *sb.*[6] (*a.*) + SIDER[2].] A left-handed person.

1926 *Amer. Speech* I. 369/2 They [*sc.* baseball players] are 'south-paws' or 'port-siders' or 'side-wheelers' when they are left-handed. **1945** *Record* (Philadelphia) 28 Oct. 8/2 We despair that portsiders will ever get their rights. **1946** *Sun* (Baltimore) 13 June 20/2 The firm had been printing check-books for Baltimore portsiders for nearly ten years. **1975** *Daily Colonist* (Victoria, B.C.) 30 July 2/1 The left-handers of my acquaintance. They're called southpaws, silly-siders and port-siders.

portsman ('pɔətsmən). [f. PORT *sb.*[1] 3 + MAN *sb.*[1]] A citizen or inhabitant of one of the Cinque Ports. (Usually in plural.)

1626 DK. BUCKHM. in Rushw. *Hist. Coll.* (1659) I. 380 When the Kings Ships, or others, be in danger on the Goodwins, and other places within the view of the Portsmen, they have refused to help with their Boats, lest the Kings ships should command them on board. **1629** in W. Boys *Sandwich* (1792) 749 The Admiralty Court doth impose fines upon portsmen. **1755** CARTE *Hist. Eng.* IV. 161 If the king's ships..have any need of pilots for the sand coasts of Flanders or the like wherein the portsmen are best experienced they will not serve without the lord Warden's..warrant. **1900** *Blackw. Mag.* Nov. 712/1 His acquaintance with the Ports and the Portsmen..is intimate and varied.

†**port-'soken.** *Old Law. Obs.* [f. PORT *sb.*[2] + SOKEN.] The jurisdiction of a port or town; hence, *spec.* the district outside a city or borough, over which its jurisdiction extended. Also *attrib.*

[*a* **1189** *Charter of Hen. II to Canterbury* in Somner *Gavelkind* (1660) 135 Infra urbem, & in Portsoka. **1200** *Rot. Chart.* (1837) 45/2 *Carta Norhamton.* Sciatis nos concessisse burgensibus nostris de Norhamton.. quietantiam murdri infra burgem et portsoka.] **1224** HEN. III *Charter to City of London* in Coke *Instit.* IV. (1648) 252 Quod infra muros civitatis, neque in portesokne nemo capiat hospitium per vim. [*a* **1272** *Charter of Hen. III* in Somner *Gavelkind* (1660) 135 Nullus de civitate vel Portsoka sua.] **1660** SOMNER *Gavelkind* 135 Portsoken, being..I take it, the same, which at this day is known there by the name of Portsoken-Ward..but in some ancient Charters of Liberties ..you may find it spreading it self to the utmost skirts and liberties of the City without the wals. **1701** MANLEY *Cowell's Interpr.*, *Portsokne*, the Soke or Liberties of any Port, i.e. City, or Town... Quietantiam murdri infra urbem & in Portsokne, i.e. within the..City, and the Liberties without the Walls.

port-town ('pɔəttaʊn).

†**1.** A market-town or borough: = PORT *sb.*[2]

c **1290** *S. Eng. Leg.* I. 307/267 He fierde ase doth a port-doggue I-norischet in port-toun.

2. A sea-port town: = PORT *sb.*[1] 2.

1601 HOLLAND *Pliny* I. 100 Gaza a port towne and farther within, Anthedon, and the mountain Angoris. **1641** EARL MONM. tr. *Biondi's Civil Warres* III. 116 Harfleur was the chiefest Port Town of all Normandy. **1705** *Royal Proclam.* 18 Jan. in *Lond. Gaz.* No. 4090/1 The Civil Magistrates at ..Our Port-Towns. **1754** FIELDING *Voy. Lisbon* Wks. 1882 VII. 88 There are many of those houses in every port-town.

†**'portuall.** *Obs. rare*[−1]. [cf. med.L. *portuālia* passes in mountains (see PORT *sb.*[1] 5), It. *portuale* 'having ports or harboroughs for ships' (Florio 1598), f. L. *portu-s* harbour, port.] Open to passage; permeable, penetrable.

1603 LODGE *Treat. Plague* (Hunter. Cl.) 16 Men of vnbrideled dyet, sanguine, and such as haue large and portuall pores.

portuary ('pɔətjuːərɪ). *arch.* [A modern formation on *portuas*, or other variant of PORTAS: perh. after *breviary*.] = PORTAS. Also *attrib.*

a **1867** (*title*) The Portuary of the Laity, containing the layman's share of the Public Offices of the Church of England. **1880** *Times* 1 Jan., The Roman Breviary..In England the more common name was Portuary. Latin 'Portiforium'. **1884** W. H. RICH JONES *Reg. S. Osmund* (Rolls) II. Gloss. 166 *Breviarium*, a breviary... Another name given to it was 'Portiforium', in English 'Portuary'.

portuas, etc., variants of PORTAS.

‖**Portugaise** (pɔrtygɛz). [Fr., = Portuguese.]

1. *Cookery.* Chiefly in phr. *à la Portugaise*, designating food prepared in a Portuguese style. Also *attrib.* or as *adj.*

1845 E. ACTON *Mod. Cookery* xx. 548 *Arocē Docē* (*or Sweet Rice. A la Portugaise*)... This is quite the best sweet preparation of rice that we have ever eaten, and it is a very favourite dish in Portugal, whence the receipt was derived. **1889** A. B. MARSHALL *Cookery Bk.* v. 54 *Clear Soup à la Portugaise.* Prepare some French plums and leeks as below, mix them and add to them sufficient clear stock, boil up all together, and serve the soup very hot. **1907** G. A. ESCOFFIER *Guide Mod. Cookery* xvi. 489 *Poularde à la Portugaise.* Stuff the pullet with three-quarters lb. of rice, combined with five oz. of peeled and *concassed* tomatoes, cooked in butter. *Poêle* the pullet. Dish it; coat it with a Portugaise sauce..and surround it with a garnish of..tomatoes, stuffed with rice 'à la Portugaise'. **1929** G. VOISIN *French Cooking for All* iv. 53 *Sole à la Portugaise*... Butter a baking-dish, lay the fish in it, scatter over it a little chopped onion and cover with sliced tomatoes. **1931** A. DE CROZE *What to eat & drink in France* ii. 10 In French cookery 'Portugaise' means that chopped meat or forcemeat is used as a bed or cover with eggs or vegetables, shell-fish, or fish. **1953** J. CONIL *Haute Cuisine* x. 171 (*heading*) Tomato sauce or Portugaise. **1964** E. BOWEN *Little Girls* I. iv. 60 An eight-egg omelette, *portugaise*, had been contrived in the kitchen. **1970** SIMON & HOWE *Dict. Gastron.* 307/2 *Portugaise, à la*, culinary French name for a dish featuring tomatoes above all else, but usually also garlic and onions.

2. = *Portuguese oyster.*

1942 E. PAUL *Narrow St.* xxv. 221 The price tags on the turquoise green Portugaises and the flat grey Marennes of incomparable flavour would have caused a traffic jam a few years before. **1962** L. DEIGHTON *Ipcress File* xxxi. 200 Scallops and flat oysters and portugaise that looked like pieces of rock. **1966** P. V. PRICE *France: Food & Wine Guide* 40 There is the..*Portugaise*..with its bumpy, longish and deep shell. **1970** *Sunday Times* 18 Oct. 21/2 The big, fat *portugais* [sic] in their craggy misshapen armour. **1978** *Observer* (Colour Suppl.) 23 July 34/4 You can eat Pacific oysters, small as the Portugais [*sic*] in Paris.

Portugal ('pɔətjʊgəl). Forms: α. 5–6 **Portyngale**, 6 **-gall**, **-ggale**, **Portingaill**, 7 **-galle**, 5–9 **-gale**, 6–9 **-gal(l**. β. 6–7 **Portugale**, **-gall(e**, 7 **-gual**, 6– **Portugal**. [a. Pg. (= Sp., F., etc.) *Portugal*, earlier *Portucal*, ad. med.L. *Portus Cale*, the port of Gaya, Oporto. Alfonso, Count of *Portucalé*, became the first king of Portugal. Cf. MDu. *Portegale*. The form *Portingale* is perh. to be compared with *nightingale* from *nihtegale*; but cf. OF. *Portingalois* Portuguese.]

1. A country in the west of the Iberian peninsula.

α. *c* **1386** CHAUCER *Epil. Nun's Pr. T.* 13 Him nedeth nat his colour for to dyghen With brasile ne with greyn of Portyngale. *c* **1435** (*title*) *Torrent of Portyngal*, Here bygynneth a good tale Of Torrente of Portyngale. ? *a* **1550** *Sir A. Barton* in *Surtees Misc.* (1888) 72 Full longe against Portingaill they weare. *a* **1618** RALEIGH *Apol.* 9 A French Shallop which he tooke in the Bay of Portingall. **1824** BYRON *Juan* XVI. xlv, With 'Tu mi chamas's' from Portingale.

β. **1553** EDEN *Treat. Newe Ind.* (Arb.) 13 The Kynge of Portugall subdued this cytie. **1588** (*title*) A true Discourse of the Armie which the King of Spaine caused to be assembled in the Hauen of Lisbon, in the Kingdome of Portugall.. against England.

†**2.** A native or inhabitant of Portugal; a Portuguese. *Obs.*

a **1497** *Acc. Ld. High Treas. Scot.* I. 383 Item,..in Dunbertane, to the Portingales in almous,..xviij.s. **1582** HESTER *Secr. Phiorav.* II. xxxii. 111 Among a number of other, I cured a Portingale. **1600** ABP. ABBOT *Exp. Jonah* 210 The late discoveries of the Portingales and the Spaniards.

β. **1542** UDALL *Erasm. Apoph.* 285 Yᵉ Portugalles, whose countree is called in latine *Lusitania*. **1624** CAPT. SMITH *Virginia* v. 196 A company of poore distressed Portugals and Spaniards. **1707** SLOANE *Jamaica* I. 253 In Ferdinando de Soto's expedition..written by a Portugal of Elvas.

†**3.** The Portuguese language. *Obs.*

1588 PARKE tr. *Mendoza's Hist. China* 251 A man, who was a Chino..and could speake Portugal. **1698** FRYER *Acc. E. India & P.* 9 Their Speech is broken Portugal.

†**4.** = PORTAGUE, the coin. *Obs.*

1546–7 *Test. Ebor.* (Surtees) VI. 255 Mʳ Palmer to have a portyngall of golde for his paynes.

†**5.** ? A sweetmeat from Portugal. *Obs. rare*⁻¹.

1560 H. MACHYN *Diary* 10 June (Camden) 237 Pepyns and marmelade, and sukett, comfets, and portynggalles and dyvers odur dyssys.

6. *attrib.* or as *adj.* **a.** = PORTUGUESE A.

α. **1498** *Acc. Ld. High Treas. Scot.* I. 388 Giffen to the Portingale man of the west see for the brokin schip that the King bocht. **1545** *Rates of Customs* C ij b, Portyngale skynnes the dossen. **1601** W. PARRY *Trav. Sir A. Sherley* 27 There came news of a Portingall fryer. **1655** (*title*) The Lusiad..written In the Portingall Language by Luis De Camoens..put into English By Richard Fanshawe.

β. **1600** J. PORY tr. *Leo's Africa* III. 178 He learned the Portugall-language most exactly. *a* **1691** BOYLE *Hist. Air* (1692) 202 A man of letters, that divers times crossed the line in great Portugal ships. **1719** DE FOE *Crusoe* (1840) I. iii. 42, I had met with the Portugal captain.

b. in names of products, esp. species and varieties of plants, as ***Portugal onion***; **Portugal crakeberry**, *Corema alba* or *lusitanicum*: see quot.; **Portugal laurel**, an evergreen shrub, *Prunus lusitanica*, native to Spain and Portugal; **Portugal onion**, a variety of onion, esp. young seedlings of this variety used as spring onions; **Portugal oyster** = *Portuguese oyster*; **Portugal peach**, **P. quince**, local varieties of these fruits.

1866 *Treas. Bot.*, *Corema*, *Portugal Crakeberry. An erect much-branched low shrub of rigid habit, closely allied to *Empetrum*. **1754** *Catal. Seeds* in *Fam. Rose Kilravock* (Spald. Club) 427 *Portugal laurel. **1839** SELBY in *Proc. Berw. Nat. Club* I. No. 7. 191 The Portugal Laurel..was not ..injured. **1914** W. J. BEAN *Trees & Shrubs Hardy in Brit. Isles* II. 241 In all but the coldest parts of Great Britain the Portugal laurel is one of the handsomest and most effective of evergreens. **1972** F. PERRY *Flowers of World* 262/1 The Portugal Laurel..makes a tree of 3–6 m (10–20 ft) with long-elliptic evergreen leaves and large racemes of dull white, heavily scented flowers. **1647** W. LILLY *Christian Astrol.* II. liv. 398, I..heavily complained to the woman for seven *Portugall Onyons which I lost; she not knowing what they were, made pottage with them, as she said. **1783** J. WOODFORDE *Diary* 21 Nov. (1926) II. 107 Mr. Priest..made me this morning a Present of a fine String of the real Portugal Onions 20 in No. **1833** *Chambers's Edin. Jrnl.* 20 Apr. 96/2 A root of rye, size of a Portugal onion. **1845** E. ACTON *Mod. Cookery* iii. 97 The meat may then be stewed ..with a Portugal onion. **1885** W. MILLER tr. *Vilmorin-Andrieux's Veget. Garden* 363 White Portugal Onion... Bulb of a dull-white colour. **1890** J. R. PHILPOTS *Oysters* I. xxiv. 570 The *Portugal oyster has appeared for the last two or three years in our markets. **1664** EVELYN *Kalendarium Hortense* in *Sylva* 72 August... Fruits in Prime... *Portugal Peach, Crown Peach, Bourdeaux Peach. **1629** J. PARKINSON *Parad.* IV. xx. 589 The *Portingall Apple Quince is a great yellow Quince... The Portingall Peare Quince is not fit to be eaten rawe like the former. **1706** EVELYN *Kal. Hort.* Nov. 120 The Suckers of the Portugal Quince. **1887** *Nicholson's Dict. Gard.*, Portugal Quince,..*Cydonia vulgaris lusitanica*.

Hence †**'Portingaler**, †**Portu'gallian**, a Portuguese; **'Portugalism**, adherence to Portugal.

a **1451** FORTESCUE *Wks.* (1869) 552 Almaner Lumbardds, ..Spaynarrds, and Portyngalers. **1479–81** *Rec. St. Mary at Hill* 95 For the Buryyng of a portyngaler. **1601–2** FULBECKE *1st Pt. Parall.* 21 The Portugallians make villaines of the Mahometistes which they sell by companies. **1676** in J. T. Wheeler *Madras* (1862) III. 419/1 [Portuguese Padrys] who used to entail Portugalism as well as Christianity on all their converts.

portugue, variant of PORTAGUE, the coin. *Obs.*

Portuguee (pɔətjʊ'giː). *U.S.* Also **Portagee**, **Portugee**. Repr. a spurious 'singular' form of PORTUGUESE *a.* and *sb.*, this being regarded as a plural.

1830 J. F. COOPER *Water Witch* II. vii. 197 It being altogether unreasonable to suppose that a Portuguee should do what an Englishman had not yet thought of doing. **1860** *Atlantic Monthly* Dec. 735/1 Somehaow I caän't help mistrustin' them Portagee-lookin' fellahs. PORTUGUESE *sb.* 1]. **1878** BESANT & RICE *Celia's Arb.* xxviii, A Portugee, as every sailor knows, is a Portugee by birth. **1880** *Harper's Mag.* Sept. 505/1 At one place was a 'Portugee' of the Western Islands. **1915** C. C. MARTINDALE *In God's Army* I. 181 China to a Portuguee was a forbidden land. **1975** J. GORES *Hammett* iii. 28 'Keep your eye on the Portagee,' said Hammett. But Dancing Frankie..put the Portuguese boy on the canvas for a six count with a roundhouse right that wasn't fooling.

Portuguese (pɔətjʊ'giːz), *a.* and *sb.* Also (6 **porteguse**), 7 **-guèze**, **-guez**, **-guise**, **-gues(s**, 7–9 **-gueze**. [ad. Pg. *portuguez*, Sp. *portugues*, It. *portoghese*, F. *portugais*, in OF. *portugalois*, med.L. *portugalensis*: see PORTUGAL and -ESE.]

A. *adj.* **a.** Pertaining to Portugal or its people. Also *spec.*, of or pertaining to Sephardic Jews whose ancestors came from Portugal.

1662 HOWELL (*title*) A New English Grammar..With som special remarks upon the Portugues Dialect,..For the service of Her Majesty. **1709** STEELE *Tatler* No. 75 ¶5 He was low of Stature, and of a very swarthy Complexion, not unlike a Portugueze Jew. **1828** C. MᶜINTOSH *Pract. Gard.* I. 67 A Portuguese settlement on the coast of Africa. **1851** [see SEPHARDI]. **1866** GEO. ELIOT *Let.* 10 Aug. (1956) IV. 298 We looked about for the very Portuguese Synagogue where Spinoza was nearly assassinated... There are..three Portuguese Synagogues now [in Amsterdam]. **1902**, etc. [see SPANISH *a.* 1 d]. **1937**, **1960** [see MANUELINE *a.*].

b. Hence in names of various things, as **Portuguese cut**, a particular form in which brilliants are sometimes cut (*Cent. Dict.* 1889); **Portuguese knot**: see quot.; **Portuguese man-of-war**: see MAN-OF-WAR 4; **Portuguese oyster**, a type of oyster, *Crasostrea angulata*, which has a bumpy, greenish shell and is native to Portugal although it is cultivated elsewhere, esp. in France; also *ellipt.*; **Portuguese parliament** *Naut. slang*, a discussion in which many speak simultaneously; hubbub; **Portuguese trade-wind**, a north-east wind felt along the coast of Portugal (*Funk's Stand. Dict.* 1895).

1871 *Routledge's Ev. Boy's Ann.* May 299 A similar band is known as the Portuguese Knot used as a lashing for sheave legs. **1890** J. R. PHILPOTS *Oysters* I. xxv. 590 The mollusc known under the name of the Portuguese oyster does not belong to the same genus as our indigenous oyster. **1928** RUSSELL & YONGE *Seas* xiv. 301 Of recent years it [*sc.* the French oyster] has been almost completely ousted in the more southern beds by the Portuguese oyster. **1960** C. M. YONGE *Oysters* ix. 166 Some Portuguese oysters are ready for sale when only two years old. **1964** E. CLARK *Oysters of Locmariaquer* i. 4 The Portuguese oyster.. has been gradually moving farther north. **1976** N. ROBERTS *Face of France* xiii. 139 The oysters of Arcachon..turn up as starters to the most modest meal, whether..the delicately flavoured 'flats' or the plumper but more commonplace Portuguese. **1897** 'F. B. WILLIAMS' *On Many Seas* 388 Of all the jabbering and wrangling and shouting to one another that I ever heard, that was the worst. It was like what sailors call a Portuguese Parliament. **1898** H. E. A. COATE *Realities of Sea Life* 133 They [*sc.* wild monkeys] could only be compared with the 'members of a Portuguese Parliament', where, according to Jack's idea, they are 'all talkers and no listeners'. **1962** GRANVILLE *Dict. Sailors' Slang* 90/2 *Portuguese parliament*, rowdy discussion in which everybody talks and nobody listens.

B. *sb.*

1. A native of Portugal. [The plural *Portugueses* (*-guezes*) was used during 17th c.: since it became obs. *Portuguese* has been sing. and pl.; in modern times a sing. *Portug(u)ee* has arisen: see PORTUGEE. Cf. CHINESE, etc.]

1622 T. ROBINSON *Anat. Eng. Nunnery* 27 Diuers Portugeses our neighbours. **1694** W. WOTTON *Anc. & Mod. Learn.* (1697) 269 The Portuguezes, who first made daring Voyages, by the Help of the Compass, into the Southern and South-Eastern Seas. **1698** FRYER *Acc. E. India & P.* 38 There being..of English and Portuguez 700. **1783** WATSON *Philip III* (1839) 133 The affairs of the Portuguese in India were more than ever neglected by the government at home.

2. The Portuguese language.

1615 T. ROE *Jrnl.* 21 July in *Embassy to Court of Gt. Mogul* (1899) I. 19 The Enterpreters were certaine Magadoxians, that spake Arabique and broken Portuguese. **1617** MINSHEU *Ductor* (title-p.), In these eleuen Languages..8. Portuguez. **1653** H. COGAN tr. *Pinto's Trav.* v. 12 A Breichman that spake very good Portugueze. **1840** MALCOM *Trav.* 35/1 These are adopted by one from the English, another from the Arabic, another from the Greek, and another from the Portuguese. **1882** W. W. SKEAT *Etym. Dict. Eng. Lang.* p. xviii, The other Romance languages..are Italian, Spanish, Portuguese, Provençal, Romansch, and Wallachian. **1933** L. BLOOMFIELD *Language* xxvi. 474 The descendants of runaway slaves who settled on the island of San Thomé off the coast of West Africa, spoke a creolized Portuguese. **1950** J. H. STEWARD *Handbk. S. Amer. Indians* VI. 168 It has been estimated that 15 percent of the vocabulary of Brazilian Portuguese is of *Tupí* origin. **1974** *Encycl. Brit. Macropædia* XV. 1031/2 Portuguese owes its importance largely to its position as the language of Brazil. **1980** G. GREENE *Dr. Fischer* viii. 47 Two letters in Portuguese were sent me to translate, although I knew no Portuguese.

†**3.** = PORTAGUE, the gold coin. *Obs.*

1586 J. HOOKER *Hist. Irel.* in *Holinshed* II. 98/1 Storing him..with seuen score porteguses. *a* **1631** DONNE *Lett.* (1651) 86 He may cast up a greater summe who hath but forty small monies, then he with twenty Portuguesses. *a* **1668** DAVENANT *News fr. Plymouth* Wks. (1673) 2 Each with a bag of Porteguez under His left arme.

†**4.** ? A kind of snuff. *Obs.*

1708 PRIOR *Mice* 84 After some thought, some Portuguese, Some wine.

Hence **Portu'guese** *v. trans.*, to make Portuguese, to assimilate to the Portuguese.

1698 FRYER *Acc. E. India & P.* 157 The Mass of the People are..Portuguezed in Speech and Manners.

‖**Portulaca** (pɔətjuː'leɪkə). Also (erron.) **portulacca**. [L. *portulāca* purslain (*P. oleracea*): taken by Tournefort, 1700, as a generic name.] A genus of plants, comprising low succulent herbs bearing white, yellow, red, or purple terminal flowers, expanding only once in direct sunshine; esp. a plant of a cultivated species of this genus.

1548 TURNER *Names of Herbes* (E.D.S.) 65 Portulaca is called in english purcellaine. **1706** PHILLIPS, *Portulaca*, Purslain, a cold and moist Herb, which stirs up the Appetite. **1866** *Harvard Mem. Biogr.*, *Savage* I. 337 My Heliotrope is magnificent and portulacas begin to make a show. **1882** *Garden* 8 Apr. 234/2 Of all annuals that can be grown out of doors I know of none more beautiful than Portulacas. **1927** M. M. BENNETT *Christison* xi. 116 They ate portulacca to keep off scurvy. **1939** R. GODDEN *Black Narcissus* xix. 173 Lupins, delphiniums..and the portulaca she had grown to love in the plains. **1942** *E. Afr. Ann.* *1941–2* 44/1 The indigenous portulaca found all round Nairobi with its masses of yellow flowers is very fascinating. **1953** *Arena* (Wellington, N.Z.) xxxv. 4 'And your lovely portulaca,' Hester said gently, 'I had forgotten you always grew it.' **1962** [see CLEOME]. **1974** J. BERRISFORD *Window Box & Container Gardening* xix. 143 The annual portulacas..are suitable for seasonal use. **1978** *Detroit Free Press* 16 Apr. (Gardening Guide) 10/1 If you want to enjoy your garden in the evening, don't plant flowers such as day lilies, morning glories and portulacca that are closed at night.

Hence **portulaceous** (-'eɪʃəs) *a. Bot.*, of or pertaining to the natural order *Portulaceæ*, comprising succulent shrubs and herbs, chiefly American, but distributed in all parts of the world.

1852 TH. ROSS *Humboldt's Trav.* I. vi. 203 Most of the portulaceous plants which grow on the banks of the gulf of Cariaco. **1858** in MAYNE *Expos. Lex.*

portulace, **-lack**. Now *rare*. Also 5 **portulake**; **portulac**. [ad. L. *portulāca* PURSLANE: see PORTULACA and cf. OF. *portulache*, *-lague*.] The common Purslane (*Portulaca oleracea*).

c **1400** *Lanfranc's Cirurg.* 240 Þe pacient schal absteine him fro fleisch & fisch & vse lactucis, portulacis. *Ibid.* 268 An enplastre as of solatri, portulace. *c* **1420** *Pallad. on Husb.* XI. 246 Yf auntes harme, a craft is ek therfore. Held on the tre the Iuce of portulake [*rime* slake] Half aysel myxt. **1770** J. R. FORSTER tr. *Kalm's Trav. N. Amer.* (1772) II. 93 Portulack (*Portulaca oleracea*) grows spontaneously here in great abundance. **1911** C. E. W. BEAN *'Dreadnought' of Darling* xxvii. 234 They helped their provisions by eating a good deal of a shrub known as portulac.

portulan, variant of PORTOLAN.

portunal ('pɔətjʊnəl). [a. Ger. *portunal*, app. ad. L. *Portūnālis* belonging to *Portūnus*: see next.] (See quots.) Also called ***portunal-flute***.

1852 SEIDEL *Organ* 101 Portunal is a very agreeable, open flute-register in the manual... Its beautiful tone is of a very peculiar quality, similar to that of the clarionet. **1876** HILES *Catech. Organ* ix. (1878) 60. **1898** STAINER & BARRETT *Dict. Mus. Terms*, *Portunal-flute*, an organ stop, the pipes of which are of wood, and are open, and larger at the top than at the mouth.

portunian (pɔ'tjuːnɪən), *a.* and *sb. Zool.* [f. mod.L. *Portūn-us* (a. L. *Portūnus* name of the god of harbours) + -IAN.] **a.** *adj.* Of or pertaining to the *Portūnidæ*, a family of swimming crabs, or to the typical genus *Portūnus*. **b.** *sb.* A crab of this family (*Cent. Dict.* 1890). So **por'tunid** = b; **por'tunoid** *a.*, akin in form to the portunians.

†**por'tunity**. *Obs. rare.* [Aphetic form of OPPORTUNITY; so OF. *portunité*.]

1508 *Kalender of Sheph.* (1892) III. App. 180 Cease whyle ye haue space and portunyte.

portuos, **portuous**, etc., variants of PORTAS.

†**porturat**, *ppl. a. Sc. Obs. rare*⁻¹. [? quasi-Latinized form of *porturit*, *-ed*; see PORTURE *v.* 3.] Fashioned, moulded, formed, made.

1489 *Barbour's Bruce* x. 281 (Edin. MS.) He was off mesurabill statur, And weile porturat at mesur.

†**porture**, *sb.*¹ *Obs. rare.* Also 4 **portoure**, 5 **porteure**. [a. OF. *port(e)ure* bearing, demeanour, that which is borne, offspring:—L.

type *portātūra, f. L. portāre, F. porter to carry: see -URE.]

1. Bearing, demeanour, behaviour.

c **1305** *St. Swithin* 25 in *E.E.P.* (1862) 44 þat he teiȝte him such portoure þat to a such child bicome. c **1400** *Laud Troy Bk.* 16604 Pirrus is knyght gode & gay, Off ffair porture, of gode aray. c **1440** *Ipomydon* 121 For thoughe a man wold all this day Hyr beaute discryue, he coude not sey All hyr worshyp ne hyr porture.

2. Offspring, progeny.

1480 CAXTON *Ovid's Met.* XIII. ix, Yet he is not fylled ne satisfyed but defowleth my porteure deed or quyke.

† **'porture**, *sb.*[2] *Obs. rare.* [f. PORTURE *v.*] A portrait, image, effigy.

1542 UDALL *Erasm. Apoph.* 88 The porture of a man in brasse or stone. *Ibid.* 115 b, The people of Athenes..made & sette vp..their ymages and portures in coppre. **1570** LEVINS *Manip.* 192/44 A Porture, *pictura, effigies.*

† **'porture, portere**, *v. Obs.* Chiefly in *pa. pple.* 4–6 portred, 5 purtred, 6 portered (-ide, *Sc.* -it), portured (-id, *Sc.* -yt), po(u)rturde, purtured. [A by-form of PORTRAY. Occurs first in pa. pple. *portred*, app. an anglicized form of OF. *portrait, portret*, pa. pple. of *portraire* to PORTRAY; from the later variants *portered, porterit, portured*, was evolved the vb. *porter, porture* in 16th c. But *portrewynge* vbl. sb. is found *a* 1400. Cf. CONSTER from *construe*.]

1. *trans.* To paint, or ornament with pictures.

c **1394** *P. Pl. Crede* 192 þat cloister..was pilered and peynt & portred well clene. c **1400** *Plowman's Tale* 135 That hye on horse willeth ryde In glitterand golde of grete aray, I-paynted and portred all in pryde. **1539** TAVERNER *Gard. Wysed.* II. 10 They haue the walles of theyr houses portered with armes.

2. To portray, depict. Also *fig.*

a **1440** *Sir Degrev.* 1448 There was purtred in ston..The story of Absolon. **1511** in Ellis *Orig. Lett.* Ser. II. I. 181 They shall present theymself with theyr names portered in theyr shyldes. **1513** DOUGLAS *Æneis* VII. iv. 70 The ancyant king Saturne thair mycht thou se..Wyth wthir prencis porturyt in that place. **1530** PALSGR. 662/2, I portyr, I make the shappe, or the portrature of a thynge, *je pourtrays*... I porter a thynge after the quycke. **1563** B. GOOGE *Eglogs*, etc. (Arb.) 114 There myght I se, with wondrous Arte, the Picture porturde playne. **1570** LEVINS *Manip.* 193/15 To Porture, *pingere.*

3. To form, fashion, mould, make: = PORTRAY *v.* 5.

1535 STEWART *Cron. Scot.* (Rolls) II. 189 Aurelius tua sisteris fair and gude,..he had of plesand pulchritude, Porterit but peir, full of formositie.

Hence † **'porturing** *vbl. sb.*

1398 TREVISA *Barth. De P.R.* XVI. xxxvii. (Tollem. MS.), Liche to golde in crownes amonge portrewynge [**1535** porturynge] and peyntoure.

portus, -e, portuus, etc., variants of PORTAS.

† **port-vein.** *Obs.* [f. PORT *sb.*[3], after F. *veine porte*, L. *vēna porta*.] = PORTAL *vein*.

1586 BRIGHT *Melanch.* vii. 30 Drawen..out of the liuer, by a braunch of the porte vayne. **1594** T. B. *La Primaud Fr. Acad.* II. 356 The first is called the port-veine, because it is as it were the doore of the liuer out of which it proceedeth. **1655** H. VAUGHAN *Silex Scint.* III. *Daphnis*, Like some great port-vein With large rich streams to feed the humble plain. **1706** PHILLIPS, *Porta*... In Anatomy, the Port-vein.

port-vent. [corresp. to a F. *porte-vent 'carry-wind', f. PORTE- + *vent* wind.] A pipe conveying the wind in an organ or bagpipe.

1727–41 CHAMBERS *Cycl.*, *Port-vent*, in an organ, is a wooden pipe, well closed, which serves to convey the wind from the bellows to the sound-board of the organ. **1877** G. MACDONALD *Mrq. Lossie* xi, Malcolm set his port vent to his mouth, rapidly filled his bag.

'port-way. Now *local.* [f. PORT *sb.*[2] + WAY *sb.*] A road leading from town to town; a public highway: a Roman road.

Used by Holland in translating various L. expressions: see quots. In the Godstow Charters c 1285 applied to a road near Cassington, Oxon. The name survives in other localities, e.g. in the Vale of the White Horse.

c **1285** (transl. c **1450**) *Godstow Reg.* 301 Of the whiche lond, v. acres (lien to-gedir) strecchen into the portwey [*se extendunt in to porteweye*]; And j. half acre, the whiche strecchith into porteweye [*portweye*] beside the lond of william Fitz Petir. **1600** HOLLAND *Livy* VII. xxx. 270 The whole multitude stand about the gates looking toward the high port-way [*via*] that leadeth from hence thither. **1610** —— *Camden's Brit.* 282 The bridges of Abbindon and Dorchester, whereby London portway [*regia via*] was turned from thence [from Wallingford]. *Ibid.* 508 The high portway or Romane Street [*via militaris*]. *Ibid.* 557 The portway or High paved street [*via Romana lapidibus constrata*] named Bath-gate [at Buxton].

'port-'wine. a. = PORT *sb.*[7] 1.

[**1692** LUTTRELL *Brief Rel.* (1857) II. 334 An English vessell..with O Porto wine and some passengers on board.] a **1700** B. E. *Dict. Cant. Crew*, *Red-fustian*, Clarret or red Port-Wine. **1759** MOUNTAINE in *Phil. Trans.* LI. 292 Six dozen of bottles of Port wine. **1836** CYRUS REDDING *Mod. Wines* viii. 220 In 1730 good port wine was sold in England at two shillings the bottle, and white wine of Portugal at the same price. **1930** H. CRADDOCK *Savoy Cocktail Bk.* 192 Port Wine Sangaree..Port Wine..sugar..ice..nutmeg. **1968** *Daily Tel.* (Colour Suppl.) 13 Dec. 41/4 Portwine is being poured over chunks of ice.

b. *attrib.* and *Comb.*, as ***port-wine colour, negus, stain, tint***; **port-wine magnolia** *Austral.*, an evergreen shrub, *Michelia figo* of the family Magnoliaceæ, native to temperate or tropical Asia and bearing scented reddish-brown or purple flowers; **port-wine mark** = NÆVUS.

1858 TROLLOPE *Three Clerks* III. ii. 38 Mrs. Davis was mixing port-wine negus as fast as her hands could make it. **1872** *Routledge's Ev. Boy's Ann.* Apr. 276/1 He has what is called a port-wine mark on the back of his neck. **1887** MRS. EWING *Peace Egg* 9 A port-wine stain on the best table-cloth. **1889** *Anthony's Photogr. Bull.* II. 123 Of a light port-wine color. **1943** K. TENNANT *Ride on Stranger* viii. 86 At Lindfield there were port-wine magnolias. **1977** *Austral. House & Garden* Jan. 17/1 Check these and spray them too if necessary: Gardenia,..Port Wine Magnolia (Michelia), Crepe Myrtle, Flowering Quince.

Hence **port-'winer**, an habitual drinker of port; **'port-'winy** *a.*, smacking of port-wine; also **port-'winily** *adv.*;

1881 MISS BRADDON *Asph.* II. 10 Those prosy port-winey old sermons of his. **1908** *Daily Chron.* 20 Oct. 5/5 A magnificently Georgian figure in his court-robes, with a red wig and generally 'port-winey' make-up. **1909** R. W. SERVICE *Ballads of Cheechako* (1910) 54, I smoked and sat as I marvelled at the sky's port-winey glow. **1920** G. E. BUCKLE *Life Disraeli* V. ii. 67 Beauchamp..warned Disraeli that the High Church party other than 'the old port-winers' were holding aloof from the political contest. **1921** A. HUXLEY *Crome Yellow* ii. 8 There was the dining-room, solidly, port-winily English, with its great mahogany table. **1923** [see CIGARY *a.*]. **1938** S. BECKETT *Murphy* 266 'A proper port-winer,' said the Coroner. 'The afterglow is unmistakable.'

'porty, *a.* [f. PORT *sb.*[7] + -Y.] Like, of the nature of, or connected in some way with port-wine: cf. prec.

1859 G. MEREDITH *R. Feverel* II. i. 7 The eloquence of that Porty reply was lost on his Client. **1892** *Pall Mall G.* 14 Dec. 1/3 As an old Academician once said, 'They [pictures] have got porty by time', and of course improved. **1906** *Macm. Mag.* Mar. 387 Gout..was suggestive of fine old porty ancestors.

portyfoliom, Portyngale: see PORTIFOLIUM, PORTUGAL.

portygewe, var. PORTAGUE *Obs.*

port-yowl (pɔːt'jaʊl). *Sc.* Also 9 portule. [f. PORT *sb.*[8] (?) + YOWL.] A doleful cry, howl: in *to sing port-yowl*, to cry out, wail, howl.

1708 M. BRUCE *Lect. & Serm.* 62 All Folks are singing Songs of Jovialty, but the people of God, they must sing Port-youl. **1722** W. HAMILTON *Wallace* iii. 161 I'll make them know they have no Right to rule, And cause them shortly all Sing up Port-yeull. **1892** *Ballymena Observer* (E.D.D.), A'll mak' you sing portule wi' the wrang side o' your lip oot.

portyr, variant of PORTURE *Obs.*

porule ('pɔərjʊl). *rare.* [f. PORE *sb.*[1] + -ULE.] A minute pore.

1846 DANA *Zooph.* (1848) 513 Porules narrow-oblong. *Ibid.* Gloss., *Cellule, Porule*, the pores in the internal texture of a corallum.

Hence **'porulose, 'porulous** *adjs.*, abounding in minute pores.

1846 DANA *Zooph.* (1848) 705 Both surfaces minutely porulose. **1858** MAYNE *Exp. Lex.*, *Porulosus*..porulous.

porvaye, obs. form of PURVEY.

porwigle, obs. variant of POLLIWOG.

† **'pory**, *a. Obs.* Also 6 powrie, 6–7 porie, poory, 7 poary. [f. PORE *sb.*[1] + -Y.] Full of or containing pores; porous.

1535 *Trevisa's Barth. De P.R.* v. xliii. 59/2 They [the reins] ben fleshely and poory [*ed.* 1582 powrie]. **1578** BANISTER *Hist. Man* I. 2 The bones of yͤ nose, and Ossicles of hearyng, are inwardly Porie. **1615** G. SANDYS *Trav.* 278 The stones hereof are so light and pory, that they will not sinke. **1654** FLECKNOE *Ten Years Trav.* 71 The body growing Cane-wise, distinguisht by several knots, out of whose poory sides, the branches issue forth in round. **1656** tr. *Comenius' Gate Lat. Unl.* §99. 33 The poary Spunge bred on the rocks under water. **1697** DRYDEN *Virg. Georg.* IV. 536 Vaulted Roofs of Pory Stone. **1826** *Blackw. Mag.* XIX. 401 They glide with ease through the pory earth.

porzy, obs. form of PURSY.

pos[1] (pɒz). *colloq.* Also 8 pozz, 8–9 poz. [Abbreviation of POSITIVE.] Positive, certain; esp. in phrase ***that's pos***. Also as *sb.*, and as *adv.* = positively.

1710 SWIFT *Tatler* No. 230 ¶5, I can't d't, that's Pozz. **1711** —— *Lett.* (1767) III. 231 'Tis very cold; but I will not have a fire till November, that's pozz. **1711** *Spectator* 4 Aug. 2/1 It is perhaps..speaking no more than we needs must, which has so miserably curtailed some of our Words, that.. they sometimes lose all but their first Syllables, as in *Mob. reb. pos.* incog. and the like. **1716** ADDISON *Drummer* III. i, I will be flattered, that's pos! **1801** SURR *Splendid Misery* II. 143 'Fie, fie, Lady Amelia', said I. 'I will, poz', replied she. **1839** THACKERAY *Catherine* ii, I will have a regiment to myself, that's poz. **1922** JOYCE *Ulysses* 418 Got a pectoral trauma, eh, Dix? Pos fact. **1930** [see *electron gun* (ELECTRON[2] 2 b)]. **1969** 'R. CRAWFORD' *Cockleburr* II. vi. 126 'Are you sure you weren't spotted?' 'Pos.' **1977** *Hot Car* Oct. 99/4 (Advt.), Smiths electronic tacho (pos earth). **1979** *SLR Camera* Mar. 34/1 Having said that, there are of course the neg/pos experts who will tell you how to produce a 20 × 16 print from a quarter inch portion of a 35mm negative.

pos[2], var. POSS *a.*

‖**posada** (pɒ'sɑːdə). Also 8 possada. [Sp., a resting place, an inn, ppl. sb. f. *posar* to lodge: see POSE *v.*[1]] **1.** A (Spanish) inn or place of accommodation for travellers.

1763 *Crt. & City Mag.* Apr. 192/2 The inside of a Spanish posada (or inn) for the night. **1827** ROBERTS *Voy. Centr. Amer.* 212 There is no passado for the reception of travellers. **1828** W. IRVING in *Life & Lett.* (1864) II. 285 The squalid miseries of the Spanish posadas. **1891** B. HARTE *1st Fam. Tasajara* II. 102 There were some Mexicans lounging about the *posada*. **1931** P. GUEDALLA *Duke* IV. vii. 236 An obliging innkeeper rode twenty miles to tell him that Clausel was safely lodged in his *posada*. **1950** G. BRENAN *Face of Spain* iv. 95, I had not reached the posada till after midnight. **1955** *Times* 4 July 12/7 Dying in poverty in a lowly *posada* in Valladolid. **1965** *New statesman* 7 May 734/1, I suppose it must have been Balzac who, when Cervantes' posadas and Fielding's coaching-inns were beginning to pall, discovered the potentialities of the boarding-house. **1966** *Listener* 4 Aug. 164/2, I was recently taken by my host in Mexico..to the ancient site of Teotihuacan,..and afterwards to lunch at a *posada* in the neighbouring village. **1974** C. LARSON *Matthew's Hand* xxvii. 161 He owns a *posada*—an inn.

2. In Mexico, each of a series of visits traditionally paid to different friends during the days before Christmas, representing Mary and Joseph's search for a lodging in Bethlehem.

1930 R. REDFIELD *Tepoztlan* vi. 128 There is time to rest now, and enjoy the Christmas *fiestas*... In many houses.. the nine *posadas* are celebrated as they are celebrated all over Mexico... The matrons of the neighborhood have arranged in whose house will take place each of the nine fiestas. **1932** CHASE & TYLER *Mexico* x. 202 December 16. Christmas fiesta. Nine days. Posadas. Processions, rodeos, singing. **1959** *Listener* 24 Dec. 1105/1 These and other decorations will take a central place in the *posadas* which go on night after night for the twelve days before Christmas. The *posadas* are supposed to represent the vain search of Mary and Joseph to find a lodging in Bethlehem. **1978** *Tucson Mag.* Dec. 105/1 You may witness a real 'Las Posadas' celebration December 12 beginning at 7:30 p.m. The candle-lighted procession of Carrillo School children will begin at the school (400 South Main) and continue through one of the city's oldest neighborhoods, in emulation of the journey of Mary and Joseph seeking shelter. The 'inn' or posada for this evening's festivities will be the school itself, where refreshments will be served and a pinata will be broken.

posadaship (pɒ'sɑːdəʃɪp). [f. POSADA + -SHIP.] The position of the keeper of a posada.

1923 *Blackw. Mag.* Nov. 700/2 The details of how from posadaship she had fallen to this minute eating-house were slurred over.

‖**posadero** (posa'dero). [Sp.] In Spanish-speaking countries: an innkeeper.

1904 CONRAD *Nostromo* I. viii. 116 The posadero in Rincon swore that on calm nights..he could catch the sound in his doorway. **1912** W. G. LAWRENCE in T. E. Lawrence *Home Lett.* (1954) 423 After lunch..Juan the Posadero came out to talk with us.

† **'posary.** *Obs. rare*[−1]. *Arch.* [app. f. med.L. *pōsāre* (whence It. *posare*, F. *poser*) to rest (see POSE *v.*[1]) + -ARY[1].] = PODIUM: see quot.

1664 EVELYN tr. *Freart's Archit.* 124 They served for Podia or posaries of a leaning-height for which they had a slight Cornice assign'd them.

‖**posaune** (po'zaʊnə). Also posaun. [G., a trumpet, trombone (= Du. *bazuin*, Da., Sw. *basun*), MHG. *busûne, -îne*, ad. OF. *buisine* BUYSINE.]

† **1.** A trombone. *Obs.*

1724 *Short Explic. For. Wds. in Mus. Bks.*, *Posaune*, a Sackbut, an Instrument of Musick made use of as a Bass to a Trumpet. **1776** HAWKINS *Hist. Mus.* IV. I. x. 150 The word Buzain is a corruption of Busaun, or, as it is now spelt Posaune, which signifies a sacbut or bass-trumpet. **1814** tr. *Klaproth's Trav.* 101 A great posaun..of brass,..in three divisions, which are pushed out in blowing.

2. A reed-stop on the organ, of a rich and powerful tone.

1843 *Civil Eng. & Arch. Jrnl.* VI. 108/1 The posaune is built on a large scale, and is by far the most powerful ever made. **1879** E. J. HOPKINS in Grove *Dict. Mus.* I. 562/2 There are some..posaunes in the pedal organ..at Doncaster.

‖**posca** ('pɒskə). *Obs.* exc. *Hist.* Also 7 pusca. [L. (Plaut.), an acidulous drink of vinegar and water, lit. drink, f. root *po-*, Gr. πο- (ποτ-), to drink: cf. *ēsca* food; so It. *posca*, in same sense.] A mixture of vinegar and water; also, weak wine diluted with water or with vinegar-water.

1541 COPLAND *Galyen's Terap.* 2 A iv b, Yf ye must wasshe the sore, take wyne or posca, that is to saye oxycraton, or the decoction of some sharpe herbe. **1640** PARKINSON *Theat. Bot.* 240 The kernells of the nuts bruised and drunke with Posca possett (that is water and vinegar mingled together). **1706** PHILLIPS, *Posca* (Lat.), a..Drink made of Vinegar and Water; also Wine diluted or mingled with Water in the Press. **1905** D. SMITH *Days His Flesh* 497 They had with them a beaker of their posca or vinegar water.

† **pose**, *sb.*[1] *Obs.* Forms: 1 ȝepos, 4–7 (8–9 *dial.*) pose, 5–6 poose, 7 pooss, poze. [OE. *ȝe-pos* a catarrh, cough, f. Brythonic **pas-* cough, whence W., Corn. *pas*, Breton *paz* cough, from

Aryan **kwes-* to wheeze, whence also Skr. *çvas-*, OE. *hwǣsan*.] A cold in the head, catarrh.

c **1000** *Sax. Leechd.* II. 54 Wiþ ȝesnote & ȝeposum ȝenim oxna lyb. *a* **1050** *Herb. Apul.* xlvi. ibid. I. 148 Wið ȝeposu [*Ad tussim gravem*]. *c* **1305** *E.E. Poems* (1862) 37 To hele him of þe pose. *c* **1386** CHAUCER *Manciple's T.* Prol. 62 He spekeþ in his nose And fneseth faste and eek he hath the pose. **1486** *Bk. St. Albans* C iij b, For the Cogh or the poose Take powdre of Bays [etc.]. **1530** PALSGR. 582/1, I have the pose, *jay la catarre* or *je suis enrimé*. **1706** PHILLIPS, *Pose*,.. a Rheum in the Head. *a* **1825** FORBY *Voc. E. Anglia*, *Pose*, a catarrh, or cold in the head.

b. in the horse.

1607 TOPSELL *Four-f. Beasts* (1658) 277 If the Horse casteth little or no matter out of his nose,.. it is a sign that he is stopped in the head, which we were wont to call the pose. **1610** MARKHAM *Masterp.* I. xxxviii. 74 The cold or poze in a horses head. **1639** T. DE GRAY *Compl. Horsem.* 59 They be most enclined to poses, rhumes, paines in the head.

pose (pəʊz), *sb.*[2] *Obs.* exc. *Sc.* Also 5 pos, 6 pois, poiss, (poess). [app., that which has been deposited or laid down, f. F. *poser* to place, lay down: see POSE *v.*[1]]

A hoard, treasure, secret store of money, etc.

c **1440** *Promp. Parv.* 410/2 Pos, or depos, *depositum*. **1549** *Compl. Scot.* xi. 89 Thir said princis gat, in the spulȝe.. the kyng of Francis pose, quhilk vas al in engel noblis. **1563** WINȜET *Wks.* (S.T.S.) II. 56 Quhat wes committit to thee, lat that remane in thy poiss. **1637** RUTHERFORD *Lett.* III. xlvii. (1881) 537 If you seek, there is a pose, a hidden treasure, a gold mine in Christ you never yet saw. **1816** SCOTT *Antiq.* xxiv, This grand pose o' silver and treasure. **1844** M. A. RICHARDSON *Hist. Table-bk., Leg. Div.* II. 91 The 'pose' was gone, the coffer had vanished.

†**pose,** *sb.*[3] *Obs.* App. a variant of POSY. (Perh. first in the plural, *posies* being taken as *poses*.)

1542 UDALL *Erasm. Apoph.* 274 b, What poses certain persones wrote under the images of Brutus & Caesar. *a* **1548** HALL *Chron., Hen. VIII* 3 b, Many subtleties, straunge deuises, with seuerall poses. **1553** T. WILSON *Rhet.* 100 b, If we purpose to dilate our cause hereby with poses and sentences. **15..** *Songs Costume* (Percy Soc.) 65 Suche garded huoes, Suche playted shoes, And suche a pose, Say y never.

†**pose,** *sb.*[4] *Obs.* [f. POSE *v.*[2]] A state of perplexity.

1616 SIR C. MOUNTAGU in *Buccleuch MSS.* (Hist. MSS. Comm.) I. 249 The Lords they say are at a pose what to do.

pose (pəʊz), *sb.*[5] [a. F. *pose*, f. *poser* to put, place: see POSE *v.*[1]] An act of posing.

1. An attitude or posture of the body, or of a part of the body, esp. one deliberately assumed, or in which a figure is placed for effect, or for artistic purposes.

1818 LADY MORGAN *Autobiog.* (1859) 170 Spencer begged the cover, and read out the letter, that my *pose* might not be disturbed. **1848** MRS. JAMESON *Sacr. & Leg. Art* (1850) 213 His idea of the pose was borrowed, as we are told, from an antique statue. **1883** B. HARTE *Carquinez Woods* i. 11 He unconsciously fell into an attitude that in any other mortal would have been a pose.

2. *fig.* An attitude of mind or conduct.

1884 J. TAIT *Mind in Matter* (1892) 311 There is difficulty in the silent pose, and meek opposition, of many of the learned in the presence of idealism, creating suspicion of partial acceptance. **1898** G. W. E. RUSSELL *Coll. & Recoll.* xiii. 176 This portentous age of reticence and pose. **1904** R. J. CAMPBELL *Serm. Individuals* vi. 109 'I thought.' He had prepared himself in his mental pose for what did not take place.

3. *Dominoes.* = DOWN *sb.*[3] 3: see quots.

1865 *Compl. Domino-Player* 11 The pose, or turn to commence the game, is determined in one particular manner in all games of dominoes. **1870** HARDY & WARE *Mod. Hoyle, Dominoes* 92 On the Continent... the person holding the highest double has the 'pose' or 'down', and he commences by playing that domino. If there should be no doubles, then the person holding the highest domino has the pose.

4. *N. Amer.* A resting place on a portage; the distance between two such rests. *Obs.* except *Hist.*

1793 J. MACDONNELL in C. M. Gates *Five Fur Traders* (1933) 96 The portage is full of hills is divided by the voyageurs into sixteen Poses or resting places. *c* **1840** D. THOMPSON *Narr. Explorations W. Amer. 1784–1812* (1916) xviii. 294 A Rest, or Pose, is the distance the cargo of a canoe is carried from place to place and then rest. **1858** *Porter's Spirit of Times* 30 Jan. 338/1 In crossing a long portage, they do not go through the whole distance with one load, but divide it into 'poses' or rests; and carry in succession each load to the first 'pose', and then carry them all to the second one, and so on, so that they can rest in walking back for the loads. **1933** C. M. GATES *Five Fur Traders* 97 Inasmuch as the same places were used as poses by all who passed, it came to be the common thing to measure the length of a portage by the number of poses along the trail. **1941** J. F. McDERMOTT *Gloss. Mississippi Valley French 1673–1850* 126 The average length of a *pose* was about one-third of a mile. **1969** E. W. MORSE *Fur Trade Canoe Routes* I. i. 5 If the portage was more than half a mile (a ten-minute carry), the voyageur, in order better to distribute his loaded and unloaded periods, dropped his packs at what was known as a *pose*, and went back for the next load. *Poses* were about half a mile apart.

†**pose,** *sb.*[6] *Obs.* [a. OF. *pose* a land measure (1336 in Godef.), Fr. Swiss *pose* an old superficial measure for meadows, fields, and forests, = half the *faux*, or 32,768 sq. feet (Godef.).] A superficial measure of land, = about three-quarters of an acre.

1759 J. MILLS *Duhamel's Husb.* II. ii. 265 This field contains, according to our measure, six poses. Each pose contains 400 square perches, and each perch nine feet. **1763** —— *Pract. Husb.* II. 306 Another field of betwixt nine and ten poses (equal to about seven acres and three roods).

pose (pəʊz), *v.*[1] *Pa. t.* and *pple.* posed: in ME. also post. [a. F. *poser* (in all the chief senses of the Eng. word):—L. *pausāre* to halt, cease, pause, in late L. to rest (see PAUSE *v.*), which subsequently acquired also through confusion with L. *pōnĕre* (*posui*, *positum*) the trans. sense to lay to rest, put or set down, place, properly belonging to the latter (so in *Leges Alam.* tit. 45, *pausant arma sua josum* they lay their arms down); so It. *posare*, Pr. *pausar*, Sp. *posar*, all trans. and intr., Pg. *pousar* intr.

The sense of *pōnere* having been restricted in the Romanic of Gaul (as shown by Fr. and Prov.) to 'lay eggs', its numerous compounds (*com-*, *de-*, *dis-*, *ex-*, *im-*, *op-*, *pro-*, *supponere*, etc.) were replaced in Fr. and Prov. by corresponding new compounds of *pausare*: see APPOSE *v.*[2], COMPOSE, etc.; It., Sp., and Pg. retain the original compounds of *ponere*. A Com. Romanic compound of the intr. *pausare* is represented by REPOSE.]

†**1.** *trans.* To place in a specified situation or condition. *Obs. rare.*

c **1380** WYCLIF *Serm.* Sel. Wks. I. 242 Noþing is better post to þe likyng of þe fend. *c* **1420** *Pallad. on Husb.* III. 495 But xxx footis pose Vche order of from other.

b. *Dominoes.* See quot. and cf. POSE *sb.*[5] 3.

1865 *Compl. Domino-Player* 40 In placing the first domino on the table, or posing, as it is called, you might [etc.].

†**2.** To suppose or assume for argument's sake. (Usually with *obj. cl.*) *Obs.*

c **1374** CHAUCER *Troylus* III. 261 (310) A[s] þus I pose a womman graunte me Here loue and seyth þat oþer wole she non. **1377** LANGL. *P. Pl.* B. XVII. 293, I pose I hadde synned so.. mouȝte I nouȝte be saued? *c* **1420** *Pallad. on Husb.* I. 285 Yet pose y that hit might amendid be. **1528** *Kalender of Sheph.* xxxvii. P vij b, Yf it were possyble that the erthe were enhabyted all aboute & pose [*earlier edd.* puttand] the case y[t] it were so.

3. a. To lay down, put forth (an assertion, allegation, claim, instance, etc.).

1512 *Helyas* in Thoms *Prose Rom.* (1828) III. 92 He made iniuriously to pose and put in faite that the said duchesse had made to empoysen her husband. **1662** GLANVILL *Lux Orient.* xi. (1682) 85 God himself in his posing the great instance of patience, Job, seems to intimate somewhat to this purpose. **1882** OWEN in *Longm. Mag.* I. 64 What is posed as the 'Neanderthal skull' is the roof of the brain-case. **1888** *Science* XI. 256/2 M. Janet.. poses the new psychology as of French origin.

b. To propound, propose (a question or problem).

1862 SALA *Accepted Addr.* 124, I don't require any answer to my question, now that I have posed it. **1873** SYMONDS *Grk. Poets* i. 14 Hesiod poses the eternal problems: what is the origin and destiny of mankind?

4. a. To place in an attitude (as an artist's model or sitter, etc.). Also *fig.*

1859 GULLICK & TIMBS *Paint.* 312 The model is posed or in other words 'set' in some particular attitude. **1868** TUCKERMAN *Collector* 70 In studied attitude, like one posed for a daguerreotype. **1878** ABNEY *Photogr.* (1881) 240 In posing a group, let it be remembered that each figure is animate, and should not be made to look as lifeless as a statue.

b. *intr.* To assume a certain attitude; to place oneself in position, esp. for artistic purposes.

1850 *Edin. Rev.* July 196 He drapes himself, and poses before you in every variety of attitude. **1885** *Truth* 28 May 834/2 Tableaux are a great improvement on drawingroom amateur theatricals,.. it is more easy to pose than to act.

c. *fig.* To present oneself in a particular character (often implying that it is assumed); to set up *as*, give oneself out *as*; to attitudinize.

1840 THACKERAY *Shabby Genteel Story* vi, He.. 'posed' before her as a hero of the most sublime kind. **1877** BLACK *Green Past.* xv, Was it true that these were the real objects which caused this man to pose as a philanthropist? **1888** BRYCE *Amer. Commw.* III. lxxxi. 70 Politicians have of late years begun to pose as the special friends of the working man.

Hence **posed** *ppl. a.*[1] *rare*, †(*a*) composed, grave, sedate (*obs.*); (*b*) placed or arranged in a pose or posture, as a sitter; (*c*) assumed as a pose; deliberately adopted or put on; whence **'posedness**; **'posing** *vbl. sb.*[1] and *ppl. a.*[1] (sense 4).

a **1693** *Urquhart's Rabelais* III. xix, An old setled Person, of a most *posed, stayed and grave Behaviour. **1891** *Anthony's Photogr. Bull.* IV. 137 Now this is not a 'posed' subject, but taken in an actual game, which makes it so much the more interesting. **1909** M. B. SAUNDERS *Litany Lane* I. iv. 43 There was also a nun-like acquiescence in her bearing, prim for her thirty-three years, and possibly a trifle posed. **1891** *Temple Bar Mag.* Mar. 442 It has the earnestness of Ingres, marred.. by his conventionality, and a certain flat *posedness. **1889** *Anthony's Photogr. Bull.* II. 88 By *posing we obtain likeness improved by beauty of outline and graceful posture. **1890** *Ibid.* III. 411 The posing chair should be a low-backed chair fastened to a platform.. on castors. This enables the operator to move the sitter to any position, without the trouble of getting up. **1888** PENNELL *Sent. Journ.* 149 Barbizon, with its picture galleries and *posing peasants.

pose (pəʊz), *v.*[2] Also 7 poase, 7–9 poze. [Aphetic form of APPOSE *v.*[1] or of OPPOSE, which was confused with it.]

†**1.** *trans.* To examine by questioning, question, interrogate: = APPOSE *v.*[1] 1, OPPOSE *v.* 1. *Obs.*

1526 TINDALE *Luke* ii. 46 They founde hym in the temple sittinge in the middes of the doctours, both hearynge them and posinge them. **1579** FULKE *Heskins's Parl.* 176 Let me pose him in his aunswere like a childe. **1612** BRINSLEY *Lud. Lit.* iii. (1627) 16 Let so many.. stand together, and then poase them without booke, one by one. **1688** BUNYAN *Dying Sayings* Wks. 50 Let us therefore be posing ourselves which of the two it will be. **1722** *Wodrow Corr.* (1843) II. 648 When posed about faith, they answered in terms of the Confession of Faith and Catechism.

2. To place in a difficulty with a question or problem; to puzzle, confuse, perplex, nonplus.

1593 DONNE *Sat.* iv. 20 A thing which would have pos'd Adam to name. **1605** VERSTEGAN *Dec. Intell.* ii. (1628) 30 Now hath Occa posed me about the countrie of India, which he expresely saith was in Africa. **1611** COTGR., *Faire quinaut*, to pose, or driue to a Nonplus. *a* **1625** FLETCHER & MASS. *Cust. Country* III. ii, What precious piece of nature To poze the world? *a* **1677** BARROW *Serm.* (1687) I. xxiii. 309 A question wherewith a learned Pharisee thought to pose or puzzle him. **1711** STEELE *Spect.* No. 113 ⁋4 You must make Love to her, as you would conquer the Sphinx, by posing her. **1807** CRABBE *Par. Reg.* I. 679 Then by what name th' unwelcome guest to call, Was long a question, and it pos'd them all. **1856** DOVE *Logic Chr. Faith* I. i. §2. 61 We have thus posed the mathematician.. and the historian.

†**b.** *transf.* To do that which puzzles (another).

1630 COWLEY *Constantia & Philetus* xxiv, She took a Lute.. And tun'd this Song, posing that harmony Which Poets attribute to heavenly spheres.

Hence **posed** *ppl. a.*[2]; **'posing** *vbl. sb.*[2] and *ppl. a.*[2]; whence **'posingly** *adv.* (Webster 1847); **'posement** *nonce-wd.*, the condition of being posed.

1820 KEATS *Hyperion* II. 244 Whether through *pozed conviction, or disdain, They guarded silence. **1850** L. HUNT *Autobiog.* III. xx. 60 Puzzlement and *posement of various sorts awaited many readers. **1556** B. GREENE in Foxe *A. & M.* (1583) 1853/1 This greate chere was often powthred with vnsauery sawces of examinations, exhortacions, *posings, and disputacions. **1841** PEACOCK *Ibid.* App. A. p. xiii. *note*, The process of examination was called apposing or posing. **1666** SPURSTOWE *Spir. Chym.* (1668) 174 Another dark and *posing thought did arise.

pose, *v.*[3] *dial.* [f. POSE *sb.*[2]] *trans.* To hoard, store *up* (money, etc.).

1866 GREGOR *Dial. Banffshire* s.v., The aul' bodie hiz a houd o' siller poset up, an's eye posin' up mair.

‖**posé** ('pəʊzeɪ), *a.* and *sb.* [Fr., pa. pple. of *poser* to place, etc., POSE *v.*[1]] **A.** *adj.* **1.** *Her.* (See quots.)

1725 COATS *Dict. Her.*, *Posé*,.. a French Term, signifying a Lyon, Horse, or other Beast standing still, with all four Feet on the Ground, to denote thereby that it is not in a moving Posture. **1882** CUSSANS *Her.* 315 *Posé*, placed: as, *Posé en bande*, bendwise.

2. Composed, poised, selfpossessed.

1858 QUEEN VICTORIA *Let.* 28 Apr. in R. Fulford *Dearest Child* (1964) 98 She.. improves so much—is become so quiet and posée. **1862** CROWN PRINCESS OF PRUSSIA *Let.* 8 Apr. in R. Fulford *Dearest Mama* (1968) 50 Valerie.. could hardly believe she was so young—so 'posée', quiet and self-possessed were her manners.

3. *Ballet.* Of a position, 'held', prolonged.

1949 A. CHUJOY *Dance Encycl.* 386/1 *Posé*, in ballet a poising of the body, made by stepping, with the knee straight, on to the pointe, or half-pointe; a ballet step 'held', such as an arabesque posé, for instance.

4. Adopted as a pose; = POSED *ppl. a.*[1] c. *rare.*

1958 L. DURRELL *Balthazar* iii. 63 A world.. which could afford to cultivate emotions *posées* by taste.

B. *sb.* **1.** *Ballet.* (See quots. 1949 and 1957.)

1927 [see JETÉ]. **1930** CRASKE & BEAUMONT *Theory & Pract. Allegro in Classical Ballet* 42 (*heading*) Posé en avant... A *Jeté sur la pointe* is a slow movement employed in *adagio*, whereas a *posé* is a quick movement used in *allegro*, executed *pied à pointe* or *pied à trois quarts*. **1949** [see sense 3 above]. **1947** G. B. L. WILSON *Dict. Ballet* 220 *Posé* (*en avant*, *en arrière*), the poising of the body (forwards, sideways, or backwards) by stepping with a straight leg on to the full or half point. *c* **1973** J. CHOLERTON *Acrobatic Enchainements* (Assoc. Amer. Dancing) (ed. 7) 18 Present your Posé devant as near as possible to a Star. Do not confuse it with Posé en avant.

2. = POSE *sb.*[5] 4.

1931 G. L. NUTE *Voyageur* 46 The length of a portage was computed by voyageurs in a characteristic way. The canoe and goods were carried about a third of a mile and put down, or *posé*, two or more trips often being required to transport all the load to this point. Then, without resting, the men shouldered their burdens and went on to the next *posé*. And so on till all the *posés* had been passed. **1961** *Canad. Geogr. Jrnl.* July 5/2 He puts down his load at a set place known as a 'posé'. **1968** *Beaver* Autumn 9/2 We.. made the traditional posés or rests after each half mile.

posed, *ppl. a.*: see POSE *v.*[1] and [2].

posedness, posement: see POSE *v.*[1], [2].

†**poselet,** *pa. pple. Obs.* ? Early form of *puzzled*.

a **1380** *Minor Poems fr. Vernon MS.* 151 Among þe pres þauh he were poselet, He spared no þing for no drede Among þe cristene til he were hoselet; Of such a child me tok non hede.

‖**pose plastique** (poz plastik). Also posé plastique. [Fr., lit. 'flexible pose'.] A type of *tableau vivant*, freq. featuring near-naked women. Also *transf.*

c **1846** J. R. PLANCHÉ *Invisible Prince* (1852) v. 25 The figure.. was alive and did both sing and speak... Ah! then it must have been a pose plastique!.. A pose plastique! what's that? **1857** DICKENS & COLLINS *Lazy Tour* v, in *Househ. Words* 31 Oct. 410/1 Poses Plastiques in the Grand Assembly Room.. at seven and nine each evening. **1859** G. A. SALA *Twice round Clock* 77 The vast shop-fronts.. offer a series of animated *tableaux* of *poses plastiques* in the shape of young ladies in morning costume, and young gentlemen.. who are.. 'dressing' the shop window. **1862** H. MAYHEW *London Labour* Extra vol. p. xxxi, The demoralizing influence of low theatres, and the licentious corruptions of the Coal Hole and Posés Plastiques, might surely afford scope for rigorous prosecutions under the Society's auspices. **1893** *N. & Q.* 7 Jan. 5/1 In 1846 Nicholson was again back at the Garrick's Head, where he added to his usual attractions *poses plastiques* and *tableaux vivants*. **1903** *Rep. R. Comm. Alien Immigration* II. 307/2 in *Parl. Papers* (Cd. 1742) IX. 1 There were *poses plastiques*—there were girls half naked. **1963** P. FRYER *Mrs. Grundy* xxvi. 242 The men of the Victorian age were enthusiastic gazers at *poses plastiques* and *tableaux vivants* (the precise distinction between these is far from clear). **1969** V. G. KIERNAN *Lords of Human Kind* iv. 136 There was a vogue of *poses plastiques*, and tableaux such as 'The Sultan's favourite returning from the bath' were popular. **1974** H. R. F. KEATING *Underside* ii. 17 The poses plastiques inside, sir, you're very welcome to step in.

poser[1] ('pəʊzə(r)). Also 8 pozer. [Aphetic form of APPOSER: see POSE *v.*[2]]

1. One who sets testing questions; an examiner; = APPOSER 1. Now *rare.*

1587 HARRISON *England* II. i. (1877) I. 35 When I consider.. the profit that ariseth at sundrie elections of scholars.. to the posers. *a* **1661** FULLER *Worthies, Norfolk* (1662) II. 258 The University.. appointed Doctor Cranmer.. to be the Poser-general of all Candidates in Divinity. **1664** PEPYS *Diary* 4 Feb., To Paul's School,.. and up to hear the upper form examined;.. Dr. Wilkins and one Mr. Smallwood, Posers. **1665** J. BUCK in Peacock *Stat. Univ. Cambr.* (1841) App. B. p. lxv, The Posers Feast was anciently kept upon the Thursday at Night the Examination or Posing was ended. **1702** C. MATHER *Magn. Chr.* III. I. i. (1852) 254 The Poser trying his Hebrew skill by the third chapter of Isaiah. **1901** RASHDALL & RAIT *New Coll.* iii. 44 The term 'Posers' is still applied to the two Fellows [of New College] who examine at Winchester.

2. A question that poses or puzzles; a puzzle.

1793 SHERIDAN in *Sheridaniana* 147 This was a pozer. **1837** DICKENS *Pickw.* x, With the air of a man who was in the habit of propounding some regular posers. **1894** *Law Times* XCVII. 387/2 Interrupting the arguments by questions in the nature of posers.

'**poser**[2]. [f. POSE *v.*[1] + -ER[1]: cf. F. *poseur.*] One who poses or attitudinizes: see POSE *v.*[1] 4.

1888 *Pall Mall G.* 24 Dec., Besides the professional posers of the studio there are.. the posers of the Row, the posers at afternoon teas, the posers in politics, and the circus posers.

‖**poseur** (pəʊzɜː(r)). [F., agent-n. f. *poser* POSE *v.*[1]: cf. prec.] One who practises an affected mental or social attitude; an affected person. The fem. ‖**po'seuse** is also occasionally used.

1872 B. JERROLD *London* xx. 174 'As one cannot go to bed in the middle of the afternoon—11.30 p.m.—it is necessary to go somewhere after the opera,' is the declaration of a well-known *poseur*. **1881** *Contemp. Rev.* May 683 The same womanish and uncontrolled *poseur*. **1887** *Athenæum* 1 Jan. 34/1 The latest attitudes in literature, art, and politics are presented in a way to make *poseurs* of all sort either laugh or wince. **1888** MRS. H. WARD *R. Elsmere* III. xliii. 260 *Poseuse*, schemer, woman of the world that she was. **1893** *Daily News* 29 Apr. 5/1 Madame de Krudener may best be regarded as the supreme 'poseuse' of history. **1930** G. B. SHAW *Apple Cart* 57 If you let yourself be beaten by that trickster and poseur, never dare to approach me again. **1977** *Times* 18 Feb. 11/3 Eleanor Bron's disastrous Elena converts that passive enchantress into an assertive Bloomsbury *poseuse*. **1977** *Time* 8 Aug. 46/3 But his life as self-styled genius and unrepentant poseur continues to tantalize.

posey, variant of POSY.

posh (pɒʃ), *sb.*[1] [dial. *posh, pash*: cf. PASH *sb.*[2] 4.]

1. *dial.* The fragments produced by a smash; a soft, decayed, rotten, or pulpy mass; a state of slush: see *Eng. Dial. Dict.*

[**1790**: see PASH *sb.*[2] 4.]

2. In full *posh-ice*: Ice broken into small fragments; brash-ice, porridge-ice.

1876 DAVIS *Polaris Exp.* iii. 75 The vessel was forced through brash or posh ice. **1885** WHYTE MELVILLE *In Lena Delta* ii, Forcing our way through a stream of posh.

†**posh** (pɒʃ), *sb.*[2] *Obs.* [App. thieves' slang (cf. Romany *posh* half).] **1.** *slang.* Money; *spec.* a halfpenny; a coin of small value.

Eng. Dial. Dict. s.v. *posh* sb.[4] provides evidence of *dial.* currency.

1830 *Sessions Papers Old Bailey, 1824–33* VI. 590/1 He had not got the *posh* (which means money) yet. **1839** H. BRANDON *Poverty, Mendicity & Crime* 164/2 *Posh*—a stiver, lowest price of money. *Ibid.* 168 The paper makers get the tats and never tip the motts a posh. [*Translation*] Thieves who pretend to belong to paper mills get the rags and never pay the women a farthing. **1846** *Swell's Night Guide* 68 As I used to doss there sometimes, her nibs got sweet on me, and in course we did our reg'lars and the dossing mongary, lush and posh. **1859** HOTTEN *Dict. Slang* 76 *Posh*, a half-penny, or trifling coin. **1886** W. NEWTON *Secrets Tramp Life Revealed* 8 Posh.. money of all kind. **1888** in Farmer & Henley *Slang* (1902) V. 261/1 They used such funny terms: 'brads', and 'dibbs', and 'mopusses', and 'posh'.. at last it was borne in upon me that they were talking about money. **1892** M. WILLIAMS *Round London* 67 That sort of patter.. is the thing to get the posh. **1905** *Daily Chron.* 2 Mar. 4/5 'But if I'd a brigh-full o' posh,' she said, 'I wouldn't parker no wedge to you.'

2. *slang.* A dandy.

Perh. a different word.

[**1867** E. FITZGERALD *Let.* 5 Jan. in T. Wright *Life E. FitzGerald* (1904) II. 81, I believe I have smoked my pipe every evening but one with Posh [*sc.* the nickname of FitzGerald's fisherman, Joseph Fletcher] at his house.] **1890** BARRÈRE & LELAND *Dict. Slang* II. 146/2 *Posh*,.. a dandy. [**1892** G. & W. GROSSMITH *Diary of Nobody* 197 Frank.. said.. he had a friend waiting outside for him, named Murray Posh, adding he was quite a swell.] **1902** in FARMER & HENLEY *Slang* V. 261/1.

posh (pɒʃ), *sb.*[3] [Etym. unknown.] Balderdash, rubbish, bosh.

1924 GALSWORTHY *White Monkey* II. xii. 214 Was he a fool? Could he not let well alone? Pity was posh! And yet! **1953** A. MILLER *Crucible* (1956) I. 20 Oh, posh!.. She took fright, is all. **1957** J. KEROUAC *On Road* (1958) I. viii. 49 You're talking absolute bullshit and Wolfean romantic posh!

posh (pɒʃ), *a. slang.* [Of obscure origin, but cf. POSH *sb.*[2] The suggestion that this word is derived from the initials of 'port outward, starboard home', referring to the more expensive side for accommodation on ships formerly travelling between England and India, is often put forward but lacks foundation. The main objections to this derivation are listed by G. Chowdharay-Best in *Mariner's Mirror* (1971) Jan. 91–2.] Smart, 'swell', 'classy'; fine, splendid, stylish; first-rate. Also *absol.* as *sb.*

The pronunciation (pəʊʃ), a supposedly 'posh' or facetious way of saying the word, is occasionally heard. Quot. 1903 may exemplify a different word.

[**1903** WODEHOUSE *Tales of St. Austin's* 37 That waistcoat.. being quite the most push thing of the sort in Cambridge.] **1918** *Punch* 25 Sept. 204 Oh, yes, Mater, we had a posh time of it down there. **1923** WODEHOUSE *Inimitable Jeeves* vii. 72 Practically every posh family in the country has called him in at one time or another. **1925** W. DEEPING *Sorrell & Son* ii. 22 Tips. Don't forget the tips. If a man's obliging—... It's a posh job. **1927** —— *Doomsday* xiv. 153 'You like it.' 'It's the poshest thing I've ever seen, old chap.' **1927** —— *Kitty* xxix. 372, I say—that's a posh show. **1927** *Daily Tel.* 24 May 9 It was a club in Ham-yard—not a very posh club. **1929** J. B. PRIESTLEY *Good Companions* II. v. 391 I'd like to have.. a very cosy car, small but frightfully posh. **1930** AUDEN *Poems* 63 To be posh, we gather, One should have no father. **1935** C. DAY LEWIS *Time to Dance* 32 For no silver posh Plane was their pigeon.. But a craft of obsolete design. **1941** BAKER *Dict. Austral. Slang* 56 *Posh, do the*, to spend lavishly, do something 'in style'. **1954** [see GROUND *sb.* 11 b]. **1957** J. OSBORNE *Look back in Anger* I. 13 *Jimmy*: Haven't you read the other posh paper yet? *Cliff*: Which? *Jimmy*: Well, there are only two posh papers on a Sunday. **1958** K. AMIS *I like it Here* viii. 98 This railway.. though posher and faster, had often reminded him of the tram-like train. **1959** *20th Cent.* Nov. 377 At the time.. none of the posh papers carried television reviews. **1970** [see CHEZ]. **1977** *Lancashire Life* Nov. 153/1 The poshest Granada Ghias.. have electric windows. **1979** E. CAVE *Blood Bond* I. iii. 35 Charles's penchant for the grand—the 'posh' as Tom would have called it.

posh (pɒʃ), *v.* [f. the adj.] *trans.* To smarten *up*. Freq. *refl.* and *pass.* Hence '**poshed-up** *a.*

1919 *War Slang* in *Athenæum* 22 Aug. 791/2 To 'posh up' was to make oneself look as smart as possible. **1932** D. L. SAYERS *Have his Carcase* xv. 197, I don't get time to posh myself up of a morning. **1955** *Times* 29 June 12/5 Beautifully 'poshed-up' for this she is, though certainly she has never been allowed to look shabby overlong. **1959** *Oxf. Mail* 1 June 3/6, I knew most of that stuff has been stolen; I wanted to posh up my old car. **1967** R. MACKAY *House & Day* 30 He was poshed up. That meant.. a trip to the town. **1967** P. PURSER *Twentymen* xvi. 104 We.. had dined at a rotten, poshed-up Thames pub. **1968** T. PARKER *People of Streets* 35 He'd.. turn up at a big state ball all poshed up. **1975** J. MCCLURE *Snake* iii. 45 Who goes to the trouble to posh himself up for the postman?

posh (pɒʃ), *adv.* [f. the adj.] In a 'posh' manner.

1957 *Listener* 7 Nov. 739/1 A device to enable you to 'write posh', as it were. You look up the 'vulgar' words, and against them you find the more elegant. **1961** P. STREVENS *Papers in Lang.* (1965) xi. 130 The recent popularity of *My Fair Lady* led to another legend, that of phonetics as a system of teaching people to 'speak posh'. **1972** 'M. INNES' *Open House* ii. 20 A crowd of electricians might well take him for a cunning crook talking posh. **1979** R. BARNARD *Posthumous Papers* iii. 33 Why do you sometimes talk Lancashire and sometimes talk posh?.. Not everyone can do the posh as well as you.

‖**po shan lu** (bo ʃan luː). Also **bo shan lu.** [Chinese.] A type of Chinese bronze censer, made during the Han dynasty and having the form of a mythical mountain of immortality.

1915 R. L. HOBSTON *Chinese Pott. & Porc.* I. ii. 12 Fig. 3 is an incense burner.... It is a variation of the more usual 'hill censer' (*po shan lu*). **1954** S. H. HANSFORD *Gloss. Chinese Art & Archæol.* 13 *Po shan lu*, hill censer; censer shaped as a stem cup with cover in the form of a mountain peak. **1973** *Genius of China* 104/2 Bronze censer in the shape of a cosmic mountain *po-shan-lu*, held up by a man seated on a monster. **1978** *Nagel's Encycl.-Guide: China* 216 The *bo shan lu* or incense-burner with a conical lid suggesting the rocks on the island where the Taosit Immortals lived.

poshet, -(o)ote, -otte, obs. ff. POSSET.

'**poshness.** *slang.* [f. POSH *a.* + -NESS.] The state or quality of being 'posh'.

1931 C. LITHGOW *Simple Sailor* xvii. 218 In his pet dark blue morning coat, with a gardenia in its buttonhole.., he was rather a splendid figure. No doubt whatever was there of 'his poshness'. **1960** C. S. LEWIS *Studies in Words* vii. 179 'A general simplicity in our dress, our discourse, and our behaviour.' Sincerity (not affectation)? Plainness (not 'poshness')? The easy (not the hard)? **1965** M. MORSE *Unattached* iv. 123 The real focus of dislike was the teachers' 'poshness', which the girls felt was often assumed in order to demonstrate that a social gap existed between teacher and pupil. **1978** R. HILL *Pinch of Snuff* xiii. 132 An extra element of 'poshness' was inherent in the 'Private Road' sign.

‖**posho** ('pɒʃəʊ). *East Africa.* [Swahili, = daily rations.] **a.** Daily rations given to porters on safari. **b.** A kind of maize flour; a porridge made from this. Also *attrib.*

1892 M. FRENCH-SHELDON *Sultan to Sultan* v. 118 The method of dealing out rice, which is carried for *posho* or rations.. is somewhat peculiar. *Ibid.*, Porters, carrying the heavy loads, are paid the least and receive the smallest *posho*. **1927** *Chambers's Jrnl.* XVII. 761/1 The safari boys were squatting round the cooking-pots, stirring their 'posho'. **1946** G. HANLEY *Monsoon Victory* x. 106 In Africa they [*sc.* askaris] ate *posho*, which is maize flour cooked into a porridge. **1964** C. WILLOCK *Enormous Zoo* ix. 157 He searched two fully occupied huts in the labour lines looking for *posho*. **1971** *E. Afr. Standard* (Nairobi) 13 Apr. 9/3 An Assistant Minister for Agriculture.. was officially opening a posho mill. **1974** *Observer* (Colour Suppl.) 28 Apr. 45/3 Posho (ground corn on the cob)... It is cooked with water to make a kind of porridge. **1975** *Times* 17 Nov. 13/7 The [Ugandan] guards were already sharing their beans and posho and lumps of lean meat with me. **1977** H. INNES *Big Footprints* II. i. 122 Sacks of maize flour they called posho.

poshteen: see POSTEEN.

posie, obs. f. POSY.

posied ('pəʊzɪd), *a.* [f. POSY + -ED[2].]

1. Inscribed with a posy or motto. *arch.*

1597 SHAKS. *Lover's Compl.* 45 Many a ring of Posied gold and bone. **1720** GAY *To Yng. Lady* 12 Some by a snip of woven hair In posied lockets bribe the fair. **1802** *Sporting Mag.* 359 The motto'd garter and the posied ring.

2. Furnished with nosegays; flowery. Now *dial.*

1797 T. PARK *Sonn.* 96 And what one corner would of flowerets yield, In posied wreaths his blooming daughter bore. **1865** E. WAUGH *Lanc. Songs* 50 It winds by a rindlin' wayter side, An' o'er a posied lea. **1894** H. SPEIGHT *Nidderdale* 393 Pleasant country houses with posied gardens are everywhere around.

posigrade ('pɒzɪgreɪd), *a. Astronautics.* [f. POSI(TIVE *a.* and *sb.* + *-grade*, after RETROGRADE *a.* and *sb.*] Of, pertaining to, or designating a small rocket that can be fired briefly to give forward thrust to a spacecraft.

1961 *Aeroplane* C. 152/1 Next, the three small 'posigrade' rockets on the blunt face of the capsule are fired to achieve separation from the booster. **1962** S. CARPENTER in *Into Orbit* 53 This sends out an electrical impulse which explodes the bolts and fires the posigrade rockets that shove the capsule and booster apart. **1965** *Time* 24 Dec. 35 To change his elliptical orbit into a circle that reached closer to Gemini 7, he made several 'posigrade' burns. **1965** *World Bk. Year Bk.* 48/2 It was also necessary to take into account.. another figure for the thrust of the small, posigrade rockets that give the spacecraft a gentle separation push away from the booster.

posil, obs. form of PUCELLE, maid, girl.

posing, posingly: see POSE *v.*[1] and [2].

posish (pəˈzɪʃ). orig. *U.S.* Also **pozish.** Colloq. abbrev. POSITION *sb.*

1862 O. W. NORTON *Army Lett.* (1903) 113 Snorting their impatience to 'get into posish', came the Monitor, the Galena and others. **1865** J. PIKE *Scout & Ranger* I. 25 Some of the managers and their wives, feeling the importance of their 'posish', put on considerable 'style'. **1914** *Dialect Notes* IV. 130 What did I tell ya about standing—Oh what a pozish! **1923** WODEHOUSE *Inimitable Jeeves* xviii. 251, I wanted to find out the general posish of affairs. **1936** —— *Laughing Gas* xiii. 139 Well, you've gone and landed yourself in a nice posish. A dashed nice posish, I don't think. **1960** J. GRANT *Come again, Nurse* x. 55 What's the coffee posish?

posit ('pɒzɪt), *v.* Also 7 -ite. [f. L. *posit-*, ppl. stem of *pōnĕre* to place, put, lay down.]

1. *trans.* To put in position; to set, dispose, or situate; to place. (Chiefly in *pa. pple.* or *passive.*)

1647 LILLY *Chr. Astrol.* To Rdr. 3 To vary their shape as they are posited in Signe and house. **1664** POWER *Exp. Philos.* III. 168 Then would those parts.. affect this.. Situation, howsoever the Loadstone was posited. *a* **1693** *Urquhart's Rabelais* III. xx. 166 He posited his left Hand wholly open. **1756** AMORY *Buncle* (1770) I. 87 To see how things were posited at home. **1871** TYNDALL *Fragm. Sci.* vi. (1872) 114 The blocks.. were moved and posited by a power external to themselves. **1886** W. GRAHAM *Soc. Problem* 161 Classes.. connected with the production of wealth or positing it where it is wanted.

2. To put down or assume as a fact; to lay down as a basis of argument, etc.; to affirm the existence of; to postulate. Chiefly in *Logic* and *Philos.*

1697 tr. *Burgersdicius his Logic* II. xii. 52 To Posit, or put the Antecedent or Consequent, is no more than to assume it. *Ibid.* xvii. 78 The Effect being posited, it follows that either there is a Cause Efficient, or else, that there has been one. **1709–29** [see POSITED]. **1847** LEWES *Hist. Philos.* IV. 167 Either the Ego must posit the Non-Ego wilfully and consciously.. or [etc.]. **1877** E. CAIRD *Philos. Kant* I. 157 In so far as anything is a cause, it posits something different from itself as an effect. **1898** J. A. HOBSON *Ruskin* 105 The crude dualism which Huxley posits.

Hence **'posited** *ppl. a.*; **'positing** *vbl. sb.* and *ppl. a.*

1665–6 *Phil. Trans.* I. 215 An account of two unusually posited Rainbows seen. **1709–29** V. MANDEY *Syst. Math., Arith.* 60 If one of the posited False Numbers is deficient from the Tree. **1854** GEO. ELIOT tr. *Feuerbach's Essence Christianity* xxii. 213 This negativing of limits by the imagination is the positing of omniscience as a divine power and reality. **1895** *Daily Chron.* 6 Nov. 2/7 His hatred of compromise, his perpetual positing of the moral dilemma—'all or nothing'. **1899** A. E. GARVIE *Ritschlian Theol.* III. iii. 82 A law, a thing posited, points back the understanding to the positing spirit and will. **1967** *Listener* 5 Oct. 430/1 If subject does not respond to direct approach try seemingly more casual positings of kindred questions at the macro-level.

posit ('pɒzɪt), *sb. Philos.* [f. the vb.] A statement which is made on the assumption that it will prove valid (see quots. 1949).

1949 HUTTEN & REICHENBACH tr. *H. Reichenbach's Theory of Probability* ix. 373 A posit is a statement with which we deal as true, although the truth value is unknown. *Ibid.*, We do not say *B* will occur, but we posit *B*... The word 'posit' is used here in the same sense as the word 'wager' or 'bet'... We do not want to say.. that it is true that the horse will win, but we behave as though it were true by staking money on it. **1953** W. V. QUINE *From Logical Point of View* ii. 45 Physical objects, small and large, are not the only posits... The abstract entities which are the substance of mathematics are another posit in the same spirit. **1976** *Sci. Amer.* Mar. 119/3 He proposed a set of five posits about the structure of the world that he believed were sufficient to justify induction.

position (pəʊ'zɪʃən, pə-), *sb.* Also 6 **posycyon, -cion, -tyon, posicion.** [a. F. *position*, ad. L. *positiōnem* a putting, placing, position; affirmation; theme, subject, etc., n. of action from *pōnĕre* (*posit-um*) to put, place, set.]

I. 1. The action of positing; the laying down or statement of a proposition or thesis; affirmation, affirmative assertion. Chiefly in *Logic* and *Philos.*

c **1374** CHAUCER *Boeth.* v. pr. iv. 125 (Camb. MS.) Ffor by grace of possession [L. *positionis gratia, ed.* **1532** posycion].. I pose þat ther be no prescience. **1604** SHAKS. *Oth.* III. iii. 234, I do not in position Distinctly speake of her. **1697** tr. *Burgersdicius his Logic* II. xii. 54 The Disjunctive Syllogism, .. if consisting of two Members immediately opposed, may proceed from a Position of one Member to an Eversion of the other. **1832** AUSTIN *Jurispr.* (1879) I. v. 175 It exists by the position or institution of its individual or collective author. **1837–8** SIR W. HAMILTON *Logic* xvii. (1866) I. 332 A disjunctive syllogism consists.. in the reciprocal position or sublation of contradictory characters, by the subsumption of one or other. **1877** E. CAIRD *Philos. Kant* II. xvi. 573 The alternate position and negation leads to an infinite series.

2. A proposition or thesis laid down or stated; something posited; a statement, assertion, tenet.

c **1500** in Peacock *Stat. Cambr.* App. A. p. xxii, The Father hath made on Argument agenst his Posytyon in the fyrst mater. **1597** BACON *Ess.* x. (Arb.) 152 It is a position in the Mathematiques that there is no proportion betweene somewhat and nothing. **1684** *Contempl. State Man* II. iii. (1699) 147 It was a Position of the Stoicks, that he was not Poor who wanted, but he who was necessitated. **1761** HUME *Hist. Eng.* I. xv. 374 An edict, which contains many extraordinary positions and pretensions. **1838–9** HALLAM *Hist. Lit.* II. II. iv. §4. 122 Hooker.. rests his positions on one solid basis, the eternal obligation of natural law. **1845** J. H. NEWMAN *Ess. Developm.* II. ii. 129, I have called the doctrine of Infallibility an hypothesis:.. let it be considered to be a mere position, supported by no direct evidence, but required by the facts of the case.

3. *Arith.* A method of finding the value of an unknown quantity by positing or assuming one or more values for it, finding by how much the results differ from the actual data of the problem, and then adjusting the error. Also called ***rule of (false) position, rule of supposition, rule of falsehood, rule of trial and error.***

1551 RECORDE *Pathw. Knowl.* II. Pref., The rule of false position, with dyuers examples not onely vulgar, but some appertaynyng to the rule of Algeber. **1704** J. HARRIS *Lex. Techn.* I, *Position*, or the *Rule of Position*, otherwise called the *Rule of Falshood*... This *Rule of False Position* is of Two kinds, viz. *Single* and *Double*. **1806** HUTTON *Course Math.* I. 135 Position is a method of performing certain questions, which cannot be resolved by the common direct rules. *Ibid.* 136 Double Position is the method of resolving certain questions by means of two suppositions of false numbers.

†4. The action of positing or placing, esp. in a particular order or arrangement; disposition. *Obs.*

1623 COCKERAM, *Position*,.. a setting or placing. **1658** PHILLIPS, *Position* (lat.), a putting. **1664** POWER *Exp. Philos.* III. 158 You may change the Polarity of many feeble Stones, by a long Position in a contrary posture. *a* **1677** HALE *Prim. Orig. Man.* III. vii. 288 In my Watch, the Law and Rule of its Motion is the Constitution and Position of its Parts by the Hand and Mind of the skilful Artist. **1735** BERTIN *Chess* iii, The Game of Chess consists of two parts, the Offensive, and Defensive;.. the Defensive [consists] in the due position of your own [forces], by guarding against your enemy's attack.

5. a. The manner in which a body as a whole, or the several parts of it, are disposed or arranged; disposition, posture, attitude. *spec.* (*a*) the disposition of the limbs in a dance step (see also *first position* (b) s.v. FIRST C, *fourth position* s.v. FOURTH C); (*b*) the posture adopted during sexual intercourse.

eastward position: the position of the officiating priest at the Eucharist, when he stands in front of the holy table or altar and faces the east.

1703 MOXON *Mech. Exerc.* 176 They should lift their Treading Leg so high, as to tire it.. after it is raised to so uncommodious a position. **1790** PHILIDOR *Chess* II. 90 In this position it is a drawn game. **1839** R. S. ROBINSON *Naut. Steam Eng.* 79 The position of the beam at half-stroke, horizontal. **1847** C. BRONTË *Jane Eyre* xiv, I cannot see you without disturbing my position in this comfortable chair. **1866** H. R. DROOP *North Side of the Table* 9 Canon law (which did not enforce an eastward position). **1874** (*title*) Reasons for opposing the (so-called) Eastward Position of the Celebrant. **1888** *Pall Mall G.* 28 Nov. 7/2 Dean Burgon never would allow the 'eastward position' to be adopted in Chichester Cathedral. **1891** FREEBOROUGH *Chess Endings* 12 There is always the general principle—the grasp of the position. **1893** BP. STUBBS *Visit. Charges, Oxford* (1907) 159, I have, ever since my ordination in 1848, used the eastward position in the Ante-Communion, and since I was ordained priest in 1850, at the consecration prayer.

(*a*) **1778** *English Mag.* Feb. 59/2 A woman who was ignorant that her first curtsey should be in the third position. **1819** M. EDGEWORTH *Let.* 17 Apr. (1971) 199 She seems evermore as if she had the fear of the five positions before her eyes. **1884** D. ANDERSON *Compl. Ball-Room Guide* 10 *Second position*, put out right foot in a straight line with left heel, right heel about four inches from left heel. **1922** [see À TERRE *adv.* and *adj. phr.*]. **1930** CRASKE & BEAUMONT *Theory & Pract. Allegro in Classical Ballet* 15 Lower the arms to the *fifth* position *en bas*. **1971** 'D. HALLIDAY' *Dolly & Doctor Bird* xi. 143 Krishtof Bey rose to his feet.. and struck the fifth position, brown arms outflung. **1979** A. MORICE *Murder in Outline* iii. 26 Carefully placing his feet, right heel to left instep, in the number two position.

(*b*) **1883** tr. *Kama Sutra of Vatsyayana* II. vi. 65 When the woman forcibly holds in her yoni the lingam after it is in, it is called the 'mare's position'. This is learnt by practice only. **1933** E. A. ROBERTSON *Ordinary Families* vi. 112, I show de shentleman de twenty-seex poseetions of lof? **1969, 1971** [see MISSIONARY *a.* 1 b]. **1974** W. GARNER *Big enough Wreath* v. 60 My pa.. always warned me about the Chinese position. **1976** *Sounds* 11 Dec. 4/1 Mickey Gallagher was being particularly adventurous one bedtime with his lady friend, and collapsed from Position Number 368 (look it up yerselves, you cheeky...) onto the floor and broke his wrist. **1977** *Times* 26 Mar. 12/5 There was actually—this was, maybe, 1938—a chapter on positions. Wow!

b. *fig.* Mental attitude; the way in which one looks upon or views a subject or question: often passing into the point of view which one occupies in reference to a subject, and so blending with 9.

1905 J. ORR *Problem O. Test.* xii. 435 A more moderate position is taken by Dr. Driver.

6. *Mus.* The arrangement of the constituent notes of a chord, with respect to their order, or to the intervals between them. (†See also quot. 1753.)

1753 CHAMBERS *Cycl. Supp.*, *Position*.. in music, is used for the putting down the hand in beating time. **1880** W. S. ROCKSTRO in Grove *Dict. Mus.* II. 17 In whatever position they may be taken, Consonant Intervals remain always consonant; Dissonant Intervals, dissonant.

II. 7. a. The place occupied by a thing, or in which it is put; situation, site, station. ***in position***, in its (his, etc.) proper or appropriate place; so ***out of position***.

1541 R. COPLAND *Galyen's Terap.* 2 H ij, Yf ye knowe parfytely the posycyon, & fygure of all the bladder. **1570** BILLINGSLEY *Euclid* I. i. 1 A poynt is materiall, and requireth position and place. **1690** LOCKE *Hum. Und.* II. xiii. §10. 77 That our Idea of Place is nothing else, but such a relative Position of any thing, as I have before mentioned. **1696** PHILLIPS (ed. 5) s.v., The Respect of a Planet in Astrological Figure, to other Planets and Parts of the Figure, is called his Position. **1727–41** CHAMBERS *Cycl.* s.v., A line is said to be *given in position*.. when its situation, bearing, or direction, with regard to some other line, is given. **1774** M. MACKENZIE *Maritime Surv.* 25 Having the Distance and Position of two Points *A* and *B*. **1840** LARDNER *Geom.* 20 The apparent position of an object is a term used in science to express the position of the object so far as it can be determined by the sight. **1850** MᶜCOSH *Div. Govt.* III. ii. (1874) 351 The view which we get of an object depends on the position which we take. **1874** In position [see POSITION *v.* 1]. **1876** TAIT *Rec. Adv. Phys. Sc.* i. (ed. 2) 14 Position is a purely space relation or geometrical conception.

b. Phrases.

angle of position: (*a*) The angle between any two points subtended at the eye; (*b*) *Astron.* The angle between the circles of declination and latitude of a celestial body; (*c*) The angle between the hour circle passing through a celestial body, and the line joining it and a neighbouring celestial body; so in *Geog.*, the angle between the meridian of a place and the great circle passing through it and some other place. ***circle of position***: any one of six great circles of the celestial sphere passing through the north and south points of the horizon. ***gun of position***: a heavy field-gun, not designed for executing quick movements. ***line of position*** or ***position line***: a line on which the observer is computed to be after having taken a bearing.

1571 DIGGES *Pantom.* I. xxviii. H iv, Notyng vppon youre slate the angle of position from the dimetient to the lyne fiduciall. *Ibid.* xxxiv. K iij b, Then turne the Diameter of your Semicircle, to euery Towne, Village, Hauen, Rode, or suche like,.. noting therewithall in some Table by it selfe the Degrees cut by the Alhidada in the Circle, which I call the Angles of Position. **1669** STURMY *Mariner's Mag.* VII. xix. 31 Circles of Position.. do all cross one another in the North and South Points of the Meridian. **1727–41** CHAMBERS *Cycl.* s.v., Circles of position, are six great circles passing through the intersection of the meridian and the horizon, and dividing the equator into twelve equal parts. **1812** WOODHOUSE *Astron.* viii. 58 Angle of Position. **1858** GREENER *Gunnery* 126 This result once secured, it is obvious that a field-piece or gun of position would become a rifle on a large scale. **1863** W. CHAUVENET *Man. Spherical & Pract. Astron.* I. viii. 428 Let the first observation give the position line *AA'* (Fig. 35), and let *Aa* represent, in direction and length, the ship's course and distance sailed between the observations. **1865** J. H. C. COFFIN *Navigation & Nautical Astron.* (ed. 2) ix. 224 The nearer the body is to the prime vertical, the more nearly the line of position coincides with a meridian. **1900** *Daily News* 10 Jan. 8/3 The 12-pounder quick-firing garrison artillery gun of 12 cwt.,.. is neither a field gun nor a gun of position. **1919** G. C. COMSTOCK *Summer Line* p. iii, The line of position, or Summer line, is generally recognized as the best method for fixing the ship's place by observation of the sun or stars. **1920** J. E. DUMBLETON *Princ. & Pract. Aerial Navigation* i. 13 Owing to small errors three position lines will rarely intersect at a point, but a small triangle is formed known as a 'cocked hat'. **1962** *Flight Handbk.* (ed. 6) xiii. 292 One bearing gives a position-line; two or more are needed for a fix. **1974** K. WILKES *Pract. Yacht Navigator* ix. 115/1 A position line from observation of a single identifiable object can be established by taking a compass bearing of it.

c. *Mil.* A site chosen for occupation by an army, usually as having a strategic value.

1781 GIBBON *Decl. & F.* xviii. II. 118 To compel his adversary to relinquish this advantageous position. **1820** SCOTT *Monast.* ii, A position of considerable strength. *a* **1839** PRAED *Poems* (1864) II. 11 On, on! take forts and storm positions. **1890** NICOLAY & HAY *Lincoln* VIII. ix. 241 General Meade.. manœuvred to select a position where he would have the advantage.

8. *Phonology.* The situation of a vowel in an open or closed syllable; *spec.* in *Gr.* and *L. Prosody*, the situation of a short vowel before two consonants or their equivalent, i.e. before a consonant in the same syllable, making the syllable metrically long, as in *in-fer-ret-que*, *con-vex-ī* = *con-vec-sī*.

In such cases it used to be said that the *vowel* was 'long by position'; but the evidence of Greek and the history of the sounds in Romanic show that the vowel remained short, while the *syllable* was metrically long. When both consonants could be taken to the following syllable, the preceding vowel might be 'in position' or not, as in *te-ne-brās* or *te-neb-rās*. In English and the modern languages generally, a long stressed vowel is often shortened by position, as in *weal, wealth*; *deem, dem-ster*; *house, husband, Lyne, Lynton*.

1580 G. HARVEY *Let. to Spenser* Wks. (Grosart) I. 106 Position neither maketh shorte, nor long in oure Tongue, but so farre as we can get hir good leaue. **1582** STANYHURST *Æneis* (Arb.) 12 And soothly.. yf the coniunction *And* were made common in English, yt were not amisse, although yt bee long by position. **1775** ASH, *Position* (in grammar) the state of a vowel placed before two consonants. **1876** KENNEDY *Public School Lat. Gram.* 512 In the words *fātō, mæstīs* both syllables are long by nature: in *fāctūs sūbsūnt* the four syllables, whose vowels are short by nature, are all lengthened by position. *H* does not give position any more than the aspirate in Greek.

9. *fig.* **a.** The situation which one metaphorically occupies in relation to others, to facts, or to circumstances; condition.

1827 DISRAELI *Viv. Grey* v. xii, Do not believe that I am one who would presume an instant on my position. **1843** PRESCOTT *Mexico* I. vi. (1864) 65 There is no position which affords such scope for ameliorating the condition of man, as that occupied by an absolute ruler over a nation imperfectly civilised. **1855** MACAULAY *Hist. Eng.* xi. III. 49 In a few weeks he had changed the relative position of all the states in Europe. **1860** TYNDALL *Glac.* I. ix. 64 The position was in some measure an exciting one. **1871** B. STEWART *Heat* §67 We are now in a position to discuss the air thermometer. **1878** BOSW. SMITH *Carthage* 392 Arms were extemporised for an adequate number of citizens, and the city was somehow put into a position to stand a siege.

b. Place in the social scale; social state or standing; status; rank, estate. *spec.* in ***social position***.

c **1832** J. S. MILL in F. A. von Hayek *J. S. Mill & Harriet Taylor* (1951) iii. 61 For a long time the indissolubility of marriage acted powerfully to elevate the social position of women. **1853** C. BRONTË *Villette* II. xxviii. 293 Pedigree, social position, and recondite intellectual acquisition, occupied about the same space and place in my interests and thoughts. **1865** TROLLOPE *Belton Est.* xi, His position in society was excellent and secure. **1868** *Digby's Voy. Medit.* Pref. 34 A man of considerable position. **1896** *Harper's Mag.* Apr. 701/2 I've got a good position now, one that I'm not ashamed to ask you to share. **1949** M. MEAD in M. Fortes *Social Struct.* 18, I found it impossible to give an adequate sociological statement which did not include the specification of each actor in terms both of his social position and of his personality. **1971** P. J. KEATING *Working Classes in Victorian Fiction* iii. 73 The physical and spiritual struggles inherent in their social position. **1976** G. BUTLER *Vesey Inheritance* vi. 176, I am a young woman of education and social position.

c. An official situation, place, or employment.

1890 *Cent. Dict.* s.v., A position in a bank. **1900** KIPLING in *Daily Express* 19 June 4/5 With a view to getting him a 'position in the city'. **1906** *Westm. Gaz.* 9 May 2/3 The old discussion as to the evolution and history of this special political position—for up to now it has been that rather than an office.

III. 10. *attrib.* and *Comb.*, as ***position-relation, -value***; **position angle** = *angle of position* (7 b); **position-artillery**, heavy field-artillery; cf. *gun of position* in 7 b; so **position-battery**; **position**

change *Genetics*, any change in the order of the genes along a chromosome; **position effect** *Genetics*, an effect on the phenotypic expression of a gene produced by a difference in its chromosomal position, esp. by its proximity to a mutant gene or to heterochromatin; **position error**, the variation of a watch when laid in certain positions; **position-finder**, an apparatus by means of which a gunner is enabled to aim a cannon at an object not visible to him; **position-finding**, the process of ascertaining one's position or that of a distant object, esp. automatically by radio or similar means; usu. *attrib.*; **position-light**, a light carried by a ship which is in company with others to indicate its course at night; **position line** (see 7 b); **position mark**, a mark made on a stone or other component part of a structure to indicate the position it is designed to occupy; **position micrometer**: see quot.; **position paper** orig. *U.S.*, a written statement of attitude or intentions; **position play** *Chess* (see quot. 1960); **position player** (*a*) *Chess*, one who adopts position play; (*b*) *Austral. Football* (see quote. 1969); †**position poet**, ? a poet who composes short pieces containing definite statements (as in commendation of a person); **position vector** *Math.*, a vector which defines the position of a point.

1893 SIR R. BALL *Story of Sun* 170 The angle between the pole projected on the Sun's disc and the north point is what we call the *position angle. **1898** E. A. CAMPBELL (*title*) Lectures on *Position Artillery. **1937** *Nature* 30 Oct. 761/2 The primary structural change of inversion gives rise to secondary changes such as reduplication and deficiency. These are changes of 'balance', and rank with intra-genic changes and *position changes as one of the three effective means of variation. **1952** C. P. BLACKER *Eugenics* x. 245 These alterations of chromosome structure resulting from one or more breakages and recombinations have been called ..position changes. **1930** *Jrnl. Genetics* XXII. 315 Since the addition of different deletions results in much the same effects, regardless of exactly where the breakage occurred, these are not '*position effects' caused by displacement of certain genes from others previously adjacent to them. **1952** SRB & OWEN *Gen. Genetics* x. 201 In many ways, the numerous position effects described in the literature of genetics appear as a bewildering array of vaguely related phenomena. **1974** *Genetic Res.* XXIII. 291 Position effect variegation is now regarded as a general phenomenon but it is in *Drosophila* that by far the largest number of cases have been described. **1884** F. J. BRITTEN *Watch & Clockm.* 24 Only the finer class of watches..are as a rule tested for *position errors. Position errors..are often confounded with a want of isochronism. **1888** *Daily News* 16 July 3/3 The sum of 25,000*l.* was paid to Major Watkin for an invention of a *position-finder. **1902** SLOANE *Stand. Electr. Dict.* 428 The Position Finder is a simplification and amplification of the Range Finder. **1918** E. S. FARROW *Dict. Mil. Terms* 463 **Position finding system*, the term applied to the system used in determining the range and direction to any target from a battery or station. **1947** CROWTHER & WHIDDINGTON *Sci. at War* 57 Another position-finding system in which, however, the aircraft 'interrogates' by sending out pulses. **1959** A. HARDY *Fish & Fisheries* vii. 160 The deep-water trawlers have been getting larger, more powerful and more efficiently equipped with echosounding and position-finding apparatus. **1897** *Daily News* 30 Aug. 6/7 When altering the course of his ship, the *position lights were omitted to be hoisted. **1928** G. G. COULTON *Art & Reformation* viii. 145 An inspection..will convince us that the rare marks found otherwise than on the surface are not banker-marks, but *position-marks. **1864** WEBSTER, **Position-micrometer*, a micrometer for measuring angles of position, having a single thread or wire which is carried round the common focus of the object-glass and eye-glass, and in a plane perpendicular to the axis of the telescope. **1965** *Guardian* 4 Sept. 9/5 Republican leavers..got out an eleven-page policy statement, called a '*position paper'. **1972** LD. GLADWYN *Mem.* xiii. 226 The idea was that all the political Under-Secretaries..should meet every so often and discuss what I suppose would now be called 'position papers'. **1977** *Time* 7 Mar. 13/1 Carter is just beginning to receive position papers from his advisers on what his policies should be. **1932** E. LASKER *Man. Chess* IV. 166/1 Whereas by combination values are transformed, they are proved and confirmed by '*position play'. Thus, position play is antagonistic to combination, as becomes evident when a 'combinative player' meets with his counterpart, the 'position player'. **1960** HOROWITZ & MOTT-SMITH *Point Count Chess* (1973) 356 *Position play* is a strategic move or plan as distinguished from a tactical (combination). **1969** EAGLESON & MCKIE *Terminol. Austral. Nat. Football* III. 4 **Position player*, a variant for *placed man* [*sc.* a player who is allocated a fixed position on the field], recorded by four informants. **1589** NASHE *Pref. Greene's Menaphon* (Arb.) 14 Epitaphers, and *position Poets haue wee more than a good many. **1881** BROADHOUSE *Mus. Acoustics* 383 The *position-relation of any two notes forming a given interval is always exactly the same. **1849** OTTÉ tr. *Humboldt's Cosmos* II. 597 Nine figures or characters, according to their *position-value, under the name of the system of the abacus. **1961** C. C. T. BAKER *Dict. Math.* 242 If *P* is the position of a point at any time, and *O* is a fixed point, the line *OP*, having length and direction, is a vector, and is denoted by $\vec{OP}$, or **OP**. If *P* is the point (*x*, *y*, *z*), the *position vector is $\mathbf{R} = \mathbf{i}x + \mathbf{j}y + \mathbf{k}z$. **1969** WADE & TAYLOR *Contemp. Analytic Geom.* vii. 243 When we speak of a position vector it is to be understood that the vector has only one representative and that the initial point of this representative is at the origin.

Hence **po'sitionless** *a.*, without a position.

1887 W. JAMES in *Mind* XII. 27 Positionless at first, it [a particular kind of feeling] no sooner appears in the midst of a gang of companions than it is found maintaining the strictest position of its own.

position (pəʊˈzɪʃən, pə-), *v.* [f. prec. sb.]

1. a. *trans.* To put or set in a particular or appropriate position; to place.

1817 COL. HAWKER *Diary* (1893) I. 151 Had I.. positioned the birds myself, I could not have had a more glorious opportunity. **1874** J. D. HEATH *Croquet Player* 15 *To Position.*—An abbreviation for 'to place in position',..'to place a ball in a proper position to make its next point in order'. **1893** *Columbus* (Ohio) *Dispatch* 23 Feb., A brace of submarine guns in the bows..positioned so as to discharge their projectiles at a depth of ten feet below the water line. **1955** *Sun* (Baltimore) 12 Jan. 12/4 The straw is baled, elevated, and positioned on an accompanying truck. **1955** *Sci. Amer.* May 124/1 You first position the hairline of the slider over the caret between the first four balls (1, 2, 3, 4) and the second four (5, 6, 7, 8) in the bottom tier of this rule. **1959** *Listener* 5 Mar. 432/3 *Il Tabarro* was directed..by Charles Rogers and produced (*i.e.* positioned, rehearsed dramatically, and so on) by Colin Graham. **1960** *Practical Wireless* XXXVI. 429/1 Beginners would be well advised to position the amplifier so that the underneath parts can be inspected while the power is on. **1967** *Times Rev. Industry* Feb. 90/3 Three two-jet engines positioned in much of the same way as the British Trident. **1979** J. WAINWRIGHT *Tension* 62 Uniformed constables had been positioned to re-direct traffic.

b. To determine the position of; to locate.

1881 H. W. NICHOLSON *From Sword to Share* vi. 40 The later geological observation,..positioning the earliest volcanic action, in this group, on the island of Kanai, and the latest on that of Hawaii.

†**2.** *intr.* To take up one's position; to lay down a position or principle. *Obs. rare.*

1678 O. HEYWOOD *Diaries*, etc. (1881) II. 196 Mr Thorp position'd on this thesis. **1703** J. RYTHER *Def. Glorious Gosp.* Pref., He had preached and position'd.

Hence **po'sitioned** *ppl. a.*, placed, situated; having or occupying a position (social or other); **po'sitioning** *vbl. sb.*, putting in position; in *Chess*, arrangement of the men in an advantageous position.

1867 F. W. COSENS in *Athenæum* 29 June 846/3 A very rich maiden more highly positioned than himself. **1896** CHESHIRE *Hastings Chess Tourn.* 348 His style of play is firm and tenacious, aiming at accurate positioning and steady crushing rather than at brilliant attacks or rapid finishes.

positional (pəʊˈzɪʃənəl, pə-), *a.* [f. POSITION *sb.* + -AL[1].] **a.** Of, pertaining to, or determined by position. *spec.* (*a*) *Linguistics* = ISOLATING *ppl. a.* 1; (*b*) *Chess*, characterized by position play.

1571 DIGGES *Pantom.* I. xxxiv, K iv, The concourse or meeting of semblable positionall lines. **1646** SIR T. BROWNE *Pseud. Ep.* II. vii. 102 A strange conceit,..ascribing unto plants positionall operations, and after the manner of the Loadstone. **1664** POWER *Exp. Philos.* III. 157 A Magnet.. acquires a new one [Magnetical vigour], according to the positional Laws in its Refrigeration. **1879** THOMSON & TAIT *Nat. Phil.* I. I. §343 A system so constituted that the positional forces are proportional to displacements and the motional to velocities. **1881** R. ELLIS in *Academy* 9 Apr. 256/1 Why has not Mr. Butler..reproduced the Greek metre exactly, or at least with that positional quantity which seems most nearly to approach it? **1883** D. H. WHEELER *By-Ways of Lit.* x. 188 The possessive form in 's stands side by side with the positional possessive,..God's love or the love of God. **1895** *Funk's Stand. Dict.*, *Positional co-ordinates* (*Mech.*), quantities, employed to fix a system, occurring explicitly in expressions for kinetic and potential energies. **1908** T. G. TUCKER *Introd. Nat. Hist. Lang.* 92 Languages which express grammar and modification of sense by position, without external or internal modification of the 'roots'..may be called *Inorganic* or *Positional*. *Ibid.* 93 The *Positional* languages include Chinese, Burmese, Anamese, and their group. *Ibid.* 117 The line of linguistic ease naturally taken by a language which finds the purely positional structure inadequate to it [*sic*] needs. **1929** *Times* 2 Nov. 6/7 Newman increased a run of 312..to 349, and then missed a positional red winner. **1937** M. EUWE *Strategy & Tactics in Chess* 18 We call games such as the preceding one, in which strategy plays such an important part, *positional* games, in contrast to *combinative* games, in which the strategy is of minor importance. **1937** J. R. FIRTH *Tongues of Men* vii. 88 Three types of language structure: (i) Meanings indicated by words; relations by position.. These were called *Isolating* and *Positional* Languages. *E.g.*, Chinese, English. **1937** *Language* XIII. 3 Not uncommonly, the same language has long consonants of different phonemic types; for example, English has long consonants both as positional variants and as geminate clusters. **1938** *Times Lit. Suppl.* 5 Mar. 157/2 It secured the dominance of the positional over the combinational school. **1945** *Diamond Track* (Army Board, N.Z.) 37/2 The Allied success..made the position of large forces of the enemy's positional infantry on our front most precarious. **1946** *Sunday Dispatch* 8 Sept. 6/2 There was no weakness in United, who played clever positional football. **1952** A. COHEN *Phonemes of Eng.* 90 'Positional diphthongs' are characterised by the preservation of the individual character of the component parts. **1960** C. BARNETT *Desert Generals* III. ii. 103 The mentality of the army's senior and rising officers could not be similarly converted by decree to suit mobile armoured warfare. The stiff, positional war of the Western Front between 1914 and 1918 was the only..influence. **1964** R. B. LEES *Gram. Eng. Nominalizations* p. xli, Subcategorization is obviously a different kind of constraint on syntactic constituents from positional constraints in a tree or domination by a certain kind of node. **1970** *Nature* 12 Dec. 1121/1 In fact, the positional accuracy achieved is typically a small fraction of the vehicle stability. **1971** *Physics Bull.* July 397/2 Three instruments incorporating laser interferometers for calibration have been built at NPL. The first of these, for measuring the positional errors of the lines on precision scales and gratings, has been in use for several years. **1972** G. GREEN *Great Moments in Sport: Soccer* iv. 58 Cohen and Ray Wilson, the full backs, overlapping down the flanks..as the whole side bamboozled Spain with mobile positional play. **1979** E. H. GOMBRICH *Sense of Order* ix. 243 Repetition devalues elements while isolation in the centre will emphasize them. In the 'field of force' we can observe the effects of 'positional enhancement'.

b. Special collocations: ***positional goods*** (Econ.): see quots.; ***positional player*** (Chess) = *position player* (a).

1976 F. HIRSCH *Social Limits to Growth* iii. 27 The positional economy..relates to all aspects of goods, services, work positions, and other social relationships that are either (1) scarce in some absolute or socially imposed sense or (2) subject to congestion or crowding through more extensive use... If..positional goods remain in fixed supply while material goods become more plentiful, the price of positional goods will rise, as consumers' relative intensity of demand for them increases in terms of material goods. **1976** *Economist* 11 Dec. 129/2 Many of the things which are valued in our society are hierarchical. They are what Professor Hirsch calls 'positional goods'. **1977** *N.Y. Times Bk. Rev.* 13 Feb. 10/3 'Positional goods'—a house at the shore, tenure on the Harvard faculty, a Picasso on the wall. **1977** *Econ. Jrnl.* Sept. 574 Positional goods are defined as those to which access is a function of an individual's income relative to other people's. **1933** M. A. SCHWENDEMANN tr. *Reti's Masters of Chess Board* 4 Typical positional players like Steinitz and Rubinstein are of the opinion that this variation of the King's Gambit is in favour of White.

Hence **po'sitionally** *adv.*

1923 C. D. BROAD *Sci. Thought* xi. 408 Some of these strands may be positionally uniform. **1961** *Times* 13 Feb. 4/1 The new open side wing forward, Rogers, was positionally at sea. **1964** *Amer. Speech* XXXIX. 35 The main adjective class is positionally any word that goes either as a prepositive or as a complement of a copulative. **1971** D. CRYSTAL *Linguistics* 190 *The*..is positionally fixed, preceding the noun it modifies. **1975** *Nature* 31 Jan. 310/2 The molecules are positionally ordered but orientationally disordered and mobile.

positioner (pəʊˈzɪʃənə(r), pə-). [f. POSITION *v.* + -ER[1].] One who or that which positions; *spec.* a device or machine for mechanically moving an object into position and keeping it there.

1934 in WEBSTER. **1957** E. B. JONES *Instrument Technol.* III. II. 133 The positioner also corrects for movements of the valve stem owing to unbalanced forces on the valve plug. **1969** *Engineering* 29 Aug. 216/1 A universal positioner,.. with vertical table adjustment under full load, has been added to the range of manipulative equipment... Capacity is from 1 to 10 tons. **1972** *Physics Bull.* June 363/1 A micrometer stage is used to traverse the resistor under an RF probe which is held by a vertical positioner.

positive (ˈpɒzɪtɪv), *a.* and *sb.* Forms: 4 **positif, -ityue, -etyve**, 4–5 **-itife**, 4–7 **-itiue**, 5 **-ityve, -ytyfe, -atyue**, 6 **-ytive, -etyfe**, 6– **positive** (4–7 **poss-**). [ME. *positif*, a. F. *positif* (13th c. in Hatz.-Darm.) characterized by laying down or by being laid down, ad. L. *positīv-us*, in grammar, positive, f. *posit-us*, pa. pple. of *pōnĕre* to place, put, lay down: see -IVE.]

A. *adj.*

I. Connected with the notion of formal, explicit, or dogmatic laying down of any statement.

1. Formally laid down or imposed; arbitrarily or artificially instituted; proceeding from enactment or custom; conventional; opp. to *natural*.

a **1300** *Cursor M.* 9433 Þe first lagh was kald 'o kind'..Þe toþer has 'positiue' to nam. *Ibid.* 9449 Þe laghes bath he þan for-lete, Bath naturel and positif. *c* **1380** WYCLIF *Wks.* (1880) 392 I-bounden oonly by a posityue lawe. **1467–8** *Rolls of Parlt.* V. 622/2 All the Lawes of the world..which resteth in thre;..the Lawe of God, Lawe of nature and posityve Lawe. **1594** W. CLERKE *Triall of Bastardie* (title-p.) A Table of the Leuitical, English, and Positiue Canon Catalogues. **1644** BULWER *Chirol.* 3 Habits of the Hand are purely naturall, not positive. **1651** HOBBES *Leviath.* II. xxvi. (1839) 271 Again, of positive laws some are human, some divine; and of human positive laws, some are distributive, some penal. *c* **1760** WARBURTON *Unpubl. Papers* (1841) 273 The question is..whether the observation of the Sabbath was a natural or positive duty? **1845** STEPHEN *Comm. Laws Eng.* (1874) II. 34 In the reign of Queen Anne it [copyright] became the subject of positive regulation. **1883** J. M. LIGHTWOOD (*title*) The Nature of Positive Law. **1902** FAIRBAIRN *Philos. Relig.* III. I. iv. 5 Positive is public law, proclaimed and upheld by some public authority... Founded religions are by the very necessities of their origin positive.

2. Explicitly laid down; expressed without qualification; admitting no question; stated, explicit, express, definite, precise; emphatic; †objectively certain.

1598 SHAKS. *Merry W.* III. ii. 49 It is as possitiue, as the earth is firme, that Falstaffe is there. **1599** —— *Hen. V*, IV. ii. 25. **1655** FULLER *Ch. Hist.* IX. vii. §27 To..give in his positive answer to the following Articles. **1670** COTTON *Espernon* II. VII. 311 [They] resolv'd in the end upon a positive night, wherein with four Companies of Swisse to surprize him in his own house. *c* **1709** LADY M. W. MONTAGU *Let. to Mrs. Hewet* Nov., Positive orders oblige us to go tomorrow. **1799** J. ROBERTSON *Agric. Perth* 437 A positive rotation of crops need not be prescribed in the lease, except to an ignorant peasantry. **1810** GOUV. MORRIS in Sparks *Life & Writ.* (1832) III. 254 Positive assertion is not always polite. **1827** JARMAN *Powell's Devises* (ed. 3) II. 7 An express and positive devise cannot be controlled by the reason assigned, nor by inference and argument from the other parts of the will. **1870** FREEMAN *Norm. Conq.* (ed. 2) I. App. 702 A strong presumption, though it does not reach positive proof.

3. Of persons: Confident in opinion or assertion; convinced, assured, very sure; also, being or expressing oneself over-sure; opinionated, cocksure, dogmatic, dictatorial.

1665 *Phil. Trans.* I. 105 He is pretty positive that..no rational Account can be given. **1702** POPE *Jan. & May* 144 Each wondrous positive, and wondrous wise. **1732** BERKELEY *Alciphr.* III. §14 He is positive as to the being of God. **1781** COWPER *Conversat.* 146 Where men of judgment creep and feel their way, The positive pronounce without dismay. **1844** LINGARD *Anglo-Sax. Ch.* (1858) I. i. 9 *note*, Ussher is positive that the visit occurred. **1875** JOWETT *Plato* (ed. 2) I. 265 Nor is Socrates positive of any-thing but the duty of enquiry. **1879** MISS BRADDON *Clov. Foot* II. i. 16 Are you sure?..Pretty positive.

II. Unqualified, unrelated, absolute.

4. *Gram.* Applied to the primary form of an adjective or adverb, which expresses simple quality, without qualification, comparison, or relation to increase or diminution. (See also B. 1.)

1447 BOKENHAM *Seyntys* (Roxb.) 161 Be twyx them tweyn owyth no more to be Than is be twyn a posatyve and a comparatyve degre. **1591** PERCIVALL *Sp. Dict.* B iv, The comparatiue exceedeth the positiue. **1669** MILTON *Grammar* Wks. (1847) 460/2 There be two degrees above the positive word itself, the comparative, and superlative. **1704** J. HARRIS *Lex. Techn.* I, *Positive* Degree of Comparison in Grammar, is that which signifies the Thing simply and absolutely, with-out comparing it with others; it belongs only to Adjectives. **1873** MORRIS *Hist. Outl. Eng. Accid.* §109 There are three degrees of comparison: the positive, *high*; the comparative, *higher*; the superlative, *highest*.

5. a. Having no relation to or comparison with other things; free from qualifications, conditions, or reservations; absolute, unconditional; opposed to *relative* and *comparative*.

1606 SHAKS. *Tr. & Cr.* II. iii. 70 Patroclus is a foole positiue. **1628** T. SPENCER *Logick* 24 A positiue argument, is that which is attributed simply, and absolutely considered in it selfe: not compared with others. **1713** BERKELEY *Hylas & Phil.* i. Wks. 1871 I. 290 You have no idea at all, neither relative nor positive, of Matter. **1721** BRADLEY *Philos. Acc. Wks. Nat.* 92 Such as feed upon raw Flesh are positive in their Ferocity. **1727–41** CHAMBERS *Cycl.* s.v., Beauty is no positive thing, but depends on the different tastes of the people. **1867** FREEMAN *Norm. Conq.* I. v. 428 Two hills of slight positive elevation, but which seem of considerable height in the low country.

b. *colloq.* That is absolutely what is expressed by the sb.: nothing less than, downright, 'perfect'; 'out-and-out'.

1802 SYD. SMITH *Wks.* (1867) I. 15 Nothing short of a positive miracle can make him an acute reasoner. **1838** GRANVILLE *Spas Germ.* 253 It is impossible for the less bold and the timid..to stem the positive mobs by which the portico and space before the Mühlbrunn are besieged. **1853** LYTTON *My Novel* x. x, You are a positive enigma. **1889** GRETTON *Memory's Harkb.* 47 The excitement, the positive panic throughout the town, when the news came.

c. Functioning for the special purpose required; having or being a well-defined and effective action.

1903 *Sci. Amer.* 21 Feb. 134/1 Instead of depending on splash lubrication alone for oiling every part of the engine, positive oil feeds are led to each of the crankshaft bearings. **1938** L. V. W. CLARK in A. E. Dunstan et al. *Sci. of Petroleum* I. IX. 434/1 Blow-out preventers of the first group have been..quite satisfactory for drilling in areas of normal pressure, but where higher pressures are encountered it becomes necessary for a positive control to be available. **1958** *Times* 1 July 6/6 The steering, which used to be somewhat indefinite, is now light and pleasantly positive in action. **1972** *Physics Bull.* Apr. 230/2 Minor but important details have been considered—the cable is five feet long and very flexible, the grip on the bench (with rubber ball feet) is positive. **1977** *Offshore Engineer* Apr. 27/2 The port has a step-down diameter which provides a positive stop during pipe pull-in. **1977** *Sci. Amer.* Aug. 106/1 The unassisted drum brakes are balanced and positive in action but require heavy foot pressure.

III. Having relation only to matters of fact.

6. a. Dealing only with matters of fact and experience; practical, realistic; not speculative or theoretical.

positive philosophy, the philosophic system of Comte: = POSITIVISM 1.

1594 CAREW *Huarte's Exam. Wits* x. (1596) 140 This selfe difference there is between the Schoole-diuine and the positiue, that the one knoweth the cause of whatsoeuer importeth his faculty; and the other the propositions which are verefied, and no more. **1642** HOWELL *For. Trav.* (Arb.) 30 The one addicts himselfe for the most part to the study of the Law and Canons, the other to Positive and Schoole Divinity. **1856** BAGEHOT *Lit. Stud.* (1879) II. 26 He [Gibbon] was what common people call a matter-of-fact reader, and philosophers now-a-days a positive reader. **1864** F. B. BARTON in *Soc. Sc. Rev.* Mar. 214 The teachers of the Positive Religion of Humanity hold that all theology has been an attempt of man to explain his relationship to the forces of nature to which he is subjected. **1875** BRIDGES tr. *Comte's Syst. Positive Pol.* I. 39 The charge of Materialism which is often made against Positive philosophy is of more importance.

b. Dealing with facts, apart from any theory; cf. OBJECTIVE *a.* 3b. *rare.*

1888 BRYCE *Amer. Commw.* II. lxxv. 619 Stating in a purely positive, or, as the Germans say, 'objective', way, what the Americans think about the various features of their system.

c. Of a conjunction: Introducing a subordinate clause which states a matter of fact, not of hypothesis; e.g. he did *as* he was told; he came *because* he was invited.

1797 *Encycl. Brit.* (ed. 3) VIII. 79/2 As to the continuatives, they are either suppositive, such as *if, an*; or positive, such as *because, therefore, as*, &c.

7. Actual, real; sensible, concrete. *rare.*

positive image = real image: see REAL *a.* 1 e.

1831 BREWSTER *Optics* ii. 18 In concave mirrors there is, in all cases, a positive image of the object formed in front of the mirror, excepting when the object is placed between the principal focus and the mirror. **1856** MRS. BROWNING *Aur. Leigh* I. 262 The skies themselves looked low and positive, As almost you could touch them with a hand. **1897** W. P. KER *Epic & Romance* 9 Its motives of action are mainly positive and sensible,—cattle, sheep, piracy, abduction, merchandise, recovery of stolen goods, revenge.

IV. Having real existence; opposed to *negative*.

8. a. Consisting in or characterized by the presence or possession, and not merely by the absence or want, of features or qualities; of an affirmative nature. Also, consisting in or characterized by constructive action or attitudes; see also *positive thinking* below. Often opposed to NEGATIVE *a.* 5.

1618 E. ELTON *Exp. Rom. vii* (1622) 456 The corruption of nature..is a positive thing, and hath a real being. **1643** PRYNNE *Sov. Power Parl.* IV. App. 130 Here all the kings of the Israelites..are strictly bound by God himself to negative and positive conditions. **1729** BUTLER *Serm.* Wks. 1874 II. 68 Ease from misery occasioning for some time the greatest positive enjoyment. **1794** J. HUTTON *Philos. Light*, etc. 134 Cold is an element as positive as heat; for, cold in bodies is the negative of heat, as much as heat is the negative of cold. **1838** DE MORGAN *Ess. Probab.* 122 The exceptions are forgotten;..it is the character of negative events to lay less firmly hold of the mind than positive ones. **1858** O. W. HOLMES *Aut. Breakf.-t.* viii, There are blondes who are such simply by deficiency of coloring matter,—*negative* or *washed* blondes... There are others that are shot through with golden light, with tawny or fulvous tinges in various degree,—*positive* or *stained* blondes, dipped in yellow sunbeams. **1867** A. BARRY *Sir C. Barry* vi. 185 Relieved by positive colour. **1930** H. CRANE *Let.* 22 May (1965) 351 The poem [*sc. The Bridge*]..is, I think, an affirmation of experience, and to that extent is 'positive' rather than 'negative' in the sense that *The Waste Land* is negative. **1961** *Oregonian* (Portland, Oregon) 24 Oct. 8 The Portland school board was asked..to take a positive stand towards developing..more plans for the city's schools in event of attack. **1971** *Times* 15 Feb. 9/3 Ireland were the more positive side throughout and the same XV has been chosen for the game against Scotland. *Ibid.* 9/4 All the positive rugby after the interval came from Ireland. **1973** *Howard Jrnl.* XIII. 310 The opportunity to have a positive experience of learning may be very significant. **1976** M. MILLAR *Ask for me Tomorrow* (1977) xvi. 132 Please try to take a more positive attitude.

b. Of a term, etc.: Denoting the presence or possession, as opposed to the absence, of a quality.

1725 WATTS *Logic* I. iv. §2 Terms are either positive or negative. **1855** BAIN *Senses & Int.* I. i. §1 (1864) 2 It is desirable to possess, in addition to this negative definition, ..a positive definition, or a specification of the quality or qualities that appertain to the phenomena designated mind. **1877** E. R. CONDER *Bas. Faith* ii. 66 Negative forms of speech and thought are continually employed to express positive ideas. 'Discord', 'disunion', 'anarchy', have a very positive meaning.

c. Designating a copy or likeness of an object with the same relief as that of the original, as opposed to the reverse relief of a mould.

1911 [see NEGATIVE *a.* 11 a]. **1931** [see NEGATIVE *sb.* 8 c]. **1940** [see NEGATIVE *a.* 11 a]. **1973** [see NEGATIVE *sb.* 8 b].

d. Psychol. ***positive thinking***: the practice or result of concentrating one's mind affirmatively on what is constructive and good, thereby eliminating from it negative or destructive thoughts and emotions; also *attrib.*; ***positive transfer***: the transfer of effects from the learning of one skill that facilitate the subsequent learning of another skill; ***positive transference***: transference in which the feelings involved are of a positive or affectionate nature.

1916 C. E. LONG tr. *Jung's Coll. Papers Analytical Psychol.* ix. 270 As long as it is a question of the so-called 'positive' transference, the infantile-erotic character can usually be recognised without difficulty. **1921** F. N. FREEMAN *Exper. Educ.* ii. 47 There is..positive transfer again from Set 3 to Set 4. **1924**, etc. [see *negative transference* s.v. NEGATIVE *a.* 8 c]. **1933** R. W. BRUCE in *Jrnl. Exper. Psychol.* XVI. 351 There is a marked positive transfer in learning to make an old response to a new stimulus. **1953** N. V. PEALE (*title*) The power of positive thinking. *Ibid.* i. 2, I listened to your speech tonight in which you talked about the power of positive thinking. **1959** N. V. PEALE *Amazing Results of Positive Thinking* p. vii, By the application of positive thinking principles to their own life situations, they have mastered fear, healed personal relationships,.. and gained strong new confidence. **1970** B. C. MATHIS et al. *Psychol. Found. Educ.* iii. 83 If the experimental group is superior to the control group on B..positive transfer of training is said to have occurred. **1970** A. JANOV *Primal Scream* xiv. 246 When the therapist is helpful and warm and offers a bit of advice, he is encouraging the 'positive' transference. **1974** *Country Life* 21 Nov. 1616/2, I believe that positive thinking can help one overcome many difficulties in life.

e. Pol. ***positive neutralism*** or ***neutrality***: a policy adopted by some of the poorer and less developed countries of maintaining relations with each of the major powers while remaining neutral in regard to their rivalry (see quot. 1968). So ***positive neutralist***.

[**1957** *Political Sci. Q.* LXXII. 266 A communiqué condemning the development of Power blocs in international affairs and urging neutralism as a positive way towards the establishment of international peace.] **1960** *Sunday Times* 28 Aug. 5/1 'We Africans are positive neutralists.'.. These phrases..have cropped up constantly in the speeches so far: 'positive neutralism' [etc.]. **1961** *NATO or Neutrality* (Fabian Soc.) iv. 20 A policy of positive neutrality would be of immense assistance in helping Britain establish good post-imperial relations with the new countries. **1968** P. CALVOCORESSI *World Politics since 1945* IV. xiii. 256 Neutralism and non-alignment, therefore, as distinct from neutrality, were the expression of an attitude towards a particular and present conflict: they entailed, first, equivalent relations with both sides and, secondly—in the phase called positive neutralism—attempts to mediate and abate the dangerous quarrels of the great.

9. a. *Alg.* Of a quantity: Greater than zero; additive: the opposite of NEGATIVE *a* 6. ***positive sign***: the sign +, used to mark a positive quantity.

1704 J. HARRIS *Lex. Techn.* I, *Positive Quantities* in Algebra, are such as are of a Real and Affirmative Nature, and either have, or are supposed to have the Affirmative or Positive Sign + before them. **1743** EMERSON *Fluxions* 74, λ is any positive whole Number greater than 0. **1827** HUTTON *Course Math.* I. 167 When a quantity is found without a sign, it is understood to be positive, or have the sign + prefixed. **1865** TYLOR *Early Hist. Man.* i. 2 Cases in which the result of progress has not been positive in adding, but negative in taking away.

b. Hence: Reckoned, situated, or tending in the direction which (naturally or arbitrarily) is taken as that of increase, progress, or onward motion. The opposite of NEGATIVE *a.* 8.

1873 MAXWELL *Electr. & Magn.* I. 24 If the actual rotation of the earth from west to east is taken positive. **1875** BENNETT & DYER *Sachs' Bot.* 677 Its negative heliotropism is..only a special case of positive heliotropism. **1893** SIR R. BALL *Story of Sun* 170 The angle between the pole projected on the Sun's disc and the north point..is reckoned as positive if it lies towards the left, that is, to the east.

c. ***positive logic***: (*a*) [tr. G. ***positive logik*** (Hilbert & Bernays *Grundlagen der Math.* (1934) I. iii. 68)] (see quots. 1943, 1947); (*b*) circuit logic in which the larger or most positive signal is taken as representing 1 and the smaller signal 0.

1943 *Mind* LII. 49 Of other 'rudimentary systems' I mention only the so-called positive logic, which does not operate with negations. **1947** *Mind* LVI. 215 Rules 4.1 to 4.5 constitute the positive logic of compound statements, that is to say, they suffice for that part of propositional logic which is independent of negation. **1955** A. N. PRIOR *Formal Logic* III. ii. 258 This segment of Heyting's calculus forming what Hilbert and Bernays have called 'positive logic'. **1958** *Proc. IRE* XLVI. 1249 In the following discussion, positive logic is used. A binary '1' is defined as the most positive signal potential, and a binary '0' as the most negative. **1962**, **1968** [see LOGIC *sb.* 4]. **1974** D. A. CALAHAN et al. *Introd. Mod. Circuit Anal.* iii. 47/2 In theory, we must be told which type of logic, positive or negative, is assumed before we can determine the function of a logical device; in practice, positive logic is assumed unless otherwise specified. **1976** BELOVE & DROSSMAN *Systems & Circuits for Electr. Engin. Technol.* xiii. 325 We shall use the positive logic convention whereby a relatively low voltage represents logical 0 and a relatively high voltage represents logical 1.

10. *Electr.* **a.** Applied to that form of electricity which is produced by rubbing glass with silk; vitreous: opposed to NEGATIVE *a.* 7. (For the reason of this use see quot. 1812.)

1755 B. MARTIN *Mag. Arts & Sci.* 322 What they had observed of positive and negative Electricity. **1770** PRIESTLEY in *Phil. Trans.* LX. 197 The result was invariably the same, whether they and the rod were loaded with positive or negative electricity. **1812** SIR H. DAVY *Chem. Philos.* 127 The terms negative and positive electricity have been likewise adopted on the idea that the phænomena depend upon a peculiar subtile fluid which becomes in excess in the vitreous and deficient in resinous bodies. **1839** *Penny Cycl.* XIV. 288/1 It will be easy to observe the analogy between the mutual relations of the two magnetisms [Austral and Boreal], and those of positive with negative electricities. **1876** PREECE & SIVEWRIGHT *Telegraphy* 3 By an arbitrary convention the electricity excited on glass has been called positive, while that excited on sealing-wax has been called negative. All electrified bodies are either positively or negatively electrified.

fig. **1831** CARLYLE *Sart. Res.* III. x, Drudgism the Negative, Dandyism the Positive: one attracts hourly towards it and appropriates all the Positive Electricity of the nation (namely, the Money thereof); the other is equally busy with the Negative (that is to say the Hunger).

b. Of or pertaining to, or characterized by the presence or production of, positive electricity; *spec.* noting that member of a voltaic couple which is most acted upon by the solution, and from which a current of positive electricity proceeds.

1808 *Med. Jrnl.* XIX. 191 Oxygen and acids..are naturally negative; hydrogen and inflammable bodies, in general, and alkalies, positive. **1812** SIR H. DAVY *Chem. Philos.* 321 Oxygene will separate at the positive surface, and small metallic globules will appear at the negative surface. **1815** J. SMITH *Panorama Sc. & Art* II. 243 If a tourmalin be cut into several parts, each piece will have its positive and negative poles, corresponding to the positive and negative sides of the original stone. **1836–41** BRANDE *Chem.* (ed. 5) 255 The conductor to which the cushion is attached is called the negative conductor; the other collects the electricity of the glass, and is called the positive conductor. **1876** PREECE & SIVEWRIGHT *Telegraphy* 12 The zinc is named the positive plate or element, the copper the negative plate or element. **1885** WATSON & BURBURY *Math. Th. Electr. & Magn.* I. 243 From 284° to 330° iron is positive to copper and negative to lead; above 330° lead is positive to copper and negative to iron. **1904** *Westm. Gaz.* 14 Dec. 10/2 The bare [rail] running down the centre of the track being the return or negative, and the protected one at the side the 'live' or positive rail.

11. *Magnetism.* Applied to the north-seeking pole of a magnet, and the corresponding (south) pole of the earth, or the direction in which such a pole is impelled by another or by an electric current.

1849 MRS. SOMERVILLE *Connex. Phys. Sc.* xxx. (ed. 8) 351 All the phenomena of magnetism, like those of electricity, may be explained on the hypothesis of one ethereal fluid, which is condensed or redundant in the positive pole. **1873** MAXWELL *Electr. & Magn.* (1881) II. 19–20 In speaking of a line of magnetic force we shall always suppose it to be traced from magnetic south to magnetic north, and shall call this direction positive. In the same way..the end of the magnet which points north is reckoned the positive end. We shall consider Austral magnetism, that is, the magnetism of that end of a magnet which points north, as positive.

b. *fig.* (from 10 and 11. Cf. POLE *sb.*^{2} 9.)

1816 COLERIDGE *Lay Serm.* 331 Of the positive pole, on the other hand, language to the following purport is the usual exponent. **1844** EMERSON *Ess., Char.* Wks. (Bohn) II. 383 Everything in nature is bipolar, or has a positive and negative pole.

12. *Optics.* **a.** Of a double-refracting crystal: Having the index of refraction of the extraordinary ray greater than that of the ordinary ray; opposed to NEGATIVE *a.* 9a.

1831 BREWSTER *Optics* xvii. §90. 147 In some [crystals] the extraordinary ray is refracted towards the axis..while in others it is refracted from the axis. In the first case the axis is called a positive axis of double refraction. *Ibid.* xxii. 196 The positive crystals, such as zircon, ice, etc. *c* **1865** J. WYLDE in *Circ. Sc.* I. 79/2 Of some bodies possessing positive axes, we may mention quartz, ice, &c.; whilst Iceland spar, ..prussiate of potass, &c., have negative axes.

b. ***positive eyepiece***: an eyepiece consisting of two plano-convex lenses having their convex sides facing each other, in which the object is viewed beyond both lenses. Cf. NEGATIVE *a.* 9b.

1842 BRANDE *Dict. Sc.*, etc s.v. *Telescope*, The two lenses are usually plano-convex, with the convex faces towards the object-glass... This eye-piece is usually called the negative eye-piece, from its having the image seen by the eye behind the field-glass [i.e. between the field-glass and the eye-glass];..Another modification..is called the positive eye-piece, because the image observed is before both lenses [i.e. between the field-glass and the object-glass]. **1867** HOGG *Microsc.* I. ii. 51 The positive eye-piece gives the best view of the micrometer.

c. Said of a visual image of the same colour or luminosity as the original sense-impression.

1899 L. HILL *Man. Hum. Physiol.* xxxv. 439 On waking in the morning in a dark room strike a match, and immediately blow it out; a positive after-image of the light persists for a moment and then gradually dies away.

13. *Photogr.* Showing the lights and shades as seen in nature. Opposed to NEGATIVE *a.* 10.

1840 SIR J. HERSCHEL in *Proc. Roy. Soc.* IV. 206 In order to avoid circumlocution the author employs the terms *positive* and *negative* to express respectively pictures in which the lights and shades are the same as in nature..and in which they are opposite; that is, light representing shade, and shade light. **1841** FOX TALBOT *Specif. of Patent* No. 8842 The portrait..is a negative one, and from this a positive copy may be obtained. **1859** GULLICK & TIMBS *Paint.* 119 The artist works upon a very faint positive 'impression',..and entirely covers it with body colour, or equally opaque coloured crayons, with the express intention of concealing the tone of the photograph. **1881** LUBBOCK in *Nature* 1 Sept. 410/2 He..by obtaining a negative rendered it possible to take off any number of positive, or natural, copied from one original picture.

V. Adapted to be placed or set down (literally).

14. ***positive organ***: a small organ, orig. app. portable, but placed upon a stand when played (as distinct from a *portative* organ, which could be played while being carried in procession); often used formerly as an addition to the large organ in a church (the same as *chair organ* or CHOIR ORGAN in its early form), and recently revived in some churches.

1727–41 CHAMBERS *Cycl.* s.v. *Organ*, Church organs consist of two parts, viz. the main body of the organ, called the great organ; and the positive, or little organ, which is a small buffet, usually placed before the great organ. **1879** STAINER *Music of Bible* 156 The positive organ in our churches and halls, and the portative barrel-organ. **1900** *Oxford Times* 26 May 7/6 Wytham. All Saints' Church. Opening of new 'positive' organ. **1905** *Athenæum* 8 July 56/1 (Church Hist. Exhib. St. Albans) The Positive organ here shown has four stops, and is *circa* 1600; this was a larger instrument, and was placed on a stand during use, but it could be moved about when required.

VI. 15. Other collocations: ***positive discrimination***, the making of distinctions in favour of groups considered disadvantaged or underprivileged, esp. in the allocation of resources and opportunities; ***positive electron***, a particle analogous to the ordinary negative electron but having a positive charge: orig. applied to the proton, now to the positron; ***positive eugenics***, an attempt to encourage the birth of children to parents having qualities considered desirable to the community; ***positive feedback*** (see FEEDBACK, FEED-BACK *sb.* a); ***positive pressure*** (Med.), pressure greater than that of the atmosphere, used to force air or oxygen into the lungs intermittently to supplement or replace natural inspiration; freq. *attrib.*; ***positive ray***, a stream of positively-charged ions which are produced in a gas discharge tube and move towards the cathode; *pl.* except when *attrib.*

1967 *Children & their Primary Schools* (Central Advisory Council for Educ.) I. v. 57 We ask for 'positive discrimination' in favour of such schools [in deprived areas] and the children in them, going well beyond an attempt to equalise resources. **1974** *Observer* 21 Apr. 14/6 Israeli educationists regard this as a challenge, and positive discrimination—in theory at least—has become an article of faith. **1977** *Film & Television Technician* Mar. 8/4 Ms Betty Lockwood, Chairman of the Equal Opportunities Commission, told a WEA seminar of trade union officials that positive discrimination inside unions and in training should be encouraged. That means discrimination in favour of either women or men, though in practice it is likely to mean women. **1978** *Daily Tel.* 28 Jan. 16 Camden Council's announcement that henceforth members of immigrant minorities, even when less qualified, will be preferred for employment to indigenous citizens will bring to the boil the simmering debate on what is euphemistically known as positive discrimination or affirmative action. **1900** LD. KELVIN in *Phil. Mag.* L. 306 For atoms of electricity, which, following Larmor, I at present call electrons, it inevitably occurs to suggest a special class of atoms... A positive electron would be an atom which by attraction condenses ether into the space occupied by its volume; and a negative electron would be an atom which, by repulsion, rarefies the ether remaining in the space occupied by its volume. **1902** [see ELECTRON^2]. **1903** O. LODGE *Mod. Views on Matter* 12 The chief defect in the electrical theory of matter at present is that the *positive* electron, if it exists, has never yet been isolated from the rest of an atom. **1921** *Phil. Mag.* XLII. 307 So far as the writer can learn, the word proton was suggested by Rutherford for use in designating the hydrogen nucleus. This will also be designated as the positive electron in the present paper. **1932** *Science* 9 Sept. 238/1 Up to the present a positive electron has always been found with an associated mass 1,850 times that associated with the negative electron. **1964** M. GOWING *Britain & Atomic Energy, 1939–1945* 18 This positive electron, or positron as it is often called, was first found in..cosmic rays. [**1907** C. W. SALEEBY in *Sociol. Papers* III. 31 We must..preserve the two-fold aspect of eugenics, the one positive—the encouragement of the better; the other negative—the discouragement of the worse.] **1909** —— *Parenthood & Race Culture* xi. 172 We must clearly divide our proposals, as the present writer did some years ago, with Mr. Galton's approval, into two classes: positive eugenics and negative eugenics. *Ibid.*, In regard to positive eugenics I..cannot believe in the propriety of attempting to bribe into parenthood people who have no love of children. **1914** [see *negative eugenics* s.v. NEGATIVE *a.* 8c]. **1952** C. P. BLACKER *Eugenics* v. 111 The statement made [by Galton] in 1901 says that positive eugenics is more *important* than negative and that made in 1908 declares that negative eugenics is more *pressing* than positive. **1970** *Sci. Amer.* Mar. 107 Conceivably a changed social climate and increased knowledge will make it possible for positive eugenics to be practiced on man. **1972** P. B. MEDAWAR *Hope of Progress* 71 The case for 'positive eugenics', that is for constructive rather than merely remedial eugenics, is based on the model of stockbreeding. **1885** I. B. YEO tr. *Oertel's Respiratory Therapeutics* II. 607 (*heading*) Action of positive pressure on the surface of the thorax. **1909** *Arch. Internal Med.* III. 369 During positive pressure respiration, the so-called artificial respiration of laboratory procedure, the blood pressure falls during inspiration and rises during expiration. **1948** *Anesthesiol.* IX. 29 Positive pressure respiration decreases the venous return, and is in effect a way of applying tourniquets not only to all four extremities but also to the head and abdomen. **1970** *Jrnl. Pediatrics* LXXVI. 183 The indications for intermittent positive pressure ventilation were asphyxia on admission, a single asphyxial attack, [etc.]. **1903** J. J. THOMSON *Conduction Electr. through Gases* xvii. 522 On the view of the discharge given in Chap. xvi. there is a stream of positively charged molecules moving towards the cathode, causing this to emit cathode rays; if the cathode is perforated, part of this stream may pass through the holes, producing in the gas behind the cathode luminosity, forming in fact the Canalstrahlen, or positive rays as we may call them, if we think this view of their constitution sufficiently established. **1920** [see *mass spectrograph* s.v. MASS *sb.*^{2} 10d]. **1922** GLAZEBROOK *Dict. Appl. Physics* II. 602/1 Positive rays were discovered by Goldstein in 1886 in electrical discharge at low pressure. **1955** C. G. DARWIN in W. Pauli *Niels Bohr* 9 Many elements in a positive-ray tube form temporary hydrides. **1968** M. S. LIVINGSTON *Particle Physics* ii. 20 Thomson's studies of the positive rays from ionized hydrogen gas were the first experiments in which the proton was isolated and identified as a particle.

16. Comb.: **positive definite** *adj. phr. Math.*, positive (formerly, positive or zero) in all cases; (of a matrix) having all its eigenvalues positive; hence **positive-definiteness**; **positive-going** *a.*, increasing in magnitude in the direction of positive polarity; becoming less negative or more positive; **positive-negative** *a.*, exhibiting both positive and negative characteristics.

1907 M. BÔCHER *Introd. Higher Algebra* xi. 150 A positive definite form is positive or zero for all real values of the variables. **1948** W. V. HOUSTON *Princ. Math. Physics* (ed. 2) vii. 120 The potential energy will be a quadratic expression in the coordinates that, if the equilibrium is stable, will be a positive definite expression. **1957** L. FOX *Numerical Solution Two-Point Boundary Probl.* vii. 179 If all the λ_r are positive, which is the case in many physical problems, and corresponds to some structure of the differential system corresponding to a positive-definite matrix *A*.., we can also assert [etc.]. **1970** G. SPOSITO *Introd. Quantum Physics* iii. 53 We further restrict this scalar product by stipulating that it be positive-definite: $(f, f) \geqslant 0$. **1968** FOX & MAYERS *Computing Methods for Scientists & Engineers* i. 6 The associated matrix may be 'general', or it may have special properties such as symmetry, with or without positive-definiteness. **1957** *Wireless World* Jan. 10/2 The area under the positive-going excursion is nearly equal to that under the negative-going excursion. **1979** *Sci. Amer.* Mar. 104/1 (*caption*) A positive-going (but not negative-going) shift in membrane voltage causes a brief outward gating current that coincides with the opening of the sodium channels. **1946** C. MORRIS *Signs, Lang. & Behavior* 82 Appraisors signify along a positive-negative continuum. **1964** E. A. NIDA *Toward Sci. Transl.* ii. 24 The differences between literal and free translating are, however, no mere positive-negative dichotomy, but rather a polar distinction with many grades between them.

B. *sb.* (absol. or ellipt. use of the adj.)

1. *Gram.* The positive degree (see A. 4); an adjective or adverb in the positive degree.

1530 PALSGR. Introd. 28 We..forme our comparatives and superlatyves out of our posytives. *c* **1620** A. HUME *Brit. Tongue* (1865) 30 The positive is the first position of the noun; as, soft, hard. **1755** JOHNSON *Dict., Gram.*, Of adjectives... The termination in *ish* may be accounted in some sort a degree of comparison, by which the signification is diminished below the positive, as *black, blackish*. **1876** MASON *Eng. Gram.* (ed. 21) §108 Some adjectives which are comparatives in origin are now used as positives.

2. That which has an actual existence, or is capable of being affirmed; a reality.

1620 T. GRANGER *Div. Logike* 93 Here is not one positiue, or being opposed to another contrarie positiue, or being,.. but the affirmation, position, being thereof, is opposed to negation, deposition, annihilation, not being thereof. **1641** R. BROOKE *Eng. Episc.* I. v. 21 White and Blacke indeed are Both positives, but so is not Evill. **1878** C. J. VAUGHAN *Earnest Words* 145 If these are not mere names and ideas, but realities, and facts, and positives.

†**3.** That which arbitrarily or absolutely prescribes or determines. *Obs.*

1685 BAXTER *Paraphr. N.T.* Rom. vii. 8 A great number of Legal Positives and Ceremonials had never obliged me. **1732** WATERLAND *Script. Vind.* III. 37 Positives.., while under Precept, cannot be slighted without slighting Morals also.

4. Elliptically or contextually for *positive quantity* (see A. 9); *positive conjunction* (see A. 6c); *positive plate, metal*, etc. (see A. 10b); *positive organ* (see A. 14); *positive colour* (see A. 8); etc.

1706 W. JONES *Syn. Palmar. Matheseos* 35 To Connect a Negative and a Positive, is to make the one destroy the other. [**1727–41** CHAMBERS *Cycl.*, *Positive*, in music, denotes the little organ usually behind, or at the foot of the organist, played with the same wind.] **1751** HARRIS *Hermes* II. ii. (1765) 244 The Suppositives denote Connection, but assert not actual Existence; the Positives imply both the one and the other. **1881** SPOTTISWOODE in *Nature* 6 Oct. 549/2 The carbon which would be connected with the copper element of a Grove battery,..and which is called the positive, is the one more rapidly consumed. **1885** A. J. HIPKINS in Grove *Dict. Mus.* IV. 303/2 The organs are Orgel (with 3 divisions of pipes), Positive (a chamber organ), Regale (a reed organ), and Portative (pipe regal). **1899** *Daily News* 7 Feb. 6/3 The picture is light in key, but though devoid of positives, save in the faint blue background, it is not really colourless.

5. *Photogr.* A picture in which the lights and shadows are the same as in nature: opposed to NEGATIVE *sb.* 8.

1853 *Fam. Herald* 3 Dec. 510/2 To obtain from those pictures good prints or positives. **1883** *Hardwich's Photogr. Chem.* (ed. Taylor) 188 Collodion Positives are sometimes termed *direct*, because obtained by a single operation.

Hence (*nonce-wds.*) **'positive** *v.*, (*a*) *trans.* to affirm positively, assert; (*b*) to produce a positive picture of; **posi'tival** *a.*, see quot.; **'positivize** *v. trans.*, to render positive or real.

1656 S. H. *Gold. Law* 43, I may safely positive it, and say, that neither his Highness..nor the Parliament..might part with their Powers. **1894** SALA *London up to Date* ii. 17 Being focussed, negatived, and positived in that apparel. **1865** J. GROVE *Moral Ideals* (1876) 13 For contrast to *ideal* in its adjective sense, I shall sometimes use the word *positival*. *Ibid.* 93 The notion of the summum bonum was very early de-idealized or positivized, and it was considered that nothing could..be considered to answer to this description except tangible, measurable, describable pleasure.

positively ('pɒzɪtɪvlɪ), *adv.* [f. prec. + -LY^2.] In a positive manner.

1. Definitely, expressly, explicitly, directly, downright; with assurance or confident assertion.

1593 NASHE *Christ's T.* 83 b, I positiuely affirme it [the Plague] is for sinne. **1642** HOWELL *For. Trav.* (Arb.) 49 Some of the approvedst Antiquaries positively hold the Originall Language of the Celts..to be Welsh. **1699** BENTLEY *Phal.* 90, I do not pretend to pass my own Judgment, or to determin positively on either side. **1730** in *Swift's Lett.* (1766) II. 121 You would not so positively affirm this fact..without knowing the certain truth. **1800** *Med. Jrnl.* IV. 139 Had he positively contradicted my assertion, I could have answered and confuted him in one word. **1849** MACAULAY *Hist. Eng.* i. I. 53 A large body of Protestants..regarded prelacy as positively unlawful.

2. Not comparatively or relatively; absolutely, simply; in itself.

1597 BACON *Coulers Good & Evill* vi. Ess. (Arb.) 146 The good or euil..may be esteemed good or euil comparatiuely and not positiuely or simply. **1871** FREEMAN *Norm. Conq.* IV. xviii. 220 The original town occupied the end of a positively small, but in that flat region, considerable, ridge of higher ground overlooking the river at its feet.

3. In an affirmative, real, or actual manner; in relation to what is, as distinguished from what is not; actually; opposed to *negatively*.

1668 WILKINS *Real Char.* 309 Prepositions..signifying some respect of Cause, Place, Time, or other circumstance either Positively or Privatively. **1683** D. A. *Art Converse* 116 They are rather not civil than positively incivil. **1776** PAINE *Com. Sense* (1791) 5 Society is produced by our wants, and government by our wickedness; the former promotes our happiness positively, by uniting our affections; the latter negatively, by restraining our vices. **1961** C. E. VINCENT *Unmarried Mothers* x. 254 Her inability to resolve these various identity crises positively. **1972** *Jrnl. Social Psychol.* LXXXVII. 34 It has generally been assumed that level of fear is related positively to response in a potential panic situation.

4. a. *Electr.* With positive electricty.

1747 FRANKLIN *Lett.*, etc. Wks. 1840 V. 186 Hence have arisen some new terms among us; we say B (and bodies like circumstanced) is electrized *positively*; A, *negatively*. Or rather, B is electrized *plus*; A, *minus*. **1770** PRIESTLEY in *Phil. Trans.* LX. 197 The result was invariably the same.. whether the jar was charged positively or negatively. **1832** *Nat. Philos.* II. *Electric.* ii. §49. 13 (U.K. Soc.) When-ever they [bodies] contain a quantity of fluid greater than this, they are said to be positively electrified, or to have positive electricity. **1873** MAXWELL *Electr. & Magn.* I. 46 A positively electrified surface.

b. In the direction taken as positive or primary.

1875 BENNETT & DYER *Sachs' Bot.* 677 In the ivy..the internodes are positively heliotropic when young, but negatively when old before growth ceases. *Ibid.* [see HELIOTROPIC].

5. Absolutely, actually, really; indeed, in truth, truly. (Qualifying the statement.) Also *colloq.* used *ellipt.* as an emphatic affirmative: yes, indeed.

17.. SHERIDAN *Sch. Scand.* I. i, So, Maria, you see your lover pursues you; positively you sha'n't escape. **1823** FOSTER in *Life & Corr.* (1846) II. 51 This edition has undergone positively the last revisal. **1859** MRS. CARLYLE *Lett.* (1883) III. 2 Positively, it took away my breath. **1886** W. J. TUCKER *E. Europe* 159 His Excellency positively hates the sight of him. **1922** H. S. WALPOLE *Cathedral* II. ii. 188 She hasn't an idea in her head. I don't believe that she knows it's Jubilee Year. Positively! **1942** PARTRIDGE *Usage & Abusage* 4/2 *Absolutely* and *positively*... In slang their meaning is *yes* (popularized by a famous vaudeville duet between 'Mr. Gallagher and Mr. Sheehan').

positiveness ('pɒzɪtɪvnɪs). [f. as prec. + -NESS.] The quality of being positive.

†**1.** Reality of existence; actuality, affirmative nature. *Obs.*

1668 WILKINS *Real Char.* II. i. §3. 28 Positiveness, Thesis. **1678** NORRIS *Coll. Misc.* (1699) 302 The Positiveness of Sins of Omission, is in the Habitude of the Will only.

2. Subjective certainty; confidence, assurance; expression of assuredness; dogmatism, obstinacy.

1679 DRYDEN *Troilus & Cress.* Ep. Ded., He was brave without Vanity, and knowing without Positiveness. **1711** *Countrey-Man's Let. to Curat* 76 Positiveness without Proof is Intolerable. **1809** W. IRVING *Knickerb.* I. iv. (1849) 58 Authors who, from the positiveness of their assertions, seem to have been eye-witnesses of the fact. **1885** RANNEY in *Harper's Mag.* Mar. 640/1 The function of these..fibres is not yet determined with positiveness.

b. Definiteness, directness, peremptoriness.

1736 CARTE *Ormonde* II. 289 If upon the literal positiveness of the King's directions we had immediately transmitted them to the commissioners.

positivism ('pɒzɪtɪvɪz(ə)m). [ad. F. *positivisme* (Comte), f. *positif, -ive*, POSITIVE: see -ISM; *la philosophie positive* being Comte's name for his system.

La philosophie positive occurs first in St. Simon *Introd. aux Trav. Scientif.*, Œuvres I. 198. Comte's *Philosophie positive* vol. I was published in 1830.]

1. A system of philosophy elaborated by Auguste Comte from 1830 onwards, which recognizes only positive facts and observable phenomena, with the objective relations of these and the laws that determine them, abandoning all inquiry into causes or ultimate origins, as belonging to the theological and metaphysical stages of thought, held to be now superseded; also a religious system founded upon this philosophy, in which the object of worship is Humanity considered as a single corporate being. Also, the name given generally nowadays to the view, held by Bacon and Hume amongst others (including Comte), that every rationally justifiable assertion can be scientifically verified or is capable of logical or mathematical proof; that philosophy can do no more than attest to the logical and exact use of language through which such observation or verification can be expressed. Also *ellipt.* for *logical positivism* (see LOGICAL *a.* (and *sb.*) 7).

1847 J. D. MORELL *Hist. View Philos.* (ed. 2) I. I. i. 88 Let those who claim Bacon as the apostle of *positivism*, give us an interpretation of this whole division of his system. **1854** BRIMLEY *Ess., Comte's Positive Philos.* 330 We are obliged to conclude, then, that positivism in M. Comte's hands, while pretending to take upon itself the regulation of human conduct, fails to furnish a guiding principle for either individuals or societies. **1865** (*title*) A General view of Positivism. Translated from the French of Auguste Comte, by J. H. Bridges. **1866** J. MARTINEAU *Ess.* I. 21 Such deification of mortals..is the avowed religion of positivism. *a* **1866** J. GROTE *Exam. Utilitarian Philos.* (1870) 2 A way of thinking about morals, which may be roughly called by the name *Positivism*; by which I mean the line of thought which endeavours to construct a system of morals..from observation and experience of fact alone. [**1868** (Nov. 8) HUXLEY *Phys. Basis Life* Lay Serm. (1883) 140 In fact M. Comte's philosophy in practice might be compendiously described as Catholicism *minus* Christianity. [Often referred to as 'Huxley's well-known description' or 'definition of Positivism'.]] **1875** BRIDGES tr. *Comte's Syst. Positive Polity* I. 264 In the conception of Humanity the three essential aspects of Positivism, its subjective principle, its objective dogma, and its practical object, are united. **1892** *Monist* II. 261 Positivism i.e. the representation of facts without any admixture of theory or mythology, is an ideal which in its purity perhaps will never be realised. **1934** W. M. MALISOFF tr. R. Carnap in *Jrnl. Philos. of Sci.* I. 16 In the following example we deal with the conflict of two theses.. which correspond more or less to positivism and to realism. **1945** K. R. POPPER *Open Society* I. v. 59 Ethical positivism ..maintains that..what is, is good. (Might is right.) **1961** M. ČAPEK *Philos. Impact Contemp. Physics* xvi. 297 The positivism prevailing amongst contemporary physicists, who insist on a consistent elimination of *all* unobservable factors. **1964** FODOR & KATZ in R. Klibansky *Contemp. Philos.* (1969) III. 303 We shall therefore examine the two dominant schools of thought in recent philosophy of language, ordinary-language philosophy and positivism. **1967** *Encycl. Philos.* VI. 415 Both share the general idea of progress, but whereas social positivism deduces progress from a consideration of society and history, evolutionary positivism deduces it from the fields of physics and biology. **1974** H. WANG *From Math. to Philos.* p. ix, The much publicized juxtaposition of logic with positivism (or empiricism or 'analytic' philosophy) has burdened logic with a guilt by association.

2. a. Definiteness, peremptoriness. **b.** Certainty, assurance: = POSITIVENESS 2.

1854 GEO. ELIOT *Feuerbach's Essence Chr.* (1881) 32 Israel is the most complete presentation of Positivism in religion. **1870** LOWELL *Among my Bks.* Ser. I. (1873) 150 The metaphysicians can never rest till they have taken their watch to pieces and have arrived at a happy positivism as to its structure, though at the risk of bringing it to a no-go. **1874** P. SMYTH *Our Inher.* v. xxi. 415 The Doctor..adopts that with positivism. **1894** E. H. BARKER *Two Summers in Guyenne* 404 The decision and positivism of the Roman character.

3. *Law.* A term derived from positive law (cf. POSITIVE *a.* 1) and applied to theories concerned with the enactment of law, the reaching of legal decisions, the binding nature of legal rules and the study of existing law; which postulate that legal rules are valid because they are enacted by the 'sovereign' or derive logically from existing decisions, and deny that ideal or moral considerations (such as those of natural law, or that a rule is unjust) should in any way limit the operation or scope of the law.

1927 M. R. COHEN in *Proc. 6th Internat. Congr. Philos., 1926* 469 (*title*) Positivism and the limits of idealism in the law. **1944** W. FRIEDMANN *Legal Theory* xv. 135 Positivism in jurisprudence comprises legal movements, poles apart in every respect. **1945** H. KELSEN *Gen. Theory Law* I. iii. 52 No sanction without a legal norm providing this sanction, no delict without a legal norm determining that delict. These principles are the expression of legal positivism in the field of criminal law. **1959** JOWITT *Dict. Eng. Law* II. 1366/2 *Positivism*, in international law, this means the method which attempts to present law as actually applied in State practice. **1961** H. L. A. HART *Concept of Law* i. 7 Some contemporary legal theory which is critical of the legal 'positivism' inherited from Austin. **1967** *Encycl. Philos.* IV. 419/1 The definition of law as the command of the 'sovereign' is no doubt the most prominent example of a form of positivism. *Ibid.*, Sometimes 'legal positivism' is used to refer to the view that correct legal decisions are uniquely determined by pre-existing legal rules. **1969** M. MORITZ in R. Klibansky *Contemp. Philos.* IV. 140 The author intends to give an empirical account of what is a legal order. He regards the distinction between natural law theory and legal positivism as being of secondary importance. **1971** *Mod. Law Rev.* XXXIV. VI. 632 Positivism regards law as a system of comprehensive and closely defined rules.

positivist ('pɒzɪtɪvɪst), *sb.* and *a.* [ad. F. *positiviste*, f. as prec.: see -IST.] **1. a.** An adherent or supporter of POSITIVISM; a Comtist. See also *logical positivist* s.v. LOGICAL *a.* (and *sb.*) 7.

1854 BRIMLEY *Ess., Comte's Positive Philos.* 324 A positivist would answer..that conscious ignorance is better than chimerical fancies, which not only themselves mislead, but prevent the growth of true doctrine. **1868** *Sat. Rev.* 25 Apr. 541/2 Christians and Positivists are agreed in acknowledging the higher virtues of self-sacrifice. **1892** [see CRITICIST]. **1936** A. J. AYER *Lang., Truth & Logic* i. 23 Some positivists have adopted the heroic course of saying that these general propositions are indeed pieces of nonsense. **1958** G. J. WARNOCK *Eng. Philos. since 1900* 58 The Positivists were also engaged in linguistic analysis, officially without metaphysical ambitions; theirs was supposed to be the two-sided task, on the one hand of exposing the muddles of metaphysicians, and on the other hand of humbly clarifying the vocabularies of the scientist and the mathematician. **1971** J. H. HADDOX *Antonio Caso* 86 To the cowardly positivists frightened by the idea of 'mental anarchy' I say, no.

b. *attrib.* or as *adj.*

1858 *Brit. Q. Rev.* LVI. 440 The smallest vestry..would be quite sufficient to hold all the Positivist worshippers in the largest county of England. **1880** *Chr. World* 8 Jan. 25/1 The Positivist creed, stated in its best form, is that man's chief end is to glorify man and to enjoy himself now. **1889** HUXLEY in *19th Cent.* Feb. 191 The incongruous mixture of bad science with eviscerated papistry, out of which Comte manufactured the Positivist religion. **1900** W. L. COURTNEY *Idea of Trag.* 61 Auguste Comte, the Positivist philosopher, added to the list of sciences the most modern of all—sociology. **1934** *Philos. of Sci.* I. 16 In using the formal mode of expression the pseudo-problem 'What is a thing?' disappears, and therewith the opposition between the positivist and the realist answer disappears. **1943** W. G. HARDY *Some Semantic Theories* in *Cornell Univ. Abstr. of Theses* 56 Bridgman's operational theory of meaning amounts to a positivist demand that meanings be assigned according to the operations performed. **1960** J. O. URMSON *Conc. Encycl. Western Philos.* 324/1 In the twenties of the twentieth century Hume's positivist arguments were revived and strengthened. **1969** F. HALLIDAY in Cockburn & Blackburn *Student Power* 298 A bid to introduce IQ tests was made, but this positivist attack was repelled when students occupied the main building of the campus for two months. **1974** *Nature* 16 Aug. 609/1 Most philosophers of science, at least within the dominant positivist schools, take the Comtean view, of physics as the paradigmatic science. **1977** *New Yorker* 9 May 145/1, I suspect that we remain, in our hearts, medieval people: our assumptions are Aristotelian, not positivist or existentialist.

2. a. An adherent or supporter of legal positivism (see POSITIVISM 3).

1927 M. R. COHEN in *Proc. 6th Internat. Congr. Philos., 1926* 469 It is therefore easy..to show that other positivists are full of hidden or unavowed natural law. **1971** *Mod. Law Rev.* XXXIV. VI. 631 Most positivists, and certainly Hart, would argue that legal rules can never be spelled out in terms of all the situations to which they might be relevant. **1973** I. M. SINCLAIR *Vienna Convention on Law of Treaties* v. 112 They [*sc.* the school of jurists led by Bynkershoek, Moser and Martens] did not wholly deny the role of natural law in filling gaps, but their emphasis on the constituent elements of positive international law gave them the title 'positivists'.

b. *attrib.* or as *adj.*

1923 R. POUND *Interpretations of Legal Hist.* iv. 78 The positivist ethnological interpretation [of legal history]..was given a comparative basis. **1944** W. FRIEDMANN *Legal Theory* xv. 135 The number and variety of positivist legal theories is as great as that of the sciences. **1963** S. I. SHUMAN *Legal Positivism* i. 11 Friedmann who speaks..of 'Austin's positivist system'. **1976** *Howard Jrnl.* XV. I. 51 The change from a classical to a positivist approach to criminology.. took the form of a belief in the biological and social causation of crime and the necessity for early prevention.

positivistic (pɒzɪtɪ'vɪstɪk), *a.* [f. prec. + -IC.] **1.** Of or pertaining to positivists; of the nature of positivism.

1875 *N. Amer. Rev.* CXX. 280 A positivistic, yet anti-Comtian spirit. **1898** *Contemp. Rev.* Sept. 421 Roberty is professedly a naturalistic, or positivistic, sociologist. **1927** M. R. COHEN in *Proc. 6th Internat. Congr. Philos., 1926* 471 The same system of legal rights and duties may be expressible in positivistic or in idealistic language. **1935** [see *anti-metaphysical* s.v. ANTI-[1] 3 b and c]. **1938** B. F. SKINNER *Bahavior of Organisms* ii. 44 So far as scientific method is concerned, the system set up..is positivistic. It confines itself to description rather than explanation. **1956** J. O. URMSON *Philos. Analysis* viii. 119 It might be thought that such a characterization of positivistic analysis embodied an illegitimate nostalgia. **1961** M. ČAPEK *Philos. Impact Contemp. Physics* xvi. 297 A similar positivistic motive is conspicuously present in the minds of physicists dealing with the problems of determinism in quantum mechanics. **1975** *Sci. Amer.* Feb. 101/1 Thinkers of a mystical turn of mind..consider it the..most fundamental of all metaphysical questions... Those of a positivistic, pragmatic turn of mind consider it trivial.

2. Characterized by positiveness. *rare.*

1893 F. ADAMS *New Egypt* 36 There was abundance of pretty red herrings here to draw themselves across the trail of a direct and positivistic pursuit of the real game.

positi'vistically, *adv.* [f. POSITIVISTIC *a.* + -LY[2].] In a positivistic manner.

1890 W. JAMES *Princ. Psychol.* I. vi. 177 Nevertheless, this formula which is so unobjectionable if taken vaguely, positivistically, or scientifically, as a mere empirical law of concomitance..tumbles to pieces entirely if we assume to represent anything more intimate or ultimate by it. **1935** *Mind* XLIV. 128 The difference between the subjective and the objective may be interpreted positivistically by the category of degree which rules the newer physics. **1946** R. G. COLLINGWOOD *Idea of Hist.* IV. ii. 182 The facts are positivistically conceived as isolated from each other. **1976** *Times Lit. Suppl.* 17 Dec. 1590/5 It is just such ordinariness that has so often been lost from psychology in its efforts to deal positivistically with isolated variables.

positivity (pɒzɪ'tɪvɪtɪ). [f. POSITIVE + -ITY, cf. F. *positivité, -eté.*] The quality, character, or fact of being POSITIVE in various senses; positiveness.

1659 H. HICKMAN (*title*) A Justification of the Fathers and Schoolmen: Shewing That they are not Selfe-condemned for denying the Positivity of Sin. **1678** GALE *Crt. Gentiles* III. 8 We grant..that sin is not a mere nothing, but has some kind of logic positivitie or notional entitie, so far as to render it capable of being the terme of a proposition. **1741** WATTS *Improv. Mind* (1801) 75 Courage and positivity are never more necessary than on such an occasion. **1842** *Fraser's Mag.* XXVI. 737 The most positive man I ever met with... There is positivity in his dark face, large eyebrows, stern features. **1858** MAYNE *Expos. Lex.*, *Positivity*, term for the state of a body which manifests the phænomena of positive electricity. **1871** MORLEY *Crit. Misc.* Ser. I. *Carlyle* 219 That truly free and adequate positivity which accepts all things as parts of a natural or historic order.

†**b.** A positive or real thing as opposed to a mere negation; an actuality. *Obs. rare.*

1681 *Relig. Clerici* 36 That Immaterial, Infinite and the like, were negatives indeed in words,..but properly and in themselves they were absolute positivities.

positon ('pɒzɪtɒn). *Physics.* [f. POSIT(IVE *a.* and *sb.* + -ON[1].] †**a.** Proposed as an alternative name for the proton. *Obs. rare*$^{-1}$. **b.** [a. G.

positon (P. Gruner 1935, in *Helvetica Physica Acta* VIII. 326.) = POSITRON.

1928 [see NEGATON]. **1937** *Chem. Abstr.* XXXI. 2917/1 The following names are proposed for corpuscles of mass approx. 10^{-27} g. (present names in parentheses): nulliton (neutrino), positon (positron), negaton (electron). **1938**, etc. [see NEGATON]. **1952** B. ROSSI *High-Energy Particles* i. 2 Positive electrons (or positons) are identical to negatons, except for their opposite sign of charge. **1956** *Nuclear Physics* I. 72 The word 'electron' applies to particles with an elementary charge of either sign. When it is desirable to emphasize the sign of the charge, the words 'positon' and 'negaton' are used. Thus the illogical phrase 'electron-positron pair' is replaced by 'electron pair', or..'positon-negaton pair'. **1960** *Ibid.* XVI. 683 (*heading*) Branching ratios of K capture to positon emission in non-unique first forbidden $2^- \rightarrow 2^+$ beta transitions. **1974** *Ibid.* A. CXXXII. 230 (*heading*) Electron capture to positon decay ratios and second-class currents.

positor ('pɒzɪtə(r)). [a. L. *positor* one who places, agent-n. from *pōnĕre*, *posit-um* to place.]

†**1.** ? An examiner: = POSER[1] 1. *Obs.*

1557 *Baxter-bks. St. Andrews* (1903) 10 James hay.. examinyt be dauid mylis positor, thomas steyne [etc.].

†**2.** One who gives security for another. *Obs. rare.*

1584 J. NEWBERY *Let. from Goa* in Hakluyt *Voy.* (1589) 211 Both the money and goods should be deliuered into the positors hands.

†**3.** One who posits, maintains, or affirms. *Obs.*

1598 FLORIO, *Positore*, a positor, an affirmer.

4. *Med.* (See quot.) Also called *repositor*.

1890 BILLINGS *Med. Dict.*, *Uterine positor*, instrument used to correct displacement of the uterus. **1895** in *Syd. Soc. Lex.*

positron ('pɒzɪtrɒn). *Physics.* [f. POSI(TIVE *a.* and *sb.* + ELEC)TRON[2].] The anti-particle of the ordinary (negative) electron, having the same mass and a numerically equal but positive charge.

1933 C. D. ANDERSON in *Science* 5 May 432/2 Experiments have been carried out which gave conclusive evidence that positrons are ejected from lead by the γ-radiation of ThC". [*Note*] The contraction positron is here used to denote the free positive electron. **1933** *Times* 9 Dec. 9/3 The unit of heavy hydrogen, the deuteron, or deuton, as it has been called, bids fair to rival in interest its recently found cousins, the neutron and positron. **1934** *Discovery* May 123/2 It appears from investigations that the earth is being bombarded by streams of positrons and electrons of very high energy. **1946** *Ann. Reg. 1945* 356 The Bethe carbon cycle (in which carbon acts as a catalyst for the conversion of hydrogen into helium and positrons). **1958** *Spectator* 13 June 778/3 When the electron and the positron meet they annihilate each other. **1960** CHALMERS & QUARRELL *Physical Examination of Metals* (ed. 2) xvi. 765 Positrons, sometimes called 'positive electrons', result from proton–neutron transitions. **1968** C. G. KUPER *Introd. Theory Superconductivity* xii. 193 The conduction electrons and holes of semiconductor theory are closely analogous to the electrons and positrons of the Dirac theory. **1974** G. REECE tr. *Hund's Hist. Quantum Theory* xv. 203 Not until the experimental observation of the positron..was the Dirac 'hole' theory generally believed.

Hence **posi'tronic** *a.*

1948 I. ASIMOV in *Astounding Sci. Fiction* Feb. 44/2 If the field were a trifle stronger, the robot would never reach the technician concerned, since its positronic brain would collapse under gamma radiations—and then we would be out one expensive and hard-to-replace robot. **1957** —— *Naked Sun* (1958) ii. 32 He knew a positronic brain..nestled in the hollow of the skull. He knew that Daniel's 'thoughts' were only short-lived positronic currents. **1968** *Punch* 23 Oct. 592/2 Barbarella (Jane Fonda), a respected astronaut in 40,000 AD, is being briefed for her mission to find an important scientist from Earth who has disappeared among the planets with his great invention the positronic ray. **1974** I. ASIMOV in George & Humphries *Robots are Coming* 5 My positronic robot stories.

positronium (pɒzɪ'trəʊnɪəm). *Nuclear Physics.* [f. prec. + -IUM.] A short-lived neutral system, analogous to an atom, consisting of a positron and a negative electron bound together.

1945 A. E. RUARK in *Physical Rev.* LXVIII. 278/1 In 1937 I conceived the idea that an unstable atom composed of a positron and a negative electron may exist in quantities sufficient for spectroscopic detection. The name positronium is suggested. The spectrum of positronium would have lines at wave-lengths twice as great as the hydrogen lines. **1957** *New Scientist* 26 Dec. 28/3 When positronium is in free (i.e., near-vacuum) conditions, spectroscopic measurement shows that it has a lifetime of about one and a half ten-millionths of a second. **1966** *McGraw-Hill Encycl. Sci. & Technol.* X. 524/1 Positronium is of particular interest because it is the two-body system to which quantum electrodynamics is applicable, and its study has served as an important confirmation of the theory of quantum electrodynamics. **1970** [see HYDROGENIC *a.* b]. **1976** *Science* 19 Nov. 826/3 If ψ were a bound system of two spin ½ particles, there could be excited levels with a spectrum similar to that of positronium (the system of electron and positron, bound to each other by the electromagnetic force).

‖**positum** ('pɒzɪtəm). [L., pa. pple. of *pōnĕre* to place, put, lay. In med. Logic, that which is laid down as a basis for reasoning, the thing supposed, assumed, or taken for granted.] The thing laid down. *lit.* or *fig.*

1730 FIELDING *Temple Beau* v. xiv, *Young P*... Suppose the *Positum* be—The woman is but half a-sleep; will it follow, *Ergo*, she is awake? *Sir Av.* The *Positum* is £20,000—ergo—I will swear any thing.

†'**positure.** *Obs.* [a. obs. F. *positure* (1547 in Godef.) ad. L. *positūra* position, posture, f. *pōnere*, *posit-* to place: cf. also POSTURE.]

1. The fact of being placed; placing, position, or situation; place, locality.

1600 HOLLAND *Livy* xxxv. xxviii. 904 To view and consider the situation and positure of the place on all sides. **1610** HEALEY *St. Aug. Citie of God* IV. xxiii. (1620) 173 A temple that should haue excelled all the rest in height of positure and magnificence of fabricke. **1658** W. BURTON *Itin. Anton.* 177 A station of very uncertain positure. **1685** H. MORE *Paralip. Prophet.* xxxii. 288 Area equal to the others, and of the like positure with the others.

2. = POSTURE *sb.* 1.

1614 RALEIGH *Hist. World* II. v. iii. §16. 451 Idols,..in such habit and positure as if they were fighting. **1625** T. GODWIN *Moses & Aaron* (1655) 63 The positure of the cherubims was such that their faces were each towards the other. **1674** PETTY *Disc. Dupl. Proportion* 122 Supposing every Body to have a Figure or Positure of its own, out of which it may be disturbed by External Force. **1706** PHILLIPS, *Positure*, Disposition, as The Positure of the Soul.

b. *Astrol.* Relative position (of the planets, etc.).

1610 HOLLAND *Camden's Brit.* I. 116 Hee attributeth all to the climate, and positure of the heavens. **1616-61** HOLYDAY *Persius* 331 The astrologers observe in that point the positure of the cœlestial constellations, that is the state of the planets amongst themselves, as also the fixed stars. **1800** COLERIDGE *Piccolom.* IV. i, Ere The scheme, and most auspicious positure Parts o'er my head.

3. A law, or principle laid down; = POSITION *sb.* 2. *rare.*

1624 J. HEWES *Surv. Eng. Tongue* A iv, The Rules and Positures of Grammar. *Ibid.* B j, The chiefe end of our Rules and Positures.

posnet ('pɒsnɪt). Now *arch.* and *dial.* Forms: 4 posti-, possy-, 4-5 poste-, 4-6 posse-, 5 poscenet, 4-6 posnette, 5-6 pos(s)enett, postnet, 5-7 possnet, posnett, 7 posnit, poss-, postnett; 4- posnet. [ME. *possenet* a. OF. *poçonnet*, *pocenet*, dim. of *poçon* pot, vase, cup. Hence W. *posnedd*.]

A small metal pot or vessel for boiling, having a handle and three feet.

1327 *Durham Acc. Rolls* (Surtees) 114, j postinet pro hostill. **1330** *Acc. Exch. K.R.* 24/18 Item vn possenet qe poise x. li. merche de mesme la merche. **1353** *Will John de Penreth* in *Test. Karleol.* 2 Cum una olla enea et parvam posnet. **1382** WYCLIF *2 Chron.* xxxv. 13 Forsothe pesible hoostis thei seetheden in posnettis, and cawdrones, and pottis. ? *c* **1390** *Form of Cury* in Warner *Antiq. Culin.* (1791) 14 Do the flesh therwith in a possynet, and styre it. **1410** *E.E. Wills* (1882) 17 Also a postnet þat y lent hym. *c* **1420** *Liber Cocorum* (1862) 10 Welle alle togedur in a posnet; In service forthe þou schalt hit sett. **1442** *Nottingham Rec.* II. 178 Unum poscenet, pretii xvj d. **1459-60** *Durham Acc. Rolls* (Surtees) 89 Item iij possenettez et iij Chawfers, etc. **1612** in *Antiquary* Jan. (1906) 28 In the Kytchin..sixe brasse potts, eighte kettles, four postnetts. *a* **1648** DIGBY *Closet Open.* (1669) 136 In a Possnet set it upon a clear lighted Char-coal-fire. **1710** STEELE *Tatler* No. 245 ¶2 A Silver Posnet to butter Eggs. **1863** MRS. TOOGOOD *Yorks. Dial.*, Set the posnet on to boil the potatoes. **1891** *Scribner's Mag.* Sept. 345/2 The great number of pewter plates,..teapots, posnets and porringers still found in old homes in New England.

posnjakite ('pɒznjəkaɪt). *Min.* [ad. Russ. *poznyakit* (Komkov & Nefedov 1967, in *Zap. Vsesoyuz. Min. Obshch.* XCVI. 58): see quot. 1967 and -ITE[1].] A hydrated basic copper sulphate, $Cu_4(SO_4)(OH)_6{\cdot}H_2O$, that occurs as dark blue crystals similar to langite.

1967 *Mineral Abstr.* XVIII. 285/2 A new mineral..is named posnjakite in honour of E. W. Posnjak (1888–1949), well known for work on copper sulphates. **1970** *Mineral. Mag.* XXXVII. 740 (*heading*) Posnjakite from Cornwall. *Ibid.*, While examining and surveying the disused workings of the Drakewalls mine, Gunnislake, we have found specimens of the recently described species posnjakite in old stopes..above the deep adit level.

poso'logic, *a.* *rare*$^{-0}$. = next.

1864 WEBSTER, *Posologic*, pertaining to posology.

posological (pɒsə'lɒdʒɪkəl), *a.* [f. F. *posologique* (in medical sense) (see POSOLOGY) + -AL[1].] Pertaining to posology (in either sense).

1. *Med.* Pertaining to quantities or doses of drugs.

1803 *Med. Jrnl.* X. 278 The Editor has..given a copious index, a reference to the cases, a posological table, and other helps. **1876** BARTHOLOW *Mat. Med.* (1879) 110 It must be given in larger doses than the posological tables authorize.

2. (In Bentham's use.) Pertaining to the science of quantity; mathematical.

1816 BENTHAM *Chrestom.* Wks. 1843 VIII. 85 Division of Somatics into Posological (Pososcopic) Somatics, and Poiological (Poioscopic) Somatics. **1831** —— *Memorandum-Bk.* ibid. XI. 72 Abstraction is—1. Posological: 2. Logical.

posologist (pəʊ'sɒlədʒɪst). *nonce-wd.* [f. next: see -IST.] One who compounds doses.

1831 SYD. SMITH *Wks.* (1850) 568 Subtle compounder, fraudulent posologist, did not you order me a drachm of this medicine?

posology (pəʊ'sɒlədʒɪ). [ad. F. *posologie* (in medical sense), f. Gr. πόσος how much + -LOGY.]

1. That department of medicine which relates to the quantities or doses in which drugs should be administered.

1823 CRABB *Technol. Dict.*, *Posology*, that part of the art of medicine which teaches the right administration of doses. **1898** *Rev. Brit. Pharm.* 57 Index and Posology.

2. Used by Bentham for the science of quantity, i.e. mathematics.

1811-31 BENTHAM *Logic* App., Wks. 1843 VIII. 287/2 By the Greek-sprung word *posology*, the science of quantity, may, it is believed, and if so, now for the first time, not inappositely be distinguished. **1816** —— *Chrestomathia*, ibid. VIII. 85 For an equivalent to Posological Somatics, may be employed the single-worded appellative Posology. **1861** *Sat. Rev.* 22 June 645 We hope that the distinguished editors..will not attempt..to substitute in their respective universities this meagre Posology for the somewhat undefined, but less empty abstractions which have hitherto passed under the name of Logic.

‖**pospolite** (pɒ'spɒlɪteɪ). [Polish *po'spolite* adj. neuter, 'general, universal', as sb. = *pospolite ruszenie* general levy.] The Polish militia, consisting of the nobility and gentry summoned to serve for a limited time.

1697 *Lond. Gaz.* No. 3333/2 That the King should call together the *Pospolite* that is, all the Gentry of the Kingdom. **1763** *Hist. Europe* in *Ann. Reg.* 46/1 Their military force consists chiefly, in the *Pospolite*, that is, the whole body of the gentry. **1822** *Edin. Rev.* XXXVII. 493 They continued ..to regard the *Pospolite*..as the impenetrable bulwark of the Commonwealth. *a* **1859** DE QUINCEY *Posth. Wks.* (1891) I. 58 But this unwieldy *pospolite* was far from meeting David's secret anxieties.

poss (pɒs), *v.* Now only *dial.* [Origin uncertain.

Possibly identical with **puss*, pa. t. *puste* (a. F. *pousser* to PUSH) which appears *c* 1300; the later form *push* appears rarely in 15th c., but is common after 1525. The form *posshen* in Langland may be either *push* or *poss*; but the vowel-change of *u* to *o* is not easily explained. The senses also coincide only partially with those of *push*; and, in sense 3, *poss* has much of the aspect of an onomatopœic formation. Perhaps it was an onomatopœic modification of the French vb.]

1. *trans.* To drive or thrust with a forcible or violent impact; to dash or toss with a blow or stroke; to knock: often expressing the action of waves on a boat, etc. Also *fig.*

c **1374** CHAUCER *Troylus* I. 415 þus possed to and fro. Al sterles with Inne a bot am I Middis the see, betwixe wyndis too. **1377** LANGL. *P. Pl.* B. Prol. 151 A cat..pleyde wiþ hem perilouslych and possed hem aboute. *c* **1385** CHAUCER *L.G.W.* 2420 (*Phillis*) The se..possith hym now vp now doun. *c* **1400** *Rom. Rose* 4479 Thus am I possed up and doun With dool, thought, and confusioun. *c* **1402** LYDG. *Compl. Bl. Knt.* 236 And thus, betwixe twayne, I possed am, and all forcast in payne. *c* **1430** *Pilgr. Lyf Manhode* IV. ix. (1869) 181 In my bal day and niht I haue more ioye þan in al my fader tauhte me..; I posse it, j handele it, j pleye þer with. **1513** DOUGLAS *Æneis* XII. v. 203 Chorineus..Syne with hys kne him possit with sic ane plat, That on the erd he spaldit him all flat. **1825** BROCKETT *N.C. Gloss.* s.v., 'Aw poss'd him ower heed'.

†**b.** To push, shove, move by pressure. *Obs.*

c **1440** *Promp. Parv.* 410/2 Posson, or schowe forthe (*K.* pocyn, *P.* pressyn, or showen), *pello*. Posson, presson, or schowe togedur, *trudo*.

2. *absol.* or *intr.* To thrust, to drive; to thrust or push *at* something with a weapon.

a **1300** *K. Horn* 1011 (Camb. MS.) þe se bigan to posse Riȝt in to Westernesse. *c* **1400** *Langland's P. Pl.* A. VII. 96 Mi plouh-pote schal be my pyk and posshen [*v.r.* to posse] atte Rootes. **1513** DOUGLAS *Æneis* X. xii. 116 Possand at hym wyth his stalwart speyr.

3. *trans.* To pound, beat down flat, squash; *spec.* to beat or stamp (clothes, etc.) in water with a heavy pestle-like instrument, or to trample or stamp them with the feet, in the process of washing.

1611 COTGR., *Mettre à la flac*, to..squash, clap, or posse downe. **1615** MARKHAM *Eng. Housew.* II. v. (1668) 138 Take it forth, posse it, rinse it, and hang it up. **1677** THORESBY *Corr.* (ed. Hunter) II. 433 Nasty women possing clothes with their feet. **1825** BROCKETT *N. C. Gloss.* (1829) s.v., To 'poss clothes' in what is called a Poss-tub. **1828** *Craven Gloss.* (ed. 2), *Poss*, to dash, to shake anything violently in the water.

†**4.** *intr.* To splash, or tramp with splashing, in wet mud or water. *Obs.*

1575 *Gamm. Gurton* I. iv, To dyg and delue in water, myre and claye, Sossing and possing in the durte. **1576** FLEMING *Panopl. Epist.* 306 This it is to posse in puddles.

Hence (*dial.*) **poss** *sb.*[1], an act of 'possing', a thrust or knock; *comb.* **poss-kit**, **poss-tub**, a large tub in which clothes are 'possed' with a **poss-stick** in washing. '**possing** *vbl. sb.*, also attrib. *possing-tub*.

1611 COTGR., *Culassé*,..that hath receiued an arse-posse, or fall on the arse. **1821** *Blackw. Mag.* VIII. 432 The good old fashion..When double-girded 'possing tubs' were made. **1825** Poss-tub [see 3]. **1855** ROBINSON *Whitby Gloss.*, *Poss-kit*, a large tub or barrel in which linen is 'possed' in hot water. The operation of possing..is performed by means of a staff with a thick knob at the immersed end, and a cross piece for a handle at the top. **1863** MRS. TOOGOOD *Yorksh. Dial.*, Give the linen a good poss in the peggy tub. **1894** *Westm. Gaz.* 26 Sept. 1/3 That her intelligence would have soared far beyond the pounding of dirty linen in 'poss' tubs.

†**poss**, *sb.*² *Obs. rare*⁻¹.

[? = post: cf. POST *sb.*¹ 1 quot. 1340; or ? = POSSE.]

a **1550** *Image Ipocr.* I. in *Skelton's Wks.* (1843) II. 419/1 With staves and crosses, With pillers and posses, With standers and banners, Without good life or manners.

poss (pɒs), *a.* Also **pos.** Colloq. abbrev. POSSIBLE *a.* Chiefly in phrases *if poss, as soon as poss.*

1886–96 in Farmer & Henley *Slang* (1902) V. 260/1 While the public morals-shaper Thinks of writing to the paper To upset the show, if pos. **1909** *Punch* 3 Mar. 160/1 People tell me I ought to have all the amusement *poss* to prevent me from brooding, so I'm making an effort. **1916** A. HUXLEY *Let.* 30 June (1969) 104 Think over this and let us have it as soon as poss. **1959** P. BULL *I know Face* i. 27, I only came back with four ambitions in mind: to learn a little about acting (if poss.), [etc.]. **1972** D. FRANCIS *Smokescreen* ii. 30 'Why the rush?' 'Well, I don't know, darling. She just said, could we come as soon as poss.'

possable, obs. Sc. form of POSSIBLE.

posse (ˈpɒsiː). Also 8 **possee**. [a. L. *posse* to be able, have power, avail, in med.L. as sb., power, armed force (1246 in Du Cange); in scholastic terminology, potentiality, capability of being. In sense 1 short for POSSE COMITATUS.]

I. 1. *Law.* = POSSE COMITATUS.

[**1314–15** *Rolls of Parlt.* I. 327/1 Mandetur Majori et Balliuis [Oxonie] quod insequantur cum toto posse suo transgressores.] **1691** *New Discov. Old Intreague* vi, Who early for the Princes Cause began: The *Posse* rais'd. **1720** MRS. MANLEY *Power of Love* (1741) 281 When Mrs. Ursula was gone down in order to raise the *Possee*, if there should be occasion. **1781** S. PETERS *Hist. Connecticut* 108 The polite New-Yorkers..sent the posse of Albany to eject the possessors. **1901** *Westm. Gaz.* 5 Dec. 11/1 A pitched battle was fought..at Rockhill, Missouri, between the Sheriff's posse and the miners on strike.

b. A force armed with legal authority; a body (of constables).

1697 DAMPIER *Voy.* (1699) 483 They need not have sent an armed *Posse* for me. **1753** *Scots Mag.* June 305/2 A posse of constables..appeared. **1800** COLQUHOUN *Comm. Thames* iii. 93 A posse of Marine Police Officers receiving information... On attempting a search [etc.]. **1884** *Graphic* 11 Oct. 371/1 An extra posse of policemen.

c. *transf.* A 'force', a strong band, company, or assemblage (of persons, animals, or things).

1645 FULLER *Good Th. in Bad T.* (1841) 13 All the *posse* of hell cannot violently eject me. **1678** BUTLER *Hud.* III. ii. 1166 No longer able To raise your Posse of the Rabble. **1697** COLLIER *Ess. Mor. Subj.* II. (1703) 85 Then you have raised the whole posse of mechanism. **1728** SWIFT *Let. Publisher Dublin Wkly. Jrnl.* 14 Sept., With these two single considerations I outbalanced the whole posse of articles that weighed just now against me. **1841** MISS SEDGWICK *Lett. Abr.* II. 71 Found her flying from a posse of cock-turkeys. **1892** STEVENSON *Across the Plains* vii, I ran..and beheld a posse of silent people escorting a cart.

II. From use in scholastic Latin.

‖**2.** The fact or state of being possible; possibility, potentiality (opposed to *esse*): esp. in phr. *in posse* opposed to *in esse*.

1583 GREENE *Mamillia* Wks. (Grosart) II. 229 She which is vicious in her youth may be vertuous in her age: I graunt indeede it may be, but it is hard to bring the *posse* into *esse*. **1592** —— *Def. Conny Catch.* Wks. (Grosart) XI. 44 To strippe him of all that his purse had in Esse, or his credyt in Posse. **1659** BAXTER *Key Cath.* xxxix. 282 If the question [of sin] be only of the posse, and not of the act. **1756** GRAY *Lett.* Wks. 1825 II. 193 You are not however to imagine that my illness is *in esse*; no, it is only *in posse*. **1877** READE *Woman Hater* v, They existed, as the school-men used to say, *in posse*, but not *in esse*.

‖**posse comitatus** (ˈpɒsiː kɒmɪˈteɪtəs, -tjʊs). [med. (Anglo) L., force of the county: see prec. and COUNTY.] 'The force of the county'; the body of men above the age of fifteen in a county (exclusive of peers, clergymen, and infirm persons), whom the sheriff may summon or 'raise' to repress a riot or for other purposes; also, a body of men actually so raised and commanded by the sheriff. (Also abbreviated to *posse*: see prec. 1).

[**1285** *2nd Stat. Westminster* c. 39 Assumpto secum posse comitatus sui est [vicecomes] in propria persona.] *a* **1626** BACON (J.), The posse comitatus, the power of the whole county, is legally committed unto him. **1628** in *Crt. & Times Chas. I* (1848) I. 453 The high sheriff of Dorsetshire had order to raise *possé comitatus*, to attack those unfencers of Gillingham forest. **1765** BLACKSTONE *Comm.* I. ix. 343 For keeping the peace and pursuing felons, he may command all the people of his county to attend him; which is called the *posse comitatus*, or power of the county. **1840** BARHAM *Ingol. Leg.* Ser. I. *Grey Dolphin*, Sheriff..of Kent..with his posse comitatus.

b. *transf.* = POSSE 1 c.

1819 BYRON *Juan* I. clxiv, With him retired his *posse comitatus*. **1860** TRISTRAM *Gt. Sahara* x. 160 On a house-top were a bevy of nut-brown maids, who..had forgotten to veil their faces. They were consequently pelted with stones by some of the *posse comitatus*, and retired in confusion.

†**po'ssede**, *v. Obs.* Also 5 **poosseede**, 6 **possed**, **posseade**, 6–7 *Sc.* **posseid**. [= F. *posséder* to possess; but this form of the Fr. vb. is not cited before the 16th c., the 15th c. form being *possider*, ad. L. *possidēre*.] = POSSESS *v.* 1, 2, 5.

a **1400–50** *Alexander* 2841 In pese & in pacience possede at he miȝt. **1426** LYDG. in *Pol. Poems* (Rolls) II. 132 Septure and crowne that he may in dede, As he hath right, in peas to possede. *c* **1430** —— *Min. Poems* (Percy Soc.) 244 Tresours of fayrye which she doth poosseede. **1484** CAXTON *Fables of Æsop* (1899) 41 The vertues [powers] which he posseded in his yong age. **1556** *Aurelio & Isab.* (1608) K v, He that loves not him selfe dothe posseade no goode. **1571** *Satir. Poems Reform.* xxvii. 70 Reid how þai forcitt the Britonis folk to flitt, And ȝitt posseidis that peoples proprietie. *a* **1641** BP. MOUNTAGU *Acts & Mon.* iii. (1642) 203 That God transport him beyond his assise, and wholly possede him.

possedie, *Sc. Obs.*: see POWSOWDY.

possess (pəˈzɛs), *v.* [a. OF. *possess-ier*, *-er* (1269 in Godef.) f. L. *possess-*, ppl. stem of *possidēre* to possess, perh. through influence of F. *possesseur* POSSESSOR, etc., the regular OF. repr. of *possidēre* being *posseer*, *-eir*, *-eoir*.]

I. Radical senses.

†**1. a.** *trans.* Of a person or body of persons: To hold, occupy (a place or territory); to reside or be stationed in; to inhabit (with or without ownership). *Obs.* (or merged in 2).

1483 CAXTON *Gold. Leg.* 431 b/2 How now..we possessen pesably our royame without ony werre. **1535** COVERDALE *Josh.* xxiv. 4, I gaue..Esau mount Seir to possesse. **1560** DAUS tr. *Sleidane's Comm.* 47 b, Colledges..were fyrst founded for the pore, but now for the most part they possesse them, which have enough besides. **1667** MILTON *P.L.* IV. 431 Dominion giv'n Over all other Creatures that possesse Earth, Aire, and Sea. **1684** BUNYAN *Pilgr.* II. 2 The City of Destruction, a populous place, but possessed with a very ill conditioned, and idle sort of People. **1713** STEELE *Guard.* No. 6 ⁋3 The whole shire is now possessed by gentlemen, who owe Sir Harry a part of Education.

absol. or *intr.* **1611** SHAKS. *Cymb.* I. v. 48 Let instructions enter Where Folly now possesses.

†**b.** Of a thing: To occupy, take up (a space or region); to be situated at, on, or in. *Obs.* (exc. with mixture of other senses).

1604 E. G[RIMSTONE] *D'Acosta's Hist. Indies* III. xiii. 159 The waves of the South sea, runne 30 leagues, and the other 70 are possessed with the billowes and waves of the North sea. *c* **1620** A. HUME *Brit. Tongue* (1865) 22 The acute [accent]..may possesse the last syllab:..the penult:..the antepenult:..and the fourth also from the end. **1712** J. JAMES tr. *Le Blond's Gardening* 205 The Addition of four Foot will be filled up and possessed by the Walls and Clay-work. **1755** B. MARTIN *Mag. Arts & Sc.* v. 22 The Solar System, in which you see the Sun possesses nearly the central Point. [**1850** ROSSETTI *Blessed Damozel* xi, When those bells Possessed the mid-day air.]

†**c.** Of a disease, etc.: To affect, infect. *Obs.*

1612 WOODALL *Surg. Mate* Wks. (1653) 90 If the palsie possesse the opposite part. **1678** PHILLIPS, *Achor*, a disease possessing the hairy scalp. **1699** BENTLEY *Phal.* 266 An error ..which has possess'd the Copies of this Play.

†**d.** To take up the attention or thoughts of; to occupy, engross. *Obs.*

1653 WALTON *Angler* vi. 134 To enjoy the former pleasures that there possest him. **1692** LOCKE *Toleration* iv. Wks. 1727 III. 464 Affairs of State which wholly possess them when grown up. **1719** DE FOE *Crusoe* (1840) II. i. 8 The..innocent amusements..which before entirely possessed me, were nothing to me.

2. a. To hold as property; to have belonging to one, as wealth or material objects; to own.

1500–20 DUNBAR *Poems* xi. 34 Thocht all this warld thow did posseid, Nocht eftir death thow sall possess. **1526** TINDALE *Luke* xii. 15 For no mannes life stondeth in the haboundaunce of the thynges which he possesseth. **1685** LADY RUSSELL *Lett.* (1819) I. 68, I was too rich in possessions whilst I possessed him. **1785** PALEY *Mor. Philos.* III. I. iv. 102 It is..'consistent with the will of God', or 'right', that I should possess that share which these regulations assign me. **1881** FROUDE *Short Stud.* (1883) IV. II. ii. 187 He could not give to others what he did not himself possess.

b. *Law.* To have possession of, as distinct from ownership; see POSSESSION 1 b.

1888 POLLOCK & WRIGHT *Possession in Com. Law* 2 The person entitled to possess is generally (though not always) the owner.

c. To have as a faculty, adjunct, attribute, quality, condition, etc. (Often meaning no more than the simple *have*.)

1576 FLEMING *Panopl. Epist.* 115 The residue of my lyfe will I lead in Rhodes, where I may possesse peace and quietnes. **1662** GERBIER *Princ.* 40 The Quarries possess more Stone, and the Woods more Timber than a Banquet Room. **1744** HARRIS *Three Treat.* III. I. (1765) 134 No Animal possesses its Faculties in vain. **1838** THIRLWALL *Greece* xxv. III. 367 Notwithstanding the ample means of information which they possest, great ignorance and many erroneous opinions prevailed. **1840** H. AINSWORTH *Tower of London* (1864) 235 'His folly has destroyed the fairest chance that ever man possessed', observed the bishop. **1860** TYNDALL *Glac.* I. vi. 46 The former may possess many times the intensity of the latter. **1889** *Times* 27 Sept. 5/4 An elaborate hidated survey, which possesses a peculiar value from its reference to the Domesday survey.

d. *fig.* in emphatic sense.

1685–6 LADY RUSSELL *Lett.* (1819) I. 81 My weakness is invincible, which makes me, as you phrase it,..possess past calamities. **1852** ROBERTSON *Serm.* Ser. III. xviii. 236 The writhings of a heart that has been made to possess its own iniquities.

e. (after F. *posséder.*) To have knowledge of or acquaintance with; to be master of, or conversant with (a language, etc.).

[Cf. quot. 1674 s.v. POSSESSOR c.]

1852 THACKERAY *Esmond* I. iii, Harry..possessed the two languages of French and English very well. **1865** M. ARNOLD *Ess. Crit.* i. 45 Every critic should try and possess one great literature, at least, besides his own.

3. a. To take possession of, seize, take; to come into possession of, obtain, gain, win. *arch.*

1526 TINDALE *Luke* xxi. 19 With your pacience possesse your soules. [**1611** BIBLE *ibid.*, In your patience possesse ye your soules. **1382** WYCLIF, ȝe schulen welde ȝoure soulis. **1881** *R.V.* ye shall win your souls]. **1586** A. DAY *Eng. Secretary* I. (1625) 45 A company of rats vpon a sudden possest his house. **1590** SPENSER *F.Q.* III. iii. 51 How to effect so hard an enterprize, And to possesse the purpose they desird. **1610** SHAKS. *Temp.* III. ii. 100 There thou maist braine him, Hauing first seiz'd his Bookes... Remember First to possesse his Bookes. **1649** CROMWELL in Carlyle *Lett. & Sp.* (1871) II. 227 Upon Thursday the One-and-thirtieth, I possessed a Castle called Kilkenny. **1764** FOOTE *Mayor of G.* I. Wks. 1799 I. 165 Turning down a narrow lane ..in order to possess a pig's stye, that we might take the gallows in flank. **1877** L. MORRIS *Epic Hades* II. 118 The strong brute forces..leap on him, and seize him and possess His life.

b. *spec.* To have sexual intercourse with (a woman). Also *absol.*

This sense, suggested in private correspondence in 1969 by Professor W. Empson, may not have been intended by the writers themselves in some of the examples that follow. —R.W.B.

1592 KYD *Sp. Trag.* I. i. 10 By duteous seruice and deseruing love, In secret I possest a worthy dame. **1600** SHAKS. *A.Y.L.* IV. i. 144 Now tell me how long you would haue her, after you haue possest her? **1680** ROCHESTER *Poems* 87 Mad to possess himself he threw, On the defenceless lovely Maid! *c* **1707** T. D'URFEY *Wit & Mirth* (1719) IV. 332 And tho' I let Loobies Oft finger my Bubbies: Who think when they kiss me, That they shall possess me. **1749** SMOLLETT tr. *Le Sage's Gil Blas* II. v. ii. 197 The four banditti expressed an equal desire of possessing the lady who had fallen into their hands, and talked of casting lots for her. **1876** *Romance of Lust* IV. 39 Her delight and surprise at finding the dear Egerton had equally desired to possess her. **1922** JOYCE *Ulysses* 72 Possess her once take the starch out of her. *Ibid.* 491 All the male brutes that have possessed her. **1961** *Partisan Rev.* XXVIII. 648 A conflict having to do with father-murder and the wish to possess the father's woman.

4. To keep, maintain (oneself, one's mind or soul) *in* a state or condition (of patience, quiet, etc.); often in allusion to Luke xxi. 19 (the proper sense being misunderstood: see quot. 1526 in 3). Also (without *in*), to maintain control over, to keep calm or steady (cf. *self-possessed*, *self-possession*).

1643 EVELYN *Mem.* 2 May, Resolving to possess myselfe in some quiet,..I built..a study,..at Wotton. **1654** BRAMHALL *Just Vind.* ii. (1661) 27 All Christians..are obliged to passiue obedience, to possess their souls in patience. **1711** STEELE *Spect.* No. 137 ⁋1 Uneasy Persons, who cannot possess their own Minds. **1749** CHESTERF. *Lett.* (1775) II. 168 A man who does not possess himself enough to bear disagreeable things, without visible marks of anger.. is at the mercy of every artful knave. **1890** MRS. LYNN LINTON in *Chamb. Jrnl.* 4 Oct. 625/1 Every man worthy of the name of man should know how to possess his soul—bearing with patience those things which energy cannot change.

5. a. Of a demon or spirit (usually evil): To occupy and dominate, control, or actuate.

1596 BP. W. BARLOW *Three Serm.* i. 23 The Hogges without leaue [of God the Father]..he coulde not possesse. **1601** SHAKS. *Twel. N.* III. iv. 95 If all the diuels of hell be drawne in little, and Legion himselfe possest him, yet Ile speake to him. **1704** HEARNE *Duct. Hist.* (1714) I. 181 Some are of Opinion that Abel slew the very same Serpent the Devil had formerly possessed. **1850** ROBERTSON *Serm.* Ser. III. ix. 113 The spirit which possessed him must be, they thought, divine. **1902** W. AXON in *Trans. Roy. Soc. Lit.* Ser. II. XXIII. 99 Belfagor undertook to possess a rich lady, and not to be exorcised, save by Matteo.

b. *pass.* (usually const. *with*, in mod. use also *by*, formerly *of*). See also POSSESSED 2.

1526 TINDALE *Matt.* iv. 24 Them that were possessed with devils. —— *Luke* viii. 36 He that was possessed of the devyll. **1612** DEKKER *If it be not good* Wks. 1873 III. 309, I am possest with the diuell and cannot sleepe. **1651** HOBBES *Leviath.* I. viii. 38 Thought by the Jewes to be possessed either with a good, or evill spirit. **1727** DE FOE *Syst. Magic* I. ii. (1840) 53 A set of people who were not possessed by, but rather, as it may be called, are possessed of the devil. **1829** W. IRVING *Conq. Granada* I. iv, One of those fanatic infidels possessed of the devil. **1854** MILMAN *Lat. Chr.* III. vii., II. 155 A woman eats a lettuce without making the sign of the cross. She is possessed by a devil.

6. Of an idea, a mental condition, or the like: To take or have hold of (a person); to hold, dominate, actuate; to affect or influence strongly and persistently. (Formerly also of bodily conditions.)

1591 SHAKS. *Two Gent.* III. i. 206 My eares are stopt, and cannot hear good newes, So much of bad already hath possest them. **1610** —— *Temp.* II. i. 199 What a strange drowsines possesses them? **1646** SIR T. BROWNE *Pseud. Ep.* I. xi. 44 Which Tuscan superstition seasing upon Rome hath since possessed all Europe. **1722** DE FOE *Plague* (1754) 3 This [suspicion] possess'd the Heads of the People very much. *a* **1814** *Gonzanga* I. i. in *New Brit. Theatre* III. 102 What can possess this young lord to be out of his bed at this hour? **1880** L. WALLACE *Ben-Hur* 31 In a mood very different from that which now possesses them.

For the passive with *with*: see 9 d.

II. Causal uses; = cause to possess.

†**7.** With *in*: To put in possession (esp. legal possession) of (lands, estates, etc.); to settle or establish in. Rarely without *in*. *Obs.*

c **1465** *Pol. Rel. & L. Poems* (1866) 4 Edwardeus Dai gracia Sithe god hathe..posseside þe in thi right Thoue hime honour with al thi myght. **1576** *Reg. Privy Council Scot.* II. 518 To enter and possess the said Nicoll in his saidis landis. **1606** G. W[OODCOCKE] *Hist. Ivstine* VIII. 39 He deposed Arimba from his kingly seat, and possessed Alexander therein. **1687** in *Magd. Coll. & Jas. II* (O.H.S.) 178 Hee thought the Bishop illegally possest. **1708** in *Phenix* II. 241 Then the Just..shall be possess'd in the fulness of their Glory.

8. a. With *of* (also †*with*): To endow with, put in possession of; to bestow (something specified) upon, give (something) to. Now *rare* or *Obs.* exc. as in b or c.

1549 *Compl. Scot.* i. 19 He possessis vthir pure pepil.. vitht the samyn reches. **1606** SHAKS. *Ant. & Cl.* III. xi. 21, I will possesse you of that ship and Treasure. **1644** MILTON *Educ.* Wks. (1847) 98/2 By possessing our souls of true virtue. **1658** *Whole Duty Man* vii. §7 By possessing his heart with this virtue of contentedness. **1789** JEFFERSON *Autobiog.* Wks. 1859 III. 45, I have thought it better to possess him immediately of the paper. **1784** SIR J. REYNOLDS *Disc.* xii. (1876) 55 It is better to possess the model with the attitude you require.

b. *refl.* To take possession *of*, take for oneself, make one's own; = 3.

1593 SHAKS. *Lucr.* Argt. 4 Lucius Tarquinius..had possessed himselfe of the kingdome. **1621** LADY M. WROTH *Urania* 546 Then possest he himselfe with his armes. **1709** STEELE *Tatler* No. 35 ¶11 My Lord Orkney received Orders to possess himself of Mortagne. **1885** SIR J. BACON in *Law Times Rep.* LII. 570/1 All that the plaintiffs did was to possess themselves..of the securities. **1888** POLLOCK & WRIGHT *Possession in Com. Law* 2 No plain man would hesitate to say that a thief possesses himself of the goods carried away.

c. *pass.* To be in possession *of*; to be endowed with; to possess (sense 2). ***possessed of*** or ***with***, having possession of, possessing.

1495 *Trevisa's Barth. De P.R.* XV. xlii (W. de W.), Creta was somtyme possessyd wyth [*Bodl. MS.* ihiȝt wiþ] an hundryd noble cytees. **1593** SHAKS. *Rich. II*, II. i. 162 The plate...and moueables, Whereof our Vncle Gaunt did stand possest. *c* **1600** —— *Sonn.* xxix, Featur'd like him, like him with friends possest. **1617** MORYSON *Itin.* II. 137 They found the Spaniards possessed of the Towne. **1791** COWPER *Iliad* III. 108 He..of her And her's possest, shall bear them safe away. **1809–10** COLERIDGE *Friend* (1865) 122 Every human being possessed of reason. **1863** GLADSTONE *Glean.* (1879) II. 197 The active vigorous English workman, possessed of all his limbs. **1888** POLLOCK & WRIGHT *Possession in Com. Law* 36 The King is not unfrequently spoken of as being seised or possessed of the crown.

9. a. With *with*: To cause to be possessed by (a feeling, idea, or the like: see 6); to imbue, inspire, permeate, affect strongly or permanently *with*; to cause to feel or entertain.

1597 MORLEY *Introd. Mus.* 180 If therefore you will compose in this kind, you must possesse yourselfe with an amorus humour. **1642** *Observ. his Maj. Answ. to City Lond. Petit.* 8 To possesse the people with a fancy against that. **1670** G. H. *Hist. Cardinals* I. I. 25 What Devil possesses them with such wicked designs? **1710** ABP. KING *Let. to Swift* 16 Sept., To possess my lord Shrewsbury and Mr. Harley with the reasonableness of the affair. **1863** GLADSTONE *Financ. Statem.* 14, I wish that I could possess the Committee with the impression..of the deep and vital importance of the subject.

b. With clause: To imbue with the notion, to persuade, convince.

1607 MIDDLETON *Michælm. Term.* I. i. 50 *Easy.* You've easily possess'd me, I am free. **1712** ARBUTHNOT *John Bull* III. iii, He had possessed the lady, that he was the only man in the world of a sound, pure and untainted Constitution. **1747** SARAH FIELDING *Lett. David Simple* I. 278 From the time I went away, my Mother had constantly possessed her, that I did so. **1828** *Craven Gloss.* (ed. 2), *Possess*, to persuade, to inform, to convince.

†**c.** Without const.: To influence the opinion of; to prepossess. *Obs.*

1591 RALEIGH *Last Fight Rev.* (Arb.) 15 Hoping to possesse the ignorant multitude by anticipating and forerunning false reports. **1605** BACON *Adv. Learn.* II. xxiii. §6 Here is observed, that in all causes the first tale possesseth much. **1681** *Trial S. Colledge* 22 *Colledge.* Mr. Attorney, I should not interrupt you, if I were not afraid this was spoken to possess the Jury.

d. *pass.* (coinciding, and in early instances often identical, with the passive of sense 6).

1576 GASCOIGNE *Steele Gl.* (Arb.) 56 A poets brayne, possest with layes of loue. *a* **1652** BROME *Queen & Concubine* II. viii, My Lord, I do presume I am unwelcome, Because you are possess'd I never lov'd you. **1661** WOOD *Life* (O.H.S.) I. 395 Being possest with a deep melancholy,..he fell, as 'twere, downe right mad. **1769** ROBERTSON *Chas. V* III. VII. 43 Henry, possessed..with an high idea of his own power and importance. **1853** MAURICE *Proph. & Kings* i. 7 He had all his life been possessed with one great conviction.

†**e.** With inverted construction: To create a possessing idea, etc., in (the mind); to infuse. *Obs. rare.*

1606 G. W[OODCOCKE] *Hist. Ivstine* IX. 42 She..possest such a superstitious toy in the heads of the people, that she made them yearly sanctifie a day and keep it holy in remembrance of him.

10. To put in possession *of*, furnish *with* (knowledge or information); to instruct *in*; to inform, acquaint, to give to understand *that*. *Obs.* or *arch.*

1596 SHAKS. *Merch. V.* IV. i. 35, I haue possest your grace of what I purpose. **1601** —— *Twel. N.* II. iii. 150 Possesse vs, possesse vs, tell vs something of him. **1607** G. WILKINS *Mis. Enf. Marriage* I. B ij b, I haue possest you with this businesse Maister Doctor. **1634** SIR T. HERBERT *Trav.* 123 If hee had any more to possesse the King, he should first acquaint him, and consequently have an answer. **1666** WOOD *Life* 3 Feb. (O.H.S.) II. 72 He beforehand possest the Vicecancellor that I would help him. **1682** *News fr. France* 9 They are very careful to possess all people in such secret methods as they dare venture on. **1771–90** FRANKLIN *Autobiog.* (1856) 91 Our debates possessed me so fully of the subject, that I wrote and printed an anonymous pamphlet on it. **1863** COWDEN CLARKE *Shaks. Char.* viii. 201 Contriving to possess her fellow-conspirators..of all the particulars of his behaviour.

possessable: see POSSESSIBLE.

possessed, possest (pəˈzɛst), *ppl. a.* [f. POSSESS *v.* + -ED[1].]

1. a. Occupied; held as property; taken possession of, seized, assumed; see POSSESS 1–3. *rare.*

1595 DANIEL *Civ. Wars* IV. xxxiii, No other crosse,..But this that toucht thy now possessed hold. **1616** J. LANE *Cont. Sqr's T.* IX. 23 Her possessd greatnes, vpstart vsurpation. **1691** tr. *Emilianne's Frauds Rom. Monks* (ed. 3) 367, I was astonish'd to see the Liberty this young Gentleman took with his Possessed.

b. Kept under control, kept calm or steady, composed. *rare*[−0]. (Implied in *possessedness*: see below. Cf. POSSESS 4 and SELF-POSSESSED.)

2. a. Inhabited and controlled by a demon or spirit; demoniac, lunatic, mad, crazy.

1534 TINDALE *Matt.* viii. 33 What had fortuned vnto the possessed of the devyls. **1577** HANMER *Anc. Eccl. Hist.* (1619) 141 By Nature possessed and frantike. **1632** LITHGOW *Trav.* I. 33, I saw an old..Frier coniuring the Diuell out of a possessed woman. **1727** GAY *Fables* I. iii. 7 She saw the Nurse, like one possess'd, With wringing hands, and sobbing breast. **1861** THORNBURY *Turner* (1862) II. 227 There were some strange weird clouds introduced, which had something demoniacal and possessed about them.

b. *absol.* A demoniac, a madman; mad folk.

1657 SPARROW *Bk. Com. Prayer* (1661) 249 After this the Catechumens, the possessed and the penitents are dismissed. **1854** MILMAN *Lat. Chr.* III. vii. (1864) II. 155 A poor peasant receives the possessed into his house.

c. See POSSESS *v.* 8 c.

d. ***like all possessed***: with great force, vehemence, energy or spirit. *U.S.*

1833 S. SMITH *Life & Writings J. Downing* 209 [He] struck his fists together like all possessed. **1916** E. PORTER *Just David* 280 He danced and laughed and clapped his hands,..an' carried on like all possessed.

3. (In instrumental combinations.) Dominated, controlled, strongly and permanently affected.

c **1620** *Convert Soul* in Farr *S.P. Jas. I* (1848) 89 Peace, catiffe body, earth possest. **1711** *Brit. Apollo* III. No. 135. 2/2 My..wo-possessed Heart.

Hence **poˈssessedness** (see 1 b), self-possession.

1676 W. ROW *Contn. Blair's Autobiog.* x. (1848) 265 A man of most calm temper with great possessedness and stayedness of Spirit.

†**poˈssessiant.** *Obs.* [a. OF. *possessant* sb., prop. pres. pple. of *possesser* to POSSESS.] A possessor.

c **1400** *Destr. Troy* 2627 Ewsebius,..Had all the crafte & conyng in his clere wit, þat pictagoras the pure god possessiant was of.

poˈssessible, *a. rare.* Also **-able.** [f. POSSESS *v.* + -IBLE.] Capable of being possessed.

1874 W. JONES *New Test. Illustr.* 278 Knowledge of divine things possessible by man. **1897** ANNE PAGE *Afternoon Ride* 9 The young beauty seemed to dissolve into more possessable mortality.

poˈssessing, *vbl. sb.* [f. POSSESS *v.* + -ING[1].] The action of the verb POSSESS; possession.

1580 SIDNEY *Ps.* XXXVII. xix, The righteous minds Shall haue the land in their possessing. **1709** *Brit. Apollo* II. No. 37. 3/1 We're cheated of the Blessing, When arriv'd at full Possessing. **17..** POPE *Imit. Swift* I Parson, these things in thy possessing Are better than the Bishop's blessing.

poˈssessing, *ppl. a.* [f. as prec. + -ING[2].]

1. Having something as a possession; *spec.* having material possessions.

1839 BAILEY *Festus* xxviii. (1852) 472 Seraphs and saints, and all-possessing souls, Which minister unto the universe. **1884** M. ARNOLD in *Pall Mall G.* I Dec. 6/1 There is in the West the possessing, the spending, and the enjoying class. **1897** *Daily News* 6 Sept. 5/6 Only representatives of the privileged and possessing classes had been convoked.

2. Inhabiting and actuating a person, as a demon or spirit; dominating as an influence.

1838–9 HALLAM *Hist. Lit.* II. II. iv. §40. 145 The political creed which actuates at present, as a possessing spirit, the great mass of the civilised world. **1902** W. M. ALEXANDER *Demonic Possession in N.T.* v. 172 Nor did He..ascribe to possessing spirits moral influence over the possessed.

Hence **poˈssessingness.**

1882 GURNEY *Tertium Quid* (1887) II. 70 We may note the degree of possessingness and permanence in the artistic impression.

poˈssessingly, *adv.* [f. POSSESSING *ppl. a.* + -LY[2].] So as to possess or captivate (one); fascinatingly.

1927 *Observer* 11 Dec. 10/4 Miss Jenkins's diary..is nothing worth in itself, but how possessingly dramatised by the identity of her correspondent!

possession (pəˈzɛʃən), *sb.* Forms: 4– **possession**; also 4–6 **-ioun, -ione, -yon,** (4 **-ioune,** 5 **-yone,** 6 **-yowne**); (4 **possescyon,** 5 **possesioon, poscescon,** 7 **pocessyon,** 6 **-ion**). [a. OF. *possessiun, -on* (12th c. in Hatz.-Darm.), ad. L. *possessiōn-em* seizing, occupation, n. of action f. *possidēre*: see POSSEDE, POSSESS.]

1. a. The action or fact of possessing, or condition of being possessed (see POSSESS 1, 2); the holding or having something (material or immaterial) as one's own, or in one's control; actual holding or occupancy, as distinct from ownership.

a **1340** HAMPOLE *Psalter* xv. 6 Merkis of my possession. **1390** GOWER *Conf.* I. 276 And yaf therto possessioun Of lordschipe and of worldes good. **1473** *Rolls of Parlt.* VI. 91/2 To the Patronage or Possession of the Church of Prescote. **1526** *Pilgr. Perf.* (W. de W. 1531) 150 But also haue sure felynge, tastynge, possessyon, and fruicyon of his goodnes. **1605** VERSTEGAN *Dec. Intell.* iv. (1628) 91 To obtaine possessions of the whole Ile. **1690** LOCKE *Treat. Govt.* II. v. §38 The same measures governed the Possession of Land too. **1813** MAR. EDGEWORTH *Patron.* xviii, I am not one of those *exigeante* mothers who expect always to have possession of a son's arm. **1875** JOWETT *Plato* (ed. 2) I. 185 Philosophy is the possession of knowledge.

b. *Law.* The visible possibility of exercising over a thing such control as attaches to lawful ownership (but which may also exist apart from lawful ownership); the detention or enjoyment of a thing by a person himself or by another in his name; the relation of a person to a thing over which he may at his pleasure exercise such control as the character of the thing admits, to the exclusion of other persons; *esp.* the having of such exclusive control over land, in early instances sometimes used in the technical sense of SEISIN.

In the Roman Law, 'possession is usually said to consist of two elements—physical control and intention to possess; but in English law the latter element does not assume the same prominence as, in the shape of the *animus domini*, it has been thought to assume in Roman law... The general rule of English law is that exclusive physical control gives legal possession, unless the apparent possessor holds only as servant or bailiff on behalf of another' (J. M. Lightwood in *Encycl. Laws Eng.* (1898) X. 229). Primarily, the term denotes a state of fact, but this fact carries with it legal advantages, and so is the source of rights. If the state of fact could always be ascertained with certainty, and if it always produced the normal legal effects, the subject of possession would present little difficulty; but it is frequently uncertain to whom the actual control of a thing is to be attributed, and, when this question is settled, the law may credit the advantages of possession to some person other than the apparent possessor... Hence arises the distinction between *actual* and *legal* possession. Actual possession denotes the state of fact; but the person to whom are credited the advantages of possession has the legal possession, whether he is the actual possessor or no. Legal possession, when not accompanied by possession in fact, is known as 'possession in law'. (*Ibid.* 228–9.) See this article; also (*inter alia*), *Essay on Possession in the Common Law* by F. Pollock and R. S. Wright, 1888, *Treatise on Possession of Land* by John M. Lightwood, 1894.

1535 *Act 27 Hen. VIII*, c. 10 Every such person..shall hensforth stond and be seasid demed and adjuged in lawfull season estate and possession of and in the same. **1559** *Rec. Monast. Kinloss* (1872) 151 We chairg..you..to pas to the ..landis..And ther gif him stait and possessioun be thak and raip as wse is. **1579** *Expos. Termes Law* 158 Possession is said two wayes, eyther actuall possession, or possession in law. Actuall possession is when a man entreth in deede into landes or tenements to him discended or otherwise. Possession in lawe, is when landes or tenements are discended to a man, and he hath not as yet really, actually, and in deede entred into them. **1706** PHILLIPS, *Unity of Possession*, is when the Possession, or Profit is united with the Property. Thus, if the Lord purchase the Tenancy held by Heriot-Service, then the Heriot is extinct by Unity of Possession, i.e. because the Seignory or Lordship and the Tenancy are now in one Man's Possession. **1766** BLACKSTONE *Comm.* II. xxv. 389 First then of property in possession absolute; which is where a man hath, solely and exclusively, the right, and also the occupation, of any moveable chattels. **1818** CRUISE *Digest* (ed. 2) III. 330 The first degree of title is the bare possession, or actual occupation of the estate, without any apparent right, or any pretence of right, to hold and continue such possession. **1837** BARON PARKE in Meeson & Welsby *Rep.* II. 331 Ownership may be proved by proof of possession, and that can be shown only by acts of enjoyment of the land itself. **1861** J. KENT *Comm. Amer. Law* (1873) II. xxxix. 493 Though the vendee acquires a right of property by the contract of sale, he does not acquire a right of possession of the goods until he pays or tenders the price. **1885** W. A. HUNTER *Roman Law* 209 Possession is the occupation of anything with the intention of exercising the rights of ownership in respect of it. **1887** LD. FITZGERALD in *Law Rep. 12 App. Ca.* 556 By possession is meant possession of that character of which the thing is capable. **1888** POLLOCK & WRIGHT *Possession in Com. Law* 1 As the name of Possession is..one of the most important in our books, so it is one of the most ambiguous. Its legal senses (for they are many) overlap the popular sense. *Ibid.* 26 The following elements are quite distinct in conception..i. physical control, detention, or de facto possession...ii. legal possession, the state of being a possessor in the eye of the law...iii. Right to possess or to have legal possession. *Ibid.* 27 Right to possess, when separated from possession, is often called 'constructive possession'. *Ibid.* 58 A servant in charge of his master's property, or a person having the use of anything by the mere licence of the owner..generally has not possession. **1894** J. M. LIGHTWOOD *Possession of Land* 2 Possession which is recognized by the law..is known as civil possession. The actual possession may be held by another on behalf of the civil possessor—by his servant or tenant, for example—and here the civil possession is still based on actual possession. **1898** —— in *Encycl. Laws Eng.* X. 232 A person holding land as a tenant for years is denied the special form of legal possession known as seisin. The English law, however, differing herein from the Roman law, does not refuse legal possession to bailees. *Ibid.* 236 In the case of goods..the mere right to possession is sometimes described as 'constructive possession', and is allowed the advantages of actual possession.

c. Phr. ***in possession***: said (*a*) of a thing, actually possessed or held; often with possessive, *in* (one's) *possession*; (*b*) of a person, usually ***in possession of***, actually possessing, holding, or occupying something. ***chose in possession***: see CHOSE. ***man in possession***, a duly authorized person who is placed in charge of chattels (furniture or the like) upon which there is a warrant for distress. ***to take possession of*** († ***take in possession***): to take for one's own or into one's control, to seize; see also TAKE *v.* 71. Conversely, ***to give possession***.

[**1308–9** *Rolls of Parlt.* I. 274/2 Mettre le dit nich' en corporele possession del avauntdit provendre.] *c* **1330** R. BRUNNE *Chron.* (1810) 239 Þe londes þat þei haue now in possessioun. **1390** GOWER *Conf.* I. 26 Cirus..tok it in possessioun. ? *a* **1400** *Morte Arth.* 2608 Of Alexandere and Aufrike, and alle þa owte landes, I am in possessione, and plenerly sessede. **1560** DAUS tr. *Sleidane's Comm.* 13 He hathe Millan nowe in possession. **1576** FLEMING *Panopl. Epist.* 417 The Queenes maiestie, nowe in possession of the English empire. **1603** OWEN *Pembrokeshire* (1892) 85 Any lande..beinge in the pocession of the Churche. **1771** *Junius Lett.* lxvii. (1820) 333 He loses the very property of which he thought he had gotten possession. **1849** *Illustr. London News* 22 Dec. 406/1 Dan Sheedey and five or six men come to tumble my house; they wanted me to give possession. I said that I would not. **1860** TYNDALL *Glac.* I. xxiv. 169, I had now the thermometers in my possession. **1886** B. L. FARJEON *Three Times Tried* I. 13/2, I..left Captain Bellwood in possession of the field. **1888** POLLOCK & WRIGHT *Possession in Com. Law* 119 When a man is away from home his household effects do not cease to be in his possession. **1897** *Daily News* 10 Dec. 3/2 (*heading*) The 'Man in Possession'. *Ibid.*, Defendant's man during the nine days only visited the house once a day and did not remain in possession. **1898** J. M. LIGHTWOOD in *Encycl. Laws Eng.* X. 237 *In possession*: as applied to an estate or interest, these words usually mean that the right is immediate, and not in reversion, remainder, or expectancy.

d. Prov. ***possession is nine*** (formerly ***eleven***) ***points*** (also ***parts***) ***of the law***: see POINT *sb.*[1] A. 12.

1650 B. *Discolliminium* 13 Possession may be 11 points of the Law. **1712** ARBUTHNOT *John Bull* IV. iii, Possession.. would make it much surer. They say 'it is eleven points of the Law!' **1813** MAR. EDGEWORTH *Patron.* (1833) III. xli. 130 Possession.. being nine parts of the law.

e. *Mining* (Derbyshire): see quots.

1653 MANLOVE *Lead Mines* (E.D.S.) 9 A cross and hole a good possession is, But for three dayes. **1681** HOUGHTON *Rara Avis* Gloss. (E.D.S.), *Possession*, the right to a *meer* of ground, which miners enjoy, by having *stows* upon that ground; and it is taken generally for the *stows* themselves; for it is the *stows* that give possession. **1802** MAWE *Min. Derbysh.* Gloss. (E.D.S.), *Stowces*, pieces of wood of particular forms and constructions placed together, by which the possession of mines is marked.

f. *U.S. colloq.* ellipt. for 'possession of narcotic drugs'.

1970 *N.Y. Times Mag.* 15 Feb. 19/1 John E. Ingersoll.. suggested that the penalty for simple possession for personal use be reduced to that of a misdemeanor. **1973** R. L. SIMON *Big Fix* x. 71 What's a few years in the cooler for possession. **1977** D. E. WESTLAKE *Enough!* i. 21 Her freak got busted on possession and went away for an extended rest.

†**2.** The action of seizing or possessing oneself *of*; capture: see POSSESS *v.* 3. *Obs. rare.*

1748 *Anson's Voy.* II. ix. 231 Our future projects..with a view to the possession of this celebrated galeon.

3. *concr.* That which is possessed or held as property; (with *a*, etc.) a thing possessed, a piece of property, something that belongs to one; *pl.* belongings, property, wealth.

a **1340** HAMPOLE *Psalter* ii. 8, I sall gif til þe genge þin heritage: & þi possession terms of erth. **1388** WYCLIF *Matt.* xix. 22 The ȝong man..wente awei sorewful, for he hadde many possessiouns. [**1429** *Act 8 Hen. VI*, c. 9 Ceux qi gardent par force lour possessions en ascuns terres on tenementz.] **1432–50** tr. *Higden* (Rolls) IV. 155 Thei occupiede the londes and possessiones of mony other peple. **1538** STARKEY *England* I. iii. 77 Such an idul sort, spendyng theyr possessyonys. **1610** HOLLAND *Camden's Brit.* (1637) 729 Masham, which was the possession of the Scropes of Masham. **1841** JAMES *Brigand* ii, Beauty is a woman's best possession till she be old. **1875** JOWETT *Plato* (ed. 2) I. 434 One of your possessions, an ox or an ass, for example.

b. In Scotland, A small farm: see quot. 1805.

1799 J. ROBERTSON *Agric. Perth* 511 The lanes include between them the breadth of two possessions only. **1805** FORSYTH *Beauties Scotl.* I. 519 [The farms] run from £30 to £1200, of £30, they are called *possessions*.

4. A territory subject to a sovereign ruler or state; now chiefly applied to the foreign dominions of an independent country.

1818 J. ADOLPHUS (*title*) The Political State of the British Empire; containing a General View of the Domestic and Foreign Possessions of the Crown. **1850** HT. MARTINEAU *Hist. Peace* II. v. xii. 377 Canada became a British possession in 1763. **1888** *Pall Mall G.* 13 Sept. 4/1 British New Guinea has very rapidly developed from the position of a protectorate into that of a possession. **1905** *Whitaker's Almanack* 512 The British Possessions in North America include the whole of the northern part of that continent excepting Alaska [etc.].

5. The fact of a demon possessing a person; the fact of being possessed by a demon or spirit (see POSSESS *v.* 5). Also in *Psychics*: see quot. 1903.

1590 SHAKS. *Com. Err.* v. i. 44 How long hath this possession held the man? **1651** HOBBES *Leviath.* I. viii. 38 Neither Moses, nor Abraham pretended to Prophecy by possession of a Spirit. **1689** C. MATHER (*title*) Memorable Providences relating to Witchcrafts and Possessions. **1746** WESLEY *Princ. Methodist* 51 If you were to suppose John Haydon..was not mad, but under a temporary Possession. **1846** TRENCH *Mirac.* v. (1862) 158 The same malady they did in some cases attribute to an evil spirit, and in others not; thus showing that the malady and possession were not identical in their eyes. **1903** MYERS *Hum. Personality* I. Gloss., *Possession*, a developed form of motor automatism, in which the automatist's own personality disappears for the time, while there is a more or less complete substitution of personality, writing or speech being given by another spirit through the entranced organism.

6. The action of an idea or feeling possessing a person (see POSSESS *v.* 6); *transf.* an idea or impulse that holds or affects one strongly; †a dominating conviction, prepossession (*obs.*).

1621 T. WILLIAMSON tr. *Goulart's Wise Vieillard* 76, I come now to speake of anger and choller, which commonly keepe possession in old men. **1728** VANBR. & CIB. *Prov. Husb.* I. i. 3, I have a strong Possession, that with this five hundred, I shall win five thousand. **1826** *New Monthly Mag.* XVI. 508 Old ideas still keep possession of old heads. **1867** LONGF. in *Life* (1891) III. 103, I have worked steadily on it, for it took hold of me,—a kind of possession.

7. The action or condition of keeping (oneself, one's mind, etc.) under control (see POSSESS *v.* 4). *rare* exc. in the compound SELF-POSSESSION.

a **1703** BURKITT *On N.T.* Luke xxi. 19 As faith gives us the possession of Christ, so patience gives us the possession of ourselves. **1710** STEELE *Tatler* No. 168 ¶4 To acquire such a Degree of Assurance, as never to lose the Possession of themselves in publick or private. **1802** MAR. EDGEWORTH *Moral T.* (1816) I. 237, I have need of that calm possession of my understanding,..necessary to convince yours. **1871** R. ELLIS *Catullus* xxxv. 12 She, if only report the truth bely not, Doats, as hardly within her own possession.

8. *attrib.* and *Comb.* **possession-man** = *man in possession*: see 1 c; **possession order**, an order made by a court of law directing that possession of a property be given to the owner.

1772 *Doc. Hist. N. York* (1851) IV. 803 The Weak pretence of Hutts hastily Built on small Spotts of Ground which they Term possession Houses. **1871** TYLOR *Prim. Cult.* xiv. II. 115 The opinion that the possession-theory is ..modelled on the ordinary theory of the soul acting on the body. **1891** *Daily News* 1 Jan. 2/6 He and 'a possession man' went with a warrant of execution to levy on the defendant's goods for a debt and costs of over 7*l.* **1897** *Ibid.* 28 Apr. 6/5 He was on drinking terms with every process-server and possession-man about the place. **1971** *Times* 24 June 3/8 Southwark council was granted possession orders against nine families squatting in eight properties in the borough in a High Court action. **1973** *Times* 11 Dec. 8/4 He granted a possession order to the GLC. The women took over the house..three weeks ago. **1977** F. BRANSTON *Up & Coming Man* ii. 17 Their large Edwardian semi-detached (three mortgages, possession orders pending on two of them).

†**possession**, *v. Obs. rare*[−1]. [f. prec. sb.] *trans.* To furnish with possessions.

1602 CAREW *Cornwall* 132 b, Sundry more Gentlemen this little Hundred possesseth and possessioneth.

po'ssessional, *a. rare.* [f. as prec. + -AL[1]; cf. *professional.*] Pertaining to possession; having possessions or property; propertied. Hence **po'ssessionalism**, the doctrine or principle of individual possession or private property; **po'ssessionalist**, one who holds this doctrine.

1872 W. R. GREG *Enigmas of Life* (1873) 48 Union among all possessional classes. **1882** OGILVIE, *Possessional*, same as *possessive*. **1903** G. R. HALL *Human Evolution* viii. 191 Some actualities of Possessionalism. *Ibid.* ix. 216 In Lower Possessionalism chattel-slavery begins to die out, industry takes on the form of serfdom... In Higher Possessionalism we find the social form of Capitalism. *Ibid.* xii. 291 Before long only two parties will exist, the Possessionalists and the Socialists... The honestly Possessionalist Cabinet.

po'ssessionary, *a.* and *sb.* [f. POSSESSION *sb.* + -ARY[1]. So obs. F. *possessionnaire* adj. (1539).]

A. *adj.* Constituted by possession; having, pertaining, or relating to possession.

1658–9 *Burton's Diary* (1828) III. 224, I do not say this, to abate any thing of his Highness's authority... He hath a possessionary right, which, I am sure, gives him power enough to call Parliaments. *Ibid.* 590 If he is but possessionary Protector, he is then hereditary and not subject to any boundings. **1739** F. BLOMEFIELD *Hist. Thetford* 52 Athelstane, Abbot of Ramsey, had a House in Theford, for then he had a Possessionary Writ, directed to the Burghers of Theford. **1809** E. S. BARRETT *Setting Sun* II. 115 The horde of possessionary and reversionary moles may deprecate an inquiry.

†**B.** *sb.* One who is in possession; = POSSESSIONER b.

1532 FRITH *Mirror* (1829) 273 It proveth our bishops, abbots, and spiritual possessionaries, double thieves and murderers, as concerning the body.

†**po'ssessionate**, *a. Obs.* [ad. med.L. *possessiōnāt-us* (in Du Cange); see POSSESSION *sb.* and -ATE[2].] Having possessions or endowments: cf. POSSESSIONER b.

1432–50 tr. *Higden, Harl. Contin.* (Rolls) VIII. 459 We wolde have destroyede..the kynge, bischopps, chanons, monkes possessionate, and alle men of churche, the frers excepte oonly. **1899** TREVELYAN *Eng. Age Wyclif* 151 The disendowment of the 'possessionate' clergy.

possessioned (-'ɛʃənd), *a.* [f. POSSESSION *sb.* + -ED[2], after F. *possessionné.*] Endowed with or holding possessions.

1794 J. GIFFORD *Reign Louis XVI* 551 That satisfaction should be given to the princes possessioned in Alsace. **1837** CARLYLE *Fr. Rev.* II. v. v, This of the Possessioned Princes, '*Princes Possessionés*', is bandied from Court to Court... The Kaiser and his Possessioned Princes will too evidently come and take compensation.

po'ssessioner. *Obs.* exc. *Hist.* [f. POSSESSION *sb.* + -ER[2].] One who is in possession, or holds possession, *of* something; a holder, occupier; a proprietor, owner; an owner of possessions.

1382 WYCLIF *Acts* iv. 34 How many euere weren possescioners [Vulg. *possessores*] of feeldis or howsis. *c* **1450** *Godstow Reg.* 89 They called before them the lordis and possessioners and tenauntis of the mylles. **1544** tr. *Littleton's Tenures* (1574) 67 b, Possessioners of a warde of the bodye of a childe within age. **1563** BONNER in Strype *Ann. Ref.* (1709) I. xxxiv. 341 Not being lawful Bishop of Winchester, but an usurper, intruder, and unlawful possessioner thereof. **1681** CHETHAM *Angler's Vade-m.* xl. §25 (1689) 299 The Owners or Possessioners thereof. **1807** BRITTON *Beauties Eng.* IX. *Linc.* 571 The sum of 1000*l.* borrowed of the king, lords, and great possessioners, till it could be levied by the commissioners of sewers. **1884** *Q. Rev.* Jan. 107 The grasping spirit of the new lords and possessioners.

b. *spec.* A member of a religious order having possessions or endowments; an endowed clergyman or ecclesiastic.

1377 LANGL. *P. Pl.* B. v. 144 Þise possessioneres preche and depraue freres. *c* **1380** WYCLIF *Sel. Wks.* I. 212 Popis and bishopis and prestis and þese new religiouse possessioneris and beggeris. **1496** *Dives & Paup.* (W. de W.) IV. vi. 167/2 Yf he be a relygyous possessyoner endewed by temporal goodes, he may releue them. **1545** BRINKLOW *Compl.* xxiv. (1874) 69 But the son of man hath not where to rest his head. Such possessionars were the bysshops of the prymatyue church! **1855** MILMAN *Lat. Chr.* VI. XIII. vi. 125 It was the villeins demanding manumission from their lords, not Wycliffe's disciples despoiling possessioners.

po'ssessionist. *nonce-wd.* [f. POSSESSION *sb.* + -IST.] One who professes to be possessed by a demon, one who holds a theory of such possession.

1726 DE FOE *Hist. Devil* II. xi. (1840) 352 The mock possessions and infernal accomplishments, which most of the possessionists of this age pretend to.

po'ssessionless, *a.* [f. as prec. + -LESS.] Destitute of possessions. Hence **po'ssessionlessness**.

1894 MRS. DYAN *All in a Man's K.* (1899) 235 How thankful you must be now that you are so possessionless. **1898** A. P. ATTERBURY tr. *Sombart's Socialism & Social Movement in 19th Cent.* i. 9 Troops of possessionless workers..herded in great undertakings. **1905** *Nation* (N.Y.) 27 Apr. 334/3 Those who shared and defended his superb possessionlessness. **1938** DYLAN THOMAS *Let.* Dec. (1966) 211 We are..completely possessionless. **1944** I. ORIGO *Diary* 24 June in *War in Val d'Orcia* (1947) 224 It is a very odd feeling to be entirely possessionless. **1969** G. LEFF *Hist. & Social Theory* ix. 174 As defined by Marxism a class is a group which stands in a certain relation to the means of production, either as possessors or possessionless or as independent of either state.

possessival (pɒsɛ'saɪvəl), *a. Gram. rare.* [f. as next, after *adjectival*, *substantival.*] Of or pertaining to the possessive case; possessive.

1873 EARLE *Philol. Eng. Tongue* (ed. 2) §572 This possessival termination ['s] detached itself, and passed into a pronoun-flexion by a sort of degeneracy, as in 'John his book'.

possessive (pə'zɛsɪv), *a.* (*sb.*) [ad. L. *possessīvus*, in grammar (Quintil.): see POSSESS *v.* and -IVE. So F. *possessif*, *-ive* (15th c. in Hatz.-Darm.).]

A. *adj.* **1.** *Gram.* Denoting possession; qualifying a thing (or person) as belonging to some other.

possessive pronoun (***possessive adjective***), a word derived from a personal or other pronoun, and expressing that the thing (or person) denoted by the noun which it qualifies belongs to the person (or thing) denoted by the pronoun from which it is derived. ***possessive case***, a name for the genitive case in modern English, ending (in nouns) in *'s*, and expressing the same relation as that expressed by a possessive pronoun.

(The name *possessive pronoun* is sometimes restricted to the absolute possessives *mine, thine, his, hers, its, ours, yours, theirs*, the adjectival forms *my, thy, his, her, its, our, your, their*, being distinguished as *possessive adjectives*. Both classes originate in or are derived from the genitive or possessive case of the personal pronouns.)

1530 PALSGR. Introd. 41 Where as we use our pronownes possessyves. **1571** GOLDING *Calvin on Ps.* xxvi. 1 The piththynesse of the Pronoune possessive (my) is to be noted. **1668** WILKINS *Real Char.* 305 Modifications of Pronouns... Possessive, denoting a relation of Propriety or Possession unto the person or thing spoken of,..as I, Mine; Who, Whose. **1712** STEELE *Spect.* No. 461 ¶3 The Poet..lets a Possessive Pronoun go without a Substantive. **1763** LOWTH *Eng. Gram.* 25 This Case answers to the Genitive Case in Latin, and may still be so called; though perhaps more properly the Possessive Case. **1824** L. MURRAY *Eng. Gram.* (ed. 5) I. 259 One substantive governs another, signifying a different thing, in the possessive or genitive case. **1870** HELFENSTEIN *Comp. Gram. Teut. Lang.* 199 The New Teutonic pronouns take the inflexions of the strong declension of the adjective, where they are used as possessive adjectives, as Germ. *mein, meine, mein*, gen. *meines, meiner, meines.* **1876** MASON *Eng. Gram.* (ed. 21) §73

The apostrophe in the possessive case singular marks that the vowel of the syllabic suffix has been lost.

2. a. Of or pertaining to possession; indicating possession. Also, showing a desire to possess or to retain what one possesses. (In quot. 1578 in sense corresp. to POSSESSION 2.)

1560 ROLLAND *Crt. Venus* I. 764 Greit Aduocat with power possessiue. **1578** *Let. Pat. to Sir H. Gilbert* in Hakluyt *Voy.* (1810) III. 175 All such our subiects and others, as shall from time to time hereafter aduenture themselues in the sayd iourneys or voyages habitatiue or possessiue. **1635** QUARLES *Embl.* v. ix. 277 What meane these liv'ries and possessive keyes? **1889** MRS. JOCELYN *Distracting Guest* II. vii. 129 His manner was kind and considerate..; perhaps a trifle too possessive; but I rejoiced just then in that very possessiveness. **1924** E. O'NEILL *Desire under Elms* I. iv, in *Compl. Wks.* II. 164 Eben..stares around him with glowing, possessive eyes... It's purty! It's damned purty! It's mine! **1931** —— *Hunted* I, in *Mourning becomes Electra* (1932) 121 You know how possessive Vinnie is with Orin. She's always been jealous of you. I warn you she'll do everything she can to keep him from marrying you. **1958** P. GIBBS *Curtains of Yesterday* xx. 170 One of those possessive women who wants to grab everything within reach. **1977** C. STORR *Tales from Psychiatrist's Couch* x. 104 A classical case of the possessive Jewish Mum... She didn't like the boy to go out of the house without telling her.

b. Having the quality or character of possessing; holding, or being in, possession.

1838 LYTTON *Leila* II. i, The life of the heir-apparent to the life of the king-possessive is as the distinction between enchanting hope and tiresome satiety. **1880** MISS BROUGHTON *Sec. Th.* III. x, Her eye, free and possessive, wanders widely round.

B. *sb. Gram. ellipt.* (*a*) for *possessive pronoun* or *adjective*; (*b*) for *possessive case*.

1591 PERCIVALL *Sp. Dict.* B iv b, Of pronounes some are primitiues... Some are deriuatiues, called also possessiues. **1704** J. HARRIS *Lex. Techn.* I, *Possessives* in Grammar, are such Adjectives as signifie the Possession of, or Property in some Thing. **1755** JOHNSON *Dict., Gram.*, The possessive of the first person is *my, mine, our, ours*. **1876** MASON *Eng. Gram.* (ed. 21) §68 The noun in the possessive is in the attributive relation to the noun which stands for what is possessed. *Ibid.* §142 *Their* retained a substantive force after the other possessives had become pronominal adjectives.

possessively (pəˈzɛsɪvlɪ), *adv.* [f. prec. adj. + -LY[2].]

1. *Gram.* In a possessive sense or relation.

1590 STOCKWOOD *Rules Construct.* 54 When the genitiue case is taken actiuely, when passiuely, and when possessiuely. **1879** WHITNEY *Sanskrit Gram.* 445 Possessively used descriptive compounds..are extremely numerous.

2. In the way of possession; in a manner indicating possession; as something possessed; as one's own.

1813 HOBHOUSE *Journey* (ed. 2) 1021 A sale by auction of the tenths belonging to the Malikiane (or fiefs held possessively), under the annual value of fifteen thousand piasters. **1901** *Westm. Gaz.* 27 Apr. 2/1 He tapped the English lady possessively on the shoulder.

poˈssessiveness. [f. as prec. + -NESS.] The quality of being possessive.

1864 *Athenæum* 10 Sept. 339/2 Its operation, its possessiveness, becomes more intense. **1883** LADY V. GREVILLE *Keith's Wife* I. 168 The man is apt to shock..by a too prompt assumption of possessiveness.

possessor (pəˈzɛsə(r)). Also 5–7 -our, 6–8 -er. [ME. and AF. *possessour*, = F. *possesseur* (14th c. in Hatz.-Darm.), ad. L. *possessor*, *-ōrem*, agent-n. f. *possidēre* to possess; with later conformation of suffix to Latin: see POSSESS and -OR[1].] One who possesses; one who holds something as property, or in actual control; one who has something (material or immaterial) belonging to him; a holder; an owner, proprietor. Const. *of*, or with *poss. pron.*

1388 WYCLIF *Acts* iv. 34 How manye euere weren possessouris of feeldis, ether of housis, thei seelden. **1477** *Rolls of Parlt.* VI. 187/1 Possessours of the Roiall Estate and Corone of Englond. **1486** *Bk. St. Albans, Her.* C vj b, The possessor of theys armys beris in latine thus [etc.]. **1535** COVERDALE *Gen.* xiv. 19 The most hye God, possessor of heauen and earth. **1596** SPENSER *F.Q.* IV. i. 29 She..their possessours often did dismay. **1667** MILTON *P.L.* I. 252 Infernal world, and thou profoundest Hell Receive thy new Possessor. **1794** MRS. RADCLIFFE *Myst. Udolpho* i, This charm was too dangerous to its possesser. **1839** LD. BROUGHAM *Statesm. Geo. III*, I. 36 Unlimited power corrupts the possessor. **1883** H. WALKER in *Leisure Hour* 501/2 The hornbeams..are the true autochthones and rightful prescriptive possessors of Epping Forest.

b. *spec.* (mainly *Law*). One who takes, occupies, or holds something without ownership, or as distinguished from the owner.

1565–6 *Reg. Privy Council Scot.* I. 432 Summond thame to compeir befoir the Lordis of Sessioun, to heir thame decernit violent possessouris. **1747** HOOSON *Miner's Dict.* N iij, Takers or Possessers have been cast and quite thrown out. **1800** ADDISON *Amer. Law Rep.* 129 The possessor remains liable to the true owner. **1818** CRUISE *Digest* (ed. 2) V. 372 Littleton..speaks of disseisins principally as between the owner and trespasser or possessor, with an eye to the remedy by assize.

c. *fig.* (*a*) One acquainted or conversant with, or master of, a subject; (*b*) One who maintains control over (himself). Cf. POSSESS *v.* 2 e, 4.

1674 PLAYFORD *Skill Mus.* Pref. 9 Whose love of this Divine Art appears by his Encouragement of it and the Possessors thereof. **1713** M. HENRY *Ordination Serm.* Wks. 1853 II. 505/2 We are most our own possessors, when we are least our own masters.

d. *Comm.* The holder (of a bill, etc.).

1682 SCARLETT *Exchanges* 63 It is the Duty of the Possessor, to take care for his Bill, and to see that the same be either accepted or protested. **1809** R. LANGFORD *Introd. Trade* 134 *Possessor*, the person who receives a foreign bill and presents it for acceptance.

poˈssessoress. *rare.* Also 6–7 -eresse. [a. obs. F. *possesseresse*, fem. of OF. *possesseur* POSSESSOR: see -ESS[1].] A female possessor.

1512 *Helyas* in Thoms *Prose Rom.* (1828) III. 11, I am the ladye and possesseresse of this londe. **1611** COTGR., *Possesseresse*, a possesseresse, a woman that possesses, holds, enioyes. **1681** W. ROBERTSON *Phraseol. Gen.* (1693) 1007 A possessoress, *domina*.

possessorial (pɒsɛˈsɔərɪəl), *a. rare.* [f. as POSSESSORY + -AL[1].] Of or pertaining to a possessor; possessory.

1594 *Mirr. Policy* (1599) 133 The parts of the House are Coniugall or Matrimoniall, Paternall or of the Parent, Seigniorall or Lordly, and Possessoriall [cf. POSSESSORY 2, quot. 1586]. **1850** LD. OSBORNE *Gleanings* 46 My friend must have had a very strong possessorial fit upon him.

poˈssessorship. [f. POSSESSOR + -SHIP.] The condition of a possessor; the holding of something as owner.

1885 STEVENSON *Pr. Otto* I. iii. 31 The joy of possessorship. **1896** *Eng. Churchm.* 16 Jan. 35/1 The long outstanding dispute touching the possessorship of the Upper Mekong Valley.

possessory (pəˈzɛsərɪ), *a.* [ad. late L. *possessōrius* adj. relating to possession, so F. *possessoire* (14th c. in Godef.): see POSSESS *v.* and -ORY.]

1. *Law.* **a.** Pertaining to a possessor; relating to possession.

possessory action, an action in which the plaintiff's claim is founded upon his or his predecessor's possession, and not upon his right or title. ***possessory interdict*** (Rom. Law), one of a class of interdicts for the acquisition, retention, or recovery of possession. ***possessory judgement*** (Sc. Law): see quot. 1838.

1425 *Rolls of Parlt.* IV. 272/2 Y^e matire possessorie, and y^u petition y^r uppon given. **1540** *Act 32 Hen. VIII*, c. 2 §2 Assice of mort auncestor..or any other action possessory. **a 1577** SIR T. SMITH *Commw. Eng.* (1609) 54 Pleas..reall, be either possessorie, to aske, or to keepe the possession: or in *rem*, which wee call a writ of right. **1766** BLACKSTONE *Comm.* II. xiii. 197 If he omits to bring this his possessory action within a competent time, his adversary may imperceptibly gain an actual right of possession, in consequence of the other's negligence. **1838** W. BELL *Dict. Law Scot.* s.v., A possessory judgment is one which entitles a person, who has been in uninterrupted possession for seven years, to continue his possession until the question of right shall be decided in due course of law. **1857** LD. CAMPBELL *Chief Justices* III. xliv. 47 In the possessory action of ejectment the legal estate shall always prevail. **1894** LIGHTWOOD *Possession of Land* i. 5 The old possessory actions which were for the recovery of possession, were founded upon seisin.

b. Arising from possession; as ***possessory interest, right, property, title***.

1615 JACKSON *Creed* IV. I. i. §1 Our personal election, predestination, salvation, or possessory right in state of grace. **1658–9** *Burton's Diary* (1828) III. 581 His possessory right, which was sufficient title for him to call a parliament, and for us to submit to it. **1708** *Termes de la Ley* s.v. *Property*, There are three manner of rights of Property; that is, Property absolute, Property qualified, and Property possessory. **1766** BLACKSTONE *Comm.* II. xxx. 453 The bailees..may..vindicate, in their own right, this their possessory interest. **1881** *Times* 14 Apr. 10/1 Throughout most parts of Ireland there has grown a tacit admission.. that the tenant has a possessory interest in his holding.

†2. That is possessed; of the nature of a possession. *Obs.*

1586 T. B. *La Primaud. Fr. Acad.* I. 464 A house..may be divided..into these foure parts: into matrimoniall, parentall, lordly or masterly, and possessorie part. **1610** GUILLIM *Heraldry* VI. iii. (1611) 260 It were an absurd thing ..that the possessorie things of the vanquished should be more priuiledged then their owners.

3. That is a possessor; holding something in possession.

1633 SIR J. BURROUGHS *Sov. Brit. Seas* (1651) 18 When the Romans had made themselves possessorie Lords of the Island. **1874** MOTLEY *Barneveld* I. i. 66 The possessory princes. **1886** J. A. KASSON in *N. Amer. Rev.* Feb. 125 Their commercial rights are to be the same as those of the possessory government.

4. Of, belonging to, or characterizing a possessor.

1659 STANLEY *Hist. Philos.* XIII. (1701) 613/1 Domestick Prudence being either conjugal and paternal, or dominative and possessory. **c 1660** *Clarke Papers* (Camden) IV. 303 The commaund I had that tyme of the army and strength of the kingdome was but a possessory and noe legall power. **1848** *Blackw. Mag.* LXIV. 6 Man's possessory instinct essentially connects itself with the future. **1879** J. BEGG *Scot. Public Affairs* 6 The possessory spirit is strong enough in man.

b. Used to render Gr. κτήσιος in Ζεὺς κτήσιος Jove the protector of property. *nonce-use*.

1850 BLACKIE *Æschylus* II. 109 A plundered house By grace of possessory Jove may freight New ships with bales that far outweigh the loss.

posset (ˈpɒsɪt), *sb.* Now only *Hist.* or *local*. Forms: 5 **posho(o)te, poshotte, poshet, possot, possyt, possate,** 5–6 **poset, possett,** 7 **possit,** *Sc.* **possat,** 5– **posset.** [ME. *poshote*, *possot*, of unascertained origin. Palsgr. (1530) gives a F. *possette*, but this is not otherwise known to French scholars. Ir. *pusoid*, posset, is from English.

Connexion with POSCA has been suggested.]

1. A drink composed of hot milk curdled with ale, wine, or other liquor, often with sugar, spices, or other ingredients; formerly much used as a delicacy, and as a remedy for colds or other affections.

14.. *Voc.* in Wr.-Wülcker 567/22 *Balducta*, a crudde, *Item dicitur*, poshet. **14..** *Metr. Voc.* ibid. 625/18 *Casius*, poshoote. **14..** *Voc.* ibid. 666/9 *Hec bedulta*, possyt. **c 1440** *Promp. Parv.* 410/2 Possot, *balducta*. **c 1460** J. RUSSELL *Bk. Nurture* 94 Milke, crayme, and cruddes, and eke the Ioncate, þey close a mannes stomak and so dothe þe possate. **1466** *Paston Lett.* II. 269 For bred, ale, and possets to the same persons, vid. **1530** PALSGR. 257/1 Posset of ale and mylke, *possette*. **1546** PHAER *Bk. Childr.* (1553) T vj, Knotgrasse..the iuice therof in a posset dronken..is excedyng good. **1605** SHAKS. *Macb.* II. ii. 6 The surfeted Groomes doe mock their charge With Snores. I haue drugg'd their Possets. **1648** HERRICK *Hesper.*, *To Phillis*, Thou shalt have possets, wassails fine; Not made of ale, but spiced wine! **1711** ADDISON *Spect.* No. 57 ¶2 [He] can make a Caudle or a Sack-Posset better than any Man in England. **1789** W. BUCHAN *Dom. Med.* xxix. (1790) 277 His supper should be light; as small posset, or water-gruel sweetened with honey, and a little toasted bread in it. **1876** F. E. TROLLOPE *Charming Fellow* II. xiii. 205, I do wish he would try a hot posset of a night, just before going to bed.

b. *attrib.*, as ***posset-ale, -basin, -bowl, -cup, -curd, -dish, -drink, -pot***.

1528 *St. Papers Hen. VIII*, I. 299 A possetale, hauing certein herbes clarified in it. **1551–60** in H. Hall *Eliz. Soc.* (1887) 152 A possett Boule of Pewter. **1596** NASHE *Saffron Walden* 125 Hee lou'd lycoras and drunke posset curd. **1606** *Sir G. Goosecappe* II. i. in Bullen *O. Pl.* III. 40 Posset Cuppes caru'd with libberds faces and Lyons heads with spouts in their mouths, to let out the posset Ale. **1612** WOODALL *Surg. Mate* Wks. (1653) 342 Plain posset drink alone, reasonable warm, will do well. **1680** *Hon. Cavalier* 11, I know some, who prefer..the Possit-Bason before the Hallowed Font. **1747** WESLEY *Prim. Physic* (1765) 59 Drink a Quarter of a Pint of Allum Posset drink. **1821** SCOTT *Kenilw.* vi, A gold posset-dish to contain the night-draught.

2. *dial.* The curdled milk vomited by a baby. (Yorksh. and Lancash. in *Eng. Dial. Dict.*)

Hence **ˈposset** *v.* †(*a*) *trans.* to curdle like a posset (*obs.*); **b.** *intr.* (*a*) to make a posset; (*b*) of a baby: to throw up curdled milk.

1602 SHAKS. *Ham.* I. v. 68 And with a sodaine vigour it doth posset And curd, like Aygre droppings into Milke The thin and wholsome blood. **1859** G. MEREDITH *R. Feverel* xxix, She broke off to go posseting for her dear invalid. **1903** *Eng. Dial. Dict.* s.v., Bless its little heart, it's possetting again. [Cited from Westmld. to South Notts.]

possibilism (ˈpɒsɪbɪlɪz(ə)m). [ad. F. *possibilisme*: see -ISM.] A possibilist doctrine or view; **a.** in *Politics*; **b.** in *Geogr.*

a. 1915 G. B. SHAW in *New Statesman* 23 Jan. 386/2 Having noticed that modern Secularism, Materialism, Rationalism: in short, Possibilism, have brought the minds of Mr Blatchford and Mr McCabe to a dead stop..they [*sc.* the Chestertons]..have frankly embraced Impossibilism. **1954** G. D. H. COLE *Hist. Socialist Thought* II. xv. 248 Paul Brousse's Possibilism, which stressed the importance of reform within capitalism, was definitely unorthodox doctrine. **1974** tr. *Wertheim's Evolution & Revolution* iii. 376, I could not endorse possibilism if it claims that all solutions have equal chances of materializing.

b. 1925 H. BERR in Mountford & Paxton tr. *Febvre's Geogr. Introd. Hist.* p. xi, He [*sc.* Febvre] has found striking formulae in which to state the question precisely. Against the geographical determinism of Ratzel he sets the possibilism of Vidal de la Blache. **1951** G. TATHAM in T. G. Taylor *Geogr. in 20th Cent.* vi. 151 The development of Possibilism is closely linked with the writings of Vidal de la Blache and Brunnes in France. **1965** H. & M. SPROUT *Ecol. Perspective Human Affairs* v. 83 The doctrine called environmental possibilism, or simply possibilism, represents an historic reversal of perspective towards man-milieu relationships. **1974** KOLARS & NYSTUEN *Geogr.* xx. 375 The message of possibilism is that the environment offers not one, but many, paths for human activities and development.

possibilist (pɒˈsɪbɪlɪst), *sb* (and *a.*). [ad. F. *possibiliste* or Sp. *posibilista*, f. L. *possibilis*: see POSSIBLE and -IST.] **1.** A member of a political party whose aims at reform are directed to what is immediately possible or practicable; *spec.* (*a*) of a party of Republicans in Spain; (*b*) of a party of Socialists in France. Also *attrib.* or as *adj.*

1881 *Daily News* 18 Aug. 5/7 The Opportunist, now called the Possibilist doctrine, that everything cannot be done in a day. **1882** *Contemp. Rev.* Sept. 459 Communists.. of the 'Possibilist' type. **1893** *Times* 8 Aug. 2/5 The Possibilists of Paris made the first notable effort to re-unite the labour parties of different countries. **1894** *Cycl. Rev. Curr. Hist.* (Buffalo, N.Y.) IV. 898 Señor Abarzuza has been virtual leader of the possibilists or moderate republicans ever since Señor Castelar announced his retirement. **1936** *Sat. Rev. Lit.* (U.S.) 15 Feb. 11/2 He [*sc.* Mazzini] was never what is called in modern phrase a 'possibilist'. He was..that most inspiring and most dangerous product of mankind, an 'idealist'. **1940, 1966** [see GUESDIST]. **1973** *Times* 26 Nov. 15/2 The Labour Party would be irreparably split between its moderate possibilists and its left-wing extremists.

2. *Geogr.* One who emphasizes man's freedom of action in cultural development and minimizes the effects and restrictions of the environment. Also *attrib.* or as *adj.*

1925 MOUNTFORD & PAXTON tr. *Febvre's Geogr. Introd. Hist.* 20 We will not ask whether there are not really any cracks in the geographical edifice, and whether it is possible to follow at the same time.. the 'determinists' after the manner of Ratzel, and what we may perhaps call the 'possibilists' after the pattern of Vidal. **1951** G. TATHAM in T. G. Taylor *Geogr. in 20th Cent.* vi. 155 Possibilists do not, nor have they ever claimed, that man can free himself from all environmental influences. *Ibid.*, Possibilist statements published during the last fifty years, make quite clear the contention that Nature does not drive man along one particular road. **1964** *Welsh Hist. Rev.* II. 275 He begins by disavowing any intention of arguing for geographical determinism and affirms his allegiance to the 'possibilist' school of geographers. rather

possibilistic (pɒsɪbɪ'lɪstɪk), *a.* [f. prec. + -IC.] Of or pertaining to possibilism.

1965 H. & M. SPROUT *Ecol. Perspective Human Affairs* v. 83 A possibilistic analysis directs attention to those factors of the milieu that may affect the operational result. **1974** *Encycl. Brit. Micropædia* III. 912/3 Contemporary environmentalists recognize that physical surroundings are only part of a total environment that includes social and economic factors... Their approach is probabilistic, rather than deterministic or possibilistic.

possibilitate (pɒsɪ'bɪlɪteɪt), *v.* [f. POSSIBILITY + -ATE³.] *trans.* To render possible.

1829 SOUTHEY in *Q. Rev.* XXXIX. 134 That this object has been *possibilitated*. **1893** *Nation* (N.Y.) 2 Feb. 90/2 Theories thus miserably imperfect have nevertheless sufficed to 'possibilitate' (as a Spaniard would say) all the great engineering works of our age.

possibility (pɒsɪ'bɪlɪtɪ). Also 4-6 with *y* for *i*, and *-e*, *-ee*, *-ie* for *-y*; (6 posabilete). [a. F. *possibilité* (13th c. in Hatz.-Darm.), ad. L. *possibilitās*, f. *possibilis* POSSIBLE: see -ITY.]

1. a. The state, condition, or fact of being possible; capability of being done, happening, or existing (in general, or under particular conditions).

by any possibility (formerly †***by possibility***): in any possible way, by any existing means, possibly; so ***by no possibility***. †***of possibility*** (quot. *c* 1374): characterized by possibility, possible.

c **1374** CHAUCER *Troylus* III. 399 (448) That kan I deme of possibilite. *c* **1386** —— *Frankl. T.* 615 Ffor wende I neuere by possibilitee That swich a Monstre or merueille myghte be. **1387-8** T. USK *Test. Love* III. iii. (Skeat) l. 112 But now thou seest.. the possibilite of thilke that thou wendest had been impossible. **1509** HAWES *Past. Pleas.* xi. (Percy Soc.) 39 That the comon wyt, by possibilitie, Maye well a judge the perfyt veritie Of theyr sentence. **1594** HOOKER *Eccl. Pol.* I. iv. §3 That high perfection of blisse, wherein now the elect Angels are without possibilitie of falling. **1641** WILKINS *Math. Magick* I. xiv. (1648) 94 To understand that assertion of Archimedes concerning the possibility of moving the world. **1709** ATTERBURY *Serm., Luke* x. 32 (1726) II. 231 Shall we be discouraged from any Attempt of doing good, by the Possibility of our failing in it? **1818** CRUISE *Digest* (ed. 2) V. 401 These continuances, therefore, take away all presumption and possibility that the judgment was given on the first day of the term. **1884** F. TEMPLE *Relat. Relig. & Sc.* vii. (1885) 193 Science and Revelation come into.. collision on the possibility of miracles. *Mod.* If I could by any possibility manage to do it, I would.

b. ***in possibility***: (*a*) not actually existing, but that may come to exist; potential: = *in* POSSE; (*b*) in relation to something possible but not actual; potentially. (See also 3 b.)

1587 GOLDING *De Mornay* iv. (1592) 45 As for God, he is not a thing in possibilitie (which is an vnperfect being) but altogether actuallie and in verie deed. **1711** ADDISON *Spect.* No. 191 ¶9 We are apt to rely upon future Prospects, and become really expensive while.. only rich in Possibility.

c. ***after possibility*** (Law): ellipt. for *after possibility of issue is extinct*, i.e. when there is no longer any possibility of issue.

[*c* **1350** *Rolls of Parlt.* II. 401/2 Dount possibilite de issue entre eux est esteinte, Maud ad fait wast, exil, vente e destruction. **1544** tr. *Littleton's Tenures* (1574) 7 b, He.. is tenaunt in the tayle after possibilitie of issue extinct.] **1596** BACON *Max. & Use Com. Law* I. xxi, If tenant after possibility make a lease for yeares, and the donor confirmes to the lessee to hold without impeachment of waste.

d. The quality or character of representing or relating to something that is possible.

1638 JUNIUS *Paint. Ancients* 63 In the phantasies of Painters, nothing is so commendable as that there is both possibilitie and truth in them. **1826** DISRAELI *Viv. Grey* II. xvi, To consult on the possibility of certain views,.. and the expediency of their adoption. **1890** RAYNER *Chess Problems* 5 The chief requisites of a problem are possibility and soundness... A possible position can be reached by a legal series of moves as in a game.

e. *Math.* The condition of being a possible or real quantity.

1673 COLLINS in Rigaud *Corr. Sci. Men* (1841) II. 555 About the constitution of incomplete equations, it is easy to observe that many of the roots lose their possibility.

2. An instance of the fact or condition described in 1; a possible thing or circumstance; something that may exist or happen. (Usually with *a*, or in *pl.*; in *pl.* sometimes nearly = capabilities: cf. 3.)

c **1400** *Beryn* 3544, I can nat wete howe To stop all the ffressh watir wer possibilite. **1588** SHAKS. *Tit. A.* III. i. 215 Oh brother speake with possibilities, And do not breake into these deepe extreames. **1699** BENTLEY *Phal.* 100 Our Examiner can give you a view of it in the Region of Possibilities. **1712** BUDGELL *Spect.* No. 539 ¶2 There is a Possibility this Delay may be as painful to her as it is to me. **1790** PALEY *Horæ Paul.* Rom. i. 10 This is spoken of rather as a possibility, than as any settled intention. **1865** TROLLOPE *Belton Est.* v. 48 Her clearer intellect saw possibilities which did not occur to him. **1883** H. DRUMMOND *Nat. Law in Spir. W.* iii. (1884) 100 Three possibilities of life.. are open to all living organisms—Balance, Evolution, and Degeneration.

†**3. a.** Regarded or stated as an attribute of the agent: The fact of something (expressed or implied) being possible to one, in virtue either of favourable circumstances or of one's own powers; hence, Capacity, capability, power, ability; pecuniary ability, means. (In quot. 1591, Possibility or chance of having something: cf. b.) *Obs.* (or merged in 1).

c **1375** *Sc. Leg. Saints* xxvii. (*Machor*) 685 Eftyr my possybilyte, Dere sone, I sal helpe þe. *c* **1450** tr. *De Imitatione* III. xxix. 99 þou shalt þan fruisshe abundance of pes after þe possibilite of þi duellyng place. **1477** EARL RIVERS (Caxton) *Dictes* 82 Liberalite is to yeue to nedi peple ..aftir the possibilite of the yeuer. **1544** *Plumpton Corr.* (Camden) 249 Consider his qualeties, his living, his posabilete, and confer al together. *a* **1550** *Hye Way to Spyttel Hous* 633 in Hazl. *E.P.P.* IV. 53 Yong brethren of small possybylyte, Not hauyng wherwith to mayntene such degre. **1552** *Reg. Privy Council Scot.* I. 133 We.. offerit us to do thairfor.. all that lay in our possibilliteis. **1579-80** NORTH *Plutarch* (1676) 75 He that maketh Laws, must have regard to the common possibility of men. **1591** SHAKS. *1 Hen. VI*, v. iv. 146 Ile rather keepe That which I haue, then coueting for more Be cast from possibility of all. **1597** —— *2 Hen. IV*, IV. iii. 39, I haue speeded hither with the very extremest ynch of possibilitie. **1648** GAGE *West Ind.* x. (1655) 33 We could not, although we proved all our possibility by night and day. **1790** PALEY *Horæ Paul.* Rom. i. 11 An instance of conformity beyond the possibility.. of random writing to produce. **1815** *Zeluca* III. 78 An object who interfered with her wishes, to a degree it was not in her possibility for any other Creature to approach to.

†**b.** ***in possibility*** (later, ***in a possibility***): in such a position that something (expressed or implied) is possible to or for one; having a prospect, expectation, or chance (*of* or *to do* something).

1523 LD. BERNERS *Froiss.* I. 794 Duke Aubert had nat bene in trewe possession of Heynalt, but in possibylite therof. **1591** HARINGTON *Orl. Fur.* Pref. ¶viij b, I be in such faire possibilitie to be thought a foole, or fantasticall for my labour. **1605** CHAPMAN *All Fooles* Wks. 1873 I. 182 That they who are alreadie in possession of it, may beare their heades aloft.. and they that are but in possibilitie, may be rauisht with a desire to be in possession. **1605** *Play Stucley* 307 in Simpson *Sch. Shaks.* (1878) I. 170, I am in possibility To marry Alderman Curtises daughter. **1682** DRYDEN *Relig. Laici* Pref., Heathens who never did.. hear of the name of Christ, were yet in a possibility of salvation.

†**c.** *sing.* and *pl.* Pecuniary prospects. *Obs.*

1592 GREENE *Upst. Courtier* D iij, A yoong gentleman of faire liuing, in issue of good parents or assured possibilitie. **1598** SHAKS. *Merry W.* I. i. 65 *Slen.* I know the young Gentlewoman, she has good gifts. *Euan.* Seuen hundred pounds, and possibilities, is goot gifts. **1637** HEYWOOD *Royall King* II. iii. (1874 VI. 25) You know I am my Fathers heire, My possibilities may raise his hopes To their first height.

4. Special Comb.: **possibility theorem** = *impossibility theorem.*

1950 [see *impossibility theorem*]. **1961** J. ROTHENBERG *Measurement of Social Welfare* ii. 24 We shall give a sketch of Arrow's proof of the General Possibility Theorem. **1964** C. E. FERGUSON *Macroecon. Theory of Workable Competition* i. 10 (*heading*) The possibility theorem and rigorous proof of the competitive optimum.

possible ('pɒsɪb(ə)l), *a.* (*sb.*, *adv.*) Also 4-6 possy-; 4 -bel, -bile, 5 -byll(e, 5-6 -bil, 6 -bill, -bul (-able). [a. F. *possible* (in OF. also *posible*, 13th c. in Godef. *Compl.*), or ad. L. *possibilis* that can be or may be done, possible, f. *posse* (for *potis esse*) to be able.]

A. *adj.* **1.** That may be (i.e. is capable of being); that may or can exist, be done, or happen (in general, or in given or assumed conditions or circumstances); that is in one's power, that one can do, exert, use, etc. (const. *to* the agent).

a. Qualifying a noun or pronoun, attributively or (more usually) predicatively.

13.. *E.E. Allit. P.* A. 452 If possyble were her mendyng. **1382** WYCLIF *Luke* xviii. 27 Tho thingis that ben vnpossible anemptis men, ben possible anemptis God. *c* **1385** CHAUCER *L.G.W.* 1020 (*Dido*), I can not seyn If that it be possible. *c* **1400** MAUNDEV. (1839) xvii. 184 And that was possible thinge. *c* **1460** FORTESCUE *Abs. & Lim. Mon.* vi. (1885) 123 We woll considre next his extra ordinarie charges, also ferre as may be possible to vs. **1526** TINDALE *Mark* ix. 23 All thynges are possyble to hym that belevith. **1541** R. COPLAND *Guydon's Quest. Chirurg.* A iij b, He ought to procede to the healyng of the pacyent in all that may lye in hym possyble. **1564** GOLDING *Justine* XI. 54 He passed the mountaine Taurus with all spede possible. **1669** STURMY *Mariner's Mag.* I. ii. 42 To make a Triangle.. whose Base shall be equal to any (possible) Number given. **1777** BURKE *Corr.* (1844) II. 150 When we speak only of things, not persons, we have a right to express ourselves with all possible energy. **1823** SCORESBY *Jrnl. Whale Fish.* p. xxxv, The manners of the Esquimaux.. being the most suitable possible to the nature of the climate. **1856** RUSKIN *Mod. Paint.* III. IV. xvii. §36 All real and wholesome enjoyments possible to man have been just as possible to him, since first he was made of the earth, as they are now. **1870** JEVONS *Logic* xxii. 187 Thomson much extends the list of possible syllogisms. *Mod.* There are three possible courses.

b. Qualifying an infinitive or other clause, usually introduced by *it*.

1340 HAMPOLE *Pr. Consc.* 6328 And if possibel ware, als es noght, þat ilk man als mykel syn had wroght, Als alle þe men þat in þe werld ever was. *c* **1386** CHAUCER *Shipman's T.* 32 In his hous as famulier was he As it is possible any freend to be. **1491** CAXTON *Vitas Patr.* (W. de W. 1495) II. 209/1 It is not vnto vs possyble for to see eche other. **1500-20** DUNBAR *Poems* lxxxiv. 29 War it possibill that in ony corce War Salamonis witt and hie sapience. **1562** TURNER *Herbal* II. 41 It is not possible to discern the one from the other. **1599** SHAKS. *Hen. V*, v. ii. 180 No, it is not possible you should loue the Enemie of France, Kate. **1705** S. CLARKE *Being & Attrib. God* x. 171 It is possible to Infinite Power, to indue a Creature with the Power of Beginning Motion. **1820** SHELLEY *Hymn to Mercury* lxix, How was it possible.. That you, a little child, born yesterday,.. Could two prodigious heifers ever flay?

c. With infinitive or other complement (nearly coinciding with 3). Cf. IMPOSSIBLE *a.* 1 b.

1706 ATTERBURY *Serm., 1 Cor.* xv. 19 (1726) II. 10 All the Advantages and Satisfactions of this World, which are possible to be attain'd by him. **1851** H. SPENCER *Soc. Stat.* 82 A limit almost always possible of exact ascertainment.

d. In elliptical phrases, as ***if possible*** = if it be (or were) possible, if it can (or could) be; ***as much as possible*** = as much as may (or might) be, as much as one can (or could).

1671 MILTON *Samson* 490 Let me here.. expiate, if possible, my crime. **1688** *Col. Rec. Pennsylv.* I. 229 Notice be given to as many of The Members as possible. **1712** ADDISON *Spect.* No. 58 ¶2, I shall endeavour as much as possible to establish among us a Taste of polite Writing. **1719** —— *Wks.* (1721) I. Ded. to Craggs 2 That they may come to you with as little disadvantage as possible. **1882** *Knowledge* II. 70 So that she might be cured, if possible.

†**e.** ellipt. for 'all possible', 'the greatest possible'. *Obs. rare.*

1596 DALRYMPLE tr. *Leslie's Hist. Scot.* x. 281 Ilk flies to his awne cuntrie with possable haist.

f. That can or may be or become (what is denoted by the sb.): as ***a possible object of knowledge*** = something that may be an object of knowledge, that can or may be known. (See also 2 b.)

1736 BUTLER *Anal.* Introd., Wks. 1874 I. 3 Nothing which is the possible object of knowledge.. can be probable to an infinite Intelligence. **1856** EMERSON *Eng. Traits, Ability* Wks. (Bohn) II. 45 The labourer is a possible lord. The lord is a possible basket-maker. **1862** STANLEY *Jew. Ch.* I. xvi, Of the three possible harbours.. they made no use.

2. a. That may be (i.e. is not known not to be); that is perhaps true or a fact; that perhaps exists. (Expressing contingency, or an idea in the speaker's mind, not power or capability of existing as in 1; hence sometimes nearly = credible, thinkable.)

1582 N. LICHEFIELD tr. *Castanheda's Conq. E. Ind.* I. lxv. 132 b, That you shoulde understand, wherefore and for what cause I remained in the Indias, for that it is possible that all you do not know. **1693** DRYDEN *Orig. & Progr. Sat.* Ess. (ed. Ker) II. 25 In such an age, it is possible some great genius may arise, to equal any of the ancients. **1734** tr. *Rollin's Anc. Hist.* (1827) VII. XVII. 300 Swept away all actual and possible debts. **1827** WHATELY *Logic* (1837) 379 This word.. relates sometimes to contingency, sometimes to power, e.g. 'It is possible this patient may recover'. **1841** ELPHINSTONE *Hist. Ind.* I. 443 The Jats, whose possible descent from the Getæ has been discussed in another place. **1860** TYNDALL *Glac.* I. xxii. 157 The thought of the possible loss of my axe at the summit was here forcibly revived.

b. That may be (what is denoted by the sb.); that perhaps is or will be.. (Cf. 1 f.)

1882 B. HARTE *Flip* i, Still less would any passing stranger have recognised in this blonde faun the possible outcast and murderer. **1884** *Manch. Exam.* 10 May 5/6 Assiduous efforts.. in whipping up every possible supporter of the Bill.

c. *Philos.* Logically conceivable; that which, whether or not it actually exists, is not excluded from existence by being logically contradictory or against reason. Freq. in phr. ***possible world***; also *attrib.* Also in gen. use, orig. with allusion to Voltaire's *Candide* (see quot. 1759).

1738 tr. *Bayle's Gen. Dict.* VI. 674/1 That cause must also be intelligent; for this world, which actually exists, being contingent, and an infinite number of other worlds being equally possible; the cause of the world must have considered all these possible worlds to pitch upon one. *Ibid.* 674/2 It will be true still.. that there is an infinity of possible worlds. **1759** W. RIDER tr. *Voltaire's Candidus* i. 3 Pangloss read Lectures in Metaphisico-theologo-cosmolonigology. He demonstrated that there can be no Effect without a Cause, that in this best of *possible* Worlds, the Baron's Castle was the finest, and my Lady the best of all possible Baronesses. **1878** S. H. HODGSON *Philos. of Reflection* I. i. 79 There is then, beside our determinate world, a world indeterminate to us, but *possible* if there should be other modes of consciousness than ours, that is possible to our thought since we imagine its condition, and *actual* to those other modes, if they are actually existing. **1900** RUSSELL *Crit. Expos. Philos. Leibniz* v. 68 It may be well, for the sake of clearness, to enumerate the principal respects in which all possible worlds agree, and the respects in which other possible worlds might differ from the actual world. **1911** G. B. SHAW *Blanco Posnet* 299 The administrative departments were consuming miles of red tape in the correctest forms of activity, and.. everything was for the best in the best of all possible worlds. **1914** —— *Misalliance* p. xlii, A life's work is like a day's work: it can begin early and leave off early or begin late and leave off late, or, as with us, begin too early and never leave off at all, obviously the worst of all possible plans. **1922** tr. *Wittgenstein's Tractatus* 127 Everything which is possible in logic is also permitted. **1924** A. HUXLEY *Little Mexican* 166 Next to the intimate and trusted friend, the perfect stranger is the best of all possible confidants. **1926** J. B. CABELL *Silver Stallion* xxvi. 112 The optimist proclaims that we live in the best of all possible worlds; and the pessimist fears this is true. **1928** R. LYND *Green Man* xviii. 147 It was impossible not to believe that this was the best of all possible worlds, for a world in which young men enjoy playing bad cricket is clearly a far happier place than a world in which young men would enjoy playing only good cricket. **1949** A. PAP *Elem. Analytic Philos.* ix. 177 Suppose there existed just one individual, *a*, that might be characterized by either one of the properties A, B and C. Then we can imagine the following 'possible worlds': (1) Aa. Ba. Ca [etc.]. **1966** R. F. ANDERSON *Hume's First Princ.* i. 3 (*heading*) Whatever is conceivable is possible. **1968** HUGHES & CRESSWELL *Introd. Modal Logic* iv. 77 This notion of one possible world's being accessible to another has at first sight a certain air of fantasy or science fiction about it. **1973** J. J. ZEMAN *Modal Logic* xv. 276 The system B, .. whose possible world semantics involve an accessibility which is reflexive and symmetrical but not transitive. **1977** *Canad. Jrnl. Linguistics 1976* XXI. II. 136 Now, we should be aware of the fact that the specific reading of (12) doesn't imply that the fish *a* which belongs to the set I(μ_1) of individuals in the possible world μ_1 belongs to the set I (μ_0) of individuals in the world μ_0 too.

†**3.** Having the power *to do* something; able, capable. *Obs. rare.* (Cf. POSSIBILITY 3.)

1512 *Helyas* in Thoms *Prose Rom.* (1828) III. 131 Yf ye be able and possible to reedifie the churches of God. **1667** MILTON *P.L.* IX. 359 Firm we subsist, yet possible to swerve. *a* **1817** JANE AUSTEN *Northanger Abbey* (1818) II. xiv. 273 The only offence against him of which she could accuse herself, had been such as was scarcely possible to reach his knowledge.

4. *Math.* = REAL *a.*[2] 1 d; opp. to IMPOSSIBLE *a.* 2.

1874 TODHUNTER *Trig.* xix. §271 (1882) 216 If *n* be even, the last term .. is possible, namely $(-1)^{\frac{n}{2}}\sin^n\theta$, and the last term but one is impossible, namely $n(-1)^{\frac{n-1}{2}}\cos\theta\sin^{n-1}\theta$.

5. With ellipsis of some qualification: Possible to deal with, get on with, understand, take into consideration, etc. (Opp. to IMPOSSIBLE *a.* 3.)

1865 M. ARNOLD *Ess. Crit.* vii. 228 He [Joubert] was more possible than Coleridge; his doctrine was more intelligible than Coleridge's, more receivable. **1929** A. HUXLEY *Let.* 26 Aug. (1969) 317 One is at 3500 feet in a rather primitive but quite possible little hotel. **1934** H. G. WELLS *Exper. Autobiogr.* I. vi. 313, I went the round of the scholastic agents, .. and I answered many impossible and some possible advertisements. **1968** A. MUNRO in R. Weaver *Canad. Short Stories* (1968) 2nd Ser. 300 Leaving Miss Marsalles and her no longer possible parties behind, quite certainly forever.

B. *absol.* or as *sb.*

1. a. *absol.* (usually with *the*): That which is possible. Phr. ***the art of the possible*** (the equivalent G. phr. *Die Politik ist die Lehre von Möglichen* is attributed to Bismarck (1867)).

1646 H. LAWRENCE *Comm. Angells* 75 If wee speake of the possible, of what may be. **1844** MRS. BROWNING *Cry Children* 135 God's possible is taught by His world's loving, And the children doubt of each. **1879** GEO. ELIOT *Theo. Such* vii. 139 The Possible is always the ultimate master of our efforts and desires. **1969** D. C. HAGUE *Managerial Econ.* i. 12 Management, like politics, is the art of the possible. **1979** *Oxf. Dict. Quotations* (ed. 3) 84/2 Politics is the art of the possible. **1979** *Guardian* 31 Oct. 4/4 Britain's strong suit is jurisprudence. France's is the art of the possible.

b. as *sb.* A possible thing: = POSSIBILITY 2. (Almost always in *pl.*)

1675 TRAHERNE *Chr. Ethics* 173 Inferior possibles are more remote, and only thought on in the second place. **1754** EDWARDS *Freed. Will* II. iii. 46 Any Thing else of all the infinite Number of Possibles. **1876** MRS. WHITNEY *Sights & Ins.* II. xiv. 448, I know .. who is a higher, and fresher, and sweeter possible of me. **1970** *Morning Star* 5 Mar. 2 Michael Parkinson looks at award-winning film possibles in 'Cinema' on Granada at 10.30 tonight. **1974** A. MORICE *Killing with Kindness* ii. 14 We were going to have a look at some boats... He'd marked one or two possibles in the local paper.

¶ **c.** ***to do one's possible*** (imitation of F. *faire son possible*): to do what is possible to one, to do one's utmost, 'to do one's endeavour'.

1792 H. MORE *Lett.* (1925) 175, I thought to have sent a line to Mr. T. but I have done my *possible* in writing for to-day. **1797** MRS. A. M. BENNETT *Beggar Girl* (1813) V. 175 He did his possible, but old Turgid was neither to be led nor driven. **1808** in Southey *Life A. Bell* (1844) II. 483, I had done my possible (in French phrase) to gratify you. **1838** SYD. SMITH in Lady Holland *Mem.* (1855) II. 408, I would however have done my possible. **1922** E. E. CUMMINGS *Let.* 26 Feb. (1969) 83 Dos's first words to me were a grim assurance that .. his possible would be done to save The Chambre énorme from any similar fate.

d. A person who possibly may have done or may do something or attain some position; a possible candidate, member of a team, sexual partner, suspect, etc.

1915 J. BUCHAN *39 Steps* vii. 180 You're in no danger from the law of this land ... they have dropped you from the list of possibles. **1923** *Daily Mail* 3 Mar. 13 C. L. Spackman .. and H. J. Still as reserve backs are possibles. **1948** *Sporting Mirror* 21 May 13/3 Olympic 'possibles', especially those recognised to be in the first flight, are going to be in great demand everywhere. **1948** 'J. TEY' *Franchise Affair* xi. 117 He hadn't even thought of her when he sat down... She just wouldn't occur to any man as a possible. **1959** *Times Lit. Suppl.* 6 Nov. p. xx/4 Most of the presidential possibles in this year are college graduates. **1973** D. WESTHEIMER *Going Public* ix. 136 Some files they rejected .. others they read through. A considerable stack of possibles began to mount. **1975** T. ALLBEURY *Special Collection* i. 4 They'd spent almost a month .. checking .. for suitable candidates. There had been three 'possibles'.

2. *slang pl.* Necessaries, means, supplies.

1823 BEE *Dict. Turf* 96 *High-tide*, plenty of the possibles; whilst 'low-water' implies empty clies. **1824** *Hist. Gaming Ho.* 61 Dick was sadly put to his trumps to raise the possibles. **1851** MAYNE REID *Scalp Hunt.* xxiv, The hunters departed, each to look after his 'traps and possibles'.

3. *colloq.* (orig. ***highest possible***): short for 'highest possible score or number of points' (in a competition, esp. in rifle practice).

1866 *York Herald* 6 Aug. 5/4 Two highest possibles were recorded, the 1st Glo'ster taking first prize on account of time; the second going to 1st Hants. **1894** *Daily News* 20 July 4/6 Despite the somewhat unfavourable conditions, three highest possibles were made. **1895** *Ibid.* 17 July 2/1 'Possibles' were also made by Private ——, 3rd East Surrey, and Captain ——, 3rd Lanark. **1896** *Westm. Gaz.* 14 July 9/1 Putting on a possible at 800 yards.

†**C.** as *adv.* = POSSIBLY. (As an intensive qualification of *can* or *could.*) *Obs.*

1542 UDALL *Erasm. Apoph.* 30 b, Crito had afore dooen all that euer he might possible dooe. **1606** G. W[ODCOCKE] *Hist. Ivstine* v. 25 He furnished a fresh Nauy of Ships, with all the hast he could possible. **1678** WALTON *Life Sanderson* 53, I wonder how a person could possible be deceived with it. *a* **1704** T. BROWN *Two Oxf. Scholars* Wks. 1730 I. 9, I shall certainly have .. as many mischievous tricks play'd me as they can possible. **1799** MRS. J. WEST *Tale of Times* II. 223 She became as cold .. in her answers as the rules of civility could possible admit.

Hence †**'possibleness**, = POSSIBILITY 1. *Obs. rare.*

1642 ROGERS *Naaman* 313 To assure me of the possiblenesse of obeying it. *Ibid.* 362 Shewing it an entrance and a possiblenesse of escape. **1727** in BAILEY vol. II.

possibly ('pɒsɪblɪ), *adv.* [f. POSSIBLE + -LY[2].]

1. In a possible manner; according to what may or can be (in the nature of things); by any existing power or means; within the range of possibility; by any possibility. (Usually, now always, as an intensive qualification of *can* or *could.*)

c **1391** CHAUCER *Astrol.* Prol. 1 Alle the conclusiouns that han ben fownde, or elles possibli myhten be fownde. **1583** STOCKER *Civ. Warres Lowe C.* I. 31 Sent .. for as much Artillery as was possiblye to be had. **1591** SHAKS. *Two Gent.* II. ii. 3 When possibly I can, I will returne. *a* **1680** BUTLER *Rem* (1759) I. 14 Every Man amaz'd anew, How it could possibly be true. **1710** ADDISON *Tatler* No. 243 ⁋ 6 He cannot possibly live till Five in the Morning. *Mod.* I cannot possibly be present. How could you possibly think so?

†**b.** Irregularly used instead of *possible* in adverbial phrases, as ***if possibly, soon as possibly, by all means possibly.*** *Obs.*

1560 INGELEND *Disob. Child* in Hazl. *Dodsley* II. 277 Therefore out of hand with all speed possibly To have a wife, methink, would do well. **1583** STOCKER *Civ. Warres Lowe C.* III. 117 b, That all South Holland, if it were possibly, might bee laide vnder the water. **1640** HABINGTON *Edw. IV* 137 Soone as possibly, he was dismist. **1654–66** EARL ORRERY *Parthen.* (1676) 701, I was somewhat moved .. if possibly, to make her think she was mistook.

†**c.** As is possible to one; according to one's ability; as much or as well as one can. *Obs. rare.*

1657 CROMWELL *Speech* 8 Apr., You have provided for every one of them as a Free Man, as a man that does possibly, rationally, and conscientiously.

2. Qualifying the statement, and expressing contingency or subjective possibility (cf. POSSIBLE *a.* 2): According to what may be (as far as one knows); perhaps, perchance, maybe. (Often as intensive qualification of *may* or *might.*)

1600 E. BLOUNT tr. *Conestaggio* 18 With greater libertie then possiblie reason woulde allowe. **1685** SOUTH *Serm.* (1697) I. viii. 362 A man by mere peradventure lights into company, possibly is driven into an House by a shower of Rain for present Shelter. **1711** ADDISON *Spect.* No. 98 ⁋ 2 The Women might possibly have carried this Gothick Building much higher. **1847** C. BRONTË *J. Eyre* iii, Possibly I might have some poor low relations. **1877** BAIN *Comp. Higher Eng. Gram.* (ed. 2) 198 We shall possibly come. **1899** T. NICOLL *Rec. Archæol. & Bible* v. 206 A Hittite woman was possibly the mother of Solomon [= it is possible that a Hittite woman was ..].

possident ('pɒsɪdənt), *a.* and *sb. rare.* [ad. L. *possidēnt-em* possessing, pres. pple. of *possidēre* to possess.]

†**A.** *adj.* Possessing, holding in possession. *Obs.*

1625 W. B. *True School War* 31 That those Countries should, by the renunciation of the possident Princes, be deliuered vp vnto him.

B. *sb.* A possessor.

1610 W. FOLKINGHAM *Art of Survey* II. ii. 49 The fensing or inclosing of the Plot appertaines to the Possident. *Ibid.* III. ii. 66 The qualities and attributes coincident to the Possident and Possession. **1885** *Pall Mall G.* 27 Oct. 6/2 One who wishes to see riches freely and equitably circulating, and looks for some adjustment between possidents and not-possidents to the ultimate advantage of peace and public safety.

possie, pozzy[1] ('pɒsɪ, 'pɒzɪ). *slang* (orig. and chiefly *Austral.* and *N.Z.*). Also **possy, pozzie.** [f. POS(ITION *sb.* + -Y[6], -IE.] A position (orig. in sense 7 c); the space a person occupies; a location; a place of residence; an appointment; an occupation. Hence as *v. trans.*

1915 T. SKEYHILL *Soldier Songs from Anzac* (1916) 15 'E climbs up stunted pine-trees, An' snipes away as us. But 'e never shows 'is pozzy. **1916** *Anzac Bk.* 10 The new sniper's pozzy down at the creek. *Ibid., Pozzy* or *Possie*, Australian warrior's short for 'position' or 'lair'. *Ibid.* 102 His mates used to take a mean advantage of his good nature, and would shunt all the work, such as sweeping out the 'possie', or trenches, on to him. **1918** *Chrons. N.Z.E.F.* 25 Oct. 149/2 We were 'possied' some distance in rear of the front line. **1919** *Ibid.* 10 Jan. 284/2 In the small hours we reached our next 'possie'—a shell-torn gully near Pusieux. **1919** W. H. DOWNING *Digger Dial.* 39 *Possy*, position; place; dugout; home. **1925** A. WRIGHT *Boy from Bullarah* 99 Quick, get a pozzy with the machine. **1926** 'J. DOONE' *Timely Tips for New Australians* Gloss., *Possie*, a slang contraction of the word position which denotes a place. A job. *c* **1926** 'MIXER' *Transport Workers' Song Bk.* 70 You'll hear him in his bar-room 'possie', As a bloke comes in for a 'wet'. **1929** A. W. WHEEN tr. *Remarque's All Quiet on W. Front* v. 101 Then we change our possy and lie down again to play cards. **1934** *Bulletin* (Sydney) 3 Jan. 21/3 A bad set in a good possie will bring nothing save an occasional adventurous doe. **1937** N. MARSH *Vintage Murder* xxi. 238 Messing about on the scene of the crime... She's going to find herself in a very, very uncomfortable .. pozzy, is Miss Caroline. **1941** *Coast to Coast* 204 S'pose you'll be after some easy stuff next time. A possie where there's a bit of fresh air. **1941** K. TENNANT *Battlers* xxvii. 301 Going to get a possie in the cannery? **1956** D. M. DAVIN *Sullen Bell* 47 'I've brought a picnic,' he said. So you watch out for a nice little pozzy while a good husband keeps his eyes on the road.' **1962** E. SALTER *Voice of Peacock* vii. 77 He couldn't have fallen into a possy like that by himself. **1970** P. WHITE *Vivisector* 620 Should have got here early—got us a good pozzy. Never be in the picture now. **1971** *N.Z. Listener* 19 Apr. 56/5 They found a possie in a bit of a trog and boiled-up.

possie, var. POZZY[2].

possody, obs. form of POWSOWDY, *Sc.*

possum ('pɒsəm), *sb.*[1] Now *colloq.* Also 7 **possown, -e, possam,** 8 **posom,** 9 **'possum.**

a. Aphetic form of OPOSSUM.

1613 A. WHITAKER *Gd. Newes fr. Virginia* 41 The female possown which will let forth her young out of her bellie. **1670** D. DENTON *Descr. New York* (1845) 7 They eat like-wise Polecats, Skunks, Racoon, Possum. **1698** G. THOMAS *Pensilvania* 14 That strange creature, the Possam. **1753** CHAMBERS *Cycl. Supp., Marsupiale*, in natural history, a name given by Tyson to the creature commonly called, the possum, or opossum. *a* **1813** A. WILSON *Foresters* Poet. Wks. (1846) 235 While owls and 'possums found concealment there. **1869** *Routledge's Ev. Boy's Ann.* 594 He's a rare dog for 'possums. **1880** 'MARK TWAIN' *Tramp Abroad* iii. 38 He cocked his head to one side, shut one eye and put the other one to the hole, like a 'possum looking down a pig. **1905** N. DAVIS *Northerner* 156 Falls ate his possum with the appetite which the ride in the cold air had given him. **1932** W. FAULKNER *Light in August* (1933) i. 19, I reckon it ain't any human in this country is going to dispute them hens with you, lessen it's the possums and the snakes. **1948** *Sat. Rev.* (U.S.) 29 May 4/2 The possum broke out of his cage. **1971** *Black World* Oct. 64/2, I suggested castor oil and fricassee possum in the milkshakes. **1975** E. WIGGINTON *Foxfire 3* 25, I wish I could get a good possum.

b. ***to play possum***: to feign, dissemble; to pretend illness: in allusion to the opossum's habit of feigning death when threatened or attacked. So ***to act possum, to come possum over.*** *colloq.* (orig. *U.S.*)

1822 W. H. SIMMONS *Notices E. Florida* 40 After being severely wounded, they have been known to lie for several hours as if dead... Hence, the expression of 'playing possum' is common among the inhabitants, being applied to those who act with cunning and duplicity. **1824** W. N. BLANE *Excursion* 134 It is a common saying in America .. that he is 'playing possum'. **1844** MRS. HOUSTON *Yacht Voy. to Texas* II. 216 When a slave is suspected by his employers of shamming sickness, to avoid his work, he is compared to this cunning little beast: 'Well, I guess he's coming 'possum over us'. **1855** HALIBURTON *Nat. & Hum. Nat.* I. 5, I will play possum with these folks. **1924** [see *death-feigning* (DEATH *sb.* 19)]. **1949** *Time* 5 Sept. 13/1 By last week, in the Senate investigation of Washington five-percenters, it became plain that John had been playing possum the whole time. **1961** G. H. COXE *Error of Judgment* iii. 26, I knew the only way I could beat you was to play possum, but it was a good try, kid.

c. Applied to the phalangers: = OPOSSUM 2.

1770 COOK *Jrnl.* (1893) 294 Here are Wolves, Possums, an Animal like a ratt, and snakes. **1864** R. HENNING *Let.* 27 Nov. (1966) 184 Several [aborigines] were carrying possums which they had caught on their way. **1869** HOARE *Figures of Fancy* 86 The 'possum prattles in the trees. **1878** *Punch* 10 Aug. 59/2 Australian beef, and kangaroos—and 'possums, wombats, and ornithorhyncusses. **1901** M. FRANKLIN *My Brilliant Career* xxx. 258 There would be more life in trapping 'possums out on Timlinbilly. **1916** J. B. COOPER *Coo-oo-ee* xii. 174 'Tim' was pushing his cold nose into Jack's hand to coax him to open the back door to let him out to race round the hut to bark at the 'possums. **1928** 'BRENT OF BIN BIN' *Up Country* i. 6 'Possums when excited by the bark of dogs at the foot of trees where they have refuge will run up and down every branch in turn. **1941** I. L. IDRIESS *Great Boomerang* xiii. 93 His arm caught in a hollow limb reaching for possum or cockatoo's nest. **1959** *Post-Primary School Bulletin* (Wellington, N.Z.) XII. III. 22 A 'possum is born only sixteen days after the egg starts developing within the mother's body. **1966** J. K. BAXTER *Pig Island Lett.* 4 He sets his trap for possums And whistles to his dog. **1966** *New Scientist* 29 Sept. 713/3 Although still popularly known as possums to distinguish them from the opossums of the New World, the Australasian family has been given the apt name of Phalangeridae. **1970** *Southerly* XXX. 303 One night a possum broke into the kitchen, through a window left just slightly ajar. **1977** D. P. GILMORE in Stonehouse & Gilmore *Biol. Marsupials* x. 171 Today the possum is probably the most numerous mammal in New Zealand.

d. *fig.* In various slang uses (see quots.).

1833 *N.Y. Mirror* 7 Sept. 80 *A 'possum*, the western phrase for a paltry fellow—a coward. **1900** *Dialect Notes* II. 51 *Possum*, a negro, or negress. **1943** BAKER *Dict. Austral. Slang* (ed. 3) 61 *Possum*, a 'ring-in'. **1945** —— *Austral. Lang.*

vi. 130 Fools of one kind and another..*flathead, possum, gammy*, [etc.]. *Ibid.* vii. 138 Thieves are described variously as..*dwelling dancers, stoops* and *possums*. *Ibid.* 142 *Jay* and *possum*, a trickster's victim.

e. ***like a possum up a gum-tree***: contented; (see also quot. 1898); ***to stir*** (or ***rouse***) ***the possum***: to stir up controversy, to liven things up. See also GUM-TREE 2. *Austral. colloq.*

1898 *Bulletin* (Sydney) 17 Dec. (Red Page), 'Like a possum up a gum tree' is not bad to express quickness or cleverness in doing anything. **1907** C. MACALISTER *Old Pioneering Days in Sunny South* 51 Sometimes..an ambitious carrier or drover would 'rouse the 'possum' by giving some long-winded ditty of the time. **1908** E. S. SORENSON *Squatter's Ward* 144, I mean to stir the 'possum in Sultan Susman from this out. **1941** BAKER *Dict. Austral. Slang* 56 *Like a possum up a gumtree*, completely happy, in the best of spirits and contentment. **1958** 'W. HENRY' *Seven Men at Mimbres Springs* (1960) viii. 94 They made 'more racket about it than six pickaninnies with a possum up a gum tree'. **1972** *Sydney Morning Herald* 31 Oct. 3 'I could be sitting in Parliament now without any great cost provided I forgot this idea of stirring the possum,' he said. **1976** *Courier-Mail* (Brisbane) 27 Mar. 18/2 Mr. Bob Hawke sees an opening to stir the possum and to step up union wage demands.

f. *attrib.* and *Comb.*, as ***possum beard, hunt*** (also as *vb. intr.*), ***hunter, hunting, -playing, rug, scalper, skin, snare, token***; **possum belly** *U.S. slang* (see quots.).

1928 'BRENT OF BIN BIN' *Up Country* xvi. 273 His 'possum beard and his slouch hat, out of which his mild blue eyes looked with incontestable simplicity. **1926** MAINES & GRANT *Wise-Crack Dict.* 12/1 *Possum belly* tent stake box carried under circus railroad cars. **1939** P. A. ROLLINS *Gone Haywire* 66 There was a sufficient supply of firewood in the 'cooney' or 'possum belly' (a baggy, dried cowhide fastened horizontally beneath the wagon box and used for carrying a reserve of fuel). **1973** *Amer. Speech 1969* XLIV. 207 *Possum belly*, livestock trailer with a drop frame to haul small animals underneath heavy cattle. **1841** *Spirit of Times* 17 July 235/1 A 'possum Hunt. **1900** *Congress. Rec.* 11 Jan. 784/1, I used to 'possum hunt. **1949** *Natural Hist.* May 223/1 According to song and story, most 'possum hunts end at the foot of a 'simmon tree. **1976** C. S. BROWN *Gloss. Faulkner's South* 154 An axe is a regular part of a possum hunt. **1869** *Routledge's Ev. Boy's Ann.* 645 A true 'possum hunter never aims except in the head. **1840** *Southern Lit. Messenger* VI. 784/1 He is fond of possum, rabbit, and coon-hunting. **1856** KANE *Arct. Expl.* I. xxix. 391 The Esquimaux..say that the dogs soon learn this 'possum-playing' habit. **1873** J. H. H. ST. JOHN *Pakeha Rambles through Maori Lands* vii. 128 With a blanket, or better still, a 'possum rug,..the traveller may jog along very comfortably. **1880** FISON & HOWITT *Kamilaroi* 197 Each lad has his head covered up in a 'possum rug. **1942** C. BARRETT *On Wallaby* iii. 36 'Fifty quid,' he said reflectively. 'More than a possum rug's worth.' **1946** F. D. DAVISON *Dusty* 164 He was a possum scalper, now. **1911** C. E. W. BEAN '*Dreadnought' of Darling* xxix. 249 They did..sometimes sew themselves sort of elementary clothes out of possum skins threaded together with kangaroo tendons. **1966** 'J. HACKSTON' *Father clears Out* 13, I remembered the honey and the fruit, the rabbits, the possum-skins, the money—all the help my little world had given me. *Ibid.* 8 Before the dawn I went round possum snares. **1961** B. CRUMP *Hang on a Minute* 145 Well, a man could sell deerskins and possum tokens.

Possum ('pɒsəm), *sb.*[2] Also **possum**. [f. the initial letters of *p*atient *o*perated *s*elector *m*echanism, after POSSUM *sb.*[1]] A proprietary name for any of various electronic devices, operated in different ways, which enable disabled persons to operate or control domestic fittings, machines, or other equipment.

1961 *New Scientist* 8 June 561/1 The basis of the device, which is known as 'Possum', is that a small steady suck or blow can operate a sensitive switch which, in turn, operates a rotary switch connected to a grid. The grid sets out letters, numbers and punctuation symbols. **1961** *Trade Marks Jrnl.* 12 July 918/1 *Possum*... All goods included in class 10 [*i.e.* surgical, medical, dental and veterinary instruments and apparatus, including artificial limbs, eyes, and teeth]. Reginald George Maling,..Aylesbury, Buckinghamshire; merchant. **1972** *Daily Tel.* 31 Oct. 18 Electronic devices with which severely disabled people can operate typewriters and other machines by mouth, finger or toe, possums.. enable the handicapped to lead useful lives. **1974** *Listener* 25 Apr. 525/3 The Possum machine with which, by sucking and blowing into a tube, she can type, telephone, open the front door..or buzz for help. **1976** *Responaut* Autumn 13/2 My window on the world, apart from my eyes, is 15 inches by 7, the size of the tilting mirror attached to my respirator. Reflected through this I can see my two Possum indicators revealing the 21 electrical devices I am able to control.

'possum, *v. U.S.* and *Austral. colloq.* [f. prec. sb.]

1. a. *intr.* To 'play possum': see prec. b.

1832 T. FLINT *Geog. Mississippi Valley* (ed. 2) I. 67 In the common parlance of the country, any one, who counterfeits sickness..is said to be 'possuming' [*ed.* 1828 oppossuming]. **1846** R. LEVINGE *Echoes from Backwoods* II. 32 'Possuming is become an idiom; a term signifying any one who is humbugging or deceiving. **1862** *Harper's Mag.* Dec. 99/2 So you see you must endure it to the end—fur thar's no possumin' thar. **1888** *Daily Inter-Ocean* 6 Feb. (Farmer), With three dangerously wounded grizzlies roaming around the immediate neighbourhood, besides the possibility of possuming among those stretched out below. **1912** W. H. THOMAS in J. F. Dobie *Rainbow in Morning* (1965) II. 4 Now when that nigger comes to, if she's been possumin', she sho' will be hungry.

b. *trans.* To feign, to simulate.

1853 J. G. BALDWIN *Flush Times Alabama* 150 All this time I was possuming sleep..as innocent as a lamb.

2. To hunt opossums. Usually in *vbl. sb.*

1869 *Routledge's Ev. Boy's Ann.* 607 To go out with him on a 'possuming expedition. **1900** H. LAWSON *Over Shiprails* 152, I promised to go 'possuming with Johnny Nowlett. **1933** *Bulletin* (Sydney) 4 Jan. 11 A short-sighted young man went out 'possuming. **1942** C. BARRETT *On Wallaby* iii. 36 He may have done a bit of cyaniding and out of season possuming.

possy, var. POSSIE, POZZY[1].

post (pəʊst), *sb.*[1] Also (4 **pos**), 5 **poost**, 5–7 **poste**, 7 **poast**. [OE. *post* a post, pillar, door-post, ad. L. *postis* a post, door-post (in med.L. also a rod, pole, beam), whence also OHG. *pfost* (Ger. *pfosten*) post, beam, MLG., LG., MDu., Du. *post* door-post; also OF. *post* (12th c. in Godef.) (mod. dial. *pôt*) post, pillar, beam, by which prob. the OE. word was reinforced in ME.

(Dialectal plurals are *posses, postès, postesses*: see Pegge *Anecd. Eng. Lang.* and *Eng. Dial. Dict.*)]

I. 1. a. A stout piece of timber, or other solid material, of considerable length, and usually of cylindrical or square shape, used in a vertical position, esp. in building as a support for a superstructure.

c **1000** ÆLFRIC *Saints' Lives* xxvi. 226 He aheng þa þæt dust on ænne heahne post. *c* **1000** *Ælfric's Voc.* in Wr.-Wülcker 164/32 *Basis*, post. *c* **1205** LAY. 28032 He bigon to hewene..and þa postes for-heou alle, þa heolden up þa halle. *a* **1300** *Cursor M.* 7258 Þe post þat al þat huse vpbare Wit bath his handes he it scok. **1340** *Ayenb.* 180 Strang and stedeuest ase a pos ine his temple. *c* **1440** *Promp. Parv.* 410/2 Poost, of an howse, *postis*. **1563** GOLDING *Cæsar* VII. (1565) 190 b, Greate postes of streight timber set on a row equally dystant a two fote space one from another. **1601** SIR W. CORNWALLIS *Ess.* xxii, Not a Poste, nor a painted cloth in the house but cryes out, Feare God. **1725** WATTS *Logic* I. iv. §6 Post is equivocal, it is a piece of timber, or a swift messenger. **1815** J. SMITH *Panorama Sc. & Art* I. 262 If it be not convenient to allow the posts in partitions to be square, which is the best form.

1795 *Sporting Mag.* V. 135 With what difficulty he gets through a crowd, or clears the postesses in the fields. **1833** MARRYAT *Peter S.* iii, I inquired of the coachman which was the best inn. He answered 'that it was the Blue Postesses, where the midshipmen leave their chestesses'.

†**b.** Formerly sometimes applied to a beam. *Obs.*

1567 GOLDING *Ovid* x. 129 Shee ryseth, full in mynd To hang herself. About a post her girdle she doth bynd. **1589** RIDER *Bibl. Schol.* 1123 A post called the browe post, which is iust over the threshold: some call it a transome.

c. As a type of lifelessness, stupidity, ignorance, deafness, or hardness: cf. BLOCK *sb.* 1 b.

between you and me and the post (or ***bed-post***): as something that no one else is to hear or know; as a secret, in confidence.

c **1412** HOCCLEVE *De Reg. Princ.* 4695 But welaway! as harde as is a post..ben hertes now! *c* **1430** *Hymns Virg.* (1867) 61 Good conscience, goo preche to þe post, þi councel saueriþ not my tast. **1617** BRATHWAIT *Drinking* 80 Till they like Posts can neither speake nor goe. **1778** MISS BURNEY *Evelina* xxxiii, They..know no more than the post. **1816** 'QUIZ' *Grand Master* Pref. 4 The fellow, stupid as a post, Believ'd in truth it was a ghost! **1832** LYTTON *Eugene A.* IV. i. 205 Between you and me and the bed-post, young master's quarrelled with old master. **1838** DICKENS *Nich. Nick.* x, And between you and me and the post, sir, it will be a very nice portrait too. *a* **1845** HOOD *T. Trumpet* iv, She was deaf as a post. **1873** MRS. ALEXANDER *Wooing o't* III. iv. 94 Between you and me and the post, I don't think they have much money.

2. a. A stake, stout pole, column, or the like, that is set upright in or on the ground, for various purposes; e.g. as a boundary mark, landmark, or monument, a stand for displaying public notices, a support for a fence, a point of attachment, etc.

poet of the post: ? one who exhibited his writings in public.

a **1300** *St. Michael* 149 in *Treat. Sc.*, etc. (Wright) 135 If ther were nou a post heȝ [*Laud. MS.* an heiȝ stepel], and a man above sete, And me seȝe him smyte an heȝ gode duntes and grete. **1417** *Searchers Verdicts* in *Surtees Misc.* (1888) 11 A party of the ferrest post of Robert of Feriby standys on Seint Leonard grunde. **1540** *Act 32 Hen. VIII*, c. 14 [They] shall..affix the same writing unto some post or other open place..in Lumberdstrete. **1640** R. WEST in Ferrand *Erotomania* b vij, And sweare, like Poets of the Post, This Play Exceeds all Iohnsons Works. **1643** MILTON *Soveraigne Salve* 40 Like Posts of direction for Travellers. *c* **1710** CELIA FIENNES *Diary* (1888) 157 At all cross wayes there are posts with hands pointing to each road. *Mod.* The boundary is marked by a line of posts. The lane is barred by posts against riding or driving.

†**b.** Formerly set up by the door of a mayor, sheriff, or other magistrate. *Obs.*

1598 BP. HALL *Sat.* IV. ii. 21 Whose sonne more iustly of his gentry boasts Then who were borne at two pide painted posts; And had some traunting Merchant to his syre. **1601** SHAKS. *Twel. N.* I. v. 157 Hee'l stand at your door like a Sheriffes post..but hee'l speake with you. **1618** *Owles Alm.*, *Painters* 57 My Lord Maiors posts must needs be trimmed against he takes his oath. **1632** ROWLEY *New Wonder* I. 7 If e'r I live to see thee Shreiffe of London, I'l gild thy painted postes. **1845** PARKER *Gloss. Archit.* s.v., Posts, planted in the ground..were formerly placed at the sides of the doors of sheriffs and municipal authorities, probably to fix proclamations and other notices to.

3. With prefixed word indicating special purpose.

draw-post, a post used in wire fences, provided with winders for tightening the wires; ***foot-post***, one of the posts at the foot of a four-post bedstead; ***kerb-post***, a post set at the edge of a pavement; ***race-post***, a starting-post or winning-post. See also BED-, CLOTHES-, DOOR-, GATE-, GOAL-, KING-, LAMP-, SIGN-POST *sb.*; also *direction-post* (DIRECTION 11), *reaching-post* (REACHING *vbl. sb.*[1]), etc.

1643 MILTON *Soveraigne Salve* 40 Like race posts quickly to be run over. **1731** W. HALFPENNY *Perspective* 32 From B and E, raise the Head-posts to the Frame L and M, also draw the Foot-posts and Rails. **1849** NOAD *Electricity* (ed. 3) 378 One end being attached to the winder at one draw-post, the wire is extended to the adjoining draw-post, and fixed to its corresponding winder at that post. **1904** *Westm. Gaz.* 25 Mar. 1/3 Four of the cannon..now fill the lowly if useful rôles of kerb-posts and lamp-posts.

4. Contextually for various specific kinds of posts.

a. A door-post or gate-post.

a **1300** *Cursor M.* 6077 On aiþer post þer hus to smer, A taken o tav [T or †] on þair derner. **1382** WYCLIF *Judg.* xvi. 3 Sampson..took both leeues of the ȝate, with her postes and lok. —— *Prov.* viii. 34 Blisful the man..that waitith at the postis of my dore. *c* **1450** *Mirour Saluacioun* 3428 Sampson..the ȝates with the postis with hym bare he away. **1671** MILTON *Samson* 147 The Gates of Azza, Post, and massie Bar.

b. A whipping-post (?).

1624 HEYWOOD *Captives* v. iii. in Bullen *O. Pl.* IV, They will spitt at us and doom us Unto the post and cart.

c. *Racing.* The post which marks the starting or finishing point; a starting-post or winning post. Also *fig.* Phr. ***first past the post***, used *attrib.* and *absol.* to designate the electoral system whereby the candidate with the largest number of votes, or the party with the largest number of seats, wins an election; ***to pip on*** (or ***at***) ***the post***: see PIP *v.*[3] 1 c.

1642 FULLER *Holy & Prof. St.* III. xii. 181 A Fool and a Wiseman are alike both in the starting-place, their birth, and at the post, their death. **1678** BUTLER *Hud.* III. i. 898 A Race, In which both do their uttermost To get before, and win the Post. **1708** *Yorkshire-Racers* 10 From diff'rent posts the various racers start. **1818** C. GRENVILLE *Let.* 19 Dec. (1920) 228 The 2nd Miss Morgan *expects* to marry Lord Rodney, if he does not again *jib at the Post*. **1885** H. SMART (*title*) From Post to Finish. **1885** *Daily Tel.* 19 Dec. 2/6 Some good horses mustered at the post. **1907** *Tribune* 23 Mar. 10/5 The hurdles... The two men were together until almost the very last fence, and then Powell shot out and won on the post. **1921** E. O'NEILL *Emperor Jones* i. 161 Den de revolution is at de post. **1935** 'N. BLAKE' *Question of Proof* x. 197 'After all,' he continued, 'the Business-As-Usual slogan gets the British middle-class where they live—it has just the right combination of backs-to-the-wall bulldog courage and commercial *savoir-faire*. In this case it will leave its only rival—the respect-for-the-dead ballyhoo—at the post.' **1949** J. D. CARR *Below Suspicion* xvii. 208 'One of the things I like about you,' commented Butler,..'is the pellucid clarity of your style. Addison is nowhere. Macaulay is left at the post.' **1952** L. OVERACKER *Austral. Party System* viii. 221 At that time the 'first past the post' system of election was in use. **1958** C. P. SNOW *Conscience of Rich* v. 37 In strength of character we were about the same. In everything but natural gifts, he had so much start that I was left at the post. **1965** *Austral. Encycl.* III. 367/1 In 1892, Queensland became the Australian pioneer of one of the chief improvements on first-past-the-post, namely the alternative or contingent vote. **1966** *Encycl. N.Z.* I. 864/2 The..first-past-the-post electoral system. Under this system, which has been in operation for most of this century, minor parties are crushed. **1976** *Times* 20 Aug. 13/1 The existing electoral system, based on the 'first past the post' principle which has shown itself to be so anomalous at Westminster.

d. *Naut.* The upright timber on which the rudder is hung; the stern-post; †hence *transf.* the stern of a ship (*obs.*).

body post, inner post: see quots. *c* 1850, 1867.

1622 R. HAWKINS *Voy. S. Sea* (1847) 22 Our ship calked from post to stem. **1682** SIR J. BERRY in *Lond. Gaz.* No. 1720/7 A terrible blow struck off the Rother, and, as was believed, struck out a blank nigh the Post. *c* **1850** *Rudim. Navig.* (Weale) 126 *Inner Post*, a piece of oak timber brought on and fayed to the fore-side of the main stern-post, for the purpose of seating the transoms upon it. **1867** SMYTH *Sailor's Word-bk.*, *Body-post*, an additional stern-post introduced at the fore-part of an aperture cut in the deadwood in a ship fitted with a screw-propeller.

e. A goal-post.

1867 [see POSTER[3]]. **1878** *Chambers's Encycl.* IV. 414/1 He will touch it down as near as he can to the goal, if possible between the posts. **1880** *Times* 15 Mar. 6/5 For some little time after this the English kept play in close proximity to their rivals' posts, causing the goalkeeper some anxiety. **1900** A. E. T. WATSON *Young Sportsman* 284 *Poster*,..a place kick which..would have hit the posts produced upward and rebounded into the field of play. **1972** G. GREEN *Great Moments in Sport: Soccer* xviii. 156 It ended with Nordahl turning Puis's chip to the near post against Wilson's upright, with the goalkeeper helpless. **1978** *Rugby World* Apr. 7/3 The Scots would..have been awarded a penalty try.., with the conversion being taken from in front of the posts, instead of from the more difficult position farther out.

f. A leg of a chair. *U.S.*

1902 W. N. HARBEN *Abner Daniel* 202 Something like a groan escaped Bishop's lips as he lowered the front posts of his chair to the floor.

†**5.** The door-post on which the reckoning at a tavern was kept; hence, the account or score. *Obs.*

1590 SHAKS. *Com. Err.* I. ii. 64 If I return I shall be post indeede. For she will scoure your fault vpon my pate. **1600–12** ROWLANDS *Four Knaves* (Percy Soc.) 11 Score it up, when God sends coyne I will discharge your poast. **1604** —— *Looke to it* 39 You that for all your diet with your Hoast, Do set your hand in Chalke vnto his Poast.

II. †**6.** *fig.* A support, prop, stay: = PILLAR 3.

c **1374** CHAUCER *Troylus* I. 1000 That þow shalt be þe best post..Of al his lay. *c* **1386** —— *Prol.* 214 Vn to his ordre he was a noble post. *c*1430 LYDG. *Min. Poems* (Percy Soc.) 29 Ful ofte a wife is a broken poste. *a*1536 *Calisto & Melibæa* (1905) 70 Now God be their guides! the posts of my life. 1579 W. WILKINSON *Confut.* 46 b, H N. and his heyre Vitels, beyng great postes in his new-found Family.

III. Transferred uses.

7. a. A vertical mass or stack of stratified rock between two 'joints' or fissures.

1712 MORTON *Nat. Hist. Northamptonshire* 127 The continued Lines are the larger Perpendicular Fissures, there called Gulfe-Joints, and sometimes Damps. The Spaces inclos'd within them are the *Posts* or *Stacks* of Stone, that are thus severed from each other by means of those Gulfe-Joints. 1772 in Picton *L'pool Munic. Rec.* (1886) II. 227 To feigh a post of stone at the said quarry.

b. Any thick compact stratum of sandstone or limestone.

1794 W. HUTCHINSON *Hist. Cumberld.* II. 443 Each key is composed of a number of layers of stone, of a different thickness, which the workmen call *posts.* 1812 R. GRAHAM *Agric. Surv. Stirling* i. §5. 52 The stratum or post, as it is here called, of this quarry, is from 10 to 15 feet thick. 1876 PAGE *Adv. Text-bk. Geol.* v. 92 The term post is frequently applied to express a thick uniform-grained stratum of sandstone. 1887 H. MILLER *Geol. Otterburn & Elsdon* iii. 10 A number of limestone bands, or 'posts', will be found at the head of Sills Burn.

c. Also ***post-stone***: Sandstone of a fine grain.

1797 *Encycl. Brit.* (ed. 3) V. 93/2 Of Post-stone. This is a free stone of the hardest kind..of a very fine texture..and when broken appears as if composed of the finest sand... Red post is generally of a dull red colour. 1883 GRESLEY *Gloss. Coal Mining, Post*,.. 2. Sandstone (fine-grained).

d. A vertical mass or pillar of coal in a mine, left uncut to support the roof of the working. ***post and stall***: = ***pillar and stall***: see PILLAR *sb.* 7.

1811 FAREY *Agric. Derbyshire* I. 188 The method of posts and stalls, or leaving large pillars and excavating chambers between them, is resorted to. 1839 URE *Dict. Arts*, etc. 979 In the post and stall system, each man has his own room, and performs all the labour in it. 1883 GRESLEY *Gloss. Coal Mining, Post*, 1. A solid block or pillar of coal.

¶ In *Paper-making*: see POST *sb.*[5] 1.

IV. 8. Phrases.

a. ***post and paling***: see quot. **b.** ***post and pan***: applied to a building or mode of construction in which the walls are formed of a framework of beams with the spaces filled in with brickwork, plaster, or the like; also called locally ***post and panel*** (Eng. Dial. Dict.), ***petrail, plaster, tan.*** **c.** ***post and railing***: see quot. 1823 and POST AND RAIL. **d.** ***from post to pillar***: see PILLAR *sb.* 11. †**e.** ***to go to the post***: = to go to the wall. **f.** ***to kiss the post*** (see KISS *v.* 6 h): to be shut out or disappointed. **g.** ***to make a hack in the post***: to use up or consume a considerable part of something, to 'make a hole in'. **h.** ***to run one's head against a post***: in fig. use. **i.** ***on the right*** or ***the wrong side of the post***, etc. (referring to posts marking the right course); hence *fig.* **j.** ***post and beam***: applied to a mode of construction in which the framework consists of upright and horizontal beams.

a. 1823 P. NICHOLSON *Pract. Build.* 590 *Post and Paling*, a close wooden fence, constructed of posts set into the ground and pales nailed to rails between them.

b. 1517 *Nottingham Rec.* III. 140 Unam domum de postis and pannes. 1788 W. MARSHALL *Yorksh.* II. Gloss. (E.D.S.), *Post-and-pan*, old half-timber buildings are said to be post-and-pan. 1842–76 GWILT *Archit.* (ed. 7) Gloss. s.v. *Pan*, Called post and pan, or post and petrail work, in the north of England. 1867 HARLAND & WILKINSON *Lanc. Folk-Lore* 263 A dwelling..of clay and wood, what is called post and petrel. 1890 *Blackw. Mag.* Oct. 462 Their 'post and tan' cottages have passed away. 1900 *Daily News* 26 Jan. 7/1 We may see the gabled post-and plaster house, of which the older part is late fifteenth-century work. 1954 S. PIGGOTT *Neolithic Cultures Brit. Isles* vi. 163 With the façade formed by orthostats ascending in height to the portals and originally linked by dry-stone walling in a 'post and panel' technique. 1975 *Country Life* 6 Feb. 319/3 Black and white timber and plaster work of the post-and-pan variety.

c. 1823 P. NICHOLSON *Pract. Build.* 590 *Post and Railing*, an open wooden fence, consisting of posts and rails only.

e. *a*1624 BP. M. SMITH *Serm.* (1632) 118 Antichrist had no sooner gotten to high strength..but the faithfull went to the post, and wandered vp and downe.

f. *c*1515–1681 [see KISS *v.* 6 h]. *a*1529 SKELTON *P. Sparowe* 710 Troylus also hath lost On her moch loue and cost, And now must kys the post. *c*1550 R. BIESTON *Bayte Fortune* B iij, The Church they despoyle, the poore the poste may kis. 1607 DEKKER *Knt.'s Conjur.* (1842) 63 The vsurer looking as hungrilie as if he had kist the post.

g. 1842 J. AITON *Domest. Econ.* (1857) 244, £25 or £30 paid all at once for one horse makes a sad hack in the post, and cannot well be spared by a minister, unless he has a nest-egg in the bank.

h. 1805 SURR *Winter in Lond.* (1806) I. 38 You have run your head against a post, as the saying is.

i. 1792–5 AIKIN & BARBAULD *Even. at Home* xxiii, At length,..Young Peer [race-horse] ran on the wrong side of the post, was distanced, and the Squire ruined. 1803 MARY CHARLTON *Wife & Mistress* IV. 94 On the right side of the Post. *a*1814 *Fam. Politics* III. iv. in *New Brit. Theatre* II. 224, I find I am on the wrong side of the post; I must flatter a little. 1852 DICKENS *Bleak Ho.* xx, Still, Tony, you were on the wrong side of the post then. 1858 TROLLOPE *Dr. Thorne* (Tauchn.) II. i. 12 Though they may possibly go astray, they have a fair chance given to them of running within the posts. 1861 —— *Framley P.* (Tauchn.) II. xxiii. 340 He had bolted from his appointed course, going terribly on the wrong side of the posts.

j. 1958 *Listener* 25 Sept. 459/1 The other structural method is the application of the simple post-and-beam technique to form a framed structure similar to that obtained by steel or reinforced concrete. 1978 *N.Y. Times* 30 Mar. c 8/2 The designer, Donald Davidson, assembled cedar slats post-and-beam style to make an armchair.

V. 9. *attrib.* and *Comb.*, as ***post-betting*** (4 c), ***-foot, -postmaker***; applied to implements for drawing, pulling up, or making a hole in the ground for, a post, as ***post-auger, -driver, -jack, -puller***; also to things fixed or mounted on a post, as ***post-box, -dial, -drill, -pump, -windlass***; ***post-legged, -like*** adjs.; †**postband**, ?a band in a panelled ceiling: = LAQUEAR 1; **post-bird, post-butt**: see quots.; **post cedar**, the white or incense cedar, *Libocedrus decurrens*; **post-driver**, (*a*) an implement for driving in posts or piles, a pile-driver; (*b*) the American bittern, the stake-driver; **post-line**, an elevated railway line (*Cent. Dict.*); †**post-metal**, the metal-work connecting a door with its post; **post-mill**, a windmill pivoted on a post, so as to be turned round to catch the wind; **post-painter**, a signpost-painter; **post-pocket**, an iron socket fixed on the outside of a railway car to receive a post; **post quintain**, a stake or post used as a quintain: = PEL; **post-retained crown** *Dentistry* = POST CROWN; **post-sitter** *Austral.* = POST-BOY 3; **post time** *N. Amer.*, the starting time for a horse-race; **post-windmill** = *post-mill*; †**post-writing**, writing on a door-post: cf. Deut. vi. 9, 24. See also POST ALONE, POST-HOLE, POST-KNIGHT, etc.

1868 *Rep. U.S. Commiss. Agric.* (1869) 354 Its practicability can..be ascertained by digging a well, or by boring with a pile or *post auger. *c*1425 *Voc.* in Wr.-Wülcker 667/19 *Hoc laquear*, *postband. *c*1475 *Pict. Voc.* ibid. 778/7 *Hoc laquiare*, postbondde. 1894 *Westm. Gaz.* 10 Apr. 7/2 It is evident that the City and Suburban will this year be a *post-betting race. 1882 *Science Gossip* XVIII. 65/1 Local Names.—(Kent)..Spotted Flycatcher..'*Post bird'; from its habit of perching on a post, watching for flies. 1884 KNIGHT *Dict. Mech.* Suppl., **Post Box*, a shafting box attached to a post. 1875 —— *Dict. Mech.*, **Post-butt*, a block inserted in the ground and having a socket to hold a post. 1669 STURMY *Mariner's Mag.* civ, *Post and Pocket Dials for any Latitude. 1546 *Yorks. Chantry Surv.* (Surtees) II. 223 Payd for a *poste fote standyng of the grounde of Robert Wodemansey, iiij[d]. 1608 ARMIN *Nest Ninn.* (1880) 48 He was gouty, bigge, *poste legged, and of yeeres something many. 1845 THOREAU *Jrnl.* 14 July in *Writings* (1906) VII. 365 A woodchopper, a *post-maker. 1582 STANYHURST *Æneis* II. (Arb.) 59 Pyrrhus..Downe beats with pealing thee doors, and *post metal heaueth. 1825 J. NICHOLSON *Operat. Mechanic* 122 To effect this [i.e. bringing the sails to the wind] two methods are in general use: the one called the *post-mill; the other the smock-mill. 1934 *Archit. Rev.* LXXVI. 165/3 The Post mill is the earliest known form of mill. The structure is box-like in shape and carries the machinery and the sails. Supporting this structure is a single upright post on which the mill revolves. 1968 J. ARNOLD *Shell Bk. Country Crafts* 169 The oldest mills, those in existence at the time of the Domesday book, were all post-mills. 1974 C. TAYLOR *Fieldwork in Medieval Archaeol.* 12 The circular mound on a hilltop may be a Bronze Age barrow, or it may be the base of a medieval post-mill, or it may be both. 1752 FOOTE *Taste* I. i, Why, thou *Post-painter, thou Dauber, thou execrable White-washer. 1801 STRUTT *Sports & Past.* III. i. §3 (1876) 186 The exercise of the pel, or *post quintain, which is spoken of at large by Vegetius. 1963 C. R. COWELL et al. *Inlays, Crowns, & Bridges* viii. 84 A *post-retained crown is commonly indicated for a root-filled anterior tooth the natural crown of which has become discoloured. 1974 C. L. STURRIDGE in Harty & Roberts *Restorative Procedures Practising Dentist* ix. 141 In the front of the mouth a post-retained crown will be the treatment of choice if the tooth is non-vital. 1901 A. J. CAMPBELL *Nests & Eggs Austral. Birds* I. 106. The Brown Flycatcher or '*Post Sitter'..begins to breed [in] September or October. 1911, etc. Post-sitter [see POST-BOY 3]. 1941 *Sun* (Baltimore) 30 Aug. 13/1 Everything is in readiness for the opening of business about an hour before *post time tomorrow. 1968 *Globe & Mail* (Toronto) 17 Feb. 42/1 (Advt.), Post time 7:45. 1884 KNIGHT *Dict. Mech.* Suppl., **Post Windlass*, a winding machine which is actuated with breaks or handspikes. 1931 *Times Educ. Suppl.* 19 Dec. (Home & Classroom Suppl.) p.iv/2 A Cambridgeshire *post-windmill..revolves in an artificial breeze to show wind-power. 1974 C. TAYLOR *Fieldwork in Medieval Archaeol.* vi. 119 A circular mound, discovered on the ground or from air photographs, can be proved to have been the site of a post-windmill if an old estate map depicts a windmill there. 1621 AINSWORTH *Annot. Pentat.* Deut. vi. 9 Whosoever hath his phylacteries on his head and on his arme,..and *post-writing on his doore, he is fortified.

post (pəʊst), *sb.*[2] Also 6–7 poste, poast, 6 *Sc.* poist. [a. F. *poste* (1477 in Godef.), in the same senses as in Eng., ad. It. *posta*, orig. the same word as *posta*, F. *poste* station, stand, late L. or Rom. *posta* sb. from *postus* (Lucretius) = *positus*, pa. pple. of *pōnĕre* to place. From It. also Sp., Pg. *posta*; from Fr. (app.), Du., Ger., Da., Sw. *post.* See Note below.]

I. †**1.** From the beginning of the 16th c., applied to men with horses stationed or appointed in places at suitable distances along the post-roads (see POST-STAGE), the duty of each being to ride with, or forward with all speed to the next stage, the king's 'packet', and at length the letters of other persons, as well as to furnish change of horses to 'thorough-posts' or express messengers riding post. ***to lay posts***, to establish a chain of such 'posts' along a route for the speedy forwarding of dispatches.

Posts were at first 'laid' temporarily only, when occasion demanded direct communication with a distant point; they were at length established permanently along certain routes. These 'posts' began in the 17th c. to be called 'postmasters' (q.v.), and were the precursors of the present local postmasters, or persons in charge of the local post offices, who receive and dispatch the local mails. In the 16th and 17th c., these 'posts' had also usually the exclusive privilege of furnishing post-horses to ordinary travellers, and of conducting the business of a posting establishment, which has since been separated from that of the Post Office.

1506 (Mar. 19) *Exch. T.R. Miscell. Bks.* 214, 46 To Gilbert Burgh one post lying at Bagshote, Thomas Anesley an other post lying at Basyngstoke [and so on, seven more to Exeter]. —— (Ap. 24) *Ibid.* 56 To the 9 posts lying betwext Bagshote and Excetour..to William Okeley riding to every of the said postes to see the ordring of them... To John Heyther..riding with letters to the postes lying at London. 1533 TUKE *Let. to Cromwell* in *St. Papers Hen. VIII*, I. 404 The Kinges pleasure is, that postes be better appointed, and laide in al places most expedient. *Ibid.* 405, I never used other ordre but to charge the townshippes to lay and appoint such a post, as they will answer for. 1536 R. SAMPSON *Let. to Cromwell* Oct., To cause Mr. Tuke diligently to lay his posts betwixt his Grace and my Lord of Suffolk, to my Lord Steward from Huntingdon, also to Ampthill, and from the North to the King. 1547 *Reg. Privy Council Scot.* I. 73 That the saidis personis..have post horsis ilk ane of thame for thair awin part, at the bailis forsaidis, to await apoun the incuming of our saidis inemeis, and the samin postis to depart fra the baile of Sanctabbis heid to the Lard of Rastalrig [etc.]. *a*1548 HALL *Chron., Hen. VIII* 37 b, [1513–14] The erle of Surrey..layed Postes euery waye, whiche Postes stretched to the marches of Wales to the counsayll there, by reason whereof, he had knowlege what was done in euery coste. 1572 in *Rep. Secret Comm. on P.O.* (1844) 34 For the wages of the ordinarie postes laide betwene London and Barwicke and elles where within hir Maiesties Realme of Englande. 1598 *Ibid.* 37 That..you take order forthwith for the speedie appointinge and layinge of the standinge and ordinarie postes againe,..betweene the Courte and Hollyheade. 1603 *Ibid.* 39 That in all places where Posts are layde for the packet, they also, as persons most fit, shall have the benefit and preheminence of letting, furnishing, and appointing of horses to all riding in poste. 1603 *Orders for the Posts* ibid. 40 Every Post, so receiving our packets,..shall, within one quarter of an houre at the most after they come to his handes, dispatch them away in Post, and shall runne there-with in sommer..after seven miles the houre. 1609 *Orders for the Pacquet* ibid. 42 All pacquets or letters..shall bee carried by the Postes in poste from stage to stage onely, and not otherwise nor further. 1609 *Orders for the thorough Postes* ibid. 42 The horsing of al through-posts, and persons riding in poste with horne or guide,..shall be performed by our standing Postes in their several stages; who..shall..have in a readinesse..a sufficient number of poste-horses. 1628 *Ibid.* 52 The humble petition of all the Posts of England, being in number 99 poore men. [Cf. POSTMASTER[1] 1 b quot. 1659.]

2. a. One who travels express with letters, messages, etc., esp. on a fixed route; *orig.* a courier, a post-rider (now chiefly *Hist.*); a letter-carrier, a postman (now chiefly *dial.*).

Applied in early times to special messengers or couriers bearing dispatches (***thorough posts***), as well as to those who carried them from stage to stage (***standing posts***: see 1). Still applied locally to a POSTMAN, who carries the mail in a vehicle, on horseback, or on foot (***foot-post***) between a principal post office and the various branch offices; sometimes also to a letter-carrier who delivers letters in a town or rural district.

1507 *Acc. Ld. High Treas. Scot.* IV. 78 To the French post quhilk com heir xxviii li. *Ibid.* 82 [see 8 h]. 1513 [see 8 b; POSTMASTER 1 a]. 1533 TUKE *Let. to Cromwell* in *St. Papers Hen. VIII*, I. 405 As to postes bitwene London and the Courte, there be nowe but 2; wherof the on is a good robust felowe. (*Ibid.* passim.) 1537 CROMWELL in *Life & Lett.* (1902) II. 110 Yt was thought meate that a post shulde be dyspaccheyd with dylygence. 1548 Flieng postes [see FLYING *ppl. a.* 4 b]. 1563 FOXE *A. & M.* 775 The prouerb sayth, that postes do bere truth in ther letters, and lyes in there mouthes. 1597 SHAKS. *2 Hen. IV*, Induct. 37 The Postes come tyring on, And not a man of them brings other newes. 1612 J. MORE in *Buccleuch MSS.* (Hist. MSS. Comm.) I. 128 The post Diston is now scarce passed Gravesend with the King's packet. 1619 SIR I. WAKE *Let.* in *Eng. & Germ.* (Camden) 142 The ordinary posts do come so slowly that I cannot expect by them anie answere of this letter in two months and more, which would be to much time. 1629 WADSWORTH *Pilgr.* iii. 27 Who deliuered it to the Poste which comes weekely from London to S. Omers. *a*1639 WOTTON *Parallel* in *Reliq.* (1651) 14 A Post came crossing by, and blew his Horn. 1684 BUNYAN *Pilgr.* II. 195 The Post presented her with a Letter. 1765 in E. E. Atwater *Hist. New Haven* (1887) 216 A special post is appointed to carry it [Gazette] out of the common post-roads. 1823 COOPER *Pioneers* xix, The man who carried the mail, or 'the post', as he was called. 1832 MACAULAY *Armada* 14 With loose rein and bloody spur rode inland many a post. 1899 *Westm. Gaz.* 15 Apr. 8/1 In early life he became post and driver of the mails, and was able to recall many interesting stories.

b. Applied to similar bearers of messages or letters in ancient times or far-off lands.

1535 COVERDALE *2 Chron.* xxx. 6 The postes [WYCLIF curours] wente with the letters from the hande of the kynge and of his rulers thorow out all Israell and Iuda, at y[e] kynges commaundement. 1600 J. PORY tr. *Leo's Africa* VIII. 321 [They] were the Soldans foote-postes that carried letters from Cairo into Syria, and trauelled on foote three-score miles a day. 1607 TOPSELL *Four-f. Beasts* (1658) 253 That gallant race of swift Horses among the Veneti: upon these ride the posts, carrying the letters of Kings and Emperors to the appointed places. 1611 BIBLE *Job* ix. 25 Now my days are swifter than a post. 1734 tr. *Rollin's Roman Hist.* (1827) II. 369 Posts and couriers. This invention is ascribed to Cyrus.

c. *transf.* and *fig.*

*c*1586 C'TESS PEMBROKE *Ps.* XCV. iv, Twise twenty times my post the sun His yearly race to end had run. 1648 BOYLE *Seraph. Love* (1660) 57 His swift Posts the Angels, when sent on Errands to us here on Earth. *c*1673 TRAHERNE *Poet. Wks.* (1906) 123 Thoughts are the priveleged posts that soar Unto His throne.

3. A vehicle or vessel used in the conveyance of the mails; a mail-coach or -cart; †a packet-boat. †Also, in early use, a post-horse. ? *Obs.* (or merged in 4, to which quots. 1785, 1848 may belong; quot. 1904 refers to Switzerland).

1597 SHAKS. *2 Hen. IV*, IV. iii. 40, I haue fowndred nine score and odde Postes. **1635** J. HAYWARD tr. *Biondi's Banish'd Virg.* 75 The poasts and vessels of intelligence.. going and coming incessantly. **1684–5** *Depos. Castle York* (Surtees) 268 'Neighbour, did you heare the post of last night?' 'Yes, I heard and saw it, but what is the newes, neighbour?' **1707** CHAMBERLAYNE *Pres. St. Eng.* III. (ed. 22) 443 The Posts in some Foreign Countries make not more Miles in a Day. **1785** CRABBE *Newspaper* 283 That day arrives; no welcome post appears. **1848** DICKENS *Dombey* xxii, The post had come in heavy that morning. **1904** *Westm. Gaz.* 23 July 4/1 It is the yellow 'post', drawn by five horses, and bound for the tops.

4. A single dispatch of letters (and other postal matter) from or to a place; also *concretely*, the letters, etc. collectively, as dispatched or conveyed, with that which carries them; the mail. Also *colloq.* the portion of a mail cleared from a receiving-house or pillar-box, or delivered at one house: *e.g.* 'The post had gone from our pillar-box'; 'I had a heavy post on Christmas morning'.

(In many of the following instances 'the post' may still have meant the bearer as in 2, or the conveyance as in 3.)

a **1674** CLARENDON *Hist. Reb.* XIV. §144 There were several Letters prepared, and made up with the dates proper for many Posts to come. **1675** EARL OF ESSEX *Lett.* (1770) 349 The post being just going, I can say no more. **1683** H. PRIDEAUX in *Lett. Lit. Men* (Camden) 184 Your letters, which came hither by the last nights post. **1711** ADDISON *Spect.* No. 127 ¶1 It is our Custom.., upon the coming in of the Post, to sit about a Pot of Coffee, and hear the old Knight read Dyer's Letter. *a* **1715** BURNET *Own Time* III. (1724) I. 444 The news of this must have been writ from London on the Saturday night's post. *Ibid.* (1766) II. 30 The state of foreign affairs varied every post. **1801** PITT in *G. Rose's Diaries* (1860) I. 429, I have but a moment to save the post. **1830** MARRYAT *King's Own* xiv, A sharp double tap at the street-door announced the post. **1891** E. PEACOCK *N. Brendon* I. 257 The post did not arrive early at Skerndale. *Mod.* How many posts have you in the day here?

5. a. The official organization or agency for the collection, transmission, and distribution of letters and other postal matter (= POST OFFICE 1); the official conveyance of letters, books, parcels, etc. Cf. GENERAL *post*, PENNY POST. Hence ***book-post, parcel-post***, the departments of this organization which carry books and parcels.

The phrases ***by post, per post***, etc., may have begun with earlier senses: cf. 8 b.

1663 PEPYS *Diary* 14 Mar., So to write by the post, and so home to supper. *a* **1674** CLARENDON *Hist. Reb.* XIII. §165 He sent it by the Post to the States. **1684** RAY *Corr.* (1848) 138, I received [your letter] by post, with the plants enclosed. **1707** CHAMBERLAYNE *Pres. St. Eng.* III. (ed. 22) 444 There is establish'd another Post, called the Penny-Post, whereby.. any Letter or Parcel.. is.. conveyed to, and from Parts.. not conveniently served by the General-Post. **1768–74** TUCKER *Lt. Nat.* (1834) I. 621 Nor have [I] sent advice with the needful per post. **1781** GIBBON *Decl. & F.* xvii. II. 58 The perpetual intercourse between the court and the provinces was facilitated by the construction of roads and the institution of posts. **1812** SHELLEY *Let. to Hookham* 17 Dec., You will receive the 'Biblical Extracts'.. by the twopenny post. **1885** *Act* 48 *Vict.* c. 15 Sched. iii. Precept §11 If a letter is addressed to him by post. **1903** *Daily Chron.* 4 Mar. 9/5 A resolution.. urging the establishment of a 'goods post' as a branch of the Post Office.

b. = POST OFFICE 2; also, the postal letter-box; e.g. 'to go to the post', 'to take a letter to the post'.

1785 J. WOODFORDE *Diary* 11 Nov. (1926) II. 214, I.. put it [*sc.* a letter] into the Post myself. **1808** R. C. DALLAS in *Corr. Ld. Byron* (1825) I. 9 If I were sure your Lordship is better pleased with its [the letter's] being put into the post than into the fire. **1835** DICKENS *Let.* 4 May (1965) I. 60, I am in great haste having scarce time to get this letter in the Post. **1848** CLOUGH *Bothie* ix, Great at that Highland post was wonder too and conjecture. **1886** *Field* 23 Jan. 91/1 Scarcely had last week's letter been dropped into the post. **1887** W. B. YEATS *Lett.* (1954) 54, I must finish to catch the post. **1921** G. B. SHAW *Back to Methuselah* II. 40 Excuse me, sir; but the letters must go to catch the post.

†6. *contextually.* The charge for the carriage of letters; postage. *Obs.*

1688 BURNET *Lett. conc. Pres. St. Italy* 95 Some give out, that the Post of the Letters, that were brought him the day in which he was seised on, rose to twenty Crowns. **1701** E. HATTON *Merch. Mag.* (title-p.), The Post of Letters to and from Foreign Countries. **1705** *Lond. Gaz.* No. 4105/3 For the Post of every single Letter from England to the said Islands not exceeding one Sheet of Paper, 1*s.* 3*d.*

II. 7. One of a series of stations where post-horses are kept for relays; a posting-house; also, the distance between two successive posting-houses; a stage. (So *poste* in mod.F.)

a **1649** DRUMM. OF HAWTH. *Poems* 133 The Sun.. Times Dispensator,.. Through Skies twelve Posts as he doth run his course. **1768** STERNE *Sent. Journ.* (1775) I. 50 (*Amiens*) 'Twill scarce be ten posts out of my way. **1779** J. MOORE *View Soc. Fr.* II. lii. 29 The ground is quite covered with snow, the roads bad, and the posts long. **1794** MRS. RADCLIFFE *Myst. Udolpho* vi, They were obliged to proceed to the next post. **1809** PINKNEY *Trav. France* 39 A post in France is six miles, and one shilling and threepence is charged for each horse.

III. 8. Phrases and senses arising out of them.

†a. ***at (the) post***: = *in post* (see d). *Obs.*

1507 *Acc. Ld. High Treas. Scot.* III. 412 To Johne Dunlop to pas our the Month to bide at post before the King. **1533** *Ibid.* VI. 131 To pas with diligence at the poist all the nycht with secret writingis fra the lordis.

b. ***by post***: †*orig.* by posting; by courier; with relays of post-horses (*obs.*); in current use, by the medium of the public postal service, through the post office: see sense 5.

1513 SIR E. HOWARD in Ellis *Orig. Lett.* Ser. III. I. 148 For Godds sake sende by post all along the coste that they brew bere, and make bisket. **1513** Q. CATHERINE *ibid.* 152 Maister Almoner I receyved your Lettre by the post, Wherby I understande of the commyng hider of the Duc. **1527** GARDINER in Pocock *Rec. Ref.* I. xxxix. 75 Passing from hence by post. **1545** *St. Papers Hen. VIII*, V. 496 We doubte not Your Lordship will take ordre for his passage by post, as apperteyneth. **1598** BARCKLEY *Felic. Man* I. (1603) 15 When he was far from the sea, then hee would eate nothing but fish brought alive by post with an excessive charge. **1652** T. FROYSELL *Gale Opportunity* 20 Letters were sent by post into all the Kings Provinces, to destroy, to kill and to cause to perish all Jewes both young and old. **1663–1885** [see 5].

c. ***by return of post*** (F. *par retour du courrier*): †*orig.* by return of the 'post' or courier who brought the dispatch (*obs.*); now, by the next mail in the opposite direction.

[**1583** STOCKER *Civ. Warres Lowe C.* III. 85 The Burrough Masters.. receiued letters from his Excellencie by the Poste, who was foorthwith sent backe.] **1737** *Col. Rec. Pennsylv.* IV. 223 Had this Government been pleased to have answered the last letter.. by the return of the Post who brought it. **1789** J. WOODFORDE *Dairy* 3 July (1927) III. 118 Received a Letter.. desiring an answer by return of Post. **1792** F. BURNEY *Jrnl.* Aug. (1972) I. 225, I wrote her my good wishes, which she answered by return of post. **1809** R. LANGFORD *Introd. Trade* 95, I beg you will freely tell me by return of post. **1980** ALEXANDER & ANAND *Queen Victoria's Maharajah* x. 183 The Maharajah replied by return of post.

†d. ***in post*** (= F. *en poste* (*a* 1500 in Littré), It. *in posta*), in the manner or capacity of a courier or bearer of dispatches, as a post; hence, at express speed, in haste: (*a*) originally qualifying *ride, go, come, send, dispatch*, and the like; (*b*) at length with verbs generally, and in *fig.* uses; whence *post* becomes = haste, full speed: see POST *adv.* *Obs.*

1525 LD. BERNERS *Froiss.* II. clxv. [clxi.] 457 Thus these four rode night and day..; they chaunged many horses; thus they rode in post. *Ibid.* ccxl. [ccxxxvi.] 741 Than the bysshoppe of Caunterbury wrote letters.. and sente them by a suffycyent man in post, who toke fresshe horses by the waye, and came to London the same daye at night. [**1536** *St. Papers Hen. VIII*, V. 52, I shulde abyde the retourne of the messanger, whom my Lorde and I sent by enposte.] **1569** *Satir. Poems Reform.* x. 208 To Dunbar that nycht scho raid in haist Behind ane man in poist, as scho war chaist. **1577** HANMER *Anc. Eccl. Hist.* (1619) 385 He was able in three days to ride in such post, as was to be wondred. **1583** STOCKER *Civ. Warres Lowe* C. IV. 1 b, Glymes was sent with ..about sixe hundred Horse in poste to surprize the Spanyardes. **1598** GRENEWEY *Tacitus' Ann.* IV. x. (1622) 105 A pesant of Temerstine.. killed him with one stroke; then fled in post to the woods. *a* **1604** HANMER *Chron. Irel.* (1809) 338 Sir Iohn de Courcy.. sent letters in post to his brother Sir Amorick Saint Laurence. **1670** MILTON *Hist. Brit.* II. Wks. 1738 II. 17 Horsemen all in post from Quintus Atrius bring word to Cæsar, that almost all his Ships in a Tempest that Night had suffer'd wreck. **1711** *Royal Proclam.* 23 June in *Lond. Gaz.* No. 4866/2 If the Post-master doth not.. furnish any Person riding in Post, with.. Horses. **1797** *Encycl. Brit.* (ed. 3) XV. 426/2 He is said to travel post, or in post, i.e. in the manner of a post.

†e. ***with post***: with speed or dispatch; cf. d.

1569 STOCKER tr. *Diod. Sic.* II. xiv. 59 The inhabitaunts.. with all possible post sent certain of their men upon Dromadaries.

†f. ***to make the post***: to provide for the transmission of the mail; to supply horses or mounted riders to convey the mail over one stage. *Obs.*

1547 *Reg. Privy Council Scot.* I. 74 The said Capitane of Dunbar to mak the post to the said Priores of Northberwik ..; and the said Priores to mak the post to the said Patrik Erle Boithuell.

g. ***to ride post*** = *to ride in post* (d): see POST *adv.*

†h. ***to run the post*** (= F. *courir la poste*, It. *correre in posta*): to run or ride as a 'post' or courier; to carry the mail. Cf. POST-RUNNER.

1507 *Acc. Ld. High Treas. Scot.* IV. 82 To Alexander Gordoun yeman of the stable his wage quhilk he wanted quhen the King was at the Month, and ran the post xxviiis. **1533** *Ibid.* VI. 154 For ij hors for him and his servand to ryn the post to Cauldstreme.

†i. ***to take post***: to start on a journey with post-horses; to travel as quickly as possible by means of relays of horses. *Obs.*

1592 SHAKS. *Rom. & Jul.* V. i. 21, I saw her laid low in her kindreds Vault, And presently tooke Poste to tell it you. **1666** PEPYS *Diary* 4 June, They.. took post about three this morning. **1714** LADY M. W. MONTAGU *Let. to Mr. W. Montagu* 9 Aug., This morning all the principal men of any figure took post for London.

IV. Transferred applications.

9. A frequent title of newspapers.

1681 (title) *The London Post.* **1708** (title) *The Flying Post* (Edinburgh). **1772** (title) *The Morning Post* (London). [See *Evening Post*, 13 Jan. 1888, 1/4.]

10. A parlour game; short for *General Post* (GENERAL *a.* 2 b (*b*)). Varieties are known as *American Post, Glasgow Post*, etc.

1868 HOLME LEE *B. Godfrey* xxxvi, Everybody was willing.. to engage in 'Post' or 'Slappy'. **1887** L. OLIPHANT *Episodes* (1888) 290 It became quite an interesting amusement to dodge about, not unlike the game of 'post'.

11. orig. **post-paper**: A size of writing-paper, the half-sheet of which when folded forms the ordinary quarto letter-paper; see quot. 1875. Also *attrib.*

1648 HEXHAM *Dutch Dict.*, *Post-pampier*, post-paper. **1678** *Ibid.*, *Post-papier*, post-paper or Venus paper. **1793** SMEATON *Edystone L.* §40 Though the separation was only by the thickness of a piece of post-paper. **1875** KNIGHT *Dict. Mech.* 1773/2 Post paper is seldom sold in the folio, that is, flat, but is cut in halves, folded, and forms quarto post, or common letter-paper.

1711 *Act 10 Anne* c. 18 §37 [c. 19 §32] For and upon all Paper usually called or knowne by the Name of Fine Large Post which shall be imported or brought in as aforesaid, the Summe of Two Shillings and Six Pence for every Reame. **1827** MACKENZIE *Hist. Newcastle* II. 727 *note*, Mr. White printed 'The Life of God in the Soul of Man' on a writing post 18mo. **1838** DICKENS *Nich. Nick.* xviii, Another book, in three volumes, post octavo. *c* **1865** J. WYLDE in *Circ. Sc.* 153/2 The plain Bath or satin post may be employed. **1875** KNIGHT *Dict. Mech.*, *Post*... A size of writing-paper, so called because its original water-mark was a postman's horn. Twelve varieties of post paper are made in England, of three sizes.. $22\frac{1}{4} \times 17\frac{1}{4}$ [to] $19 \times 15\frac{1}{4}$ inches.

V. *attrib.* and *Comb.*

12. a. Simple attributive: Of or pertaining to the post, as ***post clerk, dues, route, service***; **b.** employed in conveying the mails, or in the public conveyance of travellers by stages, as ***post-ass*** (cf. POST-HORSE), ***-calash, -caroche, -carriage, -carrier, -courier, -diligence, -driver, -equipage, -felucca, -gig, -girl, -hackney, -landaulet, -mule, -nag, -omnibus, -packet, -van, -vehicle***; **c.** belonging to a postal station or to a posting establishment, as ***post-hut, -shed, -yard***; **d.** of or pertaining to a post-road or posting route, as ***post-mile***; **e.** indicating the time at which the mail leaves or arrives, as ***post-day, -hour, -morning, -time***; **†f.** characterized by haste or speed like that of a post, as ***post-business, -expedition, -pace, -speed***: see also POST-HASTE; **g.** conveyed by post, as ***post-parcel, -tidings***.

1696 tr. *Du Mont's Voy. Levant* v. 42 At my departure from Lions I hir'd a *Post-Ass. **1613** BEAUM. & FL. *Coxcomb* IV. vi, What should this fellow be... That comes with such *post business?.. Are you the post, my friend? **1703** LUTTRELL *Brief Rel.* (1857) V. 358 Returning home by the way of Italy [they] were unhappily drowned in a *post calash. **1627** DRAYTON *Moon Calf* 296 Being to travel, he sticks not to lay His *post-caroches still upon his way. **1781** GIBBON *Decl. & F.* xix. II. 135 While the Cæsar himself, with only ten *post-carriages, should hasten to the Imperial residence at Milan. **1872** *Argosy* XIV. 208 There was no railroad then. The ladies and the girls crammed themselves into a post-carriage from the Star. **1855** *Englishwoman in Russia* 45 Our yemstchich had been a soldier..; but.. had turned *post-driver. **1859** JEPHSON *Brittany* ix. 133 The driver.. had forgotten to pay the *post-dues. **1813** A. BRUCE *Life A. Morris* iii. 57 The *post-equipage was ready. **1601** CHESTER *Love's Mart., Answ. Howell* 10 With all *post expedition, You will prepare a voyage vnto Rome. **1850** C. M. YONGE *Henrietta's Wish* v. 55 The *post girl could take the jelly. **1944** *Coast to Coast 1943* 112 Living only for the next time the postgirl's whistle sent its shrill stab through her nerves. **1977** 'J. GASH' *Judas Pair* ix. 113 There were a couple of letters.. on the doormat, so the post girl had called. **1666** WALLIS in Rigaud *Corr. Sci. Men* (1841) II. 467 The *post hour approaching allows me not time. **1753** HANWAY *Trav.* (1762) I. II. xv. 65 The *post huts on the step could not always supply us with a sufficient number of horses. **1737** J. CHAMBERLAYNE *St. Gt. Brit.* I. I. iii. (ed. 33) 10 The Shire Town is Dorchester.. 112 *Post Miles from London. **1758** J. BLAKE *Plan Mar. Syst.* 30 At the rate of fifteen post-miles each day. **1762** STERNE *Tr. Shandy* VI. xxii, On a *post-morning. **1880** C. R. MARKHAM *Peruv. Bark* xiii, 117 At Pucara I left post-houses and *post-mules behind me, for they exist only on the main roads. **1546** J. HEYWOOD *Prov.* (1867) 42 In *poste pase we past from potage to cheese. **1819** KEATS *Let.* 12 Mar. (1958) II. 71 The sail of the *Post-Packet to New York or Philadelphia. **1773** H. FINLAY *Jrnl.* (1867) 1 The *post route by lake Champlain was tedious. **1884** *Act of Congress* 1 Mar. in *U.S. Stat.* (1885) XXIII. 3 All public roads and highways while kept up and maintained as such are hereby declared to be post routes. **1904** W. M. RAMSAY *Lett. to Seven Ch.* xv. 192 No writer gives an account of the Imperial *Post-Service. **1812** SIR R. WILSON *Pr. Diary* I. 141 We came to the next *post-shed, and found all flown, so that we were obliged to proceed with the same horses. **1642** FULLER *Holy & Prof. St.* I. x. 25 Many overhasty widows.. make *post speed to a second marriage. **1628** *Brittain's Ida* v. vi, Fearefull blood From heart and face, with these *post-tydings runne. **1772** J. WEDGWOOD *Let.* 1 Sept. (1965) 133, I have been so long in these and other particulars this morning that *post time is at hand. **1836** F. WITTS *Diary* 14 July (1978) 117 B., as usual, not appearing till nearly the luncheon hour and at post time, when I received a joint letter from my wife and Edward. **1845** MACAULAY in Trevelyan *Life* (1876) II. 164, I was detained till after post-time. **1837** CARLYLE *Fr. Rev.* III. IV. v, National Convention packs them into *post-vehicles and conveyances. **1848** DICKENS *Dombey* lv, Of town and country, *postyards, horses.

13. Special Combs.: **†post-angel**, an angel who is sent post, a swift angelic messenger; **post-box**, (*a*) a box in which letters are posted or deposited for dispatch, a letter-box; (*b*) a box to which post-office mail, newspapers, etc., are delivered; (*c*) any box where papers, etc., are left for collection; **post-bus**, a post-office vehicle which also carries passengers; also *attrib.*; **post-lady** = *post-woman*; **post-letter**, a letter sent through the Post Office; **post-like** *a.*, resembling a or the post; in quot., rapid or swift in passing; **post money**, expense of travelling by post; **post-paid** *a.*, having the postage prepaid; also *fig.*; **post-paper** (see sense 11); **post-rider**, one who rides post; a mounted letter-carrier; **post-village**, a village where there is a post office; **post-warrant**, a warrant entitling a person travelling by post to accommodation, etc.; **post-woman**, a female letter-carrier; **post-worthy** *a.*, (*a*) of a letter: worth posting; (*b*) of a place: worthy to have a post office. See also POST-BAG, -BARK, etc.

1663 COWLEY *Hymn to Light* vi, Let a *Post-Angel start with Thee, And thou the Goal of Earth shalt reach as soon as He. **1754** MISS BOOTHBY in *Life Johnson* (1805) 58 The servant put my letter into the *post-box himself. **1954** J. COLLIN-SMITH *Scorpion on Stone* ii. 42, I say! I've been to the post-box. My papers have come. **1955** *Times* 3 May 5/4 Posting the letters at different post-boxes on the way. **1960** G. MARTELLI *Agent Extraordinary* v. 85 The *réseau* was entirely self-sufficient... There were no parachute drops, no wireless transmitters, no system of internal couriers or 'post-boxes'. **1963** *Times* 18 May 8/5 There were four other explosions in Westmount and one in the suburb of Pointe aux Trembles during the night, all in post boxes. **1964** L. LINTON *Of Days & Driftwood* iv. 27 The car was ready and able to take us beyond the post box for the first time in many days. **1968** 'S. JAY' *Sleepers can Kill* xv. 149 It's a post-box. The agents can deliver reports there, someone picks them up and sends them on. **1978** G. GREENE *Human Factor* III. iii. 126 Muller was on his own in a strange town, in a foreign land, where the post boxes bore the initials of a sovereign E II. **1960** *Guardian* 22 Feb. 6/4 Trains connect with *post-bus services. **1968** A. MARIN *Clash of Distant Thunder* (1969) x. 80 'How did you get to Geneva?'.. 'By post bus from Bourg,' I said. **1972** *Times* 24 Oct. 5/4 Crundale, Kent... At 6 am the new Royal Mail Post bus began its morning run. **1975** *Scottish Field* Apr. 88/3 The inauguration of the 50th Scottish postbus is a milestone in an inspired scheme by the postal service to help those who live out in the wilds. **1975** *Oxford Times* 25 July 18/5 (*heading*) *Postlady is dog's best friend!.. Mrs. Kathy Hilsdon,.. a postwoman for nearly 17 years. **1979** *Guardian* 30 Mar. 2/7 Elstead's postlady Mrs Pam Moss is confronted with one of the giant house numbers. **1656** *Jrnl. Ho. Com.* 429/2 That the *Post Letters, directed to.. Members of this House,.. be free from Postage, as formerly. **1734–5** *Ibid.* 26 Feb. **1758** in Howell *State Trials* XIX. 1369, I ring the bell in Arundel-street in the Strand for post-letters. **1837** *Act 1 Vict.* c. 30 §25 Every person.. who shall.. open or procure, or suffer to be opened, a Post Letter. **1593–4** SYLVESTER *Profit Imprisonm.* 758 Be it ne'er so long, long sure it cannot last To us whose *post-like life is all so quickly past. **1553** in *Vicary's Anat.* (1888) App. ii. 120 [Payment of £331. 7s. 4d. to] Sir gilbert Dethick.. for.. dyette and *poste mony. **1653** T. BATEMAN *Let.* 13 Dec. in H. Ellis *Orig. Lett. Illustr. Eng. Hist.* (1827) 2nd Ser. III. 373 *Post payd. **1689** in *12th Rep. R. Comm. Hist. Manuscripts* App. VII. 265 in *Parl. Papers 1889* (C. 5889) XLV. 533 Cannon bullets flew as fast as you could count them, and as soon as we took up their bulletts we sent them back again post paid. **1708** *Boston News-Let.* 11 Oct. 4/2 Whereas several persons do write upon their Letters Post paid.. without ever paying the Postage of the said Letters. **1762** GOLDSMITH *Life R. Nash* 117 This description.. must be sent in a letter post-paid. **1814** *Niles' Reg.* V. 369/1 Letters to the editor must be post-paid. **1828** WEBSTER, *Post-paid, a.*, having the postage paid on; as a letter. **1848** THACKERAY in *Scribner's Mag.* I. 393/1, I shall send them post-paid. **1926** *Scribner's Mag.* Sept. 24/1 (Advt.), Italian tooled cigarette-cases are smart and light... Colors: brown, dark red and dark green. Postpaid. **1973** *Sci. Amer.* Oct. 118/3 The Math Shop.. will supply postpaid (on prepaid orders) 100 plastic cubes. **1976** *Physics Bull.* Feb. 69/1 (Advt.), Price £6.50 postpaid. **1705** *Boston News-Let.* 19 Nov. 2/2 Strayed.. a sorrel Mare... Whoever can give any true intelligence of her to.. the *Post-rider.. shall be sufficiently Rewarded. **1759** in *Pennsylv. Gaz.* 3 May 4/3 Ludwick Bierley, Lancaster post-rider,.. informs his employers that it is now upwards of twelve months since he began to ride that stage. **1876** BANCROFT *Hist. U.S.* IV. l. 276 Six persons were chosen as post-riders, to give due notice to the country towns of any attempt to land the tea by force. **1827** A. SHERWOOD *Gazetteer Georgia* p. v, *Post Village. **1847** H. HOWE *Hist. Coll. Ohio* 264 Allensville, Middleton, Oak Hill and Charleston are small post villages. **1907** *Westm. Gaz.* 18 Jan. 12/1 Queenston, a post-village and outport of Lincoln County, Ontario. *c* **1645** HOWELL *Lett.* I. IV. xxiii. (1650) 127 For better assurance of Lodging wher I pass,.. I have a *Post Warrant as far as Saint Davids. **1834** JENKYNS in *Bye-Gones* 11 July (1894) 372 The *Postwoman called with four or five American papers. **1896** *Westm. Gaz.* 14 Jan. 8/1 A rural postwoman whose beat is from Longniddry to Seton Castle. **1827** WHEWELL in Todhunter *Acc. Writ.* (1876) II. 88 It is still uncertain whether I shall produce a letter that is *post-worthy. **1875** RUSKIN *Hortus Inclusus* (1887) 30, I shall post this to-morrow as I pass through Skipton or any post-worthy place.

[*Note.* The 'posts' in sense 1 correspond to the *equites dispositi* or 'posted horsemen' of classical and later times (cf. Cæsar *B.C.* III. ci). The earliest known use of *posta, poste*, pointing to the modern sense is by Marco Polo, 1298, who applies, in the French text, ch. xcvii. (ed. 1865, 335), *poeste*, and, in the Italian, ch. lxxxi. (ed. 1827, I. 91), *posta*, to the stations 25 miles apart on the great roads, at which the messengers of the Great Kaan or Emperor of China changed horses, and at each of which from 300 to 400 horses are said to have been kept for their service. The expression 'nous disons poeste de chevaus', i.e. 'we say post (or station) of horses', identifies the word originally with It. *posta* in the sense of POST *sb.*[3] The early course of the word in Europe is not altogether clear; but Milanese Latin documents of 1425–8 (L. Osio *Doc. Dipl. Milanesi*, 1872, II. 163. 357) have *portentur die noctuque celeriter per cavallarium postarum*, 'let them be carried day and night swiftly by a post-rider (horseman of the posts)', and *mittat eas per caballarios postarum*, 'let him send them by the horsemen of the posts'. In the second half of the 15th c. F. *poste* is found also as the appellation of the courier, and in this sense had become masculine before 1480. In English, also, the application of *poste, post*, to the courier is seen to go back practically to the earliest use of the word.]

post (pəʊst), *sb.*[3] Also 6 **poste**. [a. F. *poste* masc. (16th c. in Hatz.-Darm.), ad. It. *posto* a post, station, employment:—L. *postum* (whence also Du. *post*, Ger. *posten*), contracted from *positum*, prop. pa. pple. neut. of *pōnĕre* to place. In early use It. and Fr. had in this sense *posta, poste*, fem.]

1. *Mil.* **a.** The place where a soldier is stationed; sometimes, a sentinel's or sentry's beat or round.

1598 BARRET *Theor. Warres* IV. ii. 107 Not to giue it [the word] vnto the Sentinels, vntill the very point of their placing at their *standes* or *postes*. **1697** DRYDEN *Æneid* VI. 777 You see before the gate what stalking ghost Commands the guard, what sentries keep the post. **1713** ADDISON *Cato* II, As I watch'd the gate, Lodg'd in my post, a herald is arriv'd From Cæsar's camp. **1799** SHERIDAN *Pizarro* II. iv, I will not keep one soldier from his post. **1840** MACAULAY *Ess., Clive* (1887) 535 Clive.. was awakened by the alarm, and was instantly at his post.

b. *transf.* and *fig.* The appointed place; the place of duty.

16.. L'ESTRANGE (J.), Every man has his post assigned to him, and in that station he is well, if he can but think himself so. **1712–14** POPE *Rape Lock* II. 124 Whatever spirit.. His post neglects. **1772** MACKENZIE *Man World* I. ix, Though his virtue kept her post, she found herself galled in maintaining it. **1829** LYTTON *Devereux* II. xi, My daily post was by the bed of disease and suffering. **1849** C. BRONTE *Shirley* xvii, Mr. Hall had taken his post beside Caroline. **1872** T. L. CUYLER *Heart Th.* 63 The loftiest post of honour is the lowliest post of service.

2. *Mil.* **a.** A position taken; a place at which a body of soldiers is stationed, or the force occupying this; *esp.* a strategic position taken by a commander. Cf. OUTPOST. Also *transf.* and *fig.* ***to take post***: to occupy a position.

1692 BENTLEY *Boyle Lect.* ii. 65 Driven from all their posts and subterfuges. **1706** PHILLIPS s.v., In the Art of War, Post signifies any spot of Ground that is capable of lodging Soldiers:.. *Advanced Post* is a spot of Ground before the other Posts to secure those behind. **1734** tr. *Rollin's Anc. Hist.* (1827) II. II. ii. 2 The Gauls.. were very much surprised to find their posts in the enemy's hand. **1761** HUME *Hist. Eng.* II. xxiii. 70 Richard.. had taken post at Nottingham. **1813** WELLINGTON in Gurw. *Desp.* XI. 35 Posts will sometimes be surprised and the troops engaged be roughly handled. **1829** SIR W. NAPIER *Penins. War* II. 268 A body of two thousand men.. were.. directed to take post at the bridge of Alcantara. **1855** MACAULAY *Hist. Eng.* xii. III. 228 The line of posts which surrounded Londonderry by land remained unbroken. **1865** M. ARNOLD *Ess. Crit.* vii. (1875) 273 These processions come and take post in the theatres. **1903** *Daily Chron.* 10 Mar. 7/3 Waterholes were located at convenient intervals, and strong posts were left in occupation of them.

b. A place where armed men are permanently quartered for defensive or other purposes; a fort. Also (U.S.) 'the occupants, collectively, of a military station; a garrison' (*Cent. Dict.*); hence, the name given to a local branch of the organization of veterans called 'the Grand Army of the Republic'.

1703 *Lond. Gaz.* No. 3914/5 This Post was Garisoned by 600 Men. **1769** E. BANCROFT *Guiana* 351 Opposite this Island.. is a small Post, with several pieces of cannon. *a* **1859** MACAULAY *Hist. Eng.* xxiii. V. 2 All the troops of Charles II would not have been sufficient to garrison the posts which we now occupy in the Mediterranean Sea alone. **1890** GARDINER *Stud. Hist. Eng.* (1892) 14 Between them was the smaller post of Uriconium.

1884 *Boston* (Mass.) *Jrnl.* 6 Sept., Edwin-Humphrey Post, No. 104, G.A.R., of this town, celebrated its fifteenth anniversary by a camp-fire Friday evening.

c. *transf.* A place occupied for purposes of trade, esp. in an uncivilized or unsettled country.

1837 W. IRVING *Capt. Bonneville* III. 205 Fort Wallah-Wallah, the trading post of the Hudson's Bay Company. **1884** WHITON in *Chr. World* 4 Sept. 663/3 The dark Continent.. inviting.. schools and churches as well as trading posts.

d. *attrib.* and *Comb.*, as ***post-adjutant***, ***-commander***, ***-line***, ***-trader***; **post exchange** *U.S.*, a shop at a military post where goods and services are available to military personnel and authorized civilians.

1871 *Republican Rev.* (Albuquerque, New Mexico) 1 Apr. 2/1 Indians stole Levinsky's buggy horses from the Post trader's corral. **1873** J. H. BEADLE *Undevel. West* xxv. 525 Mr. Lionel Ayres fills the position of Post Trader. **1878** B. HARTE *Man on Beach* 96 Make a requisition on the commissary-general, have it certified to by the quarter-master, countersigned by the post-adjutant, and submitted by you to the War Department. **1887** *Pall Mall G.* 10 Aug. 14/1 A ten gallon demijohn of post trader's whisky. **1890** *Century Dict.*, *Post-trader*, a trader at a military post: the official designation of a sutler. **1892** *Ann. Rep. Secretary of War* (U.S.) I. 57 In February last, upon the ground that the term 'canteen' possibly conveyed to the public mind a meaning which, though foreign to the main purpose of the institution, has been for years associated in other armies with a place of conviviality and dissipation, the Secretary of War decided to change the name of such establishments to that of 'post exchange'. **1894** *Outing* (U.S.) XXIV. 85/2 Beside it are the company's stables and the store and house of the post-trader where we bought our provisions. **1898** *Daily News* 31 July 5/2 General Toral has sent the members of his staff ahead to notify the post commanders of the terms of surrender. **1919** *Lit. Digest* 22 Nov. 70/2 The Y.W.C.A. hostess house has been turned into a post exchange. **1973** H. GRUPPE *Truxton Cipher* iii. 25 He added that he intended to remain in the Naval Reserve so as to retain his.. post-exchange privileges.

3. An office or situation to which any one is appointed; position, place; employment.

1695–6 T. SMITH in *Lett. Lit. Men* (Camden) 239, I am very glad of the new post you are preferred to, as you write, the publick Library. **1720** HEARNE *Collect.* (O.H.S.) VII. 117 A Person of no Learning, and very unfit for this Post. **1760** in Cotton *Walton's Angler* II. p. xxviii, He was call'd away by some employment, or post, that was conferred upon him. **1849** MACAULAY *Hist. Eng.* ii. I. 223 Arlington quitted the post of secretary of state. **1879** M. ARNOLD *Mixed Ess.* 148 Those posts in the public service supposed to be posts for gentlemen.

4. *Naval.* **a.** Position as a full-grade captain, i.e. commission as officer in command of a vessel of 20 guns or more; hence, position or order of seniority in the list of captains. Used in the phrases ***to give post***, said of a ship of 20 guns or more, the officer in command of which had the rank of captain; ***to take post***, said of the officer, to receive the commission of captain of such a vessel, to date as captain; also ***to be made post***, to be appointed post captain, to be placed on the list of captains. Now *arch.* or *Hist.* Also attrib. as ***post commission***, ***post rank***; see also below.

1720 in Chamberlayne *St. Gt. Brit. for 1723*, 579–82 A General List of the Captains of His Majesty's Fleet, with the Dates of their First Commissions as Captains, from which they are allowed to take Post. [Dated] Admiralty-Office 1 March, 1720. [Here follow the] Names [in order of] Seniority. [Among these] Sir William Sanderson [and others],.. Take Post by a General Order, 1 Jan. 1712–13. **1747** *Order-in-Council* 10 Feb. (Rank and Precedence of Officers) §8 That Captains of His Majesty's Ships or Vessels, not taking Post, have rank as Majors. *Ibid.* §11 That Post-Captains, commanding ships or vessels that do not give post, rank only as Majors during their commanding such vessels. **1800** *Naval Chron.* IV. 469 Capt. Miller was made post in 1796. **1806** A. DUNCAN *Nelson* 18 Captain Nelson was made post on the 11th of June, 1779. **1849** W. R. O'BYRNE *Naval Biog. Dict.* 259/2 He was rewarded with a Post commission. **1892** BRIGHTON *Sir P. Wallis* 160 He was advanced to post rank on Aug. 12, 1819. **1907** SIR J. K. LAUGHTON *Let. to Editor*, A captain was said to *take post* from the date of his commission to a ship of not less than 20 guns: his commission to command such a ship *ipso facto* gave him *post*.

b. post captain. A captain who 'takes post': a designation formerly applied, officially and otherwise, to a naval officer holding a commission as captain, to distinguish him from an officer of inferior rank, to whom the courtesy title of captain was often given, either as being an acting captain, or as being master and commander of a vessel not rated to be commanded by a full-grade captain, and so not said to 'give post'. *Obs.* exc. *Hist.*

So far as the Naval Regulations are concerned the appellation appears to date from about 1731–47, and to have ceased in 1824, when the rule was laid down that only officers appointed to command 'ships of sixth rate and upwards shall henceforth be styled Captains'. But, in unofficial language, the courtesy use of 'Captain' for the 'Master and Commander' of a smaller vessel, and the distinctive appellation 'Post-Captain', lingered to a much later period.

1747 [see above]. **1757** J. LIND *Lett. Navy* i. 21 Both post captains and masters and commanders share alike. **1790** BEATSON *Nav. & Mil. Mem.* I. 217 For the above very gallant action, Captain Gordon was made a Post-Captain. **1796** NELSON in Nicolas *Disp.* (1846) VII. p. lxxix, Captain Miller or any other Post Captain, put into Agamemnon, and a Master and Commander acting into the Post Ship, which the Admiralty may confirm or not, as they please. **1849** COBDEN *Speeches* 86 Mr. Hume's proposal is.. that there shall be only one post-captain promoted to the rank of admiral, for every three admirals who may die, until the number of admirals is reduced to 100.

†**c. post ship.** Also 8 **ship of post**. A ship of not less than 20 guns, the commission to command which 'gave post' to a captain. *Obs.*

1731 *Regulations rel. H.M. Service at Sea*, Commanders of Fireships, Sloops, Yachts, Bomb-vessels, Hospitals, Store-ships, and other vessels, though they may have commanded Ships of Post before, shall be commanded by junior Captains in Ships of Post, while they keep company together..; but without prejudice to their seniority afterwards. **1747** *Order-in-Council* 10 Feb. (Rank & Precedence of Officers) §6 That Captains commanding post-ships, after three years from the date of their first commission for a post ship, have rank as Colonels. §7 That all other Captains, commanding Post-Ships, have rank as Lieutenant-Colonels. **1757** J. LIND *Lett. Navy* i. 21 The other rank of captains is of them, who have the command of ships of twenty guns, or upwards, which are called post ships. **1790** BEATSON *Nav. & Mil. Mem.* I. 266 The Shirley-galley was.. made a post ship in the Royal Navy, and her former commander, Mr. John Rous, appointed Captain of her. **1796** [see *post captain* above].

†**post** (pəʊst), *sb.*[4] *Obs.* Also 6–7 **poste**. [app. ad. It. *posta* 'a stake at any game; also a good hand drawen or winning at any game, namely at dice'

(Florio); prop. a sum deposited or laid down:—L. *posta, posita*, pa. pple. fem. of *pōnĕre* to place: thus orig. the same word as POST *sb.*[2] Cf. Sp. *apostar* to bet, deposit a stake.]

A term in card-playing. **a.** Name of an obsolete card-game, app. the same as *post and pair* (see below); also, a term in that game: see quots.

1528 ROY *Rede me* (Arb.) 117 In carde playinge he is a goode greke And can skyll of post and glyeke. **1565** JEWEL *Repl. Harding* (1611) 225 Hee commeth in onely with iolly brags, and great vants, as if he were playing at Poste, and should winne all by vying. **1611** COTGR., *Couche*,.. the Post, or most of a sute, at cards; also, a set, lay, or stake, at any game. *a* **1612** HARINGTON *Epigr.* IV. xii, The second game was Post, vntill with posting They paid so fast, 'twas time to leaue their bosting. **1680** COTTON *Compl. Gamester* xxii. 106 Here note, that he who hath the best Pair or the best Post is the winner. **1688** R. HOLME *Armoury* III. xvi. (Roxb.) 73/1 At Post the best cards are 21 viz.: two tens and an Ace, but a paire royall wins all, both Post, Paire and Seat.

b. post and pair. 'A game on the cards, played with three cards each, wherein much depended on *vying*, or betting on the goodness of your own hand' (Nares).

1602 *2nd Pt. Return fr. Parnass.* Prol. (Arb.) 3 You that haue beene student at post and paire, saint and Loadam. **1620** L. GERNONS *Disc. Irel.* (Stowe MS. 180), When I am playing at poste and payre, my opposite challengeth wth two counters; if I answer him wth two other, and rest, I have but a faynte game. **1688** R. HOLME *Armoury* III. xvi. (Roxb.) 73/1 Post and Paire is a game played thus, first stake at Post, then at Paire, after deale two cards, then stake at the seat and then deale the third card about [etc.]. **1808** SCOTT *Marm.* VI. Introd. 45 That night might..The lord, underogating, share The vulgar game of 'post and pair'. **1874** JEFFERIES *Toilers of Field* (1893) 41 Whist and post and pair are the staple indoor amusements. **1887** *All Year Round* 5 Feb. 66 Primero is the ancestor of such gambling games as Post and Pair, once a favourite game in the West of England.

post, *sb.*[5] [app. ad. Ger. *posten* parcel, lot, a batch of ore, ad. It. *posto*:—L. *positum* that which is put or placed: cf. POST *sb.*[2] and [4].]

1. *Paper-making.* A pile of from four to eight quires of hand-made paper fresh from the mould, laid with alternate sheets of felt ready for pressing. ***white post***: see quot. 1875.

1727-41 CHAMBERS *Cycl.* s.v. *Paper*, The coucher, who couches it upon a felt laid on a plank, and lays another felt on it; and so successively, a sheet and a felt, a sheet and a felt, till a post, i.e. one pressing, containing six quire, be made. **1766** C. LEADBETTER *Royal Gauger* xiv. (ed. 6) 370 An Heap of seven or eight Quires, which is called a Post. **1838** *Encycl. Brit.* (ed. 7) XVII. 15/1 Four to eight quires, according to the size of the paper, form a post. **1875** KNIGHT *Dict. Mech.* s.v., A white post is the pile of paper sheets when the felts are removed. **1906** R. W. SINDALL *Paper Technol.* 21 The 'coucher', who transfers the wet sheet from mould to felt and builds up the pile or 'post' of alternate wet sheets and felts. **1965** ZIGROSSER & GAEHDE *Guide to Collecting Orig. Prints* iv. 64 When 144 sheets [of paper] have been formed, they and their protective pads (the stack being known as the *post*) are conveyed to a press to squeeze out more water.

2. *Metallurgy.* A batch of ore for smelting at one time.

1839 URE *Dict. Arts* 326 The smelting *post* or charge, to be purified at once, consists of 60 cwt. of black copper. *Ibid.* 328 For example, 1 post or charge may consist of 20 cwts. of the ferruginous slate [etc.].

post (pəʊst), *sb.*[6] *Law.* [From the Lat. word *post* after, occurring in the writ: see quot. 1595.] In the phrase 'in the (†le) post', lit. 'in the (time) after (the disseisin)', esp. in the 'writ of entry sur disseisin in the post': see quot. 1895.

[**1293** *Year Bks. Edw. I* (Rolls) I. 431 Adam porta bref de entre en le post ver N., en le queus yl nad entre si noun puys la disseysine ke B. fyt a meymes cely Adam.] **1495** *Rolls of Parlt.* VI. 472/2 Severall Writtes of Entre in le Post. **1511-12** *Act 3 Hen. VIII*, c. 18 *Preamble*, Wrytte of entre uppon disseysen in the post be fore the Justices..of his Comen Benche. **1595** *Expos. Termes Law* 77 And if land bee conueid ouer to manie, or if the first disseisor bee disseised, then the writte of Entre shall be in the *Post*, that is to say that the tenaunt hath no entry but after the disseisin which the first disseisour made to the demandant or his auncestor. *Ibid.* 77 b, And the writte shall say, *in quod A. non habet ingressum nisi post disseisinam, quam B. inde iniuste & sine iuditio fecit praef. N. vel M. proauo N. cuius hæres ipse est.* **1818** CRUISE *Digest* (ed. 2) I. 399 The disseisor came in in the *post*, that is, he did not claim by or from the feoffee to uses, but came in of an estate paramount to that of such feoffee. **1895** POLLOCK & MAITLAND *Hist. Eng. Law* II. II. iv. 65 The statute of Marlborough..gave the disseisee or his heir 'a writ of entry sur disseisin in the *post*', an action, that is, in which he might allege that his adversary 'had no entry into the land save after (*post*) the disseisin' that some one or another (X) perpetrated against the demandant or his ancestor. In such an action it was unnecessary for the demandant to trace the process by which the land passed from the disseisor (X) to the tenant whom the action attacked.

post (pəʊst), *sb.*[7] [f. POST *v.*[1] 8.] An act of posting; an entry (in a ledger, etc.).

1766 W. GORDON *Gen. Counting-ho.* 6 Such post or entry in the Journal is called a simple post. [**1797** *Encycl. Brit.* (ed. 3) XV. 423/1 *Post*, an operation in book-keeping. Posting in book-keeping means simply the transferring of an article to the place in which it should be put.]

post (pəʊst), *sb.*[8] *Mil.* [app. from POST *sb.*[3] sense 1: short for 'call to post', or the like.] A bugle-call giving notice of the hour of retiring for the night. Usually ***first*** or ***last post***.

Tattoo or Watchsetting is now divided into two 'posts' sounded normally at 9.30 and 10 p.m., followed by 'Lights out' at 10.15 p.m. For many years it has been customary to sound 'Last post' by a soldier's grave after the interment.

[**1864** *Standing Orders Roy. Reg. Artill.* 134 Watchsetting. 1st post. 2nd post. 3rd post. 4th post. [A separate tune given for each.]] **1885** *City Press* 30 Sept., First post was sounded at half-past ten. **1886** *Standing Orders, Southern District* §12 Weather permitting, the 1st Post at Tattoo (in Portsmouth) will be sounded on the road opposite the Main Guard by the Drums and Fifes of the Regiment detailed..for that duty. **1900** *Daily News* 17 May 3/2 A few hours after, the 'last post' sounds over another victim to the pomp and glory of war! *Ibid.* 19 May 2/1 The brave dead were laid to their long rest in the veldt by their comrades at eventide, while 'The Last Post' wailed on the solemn air. **1901** *King's Regul. Army* §252 'Tattoo' ('last post') at 10.0 p.m. *Ibid.* §254 Which is to be sounded a quarter of an hour after 'last post' or tattoo.

‖**post,** *sb.*[9] *E. Indies.* [a. Pers. and Urdū *pōst* skin, rind, poppy-head.] The poppy-head; opium.

1698 FRYER *Acc. E. India & P.* 32 Upon an Offence they are sent by the King's Order, and committed to a place called the *Post* (from the Punishment inflicted), where the Master of the *Post* is acquainted with the heinousness of the Crime; which being understood he heightens by a Drink,.. made of *Bang*..mingled with *Dutry* (the deadliest sort of *Solanum*, or Nightshade) named *Post*, [which] after a Week's taking, they crave more than ever they nauseated. *Ibid.* 104 The inebriating Confection of the *Post.* [**1882** *Edin. Rev.* July 73 The way in which people there [in the Punjaub] talk of 'postees' or opium-eaters.]

post (pəʊst), *sb.*[10] Short for *post captain*: see POST *sb.*[3] 4; ellipt. for POST ENTRY, q.v.

post (pəʊst), *sb.*[11] U.S. slang abbrev. of POST-GRADUATE *sb.*

1900 *Dialect Notes* II. 51 *Post, n.*,..2. A post-graduate student. **1914** *Ibid.* IV. 134 It must be nice to be a *post*,—they have so many privileges. **1930** *Amer. Speech* V. 242 *Post*, post graduate.

post, *sb.*[12] *colloq.* (chiefly *U.S.*). [Abbrev. of POST MORTEM, POST-MORTEM *sb.*] An autopsy, post-mortem. Hence as *v. trans.*, to perform an autopsy on (someone).

1942 BERREY & VAN DEN BARK *Amer. Thes. Slang* §534/2 *Post*,..post-mortem examination. **1961** *Amer. Speech* XXXVI. 145 The patient died last night and will be posted this morning. **1968** J. HUDSON *Case of Need* I. v. 41 The post hadn't been started. **1969** 'F. RICHARDS' *Risky Way to Kill* (1970) xii. 147 She died last night. Overdose, probably. They're doing a post. **1979** R. COOK *Sphinx* 177 They had no internal organs. Just a shell of a body. When a post is done the shell is only cursorily examined.

post (pəʊst), *v.*[1] [f. POST *sb.*[2], or a. obs. F. *poster* (16th c. in Littré) 'courir les postes'. Cf. obs. Du. *posten* 'cursitare..discurrere' (Kilian).]

I. *intr.* **1.** To travel with relays of horses (originally, as a courier or bearer of letters).

1533 *Acc. Ld. High Treas. Scot.* VI. 123 To ane boy that postit nycht and day in the northland with lettrez. **1560** DAUS tr. *Sleidane's Comm.* 234 b, His servant..had put on the apparell of a messenger, that posteth with letters. **1598** HAKLUYT *Voy.* I. 65 Riding as fast as our horses could trot (for we had fresh horses almost thrise or four times a day) we posted from morning till night. **1683** *Brit. Spec.* 253 [He was] transported from Brighthemstead..to Feecam.. whence he posted directly to Rouen. **1706** PHILLIPS, *To Post it*, to go or ride Post. **1832** W. IRVING in *Life & Lett.* (1864) II. 465 We posted in an open carriage. **1873** HELPS *Anim. & Mast.* viii. (1875) 201 When you are posting, you must have a horse for every adult passenger.

2. To ride, run, or travel with speed or haste; to make haste, hasten, hurry.

1567 DRANT *Horace, Ep. to Mæcenas* D vj, To Philippes house al sodainly hee posteth in a brade. **1582** STANYHURST *Æneis* II. (Arb.) 53 To top hastly of turret I posted. **1595** *Blanchardyn* 208 They posted so fast [*tant cheuaucherent*], that within short time they came before the gate. **1642** FULLER *Holy & Prof. St.* III. xxi. 211 Had he seen Peter and John posting to Christs grave. **1782** COWPER *Gilpin* 214 Mistress Gilpin, when she saw Her husband posting down Into the country far away. **1851** E. FITZGERALD *Lett.* (1889) I. 214 To post about in Omnibi between Lincoln's Inn and Bayswater. **1885** STEVENSON *Child's Gard., Lamplighter* i, With lantern and with ladder he comes posting up the street.

b. *fig.*

1558 HOLLAND in Foxe *A. & M.* (1570) 2238/2 The Priestes doe so champe them and chaw them [the words of the service], and posteth so fast, that neither they vnderstand what they say, nor they that heare them. **1632** LITHGOW *Trav.* IX. 403 Gray haires come posting on. **1636** PRYNNE *Unbish. Tim.* Ded. (1661) 7 Though they greedily post and hunt after Bishopricks. **1725** POPE *Odyss.* xv. 381 He wastes away Old age, untimely posting ere his day. **1852** M. ARNOLD *Empedocles on Etna* I. ii, We see, in blank dismay, Year posting after year, Sense after sense decay.

3. *Manège.* To rise and fall in the saddle, like a post-boy, when riding.

1882 in OGILVIE.

II. †**4.** *trans.* To cause to post or hasten; to dispatch or send in haste; to hasten, hurry (a person). *Obs.*

1570 LEVINS *Manip.* 176/7 To Poste, *properare.* **1582** STANYHURST *Æneis* I. (Arb.) 27 He foorth posted.. Mercurye downeward. **1628** GAULE *Pract. The.* (1629) 68 God posts away Gabriel the Harbinger with this Message. **1694** WESTMACOTT *Script. Herb.* (1695) 184 Whom.. Saffron, by the too frequent and lavish Use thereof in the Small-Pox, hath posted to their long homes. **1700** FARQUHAR *Constant Couple* V. iii, My father..posts me away to travel. **1806-7** J. BERESFORD *Miseries Hum. Life* (1826) XVII. 101 Posting your eye down the columns, eager to see whether the alliance between Russia and Prussia is going on.

†**b.** *Oxford Univ. slang.* To summon (a candidate) for examination on the first day of a series.

1721 AMHERST *Terræ Fil.* No. 42 (1754) 224 The first and the last column in the [collector's] scheme, (which contain the names of those who are to come up the first day and the last day, and which is call'd *posting* and *dogging*,) are esteem'd very scandalous. Great application is made to them..to avoid being *posted* or *dogg'd*.

III. To convey or send by post, or post-haste.

†**5.** To carry in the manner of a post; to convey swiftly. *Obs.*

1611 SHAKS. *Cymb.* II. iv. 27 The swiftest Harts, have posted you by land; And Windes of all the Corners kiss'd your Sailes. *a* **1644** QUARLES *Sol. Recant.* Sol. iv. 24 Hath Heaven..glorifi'd thy name With honor, posted on the wings of Fame? **1682** D'URFEY *Injured Princ.* III. ii, The swiftest Racers posted you by Land.

6. †**a.** To send by special messenger. *Obs.*

1657-61 HEYLIN *Hist. Ref.* I. 32 The Roman Emperors; whose Edict for a General Council might speedily be posted over all the Province. *a* **1662** —— *Laud* II. 327 The noise of these Proceedings..being quickly posted to the Scots. **1716** B. CHURCH *Hist. Philip's War* (1867) II. 71 False Reports.. were posted home by those ill affected Officers. **1724** in G. Sheldon *Hist. Deerfield, Mass.* (1895) I. 417 News from Albany..which news I immediately posted to Deerfield and Northfield.

b. To send through the post office; to put (a letter, etc.) into a post office or letter-box for transmission by the post.

1837 *9th Rep. Post-Office* 85 If a letter or packet should be posted with a penny stamped cover. **1840** *Mulready Cover* (Instructions), It is Requested that all Letters may be fully and legibly addressed, and posted as early as convenient. **1852** MCCULLOCH *Taxation* II. vii. 317 The necessity..of paying the postage at the moment when letters are posted. **1870** E. PEACOCK *Ralf Skirl.* III. 143 His letter was posted two days later. **1886** *Law Times* LXXX. 211/1 The bills of costs were duly posted to Bouron in Paris.

IV. 7. ***to post over, off.*** †**a.** To hand over or transfer (a duty, responsibility, etc.) to another; to shift, delegate, assign; to pass off, turn off. *Obs.*

1578 TIMME *Caluine on Gen.* 104 After the example of her husband, she poasteth over the fault to another. **1578** T. WHITE *Serm.* 84 Euery body can post it [blame] off, or sport it out so prettily. **1593** NASHE *Christ's T.* 83 b, Poste ouer the Plague to what naturall cause you will, I positiuely affirme it is for Sinne. **1618** E. ELTON *Exp. Rom. vii.* 88 It is the fashion of most men to post off the fault and blame of their sinnes from themselues. *a* **1656** HALES *Gold. Rem.* (1688) 317 Nothing so well done as that which the master of the House..posts not over to his servants.

†**b.** To put off; to postpone, defer, delay. *Obs.*

1577 HANMER *Anc. Eccl. Hist.* (1619) 139 He posted over and deferred his opinion from time to time. **1586** A. DAY *Eng. Secretary* II. (1625) 58 The compasse of your writing.. maketh me post off the answere. *c* **1592** *Trag. Rich. III* (Shaks. Soc.) 69 But they that knew how innocent I was, Did post him off with many long delayes, Alleaging reasons to alaie his rage. **1642** C. VERNON *Consid. Exch.* 95 Divers good Rents and Debts have for some private ends been suffered to bee posted off, *de anno in annum.*

V. *Book-keeping*, etc. (app. related to IV.)

8. To carry or transfer (an entry) from an auxiliary book to one of more formal character, esp. from the day-book or journal into the ledger, but also from a waste-book, day-book, or cash-book into the journal; to carry (an item or entry) to the proper account; also, by extension, to enter (an item) in proper form in any of the books.

1622 MALYNES *Anc. Law-Merch.* 365 These seuen parcels are now put ouer into the Liedger which some call posted ouer. **1682** [see POSTING *vbl. sb.*[1] 5]. **1706** PHILLIPS s.v., To Post an Account, is to put an Account forward from one Book to another; as to transcribe, or enter what is written in a Merchant's Waste-Book into the Journal, etc. **1790** BURKE *Fr. Rev.* Wks. V. 158 To see the crimes of new democracy posted as in a ledger against the crimes of old despotism. **1817** J. K. PAULDING *Lett. fr. South* II. 110 Old H—— was obliged to post the proceeds of the cargo to profit and loss. **1875** POSTE *Gaius* III. Comm. (ed. 2) 407 At the end of each month the contents of the Adversaria were posted into the more formal journal, the Tabulae.

b. To complete (the ledger or other book) by transferring to it all the items in the auxiliary books, and entering them in their proper accounts; to make the proper entries in all the books, so that they contain a complete record of transactions; often *post up* (i.e. up to date, or to completion).

1707 *Providence Rec.* (1896) X. 94 So soone as Conveniently may be that ye bookes cann be posted. **1712** ARBUTHNOT *John Bull* I. x, You have not posted your books these ten years. **1745** *De Foe's Eng. Tradesman* (1841) I. xxxi. 319 He has not posted his cash-book for I know not how many months; nor posted his day-book and journal at all. *Ibid.* II. xxxiii. 62 A copy of the ledger duly posted up. **1892** STEVENSON & OSBOURNE *Wrecker* i, Take a pride to keep your books posted, and never throw good money after bad.

9. *fig.* (orig. *U.S. colloq.*) To supply with full information or latest news on a subject; to inform. Often ***post up.*** Usually in ***pass.***

1847 *Nat. Encycl.* I. 619 *Posted-up* is an Americanism for well-informed, thoroughly conversant with. **1856** G. D. BREWERTON *War in Kansas* 365 As regards the details of the defences at Lawrence, we should certainly have been 'better posted' than we are. **1862** THACKERAY *Round. Papers, De Finibus*, To improve my mind and keep myself 'posted up', as the Americans phrase it, with the literature of the day. **1868** G. DUFF *Pol. Surv.* 19, I wish our journals would keep us better posted up with regard to events in Belgium. **1883** C. D. WARNER *Roundabout Journey* 239 The lovers of the sport always post themselves as to the character of the bulls who are to perform. **1886** MISS TYTLER *Buried Diamonds* vii, Tell me..what books you had to post yourself up in for your examinations.

post (pəʊst), *v.*² [f. POST *sb.*¹: in various unconnected groups of senses.]

I. † **1.** *trans.* To square (timber) before sawing it, or in order to form it into posts. *Obs.* or *dial.*

c **1520** *Mem. Ripon* (Surtees) III. 204 Johanni Hogsson postyng tymber ad Ryso & alias per j diem, 5*d.* *Ibid.* 205 Will'mo Howyd postyng tymber for the sayd fertter per iij dies, & sawyng, 18*d.* **1600** FAIRFAX *Tasso* XIX. xxxvi, There lay by chance a posted tree therebie. **1828** *Craven Gloss.* (ed. 2) s.v., When a tree is cut into a square form, it is termed *posted*.

II. † **2.** To furnish or set with posts. *Obs. rare.*

1716 *Maldon, Essex, Borough Deeds* Bundle 147. No. 3 Wee present the sirvairs [= surveyors] of St Mary's [parish] for not posteing the foot-way.

III. 3. To attach or moor (a vessel) to a post.

1868 [see POSTING *vbl. sb.*² 1].

IV. 4. To affix (a paper, etc.) to a post or in a prominent position; to stick *up* in a public place.

1650 R. STAPYLTON *Strada's Low C. Warres* III. 62 Divers bills posted up that threatned mischief to the Judges. **1654** H. L'ESTRANGE *Chas. I* (1655) 187 A Paper was posted upon the Old Exchange..Exhorting Prentices to rise and sack his House. **1715** *Boston Rec.* (1884) II. 220 Posting up twenty of the said printed by-laws on several publick places in the said town. **1806** A. DUNCAN *Nelson's Fun.* 12 A written order.. had been..posted up. **1851** DICKENS *Repr. Pieces, Bill-sticking* (1903) 62 The old bill-stickers went to Trafalgar Square to attempt to post bills. **1874** MICKLETHWAITE *Mod. Par. Churches* 221 Boards intended for posting papers upon. **1884** *Manch. Exam.* 19 Feb. 4/7 The coalmasters..have posted a notice at the collieries intimating a reduction..in the wages of miners. **1975** *Publishers Weekly* 10 Feb. 45/1 This poster was mailed to ABA members in the hope that they will post it.

5. a. To make known, advertise, bring before the public (some fact, thing, or person) by or as by posting a placard. Also with *up*.

1633 MASSINGER *Guardian* I. i, If you take the wench now, I'll have it posted first, then chronicled, Thou wert beaten to it. **1694** SOUTH *Serm.* (1727) III. vi. 249 Those Pretences to infallible Cures, which we daily see posted up in every Corner of the Streets. **1756** C. LUCAS *Ess. Waters* I. Ded., The grateful votaries..posted up in his temple the histories of their diseases. **1828–32** WEBSTER s.v., To advertise on a post or in a public place; as, to post a stray horse. **1860** DICKENS *Uncomm. Trav.* x, Seeing him posted in the bill of the night, I attended the performance.

b. *spec.* To expose to ignominy, obloquy, or ridicule, by this means. Now *rare.*

1642 SIR E. DERING *Sp. on Relig.* xvi. 88, I may..be poasted up..as one that dares not hazard a whole Nationall Church at blind man buffe. **1650** FULLER *Pisgah* 424 Here we must have an abominable falshood.., posted, and pillored. **1684** WOOD *Life* 4 Sept. (O.H.S.) III. 108 Wright Croke..was posted up for a shark and coward in Day's coffey house. **1710** *Pol. Ballads* (1860) II. 91 Their exploits were so mean, and their actions so vain That they all deserve to be posted. **1812** *Ann. Reg., Chron.* 146/2 A criminal information against two persons for posting a merchant of London in a coffee-house for refusing a challenge. **1840** THACKERAY *Paris Sk.-bk.* (1867) 34 I'll post you for a swindler and a coward. **1884** *Law Times* 7 June 93/1 If he had not paid the bets..he would have been posted as a 'defaulter' at Tattersalls.

c. In some colleges: To place in a list, which is posted up, the names of (students who fail to pass in the college examinations).

In Cambridge colleges, said of those whose names are now subjoined to the lists of successful examinees as *not classed*.

1852 C. A. BRISTED *Eng. Univ.* 100 [At Trinity Coll., Camb.] should a man be posted twice in succession, he is generally recommended to try the air of some small college, or devote his energies to some other walk of life. **1859** FARRAR *J. Home* xix, He had been posted, in company with H. and Lord F.; *i.e.* their names had been written up below the eighth class as 'unworthy to be classed'.

d. To publish the name of (a ship) as overdue or missing.

1886 CLARK RUSSELL *Voy. to Cape* (1893) 136 My sympathy with the sailor makes me feel as often as I hear of a cargo vessel being 'posted' as if a very grave wrong were done to the memory of the drowned seamen by the unconcern with which the great mass of the public receive the news. **1896** *Times* (weekly ed.) 10 Jan. 38/3 They [the ships] were posted at Lloyd's on Wednesday as missing.

e. To achieve, 'notch up'. *N. Amer.*

1949 *Richmond* (Virginia) *Times-Dispatch* 10 Oct. 13/5 William and Mary, which Saturday posted a 54-6 decision over the Keydets to tie North Carolina for the conference lead (each has a 2-0 record), has one remaining State battle. **1968** *Globe & Mail* (Toronto) 5 Feb. 18/9 John Armstrong of Oshawa posted the longest jump of 110 feet on his way to second place. **1972** *Time* 13 Mar. 48/3 In 1944, he [*sc.* a basketball pitcher]..posted the lowest earned run average in the major leagues. **1973** *Internat. Herald Tribune* 15 June 15/3 Wise, posting his eighth victory against three defeats, struck out four, walked three and retired 14 consecutive batters at one stretch. **1975** *New Yorker* 23 June 43/1 He won nineteen games for the Pirates and lost only eight, posting an earned-run average of 2.48.

f. To announce, publish. *N. Amer.*

1961 *Los Angeles Times* 21 June IV. 6/6 Gains of 2⅜ were posted for Teleprompter and Republic Foil. **1962** *Economist* 19 May 697/2 Producer governments certainly cannot get better prices for their crude oil than those 'posted' by the companies controlled by the international groups there. **1973** *Time* 25 June 23/4 Companies that posted big price increases during Phase III will be audited. **1976** *Billings* (Montana) *Gaz.* 17 June 7-E/6 The stock market shook off Tuesday's spell of profit taking Wednesday and posted a modest gain in moderately active trading.

6. To placard (a wall, etc.) with bills, etc.

1854 DICKENS *Hard T.* III. iv, He caused the walls to be posted with it [a broadsheet]. **1887** *Pall Mall G.* 24 Dec. 2/1 We had to fall back on posting the neighbourhoods as well as we could... We put out a poster and forty-five hand-bills to every three men who registered. **1967** *Boston Sunday Herald* 26 Mar. II. 9/1 Highway arteries have been posted, warning us that stiff fines will be imposed if we toss our leavings out of the car windows. **1976** *Billings* (Montana) *Gaz.* 30 June 8-A/1 We have posted all the bars and put up signs that make it clear that no drinking is allowed in any public place.

post (pəʊst), *v.*³ [f. POST *sb.*³; so F. *poster* (16th c.) to post, station (troops, etc.).]

1. *trans.* To place, station.

1683 PENN *Wks.* (1782) IV. 316 The place of the glass-house [is] conveniently posted for water-carriage. *a* **1688** VILLIERS (Dk. Buckhm.) *Battle of Sedgmoor* Wks. (1775) 121, I suppose..that your Lordship was posted in a very strong place. **1711** BUDGELL *Spect.* No. 161 ¶3 A Country Girl, who was posted on an Eminence at some Distance from me. **1833** RITCHIE *Wand. by Loire* 166 He..posted himself at the door of the banqueting hall. **1874** GREEN *Short Hist.* v. §1. 223 A body of English horsemen, posted on a hill to the right, charged suddenly on the French flank.

b. *intr.* (for *refl.*) To station oneself, stop. *rare.*

1872 H. COWLES in Spurgeon *Treas. Dav.* Ps. xciv. 10 The question posts midway..the point of application being too obvious to need mention.

2. *Mil.* and *Naval.* To appoint to a post or command; *spec.* to appoint to command a ship which 'gave post' (see POST *sb.*³ 4); to commission as captain. Chiefly *pass.*

1800 WELLESLEY in Owen *Desp.* (1877) 555 One additional subaltern at least should be posted to every company of artillery. **1809** WELLINGTON in Gurw. *Desp.* (1838) V. 313, I am..unwilling to send Mr. Dunlop to any particular regiment lest he should not be posted to it. *c* **1815** JANE AUSTEN *Persuas.* xxiii, When I returned to England in the year eight, with a few thousand pounds, and was posted into the Laconia. **1833** MARRYAT *P. Simple* lii, I am posted, and appointed to the Semiramis frigate. **1894** *Lancet* 3 Nov. 1056/1 Surgeon-Major Tuthill, on arrival from a tour of service at Gibraltar, has been posted to Dublin. **1907** SIR J. K. LAUGHTON *Let. to Editor*, Every ship of 20 guns or more was a post-ship, and a man was ordinarily said to be *posted*, that is, appointed to command a ship which gave him post as a captain.

Hence **'posting** *vbl. sb.*³

[**1800** *Misc. Tracts* in *Asiat. Ann. Reg.* 9/1 The posting the English troops too far from his own person.] **1847** *Infantry Man.* (1854) 99 The posting of a piquet. **1880** GEN. ADYE in *19th Cent.* 701 There are palpable defects and anomalies in the Staff Corps arrangements as regards the posting of the regimental officers.

post, *v.*⁴ *Sc. dial.* [dial. var. of POSS *v.*] *trans.* To trample (clothes) in water in the process of washing them; also, to knead (clothes) with the hands for this purpose. Hence **'posting** *vbl. sb.*⁴

1820 ARMSTRONG *Gael. Dict.* s.v. *Postadh*, The Highland women put them in a tub,..[and] then, with petticoats tucked up..commence the operation of posting. **1893** N. MUNRO *Lost Pibroch* (1902) 18 The women, posting blankets for the coming sheiling, stopped their splashing in the little linn. *Ibid.* 71 A white blanket that needs no posting.

post, *v.*⁵ *slang.* [app. f. POST *sb.*³ or (?) It. *posta* a stake.] *trans.* To lay down, stake, deposit, pay down. *spec.* of bail money.

1781 C. JOHNSTON *John Juniper* II. 48 Toby having, in his own phrase, *posted the cole* (staked down the money)..lost a game or two, according to rule. **1781–1870** [see COLE *sb.*²]. **1812** J. H. VAUX *Flash Dict.*, *Post* or *post the poney*, to stake, or lay down the money. **1821** *Sporting Mag.* VIII. N.S. 233 Many..will recollect the needful was not posted. **1891** *Lic. Vict. Gaz.* 3 Apr. (Farmer), Done! post the money. **1974** *Observer* 7 Apr. 4/8 Immediately after posting five million francs..bail money..he took a private plane home from Geneva. **1974** *Progress* (Easley, S. Carolina) 24 Apr. 10/1 Arrested and charged with illegal possession and sale of piranha, the dealer posted bond and awaits trial which should come this week. **1978** S. BRILL *Teamsters* vi. 223 The other defendants flew in from around the country to plead innocent and post bail.

post (pəʊst), *adv. Obs.* or *arch.* [Originating in the phrase *ride in post* (F. *chevaucher en poste*), (POST *sb.*² 8 d), abbreviated to *ride post*, and thence extended to other verbs.] With post-horses; by post; express; with speed or haste. Cf. F. *courir la poste*, now, to run very fast.

a. With *ride*, *run*, and other verbs of motion.

1549 COVERDALE, etc. *Erasm. Par. Jas.* 37 You ryde poste to the deuil. **1588** FRAUNCE *Lawiers Log.* Ded., Riding poast towards London you chaunged horse at the vniversitie. **1593** SHAKS. *Rich. II*, v. ii. 112 Mount thee vpon his horse, Spurre post, and get before him to the King. **1613** W. BROWNE *Brit. Past.* I. i, She follow'd, flyes; she fled from, followes post. *a* **1651** CALDERWOOD *Hist. Kirk* (1843) II. 230 Madame Raillie..sent post to the comptroller, the Laird of Pittarrow,..and called for his assistance. *a* **1653** BINNING *Serm.* (1845) 377 Men begin at leisure, but they run post before all be done. **1660** *Act 12 Chas. II*, c. 35 §1 His Majestyes Post Master Generall..shall from time to time have the receiving, taking up, ordering, dispatching, sending post or with speade, and delivering of all Letters and Pacquets whatsoever. **1689** *Lond. Gaz.* No. 2485/4 A Gentleman riding Post with the Mail, was likewise taken into the said Wood. **1711** *Royal Proclam.* 23 June ibid. No. 4866/1 The Horsing of any Person..Riding Post, (that is to say) Riding several Stages upon a Post-Road, and changing Horses. **1711** *Ibid.* /2 All Letters..shall..be..delivered to the Deputy.., and..sent Post unto the..General Post-Office. **1716** *Ibid.* No. 5431/3 He set out Post for Paris. **1751** SMOLLETT *Per. Pic.* (1779) III. lxxxi. 166 Sir T—— sent his valet de chambre post with a letter. **1802** MRS. E. PARSONS *Myst. Visit* II. 176 They were to travel post. **1838** *Murray's Handbk. N. Germ.* 83 Provided..he be not journeying post to the Rhine. **1883** STEVENSON *Treasure Isl.* II. vii, So now, Livesey, come post; do not lose an hour, if you respect me.

b. With other verbs: With speed, fast; hastily.

1632 SHIRLEY *Changes* I. i. 4 'Twere no good manners to speake hastily to a Gentlewoman, to talke post (as they say) to his Mistresse. **1634** J. TAYLOR (Water P.) *Gt. Eater Kent* 4 Some haue the agilitie to ride poast, some the facilitie to runne poast, some the dexteritie to write poast, and some the abilitie to speake poast. *a* **1658** CLEVELAND *2nd Elegy to B. Jonson* 53 Scriblers (that write Post and versifie With no more Leasure than we cast a Dye).

‖**post** (pəʊst), the Latin preposition meaning 'after', occurring in certain phrases used in English contexts, as ***post meridiem***, ***post mortem***; also in

1. post bellum, after the war; also *fig.*

1874 *Southern Mag.* XIV. 37 It [*sc.* Atlanta] looks so little like a *post-bellum* town. **1883** *Standard* 17 Sept. 5/3 They were swamped by the gorgeous people of the *post bellum* epoch. **1905** *Westm. Gaz.* 30 Aug. 9/3 What the post-bellum expenses of..Japan and Russia will be during the next five, or even ten, years. **1920** *Czecho-Slovak Trade Jrnl.* Apr. 5 The post-bellum difficulties..do not yet permit her to throb with full vigour and strength. **1940** BEERBOHM *Mainly on Air* (1946) 97 The future, the post-bellum period, is to be perfectly splendid. **1974** 'M. INNES' *Appleby's Other Story* xvi. 127 A *post-bellum* relationship... That was it. Mr Charles Carter..was no longer Miss Kenterell's quarry.

2. post coitum, after sexual intercourse; also as *sb.*; *spec.* with allusion to the proverb *post coitum omne animal triste est* (and variants) 'after sexual intercourse every animal is sad'. Also *transf.*

The phrase as such does not occur in classical Latin, but cf. [Aristotle] *Problems* 877 b 9 διὰ τί οἱ νέοι, ὅταν πρῶτον ἀφροδισιάζειν ἄρχωνται, αἷς ἂν ὁμιλήσωσι, μετὰ τὴν πρᾶξιν μισοῦσιν; 'Why do young men, on first having sexual intercourse, afterwards hate those with whom they have just been associated?'; Pliny *Nat. Hist.* x. lxxxiii. homini tantum primi coitus paenitentia 'man alone experiences regret after first having intercourse'.

1762 STERNE *Tr. Shandy* V. xxxvi. 126 The oily and balsamous parts are of a lively heat and spirit, which accounts for the observation of Aristotle, '*Quod omne animal post coitum est triste.*' [**1920** A. HUXLEY *Leda* 34 Some.. Mount up on wings as frail and misty As passion's all-too-transient kiss (Though afterwards—oh, *omne animal triste*!)] **1928** *Jrnl. Morphol.* XLVI. 171 Embryos with six to ten somites are to be expected in the opossum about 8½ days post coitum. **1933** M. LOWRY *Ultramarine* iii. 158 Whether life was worth living or not was a matter for an embryo rather than a man. 'Post coitum omne animalia triste est. Omne? Supinus pertundo tunicam. **1959** *Listener* 15 Oct. 651/2 A remorseful attack of *post coitum triste*. **1966** C. M. BOWRA *Memories* xi. 246 Once Clark was visiting a college farm, and the party witnessed a bull servicing a cow. Clark..said, 'Blakeway, *omne animal post coitum triste.* There was, Blakeway, a firm of solicitors in London called Mann, Rogers, and Greaves.' **1967** *Listener* 12 Jan. 71/2 Elizabeth Sellars..had to..register such stock emotions as there was time for—fear (lover dead *post coitum*?) and gratification (*post coitum* and dialogue apparently working). **1975** M. BRADBURY *History Man* i. 6 He is in that flat state of literary post coitum that affects those who spend too much time with their own lonely structures and plots. **1979** *Guardian* 13 June 9/5 If you think there's no post coitum triste in angling, try chatting up a tench fisherman after he's spent a night by the lake.

3. post diem, after the day; in *Law*: see quots.

1607 COWELL *Interpr.*, *Post diem*, is a returne of a writ after the day assigned for the returne: for the which, the *Custos breuium* hath foure pence..: or it may be the fee taken for the same. **1658** *Practick Part of Law* 8 You are to pay 4*d.* as a *post-diem* for each of the aforesaid Processe, which you bring not into the Philizer by the day of the return. **1848** in WHARTON *Law Lex.*

4. post eventum = POST FACTUM.

1846 GEO. ELIOT tr. *Strauss's Life of Jesus* III. 166 Thus renouncing what is narrated..as composed *post eventum*. **1920** *Glasgow Herald* 13 July 6 Mr Asquith's post-eventum reproofs..leave us cold when we recall that.. he and his colleagues might have done much to make the preaching of their historic dogma on retrenchment an effective feature. **1958** *Listener* 25 Dec. 1092/2, I should have liked to put my oar, *post eventum*, into the argument. **1961** J. B. WILSON *Reason & Morals* i. 8 What seems to happen is that the philosopher arrives on the scene several centuries too late, and explains the advance of knowledge *post eventum*.

5. post festum = prec. (In quot. 1966 lit. 'after the festival'.)

1887 MOORE & AVELING tr. *Marx's Capital* I. i. 47 He begins, post festum, with the results of the process of development ready to hand before him. **1935** H. STRAUMANN *Newspaper Headlines* ii. 55 It must be kept in mind that it is an interpretation *post festum*. **1958** W. STARK *Sociol. of Knowl.* 193 They [*sc.* derivations] are merely the accompaniments of action..the *post festum* rationalizations of human conduct which, in itself, is anything but rational. **1966** *New Statesman* 11 Nov. 718/3 The reference is to a mate in 17 which the problem's author very kindly meant to mark the 17th anniversary of this column some months ago. .. So let's 'celebrate' it, even though a bit *post festum*. **1970** B. BREWSTER tr. *Althusser & Balibar's Reading Capital* (1975) II. v. 122 It begins, *post festum*, with already established givens.

6. post hoc, after this. ***post hoc, ergo propter hoc***, after this, therefore on account of this;

expressing the fallacy that a thing which follows another is therefore caused by it.

1704 Norris *Ideal World* II. iii. 221 That maxim,—*Post hoc, ergo propter hoc*,—which indeed is good logick with the vulgar,.. methinks should not pass for such with the learned. **1843** R. J. Graves *Syst. Clin. Med.* xi. 119 In the cases in which recovery is stated to have followed this practice [of mercurialization] the *post hoc* has been mistaken for the *propter hoc*. **1889** *Athenæum* 13 Apr. 468/1 We have read the whole statement without feeling convinced that 'post hoc' necessarily included 'propter hoc' in this case. **1905** *Discriminator Prosp.* 26 Inventing a dangerous post hoc explanation of a catastrophe which has surprised him.

7. post partum, after child-birth. ***post-partum depression*** = *postnatal depression* s.v. POSTNATAL *a.* Also *fig.*

1844 *Medico-Chirurg. Rev.* XLI. 267 On using the catheter, 36 hours post partum, Dr. Crosse found the uterus inverted in the vagina. **1846** *Northern Jrnl. Med.* IV. 1 (*heading*) Some suggestions regarding the anatomical source and pathological nature of post-partum hemorrhage. **1857** Dunglison *Med. Dict.*, *Post-partum*, after delivery, as, post partum hemorrhage. **1878** A. Hamilton *Nerv. Dis.* 113 The alarming condition that we occasionally meet with after post-partum hemorrhage. **1911** R. Jardine *Delayed & Complicated Labour* xiv. 185 If the third stage of labour is properly conducted, post-partum hæmorrhage can be largely prevented. **1929** *Amer. Jrnl. Psychiatry* VIII. 767, I didn't study the infanticidal impulses of many women, because these impulses are more prominent in post-partum depressions. **1957** A. Guttmacher *Pregnancy & Birth* xvi. 250 'Post partum blues', beginning a day or two after delivery and lasting several days, are frequently encountered... Your doctor.. can reassure you he has met postpartum blues.. in people whose depression cleared up. **1959** N. Mailer *Advts. for Myself* (1961) 244, I was beginning to feel the empty winds of a post-partum gloom. **1974** *Publishers Weekly* 18 Mar. 44/3 The scary-funny business of bearing a baby and coping postpartum. **1976** *Dissertation Abstr. Internat.* B. XXXVI. 5793/1 Hostile attitudes toward mother figures predispose some women toward experiences of postpartum depression. **1977** *Lancet* 28 May 1126/1 A 31-year-old woman, 6 months post-partum, complained of fatiguability.

8. post terminum (*Law*): see POST TERM *sb.*

9. With English words and phrases. [Cf. POST- B. 1 d.]

Usu. found in contexts where *after* would be equally appropriate and more agreeable.—Ed.

1965 *Listener* 16 Sept. 432/3 *Der Ferne Klang* is post-Wagnerian, and post just about everything else that was happening at the turn of the century. **1973** *Nature* 26 Jan. 273/1 Medium was replaced two days post plating and the number of foci determined on the third day. **1974** *Daily Tel.* 7 Jan. 13/3 Now, post the increase [in the price of oil],.. future gold price prospects far outweigh individual share fundamentals. **1979** *Ibid.* 19 July 21/4 Post the Geneva meeting of Opec the OECD reckons that its 24 member countries.. can expect average economic growth of only two p.c. over the next 12 months.

post, obs. form of *posed*, pa. pple. of POSE *v.*[1]

post, variant of POUST *Obs.*, power.

post- (pəʊst), *prefix*, repr. L. *post*, adv. and prep., after, behind. In L., prefixed adverbially to verbs, as *posthabēre* to hold or esteem after, *postpōnĕre* to place after, postpone, *postscrībĕre* to write after; also to pples., vbl. sbs., and other verbal derivatives, as *postgenitus* after-born, *postpositus* placed after, *postscriptus* written after, *postveniens* coming after, *postparitor* after-getter, heir. More rarely formed on the prep. and an object as, of time, *postauctumnālis* coming (*post auctumnum*) after autumn, post-autumnal; of place, *postlīminium* (a return) behind the threshold, *postscænium* (the space) behind the scenes. In English its use has received great extension, esp. in the prepositional relation, in which compounds are formed almost at will, not only on words from Latin, but also, in technical terms, from Greek, and sometimes even on English or other words, as *post-breakfast*, *post-Easter*, *post-Elizabethan*. These are often opposed to formations in *ante-* or *pre-*.

A. Words in which *post-* is adverbial or adjectival, qualifying the verb, verbal derivative, or other adj. or sb. forming, or implied in, the second element. In compounds derived or formed from L., or on L. analogies, as POST-DATE, -EXIST, -FIX, -PONE, -POSE, -POSIT, -VENE, -GENITURE, -JACENT, SCRIPT (q.v.); also in nonce-wds., sometimes formed after, and as the opposites to, words in *ante-* or *pre-* (exceptionally *pro-*).

1. Relating to time or order.

a. In adverbial relation: = After, afterwards, subsequently. (*a*) With verbs or pa. pples., or in nonce-wds. formed after verbs or pa. pples. in *pre-* (*pro-*): as ***post-determined*** (opp. to *predetermined*), ***post-disapproved***; ***post-process*** vb.; ***post-stressed*** ppl. a.; also, in nonce-wds. formed after verbs or pa. pples. in *ante-*: as ***posticipated*** (opp. to *anticipated*). **post-ac'celerate** *v. trans. Electronics*, to accelerate (an electron or electron beam) after it is deflected in a cathode-ray tube; so **post-ac'celerating** *ppl. a.*; †**post'cribrate** *v.* [see CRIBRATE], to sift afterwards; **post'multiply** *v.*, *Math.* to multiply by (or as) a *postfactor* (see b); **post-'occupied** *ppl. a.* [after *preoccupied*], ? occupied with something past; **post-'osmicate** *v. trans. Biol.*, to postfix with a solution of osmium tetroxide; †**post'place** *v.*, to place after something else; **post-pre'cipitate** *v. trans.*, to deposit by post-precipitation (see b); *intr.*, to be so deposited; **post-pro'duce** *v. trans.*, to subject (film) to post-production (see b). **ˌpost-'prophesy** *v.*, to 'prophesy after the event'; †**ˌpost'vide** *v.* [after *provide*], to provide for an event after it has happened; to take precautions too late. See also POSTJUDICED. (*b*) With adjectives, or forming the first element of adjectives: as **post'mutative** [L. *mūtāre* to change], applied to languages in which words are inflected by means of affixes placed after the stem or radical part; †**post'parative** (opp. to *preparative*: see quot.).

b. In *quasi*-adjectival relation to a sb. (chiefly a verbal sb. or noun of action) forming, or implied in, the second element: = Occurring or existing afterwards, coming after, subsequent, later: as ***post-ac'cession***, ***-act***, ***-'argument***, ***-'contract***, ***-division***, ***-fru'ition***, ***-'issue***, ***-legiti'mation***, ***-ope'ration***, ***-'pardon***, ***-'penance***, ***-'processing***, ***-'signer***, ***-'stressing***, ***-vari'ation***. Also in nonce-words formed after nouns in *pre-*, as ***ˌpost-'amble***, ***ˌpostdesti'nation*** (hence ***ˌpostdesti'narian***), ***'postface***, ***'postference***, ***post'fiction***, ***ˌpostmo'nition***: see quots. Also **post-accele'ration** *Electronics*, in a cathode-ray tube, acceleration of the electron beam after its deflection; also **post-ac'celerator**; **ˌpost-e'ternity**, eternity in the future, everlasting future existence; **post'factor**, *Math.*, the latter of two factors in non-commutative multiplication; **post-'genitive** *Gram.*, a possessive noun following the noun it qualifies; cf. *post-possessive* below; **post-'heating** *vbl. sb.*, the heating of metal after welding, in order to relieve stresses; †**'post-law**, ? a law made subsequently to, and annulling, some obligation, an *ex post facto* law; **'post-ˌmarriage**, marriage subsequent to cohabitation; **postmultipli'cation** *Math.*, multiplication by a postfactor; **postosmi'cation** *Biol.*, postfixation with a solution of osmium tetroxide; **post-po'ssessive** *Gram.*, a possessive pronoun following the noun it qualifies; cf. *post-genitive* above; **post-precipitation** *Chem.*, precipitation of a compound spontaneously following that of another for the same solution; **post-'processor** *Computers* (see quot. 1977); **post-pro'duction**, film-production effected after the completion of shooting.

1946 *Proc. IRE* XXXIV. 433/2 The intensifier electrode or electrodes, sometimes called *post-accelerating electrodes, provide acceleration after deflection. **1971** Klemperer & Barnett *Electron Optics* (ed. 3) x. 397 Electrons may be deflected while they are of very small velocity, and they may be 'post-accelerated' later on to whatever speed is required. *Ibid.*, The spot size should not be increased by the post-accelerating field. **1940** *Philips Technical Rev.* V. 245 (*heading*) A cathode ray tube with *post-acceleration. *Ibid.* 249/1 The strength of the lens increases with increasing post-acceleration voltage. **1971** Klemperer & Barnett *Electron Optics* (ed. 3) x. 399 The best post-acceleration is effected by means of fine meshes. **1956** *Proc. IRE* XLIV. 665/2 Conventional *post-accelerators, also called intensifiers, operate with conductive coatings of band or spiral shape, placed on the inside of the bulb. **1959** Rider & Uslan *Encycl. Cathode-Ray Oscilloscopes* (ed. 2) i. 20/1 The beam.. traverses the gap between the accelerator and post-accelerator areas. **1656** Stanley *Hist. Philos.* viii. (1701) 340/1 His life is not happy, for Beatitude is a *post-accession thereto. **1851** Burrill *Law Dict.* II, **Post-act*, an after-act; an act done afterwards. **1864** in Webster; and in subsequent Dicts. **1593** G. Harvey *Pierce's Super.* ***iv, He liked not ouer-long Preambles, or *Postambles to short Discourses. **1622** T. Stoughton *Chr. Sacrif.* viii. 94 This being more then an adiunct, euen a *post argument.. for confirmation of the maine argument. *a* **1610** Parsons *Leicester's Ghost* (1641) 18 It chanced that I made a *post-contract, And did in sort the Lady Sheifield wed. *a* **1631** Donne *Lett.* (1651) 308, I have cribrated,.. re-cribrated, and *post-cribrated the Sermon. **1700** C. Nesse *Antid. Armin.* (1827) 70 The Arminians.. may be called ..*post-destinarians for placing the eternal decree behind the race of man's life. **1656** T. Pierce (*title*) Prædestination .. defended against *Post-destination. **1674** Hickman *Hist. Quinquart.* (ed. 2) 160 The Doctor's Election is a Postdestination; for it then only makes men ordained to eternal life, when.. they are possessed of it. **1700** C. Nesse *Antid. Armin.* (1827) 51 To prefer time before eternity, and to set up a post-destination instead of a pre-destination. **1733** Pope *Let. to Swift* in Courthope *Life* 260 It was laboured, corrected, pre-commended, and *post-disapproved so far as to be disowned by themselves. **1628** Donne *Serm.* xxix. (1640) 287 The Schooles have made so many Divisions, and sub-divisions, and re-divisions, and *post-divisions of Ignorance. *a* **1631** —— *Serm.* vii. 71 Man hath not that, not eternity, but the Image of Eternity, that is Immortality, a *Post-eternity there is in the soule of Man. **1678** Cudworth *Intell. Syst.* 44. *a* **1680** Charnock *Attrib. God* (1834) I. 367 The promise of eternal life is as ancient as God himself.. as it hath an ante-eternity, so it hath a post-eternity. **1782** (*title*) Paris in Miniature,.. together with a Preface and *Postface by the English Limner. **1887** *Sat. Rev.* 30 Apr. 624/2 The frank admission in both preface and postface that [he] found the Japanese syllabary too many for him. **1974** *Nature* 20 Sept. 262/1 In the postface (this must be one of the few nearly Latin words invented in the twentieth century!), Eugene Skolnikoff outlines the increasing involvement.. of MIT in the field of science and public policy. **1877** Swinburne *Let.* 21 Apr. (1960) III. 326 To compare either with Shelley or Hugo for preference or *postference, is purely absurd. **1607** Harington in *Nugæ Ant.* (1804) II. 139 As for the latter predictions or rather *postfictions (since the bishops death) I willingly omit, concerning the successors of this bishop. **1922** E. Kruisinga *Handbk. Present-Day Eng.* (ed. 3) II. i. 361 Nouns preceded by a definite article are not seldom used with a *post-genitive. **1957** R. W. Zandvoort *Handbk. Eng. Gram.* II. ii. 105 The only case where an English genitive may be said to follow its headword is when it is the principal part of an *of*-adjunct to a preceding noun... The construction is known as the *post-genitive*. I gave him an old raincoat of my brother's. **1938** *Times* 4 Feb. 11/2 The *post-heating process greatly improves an already satisfactory weld by allowing the metal at the weld to recover its original structure after the severe treatment given by the welding operation. **1966** C. R. Tottle *Sci. Engin. Materials* x. 224 Temperature gradients are reduced.. in welding by preheating the parent metal or post-heating immediately after welding. **1922** Joyce *Ulysses* 663 The anticipated diamond jubilee of Queen Victoria.. and the *posticipated opening of the new municipal fish market. **1612** Chapman *Widdowes T.* II. i. Plays 1873 III. 31 Shee matching.. with some yong Prodigall: what must ensue, but her *post-issue beggerd. **1663** *Short Surv. Grand Case Pres. Ministry* 38 Oaths are sacred things, and *Post-laws are a ready Papacie to absolve them. **1780** M. Madan *Thelyphthora* (1781) I. 35 The proposers and framers of such schemes of *post-legitimation, had been convinced, that the conjugal cohabitation.. was a lawful marriage. **1785** G. A. Bellamy *Apology* II. 46 That ridicule and contempt which custom has annexed to a *post-marriage (if I may so term it). **1938** S. Beckett *Murphy* ix. 176 In the morning nothing remained of the dream but a *post-monition of calamity. **1862** *Phil. Trans. R. Soc.* CLI. 312 Every matrix of the type $n \times n$ is equivalent (by *post-multiplication) to one, and only one, of the reduced matrices included in the formula (62.). **1968** Fox & Mayers *Computing Methods for Scientists & Engineers* v. 100 For the general eigenvalue problem we can perform virtually the same operation, though with post-multiplication included to preserve similarity. **1862** *Phil. Trans. R. Soc.* CLI. 312 These numbers will remain unchanged, when the given matrix is premultiplied by any unit-matrix, and *post-multiplied by any matrix whatsoever. **1939** *Brit. Jrnl. Psychol.* XXIX. 302 After post-multiplying.. by $\hat{e}'$ we get.. [etc.]. **1978** *Nature* 20 Apr. 740/1 We are told, as though it were surprising, that pre- and post-multiplying a matrix by the matrix of its eigenvectors produces a diagonal matrix. **1899** R. C. Temple *Th. Univ. Gram.* 7 Languages are divisible into 1. pre-mutative, or those that prefix their affixes; 2. intro-mutative, or those that infix them; and 3. *post-mutative, or those that suffix them. **1876** M. Collins *Fr. Midn. to Midn.* III. iv. 8 They were for the most part silent. Lord Arthur was pre-occupied; Vance was *post-occupied. *a* **1631** Donne *Serm.* (ed. Alford) IV. 451 All my co-operation is but a *post-operation, a working by the power of that all-preventing Grace. **1965** *Jrnl. R. Microsc. Soc.* LXXXIV. 129 Sucrose was first used with formaldehyde in fixation for electron microscopy by Holt and Hicks.., who *postosmicated the tissues that had been treated this way. **1971** *Nature* 2 Apr. 334/2 Random pieces of grossly normal thyroid tissue.. were diced.., fixed in 1·5% glutaraldehyde .., post-osmicated, dehydrated and embedded in 'Araldite 502'. **1963** *Jrnl. Cell Biol.* XVII. 54/2 The final dense product could be easily referable to fine structure in sections of material embedded without *postosmication. **1581** Mulcaster *Positions* viii. (1887) 53 They that write of exercise, make three degrees in it, wherof they call the first a preparatiue,.. the next simply by the name of exercise,.. the third a *postparatiue. **1625** Donne *Serm. 3 Apr.* 37 Euery Pardon, whether a *Post-pardon, by way of mercy, after a Lawe is broken, or a Præ-pardon, by way of Dispensation, in wisedome before a Lawe bee broken. **1599** R. Linche *Anc. Fict.* G iv, I thought it fittest in this treatise to *postplace her. **1943** *Eng. Stud.* XXV. 103 The construction called by.. Curme 'double genitive', by Kruisinga 'post genitive', and, in the case of a pronoun (*a friend of mine*), '*post-possessive'. **1957** R. W. Zandvoort *Handbk. Eng. Gram.* III. ii. 140 The construction may be denoted as the post-possessive. a. I gave him an old raincoat of mine. He hated that pride of hers. b. It was no fault of theirs. **1936** Kolthoff & Sandell *Textbk. Quantitative Inorg. Analysis* viii. 105 This second phase is therefore not coprecipitated but *postprecipitated. **1939** A. I. Vogel *Text-bk. Quantitative Inorg. Analysis* i. 148 Zinc sulphide is slowly post-precipitated. **1960** Belcher & Nutten *Quantitative Inorg. Analysis* (ed. 2) x. 61 Examples of precipitates which tend to post-precipitate are zinc sulphide on mercury sulphide, and magnesium oxalate on calcium oxalate. **1932** I. M. Kolthoff in *Jrnl. Physical Chem.* XXXVI. 861 First of all, calcium oxalate precipitates and then on standing magnesium oxalate crystallizes out slowly. Therefore, we are not dealing here with a case of coprecipitation, but of *post-precipitation, the crystals of calcium oxalate being not at all or only slightly contaminated by magnesium. **1963** G. Svehla tr. *Erdey's Gravimetric Analysis* I. iii. 183 Tin (IV) sulphide tends to carry down nickel, cobalt and iron ions from a hydrochloric acid containing solution by post-precipitation. **1977** *Sci. Amer.* June 9/2 (Advt.), With the HP 5420A, you can *post-process measurement results using the four basic arithmetic functions. **1966** C. J. Sippl *Computer Dict. & Handbk.* 278 The real-time system relieves the larger system of time consuming input and output functions as well as performing preprocessing and *postprocessing functions, such as validity editing and formatting for print. **1967** *Economist* 12 Aug. 588/2 Molins, Ferranti and IBM have told the Ministry of Technology that they can jointly produce a *post-processor for the Molins machine within twelve months flat. **1977** *Gloss. Terms Data Processing* (*B.S.I.*) VII.

2/1 *Postprocessor*, a computer program that effects some final computation or organization. **1976** *Broadcast* 12 Jan. 1/1 Bring in your film and we'll *post-produce it on tape. *Ibid.* 1/2 Spend a day on *post-production using time code computer editing. **1953** K. Reisz *Technique Film Editing* i. 49 A post-production break-down of the finished sequence. **1859** F. Francis *N. Dogvane* (1888) 298 None *post-prophesied their convictions that 'this would be the end of it all', more loudly than Mr. Tom Sharp. **1819** Jefferson *Autobiog.* App., Wks. 1859 I. 121 These were the only *post-signers. **1953** *Archit. Rev.* CXIII. 377/2 (*caption*) Auditorium spanned by *post-stressed beams. **1965** *Language* XLI. 473 As many as five syllables occur prestressed, but only one syllable occurs post-stressed, except rarely when a postclitic follows a suffix. **1941** *Concrete & Constructional Engin.* XXXVI. 93/1 Dr. Abeles suggests stretching the hard steel wires after hardening and setting, which he calls '*post-stressing'. **1976** *Offshore Engineer* Mar. 26/3 The Kishorn structure departs from its smaller brothers by having a two-stage wall poststressing. The first stage will be stressed at the 15m high level, the remainder when the walls reach full height. **1650** B. *Discolliminium* 45, I and my Friends shall be allowed the full benefit of all the variations, interpretations, reservations, *postvariations, tergiversations, excusations, .. that I and my Mare can devise or possibly imagine. *a* **1661** Fuller *Worthies, Chester* (1662) I. 188 When men instead of preventing, *postvide against dangers.

2. Of local position. **a.** In advb. relation to a vbl. adj. forming the second element: = Behind, posteriorly: as POSTJACENT; also **postco'mmunicant**, communicating behind; ***p. artery***, the posterior communicating artery (Wilder). **b.** In adjectival relation to a sb. forming or implied in the second element: = Hinder, situated at the back, posterior: chiefly in terms of Anatomy and Zoology, as POSTABDOMEN, etc.; **post'choroid**, posterior choroid (artery) (Wilder); **posthippo'campal**, of or belonging to the posterior hippocampus, as in ***posthippocampal fissure***; **postsca'lene**, posterior scalene (muscle of the neck) (*Cent. Dict.* cites *Coues*); also **post-'tuberance** *nonce-wd.* [after *protuberance*], a posterior protuberance.

1868 Owen *Anat. Vert.* III. 135 The most .. important of these [fissures] in Man, has .. received the name of 'posthippocampal'. **1825** *Q. Rev.* XXXI. 466 Their beauty is proverbial in Africa, particularly for that .. quality of being singularly gifted with the Hottentot post-tuberance.

B. Compounds in which *post-* is prepositional, the object being the noun forming, or implied in, the second element.

1. Relating to time or order: = After, subsequent to, following, succeeding, later than.

a. With substantives, forming adjectives (or attributive phrases), often more or less nonce-wds., and of obvious meaning; as ***post-Ascension***, ***-attack***, ***-bop***, ***-breakfast***, ***-Christmas***, ***-coition***, ***-college***, ***-contact***, ***-crash***, ***-creole***, ***-Easter***, ***-election***, ***-erosion***, ***-experience***, ***-flu***, ***-game***, ***-harvest***, ***-holiday***, ***-Incarnation***, ***-independence***, ***-injury***, ***-language***, ***-lunch***, ***-luncheon***, ***-menopause*** (also as *sb.*), ***-midnight***, ***-Mutiny***, ***-operation*** (also as *adv.*), ***-ordination***, ***-orgasm***, ***-ovulation***, ***-publication***, ***-Reformation***, ***-Renaissance***, ***-Restoration***, ***-resurrection***, ***-Revolution***, ***-school***, ***-seizure***, ***-Sputnik*** (also as *adv.*), ***-surrealist***, ***-symbolist***, ***-Union***, ***-Watergate***, ***-World War II***, etc.; see also POST-MORTEM, POST-OBIT.

b. With adjs., or formed from *post* + a L. or Gr. sb. with an adjectival ending. Many of these are self-explaining, esp. those formed from personal names, as ***post-Adamic***, ***-Alexandrine***, ***-Aristotelian***, ***-Cartesian*** (see CARTESIAN), ***Chomskyan***, ***-Coleridgian***, ***-Constantinian***, ***-Darwinian***, ***-Davidic***, ***-Elizabethan***, ***-Hegelian***, ***-Hesiodic***, ***-Homeric***, ***-Humian***, ***-Jamesian***, ***-Kantian***, ***-Keynesian***, ***-Marxist***, ***-Mosaic***, ***-Nietzschean***, ***-Pauline***, ***-Petrine***, ***-Saussurean***, ***-Socratic***, ***-Solomonic***, ***-Wagnerian***, etc. So in geology, from the names of formations or periods, as ***post-Cambrian***, ***-cretacean***. Also terms of pathology, indicating conditions or symptoms following an attack of disease, as ***post-apoplectic***, ***-diphtheritic***, ***-epileptic***, ***-herpetic***, ***-influenzal***, ***-paralytic***, ***-paroxysmal***, ***-scarlatinal***, ***-syphilitic***, ***-typhoid*** (see also those defined below); and many others of obvious meaning, as ***post-adolescent***, ***-anæsthetic***, ***-analytic(al)***, ***-atomic***, ***-baptismal***, ***-biblical***, ***-canonical***, ***-capitalist***, ***-climacteric***, ***-cognitive***, ***-coital***, ***-collegiate***, ***-colonial***, ***-conciliar***, ***-conditional***, ***-encephalitic***, ***-eruptive***, ***-experimental***, ***-feudal***, ***-industrial***, ***-junctural***, ***-marital***, ***-mediæval***, ***-menopausal***, ***-observational***, ***-orgasmic***, ***-pagan***, ***-pausal***, ***-pentecostal***, ***-priestly***, ***-prophetic***, ***-rebellionary***, ***-resurrectional***, ***-revolutionary***, ***-romantic***, ***-talmudical***, ***-teenage***; adjs. formed as in senses 1 a and b above are occas. used *ellipt.* as *sbs.*; such adjs. may also have adverbial forms, as ***post-coitally***, ***-maritally***.

Also **posta'bortal** *Med.*, occurring or performed after an abortion; **posta'bortion** (also as *adv.*) *Med.*, (occurring or performed) after an abortion; **post-a'bortum** (also as *adv.*) *Med.* [L. *abortus* abortion] = prec.; **post-ab'sorptive** *Med.*, occurring after food has been absorbed into the body; **post-apo'stolic, -ical**, subsequent to the apostles, later than the apostolic age; **post-'cenal** (-cæn-, -cœn-) [L. *cēna*, erron. *cæna*, *cœna*, dinner], after-dinner; **post-cho'reic**, *Path.*, following an attack of chorea or 'St. Vitus's dance'; **post-co'mitial** (see quot.); **post-co'nnubial**, occurring after marriage: = POSTNUPTIAL; **post-'conquest**, applied to periods after a conquest, *spec.* (with capital), after the Norman Conquest; **post-con'questal**, founded after the Norman Conquest; **post-con'questual, -Conquestual**, after the Norman Conquest; **post-conso'nantal, -conso'nantic**, after a consonant; hence **post-conso'nantally** *adv.*; **post-con'vulsive** *Path.*, subsequent to a convulsion; **post-'cosmic** [Gr. κόσμος world], subsequent to the present world; = *postmundane*; **post'cyclic, -ical**, occurring or operating after the termination of a cycle or cycles (esp. in *Transformational Gram.*); hence **post'cyclically** *adv.*; **post-de'flection** *Electronics*, pertaining to or being acceleration of an electron beam after its deflection in a cathode-ray tube; **post-depositional** *Geol.*, occurring after the deposition of sediment; **post-dia'stolic**, *Physiol.*, following the *diastole* or dilatation of the heart in beating; **post-di'crotic**, following the dicrotic wave of the pulse; **post-dis'ruption**, subsequent to the DISRUPTION of the Ch. of Scotland and formation of the Free Ch. in 1843; **post-'embryonal, post-embry'onic**, subsequent to the embryonic stage of life or growth; **post-e'mergence**, occurring, performed, or applied after the emergence of seedlings from the soil; also *absol.*; **post-'febrile**, *Path.*, occurring after an attack of fever; **post-hemi'plegic**, *Path.*, following an attack of hemiplegia or paralysis of one side; **post-hyp'notic** (see quot. 1903); **post-'ictal** *Med.*, subsequent to a stroke or fit, esp. an epileptic fit; hence **post-'ictally** *adv.*; **post-in'fectious**, subsequent to an infection; *esp.* caused by an infection but arising after it has ceased; **Post-lap'sarian**, *Theol.* = INFRALAPSARIAN or SUBLAPSARIAN; also *gen.* (with lower case initial), after the Fall of Man; **post'literal**, following a letter of the alphabet; **post-mei'otic** *Cytology*, occurring subsequent to meiosis; **post-me'narchal, -me'narcheal** *Med.*, of, pertaining to, or designating a girl who has menstruated; **post-meta'morphic** *Geol.*, occurring or existing after metamorphism; **post-'mineral**, occurring after the formation of a mineral deposit; **post-'mortuary**, occurring, or relating to what may occur, after (some one's) death; post-mortem; **post-'mundane** [L. *mundus* world], subsequent to this present world; **postneo'natal** *Med.*, pertaining to or designating the period between the end of the neonatal period, four weeks after birth, and the end of the first year of life; **post-neu'ritic**, *Path.*, following an attack of neuritis; **post-Ni'cene** *a.*, *Ch. Hist.*, subsequent in date to the first Nicene Council (A.D. 325); also as *sb.* a Post-Nicene writer; **post-'nominal**, following a substantive or a proper name; also *ellipt.* as *sb.*; **post-'ovulative, -ovu'latory** *Med.*, subsequent to ovulation; **post-'painterly** *Art* [cf. PAINTERLY *a.*], of or characterized by a style of abstract painting that employs traditional qualities of colour, form, and texture; **post-par'turient**, *Path.* [cf. PARTURIENT 3], occurring after parturition; **post-'puberal** = next; **post-'pubertal**, subsequent to puberty; **post-'puberty** *a.* = prec.; **post-Pu'ranic**, subsequent to or later than the date of the Puranas; **post'radical** *Philol.* following a root or root-word; also as *sb.*, a postradical element or word; **post-'Raphaelite** *a.*, applied to schools of painting subsequent to the time of Raphael (died 1520): cf. PRE-RAPHAELITE; **post-re'mote**, more remote in subsequent time or order: see *pre-remote*, PRE- B. 1; **post-repro'ductive**, occurring after the period of life when a female can bear offspring; **post-'Roman**, subsequent to the Roman period; **post-sys'tolic**, following the systole of the heart; **post-tec'tonic** *Geol.*, occurring or existing after tectonic activity; **post-'temporary** *nonce-wd.* [after *contemporary*], later than the time of the actual events; subsequent in date; **post-'tonic** [see TONIC], following the accented syllable; **post-trau'matic**, *Path.* [Gr. τραῦμα wound], occurring after a wound; **post-tri'dentine** [see TRIDENTINE], subsequent to the Council of Trent; **post-'tussic** [irreg. f. L. *tussis* cough: see -IC], occurring after a cough; **post-'vaccinal**, occurring after vaccination; **post-'varioloid**, *Path.*, ? occurring after a varioloid eruption; **post-Vedic** (-'veɪdɪk), subsequent to or later than the Rig-Veda; **post-'verbal**, following a verb; hence **post'verbally** *adv.*; **postvo'calic** *Philol.*, following a vowel; hence **post-vo'calically** *adv.* See also POST-DILUVIAL, -EXILIAN, -GLACIAL, -GRADUATE, -NATAL, -PRANDIAL, etc.

c. Rarely with sbs., forming sbs., as ***postcreation***; **post-'article** *Gram.*, one of a set of words that can follow an article in a noun phrase; **post-climax** *Ecol.* [CLIMAX *sb.* 4 b], the point in a plant succession at which development has continued beyond the balanced state of climax; †**'post-noon** *Obs.*, afternoon; POST-FINE, POST TERM, etc.

d. Adjs. of the type in sense B. 1 a above are sometimes used adverbially (cf. POST *Latin prep.* 6), as *postabortion*, *-abortum*, *-operation*, *-Sputnik* above, POSTFLIGHT *adv.*

1910 *Surg., Gynecol. & Obstetr.* July 55/1 Each case of post-partum or *post-abortal infection must be studied individually. **1973** I. M. Cushner et al. in H. J. & J. D. Osofsky *Abortion Experience* vi. 147 This newer approach toward postabortal laparascopic sterilization .. may very well lead to further reduction in the need for major surgical procedures in abortion. **1963** *Amer. Jrnl. Psychiatry* CXIX. 982/2 No known attempts to document statistically the incidence of *post-abortion psychiatric illness have been found in American medical literature. **1973** E. C. Payne et al. in H. J. & J. D. Osofsky *Abortion Experience* xii. 272 In the first reported prospective study .. a single postabortion interview took place during a period of 3 to 6 months after the procedure. In even more recent studies, women have been interviewed at a relatively specific time postabortion. **1910** F. J. Taussig *Prevention & Treatm. Abortion* vi. 44 There was no fever or odor to the discharge, so that the diagnosis was clearly endometritis *post-abortum due to decidual remnants. **1950** *Proc. Soc. Study Fertility* I. 26 (*heading*) The re-establishment of ovulation, post-partum and post-abortum. **1972** *Biol. Abstr.* LIII. 5727/2 The results of treatment of 2 groups of patients with post abortum acute insufficiency of the kidneys are discussed. **1919** *Proc. R. Soc.* B. XCI. 45 The energy expenditure during sleep may be assumed .. to be only slightly smaller than that during complete muscular rest in the *post-absorptive condition, *i.e.*, 12–14 hours after the last meal. **1972** *New England Jrnl. Med.* 5 Oct. 678/1 Recordings were made in the postabsorptive state between 9:30 a.m. and noon. **1877** Dawson *Orig. World* vi. 136 The geologist finds no trace of *post-Adamic creation. **1936** *Jrnl. Pediatrics* VIII. 52 The change from the straight, boyish figure of the preadolescent girl to the more rounded, mature figure of the *postadolescent girl. **1977** *New Yorker* 29 Aug. 19/2 The new false post-adolescent authority that needs to be blown away by somebody. **1901** E. L. Hicks *Man. Grk. Hist. Inscript.* (ed. 2) Pref., An indifference to *post-Alexandrine studies too common amongst British scholars. **1910** *Practitioner* Feb. 253 The *post-anaesthetic condition. *Ibid.* Mar. 361 Ether .. rarely causes post-anaesthetic vomiting. **1965** J. Pollitt *Depression & its Treatm.* vi. 80 Patients should be carefully questioned about this to avoid the risk of post-anaesthetic vomiting. **1934** *Mind* XLIII. 136 [A sense of 'theory of knowledge'] is essentially a '*post-analytic' *evaluation*, not a description, of knowledge. **1927** J. Loewemberg in *Jrnl. Philos.* XXIV. 5 Designating by 'pre-analytical', whatever is given *for* analysis, and by '*post-analytical', whatever is given *through* analysis, we wish to ascertain whether there is any possibility of assimilating to one another these two classes of data. **1882** Farrar *Early Chr.* I. 212 *note*, Showing a *post-Apostolic date. **1882–3** *Schaff's Encycl. Relig. Knowl.* I. 493 Immediately after the *post-apostolical age. **1934** Webster, *Post-Aristotelian. **1936** J. R. Kantor *Objective Psychol. Gram.* viii. 100 The post-Aristotelian subjectivists divided the individual into soul and body. **1957** C. Vereker *Devel. Polit. Theory* i. 40 This doctrine of equality, the emergence of which is sometimes held to be the distinguishing mark of post-Aristotelian social thought. **1965** N. Chomsky *Aspects of Theory of Syntax* ii. 107 Det→(pre-Article⁀*of*) Article (*post-Article). **1971** Post-article [see *non-lexical* s.v. NON- 3]. **1895** J. Kidd *Morality & Relig.* viii. 324 The *post-ascension activity of Christ. **1905** H. D. Rolleston *Dis. Liver* 226 The patient .. passes into what may be spoken of as a *post-ascitic stage. **1948** *Britannica Bk. of Year* (U.S.) 805/2 **Post-atom*(*ic*), subsequent to the dropping of the atomic bomb. **1954** A. Huxley in *Encounter* Feb. 5/2 This .. [temple] will be standing in the Western desert, an object, to the neo-Neolithic savages, of post-atomic times, of uncomprehending reverence and superstitious alarm. **1956** Auden & Kallman *Magic Flute* (1957) 58 The form of suite For piano in a Post-Atomic Age. **1961** *Washington Post* 1 June 24 The speaker suggested that the desolation of a *post-attack world would be too awful to face. **1964** Dentler & Cutright in I. L. Horowitz *New Sociol.* 424 Our discussion of the effects of a nuclear attack on the population makes it clear that the composition of the postattack population would be so different from that of today's population that this factor alone would make for differences in the postattack society. **1976** *Sci. Amer.* Nov. 33/3 In the immediate postattack period the fallout levels could vary greatly from one place to another. **1840** G. S. FABER *Prim. Doctr. Regen.* IV. ii. 333 With respect to *postbaptismal declarations. **1882** FARRAR *Early Chr.* I. 335 The ruthless dogma that there is no forgiveness for post-baptismal sin. **1882–3** *Schaff's Encycl. Relig. Knowl.* III. 2184 The first *post-biblical author to mention Simon is Hegesippus. **1955** KEEPNEWS & GRAUER *Pict. Hist. Jazz* xix. 250 A young star who came along in the *post-bop 1950s. **1977** *Rolling Stone* 5 May 24/2 Today his style is the antithesis of classic post-bop horn players like Coltrane. **1791** COWPER *Let. to J. Newton* 22 July, All my *post-breakfast time must be given to poetry. **1879** J. JACOBS in *19th Cent.* Sept. 490 The analogous.. Triune Deity of *post-Buddhistic Brahmanism. **1875** CROLL *Climate & T.* xx. 345 The longer we suppose the pre-Cambrian periods to have been, the shorter must we suppose the *post-Cambrian to be. **1899** J. STALKER *Christology of Jesus* i. 35 The forms in which the words of Jesus appear in the earliest *postcanonical literature. **1964** I. L. HOROWITZ *New Sociol.* 81 His critique of America could only be relevant and fruitful if it was made.. with the projected hopes and ideals of a *post-capitalist era. **1976** N. O'SULLIVAN *Conservatism* v. 122 The contemporary discussion about the nature of 'post-capitalist' (or 'post-industrial') society. **1874** MIVART in *Contemp. Rev.* Oct. 782 If *post-cartesian philosophy has been so wanting in positive results. **1931** *Times Lit. Suppl.* 10 Sept. 674/2 A particularly satisfying classification of the great seminal post-Cartesian theories of knowledge. **1963** *Ibid.* 1 Mar. 150/1 The general context of post-Cartesian thought. **1848** G. F. RUXTON in *Blackw. Mag.* LXIV. 430 Augustin.. was enjoying a *post-coenal smoke. **1871** M. COLLINS *Mrq. & Merch.* II. ii. 48 In the course of their post-cænal talk. **1922** JOYCE *Ulysses* 720 A temporary concussion caused by a falsely calculated movement in the course of a postcenal gymnastic display. **1970** *Jrnl. Linguistics* VI. 130 With a side glance at some *post-Chomskyan developments. **1975** *Amer. Speech 1973* XLVIII. 154 According to the post-Chomskyan revisionist Charles J. Fillmore, however, 'there are reasons for questioning the deep-structure validity of the traditional division between subject and predicate'. **1899** *Allbutt's Syst. Med.* VII. 854 *Post-choreic paralysis is sometimes well-marked. **1959** *Encounter* Feb. 74/2 All these books are written with a light touch: just the thing for *post-Christmas hang-overs. **1961** *Wall St. Jrnl.* 23 Jan. 2/2 Steel's post-Christmas production recovery is running out of steam. **1977** *Times* 21 Dec. 17/8 The post-Christmas clearance sale. **1897** A. D. L. NAPIER *Menopause* iv. 100 Of 500 *post-climacteric cases, 36·5 per cent. had a return of hæmorrhage after the menopause had been established a year or more. **1973** E. A. MOSCOVIC tr. *J. Botella-Llusiá's Endocrinol. of Woman* xvii. 364/2 The classic concept held that in postmenopausal woman estrogenic activity had been wiped out completely by the time woman entered the postclimacteric phase. **1916** F. E. CLEMENTS *Plant Succession* vi. 110 If a change of climate results in increased water-content.. the sere.. continues the development by replacing the climax and it may be termed the *post-climax. **1928** *Jrnl. Ecol.* XVI. 26 Any well shaded ravine is occupied by *Picea albertiana* Stew. Br. which may be looked upon as a post-climax. **1964** V. J. CHAPMAN *Coastal Vegetation* ix. 215 One must regard the Plantaginatum maritimi as either a post-climax or more properly as a.. deflected climax. **1949** *Mind* LVIII. 220 A tendency to 'spatio-temporal scatter' is characteristic of paranormal cognition, the displacement manifesting itself as '*postcognitive' or 'precognitive' telepathy. **1974** *Listener* 3 Jan. 22/3 If I make a 'correct' guess before the target has appeared.. that's a pre-cognitive hit; if I get it right but several shots in arrears, that's post-cognitive. **1922** C. G. CHILD *Sterility & Conception* viii. 68 (*heading*) *Postcoital tests for sterility. **1947** E. HYAMS *William Medium* 34 Smoking a post-coital cigarette. **1975** B. GARFIELD *Hopscotch* ii. 26 'I'm distressed to see you so lackluster, old friend.' 'It's only post-coital *tristesse*.' **1968** M. R. COHEN in J. J. Gold *Textbk. Gynecol. Endocrinol.* xxv. 546 Ovulation timing.. disclosed good mucorrhea at midcycle with excellent longevity of spermatozoa *postcoitally. **1977** S. SCHOENBAUM *W. Shakespeare* (rev. ed.) vii. 85 A shotgun wedding boomed for the post-coitally chastened Will. **1953** N. TINBERGEN *Herring Gull's World* xiii. 109 There is no *post-coition display. **1893** 'MARK TWAIN' in *Century Mag.* Dec. 235/1 He.. had finished a *post-college course in an Eastern law school. **1973** *Jrnl. Genetic Psychol.* June 183 The relevance of undergraduate courses for meeting the demands of postcollege life. **1960** *Encounter* Nov. 26 A face-to-face group—the *post-collegiate fraternity of the small suburbs. **1934** WEBSTER, *Post-colonial. **1959** *Daily Tel.* 12 Dec. 6/2 It was probably inevitable that India, in the full flush of post-colonial sensitivity, should fear that association with the America of that period might involve her unnecessarily in troubles which were little to do with Asia. **1969** *Times* (Uganda Suppl.) 15 Sept. p. i/5 Behind the imposing physical presence is a mind that has been described as one of the shrewdest in post-colonial Africa. **1974** 'G. BLACK' *Golden Cockatrice* iii. 57 If there's one thing worse than.. rampant colonialism.. it's post-colonial dictatorship. **1833** ALISON *Hist. Europe* (1849) III. xvii. 505 After every session they [the Polish electors] held what were called *post-comitial diets, the object of which was to bring him to account for the vote he had given on every occasion. **1968** *Times* 24 Feb. 9/5 The *post-conciliar attitude seems to draw attention.. to the value of personal and social relationships. **1976** *Times* 9 Aug. 11/1 The post-conciliar church polishes characteristically pre-conciliar weapons. **1939** JOYCE *Finnegans Wake* (1964) II. 270 All them fine clauses in Lindley's and Murrey's never braught the participle of a present to a desponent hortatrixy,.. from her *postconditional future. **1780** BENTHAM *Princ. Legisl.* xviii. §39 *note*, By the terms connubial and *post-connubial all I mean.. is the mere physical union. **1895** in *Syd. Soc. Lex.* **1922** E. EKWALL *Place-Names Lancs.* 1 The county of Lancaster developed out of the *post-Conquest honour of Roger of Poitou. **1940** *Burlington Mag.* Aug. 56 Peruvian post-conquest tapestry work. **1959** E. A. FISHER *Introd. Anglo-Saxon Archit. & Sculpture* 94 Such post-Conquest Anglo-Saxon influence on art is outside the scope of this book. **1976** *Jrnl. Medieval Hist.* II. 1/1 The balance between French and English in post-Conquest England is still being discussed. **1880** *Sat. Rev.* 3 Apr. 439/2 Cities are the seats of *post-conquestal bishoprics. **1920** *Contemp. Rev.* Dec. 898 The manuscript is *post-conquestual. **1924** *Ibid.* Nov. 673 Welsh life in post-Conquestual days. **1934** PRIEBSCH & COLLINSON *German Lang.* II. i. 93 The position in the word (initial, *post-consonantal, inter-vocalic). **1964** Y. MALKIEL in *Archivum Linguisticum* XVI. 27 World-medial, postconsonantal *cl-*. **1953** K. JACKSON *Lang. & Hist. Early Brit.* 470 (*heading*) IE. *gʷ*. This became *b* in CC. initially except before *u*..; intervocally and preconsonantally, *g*; *post-consonantally, *b*. **1969** *Word* XXV. 25 *Tana-dg-usim had-a-n* 'towards the village', *had-a-n* 'towards it or him,' the *-a-* being a *postconsonantic variant of the post-vocalic -·. **1901** LANCIANI tr. *Athenæum* 27 July 132/1 In other baptisteries of the *post-Constantinian age. **1934** WEBSTER, *Post-contact adj. **1946** *Nature* 30 Nov. 769/2 Each article presents chronologically .. the data available from earliest times onwards through four hundred years of contact with White civilization... post-contact change and the absorption of the tribes into European civilization are revealed and traced in as much detail as possible. **1907** W. A. TURNER *Epilepsy* vi. 129 A third epileptic, whose *post-convulsive symptoms were mainly of the nature of cataleptic rigidity and dementia. **1974** E. NIEDERMEYER *Compendium of Epilepsies* xi. 187 A post-convulsive sleep may ensue for a few hours. **1891** *Riddles of Sphinx* 435 The *post-cosmic condition and end of the world-process. **1966** *Economist* 24 Dec. 1329/3 An effort to prevent *post-crash injuries by fire. **1977** *Hongkong Standard* 12 Apr. 9/3 The prevention and control of both in-flight and postcrash fuel system fires and explosions. **1922** JOYCE *Ulysses* 385 In woman's womb word is made flesh but in the spirit of the maker all flesh that passes becomes the word that shall not pass away. This is the *postcreation. **1968** D. DECAMP in *Lat. Amer. Research Rev.* III. 38 If any term is needed to distinguish the situation in Jamaica from that in Surinam and Haiti, then I suggest that we call Jamaica a **post-creole* community. **1977** *Language* LIII. 330 Speakers in a post-creole community are triply pressured: to avoid the basilect, to acquire the acrolect, and to vary the mesolect. **1880** GÜNTHER *Fishes* 21 Living and *post-cretacean forms. **1967** J. ROSS in *To Honor Roman Jakobson* III. 1672 If it cannot apply before the cycle, it must either apply in the cycle or after all cyclic rules have been applied —rules of this last type are called **post-cyclic*. *Ibid.* 1677 It is only if *pronominalization* is formulated as a post-cyclic rule that some constraint on forward pronominalization becomes necessary. **1971** J. W. BRESNAN in *Language* XLVII. 276 One might think of ordering the NSR after the entire transformational cycle but before the postcyclic transformations. **1976** *Archivum Linguisticum* VII. 138 This obviously, would call for.. an explicit formulation of the concept of 'transformation' one uses, that is whether one believes in prelexical, cyclic, precyclic, and postcyclic transformations. **1972** *Language* XLVIII. 310 Primary stress assignment must *precede* *postcyclical transformations. **1972** *Ibid.* 301 It is preferable for a rule to apply postcyclically rather than cyclically. **1899** T. VEBLEN *Theory of Leisure Class* xi. 288 The ostensibly *post-Darwinian concept of a meliorative trend in the process of evolution. **1939** *Mind* XLVIII. 528 In continuity with his previous books, Dewey is anxious to be a post-Darwinian Mill developing 'the science of evidence' in close connection with all the sciences. **1972** S. HYNES *Edwardian Occasions* 7 Much important Edwardian literature implies.. a post-Darwinian, post-Hegelian way of looking at the linear shape of time. **1890** J. MARTINEAU *Seat Authority in Relig.* II. i. 138 The *post-decretal unity seems indisputable. **1943** F. E. TERMAN *Radio Engineers' Handbk.* iv. 342 In the *post-deflection arrangement the beam is deflected at low velocity. **1950** *Electronic Engin.* XXII. 461/1 Two main advantages.. in the use of commercially available post deflexion accelerator (P.D.A.) cathode-ray tubes.. are: (i) The attainment of higher screen brightness.. and (ii) The problem of insulation in the glass pinch and the base are eased. **1959** RIDER & USLAN *Encycl. Cathode-Ray Oscilloscopes* (ed. 2) i. 18/1 These post-deflection accelerating anodes are rings or wide bands of electrically conductive material painted on the inside surface of the envelope. **1971** KLEMPERER & BARNETT *Electron Optics* (ed. 3) x. 398 Post-deflexion acceleration.. appears to offer the means to increase the sensitivity. **1949** F. J. PETTIJOHN *Sedimentary Rocks* i. 7 Diastrophism plays the dominant role in controlling the production and deposition of a sediment—and to some extent its *post-depositional history, also. **1965** G. J. WILLIAMS *Econ. Geol. N.Z.* xiii. 206/2 Post-depositional alteration is indicated by large chlorite plates that are discordant in relation to the foliation in schist pebbles. **1895** *Syd. Soc. Lex.*, **Post-diastolic*. *Ibid.*, **Post-dicrotic wave*, a secondary recoil wave some-times present, following on the Dicrotic wave of the pulse. **1897** *Allbutt's Syst. Med.* IV. 859 *Post-diphtheritic anæsthesia tends to disappear.. in the course of five or six weeks. **1889** N. KERR *Inebriety* viii. (ed. 2) 138 Though the offspring of the paternal pre-disease period showed no tendency of the kind, the paternal *post-disease child or children could only with constant supervision be kept from strong drink as soon as they began to crawl. **1906** *Daily Chron.* 16 Oct. 3/3 The men and women this preacher-poet knew in his pews in the old *post-disruption years. **1864** LUMLEY *Remin. Opera* 35 Less relished than the *post-Easter entertainment. **1962** 'K. ORVIS' *Damned & Destroyed* i. 9 His opinion would be the first *post-election one I would hear. **1976** *New Yorker* 15 Nov. 204/2 Post-election surveys show that almost ninety per cent of the Republicans who voted backed the ticket. **1883** *Harper's Mag.* Jan. 304/2 This most delightful of the *post-Elizabethan poets. **1893** TUCKEY tr. *Hatschek's Amphioxus* 151 The perforation.. falls under the *post-embryonal period of development. **1895** *Cambr. Nat. Hist.* V. 154 *Post-embryonic development, or change of form of this kind, is called metamorphosis. **1940** *Phytopathology* XXX. 334 Experience over a period of years with various chemical methods of damping-off control has emphasized the need for some soil disinfectant that will control both pre- and *post-emergence damping-off. **1955** *Sci. News Let.* 2 July 10/3 There are three prescribed methods for fighting the weed war. They are known as pre-planting, pre-emergence and post-emergence. Pre-planting treatment is made on the soil before any seed is planted in the ground. Pre-emergence control is done after seeds have been sown, but before a desired plant pushes up through the ground. Post-emergence is designed to kill undesirable plants that exist in areas where plants are already growing. **1962** *Times* 12 Nov. 17/4 Another avenue of research which is leading to useful results is that involving pre-emergence spraying of cereal crops instead of the traditional post-emergence method. **1977** *Protecting World's Crops* (Shell Internat. Petroleum Co.) 8 Crop herbicides are often divided into pre-plant, pre-emergence and post-emergence products. **1928** E. F. BUZZARD in H. French *Index Differential Diagnosis Main Symptoms* (ed. 4) 880 The tremor in *post-encephalitic Parkinsonism closely resembles that of paralysis agitans. **1932** W. BOYD *Textbk. Path.* xxx. 812 Other postencephalitic conditions.. are narcolepsy and oculogyric crises. **1961** *Lancet* 23 Sept. 683/2 Since then, she has had postencephalitic epilepsy. **1971** G. W. VOELLER in G. Birdwood et al. *Parkinson's Dis.* iii. 50 Fifteen years ago the post-encephalitic forms [of Parkinsonism] were predominant.., today, the idiopathic or arteriosclerotic forms predominate. **1875** J. H. JACKSON in *W. Riding Lunatic Asylum Med. Rep.* V. 111 The automatism in these cases is not, I think, ever epileptic, but always *post-epileptic. **1903** MYERS *Human Personality* I. 316 As the popular phrase is, the post-epileptic patient 'was not himself'. **1905** *Daily Chron.* 3 June 6/3 In a post-epileptic state, unconscious of her acts—a sleep-walking condition. **1954** L. FAIRFIELD *Epilepsy* i. 13 In some cases the post-epileptic deep sleep or 'coma', lasts an hour or more. **1899** *Allbutt's Syst. Med.* VIII. 333 Observed in *post-epileptiform paralysis. **1894** *Geol. Mag.* Oct. 449 It appears that there has been a *post-erosion subsidence to an amount from 8,000 to 12,000 feet, carrying down the Antillean plains to form the present sea-basins. **1936** *Discovery* May 148 (*heading*) *Post-eruptive movements of the earth's crust. **1946** *Nature* 19 Oct. 560/1 Some powerful beneficial influence had been at work during the post-eruptive as well as the developmental period. **1964** *Economist* 31 Oct. 502/1 The needs of the '*post-experience' students and.. immediate postgraduates. **1977** P. STREVENS *New Orientations Teaching Eng.* viii. 90 In all types of occupational ESP a distinction emerges between *pre-experience* and *post-experience* courses. **1970** *Jrnl. Gen. Psychol.* Apr. 253 All *S*s were asked in a *post-experimental questionnaire to indicate the two words they thought earned them points. **1874** BUCKNILL & TUKE *Psych. Med.* (ed. 3) 376 A prolongation of the delirium when the fever has subsided,.. intended by the term '*Post-Febrile Insanity'. **1897** *Allbutt's Syst. Med.* II. 149 The diagnosis of scarlet fever in the post-febrile stage. **1949** KOESTLER *Promise & Fulfilment* I. iii. 29 We are always apt to forget that nationalism is a product of a relatively recent, *post-feudal European development. **1970** R. STAVENHAGEN in I. L. Horowitz *Masses in Lat. Amer.* vii. 267 The Spanish Conquest was.. part of the political and economic expansion in post-feudal and mercantalistic Europe. **1918** A. HUXLEY *Let.* 25 Nov. (1969) 171 The whiskey bottle seems the only refuge from that *post-flu depression. **1971** P. D. JAMES *Shroud for Nightingale* v. 163 She had post-flu depression and she felt she couldn't cope with the baby. **1966** *Jrnl. Canad. Operational Res. Soc.* 114 *Analysis*, **post game*, use of data generated during a *game* or series of games to derive conclusions about the problems to which play was directed. **1976** *Springfield* (Mass.) *Daily News* 22 Apr. 39/1 When his club gets beaten 7–1 he is a post game press conference no-show. **1962** *Times* 20 Mar. 3/2 The study of *post-harvest physiological changes in pasture plants. **1976** *National Observer* (U.S.) 25 Dec. 1/4 Last week the FAO council called for 'prompt action.. on reducing post-harvest losses'. **1909** W. JAMES *Pluralistic Universe* v. 184 Royce makes by far the manliest of the *post-hegelian attempts to read some empirically apprehensible content into the notion of our relation to the absolute mind. **1964** P. MEADOWS in I. L. Horowitz *New Sociol.* 446 The Hegelians and the post-Hegelians (of either idealistic or materialistic breed). **1972** Post-Hegelian [see *post-Darwinian*]. **1897** *Trans. Amer. Pediatric Soc.* IX. 158 An undoubted example of *post-hemiplegic tremor. **1897** *Allbutt's Syst. Med.* II. 887 Sciatica, *post-herpetic and other neuralgias. **1960** *Farmer & Stockbreeder* 5 Jan. 16/1 A *post-holiday lull prevailed at most markets. **1976** H. FERGUSON *Confessions Long Distance Acid Head* 52 Gordon.. had brought back the usual amount of cigarettes and liquor, and another rare gift—the post-holiday feeling of exuberance. **1810** C. LAMB *Lett.* (1935) II. 97, I should suspect these personifications are the Translator's. They sound **post*-Homeric. **1846** GROTE *Greece* I. xviii. II. 17 The Post-Homeric legends are adapted to a population classified quite differently. **1959** *Encounter* July 46/1 This is the element of allegory or symbolism which so many post-homeric writers have found in the Lotus Eaters. **1909** W. JAMES *Pluralistic Universe* v. 210 This being our *post-humian and post-kantian state of mind, I will ask your permission to leave the soul wholly out of the present discussion. **1961** *Encounter* Jan. 16 The Humian and post-Humian side. **1890** *Q. Rev.* July 255 Even *posthypnotic suggestion.. was known. **1903** MYERS *Human Personality* I. Gloss., *Post-hypnotic*. Used of a suggestion given during the hypnotic trance, but intended to operate after that trance has ceased. **1941** PENFIELD & ERICKSON *Epilepsy & Cerebral Localization* (1942) ii. 19 The state in which an individual is deprived of, or released from conscious control, is called automatism. If it occurs following a seizure it may be called *post-ictal automatism. **1961** *Lancet* 29 July 242/2, 36 hours later.. the E.E.G. showed no seizure activity, but there was general post-ictal disorganisation. **1972** M. CRICHTON *Terminal Man* IV. xi. 186 He's in a post-seizure state—post-ictal, we call it. **1959** *Brain* LXXXII. 152 *Post-ictally the activity of the focus was very much reduced. **1975** *Electroencephalogr. & Clin. Neurophysiol.* XXXVIII. 601/2 Motor activity was observed to increase postictally concomitantly with the increase in EEG frequency and amplitude. **1961** *Middle East Jrnl.* Winter 3 The people were still experiencing *post-independence let-down and suffering the after effects of poor harvests in 1957. **1976** *Times Lit. Suppl.* 13 Feb. 164/2 The post-independence state is even more centralized than the colonial one. **1947** *Partisan Rev.* XIV. 230 Industrial organization and the *postindustrial state are here to stay. **1977** *Times* 21 Feb. 11/4 We are already laying the foundation for the post-industrial future. **1928** *Trans. Chicago Path. Soc.* XIII. 15 (*heading*) The pathology of *post-infectious acute toxic encephalitis in children. **1946** A. B. CHRISTIE *Infectious Dis.* xiii. 108 Encephalitis of the so-called post-infectious type occasionally occurs after chicken-pox. **1974** S. L. ROBBINS *Path. Basis Dis.* xxxii. 1532/1 Injection of brain tissue and adjuvants.. can set up a reaction in the central nervous system of experimental animals, which has a marked resemblance to post-infectious encephalomyelitis. **1898** *Allbutt's Syst. Med.* V. 294 A result of the *post-influenzal exhaustion of the nervous centres. **1951** *Postinjury [see KÜMMELL'S DISEASE]. **1976** *National Observer* (U.S.) 3 July 12/6 Whenever you injure a joint.. there is a possibility of a permanent residual stiffness or postinjury arthritis. 1960 J. BAYLEY Characters of Love iv. 258 Both D. H. Lawrence and E. M. Forster use them [sc. symbolic patterns] in a discernibly *post-Jamesian manner. 1959 E. P. HAMP in Studia Linguistica XIII. 34 Those *post-junctural syllabics which did not themselves bear a primary. 1964 Eng. Stud. XLV. 385 Postjunctural prevocalic /š/ began to be distributionally a spirant. 1843 MILL Logic I. I. iii. 79 His philosophical views are generally those of the *post-Kantian movement, represented by Schelling and Hegel. 1900 Pilot 3 Nov. 549/2 The constructive a priori post-Kantian philosophy of the great German speculative thinkers of eighty years ago. 1946 Nature 7 Sept. 322/2 James Marsh.. did much to acclimatize Kantian and post-Kantian philosophy in the United States. 1977 L. HOULDEN in J. Hick Myth of God Incarnate vi. 128 There is a strong element of post-Kantian consciousness in distinguishing the two approaches at all. 1960 New Left Rev. May—June 5/1 The more sophisticated elaboration of *post-Keynesian evolutionary theory. 1975 Times Lit. Suppl. 18 July 811/3 Post-Keynesians who instinctively treat saving and investment as different activities. 1977 Dædalus Fall 61 Post-Keynesian and econometric studies in economics. 1946 C. MORRIS Signs, Lang. & Behavior ii. 47 The latter [sc. proprioceptive stimuli] are..not themselves language signs; since they are substitute signs synonymous with language signs they are properly called *post-language symbols. 1733 NEAL Hist. Purit. II. 325 The high mysteries of..Ante- and *Post-Lapsarian doctrines. 1950 Eng. Stud. XXXI. 63 What would the corrupt post-lapsarian variety of this attitude be? 1972 Times Lit. Suppl. 29 Dec. 1587/2 A prelude..to the deplorable history of postlapsarian man. 1953 Archivum Linguisticum V. 68 He [sc. Marr] indicates.. labialization with a *postliteral circle. 1958 J. BERRY in J. A. Fishman Readings Sociol. of Lang. (1968) 742 Diacritically modified letters (i.e. 'simple' letters with e.g...postliteral circle or apostrophe). 1974 E. AMBLER Dr. Frigo III. 186 Saw patient while he was taking his *post-lunch bed rest. 1959 N. MARSH False Scent (1960) ii. 59 A long gloomy *post-luncheon talk. 1903 R. WHITEING Let. 9 Feb. in D. L. Moore E. Nesbit (1933) xi. 177 The love scenes, for such they are..though they are *post marital. 1957 V. W. TURNER Schism & Continuity in Afr. Society p. xviii, 'Uxorilocal' refers to the post-marital residence of a man in his wife's village. 1975 R. H. RIMMER Premar Experiments i. 111 They aren't fully aware of the impact that freer and open sexuality, premaritally and *postmaritally, will have on human goals and values. 1949 G. B. SHAW Buoyant Billions I. 17 In your time the young were *post-Marxists and their fathers pre-Marxists. 1963 M. H. ABRAMS in N. Frye Romanticism Reconsidered 29 It may be useful, then, to have a new look at the obvious as it appeared, not to post-Marxist historians, but to intelligent observers at the time. 1978 Bull. Amer. Acad. Arts & Sci. Jan. 35 He considers himself post-Risorgimento, post-Marxist. 1851 G. S. FABER Many Mansions 6 The principle of intellectuality..does not seem to have at all entered into the theory of our mediæval or *postmediæval Sidrophels. 1902 MISS E. SPEAKMAN in Owens Coll. Hist. Ess. 57 A great post-mediæval movement, the active monasticism of the Counter-Reformation. 1905 Q. Jrnl. Microsc. Sci. XLVIII. 490 In animals there are (normally) no *post-maiotic divisions, whereas in plants there may be, and often are, a large number. 1905 [see pre-meiotic s.v. PRE- B. 1]. 1934 L. W. SHARP Introd. Cytol. (ed. 3) xvi. 265 In certain cases evidence has been brought forward to show that the chromonema in each chromatid at the close of the second meiotic mitosis is already split 'in preparation for' the first postmeiotic division. 1973 Genetical Res. XXII. 285 A characteristic feature of recombination in Sordaria brevicollis is the relatively high proportion of recombination events which exhibit post-meiotic segregation. 1968 N. VORYS et al. in J. J. Gold Gynecol. Endocrinol. xi. 253 *Postmenarchal ovarian hypersensitivity may cause short proliferative phases. 1937 *Post-menarcheal [see premenarcheal s.v. PRE- B. 1]. 1977 Yearbk. Obstetr. & Gynecol. 332 Their mean chronological age was 13·02 years and 11 were postmenarcheal. 1928 E. NOVAK in Gynecol. & Obstetr. Monogr.: Cumul. Suppl. & Composite Index 32 (heading) *Postmenopausal bleeding with ovarian cancer. 1949 M. MEAD Male & Female viii. 180 In Bali..the post-menopausal woman and the virgin girl work together at ceremonies from which women of child-bearing age are debarred. 1975 Lancet 5 July 7/2, 11 women were postmenopausal (by at least three years); their ages ranged from forty-eight to sixty-five years of age. 1925 Practitioner July 43 *Post-menopause vulvitis is thus set up. 1975 Acta Endocrinologica LXXX. 262 Levels of plasma PRL rose with puberty and decreased during post-menopause and in elderly men. 1956 Q. Jrnl. Geol. Soc. CXII. 115 The gneiss..is transected by the Boyne Line.., and all the rocks appear to have suffered a certain amount of *post-metamorphic shearing. 1965 G. J. WILLIAMS Econ. Geol. N.Z. vi. 66/1 Grindley (1963) noted that post-metamorphic folding in southern Westland was accompanied by axial-plane cleavage on mesoscopic shear folds. 1943 L. B. LYON Evening in Stepney 18 *Post-midnight hours, be born of costlier reverence. 1970 I. PETITE Meander to Alaska II. xi. 108 A ride..ending with a postmidnight ride back on a bicycle. 1907 Technical Lit. Sept. 189/1 It is important to look for evidence of recent or *post-mineral faulting that may be connected with the secondary enrichment of the deposits. 1965 G. J. WILLIAMS Econ. Geol. N.Z. iii. 26/1 From the descriptions which are available the pattern of pre- and post-mineral faulting cannot be resolved in detail. 1893 Chicago Advance 9 Mar., He had given no one cause for *post mortuary expectations. 1882–3 Schaff's Encycl. Relig. Knowl. III. 1791 *Post-Mosaic events and customs. 1864 Realm 18 May 5 The speculative gentlemen who in mythical times transferred their *post-mundane future to Mephistopheles in exchange for immediate enjoyment. 1958 Jrnl. Amer. Med. Assoc. 21 June 937/2 Infant deaths..may be divided into two groups —deaths of infants in the neonatal period (under 28 days) and those in the *postneonatal period (28 days to one year). 1965 S. PELLER in Glass & Eversley Population in Hist. V. 93 The difference between the rates for the ruling families and for the general population..was larger during the post-neonatal period of infancy than in the neo- or peri-natal period. 1973 PUFFER & SERRANO Patterns of Mortality in Childhood v. 76 The infant period is divided into neonatal (0–27 days of age) and postneonatal (28 days through 11 months). 1899 Allbutt's Syst. Med. VII. 383 Total loss of vision dependent on *post-neuritic atrophy. 1720 WATERLAND Vind. Christ's Div. ii. 26 The *Post-Nicene Fathers Athanasius, Basil, &c. 1928 A. HUXLEY in Vogue 28 Nov. 122/3 A form which the critical intelligence of *post-Nietzschean youth can respect. 1977 N.Y. Rev. Bks. 15 Sept. 41/1 To the post-Nietzschean Bloom, these are the essential qualities of human life under the shadow of belatedness. 1935 H. STRAUMANN Newspaper Headlines ii. 51 As the word preceding it is a nominal, this position may more exactly be called *postnominal position. 1952 R.A.F. Rev. Jan. 9/2 The use of the post-nominal letters 'T.D.' is peculiar to the Territorial Army. 1961 Amer. Speech XXXVI. 159 Finally certain postnominal modifiers, such as relative clauses. 1975 Daily Tel. (Colour Suppl.) 3 Jan. 11/3 In the higher ranks of the Forces and the Civil Service the appropriate title, or post-nominal letters, almost automatically follow appointment to a senior post. 1978 E. ST. JOHNSTON One Policeman's Story xii. 287 The third problem affecting Honours..was the right of any officer holding the Queen's Police Medal to put the initials, QPM, after his name. This is technically known as wearing 'post-nominals'. 1686 GOAD Celest. Bodies I. xv. 96 At other hours of the Ante-Noon, and *Post-Noon more especially. a1866 J. GROTE Exam. Utilit. Philos. xxi. (1870) 346 The *post-observational simplicity of Copernicus and Newton. 1969 E. H. PINTO Treen 17 Operation Pegs... They are still used for plugging *post-operation tubes. 1979 Nature 25 Jan. 327/3 The nodules were found in all rats by 6 months post-operation. 1973 S. FISHER Female Orgasm vii. 190 The judgments typically portrayed the orgasm and *post-orgasm experience as having favorable..connotations. 1953 A. C. KINSEY et al. Sexual Behav. Human Female xv. 638 Sometimes, especially in youth, the *post-orgasmic relaxation is hardly more than momentary. 1973 S. FISHER Female Orgasm ix. 290 How relaxed she feels during the postorgasmic state. 1923 Amer. Jrnl. Physiol. LXVI. 325 When a bird is killed for such *post-ovulation stages care must be taken that a new ovulation stage is not initiated in the meantime. 1951 Jrnl. Clin. Endocrinol. XI. 937 Administration of chorionic gonadotropin was begun early in the postovulation period. 1933 Amer. Jrnl. Anat. LII. 610 The existence of a double uterine cycle explains the occasional appearance of intermenstrual *post-ovulative bleedings. 1968 M. R. COHEN in J. J. Gold Textbk. Gynecol. Endocrinol. xxv. 543 During the postovulative phase. 1922 H. M. EVANS in L. F. Barker et al. Endocrinol. & Metabolism II. vi. 581 In the *postovulatory period it is the corpora lutea which are responsible for further marked changes which now regularly occur in the genitalia of some other mammals. 1975 Biol. Reproduction XII. 573 The cervical epithelium of postovulatory rabbits consists of ciliated cells and nonciliated cells with bulbous apical processes. 1865 M. ARNOLD Ess. Crit. vi. (1875) 252 The new, real, immense, *post-pagan world. 1965 N.Y. Times Mag. 21 Feb. 12/2 *Post-painterly or 'hard-edge' abstraction cleaned up the gooey mess and substituted neatly defined geometrical shapes in chaste combinations. 1969 New Yorker 6 Dec. 184 At the Metropolitan, the largest displays are by so-called object-makers—'post-painterly' canvases; that is to say, smooth-surfaced, cool, and tending to blend with their setting. 1972 E. LUCIE-SMITH in Cox & Dyson 20th-Cent. Mind III. xvi. 473 The man who formed a link between Abstract Expressionism and what came to be called 'post-painterly abstraction' was Morris Louis (1912–62). 1977 P. JOHNSON Enemies of Society xvi. 218 Morris Louis, by his own description a 'post-painterly abstractionist', simply painted streaks on the edge of the canvas, leaving the rest untouched. 1876 J. H. JACKSON in W. Riding Lunatic Asylum Med. Rep. VI. 266 The temporary state of the patient immediately after the paroxysm—which will be called the *post-paroxysmal condition. 1967 Biol. Abstr. XLVIII. 7986/2 (heading) Character of the clinical progress of adolescent rheumatism in post-paroxysmal period. 1879 St. George's Hosp. Rep. IX. 464 Cases of *post-parturient anæmia. 1885 E. HATCH in Encycl. Brit. XVIII. 427/1 In the later and the probably *post-Pauline epistles the apocalyptic elements are rare. 1966 W. S. ALLEN in C. E. Bazell In Memory of J. R. Firth 11 This difficulty could be met only by assuming that, except in *post-pausal position, a high tone required a lower pitch to precede it. 1896 J. MACNEILL Spirit Filled Life xiii, We live in *post-pentecostal days. 1895 A. NUTT Voy. Bran I. 247 The *post-Prophetic phase of Judaism. 1968 A. F. FRASER Reproductive Behaviour in Ungulates v. 75 A group of bulls which were in their first *post-pubertal year. 1886 Buck's Handbk. Med. Sci. III. 396/2 The *post-pubertal falling off in growth is more rapid in girls than in boys. 1955 New Biol. XVIII. 32 It is possible that the post-pubertal mammal behaves like an insect imago.., and that the fundamental change which leads to eventual senescence has already taken place at puberty. 1978 Homes and Gardens Oct. 117/2 There are some effects of the pill which we know... Some girls suffer from post-pubertal amenorrhœa and do not conceive easily afterwards. 1943 KOESTLER in Horizon VII. 230 But that was still in his early period, a hang-over from adolescence, the nihilistic *post-puberty pose. 1964 E. A. NIDA Toward Sci. Transl. xi. 251 Incorporating *postpublication corrections into subsequent printings. 1862 MRS. SPEID Last Years Ind. 192 Among the *post-Puranic religionists of India. 1946 L. BLOOMFIELD in H. Hoijer et al. Ling. Struct. Native Amer. 121 Some roots appear in *postradical extensions... Most postradicals.. have no clear meaning. 1958 Archivum Linguisticum X. 170 In some words Postradical..elements are recognized. 1899 HOBSON Ruskin 27 The great masters of the *post-Raphaelite schools in Italy and in England. 1850 Dublin Rev. Mar. 145 The elucidation of the *post-reformation history of Ireland. 1870 Athenæum 23 Apr. 543/3 In post-Reformation times the 'prophecies'..kept the souls..of men in continual irritation. 1902 B. KIDD West. Civiliz. ix. 315 The various tendencies within the post-Reformation development. 1964 P. F. ANSON Bishops at Large i. 31 The post-Reformation Ecclesia Anglicana. 1978 R. STRONG And when did you last see your Father? 153/2 The rise of the gentry and the establishment of a new post-Reformation aristocracy. 1941 Listener 19 June 882/2 The literature of *post-Renaissance Europe. 1964 R. H. ROBINS Gen. Linguistics viii. 315 The post-Renaissance process of creating learned vocabulary from classical sources. 1978 D. DAICHES Edinburgh ii. 43 The College..was from the beginning a post-Renaissance, post-Reformation university. 1900 Q. Jrnl. Microsc. Sci. XLIV. 3 Reproductive Period.—I have used this expression to denote the whole of that period in the life of a mammal.. during which its generative organs are capable of the reproductive function; and in contrast to the Pre-reproductive and *Post-reproductive periods which severally precede and follow it, during which the generative organs are either not fully developed or are degenerative. 1963 Lancet 5 Jan. 2/1 As we reach the postreproductive years, a man's chance of dying is much greater than a woman's..so that at 60 a man has almost twice the likelihood of dying before 61 than a woman has. 1857–8 SEARS Athan. iv. 27 The *post-resurrection period. 1884 Chr. Commw. 11 Dec. 112/5 The few weeks of our Lord's post-resurrection life. 1928 Manch. Guardian Weekly 7 Sept. 73/4 The Duce's personal implication in numerous ugly stories of the *post-Revolution period. 1957 Times Lit. Suppl. 25 Oct. 685/3 Apart from a single passing reference to Zinoviev and Kamenev, Lenin, Trotsky, Stalin, Beria and Kruschev seem to be the only Bolsheviks named in the post-revolution chapters. 1814 JEFFERSON Writ. (1830) IV. 243 Our *post-revolutionary youth are born under happier stars than you and I were. 1938 Burlington Mag. June 270/1 Ducreux' post-Revolutionary style. 1966 F. SCHURMANN Ideol. & Organization in Communist China p. xxxiii, Political centralization is one of the forms that post-revolutionary organization has taken. 1970 S. L. BARRACLOUGH in I. L. Horowitz Masses in Lat. Amer. iv. 155 Where land reform has been rapid..as was the case in post-revolutionary Mexico and Bolivia—some lines of production temporarily decreased. 1865 LUBBOCK Preh. Times 51 Referring it to *post-Roman times. 1899 R. MUNRO Preh. Scot. ix. 351 Many of them were utilised in post-Roman times. 1943 Y. WINTERS Anatomy of Nonsense 19 The method of the *Post-Romantics, whether French Symbolists or American Experimentalists. 1947 A. EINSTEIN Mus. Romantic Era xvii. 330 The post-Romantic period, when these musicians can be classified roughly according to their training in Germany or in Paris. 1965 Times Lit. Suppl. 25 Nov. 1063/2 Most readers..in this post-romantic age. 1949 *Post-Saussurean [see POST-BLOOMFIELDIAN a. and sb.]. 1977 Language LIII. 394 Each of these topics is divided in turn into three parts..the last one to post-Saussurean developments. 1897 Allbutt's Syst. Med. IV. 735 *Post-scarlatinal diphtheria usually occurs at a late period of convalescence. 1934 WEBSTER, *Postschool. 1939 H. M. MINER St. Denis ix. 193 The young school child wants to have cards, ice skates, and a bicycle, because these amusements are those of postschool children. 1968 Economist 17 Aug. 17/2 The trendy thing for the past ten years has been to work on post-school education. 1975 Language for Life (Dept. Educ. & Sci.) xix. 278 Some schools do successfully guide their pupils to post-school opportunities. 1959 Brain LXXXII. 181 During the stage of *post-seizure cortical hypoxia with flattening of the EEG loud sounds failed to produce spike responses in the strychninized animal. 1882–3 Schaff's Encycl. Relig. Knowl. II. 1160 In the *post-Solomonic time, the city grew in the neighbourhood of the temple. 1957 N.Y. Herald Tribune 25 Nov. 19/1 There is no doubt that *post-Sputnik Washington is a different city and a different atmosphere. Ibid. 3 Dec. 24/1 He [sc. R. M. Nixon] has defeated the pinch-penny economizers, who, even post-Sputnik, are still in the..mood of providing too-little, too-late. 1977 Dædalus Fall 80 Many of the post-Sputnik educational programs were in fact based on this conclusion. 1938 *Post-surrealist [see muck-pot s.v. MUCK sb.[1] 5]. 1951 N. ROREM Paris Diary (1967) i. 7 She encouraged gaudy and exhibitionistic comportment..to give herself an identity with the post-surrealist gang she hung out with. 1952 KOESTLER Arrow in Blue xxiv. 224 But none of the existentialists, post-surrealists..had the guts to speak his opinion. 1953 S. SPENDER Creative Element i. 22 Writers on the Symbolists and *Post-Symbolists..note the tendency of a creative impulse which begins with a religious intensity. 1955 D. DAVIE in C. Tomlinson Necklace 1 Charles Tomlinson has taken note of the experiments and achievements of French symbolism. This does not mean that he belongs to the post-symbolist 'school' or the post-symbolist 'movement', if there are such things. 1958 J. PRESS Chequer'd Shade viii. 183 Whether the systematic employment of post-symbolist technique has weakened or strengthened poetry is likely to remain a matter of dispute. 1977 Radio Times 29 Oct.–4 Nov. 13/4 Nerval's sonnet sequences, Les Chimères..is now recognised as the source of all post-Symbolist and Surrealist poetry. 1899 Allbutt's Syst. Med. VII. 145 Drugs cannot influence a *post-syphilitic cicatrix. 1879 St. George's Hosp. Rep. IX. 159 The first sound forcible, and followed by a loud murmur (*post-systolic), which culminated at the apex. 1659 BP. WALTON Consid. Considered 113 Collected by the *post-talmudical rabbins out of several ancient Copies. 1938 Mem. Geol. Soc. Amer. No. 6. 108 The crystallization in such fabrics can be termed: pretectonic, *posttectonic, or paratectonic with reference to the particular mineral that is under consideration. 1956 Q. Jrnl. Geol. Soc. CXII. 125 The well-known post-tectonic growth of andalusite in the eastern zone may have been accompanied by recrystallization which destroyed any incipient fabric. 1971 I. G. GASS et al. Understanding Earth xx. 296/1 These granites..are both syntectonic and post-tectonic. 1973 M. AMIS Rachel Papers 22 Firstly, I assume I'm right in saying that teenage sex is quite different from *post-teenage sex? 1976 Sounds 11 Dec. 40/2 Personally, I was in the throes of extreme post-teenage depression at the total unadventurousness of yer average British audience. 1905 19th Cent. Jan. 63 That revelation through the fallible media of dead languages and *post-temporary chronicles. 1885 P. MEYER in Encycl. Brit. XIX. 860/1 In French the first of the two *post-tonic vowels of a Lat. proparoxytone always disappears; in Prov. it tends to be preserved. 1953 K. JACKSON Lang. & Hist. Early Brit. II. 268 Syncope of the post-tonic penultimate syllable. 1973 A. H. SOMMERSTEIN Sound Pattern Anc. Greek v. 123 Post-tonic vowels (not just svarita vowels, but all vowels at any distance to the right of the accent in a word). 1904 Brit. Med. Jrnl. 15 Oct. 965 The *post-traumatic disorders of the cerebro spinal system. 1845 J. H. NEWMAN Ess. Developm. 323 Nor am I aware that *Post-tridentine writers deny that the whole Catholic faith may be proved from Scripture. 1896 Allbutt's Syst. Med. I. 206 *Post-tussic suction is another highly significant sign. 1897 Ibid. II. 582 The nature, extent, and variety of *post-vaccinal eruptions. 1879 St. George's Hosp. Rep. IX. 526 An example of *post-varioloid ulceration. 1895 Daily News 10 June 6/2 The *Post-Vedic or Brahmanic period. 1934 WEBSTER, *Post-verbal. 1948 [see COMPLEMENTATION]. 1965 N. CHOMSKY Aspects of Theory of Syntax 228 A somewhat different analysis of post-Verbal Adjectives in English. 1978

Language LIV. 85 The most unmarked order of adverbs in English is generally considered to be manner, place, and time in post-verbal position. **1971** *Ibid.* XLVII. 532 The principle involved is that the experiencer in certain types of sentences cannot be extracted if the complement sentence ends up *postverbally. **1892** J. WRIGHT *Primer Gothic Lang.* i. 10 Final *postvocalic *g* and *g* in the final combination *gs* was probably a voiceless spirant. **1976** *Archivum Linguisticum* VII. 94 Icelandic words of the type *epli* being equivalent to those of the form *lappa* in having the quantitative peak on the post-vocalic consonant. **1964** R. H. ROBINS *Gen. Linguistics* iii. 101 In Scots English, /r/ occurs both prevocalically and *postvocalically (*cart*, standard /kaːt/, Scots /kart/). **1895** G. B. SHAW in *Liberty* (N.Y.) 27 July 3/1 A *post-Wagnerian reaction. **1965** *New Statesman* 7 May 736/1 The technical mêlée of..early Renaissance polyphony and sensuous post-Wagnerian harmony. **1977** *Time* 14 Mar. 26/1 The *post-Watergate Congress is in trouble with its constituents. **1978** *N.Y. Times* 30 Mar. B 5/1 Governor Carey's executive order and the city law were issued at a time of post-Watergate morality. **1957** K. REXROTH in *New World Writing* XI. 32 Many of the *post-World War II abstract expressionists..look alike, and do look like accidents. **1970** I. L. HOROWITZ *Masses in Lat. Amer.* i. 5 This definition..strangely enough became the chief ideological tool of post-World War Two 'neo-Marxism'. **1979** *Dædalus* Winter 119 The successive discard, in the post-World War II world, of the totalitarian scheme.

2. Relating to locality: = Behind, situated at the back of, posterior to. In many adjs. (rarely sbs.), chiefly *Anat.* and *Zool.*, indicating parts or organs situated behind (more rarely, in the hinder part of) other parts or organs: as **postace'tabular**, behind the acetabulum or socket of the hip-bone; **postallan'toic**, behind the allantois; **post-alve'olar**, behind the teeth-ridge; in *Phonetics* applied to a consonant articulated with the tongue against the back part of the alveolar ridge; **post'anal**, behind the anus; **postan'tennal**, behind the antennæ; **postary'tenoid**, 'behind the arytenoid cartilage or cartilages' (*Syd. Soc. Lex.*); **post'auditory**, behind the auditory nerve or chamber; **post-au'ricular**, behind the ear; **postbrachial** (-'breɪkɪəl), situated on the back of the *brachium* or upper arm: applied to a set of muscles; **postbranchial** (-'bræŋkɪəl) [see BRANCHIA], behind the gills, or a gill; **postcæcal** (-'siːkəl), behind or beyond the cæcum; **postcal'caneal**, behind the calcaneum: applied to a lobe of the interfemoral membrane in bats; **post'central**, behind the centre: applied to a convolution of the brain, also called the *posterior central convolution*; hence **post-'centrally** *adv.*; **postce'phalic**, behind or posterior to the head: applied to segments of arthropods; **postcere'bellar**, in the hinder part of the cerebellum; **post'cerebral**, (*a*) behind the cerebrum or brain; (*b*) in the hinder part of the cerebrum; **postcolu'mellar**, behind the columella (COLUMELLA 4); **post'coxal**, behind the coxa or coxæ; **post'cranial**, situated posterior to the cranium; also as *sb. pl.*, the postcranial remains of an animal; hence **post'cranially** *adv.*; **post-'cricoid**, posterior to the cricoid cartilage; **post'cruciate**, behind the cruciate fissure of the cerebrum; **post'cubital** [see CUBIT], behind, or on the back of, the fore-arm; **post'dental** [see DENTAL], behind the teeth; in *Phonetics* applied to a consonant pronounced by placing the tongue against the gum or palate just behind the teeth also as *sb.*; **post'digital**, behind the digits or toes; **post'ethmoid**, behind the ethmoid bone; **post'femoral**, situated behind the femur or thigh; **post'genital**, behind the genital pores; **post'glenoid**, behind the glenoid cavity: applied to a process of the temporal bone (*ellipt.* as *sb.*): also **postgle'noidal**; **posthumeral** (-'hjuːmərəl), behind the humerus or upper arm, or the humeri in insects (cf. HUMERAL A. 1, 3); **postischial** (-'ɪskɪəl), behind the ischium; **postmeatal** (-miː'eɪtəl) [irreg. for *postmeatual*: cf. MEATAL, and see MEATUS], behind a meatus or opening of the body; **post'median**, behind the median line or plane of the body; **post-'nasal**, behind the nose or nasal cavity; **postœso'phageal**, behind the œsophagus; **post'olivary**, behind the olivary body; **post'palatal**, (*a*) also **post'palatine**, behind the palate or palatal bones; applied to one of the pterygoid bones in certain reptiles (also *ellipt.* as *sb.*); (*b*) *Phonetics*, applied to a consonant articulated with the tip or middle of the tongue against the hard palate; also *ellipt.* as *sb.*; **postpa'rietal**, applied to certain plates behind the parietal plates in the head of a serpent (also *ellipt.* as *sb.*); **post'petiole** *sb.*, an abdominal segment in an insect immediately behind the petiole (PETIOLE 2); **postpha'ryngeal**, behind the pharynx; **postpi'tuitary**, 'situated posterior to the pituitary body' (*Syd. Soc. Lex.*); **post'pontile**, behind the pons Varolii (PONS 2); **post'rhinal** [Gr. ῥιν- nose], behind the nose (= *postnasal*), or behind the olfactory lobe of the brain; **postro'landic**, behind the Rolandic fissure of the cerebrum; **post'rostral**, behind the rostrum of a crustacean; **post'sacral**, behind the sacrum or sacral vertebræ; **post'scapular**, situated behind or below the spine of the scapula or shoulder-blade, as in *postscapular fossa*; **post'sternal**, behind the sternum or breast-bone; **post'stigmatal**, in an insect, behind the stigmata or breathing pores; **post'sylvian**, behind the Sylvian fissure of the cerebrum; **post-'tibial**, behind, or on the hinder part of, the tibia; **post-tym'panic**, behind the tympanic bone: applied to a bone, and a process of bone, in some Carnivora; also as *sb.* = *post-tympanic bone* or *process*; **post'umbonal**, behind the umbo of a molluscan shell; **post'uterine**, situated behind the uterus; **post-'velar**, behind or at the back of the velum; in *Phonetics*, applied to a consonant articulated with the tongue against the rear half of the velum or soft palate; also *ellipt.* as *sb.* Also POSTLIMINARY, -OCULAR, -ORBITAL, etc.

1866 OWEN *Anat. Vert.* II. 34 [The ilium in birds] differs in the proportions of the pre-acetabular and *post-acetabular extensions, and in the degree of divergence of the latter from the sacrum. **1904** *Brit. Med. Jrnl.* 17 Dec. 1632 The hind gut and its continuation—the *post-allantoic gut—are now without any communication with the exterior. **1932** D. JONES *Outl. Eng. Phonetics* (ed. 3) ix. 44 *Post-alveolar: articulated by the tip of the tongue against the back part of the teeth-ridge. **1964** I. DAHL in D. Abercrombie et al. *Daniel Jones* 314 [c, ɟ] are post-alveolar. **1973** *Amer. Speech 1969* XLIV. 265 Heavy retroflexion is understood to be an *r* produced by passing the breath between the underside of the apex of the tongue and the postalveolar or prepalatal region. **1888** ROLLESTON & JACKSON *Anim. Life* 335 There is generally said to be a *post-anal section of the archenteron in Vertebrata which communicates by a neurenteric canal with the neural tube. **1897** *Allbutt's Syst. Med.* II. 1034 The number and arrangement of the four pairs of pre-anal and three pairs of post-anal papillæ on the tail of the male. **1895** *Cambr. Nat. Hist.* V. 193 This structure [the pro-stemmate]..is said by Sir John Lubbock to be present in some of the Lipuridæ that have no ocelli, and he therefore prefers to speak of it as the '*post-antennal' organ. **1870** ROLLESTON *Anim. Life* 8 The *post-auditory process of the squamosal. **1875** HUXLEY & MARTIN *Elem. Biol.* (1877) 190 The Post-auditory nerves. **1903** *Ann. & Mag. Nat. Hist.* XII. 342 *Mus hypoxanthus bacchante*... Fine hairs of ears rufous; no *postauricular patch. **1934** F. STARK *Valleys of Assassins* ii. 193 The post-auricular length..is about one-third of the total length. **1977** *Proc. R. Soc. Med.* LXX. 399/1 Smaller defects in the centre of the face are therefore sometimes repaired with free grafts of full-thickness postauricular skin. **1888** J. BEARD in *Q. Jrnl. Microsc. Sc.* 179 This view..I must now also extend to the præbranchial and the sensory part of each *postbranchial nerve. **1861** HULME tr. *Moquin-Tandon* II. I. 44 The intestine is divided into the small intestine or antecæcal, and into the large intestine or *postcæcal. **1890** BILLINGS *Med. Dict.*, **Post-central convolution.* **1899** *Allbutt's Syst. Med.* VII. 310 The ascending parietal or post-central convolution. **1959** SCHVELL & JENKINS in Saporta & Bastian *Psycholinguistics* (1961) 428/2 *Verbal aphasia*, resulting from lesions of the pre- and post-central convolutions. **1967** G. M. WYBURN et al. *Conc. Anat.* vii. 193 It..separates the precentral gyrus from the postcentral gyrus. **1968** *Brit. Med. Bull.* XXIV. 202/1 A normally responsive alpha rhythm at 7-8 cyc./sec. is present *postcentrally, with slightly higher voltage on the right side. **1895** *Syd. Soc. Lex.*, **Post-cephalic*, posterior to the head or cephalic segment. **1900** MIALL & HAMMOND *Harlequin Fly* ii. 72 In a larva of one of the larger species of Chironomus the heart lies in the eleventh post-cephalic segment. **1885** WILDER in *Jrnl. Nervous Dis.* XII. 349 Cerebellaris posterior..English paronym. *Postcerebellar. **1882** *Athenæum* 14 Jan. 60/2 Not..from the archicerebrum, but from the cords connecting this with the first *postcerebral ganglion. **1885** WILDER (as above) XII. 349 Cerebralis posterior... English paronym. Postcerebral. **1880** WATSON in *Jrnl. Linn. Soc., Zool.* XV. No. 82. 91 Leaving only a central depression and a *post-columellar furrow. **1913** *Bull. Amer. Museum Nat. Hist.* XXXII. 563 The *post-cranial skeleton. **1956** *Biologia* II. 231 The skull of the common lizard..has been described in detail previously... The present paper deals with its postcranial skeleton, i.e., the vertebral column, ribs, sternum, girdles and limbs. **1971** *Nature* 5 Feb. 407/2 It has been thought for some time that Miocene hominoids differed post-cranially from living hominoids, resembling instead the cercopithecoid monkeys. But careful examination of the post-cranials of *Limnopithecus*..and the European fossil *Pliopithecus* indicates that such non-hominoid structural features as they have are ceboid-like rather than specifically cercopithecoid-like. **1978** *Sci. Amer.* July 105/1 Anatomical studies..relating respectively to the birds' postcranial skeleton and their skull. **1971** CAPPELL & ANDERSON *Muir's Textbk. Path.* (ed. 9) xviii. 485/1 There is also the relationship between the iron-deficiency anaemia..and *post-cricoid carcinoma in women. **1971** *Brit. Med. Bull.* XXVII. 34/1 Difficulty in swallowing is associated with a post-cricoid web of mucous membrane. **1885** *Alienist & Neurol.* VI. 9 That part of the cerebral cortex which corresponds to the *post-cruciate convolution. **1899** W. RIPPMANN tr. *Vietor's Elements of Phonetics* 77 As a rule the English sounds [in *thou, thin* etc.] are **postdental*, the narrowing being between the tongue point (with apical articulation) and the back of the front upper teeth. **1903** KJEDERQVIST in *Phil. Soc. Trans.* 107 The Pewsey *l* is also of two kinds; one is divided and post-dental, the other has become *o*. **1933** [see DOMAL *a.* 3]. **1933** BLOOMFIELD *Language* vi. 102 French speaks its [n] in postdental position. **1961** L. F. BROSNAHAN *Sounds of Language* vi. 138 The order of appearance of consonants is generally from back to front, in the order: glottal, velar, post-dental, palatal, labial, and labio-dental. **1891** FLOWER & LYDEKKER *Mammalia* ii. 12 The *post-digital gland of the Rhinoceros. **1870** FLOWER *Osteol. Mammalia* x. 136 The Orang agrees with Man in wanting this *postethmoid union of the frontals. **1854** OWEN *Skel. & Teeth* in *Orr's Circ. Sc.* I. *Org. Nat.* 235 The *postglenoid process in the horse is less developed than in the tapir. **1871** HUXLEY *Anat. Vertebr. Anim.* viii. 361 The squamosal [of the rhinoceros] sends down an immense *post-glenoidal process. **1906** J. B. SMITH *Explanation Terms Entomol.* 106 *Post-humeral bristles: in *Diptera*, are usually two. **1961** Post-humeral [see ACROSTICHAL *a.* 2]. **1895** MIVART in *Proc. Zool. Soc.* 373 The postaxial margin of the *postmeatal lamella. **1897** *Allbutt's Syst. Med.* IV. 714 *Post-nasal adenoid hypertrophy is a disease of early childhood. **1899** W. RIPPMANN tr. *Vietor's Elements of Phonetics* 142/1 *Postpalatal stops, etc. = back stops, etc. *Ibid.* 67 The *gutturals* (more strictly: postpalatals or velars). **1902** [see *medio-palatal* adj. s.v. MEDIO- 2]. **1925** [see *pre-palatal* s.v. PRE- B. 3]. **1942** Post-palatal [see *medio-palatal* adj. s.v. MEDIO- 2]. **1896** *Nomencl. Dis.* 133 *Post-pharyngeal abscess. **1897** *Trans. Amer. Pediatric Soc.* IX. 175 Extending from high up in the post-pharyngeal wall downwards four and a half inches as far as the fourth rib. **1885** WILDER (as above) XII. 351 Owen's prior name is *basirhinal*; the name employed by me..is **postrhinal*. **1901** *Munsey's Mag.* XXIV. 803/2 She had a spell of sneezing, and the bullet dropped out into the postrhinal cavity. **1852** DANA *Crust.* I. 114 *Post-rostral length about equal to greatest breadth. **1899** *Allbutt's Syst. Med.* VI. 72 It might be suspected from the intensity and superficialness of *post-sternal pain with tenderness. **1896** COCKERELL in *Proc. Acad. Nat. Sci. Philad.* 30 It may have the portion below the stigma (substigmatal) longer than that beyond (*poststigmatal), but usually they are about equal or the latter is longer. **1868** OWEN *Anat. Vertebr.* III. 125 A '*postsylvian fissure'..is added. **1854** —— *Skel. & Teeth* in *Orr's Circ. Sc.* I. *Org. Nat.* 236 A well-developed *post-tympanic process. **1871** HUXLEY *Anat. Vertebr. Anim.* viii. 368 [In the pig] the post-tympanic is closely appressed to the post-glenoidal process. **1934** WEBSTER, *Post-velar *a.* **1934** J. J. HOGAN *Outl. Eng. Philol.* i. 7 If the back-stops are made farther back than the normal series, they are called Post-Velars. **1942** BLOCH & TRAGER *Outl. Linguistic Analysis* ii. 16 Different points of articulation are designated by the terms *pre-velar*, *mediovelar*, and *postvelar* (or *uvular*). **1964** E. PALMER tr. *Martinet's Elem. Gen. Linguistics* ii. 50 A dorsal may also be..post-velar or uvular as in the initial sound of *rouge* in the Parisian pronunciation. **1966** M. PEI *Gloss. Linguistic Terminol.* 215 *Post-velar*, a consonant produced with the tongue farther back than the velar position, and the articulation against the rear half of the velum, or soft palate (Arabic *q*).

b. Rarely in *quasi*-adjectival relation to a sb. forming the second element: = occurring behind or posteriorly, as POSTFIXATION *sb.* 1.

postabdomen (pəʊstæb'dəʊmən). [POST- A. 2.] The posterior part of the abdomen; *esp.* in insects, crustacea, or other invertebrates, the portion posterior to the abdominal cavity. Hence **postab'dominal** *a.*, of or pertaining to the postabdomen.

1842 BRANDE *Dict. Sci.*, etc., *Post-abdomen*, the name applied by Latreille to the five posterior segments of the abdomen of Hexapod insects; and to the tail of Crustaceans, which consists of analogous but more numerous segments. **1870** ROLLESTON *Anim. Life* 108 The post-abdominal region. **1871** T. R. JONES *Anim. Kingd.* (ed. 4) 526 In all the Polyclinian group it [the ovarium] is lodged in the post-abdomen.

'postable, *a.* [f. POST *v.*[1] + -ABLE.] Capable of being posted.

[In the quotation from Mountague cited in Todd and later Dicts. 'postable' is corrected in the Errata to 'portable'.]

a **1908** in *N.E.D.* **1926** *Glasgow Herald* 23 Mar. 9/1 The £40 limitation is wholly inadequate for jewellers and others, whose goods, though of 'postable' dimensions, are of considerable value.

postabortal, -abortion, -abortum, -absorptive: see POST- B. 1 b.

post-accelerate: see POST- A. 1 a.

post-acceleration, -accelerator: see POST- A. 1 b.

postacetabular: see POST- B. 2.

post-act: see POST- A. 1 b.

post-Adamic: see POST- B. 1 b.

postage[1] ('pəʊstɪdʒ). [f. POST *sb.*[2] + -AGE.]

I. Of letters, etc.

1. The carriage or conveyance of letters, etc., by post. Now *rare*.

1590 *Acts Privy Council* XIX. 164 Sir John Norreis, knight,..hath made suit unto us to have certein allowaunces for howsrent, howshold stuff, postage and for transportacion booth in his going and coming [to Ireland]. **1609** BP. W. BARLOW *Answ. Nameless Cath.* 5 Who weekely spends fiue or six Crownes for postage of letters onely. **1617** in *Crt. & Times Jas. I* (1849) I. 465 These little pamphlets I send you for that they be of so easy postage. **1653** *Reg. Council State* XVI. 458 In the mannageing of the business of the postage of Letters. **1693** *New Hampsh. Prov. Papers* (1868) II. 100 How much a Letter [you will be pleased to allow] for postage of a single Letter from Piscataqua to Boston.

†**2.** The postal service generally; a postal service between particular points. *Obs.*

1650 *Jrnls. Ho. Comm.* 21 Mar. 385 By direction and authority of the Parliament, I erected postages for the service of the State. **1657** *Ibid.* 28 May 553/1 An Act for the Settling the Postage of England, Scotland, and Ireland. **1707** CHAMBERLAYNE *Pres. St. Eng.* III. (ed. 22) 442 The Post-Master-General.. hath annex'd, and appropriated the Market-Towns of England so well to the respective Postages, that there is no considerable Market-Town, but hath an easie and certain Conveyance for the Letters thereof, to and from the said grand Office [in London]. **1749** W. DOUGLAS *Summary* I. 466 From Piscataqua or Portsmouth, to Philadelphia, is a regular postage. **1779** HERVEY *Naval Hist.* II. 201 In the year 1653 the postage in England, Scotland, and Ireland, was farmed for ten thousand pounds yearly.

3. The amount charged for carrying a letter or postal packet; originally, that paid to a post messenger; hence, the charge made by the post-office department for the conveyance of a letter or packet, now usually prepaid by means of a POSTAGE STAMP or stamps.

1654 GAYTON *Pleas. Notes* III. viii. 119 For want of ready money, they scor'd upon his back, the postage. **1656** *Jrnls. Ho. Comm.* 429/2 That the Post Letters, directed to the several Members of this House,.. be free from Postage, as formerly. That the Letters of the several Members of this House that go to the several Parts of England, Scotland, and Ireland, be also free from Postage. **1692** T. NEALE *Patent* in *Hist. Suffolk, Mass.* (1894) II. 504 State letters, which are usually carried postage free here in England. **1787** M. CUTLER in *Life*, etc. (1888) I. 374 To forward the packets to Colonel Platt, as early as may be, free of postage. **1849** MACAULAY *Hist. Eng.* iii. I. 388 The postage increased in proportion to the weight of the packet. **1891** PHIL *Penny Post. Jubilee* 31 The postage to Aberdeen from Edinburgh was in 1777 3*d*... to Linlithgow 1*d*.

II. Of passengers.

†4. a. Travelling by means of post-horses; posting; also *transf.* a rapid journey or passage. *Obs.*

1603 in *13th Rep. Hist. MSS. Comm.* App. IV. 127 The continuance thereof hath drawn with it from this poore town the postage and recourse of merchants.. travelling to the sea coast... We pray that it would please you to erect a postage here and recommend unto you.. James Apleton, to be the postmaster. **1627–77** FELTHAM *Resolves* II. lvii. 277 All the transient.. pleasures that we fondly smack after in this postage of life in this world. **1808** *Cobbett's Wkly. Pol. Reg.* XIII. No. 25. 968 The refusal of a licence [by] the magistrates, to any innkeeper raising the price of postage.

†b. The charge for hire of a post-horse. *Obs.*

1660 *Act 12 Chas. II*, c. 35 §5 Three pence.. for each Horses hire or postage for every English mile.

†5. A station at which horses are changed; a posting house. *Obs.*

1603 [see sense 4].

III. 6. *attrib.* and *Comb.*: **postage-book**: see quot.; **postage currency**, a paper currency of denominations less than a dollar, bearing a design composed of one or more postage stamps, issued in the U.S. in 1862, to take the place of actual postage stamps, which had for some time been used instead of silver coins, when these became scarce during the Civil War: also called POSTAL *currency*; **postage envelope**: see quot.; **postage label**, early official name for a POSTAGE STAMP; so ***postage label stamp***; **postage meter** *N. Amer.* = FRANKING MACHINE; hence ***postage-metered*** adj.

1858 SIMMONDS *Dict. Trade*, *Postage-book, a memorandum-book in an office of postal expenditure. **1862** *Inscription on U.S. 5 cents bill*, *Postage Currency, Furnished only by the Assistant Treasurers and designated Depositaries of the U.S. U.S. Postage, Five Cents. *Back.* Act approved July 17, 1862. **1863** *U.S. Stat.* c. 73 §4 Be it further enacted, That in lieu of postage stamps for fractional currency, and of fractional notes, commonly called postage currency,.. the Secretary of the Treasury may issue fractional notes of like amounts. **1889** *Century Dict.* s.v. *Currency*, [On July 17, 1862], Congress authorized an issue of circulating notes called postage currency, imitating in style the stamps that had previously been used at great inconvenience, in denominations of 5, 10, 25, and 50 cents. These were superseded by the fractional currency authorized March 3d, 1863, in denominations of 3, 5, 15, 25, and 50 cents. **1860** *Murray's London* 57 (Hoppe) Others [presses] are employed in stamping the embossed medallion of the Queen on *postage envelopes. **1852** (*title*) Report from the Select Committee on *Postage Label Stamps;.. Minutes of Evidence. *Ibid.* 1 Are you [H. Archer] the Inventor and Patentee of a plan for perforating the sheets of Postage Labels, so as to effect their instant separation without the aid of any cutting instrument? *Ibid.* 20 To engrave, print, gum, and perforate the postage label stamps. *Ibid.*, For engraving, printing, and gumming the postage label sheets. **1927**, **1961** *Postage meter [see FRANKING MACHINE]. **1972** *Times* 18 May 27/1 Pitney Bowes.. claims to be the world's largest producer and marketer of postage meters and mailing machines. *Ibid.*, It was 50 years ago that Walter H. Wheeler sold the British Post Office on the idea of postage metered mail. **1974** P. GZOWSKI *Bk. about This Country* 212 I'm sort of in the same position as the stamp-licker watching a postage meter being brought in the door.

postage[2] ('pəʊstɪdʒ). *rare.* [f. POST *sb.*[1] + -AGE.] The mooring of ships to posts in a harbour; the dues charged for this.

1868 *Rep. Trial* in *Exeter & Plymouth Gaz.* 13 Mar., Nothing more than postage was paid. There were three posts as shown in the map of 1738, and three or more posts along the Parlor, which had now been removed, but to which ships were moored.

'postage 'stamp. [f. POSTAGE[1] + STAMP *sb.*] **A.** *sb.* **a.** An official stamp, either a stamp embossed on an envelope or impressed on a card or wrapper, or else (now usually) a small adhesive label having a specified face-value (in Great Britain from 1p upward), and bearing a design of a certain pattern and colour appropriated to its value, sold by or on behalf of the Post Office, to be affixed to any letter or packet sent by post, as a means of prepayment of postage, and as evidence of such payment.

The design is generally the head of the Sovereign or Ruler (whence in Great Britain the early popular appellation 'Queen's head'), or the national arms or emblems, but many countries use various symbolic or fanciful pictorial devices, historical portraits, etc.

The name *stamp* was originally applied to the marks stamped or impressed by the Post Office on letters for various purposes, among others that of stating whether they were 'prepaid', 'unpaid', 'free', partly paid, or paid by the twopenny or other post. When adhesive labels and impressed envelopes were introduced in 1840, these took the place of the 'paid' or 'prepaid' stamp, and appear to have been popularly called 'postage stamps' from the first. The official and more accurate name was *postage label*; but the popular usage prevailed; by 1850 *postage label stamp* was in official use, and finally *postage stamp* was accepted. The actual *stamps* (Ger. *briefstempel*) which continued to be impressed by the Post Office after 1840, to show the place and date of postage and arrival, and to obliterate or deface the postage-label, are now usually distinguished as *post-marks* and *obliteration-stamps* or *-marks*.

1840 *Times* 5 May 6/4 The Penny Postage Stamps... The Lords of the Treasury having fixed the 6th of May next for the issue of postage stamps. **1847** in *Rep. Sel. Comm. Postage Label Stamps* (1852) 1 The machine [Archer's] appears to be a very clever and useful invention; we are thoroughly convinced that postage stamps separated by it, having jagged edges, will adhere to letters far better than those cut from the sheets by knives or scissors. **1852** *Ibid.* 2 Mr. Bokenham told me.. he was very desirous about the sticking of the postage stamps to the letters, as there were upwards of 400 found daily loose in the bags. *a* **1862** G. H. LEWES *Let. to Parker* (in *Pearson's 76th Catal.* (1894) 39), I have read Fraser, and having read it must keep it and enclose postage stamps. **1862** *Boston Even. Transcr.* 20 July 2/1 Postage stamps have come extensively into public use during the present scarcity of silver coin. They are issued by the Post Office Departments of eight values. [**1862** S. P. CHASE *Rep. Sec. U.S. Treas.* 4 Dec. 28 It was soon discovered that stamps prepared for postage uses were not adapted to the purposes of currency.] **1862** M. BLAIR *Rep. Postmaster Gen. U.S.* 1 Dec. 133 The issue of 'postage currency' by the Treasury Department will doubtless soon displace postage stamps from circulation. **1897** O. FIRTH *Postage Stamps* 3 Every-one is.. aware of the purpose of a postage stamp, viz. to prepay postage, and to serve as an indication that the proper amount has been paid. **1907** *Post Office Guide* Jan. 139 Embossed or impressed postage stamps cut out of envelopes, post-cards, letter-cards, newspaper wrappers, or telegram forms may be used as adhesive stamps in payment of postage.

b. *transf.* and *fig.*

1908 [see DOD-]. **1930** R. GRAVES *Ten Poems More* 4 It is a large patch,.. The postage-stamp of its departure,.. closing in now To a plain countryside of less and less. **1971** M. TAK *Truck Talk* 121 *Postage stamp*, state permits in the form of a small decals that must be placed on a tractor. **1978** J. GORES *Gone, no Forwarding* vii. 42 Kearny began pacing the postage stamp of space behind his desk.

c. *attrib.* and *Comb.*, as ***postage-stamp damper***, ***size***, ***statistics***, ***system***; ***postage-stamp-sized*** adj.; *esp.* connected with the collecting of postage stamps as the objects of philatelic interest, as ***postage-stamp collecting***, ***collection***, ***collector***, ***dealer***, etc.; ***postage-stamp album***, ***catalogue***; **postage-stamp currency** (U.S.) = postage currency: see POSTAGE[1] 6.

1852 *Rep. Sel. Comm. Postage Label Stamps* 2 The efficient working of the postage-stamp system. **1862** *Boston Even. Transcr.* 1 Aug. 2/3 The Postmaster-General and the Commissioner of Internal Revenue have approved of the specimens of the postage stamp currency, which will be for five, ten, twenty-five and fifty cents. **1862** (*title*) Postage-stamp Collector's Album. **1889** *Anthony's Photogr. Bull.* II. 361 Postage-stamp damper. **1968** A. DIMENT *Gt. Spy Race* vi. 78 She wore nothing but the white, postage stamp-sized panties. **1968** 'R. RAINE' *Night of Hawk* viii. 38 A postage-stamp-sized moustache.

B. as *adj.*, used to denote something very small.

1962 *Housewife* (Ceylon) Feb. 33, I am certainly a veteran at providing the family with reasonably good food on a postage stamp budget. **1965** *New Society* 14 Oct. 5/3 Postage-stamp photos of smiling typists. **1968** J. WAINWRIGHT *Web of Silence* 137 A postage-stamp dance floor. **1971** R. BUSBY *Deadlock* iii. 32 Chrysanthemums were blooming in the postage stamp garden. **1973** 'R. MACLEOD' *Nest of Vultures* ii. 40 Spotlights were trained on a postage-stamp stage.

Hence **postage-stamped** *ppl. a.*, supplied with a postage stamp.

1942 PARTRIDGE *Usage & Abusage* 241/2 In the British Empire, a postcard may be already postage-stamped or it may require a postage stamp, in the U.S.A., it requires one, an already postage-stamped card being in the States a *postal card*.

postal ('pəʊstəl), *a.* (*sb.*) [a. F. *postal*, *-ale* (1836, 'la convention postale conclue et signée le 30 mars entre la France et la Grande Bretagne'), f. *poste* POST *sb.*[2]: see -AL[1].] **A.** *adj.* **a.** Of or pertaining to the post; relating to the carriage of mails.

1843 *Rep. Sel. Comm. on Postage* 70 Postal treaties with all the countries in the world. **1844** PRES. TYLER *to Senate U.S.* in *Messages of Presid.* (1897) IV. 315, I transmit to the Senate.. a postal convention between the United States and the Republic of New Granada, signed in the city of Bogota on the 6th of March last. **1848** CLOUGH *Bothie* IV. 235 Not for the will of the wisp.. Have even latest extensions adjusted a postal arrangement. **1885** *Act 48 & 49 Vict.* c. 58 §2 (2) Within the limit of the town postal delivery of that office. **1903** *Times* 4 May 11 Great bodies of men, such as postal servants or dockyard servants.

b. in spec. applications: **postal ballot**, a method of voting by post; also *attrib.*; **postal car**, a railway car for the carriage of mails (*U.S.*); **postal card** [cf. F. *carte postale*] = POSTCARD *sb.*; **postal clerk**, a clerk in a travelling railway post office (*U.S.*); **postal code** = POSTCODE; hence as *v. trans.*, to write a postcode on (a letter, etc.); **postal currency** = POSTAGE *currency* (*U.S.*); **postal draft**, †(*a*) in 1914 the form used at Post Offices for the payment of Navy and Army Separation Allowances, later called 'allowance form'; (*b*) a draft or cheque drawn on the Postmaster General, introduced in Jan. 1925 for the payment of National Health Insurance benefits, and later extended to certain Government Departments; **postal guide**, a handbook of information about the postal service; a post-office guide; **postal note**, (*a*) in *U.S.*, an order issued by a post office for any required sum of less than five dollars payable at any other post office; (*b*) *Austral.* and *N.Z.*, an order issued by a post office for any required sum and payable at any other post office; **postal order**, a form of money order issued by a post office of the United Kingdom: it differs from the *post-office order*, or original postal money order, in being for one of a number of fixed sums, and in being payable at any post office; **postal trade**, trade in which orders are received and goods dispatched by post; **postal tube**, trade name for a cardboard tube designed to protect documents, plans, etc., during transmission by post; **postal union**, a union of the governments of various countries for the regulation of international postage, entered into at Berne on 9 October, 1874; on 1 Feb. 1894, all countries of the world, excepting parts of Asia and Africa and certain islands, were included; **postal vote**, a vote in an election, on a resolution, etc., submitted on a special form by post; so ***postal voting*** vbl. sb.

1945 *Times* 25 May 4/1 An elaborate procedure has been devised for checking all service votes so as to eliminate any proxy vote cast on behalf of a service voter from whom a *postal ballot paper is received. **1973** A. BROINOWSKI *Take One Ambassador* i. 15 [The] returning officer for the elections.. may be able to put his hand on a postal ballot paper for you. **1974** *Times* 12 Feb. 4/8 Union members should have the opportunity of electing their leaders by postal ballot. **1873** *New York Her.* 24 Apr. 10/4 The *Postal Car Problem... Postal Car and Mail Service on Railroads. **1872** *Act of Congress U.S.* 8 *June* Stat. XVII. 304 The Postmaster-General is authorized and directed to furnish and issue to the public, with postage-stamps impressed upon them, '*postal cards', manufactured of good stiff paper. **1873** *Chicago Tribune* 17 Apr. 4/1 Postal cards, which have been used with great favor in England and Canada for a long time, will be introduced in this country on the first of next month. **1876** C. M. YONGE *Womankind* xix. 151 Do not come down to slap-dash notes and postal-cards. **1872** *Act of Congress* Stat. XVII. 310 Every route-agent, *postal clerk, or other carrier of the mail shall receive any mail-matter presented to him, if properly pre-paid by stamps. **1968** *Internat. List P.O.* (Universal Postal Union) (Eng. ed.) ii. 7 In recent years several countries have worked out *postal codes designed to facilitate the sorting, routeing and delivery of mail. **1978** S. NAIPAUL *North of South* I. ii. 63 West 11.. If we use only the postal code.. they mightn't make the connection. **1969** P. WEST *Words for Deaf Daughter* v. 139 A two-page spread.. sent postage-due, incorrectly *postal-coded from some college. **1973** *Times* 17 July 11/5 The Post Office has published a booklet with the postal codes in it. **1862** *Washington Republican* 23 Aug. 2/1 Specimens of the new *Postal Currency were received in this city this morning.., they are now for sale in exchange for specie. **1868** S. M. CLARK in *U.S. Documts.* No. 1341 The postal currency was the first government issue representing fractional parts of a dollar, and was commenced in August 1862, and closed in April 1863. **1929** *Post Office Guide* July 144 Remittances are made by certain Government Departments, etc., by means of *Postal Drafts. **1881** *Whitaker's Almanack* 1882, 367/1 *Postal Money Orders [1880 Postal Money Notes]. Unlike post office orders, they are issued for fixed sums. **1883** *Postal Telegr. & Telephonic Gaz.*, Would it not be well if the newer issue were styled '*postal notes', as in common parlance?.. 'Post-office order' and 'postal order' are too much alike in sound. **1885** *Victorian Year-Bk. for 1884–5* 481 Postal notes were first issued on the 1st January, 1885. **1926** *Austral. Encycl.* II. 318/1 In 1893 [in New South Wales] an inland and intercolonial parcels post was established and the postal-note system introduced. **1962** J. R. BERNARD in *Southerly* XXII. II. 98 A number of words compounded from standard words and attracting to themselves specific meanings are not treated at all in the dictionary. Among them are *bin-boy*, *bushfire*, *postal note*, [etc.]. **1973** *Bulletin* (Sydney) 25 Aug. 3 Enclosed please find my cheque/postal note. **1883** *Postal order [see *postal note*]. **1899** *Daily News* 23 June 8/5 Judge Emden said that.. he had no difficulty in coming to the conclusion that a postal order was not a negotiable instrument. **1916** A. HUXLEY *Let. c* 12 July (1969) 106 Business first... this postal order, is *not* for you... au contraire, for me. **1974** *Encycl. Brit. Macropædia* XIV. 887/1 Postal orders were introduced in 1881. **1902** *Encycl. Brit.* XXV. 99/2 What is called in England '*postal trade', and in America 'mail order business', is growing very rapidly. **1894** *Country Gentlemen's Catal.* 166 Postal Pockets .. Direction Labels, *Postal Tubes. **1875** (*Inscription*) Foreign Post Card for countries included in the *Postal Union. One Penny Farthing. **1876** *Brit. Postal Guide* 1 Jan., List of countries.. comprised in the Postal Union. **1945** *Times* 25 May 4/1 There will be some inevitable duplication of *postal and proxy votes. **1955** *Times* 11 May 14/4 Ministers in Argyll, who have been called to attend the General Assembly of the Church of Scotland in Edinburgh during the time they should vote in the general election, have been refused postal votes. **1971** *Oxf. Univ. Gaz.* 18 Feb. 671/2 More than fifty members of Congregation have required a postal vote on the resolution. **1974** *Times* 15 Jan. 2/6 An individual can claim a postal vote so long as he has moved from one local authority area to another. **1945** *Times* 25 May 4/1 Before these arrangements were made for postal voting by members of the forces a high proportion of them had appointed proxies. **1974** *Times* 15 Jan. 2/6 If an election is called.. all claims for postal voting must be filed.. a fortnight before election day.

B. as *sb.* **a.** *U.S. colloq.* Short for *postal card*; also for *postal note* (*Cent. Dict.* 1890). **b.** Short for *postal car*, *postal* (i.e. mail) *train*.

1871 W. DRYSDALE *Let.*, I have already, by postal,.. acknowledged receipt of your late favour. **1889** *Anthony's Photogr. Bull.* II. 193 To furnish the secretary with postals to notify the members and the press of the date of meeting. **1891** *Ann. Rep. Postm.-Gen. Washington* 583, 2 daily lines of 50-foot postals [postal railway carriages] superseding 2 lines of 40-foot. **1906** *The Missionary* (U.S.) June 249/1 The circular letter, with return postal, sent out the middle of April.

postalize ('pəʊstəlaɪz), *v.* [f. POSTAL *a.* (*sb.*) + -IZE.] To make like the postal system in respect of its fixed prices for delivery, regardless of distance. So **postali'zation**.

1893 *Review of Reviews* Oct. 394 Why not postalize Railway Traffic, and go as far as you like for 2½d? **1939** *Sun* (Baltimore) 19 Jan. 14/7 (*heading*) I.C.C. seeks order for investigating postalized rail fares. *Ibid.*, Chairman Marion M. Caskie.. suggested today that the commission be given a mandate from Congress before investigating the Hastings plan for postalization of the railroads. **1950** *Economist* 16 Sept. 472/2 There is also some pressure for extending the system of 'postalisation' whereby United Kingdom consumers as a whole bear the transport charges. **1953** *Ibid.* 27 June 894/1 It takes a good deal of economic sophistication nowadays to see anything wrong with the principle of 'postalisation'—the principle of the postal service, that the consumers in thickly populated areas who can be served cheaply should subsidise the high-cost consumers elsewhere. **1966** *Ibid.* 17 Sept. 1166/1 This American gas expert, incidentally, would suggest selling to all boards at the same price, which might certainly interest the boards remote from Britain's east coast; but this idea of 'postalising gas' seems an ancillary frill on this argument.

postallantoic: see POST- B. 2.

postally ('pəʊstəlɪ), *adv.* [f. POSTAL *a.* + -LY².] For postal purposes; in the post; as far as postal matters are concerned.

1896 *Rep. Exhib. Sheffield Philatelic Soc.*, There were two letters postally used in 1768 and 1772. **1930** *Observer* 20 Apr. 15/5 It might.. be better to show him our very latest additions to Whitehall—although they occur, postally at least, in that part of it called Charing Cross. **1970** *Daily Tel.* 17 Oct. 11/7 Those used for stamp duty, bills, receipts, licences and other fiscal purposes have *some* value, but it is very small indeed compared with the value of postally-used copies. **1972** *Police Rev.* 1 Dec. 1558/3 Neither was it acceptable to display mint (unused) stamps on the same page as those which had been postally used.

†**post a'lone**, *adv. Obs.* [f. POST *sb.*¹ + ALONE. (app. = standing alone like a post.)] Entirely or quite alone. (Very common in 16th c.)

1514 Q. MARY OF FRANCE *Let. Hen. VIII* in Ellis *Orig. Lett.* Ser. I. I. 116 Now am I left post a lone in effect. *a* **1533** FRITH *Answ. More* (1548) F j, I dare not lett him stonde post alone, least ye dispise him. **1543** GRAFTON *Contn. Harding* 454 Kyng Henry taryed poste alone in the bishoppes paleyce besyde Powles. **1567** GOLDING *Ovid's Met.* VIII. (1593) 187 He left her post alone Upon the shore. **1619** HIERON *Wks.* I. 28 To be in a manner poast alone, like a pellican in the wildernesse, or as an owle in the desart.

post-alveolar: see POST- B. 2.

postament ('pəʊstəmənt). *Arch. rare.* (Also 8 postment.) [ad. It. *postamento*, f. *postare* to post, *posta* situation, placing, setting; whence also Ger. etc. *postament*.] A pedestal, a base; also, a framing, mounting, or moulding around a bas-relief, large cameo, or the like.

1738 [G. SMITH] *Curious Relations* II. 392 All these Pyramids were railed in with Bannisters, on the Postments of every other were put Pots with Orange-Trees. **1850** LEITCH tr. *C. O. Müller's Anc. Art* §191 (ed. 2) 174 Insulated pedestals of columns (stylobates) which arose from continuous postaments (stereobates).

postanal: see POST- B. 2.

post and rail. Also hyphenated and in pl. **1.** An open wooden fence, consisting of posts and rails only; a post and rail fence. Also, materials for post and rail fencing. Cf. *post and railing* s.v. POST *sb.*¹ 8 c.

[**1641** *Rec. Colony & Plantation New Haven* (1857) 54 Fencing with.. strong and substantiall posts and rales.. nott above 18d.] **1778** 'J. H. ST. JOHN DE CRÈVECŒUR' *Sk. 18th-Cent. Amer.* (1925) 81 Our present modes of making fences are very bad... I have often observed whole lengths of posts and rails raised from the ground in the spring, and the labours of weeks thus destroyed. **1797** H. NEWDIGATE *Let.* 13 July in A. E. Newdigate-Newdegate *Cheverels* (1898) xiii. 184 As far as yᵉ Road is near the Cliff.. there is a strong post & Rail all yᵉ Way. **1823** BYRON *Don Juan* VIII. lv. 138 So was his blood stirred.. As is the hunter's at the five-bar gate, Or double post and rail. **1865** DICKSON *Poems* 98 He had fifty acres cleared, all fenced with post and rail. **1936** 'J. TEY' *Shilling for Candles* vii. 85 Flight fell with me at a post-and-rails last winter. **1959** J. VERNEY *Friday's Tunnel* xxxi. 292 The lane ended at the wood's edge in a broken post and rails.

2. *Austral. slang.* **a.** A wooden match.

a **1890** D. B. W. SLADEN in Barrère & Leland *Dict. Slang* (1890) II. 147/1 'Alf,' said a great friend of mine to a companion who was engaged with us on a shooting expedition down in Bulu-Bulu, one of the eastern provinces of Victoria, 'Have you got a match?' 'Only a post-and-rails,' was the deprecating reply, responded to with a patronising 'Never mind.' **1941** BAKER *Dict. Austral. Slang* 56 *Post-and-rails*,...(2) Wooden matches.

b. = *post-and-rail tea*.

1899 W. T. GOODGE *Hits! Skits! & Jingles!* 75 There is 'post and rails' and 'brownie' For yer breakfast now, yer know. **1904** T. PETRIE *Reminisc. Early Queensland* II. iv. 241 The tea then was all green tea, and very coarse, like bits of stick—indeed it was christened 'post and rails'. **1934** *Bulletin* (Sydney) 12 Sept. 9/2 A 'bark hut or log cabin will be erected' so that royalty may not get sunstroke while sipping his 'post-and-rail'. **1966** BAKER *Austral. Lang.* (ed. 2) iv. 85 Three old expressions are *ration tea*,..*post-and-rails* (also called *post-and-rail tea*) and *jack the painter*; the second is derived from the pieces of stalk and leaf floating on top.

c. [Rhyming slang for 'fairy tale'.] A lie.

1945 BAKER *Austral. Lang.* xv. 271 *Post-and-rail*, a lie (by rhyme on 'fairytale').

3. *attrib.* (sense 1), as *post-and-rail fence*, *fencing*, *paddock*.

1684 *Public Rec. Colony of Connecticut* (1859) III. 512 Great parte of my post and rayle fences being feched and burnt by the sowders. **1765** G. WASHINGTON *Diary* 6 Nov. (1925) I. 216 Sowing.. 19 Bushls. in ye large cut within the Post and Rail fence. **1850** H. C. WATSON *Camp-Fires of Revolution* 43 A party of our men.. pulled up a post-and-rail fence. **1914** CONRAD *Chance* I. ii. 40 She had taken the trouble to climb over two post-and-rail fences only for the fun of being reckless. **1944** M. MORRIS in *Coast to Coast 1943* 85 Bare paddocks tufted with winter-whitened grass and endless post-and-rail fences regular as printed staves of music. **1973** E. EGLETON *Seven Days to Killing* xx. 210 The post-and-rail fence at the bottom of the yard. **1786** G. WASHINGTON *Diary* 18 Mar. (1925) III. 30 Post and rail fencing lately erected as yards for my Stud horses. **1944** E. DITHMACK in *Coast to Coast 1943* 26 Inside the post-and-rail paddock the leaves of the box-trees glittered. **1976** *Horse & Hound* 3 Dec. 70/4 (Advt.), Good stabling, grazing in post-and-rail paddocks in exclusive parkland setting.

b. Special Combs., as **post-and-rail tea** *Austral.*, strong, roughy made tea with stalks, etc., floating on the top.

1851 *Australasian* 298 (Farmer) Hyson-skin and post-and-rail tea have been superseded by Mocha, claret, and cognac. **1887** *All Year Round* 30 July 66 The tea so made [in a billy can] is naturally of rather a rough and ready description, and when the stalks and coarse particles of the fragrant leaf float thickly thereon, it is sometimes graphically styled 'post-and-rails' tea. **1898** 'R. BOLDREWOOD' *Rom. Canvas Town* 33 He.. couldn't stand the rations—bad flour—post-and-rail tea and.. old ewe mutton. **1936** A. RUSSELL *Gone Nomad* iv. 48 Flour, 'post and rail' tea (the cheapest kind), black sugar, salt and meat, were the only rations provided. **1959** H. P. TRITTON *Time means Tucker* i. 10/2 We got the jobs,.. at a pound a week and tucker,.. the tucker being mutton and damper, post-and-rail tea and brown sugar.

post-angel: see POST *sb.*² 13.

post-antennal: see POST- B. 2.

post-apostolic: see POST- B. 1.

post-'Armistice, *a.* [POST- B. 1 a.] Of or pertaining to the period immediately following the Armistice of 11 Nov. 1918.

1929 *Times* 22 July 15/2 The reckless capital flotation during the short-lived post-Armistice 'boom'. **1965** G. MCINNES *Road to Gundagai* iii. 48 When Terence sat at the keyboard to 'tickle the ivories', rip-roaring post-Armistice America with all its heady intoxication came vividly alive.

post-article: see POST- B. 1 c.

post-arytenoid: see POST- B. 2.

†**'postate.** *Obs.* Aphetic form of APOSTATE.

1387 TREVISA *Higden* (Rolls) VIII. 315 And postataes and evel doers he favored strongliche. **1483** CAXTON *Cato* G viij, Euery one sholde say that ye were a postate.

†**po'station.** *Obs. rare*⁻¹. [f. L. *post* after + -ATION.] The placing of one thing after another.

1607 *Schol. Disc. agst. Antichr.* I. ii. 95 The postation of the wine doth not preiudice it, therefore the postponing of the Crosse doth not preiudice it neither.

post-auditory, -auricular: see POST- B. 2.

post-'axiad, *adv.* (*prep.*) *Anat.* [f. as next + *-ad*: cf. DEXTRAD.] In a post-axial direction (from).

1895 *Proc. Zool. Soc.* 331 These two grooves are separated by a.. ridge (narrowing postaxiad). *Ibid.* 373 The quadrate continues onwards postaxiad the dorsal margin of the zygoma.

post-axial (pəʊst'æksɪəl), *a.* *Anat.* [f. L. *post* after + AXIS, AXIAL.] Of, pertaining to, or situated on that side of a limb (in vertebrates) which is posterior to a line drawn at right angles to the body axis through the axis of the limb.

1872 MIVART *Elem. Anat.* 37 And in beasts posterior, can be spoken of as post-axial. **1875** SIR W. TURNER in *Encycl. Brit.* I. 819/2 Quite recently the term *præ-axial* has been introduced as equivalent to atlantal, and *post-axial* to sacral. **1881** MIVART *Cat* 95 The Ulna, or post-axial bone of the forearm, is longer than the humerus.

Hence **post-'axially** *adv.*, in a post-axial position or direction; also as *prep.* (cf. POST-AXIAD).

1872 MIVART *Elem. Anat.* 39 Distinct vertebræ are developed both pre-axially and post-axially to this strip. **1895** *Proc. Zool. Soc.* 331 These vertebræ.. continue on postaxially the sacral mass, narrowing as they proceed.

'post-bag. [f. POST *sb.*² + BAG *sb.*] A bag for carrying letters and other postal matter; a mail-bag; *transf.* the number of letters, etc. delivered to or sent from any house or person.

1813 MOORE *Post-bag* 284 The honour and delight of first ransacking the Post Bag. **1832** BABBAGE *Econ. Manuf.* xxviii. (ed. 3) 273 The Post-bag despatched every evening to one of our largest cities, Bristol, usually weighs less than a hundred pounds. **1855** MACAULAY *Hist. Eng.* xvi. III. 657. **1883** J. MARTIN *Remin. Old Haddington* 227 Post-bags were carried on horseback from Edinburgh to London. **1898** *Tit Bits* 23 July 322/2 The Prince of Wales has the biggest post-bag of any of the Royalties.

†**'post-bark.** *Obs.* [f. POST *sb.*² + BARK *sb.*²] = PACKET-BOAT.

1599 [see PACKET *sb.* 1]. **1600** MOUNTJOY in *Cal. Doc. rel. Irel.* 423 We find great lack of a post-bark to pass to and fro between Lough Foyle and Dublin.. we have adventured to erect a passage boat for that purpose, at the rate of 10*l.* *per mensem*, as the other post-barks have. **1650** *Cal. State Papers, Dom.* (1876) 26 The whole business of the post barks referred back to the Irish Committee. *a* **1656** USSHER *Ann.* vi. (1658) 161 Sending away neverthelesse a Post-barque to Athens, to let them know what had befallen him.

'postbase. *Linguistics.* [f. POST- B. 1 c + BASE *sb.*¹] A derivational suffix.

1958 A. A. HILL *Introd. Linguistic Struct.* viii. 121 The other class of morphemes which can follow a base, we shall call postbases... Postbases, like suffixes, are non-initial. Since more than one postbase can be added to a single base, as in *boy-ish-ness*, a postbase must be described as a morpheme which can follow a base or another postbase. **1962** *Canad. Jrnl. Linguistics* VII. II. 94 This study shows that the morphophonemics of English words having post-bases ('derivational suffixes') of learned origin can be systematized by a comparatively small number of statements of wide application. **1967** *Ibid.* XIII. I. 22 OE adverbs also fall into subsets marked by comparative and superlative postbases.

†**post-bill.** *Obs.* [f. POST *sb.*² + BILL *sb.*³]

1. See quots.

1847 WEBSTER, *Post-bill*, a bill of letters mailed by a post-master. **1858** SIMMONDS *Dict. Trade*, *Post-bill*, a post-office way-bill placed in the mail-bag, or given in charge of the guard or driver. **1864** in WEBSTER; and in later Dicts.

2. Short for *Bank Post Bill*: see BANK-BILL.

1809 R. LANGFORD *Introd. Trade* 6 Post Bills on the Bank of England.

post-Bloom'fieldian, *a.* and *sb.* *Linguistics.* [f. POST- B. 1 b + the name *Bloomfield* (see below) + -IAN.] **A.** *adj.* Subsequent to the work of the American linguist Leonard Bloomfield (1887–1949), freq. applied *spec.* to American structural linguistics in the 1950s. **B.** *sb.* An American structuralist.

[**1949** J. R. FIRTH in *Archivum Linguisticum* I. 110 Slav linguistics.. are certainly post-Saussurean and showing signs even in America of becoming post-Bloomfield.] **1961** F. W. HOUSEHOLDER in Saporta & Bastian *Psycholinguistics* 16/1 It would seem to a naive observer that the question 'what is the grammar for?' is an obvious one. Nevertheless, until recent years, no serious attempt to answer it seems to have been made by post-Bloomfieldian linguists. **1963** F. G. LOUNSBURY in J. A. Fishman *Readings Sociol. of Lang.* (1968) 63 The post-Bloomfieldian dogma in American linguistics has long upheld the desideratum of exclusion of semantic considerations from linguistics. **1965** *Foundations of Lang.* I. 92 It remains quite clear that post-Bloomfieldian linguistics was preoccupied with accounting for the corpus of speech-utterances. **1966** A. A. HILL *Promises & Limitations Newest Type Gram. Anal.* 11 Post-Bloomfieldian structuralists produced rather remarkably few grammars. **1970** *Jrnl. Linguistics* VI. II. 287 Structuralist phonemics of the so-called Post-Bloomfieldians, for instance, is only a set of practical procedures. **1970** G. C. LEPSCHY *Survey Structural Linguistics* 11 'Structural linguistics' in a more limited sense (the post-Bloomfieldians). **1971** D. CRYSTAL *Linguistics* iv. 208 The term 'structuralism' was often used, in fact, in a narrow sense to refer to the kind of emphases which characterized post-Bloomfieldian linguistics (in a broad sense, of course, *all* linguistics is structural).

post-boarding, *vbl. sb.* [f. POST- A. 1 a + BOARDING *vbl. sb.*] The shaping of a garment by heating it on a form after it is dyed, rather than before. So **post-board** *v. trans.*

1952 *Dyeing of Nylon Textiles* (I.C.I.) xii. 135 When high-temperature post-boarding techniques are employed the scarlet and blue components..are not sufficiently fast to sublimation. **1963** MEITNER & KERTESS tr. *Schmidlin's Preparation & Dyeing Synthetic Fibres* ii. 39 After..setting ..the stockings are dyed and subjected to post-boarding to impart the right type of handle. **1963, 1970** [see PREBOARD *v.*].

'post-boat. [f. POST *sb.*[2] + BOAT *sb.*] A boat or ship engaged in the conveyance of the mails, esp. on a regular route at fixed times; a packet-boat, mail-boat; also, a boat which conveys travellers between certain points; a stage-boat.

1600 SIR G. FENTON in *Cal. Doc. rel. Irel.* 340, I await [at Holyhead] for a southerly wind, and a bark to put me over, the post boat being already in Ireland. **1753** HANWAY *Trav.* (1762) I. II. xvi. 73 We found the place inhabited by some.. tartars, who ply on the river with open post boats. **1879** BATES *Egyptian Bonds* II. vi. 162 Thence by the post-boat on the canal to Port Said. **1897** *Edinb. Rev.* Oct. 455 It is sunset when one arrives by the post-boat.

† **'post-book**[1]. *Obs.* [f. POST *v.*[1] 8 + BOOK *sb.*] A book in which accounts are posted; a ledger.

1727-41 CHAMBERS *Cycl.* s.v. *Book, Ledger*, or *Leger-Book*, sometimes also called the *great book*, and the *post-book*. *a* **1734** NORTH *Lives* (1826) III. 165 Proposed a sort of post-book to be kept, in which the merchants should have their accounts.

'post-book[2]. *rare.* [f. POST *sb.*[2] + BOOK *sb.*] A book containing the regulations of a post-service.

1763 SMOLLETT *Trav.* (1766) I. viii. 135, I pulled out the post-book, and began to read..the article which orders, that the traveller who comes first shall be first served.

post-box: see POST *sb.*[1] 9, *sb.*[2] 13.

'post-boy. [f. POST *sb.*[2] + BOY *sb.*[1]]

1. A boy or man who rides post; a letter-carrier.

1588 *Cal. Border Papers* I. 320 Sum Skotes..mett with the post boay of Morpett bychanse..and tooke away his horse and pakkett. **1624** *Rutland MSS.* (1905) IV. 527 Paid to a post boy for a letter from my Lord, vjd. **1672** R. WILD *Declar. Lib. Consc.* 4, I suddenly heard the Post-boy blow his Horn near my Window. **1723** *Lond. Gaz.* No. 6137/3 The Post-Boy who was bringing the Gloucester and Bristol Mails to London. **1758** JOHNSON *Idler* No. 49 ¶13 A road through which..the post-boy every day and night goes and returns. **1881** BESANT & RICE *Chapl. of Fleet* II. vi. 122 We heard the summons of the postboy's horn, and Cicely presently ran in with a letter in her hand.

2. The postilion of a stage-coach, post-chaise, or hired carriage; = POSTILION 3.

1707 CHAMBERLAYNE *Pres. St. Eng.* III. (ed. 22) 443 If any Gentleman desire to ride Post..Post-Horses are always in readiness..only 3d. is demanded for every English Mile; and, for every Stage, to the Post-Boy 4d. for conducting. **1733** FIELDING *Tom Thumb* II. v, Tho' they should fly as swift as the gods, when they Ride on behind that post-boy, Opportunity. **1777** SHERIDAN *Trip Scarb.* I. i, Pay the postboy, and take the portmanteau. **1782** COWPER *Gilpin* 230 Away went Gilpin, and away Went postboy at his heels, The postboy's horse right glad to miss The lumbering of the wheels. **1853** LYTTON *My Novel* XII. xxxiii, The post-boys cracked their whips, and the wheels rolled away.

3. *Austral.* = *Jacky Winter* s.v. JACKY 3.

1911 J. A. LEACH *Austral. Bird Bk.* 121 Australian Brown Flycatcher, Jacky Winter, Post-boy, Post-sitter. **1931** N. W. CAYLEY *What Bird is That?* 64 Brown Flycatcher... Also called Peter-Peter, Post-boy, Post-sitter. **1969** [see *Jacky Winter* s.v. JACKY 3].

postbrachial, -branchial: see POST- B. 2.

post-butt: POST *sb.*[1] 9.

post-cæcal, -calcaneal: see POST- B. 2.

post-canonical, etc.: see POST- B. 1.

post captain: see POST *sb.*[3] 4 b.

'post-car. [f. POST *sb.*[2] + CAR *sb.*[1]] A car for the conveyance of mails; also, a car for the conveyance of travellers posting.

1694 PENN *Trav.* (1714) 203 We immediately took a Post-carr, and came next day about two in the afternoon to Cleve. **1812** SIR R. WILSON *Priv. Diary* (1861) I. 140 The boyard ..gave every aid, and a little car into the bargain for the soldiers, as being larger than the post cars.

postcard ('pəʊstkɑːd), *sb.* [f. POST *sb.*[2] + CARD *sb.*[2]] **1.** A pasteboard card of a regulation size, bearing a representation of a postage stamp or an equivalent design, officially sold to be used for correspondence. Also, since 1 Sept. 1894, a blank, private, or unofficial card of the same dimensions (*blank postcard*) to be furnished with an adhesive stamp for the proper amount of postage.

The postcard issued in Great Britain 1 Oct. 1870 cost ½*d.*; cards of higher prices from 1*d.* to 3*d.* were issued later for foreign correspondence (the first being the 1½*d.* card of 1875); from 1879 the postcard rate for countries within the postal union was 1*d.* An equivalent rate for foreign correspondence is used in most other countries; but for internal correspondence their rates differ. (*N.E.D.*) *pictorial* or *picture postcards* are cards (usually blank) bearing a picture on the reverse side, the sending and collection of which began to become prevalent shortly before 1900.

1870 Oct. 1 (*Inscription*) Post Card. The address only to be written on this side. Halfpenny. **1870** *Dame Europa's School* 16 He wrote home to his mother, on the back of a halfpenny post card, so that all the letter carriers might see how pious he was. **1872** *Punch* 3 Feb. 51/2 He gets a post-card informing him that he is proposed to the House. **1890** *Pall Mall Gaz.* 1 Feb. 2/3 The post-card was an Austrian invention, brought out in 1868, with a separate issue the following year for Hungary... We adopted the plan in 1870. **1899** Picture post-card [see PICTURE *sb.* 6 d]. **1901** *Daily News* 26 Mar. 5/1 The idea of the postcard first came to Dr. Stephan, late German Postmaster-General, who submitted his plan of a postcard, which was rejected at the time, to a German Postal Congress in 1865.

2. a. *attrib.*, as ***postcard album, flower, -monger, -photograph, poll, portrait, stand, survey, system; postcard-size*** adj.

1899 *Westm. Gaz.* 19 Aug. 8/1 They have supplied the market with a postcard album. **1907** *Yesterday's Shopping* (1969) 436c Post Card Albums. **1929** R. GRAVES *Poems* 21 Post-card flower of Kodak mud. **1938** *New Statesman* 13 Aug. 241/2 He can make his way..to..the Museums, outside which eager postcard-mongers will sell him views of Westminster Abbey and the Tower. **1920** T. P. NUNN *Education* x. 126 A postcard-photograph of a yacht. **1909** *Daily Chron.* 19 Mar. 1/6 There had been strong opposition ..to the Sunday concerts, and a postcard poll was taken. **1907** *Yesterday's Shopping* (1969) 436c These Albums have been designed to hold the Post Card Portraits now so popular. **1926** *Paper Terminol.* (Spalding & Hodge, Ltd.) 21 Post Card size... Generally applied to a board measuring 22½ x 28 in., out of which 32 official post cards may be cut. **1973** R. BUSBY *Pattern of Violence* iv. 60 A handful of postcard-size prints. **1907** *Yesterday's Shopping* (1969) 428 Post card stand. **1948** *Shell Aviation News* No. 120. 5/3 The study is based on a post-card survey of about 17,000 aircraft owners, and shows that an estimated 9,800,000 hours were flown by non-scheduled aircraft in 1946. **1897** *Westm. Gaz.* 22 Feb. 3/2 Having adopted the custom of book-retention by the post-card system.

b. Designating something picturesque, as ***postcard land, sky, view.***

1958 *Spectator* 14 Feb. 204/1 A postcard land of blossom, and bridges humped over gurgling streams. **1959** *Woman's Own* 16 May 13/1 The shining sea. The postcard sky. **1959** *Listener* 12 Mar. 459/1 He [*sc.* Utrillo] was undoubtedly clever at enlarging, squaring-up, colouring and feeling his way into postcard views of paintable *motifs*. **1979** M. A. SHARP *Sunflower* v. 45 They were crossing the Triboro Bridge, with its postcard view of the city.

c. Special Combs., as **postcard beauty,** a fashionable beauty whose picture appeared on postcards which were collected by admirers.

1924 G. B. SHAW *Let.* in *To a Young Actress* (1960) 66, I think you will gravitate towards literature after a reign as a postcard beauty. **1958** *Sunday Times* 28 Sept. 4/7 She was included among the postcard beauties of her musical-comedy days.

'postcard, *v.* [f. the sb.]

a. *trans.* To communicate with or inform by postcard. **b.** *intr.* To send a postcard.

1910 *Westm. Gaz.* 2 Feb. 5/3 (Advt.), Patterns ready for sending by return post. Postcard us to-day. **1947** *Ki-grams* (Washington, D.C. Kiwanis Club) 6 Feb., Zeddie Blackistone post-cards about the flowers, the sunshine and golf at Palm Beach.

post-caroche, to **-carrier:** see POST *sb.*[2] 12.

post-cart ('pəʊstkɑːt). [f. POST *sb.*[2] + CART *sb.*] A cart in which local mails are carried. Also *attrib.*

1826 MISS MITFORD *Village* Ser. II. (1863) 243 Here is the post-cart coming up the road at its most respectable rumble. **1884** *Manch. Exam.* 29 Nov. 4/6 The trains are all late, and the postcards do not reach their destinations. **1889** BARRIE *Window in Thrums* 151 Jamie was to..come on to Thrums from Tilliedrum in the post-cart. **1906** *Westm. Gaz.* 5 Apr. 7/1 An important post-cart service runs via Greytown and Middle Drift into the native territories. **1926** O. SCHREINER *From Man to Man* ix. 339 At half past four the postcart driver had inspanned his horses. **1949** L. G. GREEN *In Land of Afternoon* ii. 33 The old post-cart drivers used to halt between Ashton and Montagu.

postcava (pəʊst'keɪvə). *Anat.* [f. POST- A. 2 + CAVA for *vena cava.*] The inferior vena cava: so called as being behind or posterior in animals generally. Hence **post'caval** *a.*

1866 [see PRECAVAL]. **1882** WILDER & GAGE *Anat. Technol.* 331 By Owen the two are designated as the *postcaval* and *præcaval* veins... We have ventured to omit the *vena* and to designate them as simply *præcava* and *postcava.*

post-cedar: see POST *sb.*[1] 9.

postcentral, -centrally, -cephalic, -cerebellar, -cerebral: see POST- B. 2.

post-chaise ('pəʊst-ʃeɪz), *sb.* Also *colloq.* **post-chay, -shay,** PO'CHAISE, POCHAY. [f. POST *sb.*[2] + CHAISE *sb.*] A travelling carriage, either hired from stage to stage, or drawn by horses so hired: used in the 18th and earlier half of the 19th century.

In England usually having a closed body, seated for from two to four persons, the driver or postilion riding on one of the horses.

1712 *Lond. Gaz.* No. 5027/5 The Earl of Strafford arrived here in a Post-Chaise. **1756-7** tr. *Keysler's Trav.* (1760) I. 221 There is scarce any other way of travelling from Geneva to Italy than in post-chaises which will hold two persons, with a covering over head, and room for two trunks behind: they have but two wheels. **1757** F. GREVILLE *Maxims, Char. & Refl.* 19 He was told of the late invention of post-chays, of their great expedition, conveniency and cheapness. **1840** DICKENS *Old C. Shop* xlvii, Kit's mother and the single gentleman,..speeding onward in the post-chaise-and-four. **1889** G. FINDLAY *Eng. Railway* 3 At the commencement of the present century..communication between the smaller towns was by post-chaises..for the wealthy.

attrib. **1763** STONE in *Phil. Trans.* LIII. 197 Cases where the patient..caught cold, as a post-chaise boy did. **1794** W. FELTON *Carriages* I. 8 A Chariot or Post-Chaise body. These bodies differ not in the least... By the addition of a coach-box to the carriage-part, they are called Chariots.

Hence **post-chaise** *v., colloq., intr.* to travel by post-chaise; *trans.* to convey in or carry off in a post-chaise. *rare.*

1854 THACKERAY *Newcomes* xv, The Colonel delighted in post-chaising—the rapid transit through the country amused him, and cheered his spirits. **1871** [see PO'CHAISE].

post-'chariot. [f. POST *sb.*[2] + CHARIOT *sb.*] A chariot for travelling post; *spec.* a light four-wheeled carriage of the 18th and early 19th c., differing from a post-chaise in having a driver's seat in front.

1609 HOLLAND *Amm. Marcell.* 375 Messala..mounted her into a swift post-chariot, and with a maine pace rode away. **1741-70** ELIZ. CARTER *Lett.* (1808) 423 Miss Deane got into a post-chariot at Canterbury. **1762** GOLDSM. *Nash* 49 He usually travelled to Tunbridge, in a post chariot and six greys, with out-riders. **1828** PLANCHE *Descent Danube* 69 The sight of a post-chariot whirling along.

post-Chau'cerian, *a.* and *sb.* [POST- B. 1 b.]

A. *adj.* After the lifetime of Chaucer; *spec.*, of a poet: writing after, and influenced by, Chaucer. **B.** *sb.* A post-Chaucerian poet.

1933 R. TUVE *Seasons & Months* ii. 70 One may see this Lydgatean influence in most of the poets of the 'post-Chaucerian' school. *Ibid.* iii. 71 English poetry from the time of Chaucer and the post-Chaucerians to that of the eighteenth-century pastoral. **1966** *Eng. Stud.* XLVII. 172 The foregoing are the only instances of post-Chaucerian *spiced conscience* that I have been able to discover. **1967** P. J. BAWCUTT *Shorter Poems of Gavin Douglas* p. xxx, Douglas must have been well read, not only in Chaucer and the post-Chaucerian poets of the fifteenth century, but in medieval Latin poetry.

post-choreic, -choroid: see POST- B. 1, A. 2 b.

post-'Christian, *a.* and *sb.* [POST- B. 1 b.]

A. *adj.* **a.** Subsequent to the lifetime of Christ, or to the rise of Christianity. **b.** Subsequent to the decline or rejection of Christianity.

1864 PUSEY *Lect. Daniel* ix. 542 Literature,..collected in post-Christian times by the Sassanidæ. **1888** T. K. CHEYNE et al. *Bible* (Variorum Teacher's ed.) (1893) Pref., The vowel-points merely represent a valuable, but still post-Christian, exegetical tradition. **1929** H. KEYSERLING *Amer. set Free* II. 583 This is not a pre-Christian, but a post-Christian state. **1945** *Downside Rev.* LXIII. 201 He exemplifies that paralysis from which post-Christian philosophy is suffering. **1956** K. CLARK *Nude* iii. 109 The yearning for another world had entered the post-Christian spirit. **1974** *Listener* 24 Jan. 121/3 Heliogabalus..reduced Rome to a kind of post-Christian Sodom and Gomorrah.

B. *sb.* A person in a nominally Christian society who has no professed religion.

1946 *Downside Rev.* LXIV. 117 Or we may have wondered for whom the book was written, for Mgr Knox addresses sometimes the post-Christian, sometimes the 'Sunday Mass' Catholic and sometimes his fellow priests. **1958** *Spectator* 4 July 10/3 A generation of men and women who have grown up completely outside institutional Christianity. They are not lapsed Christians... But neither are they formal agnostics. They are best defined as post-Christians. **1961** *Christian Century* 18 Jan. 80/2 Australian Catholics sincerely believe that their countrymen would be better off as Catholics than as post-Christians.

post-'classic *a.* **a.** = next.

1890 in *Cent. Dict.*

b. *spec.* Usu. with initial capital. Applied to that period (*c* 900 to 1520) of Meso-American civilization succeeding the Classic.

[**1956** J. E. S. THOMPSON *Rise & Fall of Maya Civilization* ii. 96 Burials have also been found in collapsed rooms at other sites, notably a burial with pottery of post-classical types at Copan.] **1965** R. F. SPENCER et al. *Native Americans* xi. 443/1 The Post-Classic period of Mesoamerican culture history essentially amounts to reorientation in Mesoamerican cultural foci... Many of the characteristics which are typical of the Post-Classic were present in the Classic Period. **1973** *Times* 26 July 18/4 Several pottery vessels..and the architecture of the house suggested connexions with the northern part of Yucatan in the Early and the Middle Postclassic periods. **1975** *Sci. Amer.* Oct. 73/2 The most neutral of scholars' terms for this period in Middle America is Last Post-classic; many simply call it 'the decadent period'.

post-'classical, *a.* [f. POST- B. 1 + CLASSICAL.] Occurring or existing subsequent to the classical period of any language, literature, music, or art; *spec.* of the Greek and Latin.

1867 DEUTSCH *Rem.* (1874) 1 The classical and postclassical materials that lie scattered through it [the Talmud]. **1898** *Daily News* 12 Nov. 4/5 All this..suggests that gypsies, whatever their origin, were post-classical immigrants from India into Europe by way of the Levant. **1947** A. EINSTEIN *Mus. Romantic Era* xii. 167 But Bruckner did not write 'Post Classical' or Romantic church music in the style of Schubert. **1969** *Listener* 4 Sept. 320/1 In one week, between 4 and 10 September, the Proms give a most interesting perspective of post-classical symphonic development.

So **post-'classicism**, a grammatical or orthographical form of the post-classical period.

1906 *Academy* 7 Apr. 331/1 Perhaps the most remarkable post-classicism in the treatise is the appeal to the reader, as in διαγνῶθι ὅπως, 'observe how', in p. 29.

post'clavicle. *Anat.* and *Zool.* [f. POST- A. 2 b.] The posterior bone of the scapular arch of some fishes.

1888 ROLLESTON & JACKSON *Anim. Life* 416 The *Ganoidei* and *Teleostei* have investing bones known as supra-clavicle, clavicle, inter-clavicle, and post-clavicle, all derived apparently from the skin and lining membrane of the branchial cavity, and present in none of the higher Vertebrata.

So **postcla'vicular** *a.*, situated behind the clavicle; pertaining to the postclavicle.

1870 ROLLESTON *Anim. Life* 44 The clavicle overlaps a postclavicular bar.

post-climax: see POST- B. 1 c.

postclitellian (-klaɪˈtɛlɪən), *a.* (*sb.*) *Zool.* [f. POST- B. 2 + CLITELL-UM + -IAN.] Belonging to that division of earthworms in which the male genital apertures are situated behind the clitellum or thickened band. **b.** *sb.* An earthworm of this division.

[**1888** ROLLESTON & JACKSON *Anim. Life* 207.] **1888** [see INTRACLITELLIAN].

postclitic (pəʊstˈklɪtɪk). *Linguistics.* [f. POST- A. 1 b + CLITIC.] An unemphatic word stressed as part of the preceding word.

1963 BLOOMFIELD & NEWMARK *Linguistic Introd. Hist. Eng.* iv. 147 *The* is a proclitic in NE.. and *one*, as in *a bad one* or *the green one*, is a postclitic. **1965** *Language* XLI. 473 As many as five syllables occur prestressed, but only one syllable occurs poststressed, except rarely when a postclitic follows a suffix.

post-'clypeus. *Ent.* [POST- A. 2 b.] In certain insects, the upper section of a divided clypeus.

1888 J. H. COMSTOCK *Introd. Entomol.* 10 When these [*sc.* two sclerites of the clypeus] are distinct they are designated as the ante-clypeus and post-clypeus respectively. **1926** R. J. TILLYARD *Insects Australia & N.Z.* i. 12 In others [*sc.* insects] the clypeus may be divided into two parts, an anteclypeus and a postclypeus. **1937** C. LONGFIELD *Dragonflies Brit. Isles* 13 In the *Anisoptera* the frons is the most prominent portion of the two, in the *Zygoptera* it is the postclypeus. **1957** RICHARDS & DAVIES *Imm's Textbk. Entomol.* (ed. 9) I. 19 In some insects the clypeus is partially or completely divided by a transverse suture into two sclerites—the post-clypeus and the ante-clypeus.

post-coach (ˈpəʊstkəʊtʃ). [f. POST *sb.*[2] + COACH *sb.*] A stage-coach used for carrying mails, a mail-coach; a stage-coach generally.

1673 *Lauderdale Papers* (Camden) 69 The D. Hamilton and the E. of Tweedale.. goe in coch to Belford, from thence on horsback to York, and from thence by the post-coch to London. **1685** *Royal Proclam.* 7 Sept. in *Lond. Gaz.* No. 2068/1 That they presume not to set up any Foot-Post, Horse-Post, Post or Stage-Coach. **1787** *Hist. Europe* ii. in *Ann. Reg.* 32/1 A common travelling post coach or two, with a couple of hired chaises. **1849** *N. & Q.* 1st Ser. I. 33/1 A new post-coach had been set up which performed the journey to Bath in a single day. **1861** DICKENS *Gt. Expect.* xxxiii, We got into our post-coach and drove away.

postcode (ˈpəʊstkəʊd). Also with capital initial. [f. POST *sb.*[2] + CODE *sb.*[1]] A series of letters or numbers, or both, allocated to postal areas to facilitate the automatic sorting and speedy delivery of mail. Also *attrib.* Hence **'postcoding** *vbl. sb.*

1967 *Telegraph* (Brisbane) 18 May 3/1 The Post Office will allocate every city, town, suburb and small centre in Australia a four-figure postal location number called Postcode. Announcing this today, the Postmaster-General ..said the Postcode system would enable the Post Office to handle the growing volume of mail more quickly, by taking full advantage of electronic mail coding equipment. **1968** *Times* 24 July 9/7 On the back of it is stamped the instruction 'Remember to use the postcode'. **1969** *Daily Tel.* 5 June 21/6 Postcoding is to be extended to cover all of Britain's 20,000,000 addresses instead of only 75 main centres. **1969** *Guardian* 9 Aug. 8/3 The first two letters of the Postcode route the letter to the distant mail-handling centre. **1971** *Sunday Times* (Colour Suppl.) 20 June 17 A postman at the letter-coding desk has each envelope put in front of him and types out its postcode on a keyboard at his fingertips. **1973** *Guardian* 7 Feb. 1/1 Postcodes are to be put on road signs. The experiment will start in the new town of Milton Keynes, Bucks.

postcolumellar, -comitial: see POST- B. 2, 1.

post-'common. *Obs.* exc. *Hist.* [Altered from med.L. *postcommūnio*: see next, and cf. COMMON *sb.*[1] 4, *v.* 8.] = POST-COMMUNION.

a **1380** *St. Bernard* 1110 in Horstm. *Altengl. Leg.* (1878) 59 God..enspired him of an orisoun, To seyn at his post-comoun. Aftur þe post-comoun was i-songe He chaunged his orisoun. *c* **1460** in *Pol. Rel. & L. Poems* (1866) 91 When þe preste hath don his masse,..A-noþur oryson he moste say,..þe 'post comen' men don hit calle. **1493** *Festivall* (W. de W. 1515) 33 The postcomyn is not sayd [on Easter eve]. **1683** tr. *Romish Mass-bk.* 96 After the Canon and Communion then followeth the post-common with the Collects. **1879** T. F. SIMMONS *Lay Folks Mass Bk.* 307 They were to kneel again during the post-common, as was the English name for the prayer after the communion. **1882** G. H. FORBES *Misale Drummondiense* 26 This Postcommon is found without any variation in Gerbert p. 294 b.

postcommunicant: see POST- A. 2 a.

post-co'mmunion, *sb.* (*a.*) [ad. med.L. *postcommūnio, -ōn-em*; cf. F. *postcommunion* (OF. also *pocumenion*, 1287 in Godef.); see POST- B. 1 c and COMMUNION.] The or a part of the eucharistic office which follows the act of communion.

1483 CAXTON *Gold. Leg.* 442 b/1 After the preest sayth the postcommunyon whiche is so named..for thys that it is sayd after the preest hath receyued the precyous sacramente of the aulter. **1548–9** *Bk. Comm. Prayer, Communion* (Rubric), Then shall the Clarkes syng the post Communion. **1657** SPARROW *Bk. Com. Prayer* 241 The last is the Post-Communion, or, Thanksgiving, which with us is nothing but that holy Hymn [Gloria in Excelsis]. **1853** DALE tr. *Baldeschi's Ceremonial* 128 At the Post-Communion the Bishop again goes to the faldstool. **1902** *Westm. Gaz.* 11 Aug. 5/2 The Post-Communion was said by the Archbishop and the 'Gloria in Excelsis' was sung by the choir to music by Sir John Stainer.

B. *adj.* Succeeding or following the act of communion; used after communion.

1890 *Cent. Dict.* s.v., A post-communion collect. *Mod.* The post-communion address in Presbyterian churches.

post-connubial to **-cosmic:** see POST- B. 1.

postcostal (pəʊstˈkɒstəl), *a.* [f. POST- B. 2 + L. *costa*, after COSTAL.] Behind a rib; *spec.* in *Entom.* situated next behind the costal vein or nervure of the wing.

1826 KIRBY & SP. *Entomol.* III. xxxv. 608 The Intermediate Area is that which lies between the postcostal or mediastinal nervure and the anal fold of the wing. **1836–9** *Todd's Cycl. Anat.* II. 927/1 The second longitudinal nervure is the post-costal. **1895** *Syd. Soc. Lex.*, *Postcostal*, behind a rib.

postcoxal, -cranial(ly: see POST- B. 2.

postcribrate: see POST- A. 1.

post-cricoid: see POST- B. 2.

post crown. *Dentistry.* Also with hyphen and as one word. [f. POST *sb.*[1] + CROWN *sb.*] A prosthetic dental crown held in place by a post or wire sunk into the root of the tooth.

1905 G. EVANS *Pract. Treat. Artific. Crown-, Bridge-, & Porcelain Work* ii. 58 Each of these conditions causes fracture of roots carrying post or dowel crowns. **1936** J. R. SCHWARTZ *Cavity Prep. & Abutment Construction in Bridgework* xvii. 183 The earliest attempts to incorporate esthetics in the mechanical procedures of tooth restoration was the banded dowel, or postcrown, with a porcelain facing, presented by Dr. C. M. Richmond, many years ago. **1963** C. R. COWELL et al. *Inlays, Crowns, & Bridges* viii. 90 An effective temporary post-crown consists of acrylic resin on a preformed post or wire. **1974** L. J. LEGGETT in Harty & Roberts *Restorative Procedures for Practising Dentist* xvi. 216 A post crown is indicated, in a root-filled tooth, where there is insufficient bulk or strength in the remaining crown to support a jacket crown.

post-cruciate: see POST- B. 2.

post-'Cubist, *a.* and *sb.* *Art.* [POST- B. 1 b.] **A.** *adj.* Subsequent to Cubism. **B.** *sb.* A post-Cubist painter.

1927 R. H. WILENSKI *Mod. Movement in Art* 147 Imitations of..Post-Cubist art are not confined to actual works of painting. **1937** *Burlington Mag.* Dec. p. xx/1 Cubists and Post-Cubists. **1959** H. READ *Conc. Hist. Mod. Painting* v. 147 His post-Cubist development cannot be dissociated from the typical manifestations of Surrealism.

post-cubital: see POST- B. 2.

'postcure, *sb.* (and *v.*). [f. POST- A. 1 b + CURE *sb.*[1]] The action or process of further curing plastic (or an article of it) after fabrication, so as to complete the cure.

1957 B. A. DUMBROW *Polyurethanes* iii. 35 In a matter of minutes, the entire foam is produced in place and ready for post-cure, if such is necessary. **1958** D. J. DUFFIN *Laminated Plastics* iv. 75 It has been found advisable to place the part in a second oven at lower temperatures..to effect a postcure. **1967** *Electronics* 6 Mar. 324 The finished coating requires no post-cure, has very high cut-through temperature and superior resistance to high temperatures. **1968** *Encycl. Polymer Sci. & Technol.* IX. 18 A typical postcure..might involve 2 hr at 275°F, followed by 2 hr at 150°F.

So as *v. trans.*; **'postcuring** *vbl. sb.*

1956 *Brit. Plastics* XXIX. 453/1 Post curing, for example, three hours at 80°C, will eliminate all residual peroxide and bring many laminates to a stable condition. **1964** SAUNDERS & FRISCH *Polyurethanes* II. vii. 115 Postcuring of the sponge was carried out for 1 hr. at 100°C. **1969** MONROE & CHITWOOD in G. Lubin *Handbk. Fiberglass & Advanced Plastics Composites* xiv. 325 If warpage is a problem, then the part must be post-cured on a post-cure fixture which holds the part to contour. **1975** A. T. RADCLIFFE in Whelan & Brydson *Devel. with Thermosetting Plastics* v. 61 The laminate should be initially cured at 50°C and subsequently postcured at 80°C.

postcyclic(al, -cyclically: see POST- B. 1.

post-'dam, *v.* *Dentistry.* [f. POST(ERIOR *a.* and *sb.* + DAM *sb.*[1]] *trans.* and *absol.* To construct a ridge along the upper posterior border of a palatal denture, which will press against the soft palate and form a seal. So **post-'damming** *vbl. sb.*, the construction of such a ridge.

1910 J. W. GREENE *Clin. Course Dental Prosthesis* 47 We must have a way to post-dam, in such cases, without the patient's help. *Ibid.* 50 After you post-dammed its [*sc.* the impression's] rear end, it drops. *Ibid.*, You over-strained the palate in post-damming. **1945** F. W. CRADDOCK *Prosthetic Dentistry* iii. 56. Finally, the upper impression is post-dammed with a further addition of softened wax or compound across the posterior palatal edge. **1953** H. R. B. FENN et al. *Clin. Dental Prosthetics* v. 115 Post-damming is a means of increasing pressure over an area in order, either to control an impression material, or to improve peripheral seal.

Hence **post-dam** (also **post dam**) *sb.*, a ridge of this kind.

1932 E. H. MAUK in Turner & Anthony *Amer. Textbk. Prosthetic Dentistry* (ed. 6) iii. 133 Dr. J. Ewell Neal..makes special reference to the notch or groove in the bone posterior to the tuberosity on each side where the quantity and character of the soft tissue are such as to tolerate, without injury, more 'post-dam' than was usually employed. **1940** M. G. SWENSON *Compl. Dentures* xiii. 167 The anterior line of the post dam area is determined by palpating in the mouth, in order to keep the post dam pressure on soft tissue. **1945** F. W. CRADDOCK *Prosthetic Dentistry* iii. 65 The post-dam extends from tuberosity to tuberosity and will generally be about $\frac{1}{8}$ inch wide and $\frac{1}{32}$ to $\frac{1}{16}$ inch deep. **1953** H. R. B. FENN et al. *Clin. Dental Prosthetics* x. 277 Indirectly the post-dam seal influences phonation, for if it is inadequate the denture may become unseated during the formation of those sounds having an explosive effect. **1976** R. M. BASKER et al. *Prosthetic Treatm. Edentulous Patient* ix. 110 This projection, the post-dam, compresses the palatal mucosa once the denture is placed in the mouth and thus creates a border seal.

post-date (ˈpəʊstdeɪt), *sb.* [f. POST- A. 1 b + DATE *sb.*[2] So F. *postdate*, obs. *postidate.*] A date affixed to a document, or assigned to an event, later than the actual date.

1611 COTGR., *Postidate*, a Post-date. **1701** H. WANLEY in *Phil. Trans.* XXV. 1997 The reason of these Post-Dates was, because..a Book was by how much the Newer, by so much the more Valuable.

post-date (pəʊstˈdeɪt), *v.* [f. POST- A. 1 a + DATE *v.* So mod.F. *postdater* (1752 in Hatz.-Darm.); formerly *postidater* (1549 in Littré).]

1. *trans.* To affix or assign a later than the actual date to (a document, book, event, etc.).

1624 DONNE *Devotions* Medit. ix. (ed. 2) 199 This were to antidate, or to postdate their Consultation, not to giue Phisicke. **1679** C. NESSE *Antichrist* 203 Our own aptness to antedate promises, and to postdate threatnings. **1701** H. WANLEY in *Phil. Trans.* XXV. 1997 Other Books are Post dated that they might be accounted New. **1809** R. LANGFORD *Introd. Trade* 17 Knowing the same [bill] to be post-dated. **1891** C. LOWE in *19th Cent.* Dec. 861 Many of the Berlin newspapers which are published in the evening are post-dated by a day. [So with the French daily papers.]

2. To belong to a later date than (something).

1909 in WEBSTER. **1955** [see FERRICRETE]. **1971** *Daily Tel.* 5 Aug. 8/1 The mineral miracle, which post-dates his first visit to the Antipodes in 1965, has now made it clear that Australia has more to offer..than sun and surf. **1971** I. G. GASS et al. *Understanding Earth* i. 37 (*caption*) The granites post-date metamorphic rocks. **1971** *World Archaeol.* III. 170 The hearth must have post-dated the last use of the pit.

Hence **post-'dated** *ppl. a.*; **post-'dating** *vbl. sb.*

1622 DONNE *Serm.* cxii. (ed. Alford) IV. 571 Prophecy is but antedated Gospel, and Gospel is but post-dated Prophecy. **1797** GODWIN *Enquirer* I. iii. 16 A case more frequent than that of post-dated genius. **1866** CRUMP *Banking* iv. 89 Post-dated cheques, i.e. cheques bearing date subsequent to the actual drawing, are illegal [legal since 1882]. **1963** *N. & Q.* Jan. 16/2 (*heading*) A post-dating. **1968** *Times Lit. Suppl.* 11 Jan. 37/4 There are post-datings, that is, evidence for the later existence of words that OED supposes obsolete.

'post-day. [f. POST *sb.*[2] + DAY *sb.*] The day on which the post or mail is due or departs.

1670 G. H. *Hist. Cardinals* II. I. 107 Every Post-day they send them whole dozens of Pacquets of Letters. **1679** HARWELL in Jenison *Popish Plot* 27, I Have expected to hear from you these three or four post-days past. **1803** MARY CHARLTON *Wife & Mistress* IV. 215 Mrs. Aubrey,.. recollecting that it was foreign post-day, very wisely resolved to return home immediately, and write to her husband. **1890** 'R. BOLDREWOOD' *Col. Reformer* (1891) 329 This particular morning happened to be that of the bi-weekly post-day.

post-deflection: see POST- B. 1.

postdental: see POST- B. 2.

post-depositional: see POST- B. 1.

postdestination, -determined: see POST- A. 1.

post-diastolic, -dicrotic: see POST- B. 1.

postdiction (ˈpəʊstdɪkʃən). [f. POST- A. 1 b + L. *dictiōn-em* a saying, speaking, after PREDICTION *sb.*] (The making of) an assertion or deduction about something in the past. So (as a back-formation) **post'dict** *v. trans.*, to assert or imply something about (something in the past or the present).

1940 J. LAIRD *Theism & Cosmology* v. 169 If, however, the future be indeterminate before it occurs, it cannot be fixed before it occurs. For there is nothing determinate to fix. Hence inferential prediction has quite a different status from inferential post-diction. **1952** *Mind* LXI. 40 Inductive sentences may also postdict a past event, *e.g.*.. 'It is probable that Caesar crossed the Rubicon.' **1960** *Commentary* June 487/1 The Gluecks' five-factor scale in effect *post*-dicted delinquency in the Boston boys from whom it was developed. *Ibid.*, Post-diction is easier than prediction. **1966** *Amer. Speech* XLI. 208 The auxiliary of prediction *will* combines with inflectional ending of postdiction -*ed* to produce a form, *would*. **1971** *Computers & Humanities* V. 192 Discriminant analysis of 30 content variables and 192 editorials..postdicted correctly the masthead of most editorials.

post-digital: see POST- B. 2.

post-di'luvial, *a.* [f. as next + -AL^1.]
a. *Geol.* Posterior to the diluvial or drift period. **b.** *gen.* = POST-DILUVIAN.

1823 BUCKLAND *Reliq. Diluv.* 190 The diluvial and post-diluvial formations I am now speaking of. **1884** J. TAIT *Mind in Matter* (1892) 194 The postdiluvial period presents man with a knowledge of the dangerous tendencies of human nature, and the retributive consequences.

post-diluvian (pəʊstdɪˈl(j)uːvɪən), *a.* and *sb.* [f. POST- B. 1 + L. *diluvi-um* a deluge + -AN. So F. *postdiluvien* adj. (Littré).]
A. *adj.* Existing or occurring after the Flood or Noachian deluge.

1680 LAWSON *Mite into Treasury* 9 The Ante-diluvian and Post-diluvian Patriarchs, that is, the Fathers that lived before and after the Flood. **1759** WESLEY *Wks.* (1872) II. 496 Nothing on the postdiluvian earth could be more pleasant than the road from hence. **1807** G. CHALMERS *Caledonia* I. I. i. 15 The pristine ages of the post-diluvian world. **1877** DAWSON *Orig. World* xiii. 285, I have referred above only to the question of historic or postdiluvian man.

B. *sb.* One who lived, or lives, after the Flood.

1684 T. BURNET *Th. Earth* I. 221 If they allow the post-diluvians to have liv'd six hundred..years, that being clearly beyond the standard of our lives. **1710** STEELE *Tatler* No. 264 ¶5 Methusalem might be half an Hour in telling what a Clock it was; but as for us Postdiluvians, we ought to do every Thing in Hast. **1830** JAS. DOUGLAS *Truths Relig.* iii. (1832) 140 The history of the first postdiluvians has indeed passed away.

†**post-disseisin** (pəʊstdɪˈsiːzɪn). *Old Law.* [f. POST- A. 1 b + DISSEISIN.] A second or subsequent disseisin; also, a writ that lay for him who had a second time been disseised of his lands and tenements by one from whom he had recovered them by novel disseisin.

[**1308–9** *Rolls of Parlt.* I. 276/1 Le dit Henry porta bref nostre Seignur le Roi qe ore est de postdisseisine vers le dit Johan.] **1535** tr. *Natura Brevium* (1544) 128 Yf he be put out of the same tenementes by the same person agaynst whom he hath recouered then he shal haue a post disseyson, and a reddisseyson. **1607** COWELL *Interpr.*, *Post disseisin*..is a writ giuen by the statute of West. 2. cap. 26. and lyeth for him that hauing recouered lands or tenements by (*præcipe quod reddat*) vpon default, or reddition, is againe disseised by the former disseisour. **1848** in WHARTON *Law Lex.*

So †**post-di'sseisor**, one who a second time disseises another of his lands.

1647 N. BACON *Disc. Govt. Eng.* I. lxix. (1739) 183 Redisseisors and Postdisseisors found upon verdict before the Sheriff, Coroners, and Knights, shall be imprisoned. **1768** BLACKSTONE *Comm.* III. x. 188 He shall have a writ of post-disseisin against him; which subjects the post-disseisor to the same penalties as a re-disseisor.

postdoc (pəʊstˈdɒk), *sb.* and *a.* Colloq. abbrev. of POST-DOCTORAL *a.* and *sb.*

1970 *New Scientist* 21 May 368/3 In 1970 55 per cent of them are 'postdocs' as compared with 25 per cent in 1967. *Ibid.* 17 Dec. 519/3 Today the 'post-doc' appointment is referred to as a 'holding pattern'. **1971** *Ibid.* 27 Apr. 264/1 Meanwhile, the team has been enlarged by three new post-docs. **1974** *Nature* 8 Nov. p. xxix/2 (Advt.), Wanted. A postdoc in population biology interested in genetic structure of populations and species. **1978** *Ibid.* 18 May 182/1 [In the EMBL central laboratory] there is also a considerable number of 'fellows'—mainly postdocs who bring their own funds—and visiting scientists.

post-'doctoral, *a.* [POST- B. 1 b.] Of, pertaining to, or for the purpose of advanced research by persons already holding a doctor's degree. Also as *sb.*, one who is undertaking or has undertaken a period of study or research subsequent to obtaining his or her doctor's degree.

1939 WEBSTER Add., Postdoctoral *adj.* **1956** *Nature* 10 Mar. 456/1 As in Britain, there is considerable competition for the junior academic posts and post-doctoral fellowships. **1958** *Times* 8 May 2/3 (Advt.), Applications are invited for post-doctoral grants for research under the general direction of Professor R. N. Hazeldine. **1961** *Times* 26 Sept. 1/4 Postgraduate or post-doctoral work. **1966** *Rep. Comm. Inquiry Univ. Oxf.* I. 127 They [*sc.* junior research fellowships] are awarded to encourage individuals at the D.Phil. or immediate post-doctoral stage. **1971** *Nature* 10 Sept. 87/2 Physicists are the worst hit single group of scientists, with 2·9 per cent of the PhDs and 3·3 per cent of the postdoctorals out of a job. **1977** *Time* 14 Mar. 40/2 During his two-year stint as a post-doctoral fellow at the Max Planck Institute for Biochemistry near Munich, R. G., 27, impressed his boss as 'probably the most diligent man I've ever known'.

post-'doctorate, *a.* [f. POST- B. 1 a + DOCTORATE *sb.*^{1}] = POST-DOCTORAL *a.*

1939 in WEBSTER Add. **1957** [see BOOSTER 2 d]. **1959** *Times* 17 Mar. 2/5 Applicants should be graduates (preferably post-doctorate).

‖**post'dorsolum, -ulum.** *Entom.* [mod.L. f. POST- B. 2 + ***dorsulum**, dim. of *dorsum* back.] 'The middle-piece between the mesophragm and the postscutellum' (Kirby and Spence).

1826 KIRBY & SP. *Entomol.* III. xxxv. 570 The first external piece of the metathorax is the postdorsolum.

post-drill, -driver: see POST *sb.*^{1} 9, *sb.*^{2} 12.

poste, obs. f. POST; var. POUSTIE *Obs.*

‖**postea** (ˈpəʊstiːə). *Law.* [L. *postea* afterwards, lit. 'after those things'; being the first word of the usual beginning of the record.] That part of the record of a civil process which sets forth the proceedings at the trial and the verdict given.

1596 BACON *Max. & Use Com. Law* II. i. (1635) 21 Against the day they should have appeared above, to returne the verdict read in the Court above, which returne is called a *Postea.* *a* **1627** FLETCHER *Wife for Month* v. ii, *Sub-pœnas* and *posteas.* **1709** *Lond. Gaz.* No. 4508/3 A Postea, or Record of Nisi Prius, between Morris, Plaintiff, and Jordan, Defendant, was..delivered by mistake..to a Person who had no Right to receive it. **1768** BLACKSTONE *Comm.* III. xxiv. 386 Whatever, in short, is done subsequent to the joining of issue and awarding the trial, it is entered on record, and is called a *postea.* **1829** BENTHAM *Justice & Cod. Petit.* 154 Clerk of the common bails, posteas, and estreats.

post-'echo. [POST- A. 1 b.] A faint repetition of a loud sound occurring in a recording soon after the original as a result of the accidental transfer of signals in a recording medium. Cf. PRE-ECHO.

1956 G. SLOT *Hi-Fi from Microphone to Ear* xi. 151 The pre-echoes and post-echoes sometimes heard on gramophone records are usually due to this effect. **1962** *Times Lit. Suppl.* 19 Oct. 810/5 The vocal perspective is ingeniously varied to suggest the changing scene, but the fortissimo passages are occasionally marred by post-echo. **1977** *Gramophone* Mar. 1476/1 Each layer of tape tends to magnetize its recorded signal on to the adjacent layers during storage—in the process known as 'print-through'—to produce faint pre-echoes and post-echoes.

posted (ˈpəʊstɪd), *a.* [f. POST *sb.*^{1} + -ED^2.] Furnished with or having posts. Also in comb., as ***four-posted*** (see FOUR C. 2).

1572 ABP. PARKER *Corr.* (Parker Soc.) 412 This shop..is made like the terrace, fair railed and posted, fit for men to stand upon in any triumph or shew. **1614** *Inv.* in *Trans. Cumb. & West. Arch. Soc.* III. 115 One posted bedd with teaster and curtaines. **1798** *Hull Advertiser* 17 Nov. 2/2 A good and substantial wind corn posted mill. **1828** *Life Planter Jamaica* 35 The furniture consisted of a table and a chair, with a posted bed.

'posted, *ppl. a.*^{1} [f. POST *v.*^{1} + -ED^1.]
†**1.** Sent or gone away quickly like a post; departed quickly. *Obs.*

1602 MUNDAY tr. *Palmerin of Eng.* I. i, To recount thy posted pleasure and also to thinke on thy present ensuing paine.

2. Carried by or sent through the post; placed in a post-office letter-box for dispatch.

1845 MCCULLOCH *Taxation* II. vii. (1852) 318 There has been a great increase in the number of posted letters.

3. Entered in a ledger or account-book.

1771 LUCKOMBE *Hist. Print.* 268 Full-points serve..to lead and to connect the posted Article with its contingent valuation.

'posted, *ppl. a.*^{2} [f. POST *v.*^{2} + -ED^1.] Cut into the form of a post; 'squared': see POST *v.*^{2} 1.

'posted, *ppl. a.*^{3} [f. POST *v.*^{3} + -ED^1.]
1. Set in position, stationed, arranged.

1796 *Instr. & Reg. Cavalry* (1813) 144 The point where the head of a column enters an alignement, and which is marked by a posted person. **1887** RUSKIN *Præterita* II. 190 We drove under some posted field-batteries into Basle.

2. Pasted or fixed up in a prominent place, as a public notice.

1897 *Daily News* 8 June 3/3 The posted announcement that the 'jumping competitions would begin at three o'clock' brought numbers on to the grassy banks. **1898** *Ibid.* 10 May 6/6 The posted certificate at the booking-office [of the Alhambra]..ordered the dancer complete rest 'for her voice'.

post-'editor. [POST- A. 1 b.] Someone who edits text that has been produced or processed by a machine.

1953 A. D. & K. H. V. BOOTH *Automatic Digital Calculators* xvii. 206 Reiffler suggests the use of a pre-editor who need not know the (*T.L.*) at all but who, reading his own language (our *F.L.*), eliminates from the text all such alternatives... In the same way a post-editor might be used to turn the translation into acceptable *T.L.* **1960** E. DELAVENAY *Introd. Machine Transl.* 121 For each Russian polysemantic word the machine has given alternative translations; the one selected by the post-editor has been given first. **1966** D. G. HAYS in *Automatic Transl. of Lang.* (NATO Summer School, Venice, 1962) 146 Before text reaches the posteditor, it has been put through automatic dictionary lookup and automatic sentence-structure determination.

So **post-edit** *v. trans.*, to edit in such circumstances; **post-'editing** *vbl. sb.*

1957 *Year's Work Eng. Stud.* 1955 41/2 His suggestions for mechanized translation involve a much heavier reliance upon 'post-editing' than experts at present feel they need to assume. **1960** E. DELAVENAY *Introd. Machine Transl.* iii. 29 He postulated the necessity both for pre-editing texts before translation and for post-editing them when translated. **1962** *Times Lit. Suppl.* 20 Apr. 268/3 The machine output will have to be 'post-edited', before submission of the finished product to the readers. **1971** *Computers & Humanities* VI. 45 A printer's computer tape would probably require some post-editing.

postee, variant of POUSTIE *Obs.*, power.

‖**po'steen, po'stīn.** Also *erron.* poshteen, -tin. [Pers. *postīn* leathern, f. *pōst* skin, hide.] 'An Afghan leathern pelisse, generally of sheepskin with the fleece on' (Yule).

1815 ELPHINSTONE *Acc. Caubul* (1842) II. 59 At that season, they also wear brown and Grey woollen great coats, and posteens. **1862** *Punjab Trade Rep.* 65 (Y.) Otter skins from the Hills and Kashmir, worn as Postīns by the Yarkandis. **1882** MRS. B. M. CROKER *Proper Pride* II. ii. 25 The head-man of [an Afghan] village, in a richly-embroidered poshteen. **1895** KIPLING *Day's Work* (1898) 212 William, wrapped in a *poshteen*—silk-embroidered sheepskin jacket trimmed with rough astrakhan—looked out with moist eyes and nostrils that dilated joyously. **1904** *Blue bk. Papers relating to Thibet*, We would recommend that both escort and support should have clothing on winter scale with poshtins for sentries. **1910** *Encycl. Brit.* I. 314/1 Poshtins (sheepskin clothing) and the many varieties of camel and goat's hair cloth..are still the chief local products of that part of Afghanistan. **1961** P. FLEMING *Bayonets to Lhasa* xi. 151 Saved from death by his thick poshteen. **1973** 'W. HAGGARD' *Old Masters* viii. 99 Bentinck was wearing moleskin trousers and..a sort of poshteen which would keep out the cold.

post-Ein'steinian, *a.* [POST- B. 1 b.] Subsequent to the work of Albert Einstein (see EINSTEIN); involving or pertaining to concepts developed later than the theories of relativity.

1938 S. CHASE *Tyranny of Words* viii. 89 Bridgman develops various concepts for 'length' in post-Einsteinian terms. **1953** *Authentic Sci. Fiction Monthly* Apr. 137 With such rare exceptions as Bradbury, writers seem..to accept a relativity of moral standards which, while it may display a misleading harmony with the post-Einsteinian scientific outlook, is in fact simply a well of poison. **1973** B. MAGEE *Popper* vii. 97 Post-Einsteinian physics,..post-Freudian psychology,..post-Keynesian economics,..post-Frege logic.

†**postel^1.** *Obs.* Also 2–4 postle, 7 postil. [a. OF. *postel* (1160–74 in Godef. *Compl.*), mod.F. *poteau* post, dim. of OF. *post*: see POST *sb.*^{1} and -EL^2.] A door-post, gate-post.

c **1175** *Lamb. Hom.* 127 þa postles and þet ouerslaht of ure huse. *c* **1205** LAY. 1316 þa comen heo to þan bunnen þa Hercules makede mid muchele his strengðe þat weoren postles longe of marmon stane stronge. *a* **1300** *Cursor M.* 14980 Bunden þat þai soght þis ass þai fand bi a postel. **1377** LANGL. *P. Pl.* B. XVI. 54 þe powere of þis postes [*MS. C.* postles]. *a* **1631** DONNE *Serm.* cvii. (ed. Alford) IV. 459 The Blood of that Lamb is not sprinkled upon the Postils of that door.

†**postel^2.** *Obs. rare.* [ad. OF. *posterle*, *potelle* (1355, 1419 in Godef. *Compl.*):—late L. *posterula* POSTERN.] A postern or small gate.

c **1400** *Cursor M.* 7675 (Cott.) Bot micol vte bi night him lete, Vte at a priue dern postel [*Gött. & Trin.* posterne].

postem, -e, variants of POSTUME *Obs.*

postembryonal, -embryonic: see POST- B. 1.

post-emergence: see POST- B. 1.

'post 'entry, 'post-entry. [POST- A. 1 b.]
1. A subsequent or late entry.

1888 *Pall Mall G.* 31 May 10/2 The entries..show..a decrease on last year's total of 122, which may possibly be made up yet by post entries. **1888** *Daily News* 9 July 5/8 Post entries have brought the number of probable competitors up to something more than the average.

2. *spec.* **a.** An additional or supplemental entry, in the manifest of a vessel, of an item or items of dutiable merchandise omitted at the time of the entry of the vessel at the custom-house. The warrant issued on this is a **post-warrant.**

1662 *Order Ho. Comm. as to Customs* (1663) 14 Post-Entries Inward to passe without Fee under five shillings. **1725** *Lond. Gaz.* No. 6433/1 They..have been..permitted to make Post-Entries thereof with the Officer of Excise. **1812** J. SMYTH *Pract. of Customs* (1821) 18 When the Post Warrant is received, the date and number of each Post Entry must be inserted. **1832–52** MCCULLOCH *Dict. Comm.* 1047 When goods are weighed or measured, and the merchant has got an account thereof at the Custom-house, and finds his entry, already made, too small, he must make a post or additional entry for the surplusage, in the same manner as the first was done... A merchant is always in time, prior to the clearing of the vessel, to make his post.

b. A subsequent entry in book-keeping.

1798 BAY *Amer. Law Rep.* (1809) I. 33 No entry was made ..except a post entry, some time afterwards. **1847** WEBSTER, *Post-entry*..2. In *book-keeping*, an additional or subsequent entry.

post-'entry, *a.* [POST- B. 1 a.] Occurring after entry; *spec.* applied to a closed shop in which new employees are required to join a union after appointment. Cf. PRE-ENTRY *a.*

1964 [see PRE-ENTRY *a.*]. **1972** H. WILLIAMSON *Trade Unions* (ed. 2) ii. 22 In a post-entry closed shop membership of a particular union is only insisted upon after the worker has been appointed. **1976** *Milton Keynes Express* 16 July 13/2 (Advt.), Clerical Assistant (Income Section)... National conditions; superannuation; five day week; post-entry training facilities. **1978** R. TAYLOR *Fifth Estate* i. 18

Employers..have written post-entry closed-shop clauses into their collective agreements with unions.

poster[1] ('pəʊstə(r)). [f. POST *v.*[1] + -ER[1].]

1. One who travels 'post', expeditiously, or swiftly. Also *fig.* Now *rare* or *Obs.*

1605 SHAKS. *Macb.* I. iii. 33 The weyward Sisters, hand in hand, Posters of the Sea and Land, Thus doe goe, about, about. **1651** DAVENANT *Gondibert* III. vi. xxxviii, At this, Goltho alights as swiftly post As Posters mount. **1816** KEATINGE *Trav.* I. Pref. 9 A poster of roads will write rapidly; a sick man querulously [etc.]. *a* **1845** HOOD *Lament of Toby* i, O heavy day! O day of woe! To misery a poster.

†**2.** A messenger, a carrier of news. *Obs.*

1605 J. MELVILL *Diary* (Wodrow Soc.) 606 The noble poster of newis athort the world.

3. A post-horse.

1797 H. NEWDIGATE *Let.* 9 July in A. E. Newdigate-Newdegate *Cheverels* (1898) xiii. 181 A good dinner..was ready to come upon Table when yᵉ Posters arrived. **1817** T. L. PEACOCK *Melincourt* iii, Mr. Hippy's travelling chariot was rattled up to the door by four high-mettled posters from the nearest inn. **1849** THACKERAY *Pendennis* xv, There were no cattle, save the single old pair of posters.

4. One who posts a letter.

1884 *Manch. Exam.* 11 June 5/4 It will be the duty of the officer in attendance to stamp the form with the office stamp, and hand it back to the poster.

poster[2] ('pəʊstə(r)). [f. POST *v.*[2] + -ER[1].]

1. One who posts or sticks up bills; a bill-poster.

1864 [see *bill-poster*, BILL *sb.*[3] 11].

2. A placard posted or displayed in a public place as an announcement or advertisement.

pictorial or ***picture poster***, a placard consisting mainly of a picture or illustration.

1838 DICKENS *Nich. Nick.* xxx, We'll have posters out the first thing in the morning. **1861** *Illustr. Lond. News* 6 July 3/3 A most seditious 'poster' with which all the walls..were placarded. **1883** BLACK *Shandon Bells* viii, The poster, scarlet letters on a white ground, was effective. **1902** *Westm. Gaz.* 9 June 2/3 By his cartoon for a poster, 'The Woman in White', one of his biographers states that he [Fred. Walker] may be said to have started the fashion of artistic advertising in this country.

3. *attrib.* and *Comb.*, as ***poster art***, ***artist***, ***cloth***, ***-collector***, ***design***, ***-designer***, ***-designing***, ***-hoarding***, ***-making***, ***panel***, ***-pilfering***; ***poster-like*** adj.; **poster colour** = *poster paint*; **poster-maniac**, one who has a mania for collecting posters; **poster paint**, an opaque paint with a water-soluble binder such as is used on posters; **poster paper**, paper used in bills or posters; **poster session**, a meeting of scientists at which their work is represented by displayed pictures (see quot. 1977).

1920 HARDIE & SABIN *War Posters* ii. 7 *Poster art and pictorial art have essentially different aims. **1974** *Listener* 28 Feb. 283/3 Shostakovich's Twelfth Symphony. 'Poster art' it may be; but if so, some more Russian posters, please. **1896** *Daily News* 28 Nov. 6/1 Portraits of some of the leading *poster artists, with selections from their works. **1899** *Westm. Gaz.* 11 Mar. 2/1 It is said..that the new custom of *poster-collecting causes persons to strip these designs from the walls when opportunity offers. **1895** *Chap-Book* III. 471 For the benefit of *Poster Collectors a special edition of fifty copies has been printed on Japan paper. **1925** *Studio* (Art & Publicity No.) Autumn (verso front cover), The 'Kingsway' *Poster Colours..supplied in Tubes and Glass Pots. **1973** Poster colour [see POP *a.* (*sb.*[8]) 3]. **1920** HARDIE & SABIN *War Posters* ii. 14 The number of *poster designs from his hand is at least fifty. **1970** *Oxf. Compan. Art* 900/1 English poster design in the 20th c. varies between the illustrative..and the work of great merit done for Shell-Mex. **1901** W. S. ROGERS *Bk. of Poster* xix. 133 The standard of art-education amongst the *poster designers is higher than in this country. **1935** [see *copy-writer*]. **1954** T. ECKERSLEY *Poster Design* 7 The illustrations in this book are by leading poster designers. **1901** W. S. ROGERS *Bk. of Poster* ix. 129 The scope of this work does not embrace the idea of treating the subject of *poster designing at any great length. **1933** L. RICHMOND *Technique of Poster* p. v, Poster designing is a serious but most interesting art. **1906** *Athenæum* 9 June 710/1 Whose work amongst that of our own painters seemed somewhat abrupt and *posterlike. **1895** *Pall Mall G.* 16 Dec. 8/1 An exquisitely clever and amusing design, that would take the blue ribbon, judged by the points of artistic *poster-making. **1895** *Standard* 23 Nov. 5/1 There exist two or three *catalogues raisonnés* which are indispensable to the *postermaniac. **1939** W. CLEMENCE *Man. Poster-craft* xii. 92 Good quality flat *poster paints, thinned with a little turpentine..blend well, are smooth of application, and dry in excellent time and condition. **1974** I. MURDOCH *Sacred & Profane Love Machine* 103 She..laid out his coloured pencils, his poster paints, brushes, water. **1929** *Encycl. Brit.* XVIII. 319/2 On the *poster panels of to-day, in the United States, may be seen the work of Harrison Fisher. **1901** J. BEVERIDGE *Paper-makers' Pocket Bk.* i. 26 German classification and sizes of papers..Affichenpapiere (thin *poster paper). **1959** R. HOSTETTLER et al. *Technical Terms Printing Industry* (ed. 3) 130/2 *Poster paper*,..papier pour affiches. **1976** *Physics Bull.* Aug. 335/3 Although it is clear that the technique derives from the scientific exhibition, the exact origin of *poster sessions is unknown. **1977** *Sci. Amer.* Apr. 51/2 (Advt.), All contributed 'papers' are to be given in poster sessions, where from a visual display one decides whether to stop and exchange thoughts person to person.

poster[3] ('pəʊstə(r)). *Rugby Football.* [f. POST *sb.*[1] + -ER[1].] A ball that passes directly over the top of one of the goal-posts.

1867 *Routledge's Handbk. Football* 35 If the ball..rises directly over the end of one of the posts, it is called a *poster*, and is no goal. **1930** *Times* 14 Mar. 7/1 He played in three International matches, dropped a goal in two, and scoring [*sic*] a 'poster' in the other.

postered ('pəʊstəd), *a.* [f. POSTER[2] + -ED[2].] Depicted or described on posters; adorned or disfigured with posters.

1916 S. KAYE-SMITH *Sussex Gorse* III. 173 Rye electors were confronted with the postered virtues and vices of Captain Mackinnon (Radical) and Colonel MacDonald (Conservative). **1927** *Scots Observer* 7 May 9/2 The real blemishes of Glasgow are raw and postered gable-ends, untended waste grounds, [etc.].

‖**poste restante** (pɔstrɛstɑ̃t). [Fr., = remaining (at the) post office.] A direction written upon a letter which is to remain at the post office till called for; in English use, transferred to the department in a post office in which letters for travellers or visitors are kept till applied for.

1768 SARAH OSBORN *Pol. & Soc. Lett.* 9 Feb. (1890) 181 Your brother's letter to you Postrestant at Turin will acquaint you of his success. **1777** in Jesse *Geo. Selwyn & Contemp.* (1844) III. 230 You will address your answer to this to Paris, *Poste Restante.* **1816** BYRON *Let. to Moore* 5 Dec., Direct to me here, *poste restante.* **1822** W. IRVING in *Life & Lett.* (1864) II. 131 Do write to me, and direct your letters 'poste restante, Dresden'. **1844** E. FITZGERALD *Lett.* (1889) I. 129 As you give me no particular direction, I write to you at the Post Restante there [Florence]. **1880** *Brit. Postal Guide* 92 There is a Poste Restante both at the General Post Office St. Martin's-le-Grand, and at the Charing Cross Post Office, where letters 'to be called for' can be obtained between the hours of 9 A.M. and 5 P.M.

†**poster'ganeous**, *a.* *Obs.* *rare*⁻⁰. [f. L. *postergāne-us* (Cælius Aurel.) (f. *post tergum* behind the back) + -OUS.]

1656 BLOUNT *Glossogr.*, *Posterganeous*..belonging to the backside or hinder part of the body.

posterial (pɒ'stɪərɪəl), *a.* *rare.* [irreg. f. L. *poster-us* coming after or behind + -IAL.]

1. Pertaining to the hinder parts or posteriors.

1432-50 tr. *Higden* (Rolls) V. 171 His partes posterialle, or the instrumente of egestion. *Ibid.* IV. 371. **1831** CARLYLE *Sart. Res.* III. x, No license of fashion can allow a man of delicate taste to adopt the posterial luxuriance of a Hottentot.

2. Turned towards the hinder side.

1866 TATE *Brit. Mullusks* iv. 205 The apex is posterial and sinistral.

posterior (pɒ'stɪərɪə(r)), *a.* and *sb.* (*adv.*) Also 6-8 -our. [a. L. *posterior*, compar. of *poster-us* or *poster* coming after, following, future, f. *post* prep., after. Perh. repr. AF. **posteriour* = F. *postérieur* (15th c. in Hatz.-Darm.).]

A. *adj.*

1. a. Later, subsequent in time; opposed to *prior.*

1534 MORE *Treat. Passion* Wks. 1308/2 The posteriour Greekes saye, that Chryste dydde not eate his Paschall lambe in the daye appoynted by the lawe. **1653** LD. VAUX tr. *Godeau's St. Paul* A ij, The swelling criticismes, or vaine Philosophy of posteriour writers. **1756-82** J. WARTON *Ess. Pope* (ed. 4) I. iii. 125 The precepts of the art of poesy were posterior to practise. **1790** PALEY *Horæ Paul.* Rom. ii. 16 The Epistle to the Romans is posterior even to the second Epistle to the Corinthians. **1833** LYELL *Princ. Geol.* III. 68 Proofs of the posterior origin of the lava. **1884** D. HUNTER tr. *Reuss's Hist. Canon* i. 3 Found only in the literature posterior to the exile.

b. *Statistics.* Applied to the result of a calculation made subsequent to, and in consideration of, some observation(s); ***posterior probability***, the probability that a hypothesis is true, calculated in the light of relevant observations. Opp. PRIOR *a.* (*adv.*) A. c.

1921 *Phil. Mag.* XLII. 387 Even if the prior probabilities of two laws with different domains are notably different, the effect of several verifications of each is able to make the posterior probabilities of the two laws practically equal to each other and to unity. **1931** H. JEFFREYS *Sci. Inference* ii. 18 The posterior probability of p is the prior probability of p divided by the prior probability of the consequence. **1943** M. G. KENDALL *Adv. Theory Statistics* I. vii. 179 A further difficulty arises if θ can lie in an infinite range, for then Bayes' postulate apparently leads to the conclusion that prior probabilities in any finite range are zero and hence so are posterior probabilities. **1972** A. W. F. EDWARDS *Likelihood* iv. 46 The posterior odds of two hypotheses on some data is equal to the product of the prior odds and the likelihood ratio. *Ibid.* iv. 48 In practice it is determined by the fact that both the prior and the posterior distributions of θ integrate to unity. **1977** *Lancet* 13 Aug. 339/1 If the sister of a hæmophiliac initially has two unaffected boys, the 'posterior' probability of her being a carrier falls from 1/2 to 1/5.

2. Coming after in a series or order.

1626 BACON *Sylva* §115 So it is manifest, that where the anteriour body giveth way, as fast as the posteriour cometh on, it maketh no noise, be the motion never so great, or swift. **1851** NICHOL *Archit. Heav.* 286 While Man..believes..often that the line is straight—seeing neither its anterior nor its posterior convolutions.

3. Hinder; situated behind, or farther back than something else. Opposed to *anterior.*

Especially frequent in Anatomy in reference to the hinder of two organs or parts.

1632 LITHGOW *Trav.* II. 52 The belly of one ioyned with the posterior part of the other. **1741** MONRO *Anat. Nerves* (ed. 3) 47 The posterior clinoid Processes of the sphenoid Bone. **1794** S. WILLIAMS *Vermont* 90 Two bags, situated in the posterior parts of the body. **1831** BREWSTER *Optics* xxxv. 288 The two parts into which the iris divides the eye are called the *anterior* and the *posterior* chambers. **1868** DUNCAN tr. *Figuier's Insect W.* Introd. 7 The legs are called anterior, posterior, and intermediate.

B. *sb.* **1.** *pl.* Those who come after; descendants, posterity; rarely *sing.* a descendant.

1534 MORE *Treat. Passion* Wks. 1309/2 When I speake of the church of Grece in this errour: I speake but of the posteriours. **1560** *Goodli Hist. Lucres & Eurialus* (1567) G iv, Hys posteriars shall shewe for theyr noblenes a gylted bull. **1816** SCOTT *Old Mort.* xxviii, Neither he, nor his posteriors from generation to generation, shall sit upon it ony mair. **1889** in *Spectator* 9 Nov. 634/2 'No ways infarior ..And lineal postarior to Ould Aysculapius'. [Anglo-Irish.]

2. a. *pl.* The hinder parts of the body; the buttocks. Now usu. *sing.* The rump or backside (of a person). *colloq.* [After late L. *posteriōra.*]

1619 DRUMM. OF HAWTH. *Conv. B. Jonson* Wks. (1711) 225 A poor pedantick schoolmaster, sweeping his living from the posteriors of little children. *c* **1645** HOWELL *Lett.* (1650) II. 8 You know what answer the Fox gave the Ape when he would have borrowed part of his taile to cover his posteriors. **1706** E. WARD *Wooden World Diss.* (1708) 102 He drops upon his Knees or Posteriors. **1802** BINGLEY *Anim. Biog.* (1813) I. 70 The Pigmy Ape... The posteriors are naked and callous. **1936** G. B. SHAW *Simpleton* Prologue ii. 27 He shoots his foot against the E.O.'s posterior and sends him over the cliff. **1976-7** *Sea Spray* (N.Z.) Dec./Jan. 90/1 (Advt.), It is soft so that a crewman winding the spinnaker sheet winch down aft can rest his posterior on it.

†**b.** The hinder part or back side (*of* anything).

1646 G. DANIEL *Poems* Wks. (Grosart) I. 41 He oft could take Things from th' Posteriors of an Almanacke, Very behoofull to the Regimen Of health.

†**3.** *pl.* The later part. (*facetious*) *Obs.* *rare*⁻¹.

1588 SHAKS. *L.L.L.* v. i. 94 To congratulate the Princesse at her Pauilion, in the posteriors of this day, which the rude multitude call the after-noone. *Ibid.* 96.

C. *adv.* Subsequently; posteriorly.

1826 G. S. FABER *Diffic. Romanism* (1853) 43 He wrote posterior to both these Councils. **1830** PUSEY *Hist. Enquiry* II. 153 [He] wrote posterior to all these authors.

posterioric (pɒstɪərɪ'ɒrɪk), *a.* *rare*⁻¹. [f. A POSTERIORI + -IC.] Of *a posteriori* origin. Hence **posteri'orically** *adv.*, in an *a posteriori* way.

1895 *Athenæum* 7 Dec. 796/1 The knowledge acquired may be named prioric or posterioric, according as the one condition or the other is distinguished. *Ibid.*, A conclusion may be prioric though drawn from premises obtained posteriorically.

posterio'ristic, *a.* [f. POSTERIOR + -ISTIC.] Of or belonging to Aristotle's two books of Posterior Analytics; as ***posterioristic doctrine***, a doctrine contained in these; ***posterioristic universal***: see quot. Opposed to PRIORISTIC. Hence **posterio'ristically** *adv.*

c **1600** *Timon* IV. iii. (Shaks. Soc.) 67 Thou art moued formally, prioristically in the thing considered, not posterioristically in the manner of considering. **1902** *Baldwin's Dict. Philos.* II. 740/1 *Posterioristic dictum de omni* and *Posterioristic universal*: universal predication as defined by Aristotle in the fourth chapter of the first book of the *Posterior Analytics*, where it is defined as the negative of the particular:..'I call that universally predicated (*de omni*) which is not in something, in something not, nor now is, now is not'.

posteriority (pɒstɪərɪ'ɒrɪtɪ). [prob. a. AF. **posteriorité*, ad. med.L. *posteriōritās* (13th c. in Bracton), f. L. *posterior* POSTERIOR: see -ITY. Cf. F. *Postériorité* (15th c. in Littré).]

1. The state or quality of being later or subsequent in time. Opposed to *priority.*

1387-8 T. USK *Test. Love* III. iv. (Skeat) l. 166 All thinges, that been in diuers times, and in diuers places temporel, without posteriorite or priorite, been closed ther in perpetuall nowe. **1587** GOLDING *De Mornay* (1592) 131 By a certeine maner and kinde of posterioritie. **1683** CAVE *Ecclesiastici* 319 The Preposition..implies..a Posteriority in point of time. **1726** AYLIFFE *Parergon* 110 This Priority or Posteriority of Birth comes no less in enquiry to the Ordinary. **1885** SALMON *Introd. N.T.* xi. 242 To establish the posteriority of two of our Canonical Gospels.

†**b.** *Law.* See quot. 1607. *Obs.*

1523 FITZHERB. *Surv.* 23 b, If the tenaunt holde of two lordes by knight seruyce, of one by priorite and of another by posteryorite and dye, the lorde that the tenaunt holdeth of by priorite shall haue the warde of the body, be it heyre male or heyre female. **1607** COWELL *Interpr.*, *Posteriority* is a word of comparison and relation in tenure, the correlatiue whereof is *prioritie.* For a man holding lands or tenements of two lords, holdeth of his auncienter Lord by prioritie, and of his later Lord by posterioritie.

2. Inferiority in order, rank, or dignity. Now *rare.*

1534 in W. H. Turner *Select. Rec. Oxford* (1880) 123 That the..Chaun[r] and Schollers might be befor them.., and so to spite the said Mayʳ and Comminaltie from their prioritie to posterioritie. **1644** MAXWELL *Prerog. Chr. Kings* xv. 146 How can a Society be imagined without order? and how order without priority and posteriority? **1678** CUDWORTH *Intell. Syst.* I. iv. §36. 598 There must of necessity be..a priority and posteriority..of dignity as well as Order amongst them. **1704** NORRIS *Ideal World* II. xiii. 571, I mean that order of priority or posteriority, according to which this application is to be made.

†**3.** The back, the back parts of the body. *Obs.* *rare*⁻¹.

c **1532** DEWES *Introd. Fr.* II. CC iij, Moyses by the graunt of god dyd merite to se his posterioritie [F. *merita de ueoir sa posteriorité*: cf. Exod. xxxiii. 23 *mea posteriora*], the whiche is to vnderstande his workes.

posteriorly (pɒˈstɪərɪəlɪ), *adv.* [f. POSTERIOR + -LY².]

1. In a posterior position: behind; to the rear.

1597 A. M. tr. *Guillemeau's Fr. Chirurg.* * iv b, The two doe demonstrate all externall partes, as well anteriorlye as posteriorlye. **1758** J. S. *Le Dran's Observ. Surg.* (1771) 141 Below the Armpit, a little posteriorly. **1843** HUMPHREYS *Brit. Moths* 9 These stripes are blue anteriorly, and white posteriorly. **1875** HOUGHTON *Sketches Brit. Ins.* 14 An oesophagus terminating posteriorly in a widened cavity.

†**2.** At a later time, subsequently. *Obs.*

1799 KIRWAN *Geol. Ess.* 163 Rifts posteriorly choaked up. **1849** in B. Gregory *Side Lights Confl. Meth.* 457 That pledge was given.. posteriorly.

†**posteriˈorums**, *sb. pl. Obs.* [L. *posteriōrum*, gen. pl. of *posterior* later, hinder, with Eng. pl. *-s.*]

1. The Posterior Analytics of Aristotle.

1593 G. HARVEY *Pierce's Super.* Wks. (Grosart) II. 114 As very a crab-fish at an Ergo, as euer crawled-ouer Carters Logique, or the Posteriorums of Iohannes de Lapide. **1628** T. SPENCER *Logick* 29 Aristotle makes them these foure, as wee may finde, in the 11. chapter of the second booke of his Posteriorums.

2. The posteriors: see POSTERIOR B. 2. (*ludicrous.*)

1607 R. C[AREW] tr. *Estienne's World of Wonders* 262 Shewing her posteriorums which way soeuer she went. **1653** URQUHART *Rabelais* I. xliv, My Lord Posterior you shall have it upon your posteriorums.

†**poˈsterious**, *a. Obs. rare*⁻¹. [irreg. f. L. *poster-us* coming after, or *posterior*, *-ius* comp.: see -OUS.] Subsequent, posterior.

1672 *Mem. Fraser of Brae* in *Sel. Biog.* (Wodrow Soc.) II. 303 Election by the people is posterious to this call of God.

posterish (ˈpəʊstərɪʃ), *a.* [f. POSTER² + -ISH¹.] Characteristic or suggestive of a poster or posters. So **ˈposterishness**.

1930 *Aberdeen Press & Jrnl.* 25 Apr. 6 Norah Neilson Gray still seems to us to be straying too much towards a sweet but too pretty posterishness in her work. **1931** *Times Lit. Suppl.* 25 June (Suppl.) p. vi/4 Several cover-designs achieve posterish attractiveness. **1947** *Sat. Rev. Lit.* (U.S.) 1 Mar. 30 Figures in a flat, cylindrical, posterish style. **1958** *Times* 15 Dec. 3/5 There is a painting in Sickert's posterish vein. **1967** *Listener* 16 Mar. 355/2 The formalized, abstracted figures have become posterish and realistic like those in a Soviet hero painting.

posterist (ˈpəʊstərɪst). [f. POSTER² + -IST.] A designer of posters; a poster-artist.

1901 W. S. ROGERS *Bk. of Poster* p. v, If I may seem too enthusiastic on the side of Continental work, it is from no lack of sympathy with British posterists. **1968** *Times* 21 Dec. 20/4 The lack of sensitivity apparent in his academic studies ..was almost an asset to a posterist. **1972** *Guardian* 19 June 11/4 The best known posterist of the period was John Hassall... His most famous design, 'Skegness is *so* Bracing', was..designed in 1909.

posterity (pɒˈstɛrɪtɪ). [ME. *posterite*, a. F. *postérité* (14th c. in Hatz.-Darm.), ad. L. *posteritas* the condition of coming after, after time, posterity, f. *poster-us* coming after: see -ITY.]

1. The descendants collectively of any person; all who have proceeded from a common ancestor. Also *pl.* (obs.: quot. 1676); also *fig.* (quot. 1847).

1387 TREVISA *Higden* (Rolls) VII. 115 þe monk asked of þe posterite of Edward and of þe successours of reignynge. *c* **1450** *Mirour Saluacioun* 743 Crist moght noght be borne of hire posteritee. **1535** COVERDALE *Job* v. 25 Thy posterite shalbe as the grasse vpon the earth. **1553** EDEN *Treat. Newe Ind.* (Arb.) 24 They ioyne in mariage..for ye encrease of posteritie. **1676** ALLEN *Address Nonconf.* 188 The hazard we run of exposing our posterities to lose the substance by our contending for circumstance. *a* **1727** NEWTON *Chronol. Amended* i. (1728) 118 The Kingdom of Argos became divided among the posterity of Temenus. **1847** EMERSON *Repr. Men, Plato* ¶2 No wife, no children had he, and the thinkers of all civilized nations are his posterity.

2. †**a.** A later generation (with *plural*). *Obs.* **b.** All succeeding generations (collectively).

1535 COVERDALE *Ps.* lxxi[i]. 17 His name shal remayne vnder the sonne amonge the posterites, which shal be blessed thorow him. **1560** DAUS tr. *Sleidane's Comm.* 201 Hys memoryal shal endure to the last posterytie. **1581** PETTIE *Guazzo's Civ. Conv.* I. (1586) A vij b, Why should not we doe as much for the posteritie, as we haue receiued of the antiquitie? **1594** T. B. *La Primaud. Fr. Acad.* II. 29 It was necessary that some should write thereof for their good, as also for the benefit of posteritie. **1606** G. W[OODCOCKE] *Hist. Ivstine* VIII. 39 Their old household Goddes, to which many posterities had giuen their deuotion. **1609** TOURNEUR *Funeral Poem* 4 And that shall never dye But with it live to all Posteritie. **1650** S. CLARKE *Eccl. Hist.* I. (1654) 28 Yet his learning is admired by all Posterities. **1758** JOHNSON *Idler* No. 3 ¶5 The ocean and the sun will last our time, and we may leave posterity to shift for themselves. **1800** COLQUHOUN *Comm. Thames* ix. 284 They will deserve the Thanks of the Nation, and the Gratitude of Posterity. **1899** *Daily News* 2 May 6/6 'Posterity has done nothing for us. Why should we do anything for posterity?' Such is the simple creed of neo-Conservative finance.

†**3.** = POSTERIORITY 1. *Obs. rare.*

1531 *Pilgr. Perf.* (W. de W.) 199 b, In god is no accidentall thynge nor priorite or posterite, ne ony order of tyme.

posterize (ˈpəʊstəraɪz), *v. Photogr.* [f. POSTER² + -IZE.] *trans.* To print (a photograph) so that there is only a small number of different tones. Also *absol.* Hence **posteriˈzation**, the process of posterizing; **ˈposterized** *ppl. a.*, **ˈposterizing** *vbl. sb.*

1943 C. I. JACOBSON *Enlarging* (ed. 4) 278 Posterising Photographs... One method published by R. W. Wade, achieves something more than simple tone-separation. It does produce in addition, a 'posterised' picture, which is.. a picture in which all the elements are built up out of one or other of four tones only... The range of subjects suitable for posterising is practically unlimited. **1948** F. H. SMITH *Photographs & Printer* 135 The photo-engraver can readily reproduce a photograph which has already been posterised. **1950** O. R. CROY *Compl. Art of Printing & Enlarging* ii. 72 (*caption*) Posterization. The print consists only of three tones. **1977** R. HATTERSLEY *Photographic Printing* xviii. 132 Once you know how to make high-contrast negatives with Kodalith..it is relatively easy to posterize. *Ibid.* 133 With four or more tones a posterized print may not even look posterized. Instead it may look like an ordinary print with something just a wee bit odd about the tones. **1977** J. HEDGECOE *Photographer's Handbk.* 245 Posterization or tone separation means turning a normal, continuous tone photograph into an image consisting of clearly distinguished areas of flat tone.

postern (ˈpəʊstən, ˈpɒ-), *sb.* (*a.*) Also 4 postorne, 5–6 postrene, -rem, 6 -ron, -rum, -rome. [ME. a. OF. *posterne* (*Rom. de Rose* 1160–76; mod.F. *poterne*), altered from OF. *posterle*:—late L. *posterula* a back way (Ammianus *a* 400), a small back door or gate (S. Cassian *a* 450), in med.L. *posterla*, *posterna* (Du Cange), dim. of *poster-us* that is behind.]

1. A back door; a private door; any door or gate distinct from the main entrance; a side way.

c **1290** *S. Eng. Leg.* I. 196/98 þe Duyk..a-scapede a-wey bi one posterne stille liche. **13..** *K. Alis.* 4593 (Bodl. MS.) Darrie þerwhiles stale away By a Posterne [*v.r.* postorne] a pryue way. *c* **1440** *Generydes* 2559 Ther was A postrene yssuyng owt of the Citee. **1513** BRADSHAW *St. Werburge* II. 1350 Closed at euery ende with a sure postron. **1535** STEWART *Cron. Scot.* II. 524 At ane postrum, quhairof rycht few tuke cuir, The kingis cors rycht quyetlie tha buir. **1593** SHAKS. *Rich. II*, v. v. 17 It is as hard to come, as for a Camell To thred the posterne of a Needles eye. **1600** FAIRFAX *Tasso* II. xxix, And in that window made a postren wide. *a* **1654** SELDEN *Table-T.* (Arb.) 35 The other Doors were but Posterns. **1828** ELMES *Metrop. Improv.* 21 The gate..is in 3 divisions, a carriage way and 2 posterns for foot-passengers divided by stone piers. **1874** GREEN *Short Hist.* ii. §7. 98 She escaped in white robes by a postern.

b. *Fortif.* (See quots.)

1704 J. HARRIS *Lex. Techn.* I, *Postern*, in Fortification, is a false Door usually made in the Angle of the Flank, and of the Curtain, or near the Orillon for private Sallies. **1879** *Cassell's Techn. Educ.* IV. 138/2 When such a tunnel serves as the means of access to the ditch and outworks, it is called a postern.

2. *fig.* **a.** A way of escape or of refuge. **b.** An entrance other than the usual and honourable one: cf. BACK-DOOR 2. **c.** An obscure passage.

1579 TOMSON *Calvin's Serm. Tim.* 661/1 Nowe hee began with Iesus Christe, to the ende that he might be a posterne for vs all. *a* **1618** RALEIGH *Prerog. Parl.* (1628) 29 For this Maxime hath no posterne, *Potestas humana radicatur voluntatibus hominum.* **1642** FULLER *Holy & Prof. St.* III. xxv. 229 Others..not going through the porch of humane Arts, but entring into Divinity at the postern, have made good Preachers. **1672** SIR T. BROWNE *Let. Friend* §40 So closely shut up..as not to find some escape by a postern of resipiscency. **1742** YOUNG *Nt. Th.* I. 224 Thro' the dark Postern of Time long elaps'd, Led softly, by the Stillness of the Night. **1831** SIR W. HAMILTON *Discuss.* (1852) 427 Does dispensation afford a postern of escape?

†**3.** The latter or hinder part. *Obs. rare.*

1611 B. JONSON in Coryat *Crudities* Title-p., Then in the Posterne of them looke, and thou shalt find the Posthume Poems of the Authors Father. **1616** —— *Devil an Ass* v. vi, Cast care at thy posternes; and firke i' thy fetters.

B. *attrib.* or as *adj.* Placed at the back; private, side, inferior, esp. in ***postern door*** or ***gate***; also *fig.*

c **1350** *Will. Palerne* 2166 But passeden out prִueli at þe posterne gate. *c* **1400** *Gamelyn* 590 At a posterne gate Gamelyn out went. **1551** ROBINSON tr. *More's Utopia* II. (1895) 130 A posternne doore on the backsyde into the gardyne. *a* **1600** HOOKER *Eccl. Pol.* VI. v. §9 By this postern-gate cometh in the whole mart of papal indulgences. **1683** CAVE *Ecclesiastici* 92 The Bowels, and all the Intestina.. issued out of the Postern passage. **1720** STRYPE *Stow's Surv.* (1754) I. I. iv. 15/2 Just South, going down divers stone Steps, is the excellent Postern Spring, with an iron Bowl and Chain fastened to catch the Water. **1813** SCOTT *Rokeby* v. xxix, Wilfrid half led, and half he bore, Matilda to the postern door. **1873** HALE *In His Name* ix. 78 Whom he had met so unexpectedly by the postern gate of the abbey. **1886** WILLIS & CLARK *Cambridge* III. 283 A large gateway-arch flanked by a postern-arch.

b. *fig.* = 'BACK-DOOR' *attrib.*

1647 J. B[IRKENHEAD] *Assembly-Man* (1662) 6 Yet these inferiour postern Teachers have intoxicated England. **1648** HERRICK *Hesper.*, *To Weare*, A Postern-bribe tooke, or a Forked Fee.

postero- (ˈpɒstərəʊ), combining form of Lat. *poster-us* hind, hinder, prefixed to adjectives, chiefly forming anatomical terms, in the sense (*a*) 'hinder and ——', as in ***postero-external***, ***-inferior***, ***-interior***, ***-internal***, ***-medial***, ***-median***, ***-superior***; (*b*) on the back part of that which is ——, as **postero-dorsal**, on the posterior part of that which is dorsal; **postero-lateral**, placed at the posterior end of a lateral margin or part; **postero-temporal**, behind the post-temporal; **postero-terminal**, ending that which is terminal; **postero-ventral**, placed backwardly on the ventral aspect of something. Also forming advs., as **posterolaterally**, **-ventrally**.

1847 YOUATT *The Horse* xvii. 357 It is situated on the postero-external side of the haunch and thigh. **1849** DANA *Geol.* (1850) 687 Valves nearly flat, with a slight bending over the postero-dorsal margin. **1852** —— *Crust.* I. 29 The posterior portion of the Carapax consists of a postero-lateral region, and a posterior region. **1854** OWEN in *Orr's Circ. Sc.* I. *Org. Nat.* 197 The base of each neurapophysis has an antero-internal.., and a postero-internal surface. **1881** MIVART *Cat* 74 The postero-inferior margin of the malar is strongly concave. **1899** *Allbutt's Syst. Med.* VII. 10 The postero-median columns, or columns of Goll. *Ibid.* 84 The postero-parietal or superior parietal lobule [of the brain]. **1901** *Proc. Zool. Soc.* I. 263 The characteristic features of this cavity..are:—..(3) the characteristic position of its postero-medial wall, as seen from behind. **1902** *Proc. Zool. Soc.* I. 89 The blue sides are margined posteroventrally with a black line. **1959** *Bull. Mus. Compar. Zool. Harvard* CXX. 185 The segment anterior to Jacobson's organ no longer appears as a transverse slit in frontal section, but now runs anteromedially to posterolaterally. **1961** J. E. COLLIN *Empididae* I. 31 Middle femora with a comb-like row of tiny black bristles posteroventrally. **1967** G. M. WYBURN et al. *Conc. Anat.* iv. 112/2 The great wing of the sphenoid terminating posterolaterally in the spine. **1967** G. M. WYBURN et al. *Conc. Anat.* i. 28/2 The duodenal papilla—on the postero-medial aspect is the situation of the opening of the bile duct. **1974** D. & M. WEBSTER *Compar. Vertebr. Morphol.* vii. 133 The external oblique muscle..runs anterodorsally to posteroventrally.

†**ˈpostery.** *Obs. rare.* [irreg. f. L. *poster-us*, pl. *posteri*: see POSTERIOR.] = POSTERITY.

a **1548** HALL *Chron., Hen. VIII* 248 Perpetuall frendship betwene the postery both. *a* **1560** BECON *Jewel of Joy* Wks. II. 22* b, They and their postery were not onely depriued of those pleasures and commodities,..but also vtterly damned for their disobedience. **1565** *MS. Cott. Calig. B.* x. lf. 290 Continuance of their families and posteries to enjoy that which otherwise should come to them.

post-eternity, postethmoid, etc.: see POST-.

post eventum: see POST *Latin prep.*

post-exilian (pəʊstɛgˈzɪlɪən, -ɛks-), *a.* [f. POST- B. 1 + L. *exilium* EXILE *sb.* + -AN.] Of or pertaining to the period of Jewish history subsequent to the Babylonian exile. Also **post-eˈxilic** *a.*

1871 F. BOLTON tr. *Delitzsch's Comm. Ps.* cxviii. III. 223 It is without doubt a post-exilic song. **1877** MARTINEAU tr. *Goldziher's Mythol. Hebr.* ix. 308 The postexilian interpretations occurring in that of the Babylonian Isaiah. **1880** T. C. MURRAY *Origin & Growth Psalms* ii. 46 The writings of the post-exilic period. **1887** E. JOHNSON *Antiqua Mater* 163 The ideas..date from post-exilian times.

post-eˈxist, *v. rare.* [f. POST- A. 1 + EXIST *v.*] *intr.* To exist after; to live subsequently.

1678 CUDWORTH *Intell. Syst.* 37 Anaxagoras could not but acknowledge, that all Souls and Lives did Præ and Post-exist by themselves, as well as those Corporeal Forms and Qualities, in his Similar Atoms.

So **post-eˈxistence** [after PRE-EXISTENCE], existence after; subsequent existence. **post-eˈxistency**, post-existent condition. **post-eˈxistent** *a.*, existing afterwards or subsequently.

1678 CUDWORTH *Intell. Syst.* 35 That Conceit of Anaxagoras, of Præ and Post-existent Atoms, endued with all those several Forms and Qualities of Bodies. *Ibid.* 38 These two things were alwaies included together in that one opinion of the Soul's Immortality, namely its Preexistence as well as its Post-existence. **1716** M. DAVIES *Athen. Brit.* II. 422 Not denying a pre-existency to Christ's human Body (in the Arian sense..it being suppos'd to be as much a Creature as the least post-existency of a Worm). **1768–74** TUCKER *Lt. Nat.* (1834) I. 465 The spirits,..who know nothing of their pre-existence, and scarce anything of their post-existence. **1865** GROTE *Plato* III. 27 The post-existence, as well as the pre-existence of the Soul is affirmed in the concluding books. **1977** G. W. H. LAMPE *God as Spirit* iii. 71 Luke was, in fact, unable to make a simple identification of the glorified, 'post-existent' Jesus with the Spirit in the Church.

postey, variant of POUSTIE *Obs.*, power.

postface: see POST- A. 1 b.

†**ˈpostfact.** *Obs.* [ad. L. *postfactum* done afterwards.] That which is done after; a subsequent act. Phr. ***upon the post-fact***, rendering late L. *ex post facto* (in *Digest*), after the fact or event, subsequently, afterwards.

1631 HEYLIN *St. George* 91 Iust as upon the post-fact, the Normans fram'd that doughty tale of St. Romanus and the Dragon. **1641** *Proc. of some Divines* 1 Some have published, that there is a proper Sacrifice in the Lords supper, to exhibit Christs death in the Postfact, as there was a sacrifice to prefigure in the old Law, in the Antefact. **1657** SANDERSON *Serm.* Pref. ii. 4 [To] win over his affections to any tolerable liking thereof upon the Post-fact. **1687** TOWERSON *Baptism* 296 Being likely enough to be thereby dispos'd so far to acknowledge that authority and goodness, as to own them upon the postfact by confession.

postfactor: see POST- A. 1 b.

‖**post factum.** [L., = after the fact.] *adv. phr.* After the event. Also as *adj.*

1692 LOCKE *Some Considerations Money* 12 Unless you intend to break in only upon Mortgages and Contracts already made, and (which is not to be supposed) by a Law, *post factum*, void Bargains lawfully made. **1753** HANWAY *Trav.* (1762) I. I. vii. 28 Reasonings post factum, argue rather our experience than our wisdom. **1927** *Mod. Philol.* Nov. 227 New locutions..constantly replace old ones, which viewed *post factum*, would have been unintelligible, had they remained in use. **1949** KOESTLER *Insight & Outlook* p. vii, But textbooks are post-factum rearrangements of long and devious processes of inquiry. **1964** V. NABOKOV *Defence* viii. 125 I'm very glad *post factum*..but..for the moment it somehow disturbs me. **1972** *New Yorker* 16 Jan. 28/2 Not wanting to use the police emergency number—911—in a post-factum situation.

post-febrile, -femoral: see POST- B. 1, 2.

†**post'ferment.** *nonce-wd.* [f. POST- A, after *preferment.*] Removal to an inferior office; the opposite of *preferment.*

*a***1661** FULLER *Worthies, Durham* (1662) I. 294/2 Alex. Nevil..Arch-Bishop of York..was translated..to St. Andrews... This his translation was a Post-Ferment, seeing the Arch-Bishoprick of St. Andrews was subjected in that age unto York.

post festum: see POST *Latin prep.*

'post-final. *Linguistics.* [POST- B. 1 c.] In a word-final consonant cluster, a consonant following a main final consonant. Cf. PRE-FINAL *sb.*

1933, 1965 [see PRE-FINAL *sb.*].

'post-fine. *Law. Obs.* exc. *Hist.* [f. POST- B. 1 c + FINE *sb.*[1]] A duty formerly paid to the Crown for the royal licence (*licentia concordandi*) to levy a fine: = KING'S *silver* (*b*).

Called the post-fine as distinguished from the pre-fine which was due on the writ.

1607 COWELL *Interpr., Post fine,* is a duty belonging to the king for a fine formerly acknowledged before him in his court which is paid by the cognizee, after the fine is fully passed, and all things touching the same wholly accomplished. **1620** *Naworth Househ. Bks.* (Surtees) 145 For the chargeis of a post-fyne..in Candelmase tearm for 4 tone of wyne. **1758** *Act 32 Geo. II*, c. 14 §1 The Officer.. whose Duty it is to set and indorse the Pre-fine payable.., shall..at the same Time, set the usual Post Fine. **1887** *48th Rep. Dep. Kpr. Records* 642 Receipts given on behalf of the Farmers of Post Fines for the several amounts of Post Fines received from the Sheriffs of the several counties.

postfix ('pəʊstfɪks), *sb.* [f. POST- A. 1 b + FIX *v.*, after PREFIX *sb.*] A word, syllable, or letter affixed or added to the end of a word; a suffix.

1805 G. DYER *Restor. Anc. Modes bestowing Names* 43 Diminutive postfixes were added to the names of streams, &c.—*Sruth* is Gaelic for stream; *Sruthan* is little stream. **1877** SAYCE in *Trans. Philol. Soc.* 128 The Accadian postfix. **1881** A. H. KEANE in *Nature* XXIII. 220/2 The structure of the language is entirely different, being highly agglutinating, and employing both pre- and post-fixes.

Hence **post'fixal** (-'fɪxial) *a.*, of the nature of a postfix, or characterized by postfixes.

1887 SAYCE in *Jrnl. Anthrop. Inst.* Nov. 170 The postfixal languages of Central Asia. **1893** T. DE C. ATKINS *Kelt or Gael* i. 7 The expressions prefixial, postfixial, and polysynthetic are distributed among the groups.

postfix (pəʊst'fɪks), *v.* [f. POST- A. 1 a + FIX *v.*] **1.** *trans.* To affix after, or at the end; to append as a postfix (to a word, etc.).

1819 G. S. FABER *Dispensations* (1823) I. 358 See Bishop Sherlock's Dissert. i. postfixed to his Discourses on Prophecy. **1835** *Fraser's Mag.* XI. 619 How impossible it is that he should prefix a *Sir*, and postfix at the same time the *Bart.* to his name.

2. *Biol.* To fix again after a previous fixation; to treat with a second fixative.

1960 D. C. PEASE *Histol. Techniques Electron Microscopy* iii. 49 The small blocks are washed..in the buffer, and then postfixed in buffered osmium tetroxide. **1969** *Jrnl. Cell Sci.* IV. 439 After perfusion blocks were cut from the cerebral cortex which were post-fixed by placing them without washing in a 2% solution of OsO_4. **1976** *Nature* 5 Aug. 494/2 The tissue was immediately fixed in collidine-buffered glutaraldehyde and after a short buffer rinse, postfixed in osmium tetroxide.

Hence **post'fixing** *vbl. sb.*

1897 G. B. GRAY in *Expositor* Sept. 184 In post-exilic names the post-fixing occurs many times more frequently than the prefixing.

postfi'xation, *a.* and *sb.*

A. *adj. Biol.* [POST- B. 1 a.] Carried out or used after the fixation of tissue.

1958 J. R. BAKER *Princ. Biol. Microtechnique* i. 30 The fixative..may be unsuitable for indefinite preservation... In such cases a post-fixation preservative may be used. **1961** *Jrnl. Biophysical & Biochem. Cytol.* XI. 492 (*heading*) Method for obtaining increased contrast in Araldite sections by using postfixation staining of tissues with potassium permanganate. **1966** R. MAHONEY *Lab. Techniques Zool.* v. 285 (*heading*) Post-fixation preservatives.

B. *sb.* **1.** *Anat.* [POST- B. 2 b.] The state of a nerve of being postfixed (sense 2).

1953 G. A. G. MITCHELL *Anat. Autonomic Nervous Syst.* xiv. 202 The sympathetic preganglionic fibres issuing from the cord are found chiefly in all the thoracic and upper two lumbar ventral nerve roots, although occasionally prefixation or postfixation may occur in association with coincident shifts of somatic nerves. **1957** *Ann. R. Coll. Surgeons England* XXI. 367 Table II shows that..there is a much higher incidence of 'postfixation'.

2. *Biol.* [POST- A. 1 b.] Fixation of tissue that has already been treated with a fixative.

1963 *Jrnl. Cell Biol.* XVII. 28/2 For adequate post-fixation in osmium tetroxide of tissues fixed in the aldehydes ..the blocks were washed in buffered sucrose solution. **1967** *Jrnl. Cell. Sci.* II. 379 Post-fixation in osmium tetroxide was carried out for not less than 1 h. **1975** *Nature* 18 Dec. 613/2 Double fixation for blood cells with glutaraldehyde and osmium, followed by uranyl acetate postfixation, was also used.

'postfixed, *ppl. a.* **1.** [f. POSTFIX *v.* + -ED[1].] Affixed at the end of or after a word, root, or stem.

1874 SAYCE *Compar. Philol.* vii. 282 The Aryan plural is formed by a postfixed s. **1975** *Amer. Speech 1969* XLIV. 107 The endings of the English verbs have evolved in a continuing process from earliest Indo-European times, or perhaps more remotely from earliest Proto-Indo-European-Uralic-Altaic (at which time, one may surmise, they represented nothing more than postfixed pronominal forms).

2. *Anat.* [f. POST- A. 2 a + FIXED *ppl. a.*] Of a nerve: connected to the spinal cord relatively caudally. Cf. PREFIXED, PREFIXT *ppl. a.* 3.

1892 C. S. SHERRINGTON in *Jrnl. Physiol.* XIII. 635 A plexus and its trunks and branches will..be referred to as prefixed if containing spinal root-filaments attached to the cord further forward (headward) than are the root-filaments entering the corresponding trunks and branches of a converse class of plexus which will be referred to conversely as postfixed. **1931** *Proc. R. Soc.* B. CVII. 511 In animals with a 'post-fixed' sacral plexus this has been done by dividing extradurally the 6th and 7th post-thoracic dorsal roots... In animals with a normal or 'pre-fixed' sacral plexus only the 6th post-thoracic dorsal root has been divided.

3. *Biol.* [f. POSTFIX *v.* 2 + -ED[1].] Treated with a second fixative.

1968 *Jrnl. Cell Sci.* III. 579 The tissue elements in the glutaraldehyde-perfused and OsO_4 post-fixed cortex are separated by narrow extracellular spaces.

postflight, *a.* and *adv.* [FLIGHT *sb.*[1]]

A. *adj.* [POST- B. 1 a.] Existing or occurring after (a) flight. **B.** *adv.* [POST- B. 1 d.] After flight.

1970 N. ARMSTRONG et al. *First on Moon* iv. 84 There was some suspicion, lingering in the postflight shock of the first Sputnik, that this was the road the Soviet Union had chosen. **1971** *New Scientist* 29 July 249/1 Postflight there was an important development... The cosmonauts..suffered from severe orthostatic hypotension.

post'forming, *vbl. sb.* [f. POST- A. 1 b + FORMING *vbl. sb.*] Shaping of thermosetting laminated plastic carried out upon reheating before setting is complete. So **post-'formed** *ppl. a.*, **post-'form** *v. trans.*

1945 *Metals & Alloys* XXI. 392/1 (*heading*) Postformed laminated phenolic plastics. *Ibid.*, 392/2 The term of post-forming is generally used to designate the procedure by which this material is formed after the laminations have been heat-set. **1945** *Plastics* IX. 266/2 The first important reference to laminated plastics for hot post-forming was probably the announcement of 'Micarta 444' by the Westinghouse Electric and Manufacturing Co. of America. **1965** *Encycl. Polymer Sci. & Technol.* II. 53 To facilitate this postforming ability, a melamine-formaldehyde resin with an added plasticizer is used for impregnation. **1967** P. B. SCHUBERT *Die Methods* II. ii. 53 (*heading*) Designing dies for postforming thermosetting laminates. **1970** *Interior Design* Dec. 753/1 The 78 feet long, chevron-shaped post office counter is entirely clad in postforming grade Formica laminate. **1971** P. TOOLEY *High Polymers* ii. 60 Polymethyl methacrylate..softens at about 120°C and becomes quite pliable at 160°C. This enables the sheet polymer to be 'post-formed' in the fabrication of smooth streamlined shapes such as windows. **1977** *Cleethorpes News* 27 May 6/7 (Advt.), Worth a second look are..the wide range of worktops in ceramics square and postformed laminates.

‖**postfrænum, -frenum** (pəʊst'friːnəm). *Ent.* [mod.L., f. POST- B. 2 + FRÆNUM.] (See quots.)

1826 KIRBY & SP. *Entomol.* III. xxxiii. 380 *Postfrænum* (the *Postfrænum*). In *Coleoptera* the part of the *Metathorax* in which the *Postscutellum* lies... In general it may be defined, the part that intervenes between the *Postscutellum* and the *Abdomen*. *Ibid.* xxxv. 570 In the Orthoptera Order, ..the *postscutellum* and *postfrænum* are mere counterparts of the dorsolum, scutellum, and frænum.

post-free, *a.*(*adv.*) [f. POST *sb.*[2] + FREE *a.* 32: cf. Ger. *post-frei.*] Free from charge for postage, either as being officially carried free of charge or as being prepaid. Also as *adv.*, without postal charge.

1723 *Boston News-Let.* 7 Mar. 2/2 The Publisher... Desires them to send their Accounts Post-Free. **1743** POPE *Dunciad* I. 65 [*Note*] It was a practise so to give the Daily Gazetteer and ministerial pamphlets..and to send them *Post-free* to all the Towns in the kingdom. **1873** *Young Englishwoman* Apr. 202/2 Patterns sent post-free. **1882** in OGILVIE (Annandale). **1886** in *Cassell's Dict.* **1929** *Times* 1 Nov. 16/6 The post-free price for copies ordered direct from the publisher is 5s. 9d. **1980** *Radio Times* 12–18 Jan. 10/1 (Advt.), Send for Littlewoods new catalogue... Post-free. No stamp needed.

post-'Freudian, *sb.* and *a.* [POST- B. 1 b.]

A. *sb.* Someone whose psychotherapeutic ideas or practice have developed and diverged from strictly Freudian doctrine; someone whose views have been influenced as a result of Freudian theory. **B.** *adj.* Subsequent to the impact and influence of Freudian ideas. Cf. FREUDIAN *a.* (*sb.*).

1938 *Essays & Stud. 1937* XXIII. 82 He [*sc.* Balzac] had little to learn of normal psychology from the post-Freudians. **1961** J. A. C. BROWN (*title*) Freud and the post-Freudians. **1964** E. BECKER in I. L. Horowitz *New Sociol.* 114 Mills has here failed to push on to a fully post-Freudian social psychology. **1966** *Listener* 13 Jan. 64/3 We should have no post-Freudian difficulties in reconciling patience, honour, and kindness with destiny, treachery, and retribution. **1973** *Times* 29 Dec. 12/6 Heavenly rewards hereafter make us post-Freudians suspicious. **1977** R. L. WOLFF *Gains & Losses* i. 46 The emotional language frequent in nineteenth-century friendships between persons of the same sex..arouses thoughts in post-Freudian minds that sometimes were not present..in pre-Freudian minds.

postfrontal (pəʊst'frɒntəl), *a.* (*sb.*) *Anat.* and *Zool.* [f. POST- B. 2 + L. *frons, front-* forehead + -AL[1].] **a.** Situated behind the forehead, or at the back of the frontal bone. **b.** Situated in the hinder part of the frontal lobe of the brain.

1852 DANA *Crust.* I. 383 The post-frontal sutures. **1854** OWEN *Skel. & Teeth* in *Orr's Circ. Sc.* I. *Org. Nat.* 189 The post-frontal..region of the skull. **1899** *Allbutt's Syst. Med.* VII. 273 The frontal lobe..must be divided into a prefrontal and a post-frontal area.

B. *sb.* (*ellipt.* for *postfrontal process* or *bone*). The external angular process of the frontal bone, which is situated at the back part of the brim of the orbit of the eye; in some animals (not above birds) found as a distinct bone.

1854 OWEN *Skel. & Teeth* in *Orr's Circ. Sc.* I. *Org. Nat.* 194 The post-frontal..is a moderately long trihedral bone, articulated by its expanded cranial end to the frontal and parietal. *Ibid.* 206 These characters are retained in the post-frontals as well as in the mastoids of the crocodiles. **1872** MIVART *Elem. Anat.* 101 A bone exists in the skull of osseous Fishes which has often been called the 'post-frontal'.

‖**postfurca** (pəʊst'fɜːkə). *Entom.* [mod.L., f. POST- A. 2 + *furca* fork.] The hindmost of the three apodemes, or processes for attachment of muscles, in the thoracic somites of insects.

1826 KIRBY & SP. *Entomol.* III. xxxiii. 383 *Postfurca* (the *Postfurca*). A process of the *Endosternum*, terminating in three subhorizontal acute branches, resembling the letter **Y**, ..to which the muscles that move the hind-legs, &c. are affixed. **1877** HUXLEY *Anat. Inv. Anim.* vii. 404 Forked or double apodemes, the antefurca, medifurca, and postfurca, project from the sternal wall of each somite of the thorax into the cavity.

Hence **post'furcal** *a.*, pertaining to or of the nature of a postfurca.

1890 in *Cent. Dict.*

postgangli'onic, *a. Anat.* [POST- B. 2.] Of a nerve of the autonomic nervous system: running from a ganglion to the organ which it innervates.

1897 [see PREGANGLIONIC *a.*]. **1908** *Jrnl. Physiol.* XXXVII. 139 Prof. Langley remarks that according to him all reflexes in the sympathetic system isolated from the spinal cord are such axon-reflexes either in pre- or postganglionic fibres. **1946** *Nature* 19 Oct. 556/1 Giant fibres which..are distributed, one in each postganglionic stellar nerve, to the mantle musculature. **1968** PASSMORE & ROBSON *Compan. Med. Stud.* I. xxiv. 88/2 Postganglionic fibres are unmyelinated. **1974** [see PREGANGLIONIC *a.*].

Hence **postgangli'onically** *adv.*

1967 [see PREGANGLIONICALLY *adv.*].

postgenital: see POST- B. 2.

post-genitive: see POST- A. 1 b.

†**post-'geniture.** *Obs. rare.* [f. POST- A. 1 b + GENITURE.] The fact of being born after another in the same family.

1658 SIR T. BROWNE *Gard. Cyrus* i, A person of high spirit and honour,..naturally a King though fatally prevented by the harmlesse chance of post-geniture.

post-glacial (-'gleɪʃ(ɪ)əl), *a.* (*sb.*) *Geol.* [f. POST- B. 1 b + GLACIAL.] Existing or occurring subsequent to the glacial period or ice age. Also as *sb.*, a post-glacial deposit or period; **post-'glacially** *adv.*

1855 PHILLIPS *Man. Geol.* 31 Tertiary or Cainozoic Series of Strata... Formations: Postglacial... Glacial... Preglacial. **1863** *Q. Rev.* CXIV. 408 The remarkable conformity of the preglacial and postglacial fauna. **1873** J. GEIKIE *Gt. Ice Age* Pref. 7 The geological history of glacial and post-glacial Scotland. **1877** DAWSON *Orig. World* xiv. 295 Man comes in at the close of this cold period, in what is called the Post-glacial age. **1928** *Funk's Stand. Dict., Post-glacial* n., a sedimentary deposit resulting from the retreat of a continental glacier. **1937** A. L. DU TOIT *Our Wandering Continents* iv. 77 Over extensive areas the ice-front discharged into the ocean or else the sea lay not far away, as indicated by the marine post-glacials. **1949** *Bull. Geol. Soc. Amer.* LX. 1369/2 Some overlapping of ranges has taken place post-glacially, wherever reproductive isolation has gone far enough to permit it. **1957** J. K. CHARLESWORTH *Quaternary Era* II. xliv. 1231 The Dogger Bank..was post-glacially dry land or a vast freshwater fen. **1975** J. G. EVANS *Environment Early Man Brit. Isles* i. 8 We at present are in a period optimistically termed the Post-glacial, but which may be an interglacial.

postglenoid, -glenoidal: see POST- B. 2.

post-grad (pəʊst'græd), *sb.* and *a.* Colloq. abbrev. of POST-GRADUATE *a.* (*sb.*).

1950 [see GRAD[1]]. **1973** 'D. SHANNON' *No Holiday for Crime* (1974) vi. 93 Ron set up another one, one of the postgrad students. **1976** *Eastern Daily Press* (Norwich) 19 Nov. 9/6 (Advt.), Four Cambridge post-grads seek accommodation, Wymondham area. **1979** *Guardian* 26 Oct. 10/2 Best four years of your life..your postgrad days.

post-'graduate, *a.* (*sb.*) *orig. U.S.* [f. POST- B. 1 b + GRADUATE.] **A.** *adj.* Pertaining or relating to a course of study carried on after graduation. Also, *spec.* with reference to a second or further degree. Also *transf.* and *fig.*

1858 *N. York Tribune* 12 Nov. 5/5 Forming a portion of the Post-Graduate Course of Columbia College. **1886** LOWELL *Wks.* (1890) VI. 168 Special and advanced courses should be pushed on into the post-graduate period. **1900** *Dialect Notes* II. 48 *P.G.* i.e. *post-graduate*, or *pretty girl*, n. 1. A post-graduate student. 2. A pretty girl. **1901** *Daily Chron.* 15 Oct. 4/3 A new building in connection with the Post-Graduate College, of the West London Hospital. **1931** J. VAN DERNOOT (*title*) Postgraduate contract bridge: advanced points for advanced players. **1952** A. HUXLEY *Let.* 12 Oct. (1969) 657 Let it be a post-graduate school. **1955** *Publ. Amer. Dial. Soc.* XXIV. 30 Only after they [*sc.* amateur adult criminals] have been exposed to the postgraduate curriculum of prison life do a few of them make possible recruits for the ranks of the professionals. **1965** *Nursing Times* 5 Feb. p. lxii (Advt.), *Post-graduate nurses*... Applications invited for this course from S.R.N.s..and Enrolled Nurses. **1974** *Times* 31 Jan. 3/2 Strong criticism of proposals to give loans to postgraduate students to supplement state grants. **1975** *Language for Life* (Dept. Educ. & Sci.) xxiii. 338 A form of teacher training which has shown a considerable expansion in recent years is the one-year course for graduates, leading to a post-graduate certificate of education. **1978** *Time* 3 July 48/1 Beatty is also a health-food enthusiast and, as Nichols notes, 'a postgraduate hypochondriac'.

B. *sb.* A student who takes a post-graduate course, or continues his studies after graduation. Also *transf.*, and loosely, one who has received a higher degree.

1890 in *Cent. Dict.* **1900** *Congress. Rec.* 19 Feb. 1917/1 Now, the Senator is a senior, a post-graduate of great distinction of the academy of which he is now a member. **1904** M. E. WALLER *Wood-Carver of 'Lympus* 178 Marking out the work for the post-graduates..has filled my time. **1932** *Daily Express* 20 Sept. 7/2 Able young post-graduates in America..have a love of knowledge. **1959** *New Statesman* 23 May 730/2 There is the 'grand tour' of the post-graduate, working off his money at the end of a year at Harvard or Princeton. **1972** *Daily Tel.* 22 Sept. 3/7 It..was the brainchild of John Fauvel, 24, a postgraduate in mathematics. **1975** *Physics Bull.* Mar. 129/3 By issuing in both cased and paperback editions, Macmillan have ensured that post-graduates should be able to afford it.

Hence **post-gradu'ation**.

1920 H. CRANE *Let.* 14 Apr. (1965) 37 His last letter told of splenetic days following his post-graduation from Columbia.

posthabit (pəʊst'hæbɪt), *v. rare.* [f. L. *posthabēre* to place after, f. *post* (cf. POST- A. 1 a) + L. *habēre, habit-* to hold, have.] *trans.* To place after, make or hold as secondary *to*; to esteem of less importance.

1646 J. HALL *Horæ Vac.* 128 So deare ought truth to be to us that we ought to post-habite our lives to the smallest principle of it. **1856** F. E. PAGET *Owlet Owlst.* 37 Where his comfort can be increased, even in the merest trifle, she will never posthabit it to her own.

post-hackney: see POST *sb.*[2] 12.

post-haste ('pəʊst'heɪst), *sb.*, *adv.*, and *adj.* [app. from the old direction on letters 'Haste, post, haste', where the words are POST *sb.*[2] courier, and imper. of HASTE *v.*; but afterwards taken as an attrib. comb. of POST *sb.*[2] and HASTE *sb.*

1538 CROMWELL in *Life & Lett.* (1902) II. 139 From Saint James 4[to] Maij 30 R. R. Lorde Privie seal—In hast, hast, post hast. **1558** Q. MARY in R. R. Sharpe *Lond. & Kingd.* (1894) I. 480 Hast, hast post, hast, for lief, for lief, for lief, for lief.]

A. *sb.* Haste or speed like that of one travelling 'post'; great expedition in travelling. *arch.*

1545 ASCHAM *Toxoph.* (Arb.) 115 Yf he make Poste haste, bothe he that oweth the horse, and he..that afterwarde shal bye the horse, may chaunce to curse hym. *a* **1548** HALL *Chron., Edw. IV* 218 b, The Duke of Somerset, with Jhon erle of Oxenford, wer in all poste hast, flying towarde Scotlande. **1555** PHILPOT in Foxe *A. & M.* (1583) 1837/1 Farewel dear brother..written in posthast because of strait keeping. **1568** GRAFTON *Chron.* II. 724 Rode he all that poste haste, onely to blinde you? **1586** J. HOOKER *Hist. Irel.* in *Holinshed* II. 19/1 With all the hast and post hast he could, he turneth a faire paire of heeles and runneth awaie. **1681** FLAVEL *Meth. Grace* ix. 199 Messengers are sent one after another in post-haste to the Physician. **1709** HEARNE *Collect.* 13 Mar. (O.H.S.) II. 176 You did not use to write in Post-Hast. **1837** *Commodore & Daughter* I. 39 It was mainly through the interest of his uncle that he was made post with such post-haste.

B. *adv.* With the speed of a post; with all possible haste or expedition.

1593 SHAKS. *Rich. II*, I. iv. 55 Old John of Gaunt..hath sent post haste To entreat your Maiesty to visit him. **1706** E. WARD *Wooden World Diss.* (1708) 2 Such as want to ride Post-haste from one World to the other. **1709** STEELE *Tatler* No. 2 ¶2 Her Coach is order'd, and Post-haste she flies. **1839** JAMES *Louis XIV*, I. 8 This she sent post-haste to the Duke of Lorraine. **1897** 'SARAH TYTLER' *Lady Jean's Son* 258 The lad who travelled post-haste to bring the news.

†**C.** *adj.* Done with all possible speed; expeditious, speedy. *Obs. rare*[−1].

1604 SHAKS. *Oth.* I. ii. 37 The Duke..requires your haste, Post-haste appearance, Euen on the instant.

Hence †**post-'haste** *v. Obs.*, (*a*) *trans.*, to cause to hasten, to hurry; (*b*) *intr.*, to hasten with all speed.

1607 in *Hist. Wakefield Gram. Sch.* (1892) 68 He shall neither post hast them in gramer, nor dull them with exercises of writinge latine. **1628** FELTHAM *Resolves* II. xxxii. 102 The short-lyu'd Flowre, and Portion Of poore, sad life, post-hasteth to be gone.

post-heating: see POST- A. 1 b.

post-hemiplegic, etc.: see POST- B. 1.

posthetomy (pɒs'θɛtəmɪ). *Surg.* [irreg. f. Gr. πόσθη prepuce + -τομια cutting.] Circumcision. So **pos'thetomist**.

1853 DUNGLISON *Med. Lex.*, *Posthetomist*, one who performs the operation of circumcision. *Ibid.*, *Posthetomy*, circumcision. **1895** in *Syd. Soc. Lex.*

posthioplasty ('pɒsθɪəʊ,plæstɪ). *Surg.* Also postho-. [f. Gr. πόσθη (see prec.) and dim. πόσθιο-ν + -PLASTY.] Plastic surgery of the prepuce. So **posthio'plastic, postho-,** *a.*

1842 DUNGLISON *Med. Lex.*, *Posthioplastic*, an epithet applied to the operation for restoring the prepuce. **1874** VAN BUREN *Dis. Genit. Org.* 9 Absence of the prepuce.., the operation for its restoral, posthioplasty. **1890** BILLINGS *Med. Dict.*, Posthioplastic. **1895** *Syd. Soc. Lex.*, Posthoplastic..Posthioplasty, Posthoplasty.

posthippocampal: see POST- A. 2.

post-hi'storic, *a.* [f. POST- B. 1 b, after *prehistoric*.] Of, belonging to, or pertaining to, an imagined period beyond the close of recorded history or otherwise subsequent to the present historical period; also *transf.* Hence **'post-history**.

1918 S. GRAHAM *Quest of Face* i. 50 There never leaves his eyes the gleam of something beyond this time, the post-historic. **1953** S. SPENDER *Creative Element* 133 We live in an epoch without historic precedent, which may indeed be a kind of post-history. **1957** *Times Lit. Suppl.* 15 Nov. 689/3 When the scholars of post-historic China or India study English literature in the twentieth century. **1961** L. MUMFORD *City in Hist.* i. 4 His dehumanized alter ego, 'Post-historic Man'. **1977** *N.Y. Rev. Bks.* 27 Oct. 31/1 Benjamin's study of what might be called the post-history or the afterlife of works of literature has spurred the recent interest in the 'history of reception' among younger critics in Germany.

posthitis (pɒs'θaɪtɪs). *Path.* [mod.L., f. Gr. πόσθη prepuce: see -ITIS.] (See quots.)

1842 DUNGLISON *Med. Lex.*, *Posthitis*, inflammation of the prepuce. **1861** BUMSTEAD *Ven. Dis.* (1879) 97 If the disease be confined..to the membrane covering the glans, it should, strictly speaking, be called balanitis; if to the internal surface of the prepuce, posthitis.

postho-: see POSTHIO-.

postholder ('pəʊsthəʊldə(r)). [ad. Du. *posthouder*, f. *post* POST *sb.*[3] + *houder* HOLDER[1].]

1. In Dutch colonial administration: A civil official in charge of a trading settlement or post.

1812 ANNE PLUMPTREE *Lichtenstein's Trav. S. Afr.* I. 177 The house of the postholder at Mosselbay..lies directly at the upper end. **1852** H. W. PIERSON *Amer. Mission. Mem.* 270 They lodged in the house of the post-holder, a Dutch officer. **1896** *Dispute with Venezuela* in *Daily News* 23 July 5/5 The Dutch..had instituted a regular system of trading both with the Indian tribes and with their Spanish neighbours up the Orinoco; and their Postholders had special functions in controlling such trade.

2. [Reconstituted from native elements.] One who occupies a post or office; an official.

1976 *Cumberland News* 3 Dec. 32/7 (Advt.), Our Regional Officer..requires a person to look after the Carlisle office for a minimum of two months while the current postholder is away.

'post-hole. [f. POST *sb.*[1] + HOLE *sb.*] **1.** A hole made in the ground to receive the foot of a post. Also spec. *Archæol.*, a hole orig. dug to receive a wooden post and usu. packed with stones or clay to support the post. Also *attrib.* in the name of implements serving to make such holes, as ***post-hole auger***, ***borer***, ***digger***; also ***post-hole evidence***, ***pattern***.

1703 T. N. *City & C. Purchaser* 134 The Fence must be cross a Field..where it is easie digging the Post-holes. **1888** A. T. PIERSON *Evangelistic Work* xxiii. 236 [They] dug post-holes with their own hands. **1891** C. ROBERTS *Adrift Amer.* 87 The job at which I was put first was digging post holes, and..I found it rather a tough job. **1932** *Times Lit. Suppl.* 28 July 542/3 The misprint 'portholes' for 'postholes'.. should not betray the unwary reader into attributing too nautical a flavour to the Iron Age fort of Salmonsbury. **1936** *Discovery* Apr. 99/2 New house-sites were brought to light: some were of wattle-and-daub, and another with a compacted floor and post-holes was similar in plan to one discovered in 1934. **1962** H. R. LOYN *Anglo-Saxon Eng.* i. 43 Photography..and analysis of post-hole evidence have disclosed a series of royal halls. **1963** *Field Archaeol.* (Ordnance Survey) (ed. 4) 37 There are no stone settings or any indications of post-holes. **1971** *World Archaeol.* III. 120 Posthole patterns will be confused. **1977** *Antiquaries Jrnl.* LVII. 261 'Stakehole' is used here to mean the void made by the decay of timber post driven into the ground; 'posthole' means a larger hole excavated in order to insert a post.

2. A hole or well drilled to not very great depth.

1932 *Amer. Speech* VII. 269 [Language of California oil fields.] *Post-hole*, a shallow hole. *Post-hole territory*, shallow productive territory—i.e., in which the oil sands lie at depths up to 2500 feet, 'just under the grass roots'. **1965** G. J. WILLIAMS *Econ. Geol. N.Z.* ix. 133/1 The only published information directly relating to the ironsands represents the pioneering work of Nicholson, Fyfe (1958) who put down post-hole bores to depths of not more than 25 ft.

post-horn ('pəʊsthɔːn). [f. POST *sb.*[2] + HORN *sb.*] A horn formerly used by a postman or the guard of a mail-coach, to announce arrival; later often used on pleasure coaches.

1675 HEXHAM *Dutch Dict.*, *Post-horen*, Post-horn. **1677** *Lond. Gaz.* No. 1229/4 Thomas Moris a young man..with a gray Coat, and a leather pair of Breeches, and a Post-horn in his Girdle,..Rid away with a Chesnut Coloured Gelding. **1782** COWPER *Table Talk* 33 The wretch..Who, for the sake of filling with one blast The post-horns of all Europe, lays her waste. **1840** HOOD *Up the Rhine* 285 In the mean-time, the post-horn kept blowing. **1881** W. H. STONE in Grove *Dict. Mus.* III. 21 *Posthorn*, a small straight brass or copper instrument, varying in length from two to four feet, of a bore usually resembling the conical bugle more than the trumpet, played by means of a small and shallow-cupped mouthpiece.

b. *attrib.* and *Comb.*, as ***post-horn band***; **post-horn pond-snail**, *Planorbis corneus*, also called *ram's-horn*, from the form of its shell.

1864 SALA in *Daily Tel.* 16 July, A post-horn band.. performing in some unlicensed place. **1901** *Westm. Gaz.* 16 Dec. 3/1 A good purple dye may also be got from the posthorn pond snail.

post-horse ('pəʊsthɔːs). A horse kept at a post-house or inn for the use of post-riders, or for hire for the conveyance of travellers.

1527 GARDINER in Pocock *Rec. Ref.* I. 76 Now unless post-horse serve us we cannot tell how to do. **1533** TUKE *Let. to Cromwell* in *St. Papers Hen. VIII*, I. 405 Writinges, sent for provision of post horses. **1575** in W. H. Turner *Select. Rec. Oxford* (1880) 369 Neither the horses of ye Chancellor or Schollers.., nor of their servaunts,..should be taken for post horses. **1617** MORYSON *Itin.* III. 61 In England.., Post-horses are established at every ten miles or thereabouts, which they ride a false gallop after some ten miles an hower. *a* **1627** HAYWARD *Edw. VI* (1630) 100 That he intended to fly to Iernsey and Wales and laid posthorses, and men, and a boat to that purpose. **1814** SCOTT *Wav.* lxiii, From Edinburgh to Perth he took post-horses. **1835** MARRYAT *Olla Podr.* iv, With post-horses and postilions we posted post haste to Brussels.

post-house ('pəʊsthaʊs). *Obs.* exc. *dial.* [f. POST *sb.*[2] + HOUSE *sb.*[1]]

1. A post office. *Obs.* or *dial.*

1635 *Proclamation* in Rymer *Fœdera* (1732) XIX. 649/2 Which Letters to be left at the Post-house or some other House, as the said Thomas Witherings shall think convenient. **1670** MARVELL *Corr.* Wks. (Grosart) II. 324, I wrote to you two letters, and payd for them from the posthouse here. **1761** MRS. F. SHERIDAN *Sidney Bidulph* III. 77 When I go into the country a general direction to the post house may suffice. **1855** ROBINSON *Whitby Gloss.*, *Posthouse*, the post-office.

†**2.** An inn or other house where horses are kept for the use of travellers; a posting house. *Obs.*

1645 EVELYN *Diary* 28 Jan., We repos'd this night at Piperno, in the Post-house without the towne. **1712** *Lond. Gaz.* No. 5027/5 He alighted at the Post-house to change Horses. **1819** BYRON *Juan* I. ciii, They are a sort of post-house, where the Fates Change horses. **1833** L. RITCHIE *Wand. by Loire* 16 The main road running past the town.., and the post-house being at a little distance beyond.

†**'posthumary** *a. Obs.* = POSTHUMOUS. So †**'posthumate** *a.*

1652 URQUHART *Jewel* Wks. (1834) 255 He left behind him a posthumary book. **1684** T. GODDARD *Plato's Demon* 47 Charyllus, Posthumate Son to Polybita.

†**'posthume,** *a.* and *sb. Obs.* [a. F. *posthume* adj. (1560 in Godef.), ad. L. *post(h)umus* last, latest, posthumous: see POSTHUMOUS.]

A. *adj.* **a.** = POSTHUMOUS a. Also *fig.*

1591 SYLVESTER *Du Bartas* I. v. 953 Two births, two deaths, here Nature hath assign'd her, Leaving a Posthume (dead-live) seed behind her. **1659** H. L'ESTRANGE *Alliance Div. Off.* 157 This posthume Apostle..came late into Christs Livery. *a* **1661** FULLER *Worthies, Cumbld.* (1662) 221/1 Posthume Children born after the death of their Father.

b. = POSTHUMOUS b.

1611 B. JONSON in Coryat *Crudities* Title-p., In the Posterne..thou shalt find the Posthume Poems of the Authors Father. **1659** (*title*) Posthume Poems of Richard Lovelace.

c. = POSTHUMOUS c.

1597–8 BP. HALL *Sat.* IV. *Charge* 23 Oh if my soule could see their Post-hume spight. **1690** BOYLE *Chr. Virtuoso* II. 21 The posthume State of Man is so dim and uncertain, that we find even the greatest Men, among the Heathen, speak.. doubtfully [of it]. **1691** HEYRICK *Misc. Poems* 35 To claim The whole World's Curses and a Post-hume Fame.

d. Subsequent, residual. *rare.*

1662 J. CHANDLER *Van Helmont's Oriat.* 187 That the venal bloud..may be made wholly capable to be breathed thorow the pores, without a Post-hume or Future remembrance of a dreg. *Ibid.* 292 That post-hume and translated gouty character or impression, doth stick fast by a hereditary right.

B. *sb.* **a.** A posthumous child. Also *fig.*

1598 SYLVESTER *Du Bartas* II. *Sonn.* i. 14 Our dear Parent .. Who .. to thy guard his Posthumes did bequeath. **1638** W. SCLATER *Serm. Experimentall* To Rdr., They shew themselves in publike but as Posthumes, raised as it were out of almost eleven yeares of obscurity. **1692** in *Macfarlane's Genealog. Collect.* (1900) II. 142 Sir Thomas Maule .. Son to Sir Thomas the Posthume.

b. A posthumous work: cf. POSTHUMUS B. b.

1631 R. SKENE in *A. Craige's Rem.* 3 This subsequent Poësie, the Posthumes of a worthie Penne. **1676** BEAL in *Phil. Trans.* XI. 585 Sir Ken. Digby's Post-hume hath great varietie of Metheglins.

† **'posthumed,** *ppl. a. Obs. rare.* [f. as prec. + -ED¹.] Rendered posthumous, remaining after death.

a **1661** FULLER *Worthies* (1662) I. 74 A Stranger .. would hardly rally my scattered and posthumed Notes.

posthumeral: see POST- B. 2.

† **post'humial,** *a. Obs. rare*⁻¹. = POSTHUMOUS.

1605 SYLVESTER *Du Bartas, Corona Ded.*, All the Posthumiall race of that rare Spirit .. Though born, alas! after their Father's death.

† **post'humian,** *a. Obs. rare*⁻⁰. (See quot.)

1656 BLOUNT *Glossogr., Posthumian*, following or to come, that shall be.

posthumous ('pɒstjʊməs), *a.* (*sb.*) Also 8 postumous. [f. L. *postumus* last, late-born, posthumous, superl. f. *post* after; in late L. written *posthumus* through erroneous attribution to *humus* the earth, or (as explained by Servius) *humāre* to bury: see -OUS.] Used generally of anything which appears after the death of its originator.

a. Of a child: Born after the death of its father.

1619 DRUMM. OF HAWTH. *Conv. B. Jonson* Wks. (1711) 224 He [Ben Jonson] .. was posthumous, being born a month after his father's death. **1677** W. HUBBARD *Narrative* 2 North-America this posthumous birth of time. **1709** STEELE & ADDISON *Tatler* No. 110 ¶6 Some Posthumous Children, that bore no Resemblance to their elder Brethren. **1818** CRUISE *Digest* (ed. 2) VI. 574 The statute of King William, which puts posthumous children on the same footing with children born in the lifetime of their ancestor.

b. Of a book or writing: Published after the death of the author.

1668 HALE *Rolle's Abridgment* Pref. a j b, It is a Posthumous work, which never underwent the last Hand or Pensil of the judicious Author. **1796** BURKE *Regic. Peace* iii. Wks. VIII. 300 What plea .. can be alledged, after the treaty was dead and gone, in favour of this posthumous declaration? **1837–9** HALLAM *Hist. Lit.* (1847) III. 207 The posthumous volumes appeared in considerable intervals.

c. Of an action, reputation, etc.: Occurring, arising, or continuing after death.

1608 BP. J. KING *Serm. 5 Nov.* 37 A posthumous, penitent confession (after the conspirators were most of them dead, and almost rotten) of one of the complices themselves. **1642** FULLER *Holy & Prof. St.* III. v. 164 For he that was buried with the bones of Elisha, by a Posthumous miracle of that Prophet, recovered his life by lodging with such a grave-fellow. **1736** BUTLER *Anal.* I. i. Wks. 1874 I. 30 Our posthumous life .. may not be entirely beginning anew, but going on. **1808** SOUTHEY *Lett., to C. W. Williams Wynn* II. 50 It was well we should be contented with posthumous fame, but impossible to be so with posthumous bread and cheese. **1882** FARRAR *Early Chr.* I. 77 He had begged that his body might be burned without posthumous insults.

† **B.** *sb.* A posthumous child. *Obs. rare.*

a **1648** LD. HERBERT *Life* (1886) 23 My brother Thomas was a posthumous .. born some weeks after his father's death. **1718** S. SEWALL *Diary* 19 Mar. (1882) III. 177 Marry Sam. Badcock, a posthumous, and Martha Healy.

'posthumously, *adv.* [f. prec. + -LY².] In a posthumous manner, condition, or state; after death; after the death of the father or author.

1783 *Atterbury's Corr.* I. 23 *note*, The 'Register' [of bishop Kennet] was posthumously published, from his MS. Collections, in 1728. **1867** J. B. DAVIS *Thesaurus Craniorum* 15 The two latter [ancient Scottish skulls] are posthumously distorted. **1884** *Chr. Commw.* 12 June 833/2 He seems to be even more mischievous posthumously than while corporeally present.

‖ **posthumus** ('pɒstjʊməs), *a.* and *sb.* [L. *post(h)umus* POSTHUMOUS.]

† **A.** *adj.* = POSTHUMOUS *a. Obs.*

1591 LD. BURGHLEY in *Fortescue Papers* (Camden) Pref. 7 Though he be posthumus by his fathers death, being borne after. **1660** R. COKE *Just. Vind.* Pref. 5 No man that ever was born in the World, which was not a Posthumus King, but was born in subjection, not only to his Parents, or as a Servant in a Family.

B. *sb.* † **a.** (pl. -i.) A posthumous child. *Obs.*

1638 SIR T. HERBERT *Trav.* (ed. 2) 273 He was a posthumus, and the crowne set upon his mothers belly. *a* **1677** HALE *Prim. Orig. Man.* I. iv. 109 It is as evident that the Grandfather and Father and Son did as really make up a multitude, .. though the Father and Son were both *Posthumi*, as if they all had or did all now exist together.

b. *neut. pl.* **posthuma.** Posthumous writings.

1655 OWEN *Vind. Evang.* Wks. 1853 XII. 8 The passages intimated are in his *posthuma*. **1669** STURMY *Mariner's Mag.* I. ii. 35, I shall quote some more remarkable Places in *Posthuma Fosteri*. **1905** G. SAMPSON *Keats's Poems* Pref., Most reprints give the order of Keats's own three volumes with Lord Houghton's posthuma appended.

post-hypnotic: see POST- B. 1.

post-'Ibsen, *a.* [f. POST- B. 1 a + the name of Henrik *Ibsen* (see IBSENISM).] Subsequent to the life or works of Ibsen; influenced by the style or views (esp. concerning social reform) of Ibsen. Hence **post-'Ibsenist** *a.*, pertaining to or characteristic of drama subsequent to, and influenced by, Ibsen; also as *sb.*, a developer of the methods or views of Ibsen.

1913 G. B. SHAW *Quintessence of Ibsenism* (Completed ed.) 199 The post-Ibsen playwrights. *Ibid.* 206 What I have called post-Ibsenist plays. *Ibid.* 209 The post-Ibsenists. **1919** —— *Heartbreak House* p. xxxvii, The most advanced post-Ibsen plays in the most artistic settings. **1930** E. POUND *XXX Cantos* xxviii. 131 So Loica went out and died there After her time in the post-Ibsen movement.

† **'postic,** *a. Obs.* [ad. L. *postīcus* hinder, posterior, f. *post* behind; cf. *antīcus* ANTIC, ANTIQUE.] Hinder, posterior, 'back'.

a **1638** MEDE *Wks.* (1672) 237 The lowest and most postick members of all. **1646** SIR T. BROWNE *Pseud. Ep.* III. xvii. (1686) 116 The postick and backward position of the feminine parts in quadrupedes. **1664** BUTLER *Hud.* II. i. 208 A Saxon Duke did grow so fat, That Mice .. Eat Grots and Labyrinths to dwell in His postick parts without his feeling.

So **'postical** *a. rare.*

1657 TOMLINSON *Renou's Disp.* 471* Two doors; one an outward door, the other postical or inward. **1940** *Chambers's Techn. Dict.* 666/1 *Postical*, relating to or belonging to the back or lower part of a leaf or stem. **1965** F. E. ROUND *Introd. Lower Plants* viii. 105 Branching may occur at the apex or it may be intercalary. In the former, new three-sided apical cells are formed by cleavage in the leaf of initial cells —usually in the ventral half, thus eliminating the ventral (i.e. postical) lobe of the leaf.

‖ **postiche** (pɒstiʃ), *a.* and *sb.* [F., adj., ad. It. *posticcio* counterfeit, feigned:—L. type **pos(i)tīcius*, f. *pos(i)tus* placed, put.]

A. *adj.* **a.** Counterfeit, artificial. **b.** Applied to an ornament superadded to a finished work of sculpture or architecture, esp. when inappropriate.

1854 THACKERAY *Newcomes* I. xxxi. 306 Sometimes the Duchess appeared with these postiches roses, sometimes of a mortal paleness.

B. *sb.* **a.** An imitation substituted for the real thing. **b.** Counterfeiting, feigning, pretence.

1876 'OUIDA' *Winter City* ii, Fastidiousness at any rate, is very good postiche for modesty. **1885** MRS. LYNN LINTON in *Life* xviii. (1901) 251, [I] despised with loathing the .. humbug and postiche of the whole matter.

c. A piece of false hair worn as an adornment. Also *attrib.*

1886 C. E. PASCOE *London of To-day* (ed. 3) xl. 345 False tresses have been imported by cart-loads .. and postiches and other mysteries of the toilette have been brought to that perfection to which competition so greatly conduces. **1908** *Westm. Gaz.* 21 Nov. 15/2 The postiches in use must be carefully manipulated to afford the exact size demanded. **1928** *Sunday Dispatch* 9 Dec. 8 The permanent wave has already given place to the permanent curl. And the little *postiches* (buns) which have made their appearance in Paris are being eagerly adopted. **1966** J. S. COX *Illustr. Dict. Hairdressing* 120/2 *Postiche clip*, a small, flat spring clip to which are attached small postiches; used to secure them to the growing hair of a head. **1970** J. G. VERMANDEL *Dine with Devil* i. 10 Try that big hat; it might be good for a waiflike effect, very ingenue. And the postiche with .. what's that long white thing?

posticous (pɒ'staɪkəs), *a. Bot.* [f. L. *postīc-us* hinder (see POSTIC) + -OUS.] Posterior, hinder: applied variously to parts of a flower or inflorescence.

1866 *Treas. Bot.* 922 *Posticous*, turned away from the axis of a flower, as some anthers whose dehiscence takes place next the petals; also, stationed on that side of a flower which is next the axis. **1870** HOOKER *Stud. Flora* 271 Stigma obtuse, .. posticous lobe very small. **1880** GRAY *Struct. Bot.* vi. §6 (ed. 6) 253 An anther is Extrorse, i.e. turned outward, or Posticous, when it faces toward the perianth.

post-ictal(ly: see POST- B. 1.

‖ **posticum** (pɒ'staɪkəm). *Arch.* [L. *postīcum* back door, rear of a building (Vitr.), prop. neut. of *postīcus* adj.: see POSTIC.]

a. A back door or gate. **b.** A portico or apartment at the back of an ancient Greek or Roman temple, behind the *cella*, and corresponding to the *pronaos* in front: in Greek called *opisthodomos*. **c.** '*Eccl.* A reredos' (*Cent. Dict.*).

1704 J. HARRIS *Lex. Techn.* I, *Posticum* is the Postern-Gate, or Back-door of any Fabrick. **1776** R. CHANDLER *Trav. Greece* xiv. 72 In the sculpture of the posticum .. Theseus is distinguished in the same manner. **1820** T. S. HUGHES *Trav. Sicily* I. x. 286 The columns .. belonged either to the posticum or pronaos of the temple.

postie ('pəʊstɪ). *slang.* Also posty. [f. POST *sb.*² + -IE, -Y⁶.] A familiar name for a postman.

1871 S. S. JONES *Northumberland* 84/1 Tom Buglehorn, the postie, .. when he cam wi' the letters. **1886** H. BAUMANN *Londinismen* 143/2 Posty. **1892** G. STEWART *Shetland Fireside Tales* (ed. 2) 227, I mind when I saw 'Posty' come, My heart began ta beat. **1898** [see NUFF 1 b]. **1916** 'TAFFRAIL' *Pincher Martin* ix. 163 The marine postman .. was delayed... "Ere, posty!" shouted some one, 'got my *Dispatch*?' **1939** F. THOMPSON *Lark Rise* vi. 106 There was one postal delivery a day, and towards ten o'clock, the heads of the women .. would be turned .. to watch for 'Old Postie'. **1953** E. SIMON *Past Masters* II. 76 If Postie did not offer one a lift on the road—that could not be imagination. **1962** *Coast to Coast 1961–62* 73 They had a long run on outdoor workers at one stage, and it was often a cop or a postie. **1975** D. CLARK *Premedicated Murder* ii. 29 The postman would read the name rather than the number. So how did the posty .. give Harte a card addressed .. to Rencory? **1977** *S. Wales Guardian* 27 Oct. 6/2 He was missed by the upper valley residents on his transfer down to Ammanford, where he has been a 'postie' for the past 13 years.

postie, variant of POUSTIE *Obs.*, power.

† **'postify,** *v. Obs. nonce-wd.* [f. POST *sb.*¹, after *crucify*.] *trans.* To fix or nail to a post.

1624 GEE *Foot out of Snare* 29 The naile with which it was crucified or rather postified. This my new-coyned word fits their new-found Fable.

postil ('pɒstɪl), *sb.* Now only *Hist.* Forms: 5 (9) postille, (6 posthill), 6–7 postell, 6–7 (9) postill, 7 postel, postle, 5– postil. [ME. a. F. *postille* (1357 in Godef.), = It., Pg. *postilla*, Sp. *postela*, ad. med.L. *postilla* a gloss on the gospel. Of uncertain origin: Du Cange suggests, from the words '*post illa* (*verba textus*)' 'after those (words of the text)', with which the postil may have been introduced. Another suggestion is that the word is a dim. of *posta* in sense 'page': evidence is wanting. See also APOSTIL *sb.*]

1. A marginal note or comment upon a text of Scripture, or upon any passage or writing.

c **1420** *Wyclif's Bible* IV. 686 b, Prol. 1 Cor. (MS. Em. Coll. 2), A postille here.—Poul wroot this pistil to Corinthis, that ben of Acaie [etc.]. **1587** in *3rd Rep. Hist. MSS. Comm.* (1872) 283/2 Pointes of the memoriall .. with postils to the same. **1615** SIR R. COTTON in *Buccleuch MSS.* (Hist. MSS. Comm.) I. 163 The Duke's letter .. answered by way of postle .. 3 proposition[s]. *a* **1734** NORTH *Lives* (1826) I. 399 These his lordship had .. titled .. 'Impudent Assertions', to which I will annex a postil for explanation. **1891** A. M. EARLE *Sabbath in Puritan N. Eng.* xii. 166 Tender little memorial postils are frequently written on the margins of the pages.

2. A series of such comments, a commentary or exposition; *spec.* an expository discourse or homily upon the Gospel or Epistle for the day, read or intended to be read in the church service.

1483 CAXTON *Gold. Leg.* 244/1 Mayster Alysaundre .. reherseth in hys postillys upon this worde mercy and trouthe haue mette togydre. **1563–87** FOXE *A. & M.* (1596) 248/1 The said Langton also made postils vpon the whole Bible. *a* **1661** FULLER *Worthies, Northampt.* (1662) II. 290 He wrote Postills on the Proverbs, and other Sermons. **1710** tr. *Dupin's Eccl. Hist. 16th C.* I. III. 434 He wrote also .. some Postils or Homilies on the Gospels.

b. A book of such homilies.

1566 BECON (*title*) A new Postil Conteinyng most Godly and learned sermons vpon all the Sonday Gospelles. **1605** *Vestry Bks.* (Surtees) 141 Item a postell, a Comunion booke, a salter. **1888** *Bibliotheca Sacra* Jan. 136 The old prayer-books and the old Lutheran postils were still frequently used.

3. *attrib.* and *Comb.*

a **1635** SIBBES *Bowels Op.* iii. Wks. 1859 II. 40 Too much curiosity is loathsome and postill-like and calleth the mind too much from the kernel to the shell. *a* **1679** T. GOODWIN in Spurgeon *Treas. Dav.* Ps. xl. 7 Rejected, as being too like a postil gloss. **1721** STRYPE *Eccl. Mem.* III. xiii. 120 April 30 [1554] began the postil mass at St. Paul's, at five a clock in the morning every day.

† **postil,** *v. Obs.* [a. obs. F. *postil(l)er* (15th c. in Godef.), ad. med.L. *postillāre* (1243 Trivet in Du Cange), f. *postilla* POSTIL *sb.* See also APOSTIL *v.*]

1. *trans.* To make or write comments on, or marginal notes in; to comment upon, annotate.

1460 CAPGRAVE *Chron.* (Rolls) 154 Hewe a cardinal of the order of Prechoures, that postiled al the Bible. **1609** BIBLE (Douay) *Exod.* xx. Comm., Melancthon postilling the first Precept, sayth: Papistes invocate Sainctes, and worship Images. **1622** BACON *Hen. VII* 211 In some places Postilled in the Margent with the Kings hand. **1872** J. E. B. MAYOR in *Jrnl. Philol.* 290 Schoolmasters and undergraduates, who .. are accustomed to 'postil' their lexicons.

2. *intr.* To write comments.

a **1529** SKELTON *Col. Cloute* 755 To postell upon a kyry. **1617** HALES *Gold. Rem.* I. (1673) 19 That vein of postilling and allegorising on Scripture, which for a long time had prevailed in the Church.

postilion, postillion (pəʊ'stɪljən, pɒ-). Also 6–7 postillon, 7 postilian. [a. F. *postillon* (1538 in Godef.), ad. It. *postiglione* 'a postilion, a postes guide, a forerunner' (Florio), f. It. *posta* POST *sb.*² + *-iglione*, compound suffix (cf. *vermilion*); so Sp. *postillon*, Pg. *postilhão*.]

† **1. a.** (See quots.) *Obs.*

1591 PERCIVALL *Sp. Dict., Postillon*, a postillon, a guide for a post, *dux praecursoris*. **1611** COTGR., *Postillon*, a Postillon, Guide, Postes boy. **1658** PHILLIPS, *Postillon*, (French) a Post's guide, or fore-runner.

† **b.** *fig.* A forerunner. *Obs.*

a **1586** SIDNEY *Arcadia* III. (1891) 318 But when he strake, .. his arme seemed still a postillion of death. **1647** FANSHAWE tr. *Pastor Fido* I. i. 11 Seest thou yon Star of such excelling hew, The Suns Postillion?

†**2.** One who rides a post-horse, a post-boy; a swift messenger. *Obs.*

1616 BULLOKAR *Eng. Expos., Postilion*, a speedy poste or messenger. **1678** *Lond. Gaz.* No. 1281/4 It is now four days since any Vessel, Post or Postillion came from Ghent to Bruges. **1708** *Ibid.* No. 4464/6 The Postillion of Ghent is just now arrived, with Letters to Mr. de Caris.
fig. *c* **1645** HOWELL *Lett.* (1650) I. To Rdr., Those wing'd Postillions that can fly, From the Antartic to the Artic sky. *Ibid.* I. viii. 14 Those swift Postillions my thoughts find you out daily. **1685** *Gracian's Courtiers Orac.* 160 These are the Postillions of life, who to the swift motion of time, add the rapidity of their own minds.

3. One who rides the near horse of the leaders (or formerly sometimes, each of the riders of the near horses) when four or more are used in a carriage or post-chaise; *esp.* one who rides the near horse when one pair only is used and there is no driver on the box.

1623–33 FLETCHER & SHIRLEY *Night-Walker* II. iii, Thou shalt have horses six, and a postilion. **1632** MASSINGER *City Madam* II. ii, Drawn by six Flanders mares, my coachman, grooms, Postillion, and footmen. **1771** N. NICHOLLS *Corr. w. Gray* (1843) 118 The Yarmouth coach, when it has gone at all, has gone with eight horses and four postilions. **1811** WELLINGTON in Gurw. *Desp.* VIII. 286 The account of the rations issued to the post horses and mules, and postillions. **1881** BESANT & RICE *Chapl. of Fleet* III. 173 They called aloud to the postilions to stop the horses.
fig. **1656** COWLEY *Pindar. Odes, Muse* i, Let the Postilion Nature mount, and let The Coachman Art be set.

4. (*transf.* from 3.) See quot.

1888 GOODE *Amer. Fishes* 8 The use of supplementary floats, or 'postillions',..to keep the line from sinking.

5. = *postilion-basque*: see 6.

6. *attrib.* and *Comb.*, as ***postilion harness, saddle, whip***; ***postilion-wise*** adv.; in recent use applied to female costume imitating that of a postilion, as ***postilion-basque, -belt, -tab***, etc.

1676 W. PERWICH *Despatches* (Camden) 311 They..tore all his cloaths off, and with two postilion whips scurged him ..severely. **1689** *Lond. Gaz.* No. 2475/4 A Postilion Saddle of black Leather. **1794** W. FELTON *Carriages* (1801) II. 153 A postillion..harness is the same expence as either the postillion or wheel harness of the other sort. **1840** DICKENS *Barn. Rudge* lix, One of them..sat postillion-wise upon the near horse. **1872** *Young Englishwoman* Dec. 651/2 A dress of olive-brown..had a basque bodice with a postilion back. **1890** *Cent. Dict., Postilion-basque*, a woman's basque having its skirt cut at the back into short square tabs or coat-tails, after the fashion of a postilion's coat. *Postilion-belt*, a leather belt with a large buckle, worn by ladies about 1860. **1904** *Daily Chron.* 2 Jan. 8/4 The postilion tabs at the back of the bodice. *Ibid.* 28 May 8/4 The corslet belt, with postillion back.

Hence **po'stilioned, postill-** (-jənd) *a.*, provided with or ridden by a postilion; **po'stil(l)ioness**, a female postilion; **po'stilionize** *v. trans.*, to provide with a postilion, or to ride as a postilion.

1809 in *Spirit Pub. Jrnls.* XIII. 165 Then spank away drives I,..with my six greys (postilionized) against all England! **1858** B. TAYLOR *North. Trav.* xxxv. 378 At Vik.. we parted with the postillioness and with our host of Kettbo. **1879** *Daily News* 25 Nov. 5/6 Lord Rosebery,..driving down in an open barouche drawn by four magnificent horses, daintily postillioned.

† **'postillary,** *a.* *Obs. rare.* [f. med.L. **postillāri-us* (Du Cange has *postillārium* as sb.), f. *postilla* POSTIL + -OUS.] Of the nature of a 'postil'.

1653 HAMMOND *Paraphr. N.T.* Advt., Purposely abstaining from..all postillary observations.

'postillate, *v. rare.* [f. ppl. stem of med.L. *postillāre*: see POSTIL *v.* and -ATE³.] = POSTIL *v.*

1432–50 tr. *Higden* (Rolls) VIII. 235 Hewe frere of the ordre Precheours..whiche postillate alle the bible [*qui totam bibliam postillavit*], and compilede grete concordances on the bible. *a* **1864** C. KNIGHT (Webster), Tracts..which belonged to George III and in a few instances are postillated by his own hand. **1864** D. P. KIDDER *Homiletics* iv. 95 With the..Reformation both the idea and the practice of postillating were superseded by evangelical preaching.

†**b.** 'Formerly, To preach by expounding Scripture, verse by verse, in order' (Webster 1847).

Hence **posti'llation**, the writing of postils.

1847 WEBSTER, *Postillation*, exposition of Scripture in preaching. **1864** *Ibid.*, *Postillation*, the act of postillating.

postillator ('pɒstɪleɪtə(r)). Also 4 -our. [a. med.L. *postillātor*, agent-n. f. *postillāre*: see POSTIL *v.* and -OR.] = next.

1382 WYCLIF *Prol.* 58 Myche sharpliere and groundliere than manie late postillatouris, eithir expositouris, han don. **1613** SPELMAN *De non Temer. Eccl.* (1846) 38 Great Hugo Cardinalis, the first Postillator of the Bible. **1872** R. C. JENKINS in *Archæol. Cant.* VIII. 64 The Postillator on the 'Summa' of St. Raymond.

† **'postiller.** *Obs.* Also 6 postilar, 7 postillar, -iler, -eller. [f. POSTIL *v.* + -ER¹. Cf. OF. *postilleur* (1478 in Godef.).] One who makes or writes a 'postil' or 'postils'; a commentator, annotator, expositor.

1526 *Pilgr. Pref.* (W. de W. 1531) 138 Yet, after our postilars, he came agayne at yᵉ passyon of our sayd lord. **1612** T. TAYLOR *Comm. Titus* i. 7 Not drawne out of the poysoned puddles of Popish Friers, or postillars. **1621** S. WARD *Life of Faith* 99 Subtilties of School-men, sentences and conceits of Postilers. **1662** HIBBERT *Body Div.* I. 216 Shepherds (as the Roman postellers observe) must have three things, 1. scrip. 2. staffe. 3. whistle.

¶ Error for *pistoler*, PISTLER.

1891 ST. J. TYRWHITT in *Colleges of Oxford* 307 A gospeller and a postiller (Bible-clerk), eight singing clerks.

† **po'stillian,** *a.* *Obs. rare*⁻¹. [f. med.L. *postilla*: see POSTIL and -IAN.] That writes postils.

1627 PERROT *Tithes* 45 They would censure a poore Postillian Divine that should goe about to call into question the faithfulnes of Ployden.

po'stil(l)ion, *v. slang.* [f. the sb.] *trans.* To insert and manipulate a finger in the anus of (a sexual partner) as a means of sexual excitement. Hence **po'stil(l)ioning** *vbl. sb.*

1888 tr. *Tableaux Vivants* xi. 95 The fair houri was postillioning me. **1969** G. LEGMAN *Oragenitalism* i. 90 Postillioning can best be done by the middle finger.

postillion: see POSTILION.

† **'postillism.** *Obs. rare*⁻¹. [f. POSTIL + -ISM.] A production of the nature of a 'postil' or comment. So † **'postillize** *v.* = POSTIL *v.*

1622 SYDENHAM *Serm. Sol. Occ.* (1637) II. 97 If we can fleyle down the transgressions of the times by some few stolne Postellismes. **1691** WOOD *Ath. Oxon.* I. 9 Besides his postillizing the whole Doctrine of Duns Scotus.

post-im'pressionism. Freq. with capital initials. [POST- B. 1 c.] The theory or practice of the post-impressionist school in art; *spec.* a style of painting favoured in the early years of the twentieth century in which the artist sought to reveal the structural form of his subject without strict fidelity to its natural appearance; a movement or group of aims in art which constitutes a development away from impressionism.

1910 C. J. HOLMES *Notes on Post-Impressionist Painters* 11 The tradition of Post-Impressionism,..if any principles so youthful can be called a tradition, is the expression of personal vision. **1910** *Connoisseur* Dec. 315/2 The committee..wisely diluted the post-impressionism of the pictures in the entrance room by the inclusion of a dozen or more examples by Manet. **1932** *John o' London's Weekly* 30 Jan. 678/3 'Harbour of Gravelines' shows him [*sc.* Seurat] trying..to impose upon impressionism its missing sense of form. But that triumph goes to the two masters of post-impressionism, to Cezanne [*sic*] and Gauguin. **1948** R. O. DUNLOP *Understanding Pictures* iii. 20 This painter's name was, of course, Paul Cézanne, the unconscious founder of Post-Impressionism. **1957** *Observer* 3 Nov. 14/3 The deficiencies of Impressionism..were clear to many in the 1880s, and the term Post-Impressionism covers the often very different reactions of artists. **1972** S. HYNES *Edwardian Occasions* 10 Bloomsbury..supported Roger Fry's efforts to publicize Post-Impressionism. **1978** *Antiques & Art Monitor* 28 Oct. 11/3 A major exhibition entitled 'Post-Impressionism and Europe' is scheduled for the Royal Academy, London, next year.

post-im'pressionist. Freq. with capital initials. [POST- B. 1 b.] An artist whose work exhibits one or more of the facets of post-impressionism; also *transf.* and *attrib.* or as *adj.* Hence **post-impressio'nistic** *a.*, characteristic of the post-impressionists.

1910 *Poster* in *Lett. R. Fry* (1972) I. Pl. 47 Grafton Gallery. Manet and the Post-Impressionists. **1910** C. J. HOLMES *Notes on Post-Impressionists* 10 In the first Post-Impressionist painters we have a reaction from the materialism which limited the original Impressionists to the rendering of natural effects of light and colour with the greatest attainable scientific truth. **1911** *Athenæum* 28 Jan. 104/3 Post-Impressionist Sculpture. **1913** A. E. HOUSMAN *Let.* 8 Mar. (1971) 129 An exhibition of post-impressionist undergraduate art, which is calculated to frighten the Germans. **1913** *Punch* 16 July 70/1 They grumble at the ladies' skirts, The Post-Impressionistic settings. **1914** H. HOLLEY (*title*) Creation: Post-Impressionist poems. **1922** C. BELL *Since Cézanne* 81, I can't think why you don't like it: its Post-Impressionist isn't it? **1928** [see CUBISM]. **1934** C. LAMBERT *Music Ho!* III. 22 The post-impressionist harmonic experiments, the austerities and asperities of Stravinsky and Bartók. **1945** D. MACCARTHY *Memories* (1953) 181 'What was the exhibition to be called?'..At last Roger [Fry], losing patience, said: 'Oh, let's just call them post-impressionists; at any rate, they come after the impressionists.' **1957** MANVELL & HUNTLEY *Technique Film Music* iii. 70 In each sequence décor is derived from the style of one or other of the post-Impressionist painters. **1974** *Impressionism* (R. Acad.) 53/1 Increasingly affected by Post-Impressionists 1909+, with rest of Camden Town Group. **1978** *Jrnl. R. Soc. Arts* CXXVI. 701/2 Mrs. Potter Palmer had been buying Impressionist and post-Impressionist paintings with great discernment almost a century ago.

postīn: see POSTEEN.

post-infectious: see POST- B. 1.

posting ('pəʊstɪŋ), *vbl. sb.*¹ [f. POST *v.*¹ + -ING¹.] The action of POST *v.*¹ in various senses.

I. 1. a. † The dispatching of letters, etc., by a messenger riding 'post' (*obs.*). **b.** Travelling by means of relays of horses. **c.** The keeping of post-horses, -vehicles, etc., as a business.

c **1559** R. HALL *Life of Fisher* lf. 42 b, Then wanted no posting of letters betweene yᵉ kinge and yᵉ ambassadors. **1611** SPEED *Hist. Gt. Brit.* IX. xxiii. (1623) 1128 Betwixt whom were such posting of letters, such speeding to and fro. **1653** R. SANDERS *Physiogn.* 157 They [persons] will be prompt, and fit for posting. **1790** CATH. M. GRAHAM *Lett. Educ.* 141 Posting on the continent is now so much the fashion, as often to oblige a man of fortune to repeat his tour, in order to gratify his family. **1840** *Penny Cycl.* XVIII. 459/2 Posting continues in most countries to be carried on by the state, which retains the monopoly of supplying post-horses, and..of forwarding mails and diligences. *Ibid.* 460/1 Between Vienna and Pesth there is..an independent posting establishment, the speculation of peasants who drive their own horses, and called 'Bauern post'. *Ibid.* 460/2 The great superiority of English over foreign posting [shows] that..open competition in this trade is preferable to a government monopoly and control. *a* **1908** *Mod. Hotel Advt.*, Posting in all its branches.

†**2.** Speedy travelling: hastening, haste, hurry.

1589 WARNER *Alb. Eng.* VI. xxx. (1612) 149, I say, that Beautie beggeth if by posting it be got. **1599** T. M[OUFET] *Silkwormes* 12 Whereat the fearefull maide in posting flung ..Into a secret caue. **1632** LITHGOW *Trav.* IX. 500 All the Gold of the Kingdome, is daily Transported away with superfluous posting for Court.

3. The dispatching or conveying of letters and other postal matter through or by the post office; the putting of a letter, etc., into the charge of the post office, or into a post-office letter-box. Also, the (amount of) mail posted during a given period.

1871 M. COLLINS *Mrq. & Merch.* I. v. 176 [He] showed her the way to the post-office, and gave her..information as to the hours of posting. **1884** *Act 47 & 48 Vict.* c. 76 §19. (2) The due posting of a postal packet. **1900** *Daily News* 13 June 6/7 Late fee posting at pillar-boxes..is to be withdrawn on the 18th inst. **1909** *Daily Chron.* 30 Dec. 3/6 During the Christmas week of last year the postings in London alone totalled upwards of 70,000,000. **1971** D. POTTER *Brit. Eliz. Stamps* i. 14 Beginning with the Shakespeare set in 1964, special envelopes were..used. Stratford-on-Avon must have had one of their heaviest postings ever.

II. †**4.** The transferring (of responsibility, etc.) to another. Also with *off*, *over*. *Obs.*

a **1591** H. SMITH *Serm.* (1866) II. 236 There will be such a posting off of sin, that never a one will be found guilty. **1616** SURFL. & MARKH. *Country Farme* 13 Manifested by deed of Indenture, or posting ouer of the charge to another. **1617** HIERON *Wks.* II. 320 A shamelesse excusing of euill, with a posting it ouer vnto God.

5. *Book-keeping.* The carrying of an entry from the journal or other auxiliary book into the ledger; the formal entry of an item in a book of accounts; the bringing of account books up to date.

1682 SCARLETT *Exchanges* 38 In the posting of the same into his great Book, or Leidger, the Forreign Coynes must be duely exprest. **1745** *De Foe's Eng. Tradesman* (1841) I. xxxi. 323 There is no posting the books on a death-bed. **1849** FREESE *Comm. Class-bk.* 111 In order to prove the correctness of the Postings to the Ledger. **1850** *Plan for Ch. Hist. Soc.* 9 What they chiefly want is what..commercial men call 'posting up'.

III. 6. *attrib.* and *Comb.*: in sense 1, as ***posting carriage, establishment, house, inn***; in sense 3, as ***posting box, clerk***; **posting-belt**, a broad leather or other belt worn by postilions or post-boys.

1737 *Med. Ess. & Observ.* IV. 61 Our Patient..was desired to wear a posting Belt, with proper Compresses upon the Place where the Wound had been, for some time, ..that upon any violent Motion a *Hernia* might be prevented. **1836** DICKENS *Sk. Boz, Winglebury Duel*, The Winglebury Arms..is the principal Inn of Great Winglebury—the commercial inn, posting-house and excise-office. **1844** —— *Mart. Chuz.* xx, They had a posting carriage at the porch. **1876** T. HARDY *Ethelberta* (1890) 354, I think the best posting-house at this end of the town is Tempett's. **1893** *Scott. Leader* 12 June 2/1 Posting Establishment Complete. **1895** *Daily News* 31 May 3/6 The branch and sub-offices at which the posting boxes are continuously open. **1899** A. H. SAYCE *Early Israel* v. 160 Carriage roads were constructed with posting inns at intervals along them.

'posting, *vbl. sb.*² [f. POST *v.*² + -ING¹.] The action of POST *v.*² in various senses: *spec.*

1. The mooring of a vessel to a post. Also *attrib.* as ***posting dues***.

1868 *Exeter & Plymouth Gaz.* 13 Mar., Paying a small sum to the owner for 'posting'—that was for tying up the vessels to a post. *Ibid.*, He paid posting dues twenty-six years ago to Mr. Chapple, but not since. Harbour dues were paid to Mr. Chanter, Lord of the Manor of Northam.

2. a. The action of fixing a placard, notice, etc. on a post, etc., or of making anything public by this means; public advertisement by posters.

1656 EARL MONM. tr. *Boccalini's Advts. fr. Parnass.* I. xl. (1674) 54 The very night after the posting up of this defiance. **1701–3** (*title of MS.*) A Book of Postings and Sale of the Forfeited and other Estates and Interests in Ireland. **1850** HT. MARTINEAU *Hist. Peace* II. IV. ix. 412 The people would not permit the posting of notices of arrears. **1862** *Boston Transcr.* 22 Aug. 1/2 Is there no way of protection against the posting of bills about our city?

b. *attrib.* and *Comb.*, as ***posting-board, -business***; **posting-bill**, a placard: = POSTER² 2.

1802 *Naval Chron.* VIII. 436 Posting bills have been put up.., offering a bounty. **1838** *Actors by Daylight* I. 182 A pair or two of wooden posting-boards. **1884** *West. Morn. News* 30 Aug. 1/5 Particulars will appear in posting bills. **1889** *Pall Mall G.* 23 Jan. 3/1 It is now ten years ago since the picture posting business was first reduced not only to an art but almost to a science.

posting, *vbl. sb.*³ and ⁴: see POST *v.*³ and ⁴.

posting ('pəʊstɪŋ), *ppl. a.* [f. POST *v.*[1] + -ING[2].] That posts; swift, speedy, rapid; hasty, hurrying, fleeting.

posting fever, sweat, the sweating sickness, *sudor anglicanus*, of which several epidemics occurred 1481–1551.

c **1553** in Strype *Eccl. Mem.* (1721) III. vii. 72 The posting sweat, that posted from town to town thorow England, and was named 'stop-gallant'. **1575** R. B. *Appius & Virginia* D j, With posting speede, to Court I do repaire. **1611** BIBLE *Transl. Pref.* 10 Neither did we run ouer the worke with that posting haste that the Septuagint did. **1642** GAUDEN *Three Serm.* 26 A few posting and perfunctory prayers. **1718** PRIOR *Solomon* II. 827 This only object of my real care,.. In some few posting fatal hours is hurled From wealth. **1891** CREIGHTON *Hist. Epidemics* I. 276 Like dengue, influenza, and others of the 'posting' fevers of former time.

Hence **'postingly** *adv.*, hastily, hurriedly.

1636 EARL OF CORK in *Lismore Papers* (1888) Ser. II. III. 259, I could neuer see that [paper].. neither can I remember the contents of it, it was so postingly read ouer vnto me.

postique (pɒ'stiːk), *a.* [app. by-form of POSTICHE.] = POSTICHE A. b.

1727–41 CHAMBERS *Cycl.* s.v., In architecture, &c., an ornament of sculpture is said to be *postique*, when it is superadded after the work itself is done. The word is formed from the Italian, *posticcio*, added. A table of marble, or other matter, is also said to be *postique*, when it is incrustated in a decoration of architecture, &c.

postischial: see POST- B. 2.

postjacent (pəʊst'dʒeɪsənt), *a.* [f. L. *post* (POST- B. 2) + L. *jacēnt-em* lying: cf. *adjacent*.] Lying behind; posterior.

1878 BELL *Gegenbaur's Comp. Anat.* 455 A defensive arrangement, which extends over the postjacent branchial clefts.

'postjudice. *nonce-wd.* [f. POST- A. 1 b, after *prejudice*.] (See quot.) So **'postjudiced** *a.*

1886 RUSKIN *Præterita* I. vi. 174 Hence what people call my prejudiced views of things,—which are, in fact, the exact contrary, namely, post-judiced. **1905** G. K. CHESTERTON *R. Browning* v. 115 Prejudice is not so much the great intellectual sin as a thing which, we may call, to coin a word, 'postjudice', not the bias before the fair trial, but the bias that remains after.

† **'post-knight.** *Obs.* [f. POST *sb.*[1] + KNIGHT *sb.*] = KNIGHT OF THE POST, a notorious perjurer.

1594 *Merry Knack to know Knave* D j, Why, I haue bene a post knight in Westminster this xii. year. **1630** J. TAYLOR (Water P.) *Praise Hempseed* Wks. III. 73/2 The sixt a post-knight, that for fiue groats gaine Would sweare, and for foure groats forsweare 't againe.

postlapsarian, etc.: see POST- B. 1, A. 1 b.

post-'larval, *a. Zool.* [POST- B. 1 b.] Belonging or pertaining to those stages in the development of certain animals in which some larval characteristics may be retained, before the adult form is reached. So **post-'larva**, an animal, esp. a fish, during this period of its development.

1898 *Proc. Zool. Soc.* 204 (*title*) On the early post-larval stages of the Common Crab. **1929** *Amer. Naturalist* LXIII. 160 Some.. interesting discoveries.. have resulted from the writer's investigations into the habits of young postlarval lobsters. **1942** *Copeia* 126 (*heading*) The occurrence of flounder post larvae in fish stomachs. **1962** K. F. LAGLER et al. *Ichthyol.* x. 313 Differences between postlarvae and adults in some fishes are so trenchant that they have resulted from time to time in taxonomic confusion. **1967** *Oceanogr. & Marine Biol.* V. 239 The post-larval development of Copepods similarly aroused Mazza's interest. **1972** *Aquaculture* I. 179 (*caption*) Third postlarval stage with 18 mm of total length. **1973** *Ibid.* I. 363 Postlarvae and juvenile siganids are attracted by artificial light at night.

† **'postle.** *Obs.* Forms: 1 postol, 3 (Orm.) posstell, 3–6 postel, postle, 4 postyll, *Sc.* -ule, 4–5 -il, -ill(e, -ele, 6 -elle. [OE. *postol*, aphetic form of *apostol*, APOSTLE.] = APOSTLE.

c **975** *Rushw. Gosp.* Luke xxiv. 10 Ða oðre.. cwedun ðas to ðæm postolum. c **1200** ORMIN 5186 Cristess posstell, Sannt Johan. **13..** *Cursor M.* 20928 (Edin.) Siþin he com to postlis state [*Gött.* postil]. c **1375** *Sc. Leg. Saints* xxvii. (*Machor*) 1552 Ihesus his postulis xij ymang. **1377** LANGL. *P. Pl.* B. XVI. 159 Suffreth my postles in pays & in pees gange. c **1489** CAXTON *Sonnes of Aymon* x. 272 By saynt peter the postle. **1533** MORE *Apol.* 149 b, Yᵉ postle maye make some bysshoppes amonge the new brethern.

postle, variant of POSTIL, *Obs.*

postless ('pəʊstlɪs), *a. nonce-wd.* [f. POST *sb.*[2] + -LESS.] Without a postal service.

1885 MRS. INNES in *Athenæum* 12 Dec. 764 A return to our .. doctorless, bookless, milkless, postless, and altogether comfortless jungle.

post-like: see POST *sb.*[1] and [2].

postliminary (pəʊst'lɪmɪnərɪ), *a.* [f. L. *post* after + *līmen, līmin-* threshold + -ARY[1]; but in sense 1 associated with POSTLIMINIUM.

The etymological derivatives of L. *postlīminium* are *postliminiar, -iary, -iate, -iation, -ious*; and those of L. *post* + *līmen* (opposed to *preliminary*, etc.), *postliminary, -liminate, -limination, -liminous*. But in some cases erroneous use confuses the two series, and exchanges the senses.]

1. *erron.* Pertaining to or involving the right of postliminium; postliminiary.

1702 WOODROFFE *Daniel's 70 Weeks* Ep. A ij b, I trust, 'twill not be long e're the Jews themselves shall return to their Postliminary Right. **1807** WRANGHAM *Serm. Transl. Script.* 21 Admitted to the postliminary perception of her inalienable rights. **1860** WOOLSEY *Introd. Internat. Law* § 145. 333 The rights and obligation of a state restored in this postliminary way.

2. Subsequent: opposed to *preliminary*.

1826 SCOTT *Woodst.* xvi. *note*, The rere-supper was a postliminary banquet,.. which made its appearance at ten or eleven. **1827** —— *Jrnl.* 23 May I. 396, I found I had mislaid a number of the said postliminary affair.

† **post'liminate,** *v.* [f. as prec. + -ATE[3].] *trans.* To place behind, or in a subsequent place.

1690[see POSTLIMINIATE *v.* 2, quot. 1659].

† **postlimi'nation.** *Obs.* = POSTLIMINIATION.

1655 H. L'ESTRANGE *Chas. I* 45 An order that nothing should be transacted in their House, untill the Earl of Arundel were restored: upon which instantly ensued the Earls postlimination and readmittance.

† **postliminiage.** *Obs. rare*$^{-0}$. [f. as next + -AGE.] = POSTLIMINY.

1661 BLOUNT *Glossogr.* (ed. 2), *Postliminiage*.., a return of one who was thought to be dead, and so restored to his house, not by going over the threshold, but by making a hole in the wall.

† **postli'miniar,** *a. Obs. rare*$^{-1}$. [f. L. *postlimini-um* + -AR[1].] Of, pertaining to, or in accordance with the law of POSTLIMINIUM.

1681 HALLEYWELL *Melampr.* 70 It may be said, that.. the Soul may be rapt from this Terrestrial Body, and carried to remote and distant places, from whence she may make a Postliminiar return.

postli'miniary, *a. rare*$^{-0}$. [f. as prec. + -ARY[1].] A more etymological form of POSTLIMINARY in sense 1.

1882 in OGILVIE (Annandale).

† **postli'miniate,** *v. Obs.* [f. as prec. + -ATE[3].]

1. *trans.* To allow to return from banishment.

1655 H. L'ESTRANGE *Chas. I* 2 The hopes that.. his Brother.. should be postliminiated and restored to his inheritance of the Palatinate. **1659** —— *Alliance Div. Off.* 25 Just cause to wish either those Apocryphals postliminiated again, or others of the Canon to succeed them.

2. *erron.* for POSTLIMINATE. (See note s.v. POSTLIMINARY.)

1659 H. L'ESTRANGE *Alliance Div. Off.* 303 It may seem a wonder why.. this Communion Order is postliminiated [*ed.* 1690 postliminated] into that Burial Office.

Hence † **postlimini'ation**, restoration to civic rights and privileges; reinstatement. *Obs. rare*$^{-1}$.

1659 H. L'ESTRANGE *Alliance Div. Off.* 323 His postliminiation gave him liberty to approach no nearer the Altar then the Cancellum.

postliminious (pəʊstlɪ'mɪnɪəs), *a.* [f. as prec. + -OUS.]

1. Of or pertaining to postliminium. *rare.*

1656 BLOUNT *Glossogr.*, *Postliminious*, pertaining to the return of one, who was thought to be dead, or to the receiving that again, which had been alienated, or lost.

2. *erron.* Done or contrived subsequently; subsequent; = POSTLIMINOUS 2. (See POSTLIMINARY.)

1684–5 SOUTH *Serm.* (1697) I. 337 They are forced.. to strike in with things as they fall out, by post-liminious after-applications of them to their purposes. **1804** F. PLOWDEN (*title*) A Postliminious Preface to the Historical Review of the State of Ireland. **1805** W. TAYLOR in *Ann. Rev.* III. 268/1 The large work.. to which this pamphlet, with Irish aptness, is entitled a Postliminious preface. **1826** *Blackw. Mag.* XIX. 396 Every reel has a kiss by way of introduction and postliminious preface. **1850** L. HUNT *Autobiog.* II. xiv. 146 Mr. Holme Sumner.. told the House of Commons that my room had a view over the Surrey hills.. I could not feel obliged to him for this postliminious piece of enjoyment.

‖ **postliminium** (pəʊstlɪ'mɪnɪəm). [L. *postlīminium* a return 'behind one's threshold', f. *post*, POST- B. 2 + *limen, -in-* threshold.] In *Roman Law*, The right to return home and resume one's former privileges: = POSTLIMINY.

[**1611** J. CHAMBERLAIN in *Crt. & Times Jas. I* (1848) I. 146 Being.. called in question, *post-liminio* [*abl.* = 'by postliminium'], for the powder treason.] **1638** CHILLINGW. *Relig. Prot.* I. iii. § 28. 141 The Church.. afterwards, as it were by the law of *Postliminium*, hath restored their Authority and Canonicalnesse unto them. **1669** in *Evelyn's Corr.* (1852) III. 219 At my postliminium, all my hope and ambition was to exchange a shilling for three groats. **1809** *Edin. Rev.* XIII. 440 The amnestied emigrants.. enjoy.. but little of the benefits of *postliminium*. **1875** POSTE *Gaius* I. Comm. (ed. 2) 110 Postliminium is the recovery of rights by a person returned from captivity, or the recovery of rights over a person or thing recovered from hostile possession.

postliminous (pəʊst'lɪmɪnəs), *a.* [f. L. *post* after + *limen, -in-* threshold + -OUS.]

† **1.** *erron.* Of or pertaining to postliminium; = POSTLIMINIOUS 1. *Obs. rare.* (See note s.v. POSTLIMINARY.)

1640 HOWELL *Dodona's Gr.* 213 Fearing that by a postliminous way something should bee re-annexd both to Church and Crowne.

2. Subsequent; of the nature of an appendix; = POSTLIMINARY 2: opposed to *preliminary*.

1714 R. FIDDES *Pract. Disc.* II. 38 This, if I may so speak, is only a postliminous way of sinning. **1855** LD. CAMPBELL in *Life* (1881) II. 338 That he [Macaulay] should thence give a postliminous sketch of subsequent English history to correspond with the preliminary sketch, prior to the reign of James II.

postliminy (pəʊst'lɪmɪnɪ). [Anglicized form of POSTLIMINIUM.] In *Rom. Law*, The right of any person who had been banished or taken captive, to assume his former civic privileges on his return home. Hence, in *Internat. Law*, The restoration to their former state of persons and things taken in war, when they come again into the power of the nation to which they belonged.

1658 PHILLIPS, *Postliminie*, the return of one, who was thought to be dead. [*ed.* **1678** *adds*, also a return from Exile or Captivity.] **1860** WOOLSEY *Introd. Internat. Law* § 143. 331 As to limit of place modern postliminy takes effect only within the territory of the captor or his ally. **1861** J. KENT *Comm. Amer. Law* (1873) I. v. 109 Movables are not entitled, by strict rules of the laws of nations, to the full benefit of postliminy, unless [etc.]. **1875** POSTE *Gaius* II. Comm. (ed. 2) 223 If he returned from captivity his will reacquired validity by the operation of postliminy.

post-line: see POST *sb.*[1] and [3].

postliteral: see POST- B. 1.

postlude ('pəʊstl(j)uːd). [f. POST- A. 1 b + L. *lūdus* play, on analogy of *prelude, interlude*; so mod.L. *postlūdium*.] **a.** *Mus.* A concluding piece or movement played at the end of an oratorio or the like; a concluding voluntary.

1851 *Fraser's Mag.* XLIII. 460 The prelude and the postlude, in which he has enveloped Handel, are his own. **1866** ENGEL *Nat. Mus.* viii. 279 This is sung to the following tune, in which the instruments have after each verse a little postlude of three or four bars. **1891** *Sat. Rev.* 17 Oct. 441/2 The 'postlude' of the chorus. **1947** A. EINSTEIN *Mus. Romantic Era* xiv. 187 The task.. of supplying a commentary in the prelude and, particularly, the postlude. **1955** G. ABRAHAM in H. Van Thal *Fanfare for E. Newman* 26 The second version of the piano postlude to 'Schmerzen' was sent to Frau Wesendonk on a separate piece of paper. **1976** *Gramophone* Jan. 1229/1 Why the ties in the penultimate bar of the prelude and postlude of 'Pause'?

b. A written or spoken epilogue; an afterword, conclusion; an envoy.

1928 M. WILLIAMS *Catholicism & Mod. Mind* 339 (*heading*) Postlude: Easter in Gethsemani. **1934** *Punch* 2 May 503/2 Miss Bowen's 'postlude', a carefully reasoned essay in historical criticism, is a drastic and devastating but on many points convincing analysis of romantic legend. **1939** JOYCE *Finnegans Wake* (1964) 426 As the wisest postlude course he could playact, collaspsed [*sic*] in ensemble and rolled buoyantly backwards. **1959** *Times* 11 Sept. 16/6 Mr. Gerald Moore.. whose little summarizing postludes to many of the songs.. were miracles of concentrated wisdom. **1974** *Times* 15 Apr. 5/6 The rumpus was mostly caused by a very offensive postlude, spoken by one of the actors.

Hence **'postlude** *v. intr.*, to supply a postlude; **post'ludial** *a.*

1960 'A. BURGESS' *Doctor is Sick* xxi. 174 The psalmist ended, postluded. **1961** *Times* 10 Nov. 18/6 One of the poems is set twice: another has a preludial and postludial movement.

'postly, *adv. nonce-wd.* [f. POST *sb.*[2] + -LY[2].] By or in the post.

1757 MRS. GRIFFITH *Lett. Henry & Frances* (1767) IV. 244, I.. am almost tempted to write to you there, instead of suffering mine to pass you by, as they do, *postly*, at present.

postman[1] ('pəʊstmən). [f. POST *sb.*[2] + MAN *sb.*[1]]

1. A bearer or carrier of letters or other postal matter:

a. *orig.* A courier who rode 'post'. **b.** Now, One who delivers letters, etc., sent through the post, or collects them from the letter-boxes, receiving offices, etc.; a letter-carrier.

1529 *Acc. Ld. High Treas. Scot.* V. 383 David Mullray usher of the kitchen door, John Anderson, postman [etc.]. **1600** *Child-Marriages* 179 Receiued one packquet.. to be conveyed by the poste to Sir Roberte Cecill; which was, presentley vppon the receipt thereof, deliuered to the post-man to be conveyed accordingly. **1621** QUARLES *Esther* viii, By speedy Post men were the Letters sent. **1758** in Howell *State Trials* 1371, I received every one of these letters from the postman of the walk. **1783** JOHNSON 23 Mar. in *Boswell*, I may as well make a present to the postman who brings me a letter. **1785** CRABBE *Newspaper* 269 We.. wait till the post-man brings the packet down. **1839** THACKERAY *Major Gahagan* iii, As every twopenny postman knows. **1882** 'OUIDA' *Maremma* vii, The postman came over the plains.. very irregularly to Santa Tarsilla. **1900** *Westm. Gaz.* 6 Feb. 10/1 In the Franco-German war,.. pigeons did excellent service, and on the Continent experiments with these postmen of the air are going on continually.

c. *Comb.*, as *postman-like* adj. and adv.; **postman-pigeon**, the carrier pigeon.

1832 MISS MITFORD *Village* Ser. v. (1863) 410 More sins than I can remember, of forgetfulness, irregularity, and all manner of postman-like faults. **1901** *Munsey's Mag.* XXV. 421/1 In his home life, the postman pigeon is most exemplary. He is a faithful husband and a fond father.

d. In the possessive, as **postman's knock**: (*a*) a sharp knock or rap upon a door, typically made by a postman; (*b*) *transf.*, esp. a parlour game in which the participants in turn take the role of postman and deliver letters which are paid for by kisses.

1835 MARRYAT *Pirate* v, That's the postman's knock. **1837** DICKENS *Pickw.* xxix. 312 Sam Weller.. was displaying that beautiful feat of fancy sliding which is currently denominated 'knocking at the cobbler's door', and which is achieved by skimming over the ice on one foot, and occasionally giving a two-penny postman's knock upon it, with the other. **1847** *Sporting Life* 11 Dec. 204/1 The *postman's knock*—a quick rat-tap, which only a postman can execute. **1873** C. M. Yonge *Pillars of House* III. xxxii. 199 A postman's knock made her start. **1927** W. E. Collinson *Contemp. Eng.* 12, I was interested to see the kissing-forfeit game of postman's knock under the guise of 'American post'. **1928** *Daily Express* 30 July 13/6 Rose's left glove was seldom out of his opponent's face, and he often brought off a punch which in the old days was called 'The Postman's Knock'. **1954** M. Sharp *Gipsy in Parlour* xii. 125 Postman's Knock found me..maladroit: to one pimply youth who called me out I presented such a face of scorn that he never kissed me.

†**2.** A newsman, a news-writer. *Obs.*

The Postman was the name of a newspaper *c* 1700: cf. *Spectator* No. 1 ¶5, etc.

1700 Pepys *Corr.* 12 Apr., You want..some news: therefore let me be your postman, and tell you that the State has been for some time under no small convulsion in Parliament. **1709** Addison *Tatler* No. 18 ¶6, I mean the News Writers of Great Britain, whether Post-Men or Post-Boys, or by what other Name or Title soever dignified or distinguished.

†'**postman**[2]. *Obs.* [Of doubtful composition: possibly allied to post-knight, or knight of the post, and *poet of the post*: see post *sb.*[1] 2.] app. A hireling writer of libels or scurrilous falsehoods.

1599 Sandys *Europæ Spec.* (1632) 91 These men in blacking the lives and actions of the Reformers, have partly devised matter of..notorious untruth..; partly suborned other Postmen to compose their Legends, that afterwards they might cite them in proofe to the world as approved authors and histories.

†**postman**[3]. *Obs.* exc. *Hist.* [f. post *sb.*[1] + man *sb.*[1]] A barrister in the Court of Exchequer who had precedence in motions except in Crown business, till the Exchequer was merged in the Queen's Bench Division: the name was derived from the post, the measure of length in excise cases, beside which he took his stand. Cf. tubman.

1768 Blackstone *Comm.* III. iii. 28 *margin*, In the Court of Exchequer two of the most experienced barristers, called the postman and the tubman (from the places in which they sit) have also a precedence in motions. **1882** *Daily News* 15 Dec. 2/1 The last of the postmen was Mr. Charles Hall, Q.C., Attorney-General to the Prince of Wales. **1886** *Pall Mall G.* 9 Aug. 6/1 Sir R. Webster..was called to the bar (Lincoln's Inn) in 1868, held the obsolete posts of 'tubman' of the Court of Exchequer 1872–74, and 'postman' 1874–78, and took silk in 1878.

'**postmark**, *sb.* [f. post *sb.*[2] + mark *sb.*[1]] A mark officially impressed upon letters or other postal packages for various purposes; formerly *esp.* one bearing the name of the office at which the letter was posted, with the words 'paid' or 'unpaid', and the amount of postage; later also, a mark used to deface or obliterate the postage stamp; now, usually a mark giving the place, date, and hour of dispatch, or of the arrival of the mail, in the former case serving also to deface the postage stamp, or combined with a special obliteration-mark for that purpose.

Marks for various other purposes (e.g. to indicate deficient prepayment) are still in occasional use; see the work cited in quot. 1898.

1678 *Trial of Ireland*, etc. 47 *Mr. Oates*..the Post mark upon it was but Two-pence, to be paid for it. **1800** Mrs. Hervey *Mourtray Fam.* III. 94 He received a letter from Henry, without either date or post-mark. **1830** Marryat *King's Own* xiv, The post-mark is Plymouth. **1859** Lady Morgan *Autobiog.* p. vii, [Letters] with their old horrible postmarks of two-and-sixpence and two-and-tenpence (which now would be a penny a head). **1891** Smiles *J. Murray* I. xiv. 344 Letter..dated..26th December, 1814, though the post-mark shows it was not delivered until the 12th of January, 1815. **1898** J. H. Daniels (*title*) A History of British Postmarks. Illustrated. *Ibid.* 5 In 1680 William Dockwra started in London the first Penny Post, and he is also credited with the introduction of postmarks, [but] I have entire letters containing undoubted marks impressed by the General Post fifteen years previously. *Ibid.* 35 The introduction of postage-stamps took place on May 6th, 1840. The postmark used to cancel the stamp is known as the *Maltese Cross*. This was used throughout Great Britain and Ireland until 1844. *Ibid.* 2 The collecting of postmarks is gradually gaining ground as a pursuit.

'**postmark**, *v.* [f. prec. sb.] *trans.* To mark with the post-office stamp, esp. that showing place and date of posting. Almost always in *pass.* Hence '**postmarked** *ppl. a.*; '**postmarking** *vbl. sb.*

1716 *Admiralty Notice* in *Lond. Gaz.* No. 5436/3 A Letter without Date, but Post mark'd, the 24th of this Instant May. **1813** M. Cutler in *Life*, etc. (1888) II. 317 Your favor of February 3d (but postmarked the 18th). **1859** *Regul. P.-O. Department, Washington U.S.* §397 The use of the office dating or post-marking stamp as a canceling instrument is prohibited. **1883** F. M. Crawford *Dr. Claudius* i. 9 The envelope..was post-marked 'New York'.

postmaster[1] ('pəʊstmɑːstə(r)). [f. post *sb.*[2] + master *sb.*[1]: = 15th c. L. *magister postarum*, obs. F. *maître de postes*, It. *maestro delle poste*, Ger. *postmeister* (in 1491 Francis de Taxis, who superintended the Imperial mails, called himself *postmaister*).]

1. †**a.** *orig.* A master of the posts; the officer who had the charge or direction of the post-messengers, whose office gradually developed into that of postmaster general, q.v. †**b.** In the 17th and 18th c., The post-office servant at each of the stations or stages of a post-road, whose primary duty it was to carry the mails to the next stage, and subsequently, to receive and deliver or send out the letters for his own town or district; orig. called post (*sb.*[2] 1); in 1668 ***deputy postmaster***. **c.** Now, The person who has official charge of a post office, and the superintendence of all postal business there transacted.

a. 1513 in Ellis *Orig. Lett.* Ser. ii. I. 210 Whilst I have no postis at my command,..I do my dwte in wrytynge & spende monney to send my lettyrs to th' Emperours postmastir. [**1516** Francis de Taxis (the Emperor's Postmaster) *Let. to Brian Tuke* 23 Mar. (Lett. & Pap. Hen. VIII, II. 1698), [addressed] Magistro Domino meo Brianno Tuke, Magistro Postarum, Londini. **1545** *Patent Hen. VIII* in *Rep. Secret Comm. P.O.* (1844) 33 Officinam Magistri Nunciorum, Cursorum, sive postarum. **1567** *Patent Eliz.* ibid. 34 Officinam Magistri Nunciorum et Cursorum, communiter vocatam Postarum. **1572** *Ibid.*, Thomas Randolphe esquier, Maister of the Postes.] **1574–5** in W. H. Turner *Select. Rec. Oxford* (1880) 376 Item, payed for charges bestowed uppon Mr. Gasquyner the Quenes post master. [**1591** *Proclam.* in *Rep. Secret Comm. on Post Office* (1844) 36 Our Master of the Postes, or the Masters of the Postes Generall of those countreys.] **1625** in *Crt. & Times Chas. I* (1848) I. 24 Questor was overthrown this day sevennight in a suit about the postmaster's office, wherein the Lord Stanhope prevailed against him. **1708** *Lond. Gaz.* No. 4455/2 Count Paar, Post-Master of the Hereditary Countries, goes with her..Majesty as far as Holland.

b, c. 1603 in *Rep. Secret Comm. P.O.* (1844) 38 It is fit and convenient, in this time so full of busines, that the postemasters of every stage be aided and assisted with fresh and able horses. **1637** *Rutland MSS.* IV. 529 Payd to a messenger that came from the postmaster of Newarke, 2s. **1653** *Reg. Council of State* in *Rep. S.C.P.O.* 70 That the Postmasters and others employed by Mr. Prideaux, being godly and well affected, to be continued in their employments. **1659** *Jrnl. Ho. Com.* 10 June, The humble petition of the several postmasters of England in behalf of themselves, and..families, was this day read. **1668** *Lond. Gaz.* No. 322/4 Notice is hereby given, That the Post-Master-General hath contracted.., with all the respective Deputy Post-Masters, to carry from time to time all Letters directed to every particular person within Ten miles from their Stage-Towns, paying Two pence a time besides the London Post, and to bring back their Answers to the said Stage, Gratis. **1681** Boyle *Let. to Bp. H. Jones* Wks. 1772 I. p. clxxx, I resolved to dispatch them by land to Chester, to the post-master of which place I got them particularly recommended by Mr. Dowlin, post-master of Dublin. **1707** Chamberlayne *Pres. St. Eng.* iii. (ed. 22) 442 Upon this grand Office depends 182 Deputy-Post-Masters in England and Scotland, most of which keep regular Offices in their Stages, and Sub-Post-Masters in their Branches. **1771** *Chron.* in *Ann. Reg.* 98/2 The court gave judgment,..declaring, that by the several acts relating to the post-office, all letters must be delivered by the post-master of every post-town, to the persons to whom such letters are directed. **1849** Macaulay *Hist. Eng.* viii. II. 350 The letter addressed to William Lloyd, Bishop of Norwich, was, in spite of all precautions, detained by a postmaster. **1893** H. Joyce *Hist. Post Office* vi. 48 These stages [of the post roads, in 17th c.] were presided over by..postmasters, whose duty it was to carry the mails each over his own stage.

fig. **1607** Dekker *Knts. Conjur.* (1842) 33 The Post-maister of Hell plainly told them that if any so seditious a fellow as Golde were cast into prison, their fathers would never give their consent to haue him ransomed. **1647** Trapp *Comm. Matt.* xxv. 11 Epimetheus' post-masters, *semper victuri*, in Seneca's sense.

2. The master of a posting station, who provides horses for posting; one who keeps a posting establishment; = jobmaster 1.

Originally, the same person as in the earlier stage of sense 1 b; the several postmasters who carried the mails being the only persons licensed to let horses to travellers.

1581 Pettie *Guazzo's Civ. Conv.* ii. (1586) 85 The Postmaister came unto him, and called twice aloude..and forthwith there came out of the Stable a foule greate Groome..who had charge giuen him to make readie three horses. **1598** Shaks. *Merry W.* v. v. 199 It was not Anne, but a Post-masters boy. **1603, 1659** [see 1]. **1810** *Sporting Mag.* XXXV. 56 The defendant is a licenced post-master in the city of London, and had let a chaise and pair of horses for the day. **1840** *Penny Cycl.* XVIII. 461/1 That revenue can be raised on posting, without the government acting as a postmaster, we have England for an example. **1860** Spottiswoode in *Vac. Tour.* 86 The postmaster would give us no horses, as the road by which we were to proceed was not a post-road. **1865** Gladstone *Financ. Statem.* 84, I believe the largest post-masters in the kingdom are in London, and that their principal traffic is to the railway stations.

3. *Canad.* The master of a fur-trading post.

1832 in R. H. Fleming *Minutes Council Northern Dept. Rupert Land* (Hudson Bay Co.) (1940) 236 Post Masters Are a Class which ranks in the Service between Interpreters & Clerks. They are generally persons who while filling the office of common Labourers..were..raised from the 'ranks' and placed in charge of small Posts at Salys. from 35 to £45 p. Annm. **1953** A. R. M. Lower *Unconventional Voy.* 33 The postmaster at Attawapiskat..was minus the toes on his right foot.

postmaster[2] ('pəʊstmɑːstə(r)). The name given at Merton College, Oxford, from the 16th c., to the class of poor scholars instituted in 1380 by John Wyllyot; now the equivalent in that college of the term 'scholar' in general collegiate use.

For the first hundred years these appear in the College Register only as *pueri* (*M. Johannis*) *Wylyot*, 'Wylyot's boys'. But their essential characteristic was the reception of a limited weekly 'portion', *ebdomadalis portionis*; hence we find them (from 1483) styled *porcionistæ* or (1546) *portionistæ*, a term Englished in the 17th c., as by Wood, as *portionists*. The age of the term *postmaster* is not certain: it occurs in the College Records in 1593 in the established name of *Postmasters' Hall*, the dwelling opposite to the college in which the *pueri* or *portionistæ* had resided till *c* 1575, when they were moved into the college. It also appears as the appellation of the *portionistæ* in English letters of 1610 preserved in the Records. But these casual occurrences show only that it was then a long-established name. As to its origin nothing is known; it has been variously conjectured to be a corruption of *portionista*, or a rendering of **post-magister* or **post-minister*, in allusion to the fact that the *portionistæ* were at one time servitors to the Masters or Fellows, perhaps standing behind their chairs at dinner, etc. But *post-minister* does not occur in the college register, and the occurrence of *post-magister* is doubtful.

[**1380** *Ordinatio M. Joh. Wyllyott* (Merton Archives), Sic. admissus quomodo commune pretium modii frumenti 12d. non excedit, percipiat tum 7d. pro ebdomadali portione.. ebdomadalem portionem prius limitatum. **1381** *Merton Coll. Rolls Acc.* Compotus. Magister puerorum Wylyot. **1454** *Ibid.*, Pro communibus puerorum. **1483** (Dec. 31) *Merton Coll. Reg.*, Insuper porcionistarum numerum decretum est augeri sec. magistrorum numerum. **1546** (May 11) *Ibid.*, Scholaris aulæ portionistarum. **1577** (Aug. 1) *Ibid.*, Nullus portionista admittetur qui non habeat suum magistrum tutorem et in ipsius cubiculo pernoctet.]

1593 (Mar. 31) J. Leach (Chanc. Exeter Cathedr.) *Let.* in *Coll. Reg.*, By the ordinacion of my predecessor John Wiliett, founder of postmrs hall. **1610** (Aug. 1) Dr. T. Jesope *ibid.*, I have bin much sorie that I have bin so long hindered from ye performance of my long entended purpose for ye relief of the poore postmasters of Merton Colledg. [So 4 times in letter and 3 times in reply.] **1639** (May 6) Abp. Laud *ibid.*, That no Postmaster shall hold his place after that he hath gotten his grace to be a Graduate in the University. **1647** Wood *Life* 26 May (O.H.S.) I. 135 Samuel Jones was made from being a servitour of All Soules College, either a postmaster or a pro-postmaster. **1655** Fuller *Ch. Hist.* iii. vi. §8 Much honoured, in that Bishop Jewel was a postmaster before removed hence to be a fellow of Corpus Christi Colledg. **1769** *De Foe's Tour Gt. Brit.* II. 241 Merton-College... This College has a Warden, 24 Fellows, 14 Portionists or Postmasters, and 2 Clerks. **1853** 'C. Bede' *Verdant Green* i. vii, At Merton there are fourteen postmasters.

'**postmaster** '**general**. Pl. postmasters general. [f. postmaster[1] + general *a.* Called in 16th c. Latin *magister postarum* (see postmaster[1] 1 a): in 17th c. *magister generalis nunciorum et cursorum*, also *general postmaster*.] The administrative head of the postal service of a country or state, in Great Britain often, and in U.S. always, a member of the cabinet. (On 1 Oct. 1969 the office of postmaster general was abolished in Great Britain and responsibility for executing its functions was transferred to the newly constituted Post Office Board.)

1626 in *Rep. Secret Comm. P.O.* (1844) 48 The matter in controversie betwixt the Lord Stanhope and Matthew de Questir, concerning the office of Postmaster-general. **1629** *Reg. Privy Council Scot.* Ser. ii. III. 8 [Sir William Seatoun] generall postmaister to his Majestie throughout this haill kingdome. **1636** J. Taylor (Water P.) *Carriers Cosmogr.* ad fin., Let them repaire to the Generall Post-Master Thomas Withering at his house in Sherburne Lane, neare Abchurch. *c* **1638** (*title*) A discourse shewing the true State and Title of the Comptroller or Postmaster generall of England, the Lord Stanhope's right to it. **1657** [See post office 1]. **1660** *Act 12 Chas. II*, c. 35 §2 Be it further enacted..That such Post Master Generall..shall prepare and provide Horses and Furniture to lett to Hire unto all Through posts and persons rideing in post by Commission. **1663** *Commission* 29 Apr. in *Rep. Secret Comm. P.O.* (1844) 85 Officium Magistri nostri Generalis Nunciorum et Cursorum, communiter vocatum The Office of Post Master Generall. **1707** Chamberlayne *Pres. St. Eng.* iii. (ed. 22) 441 Of the Office of Post-Master General. This Office..is executed by Two Post-Masters-General. **1761** *Brit. Mag.* II. 51 The lords of the Admiralty have been pleased, at the request of the Post-master-general, to order his Majesty's sloops the Alderney and Hound, to sail to Flushing. **1846** J. Baxter *Libr. Pract. Agric.* (ed. 4) I. p. xiii, His Grace was one of the best Postmaster Generals who ever filled that important office. **1872** *Act of Congress* 8 June in *U.S. Stat.* XVII. 309 The postmaster-general shall provide for carrying the mail on all post-roads established by law.

Hence '**postmaster-**'**generalship**.

1882 E. W. Hamilton *Diary* 26 Nov. (1972) I. 365 In this list he had included..the Postmaster Generalship. **1885** *Manch. Exam.* 13 June 6/1 Lord John Manners would no doubt return to the Postmaster-Generalship.

'**post**,**mastership**[1]. [f. postmaster[1] + -ship.] The office of postmaster.

a **1603** T. Cartwright *Confut. Rhem. N.T.* (1618) 107 Howsoeuer the Iesuites take vpon them the postmastership of Angels, they are not able to tell how many miles they goe in a minute. **1623** in *Rep. Secret Comm. P.O.* (1844) 46 The office which the Lord Stanhope holdeth for Postmastership within our dominions. **1804** G. Rose *Diaries* (1860) II. 134 Lord Charles Spencer should be allowed to remain in the other joint Postmastership. **1894** *Times* 20 Sept. 4/6 [He] called at the shop of the man who had applied for the postmastership.

ˈpostˌmastership². [f. POSTMASTER² + -SHIP.] The position of postmaster at Merton College, Oxford.

1814 SOUTHEY *Lett.* (1856) II. 386 A good thing, called by the odd name of a postmastership, has been promised him at Merton, which will materially lighten the expense. **1885** *Oxf. Univ. Cal., Merton Coll.* 118 The number of postmasterships or scholarships is 18, but may be increased.

postmaˈture, *a.* [f. POST- B. 1 b; cf. PREMATURE *a.*] **1.** *Obstetrics.* = POST-TERM *a.*

1895 F. A. STAHL in *Amer. Jrnl. Obstetr. & Dis. Women* XXXI. 843, I take the liberty of suggesting the adoption of the term postmature labor to apply to labor which takes place after term. **1937** *Amer. Jrnl. Obstetr. & Gynecol.* XXXIV. 37 When pregnancy is prolonged by new corpora lutea or by progesterone, large postmature fetuses are produced. **1972** S. B. KORONES *High-Risk Newborn Infants* iv. 89 Approximately 75% to 85% of all deaths among postmature babies occur during labor.

2. Pertaining to or designating a person who is over the age of maturity.

1897 A. D. L. NAPIER *Menopause* iv. 79 In the post-mature woman it is partly in the early senile changes that we must look for a solution of the climacteric. **1941** J. S. HUXLEY *Uniqueness of Man* i. 19 A large proportion of the leaders of the community are always post-mature. **1971** *Biochim. & Biophys. Acta* CCXXXVI. 458 (*heading*) Evidence for progressive, age-related structural changes in post-mature human collagen.

Hence **postmaˈturely** *adv.*; **postmaˈturity**, the state of being postmature.

1902 *Jrnl. Obstetr. & Gynæcol.* II. 524 Neither the dimensions of the fœtus, nor the degree of development of his tissues and organs, nor the history of the pregnancy, can be taken as certain proof of postmaturity. **1933** *Jrnl. Pediatrics* II. 677 Similar factors of safety and stability seem to operate when the infant is postmaturely born, for in his behavior equipment he is advanced even though birth is postponed. **1937** *Amer. Jrnl. Obstetr. & Gynecol.* XXXIV. 36 Kaern found that there was a definite relationship between postmaturity, excessive size of the fetus, and intrauterine death. **1941** J. S. HUXLEY *Uniqueness of Man* i. 18 Another point in which man is biologically unique is the length and relative importance of his period of what we may call 'post-maturity.' **1972** E. D. MORRIS in C. J. Dewhurst *Integrated Obstetr. & Gynaecol.* xxii. 383/1 Postmaturity can, in general, be said to be present when the pregnancy has continued so long beyond term that an extra risk to the foetus exists. **1977** *Lancet* 3 Dec. 1169/2 Labour was induced, often before term, for obstetric reasons .. and also for post-maturity—which was defined as 40 weeks plus 7 days.

postmeatal: see POST- B. 2.

postmedial (pəʊstˈmiːdɪəl), *a.* (*sb.*). [f. POST- B. + MEDIAL.] Occupying a position posterior to that which is medial in place, order, or time. Also *absol.* as *sb.*

1680 H. MORE *Apocal. Apoc.* 327 The Postmedial Visions being all of them .. to come. **1852** DANA *Crust.* I. 29, 4 M, a transverse areolet, just posterior to 3 M, the *post-medial.* **1946** L. BLOOMFIELD in H. Hoijer et al. *Ling. Struct. Native Amer.* 104 Suffixes appear in divergent forms, so that we set off accretive elements: premedials, postmedials, prefinals. **1958** *Archivum Linguisticum* X. 170 In some words Postradical, Medial, Postmedial, and Prefinal elements are recognized.

post-median: see POST- B. 2.

‖**ˈpost-mediaˈstinum**. *Anat.* [See POST- A.] = *posterior* MEDIASTINUM (q.v.). So **post-mediastinal** *a.* = posterior mediastinal (arteries, etc.).

post-meiotic, -menarch(e)al: see POST- B. 1.

postˈmenstrual, *a.* *Med.* [POST- B. 1 b.] Occurring after menstruation.

1885 *Brit. Med. Jrnl.* 14 Feb. 342/2 Taking the 'menstrual period' as lasting about four days, he marked off on his temperature-charts four days before the 'show' as the 'premenstrual period', and four days after as the 'post-menstrual period'. **1901** A. E. GILES *Menstruation* ii. 17 The metabolic changes may thus be summarised: .. in the post-menstrual week, gradual return to the normal condition. **1922** JOYCE *Ulysses* 411 The postmenstrual period. **1948** *Amer. Jrnl. Obstetr. & Gynecol.* LV. 38 In other regions the endometrium was of the usual postmenstrual type, and was covered with surface epithelium.

postˈmenstruum. *Med.* [mod.L.: see POST- B. 1 c and MENSTRUUM.] The stage of the menstrual cycle which follows menstruation.

1910 *Trans. N.Y. Obstetr. Soc. 1909–11* 229 They [*sc.* Hitchmann and Adler] divide the monthly cycle into four phases. The first phase, the postmenstruum, corresponds to the picture of the normal endometrium of our text-books. The glands are small and regular, round in cross-section. **1933** *Amer. Jrnl. Anat.* LII. 564 Jaeger .. and Blumenfeld .. found conception most frequent in postmenstruum (63·6 per cent up to the fourteenth day). **1964** K. DALTON *Premenstrual Syndrome* iv. 23 Symptoms limited to the postmenstruum are extremely rare.

postmeridian (pəʊstməˈrɪdɪən), *a.* [ad. L. *postmerīdiānus* (contr. *pōmer-*) adj., in the afternoon, f. *post* after + *merīdiānus* MERIDIAN *a.*; cf. POMERIDIAN.]

1. Occurring after noon or midday; of or pertaining to the afternoon. Also *fig.*

1626 BACON *Sylva* §57 An over hasty digestion, which is the inconvenience of postmeridian sleeps. *c* **1805** W. TAYLOR in *Ann. Rev.*, The postmeridian degrees of civilization (to preserve the author's metaphor) are less favourable to the popularity of the drama. **1898** *Allbutt's Syst. Med.* V. 198 The pyrexia of tuberculosis attains its maximum .. in the post-meridian hours of the day.

2. *Geol.* Applied by Professor Rogers to the ninth of the fifteen subdivisions of the Palæozoic strata of the Appalachian chain.

1858 H. D. ROGERS *Geol. Pennsylv.* II. II. 749 These periods, applicable only to the American Palæozoic day, are the Primal .. Pre-Meridian, Meridian, Post-Meridian [etc.]. **1859** PAGE *Handbk. Geol. Terms, Post-Meridian*, .. the 'Afternoon' of the North American Palæozoics, and the equivalent, in part, of our Lower Devonians.

¶ **3. post meridian**: erron. for next.

1795 C. DIBDIN in *Life* (1803) III. 335 'Twas post meridian, half past four, By signal I from Nancy parted. **1849** JAMES *Woodman* i, About the hour of half past eleven, post meridian, the moon was shining.

‖**post meridiem**, *phr.* [L. *post merīdiem* after midday.] After midday; applied to the hours between noon and midnight; usually abbreviated P.M. or p.m.

1647 LILLY *Chr. Astrol.* iv. 34, I would erect a Figure of Heaven the sixt of January 1646, one hour thirty minutes afternoon, or P.M, that is Post Meridiem.

postmeˈridional, *a.* *humorous nonce-wd.* [f. POST- B. 1 + MERIDIONAL.] = POSTMERIDIAN 1.

1767 A. CAMPBELL *Lexiph.* (1774) 8 After our post-meridional refection.

post-metal: see POST *sb.*¹ 9.

post-metamorphic: see POST- B. 1.

post-mill: see POST *sb.*¹ 9.

postmillenarian (ˌpəʊstmɪlɪˈnɛərɪən). [f. POST- B. 1 b + MILLENARIAN.] = POSTMILLENNIALIST. So **ˌpostmilleˈnarianism** = POSTMILLENNIALISM (*Cent. Dict.* 1890).

1886 N. F. RAVELIN *Progr. Th. Gt. Subj.* v. 63 Those who think that the millennium is to precede His [Christ's] coming, are called Postmillenarians.

postmillennial (pəʊstmɪˈlɛnɪəl), *a.* [f. POST- B. 1 b + MILLENNIAL.] Of or belonging to the period following the millennium. So **postmiˈllennialism**, the doctrine that the second Advent will follow the millennium; **postmiˈllennialist**, a believer in postmillennialism; **postmiˈllennian** *a.*, postmillennial.

1851 G. S. FABER *Many Mansions* 196 The Day of the real Second Advent, which my correspondent fully admits to be postmillennial. *Ibid.* 192 The Judicial Destruction of the Man of Sin .. is acknowledged, both by Premillennialists and by Postmillennialists, to occur immediately before the commencement of the Thousand Years. *Ibid.* 205 The two Antichristian Confederacies, premillennian and postmillennian. **1879** *Princeton Rev.* Mar. 425 Dr. Seiss .. has described postmillennialism as papistic, Dr. Brookes .. branded it as the 'post-millennial heresy'.

post-mineral: see POST- B. 1.

‖**postminimus** (pəʊstˈmɪnɪməs). *Comp. Anat.* [f. POST- B. 2 + MINIMUS *sb.* 2.] An additional digit found in some mammals, outside the little toe or finger. See also quot. 1895.

1889 *Proc. Zool. Soc.* 260 In *Bathyergus maritimus* [a species of mole-rat] the præpollex and the postminimus are both very well developed. **1895** *Syd. Soc. Lex., Postminimus.* In *Anat.*, syn. for *Pisiform bone.* In *Biol.*, a supernumerary little (ulnar) finger or little (fibular) toe.

postmistress (ˈpəʊstˌmɪstrɪs). [f. POST *sb.*² + MISTRESS, after POSTMASTER¹.] A woman who has charge of a post office. Hence **ˈpostˌmistressship**, the office of postmistress.

1697 *Lond. Gaz.* No. 3299/4 Whoever gives notice of him .. to the Post-Mistress of York, .. shall be Rewarded to Content. **1816** SCOTT *Antiq.* xv, 'Tell her', said the faithful postmistress, .. 'to come back the morn at ten o'clock, and I'll let her ken; we havena had time to sort the mail letters yet'. **1884** MRS. H. WARD *Miss Bretherton* 175 At last the old postmistress .. ceased to repulse him.

1867 *Contemp. Rev.* V. 106 Women were consequently excluded from post-mistress-ships in large towns.

postmiˈtotic, *a.* *Cytology.* [POST- B. 1 b.] After mitosis; *spec.* (of a cell) having ceased (reversibly or irreversibly) to display cell division. Also *absol.*, a cell which is unlikely or unable to divide again.

1942 E. V. COWDRY *Probl. Ageing* (ed. 2) xxiv. 628 The highly specialized cells, formed from the last differentiating intermitotics at the end of the series, .. are 'end cells'. Their individual lives begin .. after the last mitosis... In a word, they are postmitotics. *Ibid.* 631 The length of life of the majority of postmitotic nerve cells can be taken to be that of the body less one year. **1962** *Lancet* 27 Jan. 211/1 The granulocytes are post-mitotic and can be ruled out, and so we are restricted to the 'mononuclears'. **1968** H. HARRIS *Nucleus & Cytoplasm* v. 92 When all the nuclei in the heterokaryon enter mitosis together, post-mitotic reconstitution may produce a single large nucleus at one step. **1971** J. Z. YOUNG *Introd. Study Man* xxii. 288 Errors in the hereditary instructions and their transcription may be of especial importance in post-mitotic cells.

post-ˈmodern, *a.* Also **post-Modern**. [POST- B. 1 b.] Subsequent to, or later than, what is 'modern'; *spec.* in the arts, esp. *Archit.*, applied to a movement in reaction against that designated 'modern' (cf. MODERN *a.* 2 h). Hence **post-ˈmodernism**, **post-ˈmodernist** *a.* and *sb.*

1949 J. HUDNUT *Archit. & Spirit of Man* ix. 108 (*heading*) Post-modern house. *Ibid.* 119 He shall be a modern owner, a post-modern owner, if such a thing is conceivable. Free from all sentimentality or fantasy or caprice. **1956** A. TOYNBEE *Historian's Approach to Relig.* II. xi. 146 Our post-Modern Age of Western history. **1959** C. W. MILLS *Sociol. Imagination* ix. 166 Just as Antiquity was followed by several centuries of Oriental ascendancy .. so now the Modern Age is being succeeded by a post-modern period. Perhaps we may call it: The Fourth Epoch. **1965** L. A. FIEDLER in *Partisan Rev.* XXXII. 508, I am not now interested in analyzing .. the diction and imagery which have passed from Science Fiction into post-Modernist literature. **1966** F. KERMODE in *Encounter* Apr. 73/1 Pop fiction demonstrates 'a growing sense of the irrelevance of the past' and Top [*sic*] writers ('post-Modernists') are catching on. **1966** N. PEVSNER in *Listener* 29 Dec. 955/2 The fact that my enthusiasms cannot be roused by .. Churchill College .., does not blind me to the existence today of a new style, successor to my International Modern of the nineteen-thirties, a post-modern style, I would be tempted to call it, but the legitimate style of the nineteen-fifties and nineteen-sixties. **1977** *N.Y. Rev. Bks.* 28 Apr. 30/3 A process that culminates, by a curious but inexorable logic, in the post-modernist demand for the abolition of art and its assimilation to 'reality'. **1979** *Jrnl. R. Soc. Arts* Nov. 743/1 Many Post-Modern architects use motifs .. in questionable taste. *Ibid.* 751/1 Post-Modernists have substituted the body metaphor for the machine metaphor, because so much research has shown that we unconsciously project bodily states into architecture. **1979** *Time* 8 Jan. 53/1 The nearest man Post-Modernism has to a senior partner is, in fact, the leading American architect of his generation: Philip Cortelyou Johnson. **1980** *Times Higher Educ. Suppl.* 7 Mar. 16/1 Postmodernism, structuralism, and neo-dada (formerly known as 'concrete poetry') all represent a reaction against modernism.

ˌpost-modifiˈcation. *Linguistics.* [POST- A. 1 b.] The qualification or limitation of the sense of one word or phrase by another coming after. Also *attrib.* Hence **post-ˈmodifier**; **post-ˈmodifying** *vbl. sb.*

1962 R. QUIRK *Use of English* xi. 181 In such units as *bravery of all kinds* or *bravery in the struggle against barbarism*, we meet .. postmodification. **1965** *Language* XLI. 205 Deictic + head + post-modifier. **1970** *Eng. Stud.* LI. 404 The category noun modification is a large one (105 instances), almost half of them with postmodifying infinitives. **1975** *Amer. Speech 1971* XLVI. 224 A postmodification rule is necessary to transform relative clauses containing an infinitive, a prepositional phrase, or an adverb.

post-money, -morning: see POST *sb.*² 13, 12.

‖**post mortem**, **post-mortem**, *adv. phr.*, *a.*, and *sb.* [L. *post mortem* after death.]

A. *advb. phrase* (*post mortem*). After death.

a **1734** NORTH *Lives* (1826) I. 132 Evidence by offices *post mortem*, charters, pedigrees. **1845** BUDD *Dis. Liver* 362 Unexpectedly made known by examination, *post mortem.* **1897** *Allbutt's Syst. Med.* IV. 222 The fistulas are but rarely found post-mortem.

B. *adj.* (*post-mortem*). Taking place, formed, or done after death. Also *transf.*

1835–6 *Todd's Cycl. Anat.* I. 806/2 The interval between spasmodic and true *post-mortem* stiffness. **1837** *Penny Cycl.* VIII. 46/1 The coroner is empowered .. to direct the performance of a *post mortem* examination. **1873** T. H. GREEN *Introd. Pathol.* (ed. 2) 325 Of a dark-red colour, and soft gelatinous consistence, closely resembling the post-mortem clot. **1888** *Pall Mall G.* 24 Apr. 11/1 Any man who held the theory of post-mortem salvation. **1909** *Westm. Gaz.* 8 June 5/1 M. Chauchard, .. who is to sleep his last sleep .. in a tomb which has cost nearly £4,000, has had many predecessors in post-mortem luxury. **1922** JOYCE *Ulysses* 609 Her brandnew arrival is on her knee, *post mortem* child. **1962** *Gloss. Terms Automatic Data Processing* (*B.S.I.*) 45 *Post-mortem routine*, a diagnostic routine which may be used to indicate the contents of selected locations after a program has stopped. **1965** in Bessinger & Creed *Medieval & Linguistic Stud.* 54 What conception of the human spirit and its *post mortem* future is implied in our inscriptions? **1969** P. B. JORDAIN *Condensed Computer Encycl.* 389 Usually, when an unexpected or inexplicable difficulty is encountered, a postmortem dump is taken to record all available information about the failed state of a program: then a postmortem analysis is made to discover the cause of the difficulty. **1979** R. RENDELL *Means of Evil* 68 Doreen Betts's denial had .. been .. a post-mortem white-washing of her mother's character.

C. *sb.* **1. a.** Short for *post-mortem examination.* (In quot. 1900 = post-mortem production.)

1850 SCORESBY *Cheever's Whalem. Adv.* iv. (1859) 53 To report a full and accurate, leisurely post-mortem of the subjects we have discussed. **1879** *St. George's Hosp. Rep.* IX. 195 Two ended fatally; but no post-mortem was obtained. **1900** *Westm. Gaz.* 27 June 10/1 By this time the genuine Strads are pretty well known—even those post-mortems made up out of the *débris* of the great man's workshop. **1903** *Edin. Rev.* July 191 Post-mortems show the cause of death.

b. *attrib.* Connected with post-mortem examinations, as ***post-mortem book***, ***record***, ***room***, ***table***.

1873 T. H. GREEN *Introd. Pathol.* (ed. 2) 345 Ascertaining in the post-mortem room the existence of the more marked structural changes. **1880** MACCORMAC *Antisept. Surg.* 205 A third .. reach the post-mortem table before the disease has contracted adhesions to the surrounding parts. **1897** *Allbutt's Syst. Med.* II. 861, 60 cases .. collected from St. George's Hospital post-mortem books.

2. *transf.* A searching (and freq. recriminatory) analysis or discussion of a past event, as an examination or card-game. Cf. INQUEST *sb.* 3 c.

In quot. 1844, a re-sit examination at Cambridge University.

1844 in Farmer & Henley *Slang* (1902) V. 264/1 I've passed the Post-mortem at last. **1907** R. DUNN *Shameless Diary of Explorer* ix. 111 Here in camp, we've been holding a post-mortem of the day. **1922** A. E. M. FOSTER *Light Side Auction Bridge* xxxvii. 155 The post-mortem fiend simply will not be denied. **1930** A. P. HERBERT *Water Gipsies* viii. 82 'I knew,' he said at the family *post mortem* in the evening. 'I knew the colt had the legs of the field, if he only had the luck.' **1943** K. TENNANT *Ride on Stranger* viii. 82 They drew in to the table and..began a family post mortem of the party. **1960** V. JENKINS *Lions Down Under* 114 The post-mortem at a team-talk in Timaru was a searching one. **1972** R. MARKUS *Aces & Places* 105 The post-mortem centred the blame on East for not ducking the jack of diamonds at trick two. **1974** L. DEIGHTON *Spy Story* xii. 119 It's all right for you... You won't have to do the post-mortem with these guys.

Hence **post-mor'temity**, the state of death (*nonce-wd.*); **post-'mortemizing** *vbl. sb.*

1851 H. MELVILLE *Moby Dick* III. ix. 67 At a certain juncture of this post-mortemizing of the whale. **1922** JOYCE *Ulysses* 387 In the nights of prenativity and post-mortemity.

post-'mortem, *v.* [f. POST-MORTEM *a.*] *trans.* To subject to a post-mortem examination. Hence **post-'morteming** *vbl. sb.*

1871 M. CLARKE *His Natural Life* (1874) III. xv. 291 'Strange that he should drop like that.'..'Yes, unless he had any internal disease... I'll *post-mortem* him and see.' **1900** *Jrnl. Compar. Path. & Therapeutics* XIII. 2 Hundreds of horses dead of horse-sickness had been post-mortemed by farriers and shoeing-smiths. **1910** H. G. WELLS *Hist. Mr. Polly* iv. 105 You didn't, I suppose, Mr. Polly, think to 'ave your poor dear father *post-mortemed*. **1934** R. A. KNOX *Still Dead* v. 67 The corpse..was taken up to the house and post-mortem'd and buried. **1971** D. E. WESTLAKE *I gave at the Office* 123 If you people in the legal department manage to distill Truth from your post-morteming you'll be better than Solomon. **1977** N. FREELING *Gadget* I. 3 Who looks twice at a couple post-morteming a traffic scrape.

post-mortuary: see POST- B. 1.

postmultiplication, -multiply: see POST- A. 1 b, a.

post-mundane: see POST- B. 1.

post-mutative: see POST- A. 1 a.

‖**postnares** (-'nɛəriːz), *sb. pl.* Rarely *sing.* **-naris.** [mod.L., f. POST- A. 2 + L. *nārēs*, pl. of *nāris* nostril.] The posterior nostrils or choanæ, the openings of the nasal chamber into the pharynx. So **post'narial** *a.*, (*a*) situated behind the nostril; (*b*) belonging to the postnares.

1866 OWEN *Anat. Vertebr.* II. 426 The disproportionate shortness of the rostral or 'prenarial' to the cranial or 'postnarial' part of the skull. **1882** WILDER & GAGE *Anat. Techn.* 513.

postnasal: see POST- B. 2.

‖**postnasus** (pəʊst'neɪsəs). *Entom.* [f. POST- B. 2 + L. *nāsus* nose.] A former name for the division of the clypeus now called the supraclypeus.

1826 KIRBY & SP. *Entomol.* III. xxxiii. 364 *Postnasus*.. that part of the *Face* immediately contiguous to the *Antennæ*, that lies behind the *Nasus*, when distinctly marked out. *Ibid.* xxxiv. 483 A triangular piece, below the antennæ and above the *nasus*..: this is the *postnasus* or after-nose.

postnatal (pəʊst'neɪtəl), *a.* [f. POST- B. 1 b + NATAL.] Subsequent to or occurring after birth. ***postnatal depression***, depression in a woman caused by a recent confinement, characterized by fatigue, irritability, and fits of crying.

*a***1859** DE QUINCEY *Posth. Wks.* (1891) I. 16 Some far halcyon time, post-natal or ante-natal he knew not. **1866** SANKEY *Lect. Mental Dis.* vi. 127 Those whose idiocy depends on post-natal diseases, and especially rickets. **1869** LECKY *Europ. Mor.* (1877) I. i. 122 Ideas which cannot be explained by any post-natal experience. **1973** *Guardian* 22 Feb. 13/2 Some 88,000 women a year were recently deemed in need of treatment for postnatal depression. **1978** J. MANN *Sting of Death* viii. 69 Anna Buxton was suffering severely from post-natal depression..a textbook case: Emmy was four months old.

Hence **post'natalist**, one who holds that the divinity of Christ was of postnatal communication; also *attrib.*; **post'natally** *adv.*, after birth.

1895 HAWEIS in *Contemp. Rev.* Oct. 599 The Postnatalists admit human parentage on both sides. *Ibid.* 604 The Prenatalist and Postnatalist theories. **1927** *Jrnl. Anat.* LXI. 321 The two parts of which the foetal suprarenal is composed—the true cortex which persists post-natally and the foetal cortex which atrophies after birth—are generally considered to have a common origin. **1934** *Times Lit. Suppl.* 29 Mar. 222/2 The child..contracts the actual disease only when post-natally brought into contact with the specific germ. **1966** *Ann. Rev. Med.* XVII. 221 The inhibition seems to disappear as the animal matures postnatally.

†**'postnate,** *a.* (*sb.*) *Obs.* [ad. med.L. *postnāt-us* (Du Cange) born after, f. *post* after + *nātus* born. See PUISNE, PUNY.] Born, produced, made, or occurring after something else; later, of later date, subsequent *to*.

1638 CHILLINGW. *Relig. Prot.* I. ii. §163. 119 Practises of the Church,..evidently post-nate to the time of the Apostles. **1672-3** GREW *Anat. Roots* I. ii. §2 Every Root hath successively two kinds of Skins... The other, Postnate, succeeding in the room of the former, as the Root ageth. **1678** CUDWORTH *Intell. Syst.* 585 Which makes.. Knowledge and Wisdom, to be but a Second or Post Nate Thing. *a***1734** NORTH *Examen* I. iii. §91 Postnate to the Narrative of Dates. **1770** SIR J. HILL *Construct. Timber* 66 It is indeed postnate and comes after them in the order of time.

B. *sb.* A production of a period later than its alleged date. *rare.*

*a***1641** BP. MOUNTAGU *Acts & Mon.* iii. (1642) 192 These and many such passages..in Sibyls Oracles,..our Philologers..would perswade us, that they were counterfaits and Post-nates, forged by Christians.

Hence †**post'nated** *a.* = POSTNATE *a.*

1659 H. L'ESTRANGE *Alliance Div. Off.* 293 The Council of Laodicea,..to which Popery is post-nated above three hundred years.

‖**post'natus,** pl. **-i.** [med.L. *postnātus* born after: see prec.]

1. One born after a particular event; *spec.* in Scotland, one born after the Union of the Crowns; in U.S., one born after the Declaration of Independence. Chiefly in pl. *postnati*.

1609 (*title*) The Speech of the Lord Chancellor of England touching the Post-nati. **1638** RAWLEY tr. *Bacon's Life & Death* (1650) 14 This Length of Life, immediately after the Floud, was reduced to a Moitie; But in the *Post-Nati*: For Noah, who was borne before, equalled the Age of his Ancestours. **1669** DK. OF LAUDERDALE in *Collect. Poems* 231 It was..solemnly adjudged, in the Case of the *Post-nati*, that those, who after the Descent of the Crown of England to King James, were born in Scotland, were no Aliens in England. **1800** LAING *Hist. Scot.* (1804) III. 14 The *postnati*, born since the death of Elizabeth, as their allegiance was indiscriminately due to James, were declared to be freely naturalized in either kingdom.

†**2.** A second son. *Obs.*

1727-41 CHAMBERS *Cycl.*, *Post-natus* is also used by Bracton, Fleta, Glanville, &c. for the second son, as distinguished from the eldest. **1730-6** BAILEY (folio), *Postnatus*, the second son, or one born afterwards. **1848** in WHARTON *Law Lex.*

postneonatal: see POST- B. 1.

post-neuritic: see POST- B. 1.

post-New'tonian, *a.* [f. POST- B. 1 b + NEWTONIAN *a.* and *sb.*] Subsequent to the life or work of Sir Isaac Newton (1642–1727); *spec.* in *Physics* (see quots. 1964, 1973).

1865 MILL *Exam. Hamilton's Philos.* xxvii. 542 Applied mathematics in its post-Newtonian development does nothing to strengthen..these errors. **1963** N. FRYE *Romanticism Reconsidered* 5 A post-Newtonian poet has to think of gravitation. **1964** *Astrophysical Jrnl.* CXL. 428 A post-Newtonian approximation, in which the effects of general relativity are treated as first-order corrections. **1973** *Nature* 31 Aug. 537/1 The only precise tests of the applicability of the theory of general relativity to the actual physical world are those long ago proposed by Einstein, and certain other tests proposed more recently that are closely related to Einstein's... They test the theory only to the so-called post-Newtonian approximation, roughly speaking to terms in $1/c^2$, where c is the speed of light. **1977** *Astrophysical Jrnl.* CCXVI. 914 The tidal radiation can be comparable to the radiation from post-Newtonian effects.

post-Nicene: see POST- B. 1.

'post-night. [f. POST *sb.*[2] + NIGHT.] A night on which letters are dispatched; a mail night.

1657 *Burton's Diary* (1828) I. 322, I am much troubled that a post-night should pass, before you come to a resolution in this business. **1686** *Lond. Gaz.* No. 2121/4 There goes a Post every Monday Night (besides the General Post-Nights) from the General Post-Office in London, to Lewis in Sussex. **1758** in Howell *State Trials* (1813) XIX. 1369, I have often received from the prisoner at the bar letters of a post-night to carry to the office in Lombard-street.

post-nominal: see POST- B. 1.

†**'post-note.** *U.S. Obs.* exc. *Hist.* [f. POST- A. 1 b + NOTE.] A note made and issued by a bank or banking association, payable not to bearer but to order, not on demand but at a future specified date, and designed as part of its circulating medium.

Issued by the banks of some of the states of U.S. during the period between 1781 and 1863.

1791 JEFFERSON in *Harper's Mag.* (1885) Mar. 534/2 Rec[d] from bank a post note..for 116⅔ D. **1807** (Oct.) *Statutes of Connecticut* (1808) I. 98 Be it enacted..That the several incorporated banks in this state be..authorized to issue post-notes, payable to order and at a time subsequent to the issuing of the same. **1824** (Dec. 24) *Laws of Alabama* 25 *margin*, The issue of Post-Notes authorized. **1839** C. RAGUET *Currency & Banking* 112 *note*, The banks of New York are prohibited from issuing post-notes. **1848** (June 5) *Barbour's Repts.* [N.Y. Supreme Court] 222 Post-notes issued by banking associations having been decided to be absolutely illegal. **1862** *Merchants' Mag.* Dec. 509 The Treasury had become a bank of deposit and of circulation for irredeemable paper money, and could issue one-year certificates, answering to old United States Bank 'post notes', without stint or limit. **1896** H. WHITE *Money & Banking* 368 Some of the States had laws forbidding the issue of post notes, but they were evaded by the device of lending notes on [certain conditions]. **1896** W. G. SUMNER *Hist. Banking in U.S.* 79, 234, 268, 296.

post'notum. *Ent.* [f. POST- A. 2 b + NOTUM.] = POSTSCUTELLUM.

1926 R. J. TILLYARD *Insects Austral. & N.Z.* i. 18 In some cases..a short posterior sclerite is also developed, called the postnotum or postscutellum. **1964** R. M. & J. W. FOX *Introd. Compar. Entomol.* ii. 52 The notum continues forward to cover the posterior part of the next segment where it is termed the postnotum.

post-'nuclear, *a.* (*sb.*) [POST- B. 1 b.]

1. *Phonetics.* Situated after a nucleus. Also *absol.* as *sb.*

1961 [see INTERNUCLEAR *a.* 3]. **1961** Y. OLSSON *On Syntax Eng. Verb* vii. 189 The variation between the post-nuclears *er* and *ee*..corresponds to a distinction between (2) and (1). **1968** *Language* XLIV. 80 Allotone 2..of the glide occurs in postnuclear syllables of the word. **1976** *Archivum Linguisticum* VII. 38 One feature both subclasses share is their insistence that any non-nuclear occurrence be in prenuclear position rather than in tail (postnuclear) position.

2. Subsequent to the development or use of nuclear weaponry.

1963 *Economist* 7 Sept. 813/2 China was dreaming of a post-nuclear heaven. **1965** *Punch* 17 Feb. 259/3 Another post-nuclear society, this time dominated by farmers.

postnuptial (pəʊst'nʌpʃəl), *a.* [f. POST- B. 1 b + NUPTIAL.] Made, occurring, or existing after marriage; subsequent to marriage. Also, subsequent to mating (of animals).

1807 VESEY *Reports Chanc.* XII. 147 That part of the Property, which is protected by the post-nuptial Settlement. **1853** JERDAN *Autobiog.* III. 31 On their post-nuptial excursion to Paris. **1877** BLACK *Green Past.* xxii, The bitter disillusionising experience of post-nuptial life. **1885** FARGUS *Slings & Arrows* 57 The large post-nuptial settlement which I proposed making. **1956** *Nature* 21 Jan. 143/1 Our experiment was begun on July 23..at about the estimated end of the postnuptial refractory period and before the next season's spermatogenesis began.

Hence **post'nuptially** *adv.*, after marriage.

1870 *Contemp. Rev.* XIV. 441 The doctor..insisted on its being postnuptially settled on his wife.

'post-oak. [f. POST *sb.*[1] + OAK.] A species of oak (*Quercus stellata*) found in sandy soil in the eastern U.S., having hard close-grained durable wood much used for posts, sleepers, etc.; also called ***iron-oak***, ***rough*** or ***box white oak***. Also *attrib.*

swamp post-oak, another species (*Q. lyrata*), growing in river-swamps in the southern U.S., with similar wood.

1775 B. ROMANS *Conc. Nat. Hist. E. & W. Florida* 18 The principal however are the following:..Virginian white oak. .. Dwarf white oak, or post oak. *a***1816** B. HAWKINS *Sk. Creek Country* (1848) 19 The trees are post oak, white and black oak, pine [etc.]. *Ibid.* 20 Between these rivers, there is some good post and black oak land. **1817** J. BRADBURY *Trav. Amer.* 257 The timber is generally..on the prairie, post oak. **1835** W. IRVING *Tour Prairies* xvii, Our march to-day lay through straggling forests of the kind of low scrubbed trees ..called 'post-oaks' and 'black-jacks'. **1836** D. B. EDWARDS *Hist. Texas* 46 They are protected..by..post-oak ridges. **1865** *Michaux's N. Amer. Sylva* I. 40 *Quercus lyrata*..is called the Swamp Post Oak, Overcup Oak, and Water White Oak. **1892** J. C. DUVAL *Young Explorers in Early Times in Texas* II. ii. 14 About noon we came to a small stream bordered by a strip of post oak woods. **1906** 'O. HENRY' *Four Million* 58 Joe Larrabee came out of the post-oak flats of the Middle West. **1945** B. A. BOTKIN *Lay my Burden Down* 263 They found the body of a white man hanging to a post oak. **1969** T. H. EVERETT *Living Trees of World* 118/2 The post oak..is widely distributed in dryish uplands from Massachusetts to Nebraska. **1975** *New Yorker* 5 May 101/1 All but six of the thirty-six holes are set off by themselves, framed by borders of post oak—a pretty tree that loses its large leaves in winter but retains its attractiveness because of the pleasing contortions of its branches.

post-obit (pəʊst'ɒbɪt, -'əʊbɪt), *a.* and *sb.* [Shortened from L. *post obitum* after decease.]

A. *adj.* **1.** Taking effect after some one's death: esp. in ***post-obit bond*** (see B. 1).

1788 H. BLACKSTONE *Reports* I. 95 This was a *post obit* bond, a security of a questionable nature, which had often been disputed with success. **1808** *Times* 26 Feb. 4/4 A Post Obit Bond for 37,000*l*, payable within three months after the death of a Gentleman, aged 67 years. **1816** SHELLEY in Dowden *Life* (1887) II. 8, I am to give a post-obit security for this sum. **1847** DISRAELI *Tancred* I. ii, By post-obit liquidation.

2. Done or made after death; post-mortem; occurring or existing after death. ? *Obs.*

1822-34 *Good's Study Med.* (ed. 4) I. 357 The real nature of the swelling..can only be determined by a post-obit examination. *Ibid.* II. 12, 99.

B. *sb.* **1.** (Short for *post-obit bond*.) A bond given by a borrower, securing to the lender a sum of money to be paid on the death of a specified person from whom the borrower has expectations.

1751 H. WALPOLE *Lett.* (1845) II. 377 They talk of fourteen hundred thousand pounds on post-obits. **1821** BYRON *Occas. Pieces, Martial*, Post-obits rarely reach a poet. **1851** D. JERROLD *St. Giles* xxvi. 267 [He] had lent ready gold, to be paid back, post-obit fashion, on a father's coffin-lid. **1899** *Daily News* 25 Jan. 5/5 A post obit..is a bond issued by an heir to property, conceding to the holder a lien on the estates after the death of the present possessor.

2. A thing which is to pass to some one after the owner's death; a legacy or heritage. *nonce-use.*

1812 SOUTHEY in Smiles *Mem. J. Murray* (1891) I. xi. 237 My intention to leave behind me my own Memoirs, as a post-obit for my family.

3. = POST-MORTEM *sb.* ? *Obs.*

1864 in WEBSTER.

post-obituary (-əʊˈbɪtjuːərɪ), *a.* [f. POST- B. 1 b + OBITUARY.] = POST-OBIT *a.*, POST-MORTEM *a.*

1816–30 BENTHAM *Offic. Apt. Maximized, Extract Const. Code* (1830) 15 Pensions, payable to any..relative of the functionary, on his decease. These may be styled post-obituary, or post-obit pensions. **1822–34** *Good's Study Med.* (ed. 4) I. 720 Abundantly established by post-obituary examinations. **1846** GROTE *Greece* I. ii. I. 93 A triple gradation of post-obituary existence, proportioned to the character of each race whilst alive.

postocular (-ˈɒkjʊlə(r)), *a.* (*sb.*) *Anat.* and *Zool.* [f. POST- B. 2 + OCULAR.] Situated behind the eye; post-orbital. **b.** *ellipt.* as *sb.* A postocular scale, as in snakes.

1877 HALLOCK *Sportsman's Gaz.* 209 Parallel curved white superciliary and postocular stripes. **1890** *Cent. Dict.* s.v., *Postocular lobes*, anterior projections of the lower sides of the prothorax [in insects], impinging on the eyes when the head is retracted.

postœsophageal: see POST- B. 2.

post office, post-office (ˈpəʊst,ɒfɪs). [f. POST *sb.*² + OFFICE.]

1. (With capital initial.) The public department charged with the conveyance of letters, etc., by post. In early use, sometimes meaning the office of the master of the posts, or postmaster (general); in other instances it is difficult to separate it from the local centre or head quarters of the department, the General Post Office in London or other capital.

The name appears first under the Commonwealth, the earlier name having been *letter-office*.

[**1635** (July 31) in Rymer *Fœdera* (1732) XIX. 649 A Proclamation for the settling of the Letter Office of England and Scotland. **1641–2** *Jrnl. Ho. Com.* 22 Mar., That Mr. Glynn do report to-morrow the matter concerning the sequestration of the letter-offices. **1646** *Jrnl. Ho. Lords* 3 Dec., All his estate and interest in the Foreign Letter-office.]

1652 *Jrnl. Ho. Com.* 19 Oct., Sir David Watkins, his claim to the foreign post-office. **1657** *Acts & Ordin. Parl.* c. 30 (Scobell) 512 From henceforth there be one General Office, to be called and known by the name of the Post-Office of England; and one Officer..nominated and appointed.. under the Name and Stile of Postmaster-General of England, and Comptroller of the Post-Office. **1666** *Lond. Gaz.* No. 85/4 The general Post-office is for the present held at the two Black Pillars in Bridges-street. **1731** GAY in *Swift's Wks.* (1761) VIII. 130 If you don't send to me now and then, the post-office will think me of no consequence. **1738–9** KING in *Swift's Lett.* (1768) IV. 223 The ill-treatment I received from the post-office; for some time I did not receive a letter that had not been opened. **1804** BP. OF LINCOLN in *G. Rose's Diaries* (1860) II. 94 Lord Charles Spencer will..resign the Post-Office. **1845** DISRAELI *Sybil* II. xv, The king granted the duke and his heirs for ever, a pension on the post-office. **1893** H. JOYCE *Hist. Post Office* vi. 46 The headquarters of the Post Office were at this time [1690] in Lombard Street. Here the postmasters-general resided.

2. a. A house or shop where postal business is carried on, where postage stamps are sold, letters are registered and posted for transmission to their destinations, and from some of which letters received from places at home and abroad are delivered.

The name is now commonly applied even to small branch offices, sub-offices, or receiving-houses, which sell stamps and receive letters for transmission, but from which letters are not delivered, this being generally done directly from the central or head office of a town or district.

General Post Office, the central or head post office of a country or state, as that in St. Martin's Le Grand, London; also popularly applied to the head post office in a city or town which has branch offices subordinate to it.

[**1657** *Acts & Ordin. Parl.* c. 30 The erecting and setling of one general Post-office. **1660**: see GENERAL *a.* 2 b.] **1675**, **1708** [see GENERAL *a.* 2 b]. **1679** OATES *Narr. Popish Plot* 46 Some of which [Letters] were delivered to the Post-office in Russel-street; others to the Post-office General. **1709** STEELE *Tatler* No. 19 ¶2, I have..looked over every Letter in the Post-Office for my better Information. **1725** *Wodrow Corr.* (1843) III. 196 You do not expect I should write a detail, since I behoved to take dinner, and at eight the post-office closes. **1802** MAR. EDGEWORTH *Moral T., Angelina* ii. (1857) I. 237 She actually discovered that there was a post-office at Cardiffe. **1825** AMELIA OPIE *Illustrations Lying* I. v. 125 He had reached a general postoffice. **1860** TYNDALL *Glac.* I. xii. 90 Money was waiting for me at the post-office in Geneva. **1867** TROLLOPE *Chron. Barset* II. lix. 168 She well remembered the number of the post-office in the Edgeware Road. **1893** H. JOYCE *Hist. Post Office* v. 41 Up to April 1680 the General Post Office in Lombard Street was the only receptacle for letters in the whole of London. *Mod. Colloq.* In Oxford the General Post Office is in St. Aldate's Street.

b. *transf.* A person who receives information and either transmits it or holds it for collection, esp. in espionage; also = DROP *sb.* 17 d. *slang.*

1885 E. W. HAMILTON *Diary* 12 Apr. (1972) II. 835 M. Lessar suggests that Brett should be asked to be the post office of the Russian Embassy. Accordingly, Lessar goes to Brett, and hands him a Memorandum... Brett forwards the Memorandum here. **1919** J. BUCHAN *Mr. Standfast* vii. 148, I had got precisely what Blenkiron wanted, a post office for the enemy... I could see the juiciest lies passing that way to the *Grosses Hauptquartier*. **1935** A. J. POLLOCK *Underworld Speaks* 90/2 *Post office*, a person who receives or delivers letters to crooks. **1945** *Tee Emm* (Air Ministry) V. 55 Beware of becoming a 'post office', simply passing on everything that comes in, happy in the knowledge that there is a higher authority behind you. **1965** D. WILLIAMS *Not in Public Interest* vii. 133 It became evident in 1911 that the hairdresser's shop of Karl Gustav Ernst was being used as a 'post office' or clearing-house for German espionage agents in this country. **1974** T. ALLBEURY *Snowball* iv. 20 Just a low-grade courier, a dead letterbox and a post office.

3. *U.S.* A parlour game in which the participants in turn act as postmaster or postmistress and pretend to deliver letters which are paid for by kisses. Cf. *postman's knock* (POSTMAN¹ 1 d (*b*)).

The sense in quot. 1851 is uncertain.

1851 J. H. GREEN *Twelve Days in Tombs* 157 How often have the professors of Christianity violated all moral principles in the..game of Post-office, where we find stationed some beautiful sister as post mistress, whose duty it is to write the names of those from whom she thinks she can secure the postage. **1855** *Quincy* (California) *Prospector* 31 Mar. 2/1 We are astonished to see men and women who are looked upon as samples for the rising generation, join in such childish plays as..'Post office', &c. **1899** *Amer. Physical Educ. Rev.* 361 Those who select love games are at the dawn of adolescence. 'Drop-the-handkerchief' and 'post-office' are the two favorites of this group. **1904** C. S. DARROW *Farmington* 163 We had to keep still, and couldn't go outdoors, and had to play 'needle's eye' and 'post-office'. **1914** B. TARKINGTON in *Cosmopolitan* Mar. 489/2 'We'd have been playing "Quaker meeting", "clap in, clap out", or "going to Jerusalem", I suppose.' 'Yes, or "post-office" and "drop the handkerchief"', said Mrs. Schofield. **1949** *Sat. Even. Post* 12 Mar. 60/3 After a time this palled and they played Post Office.

4. *attrib.* and *Comb.*, as ***post-office clerk, directory, employee, inspector, -keeper, servant, counter, door, window***, etc.; also in the names of colours associated with various Post Office services, as ***post-office green, red, yellow***; **post-office address** = postal address; **post-office annuity, insurance**, a system whereby annuities can be purchased and lives insured through the post office; **post-office box**, (*a*) a private box or pigeon-hole at a post office, in which all the letters and papers for a private person or firm are put and kept till called for; (*b*) = *post-office bridge*; **post-office bridge**, a portable self-contained form of Wheatstone bridge containing a large number of resistors which are selected by means of plugs; **post-office car**, *U.S.*, a mail-van or coach on a railway; **post-office department** = POST OFFICE 1; **post-office order**, a money-order for a specified sum, issued upon payment of the sum and a small commission at one post office, and payable at another therein named, to a person whose name is officially communicated in a letter of advice; **post-office packet** *Hist.*, a packet-boat carrying mail for the Post Office; **post-office savings-bank**, a bank having branches at local post offices where sums within fixed limits are received on government security, at a fixed rate of interest; since 1 Oct. 1969, known as the National Savings Bank; hence ***post-office savings(-bank)-book***; **post-office stamp**, a stamp officially imprinted on a letter by the post office; also the instrument used for stamping the postmark.

1901 *Tribune* (Chicago) 16 Feb., Give *postoffice address in full. **1894** W. A. PRICE *Measurement Electr. Resistance* 81 Bridge ratios of 1000 and ·001 are available in addition to those in the *Post Office box. **1914** *Phil. Mag.* XXVIII. 470 The resistances of the films of low resistance were measured by a post-office box in the ordinary way. **1965** G. A. G. BENNET *Electr. & Mod. Physics* viii. 129/2 A Wheatstone type network is connected up as shown..with the galvanometer as one of the four resistances; a Post Office box would be suitable for this purpose. **1891** H. L. WEBB *Testing of Insulated Wires & Cables* vi. 38 A small clamp for holding the battery key down permanently would be a useful addition to a *Post-office bridge. **1931** W. L. UPSON *Electr. Lab. Stud.* iii. 45 There is a second form of Wheatstone bridge known as the 'post-office bridge'. In this type there is no wire giving wide variability to the ratio of *B* to *A*, but there are fixed resistance coils so that the ratio may be made 1 to 1, 1 to 10, [etc.]. **1883** *Manch. Exam.* 30 Oct. 8/4 There is..in every train..a *post-office car, which contains..a letter box, in which letters may be deposited anywhere en route. **1866** J. REES *Foot-Prints* 326 Reed was an old *post-office clerk, who..had been in the office for twenty odd years. **1782** *Jrnls. of Congress* (1823) IV. 93 Any post-master, post-rider, or other person employed in the *post-office department. **1816** *Amer. St. Papers* (1834) XV. 50 To investigate the conduct of the General Post Office Department. **1803** *Post-Office Annual Directory: London* 3 The Editors of the *Post-Office Directory..present their most sincere and grateful Acknowledgements. **1852** DICKENS *Bleak Ho.* (1853) viii. 70 It appeared to us that some of them must pass their whole lives in dealing out subscription-cards to the whole Post-office Directory. **1963** *Ophthalmic Optician* 20 Apr. 408/1 If the hole exposes telephone services and cables, the perimeter will be lined with machinery painted in *Post Office green. **1837** DICKENS *Pickw.* ii, Mrs. Tomlinson, the *post-office-keeper, seemed..to have been chosen the leader of the trade party. **1843** DICKENS *Let.* 30 Dec. (1974) III. 617 For a *post office order there is no time. **1850** *Advt.* in 'Bat' *Cricket. Man.* 103 A remittance or Post-office order. **1865** DICKENS *Mut. Fr.* I. xvii, No Post-office order is in the interim received from Nicodemus Boffin, Esquire. **1780** A. YOUNG *Tour in Ireland* I. 342 It is much to be wished, that there were some means of being secure of packets sailing regularly ..; with the *post-office packets there is this satisfaction. **1855** DICKENS *Holly Tree Inn* in *Househ. Words* Extra Christmas No., 15 Dec. 1/2 The Post-office packet for the United States was to depart from Liverpool. **1778** MISS BURNEY *Evelina* (1791) II. xxi. 132 The *post-office people will let us know if they hear of him. **1930** *Times Educ. Suppl.* 18 Jan. (Suppl.) p. iv/2 Red offers a fertile field for flights of descriptive fancy... *Post Office red, and sealing wax red may be hackneyed words, but their tone is not in doubt. **1978** *Lancashire Life* Sept. 89/2 Newspapers, medicines, grocery orders—all are piled aboard the valley's post-office-red lifeline for delivery *en route*. **1861** *Act 24 & 25 Vict.* c. 14 *Post Office Savings Banks..An Act to grant additional Facilities for depositing small Savings at Interest, with the Security of the Government for due Repayment thereof [17th May 1861]. Whereas it is expedient..to make the General Post Office available for that Purpose. **1885** *Encycl. Brit.* XIX. 572/2 The establishment of post-office savings banks was practically suggested in the year 1860 by Mr Charles William Sykes of Huddersfield, whose suggestion was cordially received by Mr Gladstone... Half a century earlier (1807) it had been proposed to utilize the then existing..money-order branch of the post-office for the collection and transmission of savings..to a central savings bank to be established in London. **1936** M. ALLINGHAM *Flowers for Judge* xi. 172 Mr. Campion turned over the battered cardboard-backed book... 'Post Office Savings Bank?.. Whose is it?' *Ibid.* xviii. 260 One day you find her Post Office Savings Bank-book. **1966** B. KIMENYE *Kalasanda Revisited* 21 His Post Office Savings book boasted the grand total of 600s. **1973** P. MOYES *Curious Affair of Third Dog* viii. 104 A Post Office savings book showing a balance of some ten pounds. **1891** 'PHIL' *Penny Postage Jubilee* ix. 156 It was not an uncommon practice of the *post-office servants to mark the postage on the envelope with pen and red ink. **1893** H. JOYCE *Hist. Post Office* vi. 44 Out of London, the Post Office servants remained [in 1690] much as they had been ten years before, at about 239 in number, of whom all but twelve were postmasters. **1827** *Amer. St. Papers* (1834) XV. 304 William J. Stone, for *post office stamps, $128·49. **1976** *Scotsman* 15 Dec. 14/3 (Advt.), The Telecommunications showroom..is decorated internally in *Post Office yellow, with relief panels throughout in silver.

†**ˈpost-ˌofficer.** *Obs.* An officer or official of the post.

1669 *Lond. Gaz.* No. 406/4 The Post-Officers which were sent from hence into France to confer with Monsieur de Louvoy the French Postmaster,..are this day returned. **1738–9** KING in *Swift's Lett.* (1768) IV. 223 Whether those post-officers really thought me..a man of importance. **1843** *Select Comm. Postage* §2834 It was supposed that a post-officer could not pass a letter containing two coins without discovering it.

post-oˈfficial, *a.* and *sb.* [f. POST OFFICE, POST-OFFICE + -IAL, with play upon OFFICIAL *a.* and *sb.*] **A.** *adj.* Of or pertaining to a post office or its staff. **B.** *sb.* A post-office employee.

1938 DYLAN THOMAS *Let.* 31 Dec. (1966) 219, I don't know why your letter returned 'unknown', unless it was a post-official hint at the subsidence of my..reputation. *a* **1939** E. G. MURPHY in *Penguin Bk. Austral. Ballads* (1964) 209 For the Smiths rolled up..To drive the post-officials mad.

postolivary: see POST- B. 2.

post-op (pəʊstˈɒp), colloq. abbrev. of POSTOPERATIVE *a.* (*sb.*).

1971 E. CANDY *Words for Murder Perhaps* vii. 84, I can take temperatures and..make lovely beds for post-ops. **1974** *Country Life* 3–10 Jan. 58/3 Nursing Home...medical and post-op. patients. **1977** D. BENNETT *Jigsaw Man* 14 He felt he had been sawn in half. The post-op drugs took over.

postˈoperative, *a.* (*sb.*) [POST- B. 1 b.] Occurring in or pertaining to the period following a surgical operation; having recently undergone an operation. Also as *sb.*, a person who has recently had an operation.

1889 in *Cent. Dict.* **1898** *Allbutt's Syst. Med.* V. 309 In the first flush of that post-operative quiescence that we all so well recognise as a characteristic of nervous ailments. **1900** *Lancet* 20 Oct. 1152/2 A typical instance of post-operative hæmatemesis. **1925** E. HEMINGWAY *In our Time* (1926) 24 'I'm terribly sorry I brought you along, Nickie,' said his father, all his post-operative exhilaration gone. **1951** *Science* 19 Oct. 416/1 Prothrombin levels remained normal throughout the postoperative period in each animal. **1956** K. HULME *Nun's Story* x. 160 Sister Luke examined some of his post-operatives. **1962** *Lancet* 5 May 936/1 During the postoperative period he had a chest infection. **1973** R. HAYES *Hungarian Game* xiv. 332 They didn't want postoperatives to smoke. **1977** *New Yorker* 12 Sept. 114/2 Postoperative patients are always complaining about the quality of hospital food.

Hence **postˈoperatively** *adv.*, after an operation.

1908 *Practitioner* Sept. 435 The nephrectomies shown to have a normal freezing point before operation invariably demonstrated post-operatively that the kidney, which was left, was functionally adequate. **1931** *Arch. Surg.* XXII. 552 The basal metabolic rate was not determined preoperatively or postoperatively. **1961** *Lancet* 26 Aug. 491/1 Why not give sedatives postoperatively by mouth instead of by injection. **1975** *Nature* 8 May 152/2 The occurrence of ptosis and miosis postoperatively was accepted as evidence that surgery had been successful.

post-oral (-ˈɔərəl), *a. Anat.* and *Zool.* [f. POST- B. 2 + ORAL.] Situated behind the mouth:

applied to (theoretical) segments of the head in arthropods, and to certain visceral arches in the embryo of vertebrates. Opp. to PRE-ORAL.
1870 ROLLESTON *Anim. Life* 106 Besides the prae-oral or so-called 'supra-oesophageal' ganglionic mass..there are twelve post-oral ganglia in the Crayfish. **1888** ROLLESTON & JACKSON *Anim. Life* 491 [The head in *Arthropoda*] consists of a prae-oral or pro-cephalic region, to which are fused a variable number of post-oral somites. **1895** *Syd. Soc. Lex.*, *Post-oral arches*, the five subcranial plates which lie below (on the *caudal* side of) the mouth in the embryo, going to form the lower jaw and throat.

postorbital (-'ɔːbɪtəl), *a.* (*sb.*) *Anat.* and *Zool.* [f. POST- B. 2 + ORBITAL.] Situated behind, or on the hinder part of, the orbit of the eye: applied esp. to a process (usually) of the frontal bone, which forms a separate bone in some reptiles. (Cf. POSTFRONTAL.) Also *ellipt.* as *sb.* **a.** The postorbital bone or process. **b.** A scale behind the eye in snakes (= POSTOCULAR b).
1835-6 *Todd's Cycl. Anat.* I. 274/2 The post-orbital processes are most developed in the Parrots. **1866** OWEN *Anat. Vertebr.* I. 103 The bones of the dermoskeleton are—The Supratemporals..The Postorbitals..The Superorbitals [etc.]. **1882** W. K. PARKER in *Trans. Linn. Soc.* II. III. 167 Besides this antorbital rudiment, there is a large postorbital cartilage.

post-osmicate, -osmication: see POST- A. 1 a, b.

post-ovulative, -ovulatory: see POST- B. 1.

post-paid: see POST *sb.*² 13.

post-painter: see POST *sb.*¹ 9.

post-painterly: see POST- B. 1.

postpalatal, -palatine: see POST- B. 2.

post-paper: see POST *sb.*² 13.

postparative: see POST- A. 1 a.

postparietal: see POST- B. 2.

post partum: see POST *Lat. prep* 4.

post-parturient: see POST- B. 1.

†**'postpast.** *Obs.* [f. POST- A. 1 b + L. *pāstus* food, f. *pāsc-ĕre* to feed; cf. ANTEPAST, REPAST.] A small portion of food taken just after a regular meal. (Opp. to ANTEPAST.) Also *fig.*
1629 WADSWORTH *Pilgr.* iii. 16 An apple, or peece of cheese for their post past. **1657** J. SERGEANT *Schism Dispach't* 476 Who..would needs make it the post-past to his Bill of Fare.

‖**postpectus** (pəʊst'pɛktəs). *Zool.* [mod.L., f. POST- A. 2 b + *pectus* breast.] **a.** *Entom.* The underside of the metathorax. **b.** 'The hind-breast, or hinder part of the breast' (*Cent. Dict.*). Hence **post'pectoral** *a.*, pertaining to or connected with the postpectus.
1826 KIRBY & SP. *Entomol.* III. xxxiii. 382 *Postpectus*... The underside of the second segment of the alitrunk. *Ibid.* xxxv. 543 Analogous to the scapula of the medipectus and parapleura of the postpectus. *Ibid.* IV. 344 Legs... Postpectoral... The hind-legs, affixed to the *Postpectus*.

postpeduncle (-pɪ'dʌŋk(ə)l). *Anat.* [ad. mod.L. *postpedunculus*, f. POST- A. 2 b + *pedunculus* PEDUNCLE.] The inferior peduncle of the cerebellum. So **postpe'duncular** *a.*, pertaining to the postpeduncle.
1857 in DUNGLISON *Med. Dict.* **1889** *Buck's Handbk. Med. Sc.* VIII. 128/1 A caudal [pair] (postpeduncles) to the metencephal and myel. **1895** in *Syd. Soc. Lex.*

postpetiole, -pharyngeal, -pituitary: see POST- B. 2

postplace: see POST- A. 1 a.

post-Pliocene (-'plaɪəsiːn), *a.* (*sb.*) *Geol.* Also -Pleio-. [f. POST- B. 1 b + PLIOCENE.] Epithet applied to the lowest division of the Post-tertiary or Quaternary formation, immediately overlying the Pliocene or Upper Tertiary; also to the whole of the formations later than the Pliocene (so = Post-tertiary or Quaternary). Also applied to animals, etc. of this period. Also *ellipt.* as *sb.* = post-pliocene division or formation.
1841 LYELL *Elem. Geol.* (ed. 2) I. ix. 212, I have adopted the term Post-Pliocene for those strata which are sometimes called modern, and which are characterized by having all the imbedded fossil shells identical with species now living. **1851** D. WILSON *Preh. Ann.* (1863) I. ii. 51 Post-pliocene flint implements. **1863** *Q. Rev.* CXIV. 410 A cold character of climate appears to have extended through a great part of the post-pliocene period. **1865** TYLOR *Early Hist. Man.* xi. 306 In the post-pliocene of Brazil, remains have been preserved of an extinct ape. **1879** WALLACE *Australasia* iv. 64 Recent quaternary or Post-pliocene deposits.

postponable (pəʊst'pəʊnəb(ə)l), *a.* [f. POSTPONE + -ABLE.] Capable of being postponed.
1890 in *Cent. Dict. Mod.* An engagement not postponable. **1963** *Punch* 6 Feb. 206/1 So much of its expenditure is postponable. **1965** P. WYLIE *They both were Naked* I. iv. 189, I am in the middle of something. A novelette. Postponable, though. **1971** *Human World* Aug. 9 The accepted right and power of the country to decide by majority vote in free elections, not indefinitely postponable, that it has..had enough of the present government.

†**postponator.** *Obs. rare*⁻¹. [By false analogy f. POSTPONE + -ATOR.] = POSTPONER.
1775 in *N. Eng. Hist. & Gen. Reg.* (1876) XXX. 149 Rawlins postponator declares the resolution not proper to proceed from the Committee of South Carolina.

postpone (pəʊst'pəʊn), *v.* Also 6 *Sc.* postpo(y)n. [ad. L. *postpōnĕre* to put after, postpone, neglect, f. *post* after + *pōnĕre* to place, put down.
In 16th c. exclusively Sc.; rare in Eng. before 1700.]
1. a. *trans.* To put off to a future or later time; to defer. (With *simple obj.*; in 16th c., also with *inf.*)
1500-20 DUNBAR *Poems* ix. 90 Of vertew postponyng, and syn aganis nateur. **1535** STEWART *Cron. Scot.* (Rolls) II. 151 Becaus it wes so neir that tyme the nycht, Postponit all quhill on the morne wes lycht. *Ibid.* 283 This Edilfrid and Brudeus also, Postponit hes to battell for till go. **1574** *Reg. Privy Council Scot.* II. 389 The said Robert wranguslie postponis and differis to do the same. **1710** PALMER *Proverbs* 186 Every man..wou'd have all business post-pon'd for the service he expects from a patron or friend. **1726** BERKELEY *Let. to Prior* 15 Mar., Wks. 1871 IV. 124 The answer to other points you postponed for a few posts. **1836** W. IRVING *Astoria* III. 177 The project had to be postponed. **1875** HELPS *Soc. Press.* iii. 58, I propose, therefore, that we should postpone any remarks that we have to make.
absol. **1500-20** DUNBAR *Poems* xxx. 28 My brethir oft hes maid the supplicationis,..To tak the abyte, bot thow did postpone.
†**b.** To 'put (a person) off', i.e. to keep (him) waiting for something promised or expected. *Obs.*
[**1533** GAU *Richt Vay* (S.T.S.) 90 Giff vss grace to haiff pacience quhen our wil is postponit.] **1571** *Reg. Privy Council Scot.* II. 90 Thay ar..hinderit and postponit of payment of thair stipendis. *a* **1700** DRYDEN (J.), You wou'd postpone me to another reign, Till when you are content to be unjust. **1705** HEARNE *Collect.* 25 Nov. (O.H.S.) I. 98 Dr. Hudson..having many Promises from..the Bishops..was yet shamefully postpon'd by them.
c. *intr. Path.* Of ague or the like: To be later in coming on or recurring.
1843 SIR T. WATSON *Lect. Princ. & Pract. Physic* I. xl. 709 When the paroxysm thus postpones, the disease is growing milder; when it anticipates its usual period of attack, the disease is increasing in severity. **1898** P. MANSON *Trop. Diseases* ii. 42 They [i.e. malarial attacks] may occur at a later hour, in which case they are said to postpone.
2. To place after in serial order or arrangement; to put at, or nearer to, the end.
c **1620** A. HUME *Brit. Tongue* (1865) 31 We bid our inferioures, and pray our superioures, be [= by] postponing the supposit to the verb; As, goe ye and teach al nationes. **1680** G. HICKES *Spirit of Popery* Pref. 6 He hath Postponed the most scandalous part of his Speech..and put it towards the end. **1749** *Power Pros. Numbers* 66 Cicero..often postpones to the very last, that Verb or emphatical Word on which the whole Sense of the Period depends. **1774** J. BRYANT *Mythol.* I. 55 We sometimes find the governing word postponed, as in *Elizabeth*, or temple of Eliza. **1874** H. J. ROBY *Gram. Latin Lang.* II. 351 Most prepositions are prefixed to the substantive; a few are always postponed; others are occasionally but rarely postponed in prose.
3. To place after in order of precedence, rank, importance, estimation, or value; to put into an inferior position; to subordinate.
1658 PHILLIPS, *Postpone*, to set behinde, to esteem lesse then another. **1670** G. H. *Hist. Cardinals* I. II. 51 You have postpon'd the publick interest to your own. **1741** T. ROBINSON *Gavelkind* vi. 91 Females claiming in their own Right are postponed to Males. **1799** JEFFERSON *Writ.* (1859) IV. 272 Postponing motives of delicacy to those of duty. **1893** SNELL *Primer Ital. Lit.* 65 On the score of productiveness even Machiavelli must be postponed to him.
Hence **postponed** (-'pəʊnd) *ppl. a.*, **post'poning** *vbl. sb.* and *ppl. a.*
1693 LUTTRELL *Brief Rel.* (1857) III. 174 They should have their money to a farthing without any postponing. **1709** STANHOPE *Paraphr.* IV. 4 Ascribing the postponing of the Jews to their own Obstinacy. **1828** SCOTT *F.M. Perth* xxv, Anxious for the postponed explanation. **1863** READE in *All Year Round* 12 Dec. 367 [In a trial at law] the postponing swindler has five to one in his favour. **1904** *Daily Chron.* 7 June 6/7 Postponed purchases or postponed payments are the rule everywhere.

postponedly (pəʊst'pəʊnɪdlɪ), *adv. rare.* [f. POSTPONED *ppl. a.* + -LY².] At a late time; belatedly.
1851 H. MELVILLE *Moby Dick* III. xxvi. 171 He was an old man who..had postponedly encountered that thing in sorrow's technicals, called ruin.

post'poneless, *a. rare*⁻¹. [f. POSTPONE *v.* + -LESS.] That may not be postponed or averted.
c **1862** E. DICKINSON *Poems* (1955) I. 307 It's Coming—the postponeless Creature—It gains the Block—and now—it gains the Door.

postponement (pəʊst'pəʊnmənt). [f. POSTPONE *v.* + -MENT.] The action or fact of postponing.
1. The action of deferring to a later time; temporary delay or adjournment.
1818 in TODD. **1818** HAZLITT *Eng. Poets* viii. (1870) 192 Those minds..which are the most entitled to expect it, can best put up with the postponement of their claims to lasting fame. **1836** SIR H. TAYLOR *Statesman* xii. 83 The repetition of acts of postponement on any subject tends more and more to the subjugation of the active power in relation to it. **1882** MISS BRADDON *Mt. Royal* i, There was no need for the postponement of our marriage.
2. Placing after or below in esteem or importance; subordination.
1830 H. N. COLERIDGE *Grk. Poets* (1834) 274 That spirit of comparative neglect and postponement with which the maternal relationship was generally treated amongst the Greeks. **1879** H. SPENCER *Data of Ethics* §96. 251 That postponement of self to others which constitutes altruism.

postponence (pəʊst'pəʊnəns). *rare.* [f. POSTPONE + -ENCE.] = prec. 2. So †**post'ponency.** *Obs. rare*⁻¹.
1755 JOHNSON *Dict.* s.v. *Of*, Noting preference or postponence. **1845** CARLYLE *Cromwell* (1871) V. 9 It is not vain preference or postponence of one 'name' to another. **1668** WILKINS *Real Char.* 313 Whether of Prelation and preference: or Preterition and postponency.

postponer (pəʊst'pəʊnə(r)). [f. POSTPONE + -ER¹.] One who postpones, puts off, or delays.
1533 BELLENDEN *Livy* II. xix. (S.T.S.) I. 205 Of ane tribune þar war postponare of þe public weill [L. *moratorem publici commodi*]. *a* **1805** PALEY *Serm.*, *On Neglect of Warnings* (1810) 448 These postponers never enter upon religion at all, in earnest or effectually. **1880** G. MEREDITH *Tragic Com.* xiv, One of those delicious girls in the New Comedy..was called The Postponer, The Deferrer, or, as we might say, The To-Morrower.

postpontile: see POST- B. 2.

post'pose, *v.* [a. F. *postposer* (1549 in Godef.), f. *post-* POST- A. + *poser* POSE *v.*¹] *trans.* To place after or later than (something); = POSTPONE: **a.** in temporal or serial order. Now usu. *Gram.*
1598 GRENEWEY *Tacitus' Ann.* I. x. (1622) 19 Doubtfull.. which first to go to: least the other being postposed should take it in disdaine. *c* **1620** A. HUME *Brit. Tongue* (1865) 31 We utter our wil be verbes signifying the form of our wil, or postposing the supposit. **1655** FULLER *Ch. Hist.* XI. v. §24 The defense of the king's person and authority..in this Covenant is postposed to the 'privileges of parliament'. **1930** T. SASAKI *On Lang. R. Bridges' Poetry* I. i. 7 Not a single adj. in '-able' or '-ible' is postposed in Bridges. **1962** R. QUIRK *Use of English* xiv. 241 To postpose an adjective as in 'the young man carbuncular'. **1978** *Studies in Eng. Lit.: Eng. Number* (Tokyo) 106 It is obvious that there are similarities..between the rule of extraposition which postposes the string *into the heavens* in (46 b) and the one which postposes *into the clouds* in (42 b).
†**b.** in order of estimation or importance. *Obs.*
1622 DONNE *Serm.* (ed. Alford) V. 102 In postposing the Apocryphal into an inferior place [we] have testimony from the people of God. **1656** HOBBES *Six Lessons* Wks. 1845 VII. 343 Which reputation I have always postposed to the common benefit of the studious.
Hence **post'posed** *ppl. a.*; **post'posing** *vbl. sb.*
1927 O. JESPERSEN *Mod. Eng. Gram.* III. i. 19 Postposed adjectives are not in general accord with colloquial English. **1972** W. LABOV *Language in Inner City* iv. 143 There are some postposed expressions which seem quite straightforward, even unmarked. **1975** *Language* LI. 815 Passivization..may involve not one but two transformational operations—subject postposing and object preposing. **1978** *Ibid.* LIV. 76 On the other hand, response-stance verbs, and verbs that are not stance verbs at all, do not allow such postposings.

postposit (pəʊst'pɒzɪt), *v. rare.* [f. L. *postposit-*, ppl. stem. of *postpōnĕre* to POSTPONE.] *trans.* To place after; to cause to follow; to treat as of inferior importance: = POSTPONE 2, 3. Hence **post'posited** *ppl. a.*
1661 FELTHAM *On St. Luke* Resolves, etc. 390 Often in our Love to her, our Love to God is swallowed and postposited. **1892** W. M. LINDSAY in *Amer. Jrnl. Philol.* XIV. 161 The post-posited relative, to judge from the dramatists' versification, was fused with the preceding word.

postposition (pəʊstpə'zɪʃən). [n. of action f. L. *postpōnĕre*, *postposit-*: so F. *postposition* (Littré); but in sense 3, after *preposition*, with *post-* in place of *pre-*.]
†**1.** The action of postponing; postponement; delay. *Sc. Obs. rare*⁻¹.
1546 *Aberdeen Regr.* (1844) I. 229 The committer of sic recent crimes of bluid wes instantly, but [= without] postposition, causit ansuir for his offensis.
2. The action of placing after; the condition or fact of being so placed.
a **1638** MEDE *Daniel's Weeks* (1642) 36 Nor is the Postposition of the Nominative case to the verb against the use of the tongue. **1869** FARRAR *Fam. Speech* ii. (1873) 71 Its grammar, except in the postposition of the article, closely resembles that of the other Romance languages. **1928** H. POUTSMA *Gram. Late Mod. Eng.* (ed. 2) I. I. viii. 488 The influence of Latin Grammars makes itself felt in the post-position of the adjective. **1930** T. SASAKI *On Lang. R. Bridges' Poetry* I. i. 5 The postposition of two attributes joined together by means of 'and'. **1975** *Amer. Speech 1971* XLVI. 226 Simple modifiers may appear in postposition in both English and German.
3. A particle or relational word placed after another word, usually as an enclitic; *esp.* a word having the function of a preposition, which follows instead of preceding its object, as L.

tenus, versus, and Eng. *-ward(s,* as in *homewards.*

1846 *Proc. Philol. Soc.* III. 9 In some classes of languages the whole process of formation is carried on by means of postpositions, generally of a known and determinate signification. **1863** BATES *Nat. Amazon* x. (1864) 316 The feature..of placing the preposition after the noun—making it, in fact, a 'post-position'—thus: He is come the village from. **1881** *Academy* 16 Apr. 283 The case-forms in Turkish may be regarded..as parts of nouns or rather as postpositions. **1925** GRATTAN & GURREY *Our Living Lang.* I. xiii. 83 Look at the word *at* in the following sentences:— ..(*d*) These are the remarks they laughed at... We shall therefore avoid confusion of thought if we call it [*sc.* 'at'] a Postposition. **1976** J. S. GRUBER *Lexical Struct. Syntax & Semantics* II. iii. 343 In Japanese, there are some pieces of evidence..that postpositions, quantifiers, and other things which manifest left-branching..actually form one word.

4. *Music.* (See quot.)

1842 BRANDE *Dict. Sci.* etc., *Post position,* in Music, retardations of the harmony, effected by placing discords upon the accented parts of a bar not prepared and resolved according to the rules for discords.

Hence **postpo'sitional** *a.*, of, pertaining to, or of the nature of a postposition: = next; also *absol.* as *sb.*; **postpo'sitioning** *vbl. sb.*

1883 *Q. Rev.* Jan. 186 [In Corean] There are.. postpositional particles which, like the Japanese 'teniwoha', agglutinate themselves to nouns, verbs, and even sentences. **1968** *Canad. Jrnl. Linguistics* XIV. I. 50 In this example we see that the head NP is identical to the object of the postpositional phrase. **1972** *Language* XLVIII. 390, I am suggesting that the morphemes which appear as postpositionals are really functionally like verbs. **1974** L. TODD *Pidgins & Creoles* ii. 15 In the Atlantic varieties plurality can be overtly marked by the postpositioning of *dem* immediately after the noun. **1975** *Language* LI. 797 The putative specified subject can never surface, either as a subject or as a postpositional object. **1976** J. S. GRUBER *Lexical Struct. Syntax & Semantics* I. iii. 67 It appears that we always have the form with *from* to the left, but for *in* and *on* post-positioning is possible or obligatory.

postpositive (pəʊst'pɒzɪtɪv), *a.* (*sb.*) [f. L. *postposit-*, ppl. stem of *postpōnĕre*: see POSTPONE. Cf. mod.F. *postpositif* (Littré).]

A. *adj.* Characterized by postposition; having the function of being placed after or suffixed; enclitic.

1786 H. TOOKE *Purley* ix. 304 Grammarians were not ashamed to have a class of Postpositive Prepositives. **1845** *Proc. Philol. Soc.* II. 171 We..find in the Manchu itself a postpositive participle. **1854** LATHAM *Native Races Russian Emp.* 266 In the [Rumanian] word *omul* we have *homo ille*; i.e. a substantive with the postpositive article. **1877** SAYCE in *Trans. Philol. Soc.* 140 The older postpositive conjugation. **1930** T. SASAKI *On Lang. R. Bridges' Poetry* I. iv. 17 All these adjj. have been abundantly used through all the stages of English poetry... This fact appears partly to account for their frequent occurrence as postpositive attributes. **1936** *Amer. Speech* XI. 363/2 A discussion of the postpositive use of adjectives in such groups as *law ecclesiastical*. **1951** *Archivum Linguisticum* III. 24 Post-positive adjectives are in fact common in ON. **1963** [see ENCLISIS]. **1978** *Language* LIV. 281 A particular clause-modifying particle has a fixed position, either clause-initial or 'post-positive'—i.e. placed (along with indefinites and enclitic personal pronouns) immediately after the initial item in the clause.

B. *sb.* A postpositive particle or word.

1846 *Proc. Philol. Soc.* III. 13 This adjective may again be declined with all the postpositives usually employed as signs of cases.

Hence **post'positively** *adv.*

1961 R. B. LONG *Sentence & its Parts* xi. 256 Superlatives in *most* are now felt as compounds in which a modifying auxiliary pronoun has been united, postpositively, with a basic-form adjective head. **1964** *Amer. Speech* XXXIX. 36 Verbs contrast with adjectives by their ability to go postpositively.

post-possessive: see POST- A. 1 b.

†**post'posure.** *Obs. rare*⁻⁰. [f. POSTPOSE + -URE; cf. *composure.*] The action of 'postposing'; = POSTPONEMENT 2.

1656 BLOUNT *Glossogr.*, *Postposure,* a setting behind or esteeming less. Hence **1658** in PHILLIPS.

postprandial (-'prændɪəl), *a.* [f. POST- B. 1 b + L. *prandi-um* luncheon, meal + -AL[1]: cf. PRANDIAL.] Done, made, taken, happening, etc. after dinner; after-dinner. (Chiefly *humorous.*)

1820 COLERIDGE *Lett., to J. H. Green* (1895) 704 The day including prandial and post-prandial. **1846** *Life J. Guthrie* in *Lives Henderson & G.* 151 This plan, most likely of post-prandial origin, was actually attempted. **1864** *Reader* 9 July 49 A capital postprandial speaker. **1890** N. MOORE in *Dict. Nat. Biog.* XXI. 31/2 Men far advanced in post-prandial potations. *Mod.* Post-prandial oratory.

Hence **post'prandially** *adv.*, after dinner.

1851 H. D. WOLFF *Pict. Span. Life* (1853) 35 The crowd that postprandially collects thither.

post-precipitate, -precipitation: POST- A. 1 a, b.

postpre'dicament. [ad. med. Schol. L. *postprædicāmentum*, in Abelard *a* 1142, etc.; f. L. *post* after + *prædicāmentum* PREDICAMENT.] *pl.* The five relations considered by Aristotle at the end of his work on the ten predicaments or categories: viz. *opposites* (ἀντικείμενα), of four kinds; and the conceptions *before* or *priority* (πρότερον), of five kinds; *at once* or *simultaneity* (ἅμα), of two kinds; *motion* (κίνησις), of six kinds; and *having* (ἔχειν), of eight kinds.

[*a* **1280** ALBERTUS MAGNUS *De Praedicamentis* Wks. 1651 I. 173-4 Tractatus vii, *De Postpraedicamentis*..ideoque post praedicamenta oportuit sequi tractatum de his quae quidem co-ordinanda sunt sed ad unum genus praedicamenti reduci non possunt.] **1613** WITHER *Abuses Stript* B viij, He.. Handles in order the ten Prædicaments, Then Postprædicaments. **1727-41** CHAMBERS *Cycl.*, *Post-predicaments,* in logic, are certain general affections, or properties, arising from a comparison of predicaments with each other; or modes following the predicaments, and often belonging to many. **1890** in *Cent. Dict.*

post-'primary, *a.* [POST- B. 1 b.] Of education or schools: subsequent to that which is primary. Of a pupil: receiving such education.

1919 *App. Jrnls. House of Representatives N.Z.* E. VI. 15 Suffice to say the main aim we have had in view is the bringing of the post-primary work into closer touch with the vocational needs of the pupils. **1926** *Rep. Consult. Comm. Educ. Adolescent* II. 36 Is it possible..to ensure that all normal children may pursue some kind of post-primary course for a period of not less than three, and preferably four, years from the age of 11+. **1929** *N.Z. Educ. Gaz.* 1 Mar. 36/1 The teaching of French pronunciation in our post-primary schools. **1930** *Times Educ. Suppl.* 18 Jan. 21/3 A post-primary course. **1961** J. K. HUNN *Rep. Dept. Maori Affairs* (N.Z.) 23 Maori indifference to post-primary and university education. **1975** *Language for Life* (Dept. Educ. & Sci.) xiv. 213 The Hadow Report urged that there should be no sharp division between infant, junior, and post-primary stages. **1977** *Daily Times* (Lagos) 27 Aug. 4/5 The education committee would help to propagate the importance of ideal family life by organising lectures for post-primary school pupils.

post-processor: see POST- A. 1 b.

post-produce, -production: see POST- A. 1 a, b.

post-puberal, -pubertal, -puberty: see POST- B. 1.

‖**postpubis** (-'pju:bɪs). *Zool.* Pl. **-es** (-i:z). [mod.L., f. POST- A. 2 b + PUBIS.] The hinder or postacetabular part of the pubis or pubic bone, esp. when greatly developed, as in Birds and Dinosaurs. (Opp. to PRÆPUBIS.) Hence **post'pubic** *a.*, pertaining to the postpubis.

1888 ROLLESTON & JACKSON *Anim. Life* 65 The main portion of the bird's pubis is the homologue of the postpubis (so called) in the same groups [*Stegosauria* and *Ornithopoda*]. **1893** NEWTON *Dict. Birds* 862 The 'pubis' of Birds being in reality homologous with the *postpubis* of Dinosaurs and the *processus lateralis pubis* of other Reptiles.

post-puller, -pump: see POST *sb.*[1] 9.

post-Puranic: see POST- B. 1 b.

postpyramid (pəʊst'pɪrəmɪd). *Anat.* [POST- A. 2 b.] The posterior pyramid (*funiculus gracilis*) of the medulla oblongata. Hence **post-py'ramidal** *a.*[1], of or pertaining to the postpyramid; posterior to the pyramids.

1866-8 OWEN *Anat. Vertebr.* III. 83 In advance of the post-pyramids, still deeper columns of the myelon come into view. *Ibid.* I. 273 The post-pyramidal tracts diverge, expand, and blend anteriorly with the similarly bulging rectiform tracts, forming the side-walls of a triangular or rhomboedal cavity, called the 'fourth ventricle'. *Ibid.* III. 83 They expand as they enter the macromyelon, and form the 'post-pyramidal bodies'. **1890** BILLINGS *Med. Dict.*, *Post-pyramidal nucleus,* clavate nucleus. **1895** *Syd. Soc. Lex.*, *Post-pyramidal nucleus,* term for the nucleus of the *Funiculus gracilis.*

post-pyramidal (-pɪ'ræmɪdəl), *a.*[2] [f. POST- B. 1 b + PYRAMIDAL.] Subsequent to the building of the Egyptian pyramids.

1883 PROCTOR *Great Pyramid* 197 The abomination of desolation to which in our own post-pyramidal days hath been assigned the name of the 'Fifteen Puzzle'.

post-quintain: see POST *sb.*[1] 9.

post-radical, -Raphaelite: see POST- B. 1.

postre'duction. *Genetics.* [a. G. *postreduction* (Korschelt & Heider *Lehrb. der Vergleichenden Entwicklungsgeschichte der Wirbellosen Thiere* (Allgemeiner Theil) (1903) II. vi. 595): see POST- A. 1 b.] **a.** Reduction of chromosome number at the second of the two meiotic cell divisions, rather than at the first. Opp. PREREDUCTION a.

1905 *Proc. Acad. Nat. Sci. Philadelphia* LVII. 188 To the idea of postreduction we can apply the criticism 'not proven'. **1915** *Jrnl. Morphol.* XXVI. 122 In regard to the question of pre- and post-reduction, I have evidence here that the first maturation division is the reduction division. **1921** L. W. SHARP *Introd. Cytol.* xi. 245 Such tetrads separate reductionally at the second mitosis (postreduction) rather than at the first (prereduction) in certain orthopterans.

b. Separation of homologous chromatids or genes at the second of the two meiotic cell divisions, rather than at the first. Opp. PREREDUCTION b.

1934 L. W. SHARP *Introd. Cytol.* (ed. 3) xvi. 254 Disjunction in [meiosis] I is called 'prereduction'; that in II, 'postreduction'. **1950** *Adv. Genetics* III. 221 The prereductional or postreductional division of the heterozygous allele pair depends on its situation in the bivalent. Let us consider only the most common bivalent type, a bivalent with prereduction in respect to centromere, and provided with one chiasma. (In contradistinction to this, the Lecanium species have postreduction.) **1967** U. MITTWOCK *Sex Chromosomes* ix. 152 The sex chromosomes of *Apodemus* frequently exhibit postreduction, in contrast to most other mammals in which the X- and Y-chromosome show prereduction.

Hence **postre'ductional** *a.*, involving or pertaining to postreduction; **postre'ductionally** *adv.*

1905 *Proc. Acad. Nat. Sci. Philadelphia* LVII. 187 He is the solitary worker on the spermatogenesis of the Hemiptera who has taken the postreductional view. **1950** [see POSTREDUCTION b]. **1950** *Adv. Genetics* III. 221 Since the number and situation of chiasmata, as a rule, varies even in the eggs of a single female, certain parts of a bivalent and consequently the gene pairs included in them may separate either prereductionally or postreductionally depending on the number and position of chiasmata.

‖**post rem.** *Philos.* [med.L. (Albertus Magnus) lit. 'after the thing'.] Used, often post-positively, of universals considered as concepts intuited from individual instances, as opposed to their having real existence either prior to the individual instance (see ANTE REM) or only as experienced in individual instances (see *in re* (*c*) s.v. IN *Latin prep.*).

1902 W. JAMES *Var. Relig. Exper.* 523 For religion generally..the word 'judgment' here means no such bare academic verdict or platonic appreciation as it means in Vedantic or modern absolutist systems; it carries, on the contrary, *execution* with it, is *in rebus* as well as *post rem,* and operates 'causally' as partial factor in the total fact. **1927** [see ANTE REM]. **1931** S. BECKETT *Proust* 60 The Baudelarian [*sic*] unity is a unity 'post rem', a unity abstracted from plurality. **1941** E. C. THOMAS *Hist. Schoolmen* vi. 123 There remains a third aspect of Universals, generally described as Nominalist, which posits the Universal '*post rem*'. **1952** R. I. AARON *Theory of Universals* xii. 218 Nevertheless it [*sc.* the quality 'human'] is *post rem* and, to a certain degree, 'the workmanship of the mind'.

†**po'streme,** *a.* (*sb.*) *Obs. nonce wd.* [ad. L. *postrēmus* last, superl. of *posterus* coming after, following.] Last, hindmost; *absol.* one who is last.

1553 BALE *Gardiner's De vera Obed.* G j b, They were counsailed of som bodye not to contende to be called supremes, as longe as they are still postremes.

post-remote: see POST- A. 1 a.

postreproductive: see POST- B. 1.

postrhinal: see POST- B. 2.

post-rider: see POST *sb.*[2] 13.

†**po'striduan,** *a.* *Obs. rare*⁻⁰. [ad. L. *postriduān-us, -diān-us,* f. *postridie* on the next day.]

1656 BLOUNT *Glossogr.*, *Postriduan,* done the next day after or following.

'post-road. A road on which a series of post-houses or stations for post-horses is (or was) established; a road on which mails were carried.

1657 *Acts & Ordin. Parl.* c. 30 (Scobell) 513 Letters and Pacquets..to be sent forwards to the City of London, or any other place in any of the Post-Roads, from thence towards the said City. **1685** *Royal Proclam.* 7 Sept. in *Lond. Gaz.* No. 2068/2 That no man hereafter may complain for want of a setled Post in or near particular By-Towns or Places lying on the Post-Road. **1711** *Royal Proclam.* 23 June ibid. No. 4866/1 The Horsing of any Person..Riding Post, (that is to say) Riding several Stages upon a Post-Road. **1791** *Phil. Trans.* LXXXI. 108 The great post-road from hence into Italy, over Mount Cenis. **1814** SCOTT *Wav.* xlv, The common post-road betwixt Edinburgh and Haddington. **1860** SPOTTISWOODE in *Vac. Tour.* 86 When we drove into the back yard of the post-station,..the post-master would give us no horses, as the road by which we were to proceed was not a post-road. **1904** (*U.S.*) *Congress. Directory* 162 [U.S. Senate Committee on] post-offices and post-roads.

postrolandic, -Roman, etc.: see POST- B. 2, 1.

postrorse (pɒ'strɔ:s), *a.* [ad. mod.L. *postrorsus,* f. POST(E)RO- + *versus* turned: cf. ANTRORSE.] Turned or bent backward; retrorse.

1890 in *Cent. Dict.*, etc.

'post-,runner. †**a.** A 'runner' who acts as a post: see POST *sb.*[2] 2. *Obs.* **b.** One who bears messages or transports the post or mail along a certain route on foot; a post-carrier, foot-post.

1596 DALRYMPLE tr. *Leslie's Hist. Scot.* x. 403 Thir post-rinneris beginis to contemne the command. **1864** TREVELYAN *Compet. Wallah* (1866) 336 Each village in turn received a handful of chupatties or bannocks, by the hands of the post-runners, with orders to bake others, and pass them on to the next village. **1879** STEVENSON *Trav. Cevennes* 39 A cavalcade of stride-legged ladies and a pair of post-runners.

postsacral, -scalene, etc.: see POST-.

‖**postscenium** (pəʊst'si:nɪəm). *Class. Antiq.* [L. *postscænium,* f. *post* after, behind + *scæna,* a. Gr. σκηνή stage, scene.] The back part of a theatre, behind the scenes: also called *parascenium* (see PARASCENE). Cf. PROSCENIUM.

1727–41 CHAMBERS *Cycl.*, *Parascenium*, among the Romans, was a place behind the theatre, whither the actors withdrew to dress, undress, &c. more frequently called *Postscenium*. **1842–76** GWILT *Archit.* Gloss., *Postscenium* or *Parascenium*, in ancient architecture, the back part of the theatre, where the machinery was deposited, and where the actors retired to robe themselves.

postscribe (pəʊst'skraɪb), *v.* [ad. L. *postscrībĕre* (Tac.), f. *post* after + *scrībĕre* to write.]

1. *trans.* To write (something) after; to write as a postscript or appendix.

1614 T. ADAMS *Gallant's Burden* Wks. 1861 I. 325 The second is but a consequent of the first, postscribed with that word of inference, 'Now then'. **1661** J. STEPHENS *Procurations* 125 An Appendix to the former Discourse, setting forth the reason of printing that and post-scribing this. **1687** S. HILL *Catholic Balance* 133, I thought it necessary to postscribe that I bear malice to no Men or Party under Heaven.

2. *intr.* To write afterwards or subsequently; to make a written addition *to*.

c **1662** F. KERBY in *O. Heywood's Diaries*, etc. (1883) III. 26, I will not post-scribe but subscribe to Paul.

postscript ('pəʊstskrɪpt), *sb.* Also in L. form POST SCRIPTUM. [ad. L. *postscript-um*, neut. pa. pple. of *postscrībĕre* (see prec.) used as sb. Cf. obs. F. *postscript* (16–18th c.), mod.F., Du., Ger., etc., *postscriptum*, It. *poscritto*.] **a.** A paragraph written at the end of a letter, after the signature, containing an afterthought or additional matter.

1551 *Acts Privy Council* III. 409 A lettre to the Lorde Ogle..with a post script to send the sayd Irisheman by Mr. Dudley and Mr. Shelley. **1625** BACON *Ess.*, *Cunning* (Arb.) 93, I knew one, that when he wrote a Letter, he would put that which was most Materiall, in the Post-script, as if it had been a By-matter. **1655** *Nicholas Papers* (Camden) II. 191 This burthening you with Postscripts is, I confess, a rude way of writeing. **1711** STEELE *Spect.* No. 79 ⁋5 A Woman seldom writes her Mind but in her Postscript. **1806–7** J. BERESFORD *Miseries Hum. Life* x. cxxvi, It's like a Lady's Postscript, which, they tell you, contains the essence of the letter. **1873** BLACK *Pr. Thule* xxii, At the end of the letter there was a brief postscript.

b. A paragraph written or printed at the end of any composition, containing some appended matter.

1638 *Penit. Conf.* xii. (1657) 317 Towards the end whereof is an Appendix or Post-script. **1707** LUTTRELL *Brief Rel.* (1857) VI. 200 The parliament of Ireland have burnt by the common hangman the postscript to Mr. Higgins sermon. **1769** *Junius Lett.* xx. (1772) I. 142 The gentleman, who has published an answer to Sir William Meredith's pamphlet, having honoured me with a postscript of six quarto pages. **1890** MASSON *De Quincey's Wks.* IV. 321 Postscript [to *Oliver Goldsmith*]. *Ibid. note*, What is here printed as a 'postscript' appeared as a portion of De Quincey's 'Preface' to Vol. V. of his Collected Writings.

c. A thing appended; an appendage. Also, an additional or conclusory remark or action, an afterthought, a sequel.

1870 THORNBURY *Tour Eng.* I. i. 5 Brentford [was] always a mere ecclesiastical postscript to Hanwell or Ealing. **1926** C. HAMILTON in *Hutchinson's Best Story Mag.* Nov. 16/1 'We are to keep each other company until my son returns,' she added. And as a postscript, 'It is his wish.' **1932** E. V. LUCAS *Reading, Writing & Remembering* ix. 153 *The Gentlest Art* led to an amusing postscript. A firm of drapers..sent me..a specimen of epistolary gentleness of the highest order. **1949** M. MEAD *Male & Female* xvi. 340 Some couples attempt a last child, for which there are..slang phrases—'little postscript', 'little frost blossom'. **1963** A. ROSS *Australia 63* iii. 76 Benaud, who fancies these kind of brief postscripts against weary bowlers, drove Statham and hooked Coldwell. **1965** *Listener* 23 Sept. 463/3 Would he have expanded during his sixty-odd extra years, or remained as much a postscript from the 'nineties as Max?

d. A short talk broadcast after a B.B.C. radio news bulletin.

They began in 1940 and were discontinued in 1944.

1940 *Radio Times* 18 Oct. 3/1 Priestley fans in this country ..hear him only once a week, when he gives his Sunday-night postscript. **1943** *New Statesman* 20 Nov. 328 A sensible postscript by Barbara Ward. **1961** E. WAUGH *Unconditional Surrender* I. iii. 48 The BBC don't want to renew 'The Voice of Trimmer' Sunday evening postscripts. **1972** P. BLACK *Biggest Aspidistra* II. i. 95 The Postscripts began in March [1940], following the Nine O'clock News on the Home Service as a counter-attraction to Haw-Haw.

†**post'script**, *ppl. a. Obs. rare.* [ad. L. *postscript-us*, pa. pple. of *postscrībĕre*: see POSTSCRIBE.] Written after or subsequently.

1654 H. L'ESTRANGE *Chas. I* (1655) A ij, That were..to extinguish the light of all Histories.., the greatest part whereof were Postscript an age at least to the things recorded.

'**postscript**, *v. rare.* [f. POSTSCRIPT *sb.*] *trans.* To put a postscript to, to furnish with a postscript. Also, to furnish as a postscript. So '**postscripted** *a.*, 'having a postscript' (Worcester 1846 citing J. Q. Adams).

1894 A. DOBSON *18th Cent. Vignettes* Ser. II. ii. 27 Defoe prefaced and postscripted this modest effort. **1970** D. MARLOWE *Echoes of Celandine* vii. 127 He remembered writing a letter to her... *Suddenly one realizes*, he had postscripted, *that there is a sadness.*

postscriptal (pəʊst'skrɪptəl), *a.* [f. L. *postscript-um* (see POSTSCRIPT *sb.*) + -AL[1].] Of the nature of, or relating to, a postscript.

1877 MRS. OLIPHANT *Makers Flor.* xiv. 335 His life concluding with a postscriptal chapter of misery. **1891** R. BUCHANAN *Coming Terror* 82 In the postscriptal letter published this morning. **1894** MRS. OLIPHANT *Hist. Sk. Q. Anne* iv. 217 His new wife..brought him several children, a sort of postscriptal family, in his old age.

‖**post scriptum.** Also postscriptum, pl. -ta. [L. *post scriptum* (see POSTSCRIPT *sb.*).]

= POSTSCRIPT *sb.* a and b. Also *attrib.* and as *adv. phr.*

1523 WOLSEY in *St. Papers Hen. VIII*, VI. 119 Post scripta. Ye shal understonde that the Kinges Grace and his Counsail..thynke right expedient to use this way. **1535** CROMWELL in Merriman *Life & Lett.* 438 By the post scripta in myn other letteres unto youe..ye shal perceyve tharryval here of your servaunt Thwaytes. **1586** B. YOUNG *Guazzo's Civ. Conv.* IV. 191 b, And yet doubting, that she might..perceaue it, wrought underneath Post scriptum, thus, Kisse the letter. **1853** MRS. GASKELL *Cranford* v. 91 In a post-scriptum note in his handwriting, it was stated that the Ode had appeared in the 'Gentleman's Magazine', December, 1782. **1899** C. J. C. HYNE *Further Adventures Capt. Kettle* x. 191 The letter..ended in a post-scriptum tag. **1946** R. CAPELL *Simiomata* I. 11 Postscriptum.—While the April mutinies were Communist-inspired..they were not unprecedented. **1977** *Listener* 7 Apr. 447/3 A *postscriptum* has been pasted into the book registering Tambimuttu's disapproval.

‖**postscutellum** (-skjuː'tɛləm). *Entom.* Also in anglicized form **post'scutel**. [mod.L., f. POST- A. 2 + SCUTELLUM.] The fourth (hindmost) piece or sclerite of each of the segments of the thorax in an insect, situated behind the *scutellum*.

1826 KIRBY & SP. *Entomol.* III. xxxiii. 380 *Postscutellum*, ..a narrow channel running from the *Dorsolum* to the *Abdomen* in *Coleoptera*, forming an isosceles triangle reversed. **1897** W. F. KIRBY in M. Kingsley *W. Africa* 727 Postscutellum black, with a yellow dot on each side. **1899** G. H. CARPENTER *Insects* i. 21 Four distinct parts placed one behind the other can sometimes be observed; they are known as the *præscutum*, *scutum*, *scutellum*, and *postscutellum*.

Hence **postscu'tellar** *a.*, of or pertaining to the postscutellum.

1890 in *Cent. Dict.*

post-se'lection, *sb.* and *a.* **A.** *sb.* [POST- A. 1 b.] Selection, *spec.* natural selection, occurring subsequently. **B.** *adj.* [POST- B. 1 a.] Occurring after selection; of or pertaining to a time after selection.

1928 *Funk's Stand. Dict.*, *Post-selection*, natural selection carried on after the character of the animal has appeared. **1941** J. S. HUXLEY *Uniqueness of Man* ii. 56 Once the immigrants were established in the country, selection continued. This post-selection..must on the whole have encouraged and discouraged the same qualities favoured by pre-selection. **1946** *Nature* 7 Sept. 320/2 The main business of post-selection training for the Colonial Service will be carried out for the present in the Universities of Oxford, Cambridge and London. **1977** A. W. F. EDWARDS *Found. Math. Genetics* iii. 23 Starting at the point representing zygotic proportions before selection.., the population will move to the corresponding post-selection point.

†'**postship.** *Obs.* [f. POST *sb.*[2] + -SHIP.]

1. The office or position of a post or messenger; in quot. as a mock-title.

1607 DEKKER *Knts. Conjur.* vi. F iv, At the returne of his Post-ship and walking vpon the Exchange of the Worlde.. they will flutter about him, crying, What newes? what newes?

2. The office of post or local postman.

1545 *Acts Privy Council* (1890) I. 267 A letter to Mr. Mason, Master of the Postes, for the contynuaunce of Adam Gascoyne in the office of the Postship of Scrobye. **1583** *Wills & Inv. N.C.* (Surtees) II. 76 To my wiffe and my sonne Robart the postshippe of Thirlwall, towardes the maintenance of the house.

post ship: see POST *sb.*[3] 4 c.

postsphenoid (-'sfiːnɔɪd), *a.* (*sb.*) *Anat.* [f. POST- A. 2 b + SPHENOID.] ***postsphenoid bone***: the posterior part of the sphenoid bone of the skull, which forms a separate bone in (human) infancy. Also *ellipt.* as *sb.* Hence **postsphe'noidal** *a.*, pertaining to the postsphenoid bone.

1890 *Cent. Dict.*, *Postsphenoid*, *n.*, *Postsphenoidal*. **1890** BILLINGS *Med. Dict.*, *Postsphenoid bone.*

†'**post-stage.** *Obs.* [f. POST *sb.*[2] + STAGE *sb.*]

1. In 17th c., A stopping-place, station, or 'stage' on a post-road, to which the king's packet or mail was carried from the previous 'stage' and whence it was forwarded to the next; post-horses being kept in readiness for thus carrying the mail, and for the use of 'thorough-posts' or express messengers, as also for the service of private persons travelling 'post', who there took fresh horses.

1642 *Reg. Privy Council Scot.* Ser. II. VII. 327 [Order] for establishing post stages betuix Edinburgh and Portpatrik and Portpatrik and Carlill. **1685** *Royal Proclam.* 7 Sept. in *Lond. Gaz.* No. 2068/1 Not to Carry any Ship Letters.. beyond the first Post-stage to which they shall arrive in England. **1695** *Ibid.* No. 3087/4 An Act for settling Post-Stages throughout this Kingdom.

2. Short for *post stage-coach*: a mail-coach.

1771 *Boston Gaz.* 18 Feb. 3/3 The Post-stage from and to Portsmouth in New-Hampshire, lately put up at the Sign of the Admiral Vernon in King-street, Boston, is now removed to Mrs. Bean's at the Sign of the Ship on Launch.

post-'Stalin, *a.* [POST- B. 1 a.] Of Russia or of Communism subsequent to the time of Stalin (died 1953); following the death of Stalin. Hence **post-'Stalinist** *a.*

1955 H. HODGKINSON *Doubletalk* 86 Mr. Molotov's colleagues in the post-Stalin leadership. **1958** *Times Lit. Suppl.* 17 Jan. 27/1 It is not clear how much of the post-Stalinist course in the Soviet Union would fall under the same condemnation. **1964** T. B. BOTTOMORE in I. L. Horowitz *New Sociol.* 365 The post-Stalinist Communist societies. **1965** *Language* XLI. 125 The Soviet discussions on structuralism and other linguistic debates of the post-Stalin era. **1974** tr. *Wertheim's Evolution & Revolution* 332 What characterizes the post-Stalin period is that what should have been a temporary compromise is increasingly being accepted as a lasting characteristic of Soviet society.

'**post-,station.** A station on a post-road, where post-horses are kept.

1812 SIR R. WILSON *Pr. Diary* I. 141 The third post-station was also abandoned, and our cattle could do no more. **1832** G. DOWNES *Lett. Cont. Countries* I. 357 The first post-station is a solitary abode, called Torre di Mezza Via. **1901** *Wide World Mag.* VI. 445/1 At every forty or fifty versts.. the [Russian] Government has erected what are called *Poshtova Stancia*, or post-stations, where are kept a certain number of horses.

post-sternal: see POST- B. 2.

post-'stretching, *vbl. sb. Building.* [POST- A. 1 b.] = POST-TENSIONING *vbl. sb.* So **post-'stretch** *v. trans.*; **post-'stretched** *ppl. a.*

1941 *Concrete & Constructional Engin.* XXXVI. 78/2 Test results with structures post-stretched according to Mr. Hewett's method. **1946** *Ibid.* XLI. 147 Post-stretching is carried out against the hardened concrete, no immediate loss owing to elastic deformation of the concrete occurring, and that owing to shrinkage being reduced. *Ibid.* 195 The post-stretched mild steel reinforcement. **1949** P. W. ABELES *Princ. & Pract. Prestressed Concrete* xii. 92/1 Two kinds of transfer of prestress can be distinguished:—(a) instantaneous release of prestress by severing wires, previously tensioned independently of the members to be prestressed, a process which is called 'pretensioning' or 'pre-stretching', and (b) gradual release of the prestress by tensioning the wires directly against the hardened body of the member to be prestressed, a process which is called 'post-tensioning' or 'post-stretching'.

†**postsy'napsis.** *Cytology. Obs.* [POST- B. 1 c.] (See quots.)

1898 T. H. MONTGOMERY in *Zool. Jahrbücher*: *Anat. u. Ontogenie* XI. 20 The anaphase itself may be subdivided into 3 well marked periods: the early anaphase, the synapsis, and the postsynapsis. *Ibid.* 28 The postsynapsis, a term introduced here for the first time, is a well marked stage of the anaphase, distinguishable alike from the preceding synapsis as from the following telophase. **1911** *Jrnl. Morphol.* XXII. 753 My postsynapsis stage, equivalent to the diplotene.

postsy'naptic, *a.* **1.** *Cytology.* [POST- B. 1 b.] Subsequent to meiotic synapsis.

1909 [see PRESYNAPTIC *a.* 1]. **1912** *Jrnl. Exper. Zool.* XIII. 377 (*heading*) The post-synaptic spireme. Pachytene and diplotene. **1921** *Ann. Bot.* XXXV. 366 During the period when the mother-cells are in synapsis and the postsynaptic spireme stages, the tapetal cells vary greatly in appearance. **1931** *Cytologia* II. 353 Secondary association..is a post-synaptic phenomenon.

2. *Physiol.* [POST- B. 2.] Of, pertaining to, or designating a neurone that receives a nerve impulse at a synapse. Opp. PRESYNAPTIC *a.* 2.

1937, 1965 [see PRESYNAPTIC *a.* 2]. **1974** M. C. GERALD *Pharmacol.* v. 100 This interaction may produce one of two types of changes in the permeability of the postsynaptic membrane.

Hence **postsy'naptically** *adv.*

1952 *Jrnl. Physiol.* CXVII. 115 The fact that a moderate dose of curarine abolishes 'external' as well as 'internal' miniature potentials, strongly indicates that they both arise 'post-synaptically', in the end-plate. **1973** *Nature* 8 June 355/1 Lead can only block postsynaptically in conditions in which the density of ACh-receptor complexes is much lower than it is during an end-plate potential. **1978** *Ibid.* 22 June 674/1 These neurones lie postsynaptically to high densities of nerve terminals shown by immuno-histochemical techniques to contain somatostatin-like material.

post-sync(h (-'sɪŋk), abbrev. of POST-SYNCHRONIZATION, POST-SYNCHRONIZE *v.* Hence **post-'sync(h)ed** *ppl. a.*; **post-'sync(h)ing** *vbl. sb.*

1960 O. SKILBECK *ABC of Film & TV* 98 *Post Synch.*, to make apparently Synchronous sound for existing Mute film with the aid of a Guide Track, Wild track or otherwise. **1962** *Movie* June 26/1 He wasn't helped there by the post-sync sound, which was often unrelated to what was on the screen. **1963** *Movie* Jan. 21/3 The post-synching of the Italian and French versions..was done without any reference to me. **1968** J. BINGHAM *I love, I Kill* xii. 160 Doing bits and pieces of reshooting and recording the dialogue, post syncing, as they call it. **1968** *Punch* 31 Jan. 153/2 'Post-synch' may be necessary for various reasons, perhaps because the sound track of an outdoor scene has been ruined by aircraft noise, perhaps because a foreign actor's speech is so thick as to call for a substitute voice. **1972** I. HAMILTON *Thrill Machine* xiv. 58 We could always post-sync the questions or re-cut the answers. **1978** *New York* 3 Apr. 68/2 He..plays the piano with self-dramatizing virtuosity that isn't helped by the poorly matched post-synced studio sound recording. **1979** D. Lowden *Budapesti 3* iii. 22 'So tell me what you want?.. A post-synch and dubbing theatre that'll take at least eight tracks?'.. He got them [*sc.* the letters] back, neatly typed.. with the words 'dubbing tracks' and 'post-synch loops' intruding strangely in the text.

post-synchroni'zation. *Cinemat.* and *Television.* [post- A. 1 b.] The addition of a sound recording to the corresponding images of a film or video recording after the latter has been made. So **post-'synchronize** *v. trans.*; **post-'synchronizing** *vbl. sb.*

1933 A. Brunel *Filmcraft* 163 *Post-synchronise*, to add sounds, music or dialogue, after the mute film (pictorial image) has been shot. **1936** —— *Film Production* 177 For this purpose the artist, whose voice is to be used for post-synchronisation, is placed before a microphone in the studio and on to a screen is projected the scene to be post-synchronised. **1953** K. Reisz *Technique Film Editing* 275 This process involves getting the actors to speak the lines in synchronisation with the picture and is known as post-synchronising. Post-synchronisation is not used only to cover up faulty recording. *Ibid.* 276 In some Hollywood studios it has become common to post-synchronise most of the spoken lines. **1959** P. Bull *I know Face* v. 93, I.. said the two words. Two days later I was asked to post-synchronise them, as they were totally incoherent. **1960** D. Wilson *Television Playwright* 16 The advantage the director gains by retaking doubtful scenes.. by the post-synchronizing of music and sound effects. **1965** *Wireless World* July 34 (Advt.), The PRO 70 for multi-channel recording and for dubbing, post-synchronising and transfer. **1968** *Punch* 31 Jan. 153/2 Dubbing is a specialised form of post-synchronisation.

post-systolic, -tectonic: see post- B. 1.

post-'temporal, *a.* (*sb.*) *Anat.* [f. post- B. 2 + temporal.] Situated behind the temporal region of the skull: applied to a bone of the scapular arch in some fishes, also called *suprascapula* or *supraclavicle*. Also *ellipt.* as *sb.*

1890 in *Cent. Dict.*

post-temporary: see post- B. 1.

post-'tensioning, *vbl. sb. Building.* [post- A. 1 b.] Strengthening of reinforced concrete by application of tension to the reinforcing rods after the concrete has set. So **post-'tension** *v. trans.*; **post-'tensioned** *ppl. a.*

1948 *Concrete & Constructional Engin.* XLIII. 155 For post-tensioning there is no limitation of the size of the bars, but for pre-tensioning plain wires of 0·2 in. diameter are the largest that have been successfully employed. **1950** *Engineering* 13 Jan. 54/2 Adequate reasons exist to justify the claim that prestressed post-tensioned beams can successfully sustain the effects of fire. **1954** *Archit. Rev.* CXVI. 110 The gymnasium has a post-tensioned prestressed concrete frame and the changing rooms have load-bearing walls and precast concrete roof units. **1958** *Times Rev. Industry* July 25/1 Post-tensioning methods require relatively little capital expenditure. **1965** [see pre-tensioned *ppl. a.*]. **1974** Lin & Zia in B. Bresler *Reinforced Concrete Engin.* I. vi. 302 The amount of concrete posttensioned at the job site in the U.S.A... is estimated to have been about 700,000 cu yd in 1972. **1976** G. S. Ramaswamy *Mod. Prestressed Concrete Design* vii. 86 The member is post-tensioned after the concrete has sufficiently hardened.

post term, *sb. Law.* A partial rendering of L. phrase **post terminum** after the term, used *advb.*, as *adj.*, and as *sb.* for The return of a writ after term, and the fee payable for its being then filed.

1607 Cowell *Interpr.*, *Post terme*, is a returne of a writ, not onely after the day assigned.. but after the terme also..: it may be also the fee which the *Custos breuium* taketh, for the returne thereof. **1658** *Practick Part of Law* 13 In case of not filing your.. Writs, in or of the same Term they are returnable, they force you to pay when you file them.., for the *Post Terminum* of them, which is 20*d.* for every Writ. **1672** *Cowell's Interpreter*, Post terme, Post terminum. **1696** Phillips (ed. 5), *Post Term*, a Penalty taken by the Custos Brevium of the Common-pleas, for the filing any Writ by any Attorney after the usual Time. **1712** Arbuthnot *John Bull* iv. ii, To Esquire South, for *post Terminums*. **1848** Wharton *Law Lex.*, *Post terminum*, (after the term).

postterm (pəʊst'tɜːm), *a. Obstetrics.* [post- B. 1 a.] Born or occurring after a pregnancy that lasted significantly longer than normal.

1933 *Jrnl. Pediatrics* II. 677 There is a stable substrate of maturation.. which tends to keep the underweight, the preterm and the postterm infant close to his normal maturity levels in the field of behavior. **1971** Pierog & Ferrara *Approach to Med. Care of Sick Newborn* i. 7 The preterm infant is one born less than 38 weeks by gestational age from the first day of the last menstrual period; the postterm infant is one born 42 weeks or more from the first day of the last menstrual period. **1976** L. O. Lubchenco *High Risk Infant* vii. 163 There are relatively more infants who are large for gestational age in postterm deliveries than in term deliveries.

'post-'tertiary, *a.* (*sb.*) *Geol.* [f. post- B. 1 b + tertiary.] Epithet of the formations, or the period, subsequent to the Tertiary; also called Quaternary; the most recent of the whole geological series. Also applied to animals, etc. belonging to this period. Also *ellipt.* as *sb.*

1854 Page *Introd. Text-bk. Geol.* xiv. 121 The generality of post-tertiary accumulations being clays, silts, sands, gravels, and peat-mosses. **1865** Lubbock *Preh. Times* 151 Species which characterise the post-tertiary epoch in Europe. **1878** Huxley *Physiogr.* xvii. 290 By others they are called the post-tertiary series.

posttest ('pəʊsttest), *a.* and *sb. Psychol.* [f. post- + test *sb.*[1]]

A. *adj.* [post- B. 1 a.] That comes after or is subsequent to a test. **B.** *sb.* [post- A. 1 b.] A subsequent test designed to measure the effects of or changes since the initial test. Hence **post'testing** *vbl. sb.*

1966 *Jrnl. Personality & Social Psychol.* IV. 175, 60 male and female college Ss were.. tested.. in a social pressure plus reinforcement session and again in a posttest reinforcement session 2 wk. later. **1966** J. S. Bruner *Beyond Information Given* (1974) xviii. 321 This was followed by some training trials and then there was a posttest. **1972** *Jrnl. Social Psychol.* LXXXVI. 12 Endler.. observed posttest behavior consistent with his reinforcement schedules. **1973** *Jrnl. Genetic Psychol.* CXXIII. 90 The Ss were reassembled for the posttesting session, and the TAT and Test Anxiety Questionnaire were given. **1974** *Florida FL Reporter* XIII. 76/1 The recognition test of singular and plural SE forms was administered after the three-week training session and after the posttest.

post-tibial: see post- B. 2.

post-tidings, -time: see post *sb.*[2] 12.

Post Toasties. orig. *U.S.* Also with lowercase initials and sing. **Post Toasty, -ie.** The proprietary name of a breakfast cereal first marketed by Charles William *Post* (1854–1914), American manufacturer (cf. Postum). Also *transf.* and *fig.*

[**1907** *Trade Marks Jrnl.* 2 Oct. 1941 *Toasties*... [Substances used as food or as ingredients in food]. Charles William Post,.. London, England, and.. Michigan, United States of America; manufacturer.] **1908** *Official Gaz.* (U.S. Patent Office) 31 Mar. 1177/2 *Postum Cereal Co. Limited*, Battle Creek, Mich. Filed 28 Jan., 1908. *Post Toasties*... Cereal Breakfast Foods. **1914** H. W. Wiley *1001 Tests of Foods* vi. 72 Many are the letters received in regard to the cereal breakfast foods, especially for children's use. One mother writes me: 'Two small youngsters are anxiously awaiting your opinion in regard to their favorite shredded wheat, grape nuts, and post toasties.' **1926–7** *Army & Navy Stores Catal.* 2/1 *Breakfast cereals*, Post Toasties—pkt. -/9. **1943** G. Greene *Ministry of Fear* iii. iii. 202 There was milk and post-toasties and bread and marmalade. **1945** L. Shelly *Jive Talk Dict.* 31 *Post toasty*, corny character. **1950** A. Wilson *Such Darling Dodos* 134 Little pyramids of chocolate powder and post toasties.. called 'Coconut Kisses'. **1969** *Listener* 22 May 732/1 They range from chilling glimpses of the world in the next century to golden, Post-Toastie pieces of life in which.. the ancient decencies are reinforced. **1979** P. Niesewand *Member of Club* iv. 30 The economy-size box of Post Toasties on his breakfast table.

post-tonic: see post- B. 1.

'post-town. [f. post *sb.*[2] + town.]

1. A town having a (head) post office, or one that is not merely a sub-office of another. Also, a town with its own postcode.

1635 *Proclamation* in Rymer *Fœdera* (1732) XIX. 649/2 To take with them all such Letters as shall be directed to any Post-Town, or any Place near any Post-Town in the said Road. **1682** *Lond. Gaz.* No. 1761/4 All persons concerned are desired to insert at the bottom of their Letters the Post-Town nearest to the place their Letters are directed, for their speedy Conveyance. **1835** Marryat *Pacha* v, We were about five miles from any post-town. **1889** *Repentance P. Wentworth* III. 5, I walked over to the post-town for the second post. **1973** *Guardian* 7 Feb. 1/1 The Post Office will recognise Milton Keynes as a separate post town on Monday.

2. A town at which post-horses are kept. ? *Obs.*

1792 G. Wakefield *Mem.* (1804) I. ii. 54 During the necessary delay at some post-town, our contemplative parson rambled about after a bookseller's shop. **1838** *Murray's Hand-bk. N. Germ.* 252/1 Below Rheinfels lies the post-town of St. Goar.

So **post-township** (*U.S.*): see township.

1837 *Pop. Encycl.* V. 304/1 *Onondaga*; a post-township and capital of Onandaga county, New York.

post-trader: see post *sb.*[3] 2 d.

post-traumatic: see post- B. 1.

'post-treatment, *sb.* and *a.*

A. *sb.* [post- A. 1 b.] Treatment carried out subsequently. **B.** *adj.* [post- B. 1 a.] Existing or occurring after treatment.

1946 *Genetics* XXXI. 375 Studies of hatchability of eggs deposited by females that had been inseminated by males treated with.. 2000 r of X-rays.. suggest that the effect of posttreatment in reducing the frequency of chromosomal rearrangements is attributable to increased restitution. **1962** *Radiation Bot.* I. 132/2 Immediate ultraviolet post-treatments at 2967 Å.. completely overcame 1 kr X-ray depression of embryo viability. **1967** E. Chambers *Photolitho-Offset* xiii. 198 It is used mainly as a 'post treatment' after developing and before etching. **1972** *Gloss. Terms Timber* (*B.S.I.*) 25 *Post-treatment*, preservative treatment of ordinary plywood after it has been made. **1972** *Jrnl. Social Psychol.* LXXXVI. 84 Any differences in posttreatment attitude can therefore be attributed to the effects of the experimental treatment.

post-tridentine: see post- B. 1.

post-tuberance: see post- A. 2.

post-tussic to **post-velar:** see post- B.

postulancy ('pɒstjʊlənsɪ). [f. postulant: see -ancy.] The condition of being a postulant; the period during which this lasts.

1882–3 *Schaff's Encycl. Relig. Knowl.* II. 1476 Those who would enter either class undergo a postulancy of six months. **1884** *Weekly Reg.* 18 Oct. 504/2 Two years make a long postulancy.

postulant ('pɒstjʊlənt). [a. F. *postulant* ad. L. *postulāns, -āntem*, pr. pple. of *postulāre* to demand: see postulate *v.*] One who asks or petitions for something; a petitioner; a candidate for some appointment, honour, or office; *esp.* a candidate for admission into a religious order.

1759 Chesterf. *Lett. to Son* 2 Feb., That he will have one [a garter] is very certain; but when,.. is very uncertain; all the other postulants wanting to be dubbed at the same time. **1766** *Char.* in *Ann. Reg.* 28/2 There were many postulants for the abbey of Anchin. **1844** Lingard *Anglo-Sax. Ch.* (1858) I. iv. 133 The age at which the postulant might be admitted [i.e. into holy orders]. **1859** Jephson *Brittany* xv. 245 When a young man applies for admission he is taken in for two years as a postulant. **1873** F. Hall *Mod. Eng.* iv. 98 Words.. often answering to calls too subtile for analysis, are constantly presenting themselves as postulants for recognition. **1876** C. M. Davies *Unorth. Lond.* 220 The public reception of a postulant into the order of 'Our Lady of Mercy'.

†**postulary** ('pɒstjʊlərɪ), *a. Obs. rare.* [ad. late L. *postulāri-us* that demands or claims.] Of the nature of a postulate.

1637 Jackson *Serm. on Matt. ii.* 17–18 §3, I must beg one or two postulary suppositions which.. will go for maxims.

postulate ('pɒstjʊlət), *sb.*[1] [ad. L. *postulātum* (a thing) demanded or claimed: see postulatum. Cf. F. *postulat* (1771 in *Dict. Trévoux*).

In sense 1 representing classical L. *postulātum*; in 2, 3, = mod.L. *postulātum* for med.L. *petītio* rendering Gr. αἴτημα (Aristotle, Euclid). *Postulāta* (pl.) occurs in the L. transl. of *Rhet. ad Alex.* by Philelphus (died 1489) printed 1523, and is always used by Pacius *Aristot. Organ.* 1584. In L. edd. of Euclid, *postulāta* appears in Commandinus 1619.]

I. 1. A demand, a request; *spec.* a demand of the nature of a stipulation: cf. 2 d. Now *rare.*

1588 in Motley *Netherl.* (1860) II. xviii. 397 Our postulates do trouble the King's commissioners very much, and do bring them to despair. **1656** Blount *Glossogr.*, *Postulate*, a request, demand or suit. **1660** Jer. Taylor *Worthy Commun.* i. iii. 56 This St. Peter calls the stipulation of a good conscience; the postulate and bargain which man then makes with God. **1826** Scott *Diary* 4 Feb. in Lockhart *Life*, Give me my popularity, (an awful postulate) and all my present difficulties shall be a joke in four years. **1860** [see postulate *v.* 1 b].

II. 2. *Logic* and *gen.* A proposition demanded or claimed to be granted; *esp.* something claimed, taken for granted, or assumed, as a basis of reasoning, discussion, or belief; hence, a fundamental condition or principle.

1646 Sir T. Browne *Pseud. Ep.* i. vii. 25 *Ipse dixit*, or *oportet discentem credere*,.. may be Postulates very accomodable unto Junior indoctrinations; yet are their authorities but temporary. *Ibid.* iii. vii. 120 This conceit was probably first begot by such as held the contrary opinion of sight by extramission,.. and is the postulate of Euclide in his Opticks. **1653** Hales *Brevis Disquisitio* in *Phenix* (1708) II. 332 The Monk's Postulate in the fifth Proposition of the second Chapter: 'The Christian Faith excludes all doubting, and is certain and infallible'. **1715** tr. *Gregory's Astron.* (1726) I. 195 Astronomers, (who.. make it a Postulate, that any Star may be moved with any motion). **1860** Westcott *Introd. Study Gosp.* viii. (ed. 5) 400 Christianity is essentially miraculous. This is a postulate of Biblical criticism. **1884** F. Temple *Relat. Relig. & Sc.* i. (1885) 6 The Supreme Postulate, without which scientific knowledge is impossible, is the Uniformity of Nature.

b. Sometimes with special reference to its undemonstrated or hypothetical quality: An unproved assumption, a hypothesis.

1646 Sir T. Browne *Pseud. Ep.* vi. vi. 296 Which wee shall labour to induce not from postulates and entreated Maximes, but undeniable principles declared in holy Scripture. **1751** Johnson *Rambler* No. 155 ⁋2 An opinion which, like innumerable other postulates, an enquirer finds himself inclined to admit upon very little evidence. **1837** Hallam *Hist. Lit.* i. i. §23 (1847) I. 19 And as their reasonings commonly rest on disputable postulates, the accuracy they affect is of no sort of value. **1841–4** Emerson *Ess.*, *Hist.* Wks. (Bohn) I. 15 All the postulates of elfin annals.

c. Sometimes with special reference to the self-evident nature of a proposition of fact: hardly distinct from axiom.

1751 Johnson *Rambler* No. 158 ⁋1 Any settled principle or self-evident postulate. **1812** G. Chalmers *Dom. Econ. Gt. Brit.* 326 [They] had all taken it for granted, as a postulate, which could not be disputed, that a balance of trade, either favourable, or disadvantageous, enriched, or impoverished, every commercial country. **1816** Playfair *Nat. Phil.* II. 223 The postulate on which this rule proceeds is, that though each of the given equations is incorrect,.. there is nothing that determines the amount of the errors to be on one side more than another, or in excess rather than defect.

d. Something required as the necessary condition of some actual or supposed occurrence or state of things; a pre-requisite.

1841 Myers *Cath. Th.* iv. xxiii. 293 A Personal and Providential Deity—this is the necessary postulate of all Religion properly so called. **1860** Maury *Phys. Geog. Sea*

xix. §796 The low barometer, the revolving storm, and the ascending column require for a postulate the approach by spirals of the wind from circumference to centre.

3. *spec.* in *Geom.* (or derived use). A claim to take for granted the possibility of a simple operation, e.g. that a straight line can be drawn between any two points; a simple problem of self-evident nature: distinguished from AXIOM (a self-evident theorem).

The earlier Eng. term was PETITION (sense 5).

1660 BARROW *Euclid* I. (1714) 6 Postulates or Petitions. 1. From any point to any point to draw a right line... 3. Upon any center, and at any distance, to describe a circle. **1704** J. HARRIS *Lex. Techn.* I, *Postulates*, or Demands in Mathematicks, &c. are such easie and self-evident Suppositions as need no Explication or Illustration to render them Intelligible. **1814** D. STEWART *Hum. Mind* II. ii. §3. 162 (tr. *Wallis*) According to some, the difference between axioms and postulates is analogous to that between theorems and problems; the former expressing truths which are self-evident, and from which other propositions may be deduced; the latter, operations which may be easily performed, and by the help of which more difficult constructions may be effected. **1825** J. NICHOLSON *Operat. Mechanic* 681 Postulates are things required to be granted true, before we proceed to demonstrate a proposition. **1827** HUTTON *Course Math.* I. 3 A Postulate, or Petition, is something required to be done, which is so easy and evident that no person will hesitate to allow it. **1864** BOWEN *Logic* xi. 374 An indemonstrable judgment, if theoretical, is called an *Axiom*; if practical, it is styled a *Postulate*.

postulate (ˈpɒstjʊlət), *sb.*² (*a.*) *Sc. Eccl. Hist.* [ad. L. *postulāt-us*, pa. pple. of *postulāre* to ask, request, desire, etc., in med.L. to nominate or designate to a bishopric or abbacy, subject to the sanction of the Pope: see POSTULATE *v.* 2.] A person nominated by the sovereign to some superior ecclesiastical benefice, as a bishopric, etc.

'Although the Scottish kings had maintained their prerogative of appointing persons chosen by themselves to vacant Sees and Abbacies, the consent of the Pope was an indispensable form to complete an election' (Small, Wks. Gavin Douglas, I. pref. xii). A person thus nominated was in the mean time entitled 'Postulate'.

1514 *Sederunt of Council* 2 June, Gavin Douglas.. Postulat of Arbroth. **1514** *Acta Dom. Concil.* 21 Sept., The Lords ordains that a letter be written under the King's Signet requiring Gavin, Postulat of Arbroth, to deliver the keyis of the Grete Sele fra him. **1515** (July 6) *Ibid.* XXVII. lf. 26 My Lord Gouernour shew that he was informit.. that the said Postulat [Gavin Douglas] was promovit to the Bishopry of Dunkeld be the King of Inglandis writings.. the quhilk the said Postulat denyit that he knew anything off. **1566** *Reg. Privy Council Scot.* I. 463 James Erle of Mortoun.. George Dowglas callit the Postulat, sone naturall to umquhile Archibald Erle of Angus.. with diverse utheris.. delaittit of the vyle and tressonabill slauchtir of umquhile David Riccio [etc.]. **1729** in *Macfarlane's Genealog. Collect.* (1900) 11 Alexander Gordon Postulate of Galloway. **1755** in Keith *Hist. Catal. Scot. Bps.* (1824) 146 He [Bp. Foreman] was postulate of Moray in the year 1501. **1828** SCOTT *F.M. Perth* Introd., [An inaccurate explanation: see above]. **1830** R. CHAMBERS *Life Jas. I*, I. i. 20 George Douglas of Todholes.. known by the epithet of the Postulate of Aberbrothwick.

b. *attrib.* or as *adj.*

1710 RUDDIMAN *Life Douglas* in *Æneis* 5 *note*, One is said to be Postulate Bishop, who could not be canonically elected, but may through favour, and a dispensation of his superior, be admitted.

†ˈ**postulate,** *a. Obs. rare*⁻¹. [ad. L. *postulāt-us*, pa. pple. of *postulāre*: see next.] = POSTULATED.

1664 BUTLER *Hud.* II. i. 763 I'll prove that I have one: I mean by postulate illation.

postulate (ˈpɒstjʊleɪt), *v.* [f. ppl. stem of L. *postulāre* to demand, request: see -ATE³.]

1. *trans.* To demand; to require; to claim.

1593 *Hist. K. Leir* (1605) Dj, A prince perhaps might postulate my love. **1651** BIGGS *New Disp.* §282 This doth not postulate or require the Physitians consent. **1703** T. N. *City & C. Purchaser* Ded. 4 These your extraordinary Favours.. seem to Postulate from me.. a Publick Recognition. *a* **1820** W. TOOKE (Webster 1828), The Byzantine emperors appear to have exercised, or at least to have postulated a sort of paramount supremacy over this nation. **1865** MILL *Exam. Hamilton* 437 Logic, therefore, postulates to express in words what is already in the thoughts.

b. *intr.* To make a request; to stipulate.

1860 MOTLEY *Netherl.* II. xviii. 397 The excellent Doctor had not even yet discovered that the King's commissioners were delighted with his postulates [cf. 1588 in POSTULATE *sb.*¹ 1]; and that to have kept them postulating thus five months in succession.. was one of the most decisive triumphs ever achieved by Spanish diplomacy. **1893** J. FAHEY *Hist. Kilmacduagh* 438 He was.. obliged in 1866 to postulate for a coadjutor.

2. *trans. Eccl. Law.* To ask legitimate ecclesiastical authority to admit (a nominee) by dispensation, when a canonical impediment is supposed to exist (see Du Cange s.v. *Postulari*); hence, to nominate or elect to an ecclesiastical dignity, subject to the sanction of the superior authority. See POSTULATE *sb.*², POSTULATION 2. (The earliest use in Eng.)

1533-4 *Act 25 Hen. VIII*, c. 20 §1 No.. person.. to be named, elected, presented, or postulated to any archebyshopriche or bisshopriche within this realme. **1688** *Lond. Gaz.* No. 2389/4 The most.. Reverend Cardinal.. was postulated by 13 of the 24 Canons. **1710** RUDDIMAN *Life of Douglas* in *Æneis* 5 [On the death of the Bp. of Dunkeld, 15 January 1515] Andrew Stewart.. Brother to the Earl of Athole, had got himself postulated Bishop, by such of the Chapter as were present. **1762** tr. *Busching's Syst. Geog.* V. 619 From the year 1561, Princes of the electoral house of Saxony have been constantly postulated by the chapter as administrators of the bishopric. **1874** SMALL *Douglas' Wks.* I. Pref. 16 Although Douglas was postulated to it [Abbacy of Arbroath], and signed letters and papers under this designation [Postulat of Arbroth] his nomination.. was never completed. **1878** STUBBS *Const. Hist.* III. xix. 307 The chapter was then allowed to postulate the bishop of Bath.

3. To claim (explicitly or tacitly) the existence, fact, or truth of (something); to take for granted; *esp.* to assume as a basis of reasoning, discussion, or action. [med.L. *postulāre*, transl. Gr. αἰτεῖν.]

1646 SIR T. BROWNE *Pseud. Ep.* II. iv. 78 Yet do they most powerfully magnifie him [God],.. who not from postulated or precarious inferences, intreat a courteous assent, but from experiments and undeniable effects, enforce the wonder of its Maker. **1649** J. H. *Motion to Parl. Adv. Learn.* 7 They seem to be among the postulated principles of nature. **1855** H. SPENCER *Princ. Psychol.* (1872) I. II. i. 146 That which we must postulate as the substance of Mind. **1862** —— *First Princ.* I. iv. §26 (1875) 88 Every one of the arguments by which the relativity of our knowledge is demonstrated, distinctly postulates the positive existence of something beyond the relative. **1878** BOSW. SMITH *Carthage* 103 It postulated a skill in seamanship and a confidence in their own powers both of attack and defence. **1885** S. COX *Expositions* xv. 186 Reason postulates God, though it cannot prove him.

b. To assume the possibility of (some construction or operation). Cf. POSTULATE *sb.*¹ 3.

1817 COLERIDGE *Biog. Lit.* I. xii. 250 In geometry the primary construction is not demonstrated, but postulated. **1882** PROCTOR *Fam. Sc. Stud.* 16 [They] might postulate.. that such lines when finite may be indefinitely produced.

†**4.** *intr.* To plead as an advocate. (So med.L. *postulare.*) *Obs. rare*⁻¹.

1566 PAINTER *Pal. Pleas.* I. 168 In Athenes.. a yong man .. being desirous to be an orator, and a pleading aduocate, to the intent he might postulate, according to the accustomed manner of Athenes in those daies, accorded [etc.].

Hence ˈ**postulated** *ppl. a.*, claimed, required.

1646-9 [see sense 3]. **1860** FARRAR *Orig. Lang.* 208 Even if we grant the postulated length of time.

postulation (pɒstjʊˈleɪʃən). [a. F. *postulation*, †*-acion* (13th c. in Hatz.-Darm.), ad. L. *postulātiōn-em*, n. of action from *postulāre* to POSTULATE.]

1. The action of requesting or demanding; a request, demand, claim.

c **1485** *Digby Myst.* (1882) II. 44 Accordyng to your petycions that ye make postulacion. *c* **1555** HARPSFIELD *Divorce Hen. VIII* (Camden) 147 Postulation was made for the continuance of rest. **1582** N. T. (Rhem.) *1 Tim.* ii. 1 That obsecrations, praiers, postulations, thankes-gevings be made for al men. **1659** PEARSON *Creed* I. vi. 430 Presenting his postulations at the throne of God. **1864** SIR F. PALGRAVE *Norm. & Eng.* III. 375 William,.. in conforming to the constitution upon the postulation of the English acted with entire consistency.

2. *Eccl. Law.* The presentation to office of some one canonically disqualified, esp. by being already vested in a similar office, in which case the recommendation took the form of a request or appeal to the supreme authority to sanction the election. (See quot. 1688.)

1567 ABP. PARKER *Corr.* (Parker Soc.) 306 For his election, or rather postulation, is but to be presented to the Queens Highness to have her royal assent. **1688** *Lond. Gaz.* No. 2365/3 The Cardinal, as being Bishop of Strasbourg, could not, without the Pope's Dispensation, be chosen but by Postulation, which required Two Thirds of the Electors to be for him. *a* **1715** BURNET *Own Time* (1753) III. iv. 209 The Cardinals postulation was defective since he had not two thirds. **1878** STUBBS *Const. Hist.* III. xix. 307 *note*, All postulations, that is, elections of persons disqualified. **1889** *Dublin Rev.* Oct. 335 The word election comprehends postulation, nomination, and presentation.

3. *Rom. Law.* An application to the prætor for authority to bring an accusation.

1851 SIR F. PALGRAVE *Norm. & Eng.* I. 23 The postulation was the regal right of the Roman Commonwealth.

4. *Logic* and *gen.* The taking for granted of the truth or existence of something unproved, esp. as a basis of reasoning or belief; an assumption.

1648 FILMER *Anarchy Lim. & Mixed Mon.* in *Free-holder*, etc. (1679) 247 Our Author expects it should be admitted as a magisterial postulation, without any other proof than a naked supposition. **1659** STANLEY *Hist. Philos.* XII. (1701) 481/1 We know how absurd this Postulation is. **1865** MASSON *Rec. Brit. Philos.* 380 Mr. Mill cannot surely want this cumbrous allowance of postulation. **1899** *Allbutt's Syst. Med.* VII. 401 The postulation of a single separate 'centre for concepts'.

5. *Math.* (See quots.)

1869 CAYLEY *Coll. Math. Papers* VII. 225 We may say that the number of conditions imposed upon a surface of the order *n* which passes through the common intersection is the Postulation of this intersection. **1870** *Ibid.* 140 The general quadric surface.. can.. be determined so as to satisfy 9 conditions; or, as we might express it, the Postulation of the surface is = 9.

postulational (pɒstjʊˈleɪʃənəl), *a.* [f. POSTULATION + -AL.] Of or pertaining to postulation; based on or involving deduction from a set of postulates.

1926 L. BLOOMFIELD in *Language* II. 153 Nevertheless, the postulational method can further the study of language, because it forces us to state explicitly whatever we assume. **1932** M. H. STONE *Linear Transformations in Hilbert Space* i. 2 The postulational treatment was carried through only recently by J. v. Neumann. **1933** L. S. STEBBING *Mod. Introd. Logic* (ed. 2) 506 A set of primitive propositions may be called 'a set of postulates', and the system thus constructed may be called 'a postulational system'. **1956** E. H. HUTTEN *Lang. Mod. Physics* iii. 75 The three laws of motion, together with the definitions, are given [by Newton] as a postulational system. **1961** E. NAGEL *Struct. of Sci.* v. 91 A familiar example of an abstract calculus is demonstrative Euclidean geometry developed in a postulational manner.

Hence **postuˈlationally** *adv.*

1936 *Mind* XLV. 174 In general, if *x* is defined postulationally, any proposition containing *x* will *implicate* the postulational definition of *x*. **1966** H. V. GUENTHER *Tibetan Buddhism* vi. 89 The distinction between a 'co-emergent belief in things' and a 'postulationally defined belief in things'.. is concisely stated.

ˈ**postulative,** *a. rare*⁻⁰. [f. L. *postulāt-*, ppl. stem of *postulāre* to POSTULATE: see -IVE.]

1623 COCKERAM, *Postulative*, belonging to a request.

postulator (ˈpɒstjʊleɪtə(r)). [a. L. *postulātor* a claimant, agent-noun f. *postulāre* to POSTULATE.] One who postulates; one who requests or demands; *spec.* in *R.C. Ch.* a pleader for a candidate for beatification or canonization.

1863 tr. *Luquet's Life Anna Maria Taigi* 2 The undersigned Bishop of Hesebon, Postulator of the suit of the servant of God, Anna Maria Taigi. **1884** *Cath. Dict.* s.v. *Beatification*, The process is now opened, at the request of the *postulators*, or supporters of the beatification. *Ibid.* s.v. *Canonisation*, The postulator of the cause.. asks twice that the name of the servant of God whose cause he pleads may be enrolled in the catalogue of the Saints. **1973** *Times* 2 Nov. 5/5 The required proof of two miracles is said to have brought to the postulator of the cause 'an embarrassment of choices'.

postulatory (ˈpɒstjʊlətərɪ), *a.* Now *rare.* [ad. L. *postulātōri-us* adj.; see POSTULATE *v.* and -ORY²; cf. obs. F. *postulatoire* (1622 in Godef.).]

1. Making request; supplicatory.

a **1631** DONNE *Serm.* li. 509 The whole prayer is either Deprecatory.. or Postulatory. **1647** CLARENDON *Contempl. Ps.* Tracts (1727) 392 He easily recovers the courage to turn that deprecatory prayer into a postulatory one.

2. Of the nature of an assumption; hypothetical.

1646 SIR T. BROWNE *Pseud. Ep.* II. vi. 93 [He] may easily perceive in very many, the semblance is but postulatory, and must have a more assimilating phancy then mine to make good many thereof. **1853** G. JOHNSTON *Hist. Nat. E. Bord.* I. 131 The resemblance between the plant and the picture of the artist is somewhat postulatory.

‖**postulatum** (pɒstjʊˈleɪtəm). Pl. **-a**; also 7 8 **-ums** (**-a's**). [L. *postulātum* a demand, request, sb. use of pa. pple. neut. of *postulāre* to POSTULATE.

Now generally in English form, POSTULATE *sb.*¹, which see for the history of the senses.]

†**1.** A demand; a requirement. = POSTULATE 1.

1639 LAUD in Rushw. *Hist. Coll.* II. II. 981 Concerning your *Postulata*, I shall pray you to allow me the like freedom. **1663** *Flagellum, or O. Cromwell* 93 To that purpose several irreverend Postulata were put to him. **1701** DE FOE *True-born Eng.* 359 But then that King must by his Oath assent To *Postulata's* of the Government. **1703** —— in *15th Rep. Hist. MSS. Comm.* App. IV. 62 To make any postulata of future loyalty and my obedient submission.

2. = POSTULATE *sb.*¹ 2. Now *rare* or *Obs.*

a **1619** FOTHERBY *Atheom.* I. i. §4 (1622) 6 Which two *postulata*, if they be not.. presumed by the Hearer,.. there cannot possibly be any proceeding. **1672** WILKINS *Nat. Relig.* 12 In the same way and method as is used in the mathematicks, consisting of *postulata*, definitions, and axioms. **1698** NORRIS *Treat. Sev. Subj.* 42 For the Demonstration of this Proposition, I desire but this one *Postulatum.* **1767** STERNE *Tr. Shandy* IX. xxiii, It was built upon one of the most concessible postulatums in Nature. **1827** SCOTT *Hoffmann's Novels* Prose Wks. 1835 XVIII. 292 A train of acting and reasoning in itself just and probable, although the *postulatum* on which it is grounded is in the highest degree extravagant.

†**b.** *Math.* = POSTULATE *sb.*¹ 3. *Obs.*

1743 EMERSON *Fluxions* 1 Postulatum. That any Quantity may be supposed to be generated by continual Increase. *Ibid.* 5 Now by the Postulatum, these Moments will increase the Quantities *x*, *y*, which therefore will become $x + o\dot{x}$, and $y + o\dot{y}$.

†**3.** Something required to be done; a problem; a desideratum. *Obs.*

1667 *Phil. Trans.* II. 570 More easie wayes of performing this *postulatum*, are to be found in.. Tacquet's Arithmetick. **1819** *Pantologia* X. s.v. *Quadrature*, The quadrature, especially among the ancient mathematicians, was a great postulatum.

†ˈ**postule,** *v. Sc. Obs.* [a. F. *postule-r* (14th c. in Littré), or ad. L. *postulāre.*] = POSTULATE *v.* 2.

c **1425** WYNTOUN *Cron.* VII. ix. 2912 Þai postulit in til his stede Off Dunkeldyn þe bischope Ioffray: bot til hym þe pape Be na way grant waulde his gud wil.

Postum (ˈpəʊstəm). orig. *U.S.* Also **postum.** [Pseudo-Lat. formation f. the name of Charles William *Post* (see POST TOASTIES) + L. *-um.*] The proprietary name of a coffee substitute. Also *attrib.*

1895 *Official Gaz.* (U.S. Patent Office) 3 Dec. 1549/1, 27,402 *Food Drinks.* Postum Cereal Co., Limited, Battle Creek, Mich. Filed Oct. 7, 1895 *Postum Cereal.* Used since February 1895. **1912** [see INSTANT *a.* 4 c]. **1922** *Hotel World*

15 Apr. 15/2 Choice of Coffee, Tea, Milk, Postum, Cocoa. **1962** *Flight Internat.* LXXXI. 871/1 Carpenter drank normal coffee instead of postum. **1967** *Listener* 21 Sept. 370/1 His frugal breakfast—perhaps a cup of Postum coffee and some biscuits. **1977** *New Yorker* 20 June 67/1, I will have a drink of Postum or coffee. **1978** J. CARROLL *Mortal Friends* v. vi. 572 None of that cappuccino stuff, Jack... See if they have Postum, will you?.. Well, lace it with a lot of milk, will you? Make it like American.

postumbonal: see POST- B. 2.

† **'postume.** *Obs.* Also 5 postem(e, -om(me, -um, -ym(e. Aphetic form of APOSTEM.

c **1374** CHAUCER *Boeth.* III. pr. iv. 72 Catullus clepid a consul.. þat hy3t nonius postum, or boch, as who seiþ.. a congregacioun of uices in his brest as a postum is ful of corrupcioun. *c* **1380** WYCLIF *Serm.* Sel. Wks. I. 400 Alle þes newe ordris ben rotyn postumes. **14..** *Stockh. Med. MS.* II. 361 in *Anglia* XVIII. 316 It.. distroyith venym And postemys þat waxin in man. **1491** CAXTON *Vitas Patr.* (1495) 80 There engendred a postom in his legge. **1547** BOORDE *Brev. Health* xxix. 17 A Postume is no other thynge but a collection or a runnynge together of evyll humours.

postural ('pɒstjʊərəl), *a.* [f. POSTURE *sb.* + -AL[1].] **a.** Pertaining or relating to posture or position.

1857 MARSHALL HALL (*title*) On Prone and Postural Respiration in Drowning. **1895** *Syd. Soc. Lex.*, *Postural respiration*, term for the various forms of artificial respiration in which the patient is put in certain postures or positions... *Postural treatment*, treatment by position, as.. for various fractures. **1898** *Allbutt's Syst. Med.* V. 88 The use of dumb-bells or clubs, and a variety of postural exercises.

b. Path. ***postural albuminuria***, albuminuria caused by the upright posture.

1897 *Allbutt's Syst. Med.* II. 156 Cases of 'postural' or 'cyclic' albuminuria are occasionally met with. *Ibid.* VIII. 154 If there be albumin it should prove postural ('cyclical').

c. ***postural integration***, 'some form of "body work", a term that applies to various specialized kinds of massage.. that claim to bring about mental well-being through physical manipulation and body realignment' (private communication, Cyra McFadden, 15 Aug. 1979).

1977 C. MCFADDEN *Serial* xviii. 42/1 She had like *mutated* over the years through Gurdjieff.. Human Life Styling, postural integration, [etc.]. **1977** *Rolling Stone* 19 May 32/3 There was postural integration and the Alexander Technique and Aural Ecology and the Chiropractic Information Bureau and Rolfing and even one discipline called 'Prosperity Training'. **1979** *San Francisco Sunday Examiner & Chron.* (Sunday mag.) 26 Aug. 29, I used to do Gestalt therapy. I did body work, postural integration.

posturant ('pɒstjʊərənt). *nonce-wd.* [f. POSTURE *v.* + -ANT[1].] One who adopts an intellectual or æsthetic posture; a poser.

1934 E. SITWELL *Aspects Mod. Poetry* i. 19 A school of American-Greek posturants.. began to exude a thin stream of carefully chosen watery words.

posture ('pɒstjʊə(r)), *sb.* [a. F. *posture* (16th c. in Montaigne *Ess.* ii.), contr. from earlier F. *positure*, ad. L. *positūra* position, posture (so also It., Sp., Pg. *postura*): see POSITURE.]

1. a. The relative disposition of the various parts of anything; *esp.* the position and carriage of the limbs and the body as a whole; attitude, pose.

1606 SHAKS. *Ant. & Cl.* V. ii. 221, I shall see Some squeaking Cleopatra Boy my greatnesse I' th' posture of a Whore. **1633** BP. HALL *Hard Texts, N.T.* 124 The usuall forme of their posture at the Table. **1674** PLAYFORD *Skill Mus.* II. 102 In the posture of your left hand observe this Rule. *a* **1711** KEN *Serm.* Wks. (1838) 179 He draws her in three distinct postures, like a captive, like a penitent, like a conqueror. **1727** DE FOE *Syst. Magic* II. viii. (1840) 388 By mutterings and conjurings, by postures and distortions. **1804** ABERNETHY *Surg. Obs.* 231 Restlessness, which caused a constant variation of posture. **1879** LUBBOCK *Sci. Lect.* v. 155 In burials of the Stone Age the corpse was either deposited in a sitting posture or burnt.

b. Among animals, a particular pose which is a signal of a specific pattern of behaviour.

1940 H. F. WITHERBY et al. *Handbk. Brit. Birds* II. 329 In terrifying posture feathers [of long-eared owls] are ruffled up. **1953** N. TINBERGEN *Herring Gull's World* ii. 7 Some of these movements and postures are not difficult even for the human observer to appreciate. **1962** *Symp. Zool. Soc.* No. 8. 71 A rat on the defensive in the upright posture does not look at its opponent. **1964** A. L. THOMSON *New Dict. Birds* 282/1 Behaviour by which the plumage is exposed to the sun by special postures seems to be widespread in birds. **1974** I. C. J. GALBRAITH tr. *Dorst's Life of Birds* I. ix. 175 The sexes may be recognized by certain postures characteristic of each mate.

†**2. a.** The position of one thing (or person) relatively to another; position, situation. *Obs.*

1605 BACON *Adv. Learn.* II. xx. §5 In describing the fourmes of Vertue and Duty, with their situations and postures, in distributing them into their kinds, parts, Prouinces. **1650** FULLER *Pisgah* I. xi. 33 Three Provinces whose number and posture we find in the Evangelists. *a* **1662** HEYLIN *Laud* I. (1671) 63 He found.. the Communion Table standing almost in the middest of the Quire, contrary to the posture of it in his Majesties Chappel. **1695** WOODWARD *Nat. Hist. Earth* VI. (1723) 269 An imaginary.. Earth, whose Posture to the Sun he supposes to have been much different. **1764** GOLDSM. *Hist. Eng. in Lett.* (1772) I. 44 None was found.. to give intelligence of the forces, or posture of the enemy. **1835** URE *Philos. Manuf.* 54 The position of the arms.. and the connecting rods.. in one line will prevent the frame.. from moving out of the posture it was brought into.

†**b.** *Mil.* A particular position of a weapon in drill or warfare. *Obs.*

1625 MARKHAM *Souldiers Accid.* 24 The three Postures or words of Command, which are vsed for the Musquet in the face of the enemie.. are these—1. Make readie. 2. Present. 3. Giue fire. **1691** WOOD *Ath. Oxon.* II. 262 He learned.. how to handle the pike and musquet, and all postures belonging to them.

3. A state of being; a condition or situation in relation to circumstances. Also, *spec.* a military or political attitude; a condition of armed readiness.

In 19th c. chiefly in ***the posture of affairs***, and ***a posture of defence***; formerly used also of physical condition.

1642 J. M[ARSH] *Argt. conc. Militia* 11 To put the kingdome into a posture of warre. **1642** LD. WILLOUGHBY in Rushw. *Hist. Coll.* III. (1692) I. 676, I could not but give your Lordship an account in how good a Posture I found the Trained Bands of Lincoln, which was far beyond my expectation. **1659** *Clarke Papers* (Camden) IV. 293 To acquainte your Honours with the present posture of affaires here. **1666** J. DAVIES *Hist. Caribby Isles* 192 The poor Servants and Slaves.. reducing it [tobacco] to that posture wherein it is transported into Europe. **1705** tr. *Bosman's Guinea* 53 Orders came to repair and put it in a posture of Defence. *a* **1741** CHALKLEY *Wks.* (1766) 23 At Night we got our Ship into a sailing Posture. **1793** SMEATON *Edystone L.* §275 Everything put into the best posture for receiving a storm. **1871** RUSKIN *Arrows of Chace* (1880) I. 227 The present posture of affairs round Paris. **1962** *Listener* 29 Mar. 545/2 What is important about the Soviet posture is that the Soviet armed forces aim at flexibility. **1964** *Ann. Reg.* *1963* 140 The public denunciations and rigidities of the cold war appeared to have been set aside in favour of more traditional diplomatic methods and more relaxed diplomatic postures. **1974** *Times* 5 Mar. 7/1 Renewed anxiety over Nato's conventional defences was expressed today.. in the annual Pentagon 'posture' report to Congress. **1976** *National Observer* (U.S.) 1 May 16/3 DEA's mission is.. to have foreign governments in a responsive posture.

4. *fig.* A mental or spiritual attitude or condition.

1642 J. TAYLOR (Water P.) (*title*) An Apology for Private Preaching.. whereunto is annexed.. the Spirituall postures, alluding to that of Musket and Pike. **1667** PEPYS *Diary* 3 Apr., Therewith we broke up, all in a sad posture. **1690** LOCKE *Hum. Und.* III. vii. §3 [He] must.. enter into his own Thoughts, and observe nicely the several Postures of his Mind in discoursing. **1755** B. MARTIN *Mag. Arts & Sc.* I. i. 5 (Not daring to appear in a Posture of Enquiry) they knew little or nothing of the true Nature of Things. **1866** LIDDON *Bampt. Lect.* i. (1875) 5 He [Christ] insisted upon a certain morality and posture of the soul as proper to man's reception of this revelation.

5. *attrib.* and *Comb.*, as †**posture book**, applied to a drill-book: cf. 2 b; **posture-man**, one who throws his body into artificial attitudes: = POSTURE-MAKER; so ***posture-girl***.

1616 B. JONSON *Devil an Ass* III. ii. 38 Get him the posture booke, and's leaden men, To set vpon a table,.. that hee may.. shew her Finsbury battells. **1711** ADDISON *Spect.* No. 31 ¶1 In one.. there was a Rary-Show; in another, a Ladder-dance; and in others a Posture-man. **1815** *Sporting Mag.* XLVI. 267 Two.. were *dancerinas*, or posture-girls.

posture ('pɒstjʊə(r)), *v.* [f. prec. sb.]

†**1.** *trans.* To place in position; to set. *Obs.*

c **1645** HOWELL *Lett.* (1650) I. v. xxiii. 160 As pointed Diamonds being set, Cast greater lustre out of Jet, Those peeces we esteem most rare, Which in night shadows postur'd are. **1656** S. H. *Gold. Law* 41 They.. have postured him in the place and condition he now stands. **1677** GREW *Anat. Seeds* iv. §22 The Seed is postured in much a like manner, and looks just like a couple of poynted Leavs with a very long Stalk.

2. To place in a particular attitude; to dispose the body or limbs of (a person) in a particular way.

a **1628** [see POSTURING below]. **1656** S. H. *Gold. Law* 44 Both sides are Dilemma'd, and stand postured like Lots Wife. **1820** KEATS *Hyperion* I. 85 And still these two were postured motionless, Like natural sculpture in cathedral cavern.

fig. **1837** CARLYLE *Fr. Rev.* II. v. ii, There are first biennial Parliaments so postured as to be, in a sense, beyond wisdom. **1890** SARAH J. DUNCAN *Soc. Depart.* xii. 115 Three very gay little maids postured in the middle of the floor.

3. *intr.* To assume a particular posture of body; also, to put the limbs or body in artificial positions.

1851 MAYHEW *Lond. Labour* III. 102/1 Posturing.. some people call it contortionists.. is reckoned the healthiest life there is, because we never get the rheumaticks. **1865** KINGSLEY *Herew.* xxx, Laughing at the dottrel as they postured and anticked on the mole-hills.

4. *intr. fig.* **a.** To act in an artificial or affected manner; to pose for effect. **b.** To take up an artificial mental position.

1877 MORLEY *Crit. Misc.* Ser. II. 149 He.. after having postured and played tricks in face of the bursting deluge, and given the government the final impulse into the abyss of bankruptcy, was dismissed. **1880** F. G. LEE *Ch. under Q. Eliz.* I. 53 Jewell.. sometimes became witty, and occasionally postured as a buffoon. **1884** *Pall Mall G.* 11 Aug. 4/1 Burning for an opportunity to posture as a supple statesman. **1889** *Spectator* 7 Dec. 803/1 Not inventing imaginary moral burdens for the conscience, such as the duty of always so posturing to our fellow-creatures as to set them what we suppose to be a good example.

Hence **'postured**, **'posturing** *ppl. adjs.*; **'posturing** *vbl. sb.* (*a*) the action of the verb; (*b*) among birds the use of particular poses as signals of specific patterns of behaviour.

a **1628** GREVIL *Sidney* (1652) 149 With constant and obedient posturing of his body to their Art. **1650** H. MORE *Observ.* in *Enthus. Tri.*, etc. (1656) 129 Going on their heads, as if they were not inverted but rightly postured plants, or walking *stipites*. **1851** [see 3]. **1861** DICKENS *Gt. Expect.* xix, After I.. had gone through an immensity of posturing with Mr. Pumblechook's very limited dressing-glass, in the futile endeavour to see my legs. **1872** O. W. HOLMES *Poet Breakf.-t.* i, What a statue gallery of posturing friends we all have! **1898** G. MEREDITH *Odes Fr. Hist.* 22 What postured statutes barred his tread. **1929** H. E. HOWARD *Introd. Study Bird Behaviour* i. 17 Posturing.. is regarded as a manifestation of the affective aspect of the functioning of the sexual response. **1940** H. F. WITHERBY et al. *Handbk. Brit. Birds* I. 8 Display and Posturing.—Aerial evolutions.. are a feature of courtship [of the raven]. **1953** N. TINBERGEN *Herring Gull's World* ii. 7 In general, the movements playing a part in posturing are based on flattening or raising of the plumage as a whole, on eye movements and on the attitude of head, neck and wings. **1973** R. A. HINDE in D. S. Farmer et al. *Avian Biol.* III. viii. 493 Ambivalent Posturing. Sometimes the bird adopts a posture that simultaneously expresses both tendencies.

'posture-,maker. **a.** One who makes postures or contortions; a contortionist; an acrobat: = POSTURE-MASTER 1. **b.** = POSTURE-MASTER 2.

1711 STEELE *Spect.* No. 258 ¶3, I would fain ask.. Why should not Rope-dancers, Vaulters, Tumblers, Ladder-walkers, and Posture-makers appear again on our Stage? **1863** HAWTHORNE *Our Old Home* (1879) 264 Posture-makers dislocated every joint of their body. **1874** SPURGEON *Treas. Dav.* Ps. lxxxviii. 9 Men need no posture-maker, or master of ceremonies, when they are eagerly pleading for mercy.

So **'posture-,making**, (*a*) *sb.*, the art or practice of making postures or contortions of the body; (*b*) *pr. pple.*, making postures.

1837 HT. MARTINEAU *Soc. Amer.* III. 156 The posture-making of the United States is renowned. **1851** THACKERAY *Eng. Hum.* vi, He is always.. posture-making, coaxing, and imploring me.

'posture-,master.

1. A master of the art of posturing; an expert in assuming artificial postures or attitudes of the body; *esp.* an acrobat or professional contortionist.

1691 *Satyr agst. French* Ep. A ij b, Clark, the Posture-master, never knew half so many Distortions of Body, as they do. **1760-72** H. BROOKE *Fool of Qual.* (1809) III. 143 The.. posture-master, rope-dancer, and equilibrist. **1830** SCOTT *Demonol.* viii. 234 Tricks, not much different from those exhibited by expert posture-masters of the present day.

2. A teacher of postures or callisthenics.

1712 ADDISON *Spect.* No. 305 ¶9 Delivered into the Hands of their second Instructor, who is a kind of Posture-Master. This Artist is to teach them how to nod judiciously, to shrug up their Shoulders in a dubious case [etc.]. **1850** L. HUNT *Autobiog.* I. vi. 236 Deshayes.. was rather an elegant posture-master than dancer. **1854** EMERSON *Lett. & Soc. Aims* Wks. III. 174 Nature is the best posture-master.

So **'posture-,mistress**, a female expert in posturing, or teacher of postures.

1722 DE FOE *Col. Jack* (1840) 206 She was a.. posture-mistress in love, and could put herself into what shapes she pleased. **1799** *Hull Advertiser* 28 Dec. 3/2 Posture-masters and mistresses.

Posturepedic (pɒstjʊə'piːdɪk). *U.S.* Also **posturepedic.** [f. POSTURE *sb.* + ORTHO)PEDIC *a.*] The proprietary name of a Sealy mattress designed to give proper support to the relaxed body.

1952 *Official Gaz.* (U.S. Patent Office) 14 Oct. 289/2 Sealy, Incorporated, Chicago, Ill. Filed July 24, 1951. *Posturepedic.* The representation of the human figure is fanciful... For mattresses and box springs. Claims use since June 1, 1950. **1967** *N.Y. Times* 9 Apr. 63 Choose your Posturepedic at one of these fine sleep centers. **1976** *Laurel* (Montana) *Outlook* 23 June 19/5 (Advt.), Refinished walnut dining table, wooden high chair, posturepedic crib mattress. **1977** C. MCFADDEN *Serial* xxxii. 71/1 He staggered down the hall to his Posturepedic.

posturer ('pɒstjʊərə(r)). [f. POSTURE *v.* + -ER[1].] One who practises postures, or poses for effect.

1845 R. W. HAMILTON *Pop. Educ.* ix. (ed. 2) 244 It seems to treat man too much as the animal or the posturer. **1879** E. ARNOLD *Lt. Asia* I. 6 Merry crowds Gaped on the sword-players and posturers. **1896** BLACK *Briseis* xix. 244 Then there are the precious people—the posturers—strutting in front of a literary mirror and admiring themselves.

'posturist. [See -IST.] A professed posturer.

1882 in OGILVIE (Annandale). **1886** *Daily News* 19 Oct. 6/6 To point out to the mass that the performer they had received as altogether admirable appears from another point of view a mere mouther—an absurd posturist.

'posturize, *v. rare.* [f. POSTURE *sb.* + -IZE.]

1. *trans.* To compose into a particular posture, attitude, or expression.

1706 E. WARD *Hud. Rediv.* I. II. 9 When he 'ad posturiz'd his Face, And humm'd for some few Minutes Space.

2. *intr.* To assume an artificial posture, either bodily or mental; to pose.

1879 MRS. LYNN LINTON *Under which Lord?* III. xi. 254 Posturizing as a martyr, and preaching as if the Church were on the brink of persecution. **1880** F. G. LEE *Ch. under Q. Eliz.* I. p. xv, Their hired puppets caper and threaten, brag and posturize.

Hence **'posturizing** *vbl. sb.*

1862 FAIRHOLT *Up Nile* (1863) 239 There was.. a performance of vaulting and posturising, by a group of Bedouins. **1885** MRS. LYNN LINTON *C. Kirkland* II. ix. 294

There is no posturizing, no effort. **1893** A. H. S. LANDOR *Alone w. Hairy Ainu* 117 Wonderful powers of mimicking and posturising, in which grace is never lacking.

post-tussic to **post-velar**: see POST- B.

†**post'vene**, *v. Obs. rare.* [f. POST- A. 1 + L. *venire*, F. *venir* to come: cf. *convene*, etc.] *intr.* To come after, supervene. So **'postvenant** *sb. nonce-wd.* [f. F. *venant* coming], that which comes after or follows, a consequence; †**post'ventional** *a.* [cf. *conventional*] (see quot. 1678).

1656 BLOUNT *Glossogr.*, **Postvene*, to come or follow after. **1876** W. G. WARD *Ess. Philos. Theims* (1884) I. 318 We think it will be satisfactory if we use the word..'postvenant' to denote what he calls 'effect'. **1678** PHILLIPS (ed. 4), **Postventional Full Moon*, that Full Moon which comes after any grand movable Feast, or Planetary Aspect. **1706** *Ibid.*, *Postventional*, coming, or that is come after.

post-verbal(ly: see POST- B. 1.

post-Victorian, *a.* and *sb.* [f. POST- B. 1 b.] **A.** *adj.* Subsequent to the reign of Queen Victoria (died 1901) or the Victorian era (esp. in style or manners). **B.** *sb.* One who lives in the post-Victorian era.

1938 H. PALMER *Post-Victorian Poetry* p. ix, Because of the amount of space that has been taken up by the verse dating from 1900..the subject-matter seems to justify the selection of the title, *Post-Victorian Poetry*. **1960** *Times Lit. Suppl.* 24 June 400/2 Hulme was able to dress a post-Victorian change of mood in conceptual clothing which seemed..to fit. **1974** *Nature* 1 Mar. 86/2 Bowlby..offers a ..less punitive approach to the child, than is generally taken ..by the post-Victorians or the Freudians.

postvide: see POST- A. 1 a.

post-village: see POST *sb.*[2] 13.

postvocalic(ally: see POST- B. 1.

post'vocalized, *ppl. a. Philol.* [f. POST- A. 1 a + VOCALIZED *ppl. a.*] Followed (as a consonant) by a vowel.

1876 [see PREVOCALIZED *ppl. a.*].

'post-,wagon. [f. POST *sb.*[2] + WAGON, repr. Du. and Ger. *postwagen*.] A mail or stage-coach (in the Netherlands, Germany, etc.).

1677–94 PENN *Trav. Holland* 31 We..began our Journey in the common Post-waggon to Osnaburg. **1756** NUGENT *Gr. Tour, Netherl.* I. 49 There is also another carriage which goes from most of the principal towns, and is called the Post-waggon: it is..generally drawn only by three horses and is as expeditious as our stage coaches. **1830** W. TAYLOR *Hist. Surv. Germ. Poetry* I. 337 Lessing..set off in frost and snow by the post-waggon..for Kamenz.

'post-war, *a.* (*sb.*) Also **postwar**. [f. POST- B. 1 a + WAR *sb.*[1]] **A.** *adj.* Of, pertaining to, or characteristic of, the period after a war (esp. those of 1914–18 or 1939–45); ***post-war credit***, a system of additional personal taxation introduced by the British Government in 1941 to supplement wartime expenditure and repayable during the post-war period; a sum of money or promissory note associated with this scheme.

1908 *Daily Chron.* 16 July 5/1 There has been a reduction of some £2,000,000 since 1904–5, the first post-war year. **1915** *Political Q.* May 118 The plans outlined..admit most easily of deviation into whatever may approve itself as the desired norm of post-war politics and economics. **1919** J. M. KEYNES *Econ. Consequences Peace* 84 Our hypothetical calculations leave us with post-war human requirements, on the basis of a pre-war efficiency of railways and industry. **1938** *Encycl. Brit. Bk. of Year* 22/1 The sheep population reached a post-war maximum in 1932. **1942** *Times* 9 July 2/3 (*heading*) Post-War Credit Certificates. *Ibid.*, The issue of over 9,000,000 certificates for post-war credit in respect of income-tax payments for the year 1941–42 has begun. **1959** *Daily Tel.* 9 Apr. 1/7 The Trades Union Congress yesterday welcomed the Chancellor's cuts in purchase tax and his proposals to speed up post-war credit payments. **1964** F. BOWERS *Bibliogr. & Textual Crit.* I. v. 34 Some resistance to accepting the validity of post-war pioneering studies. **1972** *Times* 9 Aug. 6/6, I propose..that repayment of post-war credits to people who have not been able to produce a certificate should begin on January 1, 1973. I envisage that this final stage of the repayment should be spread over the 12 months ending December 31, 1973. **1973** D. AARON *Unwritten War* III. vi. 103 Parkman did not attempt to predict the post-War fate of the Brahmin class.

B. *ellipt.* as *sb. U.S.* The period following a war.

1944 *Sun* (Baltimore) 18 July 8/7 They will glibly write.. of projects to be undertaken 'at post war'. **1945** *Time* 24 Sept. 15/2 Management-labor unity..must be continued in the postwar. **1947** *Partisan Rev.* XIV. 454 The tank driver of the War becomes the tractor driver of the Postwar.

'postward, *adv.* Toward a post (in any sense).

1890 in *Cent. Dict.*

post-warrant: see POST *sb.*[2], and POST ENTRY.

'postwise, *adv. nonce wd.* [f. POST *sb.*[2] + -WISE.] 'Post-haste', hurriedly.

a **1734** NORTH *Lives* (1826) III. 166 Writing postwise at the same time as the dispatch was made,..they were so confounded with mistakes that they were forced to write all over again.

post-woman, -worthy, etc.: see POST *sb.*[1], [2].

posty(e, variant of POUSTIE *Obs.*, power.

posty, var. POSTIE.

postyke, -tykke, obs. ff. POTSTICK.

postzygapophysis (pəʊstzɪgə'pɒfɪsɪs). *Anat.* Pl. **-ses** (-siːz). [f. POST- A. 2 b.] A posterior zygapophysis; each of the two posterior or inferior processes (right and left) on the neural arch of a vertebra: also called *inferior* (or *posterior*) *articular process*.

1866 OWEN *Anat. Vertebr.* I. 232 The postzygapophyses of the fourth, third, and second cervicals. **1871** HUXLEY *Anat. Vertebr. Anim.* vi. 277 The neural arches have well developed pre- and postzygapophyses.

Hence **postzygapophysial** (-zɪgæpəʊ'fɪzɪəl) *a.*, pertaining to or of the nature of a postzygapophysis.

1890 in *Cent. Dict.* **1895** in *Syd. Soc. Lex.*

posy ('pəʊzɪ). Now *arch.* or *dial.* Forms: 6 **posye**, 6–9 **posey, posie**, 6– **posy**. [A syncopated form of POESY (which, even when written in full, was often pronounced in two syllables).]

I. 1. A short motto, originally a line or verse of poetry, and usually in patterned language, inscribed on a knife, within a ring, as a heraldic motto, etc. *Obs.* or *arch.*

[*c* **1430–1675**: see POESY 3.] **1533** *Coronat. Q. Anne* A v, Wafers with rose leaues, and about the wafers were written with letters of gold, this posey. **1560** DAUS tr. *Sleidane's Comm.* 160 All the stretes and waies, beyng hanged and spired with rich and costly carpets, and posies written in euery place. *a* **1569** KINGESMYLL *Godly Advise* (1580) 31 Some haue their fansie so led as though money made men: let this be your Posie rather,..Manners makes man. **1634** BP. HALL *Contempl.*, *N.T.* IV. xii, Abrahams posie is 'in monte providebitur'. **1634** SIR T. HERBERT *Trav.* 86 The rest is dried Bricks covered over with Posies of Arabique and like worke. *a* **1704** T. BROWN *Pleasant Ep.* Wks. 1730 I. 109 Our posies for rings are either immodest or irreligious. **1896** BEAUMONT *Joan Seaton* 53 Joan was reading the posy [in the ring]—'But one for me, but one for thee, but one of thee and me'.

†**b.** An emblem or emblematic device. *Obs.*

[**1530** PALSGR. 256/1 Poysy, devyse, or worde, *deuise*.] **1644** BULWER *Chirol.* 139 In all tacit posies of His ascention this figure..is most emphatically significant.

2. A bunch of flowers; a nosegay, a bouquet. Now somewhat *arch.* or *rustic*.

[**1565** GOLDING *Ovid's Met.* IV. (1567) 47 b, A gathering flowres from place to place she strayes, And (as it chaunst) the selfe same time she was a sorting gayes, To make a Poisie.] **1573** COOPER *Thesaurus* s.v. *Admoveo*, *Fasciculum ad nares admouebis*, thou shalt put the posie to thy nose. *a* **1593** MARLOWE *Passionate Sheph. to his Love* iii, And I will make thee beds of roses, And a thousand fragrant posies. **1742** SHENSTONE *Schoolmistr.* xii, Marj'rum sweet, in shepherd's posie found. **1810** WORDSW. *Scenery Lakes* ii. (1823) 51 The little garden..with its borders and patches of flowers for Sunday posies. **18..** in J. Harland *Lanc. Lyrics* (1866) 64 I'll make me a posy of hyssop,—no other I can touch.

b. A collection or 'bouquet' of 'flowers' of poetry or rhetoric. Cf. ANTHOLOGY. *arch.*

a **1569** KINGESMYLL *Comf. Afflict.* (1585) C vij, If it hath pleased almightie God any thing to refresh you with this my poore posy, his will be done. **1612** BRINSLEY *Lud. Lit.* x. (1627) 153 That booke is as a most pleasant posie, composed of all the sweet smelling flowers, picked of purpose out of all his workes. **1638** BRATHWAIT *Barnabees Jrnl.* IV. (1818) 177 Bee't so, Faustulus! there repose thee, Cheere thy country with thy posie. **1879** E. W. GOSSE in *Academy* 11 Jan. 26/1 To collect..from [these] pages a posy of funny stories and gay quips.

†**II. 3.** Sometimes in the sense of POESY 2, a poetical production. *Obs.*

1578 FLORIO *1st Fruites* 52 Gioconde was the Emperor Gratian when he read the Posies of Ausonius. **1581** PETTIE *Guazzo's Civ. Conv.* II. (1586) 63 Those, who..reade Comedies, and other posies. **1645** HARWOOD *Loyal Subj. Retiring-room* 16 Make them into a Posey.

III. 4. *attrib.* (or as *adj.*) and *Comb.*, as ***posy-bouquet***, ***-maker***; *dial.* having a flowery pattern, flowered, as ***posy gown***, ***waistcoat***; **posy-ring**, a finger-ring with a motto inside.

1626 T. H[AWKINS] *Caussin's Holy Crt.* 3 The diuine Prouidence is a skilfull Posy-maker, who knoweth artificially how to mingle all sortes of flowers, to make the Nose-gay of the Elect. **1859** THACKERAY *Virgin.* xxx, He has bought posey-rings at Tunbridge Fair. **1863** ROBSON *Bards Tyne* 89 Peg shall hev a posey gown, To mense her when she comes to town. *Ibid.* 492 A posy waiscoat aw hev got. **1896** BEAUMONT *Joan Seaton* 53 A posy-ring set with two rows of small pearls.

pot (pɒt), *sb.*[1] Forms: 2–8 **pott**, 4–7 **potte**, (5 **putte**), 3– **pot.** (Also 4–5 **poot**, 5 *Sc.* **poyt**, mod.Sc. dial. **pat, patt.**) [Late OE. or early ME. *pott*, cognate with OFris. *pot*, MDu. *pot(t*, Du. *pot*, MLG. *pot*, *put*, LG. *pot(t*; whence mod.Ger. *pott*, late ON. *potte* (*c* 1300), Sw. *potta*, Da. *potte*; also with F. *pot* (12th c. in Littré), obs. It. *potto* (Florio); cf. Sp., Pg. *pote* pot, jar. The Fr. and It. point to a late L. **pottus* (found in med.L., Du Cange); this can scarcely be identified with cl. L. *pōtus* drinking, in late L. (Fortunatus *c* 600) a drinking-cup. The relation between the German and Romanic words is undetermined; Diez and Mackel view the latter as adopted from the former; but from the absence of the word in OHG. and MHG., and its lateness in English, it cannot well be Common Teutonic. The Celtic forms, Breton *pod*, *pot*, Corn., Welsh *pot*, Ir. *pota*, Gael. *poit*, are according to Thurneysen adopted from Fr. or Eng. The original source thus remains unknown.]

1. a. A vessel of cylindrical or other rounded form, and rather deep than broad, commonly made of earthenware or metal (less commonly glass), used to hold various substances, liquid or solid, for domestic or other purposes.

Often with defining word, as ***glue-pot***, ***ink-pot***, ***jam-pot***, ***water-pot***, ***watering-pot***, etc.: see these words (also the specific uses below).

? *a* **1200** *Sax. Leechd.* I. 378 Nim readstalede harhuna & ysopo & stemp & do on ænne neowna pott, & flering of ða harhuna & oðer of ysopo..forð þæt se pott beo full. *c* **1200** *Vices & Virtues* 73 Al swo is þe pott ðe is idon on ðe barnende ofne. *a* **1300** *E.E. Psalter* xxi. 16 Dried als a pot might be Alle mi might with innen me. *a* **1300** *Cursor M.* 22937 Bot als potter wit pottes dos Quen he his neu wessel fordos. *c* **1375** *Sc. Leg. Saints* xxv. (*Julian*) 512 Thre gret poyttis..fillyt of gold to þe hals. **1463** *Bury Wills* (Camden) 23 A greet earthin potte. **1597** MORLEY *Introd. Mus.* 4, I was like a potte with a wide mouth, that receiueth quickly and letteth out as quickly. **1685** SOUTH *Serm.* (1697) I. viii. 349 Agathocles first handling the Clay, and making Pots under his Father. **1769** MRS. RAFFALD *Eng. Housekpr.* (1778) 77 Put rich melted butter in small cups or pots. **1841** LANE *Arab. Nts.* I. 79 A quantity of broken jars and pots. **1898** *Allbutt's Syst. Med.* V. 441 Blowing out the contents of each of the pipettes into a small glass pot, in which they are thoroughly stirred.

b. *spec.* Such a vessel (now usually of metal) used for cooking or boiling. Hence *transf.* the vessel with the meat or other food boiling in it; also allusively = cooking, food (as in phr. ***for the pot***); also in figurative allusions.

a **1300** *Cursor M.* 26753 (Cott.) Alle your entrailles ilkon in welland pottes sal be don. *c* **1380** WYCLIF *Sel. Wks.* III. 197 þei hackeden here children as small as morselis to here poot. *c* **1420** *Liber Cocorum* (1862) 16 Put alle in þe pot with gryþe. **1531** ELYOT *Gov.* I. xviii, Kylling of dere with bowes ..serueth well for the potte (as is the commune saynge). **1584** COGAN *Haven Health* lxiii. (1636) 75 An hearbe sometime used in Medicine, but most commonly for the Pot. **1600** J. PORY tr. *Leo's Africa* III. 141 The common sort set on the pot with fresh meat twise euery weeke. **1667** EARL TWEEDDALE in *Lauderdale Papers* (1885) II. 45 This was to me lik the spoonful that spoils the pot. **1783** BURKE *Sp. East-India Bill* Wks. IV. 129 Henry the Fourth [of France] wished that he might live to see a fowl in the pot of every peasant. **1875** JOWETT *Plato* (ed. 2) III. 38 Boiled meats which involve an apparatus of pots and pans.

fig. *a* **1225** *Ancr. R.* 368 þe wombe pot þet walleð euer of metes, and more of drunches. **1390** GOWER *Conf.* III. 32 Hote Thoght, which hath evere his pottes hote Of love buillende on the fyr. **1649** G. DANIEL *Trinarch.*, *Rich. II* cix, Gant let Glocester's pott Boyle only over, though his were as Hott. **1858** CARLYLE *Fredk. Gt.* IX. vi. (1872) III. 125 An ever-boiling pot of mutiny.

c. Such a vessel used to contain wine, beer, or any other drink; either for drinking out of (as a pewter pot for beer, etc.), or for pouring the drink into smaller vessels (as a coffee-pot or teapot). (See also 2.)

c **1440** *Alphabet of Tales* 497 þis abbot axked hym whither he went, and he said he went to giff his brethir a drynk. So he axkid hym wharto he bare so many pottis. *a* **1500** *Kyng & Hermit* 316 in Hazl. *E.P.P.* I. 25, I haue a pott of galons foure, Standyng in a wro. **1597** *1st Pt. Return fr. Parnass.* v. ii. 1527 Noe pennie, noe pott of ale. **1617** MORYSON *Itin.* III. 179 The Germans drink in peuter or stone pots, hauing little or no plate. **1837** DICKENS *Pickw.* xxiii, Shaking up the ale, by describing small circles with the pot, preparatory to drinking.

d. An earthenware vessel to hold earth in which a plant is grown; a FLOWER-POT.

[**1598–**: see FLOWER-POT.] **1615** MARKHAM *Eng. Housew.* (1660) 54 If you will set forth yellow flowers, take the pots of Primroses and Cowslips. **1856** DELAMER *Fl. Gard.* (1861) 22 It is safer to keep the bulbs in pots..in good, light, rich soil. **1887** RUSKIN *Præterita* II. iv. 141 My mother *did* like arranging the rows of pots in the big greenhouse.

e. A chamber-pot. Also, the pan of a close stool; a lavatory pan.

1598 FLORIO *Worlde of Wordes* 280/1 *Pitale*,..the pan or pot of a close stoole. **1705** OLIVER in *Phil. Trans.* XXV. 2181 He..did his necessary occasions always in the Pot. **1898** P. MANSON *Trop. Diseases* xviii. 290 There was very little in the pot except mucus tinged..with blood. **1915** *Dialect Notes* IV. 228 *Pot*,..very common for *chamber*. **1954** A. S. C. Ross in *Neuphilol. Mitt.* LV. 42 U-speakers use ['džeri]..or *pot*. **1956** *New Statesman* 8 Dec. 740/2 The old woman on the next floor fighting over who choked the cawsy by pitching cinders down the pot. **1958** [see ARTICLE 14 c].

f. Applied to various vessels or receptacles used in manufactures, etc.: see quots.

1676 *Phil. Trans.* XI. 680 The Air which has been compressed in the Pot [in a fire-engine]. **1727–41** CHAMBERS *Cycl.* s.v. *Glass*, Take of this crystal frit..set it in pots in the furnace, adding to it a due quantity of manganese. **1831** J. HOLLAND *Manuf. Metal* I. 228 These coffers, or pots, as they are called [in a steel-converting furnace]. **1839** URE *Dict. Arts* 576 The materials of every kind of glass are vitrified in pots made of a pure refractory clay. **1875** *Ibid.* III. 1011 Taken from right to left [of the figure], 1 represents the tinman's pan; 2, the tin-pot; 3, the washing or dipping pot; 4, the grease-pot; 5, the cold pot; 6, the list pot. **1875** Knight *Dict. Mech.*, Pot. 1. A perforated hogs-head in which crude sugar is placed for drainage of the molasses... 3. A brass-founder's name for a crucible. Graphite pots are most generally in use.

g. A vessel, generally of silver, given as a prize in athletic sports. Cf. pot-hunter 3. Also (*slang*) applied to any prize so given.

1885 *Cyclist* 19 Aug. 1083/2 Imagine..a three miles handicap for which the first 'pot' is a 95 guineas piano. **1886** *Ibid.* 11 Aug. 1126/2 The two best men were riding for a bigger stake than the 'pot', for were they not the representatives of rival bicycle makers? **1897** in *Windsor Mag.* Jan. 266/1 A few pots won upon playing-fields.

h. A protuberant stomach, a paunch; = pot-belly 1.

1928 'Brent of Bin Bin' *Up Country* ii. 40 Mazere..was happy that he could turn to manual work again himself, and felt the better for it. 'It's taking a little of the pot off me,' he would exclaim. **1929** Kipling in *London Mag.* Dec. 631/1 Keede patted his round little pot. **1942** D. Powell *Time to be Born* (1943) i. 22 At forty-eight..he had no pot at all due to his Yogi exercises. **1952** [see gussy *v.*]. **1959** *Encounter* Dec. 31/1 There was a time when I had a little professorial pot; later I was 'stout'..; then I became, I suppose, definitely pot-bellied. **1965** G. McInnes *Road to Gundagai* xiii. 222 The door opened carefully and revealed a tall man with a florid face, a large Roman nose,..and a big pot. **1973** 'D. Jordan' *Nile Green* xxix. 129 His pot was hanging obscenely over the lip of a pair of scarlet bathing trunks.

i. (See quots.) *slang.*

1941 *Amer. Speech* XVI. 240 *Pot*, carburetor. **1945** Baker *Austral. Lang.* viii. 160 Here is a brief list of indigenous Air Force language:..*pot*, a cylinder. **1961** Partridge *Dict. Slang* Suppl. 1230/1 *Pot*, n., a cylinder, esp. in one of the old rotary engines: R.F.C.–R.A.F.: 1914–18. They tended to split or to fly off. Hence, any aeroplane-engine cylinder. **1966** 'L. Lane' *ABZ of Scouse* 83 A pot is also a carburettor. *To tickle ther pot*: To prime a carburettor.

2. Such a vessel with its contents; hence, the quantity that fills or would fill the vessel, a potful. (Cf. cup *sb.* 8.) **a.** Const. *of* (the contents). Also allusively in *fig.* phr. ***pot of gold*** (see quot. 1895).

c **1450** *Mirour Saluacioun* 218 In a fulle potte of mans blode scho it laide. **1535** Coverdale *Bel & Dr.* 3 Sixe greate pottes of wine. **1587** in *3rd Rep. Hist. MSS. Comm.* 420/1, I have sent.. a pott of gelly which my servante made. **1621** Burton *Anat. Mel.* ii. iii. iii. (1651) 331 O that I could but finde a pot of money now. **1724** Swift *Bill for Clergy Residing on Livings* ¶ 5 No entertainment..beyond a pot of ale and a piece of cheese. **1773** *Life N. Frowde* 33 The good Woman had also kept a Pot of Tea warm for me. **1833** Ht. Martineau *Manch. Strike* i. 9 A pipe and pot of porter [were] called for. **1886** *Daily News* 9 Dec. 5/2 When a pot of coins is found by some old Roman way. **1895** *Brewer's Dict. Phr. & Fable* (new ed.) 1036/2 *Rainbow chasers*, problematical politicians and reformers, who chase rainbows, which cannot possibly be caught, to 'find the pot of gold at the foot thereof'. This alludes to an old joke, that a pot of gold can be dug up where the rainbow touches the earth. **1966** A. E. Lindop *I start Counting* xxi. 266 Matron makes a pot of tea quite late at night and lets me go and have a cup with her. **1971** *Cape Herald* 15 May 14/1 Francis Lee, the Manchester City and England striker has hit the 'pot-of-gold' in more ways than one. **1974** 'E. Lathen' *Sweet & Low* i. 11 The Japanese stock market..had been the legendary pot of gold at the end of some local rainbow. **1978** *Observer* 26 Mar. 11/7 The tendency has been to look at the North Sea in terms of its immediate isolated wealth, as a pot of gold. **1979** W. H. Canaway *Solid Gold Buddha* iii. 27 Miller..made a pot of tea.

b. *ellipt.* A pot of liquor; *transf.* liquor, drink; drinking, potation (also *pl.*). Also, a pot of tea. Cf. cup *sb.* 10.

1583 Babington *Commandm.* iv. (1637) 39 He might with great right have destroyed us, either amongst our pots, or in our dances. **1617** Brathwait *Smoaking Age* O ij b, As if no Poets Genius could be ripe Without the influence of Pot and Pipe. **1720** De Foe *Capt. Singleton* i, He carries her into a public-house to give her a pot and a cake. **1794** Southey *Botany Bay Ecl.* iii. 18, I'll wager a pot I have suffer'd more evils than fell to your lot. **1831** E. J. Trelawny *Adventures Younger Son* III. xxiii. 152 My wife always turned in three spoonsful,—one for I, one for her, and t'other for the pot. **1849** Macaulay *Hist. Eng.* viii. II. 338 The hedge alehouse, where he had been accustomed to take his pot on the bench before the door in summer. **1973** 'E. Ferrars' *Foot in Grave* ix. 166 The tea had got cold, so Christine made a fresh pot.

3. Used as a conventional quantity or measure of various commodities: cf. *barrel*, *firkin*, etc.

1530 Palsgr. 257/1 Potte, a gallon measure, *pot.* **1545** *Rates of Customs* c j b, Oyle, called baume oyle, the potte, vis. viiid. **1662** *Act 14 Chas. II*, c. 26 §1 The Pott of Butter ought to weigh Twenty pounds viz. Fourteen pounds of good and Merchantable Butter Neat and the Pott Six pounds. **1681** *Manch. Crt. Leet Rec.* (1888) VI. 123 Richard Barlow for buying twoe potts of Apples by way of forestallinge. **1775** *Chron.* in *Ann. Reg.* 143/1 A pot of sugar weighs about 70 pounds. **1825** H. M. in Hone *Every-day Bk.* I. 1344 Apples, ..from twenty to thirty pots, (baskets containing five pecks each). **1862** Ansted *Channel Isl.* iv. App. A. (ed. 2) 566 The smaller divisions are into pots (half-gallon), quarts, pints, gills, and noggins (eighth of a pint). **1943** [see handle *sb.*[1] 2 c]. **1966** G. W. Turner *Eng. Lang. Austral. & N.Z.* viii. 163 In addition Sydney has a *pony* of five ounces.., Melbourne a *pot* of ten ounces (but a pot is eleven ounces in Brisbane), Adelaide a *butcher* (six ounces) and Perth a *big pot* (fifteen ounces, which would be a *schooner* in Sydney or a *pint* in Adelaide). **1973** *Parade* (Austral.) Oct. 35/1 'Oh, yes,' said the barman. 'We like their money, but we don't have middies, we sell pots.'

4. A steel cap or small helmet, worn esp. by cavalry in the 17th c.; see also quots. 1676, *a* 1734. *Obs.* exc. *Hist.*

1639 Sir E. Verney in *V. Papers* (Camd.) 227 If I had a pott for the hedd that were pistoll proofe, it may be I would use it, if it were light. **1666** *Lond. Gaz.* No. 66/3, 4000 Landmen..with their Officers, all compleatly armed with Back, Brest, and Pot. **1676** Hobbes *Iliad* (1677) 143 To defend his head A leather cap without crest, call'd a pot. *a* **1734** North *Exam.* iii. vii. §87 (1740) 572 There were abundance of those silken Back, Breast and Potts made and sold, that were pretended to be Pistol Proof. *a* **1845** Mrs. Bray *Warleigh* xxi, Steel morions, or pots, as they were very commonly called, guarded their skulls.

5. a. A basket, tub, or box used in pairs, in the manner of panniers with a pack-saddle, to carry manure, sand, etc. *dial.*

[1388–9: see dung-pot.] **1552** Huloet, Dunge potte made of wickers. **1796** W. Marshall *West Eng.* I. 122 Dung, sand, materials of buildings, roads, etc., are carried in potts, or strong coarse panniers... The bottom of each pot is a falling door, on a strong and simple construction. **1886** Elworthy *W. Somerset Word-bk.*, *Pots*, small D-shaped boxes, placed bow side outwards on either side of a pack-saddle for carrying heavy articles.

b. A wicker basket used as a trap for fish or crustaceans; a fish-pot, lobster-pot, etc.

[*a* **1555** Fish-pot: see fish *sb.*[1] 7.] **1669** Worlidge *Syst. Agric.* (1681) 256 In several great Rivers..many have set large Pots made of Osier, with bars in them, that when the Fish are in them,..they could not get out again. **1745** Collinson in *Phil. Trans.* XLIV. 70 The Crab will live confined in the Pot or Basket some Months. **1867** F. Francis *Angling* iii. 90 Baskets called 'pots'..baited with worms.

c. The 'pound' or circular inclosed part of a pound-net; also called the *bowl* or *crib*. *U.S.*

1884 in Knight *Dict. Mech.* Suppl.

6. Applied to various things: as †**a.** A projecting band on the stem of a key, close to the bow (*obs.*); **b.** = chimney-pot; **c.** The head of a rocket.

1688 R. Holme *Armoury* iii. 301/1 Pot or *Bead*, is the round under the Bow, at the top of the Shank [of a Key]. **1703** Moxon *Mech. Exerc.* 23, H the Shank, I the Pot, or Bread,..L the Bow. *a* **1845** Hood *Town & Country* iii, He sinks behind no purple hill, But down a chimney's pot! **1873** E. Spon *Workshop Receipts* Ser. i. 126/2 The rocket being then charged, the head or pot must be fixed.

†**7. a.** ***pot of the head***: the skull, cranium, brainpan. **b.** The socket of a bone at a joint. *Obs.*

1548–77 Vicary *Anat.* iii. (1888) 27 The Bone of the Pot of the head keeping in the Braynes. **1610** Markham *Masterp.* ii. clvii. 463 As the one end of the marrow-bone [goes] into the pot of the spade-bone, and the other end into the pot of the elbow.

8. A sausage. Now *s.w. dial.*

c **1450** *Nominale* (Harl. MS. 1002) lf. 147 *Hilla*, a white pott or sawsege. **1777** *Horæ Subsecivæ* (Devonsh.) 337 (E.D.D.) The pot is a hog's black pudding..stuff'd into pits gutts or chitterlings. **1886** Elworthy *W. Somerset Word-bk.*, *Pots and puddings*, sausages made of pig's blood and fat. Same as *black-puddings*.

9. a. A large sum of money. *colloq.* (Cf. 2.)

1856 *Knickerbocker* XLVIII. 619 They had hauled down a big pot and intended henceforth to live as jolly as clams. **1871** Mrs. H. Wood *Dene Hollow* xxiv, A grandfather, who must possess pots of money laid by. **1876** F. E. Trollope *Charming Fellow* I. xvi. 219 He went to India..and came back..with a pot of money. **1897** 'Ouida' *Massarenes* v, You'll make a pot by it, as Barnum did.

b. *slang.* A large sum staked or betted.

1823 'J. Bee' *Dict. Turf* s.v., 'I shall put on the *pot* at the July meeting', signifies that the speaker will bet very high (at races), or up to thousands... Lord Abingdon once declared 'I will put on the *pot* to-day', and he did so with a vengeance—his groom, Jack Oakly, put *him* in the *pot.* **1840** *Sporting Rev.* Aug. 119 It needed only to lay against all, to insure a prize proportioned to the 'pot' put on. **1859** Lever *Davenp. Dunn* I. xiv. 124 The [horse] you have backed with a heavy pot. **1880** J. Payn *Confid. Agent* I. 214 He had solaced himself..by 'putting the pot' on at cards.

c. *Racing.* 'A horse backed for a large amount, a favourite' (Farmer *Slang*).

1823 'J. Bee' *Dict. Turf* s.v., 'Pot 8 O's', the name of a race-horse, meaning 80,000 l. or guineas. **1873** *Slang Dict.*, *Pot*, a favourite in the betting for a race. Probably so called because it is usual to say that a heavily-backed horse carries 'a pot of money'. When a favourite is beaten the pot is said to be upset. **1883** *Graphic* 17 Nov. 494/2 Medicus, the great Cambridgeshire 'pot', and Thebais, who showed well in that race, were among the runners. **1892** J. Kent *Racing Life Ld. G. C. Bentinck* ix. 201 Horses trained at Goodwood in 1842 beat great pots from Danebury.

d. A person of importance. (Usually ***big pot***.)

1880 Hardy *Trumpet-Major* I. viii. 135 When Festus put on the big pot, as it is classically called, he was quite blinded *ipso facto* to the diverting effect of that mood and manner upon others. **1885** *Punch* 12 Sept. 131/2 Oh, Yorkshire and Lancashire both are big pots. But Cricket's top honours again go to Notts. **1891** *Licensed Victualler's Gaz.* 9 Feb., Dick pointed out some of the big pots of the day. **1899** Whiteing *5 John St.* xiv, The father's some tremendous pot in the financial way. **1909** J. R. Ware *Passing Eng.* 28 Big pot (*Music-hall* 1878–82)... This phrase is probably one of the few that filter down in the world from Oxford, where, in the 50's it was the abbreviation of potentate. It referred to a college don, or a social magnate. **1947** 'A. P. Gaskell' *Big Game* 24, I don't feel at home with these big pots. **1979** R. Rendell *Make Death love Me* iii. 29 Some general at the head of it. Some big pot who means business.

e. *Cards.* 'In faro, the name given to the six-, seven-, and eight-spots in the lay-out' (*Cent. Dict.*); also, orig. U.S., the betting pool in poker and other gambling games. Also *fig.* Cf. sense 9 b, *jack-pot* s.v. Jack *sb.*[1] 34 a.

1847 J. H. Greene *Gambling Unmasked* (rev. ed.) 196 He won the first twenty '*pots*', that is to say, the stake [in poker]. **1856** G. W. Bagby *Old Virginia Gentleman* (1910) 228 He has no great faith in 'cases', but believes in betting on three cards at a time, and has a special hankering for 'the pot' [in faro]. **1868** [see keno b]. **1878** [see bullet *sb.*[1] 6]. **1889** 'Mark Twain' *Speeches* (1923) 147 What is still more irregular, the man that loses a game gets the pot. **1890** J. P. Quinn *Fools of Fortune* ii. ii. 194 In the [faro] 'lay-out'..the six, seven and eight are called the pot. **1892** [see chip *v.*[1] 8 b]. **1895** *Funk's Stand. Dict.*, *Pot*,..5. *Card-playing*, (1) The amount of stakes played for; the pool. (2) In faro, the six, seven, and eight of the layout, collectively. **1935** *Encycl. Sports* 466/2 If no player opens there is a fresh deal, each player once more contributing to the pot, and so on until the pot is opened. **1951** *Amer. Speech* XXVI. 100/1 *Open the pot*, to make the first bet after the ante [in poker]. *Ibid.* 100/2 *Pot*, the total accumulation of all bets. It rests in the centre of the table, equi-distant from each player. **1963** *Richmond* (Virginia) *Times-Dispatch* 16 Dec. 19/2 When a poker player has absolute confidence in his hand he shoves into the pot every chip he has. **1971** *Black World* June 73/1 The sergeant put up the house, got the men into the game and took half the pot. **1977** I. Shaw *Beggarman, Thief* ii. i. 118 'And if you succeed, then what?' he said. 'Russia takes the whole pot.'

f. ***old pot***: see old *a.* 1 c.

10. (Usu. spelt **pott.**) In full, **pott-paper**: A size of printing or writing paper: originally bearing the watermark of a pot (cf. *foolscap*). Also *attrib.*, as **pott-folio, -octavo, -quarto.**

The sheet measures normally $15\frac{1}{2} \times 12\frac{1}{2}$ inches.

1579 *Ludlow Churchw. Acc.* (Camden) 165, iiij[or] quiers of pott paper. *a* **1625** Fletcher *Nice Valour* iv. i, He prints my blows upon pot-paper too, the rogue! Which had been proper for some drunken pamphlet. **1712** *Lond. Gaz.* No. 5018/3 For all Paper called..Superfine Pot 2s. Second fine Pot 1s. 6d...per Ream. **1882** *Daily Tel.* 17 Jan. 5 Only four copies of the first edition, in 'pot' folio, are known to be in existence. **1890** in Webster. **1894** J. C. Jeaffreson *Bk. Recollect.* II. xxv. 229 Legal drafts on pot-paper. **1911** *Encycl. Brit.* XX. 735/1 Writing papers. Pott..$12\frac{1}{2} \times 15$. **1926** *Paper Terminol.* (Spalding & Hodge, Ltd.) 21 *Pott*, a standard size of printing paper measuring $15\frac{1}{2} \times 12\frac{1}{2}$ in. (with slight variations). The term is derived from an ancient 'pot' watermark, which represented the Sangraal. **1962** F. T. Day *Introd. to Paper* vii. 69 Sizes of paper in the United Kingdom centre round fifteen designs: Foolscap, Demy, Medium,..Pott, Elephant,..Eagle and Columbier.

11. As the name of a substance: Earthenware, stoneware; *attrib.* made of 'pot'. Also, an earthenware chimney-piece ornament; *dial.* and *local U.S.* a boy's marble of baked clay; a fragment of pottery played with in hopscotch or other games. Also, the game of hopscotch itself or a part of the game. Cf. pig *sb.*[2]

1825 J. Nicholson *Operat. Mechanic* 466 A suitable thin tool or utensil of pot, of the profile of the inside, is applied. **1861** Mayhew *Lond. Labour* I. 333/2 A street-seller who accompanied me called them merely 'pots' (the trade term), but they were all pot ornaments. Among them were great store of shepherdesses, of greyhounds [etc.]. *Ibid.* II. 396/2 The use of earthenware, clay, or pot pipes for the conveyance of liquids is very ancient. **1864** Brierley *Layrock* iii. 40 Lookin'-glasses, an' pot dolls. **1866** W. Gregor *Dial. Banffshire* 132 *Pot*,..the last division in the game of *hippin'-beds* [*sc.* hopscotch]. **1884** *Daily News* 13 Oct. 5/1 Those who kicked against ceramic art, and protested vehemently against what they called 'decoration by pot'. **1893–4** R. O. Heslop *Northumb. Words* II. 549 *Pot*, the heading written at the top of the game called 'beds', or, locally, 'hitchey dabber'... To achieve it is to get 'pot'. **1895** *Funk's Stand. Dict.*, *Pot*..*pl.* (Local, U.S.) (1) The game of hop-scotch. **1920** Webster, *Pot*.., a piece of pottery or earthenware, as a marble or piece for playing hop scotch. **1936** *Glasgow Herald* 10 Nov., 'Hopscotch', however is an English name. We Scots called it 'peever',..or 'pot', or 'the beds'... In some parts of Scotland beds 7 and 8 were called 'the kail pats', and this may be one reason why the game is sometimes called 'pot'. Another explanation is that a piece of broken pot or earthenware was often used as a peever.

12. pl. ***pots***: short for potashes.

1849 Saxe *Proud Miss Mac Bride* xvii, For John had worked in his early day, In 'Pots and Pearls' the legends say.

13. Phrases and Proverbs. **a.** ***the pot goes so long*** (or ***often***) ***to the water that it is broken at last*** (with several variations of wording). **b.** ***the pot calls the kettle black*** (etc.): said of a person who blames another for something of which he himself is also guilty; so ***to call each other pot and kettle***, etc. †**c.** ***the pot walks***: said of a drinking bout, in which the pot of liquor is passed from one to another. (See also quot. 1691.) *Obs.* **d.** ***a little pot is soon hot***: a little person is easily roused to anger. **e.** ***to boil the pot, make the pot boil***: to provide one's liveihood. (Cf. pot boiler, -boiling, potwaller.) So, in same sense, ***to keep the pot boiling***; also, to keep anything going briskly. **f.** ***to go to pot*** (formerly also ***to the pot***): to be cut in pieces like meat for the pot; to be ruined or destroyed (now *colloq.*). Also, to deteriorate, to go to pieces. So † ***to bring*** or ***send to (the) pot*** (*obs.*), ***put in the pot***, etc. †**g.** ***to have a pot in the pate***: to be the worse for liquor. *Obs.* †**h.** ***to make the pot with the two ears***: 'to set the arms akimbo' (Davies). *Obs.* **i.** ***in*** (one's) ***pots***: in a state of intoxication (cf. *in one's cups*). **j.** Various other phrases and proverbs.

a. 1340 *Ayenb.* 206 Zuo longe geþ þet pot to þe wetere, þet hit comþ to-broke hom. *a* **1450** *Knt. de la Tour* 82 It is a trew prouerbe, that 'the potte may goo so longe to water, that atte the laste it is broken'. *c* **1645** Howell *Lett.* I. i. vi, That the Pot which goes often to the water, comes home crack'd at last.

b. *a* **1700** B. E. *Dict. Cant. Crew* s.v., 'The Pot calls the kettle black A——', when one accuses another of what he is as Deep in himself. **1833** Marryat *P. Simple* xxxii, Do you know what the pot called the kettle? **1844** Dickens *Mart. Chuz* xxiv, I've been as good a son as ever you were a brother. It's the pot and the kettle, if you come to that. **1900** *Westm. Gaz.* 6 Mar. 10/1 There has been a good deal of 'pot and kettle' in the stories from the British and Boer camps since the war began.

c. 1567 Harman *Caveat* (Shaks. Soc.) 32 How the pottes walke about! their talking tounges talke at large. **1622** R. Hawkins *Voy. S. Sea* (1847) 216 The pott continually walking, infused desperate and foolish hardinesse in many. **1691** Wood *Ath. Oxon.* II. 157 Author.. of other little trivial matters meerly to get bread, and make the pot walk.

d. 1546 J. Heywood *Prov.* (1867) 25 And Christ wot It is wood at a word, little pot soon whot. **1596** Shaks. *Tam. Shr.* iv. i. 6 Now were not I a little pot, and soone hot. **1809** W. Irving *Knickerb.* ix. (1861) 137 It is an old saying, that 'a little pot is soon hot', which was the case with William the Testy. Being a little man he was soon in a passion, and once in a passion he soon boiled over.

e. [**1587** Harrison *England* ii. ii. (1877) i. 63 One of the best paire of bellowes.. that blue the fire in his [the pope's] kitchen, wherewith to make his pot seeth.] **1657–61** Heylin *Hist. Ref.* (1674) 100 So poor, that it is hardly able to keep the Pot boiling for a Parsons Dinner. **1812** Combe *Picturesque* xxiii. 18 No fav'ring patrons have I got, But just enough to boil the pot. **1825** Brockett *N.C. Gloss.*, *Keep-the-pot-boiling*, a common expression among young people, when they are anxious to carry on their gambols with spirit. **1837** Dickens *Pickw.* xxx. **1864** Carlyle *Fredk. Gt.* xvi. ii. (1872) VI. 151 A feeling that glory is excellent, but will not make the national pot boil. **1870** Lowell *Study Wind.* 139 To employ them, as a literary man is always tempted, to keep the domestic pot a-boiling. **1887** *Times* (weekly ed.) 7 Oct. 15/1 His lieutenants keep the rebellion pot boiling in.. Ireland.

f. 1542 Udall *Erasm. Apoph.* 116 The riche & welthie of his subjectes went dayly to the potte, & wer chopped up. **1552** Latimer *Serm. in Lincoln* i. 66 They that pertayne to God,.. they must goe to the potte, they must suffer here accordying to ye Scripture. **1573** *New Custom* ii. iii. C iij b, Thou mightest sweare: if I could I would bring them to the pot. **1609** W. M. *Man in Moone* (Percy Soc.) 8 All that hee can get or borrow goeth to the pot. **1641** J. Jackson *True Evang. T.* i. 32 All went to the pot [in the fourth Persecution] without respect of Sex, dignity or number. **1657** R. Ligon *Barbadoes* (1673) 120 The Sea-men.. resolv'd, the Passengers should be drest and eaten, before any of them should goe to the Pot. **1691** Wood *Ath. Oxon.* II. 552 He.. had been engaged.. to bring in K. Ch. 2. from Scotland (for which he had like to have gone to the pot). **1823** 'J. Bee' *Dict. Turf.* s.v., 'Put in the pot', said of a man who is let into a certain loss—of a wager, of his liberty or life. **1530** Tindale *Answ. More* i. xxix. Wks. (1572) 293/1 Then goeth a part of ye little flocke to pot, and the rest scatter. **1613** Purchas *Pilgrimage* (1614) 828 They had eaten sixe of his fellowes, and the next day he must haue gone to pot too. *c* **1680** Hickeringill *Hist. Whiggism* Wks. 1716 I. ii. 158 Poor Thorp, Lord Chief Justice, went to Pot, in plain English, he was Hang'd. **1699** Bentley *Phal.* xvi. 506 For if the Agrigentines had met with them, they [the letters of Phalaris] had certainly gone to pot. **1708** W. King *Cookery* 91 Ev'ry thing that ev'ry Soldier got, Fowl, Bacon, Cabbage, Mutton, and what not, Was all thrown into Bank, and went to Pot. **1789** Wolcott (P. Pindar) *Expost. Odes* xii. vii, Thousands will smile to see him go to pot. **1815** W. H. Ireland *Scribbleomania* 3 Reviewers.. Who.. send each Author to pot, That cannot proclaim he's by birth a true Scot. **1846** *Swell's Night Guide* 120/2 *Gone to pot*, become poor in circumstances, gone to the dogs. **1884** *Pall Mall G.* 16 Feb. 4/2 If it were to save the whole empire from going to pot, nobody would stay at home. **1889** *Cornh. Mag.* July 46 For the potato is really going to pot... Constitutional disease and the Colorado beetle have preyed too long upon its delicate organism. **1910** E. M. Forster *Howards End* xxv. 205 Evie heard of her father's engagement when she was in for a tennis tournament, and her play went simply to pot. **1923** S. Kaye-Smith *End of House of Alard* iv. 327 If we hung on now, still further crippled by death-duties, the land would simply go to pot. **1942** E. Paul *Narrow St.* iv. 37 The Comédie Française.. went to pot artistically and remained a travesty of its former self until reorganized about 1938. **1953** E. Simon *Past Masters* ii. 81 Discipline's gone all to pot at the camp. **1956** W. Graham *Sleeping Partner* 57 She could go in and clean up once in a while... The house wouldn't go to pot in a week or so. **1968** *Globe & Mail Mag.* (Toronto) 13 Jan. 11/3 Only a quarter of the Sames now depend on reindeer herding... Some of them, like some of Canada's native people, go to pot. **1979** *Truck & Bus Transportation* (Austral.) Apr. 65/2 It's [*sc.* the brake is] there to do its job, but it can throw a spanner in the works if the adjustment setting goes to pot.

g. 1658 Osborn *Adv. Son* (1673) 28 Especially when they have got a pot in their pate. **1737** Bracken *Farriery Impr.* (1757) II. 77 An Ox or a Cow would serve them to ride well enough, if they had only a Pot in the Pate.

h. 1675 Cotton *Burlesque upon B.* 117 See what a goodly port she bears, Making the pot with the two Ears!

i. 1618 Hornby *Sco. Dronk.* (1859) 20 There euery vpstart, base-condition'd slaue,.. A gentleman vnto his teeth will braue, And in his pots most malapertly bragge. *c* **1618** Moryson *Itin.* iv. iv. i. (1903) 340 In theire Potts [they] will promise any thinge, and make all bargaynes.

j. 1546 J. Heywood *Prov.* (1867) 81 He that commeth last to the pot, is soonest wroth. **1599** Hakluyt *Voy.* II. ii. 53 And I would not gladly so spend my time and trauell,.. and after,.. to lose both pot and water, as the prouerbe is. **1682** N. O. *Boileau's Lutrin* iv. Argt. 30 Yet so, the Fancy's richer, To end in Pot, commence in Pitcher! **1687** Montague & Prior *Hind & P. Transv.* 12 And understanding grown, misunderstood, Burn'd Him to th' Pot, and sour'd his curdled Blood. **1880** Miss Braddon *Clov. Foot* xxxviii, Don't you know that vulgar old proverb that says that 'a watched pot never boils'? **1893** Stevenson *Catriona* iii. 26 While we were all in the pot together, James had shown no such particular anxiety whether for Alan or me.

k. *Austral.* and *N.Z. slang. to put* (a person's) *pot on*: to inform against, to tell tales; to destroy the prospects of. Cf. pot *v.*[1] 6 b.

1913 A. J. Rees *Merry Marauders* xi. 206 You ought to put the Liquor Party's pot on. **1919** W. H. Downing *Digger Dial.* 40 *Put his pot on*—Report him. **1928** W. S. Smyth *Jean of Tussock Country* vi. 59 Dalton has put your pot on. **1935** Davison & Nicholls *Blue Coast Caravan* 178 He saw some blacks.. standing on the platform under guard of a policeman. 'Hullo, what's up?' One of them replied, 'Aw, somebody's been putting our pot on.' **1948** *Landfall* II. 110 'Got a ten bob rise last week,' Duggan said. 'Funny that, you know,' Larry said. 'I been there about the same time as you, Tom, and I haven't had a rise yet. Wonder if Myers put my pot on.' **1957** V. Palmer *Seedtime* 119 There's an election coming on, and there's a chance I'll be dumped... This afternoon's work has probably put my pot on.

l. *to get off the pot* (and extensions): see quot. 1972. *coarse slang* (chiefly *N. Amer.*).

1961 Partridge *Dict. Slang* Suppl. 1269/2 *Shit or get off the pot!* A Canadian Army c.p. (1939–45), directed at a dice-player unable to 'crap out'. **1966** 'A. Hall' *9th Directive* x. 90 Get some definite information for me. Tell the Ambassador to get off the bloody pot. **1972** *Dict. Contemp. & Colloq. Usage* (Eng.-Lang. Inst. Amer.) 26/2 *Shit or get off the pot*, vulgar. A command that someone either complete an action in process or abandon the attempt and give someone else the opportunity to try. **1973** W. McCarthy *Detail* ii. 112 You've got forty-eight hours, that's all. Either get it, or get off the pot. **1974** *Farm & Country* 26 Mar. 4/2 To put it bluntly: the Ottawa politicians had better perform at once or get off the pot. **1977** J. Le Carré *Hon. Schoolboy* xii. 275 You better tell some of those limousine liberals back in Langley Virginia it's time for them to shit or get off the pot.

14. *attrib.* and *Comb.*, as ***pot-grown***, ***-like***, ***-shaped*** adjs.; grown or cultivated in a pot (sense 1 d), as ***pot-flower***, ***-plant***, ***-rose***; made of 'pot' or earthenware (sense 11, q.v.); † **pot-act**, name for an Act of Parliament relating to the sale of liquor; **pot-ale**, the completely fermented wash in distillation; † **pot-ally**, a pot-mate, a companion in carousing; **pot annealing** *vbl. sb.* = *box annealing*; also *attrib.*; hence **pot-anneal** *v. trans.*; **pot-arch**, an arch in a glass-making furnace, in which the pots are annealed; † **pot-baked** *a.*, baked as pottery; † **pot-baker**, one who bakes clay into pots, etc., a potter; **pot-ball**, a dumpling; **pot-bank** *dial.*, a pottery (bank *sb.*[2] 8 b); **pot barley**: see barley 1 b; † **pot-birds**, a theatrical imitation of the notes of birds (? by blowing through a pipe in a pot or vessel of water); **pot-board**, a board upon which pots are placed or carried; **pot-bouls**, † **-bulis** *Sc.*: pot-clips: see boul 2; † **pot-brass**, a metal or alloy of which pots were made; **pot-builder**, a workman who constructs the large pots used in glass-works; **pot-bunker** *Golf*, an artificially constructed pot-shaped bunker; **pot-burial**, a prehistoric form of burial found in Crete (see quot.); **pot-butter**, *dial.*, butter salted and put up in pots; potted or salt butter; † **pot-cannon**, a pop-gun; cf. pot-gun 2; **pot-celt**, a celt with a comparatively large opening (see celt[2]); **pot-claw** = pot-clip, pot-hook; **pot clay**, clay used for making earthenware; also (freq. with capital initials), a bed of this kind of clay near the base of the English coal measures; **pot courage** = *Dutch courage* s.v. courage *sb.* 4 d; **pot-crook** = pot-hook, now *dial.*; **pot cultivation**, **pot culture**, cultivation of plants in pots; **pot cupboard**, a bedside cupboard designed to hold a chamber pot; † **pot dropsy**, diabetes (cf. 1 e); **pot-drum** (see quot.); **pot-dung**, *dial.*, farm-yard manure, carried to the field in pots: cf. sense 5 a, and *dung-pot*; hence **pot-dung** *v. trans.*, to dung with farm-yard manure; **pot-fair**, a fair at which pots and other crockery are sold; **pot-founder**, a maker of earthenware pots, a potter; **pot-fowler**, one who catches birds for the pot, i.e. for cooking; in quot. applied to a hawk; **pot-furnace**, a furnace containing pots for glassmaking; also, any furnace in which crucibles are heated; † **pot-fury**, fury or excitement caused by drinking (cf. 2 b); **pot-girl**, a girl who serves drink at a tavern, etc., a barmaid (cf. pot-boy); **pot-green** = pot-herb; **pot-gut(s)**, (*a*) = pot-belly 2; also, a pot-bellied animal; (*b*) = pot-belly 1; **pot-gutted** *a.* = pot-bellied; † **pot-hardy** *a.*, bold from the effects of drink (= pot-valiant); † **pot-harness** (*nonce-wd.*), 'harness' or armour consisting of drink (see quot.); **pot hat** (*colloq.*), a low-crowned stiff felt hat, a 'bowler'; hence **pot-hatted** *a.*; **pot-helmet** (cf. sense 4); **pot-kiln**, a small lime-kiln; † **pot-knight**, a 'knight of the pot', a pot-valiant toper; **pot-lace**, lace having the figure of a pot or vase (often containing flowers) in the pattern; **pot-ladle**, a ladle for lifting anything out of a pot; **pot-layering**, a method of propagating trees or shrubs in which a ball of soil, sometimes held within a split pot, is attached to a cut on a branch until enough roots have grown for the branch to be planted independently; † **pot-leech**, one who 'sucks', or drinks out of, a pot; a toper; **pot-licker**, **potlicker** *N. Amer.*, a mongrel dog; also *attrib.*; hence **pot-licking**, **potlicking**, toadying; **pot life**, the length of time that a glue, resin, or the like remains usable after preparation; **pot-line**, a line of retorts used for the electrolytic production of aluminium; **pot-lug**, *dial.* = pot-ear 1; **pot marigold**, the common marigold, *Calendula officinalis*, whose petals may be used to colour or flavour food; **pot marjoram**, a small shrub, *Origanum onites*, whose leaves are used to flavour food; **pot-market**, a market for pottery-ware; † **pot-mate** = pot-companion; † **pot-meal**, a drinking bout; **pot-mess** *Naut. slang*, a stew concocted from various scraps; *transf.*, a state of confusion or complete disorder; **pot-miser**, a kind of 'miser' or boring instrument (miser *sb.*[3]); **pot-paper** (see sense 10); † **pot-parliament**, ? an assembly of drinkers; **pot-plate**, a porcelain plate bearing the figure of a pot, vase, or other vessel; † **pot-proof-armour** (*nonce-wd.*), 'proof-armour' or defence supplied by the pot, i.e. by drinking; † **pot-punishment** (*nonce-wd.*), the punishment of being forced to drink; **pot-quarrel**, a quarrel 'in one's pots' (see 13 i); a drunken brawl; **pot-quern**, a pot-shaped quern or ancient hand-mill; **pot rassler**, **rastler**, U.S. var. *pot-wrestler*; so **pot rassling**, **rastling** *vbl. sb.* (see quot.); **pot-revel**, a drunken revel, a drinking bout; **pot-setting**, the process of setting or placing the pots in the furnaces in glass-making; † **pot-shaken**, **pot-sick** *a.*, †(*a*) disordered with liquor, tipsy, intoxicated; (*b*) *nonce-use*, pot-bound; cramped or starved of nutrient; **pot-sleeper**, a metal sleeper for railways of dish-like form; † **pot-smitten** *a.* (*nonce-wd.*), of a bargain, made by striking drinking vessels together; **pot-song**, a drinking song; **pot-spoon**, a large spoon for taking liquor out of a pot, a ladle; **pot stand**, a stand designed to hold pots or potted plants; **pot-steel**, ? = *cast* or *crucible steel*; **pot still**, a still to which heat is applied directly as to a pot, not by means of a steam-jacket; *attrib.* applied to whisky distilled in a pot-still; so **pot-stilled** *adj.*; † **pot-sure** *a.*, bold or confident through drink (cf. pot-valiant); † **pot-tipt** *a.* (*nonce-wd.*), of the nose, reddened at the tip by drinking; **pot-training**, *vbl. sb.*, the training of a small child to use a chamber pot; hence (as a back-formation) **pot-train** *v.*, **pot-trained** *ppl. a.*; **pot-trap**, (*a*) a pot set in the ground as a trap for moles; (*b*) a kind of trap used in drainage (? a D-trap); † **pot-vertigo** (**verdugo**) (*nonce-wd.*), giddiness induced by drinking; **pot-ware**, earthenware, crockery; **pot-washings** *sb. pl.*, food removed from pots by washing; **pot-water**, water for cooking purposes; **pot-wheel**, a wheel with pots or buckets for raising water, a noria; † **pot-wit**, one whose wit is displayed while drinking, or through drink; **pot-woman**, (*a*) a woman who sells pots; (*b*) *obs.*, a barmaid; (*c*) a woman who works at pottery; **pot-work**, an establishment where pottery or earthenware is made; † **pot-wort** = pot-herb; **pot-wrestler** (*slang*), (*a*) 'the cook on a whale-ship'; (*b*) 'a scullion (Pennsylvania)' (Bartlett); 'a kitchen-maid (*U.S.*)' (*Cent. Dict.*).; (*c*) a chef; so **pot wrestling** *vbl. sb.* See also potash, pot-luck, etc.

1737 J. Chamberlayne *St. Gt. Brit.* ii. (ed. 33) 87 Register of the Victuallers.. on Account of the *Pot-Act. **1812** *Sporting Mag.* XL. 86 Indicted for using an unlicensed still, and for having in his possession vessels containing *pot ale. **1815** J. Smith *Panorama Sc. & Art* II. 581 Feints from pot-ale (the name given to completely fermented wash). **1847** Webster, *Pot-ale*, a name in some places given to the refuse from a grain distillery, used to fatten swine. *a* **1619** Fletcher, etc. *Knt. Malta* ii. i, What can all this do? Get me some dozen surfeits.. And twenty *pot-allies. **1928** H. M. Boylston *Introd. Metall. Iron & Steel* xv. 519 Tool steels are sometimes annealed in open-type furnaces of fairly small size, but in many cases are *pot annealed. **1938** C. G. Johnson *Forging Pract.* 111 The steel is cooled very slowly either with the furnace.. or cooled in a pot surrounded by heat insulating material (pot annealed). **1925** *Jrnl. Iron & Steel Inst.* CXII. 453 A newly designed installation for the drying of wire bundles.. is.. described, in which the chambers are heated with the waste gases from *pot annealing furnaces. **1934** *Ibid.* CXXIX. 519 (*heading*) The heat conditions for the pot-annealing of steel hoops. **1839** Ure *Dict. Arts* 586 (Glass-making) Three of these arches exclusively appropriated to this purpose [annealing], are called *pot-arches. **1545** Joye *Exp. Dan.* ii. 28 b, Thou didste see the yerne mixt with *pot bakt erthe. **1621** Ainsworth *Annot. Pentat., Lev.* xi. 33 Vessels of *Pot-bakers earth. **1688** R. Holme *Armoury* iii. 293/2 A Dumpling, or *Pot-Ball, is made.. with ordinary flour and suet minced small, and mixed up with Milk or Water. *Ibid.* iii. 84/1. **1903** in *Eng. Dial. Dict.* from Lanc., Chesh., Shrops., Warw. **1888** *Sat. Rev.* LXVI. 11/1 Countless generations worked at the '*potbank'. **1894** *Westm. Gaz.* 28

Mar. 7/1 We are in the heart of the Potteries, 'the potbanks', as they call them up here. **1812** SIR J. SINCLAIR *Syst. Husb. Scot.* II. App. 50 The expence of making *pot barley..is..2s. 6d. per boll. **1621** FLETCHER *Pilgr.* v. iv. *Stage direct.*, Music afar off, *Pot-birds. **1840–1** S. WARREN *Ten Thous. a Year* (1884) 89/1 'It's a fine thing to be gentlefolk', said the boy, taking up his *pot-board. **1881** YOUNG *Ev. Man his own Mechanic* §898 A 'pot-board' on which sancepans, kettles, etc., are placed when not in use. **1519–20** *Rec. St. Mary at Hill* 307 Ress'..of hym for xxix ll of olde *potbras, the ll j d ob. **1890** W. J. GORDON *Foundry* 136 Three times has the whole mass to pass under his feet before it goes on to the *pot-builder. **1909** *Westm. Gaz.* 30 Apr. 4/2 Had its original whins been forest-trees we should not now be digging *pot-bunkers. **1963** *Times* 5 June 5/2 He..found a pot bunker and took seven which enabled Pirie..to halve. **1921** *Discovery* Feb. 33/1 A simpler form of burial, known as the '*pot-burial', was effected by trussing up the body, placing it under an inverted jar, and then burying it in the earth. *a* **1616** BEAUM. & FL. *Scornf. Lady* I. ii, One that..rose by honey and *pot-butter. **1785** *Hist. & Antiq. York* II. 109 This Market is only for Firkin or Pot-Butter. **1886** ELWORTHY *West Somers. Word-bk*, *Pot-butter*..in order to keep it, larger quantities of salt are needed. Hence *salt* and *pot* applied to *butter* are synonymous terms. **1653** URQUHART *Rabelais* II. xix, When little boyes shoot pellets out of the *pot-canons made of the hollow sticks of..an aulder tree. **1702** *Lond. Gaz.* No. 3821/8 A quantity of *Pot-Clay, and Working Tools for Bottles or Flint. **1860** E. HULL *Geol. Leicestershire Coalfield* (Mem. Geol. Survey) vi. 35 (*caption*) A. Loose breccia... B. Purple marl forming base of New Red Sandstone. C. Sandy shale. D. Coal 3 feet thick. E. Pot-clay, with rootlets stretching from the coal. **1913** *Geol. Derbyshire Coalfield* (Mem. Geol. Survey) viii. 124 Pot-clay suitable for the manufacture of stoneware occurs below a thin coal above the Alton seam. *Ibid.* 125 A bastard gannister, unsuited for use either as a pot-clay or as a gannister. **1939** tr. *E. N. Marais's My Friends the Baboons* vii. 81 Some were busy digging pot-clay from the hole with their hands while others were fashioning oxen and other animals from the clay. **1951** *Concealed Coalfield of Yorkshire & Nottinghamshire* (ed. 3) (Mem. Geol. Survey) iii. 13 The Coal Measures rest conformably on the Millstone Grit Series, the dividing line being placed, by international agreement (Jongmans 1928, p. xliv), at the Pot Clay or *Gastrioceras Subcrenatum* Marine Band. **1968** M. A. CALVER in Murchison & Westoll *Coal* viii. 173 The Pot Clay fauna lacks the typical benthonic assemblage exhibited by the other kinds of marine band. **1806** C. WILMOT *Let.* 14 Oct. in *Russ. Jrnls.* (1934) II. 231 In a fit of **Pot Courage* no doubt he stroked his paunch & felt himself a Hero! **1867** E. CUST *Lives Warriors* II. I. 190 One of the best officers..became so drunk, that in his pot-courage he wrapped the napkin about his head, and went out in this guise into the trenches to attack the foe. **1515** BARCLAY *Egloges* ii. (1570) B ij b/2 Platters and dishes, morter and *potcrokes. **1816** WOLCOTT (P. Pindar) *Middlesex Election* III. xii, E'en let'n suffer vor a rogue, A potcrook let'n veel. **1882** JAGO *Cornish Gloss.*, *Pot-crooks*, the second form in learning to write. **1845** *Florist's Jrnl.* 17 This species requires *pot cultivation. **1794** T. SHERATON *Cabinet-Maker & Upholsterer's Drawing Bk.* III. 364 This left-hand drawer is..sometimes made very short, to give place to a *pot-cupboard behind, which opens by a door at the end of the sideboard. **1973** *Country Life* 26 Apr. (Suppl.) 59/4 Late 18th century mahogany pot-cupboard. **1625** HART *Anat. Ur.* I. ii. 23 Another..dangerous disease..called *Diabete* or **Potdropsy*. **1912** *Encycl. Relig. & Ethics* V. 90/1 The *pot-drum is an earthenware vessel headed with a membrane. **1787** GROSE *Provinc. Dict.*, **Pot-dung*, farm-yard dung. *Berks.* **1794** T. DAVIS *Agric. Wilts* 107 The home arable should be manured with pot-dung. **1848** *Jrnl. R. Agric. Soc.* IX. II. 524 The land..is then *pot-dunged, and sowed with white mustard. **1836–48** B. D. WALSH *Aristoph.* 103 *note*, Certain mysterious orgies annually celebrated at Cambridge during the *Pot-fair. **1878** T. HARDY *Ret. Native* VI. i, He was looking at the *pot-flowers on the sill. **1631** *Canterb. Marr. Licences* (MS.), John Tiler of Hawkhurst, *pot-founder. **1834** MUDIE *Brit. Birds* (1841) I. 97 [The Goshawk] is nowise inferior as a *pot-fowler, if the ground for it be judiciously chosen. **1839** URE *Dict. Arts* 577 The flame that escapes from the founding or *pot-furnace is thus economically brought to reverberate on the raw materials of the bottle glass. **1905** W. MACFARLANE *Lab. Notes Pract. Metall.* II. (*heading*) Exercises in a crucible or 'pot' furnace. *Ibid.* 13 Gas coke is often good enough for a pot furnace. **1930** *Engineering* 18 Apr. 525/3 Sillimanite sieges in pot furnaces were more common. **1971** *Materials & Technol.* II. vi. 366 *Pot furnaces.* These are used for melting optical glass and other special glasses in quantities of up to half a ton at a time. **1597–8** BP. HALL *Sat.* I. iii, With some *pot-furie ravisht from their wit. **1797** LAMB *Let. to Coleridge* 5 Jan., You cannot surely mean to degrade the Joan of Arc into a *pot-girl. **1742** W. ELLIS *Mod. Husbandman* July iii. 36 They proved..sweet Eating, when no other *Pot Greens could be hardly got. **1972** *Sci. Amer.* Nov. 130/3 She studied our Southern cookbooks, too,..coming to the conclusion that 'distinctive features of Southern cooking are African in origin': gumbos and burgoo, hush puppies and pot greens, to begin with. **1915** W. L. HOWARD (*title*) Rest period studies with *pot-grown woody plants (Missouri Agric. Exper. Station Res. Bull. No. 16). **1946** G. A. R. PHILLIPS *Rock Garden* iv. 64 Pot grown plants may be planted with comparative safety at any time of the year. **1960** *Farmer & Stockbreeder* 9 Feb. 119/2 Start with small trees. In the case of *macrocarpa*, which are usually pot-grown, you could plant trees of $1\frac{1}{2}$–2 ft. **1977** C. LLOYD *Clematis* vii. 114 Pot-grown clematis have the advantage of needing very little root disturbance in the process of planting. **1909** *Dialect Notes* III. 359 **Pot-gut, n.*, a pot-bellied person. *c* **1926** 'MIXER' *Transport Workers' Song Bk.* 72 She's seated in a motor With some 'pot-gut' by her side. **1926** G. FRANKAU *My Unsentimental Journey* xiv. 182 Those little squirrels they call 'pot-guts' scuttle fatly across the well-made road. **1942** BERREY & VAN DEN BARK *Amer. Thes. Slang* §429/2 *Fat person*..pot-gut(s). **1951** R. CAMPBELL *Light on Dark Horse* 75 Then his old pot-guts would shake like a jelly. **1773** GRAVES *Spir. Quix.* IV. viii, I a vessel of broth! you *pot-gutted rascal! **1845** *Spirit of Times* 2 Aug. 267/1 *Ar* you a goin to tumtum all nite on that pot-gutted old pine box of a fiddle, *say?* **1909** *Dialect Notes* III. 359 *Pot-gutted, adj.*, pot-bellied. **1912** *Ibid.* 586 Look at that pot-gutted beer fly, will you. **1941** BAKER *Dict. Austral. Slang* 56 *Pot-gutted*, fat, paunchy. **1615** BRATHWAIT *Strappado* (1878) 3 That garland..From th' Temples sure of some *pot hardy Poet. **1622** S. WARD *Woe to Drunkards* (1627) 36 To whet their wits with wine; or arme their courage with *Pot-harnesse. **1798** JANE AUSTEN *Lett.* (1884) I. 168 She looks much as she used to do,..and wears what Mrs. Birch would call a *pot hat. **1873** *Slang Dict.*, *Pot-hat*, a low-crowned hat, as distinguished from the soft wideawake and the stove-pipe. **1898** *Westm. Gaz.* 16 Dec. 3/2 Dressed like an ordinary tourist in a tweed suit, a blue overcoat, and a pot-hat. **1899** *Daily News* 25 Sept. 7/3 A band of *pot-hatted young men linked arms, and..marched along, followed by an enthusiastic crowd. **1634** WITHER *Emblemes* 223 Some from the *pot-kilne, from the sheep cote some Hee raised hath. **1834** *Brit. Husb.* I. 304 They appear to pay dearly at present for lime, and the sorry pot-kilns by which it is manufactured are so badly managed. **1587** HARRISON *England* II. vi. (1877) I. 160 The beere..is cleere and..yellow as the gold noble, as our *potknights call it. **1865** *Pot lace [see ANTWERP]. **1960** H. HAYWARD *Antique Coll.* 15/2 The style of pattern has given this [*sc.* Antwerp lace] the name of pot lace..from the substantial two-handled vase usually prominent in it. *c* **1500** *Coventry Corp. Christi Plays* 30 Here with my *pott-ladull With hym woll I fyght. [*a* **1825** FORBY *Voc. E. Anglia*, *Pot-ladles*, tad-poles; from their shape.] **1912** A. F. BROUN *Sylviculture in Tropics* II. iv. 146 '*Pot-layering' is employed for branches which are either too high up a tree or too brittle to be bent into the ground. **1934** [see *air-layering* (AIR *sb.*[1] II)]. **1961** *Amat. Gardening* 30 Sept. (Suppl.) 2/3 Air-layering. Also known as pot-layering... A means of rooting branches or shoots. **1630** J. TAYLOR *Water-Cormorant* Wks. III. 5/1 This valiant *pot-leach, that vpon his knees Has drunke a thousand pottles vp se freese. **1932** V. RANDOLPH *Ozark Mountain Folks* 223 Jethro was splitting wood as I rode into his little clearing, heralded by a great number of *pot-licker dogs. **1947** *Clarke County Democrat* (Grove Hill, Alabama) 30 Oct. 4/3 A hound is a hound, regardless of whether he is July, Red Bone, Walker, potlicker or just plain hush-puppy. **1948** W. FAULKNER *Intruder in Dust* (1949) i. 5 A true rabbit dog, some hound, a good deal of hound, maybe mostly hound, redbone and black-and-tan with maybe a little pointer somewhere once, a potlicker, a nigger dog. **1971** W. HILLEN *Blackwater River* ii. 10 One man was walking through the village with his three pot-lickers when they met a housecat. **1929** *Potlicking [see HOLE *v.*[1] 7]. **1968–70** *Current Slang* (Univ. S. Dakota) III–IV. 95 *Pot-licking, n.* Oversolicitous behavior... He made his way to the top only by *pot-licking*. **1945** H. BARRON *Mod. Plastics* viii. 199 When the hardener is mixed into the resin then the mixture has a very limited *pot life. **1969** T. C. THORSTENSEN *Pract. Leather Technol.* xiv. 226 In this kind of finish the reactive components are usually mixed shortly before application, due to the limited pot life of the components. **1976** G. S. RAMASWAMY *Mod. Prestressed Concrete Design* vii. 86 The pot-life of the mixture was 20 to 25 minutes at an ambient temperature of 30°C. **1797** IMRIE in *Edin. Phil. Trans.* (1798) IV. 194 *Pot-like holes..hollowed out of the solid rock. [**1936** *Industr. & Engin. Chem.* Feb. 148/1 Shutting down a 'line' of aluminum cells or 'pots'..is not a difficult or lengthy operation if properly performed.] **1951** *Economist* 29 Sept. 748/1 The drought had forced the huge hydro-electric installations on the Columbia River to reduce..power to the plants that provide aluminium. Already three '*potlines' have been closed down. **1957** *Times* 12 Nov. (Canada Suppl.) p. vi/5 The power is brought down on the other side of the mountain, 10 miles away, to feed the potlines located by the deep water estuary of the Douglas channel. **1965** *Wall St. Jrnl.* 25 Feb. 32/2 Aluminum Co. of America said it will install a third 33,000-ton-a-year potline for producing primary aluminum at its Warrick County, Ind. plant. **1855** ROBINSON *Whitby Gloss.*, **Pot-lug*, the handle of a jug; the two loops at the sides of the iron porridge-pot. **1814** J. GREEN *Address on Bot. U.S.* 41/2 *Calendula officinalis.* *Pot Marygold, Common. **1883** *Encycl. Brit.* XV. 544/1 The pot-marigold..is the familiar garden plant with large orange-coloured blossoms. **1910** *Daily Chron.* 19 Feb. 9/6 Among the best annuals for town gardens are the..French and African marigolds..and the calendula or pot marigold. **1936** E. S. ROHDE *Herbs & Herb Gardening* IX. 128 Marigolds, including the old Pot Marigold.., have for some years been coming into favour again. **1966** G. B. FOSTER *Herbs for Every Garden* iii. 77 The petals of pot marigold were used to color butter, cheese, custards and sauces. **1597** *Pot marjoram [see MARJORAM a *y*]. **1629** J. PARKINSON *Parad.* II. cxxvi. 447 This kind of Marierome belongeth to that sort is called..In English Winter Marierome, or pot Marierome. **1707** MORTIMER *Husb.* 464 Of Marjoram, there are several sorts..; the vulgar sort and Pot Marjoram is raised by slips. **1936** E. S. ROHDE *Herbs & Herb Gardening* vii. 73 Pot Marjoram..is a larger and more branching plant than Sweet Marjoram. **1974** PAGE & STEARN *Culinary Herbs* 24 Pot Marjoram..is a dwarf shrub with erect densely hairy stems. **1580** HOLLYBAND *Treas. Fr. Tong*, *Vne poterie*, a *potte market, the place where pots are made. **1603** H. CROSSE *Vertues Commw.* (1878) 141 Powring it into the bosome of his *pot-mate. **1624** FORD *Sun's Darling* I. i, I will..Swagger in my *potmeals. **1914** 'BARTIMEUS' *Naval Occasions* xxiv. 238 What an awful *pot-mess my cabin is in. **1916** 'TAFFRAIL' *Carry On!* 64 "Strewth!', he murmurs under his breath, gazing at the littered floor in dismay... "ere's a fine pot mess.' **1926** *Blackw. Mag.* Dec. 835/2 The resulting pot-mess vanished all too soon. **1961** F. H. BURGESS *Dict. Sailing* 163 *Potmess*, a mixture of any- and everything; a big heap; confusion. **1962** GRANVILLE *Dict. Sailors' Slang* 90/2 *Pot mess*, kind of stew very popular on the mess decks. **1529** MORE *Dyaloge* III. Wks. 246/1 Among other such as himselfe to kepe a quot-libet and a *pot parlament vpon. **1653** URQUHART *Rabelais* I. xl. 182 It [my nose] is well antidoted with *pot-proof-armour. **1598** R. HAYDOCKE tr. *Lomazzo* T. Rdr. ¶v b, These base fellowes I leaue in their Ale-houses, to take *pot-punishment of each other. **1599** PORTER *Angry Wom. Abingd.* B iij b, Forsooth they'l call it a *pot quarrell straight. **1851** D. WILSON *Preh. Ann.* (1863) I. vii. 213 A very ancient form of hand-mill is called the *pot querne. **1894** *Nottingham. & Derbys. N. & Q.* Aug. 109 A portion of a pot-quern,..found at Breaston. **1942** BERREY & VAN DEN BARK *Amer. Thes. Slang* §460/15 *Pot rassler or rastler, a *dishwasher*. **1968** R. F. ADAMS *Western Words* (rev. ed.) 234/2 *Pot rastler*, a logger's name for a dishwasher. **1942** BERREY & VAN DEN BARK *Amer. Thes. Slang* §819/1 *Pot rassling, -rastling *or* wrestling, ..*dishwashing or cooking*. **1586** J. HOOKER *Hist. Irel.* in *Holinshed* II. 95/1 They kept such *pot-reuels, and triumphant carousing, as none of them could discerne his beds head from the beds feet. **1839** URE *Dict. Arts* 577 The *pot-setting is a desperate service. **1630** J. TAYLOR (Water P.) *Water-Cormorant* Wks. III. 5/1 Hee's *pot-shaken, or out, two and thirty. **1893** GUNTER *Miss Dividends* 195 All coming out of pot-shaped domes. **1611** FLORIO, *Brianzesco*, tipsie, drunken, *pot-sicke. **1872** HARDY *Under Greenw. Tree* I. II. iii. 157 Every morning I see her eyes mooning out through the panes of glass like a pot-sick winder-flower. **1891** KIPLING *Light that Failed* (1900) 273 Wastage of the Suakin-Berber line,..mounds of chairs and *pot-sleepers. **1900** *Engineering Mag.* XIX. 707/2 Pot Sleepers on the Great Indian Peninsula Ry. **1596** BP. W. BARLOW *Three Serm.* i. 117 Cup-shotten suertiships, and *potsmitten bargaines. **1850** P. CROOK *War of Hats* 49 *Pot-songs..bawl'd in every street and lane. *c* **1440** *Promp. Parv.* 411/1 *Potspone, or ladyl. **1907** *Yesterday's Shopping* (1969) 148/2 *Pot Stands, triangular wood..each 0/3. **1947** [see *back-drop* (BACK- B)]. **1971** *Cambr. Anc. Hist.* (ed. 3) I. II. xviii. 398 A biconical potstand has remote parallels at Büyük Güllücek, and in the Khirbet-Karak wares of the 'Amūq and Palestine. **1875** R. F. MARTIN tr. *Havrez' Winding Mach.* 10 Steel tram wheels..made of a mild '*pot steel' and annealed carefully in an oven after they are cast. [**1799** *Rep. Comm. Distilleries Scot.* in *Parl. Papers 1803* XI. 727/2 Private families distilled Whiskey for their own use; and the Still they used was a large pot, globular.] *Ibid.* 730/2 Suppose then that Fig. 5 represents an old fashioned *Pot-Still. **1890** *Daily News* 23 July 2/8 Rums and pot-still whiskies would not be so injuriously affected. **1902** *Daily Chron.* 7 Jan. 6/3 This result Professor Hewitt declared he had attained by adding certain chemical substances to the 'pot-still'. **1906** *Ibid.* 10 Apr. 3/6 This new proposal would put Lowland malt whisky and Campbeltown whisky, both made in pot-stills, on the same level as grain spirits. **1939** JOYCE *Finnegans Wake* 246 Ansighosa pokes in her potstill to souse at the sop be sodden enow and to hear to all the bubbles besaying. **1958** P. KEMP *No Colours or Crest* viii. 150 A very small, wizened old man crouched over a crude pot-still..; on the ground beside him stood a number of small flasks filled with the clear spirit. **1965** *Pot-stilled [see MAO TAI]. **1648** *Leg. Capt. Jones* 3 Arm'd against them like a man *pot-sure, They stint vaine stormes. **1638** BRATHWAIT *Barnabees Jrnl.* I. (1818) 23 With his nose *pot-tipt, most bravely. **1972** J. GATHORNE-HARDY *Rise & Fall Brit. Nanny* viii. 265 It is actually physiologically impossible to *pot train a child before the age of about six months. **1975** H. JOLLY *Bk. Child Care* I. xi. 179 You cannot truly pot train a baby before he is physically mature enough to exercise some control over his bladder and bowels. **1961** *Spectator* 17 Feb. 218 One-year-olds are *pot-trained. **1966** 'K. NICHOLSON' *Hook, Line & Sinker* 11 Three sisters, the youngest only two and a half, and not fully pot-trained. **1960** L. DURRELL *Clea* II. ii. 126 Have you managed to annul your early *pot-training? **1975** H. JOLLY *Bk. Child Care* I. xv. 217 If as a mother you never respond to your toddler's signals when he is about to wet his pants, he may give up trying to take the initiative himself and will probably be less co-operative with your efforts at pot training. **1669** WORLIDGE *Syst. Agric.* (1681) 217 The *Pot-trap..is a deep Earthen-Vessel set in the ground to the brim in a Bank or Hedge-row. **1884** G. E. WARING in *Century Mag.* Dec. 259/2 An unventilated pot-trap eight inches in diameter. *a* **1616** BEAUM. & FL. *Scornf. Lady* II. i, Haue you got the *pot verdugo? **1766** R. WHITWORTH *Adv. Inland Navig.* 42 Two, and sometimes three waggons go every week to Bridgenorth, and usually carry about eight tons of *pot-ware, to be conveyed to Bristol by water. **1912** C. N. MOODY *Saints of Formosa* ix. 195 They threatened to..feed her on the *pot-washings with which the pigs are nourished. **1796** W. MARSHALL *West Eng.* I. Gloss. (E.D.S.), **Potwater*, water for household purposes. **1886** ELWORTHY *West Somers. Word-bk.*, *Pot-water*, water used for drinking and cooking, as distinguished from *slop-water*. **1898** *Edin. Rev.* Apr. 449 Available as pot-water for domestic use. **1875** KNIGHT *Dict. Mech.*, **Pot-wheel*. **1611** COTGR. s.v. *Envaisselé*, *Vn bel esprit envaisselé*, a good *pot wit. **1802** D. WORDSWORTH *Jrnl.* (1941) I. 182 We then went to the *Pot-woman's and bought 2 jugs and a dish. **1918** *Pall Mall Gaz.* 29 June 5/4 A 'potwoman' at a public house applied for a summons for wages in lieu of notice. **1979** *Listener* 20 & 27 Dec. 854/4 The Thistle..had a three-cornered taproom. I once saw a pot-woman dance an impromptu fertility dance there. **1765** J. WEDGWOOD *Let.* 2 Mar. (1965) 29 This trade to our Colonies we are apprehensive of losing in a few years as they have set on foot some *Potworks there already. **1861** SMILES *Engineers* I. v. ii. 322 The brothers Elers..erected a potwork of an improved kind near Burslem. **1894** —— *J. Wedgwood* i. 2 There were few potworks anywhere else in that county. **1902** A. BENNETT *Anna of Five Towns* xii. 328 Behind it..was a small, disused potworks. **1965** *Punch* 17 Feb. 244/1 The potworks expose their raw materials on their open marlbanks. **1605** VERSTEGAN *Dec. Intell.* iii. (1628) 59 The colewurt, the greatest *pot-wurt in time long past that our ancestors vsed. **1860** BARTLETT *Dict. Amer.* (ed. 3) 335 **Pot-wrestler*, a scullion. Pennsylvania. **1873** *Kansas Mag.* Aug. 139/1 'Bullwhackers',.., 'pot-wrestlers' and 'ink-slingers' are but a few of the common pet English names a politician must use in addressing his audience, in order to show them he is sufficiently familiar with their language. **1889** FARMER *Americanisms* 434/2 *Pot-wrestler*, a Pennsylvanian equivalent of the English 'pot-wallopper'; a scullion. **1902** [see POTWALLOPER 2]. **1941** J. SMILEY *Hash House Lingo* 44 *Pot wrestler*, dish washer. **1947** *N.Y. Jrnl. American* 18 Mar. 17/4 The off-center meatball has been endorsed by the chefs of the old world. No less a pot-wrassler than the King's own glorified the chuckwagon croquette as the ambrosia of the parked gulp. **1942** *Pot wrestling [see *pot-rassling*].

pot (pɒt), *sb.*[2] *Sc.* and *dial.* [perh. in origin the same word as prec. (with which it is very generally identified). But used only in the north (Scotl. to Lincolnsh.) and esp. in districts where Scandinavian influence prevails; to be compared with Sw. dial. *putt*, *pott*, *pit*, water-hole, abyss, pit of hell.]

A deep hole; a pit dug in the ground; e.g. †the shaft or pit of a mine (*obs.*); a hole out of which peat has been dug; a tan-pit.

1375 BARBOUR *Bruce* XI. 364 He [Bruce] gert men mony pottis ma Of a fut breid round, and all tha Var deip vp till ane manis kne. *c* **1425** WYNTOUN *Cron.* VIII. xxiv. 46 And hyd thame in a pete-pot all. **1535** STEWART *Cron. Scot.* (Rolls) III. 227 [Bruce] Trynchis gart mak and pottis that war deip Into the erd with greit laubour and cuir. **1567–8** *Reg. Privy Council Scot.* I. 612 To serche out..the saidis..myndis [= mines], and to brek the ground, mak sinkis and pottis thairin. **1601** *Charter* in Dallas *Stiles* (1697) 769 Sinks, Syers, Gutters, Eyes, levals, Pots, Airholls. **1653** in A. Laing *Lindores Abbey* xx. (1876) 231 He had drawn leather furth of ye pott upon ane Sabboth. **1721, 1800** Peat pot [see PEAT[1] 4 d]. **1895** T. ELLWOOD *Lakeland* 45 The deep circular holes generally filled with water, from which peats have been dug, are called peat pots.

†**b.** *fig.* An abyss; the pit of hell. *Obs.*

c **1500** *Rowlis Cursing* 151 in Laing *Anc. Poet. Scotl.*, Thairfoir hy ȝow to the pott of hell. **1500–20** DUNBAR *Poems* xxvi. 119 In the depest pot [*Maitl.* pit] of hell He smorit thame with smvke. **1513** DOUGLAS *Æneis* IV. v. 128 Deip in the sorofull grislie hellis pote. **1563** WINȜET *Wks.* (1890) II. 63 The botumles potis of filthines. **1567** *Gude & Godlie B.* (S.T.S.) 149 Quhill I my self did chose the deide, To saif thé from the pot. [**1865** KINGSLEY *Herew.* i, May he be thrust down with Korah, Balaam, and Iscariot, to the most Stygian pot of the sempiternal Tartarus.]

c. A deep hole in the bed of a river or stream.

[**1533** *Aberdeen Regr.* (1844) I. 148 Euery half net of the pott..xx s.] *a* **1670** SPALDING *Troub. Chas. I* (1829) 29 About this time, a pot of the water of Brechin called Southesk, became suddenly dry, and for a short space continued so, but bolts up again. **1762** BP. FORBES *Jrnl.* (1886) 164 You walk up the North-side of the Water..till you come to a deep Pool or Pot. *a* **1800** *Earl Richard* xxii. in Scott *Minstr. Scot. Bord.* (1802) II. 48 The deepest pot in a' the linn, They fand Erl Richard in. **1884** *Nonconf. & Indep.* 31 July 746/1 The river has cut its way through the rock, carving it into hollows,..and round holes which the natives call 'pots'.

d. A natural deep hole or pit in the ground, such as are found in limestone districts.

1797 IMRIE in *Edin. Phil. Trans.* (1798) IV. 195 This pot is 940 feet above the level of the sea. **1874** BARING-GOULD *Yorksh. Oddities* (1875) II. 110, I had examined several..of those curious pots which are peculiar to the Yorkshire limestone moors. These pots..are..hideous circular gaping holes opening perpendicularly into the bowels of the mountain. **1881** JESSIE FOTHERGILL *Kith & K.* xvi, He discovered some vast and awful-looking 'pots', crevasses of limestone, sinking for unknown depths into the ground.

e. *pot and gallows* (*Sc.*), the same with pit and gallows. Aberd. (Jam.)

f. (See quot.)

1812 SIR J. SINCLAIR *Syst. Husb. Scot.* I. 48 In fields where the strata are not regular, there are often masses or *pots* of sandy soil, which absorb great quantities of water.

g. *Comb.* **pot-hole** (*local*) = c, d; in *Coal-mining*, the hole left by the fall of a pot-stone; **pot-peat**, peat dug out of a pot or deep excavation; **pot-stone**, a cone-shaped mass of stone forming the base of a fossil tree-stem in a coal-mine.

1903 in *Eng. Dial. Dict.* from Northumb., Cumb., Westmld., W. Yorksh.

†**pot**, *sb.*[3] *Obs.* Also 6 **potte**. [Agrees in form and sense with Fr. Swiss dial. *potte* (also dial. *pot*, *pout*) lip, in the phrase *faire la potte* = *faire la moue*, 'to make a lip', to pout; see POUT *v.*] A grimace; *to make a pot at*, to make a mouth at, to mow at. (In quot. 1566 applied to a popping sound.)

1532 MORE *Confut. Tindale* Wks. 638/2 They call it but a parable, and almoste make a pot at it. **1533** —— *Answ. Poysoned Bk.* ibid. 1130/1 Maister Masker..mocketh and moweth in that glasse, and maketh as many straunge faces and as many pretty pottes therein, as it were an olde rieueled ape. **1566** WITHALS *Dict.* 64 b/2 A potte made in the mouthe, with one finger, as children vse to doo, *scloppus*, vel *stlopus*.

b. *Comb.* **pot-finger** (cf. quot. 1566 above).

1592 *Arden of Feversham* IV. iii. 9 Didst thou ever see better weather to run away with another man's wife, or play with a wench at pot-finger?

pot, *sb.*[4] **a.** Short for POT-SHOT.

1888 'R. BOLDREWOOD' *Robbery under Arms* xvi, A tall man..took a cool pot at him with a revolver. **1900** POLLOK & THOM *Sports Burma* vi. 212, I got a cool pot at one [gaur], and my favourite shot behind the ribs.

b. *Rugby Football.* A dropped goal (see DROPPED *ppl. a.* 1 a). *N.Z.*

1959 *N.Z. Listener* 24 July 6/4 Five potted goals—that was when a pot was worth four points.

pot (pɒt), *sb.*[5] *slang* (orig. *U.S.*). [prob. f. Mexican Sp. *potiguaya* marijuana leaves; perhaps influenced by POT *sb.*[1]; cf. POD *sb.*[2] 1 c.]

1. = MARIJUANA 1 a.

1938 [see JAGGED *a.*[2] b]. **1951** *N.Y. Times* 13 June 24/4 Progression from sneaky pete to pot to horse to banging. **1952** *Amer. Speech* XXVII. 28 Pot,..marijuana cigarettes. .. (Maurer, *potiguaya*, marijuana leaves after pods removed.) **1959** *Oxford Mail* 9 Nov. 1/6 The detectives invited their Greenwich Village pals to a big party..with poetry readings, bongo drums and plenty of 'pot' (marijuana) to smoke. **1961** N. MAILER *Advts. for Myself* 209 In Mexico, however, down in my depression with a bad liver, pot gave me a sense of something new. **1964** S. BELLOW *Herzog* (1965) i. 87 You have to do more than take a little gas, or slash the wrists. Pot? Zero! Daisy chains? Nothing! Debauchery? A museum word. **1965** *Punch* 22 Dec. 930/3 'Like a spot of pot, Jean?' he said. 'I never touch it,' I said archly. **1966** T. PYNCHON *Crying of Lot 49* iii. 63 'But we don't repeat what we hear,' said another girl. 'None of us smoke Beaconsfields anyway. We're all on pot.' **1968** *New Scientist* 22 Aug. 371/2, I am not defending the behaviour of these students and of course I don't agree with them that 'pot' is harmless. **1972** J. L. DILLARD *Black English* vii. 289 The teacher probably should not let illusions of knowledge about the ghetto tempt him into using sentences like *John and Mary are smoking pot.* **1973** [see LSD[2]]. **1975** D. LODGE *Changing Places* ii. 63 He took an extreme radical position on all such issues as pot, sex, race. **1977** *Jrnl. R. Soc. Arts* CXXV. 464/2 His son occasionally smokes pot.

2. *attrib.* and *Comb.*, as *pot liquor*, *smoke*, *-smoker*, *-smoking* vbl. sb. and ppl. a.; **pot-head, pothead** (see HEAD *sb.*[1] 7 e); **pot party**, a party held for the smoking of marijuana.

1959, etc. [see HEAD *sb.*[1] 7 e]. **1974** *Times Lit. Suppl.* 1 Mar. 219/4 A girl..herself something of a pothead, who introduces Evans to the joys of the weed. **1970** C. MAJOR *Dict. Afro-Amer. Slang* 92 *Pot liquor*..; brew from marijuana seeds and stalks. **1967** *Boston Sunday Herald* 26 Mar. I. 40/8 Authorities said that as many as 25 teenagers attended drug sessions held twice a month at different Randolph homes by one group, and that others also held 'pot' parties. **1971** D. E. WESTLAKE *I gave at the Office* (1972) 219 The media have some leniency..as for instance when magazines stage pot parties. **1976** B. LECOMBER *Dead Weight* v. 68, I couldn't quite imagine even an Antiguan Customs officer suspecting Herr Ruchter of holding riotous pot-parties. **1978** J. KRANTZ *Scruples* iii. 66 An occasional pot party was as anti-establishment a gathering as he attended. **1966** T. PYNCHON *Crying of Lot 49* iii. 64 Their rising coils and clouds of pot smoke. **1967** *Guardian* 8 July 6/4 The bored pot-smoker looking for some better kick. **1971** *New Scientist* 11 Mar. 533/3 Pot smokers have a lowered sexual drive. **1976** H. NIELSEN *Brink of Murder* xi. 99 You must be calling on a pot smoker. Take me along? **1964** *Punch* 18 Mar. 413/1 'Pot-smoking' parties, gaming sessions. **1967** *Guardian* 3 Feb. 4/4 They said, there is no evidence of a direct link between pot-smoking and addiction to hard narcotics. **1970** G. F. NEWMAN *Sir, You Bastard* ii. 39 He didn't have the stereotype-copper look..but appeared more as one expected a pot-smoking nymphomaniac to look. **1977** *Rolling Stone* 13 Jan. 37/2 Kerr-McGee officials later quoted from the letter when they described Silkwood's pot-smoking proclivities to reporters.

pot (pɒt), *sb.*[6] Colloq. abbrev. of POTENTIOMETER.

1943 C. L. BOLTZ *Basic Radio* iii. 56 Radio workers always refer to the 'pot'. **1948** *Electronics* July 120/2 The output voltage *z* of the multiplying pot is proportional to its angular rotation. **1953** R. BRETZ *Techniques Television Production* xix. 401 The first thing the student operator learns about the audio console is that the fader dials, or 'pots', in the middle of the panel each controls [*sic*] a separate source of sound. **1967** *Electronics* 6 Mar. 311/2 (Advt.), No matter what your pot requirements, they take a turn for the better when you contact Gamewell Division.

pot (pɒt), *v.*[1] [f. POT *sb.*[1] in various senses. Cf. Du. *potten* (Kilian) to put in a pot, hoard up.]

I. To drink from a pot.

1. *intr.* To drink beer or other liquor out of a pot; to indulge in drinking; to tipple. Also *to pot it*. *Obs.* or *arch.*

1594–1863 [see POTTING *vbl. sb.*[1] 1]. **1622** S. WARD *Woe to Drunkards* (1627) 35 Oh but there are few good Wits..now a dayes but will Pot it a little for company. **1628** FELTHAM *Resolves* II. [I.] lxxxiv. 242 It is lesse labour to plow, then to pot it: and vrged Healths do infinitely adde to the trouble. **1638** BRATHWAIT *Barnabees Jrnl.* IV. I j, If thou doest love thy flock, leave off to pot. **1646** W. ELDRED *Gunner's Glasse* To Rdr., Gunners, that had rather spend their time in potting and canning.

II. To put into a pot.

2. a. *trans.* To put up and preserve (flesh, butter, or other provisions, usually salted or seasoned), in a pot, jar, or other vessel. Also, to summarize, put into 'potted' form (see POTTED *ppl. a.* 3 a). Also *absol.*

1616 R. CARPENTER *Past. Charge* 50 Manna..being potted vp for a common remembrance lasted many yeares. **1741** RICHARDSON *Pamela* (1824) I. 126, I will assist your house-keeper,..to pot and candy, and preserve. **1754** FIELDING *Voy. Lisbon* Wks. 1882 VII. 106 Stores of butter, which we salted and potted ourselves. **1870** YEATS *Nat. Hist. Comm.* 58 Prawns are potted on the South coasts.

fig. **1815** EARL OF DUDLEY *Lett.* 6 Sept. (1840) 110 Pompeii may be considered as a town potted..for the use of antiquarians in the present century. **1860** EMERSON *Cond. Life, Fate* Wks. (Bohn) II. 311 It often appears in a family, as if all the qualities of the progenitors were potted in several jars. **1927** *Year's Work Eng. Stud. 1925* 42 After preliminaries, the matter is divided into: the effect of Function upon Sound..; of Emotion upon Sound..; and of *Gliederung*... The statistics and argument can hardly be 'potted' here.

b. *Sugar Manuf.* To transfer (crude sugar) from the coolers to perforated 'pots' or hogsheads, for the molasses to drain off.

1740 *Hist. Jamaica* 321 From the Boiler the Liquor is emptied into a Cooler, where it remains till it is fit to be potted. **1750** G. HUGHES *Barbadoes* 250 About twenty-four hours after the sugar is potted, the small round hole in the bottom of each pot is unstopped. **1839–87** [see POTTING *vbl. sb.*[1] 3 b].

c. To encapsulate (an electrical component or circuit) in a liquid insulating material, usu. a synthetic resin, which sets solid.

1950 W. W. STIFLER *High-Speed Computing Devices* xvi. 426 Tests..showed that it was possible to pot printed circuits in a special casting resin in such a fashion as to permit the plugging in of the complete subassemblies. **1962** F. I. ORDWAY et al. *Basic Astronautics* vi. 279 The plastics in which electronic components are potted usually contain bacteria. **1971** J. H. SMITH *Digital Logic* i. 5 The whole assembly is usually 'potted' into a block to form a module.

3. †**a.** To put (earth) into a flower-pot (*obs.*); **b.** To set (a plant) in earth in a flower-pot for cultivation; to plant in or transplant into a pot. Also, *pot off*, to transplant seedlings into individual pots; *pot on*, to move a plant from one pot into a larger one; *pot out*, to plunge potted plants into a bed in the open garden; *pot up*, to move seedlings or larger plants into pots.

1626 BACON *Sylva* § 529 Pot that earth, and set in it stock-gilly-flowers, or wall-flowers. **1664** EVELYN *Kalendarium Hortense* April 65 Pot them [Indian tuberoses] in natural (not forc'd) earth. **1793** *Trans. Soc. Arts* (ed. 2) IV. 35, I potted them into second size pots. **1846** J. BAXTER *Libr. Pract. Agric.* (ed. 4) I. 300 The young plants require to be potted off singly into the smallest-size pots. **1870** W. ROBINSON *Alpine Flowers for Eng. Gardener* I. 63 This is a better way than sowing in pots,..from which they require to be 'potted off'. **1903** D. MCDONALD *Garden Comp.* Ser. II. 113 When in the third leaf, pot singly into 48-sized pots. **1916** M. HAMPDEN *Flower Culture* ii. 39 Now [*sc.* March] is the time for..potting up clumps of hardy plants from the garden. **1926** E. T. BROWN *Year in my Flower Garden* 58 Lift and pot roots of Solomon's Seal. **1950** *N.Z. Jrnl. Agric.* Aug. 167/1 When the leaves of the small plants touch each other in the boxes it is time to pot them up. **1950** O. SITWELL *Noble Essences* IX. vi. 139 The gentle gold of the industrial haze lay lightly on the rich beds of tulips, carnations or begonias, so neatly potted out. **1952** C. E. L. PHILLIPS *Small Garden* ix. 77 Nurselings in small pots are 'potted-on' into bigger ones when their roots have filled up the first one. **1958** *Listener* 12 June 982/2 They [*sc.* amaryllis plants] will throw off bulbils from the main bulb. These can be taken off and potted up. **1978** R. GORER *Growing Plants from Seed* v. 69 The seedlings are potted up separately in very small pots and progressively potted on.

4. *Billiards.* = POCKET *v.* 4.

1860–5 *Slang Dict.* s.v., 'Don't pot me', term used at billiards, when a player holes his adversary's ball—generally considered shabby play. **1885** *Even. Standard* 18 Dec. (Farmer), After making three he potted his opponent's ball. **1899** *Westm. Gaz.* 14 Mar. 10/1 With a gallery of gentlemen-cadets, he was too proud to pot the white.

5. a. To shoot or kill (game) for the pot, i.e. for cooking (cf. POT-HUNTER, -SHOT); to 'bag'; *gen.* to bring down or kill by a pot-shot (a man or animal). *colloq.* or *slang.*

1860 READE *Cloister & H.* viii, Martin had been in a hurry to pot her, and lost her by an inch. **1860** RUSSELL *Diary in India* I. xvii. 266, I heard a good deal of 'potting pandies', and 'polishing-off niggers'. **1881** J. GRANT *Cameronians* I. iv. 60 Sir Piers..thought it very slow work compared with ..potting a man-eater from a howdah. **1889** CLARK RUSSELL *Marooned* (1890) 235 He'll have to show himself, and if he does I'll pot him. **1899** *Westm. Gaz.* 27 Oct. 6/1 Their evident object was to pot off the gunners and the staff officers, about whom the bullets whistled viciously.

b. *intr.* To take a pot-shot, to shoot (*at.*)

1854 *Illustr. Lond. News* 11 Nov. 489/1 The French have been..sending in their skirmishers close to the walls, to *pot* at the embrasures. **1861** HUGHES *Tom Brown at Oxf.* xli, Turning out to be potted at like a woodcock. **1898** in *Globe* 4 Feb. 4/5 If..I didn't see him potting away quite cheerfully!

c. *trans.* To seize, win, secure, 'bag'. Also, in *Rugby Football* (*N.Z.*), to score (a dropped goal).

1862 W. B. CHEADLE *Jrnl. Trip across Canada* (1931) 48 Worked at harness-making & potted much money during term. **1900** H. NISBET *Sheep's Clothing* Prol. iii. 26 However, he's in with us now, since he has potted the girl. **1903** *Daily Chron.* 12 Feb. 3/1 He has the scissors of a ready book-maker, and will 'pot' extracts from Mr. Roosevelt's writings and messages 'till the cows come home'. **1904** *Ibid.* 21 Nov. 8/5 Six of the eight points have been 'potted', and not a defeat sustained. **1959** [see POT *sb.*[4] b].

III. 6. a. To outdo, outwit, deceive. Now *slang.*

1562 J. HEYWOOD *Prov. & Epigr.* (1867) 185 Pot him Iacke: pot him Iacke? nay pot him Iugge. To pot the drunkarde, the Iugge is the dugge. **1589** WARNER *Alb. Eng.* VI. xxxi. (1612) 156 The Clowne, no doubt, that potted Pan [won from him the woman whom Pan courted] lackt arte to glose and flatter. **1621** BP. MOUNTAGU *Diatribæ* 154 It is no hard matter to puzzle and to pot you with authority of Josephus in the selfesame story of Gen. 14. **1855** TAYLOR *Still Waters* ii. (Farmer), A greater flat was never potted. **1880** MILLIKIN in *Punch's Almanack* Feb., Crab your enemies,—I've got a many, You can pot 'em proper for a penny.

b. *Austral. slang.* To hand (someone) over for trial, to inform on. Cf. POT *sb.*[1] 13 k.

1911 A. WRIGHT *Gambler's Gold* 138 Why should I pot the bloke? He done me a good turn, an' th' police is no good to me. **1916** J. B. COOPER *Coo-oo-ee* ix. 108 'Yer see,' he explained, 'they've got to try to hang some cove or else they'd lose their job. The more men they pot the better they're fixed in their jobs. See?' **1945** BAKER *Austral. Lang.* II. xi. 207 A few general expressions concerned with school life:..*to pot someone* or *to put someone's pot on*, to inform on. **1953** 'CADDIE' *Sydney Barmaid* xl. 230 What dirty swine has potted me?

†**7.** To cap (verses). *Obs.*

1597 G. HARVEY *Trimming Nashe* Wks. (Grosart) III. 37 Ile teach thee howe to pot verses an houre together. **1598** STOW *Surv.* viii. (1603) 72 The boyes of diuerse Schooles did cap or pot verses.

IV. 8. 'To manufacture, as pottery or porcelain; *esp.* to shape and fire, as a preliminary to the decoration': cf. POTTING *vbl. sb.*[1] 2. Also freq. *intr.*

1914 R. FRY *Lett.* (1972) II. 377 Vanessa and I have been potting all day... We went when the potter wasn't there and got the man to turn the wheel. **1967** B. JEFFERIS *One Black Summer* (1968) i. 1 The grounds and buildings would be full of summer school students; doctors who longed to pot; dressmakers who yearned to try their hands at sculpture.

1968 *Canad. Antiques Collector* June 12/1 The Rockingham China Works..began to produce china (porcelain) in 1826. The factory ceased to manufacture towards the end of 1841. Many fine porcelain wares..were potted in this relatively brief period. **1971** J. WHITE *Left for Dead* 68 All I've got to do is to teach myself to pot... I've always been interested in making pottery. **1976** J. G. HURST in D. M. Wilson *Archaeol. Anglo-Saxon Eng.* vii. 323 Stamford ware is finely potted on a fast wheel and fired in a developed single-flue kiln.

V. 9. *colloq.* To cause (a baby or young child) to use a chamber-pot. Also *absol.*

1943 A. MEDLEY *Your First Baby* xviii. 180 With children who hardly wake up, perform with their eyes closed and drop off again, it is well worth while to pot them and to know that they will sleep dry and comfortable. **1948** B. GOOLDEN *Jig-Saw* ii. 9, I prefer them [*sc.* babies] house-trained... One feeds and pots automatically. **1957** H. CROOME *Forgotten Place* iv. 51 I'm not going to pot him or anything. I think early habit training is such a mistake. **1973** *Daily Tel.* (Colour Suppl.) 26 Oct. 7/2 She has poured the last coffee and sat back for the first time since potting the baby at 7:30 that morning.

†**pot**, *v.*² *Sc. Obs.* [f. POT *sb.*²] **a.** *trans.* To dig pits in, fill with pits. **b.** To dig a trench about; to mark off by a trench. **c.** To put in a pit.

1375 BARBOUR *Bruce* XI. 388 On athir syde the way, weill braid, It wes pottit, as I haf tald. **1595** *Aberdeen Regr.* (1848) II. 129 The said..yard dyk ascendis south eist or thairby,.. as the same was presentlie pottit and merkit. **1887** DONALDSON *Suppl. to Jamieson, To Pot, Pott,* to pit, trench, or mark off by furrow, as in boundaries of land... To plant or set in a pit, as in *potting* march stones: also, to pit and cover, as in *potting* or pitting potatoes [for] winter.

†**pot**, *v.*³ *Obs.* [f. POT *sb.*³] *intr.* To make a grimace; to mock. Hence †**'potting** *vbl. sb.*

1549 CHALONER *Erasm. on Folly* S iv, Thei on the other syde did potte at him. **1553** *Short Catech.* in *Lit. & Doc. Edw. VI* (Parker Soc.) 504 At length was he [Jesus].. mocked with potting, scorning, and spitting in his face. **1596** DANETT tr. *Comines* (1614) 326 Me they potted at, as in such cases is vsuall in Princes courts.

pot, obs. form of POTE *v.*, PUT *v.*

potability (pəʊtəˈbɪlɪtɪ). [f. late L. *pōtābil-is* (see next) + -ITY; so F. *potabilité* (Littré).] The quality of being potable or drinkable.

1671 J. WEBSTER *Metallogr.* xii. 189 That it may be brought into a condition of potability. **1873** TRISTRAM *Moab* xiii, The potability of the water.

potable (ˈpəʊtəb(ə)l), *a.* (*sb.*) (Also 7 -abile, -ible.) [a. F. *potable* (14–15th c. in Hatz.-Darm.), ad. late L. *pōtābilis* (Auson.) drinkable, f. *pōtāre* to drink: see -ABLE.]

1. Fit or suitable for drinking; drinkable.

1572 J. JONES *Bathes of Bath* II. 16 The water there is altogyther potable. *c* **1645** HOWELL *Lett.* (1650) I. 369 They bore the tree with an awger, and there issueth out sweet potable liquor. **1753** HANWAY *Trav.* (1762) II. VII. iii. 179 The water..was so corrupted.., that it was not potable. **1883** F. M. CRAWFORD *Mr. Isaacs* ix, Huge packs of provisions edible and potable.

b. *potable gold*: a preparation of nitro-muriate of gold deoxydized by some volatile oil, formerly esteemed as a cordial medicine; drinkable gold. So *potable Mars* (iron).

1576 BAKER (*title*) The Newe Iewell of Health, wherein is contayned..the vse and preparation of Antimonie, and potable Gold. **1597** SHAKS. *2 Hen. IV*, IV. v. 163 Other [gold]..is more precious, Preseruing life, in Med'cine potable. **1667** MILTON *P.L.* III. 608 What wonder then if fields and regions here Breathe forth Elixir pure, and Rivers run Potable Gold. **1694** SALMON *Bate's Dispens.* (1713) 195/1 A Tincture of Mars from Maets, which is call'd potable Mars. **1712** SWIFT *Fable of Midas* 7 He call'd for Drink; you saw him sup Potable Gold in Golden Cup. **1858** MAYNE *Expos. Lex.*, *Aurum Potabile*,..old term,..Potable gold.

†**2.** Appropriate to drinking. *Obs. rare*⁻¹.

1605 CHAPMAN *All Fooles* V. i. Plays 1873 I. 182 Come on, lets heare his wit in this potable humour.

B. *sb. pl.* Things potable; drinkables, liquor.

1623 FLETCHER *Rule a Wife* III. i, In a well-knit body, a poor parsnip will play his prize above their strong potabiles. **1651** BIGGS *New Disp.* § 287 The sick be nourished with only potables. **1791–1823** D'ISRAELI *Cur. Lit.* (1866) 268/1 He indicates the places for peculiar edibles, and exquisite potables. **1884** *Punch* 18 Oct. 190/1 The pleasant potables they would imperiously prohibit.

Hence **'potableness**, potable quality; potability.

1727 in BAILEY vol. II. **1755** JOHNSON, *Potableness*, drinkableness.

potacre, variant of PODAGRE *Obs.*, podagra.

‖**potage** (pɔtaʒ). [F. *potage*: see POTTAGE (which was the same word adopted in ME. and anglicized). Now, in this spelling, recognized as a French loan-word, found in 16th c. Sc., and in Eng. from 1660 chiefly in reference to France or French cookery.] Soup of any kind. *a potage*, a meal or mess of this.

1567 in Chalmers *Mary Q. of Scot.* (1818) I. 178 Bakyne meit to my Ladie,..with potages, after thair discretioun... Ane kyde, with potagis refarrit to the maister houshald. **1668** SHADWELL *Sullen Lovers* v. 91 Eate nothing but Potages, Fricasces, and Ragousts,..your Andoilles, your Langue de porceau, your Bisks and your Olio's. **1688** R. HOLME *Armoury* III. 84/1 Potage is strong Broth of Meat, with Herbs and Spices boiled. **1691** *Satyr agst. French* 16 Soops and Fricasies, Ragou's, Pottage, Which like to Spurs, do Nature urge to Rage. **1696** PHILLIPS (ed. 5), *Potage*, a Jumblement of several sorts of Flesh and Fowl boil'd together with Herbs, and served up in the Broth, mix'd together after the French Fashion. **1823** SCOTT *Quentin D.* Pref., The *potage*, with another small dish or two, was equally well arranged. **1842** BARHAM *Ingol. Leg.* Ser. II. *Black Mousquetaire*, He quite gave up..*potage*, or game.

†**'potager**¹. *Obs.* Forms: 4, 8 potager, 4–5 -ere, 5 -are, 6 *Sc.* **potiser**, **pottisear**. See also POTTINGER². [ME. *potager*, a. F. *potager*, in 15th c. a maker of potages (Littré), now obs. in this sense: see POTAGE, POTTAGE.] A maker of pottage or potage; one who cooks vegetables.

1377 LANGL. *P. Pl.* B. v. 157, I haue be cook in hir kichyne and þe couent serued..I was þe priouresses potagere, and other poure ladyes. *c* **1420** *Liber Cocorum* (1862) 1 Cure.. most be don in thrinne degre This, hasteler, pasteler, and potagere. **1483** *Cath. Angl.* 288/1 A Potagare, *legvminarius.* *c* **1575** *Chalmerlane Air* in *Balfour's Practicks* (1754) 585 Gif thair be ony Cuikis or Pottisearis, quha bakis pyis. *a* **1578** [see POTTINGER²]. **1727** S. SWITZER *Pract. Gard.* III. xxxiii. 177 It may be truly said, says that haughty potager [Mons. de la Quintinye, a celebrated gardener] in praise of his great master.

potager² (pɔtaʒe). [Fr.: see POTAGERE.] = POTAGERE.

c **1786** T. BLAIKIE *Diary Scotch Gardener* (1931) 199 This garden..goes with a narrow stripe of potager to the point du jour where there is another potager. **1792** A. YOUNG *Trav. France* I. 99 There is a town, and a great *potager* to remove before it would be consonant with English ideas. **1885** H. JAMES *Little Tour in France* iii. 20 Your eye wanders over the neighbouring *potagers*. **1926** *Spectator* 9 Oct. 581/2 The herb garden..lost its supremacy to the *potager* or vegetable garden less than two centuries ago. **1958** L. DURRELL *Spirit of Place* (1969) 146, I calculate that with ten chickens and the excellent *potager* out there I shall just squeeze by. **1966** A. CHRISTIE *Third Girl* iv. 35 In England..you do not love your *potager* as much as you love your flowers. **1978** J. LEES-MILNE *Round the Clock* 55 The north garden..would be called the *potager*, were it in France. Vegetables, espaliers, roses and lawns were neatly compartmented.

potager, early form of POTTINGER¹.

†**potagere.** *Obs. rare.* [a. F. *potager*, *-ère* adj. in *jardin potager*, a kitchen-garden (also *potager* sb.).] A kitchen-garden; a herb-garden.

1669 EVELYN *Diary* 2 Sept., The gardens were well understood, I mean the *Potagere*. **1699** —— *Acetaria* Pref. a vij, I content my self with an Humble Cottage, and a Simple Potagere. *Ibid.* Plan b ij, Of the Hort-Yard and Potagere.

potagerie (‖pɔtaʒri, pəʊˈtædʒərɪ). In 7–8 also anglicized **potagery**. [F. *potagerie*, †pot-herbs or kitchen-plants collectively (now a fire-place for cooking potage).] Growing herbs or vegetables collectively; a kitchen-garden.

1693 EVELYN *De la Quint. Compl. Gard.* Dict., *Potagery*, is a Term signifying all sorts of Herbs or Kitchen-plants, and all that concerns them, considered in general. **1727** S. SWITZER (*title*) Practical Kitchen Gardiner: or, a New and Entire System of Directions for Melonry, Kitchen-Garden, and Potagery. **1826** MISS MITFORD *Village* Ser. II. (1863) 318 The high ivied stone wall of the potagerie.

potagre, obs. form of PODAGRE *a.* and *sb.*

potamian (pəʊˈteɪmɪən, -ˈtæmɪən), *a.* and *sb.* *Zool.* [f. Gr. ποταμ-ός river + -IAN.] **a.** *adj.* Of or pertaining to the *Potamites* or *Trionychidæ*, the soft-shelled river tortoises. **b.** *sb.* A tortoise of this group, a river tortoise, mud turtle.

1850 BRODERIP *Notebk. Nat.* xi. (1852) 265 A good garnish of claws to enable the Potamians to scramble upon banks and logs. **1895** *Funk's Stand. Dict.*, *Potamian* adj.

potamic (pəʊˈtæmɪk), *a.* [f. Gr. ποταμ-ός river + -IC.] Of or pertaining to rivers; fluviatile.

1883 SEELEY *Expansion Eng.* 87 In the school of Carl Ritter, much has been said of three stages of civilisation determined by geographical conditions, the *potamic* which clings to rivers, the *thalassic* which grows up around inland seas, and lastly the *oceanic*. **1904** *Times* 9 Mar. 10/1 These ideas belong to the potamic stage of the naval art.

‖**Potamogale** (pɒtəˈmɒgəliː). *Zool.* [mod.L., f. Gr. ποταμό-ς river + γαλῆ weasel.] A genus of insectivorous aquatic mammals, with one species, *P. velox* of Western equatorial Africa, the ottershrew; taken as type of a family *Potamogalidæ*. Hence **pota'mogalid**, an animal of this family; **pota'mogaloid** *a.*, resembling the *Potamogale*.

1880 A. R. WALLACE *Isl. Life* iii. 43 The potamogale, a curious otter-like water-shrew. **1895** *Funk's Stand. Dict.*, Potamogalid, Potamogaloid.

‖**Potamogeton** (pɒtəməʊˈdʒiːtɒn, -ˈgiːtɒn). *Bot.* [L. *potamogēton* (Plin.), adopted by Tournefort 1700 as a generic name, a. Gr. ποταμογείτων pondweed, f. ποταμό-ς river + γείτων neighbour.] A genus of floating freshwater plants; a pondweed.

1548 TURNER *Names of Herbes* (E.D.S.) 65 Potamogeton is called in duche Samkraute, it maye be named in englishe Pondplantayne, or swymmynge plantayne, because it swymmeth aboue pondes and standyng waters. **1601** HOLLAND *Pliny* II. 250 This Potamogeton hath an adversatiue nature to Crocodiles also. **1756** J. HILL *Hist. Plants* 247 (Jod.) The oblong oval-leaved potamogeton; the potamogeton with cordated leaves surrounding the stalk. **1882** FLOYER *Unexpl. Baluchistan* 248 In front of the tent I found the English potamogeton, which I had not seen since I had left Lincolnshire. **1890** *Daily News* 24 May 5/3 He could..lament learnedly that the dropper caught in callitriche and potamogeton,..long names for water weeds.

pota'mography. [f. Gr. ποταμό-ς river + -GRAPHY.] The physiography of rivers.

1864 in Webster.

pota'mology. [f. as prec. + -LOGY.] The scientific study of rivers.

1829 (*title*) Potamology; or, the Science of Rivers: A Tabular Description of the principal Rivers throughout the World. **1872** M. COLLINS *Pr. Clarice* II. ix. 129 Nile, Ganges, Amazon..Seine, Marne, and Loire..when will there be an end of geography and potamology? **1899** *Athenæum* 2 Sept. 325/2 It is in America..that the most marked advances in the science of potamology have..been made.

Hence **potamo'logical** *a.*, of or pertaining to potamology; **pota'mologist**, one who studies or is versed in potamology.

1863 J. FERGUSSON in *Geol. Soc. Jrnl.* Aug. 322 Consequences..strangely overlooked both by engineers and potamologists. **1890** *Cent. Dict.*, Potamological.

pota'mometer. *rare.* [f. as prec. + -METER.] An instrument for measuring the force of a river current.

1895 in *Funk's Stand. Dict.*

potamophilous (pɒtəˈmɒfɪləs), *a. rare.* [f. as prec. + Gr. -φιλ-ος (see -PHIL) + -OUS.] River-loving.

1827 *Brit. Critic* I. 474 Rowed..in his public State barge, on the bosom of the Thames, in all the majesty and magnificence of a Fluviatile and Potamophilous Lord Mayor.

potamoplankton (ˌpɒtəməʊˈplæŋktən). [a. G. (C. Zimmer 1898, in *Biol. Centralbl.* XVIII. 522), f. Gr. ποταμό-ς river + PLANKTON.] Plankton found in rivers or streams.

1902 *Ann. Bot.* XVI. 584 These backwaters thus form a kind of transition from the typical Potamoplankton of the flowing river to the Heleoplankton of the ponds of the Thames valley. **1909** E. WARMING *Oecol. Plants* xxxviii. 161 Other subdivisions [of limnoplankton] may be recognized, such as potamoplankton, heloplankton, and probably several more. **1923** *Jrnl. Ecol.* XI. 209 Potamoplankton is the plankton of rivers. It is usually benthoplanktonic in character, but at times may show limnoplanktonic features. **1969** G. W. PRESCOTT *Algae* i. 17 Plankton of rivers is called potamoplankton.

potance: var. POTENCE².

pot and pan. [Rhyming slang for 'old man'.] One's father or husband.

1906 E. DYSON *Fact'ry 'Ands* xii. 153 How's yer ole pot-'n'-pan, Tutsie? **1935** A. J. POLLOCK *Underworld Speaks* 90/2 *Pot and pan*, the old man (otpay and anpay). **1938** L. ORTZEN *Down Donkey Row* 12 *Pot and Pan*, old man; meaning husband or father. **1945** BAKER *Austral. Lang.* 270 *Pot and pan*, old man. **1971** *National Times* (Austral.) 13 Dec. 20 From this handy guide you could soon establish the meaning of..'her pot and pan is in the bucket and pail'... Translated, it means '..her old man is in jail.'

potanger: var. POTTINGER¹.

potaquaine, erron. f. POTOQUANE.

†**potargo.** *Obs.* Variant of BOTARGO.

1622 FLETCHER *Sea Voy.* IV. i, Here be certain tarts of tar about me And parcels of potargo in my jerkin. **1739** 'R. BULL' tr. *Dedekindus' Grobianus* 96 If for the licqu'rish Appetite there are Mangoes, Potargo, Champignons, Caviarre.

potarite (pəˈtɑːraɪt). *Min.* [f. the name of the *Potaro* River, Guyana, where first found: see -ITE¹.] Palladium amalgam, occurring as brittle, silvery grains and nuggets and reported to consist of two distinct phases.

1925 *W. India Committee Circular* 22 Oct. 429/2 The second report deals with the occurrence of Palladium-Mercuride, a mineral new to science in British Guiana. Up to the present it has only been found in certain diamond-bearing gravels on the Potaro river; and so it was named 'Potarite'. **1928** *Mineral. Mag.* XXI. 397 He [*sc.* Sir John Harrison] proposed the name potarite (letter of April 3, 1925), but he did not himself record this name in print. **1960** *Amer. Mineralogist* XLV. 1094 Samples of PdHg which are identical with the mineral potarite may be prepared either by displacement of palladium from $Pd(NO_3)_2$ solution by mercury or by direct synthesis from powdered palladium and mercury in sealed evacuated tubes. **1968** I. KOSTOV *Mineral.* II. i. 95 Mercury group... Gold amalgam..and potarite (PdHg, tetragonal) with about 35% Pd, are rare representatives of the group.

†**potaro**, erron. variant of PEDRERO.

1665 J. FRASER *Polichron.* (S.H.S.) 374 In the Castle were ..28 brass drakes or monkeys, 2 potaros, 800 arms.

potash (ˈpɒtæʃ), *sb.* [Early mod.E. *pot-ashes* pl., app. ad. Du. *pot-asschen* (1599 Kilian, 'quod in ollis...asseruentur, ne liquescentes effluant'), mod.Du. *potasch*; so Ger. *pottasche*, Swed. *pottaska*, Da. *potaske*; also F. *potasse* (1577 *pottas*, at Liège, Godef.), It., Pg., mod.L. *potassa*, Sp. *potasa*.]

The sense-history of *potash* and its derivatives is involved in the advance of chemical knowledge. The earliest term was *pot ashes* or *pot-ashes* = Du. *pot-asschen*, applied to the crude products. The essential substance of these, when purified from extraneous matters, was spoken of in the singular as *pot-ash* or *potash*. In 1756 this was proved by Dr. Joseph Black of Edinburgh to be a compound substance, a carbonate, the removal from which of the carbonic acid left a 'caustic alkali' or 'lye' (really the hydroxide, or caustic potash, KHO), which chemists thereafter generally considered to be the true *potash* (in Fr. *potasse*). In 1807 this, in its turn, was shown by Sir H. Davy to be not a simple substance, but to contain a new metal, of which he believed it to be the oxide. To the metal (K) he gave the name *potassium*, to the oxide (on the analogy of *magnesium* and *magnesia*, *sodium* and *soda*, etc.) that of *potassa*. Next year, Dakeel gave reasons for believing that the latter contained also water, and it was subsequently shown to be the hydroxide or hydrate (KHO), the simple oxide being the anhydrous form (K_2O). The salts of potassium, in accordance with the chemical theory of the time, were viewed as compounds of the oxide, and variously named *carbonate of potassa*, *of potass*, *of potash* (= potassium carbonate, K_2CO_3), *chlorate of potassa*, *potass*, or *potash* (= potassium chlorate, $KClO_3$), etc. Commercially 'potash' is still often applied to the carbonate; by chemists usually to the hydroxide or hydrate, caustic potash, KHO, but sometimes to the anhydrous oxide, K_2O, and in names of compounds it is still often used instead of 'potassium', as *chlorate of potash* = *potassium* or *potassic chlorate*.

1. An alkaline substance obtained originally by lixiviating or leaching the ashes of terrestrial vegetables and evaporating the solution in large iron pans or pots (whence the name). Chemically, this is a crude form of potassium carbonate (more or less mixed with sulphate, chloride, and empyreumatic substances), but was long thought to be (when freed from impurities) a simple substance.

a. orig. plural, ***pot ashes***, ***pot-ashes***: now applied to the crude substance.

When purified by calcination and re-crystallization, known as *pearl ashes* or *pearl-ash*.

1648 HEXHAM *Dutch Dict.*, *Pot-asschen*, Pot-ashes. **1657** *Knaresb. Wills* (Surtees) II. 223, 50 lbs. of pott ashes. **1669** BOYLE *Contn. New Exp.* I. (1682) 37 A liquor made of the salt of Pot-ashes suffered to run in a sellar *per deliquium*. **1712** tr. *Pomet's Hist. Drugs* I. 101 We sell at Paris four Sorts of Pot-Ashes. **1714** MANDEVILLE *Fab. Bees* (1733) I. 413 Another set of [sailors] are freezing in the north to fetch potashes from Russia. **1813** SIR H. DAVY *Agric. Chem.* (1814) 112 Herbs, in general, furnish four or five times, and shrubs two or three times, as much pot ashes as trees. **1885** W. DITTMAR in *Encycl. Brit.* XIX. 588 This calcination used to be effected in iron pots, whence, the name 'potashes' was given to the product; at present it is generally conducted in reverberatory furnaces on soles of cast iron.

β. singular, ***pot-ash***, ***potash***: applied esp. to the purified carbonate, as a substance.

1751 J. HILL *Mat. Med.* 801 Potash, in general, is an impure fixed alkaline Salt, made by burning from Vegetables. We have several Kinds of it in Use. **1807** T. THOMSON *Chem.* (ed. 3) II. 22 In 1756, Dr. Black proved.. that the potash which the world had considered as a simple substance, was really a compound, consisting of potash and carbonic acid; that lime deprived it of this acid; and that it became more active by becoming more simple. **1811** A. T. THOMSON *Lond. Disp.* (1818) 320 Impure Potash. Impure Sub-Carbonate of Potash. Potashes. Pearl-ashes... This substance consists chiefly of subcarbonate of potash, mixed with some other salts. It is known in commerce by the name of potash; and is brought to us principally from the Baltic and America. **1861** MISS BEAUFORT *Egypt. Sepulchres* I. xv. 337 The 'hashish el kali'.. covered the ground: this is the plant from the ashes of which they make potash for soap.

†**b.** Used also to include the impure carbonate of soda, BARILLA. *Obs.*

1823 J. BADCOCK *Dom. Amusem.* 150 Your potash should be of that kind termed barilla.

2. *Chem.* The hydroxide or hydrate of potassium, KHO; a hard white brittle substance, soluble in water and deliquescent in air, having powerful caustic and alkaline properties; ***caustic potash***.

1800 tr. *Lagrange's Chem.* I. 171 Potash is a body, which has not hitherto been decomposed; it is of a white colour, and exceedingly caustic... This substance is prepared by burning vegetables, which all contain a greater or less quantity of potash; as we shall explain under the head Carbonate of Potash. **1846** G. E. DAY tr. *Simon's Anim. Chem.* II. 128 If.. caustic potash be added to the mass, a considerable quantity of ammonia is given off... When the acid is accurately neutralized with potash, it forms an easily-soluble salt. **1866** WATTS *Dict. Chem.* IV. 692 *Potash* .. applied sometimes to the hydrate, sometimes to the anhydrous oxide of potassium, occasionally also to the crude carbonate; it is best however to restrict it to the hydrate, either in the solid state or in aqueous solution. **1869** ROSCOE *Elem. Chem.* (1871) 198 Thrown into water, one atom of potassium displaces one of hydrogen from the water, forming potassium hydroxide, or potash. **1874** GARROD & BAXTER *Mat. Med.* (1880) 125 Caustic potash is usually moulded for medical purposes into small sticks about the size of a pencil, which should be white, but are often greenish, bluish, or reddish-brown from impurities.

b. Now sometimes applied by chemists to the anhydride or monoxide, K_2O, = POTASSA; in non-chemical works vaguely to any compound of potassium.

1843 J. A. SMITH *Product. Farming* (ed. 2) 101 The property on which this depends is, that clay invariably contains potash and soda. **1846** J. BAXTER *Libr. Pract. Agric.* (ed. 4) I. 29 Potash.. is an element in most plants. **1858** THUDICHUM *Urine* 195 There is only a very small quantity of potash present in the urine. **1866** [see 2].

c. In names of compounds = POTASSA, and now in chemical use mostly superseded by POTASSIUM.

carbonate of potash = potassium carbonate; † ***muriate of potash***, obs. name of potassium chloride; † ***oxygenated muriate of potash*** = potassium chlorate; ***sulphate of potash*** = potassium sulphate.

1791 HAMILTON *Berthollet's Dyeing* I. I. I. i. 26 Acidulous tartrite of pot-ash. **1799** *Med. Jrnl.* I. 103 Remarks on the effects of the nitrous acid, the oxygenated muriate of pot-ash, &c. **1800** tr. *Lagrange's Chem.* I. 195 Sulphate of soda may be decomposed by charcoal, phosphorus, &c. in the same manner as sulphate of potash. **1843** J. A. SMITH *Product. Farming* (ed. 2) 149 Silica enters the plant chiefly in the form of silicate of potash or soda. **1876** BRISTOWE *The. & Pract. Med.* (1878) 864 The carbonate, acetate, and citrate of potash are probably the best for the purpose.

3. Short for ***potash-water***: see 4.

1876 BESANT & RICE *Gold. Butterfly* xxxviii, They drank a whole potash-and-brandy each. **1895** *Cornh. Mag.* Oct. 396 A stiff tumbler of whisky and potash.

4. *attrib.* and *Comb.*, as ***potash-lye***, ***muck***, ***salt***, ***soap***; **potash alum**: see ALUM *sb.* 2; **potash-felspar** = ORTHOCLASE; **potash-granite**, felspathic granite; **potash greensand**, a greensand yielding potash; **potash kettle**, a large vessel employed in the manufacture of potash; **potash-lime**, see quot.; **potash-mica**, a silicate of aluminium and potassium = MUSCOVITE; **potash-water**, an aerated beverage; water impregnated with carbonic acid gas, to which is added potassium bicarbonate.

1839 URE *Dict. Arts* 39 If *potash alum is to be formed, this sulphate of alumina is evaporated to the specific gravity of 1·38. **1862** DANA *Man. Geol.* §55. 55 One [species of feldspar] has in addition potash and is a *potash-feldspar. *Ibid.* 56 Orthoclase or potash-feldspar. **1845** DARWIN *Voy. Nat.* xv. (1873) 320 Grand bare pinnacles of a red *potash-granite. **1868** *Rep. U.S. Comm. Agric.* 402 Calcareous Marls and *Potash Greensands. *a* **1817** T. DWIGHT *Trav. New Eng.* (1821) II. 256 The method of making potash in those large vessels,.. now known [as] *potash kettles. **1866** WATTS *Dict. Chem.* IV. 692 **Potash-lime*, a mixture of hydrate of potassium and quicklime. **1839–47** *Todd's Cycl. Anat.* III. 816/2 The *potash-ley will now gradually recede into the large bulb. **1865** WATTS *Dict. Chem.* III. 1011 Chemically, micas may be divided into *potash-micas, containing little or no magnesia..; and magnesia-micas. **1764** *Museum Rust.* II. xcviii. 327 The ashes, which are called *pot-ash muck, make excellent manure for some kinds of soil. **1874** GARROD & BAXTER *Mat. Med.* (1880) 123 Experiments.. have shown that the *potash salts, when introduced immediately into the blood, are extremely poisonous. **1899** *Allbutt's Syst. Med.* VIII. 861 To scrape the nail thin, and then after softening it with *potash soap, to apply chrysarobin. **1802** W. SAUNDERS in *Med. & Phys. Jrnl.* VIII. 492 [N. Paul] has introduced also the gaseous *pot-ash waters.

Hence **'potash** *v.*, *trans.* to freat or manure with potash; **po'tashery** [cf. *colliery*, *pottery*], a factory where potash is made; *pl.* potash-works.

1799 *Canada Constellation* (Niagara, Ontario) 8 Nov. 4/1 For field ashes, 9d. at the potashery, and 6d. if he goes for them. **1846** G. WARBURTON *Hochelaga* I. 263 Potasheries, tanneries, breweries, iron-works, paper-works, and others. **1860** EMERSON *Cond. Life, Power* Wks. (Bohn) II. 332 Whether to whitewash or to potash, or to prune. **1882** W. M. THAYER *From Log-Cabin to White House* 150 A pot-ashery was an establishment containing vats for leeching ashes, and large kettles for boiling the lye. **1930** *Canad. Hist. Rev.* XI. 39 The only buildings were.. two saw-mills, a carding shop, a potashery, [etc.]. **1979** *Jrnl. R. Soc. Arts* Dec. 60/2 A syndicate of Liverpool-Manchester merchants.. opened potasheries in New York and Philadelphia.

potass (pəʊ'tæs, 'pɒtæs). *Chem.* Now *rare.* [ad. F. *potasse* POTASH.] An anglicized form, variously used according to the chemical notions of the time, for potash, potassa, and (in names of compounds) potassium.

1799 *Med. Jrnl.* I. 243 To reduce the dropsical swellings .. ten or fifteen grains of potass, two or three times a day, in some bitter draught, are directed. **1815** J. SMITH *Panorama Sc. & Art* II. 388 All the mineral acids dissolve tin, and it may be precipitated from its solutions by potass; but an excess of potass will re-dissolve the metal. *Ibid.* 414 Pure potass is extremely white, and so caustic, that if applied to the hand, the skin is instantly destroyed; it is therefore in this state called caustic alkali. The potash of commerce is always combined with carbonic acid,.. this addition.. reduces it to its usual state of what is called mild alkali, or by chemists carbonate of potass, or rather sub-carbonate of potass, as it is not saturated with the carbonic acid. **1860** PIESSE *Lab. Chem. Wonders* 26 A substance of similar composition to nitrate of potass (saltpetre).

b. Potash-water: see POTASH 4.

1883 F. M. CRAWFORD *Dr. Claudius* vi, I think I will have some curaçao and potass.

c. *Comb.*: **potass-albite**, albite containing potash instead of, or besides, soda.

1850 DAUBENY *Atom. The.* xii. (ed. 2) 416 In a few instances, as in potass-albite,.. this base would seem to be partly soda and partly potass.

‖**potassa** (pəʊ'tæsə). *Chem.* [mod.L.: see POTASH.] The name appropriated by Davy to potassium monoxide, K_2O, also called *anhydrous potash*; sometimes also applied to the hydrate or hydroxide, KHO (= $K_2H_2O_2$), also called ***potassa fusa*** and ***caustic potash***.

Formerly used in names of chemical compounds in which current nomenclature uses *potassium*, as ***carbonate of potassa*** = *potassium carbonate*, K_2CO_3 (regarded as $K_2O.CO_2$).

liquor potassæ, an aqueous solution of potassium hydrate, containing about 5·84 per cent of the hydrate.

1812 SIR H. DAVY *Chem. Philos.* 324 This substance is pure potash or potassa, which was unknown in its uncombined state till I discovered potassium, but which has long been familiar to chemists combined with water in the substance which has been called pure potash; but which ought to be called the hydrat of potassa. **1813** —— *Agric. Chem.* ii. (1814) 52 Potassa or the pure caustic vegetable alkali consists of one proportion of potassium and one of oxygene. **1836–41** BRANDE *Chem.* (ed. 5) 611 The *Liquor Potassæ* of the Pharmacopœia is directed to be prepared as follows:—'Take of carbonate of potassa 15 ounces, lime 8 ounces, boiling distilled water a gallon [etc.].' **1842** BRANDE *Dict. Sc.*, etc. s.v. *Potassium*, What is called caustic potash, which is a compound of 48 potassa + 9 water. **1858** MAYNE *Expos. Lex.*, *Potassa Fusa*, fused potash; the hydrate of potash; also called *Lapis infernalis*. **1877** ROBERTS *Handbk. Med.* (ed. 3) I. 66 Liquor potassæ seems to be of use in some cases.

†**potassamide** (pəʊ'tæsəmaɪd). *Chem.* Also **potassiamide** (Ogilvie 1882). [f. POTASS-IUM + AMIDE.] An amide of potassium, formed by the substitution of one or more atoms of potassium for those of the hydrogen of ammonia (NH_3). Two of these are known, ***monopotassamide***, KH_2N, and ***tripotassamide***, K_3N: see quots.

1838 T. THOMSON *Chem. Org. Bodies* 7 Potassamide is amide of potassium. **1866** ODLING *Anim. Chem.* 16 Caustic potash and potassamide may be regarded as the hydrated and ammoniated forms of chloride of potassium. **1866** WATTS *Dict. Chem.* IV. 695 Amides of Potassium. *Monopotassamide*, KH_2N, is formed when potassium is gently heated in ammonia-gas. It is an olive-green substance. *Ibid.*, *Tripotassamide* or *Nitride of Potassium*, K_3N,.. is a greenish-black infusible substance.

potassamine (pəʊ'tæsəmaɪn). *Chem.* [f. POTASS-IUM + AMINE.] A name, preferred by some, for POTASSAMIDE: see AMIDE, AMINE.

1873 WATTS *Fownes' Chem.* (ed. 11) 233 When potassium is heated in ammonia-gas, a compound called potassamine is formed. **1880** *Libr. Univ. Knowl.* (N.Y.) XII. 373 The univalent radical, amidogen, NH_2,.. with one molecule of potassium forms potassamine, NH_2K.

†**'pota͵ssane.** *Chem.* [f. POTASS-IUM + -ANE.] Davy's proposed name for potassium chloride.

1812 SIR H. DAVY *Chem. Philos.* 327 Muriate of potash, which may be called potassane, consists of 75 of potassium and 67 of chlorine... Potassane is the only known combination of potassium and chlorine.

potassic (pəʊ'tæsɪk), *a. Chem.* [f. POTASS-A or POTASS-IUM + -IC; so F. *potassique*.]

a. Of, pertaining to, or containing potassium or potash; = ***potassium*** in comb. Also in compounds, as ***mono-***, ***dipotassic***; ***hydro-potassic*** (combined with water).

1858 MAYNE *Expos. Lex.* s.v., Berzelius termed.. the combinations of the oxide [of potassium] with acids,.. and of the metal with halogenous bodies, *Sales potassici*: potassic [salts]. **1876** HARLEY *Mat. Med.* (ed. 6) 121 Potassic Carbonate causes no precipitate. **1877** WATTS *Fownes' Chem.* (ed. 12) I. 338 Normal potassium carbonate, or Dipotassic carbonate, K_2CO_3. **1906** *Westm. Gaz.* 7 Apr. 2/2 The Prussian Government.. is a member of another 'Kartell'—that controlling the supplies of potassic salts.

b. *Geol.* Of a mineral or rock: containing an appreciable or a greater-than-average quantity of potassium, often as compared with sodium. Also applied to a metamorphic process in which such minerals are formed.

1903 W. CROSS et al. *Quantitative Classification Igneous Rocks* 227 The orthoclase may be considered as wholly potassic and reckoned as pure orthoclase. **1932** A. JOHANNSEN *Descr. Petrogr. Igneous Rocks* II. 63 The term orthorhyolite was originally suggested in 1919 for rhyolites whose only feldspar is potassic. **1967** *Amer. Mineralogist* LII. 828 The early part of the alteration sequence featured chiefly potassic metasomatism (biotite, potash feldspar), whereas the latter part was characterized by sodic metasomatism (aegirine, crocidolite). **1971** I. G. GASS et al. *Understanding Earth* i. 18/1 Two compositionally different feldspars, one more sodic and the other more potassic. **1974** P. G. HARRIS in H. Sørensen *Alkaline Rocks* VI. i. 434/1 The anomalous $^{87}Sr/^{86}Sr$ ratios of many suites of potassic rocks suggests.. a multistage origin.

potassiferous (pɒtæ'sɪfərəs), *a.* [f. POTASS-A + -(I)FEROUS.] Containing or yielding potash or potassic salts.

1890 in *Cent. Dict.*

po'tassio-, combining form of POTASSIUM, in the names of double salts of potassium and another substance, as ***po͵tassio-'platinum*** (attrib.), ***po͵tassio-'ferric*** adj., of potassium and iron, ***po͵tassio-mercuric***, ***-pla'tinic***, ***-tar'taric*** adjs., ***po͵tassio-'tartrate***, etc.

1873 RALFE *Phys. Chem.* 108 The potassio platinum chloride removed by filtration. **1876** HARLEY *Mat. Med.* (ed. 6) 308 Potassio-platinic chloride,.. insoluble in alcohol and æther. **1897** *Allbutt's Syst. Med.* IV. 403 A little tartrate of potash, or potassio-tartrate of soda may be given.

potassium (pəʊ'tæsɪəm). *Chem.* [In form, mod.L. (Davy 1807), f. POTASS or POTASH (see Note there), in accordance with the names of metals in -IUM.] **a.** One of the elements, an alkaline monad metal, the basis of POTASH; it is a highly lustrous white metal with a slight tinge of pink, soft at ordinary temperatures, of specific gravity 0·865, being the lightest solid body known except lithium; when exposed to the air it at once tarnishes or oxidizes, and when thrown upon water instantly decomposes it, uniting with the oxygen and causing the liberated hydrogen to burn with a characteristic violet flame. Symbol K (for *Kalium*); atomic weight 39·1.

1807 Sir H. Davy in *Phil. Trans.* XCVIII. 32 Potassium and Sodium are the names by which I have ventured to call the two new substances. **1812** —— *Chem. Philos.* 321 Small metallic globules will appear at the negative surface, which consist of potassium. I discovered this metal in the beginning of October 1807. **1839** Ure *Dict. Arts, Potassium* ..is a metal deeply interesting..from its having been the first link in the chain of discovery which conducted Sir H. Davy through many of the formerly mysterious and untrodden labyrinths of chemistry. **1864** H. Spencer *Princ. Biol.* I. II. x. §92. 276 Potassium alone melts at 136°, sodium alone melts at 190°, but the alloy of potassium and sodium is liquid at the ordinary temperature of the air. **1881** *Med. Temp. Jrnl.* XLVIII. 176 Bromide of potassium in large doses..has a beneficial effect [in dipsomania].

b. *attrib.* in names of chemical compounds, as ***potassium carbonate*** (also carbonate of potassium, of potassa; or of potash, potassic carbonate), K_2CO_3; so ***potassium chlorate, chloride, cyanide, hydrate, iodide, oxide***, etc.; ***potassium salt***.

1865 Mansfield *Salts* 257 Its Potassium compound. **1869** Roscoe *Elem. Chem.* (1871) 17 Formed by the action of strong sulphuric acid upon a salt called potassium permanganate. **1873** Watts *Fownes' Chem.* (ed. 11) 319 Potassium Bromide is a colourless and very soluble salt. *Ibid.* 320 Potassium Hydrate, commonly called caustic potash or potassa, is a very important substance, and one of great practical utility. *Ibid.* 324 Potassium-salts are always most abundant in the green and tender parts of plants.

c. Special comb.: **potassium-argon**, used *attrib.* to designate a method of isotopic dating, or results obtained from it, based upon measurement of the relative amounts in rock of potassium 40 and its decay (electron capture) product, argon 40.

1953 *Bull. Geol. Soc. Amer.* LXIV. 1473 (*heading*) Potassium argon studies at the University of Toronto. **1955** *Ibid.* LXVI. 1711 (*heading*) Potassium-argon ages of metamorphic and igneous rocks from the Southern Appalachians. **1968** *Times* 3 Oct. 13/5 The duration of the various magnetic reversals is known from potassium-argon dating of land rocks. **1969** Bennison & Wright *Geol. Hist. Brit. Isles* xvi. 362 Earlier pleistocene deposits can only be dated, as yet, by the use of the potassium-argon method.. which, because of the long half-life of potassium, is not suited to dating such relatively recent events. **1977** *Time* 7 Nov. 52/2 The age of a fossil can often be determined by analyzing the layer of rock or soil in which it was found and determining, often by the so-called potassium-argon method, just how old the layer is.

po'tassuretted, -eted, *a.* [irreg. f. potassa after sulphuretted: cf. carburetted.] Combined with potassium, as in ***potassuretted hydrogen***.

1815 W. Henry *Elem. Chem.* (ed. 7) I. 224 Potassureted Hydrogen Gas. This name I would propose for the solution of potassium in hydrogen gas, which,..results from the action of potassium on water. **1819** Children *Chem. Anal.* 46 We reckon at present 23 compound gases, namely, Hydruret..of carbon,..and..of phosphorus, arsenuretted, sulphuretted, telluretted, potassuretted, and selenuretted hydrogen [etc.]. **1858** Mayne *Expos. Lex., Potassureted Hydrogen*..a combination of potassium with hydrogen, forming a spontaneously inflammable gas.

† **'potate**, *a. Obs. rare*⁻¹. [ad. L. *pōtātus*. pa. pple. of *pōtāre* to drink: see -ate².] *lit.* Drunk: in quot. perh. = drinkable, liquid, liquefied.

Some take *silver potate* to be = quicksilver or mercury.

1610 B. Jonson *Alch.* iii. ii, Eight, nine, ten dayes hence He will be siluer potate; then, three dayes, Before he citronise: some fifteene dayes, The Magisterium will be perfected.

potation (pəʊ'teɪʃən). Also 5 -cioune, 5–6 -cion. [ME. a. OF. *potacion, -ation* (obs.), ad. L. *pōtātiōn-em*, n. of action from *pōtāre* to drink.]

1. Drinking; a drinking, a drink, a draught.

1479–81 *Rec. St. Mary at Hill* 97 In money yevyn to the poore peple, And for potacions to prestis and clerkes. **1483** *Cath. Angl.* 288/1 A Potacion, *potacio*. **1604** Shaks. *Oth.* ii. iii. 56 Rodorigo..To Desdemona hath to night Carrows'd Potations, pottle-deepe. **1650** Bulwer *Anthropomet.* 121 The potation of the same aliment, but liquid. *a* **1687** Cotton *Epigr., De Monsieur Cotin* (R.), Three or four hours of friendly potation. **1814** Scott *Wav.* xii, You..did rather abstain from potation. **1875** Jowett *Plato* (ed. 2) III. 78 Indulging in moderate potations.

† **b.** A drinking party, compotation, symposium.

1512 *Nottingham Rec.* III. 456 Have, make, or vse any potacions, cockfighte or drinking. **1565** *Stat. Hartlebury Sch. Worc.* in *N. & Q.* 7th Ser. IX. 90/2 The said Schoolmaster shall..take the profits of all such cock-fights and potations, as are commonly used in Schools. **1574** M. Stokys in Peacock *Stat. Cambridge* (1841) App. A. p. xiii, They have a Potation of Figgs, Reasons and Almons, Bonnes, and Beer, at the charge of the sayed Determiners. [**1890** Gross *Gild Merch.* I. 33 This gathering was called the 'potacion' or 'drinking' ('potacio').]

c. Indulgence in drinking alcoholic liquor; intemperate drinking.

1800 Weems *Washington* xi. (1877) 151 The very intemperate passions and potations of some of their officers. **1835** Marryat *Olla Podr.* viii, In stalked three..men who were..the worse for potation. **1881** Besant & Rice *Chapl. of Fleet* I. vi, His face..flushed and cheeks swollen by reason of his midnight potations.

2. Liquor for drinking; a drink, a beverage.

1426 Lydg. *De Guil. Pilgr.* 24207 Maugre hir potaciouns and dyuerse confecciouns..Maked at the potycaryes. *c* **1450** *Cov. Myst.* (Shaks. Soc.) 138 What man drynk of this potacion,..Pleyn in his face xal shewe it owth. **1772–84** Cook *Voy.* (1790) IV. 1489 The root..from whence their favourite potation is extracted. **1871** B. Taylor *Faust* (1875) I. vi. 109 He deserves thy kitchen's best potation.

† **b.** A deleterious drink or liquid; a potion. *Obs.*

1502 Arnolde *Chron.* (1811) 176 They [be accursed] that drinken potacions or do depresse or withdraw the nurisshing of the byrth within the body.

3. *attrib.* and *Comb.*: † **potation money**, money given for drink, drink-money; † **potation penny**, a contribution to the expense of a drinking entertainment; **potation-shop**, a drinking-shop.

1487–8 *Rec. St. Mary at Hill* 141 We aske alowaunce of potacions monye geven to your tenauntes in Resseyuyng of the Rentes and charges aforesaide, also in drynkkyng siluer on your werkmen. **1525** *Foundation Stat. Manch. Gram. School* 15 Apr., [The Schoolmaster or Usher shall teach the children freely] withoute any money..taking therefor, as cokke peny, victor peny, potacion peny or any other except his said stipend. **1823** *Blackw. Mag.* XIII 514 That famed potation-shop.

Hence **po'tationist** (*nonce-wd.*), one given to potations, a habitual or professed drinker.

1888 Black *Adv. Houseboat* 251 He was a powerful potationist.

potative ('pəʊtətɪv), *a. rare.* [ad. obs. F. *potatif, -ive* adj., f. L. *pōtāt-*, ppl. stem of *pōtāre* to drink: see -ive.] Addicted to drink; bibulous.

1737 Ozell *Rabelais* II. 73 *note*, The potative Bishops of his Time.

potato (pəʊ'teɪtəʊ), *sb.* Forms: α. 6 **botata**, 6–7 **bat(t)ata**: see batata. β. 6– **potato**, (6 **potaton**, 6–7 **potade, potatus**, 6–8 **patata**, 6–9 **potatoe**, 7 **partato, potado, potata, pottato, puttato**, 8– *illit.* **pertater**). γ. *dial.* and *vulg.*: see 2 d and tater, tatie, and tattie. [ad. Sp. *patata*, a variant of batata, orig. the native name in Haitian in sense 1. So, in same sense, F. *patate*, obs. It. *potata*, Ger. *potate*.]

Sense 1 is the original; the plant to which it is applied was to Gerarde, in 1597, 'the common Potatoes'; the plant in sense 2, on account of its general likeness to the other as producing esculent tubers, he called from its alleged source 'Virginia Potatoes', and (in his *Catalogue* of 1599) 'Bastard Potatoes'; but when this came to be an important object of cultivation as a food plant, it became 'the potato' par excellence; the exotic plant and tuber originally so named being distinguished by some adjunct. In 17th c. instances of the word it is often difficult or impossible to determine which plant is meant.

1. A plant, *Batatas edulis*, N.O. *Convolvulaceæ*, having tuberous roots, for which it is cultivated for food in most tropical and subtropical regions of the world; = batata. Its native region is unknown, but it appears to have been seen by the Spaniards first in the West Indies *c* 1500. Now distinguished as ***sweet*** or ***Spanish potato*** (see 3 a). **a.** The tuber.

In the 16–17th c. supposed to have aphrodisiac qualities, to which there are frequent references.

[**1555** Eden *Decades* 82 (tr. Peter Martyr, 1511–16) In Hispaniola..they dygge also..certeyne rootes growynge of theim selues, whiche they caule *Botatas* [*indigenæ batatas appellant*]... They are also eaten rawe, and haue the taste of rawe chestnuttes, but are sumwhat sweeter.] **1565** Hawkins *Voy. Florida* (Hakl. Soc.) 27 These potatoes be the most delicate rootes that may be eaten, and doe far exceede our passeneps or carets. **1577–1876** [see batata]. **1587** Harrison *England* ii. vi. (1877) i. 149 Of the potato and such venerous roots as are brought out of Spaine, Portingale, and the Indies. **1596** *Gd. Huswiues Jewell* C v b, Pare your Potaton. **1598** Shaks. *Merry W.* v. v. 21 Let the skie raine Potatoes. **1599** B. Jonson *Cynthia's Rev.* ii. i, 'Tis your onely dish, aboue all your potato's or oyster-pies in the world. *a* **1642** Sir W. Monson *Naval Tracts* iv. (1704) 452/1 The Potatoes make a delicate kind of Drink, both pleasant and wholsome. **1660** F. Brooke tr. *Le Blanc's Trav.* 183 Throughout the whole Island there growes a root they call *Igname*, or *Patata*, from whence the invention was brought to Spain. **1689** H. Pitman *Relation Gt. Suff.*, etc. 29 Of eatable Roots [in Providence Island, Bahamas] there is Partatoes, Yams, Edders, &c. **1750** G. Hughes *Barbadoes* 228 The West Indian Potatoes have all a sweetish taste.

b. The plant. (See batata, quots. 1613–1866.)

1597 Gerarde *Herbal* ii. cccxxxiv. 780 Of Potatoes. This plant..is generally of vs called Potatus or Potatoes. It hath long rough flexible branches trailing vpon the ground, like vnto Pompions... Clusius calleth it Battata, Camotes, Amotes, and Ignames: in English Potatoes, Potatus, and Potades. **1681** Chr. Jeaffreson *Let. fr. St. Kitts* 10 Nov. in *Yng. Squire 17th Cent.* (1878) I. 280 It [hurricane] broke and twisted my sugar-canes, rooted up my Cassava, and washed the graine and new-planted puttatoes. **1712** E. Cooke *Voy. S. Sea* 203 There are Patata's of four or five several Colours. **1707, 1775** [see 3 a]. **1756** P. Browne *Jamaica* 154 The Potatoe and Potatoe-slip. Both these plants are now cultivated all over America, and supply the Negroes and poorer sort of people with a great part of their food.

2. a. The plant *Solanum tuberosum*, a native of the Pacific slopes of South America, introduced into Europe late in the 16th century, and now widely cultivated for its farinaceous tubers: see b.

Described in 1553, under the name *papas*, in the *Cronica de Peru* of Piedro Cieza, cap. xl, ¶5. Introduced into Spain, it is said, from Quito, soon after 1580, and thence, *c* 1585, into Italy; in 1587 grown at Mons in Hainault, whence in 1588 two tubers were obtained and grown by the botanist Clusius, Keeper of the Botanical Garden to Maximilian II; described by him as *Papas Peruanum*. Soon grown in other botanic gardens, as at Breslau in 1590. The plant may have been brought independently to England, where Gerarde had it growing in 1596; but he was in error in his statement that he obtained it from Virginia (whence the erroneous name *Virginia Potatoes*, long kept up by English writers); for the plant is not a native of Virginia, and was not cultivated there in 16th c. In 1693 its introduction into Ireland was attributed to Sir Walter Raleigh 'after his return from Virginia' (where he never was); but no contemporary statement associating Raleigh's name with the potato has been found. See Brushfield *Raleghana* ii. in *Trans. Devonsh. Assoc.* 1898, XXX. 158–197; B. Daydon Jackson in *Gardeners' Chron.* 1900, XXVII. 161, 178.

1597 Gerarde *Herbal* ii. cccxxxv. 781 Of Potatoes of Virginia... Virginia Potatoes hath many hollowe flexible branches, trailing vppon the grounde, three square, vneuen, knotted or kneed in sundry places... The roote is thicke, fat, and tuberous; not much differing either in shape, colour or taste from the common Potatoes, sauing that the rootes hereof are..some of them round as a ball, some ouall or egge fashion..: which knobbie rootes are fastened vnto the stalkes with an infinite number of threddie strings. *Ibid.* 782 Because it hath not onely the shape and proportion of Potatoes, but also the pleasant taste and vertues of the same, we may call it in English Potatoes of America, or Virginia [*ed.* 1633 *adds* Bauhine hath referred it to the Nightshades, and calleth it *Solanum tuberosum Esculentum*]. **1599** Gerarde *Catalogus* 15 *Papus orbiculatus*, Bastard Potatoes. *P. Hispanorum*, Spanish Potatoes. [*Catal.* 1596 C 2/1 had only the Latin names]. **1629** Parkinson *Paradisus* 516 Potatoes of Virginia, which some foolishly call the Apples of youth..the flowers..somewhat like the flower of Tobacco for the forme..small round fruit, as bigge as a Damson or Bulleis, greene at the first,..like vnto Nightshade. **1678** Phillips (ed. 4), *Potatoes*, a sort of fruit, coming originally from the West Indies, but now common in English Gardens, whose Root is of great vertue, to comfort and strengthen the Body. **1707** Mortimer *Husb.* (1708) 469 Potatoes are planted in several parts of our Country,..being easily encreased by cutting the Roots into several pieces, each piece growing as well as the whole Root. **1785** Martyn *Rousseau's Bot.* xvi. (1794) 201 Potato is of this genus [Solanum], as you will be convinced, if you compare the structure of the flower with that of the other species. **1832** *Veg. Subst. Food* 128 The potato is found wild in several parts of America,..among others in Chili and Peru. **1875** W. McIlwraith *Guide Wigtownshire* 10 In 1728 Marshal Stair introduced the culture of the potatoe into Wigtownshire.

b. The tuber or underground stem of this plant, of roundish or oblong shape; now a well-known article of food in most temperate climates.

1663 in *Jrnl. Bk. of Royal Soc.* (MS.) 25 Mar., A Proposition to plant Potatoes through all the parts of England..and the benefit therof in times of scarcity of Food ..their usefulness for meat and bread. **1664** J. Forster (*title*) Englands Happiness Increased, or a Sure and Easie Remedy against all succeeding Dear Years; by a Plantation of the Roots called Potatoes. **1664** Evelyn *Kal. Hort.* Nov. 78 Take up your Potatos for winter spending, there will enough remain for stock, though never so exactly gather'd. *a* **1687** Petty *Pol. Arith.* ii. (1690) 42 Ireland being under peopled..the ground yielding excellent Roots (and particularly that bread-like Root Potatoes). **1693** *Jrnl. Bk. of Royal Soc.* (MS.) 6 Dec., Dr. Sloan related that the Irish Potatoes were first brought from Virginia, and that they were the chief subsistence of the Spanish Slaves in the mines in Peru and elsewhere. **1693** *Ibid.* 13 Dec., The President [Lord Southwell] related that his grandfather brought Potatoes into Ireland, who had them from Sir Walter Rauleigh after his return from Virginia. **1714** Gay *Sheph. Week* Monday 84 Of Irish swains potatoe is the cheer. **1778** G. White *Nat. Hist. Selborne* xxxvii, Potatoes have prevailed in this little district..within these twenty years only. **1780** A. Young *Tour Irel.* I. 18 The apple potatoe is liked best, because they last till the new ones come in. **1792** —— *Trav. France* 350 As to potatoes, it would be idle to consider them in the same view as an article of human food, which ninety-nine hundredths of the human species will not touch. **1820** Shelley *Œd. Tyr.* i. 24 Ye who grub With filthy snouts my red potatoes up. **1832** *Veg. Subst. Food* 151 Potatoes..yield a spirit of a very pure quality... They are.. cheaper..than barley from which to extract alcohol. **1869** Ruskin *Q. of Air* §76 In the potato, we have the scarcely innocent underground stem of one of a tribe set aside for evil. **1903** Joyce *Soc. Hist. Anc. Irel.* II. 497 In my grandfather's house..a big dish of laughing potatoes was always laid aside for wandering beggars.

c. ***potatoes and point***: see point *sb.*¹ C. 7.

1825 J. Neal *Bro. Jonathan* I. 75 The potatoes and point of an Irish peasant. **1831, 1897** [see point *sb.*¹ C. 7].

d. Anglo-Irish **pratie**, etc.

[*Pratie* is characteristic Anglo-Irish; the Irish name is, in Munster, *práta*, in Meath, *préata*, pl. *prat-, preataidhe*.] In quot. 1966 the use is *fig.*]

γ. **1781** W. Dyott *Diary* 8 Sept. (1907) I. 5 In short, I think them [*sc.* the Irish recruits] calculated merely to eat potatoes, or 'pratys', as they call them. **1826** 'N. Nondescript' *The* — 15 Apr. 56 'I was just thinking,' said he in a whimpering tone, 'what we poor Irish would do, if we hadn't paraties.' **1829** J. Wilson *Noct. Ambr.* (1855) II. 288

Englishmen feeding on roast-beef..or Irishmen on 'wetuns' and 'praes'. **1830** *Constellation* II. 1/1 She took my advice, and doubling herself up in the blanket, was asleep before your Honour'd say praties. **1833** MARRYAT *P. Simple* xii, You must do something to get your own dinner; there's not praties enow for the whole of ye. **1869** M. ARNOLD *Cult. & An.* (1882) 74 When all the praties were black in Ireland, why didn't the priests say the hocus-pocus over them? **1884** CUDWORTH *Yorksh. Dial. Sketches* 121 (E.D.D.) Peeling sum porates. **1927** in C. Sandburg *Amer. Songbag* 463 O, I met her in the mornin' And I'll have yez all to know That I met her in the garden Where the praties grow. **1932–53** *Whistle-Binkie* (Scot. Songs) Ser. I. 21 When evening sets in Paddy puts on the pot, To boil the dear praties and serve them up hot. **1949** C. GRAVES *Ireland Revisited* vii. 82 Nobody uses the word 'begorrah,' and a potato is a 'spud' not a 'praty'. **1966** *Listener* 12 May 687/1 A sentimental domestic melodrama—what Irish audiences..call a 'pratie', or potato. **1972** *Islander* (Victoria, B.C.) 12 Mar. 8/1 We call them 'spuds'. The Irish affectionately call them 'praties' and they sometimes call mashed potatoes 'poundies'. **1973** *Times* 29 Aug. 7/6 Do you fancy some German sausage in the garden where the praties grow?

3. With distinctive words. **a.** ***Carolina, Spanish, sweet potato*** = sense 1. **b.** ***Chilian p., Irish p.*** (now U.S.), ***white p.*** (U.S.) = sense 2. **c.** ***Virginia (-an) potato***, (*a*) = sense 2; (*b*) = sense 1.

a. **1599** [see 2]. **1629** PARKINSON *Paradisus* 517 *Battatas Hispanorum*, Spanish Potatoes. *Ibid.* 518 The Spanish Potato's are roasted vnder the embers..put into sacke with a little sugar, or without, and is delicate to be eaten. **1634** J. TAYLOR (Water P.) *Gt. Eater Kent* 12 The Spanish potato he holds as a bable. **1707** SLOANE *Jamaica* I. Pref., The Spanish Patata, eaten commonly in Jamaica, is a true Convolvulus. **1775** ROMANS *Florida* 84 They cultivate..the esculent Convolvulus, (*vulgo*) sweet potatoes. **1856** EMERSON *Eng. Traits, Voy. Eng.* Wks. (Bohn) II. 12 Shaped like a Carolina potato. **1884** *Century Mag.* Jan. 442/1 The sweet potato..is yet known in the market as the 'Carolina'.

b. **1664** J. FORSTER *Eng. Happiness Incr.* 2 The fourth sort ..are the Irish Potatoes, being little different from those of Virginia, save only in the Colour of the Flower and time of flowering. **1693** [see 2b]. **1819** WARDEN *United States* II. 213 Of esculent plants there are, in the Eastern parts, the sweet potatoe, red and white; the common, or Irish potatoe, which is in general use. **1870** YEATS *Nat. Hist. Comm.* 4 The Chilian potato has provided food for many millions of people. **1901** *Boston Morn. Jrnl.* 8/1 Irish potatoes..are called Irish from the Irish, who came in 1719, settled Londonderry, N.H., and were required to pay quit rent to the amount of a peck of potatoes... The white potato, called Irish,..did not become general until after 1800.

c. (*a*) **1597** GERARDE *Herbal* [see 2a]. **1629** PARKINSON *Paradisus* 517 (No.) 3 *Papas seu Battatas Virginianorum*, Virginia Potatoes. *Ibid.* 518 The Virginia Potato's being dressed after all these waies..maketh almost as delicate meate as the former. **1715** J. PETIVER in *Phil. Trans.* XXIX. 272 Virginia Potatoes... We are obliged to..Caspar Bauhine for a most accurate Figure..of this..Root... It was first cultivated in Ireland, and now about London, and in many Counties of Great Britain.

(*b*) **1731** CATESBY *Nat. Hist. Carolina* (1754) II. 60 The Virginian Potato. Convolvulus radice tuberosa esculenta. **1736** MORTIMER in *Phil. Trans.* XXXIX. 258 The Virginian Potato. The Roots of these Plants are the principal Subsistance of the greater Part of Africa, and the southern Parts of Asia, as well as most of the People, both black and white, in the Colonies in America.

4. Applied, with defining word, to various plants having tubers or tuberous roots, mostly edible.

Canada potato, potato of Canada, Jerusalem Artichoke, *Helianthus tuberosus*; **Cree potato** (*U.S.*), Indian or Prairie Turnip, *Psoralea esculenta*, N.O. *Leguminosæ*; **hog's potato**, the Death's Quamash of California, *Zygadenus venenosus*, N.O. *Melanthaceæ* (Miller *Plant-names*); **Indian potato**, (*a*) the genus *Dioscorea* or yams; (*b*) the American ground-nut, *Apios tuberosa*; (*c*) the American genus *Calochortus*, N.O. *Liliaceæ*; **Jerusalem potato** (*dial.*), the same as *Jerusalem Artichoke*; **native potato**, of N.S. Wales, *Marsdenia viridiflora* (Miller *Plant-names*); of Tasmania, an orchid, *Gastrodia sesamoides*; **seaside potato**, *Ipomæa biloba* (*Pes-capræ*), N.O. *Convolvulaceæ*, a tropical creeping shore-plant of both hemispheres; **Telinga potato**, *Amorphophallus campanulatus*, N.O. *Araceæ*, cultivated in India for its esculent tubers; **wild potato**, (*a*) *Convolvulus panduratus*; (*b*) of Jamaica, *Ipomæa fastigiata*.

1629 PARKINSON *Paradisus* 517 (No.) 4 *Battatas de Canada*, Potatoes of *Canada, or Artichokes of Ierusalem. **1678** PHILLIPS (ed. 4), *Jerusalem Artichokes*, a Plant so called, but more truly Battatas [**1706** (ed. Kersey), Potatoes] of Canada, because they came from Canada. **1866** *Treas. Bot.*, Potato, Canada, *Helianthus tuberosus*. **1884** MILLER *Plant-n.*, Potato, *Hog's, *Zygadenus venenosus*. **1760** J. LEE *Introd. Bot.* App. 323 Potatoe, *Indian, *Dioscorea*. **1834** ROSS *Van Diemen's Land Ann.* 131 [It] produces bulb-tubers growing one out of another, of the size, and nearly the form, of kidney potatoes... These roots are roasted and eaten by the aborigines; in taste they resemble beet-root, and are sometimes called in the colony *native potatoes. **1857** F. R. NIXON *Cruise of Beacon* 27 *Gastrodia sesamoides*, the native potato, so called by the colonists.

5. a. In various colloq. phrases, a type of what is insignificant or of little value; esp. in ***small potatoes*** (orig. *U.S.*), 'no great things', said also of persons; also in sing. and in phr. ***small potatoes and few in a*** (or ***the***) ***hill***. Also *attrib.* = petty, mean, insignificant. (to drop something) ***like a hot potato***: see HOT *a.* 12a.

1757 SMOLLETT *Reprisal* I. ii, I don't value Monsieur de Champignon a rotten potatoe. **1797** COLERIDGE *Lett.* I. 224 The London literati appear to me to be very much like little potatoes, that is no great things. **1823** BYRON *Juan* VII. iv, Who knew this life was not worth a potato. **1836** D. CROCKETT *Exploits & Adventures Texas* ii. 25 This is what I call small potatoes and few of a hill. **1839** *Boston* (Mass.) *Morning Post* 23 July 1/1 The Conservatives in Maine have held a convention and nominated F. O. J. Smith, for Governor. S.P. (small potatos). **1846** *New York Herald* 13 Dec. (Bartlett), Small potato politicians and pettifogging lawyers. **1855** HALIBURTON *Nat. & Hum. Nat.* I. 63 It's small potatoes for a man-of-war to be hunting poor game like us. **1864** SALA in *Daily Tel.* 20 July, Bananas and oranges are reckoned 'very small potatoes' indeed; you may have them for the asking. **1880** [see *ham-fatter* s.v. HAM *sb.*[1] 3]. **1885** *Harper's Mag.* Mar. 647/1 The Fourth Estate.. thinks no small potatoes of itself. **1886** *Galaxy* 1 Oct. 272 Insignificant people are 'small potatoes, and few in a hill'. **1914** 'BARTIMEUS' *Naval Occasions* xiii. 101 In the beginning he was an Assistant Clerk—which is a very small potato indeed. **1923** CONRAD *Rover* x. 160 Then indeed that corvette, the big factor of everyday life on that stretch of coast, would become very small potatoes indeed. **1926** M. J. ATKINSON in J. F. Dobie *Rainbow in Morning* (1965) 80 He's a mighty small potato in my estimation. He's mighty small potatoes and few in a hill. **1927** H. T. LOWE-PORTER tr. *Mann's Magic Mountain* II. vii. 787 If some first-class excitement doesn't come along every day, you pull a face as though you were saying: 'H'm, small potatoes *and* few in the hill!'. **1962** A. BUCHWALD *How much is that in Dollars?* 122 Mary Soo, by tradition but not contract, has the garbage concession of all United States Navy ships entering Hong Kong, which out here is no small potatoes. **1968** *Globe & Mail* (Toronto) 3 Feb. 7/6 When the conference gets around to 'other matters' on Wednesday, the current dispute over medicare should seem like small potatoes. **1973** H. NIELSEN *Severed Key* iv. 49 'Morry Sacks is going to tell the law we found a million dollars on the beach?' 'No! Morry is too small potatoes.' **1974** *Publishers Weekly* 26 Aug. 300/2 A milieu where the crime is petty and municipal corruption small potatoes. **1976** *Gramophone* July 153/3 Serenus is small potatoes by CBS or RCA standards but its albums are tastefully produced and carefully annotated.

b. Humorously applied to a person.

1815 BYRON *Let. to Moore* 8 Mar., How could you be such a potato? **1845** *Punch* VIII. 184/1 That fire-eating Milesian, that very hot potato, Mr. H. Grattan. **1868** BRIERLEY *Red Windows Hall* ii. 16 'You are Sam o' Ducky's'..'Th' same owd porrito', said Sam.

c. ***the potato***: the (very, real, or proper) thing, what is correct or excellent. Also, ***(the) clean potato***: a person or thing whose character or excellence is beyond reproach. Hence the phr. ***not (quite) the clean potato*** and vars., not completely sound or reliable; not (quite) the right or real thing. *slang.* Cf. CHEESE *sb.*[2]

1822 *Blackw. Mag.* XI. 370 The Bishop's first two volumes are not quite the potato. **1837** H. AINSWORTH *Rookwood* Pref. 31 Larry is quite 'the potato'. **1880** R. M. JEPHSON *Pink Wedding* xxiv, I am convinced he is a first-rate one—quite the clean potato, in fact. **1881** G. H. GIBSON in *Bulletin* (Sydney) 16 Mar. 8 You weren't quite the cleanly potato, Sam Holt. **1890** 'R. BOLDREWOOD' *Colonial Reformer* III. xxvii. 104 'Well,' said Mr. Cottonbush,..'it ain't quite the clean potato, of course [*sc.* to steal a neighbour's grass]; but if your sheep's dying at home, what can you do?' **1913** GALSWORTHY *Dark Flower* II. vii. 137 A suspicion he had always entertained, that Cramier was not by breeding 'quite the clean potato'. **1921** K. S. PRICHARD *Black Opal* xvi. 148, I ain't always been what you might call the clean potato. **1929** J. MASEFIELD *Hawbucks* 165 We'll shake hands, clean potato, and be good friends. **1931** M. FRANKLIN *Back to Bool Bool* 233 She was only the great-granddaughter of old Larry Healey of Little River, none so clean a potato, if rumour was correct. **1933** G. HEYER *Why shoot a Butler?* vi. 86 Not strictly the clean potato, is it?.. Guest in the man's house, you know. The Public School Spirit, and Playing for the Side, and all that wash. **1939** —— *No Wind of Blame* iv. 80 It isn't at all the clean potato. In fact, it's very dishonourable. **1941** BAKER *Dict. Austral. Slang* 56 *A clean potato*, a free or unconvicted person, one with unblemished character. **1962** T. RONAN *Deep of Sky* 42 Some of the grand old pioneers and land-takers of history were not quite the clean potato.

d. A large or conspicuous hole in a sock or stocking through which the flesh shows.

1885 *Eng. Ilustr. Mag.* June 616/1 The gladiators wore pasteboard helmets..and fleshings for legs and arms, with —what are vulgarly termed 'potatoes', that is, holes in the fleshings perceptible in many places. **1886** H. BAUMANN *Londinismen* 144/1 *Potatoes*, grosse Löcher in den Strümpfen. **1902** FARMER & HENLEY *Slang* V. 270/1 *Potato*, ..used esp. for a heel through an undarned sock or stocking. **1949** D. M. DAVIN *Roads from Home* III. iv. 241 It was a mystery the way that Paddy went through his stockings... A great big potato staring out over the heel. **1973** *Country Gentlemen's Estate Mag.* Mar. 156/1 Gumboots..will hole a 'potato' like a cannon-ball in the heels of a new pair of socks in an afternoon.

e. In pl. *U.S. slang.* Money. Occas. in more specific use, dollars ('pounds' in quot. 1939).

1931 D. RUNYON in *Collier's* 4 Nov. 8/2 'Listen, Sam,' I say, 'you have seven duckets, and we are only six, and here is a little doll who is stood up by her guy, and has no ducket, and no potatoes to buy one with, so what about taking her with us?' **1932** —— in *Collier's* 26 Mar. 7/4 Many citizens are figuring that maybe he suddenly discovers all his potatoes are counterfeit, because nobody can think of anything that will worry Sorrowful except money. **1933** *Sun* (Baltimore) 15 Sept. 1/2 Nobody gives fifteen thousand 'potatoes' to a party committee without wanting something. **1935** A. J. POLLOCK *Underworld Speaks* 90/2 *Potatoes*, money. **1939** WODEHOUSE *Uncle Fred in Springtime* i. 9 Was it conceivable..that any man, even to oblige a future brother-in-law, would cough up the colossal sum of two hundred potatoes? **1976** *National Observer* (U.S.) 8 May 14/2 Usually he [*sc.* a horse] runs with a price tag of about $3,500. With those kind of potatoes, it can be hard to get respect.

f. *Austral. slang.* Also in spelling *potater*. [Shortening of *potato peeler*, rhyming slang for SHEILA.] A girl, a woman.

1957 D. NILAND *Call me when Cross turns Over* ii. 69 Snow told him not to be a mug, the sheila had him in her sights because she thought he was a bit of all right. That would be the day, Locky retorted, when some bloody potater..had him stringing along with her. **1970** G. GREER *Female Eunuch* 266 Terms..often extended to the female herself. Who likes to be called..a *potato*? **1970** *Private Eye* 2 Jan. 12 He's been endeavouring to commit intimacy with your *potato*. **1971** *Ibid.* 2 July 16 As for this potato I must guide her footsteps back into the paths of righteousness.

6. *attrib.* and *Comb.* (almost all in sense 2); **a.** simple attrib., as ***potato-bing*** (BING *sb.*[1]), ***-bowl, -crop, -field, -fork, -garden, -graip, -ground, -harvest, -house, -land, -leaf, -merchant, -plant, -riddle, -sack, -shoot, -stem, -tuber***; in names of things made of or from potatoes, or of which the principal ingredient is the potato, as ***potato-brandy, -croquette, -flour, -fritter, -ivory, -pasty, -pudding, -soup, -starch, -sugar, -yeast***. **b.** objective and obj. gen., as ***potato-assorter, potato-chipper, -cutter, -digger, -digging, -gatherer, -grower, -lifter, -masher, -peeler, -peeling, -picker, -picking, -planter, -planting, -raiser, -roaster, -separator, -smasher, -washer*** (applied to persons and to tools).

1875 KNIGHT *Dict. Mech.*, **Potato-assorter*, a rolling screen with open meshes to allow small potatoes to be sorted from the larger merchantable ones. **1786** BURNS *Brigs of Ayr* 27 *Potatoe-bings are snugged up frae skaith. **1892** EL. ROWE *Chip-carving* (1895) 26 Numerous objects..which may thus be decorated at a small cost,..book-covers, blotters, bread-platters, *potato-bowls,..&c. **1840** HOOD *Up Rhine* 197 Mr. Kraus..found their *potato-brandy so poisonous. **1664** J. FORSTER *Eng. Happiness Incr.* 9 How to make *Potato Cheescakes. **1895** *Montgomery Ward Catal.* 436/1 *Potato Chipper, can be used as a..chopper for potatoes. **1951** *Catal. of Exhibits, South Bank Exhib., Festival of Britain* 52/1 Potato chipper; Thos. A. Nutbrown Ltd., Walker Street, Blackpool, Lancs. **1977** *Western Mail* (Cardiff) 5 Mar. 12/2 (Advt.), Hobart Potato Chipper, 40lb. per minute. Reconditioned. **1799** J. ROBERTSON *Agric. Perth* 249 When the *potatoe-crop is removed. *Note*, Potato-crop is an absurd expression, but we must use it for want of one which is more proper. **1845** *Florist's Jrnl.* 245 The disease unfortunately so very general in the potato crop. **1876** M. N. HENDERSON *Pract. Cooking* 194 *Potato Croquettes. Add to four or five mashed potatoes..the beaten yolk of one egg. **1942** C. SPRY *Come into Garden, Cook* iv. 38 The best croquettes in the world, *Potato Croquettes.* **1845** *Quincy* (Illinois) *Whig* 18 Dec. 2/5 A new *potatoe digger was recently exhibited in operation at Salem, West Jersey. **1858** J. BROWN *Let.* 13 May (1912) 160 And is the delightfullest of potato-diggers already digging? **1945** *Hardin* (Montana) *Tribune-Herald* 15 Feb. 2/4, I will sell at public auction..1 potato digger. *a* **1887** JEFFERIES in Besant *Eulogy* v. (1888) 136 Let him pass to his *potato-digging. **1822** J. WILSON *Scot. Life, Moss-side* 36 The *potatoe-field beyond the brae. **1830** *Encycl. Brit.* (ed. 7) II. 355/2 A machine for grinding *Potato-flour. **1839** *Mag. Dom. Econ.* IV. 88 The bread made of potato flour..is nutritious, wholesome, and delicate. **1906** U. SINCLAIR *Jungle* xi. 139 Potato-flour is the waste of potato after the starch and alcohol have been extracted; it has no more food value than so much wood. **1911** *Daily Colonist* (Victoria, B.C.) 4 Apr. 3/1 (Advt.), Potato Flour, Health Brand, packet 20c. **1845** E. ACTON *Mod. Cookery* xix. 417 *Potato fritters. (Entremets.) See directions for potato puddings. The same mixture dropped in fritters into boiling butter, and fried until firm on both sides will be found very good. **1966** P. V. PRICE *France* 308 Small sweetened potato fritters. **1778** PENNANT *Tour Wales* (1883) I. 22 Every Cottager has his *potatoe garden..a conveniency unknown fifty years ago. **1844** H. STEPHENS *Bk. Farm* III. 1125 There are two modes of lifting potatoes, namely, with the plough, and with the *potato-graip. **1753** W. STEWART in *Scots Mag.* Mar. 134/1 The pannel was walking from his *potatoe-ground. **1837** *Flemish Husb.* 47 in *Libr. Usef. Knowl., Husb.* III, A practice of sowing hemp in a border all round a garden or potato-ground. **1808** E. WEETON *Let.* 1 Apr. (1969) I. 78 An uncommonly *plentiful potatoe harvest. **1979** *Country Life* 2 May 1375 Mr Hurd works on the early potato harvest. **1791** W. BARTRAM *Trav. N. & S. Carolina* 192 The lowest or ground part is a *potatoe house. **1861** C. M. YONGE *Stokesley Secret* vi. 89 There was a bonfire by the potato-house. **1921** *Proc. 3rd National Country Life Conf. 1920* (U.S.) 155 Potato houses ..are isolated and located with special reference to the good of the products involved. **1970** S. TRUEMAN *Intimate Hist. New Brunswick* iii. 56 The 'potato houses' looking like dwellings that have sunk so deep into the ground that they now consist mainly of high-peaked roofs. **1883** *Cassell's Fam. Mag.* Aug. 574/2 *Potato-ivory..of creamy whiteness ..is now made from good potatoes washed in dilute sulphuric acid, then boiled in the same solution until they become solid and dense. **1780** A. YOUNG *Tour in Ireland* I. 344 Plough the *potatoe land once or twice for barley. **1855** *Trans. Amer. Inst. City of N.Y. 1854* 168 Salt..will kill grubs, and may be used to advantage on potato land. **1965** K. H. CONNELL in Glass & Eversley *Population in Hist.* xvii. 428 The practice of letting farms by auction in a country [*sc.* Ireland] where land was almost the only resource encouraged tenants to outbid one another in the tribute they offered to acquire the right to potato-land. **1858** SIMMONDS *Dict. Trade*, **Potato-lifter*, a prong; also a kind of digging machine. **1664** J. FORSTER *Eng. Happiness Incr.* 6 You must take as much Wheat or Barley Flower as your half Bushel of *Potato Meal weighs. **1858** SIMMONDS *Dict. Trade*, **Potato-pasty*, a pasty made of potatoes and flour. **1895** *Montgomery Ward Catal.* 436/1 The Peerless *Potato Peeler. This is an entirely new and novel article for peeling and slicing potatoes. **1951** *Good Housek. Home Encycl.* 610/1 Potatoes should be peeled..with either a special potato peeler or a sharp, short-bladed knife. **1961** *Which?* Mar. 61 (*heading*) Potato peelers. **1896** *Daily News* 7 Apr. 3/7 Yesterday's exhibition was enlivened by competitions in *potato-peeling, boot-blacking, cookery, and recitation. **1961** *Which?* 61/1 In this report, CA discusses five potato peeling devices on the market when our tests began. **1975** L. GILLEN *Return to Deepwater* x. 178 She impatiently brushed them [*sc.* tears] away with the back of one hand before resuming her potato-peeling. **1891** *Pall Mall G.* 29 Oct. 6/3 In the Long Sutton District..the *potato-pickers have struck work for an increase of pay. **1772** PANTON in *Phil. Trans.* LXIII. 180 The *potatoe plant has not been cultivated in any great quantities here [Anglesey] until of late years. **1857** GRAY *First Less. Bot.* (1866) 43 The subterranean growth of a Potato-plant. **1885** A. EDWARDES *Girton Girl* III. xiii. 221 The Seigneur..taking part in his *potato-planting and his vraic harvest. **1951** R. FIRTH *Elem. Social Organiz.* iv. 142 To revert to the Irish peasantry..—there is a form of non-monetary co-operation..in tasks such as..potato-planting. **1766** *Museum Rust.* VI. 396 Mashed with a trencher; as for a *potatoe pudding. **1844** H. STEPHENS *Bk. Farm* III. 1125 The *potato-riddle is made of wire. **1858** SIMMONDS *Dict. Trade*, **Potato-roaster*, a tin machine carried about by an itinerant vender, who sells hot baked potatoes. **1859** G. A. SALA *Twice round Clock* 40 There are tall *potato-sacks, propped up in dark corners. **1939** F. THOMPSON *Lark Rise* i. 4 A superannuated potato-sack thrown down by way of hearthrug. **1979** *Guardian* 28 Feb. 13/3 Ladies..manage to knit passable potato sacks to cover their nether limbs. **1875** KNIGHT *Dict. Mech.*, **Potato-separator*, an implement used for the purpose of sorting the tubers to size. **1844** H. STEPHENS *Bk. Farm* II. 690 The *potato-shoots..are fed by the matter lodged in the tuber from which the shoots proceed. **1858** SIMMONDS *Dict. Trade*, **Potato-smasher*, a cook's wooden utensil for mashing potatoes for the table. **1845** E. ACTON *Mod. Cookery* i. 20 *Potato soup. Mash to a smooth paste three pounds of good mealy potatoes..; mix with them..two quarts of boiling broth,..add pepper and salt. **1861** MRS. BEETON *Bk. Househ. Managem.* 76 *Potato soup*... When the potatoes are boiled, mash them smoothly..and gradually put them to the boiling stock [etc.]. **1906** *Macm. Mag.* July 675 Potato-soup,..pea-soup, or even chestnut-soup for the fruitarian. **1960** *Good Housek. Cookery Bk.* (rev. ed.) 72/2 *Potato soup*... Peel and slice the potatoes and chop the onion and celery. **1831** *Encycl. Brit.* (ed. 7) IV. 300/1 We have been assured, that..Indian arrowroot is nothing else than *potato starch mixed with a little gum tragacanth. **1854** *Pereira's Polarized Light* (ed. 2) 154 In all the starches which I have yet examined, viz., *tous les mois*, potato-starch, West Indian arrow-root, sago-meal [etc.]. **1844** H. STEPHENS *Bk. Farm* III. 1127 The reason why the *potato-stems are thus removed. **1882** OGILVIE (Annandale), **Potato-sugar*. **1844** H. STEPHENS *Bk. Farm* III. 780 The Heart and Dart moth ..also attack the *potato-tuber. **1800** *Naval Chron.* III. 364 Method of making *potatoe yeast.

7. Special combinations: **potato-apple**, the small fruit or berry of the potato-plant; **potato-ball**, (*a*) = *potato-apple* (Funk 1895); (*b*) pl., in *Cookery*, mashed potatoes made into balls with milk and butter, and fried; also in *sing.* and *attrib.*; **potato-bean**: see quot.; **potato-beetle**[1], a wooden beetle or pestle for mashing potatoes; **potato-beetle**[2], (*a*) the Colorado beetle, *Leptinotarsa decemlineata*, a brown beetle with black spots and stripes which attacks the leaves of the potato and related plants; (*b*) the Three-lined Leaf Beetle, *Lema trilineata*, or its larva (*Funk's Stand. Dict.* 1895); **potato blight** = *potato disease*; **potato-bogle** *Sc.*, a scarecrow in a potato-field; **potato-box**, *slang*, the mouth: cf. *potato-jaw*, *-trap*; **potato bread**, a bread made partly of the prepared flour of potatoes; **potato-bug** (*a*) = *potato-fly*; (*b*) = *potato-beetle*[2]; **potato-cake**, a small cake made of potatoes and flour; **potato chip**, (*a*) = CHIP *sb.*[1] 2 b; (*b*) *U.S.* = *potato crisp* (see also quot. 1975); also (usu. with hyphen) *attrib.*; **potato clay**, a variety of clay used by the Hopi Indians in making pigments; **potato creeper** = *potato vine* (*b*); **potato crisp** (see CRISP *sb.* 7); **potato curl**, a disease of potatoes in which the leaves and young stems curl and wither, caused by a fungus, *Verticillium atroalbum*: see CURL *sb.* 4; **potato disease**, a very destructive disease of potatoes, caused by a parasitic fungus, *Phytophthora infestans*, which attacks the leaves, stems, and tubers; also called *potato blight*, *murrain*, *rot*; **potato dumpling**, a dumpling whose ingredients include sieved cooked potatoes; **potato-eater**, a derogatory nickname usu. applied to an Irishman (see also quot. 1871); **potato-eel**, a minute threadworm found in potatoes (*Cent. Dict.* 1890); **potato-eye**, a bud of the potato-tuber: see EYE *sb.*[1] 10 a; **potato failure** = *potato famine*; **potato famine**, a dearth of potatoes caused by crop failure; *spec.* (usu. with capital initials) that which occurred in Ireland in 1846–7; **potato fern**, an Australian fern (*Marattia fraxinea*), also called HORSESHOE fern, a large part of which is edible; †**potato finger**, *fig.*, with reference to the supposed aphrodisiac quality of the sweet potato; **potato flake** (usu. in *pl.*), (see quot. 1955); **potato-fly**, one of the various blister beetles of the genus *Epicauta*, which are injurious to potato-plants in U.S. and Canada (Mayne 1858); **potato fungus**: see *potato disease*; **potato grant**: see quot.; **potato-headed** *a.*, thick-headed, dull, stupid; **potato hook**, an implement with bent tines for digging up potatoes (Knight *Dict. Mech.* 1875); **potato-jaw**, *slang*, the mouth; **potato latke** [LATKE], a pancake made with grated potato; **potato-loaf**, a loaf of *potato-bread*; **potato masher**, a device consisting of a set of wires or a perforated flat plate (formerly, a solid wooden cylinder) attached to a handle, for mashing potatoes; also *transf.*, (*a*) in full ***potato-masher grenade***, a type of hand grenade whose shape resembles that of a potato masher; (*b*) (see quot. 1945); **potato-mill**, a mill for grinding potatoes to flour; **potato moth** *Austral.* = *potato tuber moth*; **potato mould**, **potato murrain** = *potato disease*; **potato-mouth** *v. trans.*, to mutter; also **potato-mouthed** *a.* = MEALY-MOUTHED *a.*; **potato-nose**, a nose like a potato, a bottle-nose; **potato oat**, a variety of the oat; **potato oil**, an amyl alcohol derived from potato spirit; **potato onion**, a variety of the common onion, *Allium cepa*, in which new bulbs are produced at the base; **potato pancake**, a pancake in which sieved mashed potato is the basic ingredient; also, = *potato latke*; **potato patch**, a plot of ground on which potatoes are grown; **potato peelings**, strips of the peeled skin of potatoes; **potato pen**, a compartment on a ship's deck for keeping vegetables fresh during a voyage (*Cent. Dict.* 1890); **potato pie**, (*a*) a pie made with potatoes, containing meat, onions, etc.; (*b*) = *potato pit*; **potato pit**, a shallow pit, usually covered with a mound of straw and earth, in which potatoes are stored in winter; **potato puff**, a kind of potato crisp in the form of a puff (see PUFF *sb.* 5); **potato race**, a race or competitive game decided by the skill and speed with which potatoes are picked up, passed on, etc.; **potato rot** = *potato disease*; **potato salad**, pieces of cold cooked potato mixed with salad dressing and other ingredients; **potato scab**, a brown patch on the skin of the potato, caused by a fungus, or by some irritant substance in the soil (Ogilvie 1882); **potato scone**, a scone made with sieved cooked potatoes; **potato-scoop**, (*a*) a tool for cutting pieces of potatoes with 'eyes', suitable for planting; (*b*) a shovel for lifting potatoes, grated to allow loose earth to fall through (Knight *Dict. Mech.* 1875); **potato set** = SET *sb.* 23 b; **potato-shop**, a shop where fried or chip potatoes are sold; **potato-sick** *a.*, of land, exhausted by successive crops of potatoes; **potato-spirit**, alcohol distilled from potatoes; also called *potato brandy* or *whisky*; **potato-spraying**, the spraying of potato plants with some preventive against disease or insects; **potato-stalk weevil**, **potato weevil**: see quot.; **potato stick**, a small crisp potato chip; **potato-stone**: see quot. 1859; **potato straw**, a very thin stick of potato, fried until crisp; **potato-trap**, *slang*, the mouth; **potato-tree**, a small tree, *Solanum crispum*; **potato tuber moth**, the moth whose larva is the potato tuber-worm; **potato tuberworm** *U.S.*, the pinkish-white caterpillar of the moth *Gnorimoschema operculella*; **potato-vine**, (*a*) a potato plant, *Solanum tuberosum*; (*b*) one of several South or Central American climbing plants, esp. *Solanum jasminoides* or *S. wendlandii*, bearing blue or white flowers; **potato-woman**, a woman employed in gathering potatoes in the field; **potato worm** (*U.S.*), = *potato tuberworm*.

1846 J. BAXTER *Libr. Pract. Agric.* (ed. 4) II. p. v, We are ourselves curious in the fabrication of a salad,..but have never yet screwed up our courage to plunge a green *potato-apple into the bowl. **1878** tr. *von Ziemssen's Cycl. Med.* XVII. 690 A girl of fourteen died from eating green potato-apples. **1823** T. B. HAZARD *Diary* 16 May (1930) 596/1 Planted a *Potatoe Ball. **1824** M. RANDOLPH *Virginia House-Wife* 120 Potato Balls. Mix mashed potatoes with the yelk of an egg, roll them into balls, [etc.]. **1845** E. ACTON *Mod. Cooking* (ed. 2) xv. 304 English potato balls. **1846** *Jewish Manual, or Pract. Information Jewish & Mod. Cookery* v. 91 Potatoe balls are mashed potatoes formed into balls glazed with the yolk of egg, and browned with a salamander. **1850** *Rep. Comm. Patents: Agric. 1849* (U.S.) 198 In 1847, he planted a single potato-ball or apple; only one seed grew. **1877** *Rep. Vermont Board Agric.* IV. 33 Nature can make potato balls, but she couldn't make the Early Rose. **1912** M. B. BROWN *Just Use-it-Up* vi. 140 Potato balls. **1948** *Good Housek. Cookery Bk.* II. 289 Scoop out the potato balls with a Parisian potato cutter. **1963** R. CARRIER *Great Dishes of World* 213/2 Roll potato balls in flour and then in beaten egg. **1969** E. H. PINTO *Treen* 141 The hardwood handle with, at each end, a steel bowl with a hole in the base..is a potato ball maker, probably 18th-century. **1805** R. W. DICKSON *Pract. Agric.* II. 628 The dark brown-coloured excrescence that grows to the size of a large horse-bean on the haulm or straw of the potatoe..termed in some places the *potatoe bean. **1821** GALT *Ayrsh. Legatees* Let. xxvi. (1850) 261 A *potatoe-beetle is not to be had within the four walls of London. **1866** *Pract. Entomologist* I. 105/2 One day last week a gentleman left at our office a stalk from a potato hill, which was literally covered with the larva of the new potato beetle. **1868** *Amer. Entomologist* I. 44/1 It might perhaps be desirable..to get people to call it [*sc.* the Colorado potato-bug] a 'potato-beetle'. **1876** *Times* 29 Aug. 6/5 The fact of its surviving in a letter posted at Listowel, Ontario, and delivered at Stranraer, Wigtonshire, N.B., shows that the potato beetle possesses great powers of endurance. **1906** J. W. FOLSOM *Entomol.* xii. 382 From Colorado the well-known potato beetle..has worked eastward since 1840. **1931** Z. P. METCALF *Text-bk. Econ. Zool.* viii. 259 The Colorado potato beetle..often completely destroys whole fields of unsprayed potatoes. **1972** L. E. CHADWICK tr. *Linsenmaier's Insects of World* 165/2 The Colorado potato beetle..was imported accidentally into Europe from America. **1879** H. GEORGE *Progr. & Pov.* II. ii. (1881) 110 When the *potato blight came, they died by thousands. **1818** SCOTT *Rob Roy* xxxi, To be hung up between heaven and earth, like an auld *potato-bogle. **1886** STEVENSON *Kidnapped* xxvi, As if ye had stolen the coat from a potato-bogle. **1742** W. ELLIS *Mod. Husbandman* Sept. xxv. 119 **Potatoe Bread.* This Root has often been employed, like the Turnep, towards making Loaves of Bread in the scarce Times of Corn. **1766** *Museum Rust.* VI. 396 He told me, it was potatoe bread. **1831** *Encycl. Brit.* (ed. 7) IV. 299/2 Potato bread. **1915** *Chambers's Jrnl.* Oct. 661/2 There is a rather large group of words that have come at us with a rush, and cannot be classified,..that fine phrase of Mr. Lloyd George's, 'the potato-bread spirit'. *c* **1950** *Mrs. Beeton's Bk. Househ. Managem.* xxx. 695 *Potato bread.*—The adhesive tendency of the flour of the potato prevents it being baked or kneaded without being mixed with wheaten flour or meal. **1799** E. DRINKER *Jrnl.* 2 Sept. (1889) 347 They call them [*sc.* a species of Cantharides] here ..the *Potato-Bug, being numerous on the potato tops. **1838** *Hesperian* (Columbus, Ohio) I. 42/1 This company, formed for the praiseworthy purpose of encouraging the growth of potatoe-bugs, and manufacturing potato-bug oil. **1864** *Trans. N.Y. State Agric. Soc. 1863* 798 Some have been discouraged from planting potatoes, the ravages of this potato-bug have been so great. **1865** *Pract. Entomologist* I. 3/1 The new Potato Bug is not what naturalists call a Bug, but a true Beetle. **1868** *Rep. U.S. Commiss. Agric.* 10 The ravages..of the potato-bug. **1907** L. H. BAILEY *Cycl. Amer. Agric.* II. 524/1 The old-fashioned potato bug or blister-beetle..is combated in the same way as the Colorado potato-beetle. It is now rarely seen. **1908** *Springfield* (Mass.) *Republ.* 2 Sept. 14/6 Potato bugs on the rails..stalled eight trolly cars. **1949** *N.Y. Times Bk. Rev.* 5 June 14/2 It was settled that I should receive 1 cent per hundred for picking potato bugs. **1979** R. THOMAS *Eighth Dwarf* xxi. 210 The U.S. Constabulary..were swarming over the Opel plant.. like so many potato bugs. **1747** H. GLASSE *Art of Cookery* ix. 98 *Potatoe-Cakes. Take Potatoes boil them..mix them with Yolks of Eggs [etc.]. **1824** E. WEETON *Jrnl.* (1969) I. 33 Often I have..been obliged to live on potatoes and potatoe cakes for weeks. **1848** MRS. GASKELL *Mary Barton* II. xviii. 261 The potatoe-cakes she had made for her son's tea. **1884** *Chesh. Gloss.*, *Potato cake*,..a tea cake made of mashed potatoes and flour in equal parts. **1893** COUCH *Delect. Duchy* 26 Drinking cider and eating potato-cake. **1878** *Amer. Home Cook Bk.* 67 Put around *potato chips prepared as follows. **1886** [see CHIP *sb.*[1] 2 b]. **1934** WEBSTER, *Potato chips*, thin slices of raw potato fried crisp in deep fat. **1955** *Sci. News Let.* 5 Mar. 153/3 Scientists at the Eastern Laboratory are also responsible for the potato-chip bar developed primarily as a 'high-calorie, high-density military ration with taste appeal'. The potato-chip bar takes up only one twentieth the space needed for an equivalent amount of ordinary potato chips. **1972** C. WESTON *Poor, Poor Ophelia* (1973) vi. 29 Two barefoot hippies were sharing a bag of potato chips. **1975** *N.Y. Times* 30 Nov. III. 1/2 The F.D.A. gave Procter & Gamble permission to go ahead with the use of the words 'potato chips' on its product... Its potatoes are dehydrated, then turned into a mush and pressed and fried. *Ibid.* 9 Their development went a long way toward solving a basic potato-chip problem... The natural chips are easily broken. **1898** *Internat. Folk-Lore Congr. World's Columbian Exposition 1893* I. 264 The corn having boiled about three-quarters of an hour, the pot is taken from the fire and its content poured upon the sieve, through which the purple-stained boiling water is strained upon the sumac berries. Some of the talc-like substance called *potato-clay is then produced, and the operator puts a piece about the size of a walnut in his mouth, chewing it a little to soften it. **1925** H. F. MACMILLAN *Trop. Gardening & Planting* (ed. 3) 129 (*caption*) *Solanum wendlandii.* Giant *Potato-creeper. **1928** K. GOUGH *Garden Bk. for Malaya* xii. 205 Several attractive flowering creepers, sometimes called 'Potato Creepers' belong to this large genus. **1929**, etc. *Potato crisp [see CRISP *sb.* 7]. **1940** GRAVES & HODGE *Long Week-End* xiv. 231 Potato crisps were a popular new food. **1970** *New Yorker* 26 Sept. 125/1 His mum..leaves him a florin..for some ginger pop and potato crisps. **1973** J. THOMSON *Death Cap* v. 72 A stiff little breeze blew the empty potato crisp packets across the paving stones. **1976** W. TREVOR *Children of Dynmouth* v. 111 Having eaten two packets of bacon-flavoured potato crisps, he had purchased another tube of Rowntree's Fruit Gums. **1887** *Nicholson's Dict. Gard.* III. 207/2 The means employed to limit the spread of Potato Rot..are equally applicable against *Potato Curl. **1845** CLOUGH *Let.* in *Poems & Pr. Rem.* (1869) I. 104 *Potato-disease, and abolition of corn-laws. **1870** LOWELL *Study Wind.* (1886) 153 He is equally at home with the potato-disease. **1912** M. B. BROWN *Just Use-it-Up* vi. 139 *Potato dumpling. This is a very well-known dish in North Germany. **1948** *Good Housek. Cookery Bk.* II. 284 *Potato dumplings* (to serve with Meat or Vegetable Casserole). **1972** *Sat. Rev.* (U.S.) 25 Mar. 52/1 Roast-goose with potato dumplings. **1974** 'D. CRAIG' *Dead Liberty* xvii. 100 Dravier asked for roast pork and potato dumplings. **1823** W. COBBETT in *Weekly Reg.* 9 Aug. 356 Never, in this country, will the people be base enough to lie down and expire from starvation under the operation of the *extreme unction*! Nothing but a **potatoe-eater* will ever do that. **1871** J. MACKENZIE *Ten Years North of Orange River* i. 16, I have heard 'potato-eater' employed by them [*sc.* Dutch farmers] as a contemptuous term for an Englishman! **1978** *Maledicta* II. 168 *Potato-eater*, anyone from Ireland, or of Irish descent, after the Irish dietary staple. **1766** *Complete Farmer* s.v. *Potatoe*, The *potatoe-eyes cut as before directed, are placed upon this dung,..and this trench is filled up with the mould. **1845** E. S. CAYLEY *Lett. to Ld. John Russell* (1846) i. 9 The deficiency caused by the *potato failure will be in some measure compensated by the unusually large crops of oats, barley, and beans. **1846** *Times* 7 Feb. 5/1 The extreme variety in the extent of the potato failure, and the..insulated subdivisions of land in which it prevails, lead us to..doubt whether any adjustment of public works can be made to meet the need wherever it may occur. **1846** *Illustr. London News* 12 Sept. 170/3 The hon. and learned gentlemen adverted in the first place to the potato failure. **1978** R. MITCHISON *Life in Scotland* vi. 112

If we compare the state of crofting families—sustained, in squalid poverty, through the potato failure of 1846 by their landowners—with the hardships of the..urban poor..in the early 1840's [etc.]. **1875** J. O'Rourke *Hist. Great Irish Famine* vii. 196 To have met the *Potato Famine with anything like complete success, would have been a Herculean task for any government. **1881** J. A. Froude *English in Ireland* (new ed.) III. p. xiii, The potato famine, and responsibility of England. **1970** R. Lowell *Notebk.* 106 We're burnt, black chips knocked from the blackest stock: Potato-famine Irish-Puritan, and Puritan—gold made them smile like pigs once. **1974** P. Lovesey *Invitation to Dynamite Party* ii. 27 He was an Irishman whose family emigrated at the time of the potato famine. **1881** F. M. Bailey *Fern World Austr.* 24 *Potatoe Fern. **1606** Shaks. *Tr. & Cr.* v. ii. 56 How the diuell Luxury with his fat rumpe and *potato finger, tickles these together. **1955** *Sci. News Let.* 5 Feb. 89/3 To potato chips, French fries and home fries can now be added '*potato flakes', a new kind of dehydrated mashed potato... The flakes are made by drying cooked mashed potatoes on the rolls of a steam-heated double-drum drier. **1961** *Coast to Coast 1959–60* 165 A whole family of people.. had spread a rug beside the path and were drinking coloured drinks from bottles and eating potato-flakes from bags. **1806** in R. B. Thomas *Farmer's Almanack for 1807*, The *potatoe fly, or bug, appears about the first of July. **1832** W. D. Williamson *Hist. State Maine* I. 172 Potato Fly (looks like a Spanish Fly). **1854** E. Emmons *Agric. N.Y.* V. 96 *Cantharidæ*...are at times abundant upon potato vines, whence they have acquired the name of potato fly. **1857** Henfrey *Bot* §637 The common mould of paste,..the green mould of cheese... The *Potato-fungus. **1860** Bartlett *Dict. Amer.* (ed. 3), **Potato Grant*, a patch of land for growing vegetables formerly granted by the owner to each of his slaves (West Indies). **1832** G. C. Lewis *Lett.* (1870) 22 The *potato-headed jury. **1856** *Trans. Mich. Agric. Soc.* VII. 53 D. O. & W. S. Penfield..[exhibited] six Partridge's *potatoe hooks. **1874** *Ann. Rep. Vermont Board Agric.* II. 551 Then with axes, potato hooks, and bog hoes, the turf was all peeled off. **1791** Mme. D'Arblay *Diary* 4 June, 'Hold you your *potato-jaw, my dear', cried the Duke [of Clarence], patting her [Mrs. Schwellenberg]. **1927, 1974** *Potato latke [see latke]. **1831** *Encycl. Brit.* (ed. 7) IV. 302/2 The same price is taken for a *potato loaf. **1855** *Chicago Times* 16 Jan. 4/1 Butter moulds and stamps, ladles, rolling pins, *potato mashers..at Hollister's Bazaar. **1895** *Montgomery Ward Catal.* 439/3 Tinned wire Potato Masher, wood handle. **1906** *Daily Colonist* (Victoria, B.C.) 26 Jan. 4/6 (Advt.), Kitchen utilities..Potato Masher, wood. Potato Masher, metal. **1915** J. Webster *Dear Enemy* (1916) 238, I casually picked up the potato masher this morning while I was commenting upon last night's over-salty soup. **1919** H. G. Proctor *Iron Division* xii. 188 The German trench bombs were known..as 'potato mashers', because they are about the size of a can of sweet corn, fastened on the end of a short stick. **1925** Fraser & Gibbons *Soldier & Sailor Words* 229 *Potato-masher grenade*, the name given a species of German hand-grenade, resembling in form a domestic potato-masher. **1929** F. A. Pottle *Stretchers* (1930) x. 266 We saw bushels of potato-masher grenades, minenwerfer shells, and a machine gun belt of cartridges all of twenty feet long. **1929** W. T. Scanlon *God have Mercy on Us!* xxvi. 160 We had instructions on the use of every kind of grenade, including the German potato-mashers. **1945** L. Shelly *Jive Talk Dict.* 31/1 *Potato masher*, drum-stick. **1967** N. Freeling *Strike Out* 65 An old enamel saucepan,..and an oval metal affair with zigzag holes punched in it..he recognised it as a potato-masher. **1969** I. Kemp *Brit. G.I. in Vietnam* vi. 131 One..had begun to lob in grenades at us; these were of the 'potato masher' type, which sometimes failed to explode. **1969** E. H. Pinto *Treen* 141 Potato mashers were always turned from a single block,..like this one, they were often made *en suite* with a rolling pin..because in olden times, the pair was considered a lucky wedding gift. **1812** Sir J. Sinclair *Syst. Husb. Scot.* I. 339 It resembles a *potatoe-mill. **1891** *Agric. Gaz. New South Wales* II. 158 Mr. A. Bragg..and Mr. T. B. Linley.. have forwarded potatoes infested with the larvae or grubs of the *potato moth. **1926** R. J. Tillyard *Insects Austral. & N.Z.* xxviii. 426 The Potato Moth..is an introduced pest of potatoes, tomatoes and tobacco in both countries. **1965** *Austral. Encycl.* V. 88/2 The larvae of the potato-moth.. tunnel in the leaf tissue. **1930** J. Dos Passos *42nd Parallel* iv. 313 You know what we'd do if we had a man in the White House instead of a yellow-bellied *potatomouthed reformer. ..? We'd..clean this place up. **1937** *Daily Express* 17 Mar. 6/4 Lewis, square, heavy-browed, stentorian, also potato-mouthed some words, seemed bothered by having to stick to text. **1866** *Treas. Bot.* 1069/2 This *potato-murrain appears ..to be due to the presence of a fungus, *Botrytis* (or *Peronospora*) *infestans*. **1881** Miss Braddon *Asph.* I. 119 You wouldn't love a man with a *potato-nose or a pimply complexion, if he were morally the most perfect creature in the universe. **1808** W. Marshall *Review* I. 78 The '*potatoe oat',—a truly accidental variety,—being of later discovery. **1829** *Glover's Hist. Derby* I. 198 The American, or potatoe-oat, has been found to produce from seventy to eighty-four bushels per acre. **1845** J. C. Loudon *Suburban Horticulturist* III. v. 661 The *potato-onion may be planted in February. **1855, 1866** [see onion *sb.* 2 a]. **1890** E. Watts *Mod. Pract. Gardening* I. xiii. 68 The underground, or potato onion,..is so called from its habit of increasing at the bulb. **1955** W. E. Shewell-Cooper *Complete Veg. Grower* x. 135 The Potato Onion..is more difficult to get hold of today. **1935** L. Zara *Blessed is Man* I. iii. 103 She made him a heaping plateful of the fried *potato pancakes so closely associated with this holiday [*sc.* Chanukah]. **1941** L. Hellman *Watch on Rhine* II. 76, I love a good potato pancake. **1960** *Good Housek. Cookery Bk.* (rev. ed.) 535/2 *Potato pancakes*... Put the mashed potato through a sieve if at all lumpy, add seasoning, and work the flour into it to make a smooth dough. **1962** S. V. Thompson *Let.* 30 Jan. in G. Marx *Groucho Lett.* (1967) 237 Mother thinks that with this you serve potato pancakes and onions with peas. True? **1978** *Detroit Free Press* 16 Apr. (Detroit Suppl.) 28/2 With that, they bring potato pancakes which are fresh and moist on the inside, with a good crusty exterior. **1794** E. Drinker *Jrnl.* 25 June (1889) 229 John brought in a Mole he found in a *potato patch he was laying out. **1807** *Salmagundi* 15 Oct. 331 Some..enjoy the varied and romantick scenery of.. potatoe patches and log huts. **1863** A. D. Whitney *Faith Gartney's Girlhood* xxii. 207 A hollow, beyond which were the cornfields and potato-patches. **1913** J. London *Valley of Moon* 404 Hall put Billy to work on the potato patch—a matter of three acres which the poet farmed erratically. **1919** G. B. Shaw *O'Flaherty V.C.* in *Heartbreak House* 165, I.. gave him for his mother a Volumnia of the potato patch rather than an affectionate parent from whom he could not so easily have torn himself away. **1972** R. Adams *Watership Down* xxxiv. 263 The cottager..shot him [*sc.* a rabbit] as he came through the potato-patch at dawn. **1875** Trollope *Way we live Now* II. c. 314 If her future husband would consent to live on potatoes, she would be quite satisfied with the *potato-peelings. **1959** I. & P. Opie *Lore & Lang. Schoolch.* xiii. 295 Tales are told of..forcing a new boy into a box or dustbin half-filled with fish-heads, potato peelings ..and making him stay there for an hour. **1975** *Sunday Times* 16 Nov. 44/3 My husband was having fun posting old tomatoes and potato peelings down the waste disposal. **1599** B. Jonson *Ev. Man out of Hum.* II. i, Feeding on larks, sparrows, *potatoe-pies, and such good unctuous meats. **1609** Dekker *Guls Horne-Booke* i. 7 Potato-pies and Custards, stood like the sinfull suburbs of Cookery. **1646** J. Hall *Poems, To Yng. Authour*, Then hast thy finger in Potato pies. **1728** E. Smith *Compl. Housewife* (ed. 2) sig. A7ᵛ (*heading*) A Bill of Fare..For June... Second Course... Potato-Pye. **1807** *Complete Farmer* II. s.v., But the best way of storing the roots is..in what are called potatoe-pies. **1828** *Craven Gloss.* (ed. 2), *Potatoe-pie*, a small hillock of potatoes covered with straw, sods, and earth, to protect them from frost during the winter season. **1842** *Ainsworth's Mag.* I. 2 A large remnant of a potato-pie in a brown earthenware dish. **1880** Baring-Gould *Mehalah* xi, She found the parson in his garden..making a potatoe pie for the winter. **1965** in P. Jennings *Living Village* (1968) 61 Weather permitting, potato pies are opened and the potatoes sold to the merchants. **1972** K. Bonfiglioli *Don't point that Thing at Me* xviii. 152 We took a cheap night flight to Blackpool. .. I had potato pie for supper. **1883** *Girls' Own Paper* 14 July 654/1 **Potato puffs* .—Chop..some cold meat or fish. Mash some potatoes and make them into a paste with an egg. .. Fold... Fry. **1972** *V.A.T.: Scope & Coverage* (H.M. Customs) 22 Any of the following when packaged for human consumption without further preparation, namely,..potato sticks, potato puffs and similar products made from the potato. **1882** G. B. Bartlett *New Games for Parlor & Lawn* 212 The *Potato Race... This amusing out-of-door game requires a swift runner, with his feet well under control. **1946** *R.A.F. Jrnl.* May 167 The..Inter-Command Sports Meeting will include the following events..:—potato race,..relay race. **1978** 'F. Parrish' *Sting of Honeybee* i. 8 The potato race starts in three minutes. All entries to the collecting ring. *Ibid.* 9 The strange grey pony was not in the potato race. **1848** *Rep. Comm. Patents 1847* (U.S.) I. 136 The *potato rot seems likewise to have been felt to a considerable extent among the common potato. **1854** B. P. Shillaber *Life & Sayings Mrs. Partington* 43 A more disastrous havoc of potato rot has never since transpired than assailed her crops. **1858** *Penny Cycl.* 2nd Suppl. 530/1 The distress occasioned by the potato rot and bad harvests. **1885** *Times* (weekly ed.) 11 Sept. 9/1 The 'potato-rot' made a clean sweep of their little patches. **1861** Mrs. Beeton *Bk. Househ. Managem.* 593 **Potato Salad*... Cut the potatoes into slices about ½ inch in thickness; put these into a salad-bowl with oil and vinegar [etc.]. **1877** E. S. Dallas *Kettner's Bk. of Table* 399, I should weary the reader if I went on to sound the praises of the mustard and cress salad,..the potato salad, and the *salade de légumes*. **1952** B. Malamud *Natural* (1963) 185 Turkey, potato salad, cheese, and pickles. **1967** M. Gilbert *Dust & Heat* III. 246 He stopped ..at a delicatessen store in Soho where he bought..a carton of cold potato salad. **1978** J. Symons *Blackheath Poisonings* I. 39 There was a tongue..a potato salad, a Russian salad and a green salad. **1885** A. Edwardes *Girton Girl* I. vi. 136 Boiled mullet, hot *potato scones, with other indigenous Guernsey dishes. **1931** D. L. Sayers *Five Red Herrings* Foreword, We shall come back next summer to eat some more potato scones. **1973** *Perthshire Advertiser* 8 Aug. 17/6 Baking... Potato scones. **1830** *Encycl. Brit.* (ed. 7) II. 355/2 *Potato-Scoop. **1844** J. T. Hewlett *Parsons & W.* vi, In London at a *potato-shop. **1882** *Garden* 11 Mar. 164/3 The chances are it [the ground] is *Potatoe-sick. **1883** R. Haldane *Workshop Receipts* Ser. II. 12/2 *Potato-spirit is made chiefly in Germany. **1884** *St. James' Gaz.* 19 Dec. 4/1 Drinking Hamburg sherry, potato-spirit and other such poison. **1902** *Daily Chron.* 15 Apr. 8/4 The experiments in *potato-spraying were continued..with satisfactory results. **1887** *Nicholson's Dict. Gard.* III. 209/1 Still another American beetle that injures Potato crops is the *Potato-stalk Weevil (*Baridius trinotatus*). **1972** *Potato stick [see *potato puff* above]. **1859** Page *Handbk. Geol. Terms* 301 **Potato-stones*, a quarryman's term for the geodes of the mineralogist; rounded irregular concretions of various composition. **1895** J. W. Anderson *Prospector's Handbk.* (ed. 6) 97 Heliotrope.., firestone and quartz cat's eye, potato-stone, &c. **1895** M. Ronald *Century Cook Bk.* I. facing p. 82 (*caption*) Fluted knife for cutting *potato straws. *c* **1950** *Mrs. Beeton's Bk. Househ. Managem.* xxx. 692 *Potato straws*... Slice the potatoes thinly, cut them into strips about 1½ inches long... Fry the straws..until crisp. **1785** Grose *Dict. Vulg. T.* s.v. *Red rag*, Shut your *potatoe trap. **1860** Thackeray *Round. Papers* iv, And now Tom.. delivered a rattling clinker upon the Benicia Boy's potato-trap. **1892** *Insect Life* IV. 239 (*heading*) The *Potato-Tuber Moth (*Lita solanella*). **1928** Metcalf & Flint *Destructive & Useful Insects* xvi. 481 Potato tuber moth..is very destructive to potatoes in warm dry regions. **1932** *Jrnl. Econ. Entomol.* XXV. 625 During the past nine years the potato tuber moth..has caused economic losses to potato growers. **1950** *N.Z. Jrnl. Agric.* Sept. 221/3 The district is not suited to the growing of late potatoes because from January onward the potato tuber moth is very active. **1939** Metcalfe & Flint *Destructive & Useful Insects* (ed. 2) xvi. 516 *Potato tuberworm..is very destructive to potatoes in warm dry regions. **1960** *Jrnl. Econ. Entomol.* LIII. 868/1 The potato tuberworm, *Gnorimoschema operculella*.., has long been a pest of potatoes in California. **1774** P. V. Fithian *Jrnl.* 19 Sept. (1900) 257, I took a Walk thro' the Pumpkin & *Potatoe Vines. **1870** *Amer. Naturalist* III. 92 The early frosts..nearly killed the potato vines. **1902** L. H. Bailey *Cycl. Amer. Hort.* IV. 1680/2 *Solanum ..jasminoides*, Paxt. Potato Vine (from the fl[ower]s.). Fine greenhouse climbing shrub. **1939** L. & J. Bush-Brown *America's Garden Bk.* xxiv. 807 Potato Vine. Solanum jasminoides. Annual... Star-shaped, white flowers. **1947** *Southern Folklore Q.* XI. 264 Proverbial remarks disparaging to a person's character [include]..this pronunciamento from central Mississippi: 'He ought to have been hung when a potato vine would hang him.' **1963** Robertson & Gooding *Bot. for Caribbean* xxiii. 197 Climbers... Chalice Vine... Potato Vine (*Solanum wendlandii*). **1971** B. Clark in E. L. Wardman *Bermuda Jubilee Garden* i. 6 There is a very wide selection to be made from..potato-vines (*Solanum seaforthianum* and *S. wendlandii*), and chalice-vines. **1977** P. Moyes *To kill Coconut* xv. 207 Henry was eating breakfast under an arbour of potato-vines and goat's foot. **1899** Morrow *Bohem. Paris* 30 The fruit- and *potato-women came after, and then the chair-menders. **1842** T. W. Harris *Treat. Insects Injurious to Vegetation* 226 Every farmer's boy knows the *potato-worm. **1879** *Scribner's Monthly* Dec. 242/1 This white grub, which the farmers often call the 'potato worm' is..the strawberry's most formidable foe.

Hence **po'tato** *v. trans.*, to plant or crop with potatoes; **po'tatoey** *a.*, *nonce-wd.*, of the nature of a potato; **po'tatoless** *a.*, without potatoes.

1844 *Jrnl. R. Agric. Soc.* V. I. 66 The land is potatoed the following year. **1883** *Hertfordsh. Mercury* 21 July 4/2 The plan of perpetually potatoing the land. **1865** *Reader* 29 July 119/2 As potatoey as the peach over the way. **1807** Syd. Smith *Plymley's Lett.* iv. 30 Do you think that satisfaction and disaffection do not travel down from Lord Fingal to the most potatoeless Catholic in Ireland? **1845** Darwin *Voy. Nat.* xv. 324 Eating our potatoe-less breakfast.

potator (pəʊˈteɪtə(r)). *rare.* [a. L. *pōtātor*, agent-n. from *pōtāre* to drink: see -or.] A drinker, toper.

a **1660** *Contemp. Hist. Irel.* (Ir. Archæol. Soc.) I. 173 An exceedinge good potator in any liquor you please. **1834** Southey *Doctor* xliv. II. 106 Barnabee, the illustrious potator, saw there the most unbecoming sight.

potato-ring. A recent fanciful appellation for Irish dish-rings of the 18th c., now collected as objects of *virtu*.

The dish-ring was a hoop of silver, often elaborately chased, or adorned with pierced and repoussé work, used as a stand for a circular bowl or the like; in use *c* 1750–1800. The appellation 'potato-ring' is due to the suggestion or unfounded notion that the hoop was used to keep together a heap of potatoes in the middle of the dinner-table.

1893 *Times* 9 June 10/4 A number of old Irish potato-rings —one pierced with cage-pattern—45*s* per oz. **1901** *Chambers's Jrnl.* Feb. 103/2 Old Irish potato-rings are also much sought after by collectors; at recent sales they have sold for nearly £5 an ounce. **1906** *Macm. Mag.* Dec. 121 Two candles, in early Hanoverian candle-sticks, lit up the celebrated potato-ring in the centre of the table. **1907** *Daily Chron.* 1 June 4/5 Upon the tables were immense silver baskets and old silver potato rings filled with pink and red carnations. **1932** *Times Lit. Suppl.* 12 May 350/4 Certain characteristic features of Irish silver, notably the so-called 'potato' rings made in large numbers in Dublin from about 1760 to 1820. **1960** H. Hayward *Antique Coll.* 98/1 'Potato ring'... Circular silver dish or bowl stand with straight or incurved sides usually pierced and chased with pastoral or classical motifs. **1968** *Canad. Antiques Collector* Sept. 22/1 Delicate piercing [of silverware] might be suited to cake baskets, the so-called 'potato' rings, bottle coasters or the gallery of a tray. **1973** *Country Life* 8 Mar. 608/2 *Irish Silver in the Rococo Period* will..get out of his [*sc.* the average Englishman's] head that so-called potato rings have anything to do with potatoes... The fact is that such things are dish rings.

po'tato-root. [f. potato *sb.* + root *sb.*]

†**1.** A name formerly given (*a*) to the tuberous roots of the Sweet Potato, and (*b*) to the tubers of the common potato; also to these plants themselves.

1592 Greene *Disput.* 17 The Apothecaries would haue surphaling water and Potato rootes lye dead on theyr handes. **1594** *Huswifes Handmaide for Kitchin* 32 A Potaton roote well pared. **1597** *Pilgr. Parnass.* v. 549 A well disposed minde Shall no potato rootes in poets finde. **1620** Venner *Via Recta* vii. 137 Potato-roots are of a temperate quality. **1624** Capt. Smith *Virginia* v. 179 In this ship was brought [i.e. to Bermuda] the first Potata roots. **1655** Moufet & Bennet *Health's Impr.* (1746) 324 Pottato-roots are now so common and known amongst us, that even the Husbandman buys them to please his Wife.

2. *potato root*, the root of a potato-plant.

potatory (ˈpəʊtətərɪ), *a.* (*sb.*) [ad. L. *pōtātōri-us*: see potator and -ory[2].]

1. Of, pertaining to, or given to drinking.

1834 *Tait's Mag.* I. 586 I'll tame the potatory pride of this proud islander. **1839** *Blackw. Mag.* XLV. 178 His potatory prowess puts him at the head of the poll. **1860** Mrs. Byrne *Undercurrents* II. 31 Her husband's potatory tendencies.

2. Fit for drinking; potable. *rare.*

1827 Lytton *Pelham* xxxix, I helped myself to the potatory food with a slow dignity.

B. *sb.* = drinkable *sb.*

1836 E. Howard *R. Reefer* xiii, All the eatables and potatories were carried off.

‖**pot-au-feu** (pɔtofø). [Fr., = pot on the fire.] A large cooking pot of a kind common in France; the soup or broth cooked in it, *spec.* the traditional French recipe associated with this. Also *attrib.* and *fig.*

1792 C. Smith *Desmond* III. xxiii. 278 The pot *au feu* was brought forward to receive a supply of leeks. **1841** C'tess Blessington *Idler in France* I. ii. 32 Our good hostess.. served up a plentiful dinner, consisting of an excellent *pot au feu*, followed by fish, fowl, and flesh. **1868** C. M. Yonge *Chaplet of Pearls* I. xxiv. 311 To eat of the savoury mess in the great *pot-au-feu*. **1868** M. Jewry *Warne's Model Cookery* 55/2 *Pot-au-feu*, the stockpot. **1909** H. James *Novels & Tales* XV. Pref. p. xvii, We can surely account for nothing in the novelist's work that..hasn't, in that perpetually simmering cauldron his intellectual *pot-au-feu*, been reduced to savoury fusion. **1934** H. Hiler *Notes Technique Painting* iii. 183 A large glazed earthenware pot (*pot-au-feu*) which has not been used for any other purpose. **1948** 'J. Tey' *Franchise Affair* xvi. 188 The dish was a pot-au-feu chicken with all its vegetables round it. **1960** *News Chron.* 30 Mar. 6/5, I get out a vast blackened saucepan and make the old-fashioned, traditional French pot-au-feu. **1962** *Economist* 3 Nov. 485/2 This is an intimate family story, relating..Saturday evening pot-au-feu dinners. **1975** [see *New England boiled dinner* s.v. New England b].

Potawatomi (pɒtəˈwɒtəmɪ), *sb.* Also **Pattawatami, Pottiwatomie, Poutouatami,** etc. [Native name.] **a.** A member of an Algonquian Indian people located in the Great Lakes region of the northern U.S.A., principally in Michigan and Wisconsin. **b.** The language of this people. Also *attrib.* or as *adj.*

1698 tr. *Hennepin's New Discovery* I. xxiii. 74 We sent afterwards three Men to buy Provisions in the Village with the *Calumet* or Pipe of Peace, which the Poutouatami's of the Island had given us. **1722** D. Coxe *Descr. Carolana* 48 The Nations who dwell on this River, are..the Poutouatomis beforemention'd. **1789** *Deb. Congr. U.S.* 25 May (1834) 41 The treaties of Fort Harmar..with the Sachems and warriors of the Wyandot,..Pattiwatima, and Sac nations. **1805** J. Wilkinson *Let.* 12 July in *Deb. Congr. U.S.* (1852) 10th Congr. 1 Sess. 575 All hopes of the speedy recovery of their prisoners from the hands of the Pattawatamies, being at an end. **1808** Governor Harrison *Let.* 14 Apr. in *Deb. Congr. U.S.* (1853) 12th Congr. 1 Sess. 1857 A young man from the Delaware towns came to inform me that a Pottawatomie Indian had arrived at the towns. **1835** [see Kickapoo]. **1838** [see long knife 1]. **1868** *N.Y. Herald* 31 July 5/4 The Senate..ratified treaties with the Potawatamies. **1877** L. H. Morgan *Anc. Society* II. iv. 105 The Potawattamies have eight gentes of the same name with eight among the Ojibwas. **1927** L. Bloomfield in *Amer. Speech* II. 437/1 She knows only a few words of English, but speaks Ojibwa and Potawatomi fluently, and, I believe, a little Winnebago. **1933** —— *Language* 72 The Algonquian family covers the northeastern part of the continent and includes the languages of..the Great Lakes region (Ojibwa, Potawatomi..and so on). **1946** E. A. Nida *Morphol.* p. v, Linguists will readily recognize many of the problems as being drawn from Greek, Latin, French,..Potawatomi, Cherokee, and Navaho. **1965** *Language* XLI. 75 Pike and Erickson's work on Potawatomi..studies the field structures of certain lexical oppositions within given orders of Potawatomi verb affixes. **1972** *Ibid.* XLVIII. 847, 5 c [in a table of five-vowel systems] is given by Hockett for Potawatomi. **1978** *Maledicta* II. 233, I am told that the name [of Waukesha in Wisconsin] is from the Potawatomi word for 'fox'. **1979** *Tucson* (Arizona) *Citizen* 20 Sept. (Old Pueblo Suppl.) 3/1 The woman saw the 6-foot-4, 260-pound Potawatomi Indian walking down a Phoenix street.

pot-ball: see pot *sb.*[1] 14.

pot-bellied (ˈpɒtˌbɛlɪd), *a.* [Parasynthetic f. next + -ed[2].] Having a pot-belly. Also *transf.* Also, = pot-belly 2 b.

1657 W. Coles *Adam in Eden* cl. 229 Given to tame Rabbets when they are pot-bellyed through costivenesse. **1698** *Phil. Trans.* XX. 262 He would appear in all the Deformities that can be imagin'd, as Hunch Back'd, Pot Belly'd, Sharp Breasted. **1814** Scott *Wav.* lxvi, A pot-bellied Dutch bottle of brandy. **1858** Carlyle *Fredk. Gt.* IV. iii. (1872) I. 294 A gluttonous race of Jutes and Angles..lumbering about in potbellied equanimity. **1899** [see merchant *sb.* 4]. **1959** [see pot *sb.*[1] 1 h]. **1964** Mrs. L. B. Johnson *White House Diary* 21 May (1970) 143 Not only was the schoolhouse the same as the one at Fern, but there was a big pot-bellied stove inside. **1973** *Nation Rev.* (Melbourne) 31 Aug. 1455/4 He revealed an ancient potbellied stove. **1979** O. Sela *Petrograd Consignment* 5 A burly, pot-bellied Swiss.

pot-belly (ˈpɒtˈbɛlɪ). [f. pot *sb.*[1] + belly *sb.*]

1. A swollen or protuberant belly.

c **1714** Pope, etc. *Mem. M. Scriblerus* xi, He will find himself a forked stradling Animal, with bandy legs, a short neck, a dun hide, and a pot-belly. **1822–34** *Good's Study Med.* (ed. 4) IV. 224 It..gives that projecting rotundity to the abdomen which is vulgarly distinguished by the name of Pot-Belly. **1897** *Allbutt's Syst. Med.* III. 488 The pot-belly of rickety children is caused..by dilatation of the bowels with undigested food.

2. a. *transf.* A pot-bellied person.

1871 B. Taylor *Faust* (1875) I. v. 87 The baldpate pot-belly I've noted.

b. Used *attrib.* to designate a kind of domestic stove made in the shape of a barrel.

1973 L. Russell *Everyday Life Colonial Canada* vii. 76 About the middle of the nineteenth century a new kind of heating stove appeared, inelegantly known as the pot-belly stove. It was barrel-shaped, with a flat top on which a pot or kettle could be heated. **1976** *Columbus* (Montana) *News* 1 July 7/6 (Advt.), One..cast iron pot belly stove. **1976** *Morecambe Guardian* 7 Dec. 33/2 (Advt.), Wood burning or coke burning stove (pot belly type) preferably with chimney.

ˈpot-ˌboiler.

1. One who boils a pot; *spec.* in *Eng. Politics* = potwaller. *rare.*

1824 Hitchins & Drew *Cornwall* I. xvii. §17. 650 The right of election is vested at present in all the inhabitants [of Tregony] who are pot-boilers. **1826** [see potwaller].

2. *colloq.* **a.** Applied depreciatively to a work of literature or art executed for the purpose of 'boiling the pot', i.e. of gaining a livelihood: see pot *sb.*[1] 13 e; a writing, picture, or other work, made to sell. Also applied to musical compositions, plays, and films.

1864 *Sat. Rev.* 27 Aug. 275/2 Artists and novelists of a certain stamp joke about 'pot-boilers'—the name facetiously given to hasty, worthless pictures and books,..composed for the simple and sole purpose of being sold under cover of a reputation. **1864** D. G. Rossetti *Let.* 25 June (1965) II. 509 Small things and water-colours I never should have done at all, except for the long continuance of a necessity for 'pot-boilers'. **1882** J. C. Morison *Macaulay* iv. 129 Macaulay's contributions to the *Edinburgh* at this period have largely the characteristics of what are vulgarly called 'pot-boilers', though..they were written to keep, not his own but another man's pot boiling. **1884** H. D. Traill *Coleridge* iii. 53 Such..was the singular and even prosaic origin of the 'Ancient Mariner'..surely the most sublime of 'pot-boilers' to be found in all literature. **1897** W. C. Hazlitt *Four Gen. Lit. Fam.* I. iii. ii. 242 All men who have to live by their labour have their pot-boilers. **1915** W. S. Maugham *Of Human Bondage.* 256 You hear of men painting pot-boilers to keep an aged mother. **1934** C. Lambert *Music Ho!* v. 306 A certain number of works that were neither potboilers nor works of individual genius. **1973** *Times* 14 Mar. 18/7 In the next three years he directed five pot-boilers and did some screen writing. **1975** *Listener* 31 July 152/3 Ayckbourn's name could become associated with middle-brow, comedy potboilers. **1977** *Time* 10 Oct. 61/1 Condon works on his potboilers seven hours a day, seven days a week for ten weeks at a stretch.

attrib. **1879** W. L. Lindsay *Mind Lower Anim.* 20 Writing what are vulgarly known as 'pot-boiler' books.

b. A writer or artist who produces 'pot-boilers'.

1892 G. S. Layard *C. Keene* ii. 37 He never seemed to realize that he was anything more than a hard-working pot-boiler. **1900** *Pall Mall G.* 31 Aug. 1/2 The joys of matrimony have an odd way of turning all but the greatest into 'pot-boilers'.

3. *Anthropol.* (See quot. 1874.)

1874 Dawkins *Cave Hunt.* iii. 91 Among the articles of daily use were many rounded pebbles, with marks of fire upon them, which had probably been heated for the purpose of boiling water. Pot-boilers, as they are called, of this kind are used by many savage peoples at the present day. **1899** J. Kenworthy in *Essex Nat.* XI. 105 The large quantity of ashes and charcoal, with calcined pebbles and 'pot-boilers', at the bottom of the lake and upon the platform upon which the huts were built.

So (in senses corresponding to 2) **ˈpot-boil** *v. intr.*, to do pot-boiling; *trans.* to produce for sale; **ˈpot-ˌboilery** *a.* (*nonce-wd.*), of the nature of a pot-boiler; **ˈpot-ˌboiling** *sb.* and *a.* in quot. 1775, in sense 'providing for the immediate necessities of life'; cf. *boil the pot*: pot *sb.*[1] 13 e.

1775 S. J. Pratt *Liberal Opin.* cxxii. (1783) IV. 130 Send, I say, the £1. 1. just for the pot-boiling business, and who knows what tomorrow may bring forth. **1867** D. G. Rossetti *Let.* 22 Mar. (1965) II. 618, I have been pot-boiling to an extent lately that does not hold out much hope of estate buying. **1870** *Daily Tel.* 10 Feb. 5/1 The eccentric, superficial, or 'pot-boiling' qualities which degrade much of what is manufactured and sold. **1880** Howells *Undisc. Country* xx, I write and sell my work. It's what they call pot-boiling. **1881** Saintsbury *Dryden* iii. 60 A 'pot-boiling' adaptation of Troilus and Cressida was brought out. **1888** Rider Haggard *Mr. Meeson's Will* iv, He will be paid five hundred or a thousand pounds apiece for his most 'pot-boilery' portraits. **1891** *Murray's Mag.* Oct. 550 [They] saw themselves absolutely obliged to 'potboil', if I may be pardoned the phrase, in order to live. **1903** *Westm. Gaz.* 19 Mar. 4/3 To prove..that several 'old masters'..are also 'fakes', and were 'pot-boiled' in Montmartre. **1905** J. K. Jerome in *Daily Chron.* 14 July 4/4 Every barrister who accepts a brief is pot-boiling. Every clergyman who preaches a sermon is pot-boiling. The pot has got to be boiled.

ˈpot-bound, *a.* [f. pot *sb.*[1] 1 d + bound *ppl. a.*] Said of a plant growing in a flower-pot when its roots fill the pot and have no more room to expand. Also *fig.*

1850 *Florist* Nov. 262 To preserve plants in luxuriant health, they should not be allowed to become pot-bound. **1895** S. R. Hole *Tour Amer.* 100 As their roots increase and before they become 'pot-bound' they must have more room. *a* **1908** *Mod.* There is no doubt we are becoming pot-bound. **1913** Mrs. G. De H. Vaizey *College Girl* v. 66 The red-brown earth..was too tempting to be resisted when she thought of her poor pot-bound plants at home. **1919** [see *aerotropism* (aero-)]. **1925** W. Deeping *Sorrell & Son* vi. 56 You can get many a good hint from a man who dislikes you if you are not too pot-bound to soak it up. **1966** Rochford & Gorer *Rockford Bk. Flowering Pot Plants* i. 17 More frequent waterings will be required when the plant is pot-bound.

ˈpot-boy. [f. pot *sb.*[1] 1 c, 2 b + boy *sb.*[1]] A boy or young man employed at a tavern or public house to serve the customers with beer, or to carry beer to outside customers; a publican's assistant.

1795 *Chron.* in *Ann. Reg.* 2 The circumstance that led to the discovery..was that of kidnapping a pot-boy. **1852** Dickens *Bleak Ho.* xi, The potboy..having to deal with drunken men occasionally. **1877** Black *Green Past.* xi, He rose, and the publican and the pot-boy were astonished to find the difference in the appearance of this coster's face.

Hence (*nonce-wds.*) **ˈpotboydom**, the class of pot-boys; **ˈpotboyship**, the position of a pot-boy.

1841 *Fraser's Mag.* XXIII. 439 He..bestowed the pot-boyship upon the youthful Ginginbetters. **1850** Kingsley *Alt. Locke* xiii, It is a part of his game to ingratiate him-self with all pot-boy-dom.

†pot-carrier. *Obs.* A perversion of *poticary*, pothecary: cf. potter-carrier, potycaryar.

1683 Tryon *Way to Health* 532 Should the learnedst Doctor or Pot-carrier of them all tell a Country-man that the best way to preserve the strength and natural Virtues of his Hay, were to dry it in the Shade or House, he could not but Laugh at their simplicity.

potch (pɒtʃ), *sb.* Also † **potsh.** In full ***potch opal.*** Opal that has no play of colour and is of no value; also, a flat colour characteristic of this; ***potch and*** or ***with colour*** (see quot. 1971).

1897 *Jrnl. & Proc. R. Soc. New South Wales* XXX. 256 The dull, milky, and opaque stones are called 'potsh' by the miners. **1900** in J. S. Gunn *Opal Terminol.* (1971) 35 Demand for potch with color being active. **1902** *Chambers's Jrnl.* V. 494/2 'It's only potch, an' not worth a drink, the whole durned lot.'.. Occasionally I cut through seams of opal matrix carrying stones of beautiful red tints and sometimes of a peculiar blend of almost every colour. For all these Dan had but one contemptuous name, 'potch', which is the miner's term for inferior opal. **1912** *Empire Mag.* Nov. 282/1 A pocketful of 'potch-and-colour'—that is, 'potch' with a slight 'colour' of opal. **1921** [see knobby *sb.*]. **1936** A. Russell *Gone Nomad* vii. 58 The value of a pocket varied according to the size, quantity and quality of the opal stones it contained... 'Potch' or immature opal could be found by the ton. **1940** [see noodle *v.*[2]]. **1958** M. D. Berrington *Stones of Fire* 24 'What's potch?'..'Opal crystal without fire. Looks some-thing like pieces of crockery.' **1962** R. Webster *Gems* I. x. 189 The colourful precious opal is found in irregular patches in the thin veins of potch—the miners' term for opal which may be colourful but not showing the play of colour, or as they say 'not alive'—which fills the joints and bedding planes of the sandstone. **1971** J. S. Gunn *Opal Terminol.* 35 *Potch-and-colour, potch-with-colour*, opal potch with a slight colour of opal showing through. **1976** *Sci. Amer.* Apr. 94/3 The small amounts of precious opal are accompanied by an enormous quantity of valueless 'potch' opal, which looks like opal but shows no colour and is generally discarded by the miners... Electron microscopy shows that it usually consists of rounded particles of silica that are not well enough shaped, sized or ordered to form light-diffracting arrays.

potch (pɒtʃ), *v.* [ad. Yiddish *patshn*, ad. G. *patschen* to slap.] *trans.* To slap or smack; hence potch *sb.*, **ˈpotching** *ppl. a.*

1892 [see poach *v.*[2] 1 d]. **1966** R. H. Rimmer *Harrad Experiment* (1967) 150, I told you, Saul, Harry's not too old for a *potch* before he becomes a *paskudnick*. **1968** L. Rosten *Joys of Yiddish* 293 Don't be fresh or I'll potch you. **1969** K. Vonnegut *Slaughterhouse-Five* iv. 73 Her palm on his little jelly belly made potching sounds.

potch, potcher var. poach *v.*[2], poacher[1], esp. in paper-making.

pot cheese. orig. and chiefly *U.S.* [f. pot *sb.*[1] 14.] A type of cottage cheese.

1812 'H. Bull-Us' *Diverting Hist. John Bull & Bro. Jonathan* xiv. 111 Tell me, thou heart of cork,..and brain of pot-cheese. **1859** Bartlett *Dict. Amer.* (ed. 2) 420 *Smear case*,..a preparation of milk..; otherwise called Cottage-Cheese. In New York it is called Pot-cheese. **1878** *Rep. Indian Affairs* (U.S.) 19 They learn to milk and make butter and pot-cheese, which they relish highly. **1935** *Colony of Connecticut* (Connecticut Board of Educ.) (Senate Doc. 53, 74th Congr., 1st Sess.) 12 Pot cheese, Dutch cheese, and bonnyclabber were the same. These were generally sweetened with maple sugar. **1964** W. Markfield *To Early Grave* xii. 245 She has eggs for me. *And* pot cheese. **1965** T. Fitzgibbon *Art Brit. Cooking* 133 Pot cheese is a type of cottage cheese made with sour milk and butter milk..cream and salt is worked in. It is rolled into small balls.

pot-clip. *north. dial.* [f. pot *sb.*[1] + clip *sb.*[1] 2; cf. pot-kilp.] A contrivance for suspending a pot or cauldron having no 'boul', consisting of two iron rods jointed together, with hooks at the free ends to catch hold of the ears or brim of the pot.

1459–60 *Durham Acc. Rolls* (Surtees) 89, ij par del Pot-clyppez. **1465** *Ibid.* 244 Item j par de potclyps. **1567** *Wills & Inv. N.C.* (Surtees) I. 266 One broule Iron, vij speights, iiij pair of pottclipps. **1691** Ray *N.C. Words* 136 *Pot cleps*, pot-hooks, from clip or clap, because they clap or catch hold of the pot. **1825** in Brockett *N.C. Gloss.*

ˈpot-comˌpanion. [f. pot *sb.*[1] + companion *sb.*[1]] A companion in drinking; a fellow-toper.

1549 Latimer *3rd Serm. bef. Edw. VI* (Arb.) 77 Some sayed, he was a Samaritane, that he had a Deuyll wythin him, a gloser, a drincker, a pot-companion. **1636** Heywood *Love's Mistr.* I. Wks. 1874 V. 105 A pot-companion, brother to the glasse, That roars in's cups; indeede a drunken Asse. *a* **1735** Arbuthnot *Gulliver Decypher'd* Misc. Wks. 1751 I. 82 The Grand Treasurer made him his pot-companion; and the chief Secretary took him into all his pleasures. **1881** Besant & Rice *Chapl. of Fleet* II. xx, He has promised his pot-companions to bring home a wife.

Hence (*nonce-wds.*) **pot-comˈpanioning; pot-comˈpanionship.**

1549 Coverdale, etc. *Erasm. Par. Eph.* Prol., Whan was excessyue riotous bankettyng, pottecompanyonyng, and belychearynge more outragiously vsed? **1601** Dent *Pathw. Heaven* 167 As for your pot-companionship, I hate it.

‖**pot de chambre** (po də ʃɑ̃br). [Fr.] = chamber-pot. Also *attrib.*

1777 P. Thicknesse *Year's Journey* I. i. 6 The priest put the present under the side of the bed..it was only a *pot de chambre*. **1891** A. T. Ritchie *Lett.* (1924) x. 220 The Dame du Palais..escorting the King to bed, carrying a sword, a lamp and a pot de chambre. **1894** G. N. Curzon *Probl. Far East* v. 140 The national implement of Korea, a circular brass pot, with a lid, but no handle, which..serves alternately as pillow, candlestick, ashplate, spittoon, and *pot de chambre*. **1931** E. Waugh *Remote People* 65 A pedlar..with a bundle of bootlaces in one hand and an enamelled *pot de chambre* in the other. **1934** C. Lambert *Music Ho!* II. 74 Those two symbols of an alien civilization, the top hat and the *pot de chambre*. **1938** L. BEMELMANS *Life Class* 20 The *pot de chambre* humor of Regensburg. **1969** N. FREELING *Tsing-Boum* xxi. 146 It [*sc.* tea] arrived, in massive pot-de-chambre porcelain with little roses on it. **1972** 'I. DRUMMOND' *Frog in Moonflower* ii. 47 Coffee in cups like *pots-de-chambre*. **1976** [see ROUTIER[2] 2].

pote, *sb.*[1] *Obs.* exc. *dial.* See also POOT *sb.* [Connected with POTE *v.*]

1. A stick or rod for poking, thrusting, or stirring.

†**a.** In ME. ***plouh-pote***, perh. the same as ***plough-bat*** (PLOUGH *sb.*[1] 8) or PLOUGH-STAFF.

But the various readings, and the frequent variant *plough-foot*, leave the meaning doubtful.

1362 LANGL. *P. Pl.* A. VII. 96 Mi plouh-pote [*v.r.* plow-bat] schal be my pyk, and posshen atte [*v.r.* putte at þe] Rootes, And helpe my coltre to kerue, and close þe vorwes [1377 B. VI. 105 My plow-fote [*2 MSS.* plow-pote] shal be my pyk-staf, and picche atwo þe rotes].

b. A poker.

1703 THORESBY *Let. to Ray* 334 *Poit*, 'a fire-poit', an iron to stir up the fire with. **1808-25** JAMIESON, *Pout, poit*, a poker. **1828** in *Craven Gloss.* **1864** PRESTON *Poems* (W. Yorksh.) 10 (E.D.D.) An walked as stiff.. As if he'd swollud t' poyt. **1888** *Sheffield Gloss.*, Add., *Pote*, a poker for a fire.

c. 'A broad piece of wood used by thatchers to open the old thatch and thrust in the new straw. *Oxon.*' (Halliwell).

2. A kick or push with the foot.

1903 in *Eng. Dial. Dict.* from Cumberland and Lancash. to Somerset, Devon, and Cornw.

3. *Comb.* †**pote-stick** (in 4 **pootstikke**), ? a stick for stirring. But cf. POTSTICK.

c **1350** *Nominale Gall.-Angl.* (E.E.T.S.) 511 *Morter pil et mundiloun*, Morter pestelle and pootstikke.

†**pote**, *sb.*[2] *Obs. rare*[−1]. [a. MDu. *pôte*, Du. *poot*: see PAW.] A paw.

1481 CAXTON *Godeffroy* 113 The beeste..embraced hym with his potes, or feet to fore.

†**pote**, *sb.*[3] *nonce-wd.* [ad. L. *pōtus*.] Drink.

1694 MOTTEUX *Rabelais* v. 252 Our means of Life are Pote, and Cibe, and Vest.

pote, *v.* Now *dial.* Forms: 1 **potian**, 3-5 **pote(n**, 4 **pot**, 5- **pote**, (6 **poote**, **poat**; 9 *dial.* **poat**, **poot**, **pooat**, **poit(e**, **poyt**). [OE. *potian*, of uncertain etymology.]

1. *trans.* To push, thrust.

c **1000** ÆLFRIC *Hom.* I. 522 Fearra ȝelican..hi, mid leafe þære ealdan æ, heora fynd mid horne lichamlicere mihte potedon. *a* **1023** WULFSTAN *Hom.* 235 Þa deoflu hy potedon and þoddetton þa earman sawle and heton hy ut faran raðe of þam lichaman. *c* **1330** R. BRUNNE *Chron. Wace* (Rolls) 8891 [Þey] left þer pottyng many on, ȝit stirede þey nought þe leste ston. **1340** *Ayenb.* 135 Wone is of þe zoþe milde, oþren to herie and praysy, and poten him uorþ an worþssipij. **1382** WYCLIF *Mark* v. 10 He preide hym myche, that he shulde nat put [*v.r.* poten] hym out of the cuntreie. **1435** MISYN *Fire of Love* 93 Euerlastynge potand behynde, in temporall solas & bodily lufe þa seyke to florysch. *c* **1485** *Digby Myst.* (1882) III. 606 A! how pynsynesse potyt me to oppresse, that I haue synnyd on euery syde. **1530** PALSGR. 663/1, I poote. **1775** ASH, Pote (*vb. tr., a local word*), to push.

b. *esp.* (*trans.* and *intr.*) To push with the foot, to kick; also said of a horse pawing.

a **1300** *Song agst. K. of Almaigne* vii. in *Pol. Songs* (Camden) 71 Al he shulde quite here twelfmoneth scot, Shulde he never more with his fot pot To helpe Wyndesore. **1674** RAY *N.C. Words* 37 To *Pote* the Clothes off; to kick all off; to push or put out. **1828** *Craven Gloss.* (ed. 2), *Pote, Paut*, to push or kick with the feet. **1879** MISS JACKSON *Shropsh. Work-bk.* s.v., 'Them lads han poted these sheets through a'ready.' **1883** *Huddersf. Gloss.* s.v., One boy poits another out of bed... 'She were liggin on her rig a poitin.' **1884** *Cheshire Gloss.* s.v., He potes aw th' clooas off him i' bed.

2. *trans.* To poke with a stick or the like; *esp.* to poke or stir (the fire).

1709 S. BOWDICH in *Phil. Trans.* XXVIII. 266 She.. beg'd he would not poot her too hard (as she express'd it). **1828** in *Craven Gloss.* **1868** ATKINSON *Cleveland Gloss.* **1876** *Whitby Gloss.*, *Pooat*, to poke er probe into a hole. 'He now gans pooating with a stick'. **1887** *Holderness Gloss.*, *Pooat*, to poke about. **1890** *Gloucestersh. Gloss.* s.v., Pote the fire.

†**3.** To crimp or form folds in (linen) with a poting-stick; = POKE *v.*[1] 3. *Obs.*

1614 SYLVESTER *Bethulia's Rescue* v. 215 See, how hee poats, paints, frizzles, fashions him.

4. In other *dial.* uses: see *Eng. Dial. Dict.*

Hence '**poted** *ppl. a.*, crimped; '**poting** *vbl. sb.*; '**poting-stick**, †(*a*) a wooden, iron, or bone instrument for crimping linen (*obs.*); (*b*) *dial.* a stick for stirring clothes when boiling.

1600 KEMP *Nine Daies Wond.* C ij b, A boy arm'd with a poating sticke. **1609** HEYWOOD *Brit. Troy* IV. l, He..weares a formall ruffe, A nosegay, set face, and a poted cuffe. *a* **1693** *Urquhart's Rabelais* III. xxxvii. 314 Having..a bucked Ruff, raised, furrowed, and ridged, with Ponting [*sic*] Sticks of the shape and fashion of small Organ Pipes. **1892** SARAH HEWETT *Peas. Sp. Devon* 114 'Avee zeed tha poteing-stick, Mary?

pote, obs. form of PUT *v.*

pot-ear. [f. POT *sb.*[1] + EAR *sb.*[1]]

1. The 'ear' or handle of a pot.

c **1425** *Voc.* in Wr.-Wülcker 660/26 *Hec anca*, potere. **1483** *Cath. Angl.* 288/2 A Potte ere, *ansa, ansula*.

2. *Geol.* (*pl.*) See quot.

1839 MURCHISON *Silur. Syst.* I. ii. 18 The quarries.. exhibited the following beds of the Marlstone. 1. Lightish yellow micaceous sandstone full of Belemnites. 2. 'Pot-ears', bluish gray calcareous grit, quarried for troughs. 3. 'Pendle'.

pot-earth. [POT *sb.*[1]] Potter's earth, potter's clay; *Geol.* the BRICK-EARTH of the London basin.

1644 DIGBY *Nat. Bodies* xiv. §18. 125 The richest of such earth, (as pott earth and marle) will with much fire grow more compacted. **1766** ENTICK *London* IV. 201 All the hard crust of pot-earth..had been robbed by the potters. **1906** *Daily Chron.* 28 Nov. 6/7 To bridge over a weak spot from which the early potters had abstracted all the pot earth or brick earth, as we now call it.

potecarie, -cary(e, variants of POTHECARY.

poteen, potheen (pɒ'tiːn, pɒ'θiːn). Also 9 **potsheen**, **potteen**, **pottheen**. [a. Ir. *poitín* (pɔ'tjin) 'little pot', dim. of *pota, puite* POT *sb.*[1]: short for *uisge poitín* 'little-pot whisky'.] Whisky distilled in Ireland in small quantities, privately, i.e. the produce of an illicit still.

1812 MAR. EDGEWORTH *Absentee* x, Potsheen, plase your honour;—becaase it's the little whiskey that's made in the private still or *pot*; and *sheen*, becaase it's a fond word for whatsoever we'd like, and for what we have little of, and would make much of. **1820** *Blackw. Mag.* VII. 478 Whiskey too was made, They call'd Potheen, and sold so very cheap. **1856** LEVER *Martins of Cro' M.* x. 87 'That is "poteen"', Mr. Massingbred', said the host. 'It's the small still that never paid the King a farthing'. **1885** TENNYSON *Tomorrow* xvi, Yer Honour 'ill give me a thrifle to dhrink yer health in potheen.

b. *attrib.* and *Comb.*, as ***poteen still***, ***whisky***.

1826 J. BANIM *O'Hara Tales* I. xi. 273 Two [decanters] containing cold pottheen punch. **1830** M. DONOVAN *Dom. Econ.* I. 73 The smell of what, in Ireland, is called potteen whiskey. **1833** MARRYAT *P. Simple* xxxvi, There's a flaunty sort of young woman at the poteen shop there. **1903** W. B. YEATS *Celtic Twilight* 148 He supplies the potheen-makers with grain from his own fields.

poteger, early form of POTTINGER.

†**poteller**, *a.* (*sb.*) *Obs.* Also 4 **poteler**, 5 **potteler**, **potler**. [app. a. AF. **poteller*, f. med.L. type **potellāris* adj., f. *potellus* POTTLE.] Holding a pottle (qualifying *pot* or the like); hence sometimes as *sb.* = POTTLE-POT.

1390 *Earl Derby's Expedition* (Camden) 18 Pro ij ollis coreis galoners, et pro vj ollis coreis potellers. **1392-3** *Ibid.* 154, xij pottes galoners, viij pottes potelers. **1459** *Paston Lett.* I. 488 Item, iij. potteleres of lether... Item, ij pottis argenti potlers. **1465** *Mann. & Househ. Exp.* (Roxb.) 492, ij. pottes pottelers parselle gyltt, weyinge lxv. unnces.

†**potelot.** *Obs. rare.* [= G. *pottloth*, Du. *potlood* POT-LEAD[2].] Sulphuret of molybdenum.

1828 in WEBSTER, citing *Fourcroy*.

Potemkin (pəʊ'temkɪn). The name of Grigory Aleksandrovich *Potemkin* (1739–91), favourite of Empress Catherine II of Russia, used *attrib.* to designate the sham villages reputed to have been erected, on his orders, for Catherine's tour of the Crimea in 1787. Also *transf.* and *fig.*

1938 G. SOLOVEYTCHIK *Potemkin* xiv. 283 Potemkin's detractors have asserted that he built whole sham villages, with cardboard houses and paste palaces..in order to create a false picture of progress and prosperity... The originator of these stories..was the Saxon diplomat Helbig, and the legend of 'Potemkin Villages'..as a synonym of sham owes its inception to him. **1954** KOESTLER *Invis. Writing* xi. 132 This was not a Potemkin village. It was something more curious. **1965** B. PEARCE tr. *Preobrazhensky's New Econ.* 39 To lull the vigilance of..the working class, to keep it in the dark about the dangers which threaten it, and to weaken its will with Potemkin villages of childish optimism when it needs to continue to wage the heroic struggle of October. **1967** I. MARDER *Paris Bit* i. 27 Paris is above all a city of façades, an enormous Potemkin village. **1973** J. SHUB *Moscow by Nightmare* vii. 77 The new Kalinin Prospekt—the latest Potemkin Village of soaring glass and aluminium. **1974** *Guardian* 21 Mar. 3/8 It is good diplomacy..to pretend that the EEC is a political entity... But don't expect serious decisions from a political Potemkin village.

potence[1] ('pəʊtəns). [a. OF. *potence*, ad. L. *potentia* power, f. *potent-em*, pres. pple. of *posse* to be powerful or able: see -ENCE.]

1. Power, ability, strength; = POTENCY 1.

1413 *Pilgr. Sowle* (Caxton 1483) IV. xxvi. 72 That he ne may it knowen as in potence that is kyndely power. **1596** DALRYMPLE tr. *Leslie's Hist. Scot.* x. 472 Tha quha onie did excel in wisdome, or potence. **1669** GALE *Crt. Gentiles* I. I. iv. 22 His Potence, Prevalence, and Interest among the Canaanites. **1767** MRS. S. PENNINGTON *Lett.* III. 153 That there is any other being,..in the universe, which withstands the potence of God. **1850** MRS. BROWNING *Seraphim* I. 156 Where the blind matter brings An awful potence out of impotence. **1854** EMERSON *Lett. & Soc. Aims, Resources* Wks. (Bohn) III. 196 Men are made up of potences.

b. = POTENCY 1 b.

1871 B. TAYLOR *Faust* (1875) I. vi. 112 And through thy frame the liquour's potence fling.

c. Sexual power.

1885 *Law Rep. 10 Appeal Cases* 173 She..averred..that he was impotent at the date of the ceremony... The appellant averred his potence.

2. Degree of power or intensity.

1817 COLERIDGE *Biog. Lit.* xii. (1882) 135, I shall venture to use potence, in order to express a specific degree of a power, in imitation of the Algebraists. **1836-7** SIR W. HAMILTON *Metaph.* (1870) II. xxv. 120 Derivative from the principle in its lower potence or degree. **1863** MASSON in *Reader* 26 Sept. 335/2 This, then, is the first 'potence', as the Germans would call it, of that self-culture which consists in the control of thought by and within itself.

potence[2] ('pəʊtəns). Forms: 8 **potans**, (**portance**), 8-9 **pot(t)ance**, 6- **potence**. [a. F. *potence* a crutch (12th c in Hatz.-Darm.), also applied to various T- or Γ-shaped objects, as a gibbet, an armorial charge, a tactical formation, the potence of a watch, ad. L. *potentia* power, POTENCE[1], in med.L. a support (?), crutch. In sense 3, often written *pot(t)ance*. See POTENT *sb.*[1]]

†**1. a.** A cross or gibbet. *Obs.*

c **1500** *Melusine* 117 There is the potence or cros wheron the good thef Dysmas was crucefyed whan our lord was nayled to the Cros for our redempcion. **1571** *Satir. Poems Reform.* xxviii. 215 And, as I past, the Potence I espy, Quhair the anoyntit Bischop hung to dry. **1816** KEATINGE *Trav.* I. 80 *note*, One feature disfigures the landscape [in Catalonia]; the potence. The gallows appears on every hill.

b. *Engineering.* A supporting framework formed like a gallows.

1853 SIR H. DOUGLAS *Milit. Bridges* (ed. 3) 362 A vertical frame, forming a potence, or gallows, was fixed upon each of the horizontal frames, with two iron rollers on the summits, over which the two suspension cables were passed.

2. *Watchmaking.* A stud screwed to the top plate in which is made the bearing for the lower pivot of the verge; hence, any stud or fixture supporting a bearing. ***counter-potence***, a stud in which the upper pivot of the verge plays.

1678 *Lond. Gaz.* No. 1286/4 The Counter pottance [*mispr.* pettance] hath a tail that goeth a quarter of a circle. **1704** J. HARRIS *Lex. Techn.* I, *Potans*, or *Potence*, a Part of a Watch. **1705** DERHAM in *Lett. Lit. Men* (Camden) 318 One of these drilled stones they fix in the cock, the other in the bottom of the portance only to carry the ballance. **1727-41** CHAMBERS *Cycl.* s.v. *Watch-work*, The potence, or pottance, which is the strong stud in pocket-watches, whereon the lower pivot of the verge plays. **1792** *Trans. Soc. Arts* X. 219 Supported by two counter pottances upon the upper plate. **1825** J. NICHOLSON *Operat. Mechanic* 503 The potence,.. and small or counter potence.., that hold the pivots of the balance-wheel, are small cocks seen in fig. 502,..and are screwed to the top or upper plate within the frame. **1885** LOCK *Workshop Receipts* Ser. IV. 329/1 Take the potence, and..screw it in its place upon the top plate.

¶**3.** Erron. for *potent* (POTENT *sb.*[1] 1). *Obs.*

1688 R. HOLME *Armoury* III. 24/1 The Crutch is of some termed..a Crich, but more usually a Crutch Staff, which by Old Sir Geffrey Chaucer, was called a Potence.

4. A military formation, in which a line is thrown out at right angles to the main body.

1759 *Hist. Europe* in *Ann. Reg.* 40/2 The left of the English ..was formed to prevent that design in a manner which the military men call Potence, that is, in a body which presents two faces to the enemy. **1865** CARLYLE *Fredk. Gt.* XVIII. viii. (1872) VII. 243 Friedrich's line..shoots-out in mysterious Prussian rhythm, in echelons, in potences, obliquely down the Janus-Hill side.

5. (See quot. 1887.)

1887 *Jrnl. R. Archæol. Inst.* XLIV. 112 The Circular [culverhouses] were provided with a revolving machine, called a potence, by which all the nests could be conveniently got at in turn. **1978** *Erddig* (National Trust) 7 The building, shown on an estate plan of 1739, is complete with its potence (the revolving arm supporting the ladder needed to collect eggs and squabs) and several pairs of nesting fantails.

6. *attrib.* in sense 2, as ***potence file***, ***hole***.

1884 F. J. BRITTEN *Watch & Clockm.* 214 The size of the potence file most generally used is four inches long. *Ibid.* 280 The body or arbor of the verge..viewed through the follower potance hole should be seen crossing the balance wheel hole of the dovetail.

potencé ('pəʊtənseɪ), *a.* *Her.* Also **potencie**; improperly **potence**. [a. F. *potencé*, f. *potence*: see POTENCE[2]. Cf. PATONCE.] = POTENT *a.*[2]

1572 BOSSEWELL *Armorie* II. 35 Beareth Sable, a Bende Argent, with twoo double Cotizes, Potences and Counter-potences of three peces d'Or. **1602** SEGAR *Hon. Mil. & Civ.* II. xxvi. 105 That euery man..should..vpon their vppermost garment weare a blacke Crosse, voided with a Crosse potence. **1611** COTGR., *Potencé, ée*, like, or belonging, to a Gibbet, or Crutch; In Blason, potencie. **1704** J. HARRIS *Lex. Techn.* I, *Potent, or Potence*, the Term for a Cross in Heraldry, formed into this Figure. **1852** MISS YONGE *Cameos* (1877) II. xviii. 193 Richard bore on his banners the cross potence and four doves of the Saxon Saint. **1894** [see POTENT *a.*[2]].

potency ('pəʊtənsɪ). [ad. L. *potentia* power: see POTENCE[1] and -ENCY.] The quality of being potent.

1. a. Power, ability to accomplish or effect something; inherent powerfulness or capacity; authority.

1539 HEN. VIII *Instruct.* Nov., Wyatt's Wks. (1815) App. 517 Being the end and victory not in the multitude and potency, but in the hand of God. **1603** SHAKS. *Meas. for M.* II. ii. 67, I would to heauen I had your potencie, And you were Isabell. **1654** *Nicholas Papers* (Camden) II. 114 It wilbe a very great infamy and unbefittinge the potency of yͭ crowne. **1663** WOOD *Life* Apr. (O.H.S.) I. 473 Dʳ..Erbury was turned out of his fellowship of Magd. Coll. by the potency of Dʳ..Pierce the president. **1759** W. MASON *Caractacus* Poems (1774) 237 By the dread potency of every star..We do adjure thee. **1850** MERIVALE *Rom. Emp.* (1865) II. xxi. 451 The renowned name became at once a charm of magic potency. **1877** MRS. OLIPHANT *Makers Flor.* ii. 37 Inheriting the old potency of a great house. **1884** *Law Times*

1 Mar. 315/1 The decision.. has likewise a tendency to limit the potency of garnishee procedure.

b. Power to affect one physically; of liquor, etc.: overpowering or intoxicating quality; strength.

1637 J. TAYLOR (Water P.) *Drinke & Welcome* Title-p., An especiall declaration of the potency, vertue, and operation of our English Ale. **1785** SARAH FIELDING *Ophelia* II. iv, The potency of.. good October. **1786** tr. *Beckford's Vathek* (1883) 51 Suffocated by the potency of their exhalations, she was forced to quit the gallery. **1849** THACKERAY *Pendennis* xvii, You would have thought.. the very horse.. was affected by the potency of the drink.

c. *Homœopathy.* The degree of dilution of a drug, taken as a measure of its efficacy (a high dilution being regarded as more efficacious).

[**1833** J. B. GILCHRIST *Pract. Appeal* 54 Homœopathic medicines, extreme, attenuated, and minimissimised, acquire a potency in the inverse ratio of their attenuation and diminution.] **1846** C. J. HEMPEL *Homœopathic Domestic Physician* p. vii, Homœopathic drugs have now been potentialized up to the 200th and many of them up to 300th, 400th, 500th. etc., until the 2000th potency. **1906** *Homeopathic World* XLI. 109 From this tinctures of ever-augmenting potency (where disease is concerned) can be prepared. **1938** D. SHEPHERD *Magic of Minimum Dose* 4 *Nux vomica* has been a stand-by and valuable help in other cases of acute sinus trouble.., both in low potencies (1x) and high potencies. **1975** C. H. SHARMA *Man. Homoeopathy* I. iv. 29 Whether the remedy has been chosen for you or you have chosen it yourself, always keep a careful record of what it is, the potency, frequency and quantity, and the symptoms which called for it.

d. Ability to achieve orgasm in sexual intercourse. Opp. IMPOTENCE 2 b.

[**1900** *Yale Med. Jrnl.* VI. 126 There are two forms of potency—the *potentia coeundi* and the *potentia generandi*.] **1901** F. R. STURGIS *Sexual Debility in Man* x. 293 My patient was.. an ardent admirer of women, in whose company he indulged himself freely with perfect potency. **1929** G. R. SCOTT *Sex & its Mysteries* xii. 108 Anything which causes a lowering of the vitality is sufficient to induce impotence, hence the recommendation of meat, eggs and oysters for the generation of sexual potency. *Ibid.* 110 Nor does general disease affect woman's potency. **1939** G. V. HAMILTON in E. V. Cowdry *Probl. Ageing* xvi. 469 The decline in sexual potency experienced by men during the ageing period. **1966** *Listener* 10 Mar. 352/1 It may.. be true to say that young men use the car or motor-cycle as a potency symbol. **1977** E. J. TRIMMER et al. *Visual Dict. Sex* (1978) xxii. 262 Sterility is inevitable if both testes are removed... Desire and potency may be lost, but this is not inevitable.

e. *Genetics.* The extent of the contribution of an allele towards the production of some phenotypic character. Also *attrib.*

1905 *Publ. Carnegie Inst.* No. 23. 59 From these cases it seems clear that the production of partial-rough young was due to some unusual potency of the gametes bearing the smooth character. **1916** *Proc. Nat. Acad. Sci.* II. 53 The appearance of gynandromorphism in certain crosses found its right explanation in the hypothesis of a quantitatively different behavior or a different potency of the male sex-factors in the different races. **1944** *Genetics* XXIX. 528 Using the morphological guide of bristle length.. we might assign to gene b^c a potency of about 34, b^d a potency of 50, .. and b^f of 54. *Ibid.*, A potency series was set by Stern (1929b) to represent the additive effects of bobbed alleles in *D[rosophila] melanogaster.* **1955** R. B. GOLDSCHMIDT *Theoret. Genetics* III. v. 368 The potencies thus discovered.. turned out to be of the orderly type, that is, acting like dosage and thus acting in different combinations in an orderly and parallel way.

f. *Pharm.* The strength of a drug, as measured by the amount needed to produce a certain response.

1933 *Med. Res. Council Special Rep. Ser.* No. 183. 25 An approximate estimate of the potency of a preparation can be obtained by administering a series of doses, each to a single animal. **1968** A. GOLDSTEIN et al. *Princ. Drug Action* v. 351 The essential attribute we seek in a drug is not potency, but efficacy at a safe dose. **1978** F. F. COWAN *Pharmacol. for Dental Hygienist* ii. 18 The position of graded dose-response curve along the dose axis is a measure of the drug's potency, i.e., how much of the drug it takes to produce a certain intensity of response... The maximum effect, or efficacy, of a drug is of greater clinical interest.

2. *transf.* A person or body wielding power or influence; a being possessed of power; a power.

1645 W. BALL *Sphere of Govt.* 18 We may give, or Render too much to Cæsar, or Cæsars, Potentates or Potencies. **1741** *Barrow's Wks., Pope's Suprem.* v. I. 669 Before his time the Roman Episcopacy had advanced it self beyond the priesthood into a potency. **1887** C. J. ABBEY *Eng. Ch. & Bps.* I. 119 A firm believer in ghosts, witches, fairies, and such other supernatural potencies.

3. a. Capability of active development; potentiality, inherent capability or possibility.

1644 MILTON *Areop.* (Arb.) 35 Books.. doe contain a potencie of life in them to be as active as that soule was whose progeny they are. **1645** RUTHERFORD *Tryal & Tri. Faith* vi. (1845) 72 A plant is a tree in the potency. **1874** TYNDALL *Belfast Address* 55, I.. discern in that Matter.. the promise and potency of all terrestrial life.

b. *Embryol.* A capacity in embryonic tissue for developing into a particular kind of specialized tissue or organ.

1908 F. R. LILLIE *Devel. of Chick* 9 A very important property of primordia in many animals is their capacity for subdivision, each part retaining the potencies of the whole. **1926** J. S. HUXLEY *Essays Pop. Sci.* 263 The potency of forming limbs is confined to a definite area of the flank. **1958** B. M. PATTEN *Found. Embryol.* v. 108 If an area where a particular potency has been located is exposed in more detail, it is found that there is a certain central part of it from which practically all the explants exhibit the potency in question. **1968** C. W. BODEMER *Mod. Embryol.* ix. 139 During gastrulation the entire nervous system becomes limited in its potencies and can no longer develop into other structures.

4. Degree of (latent) force. Cf. POTENCE[1] 2.

a **1691** BOYLE *Hist. Air* (1692) 97 To conclude readily, what potency the bubble has, by the change of the atmosphere's weight, acquired or lost. **1871** BLACKIE *Four Phases* I. 71 The effects produced by this higher potency of the same force.

5. *Math.* (See quot. 1959.)

1906 [see FACTOR *sb.* 6]. **1959** G. & R. C. JAMES *Math. Dict.* 41/1 The cardinal number of a set is also called the potency of the set and the power of the set.

potenger, obs. form of POTTINGER.

potent ('pəʊtənt), *sb.*[1] and *a.*[2] [app. an alteration or variant of F. *potence* POTENCE[2].]

A. *sb.* †**1.** A crutch; a staff with a cross piece to lean upon; also *transf.* a crozier. *Obs.*

1362 LANGL. *P. Pl.* A. IX. 88 Dobest is a-boue boþe, And Bereþ a Busschopes cros,.. A pyk is in þe potent to punge a-doun þe wikkede. ? *a* **1366** CHAUCER *Rom. Rose* 368 So old she was that she ne wente A fote, but it were by potente. *c* **1375** *Sc. Leg. Saints* xxix. (*Placidas*) 28 For þe thryd fut hym worthis þen Haf a potent hym on to len. *Ibid.* xl. (*Ninian*) 495 His patent can [= gan] with hym ta Priuely, ore he wald ga [cf. 514 For-þi his stafe sone has he tan]. *c* **1420** LYDG. *Thebes* I. in *Chaucer's Wks.* (1561) 359 b/1 He taketh a potent, And on three feete, thus he goeth ayen. **1480** CAXTON *Ovid's Met.* XIV. xii, He.. wente with a potente or stylthe on whyche he lened.

b. *fig.* A support, stay. Cf. CRUTCH *sb.* 1 c. *Obs.* or *arch.*

1426 LYDG. *De Guil. Pilgr.* 9177 Thow art hys pyler & hys potent; And ellys he were Inpotent. *c* **1430** —— *Min. Poems* (Percy Soc.) 240 Jhesu be my staff and my potent. **1891** STEVENSON *In South Seas* (1900) 249 He was but waiting to capitulate, and looked about for any potent to relieve the strain.

†**2.** A gibbet. *Sc. Obs. rare.*

1549 *Compl. Scot.* xix. 162 [He] gart heyde them, and syne he gart hyng ther quartars on potentis at diuerse comont passagis on the feildis.

†**3.** A cross handle like the head of a crutch.

1688 R. HOLME *Armoury* III. 337/1 There is an other sort of these Dung Forks.. without a Raspe, or Potent, on the head.

B. *adj. Her.* Having the limbs terminating in potents or crutch-heads, as ***cross potent***; formed by a series of potents. ***potent (and) counter-potent***: see COUNTER-POTENT.

1610 GUILLIM *Heraldry* II. vii. (1660) 82 He bears.. a Crosse potent. **1725** COATS *Dict. Her.*, *Potent*,.. a Cross Potent, by reason of the Resemblance its Extremities bear to the Head of a Crutch. **1766–87** PORNY *Heraldry* (ed. 4) Gloss., *Potent*, *a*... said of a Cross terminating like a T, at its upper extremities. **1882** CUSSANS *Her.* (ed. 3) 54 Potent is formed by a number of figures, bearing some resemblance to crutch-heads, arranged in horizontal lines, in the same manner as Vair. **1894** *Parker's Gloss. Her.*, *Potent*,.. also gives its name to one of the heraldic furs, composed of any metal and colour: this is, however, usually blazoned *Potent counter-potent*. *Ibid.*, *Potent* is also applied to the edge of an ordinary or to a line of division, though the latter but rarely. *Ibid.* s.v. *Cross*, *Cross potent*, written sometimes *potence* (fr. potencée): so called because its arms terminate in potents,.. or like crutches. Also called a Jerusalem cross.

potent ('pəʊtənt), *a.*[1] and *sb.*[2] [ad. L. *potens*, *-ent-em* powerful, pres. part. of *posse* (*potis esse*) to be powerful or able.]

A. *adj.* **1. a.** Powerful, possessed of great power; having great authority or influence; mighty: used of persons and things, with many shades of meaning, as the power implied is political, military, social, supernatural, moral, mental, etc. (Usually a poetic or rhetorical word, felt to be stronger than *powerful*.)

a **1500** *Priests of Peblis* in Pinkerton *Scot. Poems Repr.* (1792) I. 10 Than come he hame a verie potent man; And spousit syne a michtie wyfe richt than. *a* **1550** in *Dunbar's Poems* (S.T.S.) 324 The potent Prince of joy imperiall, The he surmonting Empriour abone. **1598** SHAKS. *Merry W.* IV. iv. 89 The Doctor is well monied, and his friends Potent at Court. **1603** DRAYTON *Bar. Wars* III. viii, Thus sits the great Enchauntresse in her cell,.. With Vestall fire her potent liquor warmes. **1630** *R. Johnson's Kingd. & Commw.* 84 The potentest state there, boasting of the bravery of 200. gallies, and eight or ten galleases. **1639** N. N. tr. *Du Bosq's Compl. Woman* II. 1 The wisest and potentest of men. **1667** MILTON *P.L.* XII. 211 Moses once more his potent Rod extends Over the Sea. **1696** TATE & BRADY *Ps.* viii. 7 They jointly own his potent Sway. **1711** in *10th Rep. Hist. MSS. Comm.* App. v. 164 A smaller garrison held the town.. against a potenter host. **1783** CRABBE *Village* I. 282 A potent quack, long vers'd in human ills, Who first insults the victim whom he kills. **1813** H. & J. SMITH *Horace in Lond.* 38 Potent once at quoits and cricket, Head erect and heart elate. **1880** MCCARTHY *Own Times* IV. lxii. 375 His influence and his name were potent in every corner of the globe. **1897** W. L. CLOWES *Royal Navy* I. xi. 380 The danger of making any effort of the kind in face of a 'potent' fleet.

b. Of reasons, principles, motives, ideas: Cogent, effective, convincing.

1606 SHAKS. *Tr. & Cr.* III iii. 192 But 'gainst your priuacie The reasons are more potent and heroycall. **1679** J. GOODMAN *Penit. Pard.* III. vi. (1713) 385 Fear.. is neither so lasting a principle, nor so potent and effective a motive as hope. **1782** MISS BURNEY *Cecilia* VII. vi, An objection which, however potent, is single. **1875** HELPS *Soc. Press.* iii. 51 Ideas which should shiver into atoms some of our present most potent ideas.

2. Having strong physical or chemical properties: as a potent solvent, drug, etc.

1715 ROWE *Lady J. Gray* I. i. 25 Is there no help in all the healing art, No potent juice or drug to save a life So precious? **1756** C. LUCAS *Ess. Waters* I. 113 The most potent and probably the proper solvent of iron, is the vitriolic acid. **1807–26** S. COOPER *First Lines Surg.* (ed. 5) 242 With respect to mercury, or any other potent remedy. **1899** *Allbutt's Syst. Med.* VIII. 800 Of more potent remedies, salicylic acid is perhaps the most trustworthy.

3. Capable of orgasm in sexual intercourse: applied chiefly to men. Opp. IMPOTENT *a.* 2 b.

1893 E. MARTIN *Impotence & Sexual Weakness* 74 He.. took to himself a wife, and showed by subsequent events, that he was both potent and fertile. **1899** *Allbutt's Syst. Med.* VIII. 149 Such a man.. impotent awake, potent only in dreams. **1929** G. R. SCOTT *Sex & its Mysteries* xii. 110 So long as there is no disease or malformation of the genital organs a woman is potent until practically her dying days. **1975** L. B. HOBSON *Examination of Patient* ix. 360 Sexual arousal, erection, and even ejaculation.. are emotional as well as hormonal, and a man castrated in later life is still able to have sexual intercourse; that is, he remains potent. He is, however, sterile, since he produces no sperm.

†**B.** *sb. Obs.* **1.** Power; a power.

1512 *Helyas* in Thoms *Prose Rom.* (1828) III. 56 To praise and honour you as well for the honoure that God hath doone to you as for your noble potentes. **1631** *Celestina* VII. 88 Such a peerelesse Potent, a commanding Power, as thy imperious unparaleld beauty!

2. One who has power or authority; a potent person; a potentate.

1595 SHAKS. *John* II. i. 358 Cry hauocke kings, back to the stained field You equall Potents, fierie kindled spirits. **1642** W. BIRD *Mag. Honor* 8 There be other Potents under the King, which are called Barons.

3. A military warrant or order.

1622 F. MARKHAM *Bk. War* III. vi. 103 The Victuall-Master.. may send forth his warrants or potents for the bringing in of all manner of victualls at their ordinary prizes. **1689** G. WALKER *Siege of Derry* 15 A Fortnight later, we receiv'd a Potent to March to St. Johnstown. **1690** J. MACKENZIE *Siege London-Derry* 5/2 The Potent being more narrowly inspected, was found defective.

potent, *a.*[2]: see after POTENT *sb.*[1]

†'**potentacy.** *Obs.* [f. POTENTATE: see -ACY.] The state or rule of a potentate; supreme power.

1576 FLEMING *Panopl. Epist.* 357 The usurping potentacie, and outragious rule of thundering Tyraunts. **1681** *Whole Duty Nations* 14 Their Interests.. are preserved and kept distinct, as these are often allowed to be under some conquering Potentacy. **1701** BEVERLEY *Glory of Grace* 48 That, in which the Supreme, the Infinite Wisdom, Holiness, Dominion, Potentacy, hath placed its Glory.

potentate ('pəʊtənteɪt), *sb.* (*a.*) Also 4–6 **potentat.** [ad. L. *potentātus* (*u*-stem) power, dominion, in late L. a potentate (whence F. *potentat*), f. *potens* POTENT *a.*[1]: see -ATE[1].]

1. A person endowed with independent power; a prince, monarch, ruler.

c **1400** *Apol. Loll.* 30 Til ȝe alon wil be potentats in þe kirk. *a* **1548** HALL *Chron.*, *Hen. V* 81 b, No potentate was more piteous nor lorde more bounteous. **1591** SHAKS. *1 Hen. VI*, III. ii. 136 But Kings and mightiest Potentates must die, For that's the end of humane miserie. **1667** MILTON *P.L.* v. 706 All obey'd The wonted signal, and superior voice Of thir great Potentate. **1769** GRAY *Installation Ode* 37 High potentates and dames of royal birth. **1867** FREEMAN *N.C.* I. ii. 39 The mightiest potentate of the East.

2. A powerful city, state, or body; = POWER 6 b.

1624 CAPT. SMITH *Virginia* III. 94 Carthage grew so great a Potentate, that [etc.]. **1719** W. WOOD *Surv. Trade* 325 The best Security against any future Designs or Attempts from the French, or any other Potentate. **1855** MACAULAY *Hist. Eng.* xviii. IV. 130 Nothing indicated that the East India Company would ever become a great Asiatic potentate.

†**B.** *adj.* Powerful, ruling. *Obs.*

1556 J. HEYWOOD *Spider & F.* lxv. 54 This spider hath vsurpedlie growne To potentate state. **1597** A. M. tr. *Guillemeau's Fr. Chirurg.* 50/2 Those mighty and potentat Lordes. **1648** S. FAIRCLOUGH *Prisoner's Praises*, etc. (1650) 39 Execute.. the spirit of mortification upon your potentate and predominate sins.

'**potented,** *a. Her.* [f. POTENT *sb.*[1] + -ED[2].] (See quots.) So ‖**potentée** *a.*

c **1828** BERRY *Encycl. Herald.* I. Gloss, *Potented*, or *Potentée*, ordinaries are so termed when the outer edges are formed into *potents*, differing from what is called *potent counter-potent*, which is the forming of the whole surface of the ordinary into potents and counterpotents like the fur. *Ibid.*, *Bend potentée*, like the bend patée, is formed by one limb of the cross potent issuing from the sides. **1830** ROBSON *Brit. Herald* III, *Potented*, or *Potentée*. **1889** in ELVIN *Heraldry* 103/2.

‖**po'tentia.** [L., = power.] ***in potentia*** = in POSSE: see ‖IN 38.

1601 A. COPLEY *Answ. Let. Jesuited Gent.* 26 No compleate head in *esse* but only in *potentia*. **1612** JONSON *Alchemist* II. iii. sig. E 1 The Egg's.. a Chicken, in Potentia. **1674** N. FAIRFAX *Treat. Bulk & Selvedge* vi. 170 Gods bare Essence must be forthwith or actu, but his everlasting Essence.. must be forth-coming or in potentia. **1797** *Encycl. Brit.* XV. 441/2 Potential, in the schools, is used to denote and distinguish a kind of qualities, which are supposed to exist in the body *in potentia* only. **1948** *Mind* LVII. 486 When I claim to *know* I simply make emphatic that I am logically committed, *in potentia*, in certain determinate ways. **1957** L. DURRELL *Justine* I. 75 Life, the new material, is only lived *in potentia* until the artist deploys it in his work.

potential (pəʊˈtɛnʃəl), *a.* and *sb.* Also 4-6 -enciall. [ME. *potenciall*, ad. late L. *potentiālis* (Albertus Magnus *a* 1250, but cf. *potentiāliter* adv. 5th c., Sidon.), f. *potentia* POTENCY + -AL[1]; so OF. *potencial* (14-15th c. in Godef.), mod.F. *potentiel*.]

A. *adj.* **1.** Possessing potency or power; potent, powerful, mighty, strong; commanding. Now *rare*.

c **1485** *Digby Myst.* (1882) II. 360 The myght of the fadires potenciall deite. *a* **1529** SKELTON *Prayer to Father* 2 Celestial Father, potencial God of myght. **1604** SHAKS. *Oth.* I. ii. 13 The Magnifico is much belou'd, And hath in his effect a voice potentiall As double as the Dukes. **1796** MORSE *Amer. Geog.* I. 683 The bark, when sufficiently masticated, operates as a very potential purge and emetic. **1860** MILL *Repr. Govt.* (1865) 19/1 The nation as a whole, and every individual composing it, are without any potential voice in their own destiny.

2. Possible as opposed to actual; existing *in posse* or in a latent or undeveloped state, capable of coming into being or action; latent.

1398 TREVISA *Barth. De P.R.* XIX. viii. (Bodl. MS), Potencial liȝt þat is in a bodie medled and derke passeþ not to worke in dede but bi comynge of outeward liȝt. **1626** PRYNNE *Perpet. Regen. Man's Est.* 262 This cannot imply an actuall or a potentiall fall from the state of grace. **1657** S. PURCHAS *Pol. Flying-Ins.* I. ii. 3 The Worm or Potential Bee. **1766** BLACKSTONE *Comm.* II. xvi. 261 When he [a sole corporation] dies or resigns, though there is no actual owner of the land till a successor be appointed, yet there is a legal, potential ownership, subsisting in contemplation of law. **1861** KENT *Comm. Amer. Law* (1873) II. xxxix. 468 The thing sold must have an actual or potential existence. **1872** NICHOLSON *Biol.* 15 Life may remain in a dormant or 'potential' condition for an apparently indefinite length of time. **1897** *Westm. Gaz.* 10 Mar. 6/2 The ships..put out under steam, running eight or nine throughout the night to avoid potential torpedoes.

3. *Med.* ***potential cautery***, an agent which produces the same effects on the skin as an *actual cautery* or red-hot iron. So ***potential corrosive***.

c **1400** *Lanfranc's Cirurg.* 305 He knowiþ not þe difference bitwixe a cauterie þat is clepid actuel & potencial. **1597** A. M. tr. *Guillemeau's Fr. Chirurg.* 17 b/2 We vse nowe in these dayes potentialle corrosiues. **1612** WOODALL *Surg. Mate* Wks. (1653) 90 In which case..a potential Caustick medicament..is convenient. **1696** PHILLIPS (ed. 5), *Potential Cautery*..is that which is perform'd with Limestone or other Caustick Druggs. **1758** J. S. tr. *Le Dran's Observ. Surg.* (1771) 174, I prefer the Potential Cautery, such as the Lapis Infernalis, or the Mercurial Water. **1895** *Syd. Soc. Lex., Potential cautery*, nitrate of silver..or Potassa fusa, as distinct from the *Actual cautery*, or red-hot iron.

4. *Gram.* **a.** That expresses potentiality or possibility: ***potential mood***, a name sometimes given to the subjunctive mood, when used to express possibility; the subjunctive mood used potentially.

In French Grammar, sometimes applied to the Conditional (*j'aurais, je serais*, etc.).

[**1524** LINACRE *De Emendata Structura Latini Sermonis* (ed. Paris 1550) 30 Potentialem vocamus, quem Graeci per ἂν coniunctionem & verbum duplicis modi, alias indicatiui, alias optatiui, explicant.]

1530 PALSGR. Introd. 31 Modes: every parfyte verbe hath vi, the indicatyve, imperatyve, optatyve or potenciall, the subjunctyve, the condicionall, and the infynityve. **1612** BRINSLEY *Pos. Parts* (1669) 31 How know you the Potential Mood? It sheweth an ability, will, or duty to do any thing. **1704** J. HARRIS *Lex. Techn.* I, *Potential Mood in Grammar*, is the same in form with the *Subjunctive*; but differs in this, That it hath always Implied in it, either *Possum, Volo*, or *Debeo*; as *Roget Quis*, that is, *Rogare potest*, a Man may ask. **1824** L. MURRAY *Eng. Gram.* (ed. 5) I. II. i. 117 That the Potential Mood should be separated from the subjunctive, is evident, from the intricacy and confusion which are produced by their being blended together, and from the distinct nature of the two moods; the former of which may be expressed without any condition, supposition, etc. **1837** G. PHILLIPS *Syriac Gram.* 111, The tenses, especially the future, either alone or in connection with one or more particles, in many cases express a potential, subjunctive, or hypothetical sense. **1876** MASON *Eng. Gram.* (ed. 21) 60 To these moods [Infinitive, Indicative, Imperative, Subjunctive] many grammarians add the Potential Mood, meaning by that mood certain combinations of the so-called auxiliary verbs *may, might, can, could, must*, with the infinitive mood. This is objectionable. **1945** *Language* XXI. 2 In English what may be called the potential mode of the verb is an overt category marked by the morpheme *can* or *could*. **1946** [see HANDLE *v.*[1] 1 b]. **1964** P. HEALEY in F. W. Householder *Syntactic Theory I* (1972) III. xv. 216 It will be noted that the Potential tense may occur in the Quote of the Saying sub-type.

b. With humorous play on sense 2.

1680 T. JORDAN *London's Glory* 2 [Followed by] all Lord Mayors in the Potential Mood. **1823** BYRON *Juan* XI. xxxv, By those who govern in the mood potential.

5. *Physics.* **a.** ***potential function***: a mathematical function or quantity by the differentiation of which the force at any point in space arising from any system of bodies, etc. can be expressed. In the case in which the system consists of separate masses, electrical charges, etc., this quantity is equal to the sum of these, each divided by its distance from the point.

Introduced in 1828, by G. Green, with special reference to electricity.

1828 G. GREEN *Applic. Math. Anal. to Electr. & Magn.* in *Math. Papers* (1871) 9 Nearly all the attractive and repulsive forces..in nature are such, that if we consider any material point *p*, the effect, in a given direction, of all the forces acting upon that point, arising from any system of bodies *S* under consideration, will be expressed by a partial differential of a certain function of the co ordinates which serve to define the point's position in space. The consideration of this function is of great importance in many inquiries... We shall often have occasion to speak of this function, and will therefore, for abridgement, call it the potential function arising from the system *S*. **1882** MINCHIN *Unipl. Kinemat.* 135 The function ϕ is called the potential-function of the strain, and the curves obtained by varying the constant in the equation $\phi = C$ are called curves of equal potential. **1931** *Rev. Mod. Physics* III. 288 He..used several forms for the potential function; one in which the potential depended only upon central force fields..and others in which the potential was also a function of the apex angle. **1939** L. BAIRSTOW *Appl. Aerodynamics* (ed. 2) vii. 320 The boundary conditions to be satisfied are easily deduced; a solid boundary must be a stream-line and along it ψ must be constant or $d\phi/ds$ zero. In the case of the potential function the condition takes the form that the normal velocity, i.e. $d\phi/dh$ must be zero. **1960** HOUGHTON & BROCK *Aerodynamics* xi. 267 The velocity potential and the stream function are combined in a new function called the complex potential function. **1967** N. M. QUEEN *Vector Anal.* vii. 66 An auxiliary function from which a given vector field $\mathbf{V}$ can be derived by a suitable differential operation is sometimes called a potential function for $\mathbf{V}$; in particular, ϕ and $\mathbf{A}$ in equation (7.2) are known as the scalar and vector potentials for $\mathbf{V}$.

b. ***potential energy***: energy existing in a positional form, not as motion: see ENERGY 6.

Introduced by Rankine in 1853, *potential* being opposed to *actual*, as in sense 2; Thomson and Tait substituted *kinetic* for *actual*, making *potential energy* the opposite of *kinetic energy*. The Latin expression *vis potentialis* had been used by the two Bernoullis and Euler *a* 1750.

[**1744** EULER *Methodus inveniendi lineas curvas*, etc. 246 Quamobrem cum vir celeberrimus..Daniel Bernoulli mihi indicasset se universam vim, quae in lamina elastica incurvata insit, una quadam formula quam *vim potentialem* appellat complecti posse.]

1853 W. RANKINE *Transform. Energy* in *Sci. Papers* (1881) 203 By the occurrence of such changes, actual energy disappears, and is replaced by Potential or Latent Energy; which is measured by the product of a change of state into the resistance against which that change is made. (The vis viva of matter in motion, thermometric heat, radiant heat, light, chemical action, and electric currents, are forms of actual energy; amongst those of potential energy are those of the mechanical powers of gravitation, elasticity, chemical affinity, statical electricity, and magnetism. **1866** ODLING *Anim. Chem.* 71 We may thus render muscular force latent in a stretched bowstring, raised cannon-ball, or other instrument, for any length of time. This latent force is generally spoken of as potential energy, while the active force exertable at any moment by the flying arrow or falling ball constitutes its actual or dynamic energy. **1868** THOMSON & TAIT *Elem. Dynamics* 74 The *potential energy* of a conservative system, in the configuration which it has at any instant, is the amount of work that its mutual forces perform during the passage of the system from any one chosen configuration to the configuration at the time referred to. **1875** GAMGEE tr. *Hermann's Elem. Hum. Physiol.* Introd. 1 The human body..is an organism in which, by the chemical change of its constituent parts, *potential* is converted into *kinetic* energy. **1876** TAIT *Rec. Adv. Phys. Sc.* (1885) 364 Excellent instances of potential energy are supplied by..the wound up 'weights' of a clock .., by gunpowder, the chemical affinities of whose constituents are called into play by a spark [etc.]. **1881** MAXWELL *Electr. & Magn.* (ed. 2) I. 16 To determine the value of the potential energy when the magnet is placed in the field of force expressed by this potential.

c. ***potential temperature*** [tr. G. *potentielle temperatur* (W. von Bezold 1888, in *Sitzungsb. der K. Preuss. Akad. der Wissensch. zu Berlin* 1190)]: the temperature that a given body of gas or liquid would have if it were brought adiabatically to a standard pressure of 1 bar or 1 atmosphere.

1891 C. ABBE tr. W. von Bezold in *Mechanics of Earth's Atmosphere* xvi. 243 Von Helmholtz recognized the objection..and proposed that the word 'wärmegehalt' should be replaced by the evidently much more proper expression 'potential temperature'. When without gain or loss of heat it is adiabatically or pseudo-adiabatically reduced to the normal pressure. **1937** N. A. V. PIERCY *Aerodynamics* i. 21 An atmosphere is stable when the potential temperature is greater, the greater the altitude. **1962** W. S. VON ARX *Introd. Physical Oceanogr.* v. 128 In the very deepest part of the ocean such as in the trenches flanking island arcs, it can be shown that the potential temperature of the water is virtually uniform from the depth of the surrounding ocean floor to the bottom of the trench, even though the actual temerature increases somewhat with depth. **1967** P. GROEN *Waters of Sea* vii. 290 At 3500 meters, where the temperature is 1·6°C, the potential temperature is only 0·3°C lower. Whereas strictly speaking the temperature is not invariable even if there is no heat exchange, the potential temperature is, if the water proceeds to other depths and is therefore subjected to a different pressure.

B. *sb.* †**1.** A potential agent, a thing that gives power. *Obs. rare.*

1656 BLOUNT *Glossogr., Potentials*, things apt to breed or give power, strength or ability.

2. That which is possible, opposed to what is actual; a possibility. Also, resources that can be used or developed; freq. preceded by a defining word.

1817 COLERIDGE *Biog. Lit.* I. xii. 245 The *potential* works *in* them, even as the *actual* works on them! **1883** EDERSHEIM *Life Jesus* (ed. 6) I. 634 With this belief our highest thoughts of the potential for humanity..are connected. **1889** J. M. ROBERTSON *Ess. Crit. Method* 92 The faculty..must be held to reach its highest potential, on the side of literature, in the case of personal gift cultivated by a literary life. **1941** *Sun* (Baltimore) 24 June 10/2 The vast armored power, mobile tactics and industrial potential of the Nazi armies have been exhibited and proved in the Low Countries, France and the Balkans. **1943** *Times* 10 Dec. 5/3 The whole war potential of the German Reich. **1958** *Spectator* 14 Feb. 196/1 Industrial potential has multiplied six times since currency reform. **1958** *Listener* 27 Nov. 897/1 Mr. Cooper managed to slip the theme of indifference and its potential into this play without breaking its back. **1959** *Ibid.* 23 July 122/2 There is thought to be enormous oil potential. **1965** *Ibid.* 1 July 22/3 All collections have a built-in boredom potential. **1969** H. MACINNES *Salzburg Connection* xx. 281 His record ..has been excellent. His potential was high—very high. **1970** *Nature* 26 Dec. 1248/2 Although oceans and seas cover some 360 thousand km².., exploitation of their vast potential is only just beginning. **1978** *Observer* (Colour Suppl.) 12 Nov. 58/4 Children without these experiences.. are likely to be handicapped in terms of the development of their full potential. **1979** *Country Life* 21 June 2047/3 This ever-perceived dark potential is surely part of the reason why the cat is the intellectuals' favourite beast.

3. *Gram.* Short for *potential mood*: see A. 4.

4. *Physics.* **a.** Short for *potential function*: see A. 5 a. Hence, the amount of energy or quantity of work denoted by this, considered as a quality or condition of the matter, electricity, etc., in question. See quots. More generally, any function from which a vector field $\mathbf{F}$ can be derived by differentiation, esp. the scalar potential ϕ, where $\mathbf{F} = -\text{ grad }\phi$, and the vector potential $\mathbf{A}$, where $\mathbf{F} = \text{curl }\mathbf{A}$.

('*Potential* as the name of a function was undoubtedly introduced by Gauss in 1840' (G. F. Becker in *Amer. Jrnl. Sci.* 1893, Feb. 97). [Cf. GAUSS *Allgem. Lehrsätze d. Quadrats d. Entfernung* Wks. 1877 V. 200 Zur bequemern Handhabung..werden wir uns erlauben dieses *V* mit einer besonderen Benennung zu belegen, und die Grösse das *Potential* der Massen, worauf sie sich bezieht, nennen.])

1828 G. GREEN *On Applic. Math. Anal.* etc. in *Math. Papers* (1871) 32 This equation is remarkable on account of its simplicity and singularity, seeing that it gives the value of the potential for any point *p'*, within the surface, when $\bar{V}$, its value at the surface itself, is known, together with [etc.]. **1853** SIR W. THOMSON in *Philos. Mag.* Ser. IV. V. 288 *note*, The potential at any point in the neighbourhood of or within a charged body is the quantity of work that would be required to bring a unit of positive electricity from an infinite distance to that point if the given distribution of electricity remained unaltered. **1866** R. M. FERGUSON *Electr.* (1870) 277 Instead of the word tension, used with reference to the work that can be effected by a charge when openly insulated, or electro-motive force, the word *potential* is now used. **1867** THOMSON & TAIT *Nat. Philos.* (1883) II. 29. §483 This function [the potential] was introduced for gravitation by Laplace, but the name was first given to it by Green, who may almost be said to have in 1828 created the theory, as we now have it. *Ibid.* §485 The *Potential* at any point, due to any attracting or repelling body, or distribution of matter, is the mutual potential energy between it and a unit of matter placed at that point. **1873** J. C. MAXWELL *Treat. Electr. & Magn.* II. III. ii. 27 (*heading*) The Vector-Potential of Magnetic induction. **1876** PREECE & SIVEWRIGHT *Telegraphy* 5 Potential implies that function of electricity which determines its motion from one point to another. And the difference of potential, which determines the amount of this motion, is called electro-motive force. **1879** G. PRESCOTT *Sp. Telephone* 37 The difference..of magnetic potential existing between the diaphragm and the core is increased. **1881** MAXWELL *Electr. & Magn.* I. 76 Potential, in electrical science, has the same relation to Electricity that pressure, in Hydrostatics, has to fluid, or that temperature, in Thermodynamics, has to Heat. **1881** JENKIN *Electr.* 51 The effect of contact in producing or maintaining difference of potentials. **1892** *Pall Mall G.* 4 Feb. 6/3 (Mr. Tesla's demonstration.) Currents of these extremely high potentials appear to be absolutely without effect upon the human organism. **1902** SLOANE *Stand. Electr. Dict.* (ed. 3), The magnetic potential at any point of a magnetic field expresses the work which would be done by the magnetic forces of the field on a positive unit of magnetism as it moves from that point to an infinite distance therefrom... It is the exact analogue of absolute electric potential. **1909** J. G. COFFIN *Vector Anal.* vi. 173 We obtain $\mathbf{H} = ..\nabla \times \mathbf{Q}$... $\mathbf{Q}$ is called the potential due to the current distribution $\mathbf{q}$, or the vector-potential belonging to the magnetic force $\mathbf{H}$... The force vector $\mathbf{H}$ is obtained from the vector $\mathbf{Q}$ in a manner analogous to the way the force vector $\mathbf{F}$ is obtained from the scalar V, where..$\mathbf{F} = \nabla V$. **1933** H. B. PHILLIPS *Vector Anal.* v. 102 When the potential is known the velocity can be obtained by differentiation. If a potential exists it is simpler to describe the motion by means of it rather than the velocity. **1966** *McGraw-Hill Encycl. Sci. & Technol.* X. 540/2 If the acceleration a satisfies a relation such as..$\mathbf{a} = -\text{grad }\Phi$, the Φ is called an acceleration potential. **1971** W. HAUSER *Introd. Princ. Electromagnetism* iii. 77 Vector function $\mathbf{F}_1$ is a curl-less vector function... It is therefore expressible as the negative gradient of a scalar function of position. We thus set $\mathbf{F}_1 = -\nabla\psi(\mathbf{r})$, where the function $\psi(x, y, z)$ is referred to as the scalar potential of $\mathbf{F}_1$. *Ibid.*, The divergenceless vector function $\mathbf{F}_2$ is..expressible as the curl of a vector function $\mathbf{A}, \mathbf{F}_2 = \nabla \times \mathbf{A}$, where $\mathbf{A}$ is referred to as the vector potential of $\mathbf{F}_2$.

attrib. **1896** *Academy* 11 Apr. 399/2 The rate of leak..was no greater when the potential difference was 500 volts than when it was 5. **1898** *Engineering Mag.* XVI. 101 'High potential' electrical heat for irons, broilers, chafing dishes, and local applications. *Ibid.* 104 To run an engine dynamo ..to furnish high potential heat and light.

b. Any of a group of thermodynamic functions mathematically analogous to electric and gravitational potentials, viz. the Gibbs free energy G (or ζ), the Helmholtz free energy A (or F or ψ), the enthalpy H (or χ), the internal energy U (or E or ϵ), and the chemical potential μ.

The Gibbs and the Helmholtz functions are given respectively by $G = U + PV - TS$ and $A = U - TS$, where U is the internal energy, P the pressure, V the volume, T the temperature, and S the entropy of the system.

The chemical potential μ_i of a component i in a given phase is equal to $(\partial G/\partial m_i)_{P,T}$, where m_i is the quantity of the component present in the phase and the quantities of all other components remain constant.

1878 J. W. GIBBS in *Trans. Connecticut Acad. Arts & Sci.* III. 119 If we call a quantity μ_x, as defined by such an equation as (12), the potential for the substance S_x in the homogeneous mass considered, these conditions may be expressed as follows:—The potential for each component substance must be constant throughout the whole mass. *Ibid.* 149 If to any homogeneous mass we suppose an infinitesimal quantity of any substance to be added, the mass remaining homogeneous and its entropy and volume remaining unchanged, the increase of the energy of the mass divided by the quantity of the substance added is the potential of that substance in the mass considered... In the above definition we may evidently substitute for entropy, volume, and energy, respectively, either temperature, volume, and the function ψ; or entropy, pressure, and the function χ; or temperature, pressure, and the function ζ. **1917** G. E. GIBSON tr. *Sackur's Textbk. Thermo-Chem. & Thermodynamics* vi. 178 The component I can go spontaneously from B to A if its chemical potential in A is less than its chemical potential in B. *Ibid.* 179 In chemistry it is usual to take the mol of each component as the unit of mass, and we may then define the chemical potential.. of the component I in the solution A as the change in the thermodynamic potential of a very large mass of A when 1 mol of the component I is added to it without changing the temperature, the pressure or the masses of the other components. **1924** H. S. TAYLOR *Treat. Physical Chem.* I. ii. 67 The thermodynamic potential of all spontaneously occurring processes decreases. **1937** M. W. ZEMANSKY *Heat & Thermodynamics* xvii. 321 If a substance is not present in a phase, it does not follow that its chemical potential is zero. The chemical potential is a measure of the effect on the Gibbs function when a substance *is* introduced. **1950** E. O. HERCUS *Elem. Thermodynamics & Statistical Mech.* iv. 24 Two new thermodynamical quantities dependent only on the state of a system can be defined from the entropy. These are: Free Energy, $F = U - TS$. Thermodynamic Potential, $G = H - TS = U + pv - TS$. **1960** HALL & IBELE *Engin. Thermodynamics* x. 183 The stability of thermodynamic systems can be examined with reference to a set of quantities known as thermodynamic potentials. **1973** D. C. KELLY *Thermodynamics & Statistical Physics* viii. 147 The four thermodynamic potentials were invented to make thermodynamics 'easy'. Each potential is the natural energy variable for certain classes of physical processes.

c. Special Comb.: **potential barrier**, a region in a field of force in which the potential is significantly higher than at points either side of it, so that a particle requires energy to pass through it; *spec.* that surrounding the potential well of an atomic nucleus; **potential flow**, flow which is irrotational and for which there therefore exists a velocity potential; **potential gradient**, (the rate of) change of (electrical) potential with distance; **potential scattering** *Nuclear Physics*, elastic scattering of a particle by an atomic nucleus in which the scattering cross-section varies smoothly with the energy of the incident particle (cf. *resonance scattering*); **potential wall**, a region in a field of force in which the potential increases sharply; **potential well**, a region in a field of force in which the potential is significantly lower than at points immediately outside it, so that a particle in it is likely to remain there unless it gains a relatively large amount of energy; *spec.* that in which an atomic nucleus is situated.

1929 *Physical Rev.* XXXIII. 134 The particle in the internal region received energy sufficient to raise it over the *potential barrier. **1931** G. GAMOW *Constitution of Atomic Nuclei* ii. 37 How can such an α-particle get out from the nucleus if it has to cross on its way a potential barrier which is certainly higher than the total energy of the α-particle itself? **1966** H. J. REICH et al. *Theory & Applications Active Devices* iii. 64 An electron encounters a potential barrier in moving from left to right across the junction. **1973** V. ACOSTA et al. *Essent. Mod. Physics* xvi. 223 *(heading)* A beam of particles of kinetic energy E is incident on a potential barrier $V > E$ with a width of $OA = t$. **1937** N. A. V. PIERCY *Aerodynamics* v. 140 Irrotational flow is often called *potential flow. **1962** WALSHAW & JOBSON *Mech. of Fluids* viii. 211 'Potential' flows.. neglect viscous actions and merely provide a framework of reference against which the behaviour of a real fluid may be compared. **1975** *Sci. Amer.* Nov. 85/1 An airfoil or a wing in steady motion through the air is a device by means of which circulation is created and maintained in the form of a vortex bound to the wing. This bound vortex is then superposed on the flow pattern that the wing profile would produce in an ideal fluid. The pattern is termed the potential flow. **1895** A. DANIELL *Text-bk. Princ. Physics* (ed. 3) xvi. 585 This Electric Force on Unit Quantity, $\phi = (V' - V'') \div d$, is the Potential-Slope or *Potential-Gradient. **1931** *Discovery* July 212/1 Measurements of potential gradient have been made in balloons up to a height of nine kilometres. The gradient falls off rapidly, most of the positive charge being in the lower strata. **1963** E. V. VERNON in Zepler & Punnett *Electron Devices & Networks* i. 25 The potential gradient along the material is due to its ohmic resistance. **1973** R. BROWN *Electricity & Atomic Physics* xii. 270 There is a potential gradient in the depletion layer, positive on the *n* side and negative on the *p* side, and this represents a potential barrier. **1937** BETHE & PLACZEK in *Physical Rev.* LI. 460/2 It amounts.. to a scattering cross section $\sigma_1 = 4\pi R^2$... This part may be called *potential scattering in the narrower sense. *Ibid.* 462/1 The total potential scattering is $\sigma_{pot} = (\sigma_1{}^{\frac{1}{2}} - \sigma_3{}^{\frac{1}{2}})$. **1955** A. E. S. GREEN *Nuclear Physics* xiii. 433 Within the category of elastic scattering we may distinguish two types of processes, namely, potential scattering and resonant scattering. **1971** B. L. COHEN *Concepts of Nuclear Physics* xiii. 331 Between the resonances in Fig. 13-7 we see the effects of potential scattering only. **1931** *Proc. R. Soc.* A. CXXXIII. 238 If this theory of the resonance levels is correct, it is difficult to reconcile the results of Pose, who finds quite sharp resonance levels in Al, with the results of experiments on α-particles of sufficient energy to pass over the top of the *potential wall. **1973** V. ACOSTA et al. *Essent. Mod. Physics* xvi. 222 This situation may be treated in a simplified manner by using a thin potential wall—a potential barrier. [**1931** G. GAMOW *Constitution of Atomic Nuclei* i. 18 The potential.. must be more or less constant inside the nucleus and increase sharply at the boundary, the distribution forming a 'potential hole' of the shape shown.] **1935** *Physical Rev.* XLVII. 852/1 The positive valued parameters A and a are to be determined to fit the binding energies of the deuteron and the alpha-particle. Evidently A and $1/a_2^{\frac{1}{2}}$ are directly proportional to the depth and breadth, respectively, of the *potential well. **1952** BLATT & WEISSKOPF *Theoret. Nuclear Physics* ii. 49 Even very refined experiments at low energies do not suffice to determine more than an 'effective range' and 'depth' of the potential well, leaving the detailed shape completely indeterminate. **1972** DEPUY & CHAPMAN *Molec. Reactions & Photochem.* i. 1 Within this potential well the molecule can occupy any of a number of discrete vibrational energy levels.

potentiality (pəʊtɛnʃɪ'ælɪtɪ). [ad. med.L. *potentiālitās* (Albertus Magnus, *a* 1250), f. *potentiāl-is*: see prec. and -ITY. So F. *potentialité*.]

1. The quality of being powerful or having power: see POTENTIAL *a.* 1.

1627 HAKEWILL *Apol.* I. ii. 70 'Habent aliquid potentialitatis admixtum', as Lyra speakes, they haue some kinde of potentiality (I know not how otherwise to render his word) mixed with them. **1656** HOBBES *Liberty, Necess. & Chance* 266 Nor do I understand what derogation it can be to the Divine perfection, to attribute to it Potentiality, that is (in English) Power. **1820** COLERIDGE *Lett., Convers.* etc. I. 133, I have the power, the potentiality of walking. **1875** STUBBS *Const. Hist.* II. xvii. 514 An unlimited and unimpaired potentiality of sovereignty.

2. *esp.* The state or quality of possessing latent power or capacity capable of development into activity; possibility of action or active existence: opposed to *actuality*: see POTENTIAL *a.* 2.

1625 JACKSON *Creed* v. xiv. §2 That potentiality or aptitude which the soul hath to be linked, and made one substance with the body. **1653** H. MORE *Conject. Cabbal.* (1713) 11 By Earth you are to understand, the Potentiality or Capability of the Existence of the outward Creation. **1781** JOHNSON Apr. in Boswell, We are not here to sell a parcel of boilers and vats, but the potentiality of growing rich beyond the dreams of avarice. **1855** BAIN *Senses & Int.* III. i. §37 (1864) 378 The mental conception that we have of empty space, is *scope for movement*, the possibility or potentiality of moving. **1862** DANA *Man. Geol.* 599 Characteristics before only foreshadowed, or existing only in potentiality, come out into full expression.

b. With *a* and *pl.* An instance of this quality; a capacity or possibility, or a condition, thing, or being in which it is embodied.

1668 HOWE *Bless. Righteous* (1825) 44 By the former it hath a potentiality, by the latter an habitude in reference thereunto. **1690** LOCKE *Hum. Und.* II. xxiii. §7 (1695) 160 In this looser sense, I crave leave to be understood, when I name any of these Potentialities amongst the simple Ideas, which we recollect in our Minds, when we think of particular Substances. **1855** H. SPENCER *Princ. Psychol.* (1872) II. VIII. vi. 586 In the joy of liberty regained there are massed together the potentialities and gratifications in general. **1862** —— *First Princ.* I. ii. §11. 33 The self-creation of such a potential universe would involve over again the difficulties here stated—would imply behind this potential universe a more remote potentiality. **1875** *Encycl. Brit.* II. 522/1 The seed is the potentiality of the plant. **1879** HUXLEY *Hume* iii. 85 The conversion, by unknown causes, of these innate potentialities into actual existences.

3. *Electr.* = POTENTIAL *sb.* 4. *rare.*

1898 *Allbutt's Syst. Med.* V. 857 The individual, through whose body there is passing an electric current of not too high potentiality, generally experiences pain.

potentialize (pəʊ'tɛnʃəlaɪz), *v.* [f. POTENTIAL + -IZE.] *trans.* To make potential, give potentiality to; *spec.* in reference to energy, To convert into a potential condition. Hence **po'tentialized** *ppl. a.*, **po'tentializing** *vbl. sb.*; **potentiali'zation**, the action of making potential.

1856 P. FAIRBAIRN *Prophecy* II. III. iv. 431 *note*, The six highly potentialized—three times repeated (666) is the utmost that could be assigned him for a symbolical indication of his nature—this is the number of his name. **1865** tr. *Strauss' New Life Jesus* II. II. lxxix. 273 Neander's attempt to substitute a mere potentialization of the water for vinous properties. **1886** *Amer. Jrnl. Sci.* Ser. III. XXXI. 120 At the extreme configurations of any simple vibration, the energy of the simple movement is entirely potentialized. **1889** *Nature* 3 Oct. 562/1 With a given metal, there is large potentializing in the first stages of strain, and large dissipation in the final stages.

potentially (pəʊ'tɛnʃəlɪ), *adv.* [f. POTENTIAL *a.* + -LY[2].]

1. Powerfully, mightily; authoritatively. Now *rare.*

1549 in Foxe *A. & M.* (1583) 1381/2 The wordes of holy scripture doe worke theyr effectes potencially and thorowly by the mighty operation of the spirite of God. **1656** BLOUNT *Glossogr.*, *Potentially*, powerfully, mightily, substantially, effectually. **1878** B. HARTE *Man on Beach* ii. 53 'That settles the whole matter then,' said Bessie potentially.

2. In a potential or possible manner or state; in potentiality, possibility, or capability: opposed to *actually*.

c **1430** *Art Nombryng* 15 Seithe Boice in Arsemetrike, that vnyte potencially is al nombre, and none in act. **1597** A. M. tr. *Guillemeau's Fr. Chirurg.* 39 b/2 The matter applyed on the bodye, actuallye combureth or potentiallye, wherfore they are called actuall or potentialle Cauteryes. **1614** SELDEN *Titles Hon.* Pref. B iv, It's thought, that, in the Seed are alwaies potentially seuerall indiuiduating Qualities deriu'd from diuers of the neere ancestors. **1768–74** TUCKER *Lt. Nat.* (1834) I. 292 The doctrine of atoms actually, if not potentially, indivisible. *a* **1822** SHELLEY *Def. Poetry* Essays & Lett. (Camelot Class.) 29 The first acorn.. contained all oaks potentially. **1864** BOWEN *Logic* iv. 61 Every Concept must denote some existing object,—existing, that is, either really or potentially.

3. In the potential mood. *rare.*

1861 DICKENS *Gt. Expect.* xlv, Imperative mood, present tense: Do not thou go home, let him not go home, let us not go home... Then, potentially: I may not and I cannot go home.

So **po'tentialness**, potentiality.

1668 WILKINS *Real Char.* 28 Potentialness, Reversion, may, can. **1727** BAILEY vol. II, *Potentialness*, Powerfulness, Efficacy. **1930** G. GREENE *Two Witnesses* 135 The turning of potentialness into creative life.

po'tentiary. *nonce-wd.* [After PLENIPOTENTIARY.] One possessing power to act.

1854 THACKERAY *Newcomes* xxx, The last great potentiary had arrived who was to take part in the family congress.

potentiate (pəʊ'tɛnʃɪeɪt), *v.* [f. L. *potentia* power + -ATE[3]. In quot. 1817 after Ger. *potenzi(e)ren*.]

1. *trans.* To endow with power or potency.

1817 COLERIDGE *Biog. Lit.* xii. (1882) 135, I have even hazarded the new verb potenziate, with its derivatives, in order to express the combination or transfer of powers. **1820** —— in *Lit. Rem.* (1839) IV. 137 Of such exertions.. I do not believe a human soul capable, unless substantiated and successively potentiated by an especial divine grace. **1827–48** HARE *Guesses* (1859) 430 The true ideal is the individual, purified and potentiated, the individual freed from everything that is not individual in it.

2. To make possible.

1865 *Englishm. Mag.* Jan. 51 Before a language can arrive at that maturity which potentiates a strict art of composition, it must pass through every intermediate phase from the formless to the regular.

3. *trans.* To increase the effect of (a drug or its action); to act synergistically with; also, to promote or enhance (a physiological or biochemical phenomenon). Also *fig.*

1917 T. SOLLMANN *Man. Pharmacol.* 96 Mansfield and Hamburger.. believe.. that ether potentiates chloral or morphine, by favoring the distribution of these agents in the nervous system. **1941** *Cancer Res.* I. 107/2 Numerous experiments have shown that various exogenous influences, each in itself carcinogenic, can 'potentiate' each other's influence by simultaneous action. **1962** *Lancet* 13 Jan. 112/1 He showed that cocaine potentiated the pressor action of adrenaline. **1969** D. CLARK *Nobody's Perfect* iii. 109 Though the phenobarbitone had caused death, it had been potentiated by the alcohol. Without the alcohol he might have lived. **1973** R. G. KRUEGER et al. *Introd. Microbiol.* xix. 524/2 The membrane may serve to potentiate cell-virus association and thereby enhance infection. **1974** HAWKEY & BINGHAM *Wild Card* xi. 107 What do you intend doing to potentiate the virus's cytolytic properties? **1977** *Observer* 21 Aug. 21/5 New York potentiates music the same way that alcohol potentiates certain pills.

Hence **po'tentiated** *ppl. a.*; **po'tentiating** *ppl. a.* and *vbl. sb.*; **potenti'ation**, (*a*) the action of potentiating, endowment with power; (*b*) the phenomenon whereby the simultaneous effect of two drugs or other agents may exceed the sum of their individual effects.

a **1834** COLERIDGE *Notes & Lect.* (1849) I. 94 The energies of intellect.. in a rich and more potentiated form. **1840** J. H. GREEN *Vital Dynamics* 31 That potentiation of living existence, which we name animated. **1847** —— *Mental Dynamics* 10 This individuality.. which consists in a higher potentiation and happier combination of the human powers. **1861** *N. Brit. Rev.* No. 70. 377 A highly potentiated feeling of human brotherhood. **1914** J. T. HALSEY tr. *Meyer & Gottlieb's Pharmacol.* xviii. 576 Honigmann's experiments with mixed narcosis with ether and chloroform or ether and alcohol apparently indicate a potentiation. **1917** T. SOLLMANN *Man. Pharmacol.* 96 When several drugs are administered together, each may act independently, as if it were present alone... In many cases, however, the combined action is greater or smaller than would be calculated (potentiated and deficient summation). **1941** *Cancer Res.* I. 107/2 The 'potentiation' seen in the simultaneous action of tumor-producing virus and other carcinogenic influence. *Ibid.*, The above-mentioned 'potentiating' influence of two different exogenous influences. **1958** *Bull. Math. Biophysics* XX. 1 Two drugs may act together synergistically or they may act antagonistically. The former action we shall refer to as positive potentiation; the latter as negative potentiation. **1970** I. MURDOCH *Fairly Honourable Defeat* I. xv. 165 Her body seemed to be weighted and pinned to the sloping bank by a potentiated force of gravity. **1971** P. HUSON *Devil's Picturebk.* ii. 64 Frequent use of a complex mnemotechnic system was believed to result in the enlivening or 'potentiating' of the imagination. **1974** *Aquaculture* IV. 410 Other workers.. have also found the in vivo efficacy of a potentiated sulphonamide.. to be far superior to sulphonamide, used alone, in the treatment of furunculosis. **1974** M. C. GERALD *Pharmacol.* iii. 63 Potentiation may result from two agents acting by different mechanisms or one drug facilitating the action of the other. **1975** *European Jrnl. Pharmacol.* XXXIV. 169 *(heading)* Potentiating effect of lithium chloride on aggressive behaviour induced in mice. **1977** *Amer. N. & Q.* XV. 83/1 These properties include curative power,.. potentiation,.. and the prevention of decay or corruption.

potentiator (pəʊ'tɛnʃɪeɪtə(r)). *Pharm.* [f. prec. + -OR.] An agent that increases the effect of a drug.

1955 *Sci. News Let.* 9 July 19/3 Animals that had just recovered from a barbiturate almost immediately went back into deep hypnosis when given chlorpromazine. This shows that it is a true potentiator, and not merely a prolonger of the action of the barbiturate. **1975** *Acta Endocrinol.* LXXIX. 511 (*heading*) Normal recognition of glucose as a potentiator in subjects with low insulin response and in mild diabetes.

'potentil. *rare.* Anglicized form of next.

1884 MILLER *Plant-n.*, Potentil, Marsh, *Potentilla Comarum* (*Comarum palustre*). **1906** *Daily Chron.* 4 May 6/7 Tormentil and potentil are opening in the woods.

‖**Potentilla** (pəʊtən'tɪlə). *Bot.* [med.L. *potentilla*, f. L. *potens, -ent-em* POTENT + dim. *-illa*; applied *a* 1500 to the Garden Valerian or Phu; in 16th c. to *Potentilla anserina*, whence adopted by Linnæus as name of the genus.] An extensive genus of *Rosaceæ*, comprising herbs and undershrubs, of which the Silverweed, Cinquefoil, and Tormentil are common British species.

[*c* **1300** SIMON JANUENSIS, *Amantilla*, potentilla, fu, valleriana idem. *c* **1450** *Alphita* (Anecd. Oxon.) 150 *Portentilla*, amantilla idem. *Ibid.* 69 *Fu*, ualeriana, amantilla, ueneria, portentilla.] **1548** TURNER *Names of Herbes* H iv, Portentilla or as some write Potentilla, is named also Tanacetum syluestre.. in englishe wylde Tansey. **1578** LYTE *Dodoens* I. lix. 86. **1706** PHILLIPS, *Potentilla*, (Lat.) wild Tansey or Silver-weed; an Herb so call'd from its admirable Virtues. **1776** WITHERING *Brit. Plants* (1796) II. 477 Which confirms the opinion of those who maintain that Potentilla and Tormentilla are not distinct genera. **1867** H. MACMILLAN *Bible Teach.* ii. (1870) 30 Golden *geums* and *potentillas* gleamed like miniature suns. **1883** G. ALLEN in *Longm. Mag.* 306 The potentillas are a group of very lowly and primitive roses.

potentiometer (pəʊtɛnʃɪ'ɒmɪtə(r)). [f. L. *potentia* power (with allusion to POTENTIAL *sb.* 4) + -METER.] **1. a.** A device for measuring potential difference or an e.m.f. by balancing it against a variable potential difference of known value produced by passing a known (usu. fixed) current through a known (usu. variable) resistance.

1897 W. C. FISHER (*title*) The Potentiometer and its adjuncts. **1906** *Athenæum* 27 Oct. 517/3 The various methods of measuring resistances and a description of the uses of the potentiometer. **1922** GLAZEBROOK *Dict. Appl. Physics* II. 611/2 A Weston cell having an E.M.F. of 1·0183 volts would be balanced across 10 coils and 0·183 of the total length of the slide wire, the pressure drop across each coil of the potentiometer being then 0·1 volt. **1935** TURNER & BANNER *Electr. Measurements* xi. 127 The Crompton type is one of the most widely used potentiometers; in this, instead of a continuous slide wire covering the whole voltage range, resistance coils are used with a selector switch. **1975** D. G. FINK *Electronics Engineers' Handbk.* xvii. 6 The constant-resistance potentiometer.. uses a variable current through a fixed resistance to generate a voltage for obtaining a null with the unknown emf.

b. A voltage divider which is regulated by varying a resistance; also, *loosely*, a rheostat.

1910 G. W. PIERCE *Princ. Wireless Telegr.* xxvii. 324 The accurate adjustment of the local voltage is achieved by the use of a potentiometer. **1914** R. STANLEY *Text-bk. Wireless Telegr.* xvi. 221 Such an arrangement of battery and wire is called a potentiometer; by means of it we can obtain any voltage, to apply to our apparatus, from zero up to the full voltage of the battery. **1955** *Sci. Amer.* Aug. 96/2 Connect the power supply to the solution [in the ice-box dishes] through the carbon electrodes and adjust the potentiometer or tapped resistor to the prescribed potential of 200 volts. **1962** F. I. ORDWAY et al. *Basic Astronautics* ix. 375 The voltage in a current varies with the displacement of the mass by means of a potentiometer. **1966** *McGraw-Hill Encycl. Sci. & Technol.* X. 542/1 By using only the movable and one fixed connection, a potentiometer may be used as a rheostat. **1968** A. MARCUS *Electricity for Technicians* iv. 59 Such variable resistors are called rheostats or potentiometers.

2. *attrib.* and *Comb.*

1881 W. G. ADAMS in *Nature* 21 Apr. 582 The electrometer or potentiometer method, in which the difference of potential between two points in the circuit with a given resistance between them is directly measured. **1916** C. C. GARRARD *Electric Switch & Controlling Gear* iv. 261 Potentiometer-type regulators are used when it is desired to reduce the voltage applied to the terminals of the field coil to zero, as is the case, for example, with boosters. **1920** *Whittaker's Electr. Engineer's Pocket-bk.* (ed. 4) 434 These curves can be used for any potentiometer regulator which has a resistance 3½ times the field coil. **1922** GLAZEBROOK *Dict. Appl. Physics* II. 615/2 The total resistance of the potentiometer circuit remains unchanged whatever the setting of the dials. **1961** G. V. SADLER in G. F. Tagg *Pract. Electr. Engin.* III. 215 Special precautions must also be taken when potentiometer control is used on a crane whose d.c. supply is obtained from a static rectifier. **1962** G. A. T. BURDETT *Automatic Control Handbk.* ix. 4 Potentiometer pressure transducers are made in a number of forms. **1966** *McGraw-Hill Encycl. Sci. & Technol.* X. 543/2 Potentiometer measurement of current is accomplished by passing current through a standardized resistor of appropriate value and measuring the potential difference across this resistor. **1979** *Sci. Digest* July 35/1 When potentiometer controls are used with microprocessor games the analog voltage due to the potentiometer must be converted into a digital quantity.

Hence **potentio'metric** *a.*, of or pertaining to a potentiometer; employing, or obtained by means of, a potentiometer; *potentiometric titration*, a titration which is followed by measuring the change in potential of an electrode immersed in the sample solution; **potentio'metrically** *adv.*; **potenti'ometry**, the technique of measurement with potentiometers, esp. in chemical analysis.

1915 *Jrnl. Chem. Soc.* CVIII. II. 307 (*heading*) Potentiometric arrangement for electrochemical investigations. **1926** KOLTHOFF & FURMAN *Potentiometric Titrations* viii. 151 Everyone who has had experience with the performance of potentiometric titrations knows that, near the equivalence-point especially,.. the potential does not become constant immediately after the addition of the reagent. *Ibid.* xi. 247 Manganous salts may be titrated potentiometrically according to the Volhard-Wolff method. **1931** I. M. KOLTHOFF *Colorimetric & Potentiometric Determination of pH* vii. 129 (*heading*) Problems in potentiometry. **1946** L. MICHAELIS in A. Weissberger *Physical Methods Org. Chem.* II. xxii. 1052 Potentiometry consists of the measurement of the electro-motive force of a galvanic cell composed of two half-cells one of which is a reference half-cell of known composition; and the other an electrode immersed in the solution to be investigated. **1966** ELVIDGE & SAMMES *Course Mod. Techniques Org. Chem.* (ed. 2) xxxiv. 284 Potentiometry makes possible the titration of very weak acids and bases. **1967** *Times Rev. Industry* Oct. 49/3 The length of the cable is then determined by a potentiometric method and may be indicated at any remote control position. **1972** GRUNWALD & KIRSCHENBAUM *Introd. Quantitative Chem. Anal.* xviii. 337 A silver-silver halide electrode is used for the potentiometric titration of a mixture of halide salts with silver nitrate. **1975** D. G. FINK *Electronics Engineers' Handbk.* x. 13 Potentiometric displacement transducers are widely used because of their relative simplicity of construction and their ability to provide a high-level output. **1978** *Nature* 17 Aug. p. ix/1 Finally the controller starts the titration to titrate the free iodine potentiometrically using sodium thiosulphate.

†**po'tentional**, *a. Obs. rare*⁻¹. Erroneous form for POTENTIAL.

1651 FRENCH *Distill.* v. 162 Then.. the earth.. did specificate that potentionall salt.. into a nitrous salt.

potentiostat (pə'tɛnʃɪəʊstæt). [f. POTENTI(AL *a.* and *sb.* + -O + -STAT.] A device used to regulate automatically the potential difference between electrodes in electrolysis.

1942 A. HICKLING in *Trans. Faraday Soc.* XXXVIII. 27 The electrical circuit of the device, which will subsequently be referred to as a 'potentiostat', is shown in Fig. 1. **1949** *Analytical Chem.* XXI. 497/1 The instrument... functions as a potentiostat in automatically maintaining the potential of a working electrode constant during an electrolysis. **1965** *New Scientist* 8 Apr. 99/1 These potentiostats.. have a very rapid response to voltage fluctuations and now make the continuous control of commercial processes look very attractive. **1979** *Nature* 15 Mar. 239/1 The cinnabar electrode is connected to a platinum counter electrode and a potential of 0 V maintained between the two by means of a potentiostat.

Hence **potentio'static** *a.*, under the control of or employing a potentiostat; with the potential difference between electrodes held constant; **potentio'statically** *adv.*

1955 *Chem. Abstr.* XLIX. 5166 The potentiostatic method was compared with other methods. **1961** *Trans. Symposium Electrode Processes* (U.S. Electrochem. Soc.) 164 An attempt was made to develop apparatus in which potentiostatic conditions could be achieved in a time short enough to study the growth and decay of metal monolayers at constant potential. **1967** tr. *K. J. Vetter's Electrochem. Kinetics* (*Theoret. Aspects*) ii. 364 The potentiostatically applied overvoltage must.. be pure charge-transfer overvoltage at time t = 0. **1975** *Nature* 27 Mar. 322/2 Specimens held under potentiostatic control in the electrolyte were subjected to square wave strains in the range ±0·02 to ±0·05 at strain rates of ~0·30 s⁻¹. **1976** *Ibid.* 19 Aug. 681/1 Anodisation could be accomplished both galvanostatically and potentiostatically.

potentite ('pəʊtəntaɪt). [f. L. *potent-em* POTENT *a.*[1] + -ITE[1] 4.] Name of an explosive.

1883 V. D. MAJENDIE in *Standard* 19 Apr. 5/6 Explosives (such as dynamite, blasting gelatine,.. tonite, potentite, and detonators). **1884** KNIGHT *Dict. Mech.* Suppl., *Potentite*, an explosive used in the Cumberland and Furness mines.

'potentize, *v.* [f. L. *potent-em* powerful + -IZE, after G. *potenzi(e)ren* to potentiate.] *trans.* To make potent; *spec.* to develop the power of (a medicine) by trituration or succussion; = DYNAMIZE. Hence **'potentized** *ppl. a.* Also **ˌpotenti'zation**, dilution of a drug in order to increase its power or efficacy.

1850 C. J. HEMPEL *New Homœopathic Pharmacopœia* I. 10 By the former, these successive developments of the original substance are called dynamizations, or potentizations; by the latter, attenuations. **1857** DUNGLISON *Med. Dict.* s.v. *Dynamic*, By certain processes, called, in the aggregate, dynamization and potentizing, the dynamic powers of a medicine may be set free and developed—as by shaking the bottle in which the article is contained. **1864** *Trans. Homœopathic Med. Soc. N.Y.* 56 The administration of potentized remedies. **1881** J. G. GLOVER in *Encycl. Brit.* XII. 127/1 The most characteristic feature of Hahnemann's practice—the 'potentizing', 'dynamizing', of medicinal substances. **1892** E. HAUGHTON in *Echo* 1 Sept. 2/5 Some brand-new microbe, alive and kicking, is to be duly distilled and potentised, until a single drop of his juice, squirted under the skin of your back, will enable you to defy the foul fiend now, henceforth, and for ever. **1938** D. SHEPHERD *Magic of Minimum Dose* 7 The first law is the law of simillimum, which is followed by (2) the principle of the minimum dose, (3) the principle of potentization. **1972** D. V. TANSLEY *Radionics* viii. 80 To augment the violet one may add an ampoule of potentized onyx to the treatment. **1974** *Homoeopathy* June/July 87 Symptoms were noted when the drug was given in material and potentised doses. *Ibid.* 88 As the substance becomes more dilute with succeeding potentisations it becomes soluble.

potently ('pəʊtəntlɪ), *adv.* [f. POTENT *a.*[1] + -LY[2].] In a potent manner; powerfully, mightily.

1558 KNOX *First Blast* (Arb.) 38 With these women, I say, did God worke potentlie. **1613** SHAKS. *Hen. VIII*, v. i. 135 You are Potently oppos'd, and with a Malice Of as great Size. **1660** BOYLE *New Exp. Phys. Mech.* xvii. 129 The Air having more room.. does less potently press upon the subjacent Mercury. **1740** WESLEY *Wks.* (1872) I. 265 Idle tales, which they now potently believe. **1884** W. S. LILLY in *Contemp. Rev.* Feb. 261 A new conception.. destined most potently to influence the structure of society.

'potentness. *rare*⁻⁰. [f. as prec. + -NESS.] The quality of being potent; potency; might.

1727 BAILEY vol. II, *Potentness*, mightiness, powerfulness.

'poter. *rare.* Also 7 -our. [app. f. L. *pōt-āre* to drink, or *pōt-us* drink + -ER[1]; but cf. POTTER *sb.*[2]] A drinker, a toper.

1657 HOWELL *Londinop.* 392 They inquire after Potours, Panders, and Bawds. **1900** *Daily News* 13 Jan. 5/7, I fear I have given myself into the hands of the Philistines, whether they be total abstainers or good honest 'poters'.

potere, obs. form of POT-EAR.

‖**Poterium** (pəʊ'tɪərɪəm). *Bot.* [L. *potērium*, a. Gr. ποτήριον drinking-cup, wine-cup; also, name of a shrub. (The mod. application is said in *Treas. Bot.* to refer to the use of the Salad Burnet in flavouring Cool tankard.)] A genus of herbaceous plants of N.O. *Rosaceæ*; Salad Burnet.

1597 GERARDE *Herbal* III. xxiii. 1148, I haue sowen the seede of Poterion in April which I receiued.., that grew in my garden two yeres togither, and after perished by some mischance. **1706** PHILLIPS, *Poterium*,.. a sort of Thistle. **1753** CHAMBERS *Cycl. Supp.*, *Poterium*, a word used by many for the prickly pimpernell.

poteron, variant of POTRON *Obs.*

po'testal, *a. rare.* [irreg. f. next + -AL[1].] Of or pertaining to potestas: see next, 3.

1880 MUIRHEAD *Gaius* IV. §78 Of opinion that my action is only suspended while the child or slave is in my *potestas*, because I cannot proceed against myself, but that it revives on the potestal relationship coming to an end.

‖**potestas** (pəʊ'tɛstæs). Pl. **potestates** (-'eɪtiːz). [L. *potestās* power, used in certain connexions.]

†**1.** *Alg.* = POWER *sb.*[1] 11. *Obs.*

1656 HOBBES *Six Less.* Wks. 1845 VII. 330 The roots and potestates themselves. **1675** COLLINS in Rigaud *Corr. Sci. Men* (1841) I. 213 They will both ascend to the 18th potestas of the unknown symbol.

†**2.** Chemical or pharmaceutical power; active principle; = ESSENCE *sb.* 9. *Obs.*

1683 SALMON *Doron Med.* I. 290 That Potestates or Powers of things are as if they were the Nature. **1694** —— *Bate's Dispens.* (1713) 152/1 After the same Manner.. prepare the Potestates or Powers of other Vegetable Productions.

3. *Roman Law.* The power or authority of the head of a family over those depending on him; *esp.* parental authority.

1870 ABDY & WALKER tr. *Gaius* I. §109. 35 Whereas both males and females may be in our *potestas*, females alone come into *manus*. **1880** [see POTESTAL].

4. *Philol.* The phonetic or phonemic value of a letter in an alphabet.

1949 J. R. FIRTH in *Trans. Philol. Soc. 1948* 135 Each Arabic letter has.. syllabic value, the value or *potestas* in the most general terms being consonant plus vowel, including vowel zero, or zero vowel. **1963** *English Studies* XLIV. 4 Thus if there is a contrast.. between the North and elsewhere, then.. it is best treated as a contrast in graphemes irrespective of their phonemic 'value', or, to speak in more mediaeval terms, as a contrast in *figurae* irrespective of the *potestas* of each. **1967** R. H. ROBINS *Short Hist. Linguistics* iii. 56 Priscian worked systematically through his subject, the description of the language of classical Latin literature. Pronunciation and syllable structure are covered by a description of the letters (*litterae*), defined as the smallest parts of articulate speech, of which the properties are *nōmen*, the name of the letter, *figūra*, its written shape, and *potestās*, its phonetic value. **1972** H. BENEDIKTSSON *First Grammatical Treat.* iii. 90 He is willing to establish new letters with a value (*potestas*) of a combination of two consecutive letters.

†**'potestate.** *Obs.* Also 5–6 -at. [ad. L. *potestās, ātem* power, a ruler, supreme magistrate. So OF. *potestat* (learned form = pop. *poustee*); It. *podestà*. The pl. *potestates* is uniform with the pl. of *potestas*, and sometimes indistinguishable from it.]

1. A person possessed of power over others; a superior, potentate, ruler, lord.

c **1380** WYCLIF *Wks.* (1880) 229 Eche man owiþ to be suget to heiȝere potestatis, þat is to men of heiȝe power. *c* **1380** —— *Sel. Wks.* III. 297 Wilt þou not drede þe potestate? *c* **1386** CHAUCER *Sompn. T.* 309 Whilom ther was an Irous potestat. *c* **1470** HENRYSON *Mor. Fab.* VII. (*Lion & Mouse*) xxxvii, Ane prince or empriour, Ane potestate, or ȝit ane king with croun. **1583** STUBBES *Anat. Abus.* I. (1879) 33 Lawfull for the potestates, the nobilitie, the gentrie [etc.]. **1593** G. HARVEY *Pierce's Super.* 120 Some Potestats are queint men. *a* **1678** WOODHEAD *Holy Living* (1688) 29 They always giving a relation, or account..to their superior potestates, or to God.

2. Rendering *potestas* in the Vulgate (Eph. vi. 12, 1 Pet. iii. 22), applied to a spiritual (angelic or demonic) 'power'.

1382 WYCLIF *Eph.* vi. 12 Aȝens the princes and potestatis, aȝens gouernours of the world of thes derknessis. **1520** M. NISBET *1 Peter* iii. 22 Angels, potestatis, and virtues, ar made subiectis to him. **1542** BECON *Pathw. Prayer* xxv. L ij b, It is no man nor Aungel, but God..whome the angelike potestates do reuerently feare. **1582** N.T. (Rhem.) *Eph.* i. 21 Aboue al Principalitie and Potestate and Power, and Dominion. *c* **1610** *Women Saints* 195 They lyuing with flesh, like vnto the Potestates who want bodies, are not oppressed with the burden of their bodie.

b. *spec.*, in mediæval angelology, a member of the sixth order of angels: see ORDER *sb.* 5.

1483 CAXTON *Gold. Leg.* 255 b/2 The pryncypates armonysed, The potestates harped, Cherubyn and Seraphyn songen louynges and preysynges. **1584** R. SCOT *Discov. Witchcr.* xv. viii. (1886) 337 Thrones, dominions, principats, potestats, virtutes, cherubim and seraphim.

3. The chief magistrate in mediæval Italian towns and republics: = PODESTÀ b; *transf.* a chief magistrate in certain Turkish towns.

1456 SIR G. HAYE *Law Arms* (S.T.S.) 208 A noble marchand of Paris suld pas before thair Potestate of Florence. **1470–85** MALORY *Arthur* v. viii. 174 Whan ye shal come to Rome to the potestate and all the counceylle and Senate. *a* **1548** HALL *Chron., Hen. VIII* 187 Then folowed the potestates & gouernors of the citie [Bologna] all in Crimosyn veluet, & within a myle of the citie there met hym [Charles V] foure and twentie Cardinalles. **1585** T. WASHINGTON tr. *Nicholay's Voy.* II. viii. 41 One of the saide Mahomies is elected and created potestate, and chiefe iustice both ciuil and criminal [of Chios]. **1603** KNOLLES *Hist. Turks* (1621) 157 The potestate of Pera came by sea also with eight gallies more.

†**4.** A (collective) authority, a governing body, e.g. of a university. *Obs. rare.*

1530 *Let. fr. Venice* 1 July (*MS. Cott. Vit. B. xiii.* 92), They [all the doctors] causyd the Chaunceler of the potestate [of the University of Padua] to set his hande and seale for the approbation of the authorytye off the notarye.

†**5.** Power, authority. *Obs. rare.*

1535 STEWART *Cron. Scot.* (Rolls) I. 110 Trowand thairof that no man dar speik ill, Becaus he is ane prince of potestate.

†**pote'station.** *Obs. rare.* Also 5 -acion. [f. L. *potestās* power + -ATION; cf. *gravitation.*] Power, authorization.

c **1485** *Digby Myst.* (1882) II. 177 The prynces haue gouyn me full potestacion. **1623** COCKERAM, *Potestation*, the same that Potencie is.

potestative ('pəʊtɛsteɪtɪv), *a.* [ad. F. *potestatif*, ad. late L. *potestātīvus* adj. (Tert.) denoting or containing power, f. L. *potestāt-em* power + *-īvus*, -IVE; cf. *facultative, qualitative*, etc.]

1. Befitting a 'potestate'; having power or authority; authoritative.

1630 DONNE *Serm.* xiii. 134 So I might contemplate him in a judiciary posture, in a potestative, a soveraigne posture, sitting [etc.]. **1644** [H. PARKER] *Jus Pop.* 56 All commands are not alike binding and Potestative. **1670** BAXTER *Cure Ch. Div.* 234 The abuse of the Potestative Primality is Tyranny. **1724** R. WODROW *Life J. Wodrow* (1828) 66 A probationer only, for order's sake and without any potestative mission.

2. ***potestative condition***, a condition within the power or control of one of the parties concerned.

1652 WARREN *Unbelievers* (1654) 17 We do not..make it a potestative uncertain condition. **1671** R. MACWARD *True Nonconf.* 328 If we did hold faith, as it is our act to be required as a proper potestative foregoing condition of our acceptance. **1726** AYLIFFE *Parergon* 342 Such a Condition.. is said to be a Potestative Condition in respect of a third Person, but a Casual Condition in regard to the Person to whom such Legacy is given. **1818** COLEBROOKE *Obligations* 12 A potestative or arbitrary condition is that, which makes the execution of the agreement depend on the will of one of the contracting parties, or upon an event which it is in the power of that party to bring about or to prevent. **1853** WHEWELL *Grotius* II. 43 If the condition under which the thing may come into the power of the promiser be also potestative (such as he himself can bring about or accelerate).

pote-stick: see POTE *sb.*¹ 3.

†**po'testolate.** *Obs. nonce-wd.* ? Humorous dim. of POTESTATE.

1522 SKELTON *Why not to Court* 985 He is suche a grym syer, And suche a potestolate, And suche a potestate.

‖**pot-et-fleur** (pɔteflœr). [Fr., lit. 'pot and flower'.] A style of floral decoration using pot-plants together with cut flowers. Also *attrib.*

[**1960** V. STEVENSON in *Daily Tel.* 11 Feb. 11/2 There's a new mood afoot in flower arrangement—to combine cut flowers with indoor pot plants. I have been using this style of arrangement for ages, without finding a name for it. Can readers make any suggestions?] **1963** —— *Decorating with Flowers & Plants* vii. 71 When I wanted to describe this style of decoration about which I am writing, I invited the readers of the Woman's Page in the *Daily Telegraph* to coin a name... Our new style became pot-et-fleur, a term already recognized by the National Association of Flower Arrangement Societies of Great Britain, who have included a class in their national competition. *Ibid.* 73 You will have made your first pot-et-fleur arrangement. **1968** *Flower Arranger* Sept. 125 There were strong line arrangements in the tall slit windows behind the choir-stalls; soft arrangements, mostly *pot-et-fleur*, found here and there. **1972** *Jrnl. R. Hort. Soc.* XCVII. 375 Bonsai and pot-et-fleur are her two main techniques. **1978** T. TAYLOR *Flower Arranging* 66/1 A pot-et-fleur is a decoration that combines plants and cut flowers. The plants can be grown permanently and the flowers can be added from time to time.

[**poteuere, potewer,** scribal errors for *potener*, PAUTENER, purse. See Skeat *Notes Eng. Etym.* 227.

a **1650** *Sir Degree* 866 in Furniv. *Percy Folio* III. 47 By that sword I know thee heere; The poynt is in my poteuere [*Auchinleck MS.* aumenere]. *a* **1650** *Boy & Mantle* 21 *ibid.* II. 305 He plucked out of his potewer..a pretty mantle.]

‖**potews.** *Cookery. Obs. rare.* [a. OF. *potaus* (1387–8 in Godef.), **poteus*, pl. of *potel* a little pot, POTTLE.] A fancy dish moulded in an earthen pot, which was broken when the contents had become solid.

? *c* **1390** *Form of Cury* § 177 (1780) 80 Potews. Take Pottus of Erþe lytell of half a quart and fyll hem full of fars of pomme dorryes... Whan þey buth ynowȝ, breke þe pottus of erþe & do þe fars on þe spyt & rost hem wel.

'pot-eye. *Spinning.* [POT *sb.*¹] (See quot.)

1864 W. S. B. MCLAREN *Spinning* Gloss., *Pot-eye*, a little cup with a slit in it, set in a spinning frame for the thread to run down, and to avoid friction. **1884** *Ibid.* (ed. 2) 177 On a throstle frame the yarn is first passed through and rubbed against the 'pot-eye' of the wire-board, and then tightly wound round a hard bobbin.

†**'pot-fish.** *Obs.* Also pott-. [ad. Du. *potvisch*, in Ger. *pottfisch*, Da., Swed. *potfisk*; the first element being perh. the same as in obs. Du. *potshoofd* thick-head (Kilian), Flem. *potshoofd* an eel-pout, in reference to the huge head of this whale.] The cachalot or spermaceti whale.

1743 *Phil. Trans.* XLII. 611 In these Seas are Cachelots or Pot-fish, a sort of Whales, their Length 50 to 70 Feet. **1799** W. TOOKE *View Russian Emp.* III. 105 The Frozen Ocean.. teems with the narhwal, the pott-fish, from whose brain spermaceti is prepared.

'pot‚fisher. a. = POT-FISHERMAN. **b.** One who fishes merely 'for the pot': cf. POT-HUNTER 2.

1890 in *Cent. Dict.*

'pot‚fisherman. A fisherman who fishes while floating on the water supported by a pot, into which also he puts the fish when caught: a method practised on some Asiatic rivers; also, = *fish-potter* s.v. FISH *sb.*¹ 7.

1895 *Funk's Stand. Dict.* 1392/1 *Pot-fisherman*, one who fishes while floating buoyed up by an earthen pot, as on Asiatic rivers. **1970** *Times* 2 Sept. 10/5 A much brighter prospect has suddenly opened up for Guernsey's traditional pot fishermen, who looked as if they were doomed to go gradually out of business.

potful ('pɒtfʊl). [f. POT *sb.*¹ + -FUL.] The quantity that fills a pot; as much as a pot holds.

1362 LANGL. *P. Pl.* A. VII. 176 A potful of peosun þat pers hedde I-mad [C. IX. 182 A potful of potage þat peersses wyf made]. *c* **1450** *Mankind* 265 in *Macro Plays* 10, I was neuer worth a pottfull a wortes, sythyn I was borne. **1646** SIR T. BROWNE *Pseud. Ep.* II. v. (1686) 65 A potfull of ashes. **1881** *Scribner's Mag.* XXII. 77 A fire is started..to cook a potful of meat.

†**pot-gallery.** *Obs.* A 'gallery' of some kind on the banks of the Thames (and perhaps other navigable rivers), which often projected over the water, and was found to be an encroachment.

(Its actual nature and purpose have not been ascertained; the suggestion that it was the outside gallery or balcony of a pot-house overhanging the river (see N. & Q. 31 Aug. 1907, p. 172) appears to be set aside by the recorded dimensions of some 'pot-galleries': see the quots.)

1630 *Sir R. Ducie's Orders* §20 in R. Griffiths *Conservacy of Thames* (1746) 70 *Item*, That no Person do make or continue any Wharf, Building, Potgallery, or other Purpresture, or Incroachment into, upon, or over any Part of the Soil of the said River. **1684** *Survey of Buildings & Encroachments on Thames* (Bodl. Lib., Gough Maps 46 lf. 42), On the South Side.. 1. At Allen's Dye-house a Pott Gallery, 21 ft. E. to W., 12 ft. out into the River, Old. *Ibid.* (lf. 43), On the North Side..3. Sᵗ Katherines, from Iron Gate towards Sᵗ Katherines Dock are Pot Galleries, 620 ft. E. to W., 8 and 10 ft. out into the river, Old.

'pot-'garden. A garden of pot-herbs, a kitchen-garden. Also *attrib.*

1511 *MS. Acc. St. John's Hosp., Canterb.*, For dygyng off þᵉ beyn grownd in þe pot gardyne. **1519** HORMAN *Vulg.* 172 The knot-garden serueth for pleasure: the potte garden for profitte. **1642** *MS. Acc. St. John's Hosp., Canterb.*, Mending the locke of the potgarden gate. **1898** *Atlantic Monthly* Apr. 503/1 The cabbage and the cauliflower and most things that grow in a pot-garden are but little known to him who sees them only in the pot or on the plate.

†**'pot‚gun, 'potgun.** *Obs.* Also 6 -gonne, -goon, 6–7 -gunne. [f. POT *sb.*¹ + GUN *sb.*]

1. A short piece of ordnance with a large bore, a mortar; so called from its shape.

1549 CHALONER *Erasm. on Folly* H iv, Another striken through with a potgonne recouered. **1557** A. JENKINSON *Voy. & Trav.* (Hakl. Soc.) II. 360 They haue..a great many of morter pieces or potguns. **1599** HAKLUYT *Voy.* II. I. 81 Then the enemies were warned by the Iewe that wrote letters to them.., that the sayd potgunnes did no harme.

2. = POP-GUN *sb.* 1.

1560 WHITEHORNE *Ord. Souldiours* (1588) 30 b, One of those potgunnes of elder, that boyes vse to shoote paper and slowes in. **1611** COTGR., *Caloniere*, a pot-gunne made of a Quill, or Elder sticke. **1660** M. R. *Exact Acc. Receipts* 3, I.. wish I had been chang'd into an Elder-tree, to have been cut out into Pot-guns. **1729** SWIFT *To Dr. Delany on Libels* 14 When first in Print, you see him dread Each Pot-Gun levell'd at his Head. **1801** [see POP-GUN 1].

b. Contemptuously or ludicrously applied to a pistol or similar fire-arm; cf. POP-GUN *sb.* 2.

a **1553** UDALL *Royster D.* IV. vii. (Arb.) 75 Once discharge my harquebouse And for my heartes ease, haue once more with my potgoon. *a* **1619** FLETCHER, etc. *Knt. Malta* IV. iv, How! fright me with your pot-gun? **1659** SHIRLEY *Honoria & Mam.* I. i, When all your liveries go a-feasting By water, with your gally-foist and pot-guns.

3. *fig.* A loud talker, a mere boaster, a braggart; also, an unfounded report.

1623 WEBSTER *Duchess of Malfi* III. iii, I saw a Dutchman break his pate once For calling him pot-gun. *c* **1626** *Dick of Devon.* I. i. in Bullen *O. Pl.* II. 9, I heard such a report, But had no faith in't: a mere Potgun! **1693** CONGREVE *Old Bach.* III. viii, That sign of a man there, that pot-gun charged with wind.

4. *attrib.* and *Comb.*

1624 FORD *Sun's Darling* To Rdr., The First Season. Presents him in the Twilight of his age, Not pot-gun-proof. **1651** W. JANE *Εικων Ακλαστος* 168 These are potgun preparations for a Civill war. **1691** *New Discov. Old Intreague* xvi, Their Pot-gun Volleys charge Her Royal Ear.

†**'pot‚hanger.** *Obs.* [f. POT *sb.*¹ + HANGER².] A device for hanging a pot or kettle over the fire; a series of links, a rack, or a bar with a series of holes, on which a pot-hook or crook could be hung at different heights; = HANGER² 4 d. Mostly in *pl.*

1580 HOLLYBAND *Treas. Fr. Tong*, *Cramaillére*, the pot hanger. **1591** PERCIVALL *Sp. Dict.*, *Llares o ollares*, pot-hangers, *ollares catenæ*. **1608** WILLET *Hexapla Exod.* 235 They sate by the pot hangers, whereon they vsed to hang their pots. **1617** in W. F. Shaw *Mem. Eastry* (1870) 227 Three brass stupens [stewpans], one payer of pott-hangers. **1642** in *Archives Maryland* (1887) IV. 94, 1 Pot-hanger and potthooks. **1678–84** LITTLETON *Lat. Dict.*, *Climacter*,..pot-hanger or pot-hooks.

†**'pot‚hangings,** *sb. pl. Obs. rare.* **a.** = POT-CLIPS. **b.** = POT-HANGERS.

1521 in *Bury Wills* (Camden) 119 Item a gredyern, and a andern, a payr of poott hangyngs, and frynge pan. **1530** PALSGR. 182 *Vnes ancestes*, a payre of potte hangyngesˑ *Ibid.* 257/1 Potte hangynges, *cremilliere*.

†**'pot‚hangle.** *Obs. rare.* [f. POT *sb.*¹ + *hangle*, f. HANG *v.* + -LE, suffix of the instrument. (*Hangle* occurs otherwise only as var. of HINGLE a hinge.)] In *pl.* (const. as *sing.*) = prec. b.

1538 in *Lett. Suppress. Monasteries* (Camden) 267 Item, a fryeng panne and a peyre of pothangles sold to the seyd Scudamour vjᵈ. *Ibid.*, Item, sold to the baylyf of Staff. a potthangles vijᵈ. **1614** *MS. Stratford-on-Avon* (Nares), Item, one pothangles, price ij.s.

'pot-head. *colloq.* [POT *sb.*¹] **1.** A stupid person. So **'pot‚headed** *a.*, stupid, thick-headed.

1533 MORE *Apol.* xlvii. Wks. 920/2 These heretikes.. some potheaded postles they haue, that wander about yᵉ realme into sondry shyres. **1855** KINGSLEY *Westw. Ho!* xv, She was too good for a poor pot-head like me.

2. *Canada.* In full, ***pothead whale***. = CA'ING-WHALE, CAA'ING WHALE, *pilot-whale* s.v. PILOT *sb.* 8.

1863 *Islander* (Charlottetown, Prince Edward Island) 14 Aug. 2/3 Large numbers of Potheads are in the Bay, which probably accounts for the squid panic. **1964** *Canad. Geogr. Jrnl.* Mar. 92/3 Entire herds of 40-foot pothead whales have been known to run aground on the beaches. **1979** *Monitor* (McAllen, Texas) 16 July 2A/1 More than 170 pothead whales beached themselves on Sunday.

3. *Electr.* An insulated connector used for making a sealed joint between conductors, esp. between insulated and uninsulated lines.

1901 W. J. HOPKINS *Telephone Lines* (rev. ed.) ii. 38 (*in figure*) Pot head splice. **1903** *Phil. Mag.* V. 327 The cables were brought out to pot-heads, and each wire terminated in a screw-cup. **1930** H. P. SEELYE *Electr. Distribution Engin.* xxvi. 497 The pothead usually consists of a cast-iron tank or pot into which the cable is inserted... The conductors pass through the pot and are either brought out through porcelain bushings, or are attached to conducting terminals fixed in the bushings. The pot is then filled with insulating compound. **1963** K. NEVILLE in D. Knight *100 Yrs. Sci. Fiction* (1969) 73 Ramon Lopez, one of the truck crew, was killed today hosing down a high-voltage pothead.

4. (See POT *sb.*⁵ 2.)

†**pothecar(e, -aire.** *Sc.* and *north. Eng. dial. Obs.* Also 9 potticar. [Aphetic form of *apothecar*, = F. *apothecaire*, corresp. to Eng. *pothecary*: see next. Hence by phonetic corruption **pot(t)egar*, *potingar*, POTTINGAR.] An apothecary: = next.

c **1480** HENRYSON *Test. Cres.* 248 Spycis belangand to the pothecairis [*rime* electuairis = electuars], With mony hailsum sweit confectioun. *a* **1585** POLWART *Flyting w. Montgomerie* 231 This present from the pothecares [*rimes* wares, saires] Mee think meet to amend thee. **1825** BROCKETT *N.C. Gloss.*, *Potticar, Potecary, Pothecary*, an apothecary. **1869** *Lonsdale Gloss.*, *Pottiker*, an apothecary.

'pothecary. Now only *dial.* Forms: α. 4–5 potecarie, 4–7 -cary(e, 5 -kary, 6 -cari; 5–6 potycary(e; 6 poticarie, -carye, 6–7 (9 *dial.*) -cary; 7 pottecary, -icary. β. 6–7 pothicary, 7 pothecarie, 7–8 (9 *dial.*) -cary, 8–9 'pothecary.

See also prec. Aphetic form of APOTHECARY, formerly in common use.

c1386 CHAUCER *Pard. T.* 524 (Camb.) And forth he goth no lengere wolde he tarye In-to the toun vn-to a potecarye [so *Corp., Lansd., Harl.; Ellesm., Hengw.*, apothecarie; *Petw.* apot-]. **1426** LYDG. *De Guil. Pilgr.* 24210 Sondry lettuaryes Maked at the potycaryes. **1530** PALSGR. 257/1 Potycary that selleth medycins, *apothecayre*. **1551** TURNER *Herbal* I. Prol. A iij b, If the potecari..is ignorant in herbes. **1632** LITHGOW *Trav.* III. 98 Abundance of Alloes.., so much esteemed by our Pothecaries. **1668–9** PEPYS *Diary* 8 Feb., Going to visit Roger Pepys, at the pothecary's in King's Street. **1720** W. STUKELEY in *Mem.* (Surtees) I. 112 A league between a few doctors, poticaryes, and surgeons, who play into one anothers hands. **1820** SOUTHEY *Devil's Walk* vii, He saw a Pothecary, on a white horse, Ride by on his vocation. *a* **1825** FORBY *Voc. E. Anglia, Poticary.* **1886** ELWORTHY *W. Somerset Word-bk., Potecary*, apothecary... Not now of common use ..but I have heard it used disparagingly.

b. *attrib.* quasi-*adj.*

1540 *Act 32 Hen. VIII*, c. 40 §2 Suche poticary wares drugges and stuffes. **1558** BULLEYN *Govt. Health* 111 Who lieueth..so euill as these pothicary men? **1607** CHAPMAN *Bussy D'Ambois* v. i. Plays 1873 II. 90 If I scape Monsieurs Pothecarie Shops. **1614** MARKHAM *Cheap Husb.* To Rdr., Yet have I seene smiths so unprovided of Pothecary simples.

potheen, variant form of POTEEN.

pothel, ME. variant of *podel*, PUDDLE.

pother ('pɒðə(r), 'pʌðə(r)), *sb.* Forms: α. 7– pother; also (7 powther), 7–9 puther, 7 (9 *dial.*) poother. β. 7– pudder. [Origin unknown: appears early in 17th c. Historically *pother* rimes with *other, brother, mother, smother*, the vowel app. repr. orig. (oː); so the dial. *puther, pudder*. The current ('pɒðə(r)) appears to be a 19th c. literary innovation, after the spelling, and perh. influenced by association with *bother*. The form *pudder* is parallel to the dial. *udder, brudder, mudder, fadder*, etc. in some of which (d), in others (ð), is original.

Original identity with POWDER, though suggested by the sense 'dust', appears to be phonetically untenable.]

1. A choking smoke or atmosphere of dust. ***to kick up a pother***, to raise a choking dust.

α. **1627** DRAYTON *Nymphidia* lxxxii, The Poke Which out of it sent such a smoke, As ready was them all to choke, So greeuous was the pother. **1637** G. DANIEL *Genius of Isle* 158, I, in this smoaking pother, Had sole the want. **1886** *Cheshire Gloss.* s.v. *Poother*, What a poother tha kicks up wi' thi brush! [i.e. in sweeping a room]. **1887** T. DARLINGTON *S. Chesh. Gloss.* s.v., A puff of tobacco smoke directed into a person's face would be a poother. **1893** BARING-GOULD *Mrs. Curgenven* xlvi, There be such a pother o' smoke I doubt if that you can see her.

β. **1642** MILTON *Apol. Smect.* 4 To lay the dust and pudder in antiquity, which he and his..are wont to raise.

2. a. Disturbance, commotion, turmoil, bustle; a tumult, uproar; a noise, din. Cf. DUST *sb.*[1] 5.

α. **1591** SYLVESTER *Ivry* 71 As a Torrent..in his furious Pother Takes Land from som, and giveth more to other. **1607** (1623) SHAKS. *Cor.* II. i. 234 Such a poother, As if that whatsoeuer God, who leades him, Were slyly crept into his humane powers, And gaue him gracefull posture. **1682** N. O. *Boileau's Lutrin* II. 249 But Oh! these Chanters, Chanons make a Pother, A Dog can't rest, whilst one worries another. **1709** O. DYKES *Eng. Prov. & Refl.* (ed. 2) 308 What a Noise and Pother do our Hawkers make in a Hurry about the Streets with their News-Books. *a* **1849** HOR. SMITH *Addr. Mummy* x, Didst thou not hear the pother o'er thy head When the great Persian Conqueror, Cambyses Marched armies o'er thy tomb with thundering tread? **1898** F. T. BULLEN *Cruise Cachalot* 72 Smiting the sea with his mighty tail, making an almost deafening noise and pother.

β. **1623** *Shaks.'s Wks.*, *Lear* III. ii. 50 Let the great Goddes, That keepe this dreadfull pudder [*Qos.* I. 3 thundring; *Qo.* 2 powther] o're our heads, Finde out their enemies now. **1657** THORNLEY tr. *Longus' Daphnis & Chloe* 189 A busie noise, tumultuous pudder of carriages. **1671** CROWNE *Juliana* I. 4 Here's a pudder, ho! see if none of my cups or silver spoons be missing. **1673** in Halliwell *Pal. Anthol.* (1850) 109 'Twas uncivilly done Such a hideous pudder to keep. **1816** SCOTT *Antiq.* xv, The pony, hearing this pudder over his head, began apparently to think [etc.]. **1956** AUDEN & KALLMAN *Magic Flute* I. iv. 32 (From within the temple comes the sound of singing.).. What's that? What's that pudder? I shiver, I shudder.

b. *transf.* A verbal commotion, stir, or fuss.

α. **1631** MASSINGER *Emperor East* IV. v, All this pother for an apple! **1654** WHITLOCK *Zootomia* 481 When Heathen Authority hath kept all the Puther it can, with their Amphion and Orpheus. **1663** BUTLER *Hud.* I. i. 32 Some hold the one, and some the other, But, howsoe'er they make a Pother, The difference was so small. **1783** *Trifler* No. 13. 175 Your Sister too would make a pother, She'd never brook to call him Brother. **1850** BLACKIE *Æschylus* I. Pref. 57 With high-sounding words he will make such a pother.

β. **1609** BP. W. BARLOW *Answ. Nameless Cath.* 23 In this pudder of different opinions, recourse is had to the Great Oracle. **1759** STERNE *Tr. Shandy* II. ii, What a pudder and racket in Councils about οὐσία and ὑπόστασις! **1858** GEN. P. THOMPSON *Audi Alt.* I. lvii. 223 A mortal pudder has been raised against so harmless a proposal, as that the community should have the relief [etc.].

3. Mental perturbation or tumult; trouble, fuss; display of sorrow or grief.

1641 MILTON *Reform.* I. Wks. 1851 III. 3 Being scarr'd.. by the pangs, and gripes of a boyling conscience, all in a pudder shuffles up to himselfe such a God, and such a worship as is most agreeable to remedy his feare. **1656** S. HOLLAND *Zara* (1719) 34 Of Sorrow, making a most grievous puther [*rime* Mother]. **1738** *Gentl. Mag.* VIII. 43/1 Well! if all husbands keep so great a pother, I'll live unmarried—till I get another. **1822** HAZLITT *Table-t.* Ser. II. vii. (1869) 143 This coil and mighty pudder in the breast.

pother ('pɒðə(r), 'pʌðə(r)), *v.* Also 7 **pudder**, 9 *dial.* **puther**. [app. f. POTHER *sb.*; but sometimes app. associated with BOTHER *v.*]

1. *trans.* To put into a fuss; to fluster, worry; to confuse, perplex, trouble.

α. **1692** LOCKE *Educ.* §72 If at that Time he forces himself to it, he only pothers and wearies himself to no purpose. **1795** BIRCH *Adopted Child* I. ii, At his old employment, his pencils and his compasses, and I don't know what, pothering his poor little brains. **1860** EMERSON *Cond. Life, Wealth* Wks. (Bohn) II. 359 But how can Cockayne..be pothered with fatting..oxen? **1904** M. HEWLETT *Queen's Quair* II. x. 324 Sir James all pothered to reply; rare for him.

β. *c* **1698** LOCKE *Cond. Underst.* §13 He..will abound in contrary Observations, that can be of no other Use but to perplex and pudder him if he compares them.

b. To get *out* by worrying.

1740 J. CLARKE *Educ. Youth* (ed. 3) 167 He must pother the Meaning..out of a Dictionary.

2. *intr.* To make a fuss; to fuss, to worry.

1735 SAVAGE *Progr. Divine* 361 Detach the sense, and pother o'er the text. **1778** *Learning at a Loss* I. 32, I found the old Gentleman..pothering over the Newspaper. **1895** R. BURTON in *Forum* (N.Y.) Apr. 251 It is idle to pother with secondary causes when here is the native source.

3. *dial.* To move, pour, or roll in a cloud, as smoke or dust.

Widely used in midland dialects from Yorksh. to Warwick, Leicester, Lincoln: see *Eng. Dial. Dict.* s.v. *Puther*. Hence perh. *pothering* in 19th c. quots. below.

Hence **'pothering** *vbl. sb.* and *ppl. a.*; also **pothe'ration** (*nonce-wd.* after *botheration*), stir, turmoil, trouble; **'potherment**, *dial.* petty trouble.

1690 LOCKE *Hum. Und.* IV. iii. §30 That perplexity, puddering, and confusion, which has so much hindred Mens progress in other parts of Knowledge. **1791–1823** D'ISRAELI *Cur. Lit.* (1866) 269/1 A multitude confused of pothering odours. **1827** HARE *Guesses* Ser. I. (1873) 229 The words of their [Irish] orators are wont to roll out just like so many potatoes..rumbling, and pothering and incoherent. **1855** ROBINSON *Whitby Gloss.*, *Potherments*, perplexities, troubles. **1901** *Essex Herald* 9 Apr. 2/5 All the potheration had been purposely caused by the master of the house.

pot-herb ('pɒthɜːb). [f. POT *sb.*[1] + HERB.] A herb grown for boiling in the pot; any of the herbs cultivated in a kitchen-garden.

black pot-herb, white pot-herb, old names for Alexanders (*Smyrnium Olusatrum*) and Corn-salad (*Valerianella olitoria*) respectively. (Gerarde 1597, 243.)

1538 ELYOT, *Caulis*... Also an herbe called colewortes. It is somtyme taken for all pot herbes. **1605** *Tryall Chev.* II. i. in Bullen *O. Pl.* III. 290 E're he do my Lord any wrong, zounds Ile be cut smaller then pot-hearbs. **1644** EVELYN *Diary* 20 Nov., The Circus Maximus,..one entire heape of rubbish, part of it converted into a garden of pot-herbs. **1855** MACAULAY *Hist. Eng.* xix. IV. 369 A spot which seemed to be part of Holland, a straight canal, a terrace, rows of clipped trees, and rectangular beds of flowers and potherbs.

¶**b.** *erron.* = *pot-plant*.

1882 STEVENSON *New Arab. Nts.* (1884) 101 Flowering pot-herbs garnished the sills of the..windows.

c. *attrib.* **pot-herb butterfly**, a N. American species (*Pieris oleracea*), closely allied to the cabbage-butterfly.

1692 DRYDEN *Cleomenes* III. i, A people, baser than the beasts they worship; Below their pot-herb gods, that grow in gardens.

'pothery, *a.* [f. POTHER *sb.* + -Y.]

1. Choking, stifling; close, sultry; also *transf.* Also **puthery**.

1696 WHISTON *The. Earth* IV. (1722) 365 That Pothery and Sultry..Weather..we usually now feel. **1846** LANDOR *Imag. Conv., Southey & L.* Wks. 1853 II. 168/2 They [Shakspere's Sonnets] are hot and pothery; there is much condensation, little delicacy. **1855** MRS. GASKELL *Let.* Feb. (1966) 332 It is so *puthery* here, I can hardly walk.

2. *dial.* Of sheep: Giddy and liable to fall, through water on the brain.

Perh. a different word, related to POTTER *v.*

1839 HOLLOWAY *Dict. Provinc.*, A sheep which has water on the brain, which causes it to fall down, or move in a very weak, tottering, and uncertain manner is said to be pothery.

'pot-hole, *sb. Geol.* Also **pothole, pot hole**. [f. POT *sb.*[1] + HOLE *sb.*]

1. A deep hole of more or less cylindrical shape; esp. one formed by the wearing away of rock by the rotation of a stone, or a collection of gravel, in an eddy of running water, or in the bed of a glacier.

1826 T. L. MCKENNEY *Sk. Tour to Lakes* (1827) 54 The waters were once, in many places, some fifty feet above their present level; for their action upon the rocks is plainly seen in the pot holes, as the excavations are called, which are made by the action of pebbles upon the rocks. **1839** *Civil Eng. & Arch. Jrnl.* II. 373/1, 8 feet of the workable stone may be considered free from 'allum' or 'pot holes' containing calcareous spar, to which this stone is subject. **1862** DANA *Man. Geol.* 641 The 'Basin' in the Franconia Notch (White Mountains) is a pot-hole in granite, fifteen feet deep and twenty and twenty five feet in its two diameters. **1873** J. GEIKIE *Gt. Ice Age* (1894) 431 Large pot-holes formed on the bed of a glacier by water plunging down through crevasses. **1878** HUXLEY *Physiogr.* ix. 134 The grinding action of pebbles, when set in motion by water, is strikingly shown in the formation of potholes.

2. See quot.

1898 *Archæol. Jrnl.* Ser. II. V. 294 That the manufacture of pottery was carried on in Hayling in former times is shown by the existence of 'pot-holes', i.e. holes from which clay has been taken.

3. *N. Amer.* A pond formed by a natural hollow in the ground in which water has collected. Cf. SLEW *sb.*[1] 1, SLOUGH *sb.*[1] 4. Also *attrib.*

1902 *Saskatchewan Hist.* (1956) IX. 31 In natural depressions of the soil..water had gathered and formed so-called 'pot-holes'—circular basins of a swampy nature, generally rather shallow. The 'potholes' usually have a heavy growth of wild hay. **1938** S. C. ELLS *Northland Trails* 85 It is a land of mysterious pot-hole lakes and ponds with neither inlets nor outlets. **1946** *Sun* (Baltimore) 5 July 11/3 Experimental planting of fish with airplanes gives promise for the 'back in there' pothole lakes and spring holes. **1955** R. P. HOBSON *Nothing too Good for Cowboy* (1956) vii. 69 The pothole meadows were still some five miles away from the spruce clump. **1962** *Daily Progress* (Charlottesville, Va.) 17 Aug. 4/2 Minnesota and the Dakotas..are dotted with innumerable small ponds called 'potholes'. **1963** *Globe & Mail* (Toronto) 13 Mar. 17/1 Show me the man who doesn't get the shivers when half-a-dozen greenhead mallards start side-slipping into the pothole in front of him.

4. A depression or hollow part forming a defect in the surface of a road or track. Also *attrib.*

1909 *Westm. Gaz.* 30 Aug. 1/3 We are also beginning to see how much our urban and suburban macadam roads suffer from artificial watering and constant scavenging, for all road engineers are agreed that the uneven surfaces and pot-holes..are practically confined to the districts where the water-cart reigns supreme. **1920** *Motor Cycle* 30 Sept. 384/2 On the outward journey the pot-holes between Edinburgh and Stirling seemed appalling. **1955** *Times* 5 July 5/7 On the other hand the springing makes rather heavy going of potholes like those caused by recessed manhole covers. **1972** 'J. & E. BONETT' *No Time to Kill* v. 52 The grey car turned onto a dirt road, slowed to a crawl as it met the potholes. **1978** *New York* 3 Apr. 100/4 The locals of D.C. 37 represent social-service workers, botanical garden employees, city engineers, pothole repairmen, hospital employees, [etc.]

5. *Austral.* A shallow hole dug in the ground in prospecting for opal dirt (see OPAL 4). Also *attrib.*

1940 I. L. IDRIESS *Lightning Ridge* 90 For a time I sank pot-holes alone then went mates with little Archie Campbell. **1967** —— *Opals & Sapphires* 112 Keep the find quiet until you have sunk more potholes to prove that it is worth while pegging out.

'pot-hole, *v.* Also **pothole**. [f. the sb.]

1. *trans.* To produce pot-holes in.

1909 *Cent. Dict.* Suppl., *Pot-hole*, to produce in (a solid rock mass) a hole by the action of stones and silt whirled round in an eddy of water. **1975** *Nature* 20 Mar. 189/2 It was channelled and potholed by running water.

2. a. *trans.* To explore (pot-holes or the like). **b.** *intr.* To engage in pot-holing.

1970 *Observer* (Colour Suppl.) 25 Jan. 30/4 Its underworld labyrinth of elves and trolls consists of tunnels he potholed as a boy. **1970** *Times* 26 Oct. 4 They were with 10 others potholing on the Pennines at Casterton, near Kirkby Lonsdale.

'pot-holed, *a.* [f. as prec. + -ED[2].] Having pot-holes.

1933 AUDEN *Poems* (ed. 2) 43 By pot-holed becks. **1939** JOYCE *Finnegans Wake* 31 [He] had been meaning to inquire what, in effect, had caused yon causeway to be thus potholed. **1952** C. BARDSLEY *Bishop's Move* x. 114 It took the car of civilization away from the main road on to a bumpy, pot-holed track. **1960** I. CROSS *Backward Sex* i. 33 The lines of the tram tracks were pot-holed and rutted. **1976** *S. Wales Echo* 27 Nov. 6/3 People will have to go on putting up with a badly pot-holed road.

'pot-holer. Also **potholer**. [f. as prec. + -ER[1].] Someone who goes pot-holing.

1900 *Jrnl. Yorkshire Ramblers' Club* I. 134 The temptation to remain above ground certainly was very strong, and some of the pot-holers gazed rather wistfully after the men who, at the parting of the ways, left them for Ingleborough. **1908** *Pearson's Mag.* Mar. 282/1 To see a party of pot-holers on the warpath you would think, from the mass of spars and cordage, that they had got some idea ..of an inland voyage into their heads. **1935** *Times* 27 July 13/4 At Derby to-day cave explorers and pot-holers from several parts of England will meet to found a British Speleological Association. **1957** *Times* 10 Dec. 10/5 (*heading*) Six potholers brought out. Rescuers work all day. Community singing in cave. **1973** D. ORGILL *Jasius Pursuit* xi. 107 This kind of cat-run, in the potholers' experience, often led to a larger chamber.

'pot-holey, *a.* [f. as prec. + -Y[1].] Having many pot-holes.

1921 *Blackw. Mag.* Nov. 641/2 We lurched along over a very pot-holey road. **1925** *Motor* 15 Dec. 1001/2 Some rough stretches of wavy and pot-holey surfaces. **1936** F. CLUNE *Roaming round Darling* x. 89 Road, neither pot-holey nor unholey for thirty-five miles.

'pot-holing, *vbl. sb.* Also **potholing**. [f. as prec. + -ING[1].] **1.** The exploration of underground pot-holes.

1899 *Jrnl. Yorkshire Ramblers' Club* I. 63 The sport of cave-hunting and pot-holing, apart from its scientific interest, has fascinations and charms peculiar to itself. **1908** *Pearson's Mag.* Mar. 280/1 Subterranean mountaineering, which is, in the vernacular, pot-holing, indisputably possesses a fascination of its own. **1925** *Jrnl. Fell & Rock Climbing Club* VII. 69 An afternoon's pot-holing..was the only mountaineering done. **1935** *Times* 27 July 13/4 The pot-holing clubs of Yorkshire and Lancashire have already joined to form a rescue organization. **1967** *Potholing & Caving* (Know the Game Ser.) 12/1 The words caving and potholing are used loosely to mean the same thing... Technically a cave is an underground system which may or may not be large enough to admit a human being... A pothole is a natural hole in the ground or a cave system, containing shafts or pitches. **1975** *Times* 9 Sept. 6/2 Mr. Tony Harrison, aged 19, a member of Lancaster University's potholing team, has been killed in a fall, in a cave.

2. The formation of pot-holes.

1903 *Geogr. Jrnl.* XXI. 672 Of this [erosion] Mr. Ball thinks that at least two-thirds is accounted for by the pot-holing action. **1941** *Jrnl. Geomorphol.* IV. 71 (*heading*) Potholing of limestone by development of solution cups.

pot-hook ('pɒthʊk), *sb.* [f. POT *sb.*[1] + HOOK *sb.*[1]]

1. a. A hook suspended over a fireplace, for hanging a pot or kettle on; a crook. **b.** An iron rod (usually curved) with a hook at the end, for lifting a heated pot, stove-lid, etc.

1467 *Maldon, Essex, Court Rolls* (Bundle 43 No. 14), ii. keteles; i. rakke; i par de pottehokes. *c* **1475** *Pict. Voc.* in Wr.-Wülcker 770/14 *Hec capana*, a pothoke. **1530** PALSGR. 257/1 Potte hokes, *unes ancestes.* **1698** FRYER *Acc. E. India & P.* 296 Setting their Earthen or Copper Pots there-on, not hanging them on Pothooks as we do. **1869** MRS. STOWE *Oldtown* vi. (1870) 56 The great black crane..swung over it, with its multiplicity of pot-hooks and trammels. **1875** KNIGHT *Dict. Mech.*, *Pot-hook*, an S-shaped hook for suspending a culinary vessel from a chimney-crane.

†c. *pl.* An instrument of punishment: see quot.

1707 SLOANE *Jamaica* I. p. lviii, For running away they put..pottocks about their necks, which are iron rings with two long necks riveted to them. **1740** *Hist. Jamaica* vi. 159 The Chain and Pot-hooks are painted by his own Order in the Picture I spoke of just now. **1751** MACSPARRAN *Diary* (1899) 52 He [a runaway slave in Rhode Island] had w[t] is called Pothooks put about his Neck.

2. a. A curved or hooked stroke made in writing; a crooked stroke or character, a scrawl; now usually applied to a hooked stroke, as an element of handwriting, made by children in learning to write. (Often with *hanger*: cf. HANGER[2] 4 d.) Also *colloq. pl.* = SHORTHAND.

1611 COTGR., *Pasté*..a blurre, scraule, pothooke, or ill-fauoured whim-wham, in writing. *a* **1625** FLETCHER & MASS. *Elder Bro.* I. ii, *Bri.* What have we here? Pot-hooks and Andirons! *And.* I much pity you, it is the Syrian Character, or the Arabick. **1690** DRYDEN *Don Sebastian* II. ii, No peeping here, though I long to be spelling her Arabick scrawls and pot-hooks. **1710** SWIFT *Lett.* (1767) III. 61 You know such a pothook makes a letter; and you know what letter, and so, and so. **1738** [see HANGER[2] 4 d]. **1799** B. THOMPSON *Kotzebue's Stranger* in *Inchbald's Theatre* I. 59 I'll go for his copy-book. He makes his pothooks capitally. **1809** [see HANGER[2] 4 d]. **1846** *Swell's Night Guide* 128/1 *Pothooks and hangers*, short hand characters. **1887** G. R. SIMS *Mary Jane's Mem.* 237 She's scrawling pothooks and hangers on a dirty sheet of paper. **1937** PARTRIDGE *Dict. Slang* 653/1 *Pot-hooks and hangers*, shorthand. **1939** JOYCE *Finnegans Wake* 181 Instead of cluthoring those model households plain wholesome pothooks (a thing he never possessed of his Nigerian own) what do you think Vulgariano did but copy all their various styles of signature. **1957** R. S. HEINLEIN *Door into Summer* ii. 39 Darling, if this is a formal meeting, I guess you had better make pothooks. **1962** G. LAWTON *John Wesley's English* 239 His [*sc.* Wesley's] works are full of proverbs, pothooks, allusions, idioms, colloquialisms, and slang. **1963** C. MACKENZIE *My Life & Times* I. 156 From her I learnt to write pothooks and hangers and very soon to pass from pothooks and hangers to real letters.

b. *attrib.* in reference to crabbed or illegible writing or unintelligible characters, or to shorthand.

1674 T. FLATMAN *To Mr. Austin* 9 No more, than read that dung fork, pothook hand That in Queen's Colledge Library does stand. *a* **1683** J. OLDHAM *Charact. Old P.* Rem. (1684) 112 Nonsence and the fittest Character to write it in, that Pot-hook-hand the Devil us'd at Oxford. [See *Wood's Life & Times* (O.H.S.) I. 498.] **1914** W. OWEN *Let.* 2 Mar. (1967) 236 Thanks for the Catalogue of Pothook-books [Pitman's catalogue].

Hence (*nonce-wds.*) **'pot-hook** *v. trans.*, to curve into the shape of a pot-hook; **'pot-hooked** *a.*, having a pot-hook (sense 2); **'pot-ˌhookery**, making of pot-hooks or scrawls; **'pot-hooky** *a.*, full of or consisting of pot-hooks, scrawled.

1795 T. TWINING in *Parr's Wks.* (1828) VIII. 273 The Professor's conscribillatio is a more illegible..piece of pot-hookery than yours. **1867** *Harper's Mag.* Nov. 793 It was written in a cramped, pot-hooky hand. **1875** MAUND in *Alpine Jrnl.* May (1876) 414 After packing myself away as well as I could in the shape of a pot-hook, Martin followed and pot-hooked himself alongside me. **1898** CHR. MURRAY in *Daily News* 27 Jan. 6/2 The Dreyfus letters very commonly have a curious pothooked starting point... They curl upwards at the start. There is nothing of the sort in the *bordereau.*

‖**Pothos** ('pəʊθɒs). *Bot.* [mod.L. (Linnæus, 1737), ad. Sinhal. *pōtha*, *pōtæ.*] A genus of climbing shrubs (N.O. *Araceæ* or *Orontiaceæ*), natives of Asia, Australia, etc.: some species are cultivated as foliage plants.

1836 MACGILLIVRAY tr. *Humboldt's Trav.* xviii. 271 The pothoses, arums, and lianas, furnished so thick a covering that..they were completely sheltered. **1863** BATES *Nat. Amazon* i. (1864) 10 Climbing Pothos plants, with large, glossy, heart-shaped leaves.

'pot-house. [f. POT *sb.*[1] + HOUSE *sb.*[1]]

†1. A house where pottery is made. *Obs. rare.*

1697 *Lond. Gaz.* No. 3300/4 A very convenient Brick House to be let, having a Potthouse belonging to it, and a very fine Yard for Washing of Clay. **1761** *Chron.* in *Ann. Reg.* 95/2 A premium to..master of the stone pot-house at Fulham for..making crucibles of British materials.

2. A house where pots of beer and other intoxicants are retailed; an ale-house; a small, unpretentious, or low tavern or public-house.

1724 *Lond. Gaz.* No. 6320/3 A large well built accustomed Pot-House,..known by the Name of the Hermitage Pot-House. **1748** WARTON *Panegyr. on Oxford Ale* 27 To pot-house I repair, the sacred haunt, Where, Ale, thy votaries in full resort Hold rites nocturnal. **1861** HUGHES *Tom Brown at Oxf.* xii, The paragon of all pothouses; snug little bar with red curtains [etc.]. **1887** JESSOPP *Arcady* iii. 92 They were extremely capable men, but they could not keep from the pot-house.

b. *attrib.* Belonging to or characteristic of a pot-house; low, vulgar.

1816 SOUTHEY in *Q. Rev.* XVI. 275 The class of men for whom these pot-house epistles are written, read nothing else. **1840** DICKENS *Barn. Rudge* xxxvii, Reeking yet with pot-house odours. **1895** HOLLINGSHEAD *My Lifetime* I. xiii. 124 There was no pot-house bluster about the two combatants.

pot-housey, *a.* [f. POT-HOUSE + -Y[1].] Suggestive of or appropriate to a pot-house.

1872 HARDY *Under Greenw. Tree* I. I. viii. 105 If I strip by myself and not necessary, 'tis rather pot-housey, I own.

pot-hunt, *v.* [Back-formation f. POT-HUNTER.] *intr.* To hunt 'for the pot' (see POT *sb.*[1] 1 b); to be a pot-hunter.

1926 *Chambers's Jrnl.* July 418/1 You..prefer to pot-hunt —luckily for us, with six hefty Gurkhas and the servants to feed, as well as ourselves! **1936** AUDEN & ISHERWOOD *Ascent of F6* 46 When we were boys at school, I saw him..win the prizes... We are older now..But James..Must fill the last gap in his great collection And pot-hunt for his brother.

'pot-ˌhunter. [f. POT *sb.*[1] + HUNTER.]

†1. An opprobrious appellation: ? a sycophant, a parasite: cf. BARNACLE *sb.*[2] 3 b. *Obs.*

1592 NASHE *Four Lett. Confut.* Wks. (Grosart) II. 242 This indigested Chaos of Doctourship, and greedy pothunter after applause, is an apparant Publican and sinner. **1592** GREENE *Blacke Bks. Messenger* Wks. (Grosart) XI. 7 The verser in conny-catching is called the Retriuer And the Barnacle, the pot hunter. **1592** *Admonition Bk. Emm. Coll. Cambr.* in *4th Rep. Hist. MSS. Comm.* 420/1 Mr. Catsby..for saying my Lord [of Routland] hymself was but a child, and that he was maintained by pott-hunters..was admonished.

2. 'A sportsman who shoots anything he comes across, having more regard to filling his bag than to the rules which regulate the sport' (*Slang Dict.* 1860). Also *fig.*

1781 W. BLANE *Ess. Hunting* (1788) 102 As arrant a Pot-hunter as ever England bred, that..had not scrupled to kill a Buck or Doe at any season. **1825** *Bull baiting* I. in *Houlston Tracts* I. xxvii. 9 There's nothing a regular Shot would be sooner chafed at than being called a Pot-hunter. **1856** *Porter's Spirit of Times* 25 Oct. 126/1 It is disgusting to every lover of fair play to witness the ravages committed by the pot-hunter, who coolly murders the deer by torch-light from a dug-out or canoe. **1878** C. HALLOCK *Amer. Club List & Sportsman's Gloss.* p. ix/1 *Pot-hunter*, one who hunts or fishes for profit, regardless of close seasons, the waste of game, or the pleasure to be derived from the pursuit. **1895** J. G. MILLAIS *Breath fr. Veldt* (1899) 109 My hope is that some traveller..who is something more than a pot-hunter, may..send home to our Museum a series of the common white-quilled black Khoorhan. **1905** 'O. HENRY' in *N.Y. World Mag.* 22 Oct. 8/1 He was an old man, with a slow and limping gait, so a pot-hunter of a newly-licensed chauffeur ran him down one day when livelier game was scarce. **1922** JOYCE *Ulysses* 158 Lady Mountcashel..rode out with the Ward Union staghounds... Uneatable fox. Pothunters too. **1936** *Sun* (Baltimore) 28 Feb. 11/5 Hundreds of ducks flying northward have been slaughtered. The chief offenders..are the so-called 'pot-hunters', who hunt for profit and rent duck blinds to sportsmen.

3. One who takes part in any contest or competition merely for the sake of winning a prize. (With allusion to POT *sb.*[1] 1 g.)

1873 *Slang Dict.*, *Pot-hunter*, a man who gives his time up to rowing or punting, or any sort of match in order to win the 'pewters' which are given as prizes. *University*... Now much used in aquatic and athletic circles; and..applied, in a derogatory sense, to men of good quality who enter themselves in small races they are almost sure to win. **1883** *Pall Mall G.* 7 July 6/1 The increase..in the number of 'pot-hunters', as they are called—an epithet which originated in the early days of the Wimbledon meeting, when prizes were given 'in kind', and not as now in money. **1886** *Cycl. Tour. Club Gaz.* IV. 122 To tempt..many a 'pot-hunter' who follows racing for what he can get out of it. **1912** A. BENNETT *Matador* 22 He used to be what they called a pot-hunter, a racing bicyclist. **1942** BERREY & VAN DEN BARK *Amer. Thes. Slang* §636/21 *Contestant for a prize*, mug hunter or chaser, pot hunter.

4. One who finds or obtains objects of archaeological interest or value, esp. by unscientific or illicit methods, and for the purpose of private collection or profit.

1958 *N.Y. Times Mag.* 16 Feb. 48/3 This satisfaction..is the big distinction between the new species of digger and the acquisitive 'pot hunter', that bane of archaeological scientists. Souvenir-hunting amateurs are still with us, of course. **1966** ROBBINS & IRVING *Amat. Archaeologist's Handbk.* v. 83 This chapter might carry the subtitle: 'Pothunters, beware!' A pothunter is a person who visits a site in order to find and hoard as many 'relics' as possible. **1967** L. DEUEL *Conquistadors without Swords* iv. 52 Museum collections all over the world owe most of their treasures to disreputable pothunters. **1973** *New Yorker* 24 Mar. 102/2 Stewart L. Peckham, chief archaeologist of the Museum of New Mexico,..was distressed to find that almost all the major Mimbres sites..had been ravaged by pot-hunters.

So **'pot-ˌhunting** *sb.* and *a.* (in senses corresponding to 2, 3 and 4 above).

1808 W. COBBETT in L'Estrange *Friendships Miss Mitford* (1882) I. 43 Rush they go, the pot-hunting crew, into that manor. **1862** *Sat. Rev.* 5 July 7 The sort of pot-hunting known at Wimbledon and elsewhere as Pool, where the value of a bull's-eye is much more considered than the credit of handling with success the Queen of weapons. **1869** *Harper's Mag.* Jan. 157/1 This is regarded by many Plains men as a kind of pot-hunting, that is not entitled to the name of sport, and only to be resorted to for the purpose of securing the meat needed as food. **1881** TYLOR *Anthropology* ix. 210 The quest of food (now often contemptuously called 'pot-hunting') becomes subordinate to the excitement of the chase. **1881** *Gd. Words* XXII. 46/1 Some men are too fond of starring or pothunting at 'sports'. **1893** SINCLAIR & HENRY *Swimming* (Badm. Libr.) 369 Some swimmers seem able..to stand the strain of racing night after night... The rage for pot-hunting is apparently unconquerable. **1946** L. P. HARTLEY *Sixth Heaven* ii. 47 I'm doing a bit of pot-hunting and have to attend classes and pow-wows. **1956** A. R. KING in *Amer. Antiquity* Apr. 423/2 Scientific archaeology carries more satisfaction than 'pot-hunting' and 'treasure troving'. **1973** *New Yorker* 24 Mar. 100/3 Poverty and desperation are extenuating factors in Bangladesh, but not in the United States, where pot-hunting is a weekend hobby of the more affluent. The rise in prices for American-Indian art..has had disastrous consequences for scholarship.

poticary, obs. variant of POTHECARY.

‖**potiche** (pɒtiʃ). [Fr., in the same sense.] A large porcelain vase, usu. rounded in shape with bulging shoulders and a widish mouth freq. having a lid, originally produced in China during the Ming dynasty.

1895 in *Funk's Stand. Dict.* **1933** *Burlington Mag.* Nov. 202 (*caption*) Semi-Celadon Potiche of Chino-Sawankalōk Ware. **1935** *Ibid.* June p. xx/2 A royal potiche ornamented with a band of wave scrolls on the neck. **1960** H. HAYWARD *Antique Coll.* 226/2 *Potiche*, large broad-mouthed Chinese porcelain jar of 'baluster' shape, with cover; favoured from Ming..times. **1967** P. WHITE in *Coast to Coast 1965–66* 231 Answering back made her mistress rush at the *bibelots*, dust the *potiches* her maid neglected. **1972** *Trans. Oriental Ceramics Soc.* XXXVIII. 126 The jar of *potiche* form with broad base, short wide neck and low domed cover.

potichomania (pɒˌtiːʃəʊ'meɪnɪə). Also in Fr. form **-manie**. [ad. F. *potichomanie*, irreg. f. *potiche* an oriental porcelain vase, also a glass vase coloured in imitation + *-manie*, -MANIA.] The craze for imitating Japanese or other porcelain by covering the inner surface of glass vessels, etc., with designs on paper or sheet gelatine; the process of doing this.

1855 *Househ. Words* XI. 129 (heading) *Potichomania.* **1855** *Mechanic's Mag.* LXII. 279 *Potichomanie* is the present fashion. **1863** SALA *Capt. Slyboots* 7 He..talked about chemistry and Mr. Faraday; taught my wife *potichomanie* and modelling in wax. **1903** *Temple Bar Mag.* Feb. 152 Hence she..cared nothing for wax flowers or potichomania.

potichomanist (pɒtɪ'ʃɒmənɪst). *rare.* [f. POTICHOMANIA + -IST.] A person who practises potichomania.

1884 *Decorator's Assistant* 122 Potichomanists have found the art capable of greater results than the mere imitation of porcelain vases, by the introduction of glass panels [etc.].

‖**potin**[1] (pɒtæ̃). Also 7 pottain. [F. *potin* (13th c. in Hatz.-Darm., also *potain* 1582 in Godef.), f. *pot* POT *sb.*[1] + *-in*: cf. -INE[4].]

1. Old pot-metal (POT-METAL 1, 3).

1601 HOLLAND *Pliny* II. 505 Such pottain or old mettall which is ouerworne, and by ordinary occupying and vsing to the hand, bright-shining. **1825** J. NICHOLSON *Operat. Mechanic* 348 To work all the surface into furrows or grooves, in order that it may retain the substance called the potin, which is to be welded upon one side of the iron, to form the hard matter on which the holes are to be pierced. This potin is nothing but fragments of old cast-iron pots. *Ibid.* 349 It must be repeatedly heated and worked until the potin fixes to the iron. The workman then throws dry powdered clay upon it, in order..to soften the potin.

2. A name for an alloy of tin, copper, lead, and zinc, used in coining by the ancient Gauls.

1853 HUMPHREYS *Coin-Coll. Man.* xi. (1876) 134 Many of the coins are of base metal (potin).

‖**potin**[2] (pɒtæ̃). *rare.* [Fr.] A piece of gossip; a rumpus, a row.

1922 M. ARLEN *Piracy* II. vi. 111 He would hear of great dinners and dances and *potins.* **1938** G. ARTHUR *Not Worth Reading* vi. 86 No shred of evidence could ever be adduced to reinforce the *potin* that Fred Archer was the natural son of a peer. **1945** E. WAUGH *Brideshead Revisited* I. vi. 136 'What's going on?' 'Oh, just another boring family potin. Sebastian got tight again.'

poting, poting-stick: see POTE *v.*

potinger, obs. form of POTTINGER.

potion ('pəʊʃən), *sb.* Forms: 4–6 pocion, 5 -oun, (*Sc.* poycion), 5–6 pocyon, 6 potioun, 6– potion. [a. OF. *pocion*, *potion* (12–13th c. in Hatz.-Darm.), mod.F. *potion*, ad. L. *pōtiō-nem* a drinking, draught, potion, philtre, vbl. sb. f. *pōtāre*, *pōt-um* to drink.]

1. A dose of liquid medicine or of poison; a draught: see DRAUGHT *sb.* 15.

13.. *K. Alis.* 3509 (Bodl. MS.) He dude hym bere to pavylouns, And sauid hym wiþ pociouns. *c* 1375 *Sc. Leg. Saints* vi. (*Thomas*) 481 It is lyk to poycion men takis fore purgacione. 1432–50 tr. *Higden* (Rolls) III. 411 He hade diede anoon, but that he receyvede a pocion of Philippe his phisicion. 1548–77 VICARY *Anat.* i. (1888) 13 If a man may be cured with Dyet and Pocion, let there not be ministred any Chirurgerie. 1592 SHAKS. *Rom. & Jul.* v. iii. 244 Then gaue I her.. A sleeping Potion, which so tooke effect As I intended. 1610 HOLLAND *Camden's Brit.* (1637) 370 Bewitched by sorcerie and amorous potions. 1732 LEDIARD *Sethos* II. VII. 84 To discern the innocent.. by trials of fire and potions. 1848 MRS. JAMESON *Sacr. & Leg. Art* (1850) 435 Neither potions nor physicians can do more than postpone the evil hour.

fig. 1577 tr. *Luther's Comm. Gal.* iv. 95 He goeth about to qualify and mitigate his bitter Potion. 1597 SHAKS. *2 Hen. IV*, I. ii. 145 Your Lordship may minister the Potion of imprisonment to me. 1631 HEYWOOD *Eng. Eliz.* (1641) 108 The bitter potion of indignity. 1790 BURKE *Fr. Rev.* Wks. V. 140 To administer the opiate potion of amnesty.

†2. a. A portion of drink; a drink, a draught. b. A kind of drink; a beverage. *Obs. rare.*

1526 *Aberdeen Regr.* (1844) I. 115 Inprimis to the justice ane potioun of wyne; item to my lord chancellar, ane potioun of wyne. 1634 SIR T. HERBERT *Trav.* 150 They [Persians] vse another potion, faire water, juice of Lemmons, Sugar, and Roses.

3. *Comb.*, as ***potion-monger***.

1894 H. A. JONES in *Daily News* 7 May 6/5 The family friend, rather than the doser and potion-monger.

potion (ˈpəʊʃən), *v.* [f. prec. sb. Cf. L. *pōtiōnāre* to give to drink, f. *pōtiōn-em* drinking.] *trans.* To treat or dose with potions; to drug.

1611 SPEED *Hist. Gt. Brit.* IX. xi. §49 Hauing corrupted his Keepers, or.. hauing potioned them with a sleepy drinke, [he] escaped out of the Tower of London. 1768 FOOTE *Devil on 2 Sticks* III. Wks. 1799 II. 275 Full power.. to pill, bolus, lotion, potion,.. and poultice, all persons. 1812 L. HUNT in *Examiner* 25 May 321/1 Puff'd and potion'd up like any bladder.

†ˈ**potionate**, *v. Obs. rare*⁻⁰. [f. ppl. stem of L. *pōtiōnāre*: see prec. and -ATE³.]

1623 COCKERAM, *Potionate*, to give a medicine.

‖ˈ**potiron**. *Obs.* [F. *potiron* (dial. *potron, poturon*) a kind of large champignon; also, a kind of pumpkin: origin unknown.] A kind of pumpkin: see quots.

1719 LONDON & WISE *Compl. Gard.* 323 Citrules, or Pumpions, Harts Horn Sallet, Potirons, or flat Pumpeons, Parsnipe, Leeks, &c. keep their Places nine Months. *Ibid.* 324 Citruls or Pumpions, Potirons or comon Pumpions, Garlick and Shallots.

†ˈ**potisuge**. *Obs. humorous nonce-wd.* [f. L. *pōtus* drink (or ? POT *sb.*¹) + L. *sūgĕre* to suck.] A 'pot-sucker', toper.

1620 VENNER *Via Recta* ii. 34 How impudently would our drunken potisuges vaunt themselues.

ˈ**pot-kilp**. *north. dial.* [f. POT *sb.*¹ + KILP.] = POT-CLIP.

1542 *Richmond Wills* (Surtees) 31, ij. pare of pot kylpes, and a pare of tanges, xxd. 1611–12 *Knaresborough Wills* (Surtees) II. 20 A paire of potkilpes. 1828 *Craven Dial.* s.v. *Kelps*, The loose handle of a kale pot is called pot-kelps. 1855 ROBINSON *Whitby Gloss.*, *Pot kelps*, the loose bow or handle of a porridge-pot.

ˈ**potlatch**, ˈ**potlach(e**, *sb.* [Chinook jargon, from Nootka Indian *potlatsh, patlatsh* sb. a gift, vb. to give.] Among some N. American Indians of the Pacific coast: a. A gift, a present.

1883 T. WINTHROP *Canoe & Saddle* iv. 42 They [Klickatat Indians].. expressed the friendliest sentiments, perhaps with a view to a liberal 'potlatch' of trinkets.

b. A tribal feast at which presents are given and received, given by an aspirant to chiefship. Also, an extravagant giving away or throwing away of possessions to enhance one's prestige or establish one's position. Also *attrib.*, *transf.*, and *fig.*

1865 C. C. LEIGHTON *Jrnl.* 30 Aug. in *Life at Puget Sound* (1884) 25 There was going to be a great *potlach* at the coal-mines, where a large quantity of *iktas* would be given away, —tin pans, guns, blankets, canoes, and money... It seems that anyone who aspires to be a chief must first give a *potlach* to his tribe. 1884 *San Francisco Chron.* Sept., A potlatch is .. a sort of grand reunion and general gathering.., an occasion for the exchanging of big presents. 1890 *Amer. Antiquarian* Mar. 75 On his return he again called the people together and held a big potlatch, giving the Indians what appeared to them at that time great curiosities. 1895 *Westm. Gaz.* 18 July 8/1 In a far-away corner of British Columbia, on the occasion of the last birthday.. the Redskins held a 'pot-lach' in honour of their Great White Mother. 1902 H. L. WILSON *Spenders* xxx. 357 This life of idleness you been leadin'—one continual potlatch the whole time—it wa'n't doin' you a bit of good. 1907 C. HILL-TOUT *Brit. N. Amer.* 52 Occasions of public festivity such as potlatch gatherings. 1916 [see GIVE-AWAY 1]. 1934 R. BENEDICT *Patterns of Culture* (1935) vi. 202 A variant of this type of potlatch was that which was given upon the adolescence of the woman of highest rank. 1957 *Times* 12 Nov. (Canada Suppl.) p. v/3 Another change was the removal of the prohibition on potlatches and on some traditional religious ceremonies, an ironic measure, as they have now practically disappeared. 1965 H. KAHN *On Escalation* xiii. 270 'Potlatch' wars. Competitions in conspicuous consumption of resources or spectacular successes in such areas as space, economic growth, and 'showy' military systems are employed to gain prestige and influence events. 1969 *Times* 22 Sept. 14/3 Potlatch was an obligation to anyone caught out in a misdemeanour, or who had suffered loss of face through some mishap. Only by a parade of wealth or wild generosity or conspicuous waste could such a man regain his shattered image. 1970 *Globe & Mail* (Toronto) 26 Sept. 29/3 (Advt.), The game has become secondary to a potlatch ceremony called tailgate picknicking... This.. requires that the host participants outdo their neighbours in the quality and variety of food and drink and the elegance of serving accessories. 1976 *New Yorker* 22 Mar. 44/3 But in September the potlatch ends and there is no one left but old men and women caring for babies whose parents cannot afford to keep them abroad.

Hence ˈ**potlatching** *sb.*, holding a potlatch.

1896 *Pall Mall Mag.* Sept. 106 After two or three days of feasting and pot-latching. 1964 GOULD & KOLB *Dict. Social Sci.* 523/1 Potlatching demanded reciprocity. 1975 H. WHITE *Raincoast Chron.* (1976) 182/1 There was incessant potlatching.

ˈ**potlatch**, *v.* [f. the sb.] To give; *spec.* to establish one's name or position by the extravagant giving or throwing away of goods or by holding a feast, which entails some form of reciprocity or return.

1901 *Daily Colonist* (Victoria, B.C.) 6 Oct. 2/2 He had $120 coming to him, and he went to Mr. Landsberg and asked if he would potlatch one half of his wages to him and give the other half to the Duke. 1911 *Ibid.* 30 Apr. 8/3 The forty-one family heads of the Songhees band of Indians.. had the pleasure of collecting the last of the moneys potlached to them by the provincial government. 1934 R. BENEDICT *Patterns of Culture* (1935) vi. 203 Potlatching for an heir on the North West coast. 1943 W. H. CHASE *Sourdough Pot* xxiii. 171 The deal was closed, the butter potlatched to her father. 1958 A. R. RADCLIFFE-BROWN *Method in Social Anthropol.* I. v. 123 Amongst the Tlingit.. it is members of one moiety who potlatch against members of the other moiety. 1964 GOULD & KOLB *Dict. Social Sci.* 523/1 If.. a person were humiliated by an accident which made him appear ridiculous, or if he were taken in war and made a slave, he or his relatives must *potlatch* in his name in order to reinstate him in public esteem.

†**pot-lead**¹. *Obs.* Used to render F. *gluq*, 'a word used by Schollers of Paris, in derision of an absurd conclusion' (Cotgr. s.v. *Gluc*).

1630 LENNARD tr. *Charron's Wisd.* III. xiv. §19. 505 If he chance to speake, he entreth into a long discourse of definitions, and diuisions of Aristotle; *ergo* potlead [orig. F. *ergo gluq*].

pot-lead² (ˈpɒtlɛd), *sb.* [ad. Du. *potlood* black-lead, f. *pot* POT *sb.*¹ + *lood* lead.] A name for black-lead or graphite, esp. as used for coating the hulls of racing-yachts below the water-line so as to diminish the friction of the water. Hence ˌ**pot-**ˈ**lead** *v. trans.*, to coat with pot-lead.

1890 in *Cent. Dict.* 1894 *Outing* (U.S.) XXIV. 72/1 The racing shell, used only three times, its bottom pot-leaded, is brought out. *Ibid.* 194/1 Using very fine sandpaper and pot lead till my boat's bottom was beautifully burnished.

potleg (ˈpɒtlɛg). [app. f. POT *sb.*¹ + LEG.]

a. (?) The leg or foot of an iron pot. b. Broken scraps of cast-iron, used as shot.

1895 *Chambers's Jrnl.* XII. 738/1 Ball or shot they rarely use, but prefer a handful of broken cast-iron potleg, which at close quarters makes a ghastly wound. 1896 *Westm. Gaz.* 15 May 4/3 Their [Matabele] shot consisted of pot-legs, stones, and pieces of iron. 1900 *Longm. Mag.* Dec. 143 When the sergeant raised his officer, ragged potleg was whirring everywhere.

potler, variant of POTELLER *Obs.*

pot-lid. [f. POT *sb.*¹ + LID *sb.*]

1. The lid of a pot.

(When of iron, sometimes used as a warming-pan.)

1403 *Nottingham Rec.* II. 20, j. potlede de ligno. 1530 PALSGR. 257/1 Potlydde for a potte, *couuerlecque*. 1590 GREENE *Never too late* II. (1616) N iv b, To bed man, to bed, and we will haue a warme pot-lid [*ed.* 1590 pot-led]. 1682 T. FLATMAN *Heraclitus Ridens* No. 62 (1713) II. 134 It might be, for ought they knew, a Project for altering the Breadth of Pot-lids. 1902 *Daily Chron.* 28 Aug. 3/2 A new hobby.. is the collection of small china pot-lids; the covers of those artistic jars which long ago were used for holding shrimp-paste and meats. 1924 CLARKE & WRENCH *Colour Pictures on Pot Lids* i. 4 The collecting of pot lids and other Staffordshire pottery adorned with these pictures has gone on in a quiet way for some considerable time. 1957 MANKOWITZ & HAGGAR *Conc. Encycl. Eng. Pott. & Porc.* 181/1 Polychrome colour-printing on pottery was developed .. from 1848.. and was used extensively for the decoration of pot-lids. 1972 *Times* 7 July 14/7 These Staffordshire pot lids were a nineteenth-century packaging gimmick for products such as fish paste or cold cream.

2. *Curling.* A stone so played as to rest on the tee.

1853 WALTER WATSON *Poems & Songs* 63 (E.D.D.). 1885 'J. STRATHESK' *More Bits Blinkb.* xiv. 271 His stone landed on the Tee. 'A pat-lid', said Douce Davie. 1893–4 *Caled. Curl. Cl. Ann.* 114 A rare patlid, I fear your play is just owre guid.

3. *Geol.* Popular appellation of a concretion occurring in various sandstones and shales.

1827 FITTON *On Stonesfield-slate* in *Zool. Jrnl.* (1828) III. 416 Concretions of calcareous grit.. that form a part of almost every group... These concretions, from a coarse resemblance, are called 'Pot-lids'; and the rock which they consist of,.. bears the name of 'Pendle'.

4. *attrib.* **pot-lid valve**, 'a cap-formed valve which shuts down like a cover upon a port or the end of a pipe'; also, 'the cover of the air-pump of a steam-engine' (Knight *Dict. Mech.* 1875).

†ˈ**potling**. *Obs. humorous nonce-wd.* [f. POT *sb.*¹ + -LING¹.] ? A votary of the pot; a tippler (but cf. POETLING).

1598 B. JONSON *Ev. Man in Hum.* IV. i, You must haue your Poets and your Potlings, your Soldados and Foolados to follow you vp and down the City.

pot-liquor (ˈpɒtˌlɪkə(r)). Also (chiefly *U.S.*) pot-likker. [f. POT *sb.*¹ + LIQUOR *sb.*] The liquor in which meat has been boiled; thin broth: see also quot. 1886. Also *fig.*

1744 W. ELLIS *Mod. Husbandman* July xvii. 101 Mix fine Pollard with fresh Pot-liquor. 1773 GRAVES *Spir. Quixote* I. ix, Together with her broth or pot-liquor, he contrived to slip something more substantial into Dorothy's pipkin. 1803 HAN. MORE *Way to Plenty* 56 The pot liquor made such a supply of broth for the sick poor. 1852 DICKENS *Bleak Ho.* xxvii, Mrs. Bagnet.. sitting with every dish before her; allotting to every portion of pork its own portion of pot-liquor, greens, potatoes, and even mustard! 1886 ELWORTHY *W. Somerset Word-bk.*, *Pot-liquor*, the water in which vegetables have been boiled; sometimes called green-liquor, when cabbage or other green vegetables have been boiled in it. 1909 *Dialect Notes* III. 359 *Pot-liquor*,.. liquor from boiled greens or field peas and fat meat. 1930 *Sun* (Baltimore) 17 May 1/3 Pot likker is the best way of preventing nearly all the diseases that we are heir to. 1931 *Sun* (Baltimore) 4 Mar. 12/7 Maryland pot liquor is the liquor left over in the pot after a boiling of ham and cabbage. 1932 *Ibid.* 8 Apr. 1/4 The Louisianian contended that the corn pone should be 'dunked' into the pot likker. 1949 C. HIMES *Black on Black* (1973) 277 They sat in the hot kitchen and ate greens and side meat and rice and.. drank the pot-liquor with the corn bread. 1950 *Amer. Speech* XXV. 230 *Pot likker*, the juice in which black-eyed peas are cooked. 1963 *New Statesman* 12 July 37/3 During the years when McCarthy's briefcase was a national badge of shame, Americans looked to Britain for an example of sanity and regard for civil liberties. The present anxiety may be unfounded, but some honourable Americans succumbed to the tempting potlikker of the loyalty issue with all its hazy innuendoes. 1974 *Black World* Jan. 53 The boiler at school threatening to blow/flannel gowns and slips Pot likker and cornbread/bundles of kindling for the stove.

ˈ**pot-**ˈ**luck**. [f. POT *sb.*¹ + LUCK *sb.*] One's luck or chance as to what may be in the pot, i.e. cooked for a meal: used in reference to a person accepting another's hospitality at a meal without any special preparation having been made for him; chiefly in phr. ***to take pot-luck***. Also *transf.*

1592 NASHE *Four Lett. Confut.* Ded., That that pure sanguine complexion of yours may neuer be famisht with pot lucke. 1773 GRAVES *Spir. Quixote* IX. xii, The Gentleman said.. he should be very welcome to take pot-luck with him. 1773 MME. D'ARBLAY *Early Diary* Sept., If they have any prospect of more sport, they take pot-luck at any cottage. 1883 *Longm. Mag* July 253 Go home with this man, take pot-luck with him.. as one of the family.

attrib. 1775 MME. D'ARBLAY *Early Diary, Let.* Mar., [He] took the same kind of pot-luck company in those days when he was not so shy of London. 1894 J. C. JEAFFRESON *Bk. Recoll.* I. xv. 292 A suburban villa, at which he was in the habit of taking pot-luck dinner on Sunday.

ˈ**pot-**ˌ**maker**. Now *rare*. One who makes pots or pottery; a potter.

1535 COVERDALE *1 Chron.* iv. 23 These were potmakers, and dwelt amonge plantes and hedges. 1550— *Spir. Perle* i. (1560) 3 It is not seeming, that the pot should murmur against the potmaker. 1579–80 NORTH *Plutarch* (1595) 665 He made a herauld proclaime that all potmakers should stand vp on their feete.

†b. *spec.* A maker of pots or crucibles for the Mint. *Obs.*

1548 *Privy Council Acts* (1890) II. 177 For a smyth xxˢ; for a potmaker xxˢ. 1587 FLEMING *Contn. Holinshed* III. 1972/2 William Forleie pot-maker for the mint of the Tower of London. 1647 HAWARD *Crown Rev.* 23 Pot-maker: Fee, 10. o. o.

ˈ**pot-**ˌ**making**, *vbl. sb.* The making of pots or pottery.

1767 J. WEDGWOOD *Let.* 26 July (1965) 58, I.. am sorry to find the heat.. was much more intense than can be made use of for Potmaking. 1927 PEAKE & FLEURE *Peasants & Potters* 141 We think that they had picked up the art of agriculture, weaving and pot-making, etc. 1951 E. E. EVANS-PRITCHARD *Social Anthropol.* v. 101 A man who.. fails in some enterprise, such as pot-making, through lack of skill is responsible for the penalties or failures his actions incur. 1957 P. WORSLEY *Trumpet shall Sound* vi. 115 Malasang, the centre of the pot-making industry, ceased production.

potman (ˈpɒtmən). [f. POT *sb.*¹ + MAN *sb.*¹]

†1. A man addicted to pots of liquor; a toper.

1589 NASHE *Anat. Absurd.* Wks. (Grosart) I. 45 A man.. if lasciuious, good in some English deuise of verse, to conclude, a passing potman, a passing Poet. 1685 WOOD *Life* 23 Nov. (O.H.S.) III. 171 The pot men and juniors carry all before them.

2. A man employed at a public-house to attend to the pots and serve the liquor. (Cf. POT-BOY.)

1846 WORCESTER, *Potman*,.. a servant at a public house. 1851 MAYHEW *Lond. Labour* (1862) II. 345 He got a situation as potman to a public-house. 1860 DICKENS *Uncomm. Trav.* xiii, The potmen thrust the last brawling drunkards into the street. 1898 G. B. SHAW *You never can Tell* II. 255 He's at the Bar... A potman, eh?... No, sir: the other bar. **1925** D. GARNETT *Sailor's Return* 22 The next morning the potman came to the inn. **1936** MENCKEN *Amer. Lang.* (ed. 4) 243 *Barmaids* do the work, with maybe a *barman, potman* or *cellarman* to help. **1972** *Classification of Occupations* (Dept. Employment) II. 399/2 *Bar potmen* (wash glasses in licensed bar).

3. *dial.* A dealer in earthenware.

1889 in *N.W. Linc. Gloss.* (ed. 2).

4. In various manufacturing processes: a man who attends to the filling, emptying, firing, etc., of pots (see quots.).

1874 J. A. PHILLIPS *Elem. Metallurgy* 581 In order to desilverise by the aid of this arrangement, the potman sinks the ladle sideways to the bottom of the kettle. **1921** *Dict. Occup. Terms* (1927) §143 *Pot man* (alkali);..charges shallow iron pans with salt and sulphuric acid, attends to firing, and supervises process until product is ready for salt cake furnace. *Ibid., Pot man* (lead); puts pig and scrap lead into pot and tends and feeds fire beneath it which melts lead [etc.]. **1932** *Amer. Speech* VII. 269 *Pot man,* the man who tends the boilers in which steam is generated for drilling.

pot-metal (ˈpɒtˌmɛtəl). [f. POT *sb.*[1]]

1. An alloy of lead and copper of which pots were formerly made.

1693 POVEY in *Phil. Trans.* XVII. 736 Bell-metal being Copper and Tin, Pot-metal Copper and Lead. About 20*l.* of Lead is usually put into 100*l.* of Pot-metal. **1832** CARLYLE *Remin.* I. 38 Tinkers also, making pot metal,..often came upon the scene.

2. Stained glass coloured in the melting-pot, so that the colour pervades the whole substance.

1832 G. R. PORTER *Porcelain & Gl.* 290 Small pieces of glass coloured throughout during the process of its original manufacture..called by artists pot metal. **1898** *Daily News* 6 Jan. 6/1 Stained glass is coloured 'in the pot', by means of metallic oxides; hence 'pot metal', as the technical name for this kind of glass. **1899** *Q. Rev.* Jan. 171 In these windows pot-metal glass is used as far as possible for the larger pieces of ruby or other colour.

3. A kind of cast iron suitable for making pots.

1864 WEBSTER, *Pot-metal*... The metal from which iron pots are made, different from common pig iron. **1875** in KNIGHT *Dict. Mech.*

ˈpot-net. [f. POT *sb.*[1] + NET *sb.*[1]]

†**1.** A net in which to boil vegetables in a pot with meat; a cabbage-net. *Obs.*

1562 in H. Hall *Soc. Eliz. Age* (1886) App. 158 A brass pot and a potnet. **1599** *Acc. Bk. W. Wray* in *Antiquary* XXXII. 243 A potte nette.

2. ? A fishing-net having the form of a pot. (Cf. *pock-net* s.v. POKE *sb.*[1] 7.) ? *Obs.*

1584 in *Descr. Thames* (1758) 63 Purse Nets, Casting Nets, ..Pot Nets, Barrock Nets at Crooks, Heaving Nets. **1806** FORSYTH *Beauties Scotl.* IV. 224 A kind of pot-net, fastened to a long pole,..is used here.

potok, obs. form of PUTTOCK.

potoˈmania. [f. Gr. ποτόν drink + -MANIA.] Morbid craving for drink; dipsomania.

1858 MAYNE *Expos. Lex., Potomania,*..drink-madness. **1890** BILLINGS *Med. Dict., Potomania,* dipsomania.

potometer (pəʊˈtɒmɪtə(r)). [f. as prec. + -METER.] An instrument for measuring the amount of water absorbed by a growing plant.

1884 F. DARWIN in *Nature* 1 May 7 An ingenious instrument..the Potometer. It is a modification of Sachs' apparatus for determining the amount of water which a cut branch absorbs in a given time. **1895** in *Syd. Soc. Lex.*

‖**potoo** (pəʊˈtuː). [Echoic; from its cry.] The name given in Jamaica to one of the Nightjars (*Nyctibius jamaicensis*).

1847 GOSSE *Birds Jamaica* 42 The Potoo is not unfrequently seen in the evening..soon after sunset on some dead tree or fence-post, or floating by on noiseless wing, like an owl. *Ibid.* 47 The Potoo has become a proverb of ugliness. **1894** in NEWTON *Dict. Birds.*

‖**potoquane.** *erron.* potaquaine. The name of the Sable Antelope, *Hippotragus niger*, among the Southern Bechuana.

1850 R. G. CUMMING *Hunter's Life S. Afr.* (1902) 140/2 Potaquaines above me, seeing nothing and smelling nothing, stood bewildered until I had reloaded, lying on my side. **1900** W. L. SCLATER *Fauna S. Afr.* I. 221.

†**poˈtorious,** *a. Obs. rare*⁻⁰. [f. L. *pōtōri-us* drinking (f. *pōtor* drinker) + -OUS.]

1656 BLOUNT *Glossogr., Potorious,* of or belonging to drink, drinking.

‖**potoroo** (pɒtəˈruː). Also 8 poto roo. [Native name in New South Wales.] A small nocturnal marsupial belonging to the genus *Potorous*, esp. *P. tridactylus*, found in areas of dense vegetation in Australia; = KANGAROO-RAT 1, *rat-kangaroo* s.v. RAT *sb.*[1] 7 e.

1790 J. WHITE *Voy. N.S. Wales* 286 The Poto Roo, or Kangaroo Rat. **1839–47** *Todd's Cycl. Anat.* III. 265/2 The Potoroos..present..the same dentition as does the Koala. **1841** WATERHOUSE *Marsupialia* 172 The *Hypsiprimni*, or Potoroos, and Kangaroo-rats as they are termed, differ chiefly from the true Kangaroos, in possessing distinct canines. **1907** P. FOUNTAIN *Rambles of Austral. Naturalist* iv. 38 There are several local varieties of the potoroo. **1923** F. W. JONES *Mammals S. Austral.* 218 The remaining potoroos should be carefully protected. **1943** C. BARRETT *Austral. Animal Bk.* xi. 100 The dark rat-kangaroo, known to the natives of Port Jackson as the potoroo,..is now a rare animal. **1965** *Courier-Mail* (Brisbane) 24 Aug. 13 The potoroo is one of the rarest native animals. **1970** W. D. L. RIDE *Guide Native Mammals Austral.* 64 Potoroos apparently require the dense natural vegetation of their habitat for protection. **1975** *Nature* 8 May 141/2 The bones we exhibited included forms similar to those of living potoroos and phalangers.

ˈpot-ˌoven. [POT *sb.*[1]] **1.** (See quot. 1750.)

1750 R. POCOCKE *Trav.* (1888) 135 Pot-ovens, a round piece of iron which is heated, on which the bread is put, and then it is cover'd over with a pot, on which they heap the embers to keep in the heat. **1899** SOMERVILLE & ROSS *Irish R.M.* 189 Her potato-cakes came in hot and hot from a pot-oven.

2. A kiln in which pottery is fired.

1878 L. JEWITT *Ceramic Art Gt. Brit.* xiii. 528 In his will, dated 29th of January, 1728..this Caleb Glover 'of Pott-ovens, pott-maker'..leaves all his 'working tools belonging to the trade of a potmaker, and the pot oven'. **1971** P. C. D. BREARS *Eng. Country Pott.* 225 In 1798, John Morton & Sons assessed for their pot-ovens at Sinderhills.

†**potˈpanion.** *Obs. humorous nonce-wd.* Contraction of POT-COMPANION.

c **1580** JEFFERIE *Bugbears* III. i. in *Archiv Stud. Neu. Spr.* (1897), 'Tis Signor Amades, one of my masters pottpanions.

pot-paper: see POT *sb.*[1] 10.

pot-pie. Chiefly *U.S.* [f. POT *sb.*[1] + PIE *sb.*[2]]

a. 'A pie made by spreading the crust over the bottom and sides of a pot, and filling up the inside with meat, i.e. beef, veal, mutton, or fowls' (Bartlett *Dict. Amer.*). **b.** 'A dish of stewed meat with pieces of steamed pastry or dumplings served in it; a fricassee of meat with dumplings' (*Cent. Dict.*). **c.** 'Beef cut up into cubes, encased in dough and boiled in a pot' (*Eng. Dial. Dict.*).

1823 F. COOPER *Pioneers* i, The snow-birds are flying round your own door, where you may..shoot enough for a pot-pie any day. **18..** CARLETON *New Purchase* I. 181 (Bartlett) An enormous pot-pie,..piping hot, graced our centre, overpowering, with its fragrance and steam, the odors and vapors of all other meats; and pot-pie was the wedding dish of the country, par excellence!.. What pot could have contained the pie is inconceivable. **1883** P. E. GIBBONS in *Harper's Mag.* Apr. 658/2, I suppose it resembles chicken pot pie. **1895** *Newcastle Daily Jrnl.* 18 Feb. (E.D.D.), Four hundred pot pies and as many loaves of bread were distributed to poor people. **1906** *Amer. Illustr. Mag.* Feb. 465/1, I was out huntin' for squirrels to make a potpie out of, for squirrel potpie's just lickin' good. **1933** M. DE LA ROCHE *Master of Jalna* ii. 16 From there came the appetising smell of chicken pot-pie. **1935** A. J. CRONIN *Stars look Down* III. ix. 564, I know you've had no breakfast. Are you above eating a pit pot-pie? **1940** MENCKEN *Happy Days* iv. 59 The Rennert [Hotel] also offered an oyster pot-pie that had its points. **1975** *New Yorker* 20 Oct. 31/3 'He just bein' *prudent*,' said her father. 'Some of them non-needy chirrun might sneak in there and grab some of that chicken potpie.'

†**ˈpot-piece.** *Obs.* Also 6 pottin peice. [f. POT *sb.*[1] + PIECE *sb.* 11.] = POT-GUN 1.

a **1575** *Diurn. Occurr.* (Bannatyne Cl.) 330 Thrie houlkis of Ingland, ladunit with ane cannone ryell, four singill cannounis, ix gross culveringis, four pottin peices. *a* **1578** LINDESAY (Pitscottie) *Chron. Scot.* (S.T.S.) II. 301 Of the said xxxij thair was mony pot peices. **1637** MONRO *Exped.* II. 214 Those peeces of Cannon that are farthest hard, are called pot-peeces or Mortiers. *a* **1670** SPALDING *Troub. Chas. I* (1850) I. 223 The prouisioun laid in the castell..as granadoes, potpeices, and vtheris.

ˈpot-plant.

1. A plant grown in a pot.

1816 'A. SINGLETON' *Lett.* (1824) 63 The young Virginian ladies take pleasure in nurturing..and fostering their parlour pot-plants. **1858** GLENNY *Gard. Every-day Bk.* 187/1 Pot-plants that have been plunged, and gone by their prime, must be got up, and be replaced by others in good order. **1869** *Daily News* 14 July, Prizes..for fuchsias, geraniums, ferns, and other pot plants. **1870** W. ROBINSON *Alpine Flowers* I. 56 Our pot-plants are far before those of other countries. **1871** S. HIBBERD *Amateur's Flower Garden* xiii. 240 Well-grown pot-plants..have a much brighter, a much more artistic and finished appearance, than plants of the same kinds equally well grown in the open ground. **1914** W. F. ROWLES *Garden under Glass* xxii. 221 The loam..will be more suitable for the growth of the majority of pot plants. **1966** ROCHFORD & GORER *Rochford Bk. Flowering Pot Plants* i. 11 Flowering pot plants are usually regarded as expendable.

2. = POT-TREE 2.

1858 SIMMONDS *Dict. Trade, Pot-plant,* a name for the *Lecythis ollaria.* **1866** in *Treas. Bot.*

‖**pot-pourri** (popuri, pɒtˈpʊəri). Also 7 pot porride. [F. *pot pourri*, in same senses, lit. 'rotten pot', f. *pot* POT *sb.*[1] + *pourri*, pa. pple. of *pourrir*:—L. *putrēre* to be rotten; translating Sp. OLLA PODRIDA.]

†**1.** A dish of different kinds of meat stewed together; a stew, hotch-potch. *Obs.*

1611 COTGR., *Pot pourri*, a pot porride; a Spanish dish of many seuerall meates boyled, or stued together. **1725** BRADLEY *Fam. Dict., Pot-pourri,* a Culinary Term, signifying an Hotch-Potch.

2. a. A mixture of dried petals of different flowers mixed with spices, kept in a jar for its perfume. Also *fig.*

1749 LADY LUXBOROUGH *Let. to Shenstone* 28 Nov., It..might be called a *pot-pourri*, which is a potful of all kinds of flowers which are severally perfumes, and commonly when mixt and rotten, smell very ill. **1855** S. WHITING *Heliondé* 71 A couch, which..was made of pot-pourri, or some mixture of dried flowers peculiar to the Sun. **1863** LYTTON *Caxtoniana* II. xxii. 94 A blue china jar, filled with *pot-pourri*. **1888** *Bow Bells Weekly* 29 June 408/2 Recipes for 'Pot-pourri'... Collect rose leaves and lavender as they bloom, and place them in a jar in layers, with common or bay-salt... Add to them powdered orris-root, cloves [etc.]. **1911** D. H. LAWRENCE *White Peacock* II. ix. 344 The squire's lady has written a book filling these meadows and the mill precincts with pot-pourri romance. **1930** W. S. MAUGHAM *Cakes & Ale* iv. 51 On little Chippendale tables stood large Oriental bowls filled with pot-pourri. **1960** R. HEMPHILL *Fragrance & Flavour* 79 If the pot-pourri becomes too dry add more salt, and if too moist add more orris root powder.

b. *transf.* A container designed to hold pot-pourri.

1770 J. WEDGWOOD *Let.* 20 Aug. (1965) 94 Or have an Auction..of Statues;..Lamps, Potpouri's [etc.]. **1960** R. G. HAGGAR *Conc. Encycl. Continental Pott. & Porc.* 381/1 Faience in the Swedish/Dutch style was made, that is useful pottery.., and ornamental pieces, (pot-pourris, tureens, etc.). **1971** L. A. BOGER *Dict. World Pott. & Porc.* 268 *Potpourri*... In ceramics; the name is given to a container designed with a delicate perforated cover used to hold a mixture of potpourri. **1975** *Times* 19 Dec. 16/5 Among Minton's copies of Sèvres porcelain, a pair of *bleu-de-roi* ground pot-pourris and covers made £1,375.

3. *fig.* **a.** *Mus.* A series of airs strung together into one piece; a medley. **b.** A literary medley, or collection of miscellaneous extracts. **c.** Any diverse collection or assortment (of people or things).

1855 *Illustr. London News* 29 Dec. 755/2 The overture to the pantomime consisted of a *pot-pourri* of those popular tunes which the professors of the street-organ have been insisting on during the past year. **1864** WEBSTER, *Pot-pourri*. .. (*c*) A piece of music made up of different airs strung together... (*d*) A literary production made up of parts brought together without order, or bond of connection. **1866** G. H. LEWES Let. 1 July in *Geo. Eliot Lett.* (1956) IV. 282 There drink the sparkling water and lounge in the sun listening to the tolerable band performing overtures..pot-pourris and waltzes. **1881** in Grove *Dict. Mus.* III. 22 *Pot-pourri*, a name first given by J. B. Cramer to a kind of drawing-room composition consisting of a string of well-known airs. **1894** G. B. SHAW in *Fortnightly Rev.* Feb. 256 My first Richard III..turned out to be a wild *pot-pourri* of all the historical plays. **1898** S. R. HOLE in *19th Cent.* Apr. 647 There is no time for further enjoyment of this sweet, spicy Pot-pourri; no space for further extracts from this clever and comprehensive book. **1921** H. CRANE *Let.* 25 Dec. (1965) 75 We have a houseful of indiscriminate relatives and it has been hard to collect myself for even this potpourri. **1946** *R.A.F. Jrnl.* May 151 We blue-printed it as a *pot-pourri* of comment and opinion on Service life and manners. **1971** *World Archaeol.* III. 193 All the work, except firing, takes place..amid the characteristic potpourri of tools, vessels, mats and clutter found in such household work areas. **1977** *Time* 28 Feb. 8/2 The election of December 1973 split the Folketing among a potpourri of ten parties. **1978** F. MACLEAN *Take Nine Spies* ii. 49 A *pot-pourri* from Franz Lehar's latest opera.

4. *attrib.* and *Comb.*, as *pot-pourri bowl, jar, vase.*

1889 *Daily Tel.* 8 Mar. 3/3 There are some,..to whom the 'Two Roses' come as fresh as a bright June morning,..but some there are who,..will find instead merely a 'pot-pourri' jar full of dried rose leaves. **1875** E. METEYARD *Wedgwood Handbk.* 407 Pot-Pourri Vases. Decorated vessels for containing rose leaves and other scents were formerly much used. **1900** MARY E. WILKINS *Parson Lord* (Tauchn.) 58 Love removed the lid from a potpourri-jar. **1903** *Blackw. Mag.* Oct. 451/1 The pot-pourri-scented drawing-room led into a conservatory. **1904** *Daily Chron.* 17 June 8/3 The soft, delicate perfume of some old china pot-pourri bowl. **1957** MANKOWITZ & HAGGAR *Encycl. Eng. Pott. & Porc.* 162/1 Less frequent are such pieces as..pot-pourri vases. **1974** SAVAGE & NEWMAN *Illustr. Dict. Ceramics* 230 *Pot-pourri vase*, a vase, sometimes richly mounted in gilt-bronze, which is characterized by pierced decoration on the shoulder or cover, or both.

potrack (pəʊˈtræk), *v. rare.* [Echoic.] *intr.* To cry as a guinea-fowl.

1883 J. C. HARRIS *Nights Uncle Remus* 153 The squawking and pot-racking went on at such a rate that the geese awoke. **1886** *Pop. Sci. Monthly* Mar. 640 The dusting of chickens, cackling of geese, and 'pot-racking' of Guinea-hens.

potrero (pəʊˈtrɛərəʊ). [Sp., f. POTRO.]

1. In the S.W. United States and South America, a paddock or pasture for horses or cattle.

1848 J. A. SUTTER *New Helvetia Diary* (MS.) 7 Mar., 6 Men have been sent from the Race, on acct. having no tools, employed them to get the small potrero repaired. **1886** T. S. VAN DYKE *Southern Calif.* viii. 106 When, in the heat of day, one comes to some little *potrero* where pine-clad hills inclose a soft green meadow, [etc.]. **1892** *Dialect Notes* I. 193 *Potréro*, a pasture, generally for colts and young horses. Also a piece of land easily fenced in, situated in the bend of a stream or in a valley with a narrow pass for entrance. **1923** C. F. SAUNDERS *Southern Sierras Calif.* iii. 105 Ahead in the sun lay the Devil's *Potrero*—a verdant, wild-flowery bowl rimmed around with mountains. **1931** *Times Lit. Suppl.* 19 Mar. 214/2 He was found to be capable of milking exceptionally large numbers of untamed cows, which were driven straight from a 'potrero' into a 'corral'. **1933** A. F. TSCHIFFELY *Tschiffely's Ride* (1934) 5 Large herds of cattle grazing in the 'potreros' (paddocks). **1950** H. BACKHOUSE *Among Gauchos* xiii. 117 It is customary to kill and skin the cattle in the *consumo potrero* or paddock reserved for cattle that are to be slaughtered. **1960** G. J. BUTLAND *Lat. Amer.* xx. 287 This is the Uruguayan pastoral region *par excellence*; a land of cattle and sheep estancias with paddocks or *potreros* fenced and managed to secure the best seasonal use of the grass.

2. In the S.W. United States, a narrow steep-sided plateau or mesa.

1872 J. G. BOURKE *Diary* (MS.) 3 Dec., Hills break away in potreros. **1880** A. F. BANDELIER *Southwestern Jrnls.* (1966) I. 135 There are three ruins—one, on the Potrero de las Vacas, about one day's journey northwest. **1890** —— in *Papers Archaeol. Inst. Amer.* IV. 158 These cliffs appear like pillars or gigantic posts; hence their Spanish name 'Potreros'. The one forming the southern wall of the Cuesta Colorada gorge is an extensive plateau called Potrero Chato. **1940** E. FERGUSSON *Our Southwest* xix. 354 A potrero is a narrow ridge between canyons, and a saddle is a sag between peaks. **1953** B. P. DUTTON *Hewett's Pajarito Plateau* (ed. 2) III. iii. 104 The long, narrow potrero bounding the canyon on the north is entirely cut out for a distance of nearly a mile, thus throwing into one squarish open park the width of two small canyons and the formerly intervening mesa. **1966** in A. F. Bandelier *Southwestern Jrnls.* Gloss. 397 *Potrero*, pastureland; in New Mexico, a tongue of high ground.

‖**po'trido.** *Obs. rare*$^{-1}$. app. a corruption of *podrida*: see OLLA PODRIDA.

1651 OGILBY *Æsop* vii. 20 Breaches are made in trembling Custard large, Here a Potrido the bold sisters shatter.

‖**'potro.** [Sp., a colt, foal.] A colt, a pony; *ellipt.* pony hide, as a material.

1879 BEERBOHM *Patagonia* iii. 38 His feet were encased in potro boots tied at the knees. **1902** H. H. PRICHARD *Thro' Heart of Patagonia* xxi. 291 Boots of *potro* hide.

'pot roast. orig. *U.S.* [f. POT *sb.*[1] + ROAST *sb.*] A piece of beef or other meat cooked slowly in a closed container. Also *attrib.*

1881 F. E. OWENS *Cook Bk.* 59 Pot Roast of Beef. Get a solid piece from the round [etc.]. **1897** *Altrurian Cook Bk.* 38 (*heading*) Mutton Pot Roast. **1920** [see HAMBURGER 2]. **1929** E. WILSON *I thought of Daisy* iv. 232 The dinner was an admirable pot-roast, with onions, potatoes, and carrots. **1936** L. C. DOUGLAS *White Banners* iii. 59 'We've had breast of lamb three times in the past two weeks.'.. 'Sorry,' said Hannah. 'I'll have a pot roast to-morrow.' **1955** PRIESTLEY & HAWKES *Journey down Rainbow* 23 They are taking your order for Navy Bean soup and pot roast. **1964** *House & Garden* Nov. 100/3 Normandy pot roast chicken. *Ibid.* 100/4 French pot roast lamb. **1966** T. PYNCHON *Crying of Lot 49* iv. 82 Negroes carried gunboats of mashed potatoes, spinach, shrimp, zucchini, pot roast, to the long, glittering steam tables. **1973** G. SIMS *Hunters Point* vi. 49 Can you stay for lunch?.. Only a pot-roast but.. I make it fairly tasty. **1976** *National Observer* (U.S.) 6 Nov. 14/2 The scent of pot roast coming to a climax would drive me wild. *Ibid.*, Ma!.. I'm *starving* for a pot roast sandwich.

Hence **'pot-roast** *v. trans.*, to cook (meat) in this way; **'pot-roasted** *ppl. a.*; **'pot-roasting** *vbl. sb.*

1917 M. GREEN *Better Meals* ii. 15 *Pot roasting* is cooking in an iron kettle or earthen pot in a small amount of water, after meat has been quickly browned... Cook slowly until very tender, with or without vegetables. **1945** *ABC of Cookery* (Ministry of Food) ix. 35 Pot Roasting. This is cooking meat in a little fat in a saucepan with the lid on. **1951** N. M. GUNN *Well at World's End* xvi. 124 A solid round of cold pot-roasted venison. **1954** *Good Housek. Cookery Book* (rev. ed.) 134/2 Pot-roasted ham. *Ibid.* 553 You can boil, stew, braise, or pot-roast the meat or bird. *Ibid.*, Use the rack when pot-roasting or boiling. **1964** *House & Garden* Nov. 100/1 If he intended to pot roast, he left the lid empty. **1972** *Guardian* 9 Aug. 9/6 Pot roasting, as everyone knows, keeps juices in joints and splashes of fat off oven sides. **1979** *Country Life* 13 Sept. 806/4 Chicken pot-roasted in a case of sea salt.

†**potron** or **potrou.** *Obs. Cookery.* Also 5 poteron or -ou. [Origin and form uncertain.] A dish consisting of eggs cooked in salt.

(Cf. F. *potron-* or *patron-jaquet* in Littré; but no connexion of sense appears.)

c **1430** *Two Cookery-bks.* 53 (Harl. MS. 279), .xxviij. Potrous.—Take a schouyl of yron, & hete it brennyng hote; & þan.. fille it fulle of Salt; þan make a pitte in þe Salt..; & þan caste þin whyte & þe ȝolkys of Eyroun in-to þe hole of þe Salte, & lat seþe ouer þe fyre tyl it be half harde.. þan take a dressoure knyf, & put vnderneþe the Salt in þe panne, & hefe it vppe so fayre, þat þe cofyn with þe Eyroun breke noȝt; þan sette it on þe dyssche wyth þe Salt, & þan serue it forth. *c* **1450** *Ibid.* 93 (Harl. MS. 4016) Poterons. *c* **1440** *Douce MS.* 55 lf. 33 Potrons.

potrunk ('pəʊtrʌŋk). *Entom.* [f. L. *pō-* for POST- + TRUNK; cf. ALITRUNK.] (See quot.)

1826 KIRBY & SP. *Entomol.* III. xxxv. 532 If terms be thought necessary to designate the two intire segments into which the alitrunk is resolvable, the first may be the meditrunk (*meditruncus*), and the other the potrunk (*potruncus*).

potscar, -scarth, -shard, -share, obs. or dial. ff. POTSHERD.

pot(-)shaugh, pot(-)shaw, obs. ff. PADISHAH.

potsheen, var. POTEEN.

'pot-shell. *U.S. local.* = next.

1889 *Harper's Mag.* July 248 The pots are made of fire-clay.. mixed in varying proportions of raw and burned clay and pieces of the broken pots called 'pot shells', freed from glass and ground fine.

potsherd ('pɒt-ʃɜːd). *arch.* exc. in *Archaeol.* Forms: 4 pot-schoord (?), potszherd, 6 potsharde, -sherde, -shearde, (pottsheard), 6-8 potshard, -shard (also 9 *dial.*), (7 pottsherd), 7- potsherd; 6-7 (9 *dial.*) potshare. *β. north. dial.* 4 pot scarth, 9 potscar, -sker. [f. POT *sb.*[1] + SHERD, SHARD, OE. *sceard*, fragment, ON. *skarð*, Da. *skaar* (whence the northern *β*-forms).] A fragment of a broken earthenware pot; a broken piece of earthenware.

c **1325** *Gloss W. de Bibbesw.* in Wright *Voc.* 171 Va quere breses [*gloss* imbrers] en une teske [*gloss* a pot-schoord (*v.r.* szherd)]. *a* **1518** SKELTON *Magnyf.* 2124 A laudable Largesse, I tell you, for a lorde, To prate for the patchynge of a pot sharde! **1535** COVERDALE *Job* ii. 8 Iob.. scraped of the etter off his sores with a potsherde. **1596** SPENSER *F.Q.* VI. i. 37 They hew'd their helmes, and plates asunder brake, As they had potshares bene. **1611** BIBLE *Isa.* xlv. 9 Let the potsheard striue with the potsheards of the earth. **1639** G. DANIEL *Ecclus.* xxii. 20 He that would teach the foole, his labour's lost As he that glews a pottsherd, broke to dust. **1725** BRADLEY *Fam. Dict.* s.v. *Orange Tree*, Lay some Oister-Shells or Pot-shards at the Bottom of his Tubs, that the Water may the sooner drain away. **1857** BIRCH *Anc. Pottery* (1858) I. 64 Inscriptions were often written upon potsherds or trapezoidal fragments of vases.

β. *a* **1340** HAMPOLE *Psalter* xxi. 15 My vertu.. dried, that is, wex vile as a pot scarth, that men settis noght by. **1828** *Craven Gloss.* (ed. 2), *Pot-scar*, *Pot-shard*, a potsherd. **1868** ATKINSON *Cleveland Gloss.*, *Potsker*, a potsherd. **1869** *Lonsdale Gloss.*, *Potscar*, *Pot-share*, a potsherd.

b. *attrib.* (in quot., in allusion to Isa. xlv. 9).

a **1680** CHARNOCK *Attrib. God* (1834) II. 124 His almightiness is above.. our potsherd strength, as his infiniteness is above.. our purblind understandings.

'pot-shoot, *v. U.S.* [On analogy with POT-SHOT *sb.*[1]] *trans.* and *intr.* To take a pot-shot at (someone); to take pot-shots. Also *fig.* So **pot-shooter; pot-shooting** *vbl. sb.*

1907 C. E. MULFORD *Bar-20* xxi. 209 One hundred paces makes fine pot-shooting. **1913** —— *Coming of Cassidy* ii. 31 He.. resolved that he wouldn't take chances with a man who would pot-shoot. **1921** —— *Bar-20 Three* xiv. 166 I'm leavin' town. I ain't got a chance among buildin's again' pot-shooters. **1934** *Sun* (Baltimore) 16 Jan. 20/1 A Blue Eagle which drew the fire.. of two hunters.. brought the pot-shooters momentarily into the toils of the law. **1945** *Ibid.* 28 Nov. 1/5 What opposition has been sounded against the Socialists' proposals and the Socialists' shortcomings has been a matter of pot-shooting instead of an organized campaign. **1969** *English Jrnl.* Dec. 1309 The young men who have enjoyed pot-shooting policemen for the past few summers.

'pot-shop. [POT *sb.*[1]] **a.** A small publichouse. **b.** *local.* A crockery shop.

1837 DICKENS *Pickw.* lii, Mr. Ben Allen and Mr. Bob Sawyer betaking themselves to a sequestered pot-shop on the remotest confines of the Borough. **1889** E. PEACOCK *N.W. Linc. Gloss.* (ed. 2), *Potshop*, a shop where earthen-ware and glass are sold. *Mod.* (*Linc. dial.*), You'll get it at the pot-shop a few doors off.

'pot-,shot, *sb.*[1] [POT *sb.*[1]] **1.** A shot taken at game merely for the purpose of filling the pot for a meal, without regard to skill or the rules of sport (cf. POT-HUNTER 2), and so from any position or point of advantage. Hence *transf.* A shot aimed at a person or animal that happens to be within easy reach, without giving any chance of self-defence; e.g. at an enemy from ambush. Also, a random blow or punch.

1858 GEN. P. THOMPSON *Audi Alt.* I. xxxiii. 128 The volunteer corps began 'to take pot shots at them at nine or ten yards'. *Ibid.*, 'Pot shots'.. when a man.. shoots at partridges in a crowd upon the ground, in a way which shows a simple desire to kill for the pot. **1860** RUSSELL *Diary India* I. xvii. 265 Some dozens of the enemy.. sneak along the road.. in order to get a pot-shot at him. **1877** M. PRIOR in *Daily News* 1 Oct. 6/3 While.. looking through my telescope, a Russian sentry took a steady pot shot at us, and I had the unpleasant satisfaction of hearing the bullet flatten itself against a stone not far ahead. **1896** *Tablet* 22 Feb. 290, I was lying by my horse, taking pot-shots when I could get the chance. **1907** C. E. MULFORD *Bar-20* iii. 31 A pot shot at Hopalong sent that gentleman's rifle hurtling to the ground. **1938** *Sun* (Baltimore) 28 Jan. 1/5 He pleaded guilty to firing two 'pot' shots into the back of a loaded school bus. **1950** J. DEMPSEY *Championship Fighting* x. 49 A pot-shot with your right. **1965** C. D. EBY *Siege of Alcázar* (1966) iii. 70 A drunken *miliciano*.. took a pot shot at him. **1979** 'A. BLAISDELL' *No Villain need Be* iii. 50 Some nut.. taking potshots at couples in cars.

2. *fig.* **a.** *U.S.* A piece of criticism or verbal attack, freq. one which is random or opportunistic. **b.** A random attempt.

1926 *Forum* (N.Y.) Nov. 757 But I don't think much of the pot-shot method of refutation. **1927** *Christian Century* 7 July 828 Let him take lusty potshots, though, at some poor, prostrate ghost of bygone years, and he is hailed as brilliant, erudite, and—curiously—daring! **1942** BERREY & VAN DEN BARK *Amer. Thes. Slang* §179/2 Potshot, shot in the dark, *a wild guess.* **1943** *Commonweal* 30 Apr. 46 It is not just that Mr. Willkie is taking pot-shots at the British Empire—and please let's not swell up with anti-British self-righteousness. **1949** *Kenyon Rev.* XI. 582 It was a time when 'the intellect was at the tips of the senses' and so on. Admittedly these are literary phrases, therefore a kind of pot shot at the real point, but they seem to me good ones. **1955** *Newsweek* 7 Mar. 71 The tobacco industry is leaving no radioisotope unturned to counter medical potshots at its product and to bolster sales. **1955** *Times* 20 June 3/4 Thus certain canvases are both pot-shots at the subject and pot-shots at pictures. **1971** A. & A. SILVERMAN *Case against having Children* vi. 189 All we have done here is to take potshots at the Myth of the Working Mother.

Hence **'pot-shot** *v. trans.* and *intr.*, to take a pot-shot at (a target), to take pot-shots; **'pot-shotter; 'pot-shotting** *ppl. a.* and *vbl. sb.*

1904 P. FOUNTAIN *Gt. North-West* iv. 27 The breech-loader is the weapon of the dandy pot-shotter. **1918** E. POUND *Let.* 16 Dec. (1971) 143 And what the deuce of your punctuation?.. How much deliberate, and therefore to be taken (by me) with studious meticulousness?? How much the fine careless rapture and therefore to be pot-shotted at until it assumes an wholly demonstrable or more obvious rightness???? **1923** KIPLING *Irish Guards in Gt. War* II. 60 Snipers were forbidden to pot-shot until they could see a man's head. **1927** *Amer. Speech* III. 29 Right hand pot-shotters. **1942** BERREY & VAN DEN BARK *Amer. Thes. Slang* §394/3 *Careless person*,.. potshotter. *Ibid.* 435/7 *Potshotter*, one who shoots without taking aim. **1943** I. WOLFERT *Battle for Solomons* v. 63 However, it is likely that the battle which started as an old-fashioned 'better 'ole' kind of war has now got even more old-fashioned and become a ruthless, tracking, potshotting, Indian kind of war. **1947** HARLOW & BLACK *Pract. Public Relations* 179 Competing companies will make it their business to 'pot-shot' both purchasing and supplying organizations. **1950** *Atlantic Monthly* Apr. 21 What is really disturbing is the constant potshotting of the administrative departments from Capitol Hill. **1954** M. COWLEY *Lit. Situation* x. 178 At last he is likely to decide that the expenses are beyond his powers of computation; he will simply pot-shot at them, hoping that his guess won't be implausible. **1954** *Time* 28 June 36/3 After six years of marriage and nearly five of potshotting between their armed camps, they braced for the showdown. **1966** H. WAUGH *Pure Poison* vi. 41 She goes for the lunatic theory—like a sniper just potshotting anyone. **1970** *National Rev.* (U.S.) 30 June 685/2 Like Tocqueville, Tyrmand potshots, hit and miss, the trivial and mundane, filling space between profound insights.

†**'pot-shot, -,shotten,** *a.* (*sb.*[2]) *Obs.* [f. POT *sb.*[1] + SHOT *ppl. a.* (and *sb.*)] 'Shot' or overpowered by drink; intoxicated.

1629 WADSWORTH *Pilgr.* vi. 59 Edmunds.. being pot-shotten and perceiuing the Moone to shine bright through the windowes, said with a loud voyce, that the holy Ghost was descended. **1630** J. TAYLOR (Water P.) *Navy Land Ships* Wks. I. 83/1 When any of them are wounded, Pot-shot, Jug-bitten, or Cup-shaken. *a* **1632** T. TAYLOR *God's Judgem.* II. vii. (1642) 108 A.. Drunkard being Pot-shot and in his Cups.

B. as *sb.* **a.** A drunken person, a drunkard. **b.** Drunkenness.

1617 BRATHWAIT (*title*) A Solemne Ioviall Disputation.. Which.. Bacchus.. hath publikely expounded to his most approved and improved Fellow Pot-shots. **1630** J. TAYLOR (Water P.) *Taylors Trav.* Wks. III. 78/1 In which kind of potshot our English are growne such stout Proficients, that some of them dares bandy and contend with the Dutch.

potstick ('pɒtstɪk). Now only *dial.* Forms: see POT *sb.*[1] and STICK *sb.*; also 5 pos(s)tyke, postyk(ke. [f. POT *sb.*[1] + STICK *sb.*] A stick for stirring porridge or anything cooked in a pot. Also, a stick used for moving washing about in a pot.

c **1410** *Master of Game* (MS. Digby 182) xii, Stere it alle togyders agayne þe bothome of þe dysshe with a potstyke [*v.r.* posstyke]. *Ibid.*, Stere it wele aboute vpon þe fyre with a potstyke [*v.rr.* postykke, pottstik]. *c* **1440** *Anc. Cookery* in *Househ. Ord.* (1790) 469 When hit is boyled put in a potstik and stere hit wel. **15..** *Jack Juggler* (Grosart) 36 By cokes precious potstike, I wyll not home this night. **1612** *Proc. Virginia* 44 in *Capt. Smith's Wks.* (Arb.) 123 The next [had] in her hand a sword; another, a club; another a pot-stick... The rest, every one with their severall devises. **1847** MRS. CARLYLE in *New Lett. & Mem.* (1903) I. 236 A pair of stockings.. which seemed to have been knitted for two pot-sticks rather than for well-shaped.. woman's legs. **1869** H. USSHER in *Eng. Mech.* 3 Dec. 271/3 It beats Sir Roger de Coverley 'to potsticks'. **1894** S. R. CROCKETT *Lilac Sunbonnet* xxvii. 225 She turns roon' wi' the pat-stick i' her haund. **1903** SOMERVILLE & 'ROSS' *All on Irish Shore* 9 He.. had, in addition, boiled the meal for the hounds with a knowledge of proportion and an untiring devotion to the use of the pot-stick which produced 'stirabout' of a smoothness and excellence that Miss Barnet herself might have been proud of. **1922** JOYCE *Ulysses* 223 Maggy at the range rammed down a greyish mass beneath bubbling suds twice with her potstick and wiped her brow. **1961** F. G. CASSIDY *Jamaica Talk* v. 86 To stir cooking food one uses a *pot-stick.*

potstone ('pɒtstəʊn). [f. POT *sb.*[1] + STONE *sb.*; in sense 1, tr. L. *lapis ollāris.*]

1. A granular variety of STEATITE or SOAPSTONE.

1771 J. HILL *Fossils* 26 Potstone, Ollaris, Composed of broad, narrow, uneven flakes. **1804** R. JAMESON *Min.* I. 345 Pot Stone.. [is] soft, and sometimes very soft. **1882** GEIKIE *Text Bk. Geol.* II. II. 120 A finely felted aggregate of scales of talc, with chlorite and serpentine, is called Potstone.

2. Local name for large flints found in the chalk in Norfolk: = PARAMOUDRA.

1855 LYELL *Elem. Geol.* xvii. (ed. 5) 244 Huge flints, or potstones as they are called in Norfolk, occurring singly, or arranged in nearly continuous columns at right angles to the ordinary and horizontal layers of small flints... The pot-stones, many of them pear-shaped, were usually about three feet in height, and one foot in.. diameter.

potsy ('pɒtsɪ), *sb. Northeast U.S.* Also potsie. [Etym. obscure, but cf. POT *sb.*[1] 11.] **1. a.** The object thrown in the game of the same name. **b.** The name of a children's game similar to hopscotch.

1931 *Recreation* Mar. 672/2 *Potsy* is an adaptation of Hop Scotch, which now rivals its progenitor in popularity. The 'potsy' is a piece of tin, a rock or a puck. **1932** *Sun* (N.Y.) 26 Mar. 18/3 As any New Yorker will recognize, the potsy refers to the piece of tin can, doubled and redoubled and stamped flat with the heel, which is kicked from flagstone to flagstone of the sidewalk by the hopping, juvenile player of the game potsy. **1943** B. SMITH *Tree grows in Brooklyn* xiii. 100 Potsy was a game that the boys started and the girls finished. A couple of boys would put a tin can on the car track and sit along the curb and watch with a professional eye as the trolley wheels flattened the can... Numbered squares were marked off on the sidewalk and the game was turned over to the girls who hopped on one foot pushing the potsy from square to square. **1955** P. M. Evans *Hopscotch* 5 Then you feel around and pick up your potsie without opening your eyes. **1956** S. Bellow *Seize the Day* iii. 61, I sat down for a while in a playground..to watch the kids play potsy and skiprope. **1963** T. Pynchon *V.* v. 117 'What are you guys doing,' Profane said, 'playing potsy?'

2. The badge worn by a policeman or fireman.

1932 *Sun* (N.Y.) 26 Mar. 18/3, I recently bought a Sun which gave a vocabulary of firemen's slang, in which 'potsy' was the word for 'badge'. I have also found policemen and detectives who referred to their badges in this manner. **1936** *Baltimore News-Post* 18 Apr. 18/2 Most detectives in town never polish their gold badges (yellow potsys). **1948** Mencken *Amer. Lang.* Suppl. II. 750 *Potsy*, a fireman's badge. **1952** *N.Y. Herald Tribune* 24 Jan. 27/1 This boniface has been wearing his potsy as house dick for only a brief time. **1970** L. Sanders *Anderson Tapes* xiii. 39 Ernie goes in the lobby and flashes his potsy.

Pott (pɒt). *Med.* The name of Sir Percivall *Pott* (1713–88), English physician, used in the possessive to designate phenomena described by him, as **Pott's disease**, a form of paraplegia caused by tuberculous disease of the spine (described in *Med. & Philos. Commentaries* (1779) VI. 318–24); **Pott's fracture**, a fracture of the fibula close to the ankle, of a type described by Pott (in *Remarks on Fractures & Dislocations* (1769) 57–64) and due to eversion of the foot; *loosely*, any fracture of the lower fibula.

1835 *Lancet* 12 Sept. 775/1 Patients attacked by Pott's disease frequently die of other affections before the former has made much progress. **1897** T. L. Stedman *20th Cent. Pract.* XI. 600 The symptoms of Pott's disease may be divided into those referable to the diseased vertebræ, to the affected nerve roots of the spinal cord, and to the spinal cord itself. **1974** C. B. T. Adams in R. M. Kirk et al. *Surgery* xiv. 286 Tuberculosis (Pott's disease..of the spine) or a pyogenic extrathecal abscess may also cause cord compression. **1849** *Proc. Path. Soc. Dublin* II. 13 Mr. Robert W. Smith exhibited a remarkable specimen of Pott's fracture, taken from the body of a man, aet. 70, who had lately died in the hospital of the South Union Poor House. **1884** W. Pye *Surg. Handicraft* xiv. 209 It may be doubted whether a true Pott's fracture is ever so perfectly recovered from, that the movements of the ankle are quite free, and no deformity is noticeable. **1922** *Arch. Surg.* IV. 56 Pott's fracture, as described and pictured by himself, is a primary, nearly transverse, fracture of the fibula, attended by a subsequently produced 'partial dislocation' of the ankle joint internally. **1950** J. G. Bonnin *Injuries to Ankle* viii. 174 It has been denied by Ashurst (1922) and others that Pott's fracture, as Pott described it, ever existed... Pott's name is used more generally now to cover all fractures of the ankle by indirect violence. **1962** *Surgery* LI. 284/2, I believe that term to any and all fractures of the ankle due to external the term 'Pott's fracture' should be applied as a generic rotation violence.

pott, obs. or var. f. POT *sb.*^{1} esp. in sense 10.

pottage (ˈpɒtɪdʒ). Forms: 3–7 potage, 6– pottage, (6 -adge). [ME. *potage*, a. F. *potage*, lit. that which is put in a pot: see POT *sb.*^{1} and -AGE. Orig. stressed *poˈtage*, which was admitted in verse down to Chaucer and Lydgate, but *ˈpotage* is found in alliterative poems (and prose) in 14th c., and led to the later spelling. See also PODDISH, PORRIDGE, altered forms of this word.]

1. A dish composed of vegetables alone, or along with meat, boiled to softness in water, and appropriately seasoned; soup, *esp.* a thick soup. In ancient cookery, often a highly composite dish.

Now chiefly a literary word, historical, archaic, scriptural, or used of the soups of primitive peoples: no longer a term of English cookery. But the French form is in use in names of dishes really French or supposed to be: see POTAGE.

α. *a* **1225** *Ancr. R.* 412 Hwoso is euer feble eteð potage bliðeliche. **1297** R. Glouc. (Rolls) 8339 Wo þat misȝte weodes abbe & þe roten gnawe Oþer seþe & make potage was þer of wel vawe. *a* **1300** *Cursor M.* 3549 Esau..for his fill o þat potage, Als a wreche, has sald his heritage. **13..** *E.E. Allit. P.* B. 638 Syþen potage & polment in plater honest. **1377** Langl. *P. Pl.* B. xv. 310 Had ȝe potage and payn ynough and peny-ale to drynke..ȝe had riȝt ynough. *c* **1386** Chaucer *Monk's T.* 443 Whanne wol the Gayler bryngen oure potage? *c* **1400** Maundev. (Roxb.) xxvi. 123 Þai hafe nowþer þeise ne wortes, ne oþer maner of potagez; bot in for þaire potage þai vse broth and sothen flesch. *c* **1430** *Two Cookery-bks.* 15 A potage on fysshday.—Take an Make a styf Poshote of Milke an Ale; þan take..whyte Swete Wyne..& put Sugre..þer-to, or hony;..kepe it a[s] whyte as yt may be, & þan serue f[orth]. *Ibid.* 29 A potage on a Fysdaye.—Take an sethe an .ij. or .iij. Applys..& Flowre of Rys..whyte Wyne..Saunderys & Safroun..Roysonys of corauns..& Almaundys..; and mynce Datys Smale.., and a lytil Hony to make it dowcet, or ellys Sugre. **1531** Elyot *Gov.* I. xiii, A gentil man, er he take a cooke..wyll..examine hym, howe many sortes of meates, potages, and sauces, he can perfectly make. **1542** Boorde *Dyetary* xii. (1870) 262 Potage is not so moche vsed in al Crystendom as it is vsed in Englande. Potage is made of the lyquor in the which flesshe is soden in, with puttyng-to chopped herbes, and otemel and salt. **1604** E. G[rimstone] *D'Acosta's Hist. Indies* IV. xxi. 270 They..roast it, and make many sorts of potages. **1682** [see PLUM-POTTAGE].

β. **1530** Palsgr. 257/1 Pottage, *potage, souppe*. *Ibid.*, Pottage without herbes, *potage*. **1539** *Test. Ebor.* (Surtees) VI. 92 A whit sylver goblet that I use to ett pottadge. **1573** Tusser *Husb.* (1878) 101 Now leekes are in season, for pottage full good. **1600** J. Pory tr. *Leo's Africa* III. 142 The meat and pottage is put al in one dish; out of which euery one taketh with his greasie fists what he thinkes good. *a* **1658** Cleveland *Rel. Quaker* 24 Hadst thou sweetned thy Gumbs With Pottage of Plumbs. **1712** E. Cooke *Voy. S. Sea* 203 The Papas are either boil'd, roasted, or made into Pottage. **1747** Wesley *Prim. Physic* (1762) 85 Drink largely of Pottage made with Lentils. **1840** Barham *Ingol. Leg.* Ser. I. *Bagman's Dog*, Now just such a mess of delicious hot pottage Was smoking away when they enter'd the cottage. **1874** *Oxford Bible-Helps* 117 The red lentil is most esteemed, and is made into pottage. **1904** *Daily News* 18 Apr. 4/2 He has acquired..of the native [Kaffir] a knowledge intimate and strange, such as one can only gather by the fireside, over the pottage.

b. *fig.*: often with reference to Esau's 'mess of pottage' (MESS *sb.* 2).

1387–8 T. Usk *Test. Love* I. iv. (Skeat) l. 26 Thou..haste so mikel eaten of the potages of foryetfulnesse. *a* **1845** Mrs. Bray *Warleigh* xxi, Captain Butler..came up to the elbow of the temperate divine, and bidding him, very unceremoniously, 'leave off his pottage', shoved him aside, and stepped into his place. **1868** H. Law *Beacons of Bible* 228 You are self-slain when you prefer the pottage to Christ.

†**2.** Oatmeal porridge. *Obs.*

1683 Tryon *Way to Health* 30 Gruels and Pottage made of Oatmeal, being made thin, and quick boyled, are of an excellent Nature. **1724** in *Ramsay's Tea-t. Misc.* (1733) I. 89 There will be lang-kail and pottage And bannocks of barley-meal. **1794** Donaldson *Agric. Perth* 24 The food of the reapers..for supper, pottage of oat-meal, salt and water, with the allowance of milk made to the ploughman. **1797** *Monthly Mag.* III. 203 Oatmeal is..not unfrequently used in making pottage, among the lower classes [in the West Riding].

†**3.** A poultice. *Obs. rare*$^{-1}$.

c **1400** *Lanfranc's Cirurg.* 42 Leie þerto a potage..maad of eerbis & swynes greece & water & wheete flour.

†**4.** In proverbial phrases: ***a mess of pottage***: see MESS *sb.* 2; ***to keep one's breath to cool one's pottage***: see PORRIDGE *sb.* 4; ***to make pottage of a flint***, to be economical or parsimonious. *Obs.*

1650 H. More *Observ.* in *Enthus. Tri.*, etc. (1656) 78 Keep your breath to your self to cool your pottage. **1655** Fuller *Ch. Hist.* III. vi. §37. 85 For their fare, it was course in the quality, and yet slender in the quantity thereof. Insomuch, that they would, in a manner, make pottage of a flint.

5. *attrib.* and *Comb.*, as ***pottage dish***, ***plate***, ***pot***; ***pottage-eating*** adj.; †**pottage-ware**, materials for pottage, pot-herbs.

c **1420** *Pallad. on Husb.* VII. 57 Nowe potage ware in askes mynge, and kepe In oil barelles or salt tubbis done. **1519** *Exp. Dinners* (Misc. Philobiblon Soc. (1867–8) XIII.) 40 Pottage flesche viijd. **1526** *Pilgr. Perf.* (W. de W. 1531) 17 Remembrynge..the potage potte with flesshe, the onyons and garlyke that they were wont to eate in Egypte. **1608** Armin *Nest Ninn.* D ij, If ye meete him in your pottage-dish, yet know him. **1649** G. Daniel *Trinarch.* To Rdr. 115 You may guess Such Pottage-Eating stomackes.

Hence †ˈ**pottagy** *a.*, of the nature of pottage.

1565 J. Halle *Hist. Expost.* Table 76 Substances like a whyte potagie confection (called *Puls*).

pottager, -anger, -eger, -encher, -enger, obs. forms of POTTINGER.

†**pottagur**, obs. form of PODAGRE *a.*, gouty.

a **1450** Myrc *Festial* 271 He was pottagur; and wyth þat yse þay refreschet þe gret hete of his fete, as oft as hit was layde to.

‖**pottah** (ˈpaʊtə). *East Indies.* [ad. Hindī *paṭṭā* title-deed.] A lease, a deed certifying tenure.

1776 *Trial of Nundocomar* 101/1 My house is in Calcutta, in Huzreymull's garden... Have you got the potta? **1817** Jas. Mill *Brit. India* II. v. iii. 388 Prescribed forms of leases, in India known by the name of pottahs. **1871** Markby *Elem. Law* §357 The ryots in India appear to have frequently taken pottahs from the zemindars.

pottain, obs. form of POTIN^1.

pottance, variant of POTENCE^2 (in a watch).

potted (ˈpɒtɪd), *ppl. a.* [f. POT *v.*^{1} + -ED^1.]

1. Of meat, fish, etc.: Preserved in a closed pot or other vessel.

1646 Evelyn *Diary* 22 Mar., I was invited to excellent English potted venison. **1742** Fielding *Jos. Andrews* IV. x, The potted Partridge is potted Woodcock, if you desire to have it so. **1806** A. Hunter *Culina* (ed. 3) 106 This kind of potted meat may be recommended. **1876** Ruskin *Fors Clav.* VI. 207 Plenty of salted pork,..potted shrimps. **1922** Joyce *Ulysses* 368 Potted herrings gone stale. **1922** J. Buchan *Huntingtower* iv. 69 There was new milk..and most of the dainties which had appeared at tea, supplemented by a noble dish of shimmering 'potted-head'. **1953** *Special Sci. Rep.: Fisheries* (U.S. Dept. Interior: Fish & Wildlife Service) No. 104. 31 'Potted tuna' consisted of chunks of tuna mixed with potatoes and carrots. **1960** E. David *French Provincial Cooking* 221 As an alternative to a home-made pâté, *rillettes*, which might be described as a kind of potted pork, are quite easy to make at home. **1977** *Observer* 12 June 19/4 'I'm so excited,' she said, her expression as glazed as potted shrimp.

2. Of a plant: Planted or grown in a pot.

1849 Alb. Smith *Pottleton Leg.* xx. 176 The potted yew trees in the passage. **1883** *Harper's Mag.* Sept. 502/2 Every window was full of potted plants. **1939** A. H. Wood *Grow them Indoors* p. xi, In Carpaccio's..painting of St. Ursula's vision, two potted plants appear in the window of her room. **1976** *Times* 1 Apr. 11/4 The gorgeous store..collapsed amid a welter of potted palms and recriminatory statements.

fig. **1866** Lowell *Biglow P.* Introd., Poems 1890 II. 159 Where language is too strictly limited by convention..we get a potted literature, Chinese dwarfs instead of healthy trees.

3. *fig.* **a.** Of a piece of information, work of literature, or historical or descriptive account: put into a short and easily assimilable form; condensed, summarized, abridged. Also *transf.*

1883 *Edin. Rev.* Oct. 297 What we may call *potted* learning in the form of popular abridgments. **1901** C. H. Welch in *Westm. Gaz.* 20 May 10/1 Fed and fattened as it flows With verses scanned and potted prose. **1909** F. Gardner *Pure Folly* i. 4 Pélissier..in April, 1907..produced his first 'potted play', which he described as 'Baffles: a Peter-Pan-tomime.' Needless to say, the skit was a blend of the two plays 'Raffles' and 'Peter Pan'. **1921** —— *Days & Ways* xi. 193 *The Whip*, *Faust* and *The Chocolate Soldier* were the most popular..'potted plays'. **1929** *Morning Post* 2 Oct. 11/7 Previously such questions had merely served as an excuse for potted lectures on the iniquity of the British position. **1937** 'A. Bridge' *Enchanter's Nightshade* 32 Those little potted abstracts for the general reader. **1946** *R.A.F. Jrnl.* May 146 A potted history of the *Journal* from its infancy up to this final issue. **1957** *Listener* 24 Oct. 642/1 Even potted biographies are now usually written by experts. **1966** *Ibid.* 23 June 921/3 Photographs of all the county teams, a list of records, potted careers of most of the current players, [etc.]. **1975** *Physics Bull.* May 225/1 The first chapter..attempts to provide a very potted treatment of transport theory.

b. = CANNED *ppl. a.* b.

1928 *Melody Maker* Feb. 133/2 The delightful art of piano-playing..is in immediate danger of being usurped by the 'potted' music of wireless and gramophone. **1928** T. E. Lawrence *Let.* 23 Apr. (1938) 595 Only gramophone music, but the potted stuff is very well, for people away abroad. **1949** F. Maclean *Eastern Approaches* I. ii. 29 It was then that I grasped that the cheering was potted, synthetic cheering, issuing from loudspeakers..and conveniently obviating the need for unhygienic, insecure spectators.

4. Of pottery or porcelain, with defining adv.: (well, beautifully, etc.) fashioned or manufactured.

1902 *Encycl. Brit.* XXXI. 874/2 The ware is thin, light, beautifully potted, and of the utmost durability. **1969** *Canad. Antiques Collector* Mar. 22/2 The earlier ware of the Koryo period are thinly potted and covered with the well known celadon glaze. **1972** *Country Life* 3 Feb. 273/3 A pair of K'ang Hsi parrots..on the whole more agreeable (no pink) and I thought better potted.

5. a. *N. Amer. slang.* Drunk, intoxicated.

1924 P. Marks *Plastic Age* xiv. 149 I'd 'a' been potted about half the time. *Ibid.* xviii. 202, I don't get potted regularly. **1925** *College Humor* Aug. 125/2 Did I *ever* tell you to go getting potted like you were last night? **1943** *Sun* (Baltimore) 14 Aug. 6/4 Awful calamity at the Park bird bath..when somebody discovered the birds were potted due to some members of the Mint Julep Association having emptied their julep glasses in the fountain. **1959** *Amer. Speech* XXXIV. 156 Gators never merely drink; instead, they *sop*... They may later be..*potted*. **1974** J. Dowell *Look-off Bear* 90 He was potted, plastered, stinko.

b. *U.S. slang.* Under the influence of marijuana (cf. POT *sb.*^{5}).

1960 Wentworth & Flexner *Dict. Amer. Slang* 404/2 *Potted adj.*,.. 2 Under the influence of narcotics, esp. marijuana. **1968** Busby & Holtham *Main Line Kill* v. 48 The Jamaicans..didn't appear to be potted. **1968–70** *Current Slang* (Univ. S. Dakota) III–IV. 95 *Potted*, *v.* High on marijuana... I was *potted* out of my mind yesterday. **1972** *Dict. Contemp. & Colloq. Usage* 22/3 *Potted*..under the influence of marijuana.

6. Of an electrical component or circuit: encapsulated in an insulating material (cf. POT *v.*^{1} 2 c).

1947 *Plastics* July 71/2 Several practical applications of resin-potted circuits at the Bureau have given operation comparable to that of conventionally constructed devices. **1950** W. W. Stifler *High-Speed Computing Devices* xvi. 427 Mass production of potted plug-in units depends upon the development of complex process controls. **1955** *Brit. Plastics* XXVIII. 481/1 Extreme care must be exercised in..the removal of even traces of atmospheric moisture from the surface of the potted components. **1967** *Electronics* 6 Mar. 193/4 (Advt.), Special Assemblies. Rectifier stacks, potted bridges, [etc.].

potteen, potteler, var. POTEEN, POTELLER.

potter (ˈpɒtə(r)), *sb.*^{1} [Late OE. *pottere*, f. POT *sb.*^{1} + -ER^1.]

1. a. A maker of pots, or of earthenware vessels.

a **1100** in Birch *Cart. Sax.* III. 49 Of stenges heale on potteres leʒe. **1284** *Calr. Inq. P.M.* (1906) II. 322 [The manor..including 36*s.* 8*d.* rent of assize of the burgesses of Midhurst called] potteresgavel. *a* **1300** *Cursor M.* 22937 (Cott.) Als pottere wit pottes dos Quen he his neu wessel fordos. *a* **1340** Hampole *Psalter* ii. 9 As vessel of þe pottere þou sall paim breke. **1413** *Pilgr. Sowle* (Caxton 1483) IV. xxxvii. 84 More helply is a Carpenter or a potter than an Organer, a peynter or an ymager. *c* **1440** *Promp. Parv.* 411/1 Pottare, *ollarius, figulus*. **1597** Middleton *Wisdom Solomon* xv. 7 Thou a potter art, Tempering soft earth, making the clay to bow. **1686** Horneck *Crucif. Jesus* xxv. 838 A potter, by the motion of his wheel, and the activity of his hand, gives the clay what form and shape he pleases. *a* **1720** Sewel *Hist. Quakers* (1795) I. IV. 343 Thou and all mankind are as clay in the hand of the potter. **1867** Smiles *Huguenots Eng.* ii. (1880) 22 This wandering workman was no other than Bernard Palissy..more generally known as the great Potter.

†**b.** Applied to a maker of metal pots or vessels. *Obs. rare.*

1443 *Durham Acc. Rolls* (Surtees) 82 Willelmo Browne potter pro factura ij patenarum, j brasyn morter, ij parvarum ollarum, cum xvij libr. eris, xij s. vj d. **1549** *Compl. Scot.* i. 19 Ane pottar vil mak of ane masse of mettal diuerse pottis of defferent fassons.

2. A vendor or hawker of earthenware. *north. dial.* (Cf. south Sc. *mugger.*) Also, in northern England, a vagrant, a kind of tramp or gypsy.

c **1500** *Robin Hood & Potter* xxxiv. in Child *Ballads* (1888) III. 111 'Pottys, gret chepe!' creyed Robyn,..all that saw hem sell, Seyde he had be no potter long. **1795** Wordsw. *Guilt & Sorrow* xlvi, Rough potters seemed they, trading soberly With panniered asses driven from door to door. **1798** —— *Peter Bell* I. iii, A Potter, Sir, he was by trade. **1867** *Q. Rev.* CXXII. 378 The 'potters', a kind of indigenous gipsies, often curiously bearing the names of the great Northern families. **1881** Dixon *Craven Dales* vi. 71 [He] used to boast that 'he could.. wallop a potter, or preach a sermon with any man in the country!' **1885** *Specimens Westmoreland Dial.* 38 A com at a potter tent int' green lonnin. **1899** *West Cumberland Times* 28 Jan. 3/2 He had known the piece of waste... He had seen potters camping on it... You mean tramps or gipsies?—Yes, something of that kind. **1972** *Times Lit. Suppl.* 3 Mar. 245/3 The travellers and vagrants—gypsies, 'potters', pedlars, beggars, Irish labourers looking for work—who haunted.. the roads of Lakeland.

3. *attrib.* and *Comb.* (also with *potter's*), as ***potter craft***; **potter's asthma**, a form of fibroid phthisis to which persons exposed to the dust of the pottery industry are subject; also called **potter's bronchitis, consumption, disease, phthisis** (*Syd. Soc. Lex.* 1895); **potter's clay, potter's earth**, any plastic clay free from iron, and thus suitable for the making of earthenware, stoneware, or porcelain; **potter's field**, a name given (after Matt. xxvii. 7) to a piece of ground used as a burial place for the poor and for strangers; also *fig.*; **potter's lathe**, a frame with a horizontal disk revolvable at various speeds, on which the prepared clay is moulded into shape; **potter's lead, potter's ore**, lead ore used for glazing pottery, galena: cf. POTTERN; **potter's** (or **potters'**) **rot**, silicosis or other lung disease caused by the continued inhalation of dust in a pottery; **potter wasp**, a wasp which builds a cell or cells of clay in a cylindrical cavity, as the American species *Odynerus flavipes* and *Eumenes fraterna*; **potter's wheel**, the horizontal revolving disk of a *potter's lathe*.

1616 Surfl. & Markh. *Country Farme* 593 Sandie, stonie, grauelly, and flintie ground, as also such as consisteth of a *Potters clay in the bottome. **1796** Kirwan *Elem. Min.* (ed. 2) I. 180 *Potters Clay.* Colour, generally greyish white, and then called *pipe clay*. **1872** Ellacombe *Ch. Bells Devon* Pref. 4 Plaster of Paris casts, made from 'squeezes' taken.. with potter's clay. **1864** H. Bruce in *Daily Tel.* 15 June, The people being liable, amongst other diseases, to one peculiar to them, called '*potter's consumption'. *c* **1450** *Life St. Cuthbert* (Surtees) 444 For I can noȝt of *potter craft. *c* **1440** *Promp. Parv.* 411/1 *Pottarys erthe, *argilla*. **1670** Pettus *Fodinæ Reg.* 1 Where Clays are digged (as Fullers earth, Potters earth, etc.) we call them Pits. **1799** G. Smith *Laboratory* I. 195 Make any utensil of fine potters earth. [**1526** Tindale *Matt.* xxvii. 7 They toke counsell, and bought with them a potters felde to bury strangers in.] **1777** J. Adams in *Fam. Lett.* (1876) 259, I took a walk into the *Potter's Field, a burying ground between the new stone prison and the hospital. **1906** 'Mark Twain' in *Westm. Gaz.* 26 Nov. 4/2 When I wrote a letter.. you did not put it in the respectable part of the magazine, but interred it in that 'potter's field', the Editor's Drawer. **1727–41** Chambers *Cycl.* s.v. *Pottery*, The *potter's lathe is also a kind of wheel, but simpler and slighter. **1670** Pettus *Fodinæ Reg.* v. (1706) 21 From the Metals are produced Litharges,.. White-Lead, Read-Lead, *Potters-Lead and many other varieties. *Ibid.* vi. 25 Potters Lead is made by art from common Lead Oar. **1822** Cleaveland *Min.* (ed. 2) 634 Galena is sometimes.. called potters' Lead ore. *a* **1728** Woodward *Catal.* (1729) 213 *Potters-ore with a vein of white spar passing through the middle of it. **1908** T. Oliver *Dis. of Occupation* x. 307 As far back as the days of Ramazzini (1670), the lung troubles of the potters had been recognised and described. With the terms '*potters' rot' and 'potters' asthma' the public are quite familiar. **1966** Wright & Symmers *Systemic Path.* I. x. 405/1 Soon after calcined flint was introduced in the manufacture of porcelain, at about the middle of the 18th century, 'potter's rot' made its appearance among the workmen. **1972** G. Wigg *George Wigg* viii. 161 Silicosis, known in Stoke as 'potter's rot', was a scourge in Dudley. **1880** *New Virginians* I. 99 The little *potter-wasp makes a nest of clay, shaped like an ancient pot, which it fills with caterpillars. **1727–41** Chambers *Cycl.* s.v. *Pottery*, The *potter's wheel consists principally in its nut, which is a beam or axis, whose foot or pivot plays perpendicularly on a free-stone sole or bottom. **1832** G. R. Porter *Porcelain & Gl.* i. 5 The earliest authentic records allude to the potter's wheel as to an implement of then high antiquity.

'potter, *sb.*[2] [f. POT *v.*[1] (in various unconnected senses) + -ER[1].]

†**1.** One addicted to potting; a tippler.

1632, 1663 [see PIPER[2] 2].

2. One who pots or preserves meat, etc.

1857 J. Davy *Angler in Lake District* i. 10, I cannot do better than let you have the receipt of an experienced potter of charr.

3. One who pots at game (POT *v.*[1] 5); a pot-hunter.

1884 *Pall Mall Budget* 22 Aug. 27/2 Many a wealthy 'potter' who has.. blazed away.. at the deer.

4. Applied to some North American turtles: **a.** A fresh-water clemmyoid turtle, *Deirochelys serrata*; **b.** The red-bellied terrapin, *Pseudemys rugosa*.

1890 in *Cent. Dict.* **1890** in Webster.

potter, *sb.*[3] [f. POTTER *v.*] Trifling action or (in Scott) talk. Also, a gentle stroll or saunter. Also *fig.*

1818 Scott *Hrt. Midl.* xxxvii, That precision and easy brevity which is only acquired by habitually conversing in the higher ranks of society, and which is the diametrical opposite of that protracted style of disquisition 'Which squires call potter, and which men call prose'. **1897** *Chicago Advance* 10 June 769/1 These are little things any way, a mere potter about externals. **1901** 'L. Malet' *Hist. R. Calmady* III. v. 210 But Camp, who missing Richard, had followed his mistress out of the house for a leisurely morning potter, turned back sulkily. **1949** E. Bowen *Heat of Day* xiv. 248 A potter through the boundary woods. **1955** M. Allingham *Beckoning Lady* v. 84 The prospect of a glorious potter about was too much for Amanda. **1966** O. Norton *School of Liars* vi. 91 He'll have to go pretty steadily. No worries. No real work. A good potter for about a month. **1972** Q. Bell *Virginia Woolf* I. ii. 33 Leslie's favourite exercise was walking; he would sometimes go for what he called 'a potter', covering thirty miles or so.

potter ('pɒtə(r)), *v.* Also (6 **poder**), 9 *dial.* and *U.S.* PUTTER. [app. freq. (with shortened vowel) of POTE *v.* to thrust, push, poke.]

1. a. *intr.* To poke again and again; to make a succession of slight thrusts. Now only *dial.*

? **1530** Tindale *Expos. Matt. v.–vii.* v. 3. 16 b, Thou doest but with poderinge [*so ed. c* 1550; *Wks.* **1573** pottering] in the fyre, make the flame greater. **1646** *Topicks in Laws of Eng.* Ded., Hee will be brodding at, and pottering upon the ground, every way with his Rapier or Dagger. **1681** Cotton *Wond. Peak* (ed. 4) 64 Stooping, with our sticks t'essay, If pottering this and that way, we could find How deep it went. **1714** M. Fothergill in *Hearne's Collect.* (O.H.S.) IV. 303 Four small Coyns were.. casually found by a Shepherd, pottering upon the ground wth his Crooke. *a* **1825** Forby *Voc. E. Anglia, Potter*, to poke, pry, rummage. It seems.. to imply repetition or continuance of poking. **1865** Sleigh *Derbysh. Gloss.* (E.D.D.), Poking or pottering in the earth.

b. *trans.* To poke; to move or stir (anything) by thrusting. Now *dial.*

1747 Hooson *Miner's Dict.* Kiv b, With a Stick long enough, one might potter them down out of the Roof. **1828** *Craven Gloss.* (ed. 2), *Potter*, to poke, to push as with the end of a stick. **1877** *N.W. Linc. Gloss.* s.v., Noo then, Anne, potter that fire, or it'll be deäd oot in a minnit.

2. *trans.* To trouble, plague, perplex, worry, bother. *dial.* Cf. POTHER *v.* 1.

c **1746** J. Collier (Tim Bobbin) *View Lanc. Dial.* Wks. (1862) 40 Neaw wou'd naw sitch o Moonshine traunce Potter any body's Plucks? **1828** *Craven Gloss.* (ed. 2), *Potter*, to confuse. 'Don't potter me'. **1855** Mrs. Gaskell *North & S.* xix, By th' twenty-first, I reckon, he'll be pottered in his brains how to get them done in time. *Ibid.* xlv.

3. *intr.* To meddle, interfere, esp. where one has no business; to tamper (*with*). Now *dial.*

1655 Gurnall *Chr. in Arm.* verse 11. iii. (1669) 26/2 A Lock whose Wards have been troubled, which makes it harder to turn the Key, than if never potter'd with. **1866** Mrs. Gaskell *Wives & Dau.* I. 3 My lord's taking a fancy to go 'pottering'.. which meant that.. the earl asked his own questions of his own tenants, and used his own eyes and ears in the management of the smaller details of his property.

4. a. To occupy oneself in an ineffectual or trifling way; to work or act in a feeble or desultory manner; to trifle; to dabble (*in* something).

1740 [see POTTERING *ppl. a.* 2]. **1828** *Craven Gloss.* (ed. 2), *Potter*, to do things ineffectually. 'How thou potters'. **1832** Manning in Purcell *Life* I. 99, I suppose your husband is pottering on in his old way. **1861** Hughes *Tom Brown at Oxf.* xlvi, David pottered on at his bees and his flowers till old Simon returned. **1871** J. R. Green *Lett.* III. (1901) 294, I remember.. raving against the people who pottered over Roman roads. **1887** *Spectator* 16 Apr. 535/1 Any man.. who likes to 'potter' in zoology.

b. To talk in a trifling or desultory way.

1826 Scott *Jrnl.* 6 Sept., [They] pottered away about Persia and India, and I fell asleep.

c. *trans.* with advbs. To make *out* or work *out* by pottering; to trifle *away*, to spend, waste, or lose in or by pottering.

1853 E. FitzGerald *Lett.* (1889) I. 225, I have ordered Eastwick's Gulistan: for I believe I shall potter out so much Persian. **1883** A. Forbes in *Fortn. Rev.* 1 Nov. 664 He pottered away.. his opportunity to reach Verdun. **1893** W. A. Shee *My Contemp.* vii 188 Uncles and aunts.. were content to potter away their lives at Torquay.

5. *intr.* **a.** To move or go about poking or prying into things in an unsystematic way, or doing slight and desultory work.

1840 B. Hall *Patchwork* (1841) II. vii. 122, I pottered about in the environs of Naples. **1859** Jephson *Brittany* xiii. 220 He did not go pottering about, measuring cornices, and sticking a portico from the Parthenon here, and a pediment from somewhere else there. **1860** G. H. Lewes *Jrnl.* 26 Sept. in *Geo. Eliot Lett.* (1954) III. 349 To-day.. I wrote some letters and pottered. **1861** Hughes *Tom Brown at Oxf.* v, Pottering about in the Bodleian, and fancying I should like to be a great scholar. **1880** Miss Braddon *Just as I am* x, To potter about with your garden scissors and the watering can in the conservatories. **1922** Joyce *Ulysses* 737 He prefers pottering about the house. **1947** W. S. Maugham *Creatures of Circumstance* 94 Then he would turn his business over to his son and retire with his wife to a little house in the country where he could potter about till death claimed him at a ripe old age. **1977** *Times* 7 Dec. 12/3 Randall.. pottered about for 26 in $1\frac{3}{4}$ hours before giving a catch to gully.

b. To go about or walk slowly, idly, or aimlessly; to saunter, dawdle, loiter.

1829 Lady Granville *Lett.* 2 Apr., Balls every night. After that they all potter off to their *Campagnes*. **1835** Fonblanque *Eng. under 7 Administr.* (1837) III. 213 That lean, hobbling old fellow,.. pottering about in an incapacity for any thing but to fall to and enjoy other men's meat. **1857** T. Hughes *Tom Brown's School Days* I. ii. 32 Past the old church and down the footpath, pottered the old man and the child hand-in-hand. **1888** *Century Mag.* Dec. 219/2 The slowest of Sunday trains, pottering up to London. **1903** G. B. Shaw *Man & Superman* IV. 162 Mrs Whitefield, who has been pottering round the Granada shops, and has a net full of little parcels in her hand, comes in through the gate and sees him. **1918** Galsworthy *Five Tales* 272 He.. pottered in and out of his dressing-room. **1932** E. Waugh *Black Mischief* vii. 257 The Envoy Extraordinary finished his second cup of coffee, filled and lit his pipe, and avoiding the social life of the lawn, pottered round by the back way to the Chancery.

† **potter-carrier.** Vulgar or provincial var. of POTHECARY: cf. POT CARRIER.

1764 Foote *Mayor of G.* I. Wks. 1799 I. 161 Master Lint, the potter-carrier.

potterer ('pɒtərə(r)). [f. POTTER *v.* + -ER[1].] One who potters; one who works at things in a feeble, unsystematic, or ineffectual way; one who potters about: see the verb.

1862 Burton *Bk. Hunter* 105 A mere wayward potterer, picking up curiosities by the way for his own private individual museum. **1867** —— *Hist. Scot.* I. xi. 404 That Robertson did not throw himself into our early history, but left it to a body of dreary potterers, is the more to be regretted. **1883** A. Forbes in *Fortn. Rev.* 1 Nov. 664 He was not free from the imputation of being a potterer.

pottering ('pɒtərɪŋ), *vbl. sb.* [f. as prec. + -ING[1].] The action of the verb POTTER; feeble, unsystematic, or desultory working; sauntering about, etc.: see the verb.

? **1530** [see POTTER *v.* 1]. **1844** E. FitzGerald *Lett.* (1889) I. 140 After my usual pottering about in the midland counties of England. **1860** Emerson *Cond. Life* iii. (1861) 71 Long marches are no hardship to him... But this pottering in a few square yards of garden is dispiriting and drivelling. **1884** E. Yates *Recoll. & Exper.* II. 39 There were lovely walks and drives.. potterings about with Fenn in his sketching expeditions. **1893** E. G. Duff *Early Printed Bks.* 195 Mere antiquarian pottering or aimless waste of time.

'pottering, *ppl. a.* [f. as prec. + -ING[2].]

1. That potters: see the verb.

1826 Scott *Jrnl.* 13 June, A big.. trifle-headed, old pottering minister,.. came to annoy me about a claim [etc.]. **1842** Miall in *Nonconf.* II. 72 A plodding, pottering mind, far more expert in tinkering holes, than in forging and constructing new instruments. **1865** Miss Braddon *Only a Clod* xl, When I am a pottering old fellow of seventy, I shall have a great fortune and a handsome wife.

2. Involving or characterized by pottering.

a. Of work, etc.: Done in a feeble, unsystematic, or ineffectual way; hence, trifling, slight, paltry.

1740 J. Clarke *Educ. Youth* (ed. 3) 28 What miserable pottering Work do the poor Boys make of it. **1837** Whittock, etc. *Bk. Trades* (1842) 383 Although a small pottering business might be commenced with a much less sum. **1861** Smiles *Engineers* I. 52 Only a few pottering improvements were made.

b. Of movement: Slow, loitering; aimless, unsteady.

1821 Clare *Vill. Minstr.* II. 193 With ling'ring, pott'ring pace,.. Thou, like an old man, bidd'st the world adieu. **1873** Miss Broughton *Nancy* II. 76 The long pottering stroll that Roger and I had taken one evening.

Hence **'potteringly** *adv.*

1893 G. Meredith in *Pall Mall Mag.* II. 194 Under one aspect we appear potteringly European; under another, drunk of the East.

† **'pottern**, *a. Obs. rare.* [f. POTTER *sb.*[1], app. after *leathern*, etc.] Of or pertaining to potters: with quots. cf. *potter's lead, ore*, POTTER *sb.*[1] 3.

1661 Boyle *Unsuccessfuln. Experim.* i. Wks. 1772 I. 323 An ore, which for its aptness to vitrify, and serve the potters to glaze their earthen vessels, the miners call pottern-ore. *a* **1728** Woodward *Nat. Hist. Fossils* (1729) I. I. 188 A Spar.. that is shattery, and breaks in Squares, exactly like the finest Pottern-Lead-Ore.

pottery ('pɒtərɪ). [In 15th c. a. F. *poterie* (13th c. in Hatz.-Darm.), f. *potier* POTTER *sb.*[1]: cf. med.L. *potārius* potter, *potāria* pottery. In later use sometimes referred directly to *pot*: cf. *crockery*.

1086 *Domesday Bk.* I. 156/1 (Bladon, Oxon.), Ibi .ii. molini de .xiiii. solidis . et .cxxv. anguillis . et de ollaria [potaria *interlined*] .x. solidi.]

1. a. A potter's workshop or factory; a pot-factory.

c **1483** Caxton *Dialogues* 7/13 Pottes of erthe, Cannes of erthe For to go the watre; Thise things shall ye fynde In the potterye [F. *en le potterye*]. **1780** Howard *Prisons Eng.* 156 A prison which had been a pottery. **1867** Smiles *Huguenots Eng.* vi. (1880) 105 Two potters from Antwerp.. started a pottery, though in a very humble way.

b. In *pl.*, ***the Potteries***, a district in N. Staffordshire, including Hanley and Stoke-upon-Trent, the chief seat of the English pottery industry.

1825 J. Nicholson *Operat. Mechanic* 485 The district called 'the Potteries', is an extensive tract of country in the hundred of North Pyrehill and county of Stafford, comprehending an area of about eight miles long, and six broad. **1839** Ure *Dict. Arts* 1009 A population of 60,000 operatives now derives a comfortable subsistence within a district.. which contains 150 kilns, and is significantly called the Potteries.

2. The potter's art, ceramics; the manufacture of earthen vessels.

1727–41 Chambers *Cycl., Pottery*, the art of making earthen pots and vessels; or, the manufacture of earthen ware. **1872** Yeats *Techn. Hist. Comm.* 135 The Arabs were perfect masters of the art of pottery. **1891** Nisbet *Insanity of Genius* 236 Pottery, when he [Wedgwood] took it up, was a rude and barbarous manufacture; he raised it to the dignity of an art.

3. The products of the potter's art collectively; pottery-ware, earthenware.

1785 J. PHILLIPS *Treat. Inland Navig.* 21 Norwich goods, groceries, potteries, and other merchandise. **1825** J. NICHOLSON *Operat. Mechanic* 484 The drab pottery is useful for articles which require strength to be united to ornament, as flower-pots, water-jugs, &c. **1851** D. WILSON *Preh. Ann.* (1863) I. II. vii. 481 Primitive sepulchral pottery. **1863** LYELL *Antiq. Man* ii. 10 The pottery found associated with weapons of bronze is of a more ornamental and tasteful style than any which belongs to the age of stone. **1888** MISS BRADDON *Fatal Three* I. v, The shallow milk-pans were of Doulton pottery.

4. *attrib.* and *Comb.*, as ***pottery kiln, manufacture, market, trade, ware***; **pottery bark**, see quot.; **pottery-bark tree**, = *pottery tree*; **pottery clay** = *pot clay* s.v. POT *sb.*[1] 14, ***potter's clay*** s.v. POTTER *sb.*[1] 3; **pottery coal**, Staffordshire coal; so **pottery coalfield**; **pottery gauge**, see quot.; **pottery mould**, a 'brick' of soft stone mixed with pipeclay, used for whitening hearths, etc.; a hearthstone; **pottery tissue**, see quot.; **pottery tree**, one of various trees of the genus *Licania*, the bark of which is *pottery bark*.

1866 *Treas. Bot.* 679/2 Several undetermined species of this genus [*Licania*] afford the *Pottery bark, the ashes of which are used by the natives of the Amazon for mixing with the clay employed in the manufacture of pottery-ware, in order to enable the vessels to withstand the action of fire. **1905** *Geol. N. Staffs. Coalfields* (Mem. Geol. Survey) xii. 224 (*heading*) *Pottery clays, brick clays and marls. **1921** *S.W. Coalfield* (Mem. Geol. Survey) XIII. xii. 169 The isolated Bovey Tracey Beds of Devon, consisting in part of pottery clays..are supposed to have been laid down in a small, local lake-basin. **1962** W. STEGNER *Wolf Willow* IV. ii. 250 Floods of settlers..all figured in the dream, as did..oil, pottery clay, glass sand, and other..resources. **1867** W. W. SMYTH *Coal & Coal-mining* 58 *Pottery coals and ironstone measures..with 8 to 13 seams of coal of above two feet thick ..and 10 to 12 measures of ironstone. **1851** RICHARDSON *Geol.* (1855) 435 The Coal-fields of England and Wales... 3. North Staffordshire sometimes called the *Pottery coal-field. **1875** KNIGHT *Dict. Mech.*, **Pottery-gage*, a shaper or templet for the inside of a vessel on the wheel. **1839** URE *Dict. Arts* 821 The apparatus then resembles certain *pottery kilns. **1862** H. SPENCER *First Princ.* II. xiv. §111 (1875) 318 Witness..the absorption by Staffordshire of the *pottery-manufacture. **1853** HICKIE tr. *Aristoph.* (1872) II. 416 In the *pottery-market and the vegetable-market alike. **1876** 'OUIDA' *Winter City* iii, What pleasant lives these *pottery painters of the early days must have led. **1875** KNIGHT *Dict. Mech.*, **Pottery-tissue*, a kind of tissue-paper used to receive impressions of engravings for transference to *biscuit*. **1866** *Treas. Bot.* 679/2 s.v. *Licania*, The Indians call these trees Caraipe, but botanists have adopted that name for a genus of *Ternströmiaceæ*, owing to the *Pottery tree having at one time been supposed to belong to that order. **1847-78** HALLIWELL, **Pottery-ware*, earthenware. *West.* **1866** Pottery-ware [see *pottery-bark*].

† **'pottical**, *a. humorous nonce-wd.* [f. POT *sb.*[1], after *poetical*.] Full of, or inspired by, liquor.

1586 W. WEBBE *Eng. Poetrie* (Arb.) 37 Poets: whose potticall poeticall (I should say) heades, I would wyshe.. might..be gorgiously garnished with fayre greene Barley, in token of their good affection to our Englishe Malt. **1589** R. HARVEY *Pl. Perc.* (1590) 9 An olde sooker, that caries such Potticall verses of the State of Flanders, in a linnen bag.

pottiness ('pɒtɪnɪs). [f. POTTY *a.* + -NESS.] The state or condition of being potty.

1933 WODEHOUSE *Heavy Weather* iii. 47 It was not primarily his pottiness that led him to steal the Empress. **1935** D. L. SAYERS *Gaudy Night* v. 98 We shall all feel perfectly ghastly wondering..whether our own conversation doesn't sound a little potty. It's the pottiness, you know, that's so awful. **1957** E. HYAMS *Into Dreams* 250 He..got an impression of pottiness from the old politician's smile. **1974** *Times* 17 Jan. 7/8 The dementia of children who threw themselves upon them [*sc.* a pop group] in an orgy of enslaved pottiness. **1976** K. BONFIGLIOLI *Something Nasty in Woodshed* i. 15 This inability to see any flaws in oneself is a branch of pottiness.

potting ('pɒtɪŋ), *vbl. sb.*[1] [f. POT *v.*[1] + -ING[1].]

1. Drinking (of ale, beer, or the like); tippling. *arch.* (chiefly with allusion to Shakspere's use).

1594 LYLY *Moth. Bomb.* III. ii, What Risio, how spedst thou after thy potting? **1604** SHAKS. *Oth.* II. iii. 79, I learn'd it in England; where indeed they are most potent in Potting. **1719** D'URFEY *Pills* V. 66 Potting and sotting..Will make a good Soldier miscarry. **1864** HEMYNG *Eton School Days* viii. 95 Bird's-eye's patrons would..sit in his cottage and smoke and drink beer, for they were 'potent at potting'.

2. The making of pottery or earthenware.

1743 *N. Jersey Archives* XII. 158 This is exceedingly good for potting or any sort of Cast ware. **1877** R. BINNS (*title*) A Century of Potting in the City of Worcester, being the History of the Royal Porcelain Works from 1751 to 1851. **1894** *Westm. Gaz.* 7 May 3/1 Potting is one of the oldest industries in the world. **1970** [see MING b]. **1976** P. FLOWER *Crisscross* i. 6 How Sibyl loved it all: calling meetings..in between her potting.

3. a. The preserving of butter, meat, fish, etc. in pots or other vessels.

1615 MARKHAM *Eng. Housew.* II. vi. (1668) 147 Touching the powdering up, or potting of Butter. **1755** FARRINGTON in *Phil. Trans.* XLIX. 211 The cure and potting of charrs well. **1876** RUSKIN *Fors Clav.* VI. 254 Catching and potting of salmon on the Columbia River. **1891** *Auckland Star* 1 Oct. 4/2 Butter... Already the low price has caused many farmers to commence potting down.

b. *Sugar Manuf.* (See POT *v.*[1] 2 b.)

1839 URE *Dict. Arts* 1203 The act of transferring the crude concrete sugar from the crystallisers into these hogs-heads, is called *potting*. **1887** N. D. DAVIS *Cavaliers & Roundh. Barbados* 90 From the last copper the clarified liquor was run off into a cistern to 'cool', or become milk-warm, when the operation of 'potting' began.

c. *Woollen Manufacture.* (See quots.)

1920 J. M. MATTHEWS *Application of Dyestuffs* i. 66 An operation very similar to that of decatizing is known as potting. This is a treatment of woollen goods with steam and hot water for the purpose of producing a particular character of finish. **1927** HORSFALL & LAWRIE *Dyeing of Textile Fibres* ix. 275 Potting. This process is applied to fabrics of the faced type... The cloth is wound..on to a perforated roll which..is placed upright in a cistern in cold water. **1951** *Rev. Textile Progress* II. 329 Blowing..does not yield such good results as potting, *i.e.*, winding the cloth on a roller and heating it in water at about 160°F. for periods varying from a few hours to four days. **1961** BLACKSHAW & BRIGHTMAN *Dict. Dyeing* 137 *Potting*, a finishing process for wool cloths in which a roll of fabric is treated in water at 70–100°C. for several hours, then allowed to cool slowly, and finally immersed in cold water to set the fabric.

d. The act or process of abridging, condensing, or summarizing.

1909 *Daily Chron.* 20 Oct. 1/6 Drury Lane Dignity is down on Apollo Impudence for using the title of 'The Whip' in the 'potting' department of 'The Follies', and the seriousness of the whole business is expressed in Mr. Pelissier's startled cry to the British public: 'Hurry up! We have had a letter from Messrs. Hamilton and Raleigh's solicitors objecting to our burlesque of 'The Whip', so we may be locked up at any moment.' **1966** *Punch* 9 Oct. 521/3 The enormous subject is covered by rapid potting... The potting is efficient: the course of the 1914–18 War on the Western Front..is explained with much greater clarity than usual.

4. Planting in, or transplanting into, a pot.

1845 *Florist's Jrnl.* 83 The success of cultivation..is invariably connected with a correct arrangement and proportion of the soil, &c., in potting.

5. a. ***crab-potting***, the catching of crabs in pots: cf. POT *sb.*[1] 5 b, *crab-pot* (CRAB *sb.*[1] 13).

1891 *Pall Mall G.* 17 Aug. 3/1 We may meet a fisherman returning from crab potting. **1902** CUTCLIFFE HYNE in *Windsor Mag.* July (*title*) The Gentle Art of Crab-Potting.

b. *dial.* The catching of lobsters in pots.

1971 *Nat. Geographic* Apr. 556/2 We were out potting. Potting? Lobstering, bringing in the pots.

6. a. Shooting; taking of pot-shots: see POT *v.*[1] 5. *colloq.* or *slang*.

1884 *St. James' Gaz.* 5 Dec. 4/1 The potting of Arabs rightly struggling to be free continues merrily at Suakim. **1902** *Words Eye-witness* 43 It is commonly well on into the morning before the 'potting' swells into the rattle and roll which tells that men are hard at it 'with their coats off'.

b. *Billiards.* The act or process of knocking a ball into one of the pockets.

1909 in *Cent. Dict.* Suppl. **1935** *Encycl. Sports* 571/1 The practical application of this knowledge will make potting easy for many who find it inordinately difficult. **1950** *Hoyle's Games Modernized* (ed. 20) III. 340 The most successful [pool] player is not necessarily he who can 'pot' with the deadliest accuracy, but he who combines potting with effectively playing for position. **1956** E. GRIERSON *Second Man* iv. 59 Gilroy put an exquisite edge on his potting, though he did have a tendency to overdo it and go in off.

7. Encapsulation of a circuit or component in an insulating material (cf. POT *v.*[1] 2 c). Freq. *attrib.*

1947 *Plastics* July 57/1 During the war, exacting mechanical and electrical stability requirements of special electronic applications..necessitated the potting of the circuit components. **1955** *Rep. Progress Appl. Chem.* XL. 508 A typical potting resin comprises a mixture of 2:4-toluylene di*iso*cyanate (20–40%), monomeric styrene (up to 10%), and castor oil, lactic acid being used as a catalyst. **1962** M. C. VOLK et al. *Electr. Encapsulation* i. 5 Potting is the simplest cavity-filling process. Procedure consists of positioning the component in its container ('pot'), adding encapsulant to fill the pot, then curing to polymerize or harden the encapsulant.

8. The action or an instance of causing a baby or young child to sit on a chamber-pot.

1948 *Practitioner* Dec. 505 It is as well that the infant should suffer the experience of 'potting' quite early, and should come to appreciate that the environment reacts less encouragingly to random disposal of excreta than to its opposite. **1953** R. S. ILLINGWORTH *Normal Child* xxvii. 283 Provided that there is never a fight to keep the child on the chamber and the child does not resist, 'potting' is a harmless procedure. **1958** *Observer* 20 Apr. 8/4 Much else that controverts the views of Sir Truby King, and his 'Mothercraft' disciples, on early potting, bodily guilt, schedule feeding. **1960** *Guardian* 1 Apr. 7/1, I attended to the telephone, 'potting' of small child, and comforting child after fall. **1967** *Ibid.* 1 May 4/4 The job extends to getting the children up... No doubt the next 10 years will see minor changes—no more potting, for example. **1972** J. GATHORNE-HARDY *Rise & Fall of Brit. Nanny* viii. 265 Nearly incessant potting..produces a high..quota of wins.

9. *attrib.* and *Comb.*, as (in sense 2) ***potting business, industry, trade***; (? in sense 3) ***potting-dish***; (in sense 4) ***potting bench, compost, -house, -shed, soil***; **potting-cask**, in *Sugar Manuf.* (see POT *v.*[1] 2 b); **potting-pot**, a pot such as is used for potting meat; **potting-stick**, a flat stick used to press down the soil about the root of a plant in a pot.

1874 *Gardeners' Chron.* 17 Jan. 95/3 A movable wooden tray, shaped like the top of a *potting bench..will answer the purpose. **1935** A. G. L. HELLYER *Pract. Gardening* xxx. 185 (*caption*) The principal ingredients may well be stored in bins under the potting bench. **1766** J. WEDGWOOD *Let.* 15 Sept. (1965) 42 As our connections are to become extensive in the *Potting business, it is absolutely necessary you should visit the Manufacture. **1839** URE *Dict. Arts* 1204 [The syrup] is then transferred..into conical moulds..their capacity..is considerably less than that of the smallest *potting-casks. **1916** M. HAMPDEN *Flower Culture* ii. 38 Silver sand and old manure, chopped fine, may make up one part of the ordinary *potting compost. **1971** P. D. JAMES *Shroud for Nightingale* vi. 183 There were balls of green twine,..packets of seed,..a small plastic bag of potting compost and one of fertilizer. **1976** J. BERRISFORD *Backyards & Tiny Gardens* xv. 107 Bedding plants do well also in John Innes potting compost No. 2. **1569** *Wills & Inv. N.C.* (Surtees) I. 302 In the Hall..xix[th] peace of puder, fyue saucers, three *pottyndysshes xij[d]. **1825** CROMWELL *Hist. Colchester* 352 A Seed-shop, *Potting-house, &c. **1901** *Scotsman* 1 Apr. 7/2 The dangerous processes in use in the *potting industry. **1739** E. SMITH *Compl. Housewife* (ed. 9) 52 *Mackrel to pot*..place them close in your *potting-pots, and pour clarified butter on the top. **1747** MRS. GLASSE *Cookery* (1767) 230 When it is beat to a paste, put it into your potting-pot. **1874** *Gardeners' Chron.* 17 Jan. 95/3 The manure and compost yard should include a *potting shed. **1902** W. B. YEATS *Where there is Nothing* (1903) I. 14 Come over here to the potting shed. **1907** E. GOSSE *Father & Son* vii. 181 My Father would..bolt..round the garden into the potting-shed. **1940** J. BETJEMAN *Old Lights for New Chancels* 48 Back down the Avenue, back to the pottingshed. **1976** *Derbyshire Times* (Peak ed.) 3 Sept. 18/1 (Advt.), Detached garage, well-established gardens to front and rear, potting shed. **1908** *Daily Chron.* 29 Feb. 9/1 This material [*sc.* manure from mushroom growing] is in excellent condition for mixing with *potting soil as a fertiliser. **1936** *Forestry* X. 12 The potting soil used was a standard mixture. **1897** *Garden* 2 Jan. 9/3 They place the new compost about them, and make it firm by ramming with the *potting stick.

potting, *vbl. sb.*[2]: see POT *v.*[3]

† **'pottingar** (-gə(r)). *Sc. Obs.* Forms: 5–6 **potingar, -e, pottingar,** 6 **potingair, pothingar;** *erron.* 7 **pottinger,** 8 **potinger.** [Corrupted from **poticar*, POTHECAR, Sc. form of POTHECARY. Cf. the parallel POTTINGARY, where the intermediate forms are better seen. In the later spelling confounded with POTTINGER.] = next, 1.

1474 *Acc. Ld. High Treas. Scot.* I. 24 Potingare [see POTTINGARY 2 b]. **1489** *Ibid.* 129 Item, to Stene pottingar.. vij *li.* xv *s.* **1533** *Ibid.* VI. 88 To Francis Aikman, potingair, for sindrie droggis. **1535** STEWART *Cron. Scot.* (Rolls) II. 196 He wes ane potingar richt fyne, And had grit prattik of all medicyne. *a* **1567** DARNLEY *'Quhair Luve is kendit Confortles'* 14 (Bann. MS.) For harmes of body, handis and heid, The pottingaris will purge the panis. *a* **1585** POLWART *Flyting w. Montgomerie* 254 Passe to the pothingars againe; Some recipies does yet remaine. **1715** PENNECUIK *Truth's Trav.* in *Descr. Tweeddale*, etc. 96 The Candle-makers came and Flait, The Potingers were very Crouse. **1828** SCOTT *F.M. Perth* vii 'Pardon me', said he, 'I am but a poor pottingar. Nevertheless, I have been bred in Paris, and learned my humanities and my *cursus medendi*'.

† **'pottingary.** *Sc. Obs.* Forms: α. 5 **potigary,** 6 **potegarie.** β. 5 **potyngary,** 5–6 **pot(t)ingary,** 6 **pottingarie, -gry, potinchary.** [Corrupted from *poticary*, earlier form of POTHECARY, through the intermediate *potegary, potigary*: cf. prec., and *nihtegale, nightingale*.]

1. = APOTHECARY 1 (med.L. *apothēcārius*).

1552 ABP. HAMILTON *Catech.* Tabil (1884) 11 Potegareis that sellis corruppit drogaris. *Ibid.* 100 Pottingareis quhilk takis siluer for euil & rottin stufe and drogaris. *Ibid.* 103.

2. a. The art or practice of an apothecary; pharmacy.

c **1480** HENRYSON *Sum Pract. Med.* 16 in *Bannatyne Poems* (Hunter. Cl.) 402 My prettik in pottingary ye trow be als pure. **1500** *Exch. Rolls Scotl.* XI. 376 *note*, Oure..servitoure and potingare William Fowlare for his..service.. in his craft and science of pottingary. **1500–20** DUNBAR *Poems* xxxiii. 29 In pottingry he wrocht grit pyne, He murdreist mony in medecyne. *a* **1568** *For Helth of Body* 77 in *Bannatyne Poems* (Hunter. Cl.) 199 Thair is no raseth cumis of pottingary,.. Till all neidrent richest detray the.

b. The drugs of an apothecary, medicines.

1474 *Acc. Ld. High Treas. Scot.* I. 23 To a Flemyng of Bruges for certane potigariis coft to the King. *Ibid.* 24 Item gevin to Stephin potingare..for certane materialis and potingaris deliuerit be him to the King, v. li. **1501** *Ibid.* II. 34 Item, to William Fowlar, for potinchary tane fra him to the King..xxiij li. iij s. vj d.

pottinger[1] ('pɒtɪndʒə(r)). Now *dial.* Forms: α. 5 **poteger, pottyger,** 6 **potteger, pattecher,** 6 **potager,** 7 **pottager.** β. 5–6 **pottinger,** 6 **potenger, -ynger, pot(t)anger, pottencher,** 6–7 **-enger,** 7 **-inger.** [orig. *potager*, a. F. *potager*, f. *potage* POTTAGE; altered to *pot(t)enger, -inger* (cf. *passager, passenger, harbinger*, etc.); thence through *podenger*, PODDINGER, to *poreger*, PORRINGER, q.v.] A vessel of metal, earthenware, or wood, for holding soup, broth, or other liquid or semi-liquid food; a small basin, porringer.

α. [**1415** HEN. V *Mandate* in Drake *Eboracum* (1736) App. 17, 24 disces d'argent aunciens, només potageers de diverses formes.] **1466–7** *Abingdon Acc.* (Camden) 135, j poteger'. *c* **1500** in *Ripon Ch. Acts* (Surtees) 377, iiij pottygers. **1532** MORE *Confut. Tindale* Wks. 617/1 One sponeful of good workes should no more kil ye soule, then a potager of good wurts shuld kil & destroi y[e] bodi. **1565** in *Trans. Cumb. & West. Arch. Soc.* X. 31, iiij potteggers & xij platts. **1615** E. S. *Britain's Buss* B j b, Wodden pottagers.

β. **1494** in *Somerset Medieval Wills* (1901) 321, iiij platers iiij potingers and iiij sawcers. **1512** *Act 4 Hen. VIII*, c. 7 §7 Untrue..Workmanship of Tin or Pewter..in..Dishes, Saucers, Pottingers, Trenchers, Basons, Flaggons. **1530**

Palsgr. 257/1 Pottanger, *escuelle, avrillon.* **1563** *Wills & Inv. N.C.* (Surtees) I. 210, xij pattechers vj[s], xij saucers ij[s] vij[d], xviij old dublers in the kitchin & v pottenchers. **1570** Levins *Manip.* 80/14 A Potanger, *patella, æ.* **1594** Plat *Jewell-ho.* III. 34 In a Glasse or Stone Pottinger. **1657** Tomlinson *Renou's Disp.* 483 A Pottenger is . . a small, but patulous vessel. **1684** tr. *Bonet's Merc. Compit.* IV. 126 A Physician ordered five Pottingers of Bloud to be taken from him. **1825** Brockett *N.C. Gloss.*, *Pottinger*, a coarse earthen-ware pot, with a handle; porringer. **1828** *Craven Gloss.* (ed. 2), *Pottinger*, a small pewter mug or vessel, containing about three quarters of a pint: a porringer.

†**pottinger**[2] (ˈpɒtɪndʒə(r)). *Obs.* exc. *Hist.* [Corrupted from POTAGER: as to the form cf. prec.] A maker of pottage; a kind of cook. App. sometimes confounded with POTTINGAR, apothecary.

[*a* **1572** Knox *Hist. Ref.* Wks. 1846 I. 263 Whitther it was by ane Italiane posset, or by French fegges, or by the potage of thare potingar, (he was a French man,) thare departed fra this lyef the Erle of Cassilles, the Erle of Rothose. *a* **1578** Lindesay (Pitscottie) *Chron. Scot.* (S.T.S.) I. 337 Cuning baxteris and also excellent cuikis and potigeris [*mispr.* potiseris; MS. I, potingareis] witht confectiounis and drogis ffor thair desairtis.] **1814** Scott *Wav.* xxiv (quoting Pitscottie), Excellent cooks, and pottingars. **1820** —— *Monast.* xvi, The wafers, flams, and pastry-meat will scarce have had the just degree of fire which learned pottingers prescribe as fittest for the body. **1866** *Illustr. Lond. News* 22 Dec. 607/2 It shows that these herbs were used for seasoning by the pottingers of the period.

pottle[1] (ˈpɒt(ə)l). Forms: 4–5 **potel**, 4–7 **-ell**, 5 **-elle**, 5–7 **pottel(l**, 6– **pottle**. [ME. *potel*, a. OF. *potel* (1308 in Godef.) a little pot, a measure, f. *pot* POT *sb.*[1] + *-el*, -LE 2.]

1. A measure of capacity for liquids (also for corn and other dry goods, rarely for butter), equal to two quarts or half a gallon: now abolished.

a **1300** *Sat. People Kildare* xvii. in *E.E.P.* (1862) 155 Hail be ȝe brewesters wiþ ȝur galuns Potels and quarters ouer al þe tounes. **1389** in *Eng. Gilds* (1870) 59 Ye Alderman schal haue . . ij galons of ale; & ye dene a potel. **14..** *Tretyce* in *W. of Henley's Husb.* (1890) 54 þe thirde parte off a potell off butter. **1465** *Cov. Lt. Bk.* (E.E.T.S.), The wardens shall make a stryke, halfe stryke, hope & halfe hope, gallon & potell & quarte, the mesurs to be selyd & delyuered to the sellers of oton-meele. **1486** *Naval Acc. Hen. VII* (1896) 16 A pottell oyle for the calkers vj[d]. **1571** Digges *Pantom.* III. xii. Sj, To lerne howe many pottles or gallons is conteyned in that great vessell. **1602** Plat *Delightes for Ladies* Recipe lii, Take a pottle of damsons. **1608** Willet *Hexapla Exod.* 697 Containing each of them tenne pottels or thereabout, foure or fiue gallons. **1625** in *Naworth Househ. Bks.* (Surtees) 229 One potell of canary seck. **1657** S. Purchas *Pol. Flying-Ins.* 99 Little hony at that time of the year is ordinarily to bee had; a quart, perhaps a pottle, and this is a liberal portion. **1796** Mrs. Glasse *Cookery* xxi. 326 Take a quarter of a pound of hartshorn and put to it a pottle of water. **1869** Hazlitt *Eng. Prov.* 473 Who'd keep a cow, when he may have a pottle of milk for a penny?

b. A pot or vessel containing a pottle, or of about this capacity.

1698 Thoresby in *Phil. Trans.* XX. 311, I have . . lately procur'd a Roman Pottle from Aldbrough, which is of the Red Clay. **17..** *Anc. Poems*, etc. (Percy Soc.) 180 We'll drink it out of the pottle, my boys, Here's a health to the barley-mow! **1809** W. Irving *Knickerb.* (1849) 341 Then the Van Grolls, of Anthony's Nose, who carried their liquor in fair round little pottles. **1888** Stevenson *Black Arrow* 24 By his elbow stood a pottle of spiced ale.

c. *ellipt.* A pottle of wine or other liquor; hence, drink, liquor.

a **1700** in *Roxb. Ball.* (1874) II. 258 Yet, scrambling up, a Drunkard feels no pain, But cries 'Sirrah, hoy! t'other pottle againe'. **1850** Syd. Dobell *Roman* vii, I do not learn . . That you shall . . drink your pottle weaker at the wake.

2. A small wicker or 'chip' basket, esp. one of a conical form used for strawberries.

1771 Smollett *Humph. Cl.* 2 June Let. i, She sent us a pottle of fine strawberries. **1847** C. A. Johns *Forest Trees Gt. Brit.* I. 341 The neat-looking, but very inconvenient, basket for holding strawberries, called a pottle, is made of Beech. **1880** Disraeli *Endym.* 459 One never sees a pottle of strawberries now.

3. Name of a children's game.

1822 Southey *Lett.* (1856) III. 334, I have as little inclination to write verses as to play at pottle or whip a top.

4. *attrib.* and *Comb.*, as ***pottle bottle, draught, pitcher***; **pottle-bellied** *a.*, pot-bellied; **pottle-bodied** *a.*, stout, corpulent; **pottle-crowned** *a.* (of a hat), having a crown like a small pot; **pottle-deep** *a.*, of the depth of a pottle. See also POTTLE-POT.

1777 *Horæ Subsecivæ* 337 (E.D.D.) *Pottle-bellied. **1825** Jennings *Dial. W. Eng.* 61 *Pottle-bellied*, potbellied. **1842** Tennyson *Will Waterproof* xvii, He saw A something-*pottle-bodied boy That knuckled at the taw. **1392–3** *Earl Derby's Exp.* (Camden) 154, iiij paribus *potel botels. **1459** *Invent.* in *Paston Lett.* I. 488, j. payre of potell botellys of one sorte. *a* **1648** Digby *Closet Open.* (1677) 30 Pour this clear liquor into pottle-bottles of glass. **1604** Shaks. *Oth.* II. iii. 56 Rodorigo . . To Desdemona hath to night Carrows'd Potations, *pottle-deepe. **1784** R. Bage *Barham Downs* I. 124 The life of a Lord . . consists principally of his amours, his pottle deep potations, his politics, and his—hazards. **1639** Mayne *City Match* III. iii, I shall be glad To give thanks for you, sir, in *pottle-draughts. *a* **1529** Skelton *El. Rummyng* 402 Another . . brought a *pottel pycher, A tonnel, and a bottell.

Hence ˈ**pottled** *a.*, placed in a pottle; †savouring of the pottle or wine-cup (*obs.*).

1568 T. Howell *Arb. Amitie* 23 As potled tales they prate aloft, so thende will proue but vaine. **1845** Eliza Cook *Old Cries* ii, 'Old Cries', 'old cries' . . From 'Haut-boys', pottled in the sun, To the loud wish that cometh when The tune of midnight 'waits' is done.

†**pottle**[2]. *Obs.* (See quot.)

1689 R. Cox *Hist. Irel.* I. Expl. Index, Pottle of Land is twelve Acres.

†**pottle**[3], erron. variant of BOTTLE *sb.*[3]

1733 Fielding *Tom Thumb* II. ix, The unhappy sempstress once, they say, Her needle in a pottle, lost, of hay. **1849** James *Woodman* xvii, 'And we are to set to find a needle in the pottle of hay', replied his companion.

pottle-pot (ˈpɒt(ə)lpɒt). [f. POTTLE + POT *sb.*[1]] A two-quart pot or tankard.

1413 in *E.E. Wills* (1882) 22, Y be-quethe tho [to] William my sone, a new bras pot . . an a potel pot of peuwter. **1553** T. Wilson *Rhet.* 87 There came a man out of the towne with a pinte of wine in a pottle pot to welcome the provost of that house [King's College]. **1597** Shaks. *2 Hen. IV* II. ii. 83. **1740** Baynard *Health* (ed. 6) p. viii, Why should Men dread a Cannon Bore Yet boldly 'proach a Pottle-pot? **1841** James *Brigand* viii, Truth and my brains lie together at the bottom of the second pottle-pot.

b. *transf.* A heavy drinker, a drunkard.

1860 Sala in *Cornh. Mag.* I. 580 Edward Ward . . although a low-lived pottlepot at the best of times, makes some honest remarks concerning the barbarous treatment of the women in Bridewell.

potto (ˈpɒtəʊ). [Alleged to be from a Guinea dialect (see quot. 1705); cf. Ashanti *aˈpŏs(s)o.* (See J. Platt in *N. & Q.* 10th ser. IV. 286.)]

1. A West African lemur (*Perodicticus potto*), commonly called a 'sloth'. Also ***potto lemur.*** **b.** ***Calabar potto***, a species of lemur (*Arctocebus calabarensis*), inhabiting the district of Old Calabar.

1705 tr. *Bosman's Guinea* 250 A Creature, by the Negroes called *Potto* [*orig.* een beest, 'tgeen by de negers de naem van *potto* draegt], but known to us by the Name of Sluggard. **1868** Owen *Vertebr. Anim.* III. 405 In the Potto the sub-maxillary ducts open in the usual position, upon the free margin of the sublingual. **1901** *Q. Rev.* July 18 That most typical West African creature, the potto lemur. **1902** *Westm. Gaz.* 28 May 12/1 To a weird-looking and nocturnal creature with the eyes of a cat and the body of a tailless monkey the name of 'Bosman's Potto' has been given. **1906** Sir H. Johnston *Liberia* 685 The range of the common potto extends right across Africa from Sierra Leone to Uganda.

2. The kinkajou. Also ***potto kinkajou.***

1790 Bewick *Quadrupeds* (1824) 446 One of this species [Yellow Macauco] was shewn in London some years ago, and was said to have been brought from Jamaica, where it is called the *Potto.* **1834** McMurtrie *Cuvier's Anim. Kingd.* I. 84 This is, perhaps, the only proper place for the singular genus of the Kinkajous or Potto. . . From the warm parts of America, and from some of the great Antilles, where it is called *Potto.* **1855** H. G. Dalton *Brit. Guiana* II. 456 The Potto-kinkajou, size of a pole-cat, a pretty looking animal, is occasionally seen.

†ˈ**pottock.** *Obs. rare.* [f. POT *sb.*[1] + -OCK.] A small pot.

1694 A. de la Pryme *Diary* (Surtees) 54 They boyl it in iron pottoks till all the humidity be evaporated.

pottock, corruption of POT-HOOK.

pot-tree. 1. A tree grown in a pot.

1905 *Daily Chron.* 11 Oct. 6/4 The pot trees of . . apples are weighed down with the splendid fruit.

2. A name for the S. American tree *Lecythis Ollaria*, from the shape of its fruit; also called *monkey-pot* tree.

potty (ˈpɒtɪ), *a. colloq.* [f. POT *sb.*[1] + -Y[1].]

1. a. As a general term of disparagement: indifferent, feeble; petty, insignificant, esp. in ***potty little.***

1860 Hotten *Dict. Slang* (ed. 2) 193 *Potty*, indifferent, bad looking. [*ed. 3 (1864)*, indifferent, bad looking,—said of a rotten or unsound scheme.] **1870** *Times* 12 Aug. 10/3 Then came a single, and then a catch from a 'potty' hit. **1899** E. Phillpotts *Human Boy* 72 It is such a potty little place, hardly worth calling a wood. **1904** Kipling *Traffics & Discov.* 270 'Think they'll take you an' your potty quick-firers? **1907** Galsworthy *Country House* III. iv. 246 We stand on our petty rights here, And our potty dignity there. **1927** Chesterton *Secret of Father Brown* v. 178 Who would, or could, have killed him up in that potty little place? **1930** —— *Four Faultless Felons* 236 It was within reasonable distance of revolution; not a potty little palace revolution. **1939** G. B. Shaw *Geneva* III. 57 What I think of the mob of bagmen from fifty potty little foreign states that calls itself a League of Nations. **1980** 'M. Innes' *Going it Alone* xx. 178 They've . . smashed their way in. Just the idea I had with that potty litle motor-mower.

b. Easy to manage, accomplish, or deal with; easy, simple.

1899 E. Phillpotts *Human Boy* 127 Ferrars . . got regularly muddled over a potty question about Jacob. **1916** E. F. Benson *David Blaize* iv. 70 It was quite certain that Helmsworth would have won had not that ass Blazes . . dropped the 'pottiest' catch ever seen. **1922** *Blackw. Mag.* July 55/2 It's potty on this scaffolding . . , no end of cross-pieces to hold on to.

2. a. Crazy, mad; out of one's senses; eccentric, 'dotty'.

1920 *Cornh. Mag.* Jan. 7 Next day, at tea time, the producer of the comedy solemnly thanked Jess for saving a situation past praying for. . . In your potty part, you put 'em all to bed. How did you do it? **1921** *Chambers's Jrnl.* July 511/2 Pull yourself together. You'll be going potty if you don't get a move on. **1925** *Punch* 7 Jan. 7 Hear about Mary, Mums? Gone potty! Broke off her engagement 'cos her people disapproved. **1929** W. Faulkner *Sartoris* III. 170 Aunt Sally, a potty little woman. **1930** 'R. Crompton' *William the Bad* iv. 113 'I don't know what you're talking about,' she said. 'You seem to me quite potty today.' **1942** *Sun* (Baltimore) 25 July 8/1 Confronted, in the final scene, with the prospect of winning and wedding this incurably potty creature, he lets out an anguished yawp. **1952** [see Baconian *a.* and *sb.* 2]. **1960** *Times* 21 Sept. 3/7, I realized Floss had put the boot in. I have been going potty about this. When I 'jumped' him we didn't mean to kill or hurt him. **1976** K. Bonfiglioli *Something Nasty in Woodshed* i. 19 Violet's mother . . is, I suppose, either potty or an alcoholic. **1977** *Daily Mirror* 12 Apr. 17/1 He played the joyously potty day-dreamer.

b. Madly in love; mad *about*, gone *on* (someone or something).

1923 E. V. Lucas *Advisory Ben* xxxix. 206 I'm potty about her. **1926** *Punch* 8 Dec. 622/3, I suppose you're potty about the poor fish? **1928** 'R. Crompton' *William—the Good* ix. 228 'Hector's potty on her too,' said Ginger. **1930** A. P. Herbert *Water Gipsies* xx. 292 Jane . . confessed to herself that she was mad about Mr. Bryan—just potty. **1975** *Reveille* 20 June 11/7 Women are potty about pans—they can't resist buying them.

Hence ˈ**pottily** *adv.*

1977 *Times Lit. Suppl.* 3 June 686/3 Contributors to anthologies can pursue minor themes more selectively, if occasionally pottily.

potty (ˈpɒtɪ), *sb.* Also **pottie.** [f. POT *sb.*[1] + -Y[6].] A nursery word for a chamber-pot; occas. applied also to a lavatory.

1942 Berrey & Van den Bark *Amer. Thes. Slang* §84/14 *Chamber pot*, . . potty. **1952** C. Hayes in S. Rogers *Children & Language* (1975) IV. 283 Don't flush the soap down the potty, dear. **1959** *Observer* 22 Mar. 21/5 Pram bedding, waterproof sheets, potties. **1960** S. Foot *Emergency Exit* ii. 20 Awful little bedside tables which . . have place for potty. **1960** *News Chron.* 20 Aug. 6/8 Granny soaking her corns and Baby . . shaking his pottie. **1966** Auden *About House* 26 Lifted off the potty, Infants from their mothers Hear their first impartial Words of worldly praise. **1976** *Milton Keynes Express* 4 June 22/3 (Advt.), White baby bath and potty, £1.25.

2. *attrib.* and *Comb.*, as **potty-chair**, a child's commode; **potty-mouth** *U.S.* (see quot. 1968–70); **potty-seat** = *potty-chair*; **potty-training** *vbl. sb.*, the training of a child to use a chamber-pot; also *fig.*; hence (as a back-formation) **potty-train** *v.*; **potty-trained** *ppl. a.*

1961 Webster, Potty-chair. **1965** M. Shadbolt *Among Cinders* ii. 11 The only thing I really saw was a little kid's potty-chair. **1977** *Time* 19 Sept. 41/3 The junk in his basement, including 'one used potty-chair, a tricycle with no handle bars, one broken ski, an old door-knob and six bags of leaves'. **1968–70** *Current Slang* (Univ. S. Dakota) III–IV. 95 *Potty mouth, n.* A person who repeatedly uses foul language. **1976** *Time* 10 May 79/2 Potentially even more annoying is the widespread abuse of the channels—especially by so-called potty mouths using obscenities. **1961** L. Mumford *City in Hist.* Note to plate 10, Full of objects that bring the daily life near, from a clay sausage-griddle to a ceramic potty-seat with holes for the child's legs. **1974** E. Tidyman *Dummy* xiv. 195 He did go to school for a while, but . . he wasn't potty trained at the time. **1978** F. Weldon *Praxis* xxii. 211 Justin was not, as they said in the nursery world, 'potty-trained'. **1958** R. Martin *Before the Baby—and After* xiii. 274 The number of modern young mothers who have erroneous views on 'potty' training is amazing. **1969** *New Scientist* 13 Mar. 31/1 There is no necessary link between outstanding cleanliness and tidiness and outstanding research work. Strict potty-training is not the key to the Royal Society. **1978** P. O'Donnell *Dragon's Claw* xii. 262, I expect you suffered from poor potty training as a baby.

pottyger, early variant of *potager*, POTTINGER[1].

†ˈ**potulent,** *a.* (*sb.*) *Obs.* [ad. L. *pōtulentus* (*pōc-*) drinkable, later also drunken, f. *pōtus* a drinking; cf. POCULENT.]

1. Fit to be drunk; potable, drinkable.

1656 Blount *Glossogr.*, *Potulent*, any thing that may be drunk. **1657** Tomlinson *Renou's Disp.* 161 Potulent decoctions . . are neither safe nor gratefull. **1684** tr. *Bonet's Merc. Compit.* VI. 179 Although they be troubled with thirst . . yet they can bear no sort of potulent matter. **1775** Ash, *Potulent* . . fit to drink.

2. Given to drink; drunken.

1656 Blount *Glossogr.*, *Potulent*, . . half drunk. **1708** *Brit. Apollo* No. 37. 3/1 And Leave this potulent Profession. **1730–6** Bailey (folio), *Potulent*, pretty much in drink. Hence **1755** in Johnson, **1775** in Ash, etc.

B. as *sb.* in *pl.* Drinkables.

1706 Baynard in Sir J. Floyer *Hot & Cold Bath.* II. 315 Their way of living in Esculents and Potulents.

So †**potuˈlental** *a.*, potable, drinkable.

1620 Venner *Via Recta* viii. 182 Vnto such, liquid and potulentall meats are not profitable.

ˌ**pot-ˈvaliant,** *a.* (*sb.*) [f. POT *sb.*[1] 2b + VALIANT.] Valiant or courageous through the influence of drink.

1641 Tatham *Distracted State* III. i, You are pot-valiant, sir, it seems. **1771** Smollett *Humph. Cl.* 29 May, Like a man who has drunk himself pot-valiant. **1845** Miall in *Nonconf.* V. 181 As pot-valiant as our friend Pistol.

b. as *sb.* A pot-valiant person.

1903 *Spectator* 31 Jan. 172 The so called Irish Brigade . . composed . . chiefly of Continental pot-valiants.

Hence **pot-'valiance**, **pot-'valiancy**, **pot-'valiantry** = POT-VALOUR; **pot-'valiantly** *adv.*, with courage induced by drunkenness.

1844 W. H. Maxwell *Sports & Adv. Scotl.* xxxiii. (1855) 264 Pot-valiantly, the militia-men determined to take the road. **1845** S. Judd *Margaret* III. (1881) 410 The old man is still mercurial; but his pot-valiantry is gone. **1876** G. Meredith *Beauch. Career* I. i. 8 His bursts of pot-valiancy ..are awful to his friends. **1884** W. E. Norris *Thirlby Hall* xxxii, He had worked himself up into a condition of pot-valiance.

ˌpot-'valour. [f. as prec. + VALOUR.] Valour or courage induced by drink; 'Dutch courage'.

1627 Feltham *Resolves* I. [II.] lxxxiii. 77 To see how Pot-valour thunders in a Tauerne, and appoints a Duell. *a* **1700** Dryden *Ovid's Art of Love* I. 664 Pot-valour only serves to fright the fair. **1857** Trollope *Three Clerks* ix, Who remembered, with all the energy of pot valor, that he was not a mere clerk.

So **pot-'valorous** *a.* = POT-VALIANT.

1837 Carlyle *Fr. Rev.* I. VII. ii, Suppose champagne flowing; with pot-valorous speech. **1872** C. Gibbon *For the King* xv, Hodge was already pot-valorous.

†**pot-'walfish.** *Obs.* [? ad. Ger. *pottwallfisch*; cf. obs. Du. *pots-wal-visch* 'Cete' (Kilian); see POT-FISH, WHALEFISH.] = POT-FISH.

1694 *Acc. Sev. Late Voy.* Introd. 23 The Trumpa Whale or Spouter, may perhaps be the Physeter, and the Sperma Ceti Whale the Pot-Walfish. **1730** S. Dale *Harwich* App. 413 The Parmacitty-Whale or Pot-Wall-fish.

potwaller ('pɒtˌwɒlə(r)). [f. POT *sb.*[1] + *waller*, agent-n. from WALL *v.*, OE. *weallan* to boil.]

lit. = *pot-boiler*, the boiler of a pot: the term applied in some English boroughs, before the Reform Act of 1832, to a man qualified for a parliamentary vote as a householder (i.e. tenant of a house or distinct part of one) as distinguished from one who was merely a member or inmate of a householder's family; the test of which was his having a separate fire-place, on which his own pot was boiled or food cooked for himself and his family.

According to 18th c. statements, the test was at times abused by persons not householders, who in anticipation of an election and of receiving money for their vote, boiled a pot in the presence of witnesses on an improvised fireplace in the open air within the borough, and thus passed as potwallers.

1701 *Jrnls. Ho. Comm.* 28 May XIII. 583 Borough of Honyton:..That the Right of Election was agreed to be in the pot-wallers, not receiving Alms. **1710** *Ibid.* XVI. 479/2 [Taunton] At an Election, 40 Years ago, the Potwallers were refused, and none but Scot and Lot Men voted then. *Ibid.*, Copies of Returns..in the Years 1661, 79, 80, 88, and 1705, were produced; and it was proved..that several of the Persons, who signed those Returns, were Potwallers. **1715** *Ibid.* 30 Aug., That the Right of Election of Burgesses to serve in Parliament for the Borough of Taunton, is in the Inhabitants within the same Borough, being Pot-wallers, and not receiving Alms or Charity. **1786** *Act 26 Geo. III*, c. 100 §1 An inhabitant householder, house-keeper, and potwaller legally settled. **1826** J. Savage *Manual Electors Taunton* 17 In the Contest which took place in 1774..it was agreed that a Potwaller is a person who furnishes his own diet, whether he be a Housekeeper or only a Lodger. *Ibid.* 18 To be a Potwaller, or Pot-boiler, or to boil a Pot, was only another mode of expressing that Thomas Johnson, or any other Voter, was a man so far independent of other persons as to be visibly able to maintain himself and family by his own labour and industry. **1835** Roscoe *Rep. Munic. Corpor. Comm.* I. 649 (Tregony) Settlement in the parish, and residence as a pot-waller constitute a Burgess. **1860** Bagehot *Unref. Parl.* 7 Inhabitants of the said town [Ilchester] paying scot and lot, which the town called pot-wallers. **1895** Besant *Westminster* ix. 256 The voting qualification..was..the tenant who paid scot and lot, and the potwaller.

b. Of this term there have been various popular alterations, of which POT-WALLOPER (see next) has attained greater notoriety than the original official term; also *α.* **pot-wabbler**, **pot-wobbler**; *β.* **pot-wallader** (? mispr. for *-walloper*).

α. **1789** S. Shaw *Tour W. Eng.* 337 It appears very singular..that the Members of Parliament [for Taunton] should be chosen by electors of so strange a qualification as the following, viz. all pot-wabblers, or those who dress their own victuals, are entitled to vote. **1811** *Lex. Balatronicum*, *Pot-wabblers*, persons entitled to vote for members of parliament in certain boroughs, from having boiled their pots therein. These boroughs are called pot-wabbling boroughs. **1817** Bentham *Parl. Reform* Introd. 109 Boroughs..in which the right has the extent marked by the word householders, or by the word pot-wobblers.

β. **1790** M. Dunsford *Hist. Mem. Tiverton* IV. 180, Anno 1603. The potwalladers elected two burgesses to represent the borough of Tiverton, in the first parliament of King James I: They were returned by the portreeve.

So **'pot-ˌwalling**, also 9 **pot-wabbling**, the boiling of a pot, the being a potwaller or householder: also *attrib.* or as *adj.*

1456 *Cal. Anc. Rec. Dublin* (1889) I. 291 A sertificat [of] continuall residence and abydyng and pot wallyng wythyn any of the cytteys or towyns. **1811** [see b. *α* above].

potwalloper (pɒt'wɒləpə(r)). Forms: *α.* 8 **pot-walloner, -iner.** *β.* 8– **pot(-)walloper,** 9 **-wallopper, -wolloper.** [One of the popular alterations of POTWALLER (after WALLOP *v.* to boil with agitation), which has in general use largely supplanted the original word.

It is found first in De Foe's *Tour*, ed. 1769, as an alteration of *pot-walloner*, the form in the earlier edd. 1725–53; whether as a misprint, or as an intended correction of an erroneous form, does not appear. Thence, prob., in Grose *Dict. Vulgar Tongue*, 1785. From these works app. this form became generally known, while other forms in local use disappeared.]

1. = POTWALLER.

α. **1725** De Foe *Tour Gt. Brit.* II. II. 21 This Town [Taunton] chooses Two Members of Parliament, and their way of choosing is by those whom they call Pot-Walloners [*so edd.* **1742**, **1753**; *ed.* **1769** Pot-Wallopers], that is to say, Every Inhabitant, whether Housekeeper or Lodger, that dresses their own Victuals. ? *a* **1749** Upton *MS. Addit. to Junius* (Halliw.), Tanodunii in agro Somersetensi vocantur Pot-walliners. **1778** *Eng. Gazetteer* (ed. 2) s.v. *Taunton*, The election of members of parliament here is very singular; every pot-walloner, *i.e.* that dresses his own victuals, is intitled to vote. **1791** W. Collinson *Hist. Somerset* III. 226 Taunton..has returned members to parliament from the years 1294, 23 Edw. I. The right of choosing these members is vested in the parishioners boiling their own pot (hence called Pot-Walloners) residing within the limits of the borough, not being stated paupers.

β. **1769** [see quot. 1725 in *α*]. **1785** Grose *Dict. Vulg. T.*, *Pot-wallopers*, persons entitled to vote in certain boroughs, by having boiled a pot there. **1791** Luckombe *Beauties Eng.* I. 58 Every pot-walloper, that is, he who dresses his own victuals, is entitled to vote for members of parliament. **1831** *Blackw. Mag.* XXX. 33 The pot-wallopers of Westminster, Southwark, and Preston, are to vote alongside of the £10 householders of the Tower Hamlets, Manchester, and Birmingham. **1850** Carlyle *Latter-d. Pamph.* vi. (1872) 206 What safety will there be in..ten thousand brawling potwallopers? **1884** *Manch. Exam.* 3 Dec. 4/7 We shall become a nation of potwallopers, with the addition that every lodger is supposed to wallop his own kettle as well as householders.

b. applied as a term of reproach.

1820 *Sporting Mag.* VII. 80 Do you take me for..a pot-walloper—an ass—a fool? **1905** *Westm. Gaz.* 6 Feb. 1/3 The term potwalloper was indignantly resented as a most improper and scandalous one, which should be withdrawn.

2. (See quots.)

1860 Bartlett *Dict. Amer.*, *Pot-Walloper*, a scullion. **1890** *Cent. Dict.*, *Pot-walloper*... (*b*) A cook aboard ship; a pot-wrestler. (Slang.) (*c*) A scullion. *Bartlett.* **1902** Farmer *Slang*, *Pot-walloper*..2. (common). A scullion; a kitchen-maid; and (nautical) a cook, esp. on board a whaler: also *pot-wrestler*.

¶ **3.** Erroneously applied to something very big or clumsy. (Cf. POT-WALLOPING *a.* 2.)

1896 *Daily News* 14 Dec. 6/1 Others were father's boots —you know the sort of thing—regular potwallopers—tens —in which the tiny foot is almost lost.

pot-'walloping, *sb. nonce-wd.* [f. POT *sb.*[1] + *walloping*: see WALLOP *v.*] The boiling of a pot; in quot. the sound produced by the boiler of an engine.

1849 De Quincey *Eng. Mail Coach* §1 Wks. 1862 IV. 303 The trumpet that once announced from afar the laurelled mail..has now given way for ever to the pot-wallopings of the boiler.

pot-'walloping, *a.* [f. as prec.]

1. Boiling a pot: applied to a voter who boiled his pot, or a borough in which the voters were potwallopers (see POTWALLER).

1791–3 *Spirit Pub. Jrnls.* (1799) I. 95 Has he any close and pot-wallopping boroughs, where no property is the qualification? **1824** *Hist. Gaming* 28 A special bargain..that his bill for garden stuff..should be paid off as the price of his pot-walluping vote. **1840** Alison *Hist. Europe* (1849–50) IX. lxiv. §55. 609 'England's pride and Westminster's glory', as he [Sir F. Burdett] was termed by his potwalloping constituents in that borough. **1893** Vizetelly *Glances Back* I. i. 7 Hunt managed to get elected..for the pot-walloping borough of Preston.

¶ **2.** *erron.* for *walloping* = making vigorous but unwieldy movements. (Cf. WALLOP *v.*)

1899 Crockett *Kit Kennedy* 161 Royal lumbered through the shallows like a great pot-walloping elephant.

pot-ware to **pot-wrestler:** see POT *sb.*[1] 14.

† **'potycaryar.** *Obs.* *rare*$^{-1}$. Extended form of *potycary*, POTHECARY: cf. *mediciner*, *practitioner*, *barrister*, etc.: see -ER[1]. (Cf. POTTER-CARRIER.)

c **1533** in Ellis *Orig. Lett.* Ser. III. II. 269, I was both a groser and a potycaryar.

potynger, obs. form of POTTINGER.

potzer, var. PATZER.

pou, Sc. and north. dial. form of PULL.

pou, see POU(W).

† **'pouant.** *Obs.* *rare*$^{-1}$. [app. a. F. *puant ppl. a.* stinking.] A foul smell, stink, stench.

1600 W. Watson *Decacordon* (1602) 29 It is one thing to smell of any corruption, and an other to be infected with a pouant, or stinke of the same.

pouar, -e, obs. Sc. forms of POWER.

pouce (paʊs, puːs). [a. F. *pousse* (dial. and commerc.) dust, in 14th c. *poulce*, a deriv. of L. *pulvis*, or a by-form **pulvus*, whence also Pr. *pols* dust, F. *poussière*.]

1. Flax-dust: so called by workers in flax-mills. Hence **'poucey**, **'poucy** *a.*, affected with disease of the throat or lungs caused by pouce.

1880 *Antrim & Down Gloss.*, *Pouce*, the floating dust in rooms where flax is being dressed. *Poucy*, asthmatic, from the effects of inhaling 'pouce'. **1884** *Quiver* Mar. 299/2 Hacklers' disease..is produced by a kind of 'pouce', which being inhaled causes severe tickling in the throat. **1889** *Brit. Med. Jrnl.* 30 Mar. 703/2 The name under which the dust is known among them is 'pouce', and those suffering from its effects are said to be 'poucey'.

2. *dial.* (spelt also **pous(e, powce, pows(e, peawse**). Dust, dirt, rubbish, refuse, in various applications. Also as *adj.* Rubbishy, good-for-nothing. See *Eng. Dial. Dict.*

pouce, obs. form of PULSE *sb.*[1]

† **'poucer, 'pouser.** *Obs. rare.* [ME. (?) or AF. *pousere*, *pousir* = F. *poucier* thumb-stall, f. *pouce* thumb + *-ier*, -IER. Misread (with *n* for *u*) by modern editors as *ponser*(*e*, *ponsir*, and entered in some dicts. as *pouncer*.] In the mediæval church in England, A small cap or thimble of gold or silver worn by a bishop on his right thumb after dipping it in consecrated oil; a bishop's thumb-stall.

See Rock *Ch. of Fathers* (1849) II. vi. 167, and Latin documents there quoted. Perhaps never used in English, exc. by Rock and in mod. Dicts.

pouch (paʊtʃ), *sb.* Also 4–6 **pouche, powche,** 5 **poche,** 5–8 **powch,** 6–7 (8 *Sc.*) **poutch,** 7 **pooch,** 8– *Sc.* **pootch.** [ME. *pouche*, a. ONF. *pouche* (13th c. in Littré: cf. mod. Norm. dial. *pouchet*, in Perche *pouchon* (Godef.)), parallel form of OF. *poche* bag, pouch: see POKE *sb.*[1]]

1. a. A bag, sack, or receptacle of small or moderate size, used for various purposes, esp. for carrying small articles; a pocket as a distinct receptacle worn outside the dress.

c **1386** Chaucer *Reeve's T.* 11 A ioly poppere baar he in his pouche. *c* **1420** *Pallad. on Husb.* IV. 408 The graynes ripe,.. Putte in a poche [L. *fiscella*] of palme, and with the wrynge Let presse hem. *c* **1440** *Promp. Parv.* 411/1 Powche, *marsupium*. *c* **1496** *Serm. Episc. Puer.* (W. de W.) b iij, Ther is no vanyte in no partye of the worlde but we ben redy to bye it... Euyll fasshened garmentes & deuyllysshe shoon and slyppers of frensmen, powches and paynted gyrdels of spaynardes. **1573–80** Baret *Alv.* P 606 A Pouch: a great bag, or satchell. **1663** Butler *Hud.* I. ii. 224 By his Side a Pouch he wore Replete with strange Hermetick Powder. **1733** Neal *Hist. Purit.* II. 234 Seven pictures of God the Father in form of a little old man in a blue and red coat with a pouch by his side. **1861** *Eng. Wom. Dom. Mag.* III. 119/1 The little Pouches..still continue to be worn, suspended from the waistband by a chain and hook, and sometimes by a cord.

b. *spec.* A small bag in which money is carried; a purse. Now chiefly *arch.* or *literary*.

c **1384** Chaucer *H. Fame* III. 259 Of whiche [gold] to litel al in my pouche is. **1483** *Cath. Angl.* 289/1 A Powche, *vbi* A purse. **1515** Barclay *Egloges* iii. (1570) C iij/2 These..dare I not playnly touche, For all these crosses and siluer in my pouche. **1598** Shaks. *Merry W.* I. iii. 96 Tester ile haue in pouch when thou shalt lacke. **1678** Butler *Hud.* III. ii. 1134 Could Catechise a Money-Box, And prove all Powches Orthodox. **1824** W. Irving *T. Trav.* I. 240 Nothing so melancholy as the meditations of a poor devil without penny in pouch. **1832** Ht. Martineau *Ella of Gar.* i. 14 Out comes the pouch, as sure as I show myself to gather the rent. **1871** R. Ellis *Catullus* xiii. 8 Know he boasts but a pouch of empty cobwebs.

c. A pocket in a garment. Chiefly *Sc.*

c **1610** Sir J. Melvil *Mem.* (1735) 9 He had always a New Testament in English in his Pouch. **1686** tr. *Chardin's Trav. Persia* 87 For fear of spoiling their Caps..in the Rain, they will put 'em in their Pouches, and go Bare-Headed. **1820** Combe *Consol.* II. (Chandos ed.) 153 From his pouch his sketch-book drew. **1889** Barrie *Window in Thrums* xix. 180 She saw 'im twa or three times put his hand in his pouch. **1901** *Scotsman* 12 Mar. 5/4 Standing about..'wi' naething in his pouches but his hauns'.

d. A leathern bag or case used by soldiers for carrying ammunition. Hence *transf.* a wooden cartridge-box.

1627 Capt. Smith *Seaman's Gram.* xii. 57 You must be carefull to cleare the decks with..fire-pots, poutches of powder. **1669** Sturmy *Mariner's Mag.* I. ii. 19 Their Bandaliers fill'd with Powder, and Shot in their Pooches. **1719** De Foe *Crusoe* I. 23 He brought a great Leather Pouch which held about a Pound and half of Powder,..and another with Shot. **1810** Wellington in Gurw. *Desp.* VI. 217 A letter..complaining of certain pouches lately sent out from England for the use of the Portuguese troops. **1853** Stocqueler *Mil. Encycl.*, *Pouch*, a case of strong leather, lined with tin divisions, for the purpose of carrying a soldier's ammunition.

e. A mail-bag (also *mail-pouch*: see MAIL *sb.*[3] 4 b), esp. a smaller bag enclosed in another; also, a letter-carrier's bag.

1879 *Post Master General's Rep.* in *Parl. Papers 1878–9* (C. 2405) XXI. 197 The..number of pouches exchanged with these Travelling Post Offices..in 24 hours is now 1090. **1889** *Century Mag.* XXXVIII. 606/2 At 3 o'clock A.M. the European mails closed, and the pouches put on board the *Aller* carried the usual copies for the foreign circulation.

f. = *diplomatic bag* s.v. DIPLOMATIC *a.* and *sb.* A. 3.

1958 L. Durrell *Mountolive* vi. 140 When the Syrians want to be clever, they don't use a diplomatic courier; they confide their pouch to a lady, the vice-consul's niece. **1967** M. CHILDS *Taint of Innocence* iv. 240 He put the locked briefcase on Wyant's desk. 'Watrous said he thought you wouldn't mind sending it back to him by pouch.' **1968** D. TORR *Treason Line* 163 I've been down here for the past hour checking the airgrams for the Washington pouch. **1974** *Lebende Sprachen* XIX. 39/2 US *pouch*—BE/US *diplomatic bag*. Kuriersack, -tasche.

2. *Naut.* One of a number of divisions made by small bulkheads or partitions in a ship's hold, for stowing corn or other loose cargo.

1627 CAPT. SMITH *Seaman's Gram.* vii. 33 The Ballast will sometimes shoot, that is run from one side to another, and so will Corne and Salt, if you make not Pouches or Bulkheads. **1704** J. HARRIS *Lex. Techn.* I, *Powches*, so the Seamen call small Bulkheads made in the Hold of a Ship, to stow Corn, Goods, or the like, that it do not shoot from one side to the other.

3. Applied to a natural receptacle resembling a bag or pocket. **a.** *Anat.*, *Zool.*, *Path.* A cavity in an animal body, like a bag (usually small, and either permanent or temporary); a sac, cyst. *spec.* †(*a*) the stomach of a fish: = POKE *sb.*[1] 6 (*obs.*); (*b*) the distensible gular sac beneath the bill in certain birds, as the pelican and cormorant; (*c*) a dilatation of the cheeks in certain mammals, a cheek-pouch; (*d*) the receptacle in which marsupial mammals carry their undeveloped young; the marsupium.

c **1450** *Two Cookery-bks.* 101 Pike boyled... Slyt the pouuche, And kepe the fey or the lyuer, and kutte awey the gall. **1622** R. HAWKINS *Voy. S. Sea* (1847) 68 [The shark] is the most ravenous fish knowne in the sea... In the puch of them hath beene found hatts, cappes, shoes, shirts, leggs and armes of men. **1739** S. SHARP *Surg.* xxxvi. 205 The Spot of the Vessel.. where the Disease begins, generally recedes in such a manner from the Surface of the Artery by the force of the Blood.. pushing it outwards, as to form a large Pouch or Cyst. **1774** GOLDSM. *Nat. Hist.* (1776) V. 197 This is a pouch, the entrance of which lies immediately under the tongue, and capable of holding near seven quarts of water. **1797** M. BAILLIE *Morb. Anat.* (1807) 302 These pouches are often large enough to admit the end of the finger, and contain occasionally small calculi. **1802** BINGLEY *Anim. Biog.* (1813) I. 67 *note*, The face of this Ape is shaped somewhat like that of a Dog. The cheeks are furnished with pouches. **1834** McMURTRIE *Cuvier's Anim. Kingd.* 299 Isopoda. The females carry their ova under the second and third segments of the body, in a pouch formed of approximated scales. **1856** HUXLEY in *Q. Jrnl. Microscop. Sc.* IV. 192 The ovum passes.. into the ovicell—there as in a marsupial pouch, to undergo its further development. **1888** ROLLESTON & JACKSON *Anim. Life* 435 The respiratory system consists of gill-pouches or sacs, seven on each side in the Lampreys.

b. *Bot.* A bag-like cavity, sac, or cyst, in a plant; *spec.* a seed-vessel resembling a bag or purse, a short or rounded pod, a silicle.

1577 B. GOOGE *Heresbach's Husb.* IV. (1586) 191 b, It creepeth low by the ground,.. with a seede inclosed in little powches, like a shepheardes purse. **1776** WITHERING *Brit. Plants* (1796) III. 48 Isatis. Pouch deciduous. **1861** MISS PRATT *Flower. Pl.* I. 9 The silicle or pouch is a shorter, broader pod [than the silique]. **1862** DARWIN *Fertil. Orchids* ii. 69 As soon as the disc is drawn out of the pouch the movement of depression commences.

c. = BAG *sb.* 12 c.

1928 J. BUCHAN *Runagates Club* iv. 134 There were dark pouches under his eyes. *a* **1953** E. O'NEILL *Hughie* (1959) 8 His blue eyes have drooping lids and puffy pouches under them. **1980** P. HARCOURT *Tomorrow's Treason* I. ii. 37 Pouches under his eyes as if he hadn't slept.

†**4.** Name of some game. *Obs.*

1600 NASHE *Summers Last Will* 2048 Thou and I will play at poutch, to morrow morning for a breakfast.

5. [f. POUCH *v.* 4.] A present of money, a 'tip'. *slang* or *colloq.*

1880 DISRAELI *Endym.* III. iii. 25 Your grandfather.. pouched me at Harrow, and it was the largest pouch I ever had.

6. *attrib.* and *Comb.*, as ***pouch-belt***, ***-lid***; formed into or having a pouch-like or baggy shape, as ***pouch shirt***, ***waist***, etc.; ***pouch-like***, ***-shaped*** adjs.; **pouch-bone**, a marsupial bone (in marsupials and monotremes); **pouch-gill**, (*a*) the pouch-like gill of the *Marsipobranchii* or *Cyclostomi*; (*b*) a fish having pouch-like gills, as a lamprey; **pouch-gilled** *a.*, having pouch-like gills, marsipobranchiate; **pouch-hook** (*U.S.*), a hook on which a mail-bag is hung; **pouch-mouse**, a rodent having cheek-pouches, a POCKET-*mouse*; **pouch-toad**, a toad of the genus *Nototrema*, in which the eggs are hatched in a pouch or hole in the back of the mother. See also POUCH-MAKER, etc.

1812 *Sporting Mag.* XXXIX. 167 Cavalry uniform, a *pouch belt, and a sabre-tache. **1541** R. COPLAND *Guydon's Quest. Chirurg.* L iij, As ye wolde fasten a nedle with threde on your bosome or *pouche lid. **1835–6** *Todd's Cycl. Anat.* I. 572/2 Two prolongations.. of a *pouch-like form. **1895** S. S. BUCKMAN in *Pop. Sci. Monthly* Jan. 374 The pouchlike cheeks of a baby. **1861** J. R. GREENE *Man. Anim. Kingd.* II. *Cœlent.* 117 *Pouch-shaped processes. **1898** *St. James' Gaz.* 12 Jan. 12/1 The *pouch shirt is the last new make. **1897** *Daily News* 6 July 8/4 The modified edition of the *pouch waist as adopted by most of the Englishwomen who venture on that style.

pouch (paʊtʃ), *v.* [f. POUCH *sb.*; cf. POACH *v.*[1]]

1. *trans.* **a.** To put into or enclose in a pouch; usually, to put into one's pocket, to pocket; also *fig.* or in extended sense, to take possession of, to 'bag'.

a **1566** R. EDWARDES *Damon & Pithias* (1571) C iv, Ch a [= I've] poucht them vp all ready, they are sure in hold. **1686** F. SPENCE tr. *Varillas' Ho. Medicis* 12 He had already pouched the half ring. *a* **1774** FERGUSSON *Election* Poems (1845) 42 They pouch the gowd, nor fash the town For weights and scales to weigh them. **1832** HT. MARTINEAU *Ella of Gar.* iii. 38 He twisted their necks.. and pouched them in his plaid. **1840** MRS. F. TROLLOPE *Widow Married* ii, A pretty sum you must have pouched last night. **1890** *Sci. Amer.* 25 Jan. 55/3 They [letters] have next to be 'pouched'.. The packages of letters are thrown dexterously into the proper compartments.

b. *fig.* To 'pocket', put up with.

1819 SCOTT *Ivanhoe* xxxiii, I will pouch up no such affront before my parishioners.

c. *Cricket.* To catch (the ball); also with the batsman as object.

1910 A. A. MILNE *Day's Play* 114, I heard Slip call 'Mine' and he pouched the ball. **1963** *Times* 13 June 13/3 A series of pulls which ended with a catch at the wicket would appear in this form: 'After several cow-shots into the Great Beyond, Basher was neatly pouched by the timber-watcher.' **1970** *Times* 12 Jan. 7/7 Neither catch that Fletcher dropped was at all easy, but.. Bobby Simpson or Philip Sharpe might well have pouched them both.

2. To take into the stomach, to swallow: said of fishes (cf. prec. 3 a (*a*)), and of certain birds; also, to take into a pouch in the mouth or gullet.

1653 WALTON *Angler* vii. 154 The Pike.. will have line enough to go to his hold and powch the bait. **1774** WHITE in *Phil. Trans.* LXV. 267 Swifts when.. shot.. discover a little lump of insects in their mouths, which they pouch and hold under their tongue. **1787** BEST *Angling* (ed. 2) 13 First allowing the fish, by a little slackening the line a small time to pouch the bait. **1873** G. C. DAVIES *Mount. & Mere* xxiii. 201 He refused to pouch it.

†**3.** To swell out or protrude (the lips) into a pouch-like form; to purse the lips; to pout. *rare.*

1647 R. STAPLYTON *Juvenal* xiv. 266 If this make thee frown, And pouch thy lips out. [Cf. **1680** in *pouching* vbl. sb. below.] **1754** RICHARDSON *Grandison* (1810) V. x. 53 He pouched his mouth, and reared himself up and swelled; but answered me not.

4. [f. prec. 1 b or c.] To supply the purse or pocket of; to give a present of money to; to 'tip'. (With the person or the money as obj., or with double obj.) *slang* or *colloq.*

1810 in Dowden *Shelley* (1886) I. ii. 53 [To him [Ed. Graham] Shelley wrote.. April 1 [1810], requesting him].. to pouch those venal villains, the reviewers. **1842** W. CORY *Lett. & Jrnls.* (1897) 5, I shall not have to pouch Hawtrey or my Tutor. **1845** J. T. SMITH *Bk. for Rainy Day* 66 Charles Townley, Esq... pouched me half a guinea to purchase paper and chalk. **1864** HEMYNG *Eton School Days* i. 4 'Did your governor "pouch" you?' asked Purefoy, as they were going towards the Station. **1880** [see POUCH *sb.* 5].

5. *Dressmaking.* **a.** To make or arrange (a part of dress) so as to hang loosely in a pouch-like form. **b.** *intr.* said of the dress.

1897 *Daily News* 6 July 8/4 The muslin is lightly pouched over the belt. **1902** *Daily Tel.* 2 Aug. 3/3 The bodice is cut .. tightly fitting at the back and sides and below the waist, yet pouching over in the front.

6. *intr.* To form a pouch or pouch-like cavity. (See 5 b, and *pouching* vbl. sb.)

Hence (chiefly in sense 6) '**pouching** *vbl. sb.* (also quasi-*concr.*) and *ppl. a.*

1680 BUNYAN *Badman* Wks. (ed. Virtue) 450 He would stand gloating, and hanging down his head in a sullen, pouching manner. **1698** TYSON in *Phil. Trans.* XX. 130 The pouching or bagging out at both Extreams. **1847–9** *Todd's Cycl. Anat.* IV. 791/1 Dilations or pouchings can nowhere be seen. **1849–52** *Ibid.* V. 847/1 The great omentum is a pouching out of the meso-gastrium. **1899** *Westm. Gaz.* 16 Feb. 3/2 The balloon sleeve and the pouching bodice were all too kind to the careless.

pouched (paʊtʃt), *a.* [f. POUCH + -ED.]

1. Furnished with or having a pouch or pouches. **a.** *Zool.* (*a*) Having a gular pouch, as certain birds; (*b*) having cheek-pouches, as certain rodents, etc.; (*c*) having a pouch in which the undeveloped young are carried, marsupial: see sense 4. **b.** *Anat.* and *Path.* Having or forming pouches, cavities, or dilatations. **c.** *Dressmaking.* (See POUCH *v.* 5.)

1834 *Cuvier's Anim. Kingd.* I. 337 The Pouched Storks.. which have an appendage under the middle of the throat, resembling a thick sausage. **1849** *Sk. Nat. Hist., Mammalia* IV. 96 The Camas pouched rat is common in N. America, on the banks of the Columbia river. **1863** LYELL *Antiq. Man* xx. 401 Peopled exclusively with pouched quadrupeds. **1897** *Westm. Gaz.* 8 July 3/2 Make a simple pouched bodice of mauve and white foulard. **1899** *Allbutt's Syst. Med.* VIII. 825 The vessels are generally thin-walled, pouched and varicose.

2. [f. POUCH *v.* 1.] Put or enclosed in a pouch.

1905 *Westm. Gaz.* 12 Dec. 3/1 Home-sick Kaffirs.. trail along in Indian file with the pouched wages which are to buy wives and cattle.

3. *Comb.*, as ***pouched-lipped*** adj. (cf. POUCH *v.* 3).

1821 CLARE *Vill. Minstr.* I. 137 Where the pouch'd-lipp'd cuckoo-bud From its snug retreat was torn.

4. ***pouched mouse***, a small Australian marsupial resembling a mouse, belonging to the family Dasyuridæ, esp. the genera *Antechinus* and *Sminthopsis*; also called kangaroo-mouse.

1888 O. THOMAS *Catal. Marsupialia in Brit. Mus.* 287 Little Pouched Mouse. Size rather small, general form murine. **1896** F. G. AFLALO *Sk. Nat. Hist. Austral.* II. 28 In some of the pouched mice, the tribal badge is either replaced by a mere fold of bristles or else entirely wanting. **1907** P. FOUNTAIN *Rambles Austral. Naturalist* vi. 60 The pouched-mouse varies its habits with its locality. **1942** C. BARRETT *On Wallaby* iii. 40 There are perhaps a dozen kinds of pouched-mice, all Australian natives. **1970** W. D. L. RIDE *Guide Native Mammals Austral.* viii. 112 Kowari, Byrne's Pouched Mouse, *Dasyuroides byrnei*. Central Australia..; desert associations and grass-lands.

†'**poucher.** *Obs.* [f. POUCH *sb.* + -ER[1]: cf. *hatter*, etc.] = POUCH-MAKER.

1401 *Pol. Poems* (Rolls) II. 109 So carpenters ne sowters, card-makers ne powchers,.. this sacrament mowe treten.

pouchful ('paʊtʃfʊl). [f. POUCH *sb.* + -FUL.] As much as a pouch will hold.

1725 RAMSAY *Gentle Sheph.* III. iv, He buys some books.. And carries ay a pouchfu' to the hill.

'**pouchless,** *a. rare.* [f. POUCH *sb.* + -LESS.] Not having a pouch; in quot., not marsupial.

1888 *Pop. Sci. Monthly* Sept. 687 To be improved off the face of the earth by the keen competition of the pouchless mammals.

†'**pouch-maker.** *Obs.* [f. POUCH *sb.* + MAKER.] A maker of pouches or bags.

1362 in *Cal. Let. Bk. G. Lond.* 151 William de Thyndone, pouchemakere. **1415** in *York Myst.* Introd. 22 Pouche-makers, Botellers, Capmakers. **1533** MORE *Apol.* xxv. Wks. 890/1 In London here Bayfelde the monke, and Teurberye the powchemaker, and Baynam.

†'**pouch-mouth,** *a.* and *sb. Obs.* [f. POUCH *sb.* + MOUTH *sb.*; cf. POUCH *v.* 3.] **a.** *adj.* Having a mouth like a pouch, i.e. with thick or protruding lips; in quot. 1575 said of a word (cf. *jaw-breaking*). **b.** *sb.* A person, or a mouth, with protruding lips. So '**pouch-mouthed** *a.* = a.

1565 *Darius* (1860) 37 Thou pouchmouth knaue! Thou shalt strypes haue. *c* **1570** PRESTON *Cambyses* in Hazl. *Dodsley* IV. 179 Now, goodman pouchmouth, I am a slave with you! ? *c* **1570** in Nichols *Topographer* II. 400 A statue of a pouchemouthed squier. **1575** G. HARVEY *Letter-bk.* (Camden) 93 When I first heard that same terrible powche-mouthe and.. owtelandish worde. **1611** COTGR., *Morre*, a powch-mouth; a mouth garded with great, out-standing, or slowching lips. **1863** KIRK *Chas. Bold* II. 192 From his Polish mother, Cimburga the 'pouch-mouthed', he had inherited the large protruding under-jaw which, transmitted to his descendants, is still designated as 'the Austrian lip'.

†'**pouch-penny.** *Obs. rare*[−1]. [f. POUCH *v.* + PENNY *sb.*] One who pockets every penny; an avaricious person.

1629 GAULE *Holy Madn.* 321 Is it you (and be naught) old Pouch-penny?

†'**pouch-ring.** *Obs.* [f. POUCH *sb.* + RING *sb.*] A ring for closing a pouch or purse.

1507 *Will of Unde* (Somerset Ho.), Vnum par de powcherynges de Argento. **1584** R. W. *Three Ladies Lond.* I. D iv, Haue you any.. Powch-ringes or Buskins, to cope for new broome? *a* **1700** *Songs Lond. Prentices* (Percy Soc.) 153 Broomes for old shooes, pouch-rings, bootes and buskings! Will yee buy any new broome?

pouchy ('paʊtʃɪ), *a.* [f. POUCH *sb.* + -Y.] Having pouches; of the nature of a pouch; baggy.

1828 J. WILSON in *Blackw. Mag.* XXIV. 679 The mutterings.. have died away like so much croaking in the pouchy throats of drought-dried frogs. **1884** BURROUGHS *Pepacton* 217 Such a flaccid.. pouchy carcass, I have never before seen.

†**pouck,** obs. form of POKE *sb.*[4] 2.

1763 LINDO in *Phil. Trans.* LIII. 238 A weed called Pouck, represented to me as of a poisonous quality [in S. Carolina].

pouclesnedele: see PUCKLE *sb.*[1], PUCK-NEEDLE.

poucy: see POUCE 1.

poud, variant of POOD, Russian weight.

poudagre, variant of PODAGRE *Obs.*, gout.

pouder, -ir, -re, -ur, etc., obs. ff. POWDER.

poudesoy, obs. f. PADUASOY: see also POULT-DE-SOIE.

poudre (pu:dr). *Canad.* [Fr. *poudre* powder.] Light, powdery snow, = POWDER SNOW. ***poudre day***, a day on which light, fine snow falls.

1791 E. P. SIMCOE *Diary* 31 Dec. (1911) 71 There is little wind here, except with a snowstorm of fine snow. The French call it poudre or powdered snow, and to travel with that blowing in one's face is very disagreeable. **1873** W. F. BUTLER *Wild North Land* xiv. 152 The sun, which on one of these 'poudre' days in the North seems to exert as much influence upon the war of cold and storm as some good bishop in the Middle Ages was wont to exercise over the belligerents at Cressy or Poictiers.. muffled himself up in the nearest cloud and went fast asleep until the fight was over. **1901** G. PARKER *Right of Way* 83 It was a goodly scene .. the flowery tracery of frost hanging like cobwebs everywhere; the poudre sparkle in the air. **1951** W. O'MEARA *Grand Portage* xxxiii. 214 It was a real 'poudre day'. Only a few inches of dry, fine snow lay on the prairie.

‖**poudré** (pudre), *a.* Fem. poudrée. [Fr.] Powdered, *spec.* of the hair or a wig.

1827 DISRAELI *Viv. Grey* III. v. vi. 104 A little old, odd-looking man, with a very *poudré* head, and dressed in a costume in which the glories of the vieille cour seemed to retire with reluctance. **1852** E. RUSKIN *Let.* 24 Feb. in M. Lutyens *Effie in Venice* (1965) II. 278 Marmont poudré welcomed me. **1906** BEERBOHM *Around Theatres* (1924) II. 243 Poudrée, she sings of Brittany; and in a crinoline she warbles of Parthenay. **1909** A. LANCASTRE SALDANHA *Recoll.* iv. 34 My hair was exquisitely *poudré*.

poudre marchant: see POWDER *sb.*

‖**poudrette** (pudrɛt). [Fr. dim. of *poudre* POWDER: see -ETTE.] A manure made from nightsoil dried and mixed with charcoal, gypsum, etc.

1840 J. BUEL *Farmer's Comp.* 72 Poudrette is the contents of privies, dried, and rendered.. inodorous and inoffensive, by chemical processes. **1869** E. A. PARKES *Pract. Hygiene* (ed. 3) 113 When the poudrette is decomposing..serious consequences may certainly result.

‖**poudreuse** (pudrœz). [Fr.] A lady's dressing table of a kind made in France in the time of Louis XV (see quot. 1966).

1929 V. WOOLF *Let.* 5 May (1978) IV. 54 There are two pieces of furniture I must buy, so do mark them down—one a poudreuse, not necessarily in good condition. **1929** G. G. GOULD *Period Furnit. Handbk.* vi. 82 *Toilette-coiffeuse*, especially for powdering, new in *Régence*; later popular as *poudreuse*. **1936** *Burlington Mag.* Aug. 88/2 *Berceuses* or *poudreuses* show the delicate outlines of the curved ornament of the French cabinet-makers. **1947** *Antique Dealer* Jan. 34 (*caption*) Louis XV Poudreuse by E. J. Gibrekyer. **1959** *House & Garden* Dec.–Jan. 27/1 The so-called *poudreuse* (dreadful word) with twin adjustable mirrors and pivoting cosmetic trays. **1960** *Times* 21 June 22/7 A Louis XV marquetry poudreuse. **1966** M. M. PEGLER *Dict. Interior Design* (1967) 351 *Poudreuse*, a lady's powder or toilet table, often equipped with a mirrored lid in the center which lifts up. A Louis XV period innovation. **1973** *Country Life* 13 Dec. 32f (Advt.), An early 19th century Austrian mahogany poudreuse.

†**pou'dreye**. *Obs. rare.* Also poudré. [A derivative of *poudre*, POWDER: cf. OF. *poudroy* dust.]

13.. *K. Alis.* 2180 (Bodl. MS.) Ne þe sonne ne had ben yseye For þe dust & þe poudreye [*Weber*, poudré].

pouer(e, obs. forms of POOR, POWER.

pouerd, -ert(e, etc., obs. forms of POVERTY.

‖**pouf**[1] (pu:f). Also pouff(e. [F. *pouf*; cf. PUFF *sb.*]

1. a. A kind of elaborate female head-dress fashionable late in the 18th century. **b.** A high roll or pad of hair worn by women. Also *attrib.*

1817 MAR. EDGEWORTH *Harrington* xiii, [Describing the mode of hair-dressing *c* 1780] At the top of the mount of hair and horsehair.., there was sometimes a fly-cap, or a wing-cap, or a *pouf*. **1893** GEORGIANA HILL *Hist. Eng. Dress* II. 231 In 1825 the hair was arranged in high poufs drawn to the left side. **1902** *Westm. Gaz.* 2 Jan. 3/2 It is still the wreath of little green leaves that is most popular for wearing in the hair. These are worn now just cresting the *pouf* of the hair. **1905** *Ibid.* 9 Mar. 8/2 It must mean the elevation by pouf and curl and twist and twirl of the coiffure.

2. *Dressmaking.* A part of a dress gathered up in a projection or bunch. Also *attrib.*

1869 *Latest News* 3 Oct. 5 The enormous pouffs from the waist behind.. will be abandoned with but little regret. **1874** *Echo* 30 Dec., At the back the pouff is replaced by the skirt being closely drawn together a little distance below the waist. **1884** *Bazaar* 19 Dec. 658/1 The space being filled up by an airy little pouf of tulle. **1906** *Queen* 28 Apr. p. viii/3 A quaint pouf sleeve. **1976** *State Jrnl.* (Lansing, Mich.) 11 July D 1/6 Designed with deep *pouf* sleeves. **1977** *New Yorker* 11 July 84/3 Noelle demonstrates her virginal contempt by choosing a white strapless evening dress with a pouf of fabric.

3. A very soft stuffed ottoman or couch; now usu. a low stuffed or padded seat or cushion.

1884 *Girl's Own Paper* Feb. 211/3 A very usual seat in a drawing-room now is a Moorish or oriental *pouf*. **1894** WILKINS & VIVIAN *Green Bay Tree* I. 130 Seating himself on a low pouffe at her feet. **1919** 'C. DANE' *Legend* 32 Mrs Howe was in the chair... The Baxter girl crouched on the pouf. **1925** C. S. TAYLOR *Pract. Upholstery* xi. 96 The pouffe, or floor cushion, is much in favour. **1949** A. CHRISTIE *Crooked Horse* xiv. 106 Roger was astride a big pouffé [*sic*] by the fire-place. **1956** M. SHULMAN in *Good Housekeeping* July 51/2 You rented an apartment in Greenwich village and sat on a pouf. **1962** A. SAMPSON *Anat. Brit.* I. i. 22 Between the two sides is something which looks like a huge red pouff, with a back-rest in the middle of it: this is 'the Woolsack'. **1968** C. M. VINES *Little Nut-Brown Man* iii. 58 He held out the cutting towards me, down to where I was sitting on the pouffe, his thumbnail indicating a line of it. **1974** S. COULTER *Château* II. vi. 281 This little room.. stuffed with Algerian poufs and cushions and ottomans.

Hence **poufed** (pu:ft) *a.*, decorated with a pouf; dressed, as hair, in the form of a pouf.

1905 *Daily Chron.* 17 Apr. 8/4 This collar extends just over the poufed sleeves and the fulness of the square-cut corsage. **1906** *P.T.O.* I. 44/1 There is something to be said, also, against hair too much 'poufed' out, hats poised at too acute an angle.

pouf[2], var. POOF *sb.*[1]

pouf(f, poufter, varr. POOF *int.*, *sb.*[2] and *v.*, POOFTER.

pouff, pouffe, obs. forms of PUFF *sb.* and *v.*

†**pouffe.** *Obs. rare*$^{-1}$. ? A mattress; a bag, or bunch.

1583 FOXE *A. & M.* 1268/1 Hee lay harde vppon a pouffe of straw: course newe canuesse Sheetes.

†**pough**, *sb. Obs.* Forms: 1 **pohha, poha, pohcha, (pocca)**, 4 **powȝe, powhe, (pouge), pouhȝ**, 5–7 **poghe**, 6 **powghe**, 7 **pough.** [OE. *pohha*, app. with no exact equivalent in the cognate langs., but from the OTeut. ablaut stem *puh(h)-*, *pug(g)-* to swell up, blow, whence also EFris. *puche* a boil, MLG. *puchen*, *puggen*, LG. *puchen*, *pughen*, MDu., MFlem. *pochen*, *poghen*, Du. (G.) *pochen* to boast; also MDu. *pōghen*, Du. *pogen* to endeavour, lit. to pant from exertion. Radical connexion with POCK, POKE *sb.*[1] is uncertain.] A bag.

c **897** K. ÆLFRED *Gregory's Past. C.* xlv. 342 He legeð hie on ðyrelne pohhan [*v.r.* pohchan]. *c* **950** *Lindisf. Gosp.* Mark vi. 8 Ne poha [*Rushw.* pohha] *vel* posa ne hlaf. —— Luke ix. 3 Ne pocca [*Rushw.* pohha] *vel* posa. **1362** LANGL. *P. Pl.* A. VIII. 178 A powhe [**1377** B. VII. 191 poke, *v.r.* pouhȝ] ful of pardoun. **1388** *Pol. Poems* (Rolls) I. 276, I wolde ful were here pouge [? pouȝe] *tanti dulcedine roris*! *c* **1394** *P. Pl. Crede* 618 Þei may trussen her part in a terre powȝe! **1398** TREVISA *Barth. De P.R.* XIII. xxix. (Tollem. MS.), A fische.. when he knoweþ þat he is entrid and is within þe fischeres pouge. *c* **1450** *Douce MS.* 52 lf. 27 b, When me profereth þe pigge opon þe poghe. **1688** R. HOLME *Armoury* III. 336/1 A Sack, or Pough of Corn tyed up... It is termed a Sack when it contains about 4, 5, or 6 Measures of Corn; a Pough when it holds 1, 2, or 3.

b. A swelling of the skin.

1601 HOLLAND *Pliny* II. XXXVII. iii. 706 The people.. are subject to poghes under their throat... [Margin] This disease is called *Bronchocele* or *Hernia gutturis*.

†**pough**, *v. Obs. rare.* Forms: 1 (*pa. pple.*) **pohhed**, 4 **powȝe, pouhe, pouwe, powe**, 5 **powȝ.** [f. prec. sb.] *intr.* Of a garment: To hang loose, bag out.

c **1100** *Rule St. Benet* (Schröer 1885) 136 (MS. F.) Hy.. habbaþ side earmellan and pohhede hosa. **1297** R. GLOUC. (Rolls) 6394 Þe tailors corue so moni peces uor is robe ne ssolde powȝe [*v.rr.* powe, pouwe, pouhe, powȝ, poke].

pough, obs. form of POH *int.*

poughite ('pəʊaɪt). *Min.* [f. the name of Frederick H. *Pough* (b. 1906), U.S. mineralogist + -ITE[1].] An iron tellurite, $Fe_2(TeO_3)_2(SO_4)\cdot 3H_2O$, found as yellow orthorhombic crystals.

1968 R. V. GAINES in *Amer. Mineralogist* LIII. 1075 In 1944.. Frondel and Pough mentioned a further new iron tellurite from Honduras... This mineral had first been observed by Dana and Wells in 1890 and thought to be tellurite... Its macroscopic definition [etc.].. enabled the author to establish its identity with material found at the Moctezuma mine in Sonora, Mexico. The name poughite is proposed for this new mineral. **1968** I. KOSTOV *Mineral.* 518 Poughite is orthorhombic.. with perfect 010 cleavage.

poui ('pu:ɪ). Also pui. [Local name in Trinidad.] A tree belonging to the genus *Tabebuia*, of the family Bignoniaceæ, esp. *T. rosea*, the pink poui, and *T. serratifolia*, the yellow poui, native to the West Indies and Central America, and bearing terminal clusters of trumpet-shaped flowers; also, the wood of this tree.

1864 A. H. R. GRISEBACH *Flora Brit. W. Indian Islands* 787 *Tecoma serratifolia* Pony [*sic*]. **1924** RECORD & MELL *Timbers Trop. Amer.* II. 541 The 'pui' or 'poui'.. is one of the best known timbers of Trinidad. **1939** R. C. MARSHALL *Silviculture of Trees of Trinidad & Tobago* 182 One frequently comes across patches of young poui in the forest. **1952** S. SELVON *Brighter Sun* i. 5 In April.. pouis blossomed and keskidees sang for rain. **1962** *Times* 31 Aug. (Trinidad Suppl.) p. iv/4 The visitor will see some of the most lovely flowering trees and shrubs in the world—the bougainvillaea, the clear clean beauty of the yellow and pink poui. **1968** E. LOVELACE *Schoolmaster* I. i. 7 The poui is dropping rich yellow flowers. **1973** E. G. B. GOODING *Wayside Trees & Shrubs of Barbados* 94 The Yellow Poui was introduced into Barbados early this century.

Pouilly (puiji). Also with small initial. Any of various dry white wines produced in central France and named after villages called *Pouilly*, *spec.* (*a*) in full ***Pouilly Fumé*** (fyme), that produced near Pouilly-sur-Loire in the Nièvre department; (*b*) in full ***Pouilly-Fuissé*** (fwise), a white Burgundy produced near Pouilly-sous-Charlieu in the Mâcon region of the Loire department.

[**1814** M. BIRKBECK *Notes Journey through France* I. 29 Pouilly, [renowned] for its Vin Blanc.] **1833** C. REDDING *Hist. Mod. Wines* v. 160 Cosne is best known for its white wines called Pouilly, in considerable repute in Paris. **1924** D. H. LAWRENCE *Let.* 29 Oct. (1962) II. 816 Dinner at Coyoacán, and drank absinthe, gin, pouilly, chablis, beaune, port and whisky from beginning to end of an evening, and was not comforted. **1927** [see MOULIN-À-VENT]. **1935** M. MORPHY *Recipes of All Nations* 104 The Pouilly comes from Saône-et-Loire: it is usually sold as Pouilly-Fuissé to differentiate it from the white wines of Pouilly-sur-Loire, sold as Pouilly-Fumé. **1942** E. PAUL *Narrow St.* i. 4 Noël pointed out to me once, over a bottle of Pouilly, that men and women, like gods, choose pets in their own image. **1952** W. PLOMER *Museum Pieces* 117 A cut of salmon, some wisps of chicken, a bottle of Pouilly. **1959** E. LINKLATER *Merry Muse* iv. 81 The fish and the Pouilly fumé were succeeded by a bevy of partridges and a tenderly decanted Léoville Poyferré of 1947. **1976** *Times* 20 Mar. 3/3 (Advt.), Mâcon Blanc, a dry, very fruity wine, typified by Pouilly-Fuissé and St. Véran.

Poujadism ('pu:ʒɑ:dɪz(ə)m). Also with lower-case initial. [ad. Fr. *Poujadisme* (also used): see below.] The mainly reactionary and conservative political philosophy and methods advocated by Pierre *Poujade* (b. 1920), French publisher and bookseller, who in 1954 founded a movement for the protection of artisans and small shopkeepers (Union de Défense des Commerçants et Artisans), protesting chiefly against the French tax system then in force. Also in extended and allusive applications of similar movements acting in the interests of small-scale commercial enterprise.

1955 *Life* 18 Apr. 63/1 The mushrooming political strength of Poujadism last month forced Premier Edgar Faure's government to promise sweeping exemptions to the small shopkeepers. **1957** *Times Lit. Suppl.* 11 Oct. 607/2 The work of Chancellor Maupeou was undone.. and what was no better than an aristocratic form of Poujadism grew in power of mischief. **1961** *Listener* 7 Sept. 337/1 France presents the contrast between a strongly proletarian industrial society and a peasantry that finds its sporadic expression in Poujadism or the recent Breton uprisings. **1964** *Economist* 1 Feb. 429/1 The ensuing process of concentration in commerce and industry.. contributed to the political spread of *poujadisme* in the next few years. **1970** *Rev. Politics* XXXII. 174 Once organized Poujadism began its spread throughout France, it shared its founder's preoccupation with class defense. **1974** tr. *Wertheim's Evolution & Revolution* 149 Poujadism in France and the Farmers' Party in the Netherlands have.. been openly conservative or even reactionary. **1976** *Times* 9 Feb. 13/4 The small business sector.. is surely the very class which in other countries has.. turned to 'poujadism'.

Hence **'Poujadist**, an advocate or supporter of Poujadism; also *attrib.* or as *adj.*; **Pouja'distic** *a.*

1957 *Observer* 27 Oct. 13/2 Miss S. is not irresponsible, not a Poujadist... But the spirit of Poujadism is awake... 'The Liberal vote is a "Poujadist", disgruntlement vote.' **1958** *Economist* 6 Dec. 867/1 Electing poujadists under the name of conservatives does not mean a change. **1960** *20th Cent.* Apr. 302 In France there is a strong Poujadist element; small shopkeepers, small factory owners, the depressed bourgeoisie. **1962** *Daily Tel.* 25 June 10/2 Unless Britain is going to become Poujadist in the full sense—that is, inimical to all politicians as such—then the electorate will have to accept the sense expressed by the Prime Minister. **1967** M. DOGAN in Lipset & Rokkan *Party Syst. & Voter Alignments* iv. 181 The Poujadistic social epidemic spread particularly in the small sleepy towns. **1972** *New Statesman* 28 Jan. 100/2 Another mass movement of angry shopkeepers, the Poujadist wave of the 1950s. **1977** *Guardian Weekly* 27 Feb. 8/3 The Poujadist Progress party, led by Mr Mogens Glistrup, the controversial Copenhagen tax-lawyer, is once again the second largest party with 26 seats.

pouk, powk (pu:k). Now *dial.* [In mod. dial. written also *puke*, *peauk*, *peawk*, *pewk*, *paak*, *pahk*, *poke*, *pook*, *puck*, most of which forms point to a ME. **pouk(e*, OE. **púc-*; cf. EFris. *pûche*, *puche*, in same sense; perh. from OTeut. stem *puh(h)-*, *pug(g)-*, *puk(k)-* to swell up (Franck): cf. POCK, POUGH.] A small blister or pustule.

1611 COTGR., *Ampoule*, a small blister, weale, powke. **1657** TOMLINSON *Renou's Disp.* 338 Onely small watry powks. **1688** R. HOLME *Armoury* II. 428/1 Water Bladders, and yellow Blisters; are Powks or Tumors. **1828** *Craven Gloss.* (ed. 2), *Pouk*, a pimple.

pouk(e, obs. f. PUCK.

poukenel, obs. f. PUCK-NEEDLE.

poul, obs. f. PAUL, POLL.

‖**poulaine** (pu:'leɪn). Also 6 pullayne, 8 poleine, -eyn. [OF. *Poulaine* Poland, *souliers à la Poulaine* shoes in Polish fashion, crakows; hence the pointed beak of such shoes.] The long pointed toe of a shoe, as worn in the 14th and 15th centuries: = PIKE *sb.*[1] 4 a. (Erron. explained by some as the shoe itself: = CRAKOW.)

1464 *Act 4 Edw. IV*, c. 7 Nulle persone Cordewaner ou Cobeler.. face.. ascuns solers galoges ou husens oveqe ascun pike ou poleine qe passera la longuer ou mesure de deux poutz. **1530** PALSGR. 259/1 Pullayne, *poullane*. **1720** STRYPE *Stow's Surv.* (1754) II. v. xii. 299/2 Toes of an extraordinary Length, and sharp, called therefore Pykes, or Poleyns. **1834** PLANCHÉ *Brit. Costume* 202 No one under the estate of a lord was permitted to wear pikes or poleines to his shoes.. exceeding two inches in length.

[*erron.* **1706** PHILLIPS, *Poleine*, a sort of shooe pick'd and turn'd up at the Toe. **1877** BOUTELL in *Encycl. Brit.* VI. 469/2 The half-boots or shoes distinguished as *poulaines* continued to be long and very sharply pointed.]

poulard (pu:'lɑ:d). Also 9 poullard, poularde. [a. F. *poularde*, f. *poule* a hen + *-arde*: see -ARD.] A young hen fattened for the table; a spayed hen. (Cf. CAPON.)

1732 FIELDING *Miser* III. iii, A leash of pheasants, a leash of fat poulards. **1753** SMOLLETT *Ct. Fathom* (1784) 79/1 He bespoke a poulard for dinner. **1824** COBBETT *Cottage*

Economy §180 They [fowls] are never good for anything after they have attained their full growth, unless they be capons or poullards. *c* **1865** in *Circ. Sc.* I. 343/1 He has made capons and poulards of cocks and hens by mutilation.

poulce, obs. f. PULSE *sb.*[1]

pouldar, -er, -re, obs. ff. POWDER.

pouldavy, obs. f. POLDAVY.

pouldron (ˈpəʊldrən), **pauldron** (ˈpɔːldrən). *Obs.* exc. *Hist.* Forms: α. 5 (?)-6 polron, (5 polrond, 6 pollarone, polrynge). β. 6 poldron, (-drone, -dren, -derne, -drand, pollderon), 6- pouldron, (6-7 -dern, 7, 9 powldron). γ. 6 paleron, 6, 9 pauldron, (9 paldron). [In 15-16th c. *polron*, *pollerone*, for **poleron*, in Palsgr. 1530 *paleron*, app. aphetic forms of OF. *espauleron*, *espalleron*, f. *espaule*, mod.F. *épaule* shoulder; subseq. with *d* developed between *l* and *r*. The rare form *pauldron*, known once in 16th c., is that employed by recent writers on armour.

Palsgrave has F. *espalleron* in this sense, as = *paleron*; but the ordinary sense of OF. *espauleron* was shoulder-blade, shoulder of an animal. Mod.F. *paleron* shoulder-blade, omoplate, is referred by etymologists to *pale* blade of an oar, which does not suit the sense of the Eng. word.]

A piece of armour covering the shoulder; a shoulder-plate.

α. **1465** MARG. PASTON in *P. Lett.* II. 190 As for the harnys Wyks delyveryd it..to hym..ij payr polronds [etc.]. *c* **1550** *Clariodes MS.* (Hall.), Some only but a sure gepon Over his polrynges reaching to the kne. **1555** W. WATREMAN *Fardle Facions* II. ix. 200 Their pollerones are garnished with golde. **1579-80** NORTH *Plutarch* (1895) IV. 139 With both hands strived..to rent their polrons from their shoulders.

β. **1544** in *Lett. & Pap. Hen. VIII*, XIX. I. 465 Pollderon. *a* **1548** HALL *Chron., Hen. VIII* 82 The kyng of England.. brake his Poldron & him disarmed. **1580** HOLLYBAND *Treas. Fr. Tong, Avant bras d'vn harnois*, the polderne of an armour. **1581** STYWARD *Mar. Discipl.* I. 44 The poldrens with the Vambraces. **1590** SIR J. SMYTH *Disc. Weapons* 3 Without either pouldrons, vambraces, gauntlets or tasses. **1654** EARL MONM. tr. *Bentivoglio's Warrs Flanders* 401 There he raised three new redoubts, which were by a popular word of souldiery called Pouldrons. **1795** SOUTHEY *Joan of Arc* VIII. 454 Lifting high the deadly battle axe, Through pouldron and through shoulder deeply driven. **1840** HOR. SMITH *O. Cromwell* I. 283 Heavy cuirassiers, with helmets, breast and back pieces, poldrons and taslets.

γ. **1530** PALSGR. 251/1 Paleron, a pece of harnesse, *espalleron*. **1594** R. ASHLEY tr. *Loys le Roy* 30 Gorgets, pauldrons, vantbrasses, tasses. **1834** PLANCHÉ *Brit. Costume* 186 Shoulders..covered with overlapping plates called pauldrons. **1869** BOUTELL *Arms & Arm.* (1874) 204 When the shoulders were covered by the reinforce-plates, they were distinguished as *pauldrons*.

transf. **1603** OWEN *Pembrokeshire* (1892) 126 His [the lobster's] compleate Armour..his tases, vauntbraces, powldrons, Coushes.

†**b.** ***pouldron to pouldron***: shoulder to shoulder.

1598 BARRET *Theor. Warres* III. i. 37 Causing them to march vp close pouldron to pouldron. **1672** T. VENN *Milit. & Maritime Discipl.* vii. 15 A Rank is a Row of men uncertain in Number: Pouldron to Pouldron.

c. *attrib.*

1840 BROWNING *Sordello* v. 876 [He] flung away The pauldron-rings to give his sword-arm play.

Hence ˈ**pouldroned** *a.*, armed with a pouldron.

1688 R. HOLME *Armoury* III. xvii. (Roxb.) 109/2 He beareth Azure, a sinister Arme vambraced, and pouldroned.

‖**poule** (pul). [Fr., = 'hen'.] **1.** ***poule au pot***, in Gastronomy, a boiled chicken casserole. Also *fig.*

1884 N. LAKE *Menus made Easy* iv. 99 A fowl boiled and served with Bourgeoise sauce is called *Poule au pot*. **1930** M. T. & L. BONNEY *French Cooking for Eng. Kitchens* vii. 150 The Poule au Pot has as dignified a place on a menu as the Poussin. **1962** *Harper's Bazaar* Dec. 97/1 Chicken served as *poule au pot*. **1971** A. MIZENER *Saddest Story* xxxii. 433 An absolute monarchy committed to all Ford's favorite Tory doctrines—the *poule au pot* of the French peasant instead of the 'boiled fowls out of a pot that is no pot but a can' of American mass production.

2. *slang.* A girl or young woman, esp. one regarded as being promiscuous. Also ***poule-de-luxe***, a prostitute.

1926 E. HEMINGWAY *Sun also Rises* iii. 14 The *poules* going by, singly and in pairs. **1937** [see CHICHI *sb.*[2] and *a.*]. **1949** 'S. RUSSELL' *To Bed with Grand Music* vi. 87 All I know of the tricks used by poules-de-luxe. **1949** J. B. PRIESTLEY *Home is Tomorrow* 43 He is probably amusing himself somewhere with that little brown poule of his. **1955** D. BARTON *Glorious Life* i. 12 'If I had thought she would have understood,' said Swindlehurst, 'I would have called her to her face "the typing *poule*".' **1958** L. DURRELL *Mountolive* v. 102, I answer him in the voice of a *poule* from the Midi. **1976** *Times Lit. Suppl.* 24 Sept. 1213/3 Returns to France to find that his wife has remarried and that his daughter is in business as a *poule de luxe* and doing very well. **1979** *Ibid.* 23 Nov. 14/5 The archimandrite who regularly used the express between Sofia and Belgrade to entertain his *poules*.

poule, obs. f. PAUL, POLE *sb.*[1], POLL.

pouleine, pouler, obs. ff. PULLEN, POLLER.

†**Poules foot** = *Paul's foot*: see PAUL 6.

1468 in *Surtees Misc.* (1888) 19 Occupies xviij poules feet of ye grounde.

‖**poulet** (pulɛ). [Fr., a chicken, PULLET, also a love-letter, sometimes folded in the form of a wing.] **1.** A love-letter, a (neatly-folded) note.

1848 THACKERAY *Van. Fair* xxiv, He..sate down to pen a *poulet*..to Mademoiselle Aménaide. **1894** S. J. WEYMAN *Man in Black* ix, Even the Commissioners..found their doors beset at dawn with delicate 'poulets', or urgent, importunate applications.

2. A chicken or a chicken dish, esp. in French Gastronomy.

The spelling in quot. 1840 represents a jocular anglicization.

1840 THACKERAY *Barber Cox* in *Comic Almanack* 213 Eating, for my share,..a pully bashymall, and other French dishes. **1861** MRS. BEETON *Bk. Househ. Managem.* xxi. 474 *Poulet aux cressons*... A fowl, a large bunch of water-cresses, 3 tablespoonfuls of vinegar, ¼ pint of gravy. **1894** G. DU MAURIER *Trilby* II. v. 111 A delightful little Franco-Italian pothouse near Leicester Square, where they had..a *poulet rôti*, which is *such* a different affair from a roast fowl! **1900** C. M. YONGE *Mod. Broods* xiii. 120 Here are eggs, and some milk..four *poulets*, such as they are. **1933** D. C. PEEL *Life's Enchanted Cup* viii. 87 She made a delicious *Poulet Marengo* with a suspicion of garlic in it. **1957** P. WILDEBLOOD *Main Chance* 53 The pressure cooker burst... It suddenly went off bang and threw bits of *poulet en cocotte* all over the place like confetti. **1978** *Chicago* June 218/2 Poulet Provençal ($6.50) comes with pearl onions, fresh mushrooms, olives, tomato purée.

‖**poulette** (pulɛt). [Fr. *poulette* young hen.] In full, ***poulette sauce***. In French Gastronomy, a sauce made with butter, cream and egg-yolks.

1813 L. E. UDE *French Cook* 389 The *poulette* is made with a little *sauce tournée*, which you reduce, and next thicken with the yolks of two eggs, to which you add a little parsley chopped very fine. **1877** E. S. DALLAS *Kettner's Bk. of Table* 376 *Poulette Relish*..consists of shalots and mushrooms passed in butter, and served with chopped parsley in a Poulette sauce. **1907** A. ESCOFFIER *Guide Mod. Cookery* iii. 42 *Poulette Sauce*. Boil for a few minutes one pint of Sauce Allemande, and add six tablespoonfuls of mushroom liquor. Finish..with two oz. of butter, a few drops of lemon-juice, and one teaspoonful of chopped parsley. **1957** M. MCCARTHY *Memories Catholic Girlhood* viii. 204 Sweetbreads, with patty shells, and with a poulette sauce. **1977** ROSSANT & DAVIS tr. *Bocuse's New Cuisine* 330 *Poulette Sauce*..butter..flour..bouillon..mushroom.

poulle, -et, -ie, obs. ff. POLL, PULLET, PULLEY.

†**poulme.** *Obs. rare*$^{-1}$. [app. shortened form of next.] = next.

1561 HOLLYBUSH *Hom. Apoth.* 16b, The rotting of the poulme or lightes.

†**poulmon.** *Obs. rare*$^{-1}$. [a. obs. F. *poulmon*, mod.F. *poumon*:—L. *pulmō-nem* lung.] The lung.

1561 HOLLYBUSH *Hom. Apoth.* 16 It is conuenient for al partes of the breste and the poulmon.

poulp, poulpe (puːlp). Also 7 pulp, 7-8 pulpe. [a. F. *poulpe* in same sense:—L. *pōlypus* POLYPUS.] An octopus, cuttle-fish, or other cephalopod: = POLYP 1 a.

1601 HOLLAND *Pliny* II. 427 The Pulpe fish or Pourcuttell, maketh at the very fishooks which hee searcheth after and..claspeth hard and gripeth round about with his clees. **1681** GREW *Musæum* I. v. iv. 121 The Preke or Poulps. *Polypus*. **1835-6** *Todd's Cycl. Anat.* I. 527/1 The short round-bodied Octopi or Poulps. **1874** WOOD *Nat. Hist.* 626 The Argonaut.—The animal, or 'poulp'..is indeed a most lovely creature, despite of its unattractive form.

poulpy, poulse, obs. ff. PULPY, PULSE.

Poulsen arc (ˈpəʊlsən ɑːk). [Named after its inventor, Valdemar *Poulsen* (1869-1942), Danish electrical engineer.] An arc discharge between a carbon electrode and a water-cooled copper electrode operated in an atmosphere of hydrogen or hydrocarbon vapour and a strong magnetic field in order to make possible the emission of waves short enough to be used for radiotelegraphy.

1906 *Electrician* 21 Dec. 375/1 The physical.. circumstances of the Poulsen arc are rather forbidding. **1916** *Ibid.* 14 Jan. 535/2 In wireless telegraphy there has been a notable advance in the use of the Poulsen arc. **1931** [see KEYING *vbl. sb.* 1]. **1949** W. R. MACLAURIN *Invention & Innovation in Radio Industry* iv. 60 The patents on the Poulsen arc were held by enterprises that were competing with Marconi.

poult (pəʊlt), *sb.*[1] Forms: α. 5 pult(e, 7- poult, (7 pl. poulse), 9 polt. β. *Sc.* and *dial.* 6-8 powt(e, (6 powtt), 6- pout (7 poot, pote): see also POOT *sb.*[1] [ME. contr. f. *polet*, *poullet*, PULLET, a. F. *poulet* chicken, dim. of *poule* hen.] The young of the domestic fowl, a chicken; also of the turkey, pheasant, guinea-fowl, and various game-birds. Also *attrib.*

α. *a* **1425** *Langland's P. Pl.* A. VII. 267 (MS. U.), I haue no penyes..pultys to bugge. *c* **1440** *Prop. Parv.* 416/1 Pulte, yonge hen, *gallinella*. **1634** *Althorp MS.* in Simpkinson *Washingtons* App. p. xxii, 3 dozen pheasant poults from Oxford. **1661** LOVELL *Hist. Anim. & Min.* Introd., Pheasants, partridg, heath poulse. **1704** LOCKE in Campbell *Chancellors* (1846) IV. cxxiii. 580, 4 Turkey poults ready larded. **1810** *Sporting Mag.* XXXVI. 291 Or where the polt, in open heath, Moves in an even line from death. **1863** BARING-GOULD *Iceland* 162 Ptarmigan poults, hardly fledged.

β. **1502** *Acc. Ld. High Treas. Scot.* II. 155 To ane man brocht powtis to the King. **1550** *Reg. Privy Council Scot.* I. 95 Item the blak cok, and the gray hen vi d. Item the powttis the doosen xii d. **1575** TURBERV. *Falconrie* Commend. Hawking, When the Spanels crosse the ronne of Fesants in the wood, Or light vpon the little Poutes. **1602** CAREW *Cornwall* 24 b, Of wild [birds Cornwall hath] Quaile, Raile, Partridge..Powte, &c. **1620** in *Naworth Househ. Bks.* (Surtees) 126, 7 pootes and 2 snipes. **1633** *Ibid.* 309, 3 moorefoole and 3 potes. **1681** COLVIL *Whigs Supplic.* (1751) 125 With which they persecute those poor souls, As setting dogs do pouts and muir-fowls. **1725** BRADLEY *Fam. Dict.* s.v. *Pheasant-taking*, The old Cock and Hen [Pheasant], with all their young ones or Powts. **1784** BURNS *Epist. to J. Rankine* xi, As soon's the clockin-time is by, An' the wee pouts begun to cry. **1839** GLEIG *Only Daughter* (1859) 33 She was na comin' to see the pouts fed.

b. *transf.* A child; a youth. *colloq.* or *dial.*

1739 NICOL *Poems* 22 The meikle Trake come o'er their Snouts, That laugh at winsome kissing Pouts. **1790** J. WILLIAMS *Shrove Tuesday* in *Cabinet*, etc. (1794) 27 Bid the unbreech'd Poults and Pullets gaze. **1852** R. S. SURTEES *Sponge's Sp. Tour* xliv. 242 'He's a raw poult of a chap', replied Jack. **1897** W. D. LATTO in *Bards Angus & Mearns* 270/1 Whan I was but a feeble pout.

poult (puːlt), *sb.*[2] [Shortening of POULT-DE-SOIE.] = POULT-DE-SOIE. Also, a similar fabric manufactured from man-made fibres. Also *attrib.*

1938 *Times* 7 July 22/1 A gown..with a bodice of white poult. **1951** *Good Housek. Home Encycl.* 199/1 Nylon Fabric is now available in many different finishes, such as tricot, net, poult. **1959** *Times* 21 Sept. 12/4 A short dress of coral-coloured poult. **1960** *Woman's Own* 9 Apr. 7/1 At a dance recently I wore my poult dress. **1970** *Trafford Spring & Summer Catal.* 276 See through lace sleeves and a 40 denier Nylon poult skirt.

poult, *v. rare.* [f. POULT *sb.*[1] See also POUT *v.*[2]] *intr.* To catch chickens or poultry.

1657 R. LIGON *Barbadoes* 4 No feare of losing our hauke, by going out at Cheik, or to a village to Poult.

‖**poult-de-soie** (pudəswa). [= F. *poult-de-soie* (also *pout-de-soie*), a recent alteration of *pou-de-soie* (1667 in Littré; in OF. *poul de soie*, *pout de soye*, 1389-94 in Godef. *Compl.*), of unknown origin, which was used in England in the form *poudesoy* from 1663 to *c* 1750: see PADUASOY. After being disused for a century (exc. as consciously Fr.), it was re-introduced *c* 1850, in the current Fr. spelling, for a material identical with or similar to the 18th c. paduasoy.] A fine corded silk; 'a plain silk of rich quality in a soft and bright *grosgrain* make' (see GROGRAM); now most frequently applied to coloured goods.

[**1835** *Court Mag.* VI. p. xvii/2 Gold ear-rings of a new form. Rose-coloured *pou de soie* slippers. Black lace gloves.] **1850** *Harper's Mag.* I. 287 Robe of white poult de soie. **1900** *Daily News* 21 Apr. 6/5 A blouse made of black and white striped silk has a white poult-de-soie sailor collar.

poulter (ˈpəʊltə(r)). *arch.* Forms: 4-6 pulter, 5 -ur, 6 -ar, -or, powlter, 6- poulter (7 pulleter). [ad. OF. *pouletier* (*c* 1230 in Godef.) in same sense, f. *poulet* PULLET + *-ier*, -ER[2].]

1. a. = POULTERER. *Obs.* exc. as name of one of the London City Companies.

a **1400** in *Eng. Gilds* (1870) 353 No ffysshyere ne no pulter ne shal bygge ffysche ne pultrye for to aȝen selle, er þat vndren be y-ronge. *c* **1430** LYDG. *Min. Poems* (Percy Soc.) 166 A pulter that sellithe a fat swan, For a goselyng that grasithe on bareyn clowris. **1548** *Act 2 & 3 Edw. VI*, c. 15 §1 Bruers Bakers Poulters Cookes. **1573** TUSSER *Husb.* (1878) 56 To rere vp much pultrie, and want the barne doore, Is naught for the pulter and woorse for the poore. **1622** PEACHAM *Compl. Gent.* i. (1634) 5 Nicholas the fifth was sonne of a Poulter, Sixtus the fift, of a Hog-heard. **1633** [see POULTERER b]. **1884** *Rep. Lond. Livery Comp.* III. 688 The Poulters' Company existed by prescription as early as 1345. It was, however, incorporated by Royal Charter in the 19th year of Henry VII, on 23rd February 1504.

b. ***poulter's measure***, a fanciful name for a metre consisting of lines of 12 and 14 syllables alternately (corresponding to the modern 'short metre'): see quots.

1576 GASCOIGNE *Instruct. making Verse* in *Steele Gl.*, etc. (Arb.) 39 The commonest sort of verse which we vse now adayes (*viz.* the long verse of twelue and fourtene sillables) I know not certainly howe to name it, vnlesse I should say that it doth consist of Poulters measure, which giueth xii. for one dozen and xiiij. for another. **1586** W. WEBBE *Eng. Poetrie* (Arb.) 62 When one staffe containeth but two verses, or (if they bee deuided) foure: the first or the first couple hauing twelue sillables, the other fourteene, which versifyers call Powlters measure, because so they tall[i]e their wares by dozens. **1838** GUEST *Eng. Rhythms* II. 233. **1900** W. RALEIGH in W. E. Henley *Castiglione's Bk. of Courtier* p. xlv, The one-legged poulter's measure is not responsible for all the horrors of this. **1962** G. K. HUNTER *John Lyly* iv. 244 The case with 'fourteeners' or 'poulter's measure' is even more obvious. **1972** *Times Lit. Suppl.* 10 Nov. 1363/1 Poulter's measure (the form of verse with alternating lines of twelve and fourteen syllables).

†**2.** An officer of the royal or other household, or of a monastery, etc. who attended to the purchase of poultry and other provisions. *Obs.*

c **1450** *Bk. Curtasye* 581 in *Babees Bk.* 318 The clerke to kater and pulter is, To baker and butler bothe y-wys Gyffys seluer. *a* **1483** *Liber Niger Edw. IV* (P.R.O., Exch. T.R., Misc. Bk. 230), Anothre of these gromys ys callyd..grome surgeon, another grome pulter. **1522** *Rutland Papers* (Camden) 84 Item, to appouynt iiij pulters to serue for the said persons of all maner pultry. **1601** F. TATE tr. *Househ. Ord. Edw. II* §51 A serjant pulleter.. shal.. take thadvise of the asseour of the kinges table [etc.] what he shal bringe to court.

3. *Comb.*, as ***poulter-man***, ***-pannier***.

1424-5 *Durham Acc. Rolls* (Surtees) 620, 1 par. de Pulter-panyers. **1534** in W. H. Turner *Select. Rec. Oxford* (1880) 126 Ye s^d^ pulter man.

Hence **'poulteress**, a woman who deals in poultry, a female poulterer.

1723 *Lond. Gaz.* No. 6194/10 Elizabeth Smith,.. Poulteress.

poulterer ('pəʊltərə(r)). Also 6 pulterer, 7 polterer, poultrer. [Extended form of POULTER, perh. formed on *poultery*, POULTRY: see -ER[1] 3.]

a. One whose business is the sale of poultry (and usually hares and other game); a dealer in poultry.

(Quot. 1534 doubtful, *pulter man* occurs on same page.) [**1534** in W. H. Turner *Select. Rec. Oxford* (1880) 126 The pulterers nor other freemen of the Towne.] **1638** PENKETHMAN *Artach.* Ajb, Let Butchers, Poultrers, Fishmongers contend, Each his owne Trade in what he can defend. **1684** *Lond. Gaz.* No. 1955/4 Apprentice to Mr. Bayly, his Royal Highness's Polterer.. in the Pall-Mall. **1789** MRS. PIOZZI *Journ. France* II. 27 Poulterers hang up their animals in the feathers. **1853-8** HAWTHORNE *Eng. Note-Bks.* (1879) II. 365 An abundance of game at the poulterers.

b. Applied to the livery company of Poulters. ***poulterer's measure***, = ***poulter's measure*** s.v. POULTER 1 b. Chiefly *Hist.*

1755 STRYPE *Stow's Surv.* II. v. xiii. 303/2 The Company of Poulterers [ed. 1633, p. 632 Poulters] were incorporated in the 19th Year of Henry the Seventh. **1841** R. G. LATHAM *Eng. Lang.* v. 382 *Poulterer's Measure*,—Alexandrines and Service Measures alternately. Found in the poetry of Henry the Eighth's time. **1957** N. FRYE *Anat. Crit.* 263 There were some comparative failures, such as poulterer's measure.

poult foot, obs. form of POLT-FOOT.

poultice ('pəʊltɪs), *sb.* Forms: α. *pl.* 6 pultes, 7 poults; β. *sing.* 6 pultes, 6-7 -esse, 6-8 (9 *dial.*) pultis, pultas, 7 pultass(e, -ise, -iss, -us, 7-8 (9 *dial.*) pultess, -ice, 8 pultoss; γ. 6 poultesse, 7 poultes, -ess, -us, poltis, powltice, 7-8 poultis, -ise, 8 -iss, poltice, 7- poultice. [Ultimately from L. *puls*, *pult-em* thick pap, pottage, pulse (= Gr. πόλτος), whence It. *polta* pap (†*pulta*, Florio); F. *pulte* a poultice, in Cotgr., is unsupported. The earliest form *pultes* was app. the L. pl. *pultes* (in med.L. = pap), soon popularly taken as a sing., perh. from its collective sense. Other forms simulate Fr. suffixes *-asse*, *-esse*, *-ice*.

The form in *pult-* continued in general use till after 1750, and is still dialectal. It is difficult to account for the spelling *poult-*, which is found before 1600; the mod. pronunciation is indicated in 1645 by *poltis*.]

1. a. A soft mass of some substance (as bread, meal, bran, linseed, various herbs, etc.), usually made with boiling water, and spread upon muslin, linen, or other material, applied to the skin to supply moisture or warmth, as an emollient for a sore or inflamed part, or as a counter-irritant (e.g. a mustard-poultice); a cataplasm.

α. **1542-3** *Act 34 & 35 Hen. VIII*, c. 8 To practyse use and mynistre in and to any outwarde sore,.. any herbe or herbes oyntementes bathes pultes and emplasters. **1639** T. DE GRAY *Compl. Horsem.* 104 The poults of mallowes, &c. must be every night applyed.

β. **1544** PHAER *Regim. Lyfe* (1545) 64 b, Ye must laye vppon the payne a pultes made of herbes, and floures. **1562** BULLEYN *Bulwark, Bk. Simples* 23 b, Good to be put into glisters.. and in pultases. **1563** T. GALE *Antid.* II. 72 A Cataplasme or Pultis. **1610** MARKHAM *Masterp.* II. cxiii. 408 Couer the soare place.. with this Pultus. **1626** BACON *Sylva* §60 The Pultass relaxeth the Pores. **1633** JOHNSON *Gerarde's Herbal* I. xx. 28 Very good to be put into pultesses. **1657** W. COLES *Adam in Eden* cxix, It is used in Pultisses. **1684** tr. *Bonet's Merc. Compit.* I. 8 Apply a hot Pultess to the Throat. **1712** ARBUTHNOT *John Bull* III. x, Some were for emollient Pultas's. **1719** *Accomplisht Lady's Delight* (ed. 10) 46 Pultosses of Bran-meal. **1756** WATSON in *Phil. Trans.* XLIX. 905 Which adheres to the bottom of the vessel like pultice. **1756** C. LUCAS *Ess. Waters* II. 65 Salt.. discusses boils, in form of a pultis with raisins, hog's lard, or honey. **1828** *Craven Gloss.* (ed. 2), *Pultis*, a poultice.

γ. **1592** SHAKS. *Rom. & Jul.* II. v. 65 (Qo. 1597) Is this the poultesse for mine aking boanes? **1611** COTGR., *Pulte*, a poultice. **1612** WOODALL *Surg. Mate* Wks. (1653) 365 The hearb Crowes-foot, made into a Cataplasme or Poultis. **1643** STEER tr. *Exp. Chyrurg.* x. 44 With a little Vinegar and Honey make a Powltice. **1645** R. SYMONDS *Diary Civ. War* (Camden) 275 Make a poltis; lay it on with red flocks. **1658** A. FOX *Würtz' Surg.* I. viii. 33 There is no need of such a Poultess. **1747** WESLEY *Prim. Physic* (1762) 38 A white bread Poultis. **1875** H. C. WOOD *Therap.* (1879) 205 A hop poultice is sometimes made by simply moistening with hot water the hops contained in a gauze bag.

fig. **1576** GASCOIGNE *Steele Gl.* (Arb.) 77 That Poetrie presume not for to preache, And bite mens faults with Satyres corosiues, Yet pamper vp hir owne with pultesses. **1856** EMERSON *Eng. Traits, Ability* Wks. (Bohn) II. 35 When they have pounded each other to a poultice, they will shake hands and be friends for the remainder of their lives. **1902** *St. James' Gaz.* 19 July 8/2 His pleasing manner is the poultice to the bump which his fist has raised.

b. *attrib.* and *Comb.*: **poultice-boot**, **poultice-jacket** (see quots.); **poultice-neckerchief**, a name for the many-folded neckcloth worn c 1800; †**poultice-root** (see quot.); **poultice-shoe** = *poultice-boot*; **poultice-wise** *adv.*, in the way of a poultice.

1875 KNIGHT *Dict. Mech.*, **Poultice-boot*, a large boot used for applying poultices to horses' legs. **1896** *Allbutt's Syst. Med.* I. 434 '*Poultice' or 'Pneumonia jackets' are garments made of a strip of thin flannel or flannelette... They are lined with a layer of cotton wool.. and can easily be placed over the poultice. **1800** *Monthly Mag.* X. 242 The dress of our present beaux, their *poultice neck-handkerchiefs, pantaloons, overalls. **1788** M. CUTLER in *Life, Jrnls. & Corr.* (1888) I. 409 Several vegetables... Aspen, Black-poplar, *Poultice-root, etc. **1888** G. FLEMING in *Encycl. Brit.* XXIV. 202/1 For applying poultices to the feet [of a horse], a *poultice-shoe.. may be used with advantage. **1614** MARKHAM *Cheap Husb.* II. xxxi. (1668) 81 *Pultis-wise lay it to the offended member. **1756** C. LUCAS *Ess. Waters* II. 65 It is applied to strains with meal and honey, pultiswise.

2. *Austral. slang.* **a.** A mortgage.

1932 K. S. PRICHARD *Dark Horse of Darran* in *Kiss on Lips* 184 Mick Mallane.. sayin' if the bank wanted his farm, poultice or no poultice, it'd have to go out and take it from him, and he'd be waitin' for 'm with his gun loaded. **1934** T. WOOD *Cobbers* xi. 134 Men talked about their blister, or their poultice, which means a mortgage, with complacency. **1958** *Coast to Coast 1957-1958* 137 When the farm was free of its 'poultice', her father had promised to hand over to Sam.

b. A (large) sum of money; a bribe.

1951 E. LAMBERT *Twenty Thousand Thieves* III. xii. 235 It's only two days to pay day and I've got a poultice in that pay-book of mine. **1957** 'N. CULOTTA' *They're a Weird Mob* (1958) v. 73 'Reckon 'e pulled 'im?' 'That's wot I reckon.'.. 'Yer can't prove ut.' 'Somebody slung in a poultice, I bet.' 'They're all crooked.' **1979** *Sun-Herald* 24 June 143 A bloke who made a poultice in recent weeks when he sold Rupert a quarter of a million Channel Ten shares.

'poultice, *v.* [f. prec. sb.] *trans.* To apply a poultice to; to treat with a poultice. Hence **'poulticed** *ppl. a.*, **'poulticing** *vbl. sb.*

1730 BURDON *Pocket Farrier* (1735) 20 The same Medicine and Poulticing will cure it. **1750** *Phil. Trans.* XLVI. 441 Pultised according to the Direction of our old Female Practitioners. **1809** *Med. Jrnl.* XXI. 39 The inflammation of the wounded part had become violent, and I ordered it to be poulticed. **1875** H. C. WOOD *Therap.* (1879) 586 Brought about by continuous poulticing. **1888** *Century Mag.* XXXVI. 904 His poulticed ear and picturesque scars.

poultry ('pəʊltrɪ). Forms: α. 4-6 pultrie, -ye, 5-6 pultre, -erie, 5-7 pulletrie, -ye, 7 pultry. β. 6 poultrie, -ye, -ee, 7 poultery, powltry, 7-8 poultrey; 6- poultry. γ. *Sc.* 5-8 powtry, 7 poutry. [ME. *pult(e)rie*, a. OF. *pouletrie* (1280 in Godef.), *poulleterie*, f. *poul(l)etier* POULTER: see -ERY 1, and cf. F. *boulangerie*, Eng. *bakery*, etc.]

†**1.** The office of a 'poulter' in the royal (or a nobleman's) household (see POULTER 2); the superintendence of the purchase of fowls and other provisions; also, the room in which such provisions were stored. *Obs.*

[**1390** *Earl Derby's Exp.* (Camden) 15 Super officio pulletrie per manus eiusdem pro lacte, butiro et ouis per ipsum emptis ibidem. **1392** *Ibid.* 220 Cum conductione j domus pro officio pulleterie, j duc. v.s. **1393** *Ibid.* 241 Super officio poletrie.] **1455** in *Househ. Ord.* (1790) 22* Th' office of the Pulterie. **1541** *Act 33 Hen. VIII*, c. 12 §14 The serieant of the pultrie.. shalbe.. redie with a cocke in his hand. a **1548** HALL *Chron.*, *Hen. VIII* 74 Office[s] of houshold seruice, as Ewery,.. Buttery, Spicery, pitcher house, Larder and Poultrie. **1601** TATE *Househ. Ord. Edw. II* §42 (1876) 25 A wafrer.. shul take for his office.. egges in the pulletrie and fuel of the scullerye.

2. †**a.** A place where fowls are reared; a poultry-yard or poultry-farm. †**b.** A place where fowls are sold for food; a poultry-market. *Obs.*

1429 *Mun. Magd. Coll. Oxf.* (1882) 16 Item, j bakhous.. cum aliis parvis domibus ibidem pro yetynghous et pultrie. c **1440** *Promp. Parv.* 416/1 Pultrye, *gallinaria*. c **1483** CAXTON *Dialogues* 10/30 Goo into the pultrie, Bye poullettis, One poullet & two chekens. **1530** PALSGR. 257/2 Poultry, *poullaillerie*. **1546** LANGLEY *Pol. Verg. De Invent.* III. iii. 66 b, Pulteries of all kinde of foules wer instituted. a **1548** HALL *Chron.*, *Hen. VIII* 207 b, The Poultrees, Larders, Spicereis, and Sellars of Wine were al open. **1552** HULOET s.v. *Pultrye*, The fowles fedde in a Barton or poultry. **1570** LEVINS *Manip.* 105/30 Poultrie, *auiarium*.

c. Hence, Name of a street at the east end of Cheapside in London, where there was formerly a poultry-market.

1432-50 in *Calr. Proc. Chanc. Q. Eliz.* I. Pref. 40 Oon Richard Crewe and Nicholas Vicarye sergeaunts.. toke at divers tymes out of the said Saintuary.. and brought theym to the Counter in the Poultre of London forsaid. **1598** STOW *Surv.* 63 Powlters of late remoued out of the Powltry. **1711** J. GREENWOOD *Eng. Gram.* Title-p., Johon Lawrence at the Angel in the Poultrey.

3. Domestic fowls collectively; those tame birds which are commonly reared for their flesh, eggs, or feathers, and kept in a yard or similar inclosure, as barndoor fowls, ducks, geese, turkeys, guinea-fowls (excluding pigeons, pheasants, etc.); sometimes restricted to the barndoor fowl with its varieties; also applied to the birds as dressed for the market or prepared for food.

Usually construed as collective pl.; formerly sometimes as individual pl. after a numeral.

α. c **1386** CHAUCER *Prol.* 598 His lordes sheepe, his neet, his dayerye, His swyn, his hors, his stoor, and his pultrye [*v.rr.* pultrie, pulletrie, pultre]. **1387** TREVISA *Higden* (Rolls) III. 9 Venisoun, pultrie, and wylde foul. **1508** DUNBAR *Flyting* 157 Thow plukkis the pultre, and scho pullis off the pennis. **1550-3** *Decaye of Eng.* in *Four Suppl.*, etc. (1871) 98 Where as pultrye was wont to be breade and fedde. **1581** *Calr. Laing Charters* (1899) 255 Fowir pultrie for fowir penneis the pece. c **1640** J. SMYTH *Lives Berkeleys* (1883) I. 161 The vsuall prices of Catle, Corne, Pultry and other provisions.

β. **1545** ELYOT *Dict.*, *Pascales*, sheepe or poultrie, whiche doo feede at large. **1563** HYLL *Art Garden.* II. xxii. (1574) 63 Hennes, Cockes, Chickins, or any other Poultry sytting on the rowste. **1624** CAPT. SMITH *Virginia* IV. 164 Many more Powltry, what was brought or bred. **1656** HEYLIN *Surv. France* 202 The servant went over only to sell his Poultery. **1727** A. HAMILTON *New Acc. E. Ind.* I. xix. 237, I have seen the Portugueze Subjects bring twenty or thirty Poultry to the Market. **1807** CRABBE *Par. Reg.* III. 173 Poultry in groups still follow'd where she went. **1870** L'ESTRANGE *Miss Mitford* I. i. 31 They speak of hardly anything except the dogs and the poultry.

γ. **1486** *Exch. Rolls Scotl.* IX. 359 Onerat se.. de.. xl caponibus j^c^xlvj powtry... Summa.. lxiiij capones j^c^lxxxxiiij pultre. **1565** in J. Fraser *Polichron.* (S.H.S.) 153 Aught poutry price of the pice xij d. **1730** RAMSAY *Fables* xxii. 19 Sheep and powtry, geese and ducks.

4. *attrib.* and *Comb.*, as ***poultry-basket***, ***breeder***, ***-breeding***, ***-culture***, ***-fancier***, ***-fancy***, ***-fancying*** adj., ***-farm***, ***-farmer***, ***-farming***, ***-feather***, ***-house***, ***-keeper***, ***-keeping***, ***kind***, ***market***, ***meat***, †***-picking*** (= stealing), ***-plant*** (PLANT *sb.*[1] 6), ***-raising***, ***-rearing***, ***-run***, ***-shop***, ***-show***, ***-stall***, ***-yard***; †**Poultry Compter**, name of a prison in the Poultry in London (see 2 c and COMPTER); **poultry-feeder**, a contrivance for feeding poultry (see quots.); **poultry-flutter**, the flutter of frightened poultry; also *fig.*; **poultry-maid**, a girl employed to look after poultry; **poultry-man**, a man who sells poultry; also **poultry-woman**; †**poultry-stuff**, †**poultry-ware**, poultry as a marketable commodity.

1893 Q. [COUCH] *Delectable Duchy* (1894) 305 An old countryman, with an empty *poultry-basket on his knees. c **1882** W. COOK (*title*) Practical *poultry breeder and feeder. **1976** *Evening Post* (Nottingham) 14 Dec. 6/6 Derbyshire police advises poultry breeders to have flood lighting as a deterrent. **1816** KIRBY & SP. *Entomol.* xxvii. (1818) II. 519 Some quondam amateur of *poultry-breeding. **1715** M. DAVIES *Athen. Brit.* I. 15 [He] became at last Secondary of the *Poultry-Compter. **1894** *Daily News* 12 Dec. 6/7 The Committee.. urge that *poultry culture as a branch of our great national industry should be no longer neglected. **1865** *Atlantic Monthly* June 661/2 My experiments with chickens have been attended with a success so brilliant that unfortunate *poultry-fanciers have appealed to me for assistance. **1876** FULTON *Bk. Pigeons* 1 A poultry-fancier was apt to be fought shy of. **1891** T. HARDY *Tess* (1900) 21/1 In the management of her *poultry-farm. **1894** *Jrnl. R. Agric. Soc.* June 303 From *poultry-farmers.. the higglers obtain the millions of eggs which are sent into this country. *Ibid.*, Nothing has been said as to *poultry-farming. **1844** *Zoologist* II. 451 Its nest.. was lined with a profusion of *poultry-feathers. **1875** KNIGHT *Dict. Mech.*, **Poultry-feeder*, a device to feed grain to fowls in quantity as used. **1884** *Ibid.* Supp., *Poultry Feeder*, a revolving cylinder with coops in stories and in circuit, holding fowls which are successively presented to the attendant. **1876** G. MEREDITH *Beauch. Career* I. i. 11 We were insulted, and all in a *poultry flutter, yet no one seemed to feel it but himself! **1552** HULOET, *Pultrye house or barton, *gallinarium*,.. *viuarium*. **1819** *Amer. Farmer* (Baltimore) I. 46 Respecting the cleansing of poultry-houses from vermin, or chicken-lice. **1921** *Proc. 3rd Nat. Country Life Conf. 1920* (U.S.) 155 No argument is necessary to justify poultry houses. **1942** C. MILBURN *Diary* 11 July (1979) 145 Mr Willoughby came later with a copy of the *Smallholder* and we looked at an advertisement for a 'Utility Poultry House'. **1867** L. WRIGHT (*title*) The practical *poultry-keeper. **1935** *Discovery* Oct. 302/2 The poultry keeper and game preserver. **1960** *Farmer & Stockbreeder* 9 Feb. 123/3 Some poultry-keepers prefer to use no preventive drugs and to rely upon curative drugs, if and when an outbreak of coccidiosis occurs. **1976** *Newmarket Jrnl.* 16 Dec., He served on the committee of the allotments association and was an active gardener and poultry-keeper. **1774** GOLDSM. *Nat. Hist.* III. 83 Birds of the *Poultry kind. **1897** SARAH GRAND *Beth Bk.* xii, He went to the poultry-yard, followed by Beth.., the yard-boy, and the *poultry-maid. **1573-4** *Reg. Privy Council Scot.* II. 338 Flescheouris,.. commoun cuikis, *pultre men, and sic utheris as sellis or makis reddy flesche. **1889** *St. Landry Democrat* (Opelousas, Louisiana) 7 Dec. 2/5 Mr. Felch the well-known poultryman, has a Scotch collie dog. **1960** *Farmer & Stockbreeder* 9 Feb. 125/2 Mr. Thornber remembered that the poultryman slept for 21 days with the first mammoth they installed. **1437** *Bury Wills* (Camden) 8 In vico vocato the *Pultery market. **1960** *Farmer & Stockbreeder* 16 Feb. 79/1 The amount of *poultry meat marketed continued to shoot upwards. **1978** *Daily Tel.* 19 Sept. 19/7 Meat consumption in Britain is now at its lowest level since 1955—replaced largely by poultry meat. c **1470** HENRYSON *Mor. Fab.* IX. (*Wolf & Fox*) xvii, It is sum wyfis malisoun.. For *pultrie pyking that lichtit hes on yow. **1850** in D. J. Browne *Amer. Poultry Yard* 304 There is profit attending *poultry raising, when undertaken on a moderate scale. **1870** 'MARK TWAIN' in *Buffalo Express* 4 June 2/3 From early youth I have taken an especial interest in the subject of poultry-raising. **1896** *Rep. Vermont Board Agric.* XV. 28 Poultry raising has of late years attracted the attention of the farmer. **1916** *Daily Colonist* (Victoria, B.C.) 23 July 8/5 There is room near every industrial centre in the province for many market gardens, *poultry-runs, orchards and aviaries. **1930** R. CAMPBELL *Adamastor* 64 Heaven in which our senses swim, Aviary of aviators And poultry-run of seraphim! **1562** J. HEYWOOD *Prov. & Epigr.* (1867) 181 Thou sellest.. conies in this *pultry shoppe. **1868** M. H.

Smith *Sunshine & Shadow in N.Y.* lxxiv. 597 He has gotten up baby-shows, *poultry-shows, and dog-shows. **1873** F. Kilvert *Diary* 6 Aug. (1944) 223, I went..to Garth to attend the Garth Flower Show, Dog Show, Poultry Show, Bazaar and Athletic Sports, all in one. **1886** W. J. Tucker *E. Europe* 243 The old Jewess..used some years ago to have a *poultry-stall..on the market. **1531–2** in *Househ. Ord.* (1790) 220 He shall take noe *Poultry-stuff from noe Nobleman nor Gentleman's Servants. *Ibid.*, They shall take noe *Poultry-ware within seven myles of London. **1851** *Harper's Mag.* Apr. 662/2 The *poultry-woman must be changed. **1748** Richardson *Clarissa* I. ix. 52 You must remember the Green Lane..that runs by the side of the wood-house and *poultry-yard. **1811** Jane Austen *Sense & Sens.* III. vi. 114 The rest of the morning was..whiled away ..in visiting her poultry-yard. **1837** W. Irving *Capt. Bonneville* i. (1849) 27 Like a game-cock among the common roosters of the poultry-yard. **1847** Emerson *Poems, Threnody* v, His daily haunts I well discern,—The poultry-yard, the shed, the barn.

Hence ˈ**poultrycide** (*humorous nonce-wd.*) [-cide 2], the killing of poultry; ˈ**poultryless** *a.* [-less], destitute of poultry.

1841 *Blackw. Mag.* XLIX. 616, I..meditated all the varieties of poultrycide. **1883** 'Annie Thomas' *Mod. Housewife* 106 To a degree that drove us poultryless from her doors after an unsuccessful and prolonged parley.

poultz: see pulse *sb.*[2]

pouly, obs. f. pulley.

poum, obs. f. pome.

poume garnet(te, poum garnet, obs. ff. pomegranate.

poumil, poumle, obs. ff. pummel.

poumle, obs. f. pomely *a.*, dappled.

poumper, var. pome-pear, *Obs.*

poumysshe, obs. f. pumice.

poun, obs. f. pawn *sb.*[1] (at Chess), pound *v.*[1]

‖**pounamu** (pəʊˈnamʊ). *N.Z.* Also 9 punamu. [Maori.] Nephrite.

[**1773** J. Hawkesworth *Acct. Voy.* II. ii. vi. 400 This land ..consists of two Whennuas or islands..which he [*sc.* Cook] called Tovy Poenammoo; the literal translation of this word is, 'the water of green talc'.] **1835** W. Yate *Acct. N.Z.* (ed. 2) v. 271, I have put on board the Buffalo a mere pounamu and two garments. **1867** E. Sauter tr. *F. von Hochstetter's New Zealand* xvii. 362 A magnificent Mere punamu, a battle axe..cut out of the most beautiful, transparent nephrite. **1905** W. B. *Where White Man Treads* 39 'Pounamu' (greenstone) was only to be found in the creeks of the inland ranges of the Middle Island. **1965** G. J. Williams *Econ. Geol. N.Z.* v. 45/2 Pounamu Ultramafics occur within the rocks of this area. **1973** *Times Lit. Suppl.* 9 Feb. 141/3 The repeated word of the title, *pounamu*, however translucent to New Zealanders, will be opaque to the English reader. It means 'greenstone', a New Zealand form of jade, evocative of a past when it was the prized material of axe and ornament.

pounce (paʊns), *sb.*[1] Also 5–8 pownce, 6 pounse, *Sc.* punse, punss, 9 *dial.* punce. [Etymology obscure: no corresponding sb. is known in French or other Romanic language. The various groups of senses are parallel to those of pounce *v.*[1], the evidence for vb. and sb. beginning early in the 15th c., in one group the sb., in two the vb. appearing first. The connexion of the various groups of senses is far from clear; there may have been more than one origin. But the senses correspond to a considerable extent with those of punch *sb.*[1], and still more with those of puncheon *sb.*[1], which is found much earlier than either *pounce* or *punch*, and corresponds in form and sense to F. *poinçon* (also †*ponchon*), It. †*ponzione, punzione*:—L. or Com. Romanic *punctio, -ōnem*, f. L. *pungĕre, punct-* to prick, pierce, *puncta* point. *Pounce* and *punch* seem to have been in some way shortened from *ponson, ponchon*, puncheon, q.v.

Senses 3, 4, 5 are in puncheon from 14th c.; senses 4, 5, 7 are also in punch from 16th c.; but senses 1, 2, 6, 8 do not occur in either of these words.]

I. †**1.** A prick, sting. In quot. *fig. Obs.*

1413 *Pilgr. Sowle* (Caxton) i. xxii. (1859) 24, I haue ben with the whan thou knewe it nought, Enserchyng loo! thy pounce of conscyence.

2. The claw or talon of a bird of prey; rarely of other animals; in *Falconry* formerly restricted to the innermost of the three anterior toes or claws of a hawk, sometimes applied to any of the anterior as distinguished from the posterior claw or talon.

1486 *Bk. St. Albans* a xiij, Fyrst the grete Clees behynde that strenyth the bake of the hande ye shall call hom Talons. .. The Clees with in the fote ye shall call of right her Pownces. **1513** Douglas *Æneis* xiii. v. 118 Quhar Iovis byg fowle, the ern, With hir strang tallonys and hir punsys stern Lychtyng, had claucht the lytyll hynd calf ȝyng. **1575** Turberv. *Falconrie* 27 Festus, he is of opinion, that the Falcon is so named, bycause of hir pownces and crooked Talons, which do bend like vnto a syth, or sickle. **1596** Spenser *F.Q.* v. iv. 42 And from her griping pounce the greedy prey doth rive. **1664** Power *Exp. Philos.* i. 28 She [an insect] has two blackish claws, or pounces (at the ends of her feet,) which she can open and shut at her pleasure. **1700** Blackmore *Job* 175 Her crooked pounces bear The bloody banquet swiftly thro' the air. **1791** Cowper *Iliad* viii. 283 In his pounces strong A fawn he bore. **1863** Thornbury *True as Steel* I. 189 Had hawk ever a fuller eye, or larger pounces, or slenderer tail?

b. *nonce-use.* The paw of a lion.

a **1670** Hacket *Abp. Williams* i. (1692) 71 A Lion may be judg'd by these two Claws of his Pounce.

c. *fig.* in reference to persons. (Cf. clutch *sb.*[1])

1641 Milton *Reform.* i. (1851) 13 They must mew their feathers, and their pounces, and make but curt-tail'd Bishops of them. *a* **1734** North *Exam.* ii. iv. §84 (1740) 272 The King and the Duke (which latter they thought already in their Pounces). **1775** Burke *Sp. Conc. Amer.* Wks. III. 56 Winged ministers of vengeance, who carry your bolts in their pounces. **1782** Elphinston tr. *Martial* i. vi. 27 Say, whether gives thy wonder more to rove, The power of Caesar, or the pounce of Jove?

†**3.** *Sc.* A dagger; = puncheon[1] 2. *Obs.*

1545 *Aberdeen Regr.* XIX. (Jam.), Ane knapiscaw, and tua hand suerd, ane punss, ane sellet, ane denss aix [Danish ax], ane pair of pantars, ane coip burd.

†**4.** An engraver's burin. *Obs.*

1598 Florio, *Borino*, a small sharpe pounce that grauers vse.

II. †**5.** A die, stamp, or punch, for impressing marks on metal, etc. *Obs.*

1556 Withals *Dict.* (1566) 31/2 A pounse or printing iyorne to marke with, *rudicula*. *Ibid.* 35 b/2 A pounce to printe the money with, *tudicula*.

†**6.** A hole pinked, punched, or cut out, for the purpose of ornamenting a garment; = pink *sb.*[3]

1563 *Homilies* ii. *Excess of Apparel* (1859) 313 While one spendeth his patrimony upon pounces and cuts, another bestoweth more on a dancing shirt than might suffice to buy him honest and comely apparel for his whole body. *a* **1591** H. Smith *Wks.* (1867) II. 61 If the proud would leave their superfluity in apparel,..their vanity in cuts, guards and pounces, their excess in spangling,..and needless bravery.

III. **7.** A forcible poke with hand, elbow, foot, or stick; a thrust, push, nudge; = punch *sb.* Now *dial.*; in Sc. *esp.* a poke with the naked foot in bed.

1755 Amory *Mem.* (1766) II. 91 *note*, Giving the director a pounce, and asking him what he meant by such behavior? *c* **1821** J. W. Masters *Dick & Sal* lxxvi. (E.D.D.), I thoft I'd fedge him one more pounce, So heav'd my stick an' meant it. **1899** Crockett *Kit Kennedy* xii. 87 The command was punctuated by sundry admonitory 'punces' in the ribs. *Mod. Sc.* He gave his bed-fellow a punce with his foot to waken him.

†**8.** A padded sheath for the spur of a fighting cock. *Obs.*

1688 R. Holme *Armoury* ii. xi. 252/2 Hotts or Hutts, are the Pounces or round Balls of Leather stuffed and clapped or tied on the sharp end of the Spurs, to keep Cocks that they shall not hurt one another in sparing, or breathing themselves.

IV. †**9.** ? Pounded meat. *Obs. rare.*

1612 tr. *Benvenuto's Passenger* i. ii. 165 Of the flesh thereof [of the Tortoise] there is made pounces for sicke men [*orig.* se ne fa pesti alli infermi] to refresh..them.

V. **10.** *attrib.* (from 1): **pounce joint**, a knuckle in a hawk's toe.

1615 Latham *Falconry* (1633) 135 If it fall out that the straine do happen on any of the tallons or pownce ioynts, whereby you do perceiue that place onely to swell.

pounce (paʊns), *sb.*[2] [ad. F. *ponce* pumice, also pounce = Sp. *pómez*, Pg. *pomes*, It. *pomice*:—L. *pūmex, -icem*, pumice *sb.*]

1. A fine powder, as pulverized sandarac or cuttle-shell, used to prevent the ink from spreading in writing over an erasure or on unsized paper, and also to prepare the surface of parchment to receive writing.

[**1390** *Earl Derby's Exp.* (Camden) 19 Pro xviij pellibus pergameni..iiij s., et pro pounci, j d.] **1706** Phillips, *Pounce*, a sort of Powder strew'd upon Paper to bear Ink, or to soak up a Blot. **1714** *Lond. Gaz.* No. 5216/3 All Persons may be supply'd with..fine Pounce. **1727** W. Mather *Yng. Man's Comp.* 52 Use Pounce to Paper, if the Ink go thro'. **1753** Chambers *Cycl. Supp.*, *Pounce*, among writing-masters, a powder made of gum-sandarac, which being rubbed on the paper, makes it less apt to imbibe the ink; it is therefore used in this manner by those who are curious in the art of the pen, by which means the writing appears more precise, sharp, and determinate. **1839** Col. Hawker *Diary* (1893) II. 162 A cuttlefish, which I never saw before, (common as the shell is for pounce). **1858** Mayne *Expos. Lex.*, *Pounce*, common name for the powder of the concrete resin of the *Juniper communis*, or of pumice stone. **1861** Hulme tr. *Moquin-Tandon* ii. iii. ii. 83 The bone of the Cuttle-fish..is used..as a pounce to prevent ink from spreading after erasures. **1866** *Treas. Bot.* 198/2 *Callitris quadrivalvis*... The resin of this tree is..gum sandarach; while powdered it forms pounce. **1881** Blackmore *Christowell* xlvii, Mr. Latimer..had carefully erased with penknife and with pounce..the genuine name.

2. A fine powder, as powdered sandarac, pipeclay, or charcoal, dusted over a perforated pattern sheet to transfer the design to the object beneath; stamping-powder.

1727–41 Chambers *Cycl.*, *Pounce*, among artificers, a little heap of charcoal-dust, inclosed in some open stuff; to be passed over holes pricked in a work, in order to mark the lines or designs thereof on a paper placed underneath. **1851** Woodward *Mollusca* 76 It [the cuttle-shell] is now only used as 'pounce', or in casting counterfeits. **1853** Ure *Dict. Arts* II. 454 To obviate the difficulty and expense of drawing the pattern on every piece of a service..a 'pounce' is used. **1873** E. Spon *Workshop Receipts* Ser. i. 429/2 This powder (paper powder) makes excellent pounce.

3. *attrib.* and *Comb.*, as *pounce-bag, -box, pattern, pot, powder*; **pounce-paper**, see quot. 1858; **pounce-tree**, *Callitris quadrivalvis*.

1799 *Hull Advertiser* 29 June 2/2 Slates, inkstands, pounce-boxes, sealing-wax. **1820** Lamb *Elia* Ser. i. *South-sea Ho.*, The pounce-boxes of our days have gone retrograde. **1839** Ure *Dict. Arts* 952 Their [the moulds'] surfaces should be brushed evenly over with pounce powder (sandarach) beaten up with white of egg. **1855** W. Williams *Transparency Painting on Linen* 20 Pounce patterns..are formed of outlines perforated through the paper on which they are drawn, by a succession of small needle holes. *Ibid.* 27 The pounce-bag is made by tying a little fine, dry, black powder, in two or three squares of the muslin..used for painting on... The perforated pattern being placed on the cloth, the pounce-bag is lightly tapped on the surface, so as to force the powder..through all the perforations of the pattern. **1858** Simmonds *Dict. Trade*, *Pounce-paper*, a transparent paper for drawing, or tracing, &c. made in Carlsruhe; it is free from oily, greasy or other objectionable substance, and will therefore bear sketching and painting on. **1866** W. Davidge *Footlight Flashes* xv. 146 A pack of cards, a piece of rosin, a flute case, a pounce, or sand box, and a newspaper printed in the German language. **1884** Miller *Plant-n.*, *Pounce-tree, Callitris quadrivalvis*. **1939** *Newsweek* 13 Mar. 37/3 And (using a 'pouncebag' filled with dry pigment) [the painter] rules the outline through the perforations onto the preliminary coat of mortar. **1957** Mankowitz & Haggar *Conc. Encycl. Eng. Pott. & Porc.* 181/2 *Pounce pot*, a small box with a perforated lid for perfumes; a powder box or jar; a pierced-topped jar for sprinkling powdered pumice used to dry ink (before the popularity of blotting paper). **1971** *Country Life* 29 July 263/1 The top [of an inkstand] is inset with an ormolu tray flanked by inkpot and pounce pot.

pounce, *sb.*[3] [f. pounce *v.*[2]] An act of pouncing, as of a bird or beast on its prey; a sudden swoop or spring; quick or eager movement to an object: esp. in the phrase ***to make a pounce***. ***on the pounce***, ready to pounce, watching for an opportunity to spring upon or take one by surprise.

1841 Lane *Arab. Nts.* I. ii. 127 The Cherkh made several unsuccessful pounces. **1860** Gen. P. Thompson *Audi Alt.* III. cxxii. 69 Choosing which of them you would make a pounce upon with your collected force. **1887** E. Harrington in *Ho. Comm.* (*Pall Mall G.* 13 Sept. 8/1), You, Mr. Speaker, have been on the pounce for me since I rose, and I claim my right to speak. **1902** *Westm. Gaz.* 12 June 3/1 His enemies were on the pounce to belittle his efforts and misinterpret his motives.

pounce (paʊns), *v.*[1] Forms: (5 ponse (?), pownece), 5–6 pownse, 5–7 pounse, pownce, 5– pounce (9 *dial.* punse, punce). [Goes in form and sense with pounce *sb.*[1] Senses 1, 4, 5, 6, are found also in punch *v.* (sense 4 in Wyclif), sense 2 is found in *pounceon*, pounson *v.* (two examples in one place in Chaucer, where the MSS. are divided between *pounson* and *pounce*), a. F. *poinçonner*, OF. *ponchonner*, = It. *punzonare*. On account of the rarity of *pounson* in Eng., *pounce* and *punch* can hardly have been shortened from it; but they may have been thus formed from the Fr. vb., or in some senses from pounce *sb.*[1] Of the Romanic langs., Spanish and Portuguese alone have a corresp. vb., Sp. *punzar* 'to punch, prick, sting', Pg. and OSp. *punçar* 'to pricke, to pounce, to foine' (Minsheu 1599); but the derivation of a 14th c. word from these langs. seems out of the question. Cf. pounson *v.*, punch *v.*[1]]

I. **1.** *trans.* To emboss (plate or other metalwork) as a decoration, by raising the surface with blows struck on the under side, as in *répoussé* work. See also pounced *ppl. a.*[1] 1. *Obs.* exc. *Hist.*

[**1424** in *E.E. Wills* (1882) 57 þe keuered pece of syluer þe which was mayster Robertis Stoneham, and is pounces whith a crane.] **1430** in Rymer *Fœdera* (1710) X. 594 Bassyns of Gold..Pounsed with grete Boseletts. **1465** in Heath *Grocers' Comp.* (1869) 424 A stondynge Cuppe, cover of sylver and alle gilte, pownsed. **1530** Palsgr. 663/2, I pownce a cuppe, or a pece, as goldesmythes do. **1552** Huloet, *Pounce*. Loke in graue, and Imboce. **1570** Levins *Manip.* 220/24 To Pounce, *insculpere*. **1577–87** Holinshed *Chron.* III. 934/2 The marchionesse of Dorset gaue three gilt bolles pounced with a couer. **1849** Rock *Ch. of Fathers* II. vii. 341 As the writing, pounced on the outside of the silver-gilt rim, tells.

b. *transf.* (in *passive*) Of the surface of an animal body. **c.** *fig.* To adorn, decorate.

1576 Fleming *Panopl. Epist.* 167 Rhetoricall ornamentes, which beautifie and pounce the style of an Orator. **1705** J. Petiver in *Phil. Trans.* XXV. 1952 Its Back is variously pounc't with Sand-like Warts.

2. To ornament (cloth, etc.) by cutting or punching eyelet-holes, figures, etc.; = pink *v.*[1] 3. Also ***pounce out***. *Obs.* exc. *Hist.*

c **1386** Chaucer *Parson's T.* ¶ 344 (Hengwrt) Ther is also the costlewe furrynge in hire gownes, so muche pownsonynge of chisel to maken holes, so muche daggynge of sheris. [*Ellesm.* powsonynge, *Harl.* 1758 pounsounn-, *Petw.* pownsen-, *Egerton* 2726 pounsonyng; *c* **1425** *Harl.* 7334, *Selden* pounsyng, *Lansd.* pounseinge.] *Ibid.* ¶ 347 If.. they wolde yeue swiche pownsonyd & dagged clothynge to the pouere folk. [*Ellesm.* powsoned, *Harl.* 1758, *Petw.* pounsonede; *c* **1425** *Harl.* 7334, *Selden, Lansd.* pounsed.]

1531 ELYOT *Gov.* II. iii, To se a iuge or sergeant at the lawe in a short cote, garded and pounced after the galyarde facion. *a* **1548** HALL *Chron., Hen. VIII* 55 b, The syluer [cloth] was pounsed in letters, so that veluet might be sene through. **1591** SYLVESTER *Du Bartas* I. iii. 1143 With sumptuous silks (pinked and pounc'd, and puft). **1840** W. H. AINSWORTH *Tower of Lond.* i, Over this he wore a mantle of cloth of silver, pounced with his cipher, lined with blue velvet.

b. To cut the edges of (a garment) into points and scallops; to jag. Chiefly said in *passive*, of the cloth or garment. *Obs.* exc. *Hist.*

1542 UDALL *Erasm. Apoph.* 313 Traillyng after hym the skyrtes of his goune all pounced in cuttes and tagges. **1548** ELYOT *Dict.*, *Concido*.., to cutte in littell pieces, to hacke smalle, to iagge or pounce, to beate, to kyll or flea. **1843** LYTTON *Last Bar.* II. i, A supertunic of crimson sarcenet, slashed and pounced with a profusion of fringes.

†**c.** *passive.* Of leaves, etc.: To be laciniated with jags, points, and indentations on the edges. *Obs.*

1578 LYTE *Dodoens* IV. lviii. 519 The seconde kinde hath broade crompled leaues, al to pounced and iagged,.. and set rounde about with sharpe prickles. *Ibid.* V. xlvii. 610 The leaues.. more tenderer, and more mangled, pounsed or iagged. **1681** GREW *Musæum* I. II. i. 18 Every Plate [of the shell of an Armadillo] is about ½ Inch broad, curiously composed of small triangular or wedge-like pieces, indented one against another, and pounced or pricked all along their edges. **1705** J. PETIVER in *Phil. Trans.* XXV. 1960 Its edges are rather pounc't than notch'd.

II. †**3.** To bruise with blows; *esp.* to bruise, stamp, pound, or beat small; to comminute or reduce to powder by blows. *Obs.*

1519 HORMAN *Vulg.* 259 b, He came home with his face all to pounced [*contusa*]. **1577** STANYHURST *Descr. Irel.* in Holinshed *Chron.* (1808) VI. 8 It cutteth flegme, it.. healeth the strangurie, it pounceth the stone, it expelleth gravell. **1630** J. TAYLOR (Water P.) *Cast over Water* Wks. II. 158 I'l squeeze, and crush, and vnto poulder pounce thee. **1662** J. CHANDLER *Van Helmont's Oriat.* 106 Flowers and leaves being pounced, a ferment being snatched to them, they begin to boyl and be hot, whence ariseth a Gas.

4. To poke or thrust forcibly, esp. with the foot or a stick. Now chiefly *Sc.* (*punce*).

1577 HANMER *Anc. Eccl. Hist.* (1663) 139 He made for himself a lofty seat and high Throne,.. after the manner of the Princes of this world, smiting the thigh with the hand, pouncing the footstool with his feet. **1581** J. BELL *Haddon's Answ. Osor.* 64 And in this place our glorious Peacocke pounceth out his feathers. **1824** MACTAGGART *Gallovid. Encycl.*, *Punse*, to push and strike, as with a stick; to *punse* a brock in his lair, to push, or ratherly striking push, a badger in his den. **1863** B. BRIERLEY *Bundle o' Fents* (Lancash.) 25 Pepper Wild wantut us t' fasten him [the dummy] up theer [i.e. at the door] an' then punse th' dur an' see what Owd Johnny 'ud say when he coom eawt. *Mod. Sc.* I cannot have the child in bed with me, he punces so.

†**b.** (See quot.) *Obs.*

1708 J. C. *Compl. Collier* (1843) 11 *The way of Boreing.* We have two Labourers at a time, at the handle of the bore Rod, and they chop, or pounce with their Hands up and down to cut the Stone or Mineral, going round, which of course grinds either of them small.

5. To beat, thump, thrash (a person).

1827 CAPT. HARDMAN *Battle of Waterloo* 18 The French were pouncing us. **1847** PORTER *Big Bear*, etc. 146 He did then and there.. most wantonly and brutishly 'pounced' [sic] his old wife. **1897** RHOSCOMYL *White Rose Arno* 121 Thou got punced just the same.

III. †**6.** To prick, puncture, pierce, stab. *Obs.*

c **1440** *Promp. Parv.* 411/2 Pownson (*K.*, *P.*, poyntyn), *puncto.* **1570** FOXE *A. & M.* 125/2 Cut, pricke, and pounce hym, no longer forbeare. **1577** B. GOOGE *Heresbach's Husb.* III. (1586) 131 b, But if so be the blood be yet aboue the hoofe in the legges, you shall dissolue it with good rubbing, .. with scarifiyng, or Pouncing the skinne. **1601** HOLLAND *Pliny* II. 235 There is a juice pressed forth both of the fruit, .. and also of the root, which somtime they do pounce and prick for to let out the liquor. **1621** FLETCHER *Pilgrim* IV. ii, Out with your knives,.. pounce him lightly And, as he roars and rages, let's go deeper. *a* **1640** DAY *Peregr. Schol.* (1881) 70 Some of his profession had.. so prickt and pownct there windie reputacons with there penns.

†**7.** In primitive cultures; to prick the skin in designs as an adornment; to tattoo. Cf. PINK *v.*[1] 4. *Obs.*

1555 EDEN *Decades* 359 Theyr princes.. vse to pounse and rase theyr skynnes with prety knottes. **1613** PURCHAS *Pilgrimage* (1614) 768 The women with an Iron pownce and race their bodies, legs, thighes, and armes, in curious knots and portraitures of fowles, fishes, beasts. **1626** BACON *Sylva* §739 Barbarous People that go Naked, do not onely Paint Themselves, but they Pownce and raze their Skin, that the Painting may not be taken forth. **1650** BULWER *Anthropomet.* Pref., Painted with lists, here, naked arms behold Branded and pounc'd with colours manifold.

Hence '**pouncing** *ppl. a.*, piercing.

1798 LANDOR *Gebir* VII. 55 The wave, parted by the pouncing beak, Swells up the sides and closes far astern.

pounce (paʊns), *v.*[2] [f. POUNCE *sb.*[1] 2.]

1. *trans.* To seize, as a bird of prey, with the pounces or talons; to swoop down upon and lay hold of suddenly. *to pounce away*: to pounce upon and carry off.

1686 F. SPENCE tr. *Varillas' Ho. Medicis* 201 Whoever pounc d the state of Terra-firma. **1726** POPE *Odyss.* XIX. 631 Each fav'rite fowl he pounc'd with deathful sway. **1789** G. WHITE *Selborne* (1853) 350 They cannot pounce the quarry on the ground. **1800–24** CAMPBELL *Dead Eagle* 76 Lately when he pounced the speckled snake. **1821** CLARE *Vill. Minstr.* I. 121 And like a hawk from covert sprung It pounc'd my peace away.

2. *intr.* To make a pounce; to swoop down as a bird of prey; to spring suddenly *upon* or *at* in the way of attack.

1744 P. WHITEHEAD *Gymnasiad* III. 76 So, when a Falcon skims the airy way, Stoops from the clouds, and pounces on his prey. **1774** GOLDSM. *Nat. Hist.* (1776) VI. 74 The gannet instantly pounces down from above upon the board, and is killed or maimed. *a* **1885** HELEN H. JACKSON *Two Sundays* i, The kitten pounced.. At stealthy spiders that tried to pass.

3. *intr. to pounce on* or *upon*: *transf.* to fall upon suddenly and seize; to seize upon suddenly.

1812 H. & J. SMITH *Rej. Addr.* i, Some years ago he pounced with deadly glee on The Opera House. **1835** W. IRVING *Tour Prairies* 103 A silent, watchful, crafty people, who.. may be around us.. ready to pounce upon all stragglers. **1876** SAUNDERS *Lion in Path* x, Might not his bales be pounced upon and carried away by thievish wreckers? **1885** *Manch. Exam.* 13 Jan. 5/2 The Germans have chosen to pounce down all at once upon parts of the S. African coast.

b. *fig.* To 'lay hold of' eagerly, suddenly, or promptly.

1840 HOOD *Up Rhine* 45 He eagerly pounced upon me as one with whom he could pour out his bottled-up grievances. **1844** STANLEY *Arnold* I. iii. 142 The rapidity with which he would pounce on any mistake of grammar or construction. **1884** *Sat. Rev.* 12 July 40/1 Lord Hartington pounced upon Sir W. Barttelot's unlucky phrase.

4. *intr.* To spring or jump unexpectedly; to 'come down' (in some understood way).

1836 T. HOOK *G. Gurney* II. vi. 306 If I had not, by some misfortune or other, pounced into the old General's room by mistake for his daughter's. **1840** DICKENS *Old C. Shop* l, Mind too that I don't pounce in upon you at unseasonable hours again. **1890** *Pall Mall G.* 15 July 3/1 At a quarter past seven Mr. Smith 'pounced', and the Closure was carried by 182 to 118. **1892** *Daily News* 12 Nov. 2/2 While walking rapidly along Queen's-gate the defendant suddenly 'pounced' in front of them.

Hence '**pouncing** *vbl. sb.* and *ppl. a.*

1841 LANE *Arab. Nts.* I. ii. 126 These fine birds, in pouncing, frequently impale themselves on its sharp horns. **1869** MISS BRADDON *Lady's Mile* i, The pouncing proprietor .. has hard work to collect his rents. **1883** H. P. SPOFFORD in *Harper's Mag.* Mar. 583/1 Her face bright with a hovering triumph on the point of pouncing.

pounce (paʊns), *v.*[3] Also 6 pounse, 7 pownce. [ad. F. *poncer* (*c* 1277 in Littré) to polish or erase with pumice (:—L. *pūmicāre* to polish with pumice, f. *pūmex, -icem* PUMICE), also †to paint or powder (the cheeks), to pounce (a design for embroidery), f. *ponce* POUNCE *sb.*[2]]

1. *trans.* To smooth down by rubbing with pumice or pounce; *spec.* to smooth or finish (the surface of a hat) with pumice, sand-paper, emery-powder, or the like.

1580 HOLLYBAND *Treas Fr. Tong*, *Poncer*, to pounce [cf. COTGR., *Poncer*, to smooth, polish, rub ouer, with a Pumeise stone]. **1651** G. DANIEL *Letter* Poems (Grosart) II. 206 Though the Table, Brother, (halfe pounc't to our hands) may save some Paines. **1868** J. THOMSON *Hat-making* 48 Pouncing is a term for rubbing down the outside of a hat with a piece of pumice stone, sand paper, or emery paper. **1884** KNIGHT *Dict. Mech.* Suppl. 716/1 To sand-paper—or, as it is called in the trade, to pounce—hat-bodies when in the conical form, or, when the hat has been blocked, to pounce the brim.

2. To trace or transfer (a design) on or to a surface by dusting a perforated pattern with pounce; to dust (the perforations in a pricked pattern) with pounce; also, to imprint or copy a design upon (a surface) by means of pounce.

1594 PLAT *Jewell-ho.* III. 39 Some.. prick the pattern full of holes & so pounce it vpon another paper. **1683** CAPT. WYLDE *Let. to Pepys* in *P.'s Life* (1841) I. 422 Their patterns being drawn on paper, they prick them, and pounce them with charcoal. **1799** G. SMITH *Laboratory* I. 271 Draw or pounce what you design to emboss. **1855** W. WILLIAMS *Transparency Painting on Linen* 28 If an accident.. occur, it is only necessary to dust the powder off the muslin, to re-adjust the pattern, and again pounce in the design. **1859** GULLICK & TIMBS *Paint.* 147 Pricking through the lines,.. and pouncing the holes with red or black dust. **1960** B. SNOOK *Eng. Hist. Embroidery* 51 The design was either pricked and pounced and drawn with a clear black line, or it was printed from an engraving direct upon the linen.

†**3. a.** To sprinkle with powder; to powder, dust; *esp.* to powder (the face) with a cosmetic. **b.** To sprinkle with specks, spots, or the like. *Obs.*

1593 NASHE *Christ's T.* 71 b, How you [Ladies] torture poore olde Time with spunging, pynning and pounsing. **1610** W. FOLKINGHAM *Art of Survey* II. vi. 58 It shal not be amisse to pounce the ground with a Stainsh-Graine of burnt Allome and a double quantity of pounded Rossin both finely searced and lightly pummiced, thereby to preserue the Paper or Parchment from thorowe piercing with the Colours. **1624** DARCIE *Birth of Heresies* xii. 51 Decorations, the better to powce and set forth the great Babilonish whore. **1648** HERRICK *Hesper.*, *Julia's Petticoat*, Thy azure robe.. pounc't with stars, it shew'd to me Like a celestiall canopie. **1685** COTTON tr. *Montaigne* I. 593 They who paint, pounce and plaister up the ruins of women, filling up their wrinkles and deformities.

pounce commerce. [f. POUNCE *v.*[2] + COMMERCE *sb.* 6.] A round game of cards similar to 'grab' or 'snap'.

1864 WHYTE MELVILLE *Brookes of B.* xxiii. (*heading*), Pounce commerce. **1888** J. PAYN *Myst. Mirbridge* viii, Love is very much like the domestic game of pounce commerce —we must.. always keep changing one's hand, as the cards come round.

pounced (paʊnst), *a.* [f. POUNCE *sb.*[1] + -ED[2].] Having talons like a hawk: usually in comb.

1687 DRYDEN *Hind & P.* III. 1117 Some haggar'd Hawk .. Well pounc'd to fasten, and well wing'd to fly. **1700** — *Pythagorean Philos.* 570 The strong pounc'd Eagle and the billing dove. **1787** *Generous Attachment* III. 5 The soft doves of Venus will then flit away before the strong pounced eagle of ambition.

pounced (paʊnst), *ppl. a.*[1] [f. POUNCE *v.*[1]]

1. Of metal-work: Embossed or chased by way of ornament. *Obs.* exc. *Hist.*

[**1430**, etc.: see POUNCE *v.*[1] 1.] **1502** *Bury Wills* (Camden) 258 My best pownsyd peece. **1513** DOUGLAS *Æneis* IX. v. 94 Twa siluer coupis.. With figuris grave and punsyt ymagery. **1552** HULOET, Pounced plate, *anaglypha*, *anaglypta*. **1582** *Lanc. Wills* (1857) I. 132 A pounse [? pounsed] bolle parcell gylt.

2. Of clothing: Perforated, punctured, or laciniated for ornament; pinked. *Obs.* exc. *Hist.*

c **1386** [see POUNCE *v.*[1] 2]. *a* **1548** HALL *Chron., Hen. VIII* 11 b, All in Crymosyn Satyn, garded with a pounced garde of grene Veluet. **1589** PUTTENHAM *Eng. Poesie* III. xxiv. (Arb.) 290 Who would not thinke it a ridiculous thing to see .. a Gentleman of the Countrey among the bushes and briers, goe in a pounced dublet and a paire of embrodered hosen?

fig. *a* **1653** G. DANIEL *Idyll.* iv. 116 Wrought Pillow's bring Pownc'd Law, Stitched Common-wealth, and purled King.

†**b.** Cut or laciniated at the edges, as a leaf. *Obs.*

1681 GREW *Musæum* II. v. ii. 248 The Pounced Sea-Wrack, *Alga marina.*

†**3.** Beaten, bruised. *Obs.*

1551 *Beware the Cat* (1570) 81 The young woman to whom she shewed her pounced thies, said I was an unnatural daughter to deal so with my mother.

†**4.** Pricked, marked by pricking; tattooed. *Obs.*

1555 EDEN *Decades* 144 With a sharpe prycke made eyther of bone or elles with a thorne, they make holes in their faces: and foorthwith sprinkelynge a pouder theron, they moiste the pounced place with a certeyne blacke or redde iuise. **1610** HOLLAND *Camden's Brit.* I. 115 That their Nobilitie and Gentry thus spotted, may carrie these starres about them, in their painted pownced limmes, as badges.

pounced, *ppl. a.*[2] [f. POUNCE *v.*[3] + -ED[1].]

1. Powdered, dusted.

1619 H. HUTTON *Follie's Anat.* A viij b, And that he may obtaine his lust, compares Her eyes to starres, to Amber her pounc't hayres. **1633** PRYNNE *Histrio-m.* I. VI. xv. 546 b, Their frizled Periwigs, Love-lockes, and long effeminate pouldred pounced haire. **1683** CAPT. WYLDE *Let. to Pepys* in *P.'s Life* (1841) I. 422 Cotton yarn.. which they dip in the liquor, squeezing it gently,.. so running along the pounced work, where it turns black in a trice. **1807** CRABBE *Par. Reg.* I. 151 Tulips tall-stemm'd and pounc'd auriculas rise. **1855** W. WILLIAMS *Transparency Painting on Linen* 28 The pattern being removed, the pounced design is secured by being traced with a soft black-lead pencil, and drawn in with a reed pen.

2. Sprinkled with minute specks as if powdered.

1727 BRADLEY *Fam. Dict.* s.v. *Carnation*, The Flowers of the Picketees are always of a white Ground, spotted or pounced, as they call it, with Red or Purple. **1892** E. CASTLE *Eng. Bk.-Plates* 145 The achievements and scrolls and pounced background common to the printers' mark.

'**pounced stone,** for *pounce-stone*, F. *pierre ponce*, pumice-stone.

1585 T. WASHINGTON tr. *Nicholay's Voy.* II. xxi. 58 b, With a pounced stone hee rubbeth.. the plantes of your feete.

pounceon, var. POUNSON *Obs.*; obs. f. PUNCHEON.

pouncer[1] ('paʊnsə(r)). [f. POUNCE *v.*[1] + -ER[1].] One who or that which pounces; †a pouncing tool.

1552 HULOET, Pouncer, *anaglypharius.* **1598** FLORIO, *Punzone*.. a goldsmiths pouncer or pounce. *Ibid.*, *Siggéllo*, a kind of pouncer goldsmiths vse. **1611** *Ibid.*, *Bulino*, a kind of pouncer that grauers vse.

pouncer[2] ('paʊnsə(r)). [f. POUNCE *v.*[3] + -ER[1].] A pouncing-tool; a pounce-bag.

1881 *Sylvia's Bk. Artistic Knicknacks* 371 Place the design on the canvas and pin it down; then take your pouncer, which is filled with fine charcoal or powdered colour, and dab.. all over your perforated outline. The pouncer is.. made by half-filling a thick muslin bag with charcoal or soot, and tying it tightly round. **1960** G. LEWIS *Handbk. Crafts* 16 Using a pouncer (a roll of felt) dipped into black pounce (powdered charcoal) for light materials.. gently rub the powder through the perforations, then lift away the tracing.

pouncer, erron. f. POUCER *Obs.*, thumb-stall.

pouncet ('paʊnsɪt). [A modern appellation, app. deduced from POUNCET-BOX, and used in the same sense.] = next.

1843 JAMES *Forest Days* (1847) 263 Thou art just the height of the King's confessor, and I shall pass for his pouncet-bearer. **1899** *Westm. Gaz.* 5 Aug. 1/3 Among the baubles on the chains—.. the old pouncet, the seal, and the pencil-case—there was no knife. **1901** *Daily News* 9 Feb. 8/2 No. 29.. described as a die-shaped pouncet.

'pouncet-box. quasi-*Hist.* [Derived in some way from POUNCE *sb.*[1] or *v.*[1]: perh. orig. a misprint for *pounced-box*, i.e. pierced or perforated box.] app. A small box with a perforated lid, used for holding perfumes. A Shaksperian term revived by Scott. In quot. 1863 for *pounce-box*, i.e. box of pounce or powder.

1596 SHAKS. *1 Hen. IV*, I. iii. 38 'Twixt his Finger and his Thumbe, he held A Pouncet-box: which euer and anon He gaue his Nose, and took't away againe. **1820** SCOTT *Monast.* xxvi, Sir Piercie Shafton knelt down, and most gracefully presented to the nostrils of Mary Avenel a silver pouncet-box..containing a sponge dipt in the essence which he recommended so highly. **1842** BARHAM *Ingol. Leg.* Ser. II. *Auto-da-fé*, His pouncet-box goes To and fro at his nose. **1863** WHYTE MELVILLE *Gladiators* I. 46 She took the pouncet-box from one of the girls, and proceeded to sprinkle gold-dust in Valeria's hair. **1886** *All Year Round* 28 Aug. 80 Of far more romantic associations was the pomander, or pouncet box.

pouncheon, obs. form of PUNCHEON.

†**pouncil.** *Obs. rare*⁻¹. [ad. F. *poncille* 'the Assyrian Citron' (Cotgr.).] (See quot.)

1585 T. WASHINGTON tr. *Nicholay's Voy.* II. i. 31 b, A great barrell of muscadel,..and diuers other pouncils, citrons and oranges.

pouncing ('paʊnsɪŋ), *vbl. sb.*[1] [f. POUNCE *v.*[1] + -ING[1].] The action of POUNCE *v.*[1] in various senses. Also *attrib.*

c **1386** [see POUNCE *v.*[1] 2]. **1591** PERCIVAL *Sp. Dict.*, *Entrepunçasura*, pricking, pouncing, *interpunctio. Ibid.*, *Punçon*,..a pouncing yron,..*graphium.* **1598** FLORIO, *Broccaglio*, a bodkin or pouncing iron. **1601** HOLLAND *Pliny* Explan. Words, *Scarification*, is a kind of pouncing or opening of the skin by way of incision slightly, with the fleame or launcet. **1611** SPEED *Hist. Gt. Brit.* v. vii. §2. 38 Their going naked,..their cutting, pinking, and pouncing of their flesh with garnishments..of sundry shapes.

'pouncing, *vbl. sb.*[2] [f. POUNCE *v.*[3] + -ING[1].] The action of POUNCE *v.*[3], q.v. **pouncing-machine**, a machine used in hat-making to smooth the nap, the hat-body being caused to rotate against a revolving cylinder of sand-paper.

1593 [see POUNCE *v.*[3] 3]. **1601** DENT *Pathw. Heaven* (1831) 35 They have spent a good part of the day in pranking and pouncing. *a* **1619** FLETCHER, etc. *Knt. Malta* II. i, What can you do now, With all your paintings and your pouncings, lady? *a* **1626** BACON *Inquis. Compound. Metals* Wks 1879 I. 241/2 It may be also tried by incorporating powder of steel or copper dust by pouncing into the quicksilver. **1627** MAY *Lucan* IX. (1631) 923 As in pouncing of a picture, forth Through every hole the pressed saffron goes. **1868** [see POUNCE *v.*[3] 1].

pouncing, *vbl. sb.*[3]: see POUNCE *v.*[2]

pouncing, *ppl. a.*[1] and[2]: see POUNCE *v.*[1] and[2].

pound (paʊnd), *sb.*[1] Forms: 1–4 (*Sc.* and *n. dial.* -9) pund, (4–5 *n. dial.* punde); 3– pound, (4–6 pounde, pownd(e; pond(e). [OE. *pund* (pl. *pund*):—WGer. stem **pundo-* pound (weight), = OSax., OFris., ON., Goth. *pund* (MLG. *punt*, LG. *pund*, MDu. *pont*, Du. *pond*), OHG. *phunt* (MHG. *pfunt*, G. *pfund*), a very early adopted word, a. L. *pondo* indecl. a pound (weight), orig. instr. abl. of **pondus*, *-um* = *pondus*, *-er-* weight, in use short for *libra pondo* a pound by weight, a pound weight.]

I. 1. a. A measure of weight and mass derived from the ancient Roman *libra* (= 327·25 grams), but very variously modified in the course of ages in different countries, and as used for different classes of things; in Great Britain now fixed for use in trade by a Parliamentary standard. Denoted by *lb.* (L. *libra*).

Formerly used without change in the pl., a usage still sometimes retained after a numeral, esp. *dial.* and *colloq.*, also in *comb.* as ***a five pound note, a twenty pound shot.***

This pound consisted originally of 12 ounces, corresponding more or less to that of TROY *weight*, q.v., which contains 5760 grains = 373·26 grams. This is still used by goldsmiths and jewellers in stating the weight of gold, silver, and precious stones; but as early as the thirteenth or fourteenth century a pound of sixteen ounces was in use for more bulky commodities. This was made a standard for general purposes of trade by Edward III, and known as the pound *aveir de peis*, i.e. of merchandise of weight, now called AVOIRDUPOIS, q.v. This pound of 16 ounces, containing 7000 grains = 453·6 grams, has been since 1826 the only legal pound for buying or selling any commodity in Great Britain. In former times the pound varied locally from 12 to 27 ounces, according to the commodity, pounds of different weight being often used in the same place for different articles, as bread, butter, cheese, meat, malt, hay, wool, etc. See a list in *Old Country and Farming Words* (E.D.S.) 174–5. The Scotch pound of 16 ounces of Troy or Dutch Weight consisted of 7608·9496 grains; the Tron pound kept at Edinburgh = 9622·67 grains. *Pound* is also used to translate foreign names of weights, of cognate origin or representatives of L. *libra.* These vary greatly: in Italy between 300 and 350 grams, in Spain and Portugal, the Netherlands, and some German states between 459 and 469 grams, in other German states, Denmark, etc. between 477 and 510·22 grams. But the standard German *pfund* is now 500 grams, i.e. half a kilogram.

805–31 *Charter of Oswulf* (Sweet *O.E.T.* 444), iiii scep & tua flicca & v goes, & x hennfuȝlas & x pund caeses. *c* **1000** *Ags. Gosp* John xii. 3 Maria nam an pund deorwyrðre sealfe. *c* **1050** *Byrhtferth's Handboc* in *Anglia* VIII. 335 An uncia stent on feower and twentiȝ peneȝum. Twelf siðon twelf peneȝas beoð on anum punde. *a* **1340** HAMPOLE *Psalter* lxi. 9 Wiþ a fals punde þei begile þem þat sees þaim. **1340** *Ayenb.* 190 Uyftene pond of gold. **1362** LANGL. *P. Pl.* A. v. 155, I haue peper and piane and a pound of garlek. **1389** in *Eng. Gilds* (1870) 4 Of peyne of a pond wax to þe bretherhede. *c* **1420** *Liber Cocorum* (1862) 19 Take a pownde of ryse and sethe hom wele. **1532** *Acc. Ld. High Treas. Scot.* VI. 156, xxviij li culvering pulder, price of ilk pund iiij s. **1600** J. PORY tr. *Leo's Africa* Introd. 39 Some of them weie aboue fiue hundred pound. *Ibid.* 40 Of elephants,..some of their teeth do weigh two hundred pounds, at sixteene ounces the pound. **1602** FULBECKE *Pandectes* 71 An hundred fortie two thousand pound of siluer. **1744** BERKELEY *Siris* §22 This excellent balsam may be purchased for a penny a pound. **1749** REYNARDSON in *Phil. Trans.* XLVI. 59 At the same Time [1696] and Place, the Standard Troy Weights were compared with the Standard Avoirdepois,..which fixes the Pound Avoirdepois at 7000 such Grains, as the Troy Pound weighs 5760. *a* **1796** BURNS (*title*) The weary Pund o' Tow. **1821** J. Q. ADAMS in C. Davies *Metr. Syst.* III. (1871) 113 The time and occasion of the introduction of the avoirdupois pound into England is no better known than that of the troy weight. **1855** MORTON *Cycl. Agric.* II. 1125 Pound (Bucks.), sometimes 17 oz.; (Chesh.), 18 oz.; (Corn.), 18 oz.; (Derbys.), 17 oz.; (Devons.), 18 oz.; (Dorset), in some parts 18 oz.; (Durham), in many parts 22 oz.; etc., etc. **1895** *Model Steam Engine* 47 A common standard or 'unit of work' is obviously necessary. That..called the 'foot pound' is one pound raised through a space of one foot in one minute. **1959** *Nature* 10 Jan. 80 To secure identical values for each of these units in precise measurements for science and technology, it has been agreed [by standards laboratories in many countries] to adopt an international yard and an international pound..: the international pound equals 0·453 592 37 kgm... The yard and pound units to be used in trade are the imperial units laid down in the Weights and Measures Act, 1878. *Ibid.* 81 With regard to the pound, the values currently in use..are: 1 imperial standard pound = 0·453 592 338 kgm.; 1 Canadian pound = 0·453 592 43 kgm.; 1 United States pound = 0·453 592 4277 kgm. There is evidence that the imperial standard pound has diminished by about 7 parts in 10 millions since 1846. **1961** [see LB]. **1963** JERRARD & MCNEILL *Dict. Sci. Units* 109 In 1963 the pound was defined as being equal to '0·45359237 Kilogramme exactly' by the Weights and Measures Act... This pound is identical with the International pound adopted in 1959 by Standards Laboratories.

†**b.** A pound weight of water, forming a measure of capacity equivalent to a pint, and used in the OE. period as a standard of liquid and dry measure, in full ***water-pound.*** *Obs.*

Three Scotch pounds of the Water of Leith was the standard of the pint in Scotch liquid measure = 3 imperial pints.

c **1000** *Sax. Leechd.* II. 298 Pund eles ȝewihð xii peneȝum læsse þonne pund wætres, & pund ealoð ȝewihð vi peneȝum mare þonne pund wætres. *Ibid.* Gloss. 402 *Norma*, wæter pund.

c. *fig.* Of imponderable things; esp. in proverbial expressions.

1526, 1629, 1670 [see OUNCE *sb.*[1] 1 c]. **1607** WALKINGTON *Opt. Glass* 114 They..affirme men..to haue a pound of folly to an ounce of pollicy. *a* **1704** T. BROWN tr. *Æneas Sylvius' Lett.* lxxxii. Wks. 1709 III. II. 83 An hundred Pound of Sorrow pays not an Ounce of our Debts.

†**d.** A pound-weight, a weight. *Obs. nonce-use.*

1607 SHAKS. *Cor.* III. i. 314 This Tiger-footed-rage..will (too late) Tye Leaden pounds too's heeles.

†**e.** ***in pound***: ? in pounds, or ? in a balance. *Obs. nonce-use.*

1596 SPENSER *F.Q.* v. ii. 36 But if thou now shouldst weigh them new in pound, We are not sure they would so long remaine.

f. ***pound of flesh***: used proverbially, with reference to Shaks. *Merch. V.*: see quots.; also (with hyphens) as *phr.*

1596 SHAKS. *Merch. V.* IV. i. 99 *Shylock.* The pound of flesh which I demand of him Is deerely bought, 'tis mine, and I will haue it. *Ibid.* 308 *Portia.* Then take thy bond, take thou thy pound of flesh. **1860** KINGSLEY *Misc.* I. 23 Who would not..have given his pound of flesh to be captain of her guard? **1887** *Fortn. Rev.* Jan. 14 All the other Great Powers want their pound of flesh from Turkey. **1958** *Listener* 13 Nov. 775/2 He is entirely consistent..In the application of this pound-of-flesh attitude. **1963** AUDEN *Dyer's Hand* 228 *Pecorone* or other versions of the pound-of-flesh story.

g. ***pound and pint*** (Naut. slang), a sailor's ration as determined by the Board of Trade's Scale of Provisions. So ***pound and pinter***, a ship on which rations were provided on this scale; ***pound-and-pint idler*** (see quot. *a* 1865). *Obs.* exc. *Hist.*

a **1865** SMYTH *Sailor's Word-bk.* (1867) 540 *Pound-and-pint-idler*, a sobriquet applied to the purser. **1902** W. RUNCIMAN *Windjammers & Sea Tramps* vii. 90 Their 'whack', or to be strictly accurate, the phrase commonly used was 'your pound and pint'. **1910** D. W. BONE *Brassbounder* 168 A pound and pint ruddy limejuicer. **1938** W. E. DEXTER *Rope-Yarns* v. 31 It seemed my lot to mostly sail in what we called 'hungry-gutted ships', 'pound and pinters'. **1952** 'SINBAD' *Sargasso Sam* xxviii. 211 Wot about tucker? We never come aboard this old wagon to eat deepwater muck. Looks like we're gettin' pound an' pint and no more.

h. [from *pound of lead*, rhyming slang for 'head'.] The human head.

1933 F. RICHARDS *Old Soldiers never Die* xiv. 180 We old hands often used to remark that when we did get hit it would either be a bullet through the pound or stop a five-point-nine all on our own.

†**2.** *ellipt.* (*sc.* shot) = POUNDER *sb.*[4] 2. *Obs. rare.*

1759 ADM. HOLMES in *Naval Chron.* XXIV. 119 One carrying a 24-pound and the other a 9-pound.

II. 3. a. An English money of account (originally, a pound weight of silver), of the value of 20 shillings or 240 pence, and formerly represented by the gold sovereign; since 1971, of the value of 100 new pence. Denoted by £ before the numeral (occas. by *l.* after it), and distinguished by the epithet *sterling.*

c **975** *Rushw. Gosp.* Matt. xviii. 24 Wæs an broht, se him sceolde tyn þusend punda. *c* **1050** *Byrhtferth's Handboc* in *Anglia* VIII. 306, xx scillingas beoð on anum punde, and twelf siðon twentiȝ peneȝa byð an pund. *c* **1205** LAY. 8907 He sæl..ælche ȝere senden þreo þusend punden. *a* **1250** *Owl & Night.* 1101, & yaf for me an hundred punde. *c* **1300** *Havelok* 1633 A gold ring drow he forth anon, An hundred pund was worth þe ston. *c* **1380** WYCLIF *Wks.* (1880) 82 A litel deed leed costiþ many þousand pond bi ȝere to oure pore land. *Ibid.* 100 Many þousand pondis. *c* **1420** *Sir Amadace* (Camden) xxxii, The warst hors is worthe ten pownde. **1542** RECORDE *Gr. Artes* (1575) 198 Poundes, Markes, and shillings,..though they haue no coynes, yet is there no name more in vse than they. **1607** MIDDLETON *Five Gallants* II. iii. 232, I can lend you three pound, sir... There 'tis in six angels. *a* **1674** CLARENDON *Hist. Reb.* XIII. §33 Ten brave Spanish Horses, the worst of which cost there three hundred pounds sterling. **1712** ADDISON *Spect.* No. 445 ¶5 If my Country receives Five or Six Pounds a-day by my Labours, I shall be very well pleased. **1795** E. TATHAM *Nat. Debt* 14 Put the National funded Debt at Two Hundred Millions of Pounds. But what is a Pound: for that is the denominator. **1888** A. DOBSON *Goldsmith* 112 'Pounds' and 'guineas' were then [in the time of Dr. Johnson], as Croker points out in one of his notes, convertible terms.

b. Used as the type of a large sum of money, often in contrast with *penny*, or †associated with *mark.* Now chiefly in proverbial phrases. See PENNY 9.

a **1200** *Moral Ode* 67 Alse mid his penie alse oðer mið his punde. *Ibid.* 296 Ne sculle hi neure comen vp for marke ne for punde. *c* **1400** *Rom. Rose* 5986 That he shal, in a fewe stoundes, Lese alle his markes and his poundes. **1550** CROWLEY *Last Trump.* 1112 Thou maist for shyllinges gather poundes. **1562** MOUNTGOMERY in *Archæologia* XLVII. 240 Reamembringe that well ys spent the pennie that salveth the pounde.

†**c.** Through gradual debasement of the coinage, the 'pound Scots', originally the same as the English, was at the Union of the Crowns equal to one twelfth of a pound sterling, being divided into 20 shillings each of the value of an English penny.

1375 BARBOUR *Bruce* XVIII. 521 Lang eftir syne ransonyt wes he For twenty thousand pund to pay. **1500–20** DUNBAR *Poems* lxxxi. 75 Into this realme ȝow war worth mony ane pound. **1545** *Reg. Privy Council Scot.* I. 19 Twa hundreith pundis usuall money of this realm. **1614** B. JONSON *Barth. Fair* III. iv, What a Masque shall I furnish out, for forty shillings? (twenty pound scotch) and a Banquet of Ginger-bread? **1617** MORYSON *Itin.* I. 283 The Scots of old called 20 English pence a pound, as wee in England call 20 siluer shillings a pound. **1790** BURNS *Tam O'Shanter* 177 That sark she coft for her wee Nannie, Wi' twa pund Scots, ('twas a' her riches). **1814** SCOTT *Wav.* xviii, 'Donald would not lower a farthing of a thousand punds'—'The devil!' 'Punds Scottish, ye shall understand'.

d. Applied to the Turkish (and, formerly, Egyptian) gold pieces of 100 piastres, and to units of currency originally valued at par with the pound sterling.

1883 *Whitaker's Almanac* 371, Foreign Monies; Gold coins; Ottoman Empire, Turkish pound of 100 piastres £0. 18. 0¾. **1889** *Ibid.* 657 Egypt, 100 piastre piece (Egyptian £) £1. 0. 3½. **1949** *Britannica Bk. of Year* 364/2 On Aug. 17, 1948, a new Israeli pound..displaced the Palestine pound. **1955** *Ibid.* 141/1 Cyprus... Monetary unit: Cyprus pound (= £1 sterling). **1958** *Spectator* 15 Aug. 216/3 No one wanted to lend any money in terms of the Israeli Pound. **1975** *Times* 25 Nov. 7/1 The Israeli pound is officially fixed at seven to the dollar.

e. Phrases. ***in the pound***, † ***at pound***, reckoned at so much for each pound. ***pound and*** (or ***for***) ***pound***, one pound for another, at the same rate. ***pounds, shillings, and pence***: = money; also *attrib.* monetary; in *fig.* sense, = viewing things at their money value; matter-of-fact, realistic.

1514 WRIOTHESLEY *Chron.* (Camden) I. 9 Where was graunted to the King of all men's goodes 6*d.* in the pownde. **1545** BRINKLOW *Compl.* Table 2 b, That all creditors may have pownd and pownd alyke. **1610–11** in *North Riding Rec.* (1884) I. 209 John Raynson..using the trade of usurie, taking foure shillinges at pound. **1765** BLACKSTONE *Comm.* I. viii. 325 A new duty from 6*d.* to 1*s.* in the pound.. imposed by statutes 18 Geo. III. c. 26. and 19 Geo. III. c. 59. on every dwelling-house inhabited, together with the offices and gardens therewith occupied. **1829** SOUTHEY *Sir T. More* II. 123 Let him calculate whether he and they would have been gainers, even in this low, pounds-shillings-and-pence point of view. **1870** J. ANDERSON in *Eng. Mech.* 14 Jan. 426/2 Everything..narrows itself down into a pounds-shillings-and-pence question. **1900** *Daily News* 15 May 3/1 We claim to be a practical people, a pounds-shillings-and-pence people.

f. Five dollars; a five-dollar note. *U.S. slang.*

1935 J. HARGAN *Gloss. Prison Lang.* 6 *Pound*, a five dollar bill. **1950** *New Yorker* 25 Feb. 76 A pound off of thirty-four-fifty would still leave twenty-nine-fifty. **1970** H. E. ROBERTS *Third Ear* 11/1 Pounds, money; five dollars.

4. *attrib.* and *Comb.* **a.** simple attrib., in the senses (*a*) of a pound weight, as ***pound-butter***, sold (in quantity) by the pound, as ***pound beads***,

pins, yarn; (*b*) of the amount or value of a pound sterling, as ***pound matter, prize***. **b.** Special combs.: **pound brush**, a large paint-brush; **pound coin** (also written **£1 coin**), a coin worth one pound sterling, introduced in the U.K. on 21 April 1983 and subsequently superseding the pound note; a pound-piece; **pound-day**, see quot.; **pound-force** (pl. ***pounds-force***), a unit of force equal to the weight of a mass of 1 pound avoirdupois, esp. under standard gravity; **pound-nail**, see quot. 1727–41; **pound note**, a bank-note for one pound (see *pound coin*: pound notes are still issued in the U.K. by the Scottish banks); **pound-noteish** *a.* (*slang*), affected, pompous; **pound party** (*U.S.*), a party meeting without invitation at a friend's house, each member bringing a pound or so of some eatable ready for consumption, which is handed to the hostess to entertain the unexpected guests; also, a gathering to which each person brings a parcel of undeclared contents, which is sold by auction or otherwise to those present, the proceeds being devoted to charity; †**pound-pear**, an old name for a large variety of cooking pear; **pound-piece**, a piece of money worth a pound; **pound-pint**, a pint equal to the capacity of a pound of water: see 1 b; **pound-rate**, †**rent**, a rate of so much in the pound; †**pound-right** *obs.*, ? the right to the amount of moorland which went with a POUND-LAND; or ? a right to the moor valued at a pound; **pound rocket**, see quot.; **pound-velo**, a unit of momentum; the momentum of a body of mass 1 lb. moving with a velocity of 1 foot per second; **pound-weight** (pl. ***pounds-weight***) = *pound-force* above; **pound-worth, pound's-worth**, as much of anything as is worth or may be bought for a pound; †*spec.* a piece (of land) worth a pound a year: cf. LIBRATE *sb.* See also POUND-CAKE, etc.

1858 SIMMONDS *Dict. Trade*, **Pound-beads*, a kind of bead, white or red, used in West African trade with the natives. **1830** G. COLMAN *Random Rec.* I. ii. 35 My pictures are only sketches, and dabs of the *pound-brush. **1873** E. SPON *Workshop Receipts* Ser. I. 106/1 The large round brush, called the pound brush, and a smaller one called the tool, are those mostly used in plain work. **1886** ELWORTHY *W. Somerset Word-bk.*, **Pound-butter*, butter made up in pats of a pound each, as distinguished from..butter..in bulk. **1980** *Times* 18 July 2/5 London Transport yesterday called for a *£1 coin to cut down queues at ticket machines. *Ibid.* 12 Nov. 16/5 Anyone who travels regularly on the London Underground..will realize that a British pound coin cannot be long delayed. **1983** *Daily Tel.* 23 Apr. 21/4 The arrival of the new pound coin has triggered off something of a new 'Green Piece' movement in St. Austell, Cornwall, this week. **1986** *Sunday Tel.* 15 June 11/8, I have not found..that it is more difficult to tip a £1 coin than a pound note. **1889** *Clerks Guernsey News* 10 May 5/1 The *Pound Day at the Victoria Cottage Hospital..was a great success, the appeal for a pound weight of some kind of grocery from each donor being very..widely responded to. **1896** T. W. WRIGHT *Elem. Mech.* ii. 62 The word pound has a..variety of meanings. We speak of a pound weight, a *pound force, and of a certain body itself as 'a pound'. **1909** J. M. JAMESON *Elem. Pract. Mech.* ix. 149 These two units of force, the pound force and the gram force are sometimes called Gravitational Units of Force. **1949** W. ERNST *Oil Hydraulic Power* i. 2 The pound force imparts 32·174 feet per sec^2 to the pound mass. **1961** [see LB]. **1972** *Physics Bull.* May 285/1 The subsequent addition of small weights permits forces to be obtained directly in both tons-force and pounds-force. **1977** *Daily Tel.* 16 Dec. 2/3 As Britain moves towards complete metrication motorists will have to get used to checking their car tyre pressures in atmospheric bars instead of pounds force per square inch. *a* **1617** BAYNE *On Eph.* i. (1643) 16 We would be loath to take a slip..in a twelve-*pound matter. **1727–41** CHAMBERS *Cycl.* s.v. *Nails*, **Pound Nails*, are four-square in the shank; much used in Norfolk, Suffolk, and Essex, though scarce elsewhere, except for paling. **1845** DISRAELI *Sybil* II. x, Ah! a queer fellow; lent him a one-*pound note—never saw it again. **1936** J. CURTIS *Gilt Kid* vi. 63 Her *pound-noteish voice both annoyed and amused the Gilt Kid. **1966** AUDEN *About House* 28 When we get pound-noteish..send us some deflating Image. **1889** *Boston* (Mass.) *Jrnl.* 22 Jan. 2/3 The old-fashioned *pound party has become this winter a fashionable city entertainment. **1889** FARMER *Americanisms*, *Pound party*, very similar to *Donation party*. **1585** HIGINS *Junius' Nomencl.* 99/1 *Poire de bon Chrestien, poire de liure*,.. a *pound-peare. *a* **1667** COWLEY *Ess. in Verse & Prose*, *Greatness*, He would eat nothing but what was great, nor touch any Fruit but Horse-Plums and Pound-Pears. **1766** *Compl. Farmer* s.v. *Pear*, The pound-pear, or black-pear of Worcester. **1889** H. JOHNSTON *Chron. Glenbuckie* xxii. 261 There are twenty gouden *pound-pieces. **1865** R. HUNT *Pop. Rom. W. Eng.* Ser. II. 81 He told her to..get a packet of *pound pins. **1886** *Folk-Lore Jrnl.* IV. 126 Pins—not the well-made ones sold in papers, but clumsy things with wire heads—'pound-pins'. **1901** E. NICHOLSON in *N. & Q.* 9th Ser. VIII. 283/1 Our bushel was originally the measure containing a quantity of wheat equal to the weight of a cubic foot of water at ordinary temperature, 62·3 lb., and therefore, on the *pound-pint system, containing the same number of pints of wheat. **1773** J. NORTHCOTE *Let.* (in *Sotheran's Catal.* No 12 (1899) 39), The gentleman who won the Twenty Thousand *Pound Prize in the last Lottery. **1712** PRIDEAUX *Direct. Ch.-wardens* (ed. 4) 57 A Church-Rate..to be made..by an equal *Pound Rate. **1766** ENTICK *London* IV. 404, 125*l.* raised by a pound-rate, at 4*d.* in the pound. **1661** MARVELL *Corr.* xxvi. Wks. (Grosart) II. 62 That you ascertain in expresse words the summe that is to be raised by *pound rent. **1682** N. O. *Boileau's Lutrin* IV. 293 Item, twice fifty more Per ann. in Pound-Rents! **1586** *Wills & Inv. N.C.* (Surtees) II. 128 Two lyttell croftes..called tenter croftes, with the churche yearde of Darnton, and one *powndright of Branson moore. **1873** E. SPON *Workshop Receipts* Ser. I. 124/1 A *pound rocket will admit a leaden bullet that weighs a pound. **1887** J. B. LOCK *Dynamics* 31 We shall choose as our unit mass-velocity that of a particle of 1 lb. moving with 1 velo. We shall call this unit a *pound-velo. [**1871** J. C. MAXWELL *Theory of Heat* iv. 83 In all countries the first measurements of forces were made in this way, and a force was described as a force of so many *pounds' weight or grammes' weight. **1877** W. H. BESANT *Treat. Hydromech.* i. 9 The unit of force is 750 lbs. weight.] **1891** J. G. EASTON *First Bk. Mech.* iv. 59 It is sometimes convenient..to speak of a force as of so many pounds weight. **1907** FRANKLIN & MACNUTT *Elem. Mech.* viii. 174 (*heading*) Values of the stretch modulus of various substances. (In pounds-weight per square inch.) **1936** A. W. HIRST *Electr. & Magn.* i. 4 A force of one pound-weight = 32·2 poundals. **1960** F. LAND *Lang. Math.* vi. 71 When I buy a pound of apples, the weight of the apples is 1 pound-weight..and its mass is 1 pound mass. **1976** *Daily Tel.* 4 Mar. 2/6 The Metrication Board..warned the Government that unless it introduced a sense of urgency into replacing feet for [*sic*] metres..and pounds weight for kilogrammes, then the target of 1980 for completion of the programme could never be met. *c* **1450** *Godstow Reg.* 668 Of the yifte of Robert, Erle of leyceter, thre *pounde-worthe of lond in Halso. **1780** A. YOUNG *Tour Irel.* I. 394 The yarn spun is *pound yarn, not done in hanks at all.

pound (paʊnd), *sb.*^{2} Forms: 4–5 poonde, 5 ponde, 5–6 pounde, 6 pond, 6–7 pownd(e, 6– pound. [Not found till near the end of the ME. period:—OE. **pund*, known only in comb. *pund-fold* (in late 12th c. MS.) and early ME. *pundbreche* (Laws of Hen. I) (see POUND-BREACH), and supported by the derivatives (*ȝe-*)*pyndan* to dam up (water) (K. Ælfred), *forpyndan* to exclude, bar (Cynewulf): see PIND *v.* Origin unknown; the stem has not been certainly traced in any continental language. Of this, POND *sb.* is an anomalous parallel form; many dialects have *pound* in the sense of *pond*, and the two forms are used indifferently in sense 4 b in reference to canals.]

I. 1. a. An enclosure maintained by authority, for the detention of stray or trespassing cattle, as well as for the keeping of distrained cattle or goods until redeemed; a pinfold.

The right to impound stray cattle still exists, but in Great Britain the impounder can put the animals in his own stable or field, so that public pounds, being unnecessary, are disappearing.

1425 in *Somerset Med. Wills* (1901) 115 (Latin) [Item to mending the way between the church of Merk and the] pownde 3*s.* 4*d.* **1464** *Rolls of Parlt.* V. 559/2 All such distresse..to put in pounde. **1531** *Dial. on Laws Eng.* II. xxvii. (1638) 113 The owner may lawfully give the beasts meat and drink while they be in pound. *a* **1680** BUTLER *Rem.* (1759) I. 168 To shut them up, like Beasts in Pounds, For breaking into others Grounds. **1773** GOLDSM. *Stoops to Conq.* IV. Wks. (Globe) 668/1 I'd sooner leave my horse in a pound. **1821** CLARE *Vill. Minstr.* I. 88 While pinders, that such chances look, Drive his rambling cows to pound. **1837** DICKENS *Pickw.* xix, 'Where am I?' exclaimed Mr. Pickwick. 'In the Pound', replied the mob. **1846** LONGF. *Pegasus in Pound* v, The wise men, in their wisdom, Put him straightway into pound.

b. ***pound close*** or ***covert***, a pound to which the owner of impounded animals may not have access; ***pound open*** or ***overt***, a pound which is not roofed, and to which the owner may have access to feed his beasts.

1531 *Dial. on Laws Eng.* II. xxvii. 76 He that..hath the hurte may take the beestes as a dystresse, and put theym in a pounde ouert. **1554** *Act 1 & 2 Phil. & Mary* c. 12 §1 No Distress of Cattle shall be driven out of the Hundred.. except that it be to a Pound overt within the same Shire. **1567** *Expos. Termes Lawes* (1579) 157 b, Poundes are in two sorts, the one pounds open, the other pounds close... Pound Close is such a place, where the owner of the distresse may not come to geue them meat and drinke, with out offence, as in a close house, or whatsoeuer els place. **1768** BLACKSTONE *Comm.* III. i. 13 If a live distress, of animals, be impounded in a *common* pound overt, the owner must take notice of it at his peril; but if in any special pound-overt, so constituted for this particular purpose, the distreiner must give notice to the owner.

c. An enclosure for sheltering or in any way dealing with sheep or cattle in the aggregate; also, an enclosure in which wild animals are entrapped.

1780 A. YOUNG *Tour Irel.* I. 340 Mr. Irwin spreads it in his pound..for cattle to tread on. **1877** J. A. ALLEN *Amer. Bison* 472 The rushing of a herd over a precipice or into a pound prepared especially to entrap them. **1890** 'R. BOLDREWOOD' *Col. Reformer* (1891) 227 Two gates leading from the pound at the far end are now taken charge of by the black boys... The gate from the lane is opened and the 'ragers'..rush fiercely into the pound.

d. An enclosure in which vehicles impounded by the police are kept.

1970 P. LAURIE *Scotland Yard* iii. 75 Civilian cars that have been stolen or in accidents..stand in a pound nearby. **1970** *Globe & Mail* (Toronto) 25 Sept. 39/2 (Advt.), Permanent part time dispatcher for police auto pound, Saturday, Sunday and Monday nights. **1972** *Daily Tel.* 16 Mar. 17/6 The Vauxhall Viva had been towed to a pound because it was found parked on an urban clearway. **1974** *Times* 18 Feb. 17 I'm going to sell my car... No more police towing [it]..to a car pound.

2. *transf.* and *fig.* A place of confinement; a pen, a pent-up position; a trap; a prison for debtors or offenders; a spiritual 'fold'; in *Hunting*, a position from which escape is impossible or difficult. (See also LOB'S POUND.)

c **1380** WYCLIF *Wks.* (1880) 421 Pride of men of þe world þat wolen make hem siche poondis, is an oþer rote of consense aȝenus crist lord of þis world. **1557** *Tottell's Misc.* (Arb.) 268, I meane where you and all your flocke, Deuise to pen men in the pound. **1575** GASCOIGNE *Fruites of Warre* xix, Penne vp thy pleasure in Repentance poundes. **1575** —— *Mask for Visct. Mountacute* Wks. 49 It pleazed God to helpe his flocke, which thus in pound was pent. **1598** B. JONSON *Ev. Man in Hum.* II. i, An' hee thinke to bee relieu'd by me, when he is got into one o' your citie pounds, the Counters. **1677** W. HUBBARD *Narrative* 26 The Enemy being by this means brought into a Pound. **1684** OTWAY *Atheist* III, Well, since I am trapt thus,..There is no replevin, and I must to pound. **1727** SWIFT *Imit. Horace* 47, I hurry me in haste away, Not thinking it is levee-day; And find his honour in a pound, Hemm'd by a triple circle round. **1807** WORDSW. *White Doe* VII. 253 The grassy rock-encircled Pound In which the Creature first was found. **1886** ELWORTHY *W. Somerset Word-bk.*, *Pound*, a position from which escape seems difficult, particularly in hunting. **1887** JEFFERIES *Amaryllis* xxiv. 183 He's getting into a pound, he really is.

†**3. a.** An act or right of pounding (POUND *v.*^{2} 1).

1464 *Rolls of Parlt.* V. 540/2 The Baylewik..with Poundes, Waifes, Strayes, Herbage and Pannage.

†**b.** A seizure of cattle, etc., in a raid, etc.: cf. POIND *v.* 3. *Obs.*

c **1425** WYNTOUN *Cron.* IX. ii. 12 A cumpany gat he And rade in Ingland, for to ta A pownd, and swne it hapnyd sa That he of catale gat a pray.

II. 4. a. A body of still water, usually of artificial formation, a POND. Now *dial.* **b.** *esp.* A body of water held up or confined by a dam or the like, as in a mill-pond (now *dial.*), the reach of a canal above a lock, etc. (in which sense *pond* and *pound* are used indifferently).

1387 TREVISA *Higden* (Rolls) III. 367 Alisaundre..hadde alle maner bestes in kepyng in hyves, in layes, in fisshe weres and pondes [*MS. Cott. Tib. D. vii* poundes]. *c* **1450** *Pol. Poems* (Rolls) II. 228 Hit is a shrewde pole, pounde, or a well, That drownythe the dowghty. **1535** COVERDALE *Isa.* xix. 10 All the poundes of Egipte, all the policie of their Moates & diches shal come to naught. **1684** G. MERITON *Yorks. Dialogue* 132 (E.D.S.) Our awd Meer is slidden into'th Pownd. **1805** Z. ALLNUTT *Navig. Thames* 29 So many more Pounds and moveable Weirs as were found necessary might be erected. **1891** COTES *Two Girls on Barge* 46 First a pound and then a lock,..'pound' being a canal definition of the level reaches that lie between the locks. **1895** *Daily News* 8 Feb. 3/6 Witness said there were no indications to show that they were approaching a 'pound' (lodgment or accumulation of water). *a* **1900** E. SMITH *MS. Collect. Warwicks. Words* (E.D.D.), Where there is a separate pool, the water above the dam is called either the mill-dam or the pound.

5. An enclosure for fish. **a.** A compartment for stowing fish on board a fishing-vessel. **b.** See quot. 1867. **c.** A net trap for fish; *spec.* the last compartment of a pound net, in which the fish are finally caught; the bowl or pocket.

1809 *Naval Chron.* XXI. 21 There are pounds or enclosures made on the deck, for each fisherman to throw in what he catches. **1867** SMYTH *Sailor's Word-bk.*, *Pound*, a lagoon, or space of water, surrounded by reefs and shoals, wherein fish are kept, as at Bermuda. **1873** *Echo* 11 Mar. 2/2 Immense quantities are, however, taken in what are called 'pounds'. A pound is generally placed on the shallow flats of the bays where fish food is abundant... The fish..enter the pound, and find it impossible to get out again. **1883** S. PLIMSOLL in *19th Cent.* July 162 The haddocks..are.. stowed away in bulk in 'pound' (the pounds are like the stalls in a stable, in the hold of the ship). **1883** F. DAY *Indian Fish* 14 (Fish. Exhib. Publ.) Wicker-work labyrinths..acting like a pound in permitting the fish to enter with the flood, but precluding exit with the ebb.

6. *attrib.* and *Comb.*, as ***pound like*** adj.; **pound-boat**, a flat-bottomed centre-board boat used on Lake Erie for carrying fish from the nets (*Cent. Dict.* 1890); **pound-fee**, a fee paid for the release of cattle or goods from the pound; †**poundlose**, setting free or release from the pound: cf. LOOSE *sb.* 5; **poundman**, one employed in weir or pound fishing; **pound-master**, = POUND-KEEPER; **pound net**, an enclosure formed by nets in the sea near the shore, consisting of a long straight wall or leader, a first enclosure (the 'heart'), into which the fish are conducted by the leader, and a second enclosure (the pound, bowl, or pocket), from which they cannot escape; **pound scoop**, a scoop used in collecting fish from a pound (*Cent. Dict.* 1890).

1884 *Bull. U.S. Nat. Museum* No. 27. 700 Lake Erie *pound boat... Their peculiar construction enables them to carry large quantities of fish in shallow water and to lift the bowl of the pounds without upsetting. **1891** *Rep. U.S. Comm. Fisheries 1887* 27 The pound-boat has two tall, tapering masts. **1878** AYLWARD *Transvaal of To-Day* ii. (1881) 27 English settlers have been known in a poor neighbourhood to live almost entirely from *pound-fees and mileage, earned by continual..intermeddling with their neighbours' herds. **1898** *Westm. Gaz.* 20 Jan. 5/2 A corner is boarded off in a sort of *pound-like manner. **1622** in *Naworth Househ. Bks.* (Surtees) 197 For *poundlose of viij of the tenants' horses, iij*s*. **1888** GOODE *Amer. Fishes* 222 The *poundmen..sometimes eat them and consider them better than scup. **1792** *Southampton* (N.Y.) *Records* (1878) III. 335 John Cooper Samuel Cooper Henry Corwithe *Poundmasters. **1897** *Outing* (U.S.) XXIX. 537/1 You get my vote the next time you run for poundmaster. **1865** *Michigan Gen. Statutes* (1882) I. 577 The penalties of this section shall not apply or work injury to persons who are the present owners of *pound or trap nets. **1883** GOODE *Fish. Indust. U.S.* 12 Introduction of pound-nets or stake-nets along the sandy coasts of the Atlantic and its estuaries for the capture of the migrating summer shoals. **1897** *Outing* (U.S.) XXX. 362/1 One of the greatest nuisances.. that a seafaring man can meet with, and that is pound-nets. They lined the American shore far out into the lake. **1973** *Fisheries Fact Sheet* (Environment Canada Fisheries & Marine Service) No. 1. 4/3 Gill-nets and pound-nets are the chief gear.

pound (paʊnd), *sb.*[3] [f. POUND *v.*[1]]

I. †**1.** A pounding; *pl.* that which has been pounded. *Obs. rare.*

1562 TURNER *Herbal* II. 46 The poundes of the rootes [of Mandrag] must be put into a small firkin of swete wyne.

2. An apparatus for pounding or crushing apples for cider; a cider-mill.

1832 *Trans. Provinc. Med. & Surg. Assoc.* II. VI. 202 This mischievous part of the pound [i.e. lead basins used in cider presses] is now almost universally exploded, and in their place wooden ones are substituted. **1886** ELWORTHY *W. Somerset Word-bk.*, *Pound*,..a mill in which to grind the apples for making cider.

II. **3.** A mark caused by a severe blow; a bruise, a contusion.

1862 CAMPION *Alice* 35 [He] would frequently return [from a combat at fisticuffs] in a deluge of gore and all over pounds and bruises.

4. A heavy beating blow; a thump; also, the sound caused by this, a thud.

1890 in *Cent. Dict.* **1901** *Daily Chron.* 7 June 4/1 The breathless shout, the pound of hoofs—'The Favourite! Favourite wins!'

pound (paʊnd), *v.*[1] Forms: α. 1 **púnian, -ȝean,** 4–7 **poune, powne,** (4–5 **pone,** 8–9 *Sc.* **poon**). β. 6–7 **punne,** 6– **pun** (see also PUN *v.*). γ. 6– **pound** (9 *dial.* **pund**). [OE. *púnian* (also *ȝepúnian*, ME. IPONE):—WGer. **pûnôjan*, stem *pûn-*, whence also Du. †*puyn*, mod. *puin* 'rubbish, trash or cyment of stones' (Hexham), LG. *pün* chips of stone, building rubbish (Doorn.-Koolman). For the final *d*, cf. ASTOUND *v.*, BOUND *ppl. a.*[1], etc.]

1. a. *trans.* To break down and crush by beating, as with a pestle; to reduce to pulp or powder; to bray, bruise, pulverize, triturate.

α. *c* **1000** *Sax. Leechd.* I. 176 ȝenim þas ylcan wyrte uerbascum ȝecnucude [*v.r.* ȝepunude]. *a* **1050** *Liber Scintill.* xxiv. (1889) 95 þeah þu puniȝe [*contuderis*] stuntne on pil(an) swylce berenhula puniȝendum [*feriente*] bufan punere [*pilo*] na byð afyrred fram him dysiȝnyss his. *c* **1380** WYCLIF *Serm.* Sel. Wks. I. 89 As spicerye ȝyveþ smell whan it is powned. **1382** —— *Matt.* xxi. 44 Vpon whom it [this stone] shal falle, it shal togidre poune hym [1388 to-brise hym]. **1578** LYTE *Dodoens* I. i. 3 Sothrenwood pounde with a rosted Quince, and laide to the eyes. **1616** SURFL. & MARKH. *Country Farme* 41 Powne and temper them altogether. **1620** VENNER *Via Recta* (1650) 126 Grots pouned and sifted or strained therein. **1658** J. JONES *Ovid's Ibis* 138 Anaxarchus..being condemned..to be pound with iron pestels in a morter.

β. **1559** MORWYNG *Evonym.* 132 Then punne it in a morter. *Ibid.* 286 Pun them that be to be pund. **1600** HEYWOOD *1st Pt. Edw. IV*, I. ii, The honestest lad that ever pund spice in a mortar. **1662** H. STUBBE *Ind. Nectar* ii. 8 Cacao nut, punned, and dissolved in water.

γ. **1594** SOUTHWELL *M. Magd. Fun. Teares* (1823) 120 To feele more of their sweetnesse, I will pound these spices. **1697** DRYDEN *Virg. Georg.* I. 138 The Peasant..who pounds with Rakes The crumbling Clods. **1765** A. DICKSON *Treat. Agric.* 477 Let him..dry them, and pound them in a mortar. **1828** *Craven Gloss.*, *Pund*, to pound. **1830** M. DONOVAN *Dom. Econ.* I. 315 After the apples have been pressed, they may be economically pounded a second time. **1865** LUBBOCK *Preh. Times* xiii, A flat stone to pound roots with.

b. *fig.*

1583 STUBBES *Anat. Abus.* II. (1882) 78 The word of God is not preached vnto them, and as it were braied, punned, interpreted, and expounded. **1618** BOLTON *Florus* (1636) 101 He therefore so ground and punned Annibal, by coasting him thorow all Samnium. *a* **1677** BARROW *Serm.* Wks. 1716 II. 80 To think a gross body may be ground and pounded into rationality. **1884** *Nonconf. & Indep.* 12 June 570/1 The Lord Advocate..pounded it [the Bill] to powder.

2. a. To strike severely with the fists or some heavy instrument; to strike or beat with repeated heavy blows; to thump, to pummel. Also *fig.*

α, β. **1790** A. WILSON *Pack* Poet. Wks. (1846) 29 John swore that he wad poon you [*rimes* aboon you, spoon you]. **1903** in *Eng. Dial. Dict.* in form *pounn* in Herefordsh., *pown* in E. Lanc., *poon* (pun), *pun, punn, poan*, from Cumbld. to Glouc. and Leicester.

γ. **1700** DRYDEN *Ceyx & Alcyone* 392 With cruel blows she pounds her blubber'd cheeks. **1795** WOLCOTT (P. Pindar) *Pindariana* Wks. 1812 IV. 199 Pounds thy pate. **1839** THACKERAY *Fatal Boots* Wks. (1869) 386, I stood pounding him with my satire. **1857** HUGHES *Tom Brown* I. vi, The big boys who sit at the tables pound them and cheer. **1858** COL. K. YOUNG *Diary & Corr.* (1902) App. 328 We pounded your regiment the other day. **1874** SYMONDS *Sk. Italy & Greece* (1898) I. ix. 176 Horsed sea deities pounding one another with bunches of fish. **1875** LE FANU *Will. Die* xxviii, I danced every day, and pounded a piano, and sang a little. **1877** CLERY *Min. Tact.* xiv. (ed. 3) 189 To hang closely on their rear, pounding them with light guns. **1908** *Smart Set* June 21/2 She stopped at the door of the house and pounded the knocker vigorously. **1951** *Amer. Speech* XXVI. 230/2 St. Joseph *pounds* Mansfield. **1960** M. SPARK *Bachelors* xii. 224 The typist in the corner listlessly pounded her silent machine. **1967** *Boston Sunday Globe* 23 Apr. 17/4 Air Force and Navy jets pounded North Vietnam in 118 missions Friday. **1968** *Globe & Mail* (Toronto) 5 Feb. 17/4 Detroit..pounded Minnesota North Stars 8–1. **1972** 'E. FERRARS' *Breath of Suspicion* vii. 101 I'll be working.. pounding my typewriter.

b. *with advb. extension.* To knock (something) *in, out*, etc., by pounding; to hammer, beat.

1875 RUSKIN *Fors Clav.* li. 53 My foolishness is being pounded out of me. **1884** *Pall Mall G.* 16 Oct. 2/2 The fortifications might be pounded to pieces. **1891** KIPLING *Light that Failed* xi. (1900) 193 The big drum pounded out the tune. **1898** L. STEPHEN *Stud. Biog.* II. v. 182 He must not simply state a reason, but pound it into a thick head by repetition.

c. *U.S. Stock Exch.* To beat down the price of (stock); = HAMMER *v.* 2 d (*b*).

1901 *Munsey's Mag.* XXIV. 522/1 The bears let the opportunity to pound securities go by the board.

d. phr. *to pound one's ear*: to sleep. *slang* (orig. *U.S.*).

1899 'J. FLYNT' *Tramping with Tramps* IV. 396 *Pound the ear*, to sleep. **1900** *Dialect Notes* II. 51 [College slang] '*Pound* one's ear, or one's pillow,' to sleep. **1907** [see FLOP *v.* 2 c]. **1926** M. WALSH *Key above Door* xii. 128 'Only just awakened,' I admitted..'and how are my comrades in misfortune?'.. 'Still pounding their ears, no doubt.' **1927** C. SAMOLAR in *Amer. Speech* II. 290/2 To sleep is to *pound the ear.* I think this phrase originated with railroaders. Sleeping in a caboose on a fast-moving train actually consists of pounding one's ear. **1947** J. STEINBECK *Wayward Bus* xx. 300 Listen to the old bastard snore. He's pounding his ear.

e. To produce or turn *out* by 'pounding' a typewriter or the like.

1904 F. LYNDE *Grafters* v. 58 He sat down at the typewriter to pound out a letter to the general counsel, resigning his sinecure. **1941** B. SCHULBERG *What makes Sammy Run?* ix. 162, I was back in the old groove, pounding it out for the *Record* again. **1973** W. MCCARTHY *Detail* i. 48 He had just enough time to pound out two or three short paragraphs.

f. To walk upon; to cover (a distance or area) on foot; *spec.* of a policeman: to patrol (a beat). *colloq.* (orig. *U.S.*).

In quot. 1959 the use is *fig.* in punning allusion to the poetry of Ezra Pound (see POUNDIAN *a.*).

1906 A. H. LEWIS *Confessions of Detective* iv. 44 It's worth while to pound a beat, when one has such kindly and appreciative superiors. **1909** 'O. HENRY' *Options* (1916) 30 I'm pounding the asphalt for another job. **1923** L. J. VANCE *Baroque* vi. 33, I won't get sent back to pound sidewalks for what I'm pulling off tonight. **1935** A. J. POLLOCK *Underworld Speaks* 91/1 *Pounding the pavement*, a prostitute soliciting men on the street. **1946** [see KRIEGIE]. **1959** *Times Lit. Suppl.* 25 Sept. 546/5 An awful warning to any future translator tempted to indulge in the pleasures of what, metrically speaking, might be described as Pounding the beat. **1974** S. MARCUS *Minding Store* (1975) ii. 26 He personally pounded the pavements calling on fellow businessmen. **1978** J. GARDNER *Dancing Dodo* xxxiv. 270, I shall personally arrange for you to be back pounding the beat, in uniform.

†**3.** With inverted construction: To deliver (heavy blows) *on* some one. *Obs. rare*[−1].

1596 SPENSER *F.Q.* IV. iv. 31 An hundred knights..All which at once huge strokes on him did pound, In hope to take him prisoner, where he stood on ground.

4. a. *intr.* To beat or knock heavily, deliver heavy blows, fire heavy shot (*at, on*). ***pound away***, to continue delivering blows; to hammer away.

1815 [see POUNDING *vbl. sb.*[1] 2]. **1858–9** RUSSELL *Diary India* (1860) I. 292, I found all our guns pounding at the Martinière. **1860** EMERSON *Cond. Life, Power* Wks. (Bohn) II. 340 The chief engineer pounded with a hammer on the trunnions of a cannon, until he broke them off. **1885** *Manch. Exam.* 20 Feb. 5/2 The Opposition are anxious to have their great guns in the Upper Chamber pounding away at the same time. **1885** R. L. & F. STEVENSON *Dynamiter* ii, Within the lodging-house feet pounded on the stairs. **1895** HARE *Story of Life* (1900) VI. xxx. 400 An electric piano..goes on pounding away by itself. **1901** H. HARLAND *Com. & Err.* 60 Ferdinand Augustus's heart began to pound.

fig. **1861** J. R. GREEN *Lett.* (1901) II. 73, I spent the bulk of yesterday pounding at Dunstan in the British Museum.

b. Of a ship or boat: To beat the water, rise and fall heavily.

1903 *Daily Mail* 21 Aug. 5/7 The sea had become rough, causing the boats to pound considerably. **1906** *Westm. Gaz.* 21 Aug. 7/2 The wreck of the 'Manchuria'... The vessel is lying far inside the reef, and is pounding heavily.

5. *intr.* To walk, run, or dance with heavy steps that beat or pulverize the ground; to ride hard and heavily; *transf.* of a steamer, to force its way through the water, paddle or steam along forcibly.

1802 MAR. EDGEWORTH *Moral T.* (1806) I. viii. 51 'Look at that absurd creature!' exclaimed Forester, pointing out.. a girl, who was footing and pounding for fame at a prodigious rate. **1848** KINGSLEY *Yeast* i, A fat farmer, sedulously pounding through the mud. **1852** R. S. SURTEES *Sponge's Sp. Tour* l, He thought he saw [him]..pounding away on the chestnut [horse]. **1865** *Dublin Univ. Mag.* II. 20 So he pounds along sitting well down in his saddle. **1880** MISS BRADDON *Just as I am* xviii, I am not going to pound over half the county in a futile endeavour to come up with the hounds. **1898** G. W. E. RUSSELL *Collect. & Recoll.* xxxiv. 458 Cantering up St. James's Street..or pounding round Hyde Park. **1898** *Daily News* 23 July 7/1 She [a steamer] pounded along splendidly at over 20 knots an hour.

6. *trans.* To consolidate by beating, to beat hard; *esp.* in technical use in form *pun*, to ram down (earth, clay, or rubble) as in making a roadway or embankment: see PUN *v.*[1]

1850 *Jrnl. R. Agric. Soc.* XI. II. 706 The cows so thoroughly 'pound' the ground that in summer it is in many parts as hard as a brick.

pound (paʊnd), *v.*[2] Also 5 **pown**, 7 **poun.** [f. POUND *sb.*[2] Cf. PIND *v.*, POIND *v.*]

1. *trans.* To place or shut *up* (trespassing or straying cattle) in a pound; to impound.

c **1450** *Oseney Regr.* 44 That þey [bestes] be not Inparkid or pownyd but þey be i-founde in open harme [cf. *ibid.* 24 inparked or y-poyned; *ibid.* 86 imparkid or poyned]. **1530** PALSGR. 663/2, I pounde, I put horse, or beestes in the pynfolde. **1673** [R. LEIGH] *Transp. Reh.* 124 They exercise a petty royalty in..pounding beasts. *a* **1711** KEN *Urania* Poet. Wks. 1721 IV. 503 Your Neighbour Swains the Trespassers will pound. **1819** *Metropolis* II. 205 Law-suits for trespass, for poaching, pounding cattle,..give him notoriety in the country. **1890** 'R. BOLDREWOOD' *Col. Reformer* (1891) 87 We must not go more than half a mile away from the road, or we [i.e. our cattle] 'll be 'pounded.

fig. **1581** SIDNEY *Apol. Poetrie* (Arb.) 69 Me thinkes I deserue to be pounded, for straying from Poetrie to Oratorie. **1719** D'URFEY *Pills* (1872) V. 179 For the Heart that still wanders, is pounded at last.

2. To shut up or confine in any enclosure or within any bounds or limits, material or otherwise. Also with *up*. Also *fig.*

1589 NASHE *Pref. Greene's Menaphon* (Arb.) 12 Euen so these men..do pound their capacitie in barren Compendiums. **1608** HEYWOOD *Rape Lucrece* III. iv, Sit round: the enemy is pounded fast In their own folds. **1632** MASSINGER & FIELD *Fatal Dowry* IV. i, Married once, A man is staked or poun'd, and cannot graze Beyond his own hedge. *a* **1639** WOTTON in *Reliq.* (1651) 364 More might be said, if I were not pounded within an Epistle. **1644** MILTON *Areop.* (Arb.) 48 That gallant man who thought to pound up the crows by shutting his Parkgate. **1761** COLMAN *Jealous Wife* II. i. (1775) 22, I wish Harriot was fairly pounded [= married]. It wou'd save us both a great deal of Trouble. **1776** *Remembrancer* (1777) IV. 272/2 Hopkins, and his little navy, are safely pounded in Providence river, near Rhode Island. **1839** BAILEY *Festus* xxvii. (1848) 323 And the round wall of madness pound us in.

b. *spec.* in *Fox-hunting* (*pass.*), said of a rider who gets into an enclosed place from which he cannot get out to follow the chase. ***to pound the field***: see quot. 1886.

1827 *Sporting Mag.* XIX. 353 The whole field [i.e. the assemblage of riders] was fairly pounded. **1860** WHYTE MELVILLE *Mkt. Harb.* xvi. 135 Whenever one individual succeeds either in what is termed *pounding* a field, or in getting such a start of them that nobody shall have a chance of catching him whilst the pace holds. **1875** —— *Riding Recoll.* viii. (1879) 131 A man who never jumps at all can by no possibility be 'pounded'. **1886** ELWORTHY *W. Somerset Word-bk.* s.v., In hunting, an impassable barrier is said 'to pound the field'. So also a bold rider who clears a fence which others cannot do is said 'to pound the lot'.

fig. **1853** 'C. BEDE' *Verdant Green* ix, The pounding of the same gentleman in the middle of the first chorus. **1864** *Daily Tel.* 27 Aug., The Marquis, however, in following his leader over the agricultural plough, got..pounded with him in the political field.

3. To dam (water); dam *up*. Now chiefly *dial.*

1649 BLITHE *Eng. Improv. Impr.* (1652) b ij b, Watermills, which destroy abundance of gallant Land, by pounding up the water..even to the very top of the ground. **1770** J. BRINDLEY *Surv. Thames* 1 If they be made to pound more than five or six Feet, some of the adjacent Lands will be laid under Water. **1792** *Trans. Soc. Arts* X. 119 Which occasioned a fall for the water to run off, and prevented its being pounded up. **1879** MISS JACKSON *Shropsh. Word-bk.* s.v. *Pounded*, They'n bin gropin' fur trout I spect, I see the bruck's pounded.

4. ***to pound off***, to partition off into compartments: cf. POUND *sb.*[2] 5 a.

1887 *Fisheries of U.S.* Sect. v. II. 426 In the hair-seal fishery, on the coast of Newfoundland, the vessel's hold is 'pounded off' into bins only a little larger than the skins.

Hence '**pounded** *ppl. a.*; '**pounding** *vbl. sb.*

1621 QUARLES *Argalus & P.* (1678) 44 Here's none that can reprieve Such pounded beasts. **1641** *Boston Rec.* (1877) II. 60 The same hogg or swine..not to be fetched thence untill full satisfaction be made..for pounding and for carege. **1791** R. MYLNE *Rep. Thames & Isis* 29 The Pounding of the water by the New Locks.

pound, *v.*[3] [f. POUND *sb.*[1] I.]

†**1.** *trans.* To weigh. *Obs. rare*[−0].

1570 LEVINS *Manip.* 220/45 To Pound, *ponderare.*

2. *Coining.* To test the weight of coins (or of the blanks to be minted) by weighing the number of these which ought to make a pound weight (or a certain number of pounds), and ascertaining how much they vary from the standard.

From the earliest times, in the Indenture under which the Master of the Royal Mint produced coins for the King, a limit was assigned within which the weight was to be maintained; and as it was impossible to make every coin of the exact weight, it was customary, before 1870, to fix the number of grains variation permissible in each pound weight, taken at random from the mass of coins, this variation being termed 'remedy for the Master'. Thus, for gold coins, in which 20 troy pounds of standard gold made 934½ sovereigns, the Indenture of 1817 allows a margin of 'twelve grains in the pound weight and no more'. By the Coinage Act of 1870, the 'remedy' was fixed on the piece, as ⅕ grain on each sovereign, each of which is now separately tested by an automatic weighing apparatus of great delicacy.

1890 *Cent. Dict.* s.v., Pounding in coining. **1907** *Let. fr. Royal Mint*, The present law is far more stringent, but (for particular purposes) we still constantly resort to pounding in the Mint, and always in the case of bronze coins.

3. To weigh out or divide into pounds. *local.*
1876 *Whitby Gloss.*, *Punded*, divided into pounds. **1886** ELWORTHY *W. Somerset Word-bk.*, *Pound*, .. to make up into pats or parcels each of 1 lb. weight.

pound, *v.*[4] *slang.* [f. POUND *sb.*[1] 3.] To bet a pound, or an extravagant amount, on; esp. in phr. ***to pound it***, to wager pounds in long odds; hence, to state as a certainty or strong conviction.
1812 J. H. VAUX *Flash Dict.*, *Pound it*, to ensure or make a certainty of any thing: thus a man will say I'll pound it to be so; taken, probably from the custom of .. offering ten pounds to a crown at a cock-match, in which case, if no person takes this extravagant odds, the battle is at an end. This is termed pounding a cock. **1828** BEE *Living Pict. London* ii. 44 You'll soon be bowled out, I'll pound it. **1838** DICKENS *O. Twist* xxvi, I'll pound it, that Barney's managing properly. **1865** —— *Mut. Friend* IV. xv, I'll pound it, Master, to be in the way of school.
Hence **ˈpoundable** *a.*: see quot.
1812 J. H. VAUX *Flash Dict.*, *Poundable*, any event which is considered certain or inevitable, is declared to be poundable, as the issue of a game, the success of a bet, &c.

poundage[1] (ˈpaʊndɪdʒ). Also 5 pundage, 5–7 pondage, 7 powndage. [f. POUND *sb.*[1] + -AGE; hence med. (Anglo-) L. *pondāgium*.]
1. An impost, duty, or tax of so much per pound sterling on merchandise; *spec.* a subsidy, usually of 12 pence in the pound, formerly granted by Parliament to the Crown, on all imports and exports except bullion and commodities paying tonnage. Now *Hist.*
1399 LANGL. *Rich. Redeles* IV. 14 His puruyours toke, Withoute preiere at a parlement a poundage biside, And a fifteneth and a dyme eke. **1422** *Rolls of Parlt.* IV. 173/2 A subsidie of Tonage and Poundage .. that is to sey of every Tunne iiis; and xiid of every Pounde. *c* **1460** FORTESCUE *Abs. & Lim. Mon.* vi. (1885) 122 The kynge hath therfore þe subsidie of pondage and tonnage. **1509–10** *Act 1 Hen. VIII*, c. 20 §1 Another Subsidie called Poundage, that ys to sey: of all maner merchaundises .. caryed out of this .. Realme or brought into the same by wey of merchaundise of the value of every xxs., xijd. **1628** CHAS. I. *Speech* Wks. 1662 I. 370 As for Tonnage and Poundage it is a thing I cannot want and was never intended by you to ask. **1642** FULLER *Holy & Prof. St.* II. xxiv. 150 He knowes well that cunning is no burthen to carry, as paying neither portage by land, nor poundage by sea. **1765** BLACKSTONE *Comm.* I. viii. 315 Those [subsidies] of tonnage and poundage, in particular, were at first granted, as the old statutes (and particularly 1 Eliz. c. 19.) express it, for the defence of the realm, and the keeping and safeguard of the seas.
2. a. A payment of so much per pound sterling upon the amount of any transaction in which money passes; a commission, or fee, of so much a pound.
1599 NASHE *Lenten Stuffe* (1871) 25 There being two-hundred in it worth three hundred pounds a piece, with poundage and shillings to the lurched. **1693** SOUTHERNE *Maid's Last Pr.* III. iii, I shall be paid in crack't money, and pay poundage into the bargain. **1749** CHESTERF. *Lett.* (1775) II. 129 Pay that money .. yourself, and not through the hands of a servant, who always .. stipulates poundage. **1809** MALKIN *Gil Blas* XI. vii. (Rtldg.) 408 What cursed fools our dramatists must be, to care for anything but their poundage when their plays happen to be received! **1835** *Crompton, Meeson & Roscoe's Reports* II. 334 The sheriff is entitled to poundage on the whole amount of the goods levied. **1849** MACAULAY *Hist. Eng.* iii. I. 309 The paymaster of the forces had a poundage, amounting to about five thousand a year, on all the money which passed through his hands. **1892** E. K. BLYTH in *Law Times* XCIII. 488/2 Scandalously high court fees charged by way of poundage.
b. A percentage of the total earnings of any concern, paid as wages to those engaged in it, sometimes in addition to a fixed wage.
1892 *Labour Commission* Gloss., *Poundage*, a system in vogue in the slate industry to adjust the wages of the workmen. Every month when the claims of the slate quarrymen are made out an addition of so much in the pound is made upon the slate bill, that is, the payment due according to the standard rates. *Poundage*, the system under which the wages of tacklers or overlookers in cotton mills are based upon the output of the looms, being so much in the pound on the total earnings of the weavers under their charge. **1901** *Westm. Gaz.* 6 Sept. 8/1 The principle of poundage was agreed to by the men, who, however, prefer a higher fixed wage and less poundage.
3. A payment or charge of so much per pound weight; payment by weight.
a **1500** in Arnolde *Chron.* (1811) 100 To poundage perteynen that euery marchaundise that schalbe sold be weight brought in to London [etc.]. **1891** J. SIMSON *Hist. Thanet* 148 Under the act of 1812 the duties in those days called 'lastage' or 'poundage' were adjusted. **1904** *Westm. Gaz.* 16 Dec. 5/2 The Commonwealth Postal Department has now finally decided not to seek to renew the contract, but to rely on getting letters forwarded on a poundage basis, as provided by the Postal Union rules.
4. *Salt-making.* The number of pounds of salt contained in one gallon of brine, or (in some places) in one cubic foot of brine.
1907 *Let. to Editor fr. Cheshire*, The weight of salt contained in one gallon of brine .. is usually about 2 lb. 10 oz.; if it is as little as 2 lb. 8 oz., the brine is not worth working. The poundage is measured by a graduated hollow glass instrument, similar to that used in ascertaining the specific gravity of a fluid. (The gallon is not the imperial, but the old wine gallon. The standard poundage is thus more than 3 lb. to the imperial gallon.) The word is in constant use at the Cheshire and Staffordshire Salt Works, but is never used at Droitwich.

5. *Betting.* Extravagant odds. Cf. POUND *v.*[4], quot. 1812.
1816 *Sporting Mag.* XLVIII. 234 The poundage was here offered, but no takers. **1894** ASTLEY *50 Years Life* II. 83 At Newmarket it would have been poundage on my horse.
6. a. Weight stated in pounds. *nonce-use.*
1903 *Blackw. Mag.* Jan. 60/1 Our heaviest [fish] at that date was 20 lb., and there seemed to be a want of proportion in the business, an almost indelicate exuberance of poundage.
b. A person's weight, esp. that which is regarded as excess.
1930 WODEHOUSE *Very Good, Jeeves!* iv. 93 Women who have anything to do with opera .. always appear to run to surplus poundage. **1971** *Time* 5 Apr. 44/3 With his hair transplant and added poundage.
Hence **ˈpoundage** *v. trans.*, to impose poundage upon: whence **ˈpoundaging** *vbl. sb.* In quot. *fig.*
1644 MILTON *Areop.* (Arb.) 64 Nothing writt'n but what passes through the custom-house of certain Publicans that have the tunaging and the poundaging of all free spok'n truth.

poundage[2] (ˈpaʊndɪdʒ). Also 6 *Sc.* poindage. [f. POUND *v.*[2], *sb.*[2] + -AGE.] †**1.** The action or right of pounding stray or trespassing cattle (*obs.*); the charge levied upon the owner of impounded cattle or of anything poinded.
1554 *Act 1 & 2 Phil. & Mary*, c. 12 §2 No person .. shall take for keping in [*pr.* im-] pownde impownding or pondage of any .. Distres, above the somme of iiij d. **1576** *Reg. Privy Council Scot.* II. 524 To use the ordour of parcage or poindage establissit in the said indenture. **1660** in *1st Cent. Hist. Springfield, Mass.* (1898) I. 274 And for Swine or any Cattle that are lyable to Poundage who ever shall Pound them, they shall have foure pence a head, for yᵉ Poundage of them. **1845** S. JUDD *Margaret* II. v. (1881) 264 Molly I've known ever since she was dropt; she has brought in the strays, and many is the poundage she has saved Uncle Ket.
2. The keeping of cattle in a pound or enclosure; an enclosure in which cattle are kept.
1867 C. TOMLINSON *Cycl. Useful Arts* I. 3/2 [The slaughterman] only paying for the poundage of his beasts according to the requirements of his business. **1902** *Encycl. Brit.* XXXII. 644/1 The bye-laws usually provide .. for the poundage to have floor-space sufficient for each animal.

ˈpoundal. [f. POUND *sb.*[1]: cf. CENTAL.] See quot. (Also called *foot-poundal.*)
1879 THOMSON & TAIT *Nat. Phil.* I. I. §225 We .. define the British absolute unit force as 'the force which, acting on one pound of matter for one second, generates a velocity of one foot per second'. Prof. James Thomson has suggested the name 'Poundal' for this unit of force. **1884** A. DANIELL *Princ. Phys.* ii. 19.

pound-breach (ˈpaʊndbriːtʃ). *Law.* [f. POUND *sb.*[2] + BREACH *sb.* Early ME. *pundbreche* represents an OE. **pundbryce* not recorded.] The breaking open of a pound; hence, the illegal removal or recovery by the owner of goods lawfully impounded.
a **1135** *Laws Hen. I*, c. 40 (Schmid) Pundbreche fit pluribus modis: emissione, evocatione, receptione, excussione. **1292** BRITTON I. xxx. §3 Ceux qi ount fet prisoun en lour mesouns, ou hamsokne, ou pountbreche. **1594** WEST *2nd Pt. Symbol.* §215 Privat force .. trespas by entring into ground, .. poundbreach or otherwise. **1670** BLOUNT *Law Dict.*, *Pundbrech*, .. is the illegal taking of Cattle out of the Pound, either by breaking the Pound, picking the Lock, or otherwise. **1768** BLACKSTONE *Comm.* III. ix. 146 The distreinor has a remedy in damages .. by writ *de parco fracto*, or pound breach, in case they were actually impounded. **1891** *Carmarthen Jrnl.* 23 Jan. 3/1 At Lampeter County-court on Tuesday .. two cases of pound-breach under distress for tithes were entered for hearing.

ˈpound-cake. [f. POUND *sb.*[1] + CAKE *sb.*] A rich cake so called as originally containing a pound (or equal weight) of each of the principal ingredients, flour, butter, sugar, fruit, etc.
1747 H. GLASSE *Art of Cookery* xv. 138 Pound Cake. Take a Pound of Butter .. twelve Eggs .. a Pound of Flour .. a Pound of Sugar [etc.]. **1807** M. E. RUNDELL *New Syst. Domestic Cookery* 217 (*heading*) A good pound cake. **1841** THACKERAY *Men & Coats* Wks. 1900 XIII. 601 It will have a great odour of bohea and pound-cake. **1876** F. E. TROLLOPE *Charming Fellow* II. ix. 138 [He] begged to recommend the pound-cake, from his own personal experience. *c* **1900** *Beeton's Every-day Cook. Bk.* 396 Pound Cake.—Ingredients of large cake: 1 lb. of butter, 1¼ lb. of flour, 1 lb. of pounded loaf sugar, 1 lb. of currants, 9 eggs, 2 oz. of candied peel [etc.]. **1942** B. ROBERTSON *Red Hills & Cotton* iii. 69 We liked .. cornbread with chitterlings, ambrosia, stuffed eggs, pound cake. **1951** T. CAPOTE *Grass Harp* (1952) i. 12 Dolly, who lived off sweet foods, was always baking a pound cake. **1977** *Time* 24 Jan. 5/2 Pound cake will remain just that, no matter how many grams the ingredients weigh.

ˈpounded, *ppl. a.*[1] Forms: see the vb. [f. POUND *v.*[1] + -ED[1].] Crushed by heavy blows to small fragments or to powder; beaten small; comminuted. ***pounded meat***: *spec.* (*U.S.* and *Canad.*) the flesh of buffalo or other game cut up, dried, and pulverized into powder to form the basic ingredient of pemmican.
1600 SURFLET *Country Farm* xxviii. 181 He shall giue them parched wheate, or of pouned barly the double measure. **1771** LUCKOMBE *Hist. Print.* 33 Paper made .. with pounded cotton or reduced to a pulp. **1775** S. HEARNE *Jrnl.* 5 Sept. (1934) 177 One Cannoe came with some Dry'd & Pownded Meate. **1805** *Deb. Congress U.S.* 9th Congress 2 Sess. App. 1066 Buffalo robes, tallow, dried and pounded meat and grease. **1815** SIMOND *Tour Gt. Brit.* I. 11 The roads are well gravelled with pounded stones. **1898** F. RUSSELL *Explor. Far North* 163, I saw large quantities of pounded meat, grease, and tongues eaten. **1899** *Allbutt's Syst. Med.* VIII. 380 Pounded meat [etc.] should form the basis of the feedings. **1922** *Beaver* Nov. 51/1 Pounded meat was made from the dried meat by beating it with flails until it became as small as desired and then stored away in bags. **1956** H. S. M. KEMP *Northern Trader* 93 The meat so acquired would either be dried, converted into pounded meat, or mixed with fat and cranberries and made up as pemmican.

pounded, *ppl. a.*[2]: see POUND *v.*[2]

†**ˈpounder**, *sb.*[1] *Obs.* Forms: 5 pounder, pondre, punder. [app. f. POUND *sb.*[1]; perh. in reference to the fact that the auncel had at its end a knob of a pound weight as a counterpoise (see quot. *a* 1640 in AUNCEL). But it is also possible that the word in the form *pondre* was immediately from L. *pondus*, *ponder-* weight.] A name of the kind of balance called AUNCEL.
c **1425** *Castell Persev.* 2730 in *Macro Plays* 152 It schal þee weyen, as peys in punder [*rime* vnder]. **1429** ABP. CHICHELEY in Wilkins *Concilia* III. 516 Dicto pondere le Auncell scheft seu *pounder* .. doloso quodam stateræ genere. **1439** *Rolls of Parlt.* V. 30/1 On branche of disceit .. called a Schafte, othere wise called a Pondre, othere wise called an Hauncere, whiche greved many a trewe man. *c* **1440** *Promp. Parv.* 416/2 Punder, *librilla.*

pounder (ˈpaʊndə(r)), *sb.*[2] Also (1 púnere), 6 pouner. [f. POUND *v.*[1] + -ER[1]. Cf. OE. *púnere* a pestle, f. *púnian* POUND *v.*[1]] One who or that which pounds.
1. a. An instrument for pounding; a pestle, a crushing beetle; a beater.
a **1050** [see POUND *v.*[1] 1]. **1564** in Noake *Worcestersh. Relics* (1877) 12 A garlics morter, a pouner. **1656** W. D. tr. *Comenius' Gate Lat. Unl.* §353 They beat in a stone mortar with a rough or Greek pounder. **1799** J. ROBERTSON *Agric. Perth* 282 There were two pounders, and a third was afterwards added, all from Carron. **1830** M. DONOVAN *Dom. Econ.* I. 313 Crush them well .. with three or four strokes of the pounder. **1899** R. MUNRO *Preh. Scot.* viii. 304 With the exception of an oblong stone or 'pounder' all the stone implements were of flint.
b. A vessel for pounding in; a mortar.
1891 *Anthony's Photogr. Bull.* IV. 56 Indian women pound corn and sift the poundings, and make bread of varying grades of coarseness. A pounder is constructed of a section of a log, and is really a huge mortar, nearly three feet high.
2. a. A person who pounds.
1611 FLORIO, *Pestatore*, a stamper, a punner [1598, a stamper or beater in a morter]. **1834** DARWIN in *Life & Lett.* (1887) I. 254 A certain hunter of beetles, and pounder of rocks. **1894** B. THOMSON *S. Sea Yarns* 145 The kava-pounder paused, with stone uplifted.
b. A policeman. *U.S. slang.*
1938 *New Yorker* 12 Mar. 38/2 Letting the sickly-sweet odor of burning marijuana into the street for the first passing pounder, or patrolman, to smell. **1970** C. MAJOR *Dict. Afro-Amer. Slang* 93 *Pounder*, a policeman or detective.
c. *Surfing slang.* (See quot. 1967.)
1967 J. SEVERSON *Great Surfing* Gloss., *Pounder*, an unusually hard-breaking wave. **1970** [see GREENIE].

pounder (ˈpaʊndə(r)), *sb.*[3] Now *rare.* [f. POUND *v.*[2] + -ER[1].] One whose office it is to pound cattle; = POUND-KEEPER, PINDER, POINDER.
1622 *Canterb. Marr. Licences* (MS.), Xpoferus Hewes of St. Mary's in Dover, pownder. **1655** *Boston Rec.* (1877) II. 123 Tho. Alcock chosen Cow keeper for this yeare, .. as also to be pounder. **1848** J. KIRKPATRICK *Relig. Orders*, etc. *Norwich* 319 At a court of mayoralty, 26 Nov. 1679, the inhabitants of the Castle and Fee have liberty to erect a pound .. and the pounder to dwell upon the fee.

ˈpounder, *sb.*[4] [f. POUND *sb.*[1] + -ER[1].]
I. 1. Something of a pound weight, e.g. a fish.
1834 J. WILSON in *Blackw. Mag.* XXXV. 790 You may pick a pounder out of any black pool. **1898** *Westm. Gaz.* 29 June 5/3 A half-pound trout on this tiny lake will show as good sport as a pounder elsewhere.
II. In combination with a prefixed numeral.
2. Something weighing a specified number of pounds; *spec.* a gun carrying a shot of a specified weight; *rarely*, a projectile of a specified weight. Cf. SIX-POUNDER, TEN-POUNDER.
1684 [see FOUR C. 2]. **1695** *Lond. Gaz.* No. 3112/3 We found in the Castle of Namur .. 69 Pieces of Cannon, viz. 7 twenty four Pounders, 3 sixteen Pounders, 2 twelve Pounders, 9 ten Pounders, .. 3 three Pounders, 1 two Pounder. **1747** [see NINE *a.* 5 b]. **1756–7** tr. *Keysler's Trav.* (1760) I. 317 The French had erected a battery of twenty-four sixty pounders directly over one of the mines of the citadel. **1771** [see TWO IV. 1]. **1845** [see *one-pounder* s.v. ONE B. 35]. **1861** W. F. COLLIER *Hist. Eng. Lit.* 403 A silver-scaled twenty-pounder. **1862** *Rambler* Mar. 414 A large number of 100-pounder Armstrong guns. **1896** [see SEVEN C. 3]. **1901** *Westm. Gaz.* 10 Aug. 2/1 'Everyone must bring his own mug and a cake' .. we have carried a two-pounder at the 'handle-bar'. **1915** A. D. GILLESPIE *Let.* 14 June in *Lett. from Flanders* (1916) 196 They started with 33-pounder bombs, like a big turnip with a long handle, and we watched them sailing through the air. **1915** C. MACKENZIE *Guy & Pauline* 264 'I know a man .. who caught a four pounder with a bumble-bee.' 'I caught a six pounder at Oxford with a mouse's head myself.' **1977** F. PARRISH *Fire in Barley* ii. 25 He had sometimes seen very big trout here, three and four pounders. **1978** K. BONFIGLIOLI *All Tea in China* x. 127 The gunner ambled towards the long brass Armstrong 68-pounder.

3. a. A person possessing, having an income of, or paying (e.g. as rent) a specified number of pounds sterling; a woman having a marriage-portion of so many pounds.

1706 FARQUHAR *Recruiting Officer* III. i, I must meet a lady, a twenty thousand pounder, presently, upon the walk by the river. **1754** SHEBBEARE *Matrimony* (1766) I. 69 The eldest Daughter of..one of the richest Merchants in the City; a Seventy Thousand Pounder. **1840** THACKERAY *Catherine* iii, Rich Miss Dripping, the twenty-thousand-pounder from London.

b. A bank-note or other article of the value of a specified number of pounds sterling.

1755 JOHNSON s.v., A note or bill is called a twenty *pounder* or ten *pounder*, from the sum it bears. **1829** MARRYAT *F. Mildmay* iv, I pocketed the little donation—it was a ten-pounder. **1895** *Westm. Gaz.* 23 Feb. 2/1 It is..cheering, to discuss airily for the nonce, links which are two thousand pounders, and single pearl pins worth £1,200 each.

III. 4. *attrib.* and *Comb.*, as **pounder pear** = *pound-pear* (POUND *sb.*[1] 4); ***one-, two-*** (etc.) ***pounder cartridge, 12-*** (etc.) ***pounder gun***, etc.

1697 DRYDEN *Virg. Georg.* II. 127 Unlike are Bergamotes and pounder Pears. **1807** HUTTON *Course Math.* II. 261 What length of a 36-pounder gun [etc.]? **1828** J. M. SPEARMAN *Brit. Gunner* 362, 2-pounders take about 4 sheets of 12-pounder cartridge paper... ½-pounders, 1 sheet of 9-pounder paper. **1863** P. BARRY *Dockyard Econ.* 95 The 12-pounder Armstrong field pieces are believed by the Committee to be efficient.

†**'pounder**, *v. Obs. rare*⁻⁰. [app. freq. of POUND *v.*[1]] = POUND *v.*[1] I.

1570 LEVINS *Manip.* 78/8 To pounder, *tritumare*.

poundfalde, obs. form of PINFOLD.

'pound 'foolish, *a.* Foolish in dealing with large sums: antithetical to PENNY-WISE, q.v. So **pound-foolishness, pound-folly**: see PENNY-WISDOM.

pound garnett, obs. f. POMEGRANATE.

pound-house. [f. POUND *v.*[1] + HOUSE *sb.*] A building in which the pounding, pulverizing, or crushing of material is done: as **a.** part of a glass-works; **b.** a cider-mill.

1702 *Lond. Gaz.* No. 3821/8 A Round Bottle-Glass-House,..with all Conveniencies, a Pound House and Smith's Forge. **1796** W. MARSHALL *W. England* I. Gloss. 323, etc., Pound-house. [*Ibid.* 228 The apples being thrown into a large trough or tub, five or six persons..pounded them with large club-shaped wooden pestils... Hence, no doubt, the epithet pound is applied to the house, etc., in which the whole business of cider-making is performed.] **1899** RAYMOND *No Soul* I. vi. 122 Jacob Handsford stayed out in the pound-house..giving another screw to his apple-cheese.

Poundian ('paʊndɪən), *a.* [f. the name *Pound* (see below) + -IAN.] Of, pertaining to, or characteristic of the American writer and poet Ezra Pound (1885–1972) or his work; resembling or influenced by the style of Pound. Also *absol.* as *sb.*

1939 E. H. W. MEYERSTEIN *Let.* 4 Apr. (1959) 221, I never thought I should come round to Eliot as a poet. Here he has dropped his Poundian Babel-tongues. **1958** *N. & Q.* June 265/2 Sappho—a well-known source of Poundian inspiration. **1960** N. STOCK in *Agenda* June 1 The usual Poundian emphasis On medieval money and wages. **1965** *Times Lit. Suppl.* 25 Nov. 1070/4 Mr. Charles Olson..can often be peculiarly irritating with his Poundian mannerisms. **1971** *Guardian* 27 May 9/6 His Poundian hankerings after aristocracy. **1975** P. FUSSELL *Gt. War & Mod. Memory* ix. 313 The reader in search of innovation will find it in..Jones's Eliotic and Poundian juxtapositions. **1976** *Times Lit. Suppl.* 23 July 926/5 In this new short book he is more a Poundian than a critic.

poundiferous (paʊn'dɪfərəs), *a. rare.* [f. POUND *sb.*[3]: see -FEROUS.] Accompanied by pounding.

1871 'MARK TWAIN' *Let.* 28 Jan. (1917) I. 183 A long, vociferous, poundiferous and vitreous jingling of applause announces the conclusion.

pounding ('paʊndɪŋ), *vbl. sb.*[1] Forms: see the vb. [-ING[1].] The action of POUND *v.*[1]

1. a. Crushing or bruising into pulp or powder; trituration, pulverizing.

1591 PERCIVALL *Sp. Dict.*, *Majadura*, hammering, stamping, powning. **1601** HOLLAND *Pliny* XII. xxvii, Verjuice may be made..by punning and stamping unripe grapes in morters. **1867** BAKER *Nile Tribut.* ii. (1872) 24 Reduced by pounding in a heavy mortar. **1886** *Pall Mall G.* 20 Aug. 4/1 The juice of the apple, after being expressed by an operation called 'pounding', ferments.

b. *concr.* The proceeds of this process; pounded substance; the quantity pounded at one time.

1872 BLACKIE *Lays Highl.* p. xviii, The sea bottom, covered with the poundings of these rocks. **1893** *Daily News* 28 Apr. 5/5 A certain London firm had taken his whole year's 'pounding' [of cider].

2. Striking or beating with or as with the fist; beating, pummeling, knocking, thumping; heavy firing; an instance of this.

1815 in Scott *Paul's Lett.* (1839) 125 [Remark attributed to Wellington at Waterloo] Hard pounding this, gentlemen; let's see who will pound longest. **1858** COL. K. YOUNG *Diary & Corr.* (1902) App. D. 331 We should have given the rascals a regular pounding. **1896** T. L. DE VINNE *Moxon's Mech. Exerc., Printing* 424 The pounding of a form..with furious blows from a heavy mallet.

3. Heavy riding.

1883 JESSOPP *Arcady* iv. (1887) 116 The dreary pounding back at night in the dark, to find the baby sick.

4. *attrib.* and *Comb.*, as ***pounding house, machine, mill***; **pounding barrel**, a barrel in which clothes are pounded in water to cleanse them; **pounding match** (*slang*), a fight; also *transf.*

1869 MRS. STOWE *Old Town* xxvii, The thunder of the *pounding-barrel announced that the washing was to be got out of the way before daylight. **1656** W. D. tr. *Comenius' Gate Lat. Unl.* §353 Their work-hous was called pistrinum or a *punning-hous. **1839** URE *Dict. Arts* 813 A stamping mill or *pounding machine. **1815** WELLINGTON in Gurw. *Desp.* XII. 529 You will have heard of our battle of the 18th. Never did I see such a *pounding match... Napoleon did not manœuvre at all. **1785** T. JEFFERSON *Notes Virginia* vi. 43 A good situation on a creek for a *pounding mill. **1849** C. LANMAN *Lett. from Alleghany Mts.* i. 17 The vein gold is brought to light by means of what is called a pounding mill. **1905** 'P. PENNINGTON' *Woman Rice Planter* (1913) 142 The cows and pigs are fed on the flour, a gray substance that comes from the grain as the chaff is removed in the pounding mill.

pounding, *vbl. sb.*[2], confining in a pound: see POUND *v.*[2]

pounding, *vbl. sb.*[3], in coining: see POUND *v.*[3]

'pounding, *ppl. a.* [f. POUND *v.*[1] + -ING[2].] That pounds, in various senses of POUND *v.*[1]

1865 LE FANU *Guy Dev.* II. xi. 105 He..strode up with pounding steps to his dressing-room. **1894** B. THOMSON *S. Sea Yarns* 143 The ringing thud of the pounding kava-stones ceased. **1904** M. HEWLETT *Queen's Quair* I. viii. 113 Ah, the adventure of it, the rush of air, the pounding horse, and the safe, fierce arms!

'pound-'keeper. [f. POUND *sb.*[2] + KEEPER *sb.*] One who has charge of a public pound; a pinder.

1783 COWPER *Reports* 478 If wrongfully taken, it was at the peril of the person bringing them; not of the pound-keeper, who has no right or power to judge of the legality of the capture; but is the officer of the law, and ministerial only. **1884** *Law Times* 15 Mar. 364/1 A pound-keeper obtains a penalty before the justices against the owner of some sheep for releasing them from pound. **1886** *Even. Bell* (Auckland, N.Z.) 29 June 8/4 Borough of Newton. Written applications for Poundkeeper and Ranger will be received up to 5 o'clock on Thursday, July 1.

†**'pound-land.** *Sc. Obs.* Also pund-. [f. POUND *sb.*[1] + LAND *sb.*[1], repr. med.L. *librata terræ*.] A measure of arable land equal to four oxgangs or half a plough-land.

1547 in *Calr. Laing Charters* (1899) 139 Dowbill maill for ewerie pundland, that is to say, twentie punds money of this realm for the said ten pund land. **1575** *Reg. Privy Council Scot.* II. 468 Of every pundland of auld extent. **1585** *Decr. Sc. Exch.* in E. W. Robertson *Hist. Ess.* (1872) 136 Thirteen acres extendis and sall extend to ane oxgait of land, and four oxgait extendis and sall extend to ane pund land of auld extent. **1753** CHAMBERS *Cycl. Supp.*, *Pound land*... This is also called *librata terræ*, and is used in Scotland to denote a certain portion of arable land, containing four oxengate, or fifty-two acres.

poundlar, var. of PUNDLAR[1], steelyard.

†**'pound-law.** *Sc. Obs.* Also 6 **punlaw.** [f. POUND *sb.*[2] + LAW *sb.*[1]] Amerciament for pounded cattle or poinded goods.

1463 *Burgh Crt. Rec. Newburgh* in A. Laing *Lindores Abbey* xvi. (1876) 161 Ilka man suld hald on his awyn grys a kow or a horss in tedyr, and gyff yai war foundyn loss ye pownd-lau [*mispr.* -lan] sould be iiij. d. **1541** *Records of Elgin* (New Spald. Cl.) I. 59 For the quhi[l]k ilk auchenpart sall pay to him ane d., by [= besides] his punlaw. **1553** *Reg. Privy Council Scot.* I. 150 He mycht on na wyise eschaetit thaim, nor hald thai thame langar,..bot quhile thai had payit ane grote for the heid off ilk peax for thair poindlaw.

poundler, variant of POINDLAR *Sc. Obs.*

'poundless, *a.* [f. POUND *sb.*[1] + -LESS.] Without a pound (of money).

1891 G. MEREDITH *One of our Conq.* I. xiii. 255 I'm penniless or poundless.

†**'pound-lien.** *Sc. Obs.* In 3 ? punlayn, 6 **pundlene.** [f. POUND *sb.*[2] + LIEN[1].] Fee for the release of an animal from the pound.

c **1280** *Inquis. Miscell. Chanc.* File 67. No. 4 (P.R.O.), Dominus Thomas de Brad petiit octo denarios de punlayn de hominibus domini regis. **1533** *Aberdeen Regr.* (1844) I. 149 The prouest, bailȝeis, and counsaill..ordanit Georg Annan pvndler of thar kirk yard, and ordanit the pundlene of euery best to be four d.

†**pound-like,** *adv. Obs.* [f. POUND *sb.*[1] 3 + -LIKE I b.] By the pound; at so much per pound.

1472–3 *Rolls of Parlt.* VI. 59/1 Deduction to be made oute of every mannes apprest pownd like.

'pound-lock. Also 8–9 **pond-lock.** [f. POUND *sb.*[2] + LOCK *sb.*[2]] A lock on a river for pounding up the water; = LOCK *sb.*[2] 7.

1783 *Rules, Orders*, etc. *Thames* 13 Any of the pound-locks, lock tackle, weirs, bricks, winches. **1866** *Sat. Rev.* 21 Apr. 472/1 A century has witnessed the construction of the entire navigation of the Thames by pound-locks. **1879** *Edin. Rev.* CL. 447 In these side cuts the pound lock was introduced, with side weirs to enable the floods to escape.

'pound-meal, *adv. Obs.* exc. *dial.* [f. POUND *sb.*[1] + -MEAL.] Pound by pound; by the pound.

1362 LANGL. *P. Pl.* A. II. 198 Pardoners..senden him on sonendayes with seales to churches, And ȝaf pardun for pons, poundmele [B. poundmel, C. pound-meel] a-boute. **1903** *Eng. Dial. Dict.* s.v., The market women sell their butter by the dozen or pound-meal.

poundre, obs. form of PONDER.

†**'poundrel.** *Obs.* Also 5 **poundrelle.** [Cf. POUNDER *sb.*[1] and L. *ponderāle* the public scales.]

1. Some kind of weighing apparatus.

14.. *Nom.* in Wr.-Wülcker 714/35 *Hoc ponde*, a fowdrelle [? powndrelle]. Res sit vera staterem portate statera. *a* **1450** MYRC 712 All þat falsen or vse false measures, busshelles, galones, & potelles quartes or false wightes, poundes or poundrelles, or false ellen yerdes.

2. [perh. a distinct word.] ? A head.

1664 COTTON *Scarron.* 27 So nimbly flew away these scundrels Glad they had scap'd and sav'd their poundrels.

'poundstone. [f. POUND *sb.*[1] I + STONE.]

1. A natural stone or pebble of a pound weight, formerly often used as a weight.

1577 KENDALL *Flowers of Epigr.*, etc. *Trifles* 24 Then doth the ponderous poundstone purse Bring doune their feete againe. **1855** ROBINSON *Whitby Gloss.*, *Pundston* or *Pundstone*, a natural stone or pebble of the requisite weight, by which farmers formerly portioned their butter into pounds of twenty-two ounces or 'the lang pund'. **1860** *Athenæum* 22 Sept. 375 Echini which they called..'pound stones', as they were often used by the dairywomen for a pound-weight in the sale of butter.

2. *Coal-mining* (*local*). See quots.

1879 MISS JACKSON *Shropsh. Word-bk.*, *Poundstone*, dirt lying next under the coal,—the coal-floor. **1883** GRESLEY *Gloss. Coal Mining*, *Poundstone*, a kind of underclay.

'pound-'weight, *sb.* (*a.*) [f. POUND *sb.*[1] + WEIGHT *sb.*] A weight of one pound; *spec.* a piece of metal of the weight of a pound avoirdupois, and stamped to that effect, used in weighing.

1538 ELYOT *Dict.*, *As, assis*, a pounde weyghte. *Ibid.*, *Libralis*, a pounde weight. **1617** MORYSON *Itin.* I. 282 The pound weight English, being twelve ounces Troy, doth over-poix the pound weight of Scotland foure penny weight and nine graines English. **1706** PHILLIPS, A *Pound*-Weight of Silver-Bullion is worth 3 Pounds Sterling. **1765** BLACKSTONE *Comm.* I. vii. 274 No man can, by words only, give another an adequate idea of a foot rule, or a pound weight.

b. as *adj.* Of equal or exact weight.

1642 R. CARPENTER *Experience* IV. i. 125 Truly if my power had been pound-waight with my will.

[**poune** in *Kyng Alis.* (Weber), mispr. for *ponne* = PAN *sb.*[1]]

poungarnard, -garnet(te, -karnet, obs. ff. POMEGRANATE.

pounse, obs. form of POUNCE.

†**'pounson**, *v. Obs. rare.* [a. OF. *poinsonner, ponsonner*, Picard *ponchonner* (1324 in Godef. *Compl.*), mod.F. *poinçonner* to pounce (in goldsmith's work) = It. *punzonare* to pounce, f. OF. *poinson, ponson, ponchon*, F. *poinçon*, It. *ponzone, punzone*, PUNCHEON *sb.*[1] The Chaucer MSS. are divided between *pounson* and *pounse*. The precise sense in the quot. is not recorded for OF. or It., and does not occur in PUNCHEON *sb.*[1], but is found from 16th c. in POUNCE *v.*[1] and *sb.*[1]] *trans.* To stamp holes in (clothing) for the purpose of adornment; to PINK. Hence **'pounsoned** *ppl. a.*, **'pounsoning** *vbl. sb.*

c **1386** CHAUCER *Pars. T.* ¶344, 347 [see POUNCE *v.*[1] 2].

pouoir, obs. form of POWER.

poup, -e, pouppe, obs. ff. POOP *sb.*[1], *v.*[1], [2].

Poupart ('pu:pɑ:(r)). *Anat.* [The name of François Poupart (1661–1708), French surgeon.] ***Poupart's ligament***: the inguinal ligament which extends from the anterior superior spine of the ilium to the pubic tubercle.

1756 P. POTT *Treat. Ruptures* I. 6 What is called Poupart's or Fallopius's ligament, is nothing more than the lower border of this tendon stretched from the fore part of the os ileum or haunch bone, to the pubis. **1804** A. COOPER *Anat. & Surg. Treatm. Inguinal & Congenital Hernia* xiv. 48 On examination, a fulness could be perceived above Poupart's ligament. **1844** A. COLLES in S. Mac Coy *Lect. Theory & Pract. Surg.* I. xx. 309 In the operation for femoral hernia you should always begin your first incision at least an inch above Poupart's ligament. **1910** *Practitioner* June 848 The opening in the peritoneum was closed and the operation was concluded by suturing Poupart's ligament..to the thickened part of the pectineal fascia. **1970** I. L. LICHTENSTEIN *Hernia Repair* vi. 72 Poupart's ligament will move when the patient strains, allowing a necessary resiliency to the body's exertion.

†**poupe.** *Obs. rare*⁻¹. [? Shortened from F. *poupée* doll.] A puppet; a doll.

1530 PALSGR. 257/2 Poupe for a chylde, *povpee*.

‖**poupée** (pupe). *Obs.* [F. *poupée* baby, doll, puppet, wax figure, plaster cast, etc.] A figure used for making and exhibiting dresses, wigs, etc.

1786 *Lounger* No. 76. ¶3, I will take care to exhibit..a set of Poupées, which..will convey..a perfect idea of the reigning dress and undress of the fashionable world. **1804** *Europ. Mag.* XLV. 25/2, I do not wish to have my head and face moulded to a poupee for the embellishment of his window.

poupeton, var. PUPTON.

†ˈ**poupiets.** *Cookery. Obs.* [app. related to *poupeton*, var. PUPTON.] (See quot.)

Mispr. *poupicts* in J.; whence various errors in later Dicts. **1706** PHILLIPS, *Poupiets*, a Mess made of long and thin slices of Bacon, cover'd with Veal-stakes of the same Bigness, as also with a good Farce; in order to be roll'd up and roasted on a small Iron-Spit, wrapt up in Paper. **1721** BAILEY, *Poupiets*. **1725** BRADLEY *Fam. Dict.*, *Poupiets*, a Culinary Term. **1755** JOHNSON, *Poupicts*. **1818** TODD, *Poupicks* (erroneously citing *Bailey*). **1828** WEBSTER, *Poupies*. **1846** WORCESTER, *Poupics*.

pour (pɔə(r)), *v.* Forms: see below. [ME. *pouren*, evidenced early in 14th c.; not in OE., nor in the cognate langs.; source obscure: see Note below. The prevailing written form from the first has been *pour(e* (also spelt *powr(e, power*), in ME. (as still in Sc. and n. dial.) = (pur), in mod.Eng. till 19th c. (and still dial.) = (paʊə(r)), proved by the spelling *powre, power*, and by rimes in all the poets from Pope to Tennyson and Swinburne (these last have also pɔə(r)): see illustration of Forms. But the spelling *pore* is found in some 15th c. writings, and *poor* (perh. = puːr) in Palsgrave and Shaks. The late 18th and 19th c. (pɔə(r)), given by Nares 1784, disapproved by Walker 1791-, approved by Webster 1828, Smart 1836, is not easy to account for: it could hardly be derived from (paʊə(r)); it may be a dialectal survival of the 15th c. *pore*, though connecting evidence is wanting; it may also repr. 16th c. *poor* (puːr), altered as in *floor, door*, and vulgar *more, pore, shore, yore*, for *moor, poor, sure, your*.]

A. Illustration of Forms.

α. 4–7 poure, 5– pour. β. 5–7 powre, 6–8 power. γ. 5 pore. δ. 6 poore, 6, 9 *dial.* poor.

α. **13..** *Cursor M.* 5833 (Gött.) To þe water of þe flum þu ga, And poure [*Cott.* put, *Fairf.* putte] it vp apon þe land. *c* **1330–1549** (see B. 1, 3 b) Poure, pour. **1570** LEVINS *Manip.* 222/30 To Poure, *fundere*. **1712** POPE *Messiah* 13 Ye Heav'ns! from high the dewy nectar pour [*rime* show'r]. **1728** —— *Dunc.* II. 3 Where on her Curls the Public pours ..fragrant Grains and Golden show'rs. **1780** COWPER *Table Talk* 210 Winter invades the spring, and often pours A chilling flood on summer's drooping flowers. **1781** MORISON in *Sc. Paraphr.* xxxv. vi, Through latest ages let it pour, In mem'ry of my dying hour. **1817** SHELLEY *Rev. Islam* v. xxix. 1 A mighty crowd, such as the wide land pours..like the rush of showers. [Ibid. II. xlii. 6, x. xi. 5, etc. *rimes with* more, gore, before.] **1830** TENNYSON *Poet's Mind* 12 Holy water will I pour Into every spicy flower. [*In later poems pour'd rimes with* stored, oar'd.]

β. *c* **1420** *Liber Cocorum* (1862) 19 Be sleȝe and powre in water thenne. **1570** LEVINS *Manip.* 78/10 To Powre, *fundere*. **1597** LYLY *Woman in Moone* II. i. 25 High Ioue himselfe..Receiues more influence then he powers on thee. **1611** BIBLE *Ps.* xlii. 4, I powre out my soule in mee. **1683** SALMON *Doron Med.* I. 107 Then powring the matter upon a cold Table. **1741** WARBURTON *Div. Legat.* II. 22 The Light the Great Maimonides had powered into this enquiry.

γ. *c* **1430** *Two Cookery-bks.* 16 As a man may pore it out of þe bolle. *c* **1440** *Promp. Parv.* 409/2 Poryn in, *infundo*. *c* **1490** *Ibid.*, Poryn owt, *effundo*.

δ. **1530** PALSGR. 662/2, I poore drinke or lycoure in to a cuppe or vessell. *c* **1600** SHAKS. *Sonn.* xxxviii, Thou..that poor'st into my verse Thine owne sweet argument.

B. Signification. I. *trans.*

1. a. To emit in a stream; to cause or allow (a liquid or granular substance) to flow out of a vessel or receptacle; to discharge or shed copiously; also, to emit (rays of light). Said either of a person, or of a thing which discharges a stream. Often with advbs., *forth, out, in, down, off*, etc.

c **1330** *Amis & Amil.* 2026 The lazar tok forth his coupe of gold,..Therin he pourd that win so rich. *c* **1385** CHAUCER *L.G.W.* 648 (*Cleopatra*) He pouryth pesyn vp on the hachis sledere. **1520** M. NISBET *N.T. in Scots* (S.T.S.) III. *Prol. to Romanis* 332 Ewin as watter js powret into anne weschel. **1535** COVERDALE *Prov.* ix. 5 Drynke my wyne, which I haue poured out for you. **1600** SHAKS. *A.Y.L.* v. i. 46 Drink being powr'd out of a cup into a glasse, by filling the one, doth empty the other. **1604** E. G[RIMSTONE] *D'Acosta's Hist. Indies* v. xxix. 418 Powring foorth many teares, with great repentance and sorrow. **1614** MARKHAM *Cheap Husb.* I. iii. (1668) 34 Powre a spoonful of cold vinegar into her ear. **1666** BOYLE *Orig. Formes & Qual.* Wks. 1772 III. 62 The remaining matter..with the least heat may be poured out like a liquor. **1697** DAMPIER *Voy.* I. xi. 322 The Sky..being covered with black Clouds, pouring down excessive Rains. **1800** tr. *Lagrange's Chem.* II. 159 If potash be poured into a solution of this salt, it produces a precipitate. **1818–20** E. THOMPSON *Cullen's Nosol. Method.* (ed. 3) 206 Vesicles.. remain for several days and then pour out a thin ichor. **1819** SHELLEY *Prometh Unb.* IV. 227 Liquid darkness, which the Deity Within seems pouring, as a storm is poured From jagged clouds. **1820** W. IRVING *Sketch Bk.* II. 14 The sun had poured his last ray through the lofty windows. **1855** KINGSLEY *Westw. Ho!* iv, Campian..trying to pour oil on the troubled waters. **1860** TYNDALL *Glac.* I. xx. 138 A large wide valley into which both mountains pour their snows. **1881** MRS. J. H. RIDDELL *Senior Partner* II. x. 203 An old, old pug..took no notice of Mr. McCullagh or anything else, till Janey poured him out a glass of milk. **1893** *Times* 26 Apr. 9/4 He was obliged to pour cold water very plentifully upon the zeal of his Irish friends. **1909** E. BANKS *Mystery F. Farrington* 54 Pour me some tea, dear, and tell me about your play.

b. *nonce-use.* To send (something) down a stream.

1590 SPENSER *F.Q.* II. x. 19 But the sad virgin, innocent of all, Adowne the rolling river she did poure [*rimes* succoure, floure = floor].

c. *absol. spec.* with ellipsis of the name of the thing poured.

1539 BIBLE (Great) *2 Kings* iv. 40 So they powred out for the men to eate. **1560** (Genev.) *Ibid.* 41 Powre out for the people, that they may eat. *a* **1631** DONNE *Poems* (1650) 147 Men are spunges, which to powre out, receive. **1906** W. S. MAUGHAM *Bishop's Apron* ix. 61/1 Mrs. Railing stirred the tea, put milk in each cup, and poured out. **1919** 'C. DANE' *Legend* 5, I used to pour out when interesting people came to tea. **1925** E. H. YOUNG *William* viii. 81 Lydia immediately got into a hammock. 'I can eat here, but..I can't pour out. Dora can do that.' **1930** A. BENNETT *Imperial Palace* lvi. 420 'Will you pour?' she asked... He poured out the tea. **1956** R. FULLER *Image of Society* ix. 226 'Shall I pour?' she asked. **1962** *Woman's Own* 31 Mar. 89/2, I think Alison should pour today. **1965** R. PETRIE *Running Deep* x. 115 'Miss Fairfield poured,' Ian reminded her. **1973** 'D. HALLIDAY' *Dolly & Starry Bird* iii. 43 'I shall pour,' Johnson said, and pushed a cup under my nose. 'Black coffee and Sambucca and good intentions.'

2. Said of a river, etc.: To cause the water to flow in a flood; *refl.* to flow with strong current, to fall *into* the sea, etc.

1665 MANLEY *Grotius' Low C. Warres* 591 The Rhine mixeth and powres it self into Issell. **1790** BURNS *Tam O'Shanter* 97 Before him Doon pours all his floods. **1870** J. H. NEWMAN *Gram. Assent* II. ix. 382 As a stream might pour itself into the sea. **1894** BLACKMORE *Perlycross* 269 Every gateway poured its runnel, and every flinty lane its torrent.

3. *transf.* and *fig.* To send forth as in a stream; to send forth, emit, discharge copiously and rapidly. **a.** With material object: To send forth (persons) in a stream (also *refl.*); to discharge in rapid succession or simultaneously, as missiles; to cause (money or any commodity) to flow or pass in a constant stream; to bestow profusely.

1599 SHAKS. *Hen. V*, v. Prol. 24 How London doth powre out her Citizens. **1609** BIBLE (Douay) *1 Sam.* xxiii. 27 Make hast, and come, because the Philistijms have powred in themselves upon the land. **1617** MORYSON *Itin.* II. 83 From all partes they powred upon as great vollyes of shot. **1687** A. LOVELL tr. *Thevenot's Trav.* I. 74 When the Captain was come within distance [he] poured in two Broadsides among them. **1715–20** POPE *Iliad* II. 790 Crete's hundred cities pour forth all her sons. *c* **1764** GRAY *Triumphs Owen* 6 He nor heaps his brooded stores, Nor on all profusely pours. **1810** SCOTT *Lady of L.* VI. xviii, And refluent through the pass of fear The battle's tide was poured [*rime* sword]. **1836** MARRYAT *Midsh. Easy* xxx, At the word given, the broadside was poured in. **1849** MACAULAY *Hist. Eng.* iv. I. 495 Sixty thousand a year, little more than what was poured into the English exchequer every fortnight.

b. With immaterial object: To send *forth* or *out* as in a stream (words, music); to give free utterance or expression to (a feeling); to shed or infuse freely or continuously (an influence, etc.).

1526 TINDALE *Acts* ii. 17 Of my sprete I will poure out apon all flesshe. **1545** JOYE *Exp. Dan.* iv. 61 Daniel lykewyse cap. 9. powereth forth his herte before god. **1549** COVERDALE, etc. *Erasm. Par. Cor.* 38 Madde men whiche.. poure out wordes, whiche neyther themselues vnderstand nor other. —— *Eph.* 1 Iesus Christ..that of hys free fauour, hath powred all gentle kyndenesse vpon vs. **1557** N.T. (Genev.) *Acts* x. 45 On the Gentils also, was powred out [WYCLIF sched out, TINDALE sheed oute] the gyft of the holy Gost. **1560** DAUS tr. *Sleidane's Comm.* 58 That he alone myghte..powre out all his indignation vpon them. **1579** W. WILKINSON *Confut. Familye of Loue* 19 The essentiall nature or being of God is poured into us. **1644** *Directory for Public Worship* 11 That God would powre out a blessing. **1711** ADDISON *Spect.* No. 57 ¶4 The Charms which Nature has poured out upon them [Woman-kind]. **1733** POPE *Ess. Man* III. 33 Is it for thee the linnet pours his throat? **1789** BLAKE *Songs Innoc., Night* 23 They pour sleep on their head. **1812** J. WILSON *Isle of Palms* II. 325 Such words she o'er her lover pours As give herself relief. **1849** MACAULAY *Hist. Eng.* iv. I. 452 He frequently poured forth on plaintiffs and defendants..torrents of frantic abuse, intermixed with oaths and curses. **1871** R. ELLIS *Catullus* lxiii. 321 They.. Pour'd grave inspiration, a prophet chant to the future.

c. ***to pour (on) the coal*** (Aeronaut. slang), to cause an aircraft to accelerate; to pilot an aircraft at high speed. Also *transf.*

1937 E. C. PARSONS *Gt. Adventure* xix. 233, I poured coal into the old Hispano and lit out like a scared jack rabbit. **1944** T. H. WISDOM *Triumph over Tunisia* xxiii. 183 The bombs gone away, Jimmy put the nose down and poured on the coal to escape. **1961** J. M. FOSTER *Hell in Heavens* 58 He poured the coal to his plane and banked to avoid passing too close. **1971** M. TAK *Truck Talk* 122 *Pour on the coals*, to drive a truck at high speed.

†**4.** *fig. refl.* To give oneself up or over, yield, abandon oneself (*to*). *Obs. rare.*

c **1450** tr. *De Imitatione* II. i. 41 þe inwarde man..neuere pouriþ himself holy to outwarde þinges.

5. *spec.* in *Founding.* To make by melting; to cast, FOUND. (= L. *fundere*, F. *fondre*.) *rare.*

1873 J. RICHARDS *Wood-working Factories* 88 Whenever it is practicable, both sides of the bearings should be poured or moulded at one time.

II. *intr.* (for *refl.*)

6. a. (from 1, 2). Of liquids, etc.: To gush forth or flow in a stream; to flow strongly; of rain: to fall heavily, rain hard.

1538 ELYOT *Dict.*, *Ruo*.., to falle, to poure out. **1552** in HULOET. **1605** SHAKS. *Lear* III. iv. 18 No, I will weepe no more; in such a night, To shut me out? Poure on, I will endure. **1697** DRYDEN *Virg. Georg.* I. 174 When impetuous Rain Swells hasty Brooks, and pours upon the Plain. *Ibid.* IV. 413 The teeming Tide, Which pouring down from Ethiopian Lands, Makes green the Soil with Slime. **1737** [S. BERINGTON] *G. di Lucca's Mem.* (1738) 74 The River Nile.. running thro' the hither Ethiopia, pours down upon Egypt. **1831** WILLIS *Poem at Brown Univ.* 172 The light Of the blest sun pours on his book. **1832** TENNYSON *Dream Fair Wom.* 182 The torrent brooks..From craggy hollows pouring,.. Sound all night long. **1859** W. COLLINS *Blow up w. Brig!*, The sweat poured off my face like water. **1883** *Manch. Guard.* 22 Oct. 5/2 Sewer gas was pouring into the lavatories.

b. *impers.* To rain heavily or copiously. Often in proverb, ***it never rains but it pours***: events (esp. misfortunes) come all together or happen in rapid succession.

1726 ARBUTHNOT (*title*) It cannot rain but it pours; or London strow'd with rarities. **1809** MALKIN *Gil Blas* I. ix. ¶1 As it never rains but it pours, I was in the front of the battle. **1815** LADY GRANVILLE *Lett.* (1894) I. 79 We were to have gone with him if it had been fine, but it is pouring. **1849** THACKERAY in *Scribner's Mag.* I. 551/1 Is it pouring with rain? **1893** [see RAIN *v.* 1].

7. *transf.* and *fig.* Of persons or things: To run or rush in a stream or crowd; to come or go in great numbers, continuously, or in rapid succession; to stream, to swarm.

1573–80 BARET *Alv.* P 628 To Powre out, to come or runne forth in great companies. **1662** J. DAVIES tr. *Olearius' Voy. Ambass.* 14 The other Muscovites came pouring into the Citie. **1754** GRAY *Poesy* 11 Now the rich stream of Music winds along..Headlong, impetuous, see it pour. **1781** J. LOGAN in *Sc. Paraphr.* x. i, In streets, and op'nings of the gates where pours the busy crowd. **1848** MRS. JAMESON *Sacr. & Leg. Art* (1850) 1 The modern engravings which pour upon us daily. **1849** MACAULAY *Hist. Eng.* ii. I. 219 From every part of Germany troops poured towards the Rhine. **1860** L. V. HARCOURT in *G. Rose's Diaries & Corr.* II. vi. 204 After the announcement of Mr. Pitt's death, lamentations pour in. **1891** *Punch* 18 Apr. 185/1 Business prospered, and money came pouring in.

III. **8.** Special uses with *adv.* or *prep.*

For general uses with *forth, out*, etc., see prec. senses.

†**a. pour on** (in ME. with indirect passive). To overspread *with* something poured, to suffuse fully. [= L. *suffundĕre*.] *Obs.*

c **1450** tr. *De Imitatione* I. xxiv. 33 þe lecherovs men..shul be poured on wiþ brenyng picche & stynkyng brymston.

†**b. pour out**: to scatter, spread about. In pa. pple. ***poured out*** = L. *effusus, diffusus*, spread out diffusely. *Obs. rare.*

c **1586** C'TESS PEMBROKE *Ps.* XLIV. vi, As sheepe..we lie alone: Scattringlie by Thee out powred. **1748** THOMSON *Cast. Indol.* I. lxxi, Where, from gross mortal care and business free, They lay, poured out in ease and luxury.

[*Note.* It has been suggested that ME. *pour-e(n* was an irregular representative of F. *pur-er*:—L. *pūrāre* to purify (with religious rites). F. *purer*, now 'to scum', had in OF. the senses 'to purify, clarify, cleanse, rinse'; also in Norman 'to drip' (Lajoie revint tant moullé, qu'il puroyt de toutes parts, *c* 1560 in Godef.), so still in Guernsey (J'o l'cidre qui pure dans l'auge, 'I hear the cider dripping or pouring into the trough' Moisy), and in mod.Norman and other dialects 'to drip, drop, ooze, or flow out', in Burgundy, etc., 'to press, wring, or squeeze juice or water out of anything' (Godef.). English shows no trace of an original sense 'purify', nor even of 'press or squeeze out', and the intransitive sense 6, which comes near that of 'drip or flow out', is not of early appearance; so that the historical connexion of sense is not evident. The phonology also presents difficulty; it is doubtful whether Eng. has any certain instance of *ou* (or even *o, oo*) from Fr. *u*:—L. *ŭ*.]

pour (pɔə(r)), *sb.* [f. POUR *v.*]

1. Pouring, a pouring stream.

1790 D. MORISON *Rood Fair* xxv. Poems 23 O'er her nose the sweat in sooms, In pours began to tumble. **18..** TROWBRIDGE *The Pewee* ii. (Funk), Through rocky clefts the brooklet fell With plashy pour.

b. *fig.* A number of people streaming out or in.

1897 CROCKETT *Lad's Love* xvii, A miscellaneous pour of lads and lasses. **1898** —— *Standard Bearer* xiv. 123 There cam' a pour o' men-folk frae 'tween the lintels.

2. A heavy fall of rain, a downpour.

1814 COL. HAWKER *Diary* (1893) I. 90 A pour of rain, which turned to snow. **1831** MISS FERRIER *Destiny* xx. (D.), He..rode home ten miles in a pour of rain. **1861** WHYTE MELVILLE *Mkt. Harb.* xii. 97 Ere long, it began to rain—first of all, an ominous drizzle,..then a decided pour.

3. *Founding.* **a.** The act, process, or operation of pouring melted metal. **b.** The amount of melted metal, or other material, poured at a time.

1884 *Century Mag.* XXIX. 238/2 The 'pour' is preceded by a shower of sparks, consisting of little particles of molten steel which are projected fully a hundred feet in the direction of the open mouth of the converter. **1890** W. J. GORDON *Foundry* 102 As the pour is ended, we look into the vessel. **1899** *Edin. Rev.* Apr. 318 The core materials in each 'pipe' represent several 'pours'.

pour, obs. form of POOR, POWER.

pourable (ˈpɔərəb(ə)l), *a.* [f. POUR *v.* + -ABLE.] That may be poured; that flows easily.

1946 *Nature* 2 Nov. 636/1 The experimental preparation used was..a dilution in water prepared..in proportions to give an easily pourable, miscible oil. **1957** V. J. KEHOE

Technique Film & Television Make-Up 245 All Vinamold grades melt down to easily pourable liquids. **1959** *New Scientist* 22 Oct. 750/2 A thick syrup at room temperature, SAIB becomes pourable as the temperature is raised. **1970** *Sci. Jrnl.* May 19/1 Even with temperatures of −40°C the Astrolites did not freeze, remained pourable and were easily and safely handled.

† **pourallee.** *Old Law. Obs.* In 4 pour-, puralee, porale, puraley, 6–7 purallee, pourallee. [Anglo-Fr., f. *pur-*, *pour-*, as prefix often confused with *par-*, L. *per-* through + *alee* going, ALLEY; a literal rendering of L. *perambulātio.*] The PERAMBULATION of a forest.

a **1300** *Liber Custumarum* (Rolls) I. 197 Disantz qe nous ne voloms garder ne tenir la Grant Chartre des franchises d'Engleterre, ne la Chartre de la Foreste, ne souffrir qe la Pouralee se face. **1305** *Act 33 Edw. I*, Si aucuns de ceux, qi sount desafforestez par la puralee, voillent mieux estre dedenz forest..il plest bien au Roi quil soient a ceo rezceux. **1306** *Annales Londonienses* (Rolls) 146 Super absolutione juramenti domini regis Angliae de foresta, quae vulgariter et Anglice dicebatur *porale*. **1323–4** *Tower Roll* in Manwood *Lawes Forest* xx. (1598) 134 b, Icy comence le proces de la puraley de Winsor, fait en le Countie de Surrey.

b. Subsequently used in the sense PURLIEU, as more fully shown under the form PURALÉ, q.v.

1598 MANWOOD *Lawes Forest* title-p., Also a Treatise of the Purallee [*ed.* 1615 Pourallee], declaring what Purallee is, how the same first began, what a Purallee man may doe, how he may hunt and vse his owne Purallee. *Ibid.* xx. §3. 151 All such woods and lands, as were afforested by king Henry the second [etc.],..and were afterwards by the perambulations ..seuered from the old auncient Forrestes, and disafforested again, they were and yet still are called Pourallees... For, this woord *Pourallee* in French, is *Perambulatio* in Latin. *Ibid.* §8. 154 The Pourallee man.. must alwayes first make his course in his owne woods or lands, which he hath within the *Pourallee*, and therefore it is called *Pourlieu*, that is to say, for the place, or, for his owne woods or lands.

pourblind, obs. form of PURBLIND.

‖**pourboire** (purbwar). [F., prop. *pour boire* in order to drink, for drinking.] A gratuity to be spent on drink, drink-money; hence *gen.* a gratuity, douceur, 'tip'.

[**1815** SCOTT *Paul's Lett.* xiii. (1839) 235 There is always some Frenchman near, who, either merely to do the honours to Monsieur l'Estranger, or at most for *quelque chose pour boire*, walks with you through the collection [etc.].] **1817** H. C. B. CAMPBELL *Journey to Florence* (1951) 81 The expence of the *pour boire* at each of these places is very great... The people of the custom houses..regularly ask for it. **1836** R. LOWE in *Life* (1893) I. 116 Quarrelled with the man who led the horse because he would not go far enough. Sconsed him of his *pourboire*. **1882** SALA *Amer. Revis.* (1885) 55 No *pourboire* is expected. **1898** *Glasgow Weekly Cit.* 26 Nov. 16/3 The pourboire will figure as a considerable item when he sets his foot in the land. **1963** [see MANCIA]. **1964** *Economist* 6 June 1133/1 A *pourboire* in the shape of high rebates. **1979** *Times* 5 Dec. 14/3 Commissioners may acquire the much-coveted Cabinet boxes..if they pay for them... Until [1978]..the boxes were a kind of pourboire.

pourcelet, variant of PORCELET *Obs.*

pourchace, -chasse, obs. forms of PURCHASE.

† **'pourcuttle, pour'contrel.** *Obs.* Also 6 pourcouttell. [Origin unascertained.

The earliest cited form is *pourcouttell*, of which *pourcontrell* might easily be a misreading. The second element would then be *couttell* = *cuttle*. But *pour-* remains unexplained: it can hardly stand for an earlier *poul-* from *poulpe* or *polypus*. (Cf. POLLIWOG, *polwygle, porwiggle*.)]

An octopus.

1585 HIGINS *Junius' Nomencl.* 69/1 *Polypus*.., *poulpe, poupe*, a pourcouttell. **1591** SYLVESTER *Du Bartas* I. v. 87 Some have their heads groveling betwixt their feet (As th' inky Cuttles, and the Many-feet). [*Margin.*] Examples. The Pour-cuttle. Cuttle. **1601** HOLLAND *Pliny* I. 242 Some have a tender and soft skin,..others none at all, as the Pour-cuttle or Pourcontrell. *Ibid.* II. 427 The Pulpe fish or Pour-cuttell. **1603** FLORIO *Montaigne* II. xii. (1632) 260 The fish called a Pourcontrell, or Manie-feet, changeth himselfe into what colour he lists. **1611** COTGR., *Poulpe*,..the Pourcontrell, Preke, or many-footed fish. **1638** MAYNE *Lucian* (1664) 384 You are to eat a raw Pourcontrell, or Cuttle-fish, and so to dye. **1758** BAKER in *Phil. Trans.* L. 778 The Polypus, particularly so called, the Octopus, Preke, or Pour-contrel.

poure, obs. f. POOR, PORE, POUR, POWER, PURE.

pourehede, pourete: see POORHEAD, POVERTY.

‖**pour encourager les autres** (pur ɑ̃kuraʒe lez otr), *phr.* [Fr., 'in order to encourage the others', with reference to the execution of Admiral John Byng in 1757: cf. Voltaire *Candide* xxiii. 212 Il est bon de tuer de tems en tems un Amiral pour encourager les autres.] 'In order to encourage (or deter) the others', said of an exemplary punishment or sacrifice. Also *transf.* and in weakened senses.

1804 WELLINGTON *Disp.* (1844) II. 1032 The destruction of the band is complete, but I wished to hang some of their chiefs, *pour encourager les autres.* **1825** H. WILSON *Mem.* (ed. 2) II. 194 We talked a great deal. Hertford's subject was death, pour encourager les autres. **1896** G. B. SHAW *Let.* 29 Jan. (1965) I. 589, I am not alluding in any way to the 'Sign of the Cross' question, or to you. I have simply flicked the insect off the window pane in passing, *pour encourager les autres.* **1915** A. D. GILLESPIE *Lett. from Flanders* (1916) 118 We had another concert last night, and since some officer had to be the victim 'pour encourager les autres', I had to.. sing them the Skye boat song. **1917** T. E. LAWRENCE in *Lett.* (1938) 235 This did not fall in with our ideas, since (pour encourager les autres) we wanted the news to get about that the Arabs accepted prisoners. **1963** *New Society* 21 Nov. 20/2 So *pour encourager les autres* the institute..has just published its conclusions. **1969** Y. CARTER *Mr. Campion's Farthing* xviii. 178 A cruel gesture, made, I suppose, *pour encourager les autres.* He committed suicide? **1973** 'M. UNDERWOOD' *Reward for Defector* viii. 71, I must be punished '*pour encourager les autres*'. **1977** *Rolling Stone* 30 June 69/3 He sent the old man away to prison all the same, *pour encourager*, as Voltaire bitterly put it in another context, *les autres.*

pourer ('pɔərə(r)). [f. POUR *v.* + -ER[1].] One who or that which pours (*trans.* and *intr.*); a vessel used in pouring anything.

1594 *Mirr. Policy* (1599) 265 Saint Hierom calleth it the butler or pourer forth of water. *a* **1619** FOTHERBY *Atheom.* II. viii. §4 (1622) 287 He is not a rash powrer-out of his benefits. **1870** MORRIS *Earthly Par.* I. I. 415 The pourer forth of notes. **1881** MISS BRADDON *Asph.* II. 333 This..teapot..is not a good pourer. **1894** G. A. SMITH *Hist. Geog. Holy Land* 64 What the English Bible calls the early or former rain, literally the *Pourer*.

pourfil, obs. form of PROFILE, PURFLE.

pourge, obs. form of PURGE.

pourie ('pu:rɪ). *Sc.* Also poorie. [f. POUR *v.* + -IE, denominative, as in *cheatie*, etc.] A vessel with a spout for pouring liquid; a jug, pitcher; *esp.* a cream-jug.

1821 GALT *Ayrshire Legatees* x. 288 Miss Jenny Macbride's side-board,..where all the pepper-boxes, poories, and tea-pots..of her progenitors are set out. **1821** *Blackw. Mag.* X. 4 Mrs. M'Lecket had then the pourie in her hand to help my cup. **1823** GALT *Entail* II. iii. 23 The vera silver pourie that I gied her mysel..in a gift at her marriage.

pouring ('pɔərɪŋ), *vbl. sb.* [f. POUR *v.* + -ING[1].]

a. The action of the vb. POUR in various senses; also, the produce of this, a quantity poured at one time.

c **1374** CHAUCER *Troylus* III. 1411 (1460) Dispitous day thyn be þe pyne of helle... Thi pouryng In wol no where late hem dwelle. *c* **1440** *Promp. Parv.* 409/2 Porynge yn, *infusio. Ibid.*, Porynge owte, *effusio.* **1535** COVERDALE *2 Sam.* xxii. 16 The pourynges out of the See were sene. **1613** PURCHAS *Pilgrimage* (1614) 129 It may seeme a powring of water into the Sea. **1768–74** TUCKER *Lt. Nat.* (1834) I. 55 'Pretty bottle', says Sganarelle,..'How envied would be my lot, wert thou to keep always full for all my pourings!' **1836–48** B. D. WALSH *Aristoph.* 25 *note*, The word..literally signifies 'libations', or 'pourings out'.

b. *attrib.* and *Comb.*, as ***pouring-bottle, -machine, -vessel***; **pouring cream**, cream that flows readily; single cream; **pouring-jack**, one of the vessels used in varnish-making.

1535 COVERDALE *1 Macc.* i. 22 The table of the shewbred, the pouringe vessel, the chargers. **1737** WHISTON *Josephus, Hist.* v. xiii. §6 He did not abstain from those pouring vessels ..sent by Augustus. **1839** URE *Dict. Arts* 1266 The assistant puts three copper ladlefuls of oil into the copper pouring-jack. **1866** CRUMP *Banking* x. 227 The mint has eight melting furnaces,..two pouring machines. **1966** P. V. PRICE *France: Food & Wine Guide* 245 *Fontainebleau* is a very light cream cheese, often eaten with sugar and/or pouring cream. **1971** *Islander* (Victoria, B.C.) 13 June 8/1 Strawberries and cream go hand in hand..strawberries and pouring cream; strawberries and ice cream [etc.].

'pouring, *ppl. a.* [f. POUR *v.* + -ING[2].] That pours, in various senses; *esp.* raining heavily.

1601 B. JONSON *Poetaster* v. ii, Powring stormes of sleet, and haile. **1625** BACON *Ess., Viciss. Things* (Arb.) 570 They haue such Powring Riuers, as the Riuers of Asia, and Affrick, and Europe, are but Brookes to them. **1801** SOUTHEY *Thalaba* III. xviii, When the pouring shower Streams adown the roof. **1853** *Ecclesiologist* XIV. 358 At five o'clock on a pouring morning. **1897** M. KINGSLEY *W. Africa* 360 They marched..in a pouring rain all night long.

b. adverbially (in reference to rain).

1868 HAWTHORNE *Amer. Note-Bks.* (1879) II. 234 It rained pouring. **1900** *Daily News* 3 July 8/1 The nights had often been pouring wet.

Hence **'pouringly** *adv.*

1621 LADY M. WROTH *Urania* 363 Who..would not suddenly haue knowne whether it had rayned or no, so powringly high, and sweetely it fell like an Aprill shower.

‖**pour le sport** (pur lə spɔr), *phr.* [Fr., 'for sport'.] For fun, amusement, or sport.

1924 M. ARLEN *Green Hat* i. 6 A green hat, of a sort of felt ..being, no doubt, one of those that women who have many hats affect *pour le sport.* **1936** A. CHRISTIE *ABC Murders* xiii. 97 He kills, it would seem from his letters, *pour le sport*—to amuse himself. **1939** *Time* 22 May 10/2 He has never gained sufficient maturity to be anything more than a conscientious individualist 'pour le sport'. **1955** M. ALLINGHAM *Beckoning Lady* ii. 20 Mr. Magersfontein Lugg himself, garbed tastefully *pour le sport.* **1973** L. MEYNELL *Thirteen Trumpeters* ii. 22 Lucian had automatically made tentative exploratory investigations as to her readiness *pour le sport* and bedworthiness.

pourmenade, obs. form of PROMENADE.

‖**pourparler** (purparle), *sb.* Also in anglicized form PURPARLEY, q.v. [F. *pourparler*, subst. use of inf. *pourparler* (11th c. in Godef.) to discuss, deliberate, plot, f. *pour-* for, before + *parler* to speak.] An informal discussion or conference preliminary to actual negotiation.

1795 *Amer. St. Papers, Foreign* (1832) I. 716 (Stanf.) The *pourparlers* on foot between the two persons mentioned above. **1831** SCOTT *Jrnl.* (1890) II. 435 After some pour-parlers Mr. L——..must remain on board. **1881** JEFFERIES *Wood Magic* II. viii. 230 Another pourparler took place. **1883** *Pall Mall G.* 30 June 8/1 *Pourparlers* have commenced between the Powers for the creation of a permanent International Sanitary Commission in Egypt.

So † **pour'parle** *v. Obs.* [ad. OF. *pourparle-r* vb.: see above] *trans.* to conduct preliminary negotiations about; **pour'parler, pour'parley** *v. intr.*, to carry on a *pourparler*.

1534 *St. Papers Hen. VIII*, VII. 564 That He will for his parte kepe the sees and passages with a navie, being the saide entervieu so farre fourth pourparled and sett. **1880** *Daily Tel.* 25 Sept., Count Hatzfeldt is instructed to leave the task of pourparleying to the British representative. **1900** *Nation* (N.Y.) 11 Oct. 279/2 Meanwhile, the Powers are doing a vast amount of negotiating and pourparlering with each other.

pourpartie, pourpays, pourpensed, obs. varr. PURPARTY, PORPOISE *sb.*, PURPENSED.

‖**pour passer le temps** (pur pase lə tɑ̃), *phr.* [Fr.] To pass the time; to amuse oneself.

1681 OTWAY *Souldiers Fortune* I. i. 3 Some little inconsiderable questions *pour posser* [sic] *le temps.* **1777** P. THICKNESSE *Year's Journey* II. lii. 153 The gay part of the French women love none, but receive all, *pour passer le tems.* **1823** SCOTT *Quentin Durward* I. p. xxiv, Although he admitted he read them *pour passer le temps*, yet..it was not without execrating the tendency. **1846** GEO. ELIOT *Let.* 5 Nov. (1954) I. 225, I wanted some kind of worship pour passer le temps. **1889** E. DOWSON *Let.* 1 Apr. (1967) 59, I still scribble occasionally—pour passer le temps, and devote most of my leisure to the French Renaissance. **1895** C. M. YONGE *Long Vacation* xiii. 128 'Yet you are helping on this concern.' 'True, but partly *pour passer le temps*.' **1976** M. BIRMINGHAM *Heat of Sun* ix. 158 Cynthia asked if she could go too: '*Pour passer le temps*,' she said... 'I love riding in cars at night.'

pourpiece ('pɔəpi:s). *Typogr.* [f. POUR *v.* + PIECE *sb.*] See quot.

1885 C. G. W. LOCK *Workshop Receipts* Ser. IV. 228/1 The superfluous metal at the head called the 'tang', or 'pour-piece', is removed by a circular saw or sharp-pointed hook.

pourpoint ('puəpɔɪnt), **purpoint** ('pɜ:pɔɪnt), *sb.*[1] *Obs.* exc. *Hist.* Forms: 4 **purpont**, 5 **-peynt(e, -poynt**, 9 **pour-, purpoint.** [a. OF. *po(u)rpoint* (13th c. in Littré), prop. pa. pple., as in *gambais porpoint, cuilte purpointe* (Godef.), of *pourpoindre* to perforate, f. *pour-* (:—L. *prō-*, substituted for *par*:—L. *per* through, as in POURALLEE) + *poindre*:—L. *pungĕre* to prick.]

Something quilted. **a.** A doublet, stuffed and quilted, worn by men in the 14th and 15th centuries, both as part of civil costume and of armour.

(Sometimes misused by modern novelists.)

[*a* **1200** *Itin. Regis Rich. I* (Rolls) I. 99 Unde et vulgo perpunctum [*v.r.* parpunctum] nuncupatur. **1225** *Rot. Litt. Claus.* (1844) II. 51/1 Quos posuerunt in x. hauber-gellis et xiiij. purpuntis et xix. capellis ferreis.] **1426** LYDG. *De Guil. Pilgr.* 7232 In thy diffence..Next thy body shal be set A purpoynt or a doublet. *c* **1430** —— *Min. Poems* 245 Now smothe, now stark, now lyk an hard purpoynt.

1830 JAMES *Darnley* xxxii, His dress was a rich hunting suit,..consisting of a green pourpoint. **1843** —— *Forest Days* II. xi, A man..muffled in a large loose gabardine above his pourpoint. **1876** PLANCHÉ *Cycl. Costume* I. 403 The military pourpoint was of leather or cloth, stuffed and quilted.

† **b.** A quilt, as a bed-covering. Also in *Comb.* **pourpoint-wise** *adv. Obs.*

1390 *Will of Fillioll* (Somerset Ho.), j purpont album bonum. **1418** *Bury Wills* (Camden) 4 Item Amye Irmonger j. magnam archam j. purpeynt et j. par librarum pendentium. *c* **1440** *Promp. Parv.* 417/1 Pur-poynt, bed hyllynge.., *culcitra punctata.* **1459** *Paston Lett.* I. 483 In primis, j. feddebedde. Item, j. bolster... j. purpoynt white hangyd.

So **'pourpoint** *v. trans.*, to make in the fashion of a pourpoint, to quilt (whence **'pourpointed** *ppl. a.*, **'pourpointing** *vbl. sb.*; also **'pourpointer**, a maker of pourpoints); ‖**pourpointerie** (purpwɛ̃tri) [F.], pourpointing work, quilting.

[**1834** *Penny Cycl.* II. 370/1 Henry III's great seals afford us the earliest specimen of the *ouvrages de pourpointerie*, which came more into fashion toward the latter part of his reign. His hauberk and chausses are of this padded work, stitched.] *Ibid.*, Pourpointing, or elaborate stitching,.. became at this time [Henry III's] a trade, and there were several pourpointers in Paris and London. **1860** J. HEWITT *Anc. Armour* II. 131 The 'Jack of Defence'..was a quilted coat; or it was pourpointed of leather and canvas in many folds; or it was formed of mail. **1869** BOUTELL *Arms & Arm.* x. (1874) 194 Third Period, to about 1360.—Splinted armour..showing studs on the covering, together with studded *pourpointerie*, began to prevail. **1885** FAIRHOLT *Costume in Eng.* (ed. 3) 147 The heat and heaviness of this armour occasioned the invention of gamboised or pourpointed coverings for protection in war.

pour-point ('pɔəpɔɪnt), *sb.*[2] Also pour point. [f. POUR *v.* + POINT *sb.*[1]] The temperature below which an oil is too viscous to be poured.

1922 T. G. DELBRIDGE in D. T. Day *Handbk. Petroleum Industry* I. 660 Pour point of a petroleum oil is the lowest temperature at which this oil will pour or flow when it is drilled without disturbance under certain definite specified conditions. **1936** W. L. NELSON *Petroleum Refinery Engin.* v. 48 Since 1929..the average specified pour-point for lubricating oils has been lowered from 30 to about 10°F. **1972** *Daily Colonist* (Victoria, B.C.) 3 Feb. 12/8 The reservoir has..a low sulphur content and a pour point of minus 55 degrees Fahrenheit. **1972** L. M. HARRIS *Introd. Deepwater Floating Drilling Operations* xvi. 171 Devices for heating and treating the emulsions are helpful, particularly, with high pour-point crudes.

pourpose, pourpour(e, pourpre, pourpresture, obs. ff. PURPOSE, PURPLE, PURPRESTURE.

†**pour'prise, pur'prise,** *sb. Obs.* Also 4 purpris, -prys(e, 5 pourprys, porprise. [a. OF. *porpris* and *po(u)rprise* occupied place, enclosure, verge, sb. use of pa. pple. of *po(u)rprendre* to occupy, seize, comprehend, f. *pour* for, before + *prendre* to take.] A precinct, enclosure, circuit.

a **1325** *Body & Soul* in *Map's Poems* (Camden) 346 Thine palefreis ant steden ant al thi purpris Thou ne shalt with the beren, wrecche, ther thou lis. *c* **1400** *Rom. Rose* 3987 He hath not aright wrought, Whan that he sette nought his thought To kepe better the purpryse. **1481** CAXTON *Myrr.* II. xi. 91 Thenne followeth germanye..whiche conteyneth a grete pourprys toward thoccident. **1601** HOLLAND *Pliny* I. 139 It carrieth a pourprise or precinct of 3 miles compasse. **1612** BACON *Ess., Judicature* (Arb.) 456 Not onely the bench, but the footepace and precincts and purprise thereof ought to be preserued without scandall and corruption. **1726** *Nat. Hist. Irel.* iii. 14 Havens which..are but very little, and of a small pourprise.

So †**pour'prise** *v.* [cf. *comprise, surprise*], *trans.* to encompass, enclose, embrace, occupy.

1481 CAXTON *Myrr.* II. viii. 85 Thise barbaryns pourpryse xl Royammes. **1481** —— *Godeffroy* cc. 292 There they lodged them, and pourprised grete space of ground. **1489** —— *Faytes of A.* II. xxxv. 153 So were the walles pourprysed and sette rounde aboute wyth ladders.

‖**pour rire** (pur rir), *a.* (*adv.*) *phr.* [Fr., lit. 'in order to laugh'.] Of a kind or in a manner that causes amusement or derision, or suggests light-hearted or jocular pretence; not serious or in a serious manner.

1872 B. JERROLD *London* x. 92 The laugh is general..over Smug who swept his own office once—and is no Liberal *pour rire*. **1884** *Sat. Rev.* 3 May 562/2 The author of a motion admits that it is only a motion *pour rire*. **1909** MRS. H. WARD *Daphne* III. ix. 219 'Then there was some local scandal?'.. 'Possibly. Scandal *pour rire*! Not a soul believed that there was anything..in it.' **1926** A. HUXLEY *Jesting Pilate* I. 115 Hereditary aristocracies still exist in the West—exist, but *pour rire*. **1931** *Times Lit. Suppl.* 5 Feb. 96/4 These and other essays in the book are full of those analogies *pour rire* and elegant verbal jokes that so delight us nowadays. **1942** J. LEES-MILNE in *Ancestral Voices* (1975) 65 The King washed up after dinner, or rather carried some glasses into the pantry and made a gesture of washing up, '*pour rire*'. **1946** A. L. ROWSE *Use of Hist.* 173 They all came over in a coach... The lady who descended from it..was got up to look like one of the *louche* ladies of the Restoration Court of Charles II. It was all *pour rire*. **1959** *Punch* 25 Mar. 411/2 A flight of facetious fancy, a suggestion *pour rire*. **1980** *Country Life* 28 Feb. 609/2 The jokes about such jargon as 'a fried-chicken taste that's lip-lickin' good' have long ceased to be *pour rire*.

‖**pourriture** (purityr). Also (*rare*) pouriture. [a. F. *pourriture* a rotting, decomposition, f. *pourrir*:—L. *putrēre* to rot.]

a. Rotten or decomposed substance; a person in a 'rotten' or unwell condition.

1675 EVELYN *Terra* (1729) 17 Earth is also sometimes improv'd by Mixtures of Fern, rotten Leaves, and the pouriture of old Wood. **1890** E. DOWSON *Let.* 11 Feb. (1967) 136, I have a bad cold, leaden spirits, and in fine feel all round a pretty fair 'pourriture'.

b. *pourriture noble* [lit. 'noble rot': see NOBLE *a.* 7 f]: a common grey mould, *Botrytis cinerea*, affecting grapes, which is deliberately cultivated to perfect certain French and German wines, and Tokay; the condition of being affected by this mould; also *ellipt.* as *pourriture*.

1911 *Encycl. Brit.* XXVIII. 722/2 The peculiar character of the Sauternes, for during the latter period of ripening a specific micro-organism termed *Botrytis cinerea* develops on the grape, causing a peculiar condition termed *pourriture noble* (German *Edelfäule*). **1924, 1935** [see NOBLE *a.* 7 f]. **1951** R. POSTGATE *Plain Man's Guide to Wine* vi. 98 A full and scented wine, the product of the *pourriture noble*. **1963** *Times* 8 Feb. 12/5 Wines made from..over-ripe single grapes which are, in effect, sun-dried raisins, in a state of *pourriture noble*, or princely decay. **1966** P. V. PRICE *France: Food & Wine Guide* 175 Several great properties have begun to make dry wines again..by picking the grapes before the pourriture has started to form. **1972** *Country Life* 14 Dec. 1658/3 The *vin jaune* grapes are not harvested until November, by which time they have been withered by the *pourriture noble*..that affects Sauternes and the great sweet wines of Germany.

†**'pourry,** *a. Obs. rare.* In 5 poury. [a. F. *pour(r)i* rotten, pa. pple. of *pour(r)ir*:—**putrīre* for L. *putrēre* to rot. Cf. *pot-pourri*.] Putrid.

c **1420** *Pallad. on Husb.* I. 39 Not poury [*v.r.* moddy], but plesaunt and good to drinke.

pourselane, -slane, obs. ff. PURSLANE.

pourseut, poursiewe, -su, obs. ff. PURSUIT, PURSUE.

‖**pour-soi** (purswa). *Philos.* [F., lit. 'for itself', 'for oneself'.] A phr. used by J.-P. Sartre in *L'Être et le Néant* (1943) to designate conscious, free being; being-for-itself; contrasted with *en-soi*, being-itself.

1947 *Jrnl. Philos.* XLIV. 720 The latter [*sc.* Heidegger], seeing the given always turning again into the abstract, concludes that human existence alone is *pour soi*. **1950** *Mind* LIX. 270 Sartre..in *L'Être et le Néant*..discusses the historical character of the *pour-soi*. **1962** *Listener* 30 Aug. 317/1 Sartre sees existence in the world as a polarity, a struggle for power. To survive, the *pour-soi* or individual consciousness has to reject and deny the *en-soi* of mere identity, of being what I have to be. **1964** C. SMITH *Contemp. French Philos.* ii. 33, I doubt if Sartre would agree that there can be any possibility of 'lucidly knowing' the *pour-soi*. **1966** A. MANSER *Sartre* iii. 45 Even though Sartre distinguishes between his approach and metaphysics..his division of being into two kinds, *l'en-soi* and *le pour-soi*, together with the question he asks in his introduction..seem to indicate that what follows can only be muddled and obscure. **1977** WARREN & PONSE in Douglas & Johnson *Existential Sociol.* 304 This tension between the *en-soi* and the *pour-soi* is common in gay liberation writings and experience.

poursuivant, poursuter, var. PURSUIVANT, PURSUITOR, *Obs.*

pourte, obs. Sc. f. POVERTY.

pourtenaunce, pourtende, obs. ff. PURTENANCE, PORTEND.

pourtract, -trait, etc., **-tracture, -traiture,** etc., **-traie, -tray,** obs. ff. PORTRAIT, PORTRAITURE, PORTRAY.

pourturde, var. *portured*: see PORTURE *v. Obs.*

pourvey(e, pourveaunce, -veya(u)nce, -wiance, pourveyo(u)r, -voyer, obs. ff. PURVEY, PURVEYANCE, PURVEYOR.

poury: see POURRY.

†**pouryvyncle,** obs. form of PERIWINKLE[2].

1530 PALSGR. 257/2 Pouryvyncle a fysshe, *niuiau*.

pous, ME. form of PULSE.

‖**pousada** (pəʊ'sɑːdə). [Pg. *pousada* resting-place, f. *pousar* to rest.] An inn or hotel in Portugal, esp. one of a chain of hotels administered by the State. Also *attrib.*

1934 J. & C. GORDON *Portuguese Somersault* iv. 35 'Is there no such thing as a good *posada* [sic]?' asked Jo. 'Hotel?' said the cord porter. **1949** BRIDGE & LOWNDES *Selective Traveller in Portugal* vii. 115 Just outside the main gate of Elvas, with a fine view of the aqueduct, is one of the nicest of the Government *pousadas* or inns. **1954** G. HOGG *Portuguese Journey* 44 As we began to descend the hill into S. Tiago we passed the government pousada. **1967** *Guardian* 16 Dec. 9/2 Nights in pousadas will have to be rationed. But I have stayed in little *pensoes* and inns. **1972** *Times* 17 June (Portugal Suppl.) p. ii/4 The *pousada* restaurants cater for motorists. **1976** *Good Motoring* Jan.–Feb. 16/2 Hotel prices [in Portugal] vary enormously but the State-owned pousadas are good value.

†**pouse,** *v. Obs.* Derivation and sense obscure.

1689 in Strype *Stow's Surv.* (1720) II. v. xxviii. 382/2, 13 Item, That no Peterman shall hereafter, at any time of the Year, take the Tides, nor Pouse upon the whole River of Thames. **1757** DICKINSON *Rules, Orders*, etc. 7 (Guildhall Libr. Br. 270. 1) That no Persons shall, at any Time of the Year, take the Tides or Pouse, or use any Pousing-Net, upon the River of Thames, under the Penalty of [etc.].

pouse, var. POUZE; obs. f. PULSE.

pouse, pouss, Sc. and n. dial. ff. PUSH *v.*

poush, obs. f. PUSH *sb.*, a boil.

pousoudie, -sowdie, obs. ff. POWSOWDY.

pousse, obs. f. PULSE, pease, etc.

‖**pousse-café** (puskafe). [F., lit. 'push coffee'.] A glass of various liqueurs or cordials, in successive layers, taken immediately after coffee. Also *fig.* (Cf. *chasse-café* s.v. CHASSE[2].)

1880 *Harper's Mag.* June 25/2 There is no easier way of solving a social problem than through the medium of a mild and fragrant cigar and a *pousse-café*. **1893** KATE SANBORN *Truthf. Wom. in S. California* 136 The old Spanish, the imported Chinese, the eastern element now thoroughly at home,..each..stratum as distinctly marked as in a pousse café, or jelly cake. **1897** *N.Y. Dramatic Mirror* 27 Nov. 22/3 (Advt.), Weber and Fields' Music Hall..Next Burlesque, commencing Nov. 29, Pousse Cafe; or, the Worst Born. **1948** *Sun* (Baltimore) 1 Jan. 15/1 The sophisticate who goes to the tourist traps makes the barkeep unhappy by asking for fancy things like a pousse cafe (six different liqueurs which are poured gently to avoid mixing the colors). **1959** W. BURROUGHS *Naked Lunch* 72 Men and women in evening dress sip pousse-cafés. **1962** E. LANHAM *No Hiding Place* ii. 20 The sophisticated liqueurs of a pousse-café. **1965** *New Statesman* 24 Dec. 1011/2 The other glamour-hunter's night out was the Australian Ballet's *Raymonda*... It's tempting to be funny about..the interior of Rank's New Victoria, a storm in a pousse-café, sinking knee-deep in ice-cream kups and sweet-wrappings. **1973** *Anglican Theol. Rev.* (Evanston, Illinois) Sept. 35 In the position of Episcopalians in the sociological *pousse-café* of American life, such ecclesiastical Anglophilia was acceptable, even pleasant. **1977** *Time* 12 Sept. 46/3 Some striped jobs look like *pousse-café* or rugby sweaters gone south.

poussette (puː'sɛt), *sb.* [a. F. *poussette*, dim. of *pousse* a push; see -ETTE.] An act of poussetting: see POUSSETTE *v.*

1814 MOORE *Mem.* (1853) II. 31 Seeing the pretty tremble of her eyelids in a poussette. **1830** MARRYAT *King's Own* xxxix, The mazes of poussette and right and left. **1847** ALB. SMITH *Chr. Tadpole* xii, They gave a rapid poussette like the top and bottom people in Sir Roger de Coverley.

pou'ssette, *v.* [f. prec. sb.] *intr.* To dance round and round with hands joined, as a couple in a country dance.

1812 H. & J. SMITH *Rej. Addr., Punch's Apoth.*, Dance, Regan! dance, with Cordelia and Goneril—Down the middle, up again, poussette and cross. *a* **1839** T. H. BAYLY *Songs & Ball.* II. 283 The young poussetting, as the old survey. **1887** CLELAND *True to Type* II. 206 The motley crowd was happy—poussetted, chassied and performed feats.

fig. **1873** H. MORLEY *First Sk. Eng. Lit.* (1882) 172 Europe was little edified to see the dance..set up by the two aged popes, who poussetted to each other about France and Italy.

Hence **pou'ssetting** *vbl. sb.*

1862 CARLYLE *Fredk. Gt.* XIV. viii. (1872) V. 258 The pains he took with her elegant pirouettings and poussettings.

poussie, a Sc. spelling of PUSSY.

‖**poussin** (pusɛ̃). [Fr., a newly-born chicken.] In *Gastronomy*, a baby chicken. See also *petit poussin* s.v. PETIT *a.* (*sb.*) 5.

c **1938** *Fortnum & Mason Price List* 72/1 Poussin and Green Peas—per head 5/6. **1957** 'P. QUENTIN' *Suspicious Circumstances* vi. 64 Lunch that day was so gourmet that I thought I would choke on it... Mother took little bird pecks at her Poussin Marie Louise or whatever it was. **1964** M. KELLY *March to Gallows* vii. 72, I looked at the menu card..saw the words *half poussin*. **1969** *Daily Tel.* 11 Jan. 14/2 In Dominica try 'mountain chicken'... Well, yes, I know it's a frog, but a special frog, tasting like *poussin* when grilled. **1974** *Times* 7 Mar. 13/5 Fresh *poussins*—small chickens four to eight weeks old are available.

Poussinesque (puːsæ'nɛsk), *a.* [f. the name *Poussin* (see below) + -ESQUE.] Pertaining to or characteristic of the French landscape painter Nicolas Poussin (1594–1665) or his work; resembling or influenced by the style of Poussin.

1919 R. FRY *Let.* 9 Feb. (1972) II. 446 *La Jeune Parque* seems to me to have a quality of pure beauty—in the Miltonic Poussinesque direction that hardly any modern work possesses. **1934** *Burlington Mag.* Dec. 297/2 We hear nothing of Pierre Lamaire..whose variant of the Poussinesque landscape formula is yet quite a notable and personal one. **1944** *Ibid.* Aug. 186/2 It is no longer possible..to point to individual figures as Poussinesque. **1955** *Times* 12 May 5/5 There is a brilliant little canvas by him of women bathing in a Poussinesque landscape. **1964** *Listener* 9 Jan. 57/1 The combination of rectilinear and diagonal movements in plane and inferred space..attains a complexity and variety of such a high order that we recognize it as 'Poussinesque'. **1979** *Basildon Park* (National Trust) 18 The Poussin-esque landscape by Francisque Millet (1642–79) on the west wall.

poust (paʊst). *Sc.* and *north. dial.* [f. next, by mutescence of final *e*: cf. AVOW *sb.*] = POUSTIE.

In first quot. prob. scribal error for *poste, pouste* = next.

[*c* **1440** *York Myst.* ii. 23 So I wille my post proue.] **1819** W. TENNANT *Papistry Storm'd* (1827) 216 Wi' great poust o' arm and leg. **1832–53** R. INGLIS in *Whistle-binkie* (Scot. Songs) Ser. III. 115 The poust that's in Scottish kail-brose.

poustie, pousté ('paʊstɪ). *Obs.* (or *Sc. arch.*) Forms: 4–5 pou'ste (also 6 *Sc.*), -st'ee, pow'ste (5 -ee), poeste, poweste, poste (5 -ee), pauste (5 -i); 5 pooste, po'stey, 'pousty, 5–6 'postie, -y (6 -ye), 5 (7 *Sc.*) pausty, 7 *Sc.* powstie, 7, 9 *Sc.* poustie. [ME. a. OF. *poesté, pousté* (*a* 1000 *podestat*):—L. *potestāt-em* power.] Power; strength, might; authority. See also LIEGE POUSTIE.

in poustie, poste (quot. *c* 1450), in one's power, possible.

a **1300** *Cursor M.* 4371 (Cott.) He þat has giuen me pouste [*Fairf.* pausty] slike Godd forbedd i suld him suike. *Ibid.* 26140 To quam vr lauerd has giuen poste Bath to bind and als laus þe. **13..** *Guy Warw.* (A.) cxlv, Sumtime ich was.. An erl of gret pouste. **1375** BARBOUR *Bruce* I. 110 In-to swilk thrillage thaim held he, That he ourcome throw his powste. **1415** *York Corpus Christi Play* in *Hist. & Antiq. York* (1785) II. 130 And here I grant in your Postey Whom that ye bound, bondan shall be Ryht at your Steyne. *c* **1450** *Merlin* 610 Yef it were in poste, he wolde it not haue do for all the reme of grete Breteigne. *c* **1460** in *Pol. Rel. & L. Poems* (1866) 160, I put hem vndyr in thy poweste. **1474** CAXTON *Chesse* II. v, Whan I submysed Affrique in to your poeste. *a* **1529** SKELTON *P. Sparowe* 1330 By..all the dedly names Of infernall posty, Where soules fry and rosty. **1570** LEVINS *Manip.* 110/14 Postie, *potestas, atis*. **1606** BIRNIE *Kirk-Buriall* Ded., Statur and strength, so dexterously kythed by a peereles pausty in all campestrial prowes. **1819** W. TENNANT *Papistry Storm'd* (1827) 147 Her weary knicht's ilk limb and lith Gat tenfauld poustie, pow'r, and pith. **1845** POLSON *Eng. Law* in *Encycl. Metrop.* II. 850/1 Hence the distinction, so well known to Scotch lawyers, of death-bed and *liege poustie*—the technical terms indicating two states of competency and incompetency to burden or dispose of an estate to the prejudice of the lawful heir.

‖**pou sto** (paʊ stəʊ, *prop.* puː stɔː). [a. Gr. ποῦ στῶ 'where I may stand'; from the saying attributed to Archimedes (in Pappus 8. 11., ed. Hultsch 1060), δός μοι ποῦ στῶ, καὶ κινῶ τὴν γῆν 'give me (a place) where I may stand, and I will move the earth'. (Usually written in Greek.)] A place to stand on, a standing-place; *fig.* a basis of operation.

1847 TENNYSON *Princ.* III. 246 She..Who learns the one POU STO whence after-hands May move the world, tho' she herself effect But little. **1859** LOWELL *Biglow P.* Introd. 58 Accustomed to move the world with no ποῦ στῶ but his own two feet. **1890** E. E. C. JONES *Elem. Logic* xi. 90 The interpretation of our proposition is liable to involve us in an infinite regress; we have no ποῦ στῶ. **1911** J. WARD *Realm of Ends* iii. 67 This is the physical basis which is supposed to furnish teleology with its indispensable ποῦ στῶ. **1963** W. SELLARS *Sci., Perception & Reality* iii. 89 It is here, rather than at the level of sense contents, that we find a *pou sto* for the apparatus of hypothetico-deductive explanation. **1967** *Philos. Rev.* LXXVI. 181 The self-stultifying form appears to be shorn of its ποῦ στῶ.

pout (paʊt), *sb.*[1] Also 1 ***puta, 6 poute, 8 powt.** [OE. **púta* in *ǣle-pútan* pl., EEL-POUT = MDu. *puyt(e, pût, puut, puyde* a pout, also a frog (cf. *puytael, aelpuyt*), Du. *puit*, Flem. *puut, puud* a frog, Du. *puitaal*, EFris. *pût(-âl)*, LG. *pūt(-âl), (âl-)putt, pute*, G. *(aal-)putte* eel-pout; app. from a verbal stem **put-* to inflate: see quot. 1836 and cf. next.] A name applied to several kinds of fish, most commonly to the BIB or *whiting-pout*: see also EEL-POUT, HORN-*pout*.

[*c* **1000** ÆLFRIC *Colloq.* in Wr.-Wülcker 94 Hwilce fixas ȝefehst þu ? ælas and hacodas mynas and æleputan sceotan and lampredan.] **1591** NASHE *Prognost.* 17 If there bee few or none [eels] taken, and plentie of poutes to bee had [with pun on next]. **1706** PHILLIPS, *Powt*, a Fish otherwise call'd a Sea-Lamprey. **1809** A. HENRY *Trav.* 252 We took pouts, cat-fish, cat-heads, of six pounds weight. **1836** YARRELL *Brit. Fishes* II. 159 From a singular power of inflating a membrane which covers the eyes and other parts about the head,..it is called Pout, Bib, Blens, and Blinds. **1837** HAWTHORNE *Amer. Note-Bks.* (1883) 65 The fish caught were..three horned pouts. **1880** F. DAY *Fishes Gt. Brit.* I. 287 Bib, pout..brassie in Scotland.

pout (paʊt), *sb.*[2] [f. POUT *v.*[1]] A protrusion of the lips, expressive of pique or annoyance. ***in the pouts***, in a pouting mood, sulky.

1591 NASHE *Prognost.* 17 Plentie of poutes to bee had in all places, especiallie in those coastes and Countries where weomen haue not their owne willes. **1615** SIR E. HOBY *Curry-combe* i. 45 The fat is in the fire, she is in the powt, all a mort. **1631** R. H. *Arraignm. Whole Creature* xv. §2. 255 A Bessy Babe, that must be dandled, and in every thing humoured else she feeds all upon Poutes [with pun on prec.] **1694** MOTTEUX *Rabelais* IV. lvi, Panurge somewhat vex'd Fryar Jhon, and put him in the Pouts. **1795** *Jemima* I. 82, I could not be brought out of the pouts. **1812** H. & J. SMITH *Rej. Addr., Baby's Debut*, Jack's in the pouts, and this it is —He thinks mine came to more than his. **1892** GUNTER *Miss Dividends* 23 'Then you don't think it wise?' mutters the girl, with a pout.

b. *transf.* Protrusion, projection.

1880 BROWNING *Dram. Idylls* II. *Pan & Luna* 45 That pure undraped Pout of the sister paps.

c. *Comb.*, as ***pout-mouthing***, † ***pout puffing***.

1605 CAMDEN *Rem.* (1637) 135 Baldwin le Pettour..held his land in Suffolke, *Per saltum, sufflum & pettum, sive bumbulum*, for dancing, pout-puffing, and doing that before the King of England in Christmasse holy dayes, which the word *pet* signifieth in French. **1807** COLERIDGE *Lett., to H. Coleridge* (1895) 514 Your mad passions and frantic looks and pout-mouthing.

pout, *sb.*[3] *dial.* (Kent). [Origin obscure.] A small round stack of hay or straw; = POOK *sb.*

1686 PLOT *Staffordsh.* 15 Cattle fed in winter time at the same pout of hay... Cattle feeding at a hay-pout. **1736** PEGGE *Kenticisms, Pout*; as an hay-pout, a round stack of hay. Plot, a Kentish author, has it. **1887** *Kentish Gloss.* s.v., In the field hay is put up into smaller heaps, called cocks, and larger ones, called pouts; when carted it is made into a stack.

† **pout**, *sb.*[4] *Obs.* [perh. from POUT *v.*[1] or *sb.*[2]] A workman's name for the mount of the lens of a simple microscope, by means of which the lens is attached to a Lieberkühn.

1832 A. PRITCHARD *Microsc. Cabinet* 189 All globular bodies, having polished surfaces, reflect an image of the cups, and the pout, if there is one, appears as a dark spot in the centre. **1837** GORING & PRITCHARD *Microgr.* 31 A great deal may be done with cups having single lenses inserted in them which they do not fit, by raising or lowering their pouts or settings by means of rings of thin metal, till the focus of the lens and of the cup fall on the same point. [**1907** F. A. PARSONS (*Sec. Roy. Micr. Soc.*) in *Let.*, The term *pout* probably went out of use about 1845. I have made enquiry of all the leading Microscope makers in London, but not one has ever heard of the term.]

† **pout**, *sb.*[5] *Coal Mining. Obs.* A kind of punch: see quot.

1849 GREENWELL *Coal-trade Terms Northumb. & Durh., Pout, Punch*, a tool used by the deputies in drawing timber out of a dangerous place. It has a shank about 8 feet long, with a spade handle, and a head, pointed and slightly curved towards the handle at one side, and like a hammer at the other. It is used as a ram to knock the props down, or to draw them out after they have been knocked down.

pout, *sb.*[6] Sc. and dial. form of POULT *sb.*[1]

pout (paʊt), *v.*[1] Also 4–6 **poute**, 5–8 **powt**, 6 **powte**, **powlt**. [Known only from *c* 1300; previous history obscure. Conjectured to represent an OE. **pútian*, from a verbal stem **put-* to swell, be inflated, of which *púta*, POUT *sb.*[1], might be the agent-noun. But the evidence for this vb. in the cognate langs. is scanty: Sw. has dial. *puta* to be inflated; Sw. and Norw. *puta* pad, Da. *pude* cushion, pillow, pointing to an ON. **púta*; cf. NFris. *pütt, pute* cushion, bolster.]

1. *intr.* To thrust out or protrude the lips, esp. in expression of displeasure or sullenness; hence, to show displeasure.

?*c* **1325** *Old Age* vii. in *E.E.P.* (1862) 149 Now i pirtle, i pofte [? poffe], i poute, I snurpe, i snobbe, i sneipe on snovte, þro3 kund i comble an kelde. *c* **1460** J. RUSSELL *Bk. Nurture* 294 Be not gapynge nor ganynge, ne with þy mouth to powt. **1570** LEVINS *Manip.* 228/36 To Poute, *caperare*. **1575** CHURCHYARD *Chippes* I. *iv, Busie brains: That powlts and swels at others toils, and take themselues no pains. **1582** STANYHURST *Æneis* I. (Arb.) 18 Shee pouts, that Ganymed by Ioue too skitop is hoysed. **1592** SHAKS. *Rom. & Jul.* III. iii. 144 (Q° 5, 1637) But like a misbehav'd and sullen wench, Thou pout'st upon thy fortune and thy love [*Q°* 4, powts vpon; *Q°s* 2, 3, puts vp; *Folios*, puttest vp; Q° 1, Thou frownst vpon thy Fate that smiles on thee]. **1607** —— *Cor.* v. i. 52 The Veines vnfill'd, our blood is cold, and then We powt vpon the Morning. **1655** CAPEL *Tentations* 14 Ah, this wretched flesh of mine that can pout and swell at God our best friend. **1706** PHILLIPS, To *Powt*, to look gruff or surly, to hang out the Lip. **1866** G. MACDONALD *Ann. Q. Neighb.* v, Here the girl pretended to pout.

b. Without implication of displeasure: To swell out, to protrude, as lips.

1598, 1624, 1735 [see POUTING *ppl. a.*]. **1812** BYRON *Childe Harold* I. lviii. **1816** J. WILSON *City of Plague* I. iv. 121 Her lips would pout With a perpetual simper. **1869** MRS. HEATON *A. Dürer* I. i. (1881) 37 The full childish lips pout out as if waiting to be kissed. **1896** J. ASHBY STERRY *Tale Thames* (1903) 62/2 Sleeves closely furled to exhibit the charm Of a biceps that pouts 'neath a snowy white arm. **1897** *Allbutt's Syst. Med.* III. 980 He should note the shape of the anus, and observe whether it is pouting.

2. *trans.* To push out, to protrude (esp. the lips).

[*c* **1532** DU WES *Introd. Fr.* in *Palsgr.* 952 To powte, *poussir*.] **1784** tr. *Beckford's Vathek* (1868) 69 Gulchenrouz ..pouted out his vermilion little lips against the offer. **1798** MME. D'ARBLAY *Lett.* 28 Aug., She received me..pouting out her sweet ruby lips for me to kiss. **1842** TENNYSON *Day Dream, Sleeping Palace* iv, Her lips are sever'd as to speak: His own are pouted to a kiss. **1870** ROLLESTON *Anim. Life* 144 In a starfish which has died with its stomach pouted out.

b. To utter or say with a pout.

1877 MRS. FORRESTER *Mignon* I. 52 'Horrid old wretch' ..'I wish he had not come', pouts Mignon. **1892** GUNTER *Miss Dividends* 131 Then she pouts, 'You've had all my dances'.

pout (paʊt), *v.*[2] *Sc.* [Sc. form of POULT *v.* f. *pout*, POULT *sb.*[1]] *intr.* To shoot at poults. Hence **'pouter**, 'a sportsman who shoots young partridges or moorfowl' (Jam.); **'pouting** *vbl. sb.*, shooting at partridge or moorfowl poults; also *attrib.*, as in **pouting-net**, a net for securing poults.

a **1679** J. SOMERVILLE *Mem. Somervilles* (1815) I. 241 To take his pleasure at the poutting in Calder and Carnwath Muires. **1789** D. DAVIDSON *Seasons* 114 Now Willy..Wi' pointers on the hills did stan, The prince o' pouters. **1816** SCOTT *Antiq.* xliii, Something that will keep the Captain wi' us amaist as well as the pouting. **1840** *Contemporaries of Burns* 116 The 'pouting season', as it is called, was to her a period of more than ordinary enjoyment. **1905** *Blackw. Mag.* Jan. 123/1 'Pouting nets' were purchased for the better securing of muirfowl and partridges.

pout, *v.*[3] *dial.* (Kent.) [f. POUT *sb.*[3]] *trans.* To put up (hay, etc.) into pouts; to POOK.

1617 in *Archæol. Cant.* (1902) XXV. 15 Robert Terry [presented] for profaning of the Sabbath Day, by binding barley, and powting of podder, upon the Sabbath.

‖**poutassou** (putasu). [Provençal of Nice.] A Mediterranean species of cod, *Gadus* (or *Micromesistius*) *poutassou*.

1860 COUCH *Brit. Fishes* III. 77. **1862** GÜNTHER *Catal. Fishes Brit. Mus.* IV. 338.

poutch, obs. form of POUCH.

pouter ('paʊtə(r)), *sb.*[1] [f. POUT *v.*[1] + -ER[1].]

1. One who pouts (*intr.* or *trans.*).

1809 MALKIN *Gil Blas* XI. ix. ¶5 The pouters and ill-wishers were soon revenged. *a* **1861** D. GRAY *Poet. Wks.* (1874) 44 Sleep! Soft bedewer of infantine eyes, Pouter of rosy little lips!

2. A breed of the domestic pigeon characterized by a great power of inflating the crop: cf. POUTING *ppl. a.* quot. 1693.

1725 BRADLEY *Fam. Dict.* s.v. *Pigeon*, Such Pigeons will breed nine or ten Pair of young ones in a Year, for the little Huff of Wind thrown in from the Powter gives them Heat and Mirth. **1766** PENNANT *Zool.* I. 218 The varieties..are distinguished by names expressive of their several properties, such as Tumblers, Carriers, Jacobines, Croppers, Powters,..&c. **1840** DICKENS *Barn. Rudge* i, The wheeling and circling flights of runts, fantails, tumblers, and pouters. **1859** DARWIN *Orig. Spec.* i. (1878) 16 The pouter has a much elongated body..: its enormously developed crop, which it glories in inflating, may well excite astonishment.

3. A fish, the whiting-pout.

1889 *Lancet* 16 Nov. 1024/2 Small haddocks and rock pouters—cheap, common fish—are often..sold at a high price for whiting.

4. *attrib.*: **pouter-fish** = 3; **pouter-pigeon** = 2.

1879 *Cassell's Techn. Educ.* IV. 123/1 Specimens of the 'tumbler' but not one of the common 'pouter' pigeon. **1883** J. D. CURTIS in Moloney *W. Afr. Fisheries* 68 (Fish. Exhib. Publ.) Barracouta, porpoises, bonito,..cat-fish, and pouter-fish are to be found on the Gold Coast. **1886** J. K. JEROME *Idle Thoughts* ix. (1896) 105 Sticking out his chest, and strutting about the room like a pouter-pigeon.

pouter, *sb.*[2]: see under POUT *v.*[2]

pouter ('paʊtə(r)), *v. Sc.* Also 6 **powtter**, 9 **powter.** [Origin and sense-history obscure: cf. POTTER, POTHER. (Sense 1 may be a different word.)]

†**1.** *trans.* (?) To span with a stride. *Obs.*

a **1568** *Droichis Part of Play* 74 (Bann. MS.). The hingand brayis on adir syde Scho powtterit with hir lymmis wyde.

2. a. *intr.* To poke, to stir; 'to rummage in the dark' (Jam.); to potter.

1814 SCOTT *Wav.* lxiv, Powtering wi' his fingers amang the het peat-ashes and roasting eggs. **1832–53** CARRICK in *Whistle-Binkie* (Scot. Songs) Ser. II. 123 She would pouter a while, afore the fire could len' ony light for me to come hame wi'. **1838** A. RODGER *Poems* 281, I began to grape for 't syne, Thrang poutrin' wi' my staff, man.

b. *trans.* To poke; to get by poking or groping.

1835 CARRICK *Laird of Logan* 133 (E.D.D.) Just gang awa out and pouter a few [potatoes] frae the roots o' the shaws wi' your hands. **1892** LUMSDEN *Sheep-head* 208 He poutert the ase [poked the ashes] wi' his fore finger to see gin he couldna fin' some sma' unburned remnant.

'poutful, *a.* [f. POUT *sb.*[2] or *v.*[1] + -FUL.] Full of pouts, pouting. Hence **'poutfulness**.

1837 *New Monthly Mag.* LI. 309 So folded as to display the mouth in its most winning poutfulness. **1887** J. ASHBY STERRY *Lazy Minstrel* (1892) 31 Your pretty, poutful, child-like charm, All criticism must disarm, Miss Dimplecheek!

pouther, Sc. and obs. form of POWDER.

pouting ('paʊtɪŋ), *sb.* [f. POUT *sb.*[1] + -ING[3].] A kind of small fish; a small kind of whiting, a whiting-pout (*Morrhua lusca*).

1591 LYLY *Endym.* III. iii, For fish these; crab, carpe, lumpe, and powting. **1848** C. A. JOHNS *Week at Lizard* 247 In which were caught a few poutings, conger, and wrasse. **1883** *Fisheries Exhib. Catal.* 13 A favourite Bait for Whiting, Pouting, Codfish, &c.

pouting ('paʊtɪŋ), *vbl. sb.*[1] [f. POUT *v.*[1] + -ING[1].] The action of POUT *v.*[1]

1556 J. CARELES in Foxe *A. & M.* (1583) 1933/2 Beware in any wise of swelling, powting, or lowring, for that is a token of a cruel and vnlouing heart. *a* **1625** FLETCHER *Hum. Lieutenant* III. ii, Never look coy, lady; These are no gifts to be put off with poutings. **1716** ADDISON *Freeholder* No. 8. 45 To forbear frowning upon Loyalists, and Pouting at the Government. **1872** DARWIN *Emotions* ix. 232 With young children sulkiness is shown by pouting, or, as it is sometimes called, 'making a snout'.

b. *attrib.* as ***pouting-cloth, -crosscloth, -place***.

1589 *Pappe w. Hatchet* Divb, Ile make him pull his powting crosscloath ouer his beetle browes for melancholie. **1602** *Withals' Dict.* 275 A Crosse cloath (as they tarme it) a Powtingcloth, *plagula*. **1790** PENNANT *London* (1813) 163 It was successively the pouting-place of princes.

pouting, *vbl. sb.*[2], [3]: see under POUT *v.*[2], [3].

pouting ('paʊtɪŋ), *ppl. a.* [f. POUT *v.*[1] + -ING[2].] That pouts, in various senses of the vb.

1563 *Mirr. Mag., Hastings* xiv, Powtyng lookes. **1598** BP. HALL *Sat.* IV. i. 68 His pouting cheeks puff vp aboue his brow Like a swolne Toad touch't with the Spiders blow. **1624** K. LONG tr. *Barclay's Argenis* I. ii. 5 He had no great powting lips, nor little eyes sunke into his head. **1693** *Lond. Gaz.* No. 2853/4 There is 113 pair of Pigeons,..as Carriers, Cropers,..Shakers, Pouting Horsemen, Barbaries,..to be sold. **1727** GAY *Begg. Op.* I. viii, Yes, that you might, you pouting slut. **1735** SOMERVILLE *Chase* IV. 89 They seek the pouting Teat That plenteous streams. **1760** *Chron.* in *Ann. Reg.* 159 At a sale of powting-pigeons..one pair was sold for 16 guineas. **1863** GEO. ELIOT *Romola* x, The corners of the pouting mouth went down piteously.

Hence **'poutingly** *adv.*, in a pouting manner.

1632 SHERWOOD, Powtingly, *rechignément*. **1832** L. HUNT *Naiads* Poems 197 Like fondled things Eye poutingly their hands. **1863** GEO. ELIOT *Romola* xiv, Her lips were pressed poutingly together.

†**poutish** ('paʊtɪʃ), *a. Obs. rare.* [Allied to POUTER *sb.*[1] 2, POUTING *ppl. a.*: see -ISH[1].] Somewhat pouting; akin to a pouter-pigeon.

1725 BRADLEY *Fam. Dict.* s.v. *Pigeon*, Bastard-bred Pigeons, such as Pouting Horsemen, Poutish Dragoons, from a Powter or Cropper and a Leghorn.

pout-net ('paʊtnɛt). *Sc.* Also 5–6 polt(e-. [Origin obscure.] A small fishing-net of conical form, its mouth framed with wood or iron into a semicircle, the flat edge of which is pushed or drawn along the bottom of a stream by means of a long pole or staff.

1443 *Durham Acc. Rolls* (Surtees) 82 Item in j rethe vocat. le Polte nett xvj*d*. **1804** *Edin. Even. Courant* 16 Apr. (Jam.), Their Association..have..for protecting the fry, given particular instructions to their Water Bailiffs, to prevent, by every lawful means their shameful destruction at Mill-dams and Mill-leads with Pooks or Pout Nets. **1859** *Act 22 & 23 Vict.* c. 70 §14 To kill Salmon in or from the River by means of any Pout Net, Rake Hook, or similar Engine. **1911** A. WARRACK *Scots Dial. Dict.* 425/2 *Pout-net*, a round net fastened to two poles, thrust under the banks of a river to force out fish.

So **poutstaff**, †**poltstaff**, the detachable pole or staff of a pout-net.

c **1470** HENRY *Wallace* I. 402 Will3ham was wa he had na wappynis thar, Bot the poutstaff [*ed.* **1570** polt staff], the quhilk in hand he bar.

poutry, obs. Sc. form of POULTRY.

pouty (ˈpaʊtɪ), *a.* *U.S.* [f. POUT *sb.*² or *v.*¹ + -Y¹.] Inclined to pout (said of a person or of the mouth); hence (as a personal attribute), sullen or petulant.

1863 'G. HAMILTON' *Gala-Days* 221 They never were tired when anything was to be done, or.. peevish, or pouty, or 'offish'. **1897** R. M. STUART *In Simpkinsville* 23 This stove's ez dull-eyed and pouty ez any other woman ef she's neglected. **1912** R. A. WASON *Friar Tuck* 77 With a pouty look on his face, Tank sez: 'It's time we fixed up an' moved out into the dark.' **1971** C. FICK *Danziger Transcript* 44 Stella as in starlight was direct brown eyes and a pouty lower lip. **1976** 'O. BLEECK' *No Questions Asked* xiii. 147 She had a full red mouth that.. might have looked kissable to some, but it looked only pouty to me.

pou(w) (pəʊ). *S. Africa.* Forms: α. 9- **pouw**, **pou**, 9 **pow**; β. 9 **paauw**, **paow**, 9- **pauw**. [Afrikaans, f. Du. *paauw* peacock.] The name applied generally in S. Africa to species of Bustard. Cf. GOMPAAUW.

α. **1798** A. BARNARD *Jrnl.* 13 May in A. W. C. Lindsay *Lives of Lindsays* (1849) III. 439, I.. tied the *pow*, or wild peacock, to the waggon—a very fine bird indeed, of grave colours, but rich brown. **1858** [see DIKKOP 1]. **1872** *Routledge's Ev. Boy's Ann.* 339/1 The Bustard, which of all others the sportsman endeavours to secure in Africa, is the Pouw. **1892** *Daily News* 8 Mar. 5/3 Shooting in all two quagga, two koodoo,..and a pow,..an enormous bird, standing about 4ft. high, chiefly body. **1959** *Cape Argus Mag.* 3 Jan. 8/2 Even the beginner in bird lore would not look for..a pou in the Knysna forest. **1966** [see NARTJIE].
β. **1800** G. YONGE in G. M. Theal *Rec. Cape Colony* (1898) III. 197 Pauws or Wild Peacocks are become extremely scarce. **1838** [see GOMPAAUW, GOMPAUW]. **1850** R. G. CUMMING *Hunter's Life S. Afr.* (1902) 18/2, I.. perceived a large paow or bustard walking on the plain before me. **1879** A. FORBES in *Daily News* 28 June 5/7 Among the game of the veldt is a noble bird called a paauw—a species of wild turkey. *Ibid.*, The paauw combines the flavours of the grouse and the turkey. **1886** G. A. FARINI *Through Kalahari Desert* v. 62, I saw a large *pauw* out in the open. **1894** NEWTON *Dict. Birds* 683. **1939** S. CLOETE *Watch for Dawn* iii. 39 To make this feast there had been a great killing: of oxen,..of wildfowl, guineas, pauws, and pheasants.

pouwere, obs. form of POWER.

pouze. *local.* Also 8 pouz, 9 pouse. [Derivation doubtful: identified by some with POUCE, in dial. sense 'rubbish, refuse'.] The refuse of the crushed apples after the cider is pressed out; = POMACE 1 a.

1725 BRADLEY *Fam. Dict.* s.v. *Vinegar*, The Cyder must be drawn off as fine as may be into another vessel and a small quantity of the Must or Pouz of Apples must be added thereto. **1726** *Dict. Rust.* (ed. 3) s.v. *Cider*, The use of Must or Pouze of Apples. **1881** MISS JACKSON *Shropsh. Word-bk.*, *Pouse*..(3) The refuse of the apple pulp, when all the cider has been expressed—the 'caput mortuum'.

pover(e, obs. form of POOR.

†ˈ**poverance.** *Obs. rare*⁻¹. [f. ME. *pover-en* to become or make poor (see POOR *v.*) + -ANCE.] The action of making poor; impoverishment.

1529 H. STAFFORD in Ellis *Orig. Lett.* Ser. II. II. 24 Greate poverance and vndoing of your saide powr subject.

‖**poveˈretto.** *Obs. rare*⁻¹. [It. dim. of *povero* poor.] A poor little one.

1592 G. HARVEY *Four Lett.* iii. Wks. (Grosart) I. 206 What speciall cause the Pennilesse Gentleman hath, to bragge of his birth: which giueth the woefull poueretto good leaue,.. to reuiue the pittifull historie of Don Lazarello de Thoemes.

poverish (ˈpɒvərɪʃ), *v.* *Obs.* or *dial.* [ad. OF. *po(u)veriss-*, lengthened stem of *po(u)verir* to make poor, f. *pov(e)re* POOR. Cf. IMPOVERISH.] *trans.* To make poor, impoverish.

1382 WYCLIF *Neh.* v. 18 Forsothe the puple gretli was poueresht. **1430–40** LYDG. *Bochas* v. vii. (MS. Bodl. 263) 266/2 Bi whos absence, feeblid is Cartage, The contre porisshed [*ed.* **1554** pouerished], brouht to disencres. **1530** PALSGR. 663/1, I pouryshe, or make poure, *jappouris*. **1598** SYLVESTER *Du Bartas* II. i. I. *Eden* 156 No violent showr Poverisht the land. **1639** JOHNSTON *Diary* (1897) 72 The countrie is extremelie poverished. **1871** W. ALEXANDER *Johnny Gibb* xix, The lave.. maun be poverees't wi' sax ouks clockin'.

Hence ˈ**poverished** *ppl. a.*, ˈ**poverishing** *vbl. sb.*; also †ˈ**poverishment** [ad. obs. F. *poverissement*], impoverishment, poverty.

1484 in *Lett. Rich. III & Hen. VII* (Rolls) I. 84 To the kinges hurt and poveresshinge of his..tenantes. **1568** T. HOWELL *Arb. Amitie* (1879) 46 In pouerishment, Shee bydes and takes hir part. **1900** F. S. ELLIS *Rom. Rose* I. 57 Earth forgets her poverished drear estate.

povert, -te, obs. forms of POVERTY.

†ˈ**povertness.** *Obs. rare*⁻¹. [f. *povert*, obs. var. POVERTY + -NESS.] = next.

c **1450** R. LEYOT in Nash *Hist. Worc.* (1781) I. 421 Privey to siche matiers as my povertnesse might doo any maner of pleisir to youre goode ant bounteuouse lordship.

poverty (ˈpɒvətɪ). Forms: α. 2–5 **pouerte** (**poverte**), 4–6 **pouert**, (4 **-erd**, 5 **-ertt(e**, **powert**), **povert**. β. 3–6 **pouerte** (= *-té*), (3 **pouirte**, 4 **pouertte**, 4–5 **poerte**, 4–6 **poverte**, 5 **powerte**, **pouer-**, **povertee**, **pauuerty**, 6 **povarte**, **powertie**), 4–7 **pouertie**, 5–6 **poure-**, **povrete**, (6 **povertey**), 6–7 **povertie**, **pouerty**, 7- **poverty**. γ. 4 *Sc.* **purte**, 5 **pourte**, 6 **poorety**, *Sc.* **purtye**. [Repr. two OF. forms, (*a*) *poˈverte* or *poˈuerte*:—L. *pauˈpertās*, nominative, and (β) *poverté*, *pouerté*, *poureté*, orig. *-tet*, later F. *pauvreté*:—L. *paupertātem*, accusative, f. *pauper* poor + *-tās*, *-tātem*: see -TY. The γ forms show the early reduction of *pouerté* to *pourté*, and so to *poorty* (cf. POOR). The same reduction of the first syllable is seen in the Sc. form *purteth*, POORTITH, from OF. *pouretet*.

Here, as in the early forms of POOR, the ambiguity of *u* (*v*) before the 17th c. makes the pronunciation of many early forms uncertain. Some mod.F. dialects have *poureté*, *pauretė*, and the original *v* was prob. vocalized or suppressed in some forms of OF., as the γ forms and the doublet POORTITH show that it was from the 14th c. in some ME. dialects.]

The condition or quality of being poor. (In senses 4–6 replaced to a great extent by POORNESS.)

I. 1. a. The condition of having little or no wealth or material possessions; indigence, destitution, want (in various degrees: see POOR *a.* 1).

α. *c* **1175** *Lamb. Hom.* 143 Þer scal beon worldwunne, wiðuten pouerte. *a* **1225** *Ancr. R.* 32 Alle sorie, þet wo & pouerte þolieð. *a* **1300** *Cursor M.* 6073 (Cott.) And qua for pouert [*so Fairf., Trin.; Gött.* pouerte] es be-hind. *Ibid.* 17117, I thold pouerd [*v.r.* pouert], pine, and scame. *c* **1325** *Metr. Hom.* 3 Forthi wil I of my pouert, Schau sum thing that I haf in hert. **1362** LANGL. *P. Pl.* A. IX. 111 Was no pride on his apparail, ne no pouert noþer [B. VIII. 116 ne pouerte noyther]. **1423** JAS. I *Kingis Q.* iii, Foriugit was to pouert in exile. **1472–3** *Rolls of Parlt.* VI. 20/1 Whiche afore lyved in povert and miserye. **1550** BALE *Image Both Ch.* D vj b, Hongre, thurst, cold, pouert, care.
β. *a* **1300** *Sarmun* xli. in *E.E.P.* (1862) 5 In wo and pine and pouerte..for as i sigge so hit sal be. **13..** *Cursor M.* 19058 (Gött.) Bihald on vs and se And vnderstand vr pouertte. **1375** BARBOUR *Bruce* III. 551 And gret anoyis, and powerte [*rime* pite]. *a* **1430** *Chaucer's Melib.* ⁋598 (Harl. MS.) Þerfore clepeth Cassidore pouertee [*v. rr.* pouerte, pouert] the moder of ruyne. **1477** EARL RIVERS (Caxton) *Dictes* 33 Pouertie in surete is better than richesse in fere. **1500–20** DUNBAR *Poems* lxvii. 8 With powertie I hald him schent. **1526** *Pilgr. Perf.* (W. de W. 1531) 14 b, The thre vowes, obedyence, chastite, and wylfull pouerty. *a* **1533** LD. BERNERS *Huon* xcvi. 312 Ther is no warre but it causeth pouerte. **1562** J. HEYWOOD *Prov. & Epigr.* (1869) 165 Pouertée partth felowship, thats not trewe euer, Pouertie in beggers partth felowship neuer. **1615** W. LAWSON *Country Housew. Gard.* (1626) 9 Let no man hauing a fit plot plead pouerty in this case. **1798** MALTHUS *Popul.* III. v. (1806) II. 156 Almost all poverty is relative. **1903** *Westm. Gaz.* 23 Nov. 3/2 Mr. Rowntree explains that of the 20,000 found to be living 'in poverty' in York, 13,000 are living in what he calls 'secondary poverty', which is defined as meaning that the income of the family 'would be sufficient for the maintenance of merely physical efficiency, were it not that some portion is absorbed by other expenditure either useful or wasteful'.
γ. *c* **1375** *Sc. Leg. Saints* xxvi. (*Nycholas*) 766 Sir, purte me in sic assay Has set, þat na man wil for me Borcht na detoure noþir be. *c* **1420** *Sir Amadace* (Camden) xxxiii, He..was owte of the cuntray for pourte fledde. *c* **1568** in *Bannatyne Poems* (Hunter. Cl.) 224 Thay passit by with handis plett; With purtye fra I wes ourtane. **1589** PUTTENHAM *Eng. Poesie* III. xi. (Arb.) 173 Figures of rabbate..From the middle, as to say paraunter for *parauenture*, *poorety* for *pouertie*, *souraigne* for *soueraigne*.

†**b.** Formerly also in *pl.* (Cf. *hardships*.) *rare.*

a **1533** LD. BERNERS *Huon* lxv. 224 Yᵉ paynes, trauelles, and pouertyes that I enduryd. *Ibid.* cxxxi. 482 When I remembre the paynes, and dolours, and pouerties, that by my cause ye suffer. **1574** R. SCOT *Hop Gard.* To Rdr., It were better..that Straungers shoulde enuie our prosperities, than our Friendes shoulde pittie our pouerties.

c. *fig.* in allusion to Matt. v. 3.

13.. *E.E. Allit. P.* C. 13 Þay arn happen [= happy] þat han in hert pouerté. *c* **1394** *P. Pl. Crede* 778 Ne Helye ne Austen swiche lijf neuer vsed, But in pouerte of spirit spended her tyme. **1720** WELTON *Suffer. Son of God* I. xi. 278 Poverty of Spirit is an Abstraction of the Mind from the Mean and Despicable Trifles of the World.

d. Personified and applied to a person, or persons generally, in whom it is exemplified.

1813 BYRON *Giaour* xi, Alike must Wealth and Poverty Pass heedless and unheeding by. **1887** LOWELL *Democr.* 28 Poverty pays with its person the chief expenses of war, pestilence and famine. **1890** *Eng. Illustr. Mag.* Christmas No. 147 Several loaves..to be distributed..to whatsoever of orthodox poverty the..parish may enclose.

†**2.** *transf.* *the poverty*: the poor collectively or as a class. (Cf. *the laity*, *the quality*.) *Obs.*

1433 LYDG. *St. Edmund* III. 1487 Pray for knyhthod.. Pray for the lawe..Pray for the plowh, pray for the pouerte. *c* **1440** CAPGRAVE *Life St. Kath.* I. 731 (MS. Rawlinson) To lord & to lady, & to pouert [*MS. Arundel* povert] lowe, Full foyson was þere, to eueri man. **1537** J. LONDON in Ellis *Orig. Lett.* Ser. I. II. 80 The multytude of the poverty of the Town resortyd thedyr. **1599** MARSTON *Sco. Villanie* I. iv. 188 If to the Parish pouerty, At his wisht death, be dol'd a half-penny.

II. 3. Deficiency, lack, scantiness, dearth, scarcity; smallness of amount.

1388 WYCLIF *Prov.* vi. 32 He that is avouter schal leese his soule, for the pouert of herte. *c* **1420** *Pallad. on Husb.* XII. 331 Yf vyne abounde In leef & haue of fruyt but pouerte. **1838** PRESCOTT *Ferd. & Is.* (1846) II. xix. 180 Attributable ..to the poverty of modern literature at that time. **1895** H. P. ROBINSON *Men Born Equal* 66 The poverty and crudity of the available supply of domestic help.

4. Deficiency in the proper or desired quality; inferiority, paltriness, meanness: = POORNESS 3. (In quot. *c* 1600 = poor or inferior matter.)

1387 TREVISA *Higden* (Rolls) I. 11, I knewe myn owne pouert, and schamede..after so noble spekers..to putte forþ my bareyn speche. **1597** BACON *Ess.*, *Coulers Good & Evill* v. (Arb.) 146 By imputing to all excellencie in compositions a kind of pouertie or..a casualty or ieopardy. *c* **1600** SHAKS. *Sonn.* ciii, Alack, what pouerty my Muse brings forth, That hauing such a skope to show her pride, The argument all bare is of more worth Than when it hath my added praise beside. **1741** WATTS *Improv. Mind* I. i. §3 The poverty of your understanding. **1881** BROADHOUSE *Mus. Acoustics* 161 The peculiar quality of tone commonly called poverty, as opposed to richness, arises from the upper partials being comparatively too strong for the prime tone. **1883** MACFADYEN in *Congregat. Year Bk.* 73 The poverty of the parsonage is often reflected in the poverty of the pulpit.

5. Want of or deficiency *in* some property, quality, or ingredient; the condition of being poorly supplied with something; (of soil, etc.) the condition of yielding little, unproductiveness.

c **1420** *Pallad. on Husb.* XI. 270 And yf pouerte appere in their sellis, That robbeth hem, wel worthi go to helle is. **1871** *Routledge's Ev. Boy's Ann.* May 279 Its desolate aspect and its poverty,..although..covered with pines and scrub. **1880** HAUGHTON *Phys. Geog.* v. 209 The extraordinary poverty of north and north-eastern Africa in river-producing power.

6. Poor condition of body; leanness or feebleness resulting from insufficient nourishment, or the like.

1523 LD. BERNERS *Froiss.* I. ccclxxii. 613 Sometyme they coulde get nothynge for money, so that their horses dyed for pouertie and colde. **1523** FITZHERB. *Husb.* §69 The ewes.. wyll not take the ramme at the time of the yere, for pouertye, but goo barreyne. **1627** tr. *Bacon's Life & Death* (1651) 7 A strict Emaciating Diet..doth first bring Men to great Poverty and Leannesse by wasting the Juyces and Humours of the Body. **1731–3** MILLER *Gard. Dict.* 6 D/1 The Trees are render'd more vigorous and healthy, scarcely ever having any Moss or other Marks of Poverty. **1889** RIDER HAGGARD *Allan's Wife*, etc. 284 The ox..will..from mere maliciousness die of 'poverty'.

†**7.** Alleged name for a company of pipers. *Obs.*

1486 *Bk. St. Albans* f vj b, A Pauuerty of pypers.

III. 8. *attrib.* and *Comb.*, as ***poverty-hardened***, ***-smitten*** (= POVERTY-STRICKEN), adjs.; also in names of plants growing in poor soil, or supposed to impoverish the soil, as **poverty-grass**, (*a*) one of several North American grasses that grow on poor soil, esp. *Aristida dichotoma*; (*b*) = *poverty-plant*; **poverty level** = *poverty line*; **poverty line**, the estimated minimum income sufficient for obtaining the necessities of life; **poverty-plant**, a small North American heath-like shrub, *Hudsonia tomentosa* (N.O. *Cistaceæ*); **poverty programme** *U.S.*, a programme or policy designed to alleviate poverty; **poverty shop** (see quots.); **poverty trap**, a situation in which an earned increase to a low income is offset by the consequent loss of means-tested state benefits; **poverty-weed**, in I. of Wight, purple cow-wheat, *Melampyrum arvense*, = COW-WHEAT 1.

1832 *Boston Even. Transcript* 30 Apr. 2/3 Fields..long given up to barrenness and *poverty-grass, are now broken up in readiness to receive the grain. **1864** THOREAU *Cape Cod* 20 A moss-like plant, *Hudsonia tomentosa*..called 'poverty-grass', because it grew where nothing else would. **1884** MILLER *Plant-n.*, *Aristida dichotoma*, Poverty grass. **1906** J. C. LINCOLN *Mr. Pratt* vi. 95 He owned the sheds and barn..and the beach grass and the poverty grass. **1939** H. H. BENNETT *Soil Conservation* xvii. 418 Scores of plants, known as weeds, enter into this far-reaching cover of volunteer vegetation: goldenrod, ragweed, poverty grass, [etc.]. **1973** H. MCCLOY *Change of Heart* iii. 23 The soil is still so sandy that only scrub pine, beach plum, bayberry bushes, and poverty grass grow wild there. **1891** T. STEVENS *Through Russia* xv. 242 This, among the *poverty-hardened moujiks was..not to be expected, nor desired. **1976** *Billings* (Montana) *Gaz.* 27 June 12-G/1 Statistics for last year show that over five million persons past age 65, or one out of every six, live on a *poverty level—defined as an income of under $46 a week for a single aged person or $57 for an aged couple. **1977** *Rolling Stone* 30 June 59/1 The poverty level varies according to family status. **1901** W. S. CHURCHILL in R. S. Churchill *Winston Churchill* (1969) II. Compan. I. ii. 108 Families who cannot provide this necessary sum, or who, providing it do not select their food with like discrimination are *underfed* and come below the '*poverty' line. **1901** B. S. ROWNTREE *Poverty* iv. 114 The recipients of charity are the poor, i.e. those who from causes 'primary' or 'secondary' are below the poverty line. **1904** *Westm Gaz.* 22 Dec. 2/2 West Ham..contains a huge population of workers, many of whom are, even in normal times, very little above the poverty line. **1932** *Discovery* June 181/2, 21 shillings in Charles Booth's time..[was] the income for an 'ordinary family' at or about the poverty line. **1941** *Economist* 19 Apr. 522/1 The most fortunate group were the old age pensioners of Group C, who might..have an income of 32s., but even this, though well above the poverty line, is nowhere near the human needs level. **1968** E. BRILL *Old Cotswold* vi. 89 He had little of the sharp business acumen that goes with the making of money on a big scale, but this is not evidence that he or his family were ever on the poverty line. **1973** *Observer* (Colour Suppl.) 19 Aug. 26/2 In 1960 about 11 per cent of the population..were living below the poverty line, defined as basic National Assistance rates plus 40 per cent. **1967** *Freedomways* VII. 104 A few years ago..it seemed as if there was a real promise of hope for the poor—both black and white—through the *Poverty Program. **1970** *New Yorker* 29 Aug. 57/1 Some of the people..being in a position to welcome any kind of investment, even poverty-program investment..have decided Miller is entitled to his ideas. **1971** *Black Scholar* Apr.–May 10 Who subsist on such foreign aid programs as 'welfare' and 'poverty programs'. **1948** R. GLASS *Social Background of Plan* IV. ii. 161 Newport Road is famous for its '*poverty shops': fried fish shops, pawnbrokers and junkshops. **1956** J. M. MOGEY *Family & Neighbourhood* i. 10 It has become customary to call certain types of shops 'poverty shops': these are fried-fish shops, pawnbrokers, and junkshops. **1961** Poverty shop [see *fish and chips* s.v. FISH *sb.*[1] 7]. **1899** *Westm Gaz.* 4 Apr. 10/1 The effect of the Bill..has been to bring to the surface all the *poverty-smitten old age of the colony, all the human wrecks. **1972** *Daily Tel.* 21 Nov. 1/8 The idea was to prevent families falling into the '*poverty trap'—the situation in which a pay rise can mean the poor are worse off because they lose a disproportionate number of State benefits. **1973** *Guardian* 30 Mar. 6 The abolition of the 'poverty trap' called for the reintroduction of reduced tax rates for those near the threshold of tax. **1977** *Times* 23 Mar. 16/6 The 'poverty trap'..arises from the fact that the level of supplementary benefits judged to be the minimum..acceptable can..total more than the personal allowance against tax. **1847–78** HALLIWELL, **Poverty-weed*, purple cow-wheat. A weed growing in corn, having a fine large flower, yellow, pale red, and purple; it is very injurious, and betokens a poor, light, stony soil.

'poverty-,stricken, *a.* Stricken or afflicted with poverty; suffering from poverty; reduced to great poverty; extremely poor or destitute.

1803 M. WILMOT *Let.* 1 Oct. in *Russ. Jrnls.* (1934) I. 55 Amidst such a multitude of titles a count or countess is often the merest poverty stricken low bread [*sic*] animal that ever was known. **1844** DICKENS *Mart. Chuz.* xv, Badged and ticketed as an utterly poverty-stricken man. **1867** TROLLOPE *Chron. Barset* I. iv. 27 A wretched poverty-stricken room. **1956** *Railway Mag.* Nov. 739/2 The original promoters of the Port & Pier Railway could hardly have visualised their poverty-stricken child playing such an important role as it was destined to do!

fig. **1852** H. ROGERS *Ecl. Faith* (1853) 44 If you profess..the possession of the pure truth, do not appear to be so poverty-stricken as to array your thoughts in the tatters of the cast-off Bible. **1865** TYLOR *Early Hist. Man.* v. 101 A language so poverty-stricken as the Chinese.

'poverty struck, *a.* Now *rare* or *Obs.* = prec.

1801 D. WORDSWORTH *Jrnl.* 29 Dec. (1941) I. 98 A miserable, poverty-struck looking woman. **1813** SIR R. WILSON *Pr. Diary* II. 210 This [Fulda] is an old town,..poverty-struck by the war, pillaged by the passing enemy, and replete with misery. **1856** DELAMER *Fl. Gard.* (1861) 3 The cypress is a magnificent ornament to the gardens of the south of Europe;..is respectable in the south of England; shabby-genteel higher up the island; in the north. miserable and poverty-struck.

†**povilion**, obs. erron. f. PAVILION (sense 12).

1688 R. HOLME *Armoury* III. xvi. (Roxb.) 60/2 The Povilion, the wide end of the trumpett. *Ibid.* 62/1 The Povilion Barr.

†**povin**, obs. Sc. var. *pown*, PAWN, peacock.

1533 *Acc. Ld. High Treas. Scot.* VI. 97 For the feding of ij crannis and the povins in the castell of Striveling.

pow (pʌu, paʊ), *sb. Sc.* [A phonetic representative of earlier Sc. *poll*: see POOL *sb.*[1] Cf. Gael. *poll*, perh. the immediate source; and, for phonology, *bow, knowe, pow*, from *boll, knoll, poll* (head).] Local name for 'A slow-moving rivulet, generally in carse lands'; also a small creek where such a rivulet falls into a river or estuary, affording a landing-place for boats, esp. on the Forth; hence a wharf or quay on such a creek, as the *Pow of Alloa, of Clackmannan* (Jamieson).

(Pow in Sir W. Scott's ed. of Sir Tristram is an error for *polk*, PULK.)

[**1483** Found in place-n. *Powfoulis*, near Airth, Stirlingsh.] **1792** *Statist. Acc. Scot.* IV. 490 The country is intersected in different places by small tracts of water, called pows, which move slowly from the N. to the S. side of the carse. **1793** *Ibid.* VIII. 595 The quay..runs within the land, and forms a pow, or small creek, where the rivulet..falls into the river [Forth]. **1824** *Caledon. Mercury* 24 Jan. (Jam.), A cargo of peats from Ferintosh was discharged this week at Cambus Pow. **1866** *N.B. Daily Mail*, The only interruptions being an occasional 'pow', by which name curiously enough the streamlets are known.

pow (paʊ), *int.* orig. *U.S.* [Echoic.] The sound of a punch, blow, shot, or the like. Also *fig.*, used to denote the impact of an emotion or an idea. Also as *sb.*

1881 J. C. HARRIS in *Scribner's Monthly* June 244/1 He step en hit de hoss a rap—*pow!* De hoss 'uz dat s'prise at dat kinder doin's dat he make one jump, en lan' on his footses. **1914** B. TARKINGTON *Penrod* xxii. 207 Herman rubbed his smitten cheek. 'Pow!' he exclaimed. 'Pow-ee! You cert'ny did lan' me good one *nat* time.' **1931** *Technol. Rev.* Nov. 66/1 That class of comic-strip words like *zowie* and *pow*. **1955** H. KURNITZ *Invasion of Privacy* (1956) xxvi. 163 'A man hit him.' She went through the motion with both little fists. 'Pow!' **1961** J. HELLER *Catch-22* (1962) v. 42 He called me a wise guy and punched me in the nose..knocked me flat on my ass. Pow! Just like that. **1964** 'E. MCBAIN' *Ax* iv. 72 He got himself an axe someplace... Pow, good-bye janitor. **1968** L. DEIGHTON *Only when I Larf* i. 16 Imagine beating that typewriter..for a hundred a week and all the pencils you can take home. Pow. Not me. **1970** G. GREER *Female Eunuch* 173 Perhaps they will not fall in love all at once but feel a tenderness growing until one day *pow!* that amazing kiss. **1970** [see KER-]. **1976** *Leicester Chron.* 26 Nov. 16/3 In some cases that does not mean films which are more sanguinary, but poorly made action stuff with entire reliance on the pows and kerplunks.

pow, variant form of POU(W), S. Afr. bustard.

pow, Sc. and north. dial. var. POLL *sb.*[1] head; Sc. f. PULL; obs. f. POOH, *int.*

powah, obs. f. POWWOW.

powair, obs. Sc. f. POWER.

powaix, -ax, obs. Sc. ff. POLE-AXE.

powan ('pəʊwən, 'pəʊən). Also 8 **poan.** [A Scotch form of POLLAN, the two fishes being formerly identified.] A species of fresh-water fish, *Coregonus clupeoides*, found in Loch Lomond in Scotland (where locally known also as *Luss Herring*), in Windermere and Ulleswater (where known as the *Schelly*), in Conningham Mere, and in Bala Lake (where called *Gwyniad*). It belongs to the same genus as the Vendace and the Pollan, with which it was formerly identified, and is still often confused, under the name *Freshwater Herring*: see quots. 1774–7.

1633 MONIPENNIE *Abridgem. Scots. Chron.* N iv b, Loch [Lomond], besides abundance of other fishes, hath a kind of fish of the owne, named, Powan, very pleasant to eate. **1771** SMOLLETT *Humph. Cl.* 28 Aug., Powans [are] a delicate kind of fresh-water herring peculiar to this lake [Lomond]. **1774** PENNANT *Tour Scot. in 1769* (ed. 3) 225 Besides the fish common to the Loch [Lomond] are Guiniads, called here Poans. **1777** —— in Lightfoot *Flora Scot.* (1792) I. 61 Guiniad—Found in Loch-Mabon; called in those parts the Vendace and Juvangis; and in Loch Lomond, where it is called the Poan. [Now specifically distinguished from the Vendace of Lochmaben.] **1859** YARRELL *Brit. Fishes* I. 315 M. Valenciennes..thinks that the powan is not a continental species. *Ibid.* 317 Although agreeing in the number of fin-rays with the pollan of Ireland, this Loch Lomond fish is at once distinguished from it by the peculiar form of its mouth. **1865** COUCH *Brit. Fishes* IV. 295. **1896** *N.B. Daily Mail* 9 June 5 A powan which scaled 1lb 9oz and measured 1ft 6in in length—a record size for this species.

powar(e (Sc.), **poware**, obs. ff. POWER, POOR.

†**powart**, Sc. corr. *powhead*, POLEHEAD, tadpole.

1633 *Fife Witch Trial* in *Statist. Acc. Scot.* (1796) XVIII. App. 655 She hoped to see the powarts bigg in his hair.

powawe, obs. f. POWWOW.

powce, obs. f. PULSE *sb.*[1] (of the blood).

powch(e, obs. f. POUCH.

powder ('paʊdə(r)), *sb.*[1] Forms: 3–6 **poudre**, 4 **pudre, puder**, 4–6 **powdre**, (4 **-dir**, 4–5 **-dyr**, 5 **-dur**), 4–8 **pouder**, (4–5 **-ere**, **-ur**, 4–6 **-ir**, 5 **-ire**), 4– **powder**; also 4–6 **pouldre**, 5–6 **pulder** (6 **-dre**, *Sc.* **-dir, -dyr**), 5–7 **poulder** (6 *Sc.* **-dar**), 6–7 **powlder**. *β.* 5 **pouþer**, 5– 6 (9 *Sc.*) **pouther**, 6–7 (8 *Sc.*) **powther**. [ME. a. F. *poudre* (13th c.):—earlier OF. *poldre, puldre*:—*polre* (11–12th c.):—L. *pulver-em* (in nom. *pulvis*, whence It. *polve*, Sp. *polvo*, Pr. *pols*) dust. In 15–16th c. F. usually spelt *pouldre* (*l* re-inserted after L.); so, in 15–17th c. Eng., *poulder*, etc. With *pouther* cf. Sc. *shouther* = *shoulder*; also *father, mother, gather, hither*, with ð for d before *-er*.]

1. a. Any solid matter in a state of minute subdivision; the mass of dry impalpable particles or granules produced by grinding, crushing, or disintegration of any solid substance; dust. (Cf. DUST *sb.*[1] 1, 3 a.)

c **1290** *S. Eng. Leg.* I. 477/532 And brenden al-to poudre feor fram euerech toune. *a* **1300** *Cursor M.* 6616 (Cott.) Þis golden calf he did to brest to pudre [*Gött.* poudir]. **13..** *Ibid.* 20731 (Fairf.) Bren hit to powdre. **1390** GOWER *Conf.* I. 109 He sende, and him to pouldre smot. *c* **1400** MAUNDEV. (Roxb.) vii. 25 He brynnes him self all to powder. **1490** CAXTON *Eneydos* xii. 44 The bodyes..conuerted in-to poulder. **1526** TINDALE *Matt.* xxi. 44 He shall grynd him to powder [**1535** COVERDALE to poulder]. **1533** ELYOT *Cast. Helthe* (1539) 77 b, Fryed or layde on a burning hote stone, & made in powlder. **1542** UDALL *Erasm. Apoph.* 111 b, I will ..crushe thy hedde to powther. *Ibid.* 269 b, Sodainly crummed to dust & pouther. **1549** *Compl. Scot.* i. 21 Vas it nocht brynt in puldir ande asse? **1605** B. JONSON *Volpone* I. i, To grinde hem into poulder. **1641** J. JACKSON *True Evang. T.* I. 8 Dissected into parts, not beaten into pouder. **1662** J. DAVIES tr. *Olearius' Voy. Ambass.* 46 There is fall of water.. so violent, that breaking upon the Rocks, it is reduc'd as it were to powder. **1799** G. SMITH *Laboratory* I. 182 Clear your glass..from the powder that may lie upon it. **1853** W. GREGORY *Inorg. Chem.* (ed. 3) 226 Peroxide of Nickel... It is a black powder. **1880** G. MEREDITH *Tragic Com.* (1881) 183 If there are laws against my having my own, to powder with the laws!

†**b.** *spec.* Earth in the state of dry impalpable particles; the dust of the ground. Often in phrases denoting a condition of humiliation, or of being dead and buried. (Cf. DUST *sb.*[1] 1, 3 a, 3 c.) *Obs.*

1297 R. GLOUC. (Rolls) 7080 Vol of þe poudre of þe erþe. *a* **1325** *Prose Psalter* xliii. [xliv.] 27 Our soule is lowed in poudre. **1382** WYCLIF *Job* vii. 21 Lo, nowe in pouder [1388 dust] I slepe. —— *Isa.* xlvii. 1 Go doun, sit in pouder [1388 in dust], thou maiden doȝter of Babilon. *a* **1533** LD. BERNERS *Huon* xciii. 297 The sonne lost his lyght by reason of the pouder that rose vp in to the ayre.

†**c.** The material substance of which the animal body is regarded as created or composed, and to which it returns when decomposed; also, the mouldered remains of a dead body, or the ashes of one that is burnt. (Cf. DUST *sb.*[1] 3 a, b.) *Obs.*

a **1300** *Cursor M.* 929 (Cott.) Þou nees bot a pudre [*v.r.* pouder] plain, To puder sal þou worth a-gain. **1382** WYCLIF *Gen.* iii. 19 For powdre thow art, and into powdre thow shalt turne [1388 dust]. **1387** TREVISA *Higden* (Rolls) II. 83 Of kyng Haralde Poudre þere ȝit is halde. **1481** CAXTON *Myrr.* II. viii. 82 Out of thise asshes and pouldre groweth agayn another byrde. **1536** BELLENDEN *Cron. Scot.* (1821) I. 194 Scho departit..to Rome, berand with hir the powder of thair fader, in ane goldin poke. **1552** LYNDESAY *Monarche* 5170 Thy vyle corruptit carioun Sall..remane, in pulder small, On to the Iugement Generall.

d. Applied to the pollen of flowers, or to the spores of *Lycopodium*. (Cf. DUST *sb.*[1] 1 c.)

1676 LISTER in *Ray's Corr.* (1848) 124, I..put them [Lycopodiums] in a box, and found they shed their powder of themselves. **1857** HENFREY *Bot.* §215 The Pollen.. consists in almost all cases of a fine powder composed of microscopic vesicles. **1872** OLIVER *Elem. Bot.* I. i. 8 The fine powder is the pollen.

e. = POWDER SNOW.

1948 *Sun* (N.Y.) 30 Dec. 16 North Conway. 3 inch new powder. Skiing fair. **1973** P. A. WHITNEY *Snowfire* xii. 235 The average skier..didn't care for loose powder. But there was still powder on the steepest slope. **1973** R. HAYES *Hungarian Game* xliv. 257, I came here to ski and I'd hate to miss all this nice fresh powder. **1974** G. MOFFAT *Corpse Road* ii. 34 We had a light fall at Christmas..just powder on frozen grass.

2. A preparation in the form of powder, for some special use or purpose. (See also 3.)

a. In medicine, etc.; formerly (usually) a corrosive, stimulant, etc. for external application; in later use, a medicine, or a dose of medicine, to be taken internally, usually in some liquid or semi-liquid vehicle.

Often named after the inventor or introducer, or from the purpose, as *Dover's powder*, JAMES'S *powder*, JESUIT'S *powder*, PORTLAND *powder, worm powder*, etc.

1340 *Ayenb.* 148 Verst he ssel þerto do þe smeringes and þe plastres of zuete warningges... Þe poudres efterward and prekiinde of harde wyþniminge. **1377** LANGL. *P. Pl.* B. xx. 357 The plastres of þe persoun and poudres biten to sore. *a* **1400–50** *Stockh. Med. MS.* 143 A good powdyr. **1527** ANDREW *Brunswyke's Distyll. Waters* A j, With waters dystyllyd, all maner of confeccyons, syropes, powders, and electuaryes be myxced. **1611** B. JONSON *Catiline* II. i, Giue me some wine, and poulder for my teeth. **1615** CROOKE *Body of Man* 55 We are constrayned to inhibite and restrayne the increase with corrasiue Liniments and poulders. *a* **1641** BP. MOUNTAGU *Acts & Mon.* iv. (1642) 270 Marianme had dealt with..his Cup-bearer, to give him a powder in his wine, which she said was a Love potion. **1695** tr. *Colbatch's New Lt. Chirurg. Put out* 23 Neither Tincture, Solution, nor Pouder. **1768–74** TUCKER *Lt. Nat.* (1834) II. 235 Such an one has great faith in Ward's pill, or James' powder. **1789** W. BUCHAN *Dom. Med.* (1790) 691 The lighter powders may be mixed in any agreeable thin liquor, as tea or water-gruel. **1865** MRS. CARLYLE *Lett.* (1883) III. 265 When I had finished the antifebrile powders.

b. In alchemy or magic. *powder of* PROJECTION, *powder of* SYMPATHY: see these words.

c **1386** CHAUCER *Can. Yeom. Prol. & T.* 580, I haue a poudre heer þat coste me deere Shal make al good for it is cause of al My konnyng. **1610** B. JONSON *Alch.* I. i, You must be chiefe? as if you, onely, had The poulder to proiect with? **1663** GERBIER *Counsel* b viij b, That he doth really possess its true (and no imaginary) pouder of production, That of Hermes Trismegistos. **1706** PHILLIPS s.v. *Projection*, The pretended casting of the Powder of the Philosopher's Stone into a Crucible of melted Metal, in order to change it into Gold or Silver, is call'd Projection.

†**c.** Powdered salt, spice, or other condiment, for seasoning or preserving food. (Cf. POWDER *v.*[1] 1, 2.) Also *fig. Obs.*

13.. *Coer de L.* 3070 And soden ful hastely, With powdyr and with spysory. *c* **1460** J. RUSSELL *Bk. Nurture* 620 Þe fische in a dische..With vineger & powdur þer vppon. *a* **1555** LATIMER in Foxe *A. & M.* (1583) 1755/1 Haue I bene ..so muche, as it were seasoned with the powder of so many experiences? **1565–73** COOPER *Thesaurus* s.v. *Asseruo, Sale vel in sale asseruare carnes*, to kepe meate in pouder. **1640** C. HARVEY *Synagogue, Return* (1647) 25 He that his joyes would keep, Must weep, And in the brine of Tears And fears, Must pickle them. That powder will preserve.

d. A cosmetic in the form of powder applied to the face or skin; also HAIR-POWDER. *in powder*, wearing hair-powder; also *out of powder*.

a **1571** JEWEL *On 1 Thess.* i. 7 Wks. II. 825 Such as are bathed or perfumed with precious ointments or poulders. *a* **1639** T. CAREW *Poems* (1640) 8 For, in pure love, Heaven did prepare Those powders to enrich your hair! **1663** DAVENANT *Siege of Rhodes* Wks. (1672) 9 Our Powders and our Purls Are now out of fashion. **1758** JOHNSON *Idler* No. 5 ¶ 11 The hair has lost its powder. **1789** MRS. PIOZZI *Journ. France* I. 417, I had some grains of marechale powder in my hair. **1792** LADY TEMPLETOWN *Let.* 11 June in A. E. Newdigate-Newdegate *Cheverels* (1898) vii. 103 Mr Romney..has acquitted himself well in respect to Lady Newdigate... The hair is of an agreable *duskiness* that is neither in nor out of powder. **1839** THACKERAY *Major*

Gahagan i, We wore powder in those days. **1849** —— *Pendennis* I. xxiii. 219 Two superior officers in black..now in livery with their hair in powder. **1863** CROWN PRINCESS OF PRUSSIA *Let.* 11 May in R. Fulford *Dearest Mama* (1968) 211 We give a ball in powder tomorrow as this old Palais will have been up 100 years. **1874** L. TROUBRIDGE *Life amongst Troubridges* (1966) ix. 78 The day began hatefully by Grobee telling us that we were not to go to the Cresswells' dance in powder..what *possible* difference could it make to him whether we went with black hair or white. **1883** MRS. R. RITCHIE *Bk. Sibyls* i. 6 An oval miniature, belonging to the times of powder and of puff. **1897** R. S. HICHENS *Londoners* (1902) 8 The footman looked pleased beneath his powder. **1924** M. IRWIN *Still she wished for Company* xix. 233 Slovenly Lady Catherine Grey drove over, out of powder at four in the afternoon. **1954** H. ASHTON (*title*) Footman in powder.

e. With *of* and the name of the substance.

† ***powder of post***: the powder of a worm-eaten post; also used as the type of a neutral and worthless medicine.

1390 GOWER *Conf.* III. 96 A corde..Whan it with poudre is so besein Of Sulphre. *c* **1420** *Liber Cocorum* (1862) 30 Take powder of galingale, and temper with alle; Powder of gyngere and salt also. *c* **1440** *Douce MS.* 55 lf. 31 b, Kest ther to a litell powdre of pepyr. **1607** TOPSELL *Four-f. Beasts* (1658) 286 The powder of Myrrhe or burnt silk, felt, or cloth, or any old post. **1710** J. CLARKE *Rohault's Nat. Phil.* (1729) I. 139, I ordered the Third to put his upon the Wheel, and grind it plain..with Powder of Emery. **1769** WESLEY *Wks.* (1872) XIV. 258 Beware of swallowing ounce after ounce of indigestible powder, though it were powder of post. **1808** BENTHAM *Sc. Reform* 59 One of the powder-of-posts which the *Pharmacopœia*..is full of. **1823** J. BADCOCK *Dom. Amusem.* 95 In a tea-spoonful of honey..mix a drachm of powder of tin. **1845** S. JUDD *Margaret* (1851) II. vii. 101 The grubs of the law have gnawed into us, and we are all powder-post. **1860** MILLER *Elem. Chem.* (ed. 2) II. 639 Powder of algaroth.

†**f.** Followed by qualifying words, in names of drugs, flavouring powders, etc. *Obs.*

powder marchant, a tart kind of flavouring powder. ***powder of prelinpinpin, powder pimp a lim pimp, pimperlim-pimp, powder le pimp***, a pretended magical powder used by conjurers; hence allusively. [= F. *poudre de perlimpinpin* (in Richelet 1680 *poudre de prelinpinpin*).]

c **1386** CHAUCER *Prol.* 381 And poudre Marchant tart and galyngale. *c* **1440** *Anc. Cookery* in *Househ. Ord.* (1790) 425 Colour hit wyth saffron, and do therto pouder marchant. *Ibid.* 426 Put therto pouder douce. **1534** *Nottingham Rec.* III. 190 Powder Holand. **1688** *Vox Cleri pro Rege* 55 By virtue of their Powder pimp a lim pimp, he is changed again into a limited Prince. **1694** MOTTEUX *Rabelais* V. 238 Masters in the Art of Hocus Pocus's, Legerdemain, and Powder of Prelinpinpin [*Joüeurs de passe-passe*]. **1704** SWIFT *T. Tub* iv. 97 Peter would put in a certain Quantity of his Powder Pimperlim-pimp, after which it never failed of Success. **1737** [MORGAN] *Moral Philos.* I. 96 This clerical Religion is a new Thimble and Button, or a Powder le Pimp.

g. Denoting other preparations in the form of a powder, chiefly in cookery, hygiene, perfumery, etc., and usu. as the second element of a Comb., as *baby powder, baking powder, curry powder, flea powder, insect powder, milk powder, soap powder, talcum powder, tooth powder, washing powder*, etc.: see under the headwords.

h. Slang phr. ***to take a powder***: to depart, absent oneself; to abscond. See also RUN-OUT 4. orig. and chiefly *U.S.*

1934 J. PROSKAUER *Suckers All* xxiv. 279 The smartest guy in the office took a walk out powder this morning. **1940** J. O'HARA *Pal Joey* 72 And take a powder out of here that day. **1941** R. CHANDLER in *Street & Smith's Detective Story Mag.* Sept. 25 Why are you taking a powder? **1954** 'N. BLAKE' *Whisper in Gloom* xvi. 220 'Where's the Yank?'..'Gone. He took a powder.' **1961** J. MACLAREN-ROSS *Doomsday Bk.* v. 65 Phoned four times—no reply. Seems as if..Passman's taken a temporary powder. **1972** 'H. HOWARD' *Nice Day for Funeral* iii. 39 If he'd dumped it [*sc.* a corpse] in the river.. everybody was bound to think Frankie had taken a powder to dodge the grand jury. **1979** P. ABLEMAN *Shoestring* i. 14 The very minute that I first looked into her..eyes... Philip Marlowe took a powder and Shoestring, the womanless, took over.

3. a. = GUNPOWDER 1.

[**1339**, xxxii libræ de pulvere pro dictis Instrumentis: see GUN *sb.* 1.] *c* **1384** CHAUCER *H. Fame* III. 554 As swifte as pelet out of gonne Whan fire is in the poudre ronne. *a* **1460** *Gregory's Chron.* in *Coll. Citizen L.* (Camden) 118 Schottys, powder, gonnys. *a* **1548** HALL *Chron., Hen. VI* 141 b, Poulder failed in the fortresse. **1570** in *Satir. Poems Reform.* x. 88 Bothwell with pulder blew him in the air. **1627** CAPT. SMITH *Seaman's Gram.* xiv. 68 Fined corned Powder for hand Guns. **1795** NELSON in Nicolas *Disp.* (1845) II. 19, I have sent Officers and Men to get the powder out of the Censeur. **1818** SCOTT *Br. Lamm.* xxvi, And for the pouther, I e'en changed it, as occasion served,..for gin and brandy. **1818–25** Percussion powder [see PERCUSSION 5]. **1901** *Scotsman* 14 Mar. 7/3 The Explosives Committee..are now desirous of obtaining all the information..about the new powders that are being brought out by inventors.

b. ***powder and shot***, the matériel expended in warfare; hence, the cost or effort expended for some result; ***food for powder***: see FOOD *sb.* 1 d; ***the smell of powder***, actual experience of fighting; etc. Fig. phr. ***to keep one's powder dry***, with allusion to the advice said to have been given by Oliver Cromwell to his troops: to adopt a practical or realistic policy; to act prudentially or cautiously, be on the alert.

1579 GOSSON *Sch. Abuse, Apol.* (Arb.) 75 When I spare not to greete them with poulder and shot, answeares mee againe with a false fire. **1604** HIERON *Wks.* I. 484 [To] spend all their powder and shot to the beating downe of that, which I hope they shal neuer bee able to ouerthrow. **1620** SANDERSON *Serm.* I. 160 You..imagine that all His threatnings are but 'bruta fulmina', empty cracks and powder without shot. **1776** FOOTE *Bankrupt* II. Wks. 1799 II. 115 Meagre mechanics, fellows not worth powder and shot. **1786** BURNS *Earnest Cry and Prayer* Postscr. iii, Their gun's a burden on their shouther; They downa bide the stink o' powther. **1809** MALKIN *Gil Blas* I. x. ¶2 A novice, not yet accustomed to the smell of powder. [**1834** COL. BLACKER *Oliver's Advice* in E. Hayes *Ballads of Ireland* (1856) I. 192 The Pow'r that led great William, Boyne's reddening torrent thro',—In his protecting aid confide, and every foe defy—Then put your trust in God, my boys, and keep your powder dry.] **1845** DISRAELI *Sybil* I. iv, 'I have great faith in your canvassing,..but still, at the same time, the powder and shot—' 'Are essential', said Lady Marney, 'I know it, in these corrupt days'. [**1856** E. HAYES *Ballads of Ireland* (ed. 2) I. 191 There is a well-authenticated anecdote of Cromwell. On a certain occasion, when his troops were about crossing a river to attack the enemy, he concluded an address, couched in the usual fanatic terms in use among them, with these words—'put your trust in God; but mind to keep your powder dry'.] **1908** *Times Lit. Suppl.* 5 Nov. 383/1 In thus keeping his powder dry the bishop acted most wisely, though he himself ascribes the happy result entirely to observance of the other half of Cromwell's maxim. **1931** F. L. ALLEN *Only Yesterday* ii. 40 An inheritor of Theodore Roosevelt's creed of fearing God and keeping your powder dry. **1948** A. TOYNBEE *Civilization on Trial* x. 193 A 'Zealotism' tempered by a belief in keeping his powder dry. **1954** C. P. SNOW *New Men* ii. 17 It doesn't sound like business for this time. Still it won't do any harm to watch out and keep our powder dry. **1955** *Times* 6 Aug. 5/1 It is clear that M. Faure, to judge by what he did not say today, is keeping his powder dry. **1968** *Listener* 27 June 833/3, I seem to have been resigned most of my poetic life to the virtues of keeping one's powder dry rather than trying to fire the big guns.

†**4.** *Her.* (*pl.*) Spots or minor charges with which the field is 'powdered' (see POWDER *v.*[1] 4).

1562 LEIGH *Armorie* 131 The sixth doublyng is called Pean, whiche is the field Sable, and the pouders Or.

5. *attrib.* and *Comb.* **a.** General Combs. (chiefly in sense 3), as attrib., ***powder-barrel, -canister, -dust, -maker, mark, -measure, scales, -smoke***; instrumental, as ***powder-black, -charged, -dry, -grey, -laden, -light, -like, -marked, -pocked, -scorched, -stained, -tinged*** adjs.; (sense 2 d) ***powder bowl; powder-dusted*** adj.

1769 *Powder-barrel [see POWDER-BAG]. **1863** DICEY *Federal St.* II. 12 Children play with lucifer-matches amongst powder-barrels. **1857** THORNBURY *Songs Cavaliers & Roundh.* 20 *Powder-black, bleeding lads, hungry and torn. **1919** in G. Howell *In Vogue* (1975) 34/1 Porcelain *powder bowls, for dusting powder. **1930** 'R. CROMPTON' *William's Happy Days* ix. 218 Powder bowls and dolls and cushions. **1972** *Daily Tel.* 10 Oct. 13 Today's young people hardly know what a rose-bowl is, and few possess a cut-glass powder-bowl for loose powder and feathery puff. **1889** *Pall Mall G.* 16 Jan. 7/3 The cost and weight of guns to fire such *powder-charged shells would be so enormous. **1934** T. WOOD *Cobbers* xvi. 215 They worked themselves *powder-dry. **1942** W. FAULKNER *Go down, Moses* 100 The pale, powder-light, powder-dry dust of August. **1563** HYLL *Art Garden.* (1593) 71 They will spring in any ground, and bee nurished in fine earth like to *pouder dust. **1917** V. WOOLF *Mark on Wall* in *Two Stories* 20 The miniature of a lady with white powdered curls, *powder-dusted cheeks, and lips like red carnations. **1901** *Daily Chron.* 7 Sept. 8/3 *Powder-grey and thistle-purple sackcloth are two of his present lures. **1812** SIR J. SINCLAIR *Syst. Husb. Scot.* I. 178 The land in a *powder-like state. **1579** *Reg. Privy Council Scot.* III. 205 Quheill makaris, smythis, and *powder makaris. **1711** *Lond. Gaz.* No. 4829/4 Henry Bosseville of Hounslow,..Powder-maker. **1937** D. & H. TEILHET *Feather Cloak Murders* i. 14 The revolver bullet left a clean hole when shot close, always with *powder marks. **1975** G. LYALL *Judas Country* ix. 68 If I'd been faking a suicide, I'd've put the gun in a more obvious place. Anyway, can't you test his hand for powder marks? **1892** GREENER *Breech-Loader* 176 Adjust the *powder measure, put the powder into a basin, take up a full measure. **1976** *Shooting Times & Country Mag.* 16–22 Dec. 30/1 Whereas almost every large, local gun-dealer stocks reloading machines, very few stock *powder scales. **1857** THORNBURY *Songs Cavaliers* 19 Jenkin was *powder-scorched, black as a Turk. **1905** T. COLLINS in Murdoch & Drake-Brockman *Austral. Short Stories* (1951) 16 The explosion came off, nearly smothering me with *powder-smoke. **1899** CROCKETT *Kit Kennedy* 321 The befizzled, *powder-tinged attendant.

b. Special Combs.: **powder base** = *foundation cream* s.v. FOUNDATION 7 d; also (with hyphen) *attrib.*; †**powder-beater**, a pounder of spices, etc. (see sense 2 c); **powder beef**, powdered or salted beef; **powder-blower** (see quot.); **powder-burn**, a burn made by the hot gases emitted by a firearm; so **powder-burn** *v. trans.*; **powder cake**, a block of compressed face-powder; **powder-cart**, a covered cart for carrying gunpowder for artillery; **powder chamber**, (*a*) the cavity in a gun which contains the charge of powder; (*b*) an underground chamber in which gunpowder and bombs are stored; **powder closet** *obs.* exc. *hist.*, a small room formerly used for powdering hair or wigs; **powder colour**, (*a*) an opaque water-colour in powder form; (*b*) (see quot. 1966); **powder compact** = COMPACT *sb.*[2] e; †**powder-corn**, a grain of gunpowder; **powder division**, a division of the crew of a man-of-war detailed to supply ammunition during action; †**powder ermine**, ? the white fur of the ermine 'powdered' with black spots (cf. ERMINE *sb.* 2, 4, and POWDER *v.*[1] 5); **powder-flag**, the red flag carried by a *powder-hoy*, or hoisted on a ship when taking in or discharging gunpowder; **powder gas**, the gas evolved in the explosion of gunpowder; **powder-gun**, (*a*) = *powder-blower*, INSECT-*gun*; (*b*) a gun in which gunpowder is used, as distinguished from an airgun; **powder-hose**, a fuse for firing a mine, consisting of a tube of strong linen filled with a combustible; **powder-house**, a building for storing gunpowder; also *fig.*; so **powder-house-keeper; powder-hoy** (see quot.); †**powder-instrument**, a fire-arm; **powder keg**, a small barrel or container for holding gun powder or blasting powder; also *fig.*; **powder-knife**, a blunt knife formerly used to scrape off hair-powder from the skin; **powder-lime**, lime in the state of powder, powdered lime; **powder magazine**, a place where gunpowder is stored in a fort or on board ship: = MAGAZINE *sb.* 2 b; also *fig.*; **powder metallurgy**, the branch of metallurgy which is concerned with the production of metals as fine powders and their subsequent pressing and sintering into compact forms; hence **powder-metallurgical** *a.*; **powder metallurgist; powder-mill**, a mill for making gunpowder; **powder-mine**, a mine (MINE *sb.* 3) filled with gunpowder; **powder paint** = *powder colour* (*a*); **powder-paper**, paper impregnated with chlorate and other salts of potassium, powdered charcoal, and a little starch, used as a substitute for gunpowder; **powder pattern**, (*a*) *Cryst.* (see 5 c below); (*b*) a pattern indicative of the domain structure of a magnetized solid, formed when a colloidal magnetic powder is allowed to settle on it; **powder-plot** (now *rare*), the GUNPOWDER plot; so **powder-plotter, powder-plotting** *a.*; †**powder-poke** = POWDER-BAG; **powder-post** = *powder of post* (see 2 e); **powder-post beetle**, a small brown beetle belonging to the family Lyctidæ, the larva of which bores tunnels in seasoned timber, reducing it to powder; **powder-pot** = FIRE-POT a; **powder-prover**, an apparatus for measuring the explosive force of gunpowder, an éprouvette; **powder rag**, a piece of cloth used for applying face powder; **powder-scuttle**, a small opening in the deck of a ship for conveying gunpowder from the powder-room; **powder-shoot**, 'a canvas tube for conveying empty powder-boxes from the gun-deck of a ship to a lower deck' (*Cent. Dict.*); †**powder-shop**, a shop for the sale of hair-powder and other cosmetics, a perfumer's shop; **powder slope**, a slope covered in powder snow; **powder-spot**, a spot on the skin produced by gunpowder (cf. *gunpowder spot* s.v. GUNPOWDER 4); **powder sugar**, sugar in the form of powder, powdered or crushed sugar; hence †**powder-sugar** *v.* (*obs. nonce-wd.*), to sprinkle with powder sugar (or some similar substance); **powder-tax**, a tax upon hair-powder; †**powder-traitor**, one of the conspirators in the 'powder-treason'; †**powder-treason** (= *gunpowder treason*), the Gunpowder plot; **powder-trier** = *powder-prover*. Also POWDER-BAG, etc.

1927–8 *T. Eaton & Co. Catal.* Fall & Winter 367 A greaseless Vanishing Cream, for use as a protective or *powder base. **1932** [see BASE *sb.*[1] 11 b]. **1955** M. ALLINGHAM *Beckoning Lady* iv. 66 A good foundation of that powder-base stuff. **1972** *Vogue* 1 Mar. 52/1 An ideal powder-base—inimitable beneath modern make-up to ensure a flawless, perfectly matt finish. **1455** in *Househ. Ord.* (1790) 20* Th'office of the Spicery..Alexandre Rowton, Yoman *Pouderbeter. **1601** *Ibid.* 295 The Yeoman powder-beater hath for his fees, all the bagges and boxes,..and all the barrells once emptied. **1606** *Wily Beguiled* in Hazl. *Dodsley* IX. 291 My *powder-beef-slave, I'll have a rump of beef for thee. *a* **1660** *Contemp. Hist. Irel.* (Ir. Archæol. Soc.) I. 110 A world of carts and wagonns, loaden with powder-beefe. **1875** KNIGHT *Dict. Mech.*, **Powder-blower*, an instrument for blowing powder on to plants or into crevices infested by insects. **1884** *Ibid.* Supp., *Powder Blower.* (Surgical.) An instrument for blowing a powder upon a part. **1846** J. W. WEBB *Altowan* I. iv. 125 He might *powder-burn the bear by the nearness of the shot. **1847** in H. Howe *Hist. Coll. Ohio* 99 In this struggle, Lytle..had..his face powder burnt. **1927** *Scribner's Mag.* Feb. 176/2 In the pursuit, the Rangers literally carried out their leader's orders to 'powder-burn' them. **1969** G. MACBETH *War Quartet* 72 With his gun One braised his leg three times. The doctor saw Powder-burns there, and left him. **1975** M. BABSON *There must be Some Mistake* xx. 182 You have gloves... Put them on now. The only powder burns must be found on those two that the police may re-enact the scene. **1961** 'A. A. FAIR' *Stop at Red Light* (1962) v. 82 Parts of a *powder cake were on the floor, and bits of glass from the broken mirror. **1848** LOWELL *Biglow P.* Ser. I. VII. v, But civlyzation does git forrid Sometimes upon a *powder-cart. **1899** T. S. BALDOCK *Cromwell as Soldier* 92 A passing powder-cart blew up. **1803** *Jrnl. Natural Philos.* IV. 251 As soon as the lever has arrived at the position N, the *powder chamber P is exactly opposite the ball, and ready to be discharged against it. **1890** W. J. GORDON *Foundry* 18 The powder-chamber will..hold a charge of 900 lb. *Ibid.* 23 In all breechloaders..the powder-chamber is larger than the bore of the gun. **1905** *Pall Mall*

Mag. Dec. 746/1 Violante..lay dozing in the *powder closet which opened out of Donna Carlotta's bedroom. **1927** *Daily Express* 12 Dec. 4 Methley Park..has one or two unusual features, however; and among these are some queer old powder closets. **1929** S. Ertz *Galaxy* i. 11 The house contained a powder-closet for the dressing of ladies' hair in earlier days. **1980** *Country Life* 28 Feb. 609/1 The emergence of indecencies from the powder closet to the respectable page. **1862** *Illustr. Catal. Internat. Exhib., Industr. Dept., Brit. Div.* II. No. 5512 Colours prepared for missal-painting, and illumination in soluble *powder-colour. **1913** R. Fry *Let.* 28 Dec. (1972) II. 376 Grind up your powder colours in water very stiffly and use with the yolks of eggs. **1963** S. Marshall *Exper. in Educ.* iii. 88 Powder colour has proved its worth. **1966** J. S. Cox *Illustr. Dict. Hairdressing* 121/1 *Powder-colour*, colour rinses in powder form. **1927** *Powder compact. [see compact *sb.*² e]. **1937** D. L. Sayers *Busman's Honeymoon* xv. 259 He laid a powder-compact aside on the what-not. **1978** *Cornish Guardian* 27 Apr. 32/4 The new president, Mrs. Tippitt, presented Mrs. M. Williams, the retiring president, with a powder compact. **1610** B. Jonson *Alch.* i. i, Your complexion..Stuck full of black, and melancholique wormes, Like *poulder-cornes, shot, at th' artillerie-yard. **1534** in Peacock *Eng. Ch. Furniture* (1866) 207 A mantell for our lady of cloth of tysseu purfild aboute w *powther armyn. **1536** Wriothesley *Chron.* (Camden) I. 45 A robe of crimson velvett furred with poudre ermyns. **1872** Preble *Hist. Flag* (1880) 676 A *Powder Flag—A plain red flag hoisted at the fore, denoting the vessel is taking in or discharging powder. **1890** W. J. Gordon *Foundry* 21 To prevent the escape of *powder gas an elastic steel cap is fitted on the front of the breech-screw. **1890** *Cent. Dict.*, **Powder-gun*, an instrument for diffusing insect-powder. **1832** Southey *Hist. Penins. War* III. 420 A communication [was] formed to them with *powder hoses placed between tiles. **1834–47** J. S. Macaulay *Field Fortif.* (1851) 199 Two powder-hoses may be placed within 18 inches of one another, if covered with earth, and produce separate explosions. **1720** in *Mass. House of Representatives Jrnl.* (1921) II. 288 Daniel Powning, keeper of the *Powder-House. **1774** *Chron.* in *Ann. Reg.* 157/2 A party of troops took possession of the powder in the powder house. **1848** *Knickerbocker* XVIII. 216 The powder house, the pound, the poor-house and the county-house, are all objects of notice to the traveller. **1928** *Manch. Guardian Weekly* 7 Sept. 181/4 The spark that fired this powder-house was a letter protesting against the 'constant criticism' of the methods of Lancashire cricketers. **1789** *Rec. Early Hist. Boston* (1886) X. 183 Foster Thomas, *powder-house-keeper. **1867** Smyth *Sailor's Word-bk.*, **Powder-hoy*, an ordnance vessel expressly fitted to convey powder from the land magazine to a ship; it invariably carries a red distinguishing flag. **1613** Wither *Abuses Stript* ii. iv. S iv b, The Law, that now preuents, And bars the vse of *pouder Instruments. **1855** W. G. Simms *Forayers* iii. 39 Sinclair.. drew up an old *powder-keg by a rope-hitch, which had been made about it. **1876** 'Mark Twain' *Tom Sawyer* xxxii. 323 It was the treasure-box..along with an empty powder-keg, a couple of guns in leather cases,..a leather belt, and some other rubbish. **1893** W. K. Post *Harvard Stories* 6 One reason why they do it..is to make you flare up, you little powder keg. **1945** *Richmond* (Va.) *News-Leader* 17 Sept. 7/2 (*heading*) Argentina's militarist regime believed sitting on powderkeg. **1972** *Publishers' Weekly* 24 Jan. 21 His stories weeks before the revolt warned of the powderkeg inside the prison. **1975** *Publ. Amer. Dial. Soc. 1973* lix. 47 *Powder keg* .., a round, metal container for blasting powder, usually of twenty-five pounds capacity. **1806–7** J. Beresford *Miseries Hum. Life* (ed. 7) 243 Using a *powder-knife which has so broad an edge that it grounds the powder into your skin. **1793** Smeaton *Edystone L.* §185, I..tried a quantity of *powder-lime that had fallen from a stone imperfectly burnt. **1769** *Powder magazine [see powder-bag]. **1864** Bowen *Logic* ix. 311 To remove a lighted match from its dangerous proximity to a powder-magazine. **1890** Kipling *Departmental Ditties* (ed. 4) 98 You shouldn't take a man from Canada And bid him smoke in powder-magazines. **1933** J. Buchan *Prince of Captivity* ii. ii. 196 Birkpool is.. becoming a powder magazine. **1979** G. Latta tr. *Jacquemard-Sénécal's Eleventh Little Nigger* ii. iv. 94 The reunion of the four of them..would constitute a sort of powder-magazine: one spark and the magazine blows up. **1980** Alexander & Anand *Queen Victoria's Maharajah* i. 11 A lucky hit on the powder magazine. **1949** *Electronic Engin.* XXI. 88/1 The production of intricate structures is due to the fact that moulding powders are now made by *powder-metallurgical processes. **1975** Bram & Downs *Manuf. Technol.* iii. 79 Cemented carbides are a typical powder metallurgical product. **1949** C. G. Goetzel *Treat. Powder Metall.* I. p. vii, The final chapter of Part One covers briefly the many uses for metal powders that are somewhat beyond the sphere of interest of the *powder metallurgist. **1954** H. Udin et al. *Welding for Engineers* iii. 39 This process of spheroidization of pores or inclusions has been of great interest to powder metallurgists. **1933** *Engin. & Mining Jrnl.* CXXXIV. 373/1 What is frequently referred to as '*powder metallurgy' had its beginnings at the turn of the century when the metals tungsten and molybdenum first became commercial commodities. **1959** *Listener* 12 Mar. 453/1 Coolidge in America developed the process now known as powder metallurgy, by which a bar of compressed tungsten powder was sintered at a temperature below the melting point of the metal. **1970** *New Scientist* 12 Nov. 325/1 Powder metallurgy is commonly used to make precision components, and to fabricate exotic materials. **1650** R. Stapylton *Strada's Low C. Warres* vii. 40 These *Powder-Milles used to be distant from Townes. **1856** Emerson *Eng. Traits, Times* Wks. (Bohn) II. 118 We walked with some circumspection, as if we were entering a powder-mill. *c* **1622** Ford, etc. *Witch Edmonton* v. i, Like a swift *Powder-Mine beneath the world, Up would I blow it. **1939** L. de Lissa *Life in Nursery School* ix. 158 *Powder paints are cheap and suitable and can be obtained in good colours. **1955** E. Blishen *Roaring Boys* i. 33 How should I learn to distinguish between different types of brush, to mix powder paint? **1973** *Galt Toys Catal.* 49 *Powder paint set*.. mix up a small quantity with water as required. **1884** Knight *Dict. Mech.* Supp., **Powder Paper*, a substitute for gunpowder, invented in England... It is 5–16 stronger than gunpowder. **1934** *Physical Rev.* XLVI. 227 (*caption*) *Powder patterns with H normal to the surface. **1951** L. F. Bates *Mod. Magn.* (ed. 3) xii. 457 The main method of studying domain structure is undoubtedly the Bitter figure or powder pattern method. **1965** Craik & Tebble *Ferromagnetism & Ferromagnetic Domains* 308 The first stage in the preparation of colloids or suspensions for the powder pattern or Bitter figure technique, is the production of magnetite (Fe_3O_4) in a very finely divided state. **1616** B. Jonson *Epigrams* xcii, Of the *poulder-plot, they will talke yet. **1687–8** in Swayne *Sarum Churchw. Acc.* (1896) 348, 5th Nov. being ye Powder Plott. **1837** Carlyle *Fr. Rev.* I. v. viii, Levelled Cannon, Guy-Faux powder-plots (for that too was spoken of). **1614** Jackson *Creed* iii. xxxii. §3 If *powder-plotters, or publique Assasinates may be dignified with titles of Saints. **1653** Baxter *Worc. Petit. Def.* 34 *Powder Plotting Papists. **1532** *Acc. L.H. Tr. Scot.* VI. 155 Item, deliverit to thame [gunners] vj *pulder pokis. **1538** *Ibid.* VII. 112 For polder pokis of violat to lay amang the Kingis claithis. **1927** *Bull. U.S. Dept. Agric.* No. 1490, 7 *Powder post is that class of defects in which the larvae of insects reduce the wood fibers of seasoned or partially seasoned wood to a powderlike condition. **1905** *Yearbk. U.S. Dept. Agric. 1904* 387 (*caption*) Work of *powder post beetle..in hickory poles. **1911** *Technical Ser. Bureau Entomol., U.S. Dept. Agric.* XX. iii. 111 (*title*) A revision of the powder-post beetles of the family Lyctidæ of the United States and Europe. **1928** *Forestry* II. 42 The sapwood..has been reduced to a finely powdered, floury condition—the characteristic damage that gives the name of 'powder-post beetles' to the *Lyctus* species. **1963** *B.S.I. News* Mar. 6/1 The third British Standard will describe a test for determining the toxicity of wood preservatives to the powder post beetle, *Lyctus brunneus*. **1975** G. Evans *Life of Beetles* iv. 94 Lyctidae, the powder post beetles (e.g. *Lyctus* spp.), have larvae which produce a very fine powdery dust. **1638** Sir T. Herbert *Trav.* (ed. 2) 116 The Portugalls.. throwing on them such and so many Granadoes and burning fire-balls, *powder-pots, and scalding Lead. **1875** Knight *Dict. Mech.*, **Powder-prover*. See *Ballistic Pendulum*; *Eprouvette*. **1904** 'O. Henry' in *McClure's Mag.* Aug. 352/2 This stake comes in handier than a *powder rag at a fat man's ball. **1906** —— *Four Million* (1916) 21 Delia finished her cry and attended to her cheeks with the powder rag. *a* **1911** D. G. Phillips *Susan Lenox* (1917) II. ii. 33 Susan.. safeguarded her nose against shine; she tucked the powder rag into the stocking. **1687** T. Brown *Lib. of Consc.* in *Dk. Buckhm.'s Wks.* (1705) II. 129 You think my Trade a Nuisance, I like it better, than a *Powder-Shop. **1972** D. Haston *In High Places* xi. 115, I could put this [failure] out of my mind swooping around the *powder slopes. **1721** *Lond. Gaz.* No. 5957/3 A blue *Powder-Spot under his Left Eye. **1624** *Althorp MS.* p. lvi. in Simpkinson *Washingtons* (1860) App., *Powther sugar 2 barrells. **1707** *Curios. in Husb. & Gard.* 103 The Juices taken from Sugar-Canes are thicken'd, to make Powder Sugar. **1654** Gayton *Pleas. Notes* iii. iii. 84 She *powder-sugar'd it with a little burnt Allum. **1794** J. Moser (*title*) The Meal Tub Plot; or, Remarks on the *Powder Tax, by a Barber. **1861** Thornbury *Turner* (1862) I. 163 The powder-tax that the Tories imposed in 1795..drove out wigs. **1614** Sylvester *Parl. Vertues Royall* Wks. (Grosart) II. 123 An Act against King-Killers, *Powder-Traitors, and their Abetters. **1731** T. Cox *Magna Brit.* VI. 228/2 His Zeal in apprehending.. the Powder Traitors. **1607** Hieron *Wks.* I. 442 An euident instant whereof we haue had in the *powder-treason; a deuice, which a man would thinke the diuell himselfe should be ashamed to father. **1769** Blackstone *Comm.* IV. iv. 57 The powder-treason..struck a panic into James I. which operated in different ways. **1667** Sir R. Moray in *Phil. Trans.* II. 476 The Strength of the Powder must be examin'd by a *Powder-Tryer. **1781** Thompson *ibid.* LXXI. 298 All the eprouvettes, or powder-triers, in common use are defective.

c. With reference to the Debye-Scherrer method of X-ray crystallography (see Debye), as ***powder camera, diffraction, pattern, photograph, photography***.

1917 *Physical Rev.* X. 664 The powder photographs have an advantage..over ionization-chamber measurements, in that the intensities of reflection from different planes, as well as different orders, are directly comparable. **1924** R. W. G. Wyckoff *Struct. Crystals* vi. 178 The spectrum lines which result from these reflections of monochromatic X-rays constitute a powder photograph. *Ibid.*, Such a powder pattern can be greatly simplified by filtering the X-rays to render them essentially monochromatic. *Ibid.*, The outstanding advantage of powder diffraction methods obviously lies in their ability to treat the many crystalline materials which do not grow large single crystals. *Ibid.* 185 A more extended description of these procedures is not justified because thus far they have found little application to powder photography. **1936** *Jrnl. R. Aeronaut. Soc.* XL. 411 The powder photograph is..a powerful means of recognising alloy phases. **1945** C. W. Bunn *Chem. Crystallogr.* v. 109 A powder camera consists essentially of an aperture system to define the X-ray beam, a holder for the specimen, and a framework for holding the photographic film. **1948** K. Lonsdale *Crystals & X-Rays* iii. 76 For powder photography monochromatic radiation is used..but the specimen is a mass of tiny crystals orientated in all directions. **1962** *Times* 4 Sept. 2/6 There are four X-ray generating sets and accessory equipment includes powder cameras. **1965** Adams & Raynor *Advanced Pract. Inorg. Chem.* xvii. 155 The intersection of a curved strip of film with these diffraction cones gives the familiar powder photograph, which consists of a series of curved lines. **1969** B. E. Warren *X-Ray Diffraction* v. 67 Powder patterns are very often used for a precision measurement of the crystal axes.

ˈpowder, *sb.*² *Obs.* exc. *dial.* Also 7 pouder, 9 *dial.* pooder. [Origin unascertained. Identity with powder¹ is, from the sense, improbable; the phonology separates it from pother.] An impetus, a rush; force, impetuosity. Chiefly in phr. ***with*** (dial. ***at, in***) ***a powder***, impetuously, violently.

c **1600** *Club Law* (1907) iii. iv. 1295 Ile sett you in with a powder. ([Stage direction] *hee fells him.*) ? **1640** *New Sermon of newest Fashion* (1877) 39 If I might have my will itt should goe downe with a pouder. **1650** Fuller *Pisgah* v. v. 151 Jordan..comes down with a powder, and at set times overflowes all his bankes. **1663** Waterhouse *Comm. Fortescue* 515 Then in came the French, with a powder as we say, and everything was done and said *a la mode de France*. **1678** Butler *Hud.* iii. i. 1055 When th' heard a knocking at the Gate, Laid on in hast with such a powder, The blows grew louder still and louder. *c* **1780** in S. Gilpin *Songs* (Cumbld.) (1866) 275 Heame set he in a powder. **1878** *Cumberld. Gloss.*, *Pooder*, hurry: Off he went in sic a pooder. **1898** B. Kirkby *Lakeland Words* s.v., He was gaan at a tremendous pooder.

ˈpowder, *v.*¹ Forms: see powder *sb.*¹ [a. F. *poudre-r* to cover with powder (13th c. in Hatz.-Darm.), f. *poudre*: see powder *sb.*¹ In some senses, prob. immediately from the Eng. sb.]

I. To sprinkle or treat with powder, or something in the state of powder.

†**1. a.** *trans.* To sprinkle (food) with a condiment of powdery nature; to season, spice. *Obs.*

c **1305** *Land Cokaygne* 110 þe leuerokes..Liȝtiþ adun to manis muþ..Pudrid wiþ gilofre and canel. *a* **1440** *Sir Degrev.* 1402 Seththe sche brouȝt hom in haste, Ploverys poudryd in paste.

†**b.** *fig.* To mix with some qualifying or modifying ingredient; to 'season'; to 'alloy'. *Obs.*

a **1300** *Sarmun* vii. in *E.E.P.* (1862) 2 þi felle wiþ-oute nis bot a sakke ipudrid ful wiþ drit and ding. *c* **1380** Wyclif *Serm.* Sel. Wks. I. 58 All þis speche is poudrid with gabbinge. **1534** Tindale *Col.* iv. 6 Let youre speache be all wayes well favoured and be powdred with salt. *a* **1586** Sidney *Arcadia* (1622) 270 Framed to him a very thankefull message, powdring it with some hope-giuing phrases. *a* **1661** Fuller *Worthies, Berks.* (1662) 98 Powdering their lives with improbable passages, to the great prejudice of truth. **1790** Burke *Fr. Rev.* Wks. V. 140 The opiate potion of amnesty, powdered with all the ingredients of scorn.

2. a. To sprinkle the flesh of animals with salt or powdered spice, esp. for preserving; to salt; to 'corn'; to cure. ? *Obs.* exc. *dial.*

1389 *Durham Acc. Rolls* (Surtees) 49 In ij salmon poudrt, ijs. xd. *a* **1483** *Liber Niger* in *Househ. Ord.* (1790) 46 In beef daily or moton, fresh, or elles all poudred is more availe, 5d. **1542** Boorde *Dyetary* xvi. (1870) 271 Olde beefe.. moderatly powderyd, that the groose blode by salte may be exhaustyd. **1553** Eden *Treat. Newe Ind.* (Arb.) 27 Inuoluinge with cereclothe and pouderinge with spyces the body. **1555** W. Watreman *Fardle Facions* i. vi. 98 Thei poudre them [Locustes] with salte, and..liue by none other foode. **1577** B. Googe *Heresbach's Husb.* iii. (1586) 153 The Tubbes that you poulder in, must bee such as haue had Oyle in. *a* **1661** Fuller *Worthies, Cornwall* (1662) 194 Imploying a power of poor people..in Powdering, and Drying them [Pilchards]. **1715** Prior *Down-Hall* 79 She roasted red veal, and she powder'd lean beef. *c* **1830** Mrs. Sherwood in *Houlston Tracts* III. No. 81. 4 My good girl,..just powder me that ham, or dish me those turnips.

†**b.** *fig.* To preserve, keep, store *up*. *Obs.*

1614 R. Tailor *Hog Hath Lost Pearl* i. i. B iij, If you haue powdred vp my plot in your sconce, you may home sir. **1654** Fuller *Two Serm.* 27 All Spirituall Meat is not..for our present spending and feeding thereon, but (as good Husbands) we are to powder up some for the time to come. **1660** tr. *Amyraldus' Treat. conc. Relig.* iii. vi. 434 That horrible Leviathan which is powder'd up I know not where against the manifestation of the Messias.

3. a. To sprinkle powder upon; to besprinkle or cover *with* or as *with* some powdery substance. (In first quot., to sprinkle with dust.)

c **1350** *Story of Holy Rood* 117 in *Leg. Rood* (1871) 65 þou sal..Fall to erth and powder þe, And pray god haue mercy on me. *c* **1440** *Promp. Parv.* 411/1 Powderyd wythe powder, *pulverizatus*. **1563** Hyll *Art Garden.* (1593) 31 Which lightly couer or poulder with earth in that place where they most swarm. **1667** Milton *P.L.* vii. 581 The Galaxie, that Milkie way Which nightly as a circling Zone thou seest Pouderd with Starrs. **1883** Symonds *Ital. Byways* i. 1 Ridges powdered with light snow. **1899** *Allbutt's Syst. Med.* VIII. 870 It is a good plan after washing the feet to powder them..with boric acid.

b. To apply powder to (the hair, etc.) as a cosmetic. Also with the person as obj.; also *absol.* or *intr.* for *refl.* Phr. ***to powder one's nose***, used also *euphem.* (with reference to a woman) for 'to go to the lavatory'.

1599 [see powdering *vbl. sb.* 1]. **1609** B. Jonson *Sil. Wom.* i. i, Still to be pou'dred, still perfum'd. **1633** Ford *Love's Sacr.* ii. i, She shall no oftener powder her hair, surfell her cheeks, cleanse her teeth. **1711** Steele *Spect.* No. 2 ⁋2 He has his shoes rubb'd and his Perriwig powder'd at the Barber's. **1810** *Splendid Follies* I. 10 Edward and William were scrubbing and powdering to mount behind. **1870** Dickens *E. Drood* iii, 'A red nose..she can always powder it'. 'She would scorn to powder it', says Edwin. **1883** *Century Mag.* XXVII. 5 [One] who was not highly rouged and powdered. **1921** W. S. Maugham *Circle* i. 28, I must powder my nose, Hughie. **1924** E. O'Neill *Welded* ii. 137 You'll want to go upstairs and powder your nose. **1927** S. Ertz *Now East, now West* xvii. 261 She put no colour on her face,..which, if she powdered and didn't even redden her lips, always made people ask her if she were ill. **1930** A. Bennett *Imperial Palace* lvi. 417 That's the bathroom and so on... You can hang your overcoat in there—and powder your nose. **1938** I. Goldberg *Wonder of Words* vi. 108 We are invited to wash our hands, or, if we wear dresses, to powder our noses. **1962** *Guardian* 5 Dec. 6/5 Useful information..about where to park..dine, stay overnight, and—for women—powder one's nose in comfort. **1969** R. T. Wilcox *Dict. Costume* (1970) 88/1 Venetian gentlemen also painted, powdered and patched. **1972** L. P. Davies *What did I do Tomorrow?* 72 I'll use your bathroom. To powder my nose, as nice girls say.

c. To whiten (a fabric) by application of some white powdered substance.

1890 *Cent. Dict.* s.v., Lace which has grown yellow is powdered by being placed in a packet of white lead and beaten.

4. a. In heraldry and decorative art: To strew with a multitude of (isolated) small objects or figures of the same kind; to ornament with spots or small devices scattered over the surface; to sprinkle or spangle (a surface, etc.) *with*. Also *fig.* Usually in *pa. pple.*

13.. *Test. Christi* 221 (Vernon MS.) in Herrig's *Archiv* LXXIX. 432 A cote-armour I bar wiþ me..Poudret wiþ fyue roses rede. *c* **1430** *Syr Gener.* (Roxb.) 5680 The champe of the feld was goules, Thik y-poudred with smale foules. **1490** Caxton *Eneydos* xv. 54 The erthe taketh a newe cote.. of fyn gras, powdred with floures of a hundred thousande maners of colours. **1536** *Regr. Riches* in *Antiq. Sarisb.* (1771) 198 Many copes, powdered with Lyons Ostrages Troifoils, Flower de Luces and dyvers Armes, in number sixteen. **1580** Hollyband *Treas. Fr. Tong, Vn Chamarre broché de pourpre*, a garment poudred with purple studdes. **1612** Drayton *Poly-olb.* xv. 164 Nature..Who seemes in that her pearle [the daisy] so greatly to delight That euery Plaine therewith she powdreth to beholde. **1717** Berkeley *Tour Italy* 21 May, Delicious vineyards, gardens, &c., powdered with little white houses. **1766** Entick *London* IV. 415 Gold shoes powdered with pearls. **1882** Hare in *Gd. Words* Mar. 180 Soon the whole country becomes powdered with ruins.

b. With the decorative objects as subject.

1867 'Ouida' *C. Castlemaine* (1879) 17 Daisies powdering the turf sodden with human blood.

II. 5. To sprinkle or scatter like powder; to strew here and there in a multitude of minute particles; to disperse here and there upon a surface, as a number of small ornamental figures repeated. Usually in *pa. pple.* (Correlative to 4.)

13.. *E.E. Allit. P.* A. 44 Gilofre, gyngure & gromylyoun, And pyonys powdered ay betwene. **1483** *Act 1 Rich. III*, c. 8 *Preamble*, The Sellers of such course Clothes..usen for to powder and cast Flokkys of fynner Cloth upon the same. **1513** Douglas *Æneis* xii. ii. 40 Or quhar the schene lilleis in ony steid War pulderit wyth the vermel rosis reid. **1603** Owen *Pembrokeshire* iv. (1892) 40 As for the Irishmen they are soe powdred among the Inhabitaunts..that in euerye village you shall find the thirde, fourth, or fift housholder an Irishman. **1744** J. Paterson *Comm. Milton's P.L.* 374 Prodigious clusters of small stars,..poudered or cast close together, as it were dust sprinkled upon a floor. **1890** *Cent. Dict.* s.v., To powder violets on a silk ground.

III. To reduce or fall down to powder.

6. To reduce to powder; to pulverize.

15.. in *Vicary's Anat.* (1888) App. ix. 223 Lett all these be pouldered small, and cersed [sifted] fynely. **1605** Timme *Quersit.* i. vii. 33 The which pouldred he prescribeth to be taken in a reale egg. **1718** Quincy *Compl. Disp.* 11 In the powdering such things as Jallop, Ipecacuanha, and the like. **1862** Stanley *Jew. Ch.* (1877) I. iv. 74 The vast enclosure of its brick walls..now almost powdered into dust.

7. *intr.* To fall to powder, become pulverized.

1846 Worcester, *Powder, v.n.* to fall to dust. **1864** Webster, *Powder, v.i.*,..to become like powder; as, some salts powder easily.

IV. †8. *trans.* To charge with gunpowder; cf. powdered 5. *Obs. rare.*

1643 *Public Confider* 8 Not with..powdering our guns.

'powder, *v.*² *colloq.* and *dial.* [f. powder *sb.*²] *intr.* To rush; to hurry with impetuosity and rushing speed: said esp. of a rider.

1632 Quarles *Div. Fancies* i. lxvii, Zacheus climb'd the Tree: But O how fast,..(when Our Saviour called) he powder'd down agen! *c* **1645** T. Tully *Siege of Carlisle* (1840) 33 About 800 horse..come powdering towards the Cowes so fast. **1684** Otway *Atheist* iii. i, The Dice powd'ring out of the Box. **1694** R. L'Estrange *Fables* 3 Down comes a kite powdering upon them in the interim, and gobbles up both together. **1804** Mar. Edgeworth *Ennui* vi, You'll take four [horses]..and you'll see how we'll powder along. **1857** Thornbury *Songs Cavaliers & Roundh.* 115 And powdering fast, the men and horses Thundering swept down Frampton Hill. **1895** A. Forbes *Mem. of War & Peace* i. 13 All Belgrade, feverish for further news, rushed out into the street as I powdered along.

b. *transf.* and *fig.*

a **1734** North *Lives* (1826) III. 47 The refusal came powdering from him by wholesale. **1838** Dickens *Nich. Nick.* xxxix, 'I think I see 'un now, a powderin' awa' at the thin bread an' butther'.

powderable ('paʊdərəb(ə)l), *a. rare.* [f. powder *v.*¹ + -able.] Capable of being powdered: i.e. **a.** of being reduced to powder; friable, pulverizable; **†b.** of being salted or preserved (*obs.*).

1646 Sir T. Browne *Pseud. Ep.* iii. xxiii. (1686) 132 Nor do they become friable or easily powderable by Philosophical Calcination. **1766** Entick *London* (1776) I. 243 Corn, wine, powderable wares, fish.

†'powderal, *a. Obs. rare*⁻¹. [irreg. f. powder *sb.*¹ + -al¹.] Of the nature of powder; powdery, pulverulent.

1662 J. Chandler *Van Helmont's Oriat.* 52 No pulverous or powderall co-mixture doth tend to generation.

'powder-bag. A bag for holding powder: **†a.** ?for powdered salt or spices. *Obs.* **b.** for carrying gunpowder. **c.** for hair-powder.

1392-3 *Earl Derby's Exp.* (Camden) 152 Super officio salsarie..pro j pare powder-baggs, iiij d. **1533** *Acc. Ld. High Treas. Scot.* VI. 160 To iij careage hors to cary the gunstanis, pulder baggis, and uthir necessaris. **1769** Falconer *Dict. Marine* (1789) D dj, Cartridges..may be kept in the powder magazine.., in the empty powder-barrels and powder-bags. **1807** Southey *Espriella's Lett.* (1808) I. 7 The man who cleans boots is running in one direction, the barber with his powder-bag in another. **1867** Smyth *Sailor's Word-bk.*, *Powder-bags*, leathern bags containing from 20 to 40 lbs. of powder; substituted for petards at the instance of Lord Cochrane, as being more easily placed.

,powder-'blue, *sb.* and *a.* Also **powder blue.** [powder *sb.*¹ i.]

1. *sb.* Powdered smalt, esp. for use in the laundry.

1656 *Essex County, Mass. Probate Rec.* (1916) I. 233 Mace and Ribing, starch and poudarblu. **1707** *Lond. Gaz.* No. 4319/3 Out of the Prize, Name unknown, Smalt or Powder-Blue. **1741** *Compl. Fam.-Piece* i. ii. 194 Powder-blue, mix'd with the Saffron water, makes a Green. **1789** *Trans. Soc. Arts* I. 15 Great quantities of Smalt imported..are used under the name of Powder blue, in washing linen. **1823** J. Badcock *Dom. Amusem.* 151 A small quantity of fine powder-blue is sometimes added.

2. *adj.* Having the deep blue colour of smalt. Now also used of light blue shades. **b.** *sb.* A name for this colour.

1894 *Westm. Gaz.* 16 Aug. 3/3 A gown of powder-blue serge. **1895** Clive Holland *Jap. Wife* (ed. 11) 121 A dressing-gown robe of blue linen, with wide sleeves and an *obi* of powder-blue muslin. **1896** *Westm. Gaz.* 18 Sept. 3/2 That melton cloth boasting a whitish surface that is very happy in powder blue, greens, and dark purples. **1923** [see cyclamen c]. **1943** A. Christie *Moving Finger* xi. 130 A skin-tight powder-blue evening dress. **1967** *New Statesman* 28 July 110/3 Their powder-blue berets bob above helmets. **1970** *Cape Times* 28 Oct. 19/2 (Advt.), Rambler Rogue 1970, 12 800 miles, powder blue with black upholstery, executive's car. **1973** 'S. Harvester' *Corner of Playground* iii. i. 170 A waxed red hat with a powder-blue band. **1978** *Jrnl. R. Soc. Arts* CXXVI. 352/1 Just as there are many different shades of blue, for example powder blue,.. wedgwood blue and pacific blue, so there are many different nuances of piano tone.

3. *attrib.* or as *adj.* Applied *spec.* to a type of Chinese porcelain of the Ch'ing period having a ground of powder blue. Also as **powdered blue**.

1900 F. Litchfield *Pott. & Porc.* vii. 114 The date of what is called 'powdered blue' china is said to be the Kang-he period (1661–1722). **1906** S. W. Bushell *Chinese Art* II. viii. 36 The finely pounded pigment is blown upon the raw body to produce, when glazed, a 'powder blue', or *bleu fouetté* ground. **1911** [see Kang-Hai, Kang-He, Kang-Hi]. **1960** R. G. Haggar *Conc. Encycl. Continental Pott. & Porc.* 352/2 A powdered-blue ground colour of great depth and richness was introduced at Meissen porcelain factory before 1725. **1965** [see K'ang-Hsi]. **1971** L. A. Boger *Dict. World Pott. & Porc.* 270/1 *Powder Blue Ware*, in Chinese ceramics; porcelain of the Ch'ing period, especially of the K'ang Hsi reign, which is characterized by a beautiful and rather even ground of bright soft blue with a slightly clouded appearance.

4. *Comb.*, as ***powder-blue-grey*** adj.

1952 S. Spender *Learning Laughter* 30 Fields and fields of powder-blue-grey cornflowers.

'powder-box. A box for holding powder. **†a.** A box for powdered spice or salt. *Obs.* **b.** A box for carrying or containing gunpowder. **c.** A box for toilet-powder, usually also containing a powder-puff. **d.** A box with small holes in the lid, for sprinkling powder or sand upon writing to prevent blotting; a pounce-box.

1403 *Nottingham Rec.* II. 20, j. poudrebox. **1424** in *E. E. Wills* (1882) 57 Powderbox and salers of siluere. **1679** *Lond. Gaz.* No. 1452/4 Two silver Powder-boxes with a large buckle engraved on the lid of them. **1704** Steele *Lying Lover* iii. i. 34 Betty, bring the Powder Box to your Lady. **1713** Gay *Fan* i. 129 There stands the Toilette..The patch, the powder-box, pulville, perfumes. **1895** *Army & Navy Co-op. Soc. Price List* 172/2 Powder Boxes—Puff, ea. 7/5, 9/4, [etc.]. **1925** *Heal & Son Catal.: Glass*, Powder Box. Height 6 in. Price 9/6. **1949** *Dædalian Q.* Fall 26 Powder box, powder box, powder your nose, How many petals are in a rose? **1979** G. Latta tr. *Jacquemard-Sénécal's Eleventh Little Nigger* i. v. 46 He was still clutching his powder-box and puff in his clenched hands.

'powder-boy. A boy employed on board ship to carry gunpowder from the powder-room to the guns; a 'powder-monkey'.

1805 in Polwhele *Trad. & Recoll.* (1826) II. 577, I acted both in the capacity of a commanding officer, mate, midship-man, small-arm-man, and powder-boy. **1829** Marryat *F. Mildmay* iii, The powder-boys, each with his box full, seated on it.

'powder-chest. **a.** A chest for holding gunpowder. **b.** A kind of petard charged with gunpowder, scrap iron, old nails, etc., fastened to the deck of a ship to be discharged at a boarding enemy.

1669 Sturmy *Mariner's Mag.* v. xiii. 86 How to make Powder-Chests. **1753** Hanway *Trav.* I. ii. xxvi. 167 Our danger was the greater, as the fire was about the powder-chest. **1875** in Knight *Dict. Mech.*

'powder-,down. [f. powder *sb.*¹ + down *sb.*², rendering Ger. *puder-dunen* or *staub-dunen* (pl.), lit. powder-downs (i.e. down-plumules, 'down'), introduced 1840 by Nitzsch (*Pterylographie* vii).]

Name for peculiar down-feathers or plumules, found in various birds in definite tracts or patches: so called from the bluish-white powdery or scurfy substance into which they disintegrate; by Coues called *pulviplumes*. (Sometimes, less correctly, applied to the powder or scurf.) Also *attrib.*, as in ***powder-down feathers***, ***powder-down patch*** or ***tract***, a patch of powder-downs.

1861 A. D. Bartlett in *Proc. Zool. Soc.* 131 This has led me to the discovery of two remarkable powder-down patches. **1867** P. L. Sclater tr. *Nitzsch's Pterylogr.* vii. 38 The powder-down-feathers are intruded among the lateral feathers of the great saddle of the spinal tract. **1894** Newton *Dict. Birds* 242 The 'Downs' are almost always concealed by the Contour-feathers, and are smaller, more fluffy, and more numerous... A peculiarly modified kind are the Powder-downs. *Ibid.* 738 *Powder-downs* are so called from the powder produced by the continuous disintegration of the numerous brush-like barbs and barbules, into which the barrel is constantly splitting as it grows without forming a principal shaft.

powdered ('paʊdəd), *ppl. a.* [f. powder *v.*¹]

†1. Of food: Sprinkled or seasoned with salt or spice. Also *fig.* 'Seasoned'. *Obs.*

1563 B. Googe *Eglogs*, etc. (Arb.) 83 Our sighes, and powdred sobs with tears. **1587** R. Baynes in Turberv. *Trag. T.* To Rdr., Poets pens..Whose powdred saaes are mixt, with pleasure, and delight. **1589** R. Harvey *Pl. Perc.* 1 Reason..began this motherly, and well powdered tale.

2. a. Salted, pickled, or spiced for future use; preserved; cured; corned. ? *Obs.* exc. *dial.*

1409 *Durham Acc. Rolls* (Surtees) 53 In xvj powdret fish empt. *xs.* *c* **1460** J. Russell *Bk. Nurture* 533 Mustard is meete for brawne, beef, or powdred motoun. **1597** A. M. tr. *Guillemeau's Fr. Chirurg.* 52/2 By eatinge of pouldred or saulted meate. **1667** Denham *Direct. Paint.* ii. ix, Out of the very Beer, they sell the Malt; Powder of Powder, from powder'd Beef the Salt. **1736** Carte *Ormonde* II. 322 Powdered beef and pork imported from Ireland. **1818** Scott *Br. Lamm.* xxvi, Lord Allan, rest his saul, used to like a pouthered guse.

†b. *transf.*: cf. powdering-tub 2. *Obs.*

1603 Shaks. *Meas. for M.* iii. ii. 62 Shee hath eaten vp all her beefe, and she is her selfe in the tub... Euer your fresh Whore, and your pouder'd Bawd.

3. a. Decorated with a multitude of spots or small figures scattered over the surface; spangled.

c **1420** Lydg. *Assembly of Gods* 266 A mantell..Of blak sylke, purfylyd with poudryd hermyne. **1590** Spenser *F.Q.* iii. ii. 25 On his shield..He bore a crowned little Ermelin, That deckt the azure field with her fayre pouldred skin. **1864** Boutell *Her. Hist. & Pop.* ii. (ed. 3) 12 *Powdered* or *Poudrée* is substituted for *Semée*.

b. *Zool.* Marked with numerous minute dots or spots closely placed, as if dusted over with powder. Said esp. of moths.

1832 J. Rennie *Conspect Butterfl. & Moths* 57 The Powdered Quaker (*Orthosia sparsa*). *Ibid.* 62 The Powdered Rustic (*Caradrina superstes*). *Ibid.* 89 The Powdered Wainscot (*Simyra renosa*)... Wings..first pair hoary, sprinkled with minute black spots.

4. Of the hair or skin: Dressed with powder as a cosmetic. Also said of the person. Also in parasynthetic combination.

1655 *Songs Costume* (Percy Soc.) 146 A dresse of powdered hayre. **1716** Gay *Trivia* i. 127 The powder'd footman..Beneath his flapping Hat secures his Hair. **1848** Dickens *Dombey* vii, The greater part of the furniture was of the powdered-head and pig-tail period. *Ibid.* xxxviii, The powdered-headed ancestor. **1863** 'Ouida' *Held in Bondage* (1870) 10 The powdered servant who opened the door.

†5. [? f. powder *sb.*¹ 3 + -ed².] Charged with, or fired by, gunpowder. Also *fig.* *Obs. rare.*

1575 J. B. in *Gascoigne's Wks.* ¶¶¶¶ij b, In bloudie broyles, where pouldred shot was rife. *a* **1618** Sylvester *Tobacco Battered* Ded. to W. Loe, You'll need no Warning to avoid our Peal; Nor are in Level of our Poudred Pen.

6. Reduced to powder or dust; pulverized.

1591 Spenser *Ruines Rome* xxvii, Againe on foote to reare her pouldred corse. **1646** Sir T. Browne *Pseud. Ep.* 53 Powdered glasse emits no fume or exhalation although it bee laid upon a red hot iron. **1765** *Univ. Mag.* XXXVII. 320/2 Ground and powdered refined sugar. **1864** Bowen *Logic* x. 326 Powdered chalk..will always be insoluble.

7. Applied to foods that have been reduced to the form of a powder by dehydration.

1889 in A. Davis *Package & Print* (1967) Pl. 69 Pancake flour—self-rising mixture—..powdered milk without butter fat, corn sugar, [etc.]. **1909** *Chem. Abstr.* 933 Powdered milks are made to contain varying amounts of fat by the removal of more or less fat cream before evaporation. **1917** *Official Gaz.* (U.S. Patent Office) 2 Jan. 363/1 The Cabell Company, Baltimore, Md... Velvet *Particular description of goods.*—Powdered Egg. *Claims use* since Sept. 1, 1916. **1917** *Bakers Rev.* Nov. 13 (Advt.), *Velvet* Powdered Egg, made from selected fresh hen eggs, is entirely and instantly soluble. **1919** *N.Y. Times* 14 Dec. iii. 5/1 Dry eggs from China..include the white of egg, the yolk of egg, and powdered whole egg. **1925** T. M. Rector *Sci. Preservation Food* xii. 172 Hermetic sealing is not used in the preservation of eggs and egg products though there is certainly a field for it in 'powdered' egg. **1935** *Economist* 3 Aug. 226/2 As for powdered and condensed milk,..these imported milk products are going to be made artificially scarce. **1943** *Industr. & Engin. Chem.* XXXV. 1204/2 The losses of vitamin D in powdered whole egg during storage were studied at two temperatures, 15° and 98·6°F. **1953** *Ann. Reg. 1952* 153 The provision of powdered milk every day for over a million children. **1972** G. Durrell *Catch me a Colobus* v. 84 Complan, a sort of powdered milk which we found was very useful for rearing baby animals. **1980** *Sunday Times* (Colour Suppl.) 20 Jan. 70/1, I have orange juice..then..a cup of powdered coffee.

'powderer. *rare.* [f. powder *v.*¹ + -er¹.] One who powders: see the verb.

1555 W. Watreman *Fardle Facions* E v b, The seasoners and embalmers of the body (whome they calle poulderers).

ˈpowder-flask. A case for carrying gunpowder, formerly usually of horn (see next), later of leather or metal, usually with a special device for measuring out a charge of powder; used by soldiers and sportsmen: = FLASK *sb.*^{2} 2.

1753 CHAMBERS *Cycl. Supp.*, *Powder-flasks*, in artillery, are most commonly made of horn, of any convenient size and figure, to carry powder for priming of cannon. **1837** W. IRVING *Capt. Bonneville* (1849) 360 A powder-flask, which a clerk had purchased from a Blackfoot warrior. *a* **1845** SYD. SMITH *Wks.* (1859) II. 236/1 Irish Protestants whose.. dinner-table is regularly spread with knife, fork, and cocked pistol; salt-cellar and powder-flask.

ˈpowder-horn. A powder-flask made of the horn of an ox or cow with a wooden or metal bottom at the larger end. Sometimes applied to a powder-flask of some other material.

1533 *Acc. Ld. High Treas. Scot.* VI. 162 Item, ane pulder horne. **1695** *Lond. Gaz.* No. 3100/3 The Musket of one of them.. went off, and set his Bandeliers on fire, and they the Powder-Horns which hung in the Gun-Room. *a* **1745** SWIFT *Direct. Servants* Introd. §35 You may.. stick your candle in a bottle, or.. in a powder-horn. **1876** BANCROFT *Hist. U.S.* IV. xv. 419 The hardy backswoodsman,.. armed with a rifle, a powder-horn, and a pouch for shot and bullets. **1906** *Athenæum* 1 Dec. 687/1 Illustrations of a papier mâché powder-horn.. decorated with designs by him.

ˈpowderiness. [f. POWDERY + -NESS.] The quality or condition of being powdery; pulverulence.

1820 L. HUNT *Indicator* No. 35 (1822) I. 275 The melting powderiness of peppermint.

powdering (ˈpaʊdərɪŋ), *vbl. sb.* [f. POWDER *v.*^{1} + -ING^{1}.] The action of POWDER *v.*^{1}, or the result of this.

1. The action of sprinkling or dusting something with powder; *spec.* the application of powder as a cosmetic to the hair or face.

c **1440** *Promp. Parv.* 411/1 Powderynge, wythe powder, *pulverisacio.* **1599** B. JONSON *Cynthia's Rev.* Ded., It is not pould'ring, perfuming, and every day smelling of the taylor, that converteth to a beautiful object. **1656** *Artif. Handsom.* 78 They forbid all painting, patching, and powdering. **1855** MACAULAY *Hist. Eng.* xxi. IV. 673 [He] was very particular on his last day about the powdering and curling of his wig.

b. A deposit of powdery substance sprinkled upon a surface; a thin sprinkling (of something).

1834 ARNOLD in Stanley *Life & Corr.* (1844) I. vii. 373 We had no snow in the valleys, but frequently a thick powdering on the higher mountains. **1897** *Allbutt's Syst. Med.* II. 139 On the face and ears it [i.e. Scarlatinal peeling] usually takes the form of a fine powdering. **1902** *Westm. Gaz.* 25 Nov. 10/1 On the.. 19th and 20th a powdering of snow showed on the southern side of Monte Bignone.

2. The seasoning or preserving of food with salt or spice. Also *fig.* ? *Obs.*

c **1450** *Two Cookery-bks.* 69 Powdryng of beef, or eny other fressh flessh. **1580** HOLLYBAND *Treas. Fr. Tong*, *Salure*, poudring, or salting. **1587** GOLDING *De Mornay* xiii. (1592) 196 The Deathes of the giltlesse.. is but a powdering of their vertues, to preserue them to the vse of posteritie. **1615** [see POTTING *vbl. sb.*^{1} 3]. **1630** J. TAYLOR (Water P.) *Gt. Eater Kent* 16 Hee is profitable in.. sauing the charge of salt; for his appetite will not waite and attend the powdring.

3. Decoration with spots or small figures disposed as if sprinkled over a surface. **b.** *concr.* (usually *pl.*) Such figures themselves collectively; *esp.* the spots on a heraldic fur, or small charges (e.g. fleurs-de-lys) scattered over the field.

1405–6 *Norwich Sacrist's Roll* (MS.), In serico et in rosis de auro emptis pro powderyng. **1480** *Wardr. Acc. Edw. IV* (1830) 116 Powderings made of bogy leggs. **1505** *Acc. Ld. High Treas. Scot.* III. 41 Item for xxx^{m} powderingis to the samyn; [the Kingis rob riall] ilk hundreth iij *s.*; summa.. xlv *li.* **1602** SEGAR *Hon. Mil. & Civ.* IV. xxii. 238 A Duke's eldest sonne is borne in the degree of a Marquesse, and weares as many powdrings as a Marquesse. **1727–41** CHAMBERS *Cycl.*, *Powderings*, in building, a term some-times used for devices serving to fill up vacant spaces, in carved works: also in escutcheons, writings, &c. **1766** PORNY *Heraldry* iii. (1777) 26 Ermine is a Field Argent, with small points or spots Sable, in the form of little Triangles, which in Heraldry are generally called Powdering. **1880** *Academy* 18 Dec. 446/3 The embroiderers.. did not seek for novelty; diapers and powderings, even angel and saint, were reproduced over and over again without much change except of arrangement.

4. *attrib.* and *Comb.*: as ***powdering things***; **powdering-closet** = *powdering-room*; **powdering-dress, -gown** a garment worn over the ordinary clothes to protect them while the hair was being powdered; †**powdering-house**, a building in which meat was 'powdered' or preserved with salt or spices; **powdering-mill** a mill for pulverizing some substance (as ore, snuff); †**powdering pearls**, small pearls used for 'powdering' (see 3); **powdering-room**, a room appropriated to powdering the hair; **powdering-slipper**: see quot.; †**powdering trough**, a trough in which meat was 'powdered'. See also POWDERING-TUB.

1786 MISS E. CLAYTON in *Mrs. Delany's Life & Corr.* Ser. II. III. 399 A bed-chamber, two dressing-rooms, two *powdering-closets. **1875** MISS THACKERAY *Miss Angel* xv, There was a powdering-closet on the second story of the house. **1776** MRS. HARRIS in *Priv. Lett. Ld. Malmesbury* (1870) I. 347 In his hurry, he threw his *powdering dress over his shoulders. *c* **1770** T. ERSKINE *Barber* in *Poet. Reg.* (1810) 328 Rob'd in a flannel *powd'ring goun. **1900** DOYLE *Green Flag, Capt. Sharkey* i, He wore a loose damask powdering-gown secured by a cord round the waist. **1580** HOLLYBAND *Treas. Fr. Tong*, *Vne Saliére*, a *poudring house, a salte seller. **1606** in Nichols *Progr. Jas. I* (1828) II. 61 *note*, 10 oz. and halfe of rag *poudring pearles. *a* **1774** J. & R. ADAM *Archit.* II. pl. 1 By means of an intersol over the closet and *powdering room, we have introduced a servant's sleeping-room adjoining to this apartment. **1900** BESANT in *Daily News* 3 Sept. 6/2, I wish I could show you one room in the house. It was the old 'powdering-room'. **182.** MAR. EDGEWORTH *Parent's Assist.*, *Basket-woman* (1856) 469 'These slippers are meant ——'. 'For *powdering-slippers, miss'... 'To wear when people are powdering their hair.. that they may not spoil their other shoes'. **1786** MME. D'ARBLAY *Diary* 24 July, We help her [the Queen] off with her gown, and on with her *powdering things. **1612** in *Antiquary* Jan. (1906) 29 In the larder... Twoe *powdringe Troves with covers, a powdringe Tubbe, twoe lesser tubbes.

ˈpowdering, *ppl. a.*^{1} [f. POWDER *v.*^{1} + -ING^{2}.] That powders; that sprinkles with powder.

1799 J. ROBERTSON *Agric. Perth* 318 The powdering particles, which we see on the grass and trees. **1832–53** W. MILLER in *Whistle-binkie* (Scotch Songs) Ser. III. 107 You've come.. Wi' your crispin' an' poutherin' gear, John Frost. **1880** BLACKMORE *Mary Anerley* II. xviii. 306 Some of the powdering willow dusted her bright luxuriant locks with gold.

ˈpowdering, *ppl. a.*^{2} [f. POWDER *v.*^{2} + -ING^{2}.] Rushing impetuously; *fig.* impetuous, violent.

1619 BALCANQUAL in *Hales' Gold. Rem.* II. (1673) 73 They were called in and dismist with such a powdering speech as I doubt not.. your Lordship hath heard with grief enough.

ˈpowdering-ˌtub. [f. prec. vbl. sb. + TUB.]

1. A tub in which the flesh of animals is 'powdered', or salted and pickled.

1530 PALSGR. 257/2 Poudryng tubbe, *salover.* **1534** in Peacock *Eng. Ch. Furniture* (1866) 189 Item a powtheringe tubb with a coverynge. **1612** [see POWDERING *trough*]. **1756** NUGENT *Gr. Tour, Netherl.* I. 44 On Sunday, a piece of salt meat is usually taken out of the powdering tub. **1841–4** EMERSON *Ess.*, *Love* Wks. (Bohn) I. 77 Its gravest discourse has a savour of hams and powdering-tubs.

†**2.** Humorously applied to a sweating-tub used for the cure of venereal disease. *Obs.*

1599 SHAKS. *Hen. V*, II. i. 79 From the Poudring tub of infamy, Fetch forth the Lazar Kite of Cressids kinde, Doll Teare-sheete. **1678** BUTLER *Hud.* III. ii. 980 Whence some Tub-holders-forth have made In Powdring-Tubs, their richest Trade. **1709** O. DYKES *Eng. Prov. & Refl.* (ed. 2) 83 Pickl'd up to the very Nose in the Powdering-Tub of Sin and Salivation. **1710** *Brit. Apollo* II. No. 90. 2/2 Away to the Powdering-Tub and burnt Mutton.

powderize (ˈpaʊdəraɪz), *v.* [f. POWDER *sb.*^{1} + -IZE.] **a.** = POWDER *v.*^{1} 3 b. *rare.* **b.** = POWDER *v.*^{1} 6.

a **1800** S. PEGGE *Anecdotes Eng. Lang.* (1803) 259 Many words will admit *-ize* for the termination. A Hair-Dresser powder*izes*, while a Chemist.. pulver*izes* [etc.]. **1903** *Sci. Amer. Suppl.* 18 Apr. 22818/1 Only one thing can be done to lighten the task, and that is to powderize the soap when the mixed materials are still warm. **1978** *Nature* 20 Apr. 715/2 The material was powderised and partially attacked by a mixture of hydrofluoric and hydrochloric acids.

ˈpowderless, *a.* [f. POWDER *sb.*^{1} + -LESS.]

a. Destitute of powder; not powdered.

1887 *Atlantic Monthly* Sept. 323 His brown suit, his fur cap, his powderless hair.. betrayed him [Franklin in Paris] at once.

b. Not employing powder.

1953 *Photoengravers Bull.* XLIII. 171 The key to powderless etching in the Dow etching development lies in the chemical composition of the bath. **1959** *Times* 14 Jan. 12/4 Another precision etching system, the Lithotex powderless etcher, is being manufactured in Britain. **1967** V. STRAUSS *Printing Industry* v. 217/1 Though conventional etching methods are still used.., they are progressively replaced throughout the industry by powderless etching. **1978** *Penrose Ann.* LXXI. 162 Powderless etching is still rare [in India] and electronic engraving extremely so.

ˈpowder-man. †**a.** ? A dealer in gunpowder. *Obs.* **b.** A man who supplies the guns with powder on board a man-of-war. **c.** One who attends to the powder used in blasting operations, etc.

1669 STURMY *Mariner's Mag.* v. xii. 67 . Every Gunner may have his Peter ready made refined and in Meal at the Powder-mens, or Chandlers. **1859** F. A. GRIFFITHS *Artill. Man.* (1862) 226 Stationary powdermen are allotted to every two guns. **1886** *Sci. Amer.* LIV. 85/2 In driving the heading, each of the three shifts is made up of a boss, 4 drill men, 4 helpers on drills, 1 powder man, 1 car man, and 2 laborers.

ˈpowder-ˌmonkey. **a.** A humorous term for a powder-boy on board ship. Also *fig.* Now also (*U.S.*) a term for a member of a blasting crew; = POWDER-MAN c.

1682 SHADWELL *Medal* Ep. A iv, Heaven keep us from Juries such as will give 800 l. dammages to a Powder-monkey. **1759** *Compl. Letter-writer* (ed. 6) 225 Her powder-monkey was Dick Cummings, ogling and winking. **1815** SCOTT *Guy M.* lii, Ellangowan had him placed as cabin-boy, or powder-monkey on board an armed sloop. **1879** *Cassell's Techn. Educ.* IV. 62/1 When his son Henry was twelve years old, he was employed as a 'powder-monkey' in making and filling blank and ball cartridges. **1926** *Amer. Speech* II. 87/2 Dynamite is brought to the miner by the *powder monkey.* **1937** *Nat. Geogr. Mag.* Aug. 149/1 Hither and yon darted the 'powder monkeys', packing dynamite in the holes, shooting loose great masses of salt, which others broke up and loaded into trucks. **1939** W. FAULKNER *Wild Palms* 118 Suits from wop pick-and-shovel men and bohunk powder-monkeys and chink ore-trimmers. **1951** *Publ. Amer. Dial. Soc.* xv. 74 *Monkey* in various combinations has become a favorite term for handyman. There are *derrick monkeys, pump monkeys, boiler monkeys,* and *powder monkeys.* **1976** M. MACHLIN *Pipeline* xviii. 227 This time they wanted two powder monkeys, a couple of drillers.. and four jobs for straight camp labor.

b. (See quot. 1893.)

1882 JEFFERIES *Bevis* III. iv. 63 How to take the honey was not so easily settled, till they thought of making a powder-monkey, and so smoking them out. **1893** *Wilts. Gloss.*, *Powder-monkey*, damp gunpowder, moulded into a 'devil' or cake which will smoulder slowly, used by boys for stupefying a wasp's nest.

†**ˈpowderous,** *a. Obs. rare*$^{-1}$. [f. POWDER *sb.*^{1} + -OUS.] Apt to crumble to powder, friable.

1601 HOLLAND *Pliny* XVI. xl. I. 490 Cherry-tree wood is pliable, but drier and more powderous.

ˈpowder-puff.

1. a. A soft pad, usually of down, for applying powder to the skin. **b.** An instrument like a small bellows formerly used for powdering the hair.

a **1704** T. BROWN *Pleas. Lett. to Gent.* Wks. 1709 III. II. 16 A Powder-puff. **1841** ORDERSON *Creol.* xix. 229 This.. made him.. pass the powder-puff.. over his hair. **1851** in *Illustr. Lond. News* 5 Aug. (1854) 119/3 Occupations of People.. Powder-puff maker. **1882** MISS BRADDON *Mt. Royal* II. x. 206 Topsy and Mopsy were improved by the powder puff.

2. *transf.* **a.** ? Contemptuously applied to a man with powdered hair, a fop. **b.** Applied to a young gull with downy feathers.

1731 FIELDING *Lottery* ii, Is this the fellow for whom I am unknown? this powderpuff. **1891** *Daily News* 14 Oct. 2/8 Myriads of gulls.. sitting about, of all sizes, from tiny powder-puffs to the stately wide-winged, full grown birds.

ˈpowder-room. [f. POWDER *sb.*^{1} + ROOM *sb.*^{1}]

a. A room on board ship in which the gunpowder is stored, the powder-magazine in a ship.

1627 CAPT. SMITH *Seaman's Gram.* ii. 13 It is.. very dangerous lying ouer the Powder-roome. **1855** MACAULAY *Hist. Eng.* xviii. IV. 239 Now and then a loud explosion announced that the flames had reached a powder room.

b. = *powder closet* s.v. POWDER *sb.*^{1} 5 b.

1908 'F. DANBY' *Heart of Child* xv. 250 He liked to see.. his Staffordshire pottery en-niched in the quaint powder-room, opening out of the drawing-room. **1946** J. W. DAY *Harvest Adventure* xiv. 243 Look at the old drawings of Ockwells in Lysons' *Magna Britannica* [*sic*] and other works, and you will see that, a hundred years ago, the powder-room window was completely blocked up. **1966** M. M. PEGLER *Dict. Interior Design* (1967) 351 *Powder room*, originally a corner or small closet in the bedroom of an 18th-century house where one could go to have one's hair powdered.

c. A women's cloak-room or lavatory in a hotel or shop; *gen.* a lavatory. Also *attrib.*

1941 B. SCHULBERG *What makes Sammy Run?* xi. 272 She had just run into Laurette in the powder room. **1945** MENCKEN *Amer. Lang.* Suppl. I. 640 During the days of Prohibition some learned speak-easy proprietor in New York hit upon the happy device of calling his retiring-room for female boozers a *powder-room.* **1958** *Times Lit. Suppl.* 13 June 323/2 But there is too much of the language of powder-room chatter ('When Terry asked me to marry him, as I thought I hoped he would..') and platitude for her tale to gain and hold sympathy. **1959** D. DU MAURIER *Breaking Point* 219 The call-box was just opposite the ladies' powder room. **1977** *Time* 5 Dec. 68/3 While the play is laced with affectionately bantering humor and a gamy ration of powder-room candor, the characters are stereotypical.

powder snow. [f. POWDER *sb.*^{1} + SNOW *sb.*^{1}] A newly fallen, light, dry snow. Also *attrib.*

1929 F. SMYTHE *Climbs & Ski Runs* xi. 169 The *staublawine* or powder-snow avalanche is of little danger to the ski-runner. **1946** P. BOTTOME *Lifeline* xxiii. 253 He himself moved over the light powder snow like a soundless ghost. **1955** E. HILLARY *High Adventure* 159 High on the mountain a cloud of powder snow was being blown off the ridge. **1972** D. HASTON *In High Places* xi. 118 It was obvious what was happening—a huge powder snow avalanche was passing. **1974** *Listener* 17 Jan. 76/1 Nice sunshine, powder-snow skiing.

powdery (ˈpaʊdərɪ), *a.* [f. POWDER *sb.*^{1} + -Y.]

1. a. Of the nature or consistence of powder; consisting of fine loose particles; pulverulent; dusty.

1426 LYDG. *De Guil. Pilgr.* 10107 Wyth powdry sondys out off noumbre, Wych hyr passage so encoumbre. **1767** PERCIVAL in *Phil. Trans.* LVII. 230 A considerable portion of it.. subsided in a powdery form to the bottom of the glass. **1799** WORDSW. *Lucy Gray* vii, Her feet disperse the powdery snow, That rises up like smoke. **1884** BOWER & SCOTT *De Bary's Phaner.* 562 The cells.. forming, especially when dry, a loose, powdery mass.

b. Easily disintegrated into powder; friable.

a **1728** WOODWARD *Fossils* II. 36 A brown, powdery Spar. They say it holds Iron. Found amongst the Iron-Ore.

†**2.** Of the nature of gunpowder; inflammable, explosive. *Obs.*

1611 SPEED *Hist. Gt. Brit.* IX. xx. §14 The lighted matches of sedition found powdry spirits, and wonderfull correspondence.

3. Covered with or full of powder; having a deposit of powder; dusty.

1708 OZELL tr. *Boileau's Lutrin* 48 When from his Powdry Roost the Bird of Night.. takes his Flight. **1784** WOODWARD in *Phil. Trans.* LXXIV. 423 The powdery head is covered with a loose campanulated cap. **1872** GEO. ELIOT *Middlem.*

lix, That pollen which the bees carry off (having no idea how powdery they are). **1874** SYMONDS *Italy & Greece* 291 Delicate golden auriculas with powdery leaves and stems. **1879** *St. George's Hosp. Rep.* IX. 738 The skin is everywhere wonderfully white, in some regions raised into little powdery eminences.

4. *Comb.*, as ***powdery-looking***; **powdery mildew**, a parasitic fungus belonging to the family Erysiphaceæ, or the disease it causes in plants, characterized by a white, floury covering of conidia on the parts attacked.

1875 HUXLEY & MARTIN *Elem. Biol.* (1877) 38 Note the powdery-looking upper surface, white in young specimens. **1889** *Jrnl. Mycol.* V. 214 (*heading*) Powdery mildew of the bean. **1913** G. & I. MASSEE *Mildews, Rusts & Smuts* 36 The entire group [*sc.* Erysiphaceæ] is often spoken of as powdery mildews, on account of the dense masses of conidia that are produced, and rest on the white patches of mycelium, giving them the appearance of having been sprinkled with flour. **1936** *Jrnl. Agric. Res.* LII. 645 (*title*) The diurnal cycle of the powdery mildew *Erysiphe polygoni.* **1978** P. P. PIRONE *Dis. & Pests Ornamental Plants* (ed. 5) i. 9/2 Powdery mildews are fungi that grow superficially on the leaves and stems of their hosts.

'powdike, 'podike. *local.* Forms: 3–5 **pokediche, -dike, -dyke;** 6–8 **powdyke, -dike,** 7 **poedike,** 7–8 **podike.** [First element originally *poke*: origin unascertained; the second is DIKE *sb.*[1], sense 5 or 7, or DITCH *sb.* 4, an earthen bank.] The name of an ancient dike or embankment raised to keep the fen waters out of Marshland, in the part of Norfolk west of the Great Ouse; also of a later work, the ***new powdike***, constructed further to the south for the same purpose.

The old powdike was raised *c* 1223; it ran from W. to E. separating Marshland from Bardolph Fen. The new powdike was begun in 1423; it ran along the north brink of Well Creek, forming the southern boundary of Stow and Downham Fen. There was also a ***little powdike***, at the west end of the old powdike. See the Map in Dugdale *Hist. Imbanking & Drayning*, 1662, 1772, xlvi.

1293 *Pat. 21 Edw. I* m. 10 (P.R.O.) Forsatum quod vocatur Pokediche.. ab antiquo levatum.. pro defensione et salvacione partium ipsarum contra aquarum inundaciones. **1350** *Pat. 23 Edw. III*, pt. 1 m. 29 d, Fossatum vocatum Pokedyk in Merssheland in com. Norf. **1423** (in Dugdale, as above) Pokediche, Pokedyke. **1530–1** *Act. 22 Hen. VIII*, c. 11 Dyvers evyll dysposed personnes.. maliciously at dyverse.. times hathe.. broken vp dyvers parties of the Dyke called the newe Powdyke in Marsheland in the Countie of Norfolke, and the brokyn Dyke other wyse called Old feld Dyke by Marsheland, in the Ile of Elye. **1662** DUGDALE *Hist. Imbanking*, etc. xlvi. 245/1 Upon this occasion, by a common consent amongst them, was the old Podike first raised, about the year MCCXXIII (7 Hen. 3). *Ibid.*, The said Bank called Podike. *Ibid.* 264 (*Margin*, The making of the new Pow dike, 1 Hen. 6, 12 April) That there should be another Wall or Bank made new on the North side of Salterys lode brink, by all the Land-holders throughout Marshland. **1762** *Gentl. Mag.* 237 The old podike, the defensive bank to the country of Marshland in Norfolk, against foreign waters, was cut through by persons unknown. **1769** BLACKSTONE *Comm.* IV. xvii. 245 By statute 22 Hen. VIII. c. 11. perversely and maliciously to cut down or destroy the powdike, in the fens of Norfolk and Ely, is felony.

†powe, *int. Obs.* An imitation of a knock.

c **1580** JEFFERIE *Bugbears* III. ii. in *Archiv Stud. Neu. Spr.* (1897), I will knocke. powe! ho? who is in the house?

powe, obs. f. PAW *sb.*[1]; var. POUGH *v. Obs.*

powee, variant of POWESE, the Curassow.

Powellism ('paʊəlɪz(ə)m). [f. the name of John Enoch *Powell* (born 1912) + -ISM.] The political and economic policies advocated by J. Enoch Powell; *spec.* one of restricting or terminating the immigration of coloured people into the United Kingdom.

1965 *Economist* 17 July 217/1 In the past few months a new word has found its way into British politics: Powellism. **1968** *Guardian* 9 Sept. 6/1 Mr Enoch Powell's alternative.. is a drastic move towards laissez-faire economics and a stopping of immigration. Powellism is gaining ground within the Conservative ranks. **1972** M. WILLIAMS *Inside Number 10* x. 254 Although we realized only too well that to dissociate Labour from Powellism was not a winner in electoral terms, it was decided unhesitatingly that Harold should leave no doubt about where the Labour Party stood on matters of race. **1973** C. MULLARD *Black Brit.* II. vi. 66 It [*sc.* the Institute of Race Relations] has remained on safe, non-controversial ground, arousing as much black scorn as Powellism. **1977** M. WALKER *National Front* v. 127 The ghost of Powellism in the parliamentary party is still not laid... Powellism, Young's own ambition to lead the Club, and the bitter debates on the EEC in 1971 were.. enough to account for the crisis.

So **'Powellist** *a.* and *sb.*; **'Powellite** *a.* and *sb.*[1]

1965 *Economist* 5 June 1129/2 The Conservatives should not turn Powellite in opposition to an incomes policy. **1966** [see *blue-water school* s.v. BLUE *a.* 13]. **1968** *Guardian* 26 Apr. 22/2 (*heading*) MPs' temperatures soar as Powellite sparks fly. **1968** *Manch. Guardian Weekly* 5 Sept. 12 The Conservatives.. are likely for a year or two to be more Powellist in economics. **1968** *Peace News* 29 Nov. 8 Working-class Powellists.. are not so much thinking like colonialists, but rather as aborigines. **1977** M. WALKER *National Front* iv. 90 The NF was deeply concerned that it had missed the Powellite boat, and that it was not expanding as it should. *Ibid.* iv. 93 Stories in the press about a split in the movement between Powellites and the rest.

powellite[2] ('paʊəlaɪt). *Min.* [Named 1891, after Major J. W. Powell: see -ITE[1].] Molybdate and tungstate of calcium, of yellow colour and resinous lustre.

1897 *Amer. Jrnl. Sc.* Ser. III. XLI. 138 Powellite—calcium molybdate; a new mineral species.

Powellize ('paʊəlaɪz), *v.* [f. the name of William *Powell*, of London, who invented the process + -IZE.] *trans.* To treat (timber) by boiling in a solution of sugar so as to preserve it and reduce shrinkage. So **'Powellized** *ppl. a.*; **'Powellizing** *vbl. sb.*

1903 *Sci. Amer. Suppl.* 5 Sept. 23139/1 The London city authorities.. intend to repave the Strand thoroughfare with 15,000 Powellized blocks. **1913** *Chambers's Jrnl.* Aug. 621/1 Seeing that elm is plentiful and extremely low in price, Powellising should result in its more extended application. *Ibid.*, After being Powellised it becomes a very handsome and hard wood. **1929** *Encycl. Brit.* XXII. 222/1 Extensive tests carried out with Powellized sleepers on Indian railways give good results.

power ('paʊə(r), paʊə(r)), *sb.*[1] Forms: see below. [ME. *poër, poeir, pouer* (pu'ɛːr), a. AF. *poër, poair, pouair* = OF. *poër, poeir* (whence *poir, povoir*, mod.F. *pouvoir*), sb. use of vb. inf. *poeir, pouoir, povoir, pouvoir*:—earlier **podeir* (*podir* in *Strasb. Oaths* 842) = Pr., Sp., Pg. *poder*, It. *potere* to be able:—late pop. L. *potēre*, which, by the 8th c. in vulgar speech, supplanted *posse* (pr. pple. *potent-*, perf. *potui*) to be able: see Diez. The *v* in Fr. *povoir* was developed by hiatus in *poir*; the *w* in Eng. arose from change of *o* in *poër* to *ou, ow*. The spelling *power* has been the prevailing one from 14th c. Phonetic development (po'ɛːr, pu'ɛːr, 'puːɛr, 'paʊə(r), in north. dial. 'puːər, puːr).]

A. Illustration of Forms.

α. (3) 4 **poer, poeir,** (3) 4 **pouwer,** 4–5 **pouwere, pouer, powere,** 5 **pouere, pouoir, poweer, -eir, pouar,** 6 **powar, -are,** *Sc.* **pover,** (3) 4– **power.**

1297 R. GLOUC. (Rolls) 4523 Gret *poer of yrlonde Modred him wan al so. *c* **1330** R. BRUNNE *Chron. Wace* (Rolls) 588 Poer ynow schal come to me. **1297** R. GLOUC. (Rolls) 7639 Hii adde.. gret *poeir sone anhonde. *c* **1290** *S. Eng. Leg.* I. 127/724 Þe Erchebischop of Euerwyke fondede for-to bringe A-cord and loue bi is *pouwer bi-twene thomas and þe king. *Ibid.* 34/30 A-ȝein mine godes *pouwere. *c* **1400** *Destr. Troy* 10658 Fore to the fight with a fell *pouer. *a* **1425** *Cursor M.* 3966 (Gött.) He com egayn him wid gret pouer. *Ibid.* 9780 (Trin.) For to haue *powere þere. *c* **1420** *Anturs of Arth.* xiv, Haue petè on the pore, quyl thou hase *pouere. **1447–8** Q. MARG. in Willis & Clark *Cambridge* (1886) I. Introd. 63 To haue licence and *pouoir to ley the furst stone. *c* **1470** *Golagros & Gaw.* 412 With all thair strang *poweir. **1486** in *Exch. Rolls Scotl.* X. 100 *note*, His factouris havand *pouar of hym. **1535** STEWART *Cron. Scot.* (Rolls) II. 231 Traistand.. he micht na *powar be.. agane tha kingis thre. **1538** STARKEY *England* I. ii. 35 Conuenyent powar and strenghth. **1554–9** in *Songs & Ball.* (1860) 11 Extort *poware, whiche ys no goodly facioun. **1535** STEWART *Cron. Scot.* (Rolls) II. 624 Quhilk efter him .. Come hame agane with *pover of the new. *c* **1290** *S. Eng. Leg.* I. 20/49 Þis holi Abbod.. hadde gret *power With þe king Eadmund. **1390** GOWER *Conf.* III. 376 (Bodley MS. 902) And doth what lith in his power.

β. 4–6 **pore,** 5–6 **poure,** 5–7 **powre,** 6 ? **poore, poour,** 6–7 **pour,** 7–8 **pow'r,** 9 *Sc.* and *north. dial.* **poor** (puːr).

[**1297** R. GLOUC. (Rolls) 2049 He nom wiþ him.. gret *pore ynou.] **1461** MARG. PASTON in *P. Lett.* II. 62 Ye ar myche behold to the Meyir and to Gylberd,.. for feythfully they owe yow good wyll to ther porys. *c* **1511** *1st Eng. Bk. Amer.* (Arb.) Introd. 33/2 They haue nat the pore to come out of that deserte. *c* **1440** *York Myst.* xxi. 157 The dragons *poure.. distroyed haue I. **1555** EDEN *Decades* 36 A poure of armed men. *c* **1440** *Generydes* 15 A man of grete *powre. **1591** SHAKS. *Two Gent.* II. vi. 4 That Powre which gaue me first my oath. **1529** WOLSEY in *Four C. Eng. Lett.* (1880) 11 As my *poore shall increase. **1575** LANEHAM *Let.* (1871) 1 But also haue *poour.. to go and too see things sight worthy. **1546** *Suppl. Commons* in *Four Supplic.* (1871) 63 The *pours, whome God hathe ordeyned. **1638** Pourfull [see POWERFUL *a.* 2]. **1697** DRYDEN *Virg. Georg.* III. 500 The Western Winds with vital *Pow'r Call forth the tender Grass, and budding Flower.

B. Signification. **I.** As a quality or property.

1. a. Ability to do or effect something or anything, or to act upon a person or thing. (Cf. quot. 1690).

c **1325** *Spec. Gy Warw.* 215 And ȝaf to man fre power To chese,.. Off god and yuel shed to make. **1382** WYCLIF *John* x. 18, I haue power for to putte it, and I haue power for to take it eftsoone. **1390** GOWER *Conf.* III. 2 Him is benome The pouer bothe of hond and fot. **1470–85** MALORY *Arthur* xv. ii. 657 It shalle not lye in your power.. to perysshe me as moche as a threde. **1580** BABINGTON *Exp. Lord's Prayer* (1596) 200 That he would.. keepe vs from apposings aboue our power to satisfie. **1611** BIBLE *Transl. Pref.* 2 By his power and wisdome he built a Temple. **1690** LOCKE *Hum. Und.* II. vii. §8 Power.. is another of those simple Ideas which we receive from Sensation and Reflection. For observing in our selves, that we do and can think, and that we can, at pleasure, move several parts of our Bodies which were at rest; the effects also, that natural Bodies are able to produce in one another, occurring every moment to our Senses, we both these ways get the Idea of Power. *Ibid.* xxi. §2 Power.. is twofold, viz. as able to make, or able to receive any change: The one may be called *Active*, and the other *Passive Power.* **1713** BERKELEY *Hylas & Phil.* I. Wks. 1871 I. 287 Is it not in your power to open your eyes? **1741–2** GRAY *Agrippina* 40 The power To judge of weights and measures. **1785** REID *Let.* Wks. I. 65/2 Power to produce an effect, supposes power not to produce it; otherwise it is not power but necessity. **1853** LYNCH *Self-Improv.* v. 113 Money is power—power for bread and power for tinsel. **1858** LARDNER *Hand-bk. Nat. Phil., Hydrost.*, etc. 46 Fishes have the power of changing their bulk by the voluntary distension of an air-vessel. **1861** W. H. RUSSELL in *Morning Chron.* 3 Aug., Ready to afford any information in their power.

b. With *a* and *pl.* A particular faculty of body or mind.

1483 CAXTON *Gold. Leg.* 352/1 In theyr bodye whiche is made of four complexions and in theyr Sowle in whiche ben thre poures. **1526** *Pilgr. Perf.* (W. de W. 1531) 148 Memory, reason, & wyll. And these ben the thre powers of the soule. *c* **1540** BOORDE *The boke for to Lerne* C iij b, Moderate slepe .. doth anymat and comforte all the naturall, animall, and spyrytuall, powers of man. **1665** GLANVILL *Scepsis Sci.* xiii. 71 When we speak of Powers and Faculties of the Soul, we intend not to assert.. their real distinction from it, or each other, but only a modal diversity. **1736** BUTLER *Anal.* I. i. Wks. 1874 I. 28 Several things.. affect all our living powers, and at length suspend the exercise of them. **1869** FREEMAN *Norm. Conq.* III. xii. 81 The laureate of William taxes his powers to the uttermost to set forth the greatness of the prince.

c. Sometimes the plural does not imply different faculties, but power put forth in various directions or on various occasions.

a **1586** SIDNEY *Ps.* XX. v, I know that He heares mee, Yea, heares with powers and helps of helpfull hand. **1725** WATTS *Logic* I. vi. §9 We must consider it in its Powers and Capacities either to do or suffer. **1804** ABERNETHY *Surg. Obs.* 55 The patient, whose vital powers had long been greatly exhausted, died. **1852** R. KNOX *Gt. Artists & Gt. Anat.* 174 His powers of attention, and his educability were admirable. **1878** BROWNING *La Saisiaz* 199 Powers that fain Else would soar, condemned to grovel.

2. a. Ability to act or affect something strongly; physical or mental strength; might; vigour, energy; force of character; telling force, effect.

c **1440** *Promp. Parv.* 411/1 Power, or strengthe,.. *potestas, robur, fortitudo, nisus, vigor.* **1486** *Bk. St. Albans* d iij, The bellis that yowre hawke shall wheer, looke.. that thay be not to heuy ouer hir power to weyr. **1612** DRAYTON *Poly-olb.* iii. 209 The Bathes.. Giving that naturall power, which, by the vig'rous sweate, Doth lend the lively springs their perdurable heate. **1668** SHADWELL *Sullen Lovers* I. i, He has great power in Corranto's and Jiggs. **1738** WESLEY *Psalms* II. viii, Thou art declar'd my Son with Power. *a* **1770** WHITEFIELD in J. R. Leifchild *Cornwall Mines* (1855) 300, I rode to St. Ives, and preached to many who gladly attended to hear the word. A great power seemed to accompany it. **1838–9** FR. A. KEMBLE *Resid. in Georgia* (1863) 27 Bring them by power of lungs. **1860** LOWELL *Lett.* (1894) I. 341 More power to your elbow! God bless you! **1893** CHESNEY *Lesters* II. xxi, Mounted on an obvious screw, but in good going condition, and with plenty of power.

b. Political or national strength.

1701 Ballance of Power [see BALANCE *sb.* 13 c]. **1719** W. WOOD *Surv. Trade* 315 The excellence of our Constitution, .. would invite great Numbers over to us, exceedingly add to our Power and Strength, and make us more a Balance to the Greatness of any Country in Europe. **1753** *Scots Mag.* Jan. 28/1 Would there by any longer a balance of power in Europe? **1904** *Westm. Gaz.* 12 May 2/1 It was calculation.. based on balance-of-power considerations, which come into question now.

3. a. Of inanimate things: Active property; capacity of producing some effect; the active principle or virtue of a herb, etc. (†also *concr.*).

1592 SHAKS. *Rom. & Jul.* II. iii. 24 Within the infant rin'd of this weake flower, Poyson hath residence, and medicine power. **1690** LOCKE *Hum. Und.* II. xxiii. §10 Powers therefore, justly make a great part of our complex Ideas of Substances. He, that will examine his complex Idea of Gold, will find several of its Ideas, that make it up, to be only Powers, as the Power of being melted, but of keeping its weight in the Fire, of being dissolved in *Aq. Regia.* **1716** M. DAVIES *Athen. Brit.* II. To Rdr. 10 Bathing the parts affected with the Powers of Amber, Sage and Rosemary. **1738** GRAY *Propertius* III. 79 The Power of Herbs can other Harms remove. **1800** *Med. Jrnl.* III. 346 We have ascertained the power of the absorbents to be so great, as to take up not only such animal secretions as hog's lard, &c., but even grosser substances. **1829** *Nat. Philos.* I. *Optics* ii. 4 (U.Kn.S.) The number 1,336, which regulates the refraction of water, is called its.. co-efficient of refraction, and sometimes its refractive power. **1860** TYNDALL *Glac.* II. ii. 241 The red rays of the spectrum possess a very high heating power. **1871** JOWETT *Plato* (ed. 2) I. 26 The power of heat to burn.

b. The sound expressed by a character or symbol; the meaning expressed by a word or phrase in a particular context: = FORCE *sb.*[1] 9.

1727–41 CHAMBERS *Cycl.* s.v. *Force*, In our language the *s* between two vowels has the Force or power of a *z.* **1824** J. JOHNSON *Typogr.* II. xii. 470 There are twenty-six letters.. the names, powers, and sounds of which are as follow. **1871** EARLE *Philol. Eng. Tongue* §242 In the familiar salutation, 'How d'ye do?' we have the same verb in two powers.

c. *Mining.* Thickness or depth (of a vein).

1839 URE *Dict. Arts* 316 The power of this vein is 8 feet.

4. a. Possession of control or command over others; dominion, rule; government, domination, sway, command; control, influence, authority. Often followed by †*of*, †*on*, *over*.

1297 [see A. α]. *a* **1300** in *Leg. Rood* (1871) 28 Vorte Seint dauid þe kyng com, þat was of gret power. *c* **1306** *Exec. Sir S. Fraser* in *Pol. Songs* (Camden) 218 Muche wes the poer that him wes byreved in londe. *a* **1330** *Roland & V.* 178 Lorain & lombardye.. Schal be in þi pouwer. *c* **1400** MAUNDEV. (Roxb.) iii. 10 We trowe wele þi powere es grete apon þi subgets. **1535** COVERDALE *2 Kings* xiv. 5 Now whan he had gotten the power of the kyngdome, he smote his seruauntes which had smytten the kynge his father. **1585** T. Washington tr. *Nicholay's Voy.* iv. xxxvi. 159 They haue foure patriarches.., which doe command and haue power of the orientall churches. **1610** Shaks. *Temp.* i. ii. 55 Thy father was the Duke of Millaine and A Prince of power. **1615** W. Lawson *Country Housew. Gard.* (1626) 12 Let your plot be wholly in your owne power. *a* **1634** Coke *Inst.* iv. (1648) 36 Of the power and jurisdiction of the Parliament, for making of laws in proceeding by Bill, it is so transcendent and absolute, as it cannot be confined either for causes or persons within any bounds. **1685** Baxter *Paraphr. N.T.* Rom. xiii, An Usurper's Strength may be resisted; but Rightful Power or Authority may not. **1835** J. H. Newman *Par. Serm.* (1837) I. i. 7 Cut away by Supreme Power.

b. Authority given or committed; hence, sometimes, liberty or permission to act.

1340 Hampole *Pr. Consc.* 3844 Crist gave to Peter playn powere. *c* **1400** Maundev. (Roxb.) iii. 9 To wham Godd gaffe full powere for to bynd and to louse. *c* **1440** *Promp. Parv.* 410/1 Powere, of auctoryte, *auctoritas, jurisdictio.* **1570** B. Googe *Pop. Kingd.* (1880) 6 Graunting powre and leaue. **1700** T. Brown *Amusem. Ser. & Com.* 85, I left my self full power to drop my Indian Traveller as often as I saw convenient. **1856** Froude *Hist. Eng.* I. ii. 85 The bishops, who had power to arrest laymen on suspicion of heresy,.. had no power to imprison priests.

†**c.** The limits within which administrative power is exercised; = jurisdiction 3. *Obs. rare.*

c **1350** *Usages Winchester* in *Eng. Gilds* (1870) 355 By-þynne þe power of þe town. *Ibid.* 356 þat hit be y-lad by-þinne þe power of þe towne to selle.

d. Personal or social ascendancy, influence.

1535 Coverdale *1 Sam.* xxv. 2 The man was of great power, and had thre thousande Shepe, and a thousande Goates. **1651** Hobbes *Leviath.* i. viii. 35 Riches, Knowledge and Honour are but severall sorts of Power. **1750** Gray *Elegy* ix, The boast of heraldry, the pomp of pow'r. **1829** Mill *Hum. Mind* (1869) II. xxi. 208 A man's power means the readiness of other men to obey him. **1874** Green *Short Hist.* vii. §3. 366 The greatness of the Queen [Elizabeth] rests above all on her power over her people.

e. Political ascendancy or influence in the government of a country or state.

1833 Alison *Hist. Europe* (1847) I. ii. §70. 165 Thus, power and influence was confined to a class. **1849** Macaulay *Hist. Eng.* ii. I. 193 To employ the power which they possessed in the state for the purpose of making their king mighty and honoured. **1878** *Scribner's Mag.* XV. 613/1 The governing party has always come into power by means of revolution. **1884** *L'pool Mercury* 18 Feb. 5/2 Sinking individual opinion whenever it threatens to interfere with the tenure of power. *a* **1908** *Mod.* The party at present in power in France.

f. Used with preceding adj. or sb. to designate a movement to enhance the status of the group specified or the beliefs and activities of such a group. See also *black power*, *flower power*, etc.

1970 'J. Melville' *New Kind of Killer* ii. 32 I'm working to establish Parent Power right now. **1972** *Pride of Lions* (Columbia Univ.) Apr. 2/2 What is important is that you come out, have gay pride and leave the dance with a sense of Gay power. **1972** *Guardian* 17 May 12/1 Pupil power flexes its muscles in London today. The organisers have called on all London secondary school-children to join them in a one-day general strike. *Ibid.* 19 Sept. 12/3 Three different types of reformers: the pupil power movement: the egalitarians: and the orthodox educational reformers. **1974** *Howard Jrnl.* XIV. 38 The growth of 'pupil power' and the increase in truancy. **1974** N. Bagnall (*title*) Parent power. **1974** *Times* 7 Dec. 5/4 (*caption*) Mr Narayan: his hope lies in village power. **1975** *Times* 30 Dec. 8/8 The old form a powerful group—'grey power' to adopt Professor Wilensky's phrase.

5. a. Legal ability, capacity, or authority to act; *esp.* delegated authority; authorization, commission, faculty; *spec.* legal authority vested in a person or persons in a particular capacity.

1486 [see A. α]. **1563–4** *Reg. Pr. Counc. Sc.* I. 271 In the sycht of him, or of thame berand his power. **1568** Grafton *Chron.* II. 370 He was demaunded how he could make anye entreatye of peace, hauing no power so to do? **1771** *Junius Lett.* xlviii. (1820) 252 He was careful not to assume any of those powers which the Constitution had placed in other hands. **1818** Cruise *Digest* (ed. 2) IV. 168 Powers or authorities by which one person enabled another to do an act for him, were well known to the common law. **1859** Bright *Sp., India* 1 Aug. (1876) 55 A Bill to extend and define the powers of the Governors. **1891** *Law Times* XCII. 94/1 The borrowing powers of the company were nearly, if not quite, exhausted.

b. A document, or clause in a document, giving legal authority.

power of attorney (= *letter of attorney*), a document appointing a person or persons to act as the attorney or attorneys of the appointer. (See letter[1] 4 c, attorney[2] 2.)

1483 *Cath. Angl.* 289/1 A Powere, *apodixis.* **1706** *Lond. Gaz.* No. 4209/3 A Forged Power.. for receiving the said Money. **1747** Franklin *Lett.* Wks. 1887 II. 92 As he has your power of attorney,.. I think to put your letter to Mr. Hughes into his hands. **1836** Marryat *Midsh. Easy* xxxvii, A power of attorney will be all that is requisite. **1844** Williams *Real Prop.* ii. iii. (1845) 232 If the power should require a deed only, a will will not do.

II. As a person, body, or thing.

6. a. One who or that which is possessed of or exercises power, influence, or government; an influential or governing person, body, or thing; in early use, one in authority, a ruler, governor. Cf. It. *potestà*, podestà.

1382 Wyclif *Rom.* xiii. 1 Euery soule, or lyuynge man, be suget to hiȝer poweris. **1509** Hawes *Past. Pleas.* xxvii. (Percy Soc.) 127 O power so hye in dignitie! O prynce victorious and famous emperour! **1525** in Ellis *Orig. Lett.* Ser. ii. I. 308 The powares of Italye, withe the helpe off his Holynes, shold be able to kepe the Emperor owt off Italye. **1678** Butler *Hud.* iii. ii. 713 No power of Heav'n or Hell Can pacify Phanatick Zeal. **1738** Wesley *Psalms* iii. v, Thou hast quell'd the adverse Power. **1833** Wordsw. *Sonn., At Sea off Isle of Man*, But element and orb on acts did wait Of Powers endued with visible form, instinct With will. **1874** Mahaffy *Soc. Life Greece* xii. 282 This remarkable banker, who was evidently something of a power in Greece. **1888** Miss Braddon *Fatal Three* i. iii, Bell was a power in the house in Upper Parchment Street.

b. In late use, A state or nation regarded from the point of view of its international authority or influence.

1726 (*title*) Acta Regia: or, An Account of the Treaties, Letters and Instruments Between the Monarchs of England and Foreign Powers.. translated from the French of M. Rapin. **1790** G. Chalmers (*title*) A Collection of Treaties between Great Britain and other Powers. **1847** Mrs. A. Kerr tr. *Ranke's Hist. Servia* 448 It had been approved of by the Commissioners, whom she, as the Power in possession of the Sovereignty, had appointed. **1863** Kinglake *Crimea* I. ii. 21 All States except the five great Powers are exempt from the duty of watching over the general safety. **1872** Freeman *Gen. Sketch* xii. §17. 229 Spain.. soon became the greatest power in Europe. **1901** *N. Amer. Rev.* Feb. 182 That the United States had the capacity to be a Sea Power. *Ibid.* 183 There was no talk then of being a World Power.

c. ***the powers that be*** (after Rom. xiii. 1): the authorities concerned; the elements exercising social or political control. Also in sing.

1526 Tindale *Rom.* xiii. 1 The powers that be are ordeyned off God. **1793** W. B. Stevens *Jrnl.* 24 Feb. (1965) 70 The Selfishness and Timidities essential to his nature.. make him cling to the Powers that be. **1814** Scott *Waverley* I. xix. 281 The cautious Baillie justly observed, that.. the tenantry and villagers might become riotous in expressing their joy, and give offence to the 'powers that be', a sort of persons for whom the Baillie always had unlimited respect. **1886** Kipling *Departmental Ditties* (ed. 2) 5 Potiphar Gubbins, C.E., Is dear to the Powers that Be. **1909** *Westm. Gaz.* 11 Jan. 12/4 Perhaps next year the powers that be may take a little more trouble to discover the talent that lies outside London. **1924** Lawrence & Skinner *Boy in Bush* 15 He had to hear the end of a story against the powers-that-be. **1930** *Times* 25 Mar. 23/7 One can only express the hope that the Power-that-be in Nanking will realize the desirability for proceeding slowly and gradually. **1956** A. Wilson *Anglo-Saxon Att.* ii. ii. 331 Donald's audience was not so large as it had been for the first lectures, but even now there was a fair number.. those who had hoped that they might trap Donald into some mistake and earn a reputation for standing no nonsense from the powers that be. **1976** *Equals* Oct./Nov. 2/3, I feel that the powers-that-be have expected too much to happen too quickly.

7. A celestial or spiritual being having control or influence; a deity, a divinity. Chiefly in plural, originating in its application to the pagan divinities; often in asseveration or exclamation, as ***by (all) the powers! merciful powers!***

In quot. 1526, perh. in more general sense.

1490 Johannes de Irlandia *Meroure of Wyssdome* (1965) II. 49 He had overcummyn all their powaris of myrknes. [**1526** Tindale *Rom.* viii. 38 Nether deeth, nether lyfe, nether angell, nor rule, nether power [1577 *Genev.* powers; Gr. δυνάμεις, L. *virtutes*, Wycl. vertues], nether thynges present, nether thinges to come.. shalbe able to departe vs from Goddes love.] **1596** Shaks. *Merch. V.* iv. i. 292, I would she were in heauen, so she could Intreat some power to change this currish Iew. **1610** —— *Temp.* iii. iii. 73 For which foule deed, The Powres, delaying (not forgetting) haue Incens'd the Seas.. Against your peace. **1697** Dryden *Virg. Past.* v. 123 Such Honours as we pay to Pow'rs Divine, To Bacchus and to Ceres, shall be thine. —— *Georg.* iv. 783 And then adore the Woodland Pow'rs with Pray'r. **1725** Pope *Odyss.* iii. 192 There land, and pay due victims to the pow'rs. **1742** Gray *Adversity*, Daughter of Jove, relentless Power. **1786** Burns *To a Louse* viii, O wad some Pow'r the giftie gie us To see oursels as others see us! **1803** G. Colman *John Bull* i. i. 12 By the powers she's well enough. **1809** Malkin *Gil Blas* ii. vii. ¶ 19 No, no! by all the powers! **1835** Hood *Dead Robbery* iii, I reckon, by the pow'rs! I've lost ten pound by your not being stiffer! **1862** Thackeray *Round. Papers, Notch in Axe*, Merciful powers! I remember. **1891** T. Hardy *Tess* (1892) 153 The decline of belief in a beneficent Power. **1974** B. & R. Hill *Spirit in Stone* iii. 39 When his training period was over, he secretly painted his face in the way directed by his 'power' (i.e. spirit helper) and set out.

8. In mediæval angelology, The sixth order of angels in the celestial hierarchy; = potestate 2: see order *sb.* 5.

[Cf. **1388** Wyclif *Col.* i. 16 Ether trones, ether dominaciouns, ether princehodes, ethir poweris [1382 potestates, L. *potestates*, Gr. ἐξουσίαι].] **1667** Milton *P.L.* v. 601 Thrones, Dominations, Princedoms, Vertues, Powers. *a* **1711** Ken *Hymnotheo* Poet. Wks. 1721 III. 200 Pow'rs for Centurions in God's Hosts renown'd. **1814** Cary *Dante, Paradise* xxviii. 113[Dominations, first; Virtues, second;] and powers the third. **1846** Keble *Lyra Innoc.* (1873) 101 The Powers and Thrones above.

9. A body of armed men; a fighting force, a host, an army; = force *sb.*[1] 4; in pl. = *forces*, i.e. distinct hosts (quot. 1568), or different kinds of troops composing an army. ***power of the county***: = posse comitatus. Originally less concrete, without *a* or *pl.* Now *rare* or *arch.*

1297 [see A. β]. *a* **1300** *Cursor M.* 3966 He com again wit his poer [*v.rr.* pouer, powere]. **1390** Gower *Conf.* III. 14 He wente.. To make a werre in Orient, And gret pouer with him he ladde. *c* **1400** *Brut* 32 Come Iulius Cesar.. into þis lande, with a power of Romayns, and wolde haue hade þis lande þrouȝ strengþ. *c* **1440** *Sir Gowther* 513 My lord hath sembled a new powere. **1523** Ld. Berners *Froiss.* I. 414 As moche power of men of warre as they coude make. **1526** *Pilgr. Perf.* (W. de W. 1531) 12 b, Delyuered from the deuyll and all his hoost or power. **1553** Brende *Q. Curtius* R viij, Satibarzanes.. was with a power of horsemen entered agayne emonges the Arians. **1568** Grafton *Chron.* II. 652 They with both their powers were commyng towarde London. **1601** Shaks. *Jul. C.* iv. i. 42 Brutus and Cassius Are leuying Powers; We must straight make head. **1641** *Termes de la Ley* 262 One of them entreth into the Church with great power of Lay men, and holdeth the other out with force and armes. **1653** Dorothy Osborne *Lett.* xxiii. (1888) 116 He comes with the power of the county to demand her ..being Sheriff. **1726** Leoni *Alberti's Archit.* I. 6/2 The Albanians, who fought against Pompey with such a Power of Horse. **1805** Scott *Last Minstr.* iv. xxiv, Two hundred of my master's powers. **1819** Wordsw. *Waggoner* i. 213 His bones, and those of all his Power Slain here in a disastrous hour!

10. a. A large number, a multitude, a 'host' of persons (not a military force); **b.** A large number, quantity, or amount of things; an abundance, a great deal, 'a lot'. Now *dial.* or *colloq.*

a. *a* **1661** Fuller *Worthies* (1662) i. 194 Imploying a power of poor people, in Polling.., Gutting, Splitting, Powdering and Drying them [Pilchards]. **1706–7** Farquhar *Beaux Strat.* i. i, What other Company have you in Town? A power of fine ladies. **1801** tr. *Gabrielli's Myst. Husb.* IV. 18 They had left a power of servants at their master's. **1803** Jane Porter *Thaddeus* xi, They say there is a power of them wandering about the world. **1905** J. M. Synge *Shadow of Glen* 25 I'm thinking it's a power of men you're after knowing.

b. **1671** H. M. tr. *Erasm. Colloq.* 323 What sumptuous silken vestments were there... What a power of golden candlesticks. **1680** Crowne *Misery Civ. War* i. i, They have a power o' money. **1716** Addison *Drummer* i. i, This Spirit will bring a power of Custom to the George. **1770** Gray *Corr. w. N. Nicholls* (1843) 113 It will do you a power of good one way or other. *a* **1797** Mary Wollstonecr. *Posth. Wks.* (1798) III. vii. 17, I shall expect (as the country people say in England) that you will make a power of money to indemnify me for your absence. **1840** Dickens *Old C. Shop* liii, It has done a power of work. **1871** Mrs. H. Wood *Dene Hollow* iv, I've a power of things to do at home. **1899** O. Seaman *In Cap & Bells* (1900) 40 He was an all-round man, a scholar: knew a power of botany. **1938** B. L. Burman *Blow for Landing* 161 There's a power of music in an anvil. **1947** *Daily Mail* 22 May 3/4 There's a power of difference between farming now and when I was a lad. **1958** *People* 4 May 16/1 (Advt.), Hungry children do themselves a power of good when they polish off the sandwiches. *a* **1974** R. Crossman *Diaries* (1975) I. 400 Two days at Prescote have done me a power of good.

III. In technical uses.

11. a. †*Geom.* The square described on a given line (*obs.*) (? an error); *Math.* (in modern use), the product obtained by multiplying a number or quantity into itself a specified number of times, the number of times being indicated by an ordinal numeral.

The first power of a number or quantity is the number itself; the second power is the square, or product of the number multiplied into itself; the third power is the cube, or product of the square multiplied by the original number.

1570 Billingsley *Euclid* ii. Introd. 60 The power of a line, is the square of the same line. **1674** Jeake *Arith.* (1696) 297 Multiply alternately.. the Numbers given by the Powers of these alternate Indices for the reduced Surdes. **1743** Emerson *Fluxions* 25 If any Term be divided by the first Power of the variable Quantity; then the Fluxion of that Term must be found by itself thus. **1827** Hutton *Course Math.* I. 80, 2 is the root, or 1st power of 2. 4 is the 2d power, or square of 2.

fig. **1884** tr. *Lotze's Logic* 191 Even in cases where calculation in the strict sense is impossible we are inclined to use the term 'power' when the meaning and importance of a conception is raised in some peculiar manner.

†**b.** ***in power*** (tr. ἐν δυνάμει, Euclid): a phrase used in relation to the squares of magnitudes that are compared, as distinguished from the magnitudes themselves; thus magnitudes are *commensurable* (or *incommensurable*) *in power* when their squares are commensurable (or incommensurable). So ***equal in power***, ***of equal power***: see quots. *Obs.*

1571 Digges *Pantom.* iv. Def. vi. T j b, A lyne is sayde to be equall in power with two or moe lynes, when his square is equall to all their squares. **1655** Stanley *Hist. Philos.* i. (1701) 9/1 Pythagoras, Sacrificed a Hecatomb, having found out, that the hypothenuse of a right Angled Triangle, is of equal power to the two sides including the right angle. **1660** Barrow *Euclid* x. Def. iii, Right lines are commensurable in power, when the same space does measure their squares. **1669** Sturmy *Mariner's Mag.* i. ii. 40 How to finde two Lines, which together shall be equal in Power to any Line given.

c. ***power of a point*** with regard to a circle: the square of the distance from that point to the point of contact of the tangent drawn from it; or (equivalently) the rectangle under the segments of any chord drawn from the point.

1885 Leudesdorf *Cremona's Proj. Geom.* 58 If through a point *O* any chord be drawn to cut a circle in *P* and *Q*, the rectangle *OP* . *OQ* is called the power of the point with regard to the circle.

d. *Math.* A property of a set that is the same for any two sets whose elements can be placed in a one-to-one correspondence and that in the case of a finite set is equal to the number of elements it contains; = potency 5.

1903 B. Russell *Princ. Math.* xliii. 364 Power is synonymous with cardinal number. *Ibid.*, To prove that there are powers higher than the continuum. **1953** A. A. Fraenkel *Abstract Set Theory* i. 79 The cardinal of the continuum, often called the power of the continuum. *Ibid.* iii. 306 Cantor and many of his successors.. call cardinals in general by the neutral name of 'powers' (Mächtigkeiten). **1961** L. F. Boron tr. *Kuratowski's Introd. Set Theory & Topology* v. 61 The set of all odd natural numbers has the same power as the set of all even natural numbers. *Ibid.*, The open interval $-\pi/2 < x < +\pi/2$ has the same power as the set of all real numbers. **1968** H. SHARP *Mod. Fund. Math.* vii. 240 The power of a finite set is simply the number of elements in the set.

12. *Mech.* An instrument by means of which energy may be applied to mechanical purposes. ***mechanical*** (†***mathematical***, †***mechanic***) ***powers***: the simple machines by means of which mechanical energy may be advantageously applied; now reckoned as six, viz. the lever, wheel and axle, pulley, wedge, inclined plane, and screw: cf. MACHINE *sb.* 5.

1671 *Phil. Trans.* VI. 2286 The Five Mathematical Powers (as they are called) or noted Engines for the facilitation of Motion. **1704** J. HARRIS *Lex. Techn.* I. s.v., The Six Mechanical Faculties; the Ballance, the Leaver, the Wheel, the Pulley, the Wedge, and the Screw; which are usually stiled the Six Mechanick Powers. **1710** *Ibid.* II, *Powers Mechanick*, of these there are five usually accounted, the Lever, the Balance, the Wedge or Inclined Plane, the Screw and the Pulley. **1827** N. ARNOTT *Physics* I. 154 No mechanical power or machine generates force. **1828** J. M. SPEARMAN *Brit. Gunner* (ed. 2) 290 There are seven mechanical powers, viz.—The Lever, the Wheel and Axle, the Pulley, the Inclined Plane, the Wedge, the Screw, and the Funicular Machine. **1839** G. BIRD *Nat. Philos.* 71 Inclined plane. The action of this mechanical power depends upon the simple principle [etc.].

13. Any form of energy or force available for application to work. *spec.* **a.** Mechanical energy (as that of gravitation, running water, wind, steam, electricity), as distinguished from hand-labour; often viewed as a commodity saleable in definite quantities. In quot. 1728 = FORCE *sb.*[1] 11 a. **b.** Force applied to produce motion or pressure; the acting force in a lever or other 'mechanical power', as opposed to the *weight*. **c.** The mechanical advantage gained by the use of a machine.

1727–41 CHAMBERS *Cycl.* s.v., Power in mechanics denotes a force, which being applied to a machine, tends to produce motion... If the power be a man, or a brute, it is called an animate power; if the air, water, fire, gravity, or elasticity, an inanimate power. **1728** PEMBERTON *Newton's Philos.* 55 Caused..from the influence of the power of gravity united with the general laws of motion. **1808** J. DUNCAN *Art of Weaving* 272 Plans..for the purpose of working the weaving loom by the application of power. **1808** *Rep. High Comm. on Cartwright's Petit.* 7 The general adoption of the loom by mechanical power will operate to the prejudice of the present weavers. **1815** J. SMITH *Panorama Sc. & Art* I. 294 Three things are always to be considered..: a *weight* to be raised; the *power* by which it is to be raised; and the *instrument* or *engine*, by which that power acts upon the weight. **1825** J. NICHOLSON *Operat. Mechanic* 65 The word *power*, as used in practical mechanics, signifies the exertion of strength, gravitation, impulse, or pressure, so as to produce motion. **1830** *Mechanic's Mag.* XIV. 448, I wish to let out power, but do not know a good and certain way of measuring it. **1836** *Backwoods of Canada* 89 There is great water-power, both as regards the river and the fine broad creek which..falls into the small lake below. **1889** *B'ham Daily Post* 7 Jan. 2/3 Advt., [To let] good Shopping, with and without power.

d. Motive power or heat (as contrasted with light) obtained from an electricity supply. Usu. *attrib.*

1896 R. ROBB *Electric Wiring* v. 82 Wires that carry current for running motors, or for furnishing power in distinction from lights, are commonly called 'power-wires'. **1904** W. R. BOWKER *Dynamo, Motor & Switchboard Circuits* v. 96 (*caption*) Low-tension system for power and lighting. **1931** *Electrician* 13 Nov. 654/1 Where it is desired to instal power plugs in premises already lighted electrically a minimum of two 15A positions is demanded. **1941** E. WHITEHORNE *Elect. Wiring Specifications* vii. 98 (*caption*) Power wiring must serve specific loads and processes. **1958, 1975** [see *power point*, sense 18 below.]

14. Capacity for exerting mechanical force, as measured by the rate at which it is exerted, or the work done by it (cf. HORSEPOWER); also applied to a measurable capacity for producing some other physical effect. Also applied *concr.* to an engine that produces power.

1806– [see HORSEPOWER]. **1815** J. SMITH *Panorama Sc. & Art* I. 294 In calculating the power of a machine, it is usually considered in a state of equilibrium; that is, in the state when the power which has to overcome the resistance, just balances it. **1825** J. NICHOLSON *Operat. Mechanic* 67 The product of these two numbers 3970 will express the power of the water to produce mechanical effects. **1849** NOAD *Electricity* (ed. 3) 421 With such a battery power the sparks from the primary coil are brilliant in the extreme. **1869** *Bradshaw's Railway Manual* XXI. 399 Indian Tramway.. adapted according to local circumstances to cattle or locomotive power. **1881** *Metal World* No. 19. 297 Power is the product of force and velocity; that is to say, a force multiplied by the velocity with which it is acting is the power in operation. **1882** MINCHIN *Unipl. Kinemat.* 263 The term 'power'..signifies time-rate of doing work, and it is already in practical use in the expression 'horse power', which stands for 33,000 foot-pounds per minute. **1953** BERREY & VAN DEN BARK *Amer. Thes. Slang* (1954) §82a/1 *Motor; engine*—1. chugger, coffee grinder, mill, percolator, power, stove. **1962** *Amer. Speech* XXXVII. 134 *Power*,..all the locomotives owned by a company. The expression is heard, 'The company has lots of power.' **1973** *Ibid.* 1969 XLIV. 245 A light engine crew moves *power* from one location to another. *Ibid.* 259 *Power*, 1: Number and type of locomotives on a train. 2: Locomotives available at a given time.

15. *Optics.* The capacity of a lens (or combination of lenses) for magnifying the apparent size of an object; also *ellipt.*, the lens itself.

1727–41 CHAMBERS *Cycl.* s.v., The Power of a Glass is used by some for the distance of the convexity from its solar focus. **1831** BREWSTER *Optics* v. 49 The magnifying power, or the number of times that the apparent magnitude of the object is increased. **1854** *Pereira's Polarized Lt.* (ed. 2) 53 The light is polarized by this plate, and being then refracted by two plano-convex glasses (termed the power), is afterwards received on a semi-transparent calico screen. *c* **1865** J. WYLDE in *Circ. Sc.* I. 67/1 Another pair of lenses is generally placed between the 'power' (that is, the last lens in front of the arrangement) and the condensers. **1875** HUXLEY & MARTIN *Elem. Biol.* (1877) 21 Having found an Amœba, examine with a higher power.

IV. ¶ 16. In N.T., 1 Cor. xi. 10, a verbal rendering of Gr. ἐξουσία, L. *potestas*: see quots.

1526 TINDALE *1 Cor.* xi. 10 For this cause ought the woman to haue power in her heed, for the angels sake [COVERD. a power vpon hir heade, *Great*, *Geneva*, 1611, power on her h., *Rheims* povver vpon her head; WYCLIF 1382 a veyle [1388 an hilyng] on hir heed; *R.V.* 1881 a sign of authority on [*margin* authority over] her head; Gr. ἐξουσίαν ἔχειν ἐπὶ τῆς κεφαλῆς; *Vulg.* potestatem habere supra caput]. *c* **1550** *Vertuous Scholehous* B iv b, As Paule sayth, we go attyred and haue a power vpon our heades. And therefore must I nowe (for my louynge husband is dead) lette hange my power or vayle downewardes from my heade, hauynge no power or husbande that hath rule of me. **1625** T. GODWIN *Moses & Aaron* (1641) 236 For this cause (namely in signe of subjection) ought the woman to have power on her head, 1 Cor. 11. 10, where by power, the Apostle understandeth a veile.

V. Phrases and Combinations.

17. Phrases. †**a.** ***after, at one's power, at all one's power***: according to one's ability; to the utmost of one's ability, with all one's might. *Obs.*

c **1330** R. BRUNNE *Chron. Wace* (Rolls) 10861 þer horses at þer power runnen. **1472** *Rental Bk. Cupar-Angus* (1879) I. 165 The sade John sal kepe his land fra guld efter his powar. **1535** COVERDALE *Tobit* iv. 8 Be mercifull after ye power. Yf thou hast moch, geue plenteously. **1627** RUTHERFORD *Lett.* (1862) I. 35 Your's at all power in the Lord Jesus, S.R. *a* **1649** DRUMM. OF HAWTH. *Fam. Ep.* Wks. (1711) 138, I shall fortify and defend the true holy catholick and christian religion..at all my power.

†**b.** ***by*** (***one's***) ***power***: according to one's ability. *Obs.*

c **1290** [see A. a]. **1340** *Ayenb.* 170 þe onlosti þet byeþ slacke to godes seruice, þet ne byeþ ne wel chald be poer, ne wel hot. **1362** LANGL. *P. Pl.* A. v. 76, I haue anuyȝed him ofte,..And peired him bi my pouwer.

c. ***in power***: (*a*) in a position of authority; †(*b*) able, competent (*to do* something). *Sc.* †(*c*) in potentiality, *in posse*, as opposed to *in exercise* or *action*. †(*d*) *Math.*: see 11 b. (*e*) ***in one's power***, within one's ability, under one's control: see 1, 4.

1297 R. GLOUC. (Rolls) 7895 To drawe to him þe heyemen, þat in poer were þo. *c* **1475** *Rauf Coilȝear* 886 The tane is in power to mak that presoun. **1656** STANLEY *Hist. Philos.* v. (1701) 184/2 That Intellect which is always in act, ..is better than that Intellect which is in power. **1739** HUME *Hum. Nat.* (1874) I. I. vii. 328 They are not really and in fact present to the mind, but only in power. *a* **1908** *Mod.* [see 4 e.]

†**d.** ***of power***: able, capable, competent. *Obs.*

c **1386** CHAUCER *Melib.* ¶ 780 We be nat of power to maken hise amendes. **1486** *Hen. VII at York* in *Surtees Misc.* (1888) 53 Othre thinhabitauntes, which may not..be of power to have rede gownes. **1544** PHAER *Regim. Lyfe* (1553) I vij, If ye be of power, ye maye drinke a good draught of ypocras..after meate. **1634** MILTON *Comus* 155 Of power to cheat the eye with blear illusion.

e. †***to one's power*** (obs.), ***to the best, uttermost***, or ***extent of one's power***: as far as one is able.

[*a* **1300** in *Rolls of Parlt.* I. 241 A leur poer e a leur esseint.] **1490** CAXTON *Eneydos* xiii. 48 She..cheryssheth and enterteyneth hym to her power. **1523** LD. BERNERS *Froiss.* I. 138 The man they wolde haue defended to the best of their powers. **1568** GRAFTON *Chron.* II. 686 King Reyner did also help his daughter to hys small power. **1631** WEEVER *Anc. Fun. Mon.* 137 Three things..I remember to haue kept to my power. **1715** DE FOE *Fam. Instruct.* I. v. (1841) I. 97 To the best of my power you shall do it no more.

†**f.** ***upon one's power***: as well as one can. *Obs. rare.*

c **1380** WYCLIF *Sel. Wks.* III. 479 Doyng ȝoure bisynes upon ȝoure connynge ande powere.

†**g.** ***within power***, within range. *Obs.*

1548 PATTEN *Exped. Scotl.* N iv b, Within pour of batrie.

†**h.** ***to do*** (***make***) ***one's power***: to do one's best.

c **1412** HOCCLEVE *De Reg. Princ.* 1855 And, for to write it wel, do thi poweer [*rime* clere]. **1456** SIR G. HAYE *Law Arms* (S.T.S.) 13 He did his power to put it doun. **1523** LD. BERNERS *Froiss.* I. clxxxii. 216 Shame haue he that dothe nat his power to distroy all. **1560** DAUS tr. *Sleidane's Comm.* 42 Christierne made all his power agaynste them.

i. ***power of life and death, of pit and gallows, of the keys, of the sword***: see LIFE *sb.* 1 c, PIT *sb.*[1] 7, KEY *sb.*[1] 4, SWORD.

1560 DAUS tr. *Sleidane's Comm.* 229 b, The power of the keyes. **1609** SKENE *Reg. Maj.* I. 95 All Barons quha hes power of Pitt, and Gallous of thift. **1863** H. COX *Instit.* III. viii. 719 *note*, The power of life and death, which by martial law belonged to the Lord High Admiral.

j. ***more power to*** (someone): good luck, may fortune favour (someone). Also ***more power to one's arm***; see also ELBOW *sb.* 4 g.

1842 S. LOVER *Handy Andy* ix. 89 'More power to you, Andy,' said the Squire. **1881** CARLYLE *Reminisc.* II. 321 More power to him! **1932** E. GLASGOW *Let.* 12 Jan. (1958) 112, I read and enjoyed and admired the articles by Allen Tate. They are fine and true. More power to him. **1948** 'J. TEY' *Franchise Affair* xvi. 187 Hooray! More power to him! I begin to like the boy. **1973** P. MOYES *Curious Affair of Third Dog* viii. 107 'I'm trying to find Griselda, you see.' 'In that case, more power to your arm.'

k. ***power behind the throne***: one who exercises power behind the scenes while appearing to have no authority to do so.

[**1770** PITT *Speech* 2 Mar. in *London Museum* Apr. 249 A long train of such practices has at length unwillingly convinced me, that there is something within the court [in *Parl. Hist.* (1813) XVI. 843 something behind the throne] greater than the King himself.] **1866** MRS. LINCOLN in W. H. Herndon *Lincoln* (1889) III. 513, I told him [*sc.* Lincoln] once of the assertion I had heard coming from the friends of Seward, that the latter was the power behind the throne; that he could rule him. **1875** 'MARK TWAIN' *Old Times Mississippi* in *Atlantic Monthly* June 728/1 A power behind the throne that was greater than the throne itself. It was the underwriters! **1905** H. A. VACHELL *Hill* ix. 198 It was his habit to consult his wife in emergencies. The chief cutter.. said that Amelia was the power behind the throne. **1931** W. HOLTBY *Poor Caroline* vii. 277 I'd been..generally working in the *background*, but then I *liked* to be the power behind the throne. **1973** J. WAINWRIGHT *Devil you Don't* 8 She'd been blinded..at the possibility of controlling such a man. Of being the power behind such a throne. **1977** *Time* 8 Aug. 43/2 Anderson..will become the real power behind the throne.

18. *attrib.* and *Comb.* **a.** simple attrib., as ***power absorption, company, -distribution, -generation, group, -holder, hunger, -impulse, -instinct, logic(s, -loss, -lust, -mania, -maniac, -monger, motive, -possessor, -producer, -production, relation, -seeker, -soul, -stroke, structure, struggle, -supply, -transmission, turret, -urge, vacuum, -word, -worship***. **b.** Operated, driven, or done by mechanical power, as ***power approach, -bellows, -blast, cart, craft, -crane, ditching, drill, -engine, -forge, -hammer, hoist, -lathe, -machine, -milker, -mill, mower, -plant, -press, -pulley, saw, shovel, -vehicle, wringer***. **c.** Used in generating, distributing, or applying mechanical power, as ***power-dam, lever, -station, works***. **d.** Objective, as ***power-carrying, -craving, -generating, -giving, -handling, -holding, -losing, -loving, -propelling, -seeking, -sharing, -usurping*** (all may be used as adjs. or sbs.); ***power-greedy, -hungry, -lusting, -mad, -thirsty*** adjs. **e.** Instrumental, as ***power-crazed, -driven, -elated, -obsessed*** adjs.; ***power-feeding, -riveting, -weaving*** sbs. and adjs.; ***power-driving, -farming*** sbs., ***power-arm*** vb. **f.** Spec. Comb.: **power amplifier**, an amplifier designed to deliver an output of appreciable power into a load; **power-assistance**, (the equipment for) the application of power to assist manual operation; **power-assisted** *a.*, employing some inanimate source of power to assist manual operation; applied esp. to brakes and steering in cars where power from the engine is so used; **power bandwidth** *Electronics*, the range of frequencies over which a device can deliver a certain power or a signal with distortion less than a certain value; **power base**, a source of authority or support; **power block**, (*a*) a group of allied states, or a great power with its allies and dependencies; (*b*) *Naut.*, a power-driven pulley used to haul in a seine; **power board**, (*a*) a board or panel containing switches or meters for an electricity supply; (*b*) chiefly *N.Z.*, the controlling authority for the supply of electricity in an area; an electricity board; **power brake**, a power-assisted brake (in a motor vehicle); **power broker** orig. and chiefly *U.S.*, one who exerts influence or affects the distribution of political power by intrigue; hence **power-brokering**, **power-broking** *vbl. sbs.*; **power buzzer**, an electrical vibrator used in the war of 1914–18 to generate telegraphic earth currents; **power cable**, a cable transmitting electrical power; **power capstan**, a capstan in which the power is increased by means of gearing; **power car**, a railway carriage incorporating an engine; **power centre**, a locus of political authority; a powerful person or institution; so **power-centred** *a.*, concerned with the study, acquisition, or exercise of political authority; **power cut**, a temporary withdrawal or failure of the electricity supply; also *fig.*; **power density** *Nuclear Physics*, the power produced per unit volume of a reactor core; **power dive**, a dive made by an aircraft with its engine(s) providing thrust; also *transf.* and *fig.*; so **power-dive** *v. intr.*; **power-egg**, on an airship (rarely, an aeroplane), an ovate housing for an engine; **power élite**, a social or political group that exercises power; **power-**

ender, -ending *a.*: see quot.; **power factor** *Electr.*, (*a*) the ratio of the actual power delivery by an a.c. circuit (or a component in it) to the product of the r.m.s. values of current and voltage; (*b*) as a property of an insulating material: the power factor under specified conditions of a capacitor made with this material as dielectric; **power failure**, a failure of a power supply, esp. the electricity supply; **power frequency** *Electr.*, a frequency in the range used for alternating currents supplying power (commonly 50 or 60 Hz); **power game**, a contest for authority or influence, esp. in politics; **power-gas**, coal-gas used for supplying power, not illumination; **power law**, a relationship between two quantities such that the magnitude of one is proportional to a fixed power of the magnitude of the other; **power level**, the amount of power being transmitted, produced, etc. (in some contexts measured relative to some reference level); **power line**, a conductor supplying electrical power, often spec. one supported by poles or pylons; **power-load** *Electr.*, the amount of current delivered for use in driving machinery, as distinguished from that used for lighting; **power-loader** *Mining*, a machine which loads coal on to a conveyor belt at the coal face; hence **power-loaded** *a.*; cf. POWER LOADING *vbl. sb.*; **power-net**, a knitted stretch fabric used in women's underwear; **power oil**, oil brought up from a well and used on the spot as a source of power; **power-operated** *a.*, operated by power from an inanimate source; **power pack**, a unit for supplying power; *spec.* (*a*) one for converting an alternating current (from the mains) to a direct current at a different (usu. lower) voltage, and usu. comprising a transformer, rectifier, and capacitor, (*b*) (see quot. 1967); also *fig.*; **power package**, a self-contained source of power; **power pile** = *power reactor* below; **power play**, in sport, a concentration of players at a particular point; the style of play involving such concentrations; *spec.* in ice hockey, a group of players sent out against a depleted opposition; also *transf.*; **power point**, a point or socket (POINT *sb.*[1] A. 19 e) from which electrical machinery or heaters can be operated; also *fig.*; **power pole**, a pole used to support an overhead power line; **power reactor**, a nuclear reactor designed principally as a means of producing power; **power response** *Electronics*, the way the output power of a device depends on the signal frequency; *spec.* the power bandwidth; **power seat**, a power-assisted reclining seat; **power series** *Math.*, a series of the form . . . $+ a'_2x^{-2} + a'_1x^{-1} + a_0 + a_1x + a_2x^2 + \ldots$, where the *a*s are independent of *x*; also, a generalization of this for more than one variable; **power set** *Math.*, the set of all the subsets of a given set; **power spectrum**, the distribution of the energy of a wave-form among its different Fourier components; **power steering**, power-assisted steering (in a motor vehicle); **power stroke**, in a piston engine, a stroke during which the piston is moved by the expansion of the gases in the cylinder; **power-system**, a set of political beliefs or institutions founded or dependent upon coercion; **power take-off** (equipment for) the transmission of mechanical power from an engine, esp. that of a tractor or similar vehicle, to another piece of equipment; **power tool**, an electrically powered tool; **power-to-weight** (or **power-weight**) **ratio**, the ratio of the power an engine or motor can produce to its weight (or the weight of the vehicle, etc., containing it); **power train** *Mech.*, the mechanism that transmits the drive from the engine of a vehicle to its axle; also, this together with the engine and axle; **power transformer** *Electronics*, a transformer designed to accept a relatively large power, esp. one connected to a mains supply or power line to provide power at a lower voltage to a circuit or device; **power transistor** *Electronics*, a transistor designed to deliver a relatively high power; **power tube**, *Electronics* = *power valve* below; **power unit**, a device supplying, or controlling the supply of, power; a power plant; **power valve** *Electronics*, a valve designed to deliver a relatively high power; **power wire**, a wire transmitting electrical power.

1901 *Jrnl. Inst. Electr. Engin.* XXX. 405 If the phase difference . . had been but $3\frac{1}{2}°$ instead of 7°, the *power absorption would have been 1 H.P. and not 2 H.P. **1920** *Ibid.* LVIII. 896/1 The grid of the *power amplifier is given a negative potential. **1923** *Radio Times* 28 Sept. 36 (Advt.), Standard loud speaker . . suitable for public purposes when used with a power amplifier. **1961** G. A. BRIGGS *A to Z in Audio* 16 The final stage is the power amplifier designed to feed the loudspeaker with a few watts of audio power. **1970** J. EARL *Tuners & Amplifiers* ii. 51 The majority of power amplifiers have the push-pull output transistors driven direct from a pair of driver transistors. **1938** *Jrnl. R. Aeronaut. Soc.* XLII. 416 We may conclude, therefore, that, for the average pilot, the *power approach (or the undershoot technique) is a feasible method of approaching and landing. **1856** T. AIRD *Poet. Wks.* 139 Let the National Will *Power-arm the State. **1959** *Times* 1 Sept. 12/2 One of the technical improvements in cars that has taken place unobtrusively during the past four years has been the provision of *power-assistance for the brakes. **1970** *Commercial Motor* 25 Sept. 65/1 The steering was light even though power-assistance is not fitted. **1928** *Punch* 21 Mar. (verso front cover) (Advt.), The *power-assisted brakes give absolute control over the car under all conditions. **1950** *Gloss. Aeronaut. Terms* (*B.S.I.*) I. 38 *Power-assisted control*, a flying control in which the force needed to move the surface is provided partly by electrical or hydraulic means and partly by the pilot's physical effort. **1959** *Observer* 1 Mar. 21/5 The power-assisted steering is one of the best I have tried; it spins back swiftly after sharp corners . . and does not transmit severe road shocks. **1975** C. NESBITT *Little Love & Good Company* xviii. 226 The size of the car I was learning in terrified me to begin with. It had power-assisted steering and I wasn't happy without gears. **1965** *Wireless World* Sept. 457/2 *Power bandwidth is the curve of maximum output power (for the defined total distortion) versus frequency, plotted with logarithmic scales on both axes. **1977** *Gramophone* May 1773/2 The power bandwidth of the overall system (which is of course determined by that of the power amplifier) I found to be a little more restricted at its upper end than in some modern amplifiers. **1959** *Cambr. Rev.* 7 Feb. 311/2 This is clearly the altruistic formula for the egoistic *power-base position just discussed. **1969** J. MANDER *Static Society* i. 70 Mexico . . became the prey of rival *caudillos*, each with his geographically inaccessible power-base. **1976** *Encounter* June 79/2 Franco passed on without ever heeding the advice of his more intelligent supporters, who urged him to prepare his successor a power-base at the centre of the political spectrum. **1881** C. A. EDWARDS *Organs* 65 The pneumatic action . . by which the bulk of the pressure is taken from the key, by means of small *power-bellows. **1806** FORSYTH *Beauties Scotl.* III. 97 A *power-blast to excite the furnace fires. **1958** *Times Lit. Suppl.* 21 Nov. 675/2 The frontispiece showing the geographical arrangement of world *power blocks. **1960** M. SHARCOTT *Place of Many Winds* ii. 37 The power block has come into use so that the men no longer have to pull the net by hand. **1904** *Electr. Rev.* (N.Y.) XLV. 444 The *power-board is a handsome marble panel equipped with Weston ammeter and voltmeter arranged for taking readings. [**1918** *Statutes Dominion of N.Z.* 38 For every electric-power district there shall be an Electric-power Board.] **1938** R. FINLAYSON in D. M. Davin *N.Z. Short Stories* (1953) 242 The Power Board was brought to the pass at last of having to build a special concrete foundation for the poles. **1950** *N.Z. Jrnl. Agric.* Aug. 183/1 In New Zealand in the present [electricity] shortages there is an increasing tendency among power boards to adopt rationing. **1973** 'D. HALLIDAY' *Dolly & Starry Bird* ii. 30 The power board is on the wall of the darkroom. **1977** *Daily Tel.* 26 May 19/1 (*heading*) Power board fined over fitter's death. **1896** G. RICHMOND tr. *Lieckfeld's Gas Engines* ii. 29 The simplest and oldest of the *power brakes is that shown in fig. 3, 'The Prony Brake'. **1972** D. E. WESTLAKE *Bank Shot* ii. 16 Kelp . . stomped on the brake. It was a power brake, and the car stopped on a dime. **1961** T. H. WHITE *Making of President 1960* ii. 52 None of the young men . . could win the confidence of the aging back-room *power brokers who wield such influence in the Democratic party. **1968** W. SAFIRE *New Lang. Politics* 349/1 During his mayoral campaign and often after he was elected, Republican John Lindsay spoke scornfully, and often despairingly, of the 'power brokers' (a phrase coined by Theodore White) who ran New York behind the scenes. **1972** *Village Voice* (N.Y.) 1 June 12/5 He's not going to get the nomination in Miami without coming to some kind of arrangement with the power brokers. **1977** *Listener* 21 Apr. 498/3 Chiang Ching . . embarked on a series of intimate relationships with Yenan's power-brokers. **1975** *N.Y. Times* 10 Apr. 29/1 He . . argued that conventions were 'undemocratic' because they were subject to *power-brokering instead of the will of the people. **1977** *Guardian Weekly* 6 Nov. 9/2 The last opportunity for him [*sc.* Tito] to preside over a gathering of all the political clans and employ his power-broking to ensure an orderly succession. **1922** *Encycl. Brit.* XXXII. 489/1 The *power buzzer . . was a powerful vibrator worked by the current from a 10-volt accumulator, and connected to inconspicuous earths of insulated wire which could . . be buried 6 ft. deep . . . Detachments of troops isolated by the enemy could send out code signals which could be picked up by listening sets . . at ranges up to 3000 yd. **1923** R. STANLEY *Text-bk. Wireless Telegr.* (rev. ed.) II. xvii. 339 With a power buzzer of the 'Parleur' type on a 10-volt battery and a 100-yards earth base between the plates, in a fairly dry type of soil over chalk, good signals have been obtained over a range of 5 kilometres, the receiver being a 3-valve L.F. Amplifier connected to two earth plates 200 yards apart. **1905** HENRY & HORA *Mod. Electr.* xi. 219 Tough paper forms an excellent insulating material for electric light and *power cables. **1959** E. H. CLEMENTS *High Tension* xi. 182 One of Douglas's tall poles bearing the power-cable across the open forest. **1974** E. AMBLER *Dr. Frigo* III. 241 The body was discovered . . by workmen laying a power cable. **1936** *Discovery* Nov. 356/1 The Union Pacific RR. has two twelve-car diesel-electric trains, of which the first two coaches are the *power cars, each containing a 1,200 b.h.p. engine. **1977** *Mod. Railways* Dec. 492/1 Despite the apparently convincing case put forward for the positioning of the power car in the centre of the APT-P sets . . it is reported that options are still open regarding the formation of any subsequent production trains. **1946** *Nature* 5 Oct. 463/1 The 11,000 volt systems are in turn supplied by 33,000 volt or 66,000 volt systems, with proportionally higher *power-carrying capacities. **1971** *Power cart [see *green(s) fee* s.v. GREEN *sb.* 17]. **1961** *Sunday Express* 19 Nov. 16 By one cunning dodge after another he has kept this one-time *power centre of German militarism intact. **1962** M. MCLUHAN *Gutenberg Galaxy* 12 The Renaissance prince tended to become an exclusive power centre surrounded by his individual subjects. **1977** F. YOUNG in J. Hick *Myth of God Incarnate* ii. 28 Cyril's attack on Nestorius is related to the political struggle between the ecclesiastical power-centres of Alexandria and Constantinople. **1960** *Encounter* Oct. 4/4 A party which deals with the real problems of real men and women will become immoral, *power-centred. **1924** *Times Trade & Engin. Suppl.* 29 Nov. 239/1 With such an unusually large consumption of current, . . the electric light, heat, and *power companies can afford to sell power at a low cost. **1951** M. MCLUHAN *Mech. Bride* (1967) 136/2 This is a good record for the thousands of people who work in power companies. **1961** BIGELOW & OTIS *Manchester, Vermont* xii. 113 Manchester . . had two competing power companies until 1904. **1977** J. CLEARY *Vortex* i. 21 Get the power company out here. . . Shut off that power. **1936** *Discovery* Nov. 361/2 Part III is solely taken up by *power craft. **1954** FISHER & LOCKLEY *Sea-Birds* v. 126 The oceanic sea-birds have solved these problems of mobility by becoming sailplanes as well as power-craft. **1844** STEPHENS *Bk. Farm* II. 211 A *power-crane. **1924** P. RADIN tr. *Adler's Pract. & Theory Individual Psychol.* xix. 231 This, reduced to her line of *power-craving, meant—'I must dominate everyone, draw everybody's attention to myself.' **1914** G. FRANKAU *Et Debellare Superbos* in *Poetical Wks.* (1923) I. 185 We grasped this sword for gain's sake, caste, nor king *Power-crazed to his own people's ruining. **1952** M. ALLINGHAM *Tiger in Smoke* iv. 74 Teleprinters, radar . . when we get a *power cut the whole blessed police system is liable to go out of action. **1973** J. WAINWRIGHT *Touch of Malice* 97 It was a good clock—electric—and, apart from power cuts, it kept perfect time. **1903** *Daily Chron.* 9 Mar. 5/6 A great *power-dam belonging to the Hudson River Power Company. **1953** W. E. UNBEHAUN *Hist. & Status Exper. Breeder Reactor* (U.S. Atomic Energy Comm. AECD-3712) 40 **Power density*, a measure of the power per unit of reactor core volume. **1955** *Proc. Internat. Conf. Peaceful Uses Atomic Energy* (United Nations) III. 238/2 The power density is highest in the seed with a value of better than 200 watts/cm^3. **1967** *Technology Week* 23 Jan. 28/1 The *Phoebus 1 B* reactor . . uses a new hydrogen pump developed by North American's Rocketdyne Div. that can handle 150 lbs. of hydrogen per second for studies of operations in the higher power-density range. **1942** *Tee Emm* (Air Ministry) II. 95 The value of *power ditching is so great that the pilot should always ditch before fuel is quite exhausted. **1930** R. DUNCAN *Stunt Flying* vi. 55 In a *power dive, terrific drag is exerted on the main planes with a downward pressure on the tailplane. **1937** *Times* 14 Dec. 17/2 During these evolutions they [*sc.* Japanese bombers] 'power-dived' to within a very short distance above the Panay's decks. **1941** STEINBECK & RICKETTS *Sea of Cortez* 163 The mosquitoes . . whooped and screamed and attacked, power-diving and wheeling up and diving again. **1954** *Ann. Reg. 1953* 373 Aeroplanes flew at increasing speeds, reaching the threshold of the speed of sound in level flight and much higher speeds in power dives from high altitudes. **1973** J. WAINWRIGHT *High-Class Kill* 24 Young Shaw had chucked himself over the guard-rail and power-dived into eternity. **1961** *Motor Cycle* 16 Mar. 334/1 Nowhere is a *power drill more useful than in the garage. **1977** *36 Home Handyman Projects* (Austral. Home Jrnl.) 75/2 An economical way to buy a power drill and attachments is as a set by Black and Decker. **1835** URE *Philos. Manuf.* 334 The *power-driven machines of a factory. **1898** A. G. ELLIOTT *H. de Graffigny's Gas & Petroleum Engines* iv. 73 This motor . . has become especially famous for its application to power-driven road vehicles. **1935** *Discovery* No. 326/2 A new power-driven spray painting outfit which can be carried by hand and can be run from an ordinary lighting socket has recently been produced. **1967** KARCH & BUBER *Offset Processes* i. 4 Early Power-Driven Presses. In 1814, R. Hoe and Company built the first steam-operated press to be used for printing. **1978** J. A. MICHENER *Chesapeake* 693 Four of their power-driven boats lay off the point of Tilghman Island. **1907** *Jrnl. R. Agric. Soc.* LXVIII. 130 Seed dresser, for hand or *power driving. **1916** *Aeroplane* 1 Nov. 802/1 There is quite a long distance separating these gondolas—or '*power-eggs', as the Naval Air Service calls them—from the forward car. **1931** *Flight* 16 Jan. 49/1 The revolution counters and oil-thermometers for the outboard engines are mounted on their respective power-eggs, clearly visible for the pilots. **1961** F. K. MASON *Hawker Aircraft since 1920* 292 The two Griffon prototypes . . were to be . . replaced by Griffon 61 'power eggs' at a later date, so becoming the Tempest IV. *a* **1743** SAVAGE *Poet's Dependance* 56 See . . Meekness depress'd, and *power-elated pride. **1953** C. W. MILLS *Veblen's Theory Leisure Class* p. xiv, The major change in national glamour, in which the debutante is replaced by the movie star, and the local society lady by the military and political and economic managers—the *power elite. **1956** —— (*title*) The power elite. **1960** *News Chron.* 16 June 6/3 Behind the council lies the real power elite: The Federation of Economic Organisations. **1973** *Black Panther* 17 Mar. 7/2 The genocide, oppression, humiliation and repression this country's racist power elite has inflicted upon Native Americans, Black Americans also know. **1893** CAYLEY *Coll. Math. Papers* XIII. 267 The power-ending terms or *power-enders, bc^2, b^5, which end in a power. **1826** SCOTT *Jrnl.* 23 Nov., The people . . in great discontent on account of the *power engines. **1892** J. A. FLEMING in *Jrnl. Inst. Electr. Engin.* XXI. 606 The ninth column gives a number which it is convenient to call the *power-factor of the transformer at no load—it is the ratio of the true to the apparent watts. If the currents and pressures were simple sine functions, then the power-factor in that case would be the cosine of the angle of lag of primary current behind the primary terminal potential difference. **1912** *Ibid.* XLIX. 323 The power factor and conductance of dielectrics under alternating electromotive force of low voltage. **1930** *Engineering* 24 Jan. 97/2 It [*sc.* a generator] is rated at 30,000 kv.-a., at 80 per cent. power factor, generating at 13,900 volts, three-phase and 60-cycles, and running at 200 r.p.m. **1950** *Ibid.* 28 July 80/2 Power-factor measurements up to 250 kV root-mean-square can be made with a Schering bridge. **1967** M. CHANDLER *Ceramics in Mod. World* iv. 133 If [*sc.* zircon porcelain] has not only a low power factor, but also good electrical properties in general. **1933** *Newnes Mod. Motor Repair* 684/2 When *power failure at high revs. occurs, get someone to speed up the engine and listen at the tail pipe. **1961** *Providence* (Rhode Island) *Jrnl.* 29 Nov. 22 The impact with the utility pole caused a brief power failure in the immediate area of the accident. **1967** 'T. Wells' *Dead by Light of Moon* (1968) i. 8 Hey! The whole street is dark. .. Must be a power failure. **1974** M. Babson *Stalking Lamb* xvii. 124 'Perhaps there is a power failure.' In the darkness, Sybilla sounded older. **1952** J. W. Day *New Yeomen of Eng.* xvi. 185 Substituting cheap modern *power-farming for expensive hand and animal labour. **1971** *Power Farming* Mar. 7/1 It is just 50 years since one of the most significant innovations in the world of power farming first saw the light of day. **1873** J. Richards *Wood-working Factories* 143 This distinction.. between a *power-feeding and a hand-feeding machine. **1831** J. Holland *Manuf. Metal* I. 89 The blocks ..are prepared at the *power forges. **1950** *Engineering* 28 July 80/2 Equipment which will provide impulse voltages up to 1,400 kV peak, *power-frequency voltages up to 250 kV root-mean-square, and direct current voltages up to 200 kV. **1967** M. Chandler *Ceramics in Mod. World* iv. 130 Although excellent for insulation at power frequencies, porcelain is far from being the ideal insulating material where high frequencies..are involved. **1958** *Spectator* 1 Aug. 175/3 The landowners..the officials..and the womanisers..are all playing an elaborate and stylised *power game under the eyes of their neighbours. **1970** [see Expo]. **1975** *Guardian* 20 Jan. 8/5 Britain's puny role in the East–West power game. **1901** *Nature* 10 Jan. 257/2 On *power-gas and large gas-engines for central stations. **1956** H. Seligman in A. Pryce-Jones *New Outl. Mod. Knowl.* 159 The future will bring stream-lined *power-generating units of the type described. **1945** W. S. Churchill *Victory* 26, I repulse those calumnies..that Britain..is a selfish, *power-greedy..nation. **1941** Wyndham Lewis *Let.* 31 May (1963) 290, I mean that of the big *power-groups..we are the inhabitants or controllers of the great ocean wastes. **1977** *Listener* 17 Feb. 223/2 Directors should be appointed for their competence, not because of the power group they represent. **1875** Knight *Dict. Mech.*, **Power-hammer*, a hammer in which the weight is raised by power of machinery. **1879** *Engineer* XLVIII. 412 It professes to be a power hammer applicable, not to one class of work, but to all purposes. **1936** *Discovery* July 222/2 It is merely a question of the *power-handling capacity of amplifier and loud-speaker. **1962** Simpson & Richards *Physical Princ. Junction Transistors* viii. 174 The mesa transistor should also be competitive as far as power-handling capability and ease of fabrication are concerned. **1972** 'G. Black' *Bitter Tea* (1973) ix. 139 A contractor's lorry..with a *power hoist. **1927** A. Huxley *Proper Stud.* 29 *Power-holders to whose material advantage it would have been to wield their power ruthlessly. **1971** T. W. Robinson *Cultural Revolution in China* i. 18 On the powerholders' side were those groups and individuals having a vested interest in maintaining the status quo. **1977** A. Giddens *Stud. in Social & Polit. Theory* x. 335 All power involves a certain 'mandate'..which gives power-holders certain rights and imposes on them certain obligations. **1977** *Dædalus* Fall 87 Schools produce the docile work habits the capitalists desire and serve to provide a facade of meritocracy for what is in fact a perpetual class of power holders. **1935** Huxley & Haddon *We Europeans* ii. 37 The *power-hunger of potentates. **1946** 'G. Orwell' *James Burnham* 17 He seems to assume that power-hunger ..is a natural instinct. **1946** —— *A. Koestler* in *Crit. Ess.* 134 Spartacus, however, is not represented as *power-hungry, nor, on the other hand, as a visionary. **1960** F. Land *Lang. Math.* vi. 82 The power-hungry countries of the world are determined to remedy their situation. **1973** *Listener* 6 Sept. 307/3 There were ambitious, power-hungry men on both sides. **1936** Wirth & Shils tr. *Mannheim's Ideology & Utopia* iii. 124 Observing the mass-mind, especially its *power-impulses and their functioning. **1938** B. Russell *Power* ii. 21 Their power-impulses..seemed to themselves indubitably righteous. **1944** 'G. Orwell' in *Horizon* X. 240 *No Orchids* is aimed at the *power-instinct. **1875** Knight *Dict. Mech.* s.v. *Lathe*, The *power-lathe is driven by horse-power, water, or steam. **1919** *Phil. Mag.* XXXVIII. 637 We know of no theoretical reason for supposing that the *power-law will give a better approximate representation than any other law, *e.g.* a sine-law. **1968** *Brit. Med. Bull.* XXIV. 257/1 Davis & Zerlin..have suggested that.. the amplitude of the averaged vertex response varies with the loudness of the stimulus according to a power law with an exponent of 0·4. **1977** *Sci. Amer.* Jan. 90/2 The inverse-square power-law spectrum of crater sizes on the moon has the property that if there are enough primary craters between one kilometer and 10 kilometers in diameter to cover an entire planet, there are also enough craters between 100 and 1,000 kilometers across to cover it. **1934** A. L. Albert *Electr. Communication* iii. 50 If the amount of noise cannot be reduced, the only alternative is to raise the *power level of the speech or music being transmitted. **1945** H. D. Smyth *Gen. Acct. Devel. Atomic Energy Mil. Purposes* viii. 85 The production goal..was set at a figure which meant that the pile should operate at a power level of 1000 kw. **1953** *Language* XXIX. 91 The human brain operates on a power-level of five watts. **1975** D. G. Fink *Electronics Engineers' Handbk.* I. 52 (*heading*) Power levels of speech. **1923** G. Collins *Valley of Eyes Unseen* xiv. 305 Luckily, I had just strength enough to reach up and touch the *power-lever. **1951** M. McLuhan *Mech. Bride* (1967) 98/2 Her legs..are date-baited power levers for the management of the male audience. **1894** A. T. Snell *Electr. Motive Power* iii. 91 For very heavy *power lines, in which copper cables of about 19/16 s.w.g. are used, the stalks are forged of cast steel, sometimes galvanised. **1956** *Nature* 17 Mar. 536/2 At this remote desert location, interference due to artificial signals from electromagnetic devices and power-lines was negligible. **1970** T. Hughes *Crow* 69 It was a naked powerline, 2000 volts. **1972** *Daily Tel.* 19 June 1/3 The aircraft narrowly missed plunging into a nearby reservoir and skimmed over power lines. **1905** *Westm. Gaz.* 9 Mar. 9/2 It is only by the increase of the '*power-load' which we supply that we can hope to reduce the price of electricity for lighting purposes. **1943** *Trans. Inst. Mining Engineers* CII. 145 The point we are anxious about is whether there is mechanized machinery for taking big *power-loaded outputs from such a dip as 1 in 6. **1963** *Economist* 12 Jan. 142/1 The industry raised its average percentage of power-loaded coal from 49 to 59 per cent between the two years. **1943** *Trans. Inst. Mining Engineers* CII. 40 The present development of the Meco-Moore *power-loader differs from that of a few years ago. **1956** F. S. Atkinson in D. L. Linton *Sheffield* 269 Intensive efforts are being made to replace the hand-loading of coal on to conveyors by mechanical power-loaders. **1946** Koestler *Thieves in Night* 296 It startles me that its up-to-date, stream-lined *power logics should be accompanied by all this maudlin opera stuff. **1959** *Times Lit. Suppl.* 9 Oct. 575/3 Over large tracts of their lives the winds of the Hobbesian power-logic blow unchecked. **1951** H. Arendt *Orig. Totalitarianism* i. 5 Persecution of powerless or *power-losing groups may not be a very pleasant spectacle. **1922** Glazebrook *Dict. Appl. Physics* II. 109/1 If the condenser has internal *power loss, ..the power factor..will not be zero. **1960** *Farmer & Stockbreeder* 1 Mar. 129/2 It sharply cuts power-loss in transmission and hydraulics. **1935** *Mind* XLIV. 94 Plutarch and Lucian, experienced in the ways of *power-loving Rome. **1923** D. H. Lawrence *Kangaroo* xvi. 344 The land ..invites parasites now... What would happen if the *power-lust came that way? **1959** S. Spender tr. *Schiller's Mary Stuart* iii. iv. 61 Your uncle, the *power-lusting cardinal. **1835** Ure *Philos. Manuf.* 333 Lace made by *power-machines. **1962** *Times* 2 May 7/4 The *power-mad politicians. **1976** B. Bova *Multiple Man* xviii. 201 He was insane, sir. Crazy. Power-mad. **1971** *New Scientist* 20 May 434/1 Psychology students studying *power-mania. **1963** *Times* 26 Jan. 11/3 It would be hard to see why..even a *power-maniac wanted to leave so charming an island. **1965** *Punch* 22 Sept. 443/2 Ropy little espionage agency, riddled with power-maniacs, sends courier to Europe to pick up important information. **1886** *All Year Round* 14 Aug. 37 Now we've got the American Durand's *power-milker. **1895** *Oracle Encycl.* I. 583/2 A great number of large *power-mills have sprung up. **1654** Whitlock *Zootomia* 396 These are sawcy Truths to obtrude on the *Power-mongers..of the World. **1961** *Guardian* 16 Feb. 10/5 Intellectuals have been found flat on their faces for powermongers to walk over. **1977** *Rolling Stone* 19 May 41/2 Powermongers will undoubtedly find ways to obtain the requisite technology. **1955** P. Mullahy in H. S. Sullivan *Conceptions Mod. Psychiatry* 243 The energy of the infant, or rather its manifestations in the *power motive, become quickly modified or transformed. **1940** *Sears, Roebuck Catal.* Spring/Summer 929 *Power mower. **1957** D. Karp *Leave me Alone* xiv. 192 The young boys in the development cheerfully cut grass with power mowers but disdained raking. **1970** R. Lowell *Notebk.* 28 The lawns, the paths, the harbor—stitched with motors, Yawl-engine, outboard, power mower. **1978** J. A. Michener *Chesapeake* 836 In July he runs his power mower, pushing his lawn back year by year. **1950** *Vogue* (U.S.) 15 Nov. 150/2 (*caption*) Nylon *power net pantie-girdle..for a smooth line under, say, tight velvet..pants. **1952** *Woman's Home Compan.* Nov. 3 (Advt.), Sheer powernet corselette with the smooth fit of a glove. **1963** *Times* 17 Apr. 16/7 The company will manufacture power-net, fish-net, marquisette curtaining and other fabrics in the Natal area. **1969** *Sears Catal.* Spring/Summer 2 This bra-slip... *The power-net frame*: cool and smooth..a stretchy blend of nylon and spandex. **1963** *Times* 20 Mar. 15/6 The *power-obsessed journalist. **1957** Forbes & O'Beirne *Technical Devel. Royal Dutch/Shell* iii. 256 For correct operation it was essential that the '*power oil' should be free from impurities and it was therefore necessary to wash it thoroughly above ground. **1972** L. M. Harris *Introd. Deepwater Floating Drilling Operations* xi. 108 The direct system has individual power-oil lines from the drill vessel to the individual functions on the subsea stack. **1917** W. G. Raymond *Elem. Railroad Engin.* (ed. 3) x. 129 In the automatic block system the signal at the entrance of each block is *power-operated, usually electric. **1940** *War Illustr.* 5 Jan. 554/3 The 'Wellingtons'.. with five separate machine-gun positions, including two in power-operated turrets. **1962** *Lancet* 1 Dec. 1155/1 Conventional prosthetic limbs may in fact be incapable of substantial development, but power-operated ones seem certain to become much more practical and effective. **1937** *Jrnl. Inst. Electr. Engin.* LXXX. 194/2 This is derived from two grid-controlled rectifier valves operated from a '*power pack' of the usual construction. **1942** *Electronic Engin.* XV. 285/3 The experimental model described, together with a power pack to permit operation direct from the 50 cycle mains, can be assembled on a box chassis measuring only 6½in. × 6½in. **1958** *New Scientist* 1 May 20/2 Its thickness is controlled by plating time and current, indicated by a graduated ampere-hour meter on the power 'pack'. **1967** *Gloss. Mining Terms (B.S.I.)* viii. 21 *Power pack*, a motor-pump combination for producing power for hydraulic equipment. **1971** J. Z. Young *Introd. Study Man* iv. 69 The mitochondria carry the respiratory enzymes, and are hence called the power packs of the cell. **1972** F. Bradbury *Hydraulic Syst.* iii. 43 In a large plant..the control desk and the power pack may be separated by some distance or may be installed in separate machinery spaces. **1973** *Houston Chron.* 21 Oct. 3/1 (Advt.), Penske Road Race... It's big-time racing excitement in a box! With power pack, 2 cars and hand controls, 30-ft. of track. **1977** J. Hedgecoe *Photographer's Handbk.* 35 To produce more light a flash with a larger powerpack is needed. **1958** C. C. Adams *Space Flight* viii. 196 Auxiliaries. These include taxis and propulsion 'guns' for individual men in space suits, or reaction *power packages attached like outboard motors to large objects. **1968** *Listener* 27 June 828/1 The power supply to this satellite was a 28 lb device called SNAP/9A. This power package contained as its energy source 17 kilocuries of Plutonium 238. **1945** H. D. Smyth *Gen. Acct. Devel. Atomic Energy Mil. Purposes* vii. 70 The whole of a *power pile..has to be enclosed in very thick walls of concrete, steel, or other absorbing material. **1961** *Observer* 26 Feb. 18/1 This is now well known as *power-play, a form developed by the All-Blacks and Springboks from the simple logic of the decisiveness of forward domination. **1961** J. S. Salak *Dict. Amer. Sports* 340 *Power play* (football), a play in which the offensive team concentrates blockers at one point. *Ibid.*, *Power-play* (ice hockey), launched when a team has an extra man or is trailing in the final minutes, all players rushing into the opponent's zone, and putting on the pressure. **1968** *Globe & Mail* (Toronto) 5 Feb. 17/6 The North Stars lead the NHL in power-play goals with 37. Balon scored on the power play. **1973** L. Mosley (*title*) Power-play: the tumultuous world of Middle East oil 1890–1973. **1976** *N.Y. Rev. Bks.* 15 Apr. 34/2 The Church was making a last desperate power play (for which it is now paying dear) to keep its immigrant children in line. **1976** *Washington Post* 19 Apr. D3/2 Chicago got the first goal of the game, by Cliff Koroll on a power play. **1978** *Dumfries Courier* 13 Oct. 4/2 At No. 3 Donald Bogie, with a variation of power play and finesse, proved too much for an experienced opponent. **1951** M. McLuhan *Mech. Bride* (1967) 98/2 To the mind of the modern girl, legs, like busts, are *power points which she has been taught to tailor. **1953** K. Tennant *Joyful Condemned* xxxiii. 323 An iron was plugged in handily to a power point. **1958** C. Watson *Coffin scarcely Used* ix. 86 Purbright watched for the power points. There was one in each of the large bedrooms. **1975** G. Burdett *Do your Own Home Wiring* xiii. 124 An additional 13A power point can usually be supplied from a ring circuit in the form of a spur. **1978** *Listener* 2 Feb. 159/1 Surrealism..works that sprang into being simply by unplugging the power-points of the mind. **1959** M. Shadbolt *New Zealanders* 174 They found it [*sc.* a car], bashed and tangled, at the foot of a slanting *power pole. **1973** *Black Panther* 20 Oct. 11/2 The United Boeing severed two power poles. **1870** W. Graham *Lect. Ephesians* 98 This word represents the rulers of this world as mere *power-possessors. **1846** Worcester, **Power-press*, a printing-press worked by steam, by water, or by other power. **1906** *Chambers's Jrnl.* 27 Oct. 765/2 The internal-combustion engine is coming..rapidly into favour as a cheap *power-producer for almost every kind of work. **1909** *Westm. Gaz.* 19 Oct. 4/1 The overhead valve system of this wonderful power-producer is not uncommon to the engine employed in this firm's racing cars. **1903** *Daily Chron.* 9 Dec. 6/5 That a revolution in *power-producton might result. **1845** J. E. Carpenter *Poems & Lyrics* 65 Its *power-propelling properties were vain. **1946** *Power reactor [see burn *v.*[1] 13 h]. **1962** [see converter 3 f]. **1970** *IEEE Trans. Nuclear Sci.* XVII. i. 520 (*heading*) Silicon radiation detector monitors nitrogen 16 in a power reactor. **1958** *New Statesman* 9 Aug. 158/1 The meeting..symbolises the change in the *power-relations of the Communist world. **1977** *Dædalus* Fall 66 In this approach it was stressed that the explanation of any institutional arrangement has to be attempted in terms of power relations and negotiations, power struggles and conflicts. **1962** R. F. Graf *Mod. Dict. Electronics* 234/2 **Power response*, the frequency-response capabilities of an amplifier running at or near its full rated power. **1963** *Wireless World* July 354/1 The power response at 10W output is −3dB at 15 c/s and 15 kc/s. **1970** J. Earl *Tuners & Amplifiers* iii. 68 The latest 'quality' amplifiers.. boast a power response which is almost as good as the frequency response. **1975** *Gramophone* Nov. 953/3 Power response is taken to be the range of frequencies over which the amplifier can deliver at least half its rated power. **1960** *McGraw-Hill Encycl. Sci. & Technol.* XIV. 542/1 Bench or circular saws are the common wood-working type of *power saw. **1969** in Halpert & Story *Christmas Mumming in Newfoundland* 17 A game of cards, the loan of a power-saw ..can act as the favours that initially link two persons together. **1976** N. Thornburg *Cutter & Bone* iv. 108 The car, a late-model Buick Century, seemed to have every possible piece of optional equipment, including *power seats. **1946** 'G. Orwell' *James Burnham* 4 The English Puritans, the Jacobins, the Bolsheviks, were in each case simply *power-seekers. **1979** P. Alexander *Show me Hero* xxiii. 246 He was the perfect example of the power-seeker. .. He'd tread on anyone's face to get to the top. **1963** A. Heron *Towards Quaker View of Sex* i. 10 We see human energy that should be creative and loving deflected into activities that are coldly *power-seeking. *Ibid.* iv. 41 Our tendencies toward aggression and power-seeking. **1977** P. Johnson *Enemies of Society* xii. 169 Marxism..has a methodology of power-seeking. **1893** A. R. Forsyth *Theory of Functions of Complex Variable* iii. 56 Any one of the continuations of a uniform function, represented by a *power-series, can be derived from any other. **1938** F. E. Terman *Fund. Radio* v. 136 For electrode voltages such that the instantaneous plate current never became zero, the characteristics of a tube could be expressed in forms of the following power series. **1968** P. A. P. Moran *Introd. Probability Theory* iii. 135 $R(z)$ is a power series whose coefficients tend to zero. **1953** A. A. Fraenkel *Abstract Set Theory* ii. 96 The set of all subsets of S may..be called the *power-set of S. **1963** Selby & Sweet *Sets, Relations, Functions* i. 18 Since A contained four elements, the power set 2^A was made up of 2^4 or 16 subsets, each subset an element of the power set. **1974** *Encycl. Brit. Macropædia* I. 521/1 The power set lattice.., defined by the inclusion relation on the power set $P(U)$ of all subsets of a set U, has important special properties not shared by lattices in general. **1972** *Times* 31 Oct. 15/3 It is safe to say that that kind of enforced *power-sharing is practicable to the extent that the power to be exercised is circumscribed. **1973** *Hansard Commons* 20 Mar. 242/1 We have expressed positive views on many matters in the White Paper—for example,..on power sharing. **1978** P. Cosgrave *Margaret Thatcher* ii. 34 It was widely believed that if there had not been a general election in February 1974 his Northern Ireland 'power-sharing' executive would have worked. **1940** *Chambers's Techn. Dict.* 669/1 **Power shovel* (or *navvy*), an excavator consisting of a jib carrying a radial arm to the end of which a large bucket or scoop is attached. The bucket makes a radial cut. **1966** *McGraw-Hill Encycl. Sci. & Technol.* III. 416/2 Power shovels are made which can be rapidly converted into a dragline, crane, or backhoe by changing booms and modifying the rigging. **1971** P. O'Donnell *Impossible Virgin* iii. 57 Stacks of bricks, a concrete mixer, a power-shovel. **1922** D. H. Lawrence *Aaron's Rod* xxi. 311 Yield to the deep *power-soul in the individual man, and obey implicitly. **1944** *Bell Syst. Techn. Jrnl.* XXIII. 282 The second part is devoted principally to the fundamental result that the *power spectrum of a noise current is the Fourier transform of its correlation function. **1960** W. R. Bennett *Electr. Noise* x. 208 Many important phenomena are found to have a power spectrum even though the Fourier transform itself does not approach a limit. **1972** T. H. G. Megson *Aircraft Struct.* xii. 427 It is assumed that gust velocity is a random variable which may be regarded for analysis as consisting of a large number of sinusoidal components whose amplitudes vary with frequency. The power spectrum of such a function is then defined as the distribution of energy over the frequency range. **1901** *Daily Express* 18 Mar. 2/6 The development of *power-stations all over the country. **1932** *Automotive Industries* 10 Dec. 739/2 The greatest need for *power steering exists undoubtedly in connection with heavy trucks and buses. **1976** M. Maguire *Scratchproof* xii. 182 She gunned the vehicle forward..as she swung the power-steering into a fierce lock. **1903** *Work* 9 May 218/2 Such engines have only one *power stroke in every four. **1966** E. Rudinger *Consumer's Car Gloss.* 113 Every other stroke (the down-stroke) of the piston is a power stroke which drives the engine; whereas in a four-stroke engine, there is only one power stroke in every four. **1950** D. Riesman et al. *Lonely Crowd* xi. 255 Even those intellectuals.. who feel themselves very much out of power and who are frightened of those who they think have the power, prefer to be scared by the *power structures they conjure up. **1977** *Time* 4 July 6/1 Brezhnev already ranked No. 1 in the Kremlin power structure and was accorded the diplomatic status due a chief of state nearly everywhere he went. **1961** *Los Angeles Times* 4 Aug. iii. 4 Bitter echoes of the 1960 *power struggle.. are still audible in party circles. **1969** *New Yorker* 20 Sept. 110/1 A serious power struggle could take place in the North. **1978** *Jrnl. R. Soc. Arts* CXXVI. 669/2 The detention of the four leaders had deprived one main group in the power struggle for the succession of its principal leaders. **1906** *Westm. Gaz.* 19 Apr. 7/2 The *power-supply for the printing presses of the newspapers being cut off. **1943** J. S. Huxley *Evolutionary Ethics* vii. 59 A naked *power-system cannot tolerate tolerance or face even intellectual opposition. **1970** C. Furtado in I. L. Horowitz *Masses in Lat. Amer.* ii. 46 Allowing the landlord class to augment its share in aggregate income and to consolidate its position in the power system. **1929** *Sears, Roebuck Catal.* Spring/Summer 881 This *power take-off and clutch pulley combined makes your Fordson tractor always ready for belt power. **1943** C. G. Barger *Automotive Mech.* I. iv. 123 Power take-offs are used on such vehicles as dump trucks, fire engines, wreckers, and.. allow the accessories to be operated by the power of the engine. **1957** P. H. Wilkinson *Aircraft Engines of World* 20 (Advt.), The Lycoming 825-h.p. T53, featuring front-or-rear power take-off, is the world's first turbine designed specifically for helicopters. **1958** *Times* 1 July (Agric. Suppl.) p. viii/2 The mechanism of the trailer is driven with the power-take-off from the tractor and unloads at the rate of three tons in seven minutes. **1972** *Proc. Inst. Mech. Engineers* CLXXXIV. iii. i. 284 Power take-off systems.. supplying the power to operate various truck-mounted equipment on tipping gear, garbage packers,.. and many more applications. *Ibid.*, Power take-offs (PTOs) are necessary on most of today's trucks. **1951** H. Arendt *Orig. Totalitarianism* v. 141 Hobbes.. proceeded from this insight to a plan for a body politic best fitted for this *power-thirsty animal. **1959** *Sears, Roebuck Catal.* Spring-Summer 1299 Make your Drill a new *power tool every time you change accessories. **1961** *Times* 3 Oct. (Computer Suppl.) p. ii/5 Muscles are replaced by machines or power-tools. **1971** *New Scientist* 27 May 529/1 Other batteries still in the development stage.. include the silver oxide/zinc cell and the titanium battery, both currently under evaluation.. for application in TV, portable powertools and possibly electric vehicles. **1937** *Times* 13 Apr. (Brit. Motor Suppl.) p. vi/4 It is of 4½ litres capacity, and the *power-to-weight ratio is given at 4·2lb. a brake horse-power. **1971** *Engineering* Apr. 72 (Advt.), Reyrolle Hydraulics axial piston pumps and motors. Fixed or variable displacement, with excellent power-to-weight ratio (up to 2·8 hp/lb). **1943** C. G. Barger *Automotive Mech.* I. iv. 107 (*heading*) *Power train. **1946** W. H. Crouse *Automotive Mech.* i. 24 The power train consists of a series of gears and shafts, which mechanically connect the engine shaft with the car wheels. **1966** *Economist* 10 Sept. 1040/2 Chrysler has gained substantial sales in the United States in the past four years since it began offering a 5-year, 50,000-mile guarantee for the 'power train' (engine-transmission-rear-axle) of its American-built cars. **1976** *National Observer* (U.S.) 2 Oct. 8/2 Auto manufacturers are reluctant to offer special-engine versions of all their models and power-train combinations. **1929** K. Henney *Princ. Radio* xvi. 403 A.-c. voltages are likely to be picked up by the cores of audio transformers if they are near *power transformers carrying a.-c. currents. **1975** D. G. Fink *Electronics Engineers' Handbk.* vii. 17 Electronic power transformers normally operate at a fixed frequency. The most popular frequencies are 50, 60, and 400 Hz. **1959** K. Henney *Radio Engin. Handbk.* (ed. 5) x. 34 The increased ruggedness of the supply due to the inherently stable physical structure of the *power transistor. **1974** G. A. G. Bennett *Electricity & Mod. Physics* (ed. 2) xiv. 271/1 Power transistors are made by the same techniques as other transistors; but the collector, in which most of the heat is dissipated, is fused onto a thick metal mounting plate forming one face of the unit. **1891** *Times* 28 Sept. 13/6 A *power transmission.. from the Palmengarten.. to the exhibition, a distance of about four kilomètres. **1924** Moyer & Wostrel *Pract. Radio* vii. 103 The volume of sound may be increased by using a *power tube of, say, 5 watts of electric power, in the last stage of amplification. **1975** D. G. Fink *Electronics Engineers' Handbk.* vii. 21 Power tubes, in contrast to receiving-type tubes, handle relatively large amounts of power, and.. a major emphasis is placed on efficiency. The traditional division between the two tube categories is at the 25-W plate dissipation rating level. **1942** F. H. Joseph *Lett. home from Brit. at War* 44 Machine guns, rear *power turret having four, front power turret two. **1907** H. Allen *Gas & Oil Engines* xiv. 307 A 4-cylinder engine,.. having cylinders 8in. diam. and 8in. stroke, capable of running up to 800 revs. per minute, gives a *power unit, when using petrol, of 100 b.h.p. **1908** S. H. Moore *Mech. Engin. & Machine Shop Pract.* xix. 421 Synchronous motors are best adapted for power transmission plants and for large power units of high voltage. **1918** G. Sherwood *Farm Tractor Handbk.* vii. 110 The machine [*sc.* a Fordson tractor] is merely a power unit and transmission gear *en bloc* mounted on two pairs of wheels, together with the simplest of control and steering arrangements. **1963** *Amer. Speech* XXXVIII. 120 The auxiliary power unit supplying electrical power to the KC-97 when it is on the ground. **1967** C. J. Freezer *Model Railway Terminol.* 8/1 The power unit is a device which converts the high-voltage mains current into low-voltage currents, often with several outputs. **1922** D. H. Lawrence *Aaron's Rod* xxi. 311 But the deep *power-urge is not conscious of its aims. **1790** R. Merry *Laurel of Liberty* (ed. 2) 13 While none but *pow'r-usurping slaves are free. **1947** Koestler in *Partisan Rev.* XIV. 345 The best way to prolong the *power-vacuum to the west of the Russian bloc.. is to proclaim an independent British policy. **1976** *Times* 10 Sept. 1/1 (*heading*) Mao succession struggle. Death leaves power vacuum in China. **1919** W. D. Owen *Guide Study Ionic Valve* x. 38 *Power valves need to be very hard otherwise the plate voltage would cause a discharge across the space. **1944** *Wireless World* June 163/2 Although power valves are used, they are only lightly loaded and HT volts and current are quite low. **1909** *Chambers's Jrnl.* June 341/1 Thompson in Edinburgh introduced the first *power-vehicle running on india-rubber tires. **1916** *Ibid.* Feb. 83/1 The power-vehicle is also invaluable for communication between commanders and their units. **1831** G. R. Porter *Silk Manuf.* 266 Fabrics which *power-weaving has been found adequate to produce. **1831** *Engineering* 9 Jan. 58/3 Volumetric efficiency is important.. in that it affects the *power-weight ratio of an engine. **1950** *Times Rev. Industry* Sept. 25/2 The Swiss Federal Railways has improved the power-weight ratio of single-phase mainline types [of locomotives]. **1902** H. A. Foster *Electr. Engineer's Pocket-Bk.* 766 Special precautions of this kind must be taken where sharp angles occur, or where any wires might possibly come in contact with electric light or *power wires. **1911** W. Aitken *Man. Telephone* xx. 409 All power wires from the fuse board are now usually laid up in lead-covered cables. **1938** R. Finlayson *Brown Man's Burden* 41 The new power wires... Ten thousand volts, ehoa! **1862** Goulburn *Pers. Relig.* I. i. vi. 88 As if He had said, 'My words are *power-words indeed. They take effect'. **1941** 'G. Orwell' *England your England* in *Lion & Unicorn* i. 17 *Power-worship.. has never touched the common people. **1900** *Westm. Gaz.* 27 Apr. 5/2 The.. *power works adjacent to the river. **1921** *Electrician* 11 Mar. 304/2 In the United States where an electric ironing machine.. costs about the same as a washing machine, some women use their *power wringer as a cold mangle. **1957** *Observer* 1 Dec. 10/5 There is no national test for power wringers so test the safety release yourself before buying.

g. Designating alcoholic liquids of a grade suitable for generating mechanical power.

1919 *Rep. Interdepartmental Comm. Alcohol for Power* 4 in *Parl. Papers* (Cmd. 218) X. 117 Some sections of the community believe that the words 'industrial alcohol' refer to an inferior spirit for drinking purposes. We recommend, therefore, that all alcohol for power or traction purposes should be described as 'power alcohol'... This description has already been adopted in Australia. *Ibid.* 7 All sales.. of power alcohol should be made on the basis of a certified percentage by volume of absolute ethyl alcohol, with a minimum of 90 per cent. at a temperature of 62 deg. F. **1920** *Act 10 & 11 Geo. V* c. 18 §11 In this section the expression 'power methylated spirits' means any methylated spirits (other than mineralised methylated spirits) which are intended to be used in generating mechanical power. **1922** G. W. Monier-Williams *Power Alcohol* vii. 198 The conversion of the alcohol into power methylated spirits may be carried out only by an authorised methylator. **1934** *Proc. World Petroleum Congr. 1933* II. 693/2 It is quite a recent innovation to market a 'power' kerosine. **1939** *Sun* (Baltimore) 17 Apr. 13/3 Senator Gurney.. estimated that if farm surpluses were used to make 'power alcohol' to be mixed with gasoline, 840,000,000 bushels of grain would be diverted to that purpose annually. **1940** S. Miall *New Dict. Chem.* 330/2 Power methylated spirit is absolute ethyl alcohol, 92 volumes; benzol, 5 volumes; crude pyridine, 0·5 volume, and crude naphtha, 2·5 volumes. **1955** *Know Your Tractor* (Shell Guide) ii. 27 The cost to the farmer of gasoline and power kerosine is very variable throughout the world. **1957** *Encycl. Brit.* I. 543/1 The use of power methylated spirits practically ceased during World War II. **1961** L. M. Miall *New Dict. Chem.* (ed. 3) 446/2 *Power kerosine*, a volatile kerosine of high anti-knock value, essentially a blend of aromatic hydrocarbons, used in tractor engines and usually called tractor vaporizing oil (T.V.O.). **1975** E. M. Goodger *Hydrocarbon Fuels* vii. 134 'Power kerosine' or 'tractor vaporising-oil' denotes a kerosine blend prepared for spark-ignition engines used in agricultural tractors, which is taxed at a lower rate than that of gasoline.

h. Applied to a sportsman who applies great muscular power to his style of play; also of the style of play itself.

1958 *Observer* 15 June 24/1 The machine-like rhythm and efficiency of her power tennis. **1959** *Times* 29 May 4/7 A power player, he went for every shot. **1959** *Sunday Express* 12 July 12/1 His splendid piece of power-running. **1969** *New Yorker* 14 June 44/3 Graebner could now probably explode one. He has what is almost a setup on his power side. **1973** *Black Panther* 25 Aug. 13/1 Henry Aaron will.. establish himself unquestionably as the greatest power hitter in baseball history.

power, *sb.*² *dial.* Also 8 poor. [Etymology obscure (in reference to quot. 1836 it may be noted that *power* is not the pronunciation of *poor* in Cornwall).] The local name in Cornwall of a small species of cod, *Gadus minutus*, also called ***power-cod*** or poor-cod.

1713 Jago in *Ray's Synopsis* 163 Asellus mollis minimus. *Cornub.* Poor vel Power dictus. **1769** Pennant *Zool.* III. 150 Poor or Power. **1836** Yarrell *Brit. Fishes* II. 161 The Power, or Poor Cod, the smallest of its genus, so called, it is said, on account of its diminutive size, seldom exceeding six or seven inches in length. **1880** *E. Cornw. Gloss.*, *Power*, the fish, *Gadus minutus*.

power, *v.* [f. power *sb.*¹] †**1.** *trans.* To make powerful, empower, strengthen. *Obs. rare.*

1540 Hyrde tr. *Vives' Instr. Chr. Wom.* (1592) Kj, With silence both wisedome & chastitie be sweetly powred. **1729** Young *Merchant* v. xx, Trade gilt their titles, power'd their state.

2. *trans.* To supply with power, esp. for propulsion. Also *fig.*

1898 W. F. Durand *Resistance & Propulsion of Ships* v. 326 (*heading*) Powering ships. **1929** *Chicago Tribune* 31 Jan. 3/8 His plane is a Travelaire, powered with a whirlwind motor. **1954** *Essays in Crit.* IV. 313 Creative activity is often.. powered by the drive to accomplish. **1959** *Times* 29 June 12/7 The big traction engines that had powered the carousels. **1962** *Times* 25 Apr. 16/6 The incident.. could have powered strong conflict between faith and sex. **1973** *Sci. Amer.* Feb. 102/3 It is the gravitational energy from the falling material, rather than the rotation, that probably powers the X-ray sources. **1976** *Billings* (Montana) *Gaz.* 30 June 3-E/3 Larvell Blanks and George Hendrick each belted two-run, first-inning homers Tuesday to power the Cleveland Indians to a 4-1 victory over the Milwaukee Brewers. **1977** 'A. York' *Tallant for Trouble* iv. 53 The police launch.. was powered by two big Perkins engines.

3. *intr.* **a.** To move or travel with great speed or force.

1972 J. Mosedale *Football* ix. 129 The key play sent Nagurski powering toward the line. **1973** 'D. Rutherford' *Kick Start* ii. 46 The big bike solved all traffic problems for me, whether I was powering to the head of a two mile traffic jam or pulling it on to its stand on a yellow line. **1974** *Oxford Times* 20 Sept. 19/3 Derek Clarke powered in from the right and unleashed a superb shot. **1977** *Navy News* Aug. 38/1 At Mount Wise the following day, Civil Service powered to 256-5 off their 55 overs. **1978** *Daily Tel.* 20 June 13/2 For Michael Marshall.. diesel, electric and advanced passenger trains plainly have no appeal to compare with that of the majestic locomotives that powered along the track in the first half of the century.

b. To travel using an engine, esp. as an alternative or supplement to sail.

1975 *Daily Colonist* (Victoria, B.C.) 2 Apr. 21/2 We had to power most of the way, that's how little wind there was. **1976** 'F. Clifford' *Drummer in Dark* xv. 95 The Trident braked and powered round until it pointed down the long smeared runway. **1976** T. Heald *Let Sleeping Dogs Die* viii. 171 A seagoing cabin cruiser.. was just beginning to power towards the narrow entrance to the cove.

So **'powering** *vbl. sb.*

1898 W. F. Durand *Resistance & Propulsion of Ships* v. 340 (*heading*) Powering by the law of comparison. **1899** *Engineering Mag.* Mar. 1011/1 It is in the powering of the two vessels that the great advance in marine engineering is most apparent. *Ibid.* 1011/2 The powering of the Oceanic is.. about double that of the Great Eastern. **1976** R. Lewis *Witness my Death* i. 19 Coal and dust and slack for the powering of industrial furnaces.

power, obs. form of poor, pour.

'powerable, *a.* Now *rare.* [f. power *sb.*¹ + -able: cf. *comfortable*, *reasonable*, *peaceable*.]

†**1.** = powerful. *Obs.*

1588 Allen *Admon.* 7 Gods mighty arme that deposeth the prowde and powrable persons from their seates. **1593** G. Harvey *New Let.* Wks. (Grosart) I. 271 Howsoeuer valiant, rich, or powerable. **1605** Camden *Rem.*, *Epigr.* 14 The only powerable man of England in his time. **1608** Hieron *Wks.* I. 724 Diuers things.. very effectuall and powerable to corrupt. **1632** Holland *Cyrupædia* 131 In case our Associats.. would be willing to stay with us, more powerable we shall be to effect any thing.

†**2.** Extreme, excessive. *Obs. rare.*

1588 Allen *Admon.* 28 An unbridled powrable sinner. **1598** Grenewey *Tacitus' Ann.* iii. x. (1622) 78 The memory of Quirinius was nothing pleasing, by reason.. of the danger he brought Lepida into, and miserable niggishnes, and powerable old age [*sordidamque et præpotentem senectam*].

3. That can be effected by power; possible. $rare^{-1}$.

1860 J. Young *Prov. Reason* 172 The Infinite God.. can effect all the powerable.

Hence †**'powerableness**, powerfulness, power as a quality; †**'powerably** *adv.*, powerfully.

1581 Savile *Tacitus' Hist.* ii. xcii. (1591) 107 Powerablenesse [L. *potentia*] is neuer sure where it is too excessiue. **1593** G. Harvey *Pierce's Super.* Wks. II. 180 Powerably armed with that supreme and vncontrowlable authoritie. **1600** W. Watson *Decacordon* (1602) 49 Christ.. was both dead and buried.. and yet not corrupted as powerably preserued *per concomitantiam diuinitatis.* **1656** Heylin *Surv. France* 123 Had he.. in some measure broken the powerableness of the Princes.

'power-boat. Also power boat, powerboat. A motor-boat, esp. one with a powerful engine. Hence **'powerboater**, one who travels by power-boat; **power boating**, travel by power-boat.

1908 R. W. Chambers *Firing Line* vii. 84 Every day.. the swift power-boats sped northward to the Inlet. **1932** *World Today* LIX. 254 (*heading*) Power boating. *Ibid.* 258/2 Craft built by the British Power Boat Company have, to date, secured the championships of the world. **1953** *Richmond* (Va.) *News Leader* 2 Sept. 24/7 From the Elizabeth River at Norfolk to Gibson Island in Maryland there'll be.. more races for sailors and power boaters alike. **1966** *Listener* 28 July 144/2 That horrible vehicle, the power boat. **1971** 'E. Fenwick' *Impeccable People* xxi. 115 The powerboat owners suddenly became invisible... The local powerboaters.. remained the most unpopular minority conceivable. **1975** *Times* 17 June 14/6 Power-boat racing is the preserve of those who have a great deal of.. money. **1977** *Modern Boating* (Austral.) Jan. 71/3 Warren has set out to produce a book which will give a potential power boat buyer a complete idea of what leisure powerboating is all about.

power-cod: see power *sb.*²

'power-drive, *sb.* [f. power *sb.*¹ + drive *sb.*]

1. (Equipment for) the driving of machinery by mechanical or electrical power. Also *fig.*

1952 B. Ulanov *Hist. Jazz in Amer.* (1958) xvii. 203 Lionel Hampton.. added.. a power-drive on vibes and drums all his own. **1960** *Farmer & Stockbreeder* 15 Mar. (Suppl.) 13 The rugged, reliable AEI 'Stayrite' Single-phase power-drive has been specifically developed for arduous farming applications. **1971** P. J. McMahon *Aircraft Propulsion* iii. 78 The normal transmission efficiency of a power drive is expressed as the ratio of power output to power input.

2. The impulse to exercise power.

1954 R. F. C. Hull tr. *Jung's Pract. of Psychotherapy* in *Coll. Wks.* XVI. i. 19 The first corresponds to Freud's pleasure principle, the second to Adler's power-drive, the desire to be on top. **1964** Gould & Kolb *Dict. Social Sci.* 483/1 Some modern definitions stress the fact of the power drive of parties. **1969** J. Mander *Static Society* vi. 180 The power-drive implied in this process is an ugly thing. **1979** J. Sherwood *Hour of Hyenas* ii. 23 You are very striking-looking, but.. my power drive is far stronger nowadays than my sex drive.

powered ('paʊəd, paʊəd), *a.* [f. POWER *sb.*[1] + -ED[2].] Having power (of a specified kind or degree); utilizing mechanical power for propulsion.

1879 H. F. CRAGGS in *Daily News* 19 Apr. 3/3, I must deny ..that a small powered steamer is as seaworthy as one of good power. **1892** *Manch. Exam.* 30 Nov. 8/4 Not so heavily powered as some more modern vessels. **1903** *Motoring Ann.* 218 They are more highly powered in proportion to their weight than other cars. **1935** C. G. BURGE *Compl. Bk. Aviation* 377/2 The introduction of powered flight in 1903. **1960** *Which?* Mar. 48/1 There are two main categories of lawnmower—hand-operated and powered. **1971** *Engineering* Apr. 65 (Advt.), Straddle carriers, powered bogies,..level luffing cranes. **1974** 'D. CRAIG' *Whose Little Girl are You?* i. 5 A display of powered model aircraft.

Powerforming ('paʊəfɔːmɪŋ). Also with small initial. [f. POWER *sb.*[1] + RE)FORMING *vbl. sb.*] The name of a process for reforming petroleum using a platinum catalyst. Hence **'Powerformer**, an installation for this process.

1956 *Oil & Gas Jrnl.* 5 Mar. 62 A new catalytic-reforming process called Powerforming has been announced by Esso Research & Engineering Co. *Ibid.*, (*caption*) One of three Powerformers already operating is unit at left of picture at Carter's Billings refinery. **1958** W. L. NELSON *Petroleum Refinery Engin.* (ed. 4) xxi. 772 In catalytic reforming, only the platinum catalyst processes (Platforming,.. Powerforming, Sovaforming, etc.) are sufficiently well defined to allow the prediction of yields. **1967** BLAND & DAVIDSON *Petroleum Processing Handbk.* iii. 32 The first commercial Powerforming installation was placed on-stream in July, 1955, at Baltimore, Md., by the Esso Standard Oil Co. **1969** *Daily Tel.* 30 Dec. 2/5 (*caption*) The fire..severely damaged one of the plant's two powerformers, used in the manufacture of top grade petrol.

powerful ('paʊəfʊl), *a.* (*adv.*) [f. POWER *sb.*[1] + -FUL.] **A.** *adj.* Full of or having power.

1. Having great power; mighty, potent.

a **1400–50** *Alexander* 3242 My pure powarfull [*v.r.* power-full] gods I prestly pauoure, þine empire & þine erytage enterely þe to ȝeld. **1593** SHAKS. *Rich. II*, II. ii. 55 The Lords of Rosse, Beaumond, and Willoughby With all their powre-full friends are fled to him. **1621** DONNE *Serm.* xv. (1640) 149 [Death] is the powerfullest, the fearefulest enemy. **1727** A. HAMILTON *New Acc. E. Ind.* I. xxv. 305 He is reckoned the powerfullest King on the Sea-coast of Malabar. **1845** S. AUSTIN *Ranke's Hist. Ref.* III. 387 This powerful city had protested against the Recess of Spires.

2. Capable of exerting great force (physical or immaterial); strong, potent. (Of persons or things.)

1586 T. B. *La Primaud. Fr. Acad.* I. (1594) 80 The.. perfect understanding of the chiefest part and most powerfull beginning of himselfe, namelie of his spirit. **1593** SHAKS. *3 Hen. VI*, v. ii. 15 Whose top-branch..kept low Shrubs from Winters pow'rfull Winde. **1638** in *Hamilton Pap.* (Camden) I. 41 This is not nou to be doune uithout a pourfull force, uhich can not be rased heire. **1654–66** EARL ORRERY *Parthen.* (1676) 697 Extorting a confession from me by the powerfullest Rack. *a* **1711** KEN *Div. Love* Wks. (1838) 275 Let thy all-powerful love abound in my heart. **1802** *Med. Jrnl.* VIII. 390 By the frequent and liberal use of other powerful stimulants. **1808** SCOTT *Marm.* IV. xiii, He knew to prize Lord Marmion's powerful mind, and wise. **1847** JAMES *Convict* ii, By one of the rocks were seated three powerful men. **1876** TAIT *Rec. Adv. Phys. Sc.* vii. (ed. 2) 183 A performer with a powerful instrument (such as a cornopean).

3. a. Exerting great force or producing great effect (in quot. 1854, indicating the exertion of great force). **b.** Having power to influence greatly; impressive, convincing, telling.

1596 SPENSER *F.Q.* IV. x. 36 Had not the Ladie with her powrefull speach Him from his wicked will uneath refrayned. **1624** DONNE *Serm.* xvii. (1640) 165 Of all proofes, Demonstration is the powerfullest. **1722** DE FOE *Relig. Courtsh.* I. i. (1840) 30 There is a powerful force in a father's command. **1799** C. B. BROWN *Edgar Huntly* (1803) I. viii. 219 Features which bore at all times a powerful resemblance to those of Mrs. Lorimer. **1854** MURCHISON *Siluria* iv. (1867) 63 The line of a powerful fault. **1860** TYNDALL *Glac.* II. xxvii. 385 The sudden change of inclination producing powerful longitudinal compression. **1873** MORLEY *Rousseau* I. 124 The author of the most powerful book by which parental duty has been commended. **1899** *Allbutt's Syst. Med.* VIII. 902 A powerful fetid odour.

†**4.** Having the power *to do* something; able, capable. *Obs. rare.*

1620 T. GRANGER *Div. Logike* 108 By which the Substance is able, or powerfull to doe something.

†**5.** *Math.* Involving the square or a higher power. *Obs. rare.*

1674 JEAKE *Arith.* (1696) 614 A powerful Equation, where-in is some Figural number or other.

6. Great, in quantity or number; cf. MIGHTY *a.* 3. *dial.* and *colloq.*

1811 BYRON Let. 25 June (1830) I. 249 For a long time I have been restricted to an entire vegetable diet,..so I expect a powerful stock of potatoes, greens, and biscuit. **1822** J. WOODS *Two Years' Residence Eng. Prairie* 294, I also have got some beefs, and a powerful chance of corn. **1852** MRS. STOWE *Uncle Tom's C.* xxxiii, Dat ar Tom's gwine to make a powerful deal o' trouble. *a* **1859** CARLTON *New Purchase* II. 8 (Bartlett) This piano was sort o' fiddle like—only bigger—and with a powerful heap of wire strings. **1865** DICKENS *Mut. Fr.* I. v, [He] took a powerful sight of notice.

7. *Comb.*, as ***powerful-engined***, ***-faced***, ***-handed***.

1822 GALT *Provost* xxxvi, Pulled out of the crowd by a powerful-handed woman. **1903** *Daily Chron.* 5 Jan. 5/2 The most powerful-engined liner in the world. **1906** RIDER HAGGARD *Benita* ix. 129 A clever powerful-faced man.

B. as *adv.* In a great degree; very, exceedingly. *dial.* and *colloq.* Cf. MIGHTY *adv.*

a **1822** in *Amer. Speech* (1956) XXXI. 270 *Powerful.* This word is much used by the middling and lower class of people in the interior of So: Carolina..: instead of saying a person is very strong, they would say, *he is powerful*; or *powerful strong.* **1832** W. IRVING *Jrnl.* 10 Nov. (1919) III. 171 My gun is so powerful dirty. **1835** —— *Tour Prairies* xiii, He was powerful tired. **1848** W. E. BURTON *Waggeries* 23 He felt it tickle powerful from the top of his head to thee end of his starn-fin. **1876** BESANT & RICE *Gold. Butterfly* xviii, Rayner seems powerful anxious to get you on the paper. **1902** *Dialect Notes* II. 242 *Powerful*, adv. Very, as '*powerful* much'. **1927** *Amer. Speech* II. 362/1 Our lessons are all pow'eful hard to-day. **1942** *Morgantown* (W. Virginia) *Post* 26 Sept. 5 It does get powerful cold in those hills. **1977** F. PARRISH *Fire in Barley* III. 33 'Tes powerful hard t'temp me Mam's fancy. She d'play wi' her food, mos' times.

'powerfully, *adv.* [f. prec. + -LY[2].] In a powerful manner; with power, authority, or might; strongly, forcibly, mightily; with moving force, earnestly, impressively; greatly, exceedingly.

1602 DANIEL *Def. Rhyme* H iij, It hath stood against al the storms of factions..which so powerfully beat vpon it. **1699** BENTLEY *Phal.* 149 He is so powerfully back'd. **1766** GOLDSM. *Vic. W.* v, This well-timed present pleaded more powerfully in his favour. **1873** BLACK *Pr. Thule* i, The short, thick-set, powerfully-built man. **1880** C. R. MARKHAM *Peruv. Bark* 305 From May to November the sun shines powerfully.

'powerfulness. [f. as prec. + -NESS.] The quality of being powerful; mightiness; strength, potency; impressiveness, convincing quality.

c **1586** C'TESS PEMBROKE *Ps.* LXXXIX. iii, Who can maintaine With Thee in powrfullnes a rivall's quarrell? **1605** DRAYTON *Leg. Dk. Normandy* xxxiv, As though her words such power-fulnesse did beare. **1735–6** CARTE *Ormonde* I. 113 That by the powerfulness of some ministers of State..the Parliament had not its natural freedom. **1824** *New Monthly Mag.* XII. 249 A certain degree of want of powerfulness [of voice] in various parts of her scale. **1961** *Chicago Rev.* Summer 94 Their art is an imitation of the inescapable powerfulness of this unknown and empty world. **1975** *Listener* 24 July 109/3 The powerfulness of Queenie Leavis's mind.

'powerhouse. Also **power-house.** [f. POWER *sb.*[1] + HOUSE *sb.*[1]] **1.** A building in which power is produced on a large scale for driving machinery or for generating electricity for distribution.

Quot. 1881 refers to a building containing steam engines for pumping water.

1881 *Harper's Mag.* Mar. 597/1 He found himself in the end at that 'Power House' of which he had heard..for many a year. **1890** *Cent. Dict.*, *Power-house*,..a building especially provided to contain the prime motor or motors from which power is conveyed to the driven machinery. **1895** *Westm. Gaz.* 4 Sept. 3/3 It is intended to supply a large proportion of power from a great power-house where electricity is generated. **1901** *Chambers's Jrnl.* Mar. 206/1 In the centre of the power-house there is a raised desk, upon which are a series of press-buttons or keys. **1922** JOYCE *Ulysses* 238 The whirr of flapping leathern bands and hum of dynamos from the powerhouse urged Stephen to be on. **1922** D. H. LAWRENCE *England, my England* 175 Tall, ruined power-houses of tin-mines loomed in the darkness. **1964** LINSLEY & FRANZINI *Water Resources Engin.* xvi. 459 One of the world's largest underground plants is the Kemano powerhouse in Canada which has a generating capacity of 1,670,000 kw under a head of 2592 ft.

2. *fig.* **a.** A source of energy or inspiration; a strong person or animal; also a powerful group of people, e.g. a sports team. Also *attrib.*

1915 P. GEDDES *Cities in Evolution* xiii. 312 Before long, then, the School of Civics..must become a familiar institution in every city, with its civic library in rapid growth and widening use, and all as a veritable power-house of civic thought and action. **1916** J. BUCHAN (*title*) The power-house. **1941** *Sat. Even. Post* 1 Feb. 54/3 A thresher is one of the few powerhouses in the shark family. **1941** *Time* (Air Exp. Ed.) 15 Sept. 25/3 In the final, Powerhouse Kovacs was too much for Riggs in the first set, 7–5. **1943** *Amer. Speech* XVIII. 105 A hard hitter is known as a *distance hitter*, *power house*, *power hitter*, *slugger*, or *heavy sticker*. **1943** *Sun* (Baltimore) 20 Sept. 14/5 In the first two Saturdays of the young football season,..the mid-West and Duke again have their power-house elevens. **1952** *N.Y. World-Telegram & Sun* 29 Sept. 16/3 Michigan State, Maryland and Georgia Tech were supposed powerhouses. **1961** *Ann. Reg. 1960* 423 There continued to be no national powerhouse for [drama]. **1970** *Nature* 6 June 982/1 Although almost unreadable, it is a powerhouse of condensed factual information. **1974** E. TIDYMAN *Dummy* iii. 33 Strong? Jesus, yes. Not big, but a powerhouse. **1979** *Harvard Mag.* May–June 41 In 1972 the M.I.T. team, which had become the real powerhouse, somehow convinced the student government to give them $2,000 to go to England to play the English champions.

b. A strong hand in a card-game.

1932 *Amer. Speech* VII. 335 *Power house*, a very strong card hand. **1953** G. S. COFFIN *Acol & New Point Count* 34 The two clubs opening in Acol shows a rare powerhouse, the kind of hand you may expect to hold about once a month. **1958** *Listener* 11 Dec. 1012/2 A freak distribution resulted in South's power-house being useless against Four Spades doubled. **1967** P. ANDERTON *Play Bridge* iv. 28 An opening bid of 2 C. is reserved for the power-house and is forcing to game.

3. Applied *attrib.* or as quasi-*adj.* to loud or forceful popular music or performers of such music.

1942 BERREY & VAN DEN BARK *Amer. Thes. Slang* §578/10 *Powerhouse coda*, a strong finale. **1946** R. BLESH *Shining Trumpets* xii. 282 The hot-riff band is called in musicians' parlance a *powerhouse* band. **1952** B. ULANOV *Hist. Jazz in Amer.* (1958) xiv. 163 His brass was beginning to sound like the powerhouse sections of the swing bands. **1955** P. ROSSITER in A. J. McCarthy *Jazzbook 1955* 50 The first important revivalist group was formed..in the early 'forties ..led by..Lu Watters... The approach was powerhouse with a two trumpet, trombone and clarinet front line. **1968** *Blues Unlimited* Sept. 26 The powerhouse singing of types like Blind Roosevelt Graves. **1975** *New Yorker* 19 May 8/2 (Advt.), Power-house drummer Elvin Jones finishes up with his quintet on Sunday. **1976** *Leicester Trader* 24 Nov. 4/7 Argent's powerhouse rhythm section..have joined with John Verity who saw out the last days with the old band.

powerless ('paʊəlɪs), *a.* [f. POWER *sb.*[1] + -LESS.] Without power or ability; devoid of power; helpless.

1552 HULOET, Powerles or lackynge power, *impos, impotens.* **1596** SPENSER *F.Q.* IV. vi. 21 His powrelesse arme, benumbd with secret feare. **1726** POPE *Odyss.* XVI. 87 Powerless to relieve, I must behold it. **1860** PUSEY *Min. Proph.* 407 Human sense of right is powerless, when there is not the love of God's law.

Hence **'powerlessly** *adv.*; **'powerlessness.**

1823 *Examiner* 89/1 The doting Scrivener is not powerlessly conceived. **1833** CHALMERS *Const. Man* I. vii. II. 20 [That] the large intermediate spaces..are in fact, peopled with little worlds... Now, in the powerlessness of our existing telescopes, we do not know but it may be so. **1875** H. C. WOOD *Therap.* (1879) 535 The powerlessness of the remedy to effect such change. **1892** WESTCOTT *Gospel of Life* 17 Man feels his powerlessness in the face of physical forces.

'powerlet. [See -LET.] A petty 'power'.

1889 *Sat. Rev.* 14 Sept. 288/1 Any actual quarrel between these Powers or powerlets could only end to the disadvantage of the Sultan.

†**'powerlike,** *a. Obs. rare.* [f. POWER *sb.*[1] + -LIKE.] = POWERFUL.

1657 EARL MONM. tr. *Paruta's Pol. Disc.* 120 Rome had not..any great contestation with any powerlike Prince in her first and weakest beginning.

power 'loading, *vbl. sb.* [f. POWER *sb.*[1] + LOADING *vbl. sb.*] **1.** *Aeronaut.* The laden weight of an aeroplane divided by the total engine power.

1920 H. WOODHOUSE *Textbk. Appl. Aeronaut. Engin.* iii. 136 The lift loading of the machine per sq. ft. equals 8·3 lbs., and the power loading, 12·1 lbs. per h.p. **1927** *Observer* 12 June 17/3 The flights of the 'Horsley' have greater technical value than those wonderful American flights,..the 'Horsley' has an unprecedented high wing and power-loading. **1966** D. STINTON *Anal. Aeroplane* vii. 118 When power loading is used as a measure of merit for comparing different aircraft (W_o/P) lb/hp is used, where W_o is the all-up-weight on take-off and P the sea level horsepower.

2. *Mining.* The loading of coal on to a conveyor belt at the coal face by means of a machine (cf. *power loader* s.v. POWER *sb.*[1] 18f).

1943 *Trans. Inst. Mining Engin.* CII. 39 The films to be exhibited are shown by courtesy of the 'Power Loading' Committee, and illustrate the latest practice in power-loading in America. **1956** F. S. ATKINSON in D. L. Linton *Sheffield* 269 With thinner seams power-loading presents a difficult problem and progress has been slower. **1962** *Economist* 20 Jan. 243/1 Powerloading equipment tends to upset the whole work cycle of mining.

'power-,loom. a. A weaving loom worked by mechanical power (water, steam, etc.), as distinguished from a hand-loom. Also *fig.*

1808 J. DUNCAN *Art of Weaving* 272 The chief working parts of the different power looms. **1827** *Edin. Rev.* XLVI. 16 The power-loom..is one of the most..useful machines that has ever been constructed. **1832** BABBAGE *Econ. Manuf.* xxxii. (ed. 3) 339 A hand-weaver must possess bodily strength, which is not essential for a person attending a power-loom. **1843** *Ainsworth's Mag.* IV. 95 A stoker to the power-loom in which are weaving the future destinies of mankind. **1879** *Cassell's Techn. Educ.* IV. 259/1 Between 1785 and 1792 Cartwright matured his power-loom. **1941** J. MASEFIELD *In Mill* 6 More than a hundred power-looms were in full work. **1968** J. ARNOLD *Shell Bk. Country Crafts* xvi. 206 With the invention of the power-loom, in 1787, it became dominated by the machine.

b. *Comb.*, as ***power-loom cloth***, ***weaver***, ***weaving***.

1833 HT. MARTINEAU *Manch. Strike* i. 9 All present were spinners and power-loom weavers. **1835** URE *Philos. Manuf.* 331 Capital..expended in..the mere spinning of power-loom yarn, or the weaving of what is purchased. **1844** G. DODD *Textile Manuf.* i. 22 Power-loom weaving is combined with spinning. **1892** *Daily News* 13 Feb. 7/3 There is no change in the market for brown power-loom cloth.

'power plant. Also **power-plant, powerplant.** [f. POWER *sb.*[1] + PLANT *sb.*[1]] (An) apparatus or an installation which provides power; those parts of a machine, vehicle, or aircraft which provide power; an engine; a power station. Also *transf.*

1890 *Jrnl. Franklin Inst.* CXXIX. 270 Power Plant... Street-car work imposes a very variable load on the engines and dynamos... We require stronger engines than are needed for constant loads. **1897** E. K. SCOTT *Electr. Power in Workshops* 65 Messrs. Willans and Robinson are also laying down an extensive power plant for their new works at

Rugby. **1909** *Westm. Gaz.* 4 May 4/1 The rigid dirigible.. cannot be made to lift the weight of the power-plant necessary to render it independent of all winds. **1933** *Newnes Compl. Wireless* 595 (*heading*) Radio power plant. Notes on the uses, installation and servicing of rotary transformers, rotary converters, motor generators, and hand-driven generators. **1935** R. H. BAKER *Introd. Astron.* x. 209 Power derived from the waterfall, from the wind, and from fuel and food has its origin in the great power plant of the sun. **1942** W. FAULKNER *Go down, Moses* 207 They.. would be back once more in the little lost county seats as barbers and garage mechanics..and power-plant firemen. **1964** [see MITOCHONDRION]. **1967** *Jane's Surface Skimmer Systems 1967–68* 104/2 The powerplant is mounted at the aft end with an acoustic bulkhead and two crew rest rooms separating it from the main passenger cabin. **1973** *Nature* 16 Mar. 210/1 The remaining papers..covered gas turbine, steam and Stirling-cycle powerplants for vehicles.

'power-,politics. [f. POWER *sb.*[1] + POLITIC *sb.* 3, translating G. *machtpolitik* (f. *macht* might, power + *politik* politics).] Political action based on or backed by threats to use force. Hence **power-po'litical** *a.*, pertaining to or characterized by power-politics; **power-poli'tician**, one who practises power-politics.

1937 G. M. YOUNG *Daylight & Champaign* 135 We shall all have to..learn to talk of power-politics and art-form antecedents and the literary-critical approach, as if we had been cradled in Marburg and reared in Michigan. **1939** WODEHOUSE *Uncle Fred in Springtime* xiii. 179 The Duke's decision..to mobilize his nephew Ricky and plunge immediately into power politics was one which would have occasioned no surprise to anybody acquainted with the militant traditions of his proud family. **1940** A. HUXLEY *Let.* 9 Oct. (1969) 460, I am engaged at the moment on a strangely apposite study of Père Joseph, collaborator of Richelieu, the most astounding case of a power politician who was also a religious mystic. **1942** L. B. NAMIER *Conflicts* 21 For centuries Vienna and Paris had been the centres of European power-politics. **1942** PARTRIDGE *Usage & Abusage* (1947) 355/1 Hitler was the *protagonist* of Nazism, with its power-political ideology. **1959** *Oxf. Mag.* 4 June 448/1 The abolition of compulsory Latin was a power-political move intended to pacify the jealous monoliths of America and Russia. **1961** J. WILSON *Reason & Morals* ii. 125 If I do not use human beings as ends in themselves..it ..results in that political tyranny which tends to corrupt the power-politician or the brain-washer. **1973** J. BURROWS *Like an Evening Gone* ii. 31, I like that period... Besides—power politics of any age—it's a kind of adventure. **1977** *Church Times* 10 June 14/4 Even monasticism had been sucked into the power-political structure of the medieval Church.

powert, -te, -tie, obs. forms of POVERTY.

‖**powese** ('paʊi:s, -i:z). *Guyana.* Also 9 **powis(e, powee, powie, paui.** [a. Du. (of Surinam) *pouwies*, corrupt. of Sp. *pauxi* or mod.L. *pauxis*: see PAUXI. Mistaking of the final sibilant for a plural inflexion (as in *pease*) has brought a new sing. *powee, powie* into vulgar use.] = PAUXI.

1769 E. BANCROFT *Guiana* 175 The Peacock Pheasant of Guiana..called Powese by the Natives, from their cry, which is similar to that name. **1825** WATERTON *Wand. S. Amer.* (1882) 27 Here are also two species of the Powise, or Hocco. **1880** W. H. BRETT *Leg. & Myths Guiana* 190 The Southern Cross is supposed by many clans to represent a Paui bird. **1898** H. KIRK *Brit. Guiana* Gloss. 352 *Powis*, curassow. **1903** DES VOEUX *Col. Service* I. 73 Other birds such as powie (curassow). *Ibid.* 98.

poweste, var. POUSTIE *Obs.*, power.

powghe, powȝ, powȝe, powhe, var. POUGH *sb.* and *v.*

Powhatan ('paʊətæn), *sb.* and *a.* [Native name.] **A.** *sb.* An Algonquian people of eastern Virginia; a member of this people; their language (now extinct). **B.** *adj.* Of, pertaining to, or characteristic of this people. Hence **Powha'tanic** *a.*

1608 J. SMITH *True Relation of Occurrences in Virginia* sig. D, With a lowd oration he proclaimed me A werowanes of Powhaton, and that all his subjects should so esteeme vs, and no man account vs strangers nor Paspaheghans, but Powhatans. **1612** W. STRACHEY *Trav. Virginia* (1953) I. i. 35 There was ever Enmity..between the High-and Low Country, going by the names of Monacans, and Powhatans. **1785** T. JEFFERSON *Notes Virginia* xi. 167 We are told that the Powhatans, Mannahoacs, and Monacans spoke languages so radically different, that interpreters were necessary when they transacted business. *Ibid.* 168 The territories of the *Powhatan* confederacy, south of the Patowmac comprehended about 8000 square miles, 30 tribes, and 2400 warriors. **1860** H. R. SCHOOLCRAFT *Hist. & Stat. Information Indian Tribes* V. i. 35 Their language was so diverse from the Powhatanic dialects, which were of the Algonquin group, that not a word could be understood without interpreters. *Ibid.* 36 The older ones among them, preserve their language in a small degree, which are the last vestiges on earth, so far as we know, of the Powhatan language. *Ibid.* 37 All the sympathies of Virginians were with the Powhatanic tribes. **1907** *Amer. Anthropologist* IX. 135 When the English landed at Jamestown in 1607, the Powhatan confederacy was a thing of recent origin. **1912** T. MICHELSON in *28th Ann. Rep. U.S. Bureau Amer. Ethnol. 1906–7* (*map legend*) Languages the exact position of which is uncertain... Powhatan, Weapemeoc, Secotan, etc. **1915** J. BUCHAN *Salute to Adventurers* xxiv. 334 A voice..spoke the Powhatan language, which I knew. *Ibid.* xxvi. 355, I found some Indians..and told one who spoke Powhatan the issue of the fight. **1953** WRIGHT & FREUND *Strachey's Trav. Virginia* I. 35 The Powhatans were an Algonquian tribe and their name, which first came from the name of a town near the present Richmond, was later applied to the chief Wahunsonacock and his confederacy. **1974** *Encycl. Brit. Micropædia* VIII. 170/1 In the 1970s an estimated 3,000 Powhatan were reported, largely scattered along the Virginia coast. **1977** *Language* LIII. 259/2 Siebert places these data in the framework of Eastern Algonquian, as reconstructed by Bloomfield, and provides an English-Powhatan lexicon of 263 words.

powhead, var. POLEHEAD, tadpole.

powie, -is, -ise: see POWESE.

powin, Sc. var. PAWN *sb.*[3] *Obs.*, peacock.

Powindah ('paʊɪndə). Also **Povindah, Powandah,** ‖**pāvendeh.** [Pashto, f. Pers. *parvinda* merchandise.] A nomadic trading tribe of Afghanistan; a member of this tribe. Also *attrib.*

1851 H. B. EDWARDES *Year on Punjab Frontier* I. ix. 454 The whole of the trade between India and Central Asia is carried on by periodical caravans, which cross and re-cross the soolimânee mountains every year. They are conducted by Afghan merchants, who are generally called Lohânees, but locally in the Dérajât Powinduhs, or Povindeuhs... Lohânee is not a name applicable to either the Kharotees or the Nâssurs, so I prefer calling them Powinduhs, a name which they all acknowledge. **1880** H. W. BELLEN *Races of Afghanistan* xi. 104 During the cold weather, the Povinda is to be seen in most of the larger cities of India. *Ibid.* 105 These Povinda clans, though classed as subdivisions of the Ghilji people, differ from them in one or two important respects. **1885** E. BALFOUR *Cycl. India* (ed. 3) III. 275/2 Considering the wild and independent life the Povindahs lead, they are marvellously orderly and well-behaved when dispersed in British territory, travelling from one end of India to another. **1888** H. G. RAVERTY *Notes on Afghánistán* 489 The Naṣirs or Náṣirís, as they are also called, are about the most numerous of the Powandah tribes, and possess no land whatever of their own. **1895** [see MAHSUD]. **1920** *Blackw. Mag.* Oct. 445/1 Your car is halted at the boat bridge, to let the long Afghan powindah caravans pass. *Ibid.* 445/2 The powindahs are more often armed, each man's belt crammed with cartridges. **1934** AHMAD & AZIZ *Afghanistan* iii. 17 The Gomal pass..is much used by Povindahs on their annual migration to their winter encampments on the Indus. **1953** J. MASTERS *Lotus & Wind* xii. 158 The man.. was a Powindah horsetrader... When the Pushtu greetings were at last out of the way the Powindah said, 'Let us retire.' **1967** A. SWINSON *N.-W. Frontier* v. 104 Now the Powindahs..are great clans of warrior merchants, Ghilzais and Kharotis as well as Powindahs proper. **1974** *Encycl. Brit. Macropædia* I. 169/1 A number of nomads (*pāvendehs*) cross the eastern frontier with their herds toward their summer pastures in Pakistan. **1978** 'M. M. KAYE' *Far Pavilions* xi. 177 They were only *Powindahs*—wandering, gipsy-like folk who live in tents and are always on the move.

powk, dial. f. POKE; var. POUK.

powke-needle: see PUCK-NEEDLE.

powl, obs. f. POLE, POLL.

powlder, obs. f. POWDER.

powldoody (paʊl'du:dɪ). Also **poul-, -dowdy.** [From *Pouldoody* (? *poll Dubhda*, O'Dowd's Hole), name of the inner part of a creek near Corcomroe Abbey in Co. Clare.] A celebrated variety of Irish oyster: see quot. 1890.

1819 *Blackw. Mag.* V. 718 We had some scolloped Powldoodies for supper. **1828** *Ibid.* XXIII. 388 We are willing to bet a barrel, and make the first deposit of a dozen powldoodies at Ambrose's. **1890** *Standard* 26 Dec. 6/4 Wonderfully large supplies of exquisitely flavoured 'powldoodies'..used to be obtained from 'the..shores of the Green Isle'.

powldron, obs. form of POULDRON.

†**powle,** obs. f. POLL *sb.*[1] and *v.* In quot., nape of the neck: = POLL *sb.*[1] 2 c.

1603–4 *Act 1 Jas. I*, c. 22 §23 Any parte of any Hide.. called the Wombes, Neckes, Shanke, Flanke, Powle, or Cheeke.

powle, obs. f. POLE, POOL *sb.*[1]

powles, etc.: see PAUL.

powlt-foot, obs. var. POLT-FOOT.

powltice, powltry, obs. ff. POULTICE, POULTRY.

powm(e, obs. f. POME.

powmbe garnette, powmgarnet, obs. ff. POMEGRANATE.

pownage, erron. f. PANNAGE.

pownce, pownece, pownse, obs. ff. POUNCE.

pownch, obs. f. PAUNCH.

pownd, powne, obs. ff. POND, POUND.

powney, -nie, -ny, obs. Sc. ff. PONY.

powngarnette, obs. f. POMEGRANATE.

pownt, obs. f. POINT *sb.*[1] and *v.*[1]

†**powpe,** *sb. Obs. rare.* [perh. connected with POOP *v.*[1]] A pop-gun.

c **1440** *Promp. Parv.* 411/2 Powpe, holstykke (*S.* hole styke), *capulus.*

powpe, obs. form of POOP *sb.*[1], *v.*[1] and [2].

†**pow-penny.** *Sc. Obs. rare.* [app. f. *pow* = POLL head + PENNY.] Some payment or offering made at a funeral or on its anniversary.

1538 *Acc. Ld. High Treas. Scot.* VI. 423 Item, to the powpenny deliverit to David Lindesay, Lyoun herald, ane croune of wecht..xxs. **1539** *Ibid.* VII. 181 Expensis debursit upoun the suffrage of Quene Magdelane... Item, to the Erle of Murray till offer the pow penny, xxs.

powr, -e, obs. ff. POOR, PORE, POUR, POWER.

powrg, obs. f. PURGE.

pows, -e, obs. ff. PULSE *sb.*[1] and [2].

powsh(e, obs. ff. PUSH *sb.* and *v.*

powsowdy (paʊ'saʊdɪ), **powsoddy** (paʊ'sɒdɪ). *Sc.* and *north. dial.* Forms: 6 **possodie, -edie,** 7 **pow's-sowdy,** 7 **powsodie,** 8 **-sowdie,** 9 **-soddie, -soddy, pousoudie, -sowdie, -sowdy,** 8– **pow(-)sowdy.** [Origin obscure: see Note.]

A name given now or formerly in Scotland and the northern counties of England to various culinary preparations, not obviously related to each other; among these (in Scotland) sheep's head broth (? *obs.*); (in Cumbld. and Westmld.) an ale posset; (in north of Eng.) Yorkshire pudding (? *obs.*); a hotch-potch or heterogeneous mixture. †Also *Sc.* used as a term of endearment (*obs.*, the earliest instance of the word). Also *attrib.*

1500–20 DUNBAR *Poems* lxxv. 30 Quod he, 'My claver, and my curldodie, My hwny soppis, my sweit possodie'. *a* **1685** F. SEMPILL *Blythsum Wedding* vii, There will be.. Powsodie, and drammock, and crowdie. **1787** W. TAYLOR *Scots Poems* 24 In haf an hour hese get his mess O' crowdy-mowdy, An' fresh powsowdy. **1816** SCOTT *Antiq.* xxxv, He's hovering there making some pousowdie [*note* miscellaneous mess] for my lord, for he doesna eat like ither folk neither. **1817** *Lintoun Green* IX. 92 Pow's-sowdy, king's-hoods, mony-plies, Sheep's trotters, hot and hot. **1825** BROCKETT *N.C. Gloss.*, *Powsoddy*, suet pudding placed under a roast. **1825** HONE *Every-day Bk.* I. 53 They sit down to lobscouse, and pousoudie [*mispr.* ponsondie];..in pousoudie we recognise the wassail..of ale, boiled with sugar and nutmeg. **1857** J. SULLIVAN *Cumberld. & Westmorld.* 169 The ale-posset continues to appear at the village tavern on what is called the Powsowdy night. **1858** DE QUINCEY *Autobiog. Sk.* II. 109 The anticipation of excellent ale,..and possibly of still more excellent pow-sowdy (a combination of ale, spirits, and spices). **1894** *Northumbld. Gloss.*, *Pousowdy*, hotchpotch, disorderment, a heterogeneous dish.

[*Note. Powsoddy* has been conjected to be a comb. of *pow*, POLL *sb.*[1] head + *sodden*, boiled; also, to be a corruption of POSSET: perh. two distinct words have been confounded, as the senses seem to have little in common.]

powst(e, -tie, var. POUSTIE, power.

powt(e, obs. ff. POULT (young bird), POUT.

powter, obs. f. POUTER.

powther, obs. or dial. f. POWDER.

powtry, obs. f. POULTRY.

powwow, pow-wow ('paʊwaʊ), **pawaw** (pɑ:'wɔ:), *sb.* Forms: α. 7–9 **powah, -aw,** 7 **pouwau, powawe, -ahe,** 8 **pouwau, pow-waa,** 9 **powwaa, -waw.** β. 7–9 **pawaw, pawwaw,** 7 **pawawe, pawwau, -wawe, pauwau, -waw,** 8 **pawau, paw-waw,** 9 **pawa.** γ. 7– **powow, pow-wow,** 8 **pouwou,** 8– **powwow.** [An Algonkin (Narragansett) word, *pow'waw* or *po'wah*, the two syllables of which in colonial Eng. use were assimilated, and the stress transferred to the first, although in the form *pa'waw* also retained on the second.]

1. A priest, sorcerer, or medicine-man of the North American Indians.

α. **1624** E. WINSLOW *Gd. News fr. New Eng.* in Purchas *Pilgrims* (1625) IV. 1868 The office and dutie of the Powah is to be exercised principally in calling vpon the Deuill; and curing diseases of the sicke or wounded. **1674** JOSSELYN *Voy. New Eng.* 131 Their Physicians are the Powaws or Indian Priests. **1716** B. CHURCH *Hist. Philip's War* (1865) I. 177 The Indians reported that he was such a great Pouwau, that no bullet could enter him. **1766** C. BEATTY *Two Months' Tour* (1768) 87 Consulting their Pow-waas (a kind of prophets, who pretend to have converse with spirits). **1830** SCOTT *Demonol.* ii. 81 The tricks practised by the Powahs, or Cunning men. **1834** WHITTIER *Mogg Megone* I. 169 The Powwaw's charm. **1904** G. SMITH *Short Hist. Chr. Missions* II. xii. 138 In 1650 the first two 'powaws' or wizards were converted.

β. **1645** E. DOWNING in *Coll. Mass. Hist. Soc.* Ser. IV. VI. (1863) 65 To maynteyne the worship of the devill which theire paw wawes often doe. **1670** D. DENTON *Descr. New York* (1845) 8 The day being appointed by their chief Priest or pawaw. **1809** KENDALL *Trav.* I. ix. 101 *Pawa*, or *pawaw*, spelt also *powah*, is a word which I have not found in so general use among the Indians of New England, as it has always been among the colonists. **1832** J. DURFEE *What Cheer* VII. xliv, And oft he thought, o'er thickets brown, he saw Wave the black fox-tail of the grim Pawaw.

γ. **1634** W. WOOD *New Eng. Prosp.* II. xii. 82 Their Powwows betaking themselves to their exorcismes and necromanticke charmes. **1751** LAVINGTON *Enthus. Meth. & Papists* III. (1754) 218 The Indian Conjurer, one of those whom they call Powwows. **1858** LONGF. *M. Standish* I. 52 Let them come,..be it sagamore, sachem, or pow-wow. **1873** R. BROWN *Races Man.* I. 246 The *pow-wows* visited the sick, sang and invoked their gods, and applied their medicines.

2. A ceremony of the North American Indians, especially one where magic was practised and feasting and dancing indulged in; also, a council of Indians, or conference with them.

α, β. 1663 J. Cotton in Quincy *Hist. Harvard Univ.* (1840) I. 53 Such as join with them in the observance of their pawawes and idolatries. 1781 S. Peters *Hist. Connecticut* 215 An ancient religious rite, called the Pawwaw, was annually celebrated by the Indians. *a* 1817 T. Dwight *Trav. New Eng.*, etc. (1821) II. 263 No place could be a fitter spot for an Indian Powaw.

γ. 1788 J. May *Jrnl. & Lett.* (1873) 94 The Indians made one of their hellish pow-wows, which lasted till the hour of rising. 1820 W. Irving *Sketch Bk., Leg. Sleepy Hollow*, An old Indian chief, the prophet or wizard of his tribe, held his powwows there. 1887 *Daily News* 30 Nov. 5/5 To find the thief the Indians held the Pow-wow.

3. *transf.* Applied to any meeting compared to an Indian conference; e.g. a political or scientific congress, a friendly consultation, or a merry-making; a 'palaver' of any kind; *spec.*, a conference of senior officers. Also used occas. in general sense of 'bustle, activity'. orig. *U.S.*

1812 *Salem Gaz.* (U.S.) 5 June 3/3 The Warriors of the Democratic Tribe will hold a powow at Agawam on Tuesday next. 1840 R. H. Dana *Bef. Mast* xx. 59 The Catalina had several Kanakas on board..they had a long pow-wow, and a smoke. 1863 E. Hitchcock *Remin. Amherst Coll.* 333 The President..is located so near College that the midnight pow-wow [of the students] can hardly fail to disturb his slumbers. 1865 *Daily Tel.* 26 May, The Abolitionists are having a great pow-wow here as to whether they shall or not maintain their organisation. 1874 Huxley in *Life* (1900) I. xxviii. 411, I was not at the Cambridge pow-wow. 1892 *Spectator* 20 Aug. 253/1 Congresses and pow-wows of all descriptions are certainly a feature of the age. 1893 'Mark Twain' in *Cosmopolitan* Sept. 629/1 Without the marring additions of human pow-wow and fuss and feathers and display. 1897 —— *Following Equator* xxxviii. 346 It all helps to keep up the liveliness and augment the general sense of swiftness and energy and confusion and pow-wow. 1925 Fraser & Gibbons *Soldier & Sailor Words* 229 *Pow-wow*, a senior officers' conference, as, for instance, of a General with the Commanding Officers of units after a field-day or an operation. 1926 J. C. Lincoln *Big Mogul* vi. 112 It seems there was a great pow wow, some wanted to wear one kind of thing and some another. 1930 G. MacMunn *Behind Scenes in Many Wars* xiii. 239, I visited him here several times, and attended his rather interminable pow-wows and conferences. 1936 F. Clune *Roaming round Darling* xxii. 221 O'Hea and the bandmaster..had a private pow-wow. 1944 *Sun* (Baltimore) 17 May 18/2 Governor O'Conor..is conceded to be in control of proceedings at the Democratic pow wow. 1954 *Manch. Guardian Weekly* 28 Jan. 3/2 The associated lobbies that oppose the [St. Lawrence] seaway, the railroads, coal-owners, and Eastern port authorities, went into a round of emergency pow-wows. 1962 *Press* (Vancouver) Nov. 9 He turned up in London at a periodical pow-wow initiated by one Cyrus Eaton. 1977 *Time* 30 May 33/2 What had brought the Mob chiefs together was a series of powwows with New York City Mafia bosses about the new Mob power structure.

4. *transf.* The working of cures; 'medicine'.

1856 Kane *Arct. Expl.* II. xii. 126 After my skill in pow-wow had given me a sort of correlative rank among them.

5. *attrib.* and *Comb.*, as ***powwow-doctor***, ***-wizard***.

1843 Whittier *Agency of Evil* Prose Wks. 1889 III. 257 Without were 'dogs and sorcerers',..Powah wizards, and 'the foul fiend'. 1901 *Scribner's Mag.* III. 525 The pow-wow-doctors still repeat over many bedsides the mysterious formulas.

Hence **'powwowism**, the powwow practice.

1873 R. Brown *Races Man.* I. 235 They [*sc.* the old men] are the instructors into *pow-wowism* (or oratory), in medicine and tradition.

powwow (paʊ'waʊ), *v.* Forms: see prec. [f. prec. sb.]

1. *intr.* Of North American Indians: To practise medicine or sorcery; to hold a powwow.

1642 Lechford *Plain Dealing* (1867) 117 They will have their tomes of Powaheing, which they will, of late, have called Prayers, according to the English word. 1646 in A. S. Hudson *Hist. Sudbury, Mass.* (1889) 20 There shall be no more Powwowing amongst the Indians. And if any shall hereafter powwow, both he that shall powwow, and he that shall procure them to powwow, shall pay twenty shillings apiece. 1677 W. Hubbard *Narrative* (1865) II. 196 After the Indians..had been Powawing together. 1856 Kane *Arct. Expl.* II. xi. 118 He prescribes or powwows in sickness and over wounds.

b. *transf.* To confer, discuss, deliberate, talk, hold palaver. (Chiefly *U.S.*)

1780 J. Cochran in *N. Eng. Hist. & Gen. Reg.* (1864) XVIII. 35 He may refer the matter to Congress, they to the Medical Committee, who will probably powwow over it awhile, and no more be heard of it. 1857 Longf. in *Life* (1891) II. 334 Senator Mason of Virginia was there, pow-wowing about the Union. 1893 *Nation* (N.Y.) 13 July 32/1 Mr. Stevenson's narrative style appears to have become infected with that quality through continued pow-wowing with Samoan grandees. 1900 *Century Mag.* Feb. 600/2 She did not..sail to powwow about the dangers of the seas.

2. *trans.* To doctor, to treat with powwow.

1856 Kane *Arct. Expl.* II. xi. 116, I gave him a piece of red flannel, and powwowed him. 1905 *Athenæum* 18 Feb. 206/2 The artistic forms of the beadwork..representing the symbols of secret societies, the qualification of the worker,.. the shaman who powwowed the work.

Hence **pow'wowing** *vbl. sb.*, the practising of powwow; conference, palaver.

1642 [see 1 above]. 1650 J. Eliot in *Early Rec. Lancaster, Mass.* (1884) 27 At my first preaching at Nashaway sundry did imbrace the word, and called upon God, and Pauwauing was wholly silenced. 1764 T. Hutchinson *Hist. Mass.* I. 475 *note*, Their sweatings in their hot houses was a more rational remedy than the powowing. 1830 Scott *Demonol.* ii. 84 The magic or powahing of the North American Indians. 1893 [see 1 b above]. 1905 J. C. Lincoln *Partners of Tide* i. 8, I cal'late there must have been some high old pow-wowin' in the old house, but..they fin'lly decided 'twas their duty to take the little feller to bring up. 1928 H. W. Shoemaker in *Publ. Pennsylvania Folk-Lore Soc.* I. iv. 15 He arrived at the Little Valley with the book and tried to raise dark Cathlin's spook by pow-wowing. 1938 A. Hark *Hex marks Spot* 52 Pow-wowing is a hidden but by no means secret art among the people of Pennsylvania. 1961 D. Waldo *Beat Drum Slowly* vii. 89 There's too much pow-wowing going on hereabouts.

pow'wower. [f. prec. vb. + -er[1].] One who practises powwow; = powwow *sb.* 1.

1646 *Mass. Col. Rec.* (1854) III. 98 Such..as shall assist or countenance such pawwawing.., [to be fined] ye procurer five pounds, ye pawwawer five pounds. 1699 Wafer *Voy.* 38 That the pawawers (for so they call their conjurors) might be by themselves. 1781 S. Peters *Hist. Connecticut* 217 The inhabitants..held a conference to discover the reason why the devils and pawwawers had obeyed the prayers of one minister.

Powysian (pəʊ'ɪsɪən, paʊ'ɪsɪən), *a.* and *sb.* Also †**Powisian.** [f. *Powys* (see below) + -ian.]

A. *adj.* Of or pertaining to the historical principality of Powys in east-central Wales, or its inhabitants or dialect. **B.** *sb.* **a.** An inhabitant of Powys. **b.** The dialect of Powys.

Powys was established as the name of a Welsh county in 1974.

1868 *Coll. Hist. & Archæol. Montgomeryshire* I. 426 Powis, *Pow isa* is *the low country*, a name still given by the peasants of Montgomeryshire to the plain of Shropshire, and indeed derived from that, the only level portion of the ancient Powisian dominions. 1880 *Ibid.* XIII. 42 The men of Argoed..uphold the *brother's* right, and acknowledge not a sister's claim to inheritance... Hence we find no Boadiceas, no Cartismanduas, no queens, among the Powysians. 1897 P. Barbier *Age of Owain Gwynedd* (1908) i. 22 The death of Maredudd in 1132, and..the steadily growing power of Gwynedd..tended much to the diminution of Powysian influence. 1910 A. Jones *Hist. Gruffydd ap Cynan* 89 It was the activity of the Powysian princes, and especially of Maredudd,..that made Powys the object of attack. *Ibid.* 180 Gruffydd..threatened active hostility towards any Powysians who sought safety within his dominions. 1913 J. M. Jones *Welsh Gram.* 8 Powysian, the dialect of Powys, or North East and Mid Wales.

pox (pɒks), *sb.* [An altered spelling of *pocks*, pl. of pock *sb.*, used collectively as name of a disease (cf. *measles*, *mumps*, *rickets*, etc.), and at length as a singular.]

1. Name for several different diseases characterized by 'pocks' or eruptive pustules on the skin: see pock *sb.* 2 a. **a.** Undefined. (Usually = e (*b*) or designating any venereal disease.) Now only *colloq.*

[*c* 1325, etc.: see pock *sb.* 2 a.] 1550 Bale *Image Both Ch.* ii. xvii. S iv, Here were muche to be spoken of..saint Iobe for yᵉ pox, saint Fyacre for ague. 1604 E. G[rimstone] *D'Acosta's Hist. Indies* iii. xxii. 187 There is much of that wood which they call *Lignum sanctum*,..fit to cure the pox. 1684 tr. *Bonet's Merc. Compit.* x. 356 Treacle is the best Alexiterick against the Pox. 1726 Swift *Gulliver* iv. x, Here were no..fops, bullies, drunkards, strolling whores, or poxes. 1763 Churchill *Duellist* iii. 380 In turn to give a Pox, or take it. 1856 Emerson *Eng. Traits, First Visit* Wks. (Bohn) II. 5 He [Coleridge] said..there were only three things which the government had brought into that garden of delights [Sicily], namely, itch, pox, and famine. 1922 [see lock *sb.*[2] 18]. 1930 *Amer. Speech* V. 392 *Pox*, any kind of venereal disease. 1930 Brophy & Partridge *Songs & Slang 1914–18* 88 But now she's standing in the gutter, selling matches penny-a-box: While he's riding in his carriage With an awful dose of—[awful dose of pox *in* 1965 —— *Long Trail* 70]. 1968 [see dose *sb.* 2 d]. 1969 *Coast to Coast 1967–68* 191 'Yah! Luther stinking swine! He had the pox!' Simon..had yelled in return 'Old bugger Pope pokes the nuns!' 1976 J. O'Connor *Eleventh Commandment* viii. 101 Wally.. strangled a prostitute for giving him a dose of the pox. 1977 *Sounds* 9 July 8/4 It's still potent diz bustin' rhinostomp, a most touching lament to the pox, but it's not brash to an offensive level.

†**b.** = small-pox. *Obs.*

1621 F. Davison *Poems* Canzonet xlvi. 143 Vpon his Ladies sickenesse of the Poxe [*ed.* 1602 Sicknesse of the Small Pockes]. 1650 in H. Cary *Mem. Gt. Civ. War* (1832) II. 248 My lord's sizer and Mr. Adam's are sick of the pox; it is thought past the worst. 1685 J. Cooke *Marrow Chirurg.* vi. ii. ix. (ed. 4) 215 Their drink all the Time until the Pox begins to dye, and after..may be Small-Beer, warm at pleasure. 1819 Byron *Juan* i. cxxix, The Doctor paid off an old pox By borrowing a new one from an ox.

c. Some disease of sheep. ? *Obs.*

[1531: see pock *sb.* 3.] 1545 Elyot, *Mentigo*, the scabbe whiche is amonge shepe called the poxe. 1607 Topsell *Four-f. Beasts* (1658) 476 The Holy Fire which the Shepheards call the Pox, or the Blisters, or Saint Anthonies fire.

d. Local name for a rash or eruption to which workers in antimony are liable.

1897 *Allbutt's Syst. Med.* II. 942 This eruption which is called by the [antimony] workmen the 'pox', occurs where the skin perspire most freely. *Ibid.* 944 For the skin-eruption or 'pox' as it is called..sponging with a solution of bicarbonate or biborate of soda..is generally sufficient to give relief.

e. With qualifying words: (*a*) See chicken-pox, cow-pox, small-pox, swine-pox; (*b*) ***great***, ***French***, or ***Spanish pox***, syphilis.

1503 Frenche pox [see French A. 6]. 1529 in Ld. Herbert *Hen. VIII* (1649) 267 The foule, and contagious Disease of the Great Pox. 1584 R. Scot *Discov. Witchcr.* i. ii. (1886) 5 Our neighbours..doubted that he had the French pox. 1608 Topsell *Serpents* (1658) 616 Ointments that are prepared against the French or Spanish pox. 1731 Swift *Cassinus & Peter* 48 Say, has the small or greater pox Sunk down her nose, or seam'd her face? 1819 Byron *Juan* i. cxxx, I said the small-pox has gone out of late; Perhaps it may be followed by the great.

†**2.** In *pl.* sense = *pocks*, pustules of small-pox.

c 1672–1813 [see small-pox]. 1719 T. Boston *Mem.* (1899) 344 Jane was taken ill of the small pox... Her pox were many, and of a dangerous kind.

3. In imprecations, or exclamations of irritation or impatience. Cf. plague *sb.* 3 d. *arch.* (chiefly *Lit.*)

1588 Shaks. *L.L.L.* v. ii. 46 A Pox of that iest, and I beshrew all Shrowes. 1589 *Pappe w. Hatchet* B ij b, A pockes of that religion. 1601 Shaks. *All's Well* iv. iii. 307 A pox on him, he's a Cat still. 1647 Clarendon *Hist. Reb.* iv. §187 Some said, 'a Pox take the House of Commons, let them be Hanged'. 1695 Congreve *Love for L.* v. iv, O Pox, how shall I get rid of this foolish Girl? 1710 Mrs. Centlivre *Bickerstaff's Burying* 7 What a-pox, she wont die for the Man she hates. 1749 Fielding *Tom Jones* vii. vi, Formalities! with a pox! pooh, all stuff and nonsense! 1793 Wolcott (P. Pindar) *Pindariana* Wks. 1812 IV. 163 A pox on all sorrow! 1820 Mair *Lat. Dict.* 415 *Væ! Vah!* wo! pox on't. 1922 Joyce *Ulysses* 392 But they can go hang..for me with their bully beef, a pox on it. 1941 V. Woolf *Between Acts* 126 Hand me the mirror, girl. So. Now my wig... A pox on the girl—she's dreaming! 1963 *Sunday Times* 8 Sept. 29/3 Cool Shakespeare thrives in the sixth and phrases like 'Pox on't!' and 'Fie!' are in present usage. 1973 'A. Hall' *Tango Briefing* xiv. 184 A pox on his grave repercussions, if he meant the whole thing'd blow up..why couldn't he bloody well say so.

4. *Comb.*: ***poxfiend***; **pox-doctor** *slang*, a doctor specializing in the treatment of venereal diseases; phr. ***got up like a pox-doctor's clerk*** (and varr.), dressed smartly but in bad taste, overdressed; **pox-fouled** *a.*, infected with syphilis; **pox-rotten** *a.*, physically corrupted by syphilis; **pox-stone** = *pock-stone*: see pock *sb.* 4.

1937 D. Jones *In Parenthesis* v. 118 You feel the pack of the Ox-blood Kid—it's as light as the Rig'mentals—there's a whole lot of them that work it: the *Pox-Doctor's Clerk, for one, the chitties, and types of scullion bummers up. 1949 Partridge *Dict. Slang* (ed. 3) 1141/2 *Pox doctor's clerk, like —or got-up like—a*, in a very smart civilian suit: Naval: C. 20. 1965 E. Lambert *Long White Night* xv. 136 They was all dressed like they was at Buckingham Palace and Foran was done up like a pox doctor's clerk. 1965 P. Ferris *Doctors* iii. 57 They [*sc.* coloured doctors] can land a job in London as a pathologist or a pox-doctor, but that's about all. 1974 *Bulletin* (Sydney) 19 Jan. 13 Getting dressed up like Lord Muck and getting round kitted up like a flamin' pox doctor's clerk. 1922 Joyce *Ulysses* 419 And snares of the *poxfiend. *a* 1915 —— *Giacomo Joyce* (1968) 9 The *pox-fouled wenches and young wives that, gaily yielding to their ravishers, clip and clip again. 1682 *New Eng. Hist. & Gen. Reg.* LII. 27 A tall thin-faced fellow *pocks rotten. *c* 1700 Kennett *Lansd. MS.* 1033 lf. 305 b, Above the coal mines at Chedle in Staffordshire they have a rock of a greyish colour, called **pox-stone* so very hard, that where they doe not luckily meet with a cleft, they are forced to put fire to it, to soften it, or make it flaw.

pox, *v.* Only in vulgar use. [f. prec. sb.] *trans.* To infect with the pox (i.e., usually, with syphilis). Also in imprecations (cf. prec. 3). Also *transf.* and *fig.* Hence **poxed** (pɒkst) *ppl. a.*

1682 Dryden *Medal* 266 And the pox'd Nation feels Thee in their Brains. 1710 Swift *Jrnl. to Stella* 29 Sept., The dean friendly! The dean be pox't. 1712 Arbuthnot *John Bull* iii. iii, Jack..persuaded Peg that all mankind, besides himself, were poxed by that scarlet-faced whore. 1766 Amory *Buncle* (1770) IV. xiii. 249 She..lives..to ruin the fortune, pox the body, and for ever damn the soul of the miserable man. 1784 Prince William *Let.* 23 July in P. Ziegler *King William IV* (1971) iii. 51 Oh, for..the pretty girls of Westminster..such as would not clap or pox me every time I fucked. 1802 G. Galloway in *Admirable Crichton* 70 Tho' we were pox'd wi' poverty and law. 1846 *Swell's Night Guide* 45 These kens are tenanted by a blackguard..school of pugging shakes, whose chief fame is in..poxing a swaddy. 1933 M. Lowry *Ultramarine* i. 51 That boy got all poxed up to the eyeballs, voyage before last. .. Yes, he was poxed all away to hell. 1935 in *Sc. Nat. Dict.* (1968) VII. 225/1 When I wuz away for my breakfast my mate oot o' pure duvilment poxt the stone on me. 1961 'F. O'Brien' *Hard Life* xiv. 115 Conditions on the canal bank are nothing short of a scandal with men and women going about there poxed-up to the eyes. 1968 *Amer. Speech* 1967 XLII. 295 *Pox*, a general colloquial term for 'ruining or damaging stone through faulty handling, milling, or carving'. 1968 *Sc. Nat. Dict.* VII. 225/1 *Pox, v.*,..to botch (a job), ruin (a piece of work). 1970 G. F. Newman *Sir, You Bastard* iii. 92 The car became expedient. He was poxed with running for trains, missing trains, and worse, catching trains crowded with sickly commuters. 1977 *Sat. Rev.* (U.S.) 23 July 15/2 Wilmington, Delaware, poxed at that time by 1,200 abandoned one- and two-story homes.

poxvirus ('pɒksvaɪərəs). *Microbiol.* Also **pox virus.** [mod.L., f. pox *sb.* + virus.] Any of a group of large DNA viruses that cause smallpox and various other epidermal diseases in vertebrates.

1941 *Amer. Jrnl. Vet. Res.* II. 102/1 There are many different strains of pox virus, some of them less pathogenic than others. **1962** [see ARBORVIRUS]. **1973** R. G. KRUEGER et al. *Introd. Microbiol.* xix. 522/1 Poxviruses propagate rapidly in a wide variety of mammalian and embryo tissues *in vitro* producing cytopathic effects in 24–48 hr.

poxy ('pɒksɪ) *a.* [f. POX *sb.* + -Y[1].] Infected with pox; spotty; *fig.*, trashy, worthless. Also as a general term of abuse.

1922 JOYCE *Ulysses* 8 God knows what poxy bowsy left them off. **1950** M. PEAKE *Gormenghast* xxii. 149 Every poxy sunrise of the year, eh, that you burst out of the decent darkness in that plucked way? **1958** [see MOOR *sb.*[1] 1 b]. **1959** I. & P. OPIE *Lore & Lang. Schoolch.* ix. 171 Other unfortunates are 'Spotty Dicks'.. their friends call them: Bumps,.. Crater face,.. Pimple bonce, Poxie, and Scabby guts. **1968** BETHELL & BURG tr. *Solzhenitsyn's Cancer Ward* I. xix. 302 You know, that poxy-faced guy, the one with all the bandages. **1975** J. PIDGEON *Flame* i. 8 No more poxy weddings, no more bloody favours. **1976** J. O'CONNOR *Eleventh Commandment* ii. 31 The first tray.. was full of poxy rings worth two or three quid. **1978** K. BONFIGLIOLI *All Tea in China* III. xi. 153 My poxy friend Peter.

poy, puy (pɔɪ), *sb.*[1] Now *dial.* Also 9 powey, pooey ('poːɪ, 'puːɪ), puoy. [Etymology obscure; it has been suggested to be the same as POY *sb.*[2]; but the sense offers difficulty.]

1. A pole used to propel a barge or boat; a punting-pole; *spec.* that with an iron forked point used by keelmen on the Tyne, etc.

1486 *Nottingham Rec.* III. 243, vij. long polles for to make hokes and poyes. **1784** *Bishoprick Garland* (1834) 60 (E.D.D.). **1829** T. MARSHALL *Coll. Songs* 17 Ower the powey slap he fell. **1865** *Our Coal & Coal-fields* 72 Having walked the whole length of the vessel they pluck up the great oars, which they call puys, return hastily to the prow, put down the puys again and thrust as before. **1894** *Northumbld. Gloss.*, *Pooey, puoy, puy, powey, poy*, the pole used by keelmen to 'set' or push the keel along. Standing at the bow of the keel, the man rapidly thrusts his pooey down to the bottom of the river, where a small fork holds it in the sand [etc.].

†**2.** (See quot.) *Obs.*

1706 PHILLIPS, *Poy*, the Pole us'd by Rope-dancers to stay themselves with. **1755** in JOHNSON.

poy, *sb.*[2] Now *dial.* Also 7 poye, puoy. [perh. aphetic for **apoye*, a. OF. *apoie, appuye* 'an open and outstanding terrace or gallery, set on th' outside with railes to leane vpon' (Cotgr.). Sense 2 appears to be a distinct application of F. *appui* support.]

†**1.** (See etymology.) *Obs.*

1636 *Maldon, Essex Documents* Bundle 217 No. 22 Of Henery Adammes for his poye at his hous, 2*d.* **1656** *Maldon, Essex Borough Deeds* Bundle 87 No. 1, iid. due for quitt-rent for the poy of the howse late of Mr. Wells. **1677** *Ibid.* Bundle 100 No. 2 Paid to Mr. Finch for windowes and puoy and penthowse by him left att the howse of correction when he left itt.

2. A float used to buoy up the head of a sheep when swimming in the washing-pool. *dial.*

1863 MORTON *Cycl. Agric.* II. 720–7 s.v. (In E.D.D. from Linc. and Notts.)

poy, *v. dial.* [f. POY *sb.*[1]] *trans.* To propel (a barge or boat) with a poy; to pole, punt.

1784 *Bishoprick Garland* (1834) 60 (E.D.D.) A clever blade, I'm told, as ever poy'd a keel. **1889** *Tyneside Songster* 114 (E.D.D.) Still the twe cheps kept poweyin her reet, They powey'd till they powey'd her reet out o' seet.

‖**poya** ('pəʊjə). [Sinhalese *pōya*, f. Skr. *upavasathá* fast day.] In full, ***poya day***: a day on which the moon enters one of its four phases, observed as a day of special religious observance by Buddhists in Sri Lanka.

1853 R. S. HARDY *Man. Budhism* i. 22 When the dark póya, or day of the new moon, has come, the sun moves in one day the distance of 100,000 yojanas from the moon. *Ibid.* ii. 51 Today so many men have observed the póya (or sacred day). *Ibid.* v. 116 It was the póya day, when the prince.. went to the public alms-hall to distribute the royal bounty. **1889** M. MONIER-WILLIAMS *Buddhism* XII. 316 These preachings are generally well-attended, especially on the four Poya days. **1910** tr. *Hackmann's Buddhism as Relig.* III. ii. 116 Real preaching (not only reading of the sacred text) is done in some temples on the so-called *poya* days, the four quarters of the moon, when lay people assemble in the *vihāras* to present their gift. **1913** L. WOOLF *Village in Jungle* ii. 40 If you had come last poya, Silindu, I could have given it. **1971** *Times Weekender* (Ceylon) 3 Oct. 9/2 He had obviously stoked up in anticipation of a dry Poya day ahead.

poy-bird, obs. form of POË-BIRD.

†**poyder** ('pʏdər), obs. Sc. f. PEWTER.

1573 *Reg. Privy Council Scot.* II. 269, V dosane of Flander poyder truncheowirs... Twa lawers of Flanders poyder.

poyesye, poyet, obs. ff. POESY, POET.

†**poygné, poynyé.** *Obs.* Forms: 4–5 poygne, poyne, *Sc.* punȝe, pwnȝhe, 5 *Sc.* poynyhe, poyhne, ponyhe. [a. OF. *poignié* or *poigniee*:—late L. type *pugnāta*, f. *pugnāre* to fight.] A fight, combat, skirmish.

1375 BARBOUR *Bruce* XII. 373 For in punȝeis is oft hapnyne. *Ibid.* XVI. 307 Bot gif that ony pwnȝhe wer That is nocht for till spek of her. *c* **1400** *Laud Troy Bk.* 5565 He broght with him to that poyne Off gode knyghtes thousandes thre [*MS.* tweyne, but cf. *Destr. Troy* 6880]. *Ibid.* 12924 With hardy hert & gret fferte Come he thedur to that poygne. *c* **1425** WYNTOUN *Cron.* IX. iii. 217 Welle thre hundyr and fourty Of Inglis at that poynȝhe war tane. *Ibid.* v. 355 Poyhneis and iuperdeis of were.

poyle, poylley, obs. ff. PULLEY.

poyn, var. POIN *v. Obs.*, to prick, stitch.

poynado, poynard, obs. ff. PONIARD.

poynant, -naunt, obs. ff. POIGNANT.

poynd, obs. f. POIND; see also quot. *c* 1450 s.v. POUND *v.*[2] 1.

poynde, obs. f. POND.

poyne, var. POYGNÉ, PUNYE.

poynette, var. POIGNET *Obs.*

poyngarnette, obs. f. POMEGRANATE.

poyniard, -yard, obs. ff. PONIARD.

'**Poynings' Law.** Also (*incorrectly*) **Poyning's Law.** [f. the name of Sir Edward *Poynings* (1459–1521), Lord Deputy in Ireland, 1494–6.] The name given to a series of statutes, passed at Drogheda in 1494–5 and repealed in 1782, by which the Irish parliament was subordinated to the English Crown.

[**1612–13** in Coke *Fourth Part Institutes* (1644) lxxvi. 351 An Act made in the tenth year of H.7 called *Poynings Act.*] **1622** BACON *Henry VII* 138 But Poynings (the better to make compensation of the Meagernesse of his Seruice in the Warres, by Acts of Peace) called a Parliament; where was made that memorable Act, which at this day is called Poynings Law, whereby all the Statutes of England were made to bee of force in Ireland. **1656** BLOUNT *Glossogr.*, *Poynings Law* is an Act of Parliament made in Ireland, 10 Hen. 7, and was so called, because Sir Edw. Poynings was Lieutenant of Ireland, when that Law was made; whereby all the Statutes of England were made of force in Ireland [etc.]. **1797** *Encycl. Brit.* IX. 327/2 During his administration was enacted the law known by the name of *Poyning's Law.* **1827** H. HALLAM *Const. Hist. Eng.* II. xviii. 719 This produced the famous statute of Drogheda in 1495, known by the name of Poyning's law. **1938** D. L. KEIR *Const. Hist. Mod. Brit.* vii. 434 By Poyning's Law, in 1495, the Irish Parliament itself made applicable to Ireland all statutes lately made in England, and acknowledged the right of the King to be informed of the causes for its summons and to approve, in his Council, all bills to be introduced when it met. **1973** B. BRADSHAW in B. Farrell *Irish Parliamentary Tradition* v. 69 Essentially Poynings' Law provided that a parliament could not be validly held in Ireland without the consent of the king.. both to the convening of parliament and to the projected legislation.

poynson, obs. f. PUNCHEON.

poynt, etc., obs. ff. PAINT, POINT, etc.

Poynting ('pɔɪntɪŋ). *Physics.* The name of John Henry *Poynting* (1852–1914), English physicist, used *attrib.* and in the possessive to designate concepts in electromagnetism, as **Poynting's theorem**, the theorem that the rate of flow of electromagnetic energy through a closed surface is equal to the integral over the surface of the Poynting vector; **Poynting('s) vector**, the vector product of the electric and magnetic field strengths at any point, which can often be interpreted as representing in magnitude and direction the rate of flow of electromagnetic energy.

1893 J. J. THOMSON *Notes Recent Res. Electr. & Magn.* p. xiii, Poynting's theorem. **1913** L. SILBERSTEIN *Vectorial Mech.* i. 45 The flux of electromagnetic energy, per unit time and unit area, *i.e.* the so-called Poynting-vector. **1962** CORSON & LORRAIN *Introd. Electromagn. Fields* xi. 399 The Poynting vector for sunlight is approximately 1·4 kilowatts/meter[2] at the surface of the earth. **1971** D. A. DUNN *Models of Particles* iii. 74 The usual form of Poynting's vector, which appears in Poynting's theorem and expresses the amount and direction of power flow, is invariant to a Lorentz transformation. **1976** D. E. SOPER *Classical Field Theory* x. 150 The energy current.. and the momentum density.. are given by the familiar Poynting's vector. **1977** *Daily Tel.* 14 Nov. 8 (Advt.), You'll find a complete range of ready-prepared programs for commonly-used calculations such as.. field-strength and poynting vector due to electric dipole.

poyny(h)e, var. POYGNÉ *Obs.*

poynysse, obs. f. PUNISH.

‖**poyou** ('pɔɪuː). [Native name in Guarani.] The six-banded armadillo, *Dasypus sexcinctus.*

1834 *Penny Cycl.* II. 353/2 The *poyou*.., or yellow-footed armadillo (for thus Azara interprets the name), measures about sixteen inches from the nose to the origin of the tail. **1849** *Sk. Nat. Hist., Mammalia* IV. 195. **1896** *Cassell's Nat. Hist.* III. 185.

poyr, obs. north. f. POOR.

poyra, var. PORRAY.

poyse, obs. f. POISE.

poyse, -see, etc., obs. ff. POESY.

poysen, -son, -syn, etc., obs. ff. POISON, etc.

poyte, obs. form of POET.

poz, obs. variant of POS, short for *positive.*

poze, pozed, pozer, obs. ff. POSE, etc.

‖**pozzolana, pozzuolana** (pottso-, pottswo'lana). Also 8 puzzolane; 8–9 pouzzo-, puzzolana, 9 pozzo-, puzzolano, puozzo-, puzzuolana. Now also anglicized as **pozzolan** (pozzulan, puzzolan). [It. *pozz(u)olana*, prop. adj. (sc. *terra* earth) 'belonging to Pozzuoli' (L. *Puteolī* little springs) a town near Naples; whence F. *pouzzolane*, by which some of the Eng. spellings are affected.] A volcanic ash, containing silica, alumina, lime, etc., found near Pozzuoli, and in the neighbourhood of various volcanoes, much used in the preparation of hydraulic cement. Also, used as the name of similar artificial preparations. **pozzolan cement**, a cement made from natural or artificial pozzolan, lime, and water.

1706 PHILLIPS, *Pozzolana*, a kind of Sand found in the Territory of Pozzuolo near.. Naples. **1777** HAMILTON in *Phil. Trans.* LXVIII. 6 They grind down this sort of stone .. into a powder, which they use as a puzzolane for all their buildings under water. **1791** SMEATON *Edystone L.* §185. 111 The two substances of so much consequence in water building; viz. *Tarras* and *Puzzolana.* **1818** E. HENDERSON *Iceland* xii. II. 121 A yellowish alluvial formation resembling the tuffas or puzzuolana of Iceland. **1842** *Mech. Mag.* XXXVI. 294 The clays used in the fabrication of certain pouzzolanas. **1900** *Q. Rev.* Jan. 33 Rome is built, one may say, of pozzolana. **1907** *Chem. Abstr.* I. 1078 (*heading*) Process of manufacturing limes, cements, and puzzolans. **1947** R. H. BOGUE *Chem. of Portland Cement* xxix. 520 Only when the chemical action is completely understood will it be possible to design a 'pozzolan' of ideal composition for any particular purpose. **1951** *Econ. Geol.* XLVI. 311 Pozzolans are natural and artificial siliceous and aluminous substances which are not cementitious themselves but which react with lime in the presence of water at atmospheric temperatures to produce cementitious compounds.

attrib. **1794** SULLIVAN *View Nat.* II. 190 The catacombs of Rome are hollowed in a sort of puzzolana earth, of a brown violet colour. **1799** KIRWAN *Geol. Ess.* 45 Tartar in hogsheads of wine, and pouzzolana mortar. **1910** *Engineering News* LXIV. 597/2 The mixed Portland cement and puzzolan-cement is superior to Portland cement. **1918** R. PEELE *Mining Engineers' Handbk.* XLIII. 2217 Puzzolan cement proper is made by grinding hydrated lime and puzzolan, a volcanic material occurring near Naples. **1971** *Materials & Technol.* II. ii. 106 Pozzolan cement is made by grinding together a cement (usually Portland cement) and a powdered siliceous material.

Hence **pozzo'lanic** *a.*, of the nature of or containing pozzolana; hence also **ˌpozzola'nicity**, the property of combining with lime in the presence of water to form a cement.

1829 *Glover's Hist. Derby* I. 85 There is also pozolanic or watery limestone. **1927** F. L. BRADY *Introd. Building Sci.* xxi. 241 Mortars are used in England at the present day, which set by pozzolanic action. **1956** *Proc. Inst. Electr. Engin.* CIII. A. 225/1 Pulverized fuel fly ash from our power stations.. has the pozzolanic property of setting with lime under water. **1960** *B.S.I. News* Jan. 15 'Pozzolanic portland cements' may contain up to twenty per cent. pozzolana but need not pass the test for pozzolanicity. **1972** *Daily Tel.* 29 Apr. 17 (Advt.), Manufacturers of pozzolanic cements and grouts.

pozzy[1]: see POSSIE, POZZY.

pozzy[2] ('pɒzɪ). *Army* and Navy *slang.* Also possie, possy, pozi, pozzie. [Origin unknown.] Jam, marmalade.

1916 *Daily Mail* 1 Nov. 4/4 'Pozzy' (jam). **1919** W. H. DOWNING *Digger Dial.* 59 *Pozi*, jam. 'Who puckeroed the pozi?' 'Who took the jam?' **1929** *Papers Mich. Acad. Sci., Arts & Lett.* X. 316/1 *Possie*, jam. This seems to be a variant of pozzi (or pozzy). **1962** GRANVILLE *Dict. Sailors' Slang* 91/1 *Pozzie* (*y*), jam or marmalade.

p-process: see P III. 6.

pra, obs. Sc. f. PRAY, PREY.

praam, var. PRAM.

'**prabble,** *sb. Obs.* exc. *dial. rare.* [Dial. variant (in Shaks., a Welshman's pronunciation) of BRABBLE.] A quarrel, a squabble.

1598 [see PRIBBLE]. **1599** SHAKS. *Hen. V*, IV. viii. 69 *Fluellen*... I pray you to serue God, and keepe you out of prawles and prabbles, and quarrels and dissentions. **1883** *Almondbury & Huddersfield Gloss.* s.v., Au darn't differ wi' him for fear on a prabble.

So '**prabble** *v. trans.*, to chatter noisily.

1881 BLACKMORE *Christowell* xvi, And let the others prabble truculent philosophy.

prace, obs. form of PRESS.

prachant, variant of PRATCHANT *Obs.*

†**pract,** *v. Sc. Obs.* [f. stem of *pract-ic, -ice.*] *trans.* and *intr.* = PRACTISE *v.* (in various senses).

a **1500** *Colkelbie Sow* 121 (Bann. MS.) Yit scho callit to hir cheir On apostita freir, A peruerst perdonair And practand palmair. *Ibid.* 163 Bot presumpteouss in pryd, Practing no thing expert, In cunnyng cumpass nor kert.

practic ('præktɪk), *sb.*[1] *arch.* Forms: α. 4–6 practik, 4–7 -ike, 5 -yk, -yke, -yque, 5–9 -ique, 6–7 -icke, -icque, 6–8 -ick, 6– practic; 5 praktik, -ike; 7 pracktik. β. *Sc.* 6 pratick, -yke, 6–7 prattik, 6–8

-ick, 7–8 ique, 7 pratique; 6 prettic, -ick, -ik, -ike, -icque: see also PRATIQUE. [ME. *practik(e*, a. OF. *practike*, *-ique*, variants of *prat(t)ique* (13th c. in Hatz.-Darm.) practice, usage, intrigue, form of pleading, etc. (whence the β forms); ad. med.L. *practica*, a. Gr. πρακτική (also πρακτική ἐπιστήμη, Plato) practical (as opposed to theoretical) science, fem. sing. of πρακτικός adj.: see next.] The earlier Eng. and esp. Sc. equivalent of PRACTICE.

1. The action of practising; practical work or application of (something); practice as opposed to theory; = PRACTICE 1.

α. **1387** TREVISA *Higden* (Rolls) I. 43 Wise men and wel i-tauȝt in þe practike of gemetrie. *c* **1391** CHAUCER *Astrol.* Prol., The second partie shal teche the werken the verrey practik of the forseide conclusiouns. *a* **1460** *Pol. Poems* (Rolls) II. 241 Hatrede and praptyk of fals auctorité Al good conscience they putten owte. **1475** *Bk. Noblesse* (Roxb.) 77 To lerne the practique of law or custom of lande, or of civile matier. *c* **1480** HENRYSON *Test. Cres.* 269 Of rhetorik the praktik he micht leir. **1598** BARRET (*title*) The Theorike and Praktike of Moderne Warres. **1600** ABP. ABBOT *Exp. Jonah* 537 Thou thoughtest it so in Theorike but beleevedst it not in Practike. **1631** MASSINGER *Emperor East* II. i, He has the theory only, not the practic. **1700** WALLIS in *Collect.* (O.H.S.) I. 317 As to the practick of it; there are..consorts of music. **1853** *Fraser's Mag.* XLVII. 294 They ignored the practic and theoric of every sect. **1855** KINGSLEY *Westw. Ho!* v, Amyas..cunning as a fox in all matters of tactic and practic.

β. **1530** LYNDESAY *Test. Papyngo* 30 Boith in pratick & speculation. **1535** STEWART *Cron. Scot.* (Rolls) I. 221 In all prattik of weir he wes perqueir. **1552** LYNDESAY *Monarche* 2653 This wes the prettike of sum pylgramage. **1691** T. H[ALE] *Acc. New Invent.* p. vi, [To] obstruct their pratique in those Arts of life wherein they were expert.

†**b.** As one of the ancient divisions of Philosophy.

1390 GOWER *Conf.* III. 85 The laste science of the thre It is Practique. **1483** CAXTON *Gold. Leg.* 389 b/2 Phylosophye is deuyded in thre, in theoryque in practyque and in logyque.

c. An action, deed, work; *pl.* works, doings, deeds, practices; things practical, practical matters.

1641 'SMECTYMNUUS' *Answ.* §13 (1653) 56 Our Bishops challenge (if not in their Polemicks, yet in their Practicks) a Power that Timothy and Titus..never did. **1653** GAUDEN *Hierasp.* 204 The moralls and practiques of men, as well as their intellectuals, are much to be considered. **1748** RICHARDSON *Clarissa* (1810) III. lxii. 355 This dear lady is prodigiously learned in theories. But as to practics, as to experimentals, must be, as you know from her tender years, a mere novice. **1889** A. GISSING *Both of this Parish* II. vi. 135 Accomplished in all the practicks of tilth and tillage.

†**2.** Mode of action or operation; custom, habit, usage; = PRACTICE 2 c. *Obs.*

α. *c* **1386** CHAUCER *Wife's Prol.* 187 Telle forth youre tale ..And teche vs yonge men of youre praktike. *c* **1449** PECOCK *Repr.* II. xx. (Rolls) 269 The oolde practik of deuoute Cristen man. **1563** WINȜET *Four Scoir Thre Quest.* To Rdr., Wks. (S.T.S.) I. 57 The commoun practik of our aduersaris, to mak of obscuir mirknes a commmentare to the cleir licht. **1653** H. COGAN tr. *Scarlet Gown* Ep. Ded., Particularities of the practique..in the elections of the said Cardinalls.

β. *c* **1560** ROLLAND *7 Sages* 34 Of thair prettick to me ane point propyne.

3. Legal usage; case-law; particularly in Scots Law: see quot. 1708.

a **1533** LD. BERNERS *Gold. Bk. M. Aurel.* (1546) I i vij, To make newe offyces and to ordeyne statutes and practikes. **1565** *Reg. Privy Council Scot.* I. 353 According to the.. Actis of Parliament, lawis, and practik of this realme. *a* **1578** LINDESAY (Pitscottie) *Chron. Scot.* (S.T.S.) I. 64 The lawis and pratick of this realme. *c* **1588** in *Cath. Tractates* (S.T.S.) 253 The use and the prattik of the kirk. **1678** SIR G. MACKENZIE *Crim. Laws Scot.* I. xv. §2 (1699) 82 Albeit the manner of death is not exprest in this act, yet practick hath determined the same to be hanging. **1708** J. CHAMBERLAYNE *St. Gt. Brit.* II. III. v. (1737) 408 Upon the Civil Law the solemn Judgments in Law Cases have been collected, which are called Practiques [in Scotland], a Word of the same Import with that of Reports in England. *a* **1765** ERSKINE *Instit. Laws Scot.* I. i. §47 An uniform tract of decisions of the court of session, *i.e.* of their judgements on particular points, either of right or of form..anciently called Practics, is by Mackenzie..accounted part of our customary law. **1818** SCOTT *Hrt. Midl.* xii, What say ye to try young Mackenyie? he has a' his uncle's practiques at the tongue's end.

†**4.** Practical acquaintance; habitual intercourse or dealings; experience; = PRACTICE 3. *Obs.*

1592 WOTTON in *Reliq.* (1685) 663 A certain Florentine, of great prattick with Strangers. **1624** SIR T. ROE in *Fortescue Papers* (Camden) 206 One that hath experience and practicque with all nations. *a* **1734** NORTH *Exam.* II. iv. §140 (1740) 306 How could any one, of English Education and Prattique, swallow such a low Rabble Suggestion?

†**5.** Artful dealing, contrivance, cunning, policy; with *a* and *pl.*, an art or kind of practical skill, *esp.* an artful device or contrivance, a stratagem, trick, or deception. *Obs.*

α. *c* **1470** HENRYSON *Mor. Fab.* v. (*Parl. Beasts*) xlii, His deith be practik may be preuit eith. **1483** in *Lett. Rich. III & Hen. VII* (Rolls) I. 19 [Edw. IV] willed that my lord Dynham shuld assaie some practik therin and fele the mynde of the said lord Corder. **1513** DOUGLAS *Æneis* XI. x. *heading*, Heyr Turnus and Camylla gan devys Practikis of weir, the Troianis to supprys. **1549** *Compl. Scot.* xi. 94 He vsit the samen practik contrar irland and valis. **1583** *Leg. Bp. St. Androis* 319 Medeas practicques scho had plane, That could mak auld men young agane. **1584** LODGE *Alarm agst. Usurers*, etc. (Hunter. Cl.) 62 He brought foorth a mirrour of notable operation, a practicke in prospectiue.

β. **1500–20** DUNBAR *Poems* xxii. 13 Of quhome the gled dois prettikis preif. **1513** DOUGLAS *Æneis* XI. x. 66 A prattik of weir devys will I. **1596** DALRYMPLE tr. *Leslie's Hist. Scot.* x. 316 To occupie the toune with sum prattick or policie. **1693** *Scotch Presbyter. Eloquence* (1738) 117 Thou art always proving Pratticks.

practic (ˈpræktɪk), *a.* (*sb.*²) *arch.* Forms: 4, 6 practik, 6–7 -ike, -icke, -ique, 7–8 -ick, 7- -ic, (7 pratick). [a. obs. F. *practique*, variant of *pratique* practical, ad. late L. *practicus* (Fulgentius, *a* 550), a. Gr. πρακτικός concerned with action, practical, f. πράττειν to do, act: see prec. and -IC.]

1. Pertaining to, consisting or exhibited in practice or action; = PRACTICAL 1.

1551 RECORDE *Pathw. Knowl.* I. *heading*, The practike workinge of sondry conclusions Geometrical. **1598** BARRET *Theor. Warres* VI. i. 182 The practike rules whereof I haue ..at large set downe. **1612** WOODALL *Surg. Mate* Pref., Wks. (1653) 8 Performing the art of healing in a practick way, namely, by the hand. **1667** *Decay Chr. Piety* ix. ¶18 Our attendance on practick duties. **1732** BERKELEY *Alciphr.* v. §4 All things of a practic nature. **1813** G. COLMAN *Br. Grins, Vagaries Vind.* xlix, Witlings who in practic waggery deal. **1833** H. COLERIDGE *Poems* I. 121 Spurning the dictates of a practic creed. *a* **1849** —— *Ess.* (1851) I. 135 Its benign and sublimating influences are conveyed to the lower orb of practic works and secular relations.

b. Opposed to *theoretic*, *speculative*, or *contemplative*. (So in earliest use.) *arch.* or *Obs.*

Often applied to that department of a subject, art, or science, which relates to practice.

c **1380** WYCLIF *Serm.* Sel. Wks. I. 241 Þis cunnyng was not speculatif,..but practik, put in dede, how men shulde lyve by Goddis lawe. **1584** R. SCOT *Discov. Witchcr.* XV. ii. (1886) 322 He perfectlie teacheth practike philosophie. **1599** SHAKS. *Hen. V*, I. i. 51 The Art and Practique part of Life, Must be the Mistress to this Theorique. **1606** BRYSKETT *Civ. Life* 120 Vertues are generally deuided into Speculatiue and Practike; or we may say, into Intellectiue and Actiue. **1617** J. MOORE *Mappe Mans Mortalitie* III. x. 250 Let our skill herein not onely be contemplatiue, but practique. **1621** BURTON *Anat. Mel.* II. ii. IV. (1651) 280 What more pleasing studies can there be than the Mathematicks, Theorick or Pratick parts? **1715** HEARNE *Collect.* (O.H.S.) V. 103 Famous for his Knowledge in the Theory of Musick; in the practick part of which Faculty he was likewise very considerable. **1804** W. TAYLOR in *Crit. Rev.* Ser. III. III. 526 These were daily instructed for some hours both in the theoric and practic parts of the Pythagorean philosophy.

†**c.** Of persons or their faculties. ? *Obs.*

1610 DONNE *Pseudo-martyr* Pref. D iv, As the inuention of Gun-powder is attributed to a contemplatiue Monke; so these practique Monkes thought it belonged to them, to put it into vse and execution, to the destruction of a State and a Church. **1687** *New Atlantis* I. 375 The Practick Minds may in State Matters dive, In hidden Knowledge the Contemplative. **1798** W. TAYLOR in *Monthly Rev.* 212 The practic Essenes were mostly occupied in keeping sheep.

†**2.** = PRACTICAL *a.* 2, 4. *Obs.*

1604 R. CAWDREY *Table Alph.*, *Practique*, practising. **1620** DONNE *Serm.* lxxiv. (1640) 756 It shall do him no good, to say..that he was no speculative Atheist..if hee lived a practique Atheist. **1642** ROGERS *Naaman* 348 Practicke Atheists, who are led by sense as brute beasts.

†**3.** That has had experience in any process or course of action; experienced, practised, well-versed, skilled. *Obs.*

1596 SPENSER *F.Q.* IV. iii. 7 Right practicke was Sir Priamond in fight, And throughly skild in use of shield and speare. **1611** SPEED *Hist. Gt. Brit.* IX. xx. (1623) 981 This Ambassadour was a practicke man, of much experience. **1639** N. N. tr. *Du Bosq's Compl. Woman* I. 14 These Pamphlets, after they have made many women bold, it makes them practick in it, they finde out subtilties, with safty in them.

†**4.** Artful, crafty, cunning. *Obs.*

1585 T. WASHINGTON tr. *Nicholay's Voy.* I. viii. 8 [The corsairs] with their practick art bryng dayly too Alger a number of pore Christians, which they sell vnto the Moores. **1590** SPENSER *F.Q.* II. iii. 9 Wylie witted, and growne old In cunning sleightes and practick knavery.

†**B.** *sb.*² [absolute use of the adj.] A practical man, a man of action, as opposed to a theorist; one who practises something, as opposed to studying it; *spec.* a member of the Jewish sect of the Essenes, who took part in the active affairs of life.

1599 DANIEL *Musophilus* cxxxvii, I grant, that some unletter'd Practick may..with impious Cunning sway The Courses fore-begun with like Effect. **1625** T. GODWIN *Moses & Aaron* I. xii. 62 Of these Essenes there were two sorts, some Theorikes..; others Practicks, laborious and painfull in the daily exercise of those handy-crafts in which they were most skilfull. **1633** T. ADAMS *Exp. 2 Peter* iii. 3 They are mere sceptics, because they would not be practicks. **1650** ELDERFIELD *Tythes* 20 Two sorts of them there were; the students, and the practiques.

†ˈ**practic**, *v. Sc. Obs.* Also 5 pratik, 6 prattik, pretyk, practi(c)k -ique. [ad. F. *pratique-r*, obs. *practiquer* = med.L. *practicāre* to practise (a profession, etc.), It. *praticare*, Prov. *praticar*, Sp. *practicar*. Subseq. conformed to Gr. and L. stem.] *trans.* = PRACTISE (in various senses). **a.** To put into action or operation. **b.** To actuate or influence craftily. **c.** in *pa. pple.* Practised, versed.

a. **1456** SIR G. HAYE *Law Arms* (S.T.S.) 207 [They] pratik the granting of mark to ger resoun be done. **1533** GAU *Richt Vay* 62 Peter practik[it] his keyis in the secund chaiptur of the dedis of the apostlis, be preching of ye law he brocht the pepil to knawelege of thair sine. *c* **1588** in *Cath. Tractates* (S.T.S.) 253 To receaue the bodie and bluid of Chryst, as some tyme was prattiked in the kirkis of Scotland.

b. **1561** LETHINGTON *Let. to Cecil* 15 Aug., St. Pap. Scotl., Eliz. VI. 56 (P.R.O.) Thinking yᵗ the Quenes majesty will by some meanes practique the subiectes off this Realme she [Mary] hath written to divers..to continue thintelligence.

c. **1549** *Compl. Scot.* Prol. 15 Them that vas neuyr pretykkit in the veyris. *a* **1578** LINDESAY (Pitscottie) *Chron. Scot.* (S.T.S.) I. 160 Quhan ony ciwill insurrectioun wes in the cuntrie and specialie lesmaiestie aganis the kingis own persone quhairin he was well practicked.

practicability (ˌpræktɪkəˈbɪlɪtɪ). [f. next: see -ITY. Cf. mod.F. *praticabilité* (Littré).] The quality or state of being practicable; capability of being done or carried out in practice; feasibility. In *pl.* practicable conditions or things.

1767 SMEATON (*title*) Report..concerning The Practicability and Expence of joining the Rivers Forth and Clyde by a Navigable Canal. **1772–84** COOK *Voy.* (1790) IV. 1193 As to the existence, or at least as to the practicability of a northern passage between the Atlantic and Pacific oceans. **1816** J. SCOTT *Vis. Paris* (ed. 5) 191 Of all the practicabilities, which at present offer themselves to that country, the one that is most [promising] is the stability of the government of the Bourbons. **1875** JOWETT *Plato* (ed. 2) V. 122 He has..lost faith in the practicability of his scheme.

practicable (ˈpræktɪkəb(ə)l), *a.* [ad. F. *praticable* (*pratiquable*, 1594 in Hatz.-Darm.), f. *pratiquer* to practise: see -ABLE. Conformed in the stem to *practic*, *practice*, and med.L. *practicāre*.]

1. Capable of being put into practice, carried out in action, effected, accomplished, or done; feasible.

1670 MAYNWARING (*title*) Vita Sana & Longa. The Preservation of Health,..proved. In the due observance of Remarkable Præcautions And daily practicable Rules, Relating to Body and Mind. **1688** PENTON *Guardian's Instr.* 63 There was so much plain, practicable Truth in what he had said. **1719** DE FOE *Crusoe* I. 169, I knew not how it was practicable to get it about. **1860** TYNDALL *Glac.* I. iii. 26 Ascended the glacier as far as practicable.

2. Capable of being actually used or traversed, as a road, passage, ford, etc.

1710 *Lond. Gaz.* No. 4709/1 The Breach..being already practicable, Preparations were making for the general Assault. **1784** BELKNAP *Tour White Mts.* (1876) 16 The only practicable pass through these Mountains to the upper settlements on Connecticut River. **1828** W. IRVING in *Life & Lett.* (1864) II. 309 From Gibraltar the road to Cadiz is likewise very practicable for ladies. **1841** ELPHINSTONE *Hist. Ind.* II. 519 By the time the breach was practicable the town was distressed for provisions.

b. *Theatr.* Said of windows, doors, etc., which are capable of actual use in the play, as distinct from things merely simulated. Also (*colloq.*) *ellipt.* as *sb.*

1838 DICKENS *Nich. Nick.* xxii, He put his head out of the practicable door in the front grooves O.P. **1842** *Penny Cycl.* XXIV. 296/1 Although they [narrow passages at the back of the stage] are, in stage language, 'practicable', hardly could they have been made use of. **1856** MAYHEW *Rhine* 92 The heads of all the tinsel busts..you now find to be 'practicable', as they say in theatrical language. **1859** WRAXALL tr. *R. Houdin* xviii. 267 The machinist had put up a plank running from the stage to the end of the pit, and.. two other 'practicables', much shorter than the centre one, ran across to the boxes. **1882** MRS. OLIPHANT *Lit. Hist. Eng.* I. 362 His [Southey's] scenery and enchantments are always 'practicable', to use theatrical language.

3. *slang.* Easily practised upon or manipulated, gullible; open to connivence or collusion; facile.

1809 MALKIN *Gil Blas* V. i. ¶5 As practicable greenhorns as ever fell into the hands of a man of genius. *Ibid.* VII. xv. ¶12 You might as well be a little more practicable with the clerk of the kitchen.

Hence ˈ**practicableness**, the quality of being practicable; practicability; ˈ**practicably** *adv.*, in a practicable manner; in actual practice or operation, practically.

1643 NETHERSOLE *Proj. for Peace* (1648) 5 Without having respect to the practicablenesse thereof. **1649** *Bounds Publ. Obed.* 11 All our scruples therefore are concerning things to us practicably lawfull or unlawfull in themselves. *a* **1729** J. ROGERS (J.), The meanest capacity, when he sees a rule practicably applied before his eyes, can no longer be at a loss how 'tis to be performed. **1742** RICHARDSON *Pamela* IV. 344 Which I mention only to shew the Practicableness of a Reformation. **1883** *Christian* 1 Nov. 12/1 The question of the practicableness..of the Jordan Valley Canal scheme.

practical (ˈpræktɪkəl), *a.* (*sb.*) [f. as PRACTIC *a.* + -AL¹.]

A. *adj.* **I. 1. a.** Of, pertaining or relating to practice; consisting or exhibited in practice or action. Opp. to *speculative*, *theoretical*, or *ideal*.

Often applied to that department of a subject, art, or science, which relates to practice as distinguished from theory, as in ***practical agriculture***, ***arithmetic***, ***chemistry***, ***geometry***, ***logic***, ***music***, ***philosophy***, etc. ***practical joke***: see JOKE *sb.* 1.

1617 BP. HALL *No Peace with Rome* §8 Vnlesse it be determined (vnder some false semblance) by the verdict of our practicall iudgement, we will it not. **1620** T. GRANGER *Div. Logike* 211 Of Arts some contemplatiue, some practicall. **1657** *North's Plutarch* II. 19 The rest of Aristotles books must be referred to his Philosophy, which he divided into two parts, namely, speculative and practical. **1682** FLAVEL *Fear* 18 Hypocrisie is a lie done, a practical lie. **1715**

tr. *Gregory's Astron.* (1726) I. 282 We suppose the Maker very well versed in Practical Geometry, Mechanics and Optics. **1796** BURKE *Regic. Peace* iv. Wks. IX. 78 A Constitution, that at the time of the writing had not so much as a practical existence. **1849** THACKERAY *Lett.* 14 Sept., He said solemnly, that he did not approve of practical jokes. **1879** *Cassell's Techn. Educ.* III. 202/2 The whole system.. shows..the practical application of technical education.

b. Having, or implying, value or consequence in relation to action; available or applicable in practice; capable of being turned to account; practically useful. *spec.* of doors, windows, food, etc., forming parts of a theatrical or film set: operable; able to be used as in real life.

1642 HOWELL (*title*) Instructions for Forreine Travell. Shewing by what cours..one may arrive to the practicall knowledge of the Languages. **1673** EVELYN *Diary* 5 Mar., Time and experience may forme him to a more practical way ..of University lectures and erudition. **1701** J. JONES (*title*) Practical Phonography: or, the new Art of Rightly Spelling ..By the Sound. **1771** LUCKOMBE *Hist. Print.* 323 He should..see the joyner set and fasten it in a steady and practical position. **1858** GREENER *Gunnery* Pref. 7, I make no pretension to literary style, but have aimed to produce a practical work for practical men. **1897** *Daily News* 24 July 5/2 Practical politics is to do what you can, and not what you ought. **1898** LADY MALMESBURY in *Cycling* 93 A woman's cycling dress should be, in the first place, practical—that is, composed of materials which do not suffer from rain or dust and will stand a certain amount of hard wear. **1933** P. GODFREY *Back-Stage* iv. 47 His [*sc.* the stage-carpenter's] doors and windows never open unless he has been told to make them 'practical'. **1960** O. SKILBECK *ABC of Film & TV* 98 *Practical.* Part, or fitting, of a Set which may have to operate exactly as though real; e.g. a door, tap, or light fitting. **1974** *Some Technical Terms & Slang* (Granada Television) s.v. *Practical*, Granada gave a 'practical' banquet in its play *The Dead.*

c. *Electr.* Applied to certain units (the ampere, volt, ohm, watt, coulomb, and farad) used for practical measurements, as contrasted with the absolute units of the C.G.S. system.

They are now part of the International System of Units.

1873 J. C. MAXWELL *Treat. Electr. & Magn.* II. IV. x. 244 The practical unit of electromotive force is called the Volt. **1882** *Nature* 24 Aug. 391/2 Instead of expressing electrical quantities directly in absolute measure, the [International Electrical] Congress has embodied a consistent system, based on the Ohm, in which the units are of a value convenient for practical measurements. In this, which we must hereafter know as the 'practical system', as distinguished from the 'absolute system', the units are named after leading physicists, the Ohm, Ampère, Volt, Coulomb, and Farad. **1886** J. D. EVERETT *Units & Physical Constants* (ed. 2) xi. 151 The practical unit of capacity is the Farad. It is defined as 10^{-9} of the C.G.S. electro-magnetic unit of capacity. **1904** *Jrnl. Inst. Electr. Engin.* XXXIV. 172 He suggested that the prefix *ab* or *abs* should be used with the names of the practical units (Volt, Ampere, Ohm, etc.) to form names for the corresponding C.G.S. electro*magnetic* units. **1932** [see INTERNATIONAL *a.* (*sb.*) A. 1 c]. **1963** JERRARD & MCNEILL *Dict. Sci. Units* 12 Units based on this definition..are known as electromagnetic units (e.m.u.). The quantities defined by these units are generally of an inconvenient size for practical work so units, known as practical units, are used. The latter may be obtained by multiplying the e.m. unit by a suitable conversion factor. *Ibid.* 13 The inconvenience of having three systems of electrical units, ab units, stat units and practical units has been overcome by the introduction of the metre, kilogramme, second, ampere units (M.K.S.). In this system, the practical units have the same value as the theoretical ones.

2. a. Actually engaged in the practice of some occupation; practising, working.

1604 R. CAWDREY *Table Alph.*, *Practicall*, practising. **1765** A. DICKSON *Treat. Agric.* (ed. 2) 23 *note*, Experience has led the practical farmers into the opinion, that these things are the food of plants. **1788** JEFFERSON *Writ.* (1859) II. 546 Of all this, the practical iron men are much better judges than we theorists. **1827** *Westm. Rev.* VII. 294 Had Mongolfier not been a practical man as well as a philosopher. **1859** DARWIN *Orig. Spec.* ii. (1872) 40 The highest botanical authorities and practical men can be quoted to show that the sessile and pedunculated oaks are either good and distinct species or mere varieties.

†**b.** Actively engaged *in*; active, busy. *Obs.*

1617 MORYSON *Itin.* I. 289 They are most practicall in all kinds of businesse. **1641** SIR E. DERING *Sp. on Relig.* 13 Jan. 9 There is..scarce any of them, who is not practicall in their owne great cause in hand.

†**c.** Practised, experienced. *Obs.*

1677 YARRANTON *Eng. Improv.* 108 A Traveller..that hath given us good Discourse, and he speaks as though he were practical in things.

3. Devoted or inclined to action (as opp. to speculation, etc.); whose knowledge is derived from practice rather than theory; also, having capacity or ability for action.

1667 M. LOCKE in C. Simpson *Compendium* A v b, We poor Practical men, who doe, because we doe (as they are pleas'd to censure us). **1844** STANLEY *Arnold* I. iv. 187 He remained eminently practical to the end of his life. **1845** DISRAELI *Sybil* I. iii, The English..being a practical people, it is possible that they might have achieved their object and yet retained their native princes. **1861** BUCKLE *Hist. Civiliz.* II. 310 They..whose knowledge is almost confined to what they see passing around them, and who, on account of their ignorance, are termed practical men. **1875** JOWETT *Plato* (ed. 2) I. 76 The practical man, who relies on his own experience. **1970** P. LAURIE *Scotland Yard* 292 *Practical*, the highest police compliment; particularly of a senior officer who can still distinguish between the formal processes of law and the realities of police work. **1972** *Police Rev.* 10 Nov. 1475/3 Dickens is on the side of the angels in applauding what we now loosely term 'good practical Police work'.

4. That is such in practice or conduct (as distinguished from belief or theory); that is such in effect, though not nominally or professedly so; virtual.

1642 FULLER *Holy & Prof. St.* v. vii. 387 In a word, if he was not a practicall Atheist, I know not who was. *a* **1688** W. CLAGETT *17 Serm.* (1699) 126 Every wicked man..may indeed be called a practical atheist. **1836** J. GILBERT *Chr. Atonement* vii. (1852) 194 To suspend a law, is, in that instance, to exercise a practical veto against its being law. **1851** H. SPENCER *Soc. Stat.* xxxii. 475 We are not to be guilty of that practical atheism, which, seeing no guidance for human affairs but its own limited foresight, endeavours itself to play the god. **1882** FREEMAN *Amer. Lect.* II. v. 390 The great advantage of our practical republic over your avowed republic.

II. †**5.** That practises art or craft; crafty, scheming, artful. (Cf. PRACTIC *a.* 4, PRACTICE 6, 7.) *Obs.* (The earliest recorded sense.)

1570 FOXE *A. & M.* (ed. 2) 1906/1 Not onely perceiuing their practicall proceedings, but also much greued with their troublesome vnquietnes.

III. 6. *Comb.*, as ***practical-minded***; ***practical activity***, activity through which theory is realized and becomes actual; ***practical attitude***, an attitude that is concerned with material facts and actual events; ***practical criticism***, an analytical approach to literary criticism, advocated by I. A. Richards, which influenced and was further developed as NEW CRITICISM; ***practical nurse*** chiefly *N. Amer.*, one who has completed a course of training in nursing practice but who is not a (state-)registered nurse; also *attrib.*; hence ***practical nurse*** v. trans., ***practical nursing*** vbl. sb.; ***practical politics***, what actually takes place or is possible in political life, sometimes implying lack of moral principle (cf. REALPOLITIK); hence ***practical politician***.

1913 D. AINSLIE tr. *B. Croce's Philos. of Practical* II. i. 173 (*heading*) The *practical activity in its dialectic. *Ibid.*, We shall no longer ask, therefore, whether the practical activity precede or follow knowledge. **1935** E. BURNS *Handbk. Marxism* xiii. 213 There, where speculation ends, with real life, real positive science therefore begins, the representation of practical activity, of the practical process of the development of men. **1963** T. BOTTOMORE tr. *Marx's Early Writings* 52 The criticism of the speculative philosophy of right does not remain within its own sphere, but leads on to *tasks* which can only be solved by *means of practical activity.* **1974** R. STEVENS *James & Husserl* 177 The intentional continuity between projects of meaning and their fulfillment in practical activity. **1883** F. H. BRADLEY *Princ. Logic* 20 Not only are the genuine characteristics absent from a mere *practical attitude, but we find present there a quality which is absent from real judgment. **1902** W. JAMES *Var. Relig. Exper.* xi. 261 Our moral and practical attitude, at any given time, is always a resultant of two sets of forces within us. **1945** K. R. POPPER *Open Society* II. xxiv. 213 It may be better to explain rationalism in terms of practical attitudes or behaviour. **1962** MACQUARRIE & ROBINSON tr. *Heidegger's Being & Time* I. vi. 238 So this phenomenon by no means expresses a priority of the 'practical' attitude over the theoretical. **1970** C. A. VAN PEURSEN in J. M. Edie et al. *Patterns of Life-World* 148 Theoretical truth is of importance, but in no case does it present the origin of truth as such. The practical attitude of man, 'shunning what is harmful and pursuing what is apt to promote well-being', is of more importance. **1929** I. A. RICHARDS (*title*) *Practical criticism: a study of literary judgment. **1958** *Oxf. Mag.* 13 Nov. 94/2 'Practical criticism' itself, as a term, is unsatisfactory... What on earth is the point of any sort of criticism if it isn't practical?.. In so far as it has a clear current sense, it means the analysis, apart from their literary context, of short passages of prose and verse. **1959** *Times Lit. Suppl.* 24 Apr. 241/3 It is not merely criticism; it is 'practical criticism' of a high order and of a kind which is too rarely found in France. **1972** *Ibid.* 3 Mar. 246/3 As for the assumptions involved in the identifying of me [*sc.* F. R. Leavis] with 'Practical Criticism', my first comment is that the formula isn't mine, and,..I have been known for my insistence, when having to use it, that 'Practical Criticism is criticism in practice'. **1977** *N.Y. Rev. Bks.* 15 Sept. 40/2 His practical criticism is not much concerned with the structure of an individual poem except as an embodiment of crisis. **1881** C. GIBBON *Heart's Problem* iv, He had endured some banter from his *practical-minded friend as to the folly of thinking about love instead of law. **1906** *Daily Chron.* 14 Apr. 4/6 The practical-minded makers of modern Egypt. **1921** *Daily Colonist* (Victoria, B.C.) 1 Oct. 16/2 (Advt.), Situations Wanted—Female.. experienced *practical nurse, terms moderate. **1956** K. HULME *Nun's Story* vii. 104 Our practical nurses..can stand only a four-hour shift, but our sisters take unlimited duty. **1964** MRS. L. B. JOHNSON *White House Diary* 24 Apr. (1970) 118 To my great delight we..saw a class in practical nursing, and I told them that the world was certainly waiting for their skills. So it is, as anybody who has tried to find a practical nurse for an elderly or ill member of the family can tell you. **1971** 'A. BLAISDELL' *Practice to Deceive* v. 68 Mrs. Carstairs would be back from practical-nursing her sister. **1979** W. KIENZLE *Rosary Murders* 20 One of the orderlies and one of the practical nurses..had enjoyed a quick roll in bed. **1812** *Deb. Congress U.S.* (1853) 12th Congress 1 Sess., App. 2210 There were two circumstances, inherent in this system of coercing Great Britain by commercial restrictions, which ought to have made *practical politicians very doubtful of its result. **1961** *Times* 10 Jan. 8 The impression remains that the Liberal leader is still the diplomatist, more at home in the chancery, or the corridors of the United Nations, not the father figure, so necessary in Canadian leadership, or the practical politician, able to talk about sewage problems. **1796** *Rep. Comm. House of Commons* (1803) XIV. 38 With a view to such a knowledge of *practical Politics, as may be desired from the History of our experimental Legislation. **1826** DISRAELI *Viv. Grey* I. II. xv. 217 'Hargrave', said his lordship, 'if you want any information upon points of *practical politics*'—that was his phrase..'there is *only one* man in the kingdom whom you should consult..and that's Stapylton Toad.' **1897** [see PRACTICAL *a.* 1 b]. **1919** F. HAMILTON *Vanished Pomps of Yesterday* i. 30 As the inventor of 'Practical Politics' (*Real Politik*), Bismarck had a supreme contempt for fluent talkers and for words. **1939** I. BERLIN *Karl Marx* iv. 74 It was his [*sc.* Marx's] first experience of practical politics: he conducted his paper with immense vigour and intolerance. **1961** N. P. STALLKNECHT in Stallknecht & Frenz *Compar. Lit.: Method & Perspective* vi. 121 We may..trace the notion of individual autonomy from its manifestation in religious practice and theological reflection through practical politics and political theory into literature and the arts.

B. *sb.*

†**1.** In *pl.* **a.** Practical matters; points of practice. *Obs.*

1649 ROBERTS *Clavis Bibl.* Introd. ii. 31 How in Practicals, They Direct in wel-doing. **1653** ASHWELL *Fides Apost.* 20 Credenda, as opposed to the Agenda, or Practicalls of Christianity. **1737** M. GREEN *Spleen* 322 That tribe, whose practicals decree Small beer the deadliest heresy.

b. Practical jokes or tricks. *colloq.* ? *Obs.*

1833 M. SCOTT *Tom Cringle* xviii, Give over your practicals, Lucifer.

2. In *pl.* Practical men; persons concerned with practice.

1840 MILL *Diss. & Disc.* (1859) I. 44 The Practicals never heard of it; or if they had they disdained it as visionary theory. **1844** —— *Ess. Pol. Econ.* 142 The practicals would endeavour to determine this question by a direct induction.

3. An examination, course, or lesson devoted to practice in a subject. Also *fig.*

1934 in WEBSTER. **1955** *School Sci. Rev.* Nov. 38 For the practical paper, 93 per cent of candidates were successful —compared with 68 per cent who passed the theory, and of over 300 who passed the theory, only 7 failed the practical. **1961** *Times* 6 Nov. 14/2 Lieutenant Babington, straight out from England to take over a platoon..seems to have failed his practicals where discipline is concerned. **1966** *Rep. Comm. Inquiry Univ. Oxf.* II. 311 Nationally, the average for tutorials was much lower (1·7 hours against 6·3 hours at Oxford), while the national averages for lectures and practicals were about twice the Oxford figures. **1979** F. OLBRICH *Sweet & Deadly* xi. 125 He would get through this damned exam if it was the last thing he did... There would still be the practicals, of course.

Hence **'practicalism**, devotion to practical affairs; also, = PRAGMATISM 4; also, in Communist usage, excessive attention paid to practical matters resulting in the disregard of theory; **'practicalist**, one who devotes himself to or advocates what is practical.

1843 *Tait's Mag.* X. 146 Among the Parliamentary men belonging to Hardingston's set, there prevailed a tendency to practicalism, the origin of the sect of Utilitarians. **1856** J. GROTE in *Cambr. Ess.* 88 The very practicalism of the English has guarded them against much mistaken and superficial practicalism. **1865** MILL *Comte* 86 The theorists ..have successfully retaliated on the practicalists. **1898** W. JAMES *Philos. Concept. & Pract. Results* 5 The principle of practicalism..., as he [*sc.* C. S. Peirce] called it, when I first heard him enunciate it at Cambridge [Mass.] in the early '70s, is the clue..by following which..we may keep our feet upon the proper trail. **1898** —— *Coll. Ess. & Rev.* (1920) 424 Now the principle of practicalism says that the very meaning of the conception of God lies in those differences which must be made in our experience if the conception be true. **1951** *Britannica Bk. of Year* 686/2 *Practicalism*, a Communist term for the fault of paying too much attention to practical problems of production, etc., and not enough to ideological propaganda. **1963** R. C. TUCKER *Soviet Political Mind* ix. 181 Krushchev..has been criticized by certain elements within the Soviet Communist Party for being insufficiently so [*sc.* theory-oriented]. He has rejected their charge of 'practicalism'.

practicality (præktɪ'kælɪtɪ). [f. PRACTICAL *a.* (*sb.*) + -ITY.]

1. The quality of being practical: usually in senses 1 b and 3 of the adj.

1828 MILL *Autobiogr.* (1924) 288 It is not for me to dispute the palm of practicality with these sage and cautious persons. **1840** CARLYLE *Heroes* iii. (1858) 265 If he..had not courage, promptitude, practicality, and other suitable vulpine gifts and graces, he would catch no geese. **1883** *Contemp. Rev.* June 815 A certain prosaic practicality and hard realism. **1961** E. BECKER *Zen* iv. 107 The 'marvelous person' that is supposed to result from Zen exhibits more Chinese practicality than Indian speculation. **1972** *Physics Bull.* May 303/1 If the physicist's numeracy is combined with his practicality and technical competence one sees that he can present a formidable challenge in this market traditionally the preserve of the arts graduate.

2. A practical matter or affair. (Chiefly in *pl.*)

1854 tr. *Lamartine's Celebr. Char.* II. *Fénelon* 384 These two dreams of Fénelon have been looked upon as serious practicalities by short-sighted reasoners. **1887** MISS E. MONEY *Dutch Maiden* (1888) 303 Miss Wynyard had been educated to practicalities, and knew her own requirements.

'practicalize, *v. rare.* [f. as prec. + -IZE.]

1. *trans. nonce-use.* To subject to practical jokes. (PRACTICAL *sb.* 1 b.) Hence **practicali'zation**.

1818 KEBLE in Coleridge *Mem.* v. (1869) 74, I only hope I shall not be practicalized to death. **1869** COLERIDGE *Ibid.* 75 His fears of death by the slow process of practicalization.

2. To render practical.

1844 J. CAIRNS *Let.* in *Life* x. (1895) 225 Walker is thoroughly practicalised..more evangelically simple than heretofore. **1861** MILL *Autobiog.* i. (1874) 37 He made no effort to provide me any sufficient substitute for [the] practicalizing influences [of school life]. **1863** *Blackw. Mag.*

Sept. 289 The strong sense which practicalises the ideal to the common sympathies and comprehension of multitudes.

practically ('præktɪkəlɪ), *adv.* [f. as prec. + -LY[2].]

1. In a practical manner; in the way of, or in relation to, practice; in practice; as a matter of fact, actually. Often opposed to *theoretically*, *speculatively*, or *formally*.

1623 T. POWELL *(title)* The Attourneys Academy: or, the Manner and Forme of proceeding practically, vpon any Suite, Plaint or Action whatsoeuer, in any Court of Record whatsoeuer, within this Kingdome. **1628** DONNE *Serm.* xxiii. (1640) 233 He loves himself..Contemplatiuely, by knowing as he is known, and Practically, by loving, as he is loved. **1646** JENKYN *Remora* 12 They said not so verbally, but mentally and practically. **1732** BERKELEY *Alciphr.* II. §6 It being impossible a thing should be practically wrong and speculatively right. **1749** FIELDING *Tom Jones* IX. i, Neither physic, nor law, are to be practically known from books. **1886** *Manch. Exam.* 6 Jan. 3/1 Questions which are theoretically interesting to thoughtful people and practically interesting to every one.

2. So far as concerns practice (though not completely or formally); for practical purposes; to all intents and purposes, as good as; in effect, virtually.

1748 HARTLEY *Observ. Man* I. iii. 349 The true Root, or such an Approximation as is practically equivalent. **1834** PRINGLE *Afr. Sk.* v. 190 Their own limbs and lives..were practically altogether at their masters' mercy. **1869** TOZER *Highl. Turkey* I. 318 Thanks to its padding,..[the saddle] was practically unhurt, except for a broken girth. **1891** *Law Times* XCII. 97/2 The application was supported by practically all the creditors.

'practicalness. [f. as prec. + -NESS.] The quality or character of being practical (in various senses: see the adj.); practicality.

1710 NORRIS *Chr. Prud.* ii. 73 The practicalness of Prudence as distinct from pure Theory chiefly consists, in that it contemplates Truth for the sake of Good. **1840** MILL *Diss. & Disc.* (1859) I. 217 From it he doubtless derived the practicalness (if the word may be pardoned) in which the more purely speculative Frenchmen of the present day..are generally deficient. **1865** M. ARNOLD *Ess. Crit.* x. (1875) 425 A stringent practicalness worthy of Franklin.

'practicant. [ad. med.L. *practicans, -ant-em*, pr. pple. of *practicāre, -āri* to practise medicine; after obs. F. *praticquant* (*a* 1550 in Godef.); so mod.Ger. *praktikant*.] †a. One who practises (medicine). *Obs. rare.* b. A practitioner.

1637 BRIAN *Pisse-proph.* (1679) 66, I was then a young practicant in Physick. **1659** GAUDEN *Slight Healers* (1660) 12 This is the Patient with whose hurts, sores, bruises, wounds and sorrows, these practicants have most impudently padled. **1827** *Lancet* 17 Nov. 256/2 At some [German] universities, the clinical students are divided into *auscultants* and *practicants*. **1952** *John o' London's* 2 May 434/1 In..nutrition, we have known him as a brake on the over-enthusiasm of the practicants in that novel subject. **1974** *Spectator* 9 Nov. 591/3 Practicants of Transcendental Meditation.

†**'practicate,** *ppl. a. Sc. Obs.* Also 6 -at. [ad. med.L. *practicāt-us*, pa. pple. of *practicāre*.]

1. Practised, experienced, skilled.

c **1475** *Clariodus* (Maitl. Cl.) v. 1689 For in sik thing I am not prakticate. *a* **1578** LINDESAY (Pitscottie) *Chron. Scot.* (S.T.S.) I. 160 Quhilk he was also practicat in.

2. as *pa. pple.* Legally decided. (Cf. PRACTIC *sb.*[1] 3.)

1561 *Reg. Privy Council Scot.* I. 173 As wes practicate, for Schir Johne Grenelaw callit civilie befoir the Lordis of Sessioun. *Ibid.* 174 As wes practicate by the saidis Lordis of Sessioun contra ane Spanyeart.

'practicate, *v. rare.* [Latinized adaptation of F. *pratiquer*, after med.L. *practicāre*: see -ATE[3].] *trans.* To construct: = PRACTISE *v.* 13.

1862 *Builder* XX. 8 A great centre, from which, too, there are now two near exits actually practicated.

practice ('præktɪs). Forms: 5–6 **practyse**, 6 **-yss, praictes**, 6–7 **practis, -ize**, 6–8 **-ise**, 6– **practice**. [Formerly *practyse, -ize*, app. f. PRACTISE *v.*, substituted for the earlier PRACTIC. The later spelling *-ice* is conformed to that of the suffix in *justice, service*, etc.: see -ICE[1].] The action, or an act, of practising: and derived senses.

I. Simple senses.

1. a. The action *of* doing something; performance, execution; working, operation; method of action or working. (In quot. 1553, The bringing about, production.) *Obs.* or merged in 2. (See also 10 a.)

1553 EDEN *Treat. Newe Ind.* (Arb.) 9 Many..haue attayned to the knowledge and practise of such wonderfull effectes. **1572** MASCALL *(title)* A Booke of the Arte and maner howe to plant and graffe all sortes of trees... With diuers other newe practise, by one of the Abbey of Saint Vincent in Fraunce, practised with his owne handes. **1599** SHAKS. *Much Ado* v. i. 255 *Prin.* But did my Brother set thee on to this? *Bor.* Yea, and paid me richly for the practise of it. **1660** BARROW *Euclid* I. x. *note*, The practice of this and the precedent Proposition. **1721** PERRY *Daggenh. Breach* 121 All Vessels..may by the Practice of raising and lowering the Water in the Space between the two Pair of Gates, pass in or out of the Bason.

b. An action, a deed; *pl.* doings, proceedings. *Obs.* or merged in 2 c.

1565 *Satir. Poems Reform.* i. 237 No practise I cold vse that might vnlade my paine. **1612** WOODALL *Surg. Mate* Pref., Wks. (1653) 11 By death all mens thoughts perish, and so doth every mans private inventions and practises. **1734** *Col. Rec. Pennsylv.* III. 551 Such Practices used on the part of Maryland.

c. *Philos.* The active practical aspect as considered in contrast to or as the realization of the theoretical aspect.

c **1898** C. S. PEIRCE *Coll. Papers* (1934) V. 412 Science, when it comes to understand itself, regards facts as merely the vehicle of eternal truth, while for Practice they remain the obstacles which it has to turn, the enemy of which it is determined to get the better. **1907** F. C. S. SCHILLER *Studies in Humanism* iv. 130 It seems necessary, therefore, to conceive 'practice' more broadly as *the control of experience*. .. The aim of the doctrine of the 'subordination' of 'theory' to 'practice'..is merely *voluntarism*. **1937** C. MORRIS *Logical Positivism* v. 67 Science has integrated and utilized all of the dimensions of meaning, and may be said to walk on the three legs of theory, fact, and practice. **1969** D. CAIRNS tr. *Husserl's Formal & Transcendental Logic* 32 The distinction is after all a relative one; because even purely theoretical activity is indeed activity—that is to say, a practice (when the concept of practice is accorded its natural breadth).

d. A Marxist term for the social action which should result from and complement the theory of communism. Cf. PRAXIS 1 c.

1899 *Social-Democrat* III. 358 *(title)* Social-democratic theory and practice. ? **1924** *Communist Internat.* I. 49 The practice of the class struggle is fertilised by theory, and in its turn becomes the fruitful soil for theoretical study. **1925** N. BUKHARIN *Lenin as Marxist* 17 If Leninism in practice is not the same as Marxism, then we get just that separation of theory from practice which is specially harmful for such an institution as the Institute of Red Professors. **1966** P. HEATH tr. *Wetter's Soviet Ideology Today* I. vi. 139 It [*sc.* a theory] must issue, rather, in *correct* practice, i.e., in a practice that leads reality towards its *truth*. But the problem as to the criterion of truth is not thereby resolved. **1966** F. SCHURMANN *Ideology & Organization in Communist China* p. xlvi, By the time of Yenan, 'theory' had been canonized, and the Chinese Communists turned their attention to 'practice', namely organization and action. **1971** Z. A. JORDAN *Karl Marx* I. vi. 67 Concepts such as those of progress, of the historically restricted scope of social laws, of ideology and social engineering (practice in the Marxian terminology).

2. a. The habitual doing or carrying on of something; usual, customary, or constant action; action as distinguished from profession, theory, knowledge, etc.; conduct. (See also 9 a, b, 10 b, 11 a.)

1509 HAWES *Past. Pleas.* xi. (Percy Soc.) 43 Therto is equypolent Evermore the perfyt practyse. **1526** *Pilgr. Perf.* (W. de W. 1531) 31 b, In yᵉ sayd practyse of good moralite. **1606** WARNER *Alb. Eng.* XIV. xci. (1612) 369 Times were when Practize also preacht, and well-said was well-done. **1664** POWER *Exp. Philos.* III. 170 He..will find the Invention only pleasing in the Theory, but not in the Practice. **1717** ATTERBURY *Serm., 1 Pet.* ii. 21 (1734) I. 164 His Practice of Religious Severities. **1837** MACAULAY *Ess., Bacon* (1887) 418 It was with difficulty that he was induced to stoop from speculation to practice. **1897** E. G. CONSTANTINE *Marine Engineers* xi. 135 The amount of success attending present-day naval practice in this direction may be ascertained from the current technical press.

b. *Law.* The method of procedure used in the law-courts. (See quot. 1809.)

1623 T. POWELL *Attourn. Acad.* 1 The practice heere before this time hath bin, That no *Sub pœna* should be sued forth of the Court of Chancerie, without a Bill of Complaint first exhibited. **1656** T. FORSTER *Lay-mans Lawyer* To Rdr. A iv, This second part of the *Practice of the Law*, containing the formes of all manner of Warrants and Precepts sent out from Authority. **1780** G. CROMPTON *(title)* Practice common-placed: or, the Rules and Cases of Practice in the courts of King's Bench and Common Pleas. **1809** TOMLINS *Law Dict., Practice of the Courts.* By this is understood the form and manner of conducting and carrying on suits or prosecutions at Law or in Equity, civil or criminal..; according to the principles of Law, and the rules laid down by the several Courts. **1810** BENTHAM *Packing* (1821) 27 The oldest book of practice (such is the denomination used, among lawyers, to denote the books, in which a statement is given, of the operations and instruments in use, in the different judicatories, in the course of judicial procedure).. is *Powell's Attorney's Academy*, London, 1623.

c. A habitual way or mode of acting; a habit, custom; (with *pl.*) something done constantly or usually; a habitual action.

1568 GRAFTON *Chron.* II. 287 By this practice, the rule and regiment of the whole realme, consisted onely in the heades and orders of the Duke and the Chauncelor. **1589** *Reg. Privy Council Scot.* IV. 393 Honnest wemen,..spoted at na tyme with ony sic ungodlie practizeis. **1704** NELSON *Fest. & Fasts* (1739) 5 Grafting upon them erroneous and superstitious Practices. **1754** RICHARDSON *Grandison* I. vi. 26 A man of free principles, shewn by practices as free. **1816** SCOTT *Old Mort.* xxxvi, The privy council of Scotland in whom the practice since the union of the crowns vested great judicial powers.

3. The doing of something repeatedly or continuously by way of study; exercise in any art, handicraft, etc., for the purpose, or with the result, of attaining proficiency; hence, †the practical acquaintance with or experience in a subject or process, so gained. (See also 9 c.)

1525 LD. BERNERS *Froiss.* II. clxxxix. [clxxxv.] 577 The lorde of Coucy shewed..the great wysdome and practyse of the sayd physycion. **1553** T. WILSON *Rhet.* 3 Through practise made perfect. **1596** SHAKS. *Tam. Shr.* II. i. 165 Proceed in practise with my yonger daughter, She's apt to learne, and thankefull for good turnes. **1605** —— *Macb.* v. i. 65 This disease is beyond my practise. **1674** PLAYFORD *Skill Mus.* I. xi. 53 It was my chance lately to be in company with three Gentlemen at a Musical Practice. **1774** M. MACKENZIE *Maritime Surv.* 34 After a little Practice, an Angle may be taken more readily this way than with [etc.]. **1850** R. G. CUMMING *Hunter's Life S. Afr.* (1902) 22/1 In the forenoon we had some rifle practice at a large granite stone above the town. **1860** TYNDALL *Glac.* I. xx. 141 The ascent is a pleasant bit of mountain practice. **1899** *Allbutt's Syst. Med.* VIII. 22, I absolutely forbid any public performances which entail many hours of daily severe practice.

†4. An exercise; a practical treatise. *Obs.*

c **1541** TRAHERON *Vigo's Chirurg.* title-p., This lytell Practyce..in Medycyne is translated out of Laten in to Englysshe. **1571** DIGGES *(title)* A Geometrical Practise, named Pantometria, diuided into three Bookes. **1593** J. UDALL *(title)* The Key of the Holy Tongve..first The Hebrue Grammar..; Secondly, A practize upon the first, the twentie fift, and the syxtie eyght Psalmes, according to the rules of the same Grammar. **1712** J. JAMES tr. *Le Blond's Gard.* 87 The Manner of Tracing, reduced to Twenty Practices.

5. *spec.* The carrying on or exercise of a profession or occupation, esp. of law, surgery, or medicine; the professional work or business of a lawyer or medical man.

1576 FLEMING *Panopl. Epist.* 281 The mysteries of mingled medicines, and the practise of Physicke. **1674** R. GODFREY *Inj. & Ab. Physic* 161 He liv'd by his Practice, as other Physicians did and do. **1706** PHILLIPS (ed. Kersey), *Practice*, actual Exercise, especially that of the Profession of a Lawyer, Physician, or Surgeon; the having Clients or Patients. **1800** *Med. Jrnl.* III. 456 So valuable a branch of knowledge as the practice of physic. **1884** *Law Times* 24 May 61/2 There is no barrister in practice who is so thoroughly familiar with the ins and outs of bankruptcy practice. **1898** RIDER HAGGARD *Doctor Therne* i. 5 He sold this practice and removed into Dunchester.

6. a. The action of scheming or planning, esp. (now only) in an underhand way and for an evil purpose; machination, treachery; trickery, artifice. (The earliest recorded sense.)

1494 FABYAN *Chron.* VII. 608 The towne of Seynt Denys ..was goten by treason or practyse of one named Iohan Notice, a Knyght of Orleaunce. **1560** DAUS tr. *Sleidane's Comm.* 59 The Practise of the Deuill. **1598** GRENEWEY *Tacitus' Ann.* I. iv. (1622) 7 All sauing Lepidus, through Tiberius practise, for sundry pretended crimes were made away. *a* **1642** SIR W. MONSON *Naval Tracts* I. (1704) 201/2 The Ship..should be surrender'd without Any Practice or Treason. **1828** SCOTT *F.M. Perth* xxiii, It looks as if there were practice in it to bring a stain on my name. **1834** W. GODWIN *Lives Necromancers* 445 Keeling..inclined to the belief that it might all be practice, and that there was nothing supernatural in the affair. **1877** FREEMAN *Norm. Conq.* (ed. 3) I. v. 276 He..died a martyr's death, through the practice of the Lady Ælfthryth.

b. Dealings, negotiation, conference, intercourse; *esp.* in evil sense, Conspiracy, intrigue, collusion (*with* a person, *between* persons). *arch.*

1540 *St. Papers Hen. VIII*, VIII. 322 She ys very lothe to be knowne to have any praictes with me in any the Kinges Highnes affaires. **1572** *Reg. Privy Council Scot.* II. 156 Be ressoun of the daly traffique, practize and intelligence betuix the inhabitantis..and the declarit tratouris. **1584** R. SCOT *Discov. Witchcr.* v. viii. (1886) 85 There was not any conference or practise betwixt them in this case. **1632** MASSINGER *Maid of Hon.* I. ii, He has been all this morning In practice with a peruked gentleman-usher. **1656** EARL MONM. tr. *Boccalini's Advts. fr. Parnass.* II. xxxvi. (1674) 188 He held secret practice with all the Poets. *a* **1680** EARL OF ROCHESTER *Valentinian* v. iii, Begone and leave me I have some little practice with my soul And then the sharpest sword is welcome. **1873** BROWNING *Red Cott. Nt.-cap.* III. 945 Somehow, gloves were drawn o'er dirt and all, And practice with the Church procured thereby.

c. (with *pl.*) A scheme, plot, intrigue, conspiracy, stratagem, manœuvre, artifice, trick.

1539 CROMWELL in Merriman *Life & Lett.* (1902) II. 199 A practise which I trust shal shortely come to light. **1568** GRAFTON *Chron.* I. 415 This realme was..troubled with Ciuile sedition, and the craftie practises of the Frenchmen. *c* **1605** ROWLEY *Birth Merl.* II. ii, It may be a practice 'twixt themselves To expel the Britons. **1645** GATAKER *God's Eye on Israel* 93 How many plots and practises of the popish faction..have been discovered, defeated, and returned on the heads of those, that were either plotters of them, or imployed in them? **1728** MORGAN *Algiers* II. iii. 243 Giving them to understand, that he was not unacquainted with their Practices. **1740** JOHNSON *Sir F. Drake* Wks. IV. 414 Unable to obviate the practices of those whom his merit had made his enemies. **1871** R. ELLIS *Catullus* xii. 2 Left-hand practices o'er the merry wine-cup.

7. The action, or an act, of practising *on* or *upon* a person, etc.: see PRACTISE 11. *rare.*

1614 B. JONSON *Bart. Fair* I. ii, This is a confederacy, a meere piece of practice vpon her, by these Impostors. **1622** BACON *Hen. VII* 140 Hee thought..that the onely practise vpon their affections, was to set vp a Standard in the field. **1759** FRANKLIN *Ess.* Wks. 1840 III. 423 This menace..was also another piece of practice on the fears of the assembly.

8. *Arith.* A compendious method of performing multiplication by means of aliquot parts, in cases where one or both quantities are expressed in several denominations; e.g. in finding the value of a given number of articles at so many pounds, shillings, and pence each, or that of so many hundredweight, pounds, and ounces of something at so much a hundredweight. See quot. 1727–41.

1574 H. BAKER *Well Spring Sciences* 87 b, The third parte treateth of certayne briefe rules, called rules of practise... Some there be, which call these rules of practise briefe rules; .. There be others whiche call them the small multiplication. **1596** MELLIS *Recorde's Arith.* III. 406 Briefe Rules, called Rules of Practise... The working of Multiplication in Practise,..which is accomplished by meanes of diuision in taking the half, the third, the fourth, the fift, or such other parts of the summe which is to be multiplyed. **1671** J. NEWTON *Compl. Arith.* xxiii. (1691) 119 When the Rule of Three direct hath 1, or an Integer for the first term, it is commonly called a Rule of practice, not only for the speedy, but the practical resolution of such questions. **1727–41** CHAMBERS *Cycl.*, *Practice*, in arithmetic, *Practica Italica*, or *Italian usages*; certain compendious ways of working the rule of proportion... They were thus called from their expediting of practice and business; and because first introduced by the merchants and negotiants of Italy. **1859** BARN. SMITH *Arith. & Algebra* (ed. 6) 156 Practice is a compendious mode of finding the value of any number of articles by means of Aliquot Parts, when the value of an unit of any denomination is given.

II. Phrases and Combinations.

9. ***in practice.*** **a.** In the realm of action; practically, actually, as a fact. **b.** †In customary use, in vogue (*obs.*); practised, habitually performed. **c.** In the condition of being exercised so as to maintain skill or ability. So ***out of practice.***

1579 *Reg. Privy Council Scot.* III. 177 It is alreddy accordit and enterit in practize..that upoun the vacance of ony prelacie the kirkis thairof salbe disponit to qualifiit ministeris in titill. **1602** SHAKS. *Ham.* v. ii. 221 Since he went into France, I haue beene in continuall practice. **1631** MASSINGER *Believe as You List* IV. i, Your viper wine, So much in practise with grey bearded gallants. **1644** MILTON *Educ.* Wks. (1847) 98/2 Of attainment far more certain, than hath been yet in practice. **1693** CONGREVE *Old Bach.* III. viii, Foreigners to the fashion or anything in practice. *a* **1700** DRYDEN (J.), Obsolete words may be laudably revived, when they are more sounding, or more significant than those in practice. **1854** RONALDS & RICHARDSON *Chem. Technol.* (ed. 2) I. 322 Fyfe..believes that the heat actually made available from coal in practice, is nearly the same as ought to be produced, according to theory, by the quantity of coke which it yields. **1863** FROUDE *Hist. Eng.* VIII. vii. 53 He [Shaw] broke loose from time to time to keep his hand in practice. **1868** FREEMAN *Norm. Conq.* II. viii. 218 A saint in practice, if not in profession. **1888** BRYCE *Amer. Commw.* II. lx. 421 In practice it is but little changed. *Mod.* He played a very poor game, he was plainly out of practice.

10. ***to put in*** (or ***into***) ***practice.*** **a.** To practise, exercise, carry out in action. †**b.** To begin to practise or do, to set about (*obs.*). †**c.** To scheme, plot, attempt (*to do* something) (*obs.*). †**d.** To bring into use (*obs.*); cf. 11 b.

1559 W. CUNNINGHAM *Cosmogr. Glasse* 30 This rule will I put in practise whan the tyme of the yeare doeth insewe. **1591** SHAKS. *Two Gent.* III. ii. 89 Thy aduice, this night, ile put in practise. **1592** KYD *Murther I. Brewen* Wks. (1901) 289 She put in practise to poyson him. **1604** E. G[RIMSTONE] *D'Acosta's Hist. Indies* IV. ii. 206 Instruments, which the industry of man hath found out and put in practise. **1611** BIBLE *Transl. Pref.* 6 To haue the Scriptures in the mother-tongue..hath bene thought vpon and put in practise of old. **1706** *Royal Proclam.* 11 Apr. in *Lond. Gaz.* No. 4218/1 It is High Treason for any..Persons to put in Practise to Absolve, Perswade or Withdraw any of Our Subjects..from their..Obedience to Us. **1726** SWIFT *Gulliver* I. vi, I could never observe this maxim to be put in practice by any nation, except that of Lilliput.

11. † ***to make practice of.*** **a.** To practise, carry out in action. **b.** To make use of, use: cf. 10 d. **c.** ***to make a practice of*** (something), to do it habitually and of purpose.

1623 WEBSTER *Devil's Law Case* II. iii, What practice do they make of 't in their lives? **1634** SIR T. HERBERT *Trav.* 147 The Gun (an instrument they now make practice of). *a* **1908** *Mod.* I make a practice of walking to the train every morning. You may do so on this occasion, but you must not make a practice of it.

12. *attrib.* and *Comb.*, chiefly in sense 3, as ***practice-crew, -dress, -firing, -ground, -room, -school,*** etc.; also (in sense 2 b) ***practice direction, master***; **practice bar** *Ballet* = BAR *sb.*[1] 13 d; **practice court** (see quot. 1883); **practice-curve**, a curve or graph showing the relation of practice to progress; **practice pad**, a non-resonant pad, usu. circular and made of rubber or the like, on which to practise the art of drumming; **practice wicket**, (see quot. 1934).

1938 N. STREATFEILD *Circus is Coming* viii. 132 Using the side of the steps as a *practice bar and raising her right leg in an arabesque. **1946** —— *Party Frock* vi. 54 Sally was using the edge of the mantlepiece as a practice-bar. **1976** 'M. ALBRAND' *Taste of Terror* xiv. 78 An empty space, a practice bar, one wall mirrored. **1883** *Wharton's Law Lex.* s.v. *Queen's Bench*, Connected with the Court of Queen's Bench, and auxiliary thereto, was the *Practice Court... The Practice Court (called also the Bail Court) heard and determined common matters of practice, and ordinary motions for writs of *mandamus*, prohibition, etc. **1887** *Century Mag.* XXXIV. 178/2 Freshmen formed a *practice crew of their own. **1924** R. M. OGDEN tr. *Koffka's Growth of Mind* v. 262 New configurations are also attributable to these lower centres; as is demonstrated by the fact that the *practice curve improves by leaps which occur in learning new movements. **1956** B. R. BUGELSKI *Psychol. of Learning* xiv. 399 Learning curves are sometimes called 'practice' curves but about all that we can say for certain about such curves is that they will normally rise above a starting point if learning does take place. **1942** *Weekly Notes* 10 Jan. 19/1 (*heading*) *Practice direction... The Judges of the Chancery Division have given the following direction: [etc.]. **1968** *Weekly Law Rep.* 24 May 815 (*heading*) Practice Direction (Divisional Court: Avoidance of Delay). **1977** C. HAMPTON *Criminal Procedure* (ed. 2) viii. 212 The Lord Chief Justice issued a practice direction in July 1967 explaining the procedure. **1934** A. P. HERBERT *Holy Deadlock* 192 The young ladies of the chorus were in '*practice-dress', their plump legs naked from their 'trunks' to their ankles. **1937** M. ALLINGHAM *Dancers in Mourning* iii. 39 Her short white practice dress. **1979** K. O'HARA *Searchers of Dead* xi. 116 A scrawny girl in a practice dress..chasséed below him. **1898** KIPLING in *Morn. Post* 10 Nov. 5/3 Between the pauses of *practice-firing. **1872** *Routledge's Ev. Boy's Ann.* June 447/1 Its Cricket Club and *practice-ground. **1887** FENN *Dick o' the Fens* (1889) 93 By one rapid *practice-learned drag, the net was matched over. **1885** EMDEN & PEARCE-EDGCUMBE *Compl. Coll. Practice Statutes, Orders & Rules* 1147 (*heading*) Office Rules settled by the *Practice Masters, 1880, 1881, 1882. **1890** *Law Rep.: Queen's Bench Div.* XXV. 243 The practice masters..have at some period between 1880 and 1888 issued a direction that 'writs of summons before the Judicature Acts came into force may be renewed without an order'. **1937** *Encycl. Court Forms & Precedents* I. 13 There are eight King's Bench Masters... They have also control of the Central Office and one of them sits daily to exercise this control and to give directions with respect to questions of practice and procedure relating to the business of the Central Office... [*Note*] The Master discharging this duty (called 'the Practice Master') takes *ex parte* applications and also gives advice to solicitors on points of practice and procedure. **1966** *Masters' Practice Directions, Tables & Forms* (Supreme Court of Judicature) 1 These directions shall..supersede any Practice Masters' Rule or Direction dealing with the same subject. **1968** *New Yorker* 18 May 56, I started playing drums in junior high. I got a *practice pad and sticks and a Paul Yoder method book. **1972** *Down Beat* 16 Mar. 19/3 First of all, get a drum set, not a practice pad. Then play records. **1921** W. DE LA MARE *Crossings* 17 No more scales in that musty-fusty old *practice-room! **1922** [see BAR *sb.*[1] 13 d]. **1963** *Times* 11 June 15/3, 14 sound-proof practice-rooms. **1977** *New Yorker* 19 Sept. 54/3 A friend of Robin's, Roman Markowicz, popped out of a practice room and stopped us. **1980** *Early Music* Jan. 43/1, I agreed to come to the choir practice-room. **1895** *Daily News* 23 Apr. 6/2 Herbart founded 'a *practice school in which a few children should be instructed according to the most scientific methods'. **1871** 'THOMSONBY' *Cricketers in Council* 23 Your first lessons may well be solely in hitting. Go to your *practice wicket, and endeavour to hit hard.. every ball that is bowled to you. **1934** W. J. LEWIS *Lang. Cricket* 298 *Practice wicket*, a pitch with one wicket set up for the practice of batting or batting and bowling, usually in the nets.

practician (præk'tɪʃən), *sb.* (*a.*) Also 6 -icien, -isian, *Sc.* -iciane, 7 -itian, (6 praticiane). [a. obs. F. *practicien* (13th c. in Hatz.-Darm.), var. of *praticien*, f. L. *practica* practice + *-ien*, -IAN.] One who practises any art, profession, or occupation; a worker, practitioner; a practical man (as distinguished from a theorist, etc.).

a **1500** *Colkelbie Sow* Prohem. 62 Knawing myne vnssufficience To be comprysit praticiane [*pr.* perticiane] with prudence. **1508** DUNBAR *Poems* iv. 41 In medicyne the most practicianis, Lechis, surrigianis, & phisicianis. **1536** BELLENDEN *Cron. Scot.* (1821) I. 196 Origenes..wald dite fastar than sevin practicianis might suffice to write. **1558** WARDE tr. *Alexis' Secr.* I. 118 Wherefore many practiciens, when they wyll gylte anye woode, laye the bottome or grounde..of yelow. **1609** DOULAND *Ornith. Microl.* 4 Twixt Musitians and Practitians, oddes is great. **1678** SIR G. MACKENZIE *Crim. Laws Scot.* I. i. §4 (1699) 5 Yet is generally concluded by the practicians of all Nations, that *simplex conatus*, or endeavour, is not now punishable by death. **1818** MOORE in *Mem.* (1853) II. 245 He..was a most learned and troublesome practician, as well as theorist, in dialectics. **1899** S. COLVIN *Lett. Stevenson* I. 12 He looked..with the eye of the poet and artist, and not those of the practician and calculator.

B. *adj.* or *attrib.* Given to practical work.

1863 *N. Brit. Daily Mail* 9 Sept., The eminently adaptive and practician character of the Americans goes far to supersede the necessity of tedious drill.

practicism ('præktɪsɪz(ə)m). [f. PRACTIC(E + -ISM.] (See quot. 1957[1].)

1957 R. N. C. HUNT *Guide to Communist Jargon* xxxv. 121 Hence practicism is the tendency of party members to conduct their day-to-day work without regard to the theory which alone gives that work its justification and significance. **1957** *Economist* 26 Oct. 320/1 All the crimes in the jargon book of communist heresy—including such esoteric offences as 'practicism' (lack of clear revolutionary perspective).

'practico-, combining form of PRAXIS or PRACTICAL *a.*: = practically.., practical and.., as in ***practico-empirical, -social, -spiritual*** adjs.; **practico-inert**, Sartre's term for his hypothesis that man's present freedom of action is limited as a result of the exercise of free choice, or praxis, by previous generations in their use of the material world.

1970 B. BREWSTER tr. *Althusser & Balibar's Reading Capital* (1975) II. iii. 83 All the visible phenomena and practico-empirical concepts produced by the economic world. **1966** A. MANSER *Sartre* xiii. 207, I want to say..that all men are slaves in so far as their experience of life takes place in the realm of the *practico-inert* and in the exact measure in which this realm is originally conditioned by scarcity. **1975** B. COOPER tr. *Aron's Hist. & Dialectic of Violence* ii. 41 Alienation presupposes the moment of original freedom and translucid *praxis*. Otherwise, it would but remain the experience of the practico-inert, the activity-passivity that we live out each day, and could not be recognized as the experience of bondage. **1975** F. COPLESTON *Hist. Philos.* IX. xvii. 379 Man thus falls under the domination of the 'practico-inert' which he himself has created. Man makes the machine; but the machine then reacts on man, reducing him to the level of the practico-inert, to what can be manipulated. **1976** A. S. SMITH tr. *Sartre's Critique Dialectical Reason* 829 Practico-inert, matter in which past *praxis* is embodied. **1970** B. BREWSTER tr. *Althusser & Balibar's Reading Capital* III. 314 Ideology ..is distinguished from a science not by its falsity, for it can be coherent and logical (for instance, theology), but by the fact that the practico-social predominates in it over the theoretical, over knowledge. *Ibid.* I. 54 In the 1857 *Introduction*, Marx writes..'practico-spiritual (*praktisch-geistig*) appropriation of this world'.

†**'practicous**, *a.* *Obs. rare*[−1]. [f. L. *practic-us* PRACTIC + -OUS.] Practical.

1683 E. HOOKER *Pref. Pordage's Myst. Div.* 18 Not to mention speculativ Infidelitie, practicous Atheism, horrid Blasphemies, and all manner of Diabolism.

practicum ('præktɪkəm). *N. Amer.* [a. late L. *practicum*, neut. of *practicus*, Gr. πρακτικός practical, concerned with action. (Cf. G. *praktikum* practical training.)] A practical exercise; a course of practical training.

1904 T. F. HUNT *Cereals in Amer.* p. vi, The ideal condition involves a study of the plant in the field. Unfortunately..no systematic course of instruction can be planned that will conform with the season of crop growth and meet the exigencies of the weather. Practicums should be supplied that will as far as possible remedy this defect. **1938** KAINS & MCQUESTON *Propagation of Plants* 458 To carry out these practicums it is desirable..to have available a plot of ground of not less than one-half acre. **1973** *Arithmetic Teacher* Apr. 244/1 (Advt.), The second week will be a practicum involving children. **1974** H. L. FOSTER *Ribbin'* vii. 301 Practicum experiences involve various aspects of the community life, tutoring students, working with teachers and students, and participating in school activities. **1978** *Daily Colonist* (Victoria, B.C.) 27 Aug. 17/5 His desire for a kindergarten practicum caused a few problems..but it was arranged through the Sooke school district.

†**'practisable**, *a.* *Obs.* Also 7 -iseable, -iceable. [f. PRACTISE *v.* + -ABLE.] Capable of being practised; practicable.

1570 DEE *Math. Pref.* *j, How often, therfore, these fiue.. Operations do..differre from the fiue operations of like.. name, in our Whole numbers practisable. **1634** W. TIRWHYT tr. *Balzac's Lett.* I. 22 Certaine Vertues not practiseable by the poor. **1644** G. PLATTES in *Hartlib's Legacy* (1655) 296 The thing itself plainly appeares to be practiceable.

†**'practisant.** *Obs. rare*[−1]. [a. obs. F. *pra(c)tisant*, pr. pple. of *pra(c)tiser* to PRACTISE.] ?A plotter, conspirator (cf. PRACTISE *v.* 9); or ? performer of a stratagem (Schmidt).

1591 SHAKS. *1 Hen. VI*, III. ii. 20 *Charles.* Saint Dennis blesse this happy Stratageme, And once againe wee'le sleepe secure in Roan. *Bastard.* Here entred Pucell, and her Practisants.

practise ('præktɪs), *v.* Also 5 practis, 5–6 -ese, -yse, 5–7 -ize, 6 -ysse, *Sc.* -isse, -iz, pratize, 6–9 practice. [Known from 15th c. (or ? late 14th c.: cf. the deriv. *practisour* (PRACTISER) used by Langland and Chaucer). a. OF. *pra(c)tise-r* (14th c. in Godef.), = 15th c. L. *practizāre* (Du Cange) to practise; f. OF. *pra(c)tiquer*, med.L. *pra(c)ticāre*, by substitution of the suffix *-iser*, *-izāre* (see -IZE) for the less common *-iquer*, *-icāre*; thence also Du. *praktizeren*, G. *praktizieren*, etc. The stress, originally, as still dialectally, on *-ize* (prak'tiːz, prak'taɪz), was subseq. shifted to the first syllable, whence also the change of z to s, perh. after *practice* sb.]

1. *trans.* To perform, do, act, execute, carry on, exercise (any action or process). Now *rare*, or merged in sense 2.

c **1460** FORTESCUE *Abs. & Lim. Mon.* ix. (1885) 129 This maner off doynge hath be so ofte practised nerehande in euery reaume, þat thair cronicles be full off it. **1509** HAWES *Past. Pleas.* i. (Percy Soc.) 11 Thynges to practyse whiche should profyte be. **1559** *Mirr. Mag.*, *Dk. Clarence* xiv, Pricke the minde to practise any yll. **1591** SHAKS. *1 Hen. VI*, II. iii. 47 To thinke, that you haue ought but Talbots shadow, Whereon to practise your seueritie. **1600** (*title*) Certaine Experiments concerning Fish and Frvte: Practised by Iohn Taverner Gentleman. **1653** MARVELL *Corr.* Wks. (Grosart) II. 3 The only civility which it is proper for me to practise with so eminent a person. **1799** WASHINGTON *Lett.* Writ. 1893 XIV. 171 You shall not practise the same game with me. **1810** SCOTT *Lady of L.* v. xv, He practised every pass and ward, To thrust, to strike, to feint, to guard.

†**b.** In special uses: To work out (a problem or result); to perform, act (a play). *Obs.*

1571 DIGGES *Pantom.* I. xv. E j b, Pleasanter to practize is this than the former and moste exact for Altitudes. *Ibid.* xvi. E ij, By a Glasse heighthes may be pleasantly practized and founde on this wise. *a* **1572** KNOX *Hist. Ref.* Wks. 1846 I. 62 Frear Kyllour sett furth the Historye of Christis Passioun in forme of a play, quhilk he boith preached and practised opinlie in Striveling. **1685** DRYDEN *Alb. & Alban.* Pref., Ess. (Ker) I. 280 He [Charles II] had been pleased..to command that it should be practised before him, especially the first and third acts of it.

c. *intr.* To act, work, proceed, operate. (In quot. 1677, ? to try experiments, to experiment.)

1553 *Respublica* III. ii. 618 We reste nor daie nor night ..[To] practise and travaile for your welth and honoure. **1669** STURMY *Mariner's Mag.* VII. xiv. 23 So practice for any other Latitude. **1677** TEMPLE *Ess. on Gout* Wks. 1731 I. 135 Being little inclined to practise upon others, and as little that others should practise upon me. **1822–34** *Good's Study Med.* (ed. 4) IV. 53 Cases that require rather to be carefully watched, than vigorously practised upon.

2. *trans.* To carry on, perform, or do, habitually or constantly; to make a practice of; to put into practice, carry out in action (as distinguished from believing, professing, etc.).

1526 *Pilgr. Perf.* (W. de W. 1531) 8 b, And what ye rede, se you practise it in lyfe & dede. **1559** Bp. Scot in Strype *Ann. Ref.* (1709) I. App. vii. 17 Sute was made..to have three things graunted..to be practyssed..that is to saye, that prestes myght have wyves [etc.]. **1590** Spenser *F.Q.* ii. vi. 9 Questioned..what that usage ment, Which in her cott she daily practized. **1597** Shaks. *2 Hen. IV*, ii. iii. 23 He had no Legges, that practic'd not his Gate. **1611** Bible *Transl. Pref.* 3 Whatsoeuer is to be beleeued or practised. **1698** Norris *Pract. Disc.* IV. 76 Practice as much of Religion as you Talk, and then you have a full Licence to Talk as much of it as you Please. **1875** Jowett *Plato* (ed. 2) IV. 131 The method which Socrates had heard Zeno practise in the days of his youth.

b. *to practise religion* [after F. *pratiquer la religion*]: to perform the religious duties which the Church requires of its members; to be a practising and not merely a nominal member (esp. in *R.C. Ch.*). Also *absol.* or *intr.*

[**1615** W. Lawson *Country Housew. Gard.* (1626) 1 By religious, I meane..practising prayers.] **1808** Pike *Sources Mississ.* iii. App. 15 The catholic religion is practised in this province, after the same manner as in the other provinces. **1904** *Daily News* 5 Nov. 7 The energetic priest of a very well-organised poor parish in Paris told me that, out of forty thousand inhabitants, four thousand 'practised' religion.

c. With *inf.* To be wont or accustomed. *arch.*

1674–91 Ray *Collect. Words* 192 He hath practis'd to burn the ends of all the Posts which he sets into the ground to a Coal on the outside. **1805** Wordsw. *Prelude* ix. 488 [She] from the tower..Practised to commune with her royal knight By cressets and love-beacons.

d. *intr.* To act habitually.

1681–6 J. Scott *Chr. Life* (1747) III. 3 If we believe it, we cannot be good Christians unless we practise upon it. *a* **1716** Blackall *Wks.* (1723) I. 180 If he practises according to this Opinion, he so far renounces his Christianity. *Mod.* If he practises as well as he preaches, he must be a paragon.

3. *trans.* To work at, exercise, pursue (an occupation, profession, or art).

1560 Daus tr. *Sleidane's Comm.* 333 b, Whan they..practise coniuryng. *a* **1578** Lindesay (Pitscottie) *Chron. Scot.* (S.T.S.) I. 159 [He] wyse weill leirned in devyne syences and pratizit the samin to the glorie of god. **1608** Shaks. *Per.* ii. i. 71 *Sec. Fish.* Canst thou catch any Fishes then? *Per.* I neuer practizde it. **1727** A. Hamilton *New Acc. E. Ind.* I. xii. 131 They admit of no Trade, but practise Piracy. **1875** Jowett *Plato* (ed. 2) V. 118 No man can practise two trades, or practise one and superintend another. **1879** in *Cassell's Techn. Educ.* IV. 96/1 He endeavoured..to practise medicine, but could nowhere find patients.

†**b.** *intr.* To work (at some business or occupation). *Obs.*

1494 Fabyan *Chron.* vii. 505 Some..were holdyn in for a tyme, to practis & shewe vnto the newe how they shuld orde & guyde the sayd offyces. **1660** Bloome *Archit.* Title-p., Carvers, In-layers, Antick-Cutters, and all other that delight to practise with the Compasse and Square.

†**c.** *intr.* To perform (musically). *Obs.*

c **1430** Lydg. *Min. Poems* (Percy Soc.) 11 For to practyse withe sugrid melody, He and his scolers ther wittis did apply. **1796** Eliza Hamilton *Lett. Hindoo Rajah* I. 131 The itinerant musicians that practice in the streets.

d. *spec. intr.* To exercise the profession of law or of medicine.

1538 Starkey *England* ii. ii. 192 Only such whose.. lernyng in the law [was]..prouyd, schold be admyttyd to practyse in causys. **1645–52** Boate *Irel. Nat. Hist.* (1860) 147 Not only dwelling and practising at Dublin, but being Physician generall of the English Forces. **1768** Blackstone *Comm.* III. iv. 55 The seal was committed to the earl of Clarendon, who had withdrawn from practice as a lawyer near twenty years; and afterwards to the earl of Shaftesbury, who had never practised at all. **1867** Trollope *Chron. Barset* I. viii. 67 A medical man practising in a little village. **1883** *Law Rep. 11 Q.B. Div.* 597 A counsel practising at the bar.

†**4.** *trans.* To put into practice, carry out in action, execute (a law, command, etc.). *Obs.*

1460 Capgrave *Chron.* (Rolls) 277 This statute [of 1401] was practized in a prest, that sone aftir was brent at Smythfeld. **1560** Daus tr. *Sleidane's Comm.* 49 b, Luther vnderstode that the Emperoure, and diuerse Princes woulde practise the decree of Wormes. **1662** Stillingfl. *Orig. Sacr.* Ded. 11 If the principles be true, why are they not practised? **1718** Watts *Ps.* cxix. i. ii, Blest are the men that keep thy word, And practise thy commands. **1771** Goldsm. *Hist. Eng.* I. 81 Those [laws] which remain..under his name seem to be only the laws already practised in the country by his Saxon ancestors.

5. To perform repeatedly or continuously by way of study, in order to acquire skill; to exercise oneself in (any art, process, or act) for the purpose of attaining proficiency. Also with *obj. inf.*

c **1430** [see practising *vbl. sb.* 1]. **1590** Shaks. *Com. Err.* ii. i. 29 Ere I learne loue, Ile practise to obey. **1596** —— *Tam. Shr.* iii. ii. 253 Shall sweet Bianca practise how to bride it? **1623–4** Laud *Diary* 24 Mar., Wks. 1853 III. 150 The Earl of Oxford, practising a tilt, fell and brake his arm. **1778** Sheridan *Camp* ii. iii, To hear a march and chorus, which some recruits are practising. **1854** Thackeray *Rose & Ring* vii, She was very busy practising the piano. **1863** Mrs. Oliphant *Salem Ch.* i. 3 The young people had their singing-class, at which they practised hymns.

b. *absol.* or *intr.* To exercise oneself with the view of acquiring skill or proficiency; *esp.* in the performance of music.

1596 Shaks. *Tam. Shr.* i. i. 83 My bookes and instruments shall be my companie, On them to looke, and practise by my selfe. **1714** Addison *Spect.* No. 556 ¶11 While a Man is learning to fence, he practises both on Friend and Foe. **1796** Jane Austen *Pride & Prej.* I. xxx She will never play really well, unless she practises more. *a* **1817** —— *Lady Susan* xvii. in *Mem.* (1871) 238 Frederica spends great part of the day there, practising as it is called [at the piano]. **1888** Mrs. H. Ward *R. Elsmere* i. ix, Catherine and Agnes are at school; and Rose, I think, is practising.

6. *trans.* To exercise (any one) *in* some action in order to make him proficient in it; to train, drill.

1598 Shaks. *Merry W.* iv. iv. 65 The children must Be practis'd well to this, or they'll neu'r doo't. *a* **1656** Hales *Gold. Rem.* i. (1673) 93, I will leave this to your private considerations, to practise your wits in the depths of Christianity. **1674** *Providence Rec.* (1894) V. 292 Said william Austin Doth Couenant..and Engage..To precticе and jnstruct the Said moses Lippit in art and trade of a weauer. **1855** Trench in *Lect. to Ladies* ix. 225 We might do much..by practising the young to distinguish between words which have a near resemblance to one another. **1888** *Fortn. Rev.* Jan. 24 The captain practises his company in all the phases of war.

b. *pa. pple.* Experienced by practice; skilled, versed, proficient (*in*); †accustomed, used (*to*).

1542 Udall *Erasm. Apoph.* 30 The same officer was well practised and could good skille in that science. **1579–80** North *Plutarch* (1676) 7 The Athenians at that time were not greatly practised to the sea. **1693** *Humours Town* 35 If they..have been well practis'd in writing *Billet deux.* *a* **1715** Burnet *Own Time* (1823) I. 439 Till men were well practised in him, he was apt to impose on them. *Ibid.* II. 43 A satirical temper..which was imputed to youth and wit not enough practised to the world. **1887** Ruskin *Præterita* II. i. 17 He was..perfectly practised in all the college routine of business.

†**7.** To put to practical use; to use, make use of, employ. *Obs.*

138. in *Wyclif's Wks.* (1880) 157 þe olde testament for wynnyng of types and offryngis is sumwhat practised. *c* **1440** *Pol. Rel. & L. Poems* (1903) 288 And þorw þe grace of hevene kyng, þei practiseden medicines to helpe manky[n]d. **1549** Coverdale *Erasm. Par.* II. Ep. Ded. *ij b, The sacred Byble..set forth by your Maiesties appoyntment, to be dewly practised in all holy exercyses within your churches. **1659** Leak *Waterwks.* 26 This Engin is much practised in Germany. **1731** Pope *Ep. Burlington* 36 Proud to catch cold at a Venetian door. *Note,* A door or window so called, from being much practised at Venice, by Palladio and others. **1740** *N. Jersey Archives* XII. 29 The two most convenient Places for a speedy Transportation, of any yet practised from New-York to Philadelphia.

†**b.** To frequent, haunt [after F. *pratiquer*].

1651 *Life Father Sarpi* (1676) 73 He had always desired to have him live at Rome, because he had known him, and practised him, and knew very well how great service he was able to have done the Church. **1681** Dryden *Abs. & Achit.* i. 825 The court he practised, not the courtier's art. **1697** —— *Virg. Past.* Pref. (1721) I. 76 Several, who saw, and practis'd the World for a longer space of time. **1718** *Freethinker* No. 60 They were not in a Capacity to make any Figure by Sea; an Element, little practised by them, and less understood.

†**8.** To bring about, compass, effect, accomplish.

1550 J. Coke *Eng. & Fr. Heralds* §68 E ij, You practysed a maryage betwene the doughter and heyre of Nauerne, and Monster de la bright, countie de foyx. **1577** *F. de L'isle's Leg.* L ij, Seuen moneths before, the said Guisians had practised an other league in Guyenne, through the meanes of the lorde of Candales. **1585** T. Washington tr. *Nicholay's Voy.* i. xix. 23 They thought to practise some way for theyr suretie. **1652** Gaule *Magastrom.* 173 Suppose he intendeth..to practise the sickness, death, destruction, of man or beast. **1736** Chandler *Hist. Persec.* 318, I think he can't well be excused from practising the death of Servetus at Vienne.

†**b.** To devise means to bring about (a result); to plan, scheme, intend (something to be done). With *simple obj.* or *obj. clause.* *Obs.*

1566 Painter *Pal. Pleas.* I. 132 He doth already practise a marriage betwene the King of Hungarie and me. **1579–80** North *Plutarch* (1676) 76 Solon..began to practise that his Citizens should give themselves unto Crafts and Occupations. **1667** Milton *P.L.* xi. 802 [They] Thenceforth shall practice how to live secure. **1711** in T. W. Marsh *Early Friends in Surrey & Sussex* i. (1886) 9 A Preparative Meeting..for preserving the Reputation of our proffession blameles is Practised at Reigate.

†**c.** To exert oneself in order to effect (something); to attempt, endeavour, try. (With *simple obj.* or *inf.*) *Obs.*

1573 Tusser *Husb.* (1878) 48 This Prouerbe experience long ago gaue, that nothing who practiseth nothing shall haue. **1581** J. Bell *Haddon's Answ. Osor.* 83 b, [He] practised first to kill him selfe with his owne Dagger. **1600** Holland *Livy* xxxiii. Argt. 834 Anniball having practised in Affrick to raise war. **1679** Burnet *Hist. Ref.* I. iii. 201 The Ministers continued practising, to get further evidence for the Tryal.

9. *intr.* To lay schemes or plans, esp. for an evil purpose; to use stratagem or artifice; to scheme, plot, conspire, intrigue (*with* or *against* a person, *to do* something). Now *rare.*

1537 Latimer *Rem.* (Parker Soc.) 379 That you may see how closely in time past the foreign prelates did practise about their prey. **1572** in *Buccleuch MSS.* (Hist. MSS. Comm.) 23 Melvill..was executed..for practesing with England. **1600** Shaks. *A.Y.L.* i. i. 156 Hee will practise against thee by poyson. **1630** *R. Johnson's Kingd. & Commw.* 220 It suffereth not the one to practise against the other, upon the perill that may ensue to the offender. **1675** tr. *Camden's Hist. Eliz.* i. (1688) 136 He fell to plotting and practising with the Rebels, and attempted..to deliver the Queen of Scots out of Custody. **1861** [practising *vbl. sb.* 2].

†**b.** *trans.* To plot, conspire (some evil to be done). *Obs.*

1560 Daus tr. *Sleidane's Comm.* 247 b, They haue practised thinges against him in Germani, and in forein nations. **1581** J. Bell *Haddon's Answ. Osor.* 216 b, He practized the vtter ouerthrowe not onely of all Christian societie, but of the state of the whole world also. **1595** Shaks. *John* iv. i. 20, I doubt My Vnckle practises more harme to me. **1607** *God's Warning* in *Harl. Misc.* (Malh.) III. 64 The late papisticall conspiracie of traytors, that, with powder, practised the subuersion of this beautifull kingdome. **1634** Sir T. Herbert *Trav.* 234 Normall.. practices her owne brothers destruction.

†**c.** To endeavour to gain (favour, etc.) by arts; to aim at in an underhand way. *Obs.*

1581 Savile *Tacitus' Hist.* i. xxiii. (1591) 14 He had by al possible meanes practised the fauour and goodwill of the souldier. **1640** Habington *Q. of Arragon* i. i. in Hazl. *Dodsley* XIII. 342 What can you answer for the practising The queen's affection, when Embassador, You lay here from Castile?

10. *intr.* To have dealings or intercourse, to negotiate or treat *with* a person; *esp.* to treat or deal *with* so as to influence or gain over to some course of action. Now *rare.*

1538 *St. Papers Hen. VIII* II. 559, I practysyd soo with the sayd Bryan, and with my servaunt Stephin Apparye, that they hunted the sayd Kayr. **1555** Eden *Decades* 313 He sent to his brother Bartholomewe Colon to practise with the Kynge of Englande. **1585** T. Washington tr. *Nicholay's Voy.* iv. vi. 117, I haue seene and practised with diuers Persian gentlemen. **1683** *Pennsylv. Archives* I. 79 Practising wth all your R. Highnesses Tenants there, by fair or foul means, to turne tenants to him. **1721** Swift *Let. to Pope* 10 Jan., The grand juries of the county and city were practised effectually with to represent the said pamphlet with all aggravating epithets. **1902** A. Lang *Hist. Scot.* II. iii. 60 He and his party had long been practising with Cecil.

†**b.** *trans.* To work upon (a person, etc.), so as to persuade to some (esp. evil) course of action; 'to draw by artifice' (J.); to influence by underhand dealings, win over, 'get at', corrupt.

1570 Buchanan *Ane Admonitioun* Wks. (1892) 27 Bot Sr James..hinderit yis purpose be sum of ye Kingis familiar seruandis yat he had practisit be giftis. **1602** Warner *Alb. Eng.* Epit. (1612) 396 He allured out of Sanctuarie his fiue Neeces..whence also, to murther them,..hee had formerly practised the two yong Princes his Nephewes. **1640** in *Hamilton Papers* (Camden) App. 257 The Earle of Traquayre..did practize the jury with a good intent to finde the said Lo: guilty as aforesaid. **1678** Sir G. Mackenzie *Crim. Laws Scot.* ii. xxvi. §18 (1699) 271 A mean of corrupting Witnesses, and Assizers, who, if known, might be practised. **17..** Swift (J.), To practise the city into an address to the queen.

11. *intr.* *practise on* or *upon*: To practise tricks or artifices upon; to act upon by artifice, so as to induce to do or believe something; to play a trick upon, impose upon, delude; to work upon (a person, or his feelings, etc.).

1596 Shaks. *Tam. Shr.* Induct. i. 36 Sirs, I will practise on this drunken man. **1599** —— *Much Ado* ii. i. 398, I..will so practise on Benedicke, that..hee shall fall in loue with Beatrice. **1613** Webster *Devil's Law-Case* iv. ii, Y' are practised upon most devilishly. *a* **1715** Burnet *Own Time* (1766) II. 148 The Court practised on her..so far that she delivered up her husband's letters. **1858** Sears *Athan.* iii. ii. 268 Out of this belief papacy shaped its purgatory and practised on human credulity and fear. **1864** Tennyson *Aylmer's Field* 302 You have practised on her, Perplext her, made her..Swerve from her duty to herself and us.

b. To tamper with, to corrupt. *rare.*

1872 J. H. Newman *Tracts* (1874) 167 *note,* Photius considers his [St. Methodius'] works have been practised upon by heretics.

c. See also 1 c, 5 b.

†**12.** *trans.* To make trial of, try practically. *Obs.*

1632 Lithgow *Trav.* vi. 278, I haue seene the nature of this dust practised. **1796** J. Smyth in J. Robertson *Agric. Perth* (1799) 519 The crops I practised were 1st, oats; 2d, turnips, yams, and other potatoes; 3d, barley with grass-seeds. **1802** H. Greathead in *Naval Chron.* IX. 293, I would..recommend practising the boat.

†**13.** To construct. *Obs. rare.*

1739 H. Walpole *Let. to R. West* 11 Nov., At the end of a great road, which was practised through an immense solid rock by bursting it asunder with gun-powder. **1820** Shelley *Philos. View Reform* in Dowden *Transcr. & Stud.* (1888) 69 Most fatal of them all is that mine of unexploded mischief it has practised beneath the foundations of society.

practised ('præktɪst), *ppl. a.* [f. practise *v.* + -ed[1].]

1. That has had practice; experienced, expert, skilled, proficient. (See also practise *v.* 6 b.)

1568 Grafton *Chron.* II. 507 A companie of warlike and practised souldiours. **1638** Mayne *Lucian* (1664) 332 Your Art, of which you seem to be so practised a master. **1855** Macaulay *Hist. Eng.* xxii. IV. 714 To the practised eyes of the Kentish fishermen she looked much like a French privateer. **1871** Tyndall *Fragm. Sc.* (1879) I. vi. 209 My practised men fastened the sail at the top.

2. Executed or gone through beforehand in order to acquire proficiency in performance.

1590 Shaks. *Mids. N.* v. i. 97, I haue seene them shiuer and looke pale,..Throttle their practiz'd accent in their feares. **1611** —— *Wint. T.* i. ii. 116 Making practis'd Smiles As in a Looking-Glasse.

†**3.** Habitually used or frequented; accustomed.

1654–66 Earl Orrery *Parthen.* (1676) 658 He led us into a less practis'd walk. **1667** Milton *P.L.* iv. 945 To serve thir

Lord..with songs to hymne his Throne, And practis'd distances to cringe, not fight.

†**4.** (app.) Plotted against, made the object of conspiracy. *Obs. rare*$^{-1}$.

1602 WARNER *Alb. Eng.* x. lv. (1612) 245 Throckmorton yeat, more priuie and more practising than those,..Did mischiefes that imported more our practiz'd State disclose.

Hence **'practisedness**, the quality or fact of being practised or experienced.

1883 J. PURVES in *Contemp. Rev.* Sept. 352 Honesty he ascribes to practisedness in the world's ways.

†**'practisement.** *Obs. rare*$^{-1}$. [f. PRACTISE *v.* + -MENT.] The fact of practising, or that which is practised; a deed or practice.

1581 BURLEIGH *Let. to Walsingham* in Digges *Compl. Ambass.* (1655) 379 She speaketh of a practisement by him in the Thames mouth..that you should call it to memory.

practiser ('præktɪsə(r)). Forms: see PRACTISE; 4–5 -our (5 -ere, -ir, 6 -ure, *Sc.* -ar), 6– -er. [ME. *practisour* prob. a. AF. **practisour*, agent-noun f. OF. *pra(c)tiser*: see PRACTISE *v.* and -OUR b; the suffix being between 1450 and 1550 weakened to -ER² 3.] One who practises.

1. One who exercises a profession or occupation; a practitioner: **a.** of medicine or surgery (often opposed to one trained in the science or art).

1377 LANGL. *P. Pl.* B. XVI. 107 And did him assaye his surgerye on hem þat syke were, Till he was parfit practisoure. *c* **1386** CHAUCER *Prol.* 422 With vs ther was a Doctour of Phisik..He was a verray parfit praktisour [*Lansd. MS.* practisere]. *c* **1440** *Gesta Rom.* xx. 67 (Harl. MS.), Oon [leche]..sotill in crafte, and a good practiser. **1530** PALSGR. 257/2 Practysure, *practicien*. **1579** LYLY *Euphues* (Arb.) 133 They are like those sicke men which reiect the expert and cunning Physition,..and admitte the heedelesse practiser. **1666** W. BOGHURST *Loimographia* (1894) 30 Many ignorant practizers took upon them the name of Doctors. **1767** T. HUTCHINSON *Hist. Mass.* (1768) II. 274 Another practiser,..who had been a surgeon in the French army.

b. of law.

a **1400–50** *Alexander* 1582 Practisirs & prematis [*v.r.* practyf men in prevatez] & prestis of þe lawe. **1552** HULOET, Practiser of lawe. **1573–80** BARET *Alv.* P 641 A Chauncerie man, or practiser in the lawe, to drawe out writtes. **1647** R. STAPYLTON *Juvenal* 182 Such barbarous cruelty who ever saw Done on a duller practicer at law? **1654** GATAKER *Disc. Apol.* 33 The worthie Societie of the Professors, Practisers, and Students of the Common Law of this Land in Lincolns Inn. **1712** *Lond. Gaz.* No. 4954/1 Practicers of the Law in North Britain. **1876** BANCROFT *Hist. U.S.* I. x. 332 He had been formerly a student and practiser in the courts of common law in England.

c. *gen.* One who practises any art, science, manner of life, course of action, etc.; one who carries out a theory, principle, etc., in action.

1540–1 ELYOT *Image Gov.* (1556) 135 Philosophers were neuer good practisers in weale publike. **1586** *Praise of Mus.* 20 Her professors and practisers were not rewarded. **1607** NORDEN *Surv. Dial.* III. 136 Practizers and teachers of these Geometricall conclusions. **1762–71** H. WALPOLE *Vertue's Anecd. Paint.* (1786) I. 218 Too illustrious a lover and even practicer of the art to be omitted. **1826** C. BUTLER *Grotius* vii. 113 Councillors and practisers of schemes hostile to its welfare. **1842** MISS MITFORD in L'Estrange *Life* (1870) III. ix. 156 A believer in, if not a practiser of, animal magnetism. **1854** CDL. WISEMAN *Fabiola* II. xxxi. 340 She was..a serious, real practiser of all that she taught.

†**2.** A schemer, plotter, conspirator; a man of wicked or fraudulent devices. *Obs.*

1545 *St. Papers Hen. VIII*, X. 466 He is a gret practiser, with which honest terme we cover untrew tales tellyng, lying, dissimulyng, and flateryng. *c* **1610** SIR J. MELVIL *Mem.* (1683) 158 A perfect practiser against the quiet of this state. **1643** *5 Yrs. K. James* in *Select. Harl. Misc.* (1793) 313 That my lord of Somerset was principal practiser..in a most perfidious manner, to set a train and trap for Overbury to get into the Tower.

†**'practisie.** *Obs. rare*$^{-1}$. [irreg. f. *practise, practice*, after words etymologically in *-sy, -cy*.] Practice, action.

1573 TUSSER *Husb.* (1878) 17 To get by honest practisie, and keepe thy gettings couertlie.

practising ('præktɪsɪŋ), *vbl. sb.* [f. PRACTISE + -ING¹.] The action of the verb PRACTISE.

1. Action, performance (esp. habitual); carrying out, execution; exercise of a profession; repeated performance for the sake of becoming proficient, esp. in music.

c **1430** *Freemasonry* 229 That no mason schulde worche be nyȝth, But ȝef hyt be yn practesynge of wytte. **1581** PETTIE *Guazzo's Civ. Conv.* I. (1586) 21 That litle leasure which shalbe left you from practising on your patients. **1706** E. WARD *Wooden World Diss.* (1708) 104 By much practising in hot Countries [he] gets a Skin not much unlike a Red Herring. **1843** MRS. CARLYLE *Lett.* (1883) I. 264 The young lady..took a fit of practising on her..pianoforte. *Mod.* She must not neglect her practising.

Comb. **1903** *Westm. Gaz.* 8 Sept. 10/1 The fields..were the chief practising-grounds for the City archers.

2. Scheming, plotting; device, conspiracy, intrigue. Now *rare*.

1550 BALE *Image Both Ch.* II. 60 b, Abhominable in the practisynges of their wicked hartes. **1558** in Strype *Ann. Ref.* (1709) I. App. iv. 5 Rome..from whom nothing is to be feared, but evil will, cursing and practising. **1861** G. G. PERRY *Hist. Ch. Eng.* I. iv. 162 The continued plottings and practisings of the Jesuits were ever a source of political danger.

'practising, *ppl. a.* [f. as prec. + -ING².] That practises: in senses of the verb.

1. Exercising a profession, esp. medicine or law; engaged in practice.

1625 HART *Anat. Ur.* I. ii. 16 Most of our practising Parsons and Vicars become suddenly Physitians. **1722** DE FOE *Plague* (Rtldg.) 46 Running after..every practising old Woman, for Medicines. **1772** *Junius Lett.* lxviii. (1820) 334 The quirk and evasion of a practising lawyer. **1900** *Expositor* Sept. 236 The practising physicians seem regularly to have been Jews. **1902** *Act 2 Edw. VII*, c. 17 §10 Every woman..shall before holding herself out as a practising midwife..give notice in writing.

b. Making a practice of religious duties or observances (esp. in *R.C. Ch.*). [After F. *pratiquant*: see PRACTISE *v.* 2 b.]

1906 *Daily News* 18 Sept. 6 A 'practising' Catholic bitterly disappointed with the attitude of the Pope.

2. Plotting, scheming, intriguing. Now *rare*.

1602 [see PRACTISED 4]. **1617** MORYSON *Itin.* II. 206 A notorious Rebell..(an inward man, and a great practising instrument with Tyrone).

practitional (præk'tɪʃənəl), *a. rare.* [f. as next + -AL¹.] †**a.** Given to 'practice' or plotting; scheming, crafty. *Obs.* **b.** Relating to practice, practical.

1600 W. WATSON *Decacordon* (1602) 201 Chiefe ambitious practitionall state Iesuits. **1807** SOUTHEY *Lett.* (1856) II. 1 It is the best practitional book and the truest philosophy in existence.

practitioner (præk'tɪʃənə(r)). Also 6 practisioner, -itionere, -izioner, -ycioner, 6–7 -icioner. [Erroneously extended from †*practitian*, PRACTICIAN, as if from a n. of action in *-ition*. But cf. the obs. and dial. *logicianer*, (*-tioner*), *musicianer*, *physicianer* (*-cioner*); also *astrologer*, *astronomer*, *philosopher*, etc.: see -ER¹.]

1. One engaged in the practice of any art, profession, or occupation; a practical or professional worker in anything. **a.** *gen.*

1553 LATIMER *Serm., Lord's Pr.* vii. (1562) 56 b, Consider how long he hathe bene a practicioner: you muste consider what Satan is, what experience he hath, so yᵗ we are not able to match with him. **1566** *Pasquine in Traunce* 106 The Schole doctours, that take no payne with their doctrine,..ought to be called rather Speculatours, than Practicioners. **1571** DIGGES *Pantom.* I. xvii. E iv, The ingenious Practisioner. *Ibid.* xxxv. L iij b, The diligent practizioner. **1704** (*title*) English Dictionary..By Edward Cocker, the late famous practitioner in fair Writing and Arithmetic. **1798** W. TAYLOR in *Monthly Rev.* XXV. 568 In Cimabu, Florence boasts the first native practitioner. **1827** SOUTHEY in *Q. Rev.* XXXVI. 340 The most experienced practitioners in conscience were puzzled. **1860** EMERSON *Cond. Life, Power* Wks. (Bohn) II. 341 Hence..the worthlessness of amateurs to cope with practitioners.

b. in medicine or surgery.

general practitioner, one who practises both medicine and surgery; a doctor who treats cases of all kinds (opp. to a *consultant* or *specialist*).

1544 PHAER *Regim. Lyfe* (1553) C vij, An other singuler medecine..a thing experte of al the good practicioners. **1597** A. M. tr. *Guillemeau's Fr. Chirurg.* b iv b/2 M. Rabet, Chyrurgian at Paris,..the most experteste practitionere of his time. **1665** J. TILLISON in Ellis *Orig. Lett.* Ser. II. IV. 36 As is acknowledged by our practitioners in physic. **1791** *Gentl. Mag.* 22/2 The use of the syringe is generally recommended by medical practitioners in deafnesses. **1848** DICKENS *Dombey* i, The family practitioner opening the door for that distinguished professional. **1860** O. W. HOLMES *Prof. Breakf.-t.* i, The 'general practitioners'..had to recognize that people could get well, unpoisoned. **1898** *Allbutt's Syst. Med.* V. 503 Younger practitioners who have been alarmed at what they regarded as a sign of aneurism.

c. in law.

1598 BARCKLEY *Felic. Man* (1631) 398 Sollicitors..with all that rabblement of practitioners who devoure the substance of poore men. **1631** HEYLIN *St. George* 80 A practitioner in the Parliamentarie Court in that City. **1725** *Lond. Gaz.* No. 6384/8 John Saunders,..Practitioner of the Law. **1874** MOTLEY *Barneveld* I. x. 379 A regular practitioner at the Supreme Court of the Hague.

†**2.** One engaged in practising an art or occupation for the sake of acquiring or retaining skill in it; a learner, novice, beginner; a probationer. *Obs.*

1577 HANMER *Anc. Eccl. Hist.* (1663) 221 Certain others were late practitioners and novices in the Ministry. *a* **1625** FLETCHER *Nice Valour* IV. i, I'll fit you with my scholars, new practitioners. **1669** STURMY *Mariner's Mag.* I. ii. 6 The Practitioner in Navigation, is next to learn to know..the certain time of the Flowing and Ebbing of the Sea. **1766** ENTICK *London* IV. 341, 11 sub-engineers, and 16 practitioners. **1776** *Court & City Reg.* 166/1 Practitioner Engineers and Ensigns at 3*s.* 8*d.* a day. **1789** *Trifler* No. 33. 420 The discordant sounds of uninstructed practitioners on the harpsichord. **1801** STRUTT *Sports & Past.* III. i. 105 The practitioner was then to assail the pel, armed with sword and shield..as he would an adversary.

3. One who practises anything; one who carries on a practice or action; a habitual doer.

1548 GESTE *Pr. Masse* in H. G. Dugdale *Life* (1840) App. I. 125 Ye private masse suppers is..blasphemouse to God and annoyous to the practycioners therof. **1617** J. MOORE *Mappe Mans Mort.* III. viii. 240 Christians must be daily practicioners of Faith and Repentance. **1779** FORREST *Voy. N. Guinea* 176 A self evident virtue, of which the practitioners only know the luxury. **1888** *Pall Mall G.* 10 Nov. 4/2 The most conspicuous professor, or at any rate the most conspicuous practitioner, of the doctrine that statesmanship is superior to the trammels of moral obligation.

†**4.** One who acts on behalf of another; an agent. *Obs.*

1560 DAUS tr. *Sleidane's Comm.* 227 b, Naming also certen practicioners and messagers, by whose meanes chiefly the thing was wrought. **1561** in Strype *Ann. Ref.* (1709) I. xxiv. 243 Swadell, late Dr. Boner's servant: and yet thought to be a practitioner for him.

†**5.** One who uses artifice or trickery; a schemer, plotter, conspirator. *Obs.*

1560 DAUS tr. *Sleidane's Comm.* 44 He [Luther] is wel knowen to be such a practisioner, that there is no doubt, but suche thinges as are well written he..wil corrupt and depraue. **1601** W. WATSON *Import. Consid.* (1675) 77 Parsons and Heywood are found to be Practitioners.

Hence **prac'titionery** (*rare*), the practice of a (mere) practitioner; empiricism.

1818 *Edin. Rev.* XXIX. 267 A character compounded of confident pretence on the one hand, and the merest practitionery on the other. **1842** F. BLACK *Homœop.* i. 5 For such practitionery we know no better advice than that of the judicious Huxham..to peruse the Sixth Commandment.

†**'practive,** *a.* (*sb.*) *Obs.* [f. stem *pract-* in PRACTIC + -IVE. (After *active*, etc.)]

1. Of persons: **a.** Devoted to practice or action; active; practical.

c **1470** HARDING *Chron.* CXCIII. v, But right practyfe thei were in couetyse. **1610** BOYS *Exp. Dom. Epist. & Gosp.* Wks. (1622) 299 John doth resemble the contemplative, Peter the practive.

b. Apt to practice; adept, skilful, dexterous.

a **1400–50** *Alexander* 1582 Practyf men in prevatez, & prestez of þe lawe. **1536** *St. Papers Hen. VIII*, II. 378 Gentilmen..verey experte and practyve in the countrey there. **1593–4** SYLVESTER *Profit Imprisonment* 94 You take your Pris'ner for a practive man of Art.

2. Belonging or relating to practice or action; practical.

1526 *Pilgr. Perf.* (1531) 31 b, As well in maters speculatyue as practyue. **1613** HEYWOOD *Brazen Age* II. ii. Wks. 1874 III. 185, I am Queene of loue, There is no practiue art of dalliance Of which I am not Mistresse. **1658** SLINGSBY *Diary* (1836) 203 Not only..how to belive but for the practive part too, what to do.

B. *sb.* Practice; actual doing or working.

1396–7 in *Eng. Hist. Rev.* (1907) XXII. 298 [These] be þe uerray practyf of nigromancie rathere þanne of þe holi theologie. *c* **1460** *Play Sacram.* 591 Cunnyng yea yea & wᵗ prattife [*printed* prattise] I haue sauid many a manys lyfe. **1523** FITZHERB. *Husb.* §4 It is harde to make a man to vnderstande it by wrytynge, without he were at the operation therof, to teache the practyue. *Ibid.* §141 It is better the practyue or knowlege of an husbande man well proued.

Hence †**'practively** *adv. Obs.*, practically, in practice, actively.

1592 WARNER *Alb. Eng.* VIII. xxxix. (1612) 191 The Preachers and the people both then practiuely did thriue. **1602** *Ibid.* IX. lii, Almes deedes, and workes of Charitie we practiuely professe.

practolol ('præktəlɒl). *Pharm.* [Etym. unknown.] A white powder, $C_{14}H_{22}N_2O_3$, that is similar to propranolol in its effect on the heart but has less effect on respiratory functions.

1969 *Lancet* 14 June 1221/1 The British Pharmacopœia has issued the following supplementary list of approved names... Practolol, 4-(2-Hydroxy-3-isopropylamino-propoxy)-acetanilide. *Ibid.* 2 Aug. 227/1 Practolol..was given to forty-seven patients who had cardiac dysrhythmias after myocardial infarction. **1976** *Nature* 12 Aug. 595/2 Practolol (40 mg kg^{-1}) a β_2 receptor blocking agent that does not enter the brain in significant quantity did not inhibit hyperactivity. **1976** *Lancet* 6 Nov. 984/1 Practolol therapy may be associated with various adverse reactions. *Ibid.*, Practolol ('Eraldin') tablets were withdrawn from general use on Oct. 1, 1975.

prad (præd). *slang* (now chiefly *Austral.*). [By metathesis from Du. *paard* a horse:—late L. *paraverēdus* (see PALFREY).] A horse.

1798 TUFTS *Gloss. Thieves' Jargon*, *Prad-holder*, a bridle. **1799** in *Spirit Pub. Jrnls.* III. 352 Met Bob Blunderbuss and Ben Bounce, going out on their prads. **1838** DICKENS *O. Twist* xxxi, He's in the gig, a-minding the prad. **1882** *Sydney Slang Dict.* 10/2 He blew on Sam who frisked a lobb and the same day came it on Joe for fencing the prad got on the cross. **1895** MARRIOTT WATSON in *New Rev.* July 9 Creech..swerved..and ran his mare full face upon the struggling prads. **1916** C. J. DENNIS *Moods of Ginger Mick* 27 'E sits there while I 'arness up me prad. **1930** *Bulletin* (Sydney) 17 Sept. 21/2 Our packhorses snorted suspiciously... The prads watched, all prick ears and snorts as the axe bit into the tree. **1933** *Ibid.* 27 Dec. 20 When it [*sc.* the rope] broke, the astonished prad plunged suddenly into the dam. Two doses of that remedy and he was a reformed animal. **1977** *Courier-Mail* (Brisbane) 31 Mar. 4/5 It would surely be more appropriate for the riding [for democracy] to be done on some business man rather than on a prad.

‖**pradakshina** (prə'dʌkʃɪnə). Also **pradakshna**. [Skr. *pradakṣiṇā*, f. *pra* in front + *dakṣiṇā* right.] In Hinduism and Buddhism, circumambulation of an object in a clockwise direction as a form of worship. Also *attrib.*

1810 E. MOOR *Hindu Pantheon* 327 The respectful ceremony of *Pradakshna*, which consists in circumambulating several times the..object..to be reverenced, keeping, with closed palms, the right hand and the face towards it. **1883** M. MONIER-WILLIAMS *Relig. Thought & Life in India* I. xii. 348 A pilgrim..sets out from the source of the Ganges,..and walks by the left bank of the river to its mouth..; then, turning round, he proceeds by the right side back to Gaṅgotrī, whence he departed. This is called Pradakshinā. **1933** A. Stein *On Anc. Central-Asian Tracks* iv. 61 The ceremonial circumambulation or *pradakshina* prescribed by Indian custom. **1956** R. Pieris *Sinhalese Social Organization* ii. 84 He then..reverentially performs *pradakshinā* three times to the diagram. **1976** *Jrnl. R. Soc. Arts* CXXIV. 677/2 The apsidal temple in question could have been a temple for the Nāga cult, with the four-sided Nāga image..standing in the apse, placed there to be worshipped in the pradakṣiṇa way.

‖**Prado** ('prado). [Sp.:—L. *prātum* meadow.] The proper name of the public park of Madrid, a fashionable promenade; hence sometimes in transferred applications.

c **1645** Howell *Lett.* (1650) I. iii. xv. 60 [He] went to the *Prado*, a place hard by, of purpose to take the air. [**1657** J. Davies tr. *Voiture's Lett.* I. xxx. 58, I have not passed a fair evening in the *Prade* [Fr. fr. Sp.], but I have wished him there.] **1709** Mrs. Manley *Secret Mem.* I. 163 If a Lady be new-married, and longs to shew her Equipage, no Place so proper as the *Prado*. **1807** Southey *Espriella's Lett.* (1808) I. 80 St. James's Park, the Prado of London. **1813** *Sporting Mag.* XLII. 218 Taking their Sunday promenade upon the fashionable prado of White Conduit House.

præ-, in med.L. also pre-, a L. prep. and adv., meaning 'before'; a very frequent prefix and combining element. In Eng. the L. spelling was formerly not uncommon, but is now usual only in words that are still regarded as Latin, as *præcipe*, *præcognitum*, *præcordia*, *præmunire*, or that are terms of classical antiquity, as *prætor*. In other words PRE- is now the usual form.

There are some 17th century words that became obsolete before the *pre-* form became predominant, which are found only with the spelling *præ-*. This spelling has also been deliberately used by some writers in words commonly spelt with PRE- and so entered in this dictionary.

præacuate to **-chordal**: see PREACUATE, etc.

‖**præcipe** ('priːsɪpiː). *Law.* Also 5 pricipe, presepe, 6–8 precipe. [L. *præcipe*, imper. of *præcipĕre* to admonish, enjoin (see PRECEPT). Used as a sb. from the opening word or words of the writ, *præcipe quod reddat*, enjoin (him) that he render.]

1. (More fully ***præcipe quod reddat***.) A writ requiring something to be done, or demanding a reason for its non-performance. ***præcipe in capite***: see quots. 1535, 1607.

[**1215** *Magna Carta* c. 34 Breue quod vocatur precipe de cetero non fiat alicui de aliquo tenemento unde liber homo possit amittere curiam suam.] *a* **1500** transl. in Arnolde *Chron.* (1811) 219 A wrytte whiche is called pricipe from hensforth shall not be made too any man of ani freeholde wherthrugh a free man lese his courte. **14..** *MS. Lincoln A.* i. 17 lf. 48 (Halliw.) Standis on bakke, For here es comene a presepe, swyche menne to take. **1535** tr. *Natura Breuium* (1544) 15 This wrytte of ryghte, Precipe in capite, lyeth for the tenaunt whiche holdeth of the kynge in chefe, as of his crowne, whiche tenaunte is deforced. **1598** Kitchin *Courts Leet* (1675) 139 Plaint of a Croft is good, but Precipe of a Croft is not good. **1607** Cowell *Interpr.*, *Præcipe quod reddat*, is a writt of great diuersitie..it is called sometime a writ of *Right close*, as a *præcipe in capite*, when it issueth out of the court of common plees for a tenent holding of the King in cheife, as of his Crowne, and not of the King, as of any honour, castell or maner. **1623** T. Powell *Attorn. Acad.* 125 First draw the *Precipe* in sheetes of Paper, and Engrosse the Concord in Parchment. **1642** tr. *Perkins' Prof. Bk.* v. §381 (1657) 142 If in a *præcipe* brought against the Husband, he plead misnosmer. **1658** tr. *Coke's Rep.* iii. 6 a, Those, against whom the precipe is brought, are lawful tenants to the precipe. **1768** Blackstone *Comm.* III. xviii. 274 The *præcipe* is in the alternative, commanding the defendant to do the thing required, or shew the reason where-fore he hath not done it. **1895** Pollock & Maitland *Eng. Law* II. ii. iv. §2. 63 The simple writ of *Praecipe quod reddat*, which is the commencement of a proprietory action that is to take place from the first in the king's court.

2. A note containing particulars of a writ which must be filed with the officer of the Court from which the writ issues, by the party asking for the writ, or by his solicitor.

1848 in Wharton *Law Dict.*

attrib. **1837** Dickens *Pickw.* xx, Mr. Fogg, where is the *præcipe* book?

præcocial (priːˈkəʊʃ(ɪ)əl), *a. Ornith.* Also precocial. [f. L. *præcocēs* (C. J. Sundevall 1836, in *Kungl. Svenska Vetenskapsakademien Handlingar 1835* 70) (pl. of *præcox* early mature: see PRECOCIOUS), applied in Ornithology to a division of birds: see below.] Of or pertaining to the *Præcoces*, applied to those birds whose young are able to leave the nest and to feed themselves as soon as they are hatched; also extended to refer to the young of other animals which are independent soon after birth. Opp. to *Altricial*.

The classification of Birds into *Præcocēs* and *Altrīcēs*, as two primary divisions, introduced by Sundevall, was afterwards abandoned by him; but the adjectives founded upon these terms have been retained as useful in the classification of genera and families. See Newton *Dict. Birds*, s. vv.

1872 Coues *Key N. Amer. Birds* Index, *Præcoces*, birds that run about at birth. *Præcocial*, able to run about at birth. **1883** *Century Mag.* XXVI. 922 The young [of Wilson's Snipe] leave the nest as soon as they are hatched and follow the mother, or, as the naturalists would say, they are præcocial. **1885** *Athenæum* 1 Aug. 146/2 There is..no objection to the next in sequence being the præcocial Anseres. **1902** *Westm. Gaz.* 29 Apr. 2/1 Præcocial birds appear to have much less receptivity than altricial birds. **1932** J. S. Huxley *Probl. Relative Growth* iii. 90 The same reasoning applies to Ocypoda, whose young are similarly precocial. **1937** Allee & Schmidt tr. *Hesse's Ecol. Animal Geogr.* xxiii. 484 The young [of water-birds] are praecocial and very soon learn to forage for themselves. **1949** A. Leopold *Sand County Almanac* i. 35 The hen plover is brooding the four large pointed eggs which will shortly hatch four precocial chicks. **1974** *Nature* 30 Aug. 732/2 The subject species, *Acomys cahirinus* (spiny mouse), is a murid rodent whose precocial infants possess functional motor and sensory capabilities within hours of birth. **1978** *Sci. Amer.* July 107/1 Reid has found that the contents of the kiwi egg are 61 percent yolk, a proportion half again as large as that found in the eggs of typical precocial birds.

‖**præcognitum** (priːˈkɒgnɪtəm). Pl. -a. Also 8–9 pre-. [L., f. *præ* before + *cognitum*, neut. pa. pple. of *cognōscĕre* to know: see COGNOSCE, PRECOGNITION.] Something known beforehand; *esp.* something necessary or assumed to be known as a basis of reasoning, investigation, or study; a principle. Chiefly in *pl.*

1634 J. B[ate] *Myst. Nat.* 53 To set down some few *Præcognita* or Principles (as I may so call them). *a* **1667** Jer. Taylor *Serm. John* vii. 17 Wks. 1831 IV. 24 In this inquiry, I must take one thing for a *præcognitum*, that every good man..is 'taught of God'. **1743** Emerson *Fluxions* Pref. 16 It would be but lost Labour for any Person unacquainted with these *Precognita*, to spend any Time in reading this Book. **1846** T. Callaway *Dislocations & Fract. Clavicle & Shoulder-joint* (1849) 5 To start with certain præcognita.

præconize to **præcoracoid**: see PRECO-.

‖**præcordia** (priːˈkɔːdɪə). *Anat.* [L. pl. the midriff, diaphragm, the entrails, f. *præ* before + *cor, cord-* the heart.] The forepart of the thoracic region; the parts or region of the body about the heart.

[**1601** Holland *Pliny* xxx. v. II. 380 Now that I am come to speake of the precordiall region of the bodie, know this, That by this one word *præcordia*, I meane the inwards or entraile in man or woman.] **1681** tr. *Willis' Rem. Med. Wks.* Vocab., *Præcordia*, the parts about the heart, as the diaphragma, or midriff. **1694** Salmon *Bate's Dispens.* (1713) 234/2 Fainting Fits, Swooning, Sickness at Heart, and other Diseases of the Præcordia. **1803** *Med. Jrnl.* X. 106 An uncommon degree of oppression at the præcordia. **1863** Aitken *Pract. Med.* (1866) II. 64 A sense of fluttering in the *præcordia*, with irregular action of the heart.

Hence ‖**præcordi'algia** [Gr. ἄλγος pain], pain referred to the præcordia.

1895 in *Syd. Soc. Lex.*

præcordiac, præcordial: see PRECORD-.

‖**præ'cornu**. *Anat.* [mod.L. f. PRÆ- + *cornu* horn.] Wilder's name for the anterior horn of the lateral ventricle of the cerebellum.

1882 Wilder & Gage *Anat. Techn.* 456 Cephalad of the fornix is a marked elevation, the striatum; that part of the procœlia into which it projects is the præcornu.

præcuneus to **prædal**: see PRECUNEUS, etc.

prædella, erron. var. PREDELLA.

Praedesque (preɪˈdɛsk), *a.* [f. the name of W. M. *Praed* + -ESQUE.] In the manner or style of Winthrop Mackworth Praed (1802–39), poet, essayist, and writer of society verse. So **'Praedian** *a.*; **'Praedism**, the style of Praed's verse.

1865 *Dublin Univ. Mag.* II. 23 The best epigrams and Praedesque verses of the week. **1883** *Century Mag.* Feb. 595/1 Mr. Locker can write Praedesque poems. **1905** Mrs. H. Ward *Marriage of W. Ashe* i. ii. 29 Meanwhile the outer room gathered to hear the recitation of some *vers de société*, fondly believed by their author to be of a very pretty and Praedian make. **1927** *Observer* 15 May 6 What he was thinking of was polite badinage, Praedism, and Horatian levity.

prædormital (priːˈdɔːmɪtəl), *a. rare*$^{-1}$. [? f. PRÆ- + stem of L. *dormītiō* sleep + -AL.] = HYPNAGOGIC *a.*

1947 V. Nabokov *Bend Sinister* 11 Suddenly, with the vividness of a prædormital image or of a bright-robed lady on stained glass, she drifted across his retina, in profile, carrying something.

præfatio: see PREFACE *sb.* 1.

præfect, etc.: see PREFECT, etc.

præfervid (priːˈfɜːvɪd), *a.* [ad. L. *præfervid-us*: see PRE- A. 5 and FERVID.] Very fervid: an intentional alteration, after the L. original, of the usual PERFERVID, q.v.

[**1714** Col. Blackader *Diary* Feb. in *Life* xviii. (1834) 444 Our national temper, the praefervidum ingenium imposes upon us for zeal.] **1885** *Pall Mall G.* 13 Nov. 3/2 The praefervid Scot can tread his native heath without having to blush at the thought that [etc.]. **1890** *British Weekly* 13 June 102 The Scot..flung into the liberal principles of the great university on the Seine his own tenacious and (as Buchanan spells it) praefervid nature.

præ-fine: see PRE-FINE.

†**præ'fiscinal**. *Obs. rare*$^{-1}$. [f. L. *præfiscinē*, also *præfascinī* in security against magic (f. *præ* before, in front of + *fascin-um* bewitching, witchcraft, fascination) + -AL[1].] A charm worn as a protection against magic or witchcraft; an amulet.

1652 Gaule *Magastrom.* 192 Whether periapts [*mispr.* pericepts], amulets, præfiscinals, phylacteries,..and spels had even been used,..but for magick and astrologie?

prægnotary, var. PRENOTARY *Obs.*

præhallux: see PREHALLUX.

†**præ'labour**. *rare*$^{-1}$. [f. PRÆ-, PRE- A. 6 + LABOUR.] Intense, difficult, or immense labour.

1638 Mayne *Lucian* (1664) 201 For these prælabours, and Toyles, do not destroy the courage, but encrease, and enlarge it by provocation.

‖**præ'labrum, pre-**. *Entom.* [mod.L., f. PRÆ-, PRE- + L. *labrum* lip.] = CLYPEUS.

1895 in *Syd. Soc. Lex.*

prælect to **præm-**: see PRELECT, etc.

†**præ'metial**, *a. Obs.* [f. L. *præmētium* offering of first-fruits (to Ceres), f. *præ* before + *mētīrī* to measure.] Measured out from the first-fruits.

1621 Bp. Hall *Var. Treat.* Ded. to K. James, [To] offer to your Maiestie some præmetiall handfulls of that crop whereof you may challenge the whole haruest.

‖**præmunientes** (priːmjuːnɪˈɛntiːz). *Law.* [L. *præmūnientēs* (med.L. for *præmonentēs*, pr. pple. pl.) 'admonishing or warning' (see PRÆMUNIRE), occurring in a clause of the writ of Edw. I, 1295, summoning the spiritual estate to Parliament; hence applied attrib. to this clause and to the writ.]

præmunientes clause: the clause of the writ of 1295, in which the bishops and abbots summoned to parliament are ordered to summon representatives of the minor clergy to attend with them. So ***præmunientes writ***.

The words of the clause are 'praemunientes decanum (vel priorem) et capitulum ecclesiae vestrae, archidiaconos, totumque clerum vestrae diocesis, facientes quod..dictum capitulum per unum, idemque clerus per duos procuratores idoneos,..una vobiscum intersint' [etc.]: see Stubbs *Const. Hist.* xv. II. 195 *note*.

1700 Atterbury *Rights Convoc.* (1701) 226 The *Præmunientes* in the Bishops Writ is not an Idle Useless Clause..but a Real, and..Effectual Summons of the Clergy to Parliament. **1710** J. Harris *Lex. Techn.* II, *Præmunientes*, are writs sent to every Particular Bishop to come to Parliament, *Præmunientes*, or warning him to bring with him the Deans and Arch-Deacons within his Diocess, one Proctor for each Chapter, and two for the Clergy of his Diocess. **1888** *Q. Rev.* July 140 The part of the writ described as the Præmunientes Writ was not disused, and the Clergy are still summoned to attend Convocation, by what may be termed the Parliamentary form. **1899** *Dict. Nat. Biog.* LVII. 181/2 The movement led by Atterbury..for the revival of Convocation and the execution of the Præmunientes clause.

‖**præmunire** (priːmjuːˈnaɪəriː), *sb. Law.* Forms: 5–8 premunire, 6 -munyre, -menyre, -minire, 7 -muniri, -ie, (præ-, premonire, priminary), 6– præmunire. [L. *præmunīre* vb., pres. inf. (in cl. L., to fortify or protect in front), in med.L. confused with and used for *præmonēre* to forewarn, admonish, warn, f. *præ*, PRE- A. 1 + *monēre* to warn: cf. PREMUNITION. Occurring in the text of the writ, and thence taken as a name of the writ itself, and in various extended and transferred uses.]

1. (More fully ***præmunire facias***.) A writ by which the sheriff is charged to summon a person accused, originally, of prosecuting in a foreign court a suit cognizable by the law of England, and later, of asserting or maintaining papal jurisdiction in England, thus denying the ecclesiastical supremacy of the sovereign; also, the statute of 16th Richard II, on which this writ is based.

The words in the writ (1392–3) were (*Natura Brevium*, 1528, 150 b) 'precipimus quod per bonos et legales homines de balliua tua premunire facias prefatum propositum [A.B.] quod tunc sit coram nobis' (we command that through good and loyal men of thy jurisdiction thou do [or cause to] warn the aforesaid A.B. that he appear before us).

[**1383** *Rolls of Parlt.* III. 159/2 Ceux qi sont garniz par Brief de Premunire facias..puissent apparer par lour Attornes.] **1449** *Ibid.* V. 149/2 To have suche Processe therin, as provided in a premunire facias. *a* **1529** Skelton *Col. Clout* 108 That the premenyre Is lyke to be set a fyre In theyr iurisdictions. **1529** More *Suppl. Soulys* Wks. 291/1 He layeth that doctour Alein after that he was punished by premunyre for hys contempte committed against ye kinges temporal law, was therfore by ye bishops highly recompensed in benefices. *a* **1548** Hall *Chron., Hen. VIII* 50 Hun..takynge to hym good counsayll, sued the Curate in a preminire. **1588** *Marprel. Epist.* (Arb.) 21 A premunire will take you by the backe one day, for oppressing and tyrannizing ouer her Maiesties subiects as you doe. **1598** *Expos. Termes Law*, *Premunire* is a writ, and it lyeth where any man sueth any other in the spiritual court, for any thing that is determinable in the kings court. **1608** Day *Law Trickes* v. (1881) 75 If I haue wrongd the Prince I stand in compas of a præmonire. **1706** Tindal *Rights Chr. Ch.* 388 Bishops..being under..a Premunire oblig'd to confirm and consecrate the Person nam'd in the *Conge d'Elire*. **1769** Blackstone *Comm.* IV. viii. 115 This then is the original meaning of the offence, which we call *praemunire*; viz.

introducing a foreign power into this land, and creating *imperium in imperio*, by paying that obedience to papal process, which constitutionally belonged to the king alone. **1839** KEIGHTLEY *Hist. Eng.* I. 319 In the 16th year of this Prince [Richard II] was passed the important statute of 'præmunire'... This act received a very large interpretation from the judges and proved of great service in checking the papal usurpations. **1875** STUBBS *Const. Hist.* xvi. II. 410 The first statute of *Praemunire*, declaring the forfeiture and outlawry of those who sued in foreign courts for matters cognisable in the king's courts, was an ordinance of 1353. *Ibid.* 415 In 1365 was passed a new statute of praemunire, definitely aimed against the jurisdiction of the papal court. **1940** E. POUND *Cantos* lxx. 177 Treasons, felonies, new praemunires. **1961** E. F. JACOB *Fifteenth Cent.* VI. 253 In November, after consultation with the judges, writs under the statute of Praemunire were made out against Beaufort.

†**2.** *transf.* An offence against the statute of præmunire; also, any offence incurring the same penalties. *Obs.*

1553 *Act 1 Mary* c. 1 (*heading*), An Act repealing certayne Treasons, Felonies, and Premunire. **1621** ELSING *Debates Ho. Lords* App. (Camden) 134 That if the office were erected without warrant whether it were not a premunire, treason [etc.]. **1625** B. JONSON *Staple of N.* v. vi, Lest what I ha' done to them (and against Law) Be a Premuniri. **1678** COLEMAN in *Trial of C.* 63 That Bill which would have it a Premunire in a Sheriff not to raise the *Posse Comitatus*.

b. The penalties incurred by an offender against the statute of præmunire, which was subsequently applied to various offences not connected with its original purpose. *Obs.* exc. *Hist.*

1604 R. CAWDREY *Table Alph.*, *Premunirie*, forfeiture of goods. **1616** BULLOKAR *Eng. Expos.*, *Premunire*, a punishment wherein the offender loseth all his goods for euer, and libertie during life. **1656** BLOUNT *Glossogr.* s.v., When any man for an offence committed, shall incur a Præmunire, it is meant, he shall incur the same punishment, which is inflicted on those that transgress the Statute made Anno 16 Ric. 2 ca. 5 (commonly called the Statute of Præmunire). **1710** PALMER *Proverbs* 256 He that did not enter into one side or other, shou'd incur somewhat like a premunire; for 'twas the forfeiture of his goods and estate, as well as the banishment of his person. **1719** W. WOOD *Surv. Trade* 367 Those Merchants whose Occasions require Sums of Money to be exported,..will, to keep themselves safe, rather give these Men 3*d.* 4*d.* 5*d.* nay, 6*d.* per Ounce more for foreign Silver, than for our own coined Silver of the same Fineness, which they dare not export for fear of the Præmunire. **1724** SWIFT *Drapier's Lett.* v. Wks. 1755 V. II. 94 A judge, who upon the criminal's appeal to the dreadful day of judgment, told him, he had incurred a premunire for appealing to a foreign jurisdiction. **1902** J. GAIRDNER *Eng. Ch. 16th Cent.* viii. 141 Any subject henceforth bringing in bulls of excommunication was liable to a *præmunire*.

†**3.** A situation or condition likened (gravely or humorously) to that of one who has incurred a præmunire; a difficulty, scrape, fix, predicament.

1595 *Maroccus Ext.* 17 But how does this landlord fall into this Præmunire? **1599** MASSINGER, etc. *Old Law* v. i. 489 If the law finds you with two wives at once, There's a shrewd premunire. **1694** CONGREVE *Double-Dealer* IV. viii, I'm in such a fright! the strangest quandary and premunire! **1751** SMOLLETT *Per. Pic.* (1779) II. xlv. 81 He would not bring himself into such a premunire again for the whole kingdom. **1814** *Stock Exchange Laid Open* 22 It made them all, like every other set..of men in similar premunires, squeak out so loudly.

Hence **præmunire** (-ˈnaɪə(r)) *v. trans.*, to issue a writ of præmunire against; to convict of breach of the statute of præmunire. *Obs.* exc. *Hist.*

1681 W. ROGERS *6th Pt. Chr. Quaker* 23 Whil'st Isaac Pennington was in Prison, and in expectation of being premunired. **1708** T. WARD *Eng. Ref.* (1716) 166 Horn desir'd To have good Bonner præmunir'd. *a* **1713** ELWOOD *Autobiog.* (1885) 252 Swear, or lie In prison, premunired, until you die. **1884** A. C. BICKLEY *Fox* xix. 291 He cast the Friend into prison and praemunired him.

†**præmuˈnireal, -ial, pre-,** *a. Obs. rare.* [f. prec. + -AL[1].] Involving a breach of the statute of præmunire; liable to a præmunire. So †**præmunirized** *ppl. a.*, having incurred a præmunire.

1600 W. WATSON *Decacordon* (1602) 171 The seculars.. made it a matter of conscience, thereby to refell, infringe, and abrogate all such premunireall treachery. *Ibid.*, The seculars..clearly exempt, redeeme and keepe out themselues, from acknowledging any obedience to that already premunirized Archpriest. **1601** —— *Import. Consid.* (1831) 19 To draw you all into the same Predicament Premunirial and of Treason with him.

præmunite, -nition, etc.: see PREMUNITE, etc.

prænares: see PRENARES.

Prænestine (praɪˈnɛstiːn, priː-), *a.* and *sb.* [ad. L. *Prænestinus* f. *Præneste* Palestrina: see -INE[1].]

A. *adj.* Of or pertaining to the ancient city of Præneste or its inhabitants.

1880 *tr. Woltmann & Woermann's Hist. Painting* I. iv. 88 The engraved metal caskets of the kind commonly known as Prænestine cistæ, because they have been found for the most part at Prænestê, the modern Palestrina. **1885** *Encycl. Brit.* XIX. 654/2 Præneste was chiefly famed for its great temple of Fortune and for its oracle, in connexion with the temple, known as the 'Prænestine lots' (*sortes Prænestinæ*). **1937** *Oxf. Compan. Classical Lit.* 163/1 As regards Latin writing, in the inscription on the Praenestine *fibula*.., probably of the 6th c.,..the direction is from right to left. **1939** L. H. GRAY *Foundations of Lang.* 332 The oldest record of Italic is a Praenestine fibula of the seventh century B.C., *Manios med fhefhaked Numasioi* 'Manius me fecit Numerio'. **1970** *Oxf. Classical Dict.* (ed. 2) 873/1 Praeneste has yielded the earliest specimen of Latin, whose peculiarities confirm Festus' statement..that Praenestine Latin was abnormal. **1976** *Archivum Linguisticum* VII. 60 Praenestine *fhfhaked*..is an old reduplicated perfect remade into an aorist by the addition of *-t (> Early Latin -*d*).

B. *sb.* A native or inhabitant of Præneste.

1902 *Encycl. Brit.* XXXIII. 897/2 The Romans..were inclined to sneer at the pronunciation and idiom of the Prænestines. **1949** *Oxf. Classical Dict.* 726/1 Praenestines loyally resisted Pyrrhus..and Hannibal, and actually preferred their own status to that of Roman citizens.

Hence **Prænеˈstinian**, the extinct Latin dialect spoken by the Prænestines.

1939 L. H. GRAY *Foundations of Lang.* 333 To the [Latino-Faliscan] group also belonged the closely similar Hernician and Prænestinian. **1954** [see *Latino-Faliscan* s.v. LATINO-].

‖**prænomen** (priːˈnəʊmɛn). Also pre-. [L., a forename, f. *præ* before + *nōmen* name.]

1. In *Rom. Antiq.*, The first name, preceding the nomen and cognomen; the personal name; thus the prænomen of Marcus Tullius Cicero was Marcus. Hence, the first name of persons of other nations or times; the Christian name of later times.

1706 PHILLIPS, *Prænomen*, among the Romans, that which was put before the *Nomen*, or General Name, and signify'd as much as our Proper Name. **1745** J. WARD in *Lett. Lit. Men* (Camden) 370 Whether the C after Imp. in the others was designed for Cæsar or a prænomen, I cannot venture to assert. **1838** ARNOLD *Hist. Rome* I. 421 *note*, It need not be said, that in old times men were designated by their prænomen, rather than by their nomen, or cognomen. **1844** *Civil Eng. & Arch. Jrnl.* VII. 81/2 With reference to the dates, pre-nomens, and royal standards of the monarchs by whom the pyramids were erected. **1886** *Athenæum* 4 Sept. 313/1 The names of servants are generally prænomens only, *e.g.* 'Alicia seruiente predicti Hugonis'.

†**2.** The first of two words constituting the name of a place, as *Chipping Barnet*. *Obs. rare.*

a **1661** FULLER *Worthies, Cambr.* (1662) I. 153 It being usuall to leave out the Prenomen of a Town for brevity sake, by those of the Vicenage,..commonly calling West-chester, Chester, South-hampton, Hampton.

3. In the binominal nomenclature of Natural History, the first or generic name of a plant or animal, which precedes the specific name. *rare.*

1843 R. J. GRAVES *Syst. Clin. Med.* Introd. Lect. 28 Uva ursi is now preceded by the prænomen Arctostaphylos. **1895** *Syd. Soc. Lex.*, *Prenomen*,..*Biol.*, the first or generic portion of a compound name.

præ-notion to **præpositor**: see PREN-, etc.

†**præpositorship.** *Obs.* An incorrect rendering (cf. PREPOSITOR) of med.L. *præpositātus*, Ger. *propstei*, F. *prevôté*, the district of an ecclesiastical præpositus or *propst*, the group of parishes under one ecclesiastical superintendent; = rural deanery.

1762 tr. *Busching's Syst. Geog.* VI. 221 In the præpositorship of Bremervorde are thirteen parochial-churches. *Ibid.* 230 Its parish-churches form a distinct præpositorship.

‖**præˈpositus.** Also pre-. [L. *præpositus* prefect, president, head, chief, in med.L. provost, sb. use of pa. pple. of *præpōnĕre* to place or set over, f. *præ* PRE- + *pōnĕre* to place.] The head, chief, president, or provost, in various institutions clerical and civil. Frequent in Anglo-Latin: see PROVOST, the mod.Eng. repr.; also PREPOST.

1607–72 COWELL *Interpr.*, *Præpositus Villæ*, is some-times used for the Constable of a Town, or Petit Constable... It is used sometime for a Reve, or for a chief Officer of the King in a Town, Mannor or Village. **1627** M. WREN *Serm. bef. King* 6 Feare..'tis Gods Præpositus in the School of Graces, it sees that none of them be out of Order, or in any kinde Faulty. **1894** R. S. FERGUSON *Hist. Westmorland* 145 By the year 1217 the Præpositus or Reeve at York had been superseded by a mayor. **1906** *Athenæum* 19 May 609/3 It seems almost certain that William the 'præpositus' owed his Norman name to a godfather belonging to the Amundeville family.

præpostor, pre- (prɪˈpɒstə(r)). [Syncopated form of *præpositor*, PREPOSITOR, q.v.] The name given at various English Public Schools to those senior pupils to whom authority is delegated for the management and control of the community; elsewhere called *præfects*, or *monitors*. Cf. PREPOSITOR.

[At Eton, in the 16th c.] 'Eighteen of the senior boys were styled *Præpositi*; but inasmuch as the same term was used to designate the head of the College, the monitors soon came to be called *Præpositores*. Under the contracted form of *Præpostor*, the name has survived to our own time, though the duties..have entirely changed' (Sir H. C. Maxwell-Lyte *Hist. Eton Coll.* (1870) viii. 142).

[*a* **1518–1682**: see PREPOSITOR.] **1768** in Maxwell-Lyte *Hist. Eton* xvi. 320 Prepostors or monitors are chosen..to gather exercises, to mark the boys' names every School time and Church time, to write down the names of those who are not present at the time of absence... The sixth Form hath two Prepostors. **1813** (June) *Rugby School, Printed List* [Sixth Form called] Præpostors. **1854** T. H. GREEN *Let. fr. Rugby* Wks. 1900 III. p. xiv, It is impossible for bullying to be stopped except by praepostors. **1857** HUGHES *Tom Brown* I. v, One of the praepostors of the week stood by him on the steps. **1881** HARE in *Macm. Mag.* XLIV. 359 His rapid removal..into the fifth form at Midsummer..freeing him from the terrors of prepostors and fagging. **1887** *Athenæum* 29 Oct. 569/3 He [Rev. E. Thring] strongly encouraged self-government among the boys, and threw great responsibilities upon the præpostors.

Hence **præˈpostorial** *a.*, of or pertaining to præpostors; **præˈpostorship**, the office of præpostor.

1886 *Pall Mall G.* 10 Dec. 12/1, I should say that Percival's new model of the præpostorial system, carried out on Dr. Arnold's lines, was his greatest achievement as a head master. **1884** (Oct. 2) *Eton School Rules*, The Præpostorship must be taken in School order, unless specially excused.

præputial, præscapula, etc.: see PREP-, etc.

‖**præputium** (priːˈpjuːʃɪəm). *Anat.* [L. *præpūtium* foreskin.] The foreskin, the prepuce.

c **1400** *Lanfranc's Cirurg.* 174 In þe heed þerof is..a skyn, þat goiþ ouer & is clepid prepucium. **1693** tr. *Blancard's Phys. Dict.* (ed. 2), *Præputium*, the fore-Skin, also the Prominency of the Clytoris. **1754–64** SMELLIE *Midwif.* I. 92 The Clitoris with its praeputium is found between the Labia. **1803** *Med. Jrnl.* X. 174 To the end of each plaster, near the preputium, a tape is to be fixed.

‖**Præsepe** (priːˈsiːpiː). *Astron.* [L. *præsæpe* enclosure, stall, manger, hive, f. *præ*, PRE- + *sæpīre* to fence.] The name of a loose cluster of stars, appearing to the naked eye as a nebula, in the constellation Cancer.

1658 PHILLIPS, *Præsepe*, a constellation in 2 degrees 13 minutes of Leo. **1868** LOCKYER *Elem. Astron.* i. §71. 29 The Hyades, in the constellation Taurus, and the Præsepe or 'Beehive', in Cancer.

‖**præses, preses** (ˈpriːsiːz). Chiefly *Sc.* [a. L. *præses*, *-idem*, pl. *præsidēs*, a president, chief, guardian, prop. *adj.* presiding, f. *præsidēre* to PRESIDE.]

a. The president or chairman of a meeting.

1637–50 ROW *Hist. Kirk* (Wodrow Soc.) 285 When he was broght before the Counsell, Bishop Bancroft, the preses, comanded him to kneele. **1676** W. ROW *Contn. Blair's Autobiog.* xii. (1848) 470 Sharp is preses in that court. **1728** RAMSAY *Archers diverting themselves* 87 'My lord, your toast', the preses cries. **1763** BOSWELL *Jrnl.* 19 Jan. in *London Jrnl.* (1950) 155 It resembled a party's being worsted in the choice of praeses and clerk, at an election in a Scotch county. **1797** *The College* 51 Sir Spleen now mounted to the præses-chair. *Ibid.* 59 The Præses-knight amus'd you with his vision. **1806** FORSYTH *Beauties Scotl.* IV. 461 The Earl of Finlater is hereditary preses or provost. **1833** *Act 3 & 4 Will. IV*, c. 46 §11 (Sc.) The preses of all meetings shall ascertain the determination thereof by a show of hands. **1876** BANCROFT *Hist. U.S.* V. xiii. 484 The praeses of the Pennsylvania Lutherans. **1898** P. S. ALLEN *Let.* 10 Oct. (1939) 16 When the Praeses introduced me, the Bishop said ..'You mustn't leave me alone with a man, who makes such bold proposals, President.'

b. An academic moderator.

1841 *Rules Compilation of Catal.* in *Brit. Mus. Catal. Printed Bks.* I. p. v/1 The respondent or defender in a thesis to be considered its author, except when it unequivocally appears to be the work of the Præses. **1853** in C. C. JEWETT *Smithsonian Rep. Constr. of Catalogues of Libraries* (ed. 2) 54 The Respondent or defender in a thesis, is to be considered its author, except when it unequivocally appears to be the work of the Præses. **1931** G. S. GORDON *Let.* 19 Dec. (1943) Is it possible that there *is* no such leisure for an academic official—whether Professor or Praeses—who has a conscience about the job he's paid for? **1967** *Anglo-Amer. Catal. Rules*: *Brit. Text* 27 Enter a dissertation written for defence in an academic disputation (according to the custom prevailing in European universities prior to the 19th century) under the praeses (the faculty moderator) unless the authorship can be well authenticated.

præsidial, var. PRESIDIAL *a.*

Præsidium: see PRESIDIUM.

præsternum to **præstomium**: see PREST-.

præter *a.*, *sb.*, past (tense): see PRETER.

‖**præter-** (ˈpriːtə(r)), a L. adv. and prep. meaning 'beyond, past, besides, except', frequent in composition; in Eng. entering into many compounds, in which it is now generally written PRETER-, q.v.

A few obsolete words occur only with the spelling *præter-* which is also preferred in some words by individual modern writers; for all these see PRETER-.

‖**prætexta** (priːˈtɛkstə). *Rom. Antiq.* Also pre-. [L., short for *toga prætexta* gown bordered or fringed in front; pa. pple. fem. of *prætex-ĕre* to weave before, fringe, border.] A long white robe with a purple border, worn originally by the Roman magistrates and some of the priests, but afterwards by the children of the higher classes, viz. by boys till they were entitled to assume the *toga virilis*, and by girls till marriage.

1601 HOLLAND *Pliny* XXXIII. i. II. 455 Whiles he was under sixteene yeares of age, and as yet in his Prætexta. **1670** LASSELS *Voy. Italy* II. 153 Little boyes in the habit of a *Prætexta*. **1727–41** CHAMBERS *Cycl.* s.v., The pretexta, at first, was a robe of state, or ceremony... In continuance of time it was permitted to noblemens children; and, at length, even to all Roman children in general. *a* **1763** SHENSTONE *Progr. Taste* IV. 85 'Tis the pretexta's utmost bound, With radiant purple edg'd around. **1868** *Smith's Smaller Dict. Antiq.* 380/2 Girls wore the praetexta till their marriage.

prætor, pretor ('pri:tə(r)). Forms: 5–7 pretour, (6 *Sc.* -oir), 5– pretor, 6– prætor. [Early mod.E. *pretour* = F. *préteur*, ad. L. *prætor*, *-ōr-em* (contracted from **præ-itor*, lit. one who goes before, f. *præ* before + *ire* to go).]

Originally the title designating a Roman Consul as leader of the army; after B.C. 366, that of an annually elected Curule magistrate who performed some of the duties of the Consuls, to whom he was subordinate. Of these magistrates there were at first one, later two (*prætor urbānus*, *prætor peregrīnus*), and eventually eighteen.

c **1425** WYNTOUN *Cron.* IV. 1527 And of þe pretor[s] twenty men, And grettast of þe consel þen. **1540** PALSGR. *Acolastus* L iv, Lyke as the pretours of Rome dyd set those mens names in a table hyghest, whose causes shulde first be pleaded or dispatched. **1549** *Compl. Scot.* xvii. 147 He desirit the office of pretoir at the senat. **1601** SHAKS. *Jul. C.* II. iv. 35 The throng that followes Cæsar at the heeles, Of Senators, of Prætors, common Sutors. **1693** DRYDEN *Juvenal* iii. 219 The Prætor bids his Lictors mend their pace. **1755** JOHNSON, *Pretor.* **1781** GIBBON *Decl. & F.* xvii. II. 35 The prætors, annually created as the judges of law and equity. **1852** CONYBEARE & HOWSON *St. Paul* (1862) II. xxvi. 439 The Emperor was prætor or commander-in-chief of the troops.

b. *transf.* One holding high civic office, as a mayor or chief magistrate. In 17th–18th c., the title (= It. *pretore*) of the chief magistrate, or mayor, and of the podestà, in various parts of Italy.

1494 FABYAN *Chron.* VII. 375 No man beynge in auctorytie of any hygh offyce, as prouost, pretour, or any lyke offyce. **1591** LAMBARDE *Archeion* (1635) 72 At the pleasure of the Chancellour or Prætor onely. **1623** COCKERAM, *Pretor*, a Maior, or chiefe Officer. **1676** *Lond. Gaz.* No. 1106/2 The 30 past, the Pretor of Palermo sent to acquaint the Sieur de Haen, that the French Fleet had been seen. **1714** *Ibid.* No. 5192/2 The Prince of Scordia, Pretor of Palermo, presented him with the Book of the Constitutions and Rights of the City. **1719** D'URFEY *Pills* II. 100 And now we're in London let's pass this Affair, And praise the good Prætor now sits in the Chair. **1756–7** Prætor of Verona [see PREFECT 1 c]. **1855** MACAULAY *Hist. Eng.* xxii. IV. 705 No two of these rural prætors had exactly the same notion of what was equitable.

† '**prætoral, pretoral,** *a.* *Obs.* *rare*[−1]. [f. PRÆTOR + -AL[1].] = PRÆTORIAN.

1549 *Compl. Scot.* vi. 43 Kyngis..tuke mair delyit..to manure corne landis, nor thai did to remane in pretoral palecis or in tryumphand cities.

prætorial, pretorial (pri:'tɔərɪəl), *a.* (*sb.*) [f. L. *prætōrius* belonging to a prætor + -AL[1].] Of or pertaining to a Roman prætor; prætorian.

1579–80 NORTH *Plutarch* 917 [Vatinius] came verie arrogantly one day vnto Cicero being in his Prætoriall seate, and asked him a thing which Cicero woulde not graunt him there. **1757** BURKE *Abridgm. Eng. Hist.* I. iii. 37 Those occasional declarations of law called the prætorial edicts. **1850** MERIVALE *Rom. Emp.* (1865) I. iv. 141 Caesar.. continued to administer his praetorial functions.

†**b.** *transf.* Judicial; = PRÆTORIAN *a.* 1 b. *Obs.*

a **1688** W. CLAGETT *17 Serm.* (1699) 10 Confession to a priest, with attrition, being reckoned sufficient to receive a pretorial absolution, which shall be valid in heaven.

†**c.** ***Pretorial court***, in the colony of Maryland, a court for the trial of capital crimes, consisting of the lord proprietor or his lieutenant-general, and the council. Also called *Pretorial*. *Obs.*

1638–9 *Laws Maryland* in *Arch. Md.* (1883) I. 50 An Act For the erecting of a Pretoriall. *Ibid.* 51 This Court..Shall be a Court of Record and Shall be called the pretoriall or the pretoriall Court, and the said Pretoriall shall or may.. exercise..Jurisdictions within this Province.

prætorian, pretorian (pri:'tɔərɪən), *a.* and *sb.* [ad. L. *prætōriānus*: see PRÆTOR and -IAN.]

A. *adj.* **1.** Of, belonging, or pertaining to a Roman prætor, or to the office or rank of prætor.

1598 GRENEWEY *Tacitus' Ann.* XII. v. (1622) 161 The Consularie ornaments were giuen to Colo, and the Pretorian to Aquila. **1781** GIBBON *Decl. & F.* xviii. II. 124 Treves, the seat of Prætorian government, gave the signal of revolt, by shutting her gates against Decentius. **1861** J. G. SHEPPARD *Fall Rome* i. 23 Two prætorian fleets..patrolled the Mediterranean. **1875** POSTE *Gaius* I. § 184 Another guardian ..called a praetorian guardian, because he was appointed by the praetor of the city. **1894** GREENIDGE *Infamia* iv. 114 The only object of the praetorian infamia was to preserve the dignity of the praetor's court, and to prevent the frequent appearance in it of unworthy members of the community.

b. *transf.* Applied to a judge, court, or power analogous to that of the ancient Roman prætor, esp. to a Court of Equity. Now *rare* or *Obs.*

1622 BACON *Hen. VII* 64 In the distribution of Courts of Ordinarie Justice,..the Chancery [had] the Pretorian power for mitigating the Rigour of Law. **1677** W. HUBBARD *Narrative* (1865) I. 17 An Historian being no Pretorian Judg, his Reports cannot prejudice any peoples Jurisdiction, or persons Propriety. **1686** W. SHERLOCK *Papist not Misrepresented* 14 Attributing a Judicial and Praetorian Authority..to the Priest to forgive Sins. *a* **1709** ATKYNS *Parl. & Pol. Tracts* (1734) 237 Let not (says he) Prætorian Courts (speaking of Courts of Equity) have Power to decree against express Statutes, under Pretence of Equity.

2. Of or belonging to the body-guard of a Roman military commander or of the emperor.

Originally applied to the *prætoria cohors* or select troops which attended the person of the prætor or general of the army, subsequently to the imperial body-guard instituted by Augustus.

1432–50 tr. *Higden* (Rolls) V. 115 The knyȝhtes pretorian of Rome namede Maxentius the son of Maximian emperour. **1585** T. WASHINGTON tr. *Nicholay's Voy.* II. iii. 74 The Pretorian legions..began to become rulers ouer their maisters. **1606** HOLLAND *Sueton.* 105 Hee ordained a standing Campe at Rome, wherein the Prætorian Cohorts.. might be received. **1651** R. SAUNDERS *Plenary Possess.* 18 Augustus set up the Prætorian Guard of 10000 men. **1868** LIGHTFOOT *Philippians* (1873) 99 The great camp of the praetorian soldiers. **1881** STEVENSON *Virg. Puerisque, Æs Triplex* (1893) 159 Caligula..turned loose the Prætorian guards among the Company.

b. Of or pertaining to the prætorian soldiers.

1741–2 GRAY *Agrippina* 117 The eye of Rome, And the Praetorian camp. **1812** *Gen. Hist.* in *Ann. Reg.* 60/1 To raise a military depot in such a city as London, a sort of pretorian camp that could not but be grating to the feelings of the people.

c. *fig.* Like the prætorian cohort in venality.

1907 *Spectator* 5 Jan. 5/2 The calling into existence of a Pretorian band of pauper labour through doles for the encouragement of the unemployed.

B. *sb.* **1.** A man of prætorian rank; as an exprætor, or a legate sent as governor of a province.

1756 C. SMART tr. *Horace, Sat.* II. ii. (1826) II. 99 The prætorian Sempronius. **1856** MERIVALE *Rom. Emp.* (1865) IV. xxxii. 13 The provinces which remained under the control of the senate continued to be assigned by lot to consulars and praetorians.

fig. **1850** DOBELL *Roman* v. Poet. Wks. (1875) 71 Those proud prætorians who subverted the commonwealth of God.

2. A soldier of the prætorian guard.

1625 K. LONG tr. *Barclay's Argenis* III. iv. 163 Whom you have appointed in time of peace for Garrison souldiers or Pretorians. **1776** GIBBON *Decl. & F.* I. v. 108 These assertions..became unanswerable, when the fierce Prætorians increased their weight, by throwing..their swords into the scale. **1898** H. G. MOULE *Stud. Ep. Coloss.* vi. 120 It must have made the Praetorian wonder to see this extraordinary prisoner [St. Paul] at his prayers.

b. *fig.* One of a company whose function and interest is to defend an established power or system.

1647 WARD *Simp. Cobler* 50 The rule and reason will bee found all one, say Schoolemen and Pretorians what they will. **1829** LANDOR *Imag. Conv.* II. vii. 338 Neither would christianity have done it..without her purple and pretorians. **1844** DISRAELI *Coningsby* II. i. 162 It is in the plunder of the Church... That unhallowed booty created a factitious aristocracy, ever fearful that they might be called upon to regorge the sacrilegious spoil... These became the unconscious Prætorians of their ill-gotten domains.

Hence **præ'torianism**, a system like that of the Roman prætorian organization; military despotism, esp. when venal.

1870 *Pall Mall G.* 5 Nov. 5 M. Ernest Legouvé..had to thank Count Bismarck for several benefits—for the death of Cæsarism and pretorianism, Ultramontanism and dandyism, the fusion of classes on the ramparts, the separation of Church and State. **1901** *Speaker* 9 Feb. 514/2 Nations which believed themselves far beyond the stage of Pretorianism.

†**præ'torical, pre-,** *a.* *Obs.* *rare*[−1]. [irreg. f. PRÆTOR: cf. *oratorical*.] = PRÆTORIAN.

1639 GENTILIS *Servita's Inquis.* (1676) 857 That the Pretorical Deputy, nor any other Person assisting in the Governors place shall not be a Consultor.

‖**prætorium, pretorium** (pri:'tɔərɪəm). [L. *prætōrium* a general's tent; a provincial governor's residence, a palace; the prætorian guard; sb. use of neut. of *prætōrius* adj., belonging to a prætor.]

1. The tent of the commanding general in a Roman camp; the space where this was placed.

1600 HOLLAND *Livy* VII. xxxvi. 274 When he was come to the Pretorium, the Consull by sound of trumpet, called all the armie to an audience. **1726** LEONI *Alberti's Archit.* I. 89/2 The Prætorium, or General's Tent. **1816** SCOTT *Antiq.* iv, 'From this very prætorium'—A voice from behind interrupted his ecstatic description—'Prætorian here, prætorian there, I mind the bigging o't.' **1843** ARNOLD *Hist. Rome* III. 131 When one of their tribes first saw the habits of a Roman camp and observed the centurions walking up and down before the prætorium for exercise.

transf. **1636** MASSINGER *Bashf. Lover* IV. iii, As I rode forth With some choice troops, to make discovery Where the enemy lay... The duke's prætorium opened.

2. The official residence of the governor of a Roman province; a governor's palace or court.

1611 BIBLE *Mark* xv. 16 The souldiers led him away into the hal, called Pretorium [*mod. edd.* Prætorium], and they call together the whole band. **1706** PHILLIPS (ed. 6), *Prætorium*, the place where the Prætor administer'd Justice; ..also taken for his Palace; and sometimes for his Pleasure-House. **1877** C. GEIKIE *Christ* lx. (1879) 735 The Romans had made Herod's palace the Praetorium, or head-quarters.

b. By extension: The court or palace of an ancient king; also applied to a town-hall, etc.

1611 CORYAT *Crudities* 635 The Prætorium or rather the Stadthouse [at Nimmigen]..is a very ancient and stately place. *a* **1661** HOLYDAY *Juvenal* 205 [Hannibal] became a client to Prusias the Bithynian king; at whose prætorium, or court, he was glad to wait for a hearing. **1820** T. S. HUGHES *Trav. Sicily* I. ii. 61 This palace, or prætorium, falling into decay, was replaced by a strong Saracenic fortress.

3. The quarters of the Prætorian Guard in Rome.

1670 LASSELS *Voy. Italy* II. 96 The ruines of the Pretorium, the Quarters of the Pretorian Bands, which the Emperours lodged here. **1904** G. SMITH *Hist. Chr. Missions* II. v. 48 Paul lived in Rome and near the Praetorium.

prætorship, pre- ('pri:təʃɪp). [f. PRÆTOR + -SHIP.] The office of a Roman prætor; the term of this office.

1541 T. PAYNEL *Catiline* lii. 75 Changyng his apparel, and laying away the ornamentes of pretorship. **1581** SAVILE *Tacitus, Agric.* (1622) 186 His [Agricola's] Pretorship also he passed ouer in the same sort, with the like silence. **1641** J. JACKSON *True Evang. T.* I. 29 Trajan..delivered a sword to the Prefect of the Pretorship, bidding him, if he were good, to use it for him; if evill, against him. **1788** GIBBON *Decl. & F.* xliv. (1846) IV. 176 The praetorship of Salvius Julian, an eminent lawyer, was immortalised by the composition of the Perpetual Edict. **1880** MUIRHEAD *Gaius* I. §6 *note*, The peregrin praetorship was created in or about the year 507/247; the duty of the new magistrate being to administer justice between foreigners resident in Rome, or between foreigners and citizens.

b. *transf.* Chief magistracy; mayoralty.

1622 MIDDLETON *Hon. & Virtue* Wks. (Bullen) VII. 364 You [Lord Mayor] go From court to court before you be confirm'd In this high place, which prætorship is termed.

c. with *poss. pron.*, as title of a prætor.

1678 T. JORDAN *Triumphs of London* 12 The Governour Of this Plantation, doth present his Power, And Profits to Your Prætorship.

† '**prætory, 'pretory,** *sb.* (*a.*) *Obs.* [ME. *pretori*, a. OF. *pretorie*, *pretoire* (mod.F. *prétoire*), ad. L. *prætōrium* PRÆTORIUM; in II, ad. L. *prætōrius* one of prætorian rank.]

I. 1. A prætorium, hall, or palace.

a **1300** *Cursor M.* 16302 Pilate him ras, and forth yode Vte o þe pretory. *Ibid.* 16093. **1382** WYCLIF *Acts* xxiii. 35 He comaundide him for to be kept in the pretorie [*gloss* or moote halle], of Heroude. **1483** CAXTON *Gold. Leg.* 387 b/2 He sente secretely..for al the grete gramaryens and rethorycyens that they shold come hastelye to hys pretorye to alysaunder. **1577** HANMER *Anc. Eccl. Hist.* (1663) 235 The which Law is ingraven in a stony pillar..in the publick pretory, nigh the Emperors martial picture.

2. The prætorian guard, or their quarters.

c **1374** CHAUCER *Boeth.* I. pr. iv. 9 (Camb. MS.), I took stryf ayeins the prouost of the pretorie. **1387** TREVISA *Higden* (Rolls) V. 71 Gordianus..was y-slawe of oon Phelip, prefecte of þe pretorie, nouȝt fer from Rome. **1494** FABYAN *Chron.* IV. lxv. 44 He was Presydente of the Pretory of Rome. **1606** G. W[OODCOCKE] *Lives Emperors* in *Hist. Ivstine* H h ij, For that merit hee was called to be a souldiour, where..he arose to be the Maister of the Praetory.

3. The prætor's court. *rare.*

1594 R. ASHLEY tr. *Loys le Roy* 82 He ordained that there should be foure prefectures of the pretorie, or Courts of soueraigne authority.

II. 4. A man of prætorian rank.

1387 TREVISA *Higden* (Rolls) IV. 165 Destroyede.. senatoures, consuls, pretories, and edelynes, men of dignyte.

B. *attrib.* or *adj.* = PRÆTORIAN *a.* In quot. *transf.* Of or pertaining to a judge. *rare.*

1549 LATIMER *4th Serm. bef. Edw. VI* (Arb.) 110 Esay.. speaking of the iudgementes done..in the commune place as it myghte be Westminster hall, the gylde hall, the Iudges hall, the pretory house.

† '**præturate.** *Obs.* *rare*[−1]. [f. L. *prætūra* prætorship + -ATE[1] 1.] Prætorship.

1724 WARBURTON *Tracts* 7 In the Interim comes P. Accius Varus.., with the Character of the Præturate of Afric.

†**prag,** *sb.*[1] *Obs.* [Origin obscure: perh. earlier form of PROG.] ? A pin, nail, or spike.

1354 *Mem. Ripon* (Surtees) III. 92 In mercede fabri facientis pragges et lokats de ferro suo proprio pro fenestris figendis. *Ibid.* 92, 93 Prages, Pragges.

†**prag, pragge,** *sb.*[2] *Obs. slang.* [Origin uncertain: cf. PRIG.] ? One who 'prigs'; a thief.

1592 GREENE *Disput.* Wks. (Grosart) X. 206 More full of wyles to get crownes, than the cunningest Foyst, Nip, Lift, Pragges, or whatsoeuer that liues at this day.

†**prag,** *v.* *Obs.* or ? *dial. rare.* In 6 **pragg.** [Origin unascertained.] *trans.* To stuff, cram, fill.

1567 DRANT *Horace, Epist.* i. C j, O, neyghbours, neyghbours, first get coyne, firste hardlye pragge the purse. *Ibid.* vii. D iv, Againe With pragged paunche assayde to goe. **1866** J. E. BROGDEN *Provinc. Words Lincs.*, *Pragged with things*, having a great abundance.

†**prage.** *Obs. rare.* [Origin unascertained: cf. PRAG *sb.*[1], PROG.]

1. Perh. = PRAG *sb.*[1]

1502 ARNOLDE *Chron.* (1811) 237 Small pragys, at iiij.s'. **1545** *Rates of Customs* C ij, Prages the groce *xs.* **1583** *Ibid.* D viij, Prages the groce xvis. viiid.

2. A spear or similar weapon.

1582 STANYHURST *Æneis* I. (Arb.) 23 Theyre blades they brandisht, and keene prages goared in entrayls Of stags. **1583** STOCKER *Civ. Warres Lowe C.* III. 133 The Zealanders ..with their long rusty prages, slew euery mothers sonne of them.

† '**praggish,** *a.* *Obs.* *rare*[−1]. [? f. PRAG(MATIC) + -ISH[1].] ? = PRAGMATIC, meddlesome.

1721 AMHERST *Terræ Fil.* No. 46 (1726) 254 Sir, you ought to be hors'd out of all good company for an impudent praggish Jackanapes.

pragmatic (præg'mætɪk), *a.* and *sb.* [= F. *pragmatique*, Ger. *pragmatisch*, etc., ad. L. *pragmaticus* skilled in business, esp. law (Cic.), in late L., relating to civil affairs (also sb.), a. Gr. πραγματικός active, business-like, versed in affairs, relating to matter of fact, also sb. a man of business or action; f. πρᾶγμα, πραγματ- a deed, act, affair, state-affair, business, etc., f. πράττειν to do.]

A. *adj.* **1.** Relating to the affairs of a state or community. ***pragmatic sanction***, rendering late juridical L. (Cod. Justin.) *pragmatica sanctio* (*jussio, annotatio*), also *pragmaticum rescriptum*: 'an imperial decree referring to the affairs of a community', the technical name given to some imperial and royal ordinances issued as fundamental laws.

Applied first to edicts of the Eastern Emperors; subsequently to certain decrees of Western sovereigns, as the Pragmatic Sanction attributed to St. Louis of France, 1268, containing articles directed against the assumptions of the Papacy; those of Charles VII of France in 1438, and of the Diet of Mainz in 1439, embodying the most important decisions of the Council of Basle, the former being the basis of the liberties of the Gallican church. In more recent European history, applied particularly to the ordinance of the emperor Charles VI, in 1724, settling the succession to the Austrian throne; also, to that of Charles III of Spain in 1759, granting the crown of the Two Sicilies to his third son and his descendants.

1643 PRYNNE *Sov. Power Parl.* App. 32 In this Parliament the pragmatick sanction was restored. **1688** *Answ. Talon's Plea* 17 To abrogate and to annull at the same time, the pragmatick Sanction, and the Concordat too. **1699** BURNET *39 Art.* xxxvii. (1700) 385 Pragmatick Sanctions were made in several Nations to assert their Liberty. **1710** J. HARRIS *Lex. Techn.* II, *Pragmatick Sanction*, is a Term in the Civil Law for a Letter written to a Corporation, or any Publick Body, by the Emperour in answer to their Request to enquire or know the Law of him. **1767** *Hist. Europe* in *Ann. Reg.* 30/1 The King then published his pragmatic sanction, or royal ordinance, for the expulsion of the Jesuits. **1848** W. H. KELLY tr. *L. Blanc's Hist. Ten Y.* II. 220 The revocation of the pragmatic act which left the youthful Isabella heiress of the Spanish crown. **1858** CARLYLE *Fredk. Gt.* v. ii. I. 552 'Pragmatic Sanction' being, in the Imperial Chancery and some others, the received title for Ordinances of a very irrevocable nature, which a sovereign makes in affairs that belong wholly to himself, or what he reckons his own rights. **1885** *Encycl. Brit.* XIX. 657/1 After his [Charles VI's] death, the pragmatic sanction led to the War of the Austrian Succession.

2. Busy, active; *esp.* officiously busy in other people's affairs; interfering, meddling, intrusive; = PRAGMATICAL *a.* 3, 4.

1616 B. JONSON *Devil an Ass* I. vi, I loue to hit These pragmaticke young men, at their owne weapons. **1674** *Govt. Tongue* vi. §33 Common estimation puts an ill character upon pragmatic medling people. **1777** ROBERTSON *Hist. Amer.* II. VI. 238 Cepeda..a pragmatic and aspiring lawyer, seems to have held a secret correspondence with Pizarro. **1879** FARRAR *St. Paul* II. 282 *note*, If St. Paul said Κυρίου, the marginal Θεοῦ of some pragmatic scribe might easily have obtruded itself into the text.

3. Conceited in one's own opinion, opinionated; dictatorial, dogmatic; = PRAGMATICAL *a.* 4 b.

1638 SIR T. HERBERT *Trav.* (ed. 2) 202 It was in vaine to chalenge the pragmatique Pagan in point of honour. **1653** R. SANDERS *Physiogn., Moles* 17 It signifies her to be pragmatique, proud, and one that will domineer over her husband. **1771** FOOTE *Maid of B.* I. Wks. 1799 II. 214 She is as pragmatic and proud as the Pope. **1872** MINTO *Eng. Prose Lit.* 599 A strong contrast to the pragmatic Cobbett was the amiable, indolent, speculative Sir James Mackintosh. **1872** *Spectator* 7 Sept. 1131 To spoil by.. irrelevant and pragmatic dogmatism a very able and useful paper.

4. Treating the facts of history systematically, in their connexion with each other as cause and effect, and with reference to their practical lessons rather than to their circumstantial details. [= Ger. *pragmatisch*, after πραγματικός, πραγματεία, in Polybius.] Cf. PRAGMATISM 3.

1853 M. ARNOLD *Irish Ess.*, etc. (1882) 291 For the more serious kinds, for pragmatic poetry, to use an excellent expression of Polybius. **1864** WEBSTER, *Pragmatic history*, a history which exhibits clearly the causes and the consequences of events.

5. Practical; dealing with practice; matter-of-fact; = PRAGMATICAL *a.* 2.

1853 C. L. BRACE *Home Life Germany* 124 A strict and pragmatic people, like the mass of the Scotch. **1882-3** *Schaff's Encycl. Relig. Knowl.* II. 1613 The pragmatic school only looked at Christianity as a system of doctrine. It failed to look upon it as an historical development.

6. a. Belonging or relating to philosophical pragmatism; concerned with practical consequences or values. See PRAGMATISM 4.

1902 W. JAMES *Varieties Relig. Exp.* 518 This thoroughly 'pragmatic' view of religion has usually been taken as a matter of course by common men. **1906** *Hibbert Jrnl.* Jan. 337 Whether it is applied to knowledge or to faith, the pragmatic test is a severe one. **1907** W. JAMES *Pragmatism* 45 The pragmatic method in such cases is to try to interpret each notion by tracing its respective practical consequences. *Ibid.* iv. 136 The pragmatic value of the world's unity is that all these definite networks actually and practically exist. **1932** C. MORRIS *Six Theories of Mind* vi. 282 The pragmatic contribution to the theory of mind. **1948** *Mind* LVII. 358 These 'pragmatic paradoxes' as they have been called, are worth examination. **1964** A. W. BURKS in Moore & Robin *Stud. in Philos. C. S. Peirce* 2nd Ser. viii. 143 Peirce's pragmatic principle of meaning. **1971** G. PETROVIĆ in R. Klibansky *Contemp. Philos.* IV. 393 To the uninformed the pragmatic theory of truth seems identical with that of Marx.

b. *spec.* Relating to the practical interpretation of political or social issues. Cf. PRAGMATISM 4 b.

1961 *Mem. & Proc. Manch. Lit. & Philos. Soc.* CIII. 58 This was an explicit pragmatic democratic philosophy of an older generation. **1964** *Listener* 29 Oct. 654/2 Isn't there a danger that this kind of practical, pragmatic socialism, taking problems as they come, is going to rob you of a long-sighted view into the future. **1966** *Times* 11 Mar. 8/6 Mr. Wilson replied..that his 'policy was already very socialist and very pragmatic'. **1970** *Bull. Inst. for Study of U.S.S.R.* Aug. 17 The technocrat is more or less content with any ideology provided that it does not hamper pragmatic development. **1976** *Howard Jrnl.* XV. I. 3 Taking into account an admission of guilt or willingness to compensate for damage should only be done on the grounds that it is to the advantage of society to have the offender admit his guilt or pay for the damage. This is a very pragmatic attitude.

7. *Linguistics.* Of or pertaining to pragmatics. Cf. sense B. 4 below.

1935 B. MALINOWSKI *Coral Gardens* II. IV. iv. 52 Since it is the function, the active and effective influence of a word within a given context which constitutes its meaning, let us examine such pragmatic utterances. **1953** C. E. OSGOOD *Method & Theory Exper. Psychol.* xvi. 699 The pragmatic dimension of semiotic, the relation between signs and their users or the effect of signs upon their users. **1957** C. CHERRY *On Human Communication* vi. 226 Statistical communication theory abstracts from the semantic and pragmatic aspects of the set of signs used. **1964** E. A. NIDA *Toward Sci. Transl.* iii. 36 There is a steady tendency for many terms to shift within the pragmatic area from an ethical response to an esthetic one. **1967** R. A. WALDRON *Sense & Sense Devel.* iii. 49 The attitudes to language dealt with in the last chapter came into conflict with tradition in the stress they lay upon the pragmatic functions of language.

B. *sb.* **1.** A decree or ordinance issued by the head of a state; = *pragmatic sanction*: see A. 1.

1587 FLEMING *Contn. Holinshed* III. 1364/2 His excessiue authoritie hath beene, and still is restreined, checked and limited by lawes and pragmatikes, both ancient and new, both in France and Spaine and other dominions. **1656** BLOUNT *Glossogr.*, *Pragmatic*,..a Proclamation or Edict. **1766** *Char.* in *Ann. Reg.* 11/2 There were even two pragmatics: one that ceded the possessions of the house of Austria to the Archduchess of Poland, the other that contended they were the property of Mary Theresa. **1861** J. G. SHEPPARD *Fall Rome* vi. 286 It was a solemn occasion, and the emperor deemed it worthy of a solemn document, or 'Pragmatic', as it was called.

†**2.** One versed in business; a person deputed to represent another in business or negotiation, an agent; cf. 'man of business', BUSINESS 22 d. *Obs.*

[Cf. also obs. It. '*pragmatico*, an atturnie or practicioner in the lawe, a proctor... Also one wont to stand by a pleader or oratour instructing him in lawe points. Also one expert in doing of things' (Florio 1598).]

1589 G. HARVEY *Pierce's Super.* Wks. (Grosart) II. 150 Since those busie limmes began to rowse, and besturre them, more then all the Pragmatiques in Europe. **1611** SPEED *Hist. Gt. Brit.* IX. viii. §48. 559 Pandulphus (the Popes Pragmaticke) hauing first desired safe conduct of King John, arriues at Douer. **1625** B. JONSON *Staple of N.* I. v, My man o' Law! Hee's my Attorney and Sollicitour too! A fine pragmaticke!

3. An officious or meddlesome person; a busybody; a conceited person.

1645 MILTON *Colast.* Wks. 1851 IV. 369 These matters are not for pragmatics, and folkmooters to babble in. **1659** GAUDEN *Tears Ch.* IV. xvi. 502 Such pragmaticks..labour impertinently. **1835** *Fraser's Mag.* XII. 269 The flippants and pragmatics who infest all the highways of society.

4. *pl.* const. as *sing. Linguistics.* The study or analysis of linguistic signs as they relate to the human user and his behaviour (see quot. 1937). Also *attrib.*

1937 C. MORRIS *Logical Positivism* 4 Analysis reveals that linguistic signs sustain three types of relations (to other signs of the language, to objects that are signified, to persons by whom they are used and understood) which define three dimensions of meaning. These dimensions in turn are objects of investigation by syntactics, semantics, and pragmatics. **1952** *Mind* LXI. 205 The 'pragmatics' group would say that 'points of view' are the business of philosophers. **1954** *Ibid.* LXIII. 360 The step..from descriptive pragmatics to descriptive semantics. **1964** E. A. NIDA *Toward Sci. Transl.* iii. 35 Pragmatics, in contrast to both semantics and syntactics, deals with the relation of symbols to behavior. **1969** I. I. REVZIN in R. Klibansky *Contemp. Philos.* III. 332 In this domain there has been a general shift of interest from syntactics (the first set-theoretical and generative models) to semantics (and possibly pragmatics). **1971** *Language* XLVII. 522 The philosophical dichotomy is between 'semantics' and 'pragmatics', roughly corresponding to reference and inference respectively. **1975** *Ibid.* LI. 37 Partee..expresses reservations about the place of the referential/attributive distinction in natural language, and sees the possibility of assigning it to pragmatics. **1978** *Sci. Amer.* Nov. 82/2 The grammar of language includes rules of phonology, which describe how to put sounds together to form words; rules of syntax, which describe how to put words together to form sentences; rules of semantics, which describe how to interpret the meaning of words and sentences; and rules of pragmatics, which describe how to participate in a conversation, how to sequence sentences and how to anticipate the information needed by an interlocutor.

‖**pragmatica** (præg'mætɪkə). [Sp. *pragmatica*, a. late L. *pragmatica* (sc. *sanctio, jussio, annotatio, constitutio*) a pragmatic sanction. Cf. It. *prammatica*, F. *pragmatique*.] A royal ordinance having the force of a law; = PRAGMATIC B. 1. (Used esp. in reference to Spain.)

1652 HOWELL *Giraffi's Rev. Naples* II. 6 The Viceroy.. caus'd a Pragmatica or Proclamation to be printed and publish'd. **1838** PRESCOTT *Ferd. & Is.* (1846) III. xxvi. 418 The promulgation of *pragmaticas*, or royal ordinances. **1845** FORD *Handbk. Spain* I. 369/2 Charles V., by a Pragmatica in 1525, forbad this usage. **1879** *Encycl. Brit.* IX. 811 As the power of the Spanish crown was gradually concentrated and consolidated, royal pragmaticas began to take the place of constitutional laws.

pragmatical (præg'mætɪkəl), *a.* (*sb.*) [f. as PRAGMATIC + -AL[1]: see -ICAL.]

A. *adj.* **1.** = PRAGMATIC *a.* 1. Now *rare.*

1543 *Formul. Faith* N ij b, Sith that time, the canons pragmatical of these two counsailes, be no where used, nor yet alleged, as to be of effecte. **1593** G. HARVEY *Pierce's Super.* Wks. (Grosart) II. 274 Had he euer studied any Pragmaticall Discourse; or perused any Treaties of Confederacy, of peace, of truce, of intercourse. **1598** FLORIO, *Pragmatica*, a pragmaticall law. **1625** BACON *Ess.*, *Greatness of Kingd.* (Arb.) 481 They are sensible of this want of Natiues; as by the Pragmaticall Sanction, now published, appeareth. **1656** EARL MONM. tr. *Boccalini's Advts. fr. Parnass.* I. lxiv. (1674) 80 Peremptory or pragmatical Laws ought..to be published to the people when they themselves desire them. **1682** BURNET *Rights Princes* vi. 222 When St. Lewis by his pretended Pragmatical Sanction, restored the Liberties of Election. **1882-3** *Schaff's Encycl. Relig. Knowl.* I. 219/2 The so-called pragmatical sanction.

2. a. Of, pertaining to, or dealing with practice (as opposed to theory, etc.); practical; = PRAGMATIC *a.* 5. *Obs.* exc. as used after Ger. *pragmatisch.*

1597 J. KING *On Jonas* (1618) 157 But this knowledge of theirs was not a curious & idle knowledge,..but a pragmaticall knowledge, full of labour and business. *a* **1619** FOTHERBY *Atheom.* Pref. (1622) 17 No better, then a kinde of pragmaticall Atheists. **1704** J. HARRIS *Lex. Techn.* I, *Pragmatical*..in Physicks, or Natural Philosophy,..is some-times used in a good Signification, and signifies the same as Practical, Mechanical, or Problematical. Thus Stevinus..calls some Mechanical and Practical Experiments..by the Name of Pragmatical Examples. **1865** tr. *Strauss' New Life Jesus* I. I. i. 4 The dogmatic treatment of the Life of Jesus inevitably passed into the pragmatical. *Ibid.*, The significance of Christ in relation to modern times could only be substantiated..by treating his life as a pragmatical sequence of events on the same footing as that of other illustrious men. **1906** *Hibbert Jrnl.* Apr. 647 There is the practical or pragmatical form of Christianity usually associated with the name of James.

b. Matter-of-fact.

18.. HARE (Webster 1864), Low, pragmatical, earthly views of the gospel. **1886** *Athenæum* 14 Aug. 203/3 'In One Town', though a little pragmatical and matter of fact, is not uninteresting. It..confines itself entirely to the commonplace joys and mishaps of every-day men and women.

†**3. a.** Engaged in action; actively engaged; prone to action or work; active, busy; business-like, methodical; brisk, energetic. *Obs.*

1601 F. GODWIN *Bps. of Eng.* 427 A man of a very pragmaticall and stirring humour. **1612** T. TAYLOR *Comm. Titus* i. 16 (1619) 320 He will cling to good mens company; be pragmaticall and busie in performing many sightly duties. **1641** MILTON *Animadv.* Wks. 1851 III. 236 Can a man thus imployd, find himselfe..dishonour'd for want of admittance to have a pragmaticall voyce at Sessions and Jayle deliveries? **1661** BOYLE *Style of Script.* (1675) 212 None of these pragmatical persons..will suffer himself to be so enslaved to his business, but he will allow himself set times..for eating.

b. Experienced in business or affairs; expert, practised; skilled; shrewd. Now *rare.*

1656 BLOUNT *Glossogr.*, *Pragmatical*, that is expert in doing things, practised in the Law, and in many matters. **1665** LLOYD *State Worthies* II. (1677) 85 So pragmatical a person as this gentleman was necessary among the Custom-house men. **1822** HEBER in *Jer. Taylor's Wks.* (1839) I. p. ccciii, Political and pragmatical wisdom.

4. a. Unduly or improperly busy or forward; 'assuming business without leave or invitation' (J.); officious, meddlesome, interfering, intrusive. = PRAGMATIC *a.* 2. Now *rare.*

1611-12 BP. HALL *Impresse of God* II. Wks. (1624) 453 The absurd pragmaticall impudency of the present [Pope], in that grosse prohibition of a fauourable and naturall oath, for his Maiesties security. **1656** STANLEY *Hist. Philos.* VIII. (1701) 323/2 A wise man is not pragmatical; for he declines the doing of any thing that is beyond his office. **1794** GODWIN *Cal. Williams* iv. 29 Coming to-day in this pragmatical way, when nobody sent for you. **1829** SCOTT *Anne of G.* xiii, How he dealt with the villains of Liege, when they would needs be pragmatical.

b. Conceited, self-important; opinionated, dogmatic; doctrinaire, crotchety.

1704 HEARNE *Duct. Hist.* (1714) I. 22 Those..whose Merit wholly consists in a pragmatical peremptory way of delivering their Opinions. **1712** ADDISON *Spect.* No. 481 ¶4 Lacqueys were never so saucy and pragmatical as they are now-a-days. **1724** SWIFT *Drapier's Lett.* v. Wks. 1761 III. 92 Which..may perhaps give me the title of pragmatical and overweening. **1834** LYTTON *Pompeii* I. ii, The Romans lose both by this pragmatical affectation of refinement. **1862** BURTON *Bk. Hunter* (1863) 235 The pragmatical priggism which is the pedagogue's characteristic defect.

5. Of, pertaining, or according to pragmatism: = PRAGMATIC *a.* 6.

1903 *Hibbert Jrnl.* Mar. 577 The essentially pragmatical character of the scientific modes of ascertaining 'truth' is precisely one of the chief props of pragmatism. **1938** C. MORRIS in *Internat. Encycl. Unified Sci.* I. I. 68 The pragmatical factor which complements and completes the formal and the empirical factors.

6. Of or pertaining to pragmatics. Cf. PRAGMATIC *sb.* 4.

1939 *Mind* XLVIII. 480 It is to be noted that 'pragmatical' as it occurs throughout this paper designates the relations holding beween signs and their users or interpreters, and is not to be confused with 'pragmatic' or 'pragmatist'. **1942** R. CARNAP *Introd. Semantics* 10 Examples of pragmatical investigations are: a physiological analysis of the processes in the speaking organs..; a psychological analysis of the relations between speaking behavior and other behavior, [etc.]. **1946** C. MORRIS *Signs, Lang., & Behav.* 219 The present study has deliberately preferred to emphasize the unity of semiotic rather than break each problem into its pragmatical, semantical, and syntactical components. **1957** C. E. OSGOOD et al. in Saporta & Bastian *Psycholinguistics* (1961) 285/1 We may call the relation of signs to situations and behaviors..*pragmatical meaning*.

†**B.** *sb. Obs. rare.* **1.** A busybody; = PRAGMATIC *sb.* 3.

1593 G. HARVEY *Pierce's Super.* 100 It is..not the busie Pragmaticall, but the close Politician, that supplanteth the puissant state. **1613** R. CAWDREY *Table Alph.* (ed. 3), *Pragmaticall*, a busie body.

2. One versed in business, etc.; = PRAGMATIC *sb.* 2.

1623 COCKERAM, *Pragmaticall*, one that understands the Law.

3. A pragmatical statement.

1617 BACON *Let. Jas. I* 25 July, That..your Majesty would bestow the thanks not..upon the eloquent persuasions or pragmaticals of Mr. Secretary Winwood.

Hence **pragmati'cality**, the quality of being pragmatical (in various senses).

1846 MRS. GORE *Eng. Char.* (1852) 3 The moment an Englishman feels the pragmaticality of his native land too much for his spirits, off he goes, to relieve himself abroad. **1887** *Ch. Times* 28 Oct. 869/2 The miserable 'unsaved' pragmaticality which sends to the Independent sects a class of persons in whom there is no great relish of salvation.

prag'matically, *adv.* [f. prec. + -LY².] In a pragmatical manner: see the adj. Also, in a manner related to pragmatic philosophy, or to pragmatics.

1606 BIRNIE *Kirk-Buriall* (1833) 38 For such patrociny that Kirk-buriall procutors doe use pragmatically to pleade. **1653** GAUDEN *Hierasp.* 7 Nor..am I pragmatically suggesting, what I might foolishly imagine fittest to be done in State affairs. *a* **1716** BLACKALL *Wks.* (1723) I. 53 Not pragmatically prying into their Secrets or meddling with their concerns. **1868** G. STEPHENS *Runic Mon.* I. 94, I have tried to decipher them pragmatically, practically. **1902** W. JAMES *Varieties Relig. Exp.* 448 *note*, Pragmatically, the most important attribute of God is his punitive justice. **1909** —— *Pluralistic Universe* viii. 321 Pragmatically interpreted, pluralism or the doctrine that it is many means only that the sundry parts of reality *may be externally related.* **1933** *Mind* XLII. 246 Prof. Schlick's 'Causality in Everyday Life and in Recent Science' sets itself to discover the meaning of causality pragmatically, from its use. **1948** *Ibid.* LVII. 358 The fault is not a fault of logic in the sense that the definition is formally self-contradictory. It is merely pragmatically self-refuting. **1964** E. A. NIDA *Toward Sci. Transl.* iii. 46 Some Pentecostals respond 'pragmatically' to a passage of the Scriptures by engaging in shouting and dancing. **1969** C.-Y. CHENG *Peirce's & Lewis's Theories of Induction* xii. 129 Induction cannot be pragmatically significant in a *strong* sense.

prag'maticalness. [f. as prec. + -NESS.] The quality or character of being pragmatical; †activity, assiduity (*obs.*); officiousness, meddlesomeness; opinionativeness, dogmatism; practical or utilitarian quality; etc.: see the adj.

1643 *Let. fr. Grave Gentleman* 1 Pragmaticalnesse and want of Charity. **1655** FULLER *Ch. Hist.* VI. i. §35 Monks also hated Fryers at their hearts, because their activity and pragmaticalnesse made Monks be held as idle and uselesse. **1664** H. MORE *Exp. 7 Epist.* v. 73 The Pragmaticalnesse of whose Agents will be..ready to discover every one that dissembles his Religion. *a* **1677** BARROW *Serm.* xxii. Wks. 1741 I. 219 But pragmaticalness disturbeth the world..One busybody often (as we find by experience) is able to disturb and pester a whole society. **1731** *Gentl. Mag.* I. 526/2 The usefulness of these two noble drugs, introduc'd by Priests, atone for the pragmaticalness of those who oppos'd 'em. **1891** *Sat. Rev.* 28 Nov. 600/2 The pragmaticalness of the 'fussy Bishop'.

prag'maticism. *rare.* [f. PRAGMATIC + -ISM.]

1. = PRAGMATICALNESS.

1865 tr. *Strauss' New Life Jesus* II. II. lxxxi. Its decay as being observed by the disciples on the next [day] and not before, is pedantry and pragmaticism. **1970** *Bull. Inst. for Study of U.S.S.R.* Aug. 17 Wiles also analyses the regimes in China and Cuba, where property relations are laid down by the Party: this, in his view, will inevitably lead to a kind of pragmaticism and finally to a bureaucracy bereft of ideological impetus. **1978** J. UPDIKE *Coup* (1979) vi. 230 The development of a plausible pragmaticism.

2. *Philos.* The name given by C. S. Peirce to his pragmatic philosophy, esp. to the doctrine that concepts are to be understood in terms of their practical implications.

1905 C. S. PEIRCE in *Monist* XV. 166 So then, the writer, finding his bantling 'pragmatism' so promoted, feels that it is time to kiss his child good-by and relinquish it to its higher destiny; while to serve the precise purpose of expressing the original definition, he begs to announce the birth of the word 'pragmaticism', which is ugly enough to be safe from kidnappers. **1934** C. HARTSHORNE et al. *Coll. Papers C. S. Peirce* V. p. v, Pragmaticism (Peirce's term to indicate his divergencies from other pragmatists) was thus Peirce's way of insisting that abstractions must give an account of themselves. **1946** B. RUSSELL in J. Feibleman *Introd. Peirce's Philos.* p. xv, Peirce's pragmatism (or pragmaticism, as he came to call it) is a very different doctrine from those of James and Schiller and Dewey. **1968** E. H. MADDEN in R. Klibansky *Contemp. Philos.* II. 33 Peirce's shift..to pragmaticism and the dispositional frequency theory.

pragmatism ('prægmətɪz(ə)m). [f. Gr. πρᾶγμα, πραγματ- a deed, act (see PRAGMATIC) + -ISM. Cf. Ger. *pragmatismus.*]

1. Officiousness; pedantry; an instance of this.

1863 COWDEN CLARKE *Shaks. Char.* viii. 211 Our laughing at his pragmatisms and solemn coxcombry. **1895** E. J. HARDING in *Critic* (N.Y.) 9 Feb. 95 How refreshing it is, this absence of pragmatism, this genial resolve to take life as it is, for better for worse.

2. Matter-of-fact treatment of things; attention to facts.

1872 GEO. ELIOT *Middlem.* lxxi, Mrs. Dollop..had often to resist the shallow pragmatism of customers disposed to think that their reports from the outer world were of equal force with what had 'come up' in her mind.

†**3.** A method of treating history in which the phenomena are considered with special reference to their causes, antecedent conditions, and results, and to their practical lessons. *Obs.*

[**1832** SIR W. HAMILTON *Discuss.* (1853) 111 *note*, No word occurs more frequently in the historical and philosophical literature of Germany and Holland, than *pragmatisch*, or *pragmaticus*, and *Pragmatismus*,..the word is peculiarly employed to denote that form of history, which, neglecting circumstantial details, is occupied in the scientific evolution of causes and effects.] **1865** tr. *Strauss' New Life Jesus* I. II. xvi, I have drawn attention..to the prophetic pragmatism of Matthew. **1884** D. HUNTER tr. *Reuss's Hist. Canon* xv. 274 According to the pragmatism of history, we should now turn our attention to the influence which the reforming movement of the sixteenth century exercised on the notion of the biblical canon.

4. a. *Philos.* The doctrine that the whole 'meaning' of a conception expresses itself in practical consequences, either in the shape of conduct to be recommended, or of experiences to be expected, if the conception be true (W. James); or, the method of testing the value of any assertion that claims to be true, by its consequences, i.e. by its practical bearing upon human interests and purposes (F. C. S. Schiller). Also, the philosophical method of inquiry of C. S. Peirce; = PRAGMATICISM 2.

1898 W. JAMES *Philos. Concept. & Pract. Results* 5 The principle of practicalism or pragmatism, as he [C. S. Peirce] called it, when I first heard him enunciate it at Cambridge [Mass.] in the early '70s, is the clue..by following which..we may keep our feet upon the proper trail. *Ibid.* 6 To attain perfect clearness in our thoughts of an object, then, we need only consider what effects of a conceivable practical kind the object may involve... Our conception of these effects, then, is for us the whole of our conception of the object, so far as that conception has positive significance at all. This is the principle of Peirce, the principle of pragmatism. **1900** W. CALDWELL in *Mind* Oct. 436 In this so-called Pragmatism or Practicalism of Prof. James. **1902** F. C. S. SCHILLER *ibid.* Apr. 203 To set forth fully the doctrine which he has named *Pragmatism*, and which I would fain advance against that of Aristotle. **1902** —— *Personal Idealism* 63. **1902** C. S. PEIRCE in Baldwin *Dict. Philos. & Psychol.* II. 322/2 Synechism..is not opposed to pragmatism in the manner in which C. S. Peirce applied it, but includes that procedure as a step. **1903** *Hibbert Jrnl.* Mar. 577 Pragmatism is a new analysis of 'truth' inspired by the recent progress of psychology. **1906** SCHILLER *Humanism* 8 Pragmatism is the doctrine that 'truths' are 'values', and that 'realities' are arrived at by processes of valuation. **1906** *Academy* 4 Aug. 106/1 The most recent and (philosophically speaking) fashionable 'ism' that the new century has produced—known, by some as Humanism, and by others as Pragmatism. **1928** T. S. ELIOT *For Lancelot Andrewes* iv. 84 The great weakness of Pragmatism is that it ends by being of no *use* to anybody. **1946** B. RUSSELL in J. Feibleman *Introd. Peirce's Philos.* p. xv, Pragmatism, for Peirce, was only a method; the truths which it sought to discover were absolute and eternal. **1967** *Encycl. Philos.* VI. 432/1 Pragmatism is a method of clarifying and determining the meaning of signs. **1971** G. PETROVIĆ in R. Klibansky *Contemp. Philos.* IV. 394 We have come a great distance..from the confusion of pragmatism with Marxism. **1974** K. R. POPPER in P. A. Schilpp *Philos. K. Popper* I. 99 The tendency of English philosophers to flirt with nonrealistic epistemologies: phenomenalism, positivism,..sensationalism, pragmatism—these playthings of philosophers were in those days still more popular than realism.

b. *Politics.* Theory that advocates dealing with social and political problems primarily by practical methods adapted to the existing circumstances, rather than by methods which have been conformed to some ideology.

1951 A. B. ULAM *Philos. Found. Eng. Socialism* iii. 77 It is true that the Fabian movement and British socialism in general have been built upon foundations quite different from those of Marxism. We have here first of all a sturdy spirit of pragmatism. **1966** *New Left Rev.* Jan.–Feb. 25 Thompson at one point calls the Communist Party the 'alter ego' of the Labour and trade union Left. But he fails to see the implications of this; that the two are not so very different in nature, for they are united by a common pragmatism, which has led so often to a day-to-day accommodation. **1976** *Times* 2 Apr. 8/4 Your struggle with Adolf Hitler, when Britain cast overboard the philosophy of pragmatism, or utilitarianism—the philosophy of recognizing any group of gangsters, any puppets, as head of a country as long as they were in control of its territory. **1976** *Survey* Summer–Autumn 156 Now that Mao is dead there will no doubt be a sharp reaction towards 'pragmatism'.

pragmatist ('prægmətɪst). [f. as prec. + -IST.]

1. A pragmatical person, a busybody.

1640 BP. REYNOLDS *Passions* xvi. 176 We may [say] of Pragmatists, that their eyes looke alwaies save onely inward. **1863** COWDEN CLARKE *Shaks. Char.* viii. 209 He is a moral teetotaller, a formalist, a pragmatist.

2. a. An adherent of the doctrine called pragmatism. Also, an adherent of historical pragmatism (cf. PRAGMATISM 3).

1892 W. WALLACE tr. *Hegel's Logic* (ed. 2) 257 The motives which must be viewed by the pragmatist as really efficient. **1903** *Hibbert Jrnl.* Mar. 578 A contemporaneous review of an American pragmatist. **1906** H. JONES *ibid.* Apr. 567 It is quite true, as the Pragmatists or Personal Idealists aver, that our purposes define the meaning of things. **1907** *Ch. Times* 8 Feb. 178 The pragmatist takes religion as he finds it, a working life;..he studies the Christian life, and considers that the best way to study it is to live it;..he is content to leave many things unexplained. **1932** C. MORRIS *Six Theories of Mind* ii. 71 In this insistence that mind cannot be divorced from the world certain new realists and pragmatists are at one with the absolute idealists. **1937** —— *Logical Positivism* iv. 46 Two groups which at first sight might seem in opposition, namely: the pragmatists (or biological positivists), and the Wiener Kreis (the logical positivists).

b. *attrib.* or as *adj.* Of or according to pragmatism.

1903 *Hibbert Jrnl.* Mar. 578 The evidence for a pragmatist interpretation of the reason. **1906** W. JAMES in *Jrnl. Philos.* III. 337 (*heading*) Papini and the pragmatist movement in Italy. **1965** E. E. EVANS-PRITCHARD *Theories Prim. Relig.* iii. 48 The emotionalist explanations of primitive religion which I have discussed have a strong pragmatist flavour.

Hence **pragma'tistic** *a.*; **pragma'tistically** *adv.*

1906 W. JAMES in *Jrnl. Philos.* III. 341 Subjective factors ..are in *some* degree creative, then; and this carries with it.. the admissibility of the entire Italian pragmatistic program. **1907** —— *Pragmatism* 40 The pragmatistic philosophy.. preserves as cordial a relation with facts. *Ibid.* 281 Concretely he means..just the pragmatistically unified and ameliorated world. *Ibid.* 301 What I take the liberty of calling the pragmatistic or melioristic type of theism. *a* **1914** C. S. PEIRCE *Coll. Papers* (1958) VIII. II. ix. 247 But if this occasion did in actuality *not* arise, such habit of thought as the conditional proposition might produce would be a nullity pragmatistically and practically. **1961** *Proc. Aristotelian Soc.* LXI. 180 Basic concepts,..if chosen pragmatistically, would be like Quinian 'posits'. **1971** J. J. SHAPIRO tr. *Habermas's Toward Rational Society* v. 68 The successful transposition of technical and strategic recommendations into practice is, according to the pragmatistic model, increasingly dependent on mediation by the public as a political institution. **1974** R. A. HOCKS (*title*) Henry James and pragmatistic thought.

†**pragma'titioner.** *Obs. rare*⁻¹. [f. obs. F. *pragmaticien* (Estienne) a man skilled in law + -ER¹. Cf. *practitioner*, etc.] A man skilled in affairs; a practising lawyer; = PRAGMATIC B. 2.

1607 R. C[AREW] tr. *Estienne's World of Wonders* 129 When they [lawyers] were called *Pragmaticiens*, that is, Pragmatitioners.

pragmatize ('prægmətaɪz), *v.* [f. Gr. πρᾶγμα, πραγματ- a deed, act + -IZE. So obs. F. *pragmatiser* (1660 Oudin).] **1.** *trans.* To represent (what is imaginary or subjective) as real or actual; to materialize or rationalize (a myth).

1834 KEIGHTLEY *Tales & Pop. Fict.* v. 203 Pragmatising, or endeavouring to extract historic truth out of mythic legends. **1869** SEELEY *Lect. & Ess.* v. 136 The distinctness with which theological doctrines are pragmatised.

2. *intr.* To behave in accordance with, or give expression to, a doctrine of pragmatism.

1907 H. JAMES *Let.* 17 Oct. in R. B. Perry *Tht. & Char. W. James* (1935) I. 428, I was lost in the wonder of the extent to which all my life I have (like M. Jourdain) unconsciously pragmatised. **1966** *New Statesman* 15 Apr. 537/1 The moment the election was won he [*sc.* Mr. Wilson] was 'pragmatising' around the place like a man possessed.

Hence **'pragmatized, 'pragmatizing** *ppl. adjs.*; **pragmati'zation**, the action or process of giving practical effect to theory.

1866 FREEMAN *Hist. Ess.* Ser. I. i. (1871) 3 The old pragmatizing or Euhemeristic school of mythological interpretation. **1871** TYLOR *Prim. Cult.* I. x. 368 One of the miraculous passages..is traced..to such a pragmatized metaphor. **1950** T. WIESENGRUND-ADORNO et al. *Authoritarian Personality* xvii. 726 It is precisely this pragmatization of politics which ultimately defines fascist philosophy.

pragmatizer ('prægmətaɪzə(r)). [f. prec. + -ER¹.] One who pragmatizes.

1847 *Fraser's Mag.* XXXVI. 16 Pragmatisers, astronomers, and allegorists have worn his labours threadbare. **1866** FREEMAN *Hist. Ess.* Ser. I. i. (1871) 3 The pragmatizers take a mythical story; they strip it by an arbitrary process of whatever seems impossible, they explain or allegorize miraculous details [etc.]. **1871** TYLOR *Prim. Cult.* I. x. 368 The pragmatizer is a stupid creature, nothing is too beautiful or too sacred to be made dull and vulgar by his touch.

‖**Prägnanz** ('prɛgnants). *Psychol.* [G., = conciseness, definiteness: orig. used in this sense by M. Wertheimer 1923, in *Psychol. Forschung* IV. 317.] The tendency, noticed in experiments with Gestalts, for configurations to be given their most concise and clearly definable interpretations.

1925 *Amer. Jrnl. Psychol.* XXXVI. 359 How the configuration conforms to laws of simplicity, pregnancy or precision (Prägnanz), symmetry and the like. **1935** K. KOFFKA *Princ. Gestalt Psychol.* iv. 110 The principle was introduced by Wertheimer, who called it the *Law of Prägnanz*. **1938** *Mind* XLVII. 91 In this connection the criticism of Gestalt, and particularly of the Law of

Prägnanz, implicit in certain experiments carried out by Thouless is very relevant. **1963** J. MANN *Frontiers of Psychol.* iv. 131 The basic nature of human data-receiving and processing equipment, which organizes perceptual data without the conscious awareness of consent of the perceiver. An example of such a tendency is the law of *Prägnanz.* **1971** *Sci. Amer.* Dec. 70/2 It should be evident by now that some principle of *Prägnanz*, or minimum complexity, runs as a common thread through most of the cases.

Prague (prɑːg). [Name of capital of Czechoslovakia.] **1.** Used *attrib.* in ***Prague School*** and various associated Combs. to designate the linguistic theories, primarily in relation to phonology, developed by or associated with members of the Prague Linguistic Circle (*Cercle Linguistique de Prague*), especially during the 1920s and 1930s.

1935 [see MORPHONOLOGY]. **1936** *Eng. Stud.* XVIII. 159 Trnka is a member of the Cercle Linguistique de Prague, and his analysis may be described as an application to English of the principles of the so-called Prague phonological school. **1937** [see PHONOLOGY]. **1939** L. H. GRAY *Foundations of Lang.* 61 The phoneme..is..regarded as..a point in the psychological pattern ('phonology'; Edward Sapir and the Prague school). **1959** [see MORPHEME]. **1962** [see NEUTRALIZATION 3]. **1964** E. BACH *Introd. Transformational Gram.* vi. 135 The parallel between such incompletely specified segments and the archiphonemes of the Prague school is evident. *Ibid.* vii. 143 Such widely differing schools of linguists as the Prague circle, glossematicians, and American structuralists have all concurred in insisting that languages should be studied as structures. **1964** M. A. K. HALLIDAY et al. *Linguistic Sci.* 148 Modern theories in phonology were first developed by the 'Prague circle' founded by the Russian linguist N. S. Trubetskoy, whose work has been followed up by Roman Jakobson and many others. **1968** J. LYONS *Introd. Theoret. Linguistics* 126 The Prague school phonologists would say.. that it is not the phoneme /p/ which occurs in the word *spot*, but the archiphoneme /P/. **1976** *Archivum Linguisticum* VII. 128 The different surface realizations are due to a different functional sentence perspective. This concept has been central in the Prague School since its foundation.

2. Prague ham, a type of smoked ham (see quot. 1931).

1931 C. L. T. BEECHING *Law's Grocer's Man.* (ed. 3) 219/1 *Prague* hams (Pragerschinkers) are first salted in large vats and left in a mild brine for several months; they are smoked with beech wood and matured in cool cellars until marketed. **1959** W. HEPTINSTALL *Hors d'Œuvre & Cold Table* II. 69 For a ham to be served hot, my preference goes to the Prague hams. They are..admirable for carving, also they have an exquisite flavour. **1961** *Harrods Food News* 4/2 Sliced Hams ..Prague... lb. 12/-. **1976** T. FITZGIBBON *Food of Western World* 366/2 Prague ham..is served whole for a main course, either baked or boiled, and cold slices of it are often served as a first course.

So **'Praguean, 'Praguian** *adjs.* and *sbs.*

1968 [see MARKED *ppl. a.* 1 c]. **1972** *Language* XLVIII. 385 To use Praguean terminology, there are interlingual archiphonemes which allow, within a broad category, wide language-specific (hence speaker-specific) phonological variation for each content unit. **1973** *Ibid.* XLIX. 193 As Pragueans would put it, both writing and speech are signaling systems of the first order; in other words, one cannot dismiss writing as being the signaling system of the second order, a signal of a signal. **1974** *Trans. Philol. Soc. 1973* 64 As a result of neutralization the mark is dropped; what is left is the complex of distinctive features characterizing both members of the opposition, the *archiphoneme* in Praguian terminology.

prahm, variant of PRAM[1].

prahu, Malay boat: see PROA.

prai(e, obs. ff. PRAY, PREY.

praia (praɪə). Also **praya.** [Pg.] A beach, a sea-shore; a river-bank; a water-front.

a **1865** SMYTH *Sailor's Word-bk.* (1867) 541 *Praia*.., the beach or strand on Portuguese coasts. **1890** *Engineer* 24 Jan. 65/2 A more practical scheme is the proposed building of the whole river front of the city,..and the construction of a broad praya suitable for wheeled conveyances. **1893** KIPLING *Seven Seas* (1896) 13 Hail, Mother! Hold me fast; my Praya sleeps Under innumerable keels to-day. **1933** P. FLEMING *Brazilian Adventure* I. xv. 127 We had meant to camp that night on the sandbank (from now on all sandbanks will be referred to as *praias*). *Ibid.* 129 We slept that night on the praia, under a million stars. **1947** J. BERTRAM *Shadow of War* I. 11 Flags..streamed from the.. roof-tops of grey Victorian company offices along the *praya.* **1963** J. FLEMING *Death of Sardine* iii. 41 One day, when Trigoso Praia..was 'discovered' the road might be an important promenade but now it was tarmac and potholes.

†**praiere.** *Obs. rare.* In 4 praer, prayere. [a. OF. *pra(i)ere* (12th c. in Godef.) meadow land:—late L. *prātāria* (832 in Du Cange) prop. fem. sing. (sc. *terra*) of *prātārius* adj., of the nature of a meadow (f. *prātum* meadow); so Prov. *pradaria*, Sp. *pradera.* Cf. PRAIRIE.] A meadow.

c **1305** *Land Cokayne* 71 In þe praer is a tre Swiþe likful for to se. **13..** *Gaw. & Gr. Knt.* 768 Pyched on a prayere, a park al aboute.

praiere, praire, obs. ff. PRAYER.

‖**praire** (prɛr). [Fr.] The European clam, *Venus verrucosa*, or the North American hard-shell clam, *Mercenaria* (formerly *Venus*) *mercenaria*, which has been introduced to parts of Europe.

[**1878** P. L. SIMMONDS *Commercial Products of Sea* I. xii. 147 The 'paires doubles' [*sic*] (*Venus verrucosa*) or clams of the Mediterranean..are never as delicate in flavour as when freshly caught.] **1929** A. E. HOUSMAN *Let.* 27 Feb. (1971) 278 In the interesting menu of a Paris restaurant..there are *praires.* These may be among the shell-fish which I have eaten at Marseilles, but I do not remember them. **1960** [see PALOURDE]. **1971** M. MCCARTHY *Birds of America* 128 Sometimes I just have a dozen *praires* (which are cheaper than oysters)..for lunch. **1975** *Times* 31 May 7/3 A board.. bearing praires, clovisses, Belan oysters, langoustines.

Prairial ('prɛərɪəl, ‖prerjal). [F. (1793) f. *prairie* meadow.] The name for the ninth month of the French revolutionary calendar, extending from May 20 to June 18.

1806 *Naval Chron.* XV. 129 On the 7th Prairial [they] went to the Diamond Quarter. **1894** *Daily News* 7 June 5/4 The unfortunate Dauphin, who, according to authentic records, died in the prison of the Temple on the 20th Prairial, Year III. of the Republic (June 8th, 1795).

prairie ('prɛərɪ). Also 8, 9 **parara, pararie, praira,** 9 **praire, prairia.** [a. F. *prairie* = OF. *praerie* (12th c. in Hatz.-Darm.) a tract of meadow land = It. *prate'ria*, Sp., Pg. *pradería*:—Romanic type **prāta'ria*, f. L. *prātum* meadow (F. *pré*): see -RY.] **a.** A tract of level or undulating grass-land, without trees, and usually of great extent; applied chiefly to the grassy plains of North America; a savannah, a steppe. Also (*U.S. local*), a marsh, a swampy pond or lake.

In *salt* or *soda prairie*, extended to a level barren tract covered with an efflorescence of natron or soda, as in New Mexico, etc.; in *trembling* or *shaking prairie*, to quaking bog-land covered with thin herbage, in Louisiana.

[*a* **1682** SIR T. BROWNE *Tracts* (1684) 201 The *Prerie* or large Sea-meadow upon the Coast of Provence.] **1773** P. KENNEDY *Jrnl.* in T. Hutchins *Descr. Virginia*, etc. (1778) 54 The Prairie, or meadow ground on the eastern side, is at least twenty miles wide. *Ibid.* 55 The lands are much the same as before described, only the Prairies (Meadows) extend further from the river. **1787** J. HARMAR in E. Denny *Milit. Jrnl.* (1860) 423 The prairies are very extensive, natural meadows, covered with long grass,..like the ocean, as far as the eye can see, the view is terminated by the horizon. **1791** D. BRADLEY *Jrnl.* 19 Sept. (1935) 17 A prairia of two or three hundred acres where the grass or wild oats is 8 or 10 feet high and very thick. *Ibid.* 12 Oct. 22 Struck a large prairia in our course—found it impassable. **1794** W. CLARK *Jrnl.* 1 Aug. in *Mississippi Valley Hist. Rev.* (1914) I. 421 An open..*Pararie*..handsomly interspersed with Small Copse of Trees. **1795** J. SMITH in *Ohio Archaeol. & Hist. Q.* (1907) XVI. 380 We saw several pararas, as they are called. They are large tracts of fine, rich land, without trees and producing as fine grass as the best meadows. **1805** PIKE *Sources Mississ.* (1810) 7 Four hundred yards in the rear, there is a small prairie of 8 or 10 acres, which would be a convenient spot for gardens. **1806** *New Eng. Republican* in *Massachusetts Spy* 16 July 1/5 A venerable Philosopher sitting in the middle of an immense Map, marked with vast praires, huge rivers, and mountains of salt. **1809** A. HENRY *Trav.* 264 The Plains, or, as the French denominate them, the Prairies, or Meadows, compose an extensive tract of country. **1815** SOUTHEY in *Q. Rev.* XII. 326 A large Oak tree stands alone in a *prairie*... (*Note.* If this word be merely a French synonime for savannah, which has long been naturalized, the Americans display little taste in preferring it.) **1819** E. DANA *Geogr. Sk. Western Country* 37 The ore is dug from an open praira. *Ibid.* 108 There are two kinds of praira, the *river* and *upland.* **1834** D. CROCKETT *Narr. Life* xii. 85, I came to the edge of an open parara, and looking on before my dogs, I saw in and about the biggest bear that ever was seen in America. *c* **1834** H. EVANS in *Chron. Oklahoma* (1925) III. 181 We could look and behold..one continual large expanse of Pararie. **1861** DU CHAILLU *Equat. Afr.* xvi. 275 We were troubled..on the prairie by two very savage flies, called by the negroes the *boco* and the *nchouna.* **1874** COUES *Birds N.W.* 307 One of the few species not confined to woods, but occurring in open prairie. **1877** J. A. ALLEN *Amer. Bison* 473 It was..almost exclusively an animal of the prairies and the woodless plains. **1916** *Dialect Notes* IV. 270 *Prairie, n.*, marsh. (Barataria Bay.) **1934** *Nat. Geogr. Mag.* LXV. 601 Shallow ponds, or 'prairies', with a tropical tangle of vegetation. **1942** M. K. RAWLINGS *Cross Creek* 51 We use the word 'prairie' in a special sense. We have no open plains, but around most of the larger lakes are wet flat areas thick with water grasses, and these we call our prairies. They are more nearly marshes, yet we save the word 'marsh' for the deep mucky edges of lake and river, dense with coontail and lily pads. **1951** *Collier's* 24 Nov. 16/3 The eastern half of the Okefenokee is open. There are 'prairies', or great fields of water from one to three feet deep, covered with white or yellow water lilies, purple bladderworts, [etc.]. **1958** S. A. GRAU *Hard Blue Sky* iv. 234 'And they put the candles on squares of wood..and set 'em adrift... And the candles they draw Anton up from the bottom.'.. 'Such a big prairie to find a man in.'

b. *attrib.* and *Comb.*, as ***prairie country, craft, farm, -fever, fire, flower, fly, hay, hill, knoll, land, madness, plateau, -ranger, steppe, stream, town***, etc.; *prairie-like* adj.; **prairie-alligator**, a walking-stick insect, esp. *Diapheromera femorata*; **prairie-apple** = *prairie-turnip* (*Cent. Dict.* 1890); **prairie-bean**, *Phaseolus retusus*, of Texas; **prairie bitters**, a drink made of buffalo-gall and water; **prairie bottom**, a low-lying expanse of prairie land; **prairie-brant** = HARLEQUIN *brant*; **prairie-breaker**, a plough for cutting a wide shallow furrow, and completely inverting the furrow-slice; **prairie-breaking**, the use of a prairie-breaker; also, an area of land ploughed or broken by this means; **prairie buffalo** = *plains buffalo* s.v. PLAIN *sb.*[1] 10; **prairie-burdock**, the Rosin-weed, *Silphium terebinthaceum* (N.O. *Compositæ*); **prairie-buster** = *prairie-breaker*; **prairie clipper**, a coach traversing the prairies: cf. PRAIRIE SCHOONER; **prairie clover**, a leguminous plant of the genus *Petalostemon*; **prairie coal** *N. Amer.*, dried cattle or horse dung used as a fuel; = *buffalo-chips* s.v. BUFFALO 5; **prairie cock** = PRAIRIE-CHICKEN or *sage-grouse* s.v. SAGE *sb.*[1] 5 c; **prairie cocktail**, a raw egg, seasoned, and swallowed in vinegar or spirits (*Cent. Dict.*); **Prairie Cree** = PLAINS CREE; **prairie crocus** *Canada*, a blue- or mauve-flowered anemone, *Anemone patens*, native to northern Europe but naturalized in parts of Canada; **prairie-cup**, ? a wild flower growing on the prairie; **prairie-dock**, (*a*) = *prairie-burdock*; (*b*) *Parthenium integrifolium* (N.O. *Compositæ*) (*Syd. Soc. Lex.* 1895); **prairie-falcon**: see quot.; **prairie-formation** *Geol.*: see quot.; **prairie-fowl** = PRAIRIE-CHICKEN; **prairie fox** = KIT-FOX (*Cent. Dict.*); **prairie-goose**, *Bernicla canadensis Hutchinsii*, of North America; **prairie-grass**, (*a*) any grass growing on the prairies; (*b*) *spec.* in Australia, the grass *Bromus* (*Ceratochloa*) *unioloides*; **prairie-grouse** = PRAIRIE-CHICKEN; **prairie hare**, either of two North American hares, the varying hare, *Lepus americanus*, or the jack-rabbit, *L. townsendii*; **prairie hawk**, the American Sparrow-hawk, *Tinnunculus* or *Falco sparverius*; **prairie itch**, one of various skin affections, characterized by itching and eruption, caused by the fine dust of the prairies (Farmer *Amer.* 1889); **prairie loo**: see quot.; **prairie marmot** = PRAIRIE-DOG; **prairie-mole**, a silvery mole, *Scalops argentatus*, found on the western prairies; **prairie owl**, either of two North American owls, the burrowing owl, *Speotyto cunicularia*, or the short-eared owl, *Asio flammeus*; **prairie oyster** (*a*) = *prairie cocktail*; (*b*) calves' testicles cooked and eaten as a delicacy; **prairie pea**, a milk vetch belonging to the genus *Astragalus*, esp. *A. crassicarpus*, or its fruit; **prairie pigeon**, a name given locally in U.S. to (*a*) the American Golden Plover (*Charadrius dominicus*); (*b*) Bartram's Sandpiper (*Bartramia longicauda*); **prairie plough** = *prairie-breaker*; **prairie plover** = *prairie-pigeon* b; **prairie potato** = *prairie-turnip*; **prairie province** (also with capital initials) *Canad.*, (*a*) the province of Manitoba, *obs.* exc. *hist.*; (*b*) *pl.* the area consisting of the provinces of Manitoba, Saskatchewan and Alberta; **prairie rattler** or **rattlesnake**, one of various rattlesnakes of the prairies, as *Sistrurus catenatus* or *Crotalus confluentus*; **prairie-renovator**: see quot.; **prairie rent**: see *prairie value*; **prairie rose**, *Rosa setigera*, the American climbing rose; **prairie ship** = PRAIRIE SCHOONER; **prairie smoke**, a North American name for *Anemone patens*, a small perennial herb with blue flowers which is widely naturalized in prairie regions; also called *prairie crocus* or pasque flower; **prairie snake**, a large harmless N. American snake, *Masticophis flavigularis* (Webster 1890); **prairie snipe** = *prairie-pigeon* b; **prairie soil**, soil of the kind characteristic of the North American prairies; *spec.* in *Pedology*, a soil that is marked by a deep, dark-coloured surface horizon with a high organic content, is subject to moderate leaching, and occurs under long grass in subhumid temperate regions; **prairie squint**, a squint produced by exposure to the bright light of a prairie; also *fig.*; **prairie-squirrel**, a N. American ground-squirrel of the genus *Spermophilus*, inhabiting the prairies (in quot. 1808 applied to the PRAIRIE-DOG); **Prairie State**, the State of Illinois, U.S.; in pl. in more general sense, including Wisconsin, Iowa, Minnesota, and States to the south of these; **prairie turnip**, a hairy herbaceous plant (*Psoralea esculenta*) of N.W. America, or its edible farinaceous tuber; **prairie value** *Pol. Econ.*, the rental value of prairie land, or of any waste land; also *fig.*; **prairie wagon** = PRAIRIE SCHOONER; **prairie warbler**, a small warbler, *Dendrœca discolor*, of eastern N. America; **prairie wolf** = COYOTE; **prairie wool**, in Canada, the natural, undisturbed plant cover of prairie land, predominantly composed of grasses. See also PRAIRIE-CHICKEN, etc.

1894 Scudder in *Harper's Mag.* Feb. 456 The form.. dubbed 'stick-bogs' and '*prairie alligators', our *Diapheromera femorata.* **a1860** *Scenes Rocky Mts.* 133 (Bartlett) **Prairie Bitters*, a beverage common among the hunters and mountaineers. **1819** T. Say *Jrnl.* 24 Aug. in E. James *Acct. Expedition Rocky Mts.* (1823) I. vii. 131 Our party encamped.. in a.. beautiful and level *prairie bottom. **1834** A. Pike *Prose Sk. & Poems* 12 It is bordered by a strip of timber,.. and on the outside of this, a prairie bottom.. of exceeding rich land. **1868** *Rep. Iowa Agric. Soc. 1867* 139 On strong prairie-bottom it [*sc.* the Rio Grande bearded wheat] is liable to get down. **1888** Trumbull *Names Birds* 12 *Anser albifrons gambeli*... Known in.. the West as *Prairie Brant, Speckled Belly, and Speckled Brant,.. or Brant simply. **1884** Knight *Dict. Mech.* Suppl. s.v. *Breaker*, The timber land breaker and *prairie breaker are essentially different. **1861** *Trans. Illinois Agric. Soc.* IV. 37 The plows were running.. too deep for ordinary *prairie breaking. **1879** *Scribner's Monthly* Nov. 132/2 It is only by resorting to figures that one can reach a comprehension of the aggregate extent of these long, narrow, black strips of 'prairie-breaking'. **1886** P. G. Ebbutt *Emigrant Life Kansas* 45 Will Hopkins.. used to do a good deal of prairie-breaking, having a twenty-four inch plough and six yoke of oxen. **1806** Lewis & Clark *Orig. Jrnl. Lewis & Clark Expedition* (1905) V. 80 A species of Lizzard called by the French engages *prairie buffalo are natives of these plains as well as those of the Missouri. I have called them the horned Lizzard. **1859** H. Y. Hind *North-West Territory* xii. 105/1 That there are two kinds of buffalo appears to be still a matter of doubt; they are stated to be the prairie buffalo and the buffalo of the woods. **1951** F. G. Roe *N. Amer. Buffalo* iii. 47 The Red River hunt had had to travel increasingly long distances westward to find the ordinary Prairie buffalo. **1866** *Treas. Bot.* 1059/1 *Silphium terebinthaceum* is sometimes called the *Prairie Burdock, from its rough heart-shaped root-leaves. **1952** J. W. Day *New Yeomen of Eng.* viii. 94 On one tract.. which was recently broken up, a very good job was made by a three-furrow *prairie-buster hauled by a tracklayer. **1961** *Guardian* 8 Mar. 5/3 Open land in parks should be under planning control as protection against what are termed 'prairie busters'. **1870** D. B. R. Keim *Sheridan's Troopers* 49 The coaches or '*prairie clippers', as they are called by the denizens of the country, pitched and jolted. **1857** A. Gray *First Lessons in Botany* 95 *Petalostemon*, *Prairie Clover... Chiefly perennial herbs,.. [with] small flowers. **1870** *Amer. Naturalist* IV. 581 The prairie clovers.. are among the most interesting of the leguminose species. **1887** *Nicholson's Dict. Gard.*, *Petalostemon*,.. Prairie Clover... A genus comprising about fourteen species of pretty, hardy or half-hardy herbs. **1939** *Nat. Geogr. Mag.* Aug. 247/2 Prairie clovers may be white, pink, purple, or violet. **1968** Peterson & McKenny *Field Guide Wildflowers North-eastern & North-Central N. Amer.* 252 Prairie-clovers have pinnate leaves and dense, longish pink or white flower heads on wiry stems. **1939** C. L. Douglas *Cattle Kings of Texas* 324 He could not bring himself to relish food cooked with '*prairie coal'. **1948** *Southwest Rev.* Summer 238/1 When the permanent settlers and their families came, this 'prairie coal' became the standard fuel. **1972** J. Minifie *Homesteader* vii. 51 As he walked he collected horse-dung for his cook-fire. Weathered 'prairie coal' makes a quick, hot fire. **1805** Lewis & Clark *Orig. Jrnls. Lewis & Clark Expedition* (1905) III. xviii. 123 Send out Hunters to shute the *Prairie Cock a large fowl which I have only Seen on this river. **1846** J. W. Webb *Altowan* I. ii. 31 The prairie cock (a large species of grouse, of a pepper-and-salt colour, and long, pointed tail).. rose at their feet. **1876** J. Burroughs *Winter Sunshine* v. 115 The prairie hens or prairie cocks set up that low musical cooing or crowing. **1900** H. Garland *Eagle's Heart* 107 A belated prairie cock began to boom. **1806** *Deb. Congress U.S.* (1852) 9th Congress 2 Sess., App. 1136 The quality of the land is supposed superior to that on Red river, until it ascends to the *prairie country, where the lands on both rivers are probably similar. **1848** E. Bryant *California* iii. 34 Our march was.. through an undulating prairie-country. **1853** *Trans. Lit. & Hist. Soc. Quebec* IV. 298 The prairie country of the Saskatchewan is roamed over by countless herds of buffalo, also by the reindeer and the beautiful antelope. **1907** W. O. Lillibridge *Where Trail Divides* 152 The darkness that precedes morning has the prairie country in its grip. **1922** *Beaver* Oct. 15/1 During that time there had been two half-breed rebellions in the prairie country. **1946** J. T. Adams *Album Amer. Hist.* III. 261 Hay Burning Stoves were useful in this prairie country. **1851** Mayne Reid *Scalp Hunt.* iii, An insight into many an item of *prairie-craft. **1883** E. Petitot in *Proc. R. Geogr. Soc.* V. 649 They occupied the country between the Savanois Indians on the east and the Grandes-pagnes (also called *Prairie-Crees), on the west. **1913** F. W. Hodge *Handbk. Indians of Canada* (1971) 621/1 (Index) Plain Crees = Paskwawininiwug... Prairie-Crees = Paskwawininiwug. **1922** A. J. A. Stringer *Prairie Child* 304 *Prairie-crocuses [are] soft blue and lavender and sometimes mauve. **1951** *Chambers's Jrnl.* Aug. 505/1 The mauve prairie-crocus, really an anemone, which pushes out of grass knolls as soon as the snow melts, is the first source of pollen. **1969** N. W. Parsons *Upon Sagebrush Harp* iii. 16 The land was.. blue with furry pasqueflower, or prairie crocus. **1880** J. Hay *Pike County Ballads* 96 *Prairie-Cups are swinging free To spill their airy wine. **1874** Coues *Birds N.W.* 339 *Falco Mexicanus*, American Lanier, or *Prairie Falcon. **1893** Newton *Dict. Birds* 238 The Prairie-Falcon of the western plains of North America. **1838** H. W. Ellsworth *Valley of Upper Wabash* v. 49 A late and lamented brother of the writer, who had just finished a *prairie farm. **1884** 'Mark Twain' *Huck. Finn* vii. 46 Hogs soon went wild in them bottoms after they had got away from the prairie-farms. **1886** P. G. Ebbutt *Emigrant Life Kansas* 198, I don't think Anderson had enough energy in him to start a prairie farm for himself. **1851** Mayne Reid *Scalp Hunt.* iii, I had caught the '*prairie-fever'! **1824** W. Owen in *Indiana Hist. Soc. Publ.* (1906) IV. i. 83 We then rode on to the prairie and rode twice through the *prairie fire, which.. moved very slowly. **1836** D. B. Edward *Hist. Texas* iv. 70 Why should there be any lack of timber, when by planting it.., and preserving it afterwards from the annual prairie fires.. it would grow with such rapidity. **1852** A. Cary *Clovernook* 77 Stories of.. huge lights made by prairie fires. **1892** *Boston* (Mass.) *Jrnl.* 10 Oct. 9/3 By back-firing, the people.. saved their town from being destroyed by the great prairie-fire. **1899** *Daily News* 20 Mar. 8/3 Since 'Uncle Tom's Cabin' there has been no such prairie fire in fiction as Mr. Charles M. Sheldon's 'In His Steps'. The book.. has 'caught on'.. like a blaze in dry grass. **1922** *Beaver* Oct. 17/2 One of the most.. terrible sights of those early days was a stampede of hundreds of buffalo fleeing before a prairie fire. **1935** H. A. L. Fisher *Hist. Europe* I. xii. 144 The Moslem faith might have spread like a prairie fire through the Balkans. **1959** [see back-fire *sb.* 1]. **1963** A. Heron *Towards Quaker View of Sex* iii. 27 'The prairie fire' view of homosexual contact—that.. if it were allowed legally and morally everyone would turn to it. **1836** J. Hall *Statistics of West* iv. 56 The *prairie-flower displays its diversified hues. **1873** *Newton Kansan* 22 May 3/2 The wild prairie flowers.. are beginning to look beautiful. **1894** *Harper's Mag.* Aug. 422/1 To be sure there were patches of orange prairie flowers all about. **1922** H. L. Wilson *Merton of Movies* 69 Ain't I the little prairie flower, growing wilder every hour? **1836** W. Irving *Astoria* xliv. III 30 Their horses were.. rendered almost frantic by the stings of the *prairie flies. **1886** A. Winchell *Walks Geol. Field* 280 The *prairie-formation is a stratified formation of fine clay, sand, and alluvial matter. **1807** P. Gass *Jrnl.* 126 Our hunters killed 5 *prairie fowls. **1893** Newton *Dict. Birds* 4 Sometimes they [air-sacs] form large inflatable sacs on the throat, as, for instance, in the Prairie-fowls. **1839** Marryat *Diary Amer.* 1st Ser. I. xvii. 206 [In statistical table of furs] *Prairie fox.. 5,000. **1846** R. B. Sage *Scenes Rocky Mts.* xxviii. 241 For several nights I had a constant visitor in the shape of a prairie-fox,—a creature about twice the size of a large red squirrel. **1876** J. Burroughs *Winter Sunshine* iv. 108 The prairie fox, the cross fox, and the black or silver-gray fox, seem only varieties of the red fox. **1948** A. L. Rand *Mammals E. Rockies* 107 Kit Fox. *Vulpes velox* (Also called Prairie Fox). **1888** Trumbull *Names Birds* 4 *Branta canadensis hutchinsii*... In.. North Carolina, Marsh Goose, and on the coast of Texas, *Prairie Goose. **1812** *Connecticut Courant* 24 Nov. 2/3 In consequence of the Indians setting the *prairie grass on fire. **1890** 'R. Boldrewood' *Col. Reformer* (1891) 267 The prairie-grass of America. **1861** G. F. Berkeley *Sportsm. W. Prairies* xi. 185 Of these beautiful birds of game the *prairie grouse is the largest. **1840** E. Emmons *Rep. Quadrupeds Mass.* 58 *Lepus Virginianus*. Harlan. *Prairie Hare... This species is common throughout the New England States, and is known generally as the White Rabbit. **1866** W. R. King *Sportsman & Naturalist in Canada* 32 The Prairie Hare.. is one of the largest hares of the continent, weighing from seven to eleven pounds, and is of a grey colour tinged with yellow. **1917** H. E. Anthony *Mammals Amer.* 280/1 Although called the Prairie Hare, this species is found also on mountain slopes. **1817** E. P. Fordham *Jrnl.* 17 Dec. in *Personal Narr. Trav.* (1906) viii. 143 Saw some *prairie hawks, blue bodies, ash coloured belly and wings, tipped with black. **1856** Bryant *Prairies* 17 The prairie-hawk that, poised on high, Flaps his broad wings, yet moves not. **1898** H. S. Canfield *Maid of Frontier* 201 With a swoop like the swoop of the prairie hawk down swooping for the quail, the Paint Horse was away. **1907** W. O. Lillibridge *Where Trail Divides* 259 Swift as the swoop of a prairie hawk.. the man's arms were about her. **1835** A. Brunson *Jrnl.* 28 Oct. in *Wisconsin State Hist. Soc. Coll.* (1900) XV. 283 Here I fed myself, but could get nothing but *Prairie hay & pumpkins for my horse. **1845** *Cultivator* II. 93 Without any kind of.. comfort, except what they may gather from a poor supply of prairie hay. **1867** *Harper's Mag.* July 138/2 A little stable, near which were great stacks of prairie hay. **1878** J. H. Beadle *Western Wilds* xxviii. 433 First rate prairie hay, on which stock will keep fat all winter. **1880** D. Currie *Lett. of Rusticus* 6/2 They [*sc.* horses] are being fed with prairie hay. **1949** *Daily Oklahoman* 13 Feb. d. 4/4 More than 2,500 tons of the prairie hay used in the recent haylift operations to save icebound livestock in the western states were supplied by hay growers around Vinita, Okla. **1808** Pike *Sources Mississ.* ii. (1810) App. 4 The.. river is bounded here in a narrow bed of *prairie hills. **1844** G. A. McCall *Lett. fr. Frontiers* (1868) 418 The abrupt *prairie knolls,.. seem in the distance to elevate their rocky summits. **1807** P. Gass *Jrnl.* 34 There is handsome *prairie land on the south. **1837** Ht. Martineau *Soc. Amer.* II. 21 The green, *prairie-like, Canada shore. **1835** C. F. Hoffman *Winter in West* I. 264, I was contented to wrap myself as closely as possible in my buffalo robe, and join him in a game of *prairie loo... The game consists merely in betting upon the number of wild animals seen by either party, towards the side of the vehicle on which he is. **1912** J. Sandilands *Western Canad. Dict.* 35 *Prairie madness*, the melancholia which attacks the lonely homesteader. **1973** H. Robertson *Grass Roots* iii. 53 The loneliness and isolation which contributed to emotional breakdowns known in the West as 'prairie madness'. **1826** J. D. Godman *Amer. Nat. Hist.* II. 114 The *Prairie Marmot... Commonly called Prairie-dog. **1883** *Chambers' Encycl.* VII. 737/1 Prairie dog.. about the size of a squirrel or large rat... A more correct name would be Barking Marmot, or Prairie Marmot. **1888** *Ipswich* (Mass.) *Chron.* 15 Sept. 2/4 Usually a country that is inhabited by prairie dogs, or more properly by prairie marmots, has a thin, atmosphere. **1979** *Jrnl. R. Soc. Arts* CXXVII. 171/2 The prairie marmot at Whipsnade has been seen elsewhere in the downs. **1808** Pike *Sources Mississ.* 31 Caught a curious little animal on the prairie, which my Frenchman termed a *prairie mole. **1846** R. B. Sage *Scenes Rocky Mts.* xii. 110 The *prairie-owl and rattlesnake maintain friendly relations with these inoffensive villagers [*sc.* prairie-dogs]. **1860** C. W. Wilson *Mapping Frontier* (1970) ii. 108 Nothing to disturb me but the melancholy note of the prairie owl. **1907** W. O. Lillibridge *Where Trail Divides* 13 He would have watched the movement of a coyote or a prairie owl, for the simple reason that it was the only visible object endowed with life. **1917** T. G. Pearson *Birds Amer.* II. 101 Short-eared Owl... Other Names.—Marsh Owl; Swamp Owl; Prairie Owl. **1958** *Publ. Amer. Dial. Soc.* xxx. 9 Prairie Owl and prairie dog owl, equally frequent names for the burrowing owl,.. are expressions used by 23% of the Nebraska informants. **1883** J. F. Keane *On Blue-Water* xii. 167 We all jumped up and agreed unanimously to propose the last toast at once in the shape of a *prairie oyster—an egg broken into a cup without smashing the yolk, the toast poured in on the top of it, and the whole taken at a swallow. **1907** *Daily Chron.* 4 Feb. 4/7 A wistful pet name for an egg, duly seasoned and to be swallowed whole—the 'prairie oyster'. **1912** 'Saki' *Chron. Clovis* 275 He hurriedly ordered another prairie oyster. **1920** [see *bromo-seltzer* s.v. bromo-]. **1939** C. Isherwood *Goodbye to Berlin* 51 Would you like a Prairie Oyster? **1941** *Amer. Speech* XVI. 181 English slang metaphor also has its place, as.. *prairie oyster* for the testicles of a steer, a food morsel considered dainty. **1955** W. Foster-Harris *Look of Old West* viii. 234 Prairie or mountain oysters were an unmentionable part of a male animal. **1960** *Spectator* 25 Nov. 878 A Prairie Oyster, which is the raw yolk of an egg slipped whole into a glass containing a tablespoon of Worcester Sauce and a dash of sherry, with a flick of red pepper. **1979** A. Jute *Reverse Negative* 26 His eyes were bloodshot. His prairie oysters must have lost their potency. **1848** E. Bryant *California* ii. 28, I observed, also, a plant producing a fruit of the size of the walnut, called the *prairie-pea. **1870** *Amer. Naturalist* III. 162 One of the earliest flowers [of the Kansas plains] is the Prairie-pea. **1943** B. A. De Voto *Year of Decision* 155 They.. made spiced pickles of the 'prairie peas'. **1874** Coues *Birds N.W.* 503 In most parts of the West, between the Mississippi and the Rocky Mountains, this Tattler, commonly known as the '*Prairie Pigeon', is exceedingly abundant. **1937** *Nat. Geogr. Mag.* Aug. 200/1 The Eskimo curlew, or 'dough bird' or 'prairie pigeon', as it was called by the gunners, apparently rivaled the passenger pigeon in numbers prior to 1885. **1831** W. Sewall *Diary* 50 Apr. (1930) 136 Sat off with the team, and a *prairie plow which came on late last night with instructions, to commence breaking prairie. **1840** *Cultivator* VII. 33/1 It may be amusing to eastern readers, to hear a description of a 'prairie plow'. **1861** *Trans. Illinois Agric. Soc.* IV. 392 The sod should be broken with a prairie plow. **1875** Knight *Dict. Mech.* 1782/1 *Prairie-plow*, a large plow supported in front on wheels, and adapted to pare and overturn a very broad but shallow furrow-slice. **1851** W. Kelly *Excursion to California* I. v. 83 A stand of *prairie plover most opportunely made their appearance as we pulled up. **1888** Trumbull *Names Birds* 173 *Bartramia longicauda*... In Southern Wisconsin,.. in 1851 this bird.. was known as the Prairie Plover, and also as the Prairie Snipe. **1940** E. T. Seton *Trail of Artist-Naturalist* xxxii. 299 The white-tailed longspurs, the prairie plover, were all gone, wholly routed by the plough. **1828** J. C. Beltrami *Pilgrimage in Europe & Amer.* II. xvii. 321 Everything appeared to me delicious, even some roots which they call *prairie-potatoes, and which I had before thought detestable. **1848** E. Bryant *California* iv. 54 A root or tuber, of an oval shape, about one and one-half-inch in length.. is called the prairie potato. **1891** *Canadian Indian* Mar. 168 The prairie potato.. yields when dry a light, starchy flour, and is often cut into thin slices and dried for winter. **1917** H. Kephart *Camping & Woodcraft* II. xxi. 379 Potato, Prairie. Prairie turnip... Palatable in any form. **1876** J. C. Hamilton (*title*) The *Prairie Province: sketches of travel from Lake Ontario to Lake Winnipeg. **1881** *Progress* (Rat Portage, Ontario) 12 Nov. 4/1 The editor of the Woodstock (Ont.) *Sentinel-Review*, proposes.. to get up a huge excursion of marriageable girls in Ontario to proceed early next spring to the prairie province. **1908** M. A. Brown *My Lady of Snows* 221 The majority ruled, but the minority clamored from the prairie provinces. **1916** O. D. Skelton *Day of Sir W. Laurier* 97 The Winnipeg Board of Trade denounced the policy of 'crushing and trampling upon one hundred thousand struggling pioneers of the prairie province to secure a purely imaginary financial gain to one soulless corporation'. **1952** D. F. Putnam *Canad. Regions* 340/1 Manitoba, Saskatchewan and Alberta are known as the 'Prairie Provinces' because they include the Canadian section of the vast grass-covered interior plains of North America. **1959** *Manch. Guardian* 5 Aug. 4/4 Some of his [*sc.* Mr. John Diefenbaker's] friends in the prairie provinces think he has been clever to keep the Easterners out. **1965** *Globe & Mail* (Toronto) 5 Jan. b 5/1 All three Prairie provinces are particularly unhappy about the special incentives being offered to attract industrial enterprises. **1965** R. M. Hamilton *Canad. Quotations & Phrases* 130/2 The Prairie Province. From the title of the book which gave the phrase general circulation; after 1905 it was extended to include Saskatchewan and Alberta in 'The Prairie Provinces'. **1973** *Fisheries Fact Sheet* (Environment Canada Fisheries & Marine Service) No. 1. 4/3 The larger bodies of water in the Prairie Provinces. **1977** D. MacKenzie *Raven & Kamikaze* xi. 132 She'd come to England straight from a prairie-province university... Her father [was] a veterinarian in Saskatoon. **1878** J. H. Beadle *Western Wilds* 133 The only dangerous snakes are the little *prairie rattlers, seldom over two feet long. **1948** *Chicago Tribune* 30 May 14 A prairie rattler coils to strike; its prey is a rabbit. **1977** *New Yorker* 6 June 47/2 One.. took up pentecostalism and died from shock while caressing a prairie rattler at a revival meeting back east in Tennessee. **1817** S. R. Brown *Western Gazetteer* 31 The only venomous serpents, are the common and *prairie rattlesnake, and copper-heads. **1843** [see Missisauga 2]. **1853** Baird & Girard *Catal. N. Amer. Reptiles* i. 14 *Crotalophorus tergeminus*.. Prairie Rattlesnake, Massasanga. **1873** 'Mark Twain' & Warner *Gilded Age* 125 Prairie-rattlesnakes.. never strike above the knee. **1948** *Natural Hist.* Apr. 187/1 An extensive campaign was waged against the prairie rattlesnake. **1961** C. H. Pope *Giant Snakes* (1962) 152 In the northern United States the prairie rattlesnake may not give first birth until it is four or even five years old. **1884** Knight *Dict. Mech.* Suppl., **Prairie Renovator*, an implement with tearing harrow teeth, drawn over the surface of grass land to loosen the roots and the soil,.. and break up the matted vegetation. **1895** M. Davitt in *Westm. Gaz.* 25 Mar. 3/3 The annual value of such land, in its original or pre-reclaimed condition, would be its '*prairie rent'. **1822** J. Woods *Two Years' Residence Eng. Prairie* 303 The *prairie-roses, balm.. and sassafras-wood.. have all powerful scents. **1862** Ripley & Dana *Amer. Cycl.* XIV. 180/1 The climbing rose (*R. setigera*).. sending up shoots 10 to 20 feet high in a season; from it have originated numerous beautiful double-flowered varieties known in gardens as prairie roses. **1888** *Century Mag.* Mar. 662/2 The carpet of prairie roses, whose short stalks lift the beautiful blossoms but a few inches from the ground. **1946** E. B. Thompson *Amer. Daughter* 36 We gazed in awe upon the prairie rose, a delicate pink flower growing close to the ground, whose thorny stem belied its tender beauty. **1963** *Canad. Geogr. Jrnl.* Aug. 54/2 Later the hardy prairie rose makes its appearance and fills the air with its sweet scent. **1851** Mayne Reid *Scalp Hunt.* iii, To see the long caravan of waggons, the '*prairie ships', deployed over the plain. **1893** *Jrnl. Amer. Folk-Lore* VI. 136 *Anemone patens*, var. *Nuttalliana*... gosling, *prairie smoke, crocus. **1952** *Sun* (Baltimore) 26 Feb. 10/7 The Pasqueflower.. is a bluish open bell shaped wild flower of the prairies... Patches of the flower at a distance give the impression of a bluish haze. This gives rise to its more familiar name 'prairie smoke'. **1958** *Weekend Mag.* (Montreal) 7 June 38/1 Earliest of spring flowers, Manitoba's crocus grows so profusely in places that it looks like a low-lying mist. Hence its nickname: the 'Prairie smoke'. **1845** J. C. Frémont *Rep. Exploring Expedition* 12 A large *prairie snake..was occupied in eating the young birds. **1851** W. Kelly *Excursion to California* I. v. 80, I shot a brace of *prairie snipe. **1917** T. G. Pearson *Birds Amer.* I. 247 Upland Plover. *Bartramia longicauda*... [Also called] Prairie Snipe. **1817** S. R. Brown *Western Gazetteer* 66 The common field near the town contains nearly 5000 acres, of excellent *prairie soil. **1876** *Trans. Illinois Dept. Agric.* XIII. 288 The prairie soils are usually darker, more crude, coarser and wetter than the woodland. **1910** C. G. Hopkins *Soil Fertility* vi. 79 The undulating prairie soils vary from a gray silt loam on light clay in the older areas, to a dark brown silt loam, in the later formations, and the common flat prairie soils vary with age from drab silt loam to black clay loam. **1928** C. F. Marbut in *Proc. & Papers 1st Internat. Congr. Soil Sci.* IV. 21 The podsolic and lateritic soils of category VI have been subdivided into 8 sub-groups consisting of Tundra, Podsols, Brown Forest soils, Red soils, Yellow soils, Prairie soils (dark colored humid soils), Laterites and Ferruginous Laterites. **1974** E. A. FitzPatrick *Introd. Soil Sci.* vii. 116 In the U.S.A. and elsewhere there are prairie soils or brunizems which are similar to chernozems but they have a middle horizon with a clay maximum and are slightly less fertile. **1946** Auden *Under Which Lyre* in *Harvard Alumni Bull.* 15 June 707/1 The sophomoric Who face the future's darkest hints With giggles or with *prairie squints As stout as Cortez. **1963** R. D. Symons *Many Trails* ix. 92 He wears a grey felt hat, beneath which his tanned face is puckered in the 'prairie squint'. **1808** Pike *Sources Mississ.* II. (1810) 155 We..killed some *prairie squirrels, or wishtonwishes [cf. quot. 1808 in prairie-dog]. **1860** Bartlett *Dict. Amer.* s.v., *Spermophilus*..with great propriety called 'Prairie-Squirrels', for their true home is on the prairie. **1842** *People's Advocate* (Carrollton, Illinois) 6 Aug. 4/5 Federal Coon Whiggery extinct in the *Prairie State! **1852** Mrs. Stowe *Uncle Tom's Cabin* II. xlv. 316 Farmers of rich and joyous Ohio, and ye of the wide prairie states. **1861** O. J. Victor *Hist. Southern Rebellion* I. 166 Illinois, the 'Prairie State', then proved that she was as rich in her patriotism as in her soil and exhaustless resources. **1868** *Rep. U.S. Comm. Agric.* 127 Permitting the unparalleled soil of our prairie States to grow less and less productive. **1868** *Harper's Mag.* June 123/2 When he pronounced 'good-by' to the Prairie State, at the State line, he said, 'Behind the cloud the sun is shining still.' **1949** J. Monaghan *This is Illinois* 138 The nation began to hum the wonders of the Prairie State. **1963** R. I. McDavid *Mencken's Amer. Lang.* 691 Illinois has had many nicknames ..but *Prairie State* and *Sucker State* are the only ones surviving. **1970** *Daily Progress* (Charlottesville, Va.) 24 May 4/1 Illinois is the Prairie state. **1855** A. M. Murray *Let.* 5 Sept. (1856) II. 290 About forty miles from Chicago we passed the first *prairie town of Joliet. **1867** *Atlantic Monthly* Mar. 326/1 Chicago, for fifteen years after it began its rapid increase, was perhaps of all prairie towns the most repulsive to every human sense. **1908** Kipling in *Collier's* 28 Mar. 11/1 'If you go as far as Winnipeg, you'll see the finest hotel in all the world.' 'Nonsense!' he said. 'You're pulling my leg! Winnipeg's a prairie-town.' **1977** H. Osborne *White Poppy* viii. 68 A prairie town in a cowboy film. **1814** Brackenridge *Jrnl.* in *Views Louisiana* 249 The *prairie turnip is a root very common in the prairies, with something of the taste of turnip, but more dry. **1857** J. Palliser *Jrnls.* (1863) 38 The root..receives the name of the Prairie Turnip by the half-breeds, who, with Indians, use it as food. **1941** D. McCowan *Naturalist in Canada* 246 The Crees and the Blackfeet were glad to make a meal from the edible root of the Prairie Turnip. **1956** D. Leechman *Native Tribes Canada* 110 The Prairie Indians also ate service berries, wild cherries, red willow berries, prairie turnips, bitter root, and wild rose haws. **1851** Mayne Reid *Scalp Hunt.* xxxv, A life spent beneath the blue heaven of the *prairie-uplands and the mountain 'parks'. **1884** *Contemp. Rev.* Feb. 185 The..doctrine of '*prairie value', which has been held up to the Irish peasantry as the standard by which rent ought to be measured. **1893** Ld. Rosebery in *Daily News* 2 Mar. 6/2 We took our Colonies at prairie value, and have made them what they are. **1898** *Allbutt's Syst. Med.* V. 825 Refusing to go beyond the bare etymology—'the prairie value'—of the name. **1856** *Prairie wagon [see ambulance 3]. **1867** W. H. Dixon *New Amer.* I. iii. 37 We find that our big Concord coach has been exchanged for a light prairie waggon. **1948** *Chicago Daily News* 10 Apr. 6/2, I have an idea that too much of the squirrel rifle and prairie wagon tradition still runs in the bloodstream of most Americans. **1811** A. Wilson *Amer. Ornithol.* III. 87 [The] *Prairie Warbler..I first discovered in that singular tract of country in Kentucky, commonly called the Barrens. **1868** Wood *Homes without H.* xiii. 248 Another pensile species is the Prairie Warbler (*Sylvia minuta*). **1874** Coues *Birds N.W.* 63 *Dendrœca discolor*... Prairie Warbler. **1917** T. G. Pearson *Birds Amer.* III. 150/1 The Prairie Warbler is not very common on the prairies. **1960** R. T. Peterson *Field Guide Birds of Texas* 217 Prairie Warbler... This warbler wags its tail. **1804** Lewis & Clark *Orig. Jrnls. Lewis & Clark Expedition* (1904) I. ii. 108 A *Prarie Wolf come [*sic*] near the bank and Barked at us this evening. **1807** P. Gass *Jrnl.* 40 One of our men caught a beaver, and killed a prairie wolf. **1858** E. J. Lewis in Youatt *Dog* i. 18 The *Canis Latrans*, or prairie wolf, who whines and barks in a manner so similar to the smaller varieties of dogs. **1898** H. S. Canfield *Maid of Frontier* 39 The long howl of the prairie wolf rose on the air and hung tremulant. **1948** *Daily Ardmoreite* (Ardmore, Okla.) 18 Apr. 14/7 There are practically only two distinct kinds of wolves in America—the large gray timber wolf and the coyote or prairie wolf. **1963** R. D. Symons *Many Trails* 121 The grey jackal of the plains..we call in English the prairie wolf, but more often in corruption of its Aztec name, coyote. **1934** G. Bettany *Valley of Lost Gold* 284 She loved..every blade of *prairie wool. **1953** *Canad. Geogr. Jrnl.* June 245/1 The sheep crop the 'prairie wool'—that excellent hard forage composed of spear-grass, bunch-grass and buffalo-grass. **1970** [see *June grass*]. **1973** R. D. Symons *Where Wagon Led* I. i. 13 The prairie grass was curled and dimpled—that's why they call it 'prairie wool'.

Hence **'prairied** *a.*, containing or characterized by prairies; **'prairiedom,** **1845** (*title*) Prairiedom: Rambles and Scrambles in Texas or New Estrémadura. **1849** Whittier *Our State* i, The South land boasts its teeming cane, The prairied West its heavy grain. **1851** Mayne Reid *Scalp Hunt.* vi, (Santa Fè) The metropolis of all prairiedom. **1930** H. N. Spalding *From Youth to Age* 58 The happy cornlands of the prairied West.

'prairie-'chicken. A North American grouse found in prairie regions and belonging to one of three species of the family Tetraonidæ, *Tympanuchus cupido*, *T. pallidicinctus*, or *Pediœcetes phasianellus*. Also *fig.*

1840 *Picayune* (New Orleans) 13 Sept. 2/2 The travelling public will find..a fine table covered with white fish..and prairie chickens. **1851** Mayne Reid *Scalp Hunt.* ii, A dinner at the Planters', with its venison steaks, its buffalo tongues, its 'prairie chicken'. **1863** Dicey *Federal St.* II. 144 Dun-coloured prairie chickens whirring through the heather as we drove along. **1893** *Westm. Gaz.* 1 Apr. 6/1 The prairie chickens (sharp-tailed grouse) meet every morning at grey dawn in companies of from six to twenty. **1949** *N. Dakota Hist.* Jan. 14 The 'coo' of the prairie chicken and the twittering of the meadow-lark greet us. **1963** *Canadian Weekly* 30 Mar. 18/4 In 1945 the prairie chicken, or sharp-tailed grouse, by enactment was made an emblem of Saskatchewan. **1976** *National Observer* (U.S.) 3 July 10/6 He took Nicholson and his gang of cutthroats..and that cute little prairie chicken, Kathleen Lloyd, and made a damned good and entertaining movie. **1978** C. Harrison *Field Guide Nests, Eggs & Nestlings N. Amer. Birds* 101 Greater Prairie Chicken... Nestling. Precocial and downy. Down pattern like that of the Lesser Prairie Chicken.

'prairie-dog. A N. American rodent animal, genus *Cynomys*, of the squirrel family; *spec. C. Ludovicianus*, the Louisiana Marmot, a thickset short-tailed animal about a foot in length, and having a cry like the bark of a dog; large numbers of these animals live together in burrows, forming a 'village' or 'town'.

1774 J. R. Peyton in J. L. Peyton *Adventures of my Grandfather* (1867) xii. 121 One of the singular and interesting sights on my route was the villages of the Prairie dogs. **1807** P. Gass *Jrnl.* 37 On their return [they] killed a prairie dog, in size about that of the smallest of domestic dogs. **1808** Pike *Sources Mississ.* II. (1810) 156 *note*, The Wishtonwish of the Indians, prairie dogs of some travellers; or squirrels as I should be inclined to denominate them; reside on the prairies of Louisiana in towns or villages. **1851** Mayne Reid *Scalp Hunt.* iv, We struck through a village of 'prairie dogs'. **1859** E. H. N. Patterson in L. Hafen *Overland Routes to Gold Fields* (1942) 110 Visited a prairie dog town this evening, which covers eighty acres. **1867** [see lay-out 2 b]. **1870** Keim *Sheridan's Troopers* 301 Early in the afternoon we entered a prairie-dog town. **1902** O. Wister *Virginian* xvi. 176 There is a brown skunk down in Arkansaw. Kind of prairie-dog brown. **1914** B. M. Bower *Flying U Ranch* 135 There ain't enough grass in our lower field to graze a prairie dog. **1932** S. Zuckerman *Social Life Monkeys* ii. 23 Most writers describe the prairie dog of North America as an animal that lives in vast colonies. **1947** *Chicago Daily News* 20 Mar. 14/3 [They] make my book resemble a head of lettuce that has been gnawed by a pack of prairie dogs. **1961** *Maclean's Mag.* 29 July 23, I've seen me ..lying at the edge of a field in Saskatchewan spying on the prairie dogs. **1976** *Billings* (Montana) *Gaz.* 1 July 2-A/4 Flath contends, however, that the endangered black-footed ferret lives within prairie dog towns.

'prairie-'hen. = prairie-chicken.

1804 Lewis & Clark *Orig. Jrnls. Lewis & Clark Expedition* (1904) I. iv. 181 Capt. Lewis..Saw great numbers of Prarie hens. **1805** Pike *Sources Mississ.* (1810) 44 Killed nothing but five prairie hens, which afforded us this day's subsistence. **1841** Catlin *N. Amer. Ind.* (1844) II. xxxiii. 16 The Prairie Hen is..very much like the English grouse, or heath hen, both in size, colour, and in habits. **1888** Trumbull *Names Birds* 135 *note*, There is still another pinnated-grouse variety, found in the Southwest, and known in the books as *Tympanuchus pallidicinctus*, also as Texas Prairie Hen, Lesser Prairie Hen, and Pale Pinnated Grouse. **1909** G. Parker *Northern Lights* 336 A prairie hen rustled by with a shrill cluck. **1933** *Sun* (Baltimore) 15 Apr. 4/2 Dr. Gross considered the advisability of mating the heath hen with a Wisconsin prairie hen.

'prairie 'schooner. *N. Amer.* A fanciful name for the large covered wagons used by emigrants in crossing the N. American plains, before the construction of railways. Cf. *prairie ship* (prairie b). Also *Austral. colloq.* (see quot. 1911[1]).

1841 E. R. Steele *Summer Journey in West* 134 So much is this appearance acknowledged by the country people that they call the stage coach, a prairie schooner. **1847** T. Weed *Let.* in T. W. Barnes *Mem. T. Weed* (1884) II. 149 We found the road..occupied with an almost unbroken line of wagons, drawn generally by two yokes of oxen, bringing wheat to the city. These teams are called 'prairie schooners'. **1858** *New York Tribune* 7 June 5/6 In our streets [Lawrence, Kansas] may be seen large covered wagons, alias 'prairie schooners'... These wagons are generally drawn by oxen, otherwise by mules. **1867** [see double-decker b]. **1882** *Harper's Mag.* Dec. 5/1 The prairie schooner, or large lumbering freight wagon,..looms up in the distance. **1904** [see schooner *sb.*[1] 2]. **1911** C. E. W. Bean *'Dreadnought' of Darling* vii. 67 An old white-bearded patriarch of a fellow that had once appeared in one of the up-river towns with a 'prairie schooner'—one of those big white-hooded sort of ambulance waggons which the travelling hawkers drive from homestead to homestead over the plains in the West. **1911** *Daily Colonist* (Victoria, B.C.) 21 Apr. 4/2 Last summer one Sunday morning on the Cariboo road a prairie schooner stood by the roadside. **1949** *Amer. Speech* XXIV. 259 Hordes of treasure seekers from regions east of the mountains crossed the plains in covered wagons, the ships of the desert of the early Western emigrants. Such wagons in various regions were known as..*prairie schooners*. **1955** W. Foster-Harris *Look of Old West* vi. 159 The prairie schooners, developed from the Conestoga were smaller but still too heavy and clumsy for mountain work or badly broken country. **1957** L. Eiseley *Immense Journey* 19, I slid over shallows that had buried the broken axles of prairie schooners. **1961** [see Conestoga 2]. **1977** *Time* 14 Feb. 54/1 There it will begin tests that will culminate in flights that could do for space colonization what the prairie schooner and the railroads did for the settling of America.

prairillon (prɛ'rɪljən). Now *rare*. [dim. of *prairie*, prob. of American French origin: cf. F. *goupillon*, *vermillon*, etc.] A small prairie.

1843 J. C. Frémont *Rep. Exploration* 60 We were posted in a grove of beech,..with a narrow *prairillon* on the inner side. **1846** R. B. Sage *Scenes Rocky Mts.* 172 Interspersed among the hills are frequent openings and prairillons of rich soil and luxuriant vegetation. **1872** Schele De Vere *Americanisms* ii. 100 The *prairillon*, or little prairie, is fast disappearing from our idiom.

prais, obs. Sc. form of press *sb.*

praisable ('preɪzəb(ə)l), *a.* Now *rare*. Also 7–9 **praiseable.** [f. praise *v.* + -able.] Deserving of praise; praiseworthy, laudable, commendable.

13.. *Minor Poems fr. Vernon MS.* xlix. 314 In good tyme he was boren, I-wis, þat preisable is and not preised is. **1382** Wyclif *Lev.* xix. 24 The ferthe forsothe ȝeer al the fruyt of hem shal be halowid and preysable [1388 preiseful; *Vulg.* laudabilis] to the Lord. **1388** —— *2 Tim.* ii. 15 Bisili kepe to ȝyue thi silf a preued preisable werkman to God. *a* **1400** *Te Deum* in *Prymer* (1891) 22 The preysable nowmbre of prophetis [*L.* prophetarum laudabilis numerus]. **1509** Fisher *Fun. Serm. on C'tess of Richmond* Wks. (1876) 291 She had in maner all that was praysable in a woman, eyther in soule or in body. **1602** Segar *Hon. Mil. & Civ.* II. xviii. 91 To encourage these Gentlemen in so praiseable an enterprise. **1716** M. Davies *Athen. Brit.* II. 424 Laudable or Praisable Subsistency or Co-originating Resultancy. **1891** *Review of Rev.* 14 Nov. 517/2 This simple and praiseable quality of work.

Hence **'praisableness; 'praisably** *adv.*

1557 Cheke in T. Hoby tr. *Castiglione's Courtyer* ad fin., Then doth our tung naturallie and praisablie vtter her meaning. **1648–60** Hexham *Dutch Dict.*, *Lofwaerdigheydt*, praiseablenesse, or Laudablenesse. **1733** *Oxf. Lat. Gram.* To Rdr. A v b, No word..to be so hard..as the Scholar shall not be able praisably to enter into the forming thereof.

praisant, obs. Sc. f. present *sb.*[2]

praise (preɪz), *sb.* Forms: 5 **preyse**, 6–7 **prayse**, 6– **praise**, (6 **prease**, **prayes**, *Sc.* **prais**, **prayis(s**, 6–7 **prase**). [f. praise *v.* Not known till after 1400, and not common till after 1500. Absent from Wright-Wülcker's *Vocabs.*, *Promp. Parv.*, and *Catholicon*. See also pres *sb.*]

1. a. The action or fact of praising; the expression in speech of estimation or honour; commendation of the worth or excellence of a person or thing; eulogy; laud, laudation.

c **1430** Lydg. *Min. Poems* (Percy) 3 This citee with lawde, preyse, and glorye, For joy moustered lyke the sone beme. **1526** Tindale *John* xii. 43 For they loved the prayse that is geven off men, more then the prayse, that commeth of god. **1554–9** *Songs & Ball.* (1860) 5, I wyll not paynt to purchace prayes. **1562** Winȝet *Cert. Tractatis* i. (S.T.S.) I. 4 Albeit the time be schort, sumthing of ȝour prais man we speik. *a* **1586** Montgomerie *Misc. Poems* l. 35 Or had this nymphe bene in these dayis..Venus had not obtenit sic prayis. **1592** Kyd *Sol. & Pers.* III. i. 25 These praises..makes me wish that I had beene at Rhodes. *a* **1631** Donne *Poems* (1650) 95 He gave no prase, To any but my Lord of Essex dayes. **1651** Hobbes *Leviath.* I. vi. 30 The forme of Speech whereby men signifie their opinion of the Goodnesse of any thing, is Praise. **1742** Young *Night Th.* VII. 420 Praise is the salt that seasons right to man, And whets his appetite for moral good. **1858** Froude *Hist. Eng.* IV. xviii. 64 At the end of the conversation the king dismissed him with emphatic praise. *a* **1908** *Mod.* Those who have seen the work are loud in their praises of it.

b. Viewed as a condition or quality of the receiver: The fact or condition of being praised.

1533 *St. Papers Hen. VIII*, VII. 463 Some good meane founden..to the noo litle prease and profet of boothe [King and Pope]. **1535** Coverdale *Ecclus.* xliv. 13 For their sakes shal their children & sede contynue for euer, & their prayse [*L. gloria eorum*] shal neuer be put downe. **1610** Holland *Camden's Brit.* (1637) 632 For he the praises farre surmounts of his Progenitours. **1681–6** J. Scott *Chr. Life* (1747) III. 564 Reflecting still the same Honour, and Praise, and Glory upon it. **1849** Macaulay *Hist. Eng.* ii. I. 180 The praise of politeness and vivacity could now scarcely be obtained except by some violation of decorum.

c. A laudatory utterance; *spec.* = *praise poem*.

1861 tr. *Casalis's Basutos* II. xvii. 328 We often heard them recite, with very dramatic gestures, certain pieces... The natives called these recitations *praises*. **1901** G. M. Theal *Rec. S.-E. Afr.* VII. 202 When the king goes out he is surrounded and encircled by these *marombes*, who recite these praises to him with loud cries, to the sound of small drums, iron and bells. **1929** *Bantu Stud.* (Johannesburg) July 201 We are concerned..with 'Izibongo' as the term denoting the 'Praises' of the Zulu Chiefs. **1937** G. P. Lestrade in I. Schapera *Bantu-Speaking Tribes S. Afr.* xiii. 300 The tribal praise-poem reciter..makes a new praise from time to time. **1968** T. Cope *Izibongo: Zulu Praise-Poems* 51 The most primitive type of praise-poem is simply a collection of praises consisting for the most part of single lines or verses. **1970** R. Finnegan *Oral Lit. in Afr.* v. 111 The formalized praises which are directed publicly to kings, chiefs, and leaders, and which are composed and recited by members of a king's official entourage. **1979** G. Fortune in Hodza & Fortune *Shona Praise Poetry* 3 Fragments of the praises of individual kings of the Changamire dynasty have come down to us included in the clan praises of the Rozvi.

2. The expression of admiration and ascribing of glory, as an act of worship; *hence*, as this is chiefly done in song, the musical part of worship.

14.. in *Tundale's Vision* (1843) 127 Glorye and preyse laude and hye honoure O blisfull quene be gevon unto the. **1593** Shaks. *3 Hen. VI*, iv. vi. 44, I my selfe will lead a priuate Life, And in deuotion spend my latter dayes, To sinnes rebuke, and my Creators prayse. **1697** Dryden *Virg. Georg.* ii. 543 To Bacchus therefore let us tune our Lays, And in our Mother Tongue resound his Praise. **1750** Gray *Elegy* x, The pealing anthem swells the note of praise. **1776** Bp. Horne *Comm. on Ps.* xxxiii. 2 Music.. is of eminent use in setting forth the praises of God. **1841** Lane *Arab. Nts.* I. 114 The King rejoiced at his words, and said, Praise be to God. **1866** Newman *Hymn*, Praise to the Holiest in the height, And in the depth be praise. **1866** *Direct. Angl.* (ed. 3) 258 Praise of the Office. That portion of Matins and Even Song from the *Gloria* inclusive to the *Credo* exclusive. **1892** Bp. Talbot *Serm.* (1896) 76 Praise, like every real part of true religion, fits on to human nature...by fulfilling, I think, two great human instincts. They are the instinct of admiration and the instinct of love.

3. *transf.* **a.** That for which a person or thing is, or deserves to be, praised; praiseworthiness; merit, value, virtue. *arch.*

1526 *Pilgr. Perf.* (W. de W. 1531) 12 All this processe we haue made to shewe the prayse & dignite of grace. **1589** Puttenham *Eng. Poesie* iii. i. (Arb.) 150 The chief prayse and cunning of our Poet is in the discreet vsing of his figures. **1596** Shaks. *Merch. V.* v. i. 108 How many things by season, season'd are To their right praise, and true perfection. **1781** Cowper *Retirement* 23 A restless crowd,.. Whose highest praise is that they live in vain. **1885–94** R. Bridges *Eros & Psyche* June xix, When she should bear a boy To be her growing stay and godlike praise.

†**b.** An object or subject of praise. (Sometimes, esp. *Sc. colloq.*, put instead of the divine name.) *Obs.*

1535 Coverdale *Deut.* x. 21 He is thy prayse, & thy God. *a* **1724** *Gaberlunȝieman* v, She dancid her lane, cry'd, Praise be blest! I have ludg'd a leil poor man. **1738** Gray *Propertius* iii. 104 Of all our youth the Ambition and the Praise! **1782** Callander *Anc. Scot. Poems* 45 *note*, *Praise be blest*, God be praised. This is a common form still in Scotland with such as, from reverence, decline to use the sacred name. **1787** Skinner *Poet. Epist. to Burns* xii, But thanks to praise, ye're i' your prime.

4. *attrib.* and *Comb.*, as ***praise-folk***, ***-giver***, ***-prater***, ***-song***, ***-trap***; (in sense 2) ***praise-book***, ***-house***, ***-meeting***, ***-night***, ***-offering***, ***-portion***, ***-time***; ***praise-begging***, ***-deserving***, ***-giving***, ***-winning***, etc., adjs.; **praise-house** *U.S.*, a small meeting-house for religious services; **praise-leader** *Sc.*, the leader of the singing in a church; **praise name**, in Africa, a name or title used in ceremonial contexts; a name applied to the subject of a praise poem; **praise poem**, a laudatory poem; *spec.* one of a genre belonging to the oral tradition of certain African peoples; so ***praise poet***, ***poetry***; **praise-reciter** = *praise poet* above; **praise song**, a laudatory song; *spec.* in Africa, = *praise poem* above; so ***praise-singer***, ***-singing***; **praise-way** *adv.*, in the way or direction of praise.

1899 *Westm. Gaz.* 6 May 3/1 Giving to people who may use the Church Hymnary a guide..to use that *Praise Book with great interest and appreciation. *a* **1450** *Tourn. Tottenham* 215 (Ritson) The *prayse-folk, that hur led, Wer of the torniment. **1565** Harding in Jewel *Def. Apol.* (1611) 242 It is *praisgiuing to God, and praying for the people, for Kings, for the rest. **1862** H. Ware in E. W. Pearson *Lett. from Port Royal* (1906) 20, I went with him to the *praise-house, where he has his school. **1869** T. W. Higginson *Army Life* 20 The little old church or 'praise-house'. **1920** C. Jerdan *Scottish Clerical Stories* xviii. 370 The minister.. looked down over the side of the pulpit and said to the *praise-leader, 'Is David ill?' **1862** J. M. McKim in *N. Amer. & U.S. Gaz.* 14 July 1/8 When dey come to de *praise meeting dat night dey sing about it. **1862** H. Ware in E. W. Pearson *Lett. from Port Royal* (1906) 36 He had been up to the praise-meeting by Uncle Peter's invitation. **1863** H. G. Spaulding in *Continental Monthly* Aug. 195/1 The present opportunities for religious worship which the freedmen enjoy consist of their 'praise meetings'—similar in most respects to our prayer meetings. **1904** D. Kidd *Essential Kafir* ii. 91 If the trouble does not vanish..the people..say to the spirits, 'When have we ceased to kill cattle for you, and when have we ever refused to praise you by your *praise-names?' **1932** C. Fuller *Louis Trigardt's Trek* vii. 79 Molamoso ruled the country... This refers, however, to Legadimane, whose family or 'praise name' was Molamoso. **1935** *Critic* (Cape Town) Oct. 2 The Tswana-speaking clan called the *Ba Ra Moseki* has as its praise-name the name *Mokwena* (from *kwena*, 'crocodile', the 'totem' of the clan), and every member of that clan is addressed as *Mokwena* on suitable occasions. **1968** T. Cope *Izibongo: Zulu Praise Poems* i. ii. 26 A clan name is the personal name of its founder, and personal names are essentially praise-names. **1979** G. Fortune in Hodza & Fortune *Shona Praise Poetry* 71 The praise name is the most frequently used construction in praise poetry... Structurally the praise name is a single noun or a single complex nominal construction, one of whose constituents is a class affix. **1864** H. Ware in E. W. Pearson *Lett. from Port Royal* (1906) 253 It was not *praise-night. **1867** *Nation* (N.Y.) 30 May 432/2 But the true 'shout' takes place on Sundays or on 'praise' nights..either in the praise-house or in some cabin. *a* **1711** Ken *Edmund* Poet. Wks. 1721 I. 255 Soon as *Praise-offerings at the Throne I pay. **1935** *Critic* (Cape Town) Oct. 4 A *praise-poem..consists of a number of stanzas, following each other in different order in different versions of the same poem. **1957** S. Einarsson *Hist. Icelandic Lit.* 44 Most scholars assume that skaldic poetry originated at the courts of kings, the poems being praise poems to celebrate the deeds of these kings. **1965** I. Schapera *Praise Poems of Tswana Chiefs* 6 It is still..common for someone to..recite praise-poems. **1977** *Amer. N. & Q.* XV. 148/2 The *Prothalamion* has not been sufficiently studied in the light of Horace's *Carmina*, several of which are praise-poems. **1979** G. Fortune in Hodza & Fortune *Shona Praise Poetry* p. x, The praise poems are written in the standard Shona orthography. **1935** *Critic* (Cape Town) Oct. 7 The old *praise-poets had to compose in their heads, and had to remember as they went along. **1937** G. P. Lestrade in I. Schapera *Bantu-Speaking Tribes S. Afr.* xiii. 296 Persons of but modest rank..compose their own praise-poems,..while those of higher status have theirs composed by..the praise-poets. **1965** I. Schapera *Praise Poems of Tswana Chiefs* 5 There are..in every tribe some men who specialize in composing and reciting praises of chiefs... This they do not merely..to establish..a personal reputation as a *mmôki* (praise-poet, praise-reciter), but also in the hope of reward. **1970** R. Finnegan *Oral Lit. in Afr.* v. 111 The 'praise names'..often form the basis of formal *praise poetry. **1971** *Listener* 2 Sept. 290/3 What is nowadays called 'bardic poetry' which is a genus of praise-poetry. **1977** *Westindian World* 3–9 June 13/4 It is sheer praise-poetry. **1979** G. Fortune in Hodza & Fortune *Shona Praise Poetry* 2 Praise poetry, especially of the more formal kind, is a mode of expression that is disappearing owing to urbanization and the replacement of traditional methods of education by schools. **1610** Holland *Camden's Brit.* ii. 143 If they bestow not upon one of these *Praise-Praters the best garments they have. **1935** *Critic* (Cape Town) Oct. 7 A *praise-reciter, whose business it is to know and remember praise-poems. **1965** Praise-reciter [see *praise poet* above]. **1954** M. F. Smith *Baba of Karo* i. iii. 62 When you hear drumming, you hear the deep drum and you hear the *praise-singers—you'll give them money! **1963** W. Soyinka *Lion & Jewel* 61 And then I have to hire a praise-singer, And such a number of ceremonies Must firstly be performed. **1977** *Eastern Province Herald* (S. Afr.) 27 Apr., The installation of the new Chancellor..was a dignified affair but it is difficult to understand what relevance a Xhosa praise singer had to the function. **1957** *Africa* XXVII. 26 (*title*) The social functions and meaning of Hausa *praise-singing. **1886** Corbett *Fall of Asgard* II. 184 He made a little *praise-song about him. **1928** W. C. Willoughby *Soul of Bantu* iv. 368 Praise-songs, which make up in glory for all they lack in veracity, are chanted upon occasion by the men whom they extol. **1957** *Africa* XXVII. 29 The District Head..may request that the praise-songs of title-holders who are his particular friends..should also be sung. **1970** P. Oliver *Savannah Syncopators* 65 Bussani tribesmen in Upper Volta singing praise songs for the chief of the village of Yarkatenga. **1537** *Injunct. by Bp. of Worceter* in Abingdon *Antiq. Worcester* (1717) 162 That in *prase tyme no..body be browgth into the Church, but be browgth into the Church-yard. **1747** Richardson *Clarissa* (1811) I. xxxi. 219 Such praise-begging hypocrisy!.. Such contemptible *praise-traps! **1658** Gurnall *Chr. in Arm.* verse 16. xviii. (1669) 229/2 It was faith that tuned his spirit, and set his affections *praise-way.

praise (preɪz), *v.* Forms: 3–6 **preise**, 3–7 **preyse**, 4–7 **prayse**, 4– **praise**, (4 **preyze**, **praisse**, 4–6 **prais**, 5 **preysse**, 5–6 **prese**, **prays**, **prase**, 6 **prayes**, **prease**, **preese**, *Sc.* **preiss**, 8 (in sense 1) **praze**). [a. OFr. *preisier* (*preisant*) to price, value, prize, praise:—late L. *preci-āre*, earlier *preti-āre* (Cassiodorus *c* 550) to price, value, prize, f. *preti-um* price. At an early date in Parisian F., and afterwards also in Norman, *preisier* was levelled (under the vowel of the pres., *prise* from *prieise*) to *prisier*, mod.F. *priser*, which was also taken in Eng. in the 14th c. as *prise(n*, mod. *prize*, and here took the place of the earlier form in the more literal senses associated with the sb. *prīs*, *price*; leaving to *praise* the most topical sense = Lat. *laudare*, OE. *herian*. A little later the sb. *praise* began to be formed from the vb. in this restricted sense = Lat. *laus*; so that from the 15th c. we have *prise*, *prize* vb. beside *pris*, *price* sb., and *praise* sb. beside *praise* vb.]

I. 1. *trans.* To set a price or value upon; to value, appraise. *Obs.* or *dial.* (The late retention of this sense was probably owing to its being treated as an aphetic form of *appraise*.)

[**1292** Britton i. vi. §2 Ses chateus preyseez et deliverez a les villez.] **13..** *E.E. Allit. P.* B. 146 Þou praysed me & my place ful pouer & ful gnede. **1362** Langl. *P. Pl.* A. v. 174 Þer weore chapmen I-chose þe chaffare to preise. **1382** Wyclif *Matt.* xxvii. 9 Thritty platis of syluer, the pris [1388 prijs] of a man preysid, whom thei preysiden [1388 preiseden] of the sonys of Yrael. **14..** in *Hist. Coll. Citizen London* (Camden) 167 The whyche chalis..was praysyd at xxx. M[l] marke. **1521** *Bury Wills* (Camden) 122 Praisid at v li, x mylch kene. **1530** Palsgr. 664/1, I prayse a thynge, I esteme of what value it is, *je aprise*. **1550–51** in Willis & Clark *Cambridge* (1886) II. 561 M[r] Meres and James Goldsmyth for yer paynes in prasyng y[e] churches stuffe iij[s]. **1554** in *10th Rep. Hist. MSS. Comm.* App. v. 415 The said silver platte..to be preasid as abowe wryttin. **1556** *Inv.* in French *Shaks. Geneal.* (1869) 472, 52 shepe presid att vij li. **1653** H. Cogan tr. *Pinto's Trav.* xxi. 74 An inventory was taken..and all was praised at an hundred and thirty thousand Taels. **1713** Hearne *Collect.* (O.H.S.) IV. 252 His own Picture.. brought to London to be prazed. **1886** Elworthy *W. Somerset Word-bk.*, *Praise*, to appraise; to value.

†**2.** To attach value to; to value, esteem; to prize. *Obs.*

13.. *Cursor M.* 246 (Cott.) Selden was for ani chance Praised Inglis tong in france. *c* **1330** *Arth. & Merl.* 5348 Wawain was the better ay, Therefore y-praised, parmafay. **1402** *Pol. Poems* (Rolls) II. 46 Jakke, thi lewid prophecie I preise not at a peese. *c* **1430** *Pilgr. Lyf Manhode* ii. cxxxiii. (1869) 128 Ne hire wittes j preyse not at a budde. **1481** Caxton *Myrr.* i. xiii. 40 They preysed nothing the thinges that were erthely. *c* **1500** *Melusine* 285 Nother thou nor thy god I preyse not a rotyn dogge. **1567** *Satir. Poems Reform.* iv. 19 Sum tyme in mynde sho praisit me sa hycht, Leifand all vther.

II. 3. a. To tell, proclaim, or commend the worth, excellence, or merits of; to express warm approbation of, speak highly of; to laud, extol. (The leading current sense.)

a **1225** *Ancr. R.* 64 Ne he ne cunne ou nouðer blamen ne preisen. *c* **1290** *S. Eng. Leg.* I. 43/331 Among alle men.. mest ich preisie þe. *a* **1300** *Cursor M.* 3577 He praises al thing þat es gon O present thing he praisses non. **1387** Trevisa *Higden* (Rolls) III. 219 He is i-preysed [L. *laudatur*] for a parfite techere of philosofie. **1484** Caxton *Fables of Æsop* iii. vii, Men preysen somtyme that that shold be blamed. **1513** More *Rich. III* (1641) 219 They extolled and praysed him farre above the Starres. **1650** R. Stapylton *Strada's Low C. Warres* ix. 32 The Subjects.. praised him to the skies. **1784** Cowper *Task* iii. 702 What we admire we praise, and when we praise, Advance it into notice. **1875** Jowett *Plato* V. 151 The rewards of wicked men are often praised by poets and approved by the world.

b. In proverbial phrases.

1598 Marston *Pygmal.* i, Who now so long hath prays'd the Choughs white bill That he hath left her ne'er a flying quill. **1599** Porter *Angry Wom. Abingd.* I iv b, She doth but praise your lucke at parting. **1610** Shaks. *Temp.* iii. iii. 38 *Al.* A kind Of excellent dumbe discourse. *Pro.* Praise in departing. *a* **1633** G. Herbert *Jacula Prudentum* Wks. (1857) 304 Praise day at night, and life at the end. *Ibid.* 317 Praise a hill, but keep below. Praise the sea, but keep on land.

†**c.** To bring praise or commendation to. *rare.*

1648 Boyle *Seraph. Love* xiv. (1660) 87 As Shadows judiciously plac'd, do no less praise the Painter, than do the livelier and brighter Colours. **1649** Bp. Reynolds *Serm. Hosea* i. 24 Men shoot bullets against armour of proof, not to hurt it, but to praise it.

d. The dat. infin. *to praise* (also †*to praising* for *praisen*) used predicatively: To be praised, deserving praise. Cf. blame *v.* 6. Now *rare* or *Obs.*

1297 R. Glouc. (Rolls) 1320 Þe prinse he sede oþer king nis to preisi noȝt. **13..** *E.E. Allit. P.* A. 301, I halde þat Iueler lyttel to prayse. **1398** Trevisa *Barth. De P.R.* v. ii. (Tollem. MS.), Also yf þe heed is to gret it is not to preysynge [*ed.* **1535** it is not to prayse; L. *est illaudabile*]. *c* **1460** Ros *La Belle Dame* 631 Suche as wil say..That stedfast trouthe is nothing for to prays. **1827** *Blackw. Mag.* June 783 Yet we should have been to blame, if Shakspeare be to praise.

e. *absol.* To express approbation; to bestow praise.

c **1386** Chaucer *Parson's Tale* (1877, Ellesmere MS.) 473 Certes, the commendacioñ of the peple is somtyme ful fals and ful brotel for to triste. this day they preyse tomorwe they blame. **1609** Shakes. *Sonnet* cvi. 13 For we which now behold these present dayes, Haue eyes to wonder, but lack toungs to praise. **1879** *Fortn. Rev.* 1 Apr. 507 So Molière is read or witnessed; we laugh and we praise. **1896** *Forum* (N.Y.) Mar. 1 Whether we praise lavishly or venture to blame, two perils threaten us.

4. a. To extol the glorious attributes of (God, or a deity), especially, to sing the praises of; to glorify, magnify, laud.

a **1300** *Cursor M.* 18309 'Lauerd,' he said, 'i sal þe prais, For þou [has] tan me to þi pais.' **1398** Trevisa *Barth. De P.R.* ii. xviii. (1495) c iij/1 An angell..cessith neuer to worshyp and prayse god. **1426** Audelay *Poems* (Percy Soc.) 18 Mi pepyl praysy me with here lyppus, here hertis ben far away [cf. Isa. xxix. 13]. **1535** Coverdale *Ps.* lxvii. 5 Let the people prayse the (o God) let all people prayse the. **1693** Ken *Doxology*, Praise God from whom all blessings flow. **1697** Dryden *Virg. Georg.* i. 481 On Ceres let him call, and Ceres praise. *Ibid.* ii. 535 In jolly Hymns they praise the God of Wine. **1884** F. M. Crawford *Rom. Singer* I. i. 8 'The saints be praised', thought I.

b. Catch-phrase ***praise the Lord and pass the ammunition*** (see quots.).

1942 F. Loesser (*song-title*) Praise the Lord and pass the ammunition. **1942** *Life* 2 Nov. 43 On the cover and above are pictures of Captain William A. Maguire, the man who inspired the best of this war's songs, *Praise the Lord and Pass the Ammunition*... Legend and the song written by Frank Loesser have it that..up jumped the sky pilot, gave the boys a look And manned the gun himself as he laid aside the Book, shouting 'Praise the Lord and pass the ammunition!'. **1943** *Sun* (Baltimore) 17 Sept. 10/5 The navy..named a 35-year-old chaplain from nearby Haddonfield, N.J., as the man who first used the phrase 'Praise the Lord and pass the ammunition' during the attack on Pearl Harbor. The chaplain, Lieut. Com. Howell E. Forgy, was on his first visit home in three years. **1948** A. M. Taylor *Lang. World War II* (rev. ed.) 159 *Praise the Lord and Pass the Ammunition*: attributed to a minister at Pearl Harbor... Real author of the phrase seems to have been Naval Lieutenant Howell Forgy, Presbyterian chaplain.

Hence **praised** *ppl. a.*

14.. *Siege Jerus.* 99 Preued for a prophete þrow praysed dedes. **1552** Huloet, Praysed or valued, *estimatus*. **1650** Trapp *Comm. Deut.* x. 21 [*He is thy praise*] Thy praised one, *Psal.* 18. 3. or, thy praise-worthy one.

praiseach (prəˈʃax). Also **praisseagh**, **prashack**, **prashagh**, **prashoge**, **prassia**. [Ir., f. L. *brassica* cabbage.] **a.** A porridge made from oatmeal, sometimes flavoured with vegetables. Also *fig.*, a mess, a collection of small pieces.

1698 J. Dunton *Let.* in E. Maclysaght *Irish Life in 17th Cent.* (1969) 330 He chose rather to stay at home with Prashagh and Potatoes than hazard himself in France where he knew not that any such food grew. **1935** D. Piatt *Dialect* *in East & Mid-Leinster* 17/1 Praiseach... Secondary meaning: 'To make p. of a thing.' i.e., break in small pieces. **1969** C. CARFAX *Silence with Voices* viii. 51 Would I jam me wagon in the middle of a main road and wait to be made into *prashoge*?

b. The charlock, *Brassica arvensis*, or a related wild plant of the cabbage family.

1727 C. THRELKELD *Synopsis Stirpium Hibernicarum* s.v. Brassica, This is Praisseagh buigh in Irish, and grows plentifully in corn fields. **1859** *Ulster Jrnl. Archaeol.* VII. 278 In former times, when cabbages were not generally cultivated in Ireland, the wild kail (called in Irish *Praiseach*), was often made use of as a kitchen vegetable. **1880** T. McGRATH *Pictures from Ireland* xi. 113 The growing oat crop struggles with the perennial thistle, dock, and prassia. **1904** N. COLGAN *Flora Co. Dublin* 22 *B[rassica] Sinapis*... Prashack. Yellow Weed. Charlock. **1943** D. A. WEBB *Irish Flora* 14 *B[rassica] arvensis*... Charlock, Praiseach... Tilled fields and waste places; common.

praiseful ('preɪzfʊl), *a.* [f. PRAISE *v.* or *sb.* + -FUL. (With sense 1, cf. the earlier *worshipful*.)]

†**1.** Deserving of praise or honour; praiseworthy, laudable. *Obs.*

1382 WYCLIF *Dan.* iii. 54 Blessid art thou in the trone of thi rewme, and aboue preyseful [*Vulg.* superlaudabilis, 1388 preisable]. *c* **1450** *Mirour Saluacioun* 4037 Whare fore a praisefulle womman oure lady prefigurid. **1586** FERNE *Blaz. Gentrie* 25 Mooued certainlye, by the praisefull deedes of their kinsemen. **1598** DRAYTON *Heroic. Ep.* iv. 123 Which, if so praysefull in the meanest Men, In pow'rfull Kings how glorious is it then? **1766** G. CANNING *Anti-Lucretius* III. 161 No narrow preference for their native soil Restrains these heroes in their praiseful toil. **1818** LAMB *Poems, Salome*, The ruthless deed That did thy praiseful dance succeed.

2. Full of or abounding in praise; giving praise; eulogistic, laudatory.

1613–16 W. BROWNE *Brit. Past.* II. ii, All praisefull tongues doe waite upon that name. **1641** WITHER (*title*) Halelviah or, Britans Second Remembrancer.. in praisefull and Pœnitentiall Hymns. **1747** RICHARDSON *Clarissa* (1811) I. ix. 56 He speaks kind and praiseful things of me. **1776** MICKLE tr. *Lusiad* 86 Had other wars my praiseful lips employ'd. **1891** *Blackw. Mag.* CL. 694 Strains of praiseful lore.

Hence '**praisefully** *adv.*, '**praisefulness**.

1748 RICHARDSON *Clarissa* (1811) V. iv. 37 She must have ..heard your uncle speak praisefully of a man he is said to be so intimate with. **1867** BAILEY *Univ. Hymn* 5 Holy, and with true praisefulness inspired. **1899** CHEYNE *Chr. Use of Psalms* i. 29 Except in a general spirit of praisefulness, we cannot accompany the mass of our congregation in its jubilant singing.

praiseless ('preɪzlɪs), *a.* [f. PRAISE *sb.* + -LESS.] Without praise or honour; unpraised; undeserving of praise.

1558 PHAER *Æneid.* v. M iv b, His praiseles shyp [*sine honore ratem*] Sergestus brought. **1597** BACON *Ess., Coulers Gd. & Evil* ix. (Arb.) 151 Actions of great felicitie may drawe wonder, but prayselesse. **1632** LITHGOW *Trav.* II. 73 Death..matching the Scepter, with the Spade, and the crowned Prince with the praislesse Peasant. **1852** *Fraser's Mag.* XLV. 570 Their life is arbitrary, blameless, and praiseless.

†'**praisement**. *Obs.* [f. PRAISE *v.* + -MENT. Cf. *appraisement*.] Estimation of value, valuation, appraisement.

1497 *Naval Acc. Hen. VII* (1896) 141 Amountyng in value Aftyr the praysement of the same to cxxxvij[li]. **1511** FABYAN *Will* in *Chron.* (1811) Pref. 7 Before the praysement..of my foresaid moveables. **1638** SANDERSON *Serm.* (1657) II. vii. 143 It is beyond his..skill, to give an exact praisement of it. **1656** J. CHALONER in D. King *Vale-Royall* IV. 26 If no man will buy it, the four men are to take it by Praisment.

praiser ('preɪzə(r)). Also 5–6 praysour. [a. AF. *prei-, praisour* = OF. **preiseor*, F. *priseur*; f. *preisier, priser*, PRAISE *v.*: see -ER[1].]

†**1.** One who appraises; a valuer, appraiser. *Obs.*

1491 *Will of Stokes* (Somerset Ho.), The Bisshopes praysours. **1529** *Act 21 Hen. VIII*, c. 5 §2 Their regesters, scribes, praisers, sommoners, apparatours. **1544** in *Vicary's Anat.* (1888) App. iii. 160 Rychard Ferres..for to be one of the Comen preysers in this Cytye. **1624** in Picton *L'pool Munic. Rec.* (1883) I. 219 Oxe money..to be assessed by the foure Marchant praysers. **1707** E. CHAMBERLAYNE *Pres. St. Eng.* II. (ed. 22) 205 The Chancellor of the Exchequer..hath the Gift of the two Praisers of the Court.

2. a. One who praises, commends, or extols; a eulogist.

1382 WYCLIF *Prov.* xxvii. 21 So is preued a man in the mouth of preiseris [**1388** preyseris]. *c* **1386** CHAUCER *Melib.* ¶211 The sweete wordes of flaterynge preiseres. **1450–1530** *Myrr. our Ladye* 18 Here cometh the prayser that endyted the songe. **1573** G. HARVEY *Letter-bk.* (Camden) 30, I have bene a praiser of none save phisicians. **1620** E. BLOUNT *Horæ Subs.* 472 Let your owne conscience be your owne prayser. **1742** RICHARDSON *Pamela* III. 245 Lady Davers was one of the kind Praisers. **1863** W. W. STORY *Roba di R.* II. vii. 175 The Past never wants for praisers and apologists.

b. One who offers praise to God or a deity; a worshipper.

1610 WILLET *Hexapla Dan.* 170 They are praisers of images. **1765** J. BROWN *Chr. Jrnl.* (1814) 163 The loudest praiser of God.

c. *spec.* = *praise poet*. Cf. MBONGO.

1904 D. KIDD *Essential Kafir* ii. 92 All chiefs keep a Court Praiser, whose business it is to go in front of the chief and sing his praises. **1937** G. P. LESTRADE in I. Schapera *Bantu-Speaking Tribes S. Afr.* xiii. 299 A praiser..may..alter the order..of stanzas. **1968** T. COPE *Izibongo: Zulu praise Poems* I. ii. 26 When a man of distinction is rewarded for his services by the chief..he..establishes a great kraal and appoints a personal praiser, who will collect..and perfect his praises, so that they constitute what we call a 'praise-poem'.

Hence '**praiseress**, a female praiser. *rare*[−1].

1611 COTGR., *Louëresse*, a praiseresse, commenderesse.

†'**praiseworth**, *a.* *Obs. rare.* [f. PRAISE *sb.* + WORTH *a.*] = PRAISEWORTHY.

1591 R. W. *Tancred & Gismunda* IV. iv. F iij, This is praise-worth, not to do what you may. **1610** HOLLAND *Camden's Brit.* I. 290 Elizabeth..whose praise-worth vertues if in verse I now should take in hand.

'**praise,worthily**, *adv.* [f. PRAISEWORTHY + -LY[2].] In a praiseworthy manner; laudably, commendably.

1570 T. WILSON *Demosthenes* Pref. *j, To make an English man telle his tale praiseworthily. **1596** SPENSER *F.Q.* V. xii. 31 All That ever she sees doen prays-worthily. **1887** BROWNING *Parleyings, D. Bartoli* xv, Many a legend..Do you praiseworthily authenticate.

'**praise,worthiness**. [f. as prec. + -NESS.] The quality of being praiseworthy; laudableness.

a **1586** SIDNEY *Arcadia* (1622) 405 Quite contrary to the others praise-worthinesse. **1649** ROBERTS *Clavis Bibl.* 276 The Praise-worthinesse of God. **1747** RICHARDSON *Clarissa* (1811) II. xi. 66 Where, asks she,..is the praise-worthiness of obedience, if it be only paid in instances where we give up nothing? **1879** G. MEREDITH *Egoist* xvi, His logical coolness of expostulation..unheroic in proportion to its praiseworthiness.

†'**praiseworthly**, *adv.* *Obs.* [f. PRAISEWORTH + -LY[2]. The examples may belong to *praiseworthily*: but cf. *dearworthly*.] = PRAISEWORTHILY.

1555 W. WATREMAN *Fardle Facions* 310 The menne whiche praise worthely canne obeie shal also haue knoweledge how praise worthely to rule. *a* **1568** ASCHAM *Scholem.* 129 Some men..haue put to their helping handes, to this worke..and P. Victorius most praise-worthelie of all.

praiseworthy ('preɪz,wɜːðɪ), *a.* [f. PRAISE *sb.* + WORTHY *a.* Formerly hyphened or treated as two words: cf. b.] Worthy or deserving of praise; laudable, commendable.

1538 STARKEY *England* I. ii. 43 [He is] much more prayse-worthy, then he wych for fere and dred kepyth hymselfe in the hauen styl. **1561** T. NORTON *Calvin's Inst.* II. ii. (1634) 119 Shall we thinke anything praise-worthy or excellent, which we do not acknowledge to come of God? **1610** HOLLAND *Camden's Brit.* (1637) 489 That right good and praise-worthy man. **1699** BURNET *39 Art.* xvii. (1700) 167 All Men are so far free as to be praise-worthy or blame-worthy for the Good or Evil that they do. **1732** LAW *Serious C.* ii. (ed. 2) 21 He does not ask what is allowable.., but what is commendable and praise-worthy. **1865** SWINBURNE *Atalanta* 915 Gods, found because of thee adorable And for thy sake praiseworthiest from all men.

†**b.** *Analytically*, as ***great praise worthy***, worthy of great praise. *Obs.*

[**1556** *Aurelio & Isab.* (1608) C iij, The whiche..maketh you of so great prayse worthye.] **1570** FOXE *A. & M.* (ed. 2) 178/2 Smal prayse worthy was it in them to kepe it. **1586** J. HOOKER *Hist. Irel.* in *Holinshed* II. 52/1 Great praise-worthie was he that gaue the first aduenture.

praising ('preɪzɪŋ), *vbl. sb.* [f. PRAISE *v.* + -ING[1].] The action of the verb PRAISE. †**a.** Valuing, valuation, appraising. *Obs.*

1399 LANGL. *Rich. Redeles* I. 17 Be tallage of ȝoure townes without any werre,..By preysinge of polaxis þat no pete hadde. **1524** *Churchw. Acc. St. Giles, Reading* 22 Paid for praysyng of certayn stuff at the court..viij[d]. **1590** SWINBURNE *Testaments* 227 The registring, sealing, writing, praising, making of inuentaries.

b. Commending, commendation; the offering of praise to God. Also in *pl.*

c **1330** R. BRUNNE *Chron. Wace* (Rolls) 13401 Grete preysynge he [Arthur] made, His men to bolde, þeir hertes to glade. *c* **1380** WYCLIF *Serm.* Sel. Wks. I. 379 A litil storie is told in presing of our Ladi. **1382** —— *Prov.* x. 7 The mynde of the riȝtwise [shall be] with preisingis. **1496** *Dives & Paup.* (W. de W.) I. xi. 43/1 Theyr Pater noster, & theyr Aue maria, aud other prayers and praysynges. **1561** T. NORTON *Calvin's Inst.* IV. xviii. (1634) 711 Under the other kinde of sacrifice..are contained all..our prayers, praisings, giving of thankes. *a* **1716** SOUTH *Serm.* (1744) VIII. i. 13 Hence the very word, by which we express the praising of one, is to extol him; that is, to lift him up.

†**c.** The fact of being held worthy of praise; *transf.* that which is so held. *Obs.*

c **1330** R. BRUNNE *Chron.* (1810) 311 At conseil & at nede he [Arthur] was a skilfulle kyng, So curteis of non men rede, ne prince of more praysing Was non in Cristendam. *c* **1386** CHAUCER *Pars. T.* ¶875 The thridde manere of chastitee is virginitee..she is the preisynge of this world. **1484** CAXTON *Fables of Æsop* IV. iv, Thy..beaute is fayrer..and of gretter preysynge than the songe of the nyghtyngale.

'**praising**, *ppl. a.* [f. PRAISE *v.* + -ING[2].] That praises or expresses praise; laudatory.

1382 WYCLIF *Isa.* xxxv. 2 Buriownynge it shal burioune, and ful out ioȝen, ioȝeful and preising. *a* **1586** SIDNEY *Ps.* v. v, They ever shall send Thee their praysing voyce. **1745** *Scot. Paraphr.* xxiv. i, Ye Heavens, send forth your praising Song.

Hence '**praisingly** *adv.*, in a praising or laudatory manner; with praise.

1842 G. S. FABER *Prov. Lett.* (1844) II. 117 As that Father praisingly reminds them. **1889** G. GISSING *Nether World* III. xiii. 289 Miss Lanty..did not speak of her too praisingly.

†'**praisure**. *Obs. rare*[−1]. [f. PRAISE *v.* 1 + -URE.] Valuation, appraisement, appraisal.

1622 F. MARKHAM *Bk. War* II. iv. 55 The Clerk of the Band shall administer vpon his goods,..making a true Inuentorie or praysure thereof.

Prakrit ('prɑːkrɪt). Also 8 Pracort, 8–9 **Prácrit**, 9 **Prā-, Pracrita, Prâ-, Prā-, Prákrit.** [ad. Skr. *prākṛta* natural, unrefined, vulgar: opposed to *saṃskṛta* prepared, refined, polished (Sanskrit).] A general name for those popular languages or dialects of Northern and Central India which existed along-side of or grew out of Sanskrit. Also *attrib.* or as *adj.*

Applied primarily to the ancient vernacular dialects, the earliest traces of which go back to *c* 500 B.C.; then to the mediæval Prakrits which succeeded these; and sometimes to the modern languages Hindī, Bengālī, Marāthī, etc. Pāli is a form of primary Prakrit.

1766 J. CLELAND *Way to Things by Words* 88 The Pracort is the vulgar language, so called in contradistinction to the Sanscort. **1786** *Asiatic Miscellany* II. 502 Four unconnected Stanzas, in the Prácrit Language, which was anciently vernacular in India. **1789** SIR W. JONES tr. *Sacontalá* Pref., Wks. 1799 VI. 206 The men of rank and learning are represented speaking pure Sanscrit, and the women Prácrit, which is little more than the language of the Bráhmens melted down by a delicate articulation to the softness of Italian. **1801** COLEBROOKE *Sanscrit & Pracrit* in *Asiatic Res.* VII. 199 The Gods, &c. speak *Sanscrīta*; benevolent genii, *Prácrīta*; wicked demons, *Paísáchí*; and men of low tribes and the rest, *Mágad'hí*. *Ibid.* 200 *Prácrīt*, consisting of provincial dialects, which are less refined, and have a more imperfect grammar. **1837** C. P. BROWN *Sanscrit Pros.* 19 The Pracrita metres do not fall within the scope of the present essay. **1861** MAX MÜLLER *Sci. Lang.* Ser. IV. iv. 138 We meet the same local dialects again in what are called the Prâkrit idioms, used in the later plays, in the sacred literature of the Jainas, and in a few poetical compositions. **1875** WHITNEY *Life Lang.* x. 187 One Prakrit dialect, the Pali, became in its turn the sacred language of southeastern Buddhism. **1880**, etc. [see MAHARASHTRI]. **1883** I. TAYLOR *Alphabet* x. II. 296 The inscriptions of Asoka are written in three local Pali or Prakrit dialects, evidently derived by long continued detrition from the Sanskrit of the Vedas. **1904** *Athenæum* 18 Oct. 481/3 The literatures which were produced..by the earliest language of the Vedas, by the later classical Sanskrit, by the Pali of the Buddhist books.. and by such of the other Prakrits, or popular dialects, as attained to literary form. **1968** W. S. ALLEN *Vox Graeca* i. 14 In relatively ancient times this receives support from transcriptions into Prakrit (Middle Indian) on coins of the Greek kings of Bactria and India in the 1 and 2 c. B.C. **1971** [see INDOLOGIST].

Hence **Prak'ritic** *a.*, pertaining to Prakrit; **'Prakritize** *v.*, *trans.* to turn into Prakrit.

1875 WHITNEY *Life Lang.* x. 187 The next stage of Indian language..is called the Prakritic. **1881** R. MORRIS in *Academy* 27 Aug. 161/2 In Marâthî *muramura* = muttering, grumbling,..seems to be a prâkritised form of the Sanskrit *murmura*, which in Pâli would become *muramura* or *mummura*.

‖**pralaya** (prə'laɪjə). [Skr.] Dissolution, destruction of the world.

1922 JOYCE *Ulysses* 296 Questioned by his earthname as to his whereabouts in the heavenworld he stated that he was now on the path of pralaya or return but was still submitted to trial at the hands of certain bloodthirsty entities on the lower astral levels. **1954** G. S. RAO *Indian Words in Eng.* 134/1 *Pralaya*, destruction, esp. the destruction of the whole world at the end of a Kalpa. **1970** V. MEHTA *Portrait of India* II. 62 We Hindus say that the universe has a *pralaya*, a death —a period of withdrawal for rest. We Madrasis have our *pralaya* all the time.

pralidoxime (prælɪ'dɒksiːm). *Pharm.* [f. *aldoxime* s.v. ALDO- with arbitrary insertion of *p*, *r*, and *i* (from PYRIDINE).] (A salt of) the 2-hydroxyiminomethyl-1-methylpyridinium ion, $HO{\cdot}N{:}CH{\cdot}C_5H_4\overset{+}{N}{\cdot}CH_3$, which reactivates the enzyme cholinesterase and is used as an adjunct to atropine in the treatment of poisoning by certain cholinesterase inhibitors (as malathion and parathion).

1961 *Approved Names* (Brit. Pharmacopœia Comm.) 19 Pralidoxime Iodide, Picolinaldoxime methiodide, Protopam. **1965** *New Drugs* xlvi. 473/1 Pralidoxime chloride restores the depressed cholinesterase activity resulting from organophosphate poisoning. **1970** PASSMORE & ROBSON *Compan. Med. Stud.* II. xxxii. 2/2 Treatment of intoxication with carbamate or organophosphorus insecticides includes the use of atropine which antagonizes the muscarinic effects of acetylcholine and of pralidoxime, a cholinesterase reactivator. Pralidoxime is a quaternary ammonium compound (hydroxyiminomethyl-1-methylpyridinium) which is given slowly intravenously. **1974** M. C. GERALD *Pharmacol.* vii. 132 Normal cholinesterase activity is restored..when a cholinesterase reactivator, notably pralidoxime (2-PAM), is used as an antidote. **1978** *Daily Tel.* 23 Jan. 13/7 British soldiers and airmen are now equipped with pills which will enable them to survive three or four times the normal lethal dose of most nerve gases... The pills, produced from pralidoxime mesylate..are issued in batches for each 24 hours.

praline ('prɑːliːn). Also 8–9 **prawlin**, 9 **prawleen, prawling, praslin, praleen.** [a. F. *praline*, f. the name of Marshal Duplessis-Praslin (1598–1675), by whose cook the confection was invented.] A confection made by browning almonds or nuts in boiling sugar; also transferred to various other preparations: see quots. 1809, 1883, 1893.

1723 J. Nott *Cook's & Confectioner's Dict.* sig. B4 Almonds Fry'd, or Prawlins. **1727** Bradley *Fam. Dict.* s.v. *Almond*, Almonds fry'd, or Prawlins, a Dish prepar'd by taking a Pound of the best Jordan Almonds,..boil them to a Candy [in a syrup of loaf-sugar], constantly stirring till they are dry;..Put the Almonds again into the preserving Pan, and set them on a slow Fire, till some of their Oil comes from 'em into the Bottom of the Pan. **1770** Borella *Court & Country Confectioner* 40 We beg leave to use the words *praline* [etc.]. **1809** A. Henry *Trav.* 265, I left our fort on Beaver Lake,..provided with dried meat, frozen fish, and a small quantity of praline, made of roasted maize, rendered palatable with sugar. **1883** R. Haldane *Workshop Receipts* Ser. II. 159/1 Orange Prawlings.—Take 4 or 5 China oranges, and cut off the peel in quarters... Have about a pint of clarified sugar boiling on the fire;..put in the pieces of peel [etc.]. **1893** Mary A. Owen *Old Rabbit*, etc. iii. 39 It was the fragrance of prawleens, that compound of New Orleans molasses, brown sugar, chocolate, and butter. **1901** Winston Churchill *Crisis* I. xii, He did Miss Eugénie the honour to eat one of her praleens. **1906** *Mrs. Beeton's Bk. Househ. Managem.* 1079 (*heading*) Chocolate pralines. **1913** [see noyau b]. **1951** *People* 3 June 2/1 (Advt.), Crunchy wafers sandwiched with chocolate praline. **1971** A. R. Daniel *Bakers' Dict.* (ed. 2) 155/2 Praline sometimes consists of roasted blended whole almonds dipped in sugar boiled to the hard crack degree.

pralle, app. var. *prolle*, prowl *v.*

‖**pralltriller** (ˈpraltrɪlər). *Mus.* [G., f. *prallen* to bounce + *triller* trill.] (See quot. 1971.)

1841 J. Bishop in *Hamilton's Dict.* (ed. 13) 114 *Pralltriller* (German), a transient shake. **1876** Stainer & Barrett *Dict. Mus. Terms* 365/1 *Pralltriller*.., a transient shake. **1928** *Daily Express* 23 Feb. 3 What is a pralltriller?.. A musical ornament, performed by trilling the ornamented note with the note above it. **1971** *Everyman's Dict. Mus.* (ed. 5) 529/1 *Pralltriller* (Ger.), the rapid repetition of a note, with a note a degree higher in between.

‖**pram**[1], **praam** (prɑːm). Also 8–9 **prahm, prame**, 9 **prahme, praum.** [Du. *praam*, MDu. *praem, prame*, OFris. *prām*, Fris. *prame*, MLG., LG. *prâm, prame*; so MHG. *prâm*, G. *prahm-e*, ON. *prámr*, Da. *pram*, Norw. *praam*, Sw. *pråm*, also F. *prame*, all from Slav.; cf. OSlav. *pramŭ*, Pol. *pram*, cognate with OHG. *farm*, freight-boat, ferry: f. root *par-, per-, por-*: see fare *v.*]

a. A flat-bottomed boat or lighter, used especially in the Baltic and the Netherlands for shipping cargo, etc.

[**1390–1** *Earl Derby's Exp.* (Camden) 42 Et pro portagio dictorum piscium ad les prames, v scot [at Danzig].] **1548** [see e]. **1634** Sir T. Herbert *Trav.* 105 Some long, deepe prams, sowed together with hempe and cord (but vnpitcht or calkt). In these the Muscouian Merchants saile downe Volga, ouer the Caspian Sea. **1643** *Declar. Commons Rebell. Irel.* 49 [They] tooke a Scottish Barke and a Dover barke, and a Pram or Hute, and a Catch. **1712** *Lond. Gaz.* No. 5050/2 Danish Prams, or Flat-bottom'd Boats. **1762** *Gentl. Mag.* 251 The bason where the prames and flat-bottom boats lie. **1807** Sir R. Wilson in *Life* (1862) II. vii. 218 Three English praums had also arrived. **1817** W. Selwyn *Law Nisi Prius* (ed. 4) II. 899 The cargo..was unloaded into praams or lighters belonging to the [Russian] government. **1834** G. Crabbe in *Poetical Wks.* I. i. 9 Vessels of all sorts, from the large heavy troll-boat to the yawl and prame. **1844** *Hull Dock Act* 114 The word 'vessel' shall include ship, lighter, keel, barge, praam, boat, raft.

b. A large flat-bottomed boat mounted with guns and used as a floating battery.

1715 *Lond. Gaz.* No. 5340, 4 Prames or large Flat-bottomed Boats, one of which is to carry 20 Guns. **1761** *Chron.* in *Ann. Reg.* 126/2 There is a kind of warlike vessel called a prame..equipping in different French ports. Each ..has two decks..they are long and broad, but draw very little water, and are rigged after the manner of a ketch. **1833** Marryat *P. Simple* lviii, One of the praams mounted ten guns, and the other eight. **1845** Gresley *Frank's First Trip* 166 A large sort of gun-boats, called Praams, which were flat and wide, with three keels and three masts.

c. As name of a ship's boat.

1860 Reade *8th Commandm.* 338 His work runs into the port of annihilation quicker than pirate can launch praam to attack it. **1894** *Times* 15 Nov. 7/5 A small boat, known as a 'pram', was seen to be launched. The mate..states that.. the captain ordered the boat out to row to the shore.

d. A small sailing-boat. *U.S.*

1937 *Sun* (Baltimore) 31 July 11/8 In the pram class, Bucky Wilson..scored a surprise victory. **1956** *Ibid.* 11 Oct. 21/4 Hard luck forced Mary Sullivan and Henry White out of the competition when a boom broke on one of their prams. **1966** *Amer. Speech* XLI. 237 The smallest [sailboats] are called *Prams*, and they measure up to about 10 feet long.

e. *attrib.* and *Comb.*, as ***praam bow, brig, ship.***

1548 *Aberdeen Regr.* XX. (Jam.), For the prame [in Jam. prane] hyir havand thair gudis to the schip. **1755** Magens *Insurances* II. 278 (Ordinance of Stockholm) Disbursements and Charges..Pilotage, Anchorage, Beaconage, Prahm or Lighter-piles [etc.]. **1804** *Chron.* in *Ann. Reg.* 558/1 That part of the enemy's flotilla, consisting of two praam ships bearing the flag of chief of division and both under French colours. **1849** W. R. O'Byrne *Naval Biog. Dict.* 1237/2 An armed cutter, a praam-brig, and a gun vessel. **1902** *Rudder* Apr. 208 The fore overhang [of the Meteor] is neither the old clipper stem nor the new pram bow.

pram[2] (præm). *colloq.* [See sense 1.]

1. A shortened form of perambulator 3.

1884 *Graphic* 25 Oct. 423/2 Another favourite custom of nurses is to walk two or three abreast, chattering and laughing as they push their 'prams'. **1888** *Pall Mall G.* 25 Sept. 2/1 The Pram and the Baby. *a* **1908** *Mod. Advt.* Some Second-hand Prams to be cleared Cheap. **1916** G. B. Shaw *Pygmalion* v. 173 When I was a poor man and had a solicitor once when they found a pram in the dust cart, he got me off. **1955** *Times* 4 June 7/4 There are women who would not exchange a familiar pram with a quirk in its steering for the best new one that money could buy. **1963** [see *pram-park* below]. **1970** [see *pram-pusher* below].

2. A milkman's hand-cart for delivering milk.

1897 *Daily News* 20 Jan. 12/6 Milkman seeks Work Milking Cows, or with a pram. **1902** *Westm. Gaz.* 8 Oct. 8/2 Dairy Show..Accessories from churns and separators to milk 'prams'.

3. *attrib.* and *Comb.*, as (sense 1) ***pramful, pram-handle, -load, race, rug***; **pram-park**, (*a*) (see quot. 1963); (*b*) a space, area, etc., where prams may be left; **pram-pusher**, one who pushes a pram; *spec.* a young mother; so **pram-pushing** *ppl. a.* and *vbl. sb.*

1957 M. Frayn in *Granta* 9 Mar. 20/1 People said that an old woman had been arrested on the other side of the village, pushing a whole *pramful of stolen goods along. **1977** F. Branston *Up & Coming Man* xv. 168 A young mum and a pramful of kids. **1934** Dylan Thomas *Let.* 15 Apr. (1966) 102 Mothers are resting their bellies on *pram-handles. **1972** *Where* Oct. 273/3 Staff took to the post office two *pramloads of the report-and-appeal. **1973** *Times* 28 Feb. (Suppl. on Victoria Centre, Nottingham) p. iv/6 A flying squirrel pushes a pramload (which is a nest) of birds. **1963** *Times* 3 May 15/7 In the House of Commons on Monday Sir Robert Cary asked how one gets a pram on a bus. In New Zealand they are carried in special *pram-parks on the front of the radiators, where they seem to be safe, but nothing can be left inside, as they are hung wheels foremost. **1965** R. Rendell *To fear Painted Devil* xii. 136 We're going to have that extension done at last... A sun loggia... And a pram park! **1967** J. Wilson in L. Deighton *London Dossier* 35 Linguists wishing to meet *au pair* girls might do worse than to hang about the pram park inside Peter Jones department store. **1970** *Times* 23 Feb. 13/2 The scheme will include.. seats.and plants in the concourse, and a pram park. '**1973** *Guardian* 3 Sept. 20 Pram parks should be provided inside shops. **1935** J. L. Hodson *Harvest in North* II. i. 39 Afe on yo' are nowt but skivvies and *pram-pushers. **1963** *Guardian* 25 Jan. 8/7 The pram-pushers are always willing to discuss these, as a change from the inevitable baby-talk. **1970** A. Price *Labyrinth Makers* v. 64 Mothers bulldozing their way ahead with prams... Roskill adroitly slipped into the wake of one of the most aggressive pram-pushers. **1933** *Punch* 10 May 516/1 Possibly the *pram-pushing girl's hat caught her eye. **1964** G. Butler *Coffin in Malta* vii. 198 Most husbands were competent nannies; he fully expected to do some pram-pushing himself. **1974** *Country Life* 7 Mar. 480/1 The pram-pushing Phil's anguished claim—'he's my son!' **1968** P. Jennings *Living Village* 123 In the scrapbook there is a very good colour photograph of a Boxing Day *pram race. **1934** A. Thirkell *Wild Strawberries* ix. 196 Ivy, run and get the *pram rug and put it round her.

Pramnian (ˈpræmnɪən), *a. Gr.* and *Rom. Antiq.* [f. L. *Pramni-um (vinum)*, Gr. *Πράμνι-ος (οἶνος)* + -an.] In ***Pramnian wine***, a wine from the neighbourhood of Smyrna. Also allusively.

1601 Holland *Pliny* I. 412 The Pramnian wine (which the same Homer hath so highly commended) continues yet in credit and holds the name still: it comes from a vineyard in the countrey about Smyrna neere to the temple of Cybele. **1830** tr. *Aristoph. Knights* 57 Off, off with the cup, in the name of the Pramnian God! **1863** Ruskin *Wks.* (1872) II. 90 Pramnian wine, cheese, and flour.

pran, obs. form of prawn.

‖**prana** (ˈprɑːnə). [Skr.] In Hindu religion, the 'breath of life'; hence in extended uses, a life-giving force or inspiration; the breath, breathing. Also **pranayama**, regulation of the breath; breathing-control.

1830 H. T. Colebrooke in *Trans. R. Asiatic Soc.* II. 11 The term *prâṅa*..properly and primarily signifies respiration, as well as certain other vital actions (inspiration, energy, expiration, digestion, or circulation of nourishment); and secondarily, the senses and organs. But, in the passages here referred to, it is employed for a different signification, intending the supreme Brahme. **1875** Monier Williams *Indian Wisdom* ii. 40 Highest of all stands Prāṇa or Life. As the spokes of a wheel are attached to the nave, so are all things attached to Life. **1930** F. Yeats-Brown *Bengal Lancer* v. 66 There was a *saddhu* at Puri who claimed to be able to resurrect sparrows..by breathing *prana* into them. **1938** S. Beckett *Murphy* 196 He..trusted he would be granted Prana to finish a monograph. **1955** E. Pound *Section: Rock-Drill* (1957) xciv. 92 Above prana, the light, past light, the crystal. **1956** E. Wood *Yoga Dict.* 25/1 The shorter unit of time often mentioned in Sanskrit philosophical literature, though not used in *prānāyāma* is called the second or moment (*kshana*), and is often considered to be one quarter of the time taken up in shutting an eye. *Ibid.* 123/1 *Prana*, that Vital Air which is.. concerned with the health and strength of the heart and its work in the body. **1959** [see orgone]. **1960** J. Hewitt *Yoga* v. 70 Prana, to the Yogi, means much more than mere breath. Prana is actually the power behind and within breath. The power of the atom is Prana. Thought is Prana. .. It pervades the whole universe. **1960** Koestler *Lotus & Robot* I. iii. 117 The Yogi then demonstrated the extraordinary power of his chest muscles—the result of pranayama. **1970** *Man, Myth & Magic* v. 146/3 The idea of an astral body is very old. Ancient Indian writings describe the eight *siddhis* or supernormal powers which can be acquired through a type of yoga called *Pranayama*. **1971** 'A. Hall' *Warsaw Document* xv. 185, I took a slow breath: the answer to panic is *prana*. **1979** W. H. Canaway *Solid Gold Buddha* xi. 76 He..did some *Pranayama*, and calmed himself, through the rhythmic breathing.

prance (prɑːns, -æ-), *sb.* [f. prance *v.*]

a. The act of prancing; a prancing movement or walk.

1751 Johnson *Rambler* No. 182 ¶11 A lady..whom by the jolting prance of her gait,..he guessed to have lately buried some prosperous citizen. **1876** T. Hardy *Ethelberta* (1890) 307 Ethelberta..swept along the pavement and down the street in a turbulent prance. **1898** F. P. Dunne *Mr. Dooley in Peace & War* 184 He has th' gait proper f'r half-past six o'clock th' avenin' befure pay-day. But 'tis not th' prance iv an American citizen makin' a gloryous spectacle iv himsilf. **1904** J. G. Lorimer *Selfmade Merch. Lett. to Son* 243 I'm..as full of prance as a spotted circus horse.

†**b.** A trip, a jaunt. *Obs. nonce-use.*

1803 Dibdin *Nongtongpaw* I. xi, John Bull for pastime took a prance, Some time ago, to peep at France.

Hence **prancy** *a.*, resembling or suggestive of a prance.

1961 *New Statesman* 26 May 828/3 The 'Bohemian Jive', a prancy affair, is now an essential part of the repertoire, whether you wear points or sandals. **1963** *New Yorker* 22 June 4 The trumpeting band of Emil Coleman and the prancy one of Mark Monte.

prance (prɑːns, -æ-), *v.* Also 4–8 **praunce**, 5 **prawnce, praunse**, 5–9 **pranse**. [Appears *c* 1375: origin obscure: see *Note* below.]

1. *intr.* Of a horse: 'To spring and bound in high mettle' (J.); to rise by springing from the hind legs, either spontaneously in gaiety, excitement, or impatience, or at the rider's will; to move by a succession of such springs. Rarely, and more vaguely, of other animals.

c **1374** Chaucer *Troylus* I. 221 Than þenketh he þough I praunce al by-forn First yn þe trays ful fat and newe shorn, Yet am I but an hors. **1398** Trevisa *Barth. De P.R.* xviii. iv. (1495) 752 A lombe..lad to pasture other to deth; he grutchyth not nor prauncyth not but is obedyent and meke. *c* **1440** Lydg. *Hors, Shepe, & G.* 344 The Goos may gagle, the hors may prike & praunce. *c* **1450** Holland *Howlat* 21 Hartes in heirdis..Pransand and prunȝeand, be pair and be pair. *c* **1614** Sir W. Mure *Dido & Æneas* I. 783 Whil Phoebus' steeds abowt the Poles do praunce. *a* **1639** Wotton *Poems* in *Reliq.* (1651) 532 Here's no fantastick Mask, nor dance, But of our Kids, that frisk and prance. **1717** Lady M. W. Montagu *Let. to Mrs. Thistlethwayte* 1 Apr., I have a little white favourite [horse]..he prances under me with so much fire. **1870** Bryant *Iliad* I. vi. 208 As when some courser..Prances o'er the plain in joy of heart.

b. *trans.* (with reference to sense 3 b).

1858 Morris *Eve of Crecy* Poems 168 Look you, my horse is good to prance A right fair measure in this war-dance.

c. *trans.* To cause (a horse) to prance.

1530 Palsgr. 664/1, I praunce an horse, I make hym fetche gamboldes and to flynge, *je pourbondys*. **1609** in Hakluyt *Voy.* (1812) V. 509 He and those that went with him coursed their horses, pransing them to and fro. **1611** Cotgr., *Pourbondir*..to manage, or praunce a horse; to make him leape, or bound. **1720** Mrs. Manley *Power of Love* (1741) 119 He was provoked to see Briancon vault and praunce his Horse about the Field, as if he were certain of his Conquest. **1806** Surr *Winter in Lond.* III. 209 The marquis of Hartley and lord Barton..pranced their nags, each with two grooms behind them, close-up to the landau.

2. *intr.* Of a person: To ride (or drive) with the horse prancing; 'to ride gallantly and ostentatiously' (J.); to ride gaily, proudly, or insolently. Also † ***to prance it*** (obs.).

1390 Gower *Conf.* III. 41 Wherof this man was wonder glad, And goth to prike and prance aboute. *a* **1548** Hall *Chron., Hen. VIII* 33 b, Then vp pranced the Burgonyons and folowed the chace. **1615** G. Sandys *Trav.* 259 The Gentry delight much in great horses, whereupon they praunce continually through the streetes. **1624** Middleton *Game at Chess* III. i. 351 So make him my white jennet when I prance it After the Black Knight's litter. **1735** Somerville *Chase* III. 367 Like Troops of Amazons, the Female Band Prance round their Cars. **1802** Campbell *Lochiel's Warning* 7 Proud Cumberland prances, insulting the slain, And their hoof-beaten bosoms are trod to the plain. **1854** Thackeray *Rose & Ring* xvii, His Majesty prancing in person at the head of them all.

3. *intr.* 'To move in a warlike or showy manner' (J.); to move or walk in a manner suggestive of a prancing horse, or (more generally) in an elated or arrogant manner; to swagger. Also *fig.*

c **1400** *Beryn* 3400 They stond in altircacioune & stryff in poynt to praunce To depart yeur goodis. **1513** Douglas *Æneis* v. v. 8 Ilk ane of thaim, furth pransand lyke a lard. **1570** Levins *Manip.* 21/18 To praunce, *exultare*. **1593** Shaks. *3 Hen. VI*, II. i. 24 How well resembles it the prime of Youth, Trimm'd like a Yonker, prauncing to his Loue? *c* **1641** *Downfall of Pretended Div. Authoritie of Hierarchy* 11 How they pierck and pranse it, above all Nobilitie and Gentry. **1754** Richardson *Grandison* (1810) V. x. 60 She bid the servant tell Lord G. that she desired his company. Lord G. was [= had] pranced out. *a* **1784** Johnson in Boswell *Life* (1816) II. 68 *note*, Sir, if a man has a mind to prance, he must study at Christ-Church and All-Souls. **1848** Thackeray *Van. Fair* xvi, Rawdon..pranced off to engage lodgings with all the impetuosity of love.

b. *intr.* To dance, gambol, caper. Now *colloq.*

c **1450** *Mankind* 91 in *Macro Plays* 4 Yf ȝe wyll, ser, my brother wyll make yow to prawnce. **1790** D. Morison *Poems* 47 He tunes his win'some reed, The wee things loup and prance. **1817** *Lintoun Green* ix. 93 Whilst they touzle, ramp, and prance, The carles took their gill. **1883** Gilmour *Mongols* xxvi. 315 Two or more figures in uncouth masks.. prance about in the circle to the sound of music.

4. *trans.* To drive or frighten by prancing.

1812 L. Hunt in *Examiner* 4 May 281/1 Who thinks he has nothing to do but to put on a laced jacket and go prancing his enemies into a fit.

Hence ˈ**prancing** *vbl. sb.* and *ppl. a.*

1412–20 Lydg. *Chron. Troy* III. xxii. (MS. Digby 230) lf. 106 b/1 Furious neiȝyng of many stede, Praunsynge of hors vp on ouþer side. **1552** Huloet, Praunsynge horses, *excussores equi*. *c* **1560** *Heart's-ease* 40 in T. Rychardes *Misogonus* II, Our minds to please and live at ease, And sometimes to use praunsinge. **1611** Bible *Judg.* v. 22. —— *Nahum* iii. 2 The noise of a whip..and of the praunsing horses [**1885** (*R.V.*) and pransing horses]. **1635** Quarles *Embl.* III. ii. 22 If the fool unstride His prauncing stallion, thou may'st up and ride. *a* **1732** Gay (J.), Now rule thy prancing steeds, lac'd charioteer. **1740** C. Pitt *Æneid* XII. 465 Shook by the prancings of the thund'ring horse. **1853** Humphreys *Coin-Coll. Man.* xxii. (1876) 278 The type of the reverse is the Dioscuri on prancing horses.

[*Note.* The phonology and spelling of *praunse, pranse, praunce, prance*, suggest French origin, but no corresponding or allied word is recorded in French. Danish dialects have *prandse, pranse* (N. Jutland), 'to go in a stately, proud fashion', with an adj. *prans, pransk* 'spirited, proud, said of a horse' (Fejlberg), whence a vb. *pranske*; other dialects have *pronse*, etc. in similar senses. These resemble the Eng. word; but their age and history are unknown. Less likely to be connected are Bavar. dial. *prangezen, prangssen* to make compliments, assume airs, *prangss* assumption of airs, affected behaviour, and Swiss dial. *spranzen* to strut. Cf. also the later prank *v.*³, the identity of sense of which is remarkable, since it is difficult to equate the forms: see the Note there.]

prancer (ˈprɑːnsə(r), -æ-). [f. prance *v.* + -er¹.] One who or that which prances.

1. a. *Thieves' cant* and *slang*. A horse.

1567 Harman *Caveat* (1869) 42 A Prigger of Prauncers be horse stealers; for to prigge signifieth in their language to steale, and a Prauncer is a horse. **1622** Fletcher *Beggars' Bush* v. ii, Higgen hath prigg'd the prancers in his days. *a* **1700** B. E. *Dict. Cant. Crew, Prancer*, a Horse. **1821** Scott *Kenilw.* xxiii, I would have thought little to have prigged a prancer from the next common.

b. in general use: A mettled or prancing horse; a steed. Also *fig.*

1599 Porter *Angry Wom. Abingd.* (Percy Soc.) 19 Where stands this prawncer, in what inne or stable? **1609** W. M. *Man in Moone* (Percy Soc.) 15 'This prauncer', said Opinion, 'hath beene a wilde colt, and leaped thorough many honest men's gates in his dayes'. **1644** Evelyn *Diary* 23 Nov., Then the Captaine..of the Castle of St. Angelo upon a brave prancer. **1815** W. H. Ireland *Scribbleomania* 151 Thus corporal's guard I've review'd on their prancers. **1842** Tennyson *Sir Launcelot & Q. Guinevere* 33 She whose elfin prancer springs By night to eery warblings.

†**2.** *Old slang.* A mounted robber; a highwayman. (According to Farmer, A horse-thief.) *Obs.*

c **1600** Day *Begg. Bednall Gr.* I. iii. (1881) 21 He wo'd be your prigger, your prancer, your high-lawyer. **1673** R. Head *Canting Acad.* 192 The fifteenth a Prancer, whose courage is small; If they catch him horse-coursing he's noozed for al.

3. a. A rider on a prancing horse; *slang*, a cavalry officer. **b.** One who capers or dances.

1860 J. Nicholson *Kilwuddie*, etc. (1895) 131 (E.D.D.) My fegs, but he's a prancer..Ye ne'er saw sic a dancer. *a* **1863** Thackeray *White Squall* 120 A Prussian captain of Lancers (Those tight-laced, whiskered prancers). **1873** *Slang Dict., Prancer*,..in modern slang an officer of cavalry.

pranck(e, obs. form of prank.

†**ˈprancome.** *Obs. rare*⁻¹. [f. prank *sb.*²; see princum (-prancum).] ? Prank, freak.

1575 *Gamm. Gurton* I. ii. A iij, Gogs hart, I durst haue layd my cap to a crowne Chwould lerne of some prancome, as sone as ich came to town.

prandial (ˈprændɪəl), *a.* *affected* or *jocose*. [f. L. *prandium* a late breakfast, luncheon + -al¹.] Pertaining or relating to dinner.

1820 [see post-prandial]. **1821–30** Ld. Cockburn *Mem.* 36 Every glass during dinner required to be dedicated to the health of some one... This prandial nuisance was horrible. **1851** J. Harris in Macfarlane *Mem. T. Archer* vi. (1867) 147, I should not accept your prandial invitation. **1883** *Harper's Mag.* July 927/2 Expenses legal, medical, funereal and prandial.

Hence **ˈprandially** *adv.*, in connexion with dinner.

1837 *Fraser's Mag.* XV. 575 Any such social outrage..if prandially inflicted, is about as justifiable a proceeding. **1895** A. Stoddart *Blackie* xii. 307 Their communion, bodily and prandially, was in one of the Princes Street hotels.

†**ˈprandicle.** *Obs. rare*⁻⁰. [ad. L. *prandiculum*, dim. of *prandium* luncheon.]

1656 Blount *Glossogr., Prandicle*, a breakfast, a little dinner, a small pittance or repast. **1658** in Phillips.

Prandtl (prænt(ə)l). [Name of Ludwig *Prandtl* (1875–1953), German physicist.] ***Prandtl number***: a dimensionless parameter used in calculations of heat transfer between a moving fluid and a solid body, equal to $c_p v/k$, where c_p is the heat capacity of unit volume of the fluid, v is its kinematic viscosity, and k its thermal conductivity.

1933 W. H. McAdams *Heat Transmission* iv. 96 Prandtl number = 1/Stanton group. **1954** R. Stephenson *Introd. Nucl. Engin.* vi. 245 The ratio of the quantity of heat transferred by convection to the quantity of heat transferred by conduction is given by the value of the Prandtl number for the fluid. **1958** [see Nusselt]. **1974** F. M. White *Viscous Fluid Flow* ii. 84 Table 2-1 gives values of the Prandtl number for various fluids at 68°F. It shows that liquid metals have [a] very small Prandtl number, gases slightly less than unity, thin liquids somewhat higher than unity, and oils a very large value of *Pr*.

prane, prang, obs. ff. prawn, prong.

prang (præŋ), *sb.* *slang* (orig. R.A.F.). [etym. uncertain.] **1. a.** An accident in which an aircraft suffers damage; a crash-landing. **b.** A bombing-raid. Also *transf.* and *fig.*

1942 *Sun* (Baltimore) 7 Apr. 20/8 American flyers in the RAF Eagle Squadrons have introduced a new decoration. 'The Order of Prang'—but it never appears in official citations. 'Prang' is Eagle slang for crash. **1943** Hunt & Pringle *Service Slang* 53 'P/O Prune' is the title bestowed upon a pilot who has several 'prangs' on his record. **1945** Partridge *Dict. R.A.F. Slang* 45 *Prang*, a crash landing. (2) A bombing raid. **1946** G. Gibson *Enemy Coast Ahead* 105, I like high-level attacks..or else it must be the very low-level prang. **1948** G. Greene *Heart of Matter* III. i. 294 'There's no time like the present for a prang,' Bagster said, moving her firmly towards the bed. **1958** *Spectator* 16 May 614/1 The Prime Minister was questioned about the RAF's wizard prang on the Government's defence policy. **1979** N. Slater *Falcon* ii. 36 Tell him about your wizard prangs in the war.

2. An accident or collision involving a road vehicle; a car-crash.

1959 *Sunday Times* 1 Nov. 23/2 The grisly enormities of American stock-car racing, with an hysterical ghoul of a commentator who revelled in every prang. **1971** A. Diment *Think Inc.* ii. 26 Might have had a bad prang before they re-sprayed her.

prang, *v.* *slang.* (orig. R.A.F.). [etym. uncertain.] **1.** *trans.* **a.** To crash or crash-land (an aircraft); to damage (part of an aircraft) during a crash-landing. Also const. *down*.

1941 *Tee Emm* (Air Ministry) July 6/1 Do they give a grateful sigh and shut up shop when the last serviceable aircraft has been pranged against a hangar because its pilot would land towards obstacles? **1942** *R.A.F. Jrnl.* 18 Apr. 1 Gremlins..run down the nose of the machine and tip you up and you prang a prop. **1942** *Tee Emm* (Air Ministry) II. 143 By now he didn't give a darn—He pranged her down beside the barn. **1944** 'N. Shute' *Pastoral* v. 107 After so many operations it was an acute personal grief to him that he had pranged his Wimpey. **1977** *Belfast Tel.* 28 Feb. 9/1 (*caption*) The half of the propellor he is holding came off a Bristol fighter he 'pranged' in a schoolyard in 1925.

b. To bomb (a target) successfully from the air.

1942 [see finger *sb.* 3 a]. **1943** B. J. Hurren *Eastern Med.* 27 One can picture the..rage of the German and Italian air commanders..each verging on apoplexy that their chosen pilots should not be able to 'prang' a ship which presented a clear, long, visible deck target area of some 600 feet by 90 feet wide. **1952** M. Tripp *Faith is Windsock* v. 87 The Lancs broke off sharply at the last moment to prang Neuss. **1958** E. Hyams *Taking it Easy* I. i. 16 The RAF said they didn't know how to, they just know about pranging the Luftwaffe and the railway yard at Ham.

c. To involve (a road vehicle or other object) in an accident; to crash or 'smash up'; to collide with.

1952 E. F. Davies *Illyrian Venture* iii. 50 'What height would you like to be dropped at?' 'Would 800 feet suit you?' .. 'I think I can manage that without pranging the mountain.' **1966** T. Wisdom *High-Performance Driving* ix. 97 The driver may well have left his 'flasher' on many corners ago and is happily oblivious of the fact until you move off on his signal and 'prang' him. **1971** *Daily Colonist* (Victoria, B.C.) 26 Feb. 2/1 Recently my rather ancient Chevvy II got pranged from behind—nothing serious, just a smashed tail light. **1973** A. Mann *Tiara* ix. 79 Most of them don't drive... If they prang a car, there's always plenty of witnesses to say it's the priest's fault. **1976** *Islander* (Victoria, B.C.) 22 Aug. 11/1 We had pranged a rock getting out of Oak Bay.

2. *intr.* To crash or crash-land an aircraft. Also *transf.*

1943 P. Brennan et al. *Spitfires over Malta* ii. 55 The upwind end of the landing-path was a maze of bomb-holes. .. I was too brassed off to worry whether I pranged or not. **1961** 'J. Ross' *Last August* iii. 31 A wasp was pranging against the window. **1968** *Daily Express* 26 Feb. 4/1, I knew we were going to prang, but all I wanted to do was to make sure that we weren't killed or seriously injured.

3. *trans.* In extended uses: to break, to smash; to hit, to strike heavily (*against*). Also *fig.*

1942 J. Moore in *Observer* 4 Oct. 7/2 Now you talk..of pranging a date, meaning that you have left your popsy waiting outside the Unicorn while you continue to drink with the squadron in the Bull and Bush. **1943** Hunt & Pringle *Service Slang* 53 Jones pranged his arm at rugger to-day. **1946** *Slipstream* 38 Mind you don't prang yourselves against the table. **1948** Partridge *Dict. Forces' Slang* 147 He pranged the iron bedstead... He pranged his leg against the bedstead. **1977** F. Parrish *Fire in Barley* x. 99 He was holding a pitchfork. 'I thought I'd prang a rabbit.'

Hence **pranged** *ppl. a.*; **ˈpranging** *vbl. sb.*

1942 *Air News* Oct. 4/1 'Pranging', by the way, is a new R.A.F. expression which means smashing things up—including one's own aeroplane. **1946** Brickhill & Norton *Escape to Danger* iii. 39 A couple of 109's hacked two Hurricane down near Montreuil on the 10th of June 1940, and Eric jumped from his pranged kite and ran for it. **1959** *Times Lit. Suppl.* 7 Aug. p. iii/3 Classic understating metaphors like 'having a party', 'falling in the drink', 'pranging', and so on, had their value in time of war. **1971** R. Dentry *Encounter at Kharmel* vii. 117 Looking for the wreckage of a pranged aircraft.

†**ˈprangle**, *v.* *Obs. rare*⁻¹. [Frequentative from OTeut. vbl. stem ****prang-*** to press, squeeze, whence Goth. (*ana-*)*praggan* to oppress, Du., LG. *prangen* to pinch, etc., Du. *pranger* a barnacle for a horse: see -le 3.] *trans.* To press tightly, pinch.

c **1300** *Havelok* 639 And for keuel at þe laste, þat in mi mouth was þrist faste, Y was þe[r]with so harde prangled, þat I was þe[r]with ney strangled.

†**prank**, *sb.*¹ *Obs. rare.* [Goes with prank *v.*¹: see also prank *sb.*²] A pleat, a fold.

c **1440** *Promp. Parv.* 411/2 Prank, of prankynge, *plica, plicatura*.

prank (præŋk), *sb.*² Also 6 **pranque**, 6–7 **pranck(e**, 6–8 **pranke**. [Origin unascertained. Goes with prank *v.*², both appearing *c* 1525.

Some would connect the vb. and sb. with prank *v.*⁴, and the cognate words there mentioned, taking a 'trick' as 'an act done to show off'; but this does not appear to be supported by the early use. Others would take it as a fig. application of prank *sb.*¹ fold, pleat, comparing the fig. sense of 'wrinkle', but the evidence is not sufficient to substantiate the suggestion.]

A trick; a frolic. †**a.** In early use, a trick of malicious or mischievous nature; a trick or action deserving of reprobation; a deed of wickedness; sometimes rendering L. *scelus* or *facinus*. *Obs.*

a **1529** Skelton *Agst. Scottes* 150 Your pryde was peuysh to play such prankys. **1530** Palsgr. 658 He wyll playe me a pranke, *il me jouera dune bricolle*. **1532** More *Confut. Tindale* Wks. 665/2 Now hath it bene an old prank of heretykes, to vse that fashyon of malycyouse corruptynge the bookes of the holye scrypture. **1539** Cromwell in Merriman *Life & Lett.* (1902) II. 182 Themperour whom his grace knoweth.. more to regarde his honour and profitt then to Imagyn and Consent to so an unreasonable shame-full & dishonourable pranque. **1568** *Hist. Jacob & Esau* IV. i. in Hazl. *Dodsley* II. 230 Mother, by such a prank the matter will be worse. **1600** Holland *Livy* XXXIII. xxix. 841 At length they played these prancks [*facinora fecerunt*]..of malice unto them. **1602** Shaks. *Ham.* III. iv. 2. **1654** Trapp *Comm. Ezra* iv. 6 Infamous..for many lewd pranks (as that he killed his brother, and then his owne sister). **1727** De Foe *Syst. Magic* I. iii. (1840) 89 This was not the first of his pranks which he [the Devil] played upon mankind after the flood. **1737** Whiston *Josephus, Hist.* IV. iii. §5 They grew the more insolent upon this bold prank.

†**b.** A trick of magic, conjuring, or the like; in early times to deceive, later to surprise or amuse.

1555 J. Harpsfield in Bonner *Homilies* 49 Those prankes played by Simon Magus. **1613** Purchas *Pilgrimage* (1614) 433 Either iuggling or Magicall prankes practised by the Samoed-Coniurours or Priests. **1650** Milton *Tenure Kings* 60 Like those priests of Bel, whose pranks Daniel found out. **1756** C. Lucas *Ess. Waters* III. 329 He had the honor of playing his pranks before the whole court. **1840** Hood *Kilmansegg, Pedigree* viii, Golden bees, by alchemical prank, Gather'd gold instead of honey.

c. A trick of a frolicsome nature, or one intended to make sport; a mad frolic; a practical joke.

1576 Fleming *Panopl. Epist.* 282 Who in all his purposes and practises, playeth ranckes of puerilitie and childishnesse. **1602** Rowlands *Tis Merrie when Gossips meete* 18 But Lord the prankes that we mad-wenches playde. **1643** Burroughes *Exp. Hosea* xvi. (1652) 412 Tell tales of the pranckes of your younger dayes. *a* **1713** T. Ellwood *Autobiog.* (1765) 5 Often playing one waggish Prank or other among my fellow scholars. **1844** Emerson *Misc. Papers, Tantalus* Wks. (Bohn) III. 319 See the child..with his thousand pretty pranks, commanded by every sight and sound. **1884** Lady Verney in *Contemp. Rev.* Oct. 550 The pranks are not those of healthy schoolboys.

d. Said of capricious or frolicsome actions or movements of animals, and *fig.* of erratic actions of machines.

1692 Bentley *Boyle Lect.* 138 We appeal to observation, whether..all the various machins and utensils would now and then play odd pranks and capricio's quite contrary to their proper structures and the designs of the artificers. **1711** Addison *Spect.* No. 117 ¶5 The Cat is reported..to have played several Pranks above the Capacity of an ordinary Cat. **1784** Cowper *Task* v. 52 [The dog] Then..barks for joy. Heedless of all his pranks, the sturdy churl Moves right toward the mark.

prank, *sb.*³ *rare.* [f. prank *v.*³] Prancing, capering.

1844 Mrs. Browning *To Flush* iv, Full of prank and curveting.

†**prank**, *a.* *Obs.* [Related to prank *v.*⁴ and MLG. *prank* sb., pomp, display.] Smartly, showily, or gaily dressed.

1575 R. B. *Appius & Virginia* B ij, Ah pretie pranck parnel, the Coushen and Booke, Whereon he shoulde reade and kneele, are present here looke. **1589** R. Robinson *Gold. Mirr.* (Chetham Soc.) 58 Their children as I sayd, so pranck in pride. **1607** *Lingua* IV. vii. I iv b, If I doe not seeme pranker nowe, then I did in those dayes, Ile be hang'd. **1615** Brathwait *Strappado* (1878) 209 The 5. so pranke, he scarce can stand on ground, Asking who'le sing with him Mal Dixons round?

†**prank**, *v.*¹ *Obs.* [Goes with prank *sb.*¹, both appearing *c* 1440. Origin unascertained. There is nothing similar in form and sense in the Teutonic or the Romanic langs.] *trans.* To fold, plait, pleat, arrange in pleats.

c **1440** *Promp. Parv.* 411/2 Prankynge, *plicacio*. *a* **1529** Skelton *El. Rummyng* 69 Stytched and pranked with pletes. **1530** Palsgr. 664/1, I pranke ones gowne, I set the plyghtes in order, *je mets les plies dune robe a poynt*. **1590** Spenser *F.Q.* I. iv. 14 Some prancke their ruffes; and others trimly dight Their gay attyre.

b. *fig.* To arrange in proper order, put into order.
1676 W. Row *Contn. Blair's Autobiog.* ix. (1848) 151 Matters being in great confusion, and no appearance of pranking of them.

Hence †**pranked** *ppl. a.*, folded, pleated, adorned with pleats; †'**pranking** *vbl. sb.*
c **1440** *Promp. Parv.* 411/2 Prankyd, as clothys, *plicatus*. *Ibid.*, Prankynge, *plicacio*. *c* **1460** *Towneley Myst.* xxx. 288 Of prankyd gownes & shulders vp set, mos & flokkys sewyd wyth in. **1676** Pranking [see b above].

prank, *v.*[2] *Obs.* or *dial.* [app. f. PRANK *sb.*[2]; the sb. and vb. appear together *c* 1525.] *intr.* To play pranks or tricks, formerly sometimes wicked or mischievous, now usually in frolic; to sport.
1530 PALSGR. 664/1, I prank with one, I use craftye and subtyll maner towardes hym, *je me subtille*. *c* **1700** *Patch-Work* I. 22 Did not Somaisius and Melancton; Nay, Luther, though the Pope he prank'd on, Own him Head of the Church, ne'erless, And his Supremacy confess? **1826** HOGG *Love's Jubilee* 33 The little rays of sin That prank with the damask vein of the cheek. **1887** WILLOCK *Rosetty Ends* xii. 88 It formed a halesome lesson to him no' to prank wi' blue or red fire for a while again. **1897** *Outing* (U.S.) XXX. 456/2 A little wind, born in the gorge below, was pranking with the quaking asp leaves.

prank, *v.*[3] *Obs.* or *dial.* [Appears early in 16th c.: origin obscure: see *Note* below.]
intr. = PRANCE *v.* (in various senses, esp. with suggestion of display or arrogance); to caper; to dance. Also *to prank it*.
1519 *Interl. Four Elements* E vj b, And I can fote it by and by etc., And I can pranke it properly. *a* **1529** SKELTON *Caudatos Anglos* 57 That dronke asse..That prates and prankes. *c* **1560** *Jack Juggler* in Hazl. *Dodsley* II. 117 And a maid we have at home, Alison Trip-and-go..She simpereth, she pranketh, and jetteth without fail. **1567** GOLDING *Ovid's Met.* VI. (1593) 136 Who..With haughtie looke and stately gate went pranking vp and downe. **1570** LEVINS *Manip.* 24/25 To Pranke, *exultare, gestire*. **1587** FLEMING *Contn. Holinshed* III. 1983/1 About a mile from the English campe were the Scots horsemen verie busie, pranking vp and downe. **1842** HALLIWELL *Nursery Rhymes* (Percy Soc.) 76 His nag did kick and prank. **1870** *Daily News* 12 July, Placid infants,..who looked anything but fit for pranking it according to Offenbach.

Hence '**pranking** *vbl. sb.* and *ppl. a.*
a **1529** SKELTON *Poems agst. Garnesche* I. 19 For alle your proude prankyng, Your pride may apayere. **1904** M. HEWLETT *Queen's Quair* I. xii. 188 So the wilful lass has got her master! And a pranking rider for a bitter jade!

[*Note*. *Prank* has the appearance of a by-form of the earlier vb. PRANCE, with which, to a great extent, it coincides in sense. But its form makes the relationship difficult, *prance* and *pranke* being app. possible as parallel forms only in words from French. On the other hand, it may possibly be related to Du. *pronken* in the sense 'strut, parade', and so have the same ultimate origin as PRANK *v.*[4], although the two appear to be quite distinct words in English.]

prank (præŋk), *v.*[4] [Goes with PRANK *a.*, both being radically cognate with Du. *pronk* show, ostentation, finery, ornament, Ger. *prunk* pomp, parade, ostentation, MLG. *prank* pomp, display. (There is no corresp. sb. in Eng.) The vb. in Du. is *pronken* to show off, shine, strut, parade, in Ger. *prunken* to make a show or display, to 'show off'. Cf. also PRINK *v.*]
1. *trans.* To dress, or deck in a gay, bright, or showy manner; to decorate; *refl.* to deck oneself *out*, dress oneself *up*.
1546 BALE *Eng. Votaries* I. (1560) 22 Pranked vp with Tabernacles and lightes. **1553** —— *Vocacyon* Pref. 4 b, Not pranked vp in pompe and pleasures. **1580** LYLY *Euphues* (Arb.) 433 As willing..as you are to prancke your selues in a lookinge Glasse. **1592** NASHE *P. Penilesse* (ed. 2) 10 b, She ..spends halfe a day in pranking her selfe if she be inuited to any strange place. **1652–62** HEYLIN *Cosmogr.* I. (1682) 60 She..will be so pranked up on the Sundays..that one.. might easily mistake her for some noble Lady. **1809** W. IRVING *Knickerb.* VII. ii, All the burghers of New-Amsterdam with their wives and daughters, pranked out in their best attire. **1881** BESANT & RICE *Chapl. of Fleet* I. x, Women are fond..of pranking themselves continually in some new finery. **1895** ZANGWILL *Master* II. x, The little village was prankt and rejuvenated.
b. *fig.* To dress up.
1607 SHAKS. *Cor.* III. i. 23 They doe pranke them in Authoritie Against all Noble sufferance. **1634** MILTON *Comus* 759 Obtruding false rules pranckt in reasons garb. **1742** COLLINS *Odes* xi. 15 Science, prank'd in tissu'd vest.
c. *transf.* To deck, adorn; to brighten or set out with colours; to spangle. In various constructions, e.g. to prank (the field) with flowers, to prank (the garden or field) as a flower.
1591 SYLVESTER *Du Bartas* I. iv. 446 The least Flowr that pranks Our Garden borders or the Common banks. *Ibid.* 674 The Gardens prank them with their Flowry buds. **1652** BENLOWES *Theoph.* XII. l, When opal-colours prank the orient Tulips head. **1748** THOMSON *Cast. Indol.* I. ii, A season atween June and May, Half prankt with spring, with summer half imbrowned. **1820** SHELLEY *Sensit. Plant* I. 42 The stream whose inconstant bosom Was prankt under boughs of embowering blossom With golden and green light. **1820** —— *Question* iv, Broad flag-flowers, purple prankt with white. **1880** L. WALLACE *Ben-Hur* 200 The ground was pranked with the brightest blooms.
¶**d.** *pa. pple.* ? 'Set' (like a gem).
(App. an erroneous use, 'prankt' suggesting ideas of bespangled, begemmed.)
1817 SHELLEY *Rev. Islam* IX. i, Poplars..whose shade did cover The waning stars, prankt in the waters blue. **1821** —— *Hellas* 1049 Around mountains and islands inviolably Prankt on the sapphire sea.
2. *intr.* (for *refl.*) To show oneself off, make ostentatious show or display. Also *to prank it*.
1567 GOLDING *Ovid's Met.* VIII. P iv, Yet would I make it [a tree] ere I go To kisse the clowers with her top that pranks with braunches so. **1592** GREENE *Upst. Courtier* G j b, Hee shall not want silkes, sattins, veluets, to pranke abroade in his pomp. **1610** B. JONSON *Alch.* IV. vii, That ruffe of pride ..is the same With that, which the vncleane birds in seuenty-seuen, Were seene to pranke it with, on diuers coasts. **1649** tr. *Warn. Jac. Beem* xvi. 15 Wherewith I have not hitherto proudly prancked and vaunted. **1844** MRS. BROWNING *Romaunt of Page* ix, Or, speak she fair, or prank she gay, She is no lady of mine. **1867** M. ARNOLD *Obermann once more* i, White houses prank where once were huts.

pranked, *ppl. a.*[1], folded, pleated: see PRANK *v.*[1]

pranked, prankt, *ppl. a.*[2] [f. PRANK *v.*[4]] Decked, dressed up; decorated, bedecked.
c **1550** *Pryde & Abuse of Women* xvii. in Hazl. *E.P.P.* IV. 237 For there are some prancked gosseps every where, Able to spyll a whole countrie. **1602** WARNER *Alb. Eng.* IX. xlvii. (1612) 219 Good God, how formall, prankt, and peart became I in a trice. *c* **1610** *Women Saints* 92 Modwene.. forsooke the worlde, and all the gaye shewes and pranked profers thereof. **1877** LANIER *Florida Sunday* 65 Grays, whites and red of pranked woodpeckers.
¶ See also PRANK *v.*[4] 1 d.

'**pranker**. [f. PRANK *v.*[3] + -ER[1].]
1. = PRANCER. †**a.** *Thieves' cant.* A horse (*obs.*). **b.** A dancer.
1591 GREENE *Art Conny Catch.* II. (1592) 4 They..doe take an especiall view, where prankers or horses be. **1621** BURTON *Anat. Mel.* III. ii. VI. iii. (1651) 563 If she be a noted reveller, a gadder, a singer, a pranker or dancer, then take heed of her. **1886** G. H. BOUGHTON in *Harper's Mag.* Dec. 24 One of the most abandoned of the prankers and myself.. were tempted by cool shades of the fragrant wood to wander off.
†**2.** *pl.* Prancing action (as of a horse). *Obs.*
1636 SAMPSON *Vow-breakers* V. i. I iij, Have I practic'd my Reines, my Carree'res, my Pranckers, my Ambles, my false Trotts, my smooth Ambles, and Canterbury Paces, and shall Master Major put me besides the hobby-Horse?

'**prankful**, *a.* [f. PRANK *sb.*[2] + -FUL.] Full of pranks; mischievous, tricky; frolicsome. Hence '**prankfulness**.
1824 GALT *Rothelan* I. II. ix. 228 The prankful boy goading it with a stick, the charger reared so suddenly that the rider was unseated. **1831** *Fraser's Mag.* II. 715 Rather wounding by an unbounded prankfulness, than by a wish to inflict pain. **1839** *New Monthly Mag.* LVII. 36 Prankful squirrels, nibbling at the rind.

pranking, *vbl. sb.*[1], folding: see PRANK *v.*[1]

pranking, *vbl. sb.*[2], prancing: see PRANK *v.*[3]

pranking ('præŋkɪŋ), *vbl. sb.*[3] [f. PRANK *v.*[4] + -ING[1].] The action of PRANK *v.*[4]; decking, dressing up, 'titivating', 'making up'.
1580 HOLLYBAND *Treas. Fr. Tong*, *Attiffement*, pranking. **1594** T. B. *La Primaud. Fr. Acad.* II. 77 In all their paintings and prankings they..lift vp themselues against nature. **1612** W. PARKES *Curtaine-Dr.* (1876) 56 The nightly and nightlong prancking and pruning vp of old withered faces. **1664** H. MORE *Exp. 7 Epist.* vi. (1669) 78 Her prankings and adornings in the splendour of their Altars, and Churches, and Copes.

†'**prankingly**, *adv. Obs. rare.* [f. *pranking*, pr. pple. of PRANK *v.*[4] + -LY[2].] In a pranking or ostentatious manner, showily.
1610 BP. HALL *Apol. Brownists* xv. 43 He, his wife, and her daughter fared daintily, and went prankingly in apparell.

'**prankish**, *a.* [f. PRANK *sb.*[2] + -ISH[1].] Of the nature of a prank; inclined to pranks.
1827 HOOD *Mids. Fairies* lxxxix, My partner dear in many a prankish deed. **1868** HOLME LEE *B. Godfrey* xxxviii, She ..had quite dropt her prankish airs. **1887** MRS. HAWEIS in *Pall Mall G.* 1 Nov. 1/2 Stories concerning mischievous and prankish children.
Hence '**prankishly** *adv.*, in a prankish manner, by way of a prank; '**prankishness**, trickiness, frolicsomeness; addiction to pranks.
1881 W. M. ROSSETTI in *Art Jrnl.* 262/2 The insolent prankishness of his age. **1883** HOLME LEE *Loving & Serving* I. ix. 184 She had prankishly avoided him. **1892** *Nation* (N.Y.) 15 Dec. 456/1 If parents do not..have to trace prankishness and mischievousness to the same exemplars. **1899** *Westm. Gaz.* 15 May 1/3 If he were a very young man ..we might be indulgent to this prankishness.

prankle ('præŋk(ə)l), *v.* Now *dial.* [dim. or freq. of PRANK *v.*[3]: see -LE 3.] *intr.* To prance lightly, to move in a capering way.
a **1717** PARNELL *Fairy Tale* vii, He sees a [fairy] train profusely gay Come prankling o'er the place. **1829** W. IRVING *Conq. Granada* I. xii. 112 The prankling army of highmettled warriors issued from the ancient gates. **1903** *Eng. Dial. Dict.* (I. of Wight), *Prankle*..to prance.

pranksome ('præŋksəm), *a.* [f. PRANK *sb.*[2] + -SOME.] Addicted to pranks; prankish, frolicsome.
1810 in *Spirit Pub. Jrnls.* XIV. 148 To swell her brazen store, With one such pranksome, titt'ring booby more. **1812** BYRON *Ch. Har.* I. xiv. (Orig. Draft), And often would his pranksome prate engage Childe Harold's ear. **1876** W. H. MASON in *Macm. Mag.* XXXIV. 452 Some pranksome imp ..has turned off the hot water.
Hence '**pranksomeness**.
1899 *Daily News* 4 Nov. 7/3 The monkey-like pranksomeness of the merry, mischievous race.

prankster ('præŋkstə(r)). orig. *U.S.* [f. PRANK *sb.*[2] + -STER.] One who plays pranks; a hoaxer, a practical joker.
1927 *Amer. Speech* II. 245/1, *-ster* also, for a time, gave signs of being moribund... It is, however, found in a number of new formations...*prankster*, [etc.]. **1940** O. NASH *Face is Familiar* (1942) 14 There is at least one thing I would less rather have in the neighbourhood than a gangster, And that one thing is a practical prankster. **1951** *Mind* LX. 468 Suppose a prankster laid out some railroad tracks which..diverged in such a manner as to make them look parallel. **1957** C. RICE *My Kingdom for Hearse* i. 6 Some practical prankster had evidently left a dead horse in his nose. **1969** *Daily Tel.* 14 Nov. 36/4 Police admitted that it was an almost impossible task..to sift the bomb pranksters from the deadly serious ones. **1972** 'M. YORKE' *Silent Witness* III. 51 The key..had been turned on her... 'Some prankster, I suppose... It was a very childish trick.' **1977** *Time* 24 Jan. 37/1 Ken Waller, a not-too-merry prankster who steals bits of his opponents' costumes in order to upset their concentration before they go onstage to face the judges.

'**pranky**, *a. rare.* [f. PRANK *sb.*[2] + -Y.] Given to or full of pranks.
a **1553** UDALL *Royster D.* III. iii. (Arb.) 47 So, that is some-what like, but prankie cote, nay whan, That is a lustie brute, handes vnder your side man. **1828** *Blackw. Mag.* XXIII. 10 The strangest and most curious pranky little beings that ever were born. **1865** *Pall Mall G.* 16 Sept. 6/1 Merely a demonstration of pranky lawlessness.

pranque, obs. form of PRANK *sb.*[2]

†**pransawte**. *Obs. rare*[−1]. [? Some kind of deriv. of PRANCE *v.*] (?) Prancing, showing off.
c **1460** *Towneley Myst.* xxx. 561 Thay were sturdy and hawte..Youre pride and youre pransawte, What will it gawne? Ye tolde ilk mans defawte and forgate youre awne.

†**pran'sorious**, *a. Obs. rare*[−0]. [f. L. *pransōrius* pertaining to breakfast (f. *prandēre* to breakfast) + -OUS.]
1656 BLOUNT *Glossogr.*, *Pransorious*, of or belonging, or serving for dinner.

praoe, variant of PROA.

p'raps (præps), *adv.* Also **praps, p'r'aps, p'rhaps**. Repr. colloq. pronuncs. of PERHAPS *adv.*
1835 HOOD *Poetry, Prose, & Worse* v, He..is p'rhaps the sole Bard at this present Whose Poems are certain to pay. **1837** DICKENS *Pickw.* xxxii, 'Very good, sir,' responded Mrs. Raddle, with lofty politeness. 'Then p'raps, sir, you'll' [etc.]. **1898** G. B. SHAW *Candida* I. 93, I did think you a bit of a fool once; but I'm beginnin' to think that praps I was be'ind the times a bit. **1912** MASEFIELD *Widow in Bye St.* 24 We might go round one evening, p'raps. ? **1912** R. FRY *Lett.* (1972) I. 358 Don't leave this letter about... P'raps you'll *want* to burn it. **1955** N. MARSH *Scales of Justice* iv. 75, I know what they'll say about me. Not you, p'r'aps, but the others. **1974** 'P. B. YUILL' *Bornless Keeper* iv. 33 Praps we'd better both wait. **1976** D. CLARK *Dread & Water* vi. 126 P'raps you'll tell me what you're gunna do about it?

prasad, prasada (prə'sɑːd, -ə). *Hinduism.* [Skr. *prasāda* lit. clearness, kindness, grace, Hindi *prasād*.] **1.** A propitiatory offering of food made to a god; food which is offered to an idol and then shared among devotees.
1828 H. H. WILSON in *Asiatic Researches* XVI. 83 A *Chamár*, oh king, ministers to the *Sálagrám*, and poisons the town with his *Prasád*. *Ibid.* 96 At noon, he halted and bathed the god, and prepared his food, and presented it, and then took the *Prasád* and put it in a vessel, and fed upon what remained. **1855** —— *Gloss. Judicial & Revenue Terms* 424/2 All castes may partake of the *Prasád* of any image. **1875** MONIER WILLIAMS *Indian Wisdom* p. xxxvii, It is remarkable that the food offered to the gods, when appropriated and eaten by the priests, and the rice distributed by them to the people, are called *prasāda* (? = εὐχαριστία). **1913** J. N. FARQUHAR *Crown of Hinduism* ix. 381 In modern temples, the practice is to give every worshipper a portion of the food and of the water offered to the idol. The food is called *prasāda*, a grace-gift, and the water *tīrtha*, holy water. **1953** K. W. MORGAN *Relig. Hindus* vii. 296 The food is first offered to the Lord and what is eaten is His prasāda. **1965** 'LAUCHMONEN' *Old Thom's Harvest* x. 132 East Indians..shared out prasad, mango..and rice. **1969** *Weekly Mail* (Madras) 26 July 7/5, 90 boys..became unconscious after taking 'prasad' at a religious function at Chakasigan village. **1979** D. QUINN *Fear of God* i. 52 The Indian said, 'Prasada, the remains are food offered to the Lord... The food is Krishna himself. You should eat it all.'
2. Divine grace or favour. Also *attrib.*
1895 E. W. HOPKINS *Relig. India* xv. 429 The *prasāda* doctrine (of special grace) belongs to a much earlier literature. **1921** R. E. HUME *Thirteen Princ. Upanishads* 59 As regards speculative knowledge of Ātman, its apprehension by means of human knowledge is opposed by the doctrine of prasāda, or 'Grace', in Katha 2.20. **1964** R. ANTOINE et al. *Relig. Hinduism* xxiii. 247 This divine grace: *anugraha, prasāda, puṣṭi, kṛpā*, is *the* means which habilitates the bhakta to the obtainment and practice of the bhakti.

prase (preɪz). *Min.* [a. F. *prase*, ad. L. *prasius* (Plin.) (formerly used in Eng.), a. Gr. πράσιος leek-green, f. πράσον leek.] A cryptocrystalline or crystalline variety of translucent quartz, of a leek-green colour.

α. **1398** TREVISA *Barth. De P.R.* XVI. lxxvi. (Bodl. MS.), Prassius is a grene stone as leke. **1601** HOLLAND *Pliny* II. 619 As touching green stones..we reckon one of a Porret colour, which we cal Prasius. **1750** tr. *Leonardus' Mirr.* 218 Prassius, is so called from an Herb of its own Name. **1796** KIRWAN *Elem. Min.* (ed. 2) I. 249 *Prasium*..seems to consist of a mixture of quartz, and shoerlaceous actinolite.

β. **1788** tr. *Cronstedt's Min.* (ed. 2) I. 144 As to the prase, its name..shows it to be of a greenish-blue colour. **1797** *Encycl. Brit.* (ed. 3) XII. 82 *note*, False emeralds, or prases. **1868** DANA *Min.* (ed. 5) 194 Quartz..Cryptocrystalline Varieties..4. Prase. Translucent and dull leek-green... Always regarded as a stone of little value. The name is also given to crystalline quartz of the same color.

prase, obs. form of PRAISE.

praseodymium (preɪziːə'dɪmɪəm). *Chem.* [mod.L., f. G. *praseodym* (C. A. von Welsbach 1885, in *Monatshefte f. Chem.* VI. 490), f. Gr. πράσιος leek-green (f. πράσον leek) + G. *di)dym* DIDYMIUM: see -IUM. Named in allusion to the colour of its salts and its isolation, with neodymium, from the supposed element didymium.] A metallic element, similar to iron in appearance, which is a typical lanthanide and forms leek-green compounds in which it has a valency of three (rarely four), some of which are used to impart a yellow colour to glasses and ceramics. Atomic number 59; symbol Pr.

1885 [see NEODYMIUM]. **1905** GOOCH & WALKER *Outl. Inorg. Chem.* xix. 493 For more than fifty years the elementary character of didymium was accepted, until Auer von Welsbach, by a most laborious process of fractional precipitation of the double nitrate of didymium and ammonium, succeeded in isolating two distinctly different double nitrates..from which were prepared two different series of salts, of different elements, which were now named praseodymium and neodymium. **1922** T. M. LOWRY *Inorg. Chem.* xxxiv. 672 Praseodymium also resembles cerium in forming a dioxide, PrO_2, when the nitrate is heated with potassium nitrate at 450°. **1950** *Thorpe's Dict. Appl. Chem.* (ed. 4) X. 183/2 All cerium-bearing minerals contain some praseodymium, e.g. cerite from Arendal (Switzerland) contains up to 8% of Pr_2O_3, monazite sand from Brazil, 5·5–6·2%. **1971** J. F. LIPTROT *Mod. Inorg. Chem.* xxvi. 438 Lanthanum, cerium, praseodymium, neodymium and gadolinium may be obtained by reduction of their trichlorides with calcium at about 1000°C. **1974** *Encycl. Brit. Micropædia* VIII. 179/2 Praseodymium is about one-third as abundant as lead and about a thousand times more plentiful than gold in the igneous rocks of the Earth's crust... Natural praseodymium is all stable isotope praseodymium-141.

praseolite ('preɪziːəlaɪt). *Min.* [ad. Sw. *praseolith* (Erdmann 1840), irreg. f. Gr. πράσ-ον or πράσι-ος (see PRASE) + -LITE.] An altered form of iolite.

1864–72 WATTS *Dict. Chem.* II. 320 Hydrous Dichroite.. Praseolite from Bräkke in Norway. **1868** DANA *Min.* (ed. 5) 301 The alteration of iolite takes place so readily..that the mineral is most commonly found in an altered state..as hydrous iolite, pinite,..gigantolite, praseolite, aspasiolite.

prashack, prashagh, etc., varr. PRAISEACH.

'prasiform, *a. Min. rare.* [f. as PRASE + -(I)FORM.] Resembling prase.

1796 KIRWAN *Elem. Min.* (ed. 2) I. 392 Prasiform Porphyry of Karsten.

prasilite: see *prasolite* (s.v. PRASO-).

prasine ('preɪzɪn), *sb.* and *a.* Also 5 **prasym**, 6 **prasne**. [ad. late L. *prasina* green chalk, fem. of L. *prasinus* adj. (Plin.), a. Gr. πράσινος leek-green, λίθος πρ. leek-green stone, an emerald or other green stone: cf. F. *prasine*, adj. (*pierre prasine* leek-green stone), and in later F. sb. fem. a green earth used as a pigment.]

A. *sb.* A green-coloured mineral: †(*a*) an earth, green chalk, or verdigris; †(*b*) a precious stone, sometimes app. the emerald; (*c*) now a synonym of pseudo-malachite (Chester *Dict. Min.* 1896).

[*c* **625** ISIDORE *Orig.* XIX. xvii. §9 Prasina, creta viridis, etsi in aliquibus terris promiscue generetur, optima tamen in Libya Cyrenensi.]

[*c* **1305** *Land Cokayne* 91 in *E.E.P.* (1862) 158 Smaragde, lugre, and prassiune.] **1398** TREVISA *Barth. De P.R.* XIX. xxviii. (Bodl. MS.), Prasyn creta is grene [*Prasina creta est viridis*] & þerof is colore made grene as leke. **1491** CAXTON *Vitas Patr.* I. xlviii. (1495) 92 b/2 The partye (of the sayde chyrche) wythout forthe on the syde of the South was of the colour semblable or lyke to a precyous stone namyd Prasym. **1555** W. WATREMAN *Fardle Facions* I. iv. 43 Precious stones called the Jacinthe, and the Prasne.

B. *adj.* Leek-like; leek-green in colour. *rare.* ***prasine stone*** = A. (*b*.)

1528 PAYNEL *Salerne's Regim.* b iv b, One is called coler prassine, lyke the colour of yͤ herbe called prassion. **1665** SIR T. HERBERT *Trav.* (1677) 351 All sorts of Stones and Mines of Gold e're-while Are found there, with the choicest Prasine-stone. **1882** *Gard. Chron.* XVIII. 40 The curious prasine peduncle is covered with numerous flowers.

'prasinous, *a.* [f. L. *prasin-us* (see prec.) + -OUS.] = prec. B.

1826 KIRBY & SP. *Entomol.* IV. xlvi. 281 *Prasinous*... The colour of the leaves of leeks or onions.

‖**praskeen** (pra'skiːn). *Ir.* [a. Ir. *praiscín* apron.] An apron, *esp.* a large coarse apron.

1843 W. CARLETON *Traits* I. 24 A wooden dish, confortably covered with a clane praskeen on the well-swept hearth-stone. **1881** *Macm. Mag.* Sept. 396 Their own servants gave the same reason for wearing no caps or praskeens.

praso-, repr. Gr. πράσο-ν leek, an element in technical words. **prasochrome** ('preɪzəʊkrəʊm) [CHROME], a dull-green incrustation on chromic iron, prob. calcite coloured by oxide of chromium (Chester *Dict. Min.* 1896). †**prasocoride** *Obs.* [Gr. πρασοκουρίς, -ιδ-], a grub which destroys leeks. **prasolite** ('preɪzəʊlaɪt) (Dana) (*erron.* **prasilite**) [-LITE], a leek-green fibrous mineral, probably a variant of chlorite (Chester). **pra'sophagous** *a.* [Gr. -φαγος eating], eating leeks; hence **pra'sophagy**.

c **1420** *Pallad. on Husb.* I. 953 The Grek seith that a beest, *prosacoride [*v.r.* prasocoride] the garth ennoyeth myche. **1882** *St. James' Gaz.* 11 Feb., I should not have been *prasophagous if I had had the chance. *Ibid.*, *Prasophagy is..for a time a very cheap form of diet.

prasoid ('preɪzɔɪd), *a.* [ad. L. *prasoīdes*, a. Gr. πρασοειδής leek-green.] Resembling prase.

1849 DANA *Geol.* xvii. (1850) 632 We may distinguish it as prasoid rock. **1858** in MAYNE *Expos. Lex.*

prast, variant of PREST *a. Obs.*

prat (præt), *sb.*[1] and *a.* Now only *Sc.* Forms: 1 prætt, 1–3 præt, 3 (9 *Sc.*) pret, 5 (6 *Sc.*) pratte, 6–9 *Sc.* pratt, 7– *Sc.* prat. [OE. *prætt* guile, a trick: cf. MDu. *parte*, Du. *part* crafty trick, prank; also MDu., Flem. *perte*, Du., EFris., LG. *pret*, ON. *prettr*, Norw. *pretta* a roguish trick, etc. Ulterior origin obscure. See also PRETTY *a.*

It is remarkable that, with the exception of the instances in Layamon (which seem to be attrib. or in comb., but may be adj.), the word does not appear between OE. times and 1478.]

A. *sb.* A trick; a piece of trickery or fraud; a prank, a frolic.

c **1000** ÆLFRIC *Gram.* xliii. (Z.) 257 *Astu*, præt. *c* **1000** *Ags. Gloss.* in *Haupt's Zeitschrift* IX. 424 [*Contra mille nocendi artes*], onȝean þusendfealde deriȝende prattas. *a* **1023** WULFSTAN *Hom.* xlvii. (Napier) 245 Woȝe domas and prættas. *c* **1205** LAY. 81 Elene..þa Paris Alixandre mid pret wrenche bi-won. *Ibid.* 5302 [Hi] ðohten bi-pechen Belin mid heore præt wrenchen. **1478** SIR J. PASTON in *P. Lett.* III. 234 Iff any suche pratte scholde be laboryd, it is I hope in bettr case. **1513** DOUGLAS *Æneis* VIII. Prol. 81 Prattis ar reput policy and perellus paukis. **1596** DALRYMPLE tr. *Leslie's Hist. Scot.* VI. 338 *marg.*, Puniset for the perte and pernicious pratt thay playd to thair Bischop. **1606** BIRNIE *Kirk-Buriall* (1833) 18 When first this prat [of burying in Kirks] came in practise. **1785** FORBES *Dominie Depos'd* 33 Your prats [*ed.* 1780 pranks], she says, are now found out. **1812** CHALMERS in Hanna *Life* (1849) I. xi. 293 Of all the pratts I ever played, none was ever carried on..more gracefully. **1812** *Scotsman* 29 (Jam.) The bits o' prets, by quhilk they inveigle the public to buy their beuks.

B. *adj.* Cunning, astute.

? *a* **1200** *De Gestis Herwardi* in Michel *Chron. Anglo-Norm.* II. 51 Lefwinus Prat [id est] Astutus. *c* **1200** ORMIN 6652 Niss he nohht hinnderrȝæp ne pratt To follȝhenn ille wiless.

prat, *sb.*[2] Also **pratt**. [Origin unknown.] **1. a.** In *pl.* or (usu.) *sing.* The buttocks; the backside, rump. *slang* (orig. *Criminals'*).

1567 HARMAN *Caveat* (1869) 82 *Prat*, a buttocke. **1641** BROME *Jov. Crew* II. Wks. 1873 III. 391 First set me down here on both my Prats. *a* **1700** B. E. *Dict. Cant. Crew, Pratts*, Buttocks. **1846** [see NUT *sb.*[1] 7 a]. **1895** H. WATSON in *Chap Bk.* III. 484 To drive myself square across the way, and despatch the horses back upon their prats, setting the coachman and the post-boys yelling in a terrified hubbub. **1914** JACKSON & HELLYER *Vocab. Criminal Slang* 66 *Pratt*,.. the human rear. **1952** R. STOUT *Prisoner's Base* i. 3, I have had to spend most of my time recently sitting on my prat. **1959** E. BORNEMAN *Tomorrow is Now* ix. 93 You gimme a pain in the royal pratt. **1972** D. DELMAN *Sudden Death* iii. 65 I'm a *shmo* about tennis, so if I fall on my prat a time or two you have to bear with me.

b. A hip-pocket. *U.S. Criminals' slang.*

1914 JACKSON & HELLYER *Vocab. Criminal Slang* 66 *Pratt* .., a hip pocket. **1927** [see *prat-digging* vbl. sb.] **1936** *Detective Fiction Weekly* 12 Sept. 93/1 In spite of the fact that a pocketbook may be removed most easily from a hip pocket known as a right or left 'pratt', the majority of men carry their money there.

2. A person of no account; a dolt, fool, 'jerk'. *slang.*

1968 M. BRAGG *Without City Wall* xii. 130 He had been looking for the exact word to describe David and now he found it: *prat.* **1973** J. WAINWRIGHT *Pride of Pigs* 32 Harris was a bit of a pompous prat. **1974** N. FREELING *Dressing of Diamond* 204 Want to get an eyeful, do you, dirty-minded prat that you are. **1980** J. WAINWRIGHT *Eye of Beholder* 18 The pompous prat. The I-know-people-in-high-places nut.

3. *attrib.* and *Comb.*, as ***prat-faced*** adj.; (in sense 1 b) **prat digger**, a pick-pocket; so **prat-digging** *vbl. sb.*; **prat frisk**, the theft of a wallet from a hip-pocket; **prat-kick**, a hip-pocket; **prat leather**, a wallet kept in the hip-pocket; **prat poke**, a wallet stolen from the hip-pocket.

1935 *Amer. Speech* X. 19/2 *Prat-digger, a pickpocket, one who exploits the *prat kick.* **1955** *Publ. Amer. Dial. Soc.* XXIV. 69 Others specialize in hip pocket work and are called *prat diggers.* **1908** J. M. SULLIVAN *Criminal Slang* 19 *Pratt digging*, stealing from the hip pocket. **1916** G. A. ENGLAND *Pod, Bender & Co.* 291 It's a fact we've always been above such lays as pratt-digging. **1927** *Writer's Monthly* Nov. 390/1 The 'pratt'..is a trousers pocket. 'Pratt-digging' is stealing the 'pratt-leather' from the hip. **1976** U. HOLDEN *String Horses* i. 17 They liked to kiss each other lightly.., push each other with taunts. 'You *prat-faced les. Get off.' **1924** *Prat frisk [see *prat poke*]. **1896** I. K. FRIEDMAN *Lucky Number* 154, 'I dipped it from yer *prat-kick.'.. 'I means I took her from yer back pocket,' answered the rogue blandly. **1955** *Publ. Amer. Dial. Soc.* XXIV. 125 The hip pockets are *prat kicks.* **1908** J. M. SULLIVAN *Criminal Slang* 19 *Pratt leather*, a pocketbook in the hip pocket. **1927** Prat leather [see *prat-digging* vbl. sb.]. **1924** G. C. HENDERSON *Keys to Crookdom* 414 *Pratt poke*, purse kept in hip pocket. Pratt frisk—stealing such a purse, reefing a britch. **1955** *Publ. Amer. Dial. Soc.* XXIV. 115 When a wallet is taken from the hip pocket, it is known as a *prat poke.*

prat, *v.* Also *Sc.* pret. [app. f. PRAT *sb.*[1], but cf. PRACT *v.*] **1. a.** *intr.* To practise tricks. Hence **pratting** *vbl. sb.* trickery, and *ppl. a.* tricky, juggling. *Sc.*

1570 *Satir. Poems Reform.* xxii. 31 Quhais strenth and force consistis in pratting word, With Serpentis sting, under simplicitie. *a* **1572** KNOX *Hist. Ref.* Wks. 1846 I. 239 The Bischoppes heirat offended, said, 'What pratting is this? Lett his accusatioun be redd'. [Perhaps this is *prating*.]

b. To lark about; to trifle, romp. Freq. const. *with.*

1728 A. RAMSAY *Poems* (1953) II. 89 Some Beaus may snarl if we should prat. *a* **1835** J. AFFLECK *Posthumous Poetical Wks.* (1836) 60, I never pretit onie where At midday, night or morn. **1851** A. MACLAGAN *Sk. from Nature* 153 As for her sons, their foes will find They're no to prat wi'! **1897** C. R. *Dunning Folk-Lore* 4 Thae brownies warna to prat wi'! They played gey pliskies whiles, an' did muckle mischeef.

2. To potter *about*; to fool around, to act in a silly or annoying manner. *slang.*

1961 PARTRIDGE *Dict. Slang* Suppl. 1231/2 *Prat about*, to potter, mess about. **1973** H. MILLER *Open City* xvii. 187 Sit down and stop pratting about.

3. a. *intr.* To simulate coyness. **b.** *trans.* To feign rejection of (someone). *U.S. Blacks.*

1970 C. MAJOR *Dict. Afro-Amer. Slang* 93 *Prat*, to play coy. **1972** 'I. SLIM' in T. Kochman *Rappin' & Stylin' Out* 389 Pimping ain't no game of love, so prat 'em and keep your swipe outta 'em.

pratal ('preɪtəl), *a. Bot. rare.* [f. L. *prātum* a meadow + -AL[1].] Growing in meadows.

1847 H. C. WATSON *Cybele Britannica* I. 65 The proposed series of terms runs thus:—1. Pratal.—Plants of meadows, or rich and damp grass-land [etc.]. **1863** J. G. BAKER *N. Yorks. Stud.* 183 To designate the different kinds of locality we may employ a series of adjectives such as sylvestral, pratal, pascual, ericetal. **1883** A. FRYER in *Jrnl. Bot., Brit. & For.* 375 No hard and fast line can be drawn between Pascual and Pratal plants. **1932** G. C. DRUCE *Comital Flora Brit. Isles* 69 Meadow Crane's-bill. Pratal. British. Meadows, grassy road-borders.

†**'pratchant**, *a. Obs.* exc. *dial.* Also 7 **prachant**, 9 *dial.* **prajant**. [Origin unascertained.] Conceited, forward, swaggering.

1597 A. M. tr. *Guillemeau's Fr. Chirurg.* *vj, A Doctour might suppose me to be so pratchante and high-minded [as] that I sought to aequall my selfe with him. **1604** PARSONS *3rd Pt. Three Convers. Eng.* 433 Tymes was a Curate or deacon: but so pratchant and malepart, as he ouerwent the minister in his forwardnes of answering. **1625** USSHER *Answ. Jesuit* 72 Where a pratchant deacon, called Epiphanius, confidently avoucheth, that [etc.]. **1881** *Isle of Wight Gloss.*, *Prajant*, swaggering, conceited.

prate (preɪt), *sb.* [f. PRATE *v.* Cf. MDu. (*c* 1375), WFris. *praet*, Du., LG., NFris. *praat*, EFris. *prôt*, Da., Swed. *prat* talk, tattle, rumour.] The act or action of prating; talk; now *esp.* idle, profitless, or irrelevant talk; chatter, prattle.

1579 W. WILKINSON *Confut. Familye of Loue, Heret. Affirm.* b ij b, Have not much prate or disputation with straungers. **1592** GREENE *Def. Conny Catch.* Wks. (Grosart) XI. 98 [He] began to hold the fellow in prate, and to question whose man hee was. **1601** ? MARSTON *Pasquil & Kath.* I. 27 The common foode of prate: 'what newes at court?' **1704** S. FUACE in W. S. Perry *Hist. Coll. Amer. Col. Ch.* (1871) I. 90 'Hold your prate, Sirrah' said he..'you are an impudent Rogue'. **1728** SWIFT *Jrnl. Mod. Lady* 142 How should I, alas! relate The sum of all their senseless prate? **1860** THACKERAY *Lovel the Wid.* ii. (1869) 163 On I would go with my prate about my passion, my wrongs, and despair.

prate (preɪt), *v.* Also 6 **praite**, *Sc.* **prat(t**. [Not found before 15th c.: = MDu. *prāten* (*c* 1400), *praeten*, Du. *praten*, WFris. *præten*, *praten*, *proten*, EFris. *proten*, MLG., LG. *praten*, *proten*; thence also MHG. *braten*, *braden*, Icel., Norw., MSwed., Swed. *prata*, Da. *prate*, to talk, chatter, prate. Not known in the earlier stage of the langs.; perh. a later onomatopœic formation.]

1. *intr.* To talk, to chatter: usually dyslogistic, implying speaking much or long to little purpose; formerly also to speak insolently, boastfully, or officiously; to tell tales, blab.

c **1420** [implied in PRATER]. *c* **1430** LYDG. *Min. Poems* (Percy Soc.) 155 He may weel grucche and with his tounge prate. **1550** J. COKE *Eng. & Fr. Heralds* §62 (1877) 77, I mervayle, syr Heralde, how you dare so untruly prate agaynst your soveraygne lord the kyng of England. **1570** BUCHANAN *Chamæleon* Wks. (1892) 53 [He] prattit proudlie, vantyng ỳat his pen sould be worth ten thowsand men. **1581** J. Bell *Haddon's Answ. Osor.* 492 b, You prate hard, but you prove nought. **1605** Shaks. *Macb.* ii. i. 58 Thy very stones prate of my where-about. **1616** R. C. *Times' Whistle* iii. 992 They will prate Till they tire all men with their idle chatt. **1713** Berkeley *Guardian* No. 3 ⁋1 Sober wretches, who prate whole evenings over coffee. **1747** Richardson *Clarissa* (1811) I. viii. 54 No words! I will not be prated to. *a* **1839** Praed *Poems* (1864) II. 31 And she is prating learnedly Of logic and of chemistry. **1875** Jowett *Plato* (ed. 2) I. 212 You prate, he said, instead of answering.

b. With *at*: To scold; to 'give a lecture to'. *dial.*

1886 *S.W. Linc. Gloss.* s.v., He might have prated at him and let it go by.

2. *trans.* To utter, say, or tell in a prating manner; to tell or repeat to little purpose.

c **1489** Caxton *Sonnes of Aymon* xiv. 320 What somever ye prate, say, or crake, sayd Charlemagn, ye shall not scape me. **1575** *Gamm. Gurton* ii. iv. C j b, Auant.. syr knaue, what pratest thou of that I fynd? **1630** B. Jonson *New Inn* i. i, He prates Latin, An it were a parrot, or a play-boy. **1697** Dryden *Virg. Past.* iii. 21 What Nonsense wou'd the Fool thy Master prate. **1821** Byron *Sardan.* v. i. 292 You are sent to prate your master's will, and not Reply to mine. **1891** N. Gould *Double Event* 2 Prating mere polite nothings to a young lady fresh from school.

3. *intr.* Of hounds: To 'given tongue'. Of hens: To cluck. (*dial.*)

1592 Warner *Alb. Eng.* vii. xxxvi. 158 Loues Beagles be vncoupeld, Beautie praites And driues my Heart from out the Thicks. **1873** Spilling *Molly Miggs* i. 6 If the hen doant prate she oant lay.

ˈprate-apace. [f. prate *v.* + apace.] One who prates on; a prater, chatterbox.

1636 Heywood *Loves Mistr.* ii. i. Wks. 1874 V. 113 Prince of passions, prate-apaces, and pickled lovers. **1721** Amherst *Terræ Fil.* No. 46 (1754) 244 Mr. Prate-apace,.. nothing is more scandalous.. than your charging our university with the want of civility and good manners. **1879** Browning *Ned Bratts* 126 Well, pad on, my prate-apace!

ˈprateful, *a. rare.* [f. prate *sb.* + -ful.] Full of prate, given to prating or chattering.

1802 W. Taylor in W. Robberds *Mem.* (1843) I. 208 The French character seems to me much altered;.. the people are more circumspect, less prateful.

prately, -e, obs. forms of prettily.

ˈpratement. *rare.* [f. prate *v.* + -ment.] Prating, talking. Also allusively (quot. 1831).

1657 J. Watts *Vind. Ch. Eng.* 268 Pratements of the longest and strongest winded speaker. **1831** *Blackw. Mag.* XXIX. 982 In and out of Pratement—we beg pardon for that *lapsus linguæ*—Parliament.

†**ˈpratepye.** *Obs.* [f. prate *sb.* or *v.* + pie *sb.*[1]] A chattering magpie; a prater, chatterer.

1582 Stanyhurst *Æneis* iv. (Arb.) 101 This that prat'pye cadesse labored too trumpet in eeche place.

prater[1] (ˈpreɪtə(r)). [f. prate *v.* + -er[1]. So Du. *prater* a talker.] One who prates; an obnoxious or idle talker, one who speaks much to little purpose, a mere talker, a chatterer. Formerly also a boaster, an evil-speaker.

c **1420** Lydg. *Assembly of Gods* 674 There were bosters, braggars, & brybores, Praters, fasers, strechers, & wrythers. **1550** Bale *Apol.* Pref. 13 Though Hierome wer a great prater and boaster of virginitie, yet was he no virgine. **1622** T. Scott *Belg. Pismire* 10 He is a prater.. that never doeth any thing. *a* **1680** Butler *Rem.* (1759) II. 223 A Prater.. is like a Earwig, when he gets within a Man's Ear he is not easily to be got out again. **1704** Swift *Batt. Bks.* Misc. (1711) 258 Miscreant Prater... Eloquent only in thine own Eyes, thou railest without Wit. **1883** F. Leifchild in *Contemp. Rev.* XLIII. 51 Laertes.. a prater of moral maxims, while he is all for Paris and its pleasures.

‖**Prater**[2] (ˈprɑːtə(r)). [Ger., ad. It. *prato* meadow.] The name of a large wooded park in Vienna.

1803 C. Wilmot *Let.* 2 Aug. in *Irish Peer* (1920) 207 The Prater.. is esteem'd the most magnificent public walk and drive in Europe. **1819** M. Wilmot *More Lett.* (1935) 20 The turn out in the Prater of a Sunday Eveᵍ is Magnificent. **1870** G. H. Lewes *Jrnl.* 10 Apr. in *Geo. Eliot Lett.* (1956) V. 89 Lytton then proposed that we should drive in the Prater. **1911** *Encycl. Brit.* XXVIII. 52/1 The Prater, a vast expanse (2000 acres) of wood and park on the east side of the city, between the Danube and the Danube Canal, is greatly frequented by all classes. **1938** W. J. Turner *Mozart* xvi. 312 One fine autumn day when they were sitting in the beautiful Prater, Mozart spoke of his approaching death. **1945** C. Isherwood *Prater Violet* 33 It is a warm spring evening in the Vienna Prater. **1974** A. Goddard *Vienna Pursuit* ii. 40, I.. made a stately circuit on the Big Wheel in the Prater.

Prater John: see Prester John.

†**prate-rost.** *Obs. slang.* [f. prate *sb.* or *v.*: second element obscure.] A prater.

1671 Glanvill *Disc. M. Stubbe* Pref. A ij b, I would not have it thought, I make dealing with this Prate-rost any part of my Business. *a* **1700** B. E. *Dict. Cant. Crew.*, *Prateroast*, a Talking Boy. **1725** *New Cant. Dict.*, *Prate-Roast.*

†**ˈpratery.** *Obs. rare.* [f. prate *v.* or prater *sb.*: see -ery. Cf. Du. *praterij* talk.] Prating.

1533 Elyot *Pasquill* (1540) C v b, And lette vs leaue Pasquyll with his praterye.

pratfall (ˈprætfɔːl), *sb.* Chiefly *N. Amer. slang.* Also prat(t)-fall. [f. prat *sb.*[2] + fall *sb.*[1]]

a. *Theatr.* A comedy fall; a fall on to the buttocks.

1939 N. Coward *Play Parade* II. 108 Don't do a pratfall in your first routine. **1941** L. Rosten *Hollywood* 316 The Hollywood writers—graduates of the westerns.. masters of the chase, the 'pratt-fall'..—kept the movies moving. **1952** 'E. Box' *Death in Fifth Position* (1954) ii. 47 Some homicidal maniac.. who enjoyed seeing ballerinas take fatal pratfalls. **1960** B. Keaton *Wonderful World of Slapstick* (1967) 96 Pop's pratfalls astonished Roscoe and everybody else. **1961** *Guardian* 27 Apr. 9/4 A more intelligent form of humour—away from the pratfall type of thing. **1977** *Time* 26 Dec. 49/1 Only Saturday-morning TV addicts could possibly endure the antics of *The World's Greatest Lover*, in which characters are forever shouting their lines, bulging their eyes and stumbling through pratfalls.

b. *transf.* and *fig.*

1953 R. Bradbury *Fahrenheit 451* (1954) i. 56 Life becomes one big pratfall. **1956** D. Karp *All Honorable Men* 174 That gentlemen is in for a rude surprise some morning soon. I understand he handles government contracts. Another pratfall soon. **1971** *Guardian* 25 Nov. 17/2 Performers who write their own material often take enormous pratfalls. **1977** *Rolling Stone* 7 Apr. 43/1 Why has an important investigation so quickly degenerated into a series of pratfalls?

Hence as *v. intr.*, to fall on to the buttocks. Hence **prat-fallen, -falling** *ppl. adjs.* Also *fig.*

1940 *Time* 29 Jan. 41/1 The sight of Sonja (for the fourth time in her professional career) pratt-fallen. *Ibid.* 30 Dec. 30/1 Opera at the Met has a way of prattfalling between two stools. **1942** *Ibid.* 3 Aug. 74/2 On the way to the plate he prat-falls on the carefully laid-out row of bats in front of the dugout. **1972** *Listener* 6 July 22/1 The eloquent gamey pratfalling scapegoat. **1973** D. Lees *Rape of Quiet Town* iv. 55 As the tension built up.. it was a piece of prat-falling comedy that saved me.

prati, -ie, obs. forms of pretty.

pratic, -ick, -ik: see practic *sb.*[1] and *v.*, pratique.

pratie, dial.: see potato 2 d γ.

pratincole (ˈprætɪŋkəʊl). *Ornith.* [Named by Pennant (1773), ad. mod.L. *pratincola* (Kramer 1756), f. L. *prātum* a meadow + *incola* inhabitant.] One of several species of the genus *Glareola*, grallatorial (limicoline) birds widely distributed throughout the old world and in Australia, allied to the plovers, but regarded by some as a distinct family, resembling the swallows in appearance and habits.

1773 Pennant *Genera Birds* 48 Pratincole. Bill, short, strong, strait, hooked at the end. Nostrils, near the base, linear, oblique [etc.]. **1843** Yarrell *Hist. Birds* III. 4 The Pratincole has been arranged by some authors with the Swallows, by others near the Rails: but I believe, with Mr. Selby, that it ought to be included in the family of the Plovers. **1866** Blackmore *Cradock N.* xlvii, A woman's perception flies on the wings of the pratincole. **1903** *Westm. Gaz.* 10 July 10/1 An unfortunate black-winged pratincole that strayed from its Russian home across Central Europe to Romney Marsh has promptly been made into a specimen.

prating (ˈpreɪtɪŋ), *vbl. sb.* [f. prate *v.* + -ing[1].] The action of the vb. prate; idle chatter; †boasting, mischievous talk.

c **1460** G. Ashby *Dicta Philos.* 684 Ye aught not to haue other in hatyng, But hertely cherissh theim withoute prating. **1538** Bale *Thre Lawes* 1783 Here is a pratynge with a very vengeaunce! **1622** Bacon *Hen. VII* 164 After that these two, had by ioynt and severall Pratings found tokens of consent in the Multitude. **1706–7** Farquhar *Beaux Strat.* i. i, Hold your prating, Sirrah, do you know who you are? **1813** Byron *Corsair* i. vii, 'Peace, peace!' — He cuts their prating short.

attrib. **1593** Nashe *Four Lett. Confut.* Wks. (Grosart) II. 247 Since we are here, on our prating bench in a close roome.

ˈprating, *ppl. a.* [f. as prec. + -ing[2].] That prates, talking idly, chattering.

1567 *Triall Treas.* (1850) 11 Looke on this legge, ye prating slaues, I remember since it was no greater then a tree. **1581** Mulcaster *Positions* xxxviii. (1887) 175 There be as prating boyes, as there be pratling wenches. **1676** Bunyan *Strait Gate* Wks. (1846) 272 A prating tongue will not unlock the gates of heaven. **1754** Richardson *Grandison* III. xxii. 217 Can there be a greater torment than an officious prating Love? **1855** Macaulay *Hist. Eng.* xx. IV. 464 Montague was a brilliant rhetorician, and, therefore,.. represented by detractors as a superficial, prating pretender.

Hence **ˈpratingly** *adv.*

1755 Johnson, *Pratingly*, with tittle tattle; with loquacity.

‖**pratiquant** (pratikɑ̃), *a.* (*sb.*) [Fr.] Making a practice of religious duties or observances; practising. Also *absol.* as *sb.*

1902 G. Arthur *Let.* Mar. in *Some Lett. fron Man of No Importance* (1928) 140 If the King is not religious in the 'pratiquant' sense of the word, he has a very strong sense of religion. **1956** S. Bedford *Legacy* iii. iv. 154 Jules.. says he couldn't marry someone who wasn't a Catholic... It isn't as though *he'd* ever shewed himself the least bit *pratiquant.* **1960** *Times* 27 Feb. 7/3 Fasting is an unhealthy habit; Communists tell the people of their Muslim lands. On the contrary, urge the new *pratiquants* in Turkey and elsewhere, it is astonishing how fitter you feel at the end of Ramadan. **1965** *New Statesman* 3 Dec. 890/2 After lapsing for 15 years, she had recently tried to become *pratiquant* again.

‖**pratique** (ˈprætɪk, ‖pratik). Forms: 7 **pratticke, -ike, -iq,** 7–8 **-ick, -ic,** 7- **pratique.** [a. F. *pratique* practice, intercourse, pratique = It. *pratica*, OSp. *prática*, ad. L. *practica* (see practic); orig. spelt *pratticke* (var. of practic); subseq. conformed to F. spelling.] Permission or licence granted to a ship to hold intercourse with a port after quarantine, or on showing a clean bill of health. Especially used in connexion with the South of Europe.

1609 W. Biddulph in T. Lavender *Trav.* (1612) 4 Zante. We staied ten daies in the rode of this city, before we could get Pratticke, that is: leaue to come amongst them, or to vse traffique with them. **1615** G. Sandys *Trav.* 6 Not to suffer any to traffike or come ashore before they haue a Pratticke from the Signiors of Health. **1656** Blount *Glossogr.*, *Pratique* (from the Span. *Pratica*),.. among Merchants it is a Licence to Traffick; as in the Ports of Italy, and the Streights. **1663** Pepys *Diary* 14 Dec., To remove the inconveniences his ships are put to [at Leghorn] by denial of pratique;.. a thing that is now-a-days made use of only as a cheat. **1753** Hanway *Trav.* (1762) I. ii. xviii. 80 Ships can neither leave the port, nor be permitted to prattic but by his permission. **1817** Byron *Beppo* xxv, And when he lay in quarantine for pratique.. His wife would mount, at times, her highest attic. **1897** *Daily News* 14 Jan. 3/5 The P. and O. steamer Nubia arrived in the Thames from Plymouth yesterday afternoon... Dr. Collingridge gave the ship pratique, and the yellow flag was then hauled down amid loud cheers.

b. *attrib.* **pratique boat, house,** the boat, and house, of the quarantine officer.

1644 Evelyn *Diary* 16 Oct., We.. came on shore by the Prattiq-house [at Genoa]. **1798** Nelson in Nicolas *Disp.* (1845) III. 175 The boats.. to attend the embarkation at the Mole near the Pratique House. **1836** Marryat *Midsh. Easy* xl, The pratique boat will not come off after sunset.

Pratt (præt). The name of Felix *Pratt* (1780–1859), Staffordshire pottery-manufacturer, used *attrib.* to designate a type of cream-coloured earthenware painted in high-temperature colours and widely produced in the late eighteenth and early nineteenth centuries. So ***Pratt-type*** adj., etc.

[**1912** F. Litchfield *Pott. & Porc.* (new ed.) vii. 195 The Pottery of Felix Pratt,.. marked with the name *Pratt* and known as 'Pratt's ware', was in this district [*sc.* Fenton].] **1920** G. W. Rhead *Earthenware Collector* xi. 197 One of the most successful pieces of Pratt ware is the mug of 'Midnight Conversation' in the Hanley Museum. *Ibid.* A number of Pratt jugs have been known as Sunderland jugs. **1933** W. B. Honey *Eng. Pott. & Porc.* vii. 100 The so-called 'Pratt ware' was made by other Staffordshire potters as well as by those of Sunderland and other places in the North. **1957** Mankowitz & Haggar *Conc. Encycl. Eng. Pott. & Porc.* 182/2 *'Pratt' type*, wares made at the end of the eighteenth and beginning of the nineteenth centuries, decorated with a distinctive palette of high temperature colours. **1963** *House & Garden* May 68/2 The pottery pieces.. are mostly Pratt-ware made either just before or just after the beginning of the nineteenth century, and are part of a collection of Pratt. **1967** *Times* 14 Mar. 21/7 (Advt.), English pottery and porcelain.. including.. a Prattware grotto group. **1974** *Country Life* 21 Feb. (Suppl.) 56 Six Pratt Pot-lids and some Pratt Ware. *a* **1977** *Harrison Mayer Ltd. Catal.* 99/1 Pratt Type and Peasant enamel Wares... 20 Slides.

ˈpratted, *a. Sc.* [f. prat *sb.*[1] + -ed[2].] Having tricks or evil practices: in *Comb.* as *ill-pratted.*

1812 Chalmers in Hanna *Life* (1849) I. xi. 293 You always thought me an ill-pratted chiel.

prattelie, -ely, -ily, obs. forms of prettily.

prattie, obs. form of pretty.

prattle (ˈpræt(ə)l), *sb.* [f. prattle *v.*] The act or action of prattling; that which is prattled; idle inconsequent talk, childish chatter, small talk.

1555 W. Watreman *Fardle Facions* ii. vii. 160 As for byeng and sellyng, or any kinde of Lawe prattle, thei [Persians] vse not. **1583** Babington *Commandm.* Ded. to Earl Pembroke, There men shall be judged according to proofe,.. not according to pratles. **1600** Holland *Livy* xliv. xxii. 1184 Let him hold him there and keep his babble and prattle to himselfe. **1672** Cave *Prim. Chr.* i. iii. (1673) 35 Talkative and full of prattle. **1768–74** Tucker *Lt. Nat.* (1834) II. 629 You may soon discover this by the prattle of the children, who love to repeat what they hear. **1796** Burney *Mem. Metastasio* II. 374 [Having] since that written you a long prattle, which ought to have been forwarded to you. **1865** J. Hatton *Bitter Sweets* xxiv, Her mother was never tired of her girlish prattle.

b. *transf.* and *fig.* Applied to the voice of birds, the noise of running water, etc.

1693 Evelyn *De la Quint. Compl. Gard.* II. 179 The harmony of the pretty Birds, which a sort of extraordinary gayety and briskness at this time inspires with amorous prattle. **1856** Miss Mulock *J. Halifax* xxiii, Listening.. to the prattle of the stream, that went singing along.

prattle (ˈpræt(ə)l), *v.* Also 6 **prattel(l, prattale, prattil,** 6–8 **pratle.** [dim. and freq. of prate *v.*: see -le 3; = MLG. *pratelen, protelen* to chatter, grumble.]

1. *intr.* To talk or chatter in a childish or artless fashion; to be loquacious about trifles; formerly equivalent to prate; now chiefly said, without contempt, of the talk of young children.

1532 More *Confut. Tindale* Wks. 533/2 So he dooeth but prattle & prate of feling fayth, without the feling of any fayth at all. **1557** N.T. (Genev.) *3 John* 10 If I come, I wyl declare his dedes whych he doeth, pratteling against vs with malicious wordes. **1594** T. B. *La Primaud. Fr. Acad.* ii. 118 Those that cease not to prattle and babble about vaine and vnprofitable matters. **1692** LOCKE *Educ.* §35 He had the Mastery of his Parents ever since he could Prattle. **1722** DE FOE *Moll Flanders* (1840) 208, I talked to [the pretty little child], and it prattled to me again. **1778** JOHNSON *Let. to Mrs. Thrale* 15 Oct., I never said with Dr. Dodd that I love to prattle upon paper, but I have prattled now till the paper will not hold much more than my good wishes. **1885** CLODD *Myths & Dr.* I. viii. 134 The childhood of the race.. when it prattles of the Golden Age.

b. *transf.* and *fig.* To make an inarticulate sound resembling or likened to the talk of children: said of birds, running water, etc.

1863 B. TAYLOR *Poet's Jrnl.* III. *Under Moon*, A fountain prattles to the night. **1887** G. MEREDITH *Ballads & P.* 53 The light leaves prattled to neighbour ears.

2. *trans.* To utter in an idle, garrulous, or (now usually) childish way.

1560 BECON *New Catech.* Wks. I. 465 b, Whatsoeuer the Papistes.. pratle in this behalf, I am sure, reason sayeth, that there remaineth bothe bread & wyne. **1583** BABINGTON *Commandm.* ix. (1637) 92 If it be a vertue thus to prittle and prattle of every body uncertaine tales, but most certaine discredits. **1598** DRAYTON *Heroic. Ep.* II. 160 The little birds .. Shall learne to speake and prattle Rosamond. **1696** TATE & BRADY *Ps.* lviii. 3 They prattled Slander, and in Lies Employ'd their lisping Tongue. **1784** COWPER *Task* II. 382 Frequent in Park with lady at his side, Ambling and prattling scandal as he goes. **1887** JESSOPP *Arcady* ii. 64, I am but.. a mere chronicler of gossip that will not be prattled long.

b. To bring or drive by prattling *into*, etc.

1601 SHAKS. *All's Well* IV. i. 46 If you prattle mee into these perilles.

†ˈ**prattle-ˌbasket.** *Obs.* [f. PRATTLE *sb.* + BASKET *sb.* Cf. next.] = next.

1602 BRETON *Mother's Blessing* lxxiv, But if she be ilfauour'd, blind and old, A prattle basket, or an idle slut. **1690** SHADWELL *Amorous Bigot* II. Wks. 1720 IV. 248 Sweet prattle-basket, be quiet. **1828** *Craven Gloss.* (ed. 2), *Prattle-Basket*, a prattling child, a little young prater.

†ˈ**prattle-box.** *Obs.* [f. PRATTLE *sb.* + BOX *sb.*[2] Cf. CHATTERBOX.] A humorous name for a prattler or chatterer; a chatterbox.

1671 GLANVILL *Disc. M. Stubbe* 2 Gross Ignoramusses, Illiterate Fools, Prattle-boxes, Catch-Dotterels,.. Tories, Cheats, and poor Devils. **1696** LOCKE in Fox Bourne *Life* (1876) II. xv. 455 A very ill sign in a prattle-box of your age. **1751** R. PALTOCK *P. Wilkins* (1884) I. ii. 21 At last the old prattlebox having made a short pause to recover breath.., 'Mr. Peter', says she, 'you look as if you did not know poor Patty'.

prattlement (ˈpræt(ə)lmənt). *rare.* [f. PRATTLE *v.* + -MENT.] Idle talk, prattle, prattling: in quot. 1579, a play on *parliament*.

1579 FULKE *Heskins' Parl.* 33 He will goe immediately to his purposed matter, to bee debated in this highe Court of prattlement. **1604** HIERON *Wks.* I. 574 It were a word sufficient To ouerthrow this prattlement. **1779** COWPER *Let to Unwin* 31 Oct., The childish prattlement of pastoral compositions. **1901** J. DAVIDSON *Test. Vivisector* 9 The prattlement of amorists.

prattler (ˈprætlə(r)). [f. PRATTLE *v.* + -ER[1].] One who prattles, a talkative person; a chatterer; now *esp.* a prattling child.

1567 MAPLET *Gr. Forest* 90 One knaue or pratler will alwayes accompanie another. **1583** BABINGTON *Commandm.* ix. (1637) 93 We doe not discountenance the whispering carper, we doe not eschew the reports of peevish pratlers. **1633** G. HERBERT *Temple, Conscience* i, Peace pratler, do not lowre. **1680** OTWAY *Orphan* III. vii. 1219 Go, you're an idle Pratler. **1742** FIELDING *Jos. Andrews* IV. viii, My little prattler, the darling and comfort of my old age. **1805** WORDSW. *Prelude* IV. 204 Rosy prattlers at the feet Of a pleased grandame. **1875** JOWETT *Plato* (ed. 2) III. 140 Thousands of tragedy-making prattlers.

prattling (ˈprætlɪŋ), *vbl. sb.* [f. PRATTLE *v.* + -ING[1].] The action of the vb. PRATTLE.

1530 PALSGR. 257/2 Pratlynge, the speche of yonge chyldren, *patoys*. **1580** BABINGTON *Exp. Lord's Prayer* (1596) 233 Their priuie pratling to the hurt of their neighbours. **1605** WILLET *Hexapla Gen.* 367 Aged parents are delighted with the pratling and sport of young children. **1790** BURKE *Fr. Rev.* Wks. V. 229 This prattling of theirs hardly deserves the name of sophistry. **1877** TENNYSON *Harold* II. ii. 66 Save for the prattling of thy little ones.

ˈ**prattling,** *ppl. a.* [f. PRATTLE *v.* + -ING[2].] That prattles: see the verb.

1560 DAUS tr. *Sleidane's Comm.* 1 b, He would.. put those prattelinge pardoners to silence. **1581** N. BURNE *Disput.* in *Cath. Tractates* (S.T.S.) 170 The daft Abbottis, gukkit Prioris, guseheaddit Personis,.. and the pretland Prebendaris. **1632** LITHGOW *Trav.* I. 2 Pratling Parrots, and sounding Cymbals. **1703** ROWE *Fair Penit.* v. i. 1799 What Joys thou gav'st me in thy prattling Infancy. **1858** CAPERN *Ball. & Songs* (1859) 84 Beside that prattling brook. **1862** SALA *Accepted Addr.* 91 The prattling servants from the Priory came down town.

pratty, praty, -e, obs. and dial. ff. PRETTY.

praty, dial.: see POTATO 2 d γ.

‖**pratyahara** (prætjaːˈhaːrə). *Yoga Philos.* [Skr.] (See quots.)

1882 E. B. COWELL tr. *Âchârya's Sarva-Darśana-Saṃgraha* xv. 267 Now in this way, having his mind purified by the 'forbearances'.. the devotee is to attain 'self-mastery' .. and 'restraint' (pratyâhâra). **1899** MAX MÜLLER *Six Syst. Indian Philos.* vii. 458 We can hardly doubt that these postures and restraints of breathing.. are helpful in producing complete abstraction (Pratyâhâra) of the senses from their objects, and a complete indifference of the Yogin towards pain and pleasure. **1942** D. D. RUNES *Dict. Philos.* 248/1 *Pratyāhāra*, .. withdrawal of the senses from external objects, one of the psycho-physical means for attaining the object of Yoga. **1957** *Encycl. Brit.* XII. 251/2 The next step of *pratyāhāra* or the withdrawal of the senses from their natural outward functioning answers to what modern psychology calls introversion. **1960** J. HEWITT *Yoga* viii. 114 Sense-Withdrawal, called by the Yogis Pratyahara. **1976** *Canberra Times* 23 Aug. 2/8 The ability to transcend thought is acquired by the application of concentrated mind to a single point, pratyahara.

prau, var. PROA.

praueine, praunce, praune, obs. ff. PREVENE, PRANCE, PRAWN.

†**prave,** *a. Obs.* [ad. L. *prāvus* crooked, perverse, vicious, bad.] Vicious, evil, depraved.

1566 ADLINGTON *Apuleius* 2 That is accounted vntrew by the praue opinion of men. **1607** J. CARPENTER *Plaine Mans Plough* 189 By prave concupiscence subdued to sinne. **1689** tr. *Buchanan's De Jure Regni apud Scotos* Ep. Ded., Your Age not yet corrupted by prave opinions.

Hence †ˈ**pravely** *adv. Obs.*

1598 FLORIO, *Prauamente*, wickedly.. peruersely, prauely.

†ˈ**pravilege.** *Obs.* Also 4 pravelegie, -ylegie, 6 -ylege, 7 -iledge. [ad. med.L. *prāvilēgium* (12th c.: see quot. 1432–50), a dyslogistic alteration of *prīvilēgium* PRIVILEGE, after *prāvus* perverse, bad: see PRAVE *a.*] An evil, injurious, or worthless privilege or law.

c **1380** WYCLIF *Wks.* (1880) 482 Siche grauntis of þe pope þat ben not groundid in goddis lawe ben prauylegies, & litil worþ. **1432–50** tr. *Higden* (Rolls) VII. 409 [Pope] Paschalis the secunde.. dampnede the seide privilege in this maner.. that privilege grawntede late to themperoure, whiche may be called rather a pravilege then a privilege [orig. *illud privilegium quod potius vocandum est pravilegium*]. **1550** BALE *Eng. Votaries* II. 68 b, Dysdaynouslye changynge his pryvylege to the scornefull name of a prauylege, or writynge that stode for nought. **1613** PURCHAS *Pilgrimage* II. vii. 113 Priviledges and pravileges, whereby every John-a-Stile shall intercept the Churches due.

†ˈ**pravitous,** *a. Obs. rare*[−1]. [f. PRAVITY + -OUS: cf. *calamitous*, etc. (In quot. improperly *pravitious*.)] Characterized by pravity; evil, bad.

1648–9 OWEN *Toleration* iii. 89 Pravitious tendence of the doctrine opposed.

pravity (ˈprævɪtɪ). [ad. L. *prāvitās* crookedness, distortion, perverseness, depravity, f. *prāvus* crooked, distorted, perverse. Cf. DEPRAVITY, an analogical formation on this word.]

1. Moral perversion or corruption; wickedness, viciousness, depravity; ***original*** or ***natural pravity*** = DEPRAVITY c. Now *rare* or *Obs.*

1550 HOOPER *Serm. Jonas* Epist., To go after the prauitye and euylnes of oure owne hartes. **1618** T. ADAMS *Generation of Serpents* Wks. 1861 I. 71 Original pravity is called corruption. **1675** BAXTER *Cath. Theol.* II. I. 5 The Pelagians, who deny Original Sin, and acknowledge not the pravity of vitiated nature. **1751** SMOLLETT *Per. Pic.* (1779) II. liii. 132 The spite of their hearts, and pravity of their dispositions. **1829** SOUTHEY *Sir T. More* II. 207 The punishment.. was proportioned to the apprehended and intended consequences of the offence, not to the pravity of the offender. **1847** BUSHNELL *Chr. Nurt.* I. i. (1861) 22 The natural pravity of man is plainly asserted in Scripture.

2. *gen.* Corrupt or evil quality; badness.

1620 VENNER *Via Recta* iii. 64 The flesh is of a fishie sauour, which.. is a note of greatest prauity. **1791** BURKE *App. Whigs* Wks. VI. 99 To show this progression of their favourite work, from absolute pravity to finished perfection. **1822–34** *Good's Study Med.* (ed. 4) II. 462 Blood innutritious from scarcity or pravity of food. *Ibid.* IV. 410 Pravity of the fluids or emunctories that open on the external surface.

†**3.** Deformity, crookedness. *Obs. rare.*

1656 STANLEY *Hist. Philos.* II. VIII. 75 Defect.. whence ariseth pravity, distortion, deformity of the limbs. **1658** PHILLIPS, *Pravity*, crookednesse, deformity.

†ˈ**pravous,** *a. Obs.* [f. L. *prāv-us* (see PRAVE) + -OUS.] Corrupt, evil, depraved; = PRAVE.

1653 R. SANDERS *Physiogn., Moles* 26 It denotes a pravous, wicked, contentious nature. **1657** W. MORICE *Coena quasi Κοινὴ* 141 Ignorance.. becoming to a pravous disposition.

praw(e, Malay boat: see PROA.

prawleen, -lin(g, variants of PRALINE.

prawn (prɔːn), *sb.* Forms: 5 prayne, 5–7 prane, 6 pran, praune, prayn, 6–7 prawne, 7– prawn. [ME. *prayne, prane*, of unknown origin. No similar name found in other langs.

A suggested connexion with L. *perna*, F. *perne* ham, a ham-shaped shell-fish, a pinna, founded upon a blundered entry in Florio '*parnocchie*, Shrimps or Prawne fishes', (*parnocchia* (pl. -*ie*) being a variant of '*pernocchia*, a Nakre or Nacre [*mispr.* Narre]-fish') is opposed at once to the sense and the phonology.]

I. 1. A small long-tailed decapod marine crustacean (*Palæmon serratus*), larger than a shrimp, common off the coasts of Great Britain, and used as food. Also extended to allied species of the family.

1426 *Court Rolls Maldon*, Bundle 16 m. 2 bk. Item dicunt q[d] Margareta vxor Rob[ti] Seyken forstallauit in foro praynes qu.. emit in foro de Iohanne Gyrlfader, &c., ideo in misericordia vj d. *c* **1440** *Promp. Parv.* 411 Prane, fysche, *stingus*. *a* **1529** SKELTON *Col. Cloute* 209 Ye pycke no shrympes nor pranes. **1552** HULOET, Prane fyshe, *carides, tingus*. **1597** SHAKS. *2 Hen. IV*, II. i. 104 Telling vs, she had a good dish of Prawnes. **1620** VENNER *Via Recta* iv. 79 Pranes and Shrimps are of one and the same nature. **1788** LD. AUCKLAND *Corr.* (1861) II. 93 Within an ace of being laid low among the prawns, pebbles, and porpoises. **1840** DICKENS *Old C. Shop* v, He.. devoured gigantic prawns with the heads and tails on.

II. *transf.* and *fig.* **2.** A figure of a prawn as an ornament.

1578 T. N. tr. *Conq. W. India* 171 Two collers of redde prawnes.. and at euery one of them hanged eight shrimpes of gold, of excellent workemanship.

3. Applied to persons. **a.** Figuratively, or in a familiar manner. **b.** As a term of contempt: a fool, half-wit.

1845 DICKENS *Let.* 27 Jan. (1977) IV. 253 By the time he had finished this third dinner, his eyes protruded infinitely beyond the tip of that feature [*sc.* his nose]. You never saw such a human Prawn as he looked, in your life. **1895** W. P. RIDGE *Minor Dialogues* 207 Ah, I expect you're a saucy young prawn, Emma. **1937** PARTRIDGE *Dict. Slang* 657/1 *Prawn, silly*, a pejorative applied to persons. **1965** *Telegraph* (Brisbane) 5 July 8/4 Describing a fellow who was a bit eccentric, or one who was just plain nuts... Anyone would know what he [*sc.* an Australian] meant if he used the word .. *prawn*.

c. In phr. ***to come the raw prawn*** (***over, with,*** etc.): to attempt to deceive. *Austral. slang.*

1942 *Salt* 25 May 8 *Don't come the raw prawn*, don't try to put one over me. *c* **1948** S. L. ELLIOT in E. Hanger *Khaki, Bush & Bigotry* (1968) 36 The filthy rotten Crab, he'd better not come the raw prawn on us. **1951** CUSACK & JAMES *Come in Spinner* 306 Coupla bastards come the raw prawn over me on the last lap up from Melbourne and I done me last bob at Swy. **1959** E. LAMBERT *Glory thrown In* v. 41 Don't ever come the raw prawn with Doc, mate. He knows all the lurks. **1965** M. SHADBOLT *Among Cinders* xxi. 202 Don't you come the raw prawn with me. **1970** *Private Eye* 16 Jan. 16 Don't come the raw prawn with me. Ozzie Barry and me are just good friends.

III. 4. *attrib.* and *Comb.* **prawn cocktail**: see COCKTAIL 4; **prawn-fishing** = PRAWNING *vbl. sb.* 2; so ***prawn-fisherman***.

1611 FLORIO s.v. *Parnocchie*, Prawne fishes [1598 praunes]. **1771** MRS. HAYWOOD *New Present for Maid* 39 Craw-fish, or Prawn Soup. **1836** T. HOOK *G. Gurney* I. iii. 85 Egg-eating and prawn-picking are not delicate performances. **1883** *Fisheries Exhib. Catal.* 10 Crab, Lobster, Conger, Eel, and Prawn Pots. **1891** *Daily News* 12 June 3/3 Fine net,.. worn over prawn-pink satin. **1896** KIRKALDY & POLLARD tr. *Boas' Text Bk. Zool.* 226 The young one passes through a prawn-stage. **1921** *Chambers's Jrnl.* Sept. 590/1 Numerous are the adverse comments I've heard on the prawn fisherman and his ways. **1924** *Blackw. Mag.* Apr. 489/2 Neither the Lydons nor anybody else could make me enjoy prawn-fishing on that high walk at Galway. **1978** R. WADDINGTON *Catching Salmon* xi. 128 One cardinal principle.. applies to prawn-fishing. If in a stocked pool no fish takes or follows your bait in the first few casts, it is.. useless to continue.

Hence **prawn** *v. intr.*, to fish for prawns (orig. and chiefly in vbl. sb. or pres. pple.; see PRAWNING *vbl. sb.*); ˈ**prawner**, a fisher for prawns; ˈ**prawny** *a.*, of or pertaining to a prawn; prawn-like.

1865 *Daily Tel.* 25 Aug., Our shrimps have most prawny proportions. **1886** *Globe* 16 July The hand that prawns must be quick and steady.. Every one cannot be a successful prawner. **1905** *Daily Chron.* 30 Aug. 4/5 At the Place we prawn when the tide goes out.

prawnce, obs. form of PRANCE *v.*

prawning (ˈprɔːnɪŋ), *vbl. sb.* [f. PRAWN *v.* + -ING[1].] **1.** The action or process of fishing for prawn. Also *attrib.*

1886 *Globe* 16 July (*heading*), Prawning. *Ibid.*, A favourite prawning ground is St. Margaret's Bay. *Ibid.*, A 'fleet' of nets for prawning consists of from four to twelve of different sizes. **1973** [See *open go* s.v. OPEN *a.* 22 c]. **1978** M. GILBERT *Empty House* xxiv. 219 Spades, buckets and prawning nets should be left in the porch. **1979** *Country Life* 24 May 1658/1 The Coquet.. is a prawning and shrimping river.

2. Fishing for salmon using a prawn as bait.

1909 *Westm. Gaz.* 10 May 12/2 Prawning and spinning for salmon has begun on the Hampshire Avon. **1921** *Chambers's Jrnl.* Sept. 590/1 Prawning for salmon is looked down upon by many as being almost a form of poaching. **1931** E. TAVERNER et al. *Salmon Fishing* xxiii. 361 A rod, reel and line suitable for spinning will serve equally well for prawning.

Praxean (ˈpræksiːən), *sb.* and *a. Ch. Hist.* [f. personal name *Praxeas* + -AN.] **A.** *sb.* A follower of Praxeas (*c* 200). **B.** *adj.* Belonging to the heresy founded by Praxeas; = MONARCHIAN *sb.* and *a.*

[**1585–7** T. ROGERS *39 Art.* (1625) 6 Some doe grant and acknowledge the name of three in the God-head, but deny their persons; such were the.. Praxeneans.] **1719** WATERLAND *Vind. Christ's Div.* 83 *note*, The Praxeans.. pleaded for themselves, and against a real Trinity; *μοναρχίαν tenemus*. Tertullian tells them, that They misunderstood *μοναρχία*. **1874** J. H. BLUNT *Dict. Sects* s.v., Philaster states that the Sabellians, called also Patripassians and Praxeans, were cast out of the Church. *Ibid.*, In Praxean doctrine,.. in its second stage, we have Jesus called the Son of God, solely .. on account of a miraculous birth.

praxeology (præksɪˈɒlədʒɪ), Also praxiology, praˈxology. [ad. F. *praxéologie* (L. Bourdeau 1882, in *Théorie des Sciences* II. VII. i. 463), or directly f. Gr. πρᾶξις action: see -OLOGY.] The study of such actions as are necessary in order to give practical effect to a theory or technique; the science of human conduct; the science of efficient action. So **praxeo'logical, -iological** *a.*; **praxi'ologist**, one who studies practical activity.

1904 W. R. B. GIBSON *Philos. Introd. Ethics* ix. 190, I say 'theory of experience' instead of theory of 'knowledge' or 'epistemology', in order to include the theory of action or 'praxology'. **1911** C. A. MERCIER *Conduct & its Disorders* p. viii, Apart from the general advantage..of having a systematic knowledge of conduct as a whole; there are certain special advantages to be derived from a study of Praxiology, if I may so term it. **1944** *Philos. & Phenomenol. Res.* IV. 527 The theoretical science of human action, praxeology, and especially its hitherto best developed part, economics or catallactics. *Ibid.* 533 Praxeology does not employ the term *rational*. It deals with purposive behavior, i.e., human action. *Ibid.* 537 The technological and the praxeological methods. **1945** Z. JORDAN *Devel. Math. Logic Poland* viii. 33/2 Kotarbinski's first published papers dealt with some problems of ethics and sociology, which were to supply the foundations of a general theory of action, called by him praxeology. **1961** T. KOTARBINSKI in *Methodos* XIII. 163 (*title*) The aspirations of praxiologists. **1962** E. NAGEL et al. *Logic, Methodol. & Philos. of Sci.* 211 (*title*) Praxiological sentences and how they are proved. **1965** D. WOJTASIEWICZ tr. *Kotarbinski's Praxiology* i. 1 Considerations included in the present work come within the scope of praxiology—the general theory of efficient action. *Ibid.*, The praxiologist concerns himself with finding the broadest possible generalizations of a technical nature. **1966** HOWARD & FOX tr. *Aron's Peace & War* p. xviii (*heading*) Praxeology, the antinomies of diplomatic-strategic conduct. *Ibid.* i. 4, I must first define international relations, then specify the characteristics of the four levels of conceptualization which we call *theory, sociology, history, praxiology*. **1973** *Times Lit. Suppl.* 6 July 787/3 The synthesis of these two modes of knowledge he labels 'praxeological'. **1973** B. B. WOLMAN *Dict. Behavioral Sci.* 286/1 *Praxiology*, psychology viewed as the study of actions, and overt behavior... Any normative science, such as, e.g. education, social philosophy, ethics, etc., that sets norms and goals for human actions.

-praxia ('præksɪə), comb. form repr. Gr. πρᾶξις action in some mod.L. terms, as APRAXIA, ECHOPRAXIA, PARAPRAXIA.

praxinoscope ('præksɪnəʊskəʊp). [a. F. *praxinoscope* (M. Reynaud), irreg. f. Gr. πρᾶξις action + -SCOPE.] A scientific toy resembling the zoetrope, in which a series of pictures, representing consecutive positions of a moving body, are arranged along the inner circumference of a cylindrical or polygonal box open at the top, and having in the middle a corresponding series of mirrors in which the pictures are reflected; when the box is rapidly revolved, the successive reflexions blend and produce the impression of an actually moving object.

1882 *Nature* 16 Nov. 60/2 M. Gaston Tissandier describes in *La Nature* an ingenious adaptation of the praxinoscope,..by means of which the images are projected on a screen, and are visible to a large assembly. **1891** *Anthony's Photogr. Bull.* IV. 98 We have all heard of Mr. Eadweard Muybridge and his studies of galloping horses, etc. Some of us have even been fortunate enough to see the real things as exhibited by his praxinoscope.

praxis ('præksɪs). [a. Gr. πρᾶξις doing, acting, action, practice, n. of action f. πράττειν to do; whence med.L. *praxis* (Albertus Magnus *Metaphys.* v. v. ii, *c* 1255).]

1. Action, practice; *spec.* **a.** The practice or exercise of a technical subject or art, as distinct from the theory of it (? *obs.*); **b.** Habitual action, accepted practice, custom.

1581 SIDNEY *Apol. Poetrie* (Arb.) 39 For as Aristotle sayth, it is not *Gnosis*, but *Praxis* must be the fruit. **1644** MILTON *Educ.* Wks. 1738 I. 136 If after some preparatory grounds of speech..they were led to the praxis therof in some chosen short book. **1678** SALMON (*title*) Pharmacopœia Londinensis. Or, the New London Dispensatory..As also, The Praxis of Chymistry. **1800** COLERIDGE *Talleyrand to Ld. Grenville* Poems 1877 II. 156 In theory false, and pernicious in praxis. **1892** J. ROBERTSON *Early Relig. Israel* xv. 390 This code is merely the embodiment of praxis or the crystallisation of custom.

c. A term used by A. von Cieszkowski in *Prolegomena zur Historiosophie* (Berlin, 1838), then adopted by Karl Marx *Zur Kritik der Hegelschen Rechtsphilosophie, Einleitung* in the *Deutsch-Französische Jahrbücher* (1844), to denote the willed action by which a theory or philosophy (esp. a Marxist one) becomes a social actuality. Also *attrib.* and *transf.*

This term, frequently translated as *practice, practical ability*, or *practical activity*, has been increasingly used since the 1960s, following the translation and availability of Marx's early writings.

1933 S. HOOK *Towards Understanding K. Marx* II. ix. 76 That is why Marx claimed that only in practice (*Praxis*) can problems be solved. **1936** —— *From Hegel to Marx* viii. 281 Practice (*Praxis*) was something much wider than *practicability*. It was selective behaviour... Marx's theory of the Praxis could explain what all other philosophers recognised but which they could not begin to account for, without writing fairy-tales, viz., how knowledge could give power. **1966** L. DUPRÉ *Found. Philos. Materialism* viii. 216 But for Marx, praxis is more than a principle of consciousness: it is a prereflective unity of nature and consciousness which can be explicated in thought but not initiated. **1969** D. MCLELLAN *Young Hegelians & Karl Marx* I. ii. 10 The main agent in this transformation was not to be thought, as in Hegel's philosophy, but will, which was the motive force for that synthesis of thought and action for which Cieszkowski coined the term, so influential later, of 'praxis'. **1971** R. J. BERNSTEIN *Praxis & Action* (1972) p. xi, Marx..went on to develop a thorough, systematic and comprehensive *theory of praxis*—a theory, which I shall argue, provides the key for understanding his basic outlook from his early speculations to his mature thought. **1974** *Times Lit. Suppl.* 31 May 582/5 'The embattled imagination' and 'maimed utopia', whose values are under threat in the praxis-obsessed intellectual climate of the Federal Republic. **1976** *Survey* Summer-Autumn 255 He ascribed to Marx, not a voluntarist doctrine as the negation of determinism, but a philosophy that conceived itself as historical praxis. **1978** *Daily Tel.* 23 Nov. 8/8 The new theology is seemingly based on the Marxian concept of praxis—the involvement of the oppressed in the historical processes of change.

d. Action that is entailed by theory or a function that results from a particular structure.

1953 E. L. ALLEN *Existentialism from Within* ii. 27 The Greeks did not speak of 'things' but of *pragmata*, implying that I have to do something (*praxis*) about them. **1962** MACQUARRIE & ROBINSON tr. *Heidegger's Being & Time* II. iv. 409 What is decisive in the 'emergence' of the theoretical attitude would then lie in the *disappearance* of *praxis*. *Ibid.*, And just as *praxis* has its own specific kind of sight ('theory'), theoretical research is not without a *praxis* of its own. **1966** B. HAIGH tr. *Luria's Human Brain & Psychol. Processes* i. 42 At first glance it may appear that lesions situated in very different parts of the brain may lead to a disturbance of praxis. **1968** J. M. HEATON *Eye* iii. 46 Thus, even at this early age, praxis has emerged, i.e. the activity of looking has become meaningful, an end in itself to the infant. **1970** E. PACI in J. M. Edie *Patterns of Life-World* 131 Since instruments are extensions either of the sensing body, or of the acting body, or of the body as organ of will and praxis, they represent a fusion of the self and nature in the body. **1972** PICCONE & HANSEN tr. *Paci's Function of Sci.* III. xix. 360 Science loses its function and society hides the meaning of praxis through technistic ideology.

e. (See quot.)

1950 [see LEXIS 1].

2. a. An example or collection of examples to serve for practice or exercise in a subject, esp. in grammar.

1612 BRINSLEY *Lud. Lit.* xx. (1627) 235 Perfected and adjoyned as a praxis in the end of the Radices. **1762** LOWTH *Introd. Eng. Gram.* 173 A Praxis, or Example of Grammatical Resolution. **1779** BEATTIE *Let.* in Forbes *Life* (1806) II. 42, I..send you inclosed a little book, containing about two hundred, with a praxis at the end, which will perhaps amuse you. **1843** W. BAILLIE (*title*) The First Twelve Psalms in Hebrew, with..Grammatical Praxis.

b. A means or instrument of practice or exercise in a subject; a practical specimen or model. ? *Obs.*

1751 HARRIS *Hermes* Wks. (1841) 114 They [mathematics] are the noblest praxis of logic, or universal reasoning. **1786–97** GILLIES *Aristotle* II. 348 (Jod.) The pleadings of the Ancients were praxises of the art of oratorical persuasion. **1800** JEFFERSON *Writ.* (ed. Ford) VII. 429 It [a Parliamentary Manual] may do good by presenting to the different legislative bodies a chaste Praxis.

Praxitelean (præk,sɪtɪ'liːən), *a.* [f. Gr. Πραξιτέλει-ος, adj. f. Πραξιτέλης, Praxiteles + -AN.] Belonging to, executed by, or in the style of Praxiteles, a famous Greek sculptor of the 4th century B.C.

1819 SHELLEY *Prometh. Unb.* III. iii, Praxitelean shapes, whose marble smiles Fill the hushed air with everlasting love. **1905** *Athenæum* 4 Nov. 616/3 Works that have recently been claimed as Praxitelean originals.

pray (preɪ), *v.* Forms: 3–5 preie(n, 4–5 preye, 4–6 prey, praie, praye, 4–7 prai, 4– pray (6 *Sc.* pra, 7 prea). [ME. *preien*, a. OF. *preier* (*Eulalia a* 900), = It. *pregare*, Pg. *pregar*:—late L. *precāre* (Priscian), cl. L. *precārī* to entreat, pray. (In mod.F. *prier* the stem-vowel is levelled under that of the stem-stressed forms, *il prie*, etc.)]

I. *trans.* With personal object.

1. To ask earnestly, humbly, or supplicatingly, to beseech; to make devout petition to; to ask (a person) for something as a favour or act of grace; *esp.* in religious use, to make devout and humble supplication to (God, or an object of worship). *arch.* **a.** with personal object only.

c **1290** *S. Eng. Leg.* I. 112/200 And preide is fader wel ȝerne. **1382** WYCLIF *John* xiv. 16, I schal preie the fadir, and he schal ȝyue to ȝou another coumfortour. **1387** TREVISA *Higden* (Rolls) V. 73 Affricanus, þe writer of stories, was i-prayed and wente to Alexandria. **1567** *Gude & Godlie B.* (S.T.S.) 38 And than come furth, his Father kynde, And prayit him rycht feruentlie. **1611** BIBLE *John* iv. 31 In the meane while his disciples prayed him, saying, Master, eate. *Ibid.* xiv. 16, I will pray the Father, and hee shall giue you another Comforter [so all 16th c. vers. and *Revised* 1881]. **1819** BYRON *Juan* I. lxxvi, That night the Virgin was no further pray'd.

With various extensions:

b. *to do* a thing, or *that* a thing may be.

a **1310** in Wright *Lyric P.* xviii. 58, Y preye the thou here my bene. **13..** *Cursor M.* 17933 (Gött.) To prai vr lauerd drightin dere, To send me wid his messagere þe oyle of his merciful tre. **1390** GOWER *Conf.* III. 172 Preiende Achab,.. To hiere him speke. *c* **1430** *Life St. Kath.* (1884) 41 þey alle prayde þe preciouse virgyn þat þay myght be baptized. *c* **1450** *Merlin* 15 She wepte and cryde hem mercy, prayng hem to abyde a while. *c* **1489** CAXTON *Sonnes of Aymon* iii. 74 That we praye god that he wyll helpe vs to be auenged of the foure sones of Aymon. **1592** SHAKS. *Ven. & Ad.* 578 The poore foole praies her that he may depart. **1613–14** in *Crt. & Times Jas. I* (1848) I. 292, I pray God your friends..stick as well to you. **1637** *Documents agst. Prynne* (Camden) 66 Mr. Atturney Generall shal bee hereby prayed and required ..to proceed in examinacion..of the Warden of the Fleet and his deputy. **1712** ARBUTHNOT *John Bull* I. x, Pray God, this Hocus be honest! **1787** NELSON in Nicolas *Disp.* (1845) I. 263 Praying their Lordships to relieve him from the expenses and issue of a law-suit. **1845** M. PATTISON *Ess.* (1889) I. 22 They were sent to pray him not to show himself obstinately bent on thwarting her wish.

c. Const. *for* or *on behalf of* a person or thing; *for* (†*of*) a thing desired.

c **1330** *Assump. Virg.* 164 (B.M. MS.) My sone..I praie þee of þi blessing. *a* **1450** *Knt. de la Tour* 34 Ladies..y praie you of a bone [boon]. *c* **1450** *St. Cuthbert* (Surtees) 6956 He was besy, night and day, þe saint for synfull men to pray. **1480** CAXTON *Chron. Eng.* lii. 36 The bisshop prayd this kyng Aldroye of help and socour. **1483** —— *G. de la Tour* lxxxiv. G vij b, How..faders and moders ought euery day to pray god for theyr children.

d. with the thing asked as second object: cf. ASK *v.* 5. *rare.*

c **1586** C'TESS PEMBROKE *Ps.* LXV. i, All mens praiers to thee raised Returne possest of what they pray thee.

†**2.** To beg or entreat (a person) to come to a feast, or the like; to invite. *Obs.*

a **1300** *Cursor M.* 13987 At ete he praid him til his hus. **1387** TREVISA *Higden* (Rolls) II. 155 þey preyed to a feste al þe grete of þe Pictes. **1390** GOWER *Conf.* III. 18 Be mouthe bothe and be message Hise frendes to the feste he preide. *c* **1420** *Sir Amadace* (Camden) xix, To pray the marchand and his wife allsoe, To soupe with him that nyȝte. **1603** SHAKS. *Meas. for M.* II. i. 292, I pray you home to dinner with me.

II. *trans.* With the thing asked as object.

3. a. To ask (something) earnestly in prayer; to ask or beg (a thing) with supplication; to crave.

1387 TREVISA *Higden* (Rolls) VI. 95 What þou hast i-prayed it is [y]-graunted to þe. **1594** T. BEDINGFIELD tr. *Machiavelli's Florentine Hist.* (1595) 39 Now they were inforced to pray his aid. **1619** W. SCLATER *Exp. 1 Thess.* (1630) 218 Whether it be lawfull to pray freedome from all temptations. **1818** CRUISE *Digest* (ed. 2) VI. 359 If a conveyance had been prayed, there must have been a limitation to trustees to preserve contingent remainders. **1859** TENNYSON *Geraint & Enid* 403 Fair Host and Earl, I pray your courtesy. **1872** MORLEY *Voltaire* ii. 74 The next day Voltaire saw his man in prison with irons on and praying an alms from the passers by. **1889** RUSKIN *Præterita* III. ii. 92 He prayed permission to introduce his mother and sisters to us.

b. with inf. or obj. cl.

c **1330** R. BRUNNE *Chron. Wace* (Rolls) 7545 Preyenge ..þat he wolde ony night herberwe him wyþ. *a* **1425** *Cursor M.* 10209 (Trin.) Childe to haue þei preyed long. **1590** SHAKS. *Com. Err.* I. ii. 90 And praies that you will hie you home. **1819** SCOTT *Ivanhoe* iv, Let me also pray that you will excuse my speaking to you in my native language. **1844** H. H. WILSON *Brit. India* II. 487 [They] prayed to be exempted from the operation of the law. **1845** STEPHEN *Comm. Laws Eng.* (1874) II. 176 Praying that the proper general meetings may be convened.

4. a. with cognate object: ***to pray a prayer***, etc.

c **1350** *Will. Palerne* 163 To ȝe heiȝ king of heuene preieth a pater noster. *c* **1490** *MS. Advocates' Libr. Edin.* 18. 2. 8. 11. Colophon, Ane orisoune þat Galfryde Chauceir maid and prayit to þis lady. **1526** *Pilgr. Perf.* (W. de W. 1531) 167 The prayer of a synner, though it deserue not to be herd of god, in that he is a synner y^t prayeth it. **1603** SHAKS. *Meas. for M.* III. i. 146 Ile pray a thousand praiers for thy death, No word to saue thee. **1665** *Surv. Aff. Netherl.* 197 That they shall pray prayers twice a week. **1854** R. G. LATHAM *Native Races Russian Emp.* 57 They pray a prayer, burn a portion of the offering, and spread a portion of it over the altar.

b. With the matter of the prayer as object.

c **1586** C'TESS PEMBROKE *Ps.* LXVI. viii, Praise to him: who what I praid, Rejected not. **1681** T. FLATMAN *Heraclitus Ridens* No. 39 (1713) I. 263 They prate, they print, they pray, and preach Sedition.

III. 5. *intr.* To make earnest request or petition; to make entreaty or supplication; *esp.* to present petitions to God, or to an object of worship.

a. *simply.* To offer prayer, to engage in prayer.

a **1300** *Cursor M.* 19042 Arli þa postlis ilke dai Wente to þe tempil to praie. *c* **1375** *Sc. Leg. Saints* ii. (*Paulus*) 227 Besyd it to morne ȝe se may Twa men stannand besyd it prayand. **1382** WYCLIF *Luke* xi. 1 Lord, teche vs to preye, as and John tauȝte his disciplis. **1388** —— *Acts* ix. 11 Lo! he preieth. *a* **1400–50** *Alexander* 1477 Ilke freke & euery faunt to fast & to pray. **1533** GAU *Richt Vay* 32 Thairfor we pra al as christ hes lerit vsz in the vi chaiptur of S. Mathew. **1596** DALRYMPLE tr. *Leslie's Hist. Scot.* II. 169 At Galdies sepulchre he prayes eftir the consuetude. **1603** SHAKS. *Meas. for M.* v. i. 93 How I perswaded, how I praid, and kneel'd. **1642** MILTON *Apol. Smect.* xi, Nor is it easily credible, that he who can preach well, should be unable to pray well. **1798** COLERIDGE *Anc. Mar.* VII. xxii, He prayeth well, who loveth well Both man and bird and beast. **1828** SCOTT *Tales of Grandf.* Ser. II. xix, Claverhouse..said 'I gave you leave to pray, and you are preaching'. **1852** MRS. STOWE *Uncle Tom's C.* xxviii, 'I am dying', said St. Clare, pressing his hand; 'pray!' **1882** J. PARKER *Apost. Life* I. 83 To pray is to redeem any day from common-place.

b. Const. *to* a person, *for* a thing; also *for* (= on behalf of) a person, etc.; *spec.* to make a formal petition *for* (something); to move a prayer (PRAYER¹ 5). Also *absol.*

a **1300** *Cursor M.* 108 (Cott.) Scho prais ai for sinful men. *Ibid.* 3449 At pray to godd ai was sco prest. *a* **1340** HAMPOLE *Psalter* xv. 1 þe voice of crist in his manhed prayand til þe fadere. **1382** WYCLIF *Isa.* liii. 12 He the synne of manye toc, and for trespasseres preȝede. **1390** GOWER *Conf.* III. 15 Thanne Bachus preide To Jupiter, and thus he seide. *c* **1400** *Apol. Loll.* 26 þei prey for plentey, & pees, & swilk oþer þings. **1466** *Paston Lett.* II. 286 Every day iiij *d.*, to sing and pray for his sowle and myn. **1526** *Pilgr. Perf.* (W. de W. 1531) 2, I beseche all them..yt shall profyte by this worke to pray for me wretche. **1641** BROME *Jovial Crew* III. Wks. 1873 III. 398 That will duly and truly prea for yee. **1651** HOBBES *Leviath.* II. xxxi. 191 The People that Prayed to them [images]. **1732** BERKELEY *Alciphr.* v. §2 Shall we believe a God, and not pray to him for future benefits? **1754** ERSKINE *Princ. Sc. Law* (1809) 21 The grounds..upon which a party may pray for letters of advocation. **1875** JOWETT *Plato* (ed. 2) V. 73 A legislator..will pray for favourable conditions under which he may exercise his art. **1920** *Act 10 & 11 Geo. V.* c. 67 §1 The Council shall..determine whether to issue the order as prayed for, or to issue the order with such modifications as may appear to be necessary. **1962** HANSON & WISEMAN *Parliament at Work* viii. 211 The need for such an Order arose from the attempts of a group of Conservative back-benchers to 'harry the life' out of the Labour Government of 1950–51..by 'praying' into the small hours of the morning.

c. In the formal ending of a petition to the Sovereign, to Parliament, a petition in Chancery, etc. The words after 'pray' were at length reduced to 'etc.', which is now also usually omitted.

1429 *Petition to Parlt.* (8 Hen. VI) in *Rolls of Parlt.* IV. 346 Please it your right high and wise discretions to preye the Kyng oure soverayn Lorde, be the advis and assent of the Lord Espirituelx and Temporels of this present Parlement..to graunte his Letters Patentz undre his Great Seale [etc.]. And we shall preye to God for you. *c* **1432–43** *Petition in Chancery* in *Cal. of Proc. in Chancery* (Recd. Comm. 1827) Introd. 41 (To Ld. Chancellor) And your said pore oratours shall ever pray to God for your good Lordship. *Ibid.*, And she [Margt. Applegarth, widow] shall pray God for you. *Ibid.* 45 And thei shall truly pray for you. **1439** *Petition to King* in *Rolls of Parlt.* V. 10/1 And they shall pray to God for you perpetuelly, and for all your noble Progenitors. **1472–3** (12–13 Edw. IV) *Ibid.* VI. 20/2 And youre seid Suppliant shall ever pray to God for the preservation of your estate Roiall. **1485** (1 Hen. VII) *Ibid.* VI. 327 And he shal euer pray to God for the preservacion of your most Noble and Roiall Estate. **1575–1600** (Q. Eliz.) in *Cal. of Proc. in Chancery* (as above) Introd. 147 And the said John Hunt according to his bounden dutie shall daily praie unto God for your majesties long & prosperous raigne over us your heighnes subjectis. **1597** WEST *Symbol.* II. *Chancery* §104, And your said Orator shall daily pray vnto God for the long continuance of your H[ighness] in health and prosperitie. [Many variant forms are given.] **1727** [see ORATOR 2]. **1883** *Wharton's Law Lex.* 622 To the whole petition [to Parlt.] should be added the words, 'And your Petitioners, as in duty bound, will ever pray, etc.'; and immediately thereupon must follow the signatures. **1896** W. P. BAILDON *Select Cases in Chancery* (Selden Soc.) Introd. xxv, The familiar expression 'and your petitioner[s] shall ever pray, &c.', in its various forms, came in about the middle of the fifteenth century.

IV. Phrases and idiomatic uses.

6. *to pray in aid*: to pray or crave the assistance *of* some one. Also *fig.* See AID *sb.* 2.

For the construction, cf. *to call in the aid of*, etc.

1531 *Dial. on Laws Eng.* II. vii. 16 In like wyse he may nat pray in ayde for him onelesse he knowe the pray [*ed.* 1554 prayee] have good cause of voucher and lyon, or that he know that the pray hathe somwhat to plede that the tenaunt maye nat plede as vyllynage in the demaundaunt or suche other. **1594** PLAT *Jewell-ho.* III. 40 To drawe..by hand onely, without praying in aide of the same [perspective glass]. **1606** SHAKS. *Ant. & Cl.* v. ii. 27 A Conqueror that will pray in ayde for kindnesse, Where he for grace is kneel'd too. **1625** BACON *Ess., Friendship* (Arb.) 173 Yet, without praying in Aid of Alchymists, there is a manifest Image of this, in the ordinarie course of Nature. **1642** tr. *Perkins' Prof. Bk.* v. §310. 137 The other..prayeth in aid of his coparcener. **1768** BLACKSTONE *Comm.* III. xx. 300 In real actions also the tenant may pray in *aid*, or call for assistance of another, to help him to plead. *Ibid.*, An incumbent may pray in aid of the patron and ordinary.

7. *trans.* and *refl.* with *compl.* To bring, put, or get into some state or condition by praying. *pray down, out*: see DOWN *adv.* 17 b, OUT *adv.* 7, 8.

1643 TRAPP *Comm. Gen.* xxxii. 24 Nehemiah prayed himself pale; Daniel prayed himself sick; our Saviour also pray'd himself into an agony. **1677** I. MATHER *Prevalency of Prayer* (1864) 267 If Enemys arise, let us pray them down again. **1686** LUTTRELL *Brief Rel.* (1857) I. 371 At the queens chappell at St. James are papers stuck up..for the prayeing of persons out of purgatory. **1725** POPE *Let. to Swift* 15 Oct., I would not pray them out of purgatory. **1822** J. FLINT *Lett. Amer.* 233 One of them gifted with a loud and clear voice, drowned the other totally, and actually prayed him down. **1840** T. F. BUXTON in T. W. Reid *Life W. E. Forster* (1888) I. v. 136 All I can say is (and it applies to all cases of perplexity), pray it out.

8. † **a.** *I pray you* (*thee*): used parenthetically to add instance or deference to a question or request. So **b.** *pray you, pray thee*, etc. (Cf. PRITHEE.) **c.** *I pray*. *Obs.*

1519 *Interl. 4 Elements* B iv, Syr, I pray you, be contente, It is not vtterly myne intente Your company to exyle. **1526** *Pilgr. Perf.* (W. de W. 1531) 1 b, Ascrybe it (I praye you) to my insuffycyency and ignorauce. **1596** SHAKS. *Merch. V.* II. ii. 35 Maister yong-man, you I praie you, which is the waie to Maister Iewes? **1601** ? MARSTON *Pasquil & Kath.* III. 302 Oh, I am maz'd with ioy, I pree-thee, sweet, Vnfold to me, what said mischance it was.

b. **1524** Q. MARGARET in Mrs. Wood *Lett. Illustr. Ladies* (1846) I. 327 Pray your grace to pardon me that I write so plainly to you. **1590** MARLOWE *Edw. II*, II. ii, Pray thee let me know it. *a* **1661** HOLYDAY *Juvenal* 137 'Reward!' says one, 'why, pray y', what do I know?' **1676** HOBBES *Iliad* 91 But, brother, pra'ye, sit down and rest a while.

c. **1591** SHAKS. *1 Hen. VI*, v. v. 36 Why what (I pray) is Margaret more then that? **1630** PRYNNE *Anti-Armin.* 134, I pray, what Scripture proues it? **1704** NORRIS *Ideal World* II. xii. 457 Where, I pray, is it that we see it?

d. Contracted to *pray* (cf. PLEASE *v.* 6 c).

15.. in *Jyl of Brentford's Test.*, etc. (Ballad Soc.) 41 Pray doe it over again. **1610** SHAKS. *Temp.* III. i. 18 Pray set it down, and rest you. **1700** FARQUHAR *Constant Couple* III. i, Pray, sir, are the roads deep between this and Paris? **1707** FREIND *Peterborow's Cond. Spain* 113 Pray consider the consequences of a lost Battle. **1802** MAR. EDGEWORTH *Moral T.* (1816) I. viii. 61 Pray let me pass. **1838–9** FR. A. KEMBLE *Resid. in Georgia* (1863) 33 Now pray take notice. **1875** JOWETT *Plato* (ed. 2) III. 354 Shall I tell you why? Pray do.

9. The vb-stem in Comb. **pray-TV** *N. Amer. colloq.* [punningly after *pay-TV* s.v. PAY- 4], religious broadcasting, esp. television evangelism that dominates a time-slot or network.

1981 *N.Y. Times* 30 Aug. II 31/1 'Pray TV' (ABC)... John Ritter stars in a drama about the electronic church. **1983** *Maclean's Mag.* 10 Oct. 52/2 The commission..voted to approve 'pray TV', a national satellite-distributed religious broadcasting service. **1985** *Christian Science Monitor* 12 Apr. 25/1 There are the intertwining lives of typical Americans in politics, West Point, pray-TV.

† **pray**, *sb.*[1] *Obs. rare.* [f. PRAY *v.*] An act of praying; a prayer.

c **1325** *Spec. Gy Warw.* 68 Iesu Crist..seide: 'His preie i wole do'. *c* **1440** *Alphabet of Tales* 48 Be þi holie pray Nicholas þat I had loste hafe I getten agayn. **1470–85** MALORY *Arthur* XXI. xii. 859 They..sange & redde many saulters & prayes ouer hym. **1654** GAYTON *Pleas. Notes* II. v. 54 Father, we are for fighting, not for pray.

pray (preɪ), *sb.*[2] Now *dial.* [Deriv. unknown.] 'A wooden pin used in thatching' (E.D.D.).

1570 *Stanford Churchw. Acc.* in *Antiquary* Apr. (1888) 170 It. for hame to thatche the churche howse, v.s. iiij d. It. For prays for ye same worke..vd. It. for iiijc prays and a hundredth lydgers xij d. **1890** *Gloucesters. Gloss.*, *Prays*, the wooden pins used in thatching.

pray, erron. f. SPRAY (Douglas *Æneis* (ed. 1553) XII. Prol. 90).

pray, -e, obs. forms of PREY.

praya, var. PRAIA.

'prayable, *a.* [a. OF. *prei-, pre-, proi-, priable, f. preier to PRAY: see -ABLE.] † **a.** That may be prayed to or entreated. *Obs.*

a **1340** HAMPOLE *Psalter* lxxxix. 15 [xc. 13] Turne lord hou lange: and prayabill be abouen þi seruanits. **1382** WYCLIF *Ibid.*, Preyable be thou vp on thi seruauns [1388 able to be preied, *Vulg.* deprecabilis]. **1548** GEST *Pr. Masse* in H. G. Dugdale *Life* (1840) App. I. 116 He is then there..no lesse honourable and prayable then in heaven.

b. Of a prayer: that may be made.

1941 T. S. ELIOT *Dry Salvages* ii. 10 The hardly, barely prayable Prayer of the one Annunciation.

† **'prayant**, *a. Obs.* [f. PRAY *v.* + -ANT 1.] Praying.

1659 GAUDEN *Tears of Ch.* I. xii. 93 Fanatick Errour and Levity would seem an Euchite as well as an Eristick, Prayant as well as Predicant.

† **'pray-a'way**, *sb. Obs. nonce-wd.* One who says 'Pray, (go) away', who refuses overtures.

1601 CHETTLE & MUNDAY *Death Earl of Huntington* v. i. I iv b, The pray awayes, these trip and goes, these tits.

prayed (preɪd), *ppl. a.* [f. PRAY *v.* + -ED[1].] In *prayed-for* adj., that is sought in prayer.

1867 C. E. SMITH *Diary* 11 Mar. in C. E. S. Harris *From Deep of Sea* (1922) xvii. 224 Thank God for such a mercy! At last we are abreast of the longed-for, prayed-for Labrador. **1917** J. MASEFIELD *Lollingdon Downs* 75 In the lonely silence I may wait The prayed-for gleam—your hand upon the gate. **1952** DYLAN THOMAS *Let.* 21 July (1966) 376 I'll wait in all morning for your prayed-for call.

pray'ee. *Law.* [f. PRAY *v.* + -EE.] One whose aid is 'prayed in': see PRAY *v.* 6, quot. 1531.

prayer[1] (prɛə(r)). Forms: 3–4 preiere, 3–6 praiere, 4 preire, preyer, -or, praey-, praiyer, pray-, praior, 4–5 preyere, preier, preir, 4–6 prayere, praire, praer, prayour, 4–7 preier, prair, 5 preyȝer, prayeer, 6 prayar, 7 prayr(e, 7–8 pray'r, 4– prayer. [ME. *preiere*, a. OF. *preiere* (12th c. in Littré), 13th c. and mod.F. *prière* = Pr. *pregaria*, Sp. *plegaria*, It. *preghiera*-:—Romanic and med.L. *precāria* fem. sing., orig. neut. pl. of L. *precārius* adj., obtained by entreaty or prayer, f. *precārī* to pray. Orig. a disyllable: still so in G. Herbert.]

1. a. A solemn and humble request to God, or to an object of worship; a supplication, petition, or thanksgiving, usually expressed in words.

a **1300** *Cursor M.* 13649 (Cott.) þis es a man þat drightin heres, And helpes oþer for his praieres. *c* **1380** WYCLIF *Wks.* (1880) 317 þei passen oþere in preyeris. **1388** —— *Ps.* liv. 1 God, here thou my preier. **1393** LANGL. *P. Pl.* C. XVIII. 86 May no preiour pees make in no place, hit semeþ. *a* **1400–50** *Alexander* 1483 Putten þaim to prayers & pennance indurett. *c* **1420** *Chron. Vilod.* 3911 When þe quene hadde made hurre preyȝerus þus. *c* **1425** *Hampole's Psalter* Metr. Pref., Prayours be the which me wynneth, þe grace of god all myȝtye. **1529** MORE *Dyaloge* I. Wks. 165/1 And so would I ..knele me downe and make my speciall prayour to God. **1595** SPENSER *Col. Clout* 882 With praiers lowd importuning the skie. **1633** G. HERBERT *Temple, Church-porch* lxix, Resort to sermons, but to prayers most. *a* **1711** KEN *Hymnotheo* Poet. Wks. 1721 III. 249 His Alarum to his Midnight Pray'r. **1719** DE FOE *Crusoe* I. 106 This was the first Prayer, if I may call it so, that I had made for many Years. **1864** TENNYSON *Enoch Arden* 127 Rejoicing at that answer to his prayer. **1904** MARIE CORELLI *God's Good Man* xxix, The prayers of this congregation..are desired for Maryllia V...whose life is now in imminent peril.

b. The action or practice of praying to the Divine Being. *passive prayer*: see quot. 1727–41.

a **1300** *Cursor M.* 3138 (Cott.) þat child..was sa mani yere, Ar it was send, soght wit praiyer. **1362** LANGL. *P. Pl.* A. VIII. 104 Of preyere and of penaunce my plouh schal ben herafter. *c* **1380** WYCLIF *Wks.* (1880) 76 Preiere stondiþ principaly in good lif. **1526** TINDALE *Luke* vi. 12 He.. continued all nyght in prayer to god. **1593** SHAKS. *3 Hen. VI*, II. i. 156 He is fam'd for Mildnesse, Peace, and Prayer. **1649** JER. TAYLOR *Gt. Exemp.* II. Disc. xii. 142 Prayer is the ascent of the mind to God. **1727–41** CHAMBERS *Cycl.*, *Passive prayer*, in the language of mystick divines, is a total suspension, or ligature of the intellectual faculties, in virtue whereof the soul remains, of itself and as to its own power, impotent with regard to the producing of any effects. **1819** MONTGOMERY *Hymn*, Prayer is the soul's sincere desire, Uttered or unexprest. **1842** TENNYSON *Morte D'Arthur* 247 More things are wrought by prayer Than this world dreams of. **1883** *Catholic Dict.* s.v. *Meditation*, It is important to notice that in passive prayer 'free will exercises itself in the whole of its extent'.

c. *pl.* Petitions to God for his blessing upon some one; hence, earnest good wishes.

1597 SHAKS. *2 Hen. IV*, IV. i. 14 And concludes in heartie prayers, That your Attempts may ouer-liue the hazard. **1608** —— *Per.* III. iii. 34 Madam, my thanks and prayers. **1613** —— *Henry VIII*, III. i. 180 He..shall haue my Prayers While I shall haue my life. **1632** MASSINGER *City Madam* I. i, For it you have my prayers, The beggar's satisfaction. **1864** TENNYSON *Aylmer's Field* 751 Give me your prayers, for he is past your prayers.

d. Slang phr. *not to have* (or *have got*) *a prayer*: to have no chance.

1941 B. SCHULBERG *What makes Sammy Run?* vi. 92 Get ..back to New York. You won't have a prayer around here. **1957** R. A. HEINLEIN *Door into Summer* ii. 46 'I'm going to give you some advice.'..'Well?' 'Do nothing. You haven't got a prayer.' **1968** E. B. WHITE *Let.* 30 Dec. (1976) 574, I wish you luck. I don't think you have a prayer. **1973** A. ROSS *Dunfermline Affair* 113 He went for me... He was a big lad, and strong, but he didn't have a prayer. An amateur up against a professional almost never does. **1977** *Time* 10 Oct. 9/3 Mitterrand was prepared to sign anything back in 1972, when his party did not have a prayer of coming to power.

2. A formula appointed for or used in praying; e.g. the *Lord's Prayer* (LORD *sb.* 6 c).

1389 in *Eng. Gilds* (1870) 23 Yis bede and preyer shal bene reherside and seyde at euery tyme. **1526** *Pilgr. Perf.* (W. de W. 1531) 169 b, This prayer may be diuided in to two partes. **1545** *Primer Hen. VIII*, The Prayer of our Lord. **1548–9** (Mar.) *Bk. Com. Prayer, Communion*, The Priest..shall saie the Lordes praier. **1651** HOBBES *Leviath.* III. xl. 254 That excellent prayer, used in the Consecrations of all Churches. **1662** *Bk. Com. Prayer*, A Collect or Prayer for all Conditions of men, to be used at such times when the Litany is not appointed to be read. **1797** MRS. RADCLIFFE *Italian* x, They stopped..to repeat some prayer or sing a hymn. **1884** *Before the Altar* (1885) 60 Then the Priest kneeling says the Prayer of Humble Access, which you can follow.

3. A religious observance, public or private, of which prayer to God forms a principal part; a form of divine service; as the service of *Morning* or *Evening Prayer, family prayers*; in *pl.* with possessive, one's private or individual devotions.

a **1300** *Cursor M.* 28248 (Cott.) My prayers say was me ful lathe. **1382** WYCLIF *Acts* xvi. 13 We wenten out withoute the ȝate bisydis the flood, wher preier was seyn for to be. **1526** TINDALE *Acts* iii. 1 Peter and Ihon went vp to gedder into the temple at the nynthe houre of prayer [**1611** at the houre of prayer, being the ninth houre]. **1548–9** (Mar.) (*title*) The Booke of the Common Prayer and Administracion of the Sacramentes..after the vse of the Churche of England. *Ibid.* Pref., It may plainly appere by the common prayers in the Churche, commonlye called diuine seruice. **1552** *Ibid.* Pref., When menne say Mornyng and Euenynge prayer [1549 Matins and Euensong] priuatly. **1573** G. HARVEY *Letter-bk.* (Camden) 2 In the morning after praiers we looked for it. **1660** PEPYS *Diary* 21 July, At night..I read prayers out of the Common Prayer Book, the first time that ever I read prayers in this house. **1662** *Ibid.* 17 Aug., This being the last Sunday that the Presbyterians are to preach, unless they read the new Common Prayer. **1678** J. PHILLIPS *Tavernier's Trav.* v. iii. 205 The Assassinates found him at his prayers. **1732** LAW *Serious C.* i. (ed. 2) 1 Prayers, whether private or publick, are particular parts or instances of Devotion. **1821** CLARE *Vill. Minstr.* I. 173 The bell.. Now chimes in concert, calling all to prayers. **1846–8** ELIZ. M. SEWELL *Laneton Parsonage* vi. (1858) 50 Madeline said her prayers in haste. **1856** *Amy Carlton* 104 The servants came in, and they had prayers. *a* **1866** KEBLE *Lett. Spir. Counsel* (1870) 105 You are often hindered from the Church prayers.

4. An entreaty made to a person; an earnest supplication or appeal for some favour.

c **1350** *Will. Palerne* 996 Ful prestely for þi praire..here i graunt him grepli. *c* **1391** CHAUCER *Astrol.* Prol., As wel considere I thy bisi preyere in special to lerne the tretis of the astrelabie. *c* **1400** *Destr. Troy* 2821 Menelay..purpost vnto Pyle by prayer of Nestor, To solas hym a season. **1480** CAXTON *Chron. Eng.* 17 Atte praier of genius the quene Vaspasianus and Aruiragus were accorded. **1590** SHAKS. *Com. Err.* v. i. 115, I will fall prostrate at his feete, And neuer rise vntill my teares and prayers Haue won his grace to come in person hither. **1697** DRYDEN *Virg. Georg.* IV. 573 Unconstrain'd he nothing tells for naught; Nor is with Pray'rs, or Bribes, or Flatt'ry bought. **1858** G. MACDONALD

Phantastes ix, I held it in spite of her attempts to take it from me; yes, I shame to say, in spite of her prayers, and, at last, her tears.

5. The matter of a petition, the thing prayed for or entreated; *spec.* that part of a memorial or petition to a sovereign or public body that specifies the thing desired to be granted or done (see also quot. 1958).

c **1400** *Rom. Rose* 3450 Thus hath he graunted my prayere. **14..** *Tundale's Vis.* (Wagner) 1786 The angelle gaf hym none answere, For he wold not do his prayere. **1676** HOBBES *Iliad* I. 45 His prayer was granted by the Deity. **1836** CALHOUN *Wks.* (1874) II. 471 It is only on the question of receiving that opposition can be made to the petition itself. On all others, the opposition is to its prayer. **1937** *Hansard Commons* 4 June 1307, I undertake, if the House will allow the remaining Regulations to be passed now, to amend No 95 immediately, and the notification of the Amendment will, of course, be subject to a Prayer, just as the Regulations themselves are. **1946** *May's Treat. Parliament* (ed. 14) xiv. 286 The last item of this group consists of motions for the disallowance of statutory orders or regulations... These motions are usually in the form of addresses to the Crown praying for the annulment of orders or regulations and are hence commonly called 'Prayers'. **1958** WILDING & LAUNDY *Encycl. Parliament* 431 *Prayer*, a motion to annul a Statutory Instrument... Such motions count as Exempted Business ..and are taken at the end of the day's sitting. They must be moved during the forty days after the order is laid on the Table, at the expiration of which it automatically becomes law. **1968** *Observer* 21 Apr. 3/3 The British Medical Association..is arranging for a 'prayer' to be moved in Parliament. **1970** *Daily Tel.* 3 Nov. 2/6 Mr Enoch Powell, Conservative MP for Wolverhampton, South West, has a prayer down on the Commons Order Paper to annul the regulations. **1972** *Times* 23 Feb. 27/5 A..petitioner sought the direction of the court whether she might properly omit a prayer for costs from a petition which sought a decree of divorce. **1973** *N.Y. Law Jrnl.* 2 Aug. 5/3 Nowhere in this or any other document, has IBM denied the factual assertions, made by the United States, which are the basis for its prayer that IBM be held in contempt of court. **1975** J. P. MORGAN *House of Lords & Labour Govt.* ii. 63 Where affirmative resolution is required both Houses must give their approval before such Orders can be passed; where an Order becomes effective unless a Prayer for annulment is carried by either House (the negative resolution procedure), the Lords again enjoy the same rights as the Commons.

6. *attrib.* and *Comb.* **a.** simple attributive, as *prayer-attitude*, *-desire*, *-ground*, *-hour*, *-house*, *-life*, *-matter*, *-monger*, *-room*, *service*, *-test*, *-time*, *-union*, *-word*; **b.** obj. and obj. gen., as *prayer-answering*, *-grinding*, *-hearing*, *-lisping*, *-loving*, *-repeating*, *-saying*, etc., adjs. or sbs.; *prayer-inventor*, *-maker*; **c.** instrumental, etc., as *prayer-clenched*, *-prospering* adjs.

1770 COWPER *Hymn 'God of my life, to Thee I call'* iv, A prayer-hearing, *answering God. **1894** H. GARDENER *Unoff. Patriot* 25 Personal relationship with a prayer-answering and a praise-loving God. **1953** R. KNOX *Off Record* xliv. 148 If one does a hop from Evangelicalism to the Church the difference is not so much one of doctrines as one of *prayer-attitudes. **1857** DUFFERIN *Lett. High Lat.* (ed. 3) 396 Hands —*prayer-clenched—that would not sever. **1883** JEFFRIES *Story my Heart* 188 It is not strong enough to utter my *prayer-desire. *a* **1732** T. BOSTON *Crook in Lot* (1805) 156 The hand of a *prayer-hearing God. **1852** CONYBEARE & HOWSON *St. Paul* (1856) I. 208 All gradations..from the simple proseucha at Philippi to the magnificent *prayer-houses at Alexandria. **1856** OLMSTED *Slave States* 450 A small chapel, which the negroes call their prayer-house. **1953** R. KNOX *Off Record* xliv. 150, I should find no difficulty in accepting the doctrine as doctrine, although it would make no addition to my own *prayer-life. *a* **1847** ELIZA COOK *Future* iv, The *prayer-lisping infant. **1663** *Flagellum or O. Cromwell* 128 He was absolutely the best *prayer-maker and preacher in the Army. **1680** ALLEN *Peace & Unity* Pref. 42 By such a Form *Prayer-matter is prepared with more advantage to affect such peoples minds. **1801** SOUTHEY *Thalaba* v. xxxvi, I have led Some camel-kneed *prayer-monger through the cave. **1825** R. GORDON *Serm.* 422 Through the whole course of a *prayer-repeating life, they had never prayed at all. **1902** *Daily Chron.* 2 Oct. 7/1 There are hundreds of these little meeting-places and *prayer-rooms scattered about in the side streets and alleys. *c* **1440** *Alphabet of Tales* cxiii. 81 He went vnto Saynt Barnard agayn, and told hym what þoght come in his mynde in þis *prayer-saying. **1976** *Honolulu Star-Bull.* 21 Dec. F-2/3 Friends may call from 6 to 9 tonight at Dodo Mortuary, with *prayer service scheduled for 7:30. **1838** DICKENS *O. Twist* iii, Every evening at *prayer-time.

d. Special combs.: **prayer-bill**: see quot.; **prayer bones** *U.S.*, the knees; **prayer breakfast**, a breakfast during which prayers are offered; **prayer card**, a card used by a Member of Parliament for reserving a seat at prayers; **prayer-carpet**, a small carpet, mat, or rug used, esp. by a Moslem, when engaged in prayer; **prayer chain**, a series of people each of whom receives a written prayer with an invitation to pass it or copies of it to others; **prayer circle**, a group of people who pray together; **prayer-cloak** = *prayer-shawl*; **prayer-cure**, a cure wrought by means of 'the prayer of faith' (Jas. v. 15), a faith-cure; **prayer-cylinder** = PRAYER-WHEEL; **prayer day**, a day in Parliament on which prayers (see sense 5 above) are heard; **prayer-desk**, the desk from which prayers are read in a church; **prayer-flag**, in Tibet, a flag on which prayers are inscribed; **prayer-gong**, a gong calling people to prayer; **prayer-mat** = *prayer-carpet*; **prayer-niche**, in a mosque, a niche in the centre of a sanctuary wall indicating the direction of Mecca; **prayer-nut**, in a chaplet, a nut-shaped bead which opens to form a diptych with reliefs; **prayer-oil**: see quot.; **prayer plant**, a perennial herb, *Maranta leuconeura*, belonging to the family Marantaceæ, native to Brazil, bearing irregular, three-petalled, white flowers, and often cultivated as a house plant for the sake of its shiny, variegated leaves; **prayer ring** = *prayer circle*; **prayer rug** = *prayer-carpet*; **prayer-scarf, -shawl**, a long scarf or shawl worn round the neck or on the head by Jews when at prayer; the tallith; **prayer-stick**, a stick decorated with feathers, used by the Zuñi Indians in their religious ceremonies; **prayer stool**, a stool for kneeling on while praying; **prayer-thong**, a phylactery; **prayer ticket** = *prayer card*; **prayer-tower**, a minaret; **prayer-value**, efficacy or worth for prayer; **prayer-wall**, a wall on which prayers are inscribed; = MANI[2]. See also PRAYER-BEAD, -BELL, -BOOK, etc.

1700 T. BROWN *Amusem. Ser. & Com.* x. 123 A Number of *Prayer-Bills, containing the Humble Petitions of divers Devoto's. **1926** *Amer. Speech* II. 362 **Prayer bones* (noun phrase), knees. 'Everyone get down on his prayer bones.' *a* **1944** J. CONROY in B. A. Botkin *Treas. Amer. Folklore* (1944) IV. 531 You've got to kneel down on your prayerbones... If you kneel down to save your poor old back, the little grains of sand eat into your prayerbones. **1970** C. MAJOR *Dict. Afro-Amer. Slang* 93 *Prayer bones*, the knees. **1966** *New Statesman* 4 Mar. 285/2 The Republican governor of Oregon, is in the vanguard of a movement that sponsors '*prayer breakfasts' for politicians all around the world. **1969** *Listener* 28 Aug. 271/1 (*caption*) Billy Graham speaks at a Honolulu prayer breakfast. **1959** P. G. RICHARDS *Hon. Members* iv. 75 No permanent reservation of seats is allowed... A Member who intends to be present at prayers at the start of a sitting can place a '*prayer card' on a bench; this card has to be obtained personally from an attendant at the House at any time after eight a.m. on the same day. **1975** *Daily Tel.* 16 Apr. 16 An interesting feature of the House of Commons before the Budget statement yesterday was the number of seats bearing Prayer Cards—reservations—on the Tory side. **1861–2** R. NOEL in *Vac. Tour.* 458 The first thing that struck me was the sight of a camel, and his master kneeling on a *prayer-carpet by him. **1908** *Westm. Gaz.* 5 Oct. 4/1 Other ladies started *prayer-chains to promote or defeat the different candidates' chances of victory. **1911** *Daily Colonist* (Victoria, B.C.) 11 Apr. 4/3 We have been requested to say something about the 'prayer chain' which is being worked again... We are told that in the time of Jesus it was said that whoever copied this prayer and sent it to nine persons would have great joy, and those who did not would have great sorrow. **1880** P. DEMING *Adirondack Stories* 25 As a preliminary to the sermon, a *prayer-circle was formed. **1876** EDERSHEIM *Jewish Life Days Christ* xiii. 220 During prayer they wrap themselves in the great tallith or so-called *prayer-cloak. **1894** I. L. BISHOP *Among Tibetans* ii. 46 *Prayer-cylinders which are turned by pulling ropes. **1897** *Geogr. Jrnl.* X. 35 A prayer-cylinder revolved by the wind. **1952** *Ann. Reg. 1951* 17 A motion..to cut off alcoholic refreshment after 10 p.m. on '*prayer days'. **1843** *Ecclesiologist* II. 22 The *Prayer-desk faces east and west. **1892** J. C. BLOMFIELD *Hist. Heyford* 46 Hangings of dark blue cloth covered the pulpit, prayer-desk and clerk's desk. **1882** 'SHWAY YOE' *Burman* I. xvii. 225 These *prayer-flags ..are made of paper, cut fancifully into figures of dragons, lizards, and the like, with embroidery-work round their edges. **1897** *Geogr. Jrnl.* X. 35 Groups of prayer-flags in memory of the dead are planted beside every village. **1936** [see OBO]. **1952** [see CHORTEN]. **1955** E. HILLARY *High Adventure* 62 We sat down wearily in the snow beside a clump of Tibetan prayer-flags. **1905** E. F. BENSON *Image in Sand* ix. 135, I adore theosophy, *prayer-gongs, and letters from the ceiling. **1885** *B'ham Daily Post* 5 Jan. 6/6 The fabrics include..*prayer mats (for South America). **1937** *Burlington Mag.* Oct. 193/2 The mihrab, or *prayer-niche. **1971** *Country Life* 25 Feb. 426/1 The large construction..is an Iranian prayer-niche in coloured tin enamel tiles (*faience*). **1937** *Burlington Mag.* Aug. 98/1 She holds a little silver chain, from which hangs..a '*prayer-nut' for a chaplet, in wrought silver. **1969** E. WILKINS *Rose-Garden Game* ii. 59 The..Chatsworth paternoster..has a terminal bead that is a little hinged box, which opens to show two miniature relief carvings... The prayer-nut is usually made of boxwood. **1867** *Union Rev.* V. 190 *Prayer-oil is a sacrament in which the body of the sick believer is anointed with oil by the Priests of the Church. **1953** J. HERSEY *Garden in your Window* iv. 57 The *Prayer Plant, while a bit rare, is simple to grow. **1956** Y. FIELD *House Plants* iv. 97 The small maranta is a very beautiful foliage plant. Since this plant closes its leaves at night or almost curls them together it is known as the Prayer Plant. **1977** WARD & WELLSTED *Indoor Plants* 81/2 *Maranta leuconeura*... Prayer Plant, Rabbit's Tracks. This Brazilian plant has given rise to several spectacularly coloured foliage varieties. **1846** *Knickerbocker* XXVIII. 305 When a '*prayer ring' was to be formed, he announced it at the close of a sermon. **1898** *Atlantic Monthly* Apr. 460/2, I worshiped it in silence,..the grass a natural *prayer-rug. **1904** Prayer-rug [see KULAH[1]]. **1930** *Morning Post* 16 July 8/6 This fascinating old Koula Prayer Rug is believed to have been made for the Jewish Synagogue at Toledo. **1935** H. EDIB *Clown & his Daughter* xlviii. 277 Pembeh touched him on the shoulder and pointed to a prayer-rug spread at the threshold of the room. **1962** C. W. JACOBSEN *Oriental Rugs* 306 Tekke Prayer Rugs are available only from estates. **1979** *Guardian* 26 Oct. 15/2 The bearded Ayatollahs..[are] sweeping the most pressing problems under the prayer rug. **1867** *Ch. News* 10 July, The stole of the Deacon is called ὀραρίον which is etymologically the same with *prayer-scarf. **1905** *Daily Chron.* 10 Oct. 6/4 At the period of confession each man, wearing his four-cornered *prayer shawl, smote his breast as he enumerated his sins. **1865** TYLOR *Early Hist. Man.* v. 88, I do not know whether any of these curious *prayer-sticks are now to be seen. **1883** *Century Mag.* XXVI. 29 Symbolic slats and prayer-sticks most elaborately plumed. **1908** *Daily Chron.* 6 Apr. 1/4 As they knelt upon the wooden *prayer stool..they made no noise. **1885** *Encycl. Brit.* XIX. 1/1 Phylactery..is the name given in the New Testament to the..(tefillin) or '*prayer-thongs' of the Jews. Every Jew wears at prayer two of these thongs. **1924** J. E. MILLS *From Back Benches* ii. 9 Lady Astor..staked out the second row corner seat below the gangway, and, attending regularly.., secured her ticket from the attendant which 'booked' the seat, providing she attended prayers. All went well until Mr. Joynson Hicks, returning..after nearly a year's absence, deposited his '*prayer ticket' in..Lady Astor's seat. **1906** W. R. INGE *Truth & Falsehood in Relig.* iv. 102 It does not satisfy those who really believe in the supernatural occurences, which it is proposed to maintain in consideration of their '*prayer-value'. **1953** R. KNOX *Off Record* xliv. 149 It's no good contemplating becoming a Catholic unless you are prepared to accept doctrinal definitions which have, for you, no particular prayer-value. **1960** C. WINICK *Dict. Anthropol.* 562/2 *Mani wall* or **prayer wall*, a low long wall of mud and stone, covered with flat rocks, on which Tibetan characters are carved. Devout Tibetans walk with the mani wall to their right to get benefit from it. Such walls are frequently more than a quarter of a mile long. **1974** *Listener* 17 Jan. 76/2 As you walk up the trail, prayer-walls bisect the paths. The act of walking past the wall is a prayer in itself.

prayer[2] ('preɪə(r)). Also (for distinctness) **pray-er.** [f. PRAY *v.* + -ER[1]: cf. OF. **prei-*, *proi-*, *pri-e(o)ur*:—L. *precātōr-em*, agent-noun f. *precārī* to pray.] One who prays.

c **1440** *Promp. Parv.* 412/1 Preyare, or he that preyythe, *orator*,..*deprecator*. **1483** *Cath. Angl.* 289/2 A Prayere, ..*orator, rogator*. **1523** FITZHERB. *Husb.* §165 The trew prayers wyll worshyp the father of heuen in spyryt and with trouth. **1642** R. HARRIS *Serm.* 13 A good Engineere is not the worst Souldier; nor a good prayer the worst Parliament-man. **1705** HICKERINGILL *Priest-cr.* II. viii. 78 The Women Prayers amongst the Quakers. **1843** E. JONES *Sens. & Event* Poems (1877) 36 And still that earnest pray-er. **1863** MRS. CARLYLE *Lett.* (1883) III. 162 Anything they can say about ..this and the other preacher and pray-er.

'prayer-bead. [f. PRAYER[1] + BEAD *sb.*]

1. One of the beads of a rosary. Also *gen.*, one of a string of beads used in prayer.

1630 tr. *Camden's Hist. Eliz.* III. 110 Her prayer beades hanging at her girdle. **1852** ROCK *Ch. of Fathers* III. x. 403 Jewel-studded chains, [and] prayer-beads of precious stones. **1975** R. P. JHABVALA *Heat & Dust* 61 The white sadhu..had all his possessions with him—a bundle, an umbrella, prayer-beads, and a begging bowl. **1976** 'M. DELVING' *China Expert* iv. 47 He wore a string of Tibetan prayer beads around his neck. **1979** E. BERCOVICI *Wolf Trap* 145 Cotton pointed to the beads. 'What are those?' he asked pleasantly. 'Prayer beads,' the man answered, holding the strand out, trying to smile. 'Arab beads.'

2. A seed of the plant *Abrus precatorius*: see quot. 1861, and JEQUIRITY.

1861 BENTLEY *Man. Bot.* 528 *Abrus precatorius.*—The seeds are used as beads, for making rosaries, necklaces, &c., hence their common name of prayer-beads. **1866** in *Treas. Bot.* **1887** MOLONEY *Forestry W. Afr.* 316 Crabs' Eyes, Jequerity, Prayer Beads, Jumble Beads.

'prayer-bell. A bell rung to call a household, school, or body of worshippers, to prayer.

a **1550** *Freiris of Berwik* 76 in *Dunbar's Poems* (S.T.S.) 287 With that thay hard the prayer bell Off thair awin abbay. **1682** N. O. *Boileau's Lutrin* I. 34 They could smell The Kitchin Steams, though Deaf to th' Prayer-bell. **1846–8** ELIZ. M. SEWELL *Laneton Parsonage* xxxii. (1858) 339 The prayer bell had only just rung when I came down. **1877** A. B. EDWARDS *Up Nile* xii. 327 Echoing to the measured chime of the prayer-bell at morn and even.

'prayer-book.

1. A book of forms of prayer; *spec.* the Book of Common Prayer, containing the traditional public liturgy of the Church of England.

1596–7 in Swayne *Sarum Churchw. Acc.* (1896) 302 Prayer booke 2*d.* a Salter 4*s.* **1626–7** *Ibid.* 312 Common Prayer Booke, 7*s.* 6*d.* **1660** PEPYS *Diary* 21 July, I read prayers out of the Common Prayer Book. **1692** W. MARSHALL *Gosp. Myst. Sanctif.* xiii. (1764) 283 You must make the whole Scripture your Common-prayer-book, as the primitive Church did. **1712** STEELE *Spect.* No. 284 ¶6, I was almost the only Person that looked in a Prayer-Book all Church-time. **1824** DIBDIN *Libr. Comp.* 42 Editions of Prayer Books, beginning with the first impression in 1549, in folio. **1869** FLOR. MONTGOMERY *Misunderstood* ii, Finding the places in his prayer-book. **1892** PHILLIMORE *Eccl. Law* (ed. 2) 710 The second Prayer Book of Edw. VI omitted all reference to the manual acts, ordered in the first and last Prayer Book, attending the consecration of the holy elements.

2. *transf.* See quot.

1840 R. H. DANA *Bef. Mast* xxiii, Smaller hand-stones, which the sailors call 'prayer-books', are used to scrub in among the crevices and narrow places.

3. *attrib.* and *Comb.*

1896 *Westm. Gaz.* 22 Dec. 2/1 May I say that your lordship is a Prayer-book Churchman—by which I mean that you neither belong to the English Church Union nor the Church Association? **1899** *Ibid.* 4 Mar. 7/3 It would be much to be regretted if the influence of the Prayer-book Party were weakened by individual secessions.

prayere, variant of PRAIERE (meadow) *Obs.*

prayerful ('prɛəfʊl), *a.* [f. PRAYER[1] + -FUL.]

1. Of a person: Much given to prayer, devout.

1626 R. HARRIS *Hezekiah's Recovery* (1630) 2 Tis simply necessary in afflictions to be prayerfull, in the middest of mercies to bee thankfull. **1702** C. MATHER *Magn. Chr.* III. (1853) I. 592 He was very pious in his childhood, and, because pious, therefore prayerful. **18..** WHITTIER *Pr. Wks.* (1889) II. 153 Pious, sober, prayerful people.

2. Of speech, looks, actions, etc.: Characterized by or expressive of prayer.

1652 BENLOWES *Theoph.* Argt. I Stere home a pray'rful course to Heav'n at last. **1657** M. LAWRENCE *Use & Pract. Faith* 86 Faith puts persons into a mourning, confessing, prayerful frame. **1838** HOPE-SCOTT in Ornsby *Mem. & Corr.* (1884) I. 152 A general and prayerful reading of Scripture. **1871** PALGRAVE *Lyr. Poems* 30 With prayerful earnest eyes.

prayerfully ('prɛəfʊlɪ), *adv.* [f. prec. + -LY².] In a prayerful manner, with much prayer.

1826 G. S. FABER *Diffic. Romanism* (1853) 39 They should prayerfully examine the momentous question. **1879** CHR. ROSSETTI *Seek & F.* 160 If we sincerely, persistently, prayerfully, desire this good estate, humility will not be denied us. **1962** *Friend* 16 Mar. 326/2 The decision, like all moral decisions, can only be taken, prayerfully, on the merits of the case by the individuals concerned. **1971** 'A. GARVE' *Late Bill Smith* ii. 49 She sipped a dry martini.., raising her glass prayerfully to the success of the cruise. **1973** *Daily Tel.* 3 Mar. 3/1 Before he died of starvation, David wrote..a touching letter to his parents..talking hopefully and prayerfully about his own situation. **1977** J. F. FIXX *Compl. Bk. Running* i. 5, It is to be prayerfully hoped, but not reasonably expected, that some political leader will find the gumption to blurt out the melancholy truth.

'prayerfulness. [f. as prec. + -NESS.] The quality or state of being prayerful.

1846 in WORCESTER (citing MCKEAN). **1863** MONSELL *Hymn, 'O Worship the Lord'*, He will..Comfort thy sorrows, and answer thy prayerfulness. **1881** ILLINGWORTH *Serm. Coll. Chapel* 150 The secrets of all the fruitfulness of the fragmentary lives of old—humility and prayerfulness.

'prayering, *vbl. sb. nonce-wd.* (*contemptuous*). [f. PRAYER¹: see -ING¹.] Offering or saying of prayers.

1828 SCOTT *F.M. Perth* xii, But what is the use of all this pattering and prayering?

'prayerless, *a.* [f. PRAYER¹ + -LESS.] Without prayer; not having the habit of prayer.

a **1631** DONNE *To C'tess Bedford* Poems (1654) 160 Who prayer-lesse labours, or, without this prayes, Doth but one half, that's none. **1653** BAXTER *Chr. Concord* 26 Those that ..live ungodly, with untaught, ungoverned prayerless families. **1734** WATTS *Reliq. Juv.* lii. (1789) 163 God forbid that any house, among Christians, should be prayerless. **1866** GEO. ELIOT *F. Holt* xxxiv, Helpless and prayerless.. not thinking of God's anger or mercy, but of her son's.

b. *transf.* (Of times, places, states, etc.)

1816 J. WILSON *City of Plague* I. i. 28, I could believe That many a Sabbath had pass'd prayerless on Within its holy solitude. **1826** MILMAN *A. Boleyn* (1827) 13 Scarce a lamp Burnt on the prayerless shrines. **1855** *Fraser's Mag.* LI. 526 The usual connexion between prayerless pride and abundance of bread.

Hence **'prayerlessly** *adv.*, **'prayerlessness.**

a **1828** T. H. SKINNER (cited in Webster), Prayerlessness. **1847** WEBSTER, *Prayerlessly.* **1861** J. STEPHEN *Utterances Ps. cxix.* iv. 81 A Saviour whose Spirit can lead from prayerlessness to godliness. **1891** *Home Missionary* (N.Y.) Dec. 378 Such enthusiasts may be said to have grasped the rope carelessly and prayerlessly. **1892** DR. PIERSON in *Daily News* 1 Feb., In this apostate day—this day of unbelief and comparative prayerlessness.

'prayer-,meeting. A meeting for prayer; a religious meeting for devotion, in which several of those present offer prayer.

1780 *Arminian Mag.* III. 155 Some of these coming over to the prayer meetings at Wednesbury..were utterly astonished... Presently a prayer meeting was set up at Darlaston. **1817** W. SEWALL *Diary* 11 Jan. (1930) 7/1 Evening attended prayer meeting. **1831** A. BONAR in *Diary & Lett.* (1893) 18 In some sort a prayer-meeting over our Studies in the Bible. **1838** MCCHEYNE *ibid.* 79 This seems a fruit of our prayer-meeting, begun last Wednesday. **1877** SPURGEON *Serm.* XXIII. 446, I invite those who take part in our prayer-meetings to lay this matter to heart. **1928** J. BUCHAN *Runagates Club* xi. 298 It was the prayer-meeting, remember, which brought America into the War. **1954** D. S. DAVIS in *Ellery Queen's Mystery Mag.* June 27/1 Sue Thompson had..been..to Sunday prayer meeting. **1972** *News & Observer* (Raleigh, N. Carolina) 30 Dec. 4/3 Wednesday night prayer meeting..and the amen corner have gone with stewards who yelled out 'amen' during the sermon.

'prayer-mill. = next.

1832 J. BELL *Syst. Geogr.* V. 103 Prayer-mills, which are set in motion by wind or water. **1870** GORDON-CUMMING in *Gd. Words* 137/1 Many..walk about always with a small prayer-mill in their hand, turning it as they go. **1896** *Daily News* 16 Nov. 6/2 The pious Tibetan sets his prayer mill agoing by water-power.

'prayer-wheel. [f. PRAYER¹ + WHEEL *sb.*]

1. A mechanical aid to or substitute for prayer, used especially by the Buddhists of Tibet, consisting of a cylindrical box inscribed with or containing prayers, revolving on a spindle: see quot. 1868.

1814 tr. *Klaproth's Trav.* 102 The inscriptions in such prayer-wheels commonly consist of masses for souls, psalms, and the six great general litanies. **1868** MONTGOMERIE in *Proc. R. Geog. Soc.* 15 July 154 The Tibetans..made use of the rosary and prayer-wheel. —— 155 Each revolution represents one repetition of the prayer, which is written on a scroll inside the cylinder. **1893** EARL DUNMORE *Pamirs* I. 105 There was a Buddhist prayer-wheel being turned by water-power, and reeling off prayers at so many per hour.

2. A wheel set with bells and fastened to the ceiling of a chapel, formerly used for divination in connexion with masses or other devotional services.

1897 *Daily News* 26 July 5/1 Even now in Brittany a kind of prayer-wheels are kept in churches and set spinning by the devout.

'prayerwise, *adv.* [f. PRAYER¹ + -WISE.] After the manner or in the way of a prayer.

1583 H. D. *Godlie Treat.* 70 The like phrase praierwise.. hee vseth in his praier to the Lord. **1621** AINSWORTH *Annot. Pentat.* (1639) 63 The Greeke translates it, prayer-wise, The Lord judge. **1850** J. B. JOHNSTONE *Mem. R. Shirra* iv. 41 Be frequently sending up a thought to God prayerwise.

pray-in: see -IN *suffix*³.

praying ('preɪɪŋ), *vbl. sb.* [f. PRAY *v.* + -ING¹.]

a. The action of the vb. PRAY; prayer, earnest request.

1303 R. BRUNNE *Handl. Synne* 476 Þou mayst dreme of sum euyl þyng þat may turne to better for þy preyyng. *c* **1380** WYCLIF *Sel. Wks.* III. 519 God curseþ siche mennis blissinge and preyingis. *c* **1440** *Gesta Rom.* i. 5 (Harl. MS.) Prayinge, Almysdede, and fastyng. **1480** CAXTON *Descr. Brit.* 22 The Saxons come atte praing of the britons ayenst the pictes. **1523** FITZHERB. *Husb.* §165 There be dyuers maner of prayenges..some openly & some pryuatly. *a* **1704** DODD in M. Henry *Fam. Relig.* H.'s Wks. 1853 I. 260/1 Either praying will make a man give over sinning, or sinning will make a man give over praying. **1879** BROWNING *Ned Bratts* 253 Satan's..whisper shoots across All singing in my heart, all praying in my brain.

b. *attrib.* and *Comb.* = Used for or in prayer, as ***praying-cushion, -ground, -house, -place, -stool,*** etc.; **praying-carpet** = PRAYER-*carpet*; **praying-cylinder; praying-desk** = PRAYER-*desk*; **praying-drum** = PRAYER-WHEEL 1; **praying flag-staff,** a staff bearing a prayer flag (see PRAYER¹ 6 d); **praying jenny, machine** = PRAYER-WHEEL 1; also *transf.*; **praying mat, rug** = PRAYER-*carpet*; **praying-scarf, -shawl** = PRAYER-*scarf*; **praying-wheel** = PRAYER-WHEEL 1; **prayingwise** *adv.*, in the manner of one praying.

1844 *Mem. Babylonian P'cess* II. 201 The old Emir.. throwing his *praying carpet on the ground. **1842** MRS. CARLYLE *Lett.* (1883) I. 173, I made myself..a sort of Persian couch out of the *praying-cushions. **1884** GILMOUR *Mongols* 143 These *praying-cylinders seem to be seldom left long at rest. **1906** *Westm. Gaz.* 14 May 2/1 A *praying-desk..and a table for an altar were placed in the middle of the room, and priests carried in the sacred icon from the old house of Peter the Great. **1886** *All Year Round* 14 Aug. 34 Like a Buddhist priest's rotatory *praying-drum. **1877** T. W. R. DAVIDS *Buddhism* 211 Everywhere in Tibet these *praying flag-staffs meet the eye. **1935** Z. N. HURSTON *Mules & Men* I. ii. 39 He went way down in de swamp behind a big plantation to de place they call de *prayin' ground, and got down on his knees. **1967** W. SOYINKA *Kongi's Harvest* 55 You must hurry or the confusion Will be worse than shoes before the Praying-ground at Greater Beiram. **1976** *Sunday Times* (Lagos) 26 Sept. 3/1 (*caption*) The scene at Obalende praying ground with the Lagos Chief ..reading his address. *a* **1843** SOUTHEY *Comm.-pl. Bk.* Ser. II. (1849) 402/1 A *praying-house, or chapel. **1817** *Edin. Rev.* XXVIII. 313 The followers of the grand Lama..have invented *praying-jennies. *Ibid.*, The Kurada, or *praying machine. **1826** S. STALLYBRASS *Jrnl.* 16 July in E. Stallybrass *Mem. Mrs. Stallybrass* (1836) iv. 203 An old man ..was travelling sixty versts on foot, though not destitute of a horse, for the purpose of turning the *praying machine* for a week,..in order to atone for past misconduct and drunkenness. **1879** *Good Words* 745/1 In the great temple there is a figure of Matreya, the coming Buddha... We.. found ourselves before the top of the great praying machine, a revolving structure. **1972** C. STEPHENSON *Merrily on High* 185 Eastern [Orthodox] spiritually has tended to regard monks as primarily 'praying machines'. There has never been the tradition of 'scholar monks' which we have had in the west. **1869** 'MARK TWAIN' *Innoc. Abr.* li. 543 To step rudely upon the sacred *praying mats. **1894** MRS. DYAN *All in a Man's K.* (1899) 92 Half-reclining on a praying-mat was a young girl. **1844** *Mem. Babylonian P'cess* II. 107 The splendid marble court, studded with Mussulman *praying places. **1847** THACKERAY *Cane-Bottom'd Chair* vi, That *praying-rug came from a Turcoman's camp. **1887** *Pall Mall G.* 3 Mar. 6/2 Charged..with stealing three '*praying scarfs'..from the Jewish Synagogue, at Bayswater. **1892** ZANGWILL *Childr. Ghetto* I. 3 Their phylacteries and *praying shawls. **1887** E. GILLIAT *Forest Outlaws* 247 The *praying-stool, the whip for flagellation, and the one mat. **1871** ALABASTER *Wheel of Law* p. xlvii, The *praying-wheel, a box full of texts, the turning of which is supposed to be as efficacious as the actual repetition of them. **1889** *Century Mag.* Jan. 371/1 The praying-wheel exists in old chapels in Brittany as a religious toy, formerly used with rites half magical under the sanction of the local clergy. **1658** ROWLAND *Moufet's Theat. Ins.* 983 This Italian Mantis.. hath six feet like the Locust, but the foremost thicker and longer than the other, the which because for the most part she holds up together (*praying-wise) it is commonly called with us *Preque Dieu.* **1679** C. NESSE *Antichrist* 236 Our *praying-work which comes up as incense.

'praying, *ppl. a.* [-ING².] **a.** That prays.

1483 *Cath. Angl.* 289/2 Prayngе, *precans, precarius, precabundus. c* **1586** C'TESS PEMBROKE *Ps.* LXI. i, To thee my praying voice doth fly. **1697** M. HENRY *Life P. Henry* Wks. 1853 II. 729/2 Christ's last breath was praying breath. **1765** T. HUTCHINSON *Hist. Mass.* I. 285 A piece of revenge, which Philip caused to be taken upon John Sausaman, a praying Indian. **1892** RIDER HAGGARD *Nada* 226 The white praying man, who had come..to teach us people of the Zulu. **1931** F. L. ALLEN *Only Yesterday* iv. 80 The 'praying Colonels' of Centre College.

b. praying band = *prayer circle* s.v. PRAYER¹ 6 d; **praying-insect,** the MANTIS (****praying mantis,*** or ***praying locust***), so called from the position in which it holds its fore-legs; **praying mantis** = *praying-insect.*

1883 *Century Mag.* Sept. 788/2 The Woman's Christian Temperance Union is the lineal descendant of the Woman's Crusade of 1874, whose first '*praying band' was led..by Mrs. Thompson. **1900** C. W. WINCHESTER *Victories of Wesley Castle* ii. 41 He had seen [him]..conducting a revival meeting with a praying-band, of which he was leader. **1937** *Sun* (Baltimore) (D ed.) 25 May 4/5 On the left sits a row of younger women—the 'praying band' or 'shout band'. **1816** KIRBY & SP. *Entomol.* xxi. (1818) II. 221 The genera *Mantis* and *Phasma*—named *praying-insects and spectres. **1706** *Praying Locust [see MANTIS]. **1895** *Praying mantis [see MANTIS]. **1899** [see *mule-killer* s.v. MULE¹ 5 c]. **1961** L. VAN DER POST *Heart of Hunter* xii. 161 My old coloured nurse Klara, who had a Bushman mother..showed me my first praying mantis. **1973** M. R. CROWELL *Greener Pastures* 40 They have established a cease fire, thanks to a praying mantis.

Hence **'prayingly** *adv.*, in a praying manner.

1642 MILTON *Apol. Smect.* xi. 93 To speak prayingly.

prayn, -e, obs. forms of PRAWN.

†**'pray-pray,** *a. Obs. nonce-wd.* Of or proper to one saying 'Pray! pray!'

1754 RICHARDSON *Grandison* (1812) II. xvi. 183 'Pray, sir, forgive me'; and she held up her hands pray-pray-fashion.

prayse, obs. form of PRAISE *sb., v.*

prazosin ('preɪzəʊsɪn). *Pharm.* [Arbitrary *pr-* (sometimes interpreted as representing *piperazine*), + AZO- + *-sin.*] A drug used (as the hydrochloride) in treating hypertension, being a vasodilator whose molecular structure incorporates quinazoline, piperazine, and furyl rings.

1970 *Jrnl. Clin. Pharmacol.* X. 417/1 These data suggest that prazosin hydrochloride is an efficacious agent for the therapy of ambulatory patients with arterial hypertension, particularly when a thiazide diuretic is given in concert. **1974** *Brit. Med. Jrnl.* 11 May 298/1 Prazosin is a new hypertensive drug thought to have a peripheral action involving direct relaxation of vascular smooth muscle and sympathetic blockade. **1978** A. S. NIES in Melmon & Morrelli *Clin. Pharmacol.* (ed. 2) vi. 200/1 Prazosin produces a number of side effects, the most prominent being weakness, dizziness, headache, palpitations and lack of energy... Postural hypotension occurring within two hours of the first few doses of prazosin has resulted in loss of consciousness in some patients.

pre- (priː, prɪ) *prefix*, repr. L. *præ* adv. and prep. (of place, rank, and time) before, in front, in advance. This was commonly written *pr̨e* or *pre* in med.L., and has become *pre-* in the modern Romanic langs. In Eng. the prefix was sometimes written *præ-* after the revival of learning, but is now regularly *pre-*. In a few words recognized as Latin, and their immediate derivatives, *præ-* is now usual, though even these are frequently, esp. in America, written with *pre-*. See PRÆ-.

In L. *præ* was prefixed adverbially to a great number of verbs, as *præ-acuĕre* to sharpen in front, *præ-ambulāre* to walk before, *præclūdĕre* to shut in front, *præcognōscĕre* to foreknow, *præcurrĕre* to run before, *præ-ēminēre* to stick out before, be prominent, *præjūdicāre* to judge or pass sentence beforehand, *præmordēre* to bite off before the point or abruptly; also with verbal derivatives, as *præcentor* a leader in singing, *præcursor* a forerunner, *prædictio* foretelling, *præfātum* fore-speech, preface. Less often with adjs. and sbs., as *præcānus, præmatūrus* grey, ripe before (the time), *prævius* leading the way; *præminister* a servant standing before, *præmolestia* trouble beforehand, *prænōmen* a forename or first name. Also very frequently prefixed as an intensive to adjectives, as *prǣaltus* high before or in comparison with others, pre-eminently high, *præclārus* pre-eminently clear or bright, *præpotens* exceedingly powerful, prepotent, *prævalidus* very strong. In Latin *præ-* was rarely prefixed with prepositional force, as in *præcordia* the parts in front of the heart, *prǣripia* places in front of or near the bank of a river, *præmodum* adv. surpassing or beyond measure.

In English many Latin verbs and their derivatives in *præ-* have their representatives in *pre-*, and the use of this prefix has been greatly extended, so that it is now a living element, prefixable to almost any verb of Latin origin, and even sometimes prefixed to words of English or modern origin, as *pre-breathe, pre-embody, pre-plot, pre-sift.* Its use with adjectives or substantives, other than verbal, is less common, and the L. intensive use in *præaltus*, etc., though retained in a few words taken or imitated from L., is not a living use in Eng. But the prepositional construction, in which *pre-* governs the second element, which was so rare in L., has in English received vast extension, so as to become the second great living use, *pre-* being preferred to *ante-* as the opposite of *post-* in new formations, and often substituted for it, as in *pre-baptismal, pre-Christian, prehistoric, pre-Darwinian, pre-reformation* instead of *ante-baptismal, ante-Christian, ante-historic, ante-Darwinian, ante-reformation.* This preference of *pre-* may be partly due to its superior shortness and neatness, but is prob. largely in order to avoid the oral confusion of *ante-* with *anti-*, as in *ante-Christian, antichristian, ante-Darwinian, anti-Darwinian.*

Pronunciation. In all English formations in *pre-*, and some of those formed in Latin or French, in which the sense of 'before' is felt, the prefix is pronounced with a clear *e*, long or short ([iː], [ɪ]). In nonce-combinations, the vowel is regularly long, and more or less stressed, e.g. *pre-boil* (ˌpriːˈbɔɪl), *pre-Greek* (ˌpriːˈgriːk), *pre-telegraph* (ˌpriːˈtɛlɪgrɑːf, -æf). In words of this class of more permanent standing and more independent meaning, the *e* is long ([iː]) when stressed, and usually short ([i]), but capable of being long ([iː]), when not under stress primary or subordinate, e.g. ˌ*preaˈdamic* (priː-), *preˈadamite* (priː-). In words from Latin in which the sense 'before' is obscured or lost, *pre-*, when unstressed, is (prɪ-); when stressed, (priː-) or (prɛ-): thus, ˈ*precinct* (priː-), *preˈcinct* (prɪ-), ˈ*precipice* (ˈprɛsɪpɪs), *preˈcipitous* (prɪˈsɪpɪtəs), *preˈfer* (prɪ-), ˈ*preference* (prɛf-). But here also (prɪ-) is lengthened to (priː-) under rhetorical or factitious stress, as in 'Did you say "repair" or "*pre*pare"?' 'not the "procession" but the "*pre*cession" of the equinoxes'.

Use of Hyphen. Nonce-words and casual compounds of English formation in *pre-* are usually hyphened, as *pre-geological, pre-instil, pre-medicate*; compounds already formed in Latin or French, and their derivatives, are regularly written *indivisim*, as *precaution, predestination, prefigure*. But between these extreme types there are very many combinations in which the use varies, the hyphen being employed whenever its use appears to add to the clearness of the writer's meaning, or when it is desired to emphasize the function of the prefix, to contrast the compound with the simple word or with the analogous compound in *post-*, or the like. In this dictionary, such words are as a rule entered in the unhyphened form, though the quotations will show that both forms are freely used. But in words in which *pre-* is prefixed to a word or element beginning with *e*, the hyphen is conveniently used to separate the two *e*'s, as in *pre-eminent, pre-engage, pre-exist*. (These are sometimes printed *preëminent*, etc.)

In this dictionary, all important and established words in *pre-* are treated as main words, and will be found in their alphabetical places. But compounds of rare occurrence, chiefly obsolete, and those of obvious meaning and regular formation, are given below, under their respective classes. Nonce-words and casual combinations can be formed at will, and are unlimited in number, so that only examples showing their formation and use are required.

[*Arrangement.* A. *pre-* adverbial. I. Of time or order: 1, with vb.; 2, with sb.; 3, with adj. II. Of place: 4, with adj. or sb. III. 5, Of order, rank, importance, quality, degree. IV. 6, Intensive. B. *pre-* prepositional. I. Of time: 1, with adj.; 2, with sb. or phr. II. Of place: 3, with adj.]

A. Combinations in which *pre-* is adverbial or adjectival, qualifying the verb, adjective, or substantive, to which it is prefixed.

I. Of time or order of succession.

In casual combinations better with hyphen; but often without. *Pre-* stressed (priː).

1. With verbs, or ppl. adjs. and vbl. sbs. derived from them, in sense 'fore-, before, beforehand, previously, in advance', as PRE-ACKNOWLEDGE, -ACQUAINT, -ACT, -ADAPT, -ADMIT, etc., and in many others of obvious meaning, as ***pre-acquit, -address, -adjust, -adopt, -affect, -allege, -annex, -apprehend, -apprise, -approve, -ascertain, -assemble, -audit, -baptize, -bargain, -boil, -book, -breathe, -censure, -centrifuge, -clean, -coat, -commend, -commit, -comprehend, -compute, -conclude, -confess, -conjecture, -consolidate, -constitute, -consume, -continue, -convert, -cook, -corrupt, -counsel, -decide, -dedicate*** (***prededicate*** pa. pple.), ***-demand, -demonstrate, -describe, -devise, -devour, -direct, -dissuade, -dry, -embody, -employ, -enact, -entertain, -erect, -excuse, -extinguish, -film, -fool, -furnish, -give*** (***-given*** ppl adj.; also *absol.* as sb.), ***-grind, -imbibe, imbue, -impart, -incubate, -inhere, -instil, -ionize, -know, -let, -liquidate, -lubricate, -machine, -make, -model, -necessitate, -obtain, -own, -partake, -pattern, -perceive, -plan, -plot, -polarize, -practise, -prepare, -pressurize, -pronounce, -prove, -provide, -publish, -qualify, -receive, -resemble, -respire, -reveal, -secure, -see, -sentence, -separate, -sift, -soak, -study, -surmise, -suspect, -teach, -think, -torture, -tune, -understand, -unite, -wash, -wear, -wrap, -write***; **preˈaspirate** *Phonetics*, to aspirate (a sound) in advance of another sound; **pre-ˈbaiting**, the act or practice of accustoming vermin to harmless bait so that they will take poisoned bait more readily.

1615 T. ADAMS *Spir. Navig.* 30 Yea even doth Christ Jesus purpose..to suffer for us, and *pre-acquit his apostles with it? *a***1711** KEN *Hymnotheo* Poet. Wks. 1721 III. 23 All Sins are venial the Elect commit, Which God's Decrees Eternal pre-acquit. **1912** W. OWEN *Let.* Aug. (1967) 152, I didn't bring your *pre-addressed envelope. **1964** J. Z. YOUNG *Model of Brain* xii. 199 The particular classifying systems operating on any occasion are thus as it were pre-addressed. **1880** BURTON *Reign Q. Anne* I. v. 173 The punishment *preadjusted by the Deity. **1885** DUNCKLEY in *Manch. Exam.* 9 May 6/1 [The] result of a carefully preadjusted mechanism. **1788** D. GILSON *Serm. Pract. Subj.* x. (1807) 208 Covetous men, hastening to the grave, seem to *pre-adopt one of its qualities,—and cry out with it,—We can never have enough. **1658** BP. REYNOLDS *Lord's Supper* xix, The Spirit of God doth *preaffect the Soul with an evident taste of that glory. **1588** J. HARVEY *Disc. Probl.* 127 Any proofes, or testimonies *prealledged in the former part. **1612** T. TAYLOR *Comm. Titus* i. 12 (1619) 243 The iust causes prealledged. **1922** JOYCE *Ulysses* 713 What..causes, before rising *pre-apprehended,..did Bloom.. recapitulate? **1808** BENTHAM *Sc. Reform* 70 Of whose inability to give effect to it he is thus *pre-apprised. **1654** OWEN *Doctr. Saint's Persev.* Wks. 1853 XI. 153 Whom He foreknows, that is, *preapproves..them he predestinates. *Ibid.* 155 His preapproving of them..must be His eternal acceptation of them in Christ. **1802–12** BENTHAM *Ration. Judic. Evid.* (1827) IV. 469 Quantity being *pre-ascertained or agreed on. **1934** *Jrnl. Eng. & Gmc. Philol.* XXXIII. 191 The *preaspirated tenues in Scotland are due to the same Norse substratum. **1976** *Archivum Linguisticum* VII. 95 All geminates are held to have once been preaspirated. **1960** R. W. MARKS *Dymaxion World of B. Fuller* 21/2 It is theoretically possible..to deliver a full-size, *pre-assembled house by air. **1972** *Sci. Amer.* Oct. 118/2 The structure was prefabricated and preassembled in the carpentry shop complete with fans and electrical outlets. **1937** *Sun* (Baltimore) 2 Aug. 1/2 All *pre-auditing shall be under the control of the executive branch of the Government. **1936** *Rep. Comm. Exper. Station* (Hawaiian Sugar Planters' Assoc.) 92 It would seem that a practice of *prebaiting with unpoisoned cereal, followed by a heavy application of poisoned bait, should prove an effective means of control. **1944** J. S. HUXLEY *On Living in Revolution* x. 110 Careful study has now been made of the species [*sc.* the black rat], and this, with new methods of poisoning based on pre-baiting, is apparently providing the basis for effective control. **1973** *Times* 9 Mar. 14/1 In 1955 the anti-coagulant compounds, Warfarin and others, came on the market. No pre-baiting was needed with these. **1665** SIR T. HERBERT *Trav.* (1677) 53 Hereticks who used to baptize after death in case they were not *pre-baptiz'd. **1622** C. ARCHER in Willis & Clark *Cambridge* (1886) II. 76 Upon..which *pre-bargained pece of ground a brick wall is alreadie erected. **1903** *Motor. Ann.* 294 To obviate the trouble of *pre-boiling all the water. **1976** P. R. WHITE *Planning for Public Transport* vii. 149 The amendment also stipulated that minibuses only would be permitted, not for hire or reward, and that passengers would be *pre-booked. *Ibid.* viii. 183 The period stipulated for *pre-booking by rail appears unrealistic. **1886** *Brit. Med. Jrnl.* No. 1327. 1089/1 *Prebreathed air. **1896** *Allbutt's Syst. Med.* I. 461 [Children] are peculiarly sensitive to pre-breathed air. **1650** in H. Cary *Mem. Gt. Civ. War* (1832) II. 246 The most submissive papers were *precensured by the committee. **1976** *Nature* 15 Jan. 114/2 The homogenate was squeezed through nylon cloth and *precentrifuged at 500g for 10 min after adjusting the *p*H to 8.0. **1954** *Sun* (Baltimore) 13 Apr. B23/4 Instead of picking around through a pile at the vegetable counter,..she can buy *precleaned fresh produce of a uniform quality. **1937** *Discovery* Sept. 283/2 The press is..*precoated with fresh kieselguhr. *Ibid.*, This *precoating is done from a small vat. **1973** *Metal Finishing Jrnl.* XIX. 353 About 500,000 tonnes per year of pre-coated steel sheet was used in the UK for buildings. **1733** *Precommended [see *post-disapproved*, in POST- A. 1]. **1895** 'H. S. MERRIMAN' *Grey Lady* I. i, Their two lives had been *pre-committed to the parental care of their country. **1802–12** BENTHAM *Ration. Judic. Evid.* (1827) II. 9 To *pre-comprehend all these facts,—and on them, when so pre-comprehended, to ground a set of questions. **1948** *Amazing Sci. Fiction* Sept. 146/1 The luminous track on the radar screen had scarcely deviated from the *pre-computed path. **1956** *Jrnl. Assoc. Computing Machinery* III. 284 The method used..is to precompute between pass 1 and pass 2 this adjustment based on the count of each duplicated region. **1959** *Proc. Eastern Joint Computer Conf.* 170/1 Prior to the start of a given shut-down, a pre-computed schedule most applicable to the current situation is abstracted from a library of typical schedules. *a* **1684** LEIGHTON *Comm. 1 Peter* Wks. (1868) 132 It was *preconcluded there that the Son should undertake the business. **1855** BAILEY *Mystic* 14 Without pause, *preconfessed his sins. **1588** J. HARVEY *Disc. Probl.* 81 Might not Ælius.. probably *pre-coniecture, that Adrian should be crowned Emperor? **1845** J. PHILLIPS in *Encycl. Metrop.* VI. 542/1 Effects of sub-terranean convulsions upon the *preconsolidated strata. **1828–32** WEBSTER, *Preconstituted [citing PALEY]. **1795–1814** WORDSW. *Excursion* VIII. 288 In whom a premature necessity Blocks out the forms of nature, *preconsumes The reason. **1750** *Student* I. 43 Mahomet found most of his laws already prepared to his hands by the long *pre-continued observation of them. **1802–12** BENTHAM *Ration. Judic. Evid.* (1827) V. 80 Mendacity..*preconverted into perjury. **1946** *Fortune* Apr. 200/2 A high-priced Restaurant carrying a sideline of *precooked quick-frozen meals on plastic plates. **1964** E. BACH *Introd. Transformational Gram.* v. 92 Except with carefully 'precooked' data, there will be many conflicting ways of drawing rules together. *a* **1974** R. CROSSMAN *Diaries* (1975) I. 198 Very often the whole job is pre-cooked in the official committee to a point from which it is extremely difficult to reach any other conclusion than that already determined by the officials in advance. **1976** *Woman's Day* (N.Y.) Nov. 150/2 A step saver. No need to precook noodles. **1621** G. SANDYS *Ovid's Met.* IX. (1626) 181 She came indeede, but *pre-corrupted by Vnfriendly Iuno, life to ruinate. **1833** MRS. BROWNING *Prometh. Bound* Poems 1850 I. 186 Long ago It was looked forward to, *pre-counselled of. **1947** *Mind* LVI. 264 The meaning to be given to 'well-established' or to 'explanation', in history or the social sciences, cannot be *pre-decided by a consideration of mathematics only. **1966** G. N. LEECH *Eng. in Advertising* i. 4 It is patently false that he writes according to a predecided formula. **1889** STEVENSON *Master of B.* 169 The same day, which was certainly *prededicate to joy. **1652** J. WRIGHT tr. *Camus' Nat. Paradox* III. 55 Without preventing their commands by a *predemanded leave or any feined distast. **1664** POWER *Exp. Philos.* II. 130 You may ..*predemonstrate them, by calculation, before the senses give an Experimental thereof. **1882** *Nature* XXVI. 550 Referring back to his own *pre-described species. **1671** R. MACWARD *True Non-Conf.* 254 As much..as if they were set and *predevised. *a* **1661** FULLER *Worthies* (1840) II. 571 Where..the Queen's kindred had *pre-devoured his estate. *a* **1678** WOODHEAD *Holy Living* (1688) 28 *Predirecting us in our affairs. **1626** DONNE *Serm.* lxxviii. (1640) 797 May possibly..be *predisswaded and deprecated in all Civill consultations. **1961** *Dairy Industries* Sept. 652 Particles of the product to be dried fall in counter current to slowly rising *pre-dried air flowing at a rate of 0·05 to 1 meter per second. **1962** J. T. MARSH *Self-Smoothing Fabrics* xi. 171 The majority of the finishing ranges for the crease-resisting process..increase production and reduce costs by some form of partial *pre-drying. **1875** T. HILL *True Order Stud.* 157 Prefigured and *pre-embodied in nature. **1611** SHAKS. *Wint. T.* II. i. 49 That false Villaine, Whom I employ'd, was *pre-employ'd by him. **1825** COLERIDGE *Aids Refl.* (1848) I. 298 That every the least permissible form and ordinance.. are *pre-enacted in the New Testament. **1819** W. MORGAN in Polwhele *Trad. & Recoll.* (1826) II. 698, I *pre-entertain a high opinion of their worth. **1643** PRYNNE *Sov. Power Parl.* I. (ed. 2) 91 Were they..to institute their *preerected Principalities and Kings. **1670–98** LASSELS *Voy. Italy* Pref. 2, I have done it..to *preexcuse some things in my book. **1822** 'P. BEAUCHAMP' (Geo. Grote) *Anal. Infl. Nat. Relig.* (1875) 82 All practical improvement is thus *pre-extinguished and stifled in the birth, by the sweeping epithet of unnatural. **1960** D. WILSON *Television Playwright* 16 Does insistence on cinematic grammar imply that all television drama should be *pre-filmed? **1969** J. ELLIOT *Duel* I. ii. 38 It was to consist of three fifty-minute programmes, all prefilmed. **1633** SHIRLEY *Bird in Cage* II. i, A better project, wherein no courtier has *prefooled you. **1673** OWEN *Serm.* Wks. 1851 IX. 433 If Christ hath not pre-instructed and *pre-furnished him with gifts. **1943** M. FARBER *Found. Phenomenology* xv. 506 The theory of pre-predicative experience, which '*pre-gives' the most primitive substrates in object-evidence, represents the first portion of the phenomenological theory of judgment. **1970** B. BREWSTER tr. *Althusser & Balibar's Reading Capital* (1975) III. iv. 297 In Marx's theory..a synthetic concept of time can never be a *pre-given, but only a *result*. **1974** *Sci. & Society* XXXVIII. 395 The specific structure of 'unevenness' of the 'ever-pregiven complex whole' which is its existence. **1976** *Brit. Jrnl. Sociol.* XXVII. 296 The Rankean identification of history with pre-given past events. **1973** R. RENDELL *Some lie & Some Die* xiv. 121 He..smelt her grinding coffee beans—nothing *pre-ground out of a packet for her. **1678** OWEN *Mind of God* v. 147 *Præimbibed opinions. **1905** *Daily Chron.* 8 May 3/4 Constitutions rendered weak by pre-imbibing more dangerous stimulants. **1697** J. SERGEANT *Solid Philos.* 349 Had he not been *pre-imbued with natural notions. **1865** MASSON *Rec. Brit. Philos.* 384 Laws or rules of associability *pre-imparted to them. **1943** *Jrnl. Bacteriol.* XLVI. 383 One penicillin-containing set with and without glucose was allowed to *preincubate un-inoculated at 37°C., and a similar set at 2°C. **1977** *Lancet* 18 June 1310/1 The epithelial cells were not stained when tissue sections were preincubated in unlabelled α-B.T. before the standard reaction. **1830** COLERIDGE *Ch. & St.* (ed. 2) 235 In both..the sensibility must have pre-existed, (or rather *pre-inhered). *a* **1711** KEN *Urania* Poet. Wks. 1721 IV. 433 All Prophecies..Into the ancient Prophets *pre-instill'd. **1940** *Jrnl. Appl. Physics* XI. 471/1 Then over the *pre-ionized streamer channel the brilliant return stroke..follows at a speed of 10^{10} cm per second. **1979** *Nature* 7 June 477/3 For light ions, such long-distance propagation must be carefully arranged through a pre-ionised neutralising plasma channel, raising serious questions of possible propagation instabilities. **1867** J. S. MILL *Let.* 14 Feb. (1910) II. x. 76 Our freedom may be real though God *preknows our actions. **1976** *Field* 30 Dec. 1292/2 (Advt.), Most of our beats are *pre-let but we have one or two vacancies through late cancellation. **1802–12** BENTHAM *Ration. Judic. Evid.* (1827) IV. 302 Binding themselves..to pay a sum of money, *preliquidated or not preliquidated,..in case the plaintiff should lose his cause. **1961** *Motor Sport* Dec. 1003/1 In America Oldsmobile, Ford, Mercury, Lincoln, Plymouth, Dodge and Chrysler have adopted *pre-lubricated chassis bearings. **1976** *Lebende Sprachen* XXI. 151/2 For further information about pre-lubricated bearings see Figure 1, Detail A. **1971** *Physics Bull.* July 406/3 Deep penetration welding using electron beams is becoming quite widely used for assembling *pre-machined parts into complex assemblies as an economic alternative to forging, casting and mechanical fastening. **1977** *Offshore Engineer* Apr. 28/1 The system uses an internal clamp/welder to locate, clamp and make an inside root pass in about two minutes on a pre-machined pipe joint preparation. **1853** J. CUMMING *Foreshadows* viii. (1854) 225 He went with his mind *pre-made up to receive a certain treatment. **1691** E. TAYLOR *Behmen's Theos. Philos.* lxxiii. (1772) 470 A *premodelling or Representation. **1715** M. DAVIES *Athen. Brit.* I. 162 In Defence of their *prenecessitated Constitutions. *Mod.* Unless a license has been *pre-obtained. **1964** *Listener* 25 June 1030/3 Used cars are now referred to as *pre-owned [in the U.S.A.]. **1970** M. PEI *Words in Sheep's Clothing* ii. 12 'Pre-owned' is described as the modern euphemism for 'second-hand'. **1977** *Caravan World* (Austral.) Jan. 3 (Advt.), 2 acres of pre-owned caravans and boats can be inspected. **1861** R. QUIN *Heather Lintie* (1866) 39 [Ye] *prepartake of Hope's deliciousness. **1644** VICARS *God in Mount* 93 The great work intended and ..*pre-patterned as aforesaid. **1890** W. JAMES *Princ. Psychol.* I. xi. 444 In short, *the only things which we commonly see are those which we *preperceive*, and the only things which we preperceive are those which have been labelled for us, and the labels stamped into our mind. **1934** WEBSTER, *Preplan. **1948** *Times Rev. Industry* Aug. 18/3 Obviously continuous production must be pre-planned but thereafter is self-progressive. **1958** *Times* 11 Feb. 4/4 (Advt.), Preplanning the entire project ensures smooth continuity of operations and speedy completion. **1965** *Language* XLI. 92 Since this is not a preplanned book..there is a certain amount of repetition. **1976** *Daily Tel.* 13 Aug. 1/7 The positive anti-riot tactics, clearly pre-planned.., were introduced to counter any IRA organised trouble. **1977** J. M. JOHNSON in Douglas & Johnson *Existential Sociol.* viii. 231 None of the events described were anticipated or preplanned by the members in advance of their occurrence. **1643** PRYNNE *Rome's Master-Piece* (ed. 2) 32 A chiefe actor in this *pre-plotted Treason. **1949** *Jrnl. Acoustical Soc. Amer.* XXI. 199/1 The..temperature at which the output voltage falls to zero for a *pre-polarized specimen. *Ibid.* 200/2 The voltage gradient necessary fully to pre-polarize varies with the time allotted to polarizing. **1957** E. G. RICHARDSON *Technical Aspects Sound* II. ii. 70 The tube is metallized on the inner and outer surfaces, pre-polarized radially, and the alternating current applied in the same direction. **1655** FULLER *Ch. Hist.* XI. iii. §14 Making it necessary for others, what voluntarily they had *prepractised themselves. **1968** *Guardian* 16 Feb. 3/2 *Pre-prepared dishes, such as fish and chips. **1978** *Guardian Weekly* 29 Oct. 12/3 The President didn't deliver pre-prepared phrases, but stayed close to events. **1945** *Jrnl. Amer. Chem. Soc.* LXVII. 157/1 A current is passed through previously pressurized acid water, and bubbles form in *prepressurized water when it is quickly frozen. **1971** *Arch. Biochem. & Biophysics* CXLII. 325/2 The enzyme was prepressurized for 10 min. **1804** EUGENIA DE ACTON *Tale without Title* III. 34 We would *pre-pronounce the censure of little critics. **1849** NOAD *Electricity* (ed. 3) 280 A power, the existence of which is *pre-proved. **1655** FULLER *Ch. Hist.* IV. ix. §25 He provisionally *pre-provided

Incumbents for them. **1973** W. H. Hallahan *Ross Forgery* vi. 120 'A Lodging for the Night'—first published in a collection..under the title *The New Arabian Nights* in 1882 ..was not known to have been *pre-published separately. **1977** *Lancet* 25 June 1350/2 He asserted..that an article whose contents had already received detailed attention in the papers and on the air had..been prepublished and forfeited its claim to entry as news in a medical journal. **1980** *Times* 29 Feb. 23 (Advt.), The Irrigation Department and the Electric Power Corporation invite qualified and experienced contractors..wishing to be *pre-qualified as tenderers. **1974** *Times* 27 Apr. 14/4 The drudgery of having to *pre-qualify for [golf] tournaments. **1976** *Sunday Mail* (Glasgow) 28 Nov. 39/3 He finished in the top 25 last year, which ensured he doesn't have to prequalify this year for Turnberry in July. **1605** A. Wotton *Answ. Popish Pamph.* 27 An externall signe, or seale, of a *prereceaued grace. **1601** Bp. W. Barlow *Defence* 34 *Preresembled in those three kings or sages, which came from farre to do personall homage vnto her head, and King at Bethleem. **1852** Mundy *Our Antipodes* (1857) 213 It was certainly never *pre-revealed to me that I should spend one of the few Christmas days..at sea. **1931** Joyce *Let.* 22 Aug. (1966) III. 227 You advised me to proceed against Roth... I did though I *presaw the result. **1638** Mayne *Lucian* (1664) 236, I would know the nature of the Starres, of the Moone, and Sun himselfe, being *præsecur'd from their fires. **1643** Fuller *Serm.* 27 Mar. To Rdr., Who have unmercifully *pre-sentenced me. **1967** E. Chambers *Photolitho-Offset* iii. 30 *Pre-separated colour art work can be prepared using Bourges Colotone overlays. **1967** Karch & Buber *Offset Processes* iii. 64 Kits are useful in the preparation of pre-separated full-color process copy. *a* **1670** Hacket *Abp. Williams* (1692) 28 In weightier petitions..which was not to be *presifted by the other officers. **1919** *Science* 6 June 545/1 The *presoaked seeds are thoroughly wetted in the 1:80 solution..for ten minutes. **1974** *Indian Jrnl. Agric. Sci.* XLIII. 973/1 An experiment was laid out..in polythene bags with presoaked pumpkin seeds in different N solutions. **1919** *Science* 6 June 544/2 (*heading*) *Presoaking as a means of preventing seed injury due to disinfectants and of increasing germicidal efficiency. *a* **1661** Fuller *Worthies, Cambr.* (1662) I. 159 A most excellent preacher, who..preached what he had *prestudied some competent time before. **1664** Power *Exp. Philos.* II. 122 The effect was this (as was *pre-surmised). **1641** Best *Farm. Bks.* (Surtees) 79 If shee bee longe in lambinge, and *presuspeckted. **1721** Amherst *Terræ Fil.* No. 3 (1726) I. 13 He takes the oaths of allegiance and supremacy, which he is *prætaught to evade, or think null. **1977** E. Leonard *Unknown Man No. 89* xvii. 155 *Pre-think your options. **1966** 'A. Hall' *9th Directive* xii. 112 The Bureau..takes no action without the most serious *pre-thinking. **1960** *20th Cent.* Sept. 242 This kind of talk is not formalized or *pre-thought. **1655** Fuller *Ch. Hist.* VIII. ii. §27 Their cruelty in *pre-torturing of many, whom afterwards they put to death. **1974** Harvey & Bohlman *Stereo F.M. Radio Handbk.* iii. 41 Within this narrow band it is possible to *pre-tune the r.f. stage to 98 MHz. **1964** J. Carnochan in D. Abercrombie et al. *Daniel Jones* 399 A series of *pre-tuned reeds. **1658** *Hist. Q. Christina of Swedland* 140 Holstenius having *preunderstood that the Baron Ghirardi had thoughts of conferring with her. **1640** Bp. Reynolds *Passions* xx, It doth in some sort *preunite our souls and our blessednesse together. **1977** *Pre-wash [see program, programme *sb.* 2 g (i)]. **1976** *New Musical Express* 12 Feb. 40/1 (Advt.), Genuine 'Levi & Levi' type jeans, *preworn and shrunk, just need patches. **1934** Webster, *Pre-wrap. **1959** *Times* 9 Mar. (Britain's Food Suppl.) p. vi/4 *Pre-wrapped retail portions of natural cheese have been on the market for some years. **1963** *Economist* 29 June 1357/1 More and more cigars are.. marketed pre-wrapped in large packs. **1951** Dylan Thomas *Let.* 12 Apr. (1966) 358, I would bring great packages of new poems to read, and much more *pre-written prose to pad them in. **1969** *Computers & Humanities* IV. 106 This object code and a prewritten subroutine which searches the date item for the required elements becomes the Phase II control program.

2. With a sb., this being usually a derivative from a verb to which *pre-* is in adverbial relation: = Existing or taking place previously, placed before (something else), previous, preceding, earlier: as ***pre-accusation***, ***-adjustment***, ***-administration***, ***-advertency***, ***-appearance***, ***-approbation***, ***-approval***, ***-arrestment***, ***-ascertainment***, ***-audit***, ***-auditor***, ***-censorship***, ***-civilization***, ***-coat***, ***-collection***, ***-comprehension***, ***-concession***, ***-conclusion***, ***-connexion***, ***-consent***, ***-constituent***, ***-contemplation***, ***-conviction***, ***-decay***, ***-decision***, ***-dedication***, ***-desert***, ***-detainer***, ***-discipline***, ***-embodiment***, ***-entail***, ***-equipment***, ***-evangelism***, ***-excogitation***, ***-excitation***, ***-expectation***, ***-expounder***, ***-fecundation***, ***-hearing***, ***-impression***, ***-incubation***, ***-indisposition***, ***-inhabitation***, ***-inquisition***, ***-intelligence***, ***-knowledge***, ***-negotiation***, ***-opinion***, ***-oxygenation***, ***-polarization***, ***-pressurization***, ***-publicity***, ***-qualification***, ***-rehearsal***, ***-reluctation***, ***-remorse***, ***-representation***, ***-success***, ***-surmise***, ***-taste***, ***-taster***, ***-tincture***, ***-union***, ***-verbalization***. Also with other substantives: **pre-'adjunct** *Gram.*, an adjunct that precedes the word it modifies; also *attrib.*; **pre-an'tiquity**, previous antiquity; **pre-'aptitude**, antecedent aptitude; **pre-aspi'ration** *Phonetics*, aspiration that precedes another sound; **pre'boding**, foreboding; **pre'contour** *Phonetics*, one or more unstressed syllables which precede the peak of a contour; **pre-e'ternity**, previous eternity, eternal previous existence; **'prename**, a forename, 'Christian' name; **'pre-part**, previous or preceding part; **'prepulse**, a preliminary pulse of electricity; **prere'action**, chemical reaction occurring before some other process; **'pre-rinse**, a preliminary rinse given to something before it is washed; **pre-'scene**, an anticipatory scene; **prese'nility** *Med.*, premature senility; **pre-'shadow**, a shadow of what is coming; **'pre-soak**, (*a*) a soaking given prior to some subsequent process or treatment; (*b*) a liquid used for this; also *attrib.*; **'pre-wash**, a preliminary wash, used *spec.* as the name of a setting on an automatic washing-machine; also *attrib.*

1847 Webster, **Preaccusation*, previous accusation. **1898** *Pre-adjunct [see *head-word* s.v. head *sb.* 74]. **1914** O. Jespersen *Mod. Eng. Gram.* II. xiv. 331 There are some adjectives that are hardly ever used predicatively, and on the other hand some that are hardly ever used as pre-adjuncts. *Ibid.* 333 The averseness to pre-adjunct employment..has been transferred to other words beginning with an *a-* of a different origin. **1957** *Publ. Amer. Dial. Soc.* XXVIII. 123 *What*, *which*, *whose*, and *how* serve as pre-adjuncts: 1 What book?; 2 How far is it? **1884** Sully *Outlines Psychol.* iv. 90 The preparation or *preadjustment of attention may be said to be perfect. **1659** Pearson *Creed* x. 735 Baptism as it was instituted by Christ after the *preadministration of S. John. **1671** Woodhead *St. Teresa* I. Pref. 22 Wittingly and with a *preadvertency of it. **1855** Bailey *Spir. Leg.* in *Mystic*, etc. (ed. 2) 77 White isles whose *præ-antiquity Transcends all date. **1681** *Whole Duty Nations* 28 In Sodom and Gomorrah, was given a *pre-appearance of the final Judgment upon the World. *a* **1652** Brome *Covent Gard.* Prol., That he besought *Preapprobation though they lik't it not. **1815** Hobhouse *Substance Lett.* (1816) I. 2 *Pre-aptitude for such evil communication. **1822–56** De Quincey *Confess.* (1862) 243 The one counterworking secret for *pre-arrestment of this evil. **1816–30** Bentham *Offic. Apt. Maximized, Extract Const. Code* (1830) 36 For *pre-ascertainment of the expense. **1879** H. Spencer *Data of Ethics* xv. §104. 274 Ascertainment of the actual truth has been made possible only by pre-ascertainment of certain ideal truths. **1945** S. Einarsson *Icelandic* I. 1 Aspiration, a breath (^{h}) following or preceding (*preaspiration) the stops *p*, *t*, *k*, is indicated by an ^{h}. **1965** H. Wolter in *Proc. 5th Internat. Congr. Phonetic Sci. 1964* 595 The auditory impression of the pre-aspiration is rather like an [h], although in connection with [t] it may sound like an [f]. **1976** *Archivum Linguisticum* VII. 91 Preaspiration is not, according to Liberman, a voiceless vowel, although it does cause the end of a preceding vowel to be devoiced. **1938** *Sun* (Baltimore) 2 Apr. 6/2 It retains the principle of *pre-audit but it makes the pre-auditor amenable to Presidential authority. **1844** Tupper *Heart* x, With a nervous *pre-boding Henry took up the 'Watchman'. **1962** *Guardian* 6 Nov. 9/4 Today's issue was subjected to *pre-censorship by the State Prosecutor's office. *a* **1974** R. Crossman *Diaries* (1976) II. 663 The Lord Chancellor immediately replied that this would involve having pre-censorship all over again because if the licensees could be sued for libel then they would start controlling the plays. **1949** R. A. S. Macalister *Archæol. of Ireland* (ed. 2) p. x, It [*sc.* Ireland] has rendered to Anthropology the unique..service of carrying a primitive European **Precivilization* down into late historic times. **1946** *Precoat [see *filter aid* s.v. filter *sb.* 5]. **1664** Bp. King in Walton *Lives, Donne* (1796) 17 By which means his and your *pre-collections for that work fell to the happy manage of your pen. *a* **1849** Poe *Dickens* Wks. 1864 III. 472 Let him reperuse 'Barnaby Rudge' and with a *pre-comprehension of the mystery. **1650** R. Hollingworth *Exerc. Usurped Powers* 1 Jeroboam..had Gods *preconcession of a kingdom. **1602** Warner *Alb. Eng.* XII. lxix. (1612) 291 By *pre-conclusion Twixt him and Dorcas. **1784** R. Bage *Barham Downs* II. 219 A narrative of his *pre-connexion with Mrs. Delane. **1825** Coleridge *Statesm. Man.* App. E., Wks. 1858 I. 479 Both depend on the first, logical congruity, not indeed as their cause or *preconstituent, but as their indispensable condition. *a* **1631** Donne *Serm.* (ed. Alford) IV. 280 The very *precontemplation and predenuntiation of that Judgment..was a..distasteful bitterness to the Prophet. **1945** K. L. Pike *Intonation Amer. Eng.* iii. 29 Immediately preceding the stressed syllable of a primary contour there oftentimes will be one or more syllables which are pronounced in the same burst of speed with that primary contour but which themselves are un-stressed. These syllables may be called *precontours, and depend for their pronunciation upon the syllables which follow them. They may constitute grammatically independent words,..or they may be parts of a word. **1962** B. M. H. Strang *Mod. Eng. Struct.* 53 A contour may be preceded by one or more unstressed syllables forming a *pre-contour*; special meanings may be conveyed by varying the level of the pre-contour, but ordinarily it is spoken at pitch-level 3 unless the contour begins on level 3, which tends to lower the pre-contour. **1975** *Amer. Speech 1972* XLVII. 185 In many dialects, the medial consonant disappears in the precontour, as in *twenty-óne, United Státes*. **1867** Visct. Strangford *Select.* (1869) II. 56 Whether the antecedent facts supplied to meet their *preconvictions or fancies are sound or tainted. **1646** Sir T. Browne *Pseud. Ep.* 361 For..some *pre-decay is observable. *a* **1638** Mede *Wks.* (1672) 869 In regard of the *predecision of the Church. **1840** De Quincey *Mod. Superstit.* Wks. 1862 III. 294 Bearing a *prededication to a service. **1678** R. L'Estrange *Seneca's Mor.* (1702) 4 Some good Offices we do to Friends; others to Strangers; but, those are the noblest, that we do without *Pre-desert. *c* **1624** Lushington *Resurr. Serm.* (1659) 61 His repossession of it defrauded all the *Præ-detainers. **1894** *Daily News* 4 June 5/6 The General warmly commended the marching and *pre-discipline of both teams. **1863** Cowden Clarke *Shaks. Char.* xviii. 467 [She] seems a living *pre-embodiment of those ghastly spectres. **1678** Butler *Hud.* III. II. 70 As Forfeit Lands, Deliver'd up into his hands,..By *Pre-intail of Providence. **1865** Masson *Rec. Brit. Philos.* 377 In the shape of structural *pre-equipment for the mind. **1678** Cudworth *Intell. Syst.* I. iv. §22. 393 He seemeth, with Ocellus, to maintain the world's *Pre-eternity. **1834** *Tait's Mag.* I. 658/1 The Past, still refluent on the deepening night Of pre-eternity. **1968** F. A. Schaeffer *God who is There* v. ii. 143 *Pre-evangelism must come before evangelism... The reason we have not been reaching many of these people is because we have not taken enough time with pre-evangelism. **1951** K. S. Lashley in Saporta & Bastian *Psycho-linguistics* (1961) 186/2 Such contaminations might be ascribed to differences in the relative strength of associative bonds between the elements of the act, and thus not evidence for *pre-excitation of the elements or for simultaneous pre-excitation. **1976** *Lancet* 30 Oct. 938/2 The electrocardiographic appearances in hypertrophic cardiomyopathy may erroneously suggest the presence of pre-excitation. *a* **1560** Rolland *Crt. Venus* IV. 29 Greit argumentis, and *preexcogitatioun Of baith the Lawis. **1828–32** Webster, *Pre-expectation [citing Gerard]. **1816** Bentham *Chrestomathia* Wks. 1843 VIII. 111 That wordy and cloudy *pre-expounder of a nebulous original. **1881** *Nature* XXV. 24 A curious case of *prefecundation observed in a Spionide. **1934** Webster, *Prehearing. **1968** *Listener* 5 Sept. 315/3 The programmes were recorded in July and at a pre-hearing the impression was of an extension of current permissiveness rather than musical revolution. **1977** *Gramophone* June 95/3 On this disc the Cathedral choir,..have given an opulent preview (or pre-hearing) of some of the music for the great day. **1859** *All Year Round* No. 32. 140, M...told me..the following *pre-impression of the event, in a dream. **1943** *Jrnl. Bacteriol.* XLVI. 383 In the presence of glucose, *preincubation of the sterile solutions caused a clear-cut reduction in penicillin inhibition. **1977** *Nature* 6 Jan. 58/2 Preincubation with increasing numbers of suppressor cells yielded successively less active supernatants. **1744** Fothergill in *Phil. Trans.* XLIII. 278 Disorders, wherein, without any obvious *Præ-indispositions, Persons in a Moment sink down and expire. **1628** Donne *Serm.* xxix. (1640) 293 The pre-possession, the *preinhabitation, but not the sole possession nor sole inhabitation of the Holy Ghost. **1824** Coleridge in *Lit. Rem.* (1838) III. 416 What they all wanted was a *pre-inquisition into the mind, as part organ, part constituent, of all knowledge. **1780** *Hist. Europe* in *Ann. Reg.* 207/2 In no instance was the effect of this *pre-intelligence so ruinous as in the loss..of the British settlements on the Mississippi. **1794** G. Adams *Nat. & Exp. Philos.* II. xviii. 312 Our *pre-knowledge of the several intervening objects being equi-distant, tends still more to protract the apparent length. **1962** *Science Survey* III. 290 For many of these fish, and certainly the majority of salmon, it is the first time the journey has been made and they can have no pre-knowledge of the route or the obstacles in front of them. **1979** G. Swarthout *Skeletons* 177 Guiding myself through the gloom as much by preknowledge as eyesight. **1894** Du Maurier *Trilby* III. 31 Their names, *prenames, titles, qualities, age, address. **1900** *Daily News* 25 July 6/7 State pre-names (Christian names) of your parents. **1960** *Guardian* 22 June 9/1 The *pre-negotiations may last some days. **1967** *Economist* 25 Nov. 834/1 The idea..was to slide covertly into pre-negotiations with Britain by the device of asking the commission to talk with the British about devaluation. **1646** Sir T. Browne *Pseud. Ep.* III. xxv. (1650) 144 Some..out of a timorous *preopinion refraining very many. **1961** *Lancet* 19 Aug. 405/2 If a short-acting muscle relaxant is also used, conditions for intubation are obtained more quickly. *Preoxygenation of the patient is a wise precaution. **1961** C. F. Gell in H. G. Armstrong *Aerospace Med.* x. 145/1 Preoxygenation, or the breathing of 100 per cent oxygen at sea level, is a procedure that was utilized prior to high level flights in airplanes without pressurized cockpits or in the absence of pressurized suits. **1965** *Gloss. Aeronaut. Terms (B.S.I.)* XVII. 3 *Preoxygenation*, a process of breathing pure oxygen before flight in order to give protection against decompression sickness by eliminating nitrogen from the body tissues and fluids. **1786** J. Putnam in *Hist. Putnam Fam.* 239 The *prepart of this month. **1950** *Industr. & Engin. Chem.* Feb. 264/2 An alternating stress..is applied parallel to the direction of polarization, and conversely, expansion and contraction in the direction of an electric alternating current field superimposed parallel to the *prepolarization. **1953** *Jrnl. Acoustical Soc. Amer.* XXV. 294/2 Although polycrystalline barium titanate is basically an electrostrictive material, by prepolarization it assumes properties which make it very similar to piezoelectric materials. **1971** *Arch. Biochem. & Biophysics* CXLII. 327/2 For most of the enzymic activities the restoration or stimulation of activity by pressure was closely related to the amount of activity remaining during the *prepressurization. **1963** *Times* 19 Feb. 12/4 The sum includes *pre-publicity, brochures, and the specialist 'after-care'. **1969** *New Scientist* 23 Oct. 172/1 An unusual amount of prepublicity hinting at a good show. **1979** *Times* 1 Dec. 12/5 No lavish pre-publicity on the free plug circuit. **1978** *Nature* 2 Feb. 474/1 A 25–50-ms conditioning *prepulse was used to determine the relationship between inactivation and membrane potential before and after glyoxal treatment. **1969** *Jane's Freight Containers 1968–69* 302/3 *Pre-qualification of tenderers on an international basis for the wharf construction has been processed in liaison with the World Bank. **1979** *Daily Tel.* 19 Oct. 24 (Advt.), Kingdom of Swaziland Ministry of Works, Power and Communications. International invitation for tender prequalification. **1975** *Nature* 2 Oct. 368/2 *Prereaction did not enable him to go leaner than 3·4% methane. **1978** *Ibid.* 12 Jan. 165/2 Preincubation of the antiserum with purified β_2-μ reduced all peaks to background level, whereas pre-reaction with BSA had no effect. **1962** A. Nisbett *Technique Sound Studio* vi. 106 *Pre-rehearsals and perhaps pre-recordings of the complicated parts will be necessary. **1972** *Listener* 6 July 3/1 A good deal of pre-rehearsal often takes place away from the station, but WGBH can only offer one hour of studio rehearsal time. *a* **1631** Donne *Serm.* (ed. Alford) IV. 453 In every sin thou hast..some reluctation before thou do that sin, and that *prereluctation and *preremorse was Mercy. **1691** Beverley *Thous. Years Kingd. Christ* 19 That Great *Pre-Representation of his Kingdom. **1950** J. G. Davis *Dict. Dairying* 71 A jetting *pre-rinse which raises the temperature of the bottle at the same time. **1963** *Which?* Feb. 50/1 It was easy to give a cold pre-rinse and it improved the washing performance. **1970** *Ibid.* Oct. 293/1 For most, there was a pre-rinse and a choice of two washing programmes, depending on how dirty the dishes were. **1591** Sylvester *Du Bartas* I. vi. 1072 This Earth with blood and wrongs polluted,..the *Pre-scæne of Hell To cursed Creatures that 'gainst Heav'n rebell. **1900** Dorland *Med. Dict.* 535/1 *Presenility. **1902** *Brit. Med. Jrnl.* 16 Aug. 472/1

Another symptom of presenility is an early impairment of memory, especially of substantives. **1933** *Arch. Dermatol. & Syphilol.* XXVIII. 553 The cause of pseudoxanthoma elasticum is unknown... Jones, Alden and Bishop entertained the belief that since the disease is allied to the changes found in elastosis senilis, it is an evidence of presenility. **1972** *Albrecht v. Graefes Arch. f. klin. und exper. Ophthalm.* CLXXXIV. 314 Histologic changes in the corpus geniculatum laterale in older persons, presenility (Alzheimer's disease) and in senile dementia. **1851** MRS. BROWNING *Casa Guidi Windows* II. 560 Some *pre-shadow rising slow Of what his Italy would fancy meet To be called Brutus. **1919** *Science* 6 June 545/1 The disinfectant..must be applied at the end of the *presoak period. **1920** *Jrnl. Agric. Res.* XIX. 371 A 6-hour presoak followed by a 6-hour treatment with formalin. **1969** *Chem. & Engin. News* 3 Feb. 16/1 Makers of enzyme-active detergents and presoaks compete strongly for a place in the..home laundry products market. **1976** *Chem. in Brit.* XII. 117/1 Proteases are incorporated into presoak and heavy duty washing powders and this is the major outlet for industrial enzymes. **1891** WALT WHITMAN in *Pall Mall G.* 12 Dec. 3/1 If those *pre-successes were all—if they ended at that—..America..were a failure. **1597** SHAKS. *2 Hen. IV*, I. i. 168 It was your *pre-surmize, That in the dole of blowes, your Son might drop. **1956** E. M. FORSTER *Marianne Thornton* 18 To look out through the high glass door, upon the magnificent Tulip Tree, became a ritual, and almost a *pretaste of heaven. *a* **1974** R. CROSSMAN *Diaries* (1975) I. 329 We were a typical Labour Party gathering, which gave us a pre-taste of the Blackpool hotels when Conference starts in a few days' time. **1898** ZANGWILL *Dreamers Ghetto* I. ii. §7. 56 God's Vicegerent..who dare not take the Eucharist without a *Pretaster. **1643** *Answ. Ld. Digby's Apol.* 22, I am therefore a little jealous there might be some *pre-tincture in your Lordshipps own eye. **1653** MANTON *Exp. James* i. 2, Wks. 1871 IV. 25 A happy *preunion of their souls and their blessedness. **1959** J. C. CATFORD in Quirk & Smith *Teaching of English* vi. 188 Conscious *preverbalisation in L1, and translation into L2, may be entirely suppressed, but errors due to interference from L1 still keep breaking through. **1962** *Which?* Aug. 234/2 Up to 6 minutes *pre-wash soak or 10 minutes washing. **1966** D. V. DAVIS *New Domestic Encycl.* iv. 131 If you have a fully-automatic washing machine, use the Pre-wash or Rinse programme. **1970** *Which?* May 143/2 The Bendix LTA had a pre-wash that could be included in the automatic cycle.

3. With an adj.: as ***pre-coexistent, -combustible, -essential, -subsistent, -thoughtful***; **pre'mutative**, inflected by means of prefixes, as a language.

c **1624** LUSHINGTON *Resurr. Serm.* (1659) 61 By natural relation his body was his own, as being the essential and proper counterpart of his soul, *præ-coexistent with it in one person. **1922** JOYCE *Ulysses* 657 Fanned by a constant up-draught of ventilation between the kitchen and the chimney-flue, ignition was communicated from the faggots of *precombustible fuel to polyhedral masses of bituminous coal. **1897** CRANDALL in *Trans. Amer. Pediatric Soc.* IX. 168 *k*, That process of involution which is *pre-essential to evolution. **1899** R. C. TEMPLE *Univ. Gram.* 7 Since affixes may be prefixes, infixes, or suffixes, agglutinative and synthetic languages are each divisible into (1) *pre-mutative, or those that prefix their affixes; (2) intro-mutative ..; and (3) post-mutative. **1683** CAVE *Ecclesiastici, Eusebius* 12 [He] was preexistent and *presubsistent to the whole Creation. *a* **1851** LYTTON (Herrig's *Archiv* VIII. 269), *Prethoughtful of every chance.

II. Of local position. (Chiefly *Anat.*)

Usually without hyphen. *Pre-* stressed (ˌpriː).

4. a. In adverbial relation to an adj.: = Before, anteriorly, in front: as **precommi'ssural**, anterior to a commissure of the brain; **pre'dentate**, having teeth in the fore part of the upper jaw only, as some *Cetacea*. Also in adjectives, introduced by Wilder, etc. = 'anterior', as **precere'bellar** = anterior cerebellar (artery); so **pre'cerebral**; **pre'choroid**, anterior choroid; **preclo'acal**, belonging to the anterior portion of the cloaca; **preco'mmunicant**, anterior communicating (artery, etc.); **predi'gastric**, of or pertaining to the anterior belly of the digastric muscle; also *sb.* this anterior belly regarded as a distinct muscle; **pre'geminal**, **pre'optic**, of or pertaining to the anterior *corpora quadrigemina* or optic lobes of the brain.

b. In quasi-adjectival relation to a sb.: = 'Situated in front, anterior, fore-', esp. denoting the anterior of two or more parts of the same kind; with derivative adjs.: as **pre-ab'domen**, Latreille's name for the first five segments of the abdomen of Crustacea (*Syd. Soc. Lex.*); **predila'tator**, the anterior dilatator muscle of the nostril; **pre'forceps**, the curved anterior fibres of the *corpus callosum*, which pass into the frontal lobe of the cerebrum; **prege'niculum**, the external geniculate body; hence ***pregeniculate*** adj.; **pre-omo'sternum**, an anterior omosternum; hence ***pre-omosternal*** adj.; **prepe'duncle**, the anterior peduncle of the brain; hence ***prepeduncular, prepedunculate*** adjs.; **prepelvi'sternum**, an anterior pelvisternum; hence *prepelvi'sternal* adj.; **pre'retina**, the thin lamina representing the retina in that part of the vitreous chamber of the eye immediately anterior to the *ora serrata* (*Syd. Soc. Lex.*); hence ***preretinal*** adj.; **pre'rima**, an extension of the rima in advance of the porta in some animals, as Dipnoi; hence ***prerimal*** adj.; **prescu'tellum** *Entom.*, a sclerite sometimes appreciable between the mesoscutum and mesoscutellum; **pre'scutum** *Entom.*, the most anterior sclerite of the tergal portion of each thoracic segment in insects, etc.; hence ***prescutal*** adj.

1885 WILDER in *Jrnl. Nervous Dis.* XII. 349 Common Latin name. Cerebellaris anterior... English paronym. *Pre-cerebellar. **1890** BILLINGS *Med. Dict.*, *Precerebellar artery*. **1885** WILDER (as above), Common Latin name. Cerebralis anterior... English paronym. *Precerebral. **1890** BILLINGS *Med. Dict.*, *Precerebral artery*. **1885** WILDER (as above), Common Latin name. Choroidea anterior... English paronym. *Prechoroid. **1890** in BILLINGS. **1890** *Cent. Dict.*, **Precloacal*. **1895** *Syd. Soc. Lex.*, *Precloacal*, belonging to the anterior portion of the *cloaca*. **1896** *Q. Jrnl. Microsc. Sci.* XXXIX. 184 The cerebrum of Platypus.. conforms to the mammalian type, yet numerous features —such as..the '*precommissural area'—indicate its close Sauropsidean affinities. **1900** A. HILL tr. *Obersteiner's Anat. Central Nervous Organs* (ed. 2) 429 A small portion of the fornix which streams on to the septum pellucidum (præcommissural fibres of Huxley) ought to be reckoned as fibres of association. **1953** G. A. G. MITCHELL *Anat. Autonomic Nervous System* viii. 99 A small fascicle of fornix fibres given off near the interventricular foramen passes downwards in front of the anterior commissure... In rabbits this precommissural fascicle ends in the medial and lateral septal nuclei and in the nucleus accumbens. **1971** J. Z. YOUNG *Anat. Nervous System Octopus Vulgaris* iv. 69 There is a direct connection between the rather enigmatic precommissural region and the anterior pedal lobe. **1885** WILDER (as above), Common Latin name. Communicans anterior... English paronym. *Precommunicant. **1890** in BILLINGS. **1834** DEWHURST *Nat. Hist. Cetacea* 130 *Predentate Cetacea; or, those with teeth only in the anterior part of the upper jaw. **1895** *Syd. Soc. Lex.*, **Predigastric*, belonging to the Predigastricus. *Predigastricus*, Coues' term for the anterior belly of the digastric muscle. **1895** *Syd. Soc. Lex.*, **Predilatator*, Coues' name for the *Dilatator naris anterior*. *Ibid.*, *Preforceps..*Pregeminal. **1889** *Cent. Dict.* VI. 4694/3 **Preoptic*, anterior with respect to optic lobes; pregeminal: specifically noting the anterior pair of the optic lobes or corpora quadrigemina of the brain. **1907** J. B. JOHNSTON *Nervous System Vertebr.* xviii. 297 Surrounding the pre-optic recess is a layer of cells of very primitive character. **1970** *Jrnl. Anat.* CVII. 186 Evidence which indicates that the preoptic area is involved in the control of reproductive function. **1895** *Syd. Soc. Lex*, *Prepeduncle, -cular, -culate. **1894** GOULD *Dict. Med.* 1177/1 **Prepelvisternum*,..an anterior pelvisternum. **1887** WILDER in *Amer. Nat.* June 545 In *Ceratodus* alone..is there a **prerima*,—that is, a rima extending *cephalad* from the margin of the porta.

c. In advb. relation to a vb.; in compounds formed in L., as PRECLUDE, PREFIX, PREMUNITE.

III. Of order, rank, importance, quality, degree.

5. In sense 'before in order or importance, above, in preference to, superior to, more than, beyond'.

Common in combinations already in Latin, but rare in English use. See PRECEDE *v.*, PRECEL *v.*, PREDOMINATE *v.*, PRE-EMINENCE, PRE-EXCELLENCE, PREFER *v.*, PRE-GRAVITATE *v.*, PRE-ORDINATE *a.*, PREPONDERATE *v.*, etc., in Main words. Also **pre-epic**, surpassing the epic; **pre-Luciferian**, surpassing Lucifer.

1630 DONNE *Serm.* xxv. (1640) 250 What a superdiabolicall, what a præ-Luciferian Pride is his that will be superiour to God. **1907** *Scot. Hist. Rev.* Jan. 166 Adventures pre-epic in their vastness.

IV. With intensive force.

6. With adjs. and ppl. adjs., in the sense 'before others, pre-eminently, exceedingly, in the highest degree'; as ***pre-pious, pre-pleasing, pre-regular***: PRECLARE, PRECORDIAL[2], PRENOBLE, etc. Chiefly *Obs.*

1530 LYNDESAY *Test. Papyngo* 846 The eldest Dochter named was ryches; The secunde, Syster Sensualytie;.. Preplesande to the Spiritualytie. **1647** WARD *Simp. Cobler* 35, I had rather suppose them to powder, than expose them to preregular, much lesse to preter-regular judgements. **1657** REEVE *God's Plea* 147 Single out that præpious person, that ye think is able to convert this Age.

B. Combinations in which *pre-* is prepositional, having as its object the sb. forming, or implied in, the second element.

I. Relating to time or order of succession: in which *pre-* = before; anterior, prior, or previous to; preceding, earlier than.

These may be formed for the nonce almost at pleasure; indeed, such combinations as *pre-Alfredian, pre-Reformation, pre-reformational, pre-Shaksperian, pre-free-trade*, are rather phrases than words: *pre-Shaksperian dramatists, pre-Reformation ritual, pre-free-trade conditions*, being only a compacter way of saying 'dramatists before Shakspere', 'ritual before the Reformations', 'conditions (existing) before (the era of) free trade'.

All these are properly hyphened, but the special compounds in 1 d are often written *indivisim*. *Pre-* is always stressed (ˌpriː), and *e* long.

1. With adjectives (and their derivative adverbs and substantives), or f. *pre-* + a (Lat.) sb. + adjectival ending, as *pre-reformation-al*; forming adjectives, with derivative adverbs and substantives. Also with (Eng. or other) sbs. directly forming sbs., as *pre-cancer, -climax, -delinquency, -menarche, -myelocyte*, etc. (below). Also PREHOMINID, PREPUBERTY, etc.

Compounds of this type were not used in Latin, and they are of recent appearance in English. The earliest appears to be PRE-ADAMITE, formed in Lat. as a sb. 1655, whence in Eng. as sb. in 1662, and as adj. in 1786; thence *pre-adamitical* in 1716; *prediluvian* occurs 1804, *preprandial* 1822, *prenatal* 1826, *pre-Christian* 1828, *pre-millennian* 1828, *pre-Gothic* 1831, *prehuman* 1844, *prehistoric* 1851, *pre-glacial* 1855, *pre-scientific* 1858, *pre-Georgian* 1861, *pre-Roman* 1863. (Some of these may have been used a little earlier.)

a. Formed on proper nouns (or their adjectives), esp. on names of persons, races, nations, dynasties, and religions, as ***pre-Alfredian, -Arnoldian, -Augustinian, -Baconian, -Caroline*** [Charlemagne], ***-Cavourian, -Chaucerian, -Columbian, -Constantinian, -Copernican, -Dantean, -Darwinian, -Evite*** [Eve], ***-Galilean*** [Galileo], ***-Georgian*** [the four Georges], ***-Hieronymian*** [Hieronymus or Jerome], ***-Hitlerian, -Hitlerite, -Kantian, -Keynesian, -Linnæan, -Listerian, -Malthusian, -Mendelian, -Messianic, -Mosaic, -Muhammadan, -Newtonian, -Patrician*** [St. Patrick], ***-Pauline, -Pharaonic, -Shakespearian, -Solomonic, -Solonian, -Victorian, -Virgilian; pre-Aryan, -Assyrian, -British, -Buddhist, -Canaanitic, -Celtic, -Doric, -European, -Fascist, -Gothic, -Greek, -Han, -Hellenic, -Hispanic, -Islamic, -ite, -Israelitish, -Jewish, -Mycenean, -Nazi, -Norman, -Norse, -Roman, -Saxon, -Semitic, -Soviet, -Vedic***; etc.

b. In names of geological formations and of prehistoric periods, as ***pre-Carboniferous*** (earlier than the Carboniferous); so ***-Laurentian, -Permian, -Silurian; pre-metallic*** (before the knowledge of metals), ***pre-palæozoic***. (Cf. also PRE-CAMBRIAN *a.*)

c. In pathological terms, noting stages and symptoms in the progress of disease, as ***pre-albuminuric*** (previous to the appearance of albuminuria); so ***pre-ascitic, -cancerous, -epileptic, -fungoidal, -malignant, -paroxysmal, -pathological, phthisical, -symptomatic***, etc.

d. Formed on other adjectives (or the L. or other sbs. to which these belong): as ***pre-artistic*** (before the cultivation of art), ***-capitalist, -capitalistic, -chemical, -cinematographic, -civilized, -coitional, -colonial, -commercial, -conceptual, -conciliar, -contemporaneous, -copulative, -earthly, -elemental, -evolutionary, -experimental*** (hence ***-experimentally*** adv.), ***-fabulous, -federal, -feudal, -feudalic, -filmic, -geological, -imperial, -industrial, -industrialist, -intellectual, -koranic, -lexical, -literary, -matrimonial, -matutinal, -mediæval, -memorial, -modern, -monadic, -monarchical, -monumental, -moral, -mortal, -mythical, -nuptial, -observational, -orgasmic, -original, -paroxysmal, -personal, -philosophical, -phonemic, -political, -predicative, -prep, -preparatory, -primary, -prophetic, -rabbinical, -religious, -romanesque, -scholastic, -secular, -social, -socialist, -solar, -telegraphic, -telescopic, -theoretical, -traditional, -tragic, -transformational***, etc.; freq. in *Gram.*, as ***pre-accentual, -adjectival, -adverbial, -consonantal*** (so ***preconsonantally*** adv.), ***-infinitival, inflexional, -junctural, -pausal, suffixal, -syllabic***. Also **pre-'adult, -a'dult**, prior to the attainment of adulthood; **pre-æ'stival, -est-**, occurring before midsummer (*Cent. Dict.* 1890); **pre-'agonal, -a'gonic** *Med.*, occurring immediately before, or premonitory of, the death agony; **pre-agri'cultural** *Anthrop.*, that has not yet developed agriculture as a means of subsistence; **pre-ana'lytic, -ana'lytical**, preceding analysis; hence **pre-ana'lytically** *adv.*; **pre-'article** *sb. Gram.*, one of a set of words that can precede an article in a noun phrase; **pre-'bacillary**, prior to invasion by bacilli (*Cent. Dict.* 1890); **pre-bacterio'logic, -'logical**, previous to the discovery of the relationship of bacteria to disease; † **pre-bea'tific**, previous to the beatific vision; **pre-bro'midic**, previous to the use of bromides in medicine; **pre-'cancer** *sb. Med.*, a condition that implies an increased risk of the future development of cancer; cf. *pre-cancerous*, sense B. 1 c; **pre-carti'laginous**, preceding the development of cartilage in an embryo (*Cent. Dict.*); **pre'cellular** *Biol.*, prior to the origin of cellular life; **pre-'civil**, prior to the development of social organization; **pre'climax** *sb. Ecology*, the point in a plant succession at which development has ceased before the state of climax is reached; **pre-co'nnubial**, occurring before marriage; **precon'vulsive** *Med.*, preceding a convulsion; **pre-'cosmic**, previous to the present world; **pre-cre'ative**, existing before the Creation; **pre-'cultural**, pertaining to human existence prior to or independent of cultural development; **pre-de'linquency** *sb.*, behaviour which is likely to result in (juvenile) delinquency; hence **pre-de'linquent** *a.* and *sb.*; **pre-dia'stolic**, *Physiol.*, preceding the diastole or dilatation of the heart in beating; **pre-di'crotic**, *Physiol.*, preceding the dicrotic wave of the pulse; **pre-dy'nastic**, existing before the recognized (Egyptian) dynasties; **pre-eco'nomic**: see quot.; **pre-e'mergent** = *pre-emergence* (sense B. 2 below); **pre-erythro'cytic** *Biol.*, occurring or existing in the period between the entry of a malaria parasite into the body as a sporozoite and the subsequent entry into red blood cells of schizonts descended from the sporozoites; **pre-evo'lutional**, **-evo'lutionary**, **-evo'lutionist**, previous to the introduction of the theory of evolution; **pre-expo'nential** *Math.*, occurring as a non-exponential multiplier of an exponential quantity; **pre'gamic** *Cytology*, prior to the formation of gametes; **pre'gastrular** *Biol.*, prior to gastrulation; **pregeo'logical**, occurring in, or pertaining to, the period of the earth's history earlier than the time of formation of the oldest known rocks; hence **pregeo'logically** *adv.*; **pre'grammar** *sb. Linguistics* (see quots.); **pregra'mmatical** *Linguistics*, applied to an assumed period in linguistic communication prior to the existence of grammatical structure; **pre-hemi'plegic**, *Path.*, preceding an attack of hemiplegia or paralysis of one side (*Syd. Soc. Lex.* 1895); **pre-he'xameral**, occurring prior to the six days of Creation; **pre-'ictal** *Med.*, preceding a stroke or fit, esp. an epileptic fit; **pre-In'caic** = *pre-Incarial*; **pre-In'carial**, prior to the time of the Incas of Peru; **pre-'Latin**, designating (any of) the Italic languages older than Latin; **pre'logic** *sb.*, a mode of thought that does not yet conform to logical reasoning (cf. PRELOGICAL *a.*); **pre-ma'niacal**, preceding mania or madness; **pre-ma'terial**, prior to what is material; **pre-mei'otic** *Cytology*, occurring before meiosis; that has not yet undergone meiosis; **preme'narche** *sb. Med.*, the premenarchal period in a girl's life; **preme'narchal**, **-me'narcheal**, **-me'narchial**, of, pertaining to, or designating a girl in the few years before the onset of menstruation; **pre-'moral**, pertaining to a stage of development prior to the personal acceptance of moral responsibility; hence **pre-mo'rality** *sb.*; **pre-'mortuary**, occurring, or pertaining to what may occur, before (some one's) death; **pre-my'cosic**, *Path.*, preceding mycosis or the development of fungi in or on the body; **pre'myelocyte** *sb. Anat.* = MYELOBLAST; hence **pre,myelo'cytic**; **preneo'plastic** *Med.*, before or prefatory to the development of a neoplasm; **pre-ne'phritic**, *Path.*, preceding disease of the kidneys; **'prenoun** *sb. Gram.*, a word that generally precedes a noun and is in close syntactical relation to it; **pre-or'ganic**, prior to the existence of organic life; **pre-ovu'latory** *Med.*, before ovulation; **pre'patent** *Med.*, applied to the period between parasitic infection of a host and the time when the parasite can be first detected; so **pre'patency** *sb.*, the condition of an infected host during the prepatent period; **pre-pla'cental**, prior to the development of a placenta in gestation; **pre'planetary** *Astr.*, existing before the formation of planets; *spec.* constituting the material from which the planets were formed; **pre-'planting**, applied or performed before the crop is planted; also *absol.*; **preproinsulin** (ˌpriːprəʊˈɪnsjʊlɪn) *sb. Biochem.*, a precursor of proinsulin; **pre'puberal** = *prepubertal*; so **pre'puberally** *adv.*; **pre-'pubertal**, prior to the attainment of puberty; hence **pre'pubertally** *adv.*; **pre-re'flective**, **-re'flexive**, prior to reflection or reasoning thought; **pre-re'formatory**, prior to the Reformation; **pre-relati'vistic**, before the theory of relativity was published (in 1905 and 1915); **pre-re'mote**, more remote in previous time or order; **pre-repro'ductive**, prior to the time when an individual becomes capable of reproduction; **pre-rhota'cistic**, *Philol.*, previous to the tendency to rhotacism; **pre-'seminal**, **-'seminary**, *Phys.*, prior to insemination or fecundation; **preschizo'phrenic**, of or pertaining to the period prior to the onset of schizophrenia; as *sb.*, a person showing symptoms similar to those observed prior to schizophrenia; so **preschizo'phrenia** *sb.*; **pre'senile** *Med.*, occurring in or characteristic of the period of life preceding old age, esp. the two or three decades immediately before; **pre'solar** = *prestellar*; **pre-splenome'galic**, *Path.*, occurring before enlargement of the spleen; **pre'stellar** *Astr.*, not (yet) having formed a star or stars; **pre-'structuralist**, prior to the development of structural linguistics; **pre-syste'matic**, prior to the development of a formal system; so **pre-syste'matically** *adv.*; **pre-'temporal**, anterior to existence in time, 'before time began', antemundane; **pre-te'rrestrial**, existing before what is terrestrial; **pre'vernal**, pertaining to a season before or very early in spring; **pre-vo'litional**, existing before volition.

1965 W. S. ALLEN *Vox Latina* v. 85 *Pre-accentual loss in *disciplīna*. **1965** N. CHOMSKY *Aspects of Theory of Syntax* iv. 148 Verbs are strictly subcategorized into Intransitives, Transitives, *pre-Adjectival, pre-Sentence. **1977** *Word 1972* XXVIII. 94 From an Old Irish system of separate comparative and superlative suffixes, the language will have changed to a system of separate comparative and superlative preadjectival particles. **1902** *Buck's Handbk. Med. Sci.* (rev. ed.) IV. 527/2 The condition .. becomes manifest during the growing or *preadult period. **1974** *Sci. Amer.* Sept. 127/3 A husband, a wife and their preadult children. **1977** *Bull. Amer. Acad. Arts & Sci.* Oct. 25 Since the goals of adults tend to reflect their pre-adult formative experiences, the changing assessment of progress as it is traditionally understood may prove to be essentially an integrational phenomenon. **1976** *Archivum Linguisticum* VII. 32 Absolute-final position is the norm for final position, with *pre-adverbial positions as optional variants in sentences where non-sentence adverbials occur. **1900** *Buck's Handbk. Med. Sci.* (rev. ed.) I. 563/1 Immediately preceding death there is an intense congestion of the viscera which frequently results in an outpour of serum. This condition, when involving the peritoneal cavity, is termed *pre-agonal ascites. **1974** L. WATSON *Romeo Error* iii. 66 Professor Negovskii of the Soviet Academy of Medical Sciences calls them shock, preagonal state, agony and chemical death. **1886** *Buck's Handbk. Med. Sci.* II. 49/1 A sudden high elevation of temperature .. after a chill in a previously apyretic case, means a complication, and not a fatal issue, but a hyperpyrexia without chill, and with a profuse sweat, is *pre-agonic. **1927** *Contemp. Rev.* July 85 The moon to *pre-agricultural society was the real magic. **1947** *Sci. Amer.* Sept. 47/1 The preagricultural population .. must have been vulnerable to changes in climate .. and to the disappearance of species of prey. **1975** J. G. EVANS *Environment Early Man Brit. Isles* iii. 55 The mixed deciduous woodlands of pre-agricultural Britain. **1899** *Allbutt's Syst. Med.* VI. 338 Before the appearance of albumin in the urine .. (*pre-albuminuric stage). **1962** H. R. LOYN *Anglo-Saxon Eng.* ii. 79 The *pre-Alfredian period is rich in reference to Anglo-Saxon saints and scholars. **1929** C. I. LEWIS *Mind & World-Order* ii. 54 The acceptance of such *preanalytic data as an ultimate epistemological category would .. put an end to all worthwhile investigation. **1939** *Mind* XLVIII. 89 He holds that philosophy must begin with the pre-analytic data of experience as these are expressed in common-sense judgments. **1927** *Jrnl. Philos.* XXIV. 9 The given is for science a continual challenge, always remaining '*pre-analytical', in the sense of never condemning as bootless the task of more searching analysis. **1965** A. C. DANTO *Analytical Philos. Hist.* x. 207 From the Deduction Assumption, together with our pre-analytical notion of explanatory *in*adequacy, we may .. elicit the remainder of Hempel's Analysis. **1934** COHEN & NAGEL *Introd. Logic* xix. 385 Analysis .. may reveal many complexities in the *pre-analytically simple object or concept. **1951** *Mind* LX. 550 Something which we knew pre-analytically to be true. **1886** C. M. YONGE *Chantry House* I. iii. 22 In those *pre-Arnoldian times no lofty code of honour was even ideal among school-boys. **1965** *Pre-article [see *post-article* s.v. POST- B. 1 c]. **1971** Pre-article [see *non-lexical* s.v. NON- 3]. **1883** *Eng. Illustr. Mag.* Nov. 89/2 The silversmith's work of the late Georgian or early Victorian age which might be fairly designated the *preartistic .. period. **1865** TYLOR *Early Hist. Man.* viii. 209 Most others found in Greece are probably *præ-Aryan. **1905** H. D. ROLLESTON *Dis. Liver* 111 The early or *pre-ascitic stage of cirrhosis. **1959** J. BLISH *Clash of Cymbals* iii. 72 '*Pre-Augustinean time' came to be something that a historian could know all about, but a physicist, by definition, nothing. **1964** P. F. ANSON *Bishops at Large* i. 44 Restoring the pre-Augustinian tradition in Britain. **1865** MILL *Exam. Hamilton's Philos.* xxiv. 469 Generality of the *pre-Baconian type. **1953** K. BRITTON *J. S. Mill* v. 152 The enquiry into microscopic conditions was distinguished in pre-Baconian logic as the enquiry into *material causes*. **1902** *Buck's Handbk. Med. Sci.* (rev. ed.) IV. 391/2 It .. was long ago expressed by Alexander von Humboldt .., to be sure, in *pre-bacteriologic language. **1892** *Pall Mall Gaz.* 6 Feb. 2/1 He was educated in the *pre-bacteriological era, and had little sympathy with modern developments of medical science. **1965** S. PELLER in Glass & Eversley *Population in Hist.* v. 94 In the pre-bacteriological era, the survival rates for the ruling families were far ahead of those of the general population. *a* **1711** KEN *Hymnotheo* Poet. Wks. 1721 III. 171 He [Stephen] had of God *pre-beatifick view. **1899** *Allbutt's Syst. Med.* VII. 793 Agents of repute in the *pre-bromidic days. **1938** DORLAND *Med. Dict.* (ed. 18) 1129/2 **Precancer*, an abnormal growth which is likely to develop into cancer. **1963** *New Statesman* 19 July 71 Pre-cancer means cells which, if left untreated, will eventually develop into invasive cancer. *Ibid.*, Miscroscopic studies of the cervical smears showed .. five cases of pre-cancers. **1882** *Brit. Med. Jrnl.* 7 Jan. 5/1 (*heading*) The *pre-cancerous stage of cancer, and the importance of early operations. **1899** J. HUTCHINSON in *Arch. Surg.* X. 182 An early stage of epithelioma;—a pre-cancerous stage. **1975** *Sci. Amer.* Nov. 78/3 Screening programs have an additional shortcoming: for every cancer they detect they reveal perhaps 10 other abnormalities, many of which seem to be precancerous. **1949** I. DEUTSCHER *Stalin* vi. 194 It was, however, a formidable task to adjust their *pre-capitalist, often pre-feudal and even nomad ways of life to the Marxist, Communist policies of the central Government. **1952** V. A. DEMANT *Relig. & Decline of Capitalism* i. 28 Spontaneous social co-operation such as is universal in pre-capitalist societies. **1974** B. PEARCE tr. *Amin's Accumulation on World Scale* I. ii. 141 Non-European precapitalist societies were not fundamentally different from those of Europe. **1979** *China Now* Jan.–Feb. 22/1 Abrupt transformation of the feudal and pre-capitalist organizational structures. **1940** WIRTH & SHILS tr. *Mannheim's Ideology & Utopia* iii. 108 Two types of irrationalism .. on the one hand, *precapitalistic, traditionalistic irrationalism. **1959** *Brno Studies in English* I. 73 It would be unjust .. to explain this preference for pre-capitalistic epochs merely as a means of escape. **1894** *Geol. Mag.* Oct. 461 The South Welsh *pre-Carboniferous barrier of Hull, which forms the northern boundary of the visible Coal-fields. **1897** *Pre-Caroline [see *half-uncial* s.v. HALF- II. n]. **1934** PRIEBSCH & COLLINSON *German Lang.* ix. 356 The oldest German or rather Latin-German MS. .. is written in a pre-Caroline minuscule. **1948** D. DIRINGER *Alphabet* 545 The pre-Caroline book-hand in North Italy. **1946** *Nature* 21 Sept. 406/2 A new .. theory: that they [*sc.* bacteriophages] were the direct descendants of *precellular stages in the evolution of living forms. **1974** *Proc. Nat. Acad. Sci.* LXXI. 286/2 (*heading*) An hypothesis for the initiation of precellular evolution. **1934** S. ROBERTSON *Devel. Mod. Eng.* (1936) ii. 18 The pre-Hellenic inhabitants of Greece .. were not Indo-European, nor were the Etruscans in Italy, the *pre-Celtic peoples who inhabited Britain, or the Basques in Spain. **1953** K. JACKSON *Lang. & Hist. Early Brit.* 342 The name may very well be pre-Celtic. **1977** *Word 1972* XXVIII. 29 A pre-Celtic layer is now hardly identified with certainty through faint indices. **1909** R. BRIDGES *Let.* 29 Oct. (1940) 74, I have never studied the *pre-Chaucerian verse. **1973** P. A. COLINVAUX *Introd. Ecol.* xxix. 416 He was able to undo the mischief that contact poisons had done and leave the plantations in the security of the *pre-chemical age. **1974** M. TAYLOR tr. *Metz's Film Lang.* iii. 32 The most obvious pictorial juxtaposition, the most properly literary effect of composition, were, to hear him, prophetically *precinematographic. **1957** C. VEREKER *Devel. Polit. Theory* iii. 98 The metaphorical language used by political thinkers who posit a *pre-civil social condition is usually designated contractual. **1960** C. S. LEWIS *Studies in Words* 62 That pre-civil condition was described as *nature* or 'the state of *nature*'. **1953** S. SPENDER *Creative Element* 30 It also includes the whole universe, the unexplored, or uncivilized, or *pre-civilized areas of the map. **1956** R. REDFIELD *Peasant Society & Culture* iii. 77 Having developed out of the precivilized peoples of that very culture. **1916** F. E. CLEMENTS *Plant Succession* vi. 110 As a consequence [of reduced water-content], development would cease before reaching the climax proper, and the potential community .. may be called the *preclimax. **1929** WEAVER & CLEMENTS *Plant Ecol.* xviii. 424 The prairie itself is a preclimax to the deciduous forest with higher rainfall. **1960** N. POLUNIN *Introd. Plant. Geogr.* xi. 331 There are instances in which an apparent climax constitutes in reality a preclimax. **1959** K. E. L. SIMMONS in D. A. Bannerman *Birds Brit. Isles* VIII. 218 The ceremonies are not '*pre-coitional' in that they do not lead immediately to mating. **1961** *John o' London's* 18 May 543/2 The *pre-colonial history of Africa. **1975** A. DRUMMOND *Thames Jrnls. Vicesimus Lush* 18 No mention appears to have been made of potential goldfields in pre-colonial New Zealand. **1888** *Times* 3 Oct. 5/3 Inquirers into the *pre-Columbian history, ethnology, &c. of the American continent. **1881** W. R. SMITH *Old Test. in Jew. Ch.* xii. 348 Based on the old *precommercial state of things. **1956** J. S. BRUNER et al. *Study of Thinking* iii. 50 It is curiously difficult to recapture *preconceptual innocence. .. It is as if the mastery of a conceptual distinction were able to mask the preconceptual memory of the things now distinguished. **1967** *Sunday Times* 22 Jan. 10 Everyone tends to exaggerate the mutual isolation of *pre-conciliar days. **1976** *Times* 9 Aug. 11/1 The post-conciliar church polishes characteristically pre-conciliar weapons of censure, interdict, suspension and excommunication. **1978** *Times Lit. Suppl.* 25 Aug. 944/2 A spiritual tangle of casuistry and superstition entirely typical of pre-Conciliar Catholicism. **1887** F. R. STOCKTON *Borrowed Month*, etc. 201 *Preconnubial satisfaction of a very high order. **1951** TRAGER & SMITH *Outl. Eng. Struct.* I. 28 Most Northern Middle Western speakers have simple vowel before final or *pre-consonantal *r*. **1965** W. S. ALLEN *Vox Latina* i. 43 Before it [*sc.* h] .. the articles take their pre-consonantal rather than prevocalic form. **1976** *Archivum Linguisticum* VII. 163 He postulates the forms set down below, in which monophthongization would have been produced in pre-consonantal forms. **1953** K. JACKSON *Lang. & Hist. Early Brit.* II. 470 (*heading*) IE [*sc.* Indo-European] *gu̯*. This became *b* in CC. [*sc.* Common Celtic] initially except before *u* ..; intervocally and *preconsonantally, *g*. **1966** *Amer. Speech* XLI. 260 [R], as in SG [*sc.* Standard German], a lenis post-velar fricative, occurring preconsonantally and finally. **1977** D. CUPITT in J. Hick *Myth of God Incarnate* vii. 138 *Pre-constantinian Christian art was scarce, unofficial, of very poor quality and often somewhat ambiguous. **1907** W. A. TURNER *Epilepsy* ix. 195 He regarded the *pre-convulsive fall in alkalinity as a 'biochemical aura'. **1972** M. VERZEANO in Petsche & Brazier *Synchronization EEG Activities in Epilepsies* 178 When the preconvulsive state is reached (d), the passages of circulating activity through the network are very rhythmic, very rapid, and involve a large number of neurons discharging at a very high rate. **1964** C. S. LEWIS *Discarded Image* iii. 22 Casual statements about *pre-Copernican astronomy in modern scientists who are not historians are often unreliable. **1865** MASSON *Rec. Brit. Philos.* 170 Speculative thought, which might be debited to their *pre-Copernicanism. **1973** M. AMIS *Rachel Papers* 24 During the long *pre-copulative session I glanced downwards. **1891** *Riddles of Sphinx* 234 The *pre-cosmic conditions of the world-process. **1859** MOZLEY *Ess., Ind. Conversion* (1878) II. 328 The *praecreative or praeeternal spirit. **1927** B. MALINOWSKI *Sex & Repression in Savage Society* IV. i. 179 In a *pre-cultural condition there is no medium in which social institutions, morals, and religion could be moulded. **1963** AUDEN *Dyer's Hand* 87 Politics in every advanced society is .. not concerned with human beings as persons and citizens but with human bodies, with the precultural, prepolitical human creature. **1876–7** W. James in R. B. Perry *Tht. & Char. W. James* (1935) I. xxviii. 478 *Pre-Darwinians thought only of adaptation. They made organism plastic to its environment. **1880** *Atlantic Monthly* Oct. 444/1 Pre-Darwinian philosophers had also tried to establish the doctrine of descent with modification. **1899** A. H. Yapp *Cuckoo* iii. 189 In the case of the little birds and cuckoos we have had brought before us in the actions of the former what is decisively in the teeth of pre-Darwinian theory as of the Darwinian. **1921** G. B. Shaw *Back to Methuselah* p. viii, The pre-Darwinian age had come to be regarded as a Dark Age in which men still believed that the book of Genesis was a standard scientific treatise. **1932** Reckless & Smith *Juvenile Delinquency* vi. 168 (*heading*) Truancy as *predelinquency. **1972** *N.Y. Law Jrnl.* 24 Oct. 4/8 California's Predelinquency Statute: A Case Study and Suggested Alternatives, by Robert L. Harris. **1951** Powers & Witmer *Experiment in Prevention of Delinquency* iii. 30 If the treatment group comprised only selected *pre-delinquents.. unhappy public relations might result. *Ibid.* v. 53 No boy who showed obvious pre-delinquent trends was excluded. **1977** M. Edelman *Polit. Lang.* iv. 69 Affluent adults may be 'predelinquent' or 'prepsychotic'; but it is not behavior that governs the connotations of these terms, but, rather, the statistical chances for a group and the belief that poor children are high risks. **1853** Markham *Skoda's Auscult. & Percuss.* 213 *note*, A *prediastolic murmur is heard. **1878** Gladstone *Prim. Homer* i. 13 A poet of Asia.. would probably have called the *pre-Doric Greeks by the race-name of Hellenes. **1898** *Daily News* 14 Sept. 6/3 The Libyan stock.. can now safely be assigned to the *pre-Dynastic stock, about 5000 B.C., and even earlier. **1901** *Athenæum* 24 Aug. 256/1 A predynastic period of Egyptian history. **1848** Bailey *Festus* xix. (ed. 3) 213 Cities and fanes of diamond crown the hills.. Of this *preearthly paradise. **1876** Bagehot *Physics & Pol.* 11 A sort of *pre-economic age, when the very assumptions of political economy did not exist. **1852** Bailey *Festus* xxviii. (ed. 5) 475 That peace, Premotional, *preelemental, prime. **1959** *Times* 21 Mar. 9/3 There is no small retail pack available yet of the *pre-emergent weedkillers which are being tried extensively in commercial nurseries. **1928** L. J. J. Muskens *Epilepsy* vii. 257 The *pre-epileptic headache.. is little influenced by drugs. **1944** Huff & Coulston in *Jrnl. Infectious Dis.* LXXV. 237/2 For all the stages of the parasite [*sc. Plasmodium*] between sporozoite and erythrocytic trophozoite we shall use the term *pre-erythrocytic stages. They are, of course, exoerythrocytic in the broadest meaning of the term. **1962** J. D. Smyth *Introd. Animal Parasitol.* vii. 87 (*caption*) Pre-erythrocytic schizonts of *Plasmodium cynomolgi* and *P. vivax* in parenchymal cells of rhesus monkey and man respectively; 7 days after mosquito inoculation. **1973** R. M. Pinder *Malaria* ii. 26 This process, which constitutes the pre-erythrocytic or primary tissue stage, takes from 8 to 12 days and is essential to allow the parasites to undergo the necessary metabolic adaptation for the change from life in a poikilothermic insect to that in a warm-blooded vertebrate. **1908** *Westm. Gaz.* 7 June 2/2 In India itself the idea and word 'Indian' hardly existed in *pre-European times. **1971** *Black Scholar* June 35 We as black men are breaking loose.. becoming once again the real black man in the full tradition of our pre-European forebears. **1890** W. James *Princ. Psychol.* II. xxviii. 647 By the *pre-evolutionary naturalists, whose generation has hardly passed away, classifications were supposed to be ultimate insights into God's mind, filling us with adoration of his ways. **1885** W. R. Sorley *Ethics of Naturalism* vii. 170 A remnant of the false, *pre-evolutionist individualism. **1923** *Proc. Soc. Exper. Biol. & Med.* XX. 371 (*heading*) The influence of nutrition during the *pre-experimental period on the development of rickets in rats. **1971** *Jrnl. Gen. Psychol.* LXXXV. 157 During the pre-experimental period *Ss* were housed in group cages. **1970** *Ibid.* LXXXII. 47 It also suggests that *pre-experimentally acquired tendencies .. are important determinants of behavioral variability in experimental settings. **1966** D. G. Brandon *Mod. Techniques Metallogr.* vi. 182 Inclusion of the image term.. leads to a correction factor, *a*, in both the *pre-exponential and exponential terms. **1970** *Nature* 12 Dec. 1086/1 The Arrhenius expression is a frequently erroneous semiempirical formula, with the temperature independence of the activation energy *E* and the pre-exponential factor *A* becoming increasingly questionable as the reaction temperature range broadens. **1938** *New Statesman* 19 Feb. 276/2 It is possible.. that the present Italy willingly accepts that German domination in Central Europe which sons of the *pre-Fascist Italy spilled their blood to prevent. **1934** Webster, *Pre-feudal. **1949** I. Deutscher *Stalin* vi. 195 It was.. a formidable task to adjust their.. pre-feudal and even nomad ways of life to the Marxist, Communist policies of the central Government. **1962** H. R. Loyn *Anglo-Saxon Eng.* iii. 105 In one respect the techniques of warfare in pre-feudal England led to an inferior status on the part of the smith. **1974** M. Taylor tr. *Metz's Film Lang.* v. 114 The *iconology* (likewise *prefilmic) that organizes the denotation of those same objects. **1899** *Allbutt's Syst. Med.* VIII. 887 In this so-called '*pre-fungoidal' stage. **1880** W. James *Will to Believe* (1897) 254 The spencerian philosophy of 'Force', effacing all the previous distinctions between actual and potential energy, momentum, work, force, mass, etc., which physicists have with so much agony achieved, carried us back to a *pre-galilean age. **1952** *Mind* LXI. 417 He thinks biology is in a 'pre-Galilean' stage. **1934** *Anatomical Rec.* LX (Suppl.) 92 The most distinctive spindles are the first *pregamic figures. **1953** R. Wichterman *Biol. of Paramecium* ix. 273/1 The four micronuclear products of the first pregamic division enter quickly upon the second pregamic division without a resting stage between them.. to produce eight micronuclear products. **1894** *Biol. Lect.* (Marine Biol. Lab., Wood's Holl, Mass.) II. 2 This consideration led some morphologists to insist on the need of a more precise investigation of the *præ-gastrular stages, and the desirability of taking as a starting-point not the two-layered gastrula but the undivided ovum. **1970** *Annales Embryol. & Morphogénèse* III. 133 (*heading*) Competence and induction in the pregastrular chick blastoderm. **1882** G. H. Darwin in *Nature* XXV. 213 We must put these violent phenomena in *pregeological periods. **1899** *Geogr. Jrnl.* XIII. 233 A map of the world in early Cambrian times might show the influence of these pre-geological incidents. **1971** I. G. Gass et al. *Understanding Earth* ix. 137/2 The event which caused the loss of the primary atmosphere must have occurred fairly early in the history of the planet, presumably in pre-geological time (over 3600 million years ago). Otherwise we would expect to find some record of it in the rocks. **1899** *Geogr. Jrnl.* XIII. 234 If the ocean basins were not formed *pre-geologically, but have grown from the changes that have occurred during the long ages of geological time, then we must seek for a cause that has acted continuously, and is acting to-day. **1861** Beresf. Hope *Eng. Cathedr. 19th C.* iv. 119 The low morals of a large mass of the clergy in the Georgian or just *præ-Georgian days. **1831** *Westm. Rev.* July 31 The Siegfried's Chapel, in primeval, *Pre-Gothic architecture, not long since pulled down. **1949** *Archivum Linguisticum* I. 121 Is there anything against speaking of '*pre-grammar' as one speaks of prehistory alongside history? **1966** M. Pei *Gloss. Linguistic Terminol.* 216 *Pre-grammar*,.. research into the state of the language in its prehistoric stages, and of the grammatical categories which cannot be accounted for by logical analysis. [**1926** A. Sechehaye *Structure logique de la Phrase* i. 10 Il faut se souvenir de la différence.. qui existe entre le langage prégrammatical et le langage organisé.] **1932** A. H. Gardiner *Theory of Speech & Lang.* ii. iv. 220 Ries takes up the strange position that they [*sc.* sentences without verbs] are '*pre-grammatical, or better still extra-grammatical phrases'. **1937** J. Orr tr. *Iordan's Introd. Romance Linguistics* iv. 331 Every form of grammar has an individual origin, and has its source in some pre-grammatical or extra-grammatical act which in process of time is transformed into grammar. **1940** A. H. Gardiner *Theory of Proper Names* 12 This term [*sc.* 'name'] belongs to the pre-grammatical stage of thought. **1960** E. H. Gombrich *Art & Illusion* iv. 134 It was the Greeks who taught us to ask '*How* does he stand?' or even 'Why does he stand like that?' Applied to a *pre-Greek work of art, it may be senseless to ask this question. **1958** W. Willetts *Chinese Art* I. iv. 206 Criteria establishing the *pre-Han date of objects on which they appear. **1972** *Trans. Oriental Ceramics Soc.* XXXVIII. 13 This long survival of the most rudimentary of techniques.. contributed to the style of hard-fired pottery of the last pre-Han centuries. **1876** Gladstone *Homeric Synchr.* 214 All the passages tend to mark him as non-Hellenic or *pre-Hellenic. **1861** *Chr. Remembr.* XLI. 408 Those passages tell us far more about this *pre-hexameral period,.. than about the hexameron or six days work itself. **1919** *Proc. Soc. Antiquaries Scotl.* LIII. 24 There is no doubt that they were used as such by the *pre-hispanic tribes. **1931** *Times Lit. Suppl.* 9 Apr. 281/1 Pre-Hispanic Art in Argentina. **1963** *Times* 9 Feb. 9/7 One of the greatest obstacles to the dispersal of the thick mystery which hangs over Peru's prehispanic past is the fact that the later civilizations apparently had no form of writing. **1978** *Guardian Weekly* 26 Feb. 18/3 The pre-Hispanic Caribbean. **1959** *Encounter* July 68/1 With a broad *pre-Hitlerian gesture Napoleon destroyed her book. **1934** C. Lambert *Music Ho!* iii. 224 The earnest and thoroughgoing sense of sin that gave such a peculiar flavour to *pre-Hitlerite night life. **1958** *Electroencephalogr. & Clin. Neurophysiol.* X. 223/2 As a rule, toward the end of the attack, the record is characterized by the return of the *pre-ictal spike complex. **1969** W. Pryse-Phillips *Epilepsy* v. 17 Grand mal fits.. may be preceded by pre-ictal symptoms such as tiredness, irritability, etc. **1963** *Times* 9 Feb. 9/7 In the Machu Picchu area, at San Pedro de Cacha, an intact group of thousands of Incaic and *pre-Incaic tombs, some dating from about 1200 B.C., was found only a few weeks ago by the Peruvian archaeologist, Dr. Manuel Chavez Ballón. **1870** J. Orton *Andes & Amazons* ii. xxxv. (1876) 454 Massive monolithic monuments,.. prehistoric, *pre-incarial. **1934** A. Huxley *Beyond Mexique Bay* 251 Karl Marx went out imaginatively into the revolutionary future, Ruskin and William Morris into the *pre-industrial past. **1956** R. Redfield *Peasant Society & Culture* 71 He saw chiefly what had come into those villages from preindustrial Europe. **1969** G. Greene *Trav. with my Aunt* i. xiv. 136 Horses moved slowly along, dragging harrows. We were back in the pre-industrial age. **1977** P. Johnson *Enemies of Society* vii. 93 If there had been a powerful ecological lobby in eighteenth-century England.. the Western world would still be condemned to pre-industrial living standards. **1957** O. R. McGregor *Divorce in England* iii. 75 The peasant or domestic worker's family of *pre-industrialist days.. was largely a self-sustaining economic unit. **1877** Dods *Mohammed, Buddha & Christ* ii. (1878) 71 The *Pre-islamic condition of Arabia. **1977** *Language* LIII. 330, I will outline B's analysis of the variation in the form of the *pre-infinitival complementizer in Guyanese decreolization. **1939** L. H. Gray *Foundations of Lang.* 202 In this absence of declension we may.. see another survival of the *pre-inflexional stage. **1976** *Archivum Linguisticum* VII. 163 In this paper, having accepted a pre-inflexional phase of IE[sc. Indo-European],.. he tries to reduce the processes which give origin to the alternations I am studying. **1964** *Language* XL. 255 In speech development of the child, we can.. establish a *preintellectual stage. **1977** H. G. Burger in B. Bernardi *Concept & Dynamics of Culture* 453 Up to a certain point in time, then, a child exercises two separate mental stages: pre-intellectual and prelinguistic. **1968** *Language* XLIV. 84 The border between words constitutes a potential pause point. The features manifested at this *prejunctural spot are correlated with the difference between rapid speech forms and deliberate speech forms. **1972** *Ibid.* XLVIII. 411 Prejunctural *-j* is subsequently vocalized along with the fronting of stressed *-ō* to *-æ-*, which is unrounded in West Saxon. **1874** W. Wallace tr. *Hegel's Logic* 53 It was.. the main question of the *pre-Kantian metaphysic. **1947** *Mind* LVI. 164 It is doubtful whether any reader hitherto sunk in dogmatic slumber pre- or post-Kantian would be awakened by these rambling and inconclusive pages. **1951** W. H. Walsh *Introd. Philos. Hist.* vii. 141 Hegel saw the way the abstract conception of reason favoured by Kant and (in general) the pre-Kantian rationalists had been countered by the many philosophies of feeling. **1979** *Studies in Eng. Lit.: Eng. Number* (Tokyo) 172 Dr. Beer's present work.. is a valuable attempt to explore Coleridge's poetic intelligence with all its preoccupations coming from the poet's inborn interest in pre-Kantian Idealism and mysticism. **1959** *Ann. Reg. 1958* 88 The legislative assembly's rejection of measures to raise more local revenue illustrated some of the difficulties encountered in development—the *pre-Keynesian thinking of many local leaders, [etc.]. **1960** *20th Cent.* Aug. 99 Old-fashioned, pre-Keynesian, *laissez-faire* liberalism. **1876** W. R. Cooper *Archaic Dict.* 30 An ancient title of the Deity among the *pre-koranic Arabs. **1933** L. Bloomfield *Language* 373 *Pre-Latin *[kolnis] 'hill' gives Latin *collis*. **1975** *Language* LI. 142 *S*-stem nouns like Pre-Latin **douk* + *es* + *i* are analogically re-analysed. **1880** Ramsay in *Times* 26 Aug. 5/4 Rocks more ancient still to afford materials for.. these *pre-Laurentian strata. **1957** C. La Drière in N. Frye *Sound & Poetry* ii. 103 The concord is of natural, or at least *prelexical or paralexical, *suggestion* of the sound with its conventional reference. **1971** *Language* XLVII. 319 The Lexical Insertion Rule can insert a predicate into a prelexical terminal string only if the lexical marking of the predicate is not distinct from the feature specification of the prelexical terminal string. **1976** *Archivum Linguisticum* VII. 127 The lexical decomposition of McCawley and others yields several closely related items which differ only in one or more prelexical elements. **1903** *Pop. Sci. Monthly* Jan. 211 A correspondent.. wrote to ask if the garden would accept as a gift the large and important collection of *pre-Linnean books that it had been his pleasure to accumulate. **1936** *Discovery* Mar. 85/1 There is a rich collection of botanical incunabula, old herbals, and other pre-Linnaean items. **1962** H. R. Loyn *Anglo-Saxon Eng.* vi. 286 Botanists exercise themselves.. to give post-Linnaean forms to strongly pre-Linnaean Anglo-Saxon generalized plant names. **1928** *Daily Express* 23 Nov. 10/2 The idea of shutting out extremism by barring its representatives at the ports seems to us as obsolete as *pre-Listerian surgery. **1951** White & Hynes *Med. Bacteriol.* (ed. 5) v. 53 In pre-Listerian days the surgeon's scalpel frequently conveyed infection from one patient to another. **1931** G. Stern *Meaning & Change of Meaning* 12 *Pre-literary developments are best left aside at first.. and.. research should be restricted to periods represented by written texts. **1941** F. Klaeber *Beowulf* (ed. 3) p. lxvi, Of especial interest are the *gefrægn*-formulas, which unmistakably point to the 'preliterary' stage of poetry, when the poems lived on the lips of singers, and oral transmission was the only possible source of information. **1967** *N.Y. Rev. Bks.* 23 Feb. 33/2 The study of technology or town-planning is the same for preliterary or literary societies. **1937** R. H. Lowie *Hist. Ethnol. Theory* (1938) xii. 219 Into the notions about the dead this logical factor does not intrude, hence *prelogic here runs riot untrammeled. **1957** H. J. Uldall in Hjelmslev & Uldall *Outl. Glossematics* i. 4 All languages.. are based on this participative prelogic. **1897** *Lippincott's Med. Dict.* 824/2 *Pre-malignant. **1961** *Lancet* 29 July 250/2 It is suggested that there is a premalignant defect in the genes which control the development of the reticulo-endothelial system, and that the abnormal stem cells derived from these genes undergo further changes and become malignant. **1974** R. M. Kirk et al. *Surgery* iv. 56 Hereditary polyposis.. of the colon is pre-malignant. **1920** E. Pound in *Lett. J. Joyce* (1966) III. 9 His misspent *premalthusian youth. **1965** P. Goubert in Glass & Eversley *Population in Hist.* xix. 467 Results obtained by the second method [in the study of demography] apply to all 'pre-Malthusian' times. **1883** Maudsley *Body & Will* iii. v. 297 The *premaniacal semblance of mental brilliancy. *a* **1881** A. Barratt *Phys. Metempiric* 69 What *prematerial ages of ether beyond ether it may picture. **1863** Mansel *Lett., Lect.*, etc. (1873) 247 The genuine sensation device of a *pre-matrimonial secret. **1963** V. Nabokov *Gift* ii. 119 The river runs into the murk of the *prematutinal twilight that still hangs in the gorges. **1859** T. Parker in Weiss *Life* (1863) II. 403 The Pope is a fossil ruler, *pre-mediæval. **1905** *Q. Jrnl. Microsc. Sci.* XLVIII. 490 It is evident.. that we may group the cells that are produced in the life cycle of an animal or plant into three categories, viz. *Premaiotic, Maiotic, and Post-Maiotic respectively. *Ibid.*, The synapsis represents that series of events which are concerned in causing the temporary union in pairs of pre-maiotic chromosomes, previously to their transverse separation and distribution, in their entirety, between two daughter nuclei. **1972** *Genetical Res.* XX. 201 The sensitive stage lay between the last premeiotic mitosis and the start of DNA synthesis. **1854** *Blackw. Mag.* LXXVI. 475 Still rears its crag and heathless edge Your *praememorial wall. **1956** *Amer. Jrnl. Obstetr. & Gynecol.* LXXI. 1319 The *premenarchal girl who produces estrogen but in insufficient quantities to cause bleeding. **1975** G. S. Richardson in J. J. Gold *Gynecologic Endocrinol.* (ed. 2) v. 56/1 The premenarchal ovary is a polycystic ovary with an unscarred 'porcelain' surface. **1956** *Obstetr. & Gynecol.* XIII. 724 (*caption*) Newborn. Childhood. *Premenarche. **1958** E. & E. R. Novak *Gynecol. & Obstetr. Path.* (ed. 4) xxxv. 601 (*heading*) Pre-menarche. **1937** *Human Biol.* IX. 27 The positive slope of the regression of chest-width upon chronological age is greater in the case of *premenarcheal girls than in the case of post-menarcheal girls. **1943** *Jrnl. Pediatrics* XXII. 529 An early menarche is associated with.. greater than average height and greater than average weight during the pre-menarcheal years. **1942** Mazer & Israel *Diagn. & Treatm. Menstrual Disorders* ii. 35 A study of 175 post-menarchial and 175 *premenarchial girls. **1968** M. R. Abell in J. J. Gold *Textbk. of Gynecologic Endocrinol.* ix. 193 (*heading*) Premenarchial endometrium. **1902** W. Bateson *Mendel's Princ. Heredity: A Defence* 7 The cases are all examples of discontinuous variation: that is to say, cases in which actual intermediates between the parent forms are not usually produced on crossing. [*Note*] This conception of discontinuity is of course *pre-Mendelian. **1941** J. S. Huxley *Uniqueness of Man* iv. 121 The picture of the hereditary constitution of human groups which can now be drawn in the light of modern genetics is very different from any which could be framed in the pre-Mendelian era. **1977** Kruskal & Mosteller *Representative Sampling* (Univ. Chicago Dept. Statistics) 11 The notion is like the old pre-Mendelian genetic idea of the homunculus. **1875** E. White *Life in Christ* iii. xxii. (1878) 315 By what then were *pre-messianic believers of Israel saved? **1899** R. Munro *Preh. Scot.* xii. 449 The barrows of the *premetallic period. **1966** F. Schurmann *Ideology & Organization in Communist China* 3 Some writers assert that the economy in *premodern societies is a subsystem of a larger social system. **1970** I. L. Horowitz *Masses in Lat. Amer.* i. 7 This concept equates 'mass' to forces in the old society (old in the sense of pre-socialist, rather than pre-modern). **1977** *Sci. Amer.* Oct. 96/1 Premodern medicine blamed such failures on sepsis. **1881** *Encycl. Brit.* XIII. 403/2 *Premonarchical Israel is represented as a hierocracy and Samuel as its head. **1863** Draper *Intell. Devel. Europe* iii. (1865) 60 Traces of the prehistoric, *premonumental life of Egypt. **1858** G. Duff *Sp. at Elgin* 11 Aug., Belonging as he [Lord Palmerston] does to the *premoral, as Lord Derby says he does to the prescientific, school. **1898** L. F. Ward *Outl. Sociol.* v. 112 The evolving intellect throughout all this long pre-social and pre-moral period was exclusively devoted to the egoistic interests of individuals. **1963** L. Kohlberg in *Vita Humana* VI. 13 The six developmental types were grouped into three moral levels and labelled as follows: Level I. Pre-Moral Level. **1973** M. E. Wood *Children* 26 Children are first amoral..then enter a pre-moral stage, when social and authoritarian factors are the main restraints. **1943** *Mind* LII. 19 The pseudo-morality of sanctions lacks the inward reality of morality. It is in fact a sort of *pre-morality. **1848** Bailey *Festus* xix. (ed. 3) 201 The *premortal manhood which inhered In the conception of creative mind. **1880** Fairbairn *Stud. Life Christ* xiv. (1881) 244 A covenant may be a sort of *pre-mortuary testament. **1900** J. Hutchinson in *Arch. Surg.* XI. 195 Typical lesions in all stages and degrees..from the *pre-mycosic, figured eczema to nodosities. **1916** Jordan & Ferguson *Textbk. Histol.* viii. 221 Myeloblast (*Premyelocyte; Hemoblast, Mesameboid Cell; Primitive Blood Cell; 'Lymphocyte').—This is the parent blood-cell of bone-marrow. **1931** M. G. Wohl *Bedside Interpretation of Lab. Findings* caption facing p. 88 Abnormal leucocytes:..premyelocyte with beginning neutrophilic granules. **1964** W. G. Smith *Allergy & Tissue Metabolism* iii. 44 It is accepted that eosinophils are differentiated from the premyelocytes of the bone marrow. **1963** *Jrnl. Clin. Path.* XVI. 319 Among the acute leukaemias of the granulocytic group, acute *pre-myelocytic leukaemia is distinguished by the severity of its haemorrhages, the frequency of hypofibrinaemia, a rapidly fatal course, and an unusual cellular hyperplasia. **1854** De Quincey in 'H. A. Page' *Life* (1877) II. xviii. 84 It is not only a prehistoric, but a *premythical,..even a prefabulous and a pretraditional thesis. **1938** *New Statesman* 21 May 890/1 A record whose *pre-Nazi date can be guessed from the fact that Fritz Busch conducts the Berlin State Opera Orchestra. **1972** P. Black *Biggest Aspidistra* I. iv. 41 *Brigade Exchange*, a war play.. created by the pre-Nazi German radio. **1941** *Cancer Res.* I. 45/1 The object of these investigations was the study of the influence of irritation on the first manifestation of neoplastic transformation, which, in the case of the skin, represents the conversion of the *preneoplastic thickened epithelium into a papilloma. **1978** *Nature* 13 Apr. 635/2 Electron microscopy has shown that during the latent period only preneoplastic changes resembling those of Bowen's disease are present in rat epidermis. **1885** W. Roberts *Ur. & Renal Dis.* (ed. 4) III. iv. 472 During this *prenephritic stage, high tension is produced by the contraction of the muscular walls of the arterioles. **1873** Morley *Rousseau* II. xii. 191 *Prae-Newtonians knew not the wonders of which Newton was to find the key. **1946** L. Bloomfield in C. F. Hockett *Leonard Bloomfield Anthol.* (1970) 460 Particles (**prenouns*) appear before nouns in less variety than before verbs [in Algonquian]. **1966** G. N. Leech *Eng. in Advertising* ii. 14 The pre-noun is broken down into four chief secondary classes, determiner..numeral..adjective..and a certain range of nouns, including proper names and words denoting substances. **1869** J. Eadie *Comm. Galatians* 62 This *prenuptial condition ceased. *a* **1866** J. Grote *Exam. Utilit. Philos.* xxi. (1870) 346 The *pre-observational simplicity of the philosophers whom I have just referred to. **1897** *Nat. Sc.* Feb. 79 Strictly *preorganic or azoic rocks. **1968** R. Kyle *Love Lab.* xviii. 233 Have you ever known an orgasmic woman who wanted to go back to a *pre-orgasmic condition? **1976** *Spare Rib* Nov. 16/1, I was going to start by telling you how I came to join the pre-orgasmic group, but I suppose a lot of things preceded that step. **1980** *Time* 28 Jan. 90/1 Psychologists persistently refer to unresponsive women as 'pre-orgasmic'. **1852** Bailey *Festus* xxxiii. (ed. 5) 545 See, like clouds, the gods disperse, Into their *preoriginal nothingness. **1935** *Anat. Rec.* LXIV. Suppl. No. 1. 52 The beginning of the *pre-ovulatory enlargement coincides with the beginning of oestrus. **1975** Franchimont & Burger *Human Growth Hormone* II. iii. 175 During the first 10 days, FSH and LH fell and became stable at values similar to those encountered in the normally cycling female during the preovulatory period. **1899** *Allbutt's Syst. Med.* VIII. 343 They are more continuously noisy..in this stage than in the *pre-paroxysmal. **1907** A. W. Turner *Epilepsy* vi. 121 A form of pre-paroxysmal psychosis..is the feeling of good spirits and of exceptional well-being, which precedes the onset of an attack in some cases. **1977** *Lancet* 21 May 1095/1 *Prepatency was documented in 35 patients who..started to excrete *Giardia*. The median prepatent period was 14 days. **1926** R. W. Hegner in *Q. Rev. Biol.* I. 399/1 The *prepatent period extends from the time the infective parasites enter the body of the host until their offspring can be recovered by the usual laboratory methods. **1976** *Nature* 15 July 214/2 This highly virulent strain has a pre-patent period of 8–14 d in mice. **1897** A. D. L. Napier *Menopause* iv. 78 For a variable period, usually about two years, the physiological economy is preparing for this *pre-pathological change [*sc.* the climacteric]. **1977** M. Edelman *Polit. Lang.* v. 95 Ritualistic categorization further confuses feedback by defining a substantial proportion of the population as either pathological or pre-pathological. **1890** J. Healey *Irel. Anc. Schools* 28 Another *pre-Patrician, if not pre-Christian poet..was Torna Eigas. **1899** W. M. Ramsay in *Expositor* Jan. 40 The *pre-Pauline Church in Rome. **1941** *Language* XVII. 225 A study of post-pausal and *pre-pausal allophones reveals several recurrent differences between these and the corresponding allophones occurring elsewhere than at points of open juncture. **1973** A. H. Sommerstein *Sound Pattern Anc. Greek* v. 160 *Prepausal acute*: This phenomenon may well have nothing to do with the Acute-Grave rule; rather, it may be a feature of sentence intonation, viz. rise at end of phrase. **1948** J. L. Adams tr. *Tillich's Protestant Era* viii. 134 The dark ground of *pre-personal being..is effective in every moment of our conscious existence. **1971** *Jrnl. Gen. Psychol.* LXXXIV. 257 The body, therefore, becomes man's expression in the world, the mirror of his being at the prepersonal and preobjective level. **1977** Fontana & van de Water in Douglas & Johnson *Existential Sociol.* iii. 126 For Merleau-Ponty, consciousness was basically the anonymous, prepersonal life of the body-subject. **1933** T. S. Eliot *Use of Poetry* 21 It is true also of the change from a *pre-philosophical to a philosophical age. **1939** *Mind* XLVIII. 89 Mr. Loewenberg is a man with a mission: to rescue empiricism (*i.e.* pre-philosophical empiricism) from the empiricists. **1959** J. L. Austin *Sense & Sensibilia* (1962) vi. 55 Our ordinary, unamended, pre-philosophical manner of speaking. **1957** in *Amer. Speech 1972* (1975) XLVII. 222 To be safely *pre-phonemic, let us begin with 1874, with Whitney's 'Elements of English Pronunciation', and observe what seemed important to him. **1960** H. M. Hoenigswald *Language Change* viii. 73 The doctrine of gradual phonetic change may turn out to be a remnant from pre-phonemic days. **1889** *Amer. Nat.* Oct. 926 The *preplacental absorption of food by the embryos of placentalian mammals. **1895** in *Syd. Soc. Lex.* **1968** R. A. Lyttleton *Mysteries Solar Syst.* ii. 54 Evidence seems to suggest that the meteorites do not represent original *pre-planetary material but are a later product of the solar system. **1978** *Nature* 9 Feb. 504/1 The authors thus invoke another component—a pre-planetary disk which is accreting onto the central star. **1955** *Pre-planting [see *post-emergence* s.v. post- B. 1]. **1976** *Stillwater News* (Absarokee, Montana) 1 July 15/1 Whether pre-planting, post-plant or post-emergence herbicides are used depends upon type of crop, kinds of weeds and other conditions. **1963** *Pre-political [see *pre-cultural* above]. **1977** *Jrnl. Politics* XXXIX. 7 Hobbes' resolutive-compositive method is an early and Rawls' original position a late example of the contractarian quest for political authority's pre-political foundations. **1943** *Pre-predicative [see *pre-give*, sense A. 1]. **1950** *Mind* LIX. 264 The first section of Husserl's book deals with what he calls 'pre-predicative' experience. **1971** *Jrnl. Gen. Psychol.* LXXXIV. 259 Merleau-Ponty..spoke more than previously of the interrelation of the predicative and prepredicative levels. **1975** Ld. Hailsham *Door wherein I Went* iv. 15 My formal education began at the age of five.. when I was sent to a *pre-prep school in Rosary Gardens. **1960–1** *Where* Winter 16/1 **Pre-preparatory school*, an independent school for children under about 8. **1964** *Economist* 25 Apr. 356/1 Children do enjoy their *pre-primary schooling. *Ibid.* 356/2 The pre-primary schools—voluntary to the age of five, then compulsory for one year. **1979** *Jrnl. R. Soc. Arts* CXXVII. 483/1 A task that continues uninterrupted from the pre-primary to the post-graduate class. **1975** *Nature* 11 Sept. 89/2 The existence of an analogous precursor to insulin, a *preproinsulin, was strongly supported by the experiments of M. A. Permutt. **1979** *Ibid.* 21 June 675/1 The gene coding for preproinsulin II contained an additional intron of about 500 nucleotides between the region encoding amino acids 38 and 39 of the proinsulin II peptide chain. **1892** Montefiore *Hibbert Lect.* ii. 100 The nature of the *pre-prophetic religion was determined by the character of its God. **1942** *Endocrinology* XXXI. 673 *Prepuberal castration prevents the appearance of..physiological and behavioral reactions. **1949** *Radiology* LII. 112/1 The testes of normal chicks of this age are in the prepuberal state. **1977** *Yearbk. Obstetr. & Gynecol.* 329 Seventeen were prepuberal when leukemia was diagnosed. **1942** *Endocrinology* XXXI. 674 Male sexual behavior was shown by all 10 *prepuberally castrated females. **1947** *Physiol. Rev.* XXVII. 275 Pre-puberally castrated male chimpanzees show much more sexual activity than do similarly operated rodents. **1859** *Todd's Cycl. Anat.* V. 644/2 The individual may retain..the *pre-pubertal condition. **1898** *Amer. Jrnl. Psychol.* IX. 257 The rate of growth..decreases with fluctuations until about 10 years in girls and 12 years in boys, when the prepubertal acceleration sets in. **1932** S. Zuckerman *Social Life Monkeys* xvii. 267 Louttit holds that the nosing and circling activities of the prepubertal guinea-pig are part of its sexual responses. **1977** *Daily Colonist* (Victoria, B.C.) 19 Mar. 2/1 There may be some prepubertal girls using contraceptive pills 'to be sure'. **1978** *Bull. Amer. Acad. Arts & Sci.* Feb. 22 The eunuch or the prepubertal castrate does not develop the disease. **1937** *Nature* 3 Apr. 589/1 *Prepubertally castrated male rats are not known to mate. **1942** *Psychosomatic Med.* IV. 190/1 (*heading*) Prepubertally castrated adults. **1977** *Sci. Amer.* Jan. 100/3 Samaritan religious tradition affords a kind of telescopic glimpse of the past: the ancient Judaism of *pre-rabbinical times. **1932** *Mind* XLI. 116 We mean 'taking for granted', that state of *pre-reflective unquestioning assurance. **1966** E. S. Casey tr. *Dufrenne's Notion of A Priori* 97 Pre-reflective thought experiences the *a priori* in the *a posteriori*. **1978** S. H. Hodgson *Philos. of Reflection* I. i. ii. 107 The undistinguished unity of *primary*, pre-reflective, consciousness. **1970** J. M. Edie *Patterns of Life-World* xviii. 339 Chomsky's..own investigations lead us to what Merleau-Ponty termed the '*pre-reflexive' structures of experience. **1976** *Brit. Jrnl. Sociol.* XXVII. 360 Speaking can organize a separate mode of experience which is not simply a transmutation or decipherment of prepredicative thought. It has its own distinct phenomenological properties which exceed those of the prereflexive world. **1882–3** *Schaff's Encycl. Relig. Knowl.* 1805 In the *pre-reformatory system there were no lessons for the sixth Sunday after Epiphany. **1923** H. L. Brose tr. *Sommerfeld's Atomic Struct. & Spectral Lines* iv. 211 Coulomb's law is valid and likewise ordinary (*pre-relativistic) mechanics. **1952** Koestler *Arrow in Blue* vi. 51 In pre-Relativistic days it was still just possible for the non-specialist to keep abreast of general developments in science. **1871** Tylor *Prim. Cult.* I. xi. 378 A *præ-religious condition of the human race. **17..** E. Darwin (Webster 1828), In some cases, two more links of causation may be introduced; one of them may be termed the *preremote cause, the other the postremote effect. **1796** —— *Zoon.* II. 451 The pre-remote cause or disposition to the gout. **1900** *Q. Jrnl. Microsc. Sci.* XLIV. 3 Reproductive period.—I have used this expression to denote the whole of that period in the life of a mammal, whether male or female, during which its generative organs are capable of the reproductive function; and in contrast to the *Pre-reproductive and Post-reproductive periods which severally precede and follow it, during which the generative organs are either not fully developed or are degenerate. **1952** *New Biol.* XIII. 27 In ourselves the length of the prereproductive period of life has increased. **1977** J. L. Harper *Population Biol. of Plants* 231 The pre-reproductive period of trees is usually long. **1896** E. W. Fry in *Class. Rev.* May 184/1 The so-called contracted forms of which *ama-sse* is typical were *pre-rhotacistic presents in *-se* restrained from normal phonetic development. **1863** Lyell *Antiq. Man* ii. 21 Coins..of bronze and silver belonging to the first and *pre-Roman division of the age of iron. **1937** *N. & Q.* 6 Feb. 91/2 A *pre-Romanesque church at Quintanilla de las Viñas. **1939** *Burlington Mag.* Mar. 110/1 Stone-sculptors of the pre-romanesque epoch lacked tradition and experience. **1907** H. M. Chadwick *Origin Eng. Nation* iv. 74 It is held that the remains..date from *pre-Saxon times. **1962** H. R. Loyn *Anglo-Saxon Eng.* i. 7 Big rivers such as the Thames ..preserve their pre-Saxon names. **1958** L. Bellak *Schizophrenia* i. 54 The *pre-schizophrenic personality may be sociopathic, infantile,..brilliantly highstrung. **1964** C. M. Thompson in M. R. Green *Interpersonal Psychoanal.* xxxiii. 315 So much for the outward picture of preschizophrenia. *Ibid.* 316 It is characteristic of the preschizophrenic that all true object relationships are impossible. **1965** A. F. Korner in B. I. Murstein *Handbk. Projective Techniques* ii. 29 Conversely, frank psychotics.. often produce Rorschachs that reflect less of a schizophrenic process than do records of pre-schizophrenics. **1852** Bailey *Festus* xxxi. (ed. 5) 533 As in *presecular time emergent thence. **1874** E. R. Lankester in *Phil. Trans.* CLXV. 39 The growth of the ovarian egg and its envelopes or *præseminary development. **1897** *Lippincott's Med. Dict.* 825/2 **Presenile*, occurring before old age: as, *presenile alopecia* or baldness. **1903** *Lancet* 22 Aug. 517/2 The patients in the severe cases are men as a rule in the pre-senile stage and they present well-marked cardio-vascular lesions. **1912** *Brit. Med. Jrnl.* 16 Nov. 1379/1 He has hitherto limited the term 'melancholia' to cases occurring at the climacteric and the pre-senile period of life. **1913** *Jrnl. Nervous & Mental Dis.* XL. 386 Further investigation of the types of mental makeup out of which an involutional depression may develop..may throw light on the peculiar combination of symptoms seen in the presenile psychosis. **1950** D. B. Kirby *Surg. of Cataract* x. 193/2 The presenile soft cataract up to the fourth decade may be handled by discission. **1976** F. Warner *Killing Time* I. vi. 17 Impaired mental and motor functions, presenile dementia, usually followed by death. **1880** Swinburne *Stud. Shaks.* 247 A *pre-Shakespearean word of single occurrence in a single play of Shakespeare's. **1871** Darwin in *Life & Lett.* (1887) III. 146, I should rely much on *pre-silurian times. **1861** Maine *Anc. Law* v. (1876) 114 The *prae-social state. **1962** E. Snow *Red China Today* (1963) lxxiii. 564 All three were born the 'year of the flood', 1949, and had no memory of a *presocialist China. **1965** B. Pearce tr. *Preobrazhensky's New Econ.* 88 A country like the U.S.S.R...must pass through a period of primitive accumulation in which the sources provided by pre-socialist forms of economy are drawn upon very freely. **1855** Bailey *Spir. Leg.* in *Mystic*, etc. (ed. 2) 75 For sun and moon *præsolar light precedes. **1973** *Sci. Amer.* Apr. 61/3 The molecules might be formed in the dense environs of a 'presolar nebula', that is, in the final phases of the collapse of a protostar into a self-luminous star. **1979** *Nature* 15 Feb. 556/1 According to the second model..the presolar grains condensed in a late supernova that triggered the collapse of the solar nebula. **1937** *Sci. & Society* I. 156 We have seen that *pre-Soviet scholarship.. had given a theoretical basis for the treatment of any language as potentially capable of developing any expressions required of it. **1949** M. Mead *Male & Female* xi. 230 In pre-Soviet Russia there seems to have been extraordinarily little valuation placed on women's child-bearing character. **1957** R. N. C. Hunt *Guide to Communist Jargon* xxiii. 81 Where pre-Soviet expansionist policy was concerned, the party line changed in the middle 'thirties. **1905** H. D. Rolleston *Dis. Liver* 307 *Presplenomegalic form in which the enlargement of the liver precedes that of the spleen. **1952** C. Payne-Gaposchkin *Stars in Making* (1953) ii. 43 Nebulae like the one in Orion must represent the primitive *prestellar material. **1978** *Sci. Amer.* Apr. 112/1 The observational signpost for this pre-stellar stage is the emission by the cloud's many molecules of radio waves at wavelengths measured in millimeters. **1958** C. Rabin in *Aspects of Translation* 130 *Pre-Structuralist works on grammar recognized this fact by separating the description of forms ('accidence') from the discussion of their meaning, which appeared as part of 'syntax'. **1961** *Brno Studies in English* III. 11 Cases..were decidedly unknown to pre-structuralist study of language. **1933** L. Bloomfield *Language* 220 Some suffixes have **pre-suffixal stress*: the accent is on the syllable before the suffix. **1977** *Language* LIII. 10 If a German were to create a new word by adding the suffix *-ig* 'ish' to *Kind* 'child', the result would be [kindiç] with presuffixal *d* as in [kindər]. **1973** *Publ. Amer. Dial. Soc.* LX. 34 In such dialects, the /r/ is treated as if it were *presyllabic, as an apical alveolar consonant. **1951** *Dorland's Med. Dict.* (ed. 22) 1212/1 **Presymptomatic*, existing before the appearance of symptoms. **1966** *New Society* 12 May 7/2 Donaldson's finding that one in six 'healthy' people has presymptomatic disease. **1978** *Nature* 9 Nov. 173/1 Bubbles moving in blood vessels have been successfully detected by the Doppler method in experiments confirming their significance and presymptomatic existence. **1951** N. Goodman *Struct. Appearance* I. i. 23 Care..must be exercised..when one word..has both a systematic and a *presystematic use. For example, 'is a member of' is used in several different presystematic ways and also as the mere verbal reading of the systematic sign 'ϵ'. **1964** E. Bach *Introd. Transformational Gram.* v. 92 With..the free use of any presystematic knowledge of the language, we choose the analyses which maximize the independence of the classes set up. **1951** N. Goodman *Struct. Appearance* I. i. 22, I use '*presystematically' for 'according to ordinary usage'. **1975** *Jrnl. Philos.* LXXII. 552 Presystematically, the physicalist onto-logical position is simply put: 'Everything is physical.' **1882** Siemens in *Nature* XXVI. 393 *Pre-telegraphic days, when the letter-carrier was our swiftest messenger. **1959** *Listener* 17 Sept. 429/1 The rings were unknown in *pre-telescopic times. **1976** *Jrnl. R. Soc. Arts* CXXIV. 564/1 There were even observatories in pre-telescopic times. **1852** Bailey *Festus* xxx. (ed. 5) 500 To meditative converse most devote, And strict collation of the Spirit-book With the *pretemporal volume, writ of God. **1894** Mitchell tr. *Harnack's Hist. Dogma* App. i. 319 The pretemporal existence was a matter of certainty. *Ibid.* 322 The old idea of *preterrestrial existence with God. **1966** C. G. Hempel *Philos. Nat. Sci.* vi. 75 While the internal principles of a theory are couched in its characteristic *theoretical terms*.., the test implications must be formulated in terms..which are 'antecedently understood',..terms that have been introduced prior to the theory and can be used independently of it. Let us refer to them as *antecedently available* or **pretheoretical terms*. **1966** Y. Bar-Hillel in *Automatic Transl. of Lang.* (NATO Summer School, Venice, 1962) 8 So far, I have been using 'syntactic complexity' in its pretheoretical and unanalysed vague sense. **1968** A. J. Ayer *Origins of Pragmatism* 335 So far as anything can be, qualia are pre-theoretical. **1953** H. A. T. Reiche et al. tr. *Jaspers's Tragedy is not Enough* i. 31 *Pre-tragic knowledge is rounded out, complete, and self-contained. **1957** N. Frye *Anat. Crit.* 210 The Greek *ananke* or *moira* is in its normal, or pre-tragic, form the internal balancing condition of life. **1960** H. Read *Forms of Things Unknown* xi. 177 From this point of view Stoicism is more complete; and above all that serene code of ethics achieved in ancient China—'the feeling of security without the shadow of tragedy, a natural and sublime humanity, a sense of being at home in this world, and a wealth of concrete insights', to quote Jaspers' own description of pre-tragic knowledge. **1965** N. Chomsky *Aspects of Theory of Syntax* 213 In the syntactic component of this (*pre-transformational) grammar, indices on category symbols were used to express agreement..but not subcategorization and selectional restrictions. **1973** *Word 1970* XXVI. 396 Yet perhaps all we have to do is to rephrase Cohen's distinction between *langue bébé* and *langue adulte* by calling the former 'pre-transformational language'. Then, there would still remain the necessity of explaining how..a child suddenly employs transformations. **1908** *Westm. Gaz.* 8 July 12/2 Translated from *Pre-Vedic Sanskrit. **1935** G. K. Zipf *Psycho-Biol. of Lang.* (1936) iv. 160 In pre-Vedic Sanskrit, the accent might be on the last syllable. **1905** F. E. Clements *Res. Methods Ecol.* 321 *Prevernal, pertaining to early spring. **1908** *Science* 7 Feb. 207/1 Overtopped by the autumnal, the sublayers are successively those of the serotinal, estival, vernal and prevernal. **1926** [see aspect *sb.* 14]. **1960** N. Polunin *Introd. Plant Geogr.* x. 285 In temperate forests..the seasonal aspects are apt to be important—in particular the prevernal (i.e. before spring) one of herbs which flower before the shading tree-leaves expand. **1933** Blunden *Charles Lamb* 193 It was Lamb's instinctive utterance of indignation against the spirit of the *pre-Victorians, the tendency to make a boudoir or a Persian heaven. **1964** D. Owen *Eng. Philanthropy* (1965) 5 Victorians and pre-Victorians agitated..for more efficient employment of..charitable trusts. **1973** M. R. Booth *Eng. Plays of 19th Cent.* III. 25 The materialism of the age, its social ambition and self-seeking drive..are topics not really explored in pre-Victorian comedy. **1979** 'J. Gash' *Grail Tree* i. 17 Ceramics and pre-Victorian tapestries. **1866** S. H. Hodgson *Princ. Reform Suffrage* 103 A part of the *prevolitional nature of man.

2. a. With sbs. or phrases forming *quasi*-adjs. or attrib. phrases: ***pre-advertisement, pre-advertising*** (belonging to the days before advertising was usual), ***pre-amalgamation, -betrothal, -breakfast, -Broadway, -cession, -chloroform, -Christmas, -civilization, -Civil War, -coition, -college, -computer, -consonant, -convention, -crusade, -crusading, -development, -dinner, -dispersion, -disruption, -dynamite, -Easter, -emancipation, -employment, -enclosure, -examination, -free-trade, -game, -Inca, increase, -independence, -inscription, -invasion, -Islam, -jazz, -launch, -legislation, -liberation, -life, -log-rolling, -London, -lunch, -machine, -market, -marketing, -marriage, -Mutiny, -oïdium, -ovulation, -pause, -phylloxera, -pneumatic-tire, -police, -portraying, -pottery, -printing, -qualificative, -radio, -recognition, -railroad, -railway, -Reformation, -relativity, -remittance, -Renaissance, -retirement, -revolution, -season, -seizure, -settlement, -show, -sleep, -subject, -telegraph, -television, -theatre, -tour, -treaty, -vaccination, -vowel, -wire, -work, -world.*** The use of these appears to have begun about 1860. **b.** with personal names, meaning 'before the time or public work of': e.g. ***pre-Augustine, pre-Chamberlain, pre-Gladstone, pre-Hitler, pre-Jenner, pre-Johnson, pre-Reynolds, pre-Shakespeare,*** etc. **c.** Adjs. of the type in 2 a, b above are sometimes used adverbially (cf. pre *prep.*), as *pre-emergence* below, pre-tax, pre-war *advbs.*

pre-e'mergence, occurring, performed, or applied before the emergence of seedlings from the soil; also *absol.* and as *adv.*; **pre-'flame**, occurring in a gas flow before it reaches a flame.

1889 *Pall Mall G.* 6 Nov. 1/2 In the *pre-advertisement era a good newspaper was the exclusive luxury of the rich. **1866** *Standard* 27 Aug. 4/7 Holders of *pre-amalgamation preferences. **1861** J. G. Sheppard *Fall of Rome* xiii. 719 Early British, or *pre-Augustine Christianity. **1896** Crockett *Cleg Kelly* (ed. 2) 92 The men..answering one another in *pre-breakfast monosyllables. **1977** *Times* 19 Nov. 13/3 The musical itself is definitely an oddity of the form, and comes here with less than triumphant *pre-Broadway credits. **1920** *Chambers's Jrnl.* 13 Nov. 786/2 The natives obtained, individually or communally, land to which in the *pre-cession days they could not have established a claim. **1925** T. Dreiser *Amer. Trag.* (1926) I. ii. xxvii. 338 Clyde..was invited by her to attend a *pre-Christmas dance. **1976** *Morecambe Guardian* 7 Dec. 5/2 Getting party games organised is one of those pre-Christmas chores. **1961** *Georgia Rev.* Spring 10 In the *pre-Civil War years, the South argued that the slave was not less humanely treated than the factory worker of the North. **1966** *Eng. Stud.* XLVII. 154 Professor Parry is at his best when he is dealing with New York, either the pre-Civil War capital or the tumultuous city of the 1920's. **1953** N. Tinbergen *Herring Gull's World* iv. 120 Head-tossing is the main part of the *pre-coition behaviour. **1957** R. K. Merton *Student-Physician* 122 The greater intimacy between fathers and sons during the *precollege years. **1960** *Farmer & Stockbreeder* 29 Mar. 39/1 (Advt.), Pre-College Student, not under 18,..to acquire sound agricultural background. **1976** *Sci. Amer.* Apr. 34/2 It was in this atmosphere that the National Science Foundation precollege curricula in biology and the social sciences became the focus of extended and bitter controversy. **1961** *Times* 3 Oct. (Computer Suppl.) p. viii/3 A most efficient system of manufacturing, restocking and transport had been devised in the *pre-computer days. **1949** E. A. Nida *Morphol.* (ed. 2) ii. 20 The allomorphs are listed in a structurally corresponding fashion. First is given the *preconsonant form and secondly the prevowel form. **1977** *Time* 7 Nov. 61/1 The message and the methods are modeled after those of Billy Graham, down to *precrusade organization (by a staff of 17) and convert counseling. **1869** *Routledge's Ev. Boy's Ann.* 370 It was not an uncommon event in *pre-Davenport days for some mountebank to allow himself to be tied hand and foot. **1945** *Times* 29 June 5/6 Then there was at least a scheme in the *pre-development stage to provide the V2 rocket with wings, which had great possibilities. **1942** C. Milburn *Diary* 25 Dec. (1979) 162 The sherry..was our *pre-dinner appetiser. **1963** L. Deighton *Horse under Water* xiv. 60 We went back to H.K.'s for pre-dinner drinks. **1968** 'H. Pentecost' *Gilded Nightmare* (1969) i. iii. 46 The Trapeze Bar..is a predinner meeting place for the very rich. **1978** M. Gilbert *Empty House* x. 87 Roger..was relaxing with his pre-dinner drink. **1892** J. MacKinnon *Culture in Celtic Scot.* i. v. 51 The Celts carried with them in their wanderings from their *predisruption home, a theology. **1886** F. H. Doyle *Remin.* 26 In the happy *predynamite days. **1864** Lumley *Remin. Opera* 37 Whatever success attended the *pre-Easter season. **1940**, etc. *Pre-emergence [see *post-emergence* s.v. post- B. 1]. **1971** *Arable Farmer* Feb. 15/3 Tri-allate applied pre-emergence to wheat to control wild oat. **1977** J. L. Harper *Population Biol. of Plants* 112 In addition a 'safe site' is one from which specific hazards are absent—such as predators, competitors, toxic soil constituents and pre-emergence pathogens. **1942** *Amer. Rev. Tuberculosis* XLV. 643 The increasing adoption of *preëmployment X-ray examination. **1949** H. C. Weston *Sight, Light & Efficiency* vii. 225 Whenever a pre-employment test..is applied the examinee should wear any glasses he is in the habit of wearing. **1971** *Flying* (N.Y.) Apr. 113/3 (Advt.), Airline employment test... Pre-employment tests. **1934** Webster, *Pre-enclosure. **1945** H. J. Massingham in F. Thompson *Lark Rise to Candleford* p. ix, Intact from a pre-industrial and pre-Enclosure past. **1957** *Brit. Med. Jrnl.* 7 Sept. 551/2 *Pre-examination strain can be defined as the condition wherein the nervous tension is of such a quality that it diminishes the efficiency of study and impairs the prospects of success. **1978** S. Allan *Inside Job* i. 17 She giggled nervously in the way Sheila remembered from pre-examination tension at school. **1924** *Colliery Guardian* CXXVII. 1443/2 Experiments show that contact with a heated surface may act in two ways: generally the ignition point is raised by the absorption of heat due to *pre-flame combustion on a surface large enough to be only slightly affected itself. **1973** Boldt & Griffiths in J. P. Allinson *Criteria for Quality of Petroleum Products* v. 59 Amongst the main preflame products are the highly temperature sensitive peroxides and if these exceed a certain critical threshold concentration, the end gas will spontaneously ignite before the arrival of the flame front emanating from the sparking plug: this causes detonation or 'knocking'. **1898** *Daily News* 2 Nov. 2/2 A school to whose welfare I am still as much attached as I was when in the golden sixties I enjoyed the happiness of the *pre-flogging, pre-bullying era. **1951** *Time* 26 Feb. 78 C.C.N.Y., the heavy *pre-game favorite each time, lost to Missouri (54–37), Arizona (41–38) and Boston College (63–59). **1976** *Billings (Montana) Gaz.* 17 June 1-H/5 Saturday's game at the Metra begins at 8:00 p.m., and pregame coverage goes on the air at 7:30. **1977** J. F. Fixx *Compl. Bk. Running* xxiii. 258 If at some football training tables the pregame meal is still steak, it is only because common sense is too often no match for tradition. **1938** E. Waugh *Scoop* i. iv. 74 A volume of *pre-Hitler German poetry. **1960** *News Chron.* 4 May 5/6 Old Berlin songs that recalled carefree pre-Hitler days. **1908** *Encycl. Relig. & Ethics* I. 469/2 (*heading*) The *pre-Inca people. **1950** J. H. Steward *Handbk. S. Amer. Indians* VI. 533 In both *Inca* and pre-*Inca* Coastal sites there is found..a good deal of cotton in the seed. **1974** *Encycl. Brit. Macropædia* XIV. 133/1 The dryness of the central and southern coasts has preserved the remains of a long succession of pre-Inca peoples. **1976** *Evening Post* (Bristol) 23 Apr. 21/2 (Advt.), Mini 850, antique gold, at *pre-increase price. **1977** *Horse & Hound* 14 Jan. 44/3 (Advt.), New Rice eventer at pre-increase price, £666 on the road. **1960** *Daily Tel.* 9 July 6 The example of the Congo strengthens the case..for taking every possible precaution in our own territories to maintain law and order in the tense *pre-independence days. **1977** *Time* 15 Aug. 15/1 In preindependence days, Makarios battled the British with the legendary Colonel George Grivas. **1894** *Westm. Gaz.* 22 Jan. 3/3 Merivale..wrote in the *pre-inscription and the pre-Mommsen period. **1944** *Hutchinson's Pict. Hist. War* 27 Oct. 1943–11 Apr. 1944. 413 (*caption*) A U.S. officer pointing out a target to general Eisenhower during *pre-invasion manoeuvres by an American Armoured Unit in England. **1967** *Freedomways* VII. 111 He knows the bombing and shelling and mining we are doing are part of traditional pre-invasion strategy. **1926** Whiteman & McBride *Jazz* vii. 157 The foreign market for American music in *pre-jazz times was poor. **1934** C. Lambert *Music Ho!* iii. 198 The melodic shape is clearly the most important factor in pre-jazz popular music. **1959** 'F. Newton' *Jazz Scene* iv. 68 Most of the material thus collected was 'pre-jazz'. **1963** *IEEE Trans. Product Engin. & Production* VII. iv. 39/1 The Surveyor spacecraft is subjected to several combinations of environment during *prelaunch, boost, free flight, retro, landing and lunar operation. Vibration and shock are negligible during prelaunch operations because of careful handling. **1967** A. Battersby *Network Analysis* (ed. 2) 303 He then goes on to build up the pre-launch stock, advising M as soon as the required stock level has been reached. **1970** N. Armstrong et al. *First on Moon* ii. 45 The conversation..as always during a pre-launch breakfast, was studiedly casual. **1967** *Listener* 13 Apr. 481/1 What I should like to see is more consultation with Members of Parliament before legislation is prepared: what I call *pre-legislation committees. *a* **1974** R. Crossman *Diaries* (1976) II. 528 A few weeks ago Roy Jenkins wrote me a long minute to say that he couldn't permit a pre-legislation committee on privacy. **1962** E. Snow *Red China Today* (1963) ii. 25 Near the Hsin Ch'iao I picked one [*sc.* a two-seater pedicab] up, pumped by a neatly dressed gray-haired gentleman who said he pulled a rickshaw at the old Peking Hotel in the '*pre-liberation' days. **1974** tr. *Wertheim's Evolution & Revolution* 287 In pre-liberation China religion in the Confucianist form was associated with the establishment. **1937** R. A. Wilson *Birth of Lang.* iv. 99 The formative energy which produced the tree must..have been latent in the *pre-life matter. **1958** *Observer* 15 June 13/4 Scientists believe that pre-life processes may be occurring on the moon. **1962** F. I. Ordway et al. *Basic Astronautics* vi. 258 The search for evidence of extraterrestrial life, or at least prelife carbon compounds. **1967** J. B. Davis *Petroleum Microbiol.* ii. 19 There is no evidence of pre-life organic matter being incorporated in the sedimentary environment of geologic formations. **1887** *Pall Mall G.* 5 Jan. 4/1 The simple souls of the *pre-log-rolling era. **1959** P. Bull *I know Face* vi. 102 The Leeds incident occurred quite late in the *pre-London tour. **1961** *Nottingham Even. Post* 28 July 12 The play is on its pre-London tour. **1962** G. Butler *Coffin in Oxford* iv. 64 They had..made a film..and had now moved..to Oxford for the pre-London run. **1938** D. Kincaid *Brit. Social Life in India* xii. 276 The elderly gathered together in the clubs for *pre-lunch drinks. **1955** A. Ross *Australia 55* 131 This was the first of four successive gloomy pre-lunch sessions for England. **1974** *Times* 4 Nov. 14/4 An appropriate pre-lunch appetizer. **1957** K. A. Wittfogel *Oriental Despotism* i. 13 Temperature and surface are the outstanding constant elements of the agricultural landscape. This was true for the *pre-machine age; and it is still essentially true today. **1970** G. E. Evans *Where Beards wag All* xvi. 177 All, or nearly all, of the old terms connected with the pre-machine farming in the region are no longer used. **1963** *Wall St. Jrnl.* 9 Oct. 3/1 The council..proposed '*premarket' safety testing of cosmetics. **1977** *N.Y. Rev. Bks.* 14 Apr. 37/2 The modifications of law which constitute the subject of his book are elements of what Karl Polanya called the 'great transformation' from a pre-market to a market society. **1960** *Farmer & Stockbreeder* 5 Jan. 95/1 Results on farms throughout the country confirm the evidence of *pre-marketing trials that Dictol will protect animals against husk. **1902** *Daily Chron.* 1 Sept. 3/4 The attitude taken up by *pre-Mutiny officers towards their troops. **1920** G. Saintsbury *Notes on Cellar-Bk.* i. 7 This was *pre-oïdium and pre-phylloxera wine. **1922** *Proc. Soc. Exper. Biol. & Med.* XIX. 380 Coincident with ovulation in the pigeon there occurs an increase of the blood sugar to 25 per cent. or more above the *pre-ovulation value. **1975** *Ann. Human Biol.* II. 325 Variations in the pre-ovulation interval are also indicated by the timing of mid-cycle hormonal peaks. **1934** M. K. Pope *From Latin to Mod. French* ii. xvii. 222 The *prae-pause form of the word, the one with sounded consonant, was retained very generally. **1953** *Language* XXIX. 419 There is agreement that there are pitch factors in at least two different kinds of pre-pause terminals ('terminal junctures'). **1920** *Pre-phylloxera [see *pre-oïdium*]. **1957** R. Campbell *Portugal* 53 We may never hope to taste again the crowning glories of the best pre-phylloxera vintages. **1972** *Country Life* 25 May 1309/3 Christie's will sell over 100 small lots of mid-19th century port and pre-phylloxera claret. **1897** *Daily News* 4 Jan. 6/3 The picturesqueness of Cairo in the *pre-plaster-of-Paris age. **1864** *Realm* 22 June 5 The highwayman of our old-fashioned romances and *pre-police reports cried, 'Stand and deliver!' as he met you. **1876** Geo. Eliot *Dan. Der.* xxxvi, Old portraits stretching back..to the *pre-portraying period. **1949** W. F. Albright *Archaeol. Palestine* iii. 62 In the *pre-pottery Neolithic Age man took an important forward step in the Near East. **1960** K. M. Kenyon *Archaeol. in Holy Land* ii. 45 It may be inferred with a high degree of probability that this Pre-Pottery Neolithic A settlement of Jericho was based on a successful system of agriculture. **1977** G. Clark *World Prehist.* (ed. 3) ii. 51 Phases II and III of the Mesolithic period in the Levant, commonly termed 'Pre-pottery Neolithic A and B' in the literature. **1924** H. E. Palmer *Gram. Spoken Eng.* 183 (*heading*) Adverbs in the *pre-qualificative position... These immediately precede the qualificative... They also precede any other adverb they may modify. **1946** R. Blesh *Shining Trumpets* (1949) x. 220 The first hot records..sold by the millions and, in those *preradio days, disseminated jazz more rapidly..than a score of travelling bands. **1949** Bruner & Postman in Bruner & Krech *Perception & Personality* (1950) 26 Differential availability [of response systems]..leads to certain characteristic 'normalizing' *prerecognition responses in our incongruity experiments. **1970** *Jrnl. Gen. Psychol.* LXXXIII. 24 As a corollary of lower recognition thresholds with increased information, we can expect fewer prerecognition responses. **1900** *Daily News* 26 Nov. 8/3 Mr. Tuckwell remembers Oxford in the *pre-railway, pre-science, pre-earnestness days. **1860** Thackeray *Round. Papers, De Juventute*, We elderly people have lived in that *prae-railroad world. *Ibid.*, There will be but ten *prae-railroadites left. **1868** A. K. H. Boyd *Less. Mid. Age* 9 Only three dwellings in the city date from *pre-reformation days. **1929** Pre-Reformation [see *pre-Renaissance* below]. **1920** A. S. Eddington *Space, Time & Gravitation* ix. 149 Action is one of the two terms in *pre-relativity physics which survive unmodified in a description of the absolute world. **1946** *Mind* LV. 161 A pre-relativity physicist could use the figure..by interpreting AM and TM as curves of velocity. **1890** 'R. Boldrewood' *Col. Reformer* (1891) 281 This is my..*pre-remittance stage. **1929** T. S. Eliot *Dante* i. 19 A directness of speech which Dante shares with other great poets of pre-Reformation and *pre-Renaissance times. **1976** R. Pfeiffer *Hist. Classical Scholarship 1300–1850* i. 21 There seems to be a slight shifting of emphasis to the advantage of the classics, inconceivable in pre-Renaissance times. **1961** A. Heron *Solving New Probl.* 21 Does the evidence obtained support a rationale for adapting a *pre-retirement planning and preparation programme to the needs of older employees of different occupational levels? **1965** J. Pollitt *Depression & its Treatment* vii. 91 Older patients have greater difficulty than those of pre-retirement age in readjusting their lives after illness. **1976** *Evening Post* (Nottingham) 16 Dec. 2/6 Support for a pre-retirement course run by Gedling Borough Council was so good that plans for a second session are already in the pipeline. *a* **1902** S. Butler *Way of All Flesh* (1903) xiv. 63 The *pre-revolution French peasant. **1905** *Daily Chron.* 11 Dec. 3/3 The obvious fact about painting in England in *pre-Reynolds days was the indifference to native practitioners. **1939** H. Nicolson *Diary* 3 Apr. (1966) 394 Apparently many of their [*sc.* the Polish army's] guns are pre-Revolution guns of the Russian Army. **1978** N. Marsh *Grave Mistake* iii. 91 A pre-revolution Russian stamp that was withdrawn on the day it was issued. **1961** *Dallas Morning News* 10 Oct. 2–2 It looks as if coach Hank Stram's men will meet the Bills just as they are developing into the kind of team they were expected to be in *pre-season reckonings. **1970** N. ARMSTRONG et al. *First on Moon* vii. 144 In sports, the Houston Oilers are showing plenty of enthusiasm in their early preseason workouts. **1975** *Cricketer* May 27/2 D. J. Insole will be giving all first-class umpires a pre-season briefing. **1979** *N.Y. Post* 10 Aug. 17 In one of our most bizarre pre-season presidential campaigns, an incumbent President is being dismissed by both the opposition and large sectors of his own party as a non-person. **1926** ROWS & BOND *Epilepsy* iv. 87 In the *pre-seizure period the disturbances of consciousness often commence with a slight difficulty in the power of attention and pass through the stages of dreamy states and fugues to complete unconsciousness. **1966** *Jrnl. Neurol., Neurosurg. & Psychiatry* XXIX. 253/2 The E.E.G. appeared normal on all the pre-seizure tracings. **1926** *Glasgow Herald* 19 Oct. 9 Before the contests, there are whispers of excellent *pre-show performances of competing cows. **1960** *Farmer & Stockbreeder* 2 Feb. 84/1 Sons of several famous bulls were in competition in the showyard and their fortunes were the subject of considerable pre-show speculation. **1964** *Language* XL. 269 Nobody has made a thorough study of *presleep soliloquies before. **1970** N. ARMSTRONG et al. *First on Moon* xiii. 333 We're standing by for an exciting evening of TV and a presleep report. **1924** H. E. PALMER *Gram. Spoken Eng.* II. 182 Adverbs in the *pre-subject position. **1961** R. B. LONG *Sentence & its Parts* xx. 471 No comma is used after pre-subject adjunct clauses functioning as clause markers in assertives. **1976** *Archivum Linguisticum* VII. 32 It looks like the same pre-subject position that we called I in the 'kernel' form of the sentence. **1965** *B.B.C. Handbk.* 28 Even though BBC radio's evening audience is much less than it was in *pre-television days it is by no means inconsiderable. **1969** *Listener* 15 May 700/3 Sponsorship has entered into the scheme of things. So has advertising, which was never around in pre-television days. **1974** *Times* 17 Aug. 7/4 The older school of comedians, the pre-television comics. **1953** R. FULLER *Second Curtain* v. 74 The place was filling up: a few were eating *pre-theatre meals. **1967** A. BAILEY in L. Deighton *London Dossier* 49 This is really a lunch or pre-theatre restaurant, since it closes at 8.30 p.m. **1977** *Rolling Stone* 7 Apr. 30/2 *Pre-tour jitters are an occupational hazard the McGarrigle sisters have avoided up to now. **1897** *Allbutt's Syst. Med.* II. 184 In Great Britain during *prevaccination times, small-pox showed a periodic intensity of prevalence, every three, four, or five years. **1949** E. A. NIDA *Morphol.* (ed. 2) ii. 16 Word-initial *prevowel glottal stops. **1977** *Time* 26 Dec. 41/2 The message rings out, too, at the early morning *pre-work prayer meetings held by businessmen. **1923** D. H. LAWRENCE *Birds, Beasts & Flowers* 99 Fishes, With..their *pre-world loneliness.

II. Denoting local position: in which *pre-* = before, in front of, anterior to.

These appear to have arisen since 1825: see PREOCULAR 1826, *predorsal* 1831, *prepigmental* 1835.

These are generally written without the hyphen, which may however be used when it makes the composition clearer, as before a vowel. *Pre-* is usually (ˌpriː), but may be (prɪ) when it immediately precedes the main stress, as in *pre'vertebral*.

3. In adjs. (also sometimes used as sbs.), chiefly *Anat.* and *Zool.*, denoting parts or organs situated in front of (or, rarely, in the front part of) other parts or organs. Also occas. with sbs. directly forming sbs., as PREALBUMIN.

pre-ace'tabular, in front of the acetabulum or socket of the hip; **pre-'anal**, in front of the anus; **pre-a'ortic**, in front of the aorta; **pre-a'picial**, *Conch.*: see quot.; **pre-'auditory**, in front of the auditory nerve; **pre'basal**, in front of a base or basal part; **pre'basilar**, in front of a basilar part; **prebrachial** (-'breɪkɪəl), in front of the brachium or upper arm; applied to a group of muscles; also to a vein in the wing of some insects; **prebranchial** (-'bræŋkɪəl), in front of the gills or branchial region; **prebronchial** (-'brɒŋkɪəl), in front of the bronchi or bronchia; **pre'buccal** [L. *bucca* cheek], situated in front of the mouth or buccal cavity; = PREORAL; **pre'cardiac**, in front of or (in *Human Anat.*) above the heart; **pre'caudal**, situated in front of the caudal vertebræ; **pre'central**, anterior to the centre; applied to parts of the brain; **pre'cerebroid**, situated anterior to a cerebroid organ; **precoc'cygeal**, in front of the coccyx; **pre'condylar, -oid**, in front of the condyles; **pre'corneal**, situated on the front of the cornea (*Cent. Dict.* 1890); **pre'costal**, in front of the ribs; **pre'crucial**, anterior to the crucial sulcus of the brain; **pre'dentary**, in front of the dentary bone (in some reptiles); **pre'digital**, noting the two remiges attached to the second phalanx of the second digit; **pre'dorsal**, anterior to the dorsum or dorsal region; **pre'genital**, in front of the genital aperture or external genital organs (*Cent. Dict.*); **pre'glenoid**, in front of the glenoid fossa: applied to a process of the temporal bone (also *ellipt.* as *sb.*): also **pregle'noidal** (*ibid.*); **pre'hyoid**, in front of the hyoid bone; **pre'labial**, in front of the lips, or a labium (in an insect or crustacean); **pre'lumbar**, in front of the loins; **preman'dibular**, in front of the mandible: applied to a bone of the lower jaw in some fishes, reptiles, etc.; also as *sb.*; **pre'motor**, applied to the anterior part of the precentral area of the frontal lobe of the brain, which is concerned with the co-ordination of activities in the motor area immediately posterior to it; **preoc'cipital**, in front of the occipital lobe of the brain; **preœso'phageal**, in front of the œsophagus, or, in invertebrates, of the œsophageal ring; **pre'palatal**, in front of the palate; *spec.* in *Phonetics*, of a consonant articulated with obstruction of the airstream immediately in front of the palate; also **pre'palatine** (*Cent. Dict.*); **preparoc'cipital**, in front of the paroccipital convolution of the brain; **prepa'tellar**, situated above or in front of the patella; ***prepatellar bursitis***, inflammation of the prepatellar bursa; = *housemaid's knee* s.v. HOUSEMAID c; **preperito'neal**, in front of the peritoneum; **prepig'mental**, in front of the pigmental layer of the eye; **prepi'tuitary**, anterior to the pituitary body; **pre'pontile**, in front of the *pons Varolii* (PONS 2); **prepro'static**, in front of the prostate gland; **prepy'loric**, anterior to the pylorus or small end of the stomach; **pre'rectal**, in front of the rectum; **pre'renal**, in front of the kidney; **pre'sacral**, in front of the sacrum; **presemi'lunar**, in front of the semilunar lobe of the cerebellum; **pre'spinal**: see quot.; **prespi'racular**, in front of a spiracle; **presub'terminal**, before a subterminal; **pre'sylvian**, in front of the Sylvian fissure of the cerebrum; **presym'physial**, in front of a symphysis or point of union, usually of the jaw; **pretho'racic**, in front of the thorax; **pre'tibial**, in front of, or on the front part of, the tibia; **pre'tracheal**, in front of the trachea or windpipe; **pretym'panic**, in front of the tympanum of the ear; also as *sb.* = *pretympanic bone* or *cartilage*; **pre'vertebral**, in front of the vertebral column; **pre'vesical**, in front of the bladder (*Cent. Dict.*).

1866 *Pre-acetabular [see *postacetabular*, in POST- B. 2]. **1870** ROLLESTON *Anim. Life* 29 The presence of praeacetabular spurs. **1890** *Cent. Dict.*, **Preanal.* **1897** *Allbutt's Syst. Med.* II. 1034 The four pairs of pre-anal and three pairs of post-anal papillæ on the tail of the male. **1890** BILLINGS *Med. Dict.*, **Preaortic plexus*, aortic plexus. **1858** MAYNE *Expos. Lex.*, *Præapiciālis*,.. applied to the hinge of a bivalve shell, when, being on the back of the valve, it is before the summit: *preapicial. **1875** HUXLEY & MARTIN *Elem. Biol.* (1883) 187 The *Præauditory nerves are the following. 3. *Motores oculorum* [etc.]. **1890** *Cent. Dict.* s.v., The *prebasal plate of a myriapod. **1858** MAYNE *Expos. Lex.*, *Prebasilar. **1887** COUES & SHUTE, *Prebrachial [group of muscles] (*C.D.*). **1893** E. A. BUTLER *Househ. Insects* 179 The chief difference is in the præbrachial nervure (the third on the disc of the wing towards the tip). **1887** *Trans. Roy. Soc. Edin.* 108 The aperture in the *prebranchial zone is small. **1888** *Encycl. Brit.* XXIII. 611/2 The prebranchial zone, which separates the branchial sac behind from the branchial siphon in front. **1883** *Athenæum* 29 Dec. 870/3 The air-cells of the flamingo, which were shown to..agree with those of storks in having the *præbronchial air-cell much divided. **1858** MAYNE *Expos. Lex.*, *Præbuccalis*,.. applied to a kind of funnel which precedes the mouth..in the Holothuriæ, termed the *prebuccal cavity. **1890** *Cent. Dict.*, **Precardiac.* **1895** *Syd. Soc. Lex.*, *Precardiac*, on the cephalic side of, or superior..to, the heart. **1854** MURCHISON *Siluria* x. (1867) 238 A wide expanded *pre-caudal joint. **1890** BILLINGS *Med. Dict.*, **Præcentral sulcus*, ..furrow on convex surface of hemispheres in front of anterior central convolution, running parallel to central sulcus. **1899** *Allbutt's Syst. Med.* VII. 284 The ascending frontal or precentral convolution [of the brain]. **1870** ROLLESTON *Anim. Life* 107 Which has not any separate *præ-cerebroid ganglion frontale developed upon it as in insects. **1893** *Athenæum* 25 Mar. 382/2 The parts of the urostyle and *precoccygeal vertebræ. **1866** OWEN *Anat. Vert.* II. 78 The position..of the *precondylar groove.. helps in the determination of the bird-affinities. *Ibid.* 532 The jugular fossa is distinct from the *precondyloid and carotid foramina. **1854** —— *Skel. & Teeth* in *Orr's Circ. Sc.* I. *Org. Nat.* 197 For the insertion of the *precostal ligament. **1885** *Athenæum* 3 Jan. 20/3 A distinct and conspicuous lozenge-shaped patch of brain substance defined by the crucial and *precrucial sulci. **1889** NICHOLSON & LYDEKKER *Palæont.* II. 1155 The mandible [in the Iguanodontidæ], again, presents the peculiar feature of having a horse-shoe-like *predentary bone at the extremity of the symphysis. **1887** WRAY in *Proc. Zool. Soc.* 348 The *pre-digitals are the only other remiges of the manus which show modifications of any interest. **1831** R. KNOX *Cloquet's Anat.* 772 They.. anastomose with those of the heart and lungs, and enter the *predorsal ganglia. **1842** DUNGLISON *Med. Lex.*, *Prædorsal Region* of the vertebral column is the anterior surface of the dorsal region. **1949** I. F. & W. D. HENDERSON *Dict. Sci. Terms* (ed. 4) 351/1 **Prehyoid*, mandibulo-hyoid; *appl.* cleft between mandible and ventral parts of hyoid arch. **1974** D. & M. WEBSTER *Compar. Vertebr. Morphol.* vii. 129 In living amphibians the hypobranchial muscles can be divided into a prehyoid and a posthyoid group. **1852** DANA *Crust.* I. 24 The anterior portion of the *prælabial plate pertains to the same segment as the second antennæ. **1842** DUNGLISON *Med. Lex.* s.v., The *prelumbar surface of the spinal column is the anterior surface of the lumbar portion. **1854** OWEN *Skel. & Teeth* in *Orr's Circ. Sc.* I. *Org. Nat.* 271 There are three..laniaries at the anterior end of each *pre-mandibular bone. *Ibid.* 273 The exposed portions of the premaxillaries and premandibulars are incased by a complicated dental covering. **1900** MIALL & HAMMOND *Harlequin Fly* vi. 169 The third is the premandibular segment. **1932** *Brain* LV. 534 In the baboon forced grasping appeared five to six days after removal of the motor and *premotor areas. **1978** *Sci. Amer.* Oct. 52/2 (*caption*) The premotor area is involved in complex motor activity such as operating a typewriter. **1889** *Buck's Handbk. Med. Sc.* VIII. 152/2 *Preoccipital fovea. **1854** OWEN *Skel. & Teeth* in *Orr's Circ. Sc.* I. *Org. Nat.* 208 The *prepalatal or naso-palatal aperture. **1902**, etc. Pre-palatal [see *medio-palatal* adj. s.v. MEDIO- 2]. **1925** P. RADIN tr. *Vendryès's Language* I. i. 23 We distinguish..the pre-palatals and the post-palatals. **1934** PRIEBSCH & COLLINSON *German Lang.* II. i. 88 The *s* was more prepalatal. **1958** J. BERRY in J. A. Fishman *Readings Sociol. of Lang.* (1968) 741 Is it better..that all related languages of southern Ghana write the prepalatal affricate '*tʃ*' uniformly so, or (under cultural pressure of the trade language), '*ch*'? **1964** *Archivum Linguisticum* XVI. 22 The affricate *ch* [č] or the corresponding pre-palatal *x* [š]. **1973** *Amer. Speech 1969* XLIV. 265 An *r* produced by passing the breath between the underside of the apex of the tongue and the postalveolar or prepalatal region. **1977** *Word 1972* XXVIII. 248 Caballero..described the [ž] as a voiced prepalatal. **1882** C. B. NANCREDE in J. Ashhurst *Internat. Encycl. Surg.* II. 717 (*heading*) *Pre-patellar bursa. **1890** BILLINGS *Med. Dict.*, *Prepatellar*, in front of the patella. **1895** in *Syd. Soc. Lex.* **1900** *Lancet* 20 Oct. 1142/1 The 'deep prepatellar bursa'.. is surely a misnomer, for the bursa is not prepatellar in the least degree. **1902** R. T. FRANK tr. *Albert's Diagnosis Surg. Dis.* xxxiii. 370 Prepatellar bursitis requires but casual mention. A strictly circumscribed, elastic tense swelling directly in front of the patella is characteristic. **1927** W. C. CAMPBELL *Orthopedics of Childhood* xii. 217 Pre-patellar bursitis is commonly due to excess kneeling. The symptoms are similar to those of bursitis elsewhere. **1964** *Australasian Post* 21 May 13, I rushed off in anguish and looked up prepatellar bursitis in a medical dictionary. It was.. housemaid's knee. **1904** *Br. Med. Jrnl.* 3 Dec. 83 *Preperitoneal Fatty Tumours. **1835–6** *Todd's Cycl. Anat.* I. 553/1 We..regard [this layer]..as constituting a true *prae-pigmental retina. **1839–47** *Ibid.* III. 235/2 Certain accessory glands..called..*preprostatic. **1875** HUXLEY & MARTIN *Elem. Biol.* (1877) 132 A short '*pre-pyloric' ossicle which ascends obliquely forwards and is articulated with the anterior edge of the pyloric piece. **1877** HUXLEY *Anat. Inv. Anim.* vi. 319 With this process is articulated, posteriorly, a broad prepyloric ossicle. **1890** BILLINGS *Med. Dict.*, *Prerectal. **1878** BELL tr. *Gegenbaur's Comp. Anat.* 434 The lumbar region contains the *pre-sacral group of vertebræ. **1889** NICHOLSON & LYDEKKER *Palæont.* II. 1056 There are 29 vertebræ, of which 18 are presacral. **1842** DUNGLISON *Med. Lex.*, **Prespinal*, that which is situate before the spine. The prespinal surface of the vertebral column is the anterior surface. **1902** *Nature* 16 Oct. 604/1 The last-mentioned [*sc.* the chorda tympani] is spoken of as..*pre-spiracular in position. **1975** *Ibid.* 10 Apr. 483/3 Patterson confirms the homology between the spiracular groove of primitive actinopterygians..and the 'pre-spiracular groove' of rhipidistians. **1895** MEYRICK *British Lepidoptera* 239 Discal dot beyond median *praesubterminal not black-marked. **1868** OWEN *Anat. Vert.* III. 137 Cerebral Folds: Sylvian ..*Presylvian..Postsylvian. **1888** *Geol. Soc. Quart. Jrnl.* XLIV. 146 The largest *presymphysial bone recorded in the annals of vertebrate anatomy. **1870** ROLLESTON *Anim. Life* 108 The number..is never made up of the same *pre-thoracic, thoracic, abdominal, and post-abdominal factors. **1842** DUNGLISON *Med. Lex.*, **Pretibial*,..situate before the tibia; as the *ilio-pretibial* and *ischio-pretibial* muscles. **1897** *Allbutt's Syst. Med.* II. 457 Diminished tactile sensibility of the pretibial skin area. **1898** *Ibid.* V. 211 The glands most affected are the anterior or *pretracheal. **1854** OWEN *Skel. & Teeth* in *Orr's Circ. Sc.* I. *Org. Nat.* 178 The foremost of the two middle pieces is the '*pre-tympanic'. **1858** MAYNE *Expos. Lex.*, *Pretympanic*, applied..to the anterior subdivision of the tympanic pedicle which supports the mandible in fishes. **1880** GÜNTHER *Fishes* iii. 55 The next bone of the series is the pretympanic or metapterygoid, a flat bone forming a bridge towards the pterygoid. **1840** G. V. ELLIS *Anat.* 570 A gangliated portion situated by the side of the vertebral column, and of *prevertebral plexuses.

pre (priː), *prep.* [A further development of PRE- B. 2 c; cf. POST *Lat. prep.* 6.] = BEFORE *prep.* 8.

Usu. found in contexts where *before* would be equally appropriate and more agreeable.—R.W.B.

1973 G. SIMS *Hunters Point* xiii. 119 'Have you tried phoning David's friends in Los Angeles?'..'They are all pre my era and I don't know their names.' **1975** H. KISSINGER in *Dept. of State Bull.* 6 Oct. 532 Pre my being in office; those decisions were made in the previous Administration.

pre-abdomen, -accentual, -accusation: see PRE- A. 4, B. 1 d, A. 2.

preace, obs. by-form of PRESS *sb.*[1] and *v.*[1]

pre-acetabular: see PRE- B. 3.

preach, *sb.*[1] *colloq.* [f. PREACH *v.*; in quot. 1597 after F. *prêche* m. a Protestant sermon (16th c. in Littré), similarly f. *prêcher* to PREACH.] An act of preaching; a preachment; a discourse.

c **1500** *Wyntoun's Cron.* v. 3392 (Wemyss MS.) At Constantinople, quhare he had His duelling and his prechis [*other MSS.* prechynge] maid. **1597** HOOKER *Eccl. Pol.* v. xxviii. §3 According to this forme of theirs..No Sermon, no Seruice. Which..occasioned the French spitefully to terme Religion in that sort exercised, a meere Preach. **1643** in *7th Rep. Hist. MSS. Comm.* 445 Mr. Henderson immediately after made a thing between a speech and a preach to us. **1838** *Lett. fr. Madras* (1843) 138 [I] took the opportunity of being alone with him to give him a preach, and try to do him a little good. **1870** MRS. WHITNEY *We Girls* vi, I preached a little preach.

preach, *sb.*[2] Colloq. abbrev. of PREACHER. *U.S.*

1968 D. WILKERSON *Hey, Preach—you're comin' Through!* 9 He grabbed my arm and blurted: 'Hey, Preach—you're comin' through!' **1969** C. F. BURKE *God is Beautiful, Man* (1970) 96 Ananias..puttin' his hands on him like the preach down at the revival camp does.

preach (priːtʃ), *v.* Forms: 3–6 **preche**, 4 **preyche**, **preeche**, 4–6 (chiefly *Sc.*) **preiche**, 5–6 **prech**, 6 **preache**, 6– **preach**. [ME. *prechen*, a. F. *prêcher*, OF. *prechier*, syncopated form of *preëchier* (11th c. in Godefroy) from **predichier*, ad. L. *prædicāre* to proclaim publicly, announce, in eccl. L. to preach, f. PRÆ- + *dicāre* to proclaim.

The eccl. word *prædicāre* was adopted early in nearly all the Romanic and Teutonic langs., as It. *predicare*, Prov. *prezicar*, Sp., Pg. *predicar*; OSax. *predikôn*, OE. *predician*, OHG. *predigôn*, ON. *prédika*.]

1. a. *intr.* 'To pronounce a public discourse upon sacred subjects' (J.); to deliver a sermon or religious address (now usually from or on a text of Scripture).

a **1225** *Ancr. R.* 70 Ȝe ne schulen.. preche to none mon.. Seinte Powel uorbead wummen to prechen. *a* **1300** *Cursor M.* 175 Iesu crist.. openlik bigan to preche [*MS. F.* preyche]. *c* **1330** R. BRUNNE *Chron.* (1810) 226 Þe pape his bulle sent hider vnto þe legate, & comanded him to preche þorgh alle þe lond. **1387** TREVISA *Higden* (Rolls) V. 215 He hadde i-preched aȝenst wommen þat pleyde aboute þe ymage of Eudoxia. *c* **1425** *Cast. Persev.* 804 in *Macro Plays* 101 3a! whanne þe fox prechyth, kepe wel ȝore gees! **1500–20** DUNBAR *Poems* xiv. 6 Sic pryd with prellattis, so few till preiche and pray. *c* **1532** DU WES *Introd. Fr.* in *Palsgr.* 952 To preache, *prescher*. **1567** *Gude & Godlie B.* (S.T.S.) 45 Till all Creature for to preiche. **1644** MILTON *Areop.* (Arb.) 65 Christ urg'd it as where with to justifie himself, that he preacht in publick. **1674** PRIDEAUX *Lett.* (Camden) 6 On Sunday morneing I went to hear on Bayly of Maudlins preach. **1697** M. HENRY *Life P. Henry* Wks. 1853 II. 674/1 He preached over the former part of the Assembly's Catechism, from divers texts; he also preached over Psalm 116. **1763** JOHNSON in *Boswell* 31 July, Sir, a woman preaching is like a dog's walking on his hind legs. It is not done well; but you are surprized to find it done at all. **1853** J. H. NEWMAN *Hist. Sk.* (1873) II. I. iii. 138 The Greek clergy preached against them as heretics.

b. To utter a serious or earnest exhortation, esp. moral or religious; to talk seriously in the way of persuasion or moralizing. Now usually dyslogistic: To give moral or religious advice in an obtrusive or tiresome way.

1523 LD. BERNERS *Froiss.* I. lxxxvii. 110 They were brought to his tent, and there they were so preched to that they tourned to sir Charles parte. **1602** SHAKS. *Ham.* III. iv. 126 His forme and cause conioyn'd, preaching to stones, Would make them capeable. **1754** RICHARDSON *Grandison* (1810) V. xxv. 168 Let us.. when we are called upon to act a great or manly part, preach by action. **1806** METCALFE in Owen *Wellesley's Desp.* (1877) 807 To meet their ambition ..with the language of peace, would be to preach to the roaring ocean to be still. *a* **1834** COLERIDGE in Patmore *Friends & Acquaint.* (1854) I. 89 'Pray, Mr. Lamb, did you ever hear me preach?' 'Damme', said Lamb, 'I never heard you do anything else'. **1875** W. S. HAYWARD *Love agst. World* 45 Why do you preach to me in that manner?

c. Phr. ***to preach to the converted***: to commend an opinion to those who already assent to it.

1867 MILL *Exam. Hamilton's Philos.* (ed. 3) xiv. 319 Dr. M'Cosh is preaching not only to a person already converted, but to an actual missionary of the same doctrine. **1916** G. SAINTSBURY *Peace of Augustans* iii. 144 One may be said to be preaching to the converted and kicking at open doors in praising.. the four great novelists of the eighteenth century. **1971** *It* 2–16 June 14/4 The problem is as usual that one tends to be preaching to the converted—so the important thing is to make sure that people who don't know are informed.

2. a. *trans.* To proclaim, declare, or set forth by public discourse (the gospel, something sacred or religious). Also with *obj. cl.*

c **1290** *S. Eng. Leg.* I. 24/10 To preche cristendom. **1297** R. GLOUC. (Rolls) 1528 Seinte peter.. sende seint Marc þe ewangelist in to egypt vor to preche þen gospel þat he adde imaked. **1382** WYCLIF *1 Cor.* i. 23 Forsoth we prechen Crist crucified. **1388** —— *Rom.* x. 15 As it is writun Hou faire ben the feet of hem that prechen pees, of hem that prechen good thingis. *c* **1450** *St. Cuthbert* (Surtees) 1826 Cuthbert, sittand at þe borde, Prechid to þaim goddis worde. **1535** COVERDALE *Isa.* lxi. 1 Yᵉ Lorde hath anoynted me, and sent me, to preach good tydinges vnto the poore. **1590** SPENSER *F.Q.* II. x. 53 Joseph of Arimathy, Who brought with him the holy grayle, they say, And preacht the truth. **1651** HOBBES *Leviath.* III. xli. 263 He was to preach unto them, that he was the Messiah. **1864** TENNYSON *Sea Dreams* 21 Not preaching simple Christ to simple men.

b. To set forth or teach (anything) in the way of exhortation; to advocate or inculcate by discourse or writing; to exhort people to (some act or practice). Also with *obj. cl.*

a **1340** HAMPOLE *Psalter* cxxi. 8, I prechid pes, þat neghburs & breþere be samynd in charite. *c* **1400** *Rom. Rose* 6181 [To] preche us povert and distresse, And fisshen hemself greet richesse. **1523** LD. BERNERS *Froiss.* I. 136 [He] preched to theym that they shulde disheryte the erle Loyes. *Ibid.* 752 Than the prelates.. began to preche this voiage in maner of a crosey. **1590** SHAKS. *Com. Err.* v. i. 174 My Mʳ preaches patience to him. **1667** MILTON *P.L.* XI. 723 And to them preachd Conversion and Repentance, as to Souls In prison. **1709** PRIOR *Hans Carvel* 47 At first He therefore Preach'd his Wife The Comforts of a Pious Life. **1875** JOWETT *Plato* (ed. 2) V. 47 He practised the lesson.. which Hesiod only preached. **1906** MARIE CORELLI *Treas. Heaven* i, Are you resolved to preach copy-book moralities at me?

c. ***preach up***: to extol, commend, or support by preaching; to discourse in praise of. So ***preach down***: to decry or oppose by preaching; to discourse against; to put down or silence by preaching.

1644 J. GOODWIN *Danger Fighting agst. God* 10 [He] preacheth error up, and truth downe. **1724** A. COLLINS *Gr. Chr. Relig.* Pref. 56 Preaching down the receiv'd notions both of Jews and Gentiles. **1796** BURNEY *Mem. Metastasio* II. 190 It is easy to preach up fasting, upon a full stomach. **1855** TENNYSON *Maud* I. x. iii, Last week came one to the county town, To preach our poor little army down.

3. To utter or speak publicly, deliver (now only a sermon, a religious or moral discourse).

c **1400** *Beryn* 119 Thouȝe it be no grete holynes to prech þis ilk matere, And þat som list not to her it; ȝit [etc.]. *c* **1400** *Destr. Troy* 2207 When Priam hade his prologe preched to ende, Ector hym answarede esely and faire. **1549** (*title*) The fyrste Sermon of Mayster Hughe Latimer, whiche he preached before the Kynges Maiest. **1625** BP. HALL (*title*) A Sermon of publike Thancksgiuing preacht before his Maᵗⁱᵉ. **1706** E. WARD *Wooden World Diss.* (1708) 82 He cooks by the Hour-Glass, as the Parsons preach Sermons. **1715** DE FOE *Fam. Instruct.* I. iii. (1841) I. 58, I had such a lecture preached to me yesterday by.. our own youngest child. **1798** COLERIDGE *Fears in Solitude* 65 Words that even yet Might stem destruction, were they wisely preached.

†**4.** With personal obj. (orig. indirect): To preach to; to address in the way of exhortation (public or private); to exhort, instruct. *Obs.* **a.** on religious subjects; **b.** in any sense.

c **1290** *S. Eng. Leg.* I. 89/88 Þis holie man honourede hem þe more, And prechede heom ofte of clannesse. *c* **1290** *Beket* 1932 ibid. 162 Seint thomas.. Stod and prechede al þat folk þat mani a man i-sai. **1362** LANGL. *P. Pl.* A. Prol. 56, I Font þere Freres all þe Foure Ordres, Prechinge þe peple for profyt of heore wombes. *c* **1386** CHAUCER *Frankl. T.* 96 They prechen hire, they telle hire nyght and day That causelees she sleeth hir self allas. *a* **1450** MYRC *Festial* 82 Þys byschop had preched hym all þat he couþe, and fonde hym euer þe lengur þe wors. *c* **1500** *Melusine* xxiv. 196 How, sire knyght,.. are ye come hither for to preche vs? **1523** LD. BERNERS *Froiss.* I. 576 The foles & outragious people.. sayd howe they were preched inough. **1706** E. WARD *Wooden World Diss.* (1708) 45 He shall preach ye.. about giving Cæsar his Due. **1709** [see 2 b].

5. To bring or put by preaching into or out of some specified state; to affect in some way by preaching. (Cf. *preach down* in 2 c.)

1609 B. JONSON *Sil. Wom.* IV. iv, We had a Preacher that would preach folke asleepe still. *a* **1716** SOUTH *Serm.* (1823) IV. 427 He may preach his heart out.., and all to no purpose. *a* **1845** HOOD *Recipe Civiliz.* 88 What reverend bishop.. Could preach horn'd Apis from his temple? **1852** M. ARNOLD *Empedocles* I ii, These hundred doctors try To preach thee to their school.

Hence **preached** *ppl. a.*

1854 MARION HARLAND *Alone* ix, It did me more good than the preached sermons I have listened to since. **1891** S. MOSTYN *Curatica* 36 Both the preacher—and the preached —are too weary to do justice to them.

preachable ('priːtʃəb(ə)l), *a.* In 5 preche-. [f. PREACH *v.* + -ABLE: cf. OF. *preëschable*, L. *prædicābil-is*.] Capable of being preached, or preached about or from; affording material for a sermon or religious discourse.

c **1449** PECOCK *Repr.* I. xvi. 89 Textis and parabolis and othere precheable processis. **1895** H. R. REYNOLDS *Lamps Temple* vii. 110 It is clearly your duty and function to discern the preachable aspects of theology. **1906** H. VAN DYKE *Manhood, Faith, Courage* xi. 242 Jesus Christ is the foundation of a truly preachable and powerful Gospel.

preachee (priː'tʃiː). *nonce-wd.* [f. PREACH *v.* + -EE.] A person preached to; one to whom a sermon or exhortation is addressed.

1806 *Sporting Mag.* XXVIII. 237 The preachee and flogee, in the late assault and battery case. **1864** J. R. GREEN *Lett.* (1901) 141 Preaching implies some common understanding between preacher and preachee.

preacher ('priːtʃə(r)). Forms: 3–4 prechur, (3 -or, 4 -ore, -ure), 3–6 prechour, (4–5 -oure), 4 preychour, preichour (also 6 *Sc.*), 4–5 (6 *Sc.*) precheour, 4–7 precher, (5 -owre, 6– ar), 5–6 preachour, 6 *Sc.* preicheour, -eir, -er, 6– preacher. [ME. *precho(u)r*, a. OF. *prech(e)or*, earlier *preëch(e)or* (13th c. in Godef.), popular ad. L. *praedicātōr-em* a preacher, whence also It. *predicatore*, Prov. *prezicaire*, Sp., Pg. *predicador*: see PREACH *v.* and -ER².] One who preaches.

1. a. One who proclaims or sets forth religious doctrine by public discourse; one who delivers a sermon or sermons; *esp.* one whose occupation or function it is to preach the gospel; a minister of religion; *spec.* one licensed to preach.

a **1225** *Ancr. R.* 10 Prelaz & treowe prechures. *a* **1300** *Cursor M.* 20934 (Edin.) He firste was werrayure, eftirward bicom prechure [*v.rr.* -ur, -our, preichour]. *c* **1305** *Edmund Conf.* 314 in *E.E.P.* (1862) 79 Þe beste prechour he was ihol̃de þat me ow[h]ar vnderstode. *c* **1325** *Metr. Hom.* Prol. 3 Forthi suld ilke precheour schau The god that Godd hauis gert him knau. **1377** LANGL. *P. Pl.* B. XIX. 226 Prechoures & prestes & prentyce[s] of lawe. *c* **1380** WYCLIF *Wks.* (1880) 23 þat suche prechoris ben heretikis. *c* **1449** PECOCK *Repr.* I. xvi. 88 A famose and a plesaunt precher to peple in a pulpit. **1530** PALSGR. 34 As a famous preachour. **1548** UDALL, etc. *Erasm. Par. Matt.* iii. 28 That now was the tyme to playe the preacher. **1561–2** *Reg. Privy Council Scot.* I. 202 Sustentatioun of the precheouris and readaris. **1562** in Strype *Ann. Ref.* (1709) I. xxvii. 284 By a preacher is meant such an one as hath preached before his ordinary, and hath his approbation under seal to be a preacher. *a* **1631** DONNE *Serm.* lvii. (1640) 574 A word of the fœminine gender, not Concionator, but Concionatrix, a Shee-Preacher. **1662** PEPYS *Diary* 2 Nov., To church, and there being a lazy preacher I slept out the sermon. *a* **1774** GOLDSM. tr. *Scarron's Com. Romance* (1775) I. 289 While he rehearsed his heroics, they walked cap in hand before him, respecting him like a high-way preacher. **1859–60** J. H. NEWMAN *Hist. Sk.* (1873) III. II. ii. 232 John of Antioch.. had been the great preacher of the day. **1899** *Allbutt's Syst. Med.* VI. 887 This [paralysis] gives rise to a peculiar position of the hand which has been named 'the preacher's hand'.

b. One who exhorts earnestly; one who advocates or inculcates something by speech or writing. Also *fig.*

c **1386** CHAUCER *Wife's Prol.* 165 Now dame.. by god and by seint Iohn Ye been a noble prechour in this cas. **1599** SHAKS. *Hen. V*, IV. i. 9 They are our outward Consciences, And Preachers to vs all. **1706** SWIFT *Th. Various Subj.* Wks. 1841 II. 304/1 No preacher is listened to but Time. **1900** SPIELMANN *Ruskin* 107 The artists welcome him as a writer, and he would be taken for an art-preacher.

c. With *of*: One who preaches (something specified). So ***preacher up*** (cf. PREACH *v.* 2 c).

1377 LANGL. *P. Pl.* B. XIII. 428 Prechoures of goddes wordes. *a* **1425** *Cursor M.* 21179 (Trin.) Þese were þe apostlis twelue.. precheres [*earlier MSS.* spellers] of trouþe. **1552** ABP. HAMILTON *Catech.* (1884) 6 Precheouris of the word of God. **1611** BIBLE *Transl. Pref.* 4 The first Preachers of the Gospel. **1649** MILTON *Eikon.* xii, We have him still a perpetual preacher of his own virtues. **1860** TYNDALL *Glac.* I. xxii. 158 The precipice to my left was a continual preacher of caution. **1870** LOWELL *Study Wind.* 139 The denouncer of shams, the preacher up of sincerity.

†**2.** (In full, ***friar preacher***.) A name for the order of Dominican friars. Also ***preaching friar***: see PREACHING *ppl. a.* Cf. PREDICANT. *Obs.*

1297 R. GLOUC. (Rolls) 10105 Ther after the verste ȝer þe ordre bigan of frere prechors. *c* **1380** WYCLIF *Sel. Wks.* III. 353 Prechouris and Menours seyn þe reverse. *c* **1394** *P. Pl. Crede* 154 Þanne þouȝt y to frayne þe first of þis foure ordirs, And presede to þe prechoures to proven here wille. **1474** CAXTON *Chesse* 130 To the frere prechours an hondred pounde. **1544** tr. *Littleton's Tenures* (1574) 41 b, In the order of fryers mynoures or preachers.

3. *spec.* A name for Solomon as supposed speaker in the Book of Ecclesiastes; hence, that book itself.

1535 COVERDALE *Eccl.* i. I. 2 These are the wordes of the Preacher, the sonne of Dauid, kynge of Ierusalem. All is but vanite, saieth yᵉ preacher [*Vulg.* dixit Ecclesiastes, WYCLIF seide Ecclesiastes]. **1579** FULKE *Heskins' Parl.* 7 The book of Psalmes, the Preacher, & the song of Salomon.

4. *attrib.* and *Comb.*, chiefly appositive, as ***preacher-editor***, ***-musician***, ***-playwright***, ***-saint***, ***-teacher***; also ***preacher-like*** adj. and adv.; **preacher-in-the-pulpit**, a local N. American name of *Orchis spectabilis*; **preacher-man** *U.S. dial.*, = sense 1 a.

1884 MILLER *Plant-n.*, *Orchis spectabilis*, Preacher-in-the-pulpit, Showy Orchis of N. America. **1895** *Westm. Gaz.* 24 July 7/1 He may be described as preacher-teacher to the pitmen. **1899** in H. Wentworth *Amer. Dial. Dict.* (1944) 474/1 Preacher-man. **1900** *Westm. Gaz.* 13 Dec. 7/3 If he thought he could help the preacher-editor he would. **1904** R. SMALL *Hist. U.P. Congregations* II. 488 [He] returned to preacher life again. **1913** H. KEPHART *Our Southern Highlanders* xiii. 286 Everywhere in the mountains we hear of biscuit-bread.. preacher-man, granny-woman. **1977** *Times* 23 May 5/1 A nice, homespun preacherman who spoke with a Southern drawl.

Hence **'preacherdom**, the realm or community of preachers, preachers collectively; **'preacherless** *a.*, without a preacher; **'preacherling**, a petty or inferior preacher; **'preacherly** *a.*, of or pertaining to preachers.

1891 *Sat. Rev.* 7 Nov. 516/1 The veriest dumb dog in *preacherdom. **1893** *Boston Mission. Herald* Dec. 526 The converts from *preacherless villages are swept off their feet by the tide of persecution. **1772** NUGENT tr. *Hist. Friar Gerund* II. 27 A certain *preacherling pronounced, or was to pronounce, a funeral oration. **1905** A. LANG in *Longm. Mag.* Aug. 376 Under any despotism, lay or priestly or *preacherly.

preacheress ('priːtʃərɪs). [f. PREACHER + -ESS. Cf. OF. *proicheresse* (Godef.).] A female preacher. (Used only for distinction or emphasis.)

1649 ROBERTS *Clavis Bibl.* 365 In the Heb. this word is.. in the Feminine Gender; and so may be translated exactly, The Congregatrix, or the Preacheresse. **1671** H. M. tr. *Erasm. Colloq.* 231 How come we by this preacheress? **1880** FOWLER *Locke* vi. 101 They listened to the famous Quaker preacheress, Rebecca Collier.

preachership ('priːtʃəʃɪp). [f. as prec. + -SHIP.] The office of a preacher.

a **1656** BP. HALL *Specialities in Life* Wks. 1808 I. p. xxxii, By occasion of the public preachership of St. Edmund's Bury then offered me upon good conditions. **1757** WARBURTON *Lett. to Hurd* cxvi. (1809) 259 You have seen by the papers the disposition of the preachership to Dr. Ross. **1855** MACAULAY *Hist. Eng.* xiv. III. 459 Jeremy Collier, who was turned out of the preachership of the Rolls, was a man of a much higher order. **1900** *Westm. Gaz.* 27 Nov. 12/1 To secure a fitting successor to the Rev. T. W. Lupton, who has been Preacher of Gray's Inn for many years... The Preachership has been held by many distinguished men in the past. **1903** M. A. TUCKER in *Eng. Hist. Rev.* Apr. 283 In 1503.. the Lady Margaret preachership was founded through the influence of John Fisher, at that time vice-chancellor of the University of Cambridge.

b. With *his*, *your*, as a humorous title.

1772 NUGENT tr. *Hist. Friar Gerund* I. 483 What does his Preachership mean?

†**'preachery.** *nonce-wd. Obs.* Preaching.

1818 W. TAYLOR *Hist. Surv. Germ. Poetry* (1830) I. 107 A deistical creed.. superscribed *Poetæ Kazungali*; that is, *The Poet's Preachery*.

preachify ('priːtʃɪfaɪ), *v. colloq.* [f. PREACH *v.* + -(I)FY: cf. *speechify*.] *intr.* To preach in a factitious or a tedious way; to make a 'preachment'. Often merely contemptuous for *preach*. Hence **'preachifying** *vbl. sb.* and *ppl. a.*; also **,preachifi'cation**.

1775 S. J. PRATT *Liberal Opin.* liv. (1783) II. 147 He wrote obstinately on,..preachifying, till he piously picked my pocket of above a hundred and fifty guineas. **1828** tr. *Manzoni's Betrothed Lovers* I. vi. 180 When in his preachifying, he fixes his eyes on me, I am afraid that he will shoot out before everybody—those twenty five lira! **1843** LOCKHART in *Croker Papers* (1884) 6 Dec., Alison deserves all anybody can say..of his coxcombical pomposity and preachification. **1848** THACKERAY *Van. Fair* x, She has written to say that she won't stand the preachifying. **1869** MISS MULOCK *Woman's Kingd.* II. 137, I am going to preachify in earnest; and..it is about a very serious thing. **1916** W. OWEN *Let.* 13 July (1967) 399 His dogmatic, pig-headed, preachifying, self-sufficient manners and domineering tone. **1978** J. ANDERSON *Angel of Death* vii. 70 I'm not a great admirer of..paternalistic, preachifying Christianity.

preachiness ('priːtʃɪnɪs). *colloq.* [f. PREACHY + -NESS.] The quality of being preachy.

1861 *Illustr. Lond. News* 13 Apr. 336/1 He made a capital speech..notwithstanding the drawback of a slight preachiness—so to speak—of tone. **1892** LOUNSBURY *Stud. Chaucer* I. iv. 478 It is pervaded..by a general flavor of preachiness, not delicate but obtrusive.

preaching ('priːtʃɪŋ), *vbl. sb.* [-ING[1].]

1. The action of the verb PREACH; the delivery of a sermon or public religious discourse; the practice or art of delivering sermons.

c **1275** *Passion our Lord* 671 in *O.E. Misc.* 56 We iherden heom heryen in heore preching After vre tunge þen heoueliche kyng. **13..** *Cursor M.* 196 (Gött.) For his preching [*v.r.* sermon] þai him thrett. *c* **1400** MAUNDEV. (1839) xxii. 239 The prechynge of religiouse cristen men. *c* **1440** *York Myst.* xxi. 6 Men are so dull þat my preching Serues of noght. **1532** MORE *Confut. Tindale* Wks. 601/1 They could not beleue it at the preaching of a woman, without any other miracle. **1560** DAUS tr. *Sleidane's Comm.* 60 The preaching of the Gospell. **1673** *True Worsh. God* 45 Preaching is nothing else but Publishing, Declaring, or Pronouncing what is said to be Preached. **1681–6** J. SCOTT *Chr. Life* (1747) III. 428 By an immediate miraculous Unction of the Holy Ghost, by which they were inspired with the Gifts of Preaching. **1882** J. PARKER *Apost. Life* I. 96 Apostolic preaching was religious preaching,..and it kept itself to this one theme—the turning away men from their iniquities.

2. with *a* and *pl.* **a.** The delivering of a sermon; that which is preached, a sermon or discourse; **b.** (chiefly *Sc.*) a public religious service.

c **1449** PECOCK *Repr.* 90 For without him Grees goon on out of gree and prechingis rennen arere. **1508** DUNBAR *Tua Mariit Wemen* 71 At playis, and preichingis, and pilgrimages greit. **1523** FITZHERB. *Husb.* §155 A preachyng or a sermon is where a conuocacyon or a gatherynge of people on holy dayes..[is] in chirches or other places & tymes set & ordeyned for yᵉ same. **1535** COVERDALE *Jer.* li. 64 Thus farre are yᵉ preachinges of Ieremy. —— *Jonah* iii. 2 Preach vnto them the preachinge, which I bade the. *a* **1548** HALL *Chron., Hen. VIII* 138 b, This infamie was spoken in preachynges and euerywhere. *c* **1650** Z. BOYD in *Zion's Flowers* (1855) Introd. 50 There is not a preaching preached but some gracious pickle falleth upon some heart. **1837** HT. MARTINEAU *Soc. Amer.* III. 145 In New England, a vast deal of time is spent in attending preachings, and other religious meetings. **1861** M. PATTISON *Ess.* (1889) I. 48 We find the Germans..attending the preachings in Allhallows.

3. *attrib.* and *Comb.*, as ***preaching age, business, place, -stand, -stole, time, tour, -yard***, etc.; **preaching-cross**, see quot. 1882; **preaching-station**, a station or fixed place to which a missionary or preacher comes from time to time to hold a religious service. See also PREACHING-HOUSE.

1440–1 *Norwich Sacrist's Roll* (MS.), Pro magnis portis de le prechyngyerd juxta Carnarium. **1549** LATIMER *5th Serm. bef. Edw. VI* (Arb.) 139 *Scala cœli*, is a preachynge matter..and not a massyng matter. **1556** *Chron. Gr. Friars* (Camden) 20 Pecoke..stode at Powlles crosse,..& there he abjuryd & revokyd them in the prechenynge tyme in the presens of the byshoppe of Cauntorbury. **1571** GOLDING *Calvin on Ps.* xxix. 9 To appoint the temple as it were the preaching place of God's glory. **1641** *Arminian Nunnery* 7 By the preaching-place stood the Font. **1686** PLOT *Staffordsh.* 275 He left..3083 Sermons..accounted a prodigious number in this preaching age. **1845** A. WILEY in *Indiana Mag. Hist.* (1927) XXIII. 37 Many new neighbors were taken in as preaching places. **1848** *Wesleyan Missionary Notices* VI. 164/1 In my last I expressed a desire..to open a preaching-place in a mountain district [of Jamaica]. **1856** MRS. STOWE *Dred* I. xxiii. 314 The assembly poured in and arranged themselves before the preaching-stand. **1857** P. CARTWRIGHT *Autobiogr.* viii. 85 We took in a new preaching-place at a Mr. Moor's. **1875** W. MᶜILWRAITH *Guide Wigtownshire* 86 A preaching-station in connection with the Reformed Presbyterian Church, Stranraer. **1882** OGILVIE, *Preaching Cross*, a kind of cross formerly erected on a highway or in an open place, at which the monks and others were wont to preach. **1894** HALL CAINE *Manxman* 24 Cæsar returned home from a preaching tour. **1953** M. POWYS *Lace & Lace-Making* vi. 67 A small piece of lace like a straight collar about seven inches long and one and a half inches wide could be used as a 'protective' for a preaching stole. **1959** C. L. WRENN *Word & Symbol* (1967) 23 The association of the saintly first preachers of Christianity in religious memory with the 'preaching crosses', which the missionary first set up at his oratory, is a well-known feature of the early Celtic Church. **1960** *Church & People* Nov.–Dec. 182 Africans flocking to our Mission churches and preaching places. **1970** M. SWANTON *Dream of Rood* 13 It is clearly a preaching cross. Its message is evangelical, stating the role of Christ in the world of men. **1972** *Country Life* 17 Feb. 408/1 One such building at Sare dedicated to Saint Francis Xavier has a most unusual statue in coloured wood showing the saint in cassock, surplice and preaching stole.

'preaching, *ppl. a.* [f. PREACH *v.* + -ING[2].] That preaches: see the verb.

preaching friar, (*spec.*) a Dominican; = PREACHER 2.

1583 STUBBES *Anat. Abus.* II. (1882) 71 Are those preaching prelates,..or else reading ministers? *c* **1585** R. BROWNE *Answ. Cartwright* 12 The preaching Minister can not cause them to bee a Church of God. **1650** R. STAPYLTON *Strada's Low C. Warres* II. 35 So that nothing was done to oppose the preaching-men. **1700** TYRRELL *Hist. Eng.* II. 882 The Preaching Friars and Minors exhorted him. **1855** MACAULAY *Hist. Eng.* xii. III. 140 It was known that a preaching friar had been exerting himself to inflame the Irish population of the neighbourhood against the heretics.

Hence **'preachingly** *adv.*, in a preaching manner.

1657 J. SERGEANT *Schism Dispach't* Post-Script, Their old method of talking preachingly, quotingly and quibblingly.

'preaching-house. [f. PREACHING *vbl. sb.* + HOUSE *sb.*] A house or building devoted to or adapted for preaching; *spec.* Wesley's name for a Methodist place of worship, in frequent use among Methodists in the 18th and early 19th c.

1747 J. WESLEY *Jrnl.* 2 Nov. (1912) III. 321 Mr. J. Richards had just sent his brother word that he had hired a mob to pull down his preaching-house that night. **1760** WESLEY *Jrnl.* 16 Sept., I ordered all the windows of the preaching-house to be set open. *a* **1791** —— *Wks.* (1830) VIII. 321 Warn them..Against calling..our Houses, 'Meeting-houses': Call them plain preaching-houses, or chapels. **1763** LADY F. GARDINER in Coke & Moore *Wesley* III. ii. (1792) 414, I have never..been at the preaching-house in a morning yet, as they preach so early. **1817** S. DREW *T. Coke* iv. 49 The building of a preaching-house [in New York] was taken into serious consideration. This was ..accomplished in the year 1768, being the first Methodist preaching-house that ever presented itself to view in the western world. **1874** MICKLETHWAITE *Mod. Par. Churches* 1 The old preaching-house type of the Georgian period.

† **'preachman.** *Obs. rare.* [f. PREACH *v.* + MAN *sb.*[1]] A man who preaches, a preacher. (Usually *contemptuous.*)

c **1645** HOWELL *Lett.* II. xxxiv, Som of our Preachmen are grown dog mad, ther's a worm got into their toungs, as well as their heads. **1677** W. HUBBARD *Narrative* (1865) II. 197 Madockawando..began to demand something for Satisfaction,..not understanding before that his Father was a great Preachman, as they use to call it. **1727–8** in *Reliq. Hearnianæ* (1857) II. 675 She beareth..in a feild of sedition a crop-eared preachman.

preachment ('priːtʃmənt). [ME. *prechement*, a. OF. *prechement*, earlier *preë(s)chement* (12th c. in Godef.), ad. L. *praedicāmentum*, in med.L. a public speech; cf. PREDICAMENT, PREACH *v.*, -MENT.]

1. The fact or action of preaching; delivery of a sermon, or of a discourse or exhortation. Now usually: Obtrusive or wearisome discourse.

c **1330** R. BRUNNE *Chron.* (1810) 222 A legate Ottobon þe pape hider sent, To mak þe barons on þorgh his prechement. **13..** *Reinbrun* cviii. in *Guy Warw.* p. 667 Sire, let be þe prechement: Hit is þe meche schame. *c* **1500** *Melusine* xxiv. 196, I take my dysport in your talkyng & prechement. **1600** W. WATSON *Decacordon* (1602) 226 They rose vp presently in armes at Saint Iohns-towne (excited by Knox his preachment). **1660** H. MORE *Myst. Godl.* VI. xiv. 255 How vain a thing is it to make this Man that Angel that preached the Everlasting Gospel, whenas that Angelical Preachment was at least seven or eight hundred years before he lived. **1672** KIRKMAN *Eng. Rogue* II. 247, I..performed my Preachment and Disputation to the general satisfaction of all. **1889** D. HANNAY *Capt. Marryat* viii. 125 It [*Masterman Ready*] is didactic, and yet there is no preachment.

2. With *pl.* The delivery of a sermon; a sermon, discourse, or exhortation. Usually *contemptuous.*

c **1400** *Beryn* 1263 Is this a sermon, or a prechement? **1565** T. STAPLETON *Fortr. Faith* 51 b, To folow the preachments of a few apostat friers and monkes. **1602** WARNER *Alb. Eng.* IX. liii. (1612) 238 Making teadious Preachments, of no edifying powre. **1660** MILTON *Brief Notes on Serm.* Wks. 1738 I. 604 The rest of his Preachment is meer groundless Chat. **1742** RICHARDSON *Pamela* III. 263 There were such Preachments against Vanities, and for Self-denials. **1864** J. H. NEWMAN *Apol.* App. 9 This Volume of Sermons then cannot be criticised at all as preachments; they are essays.

preachy ('priːtʃɪ), *a. colloq.* [f. PREACH *v.* + -Y.] Inclined to preach; given to preaching; characterized by a preaching style.

1819 MISS MITFORD in L'Estrange *Life* (1870) II. 70 He was a very good man..though abundantly heavy, preachy and prosy. **1859** HOLYOAKE in *Reasoner* 27 Feb. 66/1 The Rev. Mr. M...was a little preachy and complacent. **1890** *Spectator* 15 Mar., It belongs to the class of preachy novels. **1955** A. HUXLEY *Let.* 29 May (1969) 748 If I seem to be smug and preachy, forgive me. **1966** *Word Study* Feb. 5/2 Getting so dogmatic, or preachy, or stuffy that our students rebel against us. **1978** *Time* 3 July 15/2 He is tiresomely preachy in his talks with non-Israeli leaders, repeating to the point of boredom his odd fact-and-fiction litany of Jewish biblical and legal rights, his self-justification for Irgun atrocities and his blend of self-righteous arrogance.

pre-ack'nowledge, *v.* [PRE- A. 1.] *trans.* To acknowledge beforehand or as a preliminary. Hence **pre-ack'nowledged** *ppl. a.*

1657 J. SERGEANT *Schism Dispach't* 67 A preacknowledged Infallibility strengthen'd by a long Possession. *Ibid.* 655 Had there not been some preacknowledg'd power to ground and countenance such a demand.

pre-acquaint (priːə'kweɪnt), *v.* [PRE- A. 1.] *trans.* To acquaint beforehand, inform previously. Const. *with.* So **pre-a'cquaintance**, previous acquaintance; **pre-a'cquainted** *ppl. a.*, having previous acquaintance or knowledge.

1609 B. JONSON *Sil. Wom.* II. v, You haue beene pre-acquainted with her birth, education [etc.]. **1633** SHIRLEY *Witty Fair One* I. iii, My intention was to pre-acquaint you. *a* **1670** HACKET *Abp. Williams* I. (1693) 75 The Terms of the Common Law..seem Barbarous to the vulgar Ear and had need to be familiariz'd with pre-acquaintance. **1702** STEELE *Funeral* III. i, Leave the care of Lady Charlotte to me; I'll pre-acquaint her, that she may not be frightened. **1751** HARRIS *Hermes* II. i. (1765) 223 From implying an ordinary pre-acquaintance, to presume a kind of general and universal Notoriety. **1775** T. SHERIDAN *Art Reading* 169 We are pre-acquainted with the sounds of the words.

pre-act (priː'ækt), *v.* Also 7 præact. [PRE- A. 1.] *trans.* and *intr.* To act beforehand. So **pre-'acting** *ppl. a.*; **pre-'action**, previous action.

1646 SIR T. BROWNE *Pseud. Ep.* II. ii. 61 An iron..being already informed by the Loadstone and polarily determined by its preaction. **1655** FULLER *Ch. Hist.* XI. ii. §33 Those [recreations], which, though acted after Evening-Service, must needs be preacted by the fancy..all the day before. **1660** A. SADLER *Subject's Joy* 2 She also (to acheer the King) doth..præsagingly præact his just Inauguration. **1796** C. CALDWELL *Three Phenom. Fever* 10 These phenomena can no more occur, than an effect can..take place without the pre-existence and pre-action of its cause. **1870** PROCTOR *Other Worlds* viii. 179 There is no form of force which is not the representative of some other pre-acting form of force.

† **pre'acuate**, *v. Obs. rare*[−0]. [irreg. f. L. *præ-acu-ĕre* to sharpen at the end, or to a point (f. PRÆ- before + *acuĕre* to sharpen) + -ATE[3].] (See quot.) So † **preacu'ation**.

1623 COCKERAM, *Præacuate*, to make very sharpe. *Ibid.* II, Sharpening or whetting, *preacuation*.

pread, variant of PREDE *sb.* and *v. Obs.*

pre-adamic (priːə'dæmɪk), *a.* [f. PRE- B. 1 + ADAMIC.] Anterior to Adam: = next, B. 1.

1846 in WORCESTER citing I. TAYLOR. **1855** BAILEY *Mystic* 54 To him came too from Preadamic kings The shield of power. **1875** E. WHITE *Life in Christ* II. xii. (1878) 133 By geology we have learned that there was a long pre-adamic history of the globe.

pre-adamite (priː'ædəmaɪt), *sb.* and *a.* Also without hyphen, and with capital A. [ad. mod.L. *praeadamita* (whence also F. *préadamite*): see PRE- B. 1, ADAM[1], -ITE[1].]

A. *sb.* **1.** One who lived (or one of a race held to have existed) before the time of Adam.

An appellation given by Isaac de la Peyrère in his *Præadamitæ*, 1655, to a race of men, the progenitors of the Gentile peoples, supposed by him to have existed long before Adam, whom he held to be the first parent of the Jews and their kindred only.

1662 STILLINGFL. *Orig. Sacr.* III. iv. §2 If the report given of things in Scripture bee true, the hypothesis of Præ-Adamites is undoubtedly false. **1775** ADAIR *Amer. Ind.* 11 The wild notion which some have espoused of the North American Indians being Prae-Adamites, or a separate race of men. **1879** tr. *De Quatrefage's Hum. Spec.* 31 The descendants of these Preadamites were identical with the Gentiles.

† **2.** A believer in the existence of men before Adam. *Obs.*

1710 STEELE *Tatler* No. 256 ¶4 Mr. Bickerstaff..finding Reasons, by some Expressions which the Welshman let fall in asserting the Antiquity of his family, to suspect that the said Welshman was a Præ-adamite. **1768–74** TUCKER *Lt. Nat.* (1834) II. 468 St. John had nothing of the preadamite belonging to him.

¶ **3.** ? *erron.* for ADAMITE *sb.*[1] 2.

1709 STEELE *Tatler* No. 69 ¶7 Dancing without Clothes on, after the manner of the Præ-Adamites. **1710** STEELE & ADDISON *Tatler* No. 257 ¶12 There were written on the Foreheads of these dead Men several hard Words, as Præ-Adamites, Sabbatarians, Camaronians, Muggletonians.

4. *N.Z.* An inhabitant of Canterbury Province before the settlement of 1850.

1930 L. G. D. ACLAND *Early Canterbury Runs* 1st Ser. i. 3 The old 'Pre-Adamites'..were those who had bought land from the New Zealand Company and settled here before the Canterbury settlers arrived. **1949** A. H. REED *Story of Canterbury* iii. 55 To the Hays and Sinclairs and other 'pre-Adamites'—as those few who had arrived before the 'Pilgrims' came jocularly to be called—these ships represented shops, schools, churches, roads and other amenities of which they had for so long been deprived. **1977** *N.Z. Herald* 8 Jan. 1-6/6 Any reader whose antecedents were among these 'Pre-Adamites', as they are called, is invited to send their names..to [address given].

B. *adj.* **1.** That existed before Adam; belonging to the time previous to that of Adam; prehuman.

1786 tr. *Beckford's Vathek* (1883) 142 Upon two beds of incorruptible cedar, lay recumbent the fleshless forms of the Preadamite Kings, who had been monarchs of the whole earth. **1836** LANE *Mod. Egypt.* I. x. 283 The Ginn are said to be of præ-adamite origin, an intermediate class of beings between angels and men. **1851** RICHARDSON *Geol.* (1855) 271 The bones of the *Mastodon* and *Megatherium*—those terrestrial giants of the pre-Adamite earth. **1877** DAWSON *Orig. World* xv. 356 Our knowledge of pre-Adamite and present nature. **1916** *Nature* 25 May 259/2 For imitation, a pre-Adamite simian character, plays no small part in the ostensible development, mental, moral, and otherwise, of gregarious folk.

2. Relating to the time, or to a race, previous to Adam; belonging to the Pre-adamites (sense A. 2).

1882 OGILVIE, *Preadamite, a*...2. Pertaining to the Pre-adamites: as the preadamite theory.

Hence **pre-ada'mitic, -ical** *adjs.* = PRE-ADAMITE B. 1; **pre-'adamitism**, the doctrine of the existence of pre-adamite man.

1716 *Gentleman Instr.* II. (ed. 6) 414 Upon what Memorials do you ground the Story of your Præ-adamitical Transactions? **1790** *Monthly Rev.* III. 543 The author adds a vindication of himself from an accusation of Pre-adamitism;..he insists on it, that, provided he excepts the human species, he may believe rational animals to have existed on the earth before Adam, without being guilty of this terrible heresy. **1799** KIRWAN *Geol. Ess.* 127 These, however, have been by some, ascribed to some fictitious Preadamitick periods. **1865** CDL. WISEMAN in *Ess. Relig. & Lit.* Ser. I. 26 How many human skeletons have been announced as found in preadamitic positions! Yet not one has yet been admitted as proved. **1880** A. WINCHELL *Preadamites* p. iii, The central idea of the work is human preadamitism.

preadapt (pri:ə'dæpt), *v.* [PRE- A. 1.] *trans.* To adapt beforehand; *spec.* in *Biol.*, to adapt (an organism) for life in conditions not yet available to it. Hence **prea'dapted** *ppl. a.* [in *Biol.* tr. F. *préadapté* (L. Cuénot *La Genèse des Espèces Animales* (1911) IV. 291)].

1849 SEARS *Regeneration* I. ii. (1859) 27 The same propensities in men will..preadapt the organs to every shade of meaning. **1915** *Eugenics Rev.* VII. 56 By being warm-blooded, mammals and birds are enabled to maintain their normal activity throughout a wide range of temperature, and they may therefore be said to be preadapted to all temperatures within that range. **1947** *New Biol.* III. 90 For the most part cave animals are drawn from groups habitually living in damp, dim places, such as under stones or at the bottoms of streams; they are, so to speak, preadapted to life in caves before they enter them. **1952** *Ibid.* XIII. 25 An animal adapted to living in a small isolated volume would be preadapted to captivity. **1969** J. M. WELLER *Course of Evol.* ix. 467 The evolutionary development..of these advanced and more complex feathers, whose original function was insulation, preadapted the very early birds for flight. **1970** T. H. EATON *Evolution* viii. 121 In retrospect we can say that some thecodonts were 'preadapted' in certain ways for the life of birds. **1976** *Sci. Amer.* Aug. 38/2 Such a trend, may, however, have helped to preadapt the Egyptians to a ready acceptance of food production later.

Hence **prea'daptive** *a.*, causing or characterized by preadaptation.

1915 *Eugenics Rev.* VII. 50 One can call indifferent or semi-useful, characters in a species which become evident adaptations on removal to a new habitat or on the acquirement of new habits, preadaptive or prophetic characters, or more briefly, preadaptations. **1944** G. G. SIMPSON *Tempo & Mode in Evol.* vi. 186 The direct development of adaptations in one environment may be preadaptive for another. **1969** J. M. WELLER *Course of Evol.* i. 20 Potentially preadaptive mutations..are likely to accumulate within a population as recessives.

preadap'tation. [PRE- A. 2.] Adaptation beforehand; *spec.* in *Biol.* [tr. F. *préadaptation* (L. Cuénot *La Genèse des Espèces Animales* (1911) IV. 306)], the possession or acquisition by an organism of heritable features which adapt it to an environment or mode of life which only later becomes available to it.

1886 J. WARD in *Encycl. Brit.* XX. 73/1 The movements are only more definite than those simply expressive of pain because of inherited pre-adaptation. **1915** *Eugenics Rev.* VII. 56 Versatility is an attempt at universal preadaptation, indeed at complete independence of particular circumstances. **1934** *Biol. Abstr.* VIII. 289/2 'Preadaptation': the occupation of empty regions is made by neighbouring spp. already prepared in the sense of having a necessary and sufficient adaptation. **1942** *Tee Emm* (Air Ministry) II. 144 Wear the special pre-adaptation goggles which will provide you with your hour's synthetic night before you tackle the real one. **1953** G. G. SIMPSON *Major Features Evol.* vi. 188 The term 'preadaptation' has been applied to a great variety of real or supposed evolutionary phenomena, from the appearance of a small mutation with selective value in the population in which it occurs to the sudden appearance of a form monstrous in its parental population but miraculously, one might almost say, adapted to some quite different way of life. **1978** *Sci. Amer.* Sept. 51/1 If a favored mutation does appear, it can be viewed as exhibiting a 'preadaptation' to that particular environment: it did not arise as an adaptive response but rather proved to be adaptive after it appeared.

Hence **preadap'tational** *a.*, pertaining to or characterized by preadaptation.

1940 R. GOLDSCHMIDT *Material Basis Evol.* iii. 151 A return of the subspecies at one extreme end toward the starting point could only be accomplished by retracing the steps of preadaptational mutation to its original condition. **1944** G. G. SIMPSON *Tempo & Mode in Evol.* vi. 188 The field naturalist..is not likely to be satisfied in such cases with the preadaptational axiom that animals enter a new environment simply because they can.

pre-address, see PRE- A. 1.

pre-adjectival, -adjunct: PRE- B. 1 d, A. 2.

pread'mission, *sb.* and *a.*.

A. *sb.* [PRE- A. 2.] Admission beforehand: *spec.* the admission of a certain amount of steam into the cylinder of a steam-engine before the end of the back stroke.

1887 J. A. EWING in *Encycl. Brit.* XXII. 501/2 (*Steam-engine*) An effect of lead [i.e. the condition of the valve being to a certain extent open when the piston-stroke begins] is to cause *preadmission*, that is to say, admission before the end of the back stroke. *Ibid.* 502/1 The position of the crank at which preadmission occurs.

B. *adj.* [PRE- B. 2.] Prior to admission.

1971 *Mod. Law Rev.* XXXIV. 642 The universities are to gain in both responsibility and autonomy..by assuming responsibility for pre-admission vocational training.

pread'mit, *v.* [PRE- A. 1.] *trans.* To admit beforehand. Hence **pread'mitted** *ppl. a.*

1626 DONNE *Serm.* lxviii. 694 He pre-admitted a fearfull apprehension of Death. *a* **1674** CLARENDON *Surv. Leviath.* (1676) 156 Any preadmitted power of the Pope.

preadmonish (pri:æd'mɒnɪʃ), *v.* [PRE- A. 1.]

1. *trans.* To admonish beforehand, to forewarn.

1649 CANNE *Gold. Rule* 17 Of which thing they were often preadmonished and fore-told by the prophets. **1809–10** COLERIDGE *Friend* (1866) 324 Bacon and Stewart..warn and preadmonish the sincere inquirer. **1822** T. TAYLOR *Apuleius* 311 [He should] pre-admonish him of what ought to be foreknown by him.

†**2.** To give previous notice or warning of. *Obs.*

1644 MILTON *Judgm. Bucer* xxx. Wks. 1851 IV. 322 These things thus preadmonisht, let us enquire what the undoubted meaning is of our Saviours words. **1727** BRADLEY *Fam. Dict.* s.v. *Chesnut*, However, the Beams pre-admonish the Fall of a House by their cracking.

preadmonition (pri:ædmə'nɪʃən). [PRE- A. 2.] The action, or an act, of preadmonishing; forewarning, premonition.

1652 GAULE *Magastrom.* 129 Men..stick not to accept them..as the preadmonitions of Divine Providence. **1671** FLAMSTEED in Rigaud *Corr. Sci. Men* (1841) II. 120 To continue my annual preadmonitions of the lunar appearances. **1871** M. COLLINS *Mrq. & Merch.* II. iv. 91 Whether dreams are ever preadmonitions is one of the most vexed questions of the psychologists.

preado'lescent, *a.* and *sb.* [PRE- B. 1.]

A. *adj.* **a.** Of a child: having nearly reached the beginning of adolescence. **b.** Of or pertaining to the two or three years before the beginning of adolescence.

1910 A. C. PERRY *Probl. Elementary School* x. 201 It is probably true that the preadolescent girl can pursue her school work side by side with the boy without the slightest danger. **1925** *Arch. Neurol. & Psychiatry* XIV. 215 Since the patient is usually preadolescent, a separation of the cranial sutures..is likely to be present. **1935** E. BOWEN *House in Paris* II. i. 81 His pre-adolescent mind. **1949** M. MEAD *Male & Female* xi. 232 The charming street-dance in which a little pre-adolescent girl dances to delight the men of the village. **1976** DEAKIN & WILLIS *Johnny go Home* vi. 85 Happier pre-adolescent family holidays.

B. *sb.* A preadolescent child.

1930 K. MCHALE *Pre-Adolescence* 3 Most people look upon the average pre-adolescent as one who has his second teeth..and who is not yet burdened with any difficult adjustments. **1951** *Child Devel.* XXII. 15 The opportunity to observe the play configurations of pre-adolescents was offered by the Guidance Study at the Institute of Child Welfare, University of California. **1960** *20th Cent.* Nov. 434 The idea of the unfallen, pre-adolescent has exercised an extraordinary strong appeal. **1973** *Nature* 27 Apr. 582/3 A pabulum of romanticized science digested to gibberish for consumption by pre-adolescents.

Hence **preado'lescence**, the preadolescent period or stage of development.

1930 K. MCHALE *Pre-Adolescence* 3 The brain..reaches nearly maximum size during the years of pre-adolescence. **1949** E. B. HURLOCK *Adolescent Devel.* i. 4 Because boys mature slightly later than girls, we may regard their pre-adolescence as extending from 11 to 12½ or 13, early adolescence from 13 to 17, and late adolescence from 18 to 21 years. **1972** *Sci. Amer.* July 76/2 She was able to follow the same child from birth to preadolescence.

pre-adult, -adverbial: see PRE- B. 1.

†**pre'advertise**, *v.* *Obs.* [f. PRE- A. 1 + ADVERTISE 4.] *trans.* To give previous notice to; to notify or inform beforehand; to forewarn.

1653 H. MORE *Conject. Cabbal.* (1713) 7 Wherefore Adam, being preadvertised by the vision, was presently able to pronounce, This is now bone of my bone, and flesh of my flesh. **1657** W. RAND tr. *Gassendi's Life Peiresc* I. 142 Johannes Bochartus..had already pre-advertized his Majesty thereof. **1675** WOODHEAD, etc. *Paraphr. St. Paul* Pref., It will not be amiss to preadvertise the reader.

pread'vise, *v.* [PRE- A. 1.] *trans.* To advise or warn before.

1670 COTTON *Espernon* I. III. 121 He certainly believ'd, these were the men appointed to kill him, as he had been pre-advis'd. **1845** T. W. COIT *Puritanism* 202 The Puritans had sent Simon Bradstreet and John Norton..to preadvise them of coming storms.

pre-æstival, -agonal, -agonic, -agricultural: PRE- B. 1.

preak, variant of PREKE *Obs.*

preak, preakar, obs. Sc. ff. PRICK, PRICKER.

prealbumin (pri:'ælbjʊmɪn, -æl'bju:mɪn). *Biochem.* [PRE- B. 3; so called because it appears slightly in front of albumin during electrophoresis.] A plasma protein with an electrophoretic mobility slightly greater than that of albumin; *spec.* a tetramer in human blood which binds thyroxine and the retinol-binding protein.

1955 O. SMITHIES in *Biochem. Jrnl.* LXI. 634/2 The two components migrating more rapidly than the broad albumen zone are referred to as the pre-albumins$_1$ and $_2$ ($_1$ indicating the faster-moving component). **1959** *Nature* 3 Oct. 1067/2 (*heading*) Separation of prealbumins by starch gel electrophoresis. **1975** F. W. PUTNAM *Plasma Proteins* (ed. 2) I. ii. 72 Prealbumins have been described in other species such as the mouse; the molecular weight is only about 20,000 and the function is unknown. **1976** *Sci. Amer.* Sept. 58/2 When dietary protein intake is deficient, the two proteins that play a role in the transport of vitamin A (retinol-binding protein and prealbumin) are not made by the liver in adequate amounts.

pre-albuminuric, -Alfredian: see PRE- B. 1.

preallable (prɪ'æləb(ə)l), *a. rare.* Also 9 præ-. [a. obs. F. *preallable*, now *préalable* going before, preliminary, f. OF. *preal(l)er* to precede (f. *pre-*, PRE- A. 1 + *aller* to go): see -ABLE; cf. obs. F. *al(l)able* passable (as a road).] Preceding, previous, preliminary. Hence **'preallably** *adv.*, previously, beforehand.

1603 FLORIO *Montaigne* I. xxvii. 93 Regular and remisse friendship, wherein so many precautions of a long and preallable conversation, are required. **1652** URQUHART *Jewel* Wks. (1834) 280 There are few..that have not preallably been stung with the tarantula of a preposterous ambition. **1883** H. JUTA tr. *Van der Linden's Instit. Holland* 274 It very often happens that the defendant..before answering makes one or more preliminary or praeallable applications.

preamble ('pri:æmb(ə)l, prɪ'æmb(ə)l), *sb.* [ad. F. *préambule* (13–14 c. in Hatz.-Darm.), ad. med.L. *præambulum* a preamble (whence also It. *preambolo*, Sp., Pg. *preambulo*), prop. neut. sing. of L. *præambulus* adj. (Martial) going before: see next.]

1. A preliminary statement, in speech or writing; an introductory paragraph, section, or clause; a preface, prologue, introduction.

c **1386** CHAUCER *Wife's Prol.* 831 Now dame, quod he, so haue I ioye or blis, This is a long preamble of a tale. *c* **1460** *Lydgate's Thebes* (MS. Roy. 18 D. ii, lf. 147 b/1) *Incipit Prologus.* In this preambile shortly is comprihendid A Mery conseyte of Iohn Lydgate, Monke of Bury, declarynge how he aionyde þe sege of Thebes to the mery tallys of Caunterburye. **1542–3** *Act 34 & 35 Hen. VIII*, c. 1 New testamentes, with anie suche annotacions or preambles. *a* **1626** BP. ANDREWES *Serm.* (1856) I. 107 Without any exordium or preamble here in the beginning of his Epistle he hits on the point straight. **1745** *De Foe's Eng. Tradesman* (1841) II. xxxii. 43 There needs no preamble or declaration at the head of the leaf what the meaning of the book is. **1882** FARRAR *Early Chr.* II. 29 A man..whose manner it was to say what he had to say without formula or preamble, in the fewest and simplest words.

b. *spec.* An introductory paragraph or part in a statute, deed, or other formal document, setting forth the grounds and intention of it.

1628 COKE *On Litt.* 79 a, The rehearsall or preamble of the statute is..as it were a key to open the understanding thereof. **1630** *R. Johnson's Kingd. & Commw.* 141 These French Lawes are too full of Preambles, Processes, Interims, and Provisoes. **1772** *Junius Lett.* lxviii. (1820) 345 The preamble to the statutes made by the first parliament of Edward the First. **1840** *Penny Cycl.* XVII. 277/1 If the committee allow that the allegations of the preamble have been proved, they proceed to consider the bill clause by clause... There are so many grounds upon which the preamble may fail to be proved..that [etc.]. **1863** H. COX *Instit.* I. ix. 174 Passing of Private Bills... At the close of the general case for the promoters and opponents, the committee usually decide first whether the preamble of the bill has been proved. If they decide that it has not been proved, the bill is in general lost. **1893** *Times* 8 May 9/3 Under the Standing Orders as amended in 1882 the preamble of all public Bills is reserved for consideration in Committee until after the clauses have been dealt with.

c. A (musical) prelude. *poet.*

1667 MILTON *P.L.* III. 367 With Præamble sweet Of charming symphonie they introduce Thir sacred Song. **1832** TENNYSON *Palace of Art* 174 No nightingale delighteth to prolong Her low preamble all alone, More than [etc.].

2. *gen.* A preceding or introductory fact or circumstance; a preliminary; *esp.* one betokening that which follows; a presage, prognostic.

1548 UDALL, etc. *Erasm. Par. Matt.* xxiv. 145 Of those aduersities which I haue recyted, as of certayne preambles and tokens before ye maye gesse, that the tyme is not far of. **1663** BLAIR *Autobiog.* viii. (1848) 107 This was the preamble of the great troubles that after followed. **1686** BURNET *Trav.* iii. (1750) 146 The first Step, without any Preamble or Preparative, is downright Beastliness. **1885** BAIN *Senses & Int.* III. i. §3 (1864) 336 In writing, the sight of the part last formed is the preamble to what comes next.

preamble (prɪ'æmb(ə)l), *v.* [In branch I, ad. L. *præambulāre* to walk before: see PRE- A. 1 and AMBLE *v.*; in branch II, f. prec. sb.]

I. †**1.** *intr.* To walk before or in front. *rare*$^{-1}$.

1402 *Pol. Poems* II. 56 Poerte preamblis to presse aforne Anticristis comyng, to sleen the thridde party of men.

†**2.** *trans.* To perambulate previously. *Obs.*

1647 WARD *Simp. Cobler* 15 To take a through view of those who have preambled this by-path.

II. 3. a. *trans.* To utter or deliver by way of preamble; to state in a preamble.

1621 [see PREAMBLED below]. **1667** WATERHOUSE *Fire Lond.* 164 All the execrable issues preambled in the Statute.

b. *intr.* To make a preamble or introductory statement.

1641 [see PREAMBLING below]. **1664** PEPYS *Diary* 15 July, Which, put together with what he preambled with yesterday, makes me think that my Lord do truly esteem me still. **1771** T. HULL *Sir W. Harrington* (1797) II. 199 How foolishly I preamble! **1861, 1865** [see PREAMBLING below].

4. *trans.* To make a preamble to; to preface. Also *transf.*

1628 FELTHAM *Resolves* II. [I.] xciii. 272 Some will preamble a Tale impertinently. **1951** W. SANSOM *Face of Innocence* iv. 45 She might think this was a trick of Harry's to get her away with him, to preamble the marriage-bed. **1980** *Time* 28 Jan. 90/1 Nouns continue to be overrun by the jargonaut: the New York *Times* demands stronger sourcing, meetings are preambled, situations are impacted.

Hence **pre'ambled** *ppl. a.*, **pre'ambling** *vbl. sb.* and *ppl. a.*

1621 BP. MOUNTAGU *Diatribæ* 67 [These] might haue sufficiently manifested the argument, without so long a preambled discourse. **1641** MILTON *Animadv.* Wks. 1851 III. 187 Ere a foot furder we must bee content to heare a preambling boast of your valour. **1861** *Temple Bar Mag.* III. 273 The upshot of which preambling is, that I heartily hate writing. **1865** CARLYLE *Fredk. Gt.* XXI. iv. (1872) X. 11 Well,..your account, without farther preambling.

preambular (prɪ'æmbjʊlə(r)), *a.* [f. med.L. *præambul-um* PREAMBLE + -AR; so F. *préambulaire.*] Of, pertaining to, or of the nature of, a preamble; introductory, prefatory, preliminary.

c **1645** HOWELL *Lett.* (1650) II. 9, I must begin with the fulfilling of your desire in a preambular way. **1648** *Regall Apology* 13 Their four last modest Bils, only praeambular to a personall Treaty. **1702** *Refl. Case W. Penn* 3 We shall not detain you by any preambular Discourse. **1784** R. BAGE *Barham Downs* I. 351 In the first place it was preambular.

pre'ambulary, *a.* [f. as prec. + -ARY.] = prec.

1659 PEARSON *Creed* xi. 755 These three Evangelicall resuscitations are so many preambulary proofs of the last and generall Resurrection. **1774** BURKE *Amer. Tax.* Wks. II. 363 A description of revenue not as yet known in all the comprehensive vocabulary of finance—a preambulary tax. **1882** *Edin. Rev.* July 215 Burke..scoffed at the bill..as a 'preambulary' Bill.

preambulate (prɪ'æmbjʊleɪt), *v. rare.* [f. L. *præambulāt-*, ppl. stem. of *præambulāre* to walk before: see -ATE[3].]

†**1.** *intr.* To walk or go before or in front: = PREAMBLE *v.* 1. *Obs.*

1609 *Ev. Woman in Hum.* II. i. in Bullen *O. Pl.* IV, Being mortally assaild, he did preambulate or walk off. *c* **1660** JORDAN *Poems* §§iij b, When fierce destruction followes to Hell-gate, Pride doth most commonly preambulate.

2. *intr.* To make a preamble: = PREAMBLE *v.* 3 b.

1608 PANKE *Fal of Babel* 113 Sanders..preambulateth from the matter before he come to it. **1741** RICHARDSON *Pamela* I. 71 But I will no more preambulate. **1903** *Sat. Rev.* 16 May 614 In previous articles I have preambulated somewhat to this effect.

preambulation (prɪæmbjʊ'leɪʃən). [Noun of action from prec.: see -ATION.]

1. The making of a preamble; a preamble, preface.

c **1386** CHAUCER *Wife's Prol.* 837 Now dame quod he... This is a long preamble of a tale..What spekestow of preambulacioun [*MSS. Harl.* 7334, *Camb.* perambulacioun]. **1623** COCKERAM II, The first Speech of any thing, *exordium, preambulation.* **1768** MME. D'ARBLAY *Early Diary* 27 Mar., And now I have done with preambulation. **1805** EMILY CLARK *Banks of Douro* III. 69 Introduced the subject..after a long preambulation.

2. 'A walking or going before'. *rare*[−0].

1828 in WEBSTER; hence in later Dicts.

preambulatory (prɪ'æmbjʊlətərɪ), *a.* [f. as PREAMBULATE: see -ORY[2].] Having the character of a preamble; prefatory, preliminary.

1608 T. MORTON *Preamb. Encounter* Pref., A Preambulatory Epistle vnto P.R. **1664** H. MORE *Myst. Iniq., Apol.* 551 To which, without any Preambulatory Ambages, I answer. **1808** BENTHAM *Sc. Reform* 109 Before the Circuit Court; i.e. (as explained in the preambulatory part of this section) 'the Circuit Court of Justiciary by appeal'.

†**pre'ambulous,** *a. Obs. rare*[−1]. [f. med.L. *praeambul-um* PREAMBLE + -OUS.] = PREAMBULAR.

1646 SIR T. BROWNE *Pseud. Ep.* I. x. 38 He..destroyeth the principle preambulous unto all beliefe.

pre-amp ('priːæmp), abbrev. of PREAMPLIFIER.

1957 *Practical Wireless* XXXIII. 573/1 The pre-amp and output stages make use of highly efficient miniature valves. **1968** *Times* 29 Nov. (Sound of Leisure Suppl.) p. ii/2 The cost of stereo at its best is off-putting (a second matching speaker, stereo amplifier and pre-amp., stereo head, cartridge and stylus—your old turntable will still suffice). **1975** *Hi-Fi Answers* Feb. 81/1 (Advt.), Leak 12 watt mono valve amplifier, with Rogers pre-amp. £8. **1978** *Nature* 18 May 218/2 A preamp was mounted directly on the base of the detector (bias ~ 100V) and its output was fed to an amplifier.

pre'amplifier. [PRE- A. 2.] An amplifier designed to amplify a very weak signal (as from a microphone, pickup, or similar source) and deliver it to another amplifier for further amplification.

1935 *Television* VIII. 654/1 This pre-amplifier brought R_4 signals up to consistent full loud-speaker strength. **1952** *Electronic Engin.* XXIV. 498/1 The low output signal obtained from a pick-up necessitates the use of a preamplifier. **1957** *New Yorker* 2 Nov. 95/2 Bogen RR550 DeLuxe FM-AM Receiver with built-in Preamplifier and Power Amplifier. **1965** *Wireless World* July 33 (Advt.), Transistor A.C. Microvoltmeter... Ideal as an oscilloscope preamplifier as it has a low noise level, low microphony, no hum and is independent of a mains supply. **1977** *Gramophone* June 117/1 Between the preamplifiers and the power amplifiers there are four Urei 527 A ⅓-octave equalizers.

pre'amplify, *v.* [PRE- A. 1.] *trans.* To subject to a preliminary amplification; to amplify in a preamplifier. Hence **pre'amplified** *ppl. a.*

1959 *Geophysics* XXIV. 750 The reflected signal detected by the hydrophone is pre-amplified, passed through a variable passive filter, then amplified and printed on the recorder. **1978** *Nature* 13 July 135/1 After cell contact, lock-in amplifiers sample preamplified cell potentials..at selectable phase angles. *Ibid.* 14 Sept. 111/2 The signals were preamplified and detected by two automatic gain-controlled receivers.

Hence **preamplifi'cation,** the action or result of preamplifying.

1960 *Practical Wireless* XXXVI. 397/1 The amplifier has sufficient gain for many purposes with no pre-amplification. **1971** *Melody Maker* 13 Nov. 36/5 A new concept in sound engineering..is the Mark 3 Jam-Pak series, a unique idea in pre-amplification systems. **1977** *Rolling Stone* 13 Jan. 58/2 Most ribbon mikes produce lower output signals than most dynamic types and require more preamplification.

pre-anæs'thetic, *a.* (*sb.*) *Med.* [PRE- B. 1.]

a. Occurring before the introduction of anæsthetics into surgical practice.

1892 *Pall Mall G.* 10 Mar. 3/2 In pre-anæsthetic times operations were very different to what they are now. **1916** P. J. FLAGG *Art of Anæsthesia* 1. 1 The pre-anæsthetic period ends and the anæsthetic period begins with the discovery of ether in 1842 and its general introduction in 1846.

b. Used or carried out as a preliminary to the induction of anæsthesia. Also as *sb.*, a drug so used.

1930 [see NEMBUTAL]. **1934** *Current Res. Anesthesia & Analgesia* XIII. 169 (*heading*) Pernoston as a preanesthetic in surgery. **1957** S. M. BROOKS *Basic Facts Pharmacol.* ii. 76 The most popular preanesthetic is a combination of morphine and atropine. **1974** A. FREEMAN in Lichtiger & Moya *Introd. Practice of Anesthesia* xxvii. 334 A barbiturate combined with a narcotic and a belladonna alkaloid produces suitable preanesthetic sedation in most children over 1 year of age.

Hence **pre-anæs'thetically** *adv.*

1952 V. J. COLLINS *Princ. & Pract. Anesthesiol.* vii. 64 His work indicated one of the primary objects in the use of morphine preanesthetically namely, depression of basal metabolic rate and oxygen consumption.

pre-anal: see PRE- B. 3.

pre-analytic(al, -ally: see PRE- B. 1.

pre-a'naphoral, *a.* [f. PRE- B. 1 d + Gr. ἀναφορά offering.] Preceding the *anaphora* or part of the eucharistic service containing the oblation.

1882-3 *Schaff's Encycl. Relig. Knowl.* II. 1326 That preceding the consecration of the elements (pre-anaphoral) and the *anaphora*, or sacramental service.

pre-'animism. [PRE- B. 1] Primitive belief that certain powers exist in material objects. Cf. next.

1918 A. A. BRILL tr. *Freud's Totem & Taboo* (1919) iii. 152 We have practically no further knowledge of preanimism, as no race has yet been found without conceptions of spirits. **1937** *Nature* 27 Nov. 923/1 Dr. Robert Ranulph Marett..is best known as an anthropologist, the formulator of the theory of preanimism in the study of primitive religion. **1956** E. E. EVANS-PRITCHARD *Nuer Relig.* xiii. 311 Many such origins have been propounded: magic, fetishism, manism, animism, pre-animism. **1963** S. FUCHS *Origin of Man & his Culture* xviii. 232 Andrew Lang maintained that pre-animism took two forms, that of magic and that of primitive monotheism.

pre-ani'mistic, *a.* [PRE- B. 1.] Applied to a stage of religious culture, presumed to precede animism, at which the power or spirit attributed to a material object was believed to exist in the object.

1900 R. R. MARETT in *Folk-Lore* XI. 162 (*title*) Preanimistic religion. *Ibid.* 170, I propose that we examine a few typical cases of Powers, which, beneath the animistic colour that..has more or less completely overlaid them, show traces of having once of their own right possessed pre-animistic validity as objects and occasions of man's religious feeling. **1918** A. A. BRILL tr. *Freud's Totem & Taboo* (1919) iii. 152 Our psychoanalytic view here coincides with a theory of R. R. Marett, according to which animism is preceded by a pre-animistic stage. **1949** KOESTLER *Insight & Outlook* xii. 175 Members of such very early, preanimistic types of society may be described as living in a state of original self-transcendence of consciousness. **1963** S. FUCHS *Origin of Man & his Culture* xviii. 232 It was soon necessary to assume a pre-animistic stage of religion.

preannounce (priːə'naʊns), *v.* [PRE- A. 1.] *trans.* To announce beforehand or previously. Hence **prea'nnouncer,** one who pre-announces; **prea'nnouncement,** a previous announcement.

1846 WORCESTER, *Pre-announce*, to announce before. *Coleridge.* **1852** C. WORDSW. *Occas. Serm.* Ser. IV. 57 The Prophet Isaiah..pre-announces the rising of the Sun of Righteousness. **1872** W. HANNA *Resurrect. Dead* 78 The preannouncer of a singular alteration. **1880** *Libr. Univ. Knowl.* (N.Y.) IX. 227 The pre-announcement of the betrayal, of Peter's denial.

preantepe'nult, *a.* [PRE- B. 1 d.] That precedes or stands immediately before the antepenult; the last but three. Also **preantepe'nultimate** *a.* (in same sense).

1791 WALKER *Dict.*, *Preantepenultimate*, the fourth syllable from the last. **1852** DANA *Crust.* II. 1061 The præantepenult [joint] has the anterior seta as long as the joint.

prean'ticipate, *v. rare.* [PRE- A. 1.] *trans.* To anticipate some time beforehand.

1658 FRANCK *North. Mem.* (1821) 214 Warmth..which suddenly dissolves the snow that falls preanticipating the formation of frost. **1813** SIR R. WILSON *Priv. Diary* II. 275 The approbation pre-anticipated by Lord Aberdeen on this subject, which concerns him so personally.

pre-antiquity to **-apicial:** PRE- A. 2, B. 3.

preappoint (priːə'pɔɪnt), *v.* [PRE- A. 1.] *trans.* To appoint beforehand or previously.

1633 BP. HALL *Hard Texts, N.T.* 179 Those did he preappoint and predestinate to be conformable to the image of his Son. **1768-74** TUCKER *Lt. Nat.* (1834) I. 591 By a long series of causes pre-appointed for that purpose. **1866** CARLYLE *E. Irving* 131, I remember our..visit preappointed for us by Irving.

Hence **prea'ppointed** *ppl. a.*; **prea'ppointment,** previous appointment, fore-ordination.

a **1618** SYLVESTER *Sonn. Mirac. Peace* ix, They both attain By war-like broyls their pre-appointed Reigne. **1654** H. L'ESTRANGE *Chas. I* (1655) 182 April the 13. the Parliament sate according to preappointment. **1827** CARLYLE *Misc.* (1857) I. 33 Whom wealth could not tempt..from their preappointed aims. **1850** R. I. WILBERFORCE *Doctr. Holy Baptism* 147 It is otherwise when we pass from the region of foreknowledge to that of pre-appointment.

pre-apprehend: see PRE- A. 1.

preapprehension (priːæprɪ'henʃən). [PRE- A. 2.]

1. A conception or idea formed beforehand; a preconceived notion.

1646 SIR T. BROWNE *Pseud. Ep.* II. vi. 93 Such as regarding the clouds, behold them in shapes conformable to preapprehensions. **1677** HALE *Contempl.* II. 90 The pre-apprehensions and Image that the mind makes to it self of them.

2. A preconceived fear of what may happen; fearful anticipation, foreboding.

1633 T. ADAMS *Exp. 2 Peter* iii. 18 The..preapprehension of sickness and death, is an antedating of sickness and death. **1702** C. MATHER *Magn. Chr.* III. I. App. (1852) 343 Under these pre-apprehensions it was his own endeavor to beware of abating his own first love. **1820** J. BROWN *Hist. Brit. Ch.* II. vi. 308 To see the pre-apprehensions of the protestors so fearfully verified.

pre-apprise to **pre-aptitude:** PRE- A. 1, 2.

pre'arm, *v. rare.* [PRE- A. 1.] *trans.* To arm beforehand, to fore-arm.

1615 T. ADAMS *Lycanthropy* 2 The great Bishop of our soules..heere..pre-armes them to that entertainment which the Samaritans of the world are likely to give all those whose faces looke towards Jerusalem. **1660** tr. *Amyraldus' Treat. conc. Relig.* Pref. 7 To pre-arm others against its poison.

pre-Arnoldian: see PRE- B. 1 a.

prearrange (priːə'reɪndʒ), *v.* Also with hyphen. [PRE- A. 1.] *trans.* To arrange beforehand.

1811 JANE AUSTEN *Sense & Sens.* III. vii. 133 With..the service pre-arranged in his mind, he offered himself as the messenger. **1851** J. MARTINEAU *Stud. Chr.* (1858) 281 A theatre whose scenery is not all pre-arranged. **1896** BARRIE *Marg. Ogilvy* x, A sign, prearranged between us.

So **prea'rranged** *ppl. a.*, arranged beforehand; **prea'rrangement,** action of pre-arranging or fact of being pre-arranged; previous arrangement.

1775 DE LOLME *Eng. Constit.* II. xxi. (1784) 340 By a happy pre-arrangement of things. **1875** POSTE *Gaius* IV. Comm. (ed. 2) 503 Pre-determined conditions, and pre-arranged, pre-capitulated stipulations. *Ibid.* 638 There took place, by prearrangement, a molestation of one of the litigants.

pre-article: see PRE- B. 1.

preas, prease, obs. forms of PRAISE, PRESS *sb.*[1] and *v.*[1]

preason, obs. Sc. form of PRISON.

†**pre'aspect.** *Obs. rare.* [PRE- A. 2.] An aspect beforehand, a looking forward.

1635 JACKSON *Creed* VIII. xxxiii. §8 This law had a special ..pre-aspect unto our Saviour's death upon the crosse.

†**prea'spection.** *Obs. rare.* [f. PRE- A. 2 + ASPECTION.] Previous beholding or knowledge.

1646 SIR T. BROWNE *Pseud. Ep.* IV. xi. 207 To beleeve they [pigmies] should be in the stature of a foot or span, requires the preaspection of such a one as Philetas the Poet in Athenæus, who was faine to fasten lead unto his feet lest the wind should blow him away.

preaspirate, -aspiration, -assemble: PRE- A. 1, 2.

pre-a'ssembly, *sb.* and *a.*

A. *sb.* [PRE- A. 2.] Preliminary assembly. Also *attrib.*

1958 *Engineering* 31 Jan. 140/2 From the fabrication shed the steel is moved over into the adjacent pre-assembly shed. *Ibid.* 140/3 The bulk of pre-assembly in the yard..is by welding.

B. *adj.* [PRE- B. 2.] Prior to assembly.

1977 *Design Engin.* July 37/3 This means that operations and parts are eliminated and that pre-assembly tolerances of components are relaxed.

preassume (priːə'sjuːm), *v.* [PRE- A. 1.]

†**1.** *trans.* To take previously or beforehand.

1620 VENNER *Via Recta* (1650) 315 Before the meat preassumed be well concocted. **1657** TOMLINSON *Renou's Disp.* 318 If any preassume this, lethal poyson..shall not hurt him.

2. To assume or take for granted beforehand.

1789 T. TAYLOR *Proclus' Comm.* II. 129 It is necessary to pre-assume that a b is equal to c d, in order that the circles may be also equal. **1816** COLERIDGE *Statesm. Man.* (1817) 365 All alike pre-assume, with Mr. Locke, that the mind contains only the relics of the senses.

preassurance (priːə'ʃʊərəns). [PRE- A. 2.]

1. An assurance given or received beforehand.

1635 JACKSON *Creed* VIII. xvi. §2 That great deliverance whereof the first Passover in Egypt was the pledge, or preassurance. **1645** *King's Cabinet Open.* in *Select. fr. Harl. Misc.* (1793) 342 The treaty shall be renewed upon..a pre-assurance, that the rebels will submit to reason.

2. A previous assurance or feeling of certainty in one's own mind; an assured presentiment.

1671 WOODHEAD *St. Teresa* I. Pref. 33 Who have, many times, a pre-assurance, before..their asking, of their obtaining it. **1825** COLERIDGE *Aids Refl.* (1848) I. 287 No preassurance common to a whole species does in any instance prove delusive.

preassure (priːə'ʃʊə(r)), *v.* [PRE- A. 1.] *trans.* To assure or make certain beforehand. Hence **prea'ssured** *ppl. a.*

1697 J. SERGEANT *Solid Philos.* 294 Being pre-assur'd the Thing has more Modes in it than we know. **1746** W. HORSLEY *Fool* (1748) I. 264 Being pre-assured of his returning Victorious. **1776** BENTHAM *Man. Pol. Econ.* Wks. 1843 III. 37 A preassured stock of the articles of subsistence. **1846** MRS. GORE *Eng. Char.* (1852) 155 Preassuring herself by a mysterious missive whom he will be best pleased to meet at her table.

preast(e, variant of PREST *sb.* and *a. Obs.*

pre-a'tomic, *a.* [PRE- B. 1.] Existing or occurring before the utilization of atomic energy or atomic weapons; characteristic of such a time.

1914 H. G. WELLS *World set Free* iii. 141 Originally he had been something of a thinker upon international politics,.. but the atomic bombs had taken him by surprise and he had still to recover completely from his pre-atomic opinions. **1945** R. A. KNOX *God & Atom* ii. 28 The ladder that is meant to climb heaven from our front door-step climbs it, instead, from a period world which only history recaptures for us. It is definitely pre-Atomic. **1945** *N.Y. Times* 12 Aug. 8 E/4 To talk about limited, almost parochial pre-atomic subjects, there is the important war of 1914–18. **1956** A. TOYNBEE *Historian's Approach to Relig.* 215 It [*sc.* the world] has already experienced two devastating pre-atomic wars in one lifetime.

prea'ttachment. [PRE- A. 2.] A prior or previous attachment.

1790 *Norman & Bertha* I. 150 Some ill-fated pre-attachment..had seduced her from the paths of duty. **1814** MRS. J. WEST *Alicia de Lacy* I. 318 A pre-attachment was all he dreaded.

prea'ttune, *v.* [PRE- A. 1.] *trans.* To attune beforehand.

1794 COLERIDGE *Lett., to Southey* (1895) 80, I.. preattuned my heartstring to tremulous emotion. **1839** BAILEY *Festus* xxviii. (1852) 474 The ear which hears is preattuned in Heaven.

preaty, etc., obs. forms of PRETTY, etc.

preaudience (priː'ɔːdɪəns). [PRE- A. 2.] The right to be heard before another; precedence or relative rank (of lawyers at the Bar).

1768 BLACKSTONE *Comm.* III. iii. 28 A custom has of late years prevailed of granting letters patent of precedence to such barristers, as the crown thinks proper to honour with that mark of distinction: whereby they are entitled to such rank and pre-audience as are assigned in their respective patents. **1815** *Edin. Rev.* XXV. 539 The remarkable contest for preaudience which occurred between Lord North and Lord Surry. **1884** *Times* 27 Nov. 9/4 Gradually their [Q.C.'s] right of preaudience under their royal patents accustomed Judges and litigants to look to them as constituting a separate class, like the Serjeants.

pre-audit, -auditor, -auditory: see PRE- A. 1, 2, B. 3,

†**pre'augurate,** *v. Obs.* [f. PRE- A. 1 + L. *augurāre* to augur.] *trans.* To prognosticate.

1635 PERSON *Varieties* II. 66 Seeing Comets portend drouth, they cannot likewise preaugurate inundations.

pre-Augustinian: PRE- B. 1 a.

pre-au'ricular, *a. Anat.* [PRE- B. 3.]

1. [ad. mod.L. (*sulcus*) *præ-auriculāris* (coined in Ger. by T. Zaaijer 1866, in *Natuurkundige Verhandelingen te Haarlem* XXIV. 28).] Designating a groove situated immediately anterior to the inferior margin of the auricular surface of the ilium, and better developed in the female than in the male.

[**1886** *Rep. Sci. Results Voy. H.M.S. Challenger* XVI. XLVII. 55 The most distinct examples of the sulcus præ-auricularis were found in the pelves of the Sandwich Island women.] **1897** *Lippincott's Med. Dict.* 822/2 Pre-auricular sulcus. **1911** *Anatomischer Anzeiger* XXXIX. 17 If now a dissection of the sacro-iliac joint is made in a woman, the praeauricular sulcus is seen to be entirely filled with ligamentous fibres. **1914** J. E. FRAZER *Anat. Human Skeleton* v. 132 The pre-auricular groove..is as a rule only found on female bones. **1974** *Amer. Jrnl. Physical Anthropol.* XLI. 381/1 The pre-auricular groove of the ilium is usually cited as one of the morphological features to be noted when sexing human pelves.

2. Situated in front of the ear(s).

1901 *Amer. Anthropologist* III. 38 Preauricular. **1934** *Jrnl. Anat.* LXVIII. 533 Pre-auricular fistulae and pre-auricular appendages..lie along the line of the first pharyngeal depression. **1970** *Amer. Jrnl. Ophthalm.* LXXII. 798 (*caption*) Pre-auricular lymph node showing secondary malignant melanoma.

†**prea'ver,** *v. Obs.* [PRE- A. 1.] *trans.* To aver or assert beforehand.

1591 SYLVESTER *Du Bartas* I. i. 778 Another, past all hope, doth pre-averr The birth of John, Christ's holy Harbenger.

pre-'axal, *a. Anat.* [f. PRE- B. 3 + AX-IS + -AL[1].] Situated in front of the body-axis; prechordal; pre-axial.

1890 in *Cent. Dict.*

pre-'axiad, *adv. Anat.* [f. as next + *-ad*: see DEXTRAD.] In a pre-axial direction, forward; in or towards the front.

1888 W. K. PARKER in *Proceed. Royal Soc.* XLIII. 486 Two well-marked carpals..., one of which—the radiale—lies pre-axiad and slightly proximad of the other. **1895** *Proc. Zool. Soc.* 331 The prezygapophyses..of the other two extend preaxiad more and more.

pre-'axial, *a. Anat.* [f. PRE- B. 3 + L. *axis*: cf. AXIAL.] Situated in front of the axis of the body or of a limb. Hence **pre-'axially** *adv.*

1872 MIVART *Elem. Anat.* 37 All parts which in man are relatively superior, and in beasts anterior, can be termed pre-axial in all cases. *Ibid.* 52 In the common european Terrapin we find the fourth cervical with its centrum convex pre-axially, and concave post-axially. **1875** SIR W. TURNER in *Encycl. Brit.* I. 819/2 Quite recently the term *præ-axial* has been introduced as equivalent to atlantal, and *post-axial* to sacral. **1899** *Allbutt's Syst. Med.* VIII. 169.

prebacillary to **-basilar:** PRE- A. 1, B. 1, 3.

†**pre'bearing.** *Her. Obs.* [f. PRE- A. 1 + BEARING *vbl. sb.* 3.] The fact of (a charge or device) being borne previously.

1562 LEIGH *Armorie* 200 Then the Herehaught shal.. tricke hym out a congruent cote of armes, hauing alwaies a regarde to prebearing.

prebend ('prɛbənd), *sb.* Also 5–6 **-ende**, 6 **-ente**. [a. Of. *prebende* (14–15th c. in Littré), in earlier popular forms *provende* (12th c. in Littré), *prevende*, mod.F. *prébende*, ad. med.L. *præbenda* a pension (Cassiodorus), a daily pittance, an ecclesiastical living, prebend, prop. 'things proper to be supplied', neut. pl. gerundive of L. *præbēre* to offer, grant, furnish, supply, for *præhibēre* (Plaut.), f. *præ* before, forth + *habēre* to hold.]

1. The portion of the revenues of a cathedral or collegiate church granted to a canon or member of the chapter as his stipend. Also *transf.*

c **1400** *Plowman's Tale* 721 They han greet prebendes and dere, Some two or three, and some mo. **1480** CAXTON *Descr. Brit.* 37 In pryuelege of clergy and in prebendes they knowleche hem selfe clerkis. **1502** ATKYNSON tr. *De Imitatione* III. iii. 197 For a lytell fee or prebende great Iourneys & harde labours be take an hande for such wor[l]dly lordes. **1561** T. NORTON *Calvin's Inst.* IV. v. (1634) 536 Daintie men, that get their living with singing, as Prebends, Canonships, Parsonages, and dignities, Chaplainships, and such other. **1607** COWELL *Interpr.*, *Prebend*..is the portion, which euery member, or Canon of a Cathedrall church receiueth in the right of his place, for his maintenance... Prebends be either simple, or with dignity. Simple Prebends be those, that haue no more but the reuenew toward their maintenance: Prebends with dignity are such, as haue some Iurisdiction annexed vnto them according to the diuers orders in euery seuerall church. **1845** STEPHEN *Comm. Laws Eng.* (1874) II. 674 *note*, Such canons, however, as are prebendaries, differ from such as are not, as having a prebend, or fixed portion of the rents and profits of the cathedral or collegiate church for their maintenance. **1852** HOOK *Ch. Dict.* (1871) 599 Prebend is the stipend received by a prebendary... Hence the difference between a prebend and a canonry. A canonry was the right which a person had as a member of the chapter. A prebend was the right to receive certain revenues appropriated to the place.

2. The separate portion of land or tithe from which the stipend is gathered (hence known as the *corps of the prebend*); the tenure of this as a benefice.

[**1167** *Pipe Roll 13 Hen. II* (1889) 202 Episcopatus de Bada ..Johanni Cumin .XL.S. pro prebenda sua per breue Regis. **1290** *Rolls of Parlt.* I. 33/2 Ne quis Possessionem predictarum Prebendarum ingrediatur..aut Stall' in choris Ecclesiarum..occupet.] **1422** *Ibid.* IV. 194/1 The Kyng.. had title to present unto the Prebend of Bykeleswade in the Chirche of Lincolne. **1513** BRADSHAW *St. Werburge* II. 1002 Whiche parke from Upton was distaunt a myle space A prebende to a chanon of her mynstre and place. **1711** HEARNE *Collect.* (O.H.S.) III. 141 The Bp. of Durham has given..the Golden prebend to Dr. Adams. **1844** LINGARD *Anglo-Sax. Ch.* (1858) I. App. i. 362 Where the clergy lived together, the land of the church was possessed by them in common..where separately, it was divided into prebends. **1868** FREEMAN *Norm. Conq.* II. x. 453 The Canons of Waltham..lived..each man in his own house on his own prebend.

3. = PREBENDARY 1.

1556 *Chron. Gr. Friars* (Camden) 91 The dene with alle the residew of the prebentes went but in their surples and lefte of their abbet of the universyte. **1628** *Bp. Cosin's Corr.* (Surtees) I. 151 Mr. Archdeacon and Mr. Robson, Prebends of Durham. **1661** *Colet's Serm. Conf. & Ref.* 20 And to.. these Monkes, Prebends, and Religious men, let the canons be rehearsed. **1771** SMOLLETT *Humph. Cl.* 15 July, The golden prebends keep plentiful tables. **1776** *Carlisle Mag.* 13 July 4 A college of canons, or, as we now call them, Prebends. **1872** MINTO *Eng. Prose Lit.* II. x. 615 To make him a prebend of St. Paul's.

4. *attrib.* **prebend house.**

1609 *Mem. Ripon* (Surtees) III. 334 The Parsonage or Prebend House in Stanwick.

Hence *nonce-wd.* **'prebend** *v.* [= obs. F. *prebender*, med.L. *prebendāre*] *trans.* to give a daily allowance to (a canon). **'prebendage,** name of a part of the town of Southwell, formerly under the collegiate chapter.

1868 WALCOTT *Sacr. Archæol.* s.v., When regular canons only existed, all were maintained from a common stock, from which they were prebended or fed. **1759** B. MARTIN *Nat. Hist. Eng.* II. 224 *Southwell*..is divided into two Parts, viz. the Burgage, which comprehends all that Part betwixt the Market and the Greet; and the Prebendage of the Church. The Church is both parochial and collegiate,..and has 16 Prebendaries. **1840** *Penny Cycl.* XVI. 341/1 The burgage, or burridge, the high town or prebendage (which two divisions constitute Southwell proper).

prebendal (prɪ'bɛndəl), *a.* [ad. med.L. *præbendālis*, f. *præbenda* PREBEND: see -AL[1]. So obs. F. *prebendal* (1493 in Godef.).] Of or pertaining to a prebend or a prebendary.

1751 CHESTERF. *Lett.* 11 Mar., Mr. Harte..has taken possession of his prebendal house at Windsor. **1759** J. G. COOPER tr. *Gresset's Ver-Vert* IV. Poems (1810) 535/2 No sleek prebendal priest could be More thoroughly devout than he. **1862** MRS. H. WOOD *Channings* i, Close by, were the prebendal houses,..all venerable with age.

b. *prebendal stall*, the stall of a prebendary in a cathedral; hence, the benefice of a prebendary.

1839 SIR J. STEPHEN *Eccl. Biog.* (1860) II. 17 The matricidal hands of the metropolitan of all England..were in our own days irreverently laid on her prebendal stalls. **1856** FROUDE *Hist. Eng.* II. vi. 9 He granted a prebendal stall at Wells to an Italian cardinal.

†**'prebendar.** *Obs.* Sc. f. of PREBENDARY.

1512 *Acc. Ld. High Tr. Scot.* IV. 181 For offerand to the prebendaris first mise of Striveling, v Franch crounis. **1574** *Rec. Monast. Kinloss* (1872) 159 For the Prebendar and stallaris pensioun within the Kirk cathederall of Abirdene.

prebendary ('prɛbəndərɪ), *sb.* (*a.*) [ad. med.L. *præbendārius*, f. *præbenda*: see PREBEND *sb.* and -ARY[1].]

1. The holder of a prebend; a canon of a cathedral or collegiate church who holds a prebend.

Originally, each canon had a *præbenda* or share in the funds of the church to which the clergy-house was attached; in later times when the custom grew up of assigning a particular estate for the support of a particular canon, the latter received also the designation of *prebendary* from the estate so assigned, e.g. 'Canon of St. Paul's and Prebendary of Finsbury'. By act 3 & 4 Vict. c. 113 of 1840, the members of a cathedral chapter (except the dean) are now called *canons*; but in some chapters of the Old Foundation the name *prebendary* (with a territorial addition) is retained for the titular holder of a disendowed prebend, whose status is, in most respects, similar to that of the *Honorary Canons* in cathedrals of the New Foundation.

[**1130** *Pipe Roll 31 Hen. I* (1833) 1 Et in Vestitura eorundem [xiij] Prebendariorum .lxv.s.] **1422** *Rolls of Parlt.* IV. 194 The said Philippe Morgan beyng Prebendarie of the saide Prebend, was consecrate Bisshop of Worcestre. **1432–50** tr. *Higden* (Rolls) VI. 465 Whiche putte monkes into that newe monastery callede Hide at Wynchestre, and expulsede seculer prebendaries for theire wickede life. *a* **1552** LELAND *Itin.* II. 43 This Robert made the Chapelle of S. George in the Castelle of Oxforde, and founded a College of Prebendaries there. **1675** OGILBY *Brit.* Introd. 3 The Cathedral has 30 Prebendaries. **1711** HEARNE *Collect.* (O.H.S.) III. 139 Dr. Pickering one of y[e] Golden-Prebendarys of Durham is dead. **1732** GAY in *Swift's Lett.* (1766) I. 163 You insist upon your being minister of Amesbury, Dawley, Twickenham, Richkings, and a prebendary of Westminster... You might have a good living in every one of them. **1837** SYD. SMITH *Let. Archd. Singleton* Wks. 1859 II. 256/1 Disgusted with the spectacle of rich Prebendaries enjoying large incomes, and doing little or nothing for them. **1902** *Westm. Gaz.* 13 Nov. 3/2 The greatest sticklers for the title [of Canon] are the honorary canons and prebendaries,..who revel in a title conferred upon them solely by episcopal favour.

†**2.** The office of a prebendary; a prebend. *Obs.* (The antithesis of PREBEND 3.)

1592 NASHE *P. Penilesse* Cj, Byshopricks, Deanries, Prebendaries, and other priuate dignities, animate our Diuines to such excelence. *a* **1639** SPOTTISWOOD *Hist. Ch. Scot.* II. (1677) 109 [He] founded divers Prebendaries and Canonries in the Church of Dumblane. **1725** BAILEY *Erasm. Colloq.* (1733) 239 A Prebendary was offered me, as they call it; it was a good fat Benefice, and I accepted it.

B. *attrib.* or *adj.* = PREBENDAL.

1731 *Gentl. Mag.* I. 451 Mr. Lavington, Prebendary-treasurer of Worcester, appointed one of the Residentiaries of St. Paul's. **1873** DIXON *Two Queens* IV. XIX. ii. 11 Wolsey was not satisfied with two rectories, six prebendary stalls.

Hence **'prebendaryship**, the office or benefice of a prebendary; a prebend.

1639 WOTTON in *Reliq.* (1651) 490 My Lords Grace of Canterbury hath this week sent hither to Mr. Hales very nobly a Prebendaryship of Windsor unexpected, undesired.

†**'prebendate**, *v. Obs. rare*$^{-1}$. [f. *præbendāt-*, ppl. stem of med.L. *præbendāre* to endow with a prebend.] *trans.* To present to a prebend.

1568 GRAFTON *Chron.* II. 102 Declaryng howe learned he [Stephen Langton] was in the liberall artes, and in diuinitie, insomuch as he was prebendated at Paris.

†**'prebender.** *Obs.* [A parallel form of PREBENDAR, *prebendary*: perh. ad. F. *prébendier* (1365 in Hatz.-Darm.).] = PREBENDARY *sb.* 1.

1556 *Chron. Gr. Friars* (Camden) 91 The kynge and the qwene..came in London,..and soo to Powlles; and there was goodly resevyd of the byshopp wyth the prebenders and the holi qweer of Powlles. **1583** STOCKER *Civ. Warres Lowe C.* IV. 6 The Cloysterers, and suche other like Churche men ..and their Associates, professed, or Prebenders.

†**'prebendry.** *Obs. rare*$^{-1}$. [See -RY.] = next.

1611 COTGR., *Prebende*, a Prebendrie.

†**'prebendship.** *Obs.* = PREBENDARYSHIP.

1570 FOXE *A. & M.* (ed. 2) 308/2 So that euery one of them should conferre one prebendshyp to the same fundation. *c* **1630** RISDON *Surv. Devon* §256 (1810) 264 This church..was..a prebendship to the priory. **1691** WOOD *Ath. Oxon.* I. 87 He was admitted to a Prebendship in the Church of Wells. **1715** M. DAVIES *Athen. Brit.* I. 108 Collated to the Prebendship of Bedminster and Radclyve.

prebio'logical, *a.* [PRE- B. 1.] Existing or occurring before the appearance of life; pertaining to the origin of life; = PREBIOTIC *a.*

1960 *Science* 22 July 200/3 Calvin's experiments have been criticized on the basis that the prebiological atmosphere contained only a small proportion of carbon dioxide. **1971** I. G. GASS et al. *Understanding Earth* ix. 123 Concentration of these compounds by geological processes established reservoirs of prebiological food. *Ibid.*, A prebiological environment. **1973** C. SAGAN *Cosmic Connection* vii. 54 The search for prebiological organic chemicals on the Moon, on Mars, or on Jupiter is of great importance in understanding the steps leading to the origin of life.

So **prebi'ology**, the study of the origin of life, and of conditions before this; **prebi'ologist**, a specialist in this.

1963 S. W. FOX in I. A. Breger *Org. Geochem.* ii. 40 The reaction mixture used represents..material which has significance in the context of prebiology, due particularly to the recent emphasis by Revelle..on carbon monoxide in the primitive atmosphere. **1971** I. G. GASS et al. *Understanding Earth* ix. 137/1 All the experimental evidence of prebiology points to the fact that the carbonaceous products were synthesized from gases. **1974** *Nature* 8 Mar. 180/1 Eight planetary astronomers..were assembled to meet ten practitioners interested in the origins of life (three exobiologists, two microbiologists, four chemical prebiologists and one palaeontologist).

prebi'otic, *a.* [PRE- B. 1.] = PREBIOLOGICAL *a.*

1958 *New Statesman* 23 Aug. 214/2 The dust is prebiotic, that is, before the formation of life, but with all the biochemical elements, from which life originated, waiting to be 'organised' into a chemistry of reproduction. **1962** F. I. ORDWAY et al. *Basic Astronautics* vi. 250 Lightning..may have originally been responsible for the creation of the first organic molecules from prebiotic molecules. **1968** *New Scientist* 29 Aug. 437/1 Studies on prebiotic synthesis—the way in which the chemicals of life may have originated on the primitive earth—generally have an esoteric ring to them. **1973** B. J. WILLIAMS *Evolution & Human Origins* vii. 94/1 It was a closed system containing only water, the gases assumed to be present in the prebiotic atmosphere, and an energy source.

†**pre'bition.** *Obs. rare*$^{-0}$. [ad. L. *præbitiōnem*. n. of action from *præbēre* to furnish, afford.]

1656 BLOUNT *Glossogr.*, *Prebition*, a giving, a shewing, an offering, a setting before one.

†**'preble.** *Obs.* Also 6 prebill. [Origin obscure: it has been compared with *pebble*.] Gravel.

1541 *Acts Privy Council* (1837) VII. 113 To view the workes at Dover and especially a certain barre of prebill dryven in..to the mouth of the herborough. **1577** B. GOOGE *Heresbach's Husb.* I. 17b, Varro counsels you to looke whether there be in the land eyther Stone, Marble, Sande, Grauell,..Claye, Preble [*glarea*], or Carbuncle.

pre'board, *v.* [PRE- A. 1.] *trans.* To shape by heating on a form before dyeing rather than after.

1940 *Rayon Textile Monthly* Apr. 59/1 Nylon, the new synthetic yarn..has added a new operation to the manufacture of stockings... It has been found necessary to 'set' the shape of the stocking before it is dyed... At first, various methods of 'pre-boarding', or 'setting', the stockings were tried. **1950** B. E. HARTSUCH *Introd. Textile Chem.* xi. 330 When full-fashioned nylon stockings are pre-boarded, they are mounted on metal forms of suitable shape, and these forms are heated externally with live steam for about 1 to 3 minutes. **1963** R. W. MONCRIEFF *Man-Made Fibres* (ed. 4) xliv. 660 The hosiery were seamed, pre-boarded 5 min. in 27 lb./in.^{2} steam, scoured in 2 per cent sodium lauryl sulphate + 2 per cent caustic soda. They were dyed gold, finished with a standard resin emulsion hosiery finish, and postboarded dry at 200°C. **1970** *Ibid.* (ed. 5) xlvii. 809 The cycle of operations is normally (1) pre-board, (2) dye, (3) post-board, (4) dry.

Hence **pre'boarded** *ppl. a.*, **pre'boarding** *vbl. sb.*

1940 *Rayon Textile Monthly* Apr. 59/2 Various types of pre-boarding equipment. *Ibid.* 60/1 It is not necessary to lay the pre-boarded stocking out flat, as it still has to be dyed. **1953** K. H. INDERFURTH *Nylon Technol.* viii. 208 Placing the gray stockings onto the preboarding form..must be carefully and accurately performed in order to ensure satisfactory fit, wearing qualities, and sales appeal. **1964** E. R. TROTMAN *Dyeing & Chem. Technol. Textile Fibres* (ed. 3) xxiii. 512 In the case of pre-boarding, the most convenient time for the operation is before scouring.

preboding to **pre-book**: see PRE-.

Pre'boreal, *a.* Also **pre-Boreal**, **preboreal**. [PRE- B. 1.] Applied to a European climatic period that followed the Arctic and preceded, or marked the transition to, the Boreal period, and was characterized by the spread of birch and pine forests. Also *absol.*

1924 *Jrnl. Linn. Soc.* (*Bot.*) XLVI. 497 (*caption*) Pollen-spectra... Holland (S.W. Sweden) (preboreal spectrum). **1934** *New Phytologist* XXXIII. 285 Erdtman suggests that it is partly on account of *P. montana* pollen that the pine maximum in many parts of the continent falls so much earlier than in England (i.e. in the Early Boreal or pre-Boreal). **1956** A. L. ARMSTRONG in D. L. Linton *Sheffield* vi. 101 The known [Mesolithic] moorland sites are usually upon patches of old land surface.., or in the eroded banks of streams and cloughs, where their pre-Boreal age is testified by remains of the Pennine forest lying in the peat above them. **1976** *Sci. Amer.* Feb. 94/2 Sometime between 8300 and 8000 B.C. the cold Late Dryas period was superseded by a warmer period known as the Preboreal. Pine and birch forest reinvaded the European plain from the south, and the reindeer herd, following the retreating tundra, moved off to the north and northeast.

pre-Broadway to **-buscal**: see PRE- B.

†**'precable**, *a. Sc. Obs. rare*$^{-1}$. [ad. L. *precābilis* entreating, praying, f. *precārī* to ask, beg, request: see -BLE.] That may be asked or demanded as feudal service, impost, or tax.

1587 *Sc. Acts Jas. VI* (1814) III. 505/2 Þai ar ane pair of the bodie and memberis subiect to þe payment of taxt stent watcheing warding and all vþer precable charges.

precalculate (pri:'kælkjʊleɪt), *v.* [PRE- A. 1.] *trans.* To calculate or reckon beforehand; to forecast. Hence **pre'calculated** *ppl. a.*

1841 *Blackw. Mag.* XLIX. 470 Their consequences..cannot be precalculated. **1875** MASSON *Wordsw.*, etc. 134 On what principles are they to be precalculated? **1881** —— *De Quincey* iv. 39 A carefully præcalculated opium-debauch. **1900** B. BACON in *Expositor* July 6 The Sanhedrin ..must have also relied upon a fixed precalculated calendar.

So **pre'calculable** *a.*, capable of being precalculated; **precalcu'lation**, the action of precalculating or reckoning beforehand.

1864 *Daily Tel.* 31 Aug., The tally of the unfortunate thus doomed is an absolute and precalculable figure. **1841** *Blackw. Mag.* XLIX. 469 There was no precalculation with reference to the actual events of the moment.

Pre-'Cambrian, *a. Geol.* Also **pre-Cambrian**, **Precambrian**. [PRE- B. 1.] Of, pertaining to, or designating the time before the beginning of the Cambrian period and Palæozoic era, present-day rocks of which are marked by an almost complete absence of fossils. Also *ellipt.*, the Pre-Cambrian rocks or period.

1864 J. W. SALTER in *Geol. Mag.* I. 290 The author suggests that the syenitic trap of St. David's is a part of the old pre-Cambrian land. **1875** CROLL *Climate & T.* xx. 343 The length of time embraced by the pre-Cambrian ages of geological history. **1910** LAKE & RASTALL *Text-bk. Geol.* xvii. 292 Everywhere in the British Isles there is a marked unconformity between the pre-Cambrian and the later deposits. **1915** C. SCHUCHERT *Text-bk. Geol.* II. xxvii. 540 The result..serves to make prominent the two most significant and distinctive features of the pre-Cambrian: (1) the wide-spread crustal revolutions,..and (2) the profound depth to which erosion has planed. **1921** A. W. GRABAU *Textbk. Geol.* II. xxx. 198 (*heading*) Summary of the pre-Cambrian of the Canadian region. **1951** AUDEN *Nones* (1952) 71 That the red pre-Cambrian light Is gone like Imperial Rome Or myself at seventeen. **1959** *Times* 18 June (Queen in Canada Suppl.) p. xiii/2 The gnarled Precambrian surface of the Canadian Shield, the low hills of the Mackenzie valley are all foreign to the Yukon. **1969** E. W. MORSE *Fur Trade Canoe Routes of Canada* v. 57 At the upper end of Lac des Alumettes the voyageurs came..into close contact with the granite of the Precambrian Shield, rising straight from the water. **1971** *Nature* 25 June 498/1 The Pre-Cambrian covers 85% of the total length of geological time and is the longest geological division. **1977** *Jrnl. R. Soc. Arts* CXXV. 406/1 Uranium deposits..occur in well defined provinces mainly in Precambrian terrain.

pre-cancer: see PRE- B. 1.

precant ('prɛkənt). *rare.* [ad. L. *precānt-em*, pres. pple. of *precārī* to pray: see -ANT[1].] One who prays; a pray-er.

a **1834** COLERIDGE in *Lit. Rem.* (1839) IV. 38 The efficacy of prayer relatively to the pray-er or precant himself.

precantation (pri:kæn'teɪʃən). [ad. late L. *præcantātiōn-em*, n. of action from L. *præcantāre* to foretell, later, to enchant.] †**a.** A singing before. *Obs.* **b.** A prophesying or foretelling.

1623 COCKERAM, *Præcantation*, a singing before. **1838** G. S. FABER *Inquiry* 331 These apply themselves to auguries or to signs of the heavens or to vain precantations. **1841-4** EMERSON *Ess.*, *Poet* Wks. (Bohn) I. 164 The sea, the mountain-ridge, Niagara, and every flower-bed, pre-exist, or super-exist, in pre-cantations, which sail like odours in the air.

pre-capitalist(ic), **-cardiac**: see PRE- B. 1, 3.

‖**precaria**, Feudal Law: see PRECARY *sb.* 3.

precarial (prɪ'kɛərɪəl), *a. rare.* [f. PRECARY *sb.* + -AL.] Of or pertaining to a precary.

1914 *Eng. Hist. Rev.* Jan. 137 It is also highly probable that precarial transactions were instrumental not only in the bringing together of ecclesiastical property, but also in utilizing it by means of dependent farms.

precarious (prɪ'kɛərɪəs), *a.* [f. L. *precāri-us* obtained by entreaty, depending on the favour of another, hence, uncertain, precarious (f. *prec-em* prayer, entreaty + *-ārius*, -ARY[1]) + -OUS.]

1. Held by the favour and at the pleasure of another; hence, uncertain. *precarious tenure*, a tenure held during the pleasure of the superior.

1646 SIR T. BROWNE *Pseud. Ep.* 26 With more excusable reservation may we shrink at their bare testimonies, whose argument is but precarious and subsists upon the charity of our assentments. **1656** BLOUNT *Glossogr.*, *Precarious*.., granted to one by prayer and intreaty, to use so long as it pleaseth the party, and no longer. **1673** TEMPLE *Observ. United Prov.* Wks. 1731 I. 19 Out of Indignation to see himself but a precarious Governor, without Force or Dependence. **1711** ADDISON *Spect.* No. 256 ¶10 This little Happiness is so very precarious, that it wholly depends on the Will of others. **1754** H. WALPOLE *Lett.* (1846) III. 73 Though the tenure is precarious, I cannot help liking the situation for you. **1878** W. E. HEARN *Aryan Househ.* xviii. §5. 425 His holding was, in the language of the Roman lawyers, 'precarious', that is, upon his request to the owner, and with that owner's leave.

2. Question-begging, assumed, taken for granted; unfounded, doubtful, uncertain.

1659 H. MORE *Immort. Soul* II. x. 216 That the Fabrick of the Body is out of the concurse of Atomes, is a meer precarious Opinion, without any ground or reason. *a* **1677** HALE *Prim. Orig. Man.* 9 Because it suits with that artificial and precarious Hypothesis which was before taken up and made much of. **1779** WESLEY *Wks.* (1830) IV. 148 Quite unproved, quite precarious from beginning to end. **1869** J. MARTINEAU *Ess.* II. 181 His mode of proof is precarious and unsatisfactory. **1882** FARRAR *Early Chr.* II. 506 Such an inference is most precarious.

3. Dependent upon circumstances or chance; liable to fail, insecure, unstable, uncertain.

1687 in Somers *Tracts* (1748) I. 247 When they see us owning the Exercise of our established Religion to be so precarious. **1700** DRYDEN *Ceyx & Alcyone* 44 He but sits precarious on the throne. **1700** ASTRY tr. *Saavedra-Faxardo* II. 378 His Empire is accounted precarious, and short lived. **1734** SWIFT *Pol. Tracts, Reas. agst. Bill for Tythe of Hemp* (1738) 274 The Payment of Tythes in this Kingdom, is subject to so many Frauds, Brangles, and other Difficulties, ..that they are, of all other Rents, the most precarious. **1794** S. WILLIAMS *Vermont* 136 They afforded them but a scanty and precarious support. **1838** LYTTON *Calderon* i, His health was infirm and his life precarious. **1879** ROGERS in *Cassell's Techn. Educ.* IV. 87/2 There is no article in demand the value of which is so precarious as that of a book.

4. Exposed to danger, perilous, risky.

1727 A. HAMILTON *New Acc. E. Ind.* II. xliii. 122 There are so many Banks and Rocks under Water, that Navigation is very precarious. **1827** SCOTT *Highl. Widow* v, The precarious track through the morass the dizzy path along the edge of the precipice. **1894** H. DRUMMOND *Ascent of Man* 253 The fisherman's life is a precarious life; he becomes hardy, resolute, self-reliant.

†**5.** Suppliant, supplicating; importunate. *Obs.*

1659 PEARSON *Creed* (1839) 137 'He ever liveth to make intercession for them.'.. Nor must we look upon this as a servile or precarious, but rather as an efficacious and glorious intercession. **1667** PEPYS *Diary* 6 Nov., He do endeavour to gain them again in the most precarious manner in all things that is possible. **1670** DRYDEN *1st Pt. Conq. Granada* I. i, What Subjects will precarious Kings regard? A Beggar speaks too softly to be heard. **1697** in W. S. Perry *Hist. Coll. Amer. Col. Ch.* I. 48 Sir Edmund Andros knows nothing of this right he has *jure devoluto*, or else he would not suffer the clergy to be so precarious.

†**6.** See PRECARY *sb.* 2. *Obs.*

pre'cariously, *adv.* [f. prec. + -LY[2].] In a precarious manner.

†**a.** By way of prayer or supplication; at the mercy or pleasure of another; with uncertain tenure; insecurely.

1646 Sir T. Browne *Pseud. Ep.* 42 Having once begot in our mindes an assured dependence, he makes us relye on powers which he but precariously obeyes. **1654** H. L'Estrange *Chas. I* (1655) 200 It was the 19. day precariously moved, 1. That he might be bailed. **1683** T. Hunt *Def. Charter Lond.* 45 If these Courtiers.. thought.. that all Authorities and Dignities in the Government should be held precariously of the Crown, they ought to hold their honors.. by the same tenure. **1690** Norris *Beatitudes* (1692) 21 He holds his Being as precariously as he first received it. **1728** Morgan *Hist. Algiers* I. ii. 27 Certain strangers had as much ground precariously allotted them, as they could cover with an oxe's Hide, which they, fraudulently, cut into Thongs.

b. As a thing assumed gratuitously or taken for granted; without proof; insecurely, uncertainly.

1658 Sir T. Browne *Gard. Cyrus* iii. 57 The Figures of nails and crucifying appurtenances, are but precariously made out in the Granadilla or flower of Christs passion. **1699** Bentley *Phal.* 427 Precariously suppos'd without any manner of Proof. **1705** J. Logan in *Pa. Hist. Soc. Mem.* X. 8 It is still better to have something certain than a greater share precariously. **1836** W. Irving *Astoria* III. xlv. 43 Up this river.. they kept for two or three days, supporting themselves precariously upon fish. **1896** *Current Hist.* (U.S.) VI. 822 The fragility of the basis on which the peace of Europe precariously rests.

pre'cariousness. [f. as prec. + -ness.] The quality or condition of being precarious: in various senses of the adj.; *esp.* insecurity, liability to fail.

1687 *Gd. Advice* 59 The uncertainty and precariousness of the means of their subsistance. **1693** Tyrrell *Law Nat.* 372 The weakness, or precariousness of which Hypothesis being discovered. **1705** Blair in W. S. Perry *Hist. Coll. Amer. Col. Ch.* I. 146 Assaulted and accused of countenancing the precariousness of the Clergy. **1748** Smollett *Rod. Rand.* viii, By reason of the danger of a winter voyage,.. as well as the precariousness of the wind, which might possibly detain me a great while. **1755** Johnson, *Precarious*.. is used for *uncertain* in all its senses; but it only means uncertain, as dependant on others; thus there are authors who mention the precariousness of an account, of the weather, of a die. **1798** W. Blair *Soldier's Friend* xii. 94 The precariousness and hardships of the military life. **1817** Shelley *Let. to Godwin* 11 Dec., I felt the precariousness of my life. **1859** Lang *Wand. India* 353 The precariousness of the land tenure is one of the greatest impediments to the outlay of capital by the tenant in the improvement of the land. **1881** Westcott & Hort *Grk. N.T.* Introd. §13 The complexity can evidently only increase the precariousness of printed texts.

‖**precarium** (prɪ'kɛərɪəm). *Rom.* and *Sc. Law.* [L. *precārium* a thing granted or lent upon request at the will and pleasure of the grantor, sb. use of neuter of *precārius* adj.: see precarious.] A loan granted on request but revocable whenever the owner may please.

1693 Stair *Inst.* I. xi. §10 *Precarium* is a kind of *Commodatum*, differing in this, that *Commodatum* hath a determinat time, either expresly when the use of a thing is given to such a day, or such an use, which importeth a time; .. *Precarium* is expresly lent, to be recalled at the Lenders pleasure. **1861** W. Bell *Dict. Law Scot.* s.v., The contract of *precarium* is a gratuitous loan, in which the lender gives the use of the subject in express words, revocable at pleasure.

pre-Caroline: see pre- B. 1 a.

pre-cartilaginous: see pre- B. 1.

precary ('prɛkərɪ), *sb. arch.* [See senses.]

†**1.** A grant upon request, at the will and during the pleasure of the grantor. [ad. L. *precārium*: see above.] *Obs.*

1456 Sir G. Haye *Law Arms* (S.T.S.) 132 Thare is ane othir maner of possessiounis, that ar callit precaris, that cummys for request, or lordis gevin for thair tyme, or thair will endurand. *c* **1575** *Balfour's Practicks* (1754) 458 Ane tenent beand warnit be his master at Whitsounday to flit and remove, thairefter.. sufferit be tolerance and precarie of his master to sit still and remane to ane certane day.

†**2.** See quot. [Cf. med.L. *precaria, precatoria* (Du Cange); F. *précaire* (Littré).] *Obs.*

1694 tr. *Moreri's Hist. etc. Dict.*, Precary [F. *précaire*] is a word well known in the French civil and cannon Law. Paolo saith, That the Contract called the Precary brought great Riches to the Churches... [It] consisted in a Donation that particular persons made of their Goods to the Churches. They afterwards obtained of the same Churches, by Letters which they called *precarious* or *precatorious Letters*, the same Estates again, to enjoy them by a kind of Emphyteotick Security, i.e. to improve them.

3. *Feudal Law.* = med.L. *precāria.* See quots.

[**1670** Blount *Law Dict.*, *Precariæ*, Days Works, which the Tenants of some Mannors are bound to give the Lord in Harvest,.. corruptly called *Bind days*, for *Biden days.* **1883** Seebohm *Village Commun.* 41 There are precariæ, or 'boon-days', sometimes called bene works—special or extra services which the lord has a right to require, sometimes the lord providing food for the day, and sometimes the tenant providing for himself.] **1906** N. J. Hone *Manor & Manor. Rec.* 226 A precary without dinner with three men.

†**'precary,** *a. Obs. rare.* [ad. L. *precāri-us.*] = precarious.

1631 R. Byfield *Doctr. Sabb.* 143 Holiness hath no other but a precary time, when we will borrow it of our worke.

precast ('priːkɑːst, -kæst), *a.* [pre- A. 1.]

a. Formed by casting before being placed in position; composed of units so made. **b.** Pertaining to or involving such a process.

1914 C. E. Fowler *Pract. Treat. Sub-Aqueous Foundations* xxvii. 553 The use of pre-cast piles for permanent construction at a reasonable cost is an ideal type. **1927** *Daily Express* 2 Mar. 3/6 The Concrete Products Association was formed yesterday to improve production.. of 'pre-cast' units in building. **1932** Dowsett & Bartle *Pract. Formwork & Shuttering* ii. 28 A series of rolled steel filler joists arranged to carry a pre-cast floor. **1934** *Archit. Rev.* LXXV. 15/2 The floor is in pre-cast rose and green terrazzo tiles. **1960** *Times* 6 Oct. 7/4 It may be possible to make such roofs in plastic by precast methods. **1975** *Princ. Quality Concrete* (Portland Cement Assoc.) ii. 31 British engineers were experimenting with precast residential structures as early as 1905. Following World War II, precast construction became a permanent part of the European building trades.

pre'cast, *v.*[1] *rare.* [pre- A. 1.] *trans.* To cast or calculate beforehand; to forecast. Hence **pre'casting** *vbl. sb.*

1863 H. Jennings *Rosicrucians* I. 257 The conviction that their divulgement [of future events], as the precasting of God's purposes.. is disallowed.

precast (priː'kɑːst, -kæst), *v.*[2] [pre- A. 1.] *trans.* To cast (an object, or concrete) before it is placed in position. Also *absol.*

Some passive uses are not distinguishable from a predicative use of *precast* adj.

[**1929** W. C. Huntington *Building Construction* iii. 71 Concrete piles may be precast or cast-in-place.] **1938** Wentworth-Shields & Gray *Reinforced Concrete Piling* ix. 81 The use of concrete piles which, instead of being pre-cast, are made by forming a hole in the ground and filling it with concrete.. is steadily extending. **1950** *Archit. Rev.* CVII. 333/3 A large contract, where much of the work can be precast at the site. **1956** *Nature* 4 Feb. 200/1 The art of precasting concrete has given rise to an established industry. **1974** A. Hodgkinson *AJ Handbk. Building Struct.* v. 167/2 The more difficult the in situ formwork problem, the easier is the decision to precast. **1975** *Princ. Quality Concrete* (Portland Cement Assoc.) ii. 31 Since its discovery concrete has been used to precast specialty items.

So **pre'casting** *vbl. sb.*

1938 C. E. Reynolds *Concrete Construction* xi. 484 Where unskilled labour and only a minimum of supervision are available pre-casting may allow the manufacture of the members to be localised and carried out under more convenient conditions. **1974** A. Hodgkinson *AJ Handbk. Building Struct.* v. 167/2 A quite different reason for precasting in certain parts of the UK is the local attitude of carpenters and steel fixers which may cause the contractor to limit absolutely the number of employees on site.

†**pre'cation.** *Obs.* [ad. L. *precātiō-nem*, n. of action f. *precārī* to pray. Cf. F. *précation* (15–16th c. in Godef.).] Praying; entreating, supplication.

a **1548** Hall *Chron.*, *Hen. V* 37 b, Daily praiers and continual precacions to God. *a* **1626** Bp. Andrewes *Pattern Cath. Doct.* (1642) 101 Precation is the desiring of something that is good. **1634** Jackson *Creed* vii. xxxv. §4 Mutual precations of peace and many happy days. *a* **1687** Cotton *2nd Epist. to J. Bradshaw* ix, And can you not, from your Precation And your as daily Club-Potation, To think of an old Friend find some vacation?

precative ('prɛkətɪv), *a.* [ad. late L. *precātīv-us*, f. *precārī* to entreat, pray: see -ative.] **a.** Expressing entreaty or desire; supplicatory.

In *Gram.* applied to a word, particle, or form, expressing entreaty, or the like.

1662 Gurnall *Chr. in Arm.* verse 18. i. li. (1669) 415/1, I begin with the Petitionary part of prayer, and it is three-fold, Precative, Deprecative, Imprecative. **1751** Harris *Hermes* i. viii. (1765) 144 The Requisitive.. hath its subordinate Species: With respect to inferiors, 'tis an Imperative Mode; with respect to equals and superiors, 'tis a Precative or Optative. **1845** [see adhortative *a.*]. **1872** O. Shipley *Gloss. Eccl. Terms* 5 It is a matter of controversy whether the indicative or the precative form of absolution was the earliest. **1899** Brown *Heb. & Eng. Lex.* 609 נָא attached.. to the pf. with *waw* consec., in a precative sense. **1965** *Language* XLI. 12 *Jeṣam* and *yeṣam* represent full-grade precatives. *Ibid.* 520 A precative middle paradigm is given, but nothing is said about how middle precatives are formed.

b. *precative disposition*: cf. precatory b.

1875 Poste *Gaius* ii. Comm. (ed. 2) 287 A precative disposition (a disposition in the form of entreaty) is a trust.

Hence **'precatively** *adv.*, in a precative manner.

1869 J. A. Hessey in *Contemp. Rev.* XI. 180 Sung, pronounced, or uttered precatively or authoritatively.

†**preca'torious,** *a. Obs. rare*: see precary *sb.* 2.

precatory ('prɛkətərɪ), *a.* [ad. late L. *precātōri-us*, f. *precātōr-em* one who prays, agent-n. from *precārī* to pray.] Of, pertaining to, of the nature of, or expressing entreaty or supplication.

In *Gram.*: see precative.

1636 Jackson *Creed* viii. xix. §1 Some.. would have this word *Hosanna*, to be merely precatory or optative: *The Lord send help or salvation.* **1657** Sparrow *Bk. Com. Prayer* (1661) 83 That precatory Hymn of *Veni Creator.* **1787** Sir J. Hawkins *Johnson* 270 The most perfect models of precatory eloquence and civil negotiation. **1833** Carlyle *Diderot* Misc. Ess. 1872 V. 17 Epistles precatory and amatory.. he may have written. **1842** Abp. Thomson *Laws Th.* §27 (1860) 41 Others are only precatory or exclamatory: as 'Oh that this too solid flesh would melt!' **1853** Wolfe *Heb. Gram.* 90 [The Imperative with paragogic ה] is frequently followed by the precatory particle נָא *I pray.*

b. *precatory words*, words in a will praying or expressing a desire that a thing be done. When these are deemed to have an imperative force and to bind the person to whom they are addressed, they constitute a *precatory trust.*

1782 in W. Brown *Rep. Crt. Chanc.* I. 143 The answer is that the words are precatory, not imperative. **1803** Ld. Eldon in F. Vesey *Reports* (1804) VIII. 380 Whether the terms are those of recommendation, or precatory, or expressing hope.. if the objects.. are certain.. the words are considered imperative; and create a Trust. **1890** *Will of E. W. Harcourt* (Nuneham), [The testator expresses a hope] which is not to be construed as a precatory trust, that my successors in the Harcourt estates will carry out the wishes expressed by our common benefactor, the said George Simon Earl Harcourt,.. and will use the surname of Harcourt only. **1904** *Times* 3 Feb. 2/4 The question.. was whether the bequest constituted a precatory trust.

precaudal: see pre- B. 3.

precau'sation. *rare.* [pre- A. 2.] Causation beforehand; predetermination.

1670 Baxter *Life of Faith* ii. ix. 163 By his sustentation, and universal precausation and concourse. **1768–74** Tucker *Lt. Nat.* (1834) I. 658 The ideas of precausation and fatality, of certainty and necessity, are so strongly rivetted together in men's minds.., that it is not easy to keep them asunder.

precaution (prɪ'kɔːʃən), *sb.* [a. F. *précaution* (16th c.), ad. late L. *præcautiōn-em*, n. of action from L. *præcavēre* to guard against beforehand, f. *præ* pre- + *cavēre* to beware of; see caution *sb.*]

1. As a quality or mode of action: Caution exercised beforehand to provide against mischief or secure good results; prudent foresight.

1603 Holland *Plutarch's Mor.* 128 A putting by or precaution that we should not commit any of those faults. **1658** Phillips, *Præcaution*, a fore-seeing, fore-warning, or preventing. **1782** Priestley *Corrupt. Chr.* I. Pref. 20, I have used all the care and precaution that I could. **1791** Burke *App. Whigs* Wks. VI. 20 An object of precaution to provident minds. **1823** F. Clissold *Ascent Mt. Blanc* 19 The danger in this place defies precaution.

2. An instance or practical application of this; a measure taken beforehand to ward off a possible evil, or to ensure a good result (with *a* and *pl.*).

1603 Florio *Montaigne* i. xxvii. 93 Regular and remisse friendship, wherein so many precautions of a long and preallable conversation, are required. **1748** *Anson's Voy.* ii. xi. 249 The Governor.. had taken several precautions to prevent us from forcing our way into the harbour. **1791** Mrs. Radcliffe *Rom. Forest* ii, This seemed a necessary precaution. **1856** Froude *Hist. Eng.* II. ix. 331 They believed truly that the security of the state required unusual precautions.

b. *spec.* a precaution against conception in sexual intercourse; a contraceptive device (usu. in *pl.*).

1935 N. Mitchison *We have been Warned* iv. 419 What did he do to you? Was it—rape?.. Was he using any precautions? **1941** [see it *pron.* 1 d]. **1968** B. Russell *Autobiogr.* II. ii. 97 From the first we used no precautions. **1969** G. Greene *Trav. with my Aunt* i. x. 98 If we didn't have a child together, it was purely owing to the fact that it was a late love. I took no precautions, none at all. **1975** T. Heald *Deadline* vii. 168 Neither had taken any precautions. .. Miss Morrison was pregnant.

†**3.** A caution or caveat given beforehand. *rare.*

1706 Phillips, *Precaution*, Caution, Warning, or Heed, given or us'd before-hand. **1713** Steele *Guardian* No. 17 ¶1, I should call my present Precaution A Criticism upon Fornication.

pre'caution, *v.* [a. F. *précautionner* (17th c. in Hatz.-Darm.), f. *précaution* sb.]

†**1.** *trans.* To caution (any one) beforehand *against* something; to preadmonish, forewarn.

1654 Flecknoe *Ten Years Trav.* 43 Let the Duke of Guise then be precautioned by the Duke of Alansons ill successe at Antwerp. **1768** *Woman of Honor* I. 13 She precautioned them against receiving implicitly any opinion.

2. To put (any one) upon his guard *against* something; esp. *refl.* to be on one's guard *against.*

1700 J. Welwood *Mem. Trans. Eng.* 252 They had ever the Shovel and Pickaxe in their hands, to precaution themselves against this Misfortune. **1716** M. Davies *Athen. Brit.* II. 316 Which last [Rivalling] both High and Low do Precaution themselves against. **1805** W. Taylor in *Ann. Rev.* III. 63 Precautioned by works of imperishable criticism against any real imprudence.

†**3.** To mention or say beforehand by way of caution. *Obs.*

1665 Wither *Lord's Prayer* Preamble, Therefore I have here, to that end, precautioned so much as I conceive may be pertinently extracted from the subject I have now in hand. *Ibid.* 86, I will precaution a little by the way, concerning that. **1690** Norris *Beatitudes* (1692) 215 The reason.. was not (as is already precautioned) any Absolute Merit of theirs.

†**4.** To take precautions against, guard against (a danger). *Obs. rare.*

1690 Dryden *Don Sebast.* ii. i. 30 He cannot hurt me; That I precaution'd.

Hence **pre'cautioning** *vbl. sb.* (in sense 1).

1710 *Col. Rec. Pennsylv.* II. 525 The precautioning of all witnesses.

preˈcautional, *a. rare.* [f. as next + -AL¹.] Of the nature of precaution; precautionary.

1648 W. MOUNTAGUE *Devout Ess.* I. vi. §3. 61 Wherefore this first filiall fear, is but virtuous and precautionall. **1887** *Scott. Leader* 9 Dec. 5 The precautional measures..taken by the Austro-Hungarian War Office, in view of the concentration of Russian troops on the Galician frontier.

precautionary (prɪˈkɔːʃənərɪ), *a.* (*sb.*) [f. PRECAUTION *sb.* + -ARY.]

A. *adj.* **1.** Suggesting or advising provident caution.

1757 *Herald* No. 6 (1758) I. 89 Had the planners of the scheme no precautionary forecast? **1820** CORRY *Eng. Metrop.* 103 You are startled at my first precautionary hint. **1866** GEO. ELIOT *F. Holt* xxv, Jermyn's precautionary statement that he was pursuing inquiries.

2. Of, pertaining to, of the nature of a precaution.

1807 S. TURNER *Anglo-Sax.* (ed. 2) I. IV. v. 276 The precautionary measures of Alfred. **1848** R. I. WILBERFORCE *Doctr. Incarnation* v. (1852) 125 A precautionary guard against what was afterwards the Arian heresy. **1880** FLO. MARRYAT *Fair-haired Alda* II. ix. 159 My measures were only precautionary.

†**B.** *sb.* A precautionary measure, a precaution.

1748 RICHARDSON *Clarissa* (1811) IV. 49 Thou seest, Belford, by the above precautionaries, that I forget nothing.

precautious (prɪˈkɔːʃəs), *a.* [f. PRECAUTION: see -OUS and CAUTIOUS.] Using precaution; displaying previous or provident caution or care.

1713 STEELE *Guardian* No. 147 ¶1 This precautious way of reasoning and acting has proved..an uninterrupted source of felicity. *a* **1734** NORTH *Exam.* I. ii. §116 (1740) 93 It was not the Mode of the Court, in those Days, to be very penetrant, precautious, or watchful. **1871** G. MEREDITH *H. Richmond* II. 177 She was precautious to have her giant to protect her from violence.

Hence **preˈcautiously** *adv.*, in a precautious manner, as a precaution.

a **1711** KEN *Edmund* Poet. Wks. 1721 II. 333 Jesus himself precautiously withdrew, When persecuted by the furious Jew. **1747** RICHARDSON *Clarissa* (1811) II. xii. 77 How anxious to choose and to avoid everything, precautiously, as I may say, that might make me happy, or unhappy. **1921** A. DOBSON *Later Ess.* 163 A clever critic once observed of a popular novelist that few writers had better painted the inside of certain characters—adding *precautiously* 'so far as there is any inside'. **1922** JOYCE *Ulysses* 534 Bloom. (Reflects precautiously.) **1964** M. LANE *Night at Sea* xii. 212 Ben put his injured hand precautiously behind him.

‖**precava, præ-** (priːˈkeɪvə). *Anat.* [f. PRE- A. 4b + CAVA for *vena cava*: cf. POSTCAVA.] The superior or anterior vena cava. Hence **pre-, præˈcaval** *a.* (also *ellipt.* as *sb.*).

1866 OWEN *Anat. Vert.* I. 505 The right and left precavals enter separately the auricular sinus, the left precaval opening near the postcaval vein. **1882** [see POSTCAVA]. **1884** T. J. PARKER *Zootomy* 65 A small chamber, the precaval sinus..situated in the antero-lateral angle of the abdominal cavity.

prece, obs. variant of PRESS.

†**preceˈdaneous**, *a. Obs.* Also 7 -nious, -nous; 7 precid-, 7–8 præcid-, 8 præcedaneous. [app. f. PRECEDE *v.* + *-aneous*: cf. *antecedaneous*, *succedaneous*; but perh. associated in origin with L. *præcīdāne-us* 'that is slaughtered or sacrificed before' (f. *cædĕre* to slay), which in med.L. (Du Cange), and perh. in late L., had in particular connexions the generalized sense 'preliminary, preceding'. Cf. the L. spelling *succīdāneus* beside *succēdāneus*.] Happening or existing before something else; preceding, antecedent, previous.

1647 HAMMOND *Power of Keys* iii. 19 It was but a precedaneous power, preparatory to that other of ruling. [**1656** BLOUNT *Glossogr.*, *Precidaneous*, that which goes before, or is cut or killed before.] **1697** R. PEIRCE *Bath Mem.* II. vi. 322 Precedanious to the Dropsie, are all Cachexies. **1794** T. TAYLOR *Plotinus* Introd. 16 Of goods, some are precedaneous and others preparative; and the precedaneous are such as are desirable for their own sakes, but the preparative, for the sake of other things.

Hence †**preceˈdaneously** *adv. Obs.*, previously.

1657 W. MORICE *Coena quasi Κοινή* xv. 213 There seems to result a necessity of examining Heathens precedaneously to their admission.

precede (prɪˈsiːd), *v.* Also 5 presede, 6–8 preceed, præcede, 7 precead, præceed. [a. F. *précéder* (14th c. in Littré), ad. L. *præcēdĕre* to go before, precede, excel: see PRE- A and CEDE.]

†**1.** *trans.* To go before or beyond (another) in quality or degree; to surpass, excel; to exceed.

c **1375** *Sc. Leg. Saints* xxxvi. (*Baptista*) 177 Ymang birthis þat weman bare þane Iohne baptiste vas nane mare; For he al vthyre in þat precedis, And ewine is to þame in gud dedis. **1631** WEEVER *Anc. Fun. Mon.* 150 Men in the feruencie of deuotion did not precede the weaker sex. **1760–72** H. BROOKE *Fool of Qual.* (1809) I. 84 Through the enfoldings of the stranger's modesty, Mr. Fenton discerned many things preceding the vulgar rank of men.

2. To go before in rank or importance; to occupy a position before or above; to take precedence of.

1485 CAXTON *Paris & V.* (1868) 14 The other grete lordes that shal be there precedyng your degree. **1598** BARRET *Theor. Warres* IV. i. 117 The Colonels companie preceedeth all others of his regiment. *a* **1677** BARROW *Pope's Suprem.* (1680) 285 Such a reason of precedence S. Cyprian giveth in another case, Because..Rome for its magnitude ought to precede Carthage. **1819** REES *Cycl.* s.v. *Precedence*, All the sons of viscounts and barons are allowed to precede baronets. **1839** MISS MITFORD in L'Estrange *Life* (1870) III. vii. 99, I have another short engagement, which ought to precede yours.

3. To go or come before in order or arrangement; to stand or be placed before or in front of.

1494 [see PRECEDING a]. **1530** [see 4]. *a* **1552** LELAND *Itin.* V. 56 Rethelan,..cummith of Rethe,..and Glan..; when Glan is set with a Worde præceding G is explodid. **1673** W. MOUNTAGU in *Buccleuch MSS.* (Hist. MSS. Comm.) I. 320 One for the Duchess of Portsmouth, preceded with a patent of indenization. **1756** J. WARTON *Ess. Pope* (1782) I. v. 267 Those [prologues] of Dryden..may precede any play whatsoever, even tragedy or comedy. **1879** BAIN *Higher Eng. Gram.* 145 When the adjective ends in y *preceded by* a consonant, the y is changed into i.

4. To go before, to move in front of; to walk or proceed in advance of.

1530 PALSGR. 664/1, I precede, I go byfore another to a place or in order. **1602** SHAKS. *Ham.* I. i. 122 As harbingers preceding still the fates. **1713** STEELE *Englishm.* No. 55. 352 Streamers..preceded a Cart, wherein were placed three large Figures. **1788** GIBBON *Decl. & F.* xlv. (1869) II. 677 Terror preceded his march. **1860** TYNDALL *Glac.* I. xi. 85, I sometimes preceded him in cutting the steps.

b. *Astr.* Said of a star, etc. which in the apparent diurnal rotation of the heavens rises before and moves in front of another, i.e. which is situated to the west of it. (See also PRECEDING c.)

1727–41 CHAMBERS *Cycl.* s.v. *Pisces*, Names and situation of the stars...1st of those preceding the square under the southern fish. [**1860** MAURY *Phys. Geog. Sea* (Low) vi. §313 Canopus and Sirius..are high up in their course; they look down with great splendour..as they precede the Southern Cross on its western way.]

5. To come before in time; to happen, occur, or exist before; to be earlier than or anterior to.

a **1540** BARNES *Wks.* (1573) 274/1 And Duns saith, that there is a mollifieng, that precedeth grace, whiche hee calleth attrition. **1581** NOWELL & DAY in *Confer.* I. (1584) E iij, Workes doe not preceede a man to be iustified, but doe follow him being iustified. **1653** LD. VAUX tr. *Godeau's St. Paul* 161 He told them of signes which should preceed the day of Judgement. **1772** PRIESTLEY *Inst. Relig.* (1782) I. 13 Infinite duration must have preceded the present moment. **1861** M. PATTISON *Ess.* (1889) I. 40 The century preceding the formation of the Hanseatic federation.

6. *intr.* or (now only) *absol.* (in senses 2–5): To go or come before (in rank, order, place, or time); to have precedence; to be anterior.

a **1540** BARNES *Wks.* (1573) 278/2 Whether..the will of God is alonely the cause of election, or els any merite of man precedyng afore. **1654** EARL MONM. tr. *Bentivoglio's Warrs Flanders* 123 Who..precedes now in the universal Government of Christ's flock by the name of Urban the Eight. **1667** MILTON *P.L.* x. 640 Till then the Curse pronounc't on both precedes. **1707** E. CHAMBERLAYNE *Pres. St. Eng.* II. xiv. (ed. 22) 185 The Colonel thereof is always to precede as the first Colonel. **1725** POPE *Odyss.* I. 506 To your pretence their title would precede. *Mod.* A statement different from anything that precedes or follows.

7. *trans.* in causal sense: To cause to be preceded (*by*); to preface, introduce (*with* or *by*).

1718 LADY M. W. MONTAGU *Let. to C'tess Mar* 10 Mar., The emperor precedes his visit by a royal present. **1794** MRS. A. M. BENNETT *Ellen* IV. 51 The old man..never..addressed her, without preceding Winifred with Mrs. or Miss. *a* **1834** COLERIDGE *Notes & Lect.* (1849) I. 222 No modern writer would have dared, like Shakspeare, to have preceded this last visitation by two distinct appearances. **1892** *Pall Mall G.* 31 Mar. 4/3 If it was the intention of the Government to postpone the dissolution until September or later, they would undoubtedly have to precede that by a measure of registration.

¶**8.** Erron. used for PROCEED. *Obs. rare.*

?**13..** *Cast. Love* (Halliw.) 1455 In the Fadur nome and the Sone allso, And in the Holigostys that precidit hem fro [*Vernon MS.* glit of hem bo]. **1387** TREVISA *Higden* (Rolls) VII. 89 Ageynes whom as ofte as þe kyng precede [*procederet*], þe erle Edrik counseille nouȝt [*dissuasit*] to ȝeve bataille.

precedence (prɪˈsiːdəns, ˈprɛsɪdəns). Also 5 precydence, 5–6 -sidence, 7 præ-. [prob. f. the earlier PRECEDENT *a.*: see -ENCE. Cf. F. *précédence* (16th c. in Littré).]

†**1.** = PRECEDENT *sb.* 2, 3. *Obs.* (In quots. 1484, 1541, perh. a corruption of *precedents*: cf. ACCIDENCE.)

1484 in *Lett. Rich. III & Hen. VII* (Rolls) I. 85 The bookes of accomptes..[are to] be alway in the handes of the said auditours for their presidence. **1541** in Picton *L'pool Munic. Rec.* (1883) I. 30 These presidence was corrected and drawen out of diverse old presidence. **1558** *Ibid.*, An old book of Precedences..extracted out of the elder Precedences of the town. **1546** LANGLEY *Pol. Verg. De Invent.* I. xvi. 29 b, Out of all such precedences he gathered Preceptes of Phisike.

†**b.** The being or serving as a precedent. *rare.*

1494 FABYAN *Chron.* II. 416 By precydence wherof all the great cyties & good townes of Fraunce were charged in lyke maner.

†**2.** A thing that precedes; something said or done before; an antecedent: = PRECEDENT *sb.* 1.

1588 SHAKS. *L.L.L.* III. i. 83 An epilogue or discourse to make plaine Some obscure precedence that hath tofore bin saine. **1606** —— *Ant. & Cl.* II. v. 51 *Mes.* But yet Madam. *Cleo.* I do not like but yet, it does alay The good precedence. *a* **1610** HEALEY *Epictetus' Man.* (1636) 47 Adventure upon nothing without due consideration of the precedences and consequences thereof.

3. The fact of preceding another or others in time or succession; previous existence or occurrence; priority. (Often with mixture of sense 4.)

1605 CAMDEN *Rem.* 181, I doe beseech the true King, that he would not respect the precedence in time, but devotion of my minde. **1683** TEMPLE *Mem.* Wks. 1731 I. 478 When it was ready to sign, the French Ambassadors offer'd to yield the Precedence in signing it to us as Mediators. **1828** J. BALLANTYNE *Exam. Hum. Mind* iv. 90 According to the law of Precedence, one idea acquires the power of suggesting others by immediately preceding them. **1841** D'ISRAELI *Amen. Lit.* (1867) 158 In the chronology of our poetical collectors, Gower takes precedence of Chaucer unjustly. **1884** *Manch. Exam.* 17 June 5/1 The payment of interest.. will take precedence of other Egyptian obligations.

4. The fact of preceding another or others in order, rank, importance, estimation, or dignity; higher position, superiority; the foremost place, pre-eminence, supremacy.

1658 PHILLIPS, *Præcedence*, a going before, also a surpassing, or excelling. **1694** CROWNE *Regulus* I. 8 Let me have the precedence in your heart. *a* **1719** ADDISON *Notes Ovid's Met.* III. Wks. 1721 I. 241 In which part Ovid's copiousness of invention, and great insight into nature, has given him the precedence to all the Poets that ever came before or after him. **1784** COWPER *Tiroc.* 9 That form.. Framed for the service of a free-born will, Asserts precedence, and bespeaks control. **1845** FORD *Handbk. Spain* I. xiv. 52 The Andalucian horse takes precedence of all. *a* **1902** A. B. DAVIDSON *Old Test. Proph.* x. (1903) 153 The moral everywhere takes precedence of the miraculous.

b. *spec.* The right of preceding others in ceremonies and social formalities; the occupying of a higher or more honourable place in an assembly or procession, according to one's rank; ceremonial priority. Hence in generalized sense: The order to be ceremonially observed by persons of different ranks, according to an acknowledged or legally determined system of regulations.

1598 FLORIO *Ital. Dict.* Ep. Ded. 1, I am no auctorised Herauld to marshall your precedence. ?*a* **1600** (*title*) The Copie of a Booke of Precedence of all estates and playcinge to ther degrees. **1712** ADDISON *Spect.* No. 529 ¶1 Disputes concerning Rank and Precedence. *a* **1715** BURNET *Own Time* (1766) I. 288 He moved, that a letter might be writ giving him the precedence of the Lord Chancellour. **1864** BOUTELL *Her. Hist. & Pop.* xxvii. 428 The Order of Precedence..was first established upon a definite system by a Statute of Henry VIII. **1875** JOWETT *Plato* (ed. 2) V. 123 The president of education is to take precedence of them all. **1899** *Daily News* 21 Dec. 6/1 The great precedence question, which for a while raged so fiercely in the bosoms of our Knights Bachelors, is..now satisfactorily settled.

precedency (prɪˈsiːdənsɪ). Also 7 -ie, preceed-, erron. presi-. [f. as prec. and -ENCY.]

†**1.** The furnishing of a precedent or setting an example; the being a precedent: = prec. 1 b. *Obs.*

1612 T. TAYLOR *Comm. Titus* ii. 4 (1619) 376 Let them be encouraged vnto this holy precedencie and testification of Christianity in euery word, action, and behauiour. **1615** T. ADAMS *White Devill* 5 Such..shall answere..not only for their owne sins, but for all theirs whom the pattern of their precedency has induced to the like. **1657** W. BLOIS *Mod. Policies* (ed. 7) E iv, *Fælix prædo, mundo exemplum inutile*, Happy Piracy is a thing of unhappy presidency; fortunate sins may prove dangerous temptations.

†**2.** A thing that precedes; an antecedent: = prec. 2. *Obs. rare*⁻¹.

1657 FITZ-BRIAN *Gd. Old Cause in Prim. Lustre* (1659) 6 It was an inlet, and a necessary precedency to their great mutations that were to follow.

3. Priority in time or succession: = prec. 3.

1622 PEACHAM *Compl. Gent.* xii. (1634) 106 The other two may justly claime precedency of Coines, seeing they are the ingredient simples that compound them. **1641** MILTON *Reform.* I. Wks. 1851 III. 5 The Precedencie which God gave this Iland to be the first Restorer of buried Truth. **1706** ESTCOURT *Fair Examp.* IV. i. 47 He has lov'd me long, long before you knew me, and claims a Privilege from Precedency. **1770** LANGHORNE *Plutarch* (1879) I. 83/2 Numa seems to have taken away the precedency from March,..to show his preference of the political virtues to the martial.

4. Superiority in rank or estimation: = prec. 4.

1612 *North's Plutarch* 750 You looke here, Reader, to see to which of the two I shold giue the precedencie. *a* **1613** OVERBURY *A Wife*, etc. (1638) 90 He speakes most of the precedency of age. **1682** NORRIS *Hierocles* Introd., The Pythagorick Verses deservedly call'd Golden, may justly claim the precedency. **1750** JOHNSON *Rambler* No. 81 ¶1 The precedency or superior excellence of one virtue to another. **1850** MERIVALE *Rom. Emp.* II. xii. 26 They had surrendered their ancient claim to precedency among the Gaulish states.

b. *spec.* Ceremonial priority or order: = prec. 4 b.

1599 B. JONSON *Cynthia's Rev.* II. i, One, in whom the humours and elements are peaceably met, without emulation of precedency. **1661** MORGAN *Sph. Gentry* IV. ii. 37 A controversie of precedency between the younger sons of Viscounts and Barons, and the Baronets. **1711** ADDISON

Spect. No. 119 ¶3 There is infinitely more to do about Place and Precedency in a Meeting of Justices Wives, than in an Assembly of Dutchesses. **1863** H. Cox *Instit.* I. vi. 43 Bills for granting honours or precedency.

precedent (ˈprɛsɪdənt), *sb.* Forms: α. 5 president, -cydent, 5- precedent (5 -e). β. 5-6 prese-, presy-, 7 presa-, 5-8 president (5-6 -e). [a. F. *précédent*, subst. use of the adj.: see next. The β forms arose in Eng. through practical identity of pronunciation, and consequent confusion, with PRESIDENT.]

1. A thing or person that precedes or goes before another. †**a.** That which has been mentioned just before. Usually in *pl.*: the preceding or foregoing facts, statements, etc. *Obs.*

1433 *Rolls of Parlt.* IV. 425/1 My Lord of Bedford.. nought havyng his rewarde to yᵉ said precedents offerd and agreed hym to serve yᵉ Kyng. **1494** Fabyan *Chron.* vii. 397 Whan all these presedentes were sene by yᵉ Scottes, a day was assygned of metynge at Norham. *c* **1555** Harpsfield *Divorce Hen. VIII* (Camden) 237 A fourth impediment, and worse than the precedents. **1607** Topsell *Four-f. Beasts* (1658) 105, I should here end the discourse of this beast, after the method already observed in the precedents.

b. That which precedes in time; something occurring before; an antecedent. ? *Obs.*

In first two quots. applied to a previous document, etc. serving as a guide in subsequent cases (leading to sense 2).

1450 *Rolls of Parlt.* V. 191/1 Any Graunt made by us.. of Viewe of Frauncplegge.. which we graunted to hym upon certeyn precedentez allowed in Ayer to his Aunceterz of longe time paste. **1523** Fitzherb. *Surv.* 12 But yᵉ diuersytie of these tenures.. can nat be knowen but by the lordes euydence, court rolles, rentayles, and suche other presydentes. **1691** Beverley *Mem. Kingd. Christ* 10 The mention of the Three days, and a Half as the most Immediate Precedent of their Rising. **1788** T. Taylor *Proclus' Comm.* I. 67 Things subsequent are always annexed to their precedents.

†**c.** One who goes or moves before or in advance of another; a forerunner. *Obs.*

1603 Owen *Pembrokeshire* (1892) 274 Some gaine in running vpon his precedentes, some forced to come behinde those that were once foremost. **1610** *Histrio-m.* vi. 143 Ruine and Warre, the precedents of Wrath,.. Have rid their circuit through this fertile soyle.

†**d.** The original from which a copy is made. *Obs.*

1594 Shaks. *Rich. III*, iii. vi. 7 Here is the Indictment of the good Lord Hastings,.. Eleuen houres I haue spent to write it ouer.. The Precedent was full as long a doing. **1595** —— *John* v. ii. 3 My Lord Melloone, let this be coppied out, And keepe it safe for our remembrance: [Giues Meloone the Treaty.] Returne the president to these Lords againe.

†**e.** A sign, token, earnest, indication. *Obs.*

1581 Rich *Farewell* (Shaks. Soc.) 183 He had given.. to the Kyng himself, as a president of his good will, a riche jewell. **1592** Shaks. *Ven. & Ad.* 26 With this she ceazeth on his sweating palme, The president of pith and liuelyhood.

2. a. A previous instance or case which is or may be taken as an example or rule for subsequent cases, or by which some similar act or circumstance may be supported or justified. (The prevailing sense.)

α. **1427** *Rolls of Parlt.* IV. 326/2 My Lordes your Uncles [etc.].. serched precydentes of the governaill of ye land in tyme and cas semblable. **1597** Hooker *Eccl. Pol.* v. lxv. §21 That verie precedent it selfe which they propose may bee best followed. **1627–77** Feltham *Resolves* i. xx. 37 St. Paul is Precedent for it. **1666–7** Pepys *Diary* 9 Jan., The Lords did argue, that it was an ill precedent, and that which will ever hereafter be used. **1742** Young *Nt. Th.* i. 392 Be wise to-day; 'tis madness to defer; Next day the fatal precedent will plead. **1787** Jefferson *Writ.* (1859) II. 141 They consider the North American revolution a precedent for theirs. **1832** Tennyson '*You ask me why*', etc. 12 A land.. Where Freedom broadens slowly down From precedent to precedent. **1888** F. Hume *Mme. Midas* i. i, He promptly followed the precedent set by Oxford.

β. *c* **1460** Fortescue *Abs. & Lim. Mon.* x. (1885) 134 Soche was þe sellynge off Chirke and Chirkes landes, weroff neuer manne see a president. **1537** Cromwell in Merriman *Life & Lett.* (1902) II. 102 The president were to yvel to be admytted. **1643** Milton *Sov. Salve* 4 By such a provision a dangerous president is introduced. **1663** Chas. II in Julia Cartwright *Henrietta of Orleans* (1894) 151 Considering all former presadents, who are cleerly on our side. **1733** Neal *Hist. Purit.* II. 445 His Majesty's not interposing.. was afterwards made use of as a president.

b. *Law.* A previous judicial decision, method of proceeding, or draft of a document, which serves as an authoritative rule or pattern in similar or analogous cases.

α. **1689** *Tryal Bps.* 34 Things done in particular cases in favour are not Precedents. **1765** Blackstone *Comm.* I. Introd. iii. 69 It is an established rule to abide by former precedents, when the same points come again in litigation. **1772** *Junius Lett.* Ded. Eng. Nat. 3 One precedent creates another.—They soon accumulate, and constitute law. **1874** Green *Short Hist.* viii. §5. 502 The legal research of Noy.. found precedents among the records in the Tower.

β. **1523** Fitzherb. *Surv.* 20 The lordes court rolles, the whiche is a regester to the lorde to knowe his presydentes, customes, and seruyces. **1596** Shaks. *Merch. V.* iv. i. 220 There is no power in Venice Can alter a decree established: 'Twill be recorded for a President. **1642** Chas. I *Answ. to Printed Bk.* 25 Upon pretence of Authority of Book-cases, and Presidents. **1718** S. Sewall *Diary* 5 Feb., Look'd [out] the presidents which made it good.

c. In collective or generalized sense (without article or *pl.*). ***without precedent***, unprecedented.

1622 Donne *Serm.* (ed. Alford) VI. 154 To become a precedent, govern thyself by precedent first. **1671** Salmon *Syn. Med.* Introd. 4 We will not much praise it,.. for it was wrot without President. **1750** Johnson *Rambler* No. 28 ¶7 Each comforts himself that his faults are not without precedent. **1769** *Junius Lett.* v. (1797) I. 44 Your conduct was not justified by precedent. **1858** Froude *Hist. Eng.* III. xvi. 362 The conservative English instinct, which.. ever preferred the authority of precedent to any other guide.

†**3.** *transf.* A written or printed record of some past proceeding or proceedings, serving as a guide or rule for subsequent cases. *Obs.*

1543 (*title*) A Boke of Presidentes exactly written in maner of a Register. **1625** B. Jonson *Staple of N.* i. v, Of all which seuerall [news] The Day-bookes, Characters, Precedents are kept. **1650** Weldon *Crt. Jas. I* (1651) 11 He caused a whole cartload of Parliament Presidents (that spake the Subjects Liberty) to be burnt.

†**4. a.** An example that is, or is intended or worthy to be, followed or copied; a pattern, model, exemplar. *Obs.* (exc. as in 2).

1549 Chaloner *Erasm. on Folly* Pij b, Through the abhominable president of theyr life they dooe eftsoones crucifie hym. **1565** in Strype *Ann. Ref.* (1709) I. xlvi. 472 [Thus.. did the Admonition to the Parliament charge her Chapel, viz.] as the pattern and precedent to the people of all superstition. **1607** Tourneur *Rev. Trag.* i. iv, *Piero.* That vertuous Lady! *L. Ant.* Precedent for wives! **1675** Traherne *Chr. Ethics* 299 We produce Eve only for a president.

†**b.** An example, instance, illustration, specimen.

c **1555** Harpsfield *Divorce Hen. VIII* (Camden) 217 But the most notable president of this kind of chastity is the virginity of our blessed lady.. married to good Joseph. **1600** Holland *Livy* xxviii. xliv. 704 Can there bee a president [L. *exemplum*] found more pregnant.. to prove and enforce this point, than Anniball himselfe? **1631** R. Norwood *Trigonometrie* Ep. to Rdr., Some.. who, when these tables were printing and almost finished, came to the printing house and not only tooke a sufficient view of them there, but carried away a president without the printer's leave. **1668** Rolle *Abridgm.* i. 49, I will make thee an example and president for a perjured Rogue. **1695** Woodward *Nat. Hist. Earth* ii. 103 There are so many Presidents on Record in Holy Writ of this way of proceeding, that no one can be well ignorant of them.

5. *attrib.* and *Comb.*, as ***precedent book***, ***precedent-setting***, ***-worshipping*** adjs.

1591 Nashe *Introd. Sidney's Astr. & Stella*, Although it be.. the president bookes of such as cannot see without another man's spectacles. **1853** Kingsley *Lett.* (1878) I. 374 If we can prove this point, we prove everything with precedent-worshipping John Bull. **1967** *Economist* 14 Oct. 160/3 In Boston an outspoken lawyer, in a precedent-setting challenge to the constitutionality of the Massachusetts laws against marijuana, is asking whether all the fuss over pot is really worth it. **1977** *New Yorker* 19 Sept. 50/2 Some people feel that the conductor was challenging the soloist and that she more than met the challenge, with the result that the last movement is taken at a precedent-setting speed.

precedent (prɪˈsiːdənt), *a.* Now *rare*: largely replaced by PRECEDING. Forms: α. 4- precedent, (5 ˈprecydent, 6 preˈceedent, 7 præcedent). β. 5-6 ˈpresedent, 6 ˈpresident, 7 ˈpresedentt. [a. F. *précédent* (13-14th c. in Hatz.-Darm.), ad. L. *præcēdens*, *-entem*, pres. pple. of *præcēdĕre* to PRECEDE. Originally stressed *preceˈdent*, *ˈpreced-ent* like the sb.; but in 16th c. conformed to *preˈcede*, *preˈcedence*, *preˈceding*.

(Pegge *Anecd.* 283 remarks on *precedent* having one sound when a sb., another sound when an adj.)]

1. Preceding in time; existing or occurring before something expressed or implied; previous, former, antecedent: = PRECEDING b.

c **1391** Chaucer *Astrol.* ii. §32 Fro the Midday of the day precedent. *c* **1440** *Promp. Parv.* 412/2 Presedent, *presidens* [P. *precedens*]. **1472–3** *Rolls of Parlt.* VI. 57/1 The same accompt for the first yere precedent. **1509** Hawes *Past. Pleas.* xxvii. (Percy Soc.) 123 The desteny is a thyng accydent,.. Tyll it be done it is ay precedent. *c* **1585** *Faire Em* i. 123 As if we were in our precedent way. **1598** Barckley *Felic. Man* (1631) 473 There are two sorts of ends, some are precedent, some subsequent. **1616** Sir T. Button in *Lismore Papers* Ser. ii. (1887) II. 65, I shalbe glad ..to be your tenant..and give as muche rentt..as the presedentt tenant did. *a* **1644** Quarles *Sol. Recant.* ch. i, There's nothing modern times can own, The which precedent Ages have not known. *a* **1674** Clarendon *Surv. Leviath.* (1676) 88 For there could be no Law precedent to that resignation of themselves. **16..** *Songs Costume* (Percy Soc.) 157 Our men were in precedent dayes To manly actions bent. **1787** *Minor* 201 Mr. Plodder having been busied the precedent night. **1817** Jas. Mill *Brit. India* III. vi. i. 21 The operation of control is subsequent, not precedent. **1850** Blackie *Æschylus* I. 51 A host of jarring rumours.. Each fresh recital with a murkier hue Than its precedent.

2. Preceding in order or succession; coming or placed before; esp. ***the precedent***, that coming immediately before, the foregoing: = PRECEDING a.

1483 Caxton *Cato* E iij b, To flee the false opynyons and errours of thauncient beforesayd in the iiii precedent commaundementes. **1484** —— *Fables of Æsop* v. viii, The Auctor of this booke rehercith suche another Fable.. as the precydent. **1561** Hollybush *Hom. Apoth.* 15 b, As I have taught in the precedent chapter. **1660** Barrow *Euclid* Pref. (1714) 2 The six precedent and the two subsequent [Books]. **1741** T. Robinson *Gavelkind* v. 77 The Generality of the Precedent Words. **1837** Whittock, etc. *Bk. Trades* (1842) 389 Certain provincialisms.. chiefly evinced.. in the discord of precedent, antecedent, and relative pronouns.

b. Mentioned or spoken of just before; immediately aforesaid; preceding.

1530 Palsgr. 987 The whiche may be turned lyke the verbe precedent. **1594** Plat *Jewell-ho.* iii. 63 This secrete with the preceedent I had of a Dutch mountbanke. **1597** Gerarde *Herbal* i. vii. §1. 8 The great Foxe-taile grasse.. is nothing rough in handling like the precedent. **1605** Bacon *Adv. Learn.* ii. Ded. to King §13 Another defect which I note, ascendeth a little higher than the precedent. **1705** tr. *Bosman's Guinea* 269 A Bird not above half so big as the precedent.

3. Preceding in rank or estimation; having or taking precedence.

1613 Purchas *Pilgrimage* (1614) 340 The one precedent in age and nobilitie, the other a Leader in Warre, and Lawgiuer in Peace. **1858** Bushnell *Nat. & Supernat.* x. (1864) 289 Laying his hand upon all the dearest and most intimate affections of life and demanding a precedent love.

precedent (ˈprɛsɪdənt), *v.* [f. PRECEDENT *sb.*] *trans.* To furnish with a precedent; to be a precedent for; to support or justify by a precedent. Now only in *pa. pple.*: see also PRECEDENTED.

1614 W. B. *Philosopher's Banquet* (ed. 2) 28 The examples of diuers.. kings.. do president vs in these carriages. **1652–62** Heylin *Cosmogr.* iv. (1682) 18 The Ottoman Turks were precedented by those of Egypt. **1716** M. Davies *Athen. Brit.* III. 42 Otherwise the Example might be of dangerous consequence, tho' often precedented by the Popish Monks and Jesuits in their Editions.

†**b.** *refl.* To guide or support oneself *by* a precedent; to follow as a precedent. *Obs.*

1636 Abp. Williams *Holy Table* (1637) 35 Now we are no longer to president our selves, in this kind, by the Chappell, but by the Liturgie of Queen Elisabeth. **1641** Burges *Serm.* 5 *Nov.* 63 This is a memorable Instance; and I would to God you would president your selves by it.

Hence ˈ**precedenting** *ppl. a.*, setting or serving as a precedent.

a **1693** *Urquhart's Rabelais* iii. xxxviii. 319 Prototypal and precedenting fool.

precedent, obs. Sc. form of PRESIDENT.

precedentable, *a. rare*⁻¹. [f. PRECEDENT *v.* + -ABLE.] Capable of being precedented; for which a precedent can be found.

c **1642** *Observator Defended* 4 Which power.. can never be safe either for King or people, nor is presidentable.

precedental (prɛsɪˈdɛntəl), *a. rare.* [f. PRECEDENT *sb.* + -AL[1].] Of or pertaining to a precedent; of the nature of, or constituting a precedent (= PRECEDENTIAL 1); but in quots. used as = supported by precedent, precedented (cf. PRECEDENTIAL 1 b).

1642 *Virginia Stat.* (1823) I. 237 By abollishing condemnations and censures (presidental from the time of the corporation) of the inhabitants from colonies service. **1658** *Ibid.* 499 The House humbly presenteth, That the said disolution.. is not presidentall.

preceˈdentary, *a. rare*⁻¹. [f. as prec. + -ARY[1].] Forming a precedent: = PRECEDENTIAL 1.

1887 *Blackw. Mag.* Sept. 396 Such a precedentary act as Lord Palmerston's despatch of the British fleet to the Dardanelles.

precedented (ˈprɛsɪdɛntɪd), *ppl. a.* [f. PRECEDENT *v.* or *sb.* + -ED.] Furnished with or having a precedent; in accordance with or warranted by precedent; paralleled or supported by a similar previous case or occurrence. Usually in predicate: see also PRECEDENT *v.* (Opp. to UNPRECEDENTED.)

1653 A. Wilson *Jas. I* 175 We.. with more alacrity and celerity than ever was precedented in Parliament, did address ourselves to the Service commanded unto Us. **1762** H. Walpole *Vertue's Anecd. Paint.* (1765) I. Pref. 5 When one offers to the public the labours of another person, it is allowable and precedented to expatiate in praise of the work. **1809** E. S. Barrett *Setting Sun* II. 65 This prayer is, as we have shewn before, precedented and proper. **1880** F. G. Lee *Ch. under Q. Eliz.* I. 275 Notwithstanding their extraordinary but precedented Oath of Homage.

precedential (prɛsɪˈdɛnʃəl), *a.* Now *rare.* [f. PRECEDENT *sb.* or PRECEDENCE, after *consequential*, *differential*, etc.]

1. Of the nature of or constituting a precedent; furnishing a guide or rule for subsequent cases.

a **1641** Bp. Mountagu *Acts & Mon.* (1642) 31 These were Precedentiall to their Successors. **1693** *Col. Rec. Pennsylv.* I. 404 His Excell. had made many steps of Condescention to them which he had not done in another government, and [which] was not presidentiall. **1893** *Independent* (N.Y.) 19 Oct., If he is appointed, any applicant.. can claim.. appointment on the strength of this precedential case.

¶**b.** *erron.* Supported by precedent, precedented: in comb. ***non-precedential***, unprecedented.

1642 R. Watson *Serm. Schisme* 29 They.. can fix on the same an unparallel'd, non-presidentiall interpretation.

2. Having precedence, preceding, preliminary.

1661 Blount *Glossogr.* (ed. 2), *Precedential*.. that goes before or surpasseth. **1683** Howe *Union among Protestants* Wks. (1846) 121 Negotiations.. precedential to the concord they endeavoured between the Saxon and the Helvetian Churches. **1802–12** Bentham *Ration. Judic. Evid.* (1827) III. 4 It becomes necessary to distinguish the several precedential or introductory facts..from the ultimate principal fact.

3. Relating to (social) precedence.

1836 *Fraser's Mag* XIII. 63 Charles the Fifth settled a precedential hubbub between two dames of high degree.

ˈprecedentless, *a. rare.* [f. PRECEDENT *sb.* + -LESS.] Having no precedents to follow.

1869 *Daily News* 26 May, Admitting..that his own tradition-beridden country was being slowly but surely drawn into the wake of traditionless, precedentless America.

precedently (prɪˈsiːdəntlɪ), *adv.* [f. PRECEDENT *a.* + -LY².] In the way of precedence; previously, antecedently, beforehand.

1624 FISHER in F. White *Repl. F.* 31 The mayne and substantiall points of faith are beleeued, not vpon Scripture, but vpon Tradition precedently vnto Scripture. **1678** HOBBES *Decam.* ix. 117 For precedently he had said that [etc.]. **1768** *Woman of Honor* II. 5 From what I have precedently touched to you of her character. *a* **1848** R. W. HAMILTON *Rew. & Punishm.* i. (1853) 31 Precedently to this inquiry, another claims its notice.

preceder (prɪˈsiːdə(r)). *rare* [f. PRECEDE + -ER¹.] One who or that which precedes; in quot., One who furnishes an example or precedent.

1611 SPEED *Hist. Gt. Brit.* VI. xl. 144 So desirous to be a Preceder of moderation and singularity vnto others,..that he would not permit his Empresse to weare any Iewels of high price.

preceding (prɪˈsiːdɪŋ), *ppl. a.* [f. PRECEDE + -ING².] That precedes.

a. in order or arrangement: Coming or placed before something else; *esp.* coming immediately before; given, stated, or mentioned just before; foregoing.

1494 FABYAN *Chron.* v. cxix. 95 As before is touchyd in the presedyng chapitre. **1702–3** GALE in *Pepy's Diary*, etc. (1879) VI. 258 Dr. S. gave me the preceding account. **1772** *Junius Lett.* lxviii. (1797) II. 267, I have great faith in the preceding argument. **1823** H. J. BROOKE *Introd. Crystallogr.* 127 The secondary forms belonging to the four preceding classes of primary forms, are nearly similar to each other.

b. in time: Existing, occurring, or going on before something else; previous, prior, past, anterior, former, antecedent; *esp.* occurring just before, immediately anterior, 'last'.

1601 SHAKS. *All's Well* v. iii. 196 Of sixe preceding Ancestors,..Hath it beene owed and worne. **1654** EARL MONM. tr. *Bentivoglio's Warrs Flanders* 237 They..sent them..about the end of the preceding May last [*antecedente Maggio passato*]. *a* **1720** SEWEL *Hist. Quakers* (1795) I. Pref. 16 The great difference between this last, and all the..preceding persecutions. **1875** JOWETT *Plato* (ed. 2) III. 48 Each generation improves upon the preceding.

c. in movement: *spec.* in *Astr.* said of a heavenly body, etc. situated to the west of another, and therefore moving in front of it in the apparent diurnal rotation of the heavens.

1727–41 CHAMBERS *Cycl.* s.v. *Orion*, Bright [star] in preced[ing] foot called *regel*... Preced[ing] in the girdle... Middle of three in the girdle... Third and last in the girdle. **1784** HERSCHEL in *Phil. Trans.* LXXIV. 265 The preceding side of Mars shews the flattening of the poles, while the following is terminated by an elliptical arch. **1867** SMYTH *Sailor's Word-bk.* s.v. *Quadrant*, In speaking of double stars, or of two objects near each other, the position of one component in reference to the other is indicated by the terms, north following, north preceding, south following, or south preceding, the word quadrant being understood.

preceid, obs. Sc. form of PRESIDE.

†preˈcel, *v. Obs.* Also 6 *Sc.* **presell.** [ad. L. *præcell-ĕre* to (rise above,) surpass, excel, f. *præ*, PRE- A. 5 + **cellĕre* to rise higher, to tower; cf. EXCEL. Cf. obs. F. *précellen.*]

1. *intr.* To be superior; to excel, surpass.

c **1400** *Apol. Loll.* 59 If he precelle in sciens & holines. **1430–40** LYDG. *Bochas* I. i. (MS. Bodl. 263) 13/2 As we precelle in wisdam and resoun. **1549** COVERDALE, etc. *Erasm. Par. Tim.* iii. 9 It is conueniente, that he whiche precelleth in honor, should also precelle in vertues. **1550** J. COKE *Eng. & Fr. Heralds* §54 (1877) 73 Malgo..precelled in beautye, puyssaunce, force, and strengthe, of all men in those dayes. **1552–1756** [see PRECELLING].

2. *trans.* To be superior to; to surpass, excel (another or others); = EXCEL *v.* 2.

1432–50 tr. *Higden* (Rolls) IV. 31 Bledgarec kynge precellede alle other in musike. **1530** LYNDESAY *Test. Papyngo* 26 As Phebus dois Synthia presell. **1661** CRESSY *Refl. Oathes Suprem. & Alleg.* 91 Be subject to every humane creature, to the King as precelling all others.

Hence **†preˈcelling** *vbl. sb.*

a **1532** *Remedie of Loue* Prol. v, Flouring youth, which.. a precelling haste aboue age In many a singuler commodite.

precelland, -end, obs. Sc. ff. PRECELLING.

precellence. *rare.* [ad. late L. *præcellentia* excellence, f. *præcellĕre*: see PRECEL and -ENCE. Cf. obs. F. *précellence* (16th c. in Littré).] The fact or quality of excelling; pre-eminence.

Quot. 1958 contains a rendering of Henri Estienne's title *La Précellence du langage françois* (1579).

1432–50 tr. *Higden* (Rolls) III. 159 The dedes schalle schewe the precellence of oure wifes. **1541** R. COPLAND *Galyen's Terap.* 2 G iij, Eyther by precellence & noblenes of yᵉ partye. **1669** GALE *Crt. Gentiles* I. 5 Their Divine.. Precellence beyond al human books and Records. **1737** L. CLARKE *Hist. Bible* Pref. Gosp. (1740) 9 The precellence of the Gospel will yet appear much greater, if we consider the imperfection of the Law. **1958** *Times* 6 May 12/4 When he delivers the Sir Basil Zaharoff lecture on May 20, Professor Alfred Ewert..will take as his subject 'The precellence of the French tongue'. **1978** R. SYME *Hist. in Ovid* vii. 132 There was another side to the oratorical precellence of Messalla Corvinus. Some found him prolix and lacking in bite.

†precellency. *Obs.* [f. as prec. + -ENCY.] The quality of being 'precellent'; pre-eminence; with *a* and *pl.* an instance of this.

1557 EDGEWORTH *Serm., 1 Pet.* viii. 180 b, Sainte Peter knewe no precellencye or excellencye ouer a whole realme. **1616** R. SHELDON *Rom. Mir. Antichristian* 151 Any pre-eminence or precellencie giuen. **1640** G. WATTS tr. *Bacon's Adv. Learn.* IV. iii. 207 There are many and great Precellencies of the soule of man, above the soules of beasts. **1658** W. PERCY *Compl. Swimmer* v. 9 Fishes may challenge to themselves a precellency in Swimming.

†precellent, *a. Obs.* [ad. L. *præcellent-em*, pres. pple. of *præcellĕre* to surpass (see PRECEL). So obs. F. *précellent* (*c* 1170 in Godef.).] That excels or surpasses; surpassing, pre-eminent.

1382 WYCLIF *1 Pet.* ii. 13 Be ȝe suget to..the kyng, as precellent [*gloss* or more worthi in staat]. **1432–50** tr. *Higden* (Rolls) VII. 39 Fulbertus..a man precellente in the luffe of our blissede lady. **1542** BOORDE *Dyetary* (1870) 225 To the precellent and armypotent prynce. **1660** BURNEY *Κέρδ. Δῶρον* (1661) 20 What validity is it of when precellent vertue is not valued?

b. Const. as *pres. pple.* = 'precelling', excelling.

1432–50 tr. *Higden* (Rolls) III. 219 The philosophres that were diuines were precellente alle other kyndes off philosophres.

Hence **†precellently** *adv.*

c **1557** ABP. PARKER *Ps.* cxix. 357 Proud men lyke drosse thou wilt remoue, which iet in earth so stout Precellently.

†preˈcelling, *ppl. a. Obs.* Also 6 *Sc.* **-and, -end.** [f. PRECEL + -ING².] That 'precels' or excels; excelling, excellent; surpassing, pre-eminent.

c **1430** LYDG. *Min. Poems* (Percy Soc.) 12 Ther satt a child off beauté precellyng, Middes of the trone, rayed lyke a kyng. *Ibid.* 21 Be glad, O Londone,..Citee of citees, of noblesse precellyng. **1552** LYNDESAY *Monarche* 5980 Than sall that most precelland Kyng Tyll those wrachis mak answeryng. *a* **1568** W. STEWART in *Bannatyne Poems* (Hunter. Cl.) 250 Precellend prince! havand prerogatyue As rowy royall in this regioun to ring. **1676** SHADWELL *Virtuoso* II. Wks. 1720 I. 342 Were I as precelling in physico-mechanical investigations, as you in tropical rhetorical flourishes. **1756** *Gentl. Mag.* XXVI. 308 The sacred confidence reposed in our representatives confers precelling dignity.

precellular: see PRE- B. 1.

precely, variant of PRESSLY *Obs.*, expressly.

pre-censorship: PRE- A. 2.

precent (prɪˈsɛnt), *v.* [ad. L. *præcentāre* to sing before, or back-formation from PRECENTOR.]

a. *intr.* To officiate as precentor; to lead the singing of a choir or congregation. **b.** *trans.* To lead in singing (a psalm, antiphon, etc.).

1732 R. ERSKINE *Diary* in Agnew *Theol. Consolation* (1881) 253 This day I precented for my colleague. **1824** *Blackw. Mag.* XV. 179 Owing to some misunderstanding between the minister of the parish and the session clerk, the precenting in church devolved on my father. **1872** *Sacristy* II. 224 Lifted up his voice and precented the 'Salve, Sancta Parens!' **1893** C. L. MARSON *Psalms at Work* (1894) 177/1 It is..the hymn they sang on their way to the Mount.., and Our Lord no doubt precented it by singing the first half-verse alone. **1904** R. SMALL *Hist. U.P. Congregat.* I. 669 The employment of a student to keep school and precent.

†preˈcention. *Obs. rare*⁻⁰. [ad. L. *præcentiōn-em* a singing before, a prelude, n. of action from *præcinĕre* (see next).]

1656 BLOUNT *Glossogr.*, *Precention*, a singing before; the on-set or flourish of a Song. **1658** in PHILLIPS.

precentor (prɪˈsɛntə(r)). Also 7–9 **precenter.** [a. late L. *præcentor* a leader in music, precentor, f. L. *præcinĕre, -cent-* to sing or play before (a person, etc.), also to foretell, f. *præ*, PRE- + *canĕre* to sing. So F. *précenteur* (16th c.), earlier *precentre.*] One who leads or directs the singing of a choir or congregation; *spec.* **a.** in cathedrals of the Old Foundation, a member of the chapter (ranking next to the dean), whose duties as precentor are now commonly discharged by the succentor; **b.** in those of the New Foundation, one of the minor canons (among whom he usually takes precedence) or a chaplain, who performs the duties in person; **c.** in churches or chapels in which there is no instrumental accompaniment, the officer who leads congregational singing. Also *transf.*

1613 PURCHAS *Pilgrimage* (1614) 201 The Præcentor or chiefe Chorister agaíne rising vp saith, And we know not what to doe. **1649** *Acts & Ordin. Parl.* c. 46 (Scobell) 68 That all and every person and persons, who by an Act of this Parliament..are not disabled to hold or use the Place, Function, Office, Title or Stile of Precenter, or any other Title [etc.] are and be from the Nine and Twentieth day of March..disabled to hold the same. **1659** HAMMOND *On Ps.* Pref. 2 Wherein also those Angels which shall then be our Præcentors are here pleased to follow. **1706** A. BEDFORD *Temple Mus.* iv. 73 The Business of the Præcentor was to Sing the first Verse, or at least the first Part thereof, that the rest of his Brethren might know what Tune to Sing, and what Pitch to take. **1757** in Calderwood *Dying Testimonies* (1806) 388 From pulpits or presenters seats. **1782** BURNEY *Hist. Mus.* (1789) II. i. 56 In 680 John, Praecentor of St. Peter's, was sent over by Pope Agatho to instruct the Monks of Weremouth in the art of singing. **1821** GALT *Ann. Parish* xii, The schoolmaster..was likewise session-clerk and precentor. **1840** *Act 3 & 4 Vict.* c. 113 the Precentor of the Cathedral Church of Saint David..shall be..styled Dean. **1852** HOOK *Ch. Dict.* (1871) 600 Formerly the precentor in most of the Cathedrals ranked next to the Dean. Now he is usually a minor canon. **1863** COWDEN CLARKE *Shaks. Char.* iv. 107 Observe a bevy of them seated on a door-step, joining in tiny chorus to the directing melody of an elder precentor. **1869** SPURGEON *Treas. Dav.* Ps. xxii. 22 Jesus himself leads the song, and is both precentor and preacher in his church. **1887** *Spectator* 5 Nov. 1513 [He] became a 'precentor' (or leader of the psalmody), first in a Perth Presbyterian church.

Hence **precenˈtorial** *a.*, of or pertaining to a precentor; **preˈcentory** [cf. *deanery*], the residence of the precentor in a cathedral of the Old Foundation; **preˈcentress** = PRECENTRIX.

1825 CARLYLE *Schiller* App. 313 The precentorial spirit of his father was more than reconciled, on discovering that Daniel could also preach, and play upon the organ. **1906** E. M. SYMPSON *Hist. & Topogr. Lincoln* 310 Beneath the Precentory..still exists the Roman hypocaust. **1892** STEVENSON *Lett.* (1901) II. xi. 252 Our boys and precentress ('tis always a woman that leads) did better than I ever heard them.

preˈcentorship. [f. prec. + -SHIP.] The office, position, or function of a precentor.

1819 *Blackw. Mag.* VI. 174 Saved..by the well-timed exaltation to a neighbouring precentership. **1865** T. D. HARDY *Catal. Ld. Chancellors* II. 488 Besides this canonry he [Mapes] held the precentorship of Lincoln. **1868** I. BURNS *Mem. W. C. Burns* (1870) 485 A hymn was sung by the company under his precentorship. **1886** L. O. PIKE *Yearbks. 13 & 14 Edw. III* Introd. 61 A former Bishop was seised of the advowson of the precentorship as in right of his bishopric.

precentral: see PRE- B. 3.

pre-centrifuge: PRE- A. 1.

precentrix (prɪˈsɛntrɪks). [a. med.L. *præcentrix* fem., corresp. to *præcentor* PRECENTOR: see -TRIX.] A female precentor or leader of a choir.

1706 A. BEDFORD *Temple Mus.* ii. 19 He..made his Sister Præcentrix to the Women. **1825** SCOTT *Betrothed* xix, The abbess..called on her Precentrix, and desired her to command her niece's attendance immediately. **1901** ROSA GRAHAM *S. Gilbert* 68 The Precentrix, like the Precentor, was responsible for the church services.

precept (ˈpriːsɛpt), *sb.* Also 5–6 **precepte,** 6 **presept, -ceipt,** 6–7 **præcept;** 5–7 **precep.** [ad. L. *præceptum* a maxim, rule, order, command, prop. pa. pple. neut. sing. of *præcipĕre* to take beforehand, to give rules to, advise, instruct, order, f. *præ*, PRE- A + *capĕre* to take; whence also OF. *precept* (12th c. in Littré), mod.F. *précepte.*]

†1. An authoritative command to do some particular act; an order, mandate. *Obs.*

1382 WYCLIF *Acts* xvi. 24 Whanne he hadde takyn such a precept [L. *Qui cum tale præceptum accepisset*], sente hem into the ynner prisoun. *a* **1400–50** *Alexander* 982 All þe curte kniȝtis & erles Suld put þaim in-to presens, his precep to here. *c* **1420** LYDG. *Assembly of Gods* 1682 When Adam & Eue had broke the precept. *c* **1430** —— *Min. Poems* (Percy Soc.) 18 To whom whas yoven a precepte in scripture. **1513** DOUGLAS *Æneis* XII. x. 26 Heir I command no tary nor delay Be maid of my preceptis, quhat I sal say.

2. A general command or injunction; an instruction, direction, or rule for action or conduct; *esp.* an injunction as to moral conduct; a maxim. Most commonly applied to divine commands. **†*the ten precepts*:** the ten commandments (*obs.*).

1382 WYCLIF *Ezek.* v. 6 Thei walkeden not in my preceptis [*gloss* or heestis; 1388 comaundementis]. *c* **1386** CHAUCER *Wife's Prol.* 65 Whan thapostel speketh of maydenhede He seyde that precept ther-of hadde he noon. **1495** *Trevisa's Barth. De P.R.* XIV. vi. (W. de W.) 471 Ebal is a hyll.., theron stode the vj lignages..to curse all tho that helde not the x preceptes [*Bodl. MS.* hestes]. **1526** *Pilgr. Perf.* (W. de W. 1531) 5 The x commaundementes and other preceptes of good moralite. **1547** (*title*) The Ethiques of Aristotle..preceptes of good behavoure and perfighte honestie. **1560** DAUS tr. *Sleidane's Comm.* 2 b, It is S. Paules precept, that suche as be appointed to instruct the people, should be furnished..with holsome and sounde doctrine. **1564** *Brief Exam.* Bj, Vpon the .x. preceptes. **1638** QUARLES *Hieroglyph.* i. 4 This golden Precept, *Know thy selfe*, came downe From heav'ns high Court. *c* **1670** BUNYAN *Confess. Faith* Wks. 59 Through thy preceps I get understanding. **1687** A. LOVELL tr. *Thevenot's Trav.* I. 33 Though Wine seems to be Prohibited by the Alcoran, yet the good-fellows say, that it is no more but an advice or council, and not a precept. *a* **1704** T. BROWN *Imit. Persius' Sat.* i. Wks. 1730 I. 53 Authority with all thy precepts go. **1708** PRIOR *Turtle & Sparrow* 190 Example draws where precept fails. **1865** LIVINGSTONE *Zambesi* v. 128 Teaching them, by precept and example, the great truths of our Holy Religion.

b. One of the practical rules of an art; a direction for the performance of some technical operation; a rule.

1553 T. WILSON *Rhet.* 3 In all poynctes throughly grounded and acquainted with the preceptes. **1590** RECORDE, etc. *Gr. Artes* (1646) 225 Subtraction hath the same precepts that Addition had. **1592** West *1st Pt. Symbol.* §100 D, They which haue learned by heart all the tropes, figures and precepts of Rhetoricke. **1669** Sturmy *Mariner's Mag.* vi. iii. 117, I have been the larger in this precept, that it may be a Rule of Direction. **1812** Woodhouse *Astron.* ix. 65 In the precept..for finding the length of the year. **1901** '*Knowledge*' *Diary* 11 The 'equation of time' is indicated in the Ephemeris by the precepts before or after clock.

†**3.** A written order or mandate authorizing a person to do something; a warrant. *Obs.*

1518 in Sir W. Fraser *Sutherld. Bk.* (1892) III. 69 We.. sall gif our preceppis to delyuer the saidis Jonet and Elesabeht to the seid Johune in keping. **1583** *Leg. Bp. St. Androis* 863 His precept of pensione furth he tuike, Biddand my Lord subscryve ane letter. **1596** Bacon *Max. & Use Com. Law* i. v. (1636) 26 If a warrant or precept come from the King to sell wood upon the ground whereof I am tenant. **1700** Tyrrell *Hist. Eng.* II. 907 The Pope sent his Precepts or Breves. **1762–71** H. Walpole *Vertue's Anecd. Paint.* (1786) I. 5 The king sending a precept to the sheriff of Hampshire to have a chamber in the royal castle painted.

4. *spec.* **a.** A written or printed order issued by constituted authority (as the King, a court, or a judge), to require the attendance of members of a parliament, a court, or a jury, to direct the holding of an assize, to procure the appearance, arrest, or imprisonment of a delinquent, or the production of a record, or to authorize the levying of a distress; a writ, warrant.

[**1344** *Rolls of Parlt.* II. 154/2 Et sur cel precept, meisme le jour firent un autre precept, Sicut alias, de prendre son corps.] **1444** *Ibid.* V. 110/1 Retourne uppon eny Writtes or Precepts to theyme directed. **1503–4** *Act 19 Hen. VII*, c. 15 §1 Every Shereff..to whom eny writte or precepte is.. directe. **1584** *Reg. Privy Council Scot.* III. 710 Our schiref-officiar being thair present with ane precept. **1597** Shaks. *2 Hen. IV*, v. i. 14 Marry sir, thus: those Precepts cannot bee seru'd. **1678** Sir G. Mackenzie *Crim. Laws Scot.* i. xxvi. §2 (1699) 129 Executing of any Summonds, Letters, or Precept direct by his Highness, or other Judges. **1709** *Connecticut Col. Rec.* (1890) XV. 566 Ordered, that a precept be issued to all or either of the said officers,..to bring their said prisoner..forthwith before the Governor and Council. **1868** E. Edwards *Ralegh* I. xix. 385, I have the original precept and panel of the Jury before me.

b. *Sc.* An instrument granting possession of something, or conferring a privilege. ***precept of sasine*** (***seisin***), an instrument by which the legal ownership of land is transferred. ***precept of clare constat***: see constat 3.

1515 in Sir W. Fraser *Sutherld. Bk.* (1892) III. 59 A precept of seisyne of al and haill the erldome of Sutherland ..is direct to ws in dew form be our souerane lordis chapell. **1561** *Reg. Privy Council Scot.* I. 178 It is desyrit that preceptis be grantit be hir Grace for proving of saising to hir. **1590** *Ibid.* IV. 514 His Hienes..promittis that he sall at na tyme heireftir grant ony provisioun or precept of the dewitie foirsaid..to na maner of persoun or persouns, except for [etc.]. *a* **1765** Erskine *Inst. Laws Scot.* ii. iii. §33. **1861** W. Bell *Dict. Law Scot.* s.v., A precept of sasine is the order of a superior to his bailie to give infeftment of certain lands to his vassal... There is also another precept of sasine, called a *precept of clare constat*, which is a warrant granted by a superior authorising his bailies..to give infeftment to the heir of his vassal. **1874** *Act 37 & 38 Vict.* c. 94 §4 (1) When lands have been feued..It shall not..be necessary..that he shall obtain from the superior any charter, precept, or other writ by progress. **1881** *Erskine's Princ. Law Scotl.* (ed. 16) 149 *note*, The precept of sasine is no longer a necessary part of any conveyance of land... If it should now be inserted, a short form is provided by 8 & 9 Vict. c. 35.

c. A written order to make arrangements for and hold an election; usually, that issued by the sheriff to the returning officer.

1684 *Scanderbeg Rediv.* ii. 20 Upon the Death of a King, he hath the chief Management of Affairs, and issues out Precepts for the Election of a new Prince. **1765** Blackstone *Comm.* I. ii. 177 Within three days after the receipt of this writ, the sheriff is to send his precept, under his seal, to the proper returning officers of the cities and boroughs, commanding them to elect their members. **1852–3** *Act 16 & 17 Vict.* c. 68 §3 After the receipt of the writ or precept. **1865** *Morn. Star* 3 Nov., The Earl of Powerscourt..and Lord Fermoy..are candidates for the vacant representative peerage. The precept for the election has arrived. **1878** Stubbs *Const. Hist.* III. xx. 413 The sheriffs shall send to the magistrates..a precept for the election to be made by the citizens [etc.].

d. An order for collection or demand for payment of money under a rate.

1877 Burroughs *Taxation* 262 They constitute his precept, and so long as this is correct on the face of it he may obey its commands. **1888** *Times* 20 Nov. 5/3 Altho' the amount of the precept has been thus reduced. **1894** *Daily News* 16 Oct. 5/3 Under the Equalisation of Rates Act it was left to the Local Government Board to prescribe the forms of precepts to be used... The 'equalisation charge' may be either included as an item of the ordinary precept, or made the subject of a separate precept.

pre'cept, *v.* [Found first in pa. pple. *precept*, ad. L. *præcept-us*, pa. pple. of *præcipĕre*: see prec.]

†**1.** *trans.* To seize beforehand, preoccupy, take in anticipation. *Obs. rare*$^{-1}$.

1545 Joye *Exp. Dan.* v. Ivb, In vaine wept Esau after Iacob had precept hym hys blessynge.

†**2. a.** To lay down as a precept or rule; to teach, to prescribe (something) as a duty. *Obs.*

1534 Whitinton *Tullyes Offices* i. (1540) 2 Most playnly those thynges seem to be evydent, whiche of offyce and good maner be gyve and precept of them. **1627** W. Sclater *Exp. 2 Thess.* (1629) 265 Manuall labour is amongst those acts or offices which are precepted. **1638** —— *Serm. Exper.* 133 When the duties are morally prescribed, precepted, here the vow increaseth the obligation.

b. To instruct (a person) by precepts; to give a precept to, to command, direct. *Obs.*

1627 W. Sclater *Exp. 2 Thess.* (1629) 206 Hath God.. precepted vs in vaine, to aske with assurance of audience? **1661** Feltham *Resolves* ii. xxvii. (ed. 8) 238, I do not find, but it may well become a man to..precept himself into the practice of Virtue.

3. *intr.* Of a local authority or similar body: to issue a precept; to make a demand *on* (a rating authority) for funds. Also *trans.*, to take by means of a precept. Cf. precept *sb.* 4d. So **pre'cepting** *ppl. a.* and *vbl. sb.*

1911 *Encycl. Brit.* XXII. 915/2 To distinguish the rate the name of the precepting authority is frequently added or the purpose for which it is levied specified. **1961** *Times* 30 May (I.C.I. Suppl.) p. xiv/3 The county council precepts 72 per cent of the rates. **1962** L. Golding *Dict. Local Govt.* 310 Authorities which have no rating powers are known as precepting authorities as they issue precepts, i.e., demands on the rating authority or authorities, specifying the amount required in the £ of rateable value to meet their financial requirements. Examples of precepting authorities are county councils.., joint boards, parish councils, burial boards, river boards and port health authorities. **1974** *Daily Tel.* 26 Apr. 2/2 Where percentage rises are especially high one cause is said to be the practice of some old water boards of covering a large part of their expenditure by precepting on the general rates. **1979** *Kensington & Chelsea Newslet.* Oct. 1/3 These precepting authorities are all affected by substantial salary and wage increases themselves, and they therefore are bound to precept upon local authorities a very much greater amount next year than they have in the past.

preceptacyon, obs. erron. f. precipitation.

preceptee (priːsɛp'tiː). *U.S.* [f. precept(or + -ee[1].] One who is being trained by a preceptor. Cf. preceptor 3.

1974 *Med. Times* (N.Y.) Dec. 62/2 The benefits for the preceptee are substantial. **1975** *Jrnl. Med. Educ.* May 471/2 The conference is designed to accomplish the following objectives:..discuss monitoring and evaluation methodologies appropriate for either daily preceptor-preceptee interaction or faculty-preceptorship interaction.

preceptial (prɪ'sɛpʃəl), *a. rare.* By-form of preceptual; consisting of precepts; instructive.

1599 Shaks. *Much Ado* v. i. 24 Their counsaile..Would giue preceptiall medicine to rage. **1837** D. McNicoll *Wks.* 72 It might be edifying as preceptial and declamatory.

preception (prɪ'sɛpʃən). [ad. L. *præceptiōnem* a taking beforehand, the right of receiving in advance; a preconception; a precept, an imperial rescript, n. of action f. *præcipĕre*: see precept *sb.* Cf. F. *préception* (16th c. in Littré).]

†**1.** A previous conception or notion; a preconception, presumption. *Obs. rare.*

a **1619** Fotherby *Atheom.* i. iii. §4 (1622) 19 Which Epicurus calleth a Præsumption, or Præception. **1640** G. Watts tr. *Bacon's Adv. Learn.* v. v. 255 If he have no Prenotion or Preception of that he seeketh, he searcheth..as in a maze of infinitie.

2. †**a.** A command, precept. *Obs.*

1620 Bp. Hall *Hon. Mar. Clergy* i. xviii, 'Let him be the husband of one wife'.. Leo calls these words a Preception, I did not.

b. Instruction by a preceptor; tutoring. *rare.*

1882 *All Year Round* XXIX. 448 The statement that he had 'sat at the feet of the Gamebird of Birmingham', an allusion to his preception which was not so intelligible as the rendering of other journals, 'the Gamaliel of Birmingham'.

3. *Rom. Law.* The right of receiving beforehand, as a part of an inheritance before partition.

1875 Poste *Gaius* ii. §216 Let Lucius Titius take my slave Stichus by preception (before partition). **1880** Muirhead *Gaius* Digest 529 A legacy by preception..could in strictness be bequeathed only to one of several heirs..who was thereby authorised to take and appropriate some particular item of the inheritance before it came to be divided.

preceptive (prɪ'sɛptɪv), *a.* [ad. late L. *præceptīvus* didactic, hortatory, or a. obs. F. *préceptif* (14th c. in Godef.): see precept *sb.* and -ive.]

1. Of the nature of, pertaining to, or conveying a precept. **a.** Conveying a command, mandatory.

1456 Sir G. Haye *Law Arms* (S.T.S.) 106 The pape has power preceptive apon thame. **1624** F. White *Repl. Fisher* 484 Our Sauiours words, Doe this in remembrance of me, are not Preceptiue. **1672** *Toleration not to be Abused* 15 The Law hath two parts,..the Preceptive and the Punitive. **1786** A. Gib *Sacr. Contempl.* 28 The penalty, as well as the preceptive tenor of that law, was sufficiently notified to him. **1845** Jebb in *Encycl. Metrop.* II. 687/1 The preceptive part is the law properly so called: it includes the whole of the commands and prohibitions of the lawgiver.

b. Conveying instructions or maxims; didactic, instructive.

1678 R. L'Estrange *Seneca, Epist.* iv. (1696) 483 Cleanthes allows the Parænetic, or Preceptive Philosophy, to be in some sort Profitable. **1711** Shaftesb. *Charac.* (1737) I. ii. ii. 258 The didactive or preceptive Manner. **1834** *Fraser's Mag.* X. 41 Denham's poetry must have been too grave and preceptive for the profligate gaiety of the habits of the monarch. **1884** *Friend* Dec. 297/2 The whole treatise is preceptive and hortatory.

†**2.** According to precept. *Obs. rare.*

1684 T. Hockin *God's Decrees* ix. 77 The branch..had no innate and immediate vertue to make the bitter waters sweet [at Marah], but by the preceptive use of it.

Hence **pre'ceptively** *adv.*, in a preceptive manner; in the way of precept or command.

1633 Ames *Agst. Cerem.* ii. 281 God willeth.. Ceremonies, onely permissively, not præceptively. **1651** *Rec. Communion* §7 In any thing that is held forth in the Word of God, as præceptively to worthy receiving necessary.

preceptor (prɪ'sɛptər). Also 5 -ur, 6 -our, 6–7 præ-. [a. L. *præceptor* a teacher, instructor, whence also F. *précepteur* (15th c. in Littré): see precept *sb.* and -or 2.]

1. a. One who instructs; a teacher, instructor, tutor.

c **1440** *Alphabet of Tales* 418 One þat was callid Anaximetes, þat was his preceptur & his maister. *a* **1568** Ascham *Scholem.* (Arb.) 48 The scholemaster is vsed, both for Præceptor in learnyng, and Pædagogus in maners. **1579** *Reg. Privy Council Scot.* III. 200 Maister George Buquhannane, pensionar of Corsragwell, his majesteis preceptor. **1646** Sir T. Browne *Pseud. Ep.* 277 Clemens Alexandrinus an ancient Father and preceptor unto Origen. **1771** Burke *Corr.* (1844) I. 332 History is a preceptor of prudence, not of principles. **1878** G. Smith *J. Wilson* xvii. (1879) 308 Preceptors of religion unless they purify themselves, cannot expect success to attend their labours.

b. *transf.* As title of a book containing instructions for some art. (Cf. *tutor*.)

1843 *Musical World* XVIII. 431/3 Improved Preceptor for the Cornopean.

2. The head of a preceptory of Knights Templars.

1710 J. Harris *Lex. Techn.* II. s.v. *Preceptorie*, The Knights Templars and Hospitalars sent part of their Fraternity to some Country Cell, which was govern'd by a Person whom they called a Præceptor or Commander. **1819** Scott *Ivanhoe* xxxv, This establishment of the Templars was seated amidst fair meadows.., which the devotion of the former preceptor had bestowed upon their Order.

3. *spec.* A physician or specialist who gives a medical student practical training. *U.S.*

1803 *Med. Jrnl.* IX. 410 My justly celebrated preceptor, Dr. Cullen, has been quoted. **1837** R. Dunglison *Med. Student* ii. 126 The question;—what subjects the office-student should peruse during his first year... Generally.. the preceptor gives himself but little trouble. **1864** S. Chew *Lect. Med. Educ.* p. x, Is it necessary to pay attention to Medical Auscultation? My old preceptor considered it wholly useless. **1912** *Cycl. Amer. Med. Biogr.* II. 316/1 On the death of his preceptor, Dr. A. Torrence [he] succeeded to his practice. **1925** A. Flexner *Med. Educ.* v. 107 A mere boy, fresh from school, he attended his preceptor in his office and on his visits. **1937** J. T. Flexner *Doctors on Horseback* i. 9 Morgan apprenticed himself to an experienced doctor; there was no other way of studying medicine... Preceptors were limited to repeating what they had learnt from their own preceptors. **1948** *Jrnl. Hist. Med.* Winter 96 He swept out the office, cleaned the instruments, kept the accounts... After three years of this he would, if he had his preceptor's recommendation, appear before three members of the Board of Censors of the County Medical Society. **1959** Hammond & Kern *Teaching Comprehensive Med. Care* vii. 82 Each General Medical Clinic student was assigned to a preceptorial group... Two staff physicians were assigned to each group as preceptors. **1976** *National Observer* (U.S.) 16 Oct. 10/3 A third-year Michigan State student who has served under two preceptors.

Hence **pre'ceptoral** *a.* [so F. *préceptoral*], of or pertaining to a preceptor; **pre'ceptorate** [so F. *préceptorat*], the office of preceptor or giver of instruction.

c **1847** B. Barton *Select.* (1849) 46 Free from all restraint, save that of parental or preceptoral authority and affection. **1896** *Daily News* 26 Dec. 2/2 A Society for higher female education, called the Institute of Ladies of the Christian Preceptorate, by the Vicomtesse d'Adhemar.

preceptorial (priːsɛp'tɔərɪəl), *a.* [f. med.L. *præceptōri-us* (see preceptory *a.*) + -al[1].] Of or pertaining to a preceptor. Hence **precep'torially** *adv.*

1727–41 Chambers *Cycl.* s.v. *Prebend, Preceptorial Prebend*, is that prebend whose revenues are destined for the support of a preceptor or master, who is obliged to instruct the youth of the place gratis. **1830** Carlyle *Misc.* (1857) II. 130 Without any other preceptorial nourishment. **1884** *Chr. Leader* 30 Oct. 663 Where the church catechism and the ten commandments are daily taught preceptorially.

pre'ceptorship. [f. preceptor + -ship.]

a. The office or position of a preceptor; a tutorship.

1802 W. Taylor in Robberds *Mem.* I. 448 A travelling preceptorship would suit him. **1881** R. G. Wilberforce *Life Bp. Wilberforce* II. vii. 275 In earlier life the Bishop had sought the Preceptorship to the Prince of Wales.

b. The position of one who is being trained by a preceptor (cf. preceptor 3). *U.S.*

1970 *Vital Speeches* 1 Aug. 634 In any new graduate education program we might be well advised to emphasize again a preceptorship method of training. **1972** *Science* 27 Oct. 380/2 D.O. (Osteopathy) students begin serious clinical exposure early under preceptorships with D.O.'s in family practice. **1974** *Med. Times* (N.Y.) Dec. 62/1 Students attended medical school and also went through a preceptorship with an experienced physician. **1976** *National Observer* (U.S.) 16 Oct. 10/3 In this preceptorship program, as it's called, medical students spend from 4 to 12 weeks working in a rural or community doctor's office.

preceptory (prɪ'sɛptərɪ), *sb.* [ad. med.L. *præceptōria* (*domus*?) in same sense; cf. obs. F.

preceptoirie (1598 in Godef.), mod.F. *préceptorerie*: see next.] A subordinate community of the Knights Templars, established on one of the provincial estates of the order; hence, the estate or manor supporting this, or the buildings in which it was housed. Corresponding to the COMMANDERY of the Knights of St. John of Jerusalem.

1540 *Act. 32 Hen. VIII*, c. 24 Aduousons, commanderies, preceptories, contribucions, responsions, rentes.. which appertained.. to the priours. **1633** *Sc. Acts Chas. I* (1817) V. 165/2 All templelands perteining to the preceptorie of Torphichen. **1661** WOOD *Life* 29 June (O.H.S.) I. 403 Sandford.. a house and preceptory sometimes belonging to the Knights Templars. **1722** HEARNE *Collect.* (O.H.S.) VII. 353 It was a Preceptory for the K[ts] of S[t]. John's of Jerusalem. **1878** R. W. DIXON *Hist. Ch. Eng.* v. I. 321 The establishments of the order [Templars], which bore the name of preceptories, to the number of twenty-three, were at first seized by the King and other lords, but afterwards, by a bull from the Pope and an Act of Parliament, transferred to the rival order of the Hospitallers.

pre'ceptory, *a. rare.* [ad. med.L. *præceptōrius* adj.: see PRECEPTOR and -ORY[2].] Commanding, enjoining; = PRECEPTIVE I.

1573 A. ANDERSON *Exp. Benedictus* 74 The other place.. seemeth to sundrye to stande for a law preceptorie, as well to vs now, as to the Leuits then. **1882** SPURGEON *Treas. Dav.* Ps. cxix. 142 There is nothing false about the law or preceptory part of Scripture.

preceptress (prɪ'sɛptrɪs). [f. PRECEPTOR + -ESS[1].] A female preceptor.

1784 COWPER *Task* III. 505 Experience, slow preceptress, teaching oft The way to glory by miscarriage foul. **1797** CHARLOTTE PALMER *(title)* Letters on several subjects from a preceptress to her pupils who have left school.. designed for.. Young Ladies. **1809** HAN. MORE *Cœlebs* (ed. 4) I. vi. 72 A directress for his family, a preceptress for his children, and companion for himself. **1889** RUSKIN *Præterita* III. 110 The clear insight of the fearlessly frank preceptress.

preceptual (prɪ'sɛptjuːəl), *a. rare.* [irreg. f. L. *præcept-us* (see PRECEPT *v.*) or *præcept-um* PRECEPT *sb.*, on analogy of *conceptual*, etc.] Pertaining to, consisting of, or conveying precepts. Hence **pre'ceptually** *adv.*, according to precept.

1616 J. LANE *Cont. Sqr.'s T.* I. 54 Some sonnes, livinge vnder fathers eye, may chaunce demeane them as preceptualie. **1905** P. T. FORSYTH in *Hibbert Jrnl.* Oct. 69 We leave the intellectualist and preceptual notion of revelation behind us.

precerebellar, -bral, -broid: see PRE- A. 4, B. 3.

‖**preces** ('priːsiːz), *sb. pl.* [L. *precēs*, pl. of **prex*, *prec-em* prayer.] In liturgical worship, The short petitions which are said as verse and response by the minister and the congregation alternately.

1511 FABYAN *Will* in *Chron.* (1811) Pref. 8, I will that he whiche is assigned to begyn 'De profundis' and saye the preces, have .ijd. and to euery of the other I will be given .id. **1844** LINGARD *Anglo-Sax. Ch.* (1858) I. App. 378 The preces in the Breviary. **1882** F. E. WARREN in *Encycl. Brit.* XIV. 707/1 The chief traces of Oriental affinity lie in.. the occasional presence of 'preces', a series of short intercessions resembling the Greek 'Ektene', or deacon's litany.

pre'cess, *v.* [f. L. *præcess-*, ppl. stem of *præcēdĕre* to PRECEDE.]

†**1.** *trans.* To precede, to take precedence of. *Obs. rare.*

1529 FRITH *Epist. to Chr. Rdr.* Wks. (1829) 459 Yet chiefly.. this warning precessed (in my judgment) all other words, where he exhorted us.

2. *intr.* To undergo precession.

1892 A. M. WORTHINGTON *Dynamics of Rotation* xiii. 135 The application of the couple is said to cause the spinning wheel to 'precess'. **1902** *Jrnl. Inst. Electr. Engin.* XXXII. 83 The pull of gravity on a spinning-top does not make it topple over, but makes it precess. **1942** SYNGE & GRIFFITH *Princ. Mech.* xiv. 418 A disk, 6 inches in diameter, is mounted on the end of a light rod 1 inch long and spins rapidly. It precesses once in 15 seconds. **1957** *Endeavour* Oct. 185/2 In each of these levels the nucleus precesses about the direction of H_0, but maintains its correct orientation in the field. **1971** I. G. GASS et al. *Understanding Earth* vi. 90/2 The axis of figure starts to precess about the axis of rotation. **1973** [see PRECESSION 3 c]. **1975** *Nature* 20 Feb. 590/3 When a single ^{3}He atom is placed in a magnetic field its nucleus.. precesses about the field direction in one of two permitted states, corresponding to two different energy levels. **1977** A. HALLAM *Planet Earth* 30/2 The satellites precess, or progressively change their orbiting path relative to the Earth's axis, due to these broad variations in the gravity field.

precess, obs. form of PRESES.

precession (prɪ'sɛʃən). [ad. late L. *præcessiōnem* (Boeth.) a going before, n. of action from *præcēdĕre* to PRECEDE. So F. *précession* (1690 in Hatz.-Darm.).]

¶**1.** A going forward, advance, procession. (app. in every case an error for *procession*.)

13.. *Cursor M.* 20697 (Cott.) Gas þan wit fair precessiun [*other MSS.* pro-] To ierusalem right thoru þe town. *c* **1420** *Pol. Rel. & L. Poems* (1866) 208, iij women I met with precession. **1529** RASTELL *Pastyme, Brit.* (1811) 269 The kynge, the quene, and all the lordes, vpon our Lady-day.. went a precessyon in Poules.

2. The action or fact of preceding in time, order, or rank; precedence.

a **1628** F. GREVIL *Sidney* (1652) 232 To assist her in bounding out the Imperial Meeres of all Princes by the ancient precession of Right and power. **1898** *Allbutt's Syst. Med.* V. 1020 Premising that the precession of the two sounds of tension is aortic in the earlier and pulmonic in the later phases of the disease.

3. a. *Astron.* ***precession of the equinoxes***, often ellipt. ***precession*** [*æquinoctiorum præcessio* (Copernicus): called by Hipparchus and Ptolemy μετάπτωσις mutation]: the earlier occurrence of the equinoxes in each successive sidereal year, due to the retrograde motion of the equinoctial points along the ecliptic, produced by the slow change of direction in space of the earth's axis, which moves so that the pole of the equator describes a circle (approximately: see NUTATION) around the pole of the ecliptic once in about 25,800 years. Hence commonly used to denote this motion of the equinoctial points, of the earth's axis, or of the celestial pole or equator; also the motion of the earth itself which manifests itself as the precession of the equinoxes.

As a result of the precession, the longitudes, right ascensions, and declinations of all the stars are continually changing, and the signs of the zodiac shift in a retrograde direction along the zodiac, so that they no longer coincide with the constellations from which they were named (cf. the statement s.v. CANCER *sb.* 2 b).

lunisolar precession: that part of the precession which is caused by the combined attractions of the moon and sun upon the mass of the earth (the remaining effect being due to the attractions of the other planets).

planetary precession, that part of the precession of the earth's axis caused by the gravitational attraction of the other planets.

[*a* **1530** COPERNICUS *De Revolution. Orb. Cœlest.* (1543) III. *(title)* De æquinoctium solstitiorumque anticipatione. *Ibid.* III. ii. *(heading)* Historia observationum comprobantium inæqualem æquinoctiorum conversionumque præcessionem.]

1594 BLUNDEVIL *Exerc.* III. I. xxvii. (1636) 335 Spica Virginis.. is found now to be in the eighteenth of Libra, the cause whereof is the precession of the Equinoctiall point or section. **1621** BURTON *Anat. Mel.* II. ii. III. (1676) 160/1 Whether there be such a precession of the Æquinoxes, as Copernicus holds. **1704** J. HARRIS *Lex. Techn.* I. s.v., The Equinoctial Points, or the common Intersections of the Equator and Ecliptick, do retrocede or move backwards from East to West, about 50 Seconds each Year; and this Motion backwards is by some called the Recession of the Equinox, by others the Retrocession; and the advancing of the Equinoxes forward by this means is called the Precession of them. **1796** BURKE *Regic. Peace* i. Wks. VIII. 208, I cannot move with this precession of the equinoxes, which is preparing for us the return of some very old, I am afraid no golden, æra. **1816** PLAYFAIR *Nat. Phil.* II. 89 Hipparchus discovered the precession of the equinoxes, by a comparison of his own with more ancient observations. **1863** W. CHAUVENET *Man. Spherical & Pract. Astron.* I. xi. 604 The mutual attraction between the planets and the earth tends continually to draw the earth out of the plane in which it is revolving... The planetary precession is, then, the effect of a motion of the ecliptic upon the equator... The planetary precession does not affect the declination of stars, but changes their right ascensions, their longitudes, and their latitudes. **1867** EMERSON *Lett. & Soc. Aims, Progr. Cult.* Wks. (Bohn) III. 228 Six hundred years ago, Roger Bacon explained the precession of the equinoxes. **1881** GEIKIE in *Nature* XXIII. 359/1 The alternate phases of precession, which tend to bring warmer and colder conditions of climate every 10,500 years. **1913** S. E. SLOCUM *Theory & Pract. Mech.* vii. 430 *(heading)* Precession of the earth. *Ibid.*, An important case of regular precession is that furnished by the motion of the earth. **1926** H. N. RUSSELL et al. *Astron.* I. v. 141 The motion of the ecliptic pole produces.. the planetary precession. **1939** SKILLING & RICHARDSON *Astron.* i. 16 Precession does not affect the position of the terrestrial poles upon the earth's surface. **1959** R. H. BAKER *Astron.* (ed. 7) ii. 59 The earth's precession is a slow conical movement of the earth's axis around a line joining the ecliptic poles, having a period of about 26,000 years. **1963** D. ALTER et al. *Pictorial Astron.* (ed. 2) xlvi. 211/2 This gradual north–south drift of the Southern Cross is a consequence of the precession of the earth, which produces a slow movement of the celestial pole among the stars on a circle with a radius of 23½°. **1971** BAKER & FREDRICK *Astron.* (ed. 9) ii. 49 It is the lunisolar precession that has been described... Planetary precession is the effect of other planets on the plane of the equator, so that its intersection with the ecliptic shifts slowly towards the east along the celestial equator. The result of the two precessions is the general precession.

b. *Physics.* Extended to any motion analogous to that of the earth's axis or the earth itself in the precession of the equinoxes; e.g. the slow rotation of the axis of a top spinning rapidly in a sloping position.

1879 THOMSON & TAIT *Nat. Phil.* I. I. §105 The plane through the instantaneous axis and the axis of the fixed cone passes through the axis of the rolling cone... The motion of the plane containing these axes is called the precession in any such case. **1907** FRANKLIN & MACNUTT *Elements Mech.* vii. 149 The torque required to produce precession of a spinning body depends upon the moment of inertia of the body and upon the angular acceleration which is involved in the continual change of direction of the axis of spin. **1942** *Tee Emm* (Air Ministry) June 56/1 He has a directional gyro —and should have some idea as to its rate of precession. **1958** *Engineering* 31 Jan. 132/3 If the weights are moved from one side of the point of balance to the other the direction of precession is reversed. **1962** F. I. ORDWAY et al. *Basic Astronautics* ix. 372 The antifriction motor.. applies an additional torque in the direction of precession to compensate for friction in the bearings.

c. *spec.* The rotation of the spin axis of a nucleus, electron, etc., about the direction of a magnetic or an electric field.

1927 *Physical Rev.* XXIX. 395 Predicted and observed intensity relations for a number of band spectra are in agreement if we assume that σ is an electronic quantum number which is correlated with a precession about the internuclear axis. **1928** H. S. ALLEN *Quantum* xvi. 220 As the electron has a magnetic moment, its axis will experience a precession because of the couple due to its motion in the electric field. **1960** *Dicke & Wittke Introd. Quantum Mech.* xii. 195 This torque produces a precession of the spin axis about the direction of the magnetic field; in other words, the particle acts like a gyroscope because of its spin angular momentum. **1965** *New Scientist* 1 July 36/3 This precession will alter the average area that the molecule presents to other molecules. **1973** O. HOWARTH *Theory of Spectroscopy* i. 14 The existence of precession explains why even a classical particle with a magnetic moment does not immediately align when put in a magnetic field. It precesses instead.

4. *Phonetics.* Advance in oral position.

1844 CROSBY *Gram. Gr. Lang.* I. §29. 17 Such remarkable has been this precession (præcession, going forward) of the vowels in the Greek language, that η, υ, ει, η, οι, and υι, have all lost their distinctive sounds. **1860** HALDEMAN *Analyt. Orthogr.* xi. 56 Precession (>) is a vowel change from a more open to a closer position of the organs, towards the lips or throat. The term is adopted from Crosby's Greek Grammar. **1870** MARCH *Anglo-Saxon Gram.* 26.

precession, obs. erron. f. PRESESSION.

pre-cession: see PRE- B. 2 a.

precessional (prɪ'sɛʃənəl), *a.* *Astron.* and *Physics.* [f. PRECESSION + -AL[1].] Of, pertaining to, or connected with precession (see PRECESSION 3, 3 b).

1827 G. HIGGINS *Celtic Druids* 10 They discovered the great zodiacal or precessional year of 25,920 years. **1866** PROCTOR *Handbk. Stars* 4 Corrections due to the precessional motions. **1879** THOMSON & TAIT *Nat. Phil.* I. I. §345 The second class.. may be called precessional because the precession of the equinoxes, and the slow precession of a rapidly spinning top supported on a very fine point, are familiar instances of it. **1882** PROCTOR in *Knowledge* No. 11. 218 Writers will often speak of the precessional reeling of the earth. The reeling itself is, of course, not precessional, it is but the cause of precession.

†**pre'cessor.** *Obs.* Also 5-7 -our. [a. OF. *precesseur* (15th c. in Godef.), ad. late L. *præcessōr-em*, agent-n. f. *præcēdĕre* to PRECEDE.] One who precedes another in some office or position; a predecessor.

1457 *Lichfield Gild Ord.* (E.E.T.S.) 20 Euery master of the gild, and the warden of the chapell church for the time being, shall alwayes reseyve of ther precessors the kayes, with the Indentures, of the seid cofre. **1483** *Rolls of Parlt.* VI. 257/2 The seid Master and College, or their Predecessours or Precessours. **1548–67** THOMAS *Ital. Dict.*, *Predecessore*, the precessour or foregoer. **1655** FULLER *Hist. Camb.* iii. §62. 57 Fordham was herein more Court-like.. then Thomas Arundel, his Precessour Bishop of Ely.

preche, precher, -our, etc., obs. ff. PREACH, PREACHER.

pre-chemical: PRE- B. 1 d.

prechordal, præ- (priː'kɔːdəl), *a.* [f. PRE- B. 1, 3 + CHORD + -AL[1]: see CHORDAL.]

1. *Biol.* Prior to the development of a notochord in animals, or to the evolution of the *Chordata*.

1888 *Encycl. Brit.* XXIV. 187/2 No other Vertebrata present larval forms which indicate the nature of the early ancestral history in what we may call præ-chordal times.

2. *Anat.* See quot.

1890 BILLINGS *Med. Dict.*, *Præchordal*, in front of the anterior end of the notochord.

prechoroid: see PRE- A. 4.

pre-Christian (priː'krɪstjən), *a.* [PRE- B. 1.]

1. Of or pertaining to times prior to the birth of Christ or the Christian era; before Christ.

1828 G. S. FABER *Sacr. Calend. Prophecy* II. III. i. 39 A circumstance, itself fixed.. to the middle of the seventh pre-christian century. **1885** J. M. LUDLOW in *Homilet. Rev.* Apr. 281 The Talmud and Targums.. preserve for us the records of the opinions.. of the pre-Christian age.

2. Prior to the introduction or local prevalence of Christianity.

1861 WILSON & GEIKIE *Mem. E. Forbes* i. 23 Ruins still more ancient survive from pre-Christian times. **1861** WRIGHT *Ess. Archæol.* I. vii. 110 Anglo-Saxon antiquities of the pre-Christian age.

So **pre-Christi'anic** *a. rare*[−1]. = sense 2.

1883 J. F. M'LENNAN in *Encycl. Brit.* XV. 89/2 The *loupgarou*.. fell back into his pre-Christianic position of being simply a 'man-wolf-fiend'.

preciation (priːʃɪ'eɪʃən). *rare.* [After APPRECIATION, DEPRECIATION.] The determination of price; pricing.

1893 L. COURTNEY in *19th Cent.* Apr. 624 The effect upon preciation (if I may use such a word), in any market, and in relation to any commodity, of a change in the conditions of production of gold, is a function not merely of these conditions; but [etc.]. *Ibid.* 695.

† **pre'cide**, *v. Obs.* Also 6 precyde. [a. L. *præcīdĕre* to cut off (in front), f. *præ*, PRE- A. 4 c + *cædĕre* to cut.] *trans.* To cut off, esp. from communion. (In quot. 1657, *lit.*)

1529 MORE *Dyaloge* I. Wks. 143/2 Yᵉ hole congregacion of christen people professing his name & his fayth, & abiding in yᵉ body of yᵉ same, not being precided & cut of. **1537** *Inst. Chr. Man* C j, To committe many greuous..offences.., for the whiche they deserue to be precided & excluded for a season from the communion of this holy church. **1657** *Physical Dict.*, *Precided*, cut off.

‖ **précieuse** (presjœz), *sb.* (*a.*). [F., fem. of *précieux* PRECIOUS (sense 3), used as sb.; popularized in this sense by Molière in *Les Précieuses ridicules*, 1659, a comedy in which the ladies frequenting the literary salons of Paris *c* 1650 were satirized.]

A. *sb.* A woman aiming at or affecting a refined delicacy of language and taste; usually connoting ridiculous over-refinement or over-fastidiousness.

1727 H. CROMWELL in *Pope's Lett.* (1735) I. Suppl. 6 My former Indiscretion, in putting them into the Hands of this *Pretieuse*. **1768** STERNE *Sent. Journ.* (1775) I. 5 (*Calais*) Every power..perform'd it with so little friction that 'twould have confounded the most *Physical precieuse* in France. **1830** SCOTT *Monast.* Introd., The affected dialogue of the *précieuses*, as they were styled, who formed the coterie of the Hôtel de Rambouillet. **1865** 'OUIDA' *Strathmore* I. xii. 194 There wasn't a *précieuse* in England that wouldn't have sold her pure soul to the devil and the Marquis, for his settlements.

B. *adj.* Affected after the style of *les Précieuses*; cf. PRECIOUS *a.* 3.

1785 H. WALPOLE *Let. to C'tess of Ossory* 23 July, Her conversation is natural and reasonable, not *precieuse* and affected. **1841** THACKERAY *Misc. Ess.* (1885) 203 The *précieuse* affectation of deference where you don't feel it.

‖ **précieux** (presjø), *a.* (*sb.*) [Fr.] = PRECIOUS *a.* 3. Also as *sb.* Cf. PRÉCIEUSE *sb.* (*a.*).

1891 M. S. VAN DE VELDE *French Fiction of To-day* I. IV. 109 A certain *précieux* hyper-refinement. **1939** *Burlington Mag.* Mar. p. xviii/1 The lives of other *précieux* in the stereotyped social and literary intercourse of the Salons. **1951** M. MCLUHAN *Mech. Bride* (1967) 63 Arno, Nash, and Thurber are brittle, wistful little *précieux* beside Capp. **1953** [see BAROQUE *a.* (*sb.*)]. **1964** *Eng. Stud.* XLV. 111 As a *précieux* poet, the Duke [Orsino] is an accomplished master. **1969** *Listener* 8 May 637/1 There was point in A. C. Benson's defence in 1910 of 'The May Queen', that no *précieux* writer, with a care for his reputation, could have dared to write it... Certainly mid-19th-century literature was not *précieux*: it took risks.

† **preci'nation.** *Obs. rare*⁻¹. [irreg. f. L. *præcinĕre* to sing before, utter an incantation + -ATION.] Enchantment, sorcery, divination.

1503 *Kalender of Sheph.* G iv b, Wnstabylnes, loue [of] the world, blynd thoght, loue of him self, Precynuacyon [*ed.* **1506** Precinacyon], hatrent of god, vnconsyderacion, wantonnes, wncontynens.

precinct ('priːsɪŋkt), *sb.* Forms: 5–6 -cincte, -cynct(e, 6 -cynkte, -sinkt, -sinct, -cinte, 8 -cint, 6– precinct. [ad. med.L. *præcinctum* (also *præcincta*) enclosure, precinct, subst. use of pa. pple. of L. *præcingĕre* to gird (in front), encircle, f. *præ*, PRE- A. 4 c + *cingĕre* to gird. See also the earlier PROCINCT, PURCINCT.]

1. a. The space enclosed by the walls or other boundaries of a particular place or building, or by an imaginary line drawn around it; *spec.* the ground (sometimes consecrated) immediately surrounding a religious house or place of worship.

1547 BOORDE *Brev. Health* 4 Within the precynct of S. Peters church..standeth a pyller of white marble. **1585** T. WASHINGTON tr. *Nicholay's Voy.* II. xx. 57 b, Without the presinct of the Mosquee, there are..tenementes for the poore of the citie. **1774** PENNANT *Tour Scot. in 1772*, 251 The precinct of these tombs was held sacred. **1849** MACAULAY *Hist. Eng.* ix. II. 437 In process of time not only the dwelling, but a large precinct round it, was held inviolable. **1882** MYERS *Renewal of Youth*, etc. 174 The thronged precinct of Park and Serpentine. **1915** W. S. MAUGHAM *Of Human Bondage* xvi. 60 The precincts, with the exception of a house in which some of the masters lodged, were occupied by the cathedral clergy. **1956** *Newsweek* 9 Jan. 66/3 Just a few days before Christmas, nevertheless, the 230 tenants found eviction letters under their doors. In this way they learned that their proud precincts would be converted to house between 1,100 and 1,500 students by 1957. **1961** K. J. FRANKLIN *William Harvey* 59 He was offered an official residence in the precincts of Bart's.

b. *esp.* in *pl.*, often applied more vaguely to the region lying immediately around a place, without distinct reference to any enclosure; the environs.

1485 *Surtees Misc.* (1888) 44 Ye citie of York, suburbs, or precinctes of ye same. **1612** BACON *Ess.*, *Judicature* (Arb.) 456 Not onely the bench, but the..precincts and purprise thereof ought to bee preserued without scandall. **1848** LYTTON *Harold* I. i, Once out of sight of those fearful precincts, the psalm was forgotten. **1855** BREWSTER *Newton* II. xvi. 110 From the precincts of the High Court of Commission, Newton returned to Trinity College to complete the Principia. **1921** L. STRACHEY *Queen Victoria* 415 For more than half a century no divorced lady had approached the precincts of the Court.

c. *transf.* and *fig.*

1565 T. STAPLETON *Fortr. Faith* 6 b, Brought to the faith in the precinct of this tyme. **1750** GRAY *Elegy* xxii, For who ..This pleasing anxious being e'er resign'd, Left the warm precincts of the chearful day, Nor cast one longing lingering look behind?

2. A girding or enclosing line or surface; a boundary or limit, a compass.

1542 UDALL *Erasm. Apoph.* 217 b, The bruite of..his high praise and commendacion was not to be hidden or pended within the limites and precintes of grece. **1580–1** *Act 23 Eliz.* c. 5 Wood or Underwood nowe growinge..within the Compasse and precincte of xxij myles from and above the Cyttye of London. **1654** tr. *Martini's Conq. China* 86 The enemy had passed the first Wall, and Precinct. **1703** MAUNDRELL *Journ. Jerus.* (1732) 45 Near about Sidon begin the precincts of the Holy Land. **1843** PRESCOTT *Mexico* II. ii. (1864) 80 Nor to be cooped up within the precincts of a petty island.

fig. **1550** in Foxe *A. & M.* (1563) 773/2, I haue euer bene agreable to this precinct, I haue oftentimes reasoned in it, I haue spoken & also written in it. *Ibid.* 774/1. *a* **1649** DRUMM. OF HAWTH. *Poems* 14 The Precinct's strengthened with a Ditch of Feares In which doth swell a Lake of inky Teares. **1657** OWEN *Communion* I. iii. Wks. 1851 II. 19, I intend not ..to shut up all Communion with God under these precincts, His ways being exceeding broad. **1842** MANNING *Serm.* (1848) I. 3 He might have girdled the world about with the precinct of His own holiness, so that sin should have never entered.

3. A district defined for purposes of government or representation; a district over which a person or body has jurisdiction; a province; also, a division of a city, town, or parish; *spec.* in *U.S.*, a subdivision of a county or ward for election purposes, or of a city for the purpose of police control; *ellipt.*, = *precinct-house* (*b*), *-station* (see sense 5 below).

1432–50 tr. *Higden* (Rolls) II. 97 Wapentake and hundrede be the same as the precincte of an c. townes [1387 TREVISA, þe contray of an hondred townes], whiche were wonte to yelde there weppens in the first commenge of theire lorde. **1494** FABYAN *Chron.* VI. clxxii. 168 All suche Angles as dwelled there, and within yᵉ precynct of them [the Danes], were vnder his obedyence. **1577–87** HOLINSHED *Chron.* I. 57/1 Lord lieutenant of some precinct and iurisdiction perteining to the Romane empire. **1647** N. BACON *Disc. Govt. Eng.* I. xii. (1739) 23 Dioceses have also been subdivided into inferiour Precincts, called Deanaries or Decanaries. *Ibid.*, The smallest Precinct was that of the Parish, the oversight whereof was the Presbyters work. **1672** PETTY *Pol. Anat.* iii. Tracts (1769) 311 If 100 ministers can serve all Ireland, they must have precincts of near 13 or 14 miles square. **1687** A. LOVELL tr. *Thevenot's Trav.* I. 129 All agree, that there are three and twenty thousand Precincts in Caire... A Precinct is a Quarter, and in some of them there are several Streets. **1713** S. SEWALL *Diary* 29 Oct., Ipswich Hamlet [U.S.] petitions the Genl Court to give them the Powers of a Precinct. **1735** *Amherst Rec.* (U.S.) (1884) 5/1 The Request of several freholders of the third or East Precinct of Hadley for the Calling of a precinct Meeting. **1766** ENTICK *London* IV. 17 This ward is divided into ten precincts. **1864** [see *precinct station house*]. **1882** J. D. MCCABE *New York* xxiii. 374 The city is divided into thirty-five precincts, in each of which there is a station-house. **1884** *Boston* (U.S.) *Jrnl.* 15 Sept., The precinct election officers need not necessarily vote in the precinct in which they are appointed. **1891** *San Francisco Examiner* 15 Dec. 6/4 The place of residence, giving the ward or precinct. **1894** P. L. FORD *Honorable Peter Stirling* 142, I had to go with them.. to the precinct and speak to the superintendent. **1953** W. BURROUGHS *Junkie* (1972) ix. 90 They didn't find any junk on him so they took him to the third precinct to 'hold for investigation'. *Ibid.* x. 98 They drove back to the precinct and I was locked in. This time I was locked in a different cell. **1955** W. GADDIS *Recognitions* II. vi. 555 The case you reported to us as sadism and brutality reported by you to this precinct Tuesday December 20 at 10:17 A.M. resulted in false arrest. **1971** N. FREELING *Over High Side* III. 163 Watching..the cops from the ninety-ninth precinct, on the telly. **1974** *Amer. Speech 1971* XLVI. 83 *Police station*, precinct.

fig. **1586** W. WEBBE *Eng. Poetrie* (Arb.) 71 The myddle syllables which are not very many, come for the most part vnder the precinct of Position, whereof some of them will not possibly abide the touch.

4. A part of a town or community designated for a specific purpose; *spec.* one from which motor vehicles are excluded, esp. to allow pedestrians to shop in safety.

1942 H. A. TRIPP *Town Planning & Road Traffic* vii. 75 A great number of pockets will have been created, each of which will consist of a little local system of minor roads, devoted to industrial, business, shopping or residential purposes... Each pocket represents in its way a separate little community... The best term..seems to be 'precinct'. **1943** FORSHAW & ABERCROMBIE *County of London Plan* 51 Precincts are formed which can be maintained or replanned as residential communities, business or industrial precincts. **1958** *Listener* 23 Oct. 643/1 The exclusion of wheeled traffic from the main shopping precinct. **1959** *Ibid.* 19 Mar. 509/2 The word 'precinct' implies an area free from through-traffic. *Ibid.* 22 Oct. 674/2 The Stevenage pedestrian precinct. **1961** L. MUMFORD *City in Hist.* ix. 276 In the original layout of the colleges in Oxford and Cambridge, medieval planning made its most original contributions to civic design: the superblock and the urban precinct divorced from the ancient network of alleys and streets.

5. *Comb.*, as (sense 3) ***precinct caucus***, ***level***; **precinct captain**, a leader of a political party in a precinct; **precinct court**, a court with jurisdiction over a precinct, subordinate to a county court; **precinct house**, (*a*) the headquarters of an election precinct; also *attrib.*; (*b*) a police station; **precinct sheet**, a register of eligible voters in a precinct; **precinct station** = *precinct house* (*b*) above; also **precinct station house**; **precinct worker**, one who promotes the interests of a political party in a precinct.

1954 B. & R. NORTH tr. *Duverger's Pol. Parties* I. i. 19 In the United States the caucuses formed at the county or city level co-ordinate the action of the **precinct-captains*. **1956** E. O'CONNOR *Last Hurrah* iii. 45 John, you'll see the precinct captains? **1977** *Time* 3 Jan. 38/2 Daley became a precinct captain at 21. **1976** *New Yorker* 24 May 118/2 In South Carolina *precinct caucuses last night, the highest percentage of the votes—forty-seven per cent—was for 'Uncommitted'. **1704** in *N. Carolina Colonial Rec.* (1886) I. 605 Ordered that the Marshall bring forth the body of Tho: Evans to the next *pr[e]cinct Court to answer the compl[aint]. **1943** L. E. PRICE in Boatright & Day *Backwoods to Border* 210 [Hooper] drove out to the precinct court in his rubber-tired carriage. **1863** *Rebellion Rec.* V. I. 77 The Mayor of Philadelphia..called upon all able-bodied men to assemble next morning at the *precinct-houses of the election districts. **1899** T. HALL *Tales* 171 He did very well to copy off the entries in a precinct house register or to discover the important arrivals at the hotels. **1968** *Globe & Mail* (Toronto) 13 Jan. 25/5 Imagine committing a robbery half a block from a precinct house! **1972** *Village Voice* (N.Y.) 1 June 69/3 Up the street the team went, stapling on posters, casually strolling by the precinct house with the ladder. **1974** *Nation* (Barbados) 10 Mar. 3/5 Mr. Staines wrote his neighborhood precinct house asking that his thanks be passed on to the policeman. **1954** *Newsweek* 26 July 40/3 Latin America must be approached on the '*precinct level'. Labor leaders, teachers, local politicos must be convinced that inter-American cooperation will benefit the little groups. **1957** *Time* (Atlantic ed.) 20 May 13/2 Ike seems to find something distasteful in precinct-level party politics. **1974** *Union* (S. Carolina) *Daily Times* 23 Apr. 2/3 How do you catch the fraudulent? Would there ever be an updated *precinct sheet to work from? **1936** J. STEINBECK *In Dubious Battle* ii. 12, I think I'll stop in at the *precinct station. She might of got run over. **1975** *New Yorker* 16 June 114/2 The alleged beating two weeks earlier of a twenty-seven-year-old Chinese engineer inside the Fifth Precinct station. **1864** *N.Y. Herald* 4 Apr. 8/3 The body was removed to the Fourth *precinct station house. **1952** *Time* 2 June 19/1 His deepest political instinct is party loyalty. From his start as a *precinct worker and doorbell pusher in the wards of Cincinnati,..he has been unmistakably Republican. **1976** *Washington Post* 19 Apr. B 2/3 More recently, Ray Krasnick, who headed the Tydings effort among precinct workers in Prince George's County, became Sarbanes' county co-ordinator.

precinct (prɪ'sɪŋkt), *ppl. a. rare.* [ad. L. *præcinct-us*, pa. pple. of *præcingĕre* to gird, encircle, f. *præ*, PRE- + *cingĕre* to gird.] Girt about; girdled, encompassed. Also const. as *pa. pple.*

1641 J. JACKSON *True Evang. T.* I. 38 The sixt Persecution ..[was] limited to a short time (for it was precinct with a triennial girdle). **1646** SIR T. BROWNE *Pseud. Ep.* 176 Aristotle, who..affirmeth this sound to be made, by the allision of an inward spirit upon a pellicle, or little membrane about the precinct or pectorall division of their body. **1866** J. B. ROSE tr. *Ovid's Fasti* III. 280 The lake Arician precinct is with groves.

So **pre'cinction** [ad. L. *præcinctio* lit. a girding about, a girdle] *Rom. Antiq.*, the broad landing-place running round the amphitheatre between each tier of seats; **pre'cinctive** *a.*, see quot.; **pre'cinctuary** *a. nonce-wd.*, of or pertaining to a (cathedral) precinct or close.

1730 A. GORDON *Maffei's Amphith.* 330 The first Bench or Precinction. *Ibid.* 343 The Space between one Bench or Precinction, and the other. **1900** D. SHARP in *Fauna Hawai.* II. III. 91 *note*, I use the word precinctive..in the sense of 'confined to the area under discussion'... 'Precinctive forms' means therefore forms that are confined to the area specified. **1897** *Sat. Rev.* 2 Jan. 8/2 The Dean and Chapter ..being..artistically ignorant, and socially mundane and precinctuary,..know no better.

precinctual (prɪ'sɪŋktjuːəl), *a.* [f. PRECINCT *sb.* + *-ual*, perh. after INSTINCTUAL *a.*] Of, pertaining to, or characteristic of a precinct.

1949 *Archit. Rev.* CVI. 144 The plan is clearly based on the precinctual theory, with interconnected squares, throughout which the pedestrian receives priority. **1960** *Guardian* 15 June 28/4 The road..'would be prejudicial to the precinctual character of the area'. **1965** *New Statesman* 30 July 146/1 There would be time to consider whether the Martin plan's obsession with 'enclosure' adds up to anything more than an unrevised residue of the *Architectural Review's* 'Westminster Regained'—a precinctual proposal conceived at a time of positively prelapsarian innocence.

pre-cinematographic: see PRE- B. 1 d.

preciosity (prɛʃɪ'ɒsɪtɪ). Forms: 4 preciousite, 4–5 -osyte(e, 5 preci-, precyosite, -yte, -oustee, -owste, 6 *Sc.* pretiositie, 7 -ity, 7– preciosity. [a. OF. *preciosité* (13–14th c. in Hatz.-Darm.), *precieuseté*, mod.F. *préciosité*, ad. L. *pretiōsitās*, *-tātem*, f. *pretiōsus* PRECIOUS: see -ITY.]

1. The quality of being precious or costly; preciousness, great worth, value. Now *rare* or *Obs.*

c **1380** WYCLIF *Serm.* Sel. Wks. I. 376 Crist techiþ here þe preciousite of his preching. *c* **1449** PECOCK *Repr.* V. xiii. (Rolls) 553 Gaynes preciosite or costiosenes. *c* **1470** HARDING *Chron.* CCVII. v, Iewelles in chestes, and stones of preciousstee. **1494** FABYAN *Chron.* II. 439 A relyke accomptyd of great precyosyte. **1535** STEWART *Cron. Scot.* (Rolls) III. 521 Vestimentis of greit pretiositie. **1681** H. MORE *Exp. Dan.* i. 3 The order of dignity or pretiosity in the Metals.

2. Anything very costly, an article of value. Now *rare* or *Obs.*

1485 CAXTON *Chas. Gt.* 179 Fyn gold and other precyosytees. **1646** SIR T. BROWNE *Pseud. Ep.* 185 The Index or forefinger was too naked whereto to commit their pretiosities. **1668** H. MORE *Div. Dial.* III. vi. (1713) 192 The curiosity of their application of these Preciosities. **1850** CARLYLE *Latter-d. Pamph.* vii. (1872) 225 Glittering man-mountains filled with gold and preciosities. **1864** —— *Fredk. Gt.* xv. vii. IV. 107 The Preciosities and household gods.

3. Affectation of refinement or distinction, esp. in the use of language; fastidious refinement in literary style. (See PRECIOUS *a.* 3.)

1866 CARLYLE *Remin.* I. 89 'Circle' he pronounced 'circul' with a certain preciosity which was noticeable slightly in other parts of his behaviour. **1887** H. D. TRAILL in *Macm. Mag.* July 176 The circles of Oxford preciosity. **1895** *Forum* (N.Y.) Oct. 191 The Parisian preciosity ridiculed by Molière. **1897** *Sat. Rev.* 20 Nov. 536 This..may be described as the *reductio ad absurdum* of the preciosity of Pater and Stevenson.

precious ('prɛʃəs), *a.* (*sb.*, *adv.*) Forms: 3-6 preciouse (3-4 preciuse), 4- precious (4 presci-, presi-, presh(i)-, 4-5 presy-, precy-, -ous(e, -ose, -us, -ows(e; 6-8 pretious, -os). [ME. a. OF. *precios* (11th c. in Hatz.-Darm.), mod.F. *précieux*, ad. L. *pretiōsus* costly, valuable, precious (whence also Prov. *precios*, It. *prezioso*, Sp., Pg. *precioso*), f. *pretium* price, value: see -OUS.]

A. *adj.* **1.** Of great price; having a high value; costly.

precious metals: a name including gold and silver; also sometimes platinum, and rarely mercury.

a **1300** *Cursor M.* 1040 Þei bring o paradis þe stan, Sua preciose [*v.rr.* -ious(e, -ius] es fundun nan. *c* **1305** *St. Andrew* 76 in *E.E.P.* (1862) 100 Hail beo þu swete Rode he seide, swettest of alle treo..And of ȝymmes preciouses. **13..** *E.E. Allit. P.* B. 1496 His iueles..þat presyous in his presens wer proued sum whyle. **1362** LANGL. *P. Pl.* A. XI. 12 Draf weore hem leuere þen al þe presciouse Peerles þat in paradys waxen. *c* **1380** WYCLIF *Serm.* Sel. Wks. II. 114 Trewe oynement and preshous. *c* **1449** PECOCK *Repr.* II. xiv. (Rolls) 231 Better and costioser and precioser garnementis. **1577** B. GOOGE *Heresbach's Husb.* II. (1586) 108b, The precîousest are the Cypresse, and the Cedar Tables. **1651** HOBBES *Leviath.* III. xxxv. 219 The Generalls pretious Jewel, or his Treasure. **1776** ADAM SMITH *W.N.* I. iv. (1869) I. 25 In the precious metals..even the business of weighing, with proper exactness, requires at least very accurate weights and scales. **1868** ROGERS *Pol. Econ.* iii. (1876) 26 Money is generally, but not invariably, one or both of those metals which are called precious.

2. a. Of great moral, spiritual, or non-material worth; held in high esteem.

precious blood, the blood of Christ shed for man's redemption; hence, in the names of various orders, confraternities, relics, etc.; also, the Feast of the Most Precious Blood, on the first Sunday in July. So ***precious body*** (of Christ).

a **1300** *Cursor M.* 8321 It sal be precius and prude, þe werc he sal sua semele scrude. *a* **1340** HAMPOLE *Psalter* xx. 1 He spend noght his preciouse blode in vayn on vs. **1382** WYCLIF *1 Pet.* i. 19 Not bi corruptible gold, or siluer, ȝe ben bouȝt aȝen..but bi the precious blood of..Crist Jhesu. *c* **1450** *Merlin* 11 Oure lorde Jhesu Criste, that bought vs with his precyouse blode. **1578** TIMME *Caluine on Gen.* 169 The most pretious grace of God. **1647** CLARENDON *Hist. Reb.* I. §2 Words of pretious esteem. **1703** MAUNDRELL *Journ. Jerus.* (1732) 74 Where the pretious Body of our Lord was anointed. **1875** JOWETT *Plato* (ed. 2) III. 205 Justice, which is a treasure far more precious than gold.

†**b.** in asseveration, for ***precious blood*** or ***body***. Cf. 6 b. *Obs.*

1560 INGELEND *Disob. Child* (Percy Soc.) 41 By Goddes precious, I wyll not unwysely suffre To do as I have done any longer. **1601** ? MARSTON *Pasquil & Kath.* II. 247 Gods precious! I forgot to bring my Page.

3. Aiming at or affecting distinction or choiceness in conduct, manners, language, etc.; fastidious, 'particular'; *esp.* in mod. use (after F. *précieux*: cf. PRÉCIEUSE), affecting, displaying, or using careful and fastidious delicacy or refinement in language, workmanship, etc.; often with an implication of being over-nice or over-refined.

c **1386** CHAUCER *Wife's Prol.* 148 In swich estaat as god hath cleped vs I wol perseuere, I nam nat precius. —— *Merch. T.* 718 But lest ye precious folk be with me wrooth How that he wroghte I dar not to you telle. **1712** STEELE *Spect.* No. 306 ¶7 An apparent Desire of Admiration,..a precious Behaviour in their general Conduct, are almost inseparable Accidents in Beauties. **1887** SAINTSBURY *Hist. Elizab. Lit.* iv. (1894) 145 Elaborate embroidery of precious language. **1891** *Pall Mall G.* 18 Feb. 3/1 With its brown paper cover.., its rough edges.., its twirligigs instead of spaces.., the book is everything that the most 'precious' could desire. **1894** *Athenæum* 25 Aug. 252/3 The employment of 'curious' in a somewhat precious sense at least three times.

4. *colloq.* **a.** As an intensive of something bad, worthless, or reprobated: Egregious, out-and-out, arrant; in some uses, a mere emotional intensive. (Cf. FINE *a.* 14 b.)

c **1430** LYDG. *Min. Poems* (Percy Soc.) 52 A precious knave that cast nevyr to thryve. **15..** *Jack Juggler* in Hazl. *Dodsley* II. 142 Now walk, precious thief. **1575** LANEHAM *Let.* (1871) 46 Heering and seeing so precioous ado heer at a place vnlookt for. **1605** B. JONSON *Volpone* I. i, Your worship is a precious ass. **1610** —— *Alch.* v. iv, You are a precious fiend! **1836** DARWIN in *Life & Lett.* (1887) I. 241, I find I am writing most precious nonsense. **1856** EMERSON *Eng. Traits, Cockayne* Wks. (Bohn) II. 68 This precious knave became, in good time, Saint George of England. **1857** T. HUGHES *Tom Brown* II. vii, It's hard enough to see one's way, a precious sight harder than I thought last night. **1892** CHAMBERLAIN in *Westm. Gaz.* (1898) 26 Apr. 2/3 If the Liberals got into power what a precious mess they would make of foreign policy.

b. *Ironically*, Of little worth, worthless, good-for-nothing. (Cf. FINE *a.* 12 c.)

a **1619** FLETCHER *Mad Lover* III. iii, Oh, you're a precious man! two days in town, And never see your old friend! **1777** SHERIDAN *Sch. Scand.* v. ii, *Sir O.* Well, Sir Peter, I have seen both my nephews... *Sir P.* A precious couple they are! **1781** WESLEY *Wks.* (1872) XIII. 298 Are not these precious instructers of youth?

†**5.** ? Carbuncled. *Obs.* (Cf. *precious-nosed* in D.)

1581 PETTIE *Guazzo's Civ. Conv.* I. (1586) 43 A poore old man, whose nose by some infirmitie, was become meruailous great, deformed, full of pimples, precious, and monstrous.

6. In special connexions. **a.** ***precious stone***, a stone which on account of its beauty, hardness, and rarity is prized for its use in ornamentation and jewellery and has a high commercial value; a gem.

Precious is also prefixed to some names of stones, to distinguish that which is included among gems from an inferior, opaque, or unpolishable kind of the same mineral, as in *precious* GARNET, *precious* OPAL, etc.

c **1290** *St. Brandan* 42 in *S. Eng. Leg.* I. 221 Of suete preciouse stones þat briȝtte schynen and wide. *c* **1400** MAUNDEV. (Roxb.) viii. 29 In þat ryuer er oft tymes funden many precious stanes. **1483** CAXTON *G. de la Tour* F viij, They shold gyue her..as many precious stones as she wold take of them. **1562** J. HEYWOOD *Prov. & Epigr.* (1867) 140 Folly to cast precious stones before hogs. **1655** tr. *Com. Hist. Francion* I. 18 Eyes that out-sparkled his preciousest Stones. **1870** YEATS *Nat. Hist. Comm.* 384 Precious stones are either carbonaceous, aluminous, or silicious. **1892** E. W. STREETER *Prec. Stones* (ed. 5) 286 The Almandine, or Precious Garnet. *Ibid.* 339 Any substance which can be scratched by Rock Crystal being practically of no value as a Precious Stone.

†**b.** ***precious coals***: an obsolete expletive. Cf. 2 b.

1576 GASCOIGNE *Steele Gl.* (Arb.) 80 When roysters ruffle not aboue their rule, Nor colour crafte, by swearing precious coles. **1602** *2nd Pt. Return fr. Parnass.* IV. i. (Arb.) 50 (He puls his Watch out) Precious coales, the time is at hand, I must meditate on an excuse to be gone. *Ibid.* ii. 54 Pretious coles, thou a man of worship and Iustice too?

†**c.** ***Precious John***: corruption of PRESTER JOHN.

1634 SIR T. HERBERT *Trav.* 130 The great Christian of Æthiopia, vulgarly cald Prester, Precious, or Priest-John.

d. ***precious metals***: see 1.

e. ***precious coral***, a coral belonging to the order Antipatharia, forming branching colonies resembling plants.

1906 S. J. HICKSON in Harmer & Shipley *Cambr. Nat. Hist.* I. xiii. 352 The 'precious coral' occurs in the Mediterranean. **1935** TWENHOFEL & SHROCK *Invertebr. Paleontol.* iv. 113 The compound corallum may be in the form of..bushy growths as in the precious corals. **1979** *Sci. Amer.* Aug. 115/3 The detritus feeders include the true sponges, the antipatharians ('precious corals') and the gorgonians (sea fans).

B. *sb.* Precious one, dear, darling.

1706 MRS. CENTLIVRE *Basset-Table* II. 25 With all my Heart, my Jewel, my Precious. **1755** *Mem. Capt. P. Drake* II. iii. 113 In all that time I never saw my precious but at Mrs. Jones's. **1861** DUTTON COOK *P. Foster's D.* iii, Well, my precious, and how are you?

C. *adv.* (qualifying adj. or adv.) **a.** = PRECIOUSLY.

1595 SHAKS. *John* IV. iii. 40 Or when he doom'd this Beautie to a graue, Found it too precious Princely, for a graue.

b. With intensive force: Extremely, very: ***precious few*** = few indeed. *colloq.*

1837 DICKENS *Pickw.* ii, We've got a pair o' precious large wheels on. **1839** ASA GRAY *Lett.* (1893) I. 268 While on the Continent I have received precious few letters. **1839** THACKERAY *Fatal Boots* viii, I..took precious good care to have it. **1840** DICKENS *Old C. Shop* xx, Kit..was 'precious raw' or 'precious deep'. **1886** CHAMBERLAIN *Sp. Ho. Com.* 26 Aug., Precious few of them have declared in favour of the bill before their constituents.

D. *Comb.* (parasynthetic.)

1592 SHAKS. *Rom. & Jul.* II. iii. 8 With balefull weedes, and precious Iuiced flowers. **1607** *Lingua* III. vi, There was an old..precious-nosed..slave. [Cf. sense 5 above.]

†'**precioushead.** *Obs.* *rare*⁻¹. In 5 -hed. [f. PRECIOUS + -HEAD.] = PRECIOUSNESS 1.

c **1440** *Jacob's Well* 75 Ryȝt so, lownesse excellyth in precyoushed alle oþere vertuys, & euere drawyth down to þe netherest place.

preciously ('prɛʃəslɪ), *adv.* [f. as prec. + -LY².]

†**1.** In a costly manner, at great cost or expense. *Obs.*

c **1386** CHAUCER *Wife's Prol.* 500 It nys but wast to burye hym preciously. **1547** *Homilies* I. *Good Works* II. (1859) 54 Unto whose images the people with great devotion invented pilgrimages, preciously decking and censing them, kneeling down and offering to them. **1561** T. NORTON *Calvin's Inst.* II. xvii. (1634) 250 Paul saith that we are preciously bought. **1666** DRYDEN *Ann. Mirab.* xxix, Some preciously by shattered porcelain fall, And some by aromatic splinters die.

2. Valuably; as a precious thing, as a thing of value. Now *rare* or *Obs.*

c **1400** MAUNDEV. (1839) xxi. 227 Þei worschipen the Owle. And whan þei han ony of here federes þei kepen hem fulle precyously. *c* **1450** *Mirour Saluacioun* 4935 In thilk Arche and the ymage kept was manna kept preciously. **1610** SHAKS. *Temp.* I. ii. 241 The time 'twixt six and now Must by vs both be spent most preciously. **1647** R. STAPYLTON *Juvenal* 250 A coate of armes cut in a pretious sardonix-stone, and pretiously kept.

3. Very greatly; exceedingly, extremely. *colloq.*

1607 MIDDLETON *Your Five Gallants* IV. i. 13 You're much preciously welcome. **1840** THACKERAY *Cox's Diary* Aug., Wks. 1893 VIII. 572 Captain Tagrag was my opponent, and preciously we poked each other. **1884** *Manch. Exam.* 11 June 5/1 To find out how preciously they had been befooled.

4. Fastidiously, scrupulously; with delicate workmanship.

1862 HAMERTON *Painter's Camp* I. xxix. 390 If..you fall short of this point, your art of painting from nature is not yet quite perfectly and preciously imitative.

'**preciousness.** [f. as prec. + -NESS.]

1. The quality of being precious; valuableness, costliness; value.

c **1386** CHAUCER *Pars. T.* ¶372 And eek in to greet preciousnesse of vessel, and curiositee of Mynstralcie, by whiche a man is stired the moore to delices of luxurie. *c* **1440** *Promp. Parv.* 412/1 Preciowsnesse (or preciowste), *preciositas*. **1527** R. THORNE in Hakluyt *Voy.* (1589) 252 The preciousnesse of these things is measured after the distance that is betweene vs, and the things that we have appetite vnto. **1644** EVELYN *Diary* 19 Oct., The font and pulpit..is of inestimable value for the preciousnesse of the materials. **1663-70** SOUTH *Serm.* (1727) IV. vii. 292 The Preciousness of Gospel Dispensations. **1877** BOUTELL in *Encycl. Brit.* VI. 454/2 (*Costume*) In the best period of Greek art,..the Jewellery is of value according to its workmanship; but in later times preciousness of material determined the value. **1883** RUSKIN *Fors Clav.* xci. 185 Not calculating..any of these singular powers or preciousnesses.

b. Rare beauty or excellence, such as one prizes.

1870 RUSKIN *Lect. Art* vii. 176 In some birds..the colour nearly reaches a floral preciousness.

†**2.** That which is precious. *Obs. rare.*

c **1485** *Digby Myst.* (1882) v. 33 Wysdam is better than all wordly preciousnesse.

3. Over-refinement, fastidiousness, affectation of distinction; = PRECIOSITY 3.

1884 *Harper's Mag.* Oct. 800/2 At this stage of our literature, it is wiser to turn..away from 'preciousness' of every kind. **1888** W. MORRIS in Mackail *Life* (1899) II. 206 Perhaps I am not doing the most I can, merely for the sake of a piece of 'preciousness'.

precioustee, -owste, obs. ff. PRECIOSITY.

†'**precipe.** *Obs.* Pl. pre- (præ-) cipes, -ees, -ies. [ad. L. *præcipēs*, *-cip-* (Plaut.), variant of *præceps*, *-cipit-* adj. headlong, precipitous, sb. a precipice; f. *præ* before, in front + *caput*, *-it-* head.

Chiefly in pl., which may have been meant for the L. pl. *præcipēs*; thence, perh., a sing. (? *pre-ci-pe*) was formed.]

An abrupt or steep descent; a precipice.

1621 G. SANDYS *Ovid's Met.* II. (1626) 26 Up to the fixed Starres their course they take, Now clime: now, by steep Præcipies descend. *a* **1639** WOTTON in *Reliq.* (1651) 9 On the Dukes part, we have no such abrupt strayns and precipees as these, but a fair fluent and uniform course under both Kings. **1639** S. DU VERGER tr. *Camus' Admir. Events* 41 The highest ascents make the deepest precipes. **1643** PRYNNE *Sov. Power Parl.* Ded. A ij b, Full of dangerous Precipes, Rockes,..on either hand. **1656** S. H. *Gold. Law* 15 Honours and greatness without safety is to stand on the precipe [perh. = L. *in precipe*] of a Precipice.

precipe, parallel form of PRÆCIPE.

precipice ('prɛsɪpɪs), *sb.* Also 7 præ-, (8 pri-). [= F. *précipice* (16th c. in Hatz.-Darm.), ad. L. *præcipitium* a falling headlong, a steep place, precipice, f. *præceps*, *-cipit-* headlong, steep, precipitous, or f. *præcipitāre* to throw headlong: cf. *hospitium*, *occipitium*, *flāgitium*.]

†**1.** A precipitate or headlong fall or descent, esp. to a great depth. Also *fig.* *Obs.*

1598 B. JONSON *Ev. Man in Hum.* II. iii, Precedents, which are strong, And swift, to rape youth to their precipice. **1626** BACON *Sylva* §880 There it moveth more Swiftly, and more in Præcipice; For in the breaking of the Waves there is ever a Præcipice. **1632** MASSINGER *Maid of Hon.* v. i, His precipice from goodness raising mine, And serving as a foil to set my faith off. **1635** HAKEWILL *Apol.* v. 24, I much marvell how you will accord it with her [i.e. Nature's] wholly inclining and præcipice to corruption. **1650** FULLER *Pisgah* II. ii. 81 Souldiers in the Precipice of their passion being sensible of no other stop but the bottome.

2. A vertical or very steep face of rock, etc.; a cliff, crag, or steep mountain side of considerable height.

1632 SIR T. HAWKINS tr. *Mathieu's Unhappy Prosperitie* 116 When he shall arrive on the top, he shall finde nothing but danger, and round about him a gaping precipice. **1638** SIR T. HERBERT *Trav.* (ed. 2) 146 The other side of this high hill is a precipice, downe which is no descending. **1681** DRYDEN *Spanish Friar* I. i, A Torrent, rowling down a Precipice. **1719** DE FOE *Crusoe* I. 95 To remove my Tent from the Place where it stood, which was just under the hanging Precipice of the Hill. **1856** RUSKIN *Mod. Paint.* IV. v. xvi. §1, I mean by a true precipice, one by which a plumbline will swing clear, or without touching the face of it, if suspended from a point a foot or two beyond the brow.

†**b.** The edge or brink of a cliff. *Obs.*

1644 EVELYN *Diary* 30 June, The ruins of an old..Castle ..built..on the precipice of a dreadfull cliff.

c. *fig.* A perilous situation; a hazardous position.

1651 tr. *De-las-Coveras' Don Fenise* 266 You have not seen the precipices which environ beauty. **1692** tr. *Sallust* 324 For my own part, whose years are near the Precipice of death, I do not wish one minute longer of Life. **1795** tr. *Mercier's Fragm. Pol. & Hist.* II. 134 Thus mankind wishing to avoid one precipice, fall into another.

†**3.** *transf.* (?) Precipitousness, loftiness as of a precipice. *Obs.*

1672 MARVELL *Reh. Transp.* I. 64 After he was stretch'd to such an height in his own fancy, that he could not look down from top to toe but his Eyes dazled at the Precipice of his Stature.

4. *Comb.*, as ***precipice-edge***, ***-wall***; ***precipice-writing*** adj.

1836–48 B. D. WALSH *Aristoph.*, *Clouds* v. ii, An incoherent, mouthing, loud, Harsh, precipice-writing fellow. **1898** G. MEREDITH *Odes Fr. Hist.* 85 The patience clasped, totters hard on the precipice-edge.

† **'precipice,** *v. Obs. rare.* [f. PRECIPICE *sb.*] *trans.* To dash down headlong; to precipitate.

1654 Z. COKE *Logick* Pref., Some of them..(Elevated on the wings of their Ambitions) were most ingloriously dasht and precipic'd.

'precipiced (-ɪst), *ppl. a.* [f. PRECIPICE *sb.* + -ED[2].] Having, furnished, or formed with precipices.

1873 MASSON *Drumm. of Hawth.* xx. 452 Its banks terraced and precipiced by all their wealth of shrub and foliage. **1881** SHAIRP *Asp. Poetry* i. 28 The precipiced crags and blue mountain-peaks soar aloof.

pre'cipient, *a.* [ad. L. *præcipient-em*, pr. pple. of *præcipĕre* to command, instruct: see PRECEPT.] Commanding, directing.

1828–32 in WEBSTER. **1849** in CRAIG. In mod. Dicts.

†**precipit,** *sb. Obs. rare.* In 7 precepit. [a. obs. F. *precipite* precipice (Cotgr.), ad. L. *præcipit-em* (nom. *præceps*) headlong, precipitous, a precipice: see next.] = PRECIPICE.

1613 SHAKS. *Hen. VIII*, v. i. 140 Go too, You take a Precepit for no leape of danger, And woe your owne destruction.

pre'cipit, *a. rare.* [ad. L. *præceps, -cipit-em* (see prec.), f. *præ* before, in front + *caput, capit-* head.] Headlong, steep, precipitous.

1648 EARL OF WESTMORLD. *Otia Sacra* (1879) 82 The snares of His precipit ways. **1922** JOYCE *Ulysses* 743 Not acting with precipit precipitancy.

†**pre'cipit,** *v. Obs. rare.* [ad. L. *præcipit-āre* to cast headlong, or F. *précipite-r* (15th c. in Littré).] *trans.* = PRECIPITATE *v.* 1 b.

1678 R. R[USSELL] tr. *Geber* III. ii. II. xx. 215 It will precipit you into the miserable State of Poverty.

precipitability (prɪˌsɪpɪtə'bɪlɪtɪ). [f. next + -ITY.] The quality of being precipitable; capability of being precipitated or thrown down.

1790 WEDGWOOD in *Phil. Trans.* LXXX. 315 Precipitability by water, and non-precipitation by Prussian lixivium. **1842** PARNELL *Chem. Anal.* (1845) 66 The precipitability of oxide of chromium from its solution in caustic potash by ebullition. **1881** *Nature* XXV. 142/2 The authors have examined the precipitability and precipitation of manganous and nickelous sulphates.

precipitable (prɪ'sɪpɪtəb(ə)l), *a.* [f. L. *præcipitāre* to PRECIPITATE + -ABLE.] **a.** Capable of being precipitated from solution in a liquid, or from a state of vapour.

1670 W. SIMPSON *Hydrol. Ess.* 75 Vitriol contains a greater quantity..of a precipitable ocre. **1782** KIRWAN in *Phil. Trans.* LXXIII. 78 A very saturate solution of lead is difficultly..precipitable by iron. **1878** ABNEY *Photogr.* (1890) 37 Precipitable silver compounds.

b. ***precipitable water*** (Meteorol.): the quantity of water vapour in an atmospheric column of unit cross-section, expressed as the depth it would have if condensed to a liquid or as the mass.

1928 *Mem. R. Meteorol. Soc.* III. 2 If *m* is the mass of water vapour in grams over each square centimetre of the base of the stratosphere we have *mg* = 33, *i.e.* *m* = ·034 gram. Thus the water vapour in the stratosphere is equivalent to ·34 mm. of precipitable water. **1971** *Nature* 23 Apr. 503/1 Schorn *et al.* have observed average water contents in the northern hemisphere [of Mars] of up to 25 μm of precipitable water.

precipitance (prɪ'sɪpɪtəns). [f. as next: see -ANCE.] Precipitant action or quality.

1. Very swift downward or onward movement; headlong fall or speed. *rare.*

1667 MILTON *P.L.* VII. 291 Thither they [waters] Hasted with glad precipitance. **1691** E. TAYLOR *Behmen's Theos. Philos.* 107 It was not a precipitance from a more lofty to a more low. **1827** SOUTHEY *Hist. Penins. War* II. 5 The English in the precipitance of their flight had not marched upon Ferrol. *Ibid.* 769 There had been no alarm, no confusion, no precipitance upon the march.

2. Headlong action of any kind, or the quality of such action; great haste, violent hurry; *esp.* excessive or unwise haste, hastiness, rashness.

1725 WATTS *Logic* II. iv. §5 A rashness and precipitance of judgment and hastiness to believe something on one side or the other. **1839** HALLAM *Hist. Lit.* IV. IV. iv. §49 One.. misses his mark by circuity, the other by precipitance. **1839** ALISON *Hist. Europe* (1849–50) VIII. lii. §61. 360 His precipitance and arrogance..accelerated the catastrophe. **1907** R. ELLIS *Lect. Elegiae in Mæcenatem* 11 The approbation of Augustus, who never judged with precipitance.

precipitancy (prɪ'sɪpɪtənsɪ). [f. PRECIPITANT *a.*: see -ANCY.] The quality of being precipitant.

1. The quality of a headlong descent or fall, or of a very rapid onward movement; headlong speed, violent hurry; excessive suddenness or abruptness of action or occurrence.

1646 SIR T. BROWNE *Pseud. Ep.* 231 Respecting rather the acutenesse of the disease, and precipitancy of occasion, then the rising or setting of Stars. **1797** MRS. RADCLIFFE *Italian* vii, Whence Vivaldi himself had returned with such unexpected precipitancy and consternation. **1803** JANE PORTER *Thaddeus* xxxiv, Thaddeus..with delighted precipitancy caught hold of the hand. **1868** E. EDWARDS *Ralegh* I. xxv. 614 Several conspicuous men died under his treatment, with unusual precipitancy. **1879** *Cassell's Techn. Educ.* IX. 143 He was obliged to fly with the utmost precipitancy.

2. Excessive or unwise haste in action; great want of deliberation; hastiness, rashness.

a **1619** FOTHERBY *Atheom.* I. xiii. §2 (1622) 136 Note the strange precipitancie of their tongue. **1685** *Gracian's Courtiers Orac.* 48 Precipitancy is the passion of fools, who not being able to discover the danger, act at hap-hazard. **1761** HUME *Hist. Eng.* III. l. 92 Some degree of precipitancy and indiscretion. **1865** TROLLOPE *Belton Est.* vi, He..had gone about his task with inconsiderate precipitancy.

b. An instance of this; in *pl.*, hasty or rash acts.

1665 GLANVILL *Scepsis Sci.* vii. 34 'Tis not likely, that one of a thousand such præcipitancies should be crowned with so unexpected an issue. *a* **1834** COLERIDGE *Shaks. Notes* (1849) 63 Youth with its follies, its virtues, its precipitancies.

precipitant (prɪ'sɪpɪtənt), *a.* and *sb.* [ad. L. *præcipitānt-em*, pr. pple. of *præcipitāre* to PRECIPITATE: cf. F. *précipitant* (15th c. in Godef.).]

A. *adj.* (Now *rare*: usually replaced by PRECIPITATE *a.*)

1. Falling headlong; descending vertically or steeply; headlong, directed straight downwards; falling to the bottom as a precipitate or sediment.

a **1620** [implied in PRECIPITANTLY 1]. **1667** MILTON *P.L.* III. 563 He..without longer pause Down right into the Worlds first Region throws His flight precipitant. **1708** J. PHILIPS *Cyder* II. 68 Take care Thy muddy Bev'rage to serene, and drive Præcipitant·the baser, ropy Lees. **1735** SOMERVILLE *Chase* III. 335 He [a horse]..plunging, from his Back the Rider hurls Precipitant.

2. Rushing headlong; hastening along at great speed; moving hurriedly or very swiftly onwards.

1671 GREW *Anat. Plants* vii. §25 Lest its Current should be too copious or precipitant. **1725** POPE *Odyss.* I. 213 That troop so blithe and bold,..Precipitant in fear, wou'd wing their flight. **1830** W. PHILLIPS *Mt. Sinai* II. 268 Walk'd he still erect,..quick-motion'd from the first, But not precipitant.

3. Acting or taking place with great hurry, rapidity, or suddenness; involving very rapid action; very sudden or unexpected, abrupt.

1641 CHAS. I in Rushw. *Hist. Coll.* III. (1692) I. 403 It was hard at first either to discern the Rise, or apply a Remedy to that precipitant Rebellion. **1684** tr. *Bonet's Merc. Compit.* XIV. 501 If we shall hesitate in a great and precipitant Disease, we run great dangers. **1710** LUTTRELL *Brief Rel.* (1857) VI. 625 The hasty reinforcements they are sending to Spain,..with other precipitant measures they have taken. **1803** tr. *P. Le Brun's Mons. Botte* III. 67 The precipitant departure of his uncle,..his last expressions.

4. Acting, or wont to act, with undue or unwise haste, or without any deliberation; excessively hurried; hasty, rash, headstrong. (Of persons, or their acts, etc.)

1608 T. MORTON *Preamb. Encounter* 31 Thou hast beene rash and precipitant. **1663** BP. PATRICK *Parab. Pilgr.* ix. (1668) 40 They were..hurried by their blind and precipitant passion. **1742** RICHARDSON *Pamela* IV. 222 She ..is generous—noble—but has strong Passions, and is thoughtless and precipitant. **1896** in *Westm. Gaz.* 21 Oct. 10/2 He wants reform, but it must be gradual, not precipitant.

B. *sb.* *Chem.* A substance that causes precipitation; a chemical agent which, on being added to a solution, precipitates the dissolved substance. Sometimes const. *of* (the substance precipitated). Correlative to PRECIPITATE *sb.*

1684–5 BOYLE *Min. Waters* 59 A copious Precipitate, such as might have been expected from an Alkaline Precipitant. **1756** C. LUCAS *Ess. Waters* I. 112 The most complete precipitant of copper known, is iron. **1815** J. SMITH *Panorama Sc. & Art* II. 301 The body added to the solution, in order to obtain it, is called the precipitant. **1842** PARNELL *Chem. Anal.* (1845) 32 Hydrochloric acid and chloride of sodium, the ordinary precipitants of silver, also produce a precipitate with solutions of lead.

b. *fig.* (Cf. PRECIPITATE *sb.* d, *vb.* 5 c.)

1905 *Contemp. Rev.* Oct. 503 Such impressions..seem to be little more than irritants or precipitants of consciousness.

pre'cipitantly, *adv.* [f. prec. + -LY[2].] In a precipitant manner; precipitately.

1. With headlong fall or descent; headlong. Also *fig.*

a **1620** J. DYKE *Right Receiving* (1640) Ep. Rdr., Precipitantly falling from an higher excellency then he was any way worthy of. **1642** W. PRICE *Serm.* 14 No man precipitantly falls to the worst at first. **1773** J. ROSS *Fratricide* III. 996 (MS.) To support me To the first dreadful precipice, from whence To dash myself precipitantly down.

2. With headlong movement; hurryingly, very swiftly, at great speed; suddenly, abruptly.

1660 MILTON *Free Commw.* Wks. 1851 V. 444 Returning precipitantly..back to the Captivity from whence he freed us. **1718** HICKES & NELSON *J. Kettlewell* III. xliv. 300 Being forced precipitantly to quit that Kingdom. **1753** A. MURPHY *Gray's-Inn Jrnl.* No. 23 The Suicide urges precipitantly to the Tribunal of his offended God.

3. With undue haste; hastily, rashly.

1646 S. BOLTON *Arraignm. Err.* 98 We..are to receive them as men, that is, rationally, not precipitantly, deliberately, not rashly. **1793** W. ROBERTS *Looker-on* No. 37 (1794) II. 52 It does that coolly and temperately which might otherwise be done precipitantly and lavishly. **1821** *Examiner* 8/2 We..somewhat too precipitantly declined attention to the other performance.

pre'cipitantness. *rare*$^{-0}$. [f. as prec. + -NESS.] = PRECIPITANCY.

1727 in BAILEY vol. II. **1830** in MAUNDER *Dict.*

precipitate (prɪ'sɪpɪtət), *sb.* [ad. mod.L. *præcipitātum* a precipitate, sb. use of neut. pa. pple. of L. *præcipitāre*: see PRECIPITATE *v.*] That which is precipitated; the product of precipitation.

a. *Chem.* A body precipitated from solution; any substance which, by the action of a chemical reagent, or of heat, etc. is separated from the liquid in which it was previously dissolved, and deposited in the solid state (usually in a powdery, flocculent, or cryptocrystalline form).

(Distinguished from *sediment*, a substance previously merely held in suspension, which subsides when left at rest.)

1594 PLAT *Jewell-ho.* III. 36 In the end, by a reverbatory furnesse hee turned al this great matter into a precipitate. **1666** BOYLE *Orig. Formes & Qual.* 353 A no lesse evident Example..we have in the precipitate of Gold and Mercury made by heat alone. **1790** KEIR in *Phil. Trans.* LXXX. 376 The precipitate was at first black, then it assumed the appearance of silver. **1827** FARADAY *Chem. Manip.* ii. 61 Some precipitates will be days and even weeks before they will settle. **1876** tr. *Wagner's Gen. Pathol.* (ed. 6) 89 All kinds of bacteria are indiscriminately mixed in the precipitate.

b. In *Old Chem.* and *Pharm.*, applied *spec.* to certain preparations of mercury obtained by precipitation; in later use, only with defining words:

precipitate per se [= med.L. *mercurius præcipitatus per se*], or ***red precipitate*** [= *mercurius præcipitatus ruber*], mercuric oxide or red oxide of mercury, HgO; ***sweet precipitate***, mercurous chloride or calomel, Hg_2Cl_2; ***white precipitate***, mercurammonium chloride, $HgH_6N_2Cl_2$ (*fusible white p.*), or dimercurammonium chloride, $Hg_2H_4N_2Cl_2$ (*infusible white p.*) [= *mercurius præcipitatus albus*].

1563 T. GALE *Antidot.* II. 68 The Argent Viue that is combust (whych the Alchymistes call precipitate). **1599** A. M. tr. *Gabelhouer's Bk. Physicke* 380/1 It will wexe a redde poudre which is called *Aurum vitæ*, and the aureate or goulden præcipitate. **1607** TOPSELL *Four-f. Beasts* (1658) 399 Rats-bane, Quick-silver, Sublimate, and Precipitate, and divers other things. **1696** PHILLIPS (ed. 5), *Precipitate*, a Dissolution of Mercury made by a Lamp Fire for two Months together, by which it is reduced to red and shining Powder. White precipitate is Mercury reviv'd, and Cinnaber dissolv'd in Aqua fortis of Nitre and Alum. **1704** J. HARRIS *Lex. Techn.* I, *Precipitate*... The Chymists and Writers of Pharmacy commonly give this Name by way of Eminence to Mercury dissolved in Acid Menstruums, and then afterwards precipitated down to the bottom in fine Powders. **1784** KIRWAN in *Phil. Trans.* LXXIV. 158 It may further be urged that precipitate per se yields only dephlogisticated air. **1849** D. CAMPBELL *Inorg. Chem.* 233 Oxide of mercury..reduced to a fine powder, it is changed to a yellow. It is known in pharmacy as red precipitate. **1899** *Allbutt's Syst. Med.* VIII. 516 In ointments, ammoniated mercury (white precipitate) is chiefly employed.

c. *Physics* and *Meteorol.* Moisture condensed from the state of vapour by cooling, and deposited in drops, as rain, dew, etc.

1832 CHALMERS in Hanna *Mem.* (1851) III. xvii. 321 The heat, and the vapour, and the atmospherical precipitates. **1878** HUXLEY *Physiogr.* 65 There is yet another form of atmospheric precipitate that needs a passing notice.

d. *fig.*

1851 CARLYLE *Sterling* I. iii. (1872) 24 The Sterling household shifted twice or thrice..before the vapours of Wellesley promotions and suchlike slowly sank as useless precipitate. **1890** *Spectator* 22 Nov., The proportion of his precipitate of rascaldom which can be cured..in that way, is a very small one. **1905** G. A. SMITH in *Expositor* Oct. 309 Convulsions within Jerusalem, the precipitates from which lie heavy on the later memory of the Jewish nation.

e. *attrib.* (in sense b).

1753 BARTLET *Farriery* xxv. 230 Let the dressings be changed for the precipitate medicine. **1837** SYD. SMITH *Let. to Archd. Singleton*, Finger and thumb, precipitate powder, or anything else you please. **1843** R. J. GRAVES *Syst. Clin. Med.* 391, I entered on the use of black wash, with weak precipitate ointment.

precipitate (prɪ'sɪpɪtət), *a.* Also 7 præ-. [ad. L. *præcipitātus*, pa. pple. of *præcipitāre*: see PRECIPITATE *v.*]

1. Hurled headlong; falling or descending steeply, or directly downwards; having the character of such descent; headlong.

1614 RALEIGH *Hist. World* I. iii. §7. 44 The foure Riuers (had they not fallen so precipitate) could not haue had sufficient force to haue thrust themselues vnder the great Ocean. **1703** ROWE *Ulyss.* III. i, Now like a Whirlwind, on the Shepherd's Fold He [an Eagle] darts precipitate. **1850** BLACKIE *Æschylus* II. 247 And Dadaces, the chiliarch, spear-struck fell Precipitate from his ship.

†**b.** Of a place, etc., without reference to movement: Having a steep or sheer descent; very steep, precipitous. *Obs.*

1615 G. SANDYS *Trav.* 223 Some part of it of a plaine descent, some precipitate, some clothed with trees of seuerall kinds. *c* **1630** RISDON *Surv. Devon* §225 (1810) 241 The way right down to the quay, they call it Precipitate.

2. Rushing or driven along headlong; moving or moved with excessive haste or speed, or having the character of such movement; violently hurried.

1654 tr. *Martini's Conq. China* 70 That vast and precipitate River which the Chineses call Hoang. **1703** POPE *Thebais* 191 Such was the discord of the royal pair, Whom fury drove precipitate to war. **1788** GIBBON *Decl. & F.* (1869) II. xlvi. 729 The general escaped by a precipitate flight. **1849** GROTE *Greece* II. xxxix. V. 92 This precipitate retreat produced consequences highly disastrous.

3. Performed, taking place, acting, or passing with very great rapidity; greatly hastened or hurried; exceedingly sudden or abrupt.

1658 ROWLAND *Topsell's Four-f. Beasts* Ep. Ded., That Art is long, Life short, Experience difficult, occasion precipitate, Judgement uncertain. **1703** MAUNDRELL *Journ. Jerus.* (1732) 27 Their service consisted in precipitate, and very irreverent chattering of certain Prayers and Hymns. **1845** POE *Purloined Let.* Wks. 1865 I. 280 His downfall, too, will not be more precipitate than awkward. **1899** *Allbutt's Syst. Med.* VII. 737 Besides the long and difficult labour, the quick, or, in technical language the precipitate labour.

4. a. Of persons, or their dispositions, etc.: Actuated by violent or sudden impulse, without deliberation; acting with excessive or unwise haste; over-hasty, rash, inconsiderate, headstrong.

1607 TOPSELL *Four-f. Beasts* (1658) 237 They likewise fall to be so mad and præcipitate in lust, raging both with gestures and voice. **1651** HOBBES *Leviath.* II. xxvii. 153 Men that are hasty, and præcipitate in concluding.. what to do. **1709** STEELE *Tatler* No. 112 ¶5 If I could perswade these precipitate young Gentlemen to compose this Restlessness of Mind. **1793** SMEATON *Edystone L.* §123, I was determined not to be precipitate in purchasing. **1824** W. IRVING *T. Trav.* I. 346 It was feared by some that she might be precipitate in her choice.

b. Of acts, etc.: Done in sudden haste or without deliberation; hurried, rash, unconsidered.

a **1618** RALEIGH *Mahomet* (1637) 66 His præcipitate Councels in defacing Castles and strong palaces. **1665** GLANVILL *Scepsis Sci.* xii. 68 Our senses are not in fault, but our precipitate judgments. **1791** BOSWELL *Johnson* an. 1775 (1816) II. 401 Destroyed in a precipitate burning of his papers a few days before his death. **1844** H. H. WILSON *Brit. India* I. 481 The check opposed to precipitate and indiscreet zeal was not detrimental to the ultimate extension of Christianity.

†**5.** Thrown down (*fig.*), subjected. *Obs. rare*$^{-1}$.

1627 DRAYTON *Agincourt*, etc. 216, I finde this age of oure markt with this fate, That honest men are still precipitate Vnder base villaines.

precipitate (prɪˈsɪpɪteɪt), *v.* [f. L. *præcipitāre* to throw or drive headlong, to fall, be over-hasty, f. *præceps, -cipitem* adj. headforemost, headlong, steep, rapid, violent, etc., f. *præ* before + *caput* head: see -ATE[3].]

I. 1. a. *trans.* To throw down headlong; to hurl or fling down. (Often *refl.*)

1575 R. B. *Appius & Virg.* D j b, From lofty top of Turret hie, persupetat [*sic*] me downe. **1621** BURTON *Anat. Mel.* III. iv. II. i. (1651) 692 Salmoneus, that would in derision imitate Jupiters Thunder, he was precipitated for his pains. **1687** A. LOVELL tr. *Thevenot's Trav.* II. 42 Water gushed out miraculously from the place into which he was precipitated. **1774** PENNANT *Tour Scot. in 1772*, 224 The garrison had no alternative but to perish by the edge of the sword, or to precipitate themselves into the ocean. **1839** KEIGHTLEY *Hist. Eng.* II. 36 On the brink of a precipice over which she was to be ere long precipitated.

b. *fig.* To 'hurl', 'fling', throw violently (*into* some (depressed) condition, or *upon* an object of attack).

1528 GARDINER in Pocock *Rec. Ref.* I. l. 119 He shall precipitate himself into his enemies dedition. **1662** STILLINGFL. *Orig. Sacr.* III. iii. §8 How often they are precipitated from the height of prosperity, into the depth of adversity. **1781** GIBBON *Decl. & F.* xxvi. II. 563 The invasion of the Huns precipitated on the provinces of the West the Gothic nation. **1880** G. MEREDITH *Tragic Com.* (1881) 78 A youth who could be precipitated into the writhings of dissolution, and raised out of it by a smile.

†**c.** *fig.* To cast down; to overthrow, ruin, destroy; to upset, disorder, derange. *Obs.*

1528 in Burnet *Hist. Ref.* (1679) I. *Records* II. xxii. 58 Not to suffer the Pope's Holiness, if he would thus wilfully, without reason or discretion to precipitate himself and the said See. **1609** BIBLE (Douay) *Ps.* liv. 10 Precipitate ô Lord, and divide their tongues.

†**2. a.** *intr.* (for *refl.* or *pass.*) To fall headlong; to fall, gravitate (quot. 1740). *Obs.*

1605 SHAKS. *Lear* IV. vi. 50 (So many fathome downe precipitating) Thou'dst shiuer'd like an Egge. **1740** STACK in *Phil. Trans.* XLI. 421 The Complication of these Two Forces will compel the Mobile to precipitate to the Centre.. of the Parallel it happens to be in. **1785** JEFFERSON *Corr.* Wks. 1859 I. 354 They precipitated from that height to the earth, and were crushed to atoms.

†**b.** To descend steeply, as a waterfall or river.

1644 EVELYN *Diary* 2 Nov., Aquapendente, a town situated on a very ragged rock, down which precipitates an intire river. **1793** A. MURPHY *Tacitus* (1805) VII. 8 The Rhine has its source on the steep and lofty summit of the Rhætian Alps, from which it precipitates.

†**c.** *fig.* To 'fall' or 'plunge' *into* some condition or act; to fall or come suddenly to ruin or destruction. *Obs.* (In quot. 1593, to come down from a lofty position or dignity, to condescend extremely.)

1593 LD. ESSEX in *Bacon's Wks.* (1862) VIII. 254 She [Q. Eliz.] should precipitate too much from being highly displeased with you, to give you near access. **1650** GENTILIS *Considerations* 160 Those who have such a mixture of great vices, and great vertues, sometimes precipitate and fall almost as soon as they are born. **1682** SCARLETT *Exchanges* 173 Exchanges are as variable as the Wind, and many times as if made, do precipitate without any known Cause or Reason. **1758** *Herald* No. 23 II. 116 While a nation is precipitating to its ruin.

II. 3. a. *trans.* To cause to move, pass, act, or proceed very rapidly; to hasten, hurry, urge on.

1558 WARDE tr. *Alexis' Secr.* (1568) 2 Our disordinate maner of lyfe maketh vs.. to precipitate our youth, and to abbreuiate much our lyfe. **1697** DRYDEN *Virg. Georg.* IV. 614 The Goddess.. Her self, involv'd in Clouds, precipitates her Flight. **1736** BUTLER *Anal.* II. iv. Wks. 1874 I. 204 Men are impatient, and for precipitating things. **1858** BUCKLE *Civiliz.* (1871) II. viii. 554 Men will not bide their time, but will insist on precipitating the march of affairs.

b. To bring on or cause to happen quickly, suddenly, or unexpectedly; to bring to pass hastily or abruptly; to hasten the occurrence of.

1625 BACON *Ess., Ambition* (Arb.) 227 If they bee Stout, and Daring, it may precipitate their Designes, and proue dangerous. **1670** COTTON *Espernon* I. II. 65 The Duke of Joyeuse having precipitated the Battel of Coutras,.. he there lost the Battel, with his Life. **1748** *Anson's Voy.* II. vi. 198 They could not precipitate his departure. **1837** DISRAELI *Venetia* I. vii, [He] often precipitated these paroxysms by denying his mother.. duty and affection. **1874** GREEN *Short Hist.* vi. §3. 284 Its ruin was precipitated by religious persecution.

4. a. *intr.* To rush headlong; to make great haste, to hurry; to move, act, or proceed very quickly.

1622 BACON *Hen. VII*, Wks. 1879 I. 774/2 Neither.. did their forces gather or increase, which might hasten him to precipitate and assail them. **1647** SPRIGGE *Anglia Rediv.* I. v. (1854) 39 It was brought to the King, that our army was flying to Northampton, which did occasion them the more to precipitate. **1758** JORTIN *Erasm.* I. 164, I precipitate rather than compose, and it is far more irksome to me to review than to write.

†**b.** To proceed with undue or unwise haste; to act hastily or rashly; to be precipitate in action.

1626 C. POTTER tr. *Sarpi's Hist. Quarrels* 121 They had vsed all reasons and dexteritie possible to stay the Pope that he might not precipitate. **1670** G. H. *Hist. Cardinals* III. I. 244 We are now deliberating about the Election of Gods Vice-gerent.., and shall we precipitate in this manner?

III. 5. a. *Chem. trans.* To deposit, or cause to be deposited, in a solid form from solution in a liquid, by chemical action: see PRECIPITATE *sb.* (Sometimes with the solution as object: To produce precipitation in.) Also, to cause (dust or other particulate matter in a gas) to be deposited on a surface. Formerly sometimes in wider sense: To deposit from suspension or admixture in a liquid, as sediment, etc.

1644 DIGBY *Nat. Bodies* xxxiv. §4. 290 This steame therefore, flying still to the serous bloud which passeth by, must of necessity precipitate (as I may say) the serous partes of that bloud. **1676–7** GREW *Solution Salts in Water* i. §14 They are both copiously and forthwith precipitated to the bottome of the Glass. **1790** KEIR in *Phil. Trans.* LXXX. 375 *note*, Copper and zinc readily precipitate silver from these solutions. **1800** tr. *Lagrange's Chem.* I. 96 This acid liquor precipitates lime water. **1816** FARADAY *Exp. Res.* i. 2 The filtered solution was precipitated by carbonate of potash. **1857** *G. Bird's Urin. Deposits* (ed. 5) 246 This acid readily precipitates lime from all its combinations with acids. **1911** *Jrnl. Industr. & Engin. Chem.* Aug. 543/2 Cotton-covered wire when used as a discharge electrode.. proved far more effective in precipitating the sulphuric acid mists. **1912** *Jrnl. Franklin Inst.* CLXXIV. 263 Plants.. built for precipitating the fumes from copper smelters and the dust from cement plants. **1938** *Trans. Inst. Chem. Engineers* XVI. 40/1 The gas is.. passed through an electrofitter of the dry type where the greater part of the dust is precipitated. **1975** S. MASUDA in A. R. Blythe *Static Electrification 1975* iii. 154 Particles charged by collision with unipolar ions emitted from the discharge electrode are driven by the coulombic force on to the collecting electrode, where they are precipitated.

b. *Physics* and *Meteorol.* To condense (moisture) into drops from a state of vapour, and so deposit or cause to fall, as dew, rain, etc.

1863 TYNDALL *Heat* ii. §28 (1870) 31 A very few strokes suffice to precipitate the vapour. **1869** —— in *Fortn. Rev.* 1 Feb. 235 Turning in the beam we have a second cloud, more delicate than the first, precipitated. **1878** HUXLEY *Physiogr.* 44 The mass of ice cools the surrounding air, and thus precipitates its moisture.

c. *transf.* and *fig.* in various applications; *spec.* in *Spiritualism* = MATERIALIZE 2.

1825 J. NEAL *Bro. Jonathan* II. 189 The mercury of his blood was precipitated. **1841–4** EMERSON *Ess., Nat.* Wks. (Bohn) I. 235 The world is mind precipitated. **1891** *Pall Mall G.* 1 Oct. 2/3 The assertion of a band of Mejnour and Zanoni brothers who possess the secret of dissolving their own senile bodies and precipitating them again in the prime of physical condition.

6. a. *intr.* (for *refl.*) To be deposited from solution (or from suspension); to settle as a precipitate.

a **1626** BACON *Phys. Rem.* Wks. 1879 I. 245/1 By what strong water every metal will precipitate. **1664** POWER *Exp. Philos.* I. 34 Which in a short time will precipitate and all sink down to the bottom of the glass. **1758** REID tr. *Macquer's Chem.* I. 379 It always precipitates in the form of a white calx. **1854** J. SCOFFERN in *Orr's Circ. Sc., Chem.* 403 Carbonate of lime.. precipitates.

b. To fall or be deposited as condensed vapour.

1800 VINCE *Hydrostat.* vii. (1806) 78 [The vapours] have no inclination to precipitate and fall down in drops.

preˈcipitated, *ppl. a.* [f. PRECIPITATE *v.* + -ED[1].] In senses answering to those of the verb.

1. Hastened, hurried. Now usually PRECIPITATE *a.*

1633 T. ADAMS *Exp. 2 Peter* ii. 16 Therefore was the teacher.. a stupid beast to teach him that was too precipitated. **1678** *Trans. Crt. Spain* 51 At the too precipitated death of that Gentleman of Arragon. **1688** *Lond. Gaz.* No. 2377/2 The Enemies precipitated Retreat to Sendrovia. **1749** RICHARDSON *Clarissa* IV. xlviii. 286 She set even my heart into a palpitation,.. like a precipitated pendulum in a clock case. **1845** NAPIER *Conq. Scinde* II. vii. 428 The precipitated movements of the Ameer.

2. *Chem.* and *Physics.* Deposited from solution, from a state of vapour, or from a state of suspension in a gas.

1663 BOYLE *Usef. Exp. Nat. Philos.* II. v. viii. 200 Calces of corroded and precipitated things. **1707** MORTIMER *Husb.* (1721) II. 329 You must draw it off from its precipitated Lees. **1871** TYNDALL *Fragm. Sc.* (1879) I. iv. 114 The cloud formed.., when the precipitated particles are sufficiently fine, is blue. **1899** *Allbutt's Syst. Med.* VIII. 726 A drachm of precipitated sulphur administered in milk. **1938** *Trans. Inst. Chem. Engineers* XVI. 38/1 The precipitated dust falls into hoppers below each section of the plant. **1971** M. ROBINSON in W. Strauss *Air Pollution Control* I. 267 The decline of [migration velocity] w, at.. higher gas velocities is usually accounted for by reentrainment of precipitated dust.

Hence **preˈcipitatedly** *adv.*, precipitately, hurriedly; = next, sense 2.

1770 C. JENNER *Placid Man* I. II. v. 101 [He] would have confirmed the suspicion.. by leaving the room as precipitatedly as he had entered it.

precipitately (prɪˈsɪpɪtətlɪ), *adv.* [f. PRECIPITATE *a.* + -LY[2].] In a precipitate manner.

1. With headlong fall or descent; headlong.

1632 LITHGOW *Trav.* IX. 392 An outragious Torrent; which precipitately deualleth. **1762** tr. *Busching's Syst. Geog.* I. 236 By means of this.. they secure themselves from falling precipitately upon the rocks when they dive to the bottom of the sea. **1852** MRS. STOWE *Uncle Tom's C.* xvii, Marks, heading the retreat down the rocks.., while all the party came tumbling precipitately after him.

†**b.** Steeply, precipitously. *Obs.*

1823 F. CLISSOLD *Ascent Mt. Blanc* 19 From the heights of the mountain, which precipitately rise above this Plateau, immense avalanches often descend.

2. With headlong speed; with a sudden rush; in great haste.

1728 MORGAN *Algiers* II. v. 300 The Emperor himself was forced, precipitately, to come down from the Mountain. **1778** MISS BURNEY *Evelina* (1791) I. xliii. 219 Rushing precipitately into the room. **1877** CLERY *Min. Tact.* xiv. (ed. 3) 186 If the rearguard be attacked precipitately by the first troops that arrive.

3. With hurried action, hurriedly, hastily; suddenly, abruptly; with unwise haste, rashly, inconsiderately.

1647 CLARENDON *Hist. Reb.* I. §51 A new War was as precipitately declared against France. **1676** TOWERSON *Decalogue* 517 A man may determine his will precipitately as well as considerately. **1766** GOLDSM. *Vic. W.* xviii, That state of mind in which we all are more ready to act precipitately than to reason right. **1873** MRS. H. WOOD *Mast. Greylands* ii, The.. governess had lately given warning precipitately and left.

preˈcipitateness. [f. as prec. + -NESS.] The quality or character of being precipitate; hastiness; rashness.

1669 BP. HOPKINS *Serm. 1 Pet.* ii. 12 (1685) 35 It is but precipitateness for any man to oppose himself.. defenceless against armed violence. **1884** *Manch. Exam.* 8 July 5/2 Captain Fournier.. expressed himself in similar terms with regard to General Millot's precipitateness.

precipitater: see PRECIPITATOR.

preˈcipitating, *vbl. sb.* [f. PRECIPITATE *v.* + -ING[1].] The action of the verb PRECIPITATE; usually = PRECIPITATION 5. Also *attrib.*

1664 POWER *Exp. Philos.* I. 62 By attenuating the grosser parts.. volatilizing some, precipitating of others. **1683** PETTUS *Fleta Min.* I. (1686) 83 The Philosophers do write of precipitating, by which the Silver in common tin may be put down. **1877** RAYMOND *Statist. Mines & Mining* 400 The bath after it is withdrawn from the precipitating-tanks generally contains a little copper. **1887** *Daily News* 31 Oct. 2/6 Thirteen precipitating tanks on the land side of the existing reservoir will receive the sewage.

preˈcipitating, *ppl. a.* [f. as prec. + -ING[2].] That precipitates, in various senses.

†**1.** Steep, precipitous. *Obs.*

1615 G. SANDYS *Trav.* III. 183 This Caue is..hewne out of the precipitating rocke. **1632** LITHGOW *Trav.* VI. 278 The Ponds being hewne out..from the deualling face of a precipitating mountaine.

2. Falling headlong from a height; sinking to the bottom, as a deposit from a liquid. ? *Obs.*

1756 AMORY *Buncle* (1825) II. 122 Some were covered with forest and some with precipitating streams. **1799** KIRWAN *Geol. Ess.* 40 The progressive motion impressed upon the precipitating masses.

†**3.** Coming abruptly, abrupt or sudden. *Obs.*

1638 SIR T. HERBERT *Trav.* (ed. 2) 35 Yet ere death cald for them, they were cald for, by precipitating ends.

4. Impelling headlong; hurrying violently.

1815 SHELLEY *Alastor* 321 A whirlwind swept it on, With fierce gusts and precipitating force.

†**5.** Plunging into action without consideration; acting too hastily or rashly, precipitate. *Obs.*

1681 D'URFEY *Progr. Honesty* iv, So the reverend Sire.. thus begun To pitty and instruct his just precipitating Son. **1754** RICHARDSON *Grandison* VI. xxx. 195 A man so generous, tho' so precipitating.

6. *Chem.* Causing precipitation from solution or from a gas.

1904 *Brit. Med. Jrnl.* 10 Sept. 573 The precipitating action of egg-albumen precipitin. **1912** *Jrnl. Franklin Inst.* CLXXIV. 262 The brush form of discharge from points is only a good precipitating agent when the current of gas is small.

precipitation (prɪsɪpɪˈteɪʃən). [a. F. *précipitation* (15th c. Godef. *Compl.*), ad. L. *præcipitātiōnem*, n. of action from *præcipitāre* to PRECIPITATE.] The action of precipitating.

I. 1. a. The action of casting down or falling headlong from a height; a hurling down; the fact of being hurled down; headlong fall or descent.

1607 SHAKS. *Cor.* III. iii. 102 Wee..banish him our Citie In perill of precipitation From off the Rocke Tarpeian. **1720** WELTON *Suffer. Son of God* II. xvi. 427 Under this Assurance that He might cast Himself down from the Pinnacle, but that He should be supported in His Precipitation as well as He was in His Ascent thither. **1856** STANLEY *Sinai & Pal.* x. (1858) 367 The summit of a mountain, from which summit the intended precipitation was to take place.

b. Steepness of descent; precipitousness. *rare.*

1607 SHAKS. *Cor.* III. ii. 4 Let them..pile ten hilles on the Tarpeian Rocke, That the precipitation might downe stretch Below the beame of sight. **1890** TALMAGE *Manger to Throne* 53 The hills for width and precipitation are displays omnipotent.

c. *Path.* Complete prolapsus, 'falling'.

1612 tr. *Guillemeau's Child-birth* 210 The precipitation, or comming downe of the wombe: the ligaments being loosened, and sometimes broken. **1822–34** *Good's Study Med.* (ed. 4) IV. 110 *note*, In what Madame Boivin terms *precipitation* or complete *prolapsus*..any rational scheme of relief is entitled to encouragement.

†**d.** Vertical descent (of a root). *Obs. rare.*

1669 J. ROSE *Eng. Vineyard* (1675) 18 The deepness, and fatness of the earth, contributes more to the luxury of the branches..and precipitation of the roots, than to the just, and natural stature of the stem.

II. 2. Headlong rush, violent onward motion.

1628 FELTHAM *Resolves* II. [1] x. 26 Wee goe surest, when we post not in a precipitation. **1695** WOODWARD *Nat. Hist. Earth* (J.), The hurry, precipitation, and rapid motion of the water, returning at the end of the deluge, towards the sea. **1748** *Anson's Voy.* I. viii. 76 The violence of the current, which had set us with so much precipitation to the eastward. **1822** LAMB *Elia* Ser. I. *Chimney-Sweepers*, Pacing along Cheapside with my accustomed precipitation when I walk westward.

3. a. Sudden and hurried action; sudden haste or quickness; hurry.

1502 *Ord. Crysten Men* (W. de W.) IV. vi. S ij, He therin ought to procede demeurely dyscretly, without preceptacyon [*Fr.* precipitacion] in chastysynge. **1589** PUTTENHAM *Eng. Poesie* II. xi. (Arb.) 98 Mounting and falling from note to note such as be to them peculiar, and with more or lesse leasure or precip[it]ation. **1678** *Trans. Crt. Spain* 165 That so he might undo me with greater precipitation. **1782** MISS BURNEY *Cecilia* VIII. vi, 'None, none!' interrupted she, with precipitation. **1838** DICKENS *Nich. Nick.* vii, The lady having seized it, with great precipitation, they retired.

b. Unduly hurried action; inconsiderate haste; rash rapidity.

1629 T. ADAMS *Medit. Creed* Wks. 1862 III. 119 Precipitation in our works makes us unlike to God: heady fool, art thou wiser than thy Maker? **1700** ASTRY tr. *Saavedra-Faxardo* I. 251 Precipitation is the effect of Madness, and generally the occasion of great Perils. **1794** S. WILLIAMS *Vermont* 397 Some philosophers, with great precipitation have pretended to decide it by system. **1870** DISRAELI *Lothair* xi, We must not act with precipitation.

4. The bringing on of something hastily, suddenly, or before the expected time; hastening, hurrying; acceleration.

1621 in Elsing *Debates Ho. Lords* (Camden) 109 Then the precipitacion of justice (not hearing the proofes) is hyghe injustice. **1646** SIR T. BROWNE *Pseud. Ep.* 174 The common cause alleadged..is, a precipitation or over hasty exclusion before the birth be perfect. **1769** GOLDSM. *Hist. Rome* (1786) II. 488 This, in a great measure, gave precipitation to his own downfall. **1882** FARRAR *Early Chr.* I. 557 *note*, He attributes to his death the precipitation of the ruin of Jerusalem.

III. 5. a. *Chem.* Separation and deposition of a substance in a solid (powdery or crystalline) form from solution in a liquid, by the action of a chemical reagent, or of electricity, heat, etc.; the removal and deposition of particulate matter from suspension in a gas; the separation of crystals of a solute phase from a solid solution (see also *precipitation hardening* below).

The date of first quotation is not certain: it may be 17th c.

[**1477** NORTON *Ord. Alch.* vi. in Ashm. *Theat. Chem. Brit.* (1652) 95 Longe Vessells for Precipitation.] **1612** WOODALL *Surg. Mate* Wks. (1653) 273 *Precipitation* is when bodies corroded by Aqua fortis, or Aqua Regia, and dissolved into water..are reverberated into Calx. **1660** BOYLE *New Exp. Phys. Mech.* xxxvii. 313 The precipitation of Benjamin, and some other Resinous Bodies. **1790** KEIR in *Phil. Trans.* LXXX. 374 Upon adding iron to a solution of silver in the nitrous acid no precipitation ensued. **1800** HENRY *Epit. Chem.* (1808) 12 For precipitations, and separating liquids from precipitates, the decanting-jar will be found useful. **1900** *Jrnl. Soc. Dyers* XVI. 6 The precipitation of the indigo white. **1908** F. G. COTTRELL *U.S. Patent 895,729* 2/1 The gases or vapors containing the suspended particles enter the precipitation chamber A through pipe B. **1912**, **1920** [see ELECTROSTATIC *a.*]. **1926** *Trans. Amer. Soc. Steel Treating* X. 718 The idea that the hardness of an alloy may be increased by the precipitation of a soluble constituent from solid solution was first advanced by Merica and his associates in a hypothesis to account for the age-hardening of duralumin. **1938** *Trans. Inst. Chem. Engineers* XVI. 37/2 It is unlikely that any new cement works will be designed without provision for dust separation by electrical precipitation. **1958** A. D. MERRIMAN *Dict. Metallurgy* 3/1 *Ageing*, a precipitation process, often submicroscopic, which occurs when a supersaturated solid solution is allowed to rest at atmospheric temperature after quenching. **1967** A. H. COTTRELL *Introd. Metallurgy* xx. 372 Cu-Be alloys soften rapidly by discontinuous precipitation at temperatures above about 300°C, but this can be prevented by the addition of about 0·4 wt per cent cobalt. **1974** *Encycl. Brit. Macropædia* IV. 161/1 Electrostatic precipitation is a method for the precipitation of fogs..: a high voltage is applied across the gas phase to produce electrical charges on the particles. These charges cause the particles to be attracted to the oppositely charged walls of the separator.

b. *concr.* The product of this process, a precipitated substance; a precipitate. (In quot. 1867 in extended sense.)

1605 TIMME *Quersit.* III. 154 The same coagulating force ..doth manifestly appeare in those preparations which are called precipitations. **1867** H. MACMILLAN *Bible Teach.* Pref. (1870) 12 Our forests, corn-fields, and coal-beds are the solid precipitations of unseen carbonic acid gas in the atmosphere.

c. *attrib.*

1839 URE *Dict. Arts* 37 The clear liquor should now be run off into the precipitation cistern. **1887** *Pall Mall G.* 11 Jan. 2/2 The construction of precipitation works at one of the London sewage outfalls.

6. a. *Physics* and *Meteorol.* Condensation and deposition of moisture from the state of vapour, as by cooling; *esp.* in the formation of dew, rain, snow, etc. **b.** *concr.* That which is so deposited.

1675 *Phil. Trans.* X. 468 In some..precipitations of the Air. **1692** RAY *Disc.* II. ii. (1732) 99 There was so strange a Condensation or rather Precipitation of the Vapours. **1812–16** PLAYFAIR *Nat. Phil.* (1819) I. 322 Dew is a precipitation of humidity from the lower strata of the atmosphere. **1859** R. F. BURTON *Centr. Afr.* in *Jrnl. Geog. Soc.* XXIX. 105 Thence the frequent precipitation of heavy rain, and the banks and sheets of morning cloud which veil the tree-clad peaks of the highest gradients. **1864** MARSH *Man & Nat.* 436 Marriotte found that but one sixth of the precipitation in basin of the Seine was delivered into the sea by that river. **1878** HUXLEY *Physiogr.* 179 The excess of evaporation over precipitation in the northern portion of the land hemisphere.

7. *fig.*; *spec.* in *Spiritualism* = MATERIALIZATION 2.

1891 *Pall Mall G.* 1 Oct. 2/3 A distinguished naturalist.. assured me that he had, in his own room, with no other person present save his servant, a young man of 'mediumistic' temperament, repeatedly witnessed the process of materialization (precipitation) of a human figure slowly going on under his own eyes, developing from a nebulous shape through which he could see the furniture beyond it, to a solid human form, whose hand he could grasp firmly.

8. Special Comb.: **precipitation hardening** *Metallurgy*, hardening of an alloy by heat treatment that causes the precipitation from solid solution of crystals of a solute phase; a strengthening process utilizing this phenomenon.

1926 R. S. ARCHER in *Trans. Amer. Soc. Steel Treating* X. 719 It is proposed in this paper..to develop the general theory of what may be called 'precipitation hardening'. **1931** *Jrnl. Iron & Steel Inst.* CXXIV. 671 The binary iron-boron alloys were incapable of hardening by quenching and the precipitation hardening was hardly noticeable. **1957** *Technology* Oct. 291/2 Parts made from it [*sc.* a new stainless steel] are subjected to 'precipitation hardening', a method of heat treatment designed to give increased strength by precipitating an inter-metallic compound between the metal particles. **1973** J. G. TWEEDDALE *Materials Technol.* I. vi. 169 Precipitation hardening..is a three-part treatment (1) a solution treatment at elevated temperature to dissolve the solute (2) a quenching operation to trap the solute..(3) a precipitation or ageing treatment to develop the required size of precipitate.

precipitative (prɪˈsɪpɪteɪtɪv), *a.* [f. PRECIPITATE *v.* (or its L. source): see -ATIVE.] Having the quality of precipitating (i.e. in quot., of accelerating motion).

1883 WINCHELL *World-Life* II. iv. (1889) 491 The precipitative tendencies of tidal action may exceed those resulting from resistances encountered in planetary space.

precipitator (prɪˈsɪpɪteɪtə(r)). Also 7 -er. [a. late L. *præcipitātor* a destroyer, overthrower: see PRECIPITATE *v.* and -OR.] One who or that which precipitates.

1. One who brings something to pass quickly or suddenly; a hastener.

a **1660** HAMMOND *Serm. Luke ix.* 55 Wks. 1684 IV. 590 Zealots..as it prov'd were the hastners and precipitators of the destruction of the Kingdom.

2. a. *Chem.* and *Physics.* Something that causes precipitation; a precipitant. **b.** An apparatus for precipitation; *spec.* (*a*) a tank for purifying hard water or sewage, a precipitating-tank; (*b*) an apparatus for removing particulate matter such as dust or smoke from a gas by passing it between electrodes so that the particles acquire an electric charge and are attracted to an oppositely charged surface.

1681 tr. *Belon's Myst. Physick* Introd. 20, I have found Antimony, Allum, and Coral, to be most powerful Dulcif[i]ers, Precipitaters, and Expulsers of divers sorts of Acides. **1883** HALDANE *Workshop Receipts* Ser. II. 350/1 The mother-liquor is conducted through the pipe for mother-water to the precipitators. **1886** *American* XI. 166 The slopes of elevations towards the sea are great precipitators of rain. **1919** *Jrnl. Amer. Chem. Soc.* XLI. 587 (*heading*) An electrical precipitator for analyzing smokes. **1958** *Engineering* 28 Feb. 274/3 Dust is extracted from the 'used' air by electrostatic precipitators. **1971** *Time* 7 June 61/3 Equip the plants' stacks with electrostatic precipitators and wet scrubbers that would cut air pollution by 99%.

precipitin (prɪˈsɪpɪtɪn). *Biol. Chem.* [irreg. f. base of PRECIPIT-ATE + -IN[1].] **a.** An antibody that on reacting with its antigen produces a visible precipitate. Also *fig.*

1900 *Lancet* 14 July 99/1 Experiments..with the precipitins of egg albumen and sheep's globulin were made, and in this case also one or other of the precipitins disappeared. **1903** *Brit. Med. Jrnl.* 21 Mar. 655 The same explanations hold good for the action of the..precipitins, namely those substances in immune serums which cause precipitation when added to the fluids or solutions of substances used in immunization. **1904** [see PRECIPITATING *ppl. a.* 6]. **1912** [see IMMUNOLOGIST]. **1931** *Syst. Bacteriol.* (Med. Res. Council) VI. xiii. 424 Kraus named the substance present in the bacterial filtrate precipitinogen while the term precipitin was used to denote the hypothetical substance or antibody formed or set free in the animal body in response to injections of an antigen or precipitinogen. **1966** *Lancet* 24 Dec. 1397/1 Some natives in the Territory of Papua and New Guinea who have chronic lung disease also have in their sera precipitins against a soluble substance in the roofs of their huts. **1971** 'D. HALLIDAY' *Dolly & Doctor Bird* xiii. 192, I don't think any of us felt anything: we carried our own precipitins, for the moment, against fear and danger.

b. *attrib.*, as ***precipitin reaction, technique***; **precipitin test**, a means of establishing the identity of a substance by testing whether it reacts with a particular precipitin; hence ***precipitin testing*** vbl. sb.

1958 *Immunology* I. 87 Quantitative studies of the precipitin and agglutination reactions. **1962** M. RABAEY in A. Pirie *Lens Metabolism Rel. Cataract* 310 Generally, α-crystallin has been the first lens protein which has been detected by means of precipitin techniques. **1905** F. C. WOOD *Chem. & Microsc. Diagnosis* I. ix. 255 Before applying the precipitin test to a suspected stain, the presence of blood should, if possible, be determined either by the formation of Teichmann's crystals or by the spectroscope. **1952** M. E. FLOREY *Clin. Applic. Antibiotics* I. ii. 31 They..found precipitin tests inconclusive and considered in consequence that the urticaria was not the result of an antibody-antigen reaction. **1976** *Lancet* 6 Nov. 985/1 Antibodies to thyroglobulin were detected by a precipitin test in an Ouchterlony plate. **1971** *E. Afr. Standard* (Nairobi) 13 Apr. 9/8 This will form the basis of establishing precipitin testing for East Africa.

precipitinogen (prɪˌsɪpɪˈtɪnədʒən). *Immunol.* Also †preˈcipitogen. [f. prec. + -OGEN.] A type of antigen which induces the production of a precipitin.

1904 G. H. F. NUTTALL *Blood Immunity & Blood Relationship* ii. 98 The immunifying substance, which they [*sc.* Obermayer and Pick] wrongly style 'precipitogen', as well as the precipitin they conclude are not albuminous. [*Note*] A misnomer..for the reason that it suggests a relation between precipitin and ('precipitogen') precipitable substances such as exists, for instance, between pepsin and pepsinogen, in other words that the 'precipitogen' is a forerunner of precipitin, which it is not. **1907** *Jrnl. Med. Res.* XVI. 173 Many or all of the other substances are assimilated more or less readily by the tissues, are neutralized in a relatively short space of time, and in some instances (precipitogens) definite reaction products to them may be formed. *Ibid.* XVII. 232 The complement, when incubated with antigen and low ($\frac{1}{10}$) dilution of immune serum, may..be absorbed through the union of precipitin and precipitinogen. **1931** [see prec.]. **1969** *Acta Path. & Microbiol. Scand.* LXXVII. 463 Some chemical properties of a group reactive precipitinogen from the *Fusobacterium* strain F1 have been investigated.

Hence **preˌcipitinoˈgenic** *a.*

1935 F. P. GAY *Agents of Dis. & Host Resistance* xxi. 418 Not all soluble proteins are precipitinogenic. **1970** B. G. F. WEITZ in H. W. Mulligan *Afr. Trypanosomiases* vi. 113 Cultivated trypanosomes are also agglutinogenic and precipitinogenic.

†**preci'pitious**, *a. Obs.* [f. L. *præcipiti-um* PRECIPICE *sb.* + -OUS. In sense 1 this form is more correct etymologically than *precipitous*.]

I. 1. Of the nature of a precipice: = PRECIPITOUS 4.

1635 BRATHWAIT *Arcad. Pr.* 196 But you'r specially to shunne,..To walke..Neare a precipitious place. **1658** RAY *Rem.* (1760) 196 A precipitious solid Rock. **1721** MAUNDRELL *Journ. Jerus.* Add. 6 Travelling through the Mountains, which were now somewhat more uneven and precipitious [*printed* precipititious].

b. *fig.* Involving risk of sudden fall or ruin.

1613 SHERLEY *Trav. Persia* 83 Hee cannot bee so ignorant, as to vnderstand no way to bee so precipitious for himselfe. **1654** tr. *Scudery's Curia Pol.* 60 Others have refused these royall dignities, as places too precipitious, and too full of cares and troubles.

2. Descending headlong; = PRECIPITATE *a.* 1.

1648 *Eikon Basilike* v. 35 Monarchy it self, together with Me, could not but be dashed in pieces, by such a precipitious fall as they intended. [Misquoted as *precipitous* by J.]

II. 3. Sudden, abrupt: = PRECIPITATE *a.* 3, PRECIPITOUS 2.

1676 GLANVILL *Ess.* VI. 24 Sutable to the Analogy of Nature, which useth not to make precipitious leaps from one thing to another, but usually proceeds by orderly steps and gradations.

4. Hasty, rash: = PRECIPITATE *a.* 4, PRECIPITOUS 1.

1613 DANIEL *Coll. Hist. Eng.* 141 He..stood so betweene the kingdome and the kings rigor as stayed many precipitious violencies. **1673** O. WALKER *Educ.* I. ix. 78 Cross, precipitious, despiteful, revengeful. *Ibid.* I. xiii. 178 Lust..is the mother of negligence, precipitious inconsiderateness, inconstancy.

Hence †**preci'pitiously** *adv.*, hastily, precipitately; †**preci'pitiousness**, hastiness, rashness.

1653 H. COGAN tr. *Pinto's Trav.* lxviii. (1663) 278 In regard this execution had been done precipitiously, and without any proof. **1667** *Decay Chr. Piety* viii. ¶10 Precipitiously it will on, where ever strong desire shall drive. **1673** O. WALKER *Educ.* II. iv. 261 Precipitiousness, impatience, or not staying to take the opportunity,..is frequently the ruine of many noble designs.

precipitous (prɪ'sɪpɪtəs), *a.* [ad. obs. F. *précipiteux* (16th c. in Godef.) = It., Sp., Pg. *precipitoso*, ad. late L. or Com. Rom. **præcipitōsus*, f. *præceps, præcipit-em* headlong: see -OUS.]

I. †1. Acting, or done, with excessive or undue haste; rash, headstrong: = PRECIPITATE *a.* 4. *Obs.*

1646 SIR T. BROWNE *Pseud. Ep.* I. v. 18 The attempts of some have been precipitious. **1689** SHADWELL *Bury F.* v. i, I should be censur'd for being too precipitous. *a* **1734** NORTH *Exam.* III. vii. §78 (1740) 564 This Discharge..was precipitous.., and done on Purpose to stop that Indictment.

†2. Coming on or passing very rapidly; very sudden or abrupt: = PRECIPITATE *a.* 3. *Obs.*

1646 SIR T. BROWNE *Pseud. Ep.* III. vi. 117 The small and slender time of the Beares gestation,..lasting but few dayes, ..the exclusion becomes precipitous, and the young ones consequently informous. **1666** EVELYN *Kal. Hort.* (ed. 2) 4 How precious the time is, how præcipitous the occasion, how many things to be done in their just Season.

3. Rushing headlong onwards; violently hurried or hurrying: = PRECIPITATE *a.* 2. *rare.*

1774 PENNANT *Tour Scot.* in 1772, 33 The waters are discharged with a rapid precipitous current. **1817** SHELLEY *Rev. Islam* I. viii, A course precipitous, of dizzy speed, Suspending thought and breath. **1833** LAMB *Elia* Ser. II. *Barrenness Imag. Faculty*, Precipitous, with his reeling Satyr rout about him,..Bacchus..flings himself at the Cretan. **1864** TENNYSON *En. Ard.* 588 The sweep Of some precipitous rivulet to the wave.

II. 4. Of the nature of a precipice; having a vertical, overhanging, or very steep face, as a rock or cliff; consisting of or characterized by precipices. (The usual sense: taking the place of the earlier PRECIPITIOUS.)

1806 *Gazetteer Scotl.* (ed. 2) 449 Salisbury Craig..is noted chiefly for its steep precipitous front. **1817** MOORE *Lalla R.* (1824) 271 Down the precipitous rocks they sprung. **1846** MCCULLOCH *Acc. Brit. Empire* (1854) I. 245 In the first part the shore is bold, precipitous, and picturesque. **1856** STANLEY *Sinai & Pal.* viii. (1858) 324 Up the precipitous ravines of Jericho and Ai.

b. Falling with extreme rapidity.

1897 *Allbutt's Syst. Med.* II. 360 The descent of the temperature is then rapid, even precipitous, falling 3° to 5° F. or more in a single night.

pre'cipitously, *adv.* [f. prec. + -LY².] In a precipitous manner.

1. With headlong onward movement; with a rushing violence: = PRECIPITATELY 2. *rare.*

1626 tr. *Boccalini's New-found Pol.* II. iv. 125 What hindred them from running precipitously to the acquisition of all Italie? **1864** TENNYSON *Boadicea* 58 Till the victim hear within and yearn to hurry precipitously Like the leaf in a roaring whirlwind, like the smoke in a hurricane whirl'd.

†2. With undue haste; over-hastily, rashly: = PRECIPITATELY 3. *Obs.*

1646 SIR T. BROWNE *Pseud. Ep.* III. xxi. 162 The long continuation..without any visible food, which some observing precipitously conclude they [chameleons] eate not any at all. **1673** H. STUBBE *Further Vind. Dutch War* 17 Neither is it providential for a weak Prince..to run Precipitously into a War.

3. Like or as a precipice; with a precipitous slope or face; vertically or very steeply.

1816 BYRON *Ch. Har.* III. lxxxvi, Darken'd Jura, whose capt heights appear Precipitously steep. **1869** TOZER *Highl. Turkey* II. 294 A smooth rock, which descends precipitously into the sea.

pre'cipitousness. [f. as prec. + -NESS.] The quality of being precipitous.

†1. Hastiness, rashness, precipitateness. *Obs.*

a **1660** HAMMOND *Serm. Prov.* i. 22 Wks. 1684 IV. 576 Precipitousness, as Trismegistus defines it, μανίας εἶδος, a species of madness in one place,..a kind of drunkenness in another. **1841** *Blackw. Mag.* XLIX. 572 Much of this precipitousness in judging must in candour be put down to Niebuhr's youth.

2. The quality of being precipitous as a cliff.

1833 M. SCOTT *Tom Cringle* xii. (1859) 286 The left or western bank of the narrow entrance to the harbour..ran out in all its precipitousness and beauty. **1865** GEIKIE *Scen. & Geol. Scot.* viii. 224 Where a vertical wall of granite rises into the air, it may for a long while retain its precipitousness.

precipitron (prɪ'sɪpɪtrɒn). [f. PRECIPI(TATOR + -TRON.] A kind of electrostatic precipitator.

1941 *Iron & Steel Engineer* Sept. 78 (*heading*) Precipitrons for the steel industry. **1975** E. B. CEADEL in Barr & Line *Ess. Information & Libraries* 45 It should not take him much time to find out what..services consultants mean by 'electrostatic precipitrons'.

‖**précis** ('preɪsɪ), *sb.* [F. (presi), sb. use of *précis* adj., cut short, condensed, PRECISE.] A concise or abridged statement; a summary; an abstract.

1760 CHESTERF. *Let. to Bp. Chenevix* 29 Apr., I hope you have seen Voltaire's *précis* of it in verse. **1807–8** SYD. SMITH *Plymley's Lett.* Wks. 1859 II. 165/1 Take with you, if you please, this *précis* of its exploits: eleven hundred men, commanded by a soldier raised from the ranks, put to rout a select army of 6000 men, commanded by General Lake. **1870** M. A. LOWER *Hist. Sussex* II. 90 The arguments are too lengthened for even a *précis* here. **1893** *Nation* (N.Y.) 22 June 456/2 The article is so compact as to read in parts almost like a *précis*.

b. The action or practice of précis-writing.

1886 in *Cassell's Encycl. Dict.*

c. *attrib.* and *Comb.*, as ***précis report, -writer, -writing.***

1809 G. ROSE *Diaries* (1860) II. 406 Précis-writer under his Lordship when Secretary of State. **1813** SIR R. WILSON *Priv. Diary* II. 431 To transmit home an historical *précis* detail of the operations. **1880** *Print. Trades Jrnl.* xxx. 8 The references..may be cited as the very perfection of *précis* writing.

Hence **précis** *v. trans.*, to make a précis of; to abstract, summarize; **précised** ('preɪsiːd) *ppl. a.*

1856 LD. CANNING *Let.* 2 Apr. in E. Fitzmaurice *Life 2nd Earl Granville* (1905) I. vii. 152 The lucid..way in which a heavy case is précis'd is admirable. **1863** PINKERTON in *N. & Q.* 3rd Ser. III. 181/1 The labour of..precising in a calendrical form such a vast chaos of documents may be readily imagined. **1889** *Official Notes Home Dept. India on Adulteration Food*, The replies to the circular letter will be found fully précised in the notes prefixed to the municipal proceedings. **1916** *Daily Colonist* (Victoria, B.C.) 30 July 18/4 The main work of the Canadian War Records, that of compiling and precising the all-important diaries and appendices is, of course, in arrears. **1964** P. MACKESY *War for Amer.* ii. 60 The Ministerial viewpoint on the prospects offered by the advance from Canada is précised in CO 5/253, ff. 21–30. **1972** *Islander* (Victoria, B.C.) 9 Jan. 14/1 The new book Parsons on the Plains..is actually three books precis'd down and contained in one volume. **1977** C. HUSBAND in H. Giles *Lang., Ethnicity & Intergroup Relations* ix. 223 Headlines, as precised news values, represent an expression of 'constructed reality'.

precis, obs. Sc. f. *presses*: see PRESS *v.*

precise (prɪ'saɪs), *a.* (*adv.*) Also: 6 **precyse, -syse, -sise, -size, prysyse**, 6–7 **precize**, 7 **præcise**, 9 *Sc.* **preceese.** [= F. *précis, -ise* (*prescis*, 14–15th c. in Hatz.-Darm.), ad. L. *præcisus* cut off, abrupt, shortened, pa. pple. of *præcīdĕre* to cut off (in front), cut short, abridge, f. *præ*, PRE- A. 4 c + *cædĕre* to cut.]

A. *adj.* 1. Definitely or strictly expressed; exactly defined; definite, exact; of a person, definite and exact in statement.

1526 *Pilgr. Perf.* (W. de W. 1531) 265 There shall be streyte examinacion made, & precyse accountes required for this matter. **1550** in *Vicary's Anat.* (1888) App. iii. 162 [He] hath..vntill twysdaye next, to make a precyse Aunswer. **1577** NORTHBROOKE *Dicing* (1843) 49, I must needes confesse, these reasons of theirs are sifted very depe and very harde, and marueylous precise. **1640** QUARLES *Enchirid.* xviii, That Peace is too precize, that limits the justnesse of a Warre to a Sword drawne or a Blow given. **1728** MORGAN *Algiers* I. ii. 29 It was at last agreed that each Party should, at a precise Time send away two Men on foot. **1775** HARRIS *Philos. Arrangem.* Wks. (1841) 353 It is in a sense less strict and precise, that we take the word *habit*. **1832** LEWIS *Use & Ab. Pol. Terms* Introd. 16 To be precise, it was necessary to be minute. **1868** E. EDWARDS *Ralegh* I. xxv. 638 His instructions had been precise and imperative. **1875** JOWETT *Plato* (ed. 2) III. 187 He is very precise about dates and facts. *Ibid.* IV. 80 Let us then put into more precise terms the question which has arisen.

†**b.** Of an instrument: Exact, accurate. *Obs.*

1561 EDEN *Arte Nauig.* II. xvii. 45, I made experience with a precise Astrolabie.

c. Of the voice or tone: Distinctly uttered.

1848 DICKENS *Dombey* i, In the low precise tone of one who endeavours to awaken a sleeper.

2. Strict in the observance of rule, form, or usage; formal, correct; punctilious, scrupulous, particular; sometimes, Over-exact, over-nice, fastidious. Also of a practice or action: Strictly observed.

1530 PALSGR. 321/1 Precyse, scrupulously circumspecte, *precys*. **1563** *Homilies* II. *Prayer* I. (1859) 341 As touching the precise keeping of the seventh day after the manner of the Jews. **1580** LYLY *Euphues* (Arb.) 426 So the presisest Virgins are to be won when they be young. **1587** GOLDING *De Mornay* i. (1592) 11 Mention is made of certeine presize persons, which beleeued nothing but that which they sawe. *a* **1625** *Nebuchadnezzars Fierie Furnace* (Harl. MS. 7578 lf. 50), Such fellowes proud who seem to be precise Their fantasies are onely set to please. *a* **1680** BUTLER *Rem.* (1759) I. 134 The antient Pagans were precise To use no short-tail'd Beast in Sacrifice. **1781** COWPER *Conversat.* 610 Learned without pride, Exact, yet not precise. **1847** MARRYAT *Childr. N. Forest* xiii, He..was very precise about doing his duty. **1872** *Routledge's Ev. Boy's Ann.* 65/2 An old bachelor, precise and obstinate.

b. *esp.* Strict or scrupulous in religious observance; in 16th and 17th c., puritanical.

1566 ABP. PARKER *Corr.* (Parker Soc.) 278 These precise folk would offer their goods and bodies to prison, rather than they would relent. **1589** *Marprel. Epit.* (1843) 7 In assaulting the fort of our precise brethren. **1657** SANDERSON *Serm.* (1674) 17 The hottest precisest and most scrupulous nonconformer. **1693** WOOD *Life* 15 June (O.H.S.) III. 424 He was too precise and religious. **1694** ATTERBURY *Serm., Prov.* xiv. 6 (1726) I. 195 How did they deride that Grave Preacher of Righteousness [Noah], and his Precise Family. **1827** HALLAM *Const. Hist.* (1876) I. iii. 167 Those..who favoured the more precise reformers, and looked coldly on the established church. **1860** PUSEY *Min. Proph.* 312 Men are now called 'precise', who will not connive at sin, or allow the levity which plays, mothlike, around it.

3. Exact; neither more nor less than; perfect, complete: opposed to *approximate*.

1571 DIGGES *Pantom.* B ij, A Semicircle..doth conteine.. the precise halfe of his circumference. **1651** HOBBES *Leviath.* I. iv. 15 A man that seeketh precise truth. **1753** HOGARTH *Anal. Beauty* vii. 39 The precise serpentine line, or line of grace. **1790** PALEY *Horæ Paul.* Rom. ii. 17 The coincidence is not so precise as some others. **1837–8** SIR W. HAMILTON *Logic* xxiv. (1860) II. 14 A definition..should be Precise, that is, contain nothing unessential, nothing superfluous. **1874** L. STEPHEN *Hours in Library* (1892) I. ii. 2 The precise adaptation of the key to every ward of the lock.

4. Distinguished with precision from all others; identified, pointed out, or stated, with precision or exactness; ***the precise***, the particular, the identical, the very, the exact.

1628 DIGBY *Voy. Medit.* (1868) 63 They had taken vp an euill grounded rumor, which, being traced from one to an other, euery time with some additions, came att length to vanish without finding any præcise author. **1659** PEARSON *Creed* (1839) 367 The precise day upon which he rose. **1769** ROBERTSON *Chas. V*, III. x. 221 The Protestants..insisted upon the council's copying the precise words of that instrument. **1832** BABBAGE *Econ. Manuf.* i. (ed. 3) 10 The difficulty of finding the precise angle at which the diamond cuts. **1856** SIR B. BRODIE *Psychol. Inq.* I. IV. 161 The precise character of these chemical changes we have no means of ascertaining. **1860** TYNDALL *Glac.* I. vii. 48 The precise moment at which a traveller is passing.

†**B.** as *adv.* = PRECISELY. *Obs.*

a **1400–30** *Chaucer's Astrol.* II. §45 The ȝere of ovre lord 1400, I-wryton [*v.r.* I wold wyttyn] precise, my rote. **1567** DRANT *Horace, to Mæcenas* F vij, Sum follow so precyse A learned man, that oftentymes they imitate his vyce. **1594** DANIEL *Compl. Rosamond* li, Thus stood I ballanc'd equally precize, Till my fraile flesh did weigh me downe to sin.

precise (prɪ'saɪs), *v.* [a. F. *préciser* to determine exactly, f. *précis* PRECISE *a.*] *trans.* To make precise or definite; to define precisely or exactly; to particularize. Hence **pre'cising** *vbl. sb.*

1866 T. HARPER *Peace through Truth* Ser. I. 252 Direct asseverations..which precise the meaning of terms, which might otherwise be ambiguous. **1872** *Routledge's Ev. Boy's Ann.* 139/1 Ask him, General, to precise his accusation against me. **1887** J. C. MORISON *Service Man* ix. 313 Its solution would seem to require a little more precising of what is meant by happiness, than is customary in ethical discussions.

precisely (prɪ'saɪslɪ), *adv.* Forms: see PRECISE (5–6 *erron.* percys-). [f. as PRECISE *a.* + -LY².

Known in use earlier than *precise* adj. prob. immediately translating F. *précisément*, which is also known earlier than *précis, -e* adj., and was prob. a rendering of the L. adv. *præcisē*, which was much more in use than the adj. *præcisus*.]

†1. Definitely; entirely, absolutely. *Obs.*

c **1450** in *Arnolde's Chron.* (1811) 37 From yᵉ office of aldyrmanry vtterly and percysly to cessen. **1552** ASCHAM in *Lett. Lit. Men* (Camden) 11 My purpose is preciselie bent to mynde all dewtie. **1552** HULOET, Preciselye, *obiter, precise*. **1568** GRAFTON *Chron.* II. 768 If shee percase be so obstinate and so precisely bent vpon her awne will and opinion, that [etc.]. **1630** *R. Johnson's Kingd. & Commw.* 49, I prescribe not these places so precisely, as that he may not live in others.

†**b.** In definite or precise terms; expressly. *Obs.*

1494 FABYAN *Chron.* VII. ccxlv. 287 Anon he demed yᵉ contrary, & sayd, presysely yᵗ other they must gyue batayll to theyr enemyes, or ellys they must flee wᵗ shame. **1560** A. L. tr. *Calvin's Four Serm. Song Ezech.* i. (1561) A viij b, Ther be also other more impudent, whiche..do plainly & precisely deny it to be sinne. **1577** tr. *Bullinger's Decades* (1592) 112 God doth simply offer himselfe to vs, and precisely set downe what he will be to vs ward.

†2. Particularly, specifically, in particular. *Obs.*

1532 MORE *Confut. Barnes* VIII. Wks. 782/2 As touching saint Paule, he spake not in that place precisely of yᵉ scripture. **1653** ASHWELL *Fides Apost.* 124 Cajetan there speakes of Symbolum in generall, not of the Apostles Creed precisely. **1654** WARREN *Unbelievers* 189 The matter..was ..precisely and abstractively considered. **1697** HUMFREY *Righteousn. God* IV. 55 It may be consider'd Precisely in itself, or Complexly with its Antecedents, and Consequents.

3. With strict observance of rule, form, or usage; strictly, rigorously; minutely, punctually; punctiliously, ceremoniously; properly, with propriety.

1526 *Pilgr. Perf.* (W. de W. 1531) 65 Whiche..yet to this present daye kepe the lettre of the lawe of Moyses in many thynges precysely. **1581** J. BELL *Haddon's Answ. Osor.* 501 b, Wherefore if neither this reuerend Byshopp..is able to behaue himselfe so precisely, but that he must flee dayly with vs to the mercy seate and compassion of God: where be then these glorious crakes of integrity? **1706** E. WARD *Wooden World Diss.* (1708) 26 Like a wise Philosopher, conforms to Time and Place most precisely. **1837** DISRAELI *Venetia* I. xiv, His other features small, though precisely moulded.

4. Exactly; with precise or exact correspondence; with precise identification, with exact or definite knowledge.

1567 DRANT *Horace, De Arte Poet.* A iv, Do not imitate So iumpingly so precyselie And step for step so strayte. **1610** HOLLAND *Camden's Brit.* (1637) 819 To point out precisely the very place..passeth my skill. **1783** LD. HAILES *Antiq. Chr. Ch.* ii. 39 *note*, The date is not precisely known. **1794** SULLIVAN *View Nat.* II. 156 Crystals have probably never been produced..precisely answering to the articulated basaltic pillars. **1860** TYNDALL *Glac.* II. xiv. 303 Their reports..did not always agree precisely with each other.

b. Qualifying a specified relation, time, etc., or a statement: Exactly, just; *ellipt.* just so, quite so; = EXACTLY 5 b, c.

1652 G. COLLIER *Vind. Sabbath* (1656) 39 The day Christ calls his day..is precisely the day of his birth. **1712** ADDISON *Spect.* No. 452 ¶5 It being my Design to put out my Paper every Night at Nine-o-Clock precisely. **1820** BYRON *Morg. Mag.* lxiii, Morgante at a venture shot an arrow, Which pierced a pig precisely in the ear. **1866** GEO. ELIOT *F. Holt* ii, That is precisely what I wanted to say a few words about to you. **1906** *Athenæum* 10 Mar. 289/1 Some of them might have been withheld without precisely damaging the author's reputation. **1906** H. BLACK *Edin. Serm.* 115 The apostle holds the precisely opposite view. *Mod.* 'Then you would advise me to wait a little and watch the course of events?' 'Precisely.'

preciseness (prɪˈsaɪsnɪs). [f. PRECISE *a.* + -NESS.] The quality of being precise.

1. Definiteness; exactness; minuteness, precision.

1569 GOLDING *Heminges Post.* Ded. 7 Obedience to bee performed according too the precisenesse of the word. **1576** FLEMING *Panopl. Epist.* 293 Mainteining our opinion, with the precisenesse wherof the mindes of men are amased. **1688** R. HOLME *Armoury* III. 342/1 In preciseness of Blazon..let it be called a Mill Rinde molined. **1851** HELPS *Comp. Solit.* ix. (1874) 153, I shall not tell with any preciseness where I was. **1875** WHITNEY *Life Lang.* ii. 29 A preciseness of definition which should exclude misunderstanding.

2. Strictness in behaviour, manners, morals, or religious observance; rigid propriety, primness; fastidiousness; scrupulousness, puritanical quality.

1561 T. HOBY tr. *Castiglione's Courtyer* I. E iij, I iudge it a no lesse vyce of curiositye to be in Reckelesness in lettynge a mans clothes fal of his backe, then in Preciseness to carie a mans head so like a malthorse for feare of ruffling his hear. **1598** BARCKLEY *Felic. Man* (1631) 644 Wee blame Puritanes for their affected singularitie and formall preciseness. **1612** T. TAYLOR *Comm. Titus* i. 12 (1619) 241 Godlines is made but a by-word, and a note of reproach..vnder the title of puritie and precisenesse. **1790** CATH. GRAHAM *Lett. Educ.* 94 The discipline of several of the reformed churches, is in a stile of preciseness, which does not admit of any innocent amusement. **1856** MISS YONGE *Daisy Chain* I. xviii, Dry experience, and prejudiced preciseness.

†**b.** Severity, strictness, rigorousness. *Obs.*

1581 SAVILE *Tacitus' Hist.* I. xviii. (1591) 12 His too much precisenes did harme. **1600** HOLLAND *Livy* XXVII. xxxviii. 656 The Consuls tooke musters more streightly and with greater precisenesse, than any man could remember in former yeeres. **1651** BIGGS *New Disp.* §276 By this severity and precisenesse of rules.

precisian (prɪˈsɪʒən). Also 6 pri-, 6–7 præ-; 6 -cisean, -sician, 6–7 -cision, 7 -sisian. [f. PRECISE *a.* + -IAN, after *Christian*, etc.]

One who is rigidly precise or punctilious in the observance of rules or forms. **a.** *spec.* One who is precise in religious observance: in the 16th and 17th c. synonymous with *Puritan*.

1571 ABP. PARKER *Corr.* (Parker Soc.) 377 That inconvenience that Mr. Mullyns..should openly tell the precisians that her Highness' sword should be compelled to cut off this stubborn multitude. **1572** J. JONES *Bathes of Bath* III. 24 The Puritanes, but better we may terme them piuish precisians. **1583** STUBBES *Anat. Abus.* II. (1882) 112 These presicians would haue all things remoued out of the Church which haue beene abused to Idolatrie. **1598** B. JONSON *Ev. Man in Hum.* III. ii, He's no precisian, that I'm certain of, Nor rigid Roman Catholic:..I haue heard him swear. **1612** DRAYTON *Poly-olb.* vi. 94 Like our Precisions.. Who for some Crosse or Saint they in the window see Will pluck downe all the Church. *a* **1652** BROME *Eng. Moor* V. iii, Forgiv' me for swearing, and turn Precisian, and pray I' the nose that all my brethren..spend no worse. **1725** WATTS *Logic* I. vi. §3 A profane person calls a man of piety a precisian. **1821** SCOTT *Kenilw.* vii, Here is what neither Papist nor Puritan, latitudinarian nor precisian, ever boggles or makes mouths at. **1893** FOWLER *Hist. C.C.C.* (O.H.S.) 137 Precisian as Cole was, he does not seem to have objected to card-playing.

b. Generally; or in some sphere of practice.

[**1598** SHAKS. *Merry W.* II. i. 5 Though Loue vse Reason for his precisian, hee admits him not for his Counsailour.] **1755** JOHNSON, *Precisian*, 1. One who limits or restrains. **1834** SOUTHEY *Doctor* liii. (1862) 120 A man may dwell upon words till he becomes at length a mere precisian in speech. **1862** MERIVALE *Rom. Emp.* (1865) VII. lxii. 388 He went over to the Stoics, set up for an austere precisian, and a professed opponent of the..government. **1881** *Gd. Words* XXII. 71 A precisian desires specific rules. **1894** GRAHAME *Pagan* 46 A formal precisian..during business hours.

c. *attrib.* or as *adj.*

1616 T. ADAMS *Contempl. Herbs* Wks. 1862 II. 465 A wicked politician in a ruff of precisian set. **1651** BIGGS *New Disp.* §18 Like the dull præcisian pædagogues to the ferulæ and pedantick Tyranny of the Stagirite. *a* **1882** *Sat. Rev.* (Annandale), A martyr to the political strategy of a precisian government.

Hence †**precisiˈanical** *a. Obs.*, puritanical; †**preˈcisianship** *Obs.*, the quality or action of being a (religious) precisian.

1573 ABP. PARKER *Corr.* (Parker Soc.) 436 Their manifest precisianship is too intolerable. **1574–5** *Ibid.* 476 Saving for the common precisianship in London, I hear of no sects. *a* **1652** BROME *Convent Gard.* I. i. Wks. 1873 II. 7 And what of that in your precisianical wisdom?

preˈcisianism. Also 6 *erron.* -onism. [f. prec. + -ISM.] The practice or conduct of a precisian; orig. applied to Puritanism.

1573 G. HARVEY *Letter-bk.* (Camden) 30 [If] ever I have maintainid ani od point of puritanism, or præcisionism mi self. **1599** B. JONSON *Ev. Man out of Hum.* IV. iv, 'Tis now esteem'd precisianism in wit,..to love or seek good names. **1646** BUCK *Rich. III* Ded., They will challenge the book at the very title;..the Captious and Incredulous, with their jealous præcisianismes. **1649** MILTON *Eikon.* Pref., Wks. 1851 III. 335 It must needs be ridiculous..that they.. should in this one particular outstripp all precisianism with thir scruples and cases. **1651** BIGGS *New Disp.* §272 Constrain into a precisianisme of conformity. **1884** *Jaunt in Junk* 127 To affect the precisianism of a perfect prig.

precisianist: see PRECISIONIST *sb.*

precision (prɪˈsɪʒən). [a. F. *précision* (16th c. in Godef.) or ad. L. *præcīsiō-nem* a cutting off abruptly, n. of action f. *præcīdĕre*: see PRECISE *a.*]

1. a. The fact, condition, or quality of being precise; exactness, definiteness; distinctness, accuracy.

arm of precision: a fire-arm fitted with mechanical aids, such as rifling, graded sights, etc., which make it more accurate of aim than weapons without these.

1740 CHEYNE *Regimen* Pref. 12 Precision is incompatible with Finitude. **1771** H. WALPOLE *Vertue's Anecd. Paint.* IV. i. 26 He knew how to omit exactness, when the result of the whole demands a less precision in parts. **1824** L. MURRAY *Eng. Gram.* (ed. 5) I. 438 Precision is the third requisite of perspicuity with respect to words and phrases. It signifies retrenching superfluities, and pruning the expression, so as to exhibit neither more nor less, than an exact copy of the person's idea who uses it. **1860** MOTLEY *Netherl.* (1868) I. ii. 36 A right-angled triangle of almost mathematical precision. **1877** HUXLEY *Physiogr.* Pref. 6 The precision of statement, which..distinguishes science from common information. **1906** *Lists Techn. Terms Army Schools* I. *Gunnery & Artillery* 8 Precision..[definition] Exactness, accuracy.

†**b.** With *a* and *pl.* An instance of precision; a nicety; in *pl.* exact minutiæ. *Obs. rare*⁻¹.

1691 LOCKE *Lower. Interest* Wks. 1727 II. 92, I have left out the utmost Precisions of Fractions in these Computations.

c. *Statistics.* The reproducibility or reliability of a measurement or the like; used *spec.* to denote various measures or indices of this (see quots.). [The sense is due to W. Lexis, who used G. *präcision* (now *präzision*) (W. Lexis *Zur Theorie der Massenerscheinungen in der menschlichen Gesellschaft* (1877) ii. 25).]

1885 M. MERRIMAN *Textbk. Method of Least Squares* i. 1 The comparison of observations is necessary in order to determine the relative degrees of precision of different sets of measurements made under different circumstances. **1906** *Acta Univ. Lundensis* Ny Följd I. v. 7, *k* is called the measure of precision. **1911** G. U. YULE *Introd. Theory Statistics* xiii. 253 The reliability or precision of an observed proportion varies as the square root of the number of observations on which it is based. *Ibid.* xv. 304 The use of $\sqrt{2} \times \sigma$ (the 'modulus') as a measure of dispersion, of $1/\times \sqrt{2}\cdot\sigma$ as a measure of precision, and of $2\sigma^2$ as 'the fluctuation'. **1947** O. L. DAVIES *Statistical Methods in Res. & Production* 250 The normal distribution..is given by some writers the mathematical formulation: $he^{-h^2x^2}/\sqrt{\pi}$. The parameter *h* is then called the parameter of precision, but by comparison with the usual formula it is seen that this parameter is related to the standard deviation by the identity $h = 1/\sigma\sqrt{2}$. **1949** F. YATES *Sampling Methods for Censuses & Surveys* viii. 247 The relative precision of two different methods of sampling based on the same type of sampling unit may be defined as the reciprocal of the ratio of the sampling variances of the estimates given by the two methods when the same number of units are taken. **1957** KENDALL & BUCKLAND *Dict. Statistical Terms* 224 Precision is a quality associated with a class of measurements and refers to the way in which repeated observations conform to themselves; and in a somewhat narrower sense refers to the dispersion of the observations, or some measure of it, whether or not the mean value around which the dispersion is measured approximates to the 'true' value. In general the precision of an estimator varies with the square root of the number of observations upon which it is based. **1965** R. DEUTSCH *Estimation Theory* x. 154 Precision is a measure of how close the outcome of a measurement, or a sequence of observations, clusters about some estimated value of a specified parameter. **1965** D. V. LINDLEY *Introd. Probability & Statistics* II. v. 8 We shall call the inverse of the variance, the precision. The nomenclature is not standard but is useful. **1971** *Nature* 12 Feb. 484/1 An estimate of the precision (analytical reproducibility) of each K–Ar analysis is given as a ± value. **1974** *IEEE Trans. Instrumentation & Measurement* XXIII. 278/1 The desired precision of intercomparison was set at ±0·01μV (one part in 10^8). **1974** *Nature* 8 Nov. 137/1 Radioactive isotopic dates invariably include their precision, that is, the repeatability, yet most earth scientists still take these figures as measures of accuracy.

d. In numerical work, the fineness of specification, as represented by the number of digits given and distinguished from *accuracy* (the nearness to the true value).

1948 *Math. Tables & Other Aids to Computation* III. 286 Numbers are stored to a precision of 35 binary digits. **1956** G. A. MONTGOMERIE *Digital Calculating Machines* vii. 12 Precision can be expressed in two ways: we may say that a number is correct to so many decimal places or to so many significant figures. **1962** *Gloss. Terms Automatic Date Processing* (*B.S.I.*) 14 A result may have more precision than it has accuracy, e.g. the true value of π to eight decimal figures is 3·1415927; the expression π = 3·1415249 is precise to eight figures but accurate only to about five. **1970** H. A. RODGERS *Dict. Data Processing Terms* 81/1 Strictly speaking there is a difference of precision between 1,000 and 1. × 10^3; in the first case the low-order zeros are known to have that value while in the second case all that is known is the explicit digit and the multiplier. **1972** *Physics Bull.* Aug. 459/2 To precisions varying from 1 to 0·01 parts in a million, the value of $(2e/h)_J$ does not depend on whether the effects are observed in absorption or emission.

†**2. a.** The cutting off of one thing from another; *esp.* the mental separation of a fact or idea; abstraction; in quot. 1640, a cutting short; in quot. 1683 = RESERVATION 4. *Obs.* (App. used for *prescission*, as the sb. corresponding to PRESCIND *v.*)

1640 G. WATTS tr. *Bacon's Adv. Learn.* v. v. 255 We call Prenotion a Precision of endlesse investigation. **1681** GLANVILL *Sadducismus* I. App. §8 When, from this mental Precision of Cogitation from Extension, he defined a Spirit. *Ibid.*, From the precision of our thoughts to infer the real precision or separation of the things themselves, is a very putid and puerile sophism. **1683** A. D. *Art Converse* 95 You can neither tye them by Promise, nor by Oath; for if they Promise or Swear, 'tis with a mental Precision. **1710** BERKELEY *Princ. Hum. Knowl.* Introd. §9 As the mind frames to itself abstract ideas of qualities or modes, so does it, by the same precision, or mental separation, attain abstract ideas of the more compounded beings which include several coexistent qualites.

†**b.** *transf.* A precise definition. *Obs. rare.*

1690 LOCKE *Hum. Und.* III. x. §15 The taking Matter to be the Name of something really existing under that Precision, ..has..produc'd..obscure..Discourses. **1757** MRS. GRIFFITH *Lett. Henry & Frances* (1767) II. 186 This definition I look upon to be more imperfect, and of a more dangerous tendency, than any of the three precisions he has so ingeniously proved the insufficiency of.

3. a. *attrib.* and *Comb.*, usu. implying an intended or actual precision of performance, execution, or construction.

1875 *Encycl. Brit.* III. 263/1 The theory of the common balance as we see it working in every grocer's shop, and..of the modern precision balance. **1910** *Westm. Gaz.* 6 Jan. 4/2 Those wonderful American automatic precision tools that have played so conspicuous a part in almost every European factory. **1935** *Discovery* Jan. 9/1 Continuous knife-edges and continuous knife-edge bearings such as are now used in all precision balances. *Ibid.* Dec. 368/2 The optical outfits.. consist of precision-made parts, the mere use of which teaches precision in working. **1937** *Ibid.* Apr. 112/1 These are real precision instruments,..with lens of aperture F1·9 such as the old plate cameras never knew. **1939** *War Illustr.* 16 Dec. 440/3 The barrage..gives London and other cities and vital points reasonable security from swooping raiders and precision-bombing. **1944** *Foundry* Feb. 116/1 Application of precision casting, utilizing either centrifugal or pressure methods, to the production of precision parts made from heat and corrosion resistant alloys is a recent development. **1950** *N.Y. Times Mag.* 27 Aug. 52/2 Strategic bombing as carried out by the American 8th and 15th Air Forces in Europe was 'precision bombing' directed, so far as operational accuracy permitted, against specific military targets. **1951** *People* 3 June 7/7 (Advt.), Just switch on that precision-built Arvin and discover for yourself how pleasant dry shaving can be. **1953** 'N. BLAKE' *Dreadful Hollow* 77 Yes, quite a precision-tool job. **1957** *Technology* Mar. 10/2 Other work includes..the repair of indicator gauges and other precision instruments. **1963** *New Yorker* 23 Nov. 23 (Advt.), What's low in upkeep, high in mileage,..precision-engineered with 42 hidden changes to date but looks the same every year? **1966** 'H. MACDIARMID' *Company I've Kept* viii. 187, I qualified as a precision fitter and obtained a job with a big general engineering firm. **1969** 'D. RUTHERFORD' *Gilt-Edged Cockpit* x. 172 We still think there's a market for individuality and a precision-built car. **1975** BRAM & DOWNS *Manuf. Technol.* i. 7 Gauge blocks are used as standards of measurement or reference in most precision-engineering works. **1976** J. VAN DE WETERING *Corpse on Dike* (1977) ii. 33 Mary kept her pistols in the drawer... 'Careful... They are precision instruments, both of them.'

b. Special Comb.: **precision approach radar**, a ground-based radar system used to follow accurately the approach of an aircraft and to enable landing to be supervised from the ground.

1950 *Electronics* Feb. 71/1 (*heading*) Airport surveillance and precision approach radar (GCA). **1956** *Electronic Engin.* XXVIII. 15/2 In practice, all airport radar requirements except precision approach radar..can be met. **1965** NAYLER & OWER *Aviation* xvii. 250/2 Ground Controlled Approach

.., also known as Precision Approach Radar, gives the position of an approaching aircraft in elevation, azimuth, and range relative to the touch-down point on the runway.

Hence **pre'cisional** *a.*, of or pertaining to precision; **pre'cisioner**, = PRECISIONIST *sb.*; **pre'cisionism**, practice of precision (see also PRECISIANISM); **pre'cisionize** *v. trans.*, to give precision to, state with precision or accuracy.

1874 BUSHNELL *Forgiveness & Law* II. 127 The old *precisional drill, that came so hard upon the soldier at first. **1902** *Times* 15 July 10/2 It is not an air to be breathed freely by pedants, or prudes, or *precisioners. **1868** H. KINGSLEY *Mlle. Mathilde* II. vi. 94 She had disliked André Desilles and his *precisionism all her life. **1847** SIR G. C. LEWIS *Lett.* (1870) 153 What a pity the same man does not, in the same manner, *precisionize other..questions of political morals. **1895** *Dublin Rev.* Oct. 303 To precisionise the successive whens and wheres.

pre'cisionist, *sb.* and *a.* (Also *erron*, (after *precisian*) -anist.) [f. PRECISION + -IST.]

A. *sb.* One who makes a profession or practice of precision or exactness in observance or expression; a purist; *spec.* in *Art*, one of a group of U.S. artists of the 1920s who employed a smooth, precise technique in their paintings.

1827 *Examiner* 822/1 Enjoyment which..precisianists, purists, and conventiclers would totally extinguish. **1865** BUSHNELL *Vicar. Sacr.* III. iii. 229 Must He be a precisionist in order to be passed as just? **1865** *Sat. Rev.* 21 Jan. 83/2 Well-meaning precisionists who are striving to bring back the new mongrel or mixed Romaic of the Hellenes to the purer idiom. **1873** *Spectator* 15 Feb. 203/2 Both are precisianists in utterance, and skilled in the manipulation of the finest shades of language. **1960** *Art in Amer.* III. 33/1 Its [*sc.* Cubism's] effects still prevade the most recent work of the Precisionists. **1974** *Encycl. Brit. Micropædia* VIII. 185/2 The Precisionists did not issue manifestos, and they were not a school or movement with a formal program. *Ibid.*, The Precisionists' style greatly influenced the American Magic Realists and the Pop artists. **1978** *Verbatim* Winter 6/2 And I am certain that that great precisionist intended a true rhyme.

B. *adj.* Employing or exhibiting precision as an artistic technique.

1960 *Art in Amer.* III. 32/1 The Precisionist painting process is one of continual distillation and editing. **1978** *Chicago* June 62/1 Precisionist paintings, ranging from realistic to abstract. **1979** *Jrnl. R. Soc. Arts* Nov. 747/2 Even American or German architecture looks a bit thrown together when compared with the precisionist craftsmanship of his high-gloss aluminium detailing.

Hence **pre'cisionism**, the style or technique of the precisionist painters.

1960 *Art in Amer.* III. 47 When Jefferson consciously reacted against the light, impermanent and provincial qualities of American building..it was to another and more integral kind of 'precisionism' that he turned: to a precisionism of mass. **1978** S. F. YEH *Precisionist Painters* 10 The basis for Precisionism is to be found in Cubism.

precisive (prɪ'saɪsɪv), *a. rare.* [f. L. *præcīs-*, ppl. stem of *præcīdĕre* (see PRECISE *a.*) + -IVE.]

1. That cuts off, separates, or defines one (person or thing) from another or others, as in *precisive abstraction*: see quot. 1725. (app. for *prescissive.*)

1679 PULLER *Moder. Ch. Eng.* (1843) 232 At other times our church moderates her censures,..using a moderate, gentle censure, before a precisive. **1725** WATTS *Logic* I. vi. §9 This Act of Abstraction is..either Precisive or Negative. Precisive Abstraction is when we consider those Things apart which cannot really exist apart; as when we consider a Mode without considering its Substance and Subject.

2. Characterized by precision or exactitude.

1807 GILSON *Serm. Pract. Subj.* 110 Daniel..foretold with the greatest precisive openness the exact time of our Saviour's coming. **1897** *Daily News* 22 May 5/1 [He] has made at least one definite, precisive, and particular charge.

pre-cited (priː'saɪtɪd), *ppl. a.* Also 7 præ-. [PRE- A.] Previously cited, adduced, or referred to; before-mentioned, above-mentioned.

1666 G. HARVEY *Morb. Angl.* xi. 121 This latter, besides the ordinary præcited causes, is sometimes occasioned by [etc.]. **1694** WESTMACOTT *Script. Herb.* 93 It is easie to apply to each of these precited remedies their proper virtue. **1865** VISCT. STRANGFORD *Select.* (1869) II. 138 *note*, As we read once in the pre-cited journal.

pre-civil(ization, -ized: see PRE- B. 1, A. 2.

pre-Civil War: PRE- B. 2a.

†**'preclamate**, *v. Obs. rare*$^{-0}$. [f. ppl. stem of L. *præclāmāre* to call out beforehand, f. *præ*, PRE- A. 1 + *clāmāre* to cry.]

1623 COCKERAM, *Preclamate*, to cry before.

†**precla'ration**. *Obs. rare*$^{-1}$. (?) Previous declaration or explanation.

1656 HEYLIN *Extraneus Vapulans* 16 The Arch-bishop was not..so ill a keeper of his own counsel, as to make any such preclaration of his reason for it.

†**pre'clare**, *a.* Chiefly *Sc. Obs.* Also 6 præ-, -clair. [ad. L. *præclārus* very bright, f. *præ*, PRE- A. 6 + *clārus* clear.]

1. *lit.* Very clear. *rare*$^{-1}$.

1501 DOUGLAS *Pal. Hon.* Prol. 63 A voice I hard preclair as Phebus schone.

2. Distinguished, illustrious.

1511 DUNBAR *Poems* lxxvii. 65 O potent princes, pleasant and preclair. **1535** STEWART *Cron. Scot.* (Rolls) I. 59 Richt ȝoung he wes, bayth plesand and preclair. **1596** DALRYMPLE tr. *Leslie's Hist. Scot.* I. 92 Famous & preclare exemples of men of renoume. *Ibid.* 117 Quhais myndes deip and præclair studies hes decored. **1623** COCKERAM I I, Excellent .., *preclare*. **1677** GALE *Crt. Gentiles* II. IV. 183 Do not there-fore the preclare and illustrious Institutes or Laws of Living make way to Virtue? **1819** W. TENNANT *Papistry Storm'd* (1827) 15 Lo! on Olympus' taps preclair The goddess o' men-blessing lear.

†**pre'clared**, *a. Obs.* = prec., 2; renowned.

1530 (*title*) Here foloweth the Assemble of foules.. compyled by the preclared and famous Clerke Geffray Chaucer Imprynted in london..by me Wynkyn de Worde.

†**pre'clarent**, *a. Obs. rare*$^{-0}$. [irreg. as prec.]

1623 COCKERAM, *Preclarent*, excellent.

Pre-classic, *a. Archæol.* [PRE- B. 1.] Designating a period of Meso-American culture, about 1500 B.C. to A.D. 300.

1956 G. W. BRAINERD *Morley's Anc. Maya* (ed. 3) iii. 40 Maya history may be divided into three states: (1) Pre-classic, extending from about 1500 B.C. to A.D. 317; (2) Classic, from A.D. 317 to 889; and (3) Postclassic, from 889 until 1697. **1967** L. DEUEL *Conquistadors without Swords* III. xv. 188 The emergence of an 'archaic age' in Mexican pre-history, now usually referred to as formative or pre-classic. **1970** BRAY & TRUMP *Dict. Archaeol.* 188/2 *Pre-classic* (*or Formative*) *period*, used in American archaeology for the period in which agriculture..formed the basis of settled village life. *Ibid.* 189/1 In the chronological sense..the Pre-classic period is usually taken to have ended c 300 AD. **1974** *Nature* 6 Dec. 472/1 The earliest occupation discovered belongs to the Real Xe phase of the Middle Preclassic Period... This cache was actually located beneath several preclassic floors.

pre-'classical, *a.* [PRE- B. 1 d.] Anterior to the classical age (of Greek and Roman literature). Also in extended uses.

1871 LOWELL *Study Wind.* 151 He [Thoreau]..revives the age of *concetti* while he fancies himself going back to a pre-classical nature. **1948** K. MALONE *Middle Ages* I. 28 The technic of adornment or elaboration was essentially the same in pre-classical and classical poetry. **1958** *Times* 15 Dec. 3/2 One of the first great pre-classical composers for whom general popularity seems surely destined is Monteverdi. **1976** *Observer* 16 May 1/2 He was the most brilliant and versatile of wind-players, starting as a classical bassoonist then branching out into the whole range of pre-classical wind instruments. **1978** *Early Music* Oct. 567/2 The cadenzas of the baroque and pre-classical eras were usually over a pedal point dominant rather than being the tonic six-four/dominant/tonic kind of the classical era.

preclean, -climax: see PRE- A. 1, B. 1.

pre'clinical, *a. Med.* [PRE- B. 1.] **1.** Of, pertaining to, or designating the first stage of a medical education, consisting chiefly of the necessary scientific studies without regular involvement with patients.

1930 A. FLEXNER *Universities* i. 14 Medicine stood almost still until the pre-clinical sciences were differentiated and set free—free to develop without regard to use and practice. **1948** F. ROBERTS *Med. Educ.* vii. 48 On entering the pre-clinical stage the student embarks on an intensive study of human anatomy and physiology. **1956** *Med. Press* 5 Sept. 225/1 In the more progressive medical schools it has been found of great benefit to give the pre-clinical student a series of specially selected clinical demonstrations. **1970** *Nature* 1 Aug. 431/2 In 1968–69 there were 6,017 pre-clinical and 7,024 clinical training places in medical schools in Britain. **1978** *Jrnl. R. Soc. Med.* LXXI. 373 The preclinical and paraclinical subjects that, it is widely accepted, comprise the early part of the European medical student curriculum.

2. Preceding the onset of recognizable symptoms that make a diagnosis possible.

1932 GAIGER & DAVIES *Vet. Path. & Bacteriol.* xvii. 277 The difficulty of diagnosing cases in the pre-clinical stage led to efforts to find a diagnostic agent for Johne's disease analogous to tuberculin for tuberculosis. **1943** *Brit. Jrnl. Tuberculosis* XXXVII. 98 How is the student of today going to prescribe tomorrow for the preclinical case diagnosed by mass-radiology? **1976** *Biol. Abstr.* LXI. 6389/1 (*heading*) Pulmonary cancer recognized in a preclinical phase of development.

3. Preceding clinical testing of a drug.

1962 *Folia Pharmacologica Japonica* 20 May 18* (*heading*) Consideration and some experiments of preclinical pharmacology of anti-cancer drugs. **1972** P. R. B. NOEL in Richards & Rondel *Adverse Drug Reactions* i. 3 The number of patients used..is not always very great and does not always exceed the number of animals used in the pre-clinical investigations.

preclitellian (-klaɪ'tɛlɪən), *a.* (*sb.*) *Zool.* [f. PRE- B. 3 + CLITELL-UM + -IAN.] Belonging to that division of earthworms which have the male genital apertures in front of the clitellum. **b.** *sb.* An earthworm of this division.

1888 *Encycl. Brit.* XXIV. 683/2 [see INTRACLITELLIAN].

precloacal: see PRE- A. 4.

pre'close, *v. rare.* [f. PRE- A. 1 + CLOSE *v.*; cf. PRECLUDE.] *trans.* = FORECLOSE 5.

1535 *St. Papers Hen. VIII*, II. 256 After the preclosing of the premisses, I had sure worde that O'Connor bringith with him Obrene and his power. **1898** B. GREGORY *Side Lights Confl. Meth.* 501 Dr. Bunting stoutly and successfully preclosed the question.

preclude (prɪ'kluːd), *v.* [ad. L. *præclūd-ĕre* to close, shut off, impede, f. *præ*, PRE- A. 4c + *claudĕre* to shut.]

1. *trans.* To close or shut up (a passage, etc.) against any attempt to pass; = FORECLOSE 2.

1629 MAXWELL tr. *Herodian* (1635) 133 Julian's friends counselled him to advance..and preclude the Alpine Straits. **1652** C. B. STAPYLTON *Herodian* 67 His friends advise he shall the Alpes preclude. **1653** WATERHOUSE *Apol. Learn.* 187 Preclude your ears..against all rash, rude, irrational, innovating importuners. **1751** JOHNSON *Rambler* No. 96 ¶16 Every intellect was precluded by Prejudice. **1777** ROBERTSON *Hist. Amer.* II. v. 34 Having precluded every means of escape.

b. To close beforehand; = FORECLOSE 5.

1841–4 EMERSON *Ess., Experience* Wks. (Bohn) I. 176 Shall I preclude my future, by taking a high seat, and kindly adapting my conversation to the shape of heads?

2. To 'close the door against', shut out, prevent the entrance of; to exclude, prevent, frustrate; to render impracticable by anticipatory action.

1618 T. ADAMS *Cosmopolite* Wks. 1862 II. 143 Though the desires of his mind be granted, yet this precludes not the access of new desires to his mind. **1659** in *Burton's Diary* (1828) IV. 320 As to precluding all complaints against excise, leave it to your Committee to bring in a Bill to remedy the inconveniences. **1692** RAY *Disc.* III. v. (1732) 383 If you preclude the Access of all Air. **1751** JOHNSON *Rambler* No. 105 ¶13 They hesitated till death precluded the decision. **1813** BYRON *Corsair* III. ix, Since bar and bolt no more his steps preclude. **1868** M. PATTISON *Academ. Org.* v. 120 It may be as well to preclude misunderstanding by repeating.

3. To shut out or prevent (a person) *from* something by previous action: = FORECLOSE 3.

1736 *Col. Rec. Pennsylv.* IV. 103 That they may not be precluded or foreclosed from the benefit of the Governor's Grant. **1792** BURKE *Let. to Sir H. Langrishe* Wks. VI. 320, I do not find one word to preclude his majesty from consenting to any arrangement which parliament may make. **1800** WELLESLEY in Owen *Desp.* (1877) 555 Employed in staff offices which preclude them from the performance of regimental duties. **1884** LD. COLERIDGE in *Law Rep. 12 Q. B. Div. 322* We do not preclude the duke from his remedy ..by way of action or indictment.

preclusion (prɪ'kluːʒən). Now *rare.* [ad. L. *præclūsiōn-em*, n. of action f. *præclūdĕre*: see prec. Cf. obs. F. *préclusion* (16th c. in Godef.).] The action of precluding; shutting out, or preventing the entrance or occurrence of something; prevention by anticipatory measures.

1616 T. ADAMS *Politic Hunting* Wks. 1861 I. 9 St. Augustine's preclusion of all star-predictions out of this place. **16..** DONNE *Serm.* (ed. Alford) IV. 467 Repentance of former, preclusion against future Sins. **1751** JOHNSON *Rambler* No. 95 ¶14 The extinction of parties, and the preclusion of debates. **1820** COLERIDGE in *Lit. Rem.* (1836) IV. 122 The preclusion of disturbance and indecorum in Christian assemblies.

preclusive (prɪ'kluːsɪv), *a.* [f. L. *præclūs-*, ppl. stem of *præclūdĕre* (see PRECLUDE) + -IVE.] That tends to preclude or has the effect of precluding; shutting out beforehand, preventive (*of*).

1695 *Whether Parlt. be not dissolved by Death P'cess of Orange* 41 In whom the full and entire Sovereignty..was.. settled preclusive of all others. **1804** LAING *Hist. Scot.* IV. XI. 395 Its articles..are too numerous, and on some occasions preclusive of improvement. **1809–10** COLERIDGE *Friend* (1866) 313 Obstacles the continuance of which is preclusive of all truth. **1882** STEVENSON *Fam. Stud. Men & Bks.* 347 If women's rule is not unnatural in a sense preclusive of its very existence.

Hence **pre'clusively** *adv.*

1695 *Whether Parlt. be not dissolved* 38 Preclusively from all legal Capacity and Possibility of borrowing a Duration and Continuance..from the Life of any other. **1818** TODD, *Preclusively*, with hindrance by some anticipation.

†**pre'clusory**, *a. Obs. rare*$^{-1}$. [f. L. *præclūs-*, ppl. stem of *præclūdĕre* (see PRECLUDE) + -ORY^{2}.] = PRECLUSIVE.

1609 BP. W. BARLOW *Answ. Nameless Cath.* 179 Hee takes it..to be a mandate preclusorie of the way to heauen.

precoat: see PRE- A. 1, 2.

precoccygeal: see PRE- B. 3.

precoce (prɪ'kəʊs), *a.* (*sb.*) *rare.* [a. F. *précoce*, ad. L. *præcoc-em* early ripe, premature, f. *præcoquĕre* to boil beforehand, ripen fully, f. *præ*, PRE- A. 1 + *coquĕre* to cook. Cf. PRECOQUE.]

1. Of plants: Early flowering.

1664 EVELYN *Kal. Hort.* (1729) 198 Common, double, and single Primroses, Præcoce Tulips. **1707** MORTIMER *Husb.* (1721) II. 359 The Præcoce Tulip, Winter Aconite, some sorts of Anemonies.

2. = PRECOCIOUS 2.

1689 EVELYN *Diary* 27 Jan., I had read of divers forward and precoce youths. **1868** M. COLLINS *Sweet Anne Page* I. viii. 191 Is he not a trifle too precoce?

B. as *sb.* An early plant; *spec.* = *precoce tulip*.

1699 EVELYN *Acetaria* (1729) 157 The Hot Beds for the raising of those Præcoces. **1721** MORTIMER *Husb.* II. 240, I shall begin with the Precoces or early blowing Tulips.

Hence †**pre'coceness** (precose-), precocity, earliness in flowering or fruiting. *Obs.*

1664 EVELYN *Sylva* 78 As to this extraordinary Precoseness, the like is reported of a certain Walnut-tree, as well as of the famous White-thorn of Glastonbury.

precocial, *a.* Now the usual spelling of PRÆCOCIAL *a.*

precocious (prɪˈkəʊʃəs), *a.* [f. L. *præcox, -cocem* (PRECOCE): see -IOUS.]

1. Of a plant: Flowering or fruiting early; *spec.* bearing blossom before the leaves; also said of the blossoms or fruit.

1650 SIR T. BROWNE *Pseud. Ep.* II. vi. (ed. 2) 79 Many precocious trees, and such as have their spring in the winter, may be found in most parts of Europe. *a* **1682** —— *Tracts* (1684) 72 That there were precocious and early bearing Trees in Judæa, may be illustrated from some expressions in Scripture concerning precocious Figgs. **1872** OLIVER *Elem. Bot.* II. 234 A..tree, with..precocious hermaphrodite flowers.

2. a. *fig.* Of persons: Prematurely developed in some faculty or proclivity.

1678 CUDWORTH *Intell. Syst.* I. iv. §21. 388 However it hath been of late so much decried..by..precocious and conceited wits also, as non-sence and impossibility. **1819** BYRON *Juan* I. liv, To be precocious Was in her eyes a thing the most atrocious. **1829** LYTTON *Devereux*, I. v, We were all three..precocious geniuses. **1868** E. EDWARDS *Ralegh* I. xv. 299 She was somewhat precocious in love matters.

b. Of, pertaining to, or indicative of precocity or premature development.

1672 SIR T. BROWNE *Let. Friend* §28 'Tis superfluous to live unto gray Hairs, when in a precocious Temper we anticipate the Virtues of them. **1827** MACAULAY *Machiavelli* Ess. (1887) 36 Untimely decrepitude was the penalty of precocious maturity. *a* **1863** THACKERAY *Christmas Bks.* (1872) 19 His 'Love Lays'..were pronounced to be wonderfully precocious for a young gentleman then only thirteen.

c. Of things: Of early development.

1838 DICKENS *Nich. Nick.* xx, Youthful misery stalks precocious. **1899** *Allbutt's Syst. Med.* VII. 668 'Specific' phenomena are more commonly observed within a comparatively short time from the date of infection in which case they are not rightly regarded as 'precocious' symptoms.

3. a. *Zool.* (See quot.) Contrasted with SEROTINOUS.

1900 *Quekett Microsc. Club Jrnl.* Ser. II. VII. 260 All the social or colonial Radiolarians (Polycyttaria) and most of the Acantharia are precocious, for in them the nucleus divides early in the life history of the cell.

b. = PRÆCOCIAL *a.*

1897 PARKER & HASWELL *Text-bk. Zool.* II. xiii. 382 The newly-hatched young may be..well covered with down and able to run or swim and to obtain their own food, in which case they are said to be precocious. **1970** R. A. & B. M. MAIER *Compar. Animal Behavior* ix. 193 Domestic chicks are precocious (well developed at hatching).

preˈcociously, *adv.* [f. prec. + -LY².] In a precocious manner; with premature development.

1842 ARNOLD *Hist. Rome* (1843) III. 269 A child in understanding, but with passions precociously vigorous. **1862** BURTON *Bk. Hunter* (1863) 82 He took precociously to rhyming; like Pope he lisped in numbers.

preˈcociousness. [f. as prec. + -NESS.] The quality of being precocious; = PRECOCITY.

1681 MANNINGHAM *Disc.* 10 To prevent a sawcy precociousness in Learning, [they] invite others to drudge in their methods. **1829** SOUTHEY *Sir T. More* (1831) II. 44 And as natural precocity is always to be regarded with fear, so the precociousness which art produces cannot be without its dangers. **1855** THACKERAY *Newcomes* liii, Poverty and necessity force this precociousness on the poor little brat.

precocity (prɪˈkɒsɪtɪ). [ad. F. *précocité* (17th c.), f. L. type **præcocitās*, f. *præcox*: see PRECOCE.] The quality of being precocious.

1. Of plants: Early flowering or ripeness.

1656 BLOUNT *Glossogr.*, *Precocity*, early ripeness, forwardliness in ripening, over hastiness in ripening. **1875** A. R. WALLACE in *Encycl. Brit.* I. 86/2 The grain was very fine and well grown, which gave me the idea to..see if the following year it would preserve its precocity.

2. Early maturity, premature development.

1640 HOWELL *Dodona's Gr.* 102 Imputing the cause of it [his fall] to a precocitie of Spirit and valour in him. **1682** SIR T. BROWNE *Chr. Mor.* I. §35 From such foundations thou may'st be Happy in a Virtuous precocity, and make an early and long walk in Goodness. **1820** HAZLITT *Lect. Dram. Lit.* 140 Their productions..bear the marks of precocity and premature decay. **1879** GLADSTONE *Glean.* II. vi. 267 In a happy childhood he evinced extreme precocity.

b. *transf.* One in whom this quality is exemplified; a precocious child.

1882 A. MATHESON in *Macm. Mag.* XLVI. 488/2 George Eliot's children... They are not impossible cherubs, or wingless fairies, or idealised precocities.

†**pre-coeˈtanean.** *Obs. rare*⁻¹. [f. PRE- A. 2 + COETANEAN.] An older contemporary.

a **1661** FULLER *Worthies* (1662) I. 27, I read of Petrarch, (the pre-coetanean of our Chaucer) that he was crowned with a Laurel, in the Capitol.

precog (ˈpriːkɒg). Also pre-cog. [abbrev. of PRECOGNITION.] = PRECOGNITION 1. Also, one who predicts something; a person with precognition. Also *attrib.*, = PRECOGNITIVE *a.*

1966 *Listener* 19 May 727/2 It is generally recognized that 'pre-cog' dreams take place quite often; and with the knowledge which these dream researchers provide..it may be possible to obtain quite massive evidence of precog dreaming. **1967** *Ibid.* 16 Mar. 359/3 Apart from the massive evidence of ESP in human life—what does the Professor say about 'pre-cog', I wonder—the abundance of ESP in nature must surely infuriate him. **1973** *Daily News* (N.Y.) 21 Aug. 53/1 Certain precogs prophesy the future with the buckshot approach, generalized predictions. **1977** *Sounds* 9 July 22/1 And as for the matter of whether the gent's armed with the sort of foresight Phillip K. Dick grants his 'precogs', you can just make up your own mind.

†**preˈcogitancy.** *Obs. rare.* [f. L. *præcogitānt-em*, pr. pple. of *præcogitāre*: see below and -ANCY.] Previous cogitation or thought.

c **1635** A. STAFFORD *Apol.* in *Fem. Glory* (1860) p. xxxiv, Wee speake not to Princes wthout great study, and precogitancy.

†**preˈcogitate**, *ppl. a. Sc. Obs. rare.* [ad. L. *præcōgitātus*, pa. pple. of *præcōgitāre*: see next.] = PRECOGITATED.

1573 MORTON in *Cal. Scott. Papers* (1905) IV. 516 They fund the wind favorable to the execution of thair precogitat mischeif. **1664** *Judiciary Rec.* (S.H.S.) 101 Francis Crichton without any provocation and forethought felony and precogitate malice drew his sword.

precogitate (priːˈkɒdʒɪteɪt), *v.* Now *rare.* [f. L. *præcōgitāt-*, ppl. stem of *præcōgitāre*, f. *præ*, PRE- A. 1 + *cōgitāre* to think, COGITATE: see -ATE³.] *trans.* and *intr.* To cogitate, think, or think over beforehand; to consider beforehand, premeditate. Hence **preˈcogitated** *ppl. a.*

1611 COTGR., *Precogiter*, to precogitate, premeditate, thinke of beforehand. **1639** G. DANIEL *Ecclus.* xviii. 62 Precogitate thy vowes; and doe not Say From a fantastick humor, what will rise. *a* **1652** BROME *Mad Couple* III. i. Wks. 1873 I. 56, I must come on her with a little wit though, for which I will precogitate. **1657** HAWKE *Killing is M.* Introd. It is Murder in any private Person upon precogitated malice to kill any private Man.

precogitation (priːkɒdʒɪˈteɪʃən). Now *rare.* [ad. late L. *præcōgitāti-ōnem*, n. of action f. *præcōgitāre*: see prec. Cf. obs. F. *précogitation* (16th c. in Godef.).] Previous consideration or meditation; a thinking over beforehand.

1596 J. NORDEN *Progr. Pietie* (1847) 8 We may proceed on in our progress, with this precogitation following. **1658** SIR T. BROWNE *Gard. Cyrus* v. 200 To spin out our awaking thoughts into the phantasms of sleep, which often continueth præcogitations; making Cables of Cobwebbes and Wildernesses of handsome Groves. **1809–10** COLERIDGE *Friend* (1866) 315 This purpose may have been itself excited, and this precogitation itself abstracted from the perceived likenesses and differences of the objects to be arranged.

†**preˈcognit.** *Obs. rare*⁻¹. [ad. L. *præcognitum*, pa. pple. neut. of *præcognōscĕre* to PRECOGNOSCE.] A preliminary discussion.

1654 VILVAIN *Epit. Ess.* Introd. 18 A Compend of Chronography..intended for a previous Precognit to the two insuing Tomes.

precognition (priːkɒgˈnɪʃən). Also 7 præ-. [ad. late L. *præcogniti-ōnem*, n. of action f. *præcognōscĕre*: see PRECOGNOSCE; or perh. a. obs. F. *précognition* foreknowledge (15th c. in Godef.).]

1. Antecedent cognition or knowledge; foreknowledge.

1611 COTGR., *Precognition*, a precognition. *a* **1619** FOTHERBY *Atheom.* I. viii. §2 (1622) 56 This præcognition and anticipation of God. **1651** BIGGS *New Disp.* §230 It acts without any precognition of an end. **1678** GALE *Crt. Gentiles* III. 67 God..by his determinate Counsel and precognition delivered his Son to them. **1839** BAILEY *Festus* xi. (1852) 136 O Thou!..Whom all the faiths and creeds, and rites of old ..In precognition of eternal truth Foreshadowed and foretyped. **1903** MYERS *Hum. Personality* I. 31 Here again we find also precognitions which transcend what seems explicable by the foresight of every mind such as we know. **1955** *Sci. Amer.* Oct. 116/3 The entire experimental series seemed to offer proof of some form of telepathy: 'precognition' or 'post-cognition'. **1958, 1968** [see EXTRA-SENSORY *a.*]. **1973** *Psychol. Abstr.* XLIX. 11/1 Telepathy and clairvoyance are seen as extensions of normal preceptual processes, precognition as the reverse of retrospective memory processes.

2. *Scots Law.* The preliminary examination of witnesses or persons likely to know about the facts of a case, in order to obtain, with a view to trial, a general knowledge of the available evidence; *esp.* in criminal law, an examination by a procurator-fiscal of those who can give evidence regarding a crime or offence (in older practice conducted by or before a sheriff or other judge ordinary), in order to know whether there is ground for trial and to enable a relevant libel to be prepared; also the statement itself taken down from a witness before the trial.

1661 *Sc. Acts Chas. II* (1820) VII. 22/2 That the mater of fact cannot be so well cleired at a peremptorie dyet befor the Justice without ane precognition and previous tryell of the wholl circumstances of the same. **1720** *Wodrow Corr.* (1843) II. 505 Several are taken up [= apprehended], and lawyers have taken a precognition. **1753** *Stewart's Trial* 33 We have gone thro' this libel with the greatest attention, and have taken a view of the several facts, which, after a precognition of above a thousand witnesses, are set forth to support the charge against the pannel. **1828** SCOTT *F.M. Perth* vii, The precognition of Simon Glover and Henry Gow would bear out a matter less worthy of belief. **1887** *Law Times* LXXXII. 175/1 Prisoners are not allowed to see the precognitions for the prosecution.

So **preˈcognitive** *a.*, of the nature of, or giving, foreknowledge.

1903 MYERS *Hum. Personality* I. 142, I mean precognitive dreams;—pictures or visions in which future events are foretold or depicted. **1953** P. C. BERG *Dict. New Words* 127/1 *Precognitive telepathy*,..awareness by a precipient of images and ideas occurring at some future time in the mind of a subject or agent. **1974** *Sci. Amer.* June 118/2 One is more telepathic, more clairvoyant, more precognitive. **1975** *Physics Bull.* Mar. 125/2 The author has attempted to describe and briefly to discuss a number of cases claimed to show precognitive happenings.

precognitum, variant of PRÆCOGNITUM.

precognizance, erron. f. PRECONIZANCE.

precognizant, -is- (priːˈkɒgnɪzənt), *a.* [f. PRE- A. 3 + COGNIZANT.] Having previous cognizance.

1828–40 TYTLER *Hist. Scot.* (1864) III. 404, I shall now state..the evidence upon which I have affirmed..that he [Knox] was precognisant of the intended murder [of Riccio]. **1848** CLOUGH *Bothie* iv, The wary precognisant Piper.

precognization, erron. f. PRECONIZATION.

precognize (ˈpriːkɒgnaɪz, *formerly* ˌpriːkɒgˈnaɪz), *v.* [f. PRE- A. 1 + COGNIZE.] *trans.* To know beforehand.

1612 STURTEVANT *Metallica* 34 Except that the Art.., general to all Arts & inuentions called *Heuretica* be first precognized. **1862** M. HOPKINS *Hawaii* 189 He could not.. intuitively precognize the system of Christianity. **1956** A. J. AYER *Probl. Knowl.* iv. 187 There is a tendency for them [*sc.* non-philosophers] to think that if future events were precognized, they would have to exist already... To precognize something is to know, not what *is* happening, but what *will* happen. *Ibid.*, Unless the event really were future there would be no question of one's *pre*-cognizing it. **1970** A. CAMERON et al. *Computers & Old Eng. Concordances* 29, I don't foresee the solution that you are precognizing for the simple reason that I don't think there is enough demand for any computer to be built.

precognosce (priːkɒgˈnɒs), *v. Sc. Law.* [f. PRE- A. 1 + COGNOSCE; cf. L. *præcognōscĕre* (rare) to foreknow, foresee.] *trans.* To make a preliminary examination of (witnesses), in order to enable parties to an action to set up their respective pleas and defences, and particularly in criminal suits to enable the libel to be relevantly stated and maintained: cf. PRECOGNITION 2.

1753 *Stewart's Trial* 93 The pannel's wife and his children, who, by law, cannot be called as witnesses against him, have been precognosced, or judicially examined, and.. their declarations are proposed to be produced in this trial. **1888** *Daily News* 17 July 5/2 Pending the trial of the accused, the Procurator-Fiscal 'precognosces' witnesses, and collects all available evidence, which is afterwards formulated in a detailed and printed indictment supplied to counsel, jury, and Court officials. **1901** *Scotsman* 2 Mar. 12/3 He respectfully submitted that the defence had no power to precognosce police officers.

preˈcoital, *a.* [PRE- B. 1.] Occurring or performed as a preliminary to sexual intercourse.

1935 H. M. & A. STONE *Marriage Manual* viii. 265 A long period of precoital play and a considerable prolongation of the sexual act are unsuccessful in bringing about a culmination for the woman. **1953** A. C. KINSEY et al. *Sexual Behav. Human Female* ix. 361 The pre-coital techniques in marriage are..the same. **1963** A. HERON *Towards Quaker View of Sex* Inadequacies of the love-partner during pre-coital play. **1971** 'V. X. SCOTT' *Surrogate Wife* 98 They engaged in very little precoital play. **1973** M. AMIS *Rachel Papers* 23 In normal circumstances, with her embarrassment in any kind of pre-coital conversation,..the stiff-limbed movements: you were a plaything of her unease.

Hence **preˈcoitally** *adv.*

1971 *Nature* 16 Apr. 433/2 Apocrine glands contribute to total body odour, but a smegma pheromone would be exposed precoitally with exposure of the glans.

precoition(al): see PRE- B. 2a, 1d.

pre-collection, -college, -colonial, -Columbian, -combustible: see PRE- A, B.

pre-comˈbustion. [PRE- A. 2.] In certain diesel engines, commencement of combustion of the charge before it is drawn into the main cylinder, in an adjacent small chamber; usu. *attrib.*, denoting (an engine equipped with) a chamber for this purpose.

1923 L. H. MORRISON *Diesel Engines* xx. 472 One of the first of the precombustion engines developed in the United States was the Western... The precombustion chamber is located in the cylinder head almost in line with the cylinder bore. **1932** *Mod. Diesel* v. 43 On the Continent the line of development appears to have been directed towards securing a steady and progressive burning of the fuel by a system of pre-combustion, the charge being ignited in a partially separated chamber from which the more or less controlled expansion then passes to the working cylinder. **1972** S. H. HENSHALL *Medium & High Speed Diesel Engines for Marine Use* iv. 75 Pre-combustion chamber hot member engines are characterized by their smooth running, complete combustion with clean exhaust and a tendency to high fuel consumption, together with difficulties in starting in very cold conditions.

precommissural, -communicant: see PRE- A. 4 a.

pre-co'mmunion. [PRE- B. 2.] The part of the Communion office in the Book of Common Prayer which precedes the Communion service proper; the ante-communion service.
1868 MILMAN *St. Paul's* xvii. 431 There was a full service with the pre-communion.

precompose (pri:kəm'pəʊz), *v.* [PRE- A. 1.] *trans.* To compose beforehand.
1648 HERRICK *Hesper., To Mistr. Amie Potter*, Nature has pre-compos'd us both to love. **1651** H. L'ESTRANGE *Smectymnus-mastix* 30 Every man is best able to know whether his own prayers be precomposed, or of sudden conception. **1799** C. WINTER in Jay *Mem. & Lett.* (1843) 27 It is very easy to distinguish them [sermons] which were precomposed, from others which were preached extempore.
Hence **precom'posed** *ppl. a.*
1741 *Chr. Liturgy* Pref., Those who pray extempore,.. say, that precomposed Forms stint and restrain the Spirit of God in its Operations. **1861** *Sat. Rev.* 21 Dec. 632 The professional lecturer commonly has a set of precomposed lectures,.. any of which he is ready to deliver anywhere on the receipt of his fee.

pre-com'press, *v. Building.* [PRE- A. 1.] *trans.* To compress prior to some other treatment. Hence **pre-com'pression,** *spec.* the compressive force exerted in prestressed concrete by the reinforcing rods.
1936 *Structural Engineer* XIV. 259/1 A sketch of the great 10,000 tons press constructed for the laboratory for Buildings and Public Works,.. Paris... It was constructed in concrete with only a light reinforcement, but precompressed by the tension given to the hooped wire. **1940** *Ibid.* XVIII. 629 In a pre-stressed girder the fact that the part.. has been given a pre-compression equal to or exceeding the said tension, renders it impossible for fissures to appear under normal loading or even higher loading. **1946** *Concrete & Constructional Engin.* XLI. 191 In a cracked section of a prestressed member, the precompression is either reduced or totally annulled. **1969** *Civil Engin.* (Easton, Pa.) June 45/1 In the arch section, over-compression of the upper flange was prevented by precompressing the arches: the span was made 1in. shorter at each end with hydraulic jacks. **1974** LIN & ZIA in B. Bresler *Reinforced Concrete Engin.* I. vi. 303 Prestressing imparts a precompression to a concrete member in its tension zone so as to increase its cracking resistance. **1975** KONG & EVANS *Reinforced & Prestressed Concrete* ix. 196 The precompression in the concrete tends to reduce the diagonal tension.

pre-compute, -computer: see PRE- A. 1, B. 2 a.

†**precon'ceit.** *Obs.* [f. PRE- A. 2 + CONCEIT *sb.*] A preconceived notion or opinion.
1594 HOOKER *Eccl. Pol.* Pref. iii. §9 Which.. through their misfashioned preconceit, appeared unto them no less certayne. **1647** N. BACON *Disc. Govt. Eng.* I. iii. (1739) 7 God had an eye on all this beyond all reach of pre-conceit of man. **1682** *2nd Plea Nonconf.* 79 Clear from all sinister Pre-conceits, Passion, and Disaffection to Practical.. Piety.

†**precon'ceited,** *a. Obs. rare.* [In 1, f. PRE- A. + CONCEITED *ppl. a.* In 2, f. prec. + -ED[2].]
1. Conceived beforehand, preconceived.
1600 W. WATSON *Decacordon* (1602) 330 No man on earth can tell what gouernment it is they intend to establish,.. when they come to their preconceited monarchie. **1604** EARL STIRLING *Aurora* Song ix, Whose sweet-supposed sowers Of preconceited pleasures grieu'd me most.
2. Having a previous conception or notion.
1698 tr. *Fenelon's Maxims Saints* 110 But these two things had only their Origin from Scholastick Philosophy, whereof these Mystical Men were preconceited.

preconceive (pri:kən'si:v), *v.* [PRE- A. 1.] *trans.* To conceive or imagine beforehand; to anticipate in thought.
1597 BACON *Ess., Coulers Good & Evill* (Arb.) 144 In a dead playne, the way seemeth the longer, because the eye hath preconceyued it shorter then the truth. **1701** NORRIS *Ideal World* I. i. 37 The great Architect of the world præconceived and foreknew what he would make. **1858** HAWTHORNE *Fr. & It. Note-Bks.* (1872) I. 55 The Coliseum was very much what I had preconceived it.
Hence **preconceived** (pri:kən'si:vd) *ppl. a.*
1580 *Reg. Privy Council Scot.* III. 291 Upoun preconsavit malice borne aganis hir thir mony yeris begane. *a* **1688** CUDWORTH *Immut. Mor.* (1731) 205 Anticipated and pre-conceived Ideas of Regular Lines and Figures. *a* **1704** LOCKE *Posth. Wks.* (1706) 68 We must.. not endeavour to bring things to any præ-conceived Notions of our own. **1830** LYELL *Princ. Geol.* (1875) I. II. xvi. 367 Contrary to his preconceived notions. **1875** JOWETT *Plato* (ed. 2) I. 114.

pre-concept (pri:'kɒnsɛpt). *Psychol.* [f. PRE- A. 2 + CONCEPT *sb.*] A term applied by Romanes to a higher RECEPT (q.v.), or rudimentary CONCEPT: see quot. 1888.
1888 ROMANES *Mental Evolut. Man* ix. 185 Higher Recepts, then, are what may be conveniently termed Pre-concepts: they occupy the interval between the receptual life of brute and the earliest dawn of the conceptual life of man. A pre-concept, therefore, is that kind of higher recept which is not to be met with in any brute; but which occurs in the human being after surpassing the brute and before attaining self-consciousness. **1896** *Nat. Science* Dec. 382 From this he argues that there is a logic of recepts in animals, and probably also a logic of preconcepts.

preconception (pri:kən'sɛpʃən). [f. PRE- A. 2 + CONCEPTION; cf. F. *préconception.*] The action of preconceiving; usually (with *a* and *pl.*), a conception or opinion formed and entertained prior to actual knowledge; a prepossession, a prejudice; an anticipation.
1625 DONNE *Serm.* lxvi. (1640) 667 God does nothing, Man does nothing well, without these Idea's, these retrospects, this recourse to pre-conceptions, pre-deliberations. **1711** HICKES *Two Treat. Chr. Priesth.* (1847) II. 154 Men biassed by preconceptions. **1744** HARRIS *Three Treat.* III. (1765) 286 *note*, A Pre-conception is the natural Apprehension of what is general or universal. *a* **1834** COLERIDGE in *Lit. Rem.* (1836) II. 372–3 To hear an evolving roll, or a succession of leaves, talk continually the language of deliberate reason in a form of continued preconception, Y and Z already possessed, when A was being uttered. **1843** J. MARTINEAU *Chr. Life* (1867) 175 Our preconceptions of wrong and of right. **1867** *Chronicle* 27 July 424 Mr. Longfellow's poetic reputation.. establishes a preconception in his favour. **1882** FARRAR *Early Chr.* I. 142 Human perversity has darkened the very heavens by looking at them through the medium of its own preconceptions.

pre-con'ceptional, *a.* [PRE- B. 1.] Previous to conception.
1904 *Brit. Med. Jrnl.* 17 Dec. 1644 The first, or preconceptional period of germinal life. **1933** *Jrnl. Amer. Med. Assoc.* 25 Nov. 1703/1 (*heading*) Preconceptional and prenatal influences affecting the new-born. **1957** C. T. JAVERT *Spontaneous & Habitual Abortion* xvii. 377 The author prefers to begin prenatal care on a preconceptional basis and has found this approach to be particularly effective in the management of habitual abortion patients. **1975** *Amer. Jrnl. Obstetr. & Gynecol.* CXXIII. 717/2 Preconceptional irradiation.. may impair the female reproductive capacity.

preconceptual: see PRE- B. 1 d.

pre'concert, *sb.* [f. PRE- A. 2 + CONCERT *sb.*] A previous concert, agreement, or arrangement.
1748 RICHARDSON *Clarissa* (1811) VI. xlv. 175 A book, which had there not been a preconcert, would not have taken his attention for one moment. **1834** *Blackw. Mag.* XXXV. 395 A medical man being (by preconcert) at hand.

precon'cert, *v.* [f. PRE- A. 1 + CONCERT *v.*] *trans.* To concert or arrange beforehand.
1748 RICHARDSON *Clarissa* (1811) III. vii. 59 The opportunity to effect an escape which they suppose preconcerted. **1828** D'ISRAELI *Chas. I*, I. vi. 188 With this motive we must suppose them to have preconcerted their plans. **1855** PRINCE ALBERT in *Lett. Q. Victoria* (1907) III. 134 How can the Foreign Secretary and Ambassador at Paris.. carry on their business, if everything has been privately preconcerted between the Emperor and the English Prime Minister?

precon'certed, *ppl. a.* [f. prec. vb. + -ED[1].] Concerted or agreed upon beforehand.
1766 BLACKSTONE *Comm.* II. viii. 136 Upon preconcerted marriages, and in estates of considerable consequence, tenancy in dower happens very seldom. **1774** GOLDSM. *Nat. Hist.* IV. vii. 211 They do not go singly to work, but in large companies and with preconcerted deliberation. **1840** DICKENS *Barn. Rudge* lxvii, As though the setting in of night had been their preconcerted signal.
Hence **precon'certedly** *adv.* (Worcester *Dict.* 1846 cites Dr. Allen); **precon'certedness.**
1819 COLERIDGE in *Lit. Rem.* (1836) II. 168 The rhymes.. well express the preconcertedness of Bolingbroke's scheme.

precon'certion. [irreg. f. PRECONCERT *v.*, for *preconcertation*: see CONCERTION.] The action of preconcerting; preconcert.
1846 WORCESTER cites DWIGHT. **1880** MRS. LYNN LINTON *Rebel of Family* II. 270 Bois-Duval had come to London without preconcertion as to time.

preconciliar: see PRE- B. 1 d.

precondemn (pri:kən'dɛm), *v.* [f. PRE- A. 1 + CONDEMN *v.*] *trans.* To condemn beforehand. Hence **precondemned** (-'dɛmd), **precondemning** (-'dɛmɪŋ) *ppl. adjs.*; **precondemnation** (-dɛm'neɪʃən).
a **1631** DONNE *Serm.* (ed. Alford) IV. 220 Not things which make him an unmerciful, a cruel, a precondemning God. **1633** PRYNNE *Histrio-Mastix* Ep. Ded. *iv, They will quite reject and precondemne them, ere they have once examined them. **1847** WEBSTER, Precondemnation. **1864** *Realm* 30 Mar. 2 The Judge of the Assize Court of Aix.. sate as judge, having precondemned the prisoner in his own mind. **1890** TALMAGE *Manger to Throne* 587 There stood Jesus.. the pre-condemned victim of an ecclesiastical.. mob.

precon'dense, *v.* [PRE- A. 1.] *trans.* To condense (a starting material for a polymer) so as to form a stable, low-molecular-weight intermediate which is convenient to handle and can be fully polymerized at a later stage in a process. Also **pre'condensate** [after *distillate, filtrate*, etc.], an intermediate of this nature. So **precon'densed** *ppl. a.*
1950 R. W. MONCRIEFF *Artificial Fibres* xxvii. 261 The formaldehyde and urea are pre-condensed, being allowed to react at room temperature for about five hours until the viscosity is 6 centipoises at 20°C. **1953** *Jrnl. Soc. Dyers & Colourists* LXIX. 44/2 The loss will be further accentuated by differences in molecular size of the precondensate, particularly when highly precondensed resins are used, as in some proprietary products. **1962** J. T. MARSH *Self-Smoothing Fabrics* xi. 159 These pre-condensates are probably methanol ureas which may be formed by condensing urea and formaldehyde either at room temperatures or by refluxing for a short time. **1971** S. A. HEAP et al. in H. Mark et al. *Chem. Aftertreatm. of Textiles* vi. 272 There is.. a growing tendency for finishers to purchase precondensed 'resin' in liquid form. *Ibid.* 279 The conventional process for the application of urea-formaldehyde precondensates consists of impregnating, drying, curing to bring about resinification, and washing.

precondition (pri:kən'dɪʃən), *sb.* [f. PRE- A. 2 + CONDITION *sb.*] A prior condition; a condition required to be fulfilled beforehand; a preliminary or precedent stipulation; a pre-requisite.
1825 COLERIDGE *Aids Refl.* (1848) I. 36 The ground-work and pre-condition of the spiritual state, in which the humanity strives after godliness. **1851** DE QUINCEY *Ld. Carlisle on Pope* Wks. 1859 XIII. 19 Absolute truth and simplicity are demanded by all of us as preconditions to any sympathy with moral expressions of anger or intolerance. **1877** E. CAIRD *Philos. Kant.* I. 165 The idea of God is the precondition of all thought and being. **1912** A. H. POWLES tr. *Bernhardi's Germany & Next War* 4 The conscious increase of our armaments is not an inevitable evil, but the most necessary precondition of our national health. **1923** J. W. HARVEY tr. *Otto's Idea of Holy* xi. 86 It sheds a colour.. upon the life and practice that are its precondition. **1948** *Sunday Pictorial* 18 July 7/6 He cannot accept the lifting of the blockade as a precondition. **1974** tr. *Wertheim's Evolution & Revolution* 211 Among the psychological preconditions for a revolution.. one should include a feeling among relatively large groups that avenues towards emancipation are consistently blocked.

precon'dition, *v.* [PRE- A. 1.] *trans.* To bring into a desired state or condition beforehand. Hence **precon'ditioned** *ppl. a.*, **precon'ditioning** *ppl. a.* and *vbl. sb.*
1922 JOYCE *Ulysses* 494 Self which it itself was ineluctably preconditioned to become. **1961** L. P. V. JOHNSON *In Time of Thetans* vii. 54 Second stage. Bringing reverence and servility to preconditioned humanity. **1967** *Jrnl. Compar. & Physiol. Psychol.* LXIV. 360 Significantly greater CERs.. were shown by the preconditioned groups than by control groups. *Ibid.* 360/1 Sensory preconditioning (SPC) involves the pairing of two neutral stimuli, S_1 and S_2. Following this procedure a response is conditioned to S_2. **1969** *Jane's Freight Containers 1968–69* 420/3 The fibre-board unit load device should be preconditioned for 48 hours under these conditions prior to testing. **1971** *Homes & Gardens* Aug. 19 Frying pans and baking tins should then be lightly greased with oil or cooking fat to pre-condition the non-stick coating. **1974** *Psychol. Abstr.* LI. 572/2 The strength of resultant saccharin aversions was inversely related to preconditioning saccharin familiarity.

precondylar, -condyloid, -confess: see PRE- B. 3, A. 1.

preconfigure (-'fɪgjʊə(r)), *v.* [f. PRE- A. 1 + CONFIGURE *v.*] *trans.* To configure in advance; to conform or adapt in figure beforehand.
1809–10 COLERIDGE *Friend* (1818) I. 293 It was the aweful power of Law, acting on natures pre-configured to its influences. **1835** J. HARRIS *Gt. Teacher* (1837) 237 Wherever the Bible comes, it finds our nature preconfigured to many of its truths. **1882–3** *Schaff's Encycl. Relig. Knowl.* III. 1723 The country was preconfigured to its history.
Hence **preconfigu'ration** *rare*$^{-1}$.
a **1860** in *Nonconformist*, He sees the preconfiguration of human nature to spiritual truth.

precon'form, *v.* [f. PRE- A. 1 + CONFORM *v.*] *trans.* and *intr.* To conform beforehand.
1845 DE QUINCEY *Coleridge & Opium-eating* Wks. 1859 XII. 110 There are.. two classes of temperaments as to this terrific drug—those which are, and those which are not preconformed to its power. **1847** —— in *Tait's Mag.* XIV. 103 Though the passions.. are such.. as could not have existed under Paganism; in some respects they condescend and preconform to the stage.
So **precon'formity,** antecedent conformity.
1825 COLERIDGE *Aids Refl.* (1848) I. 186 These holy and humanizing spells, in the preconformity to which our very humanity may be said to consist.

†**pre'conious,** *a. Obs. rare*$^{-0}$. [f. L. *præcōni-us* (f. *præcōn-em* crier, herald) + -OUS.]
1656 BLOUNT *Glossogr.*, *Preconious*, of or belonging to a Common-cryer; also to praise or commendation.

pre'conizance. *rare.* In 8 *erron.* precognizance. [f. med.L. *præcōnīzāre* to PRECONIZE: see -ANCE.] = PRECONIZATION 1.
1730 *St. Trials* I. 367/2 The Lord Steward, after a solemn Precognizance, commanded the Indictments to be certified and brought in.

†**pre'conizate,** *ppl. a. Obs. rare.* [ad. med.L. *præcōnīzāt-us*, pa. pple. of *præcōnīzāre* to PRECONIZE.] Summoned by proclamation. (In quots. as pa. pple.)
1529 HEN. VIII *Let.* in Burnet *Hist. Ref.* (1679) I. *Records* II. xxviii. 78 Wherefore she was thrice preconnisate, and called eft-soons to return and appear. *c* **1555** HARPSFIELD *Divorce Hen. VIII* 181 The legates caused her to be thrice preconisate and called eftsoones to return.

preconization (pri:kəʊnaɪ'zeɪʃən). [ad. med.L. *præcōnīzātiō-nem*, n. of action f. *præcōnīzāre*, see next; cf. F. *préconisation* (*preconizacion*, 1321).]
1. Public proclamation or announcement. *rare.*
1644 BP. HALL *Modest Offer* (1660) 10 A publick preconization of lawful warning affixed upon the Cathedral

Church door. **1649** —— *Cases Consc.* Add. iii. (1654) 399 The Minister in a solemne preconization, called you.. then to speake, or for ever after to hold your peace.

2. *spec.* in *R.C. Ch.* The public confirmation of an appointment (as that of a bishop) by the pope.

1692 *Lond. Gaz.* No. 2753/1 The Dispute grew very warm ..when the Pope put a stop to it, by ordering the Preconisation of the said four Bishops to go on in the usual Form. **1882-3** *Schaff's Encycl. Relig. Knowl.* 1886 Preconization..the act by which the Pope, in the assembly of the cardinals, proclaims new bishops, and assigns them their respective seats.

preconize (ˈpriːkənaɪz), *v.* Also præ-. [ad. med.L. *præcōnīzāre*, f. L. *præcōn-em* public crier, herald: see -IZE; cf. F. *préconiser* (1321 in Godef.).]

1. *trans.* To proclaim or announce publicly; to publish; to commend or extol publicly, to cry up.

c **1420** *Pallad. on Husb.* XIII. 86 Yet treste y crie Thy laude, and his honour eft preconise. **1803** W. TAYLOR in *Ann. Rev.* I. 311 Louis 14th, whose reign he preconizes as the happiest period in French history. **1847** *Blackw. Mag.* LXII. 293 [They] had all praeconised their accomplishments to us. **1902** *Contemp. Rev.* Dec. 802 Italian ecclesiastics.. undermining the monarchical principle throughout Italy,.. preconising it in Russia.

b. To call upon publicly, to summon by name.

1863 *Church Instit. Circular* II. 139 The certificates having been read, the Registrar preconized the Biships mentioned in the return from the Dean of the Province, and the Archbishop then referred to the Vicar-General to report upon the certificates transmitted by them and upon the letters of proxy. **1877** SIR T. TWISS in *Encycl. Brit.* VI. 329/2 The clergy are præconized or summoned by name to appear before the metropolitan or his commissary.

2. *spec.* in *R.C. Ch.* Of the pope: To approve publicly the appointment of (a bishop).

1692 *Lond. Gaz.* No. 2753/1 On Monday last the Pope held a Consistory, wherein the four last preconis'd French Bishops were confirmed. **1706** PHILLIPS, *Preconise*,..to make a Report in the Pope's Consistory, That the Party presented to a Benefice is qualify'd for the same. **1887** *Detroit Free Press* 21 May 2/1 After eighteen months' service in Perugia, Pope Gregory preconized him [Leo XIII] archbishop of Damietta. **1892** *Times* 23 Mar. 5/5 The Pope will preconize Dr. Vaughan at the first consistory held after Easter.

Hence **ˈpreconizing** *vbl. sb.*; **ˈpreconizer**, one who preconizes.

1703 *Pretended Indep. Lower Ho. Convocation* 40 The great end of Preconizing, is, to know who have incurr'd the Censure due to Contumacy, in not appearing pursuant to Archiepiscopal Summons. **1711** HICKES *Two Treat. Chr. Priesth.* (1847) I. 320 The great disperser and preconizer of it at home and abroad. **1804** W. TAYLOR in *Ann. Rev.* II. 240 He is commonly the panegyrist of event, the preconizer of destiny, he rows with the stream.

preconjecture, -connubial, etc.: see PRE- A. 1, 2, B. 1.

preˈconquer, *v. rare.* [f. PRE- A. 1 + CONQUER *v.*] *trans.* To conquer beforehand.

a **1661** FULLER *Worthies, Cornw.* (1662) I. 196 He [the Duke of Medina] resolved it [Mount Edgecombe] for his own possession in the partage of this Kingdome..which they had preconquered in their hopes and expectation.

ˌpre-ˈconqueror, *a.* [PRE- B. 2.] Anterior to (William) the Conqueror. So **ˌpre-ˈconquest** *a.*, preceding the (Norman) Conquest; **ˌpre-conˈquestal, -conˈquestual** *a.* [PRE- B. 1] existing in, or belonging to, times preceding the Conquest.

a **1878** SIR G. G. SCOTT *Lect. Archit.* (1879) II. 59 There were pre-conquestal Norman and post-conquestal Saxon buildings. **1880** *Sat. Rev.* 3 Apr. 439/2 The fact of the town having been a pre-conquestal see no more makes the place a city than it makes the parson a dean. **1889** *Athenæum* 10 Aug. 184/1 Dr. Stubbs..sums up strongly in favour of the antiquity of the Leet and its jury, to which he confidently assigns a pre-conquestual origin. **1900** *Edin. Rev.* July 150 A unique collection of preconquest stones. **1901** *Daily Chron.* 15 July 5/1 Royal lineage in our noble and gentle families is common enough:..most of them derive from the Plantagenet, and not from the pre-Conqueror kings. **1922** E. EKWALL *Place-Names Lancs.* 172 The example seems to indicate that Over Wyresdale was in pre-Conquest time common land to the townships round the lower Lune. **1927** J. J. HOGAN *Eng. Lang. in Ireland* 27 There is preliminary matter about pre-Conquest Ireland, then *Conquest* follows with some omissions. **1957** K. A. WITTFOGEL *Oriental Despotism* iii. 51 In pre-Conquest Mexico the various forms of land and the obligations attached were carefully depicted in codices. **1960** S. CRUDEN *Scottish Abbeys* 54 To a small pre-Conquest church..there was added on the east a square choir with a rounded apse. **1975** 'S. MARLOWE' *Cawthorn Jrnls.* (1976) xi. 87 The inevitable merging of pre-Conquest and Spanish culture in Mexico.

preconscious (priːˈkɒnʃəs), *a.* [f. PRE- B. 1 + CONSCIOUS *a.*] Antecedent to consciousness, or to conscious action of some specified kind. *spec.* in *Psychol.*, applied to memories and emotions existing at a deeper level than, or of a type different from, immediate memory or conscious thought, but which are accessible to and capable of being brought directly into consciousness; also *absol.* Cf. FORE-CONSCIOUS *a.* (*sb.*) and quot. 1958.

1860 J. D. MORELL tr. *Fichte's Contrib. to Mental Philos.* iii. 43 It is not to be denied that all the apparently abnormal phenomena with which men are seized, in somnambulism, in vision,..and in ecstasy, spring out of the same spontaneous and preconscious region, from which all involuntary impulses and inspirations take their origin. **1867** H. MAUDSLEY *Physiol. & Path. of Mind* I. i. 15 The preconscious action of the mind, as certain metaphysical psychologists in Germany have called it. **1870** E. PEACOCK *Ralf Skirl.* I. 154 A preconscious exercise of the critical faculty. **1874** CARPENTER *Ment. Phys.* I. viii. (1879) 352 The Physiological doctrine of 'Unconscious Cerebration', or, in the language of German Psychologists, the 'Preconscious Activity of the Soul'. **1876** MAUDSLEY *Physiol. Mind* vi. 366 The so-called preconscious soul, of which some philosophers have written, is truly the preconscious mental life of the race. **1891** *Antidote* 9 June 180 A yearning which is at present, except in a few cases, all preconscious, but still none the less hopeful. **1924** W. B. SELBIE *Psychol. Relig.* iv. 78 Consciousness, he [*sc.* Bergson] argues, only emerges when the individual becomes aware of his own mental states, and this allows for a preconscious or unconscious stage. **1925** J. RIVIERE tr. *Freud's Unconscious in Psycho-Anal.* in *Coll. Papers* IV. 25 We have now gained the conviction that there are some latent ideas which do not penetrate into consciousness... We may call the latent ideas of the first type preconscious. **1942, 1957** [see FORECONSCIOUS *a.* (*sb.*)]. **1958** J. STRACHEY *Freud's Compl. Psychol. Wks.* XII. 262 In the 1925 English version, throughout the paper, 'foreconscious' was altered to 'preconscious', which has.. become the regular translation of the German 'vorbewusst'. **1971** N. F. DIXON *Subliminal Perception* iv. 90 The problem is evidently one of confusing 'preconscious'—meaning antecedent physiological processes which do not have phenomenal representation—with the Freudian notion of 'a preconscious'. **1978** G. A. SHEEHAN *Running & Being* ix. 125 The preconscious..stores past preconceptions.

preˈconsciousness. [f. prec. + -NESS.] The state or condition of being preconscious; the preconscious part of the mind.

1930 W. EMPSON *Seven Types of Ambiguity* viii. 302 It is grasped in the pre-consciousness of the reader by a native effort of the mind. **1959** *Listener* 15 Oct. 624/1 This leads us to the idea of preconsciousness. That is the area of mental life in which everything we have experienced in the past, and can still remember, is stored. If consciousness is everything of which we are aware, then preconsciousness is everything which we can remember. **1970** *New Yorker* 26 Dec. 61 We learn of the 'hum' in the literal deeps of the poet's consciousness or pre-consciousness.

preconsider (priːkənˈsɪdə(r)), *v.* Also 7 præ-. [f. PRE- A. 1 + CONSIDER *v.*] *trans.* To consider beforehand or previously. Hence **preconˈsidered, preconˈsidering** *ppl. adjs.*

1647 CLARENDON *Contempl. Ps.* Tracts (1727) 393 A stubborn, pertinacious, preconsidered sin. **1670** G. H. *Hist. Cardinals* I. II. 51 They pray not for the Publick, whose interest is alwayes præ-consider'd by our Saviour. **1671** WOODHEAD *St. Teresa* I. Pref. 18 Not to go to Prayer, without preconsidering whereon to employ it. **1847** GROTE *Greece* II. xi. III. 175 The new pro-bouleutic or pre-considering senate consisted of 400 members. **1873** HOLLAND *A. Bonnic.* vi, Playing a part, thoroughly pre-considered. **1879** FROUDE *Cæsar* ii. 8 The Senate was allowed the privilege of preconsidering intended acts of legislation.

†preconˈsiderate, *a. Obs. rare.* [f. PRE- A. 3 + CONSIDERATE *a.*] That considers or deliberates beforehand; considerate beforehand.

1598 BARRET *Theor. Warres* IV. i. 98 If he be not very preconsiderate in the same, and know well the way, he runneth into these inconveniencies.

preconsideˈration. [f. PRE- A. 2 + CONSIDERATION.] Previous consideration; consideration beforehand; a preliminary consideration.

1598 BARRET *Theor. of Warres* 29 Without preuention, preconsideration, and forecast of such successes. **1656** H. PHILLIPS *Purch. Patt.* (1676) 23 Thus much for these pre-considerations: I shall now set the Tables before you. **1701** BEVERLEY *Apoc. Quest.* 25 A Second most necessary Preconsideration in the Understanding of the Beast. **1858** SIR A. GRANT in *Oxford Ess.* 94 Chrysippus said, that 'no ethical subject could be rightly approached except from the preconsideration of entire nature and the ordering of the whole'.

preconsign (priːkənˈsaɪn), *v.* [f. PRE- A. 1 + CONSIGN *v.*] *trans.* †**a.** To signify or symbolize beforehand. *Obs.* **b.** To consign or make over in advance (Bailey 1721).

1649 JER. TAYLOR *Gt. Exemp.* I. Disc. vi. § 17 St. Cyril calls baptism..'the antitype of the passions of Christ'. It does preconsign the death of Christ, and does the infancy of the work of grace, but not weakly.

preconsolidate to **-Constantinian**: see PRE- A., B.

preconˈsult, *v.* Now *rare.* [PRE- A. 1.] *trans.* and *intr.* To consult beforehand or previously.

1620 WOTTON in *Reliq.* (1672) 527 Intending in the meanwhile to preconsult with his friends. **1651** HOWELL *Venice* 14 These use to preconsult of generall matters tending to the administration of the Commonwealth..and make relation thereof to the Senat. **1683** PEPYS *Corr.* (1841) I. 336 Had my mean advice been preconsulted in it.

So **preconsulˈtation** [PRE- A. 2], previous consultation; **†preconˈsultor (præ-)**, one who advises or holds consultation beforehand.

c **1620** WOTTON *Election Dk. Venice* in *Reliq.* (1651) 187 During his Election, all Inferiour Tribunals cease, only the Colledge of the Preconsultors (as they term it) is daily open for the hearing of Ambassadours. **1631** in *Crt. & Times Chas. I* (1848) II. 144 What an honour is it to King Charles, that had an ambassador who was a præ-consultor to so lofty an action. **1656** BLOUNT *Glossogr.*, *Preconsultor*, a Pre-adviser; there is a Colledge of these at Venice. **1682** NORRIS *Hierocles* 85 Add to the other advantages of Preconsultation that it cuts off the causes of uncertain opinions.

preconˈtain, *v. rare.* [f. PRE- A. 1 + CONTAIN *v.*] *trans.* To contain beforehand.

1656 [? J. SERGEANT] tr. *T. White's Peripat. Inst.* 283 God is a most Simple Entity, precontaining in one most simple formality, the whole plenitude of Being. **1784** KIRWAN in *Phil. Trans.* LXXIV. 162 Fixed air pre-contained in the dephlogisticated.

precontemplation, -contemporaneous: see PRE- A. 2, B. 1 d.

†preconˈtest. *Obs.* [f. PRE- A. 2 + CONTEST *sb.*[1]] A former or previous fellow-witness.

c **1570** in *Durham Depos.* (Surtees) 272 One John Lawson was burying in the barn with the said Agnes brother, her precontest. **1594** *Depos. Bk. Well's Dioc. Reg.* lf. 1 b, Presente then and ther,..this Jurate, and Thomas Jeanes his preconteste.

precontour: PRE- A. 2.

pre-contract (priːˈkɒntrækt), *sb.* Also 7 præ-. [f. PRE- A. 2 + CONTRACT *sb.*] A pre-existing contract; a contract or agreement previously entered into: **a.** of marriage.

1483 *Rolls of Parlt.* VI. 241/1 Oone Dame Elianor Butteler,..with whome the same King Edward had made a precontracte of matrimonie. **1540** *Act 32 Hen. VIII*, c. 38 (*title*) An act concernyng precontractes of mariages. **1603** SHAKS. *Meas. for M.* IV. i. 72 Nor gentle daughter, feare you not at all: He is your husband on a pre-contract. **1657-8** in *Burton's Diary* (1828) II. 337 The law lies very loose as to things that are naturally essential to marriages, as to pre-contracts and dissolving of marriages. **1765** BLACKSTONE *Comm.* I. xv. 434 Of this nature are pre-contract; consanguinity, or relation by blood; and affinity, or relation by marriage. **1878** STUBBS *Const. Hist.* III. xviii. 224 Edward being already bound by a pre-contract of marriage to the lady Eleanor Butler.

b. in general sense.

1610 DONNE *Pseudo-martyr* 125 The King of Spaine had very many subiects in that Order, to whom no other Prince pretended any such precontract or interest. **1649** G. DANIEL *Trinarch., Hen. IV*, ccclxxiii, They are never safe Who weare their Titles by a Præ-contract In Treason. **1821** SCOTT *Kenilw.* v, Lawyers..to draw his contracts, his pre-contracts, and his post-contracts, and to find the way to make the most of grants of church lands, and commons, and licenses for monopoly. **1855** MACAULAY *Hist. Eng.* xvi. III. 704 The Presbyterian nonjurors..held that their country was under a precontract to the Most High, and could never ..enter into any engagement inconsistent with that precontract.

preconˈtract, *ppl. a. rare. poet.* [f. PRE- A. 1 + CONTRACT *ppl. a.*] Pre-contracted. (Used as *pa. pple.*)

1568 *Satir. Poems Reform.* ix. 205 His mother precontract Was in most solemn wise Unto the King. **1887** SWINBURNE *Locrine* I. ii. 137 Albeit their hands were precontract By Brute your father dying.

pre-contract (priːkənˈtrækt), *v.* Also 7 præ-. [f. PRE- A. 1 + CONTRACT *v.*]

1. *trans.* **a.** To engage (a person) in a previous contract of marriage; to affiance or betroth beforehand. **b.** To establish (an agreement, etc.) by contract in advance. **c.** To acquire or form (habits, etc.) beforehand. Hence **pre-conˈtracted** *ppl. a.*

1579-80 NORTH *Plutarch* (1676) 639 This Lepida had been pre-contracted unto Metellus Scipio. **1611** MIDDLETON & DEKKER *Roaring Girle* D.'s Wks. 1873 III. 209 Deere husband, pardon me, I did dissemble, Told thee I was his precontracted wife. **1631** VICARS *Eng. Hallelujah* Ps. cv. vii, That Cou'nant-good, once præ-contracted To Abraham and Isaacs Seed. **1768-74** TUCKER *Lt. Nat.* (1834) I. 613 If they would employ their talents sincerely for the public good, in preference to any private views or favourite schemes or pre-contracted prejudices. **1819** *Life & Death Jas. V of Scot.* 122 Notwithstanding she had been pre-contracted to Frederic, elector palatine of the Rhine. **1856** FROUDE *Hist. Eng.* I. ii. 167 Nor could a contract with Percy have invalidated her marriage with the king..Percy having been pre-contracted to another person.

2. *intr.* To enter into a contract beforehand; to agree or arrange in advance.

1638 SIR T. HERBERT *Trav.* (ed. 2) 88 Having precontracted with Beyrambeg and Darab-chawn, to seize him.

precontrive (priːkənˈtraɪv), *v.* [f. PRE- A. 1 + CONTRIVE *v.*] *trans.* To contrive beforehand. So **preconˈtrivance** [PRE- A. 2].

1751 WARBURTON *Pope's Wks., Ess. Man* III. 295 *note*, When the mind had the will to raise the arm to the head, the body was so pre-contrived, as to raise, at that very moment, the part required. **1840** CARLYLE *Heroes* iii. (1858) 265 Shakspeare's Art is not Artifice; the noblest worth of it is not there by plan or precontrivance.

preconveyance (priːkən'veɪəns). [f. PRE- A. 2 + CONVEYANCE *sb.*] A previous or prior conveyance (of property).

1628 *Petit. conc. Recusants* in Rushw. *Hist. Coll.* (1659) I. 517 This mystery of Iniquity patched up of colourable Leases, Contracts, and Preconveyances. **1655** FULLER *Hist. Camb.* (1840) 221 Recusant-patrons, before their conviction, had such sleights, by pre-conveyances to make over their advowsons to others.

pre-convulsive: PRE- B. I.

†**precony.** *Obs.* Also in L. form **præconium.** [ad. L. *præcōnium* the office of a public crier, a proclaiming, laudation; sb. use of neut. sing. of *præcōnius* PRECONIOUS, f. *præcōn-em* a public crier.] Public commendation; laudation, extolment.

c **1410** LOVE *Bonavent. Mirr.* viii. (Gibbs MS.), So that here is schewed a grete precony and worthy ensaumple of pouert. **1432-50** tr. *Higden* (Rolls) I. 3 Thei ar to be enhaunsede and exaltede by merite with grete preconyes. **1653** R. G. tr. *Bacon's Hist. Winds* 208 It hath been abused both by false opinions, and false Præconiums.

precook: PRE- A. I.

pre'cool, *v.* [PRE- A. I.] *trans.* To cool prior to use or some further treatment. So **pre'cooled** *ppl. a.*, **pre'cooling** *vbl. sb.* Also **pre'cooler**, a device for precooling.

1904 *Physical Rev.* XIX. 330 From the compressor, the air passes successively through an aftercooler; a separator;.. and finally through a precooler charged with broken ice or snow—reaching the liquefier at a temperature of about 2°. **1911** *Power* 14 Nov. 755/2 The Atchison, Topeka & Santa Fé Railway Company has erected at San Bernardino, Cal., a combined ice-manufacturing and precooling plant. *Ibid.* 759/1 For icing the cars, upon the completion of precooling, or for such cars as are not precooled, the ice is handled by the endless-chain conveyor. **1912** *Ice & Refrigeration* Jan. 14/1 Under some conditions the plant intended only to precool fruits before they are loaded is most advantageous while.. under other conditions car precooling after loading is preferable. **1926** *Spectator* 18 Sept. 412/1 By having a hermetically sealed compartment with the commodity pre-cooled, a low temperature is maintained until the box is opened at destination. *Ibid.*, After the cleaning the pre-cooling takes place. **1936** *Discovery* Apr. 104/1 The compressed helium is first pre-cooled by liquid nitrogen. **1958** A. LAURIE et al. *Commercial Flower Forcing* (ed. 6) xii. 328 The cases containing the bulbs are placed in storage in early October at 32 to 34°F, where they remain until shipping, which is usually in late November. Lily bulbs handled this way are referred to as precooled bulbs in contrast to bulbs sent direct to the florist immediately after digging and grading. **1958** *Times* 23 June 2/6 The more promising development is the use of precooling plants on the farms, the object being to cool the fruit quickly as soon as it is picked but before it is finally packed. **1970** *Times* 4 Sept. (Aviation Suppl.) p. ix/9 Imperial Metal Industries' Marston Excelsior subsidiary will display a range of heat exchangers, including..a precooler for the Hawker Siddeley Nimrod. **1973** *Times* 22 Sept. 13/1 We buy a quantity of double nosed Golden Harvest pre-cooled daffodils..which are delivered in the first week of October.

pre-copulative: see PRE- B. I d.

†**pre'coque**, *a.* (*sb.*) *Obs. rare.* Also 5 *pl.* **precox.** [ad. L. *præcoqu-us* (Columella), occas. equivalent of *præcox* early ripe: see PRECOCE.] Early ripe. **b.** As *sb.* Applied to an early fig.

1398 TREVISA *Barth De P.R.* XVII. clxxxi. (Bodl. MS.), Some [grapes] ben precoque..for þei ripeþ sone. *c* **1420** *Pallad. on Husb.* IV. 578 In places passyng cold, hit is most sure Precox [= precoques, L. *præcoqua*] to plaunte; her fruyt they sone enhaunce, Er shoures come.

pre'coracoid, *a.* and *sb.* [PRE- B. 3.]

A. *adj.* Situated anterior to the coracoid.

1872 HUMPHRY *Myology* 31 In Menobranch the long pre-coracoid cartilage lies upon the omo-hyoid.

B. as *sb.* A precoracoid bone or cartilage.

1870 ROLLESTON *Anim. Life* 39 The prolongation of the more perfectly developed praecoracoids. **1875** HUXLEY & MARTIN *Elem. Biol.* (1877) 221 The posterior end articulates with the præcoracoids and the clavicles.

Hence **precora'coidal** *a.* = PRECORACOID *a.* So **pre'coraco-** in comb., as *precoraco-brachial*, (a muscle) connecting the precoracoid with the arm.

1872 HUMPHRY *Myology* 33 Precoraco-brachial..arises from the whole of the outer surface of the precoracoid cartilage, with the exception of the marginal part. **1875** HUXLEY in *Encycl. Brit.* I. 761/2 (*in some copies*) The pectoral arch in the Amphibia is distinguishable into a scapular, a coracoidal, and a præcoracoidal region.

†**pre'cordiac, præ-**, (*a.*) *sb. Obs.* [irreg. f. PRÆCORDIA, perh. after *cardiac.*] = PRECORDIAL.

1671 BLAGRAVE *Astrol. Physic* 83 Proceeding from obstructions and distempers of the precordiacks and arteries.

precordial, præ- (priː'kɔːdɪəl), *a.*[1] (*sb.*) [f. PRÆCORDIA + -AL[1].]

A. *adj.* Situated in front of or about the heart; of or pertaining to the PRÆCORDIA.

1562 BULLEYN *Bulwark, Bk. Simples* 1 Against all the abundance of humours in the breaste or precordiall parts. **1601** HOLLAND *Pliny* XXII. viii. II. 119 For the midriffe and precordial parts, it is very wholsome. *Ibid.* [see PRÆCORDIA]. **1834** J. FORBES *Laennec's Dis. Chest* (ed. 4) 379 A remitting dyspnœa, attended with dry cough and precordial anxiety. **1842** DUNGLISON *Med. Lex.* s.v. Præcordia, The Præcordial Region is the epigastric region. Also, and more properly, the region of the heart [etc.]. **1880** A. FLINT *Princ. Med.* 316 It may be limited to a portion of the praecordial space. **1895** *Syd. Soc. Lex.*, *Præcordial anxiety*, a feeling of anxiety and oppression, with a sensation of constriction of the chest over the precordial region.

†**B.** *sb.* (absolute use of adj.) *pl.* The precordial parts; the parts in front of or over the heart. *Obs.*

1513 DOUGLAS *Æneis* VII. vii. 14 Amyde hir hart-pypys or precordialis lycht. **1555** EDEN *Decades* 66 The naturall heate is not dryuen from the owtewarde partes into the inwarde partes and precordials.

†**pre'cordial**, *a.*[2] *Obs. rare.* [f. PRE- A. 6 + CORDIAL *a.*] Exceedingly cordial; very hearty, warm, or sincere.

1530 LYNDESAY *Test. Papyngo* 349 Brether of court, with mynd precordial, To the gret god hartlie I commend ȝow. **1542** BECON *News out of Heaven* Prol. A iv b, Christ sayeth here playnely, that whosoeuer hath an herty & precordial [*ed.* 1560 vnfeigned] loue toward hym, kepeth his commaundementes. **1757** MRS. GRIFFITH *Lett. Henry & Frances* (1767) III. 273 Mutual Tenderness, or præcordial Sympathy.

b. *fig.* Very comforting or cheering. *Sc. rare*[−1].

a **1600** MONTGOMERIE *Misc. Poems* xxxiv. 37 Restore thairfore to glore precordiall My lif from stryf or knyf of Atropus.

Hence †**pre'cordially** *adv.*, most heartily.

c **1531** BOORDE *Let.* in *Introd. Knowl.* (1870) Forewords 47 Venerable faþer, precordyally I commend me vnto yow with thanks. **1534** —— in Ellis *Orig. Lett.* Ser. III. II. 299, I humyly and precordyally desyre yor Mastershepp to be good master..to y[r] faithfull bedmen.

†**pre'cordium**[1]. *Obs.* An error for PERICARDIUM (confused with PRÆCORDIA).

1541 R. COPLAND *Guydon's Quest. Chirurg.* Hj, Wherof is the substaunce of the coueryng of the herte?.. It is called precordium, & is of a skynny substaunce, wher to descendeth synewes as vnto other inwarde intraylles.

precordium[2] (prɪ'kɔːdɪəm). *Anat.* Formerly also **præ-**. [Sing. of PRÆCORDIA.] = PRÆCORDIA.

1892 A. E. SANSOM *Diagn. Dis. Heart & Thoracic Aorta* xvi. 128 On placing the hand over the præcordium, the observer may be sensible of a peculiar vibration occurring over a certain area and at a certain period of the heart's action. **1900** DORLAND *Med. Dict.* 533/1 *Precordium*, same as *precordia*. **1934** *Arch. Internal Med.* LIV. 341 Pulsations of the heart were felt 3.5 cm. below the epigastric notch, and sometimes a systolic thrill was felt over the precordium. **1962** *Lancet* 13 Jan. 104/2 A pericardial friction-rub was audible over the precordium, but blood-pressure was 140/170 mm. Hg and there were no signs of cardiac failure. **1970** W. DRESSLER *Clin. Aids in Cardiac Diagn.* v. 66 Fig. 24 is from a 31 year old man who showed a heaving systolic impulse in the left half of the precordium between the 2nd intercostal space and the 5th rib. **1977** J. T. WILLERSON in Willerson & Sanders *Clin. Cardiol.* 101/2 Inspection and palpation of the precordium in the patient with cardiac disease are valuable and important parts of the physical examination.

precorneal to **-costal**: see PRE- B. I d, 3.

†**pre'course**, *sb. Obs. rare.* [ad. L. *præcurs-us*: see PRECURSE *sb.*] Forerunning, anticipation, anticipatory action.

1678 MARVELL *Def. J. Howe* Wks. (Grosart) IV. 226 If God do not determine men to such wicked actions by concourse, he doth it..by precourse. **1786** A. GIB *Sacr. Contempl.* III. 470 According to the doctrine of Calvinists, there is a precourse or predetermination of the divine power in respect to every action of the Soul.

precourse (prɪ'kɔəs), *v. rare.* [f. L. *præcurs-*, ppl. stem of *præcurrĕre*: see PRECURSE *v.*] *trans.* To run before, forerun, herald, prognosticate. In quot. 1847 *intr.*, to act as a precursor.

1847 *Tait's Mag.* XIV. 643 The precursors are understood to be gentlemen in the transition state towards repeal. Some of them have, however, denied that they can be said to 'precourse' in this form. **1888** CLARK RUSSELL *Death Ship* xl, The weighty swells which had precoursed the growth of the storm had run away down the eastern waters.

pre-creative: see PRE- B. I.

pre-critical (priː'krɪtɪkəl), *a.* [PRE- B. I.] Previous to the critical treatment of a subject; in quot. 1881, previous to the development of Kant's critical philosophy as shown in his 'Critique of Pure Reason'.

1881 *Encycl. Brit.* XIII. 847/2 Belonging to the precritical period of Kant's development. **1892** MONTEFIORE *Hibbert Lect.* ii. 83 Jeroboam's revolt can no longer be estimated as in the pre-critical age.

pre-crucial, -crusade, -cultural: see PRE- B. 3, 2 a, I.

precuneus, præ- (prɪ'kjuːnɪːəs). *Anat.* [f. L. *præ* PRE- B. 3 + *cuneus*: see CUNEATE *a.*] The quadrate lobule of the brain, situated immediately in front of the cuneate lobule. Hence **pre'cuneal** *a.*, of or pertaining to the precuneus (*Cent. Dict.* 1890).

1890 in Billings *Med. Dict.* **1893** W. R. GOWERS *Man. Dis. Nerv. Syst.* (ed. 2) II. 437 Very rarely softening is limited to the paracentral region or to the precuneus. **1899** *Allbutt's Syst. Med.* VII. 308 We have found that lesion of the gyrus fornicatus, at the point where it passes into the precuneus, caused loss of sensation.

pre'cure, *v.* [PRE- A. I.] *intr.* Of a synthetic resin: to cure prematurely, making mechanical processing impossible. So **'precure** *sb.*, the premature curing of a synthetic resin; **pre'curing** *vbl. sb.*

1935 C. ELLIS *Chem. Synthetic Resins* I. xxviii. 612 Avoidance of precuring during drying is essential if the molding properties of the resin are to remain unimpaired. **1936** H. W. ROWELL *Technol. Plastics* xxiii. 170 Another form of pre-cure is due to mixing a batch of quick curing powder or already cured powder with one having a normal rate of cure. **1943** *Brit. Plastics* XV. 235/2 Precuring.. shows up on the underside of the moulding as a slight chalkiness, in which the outlines of individual moulding powder particles can be seen. **1952** J. DELMONTE *Plastics Molding* viii. 208 If preheating is carried much beyond this temperature, it [*sc.* a thermosetting resin] will begin to precure excessively and will lose its flow qualities. **1962** J. T. MARSH *Self-Smoothing Fabrics* xi. 172 Where the material is batched or plaited in a warm condition immediately after the stenter, there are dangers of what has been termed 'pre-cure' which it is essential to avoid where mechanical processing takes place before the final condensation, and which it may possibly be wise to avoid generally.

precurrent (prɪ'kʌrənt), *a.* [ad. L. *præcurrens, -entem*, pres. pple. of *præcurrĕre* to run before, precede: see PRE- A. I and CURRENT *a.*]

1. Occurring beforehand; forerunning, precursory.

1628 J. HUME *Jewes Deliv.* ii. 29 The precurrent signes of the day of Iudgement. **1799** M. UNDERWOOD *Dis. Childr.* (ed. 4) I. 192 An account of the various precurrent symptoms. **1893** *Athenæum* 2 Sept. 310/3 Precurrent symptoms of the transition to some such society.

2. *Anat.* Running or extending forward, i.e. towards the front or head. Opposed to RECURRENT.

1890 in *Cent. Dict.*

†**pre'currer.** *Obs. rare*[−1]. [f. **precur*, ad. L. *præcurr-ĕre* (see prec.) + -ER[1].] A forerunner.

1601 SHAKS. *Phœnix & Turtle* ii, Thou shriking harbinger, Foule pre-currer of the fiend.

†**pre'curse**, *sb. Obs. rare*[−1]. [ad. L. *præcurs-us* a running before, from *præcurrĕre*: see next and PRECURRENT.] Forerunning, heralding, foretokening. So **pre'cursal** *a. rare*[−1], of or pertaining to a forerunner, precursory.

1602 SHAKS. *Ham.* I. i. 121 And even the like precurse of fierce events, As harbingers preceding still the fates. **1817** G. S. FABER *Eight Dissert.* (1845) I. 262 When John began his precursal ministry.

precurse (prɪ'kɜːs), *v. rare.* [f. L. *præcurs-*, ppl. stem of *præcurrĕre* (see PRECURRENT); so F. *précurser* (15th c. in Hatz.-Darm.).] *trans.* To run or occur before; hence, to herald, foretoken, prognosticate. Hence **pre'cursing** *ppl. a.*

1865 S. WILBERFORCE *Sp. Missions* (1874) 173 This which we hear whispered there, and see spreading we know not how through the air, is just the precursing atmosphere which comes before his [Antichrist's] advent. **1891** FROUDE *Erasmus* viii. (1895) 155 You cannot regard heresy and schism and precursing antichrist as trifles.

†**pre'cursion.** *Obs. rare*[−1]. [ad. L. *præcursiōn-em* a running before, previous occurrence, n. of action from *præcurrĕre*: see prec.] = PRECURSE *sb.* Hence †**pre'cursionary** *a. Obs. rare*[−1].

1701 BEVERLEY *Apoc. Quest.* 15 That such a State of Empire, was at the change of that from Pagan to Christian as a Precursion to it. **1839** *Blackw. Mag.* XLV. 217 The landlords not named in the lists of Precursionary proscription were to be regarded popular and unattainted.

precursive (prɪ'kɜːsɪv), *a.* [f. L. *præcurs-* (see PRECURSE *v.*) + -IVE.] = PRECURSORY.

a **1814** *Sorceress* II. ii. in *New Brit. Theatre* III. 14 Does thy simple mind See the precursive harbingers of woe Like brooding guilt? **1845** *New Statist. Acc. Scot.* XIX. 281 A groundswell precursive of a storm rolls in. **1868** E. EDWARDS *Ralegh* I. xviii. 362 These rumours were..the precursive shadows which are said to be cast by coming events.

precursor (prɪ'kɜːsə(r)). Also 6-7 **præ-**; 7 **-cursoure, -curser.** [a. L. *præcursor* forerunner, advanced guard, agent-n. from *præcurrĕre* to run before; cf. F. *précurseur* (15th c.).]

1. a. One who or that which runs or goes before; a forerunner; *esp.* one who precedes and heralds the approach of another; a harbinger; *spec.* applied to John the Baptist. Also *attrib.*

1504 LADY MARGARET tr. *De Imitatione* IV. xvii. 281 The right excellent precursor Iohn Baptyste. **1612** JAS. I in Ellis *Orig. Lett.* Ser. I. III. 106, I knowe this wilbe the more wellcome that it is my præcursoure. **1792** A. YOUNG *Trav. France* I. 179 Abbé Raynal, one of the undoubted precursors of the present revolution in France. **1852** MRS. JAMESON *Leg. Madonna* (1857) 9 The Baptist is here in his character of Precursor. **1856** MISS MULOCK *J. Halifax* xxiii, Shame, the precursor of saving penitence. **1869** DUNKIN *Midn. Sky* 173 In ancient times Procyon..was called the Precursor Dog. **1871** TYNDALL *Fragm. Sc.* (1879) I. ii. 55 That dark radiation, which is the precursor..of their luminous rays.

†**b.** *Irish Politics.* See quots. *Obs.*

1847 *Tait's Mag.* XIV. 643 Conservatives 39, Repealers 37, Whigs 17, Precursors 12. The precursors are understood to be gentlemen in the transition state towards repeal. **1907** *Daily Chron.* 4 Sept. 4/7 Precursor was one of the many names that O'Connell gave to his popular organisations. The 'Precursor Society' meant that it was the precursor of O'Connell's last resource—the Repeal of the Union.

2. One who precedes in some course or office.

1792 BURKE in Ellis *Orig. Lett.* Ser. II. IV. 540 Sufferers in one Common Cause, and.. our precursors in misfortune. **1835** I. TAYLOR *Spir. Despot.* vi. 248 There is now no need that we should err as our precursors have done for want of experience. **1879** M. ARNOLD *Mixed Ess., Guide Eng. Lit.* 202 Cowper.. by his genuine love of nature was a precursor of Wordsworth.

3. *Biochem.* and *Chem.* A compound which precedes another in a metabolic pathway or a chemical synthesis, esp. a naturally occurring one.

1889 C. A. MACMUNN *Outl. Clin. Chem. Urine* iii. 36 Although we know it [*sc.* urea] is formed from proteids, we cannot trace it back through its precursors—the intermediate products of metabolism. **1890** L. C. WOOLDRIDGE tr. *G. von Bunge's Text-bk. Physiol. & Path. Chem.* vi. 102 This compound is doubtless the precursor of haemoglobin, for there is no considerable quantity of any other compound of iron in the yolk. **1948** *Jrnl. Biol. Chem.* CLXXII. 651 (*heading*) Homoserine as a precursor of threonine and methionine in *Neurospora*. **1960** [see CRYPTOXANTHIN]. **1971** *Nature* 30 July 304/1 An important feature of the process is the maintenance of the high orientation in the acrylic precursor throughout the carbonization processes. **1977** *Sci. Amer.* July 40/2 Ozone and its precursor, atomic oxygen, are destroyed by catalytic reactions that depend on H and OH.

Hence †**pre'cursorism**, the principles and practice of the Irish 'precursors' (see PRECURSOR 1 b).

1839 *John Bull* 29 Apr., Otherwise what need would there be for 'Precursorism' and 'Repeal'? **1839** *Times* 17 Sept., Precursorism has turned out to be utterly hopeless.

pre'cursorship. [f. prec. + -SHIP.]

1. The office or function of a precursor.

a **1603** T. CARTWRIGHT *Confut. Rhem. N.T.* (1618) 152 The Eremitship of Elias and Iohn Baptist, and likewise of the Precurs[or]ship of Elias. **1892** G. SAINTSBURY *Misc. Ess.* Pref. 9 Without the faintest intention of giving any fatuous hint of prophecy or precursorship.

2. Antecedence; prior occurrence.

1856 RUSKIN *Mod. Paint.* III. IV. xvii. §21 It depends for its force on the existence of ruins and traditions,.. and the precursorship of eventful history. **1867** C. J. SMITH *Syn. & Antonyms* s.v. *Antecedence*, Syn... Priority, Precursorship.

precursory (prɪ'kɜːsərɪ), *a.* (*sb.*) [ad. L. *præcursōrius*: see PRECURSOR and -ORY².]

A. *adj.* Having the character of a precursor; running before or preceding, esp. as the harbinger or presage of something to follow; preliminary, introductory. Const. *of*.

1599 SANDYS *Europæ Spec.* (1632) 125 After the kindling of many precursorie lights of knowledge. **1669** W. SIMPSON *Hydrol. Chym.* 77 Being a precursory provision to that end. **1796** *Hist.* in *Ann. Reg.* 16/1 Reprobated.. as precursory of far greater evils. *a* **1883** D. KING in *Mem.* (1885) 357, I cannot regard it [Pentecost] as the precursory advent here designed. **1899** *Allbutt's Syst. Med.* VI. 835 Another symptom which is sometimes precursory of exophthalmic goitre.

B. *sb.* (the adj. used *absol.*) A precursory fact, condition, or symptom; an antecedent.

a **1660** HAMMOND *Serm. Ezek.* xvi. 30 Wks. 1684 IV. 568 Virtue is the way to Truth: Purity of affections a necessary precursory to depth of knowledge. **1822** GOOD *Study Med.* II. 692 Yet not unfrequently the blood issues suddenly without any of these precursories.

precut ('priːkʌt), *sb.* [f. the vb.] **a.** A cut made in something prior to some other operation on it. **b.** Something that has been precut.

1948 *Trans. Inst. Mining Engin.* CVII. 242 A long bottom jib was provided to give a pre-cut and so assist in the fracturing of the coal which is rather strong. **1960** J. SINCLAIR *Winning Coal* vii. 204 A middle pre-cut has been usefully employed where a floor tends to lift and break at the bottom of the coal. **1971** *Real Estate Rev.* Fall 49/1 They are to be distinguished from pre-cuts, which involve materials cut to proper size off-site and then conventionally constructed on site.

pre'cut, *v.* [PRE- A. I.] *trans.* To cut prior to some other operation. Also *absol.* So **pre'cutting** *vbl. sb.*

1945 *Trans. Inst. Mining Engin.* CIV. 192 As with other types of loader which rely upon pre-cutting and blasting for the satisfactory preparation of the coal for loading, much difficulty was experienced. *Ibid.* 701 This roof can be a bad one if not properly controlled, and we felt we would not like to take the risk of pre-cutting and blowing coal, and thus removing all support. **1951** B. KELLY *Prefabrication of Houses* i. 4 There may be said to be various degrees of prefabrication, of which precutting might be one, the fabrication of panels another, [etc.]. **1960** J. SINCLAIR *Winning Coal* vii. 191 Two men pre-cut the face with an A.B. Fifteen Cutter. *Ibid.* 206 It may be preferable sometimes to pre-cut and load on the same shift with the separate cutter working about 40 yd ahead of the cutter-loader. **1961** M. BEADLE *These Ruins are Inhabited* (1963) xi. 160 The Co-ops are pre-cutting their meat and putting it in plastic film. **1964** A. NELSON *Dict. Mining* 343 *Pre-cutting*, a term used in machine mining where a coal-cutter makes a cut along the face in front of a cutter-loader.

Hence **pre'cut** *ppl. a.*

1946 *Fortune* Apr. 244/2 Pease makes only wall, ceiling, and floor panels in the factory; roofs are built on the site from factory precut lumber by traditional methods. **1960** *Farmer & Stockbreeder* 29 Mar. 74/3 As the mower makes a new cut, the scatterer shakes up the pre-cut swath, thereby reducing the time necessary to make the hay. **1960** *Times* 29 Aug. 15/3 The Birmingham Co-operative Society has, for some time now, been selling pre-cut and prepacked meat. **1967** KARCH & BUBER *Offset Processes* iv. 112 (*caption*) Redi-Kut display letters are pre-cut and have a pressure-sensitive backing. **1974** *Encycl. Brit. Macropædia* XIV. 966/1 One of the earliest excursions into prefabrication was the adoption of precut framing lumber pieces for walls and partitions. **1976** *Sci. Amer.* Nov. 100/2 In the commonest form of stamping, a precut metal blank is formed in a mechanical press between a set of dies that have been carefully shaped to yield the desired part.

precydence, -ent, obs. ff. PRECEDENCE, -ENT.

precydent, obs. Sc. variant of PRESIDENT.

pre'cystic, *a. Zool.* [PRE- B. I.] Applied to protozoans that are preparing to encyst.

1926 C. M. WENYON *Protozool.* I. ii. 190 It may be that.. the precystic amœbæ.. are produced by amœbæ living on the surface of the mucosa. **1938** *Archiv für Protistenkunde* XC. 405 The large majority of precystic *Colpoda* sink to the bottom to encyst. **1956** *New Biol.* XXI. 92 In preparation for this [encysting] the amoebae either digest or eject their inclusions and do not feed or grow, so that a generation of small amoebae with clear cytoplasm is produced—the precystic amoebae.

†**'predable,** *a. Obs. rare*⁻¹. [ad. med.L. *prædābilis*, f. *prædārī* (see PREDE *v.*) + -ABLE.] Liable to be preyed on or seized as prey.

1610 GUILLIM *Heraldry* III. xx. (1660) 226 Fowles.. which are Predable whereof some are Savage some Domesticall. *Ibid.* xxi. 227 From Predable Fowles that are Savage, we come to Fowles Domesticall and home-bred that are delighted with Mens Society.

†**pre'dacean.** *Obs. rare.* [f. *predace-ous*, erron. form of PREDACIOUS + -AN (after *crustacean*, etc.).] A predacious animal; a bird or beast of prey.

1835 KIRBY *Hab. & Inst. Anim.* II. xxiv. 481 The Predaceans and several others, when first born are blind. **1895** *Syd. Soc. Lex.*, *Predacean*, a syn. for *Carnivore*.

predacious (prɪ'deɪʃəs), *a.* Also erron. **predaceous.** [f. L. type **prædāx*, *-ācem* (cf. It. *predace*: f. L. *prædārī* to prey upon) + -OUS: cf. *audacious*, *voracious*, *ferocious*: see -ACIOUS.]

1. Of animals: Naturally preying upon other animals; subsisting by the capture of living prey; predatory, raptorial. Also, used of parasitic fungi which actually kill their hosts. Also *transf.*

1713 DERHAM *Phys.-Theol.* IX. i. (1727) 399 Those are endow'd with Poison, because they are predaceous. **1774** GOLDSM. *Nat. Hist.* IV. 22 These snails may be regarded as the predacious tribe among their fellows. **1789** MRS. PIOZZI *Journ. France* II. 195 One predaceous creature caught in the very act of gorging his prey. **1836** W. IRVING *Astoria* (1849) 383 They are now in a land of danger, subject to the wide roamings of a predacious tribe. **1877** COUES *Fur Anim.* iii. 60 Strictly carnivorous, predacious, and destructive to many kinds of small Mammals and Birds. **1908** C. ELIOT *Turkey in Europe* (ed. 2) iii. 73 The Turks never outgrow their ancestral character of predacious nomads. **1933** *Jrnl. Washington Acad. Sci.* XXIII. 140 Adhesion on hyphal tips ..appears to be effective in the somewhat more feebly predacious activity of a fungus bearing solitary spores. **1936** *Mycologia* XXVIII. 307 (*heading*) A new predaceous fungus. **1946** *Ecology* XXVII. 257/1 The Chelonethida are of interest as predacious arachnids. **1964** R. M. & J. W. FOX *Introd. Compar. Entomol.* xiii. 372 Some predaceous species help to control other arthropods. **1971** R. C. W. BERKELEY in Hawker & Linton *Micro-Organisms* xii. 512 The activities of the predacious fungi have been much investigated in the hope that they could provide an effective means of controlling root parasitic eelworms.

2. Of or pertaining to predatory animals.

1822–34 *Good's Study Med.* (ed. 4) IV. 509 He is as trouble-some by his sudden and predacious sallies. **1844** STEPHENS *Bk. Farm* I. 363 A barrier against the predacious attempts on the stock. **1877** COUES *Fur Anim.* iv. 128 The instincts and predacious habits of the Weasels and Stoats.

Hence **pre'daciousness** = next.

1904 BRANFORD *Ideals Sc. & Faith* 118 Characterised by, on the one hand, audacity and predaciousness, and on the other by timidity and submission.

predacity (prɪ'dæsɪtɪ). [f. as prec. + -TY; see -ACITY.] The quality or fact of being predacious.

1836–9 *Todd's Cycl. Anat.* II. 971/1 Indicatory of predacity of habits in the insect. **1853** *Tait's Mag.* XX. 314 Predacity is the order of the day. Bargains are battles, in which the greatest rogue stands the best chance. **1892** *Q. Rev.* Apr. 493 Thanks to his audacity and his predacity.

†**'predal,** *a. Obs. rare.* [f. L. *præda* prey + -AL¹.] Of or pertaining to plunder; predatory.

1737 BOYSE *Olive* i, Sarmatia, laid by prædal Rapine low. *Ibid.* xix, Allur'd, the prædal raven took his flight.

predamn (priː'dæm), *v.* Now *rare.* [ad. L. *prædamnāre*: see PRE- A. I and DAMN *v.*] *trans.* To damn or condemn beforehand.

1624 F. WHITE *Repl. Fisher* 82 The deedes.. for which the cities of Sodome and Gomorrha were predamned. **1794** J. WILLIAMS *Shrove Tuesday* in *A Cabinet*, etc. 14 Swear we're all predestin'd or predamn'd.

predamnation (priːdæm'neɪʃən). Now *rare.* [ad. late L. *prædamnātiōn-em*, n. of action from *prædamnāre*: see prec.] The action of condemning or condition of being damned beforehand.

1626 J. YATES *Ibis ad Cæsarem* II. 32 As for damnation, predamnation, &c., they are acts of iustice, and not to be thought vpon without sinne. *a* **1711** KEN *Preparatives* Poet. Wks. 1721 IV. 27 'Tis Predamnation to despair, 'Tis Bliss to trust God's tender Care. **1865** W. G. PALGRAVE *Arabia* I. viii. 367 An adequate idea of predestination, or, to give it a truer name, pre-damnation, held and taught in the school of the Coran.

predate (priː'deɪt), *v.*¹ [f. PRE- A. I + DATE *v.*]

1. *trans.* To date before the actual time; to antedate.

1864 in WEBSTER. **1902** *Edin. Rev.* Apr. 486 The tendency —found in all early as well as modern writings—to pre-date the origin of empire. **1906** *Westm. Gaz.* 9 Jan. 9/3 Mr. Gorst predates the fall of Lord Randolph Churchill.

2. To precede in date, to date before (something).

1889 *N. & Q.* 7th Ser. VII. 486/1 The Bonnington, or Law-day oak, is not a boundary tree, but it predates the times of the Tudors. **1974** *Observer* (Colour Suppl.) 19 May 14/3 Houses that pre-date the introduction of noise controls and the airport itself. **1976** *Amer. N. & Q.* XIV. 98/1 Both poems predate the letters in the authorized edition of *The Letters of Junius* published in 1772. **1978** *N. & Q.* Dec. 532/2 Deeds of the Warren estates.. provide instances in Lancashire which pre-date the above occurrence [of the name Diana] by at least three hundred years.

predate (prɪ'deɪt), *v.*² [Back-formation f. PREDATION.] **a.** *intr.* To seek prey. **b.** *trans.* Of a predator: to prey on, eat.

1974 *Trout & Salmon* Mar. 50/2 It is hoped that the stock of trout will predate sufficiently to minimise the problem [of coarse fish]. **1977** *Field* 13 Jan. 47/1 Man is a predator... To predate in person, instead of by proxy, is not unnatural. **1977** J. L. HARPER *Population Biol. of Plants* vi. 172 Wood pigeons (*Columba palumba*) cease to predate when the density of a food falls to a level at which the birds can no longer search quickly enough to pick up a sufficient quantity. **1977** *New Scientist* 27 Oct. 220/3 The eggs of many species of frogs are predated by many species of vertebrates and invertebrates.

pre'dation. Also 5–6 -acion. [ad. L. *prædātiōn-em* a taking of booty, n. of action f. *prædārī* to plunder: see PREDE *v.*]

†**1.** The action of plundering or pillaging; depredation. *Obs.*

c **1460** G. ASHBY *Dicta Philos.* 968 On erthe ther is no thing so vnsemyng As a kynge to be in predacion, Or by compulsion to be taking. *a* **1548** HALL *Chron., Hen. VIII* 143 Thys sodain visitacion or predacion, cleane shaued them. [*Margin*] Predacion, that is a robbery. **1664** EVELYN *Sylva* (1679) 20 The good Husbands expected.. that the Fruit should improve, as freed from the predations of the Hedge.

2. *Zool.* The action of one animal preying upon another. Also *transf.* and *fig.*

1932 W. L. MCATEE in *Smithsonian Misc. Coll.* LXXV. No. 7. 144 Predation takes place much the same as if there were no such thing as protective adaptations. **1937** *Ann. Rep. Board of Regents Smithsonian Inst. 1936* 243 (*heading*) What is the meaning of predation? *Ibid.*, Predation has been shown.. not to be, in a collective sense, an inexorable tax upon the luckless prey species. **1944** J. S. HUXLEY *On Living in Revolution* 61 The raids of the slave-making ants are not true war, but a curious combination of predation and parasitism. **1954** D. LACK *Nat. Regulation of Animal Numbers* xiv. 156 The small passerine birds cannot have been limited in numbers by predation. **1959** *Listener* 10 Dec. 1032/1 This predation of birds upon insects is of considerable practical importance. **1968** *Nature* 17 Aug. 694/1 Predation from vertebrates and the uncertainty associated with nests attached to palm leaves were certainly principal factors [in the death of *Scaphidura* chicks]. **1975** W. H. NESBITT in M. W. Fox *Wild Canids* xxvii. 395 They [*sc.* feral dogs] are a valuable part of the fauna by their sanitary predation activities. **1976** E. CURIO *Ethology of Predation* 1 Predation is an ecological factor of almost universal importance for the biologist. **1977** READER & CROZE *Pyramids of Life* I. 30/1 In its continuous 'predation' on plants, the elephant tears branches from trees, pulls great tufts of grass and roots from the earth. **1977** *Times* 11 Feb. 17/3 New entrants to the shipping business are said to have little chance of surviving outside the conference network because of.. the threat of predation (the practice of selling below cost to destroy competition).

predatism ('prɛdətɪz(ə)m). *Biol.* [f. PREDAT(ION + -ISM.] Predation; the mode of life of a predator.

1930 R. A. FISHER *Genetical Theory Nat. Selection* vii. 157 Though the principle of Bates is excluded when two species are actually equally acceptable or unacceptable, to demonstrate such equality with sufficient precision to exclude differential predatism, and to demonstrate it with respect to the effectual predatory population, would seem to require both natural knowledge and experimental refinement which we do not at present possess. **1946** C. T. BRUES *Insect Dietary* vi. 243 Predatism.. is a commonplace mode of sustenance among animals, including man himself. **1964** *Biol. Abstr.* XLV. 5426/2 (*heading*) A new occurrence of predatism in polychaete worms.

†**preda'titious,** *a. Obs.* [f. L. *prædātīci-us*, *-itius*, f. *prædārī*, *prædāt-*: see PREDATION and -ITIOUS¹.] Characterized by plundering or robbing; predatory.

1659 GAUDEN *Serm.*, etc. (1660) 25 Not predaticious to any, but propitious to all true Saints. **1675** EVELYN *Terra* (1729) 3 Provided no rank Weeds, or predatitious Plants (consummating their Seeds) be suffered to.. exhaust it.

predative ('prɛdətɪv), *a. rare.* [f. L. *prædāt-*, ppl. stem of *prædārī* to plunder + -IVE, after *native*, *passive*, etc.] = PREDATORY *a.*

c **1925** D. H. LAWRENCE *Virgin & Gipsy* (1930) iii. 50 She [*sc.* the gipsy-woman] was..just a bit wolfish... 'Good-morning, my ladies and gentlemen,' she said, eyeing the girls from her bold, predative eyes.

predator ('prɛdətə(r)). *Zool.* [f. L. *prædātor* plunderer (see PREDATORY *a.*); cf. mod.L. *Predatores* (W. Swainson in Swainson & Shuckard *On Hist. & Nat. Arrangement of Insects* (1840) II. iii. 115).] An animal that preys upon another.

1922 W. M. WHEELER *Social Life Insects* ii. 46 Species that behave in this manner are not true parasites, but extremely economical predators, because they eventually kill their victims. **1931** W. C. ALLEE *Animal Aggregations* xiv. 246 The struggle for existence between predators and their prey. **1945** J. STEINBECK *Cannery Row* xvii. 69 The little octopi.. prefer a bottom on which there are many caves and little crevices..where they may hide from predators. **1959** W. TRAVIS *Beyond Reefs* viii. 165 We all adopted the lazy movements and slow rhythms of these big predators [*sc.* sharks]. **1971** *Nature* 1 Oct. 345/1 Predators also show a tendency to continue to select a given type of prey, even though other types may be..more easily available.

2. *attrib.* **predator-prey** *adj. phr.*, concerning the ecological balance between a predator and its prey.

1946 *Q. Rev. Biol.* XXI. 235/2 In equations depicting predator-prey interactions in lower vertebrates, loss types may substitute naturally for each other. **1968** *Times* 2 Oct. 12/6 This clearly has considerable implications for understanding predator-prey relationships.

†**preda'torial**, *a. Obs. rare*⁻¹. [f. L. *prædātōri-us* (see PREDATORY) + -AL¹.] = PREDATORY.

c **1781** (*title*) Authentic Memoirs..from the Journal of his Predatorial Majesty, the King of the Swindlers.

†**preda'torious**, *a. Obs.* [f. as next + -OUS.] = PREDATORY (esp. in sense 3).

1640 GAUDEN *Love of Truth* (1641) 21 Interpreting that zeale, which is but naturall passion and choler, an humane, feaverish and prædatorious, not that holy, gentle, and propicious heate of love. **1659** —— *Slight Healers* (1660) 56 In complicated diseases..to give check to that, which is most accute, malignant and predatorious of the spirits. *a* **1677** MANTON *Serm. Ps. cxix.* 36 xli. Wks. 1872 VI. 379 There is a vital heat necessary to our preservation, and there are unnatural predatorious heats which argue a distemper.

predatory ('prɛdətərɪ), *a.* Also 7-8 præ-. [ad. L. *prædātōri-us*, f. *prædātōr-em* a plunderer, agent-n. f. *prædārī*: see PREDE *v.* and -ORY².]

1. Of, pertaining to, characterized by, or consisting in plundering, pillaging, or robbery.

1589 PUTTENHAM *Eng. Poesie* I. xviii. (Arb.) 53 So saith Aristotle,..that pasturage was before tillage, or fishing or fowling, or any other predatory art or cheuisance. **1673** MARVELL *Reh. Transp.* II. 30 It is a prædatory course of life. **1788** GIBBON *Decl. & F.* lxiv. (1869) III. 611 Necessity and revenge might justify his prædatory excursions by sea and land. **1803** WELLINGTON in Gurw. *Desp.* (1837) II. 203 The Marhattas have long boasted that they would carry on a predatory war against us. **1878** MACLEAR *Celts* i. 9 They for a time indulged their predatory instincts unchecked.

2. Addicted to, or living by, plunder; plundering, marauding, thieving; in modern use sometimes applied to the criminal classes of great cities.

1781 GIBBON *Decl. & F.* xxvi. (1869) II. 35 He recalled to their standard his predatory detachments. **1801** WELLINGTON in Gurw. *Desp.* (1837) I. 367 A predatory and formidable race, the Mahrattas. **1841** MACAULAY *Ess., W. Hastings* (1887) 638 The principle..is fully expressed by the old motto of one of the great predatory families of Teviotdale, 'Thou shalt want ere I want'.

†**3.** Destructive, consuming, wasteful, deleterious. *Obs.*

1626 BACON *Sylva* §299 The Evils that come of Exercise, are:..that it maketh the Spirits more hot and predatory. *Ibid.* §318 The cause is, for that all exclusion of open air (which is every predatory) maintaineth the body in his first freshness and moisture. **1686** PLOT *Staffordsh.* 32 Some sorts of it [air] being as predatory and wastful of the body, as others again are comfortable and refreshing. *a* **1711** KEN *Hymnotheo* Poet. Wks. 1721 III. 122 If of himself the Patient takes no Care, But runs into the Predatory Air.

4. Of an animal: That preys upon other animals; that is a beast, bird, or other creature of prey; carnivorous. Also, of its organs of capture.

1668 WILKINS *Real Char.* 165, I shall be content to suppose that those Animals which are now Prædatory were so from the beginning. **1861** G. F. BERKELEY *Sportsm. W. Prairies* xi. 185 They will fly from a dog or a predatory animal. **1884** SEDGWICK *Claus' Text-bk. Zool.* I. 562 The lower lip [of *Libellulidæ*] is modified to form a special predatory apparatus (the mask). *a* **1908** *Mod.* The Cicindela is one of the *Geadephaga* or predatory land beetles. **1925** *Jrnl. Mammalogy* VI. 29 The larger predatory mammals.. require for proper sustenance animal food in large quantities. **1970** R. A. & B. M. MAIER *Compar. Animal Behavior* vii. 116 Defenses against predators are necessarily less than completely effective; otherwise, predatory animals could not survive.

Hence **predatorily** ('prɛdətərɪlɪ) *adv.*, in a predatory manner (Webster 1847); **'predatoriness**, the quality of being predatory.

1890 *Cent. Dict.*, Predatoriness. **1963** *Times* 7 Mar. 13/2 The techniques of power, of political manipulation, of the predatoriness of officialdom, become even more insidiously efficient. **1979** *Listener* 30 Aug. 284/2 Poverty..makes public predatoriness irresistibly attractive.

pre-'dawn, *sb.* and *a.* **A.** *sb.* [PRE- B. 1] The period before daybreak. Also *fig.* **B.** *adj.* [PRE- B. 2.] Occurring before dawn; of or pertaining to the period before daybreak.

1946 D. C. PEATTIE *Road of Naturalist* i. 13 So now I woke, in the pre-dawn of the desert. **1951** *Jrnl. Geophysical Res.* LVI. 325 Between the post-twilight and pre-dawn, the intensity goes through a maximum which is partially localized to the north of our station. *Ibid.*, During the post-twilight period, an enhancement of intensity is observed in the western sky. In the predawn observations, no enhancement is noted in the eastern sky. **1963** J. LUSBY in B. James *Austral. Short Stories* 222 You felt the brittle pre-dawn tension of any war-time 'drome. **1965** G. MCINNES *Road to Gundagai* x. 178 The swirling pre-dawn mist lay wrapped about the feet of every illusion. **1973** G. HART *Right from Start* i. 30 On we went through October, 1970, the pre-dawn of the campaign. **1978** *Daily Tel.* 11 Nov. 11/1 A total eclipse of the sun at midday immersed the world.. in semi-gloom, as in the pre-dawn.

predazzite (prɪ'dætsaɪt). *Min.* [ad. G. *predazzit*, named 1843, f. Predazzo, in the Tyrol: see -ITE¹ 2 b.] 'A rock composed of calcite and brucite, long considered a mineral species' (Chester *Names of Minerals*).

1867 BRANDE & COX *Dict. Sc.*, etc. III, *Predazzite*, a variety of Bitter Spar mixed with Brucite, which forms mountain masses at Predazzo in the Southern Tyrol. It has a granular structure, and is white with a vitreous lustre on the planes of cleavage.

†**prede, pread**, *sb. Obs. rare.* Also 6 preede. [ad. L. *præda* booty, spoil.] Plunder, spoil, booty, prey.

1538 *St. Papers Hen. VIII*, III. 41 He was constreyned to leave behinde him the spoile and prede he had there takyn. **1542** UDALL *Erasm. Apoph.* 186 They..conspired together of all the preade & bootie that thei should geat not to bryng a iote into yᵉ kynges pauilion. **1582** STANYHURST *Æneis* I. (Arb.) 35 For we hither sayld not,..from their region with prede too gather an heardflock. *Ibid.*, etc. 139 Not a practise honest, nor a preede toe be greatlye recounted.

†**prede, pread**, *v. Obs. rare.* Also 6 preid. [ad. L. *prædārī* to plunder, spoil, f. *præda*: see prec.]

a. *trans.* To plunder, rob. **b.** *absol.* or *intr.* To seize booty, to plunder. Hence †**preding, preading**, *vbl. sb.* and *ppl. a.*

1577 STANYHURST *Descr. Irel.* in *Holinshed* (1587) II. 23/1 The inhabitants being dailie and hourelie molested and preided by their prolling mounteine neighbors. **1600** HOLLAND *Livy* III. vii. 92 To..sit still without preading, in a wast and desart countrey. **1609** —— *Amm. Marcell.* XIV. vi. 12 Crewes and troupes of preading brigands. **1632** —— *Cyrupædia* 66 Some Chaldees..that live by preading and robbing.

prede, ME. dial. form of PRIDE.

pre-decay: see PRE- A. 2.

predecease (priːdɪ'siːs), *sb.* [f. PRE- A. 2 + DECEASE *sb.*, after next. Cf. F. *prédécès* (1690 in Hatz.-Darm.).] The decease or death of one person before another.

a **1765** ERSKINE *Inst. Law Scot.* (1773) III. ix. §21 Upon the dissolution of a marriage by the predecease of the wife without issue. **1883** *Stubbs' Merc. Circular* 28 Nov. 1046/1 The same right..which the wife formerly had in the husband's [estate] on his predecease. **1888** LD. WATSON in *Law Rep., Ho. Lords* XIII. 381 Her consent had no reference to the rights accruing to her next of kin upon her own pre-decease.

predecease (priːdɪ'siːs), *v.* Also 6 præ-. [f. PRE- A. 1 + DECEASE *v.* Cf. F. *prédécéder* (16th c. in Hatz.-Darm.).] *trans.* To die before (some person, or, rarely, some event).

1593 SHAKS. *Lucr.* 1756 If children prædecease progenitours, We are their ofspring and they none of ours. **1828** SCOTT *Diary* 24 May in *Lockhart*, Burke was under the strange hallucination that his son who predeceased him was a man of greater talents than himself. **1858** GLADSTONE *Homer* III. 32 Several of the heroes who predeceased the war. **1872** JACOX *Aspects Authorsh.* xxii. 370 How continually do the words predecease (as they say in Scotland) the author of them!

b. *intr.* or *absol.* To die first or before the other.

a **1765** ERSKINE *Inst. Law Scot.* (1773) III. ix. §21 Where the husband predeceases, neither widow nor children can claim a right in any part of the heirship moveables.

Hence **prede'ceased** *ppl. a.*, previously or formerly deceased; **prede'ceaser**, one who dies before another.

1599 SHAKS. *Hen. V*, v. i. 76 Will you mocke at an ancient Tradition began vppon an honourable respect, and worne as a memorable Trophee of predeceased valor? **1880** MUIRHEAD *Gaius* Digest 506 The praetors admitted the survivor of husband or wife to *bonorum possessio ab intestato* of the predeceaser, next after cognates. *Ibid.* 520 He or she might take..the usufruct..of a third part of the predeceaser's estate.

†**prede'cess**, *v. Obs. nonce-wd.* [Back-formation from PREDECESSOR.] *trans.* To precede, be the predecessor of.

1747 H. WALPOLE *Lett.* (1846) II. 192 Lord John Sackville predecessed me here.

predecession (priːdɪ'sɛʃən). *rare.* [n. of action f. stem of PREDECESS-OR; cf. med.L. *prædēcessiōn-em* (Du Cange).] The action or condition of preceding in any position; the being a predecessor.

1647 WARD *Simp. Cobler* 51 Progenitors have had them for four and twenty predecessions. **1855** HT. MARTINEAU *Autobiog.* (1877) III. 255 How much Judaism owes to Egyptian predecession.

†**prede'cessive**, *a. Obs. rare*⁻¹. [f. as prec. + -IVE.] That has gone before; preceding.

1599 MASSINGER, etc. *Old Law* I. i, Our noble and wise prince has hit the law That all our predecessive students Have missed, unto their shame.

predecessor (priːdɪ'sɛsə(r), prɛd-). Also 6 præ-; 5-6 predy-, predi-; 4 -ur, 5 -ar, 5-7 -our, -oure, 7 -er. [ME. *predecessour* = F. *prédécesseur* (13th c. in Hatz.-Darm.), ad. late L. *prædēcessor* (Rutil. *c* 420), f. *præ*, PRE- A. + *dēcessor* one who goes away, departs, or dies, agent-n. from *dēcēdĕre* to go away, depart. Often used as the equivalent of L. *præcessor*, *antecessor*.]

1. One who has held (and ceased to hold) any office or position before the present holder; one who has preceded in the position.

[**1292** BRITTON I. i. §6 Si la fraunchise ne soit grraunté..par nous ou par nos predecessours.] *c* **1375** *Sc. Leg. Saints* x. (*Mathou*) 326 Of þi predecessare. *Ibid.* xxxi. (*Eugenia*) 416 þe emperoure Oto, þat wes predecessoure Of þe gud emperoure henry. **1494** FABYAN *Chron.* VII. 464 The newe pope..whiche also lyke to his predecessour was a Frensheman. **1560** DAUS tr. *Sleidane's Comm.* 307 b, My predecessours, Byshoppes of Rome. **1607** TOPSELL *Four-f. Beasts* (1658) 163 The Elephant..with his teeth digged up the ground and shewed her the naked body of her predecessor, intimating thereby..how unworthily she had marryed with a man, murtherer of his former wife. **1768** GRAY in *Corr. w. Nicholls* (1843) 83 Next day Hinchliffe made his speech, and said not one word (though it is usual) of his predecessor. **1861** CRAIK *Hist. Eng. Lit.* I. 83 Eadmer's immediate predecessor in the see of St. Andrews was Turgot.

b. A thing to which another has succeeded.

1742 YOUNG *Nt. Th.* II. 319 To-day is Yesterday return'd; ..Let it not share its predecessor's fate. **1853** KANE *Grinnell Exp.* xxix. (1856) 248 This is the first clear day..Compared with the gloomy haziness of its predecessors, it was cheering. **1883** *Pall Mall G.* 2 June Suppl., This Supplement..will be republished together with its predecessor.

2. An ancestor; a forefather.

c **1400** *Three Kings Cologne* 56 þe kyngis citee þe wich her predecessours and þe Chaldeys of olde tyme had byseged and destruyed. **1432-50** tr. *Higden* (Rolls) II. 199 Somme women haue childer like to theyme, somme like to the fader, and somme like to their predecessores afore tyme. **1553** EDEN *Treat. Newe India* (Arb.) 4 We may perceue such magnanimitie to haue ben in our predicessours. **1599** SHAKS. *Hen. V*, I. ii. 248 Your Highnesse..Did claime some certaine Dukedomes, in the right Of your great Predecessor, King Edward the Third. **1656** COWLEY *Verses Sev. Occas.*, *To Roy. Soc.* v, All long Errors of the Way, In which our wandring Predecessors went. **1848** R. I. WILBERFORCE *Doctr. Incarnation* xii. (1852) 323 Considering the vast number of ancestors which each individual had in the twenty-seventh generation, there can scarcely have been a Jewish parent in the time of David,..who was not, according to the flesh, a predecessor of our Lord.

†**3.** One who takes precedence. *Obs. rare.*

a **1400-50** *Alexander* 1723 Predicessour of princes & pere to þe sonn.

†**4.** One who goes before as a leader or guide.

1412-20 LYDG. *Chron. Troy* IV. xxxiii. (MS. Digby 230) lf. 154/1 þat þou shalt firste be my predecessour And goo aforn depe doun in helle. *c* **1450** tr. *De Imitatione* III. lxi. 143 He [Jesus] shal be our helpe, þat is our leder & oure predecessour. **1656** tr. *Comenius' Gate Lat. Unl.* §955 If they [Christians] knew their own priviledges, and composed themselves according to the pattern of their Predecessor.

5. *attrib.* and *Comb.*

1680 E. F. *Life Edw. II* 21 He exactly follows his Predecessor-precedent to the Life. **1683** J. WILSON in *Cloud of Witnesses* (1810) 216 That which their great doctor had yielded and their predecessor council had approven. **1723** DK. WHARTON *True Briton* No. 57 II. 498 This French Author celebrates his Predecessor Countrymen. **1858** CARLYLE *Fredk. Gt.* III. v. (1872) I. 167 'The old castle of the Schellenbergs' (extinct predecessor Line).

Hence **prede'cessoress**, †**prede'cessrix**, a female predecessor; **prede'cessorship**, the office of a predecessor.

1591 PERCIVALL *Sp. Dict.*, *Decession*, a predecessorship, *decessio*. **1640** R. BAILLIE *Canterb. Self-convict.* 119 After the example of his glorious Father and renowned predecesrix Elizabeth. **1822** *Blackw. Mag.* XII. 657 They will find no obstruction from the melodious pages of their predecessoresses.

predeclare (priːdɪ'klɛə(r)), *v. rare.* [f. PRE- A. 1 + DECLARE; cf. obs. F. *prédéclarer* (16th c.).] *trans.* To declare or announce beforehand.

1633 MASSINGER *Guardian* I. i, I do not carry An almanack in my bones, to pre-declare What weather we shall have. *a* **1711** KEN *Hymns Evang.* Poet. Wks. 1721 I. 77 For God Incarnate shalt [thou] the Way prepare, His wonderful Salvation pre-declare. **1855** MILMAN *Lat. Chr.* XIV. x. (1864) IX. 355 It is believed by few that the Priest..has the power of irrevocably predeclaring the doom of his fellow men.

predecree (priːdɪ'kriː), *sb. rare.* [PRE- A. 2.] A decree pronounced beforehand.

1831 LYTTON *Godolphin* xxvii, Of all supernatural belief, that of being compelled by a predecree,..seems the most fraught at once with abasement and with horror. **1832** ——

Eugene A. III. vi, The invisible and giant hand..at whose pre-decree we hold the dark boons of life and death.

prede'cree, *v. rare.* Also 7 præ-. [PRE- A. 1.] *trans.* To decree beforehand: to foreordain.

a **1619** FOTHERBY *Atheom.* I. vi. §1 (1622) 39 All things are prædecreed vnto men by God. *a* **1711** KEN *Hymns Festiv.* Poet. Wks. 1721 I. 374 The Force he of the promis'd Seed Had felt, in Jesus pre-decreed.

pre-dedicate, -dedication: see PRE- A. 1, 2.

predefine (priːdɪˈfaɪn), *v.* [f. PRE- A. 1 + DEFINE *v.*; cf. obs. F. *prediffinir* (15th c. in Godef.).] *trans.* To define, limit, appoint, or settle previously; to predetermine.

1542 BECON *Pathw. Prayer* xliii. Q ij b, At his tyme predefined and appoynted from euerlastynge. **1678** GALE *Crt. Gentiles* III. 29 Whatever God absolutely predefines or predestines from Eternitie he predetermines in time. *a* **1711** KEN *Hymns Evang.* Poet. Wks. 1721 I. 67 Whom thy unbounded Goodness predefin'd To be the Mighty Saviour of Mankind. **1809–10** COLERIDGE *Friend* (1865) 43 Much less can a general statute anticipate and pre-define it. **1836** G. S. FABER *Prim. Doctr. Election* II. viii. 357 The number of the predestinated is predefined and certain.

Hence **prede'fined** *ppl. a.*; **predefinite** (priːˈdɛfɪnɪt) *a.*, predetermined (in quot. 1847 = PREDESIGNATE *a.* b); **predefinition** (priːdɛfɪˈnɪʃən), predetermination.

1550 BALE *Image Both Ch.* I. L iv b, Vntill such time as the complet number..shuld be fulfilled and wholy accomplished accordinge to the eternall prediffinition of God. **1678** GALE *Crt. Gentiles* III. 25 Some distinguish between God's predefinition and his predetermination: his predefinition they restrain to his decrees, and his predetermination to his concurse. *Ibid.* 30 The decree of God..cannot have [its effect] but by efficaciously applying the create wil to the predefinite act. **1847** HAMILTON *Let. to De Morgan* 32 In the first, common, or Aristotelic meaning, definite, or more precisely predefinite (διοριστός, προσδιοριστός) is equivalent to expressed, overt, or, more proximately, to designate and pre-designate. **1929** R. BRIDGES *Testament of Beauty* IV. 124 But these philosophers ..used the abstracted terms whereby they had pre-defined distinctions. **1976** *Brit. Jrnl. Sociol.* XXVII. 302 What is offered is not the theoretical construction of an object of study, but merely the systematization of predefined data. **1977** J. D. DOUGLAS in Douglas & Johnson *Existential Sociol.* i. 63 Even Goffman..has had little to say about the self except as a 'presenter' of predefined and learned social roles.

prede'liberate (priː-), *v. rare.* [f. PRE- A. 1 + DELIBERATE *v.*; cf. obs. F. *predeliberer* (16th c. in Godef.).] *trans.* To deliberate beforehand, to premeditate. Hence **prede'liberated** *ppl. a.*, previously deliberated; premeditated. So **ˌpredelibe'ration**, previous deliberation.

1625 Pre-deliberations [see PRECONCEPTION]. **1649** BP. GUTHRIE *Mem.* (1702) 20 This Tumult was taken to be but a rash Emergent, without any predeliberation. **1671** WOODHEAD *St. Teresa* I. Pref. 2 Occasions of committing either mortal, or any voluntary and predeliberated, venial sin.

prede'lineate (priː-), *v. rare.* [PRE- A. 1.] To delineate beforehand. Hence **prede'lineated** *ppl. a.* So **predelin'eation**, previous delineation; in quot. 1879 in reference to the old theory that all the parts of the complete animal body already existed in the spermatozoon: cf. PREFORMATION 2.

1682 H. MORE *Annot. Glanvill's Lux O.* 119 The same spirit of Nature which prepares the matter by some general Predelineation. *Ibid.* 125 Such a soul as is most congruous to the predelineated Matter which it has prepared for her. **1879** tr. *Haeckel's Evol. Man* I. 37 The Animalculists, or the Believers in Sperm, looked upon the moving seminal threads as the real animal germs... Leeuwenhoek, Hartsoeker, and Spallanzani were the chief defenders of this theory of Pre-delineation.

predelinquency, -delinquent: see PRE- B. 1.

prede'livery, *a.* [PRE- B. 2.] Carried out in, or concerned with, the period preceding delivery of a baby.

1957 *Obstetr. & Gynecol.* IX. 633 (*heading*) Predelivery sedation with promazine. **1965** S. PELLER in Glass & Eversley *Population in Hist.* v. 91 Babies born out of wedlock had a perinatal mortality of 102, or 43 or 32 per 1,000.., depending on whether their mothers had been sheltered in the predelivery maternity division of the General Hospital for 0–7, 8–28, or 29–56 days.

predella (prɪˈdɛlə). Also *erron.* prædella. [a. It. *predella* (preˈdella) a stool, footstool, kneeling-stool; prob. f. OHG. *pret* a board + *-ella*, dim. suffix.]

1. The step or platform upon which an altar is placed, an altar-step, foot-pace; also, a painting or sculpture upon the vertical face of this.

DALE tr. *Baldeschi's Ceremonial* 6 All should communicate upon the edge of the predella. **1857** G. J. WIGLEY *Borromeo's Inst. Eccl. Build.* xi. §2. 26 *note*, The highest or the only step of an altar is..the Predella..the name used for this platform in all works on church ceremonies. **1873** SUSAN & JO. HORNER *Walks Florence* (1884) I. xxiv. 353 In the..predella of small figures below the altar, a priest holds up the chalice. **1926** *Trans. Scottish Ecclesiol. Soc.* VIII. II. 71 The sanctuary is, perforce, very small and the Holy Table ..is placed directly against the wall... The single step Prædella is semi-circular, and is enclosed by a beautiful tudor rail.

2. A raised shelf at the back of an altar; also (more usually) a piece of painting or sculpture on the front of such a shelf, forming an appendage to the altar-piece above it: = GRADINO.

1848 MRS. JAMESON *Sacr. & Leg. Art* (1850) 101 In a small and very curious picture which I saw at Rome, forming part of a Predella. **1859** GULLICK & TIMBS *Paint.* 307 The 'predella' or gradus was the wooden base on which the altar-piece rested, and to which it was attached. **1873** SUSAN & JO. HORNER *Walks Florence* (1884) II. i. 2 This picture formed the predella, or lower part of an altar-piece.

b. Extended to a subsidiary painting forming a similar appendage to any picture.

1882 W. SHARP *D. G. Rossetti* 252 There is a very fine predella, or lower partition, attached to the picture, which [predella] is divided by two crossbars of the frame into three divisions. **1902** *Union Mag.* Nov. 502/1 The picture is finished with a predella consisting of a kind of Dominican tree.

c. *attrib.*, as ***predella panel, picture.***

1884 *American* VIII. 202 The collection has also a small Raphael predella panel. **1884** *Athenæum* 21 June 796 The nuns of St. Anthony of Padua..sold the fine predella pictures to Christina of Sweden.

pre-demand, -demonstrate, etc.: see PRE- A. 1.

predentary, -dentate, etc.: PRE- A. 4, B. 3.

†**prede'pose**, *v. Obs. rare.* [PRE- A. 1.] *trans.* To depose, give evidence, or affirm previously. Hence †**prede'posed** *ppl. a.*

c **1560** *Durham Depos.* (Surtees) 62 As he haith predeposyd in this said matter. **1626** in *Impeachm. Dk. Buckhm.* (Camden) 29 Hee..did lade all the predeposed goods.

pre-describe, -desert, etc.: see PRE- A. 1, 2.

predesign (priːdɪˈzaɪn), *v.* Now *rare.* [f. PRE- A. 1 + DESIGN *v.*; cf. late L. *prædēsignātus.*] *trans.* To design, appoint, purpose, or contrive beforehand: see DESIGN *v.* 7, 8, 10.

1671 WOODHEAD *St. Teresa* I. Pref. 7 Her often iterated apologies..shew neither her Matter nor Method curiously pre-designed. **1688** BOYLE *Final Causes Nat. Things* iii. 87 It seems not conceivable, how they should act constantly for ends, they are not capable of predesigning. *a* **1711** KEN *Hymnotheo* Poet. Wks. 1721 III. 166 This with the spotless Soul was pre-design'd For Social Bliss and Cement to mankind.

Hence **prede'signed** *ppl. a.*

1685 BOYLE *Enq. Notion Nat.* 358 With Consciousness of what She does, and for pre-designed Ends. **1905** *Blackw. Mag.* June 825/2 A deliberate and predesigned attempt to embroil Europe in Russia's Far Eastern trouble.

predesignate (priːˈdɛsɪgnət, -ˈdɛz-), *a.* [f. PRE- A. 1 + DESIGNATE *ppl. a.*] **a.** Designated or specified beforehand. **b.** *Logic.* Of a proposition or term: Having a sign of quantity prefixed.

1837–8 SIR W. HAMILTON *Logic* xiii. (1866) I. 244 Propositions have either..their quantity..marked out by a verbal sign, or they have not; such quantity being involved in every actual thought. They may be called in the one case (a) *Predesignate*; in the other (b) *Preindesignate.* **1847** [see PREDEFINITE].

pre'designate (-neɪt), *v. rare.* [PRE- A. 1.]

1. *trans.* To designate or specify beforehand.

1823 BENTHAM *Not Paul* 153 In the calamity of dearth may be seen one of those events, of which—especially if the time of it be not predesignated with two rigid an exactness —a prediction may be hazarded.

2. *Logic.* To designate by prefixing a sign of quantity.

1864 BOWEN *Logic* v. 135 *note*, The English Exclusive particles are, *one, only, alone, exclusively, precisely, just, sole, solely, nothing but*, &c. These particles annexed to the Subject predesignate the Predicate universally, or to its whole extent.

Hence **pre'designated** *ppl. a.*

1961 J. B. WILSON *Reason & Morals* ii. 109 People do not consciously adopt a language-game for a deliberate and predesignated purpose. **1973** *Nation Rev.* (Melbourne) 31 Aug. 1449/3 Fortnightly..aficionados of the Australian pit fowl gather at the predesignated meeting place.

predesignation (priːdɛsɪgˈneɪʃən, -dɛz-). [n. of action from prec.: see -ATION.]

1. The action of predesigning, or of predesignating; previous designation, appointment, or specification.

a **1641** BP. MOUNTAGU *Acts. & Mon.* (1642) 26 For us men,..according to Promise, Prediction, Pre-designation, God to Man, in the fulnesse of time, came downe from heaven. **1701** NORRIS *Ideal World* I. i. 36 Here is an express ..prædesignation of them. **1883** C. S. PEIRCE *The. Prob. Infer.* in *Stud. Logic* viii. 162 Suppose we were to draw our inferences without the predesignation of the character *P* [for which the class had been sampled]; then we might in every case find some recondite character in which those instances would all agree.

2. *Logic.* A sign of quantity prefixed to a term or proposition.

c **1840** SIR W. HAMILTON *Logic* (1866) II. App. 273 They [logicians]..denominated a proposition *universal* or *particular*, as its subject merely was quantified by the predesignation *some* or *all.* **1864** BOWEN *Logic* v. 122 Having no sign or predesignation of Quantity affixed to it.

predesignatory (priːˈdɛsɪgnətərɪ, -ˈdɛz-), *a.* [f. PREDESIGNATE *v.* + -ORY[2].] *prop.* Having the function of predesignating; in quot. = Prefixed as a sign of quantity to a proposition (cf. prec. 2).

1853 SIR W. HAMILTON *Discuss.* App. ii. *Logical* (B) 680 Here the predesignatory words for universally affirmative and universally negative quantity are not the same.

†**pre'destin.** *Obs. rare*[−1]. [f. PRE- A. 2 + DESTIN.] = PREDESTINY.

1558 PHAER *Æneid.* VII. T j b, But we commaunded come, and by predestin seeke this ground By tokens straunge from heauen.

predestinarian (prɪdɛstɪˈnɛərɪən), *sb.* and *a.* [f. PREDESTINE *v.* + *-arian* (in *Trinitarian*, etc.).]

A. *sb.* One who believes or maintains the theological doctrine of predestination, esp. in an extreme form; a fatalist.

1667 *Decay Chr. Piety* ix. ¶20 Why does the predestinarian so adventurously climb into heaven, to ransack the celestial archives? **1741** WESLEY *Wks.* (1872) I. 302 There are several Predestinarians in our societies. **1782** W. F. MARTYN *Geog. Mag.* I. 41 The Turks being great predestinarians. **1882** W. H. FREMANTLE in *Dict. Chr. Biog.* III. 46/2 (*Hieronymus*) Jerome is not like Augustine, a thorough-going predestinarian, but a 'synergist', maintaining the coexistence of free will.

B. *adj.* Of, pertaining to, concerning, or relating to predestination; holding or maintaining the doctrine of predestination.

a **1638** MEDE *Wks.* (1672) p. xix, By way of Reply to the objected authority of S. Austin as to some part of the Predestinarian Controversie. **1701** tr. *Le Clerc's Prim. Fathers* (1702) 382 Errors to which the Divines of Marseilles gave the name of Predestinarian Heresie. **1827** HALLAM *Const. Hist.* (1876) I. vii. 402 Those who did not hold the predestinarian theory were branded with reproach by the names of freewillers and Pelagians. **1843** J. MARTINEAU *Chr. Life* (1867) 407 Every Fatalist or Predestinarian scheme destroys merit.

Hence **predesti'narianism**, the belief or doctrine of predestinarians.

1722 DE FOE *Plague* (Rtldg.) 245 A kind of a Turkish Predestinarianism. **1831** BLAKEY *Free-will* 108 Many systems and views, both in morals and religion, are maintained upon a more slender foundation than that of predestinarianism. **1882–3** *Schaff's Encycl. Relig. Knowl.* II. 896/2 The Lutheran Church..attempted to take a middle course between predestinarianism..and synergism.

†**pre'destinary**, *a. Obs. rare.* [f. PREDESTINE + -ARY[1] A.] = PREDESTINARIAN *a.*

1599 SANDYS *Europæ Spec.* (1629) 172 To professe openly they will returne to the Papacie, rather than ever admit that Sacramentarie and Predestionarie [*sic*] pestilence. *a* **1662** HEYLIN *Hist. Presbyter.* (1670) 21 The Zwinglian Gospellers..began to scatter their predestinary Doctrines in the Reign of King Edward.

predestinate (prɪˈdɛstɪnət), *ppl. a.* and *sb.* [ad. L. *prædestināt-us*, pa. pple.: see next.]

A. *ppl. a.* (as *adj.* or *pple.*) Predestined. *arch.*

1. *Theol.* Foreordained by the eternal purpose or decree of God: **a.** to salvation or eternal life.

c **1380** WYCLIF *Sel. Wks.* III. 426 If þo pope asked me wheþer I were ordeyned to be saved, or predestynate, I wolde sey þat I hoped so. *c* **1535** M. NISBET *New Test. in Scots* (S.T.S.) III. 341 To searse the boddumless secrettis of Godis predestinatiounn, quhiddir thai be predestynate or nocht. **1684** *Contempl. St. Man* I. xi. (1699) 125 The Reprobates being then in the Valley of Jehosaphat, and the predestinate in the Air. **1833** J. WATERWORTH tr. *Veron's Rule Cath. Faith* 144 Can the predestinate be lost, or the reprobate saved?

b. to any specified fate or lot in this life or after death; also of things: Foreordained by divine decree. Const. *to*, or *inf.* with *to*.

1382 WYCLIF *Rom.* i. 4 The which is predestynat [*gloss* or bifore ordeyned bi grace] the sone of God in vertu. **1433** LYDG. *St. Fremund* 618 This blissid martir..Afforn predestynat to liff that is eterne. **1526** *Pilgr. Perf.* (W. de W. 1531) 180 She that was predestynate to be the mother of God. **1582** STANYHURST *Æneis* I. (Arb) 17 Bi Gods predestinat order. **1649** A. ROSS *Alcoran* 41 In a time prescribed and predestinate. **1868** BROWNING *Ring & Bk.* III. 1044 The precious something at perdition's edge He only was predestinate to save.

2. In lighter or more general sense: Destined beforehand; fated.

c **1500** MEDWALL *Nature* (Brandl) 869 He ys predestynate to be a prynces pere. **1599** SHAKS. *Much Ado* I. i. 136 So some Gentleman or other shall scape a predestinate scratcht face. **1706** MAULE *Hist. Picts* in *Misc. Scot.* I. 40 Empires and monarchies cannot excape their predestinate ruines and fatal subversions. **1882** SWINBURNE *Tristram of Lyon.* vi. 109 The great good wizard, well beloved and well Predestinate of heaven. **1896** SIR T. MARTIN *Æneid* II. 81 There happy days, a realm, and royal bride Predestinate await thee.

B. *sb. Theol.* A person predestinated to eternal life; one of the elect.

1529 MORE *Dyaloge* II. Wks. 181/2 Yet may it be that there bee none other in it than predestinates. **1600** W. WATSON *Decacordon* (1602) 92 These Anabaptisticall heretickes, how boldly they dare censure of all others, and auouch themselues predestinates. **1905** G. G. COULTON in *Contemp. Rev.* Aug. 222 He [Newman] would have found himself in far closer and more inevitable contact with these self-elected Predestinates.

predestinate (prɪˈdɛstɪneɪt), *v.* [f. L. *prædestināt-*, ppl. stem of *prædestināre*, in cl. L. 'to appoint or resolve upon beforehand' (*prædestināre triumphos*, Livy); in Chr. L. from 4th c. (Lucifer of Cagliari *a* 370, Ambrosiaster, Vulgate (of the Epistles) *c* 384, Augustine *c* 418), rendering Gr. προορίζειν 'to determine beforehand' (Rom. viii. 29, 30); f. L. *præ*, PRE- A. 1 + *destināre* to make fast, establish, determine, appoint: see DESTINE *v.* In English the verb was first PREDESTINE (q.v.); *predestinat*, *-ate* was at first pa. pple. (= L. *prædestinātus*) and ppl. adj., later also pa. t., but became *c* 1550 the form of the finite vb. = PREDESTINE *v.* Cf. prec. and -ATE[3].]

1. *Theol.* Of God: To foreordain by a divine decree or purpose: **a.** to salvation or eternal life; to elect.

c **1450** tr. *De Imitatione* III. lxiii. 146, I preuentyed hem in blessinges of swetnes. I predestinate hem before worldes. **1530** PALSGR. 664/2 He that is predestynate is written in the boke of lyfe. **1582** N. T. (Rhem.) *Rom.* viii. 30 And whom he hath predestinated: them also he hath called. [WYCL. bifor ordeyned: TINDALE, CRANMER, *Geneva*, ordeyned before..appoynted before: 1611 did predestinate: *R.V.* foreordained.] **1704** *Collect. Voy.* (Churchill) III. 139/1 Gentiles, whom he had predestinated by the means of the Gospel.

b. to any fate or lot in this life or after death (including to elect and to reprobate); to foreordain everything that comes to pass. Const. *to*, or *inf.* with *to*.

(But many who hold the Augustinian, Thomist, or Calvinistic doctrine of God's foreordination of all things have objected to or shrunk from the use of *predestinate* and *predestination* in reference to final reprobation. Even the Westminster Confession does not so use it: see quot. 1647.)

a **1450** *Alexander* 2745 (Dublin MS.) Yff I kyd þaim ony curtasy, it Come of my-seluen..Na we pride vs for no prowez predestinate [*Ashm. MS.* predestayned] vs here. **1531** ELYOT *Gov.* I. xx, Whom god..had predestinate to be a great kyng. *c* **1560** *Petition* in Strype *Ann. Ref.* (1709) I. xxviii. 294 That God doth foreknow and predestinate all good and goodness, but doth only foreknow, and not predestinate, any evil. **1647** *Westminster Confession* iii. §§3–4 By the decree of God, for the manifestation of His glory, some men and angels are predestinated unto everlasting life, and others foreordained to everlasting death. These angels and men thus predestinated and foreordained [etc.]. *a* **1683** OLDHAM *Poet. Wks.* (1686) 44 Make Fate hang on his Lips, nor Heaven have Pow'r to Predestinate without his leave. **1849** ROBERTSON *Serm.* Ser. I. ii. (1866) 20 God does not predestinate men to fail. **1875** MANNING *Mission H. Ghost* i. 10 He predestinated them, first to grace in this world, and..to glory in the world to come. **1887** G. SALMON in *Dict. Chr. Biog.* III. 449/2 These..taught that certain were by God's foreknowledge so predestinated to death that neither Christ's passion nor baptism..could help them. **1888** BP. GORE *R.C. Claims* i. (1905) 3 *note*, Be logical,..said the Calvinist: God predestinates, and therefore man has not free will. **1901** B. J. KIDD *39 Articles* II. II. xvii. 155 [Art. XVII] declines to be committed to the doctrine of Reprobation, according to which all who are not predestinated to eternal life were held to be predestinated to eternal death.

2. To destine (as by fate); to fix beforehand by human (or animal) determination: = PREDESTINE 1 b.

1593 R. HARVEY *Philad.* 32 Infinite be that time, which is predestinated for the name of Brute and his Brutans. **1670** EACHARD *Cont. Clergy* 14 Not a few are predestinated thither [to the church] by their friends, from the foresight of a good benefice. **1730** YOUNG *Paraphr. Job* 228 And with a glance predestinates her prey. *a* **1845** HOOD *Desert-Born* iii, Predestinated (so I felt) for ever to her service.

Hence **preˈdestinated** *ppl. a.*, **preˈdestinating** *vbl. sb.* and *ppl. a.*

1593 *Tell-Trothe's N.Y. Gift* (1876) 19 To shonne his predestinated fortune. **1722** DE FOE *Plague* (1840) 13 Presuming upon their professed predestinating notions, and of every man's end being predetermined. **1737–69** CRUDEN *Concordance* (ed. 8) 535/1 Those that are so left [in their infidelity or their corruptions] are the Reprobate, and the others are the Elect or Predestinated. **1819** CHALMERS *Congregat. Serm.* (1836) I. 369 Mysteries attach to the counsels and determinations of a predestinating God. **1827** POLLOK *Course T.* VI. 204 The stagnant, dull, predestinated fool. **1956** R. MACAULAY *Towers of Trebizond* xxi. 242 The predestinating Calvinists in the Celtic mountains.

preˈdestinately, *adv.* [f. PREDESTINATE *ppl. a.* + -LY[2].] In a 'predestinate' manner; by predestination.

1579 J. JONES *Preserv. Bodie & Soule* I. xxxix. 87 All thyngs happen of fatal necessitie, predestinately. **1890** *Eng. Illustr. Mag.* Nov. 128 Mine is essentially, predestinately, and unchangeably good.

†**predestiˈnatian**, *a.* (*sb.*) *Obs. rare.* [f. L. *prædestināt-us*, *-a*, *-um* (see PREDESTINATE *v.*) + -IAN; so mod.F. *prédestinatien* (Littré).] = PREDESTINARIAN *sb.* and *a.*

1630 USSHER *Lett.* (1686) 434 Predestinatians, which was but a Nickname that the Semi-Pelagians put upon the Followers of St. Augustine. **1685** STILLINGFL. *Orig. Brit.* iv. 200 Objections..made by the Semipelagians, and not by any Predestinatian Hereticks at that time in Gaul.

predestination (prɪdɛstɪˈneɪʃən). [ad. late L. *prædestinātiōn-em* (Augustine), n. of action f. *prædestināre* to PREDESTINE: see -ATION. So F. *prédestination* (12th c. in Hatz.-Darm.).]

The action of predestinating, or fact of being predestinated; the ordaining or determination of events before they come to pass; pre-appointment by, or in the way of, fate or destiny; foreordination.

1. *Theol.*, etc. The action by which God is held to have immutably determined all (or some particular) events by an eternal decree or purpose.

'*Predestination* is a theological term, sometimes used with greater latitude to denote the decree or purpose of God by which He has from eternity immutably determined whatever comes to pass; sometimes more strictly to denote the decree by which men are destined to everlasting happiness or misery; and sometimes with excessive strictness to denote only predestination to life or election' (Marcus Dods in *Encycl. Brit.* (1885) XIX. 668/1).

a. The action of God (held by Christians generally) in foreordaining or appointing from all eternity certain of mankind through grace to salvation and eternal life. (In this sense = *election*, and opposed to *reprobation*.)

a **1340** HAMPOLE *Psalter* civ. 10, I gif heuen in heritage til anly þa þat ere takyne wiþ þe strenge of predestinacioun of god. *c* **1380** WYCLIF *Sel. Wks* III. 134 Þese two glues, of predestinacioun and of prescience of God, joynen þese two bodies. **1401** *Pol. Poems* (Rolls) II. 82 But his predestinacion may onlich save soulis, and his prevy presciens may dampne whom him list. **1562** *Articles of Religion* xvii, Of Predestination and Election. **1577** NORTHBROOKE *Dicing* (1843) 23 It is a most sure signe and token of our predestination, glad and willingly to heare the worde of God. **1579** W. WILKINSON *Confut. Familye of Loue, Brief Descr.*, The most blessed and comfortable doctrine of Predestination. **1850** BP. BROWNE *Exp. 39 Art.* xvii. (1878) 404 The Gallican clergy state, that their own belief had hitherto been that God's predestination was founded on prevision of faith. **1875** MANNING *Mission H. Ghost* i. 11 Do not misunderstand me..as if that predestination of God in any way conflicts with the perfect freedom of the human will. **1887** E. S. FFOULKES *Predestination* in *Dict. Chr. Biog.* IV. 466/1 Predestination is but another word for election,..carried out in instalments on earth, but registered in the archives of heaven in advance. **1901** B. J. KIDD *39 Articles* II. II. xvii. 157 The tenet of particular redemption, which held that God's predestination had reference not to mankind at large, but to this and that particular individual.

b. The action of God (insisted upon in some systems of doctrine, esp. those associated with the names of St. Augustine, St. Thomas Aquinas, and Calvin), in foreordaining the future lot and fate of all mankind in this life and after death (including their salvation or perdition); and, generally, His foreordaining of whatsoever comes to pass. In this sense also a doctrine of orthodox Islam.

Sometimes called *duple* or *duplex* predestination. But as to the use of the word for foreordaining to reprobation, see Note under PREDESTINATE *v.* 1 b.

c **1374** CHAUCER *Boeth.* IV. pr. vi. 104 (Camb. MS.) To maken questions of..the ordyr of destine..predestinacion diuine and of the lyberte of fre wille. **1387–8** T. USK *Test. Love* III. ix. (Skeat) l. 8 Though predestinacion be as wel of good as of badde. **1509** HAWES *Past. Pleas.* xxvii. (Percy Soc.) 123 For many one..lytell thought that tribulacion To them was ordeyned by predestinacion. **1563–87** FOXE *A. & M.* (1684) III. 292 Between Predestination and Election, this difference there is; Predestination is as well to the reprobate, as to the Elect. Election pertaineth only to them that be saved. Predestination, in that it respecteth the Reprobate, is called Reprobation: in that it respecteth the saved, is called Election. **1645** USSHER *Body Div.* (1647) 91 What is Predestination? It is the speciall decree of God, whereby he hath..fore-ordained all reasonable creatures to a certain and everlasting estate of glory in heaven, or flame in hell. **1673** MILTON *True Relig.* Wks. 1851 V. 409 The Calvinist is taxt with Predestination, and to make God the Author of Sin; not with any dishonourable thought of God, but it may be overzealously asserting his absolute power. **1689–90** TEMPLE *Ess. Heroic Virtue* Wks. 1731 I. 22 The Saracens..were animated by another Spirit, which was the Mahometan Persuasion of Predestination. **1755** JORTIN *Diss.* ii. 29 *note*, Our King James the first made an edict, that no divine, under the dignity of a bishop or a dean, should presume to preach upon the profound mysteries of Predestination. **1882** W. H. FREMANTLE in *Dict. Chr. Biog.* III. 46/2 (*Hieronymus*) He [Jerome] reduces predestination to God's foreknowledge of human determination. **1885** M. DODS in *Encycl. Brit.* XIX. 668/2 In Islam..the orthodox doctrine is thus stated by Al-Berkevi. 'It is necessary to confess that good and evil take place by the predestination and predetermination of God, that all that has been and all that will be was decreed in eternity and written on the *preserved table*. *Ibid.* 669/1 The doctrine of predestination was first formulated in the church by Augustine.

c. In reference to a similar doctrine in certain philosophies (not necessarily implying Divine action).

1858 R. A. VAUGHAN *Ess. & Rem.* I. 33 The gloomy fate of Aeschylus, and the predestination of the Stoics, were repugnant to a heart of such a temperament.

2. In lighter or more general sense: Previous determination or appointment; fate, destiny. Cf. PREDESTINE 1 b.

1631 JORDEN *Nat. Bathes* xii. (1669) 104 A natural necessity, or *fatum*, or *predestination*, that frames every member and part of the body to the best use for the creature. **1779–81** JOHNSON *L.P.*, *Pope* Wks. IV. 73 A kind of moral predestination, or over-ruling principle which cannot be resisted. **1901** SIR W. HARCOURT in *Daily Chron.* 11 July 5/6 It is what you may call political predestination, and it appears to me that it indicates a satisfactory condition of things, because by the law of Nature we younger sons are in the majority.

Hence **predestiˈnationism**, belief in predestination or the system of thought it entails; **predestiˈnationist** (*rare*) = PREDESTINARIAN A. So †**preˈdestinatist** (*Obs. rare*).

1630 G. WIDDOWES *Schysmatical Puritan* Pref., The Presuming Predestinatist is he, whose purenes is an inspired knowledge, that hee shalbe saved by Gods absolute election. **1894** MASKELYNE *Sharps & Flats* iii. 59 There is no such thing as chance, says the predestinationist. **1901** G. H. HOWISON *Let.* 21 July in R. B. Perry *Tht. & Char. W. James* (1935) II. 221 *Of course* I don't reconcile predestinationism and capricious free-will. **1937** *Mind* XLVI. 287 The unsatisfactory answer offered by Leibniz to readers frightened by *his* Predestinationism.

predestinative (prɪˈdɛstɪnətɪv), *a. rare.* [f. as PREDESTINATE *v.* + -IVE.] Having the quality of predestinating.

1833 COLERIDGE in *Lit. Rem.* (1838) III. 413 The predestinative force of a free agent's own will in certain absolute acts, determinations, or elections.

predestinator (prɪˈdɛstɪneɪtə(r)). [agent-n. in L. form f. PREDESTINATE *v.* + -OR 2; so F. *prédestinateur* (Littré), in sense 2 below.]

1. He who predestinates.

1700 C. NESSE *Antid. Armin.* (1827) 58 The act of predestination is put in the will..of the predestinated, and not in that of the divine predestinator.

2. One who believes in or maintains the doctrine of predestination; a predestinarian.

1579 W. WILKINSON *Confut. Familye of Loue, Brief Descr.*, Those that are called Frewil men (for so are they termed of the Predestinators). **1647** COWLEY *Mistress*, *My Fate* iii, Let all Prædestinators me produce, Who struggle with eternal bonds in vain. **1812** *Religionism* 29 Preachers, predestinators some, and others Arminians. **1956** R. MACAULAY *Towers of Trebizond* xxi. 240 It is the Predestinators not the Pelagians who, as it says in the 9th Article, do vainly talk.

Hence **preˈdestinatory** *a.* (*rare*) = PREDESTINATE *ppl. a.* 2.

1967 B. WRIGHT tr. *Queneau's Between Blue & Blue* xix. 203 If society gave me this predestinatory name, nature for her part provided me with peculiarly active grey matter.

predestine (prɪˈdɛstɪn), *v.* Also 5 **-en**, **-ayne**, **-yne**, 7 **-in**. [a. F. *prédestiner* (12th c. in Hatz.-Darm.), or ad. L. *prædestināre*: see PREDESTINATE *v.*]

1. *trans.* To destine beforehand; to appoint, ordain, or decree previously. **a.** *Theol.*, etc. To foreordain by an eternal purpose, in the way of a Divine decree or of fate; to appoint beforehand by destiny, or to some destiny. (Mostly in *passive*. Also *absol.*)

c **1380** [see PREDESTINING below]. *a* **1400–50** *Alexander* 305 Be-soȝt sekirly þis sire..þat scho myȝt weterly wete..Quatkyn poynt or plyte predestend hire were. **1483** CAXTON *Cato* E vj, Syth al were ordeyned and predestyned whan man shold deye. **1579–80** NORTH *Plutarch* (1595) 145 If..some bitter aduersitie and ouerthrowe be predestined vnto us. **1687** SETTLE *Refl. Dryden* 12 Heaven predestins nothing for any man that should raise him to an excess of joy or grief. **1725** POPE *Odyss.* I. 24 The day predestin'd to reward his woes. **1838** LYTTON *Leila* v. iii, The fall of Granada is predestined. **1879** FARRAR *St. Paul* II. 243 God predestines; man is free. How this is we cannot say.

b. In lighter or more general sense: To determine, settle, or fix upon beforehand; to appoint as if by fate or destiny; to fate, doom. (Usually in *passive*.)

1642 MILTON *Apol. Smect.* viii, Voluminous papers, whose best folios are predestined to no better end than to make winding-sheets in lent for pilchers. **1742** YOUNG *Nt. Th.* v. 194 Here the soul sits in council; ponders past, Predestines future action. **1845** DARWIN *Voy. Nat.* xix. (1873) 441 The white man who seems predestined to inherit the country. **1868** LYNCH *Rivulet* CLVII. iii, Within the egg how darkly lies Even the bird of paradise, Predestined for the sunniest skies!

†**2.** *loosely.* To betoken infallibly beforehand; to presage irrevocably. *Obs. rare.*

1647 COWLEY *Mistr.*, *Tree* v, Alas, poor Youth, thy Love will never thrive! This blasted Tree Predestines it.

Hence **preˈdestine** *ppl. a.* (*rare*); **preˈdestined** *ppl. a.*, destined or appointed beforehand; fated, doomed; **preˈdestining** *vbl. sb.*

c **1380** WYCLIF *Serm.* Sel. Wks. I. 179 Þe secounde persone of God..bringiþ wiþ him a grace þat clerkes clepen predestynynge. **1612** DRAYTON *Poly-olb.* ii. 26 How happie floods are yee, From our predestin'd plagues that priuiledged bee. **1624** MASSINGER *Parl. Love* IV. v, And that rich merchants, advocates, and doctors,..were Predestined cuckolds. **1740** C. PITT *Æneid* II. 169 He..Doom'd to the slaughter my predestin'd head. *a* **1825** in Hone *Every-day Bk.* I. 338 Predestinings of joy. **1867** FREEMAN *Norm. Conq.* I. iii. 158 Marked out in the eyes of all men as the predestined heirs of Charles. **1962** A. HUXLEY *Island* xiii. 204 These people are the propagandist's predestine victims.

predestiny (prɪˈdɛstɪnɪ). *rare.* Also 5 **-destiné**. [f. PRE- A. 2 + DESTINY, after PREDESTINE, etc. In Chaucer *predestiné*, a. obs. F. *prédestinée* (Cotgr.).] Preappointed destiny or fate; predestination.

c **1374** CHAUCER *Troylus* IV. 938 (966) In here merites soþly for to be, As they shul come by predestine. **1853** JERDAN *Autobiog.* IV. xiii. 229 Instead of inherent stupidity, or a predestiny to be correct. **1875** tr. *Schmidt's Desc. & Darw.* 191 Anxious to rescue design, or at least the 'purpose'—in short predestiny in the evolutionary series of Nature.

predeterminable (priːdɪˈtɜːmɪnəb(ə)l), *a. rare.* [f. PREDETERMINE + -ABLE; or f. PRE- A. 3 +

DETERMINABLE.] Capable of being predetermined; determinable beforehand. Hence **prede,termina'bility**, the quality of being predeterminable.

1835 COLERIDGE in *Fraser's Mag.* XII. 620 A privilege which it owes to the simplicity, the paucity, and the predeterminability of its processes. **1901** *Daily Mail* 31 Dec. 5 The sex of future man will be predeterminable. For a time one sex will predominate, then another.

prede'terminant, *a.* (*sb.*) *rare.* [a. F. *prédéterminant* adj., or late L. *prædēterminānt-em*, pres. pple. of *prædēterminâre* to PREDETERMINE.] **A.** *adj.* Predetermining, predestinating.

1677 GALE *Crt. Gentiles* II. IV. 520, I, as yet, cannot..see any cogent reason, why the said previous concurse may not be termed predeterminant.

† **B.** *sb.* = PREDETERMINER b. *Obs.*

1660 PEARSON *No Necess. Reform. Doctr. Ch. Eng.* 16 No man thinks a Praedeterminant or a Jansenian to be inclining to an Arminian.

predeterminate (priːdɪˈtɜːmɪnət), *a.* [ad. late L. *prædēterminăt-us*, pa. pple. of *prædēterminâre* to PREDETERMINE.] = PREDETERMINED 1.

1635 J. HAYWARD tr. *Biondi's Banish'd Virg.* 54 Not casuall, but predeterminate and certaine. **1655** BP. RICHARDSON *On O. Test.* 313 We cannot break through the bounds of Gods providence and predeterminate purpose in the guidance of them [events]. **1897** *Woman's Home Comp.* Dec., There is no predeterminate set of conditions for holiday-making that need tie adventurous hands.

Hence **prede'terminately** *adv.*

1883 GILMOUR *Mongols* xviii. 241 A Doctor of Divinity.. deliberately and predeterminately lied, that he might retain possession of a few inches of wood.

† **prede'terminate**, *v. Obs. rare.* [f. ppl. stem of late L. *prædēterminâre*.] = PREDETERMINE 1, 2. Hence † **prede'terminating** *ppl. a.*

1638 CHILLINGW. *Relig. Prot.* I. ii. §162. 118 God predeterminates men to all their Actions good, bad, and indifferent. *a* **1643** LD. FALKLAND, etc. *Infallibility* (1646) 13 They have made differences among them (as whether the Pope be infallible; whether God predeterminate every action). **1645** RUTHERFORD *Tryal & Tri. Faith* (1845) 93 The predeterminating grace of Christ.

predetermination (priːdɪtɜːmɪˈneɪʃən). [n. of action from PREDETERMINE *v.*; or (in some uses) f. PRE- A. 2 + DETERMINATION. So F. *prédétermination* (1636 in Hatz.-Darm.).] The action of predetermining; the fact or condition of being predetermined; previous determination.

1. A previous decision; a decision given beforehand, or before due examination or discussion.

1646 BP. MAXWELL *Burd. Issach.* in *Phenix* (1708) II. 287 They depose the Queen Regent; the predetermination being given, that it was lawful for them to do so, by Mr. Knox, and Mr. Wilcocks. **1794** S. WILLIAMS *Vermont* 254 That there appeared a manifest inequality, not to say predetermination, that Congress should request of their constituents power to judge and determine in the cause.

2. A previous determining or fixing of the limits or extent *of* something; = PRELIMITATION. ? *Obs.*

1637–50 ROW *Hist. Kirk* (Wodrow Soc.) 500 Aganis the predetermination and perlimitation of the Assemblie, they gave six Reasons.

3. The action of settling or ordaining beforehand what is to take place; the fact of being so settled; previous appointment; predestination.

1647 JER. TAYLOR *Lib. Proph.* Ep. Ded. 33 The Calvinists are fierce in the matters of absolute Predetermination. **1702** ADDISON *Dial. Medals* ii. 87 He makes this difference to arise from the forecast and praedetermination of the Gods themselves. **1836** H. ROGERS *J. Howe* vi. (1863) 160 Those who held extreme opinions on the subject of Divine predetermination. **1894** *Westm. Gaz.* 13 July 2/3 To impress us with the wonderful co-ordination and predetermination of natural laws.

4. A previous determination, tendency, or direction given (*to* something).

a **1716** SOUTH *Serm.* (1744) VII. v. 94 Some..assert that the creature never advances into action, but by an irresistible pre-determination of the faculty to that action.

5. A previous mental determination or resolve; an antecedent fixed intention (*to do* something).

1782 MISS BURNEY *Cecilia* VIII. iii, Hear me, then, I beg of you, with no pre-determination to disregard me. **1831** CARLYLE *Misc. Ess., Nibelungenlied* (1872) III. 134 In spite of her rigorous predeterminations, some kindness for him is already gliding in. **1897** MARY KINGSLEY *W. Africa* 369 Mr. Winwood Reade..went down..with a pre-determination to prove Du Chaillu was wrong.

prede'terminative, *a. rare.* [f. PREDETERMINE or PREDETERMINATE *v.*: see -ATIVE.]

1. Having the quality of predetermining.

a **1678** MARVELL *Def. J. Howe* Wks. (Grosart) IV. 170 If men shall also assert a predeterminative concourse of God to our wil, it seems to have too much of original perverseness. **1678** GALE *Crt. Gentiles* III. 23 This efficacious concurse, as it determines and applies the second cause to act, is both in sacred Scripture and by scholastic Theologues termed determinative and predeterminative.

2. *Gram.* Having the quality of, or acting as, a predeterminer.

1961 R. B. LONG *Sentence & its Parts* ii. 42 In *only John* the adverb *only* is essentially predeterminative exactly as it is in *only the older children.*

predetermine (priːdɪˈtɜːmɪn), *v.* [ad. Chr. L. *prædēterminâre* (Augustine), f. *præ*, PRE- A. 1 + *dēterminâre* to DETERMINE. Cf. F. *prédéterminer* (1530 in Hatz.-Darm.).] *trans.* To determine beforehand (in various senses: cf. DETERMINE).

1. *trans.* To fix, settle, or decide beforehand; to ordain or decree beforehand, to predestine. Also with *obj. cl.* or *inf.*

1625 DONNE *Serm.* lxvi. (1640) 668 That there was a concurrence of the whole Trinity, to make me in Adam, according to that Image which they were, and according to that Idea, which they had pre-determined. *a* **1667** JER. TAYLOR *Serm.* I. ix. (R.), God..prepared joys infinite and never ceasing for man before he had created him; but he did not predetermine him to any evil. **1722** DE FOE *Plague* (1840) 13 Every man's end being predetermined, and unalterably beforehand decreed. **1841** MYERS *Cath. Th.* IV. xv. 259 The Gospel was no after-thought, as it were,..but came to pass as God had predetermined. **1884** W. J. COURTHOPE *Addison* ix. 176 It had evidently been predetermined by the designers of the *Spectator* that the Club should consist of certain recognised and familiar types.

2. To give an antecedent direction or tendency to; to direct or impel beforehand (*to* something).

a **1667** JER. TAYLOR *Serm. Tit. ii.* 7 Wks. 1850 VIII. 520 We are so prepossessed and predetermined to misconstruction by false apostles without, and prevailing passions within. **1678** GALE *Crt. Gentiles* III. 16 The wil predetermined to one act has an habitual indifference or radical flexibilitie to the opposite act. **1858** BUCKLE *Civiliz.* (1873) II. viii. 576 Those general causes..were predetermining the nation to habits of loyalty and of superstition, which grew to a height fatal to the spirit of liberty.

3. *intr.* To determine or resolve beforehand or previously (*to do* something).

1823 F. CLISSOLD *Ascent Mt. Blanc* 23, I should instantly have proceeded to the summit, had I not predetermined to abide by whatever advice the guides might..give. **1848** LYTTON *Harold* VIII. vi, He had almost predetermined to assent to his brother's prayer.

Hence **prede'termining** *ppl. a.*

a **1678** MARVELL *Def. J. Howe* Wks. (Grosart) IV. 175 Another while, 'tis predetermining influence. *a* **1854** B. B. EDWARDS in Spurgeon *Treas. Dav.* Ps. cxxxix. VII. 231 If, anterior to all finite existence, his predetermining decree went forth.

predetermined (priːdɪˈtɜːmɪnd), *ppl. a.* [f. prec. + -ED[1].]

1. Determined beforehand; settled, decided, or decreed beforehand.

1660 tr. *Amyraldus' Treat. conc. Relig.* III. ix. 496 Christ was born at the predetermin'd time. **1819** G. S. FABER *Dispensations* (1823) I. 94 How shall we account..for his having beheld from afar..the predetermined day of the yet future Deliverer? **1873** HAMERTON *Intell. Life* X. v. (1875) 394 A predetermined quantity of little things.

2. Resolved beforehand (*to do* something).

1768 STERNE *Sent. Journ.* (1775) I. 6, I was predetermined not to give him a single sous. **1772** *Junius Lett.* Pref. (1820) 14 No reasonable man would be so eager to possess himself of the invidious power..if he were not pre-determined to make use of it. **1872** MINTO *Eng. Prose Lit.* II. viii. 527 An audience predetermined not to be convinced.

prede'terminer. **1.** [f. PREDETERMINE *v.* + -ER[1].] **a.** One who or that which predetermines. *rare*$^{-0}$. † **b.** A believer in predetermination (prop. *predeterminist*): = PREDESTINATOR 2 (*obs.*).

a **1678** MARVELL *Def. J. Howe* Wks. (Grosart) IV. 225 Its business here is to defend the predeterminers' opinion.

2. *Gram.* [f. PRE- B. 1 + DETERMINER[1] 3.] One of a class of limiting expressions that precede the determiner. Also *attrib.*

1959 J. SLEDD *Short Introd. to Eng. Gram.* 116 The predeterminers, finally, are rather various but limited in number. **1961** *Amer. Speech* XXXVI. 159 It is customary to describe the English nominal as consisting of a sequence of constituents: predeterminers, determiners, adjectives, [etc.]. **1961** R. B. LONG *Sentence & its Parts* ii. 40 Predeterminer modifiers generally are adverbial in function, and mensurant, selectional, differential, conjunctive, or adjunct-like in force. **1964** [see DETERMINER[1] 3]. **1965** O. THOMAS *Transformational Gram.* iv. 84 Like the other two classes of determiners, the predeterminers have a unique feature: they are invariably separated from the regular determiners by the word *of.* **1975** *Language* LI. 990 The articles are analysed with respect to..a class of modifiers sometimes known as predeterminers (*several, three,* etc.).

prede'terminism. [f. PREDETERMINE, after DETERMINISM.] The theory or doctrine that events or acts are predetermined; determinism.

1888 J. MARTINEAU *Stud. Relig.* II. III. ii. 325 This Predeterminism introduces new contradictions.

pre-development: see PRE- B. 2 a.

pre-devise, -devour: see PRE- A. 1.

predevote (priːdɪˈvəʊt), *ppl. a. rare.* [f. PRE- A. 1 + DEVOTE *a.*] Predevoted, foredoomed.

1819 SHELLEY *P. Bell 3rd* Prol., The next Peter Bell was he, Predevote, like you and me, To good or evil as may come.

predevote (priːdɪˈvəʊt), *v.* [PRE- A. 1.] *trans.* To devote beforehand. So **prede'voted** *ppl. a.*

1815 *Zeluca* I. 377 Sir John was unconsciously pre-devoted to one, and by the other Lady for the third set [of dances]. *Ibid.* III. 2 The incertitude [seemed] far more trying than conviction of Erdestone's pre-devoted affections.

predia'betic, *a.* and *sb. Path.* [PRE- B. 1.] **A.** *adj.* Of, pertaining to, or designating a person in whom it appears that diabetes mellitus is likely to develop, but who does not exhibit its full symptoms. **B.** *sb.* A prediabetic person.

1921 *Jrnl. Amer. Med. Assoc.* 8 Jan. 79/2 A prediabetic stage in fat persons has been recognized. *Ibid.* 83/2 It is to the diabetic patient and his relatives that one can look most confidently for help in preventing diabetes... Such measures, however, are but general, and they will never suffice for the prediabetic. **1954** *Jrnl. Clin. Endocrinol.* XIV. 177 The high rates of fetal loss and the production of large babies are exemplified by the pregnancies of pre-diabetic women in the Cape Town region. **1962** H. ZAROWITZ in Ellenberg & Rifkin *Clin. Diabetes Mellitus* xi. 164 Because the hereditary potential for diabetes has been firmly established, this prediabetic state can occur at any time from birth to senescence. **1970** D. M. KIPNIS in Cerasi & Luft *Pathogenesis of Diabetes Mellitus* 46 Insulin sensitivity may be *increased* rather than decreased in pre-diabetics. **1976** *Billings* (Montana) *Gaz.* 27 June 1-B/5 Our baby will most likely be pre-diabetic (genetically disposed to diabetes, but not necessarily diabetic).

So **predia'betes**, the prediabetic state.

1937 *Endocrinol.* XXI. 195 'Prediabetes' in obesity is of interest because of its possible bearing on certain problems concerning the intermediate carbohydrate metabolism in obesity. **1964** *New Scientist* 27 Aug. 482/3 'Prediabetes', or the early stages, has been found in a surprisingly high percentage of the population.., and it is now known that definite changes can be detected before there is a noticeable rise in the blood sugar level. **1970** CAMERINI-DÁVALOS & COLE *Early Diabetes* IV. 256 Prediabetes is the condition of those persons who, because of a strong hereditary tendency, have a high probability for the later development of diabetes but in whom at the time of study, all tests of carbohydrate tolerance yield normal results.

predial (ˈpriːdɪəl), *a.* (*sb.*) Also 7- **prædial.** [ad. med.L. *prædiālis*, f. L. *prædi-um* a farm, estate, manor: see -AL[1]. So F. *prédial* (16th c.).]

A. *adj.* **1.** Consisting of or pertaining to land or farms; 'real', landed; pertaining to the country, rural; agrarian.

a **1529** SKELTON *Col. Cloute* 932 For they wyll haue no losse Of a peny nor of a crosse Of theyr predyall landes. **1592** UNTON *Corr.* (Roxb.) 322, I neglect not prediall matters, though I observe most pollilicall. **1652** URQUHART *Jewel* Wks. (1834) 207 A pecunial or prædial recompense will..be very answerable to the nature of that service. **1796** W. MARSHALL *W. England* I. 100 Farm lands..having passed..from the state of common pasturage, to the predial state. **1845** R. W. HAMILTON *Pop. Educ.* iii. (ed. 2) 42 Against the quick, astute, excitable intellect, which is commonly allowed to a dense population,..many contrasts are set up in favour of the predial race.

2. Arising from or consequent upon the occupation of farms or lands; agrarian.

1641 *Lords Spiritual* 4 Because a Bishop having place in Parliament as a Peere, is, in respect of his possessions, as a prediall Nobility, and not inherent in his person. *a* **1667** JER. TAYLOR *Serm. Gunpowder Treason* Wks. 1831 IV. 282 The delinquent loseth all his right whatsoever, prædial, personal, and of privilege. **1833** *Blackw. Mag.* XXXIII. 570 To repress the predial or rural disorders of Ireland. *a* **1881** DISRAELI in *Edin. Rev.* July (1903) 204 [Politicians of every school have recognised a distinction] between political and predial sources of discontent in Ireland.

b. *predial tithe*: tithe arising or derived from the produce of the soil.

1464 *Rolls of Parlt.* V. 518/2 All maner tithes, aswell prediall as personall. **1531** *Dial. on Laws Eng.* II. lv. (1638) 169 The predial tith of trees is of such trees as bring forth fruits. **1656** BLOUNT *Glossogr.*, *Predial Tythes*, are those we call great Tythes, as of Corn and Hay. **1707** E. CHAMBERLAYNE *Pres. St. Eng.* II. (ed. 22) 128 The Priests of every particular Parish, who are commonly called the Rectors, unless the Predial Tythes are impropriated, and then they are stiled Vicars. **1834** *Brit. Husb.* I. 71 The prædial-tithe..arises from every product of the earth, whether grain, pulse, hay, plants, fruit, or wood, and becomes due whenever the crop is taken, even although there may be more than one grown upon the same land within the year.

3. Attached to farms or to the land; owing service as tenanting land, as *predial serf, slave, bondage, labour, servitude, slavery, villeinage,* etc.

1754 HUME *Hist. Eng.* I. App. i. 97 There were two kinds of slaves..household slaves..and prædial or rustic. **1757** BURKE *Abridgm. Eng. Hist.* II. i, And here these writers fix the origin of personal and predial servitude in England. **1818** HALLAM *Mid. Ages* (1872) I. ii. I. 150 Scarcely raised above the condition of predial servitude. **1839** KEIGHTLEY *Hist. Eng.* I. 300 The condition of the inferior ranks..had been that of villanage or predial bondage. **1864** KINGSLEY *Rom. & Teut.* 20 *note*, The early romancers..give pictures of Roman praedial slavery too painful to quote. **1876** DIGBY *Real Prop.* i. §3. 25 *note*, In the Domesday of St. Paul's we find that praedial services were due from three classes of persons, called villani, cotarii, bordarii.

b. *predial servitude* (*Sc. Law*): a servitude affecting heritable property; a servitude constituted over one subject or tenement in favour of the proprietor of another subject or tenement; e.g. a right of way through the property of another.

a **1765** ERSKINE *Inst. Laws Scotl.* (1773) II. ix. §5 Real or predial [servitudes are constituted] principally in favour of a tenement, and only by consequence to a person, as the owner of that tenement. **18..** W. BELL *Dict. Law Scot.* (1861) 754/1 The tenement over which a predial servitude is constituted is called the servient tenement,..that in favour of which the servitude is constituted is called the dominant tenement.

B. *sb.* (elliptical use of adj.) †A predial tithe (*obs.*); a predial slave.

1531 *Dial. on Laws Eng.* II. lv. (1638) 170 There cannot be two predials of one thing. **1844** EMERSON *Addr. W.I. Emancip.* 11 These conditions were, that the prædials should owe three-fourths of the profits of their labour to their masters for six years, and the nonprædials for four years. **1873** GARDNER *Hist. Jamaica* 293 The term of apprenticeship was limited to six years for field hands or predials, as they were termed.

Hence **'predialist**, one of a class or order of landholders; **predi'ality**, the state of being predial.

1762 tr. *Busching's Syst. Geog.* II. 14 The archiepiscopal and episcopal gentry, who are stiled praedialists, enjoy the same privileges as the Hungarian nobility. *Ibid.* 22 The gentry are termed predialists. **1897** MAITLAND *Domesday & Beyond* 28 There has been in this condition of the *theów* a certain element of prædiality.

pre-diastolic: see PRE- B. 1.

'prediatory, *a.* [ad. L. *prædiātōri-us*, f. *prædiātor* a purchaser of mortgaged lands, a dealer in landed estates, f. *prædium*: see PREDIAL.] Of or relating to the sale of land.

1727-41 CHAMBERS *Cycl.* s.v. *Debt.*, *Prædiatory Debt*, is that arising from an alienation of lands, &c. the whole purchase whereof has not been paid.

predicability (prɛdɪkə'bɪlɪtɪ). [ad. med.L. *prædicābilitās* (*a* 1280 in Albertus Magnus *De Predicabilibus*), f. *prædicābilis*: see PREDICABLE and -ITY.] The quality of being predicable.

1785 REID *Intell. Powers* v. vi. (1803) II. 178 Universals have no real existence. When we ascribe existence to them ..their existence is nothing but predicability, or the capacity of being attributed to a subject. **1965** F. SOMMERS in M. Black *Philos. in Amer.* 275, I shall use a reverse arrow to stand for the predicability relation between two terms.

predicable ('prɛdɪkəb(ə)l), *a.* and *sb.* [a. F. *prédicable* adj. and sb. (1582 in Hatz.-Darm.), or ad. L. *prædicābilis*; in med.L. that may be affirmed, predicable, neut. *prædicābile*, pl. *-bilia*, as sb. (in Lambert of Auxerre, Petrus Hispanus, and Albertus Magnus, 13th c.), whence B.; f. L. *prædicāre* to PREDICATE: see -ABLE.]

A. *adj.* That may be predicated or affirmed; capable of being asserted.

1598 FLORIO, *Predicabile*, predicable. **1667** WATERHOUSE *Fire Lond.* 51 Made that predicable of London which Florus writes of Samnium. **1722** WOLLASTON *Relig. Nat.* v. 73 It will always be predicable of him, that he was the doer of it. *c* **1730** A. BAXTER *Enq. Nat. Soul* vii. §18. 320 A thing that hath solidity, figure, &c., as properties belonging to it, or predicable concerning it, must be a solid, figured thing. **1842** ABP. THOMSON *Laws Th.* §69 (1860) 11 Predicable classes, or classes of conceptions which can stand as predicates. **1843** CARLYLE *Past & Pr.* III. xii, A people of whom great good is predicable. **1884** tr. *Lotze's Metaph.* 142 All relations which can be discovered between the two are predicable of them on exactly the same footing.

B. *sb.* In general sense: That which may be predicated.

1785 REID *Intell. Powers* v. i. (1803) II. 110 A predicable therefore signifies the same thing as an attribute. **1837** HALLAM *Hist. Lit.* I. I. iv. §79. 322 This method appears to be only an artificial disposition..of subjects and predicables, according to certain distinctions. **1906** JOSEPH *Introd. Logic* iv. 54 A predicable is merely that which can be predicated: viz. that which is universal, not an individual; all kinds, qualities, states, relations, etc., are predicable, and they are universal, because they may be exemplified in and belong to more than one individual subject.

b. *spec.* in Aristotelian Logic (in *pl.*, tr. Gr. κατηγορικά): The classes or kinds of predicates viewed relatively to their subjects, to one or other of which classes every predicated thing may be referred; second intentions of predicates considered in relation to subjects.

Of these relations Aristotle (*Topica* I. iv, v) recognized four, viz. *genus* (γένος), *definition* (ὅρος), *property* (ἴδιον), *accident* (συμβεβηκός). Under *genus* he made the subdivision of *difference* (διαφορά). The list was subsequently modified by Porphyry and by the early Schoolmen, by the omission of *definition*, and addition of *species* (εἶδος), giving the 'Five Predicables', *genus*, *species*, *difference*, *property*, *accident*.

1551 T. WILSON *Logike* 3 b, I begin with the predicables because they shewe how much every word doth comprehend in it selfe. *Ibid.*, They be called predicables because some one thing is spoken of an other. **1656** BLOUNT *Glossogr.* s.v., In Logick there are five Predicables, otherwise called Porphyries five terms. **1766** GOLDSM. *Vic. W.* vii, The essence of spirituality may be referred to the second predicable. **1864** BOWEN *Logic* v. 112 In his analysis of Judgments, Aristotle was led to consider how many kinds of Predicates there are, when viewed relatively to their Subjects; in other words, to determine the Second Intentions of Predicates considered in relation to Subjects. Thus was formed his celebrated doctrine of the Predicables ..which was considerably modified, but not improved, by his followers, Porphyry and the Schoolmen. **1906** JOSEPH *Introd. Logic* iv. 92 The Porphyrian list of predicables substitutes *Species* for *Definition*. But that difference implies a change in the point of view. *Ibid.* 96 It would be well to abandon the Porphyrian list of predicables in favour of the Aristotelian.

c. In the philosophy of Kant: see quot.

1902 *Baldwin's Dict. Philos.* II. 325/2 Kant undertook to set up his own 'predicables of the pure understanding', which were to be derivative conceptions under the categories.

Hence **'predicableness** (1727 in Bailey, vol. II); **'predicably** *adv.*

1727-41 CHAMBERS *Cycl.*, *Predicably*, *prædicabiliter*, is used in the schools in opposition to *predicamentally*.—Thus, matter is said to be united to form *predicably*, or *per accidens*; to exclude the notion of a predicamental accident.

predicament (prɪ'dɪkəmənt). Also 7 præ-. [ad. late L. *prædicāmentum* (Augustine) something predicated, a predicament, a quality (transl. Gr. κατηγορία of Aristotle), f. *prædicāre*: see PREDICATE *v.* and -MENT. So F. *prédicament* (13th c. in Hatz.-Darm.).]

1. That which is predicated or asserted; *spec.* in *Logic*, (in *pl.*) the ten categories or classes of predications formed by Aristotle: see CATEGORY 1.

c **1380** WYCLIF *Sel. Wks.* I. 195 þese foolis moten lerne predicamentis and ten kyndis of þingis, and þanne þei moun se her foli. **1451** CAPGRAVE. *Life St. Aug.* (E.E.T.S.) 11 þe book of Aristotle cleped his Cathegories, we clepe hem at þese dayes þe Predicamentis. **1579** FULKE *Refut. Rastel* 752 He remembreth what the Predicament *Vbi* meaneth. **1628** MILTON *Vac. Exerc.*, Then *Ens* is represented as Father of the Prædicaments his ten Sons. **1655** CULPEPPER *Riverius* x. ix. 308 Heat is not the chief agent in breeding of Worms, which are in the prædicaments of substance, and heat is but an accident. **1788** REID *Aristotle's Log.* vi. §1. 135 The predicaments and predicables have a like title to our veneration as antiquities. **1801** WOODHOUSE in *Phil. Trans.* XCI. 99 Bringing $x\sqrt{-1}$ under the predicament of quantity. **1864** BOWEN *Logic* v. 116 Having determined the Second Intentions of Predicates, which are the Predicables, Aristotle attempted to carry the analysis of Judgments one step farther by determining their First Intentions, and was thus led to form his celebrated list of the ten Categories or Predicaments, [in which] he inquired how many and what particular things may be predicated of any Subject.

2. A class about which a particular statement is made; = CATEGORY 2.

a **1548** HALL *Chron.*, *Edw. IV* 248 b, We beyng called reasonable creatures and in that predicament, compared and ioyned with Angelles. **1597** HOWSON *Serm.* 24 Dec. 26 Buying and selling are both in a [= one] predicament (for nothing is bought but that which is sold, & *contra*). **1618** LD. SHEFFIELD in *Fortescue Papers* (Camden) 52 Wherof some scandall hath fallne upon me as conceived to bee in the same predicamente. **1749** FIELDING *Tom Jones* IX. iii, Irish ladies of strict virtue, and many Northern lasses of the same predicament. **1845** NAPIER *Conq. Scinde* II. i. 227 The Beloochs holding the forts were part of these bands; they belonged to the same predicament.

3. State of being; condition, situation, position; *esp.* an unpleasant, trying, or dangerous situation.

1586 A. DAY *Eng. Secretary* I. (1625) 141 Supposing that ..I should still haue found you in the same predicament, without alteration. **1598** BARRET *Theor. Warres* II. i. 27 This squadron standeth in such predicament, that any Gentleman..may serue as soldier in the same. **1645** MILTON *Tetrach.* Wks. 1851 IV. 221 Sin is not in a predicament to be measur'd and modify'd, but is alwaies an excesse. **1771** *Junius Lett.* I. (1820) 260 There is a proverb concerning persons in the predicament of this gentleman. **1827** SCOTT *Highl. Widow* v, His deep sense of the deceit which had been practised on him, and of the cruel predicament to which he was reduced. **1865** CARLYLE *Fredk. Gt.* XX. vii. (1872) IX. 152 Werner finds himself suddenly in a most awkward predicament. **1882** O'DONOVAN *Merv Oasis* I. 325 Here was a predicament, inasmuch as I was in a desperate hurry.

†**4.** Preaching, 'predication'. *Obs. rare*$^{-1}$.

1765 *Mumbo Chumbo* 12 To 'stablish you in this, it is the Drift Of Solomon's most wise Predicament.

Hence **pre'dicamentist** (*humorous nonce-wd.*), one who is in a predicament.

1827 *Blackw. Mag.* XXI. 895 Of the three classes of Predicamentists, the fiercest are the Plucked.

predicamental (prɪdɪkə'mɛntəl), *a.* Also 7 præ-. [f. prec. + -AL[1].] Of or pertaining to a predicament, or the predicaments.

1601 DEACON & WALKER *Spirits & Divels* 89 They haue.. no predicamentall, but an intelligible quantity. **1661** GLANVILL *Van. Dogm.* xxiv. 240 More can be pleaded for such a Metaphysical innovation, then can for a specifical diversity among our Predicamental Opposites. **1681** R. WITTIE *Surv. Heavens* 38 God is an infinite Essence that highly transcends all Predicamental Notions. **1715** M. DAVIES *Athen. Brit.* I. Pref. 5 The whole Predicamental Climax, or different Gradations of Beings, Persons, Times and Places. **1843** MILL *Logic* I. vi. §4 From the main trunk of the Predicamental Tree, which included nothing but what was of the essence of the species.

Hence **predica'mentally** *adv.*

c **1600** *Timon* v. iv. (Shaks. Soc.) 88 Wee say thou art an asse trancendentallie, not prædicamentally. **1727-41** [see PREDICABLY].

predicant ('prɛdɪkənt), *a.* and *sb.* Also 6–7 præ-. [ad. L. *prædicāns*, *-āntem*, pres. pple. of *prædicāre* to cry in public, proclaim, in late and med.L. to preach, f. *præ* forth + *dicāre* to make known, proclaim; as sb. (sense B. 1), a. F. *prédicant* (16th c. in Hatz.-Darm.) or Du. *predikant* a Protestant preacher.]

A. *adj.* **1.** Given to or characterized by preaching; *spec.* applied to those religious orders who went about preaching, esp. the Dominicans or Black Friars.

1629 H. BURTON *Babel no Bethel* 62 But may not some predicant Frier,..by preaching, bee a meanes to saue a soule? **1710** *Managers' Pro & Con* 76 That Ecclesiastical Incendiary, and predicant Herauld, Doctor Goddard. **1850** W. D. COOPER *Hist. Winchelsea* 38 There was afterwards added, in the reign of Edw. II, a house of the Dominicans, Black Friars, or Friars Predicant. **1882-3** *Schaff's Encycl. Relig. Knowl.* I. 657 The efficacy of a predicant order.

2. 'Uttering as an affirmation' (Webster 1864).

B. *sb.* **1. a.** A preacher; *spec.* a member of a predicant religious order. Now *Hist.*

1590 GREENWOOD in L. Bacon *Genesis N. Eng. Ch.* (1874) 126 These stipendiary, roving predicants. **1598** HAKLUYT *Voy.* I. 53 Ascelline being one of the order of the Prædicants. **1625** T. GODWIN *Moses & Aaron* I. vi. 28 The difference between those three sorts of predicants mentioned by Saint Paul. **1651** W. JANE Εἰκων Ακλαστος 240 The shopps..are turned to pulpitts, and every Cooper growne a reverend Predicant. **1749** LAVINGTON *Enthus. Meth. & Papists* I. (1754) 14 These strolling Predicants have allured some itching Ears, and drawn them aside, by calumniating their proper Pastors. **1810** SOUTHEY in *Q. Rev.* IV. 503 A body of Protestant Predicants, not less intolerant in spirit, than their predecessors..in the Romish Church. **1816** T. J. HOWELL *Stranger in Shrewsbury* 130 The Dominicans, or Black Friars, were called in some places Jacobins, and in others Predicants. **1910** *Encycl. Relig. & Ethics* III. 176 The banishment of the pastors and the prohibition of public worship drove the people to private assemblies and the ministrations of lay preachers. Among the latter, who were known as 'predicants', François Vivens and Claude Brousson..were specially conspicuous. **1939** *Conc. Oxf. Dict. Eng. Lit.* 186/1 A monk of the order of the Predicants.

b. = PREDIKANT, q.v.

2. 'One that affirms any thing' (J.).

1755 in JOHNSON. Thence in TODD, WEBSTER, etc.

Hence †**'predicancy**, the action or practice of preaching; †**'predicantess**, a female predicant.

1627 HAKEWILL *Apol.* III. ix. (1630) 261 That little life of it [Rhetoric] which remained being reserved only in the predicancie of Postillars. **1647** TRAPP *Comm. Rom.* xvi. 1 A Diaconisse to minister to the sick,..not a prædicantisse, to preach or have Peters keys at her girdle. **1662** HIBBERT *Body Div.* I. 219 They were deaconisses, to minister to the sick.. not praedicantisses, to preach.

predicate ('prɛdɪkət), *sb.* Also 7–9 præ-. [ad. late and med.L. *prædicātum* (= 'quod dicitur de subjecto', that which is said of the subject, Boeth.), sb. use of neuter pa. pple. of *prædicāre* (see next). So F. *prédicat* (Oresme 1391, admitted by Acad. 1878).]

1. *Logic.* That which is predicated or said of the subject in a proposition; the second term of a proposition, which is affirmed or denied of the first term by means of the copula, as in 'this man is *my father*', 'Peter is *a man*', 'all men are *mortal*', 'the sun is *rising*'. (At first used in L. form, *prædicatum*.)

1532 MORE *Confut. Tindale* Wks. 451/1 Where the thinges that we speake of or the article of yͤ diuersitie of the word whiche is in the verbe in our englishe tonge,..maketh the matter open which of the two termes we take for *subiectum* & which for *prædicatum*. *a* **1555** RIDLEY *Treat. Error Transubst.* (1556) G iij b, It..leaueth that to be determined and tolde by that which foloweth the word (is), that is by predicatum. **1582** PARSONS *Def. Censure* 124 Nothing, but maketh a long idle speake of *prædicatum* and *subiectum*, as pertinent to the mater, as charing crosse to byllingsgate. **1612** T. TAYLOR *Comm. Titus* ii. 13 (1619) 482 The Apostle ..vseth but one article, to note but one subject, to whom both the predicates most truely and properly agree. **1651** HOBBES *Gov. & Soc.* xviii. §4. 346 The Proposition is true in which the word consequent, which by Logicians is called the Prædicate, embraceth the word antecedent in its amplitude, which they call the Subject. *a* **1688** CUDWORTH *Immut. Mor.* (1731) 95 As Aristotle observes in all Affirmation, and Negation at least, the Predicate is always Universal. **1754** EDWARDS *Freed. Will* I. iii. 16 When the Subject and Predicate of the Proposition, which affirms the Existence of any Thing, either Substance, Quality, Act or Circumstance, have a full and certain Connection, then the Existence or Being of that Thing is said to be necessary in a metaphysical Sense. **1809-10** COLERIDGE *Friend* (1818) III. 212 Existence is its own predicate [i.e. The word *is* when it means *exists* is a predicate as well as a copula]. *c* **1840** [see QUANTIFICATION]. **1867** FOWLER *Deductive Logic* II. i. 23 The term affirmed or denied is called the *predicate*, the term of which it is affirmed or denied the *subject*, the connecting verb..the *copula*. *Ibid.* iv. 34 All negative propositions distribute their predicate, whereas affirmative propositions do not. **1903** B. RUSSELL *Princ. of Math.* I. iv. 45 We shall say that 'Socrates is human' is a proposition having only one term; of the remaining components of the proposition, one is the verb, the other is a predicate... Predicates..are concepts, other than verbs, which occur in propositions having only one term or subject. **1962** A. MARTINET *Functional View of Lang.* ii. 44 *There was a riot, in the village, yesterday... There was* marks *the riot* as the predicate, i.e. as the element around which the others gravitate and in relation to which that function will be marked.

2. a. *Gram.* The statement made about a subject, including the logical copula (which in a verb is expressed by the personal suffix). Sometimes restricted to the main verb and its object or complement, to the exclusion of any adjunct. Also in *Logic* and *Math.*, freq. in wider use: an assertion or relation having one or more terms unspecified; a propositional function.

The grammatical predicate is either a simple verb, or a verb of incomplete predication with its complement. The generalization of *predicate* (G. *prädikat*) to include relations (many-place predicates) originated in Hilbert & Ackermann *Grundzüge der theoretischen Logik* (1928) 45: see quot. 1950.

a **1638** MEDE *Wks.* (1672) 81 Thus much of the Subject, 'The Righteous': Now I come to the Predicate, 'shall be in everlasting remembrance'. [**1668** WILKINS *Real Char.* II. i. §6. 46 Actions or Passions of things; (..tho it be not properly one simple part of speech, but rather a mixture of two, namely the Predicate and Copula)..Verbe.] **1852** MORELL *Anal. Sentences* I. §9. 14 The predicate affirms respecting the subject either—What it is; or, What it does; or, What it suffers. Man *is mortal*. The snow *falls*. The child *was neglected*. **1858** MASON *Eng. Gram.* §§347–8. 92 Inasmuch as the personal terminations or a verb have no existence apart from the verb itself, it is usual (and convenient) in grammar to treat the copula as a part of the predicate. Thus in the sentence 'Time flies', *time* is called the subject, and *flies* the predicate... In using the word *predicate*, we mean the predicate and copula combined. In grammar, the terms *subject* and *predicate* are used in a more restricted sense than in Logic. **1874** SAYCE *Compar. Philol.* i. 9 Every predicate must have a subject. **1892** H. SWEET *New Eng. Gram.* I. 48 In language the logical connections between words extend over a wider area than the purely grammatical ones. Thus in such a sentence as *I came home yesterday morning*, the grammatical predicate to *I* is *came*, *home* and *yesterday* being grammatically connected with the predicate only, while *morning* is an adjunct to *yesterday* only. But in thought *yesterday* is as much part of the predicate as *came* itself, *came-home-yesterday-morning* being the logical predicate which, from a grammatical point of view may be regarded either as an extended predicate or a group-predicate. **1921** E. SAPIR *Language* ii. 37 The reduced sentence resolves itself into the subject of discourse—*the mayor*—and the predicate—*is going to deliver a speech*. It is customary to say that the true subject of such a sentence is *mayor*, the true predicate *is going* or even *is*. **1961** *Archivum Linguisticum* XIII. 81 The relative priority of such class concepts as noun and verb as against such as subject and predicate. **1968** J. LYONS *Introd. Theoret. Linguistics* viii. 334 *John killed Bill in Central Park on Sunday*. The subject is *John*; the predicate is *killed Bill*; and *in Central Park* and *on Sunday* are adjuncts.

1937 S. K. LANGER *Introd. Symbolic Logic* vii. 158 'Being white' has the properties of such a relation; any term, *a*, has it or does not have it, but since there is no second term we cannot say that *a* has this relation *to* any other. Such a relation of 'monadic' degree is called a predicate. *Ibid.* 159 The sole business of predicates in logic is to define classes. **1940** W. V. QUINE *Math. Logic* i. 27 'Is true' and 'is false'.. are predicates by means of which we speak *about* statements. *Ibid.* 28 The verb 'implies'..is a binary predicate by means of which we talk *about* statements. **1943** *Trans. Amer. Math. Soc.* LIII. 42 Let us consider number-theoretic predicates, that is, propositional functions of natural numbers. **1950** tr. *Hilbert & Ackermann's Princ. Math. Logic* iii. 57 To the formula $x + y = z$ there corresponds a triadic predicate $S(x, y, z)$. The truth of $S(x, y, z)$ means that x, y, and z are connected by the relation $x + y = z$. [*Note*] Hitherto it has been customary in logic to call only functions with one argument place predicates, while functions with more than one place were called relations. Here we use the word 'predicate' in a quite general sense. **1965** HUGHES & LONDEY *Elem. Formal Logic* xxxix. 270 We shall..speak of the expressions, such as 'greater than' and 'between', which stand for two-place, three-place, etc., relations, as two-place, three-place, etc., predicates respectively. **1969** D. J. FOULIS *Fund. Concepts Math.* i. 14 Suppose that $P(x)$.. becomes a proposition whenever x takes on any particular value in U. Then $P(x)$ is called a predicate or a propositional function, and the object variable x is called its argument. **1973** H. HERMES *Introd. Math. Logic* i. 40 In the statement *The crown jewels are kept in the Tower of London, The crown jewels* and *the Tower of London* can be understood as names for individuals and *are kept in* as a name for a predicate... *are kept in* is a name for a two-place predicate... *is tall* is a name for a one-place predicate.

b. An appellation or title that asserts something.

1882–3 *Schaff's Encycl. Relig. Knowl.* 594 Nestorius refused to give Mary the praedicate θεοτόκος. **1887** *N. & Q.* 7th Ser. IV. 64/2 The noble author, head,..under the 'predicate' of Aghrim, of the eldest branch of the once princely house of Imaney.

c. A quality, an attribute.

1872 tr. *Ueberweg's Hist. Philos.* I. §106. 475 To the revealed God belong the divine predicates, and especially the predicate of reason. **1875** LEWES *Probl. Life & Mind* II. III. ii. §24. 150 For predicates—qualities—are not mere patterns on the web of a subject; they are the threads of that web.

d. (= Ger. *prädikat*.) In reference to German and other foreign universities, etc.: The judgement pronounced upon a candidate's work in an examination (e.g. 'cum laude, rite, vix satis', etc.); hence, the class or position obtained by a candidate.

1899 *Daily News* 30 May 8/5 At the examination he very often was at a loss for an answer, and received very unsatisfactory predicates.

3. *attrib.* and *Comb.*, as ***predicate accusative, adjective, -centre*** (***-centred*** adj.), ***clause, expression, marker, nominal, nominative, -part, -phrase, -position, -prefix, sentence, stress, -taking*** adj., ***term, variable, word***; **predicate calculus** [tr. G. *prädikatenkalkül* (Hilbert & Ackermann *Grundzüge der theoret. Logik* (1928) ii. 34)], any formal logic characterized by the use of existential quantifiers; cf. *propositional calculus* s.v. PROPOSITIONAL *a.* b.

1887 W. W. GOODWIN *Greek Gram.* III. 194 The predicate nominative with the passive verbs of this class represents the *predicate accusative of the active construction. *Ibid.* 196 The *predicate adjective may be connected with its noun by the copula..or by a copulative verb. **1977** *Word 1972* XXVIII. 79 In the following discussion I shall be concerned with predicate adjectives, except where otherwise noted. **1950** tr. *Hilbert & Ackermann's Princ. Math. Logic* p. ix, The terminology has been adapted to that of the *Grundlagen der Mathematik* by Hilbert and Bernays. For example, the term 'functional calculus' has been everywhere replaced by '*predicate calculus'. *Ibid.* iii. 67 We will now proceed, just as we did for the sentential calculus, to set up for the predicate calculus a system of axioms from which the remaining true sentences of the predicate calculus may be obtained by means of certain rules. **1955** A. N. PRIOR *Formal Logic* I. iv. 73 The calculus of predicational functions (often simply called the functional calculus, or the predicate calculus). **1966** *Mathematical Rev.* Jan. 7/1 (*heading*) Axiomatization of the infinite-valued predicate calculus. **1970** *Language* XLVI. 783 Whether grammatical or lexical-situational, all these relations are the linguistic counterpart of the predicate calculus. **1979** *Sci. Amer.* May 131/1 Could there exist an algorithm such that when it was given a statement written in precise mathematical language, it would report eventually whether the statement was true or false?.. For a powerful formalized language known as the predicate calculus it has been shown that no such algorithm exists. **1966** R. A. HALL *Pidgin & Creole Lang.* vi. 84 In the predicates of most pidgins and creoles, we find..virtually any type of free form of phrase, without any verb. Here are a few examples of nouns, pronouns, and adjectives as *predicate-centers. *Ibid.* 85 Examples of other types of predicate-center include those containing adverbs or adverbial phrases. **1974** *Amer. Speech 1970* XLV. 265 He differs from Becker in choosing a *predicate-centered approach in which the verb is the central element. **1966** *Eng. Stud.* XLVII. 257 Grammatically *that*-clauses..may also function as *predicate clauses. **1957** G. RYLE in M. Black *Importance of Lang.* (1962) 154 *Predicate-expressions also denote what they are truly predicable of. **1966** R. A. HALL *Pidgin & Creole Lang.* vi. 83 The predicate in many pidgins and creoles..is often set apart from what goes before, by some special syntactic marker. South Seas Pidgin English.. has a '*predicate-marker' /i-/, which is normally used when the subject..is not of the first or second person. **1965** N. CHOMSKY *Aspects of Theory of Syntax* iv. 181 'Bill is a lawyer.' The *Predicate-Nominal of the latter is not singular, in the base structure. **1887** *Predicate nominative [see *predicate accusative*]. **1957** D. L. BOLINGER in *Publ. Amer. Dial. Soc.* XXVIII. 150 This resolves the subject vs. predicate-nominative ambiguity in plain hwQs. **1924** O. JESPERSEN *Philos. Gram.* 145 We might also use the terms 'subject-part' and '*predicate-part' instead of 'primary' and 'adnex'. **1965** N. CHOMSKY *Aspects of Theory of Syntax* ii. 102 The Place and Time Adverbials that are associated with the full *Predicate-Phrase. **1955** A. N. PRIOR *Formal Logic* II. iii. 160 The Schoolmen also very freely substitute singular terms for general ones, in the *predicate- as well as the subject-position. **1966** R. A. HALL *Pidgin & Creole Lang.* vi. 83 Haitian and the other Central American French-based creoles have a series of *predicate-prefixes, which indicate negation..and tense. **1964** *Language* XL. 46 The sentences to be discussed..have *is* as their main verb. They will be referred to as *predicate sentences. **1934** PRIEBSCH & COLLINSON *German Lang.* I. iii. 60 We might term such stresses *predicate stresses, for they indicate what is the logical (if not the grammatical) predicate. **1974** *Canad. Jrnl. Linguistics* XIX. II. 153 Not only is there a problem for the analyst of knowing when to..assign a *predicate-taking adjective to an *easy* or *eager* deep structure. **1901** A. SIDGWICK *Use of Words* 157 *Predicate terms depend on artificial distinction. **1954** I. M. COPI *Symbolic Logic* iv. 67 We write the symbol for its predicate term to the left of the symbol for its subject term. **1937** A. SMEATON tr. *Carnap's Logical Syntax of Lang.* III. 84 In Language II, there are.. not only numerical variables.., but also *predicate-variables..and functor-variables. **1955** A. N. PRIOR *Formal Logic* II. iii. 158 The nearest thing to a general term-variable in the functional calculus is the predicate-variable (ϕ, etc.). **1932** A. H. GARDINER *Theory of Speech & Lang.* iv. 216 The subject-word places before the listener a thing to which he is to direct his attention, and the *predicate-word tells him what he is to perceive or think about it.

Hence '**predicateless** *a.*, of which nothing can be predicated.

1863 SHEDD *Hist. Chr. Doctr.* (1869) I. III. i. 241 There is no such dark predicateless ground; there is no such Gnostic abyss.

predicate ('prɛdɪkeɪt), *v.* Also 7 præ-. [f. ppl. stem of L. *prædicāre* 'to cry in public, proclaim', hence 'to declare, state, say', in med.L. 'to preach', and in Logic 'to assert', f. *præ* forth + *dicāre* to make known, proclaim: see -ATE³ 5.]

1. a. *trans.* To proclaim, declare; to affirm, assert; also, to set forth publicly, to preach; to preach up, extol, commend (*rare* or *obs.*).

1552 HULOET, Predicate, *prædico*. **1616** BULLOKAR *Eng. Expos.*, *Predicate*, to tell abroad, to report. **1624** ABP. ABBOT *Visib. True Ch.* 114 They doat much vpon themselues,.. who..doe predicate and magnifie their Synagogue, as the vnspotted wife and mysticall body of our most blessed Sauiour. **1635** A. STAFFORD *Fem. Glory* (1869) 66 The more her Vertue is predicated, by her Cousen, the more she humbles her selfe. **1706** PHILLIPS, *Predicate*, to publish, to cry, or preach up. **1782** V. KNOX *Ess.* (1819) II. lxvi. 43 Can all this be predicated with any regard to veracity? **1822** *Blackw. Mag.* XII. 607 Composing discourses, which.. might not have been unprofitably predicated from the pulpit. **1884** *19th Cent.* Feb. 186 Many truths may be predicated about Scripture.

b. *intr.* or *absol.* To assert, affirm; to make a statement.

1827 STEUART *Planter's G.* (1828) 111 To predicate, then, or affirm certainly, as to their respective usefulness.., is, properly speaking, more fanciful than real. **1866** J. MARTINEAU *Ess.* I. 189 To think is mentally to predicate. **1879** SALA in *Daily Tel.* 15 May, It is perilous to predicate dogmatically as to the locality.

2. a. *spec. trans.* To assert or affirm as a quality, property, or attribute (*of* something). (In quot. 1677 *absol.*, or ? *intr.* for *pass.*)

1614 SELDEN *Titles Hon.* 126 As it is inherent, and not predicated of the Person, its best exprest for its own Essence. **1628** T. SPENCER *Logick* 26 Such arguments as be essentiall vnto the thing, of which they are predicated. **1677** GALE *Crt. Gentiles* II. IV. 248 That nothing can predicate univocally of God and the Creature, is most evident, because [etc.]. **1780** BENTHAM *Princ. Legisl.* xi. §1 It has been shown..that goodness or badness cannot with any propriety be predicated of motives. **1839** HALLAM *Hist. Lit.* IV. IV. iv. §33. 170 The schoolmen..deeming it necessary to predicate metaphysical infinity of all the divine attributes. **1852** KINGSLEY *Lett.* (1878) I. 315 Of whatsoever you predicate Time you must also predicate Space.

b. *Logic.* To state or assert (something) about the subject of a proposition; also, to make (a term) the predicate in a proposition.

1570 FOXE *A. & M.* (ed. 2) 1596/2 *Substantia* may be predicated denominatiuely..or in a figuratiue locution. **1725** WATTS *Logic* III. ii. §3 There is also a fourth figure, wherein the middle term is predicated in the major proposition, and subjected in the minor. **1864** BOWEN *Logic* v. 138 To predicate..is virtually to classify, or to assign a Subject to its proper place in a class, thereby attributing to it all the Marks of that class. *Ibid.* vii. 187 The famous ..*Dictum de omni et nullo*, that whatever is predicated.. universally of any Class..may be also predicated of any part of that Class. *Ibid.* viii. 230 We prove that it is right to predicate *mortality* of Socrates, by showing that Socrates belongs to the class *man*, all the members of which are admitted to be *mortal*. **1867** FOWLER *Deduct. Logic* II. i. 23 The predicate is said to be *predicated* of the subject. *Ibid.*, In the first case the predicate is predicated affirmatively..; in the two last negatively.

c. *transf.* To convey a predication or assertion of; to connote, imply.

1718 *Entertainer* No. 28. 190 If Atheism predicates Honesty, some of the Whigs..may put in their claim to it.

3. To affirm (a statement or the like) *on* some given grounds; hence, 'to found a proposition, argument, etc. *on* some basis or data' (Bartlett); and *transf.* to found or base (anything) *on* or *upon* stated facts or conditions. orig. *U.S.*

1766 T. CLAP *Hist. Yale Coll.* 21 The Trustees..past a Vote,..predicated upon sundry former ones, wherein they finally settled the College at New-Haven. **1796** WASHINGTON *Writ.* (1892) XIII. 227 Was not the first application to you predicated on this information? **1814** M. CAREY *Olive Branch* (1815) 220 A set of measures, all predicated upon an approaching war. **1839** C. SUMNER *Lett.* (1878) II. 105 This..is predicated upon my confidence in his ability. **1876** LOWELL *Among my Bks.* Ser. II. 46 His [Dante's] moroseness, his party spirit and his personal vindictiveness are all predicated upon the Inferno. **1888** PRES. CLEVELAND in *Daily News* 10 Sept. 5/4 The reform we seek to inaugurate is predicated upon the utmost care for established industries and enterprises. **1968** *Globe & Mail* (Toronto) 5 Feb. 2/2 Mr. Diefenbaker said the federal Government had erred by predicating the conference on a bill of rights. **1973** *Times Lit. Suppl.* 20 July 836/1 A new conception of reality is demanded, predicated on dissatisfaction with formalist literature and rooted in the here and now. **1975** *High Times* Dec. 96/2 Some of the agents admitted 'they viewed routes of advancement within the DEA to be open to them predicated on the numbers of arrests they made and the amounts of narcotics they seized'. **1977** *Listener* 30 June 867/2 Crime predicated on sexual disorder I distrust.

¶**4.** *Erroneously* (as if irreg. f. L. *prædīcĕre* + -ATE³) = PREDICT *v.*

1623 COCKERAM, *Predicate*, to foretell. **1679** *N. Eng. Hist. & Gen. Reg.* (1850) IV. 131 The dark Eclipses of our lights accord To praedicate a famine of ye word. **1873–4** DIXON *Two Queens* III. XIV. vi. 101 That shrewd Venetian envoy heard enough to predicate the rising of domestic storms. **1897** *Globe* 3 Dec. 1/4 Slight falls of snow..together with the appearance of large flocks of gulls inland, is held to predicate a hard winter.

Hence '**predicated**, '**predicating** *ppl. adjs.*

1628 T. SPENCER *Logick* 19 In his doctrine of predicated arguments, hee speakes not a word of effects and subiects. **1805** EUGENIA DI ACTON *Nuns of Desert* I. 74 This predicating congress consisted of two elderly, and one young woman. **1864** BOWEN *Logic* v. 139 Any limitation of the predicated class.

predication (prɛdɪ'keɪʃən). Also 6–7 præ-. [ME. a. OF. *predicaciun* (12th c. in Hatz.-Darm.), mod.F. *prédication*, ad. L. *prædicātiōn-em*, n. of action f. *prædicāre*: see prec.]

1. The action of publicly or loudly proclaiming, declaring, or setting forth. **a.** *spec.* Preaching; an instance of this; a sermon, discourse, exhortation, oration. *Obs.* or *arch.*

c **1300** *Beket* 1969 [He] stod and prechede that folc..In his predicacioun he gan to sike sore. *c* **1386** CHAUCER *Shipm. Prol.* 14 For we shul han a predicacion This lollere here wol prechen vs somwhat. **1477** EARL RIVERS (Caxton) *Dictes* 101 The predicacion is not to be lawded that endureth ouer the power of the herkeners. **1533** J. HEYWOOD *Pard. & Friar* in Hazl. *Dodsley* I. 235 Except that the preacher himself live well, His predication will help never a dell. **1689** *Def. Liberty agst. Tyrants* 14 The tribute of God is in Prayers, Sacraments, Predications of the pure word of God. **1715** M. DAVIES *Athen. Brit.* I. 116 To bring Predications upon particular Texts of Scripture, into a regular Body of Sermons. **1827** G. S. FABER *Orig. Expiat. Sacr.* 258 Doctrines..taught and held from the very first predication of the Gospel. **1884** *Q. Rev.* Apr. 312 During half a century of uninterrupted predication.

†**b.** The action of crying up or extolling. *Obs.*

1528 ROY *Rede me* (Arb.) 84 Then with grett commendacion In their flatterynge predicacion They will their actes magnify. **1533** BELLENDEN *Livy* II. xxvi. (S.T.S.) I. 235 þe small pepil..hard þarefore þe blasonyng & predicatioun als plesandlie þan, quhen he was dede. **1628** GAULE *Pract. The. Paneg.* 8 That is our prayse and predication of God. *a* **1656** BP. HALL *Rem. Wks.* (1660) 16 This man..fell into a Hyperbolical predication of the wonderful miracles done newly by our Lady at Zichem.

†**c.** Proclamation, announcement. *Obs.*

1613–18 DANIEL *Coll. Hist. Eng.* (1626) 154 Without delay predication should be made throughout the Kingdome.

2. The action of predicating or asserting, or an instance of this; assertion, affirmation.

1579 FULKE *Heskins' Parl.* 325 Is this a proper and essentiall prædication to say, Christe is a spirituall rocke? *a* **1677** HALE *Prim. Orig. Man.* I. iv. 109 It is as true a Predication to say that these were many, as it were in case they had all coexisted. **1821** PARR *Let. to Maltby* 27 Mar., A college testimonial, wherein the word learning and all predications about it, are omitted.

b. *spec.* in *Logic*: The assertion of something of or about a subject.

a **1638** MEDE *Wks.* (1672) 253 A predication in *casu recto* is a predication of sameness, and therefore is used properly in things which are in a manner the same, as Genus and Species, *Homo est animal*. **1692** NORRIS *Curs. Refl.* 40 When ..the Predicate is said of the whole Subject according to the full latitude of its Predication. **1829** JAS. MILL *Hum. Mind* (1869) II. xiv. 4 Predication..is a name for the combination of three words, 'subject', 'predicate', and 'copula'. **1843** MILL *Logic* I. v. §3 (1856) I. 103 The most generally received notion of predication decidedly is that it consists in referring something to a class, *i.e.* either placing an individual under a class, or placing one class under another class. **1863** BAIN *Higher Eng. Gram.* (1879) 63 The Verb is the part of speech concerned in predication; that is, in affirming or denying. **1864** BOWEN *Logic* v. 126 This rule is evidently founded upon the doctrine that all predication is classification.

¶**3.** *Erroneously* = PREDICTION.

1862 *N. Brit. Rev.* May 290 The foreknowledge and predication of events.

[In CAXTON *Gold. Leg.* 198 b/1 *predycacyon* appears to be misprinted for *perdycyon*.]

predi'cational, *a.* [f. PREDICATION + -AL.] Of or pertaining to predication.

1894 J. VENN *Symbolic Logic* (ed. 2) ii. 59 It..concluded, in the predicational form,—using 'is' instead of 'is identical with'. **1921** W. E. JOHNSON *Logic* I. xiv. 237 Giving added significance to the predicational factor by bringing out the relation of an adjective to its determinable. **1922** *Ibid.* II. iii. 56 A function is called predicational when the component that determines its form is the characterising tie, which unites two variants related to one another as substantive to adjective. **1953** K. BRITTON *J. S. Mill* vi. 194 I say 'This snow is white'... The predicational form of sentence indicates this connexion [between whiteness and the other qualities of snow]: whereas 'There is snow and noise' does not—it is not asserted that the snow is noisy. **1955** [see *predicate calculus* s.v. PREDICATE *sb.* 3]. **1961** *Brno Studies in English* III. 15 The unwarranted assumption that any word taken by itself must possess an independent predicational function. **1978** *Language* LIV. 90 Quantification is often predicational (i.e. with adjectives) in Japanese.

predicatival (prɛdɪkə'taɪvəl), *a.* [f. PREDICATIV(E *a.* + -AL.] Of, pertaining to, or constituting a predicate. Also *ellipt.* as *sb.*

1891 H. A. STRONG et al. *Introd. Study Hist. Lang.* xvii. 290 A similar vacillation occurs in cases of the predicatival noun or predicatival attribute. **1937** A. H. GARDINER in *Mélanges de Linguistique et de Philologie offerts à J. van Ginneken* 310 Predicatival examples are not very frequent, e.g. *She is very Boston, Surely that knock* (i.e. at the front door) *is John*. **1958** A. A. HILL *Introd. Ling. Struct.* xvi. 274 A verb consisting of an *-ing* form..will be defined as a predicatival rather than as a predicator.

predicative (prɪ'dɪkətɪv, 'prɛdɪkeɪtɪv), *a.* [ad. L. *prædicātīv-us*: see PREDICATE *v.* and -IVE; cf. F. *prédicatif, -ive*.]

1. a. Having the quality of predicating, affirming, or asserting; of, pertaining to, or constituting a predicate. Also *ellipt.* as *sb.*

1846 *Proc. Philol. Soc.* III. 10 Thus the formation called the *casus substitutivus*, answering to the *nuncupativus* or predicative case of the Finnish and Lappish grammarians, may be employed either as an adverb or the stem of a verb. **1860** MAX MÜLLER *Chips* (1880) I. xv. 358 Words which always conveyed a predicative meaning. **1885** J. FITZGERALD tr. *Schultze's Fetichism* vi. §7 These things are all predicative of the blue vault above our heads. **1892** WESTCOTT *Gospel of Life* 103 The Divine names which are proper to the Shemitic languages are predicative and moral. **1914** O. JESPERSEN *Mod. Eng. Gram.* II. xiv. 330 As a rule words that can be used as adjuncts (pre-adjuncts) can also be used in the same form as predicatives. **1925** E. KRUISINGA *Handbk. Present-Day Eng.* (ed. 4) II. I. 235 Predicative Participles... The simple present participle is very frequently used with the copula *to be*, to form what is called the progressive. **1925** GRATTAN & GURREY *Our Living Lang.* xxi. 129 The following typical examples of Qualifiers and Predicatives. **1930** in J. T. Hatfield et al. *Curme Vol. Ling. Stud.* 46 A noun or pronoun in the subjective case may take a great variety of predicative cases. **1932** *Eng. Stud.* XIV. 129 By starting from the full meaning of the finite (or as it is now called: predicative) member of the group, the author compels us to look for a discussion of the progressive, perfect, etc., in the sections on *to be, to have*, etc. **1932** W. L. GRAFF *Lang.* ix. 328 If we emphasize the relationship of the referential parts to one another, it is noted that the Greenlandic sentence consists of a noun and its attributes, whereas the English one is formed by a subject and its predicate. Hence the further division into attributive or possessive languages and predicative ones. **1933** O. JESPERSEN *Syst. Gram.* 25 Some languages have a special case, or even two special cases in which predicatives are put: shall we say that 'a teacher' is in the 'predicative' case in 'he is a teacher' and in the 'illative' in 'he became a teacher'? **1942** R. W. ZANDVOORT in *Eng. Stud.* XXIV. 2 Only 10 of these [*sc.* forms of *to do*] are finite (predicative) forms..; the rest are non-finite (non-predicative). **1959** M. SCHLAUCH *Eng. Lang. in Mod. Times* viii. 230 He [*sc.* Deutschbein] contrasts especially the predicative sentence, which may be complicated but is apprehended as an organic whole..and the attributive sentence. **1966** *Eng. Stud.* XLVII. 50 A discussion of intransitive verbs combined with a predicative 'apposition' (e.g. *he died young; he died an admiral*).

b. In various special collocations, as ***predicative clause, syntagm***, etc.; ***predicative adjunct, appositive*** = *object complement* s.v. OBJECT *sb.* 7.

1963 Predicative adjunct [see OBJECT *sb.* 7]. **1963** F. T. VISSER *Hist. Syntax Eng. Lang.* I. ii. 182 Syntactical units of the type..'he died *a martyr*' consist of a subject, a predicate in the form of an intransitive verb, and an adjunct (called 'predicative adjunct' in this study)... Jespersen uses the term 'quasi-predicate'; Curme the term 'predicative appositive' and F. T. Wood..the term 'pseudo-complement'. **1964** E. PALMER tr. *Martinet's Elem. Gen. Linguistics* iv. 116 The syntagm *il y avait*..is not autonomous but independent. We shall call it a *predicative syntagm*. *Ibid.* 119 The predicate comprises a predicative moneme, accompanied or not by modifiers. The predicative moneme is the element around which the sentence is organized, the other constituent elements marking their function by reference to it. **1965** *Language* XLI. 136 What Saxmatov called 'predicative-attributive relations'. **1966** *Eng. Stud.* XLVII. 50 Intransitive verbs combined with a predicative 'apposition' (e.g. *he died young*..). I should prefer this term to Visser's 'predicative adjunct'. *Ibid.* 262 It is permissible to..speak of subject clause, predicate clause, predicative clause.

2. = PREDICATORY *a.* 1. *rare.*

1870 SWINBURNE *Let.* 19 Feb. (1959) II. 98, I trust you [*sc.* D. G. Rossetti] to 'cut close and deep'..if you find anything to pare away of the spouting or drawing, vociferous or predicative kind.

3. *Logic.* Of a function: of order only one greater than that of its argument of greatest order.

1906 B. RUSSELL in *Proc. London Math. Soc.* IV. 34 Norms..which do not define classes I propose to call *non-predicative*; those which do define classes I shall call *predicative*. **1910** WHITEHEAD & RUSSELL *Principia Math.* I. ii. 56 We will define a function of one variable as predicative when it is of the next order above that of its argument, *i.e.* of the lowest order compatible with its having that argument. **1936** *Mind* XLV. 498 The axiom of reducibility is adopted in *P*[*rincipia*] *M*[*athematica*]. This axiom moderates the second part of the theory by asserting that for every propositional function there is a formally equivalent one which is predicative, *i.e.*, has the lowest order compatible with its type. **1969** FEYS & FITCH *Dict. Symbols Math. Logic* v. 91 A property, of order only one greater than the order of what it applies to, is called by Russell a predicative property.

Hence **predicatively** *adv.*, as a predicate.

1875 WHITNEY *Life Lang.* xii. 233 One step from nouns used predicatively. *Ibid.* 243. **1895** *Proc. 14th Conv. Instruct. Deaf* 81 A noun or pronoun used predicatively is in the nominative case.

predica'tivity. [f. prec. + -ITY.] The fact or quality of predicating.

1963 W. V. QUINE *Set Theory* §36.265 This predicativity restriction obstructs Cantor's theorem. **1966** *Philos. Rev.* LXXV. 384 For each system in turn we examine the status of predicativity.

predicator ('prɛdɪkeɪtə(r)). [Early mod.E. *predycatour*, a. OF. *predicatour* (14th c. in Hatz.-Darm.), in 16th c. *prédicateur*, ad. L. *prædicātor* a proclaimer, praiser in public; in late and med.L. a preacher; agent-n. f. *prædicāre* to PREDICATE.] One who or that which predicates.

a. *spec.* A preacher; a preaching friar. Now *rare.*

1483 CAXTON *Gold. Leg.* 431/2 The freres predycatours and mynours. **1483** —— *G. de la Tour* cxxix, As the clerkes say, and the predycatours. **1600** HAKLUYT *Voy.* III. 123 A Monastery of Friers, of the order of the Predicators. **1632** LITHGOW *Trav.* x. 470 Two Iesuites, one of which was Predicator, and Superiour Tiatinean Colledge. **1820** J. CLELAND *Rise & Progr. Glasgow* 21 A tenement lying on the north side of the church and convent of the Predicators. **1839** YEOWELL *Anc. Brit. Ch.* iv. (1847) 41 The first predicators of the gospel may..have unfolded its saving truths in the vicinity of Glastonbury.

b. One who asserts, an assertor. *rare.*

1658 R. FRANCK *North. Mem.* (1821) 9 Our modern assertors and predicators.

c. (See quot. 1899)

1899 R. C. TEMPLE *Univ. Gram.* 36 Functionally a word is either..An integer, or a sentence in itself... An indicator. .. An explicator... A predicator, or indicative of [the] predicate [of a sentence]. **1958** [see PREDICATIVAL *a.*]. **1961** [see COMPLEMENT *sb.* 3 b]. **1966** *Amer. Speech* XLI. 204 All of the clauses here termed 'imperative' have as predicators verb forms which we can describe as present-tense subjunctives. **1966** G. N. LEECH *Eng. in Advertising* ii. 10 The elements of clause structure in English are:..P: Predicator (traditionally 'verb', but this term is needed for a class of word). **1969** *Eng. Stud.* L. 32 Clauses without a Predicator..can assume the status of independent clauses.

Hence '**predi,catress**, *rare*, a female preacher.

1669 MRS. BLOMER in Fox Bourne *Locke* (1876) I. v. 254 The impudence of the female predicatress.

†**predica'torial,** *a. Obs.* [f. late L. *prædicātōri-us* (see next) + -AL[1].] = PREDICATORY *a.* 1.

1772 NUGENT tr. *Hist. Friar Gerund* I. 469 That.. surprising monster of predicatorial excellence. **1792** G. WAKEFIELD *Mem.* (1804) I. 407 London..the most conspicuous and promising theatre for predicatorial exhibitions.

predicatory ('prɛdɪkətərɪ, -,keɪtərɪ), *a.* (*sb.*) Also 7 præ-. [ad. late L. *prædicātōrius* adj., f. *prædicātor*: see PREDICATOR. Cf. obs. F. *prédicatoire* (Godef.).]

A. *adj.* **1.** Of or pertaining to a preacher; preaching.

1611 CORYAT *Crudities* 350 A certayne Dominican Frier.. who was the chief reader of the Praedicatory family. **1645** *Sacred Decretal* 14 This is our predicatory Prowesse, when we advance to the Pulpit. **1804** MITFORD *Inquiry* 319 The most recent examples..are of the predicatory or oratorical kind. **1847** J. WILSON in G. Smith *Life* xiv. (1879) 238, I have recommenced my usual Sabbath services both predicatory and catechetical. **1877** RUSKIN *Fors Clav.* VII. lxxxi. 275 Their slightly predicatory character must be pardoned.

2. Characterized by being proclaimed or cried up.

1902 *Contemp. Rev.* Sept. 353 In his somewhat ostentatious and predicatory conversion.

†**B.** *sb.* (the adj. used *absol.*) One engaged in preaching; a preacher. *Obs. rare*[−1].

1686 J. S[ERGEANT] *Hist. Monast. Convent.* 55 The main design of their Institution being to Read, Preach, Write, and Expound the Word of God, which gives the occasion of naming them Prædicants or Prædicatories.

†'**predicature.** *Obs. rare*[−1]. [f. L. *prædicāt-*, ppl. stem of *prædicāre* to PREDICATE + -URE.] Proclamation, public declaration.

1652 *Depos. Cast. York* (Surtees) 62 For as much as the Barrons of the Exchequer..have in their predicature made a doubt whether the Parliament be dissolved or not, it is declared that the Parliament is dissolved.

pre-dicrotic: see PRE- B. 1.

†**pre'dict,** *sb. Obs. rare*[−1]. [ad. L. *prædict-um* that which is foretold, prediction: cf. F. *prédit* (obs. form *predict*).] A prediction.

c **1600** SHAKS. *Sonn.* xiv, Nor can I fortune to breefe mynuits tell; Pointing to each his thunder, raine and winde, Or say with Princes if it shal goe wel By oft predict that I in heauen finde.

predict (prɪ'dɪkt), *ppl. a. rare.* [ad. L. *prædict-us*, pa. pple. of *prædīcĕre* (see next).] Predicted. (In quot. const. as *pa. pple.*)

1839 BAILEY *Festus* xviii. (1852) 213 There is but one great sinner, human nature, Predict of every world and predicate.

predict (prɪ'dɪkt), *v.* Also 6–7 præ-. [f. L. *prædict-*, ppl. stem of *prædīcĕre* to say beforehand, foretell, give notice of, advise, charge, f. *præ*, PRE- A. 1 + *dīcĕre* to say, tell.

Cf. F. *prédire* 'to foretell, foresay, presage, diuine, prophesie' (Cotgr. 1611), It. *predire*, 'to foretell, to prophesie, to tell of a thing before it com to passe' (Florio 1598), where neither has *predict* as an English word, though both use *prediction* in explaining the corresponding noun. *Predicted* ppl. adj. was in much earlier use; but the vb. is not in Shaks., nor even in Pope; it occurs once in Milton. In dictionaries it appears in Bailey 1721.]

†**1.** *trans.* To mention previously in a discourse or document. *Obs. rare.*

[**1546, 1599**: see PREDICTED 1.]

2. a. To foretell, prophesy, announce beforehand (an event, etc.). With simple obj. or obj. clause.

[**1623**: see PREDICTED 2.] **1671** MILTON *P.R.* III. 356 Prediction still..supposes means, Without means us'd, what it predicts revokes. **1678** CUDWORTH *Intell. Syst.* I. iv. 267 We saw all those things done by, and accomplish'd in him, which were long before predicted to us by the prophets. **1679** C. NESSE *Antichrist* 210 To prophecy, not so much by prædicting future things, as by preaching the everlasting gospel. **1727** DE FOE *Syst. Magic* I. iv. (1840) 104 Thus..thou shalt predict what shall certainly come to pass. **1837** WHEWELL *Hist. Induct. Sc.* (1857) I. 113 Thales.. predicted an eclipse. **1838** LYTTON *Alice* III. viii, I predict that the beauty of next season will be a certain Caroline Lady Doltimore. **1884** F. TEMPLE *Relat. Relig. & Sc.* iii. (1885) 82 How often an observer can predict a man's actions better than the man himself.

b. *transf.* Of a theory, observation, etc.: to have as a deducible or inferable consequence; to imply.

1961 *Physical Rev.* CXXI. 1620 The theory predicts a linear dependence of M_{2p} on $[H_0/(T + \theta)]^2$, where θ is the experimentally determined Curie-Weiss constant. **1964** E. BACH *Introd. Transformational Gram.* viii. 186 General linguistic theory must provide a precise characterization of the way in which a theory can be said to 'predict' a given sentence. **1975** *Nature* 6 Feb. 442/1 Sensitivity to the taste of PTC predicts sensitivity to caffeine. **1976** *Sci. Amer.* July 39/3 The present isotopic ratios of neodymium therefore predict the total depletion in U-235. This calculation gives a result about 40 percent greater than the observed depletion. **1977** *Lancet* 24 Sept. 662/1 Running-water samples are perhaps closer to the water typically consumed in the home than are first-flush samples, and our results.. indicate that they predict blood-lead more precisely.

3. *intr.* To utter prediction; to prophesy.

1652 GAULE *Magastromancer* 196 The devil can both predict and make predictors. **1805** EUGENIA DI ACTON *Nuns of Desert* I. 315 The necromantic instruments..predicted to the company with such a relation to their circumstances, as filled every one..with the utmost astonishment. **1853** MRS. CARLYLE *Lett.* (1883) II. 225 No one can predict as to the length of her life.

4. To direct fire at with the aid of a predictor (sense 2).
1943 L. CHESHIRE *Bomber Pilot* iii. 57 They're predicting us now; looks like a barrage. **1952** M. TRIPP *Faith is Windsock* vi. 90 He saw a flak-burst below, then another, and another... 'Weave, Dig, the bastards are predicting us.'

predictable (prɪˈdɪktəb(ə)l), *a.* [f. PREDICT *v.* + -ABLE.] Capable of being predicted or foretold.
1857 BUCKLE *Civiliz.* I. i. 6 Every generation demonstrates some events to be regular and predictable, which the preceding generation had declared to be irregular and unpredictable. **1889** *Voice* (N.Y.) 10 Oct., The limit of predictable weather changes varies from two to four days.
Hence **predicta'bility**; also *attrib.*
1868 BAIN *Ment. & Mor. Sc.* IV. xi. §3 (1875) 402 The higher the constancy, the predictability of the agent, the higher the excellence attained. **1880** A. H. HUTH *Buckle* I. iv. 229 Buckle .. proves the predictability of human actions by statistics. **1954** J. H. GREENBERG in H. Hoijer *Lang. in Culture* 4 Causality should not be confused with predictability. Perhaps only a predictability relation is discerned in some cases. **1955** *Bull. Atomic Sci.* June 227/3 The concept of predictability seems in some way related to the concept of pattern. **1972** *Archivum Linguisticum* III. 4 The imperfect subjunctive occurs consistently, with equal predictability, in the language of all characters, in all situations.

predictably (prɪˈdɪktəblɪ), *adv.* [f. PREDICTABLE *a.* + -LY².] In a manner that can be or could have been predicted.
1914 J. H. SKRINE *Pastor Futurus* 88 The Pentecosts come back, as surely though not so predictably as the dawns. **1961** *Time* 13 Jan. 9/2 The British and French .. agreed to the setting up of a Communist state, North Viet Nam—which then, predictably, became a base for Communist operations. **1971** *Times* 25 Nov. (Canning Suppl.) p. ii/9 Metrication [of cans] is unlikely to be imposed, but economic pressures will probably hasten a voluntary change. Predictably, the International Organization for Standardization is busy on this and other metrication problems. **1975** *Times Lit. Suppl.* 24 Jan. 92/3 A full catalogue has been prepared by P. R. S. Moorey,.. who has already made himself the undisputed master of this field... Predictably, the commentary .. is authoritative and scholarly.

pre'dicted, *ppl. a.* [f. L. *prædict-us*, pa. pple. of *prædīcĕre* (see PREDICT *v.*) + -ED¹.]
†**1.** Before mentioned, aforesaid. *Obs.*
1546 *Rep. Gild Palmers, Ludlow*, in *Eng. Gilds* (1870) 198 The Salaries, Stipendes, or ffees of the predicted persons. **1599** A. M. tr. *Gabelhouer's Bk. Physicke* 27/2 We must vse this prædictede or fore rehearsed distilled water.
2. Prophesied, foretold, appointed beforehand.
1623 COCKERAM, *Predicted*, Foretold. **1700** DRYDEN *Pythagorean Philos.* 74 Here .. he built and wall'd The place predicted. *Mod.* At the predicted hour the eclipse took place.

prediction (prɪˈdɪkʃən), *sb.* [ad. L. *prædictiōn-em* a saying before, premising, prediction, n. of action f. *prædīcĕre* to PREDICT. Cf. F. *prédiction* (16th c.).]
1. a. The action of predicting or foretelling future events; also, an instance of this, a prophecy.
1561 FULKE (*title*) Antiprognosticon, that is to saye, Inuectiue agaynst the uaine and vnprofitable Predictions of the Astrologians, as Nostrodame, etc., translated out of Latin. **1579–80** NORTH *Plutarch* (1595) 1100 Aratus made no account of their prediction. **1625** BACON *Ess., Prophecies* (Arb.) 537 Dreames, and Predictions of Astrologie. **1704** NELSON *Fest. & Fasts* v. (1739) 62 He was born at Bethlehem according to the Prediction of the Prophet Micah. **1849** MACAULAY *Hist. Eng.* v. I. 572 The prince .. predicted that Amsterdam would raise some difficulty. The prediction proved correct. **1861** *Nat. Rev.* Oct. 430 An author who evidently identifies prophecy with prediction.
†**b.** Applied to a portent or omen. *Obs. rare.*
1601 SHAKS. *Jul. C.* II. ii. 28 Yet Cæsar shall go forth: for these Predictions Are to the world in generall, as to Cæsar.
†**2.** A statement made beforehand. *Obs. rare.*
1634 W. TIRWHYT tr. *Balzac's Lett.* (vol. I) 38, I hope it shall not be said .. that you can accuse his predictions, as erroneous, who never falsified his word with you.
3. *attrib.* and *Comb.*, as ***prediction paradox, study, table, value.***
1952 *Mind* LXI. 265, I hope Mr. O'Connor will not mind my giving his paradox the new and somewhat more appropriate name of 'the prediction paradox'. **1950** S. A. STOUFFER *Measurement & Prediction* vi. 173 Each variable in a prediction study plays one of two possible roles. **1964** M. ARGYLE *Psychol. & Social Probl.* v. 70 Is it possible to work out a grand prediction table showing what treatment each individual should have? **1961** J. B. WILSON *Reason & Morals* iii. 144 Many scientists now use the prediction-value of scientific statements as virtually the only test of their truth.
Hence †**pre'diction** *v. Obs. nonce-wd.* (*trans.*) = PREDICT *v.*; †**pre'dictional** *a. Obs.*, of, pertaining to, or of the nature of prediction.
a **1661** FULLER *Worthies, Oxford*. (1662) II. 329, I conceive it properly to intend the contests betwixt Scholars and Scholars, which were observed predictional, as if their animosities were the Index of the Volume of the Land. **1665** BRATHWAIT *Comment Two Tales* (Chaucer Soc.) 30 What this deep Soothsayer prediction'd before in jest, he now cals for in earnest.

predictionism (prɪˈdɪkʃənɪz(ə)m). [f. PREDICTION *sb.* + -ISM.] Belief in prediction or prophecy.
1919 P. H. OSMOND *Mystical Poets Eng. Church* vii. 215 He was a 'crank', dominated by extravagant notions—a victim of Predictionism and credulity. **1943** *Mind* LII. 200 The immediate issue is not Behaviourism but Predictionism, the doctrine which Professor C. I. Lewis so well sets out.

†**pre'dictious,** *a. Obs. rare*⁻¹. [f. PREDICTION: see -IOUS.] Giving predictions; prophetic; portentous, ominous.
1644 QUARLES *Sheph. Orac.* ix, There's great talk about A strange predictious Star, long since found out By learned Ticho-brachy [= Tycho Brahe].

predictive (prɪˈdɪktɪv), *a.* [ad. late L. *prædictīvus* foretelling, prognosticating, f. *prædīcĕre*: see PREDICT *v.* and -IVE.] **a.** Having the character or quality of predicting; indicative *of* the future.
1659 PEARSON *Creed* ii. 150 There is scarce an action which is not clearly predictive of our Saviour. **1791** COWPER *Odyss.* II. 243 Birds numerous flutter in the beams of day Not all predictive. **1839–40** W. IRVING *Wolfert's R.* iv. (1855) 49 That baleful and livid tint predictive of a storm. **1878** C. STANFORD *Symb. Christ* ii. 36 Using the word prophecy in its predictive sense. **1908** *Westm. Gaz.* 9 May 4/4, I can see with prophetic eyes and hear with predictive ears a development of programme-music which may in the future militate somewhat against the dominant position of the opera. **1957** *Publ. Amer. Dial. Soc. 1956* XXVI. 71 The results proved to be over 90% predictive. **1961** A. G. OETTINGER in *Proc. Symposia Appl. Math.* XII. 105 Predictive analysis yields a description of the syntactic structure of a sentence in terms consonant, although not identical, with old-fashioned parsing, immediate constituent theory .., or phrase-structure theory. **1964** E. A. NIDA *Toward Sci. Transl.* xii. 259 In contrast with this pass procedure is a 'predictive method'.., which more closely represents the mathematician's view of the language structure—one based on the expectations of what is to follow. **1966** I. RHODES in *Automatic Transl. of Lang.* (NATO Summer School, Venice, 1962) 206 Our method has become known as 'predictive analysis' and is based upon the universal habit on the part of the listener to *anticipate* the type of word which a speaker is about to utter. **1966** *Jrnl. Canad. Operational Res. Soc.* 117 *Predictive model*, a model used in a war game to predict the results of actions and interactions between opposing forces. **1972** *Jrnl. Social Psychol.* LXXXVIII. 145 Although the measures are required to compensate for educational disadvantage, they are also expected to have acceptable predictive validity in a system where all groups are competing for the limited further education places.
b. Applied to the future tense when it simply asserts, without any admixture of will or obligation.
1811–31 BENTHAM *Univ. Gram.* Wks. 1843 VIII. 350 In consequence of this modification, it required to be distinguished into two species,—1. The simply predictive future; 2. The dominative future. **1841** LATHAM *Eng. Lang.* (1850) 463 The predictive future.—*I shall be there* .. means simply that the speaker will be present... The promissive future.—*I will be there* .. means that he intends being so.
Hence **pre'dictively** *adv.*, in a predictive manner or form, by way of prediction; **pre'dictiveness.**
1840 DICKENS *Old C. Shop* xxxi, 'It was Miss Edwards who did that, I know', said Miss Monflathers predictively. **1878** C. STANFORD *Symb. Christ* vii, Anticipating the day in which we live, and predictively speaking of Christians alone. *a* **1902** A. B. DAVIDSON *Old Test. Proph.* xiii. (1903) 232 Wherein does their predictiveness consist?

predictor (prɪˈdɪktə(r)). Also -er. [a. med.L. *prædictor*, agent-n. from *prædīcĕre*: see PREDICT *v.* and -OR.]
1. a. One who (or that which) predicts or foretells.
1651 HOBBES *Leviath.* III. xxxvi. 224 *Prædictor*, .. a foreteller of things to come. **1652** [see PREDICT *v.* 3]. **1708** SWIFT *Death Partridge* Wks. 1755 II. I. 160 Whether he hath not been the cause of this poor man's death, as well as the predictor. **1859** R. F. BURTON *Centr. Afr.* in *Jrnl. Geog. Soc.* XXIX. 348 The Mganga is also a predictor and a soothsayer. **1885** *Pall Mall G.* 7 Nov. 2/1 Official predicter of the weather in the United States. **1905** *Contemp. Rev.* Apr. 545 The barometer, as a predictor, is deceptive in the ordinary way of use.
b. *spec.* in *Statistics*, a variable whose value can be used in estimation; also ***predictor variable.***
1950 S. A. STOUFFER *Measurement & Prediction* vi. 173 Each variable .. can serve as a predictor. **1966** DRAPER & SMITH *Appl. Regression Analysis* iv. 104 There are many problems in which a knowledge of more than one independent (or 'predictor') variable is necessary in order to obtain better understanding and/or better prediction of a particular response. **1974** *Nature* 9 Aug. 466/1 Students' attitudes towards scientists were strongly related to only two of the predictor variables: deference and nurturance. **1975** *Sci. Amer.* May 97/1 Later species grew up in the shade of the pioneering species, and the numerical abundance of saplings in the understory proved to be a reasonable predictor of a species' success in reaching the canopy. **1977** *Canad. Jrnl. Linguistics 1976* XXI. I. 21 Dashed lines are curves predicted on the basis of an additive model utilizing a multiple classification analysis .., which demonstrates the main effects of a given predictor (or independent variable).
2. *Mil.* An apparatus for automatically providing tracking information for an anti-aircraft gun from telescopic or radar observations.
1935 L. HART *When Britain goes to War* II. vi. 119 Greater progress has come through the invention of .. the Vickers Predictor, whereby a combined calculation of the speed, course and height of the aeroplane is automatically made and electrically transmitted to the guns. **1936** *Sphere* 30 May 363 (*caption*) Operating the predictor, a delicate instrument for determining the range of enemy 'planes. **1941** *Ann. Reg. 1940* 69 The defenders adopted new tactics, gauging the path of the raiders by means of predictors instead of using searchlights. **1944** H. HAWTON *Night Bombing* 92 Cologne's defences were massive, but with the sky thick with aircraft the searchlights were bewildered and the predictors confused. **1962** S. PUGH *Fighting Vehicles & Weapons* II. 74 The most satisfactory solution so far is this British-designed combination of Swedish Bofors 40 mm. power-operated, automatic light anti-aircraft gun, L.70, with a radar/predictor fire control equipment known as Fire Control Equipment No. 27 'Yellow Fever'. **1974** *Encycl. Brit. Macropædia* IV. 1048/2 The original electronic analogue computers arose from the needs of anti-aircraft artillery 'predictors'.

predictory (prɪˈdɪktərɪ), *a.* [f. PREDICTOR: see -ORY².] Of or pertaining to a predictor; having the quality of predicting, predictive.
1652 GAULE *Magastrom.* 48 They are .. deceived, as well as deceiving, in their presaging or predictory suggestions. *a* **1661** FULLER *Worthies, London* (1662) II. 217 Nicholas (Conquerour of his People) as his Font-name then given him, as predictory of those Victories he afterwards got. **1747** HERVEY *Medit.* II. 120, I shall scorn to ask .. any predictory Information from such senseless Masses. **1849** *Fraser's Mag.* XXXIX. 198 Arguments against the possibility of predictory power.

predigastric: see PRE- A. 4.

predigest (priːdɪˈdʒɛst, -daɪ-), *v.* [f. PRE- A. 1 + DIGEST *v.*; cf. late L. *prædīgestus* that has well digested.] *trans.* To digest beforehand (with quot. 1663 cf. DIGEST *v.* 8); *spec.* to treat (food), before its introduction into the body, by a process similar to digestion, in order to render it easily digestible. Also *fig.* Hence **predi'gested** *ppl. a.*
1663 BOYLE *Usef. Exp. Nat. Philos.* II. App. 334 Little inferiour .. to the Salt and Spirit of predigested Blood. **1890** *Cent. Dict.*, *Predigest*, to digest more or less completely by artificial means before introduction into the body. **1902** *Brit. Med. Jrnl.* 17 May 1199/1 In the case of the premature infant that is unable to suck, it has been found to be of advantage to pass predigested food directly into the stomach by means of a tube. **1905** *Westm. Gaz.* 6 May 14/1 Shakespeare .. was grappled with before our time, and has been predigested for us. **1922** 'K. MANSFIELD' *Let.* 17 July (1928) II. 229 What a relief it is to turn away from these little pre-digested books written by authors who have nothing to say! **1940** R. S. LAMBERT *Ariel & all his Quality* iv. 114 This paper [sc. *The Listener*] whose 'copy' comes to it predigested from other sources. **1975** *Country Life* 18 Dec. 1734/1 As early as 1789 Thomas Pitt, a Worcester chorister, published his pre-digested *Messiah*—ten anthems.

predigestion (priːdɪˈdʒɛstjən, -daɪ-). [f. PRE- A. 2 + DIGESTION; so F. *prédigestion.*]
†**1.** Premature or over-hasty digestion. *Obs.*
1607–12 BACON *Ess., Dispatch* (Arb.) 242 Affected dispatch .. is like that which the Phisitians call predigestion, or hastie digestion, which is sure to fill the body full of Crudities, and secrett seedes of diseases. **1698** F. MANNING *Poems* II. (1701) 21 Seeming-Wits, whose hasty Vein Betrays a Pre-digestion in the Brain.
2. Digestion (of food) by artificial means before introduction into the stomach.
1890 in *Cent. Dict.* **1897** *Allbutt's Syst. Med.* III. 135 After a time the degree of predigestion should be very gradually lessened. **1900** *Ibid.* V. 618 Milk cannot with safety be submitted for any great length of time to predigestion.

predigital, -dilatator: see PRE- B. 3, A. 4b.

‖**predikant** (prɛdɪˈkant). Also **predicant.** [Du.: see PREDICANT.] A minister of the Dutch Protestant church, esp. in South Africa.
[**1634** BRERETON *Trav. Holland*, etc. 45 On the one side, was placed the minister (the predicant).] **1849** R. MOFFAT in *Daily News* 24 Feb. (1900) 6/1 They have a measure of religious knowledge culled from the Bible and their itinerant predikants. **1889** RIDER HAGGARD *Allan's Wife* 66 Your father, the Predicant, always warned me against trekking north. **1905** *Athenæum* 25 Feb. 234/2 The first of a succession of predikants at Tuticorin [Southern India] was the noted ex-Roman Catholic priest, and subsequent translator of .. the Bible into Portuguese, João Ferreira d'Almeida.

predilect (priːdɪˈlɛkt), *a. rare.* [ad. med.L. *prædīlect-us*, pa. pple. of *prædīligĕre* to choose or love before others: see PRE- A. 1 and DILECT.] Chosen or favoured in preference to others. So †**predi'lected** *Obs.*
a **1450** *Mankind* (Brandl) 758 My predylecte sonn, where be ye? *Ibid.* 859 My predilecte specyall, ȝe are worthy to hawe my lowe. *a* **1774** W. HARTE *Charitable Mason* Poems (1810) 387/2 Heav'n to its predilected children grants The middle space 'twixt opulence and wants. **1860** MRS. BYRNE *Undercurrents Overlooked* II. 102 The felon is the predilect object of public charity in England.

predilection (priːdɪˈlɛkʃən). [a. F. *prédilection* (16th c.), ad. L. type **prædīlectiōn-em*, n. of action f. med.L. *prædīligĕre*: see prec. and

DILECTION.] A mental preference or partiality; a favourable predisposition or prepossession.

1742 HUME *Dissert.* iv. (1757) 234 It is almost impossible not to feel a predilection for that which suits our particular turn and disposition. **1768** STERNE *Sent. Journ.* (1778) I. 180 (*Translation*), I have a predilection for the whole corps of veterans. **1828** SCOTT *F.M. Perth* ix, Robert had never testified much predilection for violent exertion. **1866** CRUMP *Banking* ix. 203 Sir Robert Peel avowed his own predilection for a central bank of issue.

predi'lective, *a. rare.* [f. L. *prædīlect-*, ppl. stem of *prædīligĕre*: see PREDILECT and -IVE.] Of, pertaining to, or showing predilection.

1798 CHARLOTTE SMITH *Yng. Philos.* III. 172, I see nothing impossible in such a personage taking advantage of your predilective imprudency.

pre-diluvial (priːdɪˈl(j)uːvɪəl), *a. Geol.* [f. PRE- B. 1 + DILUVIAL.] Of or belonging to an age before that of the Diluvium or Northern Drift.

1857 B. TAYLOR *North. Trav.* xxvi. 269 The Kiöllefjord, which in the pre-diluvial times must have been a tremendous mountain gorge.

prediluvian (priːdɪˈl(j)uːvɪən), *a.* and *sb.* [f. PRE- B. 1 + DILUVIAN.] = ANTEDILUVIAN:

A. *adj.* Existing or occurring before the Noachian deluge. *rare.* B. *sb.* One who lived before the Deluge.

1804 COLLINS *Scripscrap* 169 Prediluvians, uplifted and pompous Deem'd his nautical Scheme a fantastical Dream. **1855** WYLLIE in M. Hopkins *Hawaii* (1862) 320 The original language spoken by Adam and the prediluvian race of man, if not the post-diluvian Hebrew, has disappeared. **1928** V. G. CHILDE *Most Anc. East* i. 15 The Prediluvian kings' reigns are all incredibly long. **1931** C. WILLIAMS *Place of Lion* xvi. 277 Some incantation whereby the prediluvian magicians had controlled contentions among spirits. **1981** *Times Lit. Suppl.* 26 June 731/2 Their pre-diluvian fundamentalist faith.

pre-dinner: see PRE- B. 2 a.

pre-direct, -discipline, etc.: see PRE- A. 1, 2, etc.

prediscover (priːdɪˈskʌvə(r)), *v.* [PRE- A. 1.] *trans.* To discover beforehand.

1655 FULLER *Ch. Hist.* IX. i. §52 These holy men did prudently prediscover that differences in judgements would unavoidably happen in the Church. **1766** BLACKBURNE *Confess.* (1767) 221 In his supposing them to have prediscovered the dissensions, that would happen in the church an hundred years after they were dead. **1926** *Spectator* 3 July 18/2 The poet 'prediscovers' the Einstein theory.

pre-di'scovery, *sb.* and *a.* A. *sb.* [PRE- A. 2.] Previous discovery.

1653 T. HORTON *Wisdome's Judgment* 10 To shew us them, not in the event,..but afore-hand in the pre-discoveries and apprehensions of it. **1787** SIR J. HAWKINS *Johnson* 464 A question between us and..Spain, touching the pre-discovery, and, consequently, the right of dominion over certain islands in the South seas.

B. *adj.* [PRE- B. 2.] Occurring or carried out before the discovery of something.

1946 *Nature* 9 Nov. 648/1 In the nomenclature of the time, these pre-discovery observations of Uranus are known as the 'ancient' observations. **1968** R. A. LYTTLETON *Mysteries Solar Syst.* vii. 234 LeVerrier, in his discussion, included the pre-discovery observations of Uranus going back to 1690.

predisponent (priːdɪˈspəʊnənt), *a.* and *sb.* Also 7–8 præ-. [f. PRE- A. 1, 2 + DISPONENT.]

A. *adj.* Predisposing. Now *rare.*

1649 JER. TAYLOR *Gt. Exemp.* II. Ad Sect. x. 6 These graces..are given to men irregularly and without any order of prædisponent causes. **1822–34** *Good's Study Med.* (ed. 4) III. 127 Somnambulism occurs in many persons without any manifest predisponent cause.

B. *sb.* A predisposing influence or cause.

1771 *Let. to Dr. Cadogan on Diss. Gout* 7 My neighbour is free from this prædisponent, and escapes it. **1852** *Jrnl. R. Agric. Soc.* XIII. II. 375 Secondary causes, as pre-disponents to the disease.

Hence **predi'sponency** [see -ENCY], the quality of being predisponent or causing predisposition.

a **1846** PARRY is cited by WORCESTER.

predisposal (priːdɪˈspəʊzəl). [PRE- A. 2.] Previous disposal.

1795 *Jemima* I. 119 If you had not rendered that desirable event impossible, by the predisposal of yourself,..your Jemima should have become your wife. **1830** HERSCHEL *Stud. Nat. Phil.* §26 This contemplation of possible occurrences, and predisposal of what shall happen.

predispose (priːdɪˈspəʊz), *v.* [f. PRE- A. 1 + DISPOSE: cf. F. *prédisposer* (15th c. in Hatz.-Darm.), and L. *prædisposit-us* predisposed.]

1. *trans.* To dispose (a person, etc.) beforehand; to render liable or subject *to* something; to put into a favourable or suitable frame or condition; to incline or adapt previously. Also *absol.*

1646 [see PREDISPOSED]. **1684** T. BURNET *The. Earth* I. iv. 36 Vegetable productions require the heat of the Sun, to pre-dispose and excite the Earth, and the Seeds. *a* **1716** SOUTH (J.), Unless nature be predisposed to friendship by its own propensity. **1800** *Med. Jrnl.* IV. 299 As a hot summer immediately excites the cholera, so it predisposes to diarrhœa and dysentery. **1843** BETHUNE *Sc. Fireside Stor.* 45 The relief..only predisposed him for an earlier..relapse into the same melancholy mood. **1871** BLACKIE *Four Phases* I. 147 The majority of his judges..came predisposed to condemn him. **1902** *Daily Chron.* 14 May 7/6 Hydrogen.. being mixed with a certain quantity of air, the presence of which could only help to predispose for an explosion.

2. To dispose of, give away, or bequeath before.

1666 in *10th Rep. Hist. MSS. Comm.* App. v. 20 Finding ..the office designed for him predisposed by patent. **1807** CRABBE *Par. Reg.* III. 531 Assured of wealth, this man of simple heart, To every friend had predispos'd a part.

Hence **predi'sposing** *ppl. a.*, that predisposes; that renders favourable, inclined, or susceptible.

1660 JER. TAYLOR *Duct. Dubit.* I. iv, His own purposes and predisposing thoughts. **1793** *Friendly Addr. to Poor* 21 Many things concur..to form a predisposing cause for such disorders. **1848** R. I. WILBERFORCE *Doctr. Incarnation* xiii. (1852) 362 There is one radical defect—the need of some predisposing grace on the part of God. **1904** *Brit. Med. Jrnl.* 7 Sept. 640 The end of the hot season in the tropics..is very predisposing to malaria.

predisposed (-ˈpəʊzd), *ppl. a.* [f. prec. + -ED[1].] Disposed or inclined beforehand; previously or already liable or subject.

1646 SIR T. BROWNE *Pseud. Ep.* 308 It concurreth but unto predisposed effects. **1818** HALLAM *Mid. Ages* (1872) II. vii. II. 218 Tales,..which a predisposed multitude eagerly swallowed. **1899** *Allbutt's Syst. Med.* VIII. 569 A direct transmission [of disease] from one member of a predisposed family to another.

Hence **predi'sposedness**, the quality of being predisposed; predisposition.

1645 T. COLEMAN *Hopes Deferred* 21 A praying army is a predisposednesse for successe. **1681** H. MORE *Exp. Dan.* v. 141 Whether the difference lie meerly in the predisposednesss of the persons..is a subtile piece of Philosophy.

predisposition (ˌpriːdɪspəʊˈzɪʃən). [f. PRE- A. 2 + DISPOSITION; cf. mod.F. *prédisposition.*]

1. The condition of being predisposed or inclined beforehand (*to* something or *to do* something); a previous inclination or favourable state of mind. Also, a tendency in a person to respond or react in a certain way.

1626 BACON *Sylva* §236 That the Spirits of the Teacher put in Motion, should worke with the Spirits of the Learner, a Pre-disposition to offer to Imitate. **1660** JER. TAYLOR *Worthy Commun.* II. ii. 132 St. Austin reckoning what pre-disposition is necessary by way of preparation to the holy sacrament. **1705** STANHOPE *Paraphr.* I. 259 Constituent Parts of Repentance, and necessary Predispositions to Forgiveness. **1840** MACAULAY *Ess.*, *Ranke's Hist.* (1887) 577 There had long been a predisposition to heresy. **1936** *Discovery* Aug. 254/1 All these effects..can be shown to result from psychological inhibitions and predispositions. **1949** C. I. HOVLAND et al. *Exper. Mass Communication* vii. 192 A person soon 'forgets' the ideas he has learned which are not consonant with his predispositions. **1973** G. A. DAVIS *Psychol. of Problem Solving* ii. 18 Habit and conformity are implicit in such..personality concepts as rigidity,..predisposition,..fear of the unknown and, on occasion, pigheadedness. **1980** *Sci. Amer.* Apr. 112/1 It is generally accepted that most animal characteristics are the product of an interaction between inherited predispositions and the environment.

2. *spec.* A physical condition which renders its possessor liable to the attack of disease.

1622 BACON *Hen. VII*, Wks. 1879 I. 734/1 It [the sweating sickness] was conceived..to proceed from a malignity in the constitution of the air, gathered by the predispositions of seasons. **1676** WISEMAN *Chirurg. Treat.* IV. ii. 249 External Accidents are often the occasional cause of the Kings-Evil, but they always suppose a predisposition of the Body to it. **1707** FLOYER *Physic. Pulse-Watch* 311 Table of the Pulses according to Diseases, and the Pre-Disposition to them. **1801** *Med. Jrnl.* V. 83 Predisposition to Small-pox. **1873** T. H. GREEN *Introd. Pathol.* (ed. 2) 101 Here..there may exist some special predisposition of the tissues themselves.

Hence **predispo'sitional** *a.*, of or pertaining to predisposition.

1847 BUSHNELL *Chr. Nurt.* II. i. (1861) 247 Results from predispositional state, or initially sanctified property.

predissoci'ation. *Physics* and *Chem.* [PRE- A. 2.] The passage of a molecule between a quantized vibrational and rotational state (above its ground state) and a dissociated state of the same energy that is not quantized, the occurrence of which results in certain bands in the spectrum of the molecule being diffuse instead of having the normal rotational fine structure. Freq. *attrib.*

1924 HENRI & TEVES in *Nature* 20 Dec. 895/1 The molecule can be modified in its internal structure: the atoms are driven apart, the bonds are weakened, the molecule becomes more reactive, and the rotational movements are no longer quantified. This first modification is a preliminary preparation of the molecule for its total dissociation, and it is necessary to introduce a new term for this change. We propose to denote it by the term predissociation of the molecule. **1930** *Physical Rev.* XXXV. 1028 (*heading*) Predissociation of diatomic molecules from high rotational states. **1944** GLASSTONE *Theoret. Chem.* iv. 188 In some cases the predissociation spectrum is followed by a region of continuous absorption but, in other instances, bands with fine structure are found on both long and short wave sides of the predissociation bands. **1962** P. J. & B. DURRANT *Introd. Adv. Inorg. Chem.* vii. 222 Predissociation is commonly shown only in absorption, not in emission. **1966** BARNARD & MANSELL *Fund. Physical Chem.* ii. 96 A molecule undergoing pre-dissociation will dissociate within the time of one rotation and the rotational fine structure will tend to be lost in the gas phase spectrum. **1977** *Sci. Amer.* Feb. 95/1 Instead the molecule is disassembled at a lower energy through a phenomenon called predissociation.

predi'stinguish (priː-), *v.* [PRE- A. 1.] *trans.* To distinguish by way of preference. Hence **predi'stinguished** *ppl. a.*, distinguished before or above others.

1778 *Love Feast* 25 Of saving Grace a predistinguish'd Heir. **1817** COLERIDGE *Lay Serm.* in *Biog. Lit.* (1882) 391 How shall the law predistinguish the ominous screech owl.. from the auspicious and friendly birds of warning?

†**ˌpredivi'nation.** *Obs.* [ad. L. *prædīvīnātiōn-em*, n. of action from *prædīvīnāre*: see next. Cf. obs. F. *prédivination* (1552 in Godef.).] The divining of events beforehand.

1603 *Adv. Don Sebast.* in *Harl. Misc.* (Malh.) II. 401 Many matters that he had seen take event according to his predivination. **1611** FLORIO, *Prediuinatione*, a prediuination or guessing. **1623** in COCKERAM.

†**predi'vine**, *v. Obs.* [ad. L. *prædīvīnāre* to divine beforehand, have a presentiment of: see PRE- A. 1 and DIVINE *v.* Cf. obs. F. *prédiviner* (1530 in Godef.).] *trans.* and *intr.* To divine beforehand, presage, prognosticate.

1607 WALKINGTON *Opt. Glass* 144 Which did..predivine the..eloquence of Plato. **1616** R. C. *Times' Whistle*, etc. (1871) 146 Astronomers..Can pre-divine of famines, plagues, and warres. **1622** DONNE *Serm.* 15 Sept. 42 [One who] be the intention neuer so sincere, will presage, and prognosticate, and prediuine sinister and mischieuous effects from it.

Predmost (ˈprɛdməʊst), *a.* Also **Předmost** (ˈpʒɛdmɒst). [Anglicized form of the placename *Předmost* near Brno (Brünn), in Moravia, Czechoslovakia.] Of, connected with, or relating to human or other remains, artefacts, etc., that evidence a Combe Capelle type of *Homo sapiens* of Upper Palæolithic culture, first excavated at Předmost between 1882 and 1894, and later at other sites, esp. in Central Europe and round the eastern Mediterranean; also *ellipt.* as *sb.* Hence **Pred'mostian.**

1916 H. F. OSBORN *Men Old Stone Age* iii. 257 Such very primitive forms as the Brünn or Předmost race of Upper Palæolithic times. *Ibid.* iv. 349 All these sculptures of the mammoth have in common the indication of a very small ear —similar to that in the Předmost model. **1921** M. C. BURKITT *Prehistory* x. 130 The male statuette of Brünn, if it be of the age of Předmost and not more ancient, appears to be a prolongation of the Aurignacian artistic technique. **1927** PEAKE & FLEURE *Hunters & Artists* v. 67 We may call it provisionally the Combe Capelle, or perhaps better the Predmost type by way of contrast with the Cro-Magnon type. **1931** *Times Lit. Suppl.* 23 Apr. 317/2 Sir Arthur Keith suggests that both the Cro-Magnons and the Predmostians are early Caucasians hailing ultimately from South-Western Asia. **1939** V. G. CHILDE *Dawn European Civilization* (ed. 3) i. 3 Mesolithic groups appear in general isolated and poorly equipped in contrast to Magdalenians or Předmostians. **1957** M. BULLOCK tr. *Boule & Vallois's Fossil Men* viii. 278 The long discussion of which these Predmost Men have been the object; their affinities are, above all, with the great Cro-Magnon race. **1960** W. HOWELLS *Mankind in Making* xiv. 210 There you have *Homo sapiens.* And there you have the men of the present, and the men of the Upper Paleolithic. Some of the latter, like the Předmost skulls, had rather strong brow ridges. **1977** BRACE & MONTAGU *Human Evol.* ix. 351 (*caption*) Předmost skull. Upper Paleolithic of Czechoslovakia.

prednisolone (prɛdˈnɪsələʊn). *Pharm.* [f. next with inserted *ol* (see -OL).] A synthetic steroid, $C_{21}H_{28}O_5$, which has similar properties and uses to prednisone, of which it is a reduced derivative.

1955 *Jrnl. Amer. Med. Assoc.* 21 May 166/1 Prednisolone (Meticortelone) and prednisone (Meticorten), two new synthetic steroids formerly known as metacortandralone and metacortandracin, have recently been recommended as effective in the treatment of rheumatoid arthritis. **1959** *Economist* 19 Dec. 1160/1 One of the five firms which produce the bulk of such drugs, charged chemists $17.90 for 100 tablets of prednisolone, under the brand name of Meticortelone. **1962** HARRIS & GRUBER in A. Pirie *Lens Metabolism Rel. Cataract* 379 Of the steroids, prednisolone, either as its phosphate or as the alcohol, caused the greatest reduction in cation recovery. **1966** *Lancet* 24 Dec. 1382/2 He was given the usual measures for heart-failure and antibiotics, oxygen, and prednisolone 10 mg. t.d.s. to 'buy time'. **1974** PASSMORE & ROBSON *Compan. Med. Stud.* III. xviii. 98/1 Until the prednisolone takes effect the patient's distress should be relieved by bronchodilator drugs.

prednisone (ˈprɛdnɪsəʊn). *Pharm.* [Prob. f. *pregnadiene* (f. PREGNA(NE + DIENE) + *-isone*, after CORTISONE.] A colourless, crystalline, synthetic steroid, $C_{21}H_{26}O_5$, resembling cortisone but possessing greater glucocorticoid activity, which is used as an anti-inflammatory agent and to depress immune responses, esp. in the treatment of rheumatoid arthritis.

1955 *Dis. Chest* XXVII. 515 Metacortandracin (Metacortin) used in this study and furnished by Schering Corporation, Bloomfield, New Jersey has been re-named Prednisone. **1955** [see PREDNISOLONE]. **1959** S. DUKE-ELDER *Parson's Dis. Eye* (ed. 13) xiv. 150 Prednisone and

Prednisolone, are often preferable for systemic administration since they are less liable to excite the unfortunate side-effects associated with cortisone. **1965** *Spectator* 1 Jan. 12/3 Prednisone is especially useful for easing the pain of aged arthritics. **1974** R. M. KIRK et al. *Surgery* iv. 58 Generalised disease responds to chemotherapy, usually with a combination of vincristine, mustine, procarbazine and prednisone in pulsed doses.

predominance (prɪˈdɒmɪnəns). Also 7 **præ-**. [f. as PREDOMINANT + -ANCE. Cf. F. *prédominance* (16th c.).] The fact or position of being predominant: **a.** *Astrol.* Ascendancy, superior influence.

1615 BRATHWAIT *Strappado* (1878) 112 Both haue influence from one ominous star, Which bodes our happinesse or our mischance According to the starres predominance. **1622** FLETCHER *Sea Voy.* III. i, The sullen Saturn had predominance at your nativity! *c* **1650** *Don Bellianis* 178 [A sword] which she forged under the Constellation and Predominance of such Planets, that no Enchantment might against it prevail.

b. *generally.* Prevailing or superior influence, strength, or authority; prevalence, preponderance. In early use frequently of the humours.

1602 MARSTON *Antonio's Rev.* IV. ii, Ther's not a beauty lives Hath that imperiall predominance Ore my affectes. *a* **1627** H. SHIRLEY *Mart. Soldier* III. iv, Now a Scorpion is A small compacted creature in whom Earth Hath the predominance, but mixt with fire. **1668** SOUTH *Serm.* (1727) V. xi. 420 It is really no small Argument of the Predominance of Conscience over Interest. **1791** BOSWELL *Johnson* an. 1716 (1816) I. 24 The early predominance of intellectual vigour. **1853** KANE *Grinnell Exp.* xxviii. (1856) 235 This predominance of breezes from the southward and eastward.

preˈdominancy. [f. as next + -ANCY.] The quality of being predominant; an instance of this; the fact of being predominant; = prec.

1598 FLORIO, *Predominatione*, predomination, predominancie. **1607–12** BACON *Ess., Custom & Educ.* (Arb.) 368 The predominancye of Custome is every where visible. **1611** SPEED *Hist. Gt. Brit.* IX. xi. §10 The young Queene..tooke her selfe not to be a little wronged by this vngracious mans predominancy. **1646** SIR T. BROWNE *Pseud. Ep.* IV. iii. 183 An Inflammation..Oedematous, Schirrous, Erisipelatous, according to the predominancy of melancholy, flegme, or choler. **1652** CULPEPPER *Eng. Physic.* (1809) 276 Mars claims predominancy over all these wholesome herbs. **1739** MELMOTH *Fitzosb. Lett.* (1763) 188 To be influenced in his censure or applause..by the predominancy or deficiency of his favorite beauty. **1822–34** *Good's Study Med.* (ed. 4) III. 410 Affected with a predominancy of rigid over clonic action.

predominant (prɪˈdɒmɪnənt), *a.* and *sb.* [a. F. *prédominant* (14th c. in Godef. *Compl.*), ad. L. type **prædominānt-em*, pres. pple. of **prædominārī*, *-āre*: see PREDOMINE.]

A. *adj.* Predominating.

1. Having ascendancy, power, influence, or authority over others; superior, ascendant, prevalent.

In early use a term of Astrology, also of Physiology.

predominant branch of a tree (*Math.*): see DOMINANT 5. ***predominant nerve*** (*Bot.*): the main or principal nerve, as in the leaves of mosses. ***predominant partner***: a phrase applied (after Lord Rosebery) to England among the several constituents of the United Kingdom.

1576 FLEMING *Panopl. Epist.* 279 You are not ignoraunt, yᵗ melancholy being predominant,..moueth men to madnesse. **1592** SHAKS. *Rom. & Jul.* II. iii. 29 And where the worser is predominant, Full soone the Canker death eates vp that Plant. **1601** —— *All's Well* I. i. 211 *Hel.* The warres hath so kept you vnder, that you must needes be borne vnder Mars. *Par.* When he was predominant. **1672** PETTY *Pol. Anat.* (1691) 34 Why do not the predominant Party in Parliament..make England beyond Trent another Kingdom? **1751** JOHNSON *Rambler* No. 103 ¶7 The temporary effect of a predominant passion. **1817** JAS. MILL *Brit. India* II. v. i. 315 After the power of the English became predominant. **1863** GEO. ELIOT *Romola* i, A change which was apt to make the women's voices predominant in the chorus. **1894** LD. ROSEBERY *Sp. Ho. Lds.* 12 Mar. (Hansard IV. XXII. 32), The noble Marquess [of Salisbury] made one remark on the subject of Irish Home Rule with which I confess myself in entire accord. He said that before Irish Home Rule is conceded by the Imperial Parliament, England, as the predominant Member of the partnership of the Three Kingdoms, will have to be convinced of its justice and equity. **1894** *Times* 19 Mar. 9/3 But if only a simple majority was contemplated, why the allusion to England as the predominant partner? Mr. Gladstone had a majority, and tried by its aid to carry Home Rule against the predominant partner. **1904** *Daily Chron.* 18 Mar. 6/4 If the predominant partner theory was to be carried out in the next Government.

b. More vaguely: More abundant as an element; more frequent; prevailing, prevalent.

1601 HOLLAND *Pliny* II. 488 A third [Corinthian metal] of an equall medley and temperature, wherein a man shall not perceiue any one mettall predominant. **1635** SWAN *Spec. M.* v. §2 (1643) 176 The Equator where heat is most predominant. **1709** BERKELEY *The. Vision* Ded., Those criminal pleasures so fashionable and predominant in the age we live in. **1851** D. WILSON *Preh. Ann.* (1863) II. IV. i. 179 The predominant Erse dialect. **1878** HUXLEY *Physiogr.* 47 The wet side being that towards which the predominant winds blow.

†**c.** With *of*: Domineering over, overruling. *Obs.*

1642 in Clarendon *Hist. Reb.* VI. §106 They were so presumptuous, and predominant of his Majesties Resolutions, that they forbear not those outrages.

d. *fig.* Superior in position, towering *over*.

1797 HOLCROFT tr. *Stolberg's Trav.* (ed. 2) II. xliv. 96 The Cupola..rises predominant over every object. **1867** A. BARRY *Sir C. Barry* vii. 251 Made the roofs boldly predominant.

2. *Her.* (See quots.)

1766–87 PORNY *Heraldry* Gloss., *Predominant*, this term is sometimes used in Heraldry to signify that the Field is but of one Tincture. *Ibid.* 28 When some Metal, Colour, or Fur, is spread all over the Surface or Field, such a Tincture is said to be predominant.

B. *sb.* That which predominates: **a.** A predominating person, influence, power, or authority; a predominating quality, fact, or feature.

1589 WARNER *Alb. Eng.* VI. xxxii. (1612) 163 We are Predominants, say we. **1594** *Warres Cyrus* 907 Reason, my Lord, was the predominant. **1599** B. JONSON *Ev. Man out of Hum.* III. iii, You must first haue an especial care so to weare your hat, that it oppresse not confusedly this your predominant or fore-top. *a* **1656** USSHER *Ann.* vi. (1658) 219 The Sun..was the Predominant in Greece, and the Moon in Persia. **1890** C. L. MORGAN *Anim. Life & Intell.* 349, I venture to call the prominent quality a predominant as opposed to the isolate.

†**b.** A predominating or besetting sin. *Obs.*

1633 W. STRUTHER in Spurgeon *Treas. Dav.* Ps. xxxvi. 4 Every man's predominant is a beast of Satan's saddling and providing. **1699** ELIZ. WEST *Mem.* (1865) 143, I was ill employed, pursuing after my idols and predominants.

c. *Welsh Phonology.* (See quot.)

1856 J. WILLIAMS *Gram. Edeyrn* §134 Predominants..which are f, ph, ch, ng, ngh, dd, th, l, m, n, r, mh, nh, being so called because they prevail over the umbratiles, thrust them out of the sentence, and reign by their own power in their stead.

preˈdominantly, *adv.* [f. prec. + -LY².] In a predominant manner or degree; with superior influence; preponderatingly.

1681 J. SCOTT *Chr. Life* I. iii. §2 (1684) 111 Our Wills being already predominantly inclined to follow God, and take example by him. **1773** *Life N. Frowde* 59 A Longing to view distant Climes so predominantly reigned in my Thoughts. **1884** *Manch. Exam.* 20 Aug. 5/1 Down to the beginning of the reign of George III,..the House was predominantly Whig.

predominate (prɪˈdɒmɪnət), *a.* Now *rare.* [app. a mistaken form for PREDOMINANT, prob. after such adjs. as *moderate*, *temperate*.] = PREDOMINANT.

1591 NASHE *Prognostication* To Rdr., Wks. (Grosart) II. 143 Mercury being Lord and predominate in the house of Fortune. **1597** BEARD *Theatre God's Judgem.* (1612) 509 When crueltie once beginneth to bee predominat, it is so vnsatiable that it neuer ceaseth. **1605** TIMME *Quersit.* III. 145 When salt is predominate..it produceth so many kinds of diuers ulcers. **1754** RICHARDSON *Grandison* (1810) II. xi. 136 He gave way to his predominate bias. **1800** HELENA WELLS *Constantia Neville* (ed. 2) II. 273 They commonly possessed..the predominate bad qualities of both Europeans and Africans. **1865** E. BURRITT *Walk Land's End* 331 The denomination he [Wesley] founded seems to be the standing or predominate order here.

predominate (prɪˈdɒmɪneɪt), *v.* Also 6 **præ-**. [f. med.L. **prædomināre* (prob. used in 15–16th c. L.): see PREDOMINE and -ATE³. It might also be f. F. *prédominer*, like *isolate*, etc.: see -ATE³ 6.]

†**1.** *intr. Astrol.* To have ascendancy, to exert controlling influence. *Obs.*

1597 A. M. tr. *Guillemeau's Fr. Chirurg.* 51 b/1 The astronomicall constellation which ouer vs is prædominating. **1598** SHAKS. *Merry W.* II. ii. 294, I shall awe him with my cudgell: it shall hang like a Meteor ore the Cuckolds horns: ..I will predominate ouer the pezant. *a* **1633** AUSTIN *Medit.* (1635) 147 For Saturne (principally predominating, on Saturday) disposed mens minds and bodies to a dull heavinesse.

2. *generally.* **a.** To have or exert controlling power, to lord it *over*; to surpass in authority or influence, to be superior.

1618 BOLTON *Florus* (1636) 228 Our fellowes, and allies most justly demanded equall priviledge with the Romans,..to the hope whereof Drusus had raized them upon a desire to predominate. **1623** COCKERAM II, To Gouerne or rule, ..*predominate*,..*domineere*. **1638** SIR T. HERBERT *Trav.* (ed. 2) 237 The women in those parts never predominate. **1807** S. TURNER *Anglo-Sax.* (ed. 2) I. I. viii. 87 In this period of the independence of Britain, one tyrant is said to have predominated over the rest. **1855** MILMAN *Lat. Chr.* XI. iv. V. 102 The Frenchman soon began to predominate over the Pontiff.

b. To be the stronger, main, or leading element; to prevail, preponderate.

1594 CAREW *Huarte's Exam. Wits* (1616) 83 When this element predominateth in the mixture. *a* **1687** PETTY *Pol. Arith.* i. (1691) 15 Those who predominate in Shipping, and Fishing, have more occasions than others to frequent all parts of the World. **1751** JOHNSON *Rambler* No. 141 ¶2 The desires that predominate in our hearts. **1839** MURCHISON *Silur. Syst.* I. x. 137 The hornblende for the most part predominating over the felspar. **1881** OWEN in *Nature* 1 Sept. 421/1 Since the foundation of the Museum in 1753, when the collections of printed books and manuscripts predominated.

c. To occupy a more commanding position; to tower *over*.

1814 SCOTT *Wav.* viii, A huge bear, carved in stone, predominated over a large stone-basin. **1859** GEO. ELIOT *A. Bede* v, The tall gables and elms of the rectory predominate over the tiny white-washed church.

3. *trans.* To dominate over, prevail over, control. Now *rare.*

1607 SHAKS. *Timon* IV. iii. 142 Let your close fire predominate his smoke, And be no turne-coats. **1631** *Celestina* I. 11 You happy powers that predominate humane actions, assist. **1810** *Splendid Follies* II. 95 The frailties of your nature predominated the glare of your riches. **1892** A. E. LEE *Hist. Columbus* (Ohio) II. 573 The ambition for outside effect which predominated the original plans seems to have been disdainful of interior comfort.

Hence **preˈdominated** *ppl. a.* = PREDOMINATE *a.*

1752 HUME *Ess., Parties* (1768) 36 According to that principle which is predominated and is found to have the greatest influence.

preˈdominately, *adv.* [f. PREDOMINATE *a.* + -LY².] = PREDOMINANTLY.

1594 CAREW *Huarte's Exam. Wits* xv. (1596) 271 Nature..in a woman cannot be predominatly hot. **1842** MANNING *Serm.* (1848) I. 66 In persons of a predominately worldly tone of mind. **1892** *Athenæum* 13 Feb. 212/2 Used too predominately, to the dwarfing or exclusion of other feelings. **1961** *Christian Sci. Monitor* 17 Oct. 4/7 WWRL's [*sc.* a radio station's] colorful mobile unit, cruising predominately Negro neighborhoods. **1965** C. WALSH in J. Gibb *Light on C.S. Lewis* 110 He quickly gained a wide audience..it was predominately high-brow and middle-brow. **1970** [see NON-WORD]. **1973** *Yale Rev.* Spring 452 Other indications that the *Supplement* is predominately concerned with the modern..history of the English vocabulary. **1977** *Lancet* 6 Aug. 306/2 We were fascinated by the suggestion..that in San Francisco enteric diseases are predominately sexually transmitted.

preˈdominating, *ppl. a.* [f. PREDOMINATE *v.* + -ING².] That predominates; controlling, ruling, prevailing; rarely, domineering, lording it.

1595 DANIEL *Civ. Wars* (1609) v. xciii, The pride of some predominating will. **1666** BOYLE *Orig. Formes & Qual.* 357 Not so much the Predominating as the Denominating Forme. **1866** GEO. ELIOT *F. Holt* xv, But then..that 'one' must be tender to her, not rude and predominating in his manners. **1904** *Expositor* Mar. 186 Joyousness is the predominating characteristic of Judaism.

Hence **preˈdominatingly** *adv.*

1884 BROWNING *Ferishtah, Bean-stripe* 222 Either..seems Predominatingly the colour. **1905** ORR *Probl. O.T.* vii. 196 Portions of chapters in Genesis are marked by the use exclusively or predominatingly of the divine name Elohim.

predomination (prɪdɒmɪˈneɪʃən). Now *rare* or *Obs.* [n. of action from PREDOMINE, PREDOMINATE *v.*: see -ATION.] The action, fact, or condition of predominating; predominance; ascendancy. (Often in *Astrol.* and in the doctrine of the humours.)

1586 A. DAY *Eng. Secretary* II. (1625) 105 So great a predomination hath this name of fidelity in the hearts of a number. **1612** WOODALL *Surg. Mate* Wks. (1653) 332 The colour uncertaine, according to the predomination of the humour infected. **1613** W. BROWNE *Brit. Past.* I. i, Have thy starres maligne bene such, That their predominations sway so much Over the rest? *c* **1645** HOWELL *Lett.* (1892) II. 662 The perpetual conflict of the humors within us for predomination. **1654** 'PALAEMON' *Friendship* 3 Mercury..follows the predomination of those other Planets with whom he is in Conjunction. **1783** JOHNSON 28 Apr. in *Boswell*, You would not trust to the predomination of right, which, you believe, is in your opinions.

preˈdominator. *rare*⁻¹. [agent-n. from PREDOMINATE *v.*: see -OR.] A predominating agent.

1654 GAYTON *Pleas. Notes* II. ii. 32 The chiefe predominator in the businesse was to be two grains of pulvis magneticus.

†**preˈdomine,** *v. Obs.* [app. a. F. *prédominer* (16th c. in Littré), ad. L. type **prædomināre* (which may have been used in med. or 16th c. L.), f. *præ*, PRE- A. + *dominārī*, later *-āre*, to be master, rule, f. *dominus* lord, master.

Like the other words of the group, in early use in Astrology, also in the doctrine of the humours.]

1. *intr.* = PREDOMINATE *v.* 1, 2.

1591 SYLVESTER *Du Bartas* I. ii. 104 So th' Element in Wine predomining It hot, and cold, and moist, and dry doth bring. **1596** DRAYTON *Leg.* iv. 399 To my ascendant hasting then to clime, There as the first predomining the time. **1640** R. BAILLIE *Canterb. Self-convict.* Postscr. 4 Shall partialitie so farre predomine with you, that we..must be reputed Apostates? **1678** J. BROWN *Life Faith* (1824) I. v. 109 The abounding and predomining of carnal fears.

2. *trans.* = PREDOMINATE *v.* 3.

1720 W. GIBSON *Diet. Horses* i. (1731) 2 How far these predomine or influence them, we are much at a loss to know.

†**predomiˈneer,** *v. Obs. rare*⁻¹. [f. PRE- A. 5 + DOMINEER; prob. influenced by F. *prédominer.*] *trans.* To overrule, domineer over.

1594 *2nd Rep. Dr. Faustus* iii. C ij, Being gouerned and predomineirde by that quicke and ready spirite.

†**predoˈminion.** *Obs.* [f. PRE- A. 5 + DOMINION, after *predomine*, etc.] Superior power; predominance, prevalence.

1607 WALKINGTON *Opt. Glass* vi. 77 Of the predominion of any element,..the complexion hath his..denomination. **1611** FLORIO, *Predominio*, a fore-rule or predominion. **1673** GREW *Anat. Roots* II. §70 By the predominion of the other Principles, made mild.

†pre'dominize, *v. Obs. rare*⁻¹. [f. PREDOMINE (or its source) + -IZE.] *trans.* = PREDOMINATE *v.* 3.

1648 EARL OF WESTMORELAND *Otia Sacra* (1879) 29 And so allay the Fury, stint the Rage Of madness doth predominize this age.

†pre'dominy. *Obs.* [ad. med.L. type **prædominium*: see PRE- A. 5 and DOMINIUM.] Superior power or authority; predominance.

(Used in the translation cited, but not in Trevisa.)

1432-50 tr. *Higden* (Rolls) I. 231 The Romanes made promise to Marcus, a nowble knyȝhte, that he scholde haue predominy of the cite [*urbis dominium*], and a perpetualle memory if he cowthe delyuer that cite. *Ibid.* 263. *Ibid.* 351 Obteynenge the predominy by strenȝhte and armes. **1432-50** *Harleian Contn. of Higden* (Rolls) VIII. 500 That trowble and discorde scholde not have predominy afterwarde.

predone (priː'dʌn), *ppl. a. rare*⁻¹. [f. PRE- A. 1 or (?) 6 + DONE.] Already done; or (?) completely done, fordone, exhausted.

1859 KINGSLEY in *Life* (1879) II. xviii. 99, I am..as one desperate and predone with work of various kinds at once.

predoom (priː'duːm), *v.* Also 7 præ-. [PRE- A. 1.] *trans.* **a.** To pronounce the sentence or doom of beforehand; to precondemn. **b.** To foreordain (some doom) *to.* So **predoomed** (-'duːmd), **pre'dooming** *ppl. adjs.*

1618 *Owles Almanacke* Raven 2, I haue euer been held a Prædooming Bird. **1786** *Hist.* in *Ann. Reg.* 51/2 The Sheich Mansour pretended that he was pre-doomed by the.. decrees of heaven to fill up the measure of divine revelation. **1796** COLERIDGE *Dest. Nations* 182 The indwelling angel-guide, that oft..shapes out Man's course To the predoom'd adventure. **1859** TENNYSON *Lanc. & Elaine* 725 All Had marvel what the maid might be, but most Predoom'd her as unworthy. **1882** MISS BRADDON *Mt. Royal* II. i. 10 He predooms future suffering to the innocent by a reckless indulgence of his own inclination in the present. **1885** R. BUCHANAN in *N. Amer. Rev.* May 452 Shall Man, predoom'd, Cling to his sinking straw of consciousness?

predorsal: see PRE- B. 3.

†predour. *Obs.* [a. OF. *predeur* (13th c. in Godef.), ad. L. *prædātōr-em* plunderer, pillager.] A robber, plunderer, marauder.

1577 HOLINSHED *Descr. of Irel.* 17/1 in *Chron.* I, The Earle with his bande made hoate foote after, & dogging still the track of the predours, he came to the place where the dart was hurld.

pre-dry: see PRE- A. 1.

†'predy, *a. Naut. Obs.* [Deriv. obscure: most writers have associated it in some way with *ready*.

(The suggestion has been made that the *p* was developed out of the word of command 'Make the shi*p* ready' (cf. quot. 1626). This is not impossible; though it assumes the identity of the vowel sound in *ready* and *predy*, which is not proved.)]

Prepared for action, ready.

1625 in J. S. Corbett *Fighting Instruct.* (1905) 69 That the hold in every ship should be rummaged and made predy especially by the ship's sides. **c1626** CAPT. N. BOTELER *Dialogues about Sea Services* (1685) 283 When a Ship is to be made ready for a Fight, the Word of Command is, make the Ship Predy, or make Predy the Ordnance. And a Predy Ship is when all her Decks are cleared, and her Guns and all her small Shot, and everything of that Nature, well fitted for a Fight: And likewise to make the Hold Predy is to bestow everything handsomly there, and to remove any-thing that may be troublesome. Hence **1706** in PHILLIPS.

So **†'predy** *v. Obs.*, to make ready.

1627 CAPT. SMITH *Seaman's Gram.* ix. 38 Predy, or make ready to set saile. **1704** J. HARRIS *Lex. Techn.* I, *Predy the Ship*, or *Predy the Ordnance*, is as much as to make Things ready for a Fight. **1867** SMYTH *Sailor's Word-bk.*, *Predy*, or *Priddy*, a word formerly used in our ships for 'get ready'; as 'Predy the main-deck', or get it clear.

pre-dynastic: see PRE- B. 1.

†pree, *sb.*¹ *Obs. rare*⁻¹. [a. F. *pré*:—L. *prāt-um* meadow, or a. obs. F. *prée* fem.:—L. *prāta*, pl. of *pratum*.] A meadow.

a1625 SIR H. FINCH *Law* (1636) 24 In a Writ the generall shall be put..before the speciall: as land before pree, pasture, wood, iuncary, marish, &c.

pree (priː), *v. Sc.* and *north. dial.* Also 8- prie. [A shortened form of *preive*, *preve*, by-form of PROVE *v.*; cf. Sc. *gie*, *hae*, *lee*, for *give*, *have*, *lief.*] *trans.* To make proof or trial of; to try what (a thing) is like, *esp.* by tasting. *pree the mou' of*, to kiss.

?**a1700** *Ballad*, '*Blow the winds I ho*' (in R. Bell's *Collect.* 1857), He [a horse] shakes his head above the trough But dares not prie the corn. **1724** RAMSAY *Tea-t. Misc.* (1733) I. 91 A mill of good snishing to prie. **1768** ROSS *Helenore* 103 Nae henny beik, that ever I did pree, Did taste so sweet. **1785** BURNS *Halloween* x, Rob, stownlins, prie'd her bonnie mou. **1824** SCOTT *Redgauntlet* ch. vii, I am in..haste to prie your..good cheer. **1857** *Chambers' Inform.* I. 709/2 A custom..of preeing the nets—that is, lifting out a portion of a train and examining it. **1896** BARRIE *Sent. Tommy* xix. 215 He had no thought o' preeing lasses' mouths now.

Hence **pree** *sb.*², a trial, a taste; **'preeing** *vbl. sb.*, proving, trying, tasting.

1821 GALT *Ann. Parish* xvii, The first taste and preeing of what war is. **1835** D. WEBSTER *Rhymes* 18 Sae after some drams I gat a pree, I bade gude day. **1879** J. WHITE *Jottings* 169 Gie me a pree, but no my fill. **1883** CLELAND *Inchbracken* ix. 64 The pruif o' the puddin's the preein' o' 't.

pre-earthly, -economic: see PRE- B. 1.

preeche, preede, preef, variants of PREACH, PREDE, PROOF.

pre-'echo. [PRE- A. 2.] **1.** A faint copy of a louder sound occurring in a recording shortly before the original as a result of the accidental transfer of signals in a recording medium.

1935 *Gramophone* June 42/2 It appears to be not 'an echo' in the strict sense of the word, but a 'pre-echo', as in all the examples I list below it occurs *before the actual recording grooves* are reached by the needle. **1956** [see POST-ECHO]. **1957** *N.Y. Times* 24 Feb. x. 15/1 Engineers say that a disk should not contain much more music than that;..the grooves will have to run too closely together with additional minutes;..there will be pre-echo, damage and results too ghastly to contemplate. **1962** *Times* 5 July 15/7 Prolonged storage [of tape] without rewinding..can cause 'print-through' (detectable as pre-echo on some discs). **1967** A. L. LLOYD *Folk Song in England* i. 21 The phenomenon of pre-echo on magnetic tape. **1976** *Gramophone* Sept. 445/3 It certainly avoids pre-echoes in silent bars immediately followed by fortissimi.

2. A foreshadowing or anticipation.

1948 *Mind* LVII. 375 Professor Raphael..commends Price's refutation of the 'naturalistic fallacy' (a pre-echo of G. E. Moore's). **1961** *Times* 29 May 12/7 Is this a mere pre-echo of *My Fair Lady?* **1975** *Listener* 20 Nov. 674/1 The most fascinating political pre-echo since the boy Harold Wilson had his photo taken on the steps of Number Ten. **1977** *Gramophone* July 187/2 What an extraordinary pre-echo of Brahms this second piece becomes in this performance.

pre-e'clampsia. *Path.* [PRE- B. 1.] A condition of pregnancy characterized by high blood pressure and some other of the symptoms associated with eclampsia, and formerly thought to be associated with toxæmia.

1923 *Jrnl. Michigan State Med. Soc.* XXII. 144/1 (*heading*) Toxemias of pregnancy including pre-eclampsia, eclampsia and nephritis. **1929** H. J. STANDER *Toxemias of Pregnancy* 53 Pre-eclampsia is essentially eclampsia before the outbreak of convulsions and coma. **1955** H. M. CAREY in I. Donald *Pract. Obstetr. Probl.* ix. 130 Pre-eclampsia classically is defined as the appearance, after the 28th week of pregnancy, of œdema, hypertension and albuminuria. **1974** PASSMORE & ROBSON *Compan. Med. Stud.* III. II. xlii. 17/2 The term pre-eclampsia has also been used [for hypertension in pregnancy], on the basis that women who develop hypertension in late pregnancy may, unless treated, progress to the convulsive complication known as eclampsia. **1976** *Lancet* 18 Dec. 1341/1 Maternal pre-eclampsia, birth trauma, breech delivery, and disorders of hæmostasis have also been implicated in a disorder which predominantly affects immature male infants.

pre-e'clamptic, *a.* and *sb. Path.* [PRE- B. 1.] **A.** *adj.* Characteristic of the state which precedes an eclamptic attack; of, exhibiting, or being pre-eclampsia. **B.** *sb.* A pre-eclamptic woman.

1899 J. C. EDGAR in C. Jewett *Pract. Obstetr.* xxiii. 517 Symptoms of eclampsia may be classified as those of the prodromal period, or pre-eclamptic state, and those of the attack. **1924** DE WESSELOW & WYATT *Mod. Views on Toxæmias of Pregnancy* viii. 90 It is practically certain that we are dealing with a pre-eclamptic. **1926** *Jrnl. Obstetr. & Gynæcol.* XXXIII. 21 The patient, 2-para, and seven months pregnant, was admitted for the pre-eclamptic signs of high blood-pressure, marked œdema and headache. **1960** LEVITT & ALTCHEK in Guttmacher & Rovinsky *Med., Surg., & Gynecol. Complications of Pregnancy* iv. 73/1 Clinically, the preeclamptic has more pronounced sodium and water retention than the normal gravida. **1962** *Lancet* 6 Jan. 7/1 Induction was performed in a patient with mild pre-eclamptic toxæmia. **1977** *Ibid.* 30 Apr. 923/1 Diabetic women in pregnancy often become pre-eclamptic.

pre-'edit, *v.* [PRE- A. 1.] *trans.* To edit or sort as a preliminary to later editing; to prepare for computer processing by the addition or alteration of material. Hence **pre-'edited** *ppl. a.*, **pre-'editing** *vbl. sb.*

1934 WEBSTER, Pre-edit, *v.* **1938** *Amer. Speech* XIII. 36 In pre-editing, an editor may have to consult recent books in the subject-field concerning a particular word. **1958** *N.Y. Folklore Q.* Autumn 245 The valuable *Frank C. Brown Collection of North Carolina Folklore* would have been much more valuable had Brown spent more time in arranging and pre-editing while he was alive. **1960** [see POST-EDIT *v.*]. **1968** *Amer. Documentation* Jan. 74/1 The documents are then returned to the DARE office for pre-editing and typing. **1970** A. CAMERON et al. *Computers & Old Eng. Concordances* 49 The not-so-friendly blue giant grudgingly yielded up a trial-run concordance to 1,100 pre-edited lines out of the approximately 5,500 lines of the complete gospel text. **1973** *Amer. Speech 1969* XLIV. 192 The completed field records were..preedited and encoded. **1977** J. M. SMITH in P. G. J. van Sterkenburg et al. *Lexicologie* 242 There is a need for some 'intelligent' pre-editing of input... Such pre-editing is time-consuming.

Hence **pre-'editor**, one who carries out pre-editing.

1934 in WEBSTER. **1953** [see POST-EDITOR]. **1958** *Aspects of Translation* 104 The pre-editor was to remove known ambiguities from the original text. **1960** E. DELAVENAY *Introd. Machine Transl.* 36 The role of the pre-editor would be to provide the machine with texts explicit from the graphio-semantic point of view.

pre-e'lect, *a.* Now *rare.* [ad. L. *præēlect-us*, pa. pple. of med.L. *præēligĕre* to choose before, prefer; or f. PRE- A. 1, 5 + ELECT *a.*] Chosen beforehand or before others; chosen in preference to others.

c1489 CAXTON *Blanchardyn* xxxiii. 123 Ha, noble rose, pre-elect & chosen byfore all other flouris that ben about the. **1513** BRADSHAW *St. Werburge* II. 225 This gracious virgin and preelect abbasse. **1611** FLORIO, *Preeletto*, preelect, fore-chosen. **1858** E. CASWALL *Poems* 34 Then with all perfections deck'd As this mother pre-elect. **1870** ROSSETTI *Poems* (1881) 261 This is that blessed Mary pre-elect God's virgin.

pre-elect (priːɪ'lɛkt), *v.* [PRE- A. 1.] **a.** *trans.* To elect or choose beforehand.

1570 FOXE *A. & M.* (ed. 2) 926/1 In the diuine prescience of God, whiche had chosen and preelected her before the worldes to be the mother of the Lord. **1611** COTGR., *Préeslu*, preelected, fore-chosen. **1706** PHILLIPS, *Pre-elected*, elected, or chosen before-hand. **1850** NEALE *Med. Hymns* (1867) 153 Ere the world was, pre-elected.

b. To elect to an office by anticipation. Used *spec.* of the choice of heads of colleges and of certain classes of fellows in the universities of Oxford and Cambridge.

1830 J. H. MONK *Life R. Bentley* (1833) II. 45 An appeal was also presented to the Vice-Chancellor..against the Master, who had pre-elected his son, William Bradford, to a fellowship in a College Meeting, at which only four of the twelve Fellows were present. *Ibid.* 254 Four persons, commonly deemed his inferiors in merit, were successful; two of them being pre-elected for the following year. **1977** *Daily Tel.* 28 Feb. 8/2 At Sidney Sussex, Cambridge, Miss A. P. Dowling, of Girton, has been pre-elected into a junior research fellowship. **1978** *Ibid.* 20 Jan. 14/4 At Christ's College, Prof. J. H. Plumb, Fellow of the College and Emeritus Professor of Modern English History, has been pre-elected to Mastership with effect from July 11, 1978.

pre-election (priːɪ'lɛkʃən), *sb.* Also præ-. [PRE- A. 1, 5. Cf. obs. F. *préeslection* (Godef.).]

†1. Choice of one person or thing in preference to others; selection, preference. *Obs.*

1589 PUTTENHAM *Eng. Poesie* II. xii[i]. (Arb.) 131 We must needes say, it was in many of their wordes done by pre-election in the first Poetes. **1611** A. STAFFORD *Niobe* 61 A free præelection, is not but a good, nor a free shunning but of euil. **1629** MAXWELL tr. *Herodian* III. 163 Antonine, taking small ioy in those Nuptialls, whereto hee was forcibly yoked, without any præ-election of his owne, infinitely hated both the young Lady and her Father.

2. Previous choice; an anticipatory election.

1611 FLORIO, *Preelettione*, pre-election, fore-chusing. **a1639** WOTTON in *Reliq.* (1651) 453 We shall satisfie His Majestie with a pre-Election, and yours shall have my first nomination. **1715** H. PRIDEAUX in *Life* (1748) 212 No such pre-elections shall be henceforth made in any College. **1830** J. H. MONK *Life R. Bentley* (1833) II. 257 That three scholars should be taken from Westminster every year, and that they should never be prejudiced by pre-elections. **1860** PUSEY *Min. Proph.* 596 He does not speak directly of predestination, but of præelection to temporal goods.

pre-election (priːɪ'lɛkʃən), *adj. phr.* [f. PRE- B. 1 + ELECTION.] Occurring or given before a parliamentary (or other) election.

1893 *Chicago Advance* 16 Mar., The President..refused to compromise himself by any pre-election pledges. **1896** *Atlantic Monthly* Feb. 207 Some of the preëlection tests of statesmanship. **1898** *Westm. Gaz.* 16 May 3/1 Maybe Mr. Chamberlain was remembering his pre-election promises.

pre-e'lectric, *a.* [PRE- B. 1.] Occurring or pertaining to the time before the use of electricity, esp. in the making of gramophone records. Also *ellipt.*, a gramophone record not electrically recorded. Also **pre-e'lectrical** *a.*

[**1908** *Westm. Gaz.* 29 Feb. 12/2 It was in pre-electric-light days, and I couldn't find the matches.] **1934** C. LAMBERT *Music Ho!* IV. 257 Recording will have improved on the present methods as much as the present methods have improved on the old pre-electric horn recording. **1947** *Penguin Music Mag.* May 58 The connoisseur, who has his collection of rare pre-electrical recordings carefully card-indexed. **1960** *Guardian* 8 Mar. 7/1 One has to listen to old pre-electrics with a 'creative ear'. **1968** *Listener* 22 Feb. 250/1 It is scored for..stereophonic tape.., pre-electric gramophone, percussion, [etc.]. **1977** *Gramophone* Feb. 1321/1 The first five records concern themselves almost entirely with pre-1930 (mostly pre-electric) issues.

†pre-,elemen'tation. *Obs. rare*⁻¹. [f. PRE- A. 2 + **elementation*, f. ELEMENT *v.* 3, to instruct in the rudiments of learning.] Previous elementary or rudimentary instruction or teaching.

1659 H. L'ESTRANGE *Alliance Div. Off.* 98 A duty without whose pre-elementation sermons themselves edify very little.

preem (priːm), *sb.*¹ *local.* Also 7-8 preme. [perh. a variant of PREEN *sb.*; cf. MDu., Du. *priem*, MLG. *prême*, MHG. *pfrieme*, G. *pfriem*, *pfriemen* an awl, bodkin, etc.] (See quot. 1850.)

1688 R. HOLME *Armoury* III. 289/1 The Preme is made of white Wands, this is for the opening of the Yarn..so that each thred may pass clearly through the Reed. **1726** *Dict. Rust.* s.v. *Loom.* **1850** S. BAMFORD *Dial. S. Lancs.* Gloss. 185 *Preem*, a comb used by weavers, to loosen the yarn.

preem (priːm), *sb.*² and *v.*² U.S. slang abbrev. of PREMIÈRE *sb.* or *v.*

1937 *Amer. Speech* XII. 317/2 *Preem*, first showing. **1937** [see ORK]. **1942** BERREY & VAN DEN BARK *Amer. Thes. Slang* §590/30 *Preem*, to present a premiere performance. **1945** [see HYPO *v.*]. **1945** [see PREMIÈRE *v.*]. **1948** *Variety* 25 Aug.

1/2 The mother-daughter act..has been bought by ABC and set for an Oct. 4 preem. **1952** *N.Y. Daily News* 5 Aug. 23C/5 A new hour-long radio show..which preems via ABC [network] Sunday, Aug. 17. **1961** A. BERKMAN *Singers' Gloss. Show Business* 70 *Preem* (Var.), theatre premiere.

preem (priːm), *v.*[1] *local.* [f. prec.] In textile manufacture, To clean the teasels? with a preem or comb. Hence **'preeming** *vbl. sb.*; also **'preemer** (see quot.).

1835 URE *Philos. Manuf.* 202 The next employment in the cloth manufacture for which boys are fit, is preeming; that is, cleaning the teasel-rods and handles. *Ibid.*, Preeming is much harder and more disagreeable work than carping. *Ibid.* 203 After the preeming period, the lads are put either to the gig-machines, or to the lewises in the cutting or shearing-room. **1903** *Eng. Dial. Dict.*, *Preemer*, a boy who cleans teazles. W. Yks.

preem (*Fencing*), obs. form of PRIME *sb.*

pre-embodiment, -embody: see PRE- A. 1, 2.

pre-'embryo. *Biol.* [f. PRE- B. I. + EMBRYO.] 'The inferior of the two cells opposite to the micropyle in the vegetable ovule which, by its growth and division, gives rise to the embryo' (*Syd. Soc. Lex.* 1895).

1904 *Brit. Med. Jrnl.* 15 Oct. 968 The amphibolic factor by its continued presence and influence..on the germ-cells and sperm-cells, the pre-embryo, embryo, and its primordial germ-cells, &c., renders it impossible for the germ elements..to live the charmed life of isolation.

pre-emergence, -emergent: see PRE- B. 2, 1.

preemie ('priːmɪ). *N. Amer. slang.* Also **premie, premy.** [f. PREM(ATURE *sb.* + -Y[6], -IE.] A premature birth; a baby born prematurely. Also *attrib.*

1927 *Amer. Speech* II. 314/1 A baby delivered prematurely is a 'premy'. **1942** BERREY & VAN DEN BARK *Amer. Thes. Slang* §534/6 *Premie*, a premature birth. **1949** *N.Y. Times* 25 Sept. 1. 75/2 Saving 75 per cent of the 'preemies' born. *Ibid.*, The dread eye diseases said to afflict 'preemies' are unfounded. **1968** *Trans-Action* Oct. 7/2 The prematures were more likely to be below their proper grade in school. Among white children..19·4 percent of the preemies were..in special classes. **1975** *Time* (Canada ed.) 19 May 57/1 The preemie's sense of security is further heightened by the recorded sound of a pregnant mother's heartbeat piped into the artificial womb. **1976** *Word 1971* XXVII. 61 The present-day premie nursery is the precursor of the prenatal assessment laboratory of tomorrow.

pre-eminence (priː'ɛmɪnəns). Also 5–6 prem-, 5–8 prehem-, 7–8 præem-. [ad. late L. *præēminentia* (5th c.), f. L. *præēminent-em* PRE-EMINENT: see -ENCE. Cf. F. *prééminence* (14th c. in Littré). The *h* in obs. spelling was inserted to avoid hiatus.] Surpassing or superior eminence.

1. Higher rank or distinction; priority of place, precedence; superiority.

1427 *Rolls of Parlt.* IV. 326/2 As toward any preeminence yat ye might have..as chief of Counseill. *c* **1430** LYDG. *Min. Poems* (Percy Soc.) 48 How Maria, whiche hadde a premynence Above alle women, in Bedlem whan she lay. **1526** TINDALE *3 John* 9 Diotrephes which loueth to haue the preeminence amonge them receaueth vs not. **1601** R. JOHNSON *Kingd. & Commw.* (1603) 68 As touching preheminence and dignity, he is chiefe of the Christian Princes. **1647** N. BACON *Disc. Govt. Eng.* I. i. (1739) 1 They allowed pre-eminence to their Magistrates rather than Supremacy. **1705** STANHOPE *Paraphr.* II. 10 Our Saviour is very fitly termed our Head, as that implies..Preheminence over the rest of the Body. **1872** YEATS *Growth Comm.* 97 The Venetians asserted their pre-eminence over the Genoese in a..battle.

2. Superiority in any quality; the possession or existence of a quality or attribute in a pre-eminent degree.

c **1430** LYDG. *Min. Poems* (Percy Soc.) 244 Whil they stonde in ther fresse premynence. **1486** *Hen. VII at York* in *Surtees Misc.* (1888) 54 A place to my pleasour of moost prehemynence. **1526** *Pilgr. Perf.* (W. de W. 1531) 179 b, The preemynence of his moost gracyous incarnacyon. **1612** SELDEN *Illustr. Drayton's Poly-olb.* x. 161 The East-Indian Taprobran, now called Sumatra, had preheminence of quantity before this of ours. **1781** GIBBON *Decl. & F.* xxx. III. 147 The emperor Honorius was distinguished..by the pre-eminence of fear, as well as of rank. **1883** SYMONDS *Shaks. Predecess.* ii. (1890) 46 Shakspere's pre-eminence consists chiefly in this, that he did supremely well what all were doing.

†**b.** In lit. sense of the L.: Greater stature. *Obs.*

1589 PUTTENHAM *Eng. Poesie* I. xv. (Arb.) 49 The actors..for a speciall preheminence did walke vpon those high corked shoes or pantofles.

3. With *a* and *pl.* An individual instance or case of pre-eminence: **a.** A distinction, a distinguishing privilege; **b.** A quality existing in a pre-eminent degree. Now *rare.*

a **1225** *Ancr. R.* 160 In onliche stude he beȝet þeos þreo biȝeaten [2 *MSS.* preeminences]—priuilege of prechur, merit of martirdom & meidenes mede. **1433** *Rolls of Parlt.* IV. 432/2 All the manere of preminences and duytees belangyng therto. **1597** HOOKER *Eccl. Pol.* v. lxii. §13 God, from whom mens seuerall degrees and preeminences doe proceed. **1641** EARL MONM. tr. *Biondi's Civil Warres* v. 93 The City of Auxerres, and the precincts thereof, with all the above said preheminences. **1794** BURKE *Rep. Lords' Jrnls.* Wks. 1842 II. 632 The office, the powers and preheminences annexed to it, differ very widely.

Hence †**pre-'eminenced** *ppl. a. Obs. nonce-wd.*, raised to pre-eminence; distinguished.

1661 FELTHAM *Resolves* II. xix. (ed. 8) 222 They are pre-eminenc'd before the rest of the world.

pre-'eminency. Now *rare.* Also 6 prem-, 7 præem-, 7–8 prehem-. [ad. late L. *præēminentia*, f. L. *præēminent-em*: see next and -ENCY.] The quality of being pre-eminent; = PRE-EMINENCE.

1560 BECON *Jewel of Joy* Wks. II. 20 b, Thou knowest, O lord..my necessytie, that I hate the token of prehemynencie, and glory or worshyppe, whyche I bear vpon my heade. **1672** O. PLUNKET (*title*) Jus Primatiale; or, the Ancient Right and Preheminency of the See of Armagh above all other Archbishopricks in the Kingdom of Ireland asserted. *a* **1703** BURKITT *On N.T.* Mark iii. 19 The foreman of a grand jury, has a precedency, but no pre-eminency. **1873** M. ARNOLD *Lit. & Dogma* (1876) 397 The pre-eminency of righteousness.

b. With *a* and *pl.* An instance or species of this quality; anything in which it is exhibited; a pre-eminent position.

1555 EDEN *Decades* 343 To haue certeyne priuelegies, preeminencies, and tributes. **1647–8** COTTERELL *Davila's Hist. Fr.* (1678) 4 The Royal House then enjoys two Pre-eminencies. **1757** *Herald* No. 8 (1758) I. 124 The right of precedence, which the others will not yield, notwithstanding the preheminencies of the church supersede those of blood.

pre-eminent (priː'ɛmɪnənt), *a.* Also 6–7 preh-. [ad. L. *præēminent-em*, pr. pple. of *præēminēre* (contr. *præm-*) to project forwards, rise above, excel, f. *præ*, PRE- A. 5 + *ēminēre*: see EMINENT. Cf. F. *prééminent* (15th c. in Littré).] Eminent before or above others; excelling or surpassing others; distinguished beyond others in respect of some quality.

1432–50 tr. *Higden* (Rolls) I. 7 Hauenge in possession dowerys preeminent [*dotes possidet præminentes*]. **1473** *Proclam.* 10 Nov. (Patent Roll 13 Edw. IV, pt. I. m. 2), Suche persoones as god hath called to the preeminent astate of princes. **1598** BARRET *Theor. Warres* IV. i. 118 As superior and preheminent in office, he may commaund, ordaine, do, and vndo. **1667** MILTON *P.L.* VIII. 279 Some great Maker ..In goodness and in power præ-eminent. **1812** SIR H. DAVY *Chem. Philos.* 6 In all pursuits which required only the native powers of the intellect..the Greeks were pre-eminent. **1870** LUBBOCK *Orig. Civiliz.* (1875) vi. 257 As an object of worship..the serpent is pre-eminent among animals.

b. in lit. sense of the Latin: Rising or standing out above the rest. *rare*[−1].

1827 STEUART *Planter's G.* (1828) 128 Accident may cut off or shorten either the Taproot, or the preeminent shoots of the top.

pre-'eminently, *adv.* [f. prec. + -LY[2].] In a pre-eminent manner or degree; in the highest degree; very highly, supremely.

1747 D. MALLET *Amyntor & Theodora* II. 190 From another's fate, Pre-eminently wretched, learn thy own. **1810** BENTHAM *Packing* (1821) 149 The argument of this pre-eminently learned Judge. **1865** LIVINGSTONE *Zambesi* xxix. 587 The region indicated is preeminently a cotton-field. **1884** PAE *Eustace* 83 This was pre-eminently a marriage of convenience on both sides.

So **pre-'eminentness** (Bailey vol. II, 1727).

pre-'emphasis. *Sound Recording* and *Broadcasting.* [PRE- A. 2.] A systematic distortion of a signal prior to transmission or recording, involving an increase in the relative strength of certain frequencies in anticipation of a corresponding decrease during reception or playback.

1940 *RCA Rev.* Jan. 359 The use of pre-emphasis circuit [*sic*] at the transmitter and a de-emphasis circuit at the receiver produces an overall gain in signal-noise ratio. **1942**, etc. [see DE-EMPHASIS]. **1959** K. HENNEY *Radio Engin. Handbk.* (ed. 5) xxi. 35 Below 100 cycles the characteristic of the [disk] recorder system is made constant-velocity by electric means. This tends to give preemphasis to the low frequencies... Above 500 cps a preemphasis above a constant velocity is given to the high frequencies, especially over the noise frequency range. The necessary characteristic for reproduction is the inverse of this curve. **1977** *Gramophone* Mar. 1476/3 The most important of these is the 'breathing' or 'pumping' effect as residual noise is heard rising and falling in level as the expander alters system gain in response to sudden changes in signal level... High frequency pre-emphasis, followed by mirror-image de-emphasis, reduces the effects of breathing.

So **pre-'emphasize** *v. trans.*, to subject to pre-emphasis.

1968 COOK & LIFF *Frequency Modulation Receivers* xiv. 490 Both the left (*L*) and right (*R*) channels are fed to 75-μ sec high-pass filters, where they are preemphasized. **1974** M. MANDL *Mod. Television Syst.* ii. 29 The higher audio-frequency range at the transmitter is preemphasized. **1977** *Gramophone* Mar. 1476/1 A dodge of this kind is universally employed in VHF/FM broadcasting, where high frequencies are boosted (pre-emphasized) at the transmitter and attenuated (de-emphasized) at the receiver.

pre-employ, -employment: see PRE- A. 1, B. 2 a.

pre-'empt, *sb.* [f. as next.] **1.** A pre-emptive right. *Austral. colloq.*

1890 'R. BOLDREWOOD' *Col. Reformer* xxiv. (1891) 322 My friend has the run, and the stock, and the pre-empts all in his own hands.

2. *Bridge.* A pre-emptive bid.

1939 N. DE V. HART *Bridge Players' Bedside Bk.* iii. 34 Macleod's pre-empt showed an obvious fear of both major suits, from which he was trying to shut us out. **1959** *Listener* 8 Jan. 84/2 It [*sc.* the hand] could qualify for the bolder pre-empt of *Four Clubs.* **1962** *Times* 11 July 7/1 Few players would fancy a pre-empt with a two-suiter and two primary controls. **1972** R. MARKUS *Common-Sense Bridge* II. 65 If everybody knows the strength and weakness of your pre-empts they can easily take the right counteraction. **1977** *Homes & Gardens* Feb. 17 There are two types of hand where you should respond Three No-Trumps in reply to a pre-empt.

pre-empt (priː'ɛm(p)t), *v.* orig. *U.S.* [Back-formation from PRE-EMPTION, PRE-EMPTIVE (cf. *exempt, exemption*).] **1. a.** *trans.* To obtain by pre-emption; hence (*U.S.*), to occupy (public land) so as to establish a pre-emptive title. Also *absol.*

1857 *Nat. Intelligencer* (Washington) 1 July (Bartlett), The laws of the United States give the right to any citizen who does not own three hundred and twenty acres of land in any State of the Union..to preëmpt one hundred and sixty acres, by fulfilling the detailed requirements of the act. **1870** B. HARTE *Luck Roaring Camp* (ed. Tauchn.) I. 15 To make their seclusion more perfect, the land on either side of the mountain wall that surrounded the camp they duly preempted. **1885** *Science* VI. 318 An unscrupulous 'colonist' can often preëmpt in several places at the same time. **1890** G. B. SHAW in *Fab. Ess. Socialism* 5 That specially fertile region upon which Adam pitched is sooner or later all pre-empted; and there is nothing for the new comer to pre-empt save soil of a second quality.

b. *fig.* To acquire or appropriate beforehand, pre-engage. Also *intr.*: see quot. 1889.

1855 L. OLIPHANT *Minnesota & Far West* 162 Wal, I guess, if you can find a corner that's not pre-empted, you may spread your shavings there [for a bed]. **1888** *Literature* (N.Y.) 1 Sept. 276 [The Prohibition party] had unquestionably pre-empted for itself the proud position of the party of the future. **1889** FARMER *Americanisms* s.v., Colloquially, to pre-empt is to take possession, or to qualify for. Thus a man may pre-empt for heaven. **1892** STEVENSON *Across the Plains* 283 The honours are pre-empted for other trades. **1913** J. LONDON *Valley of Moon* 11 Many [tables and benches]..were already pre-empted by family parties. **1944** AUDEN *Sea & Mirror* in *For Time Being* 15 Two wonders as one vow Pre-empting all.

2. *Bridge.* **a.** *intr.* To make a pre-emptive bid.

1914 M. C. WORK *Auction Devel.* 313 It is the exceptional case in which it is advisable to preëmpt with an original No Trump. **1920** —— *Auction Methods Up-to-Date* v. 65 His only chance is to preëmpt so strongly that his first bid will hold the declaration. **1947** S. HARRIS *Fund. Princ. Contract Bridge* I. i. 17 When North preempts but does not make a game bid, it is important for South to remember that he must not increase the contract unless he holds three quick tricks. **1964** *Official Encycl. Bridge* 435/1 The third player is best placed to pre-empt. **1972** R. MARKUS *Aces & Places* 35 South opened the bidding with 1 ♠, West doubled and North..pre-empted to 4 ♠, which became the final contract.

b. *trans.* To thwart (a player) by making a pre-emptive bid.

1964 *Official Encycl. Bridge* 435/1 The third player..knows that he cannot pre-empt his partner. **1972** R. MARKUS *Common-Sense Bridge* II. 65 Here is a hand..to show how easily you can be pre-empted into a ridiculous contract.

3. To set aside (one thing in favour of another); to preclude (something); to prevent (an occurrence); to forestall (someone).

1965 *Sun* 6 Dec. 7/7 In American TV you never, never say that a serial has been killed in favour of a new serial. It is always pre-empted. What they really mean is that it has been cancelled and a right established for the next one. **1968** *Listener* 5 Dec. 768/1, I think the Nazi regime by its own grotesque vileness pre-empted fictional effort. **1976** 'A. HALL' *Kobra Manifesto* xvi. 217 He would kill me when the showdown came unless I could pre-empt him. **1977** *B.B.C. Radio 4 News 5 p.m.* 11 May (*recorded from oral evidence*) Federal rights pre-empt State rights. **1978** *Jrnl. R. Soc. Arts* CXXVI. 675/1 The targets serve to preempt such a situation arising.

Hence **pre-'empted** *ppl. a.*; **pre-'emptible** *a.*, capable of being pre-empted; **pre-'empting** *vbl. sb.* and *ppl. a.*

1880 *Scribner's Mag.* May 102 Rival missionary boards over-run pre-empted ground and obliterate the boundaries of Christian comity. **1883** *Century Mag.* Sept. 732/1 Some public and preëmpted homestead among the surf-showered rocks. **1886** *N. Amer. Rev.* Jan. 54 As pre-emptible land recedes farther into the West. **1920** M. C. WORK *Auction Methods Up-to-Date* v. 61 With general strength, preëmpting is not necessary or advisable. *Ibid.* 63 A real preëmpting hand contains an unusual distribution of cards. **1965** H. KAHN *On Escalation* 287 It [*sc.* pre-emptive war] denotes an attack made because of a belief that the other side has determined to make an attack on the pre-empting party. **1967** *Listener* 2 Nov. 570/3 On the subject of 'pre-empting'—supplanting scheduled programmes in favour of special programmes of public interest—..he had some extremely interesting things to say.

pre-emption (priː'ɛm(p)ʃən). [ad. med.L. **præemptiōn-em*, n. of action f. **præemĕre* to buy beforehand: see PRE- A. 2 and EMPTION. Cf. F. *préemption* (1812 in Hatz.-Darm.).] **1.** Purchase by one person or corporation before an opportunity is offered to others; also, the right to make such purchase; *spec.*

a. formerly in England, the prerogative of the sovereign, exercised through his purveyor, of buying household provisions in preference to other persons, and at special rates.

b. in U.S., Australia, etc., the purchase, or right of purchase, in preference and at a nominal price, of public land by an actual occupant, on condition of his improving it; also *concr.*, land so obtained or to be obtained.

c. in *International Law*, the right of a belligerent, sometimes recognized by treaty, to seize, with indemnification of the owners, such goods of neutrals as are doubtfully or conditionally contraband.

d. ***clause of pre-emption***, in *Sc. Law*: see quot. 1861.

1602 CAREW *Cornwall* 17 Certaine persons..sought to make vse of this preemption. **1610** NORDEN *Spec. Brit., Cornw.* (1728) 16 Her late Maiestie intended to have retayned the prerogative of pre-emption. **1617** MORYSON *Itin.* I. 2 Those of Stode haue by priuiledge the preemption and choice of Rhenish Wines passing by them. **1622** MISSELDEN *Free Trade* 59 This kinde is the Preemption of Tinne here in England granted by His Maiesties gracious letters Patents to some few. **1663** F. PHILLIPS (*title*) The Antiquity..and Necessity of Pre-emption and Pourveyance, for the King. **1688** *Lond. Gaz.* No. 2379/4 The Farmers of His Majesties Coynage and Preemption of Tinn,..have affix'd the Price 10d. the Pound. **1720** *Lond. Gaz.* No. 5859/9 They have..the Pre-emption of the..Lead and Iron Oars. **1747** *First Rec. Baltimore Town* (1905) 21 Mr. Alexander Lawson applied also to enter his Preemption of making out Ground into the water. **1827** *United Empire Loyalist* (Toronto) 6 May 396/2 The first hundred purchasers of Town Lots, when they have erected a habitable house, will..be entitled to the pre-emption or privilege to purchase a Lot of Twenty-Five Acres..at..7s. 6d. per acre. **1830** GALT *Lawrie T.* IV. iv, He consented to give me the pre-emption of twenty thousand acres. *a* **1844** *Filson Club Hist. Q.* (1935) IX. 235 Each of these two men ..had a pre-emption of 1400 acres. **1859** HAWTHORNE *Fr. & It. Note-Bks.* II. 239 The Papal government..has the right of pre-emption whenever any relics of ancient art are discovered. **1860** WOOLSEY *Introd. Internat. Law* §182. 403 The harshness of the doctrine of occasional contraband brought into favor the rule of pre-emption, which was a sort of compromise between the belligerents (if masters of the sea) and the neutrals. **1861** W. BELL *Dict. Law Scot.* 172/2 Clause of Pre-emption is a clause sometimes inserted in a feu-right, stipulating, that if the vassal shall be inclined to sell the lands he shall give the superior the first offer, or that the superior shall have the lands at a certain price fixed in the clause. **1875** STUBBS *Const. Hist.* II. xvii. 537 The prerogative of purveyance included..the right of preemption of victuals. **1901** DUNCAN & SCOTT *Hist. Allen & Woodson Counties, Kansas* 582 Finding that the Indians would not settle on the Reserve, the Government, in 1860, had all of these lands offered for sale and opened to pre-emption. **1933** W. W. SPINKS *Tales Brit. Columbia Frontier* 110 Some of the land had already been pre-empted, and pre-emption amounted to an agreement by the government to sell the land to the pre-empter. **1968** R. H. PATTERSON *Finlay's River* 43, I see I have called it a homestead. Officially, in the books of the Land Registry, it is a pre-emption.

e. *attrib.* and *Comb.*

1780 in N. D. Mereness *Trav. Amer. Colonies* (1916) 643 Received a Letter and Preemption Warrant. **1784** J. FILSON *Discovery Kentucke* 37 The Settlement and preemption rights arise from occupation. **1837** HT. MARTINEAU *Soc. Amer.* II. 92 In 1830, a bill was..passed, granting a pre-emption right to squatters who had taken such possession of unsold lands. **1854** T. H. BENTON *Thirty Years' View* (1857) I. 102 The pre-emption system was established, though at first the pre-emption claimant was stigmatized as a trespasser, and repulsed as a criminal. **1901** *Daily News* 21 Feb. 5/7 The landlord buys at the pre-emption price, and sells at the market price.

2. *Bridge.* The action of making a preemptive bid.

1961 *Times* 6 Dec. 8/3 A two-suiter is not built for preemption. **1962** *Times* 7 Mar. 3/6 A preemption in one of the minor suits is even less efficacious unless the hand has two tricks on the side. **1974** *Country Life* 26 Sept. 894/1 The hand is far too good for pre-emption. **1977** *Times* 17 June 12/1, I have been making notes of unsuccessful preemptions with their effect on subsequent bidding.

3. The action or an instance of setting aside or overriding something.

1978 *Nature* 20 Apr. 664/1 The issue of Federal preemption—Federal legislation that overrides state or local initiatives—lies at the heart of the current dispute. **1979** *Arizona Daily Star* 1 Apr. (Tucson T.V. Suppl.) 12/3 CBS hasn't treated this inspirational program very kindly. It's constantly being victimized by pre-emptions, time-slot changes and disappearances for up to three weeks at a stretch.

Hence **pre-ˈemptioner**, 'one who holds a prior right to purchase certain public land' (Webster 1890, citing Abbott).

1838 *Congress. Globe* 25th Congress 2 Sess. App. 142/3 Suppose a pre-emptioner was to go there and say, Mr. President, this house is too large for you; I..claim a preemption to part of this house. **1841** *Knickerbocker* XVII. 278 They amused themselves by calling the exclusives 'squatters', 'prëemptioners', etc. **1872** [see HOMESTEADER].

pre-emptive (priːˈɛm(p)tɪv), *a.* (*sb.*) [f. med.L. **præempt-*, ppl. stem of **præemĕre* (see prec.) + -IVE.] **A.** *adj.* **1.** Relating or belonging to, or of the nature of pre-emption. Also *fig.*

pre-emptive right, the right to pre-emption; also, in Australia, land held by such right.

1855 BAILEY *Mystic* (ed. 2) 19 His, by preëmptive right, throughout all time. **1857** T. H. GLADSTONE *Englishm. in Kansas* 169 To jump a claim is to take it, notwithstanding that it is pre-occupied by one who has already given notice of his claim to a pre-emptive title. **1872** YEATS *Growth Comm.* 140 Subject to pre-emptive reservations. **1890** 'R. BOLDREWOOD' *Col. Reformer* (1891) 250 This occupation gave the selectors a legal right to about six thousand acres of 'pre-emptive right'.

2. *Bridge.* Applied to a bid made with the expectation that it is high enough to prevent opponents from bidding normally and so obtaining adequate information.

1913 F. IRWIN *Auction High-Lights* 95 A preëmptive opening-bid in a major suit means that the bidder wants no information and wishes to play the hand at his own suit. **1916** 'BASCULE' *Adv. Auction Bridge* I. 77 To what extent does it pay to make what are known as preemptive, or 'shut-out' bids? **1923** *Daily Mail* 5 May 8 The supporting bid,.. the pre-emptive raise, and 'the switch' assume a new value. **1932** *Daily Tel.* 8 Oct. 15/5 In using the term 'pre-emptive' I am not in any way ascribing the meaning of 'shut-out' to that word. **1947** S. HARRIS *Fund. Princ. Contract Bridge* I. i. 17 The most valuable pre-emptive bid..is an opening bid of four of a major suit or five of a major suit. **1952** I. MACLEOD *Bridge* v. 62 (*heading*) Pre-emptive responses. **1973** *Times* 20 Oct. 11/3 You will find plenty of opportunities for preemptive opening bids.

3. Designating an attack on an enemy who is thought to be about to make an attack himself (see also quots. 1966, 1971). Also *transf.*

1959 *Listener* 31 Dec. 1140/1 The American Strategic Air Command..might be prevented by a Russian preemptive strike from ever getting the Sword out of its scabbard. **1966** SCHWARZ & HADIK *Strategic Terminol.* 108 *Pre-emptive strike*, armed attack motivated by the conviction that an enemy attack is under way or is irreversibly imminent. Also called 'forestalling blow' or 'anticipatory attack', the pre-emptive strike differs from a so-called 'preventive' strike or war in that [etc.]. A strike or war..is preventive if the enemy still has the option of desisting from his planned aggression. **1970** *Times* 9 Oct. 15/2 December 7, 1941, when the Japanese stabbed America in the back at Pearl Harbor—or as we would say in these cooler, more euphemistic times, made their pre-emptive strike. **1971** E. LUTTWAK *Dict. Mod. War* 156/1 *Pre-emptive attack*, an attack launched in the belief that an enemy attack has already entered the executive phase, i.e. that the decision has already been made. Unless the attack actually reduces or eliminates the effect of the imminent attack, it cannot be called pre-emptive. **1976** LD. HOME *Way Wind Blows* xii. 167 There was no doubt at all about the most effective deterrent—it was the 'Polaris' submarine; which, because it was virtually undetectable, was a genuine second-strike weapon which robbed the pre-emptive attack of all its former attraction. **1978** *Times* 25 Jan. 17/2 It may well be that a guillotine is necessary... But if it is to be justified as a pre-emptive strike [etc.].

B. *sb.* Pre-emptive right; land acquired by this.

1890 'R. Boldrewood' *Col. Reformer* (1891) 321 They've got, what with their selections and pre-emptives, a tidy slice ..of Rainbar run. *Ibid.* 322 It's not worth any one else's while to come in, because they'd have no pre-emptive worth talking of. **1930** L. G. D. ACLAND *Early Canterbury Runs* 1st Ser. ii. 26 In eighteen months nearly all the run except the pre-emptives had gone.

pre-ˈemptively, *adv.* [f. PRE-EMPTIVE *a.* + -LY[2].] In a pre-emptive manner.

1917 E. BERGHOLT *Royal Auction Bridge* II. 148 By declaring 'pre-emptively', up to the full strength of his hand, Z. will no doubt be able to prevent B. from directing A. what to lead. **1952** I. MACLEOD *Bridge* vii. 84 A double is for penalties unless..(3) The double is of a suit not above the level of three (and not at the three level bid preemptively). **1959** *Encounter* Nov. 17/1 It is..easier to imagine the Soviet Union striking pre-emptively than to imagine the U.S...doing the same thing. **1968** G. JONES *Hist. Vikings* IV. iii. 392 After the death of Knut the ancient West Saxon dynasty pre-emptively reinherited England. **1975** *Sci. Amer.* Oct. 8/2 Our past practice of preemptively deploying the latest strategic weapons our technology affords us has neither forced nor persuaded the U.S.S.R. to stop deploying strategic weapons increasingly threatening to our security.

pre-emptor (priːˈɛm(p)tər). Also **pre-empter.** [f. as PRE-EMPTION + -OR; cf. med.L. *præemptor* (Gloss. Gr.-L., in L. and Sh.), agent-n. f. **præemĕre*: see PRE- A. 2 and EMPTOR.] **1.** One who acquires land by pre-emption. *N. Amer.*

1846 WORCESTER, *Pre-emptor* [citing JUDGE STOREY]. **1855** *Kansas Hist. Coll.* (1896) V. 168 A preemptor who complies with the requirements of the acts of congress cannot be prevented from obtaining his title. **1860** *Brit. Colonist* (Victoria, B.C.) 12 Jan. 2/1 Pre-emptors run the risk of having to pay twice the amount required by the American government for wild land. **1877** BURROUGHS *Taxation* 129 Land as such, in the occupancy of a pre-emptor..is not subject to taxation. **1933** [see PRE-EMPTION 1 b]. **1962** G. NICHOLSON *Vancouver Island's West Coast* 265 A kindly Norwegian pre-empter..assisted them in re-sawing and whittling the boards down to the proper dimensions by hand.

2. *Bridge.* One who makes pre-emptive bids.

1972 R. MARKUS *Common-Sense Bridge* III. 99 South.. overlooked the warning of the pre-emptor's bid and East's confident double.

Hence **pre-ˈemptory** *a.*

1895 *Funk's Stand. Dict.*, *Pre-emptory*, relating to pre-emption.

preen (priːn), *sb.* Now *Sc.* and *north. dial.* Forms: 1–3 préon, (1 préan), 3 pren, 3–6 prene, 5 preyne, 6–9 prein, 8 prine, 8– preen (prin). [OE. *préon* a pin, brooch, fastening = MDu. *priem(e*, Du. *priem* a bodkin, dagger, MLG. *prên, prêne, prême, prîm*, LG. *preen, preem* a pin, spike, awl, MGH. *pfrieme*, G. *pfriem, pfriemen* an awl, WFris. *prieme*, EFris. *prêm-e* an awl, etc., Icel. *prjónn* (found in 13th c. as prop. name) a (knitting-)pin, peg, plug, Norw. *prjona, prjöne*, Da. *preen* a bodkin, piercer. Cf. med.L. *premula*, dim. of **prema*. For interchange of *m* and *n* cf. PLUM. Gael. *prìne* pin is from Lowl. Sc.]

1. A pin; a brooch.

a **1000** in Thorpe *Charters* 530 Ic ȝeann Godan minre yldran dehter..anes bendes..and twegea preonas, and anes wifscrudes ealles. *c* **1000** ÆLFRIC *Voc.* in Wr.-Wülcker I. 152/37 *Fibula*, preon, *uel* oferfeng, *uel* dalc. *a* **1225** *Ancr. R.* 84 Þe vikelare ablent þene mon & put him preon in eien. *c* **1250** *Gen. & Ex.* 1872 Gol[d] prenes and ringes. *c* **1375** *Sc. Leg. Saints* xliii. (*Cecile*) 533 Þi poweste lik a bose of wynd Þat fillit ware, & with a prene Mocht out be latine. *c* **1420** *Anturs of Arth.* xxix. (Ireland MS.), Hur Kerchefes were curiouse, with mony a proud prene [*v. rr.* pene, pyne]. *a* **1510** DOUGLAS *K. Hart* I. xvi, For wes thair nocht..That no man micht the poynting of ane prene Repreve. **1572** *Satir. Poems Reform.* xxxii. 37 And we, agane, wald by ane Fraer of Fegges, Baith prenis and nedillis, and sell to landwart Megges. **1717** RAMSAY *Elegy on Lucky Wood* iv, She gae'd as fait as a new preen. **1725** —— *Gentle Sheph.* II. ii, O' this unsonsy pictures aft she makes O' ony ane she hates..Stuk fou o' prins. **1825** BROCKETT *N.C. Gloss.*, *Prin*, a pin. **1837** R. NICOLL *Poems* (1843) 131 My ingle she keepit as neat as a preen.

b. *fig.* As type of a thing of small value.

c **1470** HENRY *Wallace* VII. 910 Off courtlynes thai cownt him nocht a preyne. *a* **1560** ROLLAND *Crt. Venus* III. 546 For sic storyis I cuir thame not ane prene. **1728** RAMSAY *Ep. to R. Yarde* 53 Thousands a-year's no worth a Prin, When e'er this fashious Guest gets it. **1871** C. GIBBON *Lack of Gold* ii, You got to like books, and he didna care a prin for them.

2. (See quots.)

1864 ATKINSON *Provinc. Names Birds*, *Preen*, Prov. name ..for Bar-tailed Godwit, *Limosa rufa*. **1885** SWAINSON *Provinc. Names Birds* 198 Bar-tailed Godwit. Prine (Essex). From its habit of probing the mud for food.

3. See quot.: ? = PREEM.

1688 R. HOLME *Armoury* III. 290/1 *Preene*,..an Instrument used by the Clothworkers..for their Handle Dressing, or picking of the Wool Flocks,..an half round piece of Wood, with a handle..the streight side being set with Wyers like teeth.

4. *attrib.* and *Comb.*: **preen-cod, preen-cushion**, a pincushion; also *transf.*; **preen-head**, pin-head, **preen-point**, pin-point, both used *fig.* as the type of anything very small, or of small value; **preensworth**, the value of a preen or pin.

1500–20 DUNBAR *Poems* xxxii. 39 Syne said and swoir.. That he suld nocht twich hir *prenecod. **1578** *Inv. R. Wardrobes* (1815) 239 Ane preincoid of blew and yellow velvot. **1822** GALT *Provost* v, The Nabob..made [them] presents of new gowns and prin-cods. **1888** A. G. MURDOCH *Sc. Readings* Ser. II. 65 A sawdust *preen-cushion. **1825** JAMIESON s.v., 'No worth a *prein-head'. **1897** LD. E. HAMILTON *Outlaws* xviii. 207, I canna mind ae single Armstrong..worth a prein-head. **1886** A. D. WILLOCK *Rosetty Ends* vi. (1887) 42 No' carin' a *preen-point for the sorrow they left ahint them. **1887** J. SERVICE *Dr. Duguid* I. iii. 20 Lord, there's no a *preensworth but Thou kens.

preen (priːn), *v.*[1] Now *Sc.* and *north. dial.* Forms: 3 preonen, 4–6 prene, (7– prin), 8– preen. [f. prec. sb.: cf. Du. *priemen* to stab, pierce, MLG. *prünen, prunen*, LG. *prünen, prienen*, EFris. *prînen* (Doornk.-Koolman) to stitch together roughly, G. *pfriemen* to bore with an awl, Icel. *prjóna* to knit.]

†**1.** *trans.* To sew; to stitch up. *Obs.*

c **1250** *Death* 68 in *O.E. Misc.* 172 Me nimeð þe licome & preoneð in a clut. **1513** DOUGLAS *Æneis* III. vii. 26 Brusit clathis, and riche wedis, Figurit and prynnit al with goldin thredis. *Ibid.* IV. v. 163 Ane purpour claith of Tyre..Fetisly stekit with prynnit goldin thredis.

†**2.** To pierce; to transfix. *Obs.*

c **1320** R. BRUNNE *Medit.* 859 Þurgh hys herte he prened hym with mode. **13..** *Min. Poems fr. Vernon MS.* 683 Loke al ȝor loue on him beo leyd, For vs on Rode was prikket & prenet. **1388** WYCLIF *1 Sam.* xviii. 11 Forsothe Dauid harpide with his hond,..and Saul helde a spere, and caste it, and gesside that he myȝte prene [Vulg. *configere*] Dauid with the wal [*gloss* that is, perse with the spere, so that it schulde passe til to the wal]. *c* **1460** *Play Sacrament* 467 W[t] y[is] same dagger that ys so styf & strong In y[e] myddys of thys prynt I thynke for to prene..[*Stage direct.* here shalle y[e] iiij Jewys pryk y[er] daggeris in iiij quarters].

3. To fasten with a pin; to pin.

1572 *Satir. Poems Reform.* xxxiii. 22 My Coller, of trew Nichtbour lufe it was, Weill prenit on with Kyndnes and solas. **1675** in Hunter *Biggar & Ho. Fleming* ix. (1862) 96 For a dosen of great prinies to prin ye mortcloath and horscloath. **1725** RAMSAY *Gentle Sheph.* v. ii, Prin up your aprons baith, and come away. **1832–53** *Whistle-Binkie* Ser. II. 75 He took the dishclout frae the bink, And preen't it til her cockernony! **1888** DOYLE *Capt. Polestar* 25, I canna say I preen my faith in sea-bogles and the like.

preen (priːn), *v.*[2] Forms: 5 proyne, prayne, preyne, prene, 6 *Sc.* prein, 7 prain, 8 prine, 8– prin, 7– preen. [app. in origin a variant of PRUNE *v.*[1] (ME. *proyne*, etc.), assimilated to PREEN *v.*[1] (early ME. *preonen*), in allusion to the boring or pricking action of a bird's beak when it preens its plumage.]

1. *trans.* Of a bird (or duck-billed platypus): To trim (the feathers or fur) with the beak.

1486 *Bk. St. Albans* A vj, Youre hawke proynith and not pikith and she prenyth not bot whan she begynnyth at hir leggys, and fetcheth moystour like oyle at hir taill. **1681** W. ROBERTSON *Phraseol. Gen.* (1693) 989 To pick or prain, as a bird doth herself. **1691** RAY *Creation* I. (1692) 139 When.. ruffled or discomposed, the Bird..can easily preen them. **1774** G. WHITE *Selborne* 28 Sept., The feathers of these birds must be well preened to resist so much wet. **1860** G. BENNETT *Gatherings Nat. Australasia* vi. 135 Besides combing their fur to clean it when wet, I have seen them preen it with their beak (if the term may be allowed) as a duck would clean its feathers. **1884** *Leeds Mercury* Weekly Supp. 15 Nov. 8/2 A cormorant..sat watching us and preening its feathers.

2. *refl.* **a.** Of a person: To trim or dress oneself up; to smooth and adorn oneself.

c **1386** CHAUCER *Merch. T.* 768 He kembeth hym he preyneth [*v. rr.* prayneth, proynyth] hym and pyketh. **1586** *Dunbar's Tua Mariit Wemen* 374 (Maitland MS.), I wald me prein plesandlie in precious wedis. **1790** D. MORISON *Poems* 81 Ne'er price a weardless, wanton elf, That nought but pricks and prins herself. **1883** MRS. ARMYTAGE in *Fortn. Rev.* 1 Sept. 344 Egyptian beauties..sleeked and preened themselves before their brightly burnished brazen mirrors.

b. *fig.* To pride or please oneself.

1880 SHORTHOUSE *J. Inglesant* Pref. 8 They and their followers preen and plume themselves..on their aristocratic standpoint. **1907** G. B. SHAW *John Bull's Other Island* p. liv, Not so pitiable as the virtuous indignation with which Judge Lynch, himself provable by his own judgment to be a prevaricator, hypocrite, tyrant and coward of the first water, preened himself at its expense. **1926** W. & E. MUIR tr. *Feuchtwanger's Jew Süss* I. 7 The Catholics were preening themselves on the probable extinction of the Protestant line in Swabia. **1943** A. CHRISTIE *Moving Finger* xi. 131 These schools..seem to take a delight in turning out girls who preen themselves on looking like nothing on earth. They call it being sweet and unsophisticated. **1948** O. WALKER *Kaffirs are Lively* xi. 164 South Africa..sometimes preens itself on its lack of lynch-law. **1972** 'J. HERRIOT' *It shouldn't happen to Vet* i. 14 He had put one over on the young clever-pants vet and nobody could blame him for preening himself a little.

3. To trim (trees). *dial.*

1847-78 HALLIWELL, *Preen*, to prime, or trim up trees.

Hence **preened** *ppl. a.*, **'preening** *vbl. sb.*

1599 JAS. I *Βασιλ. Δωρον* (1603) 111 They should not..by their painted, preened fashion, serue for baites to filthie lechery. *Ibid.* 112 Eschewe to be effœminate in your cloathes, in perfuming, preening, or such like. **1890** E. COUES *Handbk. Field & Gen. Ornith.* II. iii. 129 Birds press out a drop of oil with the beak and dress the feathers with it, in the well-known operation called 'preening'. **1953** N. TINBERGEN *Herring Gull's World* iv. 41 Preening is a most vital occupation. **1975** J. A. G. BARNES *Titmice Brit. Isles* vii. 122 Preening must be considered almost as essential an activity as feeding.

pre-enclosure: see PRE- B. 2a.

pre-engage (ˌpriːɪnˈgeɪdʒ), *v.* Also 7 præ-, 7-8 -in-. [PRE- A. 1.] To ENGAGE beforehand.

1. *trans.* To bind in advance by a pledge or promise; to put under obligation beforehand.

1649 C. WALKER *Hist. Independ.* II. 80 Things may be legally carried..by competent Judges not preingaged. *a* **1678** in Hobbes *Decam.* Wks. 1845 VII. 141 Men have pre-engaged themselves to maintain certain principles. **1715** POPE *Lett., to Earl Burlington* (1735) I. 237 If Mr. Tonson went, he was preingaged to attend him. **1785** G. A. BELLAMY *Apology* I. 117 She pressed me to stay dinner, but..I informed her that I was pre-engaged. **1817** COLERIDGE *Biog. Lit.* (1882) 286 She is compelled by the silent entreaties of a father..to give her hand, with a heart thus irrecoverably pre-engaged, to Lord Aldobrand.

b. *spec.* To engage previously to marry, to betroth beforehand. Usually *pass.* or *refl.*

1673 *Lady's Call.* II. i. §5 That they were pre-engag'd to a better amour, espous'd to the spiritual bridegroom. **1749** FIELDING *Tom Jones* XVII. viii, If she had pre-engaged herself to any gentleman. **1823** LINGARD *Hist. Eng.* VI. 392 The princess was required to swear that she was not pre-engaged to any other person.

c. *intr.* for *refl.* To pledge oneself, guarantee, or engage beforehand. (With *inf.* or *subord. cl.*)

1654 TRAPP *Comm., Ps.* ci. Introd. (1657) II. 826 A Psalm of David, wherein he promiseth and pre-ingageth, that whenever hee came to the Kingdome, he will be a singular example. **1683** E. HOOKER *Pref. Pordage's Mystic Div.* 84, I wil præengage that the Cloze shal com off sweetly. **1905** CAPT. MAHAN *Sea Power* I. Pref. 8 Still less may they rightfully pre-engage so to do.

2. *trans.* **a.** To win over or persuade beforehand, to prepossess.

1646 J. GREGORY *Notes & Obs.* (1650) 58 Had not Pliny preengaged us to the sense of operation. **1751** EARL ORRERY *Remarks Swift* (1752) 44 They had the effect of an artful preface, and had pre-engaged all readers in his favour. **1865** BUSHNELL *Vicar. Sacr.* II. ii. (1868) 153 Something done to preengage the feeling, or raise a favoring prejudice in it.

b. To bespeak or secure for oneself beforehand.

1683 *A Match* iii. in *Third Collect. Poems* (1689) 29/1 Let trusty Monsieur preingage your ready Votes. **1712** E. COOKE *Voy. S. Sea* 134 This being a Breach of Trust to preingage his Vote.

3. To occupy beforehand; to preoccupy.

1656 OSBORNE *Adv. Son* v. §26 (1896) 124 Do not pre-engage Hope or Fear by a tedious expectation. **1659** *Gentl. Calling* vi. §12 All their time is so pre-ingaged and forestalled, that their most important interest is left forlorn. **1712** ADDISON *Spect.* No. 311 ¶5 Will..tells us, that he always found her Pre-engaged.

4. To engage in combat with beforehand.

1726 SHELVOCKE *Voy. round World* 46 If the French Captain had not pre-engaged me.

Hence **pre-en'gaged** *ppl. a.*; whence **pre-en'gagedness.**

1665 GLANVILL *Scepsis Sci.* xiv. 94 [They] owe their credit more to customary and præingaged Assent, then to any rational inducement. **1903** A. J. WILSON in *Speaker* 28 Mar. 597/1 Demands its poverty or pre-engagedness forbids it to gratify.

pre-engagement (ˌpriːɪnˈgeɪdʒmənt). [PRE- A. 2; or f. prec. vb. + -MENT.]

1. The act of pre-engaging, or fact of being already or previously engaged.

1647 N. BACON *Disc. Govt. Eng.* I. lix. (1739) 110 One that came to the Crown without pre-engagement by Promise or Covenant. **1796** LD. AUCKLAND *Corr.* (1862) III. 359 Stating to me his..pre-engagement in disposing of the present vacancy in office. **1896** 'A. HOPE' *Phroso* i, Two chairs had been tilted up in token of preëngagement.

2. An engagement previously given or made.

1647 CROMWELL in Stainer *Speeches* (1901) 44 It is such a pre-engagement that there is no need of talk of the thing. **1751** *Female Foundling* II. 35 He has no Pre-engagement, and consequently no Promise to recal. **1851** CARLYLE *Sterling* I. iii. (1872) 20 He now..opened a correspondence with the *Times* Newspaper,..voluntary Letters, I suppose, without payment or preëngagement.

b. *spec.* A previous or prior marriage engagement or betrothal.

1684 *Scanderbeg Rediv.* iii. 26 The Lady, being then very young, and asham'd to own her pre-engagement. **1815** *Zeluca* II. 146 As he prefers you, he has broken a pre-engagement with me.

†3. A previous or already existing tie, or business claiming attention; a preoccupation. *Obs.*

1646 J. WHITAKER *Uzziah* 38 That we may..lay down all preingagements at the foot of the throne of Jesus Christ. **1684-5** BOYLE *Min. Waters* 61 My want of health, and my preingagement to some Subjects that I am more concern'd for.

pre-engi'neered, *ppl. a.* [PRE- A. 1.] Constructed from prefabricated units.

1958 *Times* 29 Mar. 5 (Advt.), APEE design to any specification pre-engineered buildings which can be erected speedily and economically by unskilled labour. **1974** *State* (Columbia, S. Carolina) 15 Feb. 9-B/7 (Advt.), Need men to erect pre-engineered buildings.

preen-gland (ˈpriːnglænd). *Zool.* [f. PREEN *v.*[2] + GLAND[2].] = *oil-gland* s.v. OIL *sb.*[1] 6e. Also called the *uropygial gland.*

1923 J. A. THOMSON *Biol. Birds* ii. 12 There is a striking paucity of skin-glands, for there is usually nothing but the preen-gland at the root of the tail. **1954** FISHER & LOCKLEY *Sea-Birds* viii. 190 This waxy oil..is similar in character to the oil from the preen-glands of birds. **1962** *Listener* 15 Nov. 807/2 It was noticed long ago that the bird rubs the beak on the preen gland which is situated on its back just in front of the tail. **1975** WALLACE & MAHAN *Introd. Ornith.* (ed. 3) iii. 84 The oil or preen gland (*uropygium*) is a conical, bilobed structure, often with a tuft of tiny feathers that serve as a wick, located immediately in front of the tail.

pre-'English, *a.* and *sb.* [PRE- B. 1.]

A. *adj.* **1. a.** Designating the period before settlement of English-speakers in the British Isles.

1922 E. EKWALL *Place-Names Lancs.* 26 We expect the name of such an important river (or at least its first el[ement]) to be of pre-English origin. **1922** F. KLAEBER *Beowulf* 190 The poet was interested in the old Anglian traditions—the only legends in *Beowulf* that are concerned with persons belonging to English (i.e., pre-English) stock. **1934** *Essays & Stud.* XIX. 157 *Ærgeweorc*..referring to constructions of the pre-English period. **1966** *Eng. Stud.* XLVII. 210 The oldest river-names are of pre-English origin.

b. Pertaining to a period before the adoption of a given word into English.

1960 C. S. LEWIS *Studies in Words* vi. 133 In modern English the two meanings are not at all related as parent and child. They can be explained only by the pre-English history of the word.

2. Prior to the emergence of the English language; *spec.* of or pertaining to the West Germanic or Anglo-Frisian dialect from which English developed.

1928 C. BERGENER *Contrib. Study Conversion of Adj. into Nouns in Eng.* 1 The conversion should have taken place in English, but for the sake of greater completeness also such cases have been included where the conversion was, or may have been, pre-English. **1933** *Mod. Lang. Notes* XLVIII. 383 For names not of English origin the authors..use..*pre-English*... The..term is a most unfortunate one, since it is ordinarily used in quite another sense, viz., to denote a word form in the hypothetical Germanic dialect out of which English developed. **1936** *Anglia* LX. 367 To the Langobardish *Laiamicho* answers a pre-English trisyllabic **Lāimikô* > **Laimikô*.

B. *sb.* The West Germanic or Anglo-Frisian dialect from which English developed. Also, English before written records.

1929 *Rev. Eng. Stud.* V. 179 A large and important group of writers and speakers..use *Anglo-Saxon* not in the sense 'Old English' but in the sense 'pre-English'. **1965** *Language* XLI. 34 The allophones of /g/..reveal..both [g] and [ʒ] in pre-English.

preening (ˈpriːnɪŋ), *ppl. a.* [f. PREEN *v.*[2] + -ING[2].] That preens (see PREEN *v.*[2]); chiefly *fig.*, proud, self-confident.

1903 R. LANGBRIDGE *Flame & Flood* i. 2 The manner of Miss Lydia, as she nestled into repose upon the bench, was essentially that of the conquering fowl who, having winged her way out of the difficulties insurmountable until attained, looks back with preening self-congratulation on the terrors now safely left behind. **1959** *Times* 13 Jan. 10/6 The new, brightly preening *casa* built on the hillside by a wealthy Barcelona merchant. **1976** *Time* 27 Dec. 5/3 His preening charm and Irish good looks were also prominent in plays, films, television and supper clubs.

preent(e, prees, preest, etc., obs. ff. PRINT, PRESS, PREST *a. Obs.*, PRIEST, etc.

pre-'entry, *a.* [PRE- B 2.] Prior to entry; *spec.* applied to a closed shop in which union membership is a prerequisite of appointment to a post. Cf. POST-ENTRY *a.*

1941 [see *Air Training Corps* s.v. AIR *sb.*[1] III. 3]. **1964** W. E. J. MCCARTHY *Closed Shop in Britain* ii. 52 On the most generous of estimates the number of workers affected by the pre-entry shop in all its forms is unlikely to be more than three-quarters of a million. This means that for every worker in a pre-entry shop there are four in post-entry shops. **1969** *Gloss. Aeronaut. & Astronaut. Terms (B.S.I.)* IV. 4 *Pre-entry streamtube*, the streamtube extending to the entry of a ducted body from infinity upstream. **1972** H. WILLIAMSON *Trade Unions* (ed. 2) ii. 22 In a pre-entry closed shop, membership of a union is essential before the man is appointed to a job. **1977** J. M. JOHNSON in Douglas & Johnson *Existential Sociol.* vii. 210 Because of my preentry preparations and personal contacts, I felt more or less at ease when I addressed a joint meeting of the social workers from the two CWS units to explain the purposes of the research. **1977** *Guardian Weekly* 25 Sept. 10/2 The pre-entry closed shop (that is the kind where you need a card to get a job).

pre-ˌepileptic: see PRE- B. 1.

pre-erect, -erythrocytic, -European: see PRE- A. 1, B. 1.

pre-establish (priːɪˈstæblɪʃ), *v.* [f. PRE- A. 1 + ESTABLISH; cf. F. *préétablir* (Leibnitz 1710 in Hatz.-Darm.).] *trans.* To establish beforehand.

1643 PRYNNE *Sov. Power Parl.* IV. App. 77 Whereupon they elected him for their King..and calling him unto them, shewed him the Lawes they had pre-established. **1775** W. CRAIG *Serm.* (1808) II. 70 We have preestablished certain creeds or systems of religious belief as the truths of God. **1895** *Daily News* 23 May 6/3 What is very rare, Captain Bóttego did not exceed the sum pre-established.

Hence **pre-e'stablished** *ppl. a.*; **pre-e'stablisher,** one who or that which pre-establishes.

pre-established harmony (after F. *harmonie préétablie* Leibnitz, *Théodicée*, 1710): see HARMONY 1.

1727-41 CHAMBERS *Cycl.* s.v. *Harmony*, A pre-established harmony between the kingdoms of nature and grace. **1768-74** TUCKER *Lt. Nat.* (1834) I. 368 All the happiness.. which..the pre-established nature of things will admit. **1777** PRIESTLEY *Matt. & Spir.* (1782) I. vii. 83 Leibnitz [formed] a system which has obtained the name of the pre-established harmony. **1809-10** COLERIDGE *Friend* (1818) III. 162 [To] seek the ground of this agreement in a supersensual essence, which being at once the ideal of the reason and the cause of the material world, is the pre-establisher of the harmony in and between both. **1852** GROTE *Greece* II. lxxi. IX. 222 His preestablished reputation and the habit of obeying his orders.

pre-e'stablishment. [PRE- A. 2.] Establishment or settlement beforehand.

1755 in JOHNSON; whence in later Dicts.

Preester, obs. form of PRESTER (JOHN).

pre-'estimate, *v.* [PRE- A. 1.] *trans.* To estimate beforehand. So **pre-'estimate** *sb.*

1889 *Times* 17 Dec. 5/3 The magnitude of which it is not possible to pre-estimate. *Mod.* Your pre-estimate has been amply justified.

pre-eternity: see PRE- A. 2.

preeue, preeve, obs. forms of PROOF, PROVE.

pre-evangelism: see PRE- A. 2.

pre-evolutional, -ary, -ist: see PRE- B. 1d.

pre-exami'nation. [PRE- A. 2.] The action of examining beforehand; a previous examination.

16.. WOTTON in *Reliq.* (1651) 462 Without a pre-examination of the foresaid Giovan Battista. **1675** in *Hacket's Cent. Serm., Life* p. xxxix, To be presented..with the pre-examination of their several ministers.

pre-examination: see also PRE- B. 2a.

pre-examine (priːɛgˈzæmɪn), *v. rare.* [PRE- A. 1.] *trans.* To examine beforehand.

1659 STANLEY *Hist. Philos.* XIII. (1701) 612/2 Private Prudence consisteth..in this, that a man..deliberately pre-examin the state in which he is to spend his whole life. **1828** in WEBSTER; and in mod. Dicts.

pre-ex'cel, *v. rare.* [PRE- A. 5.] *intr.* To excel exceedingly, to be of surpassing excellence. Hence **pre-ex'celling** *ppl. a.*

1611 FLORIO, *Precellere*, to pre-excell. **1624** HEYWOOD *Gunaik.* II. 63 So farre pre-excelling is the one, as the other is vile, abject, and contemptible.

pre-'excellence. *rare.* [f. PRE- A. 5 + EXCELLENCE; cf. F. *préexcellence* (Montesquieu, 16th c.), prob. repr. a med.L. **præexcellentia*, f. **præexcellens*: see next. (L. had *præcellentia*.)] Pre-eminent excellence. So **pre-'excellency.**

1459 SIR G. HAYE *Law Arms* (S.T.S.) 270 Be all lawis, the law of nature has prerogatyf, and preexcellence. **1603** FLORIO *Montaigne* I. l. (1632) 164 A rare preexcellencie, and beyond the common reach. *Ibid.* II. xii. 255 Without any prerogative or essentiall preexcellencie.

pre-'excellent, *a. rare.* [prob. repr. a med.L. **præexcellens*; see PRE- A. 5 and EXCELLENT. (L. had *præcellens.*) Cf. obs. F. *préexcellent* (15–16th c. in Godef.).] Excellent above others; of surpassing excellence.
1611 FLORIO, *Precellente*, pre-excellent, fore-excelling. **1826** G. S. FABER *Diffic. Romanism* (1853) 50 Peter should have something preëxcellent above those who should thrice admonish.

pre-excitation: see PRE- A. 2.

pre-exilian (priːɛgˈzɪlɪən, -ɛks-), *a.* [f. PRE- B. 1 + L. *exili-um* EXILE + -AN.] Before exile; *spec.* of or belonging to the period of Jewish history before the Babylonian exile. Also, in same sense, **pre-e'xilic, pre-'exile** [PRE- B. 2], *adjs.*
1863 C. D. GINSBURG in Spurgeon *Treas. Dav.* Ps. lxxiv. 8 The only pre-exile instance. **1882–3** *Schaff's Encycl. Relig. Knowl.* II. 1160 Twenty thousand is probably too low an estimate for the pre-exilian time. **1884** *Encycl. Brit.* XVII. 303/1 The law in question is not pre-exilic. **1890** SAYCE in *Contemp. Rev.* 433 If we are ever to learn anything about pre-exilic Israel on the soil of Palestine itself, it must be by the help of the spade. **1899** *Daily News* 10 Jan. 5/5 Psalmody has its origin far back in the pre-exilian times.

pre-exist (priːɛgˈzɪst), *v.* Also 7 præ-. [f. PRE- A. 1 + EXIST; cf. F. *préexister* (1482 in Hatz.).]
1. *intr.* To exist before.
1599 [see PRE-EXISTING]. **1642** tr. *Ames' Marrow Div.* 36 Creation then produceth..out of matter that doth not præexist. **1854** OWEN *Skel. & Teeth* in *Orr's Circ. Sc.* I. *Org. Nat.* 165 The inorganic salts, defined in the tabular view of the composition of bone, pre-exist in the blood.
b. To exist before the present life.
1647 H. MORE *Præexistency of Soul* lxxxv, But that in some sort souls do præexist Seems to right reason nothing dissonant. **1699** BURNET *39 Art.* ix. (1700) 110 They.. fancied that all our Souls pre-existed in a former and purer state. **1899** J. STALKER *Christology of Jesus* ii. 62 The 'Son of Man' pre-exists with the 'Ancient of Days'.
c. To exist ideally or in the mind, before material embodiment.
1775 HARRIS *Philos. Arrangem.* Wks. (1841) 281 As there are no forms of art which did not pre-exist in the mind of man, so are there no forms of nature which did not pre-exist in the mind of God. **1839** LONGF. *Hyperion* III. v, Art preëxists in Nature, and Nature is reproduced in Art.
2. *trans.* To exist before (something).
1778 *Nat. Hist.* in *Ann. Reg.* 106/1 Inhabited by a nation, that pre-existed the formation of the marine hills. **1885** *Westm. Rev.* Jan. 27 It is necessary that the facts should pre-exist the theory.

pre-e'xistence. Also 7 præ-. [f. PRE- A. 2 + EXISTENCE; cf. F. *préexistence* (17–18th c. in Hatz.-Darm.).] Previous existence; *esp.* of the soul before its union with the body.
a **1652** J. SMITH *Sel. Disc.* iv. 91 Mere matter could never thus stretch forth its feeble force, and spread itself over all its own former pre-existences. **1662** GLANVILL (*title*) Lux Orientalis, or An Enquiry into the Opinion of the Eastern Sages, concerning the Præexistence of Souls. **1794** SULLIVAN *View Nat.* II. 107 The proofs of the antiquity and the pre-existence of nations. **1860** PUSEY *Min. Proph.* 332 It expresses præexistence, an eternal Existence, backwards as well as forwards, the incommunicable attribute of God.
Hence **pre-e'xistencist**, one who believes in the pre-existence of the soul.
1883 *Chambers' Encycl.* VII. 744/2 The followers of this opinion were termed *Pre-existencists*, to distinguish them from the *Traducianists*, who held that children received soul as well as body from their parents.

†**pre-e'xistency.** *Obs.* [PRE- A. 2.] = prec.
1642 H. MORE *Immort. Soul* III. II. i, Three apprehensions ..Concerning the souls preexistencie before into this outward world she glide. *a* **1696** SCARBURGH *Euclid* (1705) 51 This Praeexistency of the knowledge of something in the very things unknown, and sought for, is the foundation of all our Ratiocinations.

pre-existent (priːɛgˈzɪstənt), *a.* Also 7 præ-. [f. PRE- A. 3 + EXISTENT; cf. F. *pré-existant* (15th c.).] Existing beforehand, or before some person, thing, event, etc.
1624 GATAKER *Transubst.* 149 [That] the whole substance ..of bread passeth into a præexistent substance, to wit, Christ's body. *a* **1653** GOUGE *Comm. Heb.* xi. 31 There was no preexistent matter, whereof they were made. **1702** ECHARD *Eccl. Hist.* (1710) 147 According to the Jewish notion of souls sinning in some pre-existent state. **1879** *Athenæum* 19 July 83/1 Not incapable of being harmoniously combined with pre-existent beliefs.

†**pre-exi'stentiary.** *Obs.* [f. L. type **præex(s)istentia* pre-existence + -ARY[1].] One who holds the tenet of the pre-existence of souls.
1682 H. MORE *Annot. Glanvill's Lux O.* 16 A Pre-existentiary easily discerns that these Monstrosities plainly imply that God does not create souls still for every humane coition. **1698** NORRIS *Treat. Sev. Subj.* 152 According to the Hypothesis of the Preexistentiaries.
So †**pre-exi'sterian** *nonce-wd.* in same sense.
1837 F. SILVER (*title*) The Pre-Eternity of our Lord Jesus Christ denied and opposed by human pre-existerians.

†**pre-existi'mation.** *Obs. rare*[−1]. [f. PRE- A. 2 + EXISTIMATION.] Previous estimation.
1682 SIR T. BROWNE *Chr. Mor.* II. §4 Value the Judicious, and let not mere acquests in minor parts of Learning gain thy preexistimation.

pre-e'xisting, *ppl. a.* [f. PRE- A. 1 + EXISTING *ppl. a.*] That pre-exists, pre-existent.
1599 T. M[OUFET] *Silkwormes* 26 Now what are seedes and egges of wormes or foule But recrements of preexisting things. **1660** JER. TAYLOR *Duct. Dubit.* II. iii. rule 14 §9 (1676) 363 Whether all things were made of præexisting matter. **1717** PRIOR *Alma* II. 371 Our pre-existing station Before this vile terrene creation. **1871** HARTWIG *Subterr. W.* i. 2 Each of these sedimentary formations owes its existence to the disintegration of pre-existing mountain masses.

pre-expectation: PRE- A. 2.

pre-experimental(ly, -exponential: PRE- B. 1.

pre-ex'posure. [PRE- A. 2.] A preliminary or premature exposure; *spec.* in *Photogr.*, one given uniformly to a sensitive film or plate in order to increase its sensitivity.
1937 G. E. BROWN *Clerc's Photogr.* 582/1 (Index), Hypersensitizing, by pre-exposure. **1953** *Adv. Electronics* V. 77 Table VII shows..the density, *D*, of the film at optimum pre-exposure. **1967** E. CHAMBERS *Photolitho-Offset* v. 63 When double printing from positives, it is necessary to mask-out each positive in the areas where the other positive is required to print to prevent pre-exposure of the emulsion. **1979** *Nature* 24 May 341/2 Pre-exposure of human red blood cells..to dilutions of *Bufo marinus* serum followed by washing and resuspension in fresh buffer, caused a dose-dependent inhibition of subsequent ^{3}H-ouabain binding to these cells. **1979** *SLR Camera* June 73/2 The only trouble with pre-exposing the shadows in this way is that they tend to lose density in the print.
So **pre-ex'pose** *v. trans.*, to expose beforehand or in advance; *spec.* in *Photogr.*
1817 BENTHAM *Parl. Reform* Introd. 326 Brought out, pre-exposed to a damping atmosphere, and thus rendered unfit for use. **1953** *Adv. Electronics* V. 76 In order to achieve high detectivity with photographic materials, it is necessary to pre-expose the negative uniformly in order to overcome the inertia of the material. **1972** P. PETZOLD *Effects & Exper. in Photogr.* (1973) 70/2 The film should be pre-exposed for only a few shots... Further frames could be pre-exposed at higher or lower levels.

pref (prɛf). Abbrev. of *preference* (*share*) s.v. PREFERENCE 8.
1898 *Weekly Official Intelligence* 5 Mar. 145/2 Kinloch (Chas & Co.) Ord., 4/;..Pref. 3/. **1927** *Financial Times* 10 May 1/3 Mexican Nat. 1st Pref. **1971** *Financial Mail* (Johannesburg) 26 Feb. 690/3 An alternative offer for MG's pref shares can be expected soon.

pref, obs. form of PROOF, PROVE.

prefab (ˈpriːfæb), *a.* and *sb. colloq.* Also pre-fab. [Abbrev. of PREFABRICATED *ppl. a.*]
A. *adj.* Prefabricated. Also *transf.* and *fig.*
1937 *New Yorker* 27 Mar. 20 (*caption*) Darling, the Prefab Homes man was just here. **1944** *Archit. Rec.* Dec. 69/1 (*heading*) Expansible prefab house for postwar. **1958** *Times Lit. Suppl.* 21 Nov. 667/2 Wolsey's 'pre-fab.' chapel on the Field of the Cloth of Gold. **1962** J. PHILIPS *Dead Ending* (1963) II. iii. 77 That pre-fab bow tie. **1965** *New Scientist* 5 Aug. 326/2 Industrialized building is..a collection of developments. Some commentators make a division between 'light' and 'heavy', applying the former term to the progeny of the post-war 'prefab' systems, and the latter to such aids as pre-cast concrete sections of a ton or so each. **1966** T. PYNCHON *Crying of Lot 49* ii. 26 Barbed wire again gave way to the familiar parade of more beige, prefab, cinderblock office machine distributors, bottled gas works, [etc.]. **1973** C. BONINGTON *Next Horizon* xvii. 236 Neat rows of prefab huts, the homes of the Eskimos. **1977** *Rolling Stone* 24 Mar. 58/2 The temptation to follow through with prefab notions of what that audience would like..was apparently too strong to resist.
B. *sb.* A prefabricated house or building; in Britain *spec.* a light, often single-storey house of the kind built in large numbers during and after the 1939–45 war when it was necessary to rehouse many people in a short time. Also *attrib.*
1942 *Time* 16 Mar. 77/3 This year 20% of all new houses may be prefabs. **1947** 'N. SHUTE' *Chequer Board* ix. 250 Any young couple might live in a prefab when they start off first. **1949** G. COTTERELL *Randle in Springtime* 112 She continued with complaints about the people living in the new pre-fabs that had been put up where a V1 had demolished some houses in the road. **1958** *Spectator* 24 Jan. 109/2 The Crystal Palace, the first prefab in the world. **1958** U. BLOOM *Abiding City* xii. 200 England..was rising from the ashes of the bombing, with the influx of pre-fabs springing up everywhere. **1959** *Times* 24 Sept. 15/2 Active youth clubs to keep the pre-fab element out of trouble. **1972** *Daily Tel.* 7 Dec. 16/2 The last 700 prefabs in London are to be demolished.

prefab (ˈpriːfæb), *v. trans.* Colloq. abbrev. of PREFABRICATE *v.* Hence **pre-fabbed** *ppl. a.*
1959 *Observer* 4 Oct. 21/6 Prefabbed to retail on both sides of the Atlantic, the Anglo-American telefilm serial is a celluloid bastard. **1959** *Encounter* Oct. 37/2 Pre-fabbed hand-crafts and papier-maché charm. **1973** 'J. MARKS' *Mick Jagger* (1974) 67 You're still growing up in a blues environment whether you've prefabbed it or whether it's natural.

prefabricate (priːˈfæbrɪkeɪt), *v.* [PRE- A. 1.] *trans.* To manufacture (sections of a building or similar structure) in a factory or yard prior to their assembly on a site, esp. when they are larger or more complex than those considered traditional; also with the building as obj. Also *absol.* and *fig.*
1932 W. H. HAM in *Architecture* Apr. 187/1 We can prefabricate 90 per cent of a house in the factory, assemble it, and make it a permanent, attractive, useful home. **1939** *Christian Sci. Monitor* 3 Mar. 4/1 Practically every steel bridge is prefabricated, or put together in the back yard of the bridge builders before the pieces are taken apart, labeled and shipped for erection on the site. *Ibid.* 4/2 Ironwork firm, by prefabricating, makes sure that parts will join. **1941** *Times* (Weekly ed.) 23 Apr. 2 Four new plants now being erected in Nebraska, Oklahoma and Texas..will assemble annually 3,600 heavy bombers from parts pre-fabricated in automobile factories. **1944** *Hansard Commons* 7 Mar. 1906 In the most recent class of frigates at least 80 per cent. of the structure has been prefabricated. **1947** *News Chron.* 8 Apr. 2/2 The political structure which is being pre-fabricated with some success cannot be placed in position until its economic foundations have been laid. **1960** E. DELAVENAY *Introd. Machine Transl.* vii. 108 How far will it be possible to 'pre-fabricate', so to speak, this vocabulary, when preparing a programme of automatic translation, by establishing in advance a mixed vocabulary peculiar to such a translation? **1964** *Times Rev. Industry* Feb. 3/1 Five Clyde shipbuilding firms are at present prefabricating houses. **1965** R. B. WHITE *Prefabrication* III. vi. 300 The overall tendency to prefabricate has continued to make headway, particularly for buildings which form part of a national programme of expansion or modernization. **1974** *Sci. Amer.* Feb. 94/3 The Crystal Palace was the first great iron-framed building... It was also..the first for which the structural units were prefabricated.

pre'fabricated, *ppl. a.* [PRE- A. 1.] **1. a.** Of a building or similar structure: constructed by assembling a relatively small number of components which have been made elsewhere. **b.** Of a component of such a structure: made in a factory or yard prior to use elsewhere in construction.
1933 *Archit. Rev.* LXXIV. 49/2 There are a number of houses, one among them being actually of the new 'prefabricated' type. **1935** *Economist* 23 Mar. 679/1 Even the 'pre-fabricated' house, which is assembled from sections, quickly constructed, completely fitted with air-conditioning and domestic equipment..is not regarded as cheap enough to initiate the revival which is so sorely needed. **1944** *Archit. Rev.* XCVI. 30 Mr. Churchill says that we need 500,000 prefabricated houses for temporary homes in the first two years of peace. **1945** in R. W. Zandvoort et al. *Wartime English* (1957) 190 Little more than 100 yards away lie several prefabricated U-boat sections, all in an advanced state towards completion. **1951** 'J. WYNDHAM' *Day of Triffids* xvii. 298 The outbuildings are too small for our needs now—and I can't put up even prefabricated quarters singlehanded. **1959** *Listener* 17 Dec. 1072/1 Factories were built to manufacture prefabricated parts of buildings. **1963** N. MARSH *Dead Water* (1964) ii. 46 A large, prefabricated, multiple garage had been built. **1968** H. G. MILLER *Building Construction* iv. 34 These prefabricated sections, completely fitted with all doors and windows, are transported to the building site where the house can be quickly assembled on the prepared foundation. **1974** *Daily Tel.* 27 Nov. 9/1 So far about 10,000 tons of prefabricated sections of [the cruiser] Invincible have been assembled.
2. *transf.* and *fig.* Contrived, artificial.
1935 *Time* 7 Jan. 40/2 The youth is not having much success with his pre-fabricated recital. **1943** T. S. ELIOT *Reunion by Destruction* 12 The Church of South India is a pre-fabricated church. **1945** A. W. COYSH in *To start you Talking* ii. 30 The broadcast discussion is admittedly pre-fabricated. **1953** *Encounter* Oct. 14/1 This pre-fabricated public is made up not only of the more naïve party members ..but also of fellow-travellers who read nothing but the pro-Communist press. **1963** [see HAM *sb.*[1] B. 2].

prefabri'cation. [PRE- A. 2.] The manufacture or use of prefabricated components.
1932 W. H. HAM in *Architecture* Apr. 195/1 Plaster.., down to ten years ago, prohibited any advanced thought along the line of prefabrication which would create economies worth while. **1946** *Sun* (Baltimore) 8 Feb. 4/2 Prefabrication seems to be the only solution to obtaining low-cost housing for veterans. **1952** J. B. SINGER *Plastics in Building* i. 25 Prefabrication, which at one time was only intended to bridge the gap in housing shortage, has been gradually extended to cover new fields. The use of factory-produced components is universally recognized as a means to rapid and economical building. **1960** I. CROSS *Backward Sex* 13 Albertville High School was a conglomeration of brick permanence and prefabrication. **1972** *Daily Tel.* (Colour Suppl.) 17 Nov. 79/2 For the upper ten storeys, standardisation and pre-fabrication were very extensively used.

prefabricator (priːˈfæbrɪkeɪtə(r)). [f. PREFABRICAT(E *v.* + -OR.] One who, or a business which, practises prefabrication.
1933 *Fortune* Apr. 54/3 Real-estate men offer house plus land for as little as $4,400. Against this new competition what have the prefabricators to show? **1940** *Reader's Digest* July 99 Gunnison Housing Corporation, largest of prefabricators, recently sold several factory-built houses in Springfield, Ill. **1949** *Archit. Rev.* CVI. 375/1 We find a degree and a habit of uniform standardization that no American prefabricator would even attempt to impose on his customers. **1965** R. B. WHITE *Prefabrication* I. i. 4 Foster Gunnison, pioneer prefabricator of New Albany, Indiana.

preface (ˈprɛfəs), *sb.* Also 4–5 prefas, 6–7 præface. [a. F. *préface* (14–15th c. in Hatz.-Darm.), app. ad. med.L. *prefātia* (*prephatia* in

Du Cange), substituted for L. *præfātio* a saying beforehand, etc.: see PREFATION.]

I. 1. In the Liturgies of Christian Churches: The introduction or prelude to the central part of the Eucharistic service (the consecration, etc.), comprising an exhortation to thanksgiving and an offering of praise and glory to God, ending with the Sanctus. [So F. *préface de la messe*.]

Proper Preface, a variation of the Common Preface, to be used at certain seasons, including a special part proper to and varying with the particular occasion.

1387 TREVISA *Higden* (Rolls) V. 307 Gelasius..made þe comyn prefas þat is i-songe in chirches, 'Vere dignum et justum est'. *c* **1450** *Lay Folks Mass Bk.* (MS. F.) 124 The prest wil sone, in that plase, Swythe begynne the preface, That begynneth with *per omnia*. **1548–9** (Mar.) *Bk. Com. Prayer, Communion*, Here shall folowe the proper preface. **1563** FOXE *A. & M.* 896/1 The preface of the Canon from *vere dignum & inst[u]m est &c.* to *per Christum Dominum nostrum*. **1727–41** CHAMBERS *Cycl.* s.v. The preface to the mass anciently had, and still has, very different names in different churches. In the Gothic, or Gallican rite, it is called *immolation*; in the Mozarabic, *illation*; anciently among the French, it was called *contestation*; in the Roman church..it is called *præfatio, preface*. **1877** J. D. CHAMBERS *Div. Worship* 353 The Ordinary Preface, to be said daily, except in Feasts and their Octaves having Proper Prefaces. **1880** SCUDAMORE in *Dict. Chr. Antiq.* II. 1696/1 In every liturgy the eucharistic preface leads up to the angelic hymn.

II. 2. The introduction to a literary work, usually containing some explanation of its subject, purpose, and scope, and of the method of treatment.

c **1386** CHAUCER *Sec. Nun's T.* 271 And of the myracle of thise corones tweye Seint Ambrose in his preface list to seye. **1484** CAXTON *Fables of Æsop* i, Here begyneth the preface or prologue of the fyrste book. **1570** DEE *Math. Præf.* 2, I finde great occasion..to vse a certaine forewarnyng and Præface. **1642** FULLER *Holy & Prof. St.* III. xxi. 209 One shall use the preface of a mile, to bring in a furlong of matter. **1749** FIELDING *Tom Jones* Ded., I have run into a preface, while I professed to write a dedication. **1875** JOWETT *Plato* (ed. 2) V. 63 The legislator..will add prefaces to his laws which will predispose our citizens to virtue. **1895** W. A. COPINGER in *Trans. Bibliogr. Soc.* II. II. 113 The first work with a preface is the *Apuleius*, and the first with marginal notes is the *Aulus Gellius*, both works printed in 1469 at Rome by Sweynheim and Pannartz.

3. The introductory part of a speech; a prologue; an introduction or preliminary explanation.

c **1530** L. COX *Rhet.* (1899) 52 Demosthenes, in his oracyon agaynst Eschines, toke his preface out of a solempne petycyon. **1591** SHAKS. *1 Hen. VI*, V. v. 11 Tush my good Lord, this superficiall tale, Is but a preface of her worthy praise. **1667** MILTON *P.L.* XI. 251 Adam, Heav'ns high behest no Preface needs: Sufficient that thy Prayers are heard. **1725** POPE *Odyss.* XIV. 517 With artful preface to his host he spoke. **1875** JOWETT *Plato* (ed. 2) II. 249 Saying, by way of preface, that we know nothing of the truth about them.

†**b.** A prefixed epithet or title. *Obs.* ? *nonce-use.*

a **1625** FLETCHER *Love's Pilgr.* V. v, I say he is not worthy The name of man, or any honest preface, That dares report or credit such a slander.

c. A short paraphrase or practical comment upon a psalm before it was sung in church, formerly practised in Scotland: cf. PREFACE *v.* 1 b.

1869 LANDRETH *Life A. Thomson* iv. 261 A model preface would be a far nobler help to congregational praise than any choir or organ.

4. *fig.* Something preliminary or introductory.

1594 ? GREENE *Selimus* Wks. (Grosart) XIV. 234 March to Natolia, there we will begin And make a preface to our massacres. **1656** STANLEY *Hist. Philos.* V. (1701) 183/2 Mathematick is only a preface to divine things. **1746–7** HERVEY *Medit.* (1818) 222 Wasted, they are a sad preface to never-ending confusion and anguish. **1903** *Daily Chron.* 16 Mar. 3/7, I pray your readers to remember that this enhanced price of sugar has had a preface.

5. *attrib.* and *Comb.*, as ***preface-maker***, ***-monger***, ***-writer***; † **preface voice**, the particular tone of voice in which the preface (sense 1) is said or sung.

1485 *Rutland Papers* (Camden) 16 He shall chaunge his voice, and sing then in preface voice unto his words *per Christum Dominum nostrum*, which words shalbe said *in vacua voce*. **1672** MARVELL *Reh. Transp.* I. 4 Our Author is already dwindled to a Preface-monger. **1905** *Athenæum* 4 Feb. 139/3 Some occult process, which is the preface-writer's own secret.

preface ('prɛfəs), *v.* [f. prec. sb.]

1. *intr.* To make introductory or prefatory remarks; to write, speak, etc. a preface.

1619 W. SCLATER *Exp. 1 Thess.* (1630) 326 To win credence to this mystery, hee prefaceth with mention of the word of God. **1653** WALTON *Angler* i. 12, I will preface no longer, but proceed. **1720–1** *Lett. fr. Mist's Jrnl.* (1722) II. 190 Having prefaced thus much in the modern Way, I come now to apply. **1807** E. S. BARRETT *Rising Sun* I. 154 He prefaces with an account of the upright character of the panegyrist.

b. *Sc.* 'To give a short practical paraphrase of those verses of the Psalms which are to be sung before prayer' (Jamieson 1825). Also *trans.*

1727 P. WALKER *Remark. Passages* 150 He had..a singular Gift of Prefacing, which was always practised in that Day. **1824** A. THOMSON in Landreth *Life* iv. (1869) 227 This must have appeared strange to a congregation whose minister 'prefaces' the psalm for a full hour. **1869** LANDRETH *Ibid.* iv. 161 Those who have a recollection of what prefacing was.. will not soon propose its restoration. **1897** CROCKETT *Lad's Love* xv, Mind to tell me the Psalm upon which he prefaces.

2. *trans.* To write or say (something) as a preface; to state beforehand. Now *rare* or *Obs.*

1628 PRYNNE *Brief Survay* 65 That which our Author Prefaceth concerning Ember weekes..is..transcribed out of Kellams Manuall. **1664** H. MORE *Myst. Iniq.* Pref. 1 It had..been requisite to Preface something to excuse the unexpected publishing of this new Treatise. **1709** STRYPE *Ann. Ref.* I. xlviii. 483 The author thought fit to preface a very apt quotation out of S. Augustin's Epistle to Januarius. **1712** STEELE *Spect.* No. 449 ¶2 It is necessary to Preface, that she is the only Child of a decrepid Father.

†**3.** *fig.* To introduce, precede, herald. *Obs.*

1616 J. LANE *Contin. Sqr.'s T.* VIII. 36 Found they weare mingled sweete, sowr, pleasant, bitter, & praefaced ioie, but steepd in sadder licor. **1663** J. SPENCER *Prodigies* (1665) 71 That all terrible evils are prefac'd or attended with some prodigious and amazing alterations in the Creation. **1692** E. WALKER tr. *Epictetus' Mor.* ix, If thus you preface what you undertake. **1807** ANNA PORTER *Hungar. Bro.* (ed. Warne) 40 When the name of Count Leopolstat prefaced his entrance.

4. To furnish (a book, etc.) with a preface; to introduce or commence (a writing or speech) with a preface or introduction.

1691 T. H[ALE] *Acc. New Invent.* 56 That Declaration.. wherewith we Prefaced our very first Paper. **1736** SWIFT *Let. to Lady Betty Germain* 15 June, I must preface this letter with an honest declaration. **1853** ROBERTSON *Serm.* Ser. III. xxi. 277 Many..who would have prefaced that rebuke with a long speech.

5. *fig.* To place before or in front of; to front or face (*with* something).

a **1658** CLEVELAND *Gen. Poems* (1677) 24, I love to wear Clothes that are flush, Not prefacing old Rags with Plush. **1762** FOOTE *Orators* I. Wks. 1799 I. 202 A smart house, prefaced with white rails. **1880** VENABLES tr. *Berthet's Sergeant's Legacy* 137 A striped..dress, prefaced by an ample apron.

6. To precede or come before as an introduction.

1843 LYTTON *Last Bar.* I. iii, That a feat of skill with the cloth-yard might not ill preface my letter to the great earl. **1853** C. BRONTË *Villette* xxx, A depressing..passage has prefaced every new page I have turned in life.

Hence **'prefacing** *vbl. sb.*

1641 'SMECTYMNUUS' *Answ.* §1 (1653) 1 A constitution of the Areopagi, that such as pleaded before them should pleade without prefacing and without Passion. **1892** MCCRIE *Public Worship Presbyt. Scot.* 198 *note*, [He] identifies this calling on or exhorting of the congregation with prefacing.

prefacer ('prɛfəsə(r)). [f. prec. + -ER[1].] One who makes or writes a preface.

1650 [? W. SANDERSON] *Aulicus Coquin.* 89 This Prefacer stickes in their stomacks. **1678** CUDWORTH *Intell. Syst.* I. iv. §15. 272 The learned Prefacer to the late edition of Hierocles. **1758** GOLDSM. *Mem. Protestant* (1895) I. 4 The Public will scarce be influenced in their Judgment by an obscure Prefacer. **1884** *Brit. & For. Evang. Q. Rev.* Oct. 702 The Antinomianism with which Hadow charges Fisher and his prefacer.

prefacial, -tial (priː'feɪʃ(ɪ)əl), *a. rare.* [ad. med.L. *præfātia* (see PREFACE *sb.*) + -AL[1].] Of, pertaining to, of the nature of a preface; prefatory.

1888 MRS. LYNN LINTON *Thro' Long Night* III. vii, That tentative and prefatial way which means potentialities and the hereafter rather than actualities now. **1893** STEVENSON *Vailima Lett.* xxix. (1895) 262 Leaving out all the prefacial matter.

†**pre'facile,** *a. Obs. rare*$^{-0}$. [ad. L. *præfacilis*: see PRE- A. 6 and FACILE.]

1623 COCKERAM, *Prefacill*, very easie to be done.

†**'prefacive,** *a. Obs. rare*$^{-1}$. [f. PREFACE *sb.* or *v.* + -IVE.] Having the quality of prefacing; of the nature of a preface.

1650 WELDON *Crt. Jas. I* (1651) 84 All as prefacive insinuations to obtaine offices upon his future rise.

pre'factor. *Math.* [PRE- A. 2.] The first of two factors in non-commutative multiplication.

1884 J. W. GIBBS *Elements of Vector Analysis* § 131 That is, the vector $\alpha \times \beta$ as a pre- or post-factor in skew multiplication is equivalent to the dyadic $\{\beta\alpha - \alpha\beta\}$ taken as pre- or post-factor in direct multiplication.

pre-fade ('priːfeɪd), *a.* and *sb. Broadcasting.* [PRE- B. 2.] **A.** *adj.* Performed or occurring before programme material is faded up for transmission. Of apparatus: used for such monitoring. **B.** *sb.* Monitoring of programme material prior to fading it up for transmission; an instance of this; also, a technical facility for such monitoring.

1941 *B.B.C. Gloss. Broadcasting Terms* 24 *Pre-fade listening.* (1) Listening to a programme output before it is faded up for transmission. (2) Technical facilities provided for this purpose. **1949** F. FELTON *Radio-Play* ii. 19 There is also a 'pre-fade' apparatus by which the operator can listen to the record in advance. **1962** A. NISBETT *Technique Sound Studio* viii. 150 Listening to this disc on prefade it is brought into step with disc one. *Ibid.*, After a quick prefade check, the disc is once again faded up. *Ibid.* ix. 160 In the case of a typical prefade (that used for the BBC's Radio Newsreel) it is known that the duration from a certain easily recognizable point to the end of the record is exactly 1′ 17″. So the record is started exactly 1′ 17″ from the end of the programme, but not faded up. **1968** R. MILTON *Radio Programming* 313 While you are giving a talk from the studio, the technician may listen to a part of the recording he will use next, to be sure it is the right one. He will do this by using his pre-fade monitor. **1975** G. ALKIN *TV Sound Operations* 126 Gram desks are provided with a 'pre-fade' output so that the operator can listen for the cue without fading it up, so that the output is not heard by the audience. *Ibid.*, The method of cueing in discs is to play the recording on pre-fade until the cue is heard and then stop the turntable.

pre'fade, *v. Broadcasting.* [f. the sb.] *intr.* To employ pre-fade listening. Also *trans.*, to monitor (programme material) before fading it up for transmission. Hence **pre'faded** *ppl. a.*, **pre'fading** *vbl. sb.*

1962 A. NISBETT *Technique Sound Studio* viii. 149 For professional disc work..it is valuable to be able to 'prefade' (i.e. listen before fading up) while the studio loud-speaker is being used to monitor the rest of the programme. *Ibid.* ix. 160 For the close of many radio programmes prefaded music is used. *Ibid.* 161 Vocal music is not usually suitable for prefading. **1971** T. C. COLLOCOTT *Dict. Sci. & Technol.* 929/1 *Prefading*, listening to programme material and adjusting its level before it is faded up for transmission or recording.

prefalie, obs. Sc. f. PRIVILY.

prefar(re, obs. or dial. form of PREFER.

pre-Fascist: see PRE- B. 1 a.

pre'fashion, *v.* [PRE- A. 1.] *trans.* To fashion beforehand.

1614 JACKSON *Creed* III. xx. §7 Not prefashioned in mind to those descriptions the Prophets had made of his first comming in humility. **1621** BP. MOUNTAGU *Diatribæ* 147 All your thoughts prefigured, and prefashioned, by *All the spoyles*, and *onely spoyles*. **1847** BUSHNELL *Chr. Nurt.* viii. (1861) 197 It seems to be in some sense, prefashioned by what birth and nurture have communicated.

†**pre'fation.** *Obs.* Also 4–6 **prefacion.** [ad. L. *præfātiōn-em* a saying beforehand, introductory address, preface, in med.L. also = PREFACE *sb.* 1; n. of action f. *præfārī*, f. *præ* before, PRE- A. 1 + *fārī* to speak. Cf. obs. F. *prefacion* (14th c. in Godef.).] Speaking before; prefacing.

1382 WYCLIF *2 Macc.* ii. 33 Be it ynewȝ for to haue saide so myche of prefacioun [*gloss* or byfore spekyng]. **1529** MORE *Dyaloge* I. Wks. 119/2 This protestacion and prefacion made, he said that..it were well done, to do vnto saintes or their ymages dispite or dishonour. *c* **1581** in *Cath. Tractates* (S.T.S.) 252 Ye confes this your selfes in the prefatione of our new Byble. **1652** GAULE *Magastrom.* 90 Shall we attend to the præfation of irrationals and inanimate?

pre'fator. [a. L. type **præfātor*, agent-n. from *præfārī*: see prec.] A prefacer; a preface-writer.

1865 DE MORGAN *Budget of Paradoxes* (1872) 378 The prefator suspends his opinion as to the cause, though he upholds the facts. **1872** *Ibid.* 84 Fewer words would have been lost if the prefator had said at once that the work was from the manuscript preserved at Cambridge.

prefatorial (prɛfə'tɔərɪəl), *a.* [f. as PREFATORY + -AL[1].] Of or pertaining to a prefacer or a preface; prefatory. Hence **prefa'torially** *adv.*, in the character of a prefacer, by way of preface.

1799 W. GILPIN *Serm.* Pref. 6 Much prefatorial matter also may arise, before we begin the discourse. **1865** *Priory of Hexham* (Surtees) II. Pref. 5 Some prefatorial remarks.. may be of use. **1903** *Daily Chron.* 1 July 3/4 Mr. Chambers remarks prefatorially of a work which the Oxford University Press will have ready this week.

prefatory ('prɛfətərɪ), *a.* [f. L. type **præfātōrius*, f. **præfātor* PREFATOR: see -ORY[2].] Of the nature of a preface; introductory, preliminary.

1675 OGILBY *Brit.* Pref. 2 Hitherto of the Undertaking.. as Præfatory to the..Business. **1710** SHAFTESB. *Charact.* (1737) I. III. iii. 329 The anticipating Manner of prefatory Discourse is too well known. **1850** GROTE *Greece* II. lx. VII. 445 Gylippus sent the fleet out with the usual prefatory harangue. **1856** MISS MULOCK *J. Halifax* xxx, Prefatory to the customary toast. **1860** TYNDALL *Glac.* II. xxvii. 380, The Prefatory Note which precedes the volume.

Hence **'prefatorily** *adv.*, in a prefatory manner; as, or by way of, preface.

1741 RICHARDSON *Pamela* (1824) I. Pref. 4 But I think, the hints you have given me, should also prefatorily be given to the public. **1903** C. MAUDE *Haymarket Theatre* 8 This, I have already said prefatorily, is not to be regarded as a serious history.

prefect, præfect ('priːfɛkt), *sb.* Forms: 4 *Sc.* prefec, -fet(e, -feit, 4–5 -fecte, 5- prefect; 7–9 præ-. [a. OF. *prefect* (12th c.), mod.F. *préfet* = Pr. *prefeit*, Sp. *prefecto*, It. *prefetto*, ad. L. *præfect-us* an overseer, president, commander, superintendent of a public office, civil or military; in later use the governor of a province or city; sb. use of pa. pple. of *præficĕre* to set over, place in authority over, f. *præ*, PRE- A. 5 + *facĕre* to make, constitute, appoint.]

1. A person appointed to a position of command; a chief officer or magistrate; a governor, commander, superintendent, director, overseer. Applied as a title to various officers in ancient or modern times.

a. Representing L. *præfectus*, In ancient Rome and the Roman empire, the title of various officers civil and military, e.g. the prefect or chief magistrate of the city, *præfectus urbi*, the civil governor of a province, a colony, or provincial city, the commander of the pretorian troops, *præfectus prætorio*, and of the fleet, *præfectus classis*.

c **1350** *St. Ambrosius* 57 in Horstm. *Altengl. Leg.* (1878) 9/1 Ambrose of Rome was prefecte. *c* **1375** *Sc. Leg. Saints* i. (*Petrus*) 308 Fra Agrippe, þat prefet was of þat Cite, Fowre concubynis he drew a-way. *c* **1386** CHAUCER *Sec. Nun's T.* 368 Oon Maximus that was an Officer Of the Prefectes and his Corniculer Hem hente. **1447** BOKENHAM *Seyntys* (Roxb.) 13 A tyraunt, the prefect of that cuntre. **1494** FABYAN *Chron.* v. cxxiv. 103 But Clothayre..sent his sone Meroueus, vnder the gydyng of Laundry, prefect or ruler of his paleys, into Neustria. **1611** SPEED *Theat. Gt. Brit.* i. (1614) 2/2 Severus..divided the government therof into two Provinces, and placed two Prefects over the same. *a* **1719** ADDISON *Chr. Relig.* I. vii, The præfects and viceroys of distant provinces. **1781** GIBBON *Decl. & F.* xvii. II. 51 The private apartments of the palace were governed by a favourite eunuch, who, in the language of that age, was styled the *præpositus* or præfect of the sacred bed-chamber. **1868** *Smith's Dict. Gr. & Rom. Antiq.* s.v. *Ærarium*, In B.C. 28, Augustus deprived the quaestors of the charge of the treasury and gave it to two praefects, whom he allowed the senate to choose from among the praetors. **1874** GREEN *Short Hist.* i. §2. 15 York had been the capital of Britain and the seat of the Roman prefect.

b. In other countries, in ancient times: in similar uses.

1382 WYCLIF *Dan.* ii. 48 Thann the kyng..ordeynyde hym vpon alle prouyncis of Babiloyne prince and prefect. **1388** —— *1 Kings* iv. 7 Forsothe Salomon hadde twelue prefectis [*gloss* ether cheef minystrys] on al Israel. **1659** HAMMOND *Annot. Ps.* xxii. Wks. 1684 IV. 69 The Psalm thus composed by David, was committed to the Præfect of his Musick. **1850** W. IRVING *Mahomet, Successors* xvi. (1853) 72 The prefect of Ammon, with 5000 men, was near at hand.

c. In mod. Europe: A president, chief officer, chief magistrate, etc.

1540 COVERDALE *Let. to C. Hubert* Wks. (Parker Soc.) II. 507, I settled this business..in the presence and hearing of the prince, in the company of our prefect. **1629** WADSWORTH *Pilgr.* iii. 13 Father Darcy, Præfect of the *Sodalitium Beatæ Mariæ*, and the refectory. **1670** G. H. *Hist. Cardinals* I. III. 86 The office of the Prefect of the Signature of Justice, is executed by a Cardinal. **1756–7** tr. *Keysler's Trav.* (1760) IV. 64 Andrea Cornelio,..prætor of Verona, prefect of Bressia, proveditor-general of the army on the Venetian *terra ferma*.

d. *esp.* (repr. F. *préfet.*) The chief administrative officer of a department of France. ***Prefect of Police***, the head of the police administration in Paris and the department of the Seine.

1827 SCOTT *Napoleon* xxxviii, These prefects..were each the supreme governor of a department, answering to the old lieutenants and governors of counties. **1848** W. H. KELLY tr. *L. Blanc's Hist. Ten Years* I. 390 The minister of the interior wrote on the subject to the prefect of police. **1861** *Sat. Rev.* 23 Nov. 523 The experiment..seems to have satisfied the Emperor that he can rely upon his faithful prefects to supply him with a Chamber which will relieve him of the odium of extravagance without diminishing his power to squander.

e. Used to represent Chinese *chih-fu*, head or governor of a *fu* or department (cf. PREFECTURE 2 b).

1890 *Cent. Dict.* s.v. *Chih-fu*, A prefect, having general supervision of all the civil business of the hiens comprising his prefecture. **1894** [see PREFECTURAL].

f. *fig.* = Director, minister, etc.

16.. B. JONSON *Hue & Cry after Cupid* Wks. (Rtldg.) 563/1 Venus..is Præfect of Marriage. *a* **1633** AUSTIN *Medit.* (1635) 251 Angels being Prefects to particular Men; and Archangels to People or Nations.

2. *transf.* In some English public, preparatory, and secondary schools, the name given to one of the body of senior pupils to whom authority is delegated for the maintenance of order and discipline: otherwise called *præpostors*, *prepositors*, etc.

1865 W. L. C. *Etoniana* ii. 24 The senior [præpostor] was called, as he is to this day at Winchester, 'Prefect of Hall' and the two next 'Prefects of Chapel'. **1876** R. LOWE in *Life* (1893) I. 10 In the fourth year of my residence at Winchester I became a prefect. **1879** JESSOPP *One Gen. Norfolk Ho.* 102 The next two years and a half he [Henry Walpole] spent at Pont à Mousson, during which time he was 'Prefect of the Convictors'. **1891** WRENCH *Winchester Word-bk.*, *Præfects*, the senior members of the School, to whom authority is delegated for the management and control of the community. The number of Præfects was eighteen in College, three to each chamber... The 'Præfect of Tub'.. who presided over meals,..and the 'Præfect of Cloisters', are obsolete.

†**pre'fect**, *v.* *Obs.* [f. L. *præfect-*, ppl. stem of *præficĕre*: see prec.] *trans.* To appoint to a position of command or authority.

1489 *Rolls of Parlt.* VI. 428/2 Kyng Henry the VIth.. prefected and erected John then Lord Talbott..into Erle of Shrewesbury. **1534** *Act 26 Hen. VIII*, c. 3 §2 Euery suche person..nominated, elected, prefected, presented, collated or..appointed to haue any..promocion spiritual. *a* **1548** HALL *Chron.*, *Hen. VII* 52 b, Rycharde Foxe bishop of Durham, was prefected to the bishoprike of Winchestre. **1602** FULBECKE *2nd Pt. Parall.* 17 The owner of the ship is ..charged, because he prefected him, and made him Master.

prefectly ('priːfɛktlɪ), *a.* *rare.* [f. PREFECT, PRAEFECT *sb.* + -LY[1].] Characteristic of or befitting a prefect.

1927 J. ELDER *Thomasina Toddy* xxii. 218 Anne recognised them with her most prefectly twitch of the lips.

†**pre'fector.** *Obs. rare.* Erroneous equivalent of PREFECT (after agent-nouns in -OR: cf. PREFECTORIAL). Hence †**pre'fectorship** = PREFECTURE 1.

1611 SPEED *Hist. Gt. Brit.* VI. xxx. §4. 128 Yong Gordianus vnable to endure his Prefectors designes,.. complained his wrongs in open assemblies. **1790** *Bystander* 34 It is said that Sophocles was adjudged, upon a certain occasion, the prefectorship of Samos.

prefectoral (prɪ'fɛktərəl), *a.* [a. F. *préfectoral*, irreg. f. L. *præfect-us*: cf. next.] = next.

1872 *Daily News* 13 Aug., The prefectoral appointments in this day's *Officiel*. **1902** *Speaker* 9 Aug. 501/2 The results of this circular will be to restore prefectoral authority exactly as it was in the finest time of the Empire.

prefectorial (priːfɛk'tɔərɪəl), *a.* [f. late L. *præfectōri-us* (Ulpian) belonging to a prefect + -AL[1].] **1. a.** Of or pertaining to a prefect or prefects.

1883 *Century Mag.* XXV. 717 To keep up the contemptible and anti-democratic prefectorial rule in the departments. **1895** *Athenæum* 21 Sept. 381/1 At Chaot'ung, a prefectorial city, he found the people in the direst distress.

b. *esp.* in the English Public School system. (See PREFECT *sb.* 2.)

1862 *Q. Rev.* Apr. 419 Maintaining a sound and well-tempered monitorial or prefectorial system,..is involved in the true idea of a public school. **1893** *Athenæum* 22 July 130/1 It is not easy to secure..wise prefectorial authority, except by means of able boys staying out the full period of boyhood at the school.

2. Of or pertaining to a prefecture (sense 3).

1942 E. PAUL *Narrow St.* iii. 24 Hours of squinting in the dingy misplaced prefectorial light. **1963** *Times* 18 Feb. 8/3 As incumbent of the Lyons prefecture, a massive grey building typical of the 'prefectorial baroque'..he represents the central power of Paris.

Hence **prefec'torially** *adv.*, in a prefectorial capacity; by the authority of a prefect.

1895 *Westm. Gaz.* 16 Aug. 8/2 If 'rational dress' be prefectorially repressed [in Paris], and the young women compelled to resume their former coquettish costumes.

prefec'torian, *a.* *rare*[−1]. [f. as prec. + -AN.] Of or pertaining to an ancient Roman prefect.

1781 GIBBON *Decl. & F.* xxxvi. (1788) VI. 209 A decent respect was still observed for the Praefectorian rank.

prefectship ('priːfɛkt-ʃɪp). [f. PREFECT *sb.* + -SHIP.] The office of a prefect; the period of tenure of that office. (= PREFECTURE 1.)

1609 HOLLAND *Amm. Marcell.* 331 Successors after him in the Prefectship of the citie. ?**17..** TUCKER *Law Nat.* 251 (L.) Under the prefectship of Pontius Pilate.

prefectual (prɪ'fɛktjuːəl), *a.* [irreg. f. L. *præfect-us* PREFECT *sb.*] = PREFECTORIAL b.

1879 ESCOTT *England* I. 499 What is called the monitorial or the prefectual system.

prefectural (prɪ'fɛktjʊərəl), *a.* [f. PREFECTURE + -AL[1].] Of or pertaining to a prefecture. ***prefectural town*** or ***city***, the chief town or city of a prefecture, the seat of the prefect.

1811 W. TAYLOR in *Monthly Mag.* XXXII. 62 There is a prefectural nursery at Colmar. **1880** E. OPPERT *Forbid. L.* iv. 108 All prefectural officials [in Japan] are taken from the upper two degrees of this class. **1882** *Missionary Herald* (U.S.) Sept. 345 The prefectural cities Ta Tung and Sho P'ing. **1894** *Westm. Gaz.* 31 July 2/1 Nearly every prefectural town [in Korea] has its archery ground, on which in former days very frequently the Prefect would exercise his men.

prefecturate (prɪ'fɛktjʊərət). [irreg. f. PREFECTURE + -ATE[1].] = next, senses 1 and 2.

1762 tr. *Busching's Syst. Geog.* IV. 242 The upper landvogtey contains in it thirteen prefecturates. **1873** E. C. GRENVILLE-MURRAY *Men of Third Republic* 282 The rumors that arose as to a prefecturate being offered him [Edmond About] proved unfounded.

prefecture ('priːfɛktjʊə(r)). [ad. L. *præfectūra* the office or administration of a *præfectus*: see PREFECT *sb.* and -URE. So F. *préfecture* (13–14th c. in Hatz.-Darm.).]

1. The office or position of prefect, ancient or modern; administration of a governor; presidency, superintendency, directorship; the time or period during which such office is held.

1608 J. KING *Serm. St. Marys* 6 Not by way of Lieutenantship, deputation, subordinate prefecture whatsoever, but as a King over subiects. **1652** GAULE *Magastrom.* 2 All their prefecture and power [are] but derivative, subordinate, ministeriall. *a* **1654** SELDEN *Table-T.* (1689) 34 You would have some other kind of Præfeture, than a Mayoralty. **1756** NUGENT *Montesquieu's Spir. Laws* (1758) I. IV. viii. 54 Plato..says, that the præfectures of music and gymnic exercises [etc.]. **1865** MERIVALE *Rom. Emp.* VIII. lxvi. 188 He..occupied at the moment the most important of all charges, the prefecture of Syria. **1865** MAFFEI *Brigand Life* II. 34 The old officials were retained in the prefectures.

2. A district under the government of a prefect.

1577 PATERICKE tr. *Gentillet* (1602) 367 He.. commaunded they should take nothing within their prefecture or jurisdiction. **1642** JER. TAYLOR *Episc.* 303 S. Chrysostome had Pontus, Asia, and all Thrace in his parish, even as much as came to sixteen prefectures. **1762** tr. *Busching's Syst. Geog.* I. 114 The..island is divided into five Amts or Prefectures. **1841** W. SPALDING *Italy & It. Isl.* I. 108 Constantine divided the empire..into four great Prefectures.

b. = Chinese *fu*, an administrative district or division of a province; also, applied to a corresponding district in Japan: cf. PREFECT *sb.* 1 e.

1885 *Whitaker's Alm.* s.v. *Japan*, Japan..has recently incorporated Loochoo under the name of 'Prefecture of Okinawa'. **1890** HOSIE *W. China* 95 The products of the prefecture are not confined to tea. **1897** A. MACPHAIL in *Outing* (U.S.) XXIX. 325/1, 3 classes [of roads in Japan], the national roads, the prefecture roads between these [military] stations, and the village roads.

3. The official residence of a prefect or French *préfet*.

1848 W. H. KELLY tr. *L. Blanc's Hist. Ten Y.* II. 51 The insurgents..were surrounding on all sides the prefecture of police. *Ibid.* 456 A line of ramparts, along which were ranged the Hôtel-de-Ville, the prefecture, the military division and subdivision.

†**pre'fectureship.** *Obs.* Bad formation for PREFECTURE or PREFECTSHIP.

1606 G. W[OODCOCKE] *Lives Emperors* in *Hist. Ivstine* G g ij, In the time of his prefectureship. **1762** tr. *Busching's Syst. Geog.* V. 69 The lordship of Itter..constitutes a prefectureship. **1818** HOBHOUSE *Hist. Illustr.* (ed. 2) 545 We have received from the Roman people the prefectureship.

†**pre'fectury.** *Obs.* *rare*[−1]. [irreg. f. PREFECTURE + -Y.] = PREFECTURE 2; a district; ? a shire or county.

1686 PLOT *Staffordsh.* 396 These they find in Scotland in much greater plenty, especially in the prefectury of Aberdeen.

prefer (prɪ'fɜː(r)), *v.* Also (5 prefarr, profer(e), 5–7 preferre, (6 prefar(re, -phar(re, *Sc.* præfer, preffer). [a. F. *préférer* (14th c. in Hatz.-Darm.), ad. L. *præfer-re* to bear or put before or forward, prefer, advance, f. *præ*, PRE- A. 4, 5 + *fer-re* to bear.]

I. 1. a. *trans.* To put forward or advance, in status, rank, or fortune; to promote (*to* a position or office of dignity).

1388 WYCLIF *Prol.* xiii. 50 In this degre..he neither preferrith, neither makith euene himself..with the treuthe [etc.]. **1390** GOWER *Conf.* III. 180 Bot thei that wolden stonde upriht For trouthe only to do justice Preferred were in thilke office. **1429** *Rolls of Parlt.* IV. 343/2 In Benefices and Offices..when thai voiden, thoo that hath ben' Servauntz..shal be preferred therto. **1494** FABYAN *Chron.* VI. ccii. 212 The sayde Gerbres was after this preferred by one of the Othons, Emperour, vnto the Churche of Rauenne. **1526** *Pilgr. Perf.* (W. de W. 1531) 62 b, Se how our lorde preferred and promoted the great synner to the hyer dignite. **1564–78** BULLEYN *Dial. agst. Pest.* (1888) 67 If any man be prepharred by another man and made riche. **1596** DALRYMPLE tr. *Leslie's Hist. Scot.* IV. 259 Soluathie.. is to the kingdome preferit, elected, and crouned. **1607** MIDDLETON *Michaelm. Term* II. ii. 13 Being now happily preferred to a gentleman's service in London. **1610** HOLLAND *Camden's Brit.* (1637) 288 Schollers [of Eton] instructed in Grammar, and in due time preferred to the Universitie of Cambridge. *a* **1661** FULLER *Worthies, Cheshire* (1662) I. 177 (After some intermediate Dignities) he was preferred Chief Baron of the Exchequer. **1709** STEELE *Tatler* No. 4 ¶8 Happy..that he never preferred a Man who has not proved remarkably serviceable to his Country. **1878** SIMPSON *Sch. Shaks.* I. 55 To the disgust of the soldiers..he was preferred to what hitherto had always been a soldier's post.

†**b.** *refl.* To advance oneself or one's interests. *Obs.*

c **1460** FORTESCUE *Abs. & Lim. Mon.* x. (1885) 134 Ther shall non off his tenantes aliene livelod with owt is licence, wheryn he mey best preferre hym selff. **1592** TIMME *Ten Eng. Lepers* D iij, The buyer having an ambicious intent to prefer himselfe thereby. **1630** *R. Johnson's Kingd. & Commw.* 50 If hee be..a man of endeavours, and willing to preferre himselfe by service, I wish him to Historie.

†**c.** To advance or promote to a position in life; *esp.* to settle in marriage. Cf. PREFERMENT 2. *Obs.*

1559 *Mirr. Mag.*, *Dk. Glocester* ix, And after in mariage I was prefarde To a daughter of Bohan an earle honorable. **1565–6** *Child-Marriages* 136 To geve and bequethe vnto my Children, beinge not Married, and not otherwise Competentlie preferred. **1605** CAMDEN *Rem.* (1637) 142 After [being] preferred to a good marriage by his Lord.

†**d.** *fig. pass.* To be exalted or made eminent by some quality. *Obs.*

c **1430** LYDG. *Min. Poems* (Percy Soc.) 128 Nor philosophers of every regioune, Nor the prophetes preferred by Science. *Ibid.* 161 Som man is strong berys for to bynde, Anothir feeble preferryd with prudence.

e. *transf.* To promote (in various uses).

a **1533** in *More's Debell. Salem* Wks. 1008/2 It wil be hard to find any one spirituall man yt is not infect with the sayd desyre & affeccion to haue the worldlye honour of priestes exalted & preferred. **1580** LYLY *Euphues* (Arb.) 449 Alexander..pardoned his boldnesse, and preferred his arte. **1626** BACON *Sylva* §439 All Grasiers preferre their Cattel from meaner Pastures to better. **1697** DRYDEN *Virg. Georg.* III. 595 Ev'n though a snowy Ram thou shalt behold, Prefer him not in haste, for Husband to thy Fold. **1732** BERKELEY *Alciphr.* v. §33 Birds, beasts, fishes; which, upon their death, are preferred into human bodies. **1817** COLERIDGE *Biog. Lit.*

(1882) 81 The work was..preferred from the ominous cellar of the publishers to the author's garret.

†**2.** To forward, advance, promote (a result); to assist in bringing about. *Obs.*

1574 BOURNE *Regiment for Sea* xxi. (1577) 58 That effect is most preferred, if the Dragons head be in the beginning; of the figure of Aries. **1590** LLOYD *Diall Daies* 134 To prosper the corne and the cattell, and to preferre the fruites of the fields. **1600–12** ROWLANDS *Four Knaves* (Percy Soc.) 50 Thus fingring money to preferre the case. **1627–47** FELTHAM *Resolves* II. xlvii. 380 A little shaking prefers the growth of the tree.

II. †**3.** *trans.* To put or set in front or before. *Obs.*

1541 R. COPLAND *Guydon's Quest. Chirurg.* Rj b, Do nat as a folysshe iudge that forthwith gyueth his sentence, but fyrste or thou gyue it preferre God before thyne eyes, and consydre dylygently [etc.]. **1575** FENTON *Gold. Epist.* (1577) 107 He wrote speedily to Ioab..that at the time of the assault, Vrias might be preferred to the perill of his life.

4. To put, place, or set (something) before any one for acceptance; to hold out, proffer, offer, present; to introduce or recommend. *Obs.* or *arch.*

1573 L. LLOYD *Marrow of Hist.* (1653) A ij, I have here preferred to your observance and protection, a work of great Art, and of greater Industry. **1621** BURTON *Anat. Mel.* (1632) 261 Bessardus Bisantinus preferres the smoake of Juniper to melancholy persons. **1648** CRASHAW *Delights of Muses* Wks. (1904) 121 Preferre soft-Anthems to the Eares of men. **1677** EVELYN *Mem.* 13 Sept., I preferred Mr. Philips [nephew of Milton] to the service of my Lord Chamberlaine, who wanted a scholar to read to and entertain him sometimes. **1704** POPE *Summer* 53 Each am'rous nymph prefers her gifts in vain. **1725** —— *Odyss.* III. 64 He spake, and to her hand preferr'd the bowl. **1867** C. B. CAYLEY in *Fortn. Rev.* Nov. 591 Seeking what words can avail me, What numbers even, to prefer clear light to thy aspect [*præpandere lumina menti*].

5. To lay (a matter) before any one formally for consideration, approval, or sanction; to bring forward, present, submit (a statement, bill, indictment, information, prayer, etc.). Also †*prefer up*.

1559 BP. SCOT in Strype *Ann. Ref.* (1709) I. App. vii. 12 The contents of all the bills preferred and read here. **1560** DAUS tr. *Sleidane's Comm.* 162 The Marques intrateth kyng Ferdinando, that he would immediatly preferre this matter to the Emperoure. **1601** WEEVER *Mirr. Mart.* D ij b, That I preferd up Bills in Parliament, Whereto the King and Lords gaue all consent. *a* **1674** CLARENDON *Surv. Leviath.* (1676) 103 Suppose that an Information were preferr'd in the Kings Bench..against Mr. Hobbes. **1768** H. WALPOLE *Hist. Doubts* 120 The consequence of a suit preferred by him to the ecclesiastic Court. **1813** HOGG *Queen's Wake* 18 But many a bard preferred his prayer; For many a Scottish bard was there. **1850** TENNYSON *In Mem.* cii, These two have striven half the day, And each prefers his separate claim, Poor rivals in a losing game. **1884** LD. COLERIDGE in *Law Times Rep.* L. 277/1 Preferring an indictment against her for stealing his goods. **1885** *Ibid.* LIII. 51/1 An information preferred against the appellant..by the..sanitary inspector.

†**6.** To refer; to attribute, ascribe. *Obs.*

1628 WITHER *Brit. Rememb.* Concl. 35 The building of a Towne we doe preferre Unto the Mason and the Carpenter. **1658** W. BURTON *Itin. Anton.* 26 Jerome Surita..prefers this work to Antoninus the son of Severus.

III. 7. a. To set or hold (one thing) before others in favour or esteem; to favour or esteem more; to choose or approve rather; to like better. With *simple obj.*, *inf.*, or *clause*; *above*, †*before*, *to*. Now the chief sense.

1390 GOWER *Conf.* I. 268 Kinde [i.e. Nature]..preferreth no degre As in the disposicioun Of bodili complexioun. *c* **1430** LYDG. *Min. Poems* (Percy Soc.) 210 Trewe juges and sergeauntis of the lawe,..Mercy preferre alwey tofor rigour. **1502** ATKYNSON tr. *De Imitatione* III. lviii. 248 Afore all worldly thynges prefarre thou the honour & medytacion of god. **1538** STARKEY *England* I. i. 6 Hyt ys not to be preferryd therto as a thyng to be chosen and folowyd. **1552** ABP. HAMILTON *Catech.* (1884) 24, I preferre deidis of mercy abone all corporal and outwart sacrifice. **1560** DAUS tr. *Sleidane's Comm.* 24 He preferreth his owne decrees..before the Scriptures. **1661** BOYLE *Style of Script.* (1675) 165 He should not scruple to prefer the end to the means. **1680** MORDEN *Geog. Rect.* (1685) 322 We may justly prefer it before the other parts of the World. **1778** *Hist. Eliza Warwick* I. 25 He would prefer seeing his daughters dead at his feet, than behold them wedded to the worthiest men without titles and riches. **1815** J. W. CROKER in *C. Papers* (1884) 20 July, He preferred living like a Grecian, to dying like a Roman. **1882** FROUDE in *Fortn. Rev.* Dec. 734 Warlike races prefer to be under a chief. **1883** G. MOORE *Mod. Lover* II. vi. 105 There was one place he preferred above all others. **1895** LIEUT. MAGUIRE in *United Service Mag.* 378 Because the Chinese preferred the doctrines of Confucius to ordinary military common sense.

absol. **1844** BROWNING *Laboratory* vii, Let her turn it and stir, And try it and taste, ere she fix and prefer! **1902** *Edin. Rev.* Apr. 512 He prefers rather than excludes.

b. *Law.* To give preference to as a creditor. Cf. PREFERENCE 5.

1433 *Rolls of Parlt.* IV. 432/1 Yat in paiement..y preferre youre Houshold. *Ibid.* 439 Who shuld be preferred in payement. **1885** *Encycl. Brit.* XIX. 764/2 In English law the term 'preferred' than 'privileged' is generally applied to such debts.

†**8.** To be preferable to; to surpass, excel. [= OF. *préférer* to prevail, have the pre-eminence, 15th c. in Godef.] *Obs. rare.*

c **1386** CHAUCER *Wife's Prol.* 96, I graunte it wel, I haue noon envie, Thogh maydenhede preferre [*v.r.* profere] Bigamye. **1549** *Compl. Scot.* vi. 43 Sen the varld vas creat, scheiphirdis prefferrit al vthir staitis. *Ibid.* 65–6 Nor orpheus..his playing prefferrit nocht thir foir said scheiphirdis; nor ȝit the scheiphyrd pan,..nor mercurius,..none of them culd preffer thir foirsaid scheiphirdis.

preferability (ˌprɛfərəˈbɪlɪtɪ). [f. next: see -ITY.] The quality or fact of being preferable.

1802–12 BENTHAM *Ration. Judic. Evid.* (1827) IV. 482 The preferability of the less injustice to the greater would scarcely be contested. **1840** CARLYLE *Heroes* iii. (1872) 90 Good and Evil..differ not by preferability of one to the other, but by incompatibility absolute and infinite. **1962** L. J. COHEN *Diversity of Meaning* vi. 160 The preferability of one conceptual form to another. **1975** *New Yorker* 21 Apr. 96/2 The manual went on to stress the actuarial preferability of drivers leading a stable life.

preferable (ˈprɛfərəb(ə)l), *a.* (*sb.*, *adv.*) [a. F. *préférable* (Cotgr. 1611), f. *préférer*: see PREFER and -ABLE. (See also PREFERRABLE.)]

A. *adj.* **1.** Worthy to be preferred; to be chosen before or desired rather than another; more desirable.

1648 [implied in PREFERABLENESS]. **1666** S. PARKER *Free & Impart. Censure* (1667) 142 If Existence..be meerly upon this score preferable before Non-existence. **1708** J. CHAMBERLAYNE *St. Gt. Brit.* II. III. (1737) 67 A select Number..call'd Preferable Men, who are always employ'd first after the Establish'd Men. **1751** JOHNSON *Rambler* No. 177 ¶1 A condition far preferable to the fatigue, dependance, and uncertainty of any gainful occupation. **1850** HAWTHORNE *Scarlet L.* xvii. (1879) 219 Death itself,..would have been infinitely preferable. **1860** TYNDALL *Glac.* I. xxiii. 161 The cold was preferable to the smoke.

†**2.** Displaying preference; preferential. *Obs.*

1747 RICHARDSON *Clarissa* (1811) I. ix. 58 What preferable favour I may have for him to any other person. **1804** *Something Odd* III. 132 Notwithstanding her preferable affection for the brandy bottle. **1811** SHERIDAN in Moore *Mem.* (1825) II. 412, I shall as..cordially endeavour to..assist Mr. Benjamin Wyatt in the improving and perfecting his plan, as if it had been my own preferable selection.

3. = PREFERENCE 8. *attrib.*

1913 *Act 3 & 4 Geo. V* c. 20 §97 (1) Such preferable securities as existed at the date of the sequestration, and are not null or reducible.

†**B.** as *sb.* in *pl.* Things to be preferred. *Obs.*

1702 S. PARKER tr. *Cicero's De Finibus* III. 192 Unless we render both as before, *Præposita*, or *Præcipua*, Preferables; and *Rejecta*, Things Disagreeable. **1710** tr. *Werenfels's Disc. Logom.* 20 The Stoicks..denying Riches to be good things, but calling them Preferables.

†**C.** as *adv.* Preferably, in preference. *Obs.*

1683 TEMPLE *Mem.* Wks. 1731 I. 420 His entering into it with me preferable to all others. **1760–72** H. BROOKE *Fool of Qual.* (1809) III. 45 If the reader loves amusement preferable to instruction.

ˈpreferableness. [f. prec. + -NESS.] The quality of being preferable; greater desirableness.

1648 W. MOUNTAGUE *Devout Ess.* I. x. §7. 121 My purpose is not to measure or weigh the preferablenesse of severall vocations. **1711** SHAFTESB. *Charac.* (1737) II. II. II. 172 What has been said concerning the Preferableness of the mental Pleasures to the sensual. **1857** GEN. P. THOMPSON *Audi Alt.* I. xxv. 97 Firmly penetrated with the preferableness of honest commerce.

preferably (ˈprɛfərəblɪ), *adv.* [-LY².]

1. In a preferable manner; in preference to others; by preference; rather.

1729 BUTLER *Serm., Love of Neighbour* 508 Obligations, which require that we do good to some preferably to others. **1803** MARY CHARLTON *Wife & Mistress* I. 67 That I may be preferably allowed to retain the guardianship of her person. **1896** *Jrnl. R. Horticultural Soc.* Nov. 202 All fruit should be carefully placed in the basket (which is preferably lined or padded).

†**2.** In the way of preference; preferentially. *Obs.*

1782 MISS BURNEY *Cecilia* VI. ix, Even Mrs. Delvile evidently desired her absence; since..she preferably addressed herself to any one else who was present. **1818** COLEBROOKE *Import Colonial Corn* x. 179 A generous policy, which has preferably consulted the advantage of the dependent country.

prefeˈree. *rare.* In 7 preferree. [f. PREFER + -EE.] One who is preferred or receives preferment.

1676 NEEDHAM *Pacquet Adv.* 49 They [the unsuccessful candidates] resolve presently, that the Preferree is a Common Enemy, and as such to fall upon him. **1977** *Navy News* Sept. 4/3 Inevitably, there are more sea billets than preferees on the one hand while there is strong competition among the preferees for the comparatively small number of shore billets.

preference (ˈprɛfərəns). Also 7 -ferrence. [a. F. *préférence* (14th c. in Littré), ad. med.L. *præferentia* (1062 in Du Cange), f. L. *præferent-*, pr. pple. of *præferre* to PREFER: see -ENCE.]

1. a. The action of preferring or the fact of being preferred; liking for or estimation of one thing before or above another; prior favour or choice.

1656 BLOUNT *Glossogr.*, *Preference*, preferment, advancement, account before, place above, others. **1687** A. LOVELL tr. *Thevenot's Trav.* I. 257 Who (if he have a mind to keep his place) must give the same sum that the other hath offered, and so has the Preference. **1744** HARRIS *Three Treat.* Wks. (1841) 33 As to the preference which such poetic imitation may claim before musical,..the merits on each side may appear perhaps equal. **1754** EDWARDS *Freed. Will* II. vi. (1762) 56 [It] can't be that the mind is indifferent before it comes to have a choice, or till it has a Preference. **1870** FREEMAN *Norm. Conq.* (ed. 2) I. App. 626 To deny that Eadward had any preference over his half-brother.

b. *spec.*, under the system of preferential voting (see PREFERENTIAL *a.* c), the naming or numbering of candidates in the order desired by the voter; hence, the position in that order assigned to any candidate by the voter.

1908 *Westm. Gaz.* 20 Aug. 2/1 Some 272 of Haynes's supporters had not used their preference and so their votes were put aside as exhausted. **1955** E. LAKEMAN *How Democracies Vote* iv. 88 The Returning Officer either awards the appropriate number of points for each preference and adds them up, or, if each voter is obliged to number every candidate, adds up the preferences each candidate thus receives. **1965** *Austral. Encycl.* III. 367/1 In 1910 it [*sc.* Western Australia] made the marking of preferences necessary to a valid vote. **1975** *Irish Times* 10 May 1/5, I cannot dictate how my preferences should be distributed. In a democracy that is the right of the electorate.

†**2.** The quality of being preferable; preferableness; precedence, superiority. *Obs.*

1603 HOLLAND *Plutarch's Mor.* 47 A man is to aime at excellencie and preferrence before others in good and honest things. *a* **1677** HALE *Prim. Orig. Man.* 52 To discover the preference that the Humane Nature hath above the Animal Life in these most perfect faculties of Intellect. **1793** SMEATON *Edystone L.* §227 It..shewed the preference of wedging to cramping, as the cramp had failed.

3. That which one prefers; the object of prior choice; the favourite.

1864 in WEBSTER. **1873** BROWNING *Red Cott. Nt.-cap* II. 1118 And where the stretch Of barren country girdled house about, Behold the Park, the English preference! *Mod. colloq.* Of the two, this is my preference.

4. Preferment; promotion. Now *rare.*

1656 [see 1]. **1701** ROWE *Amb. Step-Mother* II. i, Is not the Elder By Nature pointed out for Preference? **1786** *Francis the Philanthropist* I. 86 Jerry, whose utmost wish was accomplished in his preference to a trust. **1893** *Harper's Mag.* Apr. 683/2 A prodigious crowd of people had flocked to the city in hope of gain or preference.

5. a. A prior claim to something; *spec.* priority of payment given to a certain debt or class of debts; a prior right to payment.

fraudulent preference, such payment made by a bankrupt with the object of preventing the equal distribution of his assets among all his creditors.

1665 *Ir. Act 17 & 18 Chas. II*, c. 2 §38 Wentworth earl of Roscommon, and Roger earl of Orrery..shall have preference and primer satisfaction of fifty thousand pounds of their own personal arrears. **1832** SIR J. B. BOSANQUET in Bingham *Reports* (1833) IX. 355 The question here is, whether the security..was given by way of fraudulent preference. [**1869** *Act 32 & 33 Vict.* c. 71 §92 Every conveyance or transfer of property..in favour of any creditor.., with a view of giving such creditor a preference over the other creditors, shall, if the person making..the same become bankrupt within three months..be deemed fraudulent and void.] **1890** *Cent. Dict.* s.v., The state has a preference for taxes. **1891** *New York Tribune* 26 Nov. 4/4 (Funk) The firm..made an assignment yesterday..giving two preferences for $600.

b. Short for *preference share*: see 8.

1890 *Pall Mall G.* 18 Sept. 7/2 This they proposed to do with 7 per cent. preferences, which at the end of three years could either fall in as ordinary or continue as preference shares. **1906** *Westm. Gaz.* 25 Jan. 11/1 This is the first time for many years that the holders of the 1889 Preference have received any dividend, but one by one the Preferences are being restored to the dividend-paying list.

6. *Pol. Econ.* The practical favouring of one customer before others in business relations; an advantage over rivals given to one of those with whom one deals; *spec.* the favouring of one country or set of countries by admitting their products at a lower import duty than that levied on those of other countries or of foreigners generally, or by levying a duty on the latter while admitting the former free. A term much used about 1900, in reference to trade between Great Britain and her colonies, as opposed to trade between either of these and foreign countries.

1887 SIR S. GRIFFITH in *Conference Blue Book* (col. 3523) 230 Whether it should not be recognized as part of the duty of the governing bodies of the Empire to see that their own subjects have a preference over foreign subjects in matters of trade. **1891** SIR J. MACDONALD *Let. to W. H. Smith* April, Canada will be quite ready to give British goods a preference of 5 or even 10 per cent. in our markets, if our products receive a corresponding preference in England. **1896** (June 3) SIR W. LAURIER in Willison *Sir W. L. & Liberal Party* II. 287 To have..a new step taken which will give to the Colonies, in England, a preference for their products over the products of other nations. **1903** (May 15) J. CHAMBERLAIN *Speeches* 13 Canada in 1898, freely, voluntarily, of her own accord..gave us a preference on all dutiable goods of 25 per cent. In 1900 she increased that preference to 33⅓ per cent. —— (Oct. 6) *Ibid.* 20 Still less am I afraid to preach to you preference with our Colonies. *Ibid.* 32, I make the same answer as Mr. Rhodes, who suggested reciprocal preference. —— (Oct. 21) *Ibid.* 111, I made two speeches..accepting the principle of Preference. **1904** *Edin. Rev.* Apr. 289 On every hand the British consumer was mulcted by colonial preference. *Ibid.* 292 When the restrictions on colonial commerce were removed, preference went with them.

7. *Cards.* **a.** In the game of Boston: The trump suit (called *first preference*) or the suit of the same colour (*second preference*). **b.** A game resembling whist in which the trump is determined by bidding; Swedish whist.

1820 *Hoyle's Games* (1830) 31 The game of Boston... During each deal, the person opposite to the dealer should shuffle another pack to be cut by his right-hand neighbour, and turn up a card for the First Preference; the suit of the same colour, whether red or black, is styled Second Preference. **1852** MRS. GASKELL *Cranford* (1853) vii. 133 We were six in number; four could play at Preference, and for the other two there was Cribbage. **1884** H. GERSONI tr. *Turgenieff's Diary Superfluous Man* 72 A great lover of preference. **1908** R. W. CHAMBERS *Firing Line* ii. 20 That kills our four at Bridge... We'll have to play Klondike and Preference now. **1977** V. S. PRITCHETT *Gentle Barbarian* v. 80 At Spasskoy he [*sc.* Turgenev]..played chess and draughts and games of Preference.

c. *Bridge*. A bid or pass by a responder indicating in which of two or more suits bid by his partner he wishes to play.

1919 R. F. FOSTER *Foster on Auction* I. 96 This bidding invariably shows a two-suiter... If he prefers the spades, he can bid two spades to indicate his preference. **1927** M. C. WORK *Contract Bridge* iii. 42 That bid would be a forced take-out and would not announce strength, merely a preference. **1958** *Listener* 4 Dec. 965/3 If..partner is two-suited it will be enough to give a spade preference when he is able to demand it.

8. *attrib.* and *Comb.*, as **preference bid** = sense 7 c above; **preference bond, share, stock**, i.e. on which dividend or interest is payable before any is paid on ordinary stock; **preference voting** = *preferential voting* s.v. PREFERENTIAL *a.* c.

1842 *Wetenhall's Course of Exch.* 15 Mar. London & Greenwich [Railw.] Preference or Privilege (Shares). [In prec. issue 11 Mar. designated Bonds.] **1852** *Times* 1 Nov. Suppl. 9/6 The second instalment of £2 per share on each and every 5½ per Cent. preference share in this undertaking [Sambre and Meuse Railway]. **1859** *Encycl. Brit.* (ed. 8) XVIII. 790/1 Interest on preference stock and loans, 27 per cent. of gross receipts. **1878** F. S. WILLIAMS *Midl. Railw.* 273 A proprietor complained that by means of certain preference shares..a priority of right would be given to outsiders over the ordinary shareholders. **1885** *Standard* 10 Apr., Egyptian Preference Bonds are largely in their hands. **1908** *Westm. Gaz.* 20 Aug. 2/1 The local Labour Party is inclined to boycott preference voting and advocate its members to plump. **1927** M. C. WORK *Contract Bridge* iii. 148 *Preference bid*, a bid made to show preference for one suit over another, rather than strength (in case partner has bid a two-suiter). **1934** G. F. HERVEY *Contract Bridge Dict.* 117 Y's bid is a preference bid showing that he prefers the hand to be played in Spades.

†**'preferency.** *Obs.* [ad. med.L. *præferentia*: see prec. and -ENCY.] = PREFERENCE 2, 4.

1579–80 NORTH *Plutarch* (1676) 993 In the great there is no preferency. **1677** GILPIN *Demonol.* (1867) 207 This is noted of Arius,..that when Alexander was chosen bishop of Alexandria, he envied him the preferency, and from thence sought occasions of contention.

preferent ('prɛfərənt), *a.* [ad. L. *præferent-em*, pr. pple. of *præferre* to PREFER.]

1. Having preference or precedence; having a right to priority of payment or consideration.

1883 H. JUTA tr. *Van der Linden's Inst. Holland* 95 In the first rank of preferent debts are funeral expenses. *Ibid.*, The holders of special mortgages..have a preferent claim on the proceeds arising from the sale of the particular property mortgaged. **1888** LD. WATSON in *Law Rep., Ho. Lords* XIII. 233 Any miner shall have a preferent right for 7 days to take possession of the ground forfeited.

2. Displaying preference; partial.

1896 *Johannesburg Weekly Times* 8 Aug. 3 To heap..shame upon his head for his supposed preferent safeguarding of the interests of the 'fighting port' to the detriment of the 'Bay'.

preferential (prɛfə'rɛnʃəl), *a.* (*sb.*) [f. med.L. *præferentia* PREFERENCE + -AL[1].]

A. *adj.* **a.** Of, pertaining to, or of the nature of preference; showing or giving, receiving or enjoying, a preference.

1849 H. MAYO *Pop. Superstit.* (1851) 76 Their preferential connection with this or that antecedent condition. *a* **1860** H. H. WILSON *Ess. & Lect.* (1862) I. 2 One division of some antiquity is the preferential appropriation of the four chief divinities to the four original castes. **1878** STUBBS *Const. Hist.* III. xviii. 78 The king was allowed a 'preferential' claim on the public revenue. **1881** J. SIMON in *Nature* 18 Aug. 373/2 That joint at once becomes a place of preferential resort to the micrococcus. **1886** *Law Times* LXXX. 148/1 Raising fresh capital by the issue of new shares, the dividends on which were to be preferential.

b. *Pol. Econ.* Of the nature of or characterized by import duties favouring particular countries, *spec.* in favour of trade between Great Britain and her colonies: see PREFERENCE 6.

1903 EGERTON *Origin & Growth Eng. Col.* 189 When..the Canadian Government gave to English manufacturers a preferential treatment of 12½ per cent.,..the measure was received with genuine gratification in Great Britain. **1903** (Oct. 20) J. CHAMBERLAIN *Speeches* 90 Now I come to the most important of all questions to my mind raised by preferential tariffs. I advocate them because, in the first place, they will stimulate colonial trade. —— (Oct. 21) *Ibid.* 111 This matter of Preferential tariffs was before both Conferences. **1904** *Edin. Rev.* Apr. 279 (*title*) Preferential Duties and Colonial Trade. *Ibid.* 289 We have now dealt with the chief articles of commerce affected by preferential duties in the past.

c. *preferential ballot, voting*, a form of voting found in various systems of proportional representation in which candidates are numbered in order of preference by the voter; the use of the alternative vote (see ALTERNATIVE *a.* 6).

1870 *Putnam's Mag.* June 717/1 Mr. Hare's scheme is one which..may be called that of *preferential* voting. It ascertains the quota by dividing the whole number of voters by the whole number of representatives... This method, which we have called that of preferential voting, is also called by the Swiss reformers that of the electoral quotient. **1908** *Westm. Gaz.* 20 Aug. 2/1 The State of Western Australia..is now attempting..preferential voting in a simple form. **1911** *Ann. Amer. Acad. Pol. & Social Sci.* XXXVIII. 760 The preferential ballot for cities is a plan to restore majority elections and true representative government. **1926** [see *alternative vote* s.v. ALTERNATIVE *a.* 6]. **1955** C. R. ADRIAN *Governing Urban Amer.* iii. 61 During their heyday—the first and second decades of the present century—reformers sponsored other organizational and procedural changes: preferential voting, such as the Bucklin and Ware systems, which did not catch on, [etc.]. **1976** J. ROGALY *Parliament for People* vi. 71 Two less satisfactory forms of preferential voting are the 'second ballot', used in France, and the 'Alternative vote'.

d. *Anthrop.* Esp. in phr. ***preferential marriage, mating***: the preference within a tribe or kinship group for marriage to take place between persons standing in a particular relationship to each other, such as cross-cousins. Cf. PRESCRIPTIVE *a.* 4 b.

1909 *Cent. Dict.* Suppl., Preferential marriage. **1920** R. H. LOWIE *Primitive Soc.* (1921) ii. 16 Among the Kariera of Western Australia the acquisition of a bride is complicated by certain rules of preferential mating. That is, a man is..practically obliged to mate with a particular type of cousin or some more remote relative. *Ibid.* 35 Cross-cousin marriage, levirate, and sororate are by no means the only terms of preferential mating. **1943** E. J. & J. D. KRIGE *Realm of Rain Queen* ix. 145 We shall turn first to the preferential marriages. A marriage is obligatory or approved, or discouraged..according as it strengthens..or conflicts with the..edifice erected by the [payment of] cattle. **1968** R. NEEDHAM tr. *Lévi-Strauss's Elem. Struct. Kinship* (1969) p. xxx, Societies which advocate marriage between certain types of kin adhere to the norm only in a small number of cases..hence the idea of calling such systems 'preferential', a name which..expresses the reality. **1971** —— *Rethinking Kinship & Marriage* p. lxviii, One should not ask whether a tribe has a prescriptive as opposed to a preferential marriage system.

e. *transf.* = PREFERRED *ppl. a.* 5.

1926 *Carnegie Scholarship Mem.* XV. 378 Since the smaller crystals grown in flat strips had no preferential orientation, none could be expected in the smaller round crystals. **1955** T. L. RICHARDS in H. S. Peiser et al. *X-Ray Diffraction by Polycrystalline Materials* xxi. 469 Preferential crystal growth in a definite crystal direction. **1968** R. RIEGER et al. *Gloss. Genetics & Cytogenetics* 161 *Selective* or *preferential fertilization*, fusion of germ cells of different genotypes from one or both sexes in combinations having nonrandom frequencies. **1977** *Lancet* 9 July 92/2 The preferential production of the IgE and IgG4 classes might..be due to structural peculiarities in the sensitising allergens.

B. *sb.* **a.** A preferential tariff rate. **b.** A preferential or privileged creditor or claim.

1903 *Westm. Gaz.* 18 May 11/1 The creditors will have received..£119,238, including £669 paid to twenty-seven 'preferentials'. *Ibid.* 15 Sept. 4/1 'Who can doubt that, but for the calamity of Mr. Chamberlain's secession, the Liberal Party would have given us "preferentials" at that time?'

prefe'rentialism. [f. prec. adj. + -ISM.] The system of giving preference in the fixing of a tariff: see PREFERENCE 6, PREFERENTIAL *a.* b.

1903 *Liberty Review* July 14 The old-fashioned protectionism, which is now popping up again under the guise of Colonial preferentialism. **1905** *Daily Chron.* 7 Sept. 3/6 This Protectionist section is coquetting with Preferentialism as a step towards a higher tariff.

So **prefe'rentialist**, an advocate of preference in tariff relations.

1903 *Westm. Gaz.* 15 Sept. 8/1 If the Inquiry is to be a mere device, under cover of which Preferentialists and Free Traders are to be enabled to assail each other to their hearts' content. **1904** *Edin. Rev.* Apr. 297 The only real strength of our new preferentialists..lies in the attitude of Canada.

prefe'rentially, *adv.* [f. PREFERENTIAL *a.* + -LY[2].] **1.** In a preferential manner, by preference.

1873 F. HALL *Mod. Eng.* 351 The same person..will..elect 'is in preparation' preferentially to 'is being prepared'. **1876** FAWCETT *Pol. Econ.* II. ix. (ed. 5) 254 One-fourth of the shares were preferentially offered to the workmen engaged in the business. **1903** L. COURTNEY in *Contemp. Rev.* Aug. 269 The dutiable imports..preferentially favoured had risen 55 per cent.

2. To a greater extent or degree.

1926 *Encycl. Brit.* II. 886/1 In the case of brass, steel and aluminium alloys, certain types of chemical reagents which act preferentially upon the material in the crystal boundaries contribute to the occurrence of such fractures. **1935** TIPSON & STILLER in Harrow & Sherwin *Textbk. Biochem.* ii. 61 The tendency is for the primary hydroxyl group to be preferentially esterified. **1957** G. E. HUTCHINSON *Treat. Limnol.* I. xvi. 851 Several crop plants assimilated ammonia preferentially above *p*H 7. **1971** *Physics Bull.* Mar. 141/3 In an equilibrium reaction these elements with greatest binding energy per nucleon are formed preferentially. **1977** *Sci. Amer.* Jan. 39/3 The black hole will therefore preferentially emit particles with charge of the same sign as itself and so will rapidly lose its charge.

preferentiate (-'rɛnʃɪeɪt), *v. rare.* [f. as PREFERENCE + -ATE[3] 7, after *differentiate*.] *intr.* To display preference, give preferential treatment; *trans.* to treat with preference.

1903 *Blackw. Mag.* Oct. 565/1 We must have a fiscal policy and a tariff suited to the occasion before we can preferentiate, differentiate, or retaliate.

preferment (prɪ'fɜːmənt). [f. PREFER + -MENT.]

I. †**1.** The action of putting or bringing forward; furtherance, promotion. *Obs.*

1454 *Rolls of Parlt.* V. 254/2 To..the good spede and preferrement of the said Rescows. **1536** *Act 28 Hen. VIII*, c. 7 §3 For the settyng forthe or preferrement of the deuorce or dissolucion therof. **1581** SAVILE *Tacitus, Hist.* II. xcii. (1591) 107 P. Sabinus and Julius Priscus were constituted captaines of the Garde; Priscus by Valens preferment [*Priscus Valentis gratia*] and Sabinus by Caecinaes.

2. Advancement or promotion in condition, status, or position in life; in early use, also, that which is done or given towards the advancement of the children of a family or the promotion of the marriage of a daughter.

1478 in *Verney Papers* (Camden) 26 For asmoch as my doughters dame Margarete Raleghe and Beatrice Danvers haue had their preferrement at their mariages of their porcions to theme belongyng of my goodes, and my sonnes John Verney and Rauf Verney haue not hadde their suche preferrement. **1522** in *Eng. Gilds* (1870) 237 Towarde the preferment and maryage of the sayd Anne. **1553** BALE tr. *Gardiner's De vera Obed.* To Rdr. A vij, Vpon hope of preferment to the diuinitie lecture in Oxforde. **1558** *Knaresborough Wills* (Surtees) I. 77 Should either dye before she come to the preferment of mariage. **1662** WOOD *Life* (O.H.S.) I. 465 There is no preferment to be had without money. **1704** NELSON *Fest. & Fasts* x. (1739) 602 For the obtaining or procuring such Ecclesiastical Preferment. **1879** FROUDE *Cæsar* xxii. 385 With their idle luxury, their hunger for lands and office and preferment.

3. An appointment or post which gives social or pecuniary advancement; chiefly, an ecclesiastical appointment.

1536 *Act 27 Hen. VIII*, c. 42 §1 Benefices and other preferrementes. **1613** SHAKS. *Hen. VIII*, v. i. 36 Further Sir, [Cromwell] Stands in the gap and Trade of moe Preferments, With which the Time will loade him. **1625** BACON *Ess., Sedition & Tr.* (Arb.) 405 When more are bred Schollers, then Preferments can take off. **1733** FIELDING *Intrig. Chambermaid* II. ix, Your interest will help him to places and preferments in abundance. **1883** LD. PENZANCE in *Law Rep. 8 Probate Div.* 197 That the defendant held no preferment within the jurisdiction.

II. †**4.** The action or fact of preferring, choosing, or favouring, as more desirable; the giving of preference; preference, advantage. *Obs.*

1526 TINDALE *Rom.* iii. 1 What preferment then hath the Jewe? [So **1557** (Genev.).] *a* **1618** RALEIGH *Maxims St.* in *Rem.* (1661) 55 To give an equality, or sometimes a preferment to the Common People. *a* **1754** E. ERSKINE in Spurgeon *Treas. Dav.* Ps. lxxxix. 16 The ground of the believer's preferment and exaltation.

b. *spec.* Priority of right, claim, or privilege; *esp.* prior right to receive payment, or to purchase or offer for anything to be sold or let. *arch.*

1451 *Rolls of Parlt.* V. 214/1 That the Act made..for youre [Hen. VI's] preferrement in payment of xx m. li...be good. **1473** *Ibid.* VI. 73/1 Rewardes, Profittes, Commodities, Preferrementes, had, made or graunted, for or by reason of the said Office. **1475** *Ibid.* VI. 124/1 That the said Priour and Covent..by the same auctorite, have preferment of and for the payment of the said vii. li. yerely. **1495** *Act 11 Hen. VII*, c. 33 §3 Persones which nowe have to ferme any of the seid Lordshippes..shall have preferrement in the takyng of the same.. befor any other. **1587** SIR C. WRAY in Willis & Clark *Cambridge* (1886) II. 365 The said Fellowes..shall alwaie haue the vse and preferment of two of the midle chambers. **1886** H. HALL *Soc. Eliz. Age* 93 He sent..to crave preferment of purchase if the place must be sold.

III. 5. *attrib.* and *Comb.*

1818 BENTHAM *Ch. Eng.* 440 Hope of translation, and thence the pursuit called preferment-hunting, scarcely even in Scotland can have been altogether without example. **1845** LD. CAMPBELL *Chancellors* (1857) IV. xcvi. 313 Parasites and preferment-hunters crowded the levee.

Hence †**pre'fermentary** (*nonce-wd.*, after *prebendary*), a recipient of preferment.

1660 WATERHOUSE *Arms & Arm.* 126 This made the Graduate Divine from a Chaplin in ordinary, become a prefermentary extraordinary.

pre-fermen'tation. *rare.* [PRE- A. 2.] A preliminary fermentation.

1743 *Lond. & Country Brewer* III. (ed. 2) 205 Molosses, or other Bodies that have not..undergone a Pre-fermentation.

†**pre'ferrable, -ible,** *a. Obs.* [f. PREFER + -ABLE. *pre'ferrable* follows the ordinary rule of English formations in *-able*: cf. *barrable*, *regrettable*. *pre'ferrible* is partly conformed to the L. analogical form **præferibilis*, which would give '*preferible*: see -BLE. Both have yielded to the French form '*preferable*.] = PREFERABLE 1.

1611 COTGR., *Preferable*, preferrable. **1662** GLANVILL *Lux Orient.* iii. (1682) 27 Will..be preferrible to both the former. **1665** BOYLE *Occas. Refl.* VI. iv, The question, Whether a publick or a private life be preferrable? *a* **1677** HALE *Prim. Orig. Man.* To Rdr. 1 The Mosaical System..is..highly preferrible before the Sentiments of those Philosophers [etc.]. **1712** STEELE *Spect.* No. 522 ¶1 He that has excellent Talents..is preferrable to him who is only rich.

preferred (prɪ'fɜːd), *ppl. a.* [f. PREFER + -ED[1].]

†**1.** Put forward, advanced, promoted. *Obs.*

1483 *Cath. Angl.* 290/2 Preferryd, *prepositus, prelatus*. **1656** STANLEY *Hist. Philos.* VIII. (1701) 328/1 We call not those things which are in the first place, the preferred or promoted, but those which are in the second.

2. That has obtained preferment or promotion.

1720 SWIFT *Fates of Clergymen* Wks. 1755 II. II. 28 Censorious upon all his brethren.. while they continued meanly preferred. **1772** BURKE *Sp. Acts of Uniformity* Wks. 1812 V. 328 They want to be preferred Clergymen in the Church of England as by Law established, but their consciences will not suffer them to conform to the doctrines and practices of that Church. **1837** ALISON *Hist. Europe* (1850) VIII. xlix. §31. 34 Individual injustice is not to be always excused by the merits of the preferred functionary.

3. a. Approved, chosen, or desired by preference.

1871 E. BURR *Ad Fidem* xiv. 273 Twist, and strain, and mutilate facts, into a preferred shape. **1887** *Lit. World* (U.S.) 23 July 228/1 His preferred plan was to betroth her to the English Prince of Wales.

b. Applied to a set of numbers or values forming an approximate geometrical progression and used to determine the officially recommended values of a dimension or other characteristic with which standard components should be made, so as to cover most efficiently the range of possible requirements.

1922 *Mech. Engin.* XLIV. 791/1 A careful study of manufactured articles shows that even when sizes are determined by utility or use value, the choice of size is largely arbitrary. It is therefore obvious that if certain numerical values are universally accepted as preferred values, and if they are so spaced and of such extent as to fit in with all requirements met in deciding on sizes to be used, the arbitrary choices may be so made as to yield sizes expressible in terms of these preferred numbers. **1936** *Proc. IRE* XXIV. 159 Preferred numbers are certain numbers that have been selected to be used for standardization purposes in preference to any others. **1962** S. HANDEL *Dict. Electronics* 269 Manufacturers and users of electrical and electronic components such as fixed resistors and capacitors find that there are advantages in standardizing component values and adopt preferred values so that each value differs from the preceding one by a constant multiplier. **1963** JERRARD & MCNEILL *Dict. Sci. Units* 110 Preferred numbers are conventionally rounded off terms in a geometrical progression whereby a tenth multiple of the initial term is obtained after a predetermined number of terms, viz: p, pq, pq^2, .. pq^{n-1}, pq^n, where p is the initial number, n is the number of terms and q a factor such that $q^n = 10$.

4. Having a prior claim to payment; privileged. ***preferred share, stock***: = PREFERENCE *share, stock*.

1864 WEBSTER s.v. *Prefer, Preferred stock*, stock which takes a dividend before other capital stock;—called, in England, *preferential stock*. **1890** *Cent. Dict.*, Preferred creditor. **1901** *N. Amer. Rev.* Feb. 201 In 1805.. he [Marshall] found .. authority for a law making the United States a preferred creditor. **1904** *Q. Rev.* Jan. 194 The preferred stock of a combination is an investment security.

5. *transf.* That is exhibited or adopted by a natural system, object, or substance more commonly than, or to the exclusion of, other apparently possible properties or modes of development; ***preferred orientation***, an orientation which crystals in a material tend to adopt or in which they tend to form, usu. because of applied stress.

1929 *Chem. Abstr.* XXIII. 1051 The detn. of the presence and the quant. description of preferred orientations in cryst. masses. **1954** R. L. PARKER tr. *Niggli's Rocks & Min. Deposits* v. 153 If the variable attribute (grain diameter, for instance) can be characterized both by size and by frequency, a mean size must first be determined. To this end the central or preferred value (modal value) in the distribution must be sought.. or the value of the arithmetic mean.. calculated. **1956** *Jrnl. Iron & Steel Inst.* CLXXXIII. 99/2 The Zn coating on galvanized wire shows no preferred orientation. **1956** *Q. Jrnl. Geol. Soc.* CXII. 123 A specimen from Logie Head.. shows no apparent preferred orientation of quartzes and the measurements are evenly scattered over the fabric diagram. **1962** E. S. GOULD *Inorg. Reactions & Struct.* (rev. ed.) iii. 64 The configuration with bond directions towards the corners of a regular octahedron.. may be shown to be preferred. **1968** M. S. LIVINGSTON *Particle Physics* x. 171 In such a plot, broad peaks are frequently observed centred about specific values of energy. Such a preferred value of energy indicates a state of the system of two particles for which decay into the final products is more probable than for lower or higher values. **1971** *Nature* 4 June 306/2 The wind has a strongly preferred direction up and down the length of the steep-sided Loch. **1974** D. M. ADAMS *Inorg. Solids* v. 97 In Chapter 4 we saw that the relative sizes of the ions in a crystal could be related to preferred coordination arrangements.

Hence **preˈferredness**.

a **1866** J. GROTE *Exam. Utilit. Philos.* iii. (1870) 51 This preferability he makes matter again of simple experience.. we should rather call it actual preferredness.

preferree, -ence, obs. ff. PREFEREE, -ENCE.

preferrer (prɪˈfɜːrə(r)). Also 6 -erer, 6–7 -errour. [f. PREFER + -ER[1].] One who prefers.

†**1.** One who promotes or advances to office, etc.; a promoter, advancer, patron. *Obs.*

a **1548** HALL *Chron., Hen. V* 35 b, Your royall person beyng my patrone & preferrer. **1575–85** ABP. SANDYS *Serm.* (Parker Soc.) 120 The preferrers unto livings are no less faulty: they choose of the worst. **1577** *F. de Lisle's Legendarie* B iv b, The Constable was the only preferer of the said Lords of Guises sister.. who by his meanes was preferred before many other both more marriageable and meete for such a man then her selfe. **1599** SANDYS *Europæ Spec.* (1632) 149 Whosoever sits in the seat, will respect more his owne safetie than the service of his preferrour. **1691** WOOD *Ath. Oxon.* I. 181 He was.. a preferrer of many, and Father to his servants.

2. One who brings a matter forward; one who submits or promotes a measure.

1536 *St. Papers Hen. VIII*, II. 318 Ye have ben, under the Kinges Highnes, a singuler patrone and preferrer of the causes of the same ['this poure lande']. **1570** FOXE *A. & M.* (ed. 2) 2033/2 Doct. Stephens Secretary, and Doct. Foxe Almosiner (who were the chief furtherers, preferrers and defendours on the kings behalfe of the sayd cause). **1579–80** NORTH *Plutarch* (1676) 625 Lycurgus and Hyperides were common speakers and preferrers of matters in Councils and Senate. **1607** COWELL *Interpr.* s.v. *Enditement*, The preferrer of the Bill in no way tyed to the proofe thereof vpon any penalty.

preferring (prɪˈfɜːrɪŋ), *vbl. sb.* [f. PREFER *v.* + -ING[1].] The action of the verb PREFER; preferment; preference.

a **1450** *Lett. Marg. Anjou & Bp. Beckington* (Camden) 140 We, desiring th'encres, firtherance, and preferring of oure welbeloved T. Bate.. pray yow [etc.]. **1575–85** ABP. SANDYS *Serm.* (Parker Soc.) 232 The preferring of true religion, the seeking of God's glory. **1642** CHAS. I in Rushw. *Hist. Coll.* III. (1692) I. 732 Since to the Power of punishing.. if the Power of preferring be added, We shall have nothing left for Us but to look on. **1675** R. BURTHOGGE *Causa Dei* 49 A Violation of the Law of God, a Preferring of Our Unruly, Profane, Unrighteous, Evil Wills before His.

†**preˈfestinate**, *v. Obs. rare*[−0]. [f. L. *præfestīnāre* to hasten before the time, hasten too much + -ATE[3]: see PRE- A. 1, 6 and FESTINATE *v.*]

1623 COCKERAM, *Prestinate*, to make too much haste.

‖**préfet** (prefɛ). [Fr.] The chief administrative officer of a department of France; = PREFECT, PRÆFECT *sb.* 1 d.

1820 M. EDGEWORTH *Let.* 22 June (1979) 168 Mme Chéron whose son is Préfet I think of Toulouse or some Provincial town. **1861** TROLLOPE *Tales of All Countries* (ser. 1) 22 And the company are all talking to him as though he were the préfet. **1869** *Bradshaw's Railway Manual* XXI. 348 Directors: C. Bart, ex-Préfet, Paris. **1872** TROLLOPE *Golden Lion* xviii. 288 Colmar.. has been accustomed to the presence of a préfet, and is no doubt important. **1908** O.E.D. s.v. *Prefecture* 3, A prefect or French *préfet*. **1942** 'A. BRIDGE' *Frontier Passage* vi. 102 They went off together to the *Préfecture* at Bayonne... Crossman's prestige.. made access to the *Préfet* easy. **1958** *Listener* 18 Sept. 431/1 While there might be scoundrels like Darnand, such could be balanced by the courage of *préfets* like Bousquet. **1974** S. COULTER *Château* I. viii. 49 'You are invited to the Préfet's. .. A reception.'.. She was impressed; the Préfet was the chief officer of the department.

‖**preˈfetto.** *Obs. rare.* [It.; see PREFECT *sb.*]

1743 POCOCKE *Descr. East* I. 147 The first account I had of it.. being from a manuscript journal, writ by the present Prefetto of Egypt. **1753** R. CLAYTON (*title*) Journal from Grand Cairo to Mount Sinai and back again, translated from a Manuscript written by the Prefetto of Egypt.

pre-feudal: see PRE- B. 1 d.

preff(e, preffer, obs. forms of PROOF, PREFER.

†**ˈprefidence.** *Obs.* [f. L. *præfīdens*: see next and -ENCE.] Over-confidence; an instance of this.

1597 R. BRUCE *Serm.* (Wodrow Soc.) 186 We leave the way of prefidence to them that presume of their own strength. **16..** T. TAYLOR *Wks.* (1659) I. 11 Some through vain prefidence of God's protection run in times of contagion into infected houses. **1677** OWEN *Justif.* Wks. 1851 V. 14 All their prefidences and contrivances do issue in dreadful horror and distress.

†**ˈprefident**, *a. Obs. rare.* [ad. L. *præfīdens, -entem*, trusting too much, over-confident, f. *præ*, PRE- A. 6 + *fīdĕre* to trust.] Over-confident, rash.

16.. BAXTER cited by WORCESTER (1846).

preˈfigurate, *ppl. a.* [ad. late L. *præfigūrāt-us*, pa. pple. of *præfigūrāre*: see next.] = PREFIGURED (as *pa. pple.* (obs.), and *ppl. a.*).

1530 PALSGR. 664/2 All the mysteryes of the passyon were prefygurate in the olde Testament. **1557** N.T. (Genev.) *Eph.* ii. 12 *note*, In Christe all things were accomplished, which were prefigurate in the Lawe. **1881** E. MULFORD *Republic of God* v. 128 The Christ is not the prefigurate, but the real, head of humanity.

prefigurate (priːˈfɪgjʊəreɪt), *v.* Now *rare.* [f. ppl. stem of late L. *præfigūrāre* to PREFIGURE: see -ATE[3].] = PREFIGURE.

1530 PALSGR. 664/2, I prefygurate, *je prefigure*. **1537** *Inst. Chr. Man* E v, Signified.. or rather prefigurated & prophecied before. **1673** T. JORDAN *London in Splendor* 7 On his Left hand standeth a well-featured Virgin who doth prefigurate Labour. **1874** M. COLLINS *Transmigr.* II. xiii. 203 Poseidon's bull can clearly prefigurate nothing but John Bull's fleet.

prefiguration (priːfɪgjʊəˈreɪʃən). [ad. late L. *præfigūrātiōn-em* (Jerome *c* 400), n. of action f. *præfigūrāre* to PREFIGURE. So F. *préfiguration*.]

1. The action of prefiguring; representation beforehand by a figure or type.

1382 WYCLIF *Pref. Ep.* vii. 68 Deutronomy forsothe the secounde lawe, and the prefiguracoun of the lawe of the euangelie. **1550** VERON *Godly Sayings* (1846) 111 Melchisedeche brought furth bread, and wyne in prefiguratyon of him. **1637** BP. HALL *Serm. Excester* 24 Aug. 43 Some [ceremonies] were of a typicall prefiguration of things to come. **1863** J. G. MURPHY *Comm. Gen.* iii. 21 Slain in prefiguration of that subsequent availing sacrifice which was to take away sin.

2. That in which something is prefigured or foreshadowed; a prototype.

a **1600** HOOKER *Eccl. Pol.* VI. vi. §11 Many of the ancient Fathers.. thought likewise their sacraments to be but prefigurations of that which ours in present do exhibit. **1652** G. COLLIER *Vindic. Sabbath* (1656) 7 Before there were any types or prefigurations of Christ. **1737** WATERLAND *Eucharist* 98 That the Legal Sacrifices were Allusions to, and Prefigurations of the Grand Sacrifice. **1851** SIR C. EASTLAKE tr. *Kugler's Schools Paint. It.* I. I. 9 The personages and events of the Old Testament were, for the most part, regarded as prefigurations of those of the New.

prefigurative (priːˈfɪgjʊərətɪv), *a.* [ad. med.L. *præfigūrātīv-us* (à Kempis *De Imitat. Chr.*): see PREFIGURATE *v.* and -IVE.]

Prefiguring, foreshadowing by a figure or type.

1504 LADY MARGARET tr. *De Imitatione* IV. i. 261 The sacryfyce of the prefyguratyue lawe that was to come. **1619** SIR J. SEMPILL *Sacrilege Handled* App. 32 These holy Feasts .. being prefiguratiue of Christ. **1685** H. MORE *Paralip. Prophet.* xxi. 189 A Dramatical show that hath a prefigurative signification of the Happiness of the millennial state of the Church. **1865** in *Reader* No. 133. 62/2 Prefigurative of the fate of his works.

Hence **preˈfiguratively** *adv.*; **preˈfigurativeness**, the quality of being prefigurative.

a **1600** HOOKER *Eccl. Pol* VII. xxii. §4 This kind of honour was prefiguratively altogether ceremonial. **1685** H. MORE *Paralip. Prophet.* xxi. 189 It may have a kind of general Prefigurativeness of the Joy and Glory of Christ's Kingdom in the Millennium. **1865** tr. *Strauss' New Life Jesus* II. II. lxxxi. 278 Jesus was supposed to have done this prefiguratively during his earthly life to a tree.

prefigure (priːˈfɪgjʊə(r), -gə(r)), *v.* [ad. late L. *præfigūr-āre* (Cyprian *a* 250): see PRE- A. 1 and FIGURE *v.* So F. *préfigurer* (13th c. in Godef.).]

1. *trans.* To represent beforehand by a figure or type.

c **1450** *Mirour Saluacioun* 1841 Cristis supere was prefigurid als in the lambe paschale. **1560** BECON *New Catech.* Wks. I. 478 b, As Melchisedech brought forthe bread and wine prefiguring him. **1651** BAXTER *Inf. Bapt.* 264 The Jews Baptisme prefigured our spiritual washing. *a* **1711** KEN *Hymns Evang.* Poet. Wks 1721 I. 83 Moses prefigur'd Bliss in Types enclos'd. **1878** B. TAYLOR *Deukalion* Argt. 9 The end of all things being prefigured in their beginnings.

2. To figure or picture to oneself beforehand.

1626 T. H. *Caussin's Holy Crt.* 24 Prefigure in your mind, that so many men.. are so many messengers of God. **1768** STERNE *Sent. Journ.* (1778) I. 153 (*Paris*) My first sensations .. were far from being so flattering as I had prefigured them. **1867** HOWELLS *Ital. Journ.* 232 He was not at all a fat priest, as I had prefigured him.

†**3.** To shape or fashion in front. *Obs. rare.*

1594 NASHE *Unfort. Trav.* 52 A wel proportioned knight .. whose head piece was prefigured lyke flowers growing in a narrowe pot.

Hence **preˈfigured, preˈfiguring** *ppl. adjs.*

1579 FULKE *Heskins' Parl.* 55 Calling the supper a true sacrament of that true and prefigured Passeouer. **1760–72** H. BROOKE *Fool of Qual.* (1809) IV. 116 The apt type and prefiguring promise of what Christ will be. **1853** DE QUINCEY *Autobiog. Sk.* Wks. I. 292 A prefiguring instinct.. of some great secret yet to come.

preˈfigurement. [f. prec. + -MENT.] The action or fact of prefiguring; representation beforehand by a figure or type; the embodiment of this.

1843 *Tait's Mag.* X. 250 No faint prefigurement of the modern steam-engine. *a* **1859** DE QUINCEY *Posth. Wks.* (1891) I. 16 In my dreams were often prefigurements of my future. **1875** DARWIN *Insectiv. Pl.* xv. 336 The prefigurement of the formation of nerves in animals.

pre-film(ic: see PRE- A. 1, B. 1 d.

ˈpre-final, *sb.* and *a.* [PRE- B. 1.]

A. *sb. Linguistics.* (See quot. 1933.) Cf. POST-FINAL.

1933 L. BLOOMFIELD *Language* viii. 132 English final clusters consist of two, three, or four non-syllabics. One can describe the combinations most simply by saying that each cluster consists of a main final consonant, which may be preceded by a pre-final, which in turn may be preceded by a second prefinal; further, the main final may be followed by a post-final. **1965** *Amer. Speech* XL. 12 There is here no specification of finals with prefinals and post-finals.

B. *adj.* Preceding the final.

1957 *Publ. Amer. Dial. Soc.* XXVIII. 114 Each of the pre-final groups.

†**ˈpre-ˌfine, præ-fine**, *sb. Law. Obs.* [f. PRE- B. 1 + FINE *sb.*[1]] (See quot. 1848.)

1641 W. HAKEWILL *Libertie of Subject* 14 When the Pre-fine is ten shillings, the Post-fine to be fifteen shillings. **1710** J. HARRIS *Lex. Techn.* II. **1758** [see POST-FINE]. **1848** WHARTON *Law Lex.*, *Præfine*, the fee paid on suing out the writ of covenant, on levying fines, before the fine was passed.

†**preˈfine**, *v. Obs.* [ad. L. *præfīnīre* (Cic.) to determine or limit beforehand, to prescribe, f.

præ, PRE- A. 1 + *fīnīre* to end, bound. So obs. F. *prefinir* (1392 in Godef. *Compl.*).]

1. *trans.* To limit or bound beforehand or by previous conditions; to define previously.

1588 LAMBARDE *Eiren.* IV. xvi. 582 The meanes by which .. penalties and forfeitures also that are certainly prefined by words of the Statutes, may be levied and brought into the Queens coffers. *a* **1619** FOTHERBY *Atheom.* II. i. §3 (1622) 173 There is not any Body, in Nature, so infinite, but that it is prefined within some bound and limit.

2. To determine or fix (a time) beforehand.

1545 JOYE *Exp. Dan.* v. K iij b, Before the which tyme prefined by gods infallible and immutable prouidence they shall not fal nor dye. **1608** J. KING *Serm. St. Marys* 24 Mar. 19 Hee dieth..in his threescore and tenth yeare, neither sooner, nor later, but the verie middle and vmbilicke of natures prefined time. **1662** HIBBERT *Body Div.* I. 187 He hath also prefined a convenient..season for every thing.

pre'finished, *a.* [PRE- A. 1.] Of metal: coated or treated at the mill so as to make finishing by a subsequent manufacturer unnecessary.

1935 H. R. SIMONDS *Finishing Metal Products* v. 41 One manufacturer of tableware is..producing highly polished products from prefinished sheets. **1963** H. R. CLAUSER *Encycl. Engin. Materials* 550/2 Except for uniformity, a plain plated or painted surface looks the same whether it is made of prefinished metal or finished after fabrication. **1974** *Industr. Finishing* Oct. 10/1 Many types of coated or laminated strip product are in fact used in the construction of motor vehicles but in the present context a prefinished material is defined as one which only requires fabrication before it can be used in its final form.

So **pre'finishing** *vbl. sb.*

1935 H. R. SIMONDS *Finishing Metal Products* v. 42 Lacquering and painting of sheets are an important part of the general prefinishing of raw materials. **1963** *Mech. World* CXLIII. 17/2 Rather than think in terms of functional or decorative coatings for pre-finishing,..it is probably more realistic to classify such pre-treatments as metallic or non-metallic.

†**prefinite,** *ppl. a. Obs.* [ad. L. *præfīnīt-us*, pa. pple. of *præfīnīre*: see PREFINE *v.*] Determined or limited beforehand. (In quot. 1555 as *pa. pple.*)

1555 EDEN *Decades* Pref. (Arb.) 50 Accordynge to the time prefinite by hym, who..hath suffered. **1601** HOLLAND *Pliny* II. 417 This poyson hath no set and prefinit time wherin it killeth any body. **1607** WALKINGTON *Opt. Glass* Ep. Ded. 4 If the prefinit tearme and limit of my life permit.

†**prefi'nition.** *Obs.* [ad. L. *præfīnītiōn-em*, n. of action f. *præfīnīre*: see PREFINE *v.*] A previous limitation or determination.

1582 N.T. (Rhem.) *Eph.* iii. 11 That the manifold wisedom of God may be notified.., according to the prefinition of worldes, which he made in Christ Jesus. *a* **1619** FOTHERBY *Atheom.* II. vii. §5 (1622) 270 A circumscription of their bounds; and a prefinition of their periods. **1661** BLOUNT *Glossogr.* (ed. 2), *Prefinition*, a determination before.

pre'fire, *v.* [PRE- A. 1.] *trans.* To fire (pottery, clay, etc.) beforehand, *spec.* before glazing. Hence **pre'fired** *ppl. a.*, **pre'firing** *vbl. sb.*

1944 E. ROSENTHAL *Porcelain & Other Ceramic Insulating Materials* I. viii. 203 Originally, pressed and other thin-walled articles were pre-fired at a temperature of between 800°–950°C. in order to give them the necessary mechanical strength so that they would not be deformed during the dipping process, but with the introduction of the aerograph for mass-production glazing pre-firing of the articles becomes superfluous. **1960** W. D. KINGERY *Introd. Ceramics* xiii. 428 The fine structure in the grog (prefired clay)..consists of fine mullite crystals in a siliceous matrix. **1961** M. FRANCIS tr. *Salmang's Ceramics* viii. 210 The grog should also be pre-fired at the temperature at which the brick will subsequently be used, so as to prevent the texture of the brick loosening owing to aftershrinkage of grog grains. **1965** G. J. WILLIAMS *Econ. Geol. N.Z.* xx. 366/1 Some use has been made of these materials for refractories at Kamo, where the shrinkage is controlled by prefiring part of the mix.

prefix ('priːfɪks), *sb.* [ad. mod.L. *præfix-um*, sb. use of neut. of *præfix-us*, pa. pple. of *præfigĕre* to fix in front: see PRE- A. 1, 4 c, and FIX *v.* So F. *préfixe* adj. and sb. (18th c. in Hatz.-Darm.).]

1. *Gram.* A verbal element placed before and joined to a word or stem to add to or qualify its meaning, or (in some languages) as an inflexional formative: strictly applied only to inseparable particles, but more loosely including also combining forms, and independent words, esp. prepositions and adverbs, used in combination.

All prefixes were originally distinct words, which have been reduced to one or two syllables, and sometimes to a single letter, as *be-* in *be-fore*, *over-* in *over-ween*, *a-* in *a-rise*, *y-* in *y-clept*, etc.

[**1614** BREREWOOD *Lang. & Relig.* ix. 63 Those adherents of words, which they call præfixa and suffixa.] **1646** SIR T. BROWNE *Pseud. Ep.* III. xxiv. 170 The Greek word *Bous*, which is a prefixe of augmentation to many words in that language. **1764** HARMER *Observ.* XIII. vi. 257 The prefix *Lamed* should in that case have been joined to the word Lips. **1845** STODDART *Gram.* in *Encycl. Metrop.* (1847) I. 77/1 The prefix *a*,..considered by some persons as necessary to distinguish Adverbs from their adjectives, as *aloud* from *loud*. **1851** J. C. BRYANT *Zulu Lang.* in *Jrnl. Amer. Orient. Soc.* I. 388 *note*, What we call the prefix in the Zulu is not something extraneous to the word and placed before it, but a part of the word itself. **1888** SWEET *Hist. Eng. Sounds* 105 [In O.E.] Substantives corresponding to verbs with separable prefixes take the stress on the particle.

2. a. A title prefixed to a person's name, as *Mr.*, *Dr.*, *Sir*, *Rev.*, *Hon.*, *Lord*, etc.

1836 TENNYSON in *Mem.* (1897) I. 158 You had promised the Marquis I would write for him something... To write for people with prefixes to their names is to milk he-goats; there is neither honour nor profit. **1865** DICKENS *Mut. Fr.* IV. xiv, Mr. Wegg expressly insisted that there should be no prefix to the Golden Dustman's name.

b. A word placed at the beginning of the registered name of a pedigree animal, esp. a dog, to indicate the establishment in which it was bred.

1893 [see AFFIX *sb.* 4]. **1922** R. LEIGHTON *Compl. Bk. Dog* 367 A Prefix or Affix shall constitute part of a name. **1954** [see AFFIX *sb.* 4]. **1961** C. H. D. TODD *Popular Whippet* 139, I remember some lovely dogs that sailed under the Poppy prefix. **1976** C. COOPER *Newfoundland* i. 31 New names were coming to join those of established breeders, among them Lt-Col. Reid-Kerr with his Gleborchd prefix.

3. The act of prefixing. *rare.*

1793 BEDDOES *Demonstr. Evid.* 7 *note*, By a prefix of the letter N, of which the primary sense is not known, is signifies *to have, to possess*. **1871** ROBY *Latin Gram.* I. Pref. 18 A language..in which, like English,..the adjective *great* requires, in order to gain the same meaning as *magni*, the prefix of the definite article, or the addition of the word *men*.

4. *attrib.* and *Comb.*, as **prefix-language**, a language inflected by means of prefixes, e.g. those of the Bantu family.

1881 WHITNEY *Mixt. Lang.* 15 If we dispute..the validity of an *à priori* claim that a prefix-language and a suffix-language—as, for example, a South African and a Hamitic tongue—might mingle in a manner seen to be impracticable in the case of two Indo-European dialects.

†**pre'fix,** *ppl. a. Obs. rare*$^{-1}$. [a. F. *préfix* (1381 in Hatz.-Darm.), ad. L. *præfix-us*, pa. pple. of *præfigĕre*: see prec.] Fixed beforehand.

c **1500** *Melusine* 336 Yf within a terme prefix none came there to be hermyte, he of the nerest Celle gooyng vpward muste entre into that other Celle so exempted.

prefix (see below), *v.* Also 7 præ-. [a. OF. *prefixer* (1392 in Godef. *Compl.*): see PRE- A. 1, 4 c, and FIX *v.*]

I. In reference to time (ˌpriː'fɪks).

1. *trans.* To fix or appoint beforehand (esp. a point or space of time).

c **1420** LYDG. *Assembly of Gods* 549 The same day Pluto had prefyxyd for a gret mater. **1432–50** tr. *Higden* (Rolls) VII. 165 The day of examinacion was prefixede. **1598** BARCKLEY *Felic. Man* (1631) 459 About the end of the time by him prefixed both the Pope and the King dyed. **1607** NORDEN *Surv. Dial.* III. 116 You prefixe too short a time farre: for Oakes are slow of growth. **1738** *Hist. Crt. Excheq.* x. 147 The first Thing is to prefix him [the sheriff] a day to account. **1770** *Amherst Records* (1884) 50/1 Voted That the Select Men be a Com'tee to Lay out and prefix sufficient boundaries to the Burying Yard. **1883** R. W. DIXON *Mano* I. i. 3 As the fatal hour prefixed drew near. **1977** *Daily Tel.* 23 Feb. 32/3 Would-be exporters can 'pre-fix' the subsidy at the present level by arrangement with the European Commission in Brussels.

†**2. a.** To fix, settle, or determine in one's mind beforehand; to set before oneself, resolve on, purpose; to make up (the mind) beforehand. *Obs.*

1523 FITZHERB. *Husb.* §157 This texte may gyue the a courage to prefyx thy mynd to make there thy purchase. **1542** UDALL *Erasm. Apoph.* 166 When he had prefixed & appoynted to take a certain castle & fortresse. **1560** DAUS tr. *Sleidane's Comm.* 194 b, This therfore dyd he pretende to bee the cause of a newe trouble and disturbaunce of the weale publicke whan he had prefixed it long before. **1610** GUILLIM *Heraldry* III. xii. (1660) 158 The order that I prefix to myself in treating of these Beasts. **1652** EARL MONM. tr. *Bentivoglio's Hist. Relat.* 109 As all Pylots prefix the haven for their end..so all war hath peace for its end.

†**b.** *pass.* To be determined or purposed. *Obs.*

1560 DAUS tr. *Sleidane's Comm.* 201 He was prefixed to haue expressed Dauid his Psalter in Frenche metre. *Ibid.* 210 b, The enemies are fully prefixed to retourne to the sege of the cassel.

3. a. To 'fix', make fast or permanent beforehand: see FIX *v.* 5.

1893 *Photogr. Ann.* 290 The troublesome and risky prefixing acid clearing bath is not necessary.

b. *Biol.* To fix with the first of two consecutively used fixatives.

1963 *Jrnl. Cell Biol.* XVII. 32 It was found that material prefixed in glutaraldehyde or acrolein..and refixed in osmium tetroxide contained numerous dense particles of diffuse contours..occupying the glycogen areas. **1971** *Nature* 29 Oct. 622/2 Even when the final suspension was prefixed by adding osmium tetroxide, damaged liposomes were not seen.

II. In reference to order and place (prɪ'fɪks, 'priːfɪks).

4. To place before or at the beginning of a book, chapter, account, or writing of any kind, esp. as an introduction or title.

1538 COVERDALE *N.T.* Ded., Wks. (Parker Soc.) II. 32, I did..direct an epistle unto the king's most noble grace; trusting that the book, whereupon it was prefixed, should afterward have been as well correct as other books be. **1551** CRANMER *Answ. Gardiner* 1 Here before the beginnyng of your boke, you haue prefyxed a goodly title. **1625** BACON *Ess.* Ded. to Dk. Buckhm., I do now publish my Essays... I thought it therefore agreeable to my affection and obligation to your Grace to prefix your name before them. **1675** OGILBY *Brit.* Introd., We have concluded it necessary to præfix an Illustration. **1782** PRIESTLEY *Corrupt. Chr.* I. Pref. 23 These Discourses are prefixed to ten..volumes. **1833** CRUSE *Eusebius* VII. xxv. 298 The evangelist does not prefix his name. **1875** JOWETT *Plato* (ed. 2) V. 9 The legislator..will prefix preambles to his principal laws.

5. In reference to place generally: To fix, fasten, or put in front. *rare.*

1604 R. CAWDREY *Table Alph.*, *Prefixed*, set in the forepart. **1616** BULLOKAR *Eng. Expos.*, *Prefixe*, to fasten before. **1805** EUGENIA DI ACTON *Nuns of Desert* I. 157 He produced a pistol, and prefixed the muzzle to his breast. **1898** *Phil. Trans. R. Soc.* B. CXC. 85 The skin and musculature of the arm of Man are somewhat prefixed as compared with *Macacus*.

6. *Gram.* To place (a word or particle) before a word, esp. in combination with it: cf. PREFIX *sb.* 1. Const. *before* (rare), *to*.

1605 CAMDEN *Rem.* 104 All which in Latine old Evidences have had *De* præfixed. **1719** WATERLAND *Vind. Christ's Div.* iii. Wks. 1823 I. II. 48 You remark, that 'the article is prefixed before Θεός, in an absolute construction, when spoken of the Father; but omitted when predicated of the Λόγος'. **1845** STODDART *Gram.* in *Encycl. Metrop.* (1847) I. 69/1 In English, we generally prefix the relative Article to the names of our rivers, but seldom to those of our mountains. **1876** PAPILLON *Manual Compar. Philol.* (1877) 162 Language seems originally to have employed.. the augment—in Sanskrit *a*, in Greek ε..prefixed to aorist, imperfect, and pluperfect tenses in both these languages.

Hence **pre'fixing** *vbl. sb.* and *ppl. a.*

1691 tr. *Emilianne's Frauds Rom. Monks* (ed. 3) 327 They have not the patience themselves to stay out the time of their own prefixing. **1893** [see 3]. **1897** [see POSTFIX *v.*].

pre'fixal, *a.* [f. PREFIX *sb.* + -AL[1].] Of, pertaining to, of the nature of, or characterized by prefixes; = PREFIXIONAL. Hence **pre'fixally** *adv.*, in the manner of a prefix.

1863 (Nov. 6) GOLDSTÜCKER (Philol. Soc.), On the Prefixal Elements of Sanskrit Roots. **1922** S. GREW *Art of Player-Piano* 86 The shorter note may be affined prefixally to the note after it. **1962** D. C. SWANSON in Householder & Saporta *Probl. Lexicogr.* 74 'Prefixal' is self-explanatory; 'co-valent' is used here (instead of non-prefixal) to refer to all other types collectively. **1964** E. A. NIDA *Toward Sci. Transl.* vi. 135 Once the verb root has been given, the selection of possible suffixes is more strictly determined than in Navajo, in which the prefixal formations do not, to the same extent, help the reader to predict either the sequence of prefixes likely to occur or the root likely to follow. **1971** *Language* XLVII. 396 Reflexive prefixal *t*-metathesizes with an immediately following sibilant and assimilates to the latter with respect to voice and pharyngealization. **1975** *Ibid.* LI. 618 The prefixal vowel in *prenatal* (but not in *pregnant*) is lengthened.

prefi'xation. I. 1. [f. PREFIX *v.* + -ATION.] The employment of prefixes in grammar.

1890 *Amer. Antiquarian* XII. 121 By prefixation and suffixation a considerable number of tenses and modes are formed in the verb. **1957** *Archivum Linguisticum* IX. 101 Hypercharacterization..of a person..is the common denominator of a wealth of processes:..the spreading prefixation of *i(l)* to the 3d sing. in modern substandard French. **1975** N. CHOMSKY *Logical Struct. Linguistic Theory* viii. 235 Any complete verb phrase can be turned into a noun phrase by prefixation of 'to'. **1978** *Amer. Speech* LIII. 64 This last observation prompts Samarin to suggest that glossolalia may provide evidence for a universal tendency to prefer suffixation to prefixation.

II. [f. PRE- + FIXATION.] **2.** *Anat.* [PRE- A. 4 b.] The state of a nerve of being prefixed (see PREFIXED, PREFIXT *ppl. a.* 3).

1953 [see POSTFIXATION *sb.* 1].

3. *Biol.* [PRE- A. 2.] The initial fixation of tissue that is subsequently to be fixed with a second fixative.

1963 *Jrnl. Cell Biol.* XVII. 32 The particles appearing when osmium tetroxide was used after glutaraldehyde or acrolein prefixation were similar to those appearing in rat liver after potassium permanganate..fixation. **1974** *Nature* 20 Dec. 722/1 The present study takes advantage of several circumstances: (i) cells could be frozen without prefixation or cryoprotectants.

prefixed, †**prefixt** (priː-, prɪ'fɪkst), *ppl. a.* [f. as PREFIX *v.* + -ED[1].]

1. Fixed, appointed, or settled beforehand.

1533 BELLENDEN *Livy* v. viii. (S.T.S.) II. 172 He admonist his army to be reddy at ane prefixt day. **1652** EARL MONM. tr. *Bentivoglio's Hist. Relat.* 5 A Council composed of a certain prefixt number of persons. **1733** TULL *Horse-Hoeing Husb.* x. 99 There is no prefix'd Time for planting Turneps. **1794** PALEY *Evid.* III. iv. §2 (1817) 312 Upon the strength of some prefixed persuasion. **1896** *Daily News* 1 Dec. 8/7 He proceeds..according to a prefixed plan.

2. Fixed or placed before something else.

1845 *Proc. Philol. Soc.* II. 172 In support of the assumed connection between the termination or prefixed sign of the genitive case and the relative. **1875** WHITNEY *Life Lang.* xii. 244 Using..suffixed instead of prefixed particles. **1898** *Daily News* 5 Mar. 6/2 Byron's signature..appears.. sometimes as 'Noel Byron', or 'N. B.', the prefixed name being assumed by him for reasons here noted.

3. *Anat.* Of a nerve: connected to the spinal cord relatively cranially. Cf. POSTFIXED *ppl. a.* 2.

1892, etc. [see POSTFIXED *ppl. a.* 2].

Hence **pre'fixedly,** †**pre'fixtly** *adv.* (*rare*), in a way fixed or determined beforehand.

1605 SYLVESTER *Du Bartas* II. iii. III. *Law* 561 Sith the holy-man Fore-tels prefixtly What and Where and When. *a* **1656** USSHER *Ann.* (1658) 429 The space of a few dayes, and those prefixedly numbred, being granted.

prefixial (priː'fɪksɪəl), *a.* [f. PREFIX *sb.*] = PREFIXAL *a.*

1975 *Verbatim* Dec. 13/2 'Bantu'..was coined in the 1850s by a philologist, Wilhelm Bleek, to characterize those peoples south of the Sahara speaking a group of related languages featuring prefixial concords, that is, a system in which the prefix is inflected to indicate grammatical case and number rather than, as in most western European languages, the suffix. **1976** *Archivum Linguisticum* VII. 136 Except for some prefixial combinations, the determinatum usually receives weak stress in English.

prefixion (priːˈfɪkʃən). [a. F. *préfixion* (1372 in Godef. *Compl.*), ad. L. type **præfixiōn-em*, n. of action f. *præfīgĕre* to PREFIX.] The action of prefixing.

†**1.** The action of fixing or appointing beforehand; preappointment. *Obs.*

day of prefixion, a fixed day on which a sheriff (or other officer) had to appear at the court of exchequer to render an account of his expenditure.

1526 *Visit. Dioc. Norwich* (Camden) 256 If my lord of Norwiche wold vysytt (according to his prefixcion). **1536** in Strype *Cranmer* II. (1694) 36 There should be as many of such as were sufficiently learned..without prefixion of any precise nombre. **1542-3** *Act 34 & 35 Hen. VIII*, c. 16 §1 Everye..shiref..shall at his daie of prefixcion..be sworne. **1563-87** FOXE *A. & M.* (1596) 404/1 Hauing this daie and place assigned you by your own consent and our prefixion. *a* **1754** CARTE in Gutch *Coll. Cur.* II. 142 The Sheriffs.. have their days of prefixion..for passing their accounts.

†**b.** A pre-appointed occasion. *Obs. rare*⁻¹.

1630 *R. Johnson's Kingd. & Commw.* 511 He that is missing at any of the prefixions, is sure to have many bastinadoes on the soles of his feet.

2. *Gram.* The placing of a word or particle before a word, esp. in combination with it; employment of a prefix.

1811-31 BENTHAM *Lang.* Wks. 1843 VIII. 324/2 The accessory word..in some instances..precedes the principal word... Hence the distinction,—accessories prefixed, or in the way of prefixion. **1894** *Nation* (N.Y.) 6 Sept. 180/3 In some categories, as in the attributive relation, prefixion is the rule. Thus, the adverb stands before the verb and not after.

Hence **preˈfixional** *a.*, characterized by prefixion; inflected by means of prefixes. *rare.*

1858 *Penny Cycl.* 2nd Supp. 377/2 The languages of the Kaffirs supply a broad distinction between them and other African races. They are prefixional and alliterational.

†**preˈfixment.** *Obs. rare*⁻¹. [f. PREFIX *v.* + -MENT.] Fixture beforehand; pre-appointment.

1614 W. B. *Philosopher's Banquet* (ed. 2) 3 Wee may lengthen out our daies with ioy..to the last periode of their prefixment.

prefixture (priːˈfɪkstjʊə(r)). Also præ-. [f. PREFIX *v.* after FIXTURE.]

1. The action of prefixing, esp. in grammar.

1824 J. WINTERBOTTOM *Two French Words* 9 Warton speaks of the prefixture of the augment *y*. **1879** J. A. H. MURRAY tr. Schiefner in *Address to Philol. Soc.* 41 In this language [Abchasian] the most interesting feature is the remarkable prefixture of the personal pronouns. For example..*ab* 'father' makes *sab* 'my father', *uab* 'thy father' (masc.), *bab* 'thy father' (fem.), *yab* 'his father', *lab* 'her father', *shab* 'your father', *rab* 'their father'.

2. A word prefixed, esp. as a title or distinction; a prefix.

1821 *New Monthly Mag.* II. 131 The ancient fiddle, with its cognomen, or monosyllabic praefixture, was, we fancy, a low instrument. **1833** T. HAMILTON *Men & Mann. Amer.* I. viii. 241 The members of the Federal Senate are addressed with the prefixture of Honourable.

preflame: see PRE- B. 2.

preˈflight, *a.* [f. PRE- B. 2 + FLIGHT *sb.*¹] **a.** Of or pertaining to the time before powered flight. *rare.* **b.** Of or pertaining to the preparations for a flight, or for flying in general.

1922 *Encycl. Brit.* XXX. 44/2 Almost all altimeters in use are based on the pre-flight aneroid in which the trade convention was to assume everywhere an atmospheric temperature of 10° C. **1942** *R.A.F. Jrnl.* 27 June 4 American boys..are to be given pre-flight aviation training. **1962** A. SHEPARD in *Into Orbit* 98 Then I went through my final pre-flight medical. **1968** J. SANGSTER *Touchfeather* xviii. 205, I could just see his head at the flight deck window as he made some of his pre-flight checks. **1970** N. ARMSTRONG et al. *First on Moon* ii. 35 She had left the Holiday Inn two hours earlier to drive to the preflight examination area.

preˈflight, *v.* [f. prec.] *trans.* To prepare (an aircraft) for a flight.

1971 *Flying* (N.Y.) Apr. 40/3 A moron could..preflight and satisfactorily steer the 172. **1975** L. D. KUSCHE *Bermuda Triangle Mystery Solved* 98 Each plane had been.. preflighted and held a full load of fuel. **1975** *High Times* Dec. 70/2 So you load up and preflight the plane. **1976** B. LECOMBER *Dead Weight* vi. 75 Simon..did want a flying lesson... I told him to pre-flight the Cherokee.

prefloration (priːflɒˈreɪʃən). *Bot.* [ad. F. *préfloraison* (Richard), f. *pré-*, PRE- B. + L. *flōs*, *flōr-em* flower: see -ATION.] = ÆSTIVATION.

1832 LINDLEY *Introd. Bot.* 409 The term estivation, or præfloration, is applied to the parts of the flower when unexpanded. **1880** GRAY *Struct. Bot.* iv. §2 (ed. 6) 132 Vernation and Æstivation—Præfoliation and Præfloration are etymologically better terms substituted by Richard.

†**prefoˈcation.** *Path. Obs.* Also præ-. [ad. L. *præfōcātiōn-em*, n. of action f. *præfōcāre* to choke, suffocate, f. *præ*, PRE- + *faux*, *faucem* throat. So F. †*préfocation* (15th c.).] Choking, suffocation; constriction.

1657 TOMLINSON *Renou's Disp.* 401 Cures the dolour and præfocation of the uterus. **1684** tr. *Bonet's Merc. Compit.* VI. 180 She suffers strangling and prefocation, because of compression about the Heart.

preˈfocus, *a.* and *v.* [f. PRE- A. 1.] **A.** *adj.* Of a bulb: constructed so that the lamp is automatically focused upon fitting of the bulb; also applied to parts of such bulbs, esp. the cap, which make possible the necessary accurate positioning of the filament during manufacture.

1944 (*title*) Dimensions of prefocus lamp-caps and lampholders (British Standards Institution). **1950** YOUNG & GRIFFITHS *Automobile Electr. Equipment* (ed. 4) vi. 181 Fine adjustment for the filament position is..essential in order to take care of slight manufacturing discrepancies in the filament distance from the bulb cap unless, of course, the bulb is of the pre-focus type now prevalent in British-made headlamps. **1967** L. HOLMES *Odhams New Motor Man.* x. 238/1 For Continental towing, British cars must have their headlamps converted to dip to the right instead of to the left, and for this purpose special pre-focus bulbs can be obtained. **1970** *A.A. Bk. of Car* 162/4 The cut-away in the flange of a pre-focus bulb ensures that it is correctly located and focused. **1972** *Gloss. Electrotechnical, Power Terms (B.S.I.)* IV. iii. 17 *Prefocus cap*, cap..which enables the luminous element to be brought into a specified position relative to the cap during the manufacture of the lamp.

B. *v. trans.* To make or adjust so that a lamp will be automatically focused when a bulb is fitted. So **preˈfocused** *ppl. a.*, **preˈfocusing** *vbl. sb.*

1951 *Philips Technical Rev.* XII. 309/1 It is of great importance that when a new bulb is fitted into a headlight its filament comes to lie exactly in the right position. This is ensured by a pre-focusing of the filament in the factory with the aid of a special adjusting device. *Ibid.* 312 (*caption*) On the base can be seen two of the three studs with which the lamp is focused: they ensure that the axis of the lamp coincides with that of the reflector, the filament being 'prefocused' with respect to the studs. **1954** A. W. JUDGE *Automobile Electr. Maintenance* (ed. 3) viii. 209 In the case of recent American-type headlamps, 'sealed-beam' units are employed. These consist of a lens, bulb, and reflector unit built into one water- and dust-proof pre-focused unit. **1970** *A.A. Bk. of Car* 162/4 *Quartz-halogen bulbs.* These are obtainable for fitting into pre-focused units in place of ordinary bulbs. **1977** *Nature* 6 Jan. 92/1 The built-in lamp turret keeps four prefocussed lamps aligned, powered and ready to work.

prefoliation (priːfəʊlɪˈeɪʃən). *Bot.* Also præ-. [a. F. *préfoliation* (Richard): see PRE- B. and FOLIATION, and cf. PREFLORATION.] = VERNATION.

1856 HENSLOW *Dict. Bot. Terms* 144 *Præfoliation*,.. synonyme for 'Vernation'. **1861** BENTLEY *Man. Bot.* (1870) 95 The arrangement of the leaves in the bud is called vernation or præfoliation. **1880** [see PREFLORATION].

prefool, preforceps: see PRE- A. 1, 4.

preform (priːˈfɔːm), *v.* [ad. L. *præformāre*: see PRE- A. 1 and FORM *v.* So F. *préformer* (18th c. Bonnet in Littré).] **a.** *trans.* To form or shape beforehand. (Chiefly in *pa. pple.*)

1601 [see PREFORMED]. **1793** HOLCROFT *Lavater's Physiogn.* xxiv. 122 If the germ exists preformed in the mother. **1858** BUSHNELL *Nat. & Supernat.* xi. (1864) 337 God's original scheme, taken as a whole, was so planned, or preformed. **1897** *Allbutt's Syst. Med.* IV. 117 Bile pigments are not preformed in the blood.

(*b*) *spec.* To form (plastic or other moulding material) into a shape, usu. one resembling a desired final shape, before some further processing. Also *absol.*

1936 H. W. ROWELL *Technol. Plastics* xx. 148 A 'tablet'.. is made in a stock size of die and is not preformed to the approximate shape of the moulding. **1943** D. W. BROWN *Handbk. Engin. Plastics* i. 9 In order to reduce the size of the powder space required in moulds, the raw material is sometimes preformed into comparatively small pellets prior to being introduced into the mould. **1968** L. K. ARNOLD *Introd. Plastics* (1969) ii. 41 The powder may be preformed, that is, pressed into pellets or disks of convenient size to reduce bulk density and facilitate charging the mold. **1975** C. A. HARPER *Handbk. Plastics & Elastomers* xii. 36 There are..transfer-type presses that will automatically feed the powder, preform, preheat, transfer, and complete the molding cycle.

b. To determine the form of beforehand; to furnish a mould or model of (a structure to be subsequently formed).

1890 *Cent. Dict.* s.v., Bone preformed in cartilage. The fetal skeleton preforms that of the adult.

Hence **preˈforming** *vbl. sb.*; also **preˈformer**, a press or similar device for preforming plastic.

1931 *Plastics & Molded Products* VII. 705 (Advt.), Trouble-free preforming and more economical production with Stokes single punch and rotary preform presses. **1952** J. DELMONTE *Plastics Molding* viii. 193 Standard single-punch preformers are illustrated in Figs. 2 and 3, and a rotary-type preforming machine is illustrated in Fig. 4. **1966** J. A. BRYDSON *Plastics Materials* x. 210 Preforming is carried out by compressing sieved powder that has been evenly loaded into a mould. **1968** *Encycl. Polymer Sci. & Technol.* IX. 26 Preformers are basically compacting presses; they may be mechanical, hydraulic, pneumatic, or rotary cam-type machines.

preform (ˈpriːfɔːm), *sb.* **1.** [f. the vb.] A moulded object which has to receive further processing to produce the final shape, which it usu. resembles.

1931 *Plastics & Molded Products* VII. 102 The test strip ..is 7½ in. long by 1 in. wide and is molded from four preforms composed of a very soft grade of phenol-plastic compound. **1935** C. ELLIS *Chem. Synthetic Resins* II. lxviii. 1317 Tablets or preforms are made from the molding powder by applying high pressure..quickly and without heat. **1945** H. BARRON *Mod. Plastics* vii. 166 Preforms are employed where the use of fairly bulky moulding powder is a disadvantage. **1962** *Gloss. Terms Glass Industry (B.S.I.)* 33 *Preform*, a small glass product, normally employed in making glass-to-metal seals, formed by dry-pressing glass powder into shape in a die, the shape being fired to consolidate the glass particles into a non-porous component. **1968** *Encycl. Polymer Sci. & Technol.* IX. 26 It is easier for an operator to pick up a preform and place it in a mold cavity or transfer pot than to have to weigh a charge of granular material. **1970** *New Scientist* 12 Nov. 326/1 A precise quantity of [metal] powder is compacted and sintered so as to produce a preform which is approximately 85 per cent dense.

2. *Philol.* [PRE- A. 2.] A linguistic form reconstructed from later evidence.

1939 L. H. GRAY *Foundations of Lang.* i. 3 If..one has such a series as English (*he*) *bears*, Old Icelandic *berr*, Gothic *bairip*.., Old High German *birit*, Old Irish *berid*, Modern Irish *bheir*..,..one may, by comparing and contrasting these forms in accordance with phonetic correspondences .., determine why they are here alike, and there unlike, and may perceive how they can all be derived from an hypothetical pre-form. **1972** *Language* XLVIII. 409 There are two possibilities for reconstructing the gen. pl. preforms of the two attested nouns.

preˈformant. *Philol. rare.* [f. PRE- A. 4 + L. *formānt-em*, pr. pple. of *formāre* to FORM: see -ANT.] = PREFORMATIVE B.

1864 PUSEY *Lect. Daniel* Notes 578 The Arabic præformant of the 3ᵈ fem. fut.

preformation (priːfɔːˈmeɪʃən). Also præ-. [f. PRE- A. 2 + FORMATION; cf. PREFORM. So F. *préformation* (18th c. Bonnet in Littré).]

1. The action or process of forming or shaping beforehand; previous formation.

1732 *Hist. Litteraria* IV. 195 It is easy to think that the Soul is a divine Automaton, still more wonderful, and that by a divine Præformation it produces these beautiful Ideas. **1819** COLERIDGE *Rem.* (1836) II. 193 The inauspicious influences on the preformation of Edmund's character. **1838** SIR W. HAMILTON *Logic* xxx. (1866) II. 129 The blind preformations of opinion. **1905** *Brit. Med. Jrnl.* 25 Feb. 442 On the other hand, the egg of Nereis..and of Beroë.. showed a high degree of 'preformation', and the early blastomeres of these eggs were not equipotential.

2. *theory of preformation* (Biol.): the theory, prevalent in the 18th c., that all the parts of the perfect organism exist previously formed in the germ, and are merely 'developed' or unfolded (not produced by accretion) in the process of reproduction. Formerly also called *theory of* EVOLUTION (6 b); opposed to that of EPIGENESIS.

1831 *Blackw. Mag.* XXIX. 68 The two styles of conversation corresponded to the two theories of generation,—one (Johnson's) to the theory of Preformation (or Evolution)—the other (Burke's) to the theory of Epigenesis. **1847** [see EPIGENESIS]. **1879** tr. *Haeckel's Evol. Man* I. ii. 40 Caspar Friedrich Wolff..with his new Theory of Epigenesis gave the death-blow to the entire Theory of Preformation. **1899** THOMSON *Sci. Life* x. 119 His [Bonnet's] central idea was the 'preformation' or asserted pre-existence of the organism and all its parts within the germ.

preforˈmationist. Also præ-. [f. PREFORMATION + -IST.] One who holds or maintains the theory of preformation (see PREFORMATION 2). Also *attrib.* or as *adj.*

1888 E. R. LANKESTER in *Encycl. Brit.* XXIV. 815/1 The so-called 'evolutionists' of the eighteenth century, better called præformationists. **1936** *Mind* XLV. 221 Boodin begins by explaining why he prefers to class the cosmological theories of Plato and Aristotle, notwithstanding certain preformationist tendencies especially in the thought of Aristotle, under the heading of creation theories. **1960** *New Biol.* XXXI. 119 As development proceeds, suitable conditions start the synthesis of a succession of new substances. This, at least, is the contemporary opinion; the Preformationists in the eighteenth century thought otherwise, but their point of view is hard to square with the atomic hypothesis. **1973** *Jrnl. Genetic Psychol.* CXXII. 326 Preformationist prejudices were so powerful that early embryologists..'saw' nonexistent miniature adults when viewing embryos through their microscopes. **1975** *Nature* 5 June 449/1 These findings fit well the expectations of the Preformationists. **1978** *Ibid.* 9 Nov. 125/1 Until this metaphor became available, the only alternative to a crude preformationist kind of innatism was a mysterious force such as Driesch's 'entelechy', which would allow the developing organism to survive the vicissitudes of the environment and the embryologist's knife.

Also **preforˈmationism**, the doctrine or theory of preformation (sense 2).

1890 *Q. Rev.* Apr. 372 Both notions have now passed along with 'preformationism' into the limbo of discarded hypotheses.

preformative (priːˈfɔːmətɪv), *a.* (*sb.*) Also præ-. [f. PRE- A. 3, 4 + FORMATIVE; cf. PREFORM.]

1. Having the quality or capacity of forming beforehand. (Sometimes with allusion to the biological theory of preformation.)

1841 MYERS *Cath. Th.* IV. §33. 342 The peculiar preformative nature of the Jewish institutions and history. **1854** *Jrnl. R. Agric. Soc.* XV. II. 305 Under the supposition that the membrane gives rise to the first production of the Dentine, and is itself obliterated by the process, it has been called the preformative membrane of the dental papilla. **1883** SCHAFF *Hist. Ch.* I. III. xxi. 199 [That] the apostolic Christianity is preformative and contains the living germs of all the following periods, personages, and tendencies.

2. *Philol.* Prefixed as a formative element: said of a letter, syllable, etc. (esp. in Semitic languages).

1821 M. STUART *Gram. Hebr. Lang.* III. (1831) 79 The præformative affixes to the Fut., would appropriately have a Sheva for their vowel-pointing. **1839** G. PHILLIPS *Syriac Gram.* 61 The præformative letters are not four as in Hebrew. *Ibid.* 62 The Infinitive of all the conjugations has Mem præformative. **1844** *Proc. Philol. Soc.* I. 269 The Georgian also employs a variety of preformative particles in conjugation.

B. *sb. Philol.* A preformative particle; a letter, syllable, etc., prefixed to a word or root in inflexion or derivation; a prefix (esp. in Semitic languages).

1821 M. STUART *Gram. Hebr. Lang.* II. (1831) 51 *Tav*, in the præformative [hit] (in Hithpael), often assimilates itself to the first radical of the verb. *Ibid.* III. 96 The Præformatives of tense and conjugation. **1837** G. PHILLIPS *Syriac Gram.* 85 The Olaph characteristic of the Aphel conjugation is sometimes retained with the preformatives. **1844** *Proc. Philol. Soc.* I. 246 One of these preformatives.. is deserving of more especial notice. **1901** J. E. H. THOMSON *Recent Comm. Daniel* 12 There are remains of eastern forms ..for instance, the use of the lamed as preformative for the yod in the Substantive Verb—a Mandaean i.e. eastern usage.

preformed (ˈpriːˌfɔːmd, *poet.* priːˈfɔːmɪd), *ppl. a.* [f. PREFORM + -ED[1], or f. PRE- A. 1 + FORMED.] **a.** Formed beforehand, previously formed.

1601 SHAKS. *Jul. C.* I. iii. 67 The true cause,..Why all these things change from their Ordinance, Their Natures, and pre-formed Faculties, To monstrous qualitie. **1866** ODLING *Anim. Chem.* 136 Alloxan, a pre-formed constituent of urine. **1869** E. A. PARKES *Pract. Hygiene* (ed. 3) 217 During baking a certain amount of preformed sugar yields carbonic acid. **1889** MIVART *Origin Hum. Reason* 116 Men do not invent concepts for preformed words, but the reverse.

b. *spec.* of plastic or other moulding material (cf. PREFORM *v.*).

1918 H. ABRAHAM *Asphalts* xxvi. 453 (*heading*) Preformed joints and washers. **1935** C. ELLIS *Chem. Synthetic Resins* II. lxviii. 1319 The charge may be used in any of three forms, powder, preformed tablets or sheets. **1943** D. W. BROWN *Handbk. Engin. Plastics* i. 9 In some cases..the shape of the article renders it impossible to use preformed materials. **1971** E. W. DUCK *Plastics & Rubbers* iv. 60 A preformed sheet of the plastic is heated and then brought on to the surface of the mould and drawn tight..by the application of a vacuum. **1977** *Gramophone* June 122/1 The enclosure is very substantially made.., being braced..and filled with pre-formed foam fittings.

preˈformism. *Biol.* [f. PREFORM *v.* + -ISM.] = PREFORMATIONISM. So **preˈformist** = PREFORMATIONIST.

1896 *Amer. Naturalist* June 449 But this is not Preformism in the old sense; since the adaptations..are novelties of function in whole or part. *Ibid.*, The case of reflex and instinctive functions as against the old preformist or Weismannist view.

†**preˈfract,** *a. Obs.* [ad. L. *præfract-us* abrupt, stern, inflexible, pa. pple. of *præfringĕre* to break off before the point or abruptly, f. *præ*, PRE- A. 4 + *frangĕre* to break.] Abrupt, stubborn, obstinate, refractory.

1555 GARDINER in Foxe *A. & M.* (1570) 1784/2 Thou wast so prefracte and stout in religion. **1597** J. KING *On Jonas* (1618) 642 Which no man could deny, that were not too prefract and obstinate. **1608** CHAPMAN *Byron's Trag.* IV. Plays 1873 II. 283 Still he stands prefract and insolent.

pre-ˈFreudian, *a.* [PRE- B. 1.] Of or characterized by attitudes, etc., that were commonly accepted prior to Freud's pioneer work in psychoanalysis.

1937 *Harper's Mag.* Nov. 563/1 With the tools of semantic analysis, the authors laid in ruin the towering edifice of classical philosophy... Psychology (pre-Freudian) emerged in little better repair. **1938** J. M. KEYNES *Two Memoirs* (1949) 100 It was not only that intellectually we were pre-Freudian, but we had lost something which our predecessors had. **1959** P. TOWNEND *Died o' Wednesday* x. 169, I had..accomplished very little, merely my duty..a matter that caused our ancestors in..pre-Freudian days no perplexity. **1970** *Eng. Stud.* LI. 489 Ward seems quite untempted by the call to psychological speculation, and the book is positively pre-Freudian. **1976** *Jrnl. R. Soc. Arts* CXXIV. 625/1 The Angst of the pre-Freudian and Freudian era.

prefrontal (priːˈfrʌntəl), *a.* (*sb.*) *Anat.* and *Zool.* Also præ-. [f. PRE- A., B. + L. *frons, front-* forehead + -AL[1], or f. PRE- + FRONTAL.]

A. *adj.* **a.** Situated in front of the frontal bone of the skull. **b.** Situated in the fore part of the frontal lobe of the brain.

1854 OWEN in *Orr's Circ. Sc., Org. Nat.* I. 194 The.. prefrontal and nasal bones. **1888** *Phil. Trans. R. Soc.* B. CLXXIX. 3 (*heading*) Results of experiments upon the prefrontal region of the hemisphere. **1899** *Allbutt's Syst. Med.* VII. 273 The frontal lobe as so defined must be divided into a prefrontal and a postfrontal area. *Ibid.* 738 That part of the brain which is probably most intimately associated with psychical processes—the præfrontal area. **1902** *Daily Chron.* 22 May 3/4 The general consensus of opinion localises what we term 'mind' in the pre-frontal lobes of the brain.

c. ***prefrontal leucotomy, lobotomy***, lobotomy of the prefrontal part of the brain.

1936, etc. [see LOBOTOMY]. **1937**, etc. [see LEUCOTOMY].

B. *sb.* (*ellipt.* for *prefrontal bone.*) A portion of the ethmoid, which forms a distinct bone in some reptiles, batrachians, and fishes.

1854 OWEN in *Orr's Circ. Sc., Org. Nat.* I. 193 There is a distinct, oval, articular surface near the anterior median angle of each frontal to which the prefrontal is attached. *Ibid.* 194 The prefrontals..are connate with the lacrymals. **1880** GÜNTHER *Fishes* 57 The prefrontals, also small, occupy the anterior margin of the orbit.

So **preˌfronto-ˈlachrymal** *a.*, at once prefrontal and lachrymal. (In quot. as *sb.*, *sc.* bone.)

1875 HUXLEY in *Encycl. Brit.* I. 759/1 This meets a curved flat bone, which bounds the orbit anteriorly and internally, and articulates with an ascending process of the maxillary bone. It may..be regarded as a prefronto-lachrymal.

†**prefruˈition.** *Obs.* [f. PRE- A. 2 + FRUITION.] Previous fruition or enjoyment; a foretaste.

a **1631** DONNE *Serm.* (1649) II. 125 Delighting in the hope of a future sin, and sin in a præfruition of his sinne, before the act. **1678** J. J[ONES] *Brit. Church* 591 To be in the Church of heaven, (while he is on earth,) by prefruition.

prefulgence (prɪˈfʌldʒəns). [f. as PREFULGENT *a.*] = PREFULGENCY.

1892 G. GISSING *Born in Exile* II. IV. iii. 227 In his most presumptuous moments he had never claimed the sexual prefulgence which many a commonplace fellow so gloriously exhibits. **1916** F. SWINNERTON *Chaste Wife* xxiii. 317 Too stupid to understand anything but physical prefulgence or absolute social convention.

†**preˈfulgency.** *Obs. rare.* [f. as next: see -ENCY.] Pre-eminent brightness or splendour.

1660 WATERHOUSE *Arms & Arm.* 31 The Patricians and Senators were so jealous of their glory and prefulgency that they allowed none participants with them. *a* **1677** BARROW *Pope's Suprem.* (1687) 57 By the prefulgency of his excellent worth and merit.

†**preˈfulgent,** *a. Obs. rare.* [ad. L. *præfulgēns, -ēntem*, pr. pple. of *præfulgēre* to shine forth or greatly: see PRE- A. 4, 6, and FULGENT.] Greatly shining; pre-eminent in brightness.

c **1560** A. SCOTT *Poems* (S.T.S.) xiv. 2 Bemis Off Phebus fair prefulgent visage bricht. **1651** *Life Father Sarpi* (1676) 105 As was said of the Images of Brutus and Cassius, that in a Funeral pomp they were more conspicuous and prefulgent, because..they were not seen among the others.

†**preˈfulgurate,** *v. Obs. rare*[-0]. [f. ppl. stem of L. *præfulgurāre* to flash forth: see FULGURATE.]

1623 COCKERAM, *Prefulgurate*, to glister before.

preg (prɛg), *a.* Colloq. abbrev. of PREGNANT *a.*[2] 1 a.

1955 W. GADDIS *Recognitions* I. v. 172 She's preg, baby. **1962** E. O'BRIEN *Lonely Girl* xvi. 188 Are you preg?..'Cos if you are, you won't be able to cycle. **1967** *London Mag.* Aug. 10 A bit of news which may just interest you, I am P-R-E-G and not by Roy. **1968** *New Society* 22 Aug. 266/1 'She's pregnant' is now used in many classes ('preg, preggy, preggers', whatever class they belonged to, are now not much used).

†**preˈgage,** *v. Obs.* [f. PRE- A. 1 + GAGE *v.*] *trans.* To pledge beforehand, pre-engage.

1655 FULLER *Ch. Hist.* IX. i. §42 The members of the Councell of Trent..were by oath pregaged to the Pope 'to defend and maintain his authority against all the world'.

pre-game: see PRE- B. 2 a.

pregamic: PRE- B. 1.

pregangliˈonic, *a. Anat.* [PRE- B. 3.] Of a nerve of the autonomic nervous system: running from the central nervous system to a ganglion.

1895 *Jrnl. Physiol.* XVIII. 280 (*heading*) Note on regeneration of præ-ganglionic fibres of the sympathetic. **1897** *Ibid.* XXII. 223 The regeneration of post-ganglionic fibres presents a somewhat similar problem to that we have considered in relation to the pre-ganglionic fibres. **1903** *Brain* XXVI. 5 The nerve fibres which leave the central nervous system are all pre-ganglionic fibres; they end in connection with nerve cells in the ganglia, and these give off post-ganglionic nerve-fibres which end in the tissues. **1946** *Nature* 19 Oct. 556/1 Single shocks at low intensity delivered to the preganglionic nerve excite a single giant fibre therein. **1972** [see INTERMEDIOLATERAL *a.*]. **1974** M. C. GERALD *Pharmacol.* v. 93 Conversely preganglionic sympathetic fibers are generally short, with long postganglionic fibers arising from the ganglion to the innervated tissues.

Hence **pregangliˈonically** *adv.*

1937 *Jrnl. Physiol.* LXXXVIII. 6 Nicotine..shortens and diminishes the *P* waves set up both antidromically and preganglionically. **1967** *Jrnl. Pharmacol. & Exper. Therap.* CLV. 37/1 The difference was statistically significant whether stimulation was carried out preganglionically or postganglionically.

pregastrular, -geological(ly): see PRE- B. 1.

pregeminal, -geniculate, -geniculum, -genital: see PRE- A. 4, B. 3.

†**preˈgerminate,** *v. Obs. rare*[-0]. [f. ppl. stem of L. *prægermināre* to bud forth early: see PRE- A. 1 and GERMINATE.]

1623 COCKERAM, *Pregerminate*, to bud before another.

pregermiˈnation. [PRE- A. 2.] The treatment of seed to start the process of germination before planting. So **preˈgerminated** *ppl. a.*, having been subjected to such treatment.

1942 H. I. BALDWIN *Forest Tree Seed* 230 Pregermination:—Germinative processes set in motion, but completion impossible because of external factors. Seed coat may or may not be broken. **1959** *Times* 7 Dec. (Agric. Suppl.) p. viii/3 Pregermination of conifer seed is practised before sowing. **1978** *Countryman* Winter 117 A new planting technique which is taking off in quite a big way is 'the fluid sowing of pre-germinated seeds'.

preggers (ˈprɛgəz), *a. slang.* [f. PREG(NANT *a.*[2] + *-ers*, as in *bonkers, crackers.*] = PREGNANT *a.*[2] 1 a.

1942 M. DICKENS *One Pair of Feet* vii. 115 Let anyone mention in her hearing that they felt sick, and it would be all over the hospital that they were 'preggers'. **1960** F. RAPHAEL *Limits of Love* I. iii. 38 'I'm preggers,' Susan said. **1964** *Times* 4 Feb. 7/3, I would only offer my seat to a woman if she were carrying a baby, if she were preggers, or if she were obviously infirm. **1968** [see PREG *a.*]. **1971** R. DENTRY *Encounter at Kharmel* vii. 115 'There was a strong suspicion that one of the women was preggers.' 'Eh?' 'Up the duff, sir.' **1980** C. FREMLIN *With no Crying* ix. 50 Preggers! Well, what do you know?

preggo (ˈprɛgəʊ), *a. Austral. slang.* Also **prego**. [f. PREG(NANT *a.*[2] + -O[2].] = PREGNANT *a.*[2] 1 a.

1951 CUSACK & JAMES *Come in Spinner* 226 Guinea's face lighted with unholy glee. 'A Parker prego? Did I hear right?' **1965** P. WHITE *Four Plays* 94 'Can't resist the bananas.' 'Yeah. They say you go for them like one thing when you're preggo.' **1971** *Guardian* 27 May 13/7 Uncommon in print, but familiar in speech, is preggo (pregnant).

preggy (ˈprɛgɪ), *a. slang.* Also **preggie**. [f. PREG(NANT *a.*[2] + -Y[1].] = PREGNANT *a.*[2] 1 a. Also *transf.*

1938 N. MARSH *Death in White Tie* v. 63 There was your bag, simply preggy with banknotes. **1961** S. PRICE *Just for Record* vi. 57 If poor little preggy Emily Nugent had lived I might never be where I am today. **1968** [see PREG *a.*]. **1970** K. GILES *Death in Church* iii. 69 She looks preggie, pretty, polite and a little sloshed. **1976** *Star* (Sheffield) 30 Nov. 2/7 Final fling for noisy Parkers shows Michael and preggie June back in England.

pre-give, -given: see PRE- A. 1.

pre-glacial (priːˈgleɪʃ(ɪ)əl), *a. Geol.* [PRE- B. 1 b.] Existing or occurring previous to the glacial period. Hence **preˈglacially** *adv.*

1855, 1863 [see POST-GLACIAL]. **1863** *Q. Rev.* CXIV. 407 Omitting the first or preglacial period, the estimate is made for the glacial and post-glacial period. **1875** *Q. Jrnl. Geol. Soc.* XXXI. 61 The small thickness of preglacially weathered rock that the brief stay of the ice at these high elevations enabled it to remove. **1882** DAWKINS in *Standard* 25 Aug. 2/4 He..felt inclined to view the river-drift man as having invaded Europe in pre-glacial times. **1903** *Jrnl. Geol.* XI. 675 To whatever state of maturity the valley development had attained preglacially, it was directly modified by the advent of the glacial epoch. **1963** D. W. & E. E. HUMPHRIES tr. *Termier's Erosion & Sedimentation* 411 A smooth preglacially eroded surface.

preglenoid, -glenoidal: see PRE- B. 3.

preˈglottalized, *ppl. a. Phonetics.* [PRE- A. 1.] Preceded by a glottalized sound. Hence **preˌglottaliˈzation**.

1964 E. J. A. HENDERSON in D. Abercrombie et al. *Daniel Jones* 419 Vichintana Chantavibulya..discovered that her pronunciation of the palatal semi-vowel in initial position is preceded by a weak glottal plosive... There is a similar pre-glottalized articulation of the labio-velar semi-vowel. **1965** *Canad. Jrnl. Linguistics* XI. I. 32 Phonological feats are possible on a paralinguistic level that seem impossible on a linguistic one,..as pre-glottalized stops and nasals. **1968** B. S. ANDRÉSEN *Pre-Glottalization in Eng. Stand. Pronunc.* 10, I shall regard the glottal stop and the following labial/alveolar/velar plosive as one phonological unit, and refer to this as a 'pre-glottalized' voiceless labial/alveolar/velar plosive. The *use* of these phones will be referred to as 'pre-glottalization'. **1969** *Eng. Stud.* L. 317 Preglottalization can be compared to other articulatory modifications of sounds, e.g. velarization of l, as in [ʃæl]. **1977** *Language* LIII. 317 Except in sentence-initial position, *b d* are either preglottalized or prenasalized, and the processes occur in complementary distribution—word-internally, pre-glottalization is the norm. **1977** *Trans. Philol. Soc. 1975* 222 For Oromo *d* represents either an alveolar implosive or a preglottalized voiced alveolar plosive.

pregnable (ˈprɛgnəb(ə)l), *a.* Forms: 5–7 prenable, 6 prenn-, prein-, preign-, preygn-, prign-, 7 prægn-, 6– pregnable. [Late ME. *prenable*, a. F. *prenable* (12th c. in Hatz.-Darm.), also in OF. *pregnable* (1306 in Godef. *Compl.*), f. *prendre* (ppl. stem *pren-*):—L. *prendĕre*, contr. from *prehendĕre*: see PREHEND and -ABLE. As to the *g* see IMPREGNABLE.] Of a fortress: Capable of being taken by assault. Also *transf.*

1435 in *Wars Eng. in France* (Rolls) II. 581 If the placis were righte prenable. **1523** LD. BERNERS *Froiss.* I. cclv. 379 They thought well the towne was preignable. *Ibid.* cclxv. 392 They sawe well that yᵉ place was prignable. **1523** *St. Papers Hen. VIII*, VI. 165 What places he supposeth there most preinable, or facile to be had. *c* **1540** tr. *Pol. Verg. Eng. Hist.* (Camden No. 29) 14 Out of hope that it was pregnable by assault. **1591** Unton *Corr.* (Roxb.) 66 It is hardlie otherwise prennable. **1603** Holland *Plutarch's Mor.* 413 *margin*, A strong hold kept by a coward is pregnable. **1632** —— *Cyrupædia* 107 Cyrus..desirous in very deed to see whether the Castle were any where prenable. **1845** Petrie *Round Towers Irel.* 371 The door alone could be pregnable. **1880** *Harper's Mag.* LX. 615 Its pregnable approaches are the portals of entrance and exit for the tube.

b. *fig.* Open to attack; assailable, vulnerable.

1836 *New Monthly Mag.* XLVIII. 334 There were but few points on which it [Libertino's character] was pregnable. **1837** Sir J. Paget in *Mem.* v. 100 A hard-headed English infidel, pregnable to neither religion nor common-sense. **1902** *Daily Chron.* 26 Apr. 3/1 He attacks Arnold's very pregnable idea that Christianity is only Stoicism 'touched with emotion'.

¶ Erroneously used for pregnant *a.*[1], [2]. *Obs.*

1607 Topsell *Four-f. Beasts* (1658) 69 In those elder times, wherein wisdom and invention was most pregnable. *Ibid.* 674 Leaving those brief and pregnable Narrations of Bellonius and Scaliger. *a* **1660** *Contemp. Hist. Irel.* (Ir. Archæol. Soc.) II. 41 These solide and pregnable reasons.

Hence **pregna'bility**, pregnable quality.

1838 S. Bellamy *Betrayal* 107 There's not a flaw In frailty coupled with defect more near Than this man's strength to pregnability.

‖**pregnada** (pre'ɲada). *Obs.* [Sp. *preñada* big with child.] A variety of lemon: see quots.

a **1691** Boyle *Hist. Air* (1692) 178 There are [in Teneriffe] oranges and lemons, especially the pregnadas, which have small ones in their bellies, from whence they are so denominated. **1772–84** *Cook's Voy.* (1790) IV. 1229 Another botanical curiosity, mentioned by him, is what they call Pregnada, or impregnated lemon. It is a perfect and distinct lemon, inclosed within another.

'pregnance. [f. pregnant *a.*[2]: see -ance.]

1. = pregnancy[1] 2–4; a pregnant quality.

1546 Langley *Pol. Verg. De Invent.* i. viii. 15 b, Poetrie.. comprehendeth al other sciences, as for that when other faculties be deuysed by the pregnaunce of mannes wytte, this art only is giuen of nature by a diuine inspiracion. **1610** W. Folkingham *Art of Survey* iv. ii. 81 Increase comprehends all profits deriued from the Pregnance and Production of the Earth. **1633** Marmion *Fine Companion* ii. vi, A sonne of..such pregnance of wit and understanding. **1645** Milton *Colast.* Wks. 1851 IV. 364 In the passage following, I cannot but admire the ripenes, and the pregnance of his native trechery. *c* **1645** Howell *Lett.* (1688) IV. 470, I doubt it not, having discover'd in your Nature so many pregnances and sparkles of innated Honor. **1959** I. Jefferies *Thirteen Days* xi. 171, I rode off early.. into the pleasant pregnance of the day.

¶ ***negative pregnance***, an erroneous rendering of the mod.L. law term ***negativa prægnans*** = ***negative pregnant***: see pregnant *a.*[2] 4 b.

1641 *Termes de la Ley* 209 The Defendant saith that it was not voyd being the temporalties in the kings hands by the death of W. this is a Negative pregnance, for it may be in the kings hands otherwise then by the death of W.

2. = Prägnanz. (But see quot. 1974.)

1948 *Brit. Jrnl. Psychol.* June 181 How little we still know of the details of this process of adaptation, of its conditions and limitations, of its relation to..'the law of pregnance'. **1969** G. N. Seagrim tr. *Piaget's Mechanisms of Perception* vi. 305 Pregnance..is only a coercive effect produced..by a form whose elements..succeed in compensating any deformations which are present. **1974** R. Arnheim *Art & Visual Perception* (rev. ed.) ii. 67 To compound the confusion, translators have rendered the German *Prägnanz* with the English *pregnance*, which means very nearly the opposite.

pregnancy[1] ('prɛgnənsɪ). [f. pregnant *a.*[2]: see -ancy.]

1. a. The condition of being pregnant, or with child or young; gestation. Also *transf.*, with reference to appearance: bigness, swollen shape.

1598 Florio, *Pregnanza*, greatnes with child, pregnancie, a being great with childe or with yoong. **1691** Ray *Creation* ii. (1692) 62 That extraordinary extension that is requisite in the time of their Pregnancy. **1777** Watson *Philip II* (1839) 9 Those appearances, which gave rise to the belief of Mary's pregnancy, were found to be nothing but the approach of a dropsy. **1801** *Med. Jrnl.* V. 132 The phænomena of mania and pregnancy will very constantly impede the progress of pulmonary consumption. **1898** *Westm. Gaz.* 25 Feb. 9/3 When Mr. Lawson Tait unravelled for himself the whole mystery of the broad ligament, the prevention of death in the awful catastrophe of tubal pregnancy was made clear to him. **1950** *Manch. Guardian Weekly* 4 May 3/4 Since Packard abolished its regal proboscis and succumbed to the epidemic pregnancy of current American models [of automobiles].

attrib. **1899** *Allbutt's Syst. Med.* VII. 799 The 'pregnancy kidney',..the chronic form of renal disease dependent on pregnancy. **1906** *Athenæum* 21 July 79/1 Mr. H. A. Rose.. describes in two papers the pregnancy observances in the Punjab, of the Hindu and Mohammedan populations.

b. *fig.* (or in *fig.* context).

a **1529** Skelton *Replycacion* 371 Suche a pregna[n]cy Of heuenly inspyracion In laureate creacyon. **1641** Milton *Ch. Govt.* vi. Wks. 1851 III. 122 Heresie begat heresie with a certaine monstrous haste of pregnancy in her birth. **1754** H. Walpole *Lett.* (1846) III. 84, I have often announced to you a pregnancy of events, which have soon after been still-born.

2. *transf.* **a.** Of the soil, etc.: Fertility, fecundity, fruitfulness; abundance.

1615 G. Sandys *Trav.* i. 21 [Mt. Ida] Famous for the iudgement of Paris, and pregnancie in fountaines. **1759** tr. *Duhamel's Husb.* i. vi. (1762) 13 [The earth] will acquire such a genuine and masculine pregnancy. **1878** *Masque Poets* 48 He knows the utmost secret of the earth, The pregnancy of every blossom's birth.

†**b.** A germinating or vitalizing quality. *Obs. rare.*

1645 Milton *Tetrach.* Wks. 1851 IV. 157 Like the eggs of an Ostrich in the dust; I do but lay them in the sun; their own pregnancies hatch the truth.

†**c.** The state or condition of being impregnated with some substance. *Obs.*

1666 G. Harvey *Morb. Angl.* iv. 31 The blood..through its pregnancy with volatil aculeous salt.

3. a. *fig.* In reference to the mind: Fertility, productiveness, inventiveness, imaginative power; quickness or readiness (*of* wit).

1550 Bale *Eng. Votaries* ii. 49 b, They perceyued in hym great copye of learnynge, pregnancy of wytt. **1597** Shaks. *2 Hen. IV*, i. ii. 192 Pregnancie is made a Tapster, and hath his quicke wit wasted in giuing Recknings. **1631** Weever *Anc. Fun. Mon.* 593 Henry the eight conceiued so good an opinion of his discreet comportement, and ingenious pregnancie, that he..made him his principall Secretary. **1647** Clarendon *Hist. Reb.* vii. §267 He [Sir H. Vane] was chosen to cozen, and deceive a whole Nation..: which he did with notable pregnancy and dexterity. **1712** Addison *Spect.* No. 309 ⁋12 The Diversions of the fallen Angels.. are described with great Pregnancy of Thought. **1833** Coleridge *Table-t.* 23 Oct., I scarcely know a more striking instance of the strength and pregnancy of the Gothic mind.

†**b.** esp. in reference to the young. *Obs.*

1599 *Broughton's Lett.* v. 16 Certaine knowledge of the Archbishops great industrie, from his youth, not pregnancie alone. **1652–62** Heylin *Cosmogr.* i. (1682) 273 A pregnancy of judgment above his years. **1671** Clarendon *Dial.* Tracts (1727) 290 He observes a pregnancy in his apprentice, which he cherishes and instructs. **1734** tr. *Rollin's Anc. Hist.* (1827) III. vii. iii. 306 Such youths as are remarkable for the pregnancy of their parts and goodness of disposition. **1852** R. Williams *Eminent Welshmen* 342 [Thos. Morgan] was.. a poor lad in a farmer's house, near Bridgewater, Somerset. The pregnancy of his genius was conspicuous, and the Rev. John Moore..offered him tuition gratis.

†**c.** *transf.* A youth of promise. *Obs.*

1655 Fuller *Ch. Hist.* vi. 340 To select yearly one, or moe, of the most promising pregnancies out of both Universities, and to breed them beyond the seas. *a* **1661** —— *Worthies, Berks.* (1662) i. 93.

4. a. In reference to speech, words, etc.: Latent fullness of meaning, significance, suggestiveness.

1841 L. Hunt *Seer* ii. (1864) 59 Not that they want the same pregnancy in our language, but because they are neither so abundant nor so musical. *a* **1884** M. Pattison *Mem.* (1885) 63 The political pregnancy of certain words in these had excited my interest.

b. In reference to events, actions, etc.: Latent capacity to produce results, potentiality.

1818 Cruise *Digest* (ed. 2) II. 401 The estate that was in them, was, by the statute, wholly transferred to serve the uses which were *in esse*, with a pregnancy and prospect to the contingent remainders, if they should arise in due time. **1883** Seeley *Expansion Eng.* 144 The true test of the historical importance of events..is their pregnancy..the greatness of the consequences likely to follow from them.

5. Special Comb.: **pregnancy test**, a test to establish whether a woman (or female animal) is pregnant; so ***pregnancy testing***.

1929 *Jrnl. Amer. Med. Assoc.* 25 May 1746/1 Their 'pregnancy test'..is based on the injection of urine into immature white mice. **1962** L. Davidson *Rose of Tibet* 313 Forcible mating begun... Army doctors followed..to make pregnancy tests. **1977** *Private Eye* 13 May 22/2 (Advt.), *Pregnancy Test Service.* Send small sample of urine & fee £3 for *reliable & strictly confidential* results by first class return post (plain sealed cover). **1977** *Times* 21 June 5/8 Scientists yesterday carried out pregnancy tests on a Colorado beetle found at the weekend on a rose bush in a garden at Peacehaven, Sussex. **1938** *Amer. Jrnl. Obstetr. & Gynecol.* XXXV. 362 A review of the most recent work in pregnancy testing is presented. **1971** *Guardian* 15 Apr. 22/4 An instant pregnancy-testing service is to be promoted in chemists' shops.

†**'pregnancy**[2]. *Obs.* [f. pregnant *a.*[1]: see -ancy.] Cogency, force, weight, of an argument; clearness of evidence or proof; a weighty reason.

1649 Milton *Eikon.* iii, All those pregnancies and just motives came to just nothing. **1650** *Vindic. Hammond's Addr.* §10. 3 On purpose..to take off from the clearnesse, and the pregnancie of the probation. *a* **1674** Clarendon *Surv. Leviath.* (1676) 45 Illustrating his definitions by instances, as he often doth with great pregnancy. **1677** Horneck *Gt. Law Consid.* iv. (1704) 106 Whatever pregnancy there may be in the motives a judicious person doth allege.

pregnane ('prɛgneɪn). *Chem.* [ad. G. *pregnan* (A. Butenandt 1930, in *Ber. d. Deut. Chem. Ges.* LXIII. 660), f. *pregnan-diol* pregnanediol (cf. -ane).] A synthetic, crystalline, saturated, tetracyclic hydrocarbon, $C_{21}H_{36}$, which has two stereoisomeric forms and from which a group of steroids, including progesterone and pregnanediol, is formally derived; *spec.* the 5β-isomer.

1932 *Ann. Rep. Progr. Chem.* XXVIII. 237 On oxidation there was formed the saturated diketone, $C_{21}H_{32}O_2$, pregnandione, and by Clemmensen reduction of the latter A. Butenandt, F. Hildebrandt, and H. Brücher have obtained the corresponding hydrocarbon, $C_{21}H_{36}$, pregnane. **1936** *Zeitschr. für Kristallogr.* XCIII. 478 Pregnane forms platy crystals elongated along the *b* axis and showing generally the *c* face only. **1959** I. L. Finar *Org. Chem.* (ed. 2) II. xi. 456 The molecular rotation of any steroid is considered as the sum of the rotation of the fundamental structure (which is the parent hydrocarbon cholestane, androstane, or pregnane) and the rotations contributed by the functional groups. **1960** L. T. Samuels in D. M. Greenberg *Metabolic Pathways* I. xi. 432 The two 21-carbon compounds are 5α-pregnane (allopregnane).. and 5β-pregnane (pregnane). **1971** M. F. Mallette et al. *Introd. Biochem.* xx. 778 Steroids are named as derivatives of the polycyclic hydrocarbons gonane, estrane, androstane, and pregnane.

pregnanediol (ˌprɛgneɪn-, ˌprɛgnən'daɪɒl). *Biochem.* and *Med.* Also **pregnandiol**. [ad. G. *pregnandiol* (A. Butenandt 1930, in *Ber. d. Deut. Chem. Ges.* LXIII. 660), f. L. *prægnan-s* pregnant + G. *di-* di-[2] + *-ol* -ol; cf. pregnane.]

A crystalline steroid containing two hydroxyl groups, $C_{21}H_{36}O_2$, which is a product of the metabolism of progesterone and occurs in the urine during pregnancy.

1930 *Chem. Abstr.* XXIV. 2785 Pregnandiol is related to the sterols and gallic acid. **1934** *Jrnl. Biol. Chem.* CVII. 324 It also seems possible that our compounds may be related to pregnandiol. **1934** *Ann. Rep. Progr. Chem.* XXX. 216 Pregnanediol..is a physiologically inactive compound found in the urine during pregnancy. **1955** *Sci. Amer.* Jan. 55/3 In pregnancy urine there was found an inactive companion of estrone, called pregnanediol. Butenandt proved that pregnanediol was related to cholic acid, a component of bile, by breaking both down to a common product. **1961** *Lancet* 5 Aug. 277/2 The relationship between myometrial progesterone and pregnanediol in the urine is even less clearly defined. **1968** Passmore & Robson *Compan. Med. Stud.* I. xxxi. 13/1 Progesterone is reduced to pregnanediol, which is excreted as sulphate or glucuronide conjugates. **1976** *Path. Ann.* XI. 240 In 1946 Smith, Smith, and Hurwitz reported that stilbestrol administered to pregnant women increased urinary pregnanediol levels.

'pregnant, *a.*[1] *arch.* Also 5 preign-, ? pren-, 5–6 -aunt(e. [a. OF. *preignant* (1572 *pregnante instance*, 15.. *preignantes raisons* Godef. *Compl.*), pr. pple. of *preindre*, earlier *priembre*, *prembre* to press:—L. *premĕre*: cf. '*preignant, pregnant*, pregnant, pithie, ripe, liuelie, forcible, strong; *raisons pregnantes*, plaine, apparent, important, or pressing reasons' (Cotgr. 1611).

The word appears in Eng. much earlier than it is actually cited in Fr., though the vb. had come down in Fr. from L. In Eng. this word ran together in form with the later pregnant *a.*[2], and it is prob. that in later times the two were viewed merely as senses of the same word, and that this was hence apt to be confused with some of the fig. uses of the next. See the quots. under ⁋.]

Of an argument, proof, evidence, reason, etc.: Pressing, urgent, weighty; compelling, cogent, forcible, convincing; hence, clear, obvious.

c **1374** Chaucer *Troylus* iv. 1151 (1179) And þis was hym a preignant [*MS. Gg.* 4. 27 ? prenaunt] argument, That she was forth out of þis world a-gon. **1534** *Act 26 Hen. VIII*, c. 4 §2 Good and pregnaunte euidence ministred to them by persons sworne before the sayde Justiciar. **1552** Huloet, Pregnant token, *auspicium liquidum*. **1601** F. Godwin *Bps. of Eng.* 276 Because my proofes are not pregnant..I will pass him ouer in silence. **1604** Shaks. *Oth.* ii. i. 239. **1621** Bp. Mountagu *Diatribæ* 538 Thus elsewhere, as is pregnant by that other example, formerly alleaged out of Diodorus. **1664** Butler *Hud.* ii. ii. 106, I doubt not, but it will appear With pregnant light. The point is clear. **1718** *Col. Rec. Pennsylv.* III. 40 That the Proofs were so Pregnant and the Crime so black. **1766** Blackstone *Comm.* II. 84 A pregnant proof that these liberties of socage tenure were fragments of Saxon liberty.

⁋The following appear also to belong here, in the preceding range of sense, though they are in some cases susceptible of being explained as pregnant *a.*[2]

1582 N.T. (Rhem.) Pref. a ij, For deciding the doubtes of these daies, more propre and pregnant then the other part not yet printed. **1592** G. Harvey *Four Lett.* iv. Wks. (Grosart) I. 227 Pregnant rules auail much; but visible Examples amount incredibly. **1602** *2nd Pt. Return fr. Parnass.* iv. i. 1546, I will shew you a place in Littleton, which is verye pregnant in this point. **1644** Digby *Nat. Bodies* xxviii. (1658) 307 The whole composure of his body throughout, were pregnant signes of a well tempered mind within. *c* **1680** Beveridge *Serm.* (1729) I. 47 We have as pregnant instances of it in the New Testament as in the Old. **1753** Smollett *Ct. Fathom* (1784) 23/1 This presage..may certainly be justified by manifold occurrences in life: we ourselves have known a very pregnant example.

pregnant ('prɛgnənt), *a.*[2] (*sb.*) Also 5 **-ante**, 5–6 **-aunt, pringnant**, 6 **preignant, -aunt.** [ad. L. *prægnāns, -ānt-em* with child, pregnant; cf. F. *prégnant* (*prégnante* fem. in Rabelais 1550).

The OF. word was *preins, preigne* = It. *pregno*, L. type **prægnus*; but in Eng. *pregnaunt* was used in 1413, and was app. common in the 15th c. in the transf. sense 3. It is remarkable that this should appear so much earlier than the literal sense. L. *prægnāns* has generally been explained as a ppl. form, from *præ* before + root *gna-* of *gnāscor, gnātus* to be born, a derivation favoured by the cognate *prægnātio* a making pregnant or being with child, and late L. *prægnāre* to be pregnant, *prægnātus* pregnant, and *prægnātus* (*u*-stem) pregnancy. On the other hand this does not explain the early collateral form *prægnās, -ātem*, (Plautus), and the connexion with root *gna-* is disputed by some: see Walde *Latein. Etymol. Wörterbuch* s.v.]

I. 1. That has conceived in the womb; with child or with young; gravid. Const. *with*, *of* (the offspring), *by* (the male parent).

1545 Raynold *Byrth Mankynde* ii. vii. 86 Hypocrates sayth: The pregnant [*edd.* 1552–65 pregnaunt, *ed.* 1598 pregnate] Woman whiche hath *Tenasmum* for the most part aborteth. **1656** Blount *Glossogr.*, *Pregnant*.., great with child or young. **1665–6** *Phil. Trans.* I. 388 Pregnant Bitches ..at certain times of their gravidation. **1667** Milton *P.L.* ii.

779 My womb Pregnant by thee, and now excessive grown Prodigious motion felt. **1774** GOLDSM. *Nat. Hist.* (1776) IV. 176 We are not certainly informed how long the females [seals] continue pregnant. *a* **1827** LD. ELDON in *Powell's Devises* (ed. 3) II. 360 The child with which A. M. is now pregnant. **1844** H. H. WILSON *Brit. India* II. 441 The widow of Ladhuba..was pregnant at the time of her husband's assassination. **1899** *Allbutt's Syst. Med.* VIII. 298 Mental changes are common in pregnant women.

b. *fig.* (or in figurative context).

c **1630** MILTON *Passion* 56 And I..Might think th'infection of my sorrows loud, Had got a race of mourners on som pregnant cloud. **1641** HINDE *J. Bruen* xxx. 93 One errour is a pregnant, and faithfull mother of many more. **1764** GOLDSM. *Trav.* 138 The pregnant quarry teem'd with human form. **1873** SYMONDS *Grk. Poets* iii. 87 Cyrnus, this city is pregnant; but I fear that it will bring forth a man to chastise our evil violence.

†**c.** *fig.* Big, laden, swelling; of a sail, bellying.

1648 HERRICK *Hesper., Oberon's Feast* 23 A pure seed-pearle of infant dew, Brought and besweetned in a blew And pregnant violet. *a* **1687** COTTON *Winter* x, With all her pregnant sails atrip.

†**2.** *transf.* **a.** Of a plant or seed: Fertilized, capable of germinating; fruitful. *Obs.*

1669 WORLIDGE *Syst. Agric.* (1681) 329 *Pregnant*, full as a Bud, or Seed, or Kernel ready to sprout. **1759** tr. *Duhamel's Husb.* I. xv. (1762) 80 May prevent the grains being render'd pregnant. **1762–9** FALCONER *Shipwr.* I. 361 There, rich with nectar, melts the pregnant vine.

†**b.** Of the soil, etc.: Fertile, fruitful; prolific, teeming. Const. *with*. *Obs.*

1615 G. SANDYS *Trav.* II. 97 The fat and pregnant slime which it [the Nile] leaueth behind it. **1715** tr. *Pancirollus' Rerum Mem.* I. IV. xix. 231 An Isle..call'd Marmora, very pregnant with Metals. **1762–9** FALCONER *Shipwr.* II. 161 The clouds, with ruin pregnant, now impend. **1789** MRS. PIOZZI *Journ. France* II. 68 This horrible volcano..seems pregnant with wonders. **1796** MORSE *Amer. Geog.* I. 614 Virginia is the most pregnant with minerals and fossils of any state in the Union.

II. In various mental or non-physical uses.

3. a. Of a person or his mind: Teeming with ideas, fertile, imaginative, inventive, resourceful, ready. Const. *of*, *in*, or *to* with *inf.* *arch.* or *Obs.*

1413 *Pilgr. Sowle* (Caxton 1483) III. x. 57 Adam was pregnaunt of vnrightwisnesse and sool disbeysaunte. **1432–50** tr. *Higden* (Rolls) III. 467 Þe mynde of man is pregnante in a feire day, and feynte in a clowdy day. **1513** BRADSHAW *St. Werburge* II. 1204 Famous in victorye, pregnant in wysdome. *Ibid.* 2024 Fyrst to maister Chaucer, and Ludgate sentencious, Also to preignaunt Barkley, nowe beyng religious, To inuentiue Skelton and poet laureate. *a* **1591** H. SMITH *Serm.* (1637) 509 Very pregnant to devise nevv shifts to keep in their almes. **1624** R. SKYNNER in *Ussher's Lett.* (1686) 352 The Jews have always been so ready and pregnant in the Scriptures, as that they need not cite the Book, Chapter, or Verse. **1632** LITHGOW *Trav.* VIII. 371 The exquisit ingeniosity of their best styles, and pregnant inuention. **1711** STEELE *Spect.* No. 136 ¶4 A Person of so pregnant a Fancy, that he cannot be contented with ordinary Occurrences. **1853** M. ARNOLD *Scholar Gypsy* iv. 34 The story of that Oxford scholar poor Of pregnant parts and quick inventive brain.

b. in *pregnant wit*, common in 16–17th c. *arch.*

1494 FABYAN *Chron.* VII. 652 A marchaunt, of pregnaunt wytte, and of good maner and speche. **1519** *Interl. Four Elem.* in Hazl. *Dodsley* I. 7 Divers pregnant wits be in this land. **1549** CHALONER *Erasmus on Folly* M ij, Who is he so pregnant witted that might grope out these misteries? [**1572** *Satir. Poems Reform.* xxx. 71 Pringnant of wit, of policie but peir. **1589** NASHE *Pref. Greene's Menaphon* (Arb.) 17 His pregnant dexteritie of wit.] **1634** HEYWOOD *Maidenhead Lost* I. Wks. 1874 IV. 106 Come, come, I know you haue a pregnant wit. *c* **1660** SOUTH *Serm., John vii.* 17 (1715) I. 241 Nor did ever the most pregnant Wit in the World bring forth any Thing great,..without some Pain and Travail.

†**c.** *esp.* of young persons, or their faculties: Apt to conceive or apprehend, quick-witted, of unusual capacity, full of promise, promising. *Obs.*

1557 *Order of Hospitalls* C viij, Suche of the children as be pregnant and very apt to learninge. **1612** DRAYTON *Polyolb.* vi. 223 Her apt and pregnant Youth sent hither yeere by yeere, Instructed in our Rites with most religious feare. **1635** BRATHWAIT *Arcad. Pr.* II. 180 Whom we no lesse truly than properly call the Muses minion, the conceits pregnantest darling. *a* **1661** FULLER *Worthies* (1662) I. 239 She was a very pregnant Lady above her age, and died in her infancy when not full four years old. **1707** CHAMBERLAYNE *Pres. St. Eng.* III. 425 Some of the most pregnant Lads are so good Proficients..that they are sent to the University.

†**d.** Apt to receive or be influenced; receptive; disposed, inclined, ready. *Obs.* (chiefly in Shaks.).

1601 SHAKS. *Twel. N.* III. i. 100 My matter hath no voice, Lady, but to your owne most pregnant and vouchsafed eare. **1602** —— *Ham.* III. ii. 66 And crooke the pregnant Hindges of the knee. **1608** —— *Per.* IV. Prol. 44 And cursed Dioniza hath The pregnant instrument of wrath Prest for this blow. **1628** DONNE *Serm.* xxix. (1640) 290 Christ places the Comfort of this Comforter, the Holy Ghost, in this, that he shall worke upon that pregnant faculty, the Memory.

†**e.** Of hearing: Keen, sharp, acute. *Obs. rare.*

1607 TOPSELL *Four-f. Beasts* (1658) 209 Their hearing is most pregnant; for the Egyptians when they signifie hearing, picture a Hare; and for this cause we have shewed you already that their ears are long like horns.

4. Of words, symbolic acts, etc.: Full of meaning, highly significant; containing a hidden sense, implying more than is obvious, suggestive; also, †full *of*, replete *with* (something significant).

c **1450** *Pol. Poems* (Rolls) II. 227 Discusse it with diligens, and telle iff hit be, This pagent is pringnant, sir Pilat, pardé. *c* **1480** HENRYSON *Test. Cres.* 270 In breif sermone ane pregnant sentence wryte. *a* **1626** BACON *Confess. Faith* Wks. 1879 I. 338/2 The continual history of the old world, and church of the Jews..is..pregnant of a perpetual allegory and shadow of the work of the redemption to follow. **1659** PEARSON *Creed* (1839) 104 The best of the Latins thought the Greek word so pregnant and comprehensive, that the Latin tongue had no single word able to express it. *a* **1661** FULLER *Worthies* (1662) I. 133 His Epithetes were pregnant with Metaphors. **1838–9** HALLAM *Hist. Lit.* III. III. vii. §41. 378 The style is what was called pregnant, leaving much to be filled up by the reader's reflection. **1860** WESTCOTT *Introd. Study Gosp.* vi. (ed. 5) 318 St. Mark compresses into this one pregnant sentence the central lesson of the trial. **1879** FARRAR *St. Paul* II. 188 It is impossible I think in fewer words to give the full interpretation of this pregnant thesis.

b. Phrases.

pregnant construction, in *Gram.* or *Rhet.*, a construction in which more is implied than the words express. ***pregnant negative***, in Logic [L. *propositio categorica negativa prægnans* in Paulus Nicolettus Venetus, 15th c., Prantl IV. 129, note 545]: see quot. 1890. ***negative pregnant***, in *Law*, a negative implying or involving an affirmative.

1607 COWELL *Interpr.*, *Negatiue pregnant*,..is a negatiue implying also an affirmatiue. As if a man being impleaded, to haue done a thing vpon such a day, or in such a place, denyeth that he did it *modo & forma declarata*: which implyeth neuer the lesse, that in some sort he did it. **1657** *Burton's Diary* (1828) II. 265 You put a negative pregnant upon a man, to say that sitting at the door is more profane than standing. **1818** CRUISE *Digest* (ed. 2) IV. 552 This general denial amounts only to a denial of personal notice to herself, and is a kind of negative pregnant. **1890** *Cent. Dict.* s.v., *Pregnant negative*, a negative proposition affected by a reduplicative, exceptive, or other expression requiring special treatment in logic: thus, 'no man, *qua* man, ever sleeps' is a pregnant negative.

5. Fertile or fruitful in results; big *with* consequences; containing important issues; momentous.

1591 FLORIO *2nd Fruites* Ep. Ded. 1 In this stirring time and pregnant prime of inuention when euerie bramble is fruitfull. *a* **1674** CLARENDON *Surv. Leviath.* (1676) 255 Error is naturally pregnant, and the more desperate it is, the more fruitful. **1783** GOUV. MORRIS in Sparks *Life & Writ.* (1832) I. 252 A critical business,..pregnant with dangerous consequences. **1820** COMBE *Consol.* (Chandos) 160 They hold a pregnant lie well told, Is worth at least its weight in gold.

†**b.** Resultant, produced. *Obs. nonce-use.*

1596 BACON *Max. & Use Com. Law* I. viii. (1636) 34 Any accessary before the fact is subject to all the contingencies pregnant of the fact, if they be pursuances of the same fact.

B. as *sb.* A pregnant woman. *rare.*

1654 WHITLOCK *Zootomia* 284 Humane Policy..forbeareth execution of a condemned Pregnant (or woman with Child). **1864** in WEBSTER [citing Dunglison, who, however, in his entry app. intends the adj.]; and in mod. Dicts.

Hence †**'pregnant** *v. trans.*, to render pregnant.

1652 SPARKE *Prim. Devot.* (1660) 407 Pray'r..Sometime descending, Pregnanteth the Womb Of Teeming Earth.

†**'pregnantly**, *adv.*[1] *Obs.* [f. PREGNANT *a.*[1] + -LY[2].] Of argument, proof, etc.: Cogently, forcibly, clearly.

c **1440** CAPGRAVE *Life St. Kath.* II. 1237 And voyd ȝour resoun well & pregnantly. **1604** T. WRIGHT *Passions* IV. ii. §1. 125 Play pregnantly prooueth passions. **1654–66** EARL ORRERY *Parthen.* (1676) 24 What more pregnantly confirm'd me he was the real Artabazus. **1765** LAW tr. *Behmen's Myst. Magnum* xliii. (1772) 254 We here see very fully and pregnantly.

'pregnantly, *adv.*[2] [f. PREGNANT *a.*[2] + -LY[2].] In a pregnant manner or state.

1. 'Fruitfully' (Johnson 1755).

b. In a form capable of development. *rare.*

1884 J. TAIT *Mind in Matter* (1892) 58 It is reiterated that all forms of life existed pregnantly in the first germs.

2. In a manner implying more than is expressed; significantly; suggestively.

1879 WHITNEY *Sanskrit Gram.* 359 Often, the *iti* is used more pregnantly. **1897** *New Eng. Dict.* III. 65/3 *A deal* is used pregnantly for *a good* or *great deal*.

†**'pregnantness.** *Obs. rare*$^{-0}$. [f. PREGNANT *a.*[1] and [2] + -NESS.] The quality of being pregnant: = PREGNANCY[1] and [2].

1727 BAILEY vol. II, *Pregnantness*, a being great with Child; also (spoken of Evidence or Proof) Strength; also (of Invention, Wit, etc.) Ripeness, Quickness.

†**'pregnate**, *a.* *Obs. rare*$^{-1}$. [ad. late L. *prægnātus* (5th cent.), pa. pple. of *prægnāre* to be pregnant.] = PREGNANT *a.*[2] 1.

1598 [see PREGNANT *a.*[2] 1, quot. 1545].

†**'pregnate**, *v.* *Obs. rare*$^{-1}$. [f. ppl. stem of L. *prægnāre*: see prec.] *intr.* Of soil: To become fertile, to promote germination or growth.

1706 LONDON & WISE *Retir'd Gard'ner* I. i. 6 Backward soils, which are long a pregnating in the Spring.

†**preg'nation.** *Obs. rare*$^{-0}$. [ad. L. *prægnātiōn-em*: see PREGNANT *a.*[2]] = PREGNANCY[1].

1623 COCKERAM, *Pregnation*, being great with childe.

†**preg'natress.** *Obs. rare*$^{-1}$. [f. as fem. of L. **pregnātor* (not found) + -ESS[1].] A (feminine) agent or power that generates or brings to birth.

1765 LAW tr. *Behmen's Myst. Magnum* vi. (1772) 26 For the Pregnatress [Ger. *Gebährerin*] of Time is a Model or Plat-form of the Eternal Pregnatress.

pregnenolone (prɛg'niːnələʊn). *Biochem.* and *Med.* [ad. G. *pregnenolon* (Butenandt & Westphal 1934, in *Ber. d. Deut. Chem. Ges.* LXVII. 2085), f. *pregn-an* PREGNANE + *-en* -ENE + *-ol* -OL + *-on* -ONE.] A synthetic steroid, $C_{21}H_{32}O_2$, which is a reduced derivative of progesterone and was formerly used in the treatment of rheumatoid arthritis.

1936 *Chem. Abstr.* XXX. 3036 Similar mixts. of III and I or III and pregnenolone (IV) met with in the prepn. of the hormone from stigmasterol can be sepd. in the same manner. **1955** *Jrnl. Amer. Med. Assoc.* 21 May 166/1 All the patients had received, at one time or another, gold salts, pregnenolone, antibiotics, [etc.]..that produced, at the most, only palliative relief. **1964** E. J. W. BARRINGTON *Hormones & Evolution* ii. 54 In this way cholesterol is thought to be transformed into progesterone, through the intermediary pregnenolone, by partial degradation of its side chain. **1967** *Martindale's Extra Pharmacopoeia* (ed. 25) 1543/2 Pregnenolone and pregnenolone acetate have been used in the treatment of rheumatoid arthritis..but their value has not been substantiated.

pregnotarie, -y, variants of PRENOTARY *Obs.*

prego, var. PREGGO *a.*

pre-'graduate, *a.* [f. PRE- B. 1, after POST-GRADUATE *a.* (*sb.*)] = UNDERGRADUATE *a.*

1937 *Discovery* Sept. p. lxxxi/1 (Advt.), The Pregraduate courses extend over three or four years and lead up to an Associateship of one of the colleges, and a B.Sc. Degree of the University of London. **1977** *Proc. R. Soc. Med.* LXX. 377/1 The knowledge and skills required to practise independently were expanding the pre-graduate curriculum to bursting point.

pre-grammar, -grammatical: see PRE- B. 1.

†**pre'grand, præ'grand**, *a.* *Obs. rare*$^{-1}$. [ad. L. *prægrand-is* very large: see PRE- A. 6 and GRAND *a.*] Extraordinarily large.

1657 TOMLINSON *Renou's Disp.* 450 Not unlike a she-goat with a prægrand body.

†**'pregravate**, *v.* *Obs. rare.* Also præ-. [f. ppl. stem of L. *prægravāre* to press heavily upon (f. *præ*, PRE- A. 5 + *gravāre* to weigh down, f. *gravis* heavy).] *trans.* To weigh down, overweight.

1652 BP. HALL *Invis. World* II. §1 The clog which the body brings with it cannot but pregravate and trouble the soul in all her performances. **1653** SCLATER *Fun. Serm.* 25 *Sept.* (1654) 12 The Soule (which is here clogg'd, and drossy, and much prægravated by the Body, subject to corruption).

Hence †**pregra'vation** *Obs. rare*$^{-0}$: see quot.

1623 COCKERAM, *Pregrauation*, great griefe.

†**pre'gravitate, præ-**, *v.* *Obs. rare.* [PRE- A. 5.] *intr.* To gravitate more (than something else).

1685 BOYLE *Enq. Notion Nat.* vi. 189 Water does gravitate in Water, as well as out of it, though indeed it does not prægravitate, because 'tis Counter-ballanc'd by an equal weight of Collateral Water, which keeps it from descending. **1722** QUINCY *Lex. Physico-Med.* (ed. 2) 187/1 Those things which do not pre-gravitate in the Air, Water, &c. the Vulgar take to have no Gravity.

†**pre'gredience.** *Obs. rare*$^{-1}$. [ad. L. type **prægredientia*, f. *prægredī*, f. *præ*, PRE- A. 1 + *gradī* to step, go.] A going before or in front.

1595 CHAPMAN *Ovid's Banq. Sence* C ij, But as the Vnicorns pregredience To venomd Pooles, doth purdge them with his horne, And after him the desarts Residence May safely drinke.

†**pre'gression.** *Obs. rare.* [ad. L. *prægressiōn-em* a going before, n. of action f. *prægredī*: see prec.] Going before, antecedence, precedence.

1623 COCKERAM, *Pregression*, a going before. **1651** BIGGS *New Disp.* ¶ 173 Medicines do not need the prægression of our heat. **1656** BLOUNT *Glossogr.*, *Pregression*,..a going before, an out-going or over-passing, a preventing.

pre-grind: see PRE- A. 1.

†**pre'gust**, *v.* *Obs. rare*$^{-0}$. [ad. L. *prægustāre* to taste before: see PRE- A. 1 and GUST *v.*[1]] To taste before. So (*nonce-wds.*) †**pre'gustant** *a.*, tasting beforehand; †**pre'gustic** = PREGUSTATOR.

1623 COCKERAM, *Pregust*, to taste before. **1824** SYD. SMITH *Wks.* (1859) II. 37/2 We must tie those prægustant punishers down by one question. **1694** MOTTEUX *Rabelais* v. xx, The Leprous were brought in by her Abstractors, Spodizators, Masticators, Pregustics [F. *Pregustes*]..and other Officers, for whom I want names.

†**pregu'station.** *Obs.* Also præ-. [n. of action f. L. *prægustāre*: see prec. So obs. F. *prégustation* (Godef.).] A tasting before, a foretaste.

1656 BLOUNT *Glossogr.*, *Pregustation*.., a tasting or assaying before. *a* **1658** A. FARINGDON *Serm.* (1674) III. 398 The Child, when he is hungry, desires milk, because he hath a kind of prægustation of milk in his very nature. **1667** WATERHOUSE *Fire Lond.* 93 Over early pregustation of Woe. **1678** A. WALKER *Character Lady Warwick* 117 In the actual exercise of prayer, by which she so often anticipated Heaven by pregustation.

†**pregu'stator.** *Obs. rare.* In 7 præ-. [a. L. *prægustātor*, agent-n. f. *prægustāre* (see PREGUST) = F. *prégustateur*.] One whose function is to taste meats and drinks before serving them.

1694 MOTTEUX *Rabelais* v. xxiii, When her Prægustators [F. *Pregustes*] had tasted the meat, her Masticators..chew'd it.

‖**prehallux, præ-** (priː'hæləks). *Anat.* and *Zool.* [mod.L., f. *præ*, PRE- B. 3 + HALLUX. Named 1885 by Bardeleben of Jena.] A rudimentary structure, osseous or cartilaginous, found on the inner side of the tarsus of some Mammalia, Reptilia, and Batrachia, and supposed to represent an additional digit.

1888 *Proc. Zool. Soc. Lond.* 150 That the pre-hallux takes on certain of the essential relationships of a digit is beyond dispute. That it really represents one is another question. **1889** *Athenæum* 18 May 635/3 Prof. Bardeleben [sent a paper] on the præpollex and præhallux of the mammalian skeleton... He also stated that he had discovered vestiges of the præhallux and præpollex in certain Reptilia. **1891** FLOWER & LYDEKKER *Mammalia* ii. 49 In the posterior limb the tibial sesamoid, and a fibular ossification corresponding to the pisiform, are regarded as representing a prehallux and a postminimus.

‖**prehalteres** (priː'hæltəriːz), *sb. pl. Entom.* [mod.L., f. PRE- B. 3 + HALTERES.] A pair of small membranous scales in front of the halteres of dipterous insects; usually called *tegulæ*.

1840 [see *pseudhalteres* s.v. PSEUDO- 2]. **1890** in *Cent. Dict.*

pre-Han: see PRE- B. 1 a.

pre'harvest, *a.* [PRE- B. 2.] Occurring before a crop is ready to be gathered.

1934 in WEBSTER. **1948** *New Biol.* V. 62 Some varieties of apple, Beauty of Bath for example, tend to fall before they are fully ripe or of good eating quality. This is known as preharvest fruit drop. **1951** [see HORMONE 2]. **1971** T. T. KOZLOWSKI *Growth & Devel. Trees* II. viii. 359 In apple, three normal periods of fruit drop occur... These include 'early drop'..and the preharvest drop.

pre-hearing: see PRE- A. 2.

pre'heat, *v.* [PRE- A. 1.] *trans.* To heat prior to use or to some other treatment.

1898 *Engineering Mag.* XVI. 245 The gas is usually not preheated, but the gas producers are set close to the furnace, so that the initial heat..is not lost. **1937** *Discovery* May 155/1 The tool having been evenly preheated is transferred to the high heat chamber. **1958** LAMBERMONT & PIRIE *Helicopters & Autogyros* 201 The ram-jets are run on propane, which is preheated before being ducted to them. **1958** *Times* 27 Oct. 11/5 Preheat the oven to 420 deg. F. (Regulo 7) and lay the hare directly on the grid. **1975** *Nature* 2 Oct. 368/2 The mixtures were preheated by an external source.

Hence **pre'heated** *ppl. a.*, **pre'heating** *vbl. sb.* and *ppl. a.*; also **pre'heater**, a device for preheating.

1898 *Engineering Mag.* XVI. 245 This method of preheating may follow either the regenerative or the recuperative system. **1910** *Encycl. Brit.* I. 445/1 What is called a 'preheater' is used to warm up the compressed air before it enters in the motor cylinder. **1911** A. REYNOLDS tr. *Dichmann's Basic Open-Hearth Steel Process* vii. 59 The second way of producing a steam-air gas with high hydrogen content, consists in the employment of superheated steam, or preheated air supply. **1931** HOFFERT & CLAXTON *Motor Benzole* viii. 221 An efficient preheater should be capable of raising the maximum flow of oil from the temperature at which it leaves the heat-exchange system to a temperature of at least 135°C. **1952** FUCHS & BRADLEY *Welding Pract.* II. iii. 65 Preheating of the parts being welded is always a help towards crack prevention. **1960** *Farmer & Stockbreeder* 15 Mar. (Suppl.) 11/1 Put the mixture into a greased and floured 6in cake tin and bake in a pre-heated fairly hot oven ..for 1 hour. **1967** KARCH & BUBER *Offset Processes* ii. 20 After one minute in an open preheater press, a reinforcement mat and backing sheet are added. Then the entire assembly is heated and later bonded. **1976** *Woman's Weekly* 6 Nov. 74/1 (Advt.), In this article she looks at preheating underblankets.

preheminence, -ent, obs. ff. PRE-EMINENCE, -EMINENT.

pre-hemiplegic: see PRE- B. 1.

pre'hend, *v.* [ad. L. *prehend-ĕre* to grasp, seize, catch, for earlier *præhendĕre* (Plaut.), f. *præ*, PRE- + **handĕre*, cognate with Gr. χανδάν-ειν to take in, hold. Sometimes perh. aphetic f. APPREHEND.] †**a.** *trans.* To seize, catch, apprehend. *Obs. rare.*

15.. STOW in *Pol. Rel. & L. Poems* (1866) Pref. 15 *note*, They were greatly blamed that prehended hym and comitted hym. *a* **1627** MIDDLETON *Mayor of Quinborough* v. i, Is not that Rebel Oliver, that Traytor to my year, Prehended yet? **1831** T. HOPE *Ess. Origin Man* II. 76 Vegetables and animals..for pursuing, prehending, and appropriating to themselves the substances they want for their further support,..want new external organs.

b. *Philos.* To apprehend with or without conscious formulation of the perceived object; to interact in time and space with an object or event. Cf. PREHENSION 3 b. Hence **pre'hended, pre'hending** *ppl. adjs.*

1925 A. N. WHITEHEAD *Sci. & Mod. World* (1926) vi. 153 Then the enduring pattern is a pattern of aspects within the complete pattern prehended into the unity of A. **1927** AUDEN & DAY-LEWIS in *Oxf. Poetry* p. vi, Emotion is no longer necessarily to be analysed by 'recollection in tranquillity': it is to be prehended emotionally and intellectually at once. **1929** A. N. WHITEHEAD *Process & Reality* 56 The essence of an actual entity consists solely in the fact that it is a prehending thing. **1933** —— *Adventures of Ideas* xiv. 268 There are the physical and the mental poles, and there are the objects prehended and the subjective forms of the prehensions. **1938** C. D. BROAD *Exam. McTaggart's Philos.* II. I. 4 When a person has repeatedly prehended certain particulars as having a certain characteristic *C* he may 'form an idea of' that characteristic. **1945** R. G. COLLINGWOOD *Idea of Nature* III. iii. 173 An iron filing prehends the magnetic field in which it lies, that is it converts that field into a mode of its own behaviour, responds to it. *Ibid.* 174 A plant prehends the sunlight. **1947** *Mind* LVI. 97 In certain circumstances, when a person 'sees' a physical object, he visually prehends that physical object... In other cases what he visually prehends is, not the physical object.., but a particular which stands in a certain relation to the visum. **1959** W. A. CHRISTIAN *Interpretation of Whitehead's Metaphysics* i. 12 It has a subject (the prehending actual entity), an object or datum that is prehended, and a subjective form. **1971** J. B. COBB in D. Brown et al. *Process Philos. & Christian Thought* xii. 220 The new occasion prehends all the entities in its past.

†**prehen'sation.** *Obs. rare.* [agent-n. f. L. *prehensāre* (*prensāre*) to seize, detain, solicit (freq. of *prehendĕre*): see prec. and cf. PRENSATION.] (?) Solicitation, suing.

1649 C. WALKER *Hist. Independ.* II. 145 The Domestick use of their Nomenclators, their Prehensations, Invitations, Clientships.

prehensible (prɪ'hɛnsɪb(ə)l), *a. rare.* [f. L. *prehens-*, ppl. stem of *prehend-ĕre* (see PREHEND) + -IBLE. So F. *préhensible*.] Capable of being grasped.

a **1832** BENTHAM *Ess. Lang.* Wks. 1843 VIII. 315 This verbal noun..which in this its separate state, becomes the name of a sort of fictitious entity, of a sort of fictitious body or substance, is, in this state, rendered more prehensible. **1947** *Mind* LVI. 101 This line has parts of two different kinds, visually prehensible and not visually prehensible.

prehensile (prɪ'hɛnsɪl, -saɪl), *a.* [a. F. *préhensile* (Buffon), f. as prec. + *-ile*, -ILE.] **a.** Capable of prehension; having the capacity of grasping or laying hold of anything. Also *fig.*

1781-5 SMELLIE tr. *Buffon's Nat. Hist.* (1791) VIII. 185 By..his prehensile tail, he [the Coaita] is easily distinguished from the monkeys. **1854** OWEN *Skel. & Teeth* (1855) 24 Not any of the limbs of fishes are prehensile. **1871** DARWIN *Desc. Man* I. iv. 142 With some savages..the foot has not altogether lost its prehensile power. **1945** R. HARGREAVES *Enemy at Gate* 23 Hungry, prehensile soldiers of fortune. **1959** *Listener* 15 Oct. 633/1 A prehensile readability. **1966** G. GREENE in *New Statesman* 25 Feb. 254/2 Martha was the plump and prehensile wife of a German correspondent who was suspected of strong Nazi sympathies. She was said to look after men's needs with a simple and indiscriminate fervour. **1976** *Time* 27 Dec. 52/3 Retailers have been eying Kong's potential with prehensile enthusiasm.

b. *Comb.*, as ***prehensile-lipped, -tailed.***

1822-34 *Good's Study Med.* (ed. 4) III. 13 M. Cuvier suspects that it [the sense of touch in the tail] has a similar existence in all the prehensile-tailed mammals. **1899** F. V. KIRBY *Sport E.C. Africa* xii. 133 The prehensile-lipped rhinoceros. **1905** *Westm. Gaz.* 18 Sept. 4/1 Prehensile-tailed creatures are, as a rule, restricted to the New World.

prehensility (priːhɛn'sɪlɪtɪ). [f. prec. + -ITY.] The quality of being prehensile, prehensiveness.

1856 EMERSON *Eng. Traits* vi. 115 Their statesmen..have invented many fine phrases to cover this slowness of perception and prehensility of tail. **1869** GILLMORE *Figuier's Reptiles* ii. 40 In..the Vipers, it [the tail] is short and without any prehensility.

prehension (prɪ'hɛnʃən). [ad. L. *prehensiōn-em* seizing, apprehending, n. of action f. *prehendĕre* (see PREHEND). So F. *préhension* (*prehencion* c 1400 in Godef.).]

1. a. The action of taking hold (physically); grasping, seizing. Chiefly *Zool.*

1828 WEBSTER, *Prehension*, a taking hold; a seizing; as with the hand or other limb. *Lawrence.* **1833** SIR C. BELL *Hand* (1834) 159 The bill of the bird..is the organ of prehension and of touch. **1884** H. SPENCER in *Contemp. Rev.* July 39 Food cannot be got without powers of prehension.

b. A taking possession, occupation, seizure. *rare.*

1880 SIR J. B. PHEAR *Aryan Vill. in India* Introd. 15 The prehension and clearing of a definite tract of ground, and.. arrangements for tilling..it.

†**2.** Seizure or arrest in the name of justice or authority; apprehension. *Obs.*

1534 *Act 26 Hen. VIII*, c. 6 §9 The nexte sessions..to be holden after the prehension or attachement of such offendour. **1581** LAMBARDE *Eiren.* I. xii. (1588) 66 The ancient Conseruator of the Peace, who had onely Coertion or Prehension in a few cases. **1802** BENTHAM *Princ. Judicial Procedure* xxii. §1 Prehension, applied to things, will be with reference to—1. A thing immoveable... 2. A thing moveable... 3. A stock of things moveable.

3. a. Grasping with the mind; mental apprehension.

1836 J. ABBOTT *Way to do Good* ix. 294 There is something in man which enables him to seize, as it were, by direct prehension, what is true and right when it is distinctly presented to him. **1899** *Blackw. Mag.* Sept. 375/2 Mr. Churchill's instinctive prehension of her claims to fashionable distinction.

b. *Philos.* Apprehension of something perceived that may or may not involve cognition; the interaction that exists between a subject and an entity or event.

1925 A. N. WHITEHEAD *Sci. & Mod. World* (1926) iv. 97 The word 'perceive' is, in our common usage, shot through and through with the notion of cognitive apprehension. So is the word 'apprehension', even with the adjective cognitive omitted. I will use the word 'prehension' for uncognitive apprehension: by this I mean apprehension which may or may not be cognitive. **1931** A. WOLF in W. Rose *Outl. Mod. Knowl.* xiii. 584 The 'interlockings' of actual occasions are called 'prehensions', and are conceived causally. Each actual occasion is generated from its prehensions of preceding occasions, and is prehended by succeeding occasions. **1938** C. D. BROAD *Exam. McTaggart's Philos.* II. I. 4, I propose to substitute the artificial term *Prehension* for 'perception' when used in McTaggart's extended sense. I think that this word avoids the objections to 'perception' and 'acquaintance', which I have pointed out. **1945** R. G. COLLINGWOOD *Idea of Nature* III. iii. 173 Everything enjoys what he calls 'prehensions', that is to say, somehow absorbs what is outside itself into its own being. **1959** W. A. CHRISTIAN *Interpretation of Whitehead's Metaphysics* i. 12 A prehension is an operation in which an actual entity 'grasps' some other entity (actual or nonactual) and makes that entity an object of its experience. **1964** I. LECLERC in Reese & Freeman *Process & Divinity* 137 Form is the object of 'conceptual prehension', not of 'physical prehension'. **1971** V. LOWE in D. Brown et al. *Process Philos. & Christian Thought* i. 7 A prehension is not so much a relation as a relating, or transition, which carries the object into the makeup of the subject.

prehensive (prɪ'hɛnsɪv), *a.* [f. L. *prehens-*, ppl. stem of *prehendĕre* (see PREHEND) + -IVE.] Capable of seizing or laying hold; = PREHENSILE; pertaining to or involving prehension, esp. in sense 3 b. Also *fig.* Hence **pre'hensiveness.**

1857 I. TAYLOR *World of Mind* xxiv. §885 Conscious of its want of a prehensive limb. **1886** J. SULLY *Teacher's Handbk. Psychol.* viii. 132 The discrimination and identification of the impression... This constitutes the first step in the process of perception. It may be marked off as the presentative or *prehensive* element. **1897** A. LANG in *Daily News* 27 Sept. 6/5 At the Raj Kumar College..'we had a higher ideal of fielding than most English schools', perhaps a greater agility and prehensiveness. **1925** A. N. WHITEHEAD *Sci. & Mod. World* (1926) iv. 90 Things are separated by space, and are separated by time: but they are also together in space, and together in time, even if they be not contemporaneous. I will call their characters the '*separative*' and the '*prehensive*' characters of space-time. *Ibid.* 98 For Berkeley's *mind*, I substitute a process of prehensive unification. **1932** D. EMMET *Whitehead's Philos. of Organism* iv. 87 Actual entities are..described as 'prehensive occasions', that is to say, events or concrete facts of becoming. **1937** J. R. FIRTH *Tongues of Men* iii. 37 The very use of likeness and differences and the habitual comparison of ordered series of words assume the principle of 'inter-related prehensiveness' which may be called implication. **1941** P. HUGHES in P. A. Schilpp *Philos. A. N. Whitehead* vi. 278 This activity of perceptual adaptation is a concrescence of prehensive processes, each of which has the quality of the act as a whole. **1966** *Punch* 13 Apr. 528/2, I shall propose to Longman to accept a work on the originality of Locke, Hobbes, and Hume, which well be as *pioneer* to a more prehensive work. **1974** *Nature* 6 Dec. 514/3 Limbless thalidomide children who carry out reaching and prehensive tasks with their mouths and teeth.

prehensor (prɪ'hɛnsə(r)). [f. as PREHENSIVE *a.* + -OR 2.] One who or that which lays hold of anything.

1829 BENTHAM *Justice & Cod. Petit.* 179 Distinguished by some such name as *prehensors* or *arrestors*. **1830** —— *Equity Disp. Court Prop.* III. vii. 41 Three different sorts of functionaries—Prehensors, Messengers, and Consignees—for carrying on the necessary intercourse, between the judge, on the one part, and things and persons, on the other.

prehensorial (priːhən'sɔərɪəl), *a.* [f. PREHENSORI(UM + -AL[1].] = PREHENSORY *a.*

1903 *Proc. Zool. Soc.* I. 51 One cannot but wonder how the spider maintains a secure hold back downwards, especially when the powerful prehensorial legs of the first and second pairs are released.

‖**prehen'sorium.** *Zool.* [mod.L., f. *prehensor*: see -ORIUM.] An apparatus or arrangement of parts adapted for prehension; *spec.* applied to a formation of the legs in some spiders and insects.

1890 in *Cent. Dict.*

prehensory (prɪ'hɛnsərɪ), *a. rare.* [ad. mod.L. *prehensōri-us*, f. as prec.: see -ORY[2].] Adapted for seizing or laying hold: = PREHENSIVE.

1826 KIRBY & SPENCE *Entomol.* III. xxxi. 240 The pupæ [of Libellulina] are furnished with a prehensory mask. **1835** KIRBY *Hab. & Inst. Anim.* II. xiii. 10 The prehensory organs or arms.

preheterocercal (priːhɛtərəʊ'sɜːkəl), *a. Ichth.* [PRE- B. 1.] Preceding the heterocercal: a supposed stage in the development of the tail in fishes.

1900 *Nature* 20 Sept. 506/1 The supposition that it represents the original 'protocercal' or preheterocercal stage.

pre-hexameral, -Hispanic: see PRE- B. 1.

prehistorian (priːhɪˈstɔərɪən). [f. as next, after *historian*.] One who studies the remains, customs, and conditions of prehistoric times.

1893 *Amer. Cath. Q. Rev.* Oct. 728 This has been either ignored or rejected..by the new school of prehistorians. **1902** *Nation* (N.Y.) 20 Nov. 398/1 Prehistorians had long known of a gentleman..who had long excavated on his own responsibility. **1936** *Discovery* Jan. 23/1 Its interest and importance are of equal..moment to prehistorian, archaeologist, and the student of religious beliefs. **1947** [see *distribution map* s.v. DISTRIBUTION 9]. **1952** G. SARTON *Hist. Sci.* I. i. 6 Prehistorians have proved beyond doubt the existence of sophisticated cultures at very early times in many places. **1970** *Nature* 12 Dec. 1019/2 The very early carbon-14 dates..for the megalithic tombs of Brittany..have been regarded suspiciously by prehistorians. **1975** *Sci. Amer.* Feb. 41/3 A major French archaeological discovery that was declared fraudulent by many prehistorians in the 1920's has now regained credibility as a result of dating studies conducted at three independent laboratories. **1980** *Early Music* Jan. 85/1 Various groups of specialists: historians of theatre-décor, pre-historians of opera, analysts of court spectacle, experts on renaissance instruments.

prehistoric (priːhɪˈstɒrɪk), *a.* [f. PRE- B. 1 + HISTORIC *a.* So F. *préhistorique*.] **a.** Of, belonging to, or existing in the period antecedent to history, or to the first historical accounts of a people. ***prehistoric archæology***: the archæology of the prehistoric period.

1851 D. WILSON (*title*) The Archæology and Prehistoric Annals of Scotland. *Ibid.* ix, The prehistoric races of Northern Europe. **1860** W. G. CLARK in *Vac. Tour.* 38 This tufa has been deposited..by some pre-historic volcano. **1863** D. WILSON *Archæol. & Prehist. Annals Scotl.* (ed. 2) I. Pref. 14 The application of the term *Prehistoric*—introduced, if I mistake not, for the first time in this work. **1878** GLADSTONE *Prim. Homer* 8 Homer and Troy lie far back in the prehistoric period. **1894** H. B. SWETE *Apostles' Creed* ii. 29 Evidence..to show that about the middle of the third century a prehistoric and premundane Sonship was ascribed by the majority of believers to Jesus Christ. **1910** *Encycl. Brit.* I. 344/2 The more serious and cautious students of prehistoric archaeology. **1932** A. R. RADCLIFFE-BROWN in *Rep. Brit. Assoc. Adv. Sci. 1931* (Centenary Meeting) 143 Another field that lies within the general field of Anthropology as now organised is that of Prehistoric Archæology. **1935** *Chambers's Encycl.* I. 387/1 Prehistoric archæology has no dates. **1948** A. L. KROEBER *Anthropol.* (rev. ed.) xix. 843 How about relations to history—with which prehistoric archaeology so obviously intergrades that no real line of demarcation can be drawn? **1974** *Encycl. Brit. Micropædia* II. 838/1 Childe was professor of prehistoric archaeology at the University of Edinburgh.

b. *transf.* and *fig.* (chiefly *joc.*).

1859 GEO. ELIOT *Let.* 17 Aug. (1954) III. 133 Pug developes new charms... I think, in the pre-historic period of his existence, before he came to me, he had led a sort of Caspar Hauser life, shut up in a kennel in Bethnal Green. **1886** KIPLING *Departmental Ditties* (1888) 15 Delilah Aberyswith was a lady..With..a little house in Simla in the Prehistoric Days. **1886** 'MARK TWAIN' *Speeches* (1910) 185, I can see that printing-office of prehistoric times yet, with its horse bills on the walls. **1924** J. BUCHAN *Three Hostages* vii. 105, I obediently sampled an old hock, an older port, and a most pre-historic brandy. **1968** M. BRAGG *Without City Wall* x. 116 It's your success story which is jaded... It's been going on for centuries... Prehistoric! **1979** *Guardian* 12 June 23/2 Red and blue looked exactly the same to anyone watching on prehistoric black and white [television].

So **prehiˈstorical** *a.*, prehistoric; hence **prehiˈstorically** *adv.*, in prehistoric times.

1862 *Parthenon* 26 July 393 From a 'prehistorical' period down to the Conquest of Tamerlane (A.D. 1398). **1863** LYELL *Antiq. Man* 11 Another class of memorials..has thrown light on the pre-historical age. **1895** *Edin. Rev.* July 137 The stream of communication set in prehistorically. **1974** *Verbatim* Dec. 1/1 Sulfur, iron,..and lead..were known to some peoples prehistorically. **1975** *Nature* 22 May 355/1 Wilkinson argues that 20th century studies on musk ox behaviour can be extrapolated back to predict the ways in which musk oxen could have been exploited prehistorically.

prehiˈstorics, *sb. pl.* [pl. of PREHISTORIC *a.*; after *economics*, *pneumatics*, etc.] Prehistoric matters as a branch of study.

1884 *Science* 4 July 212 Chinese prehistorics have not as yet been sufficiently studied to decide which metal was the first to be wrought in that distant realm. **1891** R. SEWELL in *Athenæum* 15 Aug. 226/1 A paper..on..Dravidian prehistorics in this locality, with special reference to Kapgal.

prehistory (priːˈhɪstərɪ). [f. PRE- + HISTORY, after PREHISTORIC.] **a.** The account of events or conditions prior to written or recorded history; hence, such events or facts, or the period when they occurred; prehistoric matters or times.

1871 TYLOR *Prim. Cult.* II. 401 The history and pre-history of man take their proper places in the general scheme of knowledge. **1888** *Times* 3 Oct. 8/1 The existence of the Pelasgi as a distinct and identifiable race and element in Italian or Greek history, or rather pre-history. **1902** *Nature* 30 Jan. 299/2 The clever etchings on bone and ivory of the cave-dwellers of Western Europe..are well known to all who interest themselves in the pre-history of man.

b. *transf.* Events or conditions leading up to a particular event, period, etc.

1931 N. MITCHISON in *Time & Tide* 25 July 893/1 Psychologists have come nearer to discovering its causes [*sc.* the causes of unhappiness] than politicians have, but they are mostly bad historians, inventing—as Freud has done—their pre-history to suit their theories. **1958** *Times Lit. Suppl.* 26 Dec. 746/5 The pre-history of the Civil War will not be found in the new position of the mercantile and industrial classes. **1960** K. AMIS *New Maps of Hell* (1961) i. 17 The prehistory of science fiction, up until 1914 or later, is admittedly as much British as American. **1974** *Encycl. Brit. Macropædia* X. 121/1 The latter third of the 19th century was a crucial point in the prehistory of jazz. **1977** *N.Y. Rev. Bks.* 27 Oct. 40/2 That is why the post-history of a work, the tradition it created, is as indispensable to the critic as its pre-history, its sources and the tradition it came from.

pre-Hitler: see PRE- B. 2b.

pre-Hitlerian, -Hitlerite: see PRE- B. 1a.

prehnite (ˈprɛnaɪt). *Min.* [ad. G. *prehnit* (Werner 1789), f. the name of Colonel von Prehn, who brought it from the Cape of Good Hope: see -ITE[1] 2b.] A hydrous silicate of aluminium and calcium, found in more or less globular masses of a pale green colour and vitreous lustre.

1795 *Schmeisser's Syst. Min.* I. 147 Prehnite..is called after Captain Prehn who brought it first to Europe. **1802** BOURNON in *Phil. Trans.* XCII. 282 That kind of prehnite which is composed of a mass of crystals confusedly aggregated. *a* **1882** SIR R. CHRISTISON *Life* (1885) I. 96 Finding prehnite on the way under the blastings of a trap cliff.

Hence **prehnitiform** (prɛˈnɪtɪfɔːm) *a.*, having the form of prehnite.

1843 PORTLOCK *Geol.* 152 Stilbite, both in the ordinary sheaf-shaped aggregations, and prehnitiform.

prehˈnitic, *a. Chem.* [f. prec.: see quot. 1872.] In ***prehnitic acid***: see quots.

1872 WATTS *Dict. Chem.* VI. 811 Prehnitic acid, $C_{10}H_6O_8$..crystallises..in large prisms resembling the mineral prehnite. **1875** *Ibid.* VII. 1006 Prehnitic acid..obtained by heating hydromellitic acid with strong sulphuric acid.

preˈhominid, *sb.* and *a.* [PRE- B. 1] **A.** *sb.* A creature belonging to an anthropoid genus that is considered to be an evolutionary ancestor of the hominids. **B.** *adj.* Of or pertaining to a creature of this kind.

1939 *Nature* 7 Jan. 18/1 The human affinities of his [*sc.* R. Broom's] recently discovered relics of new types of fossil prehominids. **1948** *Proc. Prehist. Soc.* XIV. 30 Several authorities refer to the Chopper-Chopping-tool Complex of the Far East as having been developed by the Prehominid stock of mankind—members of the *Pithecanthropus* group. **1959** B. WALL tr. *Teilhard de Chardin's Phenomenon of Man* III. ii. 194 To call *Pithecanthropus* and *Sinanthropus* pre-hominids might suggest that they were not yet quite man. *Ibid.* 195 Those creatures which (however pre-hominid in cranial structure) are already clearly situated *above* the point of origin..of our human race. **1968** A. S. ROMER *Procession of Life* xviii. 290 Even if a pre-hominid wished to remain a tree-dweller, his living area would be much restricted unless he were able to venture out into the open. **1978** *Nature* 26 Oct. 744/1 Among living species, the pygmy chimpanzee..offers us the best prototype of the prehominid ancestor.

prehuman (priːˈhjuːmən), *a.* (*sb.*) [PRE- B. 1.] Preceding the human; previous to the existence of man upon the earth. Also as *sb.*

1844 R. CHAMBERS *Vest. Creation, Orig. Anim. Tribes*, Throughout the whole of the pre-human period. **1883** A. WILSON in G. Allen et al. *Nature Studies* 105 That which the evolutionist and naturalist desire to know, is the nature of the forms which..must have connected the human root-stock with the pre-human root. **1900** H. MACPHERSON *H. Spencer* 117 Studying mental processes in their earlier pre-human manifestations. **1932** S. ZUCKERMAN *Social Life Monkeys* ii. 24 There is no clear reason why the social behaviour of the 'pre-humans' should be considered to have been like that of apes rather than like that of monkeys. **1958** A. R. RADCLIFFE-BROWN *Method in Social Anthropol.* II. v. 181 It is reasonable to fix the real change from pre-human to human social life by reference to the beginnings of language. **1973** G. OLIVIER in M. H. Day *Human Evolution* 94 The possibility that man..may only have appeared very late, and that the other fossils, including *Pithecanthropus*, may be only pre-human hominids.

prehyoid: see PRE- B. 3.

preiche, -our, etc., obs. ff. PREACH, PREACHER.

pre-ictal: see PRE- B. 1.

preid, var. PREDE *v. Obs.*

preie, preiȝe, obs. ff. PRAY, PREY.

preier(e, obs. ff. PRAYER.

preif, -e, preiff, obs. ff. PROOF, PROVE.

preignable, -ant, obs. ff. PREGNABLE, PREGNANT.

preignetory, -notarie, -y, var. PRENOTARY *Obs.*

pre-igˈnition. [PRE- A. 2.] Ignition of the fuel and air mixture in an internal-combustion engine before the passage of the spark.

1898 A. G. ELLIOTT *Gas & Petroleum Engines* iv. 88 This third engine has a vaporizer which..is so constructed that even if it became red-hot there would be no risk of pre-ignition. **1909** *Westm. Gaz.* 1 Apr. 4/1 The compression has been increased to the highest point compatible with safety in regard to freedom from pre-ignition. **1951** 'S. ABBEY' *Automobile Fault-Tracing* ii. 28 Pre-ignition and auto-ignition differ from detonation in that the incoming charge is ignited by an incandescent particle or surface before the sparking plug fires. **1970** *A.A. Bk. of Car* 50 Pre-ignition, like knocking, can cause extensive damage, as well as reduce engine power. **1977** I. M. CAMPBELL *Energy & Atmosphere* v. 108 Autoignition (also referred to as preignition, knock, or pinking) arises in an internal combustion engine largely on account of the finite velocity of flame propagation from the spark zone.

preik, obs. Sc. f. PRICK.

preimage (priːˈɪmɪdʒ). *Math.* [PRE- A. 2.] = *inverse image* s.v. IMAGE *sb.* 8.

1949 F. BLUM tr. *B. L. Van der Waerden's Mod. Algebra* I. i. 3 The element $\phi(a)$ is called the image of *a*, while *a* is an inverse image (pre-image) of $\phi(a)$. **1958** [see INTO *adj.*]. **1975** N. CHOMSKY *Logical Struct. Linguistic Theory* ix. 317 *T* carries the elements of its domain into strings of $\bar{p}$ which differ from one another and from their preimages in the sense of condition C6.

pre-imagine (priːɪˈmædʒɪn), *v.* [f. PRE- A. 1 + IMAGINE; cf. med.L. *præimāgināre* (1132 in Du Cange).] *trans.* To imagine beforehand; in quot. *a* 1631, to preconceive, presuppose.

a **1631** DONNE *Lett.* (1651) 274 Everie addition preimagines a beeing. **1818** MOORE *Mem.* (1856) VIII. 233, I have done it,..but, as usual, not half so well as I had pre-imagined it.

So **pre-imagiˈnation**, imagination of something before the actual existence or experience of it.

1881 SULLY *Illusions* 105 The results of definite preimagination, including what are generally known as expectations.

pre-imbibe, -imbue, -impression, etc.: see PRE- A. 1, 2.

pre-implanˈtation, *a. Biol.* [PRE- B. 2.] Occurring or existing between the fertilization of an ovum and its implantation in the wall of the uterus.

1945 W. J. HAMILTON et al. *Human Embryol.* v. 49 (*heading*) Pre-implantation period. *Ibid.* 50 The pre-implantation stages of the human ovum must be essentially the same as those of the monkey. **1968** *Nature* 9 Nov. 596/1 Mosaicism, extending to most tissues of the body in mice, was achieved by fusing pre-implantation embryos together *in vitro*. **1972** R. L. BRINSTER in Balin & Glasser *Reproductive Biol.* xx. 751 In the human, where the gestation period is 270 days, the pre-implantation period is still only 8 days.

pre-ˈimpregnate, *v.* [PRE- A. 1.] *trans.* To impregnate (a material) with something prior to mechanical processing. So **pre-ˈimpregnated** *ppl. a.*, *spec.* (*a*) of paper insulation: impregnated with oil and resin before use in electric cables; of a cable: containing such insulation; (*b*) of reinforcing material for plastics: impregnated with synthetic resin before fabrication; **pre-impregˈnation**.

1933 *Jrnl. Inst. Electr. Engin.* LXXIII. 353/2 The design conditions are extremely simple as the dielectric depends solely on the use of the pre-impregnated paper, the selection of gas-space dimensions, and the pressure of the gas. **1937** *Ibid.* LXXXI. 634/1 With proper attention to the physical properties of the impregnating medium, this pre-impregnation ensures the absolute definition of the gas spaces up to the maximum working temperature of the cable. **1958** *Times* 1 Dec. 2/5 Aeroplastics Limited..have commenced production of their new process of preimpregnating glass fabric. **1958** D. J. DUFFIN *Laminated Plastics* iv. 73 Either a dry or preimpregnated glass reinforcement is now laid in the mold. **1960** *Jrnl. Inst. Electr. Engin.* VI. 694/1 The pre-impregnated cable does not suffer from this kind of trouble because the paper is dried and impregnated in sheet form before application to the cable. **1965** *Mod. Plastics Encycl. 1966* 628/1 A preimpregnation step is frequently used, in which the reinforcing web is passed through a resin bath before lay-up. **1970** *Materials & Technol.* III. xii. 871 Mats or fabrics are pre-impregnated with resin by passing through baths containing a solution of the resin. The solvents are removed by drying and the material is worked into mouldings. **1971** *Nature* 30 July 305/2 These preimpregnated layers are then moulded together in the normal way under heat and pressure, and cured.

prein, Sc. f. PREEN.

preinable, obs. f. PREGNABLE.

†**pre-inˈanimate**, *v. Obs. rare.* [PRE- A. 1.] *trans.* To 'inanimate', vivify, or inspire beforehand.

1624 DONNE *Serm.* xlvi. (1640) 462 When he was to re-inanimate him with his spirit; rather, to pre-inanimate him; for, indeed, no man hath a soule till he have grace. *a* **1631** —— *Serm.* cvii. (ed. Alford IV. 451 That power of that Grace that prevents and preinanimates that Action.

pre-Inca: see PRE- B. 2a.

pre-Incaic, -Incarial: see PRE- B. 1.

pre-inˈcarnate, *a.* [f. PRE- B. 1 + INCARNATE *a.*] Existing previous to the Incarnation.

1868 LIGHTFOOT *Ep. Philippians* (1885) 131 Does the expression..refer to the pre-incarnate or the incarnate Christ? **1895** SALMOND *Doctr. Immortality* IV. iii. 459 Is it a ministry of the pre-incarnate Christ, the disembodied Christ, or the risen Christ?

pre-incarˈnation. [PRE- A. 2.] A previous incarnation or embodiment.

1903 MYERS *Hum. Personality* II. 136 One pre-incarnation as an Indian Princess. **1904** *Westm. Gaz.* 2 May

3/2 Can this wide-poet be a reincarnation of Swinburne? Alas! it is but Sir Thomas Overbury.

pre-incline (priːɪn'klaɪn), *v.* [PRE- A. 1.] *trans.* To incline or dispose beforehand.

1671 WOODHEAD *St. Teresa* I. Pref. 33 These Saints are.. by the Holy Spirit pre-inclined.. to ask. **1862** LYTTON *Str. Story* II. 59 Nor do I see cause for the fear to which your statement had preinclined me.

pre-increase: see PRE- B. 2 a.

†**pre-incre'pation.** *Obs. rare*$^{-1}$. [PRE- A. 2.] A previous increpation, rebuke, or reproof.

a **1631** DONNE *Serm.* lxii. (1640) 619 God armes him with a pre-increpation upon Descents, *Nolite fieri*, Goe no lesse, be not made lower.

pre-incubate: see PRE- A. 1.

pre-incubation: see PRE- A. 2.

pre-indesignate (priːɪn'dɛsɪgnət, -'dɛz-), *a. Logic.* [f. PRE- A. 3 + INDESIGNATE.] Having no sign of quantity prefixed: = INDEFINITE *a.* 4, INDESIGNATE. Opp. to PREDESIGNATE.

1837-8 [see PREDESIGNATE]. **1846** HAMILTON *Let. to De Morgan* 2 The preindesignate terms of a proposition, whether subject or predicate, are never, on that account, thought as indefinite (or indeterminate) in quantity.

pre-indicant (priː'ɪndɪkənt). *rare.* [f. PRE- A. 2 + INDICANT.] Something that indicates or betokens beforehand; a prognostic.

1659 PELL *Improv. Sea* 374 If circles about the Moon.. bee double or treble, they are.. preindicants of a.. tempest.

pre-indicate (priː'ɪndɪkeɪt), *v.* [PRE- A. 1.] *trans.* To indicate or point out beforehand.

1804 A. PIRIE in Spurgeon *Treas. Dav.* Ps. lxxxi. 3 It also pre-indicated the blowing of the gospel-trumpet. **1849** H. MAYO *Pop. Superstit.* iv. 72 For how many centuries were the laws of electricity preindicated by the single fact, that a piece of amber when rubbed would attract light bodies? **1867** *Contemp. Rev.* VI. 360 The Bishop.. preindicated the essential importance.. of the future production of the folio MS.

pre-industrial to **-intellectual**: see PRE- B. 1.

pre-inform (priːɪn'fɔːm), *v.* [PRE- A. 1.] *trans.* To inform beforehand.

1791 *Town & Country Mag.* Suppl. 593/2 Being pre-informed that it would be a very mixed assembly. **1878** H. M. STANLEY *Dark Cont.* I. xvi. 423 As couriers had pre-informed us.

pre-'instinct. *rare.* [PRE- A. 2.] A previous or pre-existing instinct.

1643 T. GOODWIN *Return of Prayers* 46 By an unerring providence and preinstinct infused by his Spirit.

pre-instruct (priːɪn'strʌkt), *v.* [PRE- A. 1: cf. OF. *preinstruict* (*a* 1500 in Godef.).] *trans.* To instruct beforehand. So **pre-in'struction**, instruction in advance.

1642 *Compl. to Ho. Comm.* 12 Sollicitation and pre-instruction in Causes. **1646** MAYNE *Serm. Unity* 16 A certaine Disciple named Ananias, pre-instructed by Christ in a vision, was sent to him. **1653** H. MORE *Conject. Cabbal., Def.* 204 As if Plato had been pre-instructed by men of the same Spirit with the Apostle.

preinte, obs. form of PRINT.

pre-intend (priːɪn'tɛnd), *v.* [PRE- A. 1.] *trans.* To intend previously; to purpose beforehand.

1649 BP. REYNOLDS *Hosea* ii. 78 Such a succession as themselves had preintended. *a* **1652** BROME *Damoiselle* v. Wks. 1873 I. 461 That Charitable use, To which I pre-intended it.

pre-interpret (priːɪn'tɜːprɪt), *v.* [PRE- A. 1.] *trans.* To interpret beforehand. So **pre-interpre'tation**, interpretation in advance.

1638 MAYNE *Lucian* (1668) 307 Our Oracles, and pre-interpretations of these Decrees. **1640** NABBES *Bride* III. i, You.. catch.. and preinterpret Thoughts that had never being.

pre-intimate (priː'ɪntɪmeɪt), *v.* [f. PRE- A. 1 + INTIMATE *v.*] *trans.* To intimate beforehand or in advance. So **pre-inti'mation**, previous intimation, a suggestion beforehand.

a **1821** T. SCOTT *Comm. Josh.* ix. 27 The transaction.. pre-intimated their admission into the church. **1828** WEBSTER cites T. SCOTT for *Preintimation.* **1896** J. E. RANKIN in *Chicago Advance* 30 Jan. 165/1 Her cheerfulness and evenness of temper.. preintimate what she may become when thoroughly taught and trained. **1923** J. W. HARVEY tr. *Otto's Idea of Holy* xx. 171 This is nothing else than the pure *impulsion* to *redemption*, and the pre-intimation and anticipation of a boded 'good'. **1925** *Law Reports: Appeal Cases* 730 Expressing the matter in my own words, I would say that a threat is a pre-intimation of proposed action of some sort.

pre-intone (priːɪn'təʊn), *v. Eccl.* [PRE- A. 1.] *trans.* To intone the introductory part of (a melody) in a low voice for the officiant, who then intones it aloud.

1853 DALE tr. *Baldeschi's Ceremonial* 67 They accompany the Officiant to his seat, and stand before him.. until the first Cantor shall have pre-intoned to him the first antiphon. *Ibid.*, The first Cantor pre-intones the Hymn for the Officiant.

pre-invasion: see PRE- B. 2 a.

pre-ionize: see PRE- A. 1.

preiotation (priːaɪəʊ'teɪʃən). [f. PRE- A. 2 + IOT(A (here standing for the palatal glide *y*) + -ATION.] In the Slavonic languages, the development of a palatal glide before a vowel. So **preioti'zation**; **prei'otized** *a.*, preceded by a palatal glide.

1877 A. H. KEANE tr. *Hovelacque's Sci. of Lang.* 281 The Lithuanian *este* becomes *jeste* in Church Slavonic; and this 'prëiotation', as it is technically called, is a leading feature of all the Slavonic tongues. **1883** W. R. MORFILL *Slavonic Lit.* i. 18 The difficulty of expressing the præiotised vowels is the same. **1887** —— in *Encycl. Brit.* XXII. 148/2 The addition of a *y* sound before vowels is one of the great characteristics of the Slavonic languages, called 'præiotization'. **1959** G. NANDRIŞ *Old Church Slavonic Gram.* 6 The Glagolitic letters for preiotized *ę* and *ǫ* are ligatures.

preire, obs. f. PRAYER.

preis(e, obs. ff. PRAISE, PRICE.

preis, -e, preiss, preist, obs. Sc. ff. PRESS, PRIEST.

preive, obs. Sc. f. PROVE.

prejacent (priː'dʒeɪsənt), *a.* (*sb.*) [a. OF. *prejacent* (15th c. in Godef.), ad. L. *præjacēnt-em*, pr. pple. of *præjacēre* to lie in front, f. *præ*, PRE- A. 4 + *jacēre* to lie.]

†**1.** Previously existing; pre-existent. *Obs.*

1546 LANGLEY *Pol. Verg. De Invent.* I. i. 2 Thales.. said that God was an understandinge that made.. all thynges of the water as matter prejacent. **1596** BELL *Surv. Popery* I. i. i. 1 Without any antecedent or prejacent matter. **1676** GARENCIERES *Corals* 46 Without any prejacent or evident cause. *a* **1703** BURKITT *On N.T.* Heb. xi. 3 The world was made, not out of any pre-jacent or pre-existent matter, but out of nothing.

2. *Logic.* Laid down previously; constituting the original proposition from which another is inferred. Hence *ellipt.* as *sb. rare.*

c **1840** SIR W. HAMILTON *Logic* App. (1860) II. 276 According to the doctrine of the logicians, conversion applies only to the naked terms themselves:—the subject and predicate of the prejacent interchange places, but the quantity by which each was therein affected is excluded from the movement; remaining to affect its correlative in the subjacent proposition.

3. Lying or situated in front. *rare.*

1762 tr. *Busching's Syst. Geog.* V. 5 With respect to its situation on the side of France, this Circle is reckoned among the four anterior and six prejacent Circles of the Empire.

pre-jazz: see PRE- B. 2 a.

prejinct, prejink, var. PERJINK *a.*, precise.

prejudge (priː'dʒʌdʒ), *v.* [ad. F. *préjuger* (16th c. in Littré), after L. *præjūdicāre* to prejudge, PREJUDICATE: see PRE- A. 1 and JUDGE *v.*]

1. *trans.* To pass judgement, or pronounce sentence on, before trial, or without proper inquiry; hence, to judge, to express or come to a judgement or decision upon (a person, cause, opinion, action, etc.), prematurely and without due consideration.

1579 *Reg. Privy Council Scot.* III. 170 That, befoir he be prejudgit thairof, he may have the ordour of the law observit to him. **1625** B. JONSON *Staple of N.* Prol., [The poet] prayes you'll not preiudge his Play for ill. **1659** H. THORNDIKE *Wks.* (1846) II. 595 The choice of religion cannot be prejudged by common sense. **1763** CHURCHILL *Epist. to W. Hogarth* Poems I. 131 When Wilkes, prejudg'd, is sentenc'd to the Tow'r. **1788** GIBBON *Decl. & F.* xliii. (1869) II. 613 The emperor had prejudged his guilt. **1845** S. AUSTIN *Ranke's Hist. Ref.* III. 259 This demand appeared to him an unauthorised attempt to prejudge the very question to be inquired into. **1878** BOSW. SMITH *Carthage* 340 She knew that the case was prejudged against her by the wolf, and that she must meet the lamb's fate.

†**b.** To judge unfavourably, condemn, or disparage in advance; to form a prejudice against. *Obs.*

1605 BACON *Adv. Learn.* I. v. §2 The expedition.. was preiudged as a vast and impossible enterprize. **1622** —— *Hen. VII* 4 It was a Title condemned by Parliament, and generally preiudged in the common opinion of the Realme.

c. To judge (a person) prematurely to be (something). *nonce-use.*

1822 BYRON *Werner* II. ii. 80 Stralenheim Is not what you prejudge him.

†**2.** To affect prejudicially or injuriously; to do something to the prejudice of; to prejudice, injure. *Sc. Obs.*

1561 *Reg. Privy Council Scot.* I. 171 That samekle dewitie hes bene payit yeirlie thairfoir, and.. suld nocht preiuge hir anent hir rycht of the saidis landis. **1600** *Burgh Rec. Glasgow* (Burgh Rec. Soc.) I. 206 The letter.. sall nocht preiuge or hurte.. ony vtheris. **1678** SIR G. MACKENZIE *Crim. Laws Scot.* I. xvii. §6 The publick Interest could not be prejudged by any connivance or Crime of the Husband. **1707** DK. OF ATHOL in *Vulpone* 20 The Barons and Burrows are also further prejudg'd in this, That.. one Commissioner will hereafter Represent several Shires or Burghs.

†**3.** To anticipate (another) in judging. *Obs.*

1626 MEADE in Ellis *Orig. Lett.* Ser. I. III. 229 That we should by this Act prejudge the Parliament. **1649** JER. TAYLOR *Gt. Exemp.* Ad Sect. xv. §5 By this time, suppose sentence given, Caiaphas prejudging all the Sanhedrim. **1719** in W. S. Perry *Hist. Coll. Amer. Col. Ch.* I. 221 That they had made a publick complaint.. which now lyes before the King; that it did not belong to our Province, either to prejudge his Majesty, or to decide the Points in difference.

Hence **pre'judged** *ppl. a.*, judged or condemned beforehand; †prejudiced; **pre'judging** *vbl. sb.*; also **pre'judger**, one who prejudges.

a **1614** DONNE *Βιαθανατος* (1644) 20 The malitious prejudged man, and the lazy affectors of ignorance, will use the same calumnies and obtrectations toward me. **1666** OWEN *Nat. & Power Indwelling Sin* Wks. 1851 VI. 273 Conscience is a man's prejudging of himself with respect unto the future judgment of God. **1785** BURKE *Corr.* (1844) III. 39 We know that we bring before a bribed tribunal a pre-judged cause. **1838** G. S. FABER *Inquiry* 113 A malignant Inquisitor, the iniquitous prejudger of his prisoner. **1882** B. HARTE *Flip* iii, As an already prejudged man.. he obtained a change of venue.

prejudgement, -judgment (priː'dʒʌdʒmənt). [ad. obs. F. *prejugement* (Cotgr.): see PRE- A. 2 and JUDGEMENT.] The action or fact of prejudging; judgement beforehand; a conclusion or decision formed before examination of the facts; prejudice.

1605 BACON *Adv. Learn.* II. xvii. §8 To remooue stronge Preoccupations and Preiudgements. **1680** *Relig. Dutch* iii. 25 Their own prejudgments have engag'd them to accommodate the Scripture to their own Erroneous Sence. **1799** BP. W. KNOX *Serm. 7 Apr.* 39 It is not free and impartial inquiry that we deprecate, it is hasty and arrogant pre-judgement. **1876** GEO. ELIOT *Dan. Der.* xl, I listen that I may know, without prejudgment.

†**pre'judicacy.** *Obs.* [f. PREJUDICATE *ppl. a.*: see -ACY.] Preconceived opinion, prepossession, prejudice.

1636 SIR H. BLOUNT *Voy. Levant* 4 Mine owne eye, not dazled with any affection, prejudicacy, or mist of education. **1652** URQUHART *Jewel* Wks. (1834) 246 Which, I cannot think, if prejudicacy be laid aside, but that.. he will acknowledge.

†**pre'judical,** *a. Obs. rare.* [app. f. L. *præjūdicāre* (see PREJUDICATE *v.*) + -AL[1]. (But perhaps only erroneous for *prejudicial*.)]

1. = PREJUDICIAL *a.*[1] 1.

1594 PARSONS *Confer. Success.* I. viii. 196 He ought to enjoy his preheminence, but yet so, that he be not preiudical therby to the whole body. **1745** *De Foe's Eng. Tradesman* v. (1841) I. 33 To be limited so as not to be prejudical to business. **1791** *St. Papers* in *Ann. Reg.* 129 Those abuses were no less prejudical to the monarch than to the nation.

2. = PRE-JUDICIAL *a.*[2]

1864 WEBSTER s.v., A prejudical enquiry or action at law.

†**pre'judicant,** *a. Obs. rare.* [ad. L. *præjūdicāns, -ānt-em*, pres. pple. of *præjūdicāre*: see PREJUDICATE *v.*] Prejudging, 'prejudicating'.

1645 MILTON *Tetrach.* Wks. 1851 IV. 163 If we.. hear him with not too hasty and prejudicant ears, we shall finde no such terror in him.

†**pre'judicate,** *ppl. a. Obs.* [ad. L. *præjūdicāt-us*, pa. pple. of *præjūdicāre*: see next.]

1. Judged, settled, or decided beforehand. (Const. as *pa. pple.*) *rare.*

1570 FOXE *A. & M.* (ed. 2) 1640/1 Neither were ignoraunt of the purpose of the aduersaries, and how ye cause was preiudicate before. **1676-7** MARVELL *Corr.* Wks. (Grosart) II. 507 The question.. should be prejudicate and decided by making this the first or second reading.

2. Formed (as an opinion) prior to knowledge or examination of the case; preconceived.

1583 STUBBES *Anat. Abus.* II. (1882) 114 A reprobate sence, and preiudicate opinion. **1677** GILPIN *Demonol.* (1867) 152 So many prejudicate prepossessions that do secretly taint the mind. **1725** WATTS *Logic* II. iv. §1 Casting away all our former prejudicate opinions and sentiments. [**1883** *Q. Rev.* Jan. 166 His treatment of civil transactions is more frequently marred by his (in Baconian phrase) prejudicate opinions.]

3. Affected by a preconceived opinion; prejudiced, prepossessed, biased.

1579 J. FIELD tr. *Calvin's Serm.* Ded. A iij, If men will come with preiudicate minds. **1599** BP. HALL *Sat.* VI. i. 122, I would repent me were it not too late, Were not the angry world prejudicate. **1646** SIR T. BROWNE *Pseud. Ep.* 27 Their reasons enforce beliefe even from prejudicate Readers. **1716** *Wodrow Corr.* (1843) II. 131 They are strangely prejudicate against the servants of Christ in this corner.

†**pre'judicate,** *v. Obs.* [f. ppl. stem of L. *præjūdicāre* to judge before, give a preliminary judgement, to prejudice, injure, f. *præ*, PRE- A. 1 + *jūdicāre* to judge.]

1. *trans.* To affect prejudicially: = PREJUDICE *v.* 1.

1553 S. CABOT *Ordinances* in Hakluyt *Voy.* (1589) 261 No particular person to hinder or preiudicate the common stocke of the companie, in sale or preferment of his owne proper wares. **1594** PARSONS *Confer. Success.* II. vii. 143 By this it is euident, that the fault of the father may preiudicate the sonnes. **1670** H. STUBBE *Plus Ultra* 41 He added, that our senses.. did prejudicate rather then qualifie us for these speculations.

b. *intr.* To act prejudicially, to do prejudice.

1565 HARDING *Confut.* IV. viii. 190 S. Gregory might call Mauritius his lord, either of courtesie, or of custome:.. Neither did S. Gregorie by that title of honour preiudicate vnto him selfe in any spirituall iurisdiction.

2. *trans.* To judge beforehand; to form an opinion of (anything) previously, *usually* hastily or rashly; to condemn in advance: = PREJUDGE 1.

[**1570**: see prec. 1.] *a* **1586** SIDNEY *Arcadia* IV. (1629) 421 To preiudicate his determination, is but a doubt of goodnesse in him, who is nothing but goodnesse. **1600** W. WATSON *Decacordon* (1602) 342 The epistle..[the Jesuits] haue rashly preiudicated to smell of an hereticall spirite. **1603** H. CROSSE *Vertues Commw.* (1878) 8 A prudent man, is so cautelous and vigillant..in prejudicating perills to come. **1660** GAUDEN *God's Gt. Demonstr.* 39 When the mists of any passions arise, either prejudicating the person for the cause, or the cause for the person. *a* **1734** NORTH *Exam.* III. vii. §29 (1740) 524 If that Vote had not prejudicated the Matter.

b. *intr.* or *absol.* To form a judgement prematurely.

c **1626** *Dick of Devon* I. iii. in Bullen *O. Pl.* II. 17, I did preiudicate Too rashly of the English. **1760–72** H. BROOKE *Fool of Qual.* (1809) I. 137 You were not placed here to prejudicate in any matter.

3. *trans.* To presage. *rare.* (Cf. *judicial astrology*, and PREJUDICE *sb.* 2 b.)

1595 *Locrine* V. iv, Behold, the circuit of the azure sky.. Prejudicating Locrine's overthrow.

4. To influence or affect (persons or their opinions) beforehand; to bias: = PREJUDICE *v.* 3.

1600 W. WATSON *Decacordon* (1602) 237 That the outward apparance..may forestall, carrie away and preiudicate mens conceits. **1654** WARREN *Unbelievers* 37 You are prejudicated against him. **1698** FRYER *Acc. E. India & P.* 129 Strange Vertigoes prejudicate Fancy.

Hence †**pre'judicated** *ppl. a.*, prejudiced, prepossessed; †**pre'judicating** *vbl. sb.* and *ppl. a.*, prejudging, prejudicing.

1581 SIDNEY *Apol. Poetry* (Arb.) 47 A minde not preiudiced with a preiudicating humor. *a* **1586** —— *Arcadia* (1622) 461 Although this were a great preiudicating of Pyrocles case, yet was he exceedingly ioyous of it, being assured of his Ladies life. **1653** GAUDEN *Hierasp.* 92 Effects, either of secular polity, or prejudicating and preposterous zeal. **1661** FELTHAM *Resolves*, etc., *Disc. Eccl.* ii. 11 (1677) 346 A prejudicated Judg, that sentences Delinquents, when yet he has not heard the cause. **1670** H. SCOUGAL *Wks.* (1765) 306 This providence to my prejudicated fancy can appear nothing less than the rod of an offended deity.

†**pre'judicately,** *adv. Obs.* [f. PREJUDICATE *ppl. a.* + -LY[2].] In a 'prejudicate' or prejudiced manner; with prejudice.

1588 J. HARVEY *Disc. Probl.* 125 We should consequently beleeue..this verie yeere to be that Fatall, yea that Finall yeere indeed, which so preiudicately it is supposed to be. **1657** G. STARKEY *Helmont's Vind.* 32, I have no personal quarrel with any, nor do I..write prejudicately. **1713** DERHAM *Phys.-Theol.* IV. iii. 126 Dr. Schelhammer prejudicately mistaketh Dr. Willis's meaning.

†**pre'judicateness.** *Obs.* [f. as prec. + -NESS.] The condition of being prejudiced; prepossession; previous bias.

1603 SIR C. HEYDON *Jud. Astrol.* xix. 398 His malicious preiudicatenes will so blynd him, that he shall keepe no euen way. **1657** J. WATTS *Dipper Sprinkled* 73 Read with impartiality, without prejudicateness.

prejudication (priːdʒuːdɪ'keɪʃən). [n. of action from L. *præjūdicāre*: see PREJUDICATE *v.*]

1. The action of 'prejudicating'; a judging beforehand; a previously formed decision or opinion.

1616 BULLOKAR *Eng. Expos.*, *Preiudication*, a iudging before hand. **1617** R. FENTON *Treat. Ch. Rome* To Rdr., Come not therefore with prejudication, either of the matter or the person. **1764** LYTTELTON *Hen. II* (1769) I. 209 A solemn determination, which assigned the precedence to the nephew of the king above his natural son was a prejudication of the right of succession in favor of the former. **1849** J. P. KENNEDY *W. Wirt* (1860) II. xvi. 273 They have come to the examination of this case under a strong prejudication of the guilt of the respondent.

2. An occasional rendering of L. *præjūdicium*: see quot., and cf. PRE-JUDICIAL *a.*[2]

1864 WEBSTER, *Prejudication*..(Roman Law), a preliminary inquiry and determination about something which belongs to a matter in dispute.

†**pre'judicative,** *a. Obs. rare.* [f. L. ppl. stem *præjūdicāt-* (see PREJUDICATE *ppl. a.*) + -IVE.] Characterized by prejudgement; prejudging.

1647 H. MORE *Song Soul* II. App., Pref. 189 A thing as ill beseeming Philosophers, as hastie prejudicative sentence [beseems] Politicall Judges. **1716** M. DAVIES *Athen. Brit.* II. 415 The irresistable Arguments and Prejudicative Prerogatives of the Law and the Testimony.

prejudicator (priː'dʒuːdɪkeɪtə(r)). *rare*[−1]. [Agent-n. on L. type, f. L. *præjūdicāre* to prejudicate: cf. L. *præjūdex*.] One who prejudges.

1821 *Blackw. Mag.* X. 679 You could have no public pretence for volunteering yourselves as my opponents, or as my prejudicators.

†**prejudicatory,** *a. Obs. rare*[−1]. [f. as prec. + -ORY[2].] = PREJUDICATIVE *a.*

1652 H. L'ESTRANGE *Amer. no Jewes* 69 To acquit my selfe from the suspected infirmity of a causelesse prejudicatory jealousy.

prejudice ('prɛdʒədɪs), *sb.* Also 4–6 -ys(e, (5 pregedys(s)e), 5–7 prejudyce, 6 -ize, 6–7 præ-. [a. F. *préjudice* (13th c. in Littré), ad. L. *præjūdicium* a preceding judgement or decision, a precedent; damage, prejudice, f. *præ*, PRE- A. 2 + *jūdicium* judgement, sentence.]

I. 1. a. Injury, detriment, or damage, caused to a person by judgement or action in which his rights are disregarded; resulting injury; hence, injury to a person or thing likely to be the consequence of some action. Now chiefly in particular phrases, as ***in prejudice of***, to the (intended or consequent) detriment or injury of; ***to the prejudice of***, to the (resulting) injury of; ***without prejudice***, without detriment to any existing right or claim; esp. in *Law*, without damage to one's own right, without detracting from one's own rights or claims: see quot. 1872.

c **1290** *Becket* 1701 in *S. Eng. Leg.* I. 155 þe king in preIudice of him, and to bi-nimen him is riȝte, Let oþur bischopes crouni is sone. *c* **1315** SHOREHAM *Poems* I. 987 ȝef hyt ne be nauȝt to þy prest Malice ne preiudice. **1389** in *Eng. Gilds* (1870) 23 To make non ordinaunce in prejudice ne lettyng of ye comoun lawe. **1426** LYDG. *De Guil. Pilgr.* 3918 Al thys I wrouhte, thorgh my myht, With-oute preiudyce of your ryht. *c* **1485** *Digby Myst.* (1882) III. 234 Be-warre ye do no pregedyse a-ȝen þe law. **1630** *R. Johnson's Kingd. & Commw.* 292 The sheepe..or their fleeces, are bought up by the Netherlands, and imployed in the making of cloth, to some prejudice of ours in England. **1660–1** MARVELL *Corr.* Wks. (Grosart) II. 43 He promised me that nothing should be done of that nature to your prejudice. **1686** tr. *Chardin's Coronat. Solyman* 10 To advance the Younger Son, in prejudice of the Eldest. *a* **1715** BURNET *Own Time* an. 1667 (1823) I. 439 It was no small prejudice to him that he was recommended by so bad a man. **1715** tr. *Gregory's Astron.* (1726) I. 184 The Fixed Stars..may be placed at different Distances, without any prejudice to this System. **1825** JEFFERSON *Autobiog.* Wks. 1859 I. 68 A material error, which I have committed in another place, to the prejudice of the Empress. **1838** in Manning & Granger *Reports C.P.* IX. 918 The above I offer without prejudice, in case it is not agreed to. **1845** MCCULLOCH *Taxation* I. i. (1852) 43 It is easy to see that it might be entirely swept off by a tax, without prejudice to the interests of any class except the landlords. **1866** G. MACDONALD *Ann. Q. Neighb.* xxxii, People will talk to your prejudice—and Mr. Walton's too. **1872** *Wharton's Law-Lex.* 763/2 *Without Prejudice*, is [said in reference] to overtures and communications between litigants..before trial or verdict. The words import an understanding that if the negotiation fails, nothing that has passed shall be taken advantage of thereafter.

†**b.** *gen.* Injury, damage, hurt, loss. *Obs.*

1539 CROMWELL in Merriman *Life & Lett.* (1902) II. 203 Veray lothe his highne[s] wold be to see any of them..to take any harme or preiudice at the papistes handes. **1563** GOLDING *Cæsar* v. (1565) 119 b, He sent hys wagoners..out of the woodes vpon our men of armes and encountred with them to their great preiudice. **1591** GREENE *Maiden's Dr.* Ded. to Lady Hatton, Whose death being the common prejudice of a present age, was lamented of most. **1600** J. LANE *Tom Tel-troth* 591 As rauening wolues that liue by preiudice. **1657** S. PURCHAS *Pol. Flying-Ins.* 135 This prejudice is chiefly caused in narrow and close grounds.. and seldome comes on hills. **1678** SIR G. MACKENZIE *Crim. Laws Scot.* I. xi. §6 (1699) 61 If the prejudice be done by the Horses foremost feet, then the Rider shall be forc'd to satisfy for the Prejudice done. **1790** BEATSON *Nav. & Mil. Mem.* I. 314 They were so well covered by a bank of sand, that the cannon of the frigates could not do them the smallest prejudice.

c. ***to terminate*** (***dismiss***, etc.) ***with extreme prejudice***: to kill, to assassinate. Hence ***termination with extreme prejudice***. *U.S. slang.*

1972 B. F. CONNERS *Don't embarrass Bureau* (1973) II. 99 'A few years ago when he wanted an agent..out of the organization he ended up dismissing him with extreme prejudice.' 'You mean he had him killed?'.. Ted nodded. **1974** W. GARNER *Big enough Wreath* x. 123 'There is no question of anyone killing anybody.' 'There is. I'm asking it... Terminate with extreme prejudice?' **1974** F. NOLAN *Oskawa Project* xvi. 105 Had he been taken out by his own people?.. He had seen some of those files with the brutal red block letters stamped diagonally across the page: *Terminate with extreme prejudice.* **1980** C. PINCHER *Dirty Tricks* i. 10 A 'termination with extreme prejudice', as the CIA called its assassination projects in those days.

II. †**2. a.** A previous judgement; *esp.* a judgement formed before due examination or consideration; a premature or hasty judgement; a prejudgement.

(Nearly always a literal rendering of L. *præjudicium*.)

1388 WYCLIF *1 Tim.* v. 21 Y preie..that thou kepe these thingis with oute preiudice [1382 withouten bifore dom; Vulg. *sine præjudicio*; 1582 N.T. (Rhem.) without preiudice; 1611 BIBLE without preferring, *marg.* prejudice; 1881 *R.V.* without prejudice, *marg.* preference]. **1483** *Cath. Angl.* 290/2 Preiudyse, *preiudicium*. *a* **1577** SIR T. SMITH *Commw. Eng.* (1609) 88 For as twelue haue giuen a preiudice against him, so twelue againe must acquit or condemne him. **1600** HOLLAND *Livy* XXVI. ii. 583 Least that they might seeme to approve the very same thing by their prejudice and dome aforehand. **1835** WHATELY in *Life* (1866) I. 313, I strongly protested against the charge of 'prejudice' in the strict sense, viz., as a *pre-judicium*, a judgment formed antecedently to knowledge.

†**b.** The action of judging of an event beforehand; prognostication, presaging. *Obs. rare.* [So F. *préjudice* in Amyot, 16th c.]

1590 SPENSER *F.Q.* II. ix. 49 That nought mote hinder his quicke prejudize. **1598** GRENEWAY *Tacitus, Descr. Germ.* ii. (1622) 261 So [they] trie their valour: and by that prejudice conjecture on whose side the victory shall fall.

3. a. Preconceived opinion; bias or leaning favourable or unfavourable; prepossession; when used *absolutely*, usually with unfavourable connotation.

1643 SIR T. BROWNE *Relig. Med.* I. §3 At a solemn Procession I have wept abundantly, while my consorts, blind with opposition and prejudice, have fallen into an excess of scorn and laughter. **1719** D'URFEY *Pills* (1872) I. 340 Who rails at faults through personal prejudice Shows more his own, than shames another's vice. **1765** A. DICKSON *Treat. Agric.* (ed. 2) 19 If a person divests himself of prejudice, and attachment to any particular opinion. **1790** BURKE *Fr. Rev.* 130 Prejudice renders a man's virtue his habit... Through just prejudice, his duty becomes a part of his nature. **1861** J. BRIGHT in *Times* 18 July, Ignorance is the mother of prejudice, whether among nations or individuals.

b. With *a* and *pl.*: An instance of this; a feeling, favourable or unfavourable, towards any person or thing, prior to or not based on actual experience; a prepossession; a bias or leaning to one side; an unreasoning predilection or objection.

1654 BRAMHALL *Just Vind.* iii. (1661) 51 God looks upon his creatures with all their prejudices, and expects no more of them then according to the talents which he hath given them. **1662** GERBIER *Princ.* 8 Being prepossessed with a prejudice. **1705** ATTERBURY *Serm.*, *Luke* xvi. 31 (1726) II. 46 Such..have had all the early Prejudices of Education on the side of Truth. **1784** J. BARRY in *Lect. Paint.* vi. (1848) 228 The works of Correggio, for which they had contracted an early prejudice. **1830** D'ISRAELI *Chas. I*, III. i. 2 He cannot ..remove the prejudices which are raised against him. **1842** DE QUINCEY *Philos. Herod.* Wks. 1858 IX. 204 When a prejudice of any class whatever is seen as such, when it is recognised for a prejudice, from that moment it ceases to be a prejudice. Those are the true baffling prejudices for man, which he never suspects for prejudices. **1894** H. DRUMMOND *Ascent Man* 5 A historian dares not have a prejudice, but he cannot escape a purpose.

†**c.** Something prejudicial. *Obs. rare*[−1].

1718 ATTERBURY *Serm.*, *Acts* xxvi. 26 (1734) I. 27 Those Articles of the Roman Catholick Faith..are to be received implicitly, without..Discussion... Now this is the greatest Prejudice imaginable against the Truth of the Doctrines of any Church.

†**4.** A preliminary or anticipatory judgement; a preconceived idea as to what will happen; an anticipation. *Obs.*

1748 *Anson's Voy.* II. ix. 225 Our former despair by degrees gave place to more sanguine prejudices. **1754–8** NEWTON *Observ. Proph. Dan.* xi. 147 Let us lay aside all [traditions] and examine what prejudices can be gathered from records of good account. **1771** LUCKOMBE *Hist. Print.* 20 The..initial letters, &c. give a prejudice at sight of their being the first production of the Art amongst us.

5. *Comb.*, as ***prejudice-born***, ***-breeding*** adjs.

1896 *Pop. Sci. Monthly* L. 270 They did not foresee such a revival of the prejudice-breeding protectionist system. **1902** *Daily Chron.* 28 Oct. 7/1 Error stupendous, sublime, indefensible, Prejudice-born, I am sadly afraid.

prejudice ('prɛdʒədɪs), *v.* Also 5 -ise, 6 -ish. [a. F. *préjudic-ier* (14th c. in Littré) to prejudice, to be injurious, f. *préjudice*: see prec.]

I. 1. *trans.* To affect injuriously or unfavourably by doing some act, or as a consequence of something done; to injure or impair the validity of (a right, claim, statement, etc.).

1472–3 *Rolls of Parlt.* VI. 25/1 That your seid Suppliant nor his heires, be in no wyse hurt nor prejudised by the same Acte. **1579** G. HARVEY *Letter-bk.* (Camden) 67 Ye have preiudishd my good name for ever in thrustinge me thus on the stage to make tryall of my extemporall faculty. **1639** FULLER *Holy War* I. ix. (1840) 14 Yet no prescription of time could prejudice the title of the King of Heaven. **1774** PENNANT *Tour Scot. in 1772*, 110 Bestowing that title should not prejudice his right to the castle and lands. **1885** *Act 48 & 49 Vict.* c. 61 §9 Nothing in this Act contained shall prejudice or interfere with any rights..vested in..the Lord Advocate.

b. To injure materially; to damage. Now *rare.*

1591 GREENE *Farewell to Follie* Wks. (Grosart) IX. 247 Watching either to preuent or preiudice the enemie. **1615** G. SANDYS *Trav.* 126 The egges being then most fit for that purpose, neither are they..preiudiced by thunder. **1653** *Clarke Papers* (Camden) III. 7 This day Vantrump.. discharged many cannons against the towne of Dover, whereby some howses were prejudiced, but noe persons slaine. **1706** HEARNE *Collect.* 9 July (O.H.S.) I. 271 The Binder has somewhat prejudic'd them. *a* **1774** GOLDSM. *Surv. Exp. Philos.* II. 22 A very convincing proof how much mines of copper may prejudice the atmosphere. **1884** *Lillywhite's Cricket. Ann.* 57 A wicket very much prejudiced by the rain.

II. †**2.** To judge beforehand; *esp.* to prejudge unfavourably. *Obs. rare.*

1570 LEVINS *Manip.* 115/22 To Preiudice, *præiudicare.* **1597** A. M. tr. *Guillemeau's Fr. Chirurg.* 33/1 We may præiudice the bones to be altered or polluted. *a* **1627** HAYWARD *Four Y. Eliz.* (Camden) 9 The Queene..desiring them,..that they would not prejudice her in their opiniones. **1642** MILTON *Apol. Smect.* Wks. 1851 III. 258 To prejudice and forecondemne his adversary in the title for slanderous and scurrilous.

3. To affect or fill with a prejudice; to prepossess with an opinion; to give a bias or bent to, influence the mind or judgement of beforehand (often, unfairly). Const. *against*, *in favour of*, †*to* (= against).

1610 WILLET *Hexapla Dan.* 360, I will not preiudice the iudgement of any. **1675** G. R. tr. *LeGrand's Man without Passion* 6 Those who..are prejudiced by passion. **1741** RICHARDSON *Pamela* II. 318 The Perverseness and Contradiction I have too often seen.., even among People of Sense, as well as Condition, had prejudiced me to the marry'd State. **1868** KINGSLEY *Hermits, St. Simon Styl.* (1880) 196, I wished..to prejudice my readers' minds in their favour rather than against them.

Hence **'prejudicing** *vbl. sb.* and *ppl. a.*

1607 HIERON *Wks.* II. 222 Without any prejudicing..of the Riches of God's grace. **1635** J. HAYWARD tr. *Biondi's Banish'd Virg.* 143 It is not knowne that ever he did any prejudicing office against any man. **1706** HEARNE *Collect.* (O.H.S.) I. 249 Those prejudicing passions which must first be removed.

prejudiced ('prɛdʒədɪst), *ppl. a.* [f. prec. + -ED[1].] Affected or influenced by prejudice; prepossessed, biased beforehand.

1579 G. HARVEY *Letter-bk.* (Camden) 60 Still to mainetayne or againe to recoover that præiudiced opinion of me amongste them, that heretofore..was conceavid. **1654** OWEN *Doctr. Saints' Persev.* Wks. 1853 XI. 375 Prejudiced men will grant it. **1739** CIBBER *Apol.* (1756) II. 55 Considering what numbers..might come to it as prejudic'd spectators. **1856** SIR B. BRODIE *Psychol. Inq.* I. vi. 234 Being in some degree a prejudiced witness. **1861** CRAIK *Hist. Eng. Lit.* II. 338 Interesting us even in its most prejudiced and objectionable passages.

Hence **'prejudicedly** *adv.*, in a prejudiced manner.

1812 SHELLEY *Proposals* Pr. Wks. 1888 I. 271 For the reasons above alleged, falsely, prejudicedly, and narrowly, will..they persecute those who have the best intentions towards them.

'prejudiceless, *a.* [-LESS.] Void of prejudice.

1830 W. TAYLOR *Hist. Germ. Poetry* II. 206 The question needs no learning, only an honest, prejudiceless heart.

†**preju'diciable**, *a. Obs.* [a. F. *préjudiciable* (14th c. in Littré), f. *préjudicier* (see PREJUDICE *v.*) + *-able*, -ABLE.] = PREJUDICIAL *a.*[1]

1429 *Rolls of Parlt.* IV. 338/2 Whether his deliverance be not prejudiciable to y[e] greet pees. **1600** J. HAMILTON in *Cath. Tract.* (S.T.S.) 243 Thairfore this heresie..is preiudiciable to the lawful standing of noble houses. **1674** tr. *Scheffer's Lapland* xiii. 66 This custom..being thought.. very prejudiciable to their herds.

prejudicial (prɛdʒə'dɪʃəl), *a.*[1] [In form corresp. to F. *préjudicial, -el* (1321 in Hatz.-Darm.) preceding judgement, and late L. *præjūdiciālis* belonging or according to a preceding judgement; but in sense belonging to PREJUDICE *sb.*: see -AL[1].]

1. Causing prejudice; of injurious tendency; detrimental, damaging (to rights, interests, etc.).

[**1304** *Year-bk. 32 Edw. I* (Rolls) 111 La quele occupacioun..ne nous deit estre prejudiciel.] **1433** *Rolls of Parlt.* IV. 472/1 The Kyng wille, that the graunte..be not prejudiciell nor hurt to the seide John. **1494** FABYAN *Chron.* VII. 351 Preiudyciall to the vnyuersall weale of the realme. **1560** DAUS tr. *Sleidane's Comm.* 44 b, Certein thinges were enacted, which they sawe should be preiudiciall to them. **1661** SANDERSON (*title*) Episcopacy.. Not Prejudicial to Regal Power. *a* **1704** T. BROWN *Praise of Wealth* Wks. 1730 I. 84 Nothing more prejudicial to great power than to own itself in the wrong. **1855** MACAULAY *Hist. Eng.* xix. IV. 360 The existing system, it was said, was prejudicial both to commerce and to learning.

†**b.** Of animals: Harmful, noxious. *Obs. rare.*

1602 ROWLANDS *Greene's Ghost* 3 Vipers,..that for their venime and poison are hated and shunned of all men, as most preiudiciall creatures.

†**c.** Liable to be prejudiced or injured. *Obs. rare.*

1682 *Lond. Gaz.* No. 1704/4 There being several great Trusts in his Name, which will be unavoidably prejudicial by his absence.

†**2.** Of the nature of prejudice; full of prejudice, prejudiced (†*to* = against), unfavourably prepossessed. *Obs.*

1535 STARKEY *Let.* in *England* (1878) p. xxx, You schold, wythout any preiudiciall affectyon taken of any man apon one parte or other..gyue your sentence. **1554** KNOX *Godly Let.* C vij b, I am not preiudiciall too Gods mercies. **1609** BP. W. BARLOW *Answ. Nameless Cath.* 169 The Emperor was.. preiudiciall in his opinion, hauing already enacted a Law for the Arrian Doctrine. **1623** T. SCOT *Highw. God* 35 Man was a Iudge preiudiciall and partiall. **1639** HOLYDAY *Serm. Obed.* (1661) 23 To look upon the actions of Princes with a prejudicial eye. **1643** MILTON *Divorce* II. ix. Wks. 1851 IV. 86 It was no time then to contend with their slow and prejudiciall belief.

Hence †**preju'dicial** *v.* (*illiterate*), to prejudice.

1633 B. JONSON *Tale Tub* II. ii, *Basket Hilts.* Take heed; the busines If you deferre, may prejudiciall you More than you thinke-for, zay I told you so.

pre-judicial (pri:dʒu:'dɪʃəl), *a.*[2] *Rom. Law.* [ad. L. *præjūdiciālis*, f. *præjūdici-um* a judicial examination previous to a trial (f. *præ* before + *jūdicium* judgement): see -AL[1].] Applied to a class of actions in Roman Law, whereby questions of right or fact, esp. as regards status, were determined, usually with a view to further proceedings.

1651 G. W. tr. *Cowel's Inst.* 223 Preiudiciall Actions also are reckoned among reall: now those are termed preiudiciall which arise from incident and emergent questions. **1670** BLOUNT *Law Dict.* s.v. *Actions*, Action is Pre-judicial (otherwise termed Preparatory) or else Principal. Prejudicial is that which grows from some question, or doubt in the Principal: As if a Man sue his younger Brother for Land descended from his Father, and it is objected, he is a Bastard... This point..must be tryed, before the cause can further proceed; and therefore is termed *Pre-judicialis, quia prius judicanda.* **1880** MUIRHEAD *Gaius* 442 Prejudicial [actions] were intended merely to settle a question of right or fact, without any immediate practical result.

preju'dicially (prɛdʒ-), *adv.* [f. PREJUDICIAL *a.*[1] + -LY[2].] In a prejudicial manner; to the prejudice of some one; injuriously, detrimentally, hurtfully; †with prejudice or prepossession (quot. 1589).

1467-8 *Rolls of Parlt.* V. 598/1 That neither this Acte, nor any other Acte..extend prejudicially, nor be prejudiciall or hurtyng unto Richard Langport. **1589** GREENE *Menaphon* (Arb.) 39 My natiue home is my worst nurserie, and my friends denie that which strangers preiudiciallie grant. **1658** SLINGSBY *Diary* (1836) 201 Those Divine contemplations, which my late converse..had so prejudicially estranged from me. **1859** MILL *Liberty* iv. (1865) 44/1 As soon as any part of a person's conduct affects prejudicially the interests of others, society has jurisdiction over it.

preju'dicialness. *rare.* [f. as prec. + -NESS.] The quality of being prejudicial; injuriousness.

1655 OWEN *Vind. Evang.* Wks. 1853 XII. 131 These.. deny his determinate decrees and purposes on the same pretence.., namely, of their prejudicialness to the free will of man. **1676** TOWERSON *Decalogue* 503 If we consider.. their prejudicialness to our neighbour. **1727** BAILEY vol. II, *Prejudicialness*, injuriousness.

†**preju'diciary**, *a.*[1] *Obs. rare.* [f. L. *præjūdici-um* PREJUDICE *sb.* + -ARY[1].] Prejudiced or biased unfavourably; = PREJUDICIAL *a.*[1] 2.

1642 *Answ. Observ. agst. King* 13 That hee will not bee froward or prejudiciary to them.

pre-'judiciary, præ-, *a.*[2] *Rom. Law.* [f. as PRE-JUDICIAL *a.*[2] + -ARY[1].] = PRE-JUDICIAL *a.*[2]

1880 MUIRHEAD *Gaius* III. §123 The sponsors and fide-promissors may..demand a praejudiciary inquiry.

preju'dicious (prɛdʒ-), *a.* Now *rare.* [f. L. *præjūdici-um* PREJUDICE *sb.* + -OUS; so OF. *prejudicieux* (1371 in Godef.); see JUDICIOUS.]

1. Injurious; = PREJUDICIAL *a.*[1] 1.

1579 TOMSON *Calvin's Serm. Tim.* 225/1 Yet doeth Gods will stande for a law, & what he establisheth amongst vs, neither may nor can be preiuditious to him. *a* **1638** MEDE *Wks.* (1672) 48 This was exceedingly prejudicious to the Jews. **1663** GERBIER *Counsel* 100 The entrance..is not so proper in the middle..; But if there be a constraint, which is most prejudicious to a Building, the entrance must be set as much towards the end as possible. **1731** S. HALES *Stat. Ess.* I. 325 [It] would turn rancid and prejudicious to the plant. **1899** [implied in PREJUDICIOUSLY].

†**2.** Full of prejudice; = PREJUDICED. *Obs. rare.*

1599 *Broughton's Let.* xiii. 44 Let him not bee paradoxically preiudicious. **1615** A. STAFFORD *Heav. Dogge* To Rdr., Either his head, his body or his taile will please thee, if modest thou art, and not prejudicious.

Hence **preju'diciously** *adv. rare.*

1899 *Harper's Mag.* Feb. 473 Why does the North seem to count for so little—and that little prejudiciously?

pre-junctural: see PRE- B. 1.

†**pre'jure**, *v. Obs. rare*[−0]. [ad. L. **præjūrāre*, f. *præ*, PRE- A. 1 + *jūrāre* to swear.] *intr.* To swear or take an oath before some one else. So †**preju'ration** [ad. L. *præjūrātiōn-em* a taking of an oath before others.]

1623 COCKERAM, *Prejuration*, a swearing before. *Prejure*, to sweare before.

prejurie, obs. erron. form of PERJURY.

prek, -e, etc., obs. Sc. and north. ff. PRICK, etc.

pre-Kantian, -Keynesian: see PRE- B. 1.

†**preke.** *Obs.* Also 7 **preak.** [Of unknown origin.] A polyp, an octopus.

1611 COTGR., *Poulpe*,..the Pourcontrell, Preke, or many-footed fish. **1639** S. DU VERGER tr. *Camus' Admir. Events* 18 Love is like honour,..like unto the Pourcontrell, or Peake [*sic*] fish, who becomes of the same colour the things are, whereon it fastens. **1681** GREW *Musæum* I. v. iv. 121 The Preke or Poulps, *Polypus.* *a* **1693** *Urquhart's Rabelais* III. xiii, You are likewise to abstain from Beans, from the Preak (by some called the Polyp) [*poulpe (qu'on nomme Polype)*]. **1758** [see POURCUTTLE].

preket, obs. f. PRICKET.

preknow: see PRE- A. 1.

pre-knowledge: see PRE- A. 2.

pre-koranic, -labial: see PRE- B. 1 d, 3.

prelacteal (pri:'læktiːəl), *a.* [f. PRE- B. 1 d + LACTEAL.] **A.** *adj.* Preceding or anticipating the milk teeth: applied to certain calcified structures in the fœtus of marsupials. **B.** *sb.* A prelacteal tooth or tooth-like process.

1897 *Q. Jrnl. Microsc. Sc.* Jan. 440 He viewed the calcified structures as the sole remains of an entire 'prelacteal' dentition which had otherwise become suppressed. *Ibid.* 441 The conviction that the deciduous premolar..must belong to the same series as the so-called 'prelacteals'.

prelacy ('prɛləsɪ). Also 5-6 **-asy, -asie.** [a. AF. *prelacie* (Rolls Parlt., 1306), ad. med.L. *prælātia* (*a* 1109 in Du Cange), f. *prælātus* PRELATE.]

1. The office, position, or dignity of a prelate; a prelatic benefice or see. †Also with possess. pron. (***his, your prelacy***), as a title (*obs.*).

[**1306** *Rolls of Parlt.* I. 219/1 La primer, des Provisions; come seinte Eglise en toutz ces estats de Prelacie soit funde par le Roi et par ces ancestres.] *c* **1325** *Metr. Hom.* 130 For it es sin quar-wit man bies Wit wer[l]des catel prelacyes. **1387** TREVISA *Higden* (Rolls) VI. 59 þis Wyn, after two ȝere of his prelacie, was i-putt oute by þe kyng. **1523** LD. BERNERS *Froiss.* I. cccxlvi. 548 The realme of France was reputed to be the chiefe fountayne of beleve of the christen faythe, bycause of the noble churches and prelasies that be therin. **1579** *Reg. Privy Council Scot.* III. 177 Upoun the vacance of ony prelacie the kirkis thairof salbe disponit to qualifiit ministeris in titill. *c* **1589** *Theses Martinianæ* 20 Praying your prelacie, if you can send one or any of my brethren any word of him. **1600** HOLLAND *Livy* x. vi. 355 Who wanted no promotions & honors, but only Sacerdotall dignities and Prelacies. **1708** *Brit. Apollo* No. 95. 4/1 The Pope had..given General Marsigli (who designs to reassume the Cardinal's Cap) a considerable Prelacy. **1827** HALLAM *Const. Hist.* (1876) III. xvii. 320 Fifty-one ministers..nominated by the king to titular bishoprics and other prelacies.

2. The order or rank of prelates; the body of prelates or of bishops collectively.

13.. *St. Erkenwolde* 107 in Horstm. *Altengl. Leg.* (1881) 268 þe primate with his prelacie was partyd fro home. *c* **1400** *Rom. Rose* 6381 That I lede right a Ioly lyf Thurgh simplesse of the prelacye. **1494** FABYAN *Chron.* VII. ccxliii. 285 The prelasy of the londe assymyled them in counceyll. **1606** WARNER *Alb. Eng.* xv. xcv. (1612) 379 The Prelacie, Nobilitie, States-men, and State betraide. **1641** R. BROOKE *Eng. Episc.* 48 Our Lordly Civill Episcopacie properly called Prelacie. **1827** HALLAM *Const. Hist.* (1876) I. ii. 73 It was no longer possible for the prelacy to offer an efficacious opposition to the reformation they abhorred.

†**3.** The authority of a prelate; ecclesiastical power, as of bishops, abbots, or priors. Also, the authority of any superior, lay or clerical. *Obs.*

a **1340** HAMPOLE *Psalter* lxxii. 17 Ofte sithis a man hafs lardeshipe & prelacy till his aughen dampnacioun. *c* **1450** tr. *De Imitatione* I. ix. 10 It is muche more sure to stonde in subieccioun þan in prelacie. **1534** MORE *Treat. Passion* Wks. (1557) 1320/2 Those..put in prelacy and auctoritie ouer other men. **1577** tr. *Bullinger's Decades* (1592) 835 They cal the power of placing of Ministers..Ecclesiasticall iurisdiction, and to consist in a certayne prelacie.

4. The system of church government by prelates or bishops of lordly rank; a term, chiefly hostile, for EPISCOPACY 2.

c **1380** WYCLIF *Wks.* (1880) 455 þis prelacye is perelous, for it is not fully groundid in crist ne in oþer of his lawis. *a* **1600** HOOKER *Eccl. Pol.* VII. xviii. §1 If these three [things] be granted, then cannot the public benefit of prelacy be dissembled. **1643** *Solemn League & Covenant* §2 That we shall..without respect of persons, endeavour the extirpation of popery, prelacy, (that is, church-government by archbishops, bishops, their chancellors and commissaries, deans, deans and chapters, archdeacons, and all other ecclesiastical officers depending on that hierarchy,) superstition, heresy, schism [etc.]. **1644** C. DOWNING (*title*) The Cleere Antithesis or diametrall opposition betweene Presbytery and Prelacy. **1849** MACAULAY *Hist. Eng.* ii. I. 184 Times had now changed: England was zealous for monarchy and prelacy. **1850** MARSDEN *Early Purit.* (1853) 35 Others.. smarting..from their..severity began to associate prelacy with popery.

†**'prelal**, *a. Obs. rare.* [f. L. *prēlum* a press + -AL[1]; but the regular L. form would be **prēlāris* 'prelar': cf. *velar, solar, stellar.*] Of or pertaining to the printing-press; typographical.

1659 FULLER *App. Inj. Innoc.* I. ix. 7 That Prelial Mistakes in Defiance of all Care will escape in the best Corrected Book. *Ibid.* 8 Prelial Faults. *Ibid.* 58 (*Errata*) There be some Press faults in this my Book, as for *Prelial* (wherever occurring) read *Prelal.* **1670** BLOUNT *Glossogr., Prelal.*

prelanguage, *sb.* and *a.* **A.** *sb.* (Stressed '*prelanguage.*) **1.** [PRE- B. 1] A form of communication preceding the emergence or acquisition of language.

1940 BRYANT & AIKEN *Psychol. of Eng.* iv. 33 What we may call 'pre-language' consisted of meaningful cries used exclusively in context to express emotions, messages, [etc.]. **1973** C. F. HOCKETT *Man's Place in Nature* xxv. 382 The lines of development we have described slowly gave rise to a vocal-auditory communicative system very different from a close call system: to an open system that we shall call *prelanguage. Ibid.*, Prelanguage was not language. **1978** *Verbatim* May 15/2 Language was supposed to begin with grammar, and prelanguage was in no way relevant to the development of speech.

2. [PRE- A. 2.] A hypothetical antecedent language.

1966 E. P. HAMP in Birnbaum & Puhvel *Anc. Indo-European Dial.* 107 This prelanguage would have arisen in Dacia.

B. *adj.* (Stressed *pre'language.*) [PRE- B. 2.] Prior to the emergence of language.

1964 *Language* XL. 240 Various prelanguage stages of development.

prelapsarian (pri:læp'sɛərɪən), *a.* [f. PRE- B. 1 d + L. *laps-us* fall, after *infralapsarian*, etc.] Pertaining to the condition before the Fall.

Quot. 1934 is taken by 'H. MacDiarmid' from an unknown source.

1879 M. D. CONWAY *Demonol.* II. IV. xix. 225 A prelapsarian perfection symbolized by nudity. **1934** 'H. MACDIARMID' *Stony Limits* 65 'The buoyant Prelapsarian naturalness of a country girl.' **1949** AUDEN *Nones* (1952) 36 Her pallid affected heroes Began their hectic quest for the prelapsarian man. **1972** *Time* 22 May 32/2 Nature unspoiled, inhabited by prelapsarian man. **1977** *Daily Tel.* 24 Mar. 15/5 Glenda Jackson's evocation of poet Stevie Smith suggests a woman of prelapsarian innocence.

prelate ('prɛlət), *sb.* Forms: 3–7 prelat, (3 *pl.* -laz, 3–4 *pl.* -las), 4– prelate, (5–6 prelatte, 6 *Sc.* -lot, *pl.* -leittis, -llattis, -lettis, 7 prælate). [a. OF. *prélat* (pl. *prelaz*) = Pr. *prelat*, It. *prelato*, Sp. *prelado*; ad. L. *prælāt-us*, sb. use of pa. pple. of *præferre* to carry or place before, PREFER; in med.L. as sb. a civil or ecclesiastical dignitary.]

1. An ecclesiastical dignitary of exalted rank and authority, as a bishop, archbishop, metropolitan, or patriarch; formerly also including the abbot or prior of a religious house, or the superior of a religious order.

c **1205** LAY. 24502 Of Rome he wes legat and of þan hirede prelat. *a* **1225** *Ancr. R.* 10 Gode religiuse beoð i þe worlde, summe nomeliche prelaz & treowe prechures. **1297** R. GLOUC. (Rolls) 3686 þe bissops & oþer prelats þat of þe londe were. **1340** *Ayenb.* 237 Alsuo is þe spot of lecherie more uouler and more perilous ine clerkes and ine prelas. *c* **1380** WYCLIF *Serm.* Sel. Wks. I. 65 Wolde God þat preelatis wolde þenke on þis now. *c* **1400** GOWER *Addr. Hen. IV* in *Pol. Poems* II. 11 The worldes princes and the prelats bothe. **14..** *Metr. Voc.* in Wr.-Wülcker 629/19 Prelatte or byschop, *antistes*. **1485** CAXTON *St. Wenefr.* 9 Hys owne moder was prelate and chyef aboue the other relygyouse nonnes. **1562** A. SCOTT *Poems* (S.T.S.) i. 46 Lat perversit prelettis leif perqueir. **1604** E. G[RIMSTONE] *D'Acosta's Hist. Indies* III. ix. 150 A reverend religious man, of the Order of Saint Dominike, and Prelate thereof. **1644** MILTON *Areop.* (Arb.) 35 This project of licencing..was catcht up by our Prelates. **1765** BLACKSTONE *Comm.* I. xi. 378 The usual method of granting these investitures, which was *per annulum et baculum*, by the prince's delivering to the prelate a ring, and a pastoral staff or crosier. **1776** HUME *Life* in *Hist. Eng.* (1812) I. Pref. 11 The primate of England,.. primate of Ireland... These dignified prelates separately sent me a message not to be discouraged. **1844** LINGARD *Anglo-Sax. Ch.* (1858) II. i. 23 The presence of at least three prelates was required at the consecration of a bishop. **1856** EMERSON *Eng. Traits, Relig.* Wks. (Bohn) II. 101 The curates are ill-paid, and the prelates are overpaid.

†**b.** Applied to a chief priest of the Jewish, or other non-Christian religion. *Obs.*

a **1400–50** *Alexander* 1529 Now passis furth þis prelate with prestis of þe temple. **1526** TINDALE *Matt.* xxvii. 41 Lykwyse also the prelates mockinge hym with the scribes and seniours sayde [etc.]. *Ibid.* xxviii. 11 The kepers.. shewed vnto the prelattes all thinges whych had hapened. **1540–1** ELYOT *Image Gov.* (1549) 2 Because he was prelate in the temple of the Son, whom the Phenices doe calle Heliogabalus. *a* **1600** HOOKER *Eccl. Pol.* VII. xviii. § 11 Moses and Aaron..the chief prince and chief prelate. **1600** HOLLAND *Livy* XXVII. vi. 630 C. Servilius the Prelate or Pontifex, was invested and installed in stead of T. Octacilius Crassus. **1601** —— *Pliny* II. 193 The Druidæ or Prelats of France aboue named, make great account of another herb.. which they name Samolus.

†**2.** A person having superiority or authority; a chief, head, principal, superior. *Obs.*

1390 GOWER *Conf.* III. 234 Bot yit a kinges hihe astat, Which of his ordre as a prelat, Schal ben enoignt and seintefied. *c* **1450** tr. *De Imitatione* I. ix. 10 To stonde under obedience & lyue under a prelate, & not be at his owne liberte. *c* **1450–60** *Bp. Grosseteste's Househ. Stat.* in *Babees Bk.* (1868) 328 ʒe, that be principalle heuede or prelate to alle ʒoure seruauntis bothe lesse and more. **1502** ATKYNSON tr. *De Imitatione* II. ii. 181 The humble subieccyon of the subiecte to the prelate. *a* **1614** DONNE *Βιαθανατος* (1644) 149 And thus dyed..These Prelates of virginitie, Captaines of Chastitie, and companions in Martyrdome. **1780** *Von Troil's Iceland* p. xvii, Dr. Von Troil..is prelate of all the Swedish orders of knighthood.

3. *attrib.* and *Comb.*, as ***prelate founder***, ***lord***, ***martyr***, ***prince***; ***prelate-like*** adj.; **prelate-Protestant**, hostile term for a Protestant of an episcopal church; **prelate-purple**, the shade of purple worn by bishops (cf. CARDINAL *a.* 8).

1746 *Acc. French Settlements in N. Amer.* 24 The *prelate-founder has his apartments in the house. ? *a* **1550** *Freiris of Berwik* 183 in *Dunbar's Poems* (S.T.S.) 291 So *prelat lyk sat he in to the chyre. *c* **1646** MILTON *New Forcers Consc.* 1 Because you have thrown of your *Prelate Lord, And with stiff Vowes renounc'd his Liturgie. **1641** MILTON *Reform.* Wks. (1847) 18/2 For those *prelate-martyrs they glory of, they are to be judged what they were by the Gospel. **1899** *Cath. Bk.-Notes* 15 Apr. 103 To many the *prelate-prince is but vaguely known. **1680** S. MATHER *Iren.* 9 Not only the Independents and the Presbyterians, but the very Papists, and *Prelate-Protestants have thought it lawful. **1895** *Daily News* 5 Feb. 6/6 The..favour in which *prelate-purple is held shows no symptom of decreasing.

†'**prelate**, *v.*[1] *Obs.* [f. prec. sb.] *intr.* To act the prelate; to perform the office of a prelate. Hence †'**prelating** *vbl. sb.* and *ppl. a.*

1548–9 LATIMER *Ploughers* B iij, Ye that be prelates loke well to your offyce, for right prelatynge is buisye labourynge and not lordyng. **1550** BALE *Apol.* Pref. 8 b, They haue counterfeted..Iudas in kyssinge, Cayphas in prelatyng, & Pilate in washinge their handes. **1642** SIR E. DERING *Sp. on Relig.* 12 Gods true Religion is violently invaded by two.. enemies;..the Papists for one party, and our Prelating faction for the other. **1656** S. H. *Gold. Law* 22 That the Presbyterie might Prelate it under the Notion of Priests, and so crush all other Sects.

†**pre'late**, *v.*[2] *Obs. rare.* [a. obs. F. *prélater* to prefer, advance, f. L. *prælāt-*, ppl. stem of *præferre* to PREFER.]

1. *trans.* To utter, pronounce. *rare.*

1547 BOORDE *Introd. Knowl.* xxiii. (1870) 179 An Englyshman, without teachyng, can not speake nor prelate the wordes of an Italyan.

2. To exalt, raise, prefer in rank or power.

1626 T. H. *Caussin's Holy Crt.* 89 To be borne into the world supereminently, prelated aboue all the creatures of the world.

3. *refl.* [transl. obs. F. *se prelater* to act the prelate, now *se prélasser*.] To affect an air of dignity and ostentatious gravity.

1685 COTTON tr. *Montaigne* III. 386, I see some, who.. prelate themselves even to the heart and liver [*orig.* qui se prelatent jusques au foye et aux intestins] and carry their state along with them, even to the close-stool.

'**prelatehood**. *rare*[−1]. [f. PRELATE *sb.* + -HOOD.] The state of a prelate; the estate of prelates.

1804 *Captive of Valence* II. x. 96 Don't deceive yourself, ..after the Friarhood will come the turn of the Priesthood, and then, my lord, that of the Prelatehood.

†**prela'teity**. *Obs. nonce-wd.* [f. PRELATE *sb.* after *hicceity*, *paneity*, etc.] The essential quality or essence of a prelate.

1641 MILTON *Ch. Govt.* II. i. 45 Neither shall I..trifle with one that would tell me of quiddities and formalities, whether prelaty or prelateity in abstract notion be this or that.

'**prelately**, *a. rare.* [f. PRELATE *sb.* + -LY[1]: cf. *kingly*, *lordly*.] Prelatical.

1550 BALE *Image Both Ch.* III. Bbb iv, Theyr copes, perrours, and chysibilles, whan they bee in theyr prelately pompous sacrifices.

prelateship ('prɛlət-ʃɪp). [f. as prec. + -SHIP.] The office of a prelate; the tenure of this office; also, with poss. pron., as a title (after *lordship*).

1570 FOXE *A. & M.* (ed. 2) 255/2 He was content that Thurstinus should safely reenter hys realme, and quietly enioye hys prelateshyp. **1654** VILVAIN *Epit. Ess.* VI. xcv, Ostia thee gav A Prelatship. **1671** H. M. tr. *Erasm. Colloq.* 406 They who in my Boat lament that they have among the living, Kingdoms, Prelateships,..do bring me [Charon] but an half-peny. **1760** *Impostors Detected* II. iii. I. 180 His prelateship very graciously uncovered himself when they entered. **1832** *Blackw. Mag.* XXXI. 547 His prelateship ordered the business of the Court to be concluded.

prelatess ('prɛlətɪs). [f. PRELATE *sb.* + -ESS.] A female prelate; an abbess or prioress: in Milton satirical; also, the wife of a prelate (*jocular*).

1642 MILTON *Apol. Smect.* Wks. 1851 III. 272 At the bordellos..raps up without pitty the sage and rheumatick old Prelatesse with all her young Corinthian Laity to inquire for such a one. **1762** tr. *Busching's Syst. Geog.* IV. 368 The abbess is also still stiled..a princess and prelatess of the holy Roman Empire. **1857** TROLLOPE *Barchester T.* xvii, Mr. Slope did not wish to have both the prelate and the prelatess against him. **1904** *Adventures of Elizabeth* vi. 181 Will no one rid me of this troublesome prelatess?

prelatial (prɪ'leɪʃ(ɪ)əl), *a. rare.* [f. med.L. *prælātia* PRELACY + -AL[1].] Of, pertaining to, or proper to prelacy or a prelate. Also, that is a prelate.

1870 DISRAELI *Lothair* xviii, It [a portfolio] was of morocco and of prelatial purple. **1886** F. G. LEE *King Edward VI* iii. 142 Both as regards what the prelatial preacher said, and what he did not say, it appeared.. unsatisfactory and..inadequate. **1903** *Bulwark* Sept. 203 The Pope receives the Ring at his election... At the Gregorian Chapel he receives cardinalitial and prelatial homage.

prelatic (prɪ'lætɪk), *a.* [f. PRELATE *sb.* + -IC.]

1. That is a prelate; of, pertaining to, of the nature or character of, or like a prelate; prelately.

1649 MILTON *Eikon.* Wks. 1738 I. 387 We..are sure that the piety of his prelatic model glister'd more upon the Posts and Pillars..than in the true works of spiritual edification. **1821** GALT *Ann. Parish* xii, A woman..of a prelatic disposition, seeking all things her own way. **1854** MILMAN *Lat. Chr.* IV. iv. (1883) II. 258 Wilfrid..blended the rigour of the monk with something of prelatic magnificence. **1871** H. S. CUMING in *Archæol. Jrnl.* Sept. 221 Egwin or Ecgwine ..whose prelatic rule extended from 693 to 717.

2. Episcopal; = PRELATICAL 2.

1642 SIR E. DERING *Sp. on Relig.* 94 Such of the Prelatick partie as are in love with..pomp and power. **1678** R. BARCLAY *Apol. Quakers* XIII. vii. 473 The Prelatick Calvinists have termed the Presbyterians Schismatical and Pertinacious. **1706** DE FOE *Jure Div.* Pref. 27 In the late Proclamation for banishing Prelatick Ministers in Scotland. **1814** SCOTT *Wav.* xiv, The prelatic clergy. **1894** CROCKETT *Mad Sir Uchtred* 183 They still held prelatic services.

pre'latical, *a.* (*sb.*) [f. as prec. + -AL[1].]

A. *adj.* **1.** = PRELATIC 1.

1634 CANNE *Necess. Separ.* (1849) 235 Their prelatical or episcopal office or ministry, is not the proper ministry of any of our church assemblies. **1660** WOOD *Life* Dec. (O.H.S.) I. 355 The most exact prelaticall garb that might be. *a* **1661** FULLER *Worthies* (1662) I. 58 Of the Prelatical Clergy, we have Francis Godwin a Bishop, the Son of a Bishop, and Doctor John King Son to his Reverend Father the Bishop of London. **1748** SMOLLETT *Rod. Rand.* ix, He rose and moved, with prelatical dignity, to the door. **1877** J. LL. DAVIES in *Dict. Chr. Biog.* I. 96 Gibbon..represents the behaviour of Ambrose as marked by a prelatical pomposity.

2. Governed by or adhering to prelates or prelacy; a hostile term for episcopal, episcopalian.

1641 R. BERNARD (*title*) A Short View of the Prælaticall Church of England. **1641** MILTON (*title*) Of Prelatical Episcopacy. **1651** BAXTER *Inf. Bapt.* 272 That the Papists and Prelaticall party do..urge Infant Baptism to be a tradition, is no wonder. **1733** NEAL *Hist. Purit.* III. 415 They insisted peremptorily on the establishment of the Presbyterian church government upon the ruins of the Prelatical. **1849** MACAULAY *Hist. Eng.* ii. I. 184 The government resolved to set up a prelatical church in Scotland.

†**B.** *sb.* in *pl.* Things pertaining to prelates or prelacy. *Obs.*

1643 W. GREENHILL *Axe at Root* 13 It's feared we stick too much to Mosaicalls, Prelaticalls, and Traditionalls.

Hence **pre'latically** *adv.*, in a prelatic or prelatical way; as a prelate; with reference to prelacy; **pre'laticalness** (Bailey vol. II, 1727).

1641 MILTON *Ch. Govt.* Concl. 53 A sort of formal outside men prelatically addicted. **1646** T. COLEMAN *Brotherly Exam. Re-exam.* 12, I feare lest the Presbyteriall government..should Prelatically tyrannize. *a* **1659** T. MORTON *Episc.* ii. §2 (1670) 30 This is as much as any Prelatically minded man could..say.

pre-Latin: see PRE- B. 1.

prelation (prɪ'leɪʃən). Now *rare* or *Obs.* [ME. *prelacioune*, a. OF. *prelacion* (13th c. in Hatz.-Darm.), F. *prélation*, ad. L. *prælātiōn-em* a preferring, preference, n. of action f. *prælāt-*, ppl. stem of *præferre* to hold forth, offer, present, prefer.]

I. †**1.** Utterance, pronunciation. *Obs. rare.*

c **1375** BARBOUR *Troy-bk.* II. 304 Tune the mater of hys sermoune As he furth mayde prelacioune. **1659** OWEN *Integr. Heb. & Grk. Text* Wks. 1853 XVI. 396 With reference to the quantity of time required to their prelation, whereby the same vowel becomes sometimes long and sometimes short.

II. 2. The action of preferring or condition of being preferred; preferment, exaltation, promotion; pre-eminence, superiority, dignity; preference.

c **1420** *Chron. Vilod.* 4610 þat he dude fiue & twenty ʒere hurre prelacione byfore. **1585** JAS. VI *Declar. to Kirk* in J. Melvill *Diary* (Wodrow Soc.) 242 Haiffing thairfor sum prelation and dignitie aboue his breithren. **1632** SIR T. HAWKINS tr. *Mathieu's Unhappy Prosperitie* 251 This Prelation offended the Emperour, and began their enmitie. **1649** ROBERTS *Clavis Bibl.* 369 A Prelation of wisdome before pleasure. **1885** EDGAR *Old Ch. Life in Scot.* iv. 189 [In] a Presbyterian Church..there is no prelacy or prelation or precedence of one presbyter over another.

†**3.** The dignity of a prelate; = PRELATURE 1. *Obs.*

1695 J. SAGE *Article*, etc. Wks. 1844 I. 108 Popish Prelates might quit their errors, not their prelations.

†**4.** The action of placing before; prefixing. *Obs.*

1701 NORRIS *Ideal World* I. v. 225 As the first consideration proves that the *an* should be before the *quid*, so the other does no less strongly plead for the prælation of the *quid* before the *an*.

†'**prelatish**, *a. Obs. rare*[−1]. [f. PRELATE *sb.* + -ISH[1].] Prelatical.

1642 MILTON *Apol. Smect.* viii. Wks. 1851 III. 310 Any congregation..perverted with Prelatish leven.

'**prelatism**. [See -ISM.] Prelacy, lordly episcopacy; adherence to this. (A hostile term.)

1611 H. BARROWE (*title*) Platform, which may serve as a Preparative to purge away prelatisme. **1641** MILTON *Prel. Episc.* 23 Five hundred years after Christ, the councils themselves were foully corrupted with ungodly prelatism. **1641** —— *Animadv.* Wks. 1851 III. 195 The Prelatism of Episcopacy which began then to burgeon, and spread.

prelatist ('prɛlətɪst). [f. PRELATE *sb.* + -IST.] A supporter or adherent of prelacy; a hostile term for an episcopalian.

1659 STEWARD *Serm. at Paris* Pref. A v, The Preacher, as great a Prelatist as any whom unkinde or jealous Brethren have ever blasted under that title. **1721** *Wodrow Corr.* (1843) II. 594 Our prelatists and Jacobites, I hear, are much chagrined. **1827** HALLAM *Const. Hist.* (1876) I. vii. 414 Tolerance..of that proscribed worship, was equally abhorrent to the prelatist and the puritan.

prelatize ('prɛlətaɪz), *v.* [f. as prec. + -IZE.]

†**1.** *intr.* To be or become prelatical. *Obs. rare.*

1641 MILTON *Animadv.* Wks. 1851 III. 195 He [Cyprian] indeed succeeded into an Episcopacy that began then to Prelatize.

2. *trans.* To make prelatical; to bring under prelatic or episcopal government.

a **1864** PALFREY (W.), Laud was busy with his more important plan of prelatizing the church of Scotland. **1873** MCDOWALL *Hist. Dumfries* xxx. 336 Efforts to prelatise the Church.

Hence '**prelatizing** *vbl. sb.* and *ppl. a.*

1641 MILTON *Reform.* II. Wks. 1851 III. 61 We may rather suspect them for some Prelatizing-spirits that admire our Bishopricks, not Episcopacy. **1882** T. A. POPE tr. *Capecelatro's Life St. P. Neri* II. 373 With all this prelatising in the Congregation we are drifting into a slavery the worse that our chains are all of gold.

prelatry ('prɛlətrɪ). [f. as prec. + -RY.] Prelacy.
1641 MILTON *Reform.* II. Wks. 1851 III. 42 The painted Battlements, and gaudy rottennesse of Prelatrie. **1653** —— *Hirelings* (1659) 21 The whole gang of prelatry. **1879** M. PATTISON *Milton* 154 There is not a hint of discontent with the prelatry, once intolerable to him.

prelature ('prɛlətjʊə(r)). [a. F. *prélature* (14th c. in Godef. *Compl.*), ad. med.L. *prælātūra* (in Du Cange): see PRELATE *sb.* and -URE.]

1. The dignity, rank, office, condition, or function of a prelate: = PRELACY 1.
1607 HARINGTON in *Nugæ Ant.* (ed. Park 1804) II. 99 One of the most eminent of his ranke, and a man that carryes prelature in his verie aspect. **1669** *Hist. Pope's Nephews* I. (1673) 70 He heaped Abbies and Prelatures upon them as many as they pleased. **1725** tr. *Dupin's Eccl. Hist. 17th C.* I. v. 99 The Bishops exercised, anciently, as they do at present, both the Prelature and the Priesthood. **1844** *Life St. Wilfrid* 149 This poor statesmanship.. filling prelatures with barely respectable mediocrity. **1876** SIR G. BOWYER in *Times* 8 Nov., [Antonelli] speedily rose to a judicial office, and then to the prelature, but still as a layman.

2. The order of prelates: = PRELACY 2.
1845 S. AUSTIN *Ranke's Hist. Ref.* I. 333 Arimbold, a member of the Roman prelature. **1855** MILMAN *Lat. Chr.* XIV. i. VI. 388 The dignity, the splendid and wealthy palaces of the Prelature.

† **'prelaty.** *Obs. rare.* [ad. med.L. *prælātia*: see PRELACY.] **1.** = PRELACY 4.
1641 MILTON (*title*) The Reason of Church-government Urg'd against Prelaty. **1642** —— *Apol. Smect.* Wks. (1847) 77/1 There be of those that esteem prelaty a figment, who yet can pipe if they can dance. **1644** —— *Areop.* (Arb.) 61 That those evills of Prelaty.. will now light wholly upon learning.

2. The office or superiority of a prelate.
1641 MILTON *Ch. Govt.* iii. Wks. 1851 III. 109 Laborious teaching is the most honourable Prelaty that one Minister can have above another in the Gospell. **1642** HALES *Schism* 12 The first I mentioned was the Prelaties of Bishops in one Sea.

pre-launch: see PRE- B. 2 a.

pre-law (priː'lɔː), *a.* (*sb.*) *U.S.* [PRE- B. 2.] Of or pertaining to subjects studied in preparation for a course in law. Also *ellipt.* as *sb.*
1961 in WEBSTER. **1971** *Mod. Law Rev.* XXXIV. 650 Their North American counterparts who have undertaken significant pre-law work in another discipline. **1976** *National Observer* (U.S.) 21 Feb. 16/1 (Advt.), Undergraduate prelaw program, premed, and other preprofessional offerings. **1976** *Billings* (Montana) *Gaz.* 17 June 3-B/1 (Advt.), [She].. plans to attend the University of Montana in Missoula to study pre-law. **1978** *Detroit Free Press* 5 Mar. 9/1 Career training offered at Madonna for deaf students includes.. pre-law and education.

prelect, præ- (prɪ'lɛkt), *v.* [f. L. *prælect-*, ppl. stem of *prælegĕre* to read to others, lecture upon, f. *præ*, PRE- A. + *legĕre* to choose, to read.]

I. † **1.** *trans.* To choose in preference to others.
1620 *Swetnam Arraign'd* (1880) 22 Thou knowst with what a generall consent Of all Sicilia I was prelected By my dread Soueraigne. **1656** BLOUNT *Glossogr.*, *Prelect*, either from *prælectus*, read before; or from *præelectus*, one chosen before another.

II. 2. *intr.* To lecture or discourse (*to* an audience, *on* or *upon* a subject); to deliver a lecture.
1785 REID *Intell. Powers* IV. iv. 384 With no greater emotion than a professor in a college prelects to his audience. **1803** *Edin. Rev.* I. 430 He then prelects upon the construction of the hearers. **1868** M. PATTISON *Academ. Org.* v. 284 The rector of a gymnasium.. sometimes yields to the temptation to prælect to his boys.. upon some abstruse point.. which is interesting himself. **1876** GRANT *Burgh Sch. Scotl.* I. i. 44 If we could ascertain the books on which our teachers prelected in the schools before the Reformation.

prelection, præ- (prɪ'lɛkʃən), *sb.* [ad. L. *prælectiōn-em*, n. of action f. *prælegĕre*: see prec.]

1. A public lecture or discourse; *esp.* a lecture by a teacher to students at a college or university.
1587 FLEMING *Contn. Holinshed* III. 1310/1 His prelections or lectures which he did read in Paules, and his poore mans librarie he caused to be imprinted. *a* **1677** HALE *Prim. Orig. Man.* I. iv. 107 Let him resort to the Prelections of Fabor, collected by Monsuerius. **1764** REID *Let.* Wks. I. 39/2, I examine for an hour upon my morning prelection. **1851** LONGF. *Gold. Leg.*, *School of Salerno*, Let us go in.. And listen awhile to a learned prelection On Marcus Aurelius Cassiodorus. *a* **1882** SIR R. CHRISTISON *Life* I. 412 The lustre which the university prelections of many members of their Church has shed on the Church itself.

2. A previous reading. (Better *pre-lection.*)
a **1655** VINES *Lord's Supp.* xii. 159 Nor could the Disciples have sung with him in consort, except we imagine such a prælection of it to them, as is used by us now. **1857** BORROW *Romany Rye* (1858) I. 271 To induce sleep, nothing could be more efficacious than a slight pre-lection of his poems.

Hence † **pre'lection** *v.*, *trans.* to make the subject of prelection; to lecture on. *Obs.* *rare*$^{-1}$.
1716 M. DAVIES *Athen. Brit.* III. 3 The next Scholastick Ascent is call'd Grammar, where are prelection'd Tully's Offices, Paradoxes, and Tusculan's Questions.

prelector, præ- (prɪ'lɛktə(r)). [a. L. *prælector* one who reads an author to others, and adds explanations, agent-n. f. *prælegĕre*: see PRELECT.] A public reader or lecturer, esp. in a college or university.

In Oxford formerly interchangeable with *professor* (as applied to all except the Regius Professors), as the *Prelector* or *Professor of Poetry*; in Cambridge applied sometimes to a college tutor or 'reader' in a subject of study; also to the college tutor or other officer who attends to the matriculation and graduation of members of his college.

1586 FERNE *Blaz. Gentrie* To Gentl. of Inner Temple, My reuerend Maysters the praelectors and Benchers of the same house. **1654** WHITLOCK *Zootomia* 385 You shall scarce meet with a Reprover that taketh not his Friend to Taske.. with the Cathedrated Authority of a Prælector, or publike Reader, to dissect him. **1779–81** JOHNSON *L.P.*, *Pope* Wks. IV. 50 Of the English Odyssey a criticism was published by Spence, at that time Prelector of Poetry at Oxford. **1881** E. R. LANKESTER in *Nature* 10 Nov. 27/1 The steadily working school of biologists which has risen around the Trinity Prælector on the banks of the Cam. **1907** *Masque Med. Learn.* in *Bk. of Words Oxf. Pageant* 56 Then as Praelector I must needs expound That ye may profit by our picturing.

Hence **pre'lectorship**, the office of a prelector; also **pre'lectress**, a female lecturer. *rare.*
1873 *Act 36 & 37 Vict.* c. 21 §2 Every.. professorship.. public readership, prelectorship, lectureship.. and exhibition.. the income of which is payable out of the revenues. **1889** *Sat. Rev.* 7 Dec. 640/2 Miss Helen Taylor and her sisterhood of itinerant Home Rule praelectresses.

pre-legislation: see PRE- B. 2 a.

pre-let: see PRE- A. 1.

prelexical: see PRE- B. 1 d.

† **'prelial,** *a. Obs. rare*$^{-1}$. [ad. late L. *prœliāl-is*, f. *prœlium* a battle: see -AL^{1}.] Of or pertaining to battles; warlike, fighting.
1637 R. HUMPHREY tr. *St. Ambrose* I. 97 These may give them tast.. of the preliall vertue, and victories of Gods people.

† **preli'ation.** *Obs. rare.* Also 7 prœ-, (præ-). [ad. late L. *prœliātiōn-em* a battling, n. of action f. *prœliāre* to fight.] Fighting, contention; a battle.
1651 HOWELL *Venice* 204 In their preliations and quarrells. **1660** —— *Parly of Beasts* iii. 33 We have stirred the humors of the foolish Inhabitants of the earth to insurrections, to warr and præliation. **1678** SIR J. SPELMAN *Alfred Gt.* (1709) 32 Their war being mostly Inroads, Foraging and Spoil, subject to Skirmishes and unexpected Prœliations.

† **'prelibate,** *v. Obs.* Also præ-. [f. ppl. stem of L. *prælībāre* (f. *præ*, PRE- A. 1 + *lībāre* to taste).] *trans.* To taste beforehand; to give a foretaste.
1623 COCKERAM, *Prelibate*, to taste first. **1645** OUGHTRED in Rigaud *Corr. Sci. Men* (1841) I. 63, I received information by a letter from Paris, wherein was prælibated only a small taste thereof.

prelibation (priːlaɪ'beɪʃən). Also 7 præ-. [ad. late L. *prælībātiōn-em* a tasting beforehand, an offering of the first-fruits, n. of action f. *prælībāre*: see prec. So F. *prélibation.*]

1. A tasting beforehand or by anticipation; a foretaste. Chiefly *fig.*
1526 *Pilgr. Perf.* (W. de W. 1531) 296 As prelibacyons or foretastynges of that endlesse glory. **1633** T. ADAMS *Exp. 2 Peter* i. 19 The wicked have a prelibation of that darkness they shall go unto hereafter. **1742** YOUNG *Nt. Th.* IX. 2370 Rich prelibation of consummate joy! **1841** *Blackw. Mag.* XLIX. 287 That mysterious ante-dawn—that prelibation of the full daylight, which, under the name of the Zodiacal light, perplexes the oriental surveyor of the heavens. **1874** H. R. REYNOLDS *John Bapt.* vii. 415 Their master had been taken from them, a sad prelibation of the deeper agony which His own true disciples would experience.

2. An offering of first-fruits, or of the first taste, of anything. Now *rare.*
1635–56 COWLEY *Davideis* II. Note 22 Why may we not say.. that before the men were refresht by bread and wine, there was an offering or prelibation of them to God? **1649** JER. TAYLOR *Gt. Exemp.* Ad Sect. v. §1 Offering them [the first-fruits of his blood] to God like the prelibation of a sacrifice. **1805** WORDSW. *Prelude* v. 245 Like a stallèd ox.. that may not taste A flower till it have yielded up its sweets A prelibation to the mower's scythe.

So **pre'libatory** *a.*, of the nature of or affording a foretaste; preliminary. *rare*$^{-1}$.
1826 G. S. FABER *Diffic. Romanism* (1853) 201 Set forth, not as a transient preparatory purgatory, but as a dungeon of fearful prelibatory punishment to receive its completion in gehenna.

pre-liberation, -life: see PRE- B. 2 a.

prelim (prɪ'lɪm, 'priːlɪm), colloq. abbrev. of PRELIMINARY *sb.* and *a.* **a.** A preliminary practice, examination, contest, inquiry, or report. Also *transf.*, a student in a preliminary class and *attrib.*
1891 C. DAWSON *Let.* 19 Feb. in R. S. Churchill *Winston S. Churchill* (1967) I. Compan. I. v. 228, I was so glad to hear you had successfully passed the 'Army Prelim', allow me to congratulate you. **1901** *Daily News* 1 Apr. 5/6 We arrived at Putney, just in time to see Oxford come out for their 'prelim'. **1902** *Daily Chron.* 19 Dec. 5/2 The English public school boy goes north for months of special tutoring for his 'prelim.'; thereat, probably, to fail in his English paper. **1904** *Daily News* 28 Dec. 6 While yet in the preliminary class,.. she.. said, 'I want a canvas six feet long.' 'What does she want with a six-foot canvas?.. She's only a "prelim"!' **1923** L. J. VANCE *Baroque* xxvii. 173 A fight that'd make the Dempsey-Carpenteeyay bout look like a cooked prelim. **1928** *Collier's* 18 Aug. 25/2 You're nothin' but a has-been, staggerin' around like some prelim boy. **1958** *Times* 17 Oct. 3/5 The general college rule which stipulates that undergraduates who twice fail 'prelims' should be sent down or rusticated. **1965** D. FRANCIS *Odds Against* vi. 86 I'll put one of the boys on to it and let you have a prelim. Is it urgent? **1974** N. FREELING *Dressing of Diamond* 41 I've been waiting to hear from you to set a prelim afoot. **1977** P. COSGRAVE *Cheyney's Law* ii. 17 Tommy went to Cambridge. .. His prelims were only fair.

b. Usu. in *pl.* The preliminary matter of a book. Cf. PRELIMINARY *sb.* c.
1927 *Observer* 18 Dec. 4 He tells.. about signatures, prelims, end-papers, uncut and unopened pages, issues and imperfections. **1932** *Times Lit. Suppl.* 7 Jan. 13/2 When, with the 'prelims' of 'The Painted Veil', he [*sc.* W. S. Maugham] comes up against a more important bibliographical problem, his description is confused. **1957** *Ibid.* 1 Nov. 664/3 Besides a few corrections in the text there are some notes in pencil among the prelims.. and in ink on the back endpaper. **1960** [see BLAD *sb.*^{2} 2 c]. **1976** *Indexer* Oct. 93/2 The index.. should be provided by the publisher much as he provides prelims and jacket copy.

prelimen (prɪ'laɪmən). [f. L. *præ* before + *līmen* threshold.] A preliminary step.
1898 C. S. SHERRINGTON in *Phil. Trans. R. Soc.* B. CXC. 50 The requisite prelimen to the original aim of the inquiry [having been] carried through, the examination of certain spinal reflexes has been proceeded to.

pre'liminarily, *adv.* [f. next + -LY^{2}.] In a preliminary manner; as an introduction.
1768 *Woman of Honor* II. 29 His reason.. for not preliminarily addressing himself to Clara. **1849** H. MAYO *Pop. Superstit.* (1851) 188, I went over preliminarily my schoolboy recollections. **1891** G. MEREDITH *One of our Conq.* II. viii. 207 So must we.. preliminarily do something.

preliminary (prɪ'lɪmɪnərɪ), *sb.* and *a.* (*adv.*) Also 7 præ-. [ad. F. *préliminaire* or mod.L. *prælīmināris* (both used in Treaties of Westphalia, 1648), f. L. *præ* before + *līmen*, *-in-*, threshold; cf. L. *līmināris* of or belonging to a threshold. The L. *prælīmināris* was prob. in earlier use.]

A. *sb.* **a.** A subordinate step, measure, statement, etc., that precedes another to which it is introductory or preparatory. Chiefly in *pl.* = preparatory measures or arrangements.
1656 CROMWELL *Lett.* 6 May in *Carlyle*, There were some preliminaries to be performed by him before we could enter upon the whole body of a treaty. **1661** GLANVILL *Van. Dogm.* Pref. B j b, Sensible of the tædium of long præliminaries. **1693** LUTTRELL *Brief Rel.* (1857) III. 24 The lords were taken up in adjusting the preliminaries for the lord Mohuns tryall. **1762** SYMMER in Ellis *Orig. Lett.* Ser. II. IV. 449 This is not the Ratification of Preliminaries simply as such, but indeed of the Treaty of Peace. **1792** BURKE *Corr.* (1844) IV. 3 The petition to the king I hold an essential preliminary. **1857** DICKENS *Lett.* (1880) II. 19 The general manager.. will arrange all the preliminaries for me. **1885** *Law Times* LXXIX. 159/1 The value of systematic teaching as a preliminary to professional work.

b. (*ellipt.* use of adj.) Preliminary examination.
1882 EDNA LYALL *Donovan* xxiv, He passed his preliminary successfully.

c. Usu. in *pl.* The preliminary matter of a book. Cf. PRELIM b.
1888 C. T. JACOBI *Printers' Vocab.* 103 *Preliminary*, any matter coming before the main text of a work—title, preface, contents, etc. **1903** A. E. HOUSMAN *Let.* 12 Feb. (1971) 64, I don't quite know the meaning of 'the preliminary', but I enclose the dedication which is to follow the title page. **1977** *N. & Q. for Somerset & Dorset* Sept. 301 The list of abbreviations on p. 70 would have been more usefully placed in the preliminaries.

B. *adj.* Preceding and leading up to the main subject or business; introductory; preparatory.
a **1667** JER. TAYLOR *Serm. Jas. ii. 24* Wks. 1831 III. 307, I shall premise some preliminary considerations, to prepare the way of holiness. **1709** ADDISON *Tatler* No. 20 ¶8 The Articles Preliminary to a general Peace were settled. **1759** ROBERTSON *Hist. Scotl.* III. Wks. 1813 I. 241 After these preliminary steps, Mary ventured to call a meeting of Parliament. **1828** D'ISRAELI *Chas. I*, I. iv. 89 The restoration of the Palatinate was insisted on as a preliminary article of the treaty. **1890** A. R. WALLACE *Darwinism* 1 It is for want of this preliminary knowledge.

C. as *adv.* = PRELIMINARILY.
1748 RICHARDSON *Clarissa* (1811) III. 329 But that you had preliminary bound me under a solemn vow. **1897** *Outing* (U.S.) XXIX. 438/1 [He] gathered the leashed hounds about him preliminary to a start.

Hence **pre'liminarize** *v.*, *trans.* to put forward as a preliminary.
1844 TUPPER *Crock of Gold* xiii, Let us preliminarize a thought or two.

† **prelimi'nation.** *Obs. rare.* [f. as prec. + -ATION.] A preliminary action or performance.
1667 WATERHOUSE *Fire Lond.* 16 These preliminations ushered in Laws of purgation.

prelimit (priː'lɪmɪt), *v.* Also 7 præ-. [PRE- A. 1.] *trans.* To limit or set bounds to beforehand; to confine within limits previously fixed.
a **1649** DRUMM. OF HAWTH. *Hist. Jas. II*, Wks. (1711) 25 The commissioners are chosen.., prepared, instructed, prelimited by him. **1693** *Apol. Clergy Scot.* 81 Who have prelimited the Assembly, by their Letter and Act. **1784** J. BROWN *Hist. Brit. Ch.* (1820) II. vi. 288 The free election of Commissioners had been prelimited by the letter and act of the Commission. **1880** MASSON *Milton* VI. II. ii. 412 A royalty duly prelimited and constrained into respectability.

Hence **pre'limited** *ppl. a.*; **pre'limiting** *vbl. sb.* **1637-50** Row *Hist. Kirk* (Wodrow Soc.) 248 To thir Articles the ministers consented..for the tyme, even to be silent,..and to have a prælimited Assemblie, feareing, that if they had made any opposition, neither should a Generall Assemblie have been obtained. *a* **1715** Burnett *Own Time* an. 1687 (1753) III. iv. 147 The prelimiting and the packing of a parliament. **1784** J. Brown *Hist. Brit. Ch.* (1820) II. vi. 293 The prelimiting and corrupting of the General Assembly.

pre'limitate, *v. rare.* [f. pre- A. 1 + limitate *v.*] *trans.* = prelimit.
1901 W. Morison *Johnston of Warriston* viii. 58 Her refusal to approve the Acts of the Glasgow Assembly prelimitated the next Assembly.

prelimi'tation. [f. pre- A. 2 + limitation.] The action of prelimiting; an instance of this.
1637-50 Row *Hist. Kirk* (Wodrow Soc.) 35 To prepare maters for the Assemblie ensueing.., without prejudice or prælimitation of the Assemblie alwayes. **1661** R. L'Estrange *Interest Mistaken* 15 The Royal Party press'd for a Free Choice and Convention, without Prelimitation.

prelingual (pri:'lɪŋgwəl), *a.* a. [pre- B. 1] Antecedent to the development or acquirement of language.
1873 F. Hall *Mod. Eng.* 334 Theoretical admirers of the prelingual period are, possibly, scattered here and there, to this day. **1881** J. Owen *Even. w. Skeptics* II. x. 364 The prelingual state, in which impressions of outward objects exist in the mind as inarticulate, voiceless concepts. **1924** R. M. Ogden tr. *Koffka's Growth of Mind* v. 322 The behaviour of the child during his pre-lingual period. **1976** *Word 1971* XXVII. 132 What constitutes semantic salience for the pre-lingual child?
b. [pre- B. 3.] Located in front of the tongue.
1953 *Archivum Linguisticum* V. 69 According to their articulating points Marr's consonants fall into labial, 'prelingual' (dentialveolar and palatal), and 'postlingual' (velar and ultravelar).

prelin'guistic, *a.* and *sb.* [pre- B. 1.] A. *adj.* = prelingual *a.* a.
1900 H. Sweet *Hist. Lang.* iv. 39 Even in the pre-linguistic stage in which gesture predominated, there must have been some principles of order. **1901** [see inner *a.* 2 b]. **1919** M. K. Bradby *Psycho-Anal.* x. 133 A dream does.. sometimes belong to a pre-linguistic stage of mental experience. **1941** *Mind* L. 421 Mathematics will vanish with the rest of our intellectual heritage if we revert to our pre-linguistic apehood. **1951** Trager & Smith *Outl. Eng. Struct.* 13 Prelinguistic data are now available. **1963** Ervin & Miller in J. A. Fishman *Readings Sociol. of Lang.* (1968) 70 The prelinguistic sounds of deaf and hearing children are indistinguishable in the first three months. **1972** *Language* XLVIII. 487 The identification of a prelinguistic stage has for decades rested on the intuition that everything which precedes the first utterance identifiable as a word is non-linguistic. **1979** N. Lash *Theol. on Dover Beach* ii. 29, I am not suggesting that there is..any such thing as pre-linguistic or non-linguistic human experience.
B. *sb. pl.* [-ic 2.] The study of biological and physiological aspects of speech.
1949 [see microlinguistics *sb. pl.*]. **1953** *Internat. Jrnl. Amer. Linguistics Memoir* viii. 28 'Prelinguistics' studies the physical and biological aspects of speech. **1959** M. Joos in J. A. Fishman *Readings Sociol. of Lang.* (1968) 186 This line, along which he [*sc.* the linguistic analyst] can shift items into the 'past' or the 'future' as he moves from pre-linguistics towards metalinguistics. **1964** Crystal & Quirk *Syst. Prosodic & Paralinguistic Features in Eng.* ii. 27 Speech results from activities which create a back-ground of voice set ('the idiosyncratic, including the specific physiology of the speakers, and the total physical setting'). This is in the area of 'prelinguistics'.

pre-Linnean, -Listerian, -literary: see pre- B. 1.

prelinpinpin, in *powder of prelinpinpin*: see powder *sb.*[1] 2 f.

preliography, prœli-. [f. L. *prœli-um* battle + -(o)graphy.] 'A description of battles.'
1846 Worcester cites Harris.

pre'literate, *a.* [pre- B. 1.] Applied to social groups or cultures which have not acquired a form of writing. Also as *sb.*, a person belonging to such a group or culture. Cf. non-literate *a.*
1925 E. Faris in *Amer. Jrnl. Sociol.* XXX. 710 For some time the writer has been using..the term 'pre-literate' to designate the peoples of the *sociétiés inferieures*, as Lévy-Bruhl calls them. *Ibid.* 712 Pre-literate man is...one in whose culture there is no written literature. *Ibid.*, Pre-literates do not have cities. **1933** A. R. Radcliffe-Brown in *Encycl. Social Sci.* IX. 202/1 The confusion which has resulted in the attempt to apply to preliterate societies the modern distinction between criminal law and civil law can be avoided. **1957** *Antiquity* XXXI. 211 Rubbish deposited in superimposed layers by preliterate men. **1962** E. R. Service *Primitive Social Organization* i. 8 Where an Arunta-like way of life is not yet significantly altered by modern influences it is a culture that is primitive, ancient, and preliterate. **1966** E. G. Stanley *Continuations & Beginnings* 127 To understand the use of tags and set phrases, whole half-lines of verse used repeatedly, it is useful to know about some kinds of preliterate composition. **1967** *N.Y. Rev. Bks.* 23 Feb. 33/3 He writes about the last 8000 years of pre-literate Europe, which means that he excludes Greeks and Romans. **1970** [see non-literate *a.*].
Hence **pre'literacy,** the quality or state of being preliterate.
1957 G. Clark *Archaeol. & Society* (ed. 3) i. 22 Clearly.. some difference of opinion is likely to exist as to precisely at what stage preliteracy gives way to literacy. **1967** *N.Y. Rev. Bks.* 23 Feb. 33/1, I wish I knew who invented the word 'preliteracy' to indicate the illiteracy of certain extinct or living cultures... Preliteracy points to literacy as the next step in human evolution... In the latter part of the nineteenth century illiteracy was still illiteracy—not preliteracy.

†**prelleds,** some obsolete game.
1448 [see *quarter-spells*, quarter *sb.* 31].

pre-load, *sb.* [pre- A. 2.] A load applied beforehand; *spec.* (*a*) one in a bearing or machine part (see preload *v.*); (*b*) the tension in heart muscle at the end of diastole.
1941 *Motor Commerce* July 25/3 Adjust the pinion assembly to the correct bearing pre-load of 12 to 17 in.-lbs., and lock the adjusting nuts in position by a lock-washer. **1954** *Sun* (Baltimore) (B ed.) 3 Nov. 36/4 This earth pile acts as a preload or surcharge on the subsoil... The preload or surcharge is to get a settlement of the earth before the towers are constructed. **1962** *Amer. Jrnl. Physiol.* CCII. 936/1 Theoretically, with no load on the muscle, the velocity of shortening is maximal... Experimentally, the closest one can approach such a condition with heart muscle is to use the smallest preload from which a contraction occurs that produces analysable data. **1970** *Circulation Res.* XXVI. 114/1 The muscle is pre-stretched to a certain initial length using a 'preload', P, and temporarily fixed at that length. **1971** J. J. Gregory in Ayres & Gregory *Cardiol.* xii. 225 Just as ventricular function may be evaluated by change in afterload, interventions that alter preload may also be utilized to test myocardial function. **1971** *Power Farming* Mar. 71/1 Dynamic loading in a tightened bolt may vary from no stress at all to that exceeding the bolt's preload. **1972** H. E. Ellinger *Automechanics* xxiii. 400 Pinion preload is sufficient to eliminate any end play in the pinion shaft and still low enough to prevent bearing damage. **1976** *Circulation* LIII. 298/2 In the intact heart it is impossible to completely separate preload from afterload.

pre'load, *v.* [pre- A. 1.] *trans.* To load beforehand; *spec.* in *Engin.*, to design or make (a bearing or machine part) in such a way that there are internal loads independent of any working load (e.g. to reduce noise in operation).
1945 R. K. Allan *Rolling Bearings* x. 253 Another method..is to preload the bearings by axial adjustment. **1950** O. J. Horger in M. Hetényi *Handbk. Exper. Stress Analysis* xi. 556 Seeger investigated the fatigue resistance of hollow shafts which were preloaded axially so as to produce compressive prestress below yield-strength value of the steel. **1952** C. H. Dix *Seismic Profiling for Oil* iii. 44 In some cases it is desirable to drill several shot holes, preload each one of them, and not plan to reshoot any of them. **1969** W. Wrigley et al. *Gyroscopic Theory* xiv. 324 When two ball bearings are preloaded against each other, the result is a much stiffer assembly. **1969** *Jane's Freight Containers 1968-69* 439 (*caption*) They are pre-loaded and sealed by shippers.
So **pre'loaded** *ppl. a.*, **pre'loading** *vbl. sb.*
1936 *Brit. Pat. 471,989*, The object of our invention is to provide improved brake-operating mechanism which permits a pre-loaded spring to be used in conjunction with compensation between the brakes on the front and rear wheels of a vehicle for normal braking. **1941** *Automobile Engineer* XXXI. 180/3 Owing to the substantial design of the housing it has not been found necessary to employ pre-loading of the bearings. **1945** R. K. Allan *Rolling Bearings* x. 235 The primary object of preloading is to eliminate.. radial and/or axial movements in a bearing when it is functioning in a machine. **1962** *John o' London's* 22 Feb. 182/2 The dice are, as it were, already pre-loaded. **1969** W. Wrigley et al. *Gyroscopic Theory* xiv. 324 Under the preloaded condition, the pair of bearings have axial and radial stiffnesses vs. load which are very nearly constant. **1971** B. Scharf *Engin. & its Lang.* xii. 137 Pre-loading is frequently used in high precision work and in order to ensure noiseless running. **1976** Attewell & Farmer *Princ. Engin. Geol.* xi. 826 Any pre-loading or the application of consolidation pressure must..start with the condition that the initial stresses applied to the soil are less than the existing shear strength of the soil.

†**prelo'cutor.** *Sc. Obs.* Also 7 preloquutour. [a. med.L. *prælocūtor* (f. L. *præloquī* to speak beforehand or before another), sometimes erron. used in med.L. for *prolocutor* (see Du Cange).] = prolocutor; an advocate, a pleader.
1573 *Reg. Privy Council Scot.* II. 254 Comperand personalie with Maister Alexander Sym prelocutor. **1609** Skene *Reg. Maj.*, *Stat. Rob. I* 23 The defender or his preloquutour sould not answer; before the complainer or his preloquutour hes spoken and said all.

pre-logic: see pre- B. 1.

pre'logical, *a.* [pre- B. 1.] Preceding or prior to logic or logical reasoning; chiefly in *Anthrop.*, applied to the thinking of persons or cultural groups which is based on myth, magic, etc. Also *transf.* and *absol.*
1893 C. S. Peirce *Coll. Papers* (1933) IV. i. iv. 62 The whole of the theory of numbers belongs to logic; or rather, it would do so, were it not, as pure mathematics, *prelogical*, that is, even more abstract than logic. **1923** L. A. Clare tr. *Lévy-Bruhl's Primitive Mentality* ii. 91 To prelogical mentality, cause and effect present themselves in two forms, not essentially different from one another. **1926** —— tr. *Lévy-Bruhl's How Natives Think* i. ii. 78 By designating it [*sc.* the mentality of primitives] 'prelogical' I merely wish to state that it does not bind itself down, as our thought does, to avoiding contradiction. **1933** H. Read *Art Now* i. 34 Art conceived as a stage in the ideal history of mankind, as a pre-logical mode of expression, as something necessary and inevitable and organic. **1935** *Mind* XLIV. 544 Insistence on the alogical, or prelogical, character of the aesthetic consciousness. **1943** *Amer. Speech* XVIII. 220 The first stage of human development..is that of the savage, prelogical mentality, with a one-valued semantics (or system of evaluations), in which..'everything is everything else' by 'mystic participation'. **1959** *Spectator* 11 Sept. 339/3 If we seek the pre-logical and oppose the march of intellect, we are the enemies of science..and the worshippers of myth. **1967** C. L. Markmann tr. *Fanon's Black Skin, White Masks* (1968) vi. 159 The prelogical thought of the phobic has decided that such is the case. **1977** G. W. Hewes in D. M. Rumbaugh *Lang. Learning by Chimpanzee* i. 28 Early language was also characteristically 'prelogical'.

[**preloke** *v.* in passage cited, evidently some error.
a **1547** Surrey *Ps.* lv, The bloody compackts of those That preloked on with yre, to slaughter me and myne. (? For *prikked*; the editor of 1815 (pp. 84, 397) suggests *pressed*.)]

pre-London: see pre- B. 2 a.

pre-lubricate: see pre- A. 1.

†**pre'lucent,** *a. Sc. Obs. rare.* Also 6 preluciand. [ad. L. *prælūcēns, -ēnt-em*, pres. pple. of *prælūcēre* to shine forth: see pre- A. 4 c and lucent.] Shining, resplendent.
1560 Rolland *Crt. Venus* ii. 474 Till he come till ane Palice prelucent. *c* **1560** A. Scott *Poems* (E.E.T.S.) iv. 3 Preluciand bemes befoir þe day.

prelude ('prɛlju:d, 'pri:lju:d, -lu:d), *sb.* Also 6 preludie, 6-7 prælude. [a. F. *prélude* (Rabelais, 1532), ad. late or med.L. *prælūdium*, f. *prælūdĕre*: see next. The first pronunciation prevails in Great Britain.]
†**1.** Preliminary play, before the real performance.
[Cf. *Thomæ Thes. nov. Lat.* in Quicherat *Addenda*, Præludium, parvus ludus, majorem præcedens.]
1599 B. Jonson *Cynthia's Rev.* v. ii, *Cri.* It is the sute of the strange opponent..to see some light stroke of his play, commenced with some other... *Amo.* Is it your sute Monsieur, to see some prælude of my scholer?
2. A preliminary performance, action, event, or condition, coming before and introducing one of more importance; an introduction, preface (to a literary work).
1561 Daus tr. *Bullinger on Apoc.* lxi. 435 *margin*, The begynninges and preludies of the Empyre translated. **1583** Golding *Calvin on Deut.* xxxviii. 227 It is well knowen that dancing can be no better but a prelude to whoredome, to open an entrie purposely vnto Satan. **1637-50** Row *Hist. Kirk* (Wodrow Soc.) 220 To bring this Kirk of Scotland backward to them [Popish ceremonies], (a prelude whereof wes vote in Parliament so eagerlie gone about by the King). **1682** Dryden *Mac Fl.* 37 My warbling lute..Was but the prelude to that glorious day. *a* **1704** T. Brown *Praise of Poverty* Wks. 1730 I. 97 Their smiles are but the preludes of their hate. **1844** Dickens *Lett.* (1880) I. 115 They say it is the prelude to clear weather. **1869** Freeman *Norm. Conq.* (1875) III. xii. 214 A sort of prelude to the still greater work which he had to do. **1889** *Mod. Lang. Notes* IV. 350 Grein's sixteenth Canto of the 'Christ'.., is a transitional passage... The whole passage forms a kind of interlude, while it is also a prelude to Part III. **1892** J. Earle *Deeds of Beowulf* p. xxiv, It is not easy to account for this Prelude, which really throws no light on the poem, nor in any way helps the narrative. **1899** *Allbutt's Syst. Med.* VIII. 722 Functional changes [in glands]..generally form a prelude to structural changes.
3. *Mus.* A movement or piece forming the introduction to a musical work; *esp.* such a movement preceding a fugue or forming the first piece of a suite.
1658 Phillips, *Prælude*,..in Musick it is taken for a voluntary or flourish upon any instrument. *a* **1679** Hobbes *Rhet.* (1840) 500 In some kinds of orations it resembles the prelude of musicians, who first play what they list, and afterwards the tune they intended. **1685** *Lond. Gaz.* No. 2081/4 Airs for the Violin: To wit, Preludes, Fuges, Allmands, Sarabands. **1880** Tennyson *Ballads & P.*, *Sisters* 2 By their clash, And prelude on the keys, I know the song. **1881** H. F. Frost in Grove *Dict. Mus.* III. 28 *Prelude*, ..a preliminary movement, ostensibly an introduction to the main body of a work, but frequently of intrinsic and independent value and importance.
fig. **1749** Smollett *Regicide* iii. ii, O welcome messenger! How sweetly sounds Thy prelude! **1845-6** Trench *Huls. Lect.* Ser. ii. iii. 179 The world, with all its discords, has had also its preludes to the great harmonies of redemption. **1871** R. Ellis *Catullus* lxiv. 382 In such prelude old..Sang their deep divination.
attrib. *a* **1845** Hood *Storm at Hastings* x, So the hoarse thunder Growl'd long—but low—a prelude note of death. **1887** J. W. Ebsworth in *Roxb. Ball.* VI. 254 *note*, Also to the same tune is marked, 'The Sweet Salutation on Primrose-Hill; or, I know you not'... It has the prelude versicle:—'I know you not! What, doth the times so change? [etc.].'

prelude (see below), *v.* [ad. L. *prælūd-ĕre* to play beforehand, prelude, preface, f. *præ*, pre- A. 1 + *lūdĕre* to play; so F. *préluder* (17th c. in Hatz.-Darm.). All the verse quots. and the dictionaries down to *c* 1830 have (pri:'lju:d); Smart 1836 has ('prɛlju:d), after the sb., and this is now usual, esp. in the musical sense 3. Tennyson has both: see quots.]
1. a. *trans.* To precede as a prelude or preliminary action; to serve as a prelude to; to prepare the way for, introduce; to foreshadow.
1655 H. Vaughan *Silex Scint.* i. *Rules & Lessons*, The Sun now stoops, and hastes his beams to hide Under the dark and melancholy Earth. All but preludes thy End. *a* **1700** Dryden *Ovid* xv. (1810) 549/2 When the gray Of morn preludes the splendour of the day. **1703** Rowe *Ulyss.*

II. i. 822 The gath'ring Storm That grumbles in the Air, preluding Ruin. **1768** PENNANT *Zool.* II. 252 Their immersion was preluded by a dirge of a quarter of an hour's length. **1832** TENNYSON *Dream Fair Wom.* 7 Dan Chaucer, the first warbler, whose sweet breath Preluded those melodious bursts. **1898** P. MANSON *Trop. Diseases* xxvi. 392 Being.. preluded by an outburst more severe than usual of fever.

b. Of a personal or other agent: To introduce with a prelude or preliminary action.

1697 DRYDEN *Æneid* XII. 160 Proudly he bellows, and preludes the fight. **1841** CATLIN *N. Amer. Ind.* (1844) II. lviii. 252 He also preludes his work by saying [etc.]. **1860** ADLER *Fauriel's Prov. Poetry* v. 109 A priest preluded with some prayer or pious ceremony these rounds and these profane songs. **1879** H. SPENCER *Data of Ethics* vi. §38. 95 The necessity for preluding the study of moral science, by the study of biological science. **1915** J. BUCHAN *Nelson's Hist. War* II. ix. 34 Von Kluck preluded it [*sc.* an enveloping movement] by a heavy bombardment of Binche and Bray.

†**c.** To compose as a prelude. *Obs. rare.*

1785 *Eng. Rev.* VI. 204 'May I ask what subject employs your thoughts?' 'I am preluding a preface'.

2. a. *intr.* To give a prelude or introductory performance *to* some later action.

1660 INGELO *Bentiv. & Ur.* II. (1682) 16 They prelude to them with Tears. **1697** DRYDEN *Virg.* (1721) I. Ded. 9 He found the strength of his Genius betimes, and was even in his Youth preluding to his Georgics, and his Æneis. *a* **1729** CONGREVE tr. *Ovid's Art of Love* III. Wks. 1773 III. 279 So love, preluding, plays at first with hearts, And after wounds with deeper piercing darts. **1854** DE QUINCEY *Autobiog. Sk.* Wks. II. 164 He had also preluded to this great work, in a little English medical tract.

b. To form a prelude, to be introductory (*to*).

1838–43 ARNOLD *Hist. Rome* III. xliii. 140 The skirmishing of the light-armed troops preluded as usual to the battle. **1865** GROTE *Plato* I. xvii. 482 Much dramatic incident.. preluding to the substantive discussion.

3. *Music.* **a.** *intr.* To play a prelude or introductory movement before the main composition.

1678 DRYDEN *Limberham* I. i, As a good musician always preludes before a tune. **1824** MISS FERRIER *Inher.* xxxiii, She .. seated herself at the harp, and began to prelude. **1825** SCOTT *Talism.* xxvi, So soon as he began to prelude,.. his countenance glowed with energy and inspiration. *a* **1945** E. R. EDDISON *Mezentian Gate* (1958) xxxix. 214 The musicians tuned their instruments, preluded and, when the murmur of talk was stilled.., struck up a cavatina.

b. *trans.* (*a*) To play as a prelude; (*b*) to introduce with a prelude.

1795 MASON *Ch. Mus.* i. 63 If the Organist preludes an Anthem of Praise or Thanksgiving, a spirited movement is certainly in its place. **1850** TENNYSON *In Mem.* lxxxviii, And I—my harp would prelude woe—I cannot all command the strings. **1856** KANE *Arct. Expl.* II. xii. 128 The accuser rises and preludes a few discords.. on a tom-tom or drum. He then passes to the charge.

Hence **preluding** *vbl. sb.* and *ppl. a.*; **preluder**, one who plays or performs a prelude; **pre'ludingly** *adv.*, in a prelusive manner (*rare*).

a **1700** DRYDEN *Cinyras & Myrrha* 220 At last.. she.. drew a long preluding sigh, and said, O happy mother in thy marriage bed! **1794** MATHIAS *Purs. Lit.* (1798) 175 Bates sounds the soft preluding symphony. **1795** MASON *Ch. Mus.* i. 60 Invention, science and execution, which Rousseau requires in a good Preluder. **1834** PRINGLE *Afr. Sk.* vi. 214 Which much resembled the preluding quaver of the woodlark. **1841** H. F. CHORLEY *Music & Manners* (1844) III. 246 Classical preluders and steady fuguists will come in time. **1847** BUSHNELL *Chr. Nurt.* viii. (1861) 212 To act the preluding of the Christian love. **1858** CARLYLE *Fredk. Gt.* v. ii. (1872) II. 66 The needful Parliamentary preludings are gone through. **1932** J. JOYCE in *New Statesman* 27 Feb. 261/1 Preludingly he conspews a portugaese into the gutter, recitativing.

preludial (prɪ'l(j)uːdɪəl), *a.* [f. late or med.L. *prælūdi-um* PRELUDE *sb.* + -AL[1].] Pertaining to, or of the nature of, a prelude; serving to introduce.

1649 AMBROSE *Media* i. (1652) 2 The second is the fruit of the first, and the preludial assurance of the last. **1657** W. MORICE *Coena quasi Κοινή* xix. 341 Preludial beames of the Sun of Righteousness. *a* **1711** KEN *Anodynes* Poet. Wks. 1721 III. 394 Preludial Scorchings of eternal Fire. **1856** J. GROTE in *Cambr. Ess.* 88 To have.. no preludial education, but to begin a thing in earnest.

†**pre'ludiately**, *adv. Obs. rare.* [f. as prec. + -ATE[2] + -LY[2].] By way of a prelude.

1593 NASHE *Christ's Tears* Ep. Ded., Giue mee leaue with the Sportiue Sea Porposes, preludiatelie a little to play before the storme of my Teares. **1623** COCKERAM, *Preludiately-done*, done as a Prologue.

Preludin (prɪ'l(j)uːdɪn). *Pharm.* Also **preludin**. A proprietary name for phenmetrazine hydrochloride.

1954 *Trade Marks Jrnl.* 17 Mar. 270/1 *Preludin*... All goods included in class 1 [*i.e.* chemical products used in industry, science, etc.]. Albert Boehringer, [*et al.*].., trading as C. H. Boehringer Sohn, Ingelheim am Rhein.., Germany; manufacturers. **1955** *Official Gaz.* (U.S. Patent Office) 13 Sept. TM59/2 C. H. Boehringer Sohn, Ingelheim am Rhein, Germany.. *Preludin.* For anti-depressant and anti-obesity drug. Use since April 1, 1954. **1955** *Chem. Abstr.* XLIX. 8566 (*heading*) Identification of Preludin (2-phenyl-3-methylmorpholine) and Ritalin.. before and after passage through the body. **1957** *Brit. Med. Jrnl.* 5 Jan. 30/2 'Preludin', a new drug for controlling the appetite, is, I believe, gaining popularity among those who.. try to slim. It was discovered in 1953 and first marketed in Germany in 1954. **1959** [see PHENMETRAZINE]. **1960** *Spectator* 22 July 120/3 A few weeks ago we criticised the irrationality of the campaign then being waged by some newspapers against the pep-pill Preludin. **1970** PASSMORE & ROBSON *Compan. Med. Stud.* II. v. 39/1 Appetite suppressant drugs include phenmetrazine (preludin), chlorphentermine and diethylpropion (tenuate). Their value in this respect is limited and emotional dependence has been reported. **1974** M. C. GERALD *Pharmacol.* xv. 286 Phenmetrazine (Preludin) swept the market in Sweden after its introduction .. in 1955. This drug.. continues to be the abused drug of choice in Sweden. **1976** D. HARE *Teeth 'n' Smiles* i. 20 *Anson*: Is that heroin? *Peyote*: Preludin. *Anson*: Ah. Preludin is a fuck-pump... It enlarges your sexual capacity.

‖**pre'ludio.** *Music. rare.* [It., ad. late or med.L. *prælūdium* PRELUDE *sb.*] = PRELUDE *sb.* 3.

1724 *Short Explic. For. Words in Mus. Bks.*, *Preludio*, a Prelude; the first Part or Beginning of a Piece of Musick.. much the same as *Overture*. **1810** S. GREEN *Reformist* I. 236 She played a preludio on the fine-toned instrument. **1823** BYRON *Juan* XII. liv, These first twelve books are merely flourishes, Preludios, trying just a string or two Upon my lyre.

preludious (prɪ'l(j)uːdɪəs), *a.* [f. late or med.L. *prælūdi-um* PRELUDE *sb.* + -OUS.] Of the nature of a prelude; introductory, preparatory.

1651 CLEVELAND *Senses' Festival* vi, Yet, that's but a preludious bliss; Two souls pickearing in a kiss. **1681** H. MORE *Exp. Dan.* iii. 78 We see the Angel Gabriel.. to have a preludious mission, as of an Apostle, to preach to Daniel. **1812** NOTT *Dekker's Gull's Horn-bk.* 142 *note*, Trumpets were then the preludious instruments to a play. **1887** CLARK RUSSELL *Frozen Pirate* II. viii. 146 Sharp cubbish snarlings preludious of the lion's voice.

Hence **pre'ludiously** *adv.*

1653 H. MORE *Conject. Cabbal.* (1713) 150 Afterward did he shew himself upon Earth, and conversed with men: Preludiously in the Cloud and in the Bush.

‖**preludium, præ-** (priː'l(j)uːdɪəm). Now *rare.* [Late or med.L. *prælūdium* PRELUDE *sb.*] A prelude or introduction; a preliminary.

1570 FOXE *A. & M.* (ed. 2) 1594/2 So the disputation began to be set a worke by yᵉ Prolocutor with a short *Præludium.* **1620** VENNER *Via Recta* viii. 178 Euery inequality of concoction is a *præludium* of crudity. **1646** CRASHAW *Poet. Wks.* (1857) 21 This knife may be the spear's præludium. **1678** NORRIS *Coll. Misc.* (1699) 66 The Birds in short præludiums tune their throat. **1712** M. HENRY *Comm. with God* (1822) 360 An earnest of the blessedness of heaven .. and a preludium to it. *a* **1734** NORTH *Examen* II. iv. §91 (1740) 276 A devillish Invention.. which from the Preludiums of the Business, may be ascribed to the Lord Howard. **1885** COUPLAND *Spirit Goethe's Faust* ii. 48 The preludium prefixed to the Indian play.

preludize ('prɛl(j)uːdaɪz), *v.* [f. PRELUDE *sb.* + -IZE.] *intr.* To play or write a prelude.

1842 J. R. PLANCHÉ *White Cat* I. 9 The leader preludizes on the violin. **1845** C. H. J. ANDERSON *Swedish Brothers* 38 Preludising for a few moments with the air of one who is accustomed to sing. **1878** in Grove *Dict. Mus.* I. 372 Mozart then began to preludise, and played some variations. **1902** *Nation* (N.Y.) 19 June 488/1 The chief fault of Mr. Young's book is a tendency to verbose preludizing. **1978** *Gramophone* Feb. 1389/3 When at a recital Hans von Bülow had to follow a singer of whom he thought little he would sometimes sit at the piano and preludize for a moment or two on the passage from Beethoven's Ninth Symphony.

prelumbar: see PRE- B. 3.

pre,lumirho'dopsin. *Biochem.* [PRE- A. 2.] An isomer of rhodopsin, stable only at very low temperatures, which is formed by the action of light on rhodopsin and changes spontaneously to lumirhodopsin.

1963 YOSHIZAWA & WALD in *Nature* 30 Mar. 1280/1 The intermediate was shown to be stable to about −140°, above which it forms lumirhodopsin. We shall call it prelumirhodopsin. **1968** A. WHITE et al. *Princ. Biochem.* (ed. 4) xl. 904 After pre-lumirhodopsin is formed by the isomerization of one double bond, all subsequent steps proceed spontaneously. **1976** *Nature* 5 Feb. 424/2 The results of a picosecond study indicated that the formation of prelumirhodopsin when rhodopsin is irradiated probably involves a restricted change in the geometry of retinal rather than a complete isomerisation. *Ibid.* 22 Apr. 726/2 In the photolysis of the visual pigment rhodopsin the intermediate first observed is bathorhodopsin (formerly called prelumirhodopsin).

pre-lunch: see PRE- B. 2 a.

pre-'luncheon, *sb.* and *a.* **A.** *sb.* [PRE- A. 2.] A light mid-day meal preceding luncheon.

1873 C. M. YONGE *Pillars of House* II. xvi. 110 A pre-luncheon or nooning of cake and wine within an hour of the meal of the day.

B. *adj.* [PRE- B. 2.] Held or occurring before luncheon.

1975 *N.Y. Times* 29 Aug. 29/1 The four actors.. did a jungle scream in unison for the press at a preluncheon cocktail party.

prelusion (prɪ'l(j)uːʒən). [ad. L. *prælūsiōn-em*, n. of action f. *prælūdĕre* to PRELUDE.] The performance of a prelude; a prelude or introduction.

1597 J. KING *On Jonas* (1618) 592 Your liues.. should bee prelusions and preparations for a better life to come. **1660** H. MORE *Myst. Godl.* IV. ii. 102 It was a prelusion to & prefiguration of the forwardness of the Gentiles.. to receive Christ as their Soveraign and Redeemer. **1838** *Blackw. Mag.* XLIII. 3 So sudden and so early a prelusion of summer.. could not last. **1871** MORLEY *Crit. Misc.* 314 Of the nature of a prelusion in the art of logical division.

prelusive (prɪ'l(j)uːsɪv), *a.* [f. L. *prælūs-*, ppl. stem of *prælūdĕre* to PRELUDE + -IVE.] Of the nature of or serving as a prelude; preliminary or introductory to that which is to follow.

1605 BACON *Adv. Learn.* II. ii. §8 This monarchy before it was to settle in your Maiestie and your generations.. had these prelusiue changes and varieties. **1728–46** THOMSON *Spring* 174 The clouds.. softly shaking on the dimpled pool Prelusive drops. **1807** WORDSW. *White Doe* I. 36 And scarcely have they disappeared Ere the prelusive hymn is heard. **1895** SALMOND *Chr. Doctr. Immort.* III. ii. 300 Christ speaks of His return as intimated by certain prelusive tokens.

Hence **pre'lusively** *adv.*, in a prelusive manner, by way of prelude.

1833 *Blackw. Mag.* XXXIV. 451 He has but been prelusively flourishing his tool.

prelusory (prɪ'l(j)uːsərɪ), *a.* [f. as prec. + -ORY[2].] = prec.

1640 *Consid. touching Ch. of Eng.* 33 A precursorie or prelusorie judgement of Christ. **1650** *Vind. Dr. Hammond's Addr.* 37 That Argument.. is but prælusory and preparative. **1659** *Gentl. Calling* Pref. §12 These are but the light prelusory skirmishes to a more dismal slaughter. **1876** BANCROFT *Hist. U.S.* V. lxix. 315 Without some prelusory trials of our strength, we ought not to commit our country.

Hence **pre'lusorily** *adv.*

1847 in WEBSTER; and in later Dicts.

prem (prɛm), *sb.* and *a.* [Abbrev. of PREMATURE *a.* or *sb.*] **A.** *sb.* A premature baby. **B.** *adj.* Premature; of or pertaining to premature babies.

1953 BAKER *Australia Speaks* vi. 142 *Prem*, a hospital term for a premature baby. **1960** *News Chron.* 18 Mar. 8/6 Children's specialists are improving the outlook for 'prems' —frail, under-developed babies, some born too soon. **1961** *News of World* 23 Apr. 13 My last was three months prem. **1962** G. BUTLER *Coffin in Oxford* ix. 126 Father Mahoney was standing.. at the end of the corridor by the nursery and 'prems' block. **1963** L. DIACK *Labrador Nurse* xxix. 142 I've got a lovely prem. Four pounds. **1972** R. LEWIS *Fool for Client* ii. 44 My daughter.. was took bad in the night and they think the baby is going to be a prem. **1976** 'D. HALLIDAY' *Dolly & Nanny Bird* iii. 41 The last time I heard her whisper like that, the incubator lights had cut out in a prem ward.

pre-machine: see PRE- A. 1, B. 2 a.

pre-'make-ready. *Printing.* [PRE- A. 2.] (See quots.)

1948 R. R. KARCH *Graphic Arts Procedures* x. 256 Premakeready includes those operations done in advance of placing the form on the printing press. **1964** *Gloss. Letterpress Rotary Printing Terms* (*B.S.I.*) 16 *Pre-make ready*, the operations relating to the obtaining of a good printing result which take place before the printing plates or formes go to the press. **1967** V. STRAUSS *Printing Industry* vii. 423/2 Pre-makeready is.. that part of quality control in letterpress which deals with the printing-image carrier and has the purpose of reducing to a minimum the time spent for makeready of type forms on the press.

premalignant, -Malthusian: see PRE- B. 1.

pre-man, *sb.* and *a.* **A.** *sb.* [PRE- B. 1] (Stressed '*pre-man.*) A hominid or man-like creature that lived before the appearance of man, *Homo erectus* and *H. sapiens.* **B.** *adj.* [PRE- B. 2.] (Stressed *pre-'man.*) Occurring or belonging to the time before the appearance of man.

1921 H. G. WELLS *Short Stories* (1927) 687 Men, our ancestors, had their first glimpse of the pre-men of the wilderness. **1947** *Sci. Illustr.* Sept. 60/1 Desert so devoid of life that it takes the visitor back to pre-man time on earth. **1953** J. S. HUXLEY *Evolution in Action* vi. 136 We can distinguish.. three stages in the physical evolution of man. First, the deployment of the pre-men. **1971** J. Z. YOUNG *Introd. Study Man* xxxiii. 457 Up to the stage that may be called pre-man (*Australopithecus*) the changes were gradual. **1977** *Time* 7 Nov. 48/1 Leakey has found more and better pre-man and early man fossils than any other anthropologist.

premandibular, -maniacal, -material, etc.: see PRE- B.

Premarin (prɪ'mɛərɪn). *Pharm.* Also **premarin**. [f. PRE(GNANT *a.*[2] + MAR(E[1] + -IN[1].] A proprietary name for a mixture of œstrogenic compounds obtained from the urine of pregnant mares and used in the treatment of various conditions, esp. those caused by or involving œstrogen deficiency.

1942 *Official Gaz.* (U.S. Patent Office) 21 July 498/1 Ayerst, McKenna & Harrison (United States) Limited, Rouses Point, N.Y... *Premarin.* For pharmaceutical preparations for the treatment of ovarian deficiencies. Claims use since Feb. 24, 1942. **1944** *Jrnl. Amer. Med. Assoc.* 19 Aug. 1098/2 Premarin.—An amorphous preparation containing the naturally occurring, water soluble, conjugated forms of the mixed estrogens obtained from the urine of pregnant mares. *Ibid.*, Premarin Tablets. **1956** *Trade Marks Jrnl.* 2 May 312/1 *Premarin*... Estrogenic preparations. Ayerst, McKenna & Harrison, Limited.., St. Laurent, Quebec, Canada; manufacturers and merchants. **1961** *Lancet* 2 Sept. 504/2 In these patients continued administration of premarin resulted in a suggestive, though inconclusive, improvement in mortality as compared with a comparable control group. **1977** *Ibid.* 19 Nov. 1063/1 A two to three fold increase in the incidence of ovarian cancer was recorded in women treated for menopausal symptoms with 'Premarin' (conjugated equine œstrogens) usually combined with stilbœstrol.

pre'marital, *a.* [PRE- B. 1.] Occurring before marriage.

1886 *Manch. Exam.* 10 Nov. 3/1 The premarital correspondence of Carlyle and Miss Welsh. **1915** T. F. A. SMITH *Soul of Germany* v. 97 During his pre-marital years he may form many such irregular acquaintanceships. **1937** A. HUXLEY *Let.* 17 Dec. (1969) 430 As to pre-marital continence, there is a great deal of evidence that this is important if there is to be higher education. **1951** M. MCLUHAN *Mech. Bride* (1967) 32/1 The tendency of the modern housewife, after a premarital spell in the business world, to embrace marriage and children but not housework. **1963** A. HERON *Towards Quaker View of Sex* i. 6 An increase in transient pre-marital sexual intimacies. **1976** *Drum* (E. Afr. ed.) Nov. 26/1, I think your girl is one of those sensible ones who do not like to indulge in pre-marital sex. **1980** 'R. DEACON' *Spy!* iii. 70 It was essential to cover up this pre-marital affair.

Hence **pre'maritally** *adv.*

1973 S. FISHER *Understanding Female Orgasm* ii. 34 Religiosity plays a role in how sexually active women are premaritally. **1975** R. H. RIMMER *Premar Experiments* (1976) i. 108 They aren't fully aware of the impact that freer and open sexuality, premaritally and postmaritally, will have on human goals and values.

pre-market(ing): see PRE- B. 2 a.

premate, premative, obs. ff. PRIMATE, PRIMITIVE.

†**prema'turance**. *Obs. rare.* [f. as next + -ANCE.] Early ripening.

1610 W. FOLKINGHAM *Art of Survey* I. iii. 6 In Grouth, the thriuage, verdure, fruitage, prematurance &c. of particular Vegetables are regardable.

†**prema'turate**, *a. Obs. rare*⁻¹. [f. mod.L. **præmātūr-āre* + -ATE²: cf. MATURATE *a.*] Done before the due time.

1570 FOXE *A. & M.* (ed. 2) 479/1 It is thought also by some, that the reuoking backe agayne.. was premature, or done all out of time.

prematuration (prɛmətjʊ'reɪʃən, ˌpriːmætjʊ'reɪʃən), *sb.* [f. PREMATUR(E *a.* (*adv.*) + -ATION.]

1. The fact of making or becoming mature unnaturally early.

1909 *Westm. Gaz.* 3 Feb. 2/1 The systems followed in the schools of the leading civilised races of the world make for prematuration.

2. [after F. *prématuration* premature birth.] = PREMATURENESS. *rare*⁻¹.

1977 A. SHERIDAN tr. *Lacan's Écrits* iv. 137 This is a point that I think I have myself helped to elucidate by conceiving the dynamics of the so-called *mirror stage* as a consequence of a prematuration at birth.

prematuration (priːmætjʊ'reɪʃən), *a.* [f. PRE- B. 2 + MATURATION.] Occurring before maturation.

1919 T. H. MORGAN *Physical Basis Heredity* xii. 142 Most of the eggs pass through this early prematuration stage in the larvæ and some of them may reach the maturation stage in the pupa. **1974** *Austral. Jrnl. Agric. Res.* XXV. 883 Only in one cultivar.. could a difference in rate of development between samples be attributed with any confidence to pre-maturation cold acquisition.

premature (ˌpriːmə'tjʊə(r); 'priː-, 'prɛmətjʊə(r), in predicative use prɛmə'tjʊə(r)), *a.* (*adv.*, *sb.*) Also 6 pri-, 7 præ-. [ad. L. *præmātūr-us* very early, too early, premature, f. *præ*, PRE- A. + *mātūrus* MATURE *a.* The last pronunciation is now common in Great Britain, esp. in connexions in which there is no mental association with *mature*; the first is favoured by American dicts.]

A. *adj.* †**1.** Ripe before the proper season. *Obs. rare.*

1656 BLOUNT *Glossogr.*, *Premature*, ripe before other, or ripe before due time and season. **1658** in PHILLIPS.

2. a. Occurring, existing, or done before the usual, proper, or appointed time; arriving or adopted too soon; too early; over-hasty.

c **1529** in Fiddes *Wolsey* II. (1726) 171 His so primature deathe was imputed only to nimio coitu. **1654** HAMMOND *Fundamentals* xiii, 'Tis hard to imagine what.. should be able to perswade him to repent, til he hath deposited that premature perswasion of his being in Christ. **1758** JOHNSON *Idler* No. 7 ¶15 The account of the engagement.. was premature. **1813** SIR H. DAVY *Agric. Chem.* (1814) 219 Too rapid growth and premature decay seem invariably connected. **1829** LYTTON *Devereux* I. v, The constant company.. made us premature adepts in the manners of the world. **1838** THIRLWALL *Greece* II. xiv. 228 His birth was premature. **1874** GREEN *Short Hist.* vii. §7. 426 Indications that he already felt the advance of premature age.

b. *Obstetrics.* Born or occurring before full term (but usu. after the stage when the fœtus normally becomes viable).

1754 W. SMELLIE *Coll. Cases & Observations in Midwifery* II. xiii. 213 (*heading*) On the situation of the child during pregnancy, the signs of conception and premature labour. **1775** A. HAMILTON *Elem. Pract. Midwifery* 122 When a woman miscarries in early Gestation, *this* they consider as an Abortion; but, if in the later Months, *that* they term a Premature Birth. **1800** *Med. Facts & Observations* VIII. 190 She has since borne six children by premature labour. **1840** [see INDUCTION 9]. **1878** *Obstetr. Jrnl.* VI. 163 (*heading*) Case illustrating the viability of extremely small premature children. **1923** J. H. HESS *Premature & Congenitally Diseased Infants* iii. 40 Heat regulation is one of the least developed functions of the premature infants. **1924** C. MACKENZIE *Heavenly Ladder* xviii. 244 The shock brought on a premature travail, and she was delivered of a boy in the Vicarage. **1969** D. BAIRD *Combined Textbk. Obstetr. & Gynæcol.* (ed. 8) xxxiii. 544 By international agreement a 'premature' infant has been defined as one weighing 2,500 g. (5½ lb.) or less at birth. **1973** *Sci. Amer.* May 27/2 Most of the mothers in the experimental group had had a premature baby (gestation period less than 38 weeks).

c. ***premature ejaculation*** (see quot. 1974); = EJACULATIO PRÆCOX.

1910 A. ABRAMS *Diagnostic Therapeutics* iii. 230 Occasionally onanism is followed by various grades of impotency (usually psychic) and premature ejaculation. **1925, 1928** [see EJACULATIO PRÆCOX]. **1942** T. P. WOLFE tr. *Reich's Function of Orgasm* v. 138 Hysterical men suffer either from erective impotence or premature ejaculation. **1968** T. WISEMAN *Quick & Dead* 140, I with my quick grin and premature ejaculations. **1974** PASSMORE & ROBSON *Compan. Med. Stud.* III. xxxv. 34/1 Partial impotence is common and may take the form of a failure to ejaculate or ejaculation before entry into the vagina or before orgasm is reached, i.e. premature ejaculation.

B. as *adv.* = PREMATURELY. (Only *poet.*)

1791 COWPER *Iliad* I. 4 Achilles.. who.. sent many a soul Illustrious into Ades premature.

C. as *sb. Obstetrics.* A child born before full term.

1900 in DORLAND *Med. Dict.* **1923** J. H. HESS *Premature & Congenitally Diseased Infants* xiv. 313 In the premature especially the skin is delicate, lacking the horny layer. **1960** A. K. GEDDES *Premature Babies* iii. 18 An irregular respiratory rhythm is normal for prematures.

premature ('prɛmətjʊə(r)), *v. Mil.* [f. PREMATURE *a.*] *intr.* Of a shell or other projectile: to explode prematurely. Of a gun: to fire a shell that explodes prematurely. Hence **'prematuring** *ppl. a.*

1916 'BOYD CABLE' *Doing their Bit* v. 83 A shrapnel prematuring at the muzzle, and the bullets that should have gone lifting high and clear inside the case smashing, perhaps, into the open rear of a gun-emplacement or a battery a few hundred yards in front of the prematuring gun. **1918** G. FRANKAU *Judgement of Valhalla* 49 Behind, a cratered slope, with batteries Crashing and flashing, violet in the dusk, And prematuring every now and then.

†**prema'tured**, *a. Obs. rare.* [f. PRE- A. 1 + MATURED; cf. prec.] = PREMATURE *a.*

1768 *Woman of Honor* II. 12 Its being a little prematured was of no great moment.

prematurely, *adv.* [f. PREMATURE + -LY².]

a. In a premature manner; before the proper time; too soon, too hastily.

1650 BULWER *Anthropomet.* 189 When Nurses prematurely, and without regard, commit weaker Infants to their Feet. **1748** HARTLEY *Observ. Man* II. ii. 136 Man's Wisdom.. would have rushed forward upon it prematurely. **1841** D'ISRAELI *Amen. Lit.* (1867) 367 Ascham.. died prematurely. **1873** BLACK *Pr. Thule* ii, His hair was becoming prematurely grey. **1878** R. W. DALE *Lect. Preach.* ii. 39 Taking care not to exhaust the interest of your audience prematurely.

b. *spec.* in *Obstetrics.*

1812 *Medico-Chirug. Trans.* III. 137, I have however now before me, a list of *seventy-eight* labours occurring prematurely, either from the spontaneous action of the womb, or from accidental violence. **1902** *Brit. Med. Jrnl.* 17 May 1197/2 The dry mouth and the weak digestion, and the frequency of gastro-intestinal disorders in the prematurely born are matters of every-day observation. **1943** *Lancet* 9 Dec. 320/1 An infant, prematurely born, is, although in a normal stage of development, inadequately prepared to contend against the operation of external agents.

prematureness. [f. as prec. + -NESS.] The quality of being premature.

1727 BAILEY vol. II, *Prematureness*, early Ripeness, or Ripeness before the Time. **1796** HARGRAVE *Hale's Jurisdict. Ho. Lds.* Pref. 181 [One] whose prematureness of fate.. caused an almost unsuppliable interstice in the science of English equity. **1883** A. FORBES in *Fortn. Rev.* 1 Nov. 671 What dealings he held with the enemy did not result in a prematureness of surrender.

prematurity (ˌpriː-, prɛmə'tjʊərɪtɪ). [ad. F. *prématurité* (16th c. in Littré): see PRE- A. 2 and MATURITY.] The quality or fact of being premature.

†**1.** Of plants: Early ripening or flowering. *Obs.*

1611 COTGR., *Prematurité*, prematuritie; hastie ripenesse, quicke ripening, forward or timelie growth. **1707** *Curios. in Husb. & Gard.* 265 Their Pre-maturity is very desirable.

2. a. Early development, esp. of mental or physical faculties; = PRECOCITY 2.

1778 WARTON *Hist. Eng. Poetry* (1840) II. xxvi. 359 He [Chatterton] will appear to have been a singular instance of a prematurity of abilities; to have acquired a store of general information far exceeding his years. **1779** BURNEY in *Phil. Trans.* LXIX. 199 Another wonderful part of his prematurity was the being able at two years and four months old to transpose into the most extraneous and difficult keys whatever he played. **1823** W. FAUX *Mem. Days in Amer.* 121 Unnatural prematurity is here very common. Boys look grave, and talk, act, and dress like men. **1907** *Q. Rev.* Apr. 455 Prematurity of thought and feeling has often an early grave.

b. An example of premature development.

1812 COLERIDGE in *Lit. Rem.* (1836) I. 381 Of the few, the greater part are pre-maturities.

3. Undue earliness or haste (of any action or event); hastiness, precipitancy.

1706 PHILLIPS, *Prematurity*, the State, or Condition of that which is premature. *a* **1797** H. WALPOLE *Mem. Geo. II* (1847) II. iii. 81 The only prematurity was in getting the Bill ready against it was necessary. **1825** WADDINGTON *Visit to Greece* Introd. 58 The prematurity and consequent failure of Ypsilanti's expedition. **1876** BRISTOWE *The. & Pract. Med.* (1878) 12 Their early sickliness and prematurity of death. **1899** *Westm. Gaz.* 21 Aug. 6/1 There is a good deal of prematurity.. about most of the rumours. **1927** *Times Lit. Suppl.* 10 Feb. 90/3 Our advice is to save this book for a dismally wet afternoon: tea will arrive with a startling prematurity. **1961** E. A. POWDRILL *Vocab. Land Planning* iii. 45 The term 'prematurity' is used by planners, very often as a sort of delaying action in grounds of refusal. *Ibid.* 46 Thus, the term 'prematurity', used in the sense of preventing something from happening in advance of the proper time, also implies that at some future date the proposal could be approved.

4. *Obstetrics.* The birth of a baby before full term.

1875 *Trans. Edin. Obstetr. Soc.* III. 260, I have seen nothing to warrant me viewing prematurity—that is, at and after the seventh month—as necessarily convertible with debility. **1902** *Brit. Med. Jrnl.* 17 May 1196/2 In this contribution the type of prematurity which is considered is that of the infant expelled from the uterus at the seventh month of intrauterine life. **1937** A. TOW *Dis. of Newborn* iii. 63 More careful antepartum care has definitely lowered the incidence of prematurity. **1971** *Sci. Amer.* Oct. 118/2 Prematurity from spontaneous abortion, affecting approximately one pregnancy in 10, is the main source of mortality.

pre-matutinal: see PRE- B. 1 d.

prematyue, obs. form of PRIMITIVE.

‖**prema'xilla, præ-**. *Zool.* [mod.L., f. PRE- B. + MAXILLA, after next.] The premaxillary bone.

1866 HUXLEY *Preh. Rem. Caithn.* 95 The alveolar surface of the premaxillae is nearly perpendicular. **1872** MIVART *Elem. Anat.* 115 The second element of the human maxillary bone.. is termed in zootomy the pre-maxilla.

premaxillary (priːmæk'sɪlərɪ), *a.* and *sb.* [f. PRE- B. 3 + MAXILLARY.] **A.** *adj.* Situated in front of the maxilla or upper jaw. **B.** *sb.* the premaxillary bone. So **prema'xillo-ma'xillary** *a.*, connecting or lying between the premaxillary and the maxillary bones.

1854 OWEN *Skel. & Teeth* in *Orr's Circ. Sc.* I. *Org. Nat.* 196 The premaxillary bone is edentulous. *Ibid.* 271 The premaxillary teeth [in the wolf-fish] are all conical, and arranged in two rows. *Ibid.* 273 The exposed portions of the premaxillaries and premandibulars. **1866** HUXLEY *Preh. Rem. Caithn.* 102 Only the faintest traces of the premaxillo-maxillary suture are to be seen in any of the skulls.

preme, obs. form of PREEM *sb.*

pre-med (priː'mɛd), *a.* (*sb.*¹) Chiefly *U.S.* Colloq. abbrev. of PREMEDICAL *a.* (*sb.*).

1962 E. SNOW *Red China Today* (1963) xxxv. 263, I finished my pre-med work in three years and won a scholarship to the American University in Beirut. **1971** 'S. RANSOME' *Trap 6* (1972) iii. 27 He's about to begin his premed courses and he's not sure whether he'll make it all the way through to his M.D. **1972** W. P. MCGIVERN *Caprifoil* (1973) xiii. 212 London told us you did a year of pre-med at Birmingham University. **1977** *Time* 28 Mar. 70/3 After high school Lily entered Detroit's Wayne State University as a premed student because 'I wanted to be a doctor'. **1978** *Detroit Free Press* 5 Mar. 9/1 Career training offered at Madonna for deaf students includes art, journalism, public relations, pre-med and pre-dentistry [etc.].

pre-med (priː'mɛd, 'priːmɛd), *sb.*² Colloq. abbrev. of PREMEDICATION. Also *attrib.*

1964 D. FRANCIS *Nerve* vi. 64 A brisk nurse told us he was going to the operating theatre within minutes and not to disturb the patient, as he had been given his pre-med. **1974** C. FREMLIN *By Horror Haunted* 110 The shaving, the marking-up, the pre-med injections. **1977** *Observer* 4 Sept. 22/1 You'll get a pre-med, a jab to make you drowsy, at about ten.

pre'medial, præ-, *a.* (*sb.*) [f. PRE- B. 3 + MEDIAL.] Situated in front of the medial line or position. So **pre'median** *a.*

1852 DANA *Crust.* I. 246 The præmedial and extramedial [areolets] are usually coalescent. *Ibid.* 334 Præmedian margin abrupt. *Ibid.* 343 Breadth [of carapax] to præmedials, about one line.

†**pre'mediate**, *v. Obs. rare.* [f. obs. F. *prémédier*, f. L. *præ* before, in front + *mediārī* to MEDIATE.] **a.** *intr.* To be a mediator or intermediary. **b.** *trans.* To mediate in (a dispute, etc.); to plead or advocate (a cause).

1530 PALSGR. 664/2, I premedyate for him, I am meane for one, *je premedie.* It shall be no wysedome to put thyselfe to moche in prease tyll thou have some body to premedyat thy cause. **1847–78** HALLIWELL, *Premediate*, to advocate one's cause.

pre'medical, *a.* (*sb.*) Chiefly *U.S.* [PRE- B. 1.] Of, pertaining to, or designating subjects studied in preparation for a medical course. Also *ellipt.*, a premedical course of studies. Cf. PRE-MED *a.* (*sb.*¹).

1904 *Bot. Gaz.* XXXVII. 225 This general text-book of botany is written for premedical and pharmaceutical students in particular. **1928** *Brit. Med. Jrnl.* 1 Sept. 363/2

The elementary sciences, and pre-medical subjects of chemistry, physics, biology, and botany, are in the curriculum to familiarize the student with the structure and behaviour of the materials with which, and upon which, he will have to work. **1940** A. Huxley *Let.* 7 July (1969) 455 Matthew has got through his second year of pre-medical quite well. **1961** *Lancet* 26 Aug. 484/1 Major Titov's first question, on returning from Space recently, concerned his wife's premedical examination results. **1976** *New Yorker* 16 Feb. 41/3 They reserved their serious efforts for the medievalists, true scientists, linguists, pre-law and pre-medical students, other scholars.

pre'medicant. [PRE- A. 2.] A drug given as premedication. Also *attrib.*

1960 *Proc. R. Soc. Med.* LIII. 673/1 The sister in charge administered the premedicant combinations in rotation, leaving the anaesthetist and the assessor in ignorance of the drugs given to particular patients. **1964** *Brit. Jrnl. Anaesthesia* XXXVI. 703/1 When evaluating the effects of various premedicants, the authors were impressed with the very high incidence of pre-operative vomiting and nausea which occurred when pethidine 100 mg was given alone. **1971** Pryor & Macalister *Gen. Anaesthetic & Sedation Techniques for Dentistry* ix. 60 The description of premedicant drugs earlier in this chapter should enable the anaesthetist to select appropriate combinations for any particular circumstance. **1977** *Lancet* 10 Dec. 1229/2 Anæsthetic premedicants include the minor tranquillisers (e.g., diazepam), major tranquillisers (e.g., droperidol), barbiturates, and opiates, but all possess undesirable side-effects.

pre'medicate, *v.* [PRE- A. 1.] *trans.* To give preparatory medication to, now esp. before anæsthesia. Hence **pre'medicating** *vbl. sb.*

1846 Grote *Greece* I. xiii. I. 324 The body of Jasôn having been thus pre-medicated, became invulnerable. **1940** MacIntosh & Pratt *Essent. Gen. Anæsthesia* x. 91 The dose of premedicating drug a patient will require can often be roughly gauged by his resistance to alcohol. **1972** *Nature* 15 Dec. 411/1 Before the injection..patients were premedicated with 100 mg of pethidine.

Hence **premedi'cation,** medication given prior to or in preparation for the main treatment; *spec.* a pre-anæsthetic. Cf. PRE-MED *sb.*[2]

1926 *Surg., Gynecol. & Obstetr.* XLIII. 103/2 All patients received as a premedication half a gram of veronal and 2 centigrams of morphine. **1932** *Brit. Jrnl. Anaesthesia* IX. 41 For the purpose of this discussion, by *premedication* is understood a new conception of preanaesthetic medication, whereby the patient is rendered unconscious in his bed before the administration of the anaesthetic. **1965** J. Pollitt *Depression & its Treatment* iv. 57 If an emergency operation must be performed.., the combination of chlorpromazine..and a barbiturate..is effective as premedication.

†**pre'meditate,** *a. Obs.* [ad. L. *præmeditātus*, pa. pple. (with passive sense, Cic.) of *præmeditārī* to premeditate: see PRE- A. 1 and MEDITATE *a.*]

1. = PREMEDITATED *ppl. a.* 1.

1555 Bradford in Strype *Eccl. Mem.* (1721) III. App. xlv. 128 Neverthelesse I shall declare the premedytate myschiffe. **1581** Lambarde *Eiren.* II. vii. (1588) 239 Manslaughter upon premeditate malice. **1642** Fuller *Holy & Prof. St.* II. ix. 82 Not making odious comparisons betwixt ..Publick prayer and Private, Premeditate prayer and Extempore. **1752** J. Louthian *Form of Process* (ed. 2) 80 From a propense and premeditate Malice.

2. Using premeditation or previous deliberation; considerate, deliberate.

1592 G. Harvey *Four Lett.* Wks. (Grosart) I. 177 A premeditate, and resolute minde lightly shaketh off the heauiest crosses of malice. **1597** J. Payne *Royal Exch.* 40 Studiouse labourers, as premeditate for doctrine and exhortation, and as carefull for good lyfe and conversation.

premeditate (pri:'mɛdɪteɪt), *v.* Also 6 premydytatt, *pa. pple.* premiditat. [f. ppl. stem of L. *præmeditārī*, or f. PRE- A. 1 + MEDITATE *v.*; cf. F. *préméditer* (14th c.)] To meditate beforehand.

1. a. *trans.* To ponder upon or study with a view to subsequent action, to think out beforehand; now *esp.* to plan or contrive previously.

a **1548** Hall *Chron., Edw. IV* 220 That they shoulde before hande premeditate with themselues maturely and deliberatly these thynges by her moued. **1579–80** North *Plutarch* (1676) 593 Cæsar..made an oration penned and premeditated before. **1653** H. Cogan tr. *Pinto's Trav.* xli. (1663) 161 Mendez, who had long before premeditated his answer. **1719** De Foe *Crusoe* I. 217, I began now to premeditate the Destruction of the next that I saw there. **1832** Austin *Jurispr.* (1879) I. xx. 444 When the act is done the party contemplates the consequence, although he has not premeditated the consequence or the act. **1929** S. Leslie *Anglo-Catholic* xvi. 231 Your Aquin often premeditated modern theories, but he is generally truest..when his followers or commentators try their hardest to explain him away. **1965** K. Sisam *Struct. Beowulf* 3 *Beowulf*, with more lapses and more use of devices that help an improviser, has many of the marks of premeditated art.

†**b.** To think of or consider in anticipation. *Obs.*

1566 *Reg. Privy Council Scot.* I. 473 That all troubill and occasioun of disordour be afoirhand foirsene and premiditat.

2. *intr.* To think deliberately beforehand or in advance (*on* or *of* something).

1586 B. Young *Guazzo's Civ. Conv.* IV. 204 b, While the men propowned their conceites, you (faire Ladies) may haue time to premeditate and thinke on yours. **1647** in *Bury Wills* (Camden) 195 It is the dutie therefore of euerie christian soe to premeditate of that day, and soe to dispose of his earthly affaires, that he may be allwayes in a readinesse. **1685** Cotton tr. *Montaigne* (1711) I. xix. 98 To premeditate is doubtless a very great advantage. **1849** James *Woodman* xi, I never premeditate, dear lady.

†**3.** To form a (specified) opinion beforehand; to think (well or ill) *of* previously. *Obs. rare*$^{-1}$.

1590 in Tolstoy *1st 40 Yrs. Interc. Eng. & Russ.* (1875) 368 We take hold of your loving consideracion..and will premydytatt the best of you.

Hence **pre'meditating** *ppl. a.*; whence **pre'meditatingly** *adv.*, with or by premeditation.

1839 Lady Lytton *Cheveley* (ed. 2) III. v. 107 He was determined religiously to adhere to his promise to Julia, of not premeditatingly putting himself in her way.

pre'meditated, *ppl. a.* [f. prec. + -ED[1].]

1. Considered, contemplated, or composed beforehand; previously contrived or planned.

1590 Shaks. *Mids. N.* v. i. 96 Great Clearkes haue purposed To greete me with premeditated welcomes. **1593** *Tell-Troth's N.Y. Gift* (1876) 18 Their premeditated mischief. **1638** R. Baker tr. *Balzac's Lett.* (vol. III.) 75 You shall receive from me no premeditated excuses, I had rather confess my fault. **1709** Steele *Tatler* No. 36 ¶3 A premeditated Quarrel usually begins and works up with the Words, *Some People.* **1870** Mrs. Riddell *A. Friars* iii, Her going was not the result of a premeditated plan.

†**2.** Of a person: Prepared by premeditation; = PREMEDITATE *a.* 2. *Obs. rare*$^{-1}$.

1651 *Life Father Sarpi* (1676) 10 To argue to some conclusion, wherein it was impossible he should be premeditated.

Hence **pre'meditatedly** *adv.*, with premeditation, advisedly, deliberately; **pre'meditatedness,** the quality or fact of being premeditated.

1727 Bailey vol. II, *Premeditatedly. **1748** Richardson *Clarissa* (1811) IV. xxxv. 230 Resolutions so premeditatedly made. **1817** J. W. Croker in *C. Papers* 26 Nov., Some blunders crept in accidentally, and one or two were premeditatedly added. **1659** Gauden *Tears Ch.* I. xii. 89 Its order, *premeditatedness, and constancy of devotion was never forbidden or disallowed by God. **1825** Bentham *Offic. Apt. Maximized, Indic.* (1830) 58 Premeditatedness—is it not in possession of being regarded as operating in extenuation of moral guilt?

†**pre'meditately,** *adv. Obs.* [f. PREMEDITATE *a.* + -LY[2].] = PREMEDITATEDLY.

1648 Heylin *Relat. & Observ.* I. 42 This was cunningly and premeditately contrived, to encrease the scandall upon the City. **1678** Sir G. Mackenzie *Crim. Laws Scot.* II. xxviii. §3 (1699) 274 Remissions should not be granted for Slaughter committed premeditatly. **1785** Sarah Fielding *Ophelia* II. xvi, A woman who did one imprudent thing premeditately. **1803** *Forest of Hohenelbe* I. 302 The natural ingenuousness of her disposition was wounded, by acting thus premeditately.

premeditation (pri:mɛdɪ'teɪʃən). Also 7 præ-. [ad. L. *præmeditātiōn-em*, n. of action f. *præmeditārī* to PREMEDITATE. So F. *préméditation* (-cion 14th c.).] The action of premeditating; previous meditation. **a.** Previous deliberation upon or thinking out of something to be done; now *esp.* designing, planning, or contrivance to do something.

1432–50 tr. *Higden* (Rolls) IV. 313 Moore scharpe and apte to an answere withowte deliberacion then with premeditacion. **1651** Hobbes *Leviath.* II. xxvii. 158 A Crime,..he that doth it with præmeditation, has used circumspection [etc.]. **1707** Mortimer *Husb.* (1721) I. 368 Premeditation being a very necessary Preliminary to Building. *a* **1832** Mackintosh *Revol. of 1688*, Wks. 1846 II. 40 There are probably few instances where, with so much premeditation and effrontery, the spoils of an accused man were promised..to the judge, who might have tried him. **1863** Geo. Eliot *Romola* xxxix, The passionate words were like blows—they defied premeditation. **1892** Zangwill *Bow Mystery* (1895) 124 The prisoner murdered his friend and fellow-lodger..in cold blood, and with the most careful premeditation.

†**b.** The action of thinking of or considering something beforehand or previously (without implication of purpose). *Obs.*

a **1450** *Mankind* 44 in *Macro Plays* 2, I be-sech yow hertyly, haue þis premedytacyon. **1526** *Pilgr. Perf.* (W. de W. 1531) 36 Somtyme dremes may come of some premeditacyon or thought that a persone hath had þe daye before. **1685** Cotton tr. *Montaigne* (1877) I. 82 The premeditation of death is the premeditation of liberty; he who has learned to die has unlearned to serve.

premeditative (pri:'mɛdɪteɪtɪv), *a. rare.* [f. as PREMEDITATE *v.* + -IVE.] Given to or characterized by premeditation.

1858 Bushnell *Nat. & Supernat.* vii. (1862) 137 Every first thing accordingly shows some premeditative token of every last. **1904** *Westm. Gaz.* 23 Apr. 2/1 A telling meeting of extremes—the most premeditative classic revivalists by the most 'instantaneous' of the moderns.

pre'meditator. [Agent-n. from PREMEDITATE *v.*: see -OR.] One who premeditates. So **premedi'tatrix,** a female premeditator. *rare.*

1853 Miss Hardy *The Confessor* xx. 200 The old woman at Amboise was a premeditatrix.

pre-meiotic to **-Mendelian:** see PRE- B. 1.

pre-memorial: see PRE- B. 1.

premeno'pausal, *a. Med.* [PRE- B. 1.] Of or pertaining to the years preceding the menopause.

1939 *Jrnl. Clin. Investigation* XVIII. 177/2 The pituitaries from premenopausal individuals were low in gonadotropic potency. **1944** *Jrnl. Clin. Endocrinol.* IV. 577/1 While anovulatory cycles may occur at any age, it seems certain that they are far more common in the premenopausal years than they are in younger women. **1956** C. F. Fluhmann *Managem. Menstrual Disorders* xxv. 322 A series of 173 hospital patients over forty years of age with various types of abnormal uterine bleeding are illustrative of the 'premenopausal' period. **1975** *Lancet* 5 July 7/2, 6 women were premenopausal, with ages ranging from thirty-two to forty-four years.

So **pre'menopause,** the stage of a woman's life immediately preceding the menopause.

1941 Mazer & Israel *Diagn. & Treatm. Menstrual Disorders* xxi. 308 A number of clinicians reported favorably on the use of testosterone propionate in cases of dysfunctional uterine bleeding, especially that of the premenopause. **1957** *Amer. Jrnl. Obstetr. & Gynecol.* LXXIII. 985 Since the average age of menopause in the American white woman is 46, it appears that age 40 would be the beginning of the premenopause. **1968** R. W. Kistner in Astwood & Cassidy *Clin. Endocrinol.* II. vi. ix. 697 Effective treatment of the premenopause should..produce regular, but not excessive, uterine bleeding.

pre'menstrual, *a.* [PRE- B. 1.] Occurring before menstruation; ***premenstrual tension,*** tension felt prior to menstruation. Also *transf.*

1885 [see POSTMENSTRUAL *a.*]. **1928** *Jrnl. Amer. Med. Assoc.* 14 Jan. 109/1 With Premenstrual Tension.—This was shown by a considerable group of women and manifesting [*sic*] itself by extreme nervousness, symptoms of autonomic imbalance, irritability, psychic changes and a feeling of tremendous tension. **1943** *Amer. Jrnl. Dis. Children* LXV. 302 The premenstrual state persisted, and fifteen months later the child menstruated. **1954** G. I. M. Swyer *Reproduction & Sex* iv. 43 The 'premenstrual tension' of which some women complain. **1970** R. Lowell *Notebk.* 72 Revolution, Drugging her terrible premenstrual cramps, Marches..to storm the city. **1974** J. Cooper *Women & Super Women* 11 Other occupations are.. smashing crockery from pre-menstrual tension. **1978** F. Weldon *Praxis* xxii. 203 You're hysterical. I expect you're pre-menstrual.

Hence **pre'menstrually** *adv.*

1931 *Arch. Neurol. & Psychiatry* XXVI. 1054 The blood of this patient showed twice the amount of female sex hormone that is normally found premenstrually. **1973** J. Zubin *Contemp. Sexual Behaviour* viii. 160 Mean levels of hostility are highest premenstrually.

pre'menstruum. *Med.* [f. PRE- B. 1 + MENSTRUUM.] The stage of the menstrual cycle which precedes menstruation.

1910 *Trans. N.Y. Obstetr. Soc. 1909–11* 229 In the third stage called by them [*sc.* Hitchmann & Adler] the premenstruum, the mucous membrane which is now thick and velvety, can be divided into a superficial, compact, and deeper, spongy layer. **1938** *Jrnl. Amer. Med. Assoc.* 21 May 1722/1 During the premenstruum, the concentration of estrogen in the blood rises and affects the sympathetic nervous system. **1969** *Sunday Times* 14 Sept. 54/3 Crimes of violence by women, most often involving their own families, are more often committed during the premenstruum. **1977** *Lancet* 24/31 Dec. 1330/2 It is common knowledge that exacerbations of acne and skin allergies occur during the premenstruum.

†**'prement.** *Obs. rare*$^{-1}$. [ad. L. *prement-em*, pres. pple. of *premĕre* to press.] That which presses.

1700 *Phil. Trans.* XXII. 569 Any exteriour Body which may compress the Fibres..As for external Prements [etc.].

pre-'mention, *sb. rare.* [PRE- A. 2.] Mention beforehand, previous notice.

a **1651** Calderwood *Hist. Kirk* (Wodrow Soc.) II. 46 The admissioun of ministers, elders, and deacons, is ordeaned to be made publicklie in the kirk, and pre-mentioun to be made upon the Lord's day preceding.

pre-'mention, *v. rare.* Also 7 præ-. [f. PRE- A. 1 + MENTION *v.*; so obs. F. *prémentionner* (1588 in Godef.).] *trans.* To mention previously or beforehand. Hence **pre-mentioned** *ppl. a.*, before-mentioned.

1647 Ward *Simp. Cobler* 21 That the prementioned Planters, by Tolerating all Religions, had immazed themselves in the most intolerable confusions and inextricable thraldomes the world ever heard of. **1660** *Charac. Italy* 4 Arguments..of greater solidity and weight than the præmentioned. **1705** Hauksbee in *Phil. Trans.* XXV. 1866 A small quantity of the pre-mention'd Ingredients. **1793** J. Williams *Life Ld. Barrymore* 43 To build a room..for the purpose of debating upon a pre-mentioned subject.

premenyre, premere, obs. ff. PRÆMUNIRE, PRIMER.

premeridian (pri:mə'rɪdɪən), *a.* [PRE- B. 1 a.] Occurring before noon; in *Geol.*, applied by H. D. Rogers to the seventh of his fifteen subdivisions of the Palæozoic strata of the Appalachian chain.

1858 [see POSTMERIDIAN *a.* 2]. **1859** Page *Geol. Terms.*

premerit (priːˈmɛrɪt), *v. rare.* [PRE- A. 1.] *trans.* To merit or deserve beforehand.

a **1628** PRESTON *New Covt.* (1634) 107 He that is capable of no gift, there can be nothing done to him, to premerit any thing. **1648** *Eikon Bas.* viii. 56 Nor is it strange that they.. should not finde mercy enough to forgive him, who so much premerited of them. **1850** MARSDEN *Early Purit.* (1853) 389 That eternal life was the free gift of God through Christ, and not procured or pre-merited.

preˈmetallize, *v.* [PRE- A. 1.] *trans.* To convert (a dye) before use into a metal chelate form by treatment with a metal salt, usu. in order to improve fastness properties. Hence **preˈmetallized** *ppl. a.*

1948 KIRK & OTHMER *Encycl. Chem. Technol.* II. 252 The formation of the metallic complex can be accomplished as an after-treatment, or the dye can be premetallized and applied to the fiber in the form of its soluble alkali salt. **1949** *Jrnl. Soc. Dyers & Colourists* LXV. 490/2 Ultralan Orange RS —This is a premetallised dye giving bright oranges when applied from strongly acid dye-baths, under which conditions the most level dyeings are obtained. **1963** A. J. HALL *Textile Sci.* ii. 82 Nylon can also be dyed with wool and cotton dyes (notably the acid wool dyes, pre-metallised dyes and direct cotton dyes). **1963** *Times* 31 May 19/6 The use of premetallised dyes for wool has also increased.. despite the poor trading conditions in the textile printing industry.

premetive, obs. Sc. form of PRIMITIVE.

†**ˈpremiable,** *a. Obs. rare*$^{-1}$. [ad. L. type **præmiābil-is*, f. *præmiārī*: see PREMIATE and -ABLE.] Deserving of reward. Hence †**premiaˈbility,** deservingness of reward. *Obs. rare*$^{-1}$.

a **1450** *Mankind* (Brandl) 854 Your merytes were not premyabyll to þe blys abowe. **1675** BAXTER *Cath. Theol.* II. xii. 271 What word can you find? Premiability and Rewardableness are long and unhandsome, and I remember no other, without using many words.

†**ˈpremial,** *a. Obs. rare*$^{-1}$. [ad. late L. *præmiālis* (August.) used as a reward, f. *præmium* reward: see -AL[1].] Of the nature of a reward.

a **1680** J. CORBET *Free Actions* III. xxxi. (1683) 50 If Gods Positive Denegation of further Grace be penal, why may not his conferring of further Grace be premial?

†**ˈpremiant,** *a. Obs. rare.* [ad. L. *præmiānt-em*, pres. pple. of *præmiārī*: see next.] Rewarding; prescribing or conferring a reward.

1675 BAXTER *Subst. Cartwright's Excep.* 32 From the condition of premiant or penal acts. **1675** —— *Cath. Theol.* II. ii. 40 Of the latter, there is a flat Promise, and premiant Law or Covenant made by God.

premiate (ˈpriːmɪeɪt), *v. rare.* Also 7 *pa. pple.* premiate. [f. ppl. stem of L. *præmiārī* to stipulate for a reward, also (?) to reward (f. *præmium* reward). Cf. OF. *premier* vb. (1410 in Godef.).] *trans.* To reward; to award a prize to. Hence **ˈpremiated** *ppl. a.*

1537 POLE *Let. to Cromwell* in Strype *Eccl. Mem.* (1721) I. App. lxxxiv. 222 If ony man had been premiate to do him service none could have don more. *a* **1651** CALDERWOOD *Hist. Kirk* (Wodrow Soc.) III. 254 So she premiated and rewarded him. **1858** *Sat. Rev.* 4 Sept. 230/2 Of all the premiated competitors Mr. Scott has proved himself to be the best man. **1892** *Athenæum* 3 Sept. 326/3 A model of the arch.. was tried over each of the premiated models.

premiation (priːmɪˈeɪʃən). *rare.* [f. as PREMIATE *v.*] Reward; the act of rewarding, a prize-giving.

a **1490** JOHANNES DE IRLANDIA *Meroure of Wyssdome* (1965) II. 53 And þocht euirilk man and ressonable creatur incontinent eftir þar deid and partyn furth of the waurld have certane knaulage of þar dampnacioun or premiacioun [etc.]. **1930** J. RITCHIE in *Scots College, Rome* iii. 93 We witnessed two great functions. The first was a premiation at the Gregorian University when.. we saw John Joseph Dyer ..marching up for his gold medals.

premices, var. PRIMICES *Obs.*, first-fruits.

†**ˈpremie.** *Obs.* Also -ye. [a. obs. F. *premie* (rare, 16th c. in Godef.), ad. L. *præmi-um*: see PREMIUM.] A reward, prize; a gift.

c **1550** BALE *K. Johan* (Camden) 85 The cytie of London, through his mere graunt and premye, Was first privyleged to have both mayer and shryve. **1550** —— *Image Both Ch.* Pref. A iij b, It manifesteth also what premyes, what crownes, and what glory the sayd congregation shall haue.

premie, var. PREEMIE.

premier (ˈprɛmɪə(r), ˈpriːmɪə(r)), *a.* and *sb.* Forms: 5, 7–8 **primier,** 8 **premiere,** 7– **premier.** [a. F. *premier* first:—L. *prīmāri-us* of the first rank, PRIMARY, f. *prīm-us* first.

(The first pronunciation (in Smart 1836) is now the more frequent in England. A third pronunciation (prɪˈmɪə(r)), formerly in use, is evidenced in various poems.)]

A. *adj.* **1. a.** First in position, importance, or rank; chief, leading, foremost.

c **1470** ASHBY *Active Policy* 2 Maisters Gower, Chauucer & Lydgate, Primier poetes of this nacion. **1610** HOLLAND *Camden's Brit.* I. (1637) 335 The Captain of the primier band of the Vetasians. **1614** CAMDEN *Rem.* 5 The Spaniard ..challengeth the primier place in regard of..his dominions. **1621** BP. MOUNTAGU *Diatribæ* 575 That Power which is primierepresident amongst them desireth to be accounted the supreme God. *c* **1630** RISDON *Surv. Devon* §293 (1810) 303 One of the premier knights of the order of the garter. **1762** H. WALPOLE *Vertue's Anecd. Paint.* (1765) I. ii. 43 Henry Beauchamp, son of Richard and Isabel, was at the age of nineteen created premier earl of England. **1833** MARRYAT *P. Simple* xxxi, The premier violin, master of the ceremonies and ballet-master. **1889** *Pall Mall G.* 3 Dec. 2/3 The six principal exports of Brazil... Coffee takes the premier place. **1905** *Daily Chron.* 6 Dec. 6/3 The Prime Minister is to be not only the premier Commoner, but to take precedence over all Dukes.

†**b.** ***premier minister, minister premier*** [cf. F. *premier ministre*]. = B. *Obs.*

1686 EVELYN *Diary* 19 Feb., Lord Sunderland was now Secretary of State, President of the Council, and Premier Minister. **1691** BEVERLEY *Mem. Kingd. Christ* 1 The Angel ..was the Primier Minister of Prophecy from Christ, to the Apocalyptical Apostle John. **1703** *Royal Resolutions* xii. in *Marvell's Wks.* (Grosart) I. 433 My pimp shall be my minister primier. **1731** SWIFT *To Gay* Wks. 1755 IV. I. 172 Thus families like realms with equal fate Are sunk by premier ministers of state. *a* **1734** NORTH *Exam.* III. vii. §15 (1740) 515 The Duke of Buckingham was potent, being, as I said before, a sort of primier Minister.

2. First in time; earliest.

1652 HEYLIN *Cosmogr.* To Rdr. A iv, Vouching the legal Interess of the English Nation, in Right of the first Discovery or Primier Seisin, to Estotiland. **1768** [W. DONALDSON] *Life Sir B. Sapskull* II. xx. 161 The venerable dame of antiquity, who was recommended..to superintend my premiere actions, till I should grow into power to assist myself. **1882** J. ASHTON *Soc. Life Q. Anne* II. xxvi. 28 The premier advertisement of opera in England. **1889** *Queen* 30 Mar., A woman, who, we may imagine, was no longer in her premier youth. **1898** *Whitaker's Titled Persons* 85 Sir Hickman Beckett Bacon..Premier Baronet. **1899** *Westm. Gaz.* 19 June 6/1 The committee of the Post Office Savings Bank refreshment department have just issued their premier statement of accounts and balance-sheet.

B. *sb.* [Short for *premier minister.*] **a.** *generally.* The first or chief minister of any ruler; the chief officer of an institution.

1711 HICKES *Two Treat. Chr. Priesth.* (1847) II. 23, I had rather be the poor deprived priest..than be premier, or plenipotentiary to the greatest monarch. **1739** HILDROP *Contempt of Clergy* 61 He..makes him not only his Premier in Temporals, but his Vice-gerent in Spirituals. **1784** D. HERD *Let.* in *Songs* (1904) 50, I am determined to give up.. this name of Premier [head of the Cape Club, Edinburgh].

b. The first minister of the Crown, the PRIME MINISTER of Great Britain or one of its (former) Colonies.

This sense is now *obs.* in *Austral.* and *Canad.* usage: cf. sense B. c below and note *s.v.* PRIME MINISTER 3 b.

1726 W. STRATFORD *Let.* 23 June in *Rep. MSS. Dk. Portland* (Hist. MSS. Comm. 1901) VII. 439 The Premier and his brother of All Souls called on me last week on their way to young Bromley's. **1727** LADY E. LECHMERE in *15th Rep. Hist. MSS. Comm.* App. VI. 53 Our Premier..is in as great favour with the King as with the Queen. **1746** DK. OF CUMBERLAND in Coxe *Mem. Administr. Pelham* (1829) I. 486, I should be much better pleased..if the Premier moved it... I am fully convinced of the Premier's goodwill to me. **1799** MME. D'ARBLAY *Let.* in *Diary* VI. 193 How can the Premier [Pitt] be so much his own enemy in politics as well as in happiness? **1847** TENNYSON *Princ.* Concl. 102 A shout More joyful than the city-roar that hails Premier or king! **1883** *Brandon* (Manitoba) *Daily Mail* 29 Jan. 2/1 It says that several of those roughly classed as Ministerialists will in all probability vote 'no confidence' in the present Premier. **1888** HENLEY *Bk. Verses, If I were King*, If I were King, my pipe should be premier. The skies of time and chance are seldom clear. **1902** *Edin. Rev.* Oct. 472 The colonial premiers of Canada and Australia..have set their face against any closer linkage of the Empire as a whole. **1916** A. BRIDLE *Sons of Canada* 14 It is of prime importance to remember how..so impersonal a figure ever came to be Premier of Canada.

c. *Austral.* and *Canad.* The chief minister of a State or Province.

1853 *Hamilton* (Ontario) *Gaz.* 3 Oct. 2/6 In the prosecution of this singularly dignified scheme—we shall say nothing of its abstract honesty—the Premier scruples not to employ the influence which his position invests him with. **1902** *Parl. Debates Austral.* 1901–2 XI. 14528/2 Is it the case, as stated by the Premier of Queensland, that he (the Premier) has made repeated applications for a detailed statement of the receipts and expenditure of the departments transferred to the Commonwealth, and that such statement has not yet been supplied to him. **1917** N. MCNEIL in J. O. Miller *New Era in Canada* 197 Why did Honoré Mercier, as Premier of Quebec, place a reference to the Pope in the preamble of his Jesuits Estates Bill? **1929** M. DE LA ROCHE *Whiteoaks* xi. 151 Look at the situation in the Province of Quebec! There the women have no vote. 'We are Latins!' their Premier exclaims. **1930** W. K. HANCOCK *Australia* x. 209 In 1916 a Labour Premier of New South Wales..handed his resignation, not to the official head of the State, but to caucus. **1969** T. JENKINS *We came to Australia* I. ii. 30 Australia has a Prime Minister in the capital, Canberra, but..each of its six States has its own 'local' Prime Minister, known as a Premier. **1972** *Ann. Reg. 1971* 79 On 21 October the Progressive Conservative Party in Ontario under a new Premier, Mr William Davis, retained power with an increased majority winning 78 seats.

d. *U.S.* The Secretary of State. ?*Obs.*

1855 *N.Y. Herald* 22 Nov. 4/4 The casting vote between the Premier and the Kitchen is subject to the caprices and vacillations of the President, whose official position makes him supreme over both the action of the premier and the counsels of the Kitchen. **1878** *Harper's Mag.* Mar. 490/2 The diplomatic anteroom, where foreign dignitaries await audience with the Premier, is handsome in its appointments. **1886** E. ALTON *Among Law-Makers* vii. 68 The Secretary of State..is sometimes (though not accurately) referred to as 'The Premier'. **1905** *Washington Post* 21 Mar. 4 Elihu Root ..is ideally equipped for the duties of the Department of State, but it is considered unlikely that he could be induced to return to the Cabinet, even as premier. **1925** W. H. SMITH *Hist. Cabinet U.S.A.* 28 He [*sc.* the Secretary of State] is frequently spoken of as the 'premier' of the cabinet, but there is no such title or designation known to our laws.

e. The Prime Minister of a country other than Great Britain or one of its colonies or a nation belonging to the British Commonwealth. Also used as a title prefixed to the surname of a premier.

1936 [see MEIJI]. **1942** W. S. CHURCHILL *End of Beginning* (1943) 14 We sent Premier Stalin—for that I gather is how he wishes to be addressed..—exactly what he asked for. **1961** *N.Y. Times* 21 May IV. 1 Premier Khrushchev has made propaganda capital out of that fact. **1976** *Daily Tel.* 20 July 4/1 This is assumed to refer to some sort of demonstration similar to April's Peking riot by supporters of Teng and the late Premier Chou En-lai.

Hence (*nonce-wds.*) **ˈpremier** *v. intr.*, to play the premier, to govern as prime minister; **ˈpremieral** *a.*, pertaining to a premier; **ˈpremieress,** the wife of a premier.

1790 BURNS *Addr. Beelzebub* 22 Nae sage North, now, nor sager Sackville, To watch and premier o'er the pack vile. **1894** *Spectator* 24 Mar. 400 Monarchy, now being replaced everywhere, more or less, by Premieral Government. **1865** *Pall Mall G.* 9 Nov. 11 A gentleman who 'goes regularly into Society', 'attends the Premieress's soirées', and 'knows all the best people'.

‖**premier cru** (prəmje kry). Also **premier crû.** Pl. **premier(s) crus.** [Fr., lit. 'first growth'.] A wine of the best quality. Also *transf.*, *fig.*, and *attrib.* Cf. CRU, GROWTH[1] 1 d.

1868 E. L. BECKWITH *Pract. Notes Wine* x. 47 The old, well-known *premiers crûs*, or first growths, retain their ancient and honoured places at the head of French wines. **1875** H. VIZETELLY *Wines of World* I. 13 Branne-Mouton, next-door neighbour to Château Lafite, and noted for its nutty aroma,..is deserving..of being ranked among the *premiers crûs*. **1928** P. M. SHAND *Bk. French Wines* ii. 58 Château Haut-Brion ranks..as the peer of the three great *Premiers Crus* of the Médoc. **1951** [see CRU]. **1965** P. O'DONNELL *Modesty Blaise* i. 16 He has a wonderfully varied list of girl-friends. From *premier cru* to honest *vin du pays*. **1970** *Guardian* 21 May 13/1 The American demand begins at the top with the five Premiers Crus, and moves steadily down the 1855 classification of the Médoc wines. **1976** *Time* 20 Dec. 27 (Advt.), The best cognacs come only from the Grande and the Petite Champagne districts, the 'premiers crus' of the Cognac region. **1978** L. PRYOR *Viper* (1979) ii. 31 The Long Beach race..the United States' only true road race..lacks the *premier cru* quality of Monaco.

‖**premier danseur** (prəmje dɑ̃sœr). Pl. **premiers danseurs.** [Fr., lit. 'first dancer'.] A leading male dancer in a ballet company. Cf. PREMIÈRE DANSEUSE.

1828 [see DANSEUR]. **1860** THACKERAY *Roundabout Papers* iii, in *Cornh. Mag.* May 634 Sir Alcide Flicflac (premier danseur of H.M. Theatre)! **1930** C. W. BEAUMONT *Hist. Ballet in Russia* VII. 49 Dutac was honoured with the position of *premier danseur* during the reign of Alexander I. **1930** —— tr. *Noverre's Lett. on Dancing & Ballets* 21 If he [*sc.* the *maître de ballet*] concentrate his attention of the *premières danseuses* and *premiers danseurs*, the action becomes tedious. **1938** A. L. HASKELL *Ballet* ii. 20 The field-marshal de Bassompière, [was] a *premier danseur* between campaigns. **1969** *Times* 11 Nov. 9/3 The vicissitudes of a *premier danseur* only half the size of his ballerina partner are worthy of consideration. **1973** R. HAYES *Hungarian Game* xxxv. 211, I watched a traffic cop directing sluggish cars like a *premier danseur* in a cattle pen. **1978** *Chicago* June 26/3 Jacques d'Amboise, premier danseur of the New York City Ballet, returns to choreograph a special number for the evenings.

‖**première** (prəmjɛr, ˈprɛmɪɛə(r), *U.S.* prɪˈmɪə(r)), *sb.* Also **premier, preemeer.** [F., short for *première représentation.*] A first representation or performance of a play, etc.; a 'first night'. Also *transf.*

1889 'F. LESLIE' *Let.* 9 Feb. in W. T. Vincent *Recoll. Fred Leslie* (1894) II. xxii. 81 It upset all of us and made us more nervous than a *première*. **1890** G. B. SHAW *Let.* 28 Feb. (1965) I. 244 This does not..include the expenses of the *première* at Amsterdam. **1895** *Punch* 26 Jan. 37/1 It was a pleasant sight, on the *première* of 'King Arthur' to see [etc.]. **1896** A. W. À BECKETT in *Daily News* 14 Feb. 6/2 The day before the date fixed for our premiere arrived, and I duly reported progress. **1897** 'OUIDA' *Massarenes* xxvi, [He] never misses a season at Bayreuth, or a *première* of Saint-Saëns's. **1915** *Sat. Even. Post* 9 Oct. 62/2 She always accompanies me to our premières. **1930** E. MANNIN *Confessions & Impressions* II. iv. 137 He complimented me on my literary *première* and told me to keep on writing. **1937** *New Republic* 19 May 48/1 Miss Gaynor [arrives] at another preemeer in smart mourning. **1941** *Commonweal* 10 Jan. 294/1 The movie première—pronounced pre-meer, with heavy emphasis on the second syllable—is a national phenomenon. **1957** *Times* 9 Sept. 11/4 Each season, when Balmain finally settles down to the production of a new collection of some 150 models, Ginette Spanier is sent away for three weeks' holiday, returning only a few days before the all-important *première*. **1968** S. CHALLIS *Death on Quiet Beach* viii. 115 Fane was due to attend a late premier of his current movie. **1978** J. ANDERSON *Angel of Death* xiii. 144 'I'll be the only actress in the world who could do it justice.' ..'I'll come to the premiere.'

première (ˈprɛmɪɛə(r), prɪˈmɪə(r)), *v.* Also **premier.** [f. prec.] *trans.* To present or perform (a play, film, programme, or the like) for the first time; to reveal (a new product). Also *absol.* and *intr.* for *pass.* Hence **premiˈered, premiering** *ppl. adjs.*

1940 *Winchell Coll.* (Topeka, Kansas) *Jrnl.* 11 Dec. 4/6 There's irony in the request of Grinnell college's alumni that Frank Capra should premiere 'Meet John Doe' there.

1941 W. C. HANDY *Father of Blues* v. 70 With..Gordon Collins, Lew Hall, all-time end men, premiering on the flanks, you'd feel a strange enchantment creeping over you. **1943** *Newsweek* 13 Sept. 101 Keepsakes, a new Sunday program..premièred on Blue Sep. 5, 8–8:30. **1945** G. ANTHEIL *Bad Boy of Music* ii. 16 This symphony, my 'First Symphony', was later to be premiered in Berlin. **1945** MENCKEN *Amer. Lang.* Suppl. I. 387 A few of its [sc. *Variety's*] characteristic inventions will suffice:..*to premier* (often shortened to *to preem*). **1952** 'E. Box' *Death in Fifth Position* (1954) i. 2 My company is going to première an important new ballet tonight. *Ibid.* vii. 181 By the time *Eclipse* was to be premièred, Ella had infuriated Miles..by threatening to leave the company. **1955** L. FEATHER *Encycl. Jazz* 141/1 He [sc. W. G. Fuller]..was co-composer and arr. of..*The Swedish Suite* premiered at Carnegie Hall '48. **1967** *N.Y. Herald Tribune Internat.* 11–12 Feb. 5/4 André Kostelanetz, who commissioned the work and premiered it 25 years ago, asked Mr. Lindsay to do the reading and will conduct the performance. **1973** *Times* 11 Apr. 12/7 In Frankfurt the Theater am Turm, which has premiered most of Peter Handke's plays, is run on similarly cooperative lines. **1975** *Publishers Weekly* 1 Dec. 62/3 He managed to keep the title in the public eye until the film premiered in December 1939. **1976** *National Observer* (U.S.) 10 Apr. 20/2 The premiere of a bizarre Scots drama, Menzies McKillop's *Future Pit*, now joined in repertory by a premiering trio of one-acters: Frank B. Ford's *Waterman*, Gladden Schrock's *Glutt*, and Michael Casales' *Cold*. *Ibid.* 16 Oct. 10/3 The ABC Evening News..premiered last week ..and was notable in at least two respects. **1977** *Custom Car* Nov. 13/4 Saab premiered their long-rumoured Turbo 99.

‖**première danseuse** (prəmjɛr dɑ̃søz). Also *ellipt.* **première**. Pl. **premières danseuses**. [Fr., fem. of PREMIER DANSEUR.] A leading female dancer in a ballet company; a ballerina.

1828 [see DANSEUSE]. **1846** R. FORD *Gatherings from Spain* xxiii. 327 Egyptians, whose women are the premières danseuses of these occasions, in which [gipsy] men never take a part. **1867** *Galaxy* Aug. 441 The dancer who has passed the chrysalis ballet-girl stage, and is now a full-fledged, butterfly *première*. **1887** J. PAYN *Holiday Tasks* 13 But here his eye wanders..from the photo of the *première danseuse* at the Frivolity Music Hall. **1890** G. B. SHAW *London Music 1888–89* (1937) 314 Many a *première danseuse* holds her position in spite of a neck and wrists which are, dancingly considered, dead as doornails. **1911** [see BALLERINA]. **1930** [see PREMIER DANSEUR]. **1942** L. KIRSTEIN *Bk. of Dance* xiv. 319 The great..artist Vaganova,.. frequently shines as its *première* [in the *Lac des Cygnes*]. **1974** *Sat. Rev. World* (U.S.) 19 Oct. 40/2 The *première danseuse étoile* of the Opéra in Paris. **1978** LD. DROGHEDA *Double Harness* xx. 261 In 1919, she [*sc.* Ninette de Valois] was engaged as *première danseuse* for the season of international opera at Covent Garden.

premiership ('prɛmɪəʃɪp, 'priːm-). [f. PREMIER *sb.* + -SHIP.]

1. a. The office of a premier or prime minister.

1800 HAZLITT *Pol. Ess.* (1819) 398 An inherency of the office in the person of the King, which made the office itself a nullity, and the Premiership, with its accompanying majority, the sole and permanent power of the State. **1806** MOORE *Mem.* (1853) I. 187 The King will certainly offer the premiership to Addington. **1873** *Spectator* 9 Aug. 1001/1 Mr. Gladstone..takes the control of the Exchequer as well as the Premiership. **1893** F. ADAMS *New Egypt* 125 The premiership of Fakhry Pasha was never gazetted.

b. *U.S.* The office of Secretary of State. Cf. PREMIER *sb.* d. ? *Obs.*

1928 H. MINOR *Story Democr. Party* 69 Madison had cabinet troubles, too. Monroe accepted the premiership in March 1811.

2. The state of being first in position or rank, as in a competition. Also *attrib.*

1870 ANDERSON *Missions Amer. Bd.* II. xvii. 138 Kinau was succeeded in the premiership by..her half-sister. **1883** *Standard* 26 Feb. 2/6 Lowland Chief maintains the Premiership in the Lincolnshire Handicap betting. **1897** *Daily News* 9 July 6/2 He also took a special prize as a 'premiership dog'.

pre-'milking. [PRE- A. 1.] The removal of milk from a cow's udder before the birth of her calf.

1953 K. RUSSELL *Princ. Dairy Farming* xiii. 157 Premilking can be done either by hand or machine. **1960** *Farmer & Stockbreeder* 5 Jan. 101/3 Too many concentrates before calving can result in pre-milking being necessary. **1970** W. H. PARKER *Health & Dis. in Farm Animals* xiii. 167 Premilking..is a severe handicap to the calf.

premillenarian (ˌpriːmɪlɪ'nɛərɪən), *sb.* and *a.* [f. PRE- B. 1 + MILLENARIAN: cf. next.]

A. *sb.* One who believes that the Second Advent of Christ will precede the millennium; = PREMILLENNIALIST. **B.** *adj.* Of or pertaining to this belief or its holders. Hence **premille'narianism**, the premillenarian doctrine; = PREMILLENNIALISM.

1844 G. S. FABER *Eight Dissert.* (1845) I. Pref. 10 The usual argument of premillennarian expositors, deduced from a combination of Dan. vii. 9–14, 25–27.. is wholly inconclusive. *Ibid.* Pref. 17 The prediction of St. Peter is the millstone suspended from the neck of Premillennarianism, which no effort and no ingenuity can shake off. *Ibid.* 8 His paraphrase..expresses my own view, though it stands opposed to that of the Premillennarians. **1879** *Princeton Rev.* Mar. 419 The rejection of the pre-millenarian advent. **1883** R. W. PATTERSON in *Chicago Advance* 6 Sept., In some respects, these Adventists agree with the pre-millenarians.

premillennial (ˌpriːmɪ'lɛnɪəl), *a.* [f. PRE- B. 1 + MILLENNIAL *a.*] Occurring before the millennium; particularly said of the Second Advent of Christ; also, pertaining to the world as it now is before the millennium.

1846 G. OGILVY (*title*) Popular Objections to the Premillennial Advent considered. **1848** G. S. FABER *Many Mansions* Pref. (1851) 21 If we admit the conclusion, we shall have..a literal Premillennial Second Advent; a literal Reign, upon Earth, of the literally resuscitated Saints and Martyrs. **1868** VISCT. STRANGFORD *Select.* (1869) II. 304 A statesman who objects to our common work-a-day premillennial logic as an instrument of human education.

Hence **premi'llennialism**, the doctrine or belief that the Second Advent will precede the millennium; **premi'llennialist**, one who holds this doctrine; **premi'llennialize** *v. intr.*, to preach premillennialism; hence ***premi'llennializing*** ppl. adj.; **premi'llennially** *adv.*, prior to the millennium.

1848 G. S. FABER *Many Mansions* Pref. (1851) 23 The Scheme of Mr. Mede and the Premillennialists. *Ibid.* 178 A want of attention to it has led our premillennialising friends to bring forward a very inconclusive argument in support of their speculation. *Ibid.* 196 This prophecy, instead of being invincibly demonstrative of Premillennialism, is absolutely fatal to it. **1851** ELLIOTT *Horæ Apoc.* (1862) IV. 157 The martyrs and saints spoken of just before, as raised premillennially to live and reign with Christ. **1878** H. G. GUINNESS *End of Age* (1880) 92 All the primitive expositors and teachers were premillennialists. **1882–3** *Schaff's Encycl. Relig. Knowl.* III. 1888 From the death of the apostles till the time of Origen, premillenialism was the general faith of ..orthodox Christians.

premi'llennian, *a.* [f. PRE- B. 1 + MILLENNIAN *a.*] = PREMILLENNIAL *a.*

1828 G. S. FABER *Sacr. Calend. Prophecy* III. vi. viii. 449 The two theories of the literal premillennian second advent and of the universal premillennian conflagration stand or fall together. **1848** —— *Many Mansions* Pref. (1851) 205 When each of the two Anti-christian Confederacies, premillennian and postmillennian, is destined to perish.

preminire, obs. form of PRÆMUNIRE.

‖**'premio.** *Obs.* [It., ad. L. *præmium* a reward, PREMIUM.] = PREMIUM; *esp.* the earlier term for an insurance premium; also, a reward or prize; a bonus added to interest or to a payment.

1622 MALYNES *Anc. Law-Merch.* 150 Concerning the price of Assurances or *Premio* (as the Spaniards call it) it is differing in all places. *Ibid.* 160 Not to assure for vnlawfull places of trade..vnlesse a good *premio* bee giuen. **1638** *Insurance Policy* in R. G. Marsden *Sel. Pl. Crt. Admir.* (Selden) II. 59 All in good faith without fraud or guyle the Premio is paid as aforesaid. **1703** DE FOE *Villainy Stockjobbers* in *Misc.* 256 The Money'd Men, who obtain'd the Discount as a *Premio* added to the Interest upon the Originals. **1728** NORTH *Mem. Music* (1846) 117 A contribution..to be given as a premio to him that should best entertain them in a solemne consort. *a* **1734** —— *Exam.* III. vi. §91 (1740) 490 It is just as if the Ensurers brought in a Catalogue of ensured Ships lost, taking no Notice of Ships arrived and Premios.

†**'premiour.** *Obs. rare*$^{-1}$. [a. AF. *premiour*, corresp. to late L. *præmiātor* rewarder, f. L. *præmium* a reward, PREMIUM: see -OUR.] A rewarder.

1493 *Festivall* (W. de W. 1515) 123 b, Ihesus is and perpetually shall be to his louers rewarde and premyour.

'premious, *a. rare*$^{-0}$. [ad. L. *præmiōs-us* rich, f. *præmium* reward: see -OUS.] Rich in gifts.

1855 in CLARKE. Hence **1864** in WEBSTER, etc.

premisal (prɪ'maɪzəl). [f. PREMISE *v.* + -AL[1].] The action of premising; the making of a prefatory or introductory statement; stating (of something) as a premiss.

1652 N. CULVERWELL *Mount Ebal* Treat. (1654) 90 Here by way of premisal; 1. It must be in a lawful and warrantable way. **1701** BEVERLEY *Glory of Grace* 22 To this Premisal of the Efficient Cause from Eternity; and the Final Cause to Eternity;..I would add the Consideration of our Being placed into Christ. **1701** NORRIS *Ideal World* I. Pref. 10 Whether a conclusion may not immediately follow upon the premisal of one single proposition. **1912** *Catholic Encycl.* XIV. 75/1 Ethics may not be divided from psychology and theodicy, any more than from deductive logic. With the proper premisals then from the one and the other here assumed, we say that the Creator could not have given man a fixed nature, as He has, without willing man to work out the purpose for which that nature is framed.

premise, premiss ('prɛmɪs), *sb.* [a. F. *prémisse* (Oresme, 14th c.), also obs. and less usual *premise* ('a foreplacing, a setting before' Cotgr.), ad. med.L. *præmissa* (*propositio*, *sententia*), in Logic, a proposition set in front, a premiss, pa. pple. fem. of *præmittĕre* to put before: see PREMIT.

The etymological spelling is *premiss*, pl. *premisses*, formerly used in all senses, and still frequent (but by no means universal) in sense 1; in other senses *premises* (sing. *premise*), which appears early in 16th c., is now in use. This may have been influenced by *promise*, *-ises*, or possibly by the 16th c. Fr. variant *prémise*.]

I. in *Logic*. (Often *premiss*.)

1. A previous statement or proposition from which another is inferred or follows as a conclusion; *spec.* in *pl.* the two propositions from which the conclusion is derived in a syllogism. (The sing. is late (17th c.) and less common.)

The two propositions in a syllogism were formerly called, collectively, the *premisses*; individually, the *major proposition* or simply the *proposition* (πρότασις, Aristotle), and the *minor proposition* or *assumption* (πρ. ἡ ἑτέρα or ἡ τελευταία); the singular terms *major premiss* and *minor premiss* are not instanced before the 19th c.

The πρότασις of Aristotle was orig. rendered in Latin by *propositio* (Boethius, etc.). *Præmissæ* (plural) appears first in 12th c. L. translations from the Arabic versions of Aristotle. Prantl (II. 310, n. 48) cites *duæ præmissæ* from Pseudo-Averroës (*a* 1200); *altera præmissārum* occurs in Albertus Magnus *Prior. Analyt.* I. v. 3. *Duæ præmissæ* represents the Arabic *muqaddamatāni* (quoted, in a MS. of 1200, from Avicenna *a* 1037), dual of *muqaddamah* '(that which is) put before', passive pple. of *qadama*, to go before, put before, etc.; as sb. it stands for *qaḍiyyah muqaddamah*, 'propositio præmissa'. The *Mafātīḥ al 'ulūm* (Keys of the Sciences) *c* 970, in the account of the Analytics, has 'the *muqaddamah* (præmissa) is the *qaḍiyyah* (propositio): it is put before in making the deduction' (Prof. Margoliouth).

α. *c* **1374** CHAUCER *Boeth.* III. pr. x. 71 (Camb. MS.), I se wel þat it folweth by strengthe of þe premysses [*Addit. MS.* premisses]. **1398** TREVISA *Barth. De P.R.* II. ii. (1495) b j b/1 Yf he knowe the forsayd two premisses he knoweth the conclusyon by the premysses, for he concludeth that one of that other. **1426** LYDG. *De Guil. Pilgr.* 10717 Thy premysses for to make Ful ffayre exaumples thow kanst take. **1530** PALSGR. 257/2 Premysses that cometh in an argument, *premisse*. **1588** FRAUNCE *Lawiers Log.* I. iii. 19 b, The premisses, as they terme them, that is, the proposition and the assumption, must bee prooued and confirmed. **1614** RALEIGH *Hist. World* II. (1634) 485 They lay hold upon the conclusion, and by shaking that into pieces, hope to overthrow all the premisses upon which it is inferred. **1713** SWIFT *Cadenus & Vanessa* 280 Her foe's conclusions were not sound, From premisses erroneous brought. **1827** [see MINOR A. 4]. **1843** CARLYLE *Past & Pr.* II. x, Putting consequence on premiss. **1855** H. SPENCER *Princ. Psychol.* II. VI. ii. 11 What here are the premisses and inference? **1884** tr. *Lotze's Logic* 5 In expressing a universal truth in the major premiss, and bringing a particular instance under it in the minor.

β. **1628** T. SPENCER *Logick* 147 Vpon these premises, we may wel conclude [etc.]. **1660** BARROW *Euclid* I. Definitions, A Lemma is the demonstration of some premise whereby the proof of the thing in hand becomes the shorter. **1725** WATTS *Logic* III. iii. §1 In the premise all animals signifies every kind of animals. **1796** BURKE *Regic. Peace* III. Wks. VIII. 270 The premises in that piece conduct irresistably to the conclusion. **1827** WHATELY *Logic* I. i. §2 23 Every conclusion is deduced..from two other propositions (thence called Premises). **1864** BOWEN *Logic* v. 134 Here the second premise is materially false.

II. in *Law* and *gen.* (Now always *premise*(*s.*)

2. *pl.* The matters or things stated or mentioned previously; what has just been said; the aforesaid, the foregoing. Often in legal phraseology: see also 3, 4. Rarely in *sing.* (quot. 1683 in *β*). Now *rare* or *Obs.* exc. in technical use.

α. **1429** *Rolls of Parlt.* IV. 352 Plese itt to youre noble discretions to considere the premisses. **1494** FABYAN *Chron.* v. cxl. 126 As by the redynge of the premysses ye maye well perceyue and know. *c* **1550** LLOYD *Treas. Health* X vj, Take mouse ears, betony, Sanamund, sage,..make a pouder therof & boile the premisses in wine. *c* **1555** HARPSFIELD *Divorce Hen. VIII* (Camden) 29 Now after these premisses let us..commence the matter itself. **1631** WEEVER *Anc. Fun. Mon.* 646, I found since I writ the premisses, that Edward the Confessour was the prime cause. **1713** WARDER *True Amazons* (ed. 2) 61 But must be fully satisfy'd in the Premisses by ocular Demonstration.

β. **1529** WOLSEY in *Four C. Eng. Lett.* (1880) 10 Yf yt wold please you of your cherytable goodnes to shewe the premyses. **1570** *Homilies* II. *Agst. Disobedience* I, Of whiche all and singuler the premises, the holy Scriptures doo beare recorde in sundrie places. **1683** *Pennsylv. Archives* I. 63 Renouncing all Claims or Demands of anything in or for ye Premise for ye future from Him. **1696** *Vestry Bks.* (Surtees) 261 For the better inforceing the observacion of the premises. **1794** *Bloomfield's Amer. Law Rep.* 30 The Court having considered the Premises are of Opinion [etc.]. *a* **1830** in Trevelyan *Macaulay* (1876) I. iii. 137 To discuss questions conformably to the premises thus agreed on. **1844** WILLIAMS *Real Prop.* (1877) 15 The word premises is frequently used in law in its proper etymological sense of that which has been before mentioned.

3. *Law.* (*pl.*) That part in the beginning of a deed or conveyance which sets forth the names of the grantor, grantee, and things granted, together with the consideration or reason of the grant.

1641, **1818** [see HABENDUM]. **1642** tr. *Perkins' Prof. Bk.* ii. §161. 72 If the 'Habendum' etc. cannot stand with the Premisses but is repugnant to their premisses. **1749** E. WOOD *Compl. Body Conveyancing* I. v. §2. 236 The premisses of a Deed is all the Forepart of the Deed, or all that is written before the *Habendum*. **1837** T. D. HARDY *Rot. Chart.* Pref. 11 The *Premises* of a Charter comprehend all that precedes the Habendum, and contain the name and titles of the grantor, the address, the name and quality of the grantee, the description of the thing granted, and the reason or consideration of the grant being made.

4. *Law.* (*pl.*) (*spec.* use of 2.) The subject of a conveyance or bequest, specified in the premises of the deed: so expressed when referred to collectively in the later part of the document; = the houses, lands, or tenements above-said or before-mentioned.

α. **1480** *Bury Wills* (Camden) 56 That..my executourrez have and resseyve alle the issuez and profytys of alle the seyd meese londys and rentys and other premissez. **1508** in Nichols *Royal Wills* 379 All which maners, londs, and tenements, and other the premisses, we late purchased. **1547** in *Newminster Cartul.* (Surtees) 311 All grett Trees & Woodds growyng in & uppon the premyssez, all & syngler which premyssez aboue expressed & specified. **1609** *Mem.*

Ripon (Surtees) III. 334 The said Tythe Corn Hay Lamb and Wool in Allerthwaite Markinton and Ingerthorpe and other the Premisses..which premisses so sold..is now worth p. Ann. 60 *l.* **1774** in *Brasenose Coll. Doc.* I. 48 The Purhcase money to be paid Mr. B. for Premisses.

β. **1818** CRUISE *Digest* (ed. 2) VI. 526 Alice Higgins devised the premises, being a term for 999 years, to trustees, in trust for herself for life, remainder to H. Higgins her son and Mary his wife. **1827** JARMAN *Powell's Devises* II. 187 Where a testator devised a certain messuage and the furniture in it to A. for life, and after his decease he gave the said messuage and premises to B. the latter devise was held to carry the furniture as well as the messuage to B. on the principle that the word premises included all that went before.

5. *pl.* (from 4.) A house or building with its grounds or other appurtenances.

α. **1730** *Lond. Gaz.* No. 6922/2 The Committee for Letting the Cities Lands..give Notice That they intend to Lett by several Leases the Premisses hereafter mentioned. **1764** HARMER *Observ.* VIII. v. 217 The Eastern villagers now have oftentimes little [wood] or none on their premisses.

β. **1766** BLACKSTONE *Comm.* II. xx. 312 An actual seisin, or entry into the premises, or part of them. **1782** MISS BURNEY *Cecilia* x. iii, Till it suits you..to quit the premises. **1817** W. SELWYN *Law Nisi Prius* (ed. 4) II. 685 The wife being served, on the premises, or at the dwelling house of the husband. **1851** HAWTHORNE *Ho. Sev. Gables* xiii, Allowed to make it his home for the time being, in consideration of keeping the premises in thorough repair. **1902** *Act 2 Edw. VII*, c. 28 §21 Nor shall any coroner's inquest be held on such licensed premises. *Mod.* Licensed to retail beer, wine, spirits, and tobacco to be consumed on the premises. All repairs done on the premises.

†**6.** *pl.* Previous circumstances or events; things happening before. *Obs.*

1613 SHAKS. *Hen. VIII*, II. i. 63 The Law I beare no mallice for my death, T'has done vpon the premises, but Iustice. **1642** ROGERS *Naaman* 42 As he meant to scatter those ten Tribes..so he orders the whole frame of premises tending thereto. **1759** ROBERTSON *Hist. Scotl.* VIII. Wks. 1813 II. 86 So after these premises, the murder of the king following, we judge, in our consciences [etc.].

premise (prɪˈmaɪz), *v.* Also 6 **premyse, -mysse,** 7 **præmise, premize.** [f. prec. sb.; or f. 15–16th c. F. *premis, -mise*, pa. pple. of *premetre, prémettre* to place or put forth before: cf. PREMIT.]

1. *trans.* To state, set forth, or mention before something else; to say or write by way of preface or introduction to the main subject. (With *simple obj.* or, now usually, *obj. clause.*)

1526 *Pilgr. Perf.* (W. de W. 1531) 195 Whan almyghty god forbade the iewes to make..ydolles, he premysed & put before these wordes, sayenge: Thou shalt haue no god but me. **1571** DIGGES *Pantom.* I. vi. C iij, I thinke it not amisse ..to premise certaine Theoremes. **1606** HOLLAND *Sueton.* To Rdrs., With some few advertisments præmised. **1669** W. SIMPSON *Hydrol. Chym.* 34 What we have already said to that point being premiz'd. **1781** EARL MALMESBURY *Diaries & Corr.* I. 453, I can venture to premise that he will..be deprived of every possible means of doing harm. **1804–6** SYD. SMITH *Mor. Philos.* (1850) 367 Having premised these observations, I proceed to consider [etc.]. **1852** MISS YONGE *Cameos* (1877) II. xv. 162 He finally gave way, and accepted the commission, premising that he would only submit to it for twelve months.

absol. or *intr.* **17..** SWIFT (J.), I must premise with three circumstances.

†**b.** To put before, prefix (words, etc.) *to* a writing, speech, etc. *Obs.* except as involved in prec.

1626 R. HARRIS *Hezekiah's Recovery* (1630) 2 Neither is there any necessitie of premising petitions to each particular thanksgiving. **1681** BOYLE *Let. to Bp. H. Jones* 8 Apr., Wks. 1772 I. Life 173 The preface that the Jansenists have premised to their translation of the new testament. **1707** SLOANE *Jamaica* I. Pref., An Introduction,..which seemed necessary to be premised to the History itself. **1828** PUSEY *Hist. Enq.* I. 36 Premising to each article a definition.

†**c.** To imply beforehand; to presuppose. *Obs.*

1657–83 EVELYN *Hist. Relig.* (1850) I. 165 The very notion of the Soul's regeneration premising a generation.

d. *Logic.* To state in the premises. Also *absol.*

1684 BURNET *The. Earth* I. iv. 48 The Apostle's discourse here was an argumentation..'tis an answer upon a ground taken, he premiseth and then infers. **1864** BOWEN *Logic* vii. 182 For if only *some* is premised, we cannot conclude *all*.

2. To make, do, perform, or use beforehand; *esp.* in *Surg.* and *Med.* to perform (an operation) or administer (a remedy) as the beginning of a course of treatment.

1542 UDALL *Erasm. Apoph.* 142 When Antonie (the signe of the holy crosse premised) had in the name of God demaunded. **1635** PAGITT *Christianogr.* I. iii. (1636) 122 This solemne prayer being ended,..and the Lords prayer premised, all communicate. **1651** WITTIE *Primrose's Pop. Err.* III. 171 They forbid to use them,..before that purging be premised. **1736** AMYAND in *Phil. Trans.* XXXIX. 337 The Limb was immediately cut off.., having first premised a Ligature about the Flesh surrounding the Vessels. **1787** J. COLLINS in *Med. Commun.* II. 367 After premising a few drops of the antimonial wine,..I had recourse to the bark. **1836** J. M. GULLY *Magendie's Formul.* (ed. 2) 209 In the first case, of ulcers, I premised a seton in the arm.

3. *transf.* To preface or introduce (*with, by* something else).

1823 CHALMERS *Serm.* I. 448 Let me premise this head of discourse by admitting that I know nothing more hateful than the crouching spirit of servility. **1847** MEDWIN *Shelley* I. 283, I shall premise it [the history] with a few observations.

†**4. a.** To send before or in advance. **b.** To send or bring before the time. *Obs. rare.*

c **1540** tr. *Pol. Verg. Eng. Hist.* (Camden No. 29) 104 The King premised certaine horsemen to beset all the sea coast. **1593** [see PREMISED 2].

premised (prɪˈmaɪzd), *ppl. a.* [f. prec. + -ED¹.]

1. Stated or mentioned previously; aforesaid.

1546 *Yorks. Chantry Surv.* (Surtees) II. 247 Fre rente goinge furth of the premyssed landes. **1599** H. BUTTES *Dyets drie Dinner* A iv b, All these premised words..inferre thus much. **1667** BOYLE in *Phil. Trans.* II. 612, I shall conclude your trouble with the premised Note. **1701** NORRIS *Ideal World* I. vi. 326 The premised general notion of eternal truths.

†**2.** Sent before the time. *Obs. rare.*

1593 SHAKS. *2 Hen. VI*, v. ii. 41 O let the vile world end, And the premised Flames of the Last day, Knit earth and heauen together.

premisory (prɪˈmaɪzərɪ), *a. rare*⁻¹. [irreg. f. PREMISE *v.* + -ORY².] Introductory, antecedent.

1844 BABINGTON tr. *Hecker's Epidemics Mid. Ages* 190 The Sweating Sickness of 1485 did not make its appearance without great and general premisory events.

†**preˈmission.** *Obs.* [a. obs. F. *prémission* (*-icion* 15th c.), ad. late L. *præmissiōn-em* (*Pompej. gr.* p. 31, in Quicherat), n. of action from L. *præmittĕre*: see next.] A sending before or in advance.

1609 BP. W. BARLOW *Answ. Nameless Cath.* 247 There was a premission of him [Joseph] into Egipt. **1656** BLOUNT *Glossogr.*, *Premission*,..a sending before.

†**preˈmit,** *v. Obs.* [ad. L. *præmittĕre* to send or set before, f. *præ*, PRE- A. + *mittĕre* to send.]

1. *trans.* = PREMISE *v.* 1.

1540 in *10th Rep. Hist. MSS. Comm.* App. v. 385 That the said statute to be allwaye keapte..as it is premitted. **1608** WILLET *Hexapla Exod.* 84 Certaine generall questions are to bee premitted. **1681** R. FLEMING *Fulfill. Script.* (1801) I. 263, I would premit here some few things. **1784** J. BROWN *Hist. Brit. Ch.* (1820) II. vi. 218 After premitting a declaration of their peaceful intentions, the Covenanters took possession of Newcastle.

2. = PREMISE *v.* 2.

1662 [see PREMITTED below]. **1670** MAYNWARING *Physician's Repos.* 37 Purgation is necessary to be premitted.

3. To send forth. *rare.*

1677 GALE *Crt. Gentiles* II. IV. 50 Seneca would needs persuade us..that Virtue doth premit its light into the minds of al.

Hence †**preˈmitted** *ppl. a. Obs.*

1662 GUNNING *Lent Fast* 100 The Church..directed the Catechumeni to prepare themselves by premitted solemn fastings for the reception of holy Baptism.

premities, irreg. var. PRIMICES *Obs.*, first-fruits.

premium (ˈpriːmɪəm). Also 7–8 **præmium.** Pl. **-iums, -ia.** [a. L. *præmium* booty, profit from booty, profit, advantage, reward, f. *præ*, PRE- A. I + *emĕre* to buy, orig. to take.]

1. A reward given for some specific act or as an incentive; a prize.

1601 A. COPLEY *Answ. Let. Jesuited Gent.* 107 Their martyrdomes being to them as a *præmium* for the one, and.. a sufficient *Piaculum* for the other. **1612** BRINSLEY *Lud. Lit.* xxviii. (1627) 283 Those [scholars] who doe best, would be graced with some *Præmium* from them: as some little booke, or money. [*Margin*] Some *Præmia* giuen. **1661** BLOUNT *Glossogr.* (ed. 2), *Premium*..is used in Schools, for a reward given to that Schollar that says his Lesson, or performs his Exercise well. **1716** B. CHURCH *Hist. Philip's War* (1865) I. 152 The Captain with his Company..received their Praemium, which was Thirty Shillings per head, for the Enemies which they had killed or taken. **1765** T. HUTCHINSON *Hist. Mass.* I. ii. 305 He knew the premium set upon his head. **1770** SMALL in J. P. Muirhead *Life Jas. Watt* xvi. (1858) 223 The French..offer large præmia for time-keepers. **1785** W. TOOKE in *Lett. Lit. Men* (Camden) 429 The præmiums annexed, as incitements to Philosophical industry. **1797** *Monthly Mag.* III. 486/1 It was resolved, that a premium of twenty guineas should be paid to the owner who shall exhibit the best three-year-old bull. **1880** WARREN *Book-plates* xiv. 168 A premium of Trinity College, Dublin. **1898** *Daily News* 9 Mar. 4/4 After all premiums had been awarded, and the winners had been paraded,..the hunter classes had their chance.

fig. **1835** LYTTON *Rienzi* x. vi, Misplaced mercy would be but a premium to conspiracy. **1860** R. A. VAUGHAN *Mystics* I. 208 Such an abandonment..as should be a premium on his indolence.

2. The amount agreed on, in an insurance policy, to be paid at one time or from time to time in consideration of a contract of insurance (formerly *premio*): see INSURANCE 4, POLICY *sb.*² 1.

[**1622, 1638**: see PREMIO.] **1661** BLOUNT *Glossogr.* (ed. 2), *Premium*... Among Merchants it is used for that sum of money..which the Ensured gives the Ensurer for ensuring the safe return of any Ship or Merchandize. **1681** *Lond. Gaz.* No. 1668/4 The Insurers will oblige Themselves..to accept of a Surrender, and repay their Premium, only deducting a Proportion for the time Insured. **1766** ENTICK *London* IV. 262 The conditions of insurance are 2s. per cent. premium. **1835** SIR J. ROSS *Narr. 2nd Voy.* xxxiv. 480 The premium that might be demanded at Lloyd's. **1907** *Westm. Gaz.* 16 Jan. 8/1 This seemed to him to sufficiently define 'the premiums of the company',..the periodical sums required to be paid in respect of policies issued by the company in order to maintain such policies against the company.

3. a. A sum additional to interest, price, wages, or other fixed remuneration; a bonus; a bounty on the production or exportation of goods. *spec.*, a sum paid in addition to the rent on a leased property. †Formerly sometimes applied to interest on a loan.

1695 C. MONTAGU in Cobbett *Parl. Hist. Eng.* (1809) V. 968 The supplies..being so much diminished..by the unequal change, and exorbitant Premiums, before they reached the camp. **1698** LUTTRELL *Brief Rel.* (1857) IV. 340 An account..what imprest money has been paid to Mr. Burton and Mr. Knight for premiums for advancing money, &c., since May 95. **1729** *N. Jersey Archives* XI. 183 Any Person importing Masts into Great Britain, to be intituled to the Bounty or Praemium, must produce a Certificate. **1731** SWIFT *To Mr. Gay* 69 With Int'rest, and a Præmium paid beside, The Master's pressing Wants must be supply'd. **1748** H. ELLIS *Hudson's Bay* 103 Besides the extraordinary Wages..given, Premiums were settled in Case of Success, proportionable to the Rank of all the Persons on board. **1766** BLACKSTONE *Comm.* II. xxx. 456 If no premium were allowed for the hire of money, few persons would care to lend it. **1859** GEO. ELIOT *Let.* 19 Feb. (1954) III. 14 There was a house after my own heart at Mortlake..but it turned out to have a premium affixed to the lease, which made it too expensive. **1897** MARY KINGSLEY *W. Africa* 649 A captain is..sure to get their passage money and a premium for them. **1924** A. CHRISTIE *Poirot Investigates* iii. 71 'We've got a flat —at last!.. It's dirt cheap. Eighty pounds a year!'.. 'Big premium, I suppose?' **1966** *New Statesman* 21 Jan. 71/2 If railwaymen work genuinely longer or more difficult hours, and get overtime or shift premia in compensation, this is fair enough. **1966** *Economist* 29 Jan. 386/1 The case for higher night premia would be 'examined' in a later report, but he most definitely did not recommend them now. **1970** M. GREENER *Penguin Dict. Commerce* 263 Very often when property is leased, the lessee, in addition to paying a rent for an agreed period, pays a lump sum. This is known as a premium, or sometimes as 'key money', and was once intended to avoid taxation and disguise the true rent. **1974** M. B. BROWN *Econ. of Imperialism* viii. 177 Some foreign issues [of stocks] were certainly made more attractive because of the premiums at which they were issued.

b. *Comm.* (See quot. 1928.)

1928 *Funk's Stand. Dict.* II. 1956/3 *Premium*,..any object offered free to those who purchase goods to a certain value, as a set of books given free as an inducement to subscribe to a magazine. **1930** LUCAS & BENSON *Psychol. for Advertisers* xii. 204 $1,502,000,000 is spent annually on advertising. This is divided as follows: Newspapers..$690,000,000.. Premiums, programs and directories..25,000,000. **1954** R. J. SCHWARTZ *Dict. Business & Industry* 392/1 *Premium*, something given free or at a nominal price to induce an actual sale or to promote interest in a product. **1963** *Sunday Times* 17 Nov. 11/1 A rapidly-growing little specialist industry is growing round the 'take-a-plastic-daffodil-madam' school of retailing... A premium, in their jargon, can be anything given away or sold cheap to persuade people ..to buy, stock, sample or re-order a product. **1974** *Encycl. Brit. Micropædia* VIII. 191/1 Until the 1900s the most popular premiums were pictures and trade cards.., which were collected and exchanged by enthusiastic consumers whose collections became quite valuable.

c. *Finance.* The excess of the forward price of a currency or a commodity over the spot price.

1933 B. ELLINGER *This Money Business* x. 101 In normal times the difference between 'spot'—i.e. the rate for immediate delivery—and 'forward' rates depends on the rates of interest in the respective countries, but in abnormal times merchants may find a growing premium or discount on the forward rate over the spot rate. **1957** [see FORWARD *a.* 4]. **1971** R. F. PITHER *Man. Foreign Exchange* (ed. 7) x. 138 Forward rates of exchange are quoted as a 'margin' or 'difference' against the 'opot' rate of the currency concerned, or as a 'premium' or 'discount' on the 'spot' rate, or they may be quoted 'outright'. **1978** R. G. F. CONINX *Foreign Exchange Today* viii. 111 Forward margins are referred to as *premiums* or *discounts*. *Ibid.* 113 With indirect quotations, premiums indicate that the home currency enjoys higher interest rates than the quoted currency.

4. A fee paid for instruction in a profession or trade.

1765 BLACKSTONE *Comm.* I. xiv. 426 Sometimes very large sums are given with them [apprentices], as a premium for such their instruction. **1812** H. & J. SMITH *Rej. Addr.*, *The Theatre* 86 He would have bound him to some shop in town, But with a premium he could not come down. **1878** JEVONS *Prim. Pol. Econ.* vii. 58 To learn a profession, like that of an architect or engineer, it is requisite to pay a high premium, and become a pupil in a good office.

5. The charge made for changing one currency into another of greater value; agio; hence, the excess value of one currency over another.

1717 NEWTON in Rigaud *Corr. Sci. Men* (1841) II. 425 At home they make their payments in gold, but will not pay in silver without a premium. **1757** JOS. HARRIS *Coins* 121 A country which oweth a ballance to another must pay a præmium upon all the bills.

6. a. *at a premium*: at more than the nominal or usual value; above par; *fig.* in high esteem. (Opp. to *at a* DISCOUNT.)

1828 *Harrovian* 191 John Lyon put their charms at a premium. **1833** HT. MARTINEAU *Vanderput & S.* iii. 51 It answers our purpose better to sell our claim for this money at a premium. **1856** READE *Never too late* xxv, Suicide is at a premium here. *Ibid.* [see DISCOUNT *sb.* 4]. **1861** [see DISCOUNT *sb.* 4]. **1863** FAWCETT *Pol. Econ.* III. ix. (1876) 421 When the exchange is unfavourable, and bills at a premium, this premium..varies from day to day. **1882** BITHELL *Counting-ho. Dict.* (1893) 237 If £100 of Russian Stock is issued at the price of £94, then, if the quoted price on the Stock Exchange is 95½, it is said to be at 1½ premium. **1906** GALSWORTHY *Man of Property* xxiv. 295 When Mrs. MacAnder dined at Timothy's, the conversation..took that wider, man-of-the-world tone current among Forsytes at large, and this, no doubt, was what put her at a premium there. **1932** *Time* 28 Mar. 30/2 The news put Philharmonic subscriptions back at a premium last week. **1974** *Times* 14 Mar. 11/2 Sadly, space is at a premium in most department stores.

b. *fig.* ***to put*** (or ***place***) ***a premium on*** (something) and varr., to put a high value on something esp. as an inducement or incentive.

1907 G. B. SHAW *John Bull's Other Island* p. xvi, In short, our circumstances place a premium on political ability whilst the circumstances of England discount it; and the quality of the supply naturally follows the demand. **1911** —— *Getting Married* 142 Our democratic and matrimonial institutions.. put a premium on want of self-respect in certain very important matters. **1933** J. W. N. SULLIVAN *Limitations of Sci.* iv. 132 The struggle for existence takes the place of the human breeder. Nature sets a premium upon certain varieties as compared with others. **1939** A. HUXLEY *After Many a Summer* I. xi. 147 He's been greedy and domineering, among other reasons, because the present system puts a premium on those qualities. **1959** [see PEARL HARBOUR].

7. a. *attrib.* and *Comb.*, as ***premium*** (= prize) ***bull, tulip***, etc.; (sense 3 b) ***premium promotion, selling; premium-hunter, -winner; premium-fed, -paying*** adjs.: **premium apprentice**, an apprentice who has paid a premium for instruction in his intended trade; **premium bonus system, premium system**, a system by which a bonus is paid in addition to wages in proportion to the amount or value of work done.

1855 J. R. LEIFCHILD *Cornwall Mines* 249 The mine rose in value to the *premium amount of £24,000 in a few days. **1927** F. H. SHAW *Knocking Around* vi. 54 My greatest efforts of all should be expended in an endeavour to ameliorate the lot of that hard-lying ocean Ishmael, the *premium apprentice. **1979** *Jrnl. R. Soc. Arts* Dec. 36/2 When I left school,.. I put in a happy period as a premium apprentice at the Sentinel Waggon Works at Shrewsbury. **1902** *Daily Chron.* 17 Oct. 3/3 The *premium bonus system, as provisionally agreed to, seems to Mr. Webb to be an admirable expedient. **1905** *Ibid.* 30 Jan. 3/7 Parents and guardians often pay a premium to a Canadian farmer. But the best farmers will not take a *premium boy. **1895** *Daily News* 4 Feb. 5/7 What an incubus the pampered and *premium-fed merchant navy is upon national finances. **1899** *Westm. Gaz.* 8 June 8/1 A sign that many *premium-hunters will be left out in the cold. **1962** S. STRAND *Marketing Dict.* 562 **Premium promotion*, the use of premiums (inexpensive gifts) in the promotion of the sale of products or services. **1974** *Encycl. Brit. Micropædia* VIII. 191/2 *Premium promotion*, an advertisement, often part of the product package, that induces prospective purchasers to buy the product by offering a free gift or a reduced price. **1966** *Lebende Sprachen* XI. 109/1 **Premium selling*, offering an item with the purchase of another product, either free or for a nominal additional payment, as an inducement to buy the product. **1901** *Westm. Gaz.* 5 Sept. 8/1 Brief descriptions were given of the working and general results of the *premium system. **1844** DICKENS *Mart. Chuz.* xiii, 'I am, sir', said Mr. Tigg,..'a *premium tulip, of a very different growth and cultivation'.

b. Passing into *adj.* Of a commodity, etc., esp. petrol: superior in quality and therefore commanding a higher price; of a price: such as befits an article of superior quality; higher than usual. orig. *U.S.*

1928 *National Petroleum News* 24 Oct. 115 (Advt.), This is our anti-knock gasoline, a premium motor fuel. **1931** *Economist* 5 Sept. 422/2 The profit to the garage on the sale of petrol.. is now 2d a gallon on national 'commercial' grades and 2½d on national 'premium' grades. **1945** H. S. BELL *Amer. Petroleum Refining* (ed. 3) xviii. 278 The refiner cannot approach the desired knock rating of 80 for premium motor fuels.. by simple skimming and thermal cracking except by a material reduction of the end point of his product. **1961** I. L. HOROWITZ *Philos., Sci. & Sociol. of Knowledge* v. 54 A world which pays a premium price for technological manipulation. **1965** *New Statesman* 23 Apr. 634/1 There were the garages selling the well-known, branded petrols, each in three main grades—Super, Premium and Regular. **1970** *Daily Tel.* 30 Jan. 19/1 All supersonic travellers would fly 'premium class' at a slightly lower rate than that paid at present by first-class passengers, but with the same comfort. **1977** *Listener* 1 Dec. 708 Qube [*sc.* U.S. cable television] has ten 'premium' channels where you pay per programme. **1979** *Guardian* 22 June 9/8 Trout will for some time still be a premium fish, selling at about £1 each.

Hence **premiumed** ('pri:mɪəmd) *a.*, that has gained a premium or prize; that has paid a premium; **'premiumless** *a.*, without (the means of paying) a premium.

1799 J. ROBERTSON *Agric. Perth* 305 A breed of these premium'd bulls. **1796** COLERIDGE *Lett., to T. Poole* (1895) 189 He was too young and premiumless, and no one would take him. **1927** *Daily Express* 5 July 5/5 The trade may also be entered as a premiumed apprentice or as a beginner at a nominal wage.

premium bond. Also Premium Bond. [f. PREMIUM + BOND *sb.*[1]] A debenture earning no interest but eligible for lotteries; *spec.* (in full ***Premium Savings Bond***) since 1956, a British government bond not bearing interest but with the periodic chance of a cash prize. Also *attrib.* (See also ERNIE.)

[**1882** R. BITHELL *Counting-House Dict.* 237 A number of Lottery Loans of the worst class have been started in some of the German States, and also in Austria... It would be impossible to get subscriptions to them to any great extent in this country if called by their proper name. The name of Premium-Loans.. has therefore been substituted.., and the money that has been extracted from the pockets of unfortunate dupes by these means is enormous. **1908** *Westm. Gaz.* 29 Aug. 2/2 Two of the largest of these lotteries, the Panama and Congo premium-bearing loans, are two of the most scandalous pieces of finance which Europe has ever witnessed. Here is an exciting chance of winning a fortune by gambling; let us get the money somehow to buy half a dozen of the bonds, and work no more!] **1908** *Economist* 12 Sept. 477/2 The practical man in the street who knows anything about premium bonds is quite aware that they are in their nature and intention lotteries. **1918** *Ibid.* 19 Jan. 79/2 The report of the Select Committee on Premium Bonds.. concludes with the following paragraphs:—'.. We do not, therefore, advise that an issue of Premium Bonds be made at the present time.' **1931** *Star* 8 May 6/3 Every trick—from premium bonds to guessing the number of beans in a bottle—seems to have been tried. **1940** GRAVES & HODGE *Long Week-End* v. 77 He [*sc.* Horatio Bottomley] was then launching new prize schemes—the Premium Bond Scheme of 1918, for example, to which his readers subscribed £90,000. Out of this he had agreed to pay £10,000 in prizes. **1956** H. MACMILLAN in *Times* 18 Apr. 5/2 Finally, I have something completely new for the saver in Great Britain—a premium bond. **1957**, etc. [see ERNIE]. **1957** *Observer* 25 Aug. 9/3 New National Savings reported last week totalled £26,689,000 (including £1,200,000 Premium Bonds and £2,566,000 accrued interest). **1958** *Times Lit. Suppl.* 15 Aug. p. x/3 He also prefers pools to premium bond gambling—in which a bloke can't choose his own combination of numbers, so how does one know that it's on the level? **1962** H. O. BEECHENO *Introd. Business Stud.* xiv. 140 The Premium Savings Bond scheme has taken advantage of our national love of a gamble, holding out the possibility of a reward for the few much higher than other savings methods would give. **1974** *Guardian* 27 Mar. 1/1 Another £500,000 a month added to Premium Bond prizes.

pre'mix, *v.* [PRE- A. 1.] *trans.* To mix beforehand.

1934 in Webster. **1966** *Gloss. Terms Internal Plastering* (*B.S.I.*) 17 A plaster in which a lightweight aggregate has been pre-mixed dry with a gypsum plaster to give a low density. **1966** *McGraw-Hill Encycl. Sci. & Technol.* V. 292/1 Gaseous fuels can be premixed with air or oxygen, in which case the mixture can be fed to a flame holder and burned in a very efficient manner. **1972** [see PREMIX *sb.*]. **1976** *Nature* 20 May 259/2 Rattlesnake venoms are neutralised also when premixed *in vitro* with either rattlesnake plasma or commercial antivenin.

Hence **pre'mixed** *ppl. a.*, **pre'mixing** *vbl. sb.*

1941 *Engineers' Digest* II. 417 (*heading*) Premixed combustion of gaseous fuel for steel finishing operations. *Ibid.*, Premixing provides accuracy of air to fuel-gas proportioning over the widest conceivable operating range. **1945** H. BARRON *Mod. Plastics* vii. 163 (*caption*) Rotary premixing machines in which powdered phenolic resins (Novolak) is mixed with hexamethylenetetramine, wood flour, and colouring material. **1959** *Economist* 31 Jan. 431/2 A 'flexible' type of road carriageway base incorporating premixed water-bound macadam. **1960** *Farmer & Stockbreeder* 8 Mar. 75/1 The idea being that two different fertilizers can be applied at the same time without pre-mixing. **1963** A. M. NEVILLE *Properties of Concrete* iv. 205 If instead of being batched and mixed on the site concrete is delivered ready for placing from a central plant it is referred to as ready-mixed or pre-mixed concrete. **1978** *Sci. Amer.* Apr. 155 In a premixed flame the gases are mixed prior to the burning and the rate of combustion depends on the flow rate.

premix ('pri:mɪks), *sb.* and *a.* [PRE- A. 2.] **A.** *sb.* A mixture prepared beforehand; *spec.* (*a*) *Agric.*, a powder or granular preparation into which a drug or the like has been incorporated and which is mixed with animal feed to introduce the drug, etc., into it in suitably low concentrations; (*b*) synthetic resin to which various substances have been added to make it suitable for moulding; (*c*) (see quot. 1976).

1957 *Times* 2 Dec. (Agric. Suppl.) p. vi/4 A source of greater fear to those familiar with oestrogen effects is the inhalation of dust from a concentrated premix, which would present a definite hazard. **1960** O. SKILBECK *ABC of Film & TV* 98 *Premix*, when dubbing is likely to prove especially difficult, or when insufficient heads are available for the number of tracks involved, some tracks may be combined at a first premix stage and added to the remainder later. **1963** H. R. CLAUSER *Encycl. Engin. Materials* 519/1 The unsaturated resin is first mixed with fillers, fibers, and catalyst to provide a nontacky compound... The premix is molded at pressures of 150 to 500 psi and at temperatures ranging from 250–310 F. **1963** *Poultry Sci.* XLII. 1264/2 Premixes containing menadione sodium bisulfite complex (16 gm./lb.) were made employing soybean meal or corn as the carrier. **1967** SIMONDS & CHURCH *Encycl. Basic Materials for Plastics* 58/2 Premix is a damp, sometimes sticky variation of molding compound differing technically from so-called 'molding compound' only in the ratio of monomer which is used. **1971** *Farmer & Stockbreeder* 23 Feb. 25/1 Emtryl is available in two forms, as a soluble powder and as a premix. **1972** QUICK & LABAU *Handbk. Film Production* xviii. 201 In the event of an extremely complex mix, pre-mixes may be desirable. This is where a few of the tracks are mixed to a desired level and then that master track mixed with the remaining channels of information. The director makes decisions concerning whether or not to pre-mix his film. **1976** B. ARMSTRONG *Gloss. TV Terms* 71 *Premix*, a preliminary dub of certain sound tracks, usually music and effects, before the final mix.

B. *adj.* Premixed.

1963 H. R. CLAUSER *Encycl. Engin. Materials* 537/2 Premix molding materials are physical mixtures of a reactive thermosetting resin.., chopped fibrous reinforcement.. and powdered fillers (usually carbonates or clays). **1968** P. I. SMITH *Plastics as Metal Replacements* i. 45 The manufacturer makes available to the moulder either conventional pre-mix compounds or pre-impregnated chopped strand glass mat all ready for moulding. **1975** *Petroleum Rev.* XXIX. 96/1 A semi-closed circuit deep sea diving breathing set, using air or a pre-mix gas. **1976** P. HILL *Hunters* xii. 176 A huge pre-mix concrete lorry was disgorging its load. **1977** *Evening News* 11 June 11/6 Producer and artist then live with these 'pre-mix' tapes for about two months.

pre'mixture. [PRE- A. 2.] A mixture prepared beforehand.

1934 in WEBSTER. **1972** *Physics Bull.* Jan. 20/2 Two separate arrays of injector tubes are used to introduce premixtures of fluorine with helium and nitric oxide with carbon dioxide at the upstream end.

pre-modern: see PRE- B. 1 d.

pre'modify, *v.* *Linguistics.* [PRE- A. 1.] *trans.* To modify (a word or phrase) by an immediately preceding word or phrase. So **pre'modifying** *ppl. a.*; **premodifi'cation, pre'modifier.**

1962 R. QUIRK *Use of English* x. 164 The premodification of nouns by nouns was a common feature of English before Germans studied science or America was discovered. **1966** G. N. LEECH *English in Advertising* xiv. 127 In advertising language, the interesting part of the noun group is the pre-modifying part... Noun groups with lengthy pre-modifications are italicised. *Ibid.* 128 Pre-modifiers which can have the designative, or categorising function are nouns, adjectives and compounds. **1972** *Language* XLVIII. 456 The relatively empty *do* [in the ungrammatical sentence *He had well done it*] does not permit a premodifier *well*, but with a richer verb pre-modification is normal, e.g. *He has well revealed the causes.* **1973** G. W. TURNER *Stylistics* iii. 81 Words preceding the head word in a group are conveniently called 'modifiers' (sometimes 'premodifiers'). **1976** *Amer. Speech 1974* XLIX. 82 It [*sc. much*] collocates with *like* in an affirmative sentence if it is premodified, hence *I like him very much.*

premolar (pri:'məʊlə(r)), *sb.* (*a.*) [f. PRE- B. 3 + MOLAR. Cf. F. *pré-molaire.*] **A.** *sb.* One of the set of molar teeth in front of the true molars, replacing the molars or grinders of the milk dentition; a false molar, in man called 'bicuspid'.

(Sometimes erroneously applied to a molar of the deciduous dentition.)

1842 OWEN in Brande *Dict. Sci.*, etc. 326/2 The teeth.. which are analogous to the bicuspids in man are called 'præmolars' or spurious molars [in mammalia generally]. **1849–52** *Todd's Cycl. Anat.* IV. 903/1 Those grinders which succeed the deciduous ones.. are called 'premolars'. **1861** HULME tr. *Moquin-Tandon* II. III. ii. 114 The Civet.. is characterized by the possession of three false molars (premolars of Owen). **1863** HUXLEY *Man's Place Nat.* ii. 81. **1872** MIVART *Elem. Anat.* vii. 253 The bicuspid molars of man.. are in zootomy termed premolars because they are placed in front of the true molars. **1897** [see PRELACTEAL].

B. *adj.* Situated in front of the (true) molars; that is a premolar.

1880 HAUGHTON *Phys. Geog.* vi. 283 The last premolar tooth has gone over to the molar series.

†**premo'llition.** *Obs.* *rare*[−1]. [n. of action from L. *præmollīre* to soften beforehand: see -TION.] A previous softening or mitigation.

1682 NORRIS *Hierocles* Pref. 4 Sometimes without any Premollition at all, they are downright sins.

premonarchical: see PRE- B. 1 d.

premonish (pri:'mɒnɪʃ), *v.* Now *rare.* [f. L. *præmonēre* to forewarn, foreshow, after MONISH, ADMONISH.] *trans.* To forewarn; to advise, caution, notify, or admonish beforehand.

1526 *Pilgr. Perf.* (W. de W. 1531) 201 b, Thou art agayn premonysshed, aduysed & warned neuer to.. ymagyn in thy fantasy ony suche. **1599** B. JONSON *Cynthia's Rev.* II. iii, Fye, I premonisht you of that. **1640–1** *Kirkcudbr. War-Comm. Min. Bk.* (1855) 153 The said Committie of Estaites of Parliament doe heirby warne, premoneis and requyer all Commissares and Collectores.. that they prepare thair comptes and present thame befoire the auditors. **1742** J. WILLISON *Balm of Gilead* i. (1800) 60 Got doth premonish us that a storm is coming. **1876** LOWELL *Among my Bks.* Ser. II. 191 Of whose haunting presence the delicacy of his senses had already premonished him.

b. *intr.* or *absol.* To give warning beforehand.

1550 HOOPER *Serm. Jonas* i. 12 b, He is yet so mercyfull that he premonysheth & forewarneth of hys scourge to come, by hys prophets. **1625** SHIRLEY *Love Tricks* II. ii, Were it otherwise, I should elect, as you pre-monish, youth And prodigal blood. *a* **1703** BURKITT *On N. Test.* Matt. xxiv. 30 Got premonishes before he punishes. **1894** F. P. BADHAM in *Academy* 15 Dec. 513/2 The mention of women in the genealogy.. premonishes that some peculiar importance will attach to Christ's mother.

†**pre'monishment.** *Obs.* [f. prec. + -MENT.] The act of premonishing; premonition.

1550 BALE *Image Both Ch.* i. B v b, To obserue the rules, and take the premonishementes of Godly doctrine. *Ibid.* B vij, Without premonishement or warning. **1624** WOTTON *Archit.* in *Reliq.* (1672) 40 Now, after these premonishments I will come to the Compartition itself. **1788** GILSON *Serm. Pract. Subj.* vii. (1807) 133 We are not given to know what premonishment Elijah had received.

premonition (pri:məʊ'nɪʃən, prɛ-). [ad. obs. F. *premonicion* (15th c. in Godef.), *-ition*, ad. late L. *præmonitio* a forewarning, n. of action f. L. *præmonēre*: see PREMONISH. In med.L. the word was identified in form with *præmūnītio* (prop. a fortifying in front), so that the earlier form in Eng. was PREMUNITION, q.v.] The action of premonishing or forewarning; a previous notification or warning of subsequent events; a forewarning.

[1456–1693: see PREMUNITION 2.] **1545** JOYE *Exp. Dan.* Argt. 8 It is necessarye to note this premonicion teaching vs how we shulde knowe the chirche of God. **1577–8** *Reg. Privy Council Scot.* II. 666 Upoun sic schort and unlauchfull premonitioun. **1652** NEEDHAM tr. *Selden's Mare Cl.* 465 Wee have thought good (by way of friendly premonition) to declare unto them all as followeth. **1785** REID *Intell. Powers* II. iii. 250 In the premonition to the reader prefixed to the second edition of his Optics. **1869** *Act 32 & 33 Vict.* c. 116 §7 The lands.. should be redeemable by the grantor.. upon premonition of three months. **1876** FARRAR *Marlb. Serm.* xx. 195 It will be the creeping premonition of paralysis to come.

premonitive (priːˈmɒnɪtɪv), *a. rare.* [f. L. *præmonit-*, ppl. stem of *præmonēre* (see next) + -IVE.] Of or pertaining to premonition; premonitory.

1861 I. TAYLOR *Spir. Hebr. Poetry* 291 The present trouble.. may be interpreted as premonitive of a renewed life.

premonitor (priːˈmɒnɪtə(r)). [a. L. *præmonitor*, agent-n. f. *præmonēre* to forewarn: see PREMONISH.] One who or that which forewarns; a premonitory sign or token.

a **1656** BP. HALL *Soliloquies* lxxix, Some such like uncouth premonitors; which the great and holy God sends purposely to awaken our security. **1822** T. TAYLOR *Apuleius* 311 A premonitor in things dubious. **1844** STEPHENS *Bk. Farm* I. 245 Of these the Clouds are eminent premonitors. **1866** J. B. ROSE tr. *Ovid's Met.* 464 Premonitors of crime.

premonitory (priːˈmɒnɪtərɪ), *a.* (*sb.*) [ad. late L. *præmonitōri-us*, f. *præmonitor*: see prec. and -ORY[2]. Cf. F. *prémonitoire.*] **A.** *adj.* Giving or conveying premonition; serving to warn or notify beforehand.

1647 WARD *Simp. Cobler* 43 In premonitory judgements, God will take good words, and sincere intents; but in peremptory, nothing but reall performances. **1686** GOAD *Celest. Bodies* II. iv. 213 A Comet.. following an Earthquake, though it looseth the Praemonitory part, yet it looseth not the Nature of a Sign. **1822** LAMB *Elia* Ser. I. *Diss. Roast Pig*, A premonitory moistening.. overflowed his nether lip. **1846** J. BAXTER *Libr. Pract. Agric.* (ed. 4) I. 429 We are warned of approaching danger, by certain premonitory symptoms. **1868** BROWNING *Ring & Bk.* IV. 1356 Signs and silences Premonitory of earthquake.

B. *ellipt.* as *sb. pl.* Premonitory symptoms.

1834 *Knickerbocker* IV. 307 The premonitories seize me before I have time to run to the doctors for relief. **1853** KANE *Grinnell Exp.* xxxiv. (1856) 308, I am down myself today with all the premonitories.

Hence **preˈmonitorily** *adv.*

1847 in WEBSTER. **1880** G. MEREDITH *Tragic Com.* viii, Shaking her own head premonitorily.

†**Preˈmonster,** *a.* and *sb. Obs. rare.* Shortened from PREMONSTRATENSIS.

c **1425** WYNTOUN *Cron.* VII. 1111 (Cotton MS.) And of þe ordyr Premonster lyk Qwhit chanownys coyme þan to Alnewyk. *c* **1440** *Promp. Parv.* 412/1 Premoster, whyȝte chanon (*H., P.* Premonster), *Premonstrensis.*

†**preˈmonstrance.** *Obs.* [a. obs. F. *premonstrance* (16th c. in Godef.), f. OF. *premonstrer*: see -ANCE.] A showing beforehand; foreshowing.

1594 NASHE *Terrors of Nt.* F ij b, Dreames.. if they haue anie premonstrance in them, the preparatiue feare of that they so premonstrate.. is far worse than the mischiefe itselfe by them denounced and premonstrated. **1633** T. ADAMS *Exp. 2 Peter* i. 14 Our apostle had some special premonstrance of the nearness of his end.

Premonstrant (priːˈmɒnstrənt), *sb.* and *a. Eccl. Hist.* [In form pres. pple. of OF. *premonstrer* to foreshow: used to represent med.L. PREMONSTRATENSIS.]

A. *sb.* = PREMONSTRATENSIAN *sb.*

1700 TYRRELL *Hist. Eng.* II. 853 The Orders of the Cistercians and Præmonstrants. **1747** *Gentl. Mag.* 570/2 Abbeys of Benedictins, Cistercians, regular Canons, and Premonstrants, to which the king nominates.

B. *adj.* = PREMONSTRATENSIAN *a.*

1895 E. MARG. THOMPSON *Hist. Somerset Carthusians* 71 He had been Abbot of the Præmonstrant Abbey of Dryburgh. **1896** LINA ECKENSTEIN *Woman under Monast.* 195 There were also two settlements of Premonstrant nuns in England.

†**Preˈmonstrate,** *sb. Obs. rare.* A shortened equivalent of PREMONSTRATENSIAN.

1550 BALE *Eng. Votaries* II. H iv, About this time arose other sectes of perdicion, as the.. Premonstrates. **1631** WEEVER *Anc. Fun. Mon.* 283 White Canons premonstrates.

†**preˈmonstrate,** *ppl. a. Obs. rare*[−1]. [ad. L. *præmonstrāt-us*, pa. pple. of *præmonstrāre*: see next.] 'Premonstrated', foreshown. (Const. as *pa. pple.*)

1654 Z. COKE *Logick* 10 When they are ordinative, methodical, and by conclusion, as is premonstrate.

preˈmonstrate, *v. rare.* [f. ppl. stem of L. *præmonstrāre* to show beforehand, f. *præ*, PRE- A. 1 + *monstrāre* to show.] *trans.* To point out or make known beforehand; to foreshow, portend.

1588 J. HARVEY *Disc. Probl.* 104 The same coniunction againe infusing, doth out of all doubt premonstrate the second coming of the sonne of God and man in the maiestie of his glorie. **1594** [see PREMONSTRANCE]. **1652** WHARTON tr. *Rothman's Chirom.* Wks. (1683) 550 They premonstrate Happiness to the Man in his Journeys and Messages. **1679** C. NESSE *Antichrist* 132 It is not the manner of Holy Scripture to premonstrate any certain periods. **1857** A. MATHEWS *Tea-Table Talk* I. 251 Marks, natural or acquired, premonstrate a talent for locomotion.

Premonstratensian (priːmɒnstrəˈtɛnsɪən), *sb.* and *a. Eccl. Hist.* Also 7 præ-. [f. med.L. *Præmonstrātensis* (see next) + -AN.]

A. *sb.* A member of the Roman Catholic order of regular canons founded by St. Norbert at Prémontré, near Laon, Île de France, in 1119. Also called *Premonstrants, Norbertians*, and, from the colour of their dress, *White Canons.* Also, a member of a corresponding order of nuns.

1695 T. TANNER *Notitia Monastica* Pref. a vj b, Concerning the introducing of the Benedictine Order into this Kingdom,.. as also of the Regular Canons, Austins, Præmonstratensians, Gilbertines, &c. **1839** *Penny Cycl.* XV. 290/2 The Premonstratensians procured a constitution, which was confirmed by Pope Innocent III, that all the abbots of their order should wear them [*sc.* mitres]. **1885** *Cath. Dict.* 658/2 More recently a community of French Premonstratensians has been established at Storrington.

B. *adj.* Of or belonging to this order.

1695 T. TANNER *Notitia Monastica* 123 Newhouse or Newsom. The first Monastery of the Præmonstratensian Order in England, built by Petr. de Gousla A.D. 1146. *Ibid.* Pref. b v, The Austin, Premonstratensian and Gilbertine Nuns,.. were instituted by the same as the Monks of those Orders. **1864** *Churchman* 3 Nov. 64 Bishop Maxe, the general visitor of the Premonstratensian order. **1885** *Cath. Dict.* 685/1 There were at one time, according to Hélyot, a thousand Premonstratensian abbeys.. and five hundred houses of nuns.

‖**Premonstraˈtensis, Præ-,** *a.* and *sb.* [med.L. 'belonging to Prémontré', med.L. (*locus*) *Præmonstrātus* 'the place foreshown' (see PREMONSTRATE *v.*), so called because the site is said to have been prophetically pointed out by St. Norbert.] = PREMONSTRATENSIAN *a.* and *sb.* Hence †**Premonstraˈtense,** *contr.* **Premonstrense,** *a.* and *sb.*; †**Premonstraˈtenser** *sb.*; †**Premonˈstrensian** *a.*

1387 TREVISA *Higden* (Rolls) VII. 459 Aboute þis tyme began þe ordre Premonstratensis [*MS.* -censis], þat is þe ordre of white chanouns. **1432–50** *Ibid.*, The ordre Premonstratense [*MS.* -cense] began abowte this tyme. *c* **1425** WYNTOUN *Cron.* VII. 806 (Wemyss MS.) And in þe nixt ȝere efter þan The ordre Premonstrense [*Cott. MS.* Premonstrans; *Auchinleck* of Premonstratens] he began, That is to say of channons quhite. *c* **1440** *Alphabet of Tales* 412 Þer was a blak monk þat fell in apostasye, & syne he was a Premonstratence [*MS.* -cence] & went oute. **1550** BALE *Eng. Votaries* II. 78 The Premonstratensers or white chanons, came in to the realme & buylded at Newhowse in Lyncolne dyocese in the yeare of our lord a M, a C, and xlv. *c* **1630** RISDON *Surv. Devon* §134 (1810) 146 Canons of the order of Præmonstretenses. **1715** M. DAVIES *Athen. Brit.* I. 142 This was answered by Father Hugo, a Regular Premonstratensian Prebendary. **1805** FORSYTH *Beauties Scotl.* II. 18 Patrick, of the reformed order of Premonstratenses of Dryburgh.

premonˈstration. *rare.* [ad. late L. *præmonstrātiōn-em*, n. of action f. *præmonstrāre*: see PREMONSTRATE *v.*] The action of premonstrating or showing beforehand; a showing forth, making known, indication, or manifestation beforehand.

c **1450** *Mirour Saluacioun* 44 The fift Chapitle vs telles oure ladys oblacionne In the temple by thre figures of premonstracionne. **1581** MARBECK *Bk. of Notes* 215 The Church by premonstration declareth what is the word of God. **1610** WILLET *Hexapla Dan.* 59 This dreame beeing a premonstration of things to come. **1623** COCKERAM, *Premonstration*, a fore-shewing. **1920** E. H. BEGBIE *Mirrors of Downing St.* i. 9 His intuitions are amazing. He astonished great soldiers in the war by his premonstrations.

ˈpremonˌstrator. *rare.* [a. L. *præmonstrātor*, agent-n. f. *præmonstrāre*: see PREMONSTRATE *v.*] One who or that which shows beforehand.

1846 in WORCESTER, citing KIRBY. Hence in later Dicts.

pre-moral(ity): see PRE- B. 1.

preˈmorbid, *a. Med.* [PRE- B. 1.] Preceding the occurrence of symptoms or disease.

1939 *Amer. Jrnl. Psychiatry* XCV. 1041 A number of factors were included: age, sex, physical build, premorbid personality.. and permeability quotients. **1953** *Jrnl. Nerv. & Mental Dis.* CXVII. 516 The scale was used to evaluate each patient in.. the following three areas: (a) the premorbid history; (b) possible precipitating factors; (c) signs of the disorder. **1969** *Jrnl. Amer. Med. Assoc.* 18 Aug. 1085/2 Marihuana may have a psychotogenic effect even in an individual with a healthy premorbid personality.

premorse (priːˈmɔːs), *a. Bot.* and *Entom.* Also præ-. [ad. L. *præmors-us*, pa. pple. of *præmordēre* to bite (off) in front, f. *præ*, PRE- A. 4 c + *mordēre* to bite.] Having the end abruptly truncate, as if bitten or broken off.

1753 CHAMBERS *Cycl. Supp.* s.v. *Leaf, Præmorse Leaf*,.. a leaf which is truncated and terminated by an acute sinus at the summit. **1826** KIRBY & SP. *Entomol.* IV. xlvi. 295 *Premorse*.., terminating in an irregular truncate apex, as if bitten off. **1861** MISS PRATT *Flower. Pl.* III. 192 Its root is premorse or bitten. **1872** OLIVER *Elem. Bot.* II. 192 Blue Scabious.. Herb with a præmorse (abrupt) rootstock. **1887** *Amer. Naturalist* XXI. 529 The types of the modern carrot are the tap-rooted and the premorse-rooted.

premortal to **-Mosaic:** see PRE- B. 1.

pre-ˈmortem, *a.* (*sb.*) [a. L. *præ mortem* before death.] Taking place or performed before death: opposed to *post-mortem.* Also as *sb.* in *fig.* use.

1892 *Chicago Advance* 21 July, To see himself as others see him through the kindly medium of pre-mortem obituary notices. **1893** W. R. GOWERS *Dis. Nerv. Syst.* (ed. 2) II. 339 The pre-mortem rise in temperature is usually attended by extreme frequency of pulse. **1971** *Listener* 7 Jan. 18/1 'The death of the symphony orchestra' was discussed on Radio 4, in a kind of pre-mortem. **1972** F. WARNER *Lying Figures* III. 33 What of love? *Guppy.* A post-prandial pre-mortem.

premotion (priːˈməʊʃən). [ad. med.L. *præmōtiōn-em*, n. of action f. late L. *præmovēre* to move (anything) beforehand: see PREMOVE. So F. *prémotion* (1713 in Hatz.-Darm.).] Motion or impulse given beforehand; *esp.* applied to divine action held to determine the will of the creature.

a **1643** LD. FALKLAND, etc. *Infallibility* (1646) 133 They contend.. whether with this freedome of will.. Physicall predeterminations or præmotions can consist. *a* **1680** J. CORBET *Free Actions* II. vii. (1683) 18 It being to a good act, it is a Premotion perfective of our Nature, and to its well-being. **1727–41** CHAMBERS *Cycl.* s.v., Physical premotion, according to Alvarez, Lemos, etc., is a complement of the active power, whereby it passes from the first act to the second; i.e. from a complete, and next power, to action. **1867** [see PREMOVEMENT]. **1885** *Catholic Dict.* 384/2 [About 1580] Bannez, a Dominican professor at Salamanca,.. represented efficacious grace as determining the free consent of the will by 'physical premotion', and this premotion which was infallibly followed by the consent of the will came, as he alleged, from God's absolute decree that the person so moved by grace should correspond to it. **1887** *Mind* Apr. 266 This thesis is nothing more than the mere denial of 'physical premotion'.

preˈmotional, *a. nonce-word.* [f. PRE- B. 1 d + MOTION *sb.* + -AL[1].] Existing before motion.

1852 BAILEY *Festus* xxviii. (ed. 5) 475 At the first creation, in that peace, Premotional, preelemental, prime.

premotor: see PRE- B. 3.

preˈmoult, *a.* and *sb. Zool.* **A.** *adj.* [PRE- B. 2.] Existing or occurring just before a change of plumage in birds or the shedding and replacement of the integument of insects, crustaceans, or reptiles. **B.** *sb.* [PRE- B. 1.] A premoult stage or period.

1957 R. A. H. COOMBES in D. A. Bannerman *Birds Brit. Isles* VI. 312 (*heading*) The pre-moult migration of the sheld-duck. **1964** *Oceanogr. & Marine Biol.* II. 303 At moult [of the crab, *Carcinus maenas*], uptake of water, averaging 66·3% of the premoult weight, takes place. **1967** P. A. MEGLITSCH *Invertebr. Zool.* xvi. 681/1 The physiology of most of the body parts [of arthropods] is affected by premolt. **1973** *Nature* 9 Mar. 133/2 An insect does not enter premoult if its thoracic glands have been removed.

premove (priːˈmuːv), *v. rare.* [ad. late L. *præmovēre* to move (anything) beforehand, f. *præ*, PRE- A. 1 + *movēre* to MOVE.] *trans.* To move or influence beforehand; to impel or incite to action.

1598 FLORIO, *Premosso*, promoted, preferred, premooued. **1663** BAXTER *Divine Life* 141 It followeth that we have no certainty when God premoveth an Apostle or Prophet to speak true, and when to speak falsly. **1675** —— *Cath. Theol.* II. viii. 190 It performeth that Act because it is premoved to it. **1867** W. G. WARD *Ess. Philos. Theism* (1884) II. 187 *note*, Let it be assumed, then, that God does premove earthly phenomena.

Hence **preˈmovement.** *rare.*

1867 W. G. WARD *Ess. Philos. Theism* (1884) II. 172 It does not follow.. because they are fixed that they proceed independently of God's constant and unremitting 'premovement'. [*Note*] We do not say 'premotion', because this word has a special sense in the Thomistic philosophy, totally distinct from that here intended.

premultipliˈcation. *Math.* [PRE- A. 2.] Multiplication by a prefactor.

1862 *Phil. Trans. R. Soc.* CLI. 316 Let that maxtrix be reduced by premultiplication with a unit-matrix. **1972** *Computer Jrnl.* XV. 250/2 Pre- and post-multiplication is preserved.

preˈmultiply, *v. Math.* [PRE- A. 4 c.] *trans.* To multiply by (or as) a PREFACTOR, q.v.

1862 [see *post-multiply* vb. s.v. POST- A. 1 a]. **1890** in *Cent. Dict.* **1972** ROBERTS & SHIPMAN *Two-Point Boundary Value Probl.* viii. 223 If each side of (8.8.12) is premultiplied by the square partitioned matrix of order $n(m+1)$,.. the following partitioned matrix is obtained. **1978** [see *post-multiply* vb. s.v. POST- A. 1 a].

†**premunˈdation.** *Obs. rare*[−1]. In 7 præ-. [n. of action f. L. *præmundāre*, repr. by *præmundātus* cleansed beforehand, f. *præ*, PRE- A. 1 +

mundāre to cleanse: see -ATION.] A cleansing or purification beforehand.
*a*1660 HAMMOND *19 Serm.* ix. Wks. 1684 IV. 619 A præmundation or præsanctification of them that sued to be admitted higher.

†**pre'mune**, obs. colloq. contraction of PRÆMUNIRE (in sense 3).
1758 MRS. LENNOX *Henrietta* III. i, 'Nay, for that matter, ..I may draw myself into another premune perhaps: after what I have suffered I ought to be cautious.'

premunire, -eal, -ize, etc.: see PRÆMUNIRE, etc.

†**premu'nite**, *v. Obs.* [f. ppl. stem of L. *præmūnīre* (see next). Cf. F. *prémunir* (14th c.).] *trans.* To fortify or guard in front or beforehand.
*a*1619 FOTHERBY *Atheom.* Pref. (1622) 12 For the better removing of the exception..I thought good to præmunite the succeeding Treatise, with this præceding Preface. 1679 V. ALSOP *Melius Inquirendum* I. i. 53 King James sent thither [to Dort] several of his most learned and eminent divines, premunited with an instrument.

premunition (priːmjuː'nɪʃən). [ad. late L. *præmūnītiōn-em*, n. of action f. *præmūnīre* to fortify or protect in front, f. *præ*, PRE- A. 4 c + *mūnīre* to fortify, defend. In med.L. *præ-*, *pre-* 'before' was referred to time, and the verb confounded with *præmonēre* to warn beforehand, so that with the form of *præmunīre* it had the sense of *præmonēre*; whence the sb. PRÆMUNIRE, and sense 2 here (the earlier use in English).]

1. The action of fortifying or guarding beforehand; a previous securing of immunity against attack or danger; a forearming. Now *rare*.
1607 *Schol. Disc. agst. Antichr.* I. iv. 177 We premise these two prouisoes and premunitions for our selues. 1622 S. WARD *Life of Faith in Death* (1627) 49 Let mee tell thee præuision is the best preuention, and præmonition the best præmunition. 1874 H. N. HUDSON *Wordsw.* i. (1884) 7 (Funk) That issue was to be forestalled by timely premunition.

2. Used, by confusion, in the sense of PREMONITION. (The earlier use). *Obs.* exc. as in quot. 1875, referring to PRÆMUNIENTES: cf. next.
[1389 *Rolls of Parlt.* III. 267/1 Soit tiel conviction ou atteindre envers luy par Brief de Premunition.] 1456 *Cov. Leet Bk.* (E.E.T.S.) 296 That all the churche-wardens..be redy to accompt ȝerely aftur premunicion made vnto theym. 1546 *Reg. Privy Council Scot.* I. 62 Upoun the premunitioun of xx[ti] dayis to compeir befoir thaim. 1629 LYNDE *Via Tuta* 49 Letters of aduertisement or premunition were written.. and were sent by the Orthodox Bishops and Pastors to other parts and sound Members of the Catholique Church. 1693 R. FLEMING *Disc. Earthquakes* 103 An experimental Knowledge of the Truth of Divine Premunitions, when it's too late..will be very sad. 1875 STUBBS *Const. Hist.* xv. II. 195 The whole body of beneficed clergy..was organised by Edward I as a portion of his parliament, by the clause of premunition inserted in the writ of summons addressed to the bishops.

3. *Med.* [ad. F. *prémunition* (E. Sergent et al. 1924, in *Bull. de la Soc. de Path. exotique* XVII. 38).] (The production of) a resistance to disease due to the presence of the causative agent in the host in a harmless or tolerated state.
[1924 *Tropical Dis. Bull.* XXI. 492 For absolute immunity the distinguishing term proposed is 'immunity'..and for relative immunity, 'premunition' brought about by a process of 'premunition', with corresponding verb. (Unfortunately English words corresponding with 'premunition' and 'premunir' do not at present exist.)] 1934 T. W. M. CAMERON *Internal Parasites of Domestic Animals* IV. 218 In..premunition, removal of the latent infection may permit of re-infection. 1951 G. LAPAGE *Parasitic Animals* vii. 205 Some experts believe that the greater resistance of the negro race to human malarial parasites..is really premunition. 1971 P. C. C. GARNHAM *Progress in Parasitol.* vi. 101 Host and parasite eventually settle down together in the state of premunition. 1975 *Tropical Animal Health & Production* VII. 125 (*heading*) The premunition of adult cattle against Babesiosis.

pre'munitory, *a.* [f. L. *præmūnīt-*, ppl. stem of *præmūnīre*, in med.L. used for *præmonēre* (see prec. and PRÆMUNIRE) + -ORY².] Used, by confusion, for PREMONITORY *a.* ***premunitory clause*** = PRÆMUNIENTES *clause*.
1700 ATTERBURY *Rights Eng. Convoc.* (1701) 227, I..shall ..endeavour to give some account of the Original of the Premunitory Clause. *Ibid.* 241 The Præmunitory Clause. 1854 THIRLWALL *Rem.* (1877) I. 211 The præmunitory clause though seemingly become a dead letter, was really carried into effect in its spirit.

premunity (priː'mjuːnɪtɪ). *Med.* [f. PREMUN(ITION + -ITY, after *immunity*.] (See quot. 1938.) So **pre'mune** *a.*, exhibiting premunity.
1938 G. O. DAVIES *Vet. Path. & Bacteriol.* (ed. 2) vii. 145 Premunity denotes a state of resistance or tolerance to infection which only lasts so long as the infecting organism is present in the tissues of the host. 1948 U. F. RICHARDSON *Vet. Protozool.* i. 7 The more uniform 'premunity' of animals to protozoa in an infected area is mainly due to the more uniform exposure to infection and reinfection. *Ibid.* iv. 86 Infection derived from a premune animal is less severe than that from an active case.

premunization (ˌpriːmjuːnaɪ'zeɪʃən). *Med.* [f. PREMUN(ITION + -IZATION, after *immunization*.] The action or result of premunizing; premunition (sense 3).
1941 J. T. CUTHBERTSON *Immunity against Animal Parasites* iv. 49 Resistance to reinfection with the malarias of monkeys, birds, and dogs have all been shown to depend in part on premunization. 1975 *Tropical Animal Health & Production* VII. 126 Premunisation was effected by the injection of infected blood and control of the subsequent infection with drugs.

premunize ('priːmjuːnaɪz), *v. Med.* [f. PREMUN(ITION + -IZE, after *immunize*, as anglicization of F. *prémunir* (E. Sergent et al. 1924, in *Bull. de la Soc. de Path. exotique* XVII. 37).] *trans.* To introduce pathogens into (a host) so as to produce premunition. Hence **'premunized, 'premunizing** *ppl. adjs.*
1925 E. SERGENT et al. in *Trans. R. Soc. Tropical Med.* XVIII. 384 We ask our British colleagues to..consider whether it is possible to give currency to the verb 'to premunize' and to Anglicize the word 'premunition'. 1934 T. W. M. CAMERON *Internal Parasites of Domestic Animals* II. 45 Immune animals..are premunized and may act as carriers. 1938 *Proc. R. Soc. Med.* XXXI. 1301 When a premunized host is superinfected..little apparent effect is produced. 1963 E. SERGENT in P. C. C. Garnham et al. *Immunity to Protozoa* iii. 44 A typical example of a premunizing vaccine is the antitubercular vaccine, BCG. 1975 *Tropical Animal Health & Production* VII. 125 Twenty-five cattle..were premunised with virulent *Babesia bigemina*. *Ibid.*, The results of haematological and serological immune responses of premunised cattle..are reported.

premutative, -mycosic, -mythical: see PRE- A. 3, B. 1.

premy, var. PREEMIE.

premye: see PREMIE.

premyelocyte, -cytic: see PRE- B. 1.

†**pre'nade**. *Obs.* Name of a dish in old cookery.
*c*1450 *Two Cookery-bks.* 91 Prenade [*Douce MS.* Brewes]. —Take wyn,..and clarefied honey, sawndres, pouder of peper, Canel, Clowes, Maces, Saffron, pynes, my[n]ced dates, & reysons, And cast thereto a litul vinegre, and sette hit ouer the fire, and lete hit boyle [etc.].

prename, -nasal: see PRE- A. 2, B. 3.

‖**prenares, prænares** (priː'nɛəriːz), *sb. pl. Anat.* Also in sing. -naris. [mod.L., f. *præ* before + L. *nārēs*, pl. of *nāris* nostril.] The anterior nares or openings of the nasal cavity; the nostrils (as opposed to the POSTNARES).
1882 WILDER & GAGE *Anat. Techn.* 513 There is a tolerably direct passage from the *prænaris* to the *postnaris* through the so called *meatus ventralis* (inferior).

Hence **pre-, prænarial**, *a.*¹, belonging to the prenares.
1890 *Cent. Dict.*, Prænarial. 1895 *S.S. Lex.*, Prenarial.

prenarial (priː'nɛərɪəl), *a.*² *Anat.* [f. PRE- B. 3 + L. *nāris* nostril + -AL¹.] Situated in front of the nostrils.
1866 OWEN *Vertebr. Anim.* II. 426 *Euphysetes simus* shows the opposite extreme to *Balæna* and *Physeter*, in the disproportionate shortness of the rostral or 'prenarial' to the cranial or 'postnarial' part of the skull.

pre'nasal, *a.* and *sb.*
A. *adj.* **1.** *Anat.* and *Zool.* [f. PRE- B. 3 + NASAL *a.*] In front of the nose or nasal region.
1875 HUXLEY & MARTIN *Elem. Biol.* (1883) 170 The lateral angles of this truncated face are produced outwards and forwards into two flattened præ-nasal processes. 1891 FLOWER & LYDEKKER *Mammals* ix. 282 A peculiar prenasal bone is developed at the anterior extremity of the mesethmoid, which serves to strengthen the cartilaginous snout [in the *Suidæ*].

2. *Linguistics.* [f. PRE- B. 2 + NASAL *sb.*] Occurring before a nasal consonant.
1973 J. M. ANDERSON *Struct. Aspects Lang. Change* 137 Modifications in French, revolving around nasalization of prenasal vowels.

B. *sb. Linguistics.* [f. PRE- A. 2 + NASAL *sb.*] A prenasalized consonant.
1948 R. A. D. FORREST *Chinese Lang.* v. 93 The Heh-Miao ..have rid their language of all compound consonants (except the prenasals). *Ibid.* 94 The irregular representation of the initials with prefixed homorganic nasals ('prenasals') is puzzling.

Hence **prena'sality**, the quality or state of being prenasalized.
1976 *Language* LII. 332 Another class of consonants involving nasality..argues against any solution to the problem of prenasality in which a single feature has the entire segment as its domain.

pre'nasalize, *v. Linguistics.* [PRE- A. 1.] *trans.* To pronounce (a consonant) with initial nasalization. Chiefly as pa. pple. or ppl. adj. Hence **prenasali'zation**.
1956 JAKOBSON & HALLE *Fund. of Lang.* iv. 43 Such relatively rare phonemes as the discontinuous nasals (the so-called prenasalized stops). 1961 WEBSTER, Prenasalization. 1973 J. M. ANDERSON *Struct. Aspects Lang. Change* 119 Some consonants..may become aspirated, pre-aspirated, glottalized, prenasalized, [etc.] 1976 *Language* LII. 331 Another class of segment is much more common..: this is the type generally described as 'prenasalized stops'. 1977 *Ibid.* LIII. 317 Prenasalization of these consonants, while common, is limited in the following ways: except in sentence-initial position, *b d* are either preglottalized or prenasalized, and the processes occur in complementary distribution.

prenatal (priː'neɪtəl), *a.* [f. PRE- B. 1 d + NATAL *a.*¹] Existing or occurring before birth; previous to birth; antenatal. Also = ANTENATAL *a.* 2.
(In quot. 1895 with reference to the prenatal divinity of Christ.)
1826 SOUTHEY *Vind. Eccl. Angl.* 172 For his prenatal performances, and the other miracles of his early life,.. St. Fursey is as little entitled to discredit as to honour. 1874 H. R. REYNOLDS *John Bapt.* ii. 103 *note*, The idea of John's prenatal inspiration;..the supposed inspiration of the unborn John. 1895 HAWEIS in *Contemp. Rev.* Oct. 599 There are what I may call the Prenatal Infusion clergy and the Postnatal Transfusion clergy. 1899 *Allbutt's Syst. Med.* VIII. 233 The principal causes [of idiocy and imbecility] may be grouped as pre-natal and post-natal. 1909 CHESTERTON *Orthodoxy* iv. 94 This proves that even nursery tales only echo an almost pre-natal leap of interest and amazement. 1938 *New Statesman* 19 Feb. 298/2 Pre-natal clinics are increasing. 1960 C. MACINNES *Mr. Love & Justice* 207 Step up to the pre-natal clinic, darling. See what they have to say.
fig. 1877 TYNDALL in *Daily News* 2 Oct. 2/4 Pre-natal intimations of modern discoveries and results are strewn through scientific literature. 1909 *Westm. Gaz.* 19 Apr. 2/3 In some forgotten strange pre-natal world, Where rose-crowned summer smiled on placid seas.

Hence **pre'natalist**, one who believes in the prenatal divinity of Jesus Christ (also *attrib.*); **pre'natally** *adv.*, in the prenatal stage or period.
1879 TOURGEE *Fool's Err.* xxxix. 286 That they were prenatally infected with the seeds of fatal disease. 1895 HAWEIS in *Contemp. Rev.* Oct. 599 The Prenatalists admit human parentage on one side only. *Ibid.* 604 [see POSTNATALIST]. 1953 R. LEHMANN *Echoing Grove* II. 73 Already mid-summer dawn fainted pre-natally in the high uncurtained windows. 1965 *Science* 15 Jan. 306/3 This period of neural differentiation occurs prenatally in guinea pigs..and during the 1st week of postnatal life in rats. 1976 *Lancet* 18 Dec. 1352/2 Of interest was the occurrence of measles prenatally in the mother of 1 patient..during the third trimester of gestation.

pre-Nazi: see PRE- B. 1 a.

prence, obs. form of PRINCE.

†**prend**, *sb. Obs.* [? for **reprend*, from F. *reprendre* to join broken parts.] ? A repaired crack.
1479 *Paston Lett.* III. 272 Item, a grete maser with a prend in the botom, and the armes of Seint Jorge... Item, a nother maser sownde in the botom and a sengilbonde.

†**prend**, *v. Obs. rare.* [ad. F. *prend-re*:—L. *prendĕre*, contracted form of *prehendĕre* to take: see PREHEND.] *trans.* To take.
1447 BOKENHAM *Seyntys* (Roxb.) 149 In hym thou prendyddyst thi symylytude.

prender ('prɛndə(r)). *Law.* [sb. use of F. *prendre*, inf., to take.] The power or right of taking a thing without its being offered.
1597 WEST *2nd Pt. Symbol.* §126 The Lord..shal haue such things, as lye in *prender*: as the warde of the bodie of the heire and of the land, escheates &c. 1607 COWELL *Interpr.* s.v. *Render*, There be certaine things in a maner that lie in *prender*..and certaine that lie in *Render*. *a*1625 SIR H. FINCH *Law* (1636) 138 A reseruation of things in prender or vser, as to haue common for four beeues, or foure cart loads of wood, maketh no tenure. 1768 BLACKSTONE *Comm.* III. i. 15 Heriot custom (which Sir Edmund Coke says, lies only in prender, and not in render).

prene, obs. form of PREEN.

‖**prenegard**. *Obs.* The Fr. phrase *prenez garde*, take care.
*c*1400 *Songs Costume* (Percy Soc.) 50 Prenegard, prenegard, thus bere I myn baselard.

prenegotiation: see PRE- A. 2.

preneoplastic, -nephritic: see PRE- B. 1.

pre'neural, *a.* and *sb. Zool.* [PRE- B. 3.] **A.** *adj.* In chelonians, applied to a skeletal element that lies between the nuchal bone and the neural bones. **B.** *sb.* A bone in this position.
1904 *Amer. Jrnl. Sci.* CLXVIII. 274 There is a pre-neural bone, whose anterior border has occupied a notch in the hinder border of the nuchal. 1957 *Bull. Mus. Compar. Zool. Harvard* CXV. 171 The very similar term 'pre-neural' has long been in use for an element that is immediately posterior to the nuchal. 1969 R. ZANGERL in C. Gans *Biol. Reptilia* I. vi. 333 Most of the Mesozoic genera retain some amphichelydian characters,..but..the occurrence of a preneural is erratic. *Ibid.* 334 Pre-neural elements occur occasionally.

prenex ('priːnɛks), *a. Logic.* [ad. late L. *praenex(us* tied or bound up in front: see PRE- A. 1 and NEXUS.] Of or relating to a quantifier placed initially in a formula whose scope affects the whole formula; *spec.* in phr. ***prenex normal form*** (see quot. 1944).
1944 A. CHURCH in *Ann. Math. Stud.* XIII. 60 Thus we have that a w.f.f. is in prenex normal form if and only if all

its quantifiers are initially placed, no two quantifiers are upon the same variable, and every variable occurring in a quantifier occurs at least once within the scope of that quantifier. *Ibid.* 61 Use of the prenex normal form was introduced by C. S. Peirce, although in a different terminology and notation. **1950** W. V. QUINE *Methods of Logic* (1952) IV. 226 Let us speak of a quantifier as prenex in a sentence when.. it is initial.. and its scope reaches to the end of the sentence. *Ibid.* 243 The prenex universal quantifiers.. are dropped for ease in reading. **1951** *Jrnl. Symbolic Logic* XVI. 32 For any formula *F* of our *m*-valued formalization there is a formula *G* in prenex normal form which is weakly equivalent to *F*. **1965** HUGHES & LONDEY *Elem. Formal Logic* xli. 297 A wff in which all the quantifiers occur at the beginning, all are affirmative, and in which their scope extends to the end of the whole wff, is said to be in Prenex Normal Form. **1974** BOOLOS & JEFFREY *Computability & Logic* ix. 112 Thus.. F_2 is in prenex form but F_1 is not; since F_2 is a prenex formula logically equivalent to F_1, F_2 is a prenex form of F_1.

prengte, prenk: see PRINK *v.*

prennable, obs. f. PREGNABLE.

prenoble (priːˈnəʊb(ə)l), *a. nonce-wd.* [f. PRE- A. 6 + NOBLE *a.*] Pre-eminently noble. So †preˈnoble *v. Obs., trans.* to ennoble pre-eminently.

1657 REEVE *God's Plea* 40 We should prenoble priority with honourable actions. **1812** SOUTHEY *Omniana* II. 96 One of these prenoble and reverend Doctors of Theology.

prenominal (priːˈnɒmɪnəl), *a.* (*sb.*) [f. L. *prænōmin-*, stem of PRÆNOMEN + -AL[1]: cf. NOMINAL.] **a.** Pertaining to the *prænomen* or personal name, as distinguished from the surname; also, to the first word in binominal specific names.

1646 SIR T. BROWNE *Pseud. Ep.* II. vii. 102 So are they deceived in the names of Horse-raddish, Horse-mint, Bull-rush and many more: conceiving therein some prenominall consideration, whereas indeed that expression is but a Grecisme, by the prefix of *hippos* and *bous*.. intending no more then great. **1847** SAXE *Rape of Lock* xxi, The patronymical name of the maid Was so completely overlaid With a long prænominal cover. **1882** *Cornh. Mag.* Feb. 219 Many other prenominal absurdities.

b. Preceding a substantive. Also as *sb.*

1961 *Amer. Speech* XXXVI. 163 Roughly speaking, the prenominal adjectivals will be only single, simplex (descriptive) adjectives. **1964** *Language* XL. 45 As a prenominal the genitive has two unique characteristics. **1965** *Ibid.* XLI. 283 Prenominal and postnominal modifiers. **1978** *Ibid.* LIV. 26 A prenominal numeral like *cinq* 'five' may be pronounced with a final consonant in all positions.

†preˈnominate, *a. Obs.* [ad. L. *prænōmināt-us*, pa. pple. of *prænōmināre*: see next.] Before-named, above-named; = PRENOMINATED.

1513 BRADSHAW *St. Werburge* II. 141 In short tyme after the prenominate pagans At tamysmouth reentred this realme agayne. *Ibid.* 1486 After the decesse of Hug. Lupe prenominate. **1602** SHAKS. *Ham.* II. i. 43 Hauing euer seene, in the prenominate crimes The youth you breath of guilty.

†preˈnominate, *v. Obs.* [f. late L. *prænōmināre* to name in the first place + -ATE[3]; see PRE- A. 1 and NOMINATE *v.*] *trans.* To name beforehand, to mention previously. Hence **†preˈnominated** *ppl. a.*, previously mentioned, aforesaid; aforenamed, above-named.

1547 BOORDE *Brev. Health* xxv. 15 b, For al such matters loke in ye chapitres of the prenominated infirmities. **1597** A.M. tr. *Guillemeau's Fr. Chirurg.* 53/1 Those præcedent or prænominated occasions. **1606** SHAKS. *Tr. & Cr.* IV. v. 250 Think'st thou to catch my life so pleasantly, As to prenominate in nice coniecture Where thou wilt hit me dead? **1670** *Conclave wherein Clement VIII was Elected Pope* 3 Some.. did not only refuse all the prenominated persons, but would have introduced others.

†ˌprenomiˈnation. *Obs.* [n. of action from prec. vb.]

1. Prior nomination; naming first; forenaming.

1575 in H. Swinden *Gt. Yarmouth* (1772) 222 We have lately tollerated youre baylives to have prenominacion to oure discredytt. **1646** SIR T. BROWNE *Pseud. Ep.* III. xxiv. 170 In strict reason the watery productions should have the prenomination: and they of the land rather derive their names, then nominate those of the sea. **1658** PHILLIPS, *Prænomination*, a forenaming.

2. The giving of a prænomen; a first name or appellation.

1599 NASHE *Lenten Stuffe* 16 All Common wealths assume their prenominations of their common diuided weale, as where one man hath not too much riches, and another man too much pouertie.

†preˈnostic, *sb. Obs.* In 4 -ik, -yk, 5 -ike. [ad. med.L. *prænosticus*, partially Latinized form of *prognōsticus*: so *prænosticāre* vb. (Du Cange), and OF. *prenosticable* (Godef.).] = PROGNOSTIC.

1390 GOWER *Conf.* I. 219 He seith, for such a prenostik Most of an hound was to him lik. *c* **1398** CHAUCER *Fortune* 54 Prenostik is thow wolt hir towr asayle. **1481** BOTONER *Tulle on Old Age* (Caxton) e vj, The dayes callid Dies cretici and dies of prenostikes of good determynacions of the passions of a mans sikenesse or the contrarye.

So **†preˈnostic**, **†preˈnosticate** *v. trans.* = PROGNOSTICATE; **†preˈnosticate** *sb.*, **†preˈnosticative** = PRENOSTIC *sb.*; **†prenostiˈcation**, **†preˈnosticature** = PROGNOSTICATION (in quot. 1432–50, foreknowledge).

1480 CAXTON *Ovid's Met.* XII. xvii, Ffor that day was hys deth *prenostyked, yf he wente to batayile. **1432–50** tr. *Higden* (Rolls) V. 169 Men.. seide that hit was a *prenosticate and a signe that he sholde reioyce thempyre. *Ibid.* II. 283 If thay fynde the horne fulle at that tyme thei prenosticate grete habundaunce of goodes. **1513** DOUGLAS *Æneis* III. vi. 209 Eftir that this prophet.. Thir devyne answeris thus prenosticate. *c* **1400** MAUNDEV. (1839) xv. 167 The *prenosticaciouns of thinges that felle aftre. **1432–50** tr. *Higden* (Rolls) II. 317 A scribe, hauenge prenostication of thynges to comme [L. *præscius futurorum*]. *Ibid.* VI. 217 In whiche yere ij horrible blasynge sterres apperede;.. as a *prenosticatyve of grete destruccion. **1490** CAXTON *Eneydos* xxii. 80 Dyuynacions presagyous & aruspycyous, vnto her tolde,.. by the auguryes & *prenostycatures of her harde and aduerse fortunes.

†preˈnotary. *Obs.* Forms: 5 prenotarye, 6 -arie, preignetory, prignatory, 7 pre(i)gnotarie, -ry, prægnotary, pregnotory, prenotory. [ad. med.L. *prænotārius*, app. a latinized synonym of *prōtonotārius* PROTONOTARY: cf. AF. *preno'tarie* (Britton 1292), *preignatorie*. Prob. at first stressed *ˌpreno'tarie*, whence *'prenŏtary*, *-nătorie*, *-nĕtory*, etc., and *pregn-* for *pren-*.] The chief clerk of a court of law; a protonotary. Also *fig.*

[*c* **1250** BRACTON *De Leg. Angliæ* (Rolls) III. 188 Tunc legat prothonotarius virtutem brevis ad instructionem juratorum. *c* **1290** FLETA IV. ix. (1647) 230 Tunc legat prænotarius virtutem Juratorum. **1292** BRITTON II. xxi. §5 Adounc lour seit bref leu par le clerc prenotarie, qi dirra en ceste manere.]

c **1450** LYDG. & BURGH *Secrees* 2399 Prenotaryes to haue I the Advyse. **1535** CROMWELL in Merriman *Life & Lett.* (1902) I. 398 John Joyner the kinges Preignetory of his graces comen bench at Westminster. **1542–3** *Act 34 & 35 Hen. VIII*, c. 27 §43 Vpon euery fine.. shalbe paied.. twoo shillynges.. Wherof.. the Prenotarie, entring the same, shall haue two pens. **1600** *Maldon, Essex, Doc.* Bundle 162 lf. 8 Vnto serjeants, prignatoryes, atturneys, and councelors. **1651** tr. *De-las-Coveras' Don Fenise* 20 The Judge of the towne assisted by the Pregnotory and serjeants came into the house. **1658** PHILLIPS, *Prægnotaries*,.. in Common law, the chief Clerks of the King's Court, whereof three are of the Common pleas, and one of the King's Bench. *a* **1693** *Urquhart's Rabelais* III. xlii. 345 Sequestrators,.. Tabellions,.. Pregnatories, Secondaries.

prenotation (priːnəʊˈteɪʃən). In quot. præ-. [f. PRE- A. 2 + NOTATION; see next. Cf. late L. *prænotātio* a first notion (Ennod. in Quicherat).] Noting beforehand; prediction, prognostication.

1861 I. TAYLOR *Spir. Hebr. Poetry* Pref. 13 Attested by.. the Divine præ-notation of events.

†preˈnote, *v. Obs.* [ad. L. *prænotāre* to mark before, in late L. to predict: see PRE- A. 1 and NOTE *v.* So obs. F. *prénoter* to note before.]

1. *trans.* To note or make mention of previously.

1570 FOXE *A. & M.* (ed. 2) 178/1 This blinde ignorance of that age, thus aboue prenoted.

2. To denote or betoken beforehand, to prognosticate; to predict, foretell.

1641 H. L'ESTRANGE *God's Sabbath* 63 It was not typicall; it did not prenote any thing to ensue or be accomplisht. **1647** LILLY *Chr. Astrol.* xxvii. 173 In what House you find Cauda Draconis, it prenotes detriment. *a* **1711** KEN *Hymnarium* Poet. Wks. 1721 II. 143 How Prophets clearly could prenote Events remote.

pre-ˈnotice. *rare.* [PRE- A. 2.] Previous notice or intimation.

a **1680** CHARNOCK *Attrib. God* (1834) I. 225 He judged it expedient to give some pre-notices of that Divine incarnation. **1814** COLERIDGE in J. Cottle *Early Recoll.* (1837) II. 218 With silent wishes, that these explanatory pre-notices may be attributed to their true cause.

prenotifiˈcation. *rare.* [PRE- A. 2.] Previous notification.

1765 STERNE *Tr. Shandy* VIII. iv, Bridget's pre-notification of them to Susannah.. made it necessary for my uncle Toby to look into the affair. **1884** J. TAIT *Mind in Matter* (1892) 197 By divine prenotification, Noah saved himself and family.

prenotion (priːˈnəʊʃən). Now *rare.* [ad. L. *prænōtiōn-em* a previous notion, preconception, innate idea (Cic.), transl. Gr. πρόληψις of the Epicureans: see PRE- A. 2 and NOTION. So F. *prénotion* (16th c.).]

1. A notion or mental preception of something before it exists or happens. Also (without *a* or *pl.*), foreknowledge, prescience; in quot. 1652, prognostication.

1588 J. HARVEY *Disc. Probl.* 77 Euen in such prenotions and premonitions.. they may prouidently and reasonably foresee the consequence of Naturall or Morall effects. **1605** BACON *Adv. Learn.* II. xi. §2 That the mind when it is withdrawn and collected into itself.. hath some extent and latitude of prenotion. *a* **1607** BRIGHTMAN *Predict.* (1641) 2 Whosoever.. may be amply satisfied, what prevalence his prenotions had. **1652** GAULE *Magastrom.* 341 Many soothsaying astrologers.. had gathered themselves together, to consult about the prænotion of Valens his successor. **1709** BERKELEY *The. Vision* §148 Some glimmering analogous prænotion of things, that are placed beyond the certain discovery.. of our present state. **1856** R. A. VAUGHAN *Mystics* (1860) I. 218 The belief that the soul, when by abstinence and observances it has been purified and concentrated, has a certain extent and latitude of prenotion.

2. A notion of something before actual experience of or acquaintance with it; a previous notion; a preconceived idea.

1605 BACON *Adv. Learn.* II. xv. §3 This art of memory is but built upon two intentions; the one prenotion, the other emblem. **1614** JACKSON *Creed* III. xxi. §22 Were we well acquainted.. with.. those prænotions the Apostle supposed as known [etc.]. **1672** WILKINS *Nat. Relig.* 42 What kind of men are there any where, who have not of themselves this prenotion of a Deity? **1846** SIR W. HAMILTON *Dissert.* in *Reid's Wks.* App. 762 Anticipations—Presumptions—Prenotions.

Hence **preˈnotional** *a.*, pertaining to a preconceived notion.

1872 DE MORGAN *Budget of Paradoxes* 383 They might have gone so far, for example, under pre-notional impressions, as the alliterative allopath, who,.. opposing the progress of science called vaccination, declared that some of its patients coughed like cows, and bellowed like bulls.

pre-noun: see PRE- B. 1.

prenova (priːˈnəʊvə), *a.* and *sb. Astr.* **A.** *adj.* [PRE- B. 2.] Preceding development of a star into a nova. **B.** *sb.* [PRE- B. 1] A star prior to its becoming a nova.

1939 D. B. MCLAUGHLIN in *Pop. Astron.* XLVII. 418 The pre-nova stage. During this portion of its life, the star is either constant or irregularly variable through a small range. **1943** *Publ. Observatory Univ. Michigan* VIII. 188 In the pre-nova state the star is very hot, probably 50,000° to 60,000° K. **1956** Z. KOPAL in A. Beer *Vistas in Astron.* II. 1499 (*heading*) Internal constitution of the pre-novae. **1957** C. PAYNE-GAPOSCHKIN *Galactic Novae* xi. 313 The pre-nova is regarded as a hydrogen-poor sub-dwarf with contraction the main source of energy. **1976** *Nature* 22 Jan. 172/3 First indications that the nova was unusual came when a search for the prenova on the Palomar Sky Survey plates showed no star at the nova's position.

†prenˈsation. *Obs. rare.* [ad. L. *prensātio*, n. of action f. *prensāre*, contr. f. *prehensāre*: see PREHENSATION.] Seizing; laying hold.

1620 J. KING *Serm. 24 Mar.* 22 How would I vrge vnto you.. the presentest prensation and pursuit of the very forelock of time? *a* **1677** BARROW *Pope's Suprem.* (1680) 149 By ambitious prensations, by Simoniacal corruptions,.. by all kinds of sinister ways, men crept into the place.

So **†ˈprensile** *a. Obs. rare*, perh. error for PREHENSILE; **prension** (*rare*) = PREHENSION (sense 3).

1825 WATERTON *Wand. S. Amer.* IV. ii. 322 The large red monkey of Demerara.. having a long prensile tail. [*Note*] I believe prensile is a new-coined word. I have seen it, but do not remember where. [*Prehensile* was a recent word.] **1836–48** B. D. WALSH *Aristoph.*, *Clouds* I. iv, Verboseness, and pulsion, and prension.

prent, -e, obs. f. PRINT *sb.* and *v.*; obs. pa. pple. of PRINK *v.*

prentice (ˈprɛntɪs), *sb.* Now *arch.* or *dial.* Forms: 4–6 prentis, -ys, -yse, -yce, -iz, *Sc.* -eis, (4 -yss, -ese, prenttis, printiz, -yce, preyntyce, 5 prentez, -isse, 5–6 -es, 6 -esse, *Sc.* -eiss), 4–7 prentise, *Sc.* printeis, 6–7 prentize, 5– prentice, (8– ˈprentice). [Aphetic form of APPRENTICE. The pl. was sometimes *prentis*, *prentes*, *-ez*, etc.]

1. a. = APPRENTICE *sb.* 1.

to send or ***put to prentice***, to bind as apprentice.

a **1300** *Cursor M.* 12233 Als printiz [*v.rr.* prentiz, prentis] wend i him haf ouer-cummen. **1362** LANGL. *P. Pl.* A. v. 116, I serued Simme atte noke, And was his pliht prentys his profyt to loke. **1453–4** *Cal. Anc. Rec. Dublin* (1889) I. 280 Irysh jornaymen, Irysh prentesys. *a* **1548** HALL *Chron.*, *Hen. VIII* 61 b, Then all the young men resisted the Alderman.. and cryed prentyses and clubbes. **1556** *Chron. Gr. Friars* (Camden) 30 Thys yere was yell May day, that yong men and prentes of London rose in the nyght. **1593** SHAKS. *2 Hen. VI*, II. iii. 71 Be merry Peter, and feare not thy Master, Fight for credit of the Prentices. **1611** *Glasgow Burgh Rec.* (1876) I. 318 That na printeis heireftir salbe admittit burges except his maister compeir with him. **1711** STEELE *Spect.* No. 107 ¶7 Sir Roger.. sent his Coachman's Grandson to Prentice. **1721** AMHERST *Terræ Fil.* No. 38 (1754) 202 City 'prentices and lawyers clerks. **1857** RUSKIN *Pol. Econ. Art* 31 Stupid tailor's 'prentices who are always stitching the sleeves in the wrong way upwards.

†b. A learner generally; a disciple. *Obs.*

[**1292** BRITTON VI. iii. §3 En eyde des prentiz [for the assistance of learners].] *c* **1375** *Sc. Leg. Saints* ii. (*Paulus*) 248 A woman.. þat.. to petir printeis had bene. *Ibid.* iii. (*Andreas*) 479 þu tak to þe þe forme of prenttis, gyf þat þu Wil knaw it þat þou speris now!

†2. *Law.* = APPRENTICE *sb.* 2. *Obs.*

1377 LANGL. *P. Pl.* B. XIX. 226 Prechoures & prestes & prentyces of lawe. **1399** —— *Rich. Redeles* III. 350 Ffor selde were þe sergiauntis souȝte ffor to plete, Or ony prentise of courte preied of his wittis. **1460** CAPGRAVE *Chron.* (Rolls) 277 Glendore.. was first a prentise at Cort, and than a Swyere of the Kingis hous. **1484** in J. S. Davies *Hist. Southampton* (1883) 474 There was ayenst us ij sergeauntez and iiij prentez. **1530** PALSGR. 258/1 Prentyce in lawe a lerned man: they [French] use no suche order.

†3. *fig.* = APPRENTICE *sb.* 3. *Obs.*

1489 CAXTON *Faytes of A.* I. xvi. 47 He shal not be noo prentiz.. in puttyng his oost in fayre ordenance. **1549** COVERDALE, etc. *Erasm. Par. Gal.* 8 Assone as.. I became prentice to the spirituall lawe of fayth. *a* **1586** SIDNEY *Astr. & Stella* lxx, Sonets be not bound prentise to annoy.

4. *attrib.* and *Comb.*, as ***prentice-boy***, ***-girl***, ***-lad***, ***-player***, ***-years***; often implying inexperience as of a novice or beginner, as

prentice ear, hand, stroke, work; ***prentice-like*** adj.

1594 NASHE *Unfort. Trav.* Wks. (Grosart) V. 63 Did neuer vnlouing seruant so prentiselike obey his neuer pleased mistres. **1598** SYLVESTER *Du Bartas* II. i. IV. *Handicrafts* 596 My Prentice ear doth oft reverberate. **1633** P. FLETCHER *Pisc. Ecl.* II. xi, When Thelgon here had spent his prentise-yeares. **1666** PEPYS *Diary* 3 Sept., Saying that she was not a 'prentice girl, to ask leave every time she goes abroad. **1745** *De Foe's Eng. Tradesman* v. (1841) I. 32 There is nobody to serve but a prentice-boy or two. **1784** BURNS *Green grow the Rashes* v, Her prentice han' she tried on man, An' then she made the lasses, O. **1839** C. J. LEVER *Confessions H. Lorrequer* vi. 47 A red-hot orangeman,.. vice-chairman of the ''Prentice Boys'. **1849** CLOUGH *Dipsychus* II. iv. 74 In the deft trick Of prentice-handling to forget great art. **1852** DICKENS *Bleak Ho.* (1853) i. 1 Fog cruelly pinching the toes and fingers of his shivering little 'prentice boy on deck. **1860** MOTLEY *Netherl.* I. 212 There was likely to be no prentice-work. **1881** 'MARK TWAIN' *Prince & Pauper* xxii. 269 His frantic and lubberly 'prentice-work found but a poor market for itself. **1898** Prentice hand [see ELEVEN *a.* 2c]. **1907** 'MARK TWAIN' *Christian Sci.* II. iii. 127 They seem to me to prove the presence of the 'prentice hand. **1963** *Times* 7 May 8/7 How fine it would be to hear Sir John Gielgud on a stage where Edmund Kean was a prentice player. **1975** *Times Lit. Suppl.* 29 Aug. 963/1 It is unfair to print such academic prentice-work cheek by jowl with the work of experienced professionals. **1980** *Times* 12 Jan. 10/6 Breaded scallops and fragile wun-tun came from an expert, not a prentice, hand.

'prentice, *v.* Now *arch.* or *dial.* [f. prec. sb.] *trans.* = APPRENTICE *v.*

1598 MARSTON *Sco. Villanie* II. ix. G viij, But when to seruile imitatorship Some spruce Athenian pen is prentizèd, Tis worse then Apish. **1608** DAY *Law Trickes* I. ii, Thou wouldst not prentise thy affections Nor tie thy fortunes to a strangers loue. **1716** HEARNE *Collect.* (O.H.S.) V. 278 His Father was a Bookseller in Oxford, prenticed to old Hen. Davies. **1896** A. E. HOUSMAN *Shropshire Lad* xlvii, 'Prenticed to my father's trade.

† **'prenticeage.** *Obs.* Also 7 -isage. Aphetic f. APPRENTICEAGE; also analysed as ***prentice-age.***

a **1586** SIDNEY *Arcadia* (1622) 270 Must I be the exercise of your prentice-age? **1624** *Trag. Nero* II. ii. in Bullen *O. Pl.* I. 35 Full blowne Inspire me with Machlæan rage That I may bellow out Romes Prentisage. **1657** J. SERGEANT *Schism Dispach't* 2 To make the confutation of that Treatise the prentisage of his endeavours in controversie.

† **'prenticehead.** *Obs.* [f. PRENTICE *sb.* + -HEAD.] = next.

1423 JAS. I *Kingis Q.* clxxxv, On way, In gude tyme and sely to begynne Thair prentissehed. **1463** in *Bury Wills* (Camden) 16 He to haue his indentour of his prentished. **1526** *Pilgr. Pref.* (W. de W. 1531) 142 Than we shall be delyuered out of our prentyshed, and be made free men.

† **'prenticehood.** *Obs.* [f. as prec. + -HOOD; cf. APPRENTICEHOOD.] = next, 1.

1377 LANGL. *P. Pl.* B. v. 256, I..haue ymade many a knyȝte bothe mercere & drapere, þat payed neuere for his prentishode nouȝte a peire gloues. *c* **1386** CHAUCER *Cook's T.* 36 This ioly prentys with his maister bood Til he were ny out of his prentishood. **1467** in *Eng. Gilds* (1870) 390 Fulle vij. yere of prentishode. **1554** in *Bury Wills* (Camden) 145 When he commith out of his yeres of prentiswood. **1568** FULWELL *Like will to Like* in Hazl. *Dodsley* III. 310 So soon as my prenticehood was once come out. **1648** J. BEAUMONT *Psyche* II. xliii, I serv'd no prentisehood to any Rod.

prenticeship ('prɛntɪsʃɪp). Now *arch.* or *dial.* Forms: see PRENTICE; also contr. 6 **prentyship, prent'ship,** *Sc.* **prentischip,** 6–7 (9 *dial.*), **prentiship.** [f. as prec. + -SHIP.]

1. = APPRENTICESHIP 1, 2.

1535 LYNDESAY *Satyre* 3884 He man gang till his prentischip agaïne. **1581** MULCASTER *Positions* xxxvii. (1887) 154 To abide the paines of some more laborious prenticeship. **1599** BP. HALL *Sat.* VI. i. 86 Of late did many a learned man Serue thirtie yeares Prenti-ship with Priscian. *a* **1659** OSBORN *Misc.* 81 Of too noble a nature to be learned under a Prentiship. **1737** POPE *Hor. Epist.* II. i. 181 He serv'd a 'Prenticeship, who sets up shop. **1822** T. MITCHELL *Aristoph.* II. 273 In perils and alarms Was his prenticeship of arms.

2. = APPRENTICESHIP 3, 4; *transf.* a space of seven years.

1553 ASCHAM in *Lett. Lit. Men* (Camden) 16, I have allready served out three prentyships at Cambrige. **1632** MASSINGER *Maid of Hon.* III. i, I served two prenticeships, just fourteen years, Trailing the puissant pike. **1702** C. MATHER *Magn. Chr.* VII. v. (1852) 545 Men [who] had spent whole prenticeships of years in the faithful service of the churches. *a* **1845** HOOD *Sniffing a Birthday* i, Three 'prenticeships have past away,.. Since I was bound to life!

† **'prenticewick.** *Obs.* *rare*$^{-1}$. [f. as prec. + -WICK.] = prec. 1.

1462 *Litt. Red Bk. Bristol* (1900) II. 129 At that tyme they beyng in theyre prentiswyke.

pre-'nuclear, *a.* [PRE- B. 1.] **1.** *Phonetics.* That occurs before a nucleus.

1952 W. JASSEM *Intonation of Conversational Eng.* vi. 61 The distinctive feature of the prenuclear tunes is..the relation of the final tone of the tune to the initial tone of the following tune. **1961** [see INTERNUCLEAR *a.* 3]. **1966** J. E. BUSE in C. E. Bazell *In Memory of J. R. Firth* 54 Of the four pre-nuclear classes, prepositions, determinatives and number particles are mutually exclusive with..the tense particles. **1976** *Archivum Linguisticum* VII. 38 One feature both subclasses share is their insistence that any non-nuclear occurrence be in prenuclear position rather than in tail (postnuclear) position.

2. Preceding the development of nuclear weapons.

1960 *Guardian* 14 Sept. 10/5 In the pre-nuclear age power was physical violence. **1965** *Economist* 11 Dec. 1181/1 Mr Kosygin's attitude is frightening because it is so stunningly out of date. It is pre-nuclear, pre-coexistence. **1968** *Punch* 10 Apr. 543/3 A strange, pre-nuclear atmosphere prevailed.

† **pre'nunce,** *v.* *Obs.* *rare*$^{-1}$. [ad. OF. *prenoncer* (Froissart), or ad. L. *prænuntiāre* (*-nunciāre*) to foretell, f. *præ* PRE- A. 1 + *nuntiāre* to announce.] *trans.* = PRENUNCIATE *v.*

1580 *Hay's Demandes* in *Cath. Tractates* (S.T.S.) 48 The cleane sacrifice quhilk Malachias did prenunce and forespeake.

† **pre'nunciate, -nuntiate,** *v.* *Obs.* [f. ppl. stem of L. *prænuntiāre*: see prec.] *trans.* To announce beforehand; to foretell; to predict.

1623 COCKERAM, *Prenunciate*, to foreshew. *a* **1636** FITZ-GEFFRAY *Compassion Captives* Ded. Ep. (1637) 2, I come.. not as the sea-porpesses to prenuntiate a storme, but..to procure a calme. **1652** GAULE *Magastrom.* 94 If the.. conjunctions of the stars be sufficient to prognosticate and prenuntiate all manner of mutations.

So † **prenunci'ation,** announcement beforehand, foretelling, prediction, prognostication; † **pre'nunciative** *a.*, † **pre'nuncious** *a.* (*rare*$^{-0}$), announcing beforehand, presaging; **pre-'nuntiate** *nonce-wd.*, used to render L. *prænuntius* masc., *prænuntia* fem., foreteller, harbinger.

1623 COCKERAM II, Fore-shewing..**prenunciation.* *a* **1626** W. SCLATER *Exp. 4th ch. Rom.* (1650) 152 Propheticall prenunciations all verified by events. **1652** GAULE *Magastrom.* 67 To cause a falsehood in the pronuntiation, prenuntiation, or prediction. **1555** BONNER *Necess. Doctr.* L iv, The fyrste Sacramentes..were *Prenuncyatyue of Chryst to come. **1843** G. S. FABER *Eight Dissert.* (1845) I. 47 Typical and prenunciative of the one efficacious piacular devotement of the Lamb of God. **1656** BLOUNT *Glossogr.*, **Prenuncious*,..the first brings tidings, that goes afore and tells news. **1866** J. B. ROSE tr. *Ovid's Fasti* II. 825 But now the bird *prenuntiate of day [L. *lucis praenuntius ales*] Proclaims the morning. *Ibid.* VI. 244 The herald priest, with javelin in hand, Prenuntiate of warfare [L. *belli praenuntia*].

† **prenzie,** *a.* *Obs.* A doubtful word in the following passage; prob. an error.

1603 SHAKS. *Meas. for M.* III. i. 94, 97 *Cla.* The prenzie Angelo? *Isa.* Oh 'tis the cunning Liuerie of hell, The damnest bodie to inuest, and couer In prenzie gardes.

† **pre-ob'ject,** *v.* *Obs.* *rare*$^{-0}$. [f. PRÆ-, PRE- A. 1 + OBJECT *v.* 3.] *trans.* To bring forward or offer in advance. So † **pre-ob'jected** *pa. pple.*, previously offered.

1636 PRYNNE *Humb. Remonstr.* (1643) 31 For any other pretended Presidents (or Records) that may be alleadged to prove the lawfulnesse of this Tax, we intend not here..to trouble your Majestie with particular answers to them, they being all fully answered in those præobjected.

pre-ob'jectal, *a.* *rare.* [f. PRE- B. 1 d + OBJECT *sb.* + -AL[1].] Existing before becoming an object of knowledge.

1865 J. GROTE *Explor. Philos.* I. 67 Knowledge..is the mingling of our own consciousness with a certain (so to call it) præ-objectal matter of knowledge, of which we are so far conscious, as that it is that by distinction from which we know ourselves.

pre-o'blige, *v.* *rare.* [PRE- A. 1.] *trans.* To oblige beforehand; to bind by previous obligation.

1644 HUNTON *Vind. Treat. Monarchy* iii. 17, I grant a people (not preobliged) fully overcome should much sin against Gods providence by obstinacie. **1668** FRANCO *Truth Springing* 25 Onely the two last were commanded to Noah (to the other five he was preobliged). *a* **1694** TILLOTSON *Serm.* lxxxv. (1742) VI. 1363 Nor lastly, was he pre-obliged by any kindness or benefit from us.

preobrazhenskite (priːəʊbrə'ʒɛnskaɪt). *Min.* [ad. Russ. *preobrazhenskit* (Ya. Ya. Yarzhensky 1956, in *Doklady̆ Akad. Nauk SSSR* CXI. 1087), f. the name of P. I. *Preobrazhensky* (1874–1944), investigator of Russian salt deposits: see -ITE[1].] A hydrated magnesium borate found as nodules in salt deposits in Kazakhstan.

1957 *Amer. Mineralogist* XLII. 704 *Preobrazhenskite*... It occurs in colorless, lemon-yellow, and dark gray nodules in fine-grained halite-polyhalite rock. **1972** *Soviet Physics: Doklady* XVI. 519/1 The equation of preobrazhenskite so obtained corresponded to the chemical composition $3MgO.5{\cdot}5B_2O_3.4{\cdot}5H_2O$, but not $3MgO.5B_2O_3.4{\cdot}5H_2O$ as originally proposed. *Ibid.*, The most important crystal-chemical complex in the structure of preobrazhenskite comprises a set of infinite boron-oxygen chains perpendicular to the b axis with a new type of radical; the repeated link in each chain comprises four triple boron-oxygen rings..and two additional $BO_2(OH)_2$ tetrahedra.

pre-observational: see PRE- B. 1 d.

pre-ob'serve. *rare.* [PRE- A. 1.] *trans.* To observe beforehand.

1664 POWER *Exp. Philos.* I. 11 As hath been pre-observ'd in other Insects. *Ibid.* III. 160 As has been præobserved by all Magnetick Writers. **1675** HAN. WOOLLEY *Gentlewoman's Comp.* 193, I shall give you an account of what must be pre-observed in the keeping of a Dayry.

pre-obtain, -occipital: see PRE- A. 1, B. 3.

preoccupancy (priː'ɒkjʊpənsɪ). [f. PRE- A. 2 + OCCUPANCY; cf. PREOCCUPY.]

1. The fact of occupying previously; previous or earlier occupancy; = PREOCCUPATION 3.

1755 JOHNSON, *Preoccupancy*, the act of taking possession before another. **1796** MORSE *Amer. Geog.* I. 632 The Indians had an undisputed title to the..territory, either from pre-occupancy or conquest. **1832** LYELL *Princ. Geol.* II. 167 That powerful barrier against emigration [of plants]—pre-occupancy.

2. The state of being preoccupied or engaged.

1893 *Argosy* Sept. 202 An endless restless preoccupancy vaguely followed by fear of satiety. **1898** *Daily News* 22 Jan. 2/6 He..declined repeated offers of a seat in Parliament.. on the ground of his preoccupancy in the administration of Owens College.

preoccupant (priː'ɒkjʊpənt), *a.* and *sb.* [f. PRE- A. 3 + OCCUPANT.]

A. *adj.* Previously occupying; preoccupying.

1654 tr. *Scudery's Curia Pol.* 56 Least a preoccupant fear possess their spirits.

B. *sb.* One who occupies (a place or region) before others; a previous or earlier occupant.

c **1826** T. ALDEN in *3 Mass. Hist. Coll.* (1837) VI. 152 Tools, made of iron,..which, no doubt, were obtained by the tawny pre-occupants of this region from the French. **1832** LYELL *Princ. Geol.* II. 173 Invasions of this kind, attended by the expulsion of the pre-occupants, are almost instantaneous.

† **'preoccupate,** *a.* *Obs.* *rare*$^{-0}$. [ad. L. *præoccupāt-us*, pa. pple. of *præoccupāre* to PREOCCUPY.] = PREOCCUPATED.

1656 BLOUNT *Glossogr.*, *Preoccupate*, prevented, overreached, taken aforehand.

† **'preoccupate,** *v.* *Obs.* [f. ppl. stem of L. *præoccupāre* to PREOCCUPY: see OCCUPATE *v.*]

1. *trans.* To take possession of or seize upon beforehand or before another; to usurp.

1586 FERNE *Blaz. Gentrie* 311 If..any other Captayne shall with hys insigne preoccupate the place of honor. **1592** NASHE *Strange Newes* L j b, My heart is præoccupated with better spirits, which have left no house roome. **1628** HOBBES *Thucyd.* (1822) 76 The Thebans foreseeing the war, desired to preoccupate Platea. **1727** *Philip Quarll* 252 The late Omen of approaching Evil had preoccupated his Thoughts.

2. To take at unawares, surprise, overtake.

1582 N.T. (Rhem.) *Gal.* vi. 1 If a man be preoccupated in any fault, ye that are spiritual, instruct such an one in the spirit of lenitie. **1630** LENNARD tr. *Charron's Wisd.* (1658) 59 The Spirit being preoccupated, tainted and overcome. **1650** TRAPP *Comm. Deut.* xxxii. 5 They are preoccupated, taken at unawares. **1654** *Ibid.*, *Ps.* li. 14 If Davids adultery was a sin of infirmity (he was preoccupated, as Gal. 6. 1).

3. To take possession of the mind beforehand; to prepossess; to influence, bias, prejudice.

1582 N.T. (Rhem.) Pref. b ij b, If the preiudice of any erroneous persuasion preoccupate the mind. **1624** WOTTON *Archit.* in *Reliq.* (1651) 256 Lest the pleasure of the Eye preoccupate the Judgment. **1647** TRAPP *Comm. Acts* xxv. 11 A corrupt Judge, notoriously forestalled and preoccupated. **1681** HICKERINGILL *Vind. Naked Truth* 2 To preoccupate and prepossess his Readers with an opinion of his Modesty.

4. To meet in advance; anticipate; forestall.

1588 *Reg. Privy Council Scot.* IV. 287 Drawing in of strangearis, and, to preoccupat thair arryvall, hes causit his speciall kynnismen and houshald servandis surprise and occupy his Hienes awne houssis. **1607–12** BACON *Ess.*, *Death* (Arb.) 384 Revenge triumphes over death, love esteemes it not..greif flyeth to it, feare preoccupateth it. **1678** CUDWORTH *Intell. Syst.* 258 This objection is thus preoccupated by Plato.

5. To cause to seize *upon* beforehand. *rare*$^{-1}$.

1603 FLORIO *Montaigne* (1634) 503 Why is not some one of them possessed with the humor to preoccupate on his companions the glory of this chaste love?

Hence † **pre'occupated** *ppl. a.*; † **pre'occupating** *vbl. sb.* and *ppl. a.*

1591 R. TURNBULL *Exp. St. James* 128 The mocking and ironicall preoccupating and preuenting of the objection. **1651** H. L'ESTRANGE *Answ. Mrq. Worcester* 77 We should leave the deciding of the sense..to the pre-occupated understanding of one of the Advocates. **1651** tr. *Bergerac's Satyr. Char.* xiii. 52 For fear, least the pre-occupated should conclude, that 'tis the devill that speaks in him.

† **pre'occupately,** *adv.* *Obs.* *rare*$^{-1}$. [f. PREOCCUPATE *a.* + -LY[2].] In a preoccupied manner; in quot., so as to preoccupy.

a **1628** F. GREVIL *Hum. Learn.* xii, Abstracts the imagination or distasts With images preoccupately plac'd.

preoccupation (priːɒkjʊ'peɪʃən). [ad. L. *præoccupātiōn-em*, n. of action from *præoccupāre*: see prec. So F. *préoccupation* (15th c. in Godef. *Compl.*).] The action of preoccupying.

† **1.** The meeting of objections beforehand. In *Rhet.* A figure of speech in which objections are anticipated and prevented; anticipation, prolepsis.

(In quots. 1538 and thence in 1552, erroneously explained as = *paralipsis*, app. by confusing this with *prolepsis*.)

[**1538** ELYOT, *Preoccupatio*, a fygure in Rhetorike, whan we wyll saye that we will not tell a thinge, and yet therby couertly we wil declare the matter, or make it suspected. **1552** HULOET, *Preoccupation*..is also a certayne fygure in rethorycke, or a darke speakynge, as when we wyll saye, I wyll not tell all (etc.).] **1584** R. SCOT *Discov. Witchcr.* II. viii.

(1886) 23 They prevent us with a figure..prolepsis or præoccupation. **1611** W. Sclater *Key* (1629) 340 The words haue in them a preoccupation, of what might be obiected against the former Doctrine. **1683** E. Hooker *Pref. Pordage's Mystic Div.* 64 By waie..of obviation, prævention, præoccupation and anticipation.

2. Prepossession of the mind which gives it a certain disposition or tendency; bias; prejudice.

1603 Florio *Montaigne* II. xii. (1632) 247 These [Atheists] have some preoccupation of judgements that makes their taste wallowish and tastlesse. **1613** Sherley *Trav. Persia* 135 Let not your desires of promoving this great..businesse, blind you from foreseeing all sorts of preoccupations, which..you..may perchance find greater. **1696** Locke *Lett.* (1708) 156 'Tis your preoccupation in favour of me, that makes you say what you do. **1875** E. White *Life in Christ* IV. xxiv. (1878) 346 Starting as we believe without pre-occupation.

3. Actual occupation (of a place) beforehand.

1658 Phillips, *Præoccupation*, a possessing before hand. **1706** *Ibid.* (ed. Kersey) s.v., That Land was in his Preoccupation. **1859** Darwin *Orig. Spec.* xiii. (1873) 357 Preoccupation has probably played an important part in checking the commingling of the species.

4. Occupation that takes precedence of all other; 'first business'.

1873 Symonds *Grk. Poets* vi. 166 The first preoccupation of every Greek who visited Olympia, was to see the statue of Zeus. **1883** *Manch. Guard.* 13 Oct. 7/2 The fixed preoccupation of our agents on the spot..is to maintain the peace. **1885** *Pall Mall G.* 27 June 4/1 Marrying and giving in marriage is now and always has been the great preoccupation of man and womankind.

5. The condition of being preoccupied; mental absorption or engrossment.

1854 Milman *Lat. Chr.* VIII. i. III. 264 The preoccupation of men's minds with this absorbing subject. **1866** Geo. Eliot *F. Holt* xiv, The stamp of gravity and intellectual preoccupation in his face and bearing.

pre'occupative, *a. rare.* [f. as PREOCCUPATE *v.* + -IVE.] Characterized by preoccupying. Hence **pre'occupatively** *adv.*

1860 Sala *Looking at Life* 147 Mercy allows the present necessity to overshadow and pre-occupatively overcome the contingent emergency.

preoccupied (priːˈɒkjʊpaɪd), *ppl. a.* [f. PREOCCUPY *v.* + -ED[1].] Occupied previously.

a. Absorbed in thought, abstracted. **b.** *Zool.* and *Bot.* Of a name: already occupied or used for something else.

1842 *Rep. Brit. Assoc. Adv. Sci.* 113 The genus of birds, *Plectorhynchus*, being preoccupied in Ichthyology, is changed to *Plectorhamphus*. **1849** C. Bronte *Shirley* viii, The pre-occupied, serious face. **1891** T. Hardy *Tess* xviii, Something nebulous, preoccupied, vague, in his bearing and regard, marked him as one who probably had no very definite aim or concern about his material future. **1898** [see BENTONITE]. **1903** *Westm. Gaz.* 12 Feb. 1/3 In the further corner..a preoccupied-looking band is exploiting the musical comedies. **1913** [see BALUCHITHERIUM]. **1967** J. R. & P. H. Napier *Handbk. Living Primates* III. 377 The subgeneric name *Lyonogale* is substituted for the preoccupied *Tana* Lyon.

Hence **pre'occupiedly** *adv.*, in a preoccupied manner; with preoccupation of thought.

1884 J. Hawthorne *Pearl-shell Necklace* xi, 'Ay, surely..', said Poyntz, puffing his pipe preoccupiedly.

preoccupier (priːˈɒkjʊpaɪə(r)). [f. next + -ER[1].] One who preoccupies.

1863 Cowden Clarke *Shaks. Char.* xvii. 430 Is he not almost the sole preoccupier of the mind whenever it recurs to these plays?

preoccupy (priːˈɒkjʊpaɪ), *v.* [f. PRE- A. 1 + OCCUPY, after L. *præoccupāre* to seize beforehand. Cf. F. *préoccuper* (14th c. in Hatz.-Darm.).]

1. *trans.* To occupy or engage beforehand; to engross to the exclusion of other things; †to prepossess, to bias.

1567 Drant *Horace, Epist.* To Rdr., Amarouse Pamphlets haue so preoccupyed the eyes and eares of men. **1607** Shaks. *Cor.* II. iii. 240 Say..that Your minds pre-occupy'd with what you rather must do, Then what you should, made you against the graine To voice him Consull. *a* **1735** Arbuthnot (J.), I think it more respectful to the reader to leave something to reflections, than preoccupy his judgment. **1856** Emerson *Eng. Traits, Voy. Eng.* Wks. II. 13 The inconveniences..of the sea are not of any account to those whose minds are pre-occupied.

2. To occupy or take possession of beforehand or before another; to appropriate for use in advance.

1622 Malynes *Anc. Law-Merch.* 240 The places of these Ships which by them should haue been preoccupied, may be filled vp yearely with good fish. **1795** Southey *Lett. fr. Spain* (1799) 69 We found the posada pre-occupied by a Marquis and his retinue. **1837** Carlyle *Fr. Rev.* (1872) III. I. vii. 44 A Mountain-wall of forty miles..which he should have preoccupied. **1865** M. Arnold *Ess. Crit.* x. (1875) 409 The name of Antoninus being preoccupied by Antoninus Pius.

b. To occupy or fill (a thing) *with* (something) beforehand.

1822–34 *Good's Study Med.* (ed. 4) III. 307 It has..been proposed..to fight off the poison of lyssa by preoccupying the ground with the poison of a viper. **1868** Browning *Ring & Bk.* IX. 1240 If field with corn ye fail preoccupy, Darnel for wheat and thistle-beards for grain..Will grow apace.

†**3.** To possess by anticipation. *Obs.*

1638 Junius *Paint. Ancients* 123 That they should in their life time preoccupie a lively feeling of an everlasting name. *a* **1677** Manton *Exp. Lord's Pr.* Matt. vi. 11 Wks. 1870 I. 166 We need not anticipate and pre-occupy the cares of the next day.

†**4.** To anticipate, forestall. *Obs. rare.*

a **1677** [cf. 3]. **1785** Warton *Milton's Poems* 306 *note*, I have been preoccupied by Dr. Jortin in noting this parallel.

†**5.** To wear beforehand. **b.** *pass.* To be dressed *in* beforehand. *Obs. rare.*

1630 B. Jonson *New Inn* Argt. IV, The tailor's wife, who was wont to be pre-occupied in all his customers' best clothes. *a* **1637** —— *Underwoods* lx, Whose like I have known the tailor's wife put on..ere 'twere gone Home to the customer: his letchery Being the best clothes still to pre-occupy.

pre'occupying, *ppl. a.* [f. prec. + -ING[2].] That preoccupies (in various senses of the vb.).

1642 Milton *Apol. Smect.* Wks. 1851 III. 259 So little can he suffer a man to measure..what is short or what tedious without his preoccupying direction. **1863** Geo. Eliot *Romola* x, A smile..was soon quenched by some pre-occupying thought. **1893** W. G. Collingwood *Ruskin* II. 151 His patience in the midst of pre-occupying labour and severest trial.

preocular (priːˈɒkjʊlə(r)), *a.* (*sb.*) Also præ-. [f. PRE- B. 3 + L. *ocul-us* an eye + -AR[1].] **A.** *adj.* Situated in front of the eye: *spec.* applied to certain plates in the head of a reptile.

1826 Kirby & Sp. *Entomol.* IV. xlvi. 316 *Preocular*... When antennæ are inserted before the eyes. **1852** MacGillivray *Hist. Brit. Birds* V. 522 The preocular bristly feathers blackish.

B. as *sb.* One of the preocular plates of a scaled reptile, as a snake or lizard.

1890 in *Cent. Dict.*

pre-Œdipal (priːˈiːdɪpəl), *a. Psychoanalysis.* Also preœdipal. [f. PRE- B. 1 + ŒDIPAL *a.*] That is prior to the onset of the Œdipal phase of development. Also **pre-'Œdipus** *attrib.*

1932 *Internat. Jrnl. Psycho-Anal.* XIII. 282 Our insight into this early, pre-Oedipal, phase in the little girl's development comes to us as a surprise. **1958** *Ibid.* XXXIX. 516 (*title*) The preoedipal attachment to the mother. **1961** J. Strachey et al. tr. *Freud's Compl. Psychol. Wks.* XXI. 230 The phase of exclusive attachment to the mother, which may be called the pre-Oedipus phase, possesses a far greater importance in women than it can have in men. **1974** G. & R. Blanck *Ego Psychol.* ii. 36 The beginning introjections, incorporations, and identifications are variously described in the literature as primitive, archaic forms of superego, or as..preoedipal super-ego.

pre-œsophageal: see PRE- B. 3.

pre-oïdium: see PRE- B. 2 a.

†**pre'ominate**, *v. Obs. rare.* [PRE- A. 1.] **a.** *intr.* To have a foreboding, to augur. **b.** *trans.* To be an omen of, to portend.

1594 Nashe *Terrors Nt.* Wks. (Grosart) III. 255 One may aswel..by paraphrasing on smokie dreames præominate of future euents. **1646** Sir T. Browne *Pseud. Ep.* v. xxii. 264 Because many Ravens were seen when Alexander entered Babylon they were thought to pre-ominate his death.

Hence †**preomi'nation**, augury, foreboding.

1660 A. Sadler *Subject's Joy* 8 In an holy Preomination of the years succeeding.

pre-omosternum, -omosternal: see PRE- A. 4.

pre-op (priːˈɒp), colloq. abbrev. of PREOPERATIVE *a.* Also as *sb.*, ellipt. for *preoperative preparation* or the like.

1934 S. Kingsley in *Famous Plays of 1934* 159, I was kind of worried about that preop insulin. **1956** K. Hulme *Nun's Story* x. 162 All pre-op medication given. **1972** M. Crichton *Terminal Man* I. v. 44 Pre-op patients..often didn't want to see people. **1976** 'R. Gordon' *Doctor on Job* iv. 34 The razor's a bit ropey. It's the one they use for the ward preops. **1977** *Lancet* 5 Feb. 301/2 His details are entered in the book for the agreed date, with comments such as 'very fat' or 'needs pre-op physio'.

pre-'operate, *v. rare.* [PRE- A. 1.] *intr.* To operate or work before or in front.

1658 Bp. Reynolds *Van. Creature* Wks. (1677) 46 Grace must prevent, follow, assist us, pre-operate and co-operate.

pre-ope'ration, *sb.* and *a. rare.* **A.** *sb.* [PRE- A. 2.] **1.** Operation or working beforehand.

1622 Donne *Serm.* (ed. Alford) V. 109 So there is a good sense of co-operation, and post-operation; but pre-operation, that we should work, before God work upon us, can admit no good interpretation. **1655** *Nicholas Papers* (Camden) II. 248 He reasons that such a determinacion could not be grounded on what the former printes spake, and accordingly he makes pre-operation. *a* **1779** Warburton *Div. Legat.* IX. i. Wks. 1788 III. 649 It would be trifling to speak of a pre-ordination, which was not to be understood of a pre-operation.

2. A preoperational activity.

1971 *Nature* 13 Aug. 456/1 For some time, it has been believed that young children are unable to form transitive inferences about quantity until they pass the stage of logical preoperations at about 7 yr old.

B. *adj.* [PRE- B. 2.] Prior to a surgical operation.

1976 J. Snow *Cricket Rebel* 107, I relaxed as the pre-operation drugs took effect and I moved into another world. **1978** *Detroit Free Press* 16 Apr. D4/2 This way, except for a pre-operation visit, 'I just see them unconscious.'

preope'rational, *a. Psychol.* [PRE- B. 1.] That precedes operational thought, usu. typified by the mental processes of children aged between 2 and 7. (Cf. OPERATION 4 b.)

1953 Mays & Whitehead tr. *Piaget's Logic & Psychol.* ii. 12 Starting from the postulate that all logical problems arise in the first place from manipulations of objects, we can now say that this period is pre-operational. **1960** J. S. Bruner *Process of Educ.* iii. 34 In this so-called preoperational stage, the principal symbolic achievement is that the child learns how to represent the external world through symbols established by simple generalization; things are represented as equivalent in terms of sharing some common property. **1964** Lunzer & Papert tr. *Inhelder & Piaget's Early Growth of Logic in Child* 291 Whether or not the co-ordination is complete, operations and pre-operational co-ordinations enter into the most diverse kinds of behaviour. **1975** M. D. Smith *Educ. Psychol.* ii. 40 Pre-operational two to seven uses egocentric speech.

preoperative (priːˈɒpərətɪv), *a. Med.* [PRE- B. 1.] Given or occurring before a surgical operation.

1904 *Brit. Med. Jrnl.* 10 Sept. *Epit. Med. Lit.* 35 Pre-operative and Post-operative Treatment in Abdominal Section. **1954** Martin & Hynes *Clin. Endocrinol.* (ed. 2) iii. 69 The use of pre-operative iodine or anti-thyroid drugs..adds further difficulty in the histological diagnosis of thyroidectomy specimens. **1957** *New Biol.* XXIV. 54 Without preoperative treatment with heparin there would be every likelihood of the blood clotting within the operated blood vessel. **1977** *Lancet* 25 June 1352/1 In preoperative preparation of the bowel most surgeons used neomycin for 1–3 days, or phthalylsulphathiazole for 3–10 days.

Hence **pre'operatively** *adv.*, before an, or the, operation.

1931 [see POSTOPERATIVELY *adv.*]. **1957** *Ann. R. Coll. Surgeons* XXI. 368 The visual defect pre-operatively affected both eyes nearly equally. **1976** *Lancet* 27 Nov. 1205/2 All the patients feel well, and there have been no occlusive vascular episodes postoperatively. However, in the only patient (no. 2) whose electrocardiogram was abnormal preoperatively, no change has occurred.

pre-o'percle. Also -cule. Anglicized form of PRE-OPERCULUM.

1858 Mayne *Expos. Lex.* s.v., A bony formation on which the *operculum*, or lid of the gills play: the preopercule. **1886** *Cassell's Encycl. Dict.*, Preopercle. So *Cent. Dict.*, etc.

pre-opercular, præ- (priːəʊˈpɜːkjʊlə(r)), *a.* (*sb.*) [f. PRE-OPERCUL-UM + -AR[1].] Of or pertaining to the pre-operculum. Also *absol.* or as *sb.* The pre-opercular bone, the pre-operculum.

1854 Owen *Skel. & Teeth* in *Orr's Circ. Sc.* I. *Org. Nat.* 178 The appendage..consists of four bones; the one articulated to the tympanic pedicle is called 'preopercular'. **1858** Mayne *Expos. Lex.*, *Pre-opercular*, term applied by Prof. Owen..to the first or proximal segment of the radiated appendage of the tympano-mandibular arch. **1866** Owen *Vertebr. Anim.* I. 105 The preopercular,..runs parallel with, strengthens, and connects together the divisions of the tympanic pedicle.

pre-operculum, præ- (priːəʊˈpɜːkjʊləm). [f. *præ*, PRE- A. 4 + OPERCULUM.]

1. *Ichth.* The foremost of the four bones forming the operculum in fishes.

1828 Stark *Elem. Nat. Hist.* I. 454 Head scaly; operculum with spines, and the preoperculum with dentations. **1880** Günther *Fishes* 80 The side of the skull, in front of the operculum, is covered by a large irregularly-shaped bone, held by some to be the præoperculum.

2. *Bot.* = OPERCULUM 2.

1864 Webster, *Preoperculum, Bot.*, the fore-lid or operculum in mosses. (Also in later Dicts.)

pre-opinion, -optic: see PRE- A. 2, 4.

pre-option (priːˈɒpʃən). [PRE- A. 2.] An option before any one else; right of first choice.

1666 Bp. Reynolds *Serm. Westm. Abbey* 7 Nov. 19 He gave unto Lot the praeoption of what part of the Land he would live in. **1732** Stackhouse *Hist. Bible* (1752) I. v. iv. 723/2 Agamemnon, as General, had the Preoption of what Part of the Booty he pleas'd. **1830** J. H. Monk *Life R. Bentley* (1833) II. 98 *note*, The right of the senior graduates to the preoption of livings.

pre-oral, præ- (priːˈɔərəl), *a.* [f. PRE- B. 3 + ORAL, f. L. *ōs*, *ōr-* mouth.] Situated in front of the mouth.

1870 Rolleston *Anim. Life* 106 The prae-oral or so-called 'supra-oesophageal' ganglionic mass. **1875** Huxley & Martin *Elem. Biol.* (1877) 130 The labrum and the metasterna are median growths of the sterna of the præoral and post-oral somites. **1893** Tuckey tr. *Hatschek's Amphioxus* 149 This diverticulum..breaks through on the left side of the body with a small opening outwards—the preoral pit.

Hence **pre-'orally** *adv.*

1888 *Huxley & Martin's Elem. Biol.* 184 The three anterior pairs having coalesced preorally to form the brain.

pre-orbital (priːˈɔːbɪtəl), *a.* (*sb.*) *Anat.* and *Zool.* Also præ-. [f. PRE- B. 3 + ORBIT *sb.* + -AL[1].] **A.** *adj.* Situated in front of the orbit or eye-socket.

1852 Dana *Crust.* I. 93 Præorbital tooth acute. **1881** Mivart *Cat* 64 Each frontal bifurcates laterally into a sharp pointed 'nasal process' and a more obtuse 'pre-orbital process'. **1886** Guillemard *Cruise Marchesa* I. 214 The slight development of the pre-orbital fossa.

B. *sb.* The pre-orbital bone or process.

1897 GÜNTHER in M. Kingsley *W. Africa* App. iii. 709 Præorbital about half the area of the orbit.

pre-ordain (priːɔːˈdeɪn), *v.* Also *Sc.* in 6 preordine. [f. PRE- A. 1 + ORDAIN *v.*; = late L. *præordināre* (Vulg.), OF. *preordiner* (15th c. in Godef.), F. *préordonner.*] *trans.* To ordain or appoint beforehand; in *Theol.* to foreordain.

1533 GAU *Richt Vay* 68 Quhen yᵉ time is cum preordinit be God. **1576** FOXE *A. & M.* (ed. 3) 102/2 No aduersitie or perturbation happeneth..which his prouident wisedome dooth not foresee before and preordaine. **1582** N.T. (Rhem.) *Acts* xxii. 15 [14] The God of our fathers hath prëordained thee, that thou shouldest know his wil. **1671** MILTON *P.R.* I. 127 Unweeting he fulfill'd The purpos'd Counsel pre-ordain'd and fixt Of the most High. **1791** COWPER *Iliad* III. 372 This day is preordain'd the last. **1863** KINGLAKE *Invas. Crimea* I. xiv. 295 Having preordained the question to be put to the people. **1894** PARRY *Stud. Gt. Composers, Schubert* 226 In Italian works, the form was, as it were, pre-ordained.

Hence **pre-orˈdained** *ppl. a.*; **pre-orˈdainer**; **pre-orˈdaining** *vbl. sb.* and *ppl. a.*; **pre-orˈdainment**, pre-ordination.

1651 HOBBES *Leviath.* IV. xlvi. 374 God's Will, and Præordaining of things to come. **1842** I. WILLIAMS *Baptistery* II. xxx. (1874) 165 Deep plans of preordaining thought. **1855** BADEN POWELL *Ess.* 479 Imagined interruptions of pre-ordained order for the introduction of new forms of life. **1855** G. MEREDITH *Shav. Shagpat* (1856) 377 So was shaved Shagpat,..according to preordainment. **1890** J. MARTINEAU *Seat Authority in Relig.* IV. iii. 480 The preordainer of the whole world-scheme through its series of ages.

pre-ˈorder, *v. rare.* [PRE- A. 1.] *trans.* To order, arrange, or appoint beforehand. Hence **pre-ˈordered** *ppl. a.*; **pre-ˈordering** *vbl. sb.*

1638-48 G. DANIEL *Eclog* v. 264 Scepters, to præordred Ends must fall. **1726** LEONI *Alberti's Archit.* I. 1/2 A.. graceful pre-ordering of the Lines and Angles. **1829** LYTTON *Devereux* I. viii, Do you believe that Heaven preorders as well as foresees our destiny? **1832** —— *Eugene A.* I. iv, Shall we see..each marvel fulfilling its pre-ordered fate?

†**pre-ˈordinance.** *Obs.* [f. PRE- A. 2 + ORDINANCE; cf. obs. F. *preordonnance* (16th c. in Godef.).] Previously established ordinance or rule.

1387-8 T. USK *Test. Love* III. ii. (Skeat) l. 144 If it wer nat in mannes own liberte of fre wil to do good or bad but to the one teied by bonde of goodes preordinaunce. **1486** *Surtees Misc.* (1888) 56 God so disposith of His preordinaunce. **1571** DIGGES *Pantom.* Pref. A ij, The skilfull in Architecture can applye the Stereometria..in preordinance and forecasting both of the charges, quantities and proportion of ..any kinde of buyldings. **1601** SHAKS. *Jul. C.* III. i. 38 These couchings, and these lowly courtesies Might..turne pre-Ordinance, and first Decree Into the law [*pr.* lane] of Children.

pre-ˈordinate, *a.* [f. PRE- A. 5 + ORDINATE *a.*, f. L. *ordo, ordinem* order, rank. After *subordinate.*] Superior in rank, importance, or degree (*to*). Opposed to *subordinate*, and *co-ordinate*.

1801 JEFFERSON *Writ.* (1830) III. 473 In other cases..the general executive is certainly pre-ordinate. **1863** J. G. MURPHY *Comm. Gen.* i. 1 The stars which are co-ordinate with the sun, and pre-ordinate to the moon.

pre-ˈordinate, *ppl. a. arch.* [ad. late L. *præordināt-us*, pa. pple. of *præordināre*: see PRE-ORDINATE *v.*] Foreordained, pre-appointed, pre-destined. Formerly construed also as *pa. pple.*

1426 LYDG. *De Guil. Pilgr.* 17096 Folk predestynaat, And swych as be preordynaat To kome vn-to savacioun. *c* **1470** HARDING *Chron.* Proem. xxi, Kyng Richarde..whom, for his mede Kyng Henry quyt with death preordinate. **1526** *Pilgr. Perf.* (W. de W. 1531) 181 This holy name was preordynate & gyuen of god. **1570** FOXE *A. & M.* (ed. 2) 139/1 According to the preordinate counsayle of God. **1582** N.T. (Rhem.) *Acts* xiii. 48 As many as were preordinate to life euerlasting. **1643** SIR T. BROWNE *Relig. Med.* I. §17 The will of His Providence, that disposeth her favour to each Country in their pre-ordinate season.

Hence **pre-ˈordinately** *adv.*, by pre-ordination.

1894 W. D. SPELMAN in *Voice* (N.Y.) 22 Nov. 6/3 The Countess..should be summoned to court as soon as [etc.].. which time, however, preordinately, should never come.

†**pre-ˈordinate**, *v. Obs.* [f. ppl. stem of late L. *præordināre* to order beforehand, pre-ordain; f. *præ*, PRE- A. 1: see ORDINATE *v.*] *trans.* To foreordain, predestine.

1565 STAPLETON tr. *Bede's Hist. Ch. Eng.* 68 They beleaued him..who were preordinated to lyfe euerlasting. **1654** OWEN *Saints' Persev.* Wks. 1853 XI. 156 To preordinate, I fear, in Mr. Goodwin's sense, is but to predispose men by some good dispositions in themselves. *a* **1693** *Urquhart's Rabelais* III. xxviii. 230 It was preordinated for thee.

pre-ordiˈnation. Now *rare.* [= late L. *præordinātio* (Hilary *c* 350), F. *preordination* (16th c. in Godef. *Compl.*), n. of action from L. *præordināre* to PRE-ORDAIN.] The action of pre-ordaining, or settling beforehand, what is to take place; the condition of being pre-ordained; predestination.

1550 BALE *Image Both Ch.* II. xvi. Qj b, Yt ys..to be mynystred vnto them by the preordynacyon of God. **1582** N.T. (Rhem.) *Acts* xiii. *margin*, They beleeued specially by Gods grace and preordination. **1678** MARVELL *Def. J. Howe* Wks. (Grosart) IV. 213 Many who grant prescience, deny preordination. *a* **1779** [see PRE-OPERATION *sb.*]. **1948** *Mind* LVII. 180 The well-worn antagonisms of the immanent and transcendent, of finite sinfulness and divine perfection and preordination, which centuries of theological brooding have failed to dissipate.

pre-organic, -original: see PRE- B. 1, 1 d.

pre-orgasmic, -ovulatory: see PRE- B. 1.

preost, preoue, obs. ff. PRIEST, PROVE, PROOF.

†**preostend**, *v. Obs. rare*⁻¹. [ad. late L. *præostend-ĕre* (Augustine), f. *præ*, PRE- A. 1 + *ostendĕre* to OSTEND.] *trans.* To show or reveal beforehand.

c **1450** *Mirour Saluacioun* 3339 This delyvraunce of man also godde preostendid When he Patriarche abraham fro hurr of Caldee delyvrid.

pre-ovulation: see PRE- B. 2 a.

pre-own: see PRE- A. 1.

pre-oxygenation: see PRE- A. 2.

prep (prɛp), *sb.* and *a. slang* (orig. *School* and *College*).

1. *sb.* Short for PREPARATION. **a.** In sense 1 c; esp. lessons and exercises to be done by a pupil after school hours, either at school or as homework (see HOMEWORK 2). Also *attrib.*

1862 [see PREPARATION 1 c]. **1899** E. PHILLPOTTS *Hum. Boy* 119 Murdoch he let crib off him in 'prep' three times. **1900** *Dialect Notes* II. 51 (College Words and Phrases) *Prep.* .. Preparation. **1901** 'IAN MACLAREN' *Yng. Barbarians* xv, The recreations which enliven 'prep'. **1911** BEERBOHM *Zuleika D.* xxii. 313 With his elbows on the kitchen table.. sat Clarence, intent on belated 'prep'. **1939** R. C. WOODTHORPE *Rope for Convict* v. 51 I've just remembered I haven't done the prep. he sent me. **1961** E. S. TURNER *Phoney War* vii. 28 At prep time, they were not allowed to use ink, for fear of damaging the art treasures on the walls. **1972** *Where* Sept. 237/3 The standard half-hour homework, or 'prep' as it is called in some schools, is purely notional. **1976** *Daily Times* (Lagos) 4 Sept. 19/2 (Advt.), Boarding with daily coaching, strict attention, and Prep Supervision for: Forms One to Five male and female in Lagos. **1977** J. I. M. STEWART *Madonna of Astrolabe* i. 8 Two of her boys ..must be got home in time to be calmed down and persuaded to do their prep. **1979** *Homes & Gardens* June 97/2 There is a general shuffling, an air of impatience, boredom even, of the sort you find at prep. time in public schools.

b. In various other senses. Also *attrib.*

1925 D. H. LAWRENCE *Let.* ? 17 Dec. (1962) II. 870 Tell Achsah, lest she make any preps for me. **1934** *Amer. Speech* IX. 237/2 The curtailed word or back-shortening *prep*... In this sentence, *The team had an intensive prep yesterday afternoon*, it has the same connotation as *drill* or *practice*. **1976** M. MILLAR *Ask for me Tomorrow* (1977) xvi. 127 A little too perfectly groomed, as if he'd just been given the full treatment in..a mortician's prep room. **1976** *Amer. Speech* 1973 XLVIII. 204 He is given a *prep* 'surgical preparation'. **1977** *Hot Car* Oct. 69/1 (*caption*) Persevere with this as it is an important prep stage for the paint.

c. *Horse-racing.* A race that is a preparation for a more important event. *U.S.*

1944 *Sun* (Baltimore) 4 Mar. 9/4 A better-than-fair horse, which he..guided to second place..in the $7,500-McClennan, the widener prep won by Sun Again. **1975** *New Yorker* 15 Sept. 110/2 It isn't often that a hundred-thousand-dollar race is a prep for a two-hundred-and-fifty-thousand-dollar one. **1977** *Ibid.* 3 Oct. 112/1 Quiet Little Table..won the prep, running head-and-head down the stretch with Wise Philip and Jatski.

2. Short for PREPARATORY *a.* orig. *U.S.*

a. *adj.* In sense 2 a.

1895 J. L. WILLIAMS *Princeton Stories* 128 After awhile he found himself walking with the freshman way out toward the Prep. school. **1903** *Chicago Record-Herald* 7 June III. 1/1 A crowd of nearly 4,000 university, 'prep' school and grammar school rooters cheered from the bleachers. **1905** *McClure's Mag.* June 123/2 The commercial class of prep school athletes admire their prototypes in the colleges. **1906** M. NICHOLSON *Ho. w. 1000 Candles* i. 3, I had thrashed him soundly at the prep school. **1930** [see FACT *sb.* 4 f]. **1934** C. LAMBERT *Music Ho!* v. 298 They are..as childish as the hidden rivers and prep school puns that adorn Joyce's *Anna Livia Plurabelle*. **1943** *Scrutiny* XI. 287 His [*sc.* Wodehouse's] humour is a cross of Prep-school and *Punch*. **1959** T. S. ELIOT *Elder Statesman* II. 63 You were expelled from your prep school for stealing. **1971** *New Yorker* 15 May 51/2 Dulwich College—what the English call a public school and we call a prep school. **1974** *Listener* 14 Mar. 339/3 The prep-school language and the note of petulance nicely convey the immaturity..of this band of heroes. **1976** *National Observer* (U.S.) 17 Apr. 10/4 It was not the Vietnam War that pinched the adolescent rush to prep schools.

b. *sb.* Short for *preparatory school*. Also *attrib.*

1895 J. L. WILLIAMS *Princeton Stories* 244 Charlie Symington was a well-built prep. boy who had been known to strike out three men with the bases full. **1924** H. DE SÉLINCOURT *Cricket Match* v. 158 To know whose call it is ..was driven into me at the prep. **1927** W. E. COLLINSON *Contemp. Eng.* 21 My attendance at Dulwich College Preparatory School (the Prep.) coincided with the South African war. **1934** *Amer. Speech* IX. 237/2 In the following sentence the term refers to high schools, *Nebraska Preps Have Major Encounters this Week.* **1969** *Eugene* (Oregon) *Register-Guard* 3 Dec. 2D/1 The Eagles thought, to win the state B prep football title, they'd have to throw more than they did. **1976** *Honolulu Star-Bull.* 21 Dec. H-2/1 Going back to last Saturday's game, it was great to see just how far Russ Francis has come since his prep days at Kailua High.

c. *sb.* A student at a preparatory school, or who is preparing for college (*Cent. Dict.* 1890). *U.S.*

1899 A. H. QUINN *Pennsylvania Stories* 117 He was going to tell all those people, from the Governor down to the prep in the gallery, who came from his own old school, just what the College had done for *him*. **1948** *Chicago Daily News* 6 Dec. 23/4 (*caption*), 2 preps die in Oregon bush crash. **1978** *Maledicta* 1977 I. 223 A stout prep who wore saucer-shaped glasses.

prep (prɛp), *v.*¹ *U.S. slang.* [f. prec., sense 2.] *intr.* To attend a preparatory school, be a preparatory school student.

1915 *Dialect Notes* IV. 236 *Prep*, preparatory: used as a verb 'to attend a preparatory school'. **1920** F. SCOTT FITZGERALD *This Side of Paradise* ii. 43 Where'd you prep? **1936** L. C. DOUGLAS *White Banners* xiv. 305 Thomas and this Colonel Livingstone had prepped together at this academy. **1967** *Boston Sunday Herald Mag.* 16 Apr. 8/2 What school do you go to?.. Where did *you* prep? **1977** *New Yorker* 23 May 91/1 A native of Peoria, Illinois, who prepped at Lawrenceville, Davis graduated from Princeton with highest honors in history.

prep (prɛp), *v.*² *slang* (orig. *U.S.*). [f. PREP *sb.* 1, or shortening of PREPARE *v.*] **a.** *trans.* To prepare (someone or something); to train (an animal) for racing; to prime (a witness); *spec.*, in hospital terminology, to prepare (a patient) for an operation. Also *absol.*

1927 *Amer. Speech* II. 313/1 Ask whether the 'ten-thirty appendectomy has been prepped yet?' For some reason a patient's abdomen is not shaved, it is 'prepped', that is, prepared for the surgeon. **1936** *Esquire* Sept. 160/3 *Little Lord Fauntleroy* and *Dodsworth* [*sc.* two films] have been 'prepping prod.' (preparing production) for some time. **1937** 'J. BELL' *Murder in Hospital* vii. 133 Macdonald started to prep him. *Ibid.*, She gave him his atropine for the operation when she had finished prep'ing the leg. **1943** *Sun* (Baltimore) 12 Oct. 16/5 (*heading*) Attention [*sc.* a horse] being prepped for New Orleans 'Cap. **1961** 'K. NORWAY' *Waterfront Hosp.* i. 19, I told Nurse David, 'Five minutes —we'll have to prep on the table.' **1965** *Eng. Stud.* XLVI. 461 *Prepster* 'one who is being prepped; trainee'. **1967** *Boston Sunday Herald* 14 May II. 3/1 Anyone planning to enter greyhound racing should know it costs close to $600 to prep each dog for the races. **1968** J. D. MACDONALD *Pale Grey for Guilt* (1969) xii. 145 Somebody prepped her pretty good, Sheriff. I might even have thought she saw somebody she sincerely mistook for me. **1969** I. KEMP *Brit. G.I. in Vietnam* v. 110 The gun-ships must have done a thorough job of 'prepping' the L.Z. because, apart from sporadic sniper fire,..we met no opposition there. **1972** M. GOLDBERG *Karamanov Equations* xxiii. 226 Have the nurse prep him... Neck, chest, and groin. **1975** *Globe & Mail* (Toronto) 18 Sept. 5/1 Looking as Tory as the advance men who precede the Premier to prep the crowd, he strolled through the market.

b. *intr.* for *refl.* To prepare oneself (for an event); to practise, to train (esp. in sport). *U.S.*

1934 *Amer. Speech* IX. 237/2 Verbal use of the word appears in *Beavers Arrive in Omaha to Prep for Husker Fray.* **1937** *Sun* (Baltimore) 22 Apr. 17/1 (*heading*) Track preps for Ky. Derby. **1941** *Ibid.* 3 July 16/1 The latter..was prepping for the New Castle Handicap to be run on Saturday. **1949** *N.Y. Times* 4 Sept. v. 2/6 A pitcher, who had prepped earnestly for many years in the minors..was cut from the roster. **1972** *Newsweek* 10 Jan. 24/3 Mrs. Nixon has been prepping for the trip for weeks. **1977** *Time* 28 Nov. 66/1 Akers had prepped as a Royal assistant before moving into the head coaching job at Wyoming in 1975.

pre-ˈpack, *v.* [PRE- A. 1.] *trans.* To pack or wrap (an article, usu. of food) on the site of production or before retail. Also *fig.* So **ˈpre-packed** *ppl. a.*, **pre-ˈpacking** *vbl. sb.* Also **pre-ˈpacker**.

1928 *Daily Express* 23 Mar. 3/1 The public..would abandon bread altogether in favour of pre-packed foods, all of them comparatively expensive. **1931** J. W. WINGATE *Man. Retail Terms* xv. 344 *Prepacking*, merchandise packed by the store in advance of sale. **1952** *Times* 6 Aug. 2/2 Describing the method of pre-packing butter in most machines, the report states that..the rate of delivery is between 60 and 80 packets a minute. **1957** *Times* 2 July (Agric. Suppl.) p. v/4 These requirements..have done much to encourage prepacking on the farm in units ready for retail sale without further wrapping or weighing. **1962** H. O. BEECHENO *Introd. Business Stud.* ii. 14 Now we have the ability to pre-pack, preserve and store the vast majority of the goods available on the market. **1974** 'E. ANTHONY' *Malaspiga Exit* i. 14 The average pre-packed American beauty. **1976** C. BERMANT *Coming Home* II. iii. 149 The reasoning seemed to be pre-packed and clogged with clichés and slogans. **1976** *Milton Keynes Express* 23 July 23/3 (Advt.), Wholesale fruit and vegetable merchants and pre-packers of quality produce. **1977** *Oxf. Diocesan Mag.* July 14/2 We have exciting new concepts of mission—no longer seeing the Church as going out with a prepacked Gospel to sell.

ˈpre-pack, *sb.* [PRE- A. 2.] A container or wrapper in which an article (usu. of food) is enclosed on the site of production or before retail.

1957 *Daily Mail* 26 Sept. 8/5 Business is growing so fast that the sale of pre-packs is expected to increase by 70,000,000 a year. **1973** *Times* 1 Feb. 4/2 Prepacks containing 'A' grade eggs may be decorated with a red band. **1976** *Oxf. Consumer* Mar. 8/2 Prepacks of biscuits and shortbread must be marked with their weights if they weigh more than 50g.

pre-'packaged, *a.* [PRE- A. 1.] Packaged on the site of production or before retail. Also *fig.* So **pre-'packaging** *vbl. sb.* Also **pre-'package** = PRE-PACK *sb.*

1944 R. E. LEE *Television* 179 Local stations will transmit pre-packaged variety shows. **1945** *Business Week* 18 Aug. 91 An ill-timed effort to market prepackaged frozen meat. **1947** *Printers' Ink* 3 Jan. 70 (*heading*) Produce marketers survey pre-packaging to stem competition from frozen foods. **1957** *Times* 2 July (Agric. Suppl.) p. vii/2 The growing popularity of pre-packaged foods, of self-service shopping, of refrigerators. **1960** *News Chron.* 22 Sept. 13/1 The pre-package industry was born. **1963** *Supermarket & Self-Service* (Johannesburg) Nov./Dec. 9/1 Place a mass display of pre-packaged cheese on a dump table in the middle of a side aisle. **1965** *Wireless World* July 345/2 (*heading*) Pre-packaged semiconductors for the retail market. **1966** *Rep. Comm. Inquiry Univ. Oxf.* II. 470 To establish a system of required lectures would..place a disastrous emphasis on prepackaged instruction. **1976** *Times* 1 May (Food Suppl.) p. iii/6 Prepackaging..has..been used for cuts of fresh meat.

prepaid: see PREPAY.

prepalæolithic (ˌpriːpæliːəʊˈlɪθɪk), *a.* *Anthropol.* [PRE- B. 1 b.] Preceding or anterior to the Palæolithic or Early Stone Period of human history. So **pre'palæolith**, a stone used in this period, as a weapon or implement.

1895 H. STOPES in *Athenæum* 7 Sept. 325/3 The stones used throughout this transition or prepalæolithic time are frequently very large, generally left-handed, and nearly always rough. *Ibid.* 325/1 Some of these prepalæoliths..are found in many positions in Swanscombe.

pre-palæozoic, -palatal, -ine: see PRE- B. 1 b, 3.

preparable (ˈprɛpərəb(ə)l), *a. rare.* [a. F. *préparable* (*c* 1500 in Godef.): see PREPARE *v.* and -ABLE.] Capable of being prepared.

1663 BOYLE *Usef. Exp. Nat. Philos.* II. App. 363 More costly Spirits, scarce any of which being preparable by so safe, and compendious a way. **1669** W. SIMPSON *Hydrol. Chym.* 167 All such preparable remedies. **1685** BOYLE *Enq. Notion Nat.* vii. §6 Wks. 1772 V. 240 If there be any such medicine preparable by art. **1837** CARLYLE *Fr. Rev.* III. IV. i, 'Day of the Preparation of Peace?' Alas, how were peace possible or preparable?

†**prepa'rado.** *Obs. rare*[−1]. [ad. Sp. *preparada*, or a fanciful imitation of Sp., after *armado*, etc.: see -ADO.] Preparation.

1610 ROWLANDS *Martin Mark-all* 21 Such as shall..haue right and title there..may make a preparado to haue passage when the winde shall sit faire for that place.

†**'preparance.** *Obs.* [a. OF. *preparance* (14th c. in Godef.), f. *préparer* to PREPARE: see -ANCE.] The action of preparing; preparation.

1543 GRAFTON *Contn. Harding* 452 He herde his enemies made no greate preparaunce or haste. **1583** STUBBES *Anat. Abus.* I. (1879) 72 Preparaunce was made for her buriall. **1602** CAREW *Cornwall* 158 b, Small troops of ours..after forewarning and preparance, have wonne, possessed,..captived and carried away the townes, wealth and inhabitants.

†**'preparate,** *ppl. a. Obs.* Also 4–6 -at. [ad. L. *præparāt-us*, pa. pple. of *præparāre* to PREPARE.] Prepared. (Const. as *pa. pple.*)

c **1386** CHAUCER *Can. Yeom. Prol. & T.* 257 Sal tartre Alkaly and sal preparat. **1460–70** *Bk. Quintessence* 5 Birie it al in hors dounge, preparate as it is seid hereafter. **1513** BRADSHAW *St. Werburge* I. 3073 All thynges were redy preparate. **1575** TURBERV. *Venerie* 225 Two drams and a halfe of scamony preparat in white vineger.

†**'preparate,** *v. Obs.* [f. ppl. stem of L. *præparāre* to PREPARE: see -ATE[3].] *trans.* To prepare (esp. a drug or compound); to make a preparation of. Hence †**'preparated** *ppl. a.*

1460–70 *Bk. Quintessence* 8 Who so coude reparale and preparate kyndely þis fier. **1569** R. ANDROSE tr. *Alexis' Secr.* IV. I. 15 Into which is put a little of preperated Tutia. *Ibid.* II. 54 In like maner preperate Oripigment.

preparation (prɛpəˈreɪʃən), *sb.* [a. F. *préparation* (13–14th c. in Hatz.-Darm.), ad. L. *præparātiōn-em*, n. of action f. *præparāre* to PREPARE.]

1. a. The action of preparing, or condition of being prepared; previous putting or setting in order for any action or purpose; making or getting ready; fitting out, equipment.

1390 GOWER *Conf.* III. 133 After the preparacion Of due constellacion. **1530** PALSGR. 258/1 Preparation, *apareil.* **1531** ELYOT *Gov.* II. i, Nowe will I traicte of the preparation of suche personages, whan they firste receyue any great dignitie. **1601** SHAKS. *Twel. N.* III. iv. 245 Be yare in thy preparation, for thy assaylant is quick, skilfull, and deadly. **1711** SHAFTESB. *Charac.* (1737) III. Misc. v. iii. 328 They are in use..as well for Church-Service as Closet-Preparation. *a* **1880** GLADSTONE in *Might of Right* (U.S.) 206 It is in and by freedom only, that adequate preparation for fuller freedom can be made.

b. An act or proceeding that serves to prepare for something; usually in *pl.*: Things done by way of making ready *for* something; preparatory actions, proceedings, or measures.

1560 BIBLE (Genev.) *Prov.* xvi. 1 The preparations of the heart are in man: but the answer of the tongue is of the Lord. **1687** A. LOVELL tr. *Thevenot's Trav.* I. 233 On Thursday..we went to Boulac, to see the preparations that were making for the cutting of the Khalis. **1725** DE FOE *Voy. round World* (1840) 38, I..made mighty preparations for the feast. **1856** FROUDE *Hist. Eng.* (1858) II. vii. 143 The preparations for the marriage were commenced. *Mod.* A good life here is the best preparation for a future life.

c. The action of getting ready a lesson, speech, etc., by preliminary study; *spec.* the preparing of lessons, as a part of the routine of school work (in school slang abbreviated *prep*: see PREP 1).

1862 ['Used at Clifton College, from the beginning, the boys..calling it *Prep.*' (Bp. Percival).] **1875** A. R. HOPE *My Schoolboy Fr.* 181, I had to go downstairs to preparation. **1879** LUBBOCK *Addr. Pol. & Educ.* iii. 52 As regards..hours of work per week, I found that, including preparation they might be taken as not less than thirty eight. *Mod.* One of the Assistant Masters who took preparation in the Long Class-room. **1914** 'I. HAY' *Lighter Side School Life* iv. 114 A prefect..awarded both signallers fifty lines for creating a disturbance in Preparation. **1971** *Black Scholar* Jan. 64/1 (Advt.), Teaching load each semester is 7 to 8 hours with two preparations.

2. The action or special process of putting something into proper condition for use; preparatory treatment; working or making up; dressing and serving up (*of* food); composition, manufacture (*of* a chemical, medicinal, or other substance); drawing up (*of* a document).

1495 *Trevisa's Barth. De P.R.* VI. xx. n iv b/1 In meete preparacion [*Bodl. MS.* greiþing] gooth tofore and thenne comyth chewynge. **1615** CROOKE *Body of Man* 474 The Animall spirit is generated of the vitall spirit and the aire breathed in; whose preparation is in the labyrinthian webs of the small arteries, & in the vpper or forward ventricles. **1663** BOYLE *Usef. Exp. Nat. Philos.* II. App. 363 The Easinesse of the preparation..will much indear it [a medicine] to me. **1856** MILLER *Elem. Chem.* II. 625 Owing to the unstable character of the binoxide of hydrogen (HO_2), its preparation is attended with great difficulty. **1863** H. COX *Instit.* III. v. 657 The preparation..of Bills and Orders in Council. **1865** LIVINGSTONE *Zambesi* xxvi. 544 Another part of the work of women is in the preparation of beer. **1895** *Bookman* Oct. 15/1 A new edition is in active preparation.

3. *concr.* **a.** That which is prepared for any action, esp. for warfare; an equipment; a force or fleet fitted out for attack or defence; an armament. ? *Obs.*

1583–4 *Reg. Privy Council Scot.* III. 639 How far his Hienes munitioun houssis, ordinance, cairtis, and utheris preparationis of weir, ar demountid and decayit. **1599** SHAKS. *Hen. V*, II. iv. 18 Defences, Musters, Preparations Should be maintain'd, assembled, and collected. **1604** —— *Oth.* I. iii. 221 The Turke with a most mighty Preparation makes for Cyprus. **1781** GIBBON *Decl. & F.* xxxvi. (1869) II. 327 The preparations of three years were destroyed in a single day. **1781** JEFFERSON *Corr.* Wks. 1859 I. 303 Their preparation of boats is considerable.

b. *Spinning.* (See quot.)

1851 L. D. B. GORDON in *Art Jrnl. Illustr. Catal.* p. iv**/2, 160 pounds [of wool] constitute a preparation, which is confined to a given set of cards, drawers, and roving frames. One man superintends four such preparations.

†**4.** A personal capacity gained by previous instruction or training; an accomplishment. *Obs.*

1598 SHAKS. *Merry W.* II. ii. 237 You are a gentleman of excellent breeding, admirable discourse,..generally allow'd for your many war-like, court-like, and learned preparations.

†**5.** An introduction, preface (to a book, etc.).

1526 *Pilgr. Perf.* (W. de W. 1531) 1 The two first [books] be but as prefaces, preparacyons and declaracyons to the thyrde boke. **1646** *Suckling's Poems* Pref. 1 While Sucklin's name is in the forehead of this Book, these Poems can want no preparation.

6. *concr.* **a.** A substance specially prepared, or made up for its appropriate use or application, e.g. as food or medicine, or in the arts or sciences.

1646 SIR T. BROWNE *Pseud. Ep.* I. vii. 28 The Chymistes ..overmagnifying their preparations. **1732** ARBUTHNOT *Rules of Diet* in *Aliments*, etc. 263 Express'd Oils of ripe Vegetables, and all Preparations of such. **1828** SCOTT *F.M. Perth* xxviii, There were also various preparations of milk which..were eaten out of similar vessels. **1836** J. M. GULLY *Magendie's Formul.* (ed. 2) 25 The most commonly used preparations of opium. **1875** H. C. WOOD *Therap.* (1879) 17 A chapter on preparations, with directions for their manufacture. **1960** *Harper's Bazaar* Oct. 117/2 The..unfussy packaging of men's preparations. **1964** *New Statesman* 6 Mar. 354/1 In this country a doctor can prescribe from a list of about 5,000 'preparations', mostly mixtures of drugs. **1972** *Guardian* 7 Nov. 11/3 The Vichy preparations include complete ranges of cleansers, toners, moisturisers, night creams.

b. A specimen of a natural object specially prepared or treated for some scientific purpose; *esp.* an animal body or part of one prepared for dissection, or preserved for examination.

1753 CHAMBERS *Cycl. Supp.* s.v. *Insects*, Those [animals] which so elegantly eat away the fleshy parts from the injected anatomical preparations. *a* **1862** BUCKLE *Civiliz.* (1869) III. v. 433 It contained upwards of 10,000 preparations illustrative of the phenomena of nature.

7. The acts or observances preliminary to the celebration of the Jewish sabbath or other festival; hence *transf.* (= *day of preparation*) the day before the sabbath or other festival.

1557 N.T. (Genev.) *Matt.* xxvii. 62 The next day that folowed the day of Preparation *of the Sabbath* [μετὰ τὴν παρασκευήν; 1539 (Great) the daye of preparinge, **1611** the day of the preparation]. **1611** BIBLE *John* xix. 14 And it was the preparation of the Passeouer. *Ibid.* 31. **1625** T. GODWIN *Moses & Aaron* (1641) 99 In old time they proclaimed the Preparation with noise of Trumpets, or hornes.

8. In devotional use: The action of preparing for Holy Communion; a set of prayers used before a celebration by the officiant and his ministers, or by a person intending to communicate; also, the first part of the Communion Office.

1650 JER. TAYLOR *Holy Living* iv. §10 (*heading*) A Prayer of Preparation or Address to the Holy Sacrament. **1855** PROCTER *Hist. Bk. Com. Prayer* II. iii. 334 [The Office of Holy Communion] consists of three general divisions: the Preparation, the Office itself, and the service of Thanksgiving. The first part of the Preparation incites the whole congregation to the exercise of repentance, by the Lord's Prayer, the Collect for purity, and the Ten Commandments. **1880** SCUDAMORE in *Dict. Chr. Antiq.* 1060/2 This occurs in a prayer or preparation said before the priest places himself at the altar in the liturgy of St. James. **1885** *Before the Altar* 30 In using the prayers of preparation. **1890** BP. W. WALSHAM HOW *Holy Communion* I. 21 The following Prayer on the Passion may..be used during the preparation on Friday.

9. *Mus.* The preparing of a discord: see PREPARE *v.* 8 a. Opposed to *percussion* and *resolution.*

1727–41 CHAMBERS *Cycl.* s.v. *Discord*, These Discords are introduced into the harmony with due preparation, and must be succeeded by concords; which is commonly called the *resolution of the Discord.* **1869** OUSELEY *Conterp.* v. 24 The resolution of one dissonance may serve as the preparation for the next. **1877** STAINER *Harmony* vii. §91 The note of preparation is generally heard in the same part as the dissonant note.

10. *attrib.* and *Comb.*: (sense 1 c) *preparation book*; (sense 8) *preparation sermon*; **preparation day**: see 7.

1896 E. TURNER *Little Larrikin* viii. 76 The diminution of the pile of *preparation books. **1693** DRYDEN *Juvenal* vi. (1697) 145 But e're she sup, Swallows a swinging *Preparation-Cup; And then to clear her Stomach, spews it up. **1557** N.T. (Genev.) *John* xix. 42 There then layd they Iesus, because of the Iews *Preparation day [so 1611; 1539 (Great) the preparing of the Sabbath of the Iewes]. **1683** J. MASON *Hymn*, '*My Lord, my Love was crucified*', These are my preparation days. **1843** *Knickerbocker* XXI. 261 On the very day of the *preparation sermon at Tinnecum, a number of young persons were assembled.

Hence †**prepa'ration** *v.* (*Obs. nonce-wd.*) *intr.*, to make preparations.

1770 MME. D'ARBLAY *Early Diary* 10 Jan., All Monday we passed in preparationing for the evening.

preparationist (prɛpəˈreɪʃənɪst). *temporary.* [f. PREPARATION *sb.* + -IST.] One who favours naval and military preparedness.

1915 A. L. LOWELL in *World's Work* (N.Y.) XXX. 719/1 The preparationists..fix their attention primarily on the means of securing the safety of our own land from injury by war. *Ibid.*, To the preparationists..the suggestion of a league to enforce peace ought to appeal as a means of doing on an international scale the thing they are seeking to do for the United States.

preparative (prɪˈpærətɪv), *a.* and *sb.* [ME. *preparatif*, a. F. *préparatif*, *-ive* adj. and sb. (14–15th c. in Hatz.-Darm.), ad. med.L. *præparātīvus* (in Albertus Magnus (*a* 1255) and Aquinas): see PREPARE *v.* and -ATIVE.]

A. *adj.* **1.** Having the function or quality of preparing; serving as a preparation; preliminary, introductory; preparatory.

1530 PALSGR. 321/1 Preparatyfe, *preparatif.* **1607** R. C[AREW] tr. *Estienne's World of Wonders* Title-p., A Preparatiue Treatise to the Apologie for Herodotvs. **1646** SIR T. BROWNE *Pseud. Ep.* (1650) 206 After he had washed the Disciples feet, and performed the preparative civilities of suppers. **1806** *Med. Jrnl.* XV. 355 A subsequent statute is so particular as to prescribe the preparative qualification of the physician. **1872** BUSHNELL *Serm. Living Subj.* 58 Having a certain relationship and preparative concern.

b. *spec.* Of medicine, etc.: Serving to prepare the system for a course of treatment. Also applied to drink taken before a meal. ? *Obs.*

1612 WOODALL *Surg. Mate* Wks. (1653) 385 It were also fitting that there were prescribed..some preparative medicaments. **1747** tr. *Astruc's Fevers* 323 The preparative remedies of both are the same.

c. *preparative meeting* (in the Society of Friends): a local 'meeting' acting in matters of business or discipline, which is preparatory and subordinate to the 'monthly meeting'. (Cf. MEETING *vbl. sb.* 3 b.)

1711 in T. W. Marsh *Early Friends in Surrey & Sussex* i. (1886) 9 A Preparitive Meeting Recommended by a former meeting for preserving the Reputation of our proffession blameles is Practised at Reigate. **1831** *Weeks's Southern Quakers & Slavery* 300 Not a school..that is under the care of a committee of either monthly or preparative meeting.

d. quasi-*adv.* In preparation, by way of preparation: = PREPARATORY A. 1 b.

1632 TATHAM *Love Crowns the End* Prol., Our wit's the meat, Preparative to which we bid you eat. **1651** EVELYN *Diary* 31 Dec., The Holy Communion, which I received also, preparative of my journey. **1771** GOLDSM. *Hist. Eng.* III. 120 Such notes as she had taken preparative to her trial.

2. Used in or for preparing. *rare.*

1745 in *6th Rep. Dep. Kpr.* App. II. 122 Furnaces and preparative pans for boiling sea-water. **1785** *Hist. & Antiq. York* II. 376 [In the Assembly Rooms] To the Right and Left Hand are Preparative Rooms.

†3. *Gram.* = DESIDERATIVE *a.* 2. *Obs. rare*⁻¹.
1552 HULOET A aj, All verbes endynge in *Turio*, as *Amaturio*..and suche other, be as verbes preparatyues, hauynge desyre and entente to do that theyr..significations meane.

B. *sb.*

1. A preparative act, proceeding, or circumstance; something that prepares the way for something else; a preliminary; a preparation.
In first two quots., Something that inclines or disposes one to a course of action, an incentive.
c **1440** *Alphabet of Tales* 440 Hym had lyffer be deformyd ..þan daylie be a preparatyfe to oþer folk luste & syn. **1526** *Pilgr. Perf.* (W. de W. 1531) 76 b, These examples or preparatyues to vertues, put before. **1553** [see PREPARER 1 b]. *c* **1580** JEFFERIE *Bugbears* III. ii. in *Archiv Stud. Neu. Spr.* (1897), The grene sicknes, a preparatyve to the dropsie. **1624** CAPT. SMITH *Virginia* 193 Those are but as daies of hearing, and as preparatiues against their Courts. **1707** FREIND *Peterborow's Cond. Sp.* 183 The preparatives against France are so terrible in Italy. **1820** W. IRVING *Sketch Bk.*, *Voyage* §1 To an American visiting Europe, the long voyage he has to make is an excellent preparative. **1865** CARLYLE *Fredk. Gt.* XX. x. (1872) IX. 179 Levying the severe contributions; speeding all he can the manifold preparatives.

b. *Med.* Something administered before medicine, or before a course of treatment, to prepare the system for it. Often in fig. or allusive use. Also, a draught of liquor taken before a meal. ? *Obs.*
a **1500** MEDWALL *Nature* (Brandl) II. 1086 Lo, thys be preparatyfys most souerayn Agaynst thy sores. *a* **1591** H. SMITH *Lord's Supper* (1611) 82 Preparatiues are ministred alwaies before physicke. *a* **1656** BP. HALL *Rem. Wks.* (1660) 179 He that takes the preparative but refuses the medicine. **1744** BERKELEY *Siris* §2 Cold infusion of tar hath been used ..as a preservative or preparative against the smallpox. **1778** R. JAMES *Diss. Fevers* (ed. 8) 121, I have advised the Powder by way of alterative, or preparative.

†**2.** ? An omen, prognostic; a warning. *Obs.*
c **1430** LYDG. *Min. Poems* (Percy Soc.) 168 A preparatif that they shul never the. **1588** J. HARVEY *Disc. Probl.* 130 Some apparant significations, or preparatives, of a Tragedy insuing.

†**3.** An act or circumstance serving as an example for subsequent cases: = PRECEDENT *sb.* 2. *Sc. Obs.*
1565–6 *Reg. Privy Council Scot.* I. 432 Gif the King and Quenis Majesteis..sall permit this preparative of removing of kyndlie tenentis to cum in the Bordouris, it salbe far aganis the communweill. **1571–2** *Ibid.* II. 115 This salbe na preparative to uther the lyke thingis heiraftir. **1637–50** ROW *Hist. Kirk* (Wodrow) 237 Bidding them take heed that they made not a preparative of poore Andro Melvill.

4. A military or nautical signal sounded on a drum, bugle, etc., as an order to make ready.
1635 BARRIFFE *Mil. Discip.* xv. (1643) 376 The Drum begins to beat a preparative. **1688** R. HOLME *Armoury* III. xix. (Roxb.) 153/2 The drumer is to beat all maner of beats, as a Call,..a Preparative, a Battalia. **1847** *Infantry Man.* (1854) 40 At the close of the preparative, the first file will begin. **1875** BEDFORD *Sailor's Pocket Bk.* vii. (ed. 2) 268 When the preparative is made with this signal, the bowmen are to lay their oars in.

pre'paratively, *adv.* [f. prec. + -LY².] In a preparative manner; in the way of preparation.
1619 W. SCLATER *Exp. 1 Thess.* (1630) 71 Aliens, he thinks, may be won; preparatiuely at least, to thinke well of that doctrine. **1748** RICHARDSON *Clarissa* (1811) IV. xviii. 95 Can I be more preparatively condescending? **1870** DISRAELI *Lothair* xlvii, At noon..preparatively preceded by Mr. Putney Giles.., the guardians..waited on Lothair.

preparator ('prɛpəreɪtə(r)). [a. late L. *præparātor*, agent-n. f. *præparāre* to PREPARE.] One who makes a preparation; a preparer (of medicine, specimens, etc.).
1762 GOLDSM. *Cit. W.* lxviii, Next..is Doctor Walker, preparator of his own medicines. **1864** WEBSTER, *Preparator*, one who prepares beforehand, as subjects for dissection, specimens for preservation in collections, and the like. *Agassiz.* **1882** *Smithsonian Inst. Rep.* 103 In connection with the work of the preparators. **1884** *Science* 11 Apr. 443 While, however, the use of the photograph for outlines diminishes the labor of the artist about one-half, it increases that of the preparator. **1931** A. A. MORRIS *Digging in Yucatan* xvii. 267 A phenomenally skillful Japanese artist preparator who was then working for the American Museum of Natural History. **1937** *Nature* 2 Jan. 16/1 The [preservation] process was repeated once, and the bones were then ready for the preparators, who mended cracks and other deficiencies. **1938** *Times* 18 Jan. 15/5 In addition the Museum preparators have made use of skeletons already in the collection.

preparatorily (prɪ'pærətərɪlɪ), *adv.* [f. next + -LY².] In a preparatory manner; in or by way of preparation; as a preliminary (*to* an action).
a **1631** DONNE *Serm.* lviii. (1640) 583 Preparatorily in himself, and then declaratorily towards God. **1685** BAXTER *Paraphr. N.T.* Matt. iii. 11, I do but baptize you preparatorily with water to repentance. **1809** *Hist.* in *Ann. Reg.* 169/2 To submit certain motions, preparatorily to a measure which he had had..in contemplation. **1886** *Nature* 8 Apr. 540/1 When we get the chromosphere agitated preparatorily to one of these tremendous outbursts.

preparatory (prɪ'pærətərɪ), *a.* and *sb.* [ad. med.L. *præparātōrius* (Digest), f. *præparātor* a preparer: see -ORY². In quot. 1413, prob. ad. F. *préparatoire* (1322 in Hatz.-Darm.).]

A. *adj.* **1. a.** That prepares or serves to prepare for something following; preliminary, introductory.
1413 *Pilgr. Sowle* (Caxton 1483) v. viii. 99 This feste was but as an assaye and preparatory as an exampler to these other feestes. **1649** JER. TAYLOR *Gt. Exemp.* III. Ad Sect. xv, Considerations of some preparatory accidents before the entrance of Jesus into his Passion. **1686** GOAD *Celest. Bodies* II. i. 152 The Sun and Moon alone..cannot be the Causes preparatory or determinant of a Showre. **1745** J. MASON *Self Knowl.* I. viii. (1853) 61 The previous steps and preparatory Circumstances. **1838** DICKENS *Nich. Nick.* xv, [He] had indeed swallowed a preparatory glass of punch. **1868** OUSELEY *Harmony* iv. (1875) 61 The leading note would be simply a preparatory note, introducing a Scale of the compass of a hexachord.

b. quasi-*adv.* = PREPARATORILY. Const. *to.*
1649 EVELYN *Diary* 10 June, I receiv'd the Blessed Sacrament preparatory to my journey. **1810** COLERIDGE *Lett., to T. Poole* (1895) 557, I will, preparatory to writing.., consider whether it can be treated popularly. **1877** LADY BRASSEY *Voy. Sunbeam* xiv. (1878) 240 They were weighing it preparatory to sending it to town.

2. a. *U.K.* Applied to a junior school in which pupils are prepared for a higher school or college. *U.S.*, applied to a (usu. private) school in which pupils are prepared for college entrance.
1822 M. EDGEWORTH *Let.* 23 Jan. (1971) 328, I have asked all your questions my dear mother about the preparatory school for Pakenham... Mr. Malthus and Dr. Batten declared that they should prefer having a boy sent to them from the Charter-House to having him from any lesser preparatory school. **1828** E. IRVING *Last Days* 87 The children of the rich are sent to preparatory schools. **1848** THACKERAY *Bk. Snobs* v, The Reverend Otto Rose, D.D., Principal of the Preparatory Academy for young noblemen and gentlemen,..took this little Lord in hand. **1848** *Indiana Gen. Assembly Doc.* (1849) II. 279 Connected with the Institution is a flourishing Grammar School, which serves the double purpose of a Normal School and a Preparatory Department. **1851** C. CIST *Sk. Cincinnati in 1851* iii. 69 The Classes in the course of study in the Preparatory Department, are divided among the Adjunct Professors of Mathematics and Languages and the Professor of Modern Languages. **1865** DICKENS *Mut. Fr.* II. i, The streets being for pupils of his degree the great Preparatory Establishment in which very much that is never unlearned is learned without and before book. **1879** *Scribner's Monthly* Dec. 207 The Johns Hopkins is seeking..to penetrate downward into the preparatory schools. **1903** *World's Work* (N.Y.) Sept. 3884/1 The preparatory school..take[s] boys from twelve to fourteen years of age to fit them in from three to six years for entrance to our best colleges. *a* **1909** *Mod.* Scholarships won by pupils of the Oxford Preparatory School. **1924** *Granta* 25 Apr. 361/2 At the age of eight, he arrived at his Preparatory School, 'The Wick', in Sussex. **1949** *Manch. Guardian Weekly* 20 Jan. 5/2 The son of a bishop, he went through a fashionable preparatory (that is, public) school. **1954** A. S. C. Ross in *Neuphilol. Mitt.* LV. 26 School-boys at their preparatory school..should be addressed as *Master*. **1963** [see *junior college* s.v. JUNIOR *a.* (*sb.*) 5]. **1969** *Listener* 9 Jan. 41/3 Such a young man..can often command a tiny handout to tide him over by entering the profession of preparatory schoolmaster, purely as a temporary measure. **1972** *Lebende Sprachen* XVII. 35/2 US preparatory school—BE private secondary school. **1976** *Southern Even. Echo* (Southhampton) (Advt. Suppl.) 6 Nov. 7/6 Resident matron required for January for Boys' Preparatory School.

b. *U.S.* Applied to a scholar at a preparatory school, or engaged in a preparatory course of study.

B. *sb.*

1. a. = PREPARATIVE B. 1. Now *rare* or *Obs.*
1620 BRENT tr. *Sarpi's Counc. Trent* v. 420 He..would bee sure of the necessary preparatories, that the desired fruit might succeede. **1691** NORRIS *Pract. Disc.* 196 The best Preparatory for Heaven. **1785** TRUSLER *Mod. Times* I. 105 To a villain it was a good preparatory to his arraignment at the Old Bailey. **1824** SOUTHEY *Bk. of Ch.* (1841) 321 After these preparatories the fiery process began.

b. = PREPARATIVE B. 1 b. ? *Obs.*
1756 C. LUCAS *Ess. Waters* III. 164 The simplest and best preparatory..is..water.

2. Short for *preparatory school*: see A. 2.
1907 *Athenæum* 20 Apr. 472/1 He ought to have attacked ..the 'preparatories' where the little dears have Turkey carpets for their small feet and port for their small stomachs.

†**pre'parature.** *Obs. rare.* [a. obs. F. *preparature* (16th c. in Godef.), or ad. late L. *præparātūra*, f. *præparāre* to PREPARE: see -URE.] The action or process of preparing; preparation.
1563 FOXE *A. & M.* 1549/2 They..partly detested and abhorred thextreme cruelty of the Commissioners.., and partlye laughed at theyr folly in making such preparature.

†**pre-'pardon.** *Obs. rare.* Also 7 præ-. [f. PRE- A. 2 + PARDON *sb.*] Pardon beforehand; pardon for an offence before it is committed.
1625 DONNE *Serm.* 3 Apr. 38 A Præ-pardon, by way of Dispensation, in wisedom before a Lawe bee broken, is not a Destroying of this foundation. **1642** CHAS. I *Declar.* 12 *Aug.* 15 With a prepardon for whatsoever they should do under colour of these Offices.

pre'pare, *sb.* [f. PREPARE *v.*]

1. The act of preparing; preparation. *Obs.* or *dial.*
1535 STEWART *Cron. Scot.* (Rolls) II. 24 Beseikand him that he wald mak prepair In Albione sen he wes prince and air. *a* **1548** HALL *Chron.*, *Hen. VIII* 17 b, Shortly such prepare should be made, that he should see and proue, that [etc.]. **1593** SHAKS. *3 Hen. VI*, IV. i. 131. **1594** T. BEDINGFIELD tr. *Machiavelli's Florentine Hist.* (1595) 73 You see the prepare of your adversaries. **1633** EARL MANCH. *Al Mondo* (1636) 112 Delay not thy prepare for death. *a* **1810** TANNAHILL *Meg o' the Glen* Poems (1846) 143 Meg o' the glen set aff to the fair, Wi' ruffles, an' ribbons, an' meikle prepare.

2. A substance used to prepare stuff for a dye.
1874 W. CROOKES *Dyeing & Calico-print.* II. vii. 542 As 'prepares' for steam-colours, all the antimonial compounds hitherto tried have shown themselves inferior to tin. **1893** THORPE *Dict. App. Chem.* III. 57/1 It is also used as a 'prepare' for steam colours in calico-printing.

prepare (prɪ'pɛə(r)), *v.* Also (chiefly *Sc.*) 6 præpare, prepayre, 6–8 prepair. [a. F. *préparer* (14–15th c. in Hatz.-Darm.), ad. L. *præparāre* to make ready beforehand, prepare, f. *præ*, PRE- A. 1 + *parāre* to make ready.]
As in other verbs denoting a process (e.g. *bake, build, cook, make*) the construction *is* or *was preparing* (†*in* or *a-preparing*, = *in preparation*) to form progressive tenses of the passive voice = *is* or *was being prepared*, was very common in the 17th and 18th c., and is still in colloquial use. (See PREPARING *vbl. sb.*, and -ING².)

1. a. *trans.* To put beforehand into a suitable condition for some action; to set in order previously for some purpose; to get ready, make ready, put in readiness; to fit out, equip.
1466 in *Archæologia* (1887) L. 1. 49 Many moo small thingis as syngyng and Redyng and preparing the bookis and Turnyng theroff to the dyvine service afore it begyne. **1526** TINDALE *Luke* iii. 4 The voyce off a cryar in wyldernes, prepare the waye off the lorde, make hys pathes straight. **1605** SHAKS. *Lear* I. iv. 280 Prepare my Horses. **1616** T. GATAKER in *Ussher's Lett.* (1686) 37, I should be glad to hear ..that the second part..were preparing, or fully prepared for the Press. **1703** MAUNDRELL *Journ. Jerus.* (1732) 74 Anointed and prepair'd for the Burial. **1793** SMEATON *Edystone L.* §241 While the center plug of this course was preparing to be fixed. **1846** J. BAXTER *Libr. Pract. Agric.* (ed. 4) II. 326 In choosing and preparing the bud, fix on one seated at about the middle of a healthy shoot of the midsummer growth.

b. To bring into a state of mental or spiritual readiness; to incline or dispose beforehand; to make mentally ready or fit for something.
1526 *Pilgr. Perf.* (W. de W. 1531) 162 b, Prepare our hertes to god, makyng inuocacyon for grace. **1561** DAUS tr. *Bullinger on Apoc.* (1573) 217 These thynges..prepare also the reader and hearer to the treatise now followyng. **1667** MILTON *P.L.* XI. 555 And now prepare thee for another sight. *a* **1703** BURKITT *On N.T.* Mark xiv. 72 His sinful equivocation prepared him for a downright denial. **1898** EDNA LYALL *Hope the Hermit* xxx, You do not understand. .. I am trying to prepare you... He is dead.

c. To get ready by previous study, as a speech or sermon for delivery, a piece for recitation, a lesson for repetition or inspection; to 'get up'. Also *absol.* (Sometimes passing into 7 b.)
1683 WOOD *Life* 21 May (O.H.S.) III. 53 Peter Lancaster, a student of Civill Law, read a copie of English verses (for they had not time enough given to prepare). **1886** G. MACDONALD *Ann. Q. Neighb.* xiii, In this manner I prepared almost all my sermons that summer. *Mod.* The boys are preparing their lessons. The speech was not well prepared.

d. To fit or get ready (a person) by preliminary instruction or training (*for* college, an examination, etc.).
1891 *Spectator* 5 Dec. 817 Advt., Boys from 8 to 14 years of age are prepared for the Public Schools. **1900** *Academy* 15 Sept. 216/2 For ten years he has 'prepared' (*Anglice*, crammed) pupils for Army and other examinations.

e. *to be prepared*: to be in a state of readiness, ready; to be mentally ready, inclined, disposed (*for*, †*to* a thing); to be in a condition or position *to do* something. Also in extended sense, to be willing or determined *to do* something. ***be prepared***, the motto of the Scout and Guide organizations.
1579 *Poore Knights Palace* C iij b, Who caryed forth the Amner's hutch unto the Porters gate, And freely gave unto the poore which were preparde therat. **1591** SHAKS. *1 Hen. VI*, I. ii. 98, I am prepar'd: here is my keen-edg'd Sword. **1687** A. LOVELL tr. *Thevenot's Trav.* I. 48 The rest who are washed and prepared to pray. **1790** WASHINGTON *Sp. to both Ho. Congress* 8 Jan., To be prepared for war is one of the most effectual ways of preserving peace. **1895** *Pall Mall G.* 8 Oct. 1/3 He was prepared to deal with every..question on its merits. **1902** G. B. SHAW *Mrs Warren's Profession* Pref. p. ix, Nor am I prepared to accept the verdict of the medical gentlemen who would compulsorily sanitate and register Mrs Warren. **1908** R. S. S. BADEN-POWELL *Scouting for Boys* I. 20 The badge..of the first class scout consists of a brass arrow head with the motto on it '*be prepared*'. *Ibid.* 48 The scouts' motto is founded on my initials, it is: *be prepared. Ibid.* 49 A scout..must Be Prepared at any time to save life. **1939** G. B. SHAW *Geneva* I. 13, I came here to place it before a body of persons of European distinction. I am not prepared to discuss it with an irresponsible young woman. **1948** E. GOWERS *Plain Words* vi. 40 The recipient of a letter may feel better..if he is told that the Minister 'is not prepared to approve' than he would have done if the letter had said 'the Minister does not approve'. *Ibid.* 41 'The Board have examined your application and they are prepared to allocate 60 coupons for this production. I am accordingly to enclose this number of coupons.'.. *Prepared to allocate* should be *have allocated*. Since the coupons are enclosed, the preparatory stage is clearly over. **1961** NEW ENG. BIBLE *Acts* x. 47 Is anyone prepared to withhold the water for baptism from these persons? **1963** A. CHRISTIE *Clocks* xxvii. 229 What I say to you is: 'Be prepared.' And I don't mean it in the Boy Scout sense. **1972** J. POYER *Chinese Agenda* (1973) xiv. 190 It's better to be prepared.. that's what they taught us in the Boy Scouts. **1976** *Daily Tel.* 20 July 2/1 The Government was not prepared to fight for realistic exclusive zones for British fishermen.

2. *intr.* for *refl.* To put oneself, or things, in readiness; to get ready, make preparation.

1509 HAWES *Past. Pleas.* xi. (Percy Soc.) 43 Nothyng prepensyng how they dyd prepare To scourge them selfe and bryng them in a snare. **1599** SHAKS. *Hen. V*, v. ii. 398 Prepare we for our Marriage. **1611** BIBLE *Amos* iv. 12 Prepare to meete thy God, O Israel. **1634** SIR T. HERBERT *Trav.* 86 When they prepare to prayer. **1741** RICHARDSON *Pamela* (1824) I. xlix. 377 A prudent mind will be always preparing till prepared. **1791** MRS. RADCLIFFE *Rom. Forest* iv, And bade her prepare to quit the abbey. **1889** *Spectator* 19 Oct., The war against which he..incessantly prepares. **1906** D. W. FORREST *Author. Chr.* III. ii. 122 He [God] has prepared from of old for the emergencies of every passing hour.

†**3.** *refl.* and *intr.* To make preparation for a journey; to get ready to go (*to, into*, etc. a place); hence, to go, repair. *Obs.*

1510 *Virgilius* (1812) 1 He raysed a great armey..and prepared hym towarde the towne. **1570** FOXE *A. & M.* (ed. 2) 377/2 Vnles he would prepare hymselfe into Asia. *c* **1585** PEELE *Sir Clyomon* Wks. (Rtldg.) 506/2 To Denmark will I straight prepare. *a* **1662** HEYLIN *Hist. Presbyt.* v. (1670) 220 With these Instructions he prepares to the Court of Scotland. **1784** R. BAGE *Barham Downs* II. 250 We are actually preparing for England.

4. a. *trans.* To get or have in readiness beforehand; to provide, furnish. Now *arch.* or merged in 1.

1535 COVERDALE *Ps.* lxiv. [lxv.] 9 Thou preparest man his corne [**1611** Thou preparest them corne; **1885** *R.V.* Thou providest them corn]. **1697** DRYDEN *Virg. Georg.* I. 247 The Sled, the Tumbril, Hurdles and the Flail... These all must be prepar'd, if Ploughmen hope The promis'd Blessing of a Bounteous Crop. **1859** TENNYSON *Lancelot & Elaine* 1115 Let there be prepared a chariot-bier To take me to the river, and a barge..clothed in black.

†**b.** With inverted construction: To provide (oneself) preparatorily *with* something. *Obs. rare.*

1625 PURCHAS *Pilgrims* VII. vii. §5. 1167 To prepare our selues with things necessarie for the Warre, especially of Powder.

5. To make ready (food, a meal) for eating; to cook or dress and serve up.

1490 CAXTON *Eneydos* xxiii. 85 She..prepared to hym his mete, alle after his complexion. **1526** TINDALE *Luke* xxii. 8 Goo and prepare vs the ester lambe, that we maye eate. **1566** PAINTER *Pal. Pleas.* II. 498 During the time that supper was preparyng. **1671** MILTON *P.R.* II. 273 He found his Supper on the coals prepar'd. **1755** AMORY *Mem.* (1766) II. 60 Our repast was preparing. **1794** MRS. RADCLIFFE *Myst. Udolpho* iv, They were preparing their supper. **1860** TYNDALL *Glac.* I. xi. 72 Breakfast was soon prepared.

6. To bring into proper state for use by some special or technical process; to work up; to dress.

In quot. 1722, To put in proper order, make tidy.

1722 DE FOE *Plague* (1756) 53 That every Householder do cause the Street to be daily prepared before his Door. **1753** CHAMBERS *Cycl. Supp.* s.v. *Insects*, Skeletons..have been prepared by burying them in an ant-hill. **1825** J. NICHOLSON *Operat. Mechanic* 484 Pure clay..is always opaque, and the flint..always transparent; but both are prepared previously to being used. **1879** *Cassell's Techn. Educ.* IV. 90/1 Sheep-skins are sometimes prepared to imitate morocco.

7. a. To make, produce, or form for some purpose; in mod. use *esp.* 'to make by regular process' (J.), to manufacture, to make or compound (a chemical product, a medicinal or other 'preparation', etc.).

1535 COVERDALE *Ps.* xciv. [xcv.] 5 The see is his for he made it, and his hondes prepared the drie londe. **1567** *Gude & Godlie B.* (S.T.S.) 51 Prepair thy creddill in my Spreit. **1712** BLACKMORE *Creation* II. 77 In vain the Author had the Eye prepar'd With so much Skill, had not the Light appear'd. **1799** G. SMITH *Laboratory* I. 34 The stars and sparks..are prepared in the following manner. **1809** *Med. Jrnl.* XXI. 356, I suggested to the apothecary..to prepare some pills of five grains each. **1856** MILLER *Elem. Chem.* II. 451 The most convenient methods of preparing nitrogen are based upon the removal of oxygen from atmospheric air. **1865-8** WATTS *Dict. Chem.* III. 193 Hydrogen prepared by dissolving zinc or iron in sulphuric acid. **1875** *Ure's Dict. Arts* II. 914 Writing Ink may be..prepared in many different ways.

b. To compose and write out in proper form for use; to draw up (a writing or document).

1797 MRS. RADCLIFFE *Italian* xi. Do you prepare a few lines to acquaint Vivaldi with your consent to his proposal. **1818** CRUISE *Digest* (ed. 2) IV. 271 The deed of settlement having been prepared and engrossed by the direction of Lord Coventry. **1854** J. S. C. ABBOT *Napoleon* (1855) I. xxxvii. 577 A code is preparing for the regulation of commerce. *a* **1873** WILBERFORCE *Ch. & Empires* (1874) 306 The Bulls were being prepared as speedily as was possible.

8. *Mus.* **a.** To lead up to (a discord) by sounding the dissonant note in it as a consonant note in the preceding chord. **b.** To lead up to (a shake or other grace) by a preliminary note, turn, etc.

1727-41 CHAMBERS *Cycl.* s.v. *Discord*, The Discord is prepared by subsisting first in the harmony in quality of a concord. **1869** OUSELEY *Counterp.* v. 24 Always let the dissonant note be heard as a concord in the preceding chord. This is called preparing it.

prepared (prɪˈpɛəd, *poet.* prɪˈpɛərɪd), *ppl. a.* [f. prec. + -ED[1].] **a.** Made ready, got ready, fitted or put in order beforehand for something.

For *to be prepared* in reference to persons see prec. 1 e.

1526 *Pilgr. Perf.* (W. de W. 1531) 73 In a prepared or disposed soule he maketh yᵉ fyrst beame of loue to shyne. **1574** HELLOWES *Gueuara's Fam. Ep.* 11 To resist a prepared vice. **1606** SHAKS. *Ant. & Cl.* IV. xii. 38 Let Patient Octauia plough thy visage vp With her prepared nailes. **1783** BURKE *Sp. Fox's E. Ind. Bill* Wks. IV. 32 Even in the prepared soil of a general pacification. **1882** J. PARKER *Apost. Life* I. 74 A prepared pulpit should be balanced by a prepared pew.

b. Treated for some purpose by a special process; made or compounded by a special process: see PREPARE *v.* 6, 7. spec. ***prepared core*** Archæol. (see CORE *sb.*[1] 5), ***food, piano*** (see quot. 1960).

1663 BOYLE *Usef. Exp. Nat. Philos.* II. i. 23 Taking out the more corruptible parts, and stuffing their prepar'd Skins with any convenient Matter. **1694** SALMON *Bate's Dispens.* (1713) 437/2 The former prepared Pouder of our Author. **1849** NOAD *Electricity* (ed. 3) 457 The nerve of a prepared frog's leg was laid on the bared muscle of the thigh of a living rabbit. **1918** A. HUXLEY *Let.* 12 Aug. (1969) 160 Thirty-two quintals of sugar and prepared foods. **1946** *Mod. Music* Summer 205 *Four Sonatas* for prepared piano by John Cage were also heard. **1952** *Musical Q.* XXXVIII. 124 Cage's pieces for what he calls the 'prepared piano' offer an array of tightly organized little sounds of many colors. **1959** J. D. CLARK *Prehist. S. Afr.* vi. 142 The characteristic technique of the Middle Stone Age times is the prepared core and specially prepared flake with thin section and faceted butt. *Ibid.* 157 The same basic prepared-core technique. **1960** *20th Cent.* Apr. 348 Cage, an American, is the originator of the 'prepared piano',..in which the pitch and timbre of certain notes are altered by attaching..metal, rubber, wood, etc., to the strings at various distances from the point at which the hammer strikes. **1964** H. HODGES *Artifacts* vii. 102 The core may be very carefully flaked in preparation so that ultimately one final blow will detach a flake tool of the required shape, and these prepared cores are generally the result of hammer, punch or pressure flaking. **1972** *Listener* 7 Sept. 292/3 Further rapid growth [is] expected in the prepared-foods trade. **1977** *Belfast Tel.* 24 Jan. 9/3 The same professionalism marked John Cage's sonata for prepared piano. For this another small grand piano had been fitted out in advance with an assortment of bolts, nuts and rubber wedges according to a carefully specified plan.

c. *Mus.* Of a discord, or a shake, etc.: see PREPARE *v.* 8.

1867 MACFARREN *Harmony* (1892) 76 A prepared 7th may be added to the chord of the dissonant 5th. **1898** STAINER & BARRETT *Dict. Mus. Terms* 403/2 A shake which commences with a turn is called a prepared shake.

preparedly (prɪˈpɛərɪdlɪ), *adv.* [f. prec. + -LY[2].] In a prepared manner or condition; in a state of readiness.

1606 SHAKS. *Ant. & Cl.* v. i. 55 That she preparedly may frame her selfe To' th' way shee's forc'd too. **1647** TRAPP *Comm. 1 Cor.* xi. 28 But can they..at that age..examine themselves, and receive preparedly?

preparedness (prɪˈpɛərd-, prɪˈpɛərɪdnɪs). [f. as prec. + -NESS.] The state or condition of being prepared; readiness.

1590 GREENWOOD *Answ. Def. Read Prayers* 25 Except you can make all assemblies..in the same preparednes to aske,.. you can make no stinted prayers for them. **1654** H. L'ESTRANGE *Chas. I* (1655) 265 Then..having prayed awhile, he gave the Executioner the token of his preparednesse, whereat the Heads-man..severed his head from his body. **1736** BOLINGBROKE *Patriot.* (1749) 58 Information, knowledge, and a certain constant preparedness for all the events that may arise. **1849** MACAULAY *Hist. Eng.* x. II. 564 Before two the capital wore a face of stern preparedness which might well have daunted a real enemy.

†**pre'parement.** *Obs. rare.* [f. PREPARE *v.* + -MENT, or ad. obs. F. *preparement* (15–17th c. Godef.).] The action of preparing; preparation.

1627 FELTHAM *Resolves* I. [II.] xl. 126 The souldier that dares not fight affoords the enemy too much advantage; for his preparement, both for directing his souldiers, plotting his stratagems [etc.].

preparer (prɪˈpɛərə(r)). [f. as prec. + -ER[1].]

1. One who or that which prepares.

1548 UDALL *Erasm. Par. Luke* iii. 32 b, I am no more but a preparer of you to a baptisme of more efficacie and vertue. **1636** PRYNNE *Remonstr. agst. Shipmoney* 11 The King hath not before this time given no wages to the said Preparers, or Counties, nor Souldiers whom they have brought. **1738** WARBURTON *Div. Legat.* II. II. App. 28 The Preparer of the Way to pure Pagan Philosophy. *a* **1890** J. BROWN *Serm.* (1892) 100 For that day of wrath, that day of hope there was to come a preparer.

b. *spec.* One who prepares, dresses, or makes up (food, medicine, manufactured articles, etc.): see PREPARE *v.* 5–7.

1553 *Primer* in *Liturgies Edw. VI* (Parker Soc.) 377 In thy faithful prayers remember Thomas Cottesforde the preparer of this preparative. *a* **1639** SPOTTISWOOD *Hist. Ch. Scot.* VII. (1677) 525 The preparers of the poison.. confessed every thing. **1753** *Act 26 Geo. II*, c. 20 §2 The Growers, Preparers and Spinners of such Flax. **1762** tr. *Busching's Syst. Geog.* V. 441 Cloth and stuff-makers, cloth-shearers and preparers. **1891** *Labour Commission* Gloss., *Preparers*, persons employed at the drawing and roving frames in preparing the wool previous to spinning: term used locally at Leicester.

2. A thing used for preparing; †*spec.* a medicine administered preliminarily to a course of treatment (= PREPARATIVE B. 1 b).

1610 MARKHAM *Masterp.* I. xciii. 182 Preparatiues or preparers of the body to entertaine more stronger medicines. **1632** tr. *Bruel's Praxis Med.* 60 Preparers... Wormwood and Apples. **1707** MORTIMER *Husb.* (1721) I. 157 Rape and Cole-Seed..'Tis a very good Preparer of Land for Barley or Wheat.

preparing (prɪˈpɛərɪŋ), *vbl. sb.* [f. as prec. + -ING[1].] The action of the verb PREPARE; preparation. (With quot. 1535 cf. PREPARATION 3.)

1497 *Naval Acc. Hen. VII* (1896) 141 The preparing and reparacion with other necessaries for the Kynges..shippe. **1535** COVERDALE *Judith* vii. 2 There were..two & twentie thousande horsmen, besyde the preparynge [WYCLIF redi cumpanyes] of them yᵗ were wonne. **1586** D. ROWLAND *Lazarillo* II. (1672) 75 Whilst dinner was in preparing, they sported with the Gentlewoman. *a* **1648** LD. HERBERT *Hen. VIII* (1683) 52 While these things were in preparing, Mary the French Queen was..Crowned in St. Denis. **1748** *Anson's Voy.* III. iii. 325 The killing and preparing of provisions. **1865** DICKENS *Mut. Fr.* II. i, My sister..wants no preparing.

b. *attrib.* and *Comb.*, as ***preparing-box, -table***.

1884 W. S. B. MᶜLAREN *Spinning* (ed. 2) 81 This is..not unlike Clough's preparing-boxes, which first partially open the wool by slow-going fallers, before the quicker fallers. *c* **1890** W. H. CASMEY *Ventilation* 10 The fresh air..passes over the preparing machinery, carrying any little dust away with it over the cards to the fans. **1894** ELIZ. L. BANKS *Camp. Curiosity* 175, I was sent to the 'preparing-table' to sprinkle and fold some print dresses. Agnes, the head preparer, taught me.

pre'paring, *ppl. a.* [f. as prec. + -ING[2].] That prepares; preparatory; preliminary.

†*preparing vessels* (Physiol.), a rendering of L. *præparantia vasa*, applied to the blood-vessels which supply a gland and 'prepare' its secretion, as the spermatic arteries.

1615 J. STEPHENS *Ess. & Char., Worthy Poet* (1857) 145 That mountebanks preparing oyle which kept his hands unscalded. **1667** N. FAIRFAX in *Phil. Trans.* II. 549 The Preparing Vessels arise on the right side, out of the Cava. **1675** COTTON *Scoffer Scoft* 35 After a few preparing rings, He makes his stoop. **1693** tr. *Blancard's Phys. Dict.* (ed. 2), *Præparantia vasa*, the preparing Vessels, are Veins and Arteries which go to the Testicles and Epididymes. **1864** 'E. WETHERELL' *Old Helmet* I. i. 21 The other figures, the dark walls and ivy, the servants and the preparing collation, were only a rich mosaic of background for those two.

Hence **pre'paringly** *adv.*, in the way of preparation, preparatorily.

1816 L. HUNT *Rimini* IV. 244 'A noble word', exclaimed the prince, and smote Preparingly on earth his firming foot.

preparoccipital, -patellar: see PRE- B. 3.

pre-paroxysmal: see PRE- B. 1 d.

pre-part: see PRE- A. 2.

pre-partum (priːˈpɑːtəm), *a.* [L. phr., 'before birth', used *attrib.*] = ANTE-PARTUM *a.*

1858 R. BARNES *Physiol. & Treatm. Placenta Prævia* ii. 71, I believe these considerations present a rational explanation of a multitude of cases of præ-partum hæmorrhage, [etc.]. **1950** *Amer. Jrnl. Obstetr. & Gynecol.* LIX. 1116 In cases of prepartum bleeding, cesarean section to facilitate abdominal exploration was practically always necessary. **1978** J. UPDIKE *Coup* (1979) v. 186 'My goodness, you're touchy these days.' 'Pre-partum blues,' he suggested.

prepatency, -patent, -pathological, -pausal: see PRE- B. 1.

pre-pause: see PRE- B. 2 a.

prepay (priːˈpeɪ), *v.* [f. PRE- A. 1 + PAY *v.*[1] Cf. OF. *prepayer*, 1305 in Godef.] *trans.* To pay (a charge) beforehand; *esp.* to pay (the postage of a letter or parcel) before dispatching it (as by affixing a postage stamp). Also *transf.* with the letter, etc., as object.

1839 *Treasury Minute* 12 Nov. (L.), All letters and packets exceeding the weight of one ounce to be prepaid, and delivered in at the window; if not so prepaid, and delivered, to be charged double postage. **1858** R. S. SURTEES *Ask Mamma* lxxviii, Pre-paying a letter..used to be thought little short of an insult. **1899** A. E. W. MASON *Miranda of Balcony* xv. 216 He wires me..and prepays the reply. *a* **1908** *Mod.* The school fees must be prepaid. The subscription for each half-year must be prepaid. The parcel was sent by passenger-train, carriage prepaid. **1973** *Philadelphia Inquirer* (Today Suppl.) 7 Oct. 42/2 He'll be in to prepay.

Hence **pre'paid** *ppl. a.* (also as *sb.* = prepaid letter or parcel); **pre'payable** *a.*, that may or must be prepaid; **pre'payment**, the act of prepaying, payment in advance; also *attrib.*

1854 FONBLANQUE in *Life* (1874) vi. 508 In a lecture on education, Dr. Whewell..cites the word **prepaid*, now in common and barbarous use... 'Prepaid' was introduced with the penny postage. **1885** *Act 48 & 49 Vict.* c. 54 §15 Every notice..sent through the post in a prepaid registered letter. **1926** C. CONNOLLY *Let.* Sept. in *Romantic Friendship* (1975) 172, I..sent a prepaid wire. **1977** *Modern Railways* Dec. 465/2 Urgent introduction of a wide-ranging system of pre-paid bus tickets. **1899** *Westm. Gaz.* 16 Jan. 4/1 Letters sent from this country to her Majesty's ships in any part of the world are now *prepayable at the rate of 1*d.* per half ounce. **1838** in *Rep. Sel. Comm. Postage* 62 The distinctive feature of your [R. Hill's] plan..is the compulsory *pre-payment and one rate of postage. **1876** GRANT *Burgh. Sch. Scotl.* II. xiii. 469 Some parents refused prepayment [of school fees]. **1899** *Westm. Gaz.* 28 Sept. 9/1 The pioneer of the prepayment gas-meter. **1903** *Rep. West Ham Gas Co.*, The Prepayment Meter System of Supply has been put in operation. **1906** Prepayment [see *coin-box*]. **1970** *Which?* Mar. 90/1 Fire meters had defective prepayment mechanisms. **1977** *Wandsworth Borough News* 16 Sept. 14/3 Cash from pre-payment meters, believed to be £107, was stolen from the home.

pre-peduncle, -cular, -culate, prepelvisternal, -num: see PRE- A. 4.

prepend (prɪ'pɛnd), *v. rare.* [f. PRE- A. 1 + L. *pendĕre* to weigh.] *trans.* To weigh mentally, ponder, consider; to premeditate. (But app. often used by confusion for PERPEND.)
a **1568** WEDDERBURN in *Bannatyne Poems* (Hunter. Cl.) 839 And als ye sowld prepend bayth day and houris, To grit mischeif, misery and neid, Fra paramouris dois evir mair succeid. **1621** BOLTON *Stat. Irel.* 128 (Act 28 Hen. VIII), The kings majestie..prepending and waying..how much it doth more conferre to the induction of rude and ignorant people to the knowledge of Almightie God. **1890** *Scots Observer* 4 Jan. 179 There are still amongst us people who prepend the Sphinx-torpedo question.
Hence **pre'pended** *ppl. a.*, premeditated; = PREPENSE *a.* (*nonce-use.*)
1831 LAMB *Elia* Ser. II. *Newspapers* 35 *Years Ago*, To get up, moreover, to make jokes with malice prepended.

†**pre'pendent,** *a.* (*sb.*) *Obs.* [ad. L. *præpendent-em*, pr. pple. of *præpendē-re* to hang down in front, f. *præ*, PRE- A. 4 + *pendēre* to hang: cf. PENDENT.] **A.** *adj.* Hanging down in front; overhanging. **B.** *sb.* The male member.
1592 R. D. *Hypnerotomachia* 20 b, Upon the which they placed a chapter with prependent folding. **1593** NASHE *Christ's T.* Wks. (Grosart) IV. 103 Like an ouer-hanging Rocke eaten on with the tyde,..so did theyr prependant breast-bones imminent-ouercanopy theyr bellies. **1610** HEALEY *St. Aug. Citie of God* 252 Priapus..was expelled from Lampsacum..for the hugeness of his pre-pendent.

‖**prepenna** (priː'pɛnə). *Ornith.* Pl. -æ. [mod.L., f. *præ*, PRE- A. 2 + *penna* feather.] A neossoptile or primitive feather of a bird.
1901 *Ibis* Apr. 343 In Apteryx the first definite feathers do not thrust out the prepennæ.

prepense (priː'pɛns), *a.* [Substituted for earlier *prepenst*, PREPENSED (orig. *purpensed*, OF. *purpense*), either by simple phonetic reduction, or after F. pa. pple. *-pensé*, or corresp. L. pple. *-pens-us.*] Considered and planned beforehand; premeditated, purposed; intentional, deliberate.
a. (*a*) in ***malice prepense*** (*Law*): malice premeditated or planned beforehand; wrong or injury purposely done.
1702 ADDISON *Dial. Medals* ii. 50 Our English poets.. show a kind of malice prepense in their Satires. **1752** W. MILLER in *Scots Mag.* May (1753) 232/1 Such prepense malice. **1769** BLACKSTONE *Comm.* IV. xiv. 202 The benefit of clergy is taken away from murder through malice prepense. **1852** MISS YONGE *Cameos* (1877) IV. xii. 137 This..was set down to malice prepense on his side. **1862** GOULBURN *Pers. Relig.* III. ii. (1873) 166 To kill a man in wrath of malice prepense is murder. **1877** LONGF. in *Life* III. 277 The article..is certainly written with malice prepense.
(*b*) *humorously* and *poet.*
[**1792** BURKE *Let. Sir H. Langrishe* Wks. 1842 I. 543 You see by the paper I take that I am likely to be long, with malice prepense.] **1857** HUGHES *Tom Brown* II. v, I have put in this chapter on fighting of malice prepense,..partly because of the cant and twaddle that's talked of boxing and fighting with fists now-a-days. **1874** L. STEPHEN *Hours in Library* (1892) I. vii. 255 He..plunges into slang, not irreverently..but of malice prepense. **1884** J. PAYN *Some Lit. Recoll.* 98, I went up to Lakeland..with the avowed intention and malice prepense of writing my second volume of poems. **1923** D. H. LAWRENCE *Birds, Beasts & Flowers* 128 Full of malice prepense, and overweening.
b. In other connexions.
1770 *Junius Lett.* xxxix. (1797) II. 23 From that period, whatever resolution they took was deliberate and prepense. **1816** KEATINGE *Trav.* I. 268 Travelling is seldom a very prepense undertaking. **1886** SWINBURNE *Misc.* 143 When least meditative with any prepense or prefixed purpose.
c. Of a person: Acting with intention, deliberate. *rare.*
1879 G. MACDONALD *Sir Gibbie* III. ix. 160 He was an orator wilful and prepense, choice of long words, fond of climaxes. **1919** W. B. YEATS *If I were Four & Twenty* in *Irish Statesman* 23 Aug. 212/1 For he [*sc.* Claudel] is prepense, deliberate.
Hence **pre'pense** *sb.*, forethought, purpose, intention, design. *rare.*
1847 GILFILLAN in *Tait's Mag.* XIV. 362 Her poetry is not, of prepense and purpose, the express image of her religious thought.

†**pre'pense,** *v. Obs.* [Altered from earlier PURPENSE, OF. *purpenser*, after words in PRE-; so in early 16th c. F. *prepenser* to think of before: see PRE- A. 1 and PENSE *v.*
In later edd. of 15th and early 16th c. documents, e.g. the *Paston Letters* and *Acts of Parlt.*, *purpense* of the original is often altered to the mod. *prepense*.]
1. *trans.* To plan, devise, or contrive beforehand.
[*c* **1400–1512**: see PURPENSE *v.*]
1509 HAWES *Past. Pleas.* XXX. xix, Prepence [*so edd.* 1517–1555] nothynge vnto her dyshoneste. **1525** LD. BERNERS *Froiss.* II. clxxxvi. 232/2 It was a thing prepensed by false traitoures to put the realme to trouble. **1633** T. ADAMS *Exp. 2 Peter* ii. 15 It is one thing to forsake, another to propose and prepense a forsaking.
2. To weigh or consider beforehand.
1509 HAWES *Past. Pleas.* XI. xxix, For to reuolue vnderstande and prepence [*so edd.* 1517–1555]..The begynnynge and the myddle certaynly With the ende or thou put it in vre. **1531** ELYOT *Gov.* I. xxv, All these thinges prepensed and gathered together seriously. **1590** SPENSER *F.Q.* III. xi. 14 Ever in your noble hart prepense, That all the sorrow in the world is lesse Then vertues might and values confidence. *a* **1656** BP. HALL *Via Media* Wks. 1808 IX. 835 A consequent will,..whereby, all circumstances prepensed, God does simply will this or that particular event, as simply good to be.
b. *intr.* or *absol.* To meditate beforehand.
1531 ELYOT *Gov.* III. xxiv, His [the soul's] office is, before that any thynge is attempted, to thinke, consydre, and prepence.

†**pre'pensed,** *ppl. a. Obs.* Also prepenst. [f. prec. vb. + -ED^1; substituted early in 16th c. for the original PURPENSED; subsequently reduced to PREPENSE *a.*] **a.** esp. in legal phraseology in ***malice prepensed, prepensed malice***, malice prepense: see PREPENSE *a.*
[**1436–1548**: see PURPENSED.]
1530–1 *Act 22 Hen. VIII*, c. 14 Manslaughter by chaunce medley, and not murder of malyce prepensed. **1531** in W. H. Turner *Select. Rec. Oxford* (1880) 104 Intendyng of malyce prepenced to putte..Govnter to..trobyll. **1603** HOLLAND *Plutarch's Mor.* 664 We take more to the heart, a mocke or scornfull flout, as comming from a prepensed malice. **1607** COWELL *Interpr.* s.v. *Murder*, Murder.. signifieth in our common lawe, a wilfull and felonious killing of any other vpon prepensed malice. **1659** THORNDIKE *Wks.* (1846) II. 639 What fault soever may have come..it cannot be presumed to have come upon prepensed malice. **1704** J. HARRIS *Lex. Techn.* I. s.v., If there were Malice prepensed formerly between them, it makes it Murder; as it is called in some Statutes Prepensed Murder.
b. In other connexions: = PREPENSE *a.* b.
a **1529** SKELTON *Replyc.* 300 *heading*, An ineuytably prepensed answere to all waywarde or frowarde altercacyons. **1553** T. WILSON *Rhet.* 73 If the offence be committed vpon a prepensed mynde and wilfully. **1600** HOLLAND *Livy* XXXVII. vii. 948 Having no time to put any prepensed plot in practise. **1670** PENN *Truth Rescued fr. Impost.* 40 With what prepenst Unkindness and disdainful Ketch he was treated.
Hence †**pre'pensedly** *adv.* = PREPENSELY.
1583 STUBBES *Anat. Abus.* II. (1882) 14 If it were proued that he killed him wittingly, willingly, and prepensedly.

pre'pensely, *adv.* [f. PREPENSE *a.* + -LY^2.] In a prepense manner; with deliberation or premeditation; deliberately, purposely, designedly.
1837 LANDOR *Pentameron, 2nd Day's Interv.* Wks. 1853 II. 320/1, I never could see why we should designedly and prepensely give to one writer more than his due, to another less. **1880** W. MORRIS in Mackail *Life* (1899) II. 13 Sonning, a village prepensely picturesque. **1880** SWINBURNE *Stud. Shaks.* iii. (ed. 2) 201 Shakespeare..has set himself as if prepensely to brutalise the type of Achilles.

†**pre'pensity.** *Obs. rare*$^{-1}$. In 8 præ-. [f. PREPENSE *a.* + -ITY: cf. *immensity*.] Premeditation.
1757 MRS. GRIFFITH *Lett. Henry & Frances* (1767) II. 43 Montaigne observes,..upon the subject of death, 'that the philosophy of the schools but increases, by præpensity, the terrors of it'.

†**pre'pensive,** *a. Obs. rare*$^{-1}$. Factitious formation for PREPENSE *a.*
1752 FIELDING *Amelia* I. x, Carrying the penknife drawn into the room with you..seems to imply malice prepensive, as we call it in the law.

†**pre'pention.** *Obs. rare*$^{-1}$. [For **prepension*, n. of action from L. *præpendēre* to hang down in front.] A part hanging down in front.
1592 R. D. *Hypnerotomachia* 86 Where the axeltree was.. ouer the naue of the wheele, there came downe a prepention ioyning to the Plynth.

preperceive: see PRE- A. 1.

ˌ**preper'ception.** [PRE- A. 2.] Previous perception; a condition preceding perception.
1871 FRASER *Life Berkeley* x. 402 *note*, Kant's preperception of space differs from Berkeley's, in recognising it as necessary *à priori* to all sense experience as such. **1881** J. SULLY in *Nature* XXIV. 185/2 A 'stage of preperception', during which the mind receives the impression of sense, but has not yet interpreted the impression into a coherent percept. **1896** *Educ. Rev.* Mar. 278 Prof. James has illustrated and emphasized the importance of preperception.
So **preper'ceptive** *a.*, characterized by preperception.
1907 *Hibbert Jrnl.* Jan. 421 The suggested topic defines my purpose, gives it its orientation and its preperceptive and selective tendencies.

preperitoneal: see PRE- B. 3.

prepersonal to **-phonemic:** see PRE- B. 1.

†**pre-pe'tition.** *Obs. rare*$^{-1}$. [PRE- A. 2.] Petition beforehand, previous petition.
1540 in I. S. Leadam *Sel. Cas. Crt. Requests* (Selden) 50 Your said oratours vppon prepeticion made vnto Sir Thomas Denys knighte [etc.], concernyng the same [etc.].

pre-phylloxera: see PRE- B. 2 a.

prepigmental, -pituitary: see PRE- B. 3.

pre-pious: see PRE- A. 6.

pre-placental: see PRE- B. 1.

preplan: see PRE- A. 1.

preplanetary, -planting: see PRE- B. 1.

pre-pleasing, -plot: see PRE- A. 6, 1.

prepolarization: see PRE- A. 2.

prepolarize: see PRE- A. 1.

†**pre'poll,** *v. Obs. rare*$^{-1}$. [ad. L. *præpoll-ēre* to exceed in power or strength, f. *præ*, PRE- A. 5 + *pollēre* to be strong.] *intr.* To excel in power or importance; to be prepollent, to preponderate.
1657 TOMLINSON *Renou's Disp.* 229 Is thought to prepoll in the same faculties.

pre'pollence. Now *rare* or *Obs.* [ad. late L. *præpollentia*, f. *præpollĕnt-em*: see PREPOLLENT and -ENCE.] The fact of being prepollent; greater prevalence.
1748 HARTLEY *Observ. Man.* I. iii. 322 The Prepollence of agreeable Tastes upon the Whole. *Ibid.* II. i. 28 The infinite Prepollence of Happiness above Misery.

pre'pollency. Now *rare* or *Obs.* [f. as prec.: see -ENCY.] The quality or fact of being prepollent.
1681 tr. *Willis' Rem. Med. Wks.* Vocab., *Præpollency*, of very great force, strength, excellency, or virtue. **1684** tr. *Bonet's Merc. Compit.* XVI. 576 Such things as destroy the prepollency of an acid Salt in the Blood. **1802** PALEY *Nat. Theol.* xxvi. (1819) 410 The prepollency of good over evil.

prepollent (prɪ'pɒlənt), *a.* Now *rare.* Also præ-. [ad. L. *præpollĕnt-em*, pr. pple. of *præpollēre*: see PREPOLL.] Having superior power, weight, or influence; predominating, prevailing.
1657 TOMLINSON *Renou's Disp.* 130 Now the basis is.. more prepollent in quality. **1685** BOYLE *Eng. Notion Nat.* v. 146 The præpollent gravity of some [bodies], sufficing to give others a comparative or respective lightness. **1752** *Gentl. Mag.* 154 Other evidence..such as has been always deemed prepollent to any other. **1825** R. P. WARD *Tremaine* III. xiii. 239 The question..whether the evil or good is præpollent. **1901** *Dublin Rev.* Apr. 293 It had nowhere any current or prepollent vogue.

‖**pre'pollex, præ-.** *Anat.* and *Zool.* [mod.L. f. *præ*, PRE- B. 3 + POLLEX.] A rudimentary structure, sometimes osseous, similar to the prehallux, found in certain animals on the radial border of the hand or fore-foot, and supposed to represent an additional digit.
1889 [see PREHALLUX]. **1891** FLOWER & LYDEKKER *Mammalia* 49 Occasionally, as in *Pedetes caffer*, the so-called prepollex consists of two bones, of which the distal one bears a distinct nail-like horny covering.

pre'polymer. [PRE- B. 1.] An intermediate in a process of polymerization which is convenient for manipulation and can be fully polymerized at a later stage in the process.
1956 *Mod. Plastics* July 111/3 If this thickening process is interrupted at the appropriate point, the prepolymer or sirup has about the same consistency as molasses (in June, not January!). **1962** *New Scientist* 25 Oct. 205/1 The state of polymerization of special synthetic fluids such as aviation turbine oils or polypropylene glycol (the latter a prepolymer used in the manufacture of polyurethane foams). **1971** *Penrose Ann.* LXIV. 23 The second [solventless ink] system uses liquid photo-sensitive pre-polymers which are polymerized and solidified immediately by exposure to high doses of ultra-violet light. **1978** *Sci. Amer.* June 107/1 The third method of consolidating stone is to treat it with organic monomers and prepolymers.
So **pre,polymeri'zation**; **pre'polymerize** *v. trans.*, to convert (a monomer) into a prepolymer.
1949 B. L. DAVIES *Technol. Plastics* ix. 151 If the prepolymerization of the resin is carried too far, the flow in the mould is restricted so that only a limited range of mouldings can be produced. **1956** *Mod. Plastics* July 111/3 (*heading*) Prepolymerization. *Ibid.* 114/1 Thermosetting resins cannot be prepolymerized to any useful degree in this manner, since they set up to a firm gel at a relatively low degree of cure. **1967** MARGERISON & EAST *Introd. Polymer Chem.* iv. 200 If all traces of inhibitors..are not removed from the monomer, irreproducible rates of polymerization are often found; for this reason it is the practice to 'pre-polymerize' 1 or 2% of the monomer before use.

pre'pond, *v.* Short for next or *preponderate.*
a **1854** CAROLINE B. SOUTHEY *Birthday* II. Poet. Wks. (1867) 50 If a mote, a hair, a dust prepond..On Inclination's side, down drops the scale.

preponder (prɪ'pɒndə(r)), *v.*^{1} Now *rare.* [a. OF. *prépondér-er* (16th c. in Hatz.-Darm.), or L. *præponderāre* to outweigh, be of greater weight: see PRE- A. 5 and PONDER *v.*]
†**1.** *trans.* To attribute greater weight or importance to. *Obs. rare.*
1502 ATKYNSON tr. *De Imitatione* III. vii. 202 He.. prepondereth the gyuer before all thynges gyuen.
2. To outweigh in importance, to preponderate over.
1624 WOTTON *Archit.* in *Reliq.* (1651) 236 [Channelled pillars] ought..not to be the more slender, but the more corpulent, unlesse apparances preponder truths. *a* **1661** FULLER *Worthies, Surrey* (1662) III. 76 Though the transporting thereof be by Law forbidden, yet private profit so prepondereth the publick, that Ships ballasted therewith are sent over into Holland, where they have..Magazins of this Earth.
3. *intr.* To exceed in weight, number, etc.; = PREPONDERATE *v.*^{1} 1.

1676 BEAL in *Phil. Trans.* XI. 601, I found not so much difference, as could clear me from suspecting a prepondering fancy. **1820** J. CLELAND *Glasgow* 39 The Trades' Burgesses have prepondered. **1893** *Scribner's Mag.* June 749/1 As it is, the embellishments preponder over constructive ability.

† pre-ˈponder, *v.*[2] *Obs. rare.* [f. PRE- A. 1 + PONDER *v.*] *trans.* To ponder beforehand.

1610 NORDEN *Spec. Brit., Cornw.* (1728) 92 Thowgh the continuance..manie thowsande yeares may importe suffitient warrant, it will not now fall..; yet the prepondering minde of future daungers may vpon the view be easelye perswaded of perill in standinge nere it.

preponderance (prɪˈpɒndərəns). [f. PREPONDERANT *a.*: see -ANCE, and cf. F. *prépondérance* (18th c. in Hatz.-Darm.).]

1. The fact of exceeding in weight; greater heaviness.

1681 GREW *Musæum* I. v. ii. 106 Little light Boats.. To the side whereof, this Fish [remora] fastening her self, might easily make it swag, as the least preponderance on either side will do. **1742** YOUNG *Nt. Th.* IX. 1499 Close with the side where one grain turns the scale; What vast preponderance is here! **1831** LARDNER *Pneumat.* iv. 259 The preponderance of the iron ball assists the atmospheric pressure in sustaining the column.

b. *Gunnery.* The excess of weight of that part of a gun which is to the rear of the trunnions over that in front of them. (So F. *prépondérance*, Littré.)

It is measured by the force (expressed in pounds) which must be applied under the rear end of the base-ring or neck of the cascabel in order to balance the gun with the axis of the bore horizontal, when supported freely on knife-edges placed under the trunnions.

1864 in WEBSTER. **1871** C. H. OWEN *Mod. Artillery* (1873) 2 The excess of weight in rear of the trunnions is termed the preponderance. **1875** KNIGHT *Dict. Mech.* 1783/2 The preponderance of a gun is usually $\frac{1}{20}$ of its weight. **1887** *Text Bk. Gunnery* 81 The trunnions..are generally placed a very little way in front of the centre of gravity to allow of elevating with ease; this causes a statical pressure on the elevating gear called *preponderance*, which is necessary for steadiness.

2. Superiority or excess in moral weight, power, influence, or importance.

1780 BENTHAM *Princ. Legisl.* xiv. §3 The good would have an incontestible preponderance over the evil. **1808** WELLINGTON in Gurw. *Desp.* (1837) IV. 55 It would give Great Britain the preponderance in the conduct of the war in the Peninsula. **1883** SIR T. MARTIN *Ld. Lyndhurst* xi. 299 The Ministry had the great preponderance of popular opinion at their back.

3. Superiority in number or amount.

1845 MᶜCULLOCH *Taxation* I. i. (1852) 158 A consequence ..of their immense preponderance in point of numbers. **1862** DANA *Man. Geol.* 516 The collection of animals has a strikingly Oriental character, except in the preponderance of Ungulates. **1894** H. DRUMMOND *Ascent Man* 305 The more social animals are in overwhelming preponderance over the unsocial.

preˈponderancy. Now *rare.* [f. as prec. + -ANCY.] The quality or fact of being preponderant; an instance of this.

1. Superiority of physical weight.

1646 SIR T. BROWNE *Pseud. Ep.* IV. vii. 196 Whereas men affirme they perceave an addition of ponderosity in dead bodies,..this accessionall preponderancy is rather in appearance then reality. **1692** RAY *Disc.* II. ii. (1732) 86 By reason of the Preponderancy of the Earth. **1772** HUTTON *Bridges* 58 The pointed projections..will be a sufficient addition to the pier, to give it the necessary preponderancy. *fig.* **1802** *Edin. Rev.* I. 200 The permanent restoration of the balance of trade to its accustomed preponderancy in our favour.

2. Superiority of power, influence, or importance.

1692 LOCKE *Toleration* iv. Wks. 1727 III. 468 If..all Magistrates saw the Preponderancy of the Grounds of Belief, which are on the Side of the true Religion. **1777** PRIESTLEY *Disc. Philos. Necess.* iv. 40 The final preponderancy of desire is called a will, or wish to obtain it. **1828** D'ISRAELI *Chas. I*, I. v. 104 Coalition of interests.. were to strike at the preponderancy of Imperial Austria.

3. Greater prevalence; = prec. 3.

1845 A. DUNCAN *Disc.* 159 The evident preponderancy of good, however unable they might be to explain the origin of evil, testified against them.

preponderant (prɪˈpɒndərənt), *a.* [ad. L. *præponderānt-em*, pr. pple. of *præponderāre*: see PREPONDER. Cf. F. *prépondérant* (1723 in Hatz.-Darm.).] Preponderating.

1. Surpassing in weight; outweighing, heavier.

1664 POWER *Exp. Philos.* II. 136 The internal Cylinder of Quicksilver in the Tube is not held up by the preponderant Ayr without.

2. Surpassing in influence, power, or importance; predominant.

1660 tr. *Amyraldus's Treat. conc. Relig.* II. ii. 180 If he judge the reasons which disswade the thing..to be preponderant, then he will..abstain from doing it. **1799** S. TURNER *Anglo-Sax.* II. i. 171 Ella is commemorated as the preponderant Saxon chief. **1849** MACAULAY *Hist. Eng.* ii. I. 239 The Roundhead party was now decidedly preponderant. **1899** *Allbutt's Syst. Med.* VIII. 77 Flexion at the metacarpo-phalangeal joints..from preponderant contraction of the interossei.

preˈponderantly, *adv.* [f. prec. + -LY[2].] In a preponderating degree; predominantly.

1823 BENTHAM *Not Paul* 392 Becoming established, it [religion] became noxious,—preponderantly noxious. **1836-7** SIR W. HAMILTON *Metaph.* xlii. (1870) II. 443 The powers..are either preponderantly strong by nature, or have become preponderantly strong by habit. **1886** H. JAMES *Bostonians* I. ix, So preponderantly intellectual a nature.

preponderate (prɪˈpɒndərət), *a. rare.* [f. pa. pple. of L. *præponderāre* (see PREPONDER) + -ATE[2]. For sense cf. PREDOMINATE *a.*] = PREPONDERANT.

1802 BENTHAM *Princ. Judic. Procedure* Wks. 1843 II. 8/2 What security can, without preponderate hardship, be provided against falsity uttered by an individual coming in the character of a pursuer. **1818** *Gen. Hist.* in *Ann. Reg.* 166/1 Unless the fate of mankind takes some preponderate determination, it will not be easy to pronounce whether good or evil will be the final result. **1889** SEXTON *Sp.* in *Daily News* 11 Apr. 8/2 A preponderate majority of elected representatives.

Hence **preˈponderately** *adv.*, predominantly.

1820 BENTHAM *Liberty of Press* Wks. 1843 II. 290/1 Nothing will be done but what is bad,—absolutely bad, or at least,..preponderately bad. **1882** *Society* 11 Nov. 27/2 Whether the style..is not preponderately heavy.

preponderate (prɪˈpɒndəreɪt), *v.*[1] Also 7 præ-. [f. ppl. stem of L. *præponderāre*: see PREPONDER *v.* and -ATE[3].]

I. Intransitive senses.

1. To weigh more; to be heavier; to incline the balance; to turn the scale.

1623 COCKERAM, *Preponderate*, to weigh downe more. **1660** BOYLE *New Exp. Phys. Mech.* xxxiv. 259 The Bladder appear'd to preponderate. **1672** WILKINS *Nat. Relig.* 37 Where neither side doth preponderate, the balance should hang even. **1785** IMISON *Sch. Art* I. 125 The cork will preponderate, and show itself to be heavier than the lead. **1800** VINCE *Hydrostat.* ii. (1806) 26 If two bodies of the same weight in air be put into a denser fluid, the smaller body will preponderate.

b. *fig.* To have the greater moral or intellectual weight.

1659 FULLER *App. Inj. Innoc.* (1840) 288 These last reasons did preponderate with me. **1690** LOCKE *Hum. Und.* IV. xvi. §9 As the Arguments..shall to any one appear, upon the whole matter, in a greater or less degree, to preponderate on either side. **1818** SCOTT *Hrt. Midl.* iii, The verdict of the jury sufficiently shows how the evidence preponderated in their minds. **1874** STUBBS *Const. Hist.* I. i. 8 One influence preponderates in the language, the other in the policy.

c. To exceed or be superior in power, force, or influence; to exceed in amount, number, etc.; to predominate.

1799 S. TURNER *Anglo-Sax.* II. vii. 298 Oswy is ranked by Bede the seventh..of the kings who preponderated in the Anglo-Saxon octarchy. **1838** DICKENS *Nich. Nick.* vi, The good in this state of existence preponderates over the bad. **1862** DANA *Man. Geol.* II. i. 481 But the relics of Ferns, Conifers and Cycads greatly preponderate. **1867** *Pall Mall G.* 19 July 16 In milk,..the heat-sustaining element preponderates largely over the nitrogenous or tissue-forming.

2. To descend or incline downwards, as one scale or end of a balance, or account of greater weight; to weigh or be weighed down; to show a preponderance. Also *fig.*

1678 HOBBS *Decam.* viii. 92 In a pair of Scales equally charged with Quicksilver, the addition of a little Oyl to either Scale, will make it praeponderate. **1725** JEFFERSON in *Athenæum* 25 June (1892) 825/1 When these have been withdrawn from us..the balance of pain preponderates unequivocally. *a* **1774** GOLDSM. *Surv. Exp. Philos.* (1776) I. 212 Suppose I take..a walking cane,..and attempt to balance it across my finger; I shall at last find some one particular part in it which being supported, neither of the ends will preponderate. **1831** LARDNER *Hydrostatics* v. 83 By the weight of this quantity the dish [of a balance] will now preponderate. **1844** LD. BROUGHAM *Brit. Const.* iii. (1862) 45 It appears that the balance of probability preponderates in favour of the position.

b. To gravitate or incline more strongly. *rare.*

1692 BENTLEY *Boyle Lect.* vii. 255 They cannot be evenly attracted on all sides, but must præponderate some way or other. **1757** EDWARDS *Orig. Sin* iii. (1837) 24 The question ..is not whether he is not inclined to perform as many good deeds as bad ones; but which of these two he preponderates to.

II. Transitive senses.

†3. To weigh more than, exceed in weight; to turn the scale when weighed against (something else); to outweigh. *Obs.*

1651 H. MORE *Second Lash* in *Enthus. Tri.*, etc. (1656) 268 The greater number of the lincks of a chain preponderating the lesse number. **1661** GLANVILL *Van Dogm.* 137 An inconsiderable weight by vertue of its distance from the Centre of the Ballance, will preponderate much greater magnitudes. **1755** B. MARTIN *Mag. Arts & Sc.* III. xii. 394 You see the Cork preponderate the Gold, as far as the Beam will admit.

†b. *fig.* To outweigh in importance, value, or influence. *Obs.*

1611 SPEED *Hist. Gt. Brit.* IX. vi. §10 All which and some other,..must not preponderate the handling of things more rare and considerable. *a* **1652** J. SMITH *Sel. Disc.* VII. iii. (1821) 324 His merits preponderate his demerits. **1699** BURNET *39 Art.* xxv. (1700) 280 The evil does so far preponderate the good. **1768-74** TUCKER *Lt. Nat.* (1834) I. 607 That the good must greatly preponderate the evil.

†4. To cause to descend, as one scale of a balance, by reason of greater weight; to weigh down. Also *fig.* To cause to incline more strongly.

1642 FULLER *Holy & Prof. St.* IV. xvi. 324 Desiring to spare Christian bloud, preponderates him for Peace. **1658** GURNALL *Chr. in Arm.* II. 360 They need not, when cast into the scale of thy thoughts, preponderate thee either way. **1660** INGELO *Bentiv. & Ur.* I. (1682) 117 Is not our Will.. given us to preponderate our powers to such Actions as Reason pronounceth good? **1796** JEFFERSON *Writ.* (1859) IV. 150 The addition of my wish may have some effect to preponderate the scale.

† pre-ˈponderate, *v.*[2] *Obs.* [f. PRE- A. 1 + PONDERATE *v.* 6.] To ponder previously; to weigh mentally or consider beforehand; = PREPONDER *v.*[2]

a. *trans.*

1599 *Life Sir T. More* in Wordsw. *Eccl. Biog.* (1853) II. 106, I have considered and preponderated all my affairs and doings. **1632** LITHGOW *Trav.* I. 7 Preponderate seriously this consequent. **1711** SHAFTESB. *Charact.* (1737) II. II. iv. 308 How many things do they preponderate? How many at once comprehend?

b. *intr.* or *absol.*

1681 P. THACHER in *New Eng. Hist. & Gen. Reg.* (1868) XXII. 260, I have diligently weighed and preponderated, seriously consulted with Others. **1742** FIELDING *Jos. Andrews* III. vi, The squire and his company thought proper to preponderate, before they offered to revenge the cause of their..allies. **1838** *Fraser's Mag.* XVII. 263 Deeply began she to preponderate Whether she'd cut her throat.

Hence **† pre-ˈponderated** *ppl. a.*

1653 *Nissena* 102 The first [step] required well weighed determinations and preponderated execution.

preˈponderating, *ppl. a.* [f. PREPONDERATE *v.*[1] + -ING[2].] That preponderates, or is superior in weight, influence, power, amount, number, etc.

1674 BOYLE *Excell. Theol.* II. i. 115 Her excellencies, though solid and weighty, are less so, than the preponderating ones of Theology. **1797** BURKE *Regic. Peace* iii. Wks. VIII. 325 That very preponderating part of the nation, which had always been..adverse to the French principles. **1886** TUCKER *E. Europe* 211 Your mastery over a preponderating number of alienated races.

Hence **preˈponderatingly** *adv.*, in a preponderating or surpassing degree; predominantly.

1840 MILL *Diss. & Disc., Democr. in Amer.* (1859) II. 71 In each of them some one element..existed exclusively or so preponderatingly as to overpower all the others. **1891** *Times* 6 Oct. 8/2 [Comparative Philology] had been all along preponderatingly the science of comparing the Aryan languages with one another. **1899** *Allbutt's Syst. Med.* VIII. 332 The small pyramidal cells..have been assumed to be preponderatingly sensory in feature and function.

prepondeˈration. Now *rare* or *Obs.* [n. of action f. L. *præponderāre* to PREPONDER; in late L. *præponderātio* (*Gloss. Lat. Gr.*, in Lewis & Sh.).]

1. The action or fact of preponderating or exceeding in weight; preponderance.

1653 BAXTER *Peace of Consc.* 103 If..the scales be turned but with one grain,..its preponderation is with great wavering and mobility. **1741** WATTS *Improv. Mind* I. xviii. §21 See on which side the preponderation falls. **1821** *Examiner* 77/1 We are scarcely conscious of the defects that are involved in the large preponderation of excellence.

2. The adding of weight to one side; greater inclination or bias.

1653 A. WILSON *Jas. I* 201 Which preponderation of His puts them in Æquilibrio. **1667** WATERHOUSE *Fire Lond.* 25 The only probable ballance to their mutinous preponderations. **1754** EDWARDS *Freed. Will* I. i. (1762) 4 In every Act, or going forth of the Will, there is some Preponderation of the Mind or Inclination one way rather than another. **1799** C. WINTER in W. Jay *Mem. & Lett.* (1843) 43 In such a state of preponderation as to be uncertain which way the balance will turn.

† preˈponderer. *Obs. rare*[−1]. [f. PREPONDER *v.* + -ER[1].] That which outweighs; in quot. an overbalancing branch.

1679 EVELYN *Sylva* xxvii. (ed. 3) 141 Crooked Trees are reform'd by taking off or topping the præponderers, whilst charg'd with Leaves or Woody and hanging counterpoises.

preˈponderous, *a. rare.* [f. PRE- A. 5 + PONDEROUS, after PREPONDERATE, etc.] Exceeding in weight, amount, or number; having the preponderance.

1700 S. PARKER *Six Philos. Ess.* 53 When once gathered to a preponderous Body they [vapours] return, and become the material Cause of our extraordinary Showers of Rain. **1900** *Yorks. Post* 5 Jan. 7/1 We are in a position to-day of being sufficient throughout and preponderous nowhere.

preˈponderously, *adv. rare.* [f. PREPONDEROUS *a.* + -LY[2].] To a preponderous degree; excessively.

1921 *Public Opinion* 5 Aug. 133/1 Is it a city or merely a village preponderously overgrown?

prepontile: see PRE- B. 3.

† preport, obs. erron. f. PURPORT *sb.* and *v.*

1583 STOCKER *Civ. Warres Lowe C.* IV. 16 Accordyng to the tenure and preporte of the saied pointes. **1616** *Withals' Dict.* 575 *Poraustæ* [v.r. *pyr*] *gaudes gaudium*, your inconstant ioy preports annoy.

preˈpose, *v.* Also 6 præ-. [a. F. *préposer* (15th c. in Godef. *Compl.*) after L. *præpōnĕre* to put before: see PRE- A. and POSE *v.*[1]]

† 1. *trans.* To set over; to appoint as chief or superior. (Cf. PRÆPOSITUS.) *Obs.*

1491 CAXTON *Vitas Patr.* (W. de W. 1495) I. xcii. 127b, The holy man..ordeyned there relygyouses, to the whyche he preposed & gaaf for abbot the holy man Samuell. **1655** FULLER *Waltham Abb.* (1840) 258 A dean, in Latin, *decanus*, hath his name from δεκα, 'ten', over which number he is properly to be preposed.

2. To place before or in front of something else; to preface, prefix.

1541 R. COPLAND *Galyen's Terap.* 2 D iv b, But yf any thynge be done presently thou shalt prepose two fynalytees of curacyon. **1594** W. PERCY *Sonn.* To Rdr. A ij, I did deeme it most conuenient to præpose mine Epistle, onely to beseech you to account of them [poems] as of toyes. **1662** HIBBERT *Body Div.* I. 218 It is either prefixed or preposed to a sentence. **1669** GALE *Crt. Gentiles* I. II. iv. 37 To words beginning with a vowel, the Æoles were wont to prepose a Digamma. **1946** O. JESPERSEN *Mod. Eng. Gram.* V. xv. 220 *Well to do* = 'well off, living in easy circumstances' is often preposed, generally written with hyphens: *a well-to-do farmer.* **1951** W. K. MATTHEWS *Languages U.S.S.R.* iv. 53 Syntactically Altaic follows the rule of subordinating, in this case preposing, secondary to principal categories. **1971** *Language* XLVII. 276 The former [example] would result if the NSR preceded the postcyclic transformation which preposes *away.* **1975** *Ibid.* LI. 386 Truncated passives can be generated transformationally..by a rule which obligatorily preposes the underlying object..into underlying subject position. **1978** *Studies in Eng. Lit.: Eng. Number* (Tokyo) 106 It is obvious that there are similarities between the rule which preposes *higher into the heavens* in (46 a) and the one which preposes, for example, *up into the clouds* in (42 b).

b. To put forward. *rare.*

1607 MARKHAM *Caval.* II. (1617) 27 So that I conclude, and dare..prepose myselfe against anie man of contrarie opinion.

†**3.** To propose, purpose, or intend.

(Perh. in most cases an error for *propose, purpose.*) *Obs.*

1508 KENNEDIE *Flyting w. Dunbar* 458 Foul brow in holl thow preposit for to pas. **1513** BRADSHAW *St. Werburge* I. 3202 Tho mankynde prepose his mynde to fulfyll, Yet god dysposeth all thynge at his wyll. **1597** WARNER *Alb. Eng.* XI. lxii. 271 And Prizes were preposde for such whose Champions bore them best At Tilts and Turnies. **1635** J. HAYWARD tr. *Biondi's Banish'd Virg.* 187, I then would.. never have presumed to have preposed you your flight.

Hence **pre'posed** *ppl. a.*, placed in front; also **pre'posing** *vbl. sb.*

1608 B. JONSON *Masque Ld. Haddington's Marriage* Wks. (1692) 340/1 With this preposed part of Judgment. **1888** *Trans. & Proc. Mod. Lang. Assoc. Amer. 1887* III. 39 It is a characteristic of Anglo-Saxon poetry..to introduce an idea with a pronoun... This preposed pronoun is noticed by all writers upon A.-S. style as frequently standing at the head of the sentence. **1928** O. JESPERSEN *Internat. Lang.* II. 153 Word-order with preposed subject (as in E[nglish] 'Are you ill?') cannot well be used in an I.A.L. **1970** B. M. H. STRANG *Hist. English* v. 290 A strongly falling pattern overall, which has been less general in later English because of the increase in preposed weak particles. **1975** *Language* LI. 815 Passivization..may involve not one but two transformational operations—subject postposing and object preposing. **1976** J. S. GRUBER *Lexical Struct. Syntax & Semantics* I. iii. 70 The preposing..seems to add emphasis to the phrase, changing the meaning slightly. **1978** *Language* LIV. 174 Bernard Mohan..presents some formulas and the results of a 'grammaticality' test..for various sentences with adverb-preposing or topicalization below and above a set of predicates. *Ibid.* 283 These failures are also significant facts about the speech of Achilles:..(d) Syntax: sentence length; clause length; preposed relative clauses.

†**pre'posital**, *a. rare.* [f. L. *præposit-*, ppl. stem of *præpōnĕre* (see prec.) + -AL[1].] Prepositional.

1652 URQUHART *Jewel* Wks. (1834) 203 In the contexture of nouns, pronouns, and preposital articles, united together.

preposition (prɛpə'zɪʃən), *sb.* [ad. L. *præpositiōn-em* a putting before, a preposition, n. of action f. *præpōnĕre* to put before: see PRE- and POSITION. So F. *préposition* (*preposicion*, 15th c. in Godef.).

L. *præpositio* rendered Gr. πρόθεσις, both terms having the wider sense, 2 below; thus, such particles as εὐ- well, and *in*- not, were included among prepositions.]

1. *Gram.* One of the Parts of Speech: an indeclinable word or particle serving to mark the relation between two notional words, the latter of which is usually a substantive or pronoun; as, sow *in* hope, good *for* food, one *for* you, Stratford *on* Avon, late *in* time. The following sb. or pron. is said to be 'governed' by the preposition, and in inflected languages stands in an oblique case. Originally, and still often, the term was applied also to the same words when combined as prefixes with verbs or other words, and to certain other particles of similar force which are used only in combination (***inseparable prepositions***).

postpositive preposition (= POSTPOSITION 3), a word or particle, having the same function as a preposition, which follows its sb., as 'he goes home*wards*'; L. 'domum *versus*', Ger. 'meinet*wegen*'. In English, when the object is an interrogative or relative pronoun, the verb follows this pronoun, and the preposition, instead of preceding the pronoun, often follows the verb, as Whom did you go *with?* the town that he lives *in*, the place (that) he came *from*. With the relative *that* no other construction is possible.

[*c* **1000** ÆLFRIC *Gram.* xlvii. (Z.) 267 Praepositio est pars orationis indeclinabilis. Praepositio mæg beon gecweden on englisc *foresetnys*, forðan ðe he stent ǽfre on foreweardan, swa hwær swa he byð, beo he gefeged to oðrum worde, ne beo he.] **1388** WYCLIF *Prol.* 60 Manie such aduerbis, coniunccions, and preposicions ben set ofte oon for another, and at fre chois of autouris sumtyme. **1530** PALSGR. Introd. 40 They take awaye the preposytion and say, *la robbe mon maistre.* **1661** MILTON *Accedence* Wks. 1738 I. 620 A Preposition is a part of Speech most commonly, either set before Nouns in Apposition, as *ad patrem*, or join'd with any other words in Composition, as *indoctus.* **1672** DRYDEN *Def. Epilogue* Ess. (Ker) I. 168 The preposition in the end of the sentence; a common fault with him. **1704** J. HARRIS *Lex. Techn.* I. s.v., 'Tis called *Præposition*, because 'tis most frequently in the Latin Tongue placed before other Words; and then either separately, as *Ad patrem*; or conjunctively, as *Admiror.* **1843** *Proc. Philol. Soc.* I. 66 The speaker made the prepositions do the work of the lost inflexions. **1845** STODDART *Gram.* in *Encycl. Metrop.* (1847) I. 124/1 These and other examples of a like kind induced some authors to make a class of postpositive prepositions;..there are languages in which all the prepositions, if we may so speak, are postpositive. *a* **1854** H. REED *Lect. Eng. Lit.* iii. (1878) 102 The peculiarly characteristic arrangement, which puts a preposition at the end of a sentence, is eminently an English idiom. **1874** I. TAYLOR *Etruscan Res.* vii. 247 Qualifying words, which in Aryan languages would appear as prepositions or..are in the Ugric languages glued on as postpositions. **1875** LELAND *Fusang* x. 102 Those Asiatic languages have, moreover, no prepositions, but only *post*positions. So likewise, has the Dakota tongue.

†**2.** More widely: Any word or particle prefixed to another word; a prefix. *Obs.*

1565 *Kyng Daryus* (Brandl) 838 That Preposition *In* is a pestilent fellow For it is that which maketh this variance betwene mee and you: My name is called *Iniquitee*, And thy name is called mayster *Equytie.* *a* **1653** GOUGE *Comm. Heb.* xi. 5 The preposition (εὐ), with which the verb (εὐηρεστηκέναι) is compounded, signifieth 'well'. **1661** [see 1].

3. a. The action of placing before; the fact of being so placed; position before or in front.

Now usu. hyphened in this sense.

1586 WEBBE *Eng. Poetrie* (Arb.) 71, I am constrayned to straine curtesy with the preposition of a worde compounded or such like, which breaketh no great square. **1656** BLOUNT *Glossogr.*, *Preposition*, a putting or setting before. **1885** *Amer. Jrnl. Philol.* Oct. 346 Contrasting the English preposition with the French postposition of the adjective. **1901** M. CALLOWAY in *Publ. Mod. Lang. Assoc. Amer.* XVI. 153 In Anglo-Saxon the appositive participle regularly follows its principal (post-position), though occasionally it precedes (pre-position). **1930** T. SASAKI *On Lang. R. Bridges' Poetry* 26 In French, where postposition, and not pre-position, of the adj. attrib. is the general rule. **1946** O. JESPERSEN *Mod. Eng. Gram.* V. xxi. 392 Historically, however, *for* was a subordinating conjunction, as shown (1) by the possibility of pre-position. **1961** *Moderna Språk* LV. 243 Another theory advanced by Jespersen is that some words cannot be freely used in pre-position because their signification demands a complement; thus *ashamed* (of something, to do something). **1963** F. T. VISSER *Hist. Syntax Eng. Lang.* I. i. 19 The extreme scarcity, however, of examples, in Old English with pre-position of the clause.. renders the correctness of this interpretation doubtful.

†**b.** Something placed before. *Obs.*

1635 WITHER *Emblemes* (ad. init.), A preposition to this Frontispiece. **1811** BUSBY *Dict. Mus.* s.v. *Sharp*, A character, the power of which is to raise the note before which it is placed half a tone higher than it would be without such a preposition.

†**4.** A setting forth; a proposition or exposition. *Obs.* [Due to early confusion of *pre-* and *pro-*.]

1494 FABYAN *Chron.* v. cxxxii. 116 Dagobert..made a longe preposicion & oracion concernynge yᵉ allegiaunce which he exortyd his lordes to owe & bere to hym. **1525** LD. BERNERS *Froiss.* II. cxcvi. [cxcii.] 605 This preposycion that the vnyuersite hadde made before the kynge, pleased right well the kynge. **1568** GRAFTON *Chron.* II. 390 The said Sir Iohn Bushe in all his prepositions to the king, did not onely attribute to him worldly honours, but diuyne names.

5. *pl.* Premises: see PREMISE *sb.* 1.

1646 FULLER *Wounded Consc.* iii. 19 Gods children by better logick, from the prepositions of Gods former preservations, inferre his power.

pre-position (priːpəʊ'zɪʃən), *v.* [PRE- A. 1.] *trans.* To position (esp. military equipment) in advance. So **pre-po'sitioning** *vbl. sb.*

1962 *Daily Tel.* 7 May 22/6 The area was selected as one where climatic conditions would provide the maximum test for seaborne military 'pre-positioning'... Stockpiling of military equipment, or as military experts call it, pre-positioning, has been accelerated in Europe. **1972** C. JOHNSTON *Brink of Jordan* I. iv. 23 This gave the unsettling impression that they [*sc.* Saudi and Syrian forces] were simply pre-positioned there so as to ensure the best results for their countries in an eventual carve-up of Jordanian territory. **1979** *Sci. Amer.* Jan. 9/3 Indeed, our own proposals improve the quick-reaction defense of Europe by prepositioning more armor in Europe and rebasing most of the powerful combat air strength now held on the carriers to land bases in support of NATO.

prepo'sitional, *a.* [f. PREPOSITION *sb.* + -AL[1].] Of, pertaining to, or expressed by a preposition; formed with a preposition; serving as, or having the function of, a preposition.

a **1831** BENTHAM *Univ. Gram.* Wks. 1843 VIII. 346/1 In the singular number, besides the prepositional genitive, there is the inflexional formed as above by *'s.* **1846** *Proc. Philol. Soc.* II. 212 The pronominal and prepositional roots constitute a class apart. **1940** C. C. FRIES *Amer. Eng. Gram.* 130 The prepositional infinitive was made up of the preposition or function word *to* and the dative case of a verbal noun. **1961** R. B. LONG *Sentence & its Parts* iii. 71 The prepositional adverbs *but* and *like* sometimes enter into subordinate clauses (then best regarded as interrogative in type) instead of preceding them and functioning as prepositions with declarative-clause objects. *Ibid.* viii. 185 Prepositional units used as subjects are assigned singular force. *Over the fence* is out. *To admit the truth* would be to endanger the whole enterprise. **1963** F. T. VISSER *Hist. Syntax Eng. Lang.* I. iv. 390 This object is traditionally called 'the prepositional object';..it would be more correct to call it a 'direct object dependent on a prepositional group-verb'... Other terms for 'prepositional group-verbs' are 'phrasal verbs'..'group verbs'..'compound verbs'. **1965** N. CHOMSKY *Aspects of Theory of Syntax* ii. 101 It is well known that in Verb-Prepositional-Phrase constructions one can distinguish various degrees of 'cohesion' between the Verb and the accompanying Prepositional-Phrase. **1965** *Language* XLI. 158 Prepositional object: *John is looking at her* (actually this is not what is usually called a prepositional object, but the object of a prepositional verb-unit *look at.*). **1966** G. N. LEECH *Eng. in Advertising* ii. 12 Prepositions are a class of words which occur in initial position in a type of adverbial group, the 'prepositional phrase'.

prepo'sitionally, *adv.* [f. prec. + -LY[2].] In a prepositional manner; with the force or meaning of a preposition.

1845 STODDART *Gram.* in *Encycl. Metrop.* (1847) I. 130/1 The same must be said of the word *along* prepositionally used by old writers to signify the relation of an effect to its cause. **1879** WHITNEY *Sanskrit Gram.* 366 Words are used prepositionally along with all the noun-cases excepting the dative.

prepo'sitionless, *a.* [f. PREPOSITION *sb.* + -LESS.] Lacking or without a preposition.

1956 A. H. SMITH *Eng. Place-Name Elements* I. 6 The normal syntax demanded a prepositionless nominative. **1963** F. T. VISSER *Hist. Syntax Eng. Lang.* I. iv. 328 To the general replacement..of the prepositionless complements by prepositional complements there are a few exceptions. **1965** *Language* XLI. 133 The subchapter on direct (i.e. prepositionless) verbal government includes..'The accusative of price, measure and quantity'. **1966** *Eng. Stud.* XLVII. 54 The traditional and vague term *direct object*.. which corresponds to an OE complement in the accusative form and, later on, to a postverbal prepositionless stem-form.

prepositive (prɪ'pɒzɪtɪv), *a.* (*sb.*) [ad. late L. *præpositīv-us* (Diomedes) that is set before (in gramm.), f. ppl. stem of *præpōnĕre* to put before: see -IVE; cf. F. *prépositif* (14th c. in Hatz.-Darm.).] **A.** *adj.* Proper to be placed before or prefixed.

1583 FULKE *Defence* i. (1843) 139 It is a common thing in the Greek tongue, that the article prepositiue is taken for the subjunctiue. **1691** RAY *Collect. Words, Acc. Errors* 161 What is the prepositive Letter in this Diphthong is doubtful. **1755** JOHNSON *Dict. Gram.* c j, The prepositive particles *dis* and *mis.* **1808** T. F. MIDDLETON *Grk. Article* (1855) 3 Theodore Gaza..gives in his [Greek] Grammar the following account: The Article is a declinable part of speech prefixed to Nouns. It is indeed divided into the prepositive and the subjunctive; but properly speaking the prepositive only is the article. **1845** *Proc. Philol. Soc.* II. 169 Many instances where the postfixes of older languages have become prefixes or distinct prepositive words in more recent ones. **1874** DAVIES tr. *Gesenius's Hebr. Gram.* 50 Some [accents]..stand only on the first letter of a word (*prepositive*), others only in the last letter (*postpositive*).

B. *sb.* A prepositive word or particle.

1693 CHAUNCY *Enq. Gosp. New Law* 38 It were easie to shew upon what probable Reasons the Prepositive is added or omitted, in other places. **1786** [see POSTPOSITIVE *a.*].

Hence **pre'positively** *adv.*, by placing in front.

1873 F. HALL *Mod. Eng.* 50 As concerns a substantive, its subjective genitive, universally, and its objective genitive, very often, may be expressed prepositively.

prepositor[1], **præ-** (prɪ'pɒzɪtə(r)). Also 6 -er, -our. [Alteration of L. PRÆPOSITUS: see note s.v. PRÆPOSTOR.]

1. The name given in some English public schools to those senior boys who are entrusted with much of the discipline of the school, esp. out of the classroom; now usually PRÆPOSTOR, q.v. Also *fig.* and in *fig.* context.

a **1518** SKELTON *Magnyf.* 1941, I am Goddys Preposytour; I prynt them with a pen; Because of theyr neglygence and of theyr wanton vagys. **1519** HORMAN *Vulg.* 92b, I am preposyter of my boke, *duco classem.* **1581** J. BELL *Haddon's Answ. Osor.* 259b, And who hath made you usher I pray you, or prepositour of Ciceroes schoole? **1606** J. CARPENTER *Solomon's Solace* i. 2 For this end had King Solomon those prudent and meete prepositours. **1649** HEYLIN *Relat. & Observ.* II. 30 A meer Free-schoole, where Cromwell is Head-school-master, Ireton Usher, and..Fairfax a Prepositor. **1681–2** *Verney Lett.* in R. T. Warner *Winchester* iv. (1900) 43 He is one of the best, if not the best scholar in the Schoole of his standing, though Hee Bee not yet a Praepositor. **1706** PHILLIPS, *Prepositor*, (School-Term) a Scholar appointed by the Master, to over see the rest; such a one is otherwise call'd *Observator* and *Monitor.* **1855** LADY HOLLAND *Sidney Smith* I. i. 8 Whilst at Winchester he had been one year Præpositor of the College, and another, Præpositor of the Hall. **1894** ASTLEY 50 *Years Life* I. 16 It was eight or ten days before he came under the Prepositor's ken [at Eton].

β. in corrupt form **propositor.**

1633 E. VERNEY *Let. fr. Winchester* in *Verney Mem.* (1892) I. 156 His schoole master being at London, the propositors begin to affront mee. **1702** C. MATHER *Magn. Chr.* III. I. iii. (1852) 303 He made such proficiency that while he was the least boy in the school he was made a propositor.

†**2.** The master, director, or manager (of a house, etc.); the president or head (*præpositus*) of a monastic house. *Obs.*

1698 FRYER *Acc. E. India & P.* 343 The Prepositor of each [Bathing] House [in Ispahan] gives Notice to all Comers by blowing a Horn, when the Houses are ready. **1881** *Blackw. Mag.* Apr. 489 The fame for sanctity of their leader—or praepositor as he was called at first—spread throughout the land.

Hence **preposi'torial** *a.*, of or pertaining to prepositors in schools.

1844 MOZLEY *Ess.* (1878) II. 14 Their prepositorial authority, as well as the fagging system, having been part of the old school plan, which he found going on when he came to Rugby. **1859** HODSON *12 Yrs. Soldier's Life in India* 3 Though he immediately re-established the shattered prestige of præpositorial power he contrived to make himself very popular with various classes of boys.

‖**pre'positor²**, **præ-**. *Roman Law.* [L. agent-noun from *præpōnĕre* to appoint over, charge with the management of an affair; f. *præ* before, in front + *pōnĕre* to place.] The principal who deputes the management of any business or commercial undertaking to a factor, consignee, or *institor*. (Formerly used in *Scotch Law.*)

1681 STAIR *Instit. Law Scot.* I. x. §47 By the Contracts of Institors in relation to that wherein they were intrusted, their prepositors are oblieged, as Exercitors are as to Maritime matters; so Prepositors are correspondent in Trafficque at Land. **1754** ERSKINE *Princ. Law Scot.* III. iii. §14 Tho' the institors be pupils, and so cannot bind themselves, the prepositor.. stands obliged by their deeds. **18..** W. BELL *Dict. Law Scot.* (1861) 451/2 Prepositors are liable for the acts of the institor.

†**pre'positure, præ-**. *Obs.* [ad. late L. *præpositūra* the office of an overseer, in med.L. in eccl. sense, f. *præpositus*: see PRÆPOSITUS and -URE.] The office of a præpositus or provost of a collegiate church or priory.

a **1425** *Found. St. Bartholomew's* (E.E.T.S.) 34 The tyme of a ȝere turnyed abowte, succedid in-to the prepositure and the dignyte of the priore of this new plantacioun. **1617** MORYSON *Itin.* III. 280 Which dignitie is tied to the Prepositure of Bruges Church. *a* **1641** BEDELL in *Fuller's Abel Rediv., Erasmus* (1867) I. 82 In the interim he sent him a collation to the præpositure of Daventry. **1758** LOWTH *Life of Wykeham* i. 28 The King gave him.. the Prepositure of Wells with the Prebend annexed.

prepositus, variant of PRÆPOSITUS.

prepossess (priːpə'zɛs), *v.* [f. PRE- A. 1 + POSSESS.]

1. *trans.* To take or get possession of beforehand, or before another; to have prior possession of. Now *rare.*

1614 RALEIGH *Hist. World* II. v. iii. §11 408 All passages out of there Campe, Martius hath prepossessed, so that there is no way to escape. **1640** BP. REYNOLDS *Passions* xvii. 186 Honours seldome come to us but by the mortality of those that prepossessed them. **1665** MANLEY *Grotius' Low C. Warres* 349 The Enemy had prepossessed all the places more inward. *a* **1716** SOUTH *Serm.* (1744) X. 42 Hope is that which antedates and prepossesses a future good.

†**b.** *refl.* with *of* or *with*: To possess oneself of beforehand; to take for oneself or make one's own beforehand; also in pass. *to be prepossessed. Obs.*

a **1656** USSHER *Ann.* (1658) 855 Pilate prepossessing himself with his horse and foot at the top of the hill. **1692** R. L'ESTRANGE *Josephus, Antiq.* XIV. viii. (1733) 368 Without more ado they prepossess'd themselves of the Temple. **1738** tr. *Guazzo's Art Conversation* 79 Some.. eagerly push for the chief Place, and are mightily chagrin'd if another is prepossessed of that silly Pre-eminence.

2. To possess (a person) beforehand or cause (him) to be preoccupied or pre-engaged *with* or *by* a feeling, notion, etc.; to imbue, inspire, or affect strongly beforehand. Chiefly in *pass.*

1639 FULLER *Holy War* II. xx. (1840) 75 Being prepossessed with this intent to dispossess him of his place. **1642** MILTON *Apol. Smect.* Prol., Wks. 1851 III. 258 Seeking thus unseasonably to prepossesse men of his modesty. **1657** *North's Plutarch* Add. Lives (1676) 16 They were.. prepossest with an ill opinion of him. **1730** A. GORDON *Maffei's Amphith.* 288 Having been prepossessed in the Opinion, that they were all equal. **1738** tr. *Guazzo's Art Conversation* 53 They prepossess their Auditors of their own Sincerity,.. and under that Covert say the most spiteful Things. **1836** KEBLE *Serm.* viii. (1848) 201 The Creed.. had prepossessed them with these truths, before ever they thought of proving them from Holy Writ. **1862** S. LUCAS *Secularia* 375 The result of a disposition by which it [the French nobility] was fatally prepossessed.

†**b.** with the notion expressed by a clause. *Obs.*

a **1677** HALE *Prim. Orig. Man.* I. ii. 69 This brief Inventory I have here given.. to pre-possess the Reader, 1. That [this] is no contemptible or unworthy enquiry. *a* **1732** GAY *Fables* II. iii. 9 We're prepossest my Lord inherits, In some degree, his grandsire's merits. **1797–8** JANE AUSTEN *Sense & Sens.* xxxiii, Fanny and Mrs. Ferrars were both strongly prepossessed that neither she nor her daughters were such kind of women.

3. *spec.* To cause (a person) to have a feeling or opinion beforehand against or in favour of a person or thing; to bias, prejudice; now chiefly, To impress favourably beforehand. Chiefly in *pass.*

1647 TRAPP *Comm. 1 Cor.* i. 22 The reason of their rejecting the Gospel is, they are prepossessed against it. **1654** FULLER *Comm. Ruth* (1868) 129 Who have taken bribes to prepossess the Judge. **1700** T. BROWN *Amusem. Ser. & Com.* 141 An Outside so Prepossessing us in his Favour. **1846** POE *Anthon* Wks. 1864 III. 45 An attempt was made.. to prepossess the public against his 'Classical Dictionary'. **1849** EASTWICK *Dry Leaves* 123, I was quite pre-possessed by his appearance. **1866** G. MACDONALD *Ann. Q. Neighb.* xiii, His talk prepossessed me still more in his favour.

Hence **prepo'ssessed** *ppl.*, possessed by a preconceived idea; prejudiced, biased.

1633 PRYNNE *Histrio-M.* I. VI. xvi. 549 The sight of one onely Stage-play, though with a prepossessed opinion against it, will draw men on to frequent, applaud, and admire others. **1670** COTTON *Espernon* I. II. 50 What reasons can prevail with a pre-possess'd, and exasperated multitude? **1774** FLETCHER *Ess. Truth* Wks. 1795 IV. 131 Come then my prepossessed brethren, show yourselves the children of Abraham.

prepo'ssessing, *ppl. a.* [f. prec. + -ING².] That prepossesses.

1. Biasing; causing prejudice.

1642 H. MORE *Song of Soul* II. i. I. xxii, I'll purge out the strong steem Of prepossessing prejudice. **1711** SHAFTESB. *Charac.* (1737) III. Misc. III. i. 154 A very prepossessing Circumstance against our Author. **1754** EDWARDS *Freed. Will* III. vi. (1762) 182 Every pre-possessing fix'd Bias on the Mind brings a Degree of moral Inability for the contrary. **1773** GOLDSM. *Stoops to Conq.* II. i, This awkward prepossessing visage of mine.

2. *spec.* That predisposes favourably; causing an agreeable first impression; attractive, pleasing.

1805 SURR *Winter in Lond.* (1806) III. 92 Nature had bestowed upon him a fair and prepossessing exterior. **1838** DICKENS *Nich. Nick.* iv, Squeers's appearance was not prepossessing. **1853** LYTTON *My Novel* IX. vi, Its expression was eminently gentle and prepossessing.

Hence **prepo'ssessingly** *adv.*, **prepo'ssessingness**.

1819 *Blackw. Mag.* V. 681 A way prepossessingly earnest. **1876** *Contemp. Rev.* XXVII. 390 That which has an air of consummate truth and likelihood, the prepossessingness of that which has this air. **1883** M. ARNOLD *Lit. & Dogma* Pref. 11 His prepossessingness, his grace and truth.

prepossession (priːpə'zɛʃən). [n. of action f. PREPOSSESS *v.*; see PRE- A. 2 and POSSESSION.]

1. The having or taking of possession beforehand; prior possession or occupancy. Now *rare.*

1648 BOYLE *Seraph. Love* xxv. (1660) 151 Affording them a full Præpossession of all the Objects of Desire. **1654** HAMMOND *Fundamentals* viii, To give piety the prepossession, before other competitors.. should be able to pretend to him. **1733** W. CRAWFORD *Infidelity* (1836) 208, I have heavenly qualities and joys already begun in me; I have a prepossession of heaven. **1820** MAIR *Tyro's Dict.* (ed. 10) 378 *Praesumptio*,.. prepossession, pre-occupation.

b. A previous or former possession.

1646 SIR T. BROWNE *Pseud. Ep.* 331 In after Ages many Colonies dispersed, and some thereof upon the coasts of Africa, and the prepossessions of his [Ham's] elder brothers.

2. The condition of being mentally prepossessed; a preconceived opinion which tends to bias the mind; unfavourable or favourable antecedent opinion; prejudice, predisposition, liking.

1649 JER. TAYLOR *Gt. Exemp.* I. Ad Sect. v, God.. blesses holy Meditations with results of Reason, and prepossessions dogmatically decreeing the necessity of Vertue. *a* **1680** BUTLER *Rem.* (1759) I. 202 It is the noblest Act of human Reason To free itself from slavish Prepossession. **1702** *Eng. Theophrast.* 173 The prepossessions of the Vulgar for men in power and authority are blind. **1786** MME. D'ARBLAY *Lett.* 19 June, The prepossession the Queen has taken in my favour is truly extraordinary. **1863** H. COX *Instit.* I. x. 247 The King's strong personal prepossessions against the ministers of the late Queen. **1871** MORLEY *Carlyle* in *Crit. Misc.* Ser. I. (1878) 163 To chime in most harmoniously with prepossessions.

Hence †**prepo'ssessionary** *a.*, having possession beforehand, of the nature of a prepossession.

1757 *Herald* No. 7 (1758) I. 106 Valour commonly carries with it a prepossessionary excuse, even for actions of temerity.

pre-po'ssessor. *Obs.* or *rare.* [f. PRE- A. 2 + POSSESSOR.] A previous possessor.

1684 R. BRADY *Introd. O. Eng. Hist.* Gloss. 18 They signifie only a bare Præpossessor, one that possessed the Land before the present Possessor.

†**prepost.** *Obs. rare.* [ad. L. *præpost-us*, contr. f. *præposit-us*, sb. use of pa. pple. of *præpōnĕre* to place before.] = PRÆPOSITUS; an overseer, steward, superintendent, provost.

1382 WYCLIF *Dan.* i. 3 Aphanet, prepost [*gloss* or souereyne; Vulg. *præposito*] of his geldingus. —— *Acts* vii. 10 He ordeynede him prepost [*gloss* or souereyn; *v.r.* prouoost; Vulg. *præpositum*] on Egipt, and on al his hous.

preposter, erron. form of PRÆPOSTOR.

†**pre'posterate**, *v. Obs.* [f. L. *præposterāre* to reverse, thwart (f. *præposter-us* PREPOSTEROUS) + -ATE³. Cf. obs. F. *prepostérer* (Cotgr.).] *trans.* To make 'preposterous'; to reverse, invert; to overturn; to pervert.

1566 PAINTER *Pal. Pleas.* I. 127 Before the warres had preposterated the order of auncient government. **1607** *Schol. Disc. agst. Antichr.* I. iii. 147 This sinceritie of the election, the crosse preposterateth first of all, in that it is chosen being an vnlawfull ceremonie before those that are lawfull: being a tradition of mans before Gods precept. **1628** R. HUBERT *Edw. II* clxxi, Never did princes more preposterate Their private lives.

So †**preposte'ration** [ad. late L. *præposterātiōn-em*], reversal, perversion.

1607 *Schol. Disc. agst. Antichr.* I. iii. 146 The hypocrisie and preposteration of the Crosse, in the Will, in respect of the meanes for attayning to the right end. *Ibid.* 147 Is there not a preposteration to renewe a Crosse so zealously, while we burry so carelessly this auncient custome? raysing vp in the roome thereof newe courses of our owne which doe no good.

preposterous (prɪ'pɒstərəs), *a.* Also 7 -postrous. [f. L. *præposter-us* reversed, perverted, absurd (f. *præ* before + *poster-us* coming after, following) + -OUS. Cf. obs. F. *prépostère* (Cotgr.).]

1. Having or placing last that which should be first; inverted in position or order. Now *rare.*

1552 HULOET, Preposterouse, out of order, ouerthwarth, transuerted, or last done which should haue ben first. **1583** STUBBES *Anat. Abus.* II. (1882) 59 This is preposterous geare, when Gods ordinance is turned topsie turuie, vpside downe. **1589** PUTTENHAM *Eng. Poesie* III. xx. (Arb.) 262 The preposterous is a pardonable fault... We call it by a common saying to *set the carte before the horse.* **1657** HAWKE *Killing is M.* 56 Though the Monster lurk in Cacus cave, yet notwithstanding his preposterous steps will be discovered. **1725** BRADLEY *Fam. Dict.* s.v. *Tulip*, Which would certainly do them harm, by reason of the preposterous Motion it might give the Sprout when the Season for planting the Bulbs is come. **1809–10** COLERIDGE *Friend* (ed. 4) I. 224 It is, indeed, in the literal sense of the word, preposterous. **1856** FERRIER *Inst. Metaph.* Introd. §62 The fatal effects of this preposterous (in the exact sense of that word) procedure.

†**b.** Having the eyes set behind. *Obs. rare*⁻¹.

1665 GLANVILL *Scepsis Sci.* xvii. 102 Thus our Eyes like the preposterous Animals are behind us.

2. Contrary to the order of nature, or to reason or common sense; monstrous; irrational; perverse, foolish, nonsensical; in later use, utterly absurd.

1542 UDALL *Erasm. Apoph.* (1877) 14 He checked the preposterous & ouerthwarte iudgemente, that the common sort of people haue of thinges. **1584** R. SCOT *Discov. Witchcr.* x. vii. (1886) 148 Dreames in the dead of the night are commonlie preposterous and monstrous. **1593** SHAKS. *3 Hen. VI*, v. vi. 5 Good Gloster, and good Deuill, were alike, And both preposterous. **1641** MILTON *Judgm. Bucer* xxii. Wks. 1738 I. 281 Austin and some others, who were much taken with a preposterous admiration of single life. **1713** GAY *Guardian* No. 149 ¶12 The muff and fur are preposterous in June. **1789** W. BUCHAN *Dom. Med.* i. (1790) 2 Nothing can be more preposterous than a mother who thinks it below her to take care of her own child. **1809** W. IRVING *Knickerb.* (1861) 103 To exclaim at the preposterous idea of convincing the mind by tormenting the body. **1863** P. BARRY *Dockyard Econ.* 126 America has constructed, and is still constructing, ships of war of preposterous tonnage, simply because England is constructing ships of war of preposterous tonnage. **1879** FROUDE *Cæsar* xxviii. 480 The very notion is preposterous.

pre'posterously, *adv.* [f. prec. + -LY².] In a preposterous order or manner.

1. In an inverted or reversed order or position; with the latter part being the former; hind-side before. Now *rare.*

1576 FLEMING *Panopl. Epist.* 269 So the sense inferreth albeit the wordes be somewhat preposterously placed. **1589** NASHE *Anat. Absurd.* Dij, Those that are called Agrippæ being preposterously borne with their feete forward. **1676** *Phil. Trans.* XI. 767 So preposterously are those Books ranged in this Catalogue. *a* **1716** SOUTH *Serm.* (1744) XI. 3 Some indeed preposterously misplace these, and make us partake of the benefit of Christ's priestly office.. before we are brought under the scepter of his kingly office. **1829** SIR W. HAMILTON *Discuss.* (1853) 17 Preposterously.. deducing the laws of the understanding from a questionable division of logical propositions.

2. Unnaturally, irrationally; perversely; absurdly.

c **1540** tr. *Pol. Verg. Eng. Hist.* (Camden) I. 39 His brother Archigallo.. didd preposteruslie exalte and honor the moste obscure and servile persons. **1599** SHAKS. *Hen. V*, II. ii. 112 Whatsoeuer cunning fiend it was That wrought vpon thee so preposterously, Hath got the voyce in hell for excellence. **1615** W. LAWSON *Country Housew. Gard.* (1626) 9 They doe preposterously, that bestow more cost and labours,.. vpon a Garden than vpon an Orchard. **1661** BOYLE *Style of Script.* (1675) 141 Our preposterously partial Memories. **1786** tr. *Beckford's Vathek* (1883) 123 She is preposterously sighing after a stripling with languishing eyes and soft hair, who loves her. **1868** FARRAR *Seekers* III. iii. (1875) 299 Preposterously regarded as a sure criterion of truth. **1873** BLACK *Pr. Thule* viii, He got up at preposterously early hours.

pre'posterousness. [f. as prec. + -NESS.] The quality of being preposterous; inversion of the natural or rational order (now *rare*); perversity; unreasonableness; absurdity.

1607 *Schol. Disc. agst. Antichr.* I. iii. 137 From this preposterousnesse of the Crosse setting the sense before the spirite, come wee to his Vacuitie for his inwarde Devotion. **1678** CUDWORTH *Intell. Syst.* 176 We shall.. choose rather to break those laws of method.. and subjoyn them immediately in this place, craving the readers pardon for this preposterousness. **1727** BAILEY vol. II, *Preposterousness*, the having the wrong End forward, Absurdness, contrariety to Nature or Custom. **1862** F. HALL *Hindu Philos. Syst.* I. vi. 106 So they go on, rearing one thing upon another, utterly regardless of the preposterousness of their conclusions.

prepostor, variant of PRÆPOSTOR.

prepotence (priː'pəʊtəns). [a. F. *prépotence*, ad. L. *præpotentia*: see next.] The fact of being prepotent or of predominating; = next, 1.

1829 LANDOR *Imag. Conv.* Ser. II. II. 305 The consciousness of having mastered some prepotence of passion. **1857** SIR F. PALGRAVE *Norm. & Eng.* II. 81 Henry.. enforced his claims with stern prepotence. **1888** J. T.

GULICK in *Linn. Soc. Jrnl., Zool.* XX. 245 It may at first appear that a slight degree of prepotence will prevent crossing as effectually as a higher degree. **1896** *Edin. Rev.* Jan. 265 Challenging the prepotence on land of so mighty an empire.

prepotency (priːˈpəʊtənsɪ). [ad. L. *præpotentia* superior power, f. *præpotent-em*: see PREPOTENT and -ENCY.]

1. a. The quality of being prepotent; superior power or influence; predominance, prevalence.

1646 SIR T. BROWNE *Pseud. Ep.* IV. v. 187 If there were a determinate prepotency in the right [hand]. **1651** HOWELL *Venice* 178 Prepotency of plundring did facilitat the way to dispossesse me of mine own. **1815** *Zeluca* I. 135, I shall not fall into the sullens at his present prepotency. **1887** *Edin. Rev.* CLXV. 307 The destruction of that Russian prepotency.

b. *Psychol.* The quality inherent in a particular stimulus or response that makes it prepotent (cf. next).

1928 *Psychol. Rev.* XXXV. 420 What response the animal will make at a given moment depends upon the prepotency of the stimuli. **1953** B. F. SKINNER *Sci. & Human Behav.* xiv. 220 When two responses are strong at the same time, only one can be emitted. The appearance of one response is called 'prepotency'.

2. *Biol.* The prepotent power of a parent organism to transmit special characteristics to offspring.

1859 DARWIN *Orig. Spec.* viii. 274 The prepotency runs more strongly in the male ass than in the female. **1868** —— *Anim. & Pl.* II. 71 The subject of prepotency is extremely intricate—from its varying so much in strength, even in regard to the same character, in different animals. **1877** —— *Forms of Fl.* vi. 258 The prepotency of pollen from another individual over a plant's own pollen. **1893** *Nat. Observ.* 8 Apr. 523/2 Attributed to the Anglo-Saxon prepotency of transmission in the racial struggle.

prepotent (priːˈpəʊtənt), *a.* [ad. L. *præpotent-em*, pr. pple. of *præposse* to be more or very powerful, to have the superiority, f. *præ*, PRE- A. 5, 6 + *posse* to be able, have power: see POTENT.]

1. a. Having great power, force, influence, or authority; pre-eminent in power.

a **1450** *Mankind* (Brandl) 759 My prepotent father, when ȝe sowpe, sowpe owt ȝowur messe. **1468** *Hen. VII at York* in *Surtees Misc.* (1888) 56 Most prepotent prince of power imperiall. **1591** R. TURNBULL *Exp. St. James* 166 b, Excellent for wisdome, prepotent in power, renowmed for vertue. **1657** *Physical Dict.*, *Præpotent*, strong, effectual, potent, above or before others. **1826** G. S. FABER *Diffic. Romanism* (1853) 300 To borrow his prepotent bolt from the armoury of his predecessor. **1885** MRS. LYNN LINTON *Stabbed in Dark* iii, Some vague, intangible, but prepotent barrier had risen up between him and them.

b. Excelling in potency, more powerful than others; predominant.

1641 R. B. K. *Parallel of Liturgy w. Mass-Bk.*, etc. Pref. 6 Overswayed by the prepotent Popish faction. **1880** P. GREG *Errant* II. v. 59 What was the attraction prepotent over all the charms of the ball-room? **1881** PALGRAVE *Visions of Eng.* 153 After the ruin of the prepotent influence of Spain.

c. *Psychol.* Applied to the effective stimulus and its response when stimuli with different, conflicting, responses occur together.

1906 C. S. SHERRINGTON *Integrative Action Nervous Syst.* vi. 228 It is those stimuli which.. are most fitted to excite pain which, as a general rule, excite in the 'spinal' animal.. the prepotent reflexes. **1928** *Psychol. Rev.* XXXV. 420 The animal behaves as it does because a certain prepotent stimulus in the environment has forced it that way. **1948** W. MCDOUGALL *Introd. Social Psychol.* (ed. 29) 459 The 'prepotent reflexes' of sex, fear, and rage. **1953** B. F. SKINNER *Sci. & Human Behav.* xiv. 220 The prepotent response does not, merely by virtue of its having been emitted, alter the strength of the dispossessed response. **1960** HINSIE & CAMPBELL *Psychiatric Dict.* (ed. 3) 571/2 In general, nociceptive reflexes, such as the flexion reflex, are prepotent to all other types of reflex competing for the final common pathway.

2. *Biol.* Having a greater power of transmitting hereditary features or qualities; having a stronger fertilizing influence.

1859 DARWIN *Orig. Spec.* iv. 99 A plant's own pollen is always prepotent over foreign pollen. *Ibid.* viii. 274 When two species are crossed, one has sometimes a prepotent power of impressing its likeness on the hybrid. **1878** STEWART & TAIT *Unseen Univ.* v. §168. 173 There seems to be in many instances a prepotent influence about a newly arisen variety. **1888** J. T. GULICK in *Linn. Soc. Jrnl., Zool.* XX. 239 If.. individuals so varying as to be prepotent with each other are very few.. they will fail of being segregated through failing to receive any of the prepotent pollen.

3. [PRE- A. 3.] Previously endowed with power or potentiality.

1874 TYNDALL *Addr. Brit. Assoc. Belfast* 58 It is by the operation of an insoluble mystery that life is evolved, species differentiated, and mind unfolded from their prepotent elements in the immeasurable past.

Hence **preˈpotently** *adv.*, in a prepotent manner; with overwhelming power.

1899 W. JAMES in *Talks on Psychol.* 88 A single exciting word may call up its own associates prepotently.

prepotential (priːpəʊˈtɛnʃəl), *a.* (*sb.*) [f. PRE- A. 3 + POTENTIAL.]

1. Having a prior or superior power; prepotent.

1888 *Academy* 24 Nov. 329/3 What a contrast between those days.. and our times of 'telegraphic ambassadors' and a prepotential 'clerkery'!

2. *Math.* (See quot.) Also as *sb.* A prepotential function.

1875 CAYLEY *Memoir on Prepotentials* in *Coll. Math. Papers* IX. 318 The present Memoir relates to multiple integrals expressed in terms of the $(s + 1)$ ultimately disappearing variables $(x, \ldots, z, w)$, and the same number of parameters $(a, \ldots, c, e)$... Such an integral, in regard to the index $\frac{1}{2}s + q$, is said to be 'prepotential', and in the particular case $q = -\frac{1}{2}$ to be 'potential'. *Ibid.* 324 The prepotential of the whole surface in regard to the indefinitely near point P is thus equal to the prepotential of the disk.

pre-pottery: see PRE- B. 2 a.

prepper (ˈprɛpə(r)). *School* and *College slang.* [f. PREP *sb.* and *a.* 2 + -ER[1], [6].] **a.** *U.S.* A preparatory sports team or a member of such a team. **b.** A preparatory school (PREPARATORY *a.* 2 a).

1945 *Richmond* (Virginia) *Times-Dispatch* 10 Oct. 18/4 (*heading*) T[homas] J[efferson High School] leads off heavy slate for preppers. **1956** 'M. INNES' *Appleby plays Chicken* I. i. 16 My public school was.. nothing to my prepper. **1962** 'R. GORDON' *Doctor in Swim* xi. 73 'Actually, I'm a stinks beak in a prepper,' he confessed. **1974** *Anderson* (S. Carolina) *Independent* 19 Apr. 5B/3 Audie Mathews, 6-4, of Chicago Heights, Ill., one of the nation's most coveted preppers, is reported to be considering North Carolina State, Illinois, Oregon, Purdue and UCLA. **1974** *Times* 29 Oct. 16/4 Cheam is demonstrably the oldest prepper in the business, having started in the Surrey suburb in 1645.

preppy (ˈprɛpɪ), *a.* *U.S. School* and *College slang.* Also **preppie**. [f. PREP *sb.* and *a.* + -Y[1].] Of, pertaining to, or characteristic of a pupil at a preparatory school (see PREPARATORY *a.* 2 a); immature; (see also quot. 1980). Also as *sb.*, a pupil at a preparatory school. Hence **ˈpreppiness**.

1900 *Dialect Notes* II. i. 51 *Preppy*, silly, immature. **1970** *New York* 16 Nov. 52/3 His first year as a preppie had left Junius feeling like a pound of plaster of Paris. **1971** M. MCCARTHY *Birds of Amer.* 10 When he finally did ask,.. it was in a casual preppy voice. **1975** B. MEGGS *Matter of Paradise* I. iii. 30 All you preppies had those funny names. *Ibid.* III. vi. 98 Bubbling along now in his keen preppie way. **1977** *New Yorker* 11 July 80/2 They are wearable, stylish, practical translations of the all-American look—of preppiness and of L. L. Bean. **1978** *N.Y. Times* 6 May 12/4 The pair of loafers my sons refuse to own because they're too preppy. **1980** W. SAFIRE in *N.Y. Times Mag.* 30 Mar. 9 The word that sums up the rage of the fashion world is 'preppie'. .. Suddenly, neatness counts, the buttons are down, the sweaters and skirts are back.

pre-practise: see PRE- A. 1.

pre-prandial (priːˈprændɪəl), *a.* [f. PRE- B. 1 + L. *prandium* luncheon (see PRANDIAL) + -AL[1].] Done, made, taken, happening, etc. before dinner; before-dinner.

1822 LAMB *Let. to Coleridge* Wks. (1865) 25, I have no quarrel with you about praeprandial avocations. **1862** MRS. N. CROSLAND *Mrs. Blake* II. 101 The 'pre-prandial' hour or two of winter darkness. **1875** HELPS *Soc. Press.* xviii. 269 That charming invention of modern days, the pre-prandial tea.

pre-precipiˈtation, *a. Metallurgy.* [PRE- B. 2.] Applied to phenomena occurring at or immediately before the onset of precipitation from solid solution in alloys, esp. the separation of submicroscopic particles from which crystals later develop.

1936 M. COHEN in *Metals Technol.* Oct. 14 (*heading*) Pre-precipitation behavior of the alloy. *Ibid.* 15 The resistance and dilation curves indicate knot formation even at 200°, although there is no pre-precipitation hardening at this temperature. **1949** J. E. GARSIDE *Process & Physical Metall.* xii. 213 This process of age-hardening consists of two stages —(i) Pre-precipitation stage resulting in the formation of nuclei; (ii) Growth of the nuclei, first into particles of ultramicroscopic size, and then of microscopic size. **1959** B. CHALMERS *Physical Metall.* viii. 391 The desirable results of precipitation are almost always obtained when a very large number of precipitate particles or pre-precipitation zones are formed. **1965** HUNSICKER & STUMPF in C. S. Smith *Sorby Centennial Symposium Hist. Metall.* xviii. 287 In the face of mounting evidence the conviction became widespread that some sort of 'pre-precipitation' structure was developed at low temperatures and possibly at higher temperatures prior to and preparatory to actual precipitation.

pre-predicative: see PRE- B. 1 d.

pre-ˈpreference, *a.* [PRE- B. 2.] Ranking before preference bonds, shares, claims, etc., in security, payment of dividend or interest. Cf. PREFERENCE 8.

1869 *Bradshaw's Railway Manual* XXI. 128 New capital .. was created as a 4½ per cent. pre-preference or debenture stock, the first preference being made second. **1882** BITHELL *Counting-ho. Dict.* 236 The new series of Bonds.. distinguished from all the others by the name of pre-preference bonds. **1896** *Westm. Gaz.* 3 Mar. 6/1 The directors.. announce the issue of 6,000 Five and a-Quarter per Cent. Cumulative Pre-preference £10 shares at a premium of 10*s.* each. **1900** *Ibid.* 5 Mar. 11/1 The shareholders.. would not have it [the new issue] in the form of pre-preference shares, and now apparently the directors are determined to make it more pre than ever [by an issue of debentures].

So **pre-prefeˈrential** *a.*

1885 *Manch. Exam.* 21 Jan. 4/7 We might.. guarantee the whole loan.. instead of guaranteeing only five and raising the other four by pre-preferential bonds.

ˈprepreg, *sb.* (*a.*) [f. PRE-(IM)PREG(NATED *ppl. a.*] A fibrous material (e.g. glass or carbon fibres) that is pre-impregnated with synthetic resin for use in the manufacture of reinforced plastics. Freq. *attrib.* or as *adj.*

1954 R. H. SONNEBORN *Fiberglas Reinforced Plastics* iii. 63 The pre-preg materials are fabrics or mats that are pre-loaded, using resin mixtures that are essentially the same as are used in standard molding operations. **1958** D. J. DUFFIN *Laminated Plastics* iv. 72 Although more expensive than standard materials, prepregs are widely used in the aircraft industry and elsewhere because of the considerable savings in time—and therefore labor—costs. **1965** *Mod. Plastics Encycl. 1966* 167/3 Pre-preg laminates are made by pre-impregnating glass cloth with a resin solution. **1969** *Sci. Jrnl.* Feb. 43/3 Prepreg is made by dripping numerous tows or groups of fibres in a dilute solution of resin in acetone and then laying them down side by side.. on a firm flat surface. **1972** *Physics Bull.* Nov. 664/3 Fibre-polymer systems for the fabrication of composite parts are used either as prepregs, in which fibre and polymer are precombined and are ready for the fabrication operation, or as wet systems in which the dry fibre and the polymer are brought together during the moulding process.

Hence **ˈprepreg** *v. trans.*, to pre-impregnate with synthetic resin; **preˈpregged** *ppl. a.*; **preˈpregging** *vbl. sb.*

1964 OLEESKY & MOHR *Handbk. Reinforced Plastics* II. iii. 77/2 Epoxy resins may be readily adapted to pre-pregging using glass fabrics or roving. *Ibid.* IX. ii. 545/1 The general specifications governing roving for filament winding also apply to roving to be prepregged. **1970** *Encycl. Polymer Sci. & Technol.* XII. 26 'Sheet moulding compounds' is the term used by the Society of the Plastics Industry to identify these new reinforced, basically pre-preged sheet compounds.

pre-prep(aratory: see PRE- B. 1 d.

pre-prepare: see PRE- A. 1.

pre-pressurization: see PRE- A. 2.

pre-pressurize: see PRE- A. 1.

pre-primary: see PRE- B. 1 d.

preˈprimate. [PRE- B. 1.] An evolutionary ancestor of the primates, or an animal showing characteristics that are more highly developed in the primates.

1931 E. A. HOOTON *Up from Ape* II. 67 Our arboreal pre-primate ancestors must have been very closely similar to the existing tree shrews of the Order Insectivora. *Ibid.* 69 When the insectivorous pre-primate became a hand-feeder and a manipulator of objects, it opened up for its descendants a new route of evolutionary progress. **1971** G. H. BOURNE *Ape People* xiii. 322 The slope of the jaw seemed to be more like that of a modern preprimate known as the tarsier.

preprint (ˈpriːprɪnt), *sb.* [PRE- A. 2.] Something printed in advance; a portion of a work printed and issued before the publication of the whole. Also *attrib.*

1889 *Academy* 1 June 385/2 Dr. Charles Waldstein.. has made arrangements with the American Journal of Archaeology.. to issue these papers independently in a series of 'preprints'. **1903** *Dial* (Chicago) 1 Feb. 93/1 A preprint from the Decennial Publications of the University of Chicago... Other preprints in this series are as follows. **1929** E. C. BINGHAM *Some Defs. Rheology* 1 This paper is issued in preprint form primarily to stimulate discussion. **1955** J. A. WHEELER in *Niels Bohr* 174 A paper.. seen in preprint form through the kindness of the authors. **1961** D. J. BOORSTIN *Image* iv. 141 They [*sc.* scientists] now use the device of the 'preprint'. This is a version of an article made available *before* its 'publication'. **1970** *Nature* 26 Dec. 1356/2 We can show how well connected we are by giving references to a large number of preprints.

preˈprint, *v.* [PRE- A. 1.] *trans.* To print in advance, *spec.* to print and issue (part of a work) before publication of the whole. Hence **preˈprinted** *ppl. a.*

1928 E. D. P. EVANS (*title*) Meaning of minster in place-names. (Preprinted from the Philological Society's Transactions, 1925–28, part I.) **1958** *Practical Wireless* XXXIV. 72/2 It is provided with interchangeable paper on plastic shields which can be supplied either pre-printed or blank. **1964** *Economist* 11 July 165/1 The answer has been preprinted colour gravure. **1965** L. W. BECK *Stud. Philos. Kant* vii. 108 This paper.. is preprinted here by kind permission. **1970** A. DAVIDSON *Returns of Love* ii. 21 You pick up the little card which pops out of the slot, knowing that it's been pre-printed. **1977** *It* May 6/1 You can purchase books of 25 pre-printed slips at two pence per book.

preˈprocess, *v.* [f. PRE- A. 1 + PROCESS *v.*[1]] *trans.* To subject to a preliminary processing. Hence **preˈprocessing** *vbl. sb.* Also **preˈprocessor**, a machine for preprocessing.

1964 *Ann. N.Y. Acad. Sci.* CXV. 568 The use of some analog equipment, such as filters, to preprocess data. **1965** *Proc. Internat. Fed. Information Processing Congr.* II. 329/1 (*heading*) ISODATA—a self-organizing computer program for the design of pattern recognition preprocessing. **1966** [see *post-processing* s.v. POST- A. 1 b]. **1967** E. R. LANNON in Cox & Grose *Organiz. Bibliogr. Rec. by Computer* IV. 83 In order to reduce errors.. the system provides for a preprocessing and storage of a data base description.. in secondary storage. **1967** *Computer Jrnl.* IX. 360/1 The preprocessor was.. designed to translate these two dialects into a form acceptable to the Atlas compiler. **1970** A. CAMERON et al. *Computers & Old Eng. Concordances* 68 Some preprocessing of the concordances is a desirable prerequisite to editing. **1976** *Nature* 29 Jan. 294/2 The three detected voltages were digitised, pre-processed and recorded on magnetic tape for later computer processing.

pre'processed, *ppl. a.* [PRE- A. 1.] Of food: processed before being offered for sale; needing little preparation.

1961 M. BEADLE *These Ruins are Inhabited* (1963) viii. 107 Englishwomen..can't afford the extra cost of preprocessed food or commercial laundry charges. **1962** F. I. ORDWAY et al. *Basic Astronautics* xiii. 520 Fresh meat and vegetables under conventional refrigeration obviously cannot be considered. However, some preprocessed, small bulk, frozen foods are a possibility.

pre-production, *sb.* and *a.* **A.** *sb.* **1.** [PRE- A. 2.] (A) preliminary or trial production.

1938 *New Statesman* 20 Aug. 282/1, I have seen pre-productions, for the Festival, of this week's naturalistic plays. **1947** CROWTHER & WHIDDINGTON *Science at War* I. 49 The General Electric Company worked out a method of pre-production, by which small quantities of new valves could be produced by formerly unskilled women workers, while the problems of mass-production were being worked out.

2. [PRE- B. 1.] Work prior to production; preparation for production.

1976 *Time* 20 Dec. 63/1 We're here in New York doing preproduction. **1979** D. LOWDEN *Boudapesti 3* xviii. 100 In films, 80% of scripts written never reached the stage of pre-production.

B. *adj.* [PRE- B. 2.] Prior or preliminary to (a) production.

1946 *Nature* 21 Dec. 897/2 An extremely active development department using a larger number of pre-production machines. **1959** *Times* 19 Feb. 2/4 Testing of valves up to pre-production stage. **1959** P. BULL *I know Face* iv. 66 Other pre-production costs included advance payment to producer. **1967** *Jane's Surface Skimmers Systems 1967–68* 133/1 The design team..is based in a factory at Zaporojie.., where all prototypes and pre-production engines..are developed and built. **1970** M. TORMÉ *Other Side of Rainbow* (1971) iii. 34 Nearly every television variety show operates in a three-phase pattern. First, there is a preproduction period in which songs are chosen, scripts are written, [etc.]. **1973** *Times* 12 Nov. 2/5 Noise measurements on the 02 preproduction aircraft had been disappointing. **1977** *Engin. Materials & Design* Aug. 17/1 The results obtained were comparable with those expected from a pre-production run of conventionally designed radiators.

pre-pro'fessional, *a.* and *sb.* [PRE- B. 1.]

A. *adj.* Prior or preliminary to professional training.

1948 *Mind* LVII. 387 University instruction in psychology should serve..as a preparation for other fields (*e.g.* law, medicine, engineering), in the form of pre-professional courses. **1975** *N.Y. Times* 28 Dec. IV. 12/4 New pre-professional (a currently popular term in education) programs, such as Mills's prelaw 'Administration and the Legal Process'.

B. *sb.* One who is training for a profession.

1970 *Jrnl. Gen. Psychol.* LXXXIII. 140 When I speak to audiences, I find that the myth is still believed firmly, even by preprofessionals. **1977** *Early Music* Apr. 263/1 The conference was designed to draw together professionals and college-age pre-professionals.

pre'program, *v.* Also preprogramme. [PRE- A. 1.] *trans.* To program (a computer or calculator) beforehand. Also *transf.* and *fig.* So **pre'programmed** *ppl. a.*, **pre'programming** *vbl. sb.* (*U.S.* also **-gramed, -graming**).

1964 *Economist* 16 May 746/2 Ships operated entirely by pre-programmed computer are practicable. **1965** H. KAHN *On Escalation* viii. 166 Deterioration in international relations will provoke a pre-programed crash defense program. **1970** *Computers & Humanities* IV. 355 Produce a number of specific movies, then use the experience gained to develop appropriate software for combined interactive and preprogrammed modes of operation. **1971** J. Z. YOUNG *Introd. Study Man* p. viii, His brain may indeed be pre-programmed to operate in this way. **1973** P. EVANS *Bodyguard Man* xvii. 110 It was as though his thought-processes had been pre-programmed, as though this was a situation that he had foreseen. **1974** HAWKEY & BINGHAM *Wild Card* xv. 129 Because of the preprograming..all I have to do is transmit the starting instructions. **1977** J. D. DOUGLAS in Douglas & Johnson *Existential Sociol.* i. 60 Even the simplest of human activities, such as walking down the street, cannot be preprogrammed without danger of catastrophe. **1977** *Sci. Amer.* Apr. 94/1 (Advt.), A series of preprogrammed hand-held calculators that virtually revolutionized numerical data processing.

Hence as *sb.*, an already existing program.

1971 J. Z. YOUNG *Introd. Study Man* p. vii, The whole structure of our language and thought is limited by a pre-programme in the organization of the brain.

preproinsulin: see PRE- B. 1.

†**pre'properate,** *v. Obs. rare*$^{-1}$. [f. ppl. stem of late L. *præproperāre* to hasten greatly (Gloss. Philox.): see PRE- A. 6 and PROPERATE.] *trans.* To hasten unduly or in excess. So †**,prepropeˈration,** the action of hastening unduly. *Obs. rare*$^{-1}$.

1647 WARD *Simp. Cobler* 37 The importunity of some impatient..mindes, will put both Parliament and Assembly upon some prepropeations, that will not be safe in Ecclesiasticall Constitutions. **1651** J. ROCKET *Chr. Subject* viii. (1658) 77 To prevent the preproperating our misery, or lessen those evils into which..we have cast ourselves.

†**pre'properous,** *a. Obs.* [f. L. *præproper-us* too quick or hasty (f. *præ*, PRE- A. 6 + *proper-us* speedy, quick) + -OUS.] Over-hasty, precipitate.

1555 J. PROCTOR *Hist. Wyat's Rebell.* 62 Vnaduised hardinesse and preproperous haste in mooste matters haue these twoo companions: Errour in the beginning, and Repentaunce in the ende. *a* **1661** FULLER *Worthies, Leicestersh.* (1662) II. 133 By such preproperous Couling of Boyes, and vailing of Girles, Parents were cozened out of their children. **1670** RAY *Proverbs, Devon.* 226 Administring preposterous and preproperous justice.

Hence †**pre'properously** *adv.*, over-hastily.

1637 R. HUMPHREY tr. *St. Ambrose* I. 31 Why dost preproperously call for a crowne before thou overcommest?

preprostatic: see PRE- B. 3.

pre-prove, pre-provide: see PRE- A. 1.

prepster ('prɛpstə(r)). *U.S.* [f. PREP *sb.* and *a.* 2 + -STER.] (See quot. 1965.)

1965 *Eng. Stud.* XLVI. 464 *Prepster* not only denotes a preparatory student in collegiate slang but also a trainee. **1974** *Sumter* (S. Carolina) *Daily Item* 22 Apr. 1B/1 His credentials—23 points per game and a fantastic field goal average of 80 per cent, plus nine rebounds per game and seven assists per outing as a senior—as a prepster.

prepsy'chotic, *a.* (*sb.*) *Psychol.* [PRE- B. 1.] Of or relating to symptoms, or to the period of time, prior to the onset of a psychosis. Also as *sb.* Hence **prepsy'chotically** *adv.*

1927 HENDERSON & GILLESPIE *Text-bk. Psychiatry* ix. 218 Are there certain pre-psychotic traits which indicate a severer grade of disturbance in the event of a psychosis developing? **1931** *Internat. Jrnl. Psycho-Anal.* XII. 298 (*title*) Ego defence and the mechanism of oral ejection in schizophrenia: the psycho-analysis of a pre-psychotic case. **1935** *Brit. Jrnl. Med. Psychol.* XV. 140 By 'pre-psychotic' I mean someone who is showing ominous signs of an impending psychosis but who is not yet frankly psychotic. **1941** *Jrnl. Amer. Med. Assoc.* 16 Aug. 522/1 A severe hypotension, which existed prepsychotically as well as during the course of the psychosis, has been improved. **1959** H. NIELSEN *Fifth Caller* iii. 48 There was a tragic case—a man, prepsychotic, who needed expert attention. **1977** *Time* 4 Apr. 41/2 Tom Verlaine..delivers raw, jabbing vocals in a declamatory, prepsychotic style similar to Patti Smith's. **1977** *Lancet* 27 Aug. 449/1 There are no doubt prepsychotics who abuse alcohol.

prepuberal(ly, -pubertally: see PRE- B. 1.

pre-pubertal: see PRE- B. 1.

pre'puberty. [PRE- B. 1.] The period of life preceding puberty, esp. the two or three years immediately before. Also *attrib.*

1922 R. T. FRANKS *Gynecol. & Obstetr. Path.* iv. 74 Pre-puberty.—Practically it begins with the time at which 'budding into womanhood' is first noticed and ends with the onset of the first menstruation. *Ibid.* 75 In some instances ..in which the menstruation is delayed or remains in abeyance, although ovulation occurs, the prepuberty and the puberty stage cannot be differentiated clinically. **1932** *Amer. Jrnl. Dis. Children* XLIII. 329 We firmly believe that there is a prepuberty rise in basal metabolism. **1941** *Jrnl. Pediatrics* XIX. 291 Adolescence lasts from the time of puberty until about 21 years. Today we are not discussing this whole subject, only certain phases of it and perhaps particularly that part of adolescence which we might call prepuberty and puberty. **1949** M. MEAD *Male & Female* xiii. 280 For the old institutionalized hostilities of..girls' tears and boyish pranks, the new pre-puberty dating pattern is being substituted. **1976** *Times* 1 Sept. (Fashion Suppl.) p. vii/1 All three categories of clothing—male, female and pre-puberty.

prepu'bescent, *a.* [PRE- B. 1.] = *pre-pubertal* adj. s.v. PRE- B. 1.

1904 G. S. HALL *Adolescence* I. p. x, Rousseau would leave prepubescent years to nature..and allow the fundamental traits of savagery their fling till twelve. **1932** R. F. FORTUNE *Sorcerers of Dobu* ix. 276 The pre-pubescent girls of his own age have lain with boys older than he. **1965** F. SARGESON *Mem. Peon* vi. 174 A pre-pubescent male was..demanding ..that 'you leave my mother alone'. **1978** J. HYAMS *Pool* v. 61 This prepubescent midget has put me on the defensive.

Hence **prepu'bescence** = PREPUBERTY.

1916 *Arch. Internal Med.* XVII. 887 We may consider boys in the period of prepubescence as individuals of adult form but of small size, growing rapidly, and as yet scarcely influenced by the internal secretions of the sex glands. **1950** *Psychiatric Q.* XXIV. 495 It would appear that any study of attitudes towards death during pre-pubescence or adult life, would throw further light on the psychodynamics of human behavior. **1977** *N.Y. Rev. Bks.* 29 Sept. 13/1 During Baum's prepubescence the Civil War took place.

prepubic, præ- (priːˈpjuːbɪk), *a.* [f. next + -IC; in b, f. PRE- B. 3 + PUBIC.] **a.** Pertaining to the prepubis. **b.** Situated in front of the pubis.

1871 HUXLEY *Anat. Vertebr. Anim.* v. 270 A large spatulate bone..seems to be an exaggeration of the pre-pubic process. **1872** HUMPHRY *Myology* 13 It extends over the side of the abdomen to the middle line and the edge of the prepubic shield and cornu. **1918** *Bull. Amer. Mus. Nat. Hist.* XXXVIII. 521 In the ornithischian dinosaurs the expanded prepubic process appears to have served as a base for a forward extension of the pubi-ischio-femoralis. **1934** *Anatomischer Anzeiger* LXXVIII. 44 The prepubic skeletal element [of *Ascaphus truei*] is cartilaginous. **1974** D. & M. WEBSTER *Compar. Vertebr. Morphol.* v. 102 In prototherian and metatherian (but not eutherian) mammals there is a fourth skeletal element on each side [of the pelvic girdle], called the marsupial or prepubic bone.

‖**prepubis, præ-** (ˌpriːˈpjuːbɪs). *Anat.* Also **-es.** [PRE- A. 4.] **1.** The pre-acetabular portion of the pubis, esp. in Dinosaurs.

1888 ROLLESTON & JACKSON *Anim. Life* 65 This process appears to be the homologue of the prae-pubis (so-called) in the *Stegosauria* and *Ornithopoda* among *Deinosauria*. **1895** *Syd. Soc. Lex.*, Prepubes. **1896** NEWTON *Dict. Birds* 862 The..anterior process of the *os pubis*, often called the pectineal,..is the element which in Dinosaurs is described as the 'præpubis', while in recent Reptiles it is represented by the pubis proper. **1956** A. S. ROMER *Osteol. Reptiles* vii. 328 In this case [*sc.* the pterosaur skeleton] the majority opinion is that the true pubis is included in the plate and that this anterior element is a neomorph, a prepubis.

2. = EPIPUBIS.

1931 G. K. NOBLE *Biol. Amphibia* x. 240 A prepubis may have been a primitive character of modern Amphibia. **1969** *Nature* 14 June 1091/1 Here I report the presence of the so-called marsupial bone (praepubis or epipubis) in the skeleton of *K[ryptobaatar] dashzevegi*. This bone has never before been found in fossil Multituberculata material. **1975** *Nature* 26 June 698/1 Marsupial bones (epipubes, prepubes) occur in Marsupialia, Monotremata and have also been found in Cretaceous Multituberculata.

prepubli'cation, *a.* and *sb.* [PRE- B. 2.]

A. *adj.* Produced, issued, or occurring in advance of publication.

1922 F. SCOTT FITZGERALD *Let.* 6 Feb. (1964) 332 A pre-publication review which contained private information destined..to hurt the sale of my book. **1936** *Amer. Speech* XI. 171/1 The prepublication announcement and the blurb on the jacket of his recent book. **1964** F. BOWERS *Bibliogr. & Textual Crit.* III. iv. 78 It constituted a pre-publication state decided on before public sale could have offered any opportunity for objections. **1977** *Time* 13 June 60/2 Seldom has an anthology of critical essays aroused so much prepublication anxiety as Diana Trilling's *We Must March My Darlings*.

B. *sb.* [PRE- A. 2.] The action or fact of publishing beforehand; publication in advance.

1971 *Nature* 30 Apr. 547/3 In the opinion of the editor.. an article about the paper that had appeared in *Medical World News* contained so much of its substance..as to constitute prepublication and disqualify its claims for space in a journal that aims to publish original material. **1975** P. HARCOURT *Fair Exchange* II. iii. 105 This book..where did you get it?..you realize it's pre-publication?

prepublicity, -publish: see PRE- A. 2, 1.

prepuce ('priːpjuːs). [a. F. *prépuce* (15th c. in Godef. *Compl.*):—L. *præpūtium*.] The loose fold of integument which covers the glans penis (or the glans clitoridis); the foreskin.

c **1400** MAUNDEV. (Roxb.) xi. 42 In þis temple was Charlemayne, when þe aungell broght him þe prepuce of oure Lord, when he was circumcised. **1541** R. COPLAND *Guydon's Quest. Chirurg.*, etc. Kj b, The heade hyght prepuce. *c* **1618** MORYSON *Itin.* IV. v. vi. (1903) 495 Then the prepuce or foreskinne was taken out, and putt into a box of salt to be buryed after in the Churchyearde. **1767** GOOCH *Treat. Wounds* I. 433, I have divided the Prepuce several times in Phimoses, without any ill accidents supervening. **1878** BELL *Gegenbaur's Comp. Anat.* 623 The end of the clitoris is generally provided with a gland, and is also covered by a prepuce.

†**b.** *transf.* (*a*) The state of the uncircumcised, uncircumcision. (*b*) See quot. *a* 1682. *Obs.*

c **1400** *Apoll. Loll.* 84 Poul seiþ, Noiþer prepuce nor circumcicoun is out, nor out worþ, not but keping of þe biddingis of God. **1582** N.T. (Rhem.) *Rom.* ii. 25 If thou be a preuaricatour of the Law, thy circumcision is become prepuce. *a* **1682** SIR T. BROWNE *Tracts* (1684) 64 As the vulgar expresseth it to take away the prepuces from such trees. [Vulgate *Lev.* xix. 23 Auferetis præputia eorum: poma quæ germinant, immunda erunt vobis.]

†'**prepucy.** *Obs.* [ad. L. *præpūtium*: see prec. and -CY.] The foreskin. Also *transf.* The state of the uncircumcised; uncircumcision.

1382 WYCLIF *Acts* xi. 3 Whi entridist thou to men hauynge prepucie? [Vulg. *ad viros præputium habentes*]. —— *Rom.* ii. 25 If thou be a trespassour of the lawe, thi circumcisioun is maad prepucie [Vulg. *circumcisio tua præputium facta est*]. **1388** —— *Deut.* x. 16 Therfor circumcide ȝe the prepucie [*gloss* ethir vnclennesse] of ȝoure herte [Vulg. *præputium cordis*]. **1483** CAXTON *Gold. Leg.* 392/1 That I may haue the prepucye vndefouled.

prepulse: PRE- A. 2.

pre'punched, *ppl. a.* [PRE- A. 1.] Of a card or the like: having holes already punched in it. Of information: already stored or represented as a pattern of holes. So **pre'punch** *v. trans.*

1953 *Proc. IRE* XLI. 1274/1 While at his desk the programmer may then assemble into a single deck of cards some prepunched library programs together with cards especially punched for the problem to be solved. **1957** *Practical Wireless* XXXIII. 705/1 Pre-punched holder plates take such focal components as valves, etc. **1964** T. W. MCRAE *Impact of Computers on Accounting* ii. 47 We are likely to see a great deal more of inter-business documentation in the form of machine-sensible input, such as sending a purchase order as a pre-punched card. **1965** *New England Jrnl. Med.* CCLXXII. 1211/2 The clerk.. obtained a deck of data-processing cards that had been prepunched with the patient's file number.

pre'punctual, *a. rare.* [f. PRE- A. 5, 6 + PUNCTUAL.] More than punctual; coming earlier than the appointed time. So **prepunctu'ality,** anticipative punctuality, the fact of arriving before the precise time; **pre'punctually** *adv.*, more than punctually.

1870 Helps in *Macm. Mag.* July 239/2 Our conjoint prepunctualities brought us to the station a good half-hour before the time. **1882** *Society* 9 Dec. 8/1 So far was prepunctuality..carried, that..Her Majesty was ten minutes before time. **1890** *Cent. Dict.*, Prepunctual. **1894** *Story of My Two Wives* 110 We were at the agent's prepunctually.

prepupa (priːˈpjuːpə). *Ent.* [pre- B. 1.] An insect late in its larval development, during a relatively quiescent phase in which preparations for the transformation into a pupa take place; also, in certain beetles, a distinct instar preceding the pupa stage.

1925 A. D. Imms *Gen. Textbk. Entomol.* 186 The prepupa represents a greatly abbreviated instar. **1955** P. A. Buxton *Nat. Hist. Tsetse Flies* xi. 380 Generally speaking one measures the duration of life of the puparium in an inclusive way, from the time when the larva becomes immobile, through the life of prepupa and pupa, to the emergence of the adult. **1959** E. F. Linssen *Beetles Brit. Isles* II. 85 After the third moult..it [*sc.* a meloid beetle] turns into what is called a pre-pupa. **1975** *Nature* 17 Apr. 592/2 In such specimens..there is no visible response to background, whether the caterpillars or prepupae are exposed to long or short hours of daylight.

prepupal (priːˈpjuːpəl), *a. Ent.* [pre- B. 1.] Immediately preceding a larval insect's change into a pupa.

1906 J. B. Smith *Explanation Terms Entomol.* 108 Prepupal: that stage in the larva just preceding the change to pupa. **1925** A. D. Imms *Gen. Textbk. Entomol.* 185 A brief period of quiescence follows which marks the prepupal instar. **1933** *Jrnl. R. Hort. Soc.* LVIII. 233 The excellent photographs..illustrate the adult sawflies..and the larval, prepupal and pupal stages. **1971** Borror & DeLong *Introd. Study Insects* (ed. 3) iv. 69/1 The other changes begin in the prepupal stage of the last larval instar.

preputial (prɪˈpjuːʃ(ɪ)əl), *a.* [f. L. *præpūti-um* præputium + -al¹; so mod.F. *préputial.*] Of or pertaining to the prepuce.

1611 Corbet in Coryat *Crudities, Panegyr. Verses*, Thy observations..Have stuft thy massie and voluminous head With Mountaines Abbies Churches Synagogues Preputiall Offals and Dutch Dialogues. *a* **1682** Sir T. Browne *Tracts* (1684) 65 Those sprouts and buds which..resembleth the preputial part. **1846** G. E. Day tr. *Simon's Anim. Chem.* II. 461 Preputial and urethral calculi. **1971** [see fixative *sb.* 3]. **1976** *Lancet* 20 Nov. 1107/2 Culture of swabs from the preputial sac, and comparison with matched controls, suggested that the source of infection in boys is the prepuce or urethra rather than the bowel as in girls.

prepyloric: see pre- B. 3.

prepyramid (ˌpriːˈpɪrəmɪd). *Anat.* [pre- A. 4.] The anterior pyramid of the medulla oblongata. So **ˌprepyˈramidal** *a.*, pertaining to the prepyramids, or situated in front of the pyramids.

1866 Owen *Vertebr. Anim.* I. 273 A narrower median 'pre-pyramidal' tract. *Ibid.* 276 The 'commissura ansulata', which crosses the pre-pyramids just behind the 'hypoaria'. **1868** *Ibid.* III. 83 The prepyramids..are long, narrow, flat, and contract as they approach the pons. *Ibid.* 86 The prepyramidal columns.

prequalification, -ative: see pre- A. 2, B. 2 a.

prequalify: pre- A. 1.

prequel (ˈpriːkwəl). [f. pre- A. 2 + se)quel *sb.*] A book, film, etc., the events portrayed in which or the concerns of which precede those of an existing completed work.

1973 *Britannica Bk. of Year 1972* 732/3 *Prequel*, a literary work whose narrative sequentially precedes that of an earlier work. **1977** *National Observer* (U.S.) 1 Jan. 1/4 Cammer.. has just written a book, *Freedom from Compulsion*... He calls it a 'prequel' to his earlier book, *Up from Depression.* '"Prequel" is a word I coined', he explains. 'It's a sequel except it's on a subject that comes before.' **1977** *Globe & Mail* (Toronto) 17 Sept. 37/5 The Silmarillion, for which Tolkien coined the term Prequel, describes not only the creation of Middle Earth, but of the universe. **1979** *Films & Filming* Mar. 11 In this 'prequel' Tom Berenger stars as Butch Cassidy and William Katt as Sundance.

prerabbinical, -radio: see pre- B. 1 d, 2 a.

Pre-Raph. (priːˈræf), *a.* (*sb.*) Colloq. abbrev. of Pre-Raphaelite *sb.* and *a.* (senses A. 1 and B. 1). Hence **Pre-ˈRaphly** *adv.*

1874 L. Troubridge *Life amongst Troubridges* (1966) 80 A new rage..painting the panels of the shutters of our bedrooms,..you can't think how pre-Raph. they look. Pale blue ground..and in each panel droops a flower, of course very pre-Raphly done. **1944** J. Lees-Milne *Prophesying Peace* (1977) 54 These flowers are madly Pre-Raph. Do you suppose William [Morris] planted these? **1970** *Listener* 27 Aug. 291/2 The diaries of Laura Troubridge written when she was 'a madly Pre-Raph' young Victorian. **1975** *Times* 25 Sept. 13/5 William Gaunt's brilliant little 1940s book at that time contained all that most of us knew..about the Pre-Raphs.

Pre-Raphael (priːˈræfeɪɛl), *a.* (*sb.*) [pre- B. 2.] Previous to Raphael; a painter (or painting) before the time of Raphael. **b.** = Pre-Raphaelite. Hence **Pre-ˈRaphaelly** *adv. rare.*

1850 W. M. Rossetti *The P.R.B. Jrnl.* July in *Præraphaelite Diaries & Lett.* (1900) 275, I reverence—indeed almost idolize—what I have seen of the Pre-Raphael painters. **1850** *Germ* May 158 Mediæval, or pre-Raffaele art is seen in his youthful timid darings. **1850** Dickens in *Househ. Words* I. 266/1 That the Pre-Raphael Brother is indisputably accomplished in the manipulation of his art. *Ibid.* 265/2 As befits such a subject—Pre-Raphaelly considered. **1853** D. G. Rossetti in *D. G. R.'s Family Letters* (1895) II. 122 Fattening on ill-got pictures in his sleep, Till some Præraphael prove for him too deep. **1878** Grosart in *H. More's Poems* Mem. Introd. 29/1 Its pre-Raphael-like studies of nature.

Pre-ˈRaphaelism, preˈraph-, præ-. [f. as prec. + -ism.] The artistic principles of the Pre-Raphaelite Brotherhood (= Pre-Raphaelitism); by Ruskin and others applied, by way of distinction, to the art of the painters who preceded Raphael; see quot. 1882 s.v. Pre-Raphaelitism.

1852 Geo. Eliot *Let.* 24–25 July (1954) II. 48 The British Q[uarterl]y..have one subject of which I am jealous—'Pre-Raphaelism in Painting and Literature'. **1853** W. M. Rossetti in *Præraph. Diaries & Lett.* (1900) 308 Though both Præraphaelism and Brotherhood are as real as ever. **1859** Gullick & Timbs *Paint.* 231 Pre-Raphaelism, though open to the charge of mannerism, was a revulsion and protest against the unmanly conventionalisms into which a portion of the English school had fallen. **1862** 'Shirley' *Nugæ Crit.* viii. 356 Fra Angelico da Fiesole..is almost the only one of the præ-Raphaelites, whom a man who does not believe in præ-Raphaelism can thoroughly relish. **1882** [see Pre-Raphaelitism].

So **Pre-Raphaeˈlistic** *a.* = next, B.

1884 R. Buchanan *Foxglove Manor* II. xvi. 38 One of your detestable pre-Raphaelistic drawings.

Pre-Raphaelite, preraphaelite, præ- (priːˈræfeɪəlaɪt), *sb.* and *a.* Also **-Raffael-**. [f. pre- B. 1 + the proper name *Raphael* (It. *Raffaello, Raffaele*) + -ite¹.]

A. *sb.* **1.** An artist who aims at producing work in the spirit which generally imbued art before the time of Raphael (or, more especially, before his later work and that of his successors); *spec.* one of the group of English artists, including Holman-Hunt, Millais, and D. G. Rossetti, who *c* 1848 called themselves the 'Pre-Raphaelite Brotherhood' (P.R.B.).

1849 W. M. Rossetti *The P.R.B. Journal* in *Præraph. Diaries & Lett.* (1900) 209. —— *Ibid.* 19 Nov., ibid. 231 Tonight was a P.R.B. meeting at Millais's, at which we were all present with the exception of Woolner. **1849** D. G. Rossetti *Let. to J. Collinson* 25 Oct., ibid. 13 Dear P.R.B. [= Brother], On the road hither last night I [etc.]. **1850** *Blackw. Mag.* July 82/1 The mountebank proceedings of a small number of artists, who..are endeavouring to set up a school of their own. We allude to the pre-Raphaelites. **1851** Ruskin *Pre-Raphaelitism* 27 The Pre-Raphaelites imitate no pictures: they paint from nature only. **1854** Fairholt *Dict. Terms Art*, *Pre-Raphaelites*, a school of modern artists, who profess to follow the mode of study and expression adopted by the early painters who flourished before the time of Raphael, and whose principal theory of action is a rigid adherence to natural forms and effects. **1862** 'Shirley' *Nugæ Crit.* vi. 271 We are all præraphaelites. Mr. Millais' gawky girls, and Mr. Dyce's skinny saints, have gained the day. **1875** Helps *Ess.* 107 The luxuriance and beauty of the water-weeds and of the bulrushes..would have given work to a pre-Raffaelite for a year. **1882** W. Hamilton *Æsthetic Movement* (ed. 3) 11 It pleased Mr. Buchanan, in his attack on the Pre-Raphaelites and Æsthetes, to stigmatise The Germ as an unwholesome publication. **1907** W. M. Rossetti in *Let. to Editor*, I myself write the words thus, *Præraphaelite* and *Præraphaelitism.*

2. One of the painters who preceded Raphael.

1862 [see Pre-Raphaelism].

B. *adj.* (or attrib. use of sb.)

1. Of, belonging to, or characteristic of the Pre-Raphaelites, or their principles and style.

1849 [see A. 1]. **1851** *Art Jrnl.* 1 July 185/1 The attempts of a few young men who style themselves the Pre-Raffael-ite school, but more properly might be called the Gothic school. **1851** Ruskin *Pre-Raphaelitism* 27 The Pre-Raphaelite pictures are just as superior to the early Italian in skill of manipulation, power of drawing, and knowledge of effect, as inferior to them in grace of design. **1853** —— *Lect. Archit.* iv. §132 Every Pre-Raphaelite landscape background is painted to the last touch, in the open air, from the thing itself. **1857** *Athenæum* 7 Feb. 176/3 If our Crabbe be a poet (and a Pre-Raphaelite poet Crabbe was, long ere the Pre-Raphaelite style was dreamed of). **1860** Hawthorne *Marb. Faun* xxxii, A pre-Raphaelite artist.. might find an admirable subject in one of these Tuscan girls. **1873** Hamerton *Th. about Art* xiii. 184 The Pre-Raphaelite movement is understood to have combined two very distinct aims: first, the intellectual elevation of art by the choice of noble and original subjects, and, secondly, its technical advancement by a new and minute analysis of nature. **1905** Holman-Hunt *Pre-Raphaelitism* I. 101 In our final estimation this picture [Raphael's Transfiguration] was a signal step in the decadence of Italian art. When we had advanced this opinion to other students, they, as a *reductio ad absurdum*, had said, 'Then you are Pre-Raphaelite'. Referring to this as we worked side by side, Millais and I laughingly agreed that the designation must be accepted.

2. Existing before Raphael.

1855 Motley *Corr.* (1889) I. vi. 182 In these pre-Raphaelite productions Florence is very rich. **1882** W. Hamilton *Æsthetic Movement* 1 Enthusiastic in their admiration of early Italian art and the mediaeval Pre-Raphaelite painters.

Pre-Raphaelitic, preraph-, præ- (-ˈɪtɪk), *a.* [f. prec. + -ic.] Of, pertaining to, or after the manner of the Pre-Raphaelites; = prec. B. 1.

1877 T. Sinclair *Mount* (1878) 5 To note the baldness of Cæsaric heads without specially organised education in this pre-Raphaelitic direction. **1881** W. G. Palgrave in *Macm. Mag.* XLV. 23 A lofty tree of præ-Raphaelitic slenderness and grace.

ˌPre-Raphaeˈlitically, preraph-, præ-, *adv.* [f. Pre-Raphaelitic *a.* + -al + -ly².] In a manner suggestive of the Pre-Raphaelites.

1895 G. B. Shaw *Let.* 1 Mar. (1965) I. 490 You are glad to..come back PreRaphaelitically to Giotto again. **1927** *Glasgow Herald* 7 July 4/6 The drabness of Arnold Bennett's pre-Raphaelitically accurate Five Towns.

Pre-ˈRaphaelitish, preraph-, præ- (-aɪtɪʃ), *a. rare.* [f. as prec. + -ish¹.] Resembling the work of the Pre-Raphaelites.

1854 A. Thackeray *Jrnl.* Feb. in H. Ritchie *Lett. A. T. Ritchie* (1924) v. 61 Mr. Millais was there, a tall good-looking Pre-Raphaelitish young man. **1865** Miss Mulock *Christian's Mistake* ii. (1866) 38 That pale, prim, pre-Raphaelitish dame who was represented all over the College. **1889** *Art Jrnl.* Aug. 222 A picture, which he describes as very pre-Raphaelitish indeed, of a cornfield.

Pre-ˈRaphaelitism, preraph-, præ-. [f. Pre-Raphaelite + -ism.] The principles, methods, or style of painting adopted by the Pre-Raphaelite Brotherhood and their followers; sometimes applied to a similar tendency in poetry and other arts.

1851 Ruskin (*title*) Pre-Raphaelitism. **1853** *N. Brit. Rev.* 303 Pre-Raphaelitism is in painting very much what the reform led by Wordsworth was in poetical literature. **1853** Ruskin *Lect. Archit.* iv. §132 Pre-Raphaelitism has but one principle, that of absolute, uncompromising truth in all that it does, obtained by working everything, down to the most minute detail, from nature, and from nature only. **1858** *Edin. Rev.* July 206 Pre-raphaelitism, both of the pen and brush, is a useful correction of a previous morbid tendency. **1882** Ruskin *Let. to Chesneau* 20 Dec. (Ashley Libr. 1894), Pre-Raphaelism would properly express the method or manner of the painters who actually lived before Raphael—as 'Raphaelism' might generally be applied to the style of all his school, at every subsequent date. Pre-Raphaelitism is, it seems to me, the proper term to express the peculiar tenets of the sect you have been examining, who called itself 'Pre-Raphaelite'; or, with still greater exclusiveness, 'The Pre-Raphaelite Brethren'. **1974** J. Christian *Pre-Raphaelites in Oxford* 5 In the history of Pre-Raphaelitism nowhere played a more important part than Oxford. **1978** *Bodl. Libr. Rec.* X. 52 In view of Oxford's strong connections with Pre-Raphaelitism, it is doubly gratifying to be able to record that the Bodleian Library has proved a comparatively rich quarry.

pre-ˈrational, *a.* [pre- B. 1.] Intuitive, instinctive, based on mental processes more primitive than reason.

1903 C. A. Strong *Why Mind has Body* xi. 274 Not reasoning, but some deep pre-rational instinct..is the basis of our belief in other minds. **1919** M. K. Bradby *Psycho-Anal.* iii. 39 In our intuitive pre-rational unconsciously based convictions we shall rediscover the beliefs of primitive man. **1921** E. Sapir *Language* ii. 39 We have been assuming that the material of language reflects merely the world of concepts and, on what I have ventured to call the 'pre-rational' plane, of images, which are the raw material of concepts. **1936** Wirth & Shils tr. *Mannheim's Ideology & Utopia* iii. 108 A mode of thought is thus created which conceives of history as the reign of pre- and super-rational forces. **1941** *Mind* L. 378 It is, however, pertinent to one central topic, morality as pre-rational, rational, and post-rational. **1948** P. Tillich *Protestant Era* p. xxiv, The trend of the younger generation in Europe toward the vital and prerational side of the individual and social life. **1957** J. S. Huxley *Relig. without Revelation* (rev. ed.) iii. 52 This pre-rational phase of individual mental life.

prereaction: see pre- A. 2.

pre-ˈreader. [pre- B. 1.] **a.** A book designed for students who cannot yet read. **b.** A person who cannot yet read. Also **pre-ˈreading** *ppl. a.* and *vbl. sb.*

1965 *Language* XLI. 548 There is no reason to believe that prereading training on Latin phonology would be of any benefit. **1966** J. Derrick *Teaching Eng. to Immigrants* ii. 104 A set of pictures is published for use at this pre-reading stage. *Ibid.* v. 182 There is preparatory work even to this—work which may be called 'pre-reading' and which is aimed at familiarizing the pupils with the notion of reading and with some of the musculo-sensory activities that are involved in the whole process. *Ibid.* 183 Many elementary courses do in fact include a pre-reader or picture book which can be used with the class if pupils' copies are available. **1972** *Sci. Amer.* Dec. 114/3 Pre-readers will like the action just fine; small sophisticates in the early grades will find the challenge interesting. **1976** *Word 1971* XXVII. 501 This spontaneously developed ability of the prereader has been noted only sporadically.

prerecognition: see pre- B. 2 a.

pre-reˈcord, *v.* [pre- A. 1.] *trans.* To record for subsequent use, esp. in film-making and broadcasting. So **pre-reˈcorded** *ppl. a.* (***pre-recorded tape***, magnetic tape on which sound has been recorded prior to its sale); **pre-reˈcording** *vbl. sb.*

1937 M. Steiner in N. Naumburg *We make Movies* xiv. 233 Pre-recording means pre-scoring, pre-playing with an orchestra, piano, or whatever is required of the song or dance number to be used in the picture. **1941** *B.B.C. Gloss. Broadcasting Terms* 24 *Pre-Record* (*v. trans.*), to record a programme on a closed circuit for subsequent reproduction. **1954** *Newsweek* 11 Oct. 55/2 In TV, as in the movies, it is not unusual to pre-record musical numbers, but this is generally done a few days before the performance. **1958** *Sunday Times* 3 Aug. 3/6 Now that the station has brought a new record-player and gets all its music in prerecorded tapes, the personal touch is all but gone. **1962** *Times* 5 July 15/4 Pre-recorded tapes have been issued in some quantity in Great Britain. **1965** *Listener* 30 Dec. 1087/3, I can only say that pre-recording again ruined what might have been a delightful three-quarters of an hour. **1972** *Daily Tel.* 6 Jan. 1/2 Mr Wilson, Leader of the Opposition, visited a television studio yesterday morning to pre-record his contribution to the programme. **1978** *N.Y. Times* 30 Mar. B22/6 (Advt.), The synchronized cassette player lets you make perfect pre-recorded presentations. **1978** *Lancashire Life* Sept. 131/1 Few people feel that the pre-recorded cassette is of comparable quality to the long playing record.

prerectal: PRE- B. 3.

prere'duction. *Genetics.* [ad. G. *praereduction* (Korschelt & Heider *Lehrb. der Vergleichenden Entwicklungsgeschichte der Wirbellosen Thiere* (Allgemeiner Theil) (1903) II. vi. 586): see PRE- A. 2 and REDUCTION.] **a.** Reduction of chromosome number at the first of the two meiotic cell divisions, rather than at the second. Opp. POSTREDUCTION a.

1905 *Proc. Acad. Nat. Sci. Philadelphia* LVII. 186 He has to assume a complex axial metamorphosis, which is wholly unnecessary on the basis of a prereduction. **1915, 1921** [see POSTREDUCTION a].

b. Separation of homologous chromatids or genes at the first of the two meiotic cell divisions, rather than at the second. Opp. POSTREDUCTION b.

1934, etc. [see POSTREDUCTION b].

Hence **prere'ductional** *a.*, involving or pertaining to prereduction; **prere'ductionally** *adv.*

1905 *Proc. Acad. Nat. Sci. Philadelphia* LVII. 187 He describes a prereductional division of the bivalent chromatin nucleolus. *Ibid.* 195 Whenever the heterochromosomes occur in pairs in the spermatogonia.. their univalent components become separated in the first maturation mitosis, *i.e.*, divide prereductionally. **1950** [see POSTREDUCTION b]. **1950** [see POSTREDUCTIONALLY *adv.*].

pre-reflective, -reflexive: see PRE- B. 1.

pre-reformatory, etc.: PRE- B. 1, etc.

pre-'registered, *ppl. a.* [PRE- A. 1.] Registered in advance; *spec.* in *Printing*, brought into alignment or coincidence beforehand (cf. REGISTER *v.* 4 b).

1967 KARCH & BUBER *Offset Processes* vi. 219 For multicolor work, cross-hair register marks sight the original material in precision-notched and pre-registered frames. **1973** *LSA Bull.* Mar. 24 The 13 countries with the largest numbers of pre-registered members (all with 20 or more)... The U.S.A... had 189 pre-registered participants.

preregi'stration, *a.* and *sb.* **A.** *adj.* [PRE- B. 2.] Of or pertaining to the period of a doctor's training between qualification and registration (cf. HOUSEMAN 6).

1922 *Brit. Med. Jrnl.* 2 Sept. 423/2 After January 1st, 1923, prospective medical students will also be required to pass a pre-registration examination in chemistry and physics. **1962** 'D. MARGERSON' *Med. as Career* x. 67 House officer posts, including the two obligatory preregistration appointments, will usually take up eighteen months to two years. **1964** *Lancet* 5 Sept. 519/2 If.. the two-year clinical course were followed by graduation and two years' preregistration house-appointments, hospitals in the 'network' would get preregistration doctors a year earlier than they do now. **1977** *Daily Tel.* 22 July 6 (Advt.), You'll get £2,636 to continue your normal medical studies. And £4,429 during your pre-registration period.

B. *sb.* [PRE- A. 2.] Registration in advance, *spec.* in *Printing*, the action of bringing into register in advance.

1967 E. CHAMBERS *Photolitho-Offset* vi. 68 Loading and pre-registration are carried out on a separate appliance, thereby enabling subjects to be prepared in advance. **1973** *LSA Bull.* Mar. 24 Pre-registrations for the Congress.

†**pre'regnant.** *Obs. rare.* [f. PRE- A. 2 + REGNANT.] One who reigns before another; a predecessor in the kingdom.

1589 WARNER *Alb. Eng.* IV. xxii. 99 Edward, King Harolds Preregnant, of this same Change foretold. **1602** *Ibid.* Epitome 376 William and Edward the Confessor Harolds Preregnant were, by the father's side, Cosen Iarmaines.

pre-rehearsal: see PRE- A. 2.

pre-relativistic: PRE- B. 1.

pre-relativity: PRE- B. 2 a.

pre-re'lease, *a.* (*sb.*) [PRE- B. 2.]

1. a. Designating a period before the date fixed for release of a film.

1927 *Glasgow Herald* 15 Nov. 9/7 An amendment.. providing that pre-release cinema shows should take place in provincial centres as well as in London was agreed to without a division. **1928** *Daily Express* 9 July 9 There is a pre-release presentation of Dolores del Rio in 'The Gateway of the Moon', at the Kensington Kinema. **1973** *Times* 11 May 2/6 The film.. had only been booked for five prerelease test runs at cinemas in Leeds. **1976** L. ST. CLAIR *Fortune in Death* vii. 68 He's made.. a Near East thriller. They wanted some pre-release publicity.

b. Of or pertaining to the period before release of a suspect or prisoner.

1958 F. NORMAN *Bang to Rights* III. 106 You have to atend [*sic*] what they call a prerelease course. **1959** *New Statesman* 7 Mar. 335/2, I am very glad that Critic called attention to the scheme for pre-release leave to selected prisoners. **1961** *Lancet* 22 July 204/1 Such measures as the open prison and the pre-release hostel were proving invaluable. **1971** R. CROSS *Punishment, Prison & Public* ii. 68 Attached to some prisons are pre-release hostels from which the inmates go out to daily regular work. **1976** *Newmarket Jrnl.* 16 Dec., The first mention of any possible charge relating to drink-driving came after he had given a blood sample and a pre-release breath test.

2. *ellipt.* as *sb.* A film or record given restricted availability before being generally released.

1929 *Sunday Dispatch* 13 Jan. 16/3 We, in London, have been privileged to view many pre-releases. **1978** *Sunday Times* 29 Jan. 43/3 'Top Ranking' started life in Britain as a status single, available only as an imported 'pre-release'.

pre-re'lease, *v.* [PRE- A. 1.] *trans.* To release beforehand.

1968 *Punch* 24 Apr. 589/1 There's a lot to be said for pre-releasing the decimal coinage at the lower end of the scale. *a* **1974** R. CROSSMAN *Diaries* (1975) I. 147 We had pre-released the news to the *Daily Express*, the *Guardian* and the *Evening Standard.* **1976** *Church Times* 2 Apr. 10/1 He persistently declines to extend to the Press that assistance (such as circulating in advance scripts of major speeches, or sticking to the text of speeches thus pre-released) which so greatly facilitates newspaper production.

pre-remote, -renal, etc.: see PRE- B. 1, 3, etc.

pre-reproductive: see PRE- B. 1.

†**pre'rept,** *v. Obs. rare.* [f. L. *prærept-*, ppl. stem of *præripĕre* to snatch away in front of another, f. *præ*, PRE- A. 4 c + *rapĕre* to seize. Cf. CORREPT *v.*] *trans.* To snatch away in front of any one; to anticipate or forestall in seizing.

(Known only in pa. pple. *prerept*, after L. *prærept-us.*)

1545 JOYE *Exp. Dan.* v. 69 b, In vayne wept Esau aftir Iacob had prerept him his blyssinge.

†**pre'reption.** *Obs. rare.* In 7 præ-. [n. of action from L. *præripĕre, prærept-*: see prec.] The action of seizing or snatching away in front of one.

1648 *Eikon Bas.* x. 79, I have none to defend my selfe, or to preserve what is mine own from their præreption.

prerequire (priːrɪ'kwaɪə(r)), *v.* Also 7 præ-. [PRE- A. 1.] *trans.* To require beforehand.

1620 BP. HALL *Hon. Mar. Clergy* I. iii, All other Churches ..prerequire a necessity of Mariage in the persons to be ordained. **1654** WARREN *Unbelievers* 223 Union..prerequireth existence. **1696** LORIMER *Goodwin's Disc.* vii. 62 Repentance is pre-required, and always was pre-required as a necessary Condition whereby a Sinner is qualified and made meet to receive the Pardon of his Sins. **1793** W. ROBERTS *Looker-on* No. 69 (1794) III. 79, Z will not be able to move till A moves,.. neither will A be able to move.. till Z hath: so that the motion of every part will be prerequired to itself. **1975** *Christian* II. 228 There are two levels of psychotherapy, the second prerequiring the first.

Hence **prere'quired** *ppl. a.*, prerequisite.

1661 GLANVILL *Van. Dogm.* 213 Every single motion ..[owes] a dependence on.. a Syndrome of prae-required motors. **1696** LORIMER *Goodwin's Disc.* vii. 62 The pre-required Condition.

prerequisite (priː'rɛkwɪzɪt), *a.* and *sb.* [f. PRE- A. 3 + REQUISITE *a.* and *sb.*]

A. *adj.* Required beforehand; requisite as a previous condition.

1651 BAXTER *Inf. Bapt.* 90 A condition prerequisite in the subject of sanctification. **1696** WHISTON *Th. Earth* IV. (1722) 382 This breaking up of the Fountains of the Deep was a prerequisite Condition. **1817** COLERIDGE *Biog. Lit.* II. xvi. 39 For the human soul to prosper in rustic life, a certain vantage-ground is pre-requisite. **1884** J. BURROUGHS *Birds & Poets* 185 Something.. which is prerequisite to any deep and lasting success.

B. *sb.* That which is required beforehand; a condition previously necessary.

1633 T. ADAMS *Exp. 2 Peter* ii. 20 Knowledge is but a prerequisite to the main of obedience. **1758** *Monthly Rev.* 378 Prerequisites.. expedient at least, if not wholly indispensable. **1830** MACKINTOSH *Eth. Philos.* Wks. 1846 I. 158 All the changes in the organs.. are nothing more than antecedents and pre-requisites of perception, bearing not the faintest likeness to it. **1881** WESTCOTT & HORT *Grk. N.T.* Introd. §226 The essential prerequisites for striking the balance.

†**prerequi'sition.** *Obs. rare.* [PRE- A. 2.] Requisition beforehand, previous requirement.

1651 BAXTER *Inf. Bapt.* 292 That the giving of the Holy Ghost in ordinary for Regeneration, was one stated end of Baptism,.. from the constant prerequisition of repentance and faith is evident to be a mistake.

pre-re'solve, *v.* Now *rare.* Also 7 præ-. [PRE- A. 1.] **a.** *pa. pple.* Previously resolved; having made up one's mind beforehand. **b.** *intr.* To resolve beforehand.

1633 PRYNNE *Histrio-M.* II. IV. ii. 950 No man goes thus pre-resolved to a Play. **1642** SIR E. DERING *Sp. on Relig.* xvi. 83, I am confident you are herein præ-resolved as I wish. *a* **1657** W. BURTON *Itin. Anton.* (1658) 79 They came præ-resolved, by study, of what they soon acted in the Counsel. **1786** MRS. A. M. BENNETT *Juvenile Indiscr.* II. 153 He had pre-resolved to send Henry from Ether.

preretina: see PRE- A. 4.

pre-retirement, -revolution: see PRE- B. 2 a.

pre-revo'lutionary, *a.* and *sb.* [PRE- B. 1.]

A. *adj.* **1.** Existing before a (particular) revolution.

1861 MAINE *Anc. Law* iv. (1876) 85 The præ-revolutionary jurists. **1867** H. W. BEECHER in *N.Y. Ledger* 7 Sept. 2/3 Planted in 1646, it was more than a hundred years old when the pre-revolutionary excitements were taking place in Boston. **1874** T. B. ALDRICH *Prudence Palfrey* x. 166 Since the hanging of a witch or two in pre-revolutionary days, the office of sheriff there has been virtually a sinecure. **1936** *Burlington Mag.* Mar. 130/2 Baroque paintings of the pre-Revolutionary decades in France. **1961** *Times* 29 Dec. 11/1 Pre-revolutionary St. Petersburg. **1976** *New Yorker* 15 Nov. 213/1 Some extraordinarily rich evocations of pre-revolutionary village life in China.

2. Of a society or its condition: verging on social or political revolution.

1964 R. D. HOPPER in I. L. Horowitz *New Sociol.* xix. 313 In pre-revolutionary societies, there is formed a group that is marginal to the structure of political power and social prestige. **1972** 'H. BUCKMASTER' *Walking Trip* 85 It is a prerevolutionary situation I'm told by a white politician in Salisbury, and he thinks the next step is violence. **1974** *Listener* 24 Jan. 108/3 An artist in a pre-revolutionary situation concentrates upon actually producing art. **1975** A. BEEVOR *Violent Brink* vii. 165 England, the despair of Marx, seemed at last about to move into a pre-revolutionary situation.

B. *sb.* One who prepares the way for a revolution.

1937 *Times Lit. Suppl.* 1 May 323/2 Mr. Stephen Spender's 'The Destructive Element', with its presentation of Henry James as a master pre-revolutionary.

pre-rhotacistic: see PRE- B. 1.

pre-rinse: see PRE- A. 2.

†**prerogancy.** *Obs. rare*$^{-1}$. [f. L. *prærogā-re* to ask first or before + -ANCY.] The possession of privilege; prerogative.

[Cf. **1292** BRITTON IV. i. §3 Nul parcener neqedent ne porra presenter sauntz autre par nule prerogaunce de einznescerie.] **1432-50** tr. *Higden* (Rolls) VI. 205 The privilege or immunite of whiche place encreasede to grete prerogancy [*ad magnam prærogativam*].

prerogatival (-'taɪvəl), *a. rare.* [f. next + -AL[1].] Of or pertaining to prerogative.

1619 SIR J. SEMPILL *Sacrilege Handl.* 73 So must it not remaine still ἐν αὐτῷ, but returne ἐπὶ χριστόν. All these prerogatiual Prepositions end euer in Christ.

prerogative (prɪ'rɒgətɪv), *sb.* [a. F. *prérogative* (14th c. in Littré) a prerogative, ad. L. *prærogātīva* a previous choice or election; a foretoken, prognostic; preference, privilege, prerogative; prop. fem. sing. of *prærogātīvus* adj. (see next) agreeing with *tribus* or *centuria*, applied to the tribe or century to which it fell by lot to give its vote first in the Roman comitia.

'The box being shaken, so that the lots might lie equally, ..the century which came out first gave its vote first, and hence was called *Prærogativa*... Its vote was held of the greatest importance... Hence *prærogativa* is put for a sign or pledge, a favourable omen or intimation of any thing future;.. for a precedent or example,.. a choice,.. or favour, ..and among later writers for a peculiar or exclusive privilege' (Adam *Rom. Antiq.* (1801) 91).

(As the sense-development took place before the word was taken into English, the chronological order here, as will be seen, does not correspond with it; the original or etymological sense is of late use: see 3.)]

1. A prior, exclusive, or peculiar right or privilege.

a. *esp.* in *Constitutional Hist.* That special pre-eminence which the sovereign, by right of regal dignity, has over all other persons and out of the course of the common law, the ***royal prerogative***, a sovereign right (in theory) subject to no restriction or interference.

In Great Britain, the extent of the royal prerogative has been a matter of discussion, more especially since the 17th century: see the quots. At present it includes the right of sending and receiving ambassadors, of making treaties, and (theoretically) of making war and concluding peace, of conferring honours, nominating to bishoprics, and giving all commissions in the army and navy, of choosing ministers of state, summoning Parliament, and refusing assent to a bill, of pardoning those under legal sentence; with many other political, ecclesiastical, and judicial privileges. The exercise of many of these prerogative rights is practically limited by the rights of parliament or of other bodies or persons, the constitutional obligation to take the advice of ministers, and the need to secure the general approval and support of the nation.

[**1293** *Rolls of Parlt.* I. 117/1 Quod Dominus Rex Presentationem suam ratione Prerogative sue,.. ad predictam Vicariam habeat. **1308-9** *Ibid.* 274/1 Pur la Prerogative & le droit le Roy.] **1404** *Ibid.* III. 549/1 By the lawe of his [the King's] land, or by his prerogatif. **1494** FABYAN *Chron.* VII. 343 The wood or madde parlyament;.. at this Counceyll, were made many actis agayn the Kynges prerogatyue and pleasure, for the reformacion of the state of the land. **1553** T. WILSON *Rhet.* 87 b, The kynges prerogatiue declareth his power royall aboue all other. **1637** *Documents agst. Prynne* (Camden) 88, I heare all the Judges ..have concluded the Bishopps have noe whitt incroacht uppon the King's prerogative or the subject's liberties. **1678** MARVELL *Growth Popery* Wks. (Grosart) IV. 249 His [the king of England's] very Prerogative is no more than what the Law has determined. *a* **1680** BUTLER *Rem.* (1759) I. 210 Princes had Prerogative to give Convicted Malefactors a Reprieve. **1690** LOCKE *Govt.* II. xiv. §160 This Power to act according to discretion for the Publick Good, without the Prescription of the Law, and sometimes even against it, is that which is called *Prerogative.* **1765** BLACKSTONE *Comm.* I. vii. 257 The king has also the sole prerogative of making war and peace. For it is held by all the writers on the law of nature and nations, that the right of making war, which by nature subsisted in every individual, is given up by all private persons that enter into society, and is vested in the sovereign power. **1769** *Junius Lett.* viii. (1797) I. 52 Every ungracious or severe exertion of the prerogative should be placed to the account of the minister. **1839** KEIGHTLEY *Hist. Eng.* I. 410 The parliament by perseverance, and by taking advantage of foreign wars, disputed successions and other circumstances, gradually set limits to prerogative. **1863** H. COX *Instit.* III. ii. 592 Writers on the constitution have frequently used the word 'prerogative' in a restricted sense, confining it to those political powers of the Crown which are not conferred by statute; and in this sense the word will be here employed. **1887** *Spectator* 27 Aug. 1143 The exercise of the prerogative of mercy is no easy or pleasant duty.

b. *generally.* The peculiar right or privilege of any person, class, or body of persons; as the prerogatives of parliament, of a peer, of a manor, of a free man, etc.

14.. [see next, 2]. **1494** FABYAN *Chron.* VII. 330 The kynge consyderynge the great prerogatyues belongynge to that erledome. **1495** *Act 11 Hen. VII*, c. 34 §1 The same Manoris ..with all liberties prerogatyves and fraunchises in the same. **1538** STARKEY *England* II. i. 151 Thys thyng schold much intyse men to maryage, specyally yf we gaue vnto them also certayn pryuylegys and prerogatyf. **1623** GOUGE *Serm. Extent God's Provid.* §8 The Church, and every member of it..challengeth the speciall care of God, as a prerogative to itselfe. **1655** M. CARTER *Hon. Rediv.* (1660) 60 The Crown set on his head by the Archbishop of Canterbury, a Prerogative to that See. **1685** DRYDEN *Thren. August.* 301 Freedom, an English subjects sole prerogative. **1751** JOHNSON *Rambler* No. 180 ¶2 Every one must have remarked, what powers and prerogatives the vulgar imagine to be conferred by learning. **1757** SMOLLETT *Reprisal* I. ii, The prisoners to be plundered, which you know is the prerogative of pirates and privateers. **1850** MERIVALE *Rom. Emp.* (1865) I. i. 13 It was for their existence rather than their prerogatives that the Romans had to contend. **1875** JOWETT *Plato* (ed. 2) I. 52 Will he not entrust to us the prerogative of making soup, and putting in anything that we like?

2. *fig.* A faculty or property by which a being (or formerly a thing) is specially and advantageously distinguished above others; a natural or divinely-given advantage or privilege.

1387 TREVISA *Higden* (Rolls) II. 213 In many poyntes of manis condicioun, of his prerogatif and his worþynesse [*orig.* in nonnullis conditionis prærogativis; **1432–50** [*Harleian tr.*] in mony prerogatifes of his condicion]. *c* **1400** *Laud Troy Bk.* 3778 Thei are at home In here contre And that is hem [*MS.* tyme]—so mote I thryue—A wondir gret prerogatyue. *c* **1407** LYDG. *Reson & Sens.* 6444 [The panther] hath a prerogatyf That al[le] bestys specialy Desire of kynde hys companye And to be in his presence. **1485** CAXTON *St. Wenefr.* 1 This prouynce..was embellisshed and decorate with innumerable prerogatyuys. **1526** *Pilgr. Perf.* (W. de W. 1531) 123 b, The gyfte of prerogatyue called discrecyon or discernynge of spirytes is but in fewe persones. **1555** EDEN *Decades* 166 Other prerogatiues whiche nature hath plentifully giuen to this blessed Iland. **1665** BOYLE *Occas. Refl.* v. iv. (1848) 309 Rare Qualities may sometimes be Prerogatives, without being Advantages. **1773** MONBODDO *Lang.* (1774) I. Introd. 1 This distinguishing prerogative of our Nature. **1845** CORRIE *Theol.* in *Encycl. Metrop.* 861 It is man's high prerogative to be endowed with reason and conscience. *a* **1862** BUCKLE *Misc. Wks.* (1872) I. 37 It is the peculiar prerogative of certain minds to be able to interpret as well as to originate.

†**b.** Precedence, pre-eminence, superiority. *Obs.*

c **1407** LYDG. *Reson & Sens.* 4422 Hyt hath swych A prerogatyf And of vertu so grete myght. **1412–20** —— *Chron. Troy* (E.E.T.S.) 2600 For trewly ȝe.. In bewte han a prerogatyfe, Passyng echon,..Amongis flouris as doth þe rede rose. **1555** EDEN *Decades* 340 The moste noble..metals haue obteyned the prerogatiue to be estemed aboue other. **1588** J. READ *Compend. Method* 62 This medicine hath a great prerogatiue in healing the French poxe. **1605** CAMDEN *Rem.* (1637) 37 The Greek and Latin have always borne away the prerogative from all other tongues. **1624** CAPT. SMITH *Virginia* 22 A country that may haue the prerogatiue over the most pleasant places knowne, for large and pleasant navigable Rivers. **1671** J. WEBSTER *Metallogr.* iii. 41 What prerogative have Vegetables over Metals.

3. The right of giving the first vote and thus of serving as a guide or precedent to the votes that follow. (Only an etymological use in English.)

1600 HOLLAND *Livy* XXIV. 513 When it hapned that the centurie of the younger sort was drawne out first by lot, and had the prerogative. **1897** *Daily News* 20 May 5/1 Tomorrow the vote will be given, and..Cambridge has, in this instance, to use an old word in its original sense, the prerogative. If Cambridge gives women degrees, Oxford cannot continue to withhold them. **1906** *Daily Chron.* 4 Jan. 6/6 The..attempt to get the Birmingham pollings fixed for an earlier date,..was an effort for 'prerogative' in its original sense.

4. Short for *prerogative court*: see 6.

1603 *Constit. & Can. Eccl.* xcii, The Probate..under the seal of the Prerogative.

5. *attrib.* and *Comb.*, as ***prerogative-monger***, ***notion***, ***party***; **prerogative case**, a cause within the jurisdiction of the prerogative court (see 6); **prerogative copy**, a book of which the copyright is a prerogative of the crown; **prerogative lawyer**, a lawyer retained in behalf of the royal prerogative; **prerogative man**, an advocate or supporter of prerogative; **prerogative office** = *prerogative court*: see 6.

1589 NASHE *Martins Months Minde* 51 My will, being a *prerogatiue case..will hardlie passe with such expedition, as is conuenient. **1596** HARINGTON *Metam. Ajax* (1814) 62, I have small skill in the law especially in prerogative cases. **1667** *Modern Rep.* I. 257 The almanack that is before the common-prayer proceeds from a public constitution..and is under the government of the Archbishop of Canterbury, so that almanacks may be considered *prerogative copies. **1766** BLACKSTONE *Comm.* II. xxvii. 410. **1681** NEVILE *Plato Rediv.* 120 If a Controversie should arise..between the House of Commons and the *Prerogative Lawyers, about the choice of their Speaker. *a* **1797** H. WALPOLE *Mem. Geo. II* (1847) II. iv. 118 Beckford finished the Debate with reflections on the notorious ductility of prerogative lawyers. **1710** M. HENRY *Comm. Bible, John* iv. 46 He was an Herodian, a royalist, a *prerogative man. **1747** RICHARDSON *Clarissa* (1811) II. xxiii. 152 That little piddling part of the marriage-vow which some *prerogative-monger foisted into the office. **1716** M. DAVIES *Athen. Brit.* II. 136 In the *Prerogative Office of the Province of Canterbury. *a* **1850** CALHOUN *Wks.* (1874) II. 399 That most dangerous spectacle in a country like ours, a *prerogative party, who take their creed wholly from the mandate of their chief.

6. prerogative court. The court of an archbishop for the probate of wills and trial of testamentary causes in which effects to the value of five pounds had been left in each of two (or more) dioceses within his province; its jurisdiction was transferred in 1857 to the Court of Probate. **b.** In New Jersey, U.S.A.: A court held by the chancellor sitting as ordinary, in which probate and similar causes are determined.

[**1603** *Constit. & Can. Eccl.* xcii, Apparitors, both of inferior courts, and of the courts of the Archbishop's Prerogative. *Ibid.*, To prove the said will..in the court of the said Prerogative.] *Ibid.*, The Apparitor of the Prerogative Court. **1610** HOLLAND *Camden's Brit.* (1637) 181 The Prerogative Court, in which the Commissarie sitteth upon Inheritances fallen either by the Intestate, or by will and testament. *a* **1613** OVERBURY *Charac.*, *Vertuous Widow* Wks. (1856) 138 She would doe it were there no prerogative court. **1766** BLACKSTONE *Comm.* II. xxxii. 509 The court where the validity of such wills is tried, and the office where they are registered, are called the prerogative court, and the prerogative office, of the provinces of Canterbury and York [Abbrev. P.C.C. and P.C.Y.]. **1846** MCCULLOCH *Acc. Brit. Empire* (1854) II. 187 The Prerogative Court has jurisdiction of all wills and administrations of personal property left by persons having *bona notabilia*, or effects of a certain value, in divers jurisdictions within the province. **1857** *Act 20 & 21 Vict.* c. 79 §7 (Ireland), The Person who..may be the judge of the Prerogative Court, shall be the First Judge of His Majesty's Court of Probate.

7. prerogative writ. A writ issued on extraordinary occasions in the exercise of the royal prerogative: see quots.

1759 LD. MANSFIELD in Burrows *Reports* II. 855 Writs, not ministerially directed, (sometimes called *prerogative* writs, because they are supposed to issue on the part of the king,) such as writs of *mandamus, prohibition, habeas corpus, certiorari*, are restrained by no clause in the constitution given to Berwick. **1771** *Junius Lett.* lxiv. (1797) II. 225 Prerogative writs,..though liable to the greatest abuses, were never disputed. **1898** G. H. B. KENRICK in *Encycl. Laws Eng.*, Prerogative writs..are issued upon cause shown in cases where the ordinary legal remedies are inapplicable or inadequate. *Ibid.*, The prerogative writs in present use are the writs of *habeas corpus, mandamus, prohibition, certiorari, procedendo.*

prerogative (prɪˈrɒgətɪv), *a.* [ad. L. *prærogātīv-us* characterized by being asked first, deriv. of *prærogāt-us*, pa. pple. of *prærogāre* to ask before (others), f. *præ*, PRE- A. 1 + *rogāre* to ask: see prec. and -IVE. So F. *prérogatif, -ive.* The example from Wyntoun in sense 2 stands quite alone in date.]

1. *Rom. Hist.* Characterized by having the right to vote first. Of a vote: Given first and serving as a precedent for those that follow. Also *transf.*

prerogative century: see quot. 1850.

1600 HOLLAND *Livy* XXVI. 601 This fore-dome & choise of the prerogative centurie, all the rest followed after, and by their suffrages confirmed. **1656** J. HARRINGTON *Oceana* (1658) 76 The Lord High Sheriff, who..is the first Magistrate of the Phylarch, or prerogative Troop. **1783** W. GORDON *Livy* v. xviii. (1823) 425 Licinius Calvus was by the prerogative tribes chosen military tribune. **1850** MERIVALE *Rom. Emp.* (1865) I. ix. 387 *note*, The prerogative century was chosen by lot from the hundred and ninety-three which constituted the whole number, to give its decision first. **1885** *Pall Mall G.* 3 Nov., The municipal elections..do not constitute a 'prerogative' vote in favour of the Tories.

2. Of, pertaining to, or arising from prerogative or special privilege; held, enjoyed, or exercised by exclusive prerogative or privilege; privileged.

14.. WYNTOUN *Cron.* (Wemyss MS.) IV. 1809 To þis fredome þan, And dignite prerogative, Foroutin ganecalling or strive The Scottis fra þe Pichtis wan [*Cott. MS.* þis prerogatywe þan þe Scottis fra þe Peythtis wan].

1622 T. STOUGHTON *Chr. Sacrif.* ii. 18 He arrogateth the prerogatiue title of Christ Iesus, styling himselfe King of Kings and Lord of Lords. **1768** BLACKSTONE *Comm.* III. xvii. 258 Much easier and more effectual remedies are usually obtained by such prerogative modes of process, as are peculiarly confined to the crown. **1854** MILMAN *Lat. Chr.* VI. iii. (1864) III. 425 It established a kind of prerogative right in the Roman clergy to the Pontificate. **1863** H. COX *Instit.* I. v. 28 Many of the prerogative Orders in Council have a legislative character. **1906** BP. GORE in *Westm. Gaz.* 1 Sept. 8/3 This means the establishment in the public schools of one kind of religious teaching in the prerogative position.

3. Having precedence or priority; having the right to lead, leading; pre-eminent. *rare.*

1646 SIR T. BROWNE *Pseud. Ep.* 27 The affirmative hath the prerogative illation, and Barbara engrosseth the powerfull demonstration. **1894** M. W. MACCALLUM *Tennyson's Idylls* 87 It might have been expected that the adapter of knightly stories like *Palamon and Arcite*..would above all be attracted to the prerogative romances of chivalry.

prerogatived (prɪˈrɒgətɪvd), *ppl. a.* [f. PREROGATIVE *sb.* + -ED^{2}.] Endowed with or possessed of a prerogative. Sometimes construed as pa. pple.

a **1603** T. CARTWRIGHT *Confut. Rhem. N.T.* (1618) 178 The most priuiledged and prerogatiued man that is in the world. **1604** SHAKS. *Oth.* III. iii. 274. **1661** FELTHAM *Lett.* vii. in *Resolves*, etc. 71 Prerogativ'd at once to Create both a City and Church. **1835** *Tait's Mag.* II. 182 The flattering attentions of one so privileged and so prerogatived as his capricious Lordship. **1879** BROWNING *Tray* 38 Somebody, prerogatived With reason, reasoned.

preˈrogatively, *adv. rare.* [f. PREROGATIVE *a.* + -LY^{2}.] As a prerogative or distinctive privilege.

a **1641** BP. MOUNTAGU *Acts & Mon.* (1642) 32 Of these times it was said prerogatively by Esay 54. 13. 'All shall bee then taught by God'.

†**preˈrogativeship.** *Obs. nonce-wd.* [f. PREROGATIVE *sb.* + -SHIP.] With possessive pronoun, as a satirical title for a holder of a prerogative.

1645 *Sacred Decretal* 23 No Petition or Remonstrance.. can have a free passage for Redresse unto the Parliament, but what pleaseth their Prerogativeship.

†**preroˈgator.** *Obs. rare*$^{-1}$. [a. med.L. *prærogātor* 'dispensator' (Gloss. Isid.), agent-n. from *prærogāre* to ask first: see PREROGATIVE.] (?) One who gives a prognostic.

1652 GAULE *Magastrom.* 237 Such a significator, such a promissor,..such a prerogator, such a dispositor.

pre-romanesque: PRE- B. 1 d.

pre-Romantic, *a.* (*sb.*) *Mus.* and *Lit.* Also **pre-romantic.** [PRE- B. 1.] Pertaining to or characteristic of the period before the Romantic Movement. As *sb.*, a composer or writer of that period.

1934 C. LAMBERT *Music Ho!* I. 57 Purcell, the most picturesque of the pre-Romantic composers. **1938** C. CONNOLLY in *New Statesman* 6 Aug. 223/1 The English pre-romantics..balanced their love of childhood by their hope of heaven. **1947** A. EINSTEIN *Mus. Romantic Era* xi. 134 One can find examples of it, particularly in the opera, even in pre-Romantic opera. **1959** *Brno Studies in English* I. 104 Bulwer attempted to follow in the steps of the great representatives of the English pre-romantic and romantic period, especially of William Godwin and Lord Byron. **1962** *Times* 16 Feb. 15/3 Mozart is observed..as the clever pre-romantic tune-spinner. **1963** N. FRYE *Romanticism Reconsidered* 9 It is obvious that in pre-Romantic poetry there is a strong affinity with the attitude that we have called sense... But the pre-Romantic structure of imagery belonged to a nature which was the work of God. **1978** D. GRYLLS *Guardians & Angels* iv. 112 In her treatment of parent-child relations Jane Austen is pre-Romantic. **1980** *Church Times* 25 July 6/4 The enormous revolution in literary taste which began in the 'twenties..demoted Spenser, the tribe of Ben Jonson, and the eighteenth-century pre-romantics.

prerupt (prɪˈrʌpt), *a. rare.* Also 7 **præ-** [ad. L. *prærupt-us* broken or torn off, steep, abrupt, rash, pa. pple. of *prærumpĕre* to break off before (the point), f. *præ*, PRE- A. 4 c + *rumpĕre* to break.]

1. Broken off before the end, or (in quot.) having the beginning broken off or lost.

1600 HOLLAND *Livy* XLI. 1096 The beginning of this booke, and the greater part thereof immediatly ensuing, is lost..thus it sheweth a prærupt and broken front as ye see.

2. Abruptly broken away; precipitous; = ABRUPT *a.* 4.

1603 HOLLAND *Plutarch's Mor.* 1282 Prerupt and craggy rocks. **1819** *Blackw. Mag.* IV. 729 Yon craigs prerupt, which o'er the murky glare Of crimsoned smoke, their gloomy ledges shoot. **1831** J. WILSON *Unimore* vii. 254 Disjoined with horrid chasms prerupt.

3. Sudden, unexpected; = ABRUPT *a.* 3.

1831 SCOTT *Ct. Robt.* Intr., Transferring the said calumnious reports to my ears in a prerupt and unseemly manner.

†**preˈruption.** *Obs. rare*$^{-1}$. [n. of action from L. *prærumpĕre, prærupt-*: see prec.] An abrupt breaking off, a cutting off at one stroke.

a **1653** GOUGE *Comm. Heb.* xi. 32 Self-murther is a violent preruption of the place, time and means of ones own repentance.

†**pres, prese.** *Obs. rare.* [Etymology obscure: see NOTE.] ? Praise. Phr. ***to hold in pris and***

pres, to hold in esteem and (?) praise. (Cf. PRICE *sb.*)

a **1300** *Cursor M.* 6358 Fra þan forth heild sir moyses þis [*v.rr.* þa, þer] wandes bath in pris and pres. ? *a* **1375** *E.E. Allit. P.* A. 419 Hys prese, his prys, and hys parage, Is rote and grounde of alle my blysse.

[Usually taken as a form of PRAISE *sb.*, which in both passages fairly makes sense. But it is difficult to bring *prēs* (riming in *Cursor M.* with *Moysēs*) into phonetic relation with *preyse*, *praise*, which is moreover unknown till after 1400. The final *e* in *E.E. Allit. P.* is not etymological.]

pres, obs. collateral form of PRESS.

pres: see PREZ[1], [2].

‖**presa** (ˈpreza). *Mus.* [It., = a taking, from *presa*, pa. pple. fem., taken.] (See quot. 1898.)

1724 *Short Explic. For. Words in Mus. Bks.*, *Presa*, is a Character in Musick called a Repeat. **1898** STAINER & BARRETT *Dict. Mus. Terms*, *Presa*,..a character or mark used generally in continuous fugues or canons to mark the point of entry for the voices or instruments; a lead.

presacral: see PRE- B. 3.

presage (ˈprɛsədʒ, ˈpriː-, formerly prɪˈseɪdʒ), *sb.* Also 7 præ-. [a. F. *présage* (15–16th c. in Hatz.-Darm.), ad. L. *præsāgium* a foreboding, prognostic, f. *præsāgīre* to forebode, f. *præsāg-us* foreboding, f. *præ*, PRE- A. 3 + *sāg-us* predicting, divining. (In Gower perh. direct from Latin.)]

1. Something that portends, foreshows, or gives warning of that which is about to happen; an indication of a future event; an omen, sign, portent.

1390 GOWER *Conf.* I. 219 And seide how that was a presage..Of that fortune him scholde adverse. **1579–80** NORTH *Plutarch* (1595) 1112 A very euil signe and presage for him, to enter into Rome with such bloudshed. **1595** SHAKS. *John* III. iv. 158 They will..call them Meteors, prodigies, and signes, Abortiues, presages, and tongues of heauen. **1664** BUTLER *Hud.* II. III. 686 Do not the Hist'ries of all Ages Relate miraculous presages Of strange turns in the World's affairs? **1669** WORLIDGE *Syst. Agric.* (1681) 313 The coming of the Swallow is a true presage of the Spring. **1704** DENNIS *Faction Display'd* xvii, When Health and Vigour with a kind presage, Promis'd the hoary happiness of Age. **1725** POPE *Odyss.* II. 188 [He] drew A sure presage from ev'ry wing that flew. **1774** PENNANT *Tour Scot. in 1772*, 312 The dread of Mariners who draw a certain presage of a Storm from their appearance. **1866** J. H. NEWMAN *Gerontius* iii. 25 A presage falls upon thee, as a ray Straight from the Judge, expressive of thy lot.

b. Without *pl.* Indication of the future; chiefly in phr. ***of evil*** (etc.) ***presage***, of (evil) omen, that presages (evil).

1671 MILTON *Samson* 1387 If there be aught of presage in the mind, This day will be remarkable in my life By some great act, or of my days the last. **1691** EVELYN *Let to Bp. of Lincoln* 15 Oct., Those furious ravages..I looke on..as..of evil præsage. **1698** CONGREVE *Semele* I. i, This dreadful Conflict is of dire Presage. **1797** BURKE *Regic. Peace* iii. Wks. VIII. 395 These birds of evil presage, at all times, have grated our ears with their melancholy song. **1871** B. TAYLOR *Faust* (1875) I. i. 32 Filled with mystic presage chimed the church bell slowly.

2. An utterance foretelling something future; a prediction, prognostication. Now *rare*.

1595 MARKHAM *Sir R. Grinvile* cxxxix, Misfortune hearing this presage of life. **1605** VERSTEGAN *Dec. Intell.* iii. (1628) 67 Presages or fore-tellings of their good or euill fortune. **1647** CLARENDON *Hist. Reb.* II. §103 He might reasonably have expected as ill a presage for himself from those Fortune tellers. **1681** GLANVILL *Sadducismus* I. (1726) 68 An ingenious Presage, but not true. **1871** ROSSETTI *Dante at Verona* vi, Shall not his birth's baptismal Town One last high presage yet fulfil?

3. A presentiment, a foreboding; a feeling of what is going to happen; an intuition of the future.

1593 SHAKS. *Rich. II*, II. ii. 142 Farewell, if hearts presages be not vaine, We three here part, that neu'r shall meete againe. **1631** WEEVER *Anc. Fun. Mon.* 9 The presage or forefeeling of immortalitie, implanted in all men naturally. **1736** BUTLER *Anal.* I. iii. 64 The natural presages of Conscience. **1812** J. HODGSON in J. Raine *Mem.* (1857) I. 115 He had a strong presage upon his mind that he had only a very short time to live. **1847** TENNYSON *Princess* IV. 427. **1852** LD. COCKBURN *Jeffrey* I. 61, I have very often deep presages that the law will not hold me.

4. *Comb.* **presage-woman**, a fortune-teller.

a **1693** *Urquhart's Rabelais* III. xvi. 135 The customary style of my Language alloweth them the Denomination of Presage Women.

presage (ˈprɛsədʒ, prɪˈseɪdʒ), *v.* Also 7 præ-. [a. F. *présager* (16th c. in Hatz.-Darm.), f. *présage* PRESAGE *sb.* The form *presagier*, ad. L. *præsāgīre* was common in 16th c. French (Hatz.-Darm.).]

1. *trans.* To signify beforehand (supernaturally); to portend, foreshadow.

1562 BULLEYN *Bulwark, Sicke Men* 54 Thei dooe presage, deuine, or shewe before, what thynges doe folowe. *c* **1595** CAPT. WYATT *R. Dudley's Voy. W. Ind.* (Hakl. Soc.) 56 If but one fyre is sene, it presageth a most cruell, daingerous and tempestuous storme. **1672** SIR T. BROWNE *Let. Friend* §16 Hippocrates wisely considered Dreams as they presaged Alterations in the Body. **1711** ADDISON *Spect.* No. 1 ¶2, I am not so vain as to think it [a dream] presaged any Dignity that I should arrive at. *a* **1816** JOYCE *Sci. Dial.* xv. (1846) 105 Have not eclipses been esteemed as omens presaging some direful calamity?

b. *transf.* To point to or indicate beforehand; to give warning of (by natural means).

1591 SHAKS. *1 Hen. VI*, IV. i. 191 This iarring discord of Nobilitie,..doth presage some ill euent. **1596** *Edw. III*, I. ii, Whose habit rude, and manners blunt and plain, Presageth nought. **1671** SALMON *Syn. Med.* II. li. 326 If the Feaver continue to the third Crisis, it presages Bleeding at the Nose. **1748** GRAY *Alliance* 33 Th' Event presages, and explores the Cause. **1822** IMISON *Sc. & Art.* (ed. Webster) I. 150 The rising of the mercury presages, in general, fair weather. **1871** B. TAYLOR *Faust* (1875) I. 399 *note*, The confusion of Margaret's thoughts, presaging her later insanity.

2. Of a person: To augur, predict, forecast. †By Spenser used for To point out, make known.

1578 LYTE *Dodoens* VI. lxviii. 746 If they finde..a Spider, they presage pestilence. **1590** GREENE *Orl. Fur.* (1599) 12 Seest thou not all men presage I shall be King? **1590** SPENSER *F.Q.* I. x. 61 Then seek this path that I to thee presage, Which after all to heaven shall thee send. *a* **1680** BUTLER *Rem.* (1759) I. 174 Like Prophecy, that can presage Successes of the latest Age. **1770** GOLDSM. *Des. Vill.* 209 Lands he could measure, terms and tides presage. **1865** MERIVALE *Rom. Emp.* VIII. lxiv. 95 *note*, The author presaged from this vision that he should write no more than the emperor had read.

b. *intr.* To form or utter a presage or prediction.

1592 *Doctor Faustus* in Thoms *E.E. Prose Rom.* (1858) III. 199 Which learned him to presage of matters to come. **1665** J. SPENCER *Vulg. Proph.* 5 Men..are apt to believe as they affect, and then to presage as they believe. **1697** DRYDEN *Virg. Georg.* I. 483 By certain Signs we may presage Of Heats and Rains, and Wind's impetuous rage. **1871** R. ELLIS *Catullus* lxviii. 87 Which not long should abide, so presag'd surely the Parcae. **1876** MOZLEY *Univ. Serm.* iv. 73 Prophecy would fain presage auspiciously.

3. *trans.* To have a presentiment or prevision of.

1594 *1st Pt. Contention* (1843) 27 My mind presageth I shall live To see the noble Duke of Yorke to be a King. **1598** TOFTE *Alba* G v, My misgiving minde presaging to me ill. **1675** tr. *Camden's Hist. Eliz.* II. (1688) 145 William Herbert Earl of Pembroke,..presaging some Disaster to himself, departed this life in his Climacterical year. **1797** MRS. A. M. BENNETT *Beggar Girl* (1813) V. 146 God forgive me if I don't presage some mischief to poor Miss Rosy. **1879** TOURGEE *Fool's Err.* xxv. 154 That great experiment, from the preliminaries of which he was only able to presage danger and disaster.

b. *intr.* To have a presentiment.

1586 WARNER *Alb. Eng.* I. vi. (1612) 22 Where, like as did his minde presage, He found it very so. **1670** G. H. tr. *Hist. of Cardinals* II. III. 181 It succeeded as they presag'd.

presageful (prɪˈseɪdʒfʊl), *a.* [f. PRESAGE *sb.* + -FUL. (The pronunc. retains the earlier stress.)]

1. Full of presage; portentous, ominous.

1591 SYLVESTER *Ivry* 182 O Princely Port! Presagefull Countenance Of Hap at hand! **1605** —— *Du Bartas* II. iii. III. *Law* 179 Presagefull rays of somwhat more divine. **1726–46** THOMSON *Winter* 70 The brawling brook, And cave, presageful, send a hollow moan, Resounding long in listening Fancy's ear. **1820** L. HUNT *Indicator* No. 62 (1822) II. 75 The presageful nature of the meteor. **1888** BRYCE *Amer. Commw.* II. III. lxxi. 584 A better chance of winning the preliminary canter, and thereby securing the advantage of a presageful victory.

2. Full of presentiment or foreboding.

1729 SAVAGE *Wanderer* v. 142 No sad, presageful Thought preluded Fate. **1796** COLERIDGE *Sonn., to Friend who asked how I felt*, etc. 10 Dark remembrance and presageful fear. **1859** TENNYSON *Vivien* 293 Ev'n such a wave,..Dark in the glass of some presageful mood, Had I for three days seen.

Hence **preˈsagefully** *adv.*

1844 BROWNING *Colombe's Birthday* III, Presagefully it beats, presagefully, My heart.

†**preˈsagement**. *Obs.* [f. PRESAGE *v.* + -MENT.] The action or fact of presaging. **a.** Foreshowing, prognostication; an omen, a portent.

c **1595** CAPT. WYATT *R. Dudley's Voy. W. Ind.* (Hakl. Soc.) 55 A fyre..called Santelmo or Corposantie; the which appeareth before anie tempestuous weather as a presagement of a most dainegerous storme. *a* **1639** WOTTON *Dk. Buckhm.* in *Reliq.* (1651) 118, I have spent some enquiry, whether he had any ominous presagement before his end. **1646** SIR T. BROWNE *Pseud. Ep.* v. xxi. 265 The falling of Salt is an authenticke presagement of ill lucke.

b. Presentiment; foretelling power; prevision.

1637 JACKSON *Serm. on Matt.* ii. 17, 18, §8 Her own prediction or good ominous presagements of Joseph's name. **1646** SIR T. BROWNE *Pseud. Ep.* I. x. 40 His reservednesse had contrived answers, whose accomplishments were in his power, or not beyond his presagement.

presager (prɪˈseɪdʒə(r)). [f. PRESAGE *v.* + -ER[1].] One who or that which presages or portends.

1591 *Troub. Raigne K. John* xiii. 141 Vnvsuall signes, Presagers of strange terrors to the world. *c* **1600** SHAKS. *Sonn.* xxiii, O let my books be..domb presagers of my speaking brest. **1698** [R. FERGUSON] *View Eccles.* Pref., A Presager and Prophet, of the Fate and Destiny which did await him. **1743** tr. *Heister's Surg.* 188 An able Presager in the Events of this kind of Inflammation.

†**ˈpresagie**. *Obs. rare*[−1]. [ad. L. *præsāgium* PRESAGE: for the form, cf. *prodigy*.] = PRESAGE *sb.*

1581 STUBBES *Two Examples* (N.), Thinke thou this is a presagie of God's fearce wrath to thee.

†**preˈsagient**, *a.* *Obs. rare.* Also præ-. [ad. L. *præsāgient-em*, pr. pple. of *præsāgīre* to presage: see PRESAGE *sb.* Cf. obs. F. *presagiant* (Cotgr.).] Having presentiment or foreboding.

1648 W. SCLATER *Comm. Malachy* (1650) Ep. Ded., As it were forespeaking, and (after Zanchy's expression) præsagient, conjecturing natures. **1668** H. MORE *Div. Dial.* II. xi. (1713) 120 There not being..so comprehensive and presagient an Anxiety..in Brutes.

presaging (prɛˈsədʒɪŋ, prɪˈseɪdʒɪŋ), *vbl. sb.* [-ING[1].] The action of the vb. PRESAGE; prognostication.

1598 FLORIO, *Presagia*, the arte of presaging or diuination. **1652** GAULE *Magastrom.* 241 When or where their divinations and presagings were most received. **1744** BERKELEY *Siris* §252 Plotinus observes..that the art of presaging is in some sort the reading of natural letters denoting order. **1906** *Hibbert Jrnl.* Jan. 246 Destined to fulfil in his person the presagings of the nation's seers.

preˈsaging, *ppl. a.* [-ING[2].] That presages.

a. Foreboding, portending, giving augury.

1606 HOLLAND *Sueton.* 242 Presaging tokens which I will now relate. **1704** *Hymn Vict.* lix, We had presaging Tokens of Success. **1846** TRENCH *Mirac.* xviii. (1862) 299 The very name of the pool having in his eyes a presaging fitness.

b. That has presentiment or prevision.

1632 LITHGOW *Trav.* x. 459 The portending heauinesse of my presaging soule. *a* **1664** KATH. PHILIPS *In Mem. F. P.* Poems (1667) 40 No, thou art gone, and thy presaging Mind. **1713** YOUNG *Force Relig.* II. 114 [He] wondring sees in sad presaging thought. **1893** *Standard* 14 June, So much for the presaging intelligence which first invented the fable.

Hence **preˈsagingly** *adv.*, in a presaging manner.

1612 R. SHELDON *Serm. St. Martin's* 48 How often..haue I heard Robert Parsons..presagingly hope for such contentions vpon vnion of the two kingdomes. **1660** A. SADLER *Subject's Joy* 2 The Younger is a Masquer; and she also..doth..præsagingly præact his just Inauguration. **1846** *Chambers' Misc.* XI. *Alex. Andrayne* 5 The jailer opened a little door studded with iron, on which my eyes had been from the first presagingly fixed.

†**preˈsagious**, *a.* *Obs.* [f. L. *præsāgi-um* PRESAGE + -OUS; cf. obs. F. *presagieux* (Cotgr.).]

a. Of the nature of a presage; ominous, portentous. **b.** Having a presage or presentiment.

a **1586** SIDNEY *Arcadia* (1622) 204 Strange visions,..confirmed with presagious chances. **1663** *Flagellum, or O. Cromwell* (1672) 9 Nor were there any presagious dreams or fearful divinations. **1702** C. MATHER *Magn. Chr.* III. IV. vii. (1852) 603 That holy..minister of the gospel at length grew very presagious that his labours..drew near unto an end.

†**presaˈgitian**. *Obs. rare*[−1]. In 7 præ-. [app. for **presagician*, f. PRESAGE after *magician*, *practician*, etc.] A professor of presages; an augur, prognosticator.

1652 GAULE *Magastrom.* 293 Augustus had..such a confidence in this fatidical praesagitian, that he divulged his natalitial Theme.

†**presaˈgition**. *Obs.* [ad. L. *præsāgītiōn-em*, n. of action f. *præsāgīre* to presage: see PRESAGE *sb.*] A presaging, a presage.

c **1540** tr. *Pol. Verg. Eng. Hist.* (Camden) I. 228 A presagition and token, wherebie this Edgina conceaved hope to bringe forthe a childe, which in tyme to comme showlde reigne. **1652** GAULE *Magastrom.* 52 Have not beasts..a more perfect presagition, by their senses, than men, with all their reason, can attain unto?

‖**pré salé** (pre sale). Also **pré-salé**. [Fr.] A salt meadow, *spec.* one on which sheep are reared; freq. used *attrib.* or *ellipt.* to designate the flesh of sheep reared on a salt meadow.

1839 F. A. KEMBLE *Let.* 21 July in *Rec. Later Life* (1882) I. 255 That peculiar close short turf which creates South Down and Pré Salé mutton. **1903** J. M. FALKNER *Nebuly Coat* i. 3 The low-lying meadows..where as good-tasting mutton is bred as on any *pré-salé* on the other side of the Channel. **1930** A. BENNETT *Imperial Palace* xxiii. 145 It was a man's menu... Turtle soup. Sole *Palace*. Pré-salé with two vegetables. **1935** M. MORPHY *Recipes of All Nations* 54 It is an error to imagine that French mutton and lamb are inferior to English meat. Their *pré-salé* is equal to any. **1966** P. V. PRICE *France: Food & Wine Guide* 48 The most vaunted type of lamb comes from flocks that feed on pastures by the sea, which gives the meat a special delicacy; this type is known as *pré salé* (salty meadow) and has an *Appellation Contrôlée*.

preˌsanctifiˈcation. Also 7 præ-. [In a, f. PRE- A. 2; in b, n. of action from prec.]

a. A previous sanctification. **b.** Consecration of the eucharistic elements at a previous celebration.

a **1660** HAMMOND *19 Serm.* ix. Wks. 1684 IV. 619 A præmundation or præsanctification of them that sued to be admitted higher. **1872** O. SHIPLEY *Gloss. Eccl. Terms* 128 It is doubtful what the usage of the English Church, in the abeyance of presanctification, ought to be.

presanctify (priːˈsæŋktɪfaɪ), *v.* *rare.* [PRE- A. 1.] *trans.* To sanctify previously or beforehand. Chiefly in **presanctified** *ppl. a.* [after med.L. *præsanctificāta* the presanctified (elements), *missa præsanctificātōrum* the mass of presanctified (elements); so F. *la messe des présanctifiés*], sanctified or consecrated beforehand. ***Liturgy*** or ***Mass of the Presanctified***, an office said in the Roman

Catholic Church and in some Anglican churches on Good Friday, and in the Greek Church throughout Lent (except on Saturdays and Sundays and the Feast of the Annunciation), at which the elements used have been consecrated at a previous celebration.

1758 S. Redford *Important Inquiry* (ed. 2) App. 397 They offer up and shew the people the Sacrament reserved on those two solemn days, which they call the *imperfect* Mass, or the Mass of the *presanctified*. *a* **1773** A. Butler *Feasts Catholic Church* (1774) vi. iv. 355 This is called the 'Mass of the Pre-sanctified Mysteries, *Missa præsanctificatorum*'. **1839** *Penny Cycl.* XIV. 57/2 In the Greek or Constantinopolitan church three Liturgies are in use, those of Basil, Chrysostom, and the Liturgy of the Præ-sanctified. **1853** Rock *Ch. of Fathers* III. ii. 242 The mass of the presanctified was celebrated. **1866** Felton *Anc. & Mod. Gr.* II. ii. iv. 336 These two, with a third, called the Liturgy of the Presanctified, .. constitute the general liturgy of the Greek Church down to the present day. **1872** O. Shipley *Gloss. Eccl. Terms* 128 The custom .. of not consecrating but only of receiving the presanctified Host consecrated on Maundy Thursday. **1909** *Daily Chron.* 10 Apr. 5/4 At Westminster Cathedral yesterday morning the Mass of the Presanctified was solemnised in the presence of Archbishop Bourne. **1957** *Oxf. Dict. Chr. Ch.* 1101/1 In the Middle Ages all present at the Mass of the Presanctified received Holy Communion. **1965** C. E. Pocknee *Parson's Handbk.* (ed. 13) 156 In some churches the Mass of the Pre-sanctified has been reintroduced with a general Communion from the reserved sacrament. **1978** C. Jones et al. *Study of Liturgy* 409 Communion from the reserved sacrament, the so-called Mass of the Pre-Sanctified.

presand, -ant, -aunt, etc., obs. ff. present.

pre-sar'torial, *a. nonce-wd.* [pre- B. 1.] Anterior to the rise of the 'sartorial art' or tailoring.

1871 Lowell *Study Wind., Thoreau* 145 Bran had its prophets, and the presartorial simplicity of Adam its martyrs, tailored impromptu from the tar-pot of incensed neighbours.

†**pre-'say,** *v. Obs. rare.* [f. pre- A. 1 + say *v.*] *trans.* To say before; to preface with something said.

1722 S. Sewall *Diary* 25 Sept., Sung 4 Staves of the 80th Psalm, the last of it; only pre-said it with, From Egypt, &c., four Lines.

presbycousis (prɛzbɪ'kuːsɪs). *Med.* Also **presby(a)cusis, -ac(o)usia** (-ə'kuːzɪə), **-kousis.** [mod.L., f. Gr. πρέσβυς an old man (cf. presbyopia) + ἄκουσις hearing (ἀκούειν to hear).] Loss of acuteness of hearing due to age.

1890 Billings *Med. Dict.* II. 386/1 Presbykousis. **1892** F. P. Foster *Med. Dict.* IV. 2640/2 Presbycusis. **1896** *Syd. Soc. Lex.*, Presbycousis. **1900** *Lancet* 18 Aug. 538/2 To this last belonged the progressive deafness which came on between the ages of 40 and 50 years, and which had been called presbyacousia. **1911** Stedman *Med. Dict.* 703/1 Presbyacusia. **1958** *Times Rev. Industry* Aug. 13/1 Gradual blunting of auditory acuity with the increasing age of the worker .. is known as 'presbycusis'. **1970** *Brit. Med. Jrnl.* 30 May 524/2 It is possible that the high level of everyday noise in industrial countries plays some part in the development of presbyacusis. **1976** *Listener* 2 Sept. 279/1 Presbycousis has not yet set in. Most people over 30, said Jeremy Bugler, .. lose some of their hearing.

presbyope ('prɛsbɪəʊp, 'prɛz-). [f. as next + Gr. -ωπος seeing.] A person affected with presbyopia.

1857 in Dunglison. **1880** L. Owen tr. *Giraud-Teulon's Elem. Treat. Function of Vision* ii. 30 The presbyope presents himself generally under the following aspect: he has always enjoyed excellent distant vision... But he is drawing near to forty-five or fifty and begins to experience a certain difficulty in reading small type. **1900** C. H. May *Man. Dis. Eye* xxiv. 332 The presbyope is compelled to hold reading, writing, sewing, and other forms of near work farther away than the usual distance, making such efforts uncomfortable. **1937** *Jrnl. Optical Soc. Amer.* XXVII. 332/1 Presbyopes should invariably wear their reading correction (reading spectacles). **1974** *Nature* 25 Oct. 729/2 It is known that convergence can bring about accommodation; and it seems likely that in a presbyope, devoid of accommodative ability, convergence would still be accompanied by a central command for accommodation.

‖**presbyopia** (prɛs-, prɛzbɪ'əʊpɪə). Rarely in anglicized form **'presbyopy.** [mod.L., f. Gr. πρέσβυς an old man + -ωπία (as in ἀμβλυωπία amblyopia), f. ὤψ, ὠπ- eye.] An affection of the eyes incident to old or advancing age, in which the power of accommodation to near objects is lost or impaired, and only distant objects are seen distinctly; a form of long-sightedness.

1793 Young in *Phil. Trans.* LXXXIII. 178 The central part of the crystalline becomes rigid by age, and this is sufficient to account for presbyopia. **1822–34** *Good's Study Med.* (ed. 4) III. 151 The third variety, or that produced by old age, constitutes the presbytia and presbyopia of medical writers. **1869** G. Lawson *Dis. Eye* (1874) 233 Presbyopia or Long Sight is one of the first of the legion of troubles which advancing years bring upon all of us. **1881** Le Conte *Sight* i. iii. 49 The remedy for presbyopy is the use of convex glasses. *Ibid.* 50 Myopy is a structural defect; presbyopy is a functional defect.

presbyopic (-'ɒpɪk), *a.* (*sb.*) [f. as prec. + -ic.] Pertaining to or affected with presbyopia. (In the same sense ‖**presbyops** has been used).

1801 Home in *Phil. Trans.* XCII. 6, I adapted the optometer .. to presbyopic eyes. [**1803** tr. *Heberden's Comm.* lxvi. (ed. 2) 330 A violent giddiness has suddenly made a person presbyops, or long sighted.] **1881** Anderson in *Nature* 27 Oct. 618/2 Suppose a man has become presbyopic, *i.e.* his accommodation has gradually become stiff, and its range reduced.

b. as *sb.* A person affected with presbyopia.

1864 tr. *Donders' Accom. & Refract. Eye* 308 Often hyperpresbyopics and presbyopics are met with in this group.

presby'otic, *a. nonce-wd.* [f. as prec. + Gr. οὖς, ὠτ- ear, -ωτος -eared + -ic.] Dull of hearing in consequence of old age.

1890 Humphry *Old Age* 152 To meet the auditory defects which may be attributed to a presbyotic condition.

'presbyte. [ad. Gr. πρεσβύτης an old man (Aristotle, *Prob.* 31. 25). So F. *presbyte*, mod.L. *presbyta*.] = presbyope.

(The modern use is not that of Aristotle, who only raises the question *why* an old man (πρεσβύτης) is long-sighted. Nor is it recognized even in the 1762 ed. of Castelli *Lex. Med.* I. Bywater.)

[**1704** J. Harris *Lex. Techn.* I, *Presbitæ*, are those Men who by Old Age, or other Accidents, have the Globe of the Eye so flat, that the produced Visual Rays pass the Retina before they unite. **1727–41** Chambers *Cycl.* s.v., If the distance between the retina and the crystalline be too small, the person will likewise be a presbyta.] **1846** Worcester cites Prof. Farrar for *Presbyte*.

†**Presby'teer.** *Obs. rare*$^{-1}$. Derisive abbreviation of Presbyterian *sb.*, after *pulpiteer*, etc. Hence †**Presby'teering** *vbl. sb.*, acting the Presbyterian; practice of Presbyterianism.

1708 T. Ward *Eng. Ref.* (1716) 112 The Wars that were begun In sixteen hundred forty one 'Tween Protestants and Presbyteers. **1684** *Roxb. Ball.* (1885) V. 461 Then leave your rebellious and damn'd Presbyteering, Or you may be glad of Poor-Jack and Red-Herring.

presbyter ('prɛs-, 'prɛzbɪtə(r)). Also 6 **presbiter.** [a. late L. *presbyter* (Tertullian), ad. Gr. πρεσβύτερος, in N.T. an elder of the Jewish council or Sanhedrim, an elder of the apostolic church; prop. adj. 'older, elder', compar. of πρέσβυς an old man. So F. *presbytre*.

The Vulgate regularly renders Gr. πρεσβύτερος, -οι by *senior, seniores*, exc. in Acts xx. 17, xxii. 5, where it has *majores natu*, and in Acts xiv. 23, xv. 2, 1 Tim. v. 17, 19, Titus i. 5, Jas. v. 14, where the Gr. is retained as *presbyter, -eri*. The same men who in Acts xv. 2 are called *apostoli et presbyteri*, are denominated in verses 4, 6, 22, 23 *apostoli et seniores*; the Gr. having uniformly ἀπόστολοι και πρεσβύτεροι. Wyclif faithfully renders these Latin equivalents by 1) *elder man, eldre, eld(e)re men* (twice, in Rev., *senyoures*), 2) *the more thorw* (or *in*) *birth*, and 3) *prestis*. The 16–17th Eng. versions from the Greek, and the Revised, have uniformly *elder, -s*, in every instance. The Rhemish N.T. has *priest* wherever the Vulgate has *presbyter*; in other places regularly *auncients*; but, from 1 Peter onward (18 places) *senior, seniors*.

Notwithstanding the prevalence of *senior* in the Vulgate, *presbyter* became the official name of the ecclesiastical order, whence also the Com. Romanic *prêster*, OF. and Prov. *prestre*, F. *prêtre*, Sp. and Cat. *preste*, It. *prete*; WGer. **prêster*, OS. *prêstar*, OFris. *prêstere*, MDu. and Du. *priester*, OHG. *prêstar, prêst, priast*, ON. *prestr, prest-*, OE. *preost*, Eng. *priest* (as an order in the Latin and Anglican churches): see priest.]

1. An elder in the Christian church. **a.** In the early church: One of a number of officers who had the oversight and management of the affairs of a local church or congregation, some of them having also the function of teaching. (Cf. bishop *sb.* 1 a.)

1597 Hooker *Eccl. Pol.* v. lxxviii. §4 The historie doth make no mention by what occasion Presbyters were instituted in Ierusalem, onely wee reade .. how the like were made afterwards else where. **1651** C. Cartwright *Cert. Relig.* ii. 64 All agree in this, that in the Apostles time there was no difference betwixt Bishops and Presbyters. **1781** Gibbon *Decl. & F.* xxxi. III. 261 After receiving, by the imposition of hands, the sacred character of a Christian Presbyter, he ventured to open the gates of the city. **1820** Southey *Wesley* II. 437 [Wesley] proposed, in his character of presbyter, which, he said, was the same as bishop, to invest him [Dr. Coke] with the same presbytero-episcopal powers. **1852** Conybeare & H. *St. Paul* (1862) I. xiii. 406 The office of the Presbyters was to watch over the particular church in which they ministered, in all that regarded its external order and internal purity.

b. In Episcopal churches: A minister of the second order, ranking below a bishop and above a deacon; a priest or pastor. (In modern use, not an official or ordinary term, but used occasionally instead of *priest*, to connote identity with sense a, or distinction from the sense of 'a sacrificing priest' (= Gr. ἱερεύς, L. *sacerdos*): see priest).

1597 Hooker *Eccl. Pol.* v. lxxviii. §2 The Cleargie are either Presbyters or Deacons. *Ibid.* §3 In truth the word Presbyter doth seeme more fit, and in proprietie of speech more agreeable than Priest with the drift of the whole Gospell of Iesus Christ. **1635** *Canons Eccles. Ch. Scot.* xviii. 39 If anie .. confesse the same to the Bishop, or Presbyter, .. hee shall not make knowne, nor reveale what hath beene opened to him in Confession. **1706** Phillips, *Presbyter*, .. a Priest; as a Presbyter of the Church of England. **1820** [see a]. **1846** Sharpe *Hist. Egypt* xiv. 443 Origen afterwards removed to Palestine, and fell under the displeasure of his own bishop for having been there ordained a presbyter.

c. In Presbyterian churches: An occasional name for an elder (see elder *sb.*[3] 4, Presbyterian *a.* 1); *esp.* one who is a member of a presbytery.

1615 Heywood *Foure Prentises* i. xviii. Wks. 1874 II. 207 Should Soldan, Sophy, Priest or Presbyter, Or gods, or Diuels, or men, gaine-say our will. *c* **1646** Milton *New Forcers Consc.* 20 When they shall read this clearly in your charge: New Presbyter is but Old Priest writ Large. **1821** Galt *Ann. Parish* xii, She considered the comely humility of a presbyter as the wickedness of hypocrisy. **1858** Buckle *Civiliz.* (1869) II. v. 197 The main object was, to raise up presbyters, and to destroy bishops.

†**2.** A Presbyterian. *Obs.*

1647 in Rushw. *Hist. Coll.* iv. (1701) II. 1033 He .. prest him to tell him whether he was an Independent or a Presbiter? The Gentleman answered, Neither, for he was a Protestant. **1655** Evelyn *Diary* 25 Dec., The mournfullest day that in my life I had seene, or the Church of England herselfe since the Reformation; to the greate rejoicing of both Papist and Presbyter. **1660** J. C[rouch] *Return Chas. II* 10 Monck was not so much Presbyter. **1681** Wood *Life* 5 Nov. (O.H.S.) II. 558 Westminster School-boyes burn'd Jack Presbyter instead of the pope. **1827** Pollok *Course T.* viii. 96 Episcopalian none, nor presbyter.

3. *attrib.* and *Comb.*: **presbyter-abbot**, an abbot who was a presbyter; **presbyter-bishop** = sense 1 a, identified with bishop *sb.* 1 a; †**presbyter dissent**, app. a dissent on the part of presbyters or priests; †**Presbyter John**: see Prester John; †**presbyter Scot**, a Presbyterian Scot, or ? a Scottish Presbyterian elder.

1839–47 Yeowell *Anc. Brit. Ch.* ix. 97 The monastery of Iona had for its governor a *Presbyter-Abbot, to whose authority .. the whole province, and also the bishops themselves were bound to be subject. **1903** *Union Mag.* Aug. 364/2 *Presbyter-bishops were in existence before the single bishop was thought of. **1690** Evelyn *Diary* 9 Mar., He observed that the first *Presbyter dissents from our discipline were introduc'd by the Jesuites order, about the 20 of Queene Eliz. **1649** Milton *Eikon.* xxvii, While the *presbyter Scot that woos and solicits him, is neglected and put off. **1669** Pepys *Diary* 14 May, A mockery, by one Cornet Bolton, .. that .. did pray and preach like a Presbyter Scot.

presbyteral (prɛs-, prɛz'bɪtərəl), *a.* Also 7 **-bit-**. [a. F. *presbytéral* (14th c. in Hatz.-Darm.), ad. med.L. *presbyterālis* (*c* 984 in Du Cange): see prec. and -al[1].]

1. Of or pertaining to a presbyter or priest; consisting of presbyters.

1611 Cotgr., *Presbiteral*, Presbiterall, Priestlie, belonging to a priest. **1620** Brent tr. *Sarpi's Counc. Trent* vii. 652 According to the Councell of Chalcedon, at which time a presbyterall title without an Office was not heard of. **1725** tr. *Dupin's Eccl. Hist. 17th C.* I. v. 176 Neither the Unction, nor the Delivery of the Consecrated Vessels, are the Matter of Presbyteral Ordination. **1776** Gibbon *Decl. & F.* xv. I. 490 These powers, during a short period, were exercised according to the advice of the presbyteral college. **1885** Lightfoot *Ep. Philippians* (ed. 8) 350 [In the *Doctrine of the Twelve Apostles*] There is no trace of the episcopal office as distinct from the presbyteral.

2. = Presbyterian *a.* 1.

1651 W. Jane Εικων Ακλαστος 193 The Directory, Extemporall devotions, independent, or Presbiterall platformes. **1688** *Andros Tracts* II. 12 Dissenting Ministers in and about London, that go under the Denomination of Presbiteral and Congregational. **1716** M. Davies *Athen. Brit.* III. 49 Calvin's Presbyteral Order. **1807** W. Taylor in *Ann. Rev.* V. 577 Zeal for a presbyteral, rather than an episcopal organization of Church government. **1902** T. M. Lindsay *Ch. Early Cent.* v. 194 There is no indication that he is upholding the episcopal against any other form of church government, as for instance the presbyteral.

presbyterate (prɛs'bɪtərət, prɛz-), *sb.* [ad. med.L. *presbyterātus* (755 in Du Cange): see presbyter and -ate[1].]

1. The office of presbyter; presbytership, eldership.

1642 Jer. Taylor *Episc.* (1647) 82 Why should a Deaconship, or a Presbyterate consist with the office of an Evangelist, more then a Bishoprick? **1683** Corbet *Nonconf. Plea* 12 The Ministry that I have received, is the sacred office of Presbyterate. **1833–6** J. H. Newman *Hist. Sk., Prim. Chr., Apollinaris* (1872) 392 His father .. rose to the presbyterate in the Church of that city [Laodicea]. **1881** Stanley *Chr. Instit.* (1884) 36 As the Episcopate became more separate from the Presbyterate.

2. A body of presbyters; the order of presbyters.

1641 R. Brooke *Eng. Episc.* ii. iii. 74 As appears by that of Paul to Timothy, on whom were laid the Hands of the Presbytery; not of the Presbyterate, or one Presbyter. **1725** tr. *Dupin's Eccl. Hist. 17th C.* I. v. 165 The distinction of the Episcopate and Presbyterate, as of two separate Orders. **1879** Farrar *St. Paul* II. App. 618 The mild and natural authority which the Apostle assigns to a representative presbyterate.

pres'byterate (-ət), *a.* [Short for *presbyterated*: see next.] Constituted of presbyters or elders.

1853 D. King *Def. Presbyt. Ch. Govt.* vi. iii. (1854) 349 The sole or chief use of presbyterate gathering is to settle disputes.

pres'byterate (-eɪt), *v.* Also 9 **-trate.** [f. presbyter + -ate[3] 7.] *trans.* To constitute or organize according to the Presbyterian system. Chiefly in **pres'byterated** *ppl. a.*

1702 C. MATHER *Magn. Chr.* v. ii. (1852) 208 A presbyterated society of the faithful. **1900** W. A. SHAW *Hist. Eng. Ch.* II. 126 All the Parliamentary ordinances for the county classes which have survived, only presbytrated or united into the classes, the parish churches or chapels.

‖**presbytère.** [F., ad. late L. PRESBYTERIUM.] A Roman Catholic priest's house; = PRESBYTERY 6.

1844 LEVER *T. Burke* II. 165, I took him home with me to my presbytère at Sevres, for that was my parish. **1857** G. OLIVER *Coll. Hist. Cath. Relig. Cornwall*, etc. 27 A convenient site was purchased..for a church, school, and presbytère. **1860** *All Year Round* No. 63. 306 At the entrance of the..village street,..stood the church, and..the presbytère and its apple garden.

presbyteress ('prɛs-, 'prɛzbɪtərɪs). [ad. med.L. *presbyterissa* (*Ordo Rom.* in Du Cange, Duns Scotus *Sentent.* 4. 25. 2–6); in sense 2 for earlier L. *presbytera*: see PRESBYTER and -ESS.]

†**1.** The wife of a presbyter or priest. *Obs.*

1546 BALE *Eng. Votaries* I. (1550) 71 Marianus sayth, she was a presbyteresse or a prestes leman, to saue the honoure of that ordre, bycause he was a monke hys selfe. [**1563** FOXE *A. & M.* 21/2 Priestes then in those daies [*c* 1074] had wiues openly and lawfully..as appeareth by the dedes and writynges of their chapter seales..and were called, by their name, presbyterisse.] **1672–5** COMBER *Comp. Temple* (1702) 240 So it was in Germany long after, where the Priests Wife had the Title of Presbyteress.

2. A female presbyter; one of an order of women in the early church, having some of the functions of presbyters.

They were either widows, or matrons who had with their husbands' consent left the estate of matrimony, to devote themselves to divine service. (See Du Cange.)

1651 JER. TAYLOR *Clerus Dom.* 15 The Presbyteresses who were the..governesses of women, in order to manners and religion. **1682** *Weekly Mem. Ingen.* 342 To enquire into the quality of these Presbyteresses of the primitive church. **1901** J. WORDSWORTH *Ministry of Grace* v. 271 In these [*sc.* the 'Didascalia' and the 'Constitutions'] and similar books the elders Widows are sometimes mentioned under the title of πρεσβύτιδες, a name for which we have no nearer equivalent than the somewhat ambiguous and inexact 'Presbyteresses'. .. The Virgins, Widows and Presbyteresses have the first place among the women in church.

presbyterial (prɛs-, prɛzbɪ'tɪərɪəl), *a.* (*sb.*) Also 6–7 -bit-. [f. late L. *presbyteri-um* PRESBYTERY + -AL[1].]

1. Of or pertaining to a presbytery or body of presbyters or elders: **a.** generally.

a **1600** HOOKER *Eccl. Pol.* VI. i. §4 Treatises..whereby they have laboured to void the rooms of their spiritual superiors before authorized, and to advance the new fancied sceptre of lay presbyterial power. **1641** R. BROOKE *Eng. Episc.* 81 Timothy received his Evangelicall Gift by the Imposition of Presbyteriall hands. **1706** DE FOE *Jure Div.* Pref. 34 The Disputes about the *Jus Divinum*, of several sorts of Power, whether Regal, Episcopal, or Presbyterial, have had fatal Effects in their several Turns. **1840** GLADSTONE *Ch. Princ.* 410 A question of pure fact,..whether the sufficiency of Apostolical powers has been historically transmitted in the Presbyterial as well as in the Episcopal line.

b. of a local PRESBYTERY (sense 4).

1717 DE FOE *Mem. Ch. Scot.* 16/1 The Assembly of Ministers, either General, Synodical, or Presbyterial. **1796** MORSE *Amer. Geog.* I. 271 The Presbyterian churches are governed by congregational presbyterial and synodical assemblies. **1832** CHALMERS in Hanna *Mem.* (1851) III. xvii. 317 Men will not suspend their secular business on the Presbyterial fast-day. **1852** BLACKIE *Stud. Lang.* 25 Passing the entrance trials..and Presbyterial examinations.

2. (Usu. with capital initial.) = PRESBYTERIAN *a.* 1. (Common in 17th c.; now *rare.*)

1592 (*title*) Conspiracie for Pretended Reformation: viz. Presbyteriall Discipline. **1593** ABP. BANCROFT (*title*) Davngerovs Positions and Proceedings, published and practised within this Iland of Brytaine, vnder pretence of Reformation, and for the Presbiteriall Discipline. **1641** MILTON *Ch. Govt.* Pref., This government, whether it ought to be presbyterial or prelatical. **1642** SIR E. DERING *Sp. on Relig.* xvi. 82 The next is the Presbyteriall way... I can poynt out when it began. **1646** CHAS. I in Ellis *Orig. Lett.* Ser. II. III. 326 Many persuasions and threatnings that hath been used to me for making me change Episcopal into Presbiterial Government. **1681–6** J. SCOTT *Chr. Life* (1747) III. 388 The two main Rival Forms of Church Government pretending to divine Institution, are the Presbyterial and Episcopal. **1904** *Westm. Gaz.* 6 June 3/2 The petitioners were departing from the constitution of the Presbyterial system and were going on the worst lines of a Congregationalism no one could defend.

†**b.** as *sb.* = PRESBYTERIAN *sb. Obs.*

1647 G. PALMER *Sectaries Unmasked* 23 Another point in difference between the Presbyterialls and some of the Sectaries.

Hence †**Presby'terialist**, a Presbyterian; **presby'terially** *adv.*, †(*a*) according to the Presbyterian system of church government (*obs.*); (*b*) by or on the part of a (or the) presbytery.

1647 G. PALMER *Sectaries Unmasked* 2 Conversations between those that stand for the Presbyterialists government (or at least nearest it) and those that dissent from it. **1655** S. ASHE in *R. Baillie's Lett. & Jrnls.* (Bannatyne Club) III. 307 Many act presbyteriallie in London, and in many counties, both in reference to ordination and admission to the sacrament. **1904** R. SMALL *Hist. U.P. Congregat.* I. 281 The congregation was visited presbyterially in the end of 1773.

Presbyterian (prɛs-, prɛzbɪ'tɪərɪən), *a.* and *sb.* Also 7 -bit-; occas. with lower-case initial. [f. L. *presbyteri-um* PRESBYTERY + -AN; cf. F. *presbytérien* (in 15th c. an almoner, Froissart). For form cf. *episcopalian*.]

A. *adj.* **1.** Pertaining to, or characterized by, government by presbyters or presbyteries; applied to a form or system of church polity (see below); belonging to or maintaining this system.

In Presbyterian Churches no higher order than that of presbyter or elder is recognized, the 'bishop' and 'elder' of the N.T. being held to be identical. All elders are ecclesiastically of equal rank; but, in their function in the church, while some are 'ruling and teaching elders' or 'ministers', others are only 'ruling elders' (popularly called 'lay elders', but erroneously, since all elders are ordained or 'in orders'). Each congregation is governed by its session, consisting of the minister and the other elders (see KIRK-SESSION, also CONSISTORY 9); the sessions are subordinate to the PRESBYTERY (see also CLASSIS), the presbyteries to the SYNOD, and (in most Presbyterian Churches) the synods to the General Assembly of the Church (see ASSEMBLY 5 b).

1641 SIR T. ASTON *Remonstr. Presbitery* Title-p., A Short Survey of the Presbyterian Discipline. **1647** CLARENDON *Hist. Reb.* I. §172 In Scotland..though there were Bishops in name,..they themselves were..subject to an Assembly, which was purely Presbyterian. **1651** BAXTER *Inf. Bapt.* 228, I am confidently perswaded, That the true way of Christ's Discipline, is parcelled out between the Episcopal, Erastian, Presbyterian, and Independents; and that every party hath a piece of the Truth in peculiar. **1663** BUTLER *Hud.* I. i. 191 For his Religion it was fit To match his Learning and his Wit: 'Twas Presbyterian true Blew. *a* **1715** BURNET *Own Time* (1823) V. VII. 281 After the general vote was carried for the union [of England and Scotland], before they entered on the consideration of the particular articles, an act was prepared for securing the presbyterian government. **1750** J. EDWARDS *Wks.* (1834) I. xvii. p. clxiii/1 The presbyterian way has ever appeared to me most agreeable to the word of God and the reason and nature of things. **1817** J. EVANS *Excurs. Windsor*, etc. 10 For this purpose they erected a Presbytery at Wandsworth [1572]... This was the first Presbyterian church in England. **1820** SOUTHEY *Wesley* II. 365 He died at Newbury-Port, in New-England, and..was buried before the pulpit, in the Presbyterian church of that town. **1853** KILLEN *Hist. Presbyt. Ch. Irel.* III. xxxi. 585 On Friday, the 10th of July 1840,..the court was regularly constituted under the title of 'The General Assembly of the Presbyterian Church in Ireland'. **1876** *Proc. Union Synod* in Drysdale *Hist. Presbyt. Eng.* III. (1889) 626 *note*, That the name of the Church shall be 'The Presbyterian Church of England'. **1901** M[c]CRIE *Church of Scot. Divisions & Reunions* ii. 33 The polity of the Societies was presbyterian.

b. ***Reformed Presbyterian***, of or pertaining to those Presbyterians who protested against the constitution of Church and State in Scotland at the Revolution Settlement in 1689, and claimed to be the true representatives of the Covenanters of the seventeenth century; also popularly called CAMERONIAN, q.v.

They consisted of members of the 'United Societies' formed in 1681, and in 1743 organized themselves under the name of *The Reformed Presbytery*, known at a later date as the 'Reformed Presbyterian Church'. In 1876 the greater part of this body in Scotland united with the Free Church; but some held out, and still constitute a separate denomination.

[**1701**: see B. **1744** A. MARSHALL in Hutchinson *Ref. Presb. Ch.* 187 The Rev. Mr. John M'Millan and I,..with certain elders, upon the 1st August 1743, did erect ourselves into a Presbytery under the name of 'The Reformed Presbytery'.] **1806** (*title*) Reformation Principles exhibited by the Reformed Presbyterian Church in the United States of America. **1860** J. GARDNER *Faiths of World* II. 745/2 A fully organized and independent section of the Reformed Presbyterian Church was formed in the sister isle. **1893** HUTCHINSON *Ref. Presbyt. Ch.* ii. 25 The persecuted Presbyterians, of which the Reformed Presbyterian Church has always claimed to be the legitimate ecclesiastical successor.

c. ***United Presbyterian***, of or pertaining to the united church or denomination formed in Scotland in 1847 by the union of the United Secession and Relief churches. (Abbreviated U.P.) In 1900 this body united with the (main body of the) Free Church of Scotland, to form the denomination then named the United Free Church of Scotland.

1847 *Proc. United Presbyt. Synod* 14 May 13 That the Name of the Church under the authority and inspection of this Synod be *The United Presbyterian Church*; and that the Name of this Synod be *The Synod of the United Presbyterian Church*, composed of the United Associate Synod of the Secession Church and of the Synod of the Relief Church. **1900** ROSS TAYLOR in *Proc. Assembly United Free Ch. Sc.* 64, I declare the Act of Union finally adopted, and that the Free Church of Scotland and the United Presbyterian Church are now one Church in Christ Jesus, under the designation of the United Free Church of Scotland.

2. Characteristic of a Presbyterian. *nonce-use.*

1699–1700 EARL OF BELLOMONT *Let. to Sir. J. Stanley* 5 Mar. (Welbeck MSS.), He gave me a terrible hard presbyterian gripe in the articles between him and me. —— *Let. to Vernon* 7 Mar. (Ibid.), When he had made me depend on him for advancing the money..he then gave me a Presbyterian gripe and fettered me in the writeings between us.

3. Of or pertaining to presbyters or priests, or the priestly order. *rare.*

1881 STANLEY *Chr. Inst.* vii. (ed. 2) 147 The texts on which the theory of Episcopal or Presbyterian absolution rests.

B. *sb.* One who maintains the Presbyterian system of church government; a member or adherent of a Presbyterian church.

Reformed Presbyterian, United Presbyterian, a member or adherent of the religious denominations so called: see A. 1 b, c.

1641 SIR T. ASTON *Remonstr. Presbit., Survey Presbyt. Discipl.* Table, Sectio 7. The Presbyterians must not be prescribed in doctrine. *Ibid.* xiii. I iij, The inordinate violence of the Presbyterians. *c* **1645** HOWELL *Lett.* (1753) 478 Those unhappy separatists, the Puritans,..who since are called 'Presbyterians', or 'Jews of the New Testament'. **1655** FULLER *Ch. Hist.* IX. vii. §21 A Synod of the Presbyterians, of the Warwickshire Classis, was call'd at Coventry. **1673** *Essex Papers* (Camden) I. 77 The Pow'r and Interest of y[e] Non-Conformists here [Ireland], and their greatest strength, is certainly that of y[e] Presbiterians, who are of y[e] Scotch nation. **1701** SIR R. HAMILTON in Hutchinson *Ref. Presbyt. Ch.* v. (1893) 138, I die a true Protestant, and to my Knowledge a Reformed Presbyterian. **1732** E. ERSKINE *Synod Sermon* Wks. 1871 I. 504 All sound Presbyterians, who read the history of our forefathers, generally approve of the practice of Mr. Samuel Rutherford ..and other ministers of this church. **1824** BYRON *Juan* XV. xci, For I was bred a moderate Presbyterian. **1867** T. S. JAMES *Hist. Litigation resp. Presbyt. Chapels* 191 Milton, whatever he was, was no Presbyterian. **1874** J. H. BLUNT *Dict. Sects* (1886) 98/2 Under the name of *Reformed Presbyterians* the society still exists, claiming to be the representative of the old Covenanters in maintaining the Solemn League and Covenant as one of the standards, and still deploring the constitution of Church and State..as established at the Revolution of 1688 and at the Union. *Ibid.* 609/2 The United Presbyterians carry on missions..in the East and West Indies, and in Africa, together with medical missions to China. **1885** W. D. JEREMY *Presbyt. Fund & Dr. Williams's Trust* Introd. 8 *note*, In the eighteenth century, wind-guards fixed on chimney-pots were called Presbyterians, in derisive allusion to the want of fixedness in the theological opinions of the Denomination of that name.

Presby'terianism. [f. prec. + -ISM; cf. F. *presbytérianisme.*] The Presbyterian system of church government: see prec. A. 1.

1644 GILLESPIE (*title*) A Recrimination charged upon Mr. Goodwin, in defense of Presbyterianism. **1661** K. W. *Conf. Charact., Univ. Beadle* (1860) 72 The favorites of independing presbyterianisme. **1716** ADDISON *Freeholder* No. 54 ¶3 The Tories tell us, that the Whig-Scheme would end in Presbyterianism and a Commonwealth. **1809** PINKNEY *Trav. France* 3 A more pious Christian, but without presbyterianism, did not exist than Captain Eliab. **1871** RAINY & MACKENZIE *Life Cunningham* xii. 164 The ineradicable Presbyterianism of the Scottish people.

Presby'terianize, *v.* [f. as prec. + -IZE.]

a. *trans.* To make Presbyterian; to organize according to the Presbyterian system. **b.** *intr.* To act as a Presbyterian, or in a way tending towards the Presbyterian system or doctrine. Hence **Presby'terianized** *ppl. a.*; **Presby'terianizing** *ppl. a.*

a **1843** SOUTHEY *Com.-pl. Bk.* Ser. II. (1849) 192/1 Cromwell's policy with the Independents, setting them to prepare a Confession of faith,—which would, ipso facto, have Presbyterianized them. *c* **1878** PUSEY in Liddon *Life* (1897) IV. xiii. 315 Our Bishops seem paralyzed by our Presbyterianizing Archbishop of Canterbury. **1885** *Ch. Q. Rev.* Jan. 494 The reaction from the unwise step of Archbishop Laud led them [Scottish Episcopalians] to all but Presbyterianize their worship at the..restoration..in 1660. **1886** BRODRICK *Hist. Univ. Oxford* 145 These bodies were equally resolved to Presbyterianise the University. **1889** DRYSDALE *Hist. Presbyt. in Eng.* 592 The need of.. submitting to some more Presbyterianized development.

Presby'terianly, *adv.* [f. as prec. + -LY[2].] In a Presbyterian manner or direction.

1656 EVELYN *Diary* 2 Nov., Tho' the Minister was Presbyterianly affected, he yet was..duly ordain'd. **1691** WOOD *Ath. Oxon.* II. 255 This person [Thos. Vaughan] tho' presbyterianly affected, yet he had the Kings ear. **1894** W. WALKER *Hist. Congreg. Ch. U.S.* 171 This extension of the communion was not put in practice..during the first half-century..save at Presbyterianly inclined Newbury.

'Presbyterism. *rare.* [f. PRESBYTER + -ISM.]

†**a.** = PRESBYTERIANISM. *Obs.* **b.** The office or rank of a presbyter.

1659 GAUDEN *Tears Ch.* 564 Anabaptisme, or Presbyterisme, or Independentisme. *a* **1670** HACKET *Abp. Williams* II. (1692) 197 It looks not all like Popery that Presbyterism was disdained by the king; his father had taught him that it was a sect so perfidious, that he found more faith among the Highlanders. **1826** G. S. FABER *Diffic. Romanism* (1853) 407 The consecration..of Archbishop Parker, even if we concede the mere Presbyterism of Barlow, will be more canonical than that of Pope Pelagius, by the precise amount of one Bishop.

‖**presby'terium, -ion.** [Christian L. (Cyprian, *a* 250), ad. Gr. πρεσβυτέριον, -τερεῖον (N.T.) a council of elders, Jewish or Christian; in eccl. Gr. the office of a presbyter, also the meeting-place of presbyters or elders.]

1. = PRESBYTERY 1.

1565 JEWEL *Repl. Harding's Answ.* III. xxvi. 196 The Quier was then..called *Cancelli*, a Chauncel, and commonly of the Greekes *Presbyterium*, for that it was a place specially appointed vnto the Priestes, and Ministers, and shut vp from al others. **1701** *Cowell's Interpr.*, *Presbyterium*, the Presbytery *i.e.* The Quire or Chancel so called, because it was the place appropriated to the Bishop and Priests, and other Clergy.

2. = PRESBYTERY 3.

a **1886** J. KER *Lect. Hist. Preaching* iii. (1888) 46 Next was a space occupied by the Presbyterion or body of Presbyters.

1896 E. BECK in *Dublin Rev.* July 82 The college of cardinals represents the ancient *presbyterium*, or council, by which the bishop of Rome, as every other bishop, was assisted. **1902** T. M. LINDSAY *Ch. & Min. in Early Cent.* v. 196 According to the conception of Ignatius, every Christian community ought to have at its head a bishop, a presbyterium or session of elders, and a body of deacons.

pres'bytero-e'piscopal, *a. nonce-wd.* Of or pertaining to a presbyter-bishop.
1820 [see PRESBYTER 1 a].

'presbytership. [See -SHIP.] The office or rank of presbyter; = PRESBYTERATE 1.
1597 HOOKER *Eccl. Pol.* v. lxxviii. §3 Let them vse what dialect they will, whether we call it a Priesthood, a Presbytership, or a Ministerie, it skilleth not. **1635** PAGITT *Christianogr.* 84 That no Deaconship or Presbytership is given among them, except first they have contracted a Virgin. **1656** TRAPP *Comm. 1 Tim.* iii. 13 A fair step to a higher order, i.e. to a bishoprick or presbyter-ship. **1882–3** *Schaff's Encycl. Relig. Knowl.* I. 298/1 In chapter 47 he [Clement] speaks of the dignity of presbytership. **1885** E. S. FFOULKES *Prim. Consecr.* ix. 470 Thy servants, whom we dedicate to the honour of the presbytership.

presbytery ('prɛs-, 'prɛzbɪtərɪ). Also 5 presbetory, -bytory, 6–7 -beterie, -y, biterie, -bytrie, 6–8 -bitery. [a. OF. *presbiterie* (12th c. in Littré) a priest's house, ad. late L. *presbyterium*: see PRESBYTERIUM.]

1. A part of a church, esp. of a cathedral or other large church, reserved for the clergy; formerly, the three seats or *sedilia* on the south side of the eastern part of the chancel, the remnant of the bench which in earlier times ran all round; hence, the whole of the eastern part of the chancel beyond the choir, in which the altar is placed; the sanctuary.
1412 in Raine *Catterick Church* (1834) 9 A high awter.. with three Prismatories [*sic*] convenably made be mason crafte. **1466** *Inv.* in *Archæologia* L. 34, j cloth of grene bokrame lyned for the presbetory. **1483** *Cath. Angl.* 291/1 A Presbytory, *presbiterium*. *c* **1510** *Inv.* in *Papers Norf. & Norw. Archæol. Soc.* XIV. 194 Itm. iij old qwishons daily lying in the presbitery. *a* **1552** LELAND *Itin.* II. 77 A Noble Man caullid Philip Fitz Payne was buryed.. under an Arch on the North side of the Presbyterie. **1845** PARKER *Gloss. Archit.*, *Presbytery*,.. the part of a church in which the high Altar is placed; it forms the eastern termination of the choir, above which it is raised by several steps, and is occupied exclusively by those who minister in the services of the Altar. **1848** *Rickman's Archit.* (ed. 5) p. xlvii, Clerestory of the presbytery, a fine rich example. **1874** MICKLETHWAITE *Mod. Par. Churches* 8 The nave, or body of the church; the choir, and the sanctuary or presbytery.

†**2.** The office of a presbyter; eldership or priesthood; = PRESBYTERATE 1. *Obs.*
1604 R. CAWDREY *Table Alph.*, *Presbytery*, eldership. **1623** COCKERAM, *Presbyterie*, Priesthood. **1630** BRATHWAIT *Eng. Gentlem.* (1641) 196 Those precise schismatics.. cannot endure any precedency or priority of place to be in the church, but an equality of Presbyterie. **1634** SIR T. HERBERT *Trav.* 74 He.. ransacks the Temples or Houses of Christian Deuotion, trampling vnder-foot.. all reliques and vsefull Ornaments, belonging to Presbytery [among the Georgian Christians]. **1660** R. COKE *Power & Subj.* 89 The next order in the Church of Christ to Apostles and Bishops is that of Presbytery or Priesthood. **1704** NELSON *Fest. & Fasts* II. vii. (1739) 539 If the Word.. Presbytery.. signifies not a College of Presbyters, but the Office.

3. A body of presbyters or elders (in the early church; also in a general sense, usually with allusion to 4).
1611 BIBLE *1 Tim.* iv. 14 Neglect not the gift.. which was giuen thee by prophesie, with laying on of the hands of the Presbyterie [τοῦ πρεσβυτερίου, *presbyterii*, WYCLIF of prestis or presthod, TINDALE an elder, CRANMER presthode, *Geneva* the Eldership, *Rheims* priesthod, *Revised* the presbytery]. **1641** MILTON *Reform.* I. Wks. 1851 III. 32 The bosome admonition of a Friend is a Presbytery, and a Consistory to them. **1650** BAXTER *Saints' R.* II. vi. §1 (1651) 254 Even the Bishop with his Presbyterie was in each particular Church. **1709** J. JOHNSON *Clergym. Vade M.* II. p. li, When Alexander, bishop of Alexandria, called a Presbytery to condemn Arius, he had Deacons present with him, as well as Bishops and Priests. **1833** *Tracts for Times* No. 7. 4 The Bishops have no where committed it to the Presbytery. **1853** D. KING *Def. Presbyt. Ch. Govt.* v. vi. (1854) 269 The early Christian fathers frequently call the deliberative council of a particular church its presbytery.

4. In the Presbyterian system: A body or assembly of presbyters or elders, consisting of all the ministers, and one ruling elder (or sometimes two) from each parish or congregation within a particular local area, constituting the ecclesiastical court next above the kirk-session and below the synod (see PRESBYTERIAN *a.* 1).
1578 *2nd Bk. Discipl. Ch. Scot.* xi. §11 Na man aucht to have the office of visitation [i.e. be a Superintendent] bot he that is lawfully chosin be the Presbytrie thereunto. **1582** *Reg. Privy Council Scot.* III. 476 Patrik Gillespie, moderatour of the haill presbiterie of Striveling. **1640–1** *Kirkcudbr. War-Comm. Min. Bk.* (1855) 25 Some must be appoyntit in everie Presbytrie, by the Committee thairof. **1761** HUME *Hist. Eng.* III. liii. 138 *note*, A presbytery in Scotland is an inferior ecclesiastical court, the same that was afterwards called a classis in England. **1806** *Gazetteer Scotl.* (ed. 2) p. xviii, The General Assembly.. consists of commissioners, some of whom are laymen, under the name of ruling elders, from presbyteries, royal boroughs, and universities. **1828** E. IRVING *Last Days* p. viii, Having received ordination from the Presbytery,.. I set out on this very morning six years ago, on my way to London. **1876** GRANT *Burgh Sch. Scotl.* II. i. 83 In 1706 the Assembly recommended presbyteries to visit all public grammar schools within their bounds.
attrib. **1629** *Reg. Privy Council Scot.* Ser. II. III. 22 That they.. make thair addresse to the severall presbytereis upoun the first presbyterie day after the charge.

b. *transf.* The district comprising the parishes or congregations represented by a presbytery.
1581 *Reg. Privy Council Scot.* III. 383 That thaireftir presbitereis or elderschippis may be constitute. **1591** *Ibid.* IV. 628 Maist pairt of the kirkis within the said presbiterie. **1640–1** *Kirkcudbr. War-Comm. Min. Bks.* (1855) 48 Thair are ten kirkes of the presbytrie of Drumfries. *a* **1817** T. DWIGHT *Trav. New Eng.*, etc. (1821) II. 112 He lived within the bounds of the Presbytery of Albany [U.S.]. **1840** *Penny Cycl.* XVIII. 500/1 In the Established Church of Scotland .. there are 69 Presbyteries, each consisting of parishes in number not more than 24 nor fewer than 12. The Provincial Synods, of which there are 15,.. are composed of the Presbyteries within the provinces which give name to the Synods. *Mod.* The churches in the London Presbytery.

c. By early writers, sometimes applied to the body of elders of an individual parish church (corresponding to the actual kirk-session).
[**1573** SANDYS *Let. to Bullinger* 15 Aug. in *Zurich Lett.* (Parker Soc.) I. II. 173 Ecclesia Christi non admittit aliam gubernationem, quam illam solum, quæ fit per presbyterium: scilicet per ministrum, seniores et diaconum. *Ibid.*, Habeat unaquæque parochia suum proprium presbyterium. *transl.* ibid. I. I. 295–6 The church of Christ admits of no other government but that by presbyteries; viz. by the minister, elders, and deacon... Each parish should have its own presbytery.] **1655** FULLER *Ch. Hist.* IX. iii. §8 The Nonconformists though over-powred for the present [1572] in Parliament.. after the dissolution thereof,.. presumed to erect a Presbitery at Wandsworth in Surrey... This was the first-born of all Presbyteries in England, and *secundum usum Wandesworth*, as much honoured by some, as *secundum usum Sarum* by others. **1889** A. H. DRYSDALE *Hist. Presbyt. in Eng.* 121 A Congregational Eldership or parochial Presbytery, to which the Elizabethan Puritans attached prime importance. *Ibid.* 146 The Presbytery which was set up at Wandsworth was a local or parochial eldership. [But some question this view, and hold that the Wandsworth Presbytery was at least an approach to what is still known in Scotland as a presbytery (sense 4).]

†**d.** The ministers and elders collectively forming the administrative body of the Presbyterian church of a country. *Obs.*
1628 WITHER *Brit. Rememb.* VIII. 1705 In Scotland if I liv'd, I would deny No due respect to their Presbyterie. **1651** HOBBES *Leviath.* xliv. 341 The Presbytery hath challenged the power to Excommunicate their owne Kings, and to bee the Supreme Moderators in Religion, in the places where they have that form of Church government.

e. ***Reformed Presbytery***, the presbytery or court of the Reformed Presbyterian church: see PRESBYTERIAN *a.* 1 b.
1744 [see PRESBYTERIAN *a.* 1 b]. **1860** GARDNER *Faiths of World* II. 745/2 There being now two ministers, a meeting was held at Braehead on the 1st of August 1743, when a presbytery was the first time formed under the name of the *Reformed Presbytery*. *Ibid.* 749/2 The formation of the Reformed Presbytery in Scotland in 1743 was productive of much advantage to the Cameronians in Ireland.

5. The Presbyterian polity or system; Presbyterianism. (Contrasted with *episcopacy* or *prelacy*, and with *independency*.) Common in 17th c.; now *rare*.
1590 NASHE *Pasquils Apol.* Wks. (Grosart) I. 239 Thys beeing a place vppon which they haue built theyr Presbiterie, if they pull but one straw out of the nest, al their egges are broken. **1622** BACON *Hist. Gt. Brit.* Mor. & Hist. Wks. (Bohn) 499 The ministers, and those which stood for the presbytery, thought their cause had more sympathy with the discipline of Scotland than the hierarchy of England. **1641** MILTON *Reform.* II. Wks. 1851 III. 66 In France.. the Protestants.. carry the name of the best Subjects the King has; and yet Presbytery, if it must be so call'd, does there all that it desires to do. **1647** *Case Kingd.* 10 Presbyterie is the Rivall of Episcopacie. **1716** M. DAVIES *Athen. Brit.* III. *Diss. Drama* 2 The Independants pretend to refine upon Presbitery (as that did upon the Church). **1846** MCCULLOCH *Acc. Brit. Empire* (1854) II. 283 The Act of William and Mary, re-establishing Presbytery, passed in 1690. **1872** O. SHIPLEY *Gloss. Eccl. Terms* 264 Prelacy was re-established 1610,.. but Presbytery became finally triumphant.

6. A presbyter's or priest's house; a parsonage. (Now only in *R.C. Ch.*) Also ***presbytery-house***.
1825 SOUTHEY in *Q. Rev.* XXXIII. 136 The presbytery of the Moderator differed little either in construction or size from the hovels by which it was surrounded. **1896** *Westm. Gaz.* 3 Mar. 8/3 He dated his communication from 'The Presbytery', as is usual among Roman Catholic clergy. **1902** N. MUNRO in *Blackw. Mag.* Nov. 584/1 They walked together to the presbytery-house.

‖**presbytia** (-'bɪtɪə). [mod.L., f. Gr. πρεσβύτης: see PRESBYTE. Cf. F. *presbytie*.] = PRESBYOPIA. So **pres'bytic** *a.*, **'presbytism**.
1706 PHILLIPS (ed. 6), *Presbytia*, a dimness of Sight, when the Ball of the Eye is so flat, that the Visual Rays pass the Retina, or Net-like Coat before they are united. **1822–34** Presbytia [see PRESBYOPIA]. **1857** DUNGLISON *Dict. Med.*, *Presbytic*, presbyopic. **1863** ATKINSON tr. *Ganot's Physics* VII. vi. §509. 461 The most usual affections of the eye are myopy and presbytism, or short sight and far sight.

pre'scaler. *Electronics.* [PRE- A. 2.] A scaling circuit employed to scale down the input to a counting or other scaling circuit so that it can deal with high counting rates.
1954 E. H. W. BANNER *Electronic Measuring Instruments* xi. 277 When very short resolving times are essential, it is necessary to use a hard-valve pre-scaler in front of a scaler using these new tubes. **1967** *Electronics* 6 Mar. 152 (*caption*) The counter is used in pairs as a prescaler. **1972** *Physics Bull.* Feb. 114/1 A new high performance, low priced scaler timer for use in schools and technical colleges... It features a fast (1 μs) prescaler of integrated circuit construction with a bold two digit read out of counts. **1976** *CB Mag.* June 72/2 Because the VHF prescaler is built-in, the decimal point is placed properly on the display. **1977** *Design Engin.* July 81/3 A prescaler extends this range to 800 MHz.

‖**prescapula** (priː'skæpjʊlə). *Anat.* [PRE- A. 4 b.] That part of the scapula or shoulder-blade above (or in quadrupeds, anterior to) its spine or median axis. Hence **pre'scapular** *a.*, anterior to the spine or long axis of the shoulder-blade; *sb.* the *prescapularis* or *supraspinatus* muscle.
1890 BILLINGS *Med. Dict.*, *Prescapular fossa*, supraspinous fossa.

pre-scene, -scholastic: see PRE- A. 2, B. 1 d.

preschizophrenia, -ic: see PRE- B. 1.

preschool, *a.* and *sb.* **A.** *adj.* [PRE- B. 2.] (Stress variable.) Of or pertaining to the time before a child is old enough for school.
1924 *Jrnl. Amer. Med. Assoc.* 5 Jan. 1/1 We weigh our preschool children nude on their birthdays. **1934** [see ATTENTIVE *a.* 1 b]. **1946** *Nature* 23 Nov. 737/1 They [*sc.* defects] develop during the pre-school age, and accurate knowledge concerning them is lacking. **1958** *Word* XIV. 170 In this experiment, preschool and first grade children.. were presented with a number of nonsense words. **1960** *Guardian* 29 Apr. 6/4 Dr Tizard suggested the opening of pre-school centres for mentally handicapped children. **1979** *Dædalus* Spring 76 Participation rates for mothers with children of preschool age increased from 18 to 27 percent between 1966 and 1976.

B. *sb.* [PRE- B. 1] (Stressed '*preschool*.) A kindergarten or nursery school for children of preschool age.
1934 in WEBSTER. **1937** S. V. BENÉT *Thirteen o' Clock* (1938) 275 Nope, that doesn't work any more, what with pre-schools, automats and movies. **1958** *Word* XIV. 159 The oldest children at the Preschool were five years old. **1966** BEREITER & ENGELMANN *Teaching Disadvantaged Children in the Preschool* i. 3 This is a 'successful' preschool for disadvantaged children. **1977** *Caravan World* (Austral.) Jan. 67/3 Sue drops their young son at pre-school every morning.

Hence **pre-'schooler**, a child who is too young to attend school; a child who attends preschool; **pre-'schooling** *vbl. sb.*, the education of a preschool child.
1954 *Recreation* Apr. 241/1 Remember that pre-schoolers are people. **1958** *Word* XIV. 159 First graders did significantly better than preschoolers. **1960** *Parents' Mag.* July 92/2 Brevity.. produces good results with preschoolers. **1965** *Economist* 4 Sept. 883/1 Even as pre-schoolers, these children do not lack experiences. **1971** *Daily Colonist* (Victoria, B.C.) 28 Aug. 18/1 Sesame Street, for preschoolers, to date has gotten few brickbats. **1972** *Guardian* 11 Aug. 12/1 Preschooling is the outstanding economical and effective device in the general approach to raising educational standards in EPAs. **1974** *Ibid.* 19 Mar. 20/2 The schools would be there to offer gipsy children preschooling opportunities. **1979** *Guardian* 5 June 11/3 Pre-schoolers should know their full name by $2\frac{1}{2}$.

prescience ('priːʃɪəns). [a. F. *prescience* (13th c.), ad. late L. *præscientia* (Tertull.) foreknowledge: see PRESCIENT *a.* and -ENCE.] Knowledge of events before they happen; foreknowledge.

a. esp. as a divine attribute.
c **1374** CHAUCER *Troylus* IV. 974 (998) They seyn right þus þat þyng is not to come For þat þe prescience hath seyghen by-fore. **1382** WYCLIF *1 Pet.* i. 2 Up the prescience [*gloss* or bifore knowinge; Vulg. *secundum præscientiam*] of God, the fadir. *c* **1491** *Chast. Goddes Chyld.* 17 Thus it fareth by hem also that wyll ymagyne of predestynacyon and of the prescience or of the foreknowinge of god. **1532** MORE *Confut. Barnes* VIII. Wks. 787/1 Prescyence of God putteth no necessitie in thinges of their nature conuenient vnto free wyll of man. **1674** OWEN *Holy Spirit* (1693) 106 It is utterly inconsistent with his Prescience and Omniscience. **1791** BOSWELL *Johnson* an. 1769 (1816) II. 100 Predestination, or what is equivalent to it, cannot be avoided, if we hold an universal prescience in the Deity. **1835** I. TAYLOR *Spir. Despot.* vii. 331 If we attribute it to the divine prescience.

b. as a human faculty or quality: Foresight.
1412–20 LYDG. *Chron. Troy* II. x. (MS. Digby 230), Cassandra.. in eche arte had experience Of þinges future fully prescience To telle aforn what that shal betide. **1530** LYNDESAY *Test. Papyngo* 962 O prudent prelatis, quhare was your presciance, That tuke on hand tyll obserue Chaistytie, But austeir lyfe, laubour, and abstenance? **1615** G. SANDYS *Trav.* 100 Nature hauing endued them with that wonderfull prescience, to auoide the inconueniences, and yet to enioy the benefit of the riuer. **1791** BURKE *Let. to Memb. Nat. Assemb.* Wks. VI. 54 Statesmen of a more judicious prescience, look for the fortunate moment too. **1856** KANE *Arct. Explor.* II. iv. 55 Resources.. contingent certainly, so far as our prescience goes.

c. With *a* and *pl.* An instance of this. *rare*$^{-1}$.
a **1763** SHENSTONE *Ess.* (1765) 148 We.. deny ourselves.. natural gratifications, through speculative presciences and doubts about the future.

presciencelessness ('prɛsɪənslɪsnɪs). *rare*$^{-1}$. [f. PRESCIENCE + -LESS + -NESS.] The state or condition of lacking prescience.
1928 HARDY *Winter Words* 5 Led by sheer senselessness And presciencelessness Into unreason.

†**'presciency.** *Obs. rare.* [f. as PRESCIENCE: see -ENCY.] = PRESCIENCE.

1572 R. T. *Discourse* 16 Partly by the Naturall motions of their myndes,.. partly by the presciencie and foreknowledge of the thinges to comme.

prescient ('priːʃɪənt), *a.* Also 8 præ-. [a. F. *prescient* (15th c.), ad. L. *præscientem*, pr. pple. of *præscīre* to know before, f. *præ*, PRE- A. 1 + *scīre* to know.] Having foreknowledge or foresight; foreseeing.

a **1626** BACON *Hist. Gt. Brit.* Wks. 1879 I. 796/1 The providence of king Henry the seventh was in all men's mouths; who..showed himself sensible and almost prescient of this event. **1733** POPE *Ess. Man* III. 101 Præscient, the tides or tempests to withstand. **1798** CANNING, etc. *New Morality* 123 in *Anti-Jacobin* 9 July, Or, like the *anagallis*, prescient flower, Shuts her soft petals at the approaching shower. **1845** DISRAELI *Sybil* VI. xi, Gerard prescient that some trouble might in consequence occur there. **1888** BRYCE *Amer. Commw.* I. iv. 46 James Harrington, one of the most prescient minds of that great age.

b. Of, pertaining to, or arising from prescience.

1860 W. COLLINS *Wom. White* I. x, The prescient sadness of a coming and a long farewell.

So †**pre'sciential, præ-**, *a.* = prec.

a **1699** J. BEAUMONT *Love's Eye* ii. Poems (Grosart) II. 243/1 Love..into dark Futurity With præsciential Rays doth press.

prescientific (priːsaɪən'tɪfɪk), *a.* [In 1, irreg. f. PRESCIENCE after *scientific*; in 2, f. PRE- B. 1 + SCIENTIFIC (prob. after *prehistoric*).]

I. †**1.** Of or belonging to prescience; ***conditional prescientific***, making (the divine) prescience conditional. *Obs. rare.*

1836 G. S. FABER *Prim. Doctr. Election* II. iii. 265 Ireneus ..has also been claimed as an advocate of the same Conditional Prescientific System: but, in truth,..he really maintained a directly opposite Scheme of causation. *Ibid.* 267 Ireneus never maintains the Conditional Prescientific Scheme.

II. 2. Of or pertaining to times prior to the rise of modern science, or to the application of the scientific method.

1858 G. DUFF *Sp. at Elgin* 11 Aug., Belonging as he [Lord Palmerston] does to the premoral, as Lord Derby says he does to the prescientific, school. **1868–70** MILL *Ess. Relig.* (1874) 241 In prescientific times men always supposed that any unusual faculties which came to them they knew not how, were an inspiration from God. **1879** *Times* 5 June 9 Their expeditions should not be regarded as either unscientific or prescientific.

presciently ('priːʃɪəntlɪ), *adv.* [f. PRESCIENT + -LY².] In a prescient manner: with prescience.

1791–1823 D'ISRAELI *Cur. Lit.* (1858) III. 454 On this memorable day a philosophical politician might have presciently marked the seed-plots of events. **1844** DE QUINCEY *Greece under Romans* Wks. 1858 VIII. 346 He legislated well and presciently, they imagine, for the interests of a remote posterity.

prescind (prɪ'sɪnd), *v.* [ad. L. *præscindĕre*, *præsciss-* to cut off in front, f. *præ*, PRE- A. + *scindĕre* to cut.]

1. *trans.* To cut off beforehand, prematurely, or abruptly; to cut away or remove at once.

1636 BRATHWAIT *Rom. Emp.* 20 The brevity of his reigne prescinded many and great hopes of his good government of the whole Empire. **1657** TOMLINSON *Renou's Disp.* 284 Therefore these surcles are prescinded, that a new spring.. may follow. **1689** *Consid. conc. Succession & Alleg.* 17 The Crown may be so entailed..to some Persons, as to bar and prescind the Title of others. **1718** *Entertainer* No. 29. 196 Kings ought..if they do fall into Mischiefs to prescind the Occasions of them, as soon as they are discovered. **1850** O. BROWNSON *Wks.* VII. 218 The ingenious writer is not at liberty to prescind from divine revelation all that he is not sure of by his own instincts.

2. To cut off, detach, or separate *from*; to abstract.

1660 H. MORE *Myst. Godl.* To Rdr. 25 Nothing..but a mere Phrase, if you prescind it from what is comprized in Remission of sins. **1710** BERKELEY *Princ. Hum. Knowl.* I. §100 An abstract idea of happiness, prescinded from all particular pleasure. **1744** —— *Siris* §225 If force be considered as prescinded from gravity and matter, and as existing only in points or centers, what can this amount to but an abstract spiritual incorporeal force? **1856** FERRIER *Inst. Metaph.* VII. 475 Nor have universal things prescinded from the particular any absolute existence.

3. *intr.* (for *refl.*) with *from*: **a.** To withdraw the attention *from*; to leave out of consideration. †**b.** To separate itself, withdraw *from* (*obs.*). †**c.** ***prescinding from***, apart from (*obs.*).

1650 H. BROOKE *Conserv. Health* A ij, They would not be prejudiced by Custom,..but prescinding from that, give their understandings. **1686** GOAD *Celest. Bodies* I. ii. 6 The Air..must be defin'd, prescinding from all Admistions that are extraneous to it. *Ibid.* I. xii. 48 The Observer shall never find it worth while to observe Lunar Semisextiles or Quincunxes, either prescinding from their Principals. **1687** NORRIS *Coll. Misc.* 362 A bare act of Obliquity does not only prescind from, but also positively deny such a speical dependence of it upon the will. **1713** BERKELEY *Alciphr.* VII. §5 The abstract general idea of man prescinding from, and exclusive of all particular shape, size, complexion, passions, faculties, and every individual circumstance. **1890** W. S. LILLY *Right & Wrong* 98 In what I am about to write I prescind entirely from all theological theories and religious symbols.

Hence **pre'scindent** *a.*, prescinding, abstracting.

1715 CHEYNE *Philos. Princ. Relig.* II. 101 Which no Body who knows the prescindent Faculties of the Soul..can deny.

†**'prescious,** *a. Obs.* [f. L. *præsci-us* foreknowing (f. *præscīre* to foreknow: see PRESCIENT) + -OUS.] = PRESCIENT.

1643 SIR T. BROWNE *Relig. Med.* I. §11 Predestination.. is in respect to God no prescious determination of our Estates to come, but a definitive blast of His Will already fulfilled. **1697** DRYDEN *Æneid* XI. 242 Thrice happy thou,.. Prescious of ills, and leaving me behind, to drink the dregs of life by fate assign'd. **1765** C. SMART *Phædrus* III. ix, Cassandra's prescious care Sought, but obtain'd no credence there.

prescission (prɪ'sɪʃən). *rare.* [n. of action from PRESCIND.] The action of prescinding.

1589 NASHE *Almond* 2 If, in comparing thy knauery, my full points seeme as tedious to thy puritane perusers as the Northeren mans mile and a waybitte to the weary passenger ..till I see what market commission thou hast to assist any mans sentences, I will neuer subscribe to thy periode prescission [*printed* prescisme]. **1890** *Cent. Dict.*, Prescission. [See also PRECISION 2.]

†**prescit,** *a. Obs. rare*$^{-1}$. [ad. L. *præscīt-us*, pa. pple. of *præscīre* to foreknow (see PRESCIENT), in med.L. = reprobate (see Du Cange).] Foreknown (to be damned); hence, condemned, reprobate. So †**pre'scited** *a.*

(*Præscītus* 'foreknown' was evidently employed to avoid *prædestinātus*; but the latter being commonly restricted to the sense 'presdestinated to salvation', *præscitus* came to be = 'foreordained to perdition, condemned, reprobate'.)

c **1400** *Apol. Loll.* 7 þe pope wat not, ne of himsilf, if he be sauid of God, or prescit to be dampnid, þat if he be prescit, silk indulgencis rennun not forþ aȝen þe ordinaunce of God. *a* **1660** *Contemp. Hist. Irel.* (Ir. Archæol. Soc.) I. 276 The deuout penetent and humble publican, whoe by our Sauiours verditt,..was justified, and the other, your examplare and his antigoniste, prescited, by those words *qui se humiliat exaltabitur, et qui se exaltat humiliabitur.*

prescle, erron. form of PRESLE *Obs.*

pre-score, *v.* [PRE- A. 1.] *trans.* To score or inscribe beforehand.

1977 *Engin. Materials and Design* Aug. 29/3 A diamond tool to scribe the fired material, or a system that prescores the ceramic alumina in its green state.

pre-'scoring, *vbl. sb. Cinemat.* [PRE- A. 1.] The recording of a sound track in advance of the shooting of the film it is to accompany.

1937 *Jrnl. Soc. Motion Picture Engineers* XXIX. 356 We do not record songs or orchestras on the set... We record them in advance, usually before the picture goes into production. This we call pre-scoring. **1937** [see PRE-RECORD *v.*]. **1948** E. LINDGREN *Art of Film* I. ii. 31 The flexibility of sound-recording methods is well illustrated by the device known as pre-scoring. **1949** B. WOODHOUSE *From Script to Screen* vii. 111 The principle known as pre-scoring is used extensively.

pre'screen, *v.* [PRE- A. 1.] *trans.* To screen (in any sense) beforehand. Hence **pre'screened** *ppl. a.*, **pre'screening** *vbl. sb.*

1967 KARCH & BUBER *Offset Processes* v. 167 Although no claim is made that the use of this screen will improve the quality of the picture, this new technique will reduce the cost of prescreening the photographs and then stripping the half-tone negative into the flat. **1967** E. CHAMBERS *Photolitho-Offset* xi. 174 With a prescreened film the contact screen is absent, and..the sensitivity of the film itself is varied in the form of a dot pattern. **1977** *Time* 20 June 48/2 The microwave detector could at the very least be used for pre-screening women—epecially those under 35 who are ordinarily not encouraged to have mammograms unless they have a family history of breast cancer or symptoms of the disease. **1977** *Jrnl. R. Soc. Arts* CXXV. 241/1 Careful prescreening for human health hazards will have taken place. **1978** *New York* 3 Apr. 84/1 College Background Singles Only—Newsletter of pre-screened, higher quality singles events plus our own tennis and theatre parties.

prescribable (prɪ'skraɪbəb(ə)l), *a.* [f. PRESCRIBE *v.* + -ABLE.] That can or may be prescribed; capable of being prescribed.

1967 *Economist* 25 Feb. 708/1 The Central Health Services Council's committee on the classification of proprietary preparations has laid down for doctors' guidance its views on when a food is a food and not a drug and therefore not prescribable. **1977** *Lancet* 24/31 Dec. 1360/1 Only a fraction of these are prescribable.

prescribe (prɪ'skraɪb), *v.* Also 7 præ-. [ad. L. *præscrībĕre* to write before, to appoint or direct in writing; in law, to bring an exception against, demur to, etc.; f. *præ*, PRE- A + *scrībĕre* to write.]

I. †**1. a.** *trans.* To write first or beforehand; also, to write with foreknowledge; to predict in writing; to describe beforehand. *Obs.*

1545 LELAND *New Year's Gift* (1549) D iij, There hath bene to the nombre of a full hundreth or mo, that..hath.. prescribed the actes of your moste noble predecessours. **1570** DEE *Math. Pref.* d ij, So to Paint, and prescribe the Sunnes Motion, to the breadth of a heare. **1612** BRINSLEY *Lud. Lit.* (1627) To Rdr., For the manner of proceeding used in this worke, it is prescribed in the preface. **1651** C. CARTWRIGHT *Cert. Relig.* I. 133 Except you rightly understand the words of Berengarius, (hee might have said of Pope Nicolas, who did prescribe them). **1653** H. WHISTLER *Upshot Inf. Baptism* 102 Esaias prescribed it excellently; The wolf shall dwell with the Lamb.

†**b.** To inscribe on the front or forepart. *Obs.*

1608 CHAPMAN *Byron's Conspir.* Ded., (Hauing heard your approbation of these in their presentment) I could not but prescribe them with your name.

2. a. To write or lay down as a rule or direction to be followed; to appoint, ordain, direct, enjoin. Const. *to* or dative; with simple obj. or obj. cl.

1535 *Goodly Primer* (1834) 204 Let us prescribe him no time, but ever submit our wills to his. **1538** CROMWELL in Merriman *Life & Lett.* (1902) II. 153 The workes of charite marcy and faithe specially prescribed and commaunded in scripture. **1551** ROBINSON tr. *More's Utop.* II. (1895) 249 What soeuer is prescribed vnto him that killeth any of the proclamed persons. **1576** FLEMING *Panopl. Epist.* 93 Reason prescribeth..that Whatsoeuer we attempt in the course of our life, blame may be auoyded. *a* **1648** LD. HERBERT *Hen. VIII* (1683) 227 Your master ought not to prescribe me what I am to do. **1724** SWIFT *Drapier's Lett.* iv. Wks. 1761 III. 64 Wood prescribes to the news mongers in London what they are to write. **1778** JOHNSON in Boswell 17 Apr., Verses..prescribed as an exercise. **1843** SIR J. T. COLERIDGE in Stanley *Arnold* (1844) I. i. 9, I know not whether the statutes prescribe the practice. **1884** tr. *Lotze's Metaph.* 415 Not even Religion should presume to prescribe to God the course which the world's development must have followed subsequently to its creation.

b. in *indirect pass.* with the person as subject.

1609 B. JONSON *Sil. Wom.* IV. iv, So they were prescrib'd to goe to Church. **1879** BROWNING *Ned Bratts* 37 And ten were prescribed the whip, and ten a brand on the cheek.

c. *absol.* or *intr.* To lay down a rule; to dictate, appoint, direct. Of a law or custom: To be of force.

1564 *P. Martyr's Comm. Judges* 189 b, These prescribe not, when as they are manifestly vicious and euyll. But that custome prescribeth, which is neither against the woord of God, nor the law of nature, nor the common lawe. *c* **1586** C'TESS PEMBROKE *Ps.* CV. vi, He rulers rules,..prescribes, and all obey. **1610** BP. CARLETON *Jurisd.* 278 This Synode prescribed against the Pope's jurisdiction. *a* **1716** SOUTH *Serm.* (1727) IV. ix. 387 Nothing..being so tyrannical as Ignorance, where Time and long Possession enables it to prescribe. **1961** *Parthenon* (Marshall Univ., W. Va.) 10 Nov. 3/3 The '*Third Unabridged*' does not, of course, pretend to prescribe. It seeks, rather, to describe. **1978** *Amer. Speech* LIII. 70 Conceived as a modern dictionary that describes but does not prescribe, *Webster's Third New International Dictionary of the English Language* brought forth a deluge of adverse criticism and scathing reviews.

3. *Med.* **a.** *trans.* To advise or order the use of (a medicine, remedy or treatment), with directions for the manner of applying it. Const. as in 2.

1581 PETTIE *Guazzo's Civ. Conv.* II. (1586) 54, I prescribe for his health this medicine. **1607** TOPSELL *Four-f. Beasts* (1658) 178 Pliny prescribeth a man which twinkleth with his eyes, and cannot look stedfastly, to wear in a chain the tongue of a Fox. **1676** W. HUBBARD *Happiness of People* 40 To prescribe to the people poysonous Drugs instead of wholsome food or physick. **1758** J. S. *Le Dran's Observ. Surg.* (1771) 324 He was..prescribed a..Ptisan. **1806** BOSANQUET & PULLEN *New Rep.* I. 196 The Defendant as apothecary made up the medicines prescribed by the Plaintiff for the patient. **1843** R. J. GRAVES *Syst. Clin. Med.* ix. 97 To leech his head and prescribe tartar emetic.

b. *absol.* or *intr.* Also *fig.*

1598 SHAKS. *Merry W.* II. ii. 249 Methinkes you prescribe to your selfe very preposterously. **1607** —— *Timon* V. iv. 84, I will..make each Prescribe to other, as each others Leach. **1674** R. GODFREY *Inj. & Ab. Physick* 200 This Doctor.. Prescribes, and..gives order for a Preventive Purge to be taken next morning. **1737** WEST *Let.* in *Gray's Poems* (1775) 27 If..'Friendship be the physic of the mind', prescribe to me, dear Gray,..I shall be a most obedient patient. **1899** *Daily News* 13 Mar. 7/1 His motto was that no statesman should prescribe until he was called in. *Mod.* The physician was asked to prescribe for him.

4. *trans.* To limit, restrict, restrain; to confine within bounds.

1596 DRAYTON *Leg.* i. 601 Prescrib'd to one poore solitary place, Who should have progress'd all a Kingdomes space. **1688** PRIOR *Exodus iii.* 14 vii, Laws to his Maker the learn'd wretch can give: Can bound that Nature, and prescribe that Will, Whose pregnant word did either ocean fill. **1726** DE FOE *Hist. Devil* II. iii. (1840) 197 The faculties of man..are prescribed on the other hand, and cannot sally out without leave. **1919** K. ROUTLEDGE *Mystery of Easter Island* viii. 116 As both the lifeboat and the cutter were carried in the waist of the ship when we were at sea, the space available for 'constitutionals' was prescribed.

II. *Law.* †**5.** *trans.* **a.** To hold by PRESCRIPTION (sense 4 b). **b.** To claim by prescription. *Obs. rare.*

1455 *Rolls of Parlt.* V. 337/1 (Anc. Pet. 1387, P.R.O.) Not withstonding that by the olde liberte and fredome of the Comyne of this londe had, enjoyed and prescribed, frõ the tyme that no mynde is, alle such persones as..beene assembled in eny parlement..ought to haue theire fredome to speke and sey in the hous of theire assemble..he was.. arrested, and..led to the Toure of London. **1607** COWELL *Interpr.* s.v. *Prescription*, A seruant prescribeth liberty after a yeare.

6. *intr.* To make a claim by prescription; to assert a prescriptive right or claim (*to* or *for* something; also with *inf.* or *clause*).

1531 *Dial. on Laws Eng.* II. l. 104 b, If a hole countrey prescribe to pay no tythes for corne, or hey or suche other, [shewe me] whether thou thynke that that prescripcion is good. **1544** tr. *Littleton's Tenures* II. xi. 42 b, A man may not prescrybe in a vyllayne in grosse without shewynge of wryttynge but in hymselfe that claymeth the vyllayne and in his auncesters whose heyre he is. *Ibid.* 47 b, If a lord of a manour wyl prescrybe that it hath ben accustomed within his manoure tyme out of mynde that euery tenaunt [etc.].

1712 PRIDEAUX *Direct. Ch.-wardens* (ed. 4) 75 The Lord of a Manor.. may prescribe to a Seat in the Body of the Church, which he and his Ancestors have immemorially used. **1766** BLACKSTONE *Comm.* II. xvii. 264 Formerly a man might, by the common law, have prescribed for a right which had been enjoyed by his ancestors or predecessors at any distance of time. **1817** W. SELWYN *Law Nisi Prius* (ed. 4) II. 1119 If the party has a general common, and prescribes for common for any particular sort of cattle, this will be good. **1844** WILLIAMS *Real Prop.* (1875) 450 A man might.. prescribe that he and his ancestors had from time immemorial exercised a certain right in gross.

fig. *a* **1619** FOTHERBY *Atheom.* I. ix. §2 (1622) 62 Time, which prescribeth against all humane inuentions, and which chalengeth the honour of Antiquity from them. **1650** FULLER *Pisgah* II. xii. 260 Presuming on their former victories, that in so fortunate a place they might prescribe for conquest.

†**7.** *intr.* Of a person: To plead prescription of time (PRESCRIPTION 4) *against* an action, statute, or penalty; to cease to be liable on account of the lapse of the prescribed time. *Obs.*

1595 *Expos. Terms Law* 145 b, But one may not prescribe against a statute except he haue an other statute that serueth for him. **1670** BLOUNT *Law Dict.* s.v. *Prescription* A Judge or Clerk convicted for false entring of Pleas, &c. may be Fined within two years; the two years being past, he prescribes against the punishment of the said Statute. **1672** *Cowell's Interpr.* s.v. *Prescription*, Whosoever offendeth against any such Statute, and escapes unquestion'd for two years or three.. may justly be said to have prescribed against that Action.

8. *Sc. Law. intr.* Of an action: To suffer prescription; to lapse, to become invalid or void by passage of time. Of a crime, debt, etc.: To be no longer capable of prosecution.

1617 *Sc. Acts Jas. VI*, c. 12 All actions of warrandice.. shall not præscrybe [*ed.* 1816 prescryve], from the date of the band.. but only from the date of the distresse. **1678** SIR G. MACKENZIE *Crim. Laws Scot.* II. xxix. §1 (1699) 276 According to the Civil Law, Crimes did prescribe in twenty years. **1751** HUME *Ess., Justice* (1817) II. 235 Bills of exchange and promissory notes, by the laws of most countries, prescribe sooner than bonds, and mortgages. **1838** W. BELL *Dict. Law Scot.* 773 By the act 1579, c. 82, actions of removing prescribe within three years from the term at which the tenant has been warned to remove. **1874** *Act 37 & 38 Vict.* c. 94 §42 All inhibitions.. shall prescribe on the lapse of five years from the date.

fig. **1847** DE QUINCEY *Sp. Mil. Nun* xv. Wks. 1853 III. 37 The grasp of the church never relaxed, never 'prescribed', unless freely and by choice.

Hence **pre'scribing** *vbl. sb.*; †**pre'scribement**, prescription, prescribing. *Obs. rare*$^{-1}$.

1542 N. UDALL *Erasmus's Apophthegmes* sig. N5ᵛ, Signifying, not to bee any prescribyng to the Romaines, how ferre thei ought to extend their empier. **1563** FOXE *A. & M.* 26/2 The matter being decised betwixt them after the popes own prescribement, themperour taketh his iourny to Papia. **1618** M. BARET *Horsemanship* I. 65 By practise it may bee better perceiued then by prescribing. *a* **1704** T. BROWN *Sat. on Quack* Wks. 1730 I. 63 Whole nations might be killed by thy prescribing.

prescribe, formerly frequent for PROSCRIBE.

prescribed (-'skraɪbd), *ppl. a.* [f. PRESCRIBE *v.* + -ED¹.] Laid down, appointed, or fixed beforehand; ordained, appointed, set, fixed, defined.

1577 tr. *Bullinger's Decades* (1592) 562 They.. which after a prescribed manner of punishment doo penance for their sinnes. *a* **1610** HEALEY *Epictetus' Man.* (1636) 49 To drink no colde water nor wine, but at prescribed seasons. **1728** MORGAN *Algiers* II. iv. 276 Two of them seizing each prescribed Criminal. **1855** MACAULAY *Hist. Eng.* xxii. IV. 775 On the prescribed day, the Sheriff's officers ventured to cross the boundary. **1863** E. V. NEALE *Anal. Th. & Nat.* 193 Within its prescribed limits, and under its prescribed conditions, the operations of instinct are certain.

prescriber (prɪ'skraɪbə(r)). [f. as prec. + -ER¹.] One who prescribes.

1. One who appoints or ordains.

1548 UDALL *Erasm. Par. Luke* Pref., The physycians of the bodyes, haue practycioners, and potycaryes that dooe ministre theyr arte vnder theym: and themselfes are the prescrybers and appoyncters what it is that muste bee geuen to the sycke. **1557** *Pet.* in H. Swinden *Hist. Gt. Yarmouth* (1772) 428 Not as prescribers, but humbell submitters. **1630** LORD *Banians* 71 The first Prescriber of their rites. **1760–72** H. BROOKE *Fool of Qual.* (1809) IV. 63, I was impelled to.. your destruction.. by the bloody prescribers of custom. **1907** in *Westm. Gaz.* 2 Oct. 6/3 Prescription is all very well if you are satisfied as to the infallibility of the prescriber.

2. One who writes a medical prescription. Also *fig.*

[**1548**: see sense 1.] *a* **1660** HAMMOND *xix Serm.* xiii. Wks. 1684 IV. 652 Hence is neither the physick to be under-prized, nor the Prescriber. **1756** C. LUCAS *Ess. Waters* I. Pref., The best prescriber can hardly confide in his own prescriptions. **1851** J. CUMMING *Foreshadows* viii. (1854) 233 The cure is not in the prescription, but in the prescriber.

3. One who holds or claims by prescription. *rare.*

1717 in Keble *Life Bp. T. Wilson* x. (1863) 348 Being thoroughly convinced of the Divine right of paying tithes in kind, and being one of the ancient prescribers in this isle, [he] did freely.. give up the said prescription into the hands of the Bishop.

prescript ('priːskrɪpt, † prɪ'skrɪpt), *sb.* Also (in sense 3) præscript. [ad. L. *præscript-um* something prescribed, a copy, task, precept, rule, etc., sb. use of pa. pple. neut. of *præscrībĕre* to PRESCRIBE. So F. *prescript.*]

1. That which is prescribed or laid down as a rule; an ordinance, rule, law, precept, command; a regulation, direction, instruction.

c **1540** tr. *Pol. Verg. Eng. Hist.* (Camden) I. 19 Emonge artificers and husbandmen it is receaved as a prescripte that thei should sweate bie noe meanes. **1543** BECON *Policy of War* Wks. 1560 I. 128 b, They worshipped and serued him.. according to the prescripte of his holy worde. **1683** TRYON *Way to Health* 624 To conduct the rest of their Lives according to the Prescripts of Chastity and Virtue. **1797** BURKE *Regic. Peace* iii. Wks. VIII. 359 The legitimate contributions which he is to furnish according to the prescript of law. **1898** *Westm. Gaz.* 30 Aug. 5/1 Whether the French Government was consulted before the issue of the Prescript.

2. Medicine prescribed; also *transf.* a medical prescription. Now *rare.*

1603 HARSNET *Pop. Impost.* 45 Your prescript is compounded of these delicate simples, Brimstone, Assa fœtida, Galbanum, S. John's Wort, and Rue. **1647** TRAPP *Comm. Matt.* xxiii. 5 Like unto the foolish patient, which when the physician bids him take the prescript, eats up the paper. **1710** T. FULLER *Pharm. Extemp.* Title-p., A Body of Medicines, containing a thousand select prescripts. **1749** SHENSTONE *Ode after Sickness* 52 The nymphs that heal the pensive mind, By prescripts more refin'd. **1891** G. MEREDITH *One of our Conq.* (1892) 205 A medical prescript, one of the grand specifics.

3. *nonce-use.* That which is written beforehand or in the forepart (of a book, etc.); a preface, introduction.

1862 LD. STANHOPE *Pitt* III. 408 He proposed that the paper should be sent unsigned, and with a Preface or Præscript as follows.

¶ In the following, app. a misprint of the early edd. for PRESCRIPTION 4 b:

1596 BACON *Max. & Use Com. Law* II. (1629) 85 In those cases prescripts will not serue, except it bee so ancient, that it hath had allowance before the Iustices in Eyre.

prescript (prɪ'skrɪpt), *a.* [In I., ad. L. *præscript-us*, pa. pple. of *præscrībĕre* to PRESCRIBE. So obs. F. *prescript* adj. (*a* 1430 in Godef.), F. *prescrit.* In II., f. PRE- B. 1 + L. *script-us* written.]

I. 1. Prescribed or laid down beforehand as a rule; ordained, appointed, fixed, settled. Now *rare.*

c **1460** *Oseney Reg.* 161 Of oolde & laudabile and lawfully prescripte custome. **1551** ROBINSON tr. *More's Utop.* I. (1895) 108 A prescripte and appointed some of money. **1586** *Exam. H. Barrowe* in *Harl. Misc.* (Malh.) II. 19 Whether he thinketh that any leitourgies or prescript formes of prayer may be imposed vpon the church. *a* **1693** *Urquhart's Rabelais* III. xxxiv. 290 The Prescript Rule of Hippocrates. **1792** BURKE *Corr.* (1844) IV. 13 The prescript form to which the Church of Rome binds its clergy. **1877** KINGLAKE *Crimea* VI. viii. 482 Trying to make prescript words perform the task of a General.

†**2.** Circumscribed, limited. *Obs. rare*$^{-1}$.

1645–7 PAGITT *Heresiogr.* 59 A prescript place like a Tub.

†**3.** Acquired by or based on prescription; prescriptive. *Obs. rare*$^{-1}$.

1652 NEEDHAM tr. *Selden's Mare Cl.* 7 If any Doctors should.. say, that the Republick hath a prescript Dominion over the Adriatick Sea, with a long possession, notwithstanding they prove it not.

II. 4. Prior to the age of writing. *nonce-use.*

1883 T. KERSLAKE in *N. & Q.* 6th Ser. VII. 283/1 The earlier southern incursions of the Patrician school [i.e. that of St. Patrick] through the estuary of the Severn, were in a darker and prescript age.

pre'scriptible, *a. rare.* [f. L. ppl. stem *præscript-* (see prec.) + -IBLE; so F. *prescriptible* (*prescrittible* 16th c. in Littré), It. *prescrittibile.*] Liable or subject to prescription; derived from or founded on prescription.

1542 HENRY VIII *Declar. Scots* D iij b, The hole prescription of the Scottis, if the matier were prescriptable, is thus deduced euidentely to .xiii. yere. **1688** *Answ. Talon's Plea* 31 A Sovereign Power, that neither suffers attaint, nor is prescriptible. **1795** WYTHE *Decis. Virginia* 97 That the demand of the plaintiffs is in its nature prescriptible.

Hence **prescripti'bility**, the quality of being prescriptible.

a **1843** JUDGE STORY cited in WORCESTER.

prescription¹ (prɪ'skrɪpʃən). [a. F. *prescription* (13th c. in Hatz.-Darm.), or ad. L. *præscriptiōn-em* a writing before or in front, a title, introduction; a pretext, pretence; a precept, rule; in law, as in sense 4; n. of action f. *præscrībĕre* (ppl. stem *præscript-*) to PRESCRIBE.]

I. 1. The action of prescribing or appointing beforehand; that which is prescribed or appointed; written or explicit direction or injunction.

1542 N. UDALL *Erasmus's Apophthegmes* sig. f4ᵛ, The moste parte of people is barred from offendyng, onely by prestripcions [*sic*] of lawes, but a philosopher accoumpteth and vseth reason in stede of lawes. **1549** LATIMER *1st Serm. bef. Edw. VI* (Arb.) 37 Suerlye, we wyll not exchange oure fathers doynges and tradicions,.. but chiefely lene vnto them and to theyr prescription. **1589** PUTTENHAM *Eng. Poesie* II. xiv. (Arb.) 137 Your feete of three times by prescription of the Latine Grammariens are of eight sundry proportions. **1641** 'SMECTYMNUUS' *Answ.* §2 (1653) 8 Their prayer was not of Regular prescription, but of a present Conception. *a* **1716** BLACKALL *Wks.* (1723) I. 4 To lead his Life according to those Rules and Prescriptions which are here given by our Saviour. **1874** SIDGWICK *Meth. Ethics* I. ix. 95 In the recognition of conduct as 'right' is involved an authoritative prescription to do it. **1888** *Pall Mall G.* 30 Apr. 7/1 Provinces.. where the prescriptions of the Berlin Treaty are still unfulfilled. **1960** J. O. URMSON *Conc. Encycl. Western Philos.* 143/1 Moral judgements, on this view [*sc.* the prescriptivist's], share with imperatives the characteristic that to utter one is to commit oneself, directly or indirectly, to some sort of precept or prescription about actual or conceivable decisions or choices. **1963** *English Jrnl.* May 337/2 Note that this statement [from Sir James Murray's preface to the Dict.] contains not one word about fixing the language, about proscription or prescription of any kind. **1968** J. LYONS *Introd. Theoret. Linguistics* i. 43 It should be stressed that in distinguishing between description and prescription, the linguist is not saying that there is no place for prescriptive studies of language.

2. A direction or formula (usually) written by a physician for the composition and use of a medicine; a recipe; *transf.* the medicine prescribed. In early use, more widely, any course of hygiene ordered by a physician, 'doctor's orders'.

1579 FENTON *Guicciard.* x. (1599) 413 Eating.. raw apples and things contrary to the prescription of Physicke. **1601** SHAKS. *All's Well* I. iii. 227 You know my Father left me some prescriptions Of rare and prou'd effects. **1650** BULWER *Anthropomet.* 188 The best prescription.. is to use such exercises as gently dilate and extend the Breast. **1679** *Hist. Jetzer* 15 This Prescription the Sub-prior faithfully made up, and put into Phials for use. **1700** RYCAUT *Hist. Turks* III. 131 The Elector of Bavaria.. remained at Brin to take the Air by the prescription of his Physitians. **1777** FLETCHER *Bible Armin.* Wks. 1795 IV. 263 Physicians, who write their prescriptions in Latin. **1861** FLO. NIGHTINGALE *Nursing* 93 Women who will write to London to their physician,.. and ask for some prescription from him, which they 'used to like'.

†**3.** Restriction, limitation, circumscription. *Obs.*

1604 R. CAWDREY *Table Alph., Prescription*, limitation, or appointing a certaine compasse. **1649** MILTON *Eikon.* ix. Wks. 1851 III. 405 To limit and lay prescription on the Laws of God and truth of the Gospel by mans establishment. *a* **1718** PENN *Tracts* Wks. 1726 I. 451 If Men be restricted by the Prescriptions of some Individuals.

II. *Law.* **4. a.** Limitation or restriction of the time within which an action or claim can be raised. [L. *præscriptio*, in law, An exception, objection, demurrer; a limitation of the subject-matter in a suit; limitation as to time (*Digest* 18. I. 76).] Now commonly called ***negative prescription***.

[**1292** BRITTON I. xix. §7 En tel cas voloms nous qe.. prescripcioun de tens courge encountre nous cum encountre autre del poeple. *a* **1377** *Rolls of Parlt.* II. 409/1 La ou il ne poit assigner la dite Assise estre par prescription de temps.] **1474** *Sc. Acts Jas. III* (1814) II. 107/1 Anentis þe act maide of befor of prescripcione of obligacionis it is ordanit [etc.]. **1542** HENRY VIII *Declar. Scots* D iij b, The passing ouer of tyme not commodious for the purpose, is not allegable in prescription for the losse of any right. **1605** *Tryall Chev.* I. i. in Bullen *O. Pl.* (1884) III. 268 Yeres limit not a Crowne; There's no prescription to inthrall a King. **1639** FULLER *Holy War* I. ix. (1840) 14 No prescription of time could prejudice the title of the King of Heaven. **1797** tr. *Vattel's Law Nat.* II. xi. 187 *Prescription* is the exclusion of all pretensions to a right—an exclusion founded on the length of time during which that right has been neglected. **1838** W. BELL *Dict. Law Scot.* 768 The negative prescription of obligations, by the lapse of forty years, was first introduced [into Scotland] by the statute 1469, c. 29. *Ibid.* 774 By 7 Will. III, c. 3 §5, high treason committed within the Queen's dominions suffers a triennial prescription, if indictment be not found against the offender by a grand jury within that time.

b. Uninterrupted use or possession from time immemorial, or for a period fixed by law as giving a title or right; hence, title or right acquired by virtue of such use or possession: sometimes called ***positive prescription***.

c **1380** WYCLIF *Sel. Wks.* III. 294 3if coveitouse prestis han be in possession of oþere mennus goodis fourty 3eer or þritti, wrongfully,.. þei may not be taken from hem..; þe vertu of prescripcion, bi long custom of synne, haþþe made hem lordis. **1483** *Act 1 Rich. III*, c. 6 §1 Divers Fairs have been holden.. by Prescription allowed afore Justices in Eyre. **1523** FITZHERB. *Surv.* 6 This is commen appurtenaunte by prescripcyon, bycause of the vse out of tyme of mynde. **1590** SWINBURNE *Testaments* 221 Where the probation and approbation of testamentes of the tenaunts there dwelling, dooth by prescription appertaine to the principall Lord. **1650** FULLER *Pisgah* II. xiii. 269 His title to this plain.. is made lawfull by the prescription of three thousand years possession. **1682** *Enq. Elect. Sheriffs* 32 Nor were these Charters.. Original Grants, but only Confirmations of what the City had by prescription possess'd and enjoy'd long before. **1726** AYLIFFE *Parergon* 194 'Tis said in our Law Books, that the Publick acquires a Right by Custom, but only private Persons acquire it by Prescription. **1790** BURKE *Fr. Rev.* Wks. V. 276 If prescription be once shaken, no species of property is secure, when it once becomes an object large enough to tempt the cupidity of indigent power. **1818** CRUISE *Digest* (ed. 2) III. 467 This mode of acquisition was well known in the Roman law by the name of *usucapio*... In the English law it is called prescription. **1838** W. BELL *Dict. Law Scot.* 766 The positive prescription was introduced [into Scotland] by the act 1617, c. 12. **1876** DIGBY *Real Prop.* iii. §18. 156 *note*, Prescription is where a person possesses a right by reason of the fact of long and uninterrupted enjoyment, as of right, either by himself and his ancestors, or by himself and his predecessors in title. **1895** POLLOCK & MAITLAND *Hist. Eng. Law* II. II. iv. 81 Our law [in 13th c.] knew no acquisitive prescription for land, it merely knew a limitation of actions. *Ibid.* 140 Many incorporeal things can be acquired by prescription, by long-continued user. In particular we may see this in the case of rights of common.

c. *transf.* and *fig.* (*a*) Ancient or continued custom, esp. when viewed as authoritative. (*b*) Claim founded upon long use.

(*a*) **1589** Horsey *Trav.* (Hakl. Soc.) App. 301 Yt was not fytte his Majestie should be bound to geve his letteres of protectyon by prescriptyone, but as seemed his Kyngly pleasure beste. **1605** Camden *Rem.* (1637) 109 Yet Plantagenet, Steward, Valoys, Borbon, Habsburg, &c. by prescription of time haue preuailed so farre, as they are now accounted surnames. **1652** Needham tr. *Selden's Mare Cl.* 170 Almost all the Principal Points of the Intervenient Law of Nations..do depend upon Prescription or antient Custom. *a* **1704** T. Brown *Praise of Wealth* Wks. 1730 I. 83 Your love to my order is of antient date and very long prescription. **1750** Johnson *Rambler* No. 1 ¶1 Some easy method..which..might enjoy the security of prescription. **1850** Merivale *Rom. Emp.* (1865) I. ii. 68 His temper was moulded to the love of precedent and prescription. **1881** Westcott & Hort *Grk. N.T.* Introd. §19 The..modified texts that reigned by an accidental prescription.

(*b*) **1625** Bacon *Ess., Negotiating* (Arb.) 91 Vse also such, as haue..Preuailed before in Things wherein you haue Emploied them; For that breeds Confidence, and they will striue to maintaine their Prescription. **1682** Sir T. Browne *Chr. Mor.* III. §17 Narrow self-ended Souls make prescription of good Offices. **1855** Macaulay *Hist. Eng.* xix. IV. 334 The country gentlemen and the country clergymen [had been] on the side of authority and prescription.

†**5.** The action of 'prescribing' or claiming by prescription (see PRESCRIBE *v.* 6). *Obs.*

1531 [see PRESCRIBE *v.* 6]. **1641** *Termes de la Ley* 222 Prescription is when a man claimeth any thing, for that he, his ancestors, or predecessors,..have had, or used any thing all the time, whereof no mind is to the contrary. **1818** Cruise *Digest* (ed. 2) III. 65 A prescription *de non decimando* is a claim to be entirely discharged from tithes, and to pay no compensation for them.

III. 6. *attrib.* and *Comb.*, as ***prescription-book, charge, pad, -writing***; **prescription-glass**, (*a*) a glass vessel with measures marked on it (*Cent. Dict.*); (*b*) a lens ground according to an oculist's prescription.

1793 Beddoes *Calculus* 190 The art of pharmacy and the science of prescription-writing will become useless. **1887** J. C. Harris *Free Joe*, etc. (1888) 155 Dr. Buxton, prescription-book in hand, gazed at her..over his old-fashioned spectacles. **1888** *Sci. Amer.* 28 Apr. 259/1 The lens-grinding room..is devoted almost exclusively to making what are known as 'prescription glasses'. **1928** E. O'Neill *Strange Interlude* II. 61 He..goes to the table and taking a prescription pad from his pocket, hastily scratches on it. **1961** *Daily Herald* 9 Feb. 9 Of the doubled prescription charge his argument was: 'It is ludicrous exaggeration to say that by and large a 2/os. charge is any more of a burden than a 1/os. charge was in 1949.' **1965** *Ann. Reg. 1964* 47 Medical prescription charges would be abolished (at a cost of £25 million a year) and pensions would be increased. *a* **1974** R. Crossman *Diaries* (1975) I. 35 Kenneth Robinson gave the case for abolishing prescription charges. **1975** M. Simpson *Chrome Connection* iii. 61 The indentations on the prescription pad bore witness to his complicity.

Hence †**pre'scriptionary** *a.*, arising from prescription of time, prescriptive.

1728 Earbery tr. *Burnet's St. Dead* I. 80 We may safely, therefore, explode that old prescriptionary Maxim.

†**prescription²**, a frequent early form of PROSCRIPTION. [Due to confusion of *præ-* and *pro-*.]

c **1400** *Apol. Loll.* 19 Lawful cursing..is dede of þe kirk; for it is a prescripcoun fro comyning of feipful men. **1432–50** tr. *Higden* (Rolls) IV. 129 Grete treasones, destruccion of citesynnes, robbenge and prescriptiones folowede [L. *proscriptiones*; 1387 exilynge]. **1560** Daus tr. *Sleidane's Comm.* 275 The same outlawing or prescription is against the lawes. **1639** Drumm. of Hawth. *Prophecy* Wks. (1711) 181 Nothing was heard but Prescriptions, Banishments, Assasinations, Treasons.

prescriptionist (prɪ'skrɪpʃənɪst) [f. PRESCRIPTION¹ + -IST.] **a.** One who writes prescriptions. *Obs.* **b.** One who makes up medicines in accordance with prescriptions; a dispenser.

1716 M. Davies *Athen. Brit.* III. Diss. Physick 12 All comprehended in the honourable Tetrarchy of Physicians or Doctors (κατ' ἐξοχὴν, or Præscriptionists), Chirurgians, Apothecaries, and Chymists. **18..** *Sanitarian* XVIII. 427 (Cent. D.) The apparent deterioration was due to the dishonesty of the retail druggist or prescriptionist. **1906** *Dialect Notes* III. 151 (*Arkansas*) Mr. H. B. Mayes has accepted a position as *prescriptionist* for James S. Robinson, one of the most prominent druggists of Memphis.

c. = PRESCRIPTIVIST *sb.*

1954 *Mind* LXIII. 258 It would be correct to call him an ethical 'prescriptionist'. **1964** C. Barber *Ling. Change Present-Day Eng.* i. 8 In fact they become moralists or prescriptionists, intent on telling us how we ought to talk.

Hence **pre'scriptionism** = PRESCRIPTIVISM 2.

1962 *Amer. Speech* XXXVII. 215 Long's expressed dissatisfaction with school grammars..as well as his impatience with common proscriptions like *everybody they* indicate his rejection of traditional prescriptionism.

prescriptive (prɪ'skrɪptɪv), *a.* [ad. late L. *præscrīptīv-us* of or relating to a legal exception or demurrer: see PRESCRIPT *sb.* and -IVE.]

1. a. That prescribes or directs; giving definite, precise directions or instructions. Now also *spec.* in *Linguistics.* (Opp. DESCRIPTIVE *a.* 3 b: cf. *normative grammar* s.v. NORMATIVE *a.* b.)

1748 Richardson *Clarissa* (1811) VII. xviii. 93 A will to be executed by a father for a daughter..carries somewhat daring and prescriptive in the very word. **1788** *Trifler* No. 10. 126 Prescriptive rules for the preservation of health. **1849** Robertson *Serm.* Ser. I. vi. 92 Thus the spirit of the prescription may be still in force when the prescriptive authority is repealed. **1933** O. Jespersen *Essent. Eng. Gram.* i. 19 Of greater value, however, than this *prescriptive* grammar is a purely *descriptive* grammar. **1963** *Eng. Jrnl.* May 338/1 An accurate description of the language as it is actually used, kept simple by the relative absence of variants..will in itself serve prescriptive purposes. **1968** J. Lyons *Introd. Theoret. Linguistics* i. 43 Linguistics..is *descriptive*, not *prescriptive* (or normative). **1977** *Time* 4 Apr. 5/3 The point to be made to Ms. Spaak, the Académie Francaise and all other prescriptive-normative institutions that would like to see language spoken in a certain way: c'est impossible.

b. *Philos.* Having or implying an imperative force. Also *absol.*

1946 *Jrnl. Philos.* XLIII. 35 The issue is whether a definition shall be taken as prescriptive in empirical enquiry or used as a convenient tool constantly responsible to facts. A nominal definition is by definition prescriptive. **1951** [see DESCRIPTIVE *a.* 3 a]. **1952** R. M. Hare *Lang. Morals* i. 2 If moral language belongs to the genus 'prescriptive language', we shall most easily understand its nature if we compare and contrast first of all prescriptive language with other sorts of language. **1961** I. L. Horowitz *Philos., Sci. & Sociol. of Knowl.* vii. 88 Whatever the ratio of descriptive and prescriptive elements in an ideology, it is clearly a different qualitative entity than either religion or science. **1963** R. M. Hare *Freedom & Reason* v. 72 If moral judgements were *singular* prescriptives.., there would be less difficulty. **1967** *Encycl. Philos.* II. 314/2 All the views of definition that have been proposed can be subsumed under three general types of positions... These three general positions will be called 'essentialist', 'prescriptive', and 'linguistic' types. **1976** T. D. Perry *Moral Reasoning & Truth* 176 Every moral statement is prescriptive in the sense that it entails a certain imperative.

†**2.** Appointed or fixed by prescription. *Obs.*

1765 Blackstone *Comm.* I. xviii. 485 Directions are given for appointing a new officer, in case there be no election, or a void one, made upon the charter or prescriptive day.

3. Derived from or founded on prescription or lapse of time, as ***prescriptive right*** or ***title***.

1766 Blackstone *Comm.* II. xxxii. 494 Lords of manors..who have to this day a prescriptive right to grant administration to their intestate tenants and suitors. **1782** Burke *Reform Representation* Wks. 1842 II. 487 Our constitution is a prescriptive constitution; it is a constitution, whose sole authority is, that it has existed time out of mind. **1876** Grant *Burgh Sch. Scot.* II. v. 182 The ancient holiday, to which the scholars believed they had acquired a prescriptive title from immemorial usage.

4. a. Arising from or recognized by long-standing custom or usage; prescribed by custom.

1765 Johnson *Preface* in *Plays of Shakespeare* I. p. vii, The Poet, of whose works I have undertaken the revision, may now begin to assume the dignity of an ancient, and claim the privilege of established fame and prescriptive veneration. **1775** Johnson *Let. to Mrs. Thrale* 11 June, Unusual compliments, to which there is no stated and prescriptive answer, embarrass the feeble,..and disgust the wise. **1805** Roscoe *Leo X*, II. 23 A work, which does not implicitly adopt prescriptive errors. **1837** Hawthorne *Twice-told T.* (1851) II. i. 9 To have his regular score at the bar..and his prescriptive corner at the winter's fireside. *a* **1854** H. Reed *Lect. Brit. Poets* (1857) II. x. 14 To have the sun called by his simple almanac name, instead of the loftier prescriptive title of Phœbus.

b. *Anthrop.* Applied to marriage traditionally considered obligatory between persons in certain categories of relationship to each other within a tribe or kinship group. (Cf. PREFERENTIAL *a.* d.)

1958 *Amer. Anthropologist* LX. 75 Prescriptive marriage rules entail enduring affinal ties between groups. **1961** E. Leach *Rethinking Anthropol.* iii. 54 Needham..claims to have demonstrated that a rule of prescriptive patrilineal cross-cousin marriage is an impossibility. **1968** R. Needham tr. *Lévi-Strauss's Elem. Struct. Kinship* (1969) p. xxxi, Exceptional cases apart, they do what they say they must, hence the reason for calling their marriage system 'prescriptive'. **1971** F. Korn in R. Needham *Rethinking Kinship & Marriage* 113 The terms can be consistently arranged in an asymmetric prescriptive terminology.

5. Giving or recognizing prescription or prescriptive right. *rare.*

1785 Burke *Nabob of Arcot's Debts* Wks. IV. 226 This venerable patriarchal job,..hoary with prescriptive years. **1796** —— *Let. Noble Ld.* ibid. VIII. 48 The duke of Bedford will stand as long as prescriptive law endures.

Hence **pre'scriptively** *adv.*, by prescription; by recognized custom; **pre'scriptiveness**, prescriptive character or quality.

1780 Burke *Œcon. Reform* Wks. III. 272 The forest lands, in which the crown has (where they are not granted or prescriptively held) the dominion of the soil, and the vert and venison. **1826–7** De Quincey *Lessing* Wks. 1859 XIII. 298 The cards themselves, by their gay colouring, and the antique prescriptiveness of the figures..throw an air of brilliancy upon the game. **1858** Hawthorne *Fr. & It. Note-bks.* I. 178 We continue to admire pictures prescriptively and by tradition.

prescriptivism (prɪ'skrɪptɪvɪz(ə)m). [f. PRESCRIPTIVE *a.* + -ISM.] **1.** *Linguistics.* The practice or advocacy of prescriptive grammar; the belief that the grammar of a language should lay down rules to which usage must conform.

1954 *College English* XV. 395/1 Professor Bloomfield comes to the conclusion that what is taught in an English class must be some form of..prescriptivism, checked by the limits of fact as established by linguistics. *Ibid.* 395/2 Bloomfield defends prescriptivism first because it has social utility. That is, the public judges..our students by the language they use. **1957** *Eng. Lang. Teaching* XII. 1. 10 It is not for their prescriptivism as such that the older teaching grammars stand condemned. **1964** *Word* XX. 289 The charge of prescriptivism is also made against Chomsky. **1971** *Archivum Linguisticum* II. 54 We are probably all aware of the operation of even weaker collocational constraints as we search for the 'right' choice among, say, *achieve, accomplish, effect*,..etc. to associate with *plan* or *project* or *proposal*.., and a certain inescapable 'prescriptivism' informing language choices is perhaps worthy of note in passing. **1976** *Amer. Speech 1973* XLVIII. 264 Prescriptivism is wrong, the reader is told again.

2. *Philos.* The theory that (moral) judgements have prescriptive force akin to that of imperatives; freq. contrasted with DESCRIPTIVISM 1.

1963 R. M. Hare *Freedom & Reason* ii. 16 Let me refer to the type of doctrine..as 'universal prescriptivism'. **1963** I. L. Horowitz *Power, Politics & People* 15 His [*sc.* Mills's] role in sociology as a contributor to its debates on descriptivism and prescriptivism. **1967** *Encycl. Philos.* II. 317/2 There are two main varieties of prescriptivism. The nominalist variety explains definitions as semantic rules for assigning names to objects, while the formalist variety regards definitions as syntactic rules for abbreviating strings of symbols. **1973** *Heythrop Jrnl.* XIV. 136 (*title*) Prescriptivism in theory and practice. **1976** T. D. Perry *Moral Reasoning & Truth* i. 33 Moore's famous doctrine of the 'naturalistic fallacy' which has been accepted in principle by three of the four major tendencies in analytical ethics: intuitionism, emotivism, prescriptivism.

prescriptivist (prɪ'skrɪptɪvɪst), *a.* and *sb.* [f. as prec. + -IST.] **A.** *sb.* An adherent or advocate of prescriptivism. **B.** *adj.* Of, pertaining to, or characteristic of prescriptivism.

1952 T. Pyles *Words & Ways Amer. Eng.* xi. 272 But he is likely not to see any reason why absolute uniformity, the desideratum of the prescriptivist, should be any particular concern of the student of language even if it were possible of attainment. **1959** *Aristotelian Soc. Suppl. Vol.* XXXIII. 167 It seems to me that only prescriptivist prejudice can deny that we have here a morality. **1960** J. O. Urmson *Conc. Encycl. Western Philos.* 143 To call a thing good is thereby to offer guidance about choices; and the same might be said of the other moral terms. Descriptivists, however, refuse to admit that this feature is part of the *meaning* of moral terms. Their principal opponents, who may be called 'prescriptivists', hold that it *is* part of the meaning. **1964** E. Bach *Introd. Transformational Gram.* v. 90 But the decision to edit..has nothing in common with the prescriptivist's zeal. **1967** *Encycl. Philos.* II. 317/2 The prescriptivist assimilates definitions to imperative sentences rather than to declarative sentences. **1973** *Heythrop Jrnl.* XIV. 139 His normative views are no more arbitrary or relativist than those of any utilitarian, despite his non-naturalist and prescriptivist theory of meta-ethics. **1976** T. Eagleton *Crit. & Ideology* v. 174 It is this purely prescriptivist morality..which finds a later echo in the moral ideology of Kant. **1977** *Publ. Amer. Dial. Soc. 1974* LXI/LXII. 8 The English teacher who..is suddenly bereft of her prescriptivist techniques and her substitution drills.

prescriptivity (,prɪskrɪp'tɪvɪtɪ). [f. PRESCRIPTIVE *a.* + -ITY.] = PRESCRIPTIVENESS.

1963 R. M. Hare *Freedom & Reason* i. 6 The prescriptivity of moral judgements explains both why there should be thought to be a problem about moral freedom, and how to approach its solution. **1966** *Amer. Philos. Q.* III. 305/2 We questioned the 'prescriptivity' of the deduced conclusion of normative syllogisms. **1976** T. D. Perry *Moral Reasoning & Truth* 9 When we point out to our interlocutor what other moral judgements his present judgement commits him to in view of its universalizability and 'prescriptivity' we shall often be able to force him to withdraw it.

prescriptorial (,priːskrɪp'tɔərɪəl), *a. rare.* [f. PRE- B. 1. + SCRIPTORIAL *a.*] Existing before the use of writing.

1897 J. W. Powell in *16th Ann. Rep. U.S. Bureau Amer. Ethnol. 1894–95* p. xcvi, The names are associative or symbolic in the vague fashion characteristic of prescriptorial ideation.

†**pre'scrive**, *v. Sc. Obs.* Also 6 præ-, 5 -scrife. [ad. F. *prescriv-*, full stem of *prescrire* (15th c. in Godefroy *Compl.*), ad. L. *præscrībĕre* to PRESCRIBE, after *écrire*:—*scrībĕre*. Cf. DESCRIVE.]

1. *trans.* = PRESCRIBE *v.* 2.

1563 Winȝet *Four Scoir Thre Quest.* lxxxi. Wks. (S.T.S.) I. 129 Of prayar at præscrivit tymes in the Kirk. **1596** Dalrymple tr. *Leslie's Hist. Scot.* IX. 236, I prescriue him na law. **1597** Skene *De Verb. Sign.* s.v. *Annuel*, Prescrived and appoynted be the law of this realm. **1640–1** *Kirkcudbr. War-Comm. Min. Bk.* (1855) 97 At the expyering of everie ane of the dyets prescryvit be thir instructiones.

b. = PRESCRIBE *v.* 3.

1861 Davidson *Poems* 77 (E.D.D.) My grannie may prescrive an herb for me.

2. (?) *intr.* To become valid by prescription.

1456 Sir G. Haye *Law Arms* (S.T.S.) 80 Thair possessioun..is of sa lang tyme bygane prescrivit and passit prescripcioun.

3. *intr.* Of a right or claim: To cease to be valid, to lapse by prescription of time; = PRESCRIBE *v.* 7; also said of the prescribed period: To elapse, run out.

1456 Sir G. Haye *Law Arms* (S.T.S.) 262 Efter xxxti ȝeris he aw nouthir till ansuer bataill na othir process, for the tyme prescryvis of lawe. **1469** *Sc. Acts Jas. III* (1814) II. 95/1 þe obligatione..sall prescrife & be of nain avail þe said fourtj ȝeris beand Ronnyng & vnpersewit be þe law. **1474** *Ibid.* 107/1 In tyme to cum all obligacionis maid or to be maide þt beis not folowyt w in xl ȝeris sall prescrive and be of na awaill. **1540** in *Balfour's Practicks* (1754) 147 Comprysit landis expiris and prescryvis sevin ȝeiris being bypast; bot landis annalȝeit under reversioun prescryvis nevir. **1678** SIR G. MACKENZIE *Crim. Laws Scot.* I. vi. §22 (1699) 29 If these pursuits should not prescrive with us in five years, as they do by the common Law.

¶ **4.** *trans.* To condemn, prohibit, PROSCRIBE. *rare*$^{-1}$.

[Due to med.L. confusion of *præ-* and *pro-*.]

1562 A. SCOTT *Poems* (S.T.S.) i. 58 Bot wyte the wickit pastouris wald noᵗ mend Thair vitious leving all þᵉ warld prescryvis.

†**pre'scriver.** *Sc. Obs.* [f. prec. + -ER[1].] = PRESCRIBER 1.

1639 BALCANQUHAL *Declar. Chas. I Tumults Scot.* 347 Albeit by the meaning of the prescriver of an oath, the swearer were tacitly bound to maintaine Episcopacie. *a* **1653** BINNING *Serm.* (1845) 408 What is the service of him that may be called religion indeed? Should we be the prescrivers of it?

prescutal, -scutellum, -scutum: PRE- A. 4.

Presdwood ('prɛstwʊd). Also presdwood. [Alteration of *pressed wood.*] (See quot. 1940.)

A proprietary name in the U.S.

1940 *Chambers's Techn. Dict.* 671/1 *Presdwood*.., trade-name for a strong building-board having water-resisting properties. **1946** *Amer. Jrnl. Roentgenol.* LV. 198/2 The procedure was repeated using tempered presdwood phantoms. **1949** *Official Gaz.* (U.S. Patent Office) 5 Apr. 36/1 Masonite Corporation, Chicago... *Presdwood*... For fiberboard, insulating board, composite board, [etc.]... Claims use since Oct. 6, 1926. **1951** R. MAYER *Artist's Handbk.* v. 193 In the majority of instances Presdwood is superior to wooden panels.

prese, obs. f. PRAISE, PRESS, PRIZE.

†**'preseance.** *Obs.* [a. F. *préséance* (*presseance* 1595 in Godef. *Compl.*), f. *pré-*, PRE- A. 2 + *séance* a sitting (see SÉANCE), after OF. *preseer* to preside.] Presidence, presidency.

1581 SAVILE *Tacitus, Hist.* IV. lxix. (1591) 222 Yet were they at discorde brawling about the preseance. **1602** CAREW *Cornwall* 71 Who..may for their discrete judgement in precedence, and preseance, read a lesson to our civilest gentry. [**1826** H. BEST *Four Yrs. France* 27 To allow to the bishop of that city a préséance above all other bishops.]

pre-season: see PRE- B. 2a.

presede, obs. form of PRECEDE.

presedent(e, obs. ff. PRECEDENT, PRESIDENT.

presee: PRE- A. 1.

[**preseeing,** misreading of *foreseeing* (in MS.). In *Leycester Corr.* (Camden) 170; whence in Motley, *Cent. Dict.*, etc.]

†**presegme.** *Obs. rare*$^{-0}$. [ad. L. *præsegmen* a piece cut off, paring.]

1623 COCKERAM, *Presegme*, the paring of ones nailes.

pre-seizure: see PRE- B. 2a.

prese'lect, *v.* [PRE- A. 1.] *trans.* To select in advance.

1864 WEBSTER s.v., Stars preselected for simultaneous observation. **1910** *Proc. Amer. Inst. Electr. Engin.* XXIX. 189 The secondary switches are inserted between the line-switches and the first selectors in such a way that the primary line switches pre-select idle secondaries and the secondaries pre-select idle first selectors. **1941** J. S. HUXLEY *Uniqueness of Man* ii. 56 Immigrants were pre-selected for.. the qualities making up the pioneer spirit. **1961** *Which? Reports on Cars* 7 The cars tested..are in no way pre-selected by the dealer or especially inspected by the manufacturer. **1974** *Country Life* 28 Nov. 1673/1 Four pushbuttons..can be set to pre-select any given four FM stations.

Hence **prese'lected, -se'lecting** *ppl. adjs.*

1910 *Proc. Amer. Inst. Electr. Engin.* XXIX. 184 A line switch always uses a pre-selected idle trunk instead of making a selection after a subscriber starts to call as the Strowger selector switches do. **1924** H. H. HARRISON *Introd. Strowger Syst. Autom. Telephony* i. 16 The combination of such pre-selecting switches with the trunking methods..made the large capacity exchange system a commerical possibility. **1933** AUDEN in *Rev. Eng. Stud.* (1978) Aug. 305 The pre-selected gear adjusted. **1962** J. RIORDAN *Stochastic Service Syst.* vi. 126 A. B. Clarke.. proposed..that the process be observed, in the stationary condition, for a preselected busy time τ. **1974** D. KYLE *Raft of Swords* iii. 19 A short-range missile..capable of being fired at pre-selected targets. **1977** *Offshore Engineer* June 60/3 A computer program..carried out a complete fatigue analysis of pre-selected joints of the tower.

pre-select: see PRE- A. 1.

prese'lection, *sb.* and *a.* **A.** *sb.* [PRE- A. 2.] Selection in advance; *spec.* the operation or use of a preselector.

1924 H. H. HARRISON *Introd. Strowger Syst. Autom. Telephony* 145/2 (Index), Pre-selection. **1930** W. K. HANCOCK *Australia* x. 207 Members of branches join with the unionists who live in the same area to choose by a pre-selection ballot the local party candidate, and to elect delegates to attend the State conference of the party. **1941** J. S. HUXLEY *Uniqueness of Man* ii. 55 Pre-selection was at work on the pioneers. The human cargo of the *Mayflower* was certainly not a random sample of the English population. **1948** R. V. POUND *Microwave Mixers* i. 28 Since most of the circuits..were designed for use in pulse-radar systems, preselection is achieved by means of the resonant TR cavity of the duplexer that precedes the converter. **1950** J. ATKINSON *Herbert & Procter's Telephony* (new ed.) II. xviii. 572/1 The trunking between the subscribers' lines and the 1st group selectors makes use of two stages of preselection by means of 10-outlet unidirectional mechanisms. **1957** *Railway Mag.* Nov. 758/2 Route-setting is used, with pre-selection facility.., the controls remaining stored until conditions allow of their becoming effective. **1962** *Lancet* 6 Jan. 23/2 All cases with chorioretinitis or cerebral calcification, were excluded. There was no other preselection. **1976** [see PRESELECTOR a]. **1979** *Daily Tel.* 24 Sept. 4/8 Mr Bob Hawke, president of the Australian Council of Trade Unions and former President of the Australian Labour party, announced yesterday that he would be a contender for pre-selection for the safe Labour seat of Wills at the next Federal election.

B. *adj.* [PRE- B. 2.] Occurring before selection.

1977 *Daily Tel.* 7 Nov. 2 The Service's Ground Branch is most seriously affected, with one in three group captains nominated for command making it known at preselection stage that they are not interested in taking over their own stations.

prese'lective, *a.* [PRE- A. 3.] That preselects or permits preselection.

1925 *Jrnl. Inst. Electr. Engin.* LXIII. 660/2 If there are switches with a large number of outlets the problem does not arise; neither would it arise if one could use pre-selecting outgoing secondary switches, i.e. switches which themselves found the line before it was wanted... Such a circuit will no doubt arrive and, when it does, outgoing switches of a pre-selective type will for 10-point switches..completely sweep the board. **1930** *Engineering* 17 Oct. 498/3 The pre-selective device consists of an arrangement whereby the gear-control lever can be set for any gear, but the selected gear will not actually be engaged until a pedal is depressed. **1941** J. S. HUXLEY *Uniqueness of Man* ii. 54 Pre-selective influences are those which attract certain types into an environment and discourage others. **1955** *Times* 16 Aug. 2/6 The Conquest Century has the characteristic Daimler transmission, which comprises a fluid flywheel and a preselective epi-cyclic gearbox. **1971** B. SCHARF *Engin. & its Lang.* xvi. 234 More sophisticated overhead chain conveyors are provided with a mechanism by means of which any one of a number of discharge points can be preselected at any loading station. The material will then be automatically discharged or moved on to a side line... These conveyors are termed preselective overhead chain conveyors.

prese'lector. [PRE- A. 2.] **a.** *Teleph.* A switch which when a subscriber lifts his receiver automatically connects the calling line to an idle trunk by a hunting action, independently of impulses produced by dialling; formerly also = *line finder* s.v. LINE *sb.*[2] 32.

1912 J. POOLE *Pract. Telephone Handbk.* (ed. 5) xxxii. 535 The line-switch used by Siemens is a specially neat arrangement... It is called a 'pre-selector' by Messrs Siemens, and each switch is complete in itself. *Ibid.* 536 Secondary line-switches or pre-selectors are used in both systems to facilitate and economise the connections. **1921** W. AITKEN *Autom. Telephone Syst.* I. 3 A preselector is a switch that automatically selects an idle line of a group when the receiver is lifted. **1924** [see HUNT *v.* 9]. **1950** J. ATKINSON *Herbert & Procter's Telephony* (new ed.) II. xviii. 572/2 The 1st preselectors are arranged in groups, so that each group carries..an equal volume of traffic. The preselectors of one group are trunked via 2nd preselectors to a maximum of 100 1st selectors. **1976** T. H. FLOWERS *Introd. Exchange Syst.* iv. 89 The choice between preselection and line-finding is mostly a question of economics. The first needs one exchange switch, or exchange line, and the second one switch per cord circuit. The quantity of switches needed as line finders is thus much less than the quantity as pre-selectors, but whereas line finders must be full-sized exchange switches to achieve satisfactory traffic loading, pre-selector switches may have as few as ten contacts in the banks.

b. *Telecommunication.* A tuned circuit preceding the first mixer in a superheterodyne receiver; an analogous filter in a microwave receiver.

1930 *Electronics* Sept. 279/1 (*heading*) An improved preselector circuit for radio receivers. *Ibid.* 308/1 The essential features of this preselector are shown in Fig. 6. **1951** A. SHEINGOLD *Fund. Radio Communications* xv. 307 The preselector, when present, helps to maintain a favorable signal-to-noise ratio and minimizes interference effects. **1971** M. G. SCROGGIE *Found. Wireless & Electronics* xxii. 396 Because the i.f. amplifier is relied upon for most of the selectivity, the preselector tuning circuits do not have to be very sharp, so slight errors in gauging are not serious. **1975** D. G. FINK *Electronics Engineers' Handbk.* xxv. 72 Narrow-band filters in the receive path, often called preselectors, are built using mechanically tuned cavity resonators or electrically tuned YIG resonators. Preselectors can provide up to 80 dB suppression of signals from other radar transmitters in the same rf band but at a different operating frequency.

c. A gearbox that enables a driver to select the next gear at any time before the change is actually made (by means of a separate pedal). Usu. *attrib.*

1930 *Engineering* 17 Oct. 498/2 There is one cam for each gear, all mounted on a common shaft coupled to the pre-selector lever. **1935** *Economist* 7 Dec. 1144/1 It is a natural step from the power unit to the transmission, where most important developments have centred round such features as the fluid flywheel and the pre-selector gear. **1969** *Driving* (Ministry of Transport) xvi. 198 'Pre-selector' transmissions, mostly found on buses and coaches, have a lever by which the driver can select gears in advance, ready for later changes... No gear change takes place until a gear-change pedals is pressed and released. **1979** J. LEASOR *Love & Land Beyond* i. 13 An electrical gear change which could be used as an ordinary box or as a preselector.

presell, Sc. var. PRECEL *Obs.*

pre-'sell, *v. Comm.* [PRE- A. 1.] *trans.* To promote (a product) before it is available to the consumer; to persuade (the consumer) in advance to buy a product. Also *transf.* So **pre-'selling** *vbl. sb.* and *ppl. a.*, **pre-'sold** *ppl. a.*

1950 in WEBSTER Add. **1958** *Washington Post* 22 Sept. A2/1 Campaign organizers and the American Heritage Foundation public services advertising campaign has already done much to 'pre-sell' the public. **1959** *Times* 7 Apr. 14/4 It is the turn of the television programme to provide pre-sold material for cinema films. **1959** P. WOOD in S. Spender tr. *Schiller's Mary Stuart* 8 English audiences are far less indulgent to her than foreign ones, who are pre-sold on the pathos of her situation. **1960** *Times* 26 Oct. 4/2 Plays expanded from television originals are also, in a sense, pre-sold. **1961** *Economist* 11 Mar. 984/1 Others believed.. that the 'pre-selling' of the major products by advertising direct to the consumer would have a much more potent effect when the barrier of the counter had been removed and she had nothing to do but pick them up. **1962** E. GODFREY *Retail Selling & Organization* iv. 33 Pre-sold goods. In some cases the preliminary stages of the sale will have been completed before the customer comes into the department, through advertising. **1967** *Guardian* 21 July 3/2 We deliberately avoided preselling the film to America. **1973** *Publishers Weekly* 30 Apr. 50/3 The recent January issue.. was so relatively 'with it' that the entire issue was presold. **1977** *Daily Tel.* 2 Dec. 19/1 The interviews..have been pre-sold to the United States and other foreign countries.

presemilunar, -seminal, -ary: see PRE- B. 3, 1.

presence ('prɛzəns). Also 4-6 presens, -ense, 5 -ance, 6 -enss, præsence, 7 præsens. [a. OF. *presence* (12th c. in Littré) (mod.F. *présence* after new formations in *pré-*):—L. *præsentia* presence, f. *præsens* PRESENT *a.*: see -ENCE.]

1. a. The fact or condition of being present; the state of being before, in front of, or in the same place with a person or thing; being there; attendance, company, society, association. Usually with *of* or possessive indicating the person or thing that is present.

a **1340** HAMPOLE *Psalter* xvii. 47 þe folke þat i visited noght with bodily presens. **1340** *Ayenb.* 161 Of blisse of þe presense of Iesu crist, and of þe uelinge of þe holy gost. *c* **1400** *Destr. Troy* 7936 þou partid our presens with þi prise wepyn, þat with faith and affynité were festinyt togedur. *a* **1533** LD. BERNERS *Huon* lxi. 211 Ye shall se Huon, whose presence ye so sore desyre. **1560** DAUS tr. *Sleidane's Comm.* 231 Hys presence and persone is to them ryghte acceptable. **1651** HOBBES *Leviath.* I. vi. 24 By Aversion, we signifie the Absence; and by Hate, the Presence of the Object. **1671** MILTON *Samson* 1321 Our Law forbids at thir Religious Rites My presence; for that cause I cannot come. **1781** GIBBON *Decl. & F.* xvii. II. 2 They were seldom honoured with the presence of their new sovereign. **1836** E. OSLER *Hymn*, O God, unseen, yet ever near, Thy presence may we feel. **1839** DE LA BECHE *Rep. Geol. Cornwall*, etc. ii. 31 The junction of the..rocks..is marked by the presence of a conglomerate with a calcareo-magnesian cement. **1893** LIDDON, etc. *Life Pusey* I. xii. 288 Pusey..delighted in the presence of God manifested in nature.

†**b.** With *pl.* An instance of being present. *rare.*

a **1635** SIBBES *Emanuell* ii. (1638) 10 There were divers presences of Christ, before Hee came.

c. In reference to the manner in which Christ is held to be present in the Eucharist. (See also REAL *a.*[2] 2b.)

[*c* **1420** LYDG. *Assembly of Gods* 1438 When they sy the bodyly presence Of that hooly Eukaryst, lowly gan they lowte.] **1552** *Bk. Com. Prayer, Communion* ad fin., It is not ment thereby [kneeling], that any adoracion is doone..unto anye reall and essencial presence there beeyng [1662 any Corporal Presence] of Christs naturall fleshe and bloude. ? *a* **1555** [? LATIMER] in Foxe *A. & M.* (1563) 979/1 This same presence may be called moste fitly, a reall presence, that is a presence not fained, but a true and faythfull presence. **1559-1882** [see REAL *a.*[2] 2b]. **1560** DAUS tr. *Sleidane's Comm.* 369b, The doctrine of the corporall presence of Christ in the Sacrament. *c* **1683** BURNET *Orig. Mem.* (1902) 52 He [Jas. Dk. of York] was bred to believe a mysterious sort of real presence in the sacrament. **1851** S. WILBERFORCE in R. G. Wilberforce *Life* (1881) II. iii. 105 This seems to me wholly different from speaking of the 'Presence' as the result of the faith of the receiver. **1866** R. W. DALE *Disc. Spec. Occas.* iv. 93 The presence of Christ is not in consecrated bread but in regenerated souls. **1875** TENNYSON *Q. Mary* I. ii, You do not own The bodily presence in the Eucharist, Their wafer and perpetual sacrifice. **1901** B. J. KIDD *39 Articles* II. xxviii. §3 The presence, as being thus a spiritual presence, is at once a real presence and not a 'gross or sensible' one. **1901** BP. GORE *Body of Christ* iv. §2 (1907) 232 The doctrine of the objective presence in, under, or with, the consecrated elements. **1903** J. P. WHITNEY in *Cambr. Mod. Hist.* II. x. 332 In spite of varying views as to the exact nature of the Presence, its reality had always been admitted.

d. The quality in reproduced sound that gives a listener the impression that the recorded activity is occurring in his presence (see also quot. 1950).

1950 *Audio Engin.* Sept. 33 In motion picture work presence refers to the lack of localization of the reproduced sound, so that the eye is beguiled into believing that the sound issues from the location the eye follows... A second use of the term *presence* indicates the degree of intimacy achieved... A third type of presence is detail presence, in which an auditor is able to pick out an individual instrument or soloist, and more or less easily follow its melodic line throughout the changing mass of sound. **1952** H. F. OLSON

Musical Engin. vii. 262 The reverberation-frequency characteristic has a marked effect upon presence. Excessive reverberation in the low-frequency range reduces presence. A uniform directional pattern in the directivity characteristic of a loudspeaker enhances the presence. **1957** *IRE Trans. Audio* V. 106/2 If the need for great 'presence' calls for a very close microphone position, the reproduction may cause a solo instrument to sound much too large, and this can be corrected by attenuating the difference channel relative to the sum. **1958** *Proc. Inst. Electr. Engin.* CV. B. 609/1 The second observation concerns the critical nature of the frequency band in the region 2–4 kc/s... Deficiency in this band gives a distant impression; slight excess gives a forward quality, sometimes referred to as 'presence'. **1974** HARVEY & BOHLMAN *Stereo F.M. Radio Handbk.* v. 127 (*caption*) Curves showing prominence given to mid-range and bass frequencies by the presence control. **1976** G. ALKIN in J. Borwick *Sound Recording Pract.* xxiv. 364 Some types of Lavalier microphone have a non-linear frequency response which peaks in the 'presence' region (between about 4 and 6 kHz) to restore clarity of diction.

e. *Politics.* The maintenance by a nation of political interests and influence in another country or region; *spec.* the maintenance of personnel, esp. armed forces, on the soil of an allied or friendly state; *concr.*, armed forces stationed in this way. Also *transf.*, denoting the representation of a nation's interests at an event.

Cf. Fr. *présence*, in same sense as in quot. 1955.

[**1955** *Times* 4 Aug. 5/3 Times had changed, he said, and there was no longer any need for outmoded oriflamme to guarantee the *présence française*, or rather the *permanence française*, which could only exist 'if we respond to the wishes of the peoples oversea'.] **1958** *Spectator* 7 Feb. 176/2 The 'presence of France' must be maintained. **1961** *Listener* 21 Dec. 1058/1 As Britain and France step back on to the side-lines [in Africa], the United States steps forward to join them there. This new presence...was not at first easy for Britain to accept. **1963** *Ann. Reg. 1962* 319 An effective United Nations 'presence' in South West Africa. **1966** *Punch* 22 June 898/1 How small can a 'presence' be, of the sort we are going to maintain East of Suez?.. The Americans have a presence of 380,000 men in Vietnam alone, and regard that as barely enough. **1972** *Times* 18 Mar. 12/4 Setbacks in the Arab world that followed his liquidation of the guerrilla presence in Jordan. **1975** *Listener* 25 Sept. 390/1 They were known as the Trucial States. When the British presence was withdrawn in 1971, they became a federation called the United Arab Emirates. **1977** *Time* 10 Oct. 11/3 Working out a formula that would allow some Palestinian presence at Geneva was the focus all week long of intense bargaining.

2. a. In certain connexions, used with a vague sense of the place or space in front of a person, or which immediately surrounds him. With *of* or possessive; usually preceded by a prep. (*in*, *before* (arch.), *into*, *to*, *from*, *out of*, etc.); also as obj. of certain verbs, as *forsake*.

in his presence = before or with him, where he is, in his company; ***from his presence*** = from being with him, from where he is, out of his company, etc.; also *poet.* and *rhet.* with demonstrative and other adjs. which in effect qualify the person or persons implied: e.g. ***in this (august) presence*** = in the presence of this (august) personage.

13.. *Seuyn Sag.* (W.) 329 That emperour het,..that thai brinngge him sket, To Rome toun, to his presens. **1340** HAMPOLE *Pr. Consc.* 5441 First sal þair awen conscience, Accuse þam þan in Cristes presence. **1390** GOWER *Conf.* III. 288 He..goth to aproche The kinges Court and his presence. *c* **1420** LYDG. *Assembly of Gods* 174 That he myght come vnto hys presence. **1493** *Petronilla* 92 This proude knight Made him redy to come to hir presence. *c* **1500** *Melusine* 322 Thenne came tofore the presence of Raymondyn the barons of the land. **1526** TINDALE *Luke* xv. 10 Ioye shalbe in the presence off the angels off God over one synner that repenteth. *a* **1533** LD. BERNERS *Huon* lxx. 240 The duke caused them to appere before the kynges presence. *c* **1600** J. LEACH in *Lett. Lit. Men* (Camden) 74 Peregrination from the presens of your Worship. **1781** GIBBON *Decl. & F.* xxviii. III. 92 *note*, A man, who even in his presence would swear by Jupiter. **1809** W. IRVING *Knickerb.* I. v. (1849) 71 The five..monsters, which we have brought into this august presence. **1845** M. PATTISON *Ess.* (1889) I. 22 Being admitted to his presence they saluted him in the queen's name. **1878** BROWNING *Poets Croisic* xlii, René..palely found Way of retreat from the pale presence. *Mod.* He was always very collected in the presence of danger.

b. Without *of* or possessive; usually preceded by prep., as ***in (the) presence*** (†often = present), ***to (the) presence***, etc.; *spec.* (now only) in reference to ceremonial attendance upon a person of superior, esp. royal, rank; formerly also = 'company', (polite) society.

1375 BARBOUR *Bruce* I. 20 For aulde storys..Representis..the dedys Of stalwart folk þat lywyt ar, Rycht as þai þan in presence war. **1390** GOWER *Conf.* III. 154 When the court was plein, When Julius was in presence. *a* **1400–50** *Alexander* 3328 þe maistirs of Persy þan put þam in-to presens, as þeprose tellis. **1514** BARCLAY *Cyt. & Uplondyshm.* (Percy Soc.) 13 Thus all the chyldren than beynge in presence He set in honour, & rowme of excellence. *c* **1560** A. SCOTT *Poems* (S.T.S.) iii. 14 And preiss ȝow ay in presenss to repair. **1593** SHAKS. *Rich. II*, IV. i. 62 'Tis very true: You were in presence then, And you can witnesse with me, this is true. **1630** *R. Johnson's Kingd. & Commw.* 20 The King of China gives not presence, but rarely at the great suit of his people. *a* **1655** VINES *Lord's Supp.* (1677) 379 His fathers corpse lying in presence in a coffin or bier. *c* **1730** BURT *Lett. N. Scotl.* (1818) I. 176 They would not have done it in the presence at St. James's. **1760–72** H. BROOKE *Fool of Qual.* (1809) III. 134 The master of the ceremonies..led Harry up to the presence. **1823** SCOTT *Quentin D.* xxii, A flock of sheep which, when a stranger dog is in presence may be..seen to assemble in the rear of an old belwether. **1889** *Daily News* 28 June 5/8 Eight-and-twenty gentlemen,.. bent low to receive them, and backed out of the Presence as best they could with their prizes.

†c. Hence, A place prepared for ceremonial presence or attendance; a presence-chamber. *Obs.*

a **1548** HALL *Chron., Hen. VIII* 86 Shortly after was made in Westmynster hall a scaffolde for the lordes and a presence for a Iudge railed and counter railed about, and barred with degrees. **1613** SHAKS. *Hen. VIII*, III. i. 17 And 't please your Grace, the two great Cardinals Wait in the presence. **1735** POPE *Donne Sat.* IV. 238 The Presence seems, with things so richly odd, The mosque of Mahound, or some queer Pagod.

†d. In same sense, ***chamber of presence***. *Obs.*

1565 EARL OF BEDFORD in Ellis *Orig. Lett.* Ser. I. II. 210 David [Rizzio] was thruste owte of the Cabinet thorowe the bede chamber into the Chamber of Presens. **1587** FLEMING *Contn. Holinshed* III. 1582/1 Hir Maiesties most gratious answer, deliuered by hir selfe..in hir chamber of presence at Richmond. **1643** EVELYN *Diary* 5 Dec., He had audience of the French King..in the golden chamber of presence.

†3. *concr.* Those who are present; a number of persons assembled; an assembly, a company. *Obs.* (See also note to 2.)

c **1400** *Destr. Troy* 4560 When all the pepull were pesit, þe presens full still, Calcas to the kynges carpes thies wordes. **1542** UDALL *Erasm. Apoph.* 216 Suche persones..forgetten theimselfes..& maken all the presence to laughe at theim. **1588** SHAKS. *L.L.L.* v. ii 536 Here is like to be a good presence of Worthies. **1624** BP. MOUNTAGU *Immed. Addr.* A ij b, I preached in English, vnto an English Auditorie, though composed then of Royall and Noble presence. **1674** GREW *Anat. Trunks* II. iv. §13 In this Honourable and Learned Presence, I have formerly had occasion to shew the Experiment. **1705** STANHOPE *Paraphr.* I. 192 Choosing to.. have his first Presence composed, of a few humble Shepherds. **1788** JEFFERSON *Writ.* (1859) II. 462 The presence was so numerous, that little could be caught of what they said to the King.

4. a. With possessive, denoting the actual person (or thing) that is present (*his presence* = his present self, himself being present); hence sometimes nearly = embodied self, objective personality. Chiefly *poet.*

c **1430** LYDG. *Min. Poems* (Percy Soc.) 7 Where that ever [she] schewithe her presence, Sche bryngithe gladnes to citees and tounnes. **1595** SHAKS. *John* I. i. 377 Your Royall presences be rul'd by mee. **1671** MILTON *Samson* 28 As in a fiery column charioting His Godlike presence. **1728** POPE *Dunc.* I. 261 Her ample presence fills up all the place. **1821** SHELLEY *Epipsychidion* 325 And from her presence life was radiated Through the grey earth and branches bare and dead. **1844** MRS. BROWNING *Lost Bower* xviii, And the blue-bell's purple presence signed it worthily across.

b. Hence, A person who is corporally present; usually with implication of impressive appearance or bearing (see 5); sometimes merely, a person of good 'presence' or aspect.

1826 DISRAELI *Viv. Grey* II. xii, In an awkward retreat to make way for the approaching presence. **1847** WORDSW. *Ode Install. Pr. Albert* ad fin., That Presence fair and bright,.. The pride of the Islands, Victoria the Queen. **1871** BROWNING *Balaustion* 1814 And over him, who stood but Herakles? There smiled the mighty presence, all one smile. **1896** 'M. FIELD' *Attila* II. 37 Our envoy owns the Hun, When mounted on his wiry steed, a presence To pause before admiring.

5. a. Demeanour, carriage, or aspect of a person, esp. when stately or impressive; nobleness, majesty, or handsomeness of bearing or appearance. Also *transf.*

1579 PUTTENHAM *Partheniades* viii, Affable grace, speeche eloquent, and wise; Stately præsence, suche as becometh one Whoe seemes to rule realmes by her lookes alone. **1590** SHAKS. *Com. Err.* III. ii. 166 Her faire sister..Of such inchanting presence and discourse. **1660** PEPYS *Diary* 22 Nov., The Queene a very little plain old woman, and nothing more in her presence..than any ordinary woman. **1762–71** H. WALPOLE *Vertue's Anecd. Paint.* (1786) I. 210 More was a man of a stately and handsome presence. **1861** J. BROWN *Horæ Subs.* (1863) 120 He must have what is called a 'presence'..his outward man must communicate.. at once and without fail, something of indwelling power. **1899** J. G. MILLAIS *Life Sir J. E. Millais* I. i. 1 He was a man of fine presence and undeniable talent. **1959** *Sunday Times* 18 Jan. 16/8 For a painter to have a presence is already an achievement. By 'presence' I mean the variously-definable something that bids a visitor pause and is one of the signs of greatness. **1977** 'E. ANTHONY' *Silver Falcon* vii. 135 The chestnut..had that indefinable quality known in the horse world as presence.

†b. Carriage (of the body) in dancing. *Obs.*

1706 J. WEAVER *Art Dancing* 3 The Posture or Presence of the Body, is to have respect to that part of the Room, to which the Face or Fore-part of the Body is directed.

6. Something present, a present being (see also 4 b); a divine, spiritual, or incorporeal being or influence felt or conceived as present.

1667 MILTON *P.L.* x. 144 To whom the sovran Presence thus repli'd. Was shee thy God, that her thou didst obey Before his voice? **1718** PRIOR *Knowledge* 589 How can good angels be in Heaven confin'd, Or view that Presence which no space can bind? **1798** WORDSW. *Lines Tintern Abbey* 44 And I have felt A presence that disturbs me with the joy Of elevated thoughts. **1857–8** SEARS *Athan.* vi. 48 Divine and celestial presences. **1876** J. PARKER *Paracl.* I. ii. 17 He caused Himself to be succeeded by an eternal Presence, 'even the Spirit of Truth, which abideth for ever'.

7. *presence of mind* (= L. *præsentia animi*): the state or quality of having one's wits about one, or of having full control over oneself, esp. in peril or emergency; calmness and self-command in trying or dangerous circumstances; freedom from embarrassment, agitation, or panic. Cf. *present mind*, PRESENT *a.* 4.

1665 J. SPENCER *Vulg. Proph.* 38 Great courage and presence of mind. **1704** N. N. tr. *Boccalini's Advts. fr. Parnass.* III. 96 The Commander..never wanted Presence of Mind in the most immergent Dangers. **1754** RICHARDSON *Grandison* III. xix. 168, I had besides been led into a presence of mind, by being made a person of some consequence. **1837** DISRAELI *Venetia* IV. i, I lost my presence of mind. **1883** J. G. MCKENDRICK in *Encycl. Brit.* XV. 281/2 What is called 'presence of mind' really means that power of self-control which prevents the bodily energies being paralysed by strong sensory impressions.

¶8. *Catachr.* ***this presence***: the present writing or document (corruption of *these presents*: see PRESENT *sb.*[1] 2 b). *Obs.*

1464 *Rolls of Parlt.* V. 544/1 Expresse mencyon of the verey yerly valure..in this presence is not made. **1617** in *Bury Wills* (Camden) 165 The..writinge before in this presence conteyned.

9. *attrib.* and *Comb.*, as ***presence-affirming*** adj., ***-list***, ***-token***; **presence-lobby**, the lobby or anteroom of a presence-chamber; **presence-room** = PRESENCE-CHAMBER.

1633 FORD *Broken H.* II. ii, She sits i'th presence-lobby fast asleep, sir. **1690** LOCKE *Hum. Und.* II. iii. §1 To convey them..to their Audience in the Brain, the mind's Presence room. **1829** JAS. MILL *Hum. Mind* (1869) II. xiv. 104 Presence-affirming terms. **1836** KEBLE in *Lyra Apost.* (1849) 178 Since holy Gabriel to meek Mary bore The presence-token of th' Incarnate Son. **1847** TENNYSON *Princ.* I. 50 That morning in the presence room I stood With Cyril and with Florian, my two friends. **1904** H. HECHT *Herd's Songs* 47 The presence-lists show that Fergusson seldom missed the meetings of the Cape.

Hence **ˈpresenced** (-ənst) *a.*, (in comb.) having (such and such) a 'presence', personality, or aspect; **ˈpresenceless** *a.*, not accompanied by the presence of any one; **†ˈpresencing** *vbl. sb.* (as if from a vb. *presence*), causing to be present.

a **1638** MEDE *Wks.* (1672) 392 Temples..Places whereunto the Gods..were confined and limited, and for the presencing of whom a Statue was necessary. **1877** IZA D. HARDY *Glencairn* VI. xx, It chilled him as if a presenceless voice had spoken. **1886** RUSKIN *Præterita* I. xi. 375 One of the rarest types of nobly-presenced Englishmen.

ˈpresence-ˌchamber. [Cf. prec. 2 c, d.] The chamber in which a sovereign or other great personage receives guests, or persons entitled to appear before him; a reception-room in a palace or great house. Also *fig.*

[**1565–1643** Chamber of presence: see prec. 2 d.] **1575** LANEHAM *Let.* (1871) 47 The Parcæ..at high midnight, gate them gigling..into the prezens Chamber. *a* **1649** DRUMM. OF HAWTH. *Consid. Parlt.* Wks. (1711) 186 That no man stand bare-headed in the presence-chamber or parliament-house of Scotland, or before any chair of state. **1667** POOLE *Dial. betw. Protest. & Papist* (1735) 143 We shew our Reverence to the King in being uncovered in his Presence Chamber, though the King be not there. **1827** HALLAM *Const. Hist.* (1876) I. v. 251 The peers..were excluded the presence-chamber till they made their submission. **1885** W. F. MARTIN *Mem.* vii. 160 Her closet was the presence-chamber of Deity.

†ˈpresency. *Obs. rare.* [ad. L. *præsentia*: see -ENCY.] = PRESENCE.

1542 *Test. Ebor.* (Surtees) VI. 169 In the prescencie of Sir Robert Gell. **1641** SIR E. DERING *Sp. on Relig.* (1642) 97 You give us..a promise of a Nationall Synod; I doe still wish the presency thereof.

presenile, -senility: see PRE- B. 1, A. 2.

presenium (priːˈsiːnɪəm). *Med.* [f. PRE- B. 1 + L. *senium* feebleness of age.] The period of life preceding old age.

1926 *Lancet* 16 Oct. 820/2 Presenile Mental Disorders. In this article the term presenile is applied to mental disorders arising in the period of life beginning in the late 'forties and extending to the early 'sixties. This period includes the climacterium in women, and certain common mental disorders met with in both sexes during the years which precede the actual period of old age or senility. The more frequent clinical types of mental disorders that are encountered during the presenium are as follows. **1976** SMYTHIES & CORBETT *Psychiatry* vii. 132 Dementia occurring in the presenium demands thorough and complete investigation.

presensation (priːsɛnˈseɪʃən). [f. PRE- A. 2 + SENSATION.] = next.

1653 H. MORE *Conject. Cabbal., Def.* 219 The presage and presensation of it, has in all ages been a very great Joy and Triumph to all holy men and Prophets. **1711** SHAFTESB. *Charac.* (1737) II. II. iv. 307 Beasts..have indeed Perceptions, Sensations, and Pre-sensations (if I may use the Expression). **1807** JAS. HALL *Trav. Scot.* II. 436 Many believe in the prescience or presensation of magpies. **1890** *Q. Rev.* July 256 Concerning the faculty of presensation, it is worth while to say a little more.

presension (priːˈsɛnʃən). Now *rare* or *Obs.* Also 7–8 -tion. [ad. L. *præsensiōn-em* (Cic.) a foreboding, presentiment, n. of action f. *præsentire*, ppl. stem *præsens-*, to feel beforehand.] Feeling or perception of something before it exists, occurs, or manifests itself; foreknowledge, foresight; presage, presentiment.

1597 J. KING *On Jonas* (1618) 125 They had many sorts of predictions, presensions, forseeings. **1646** SIR T. BROWNE *Pseud. Ep.* 128 In sundry animalls, we deny not a kinde of naturall Astrologie, or innate presention both of wind and weather. *a* **1677** BARROW *Serm.* (1683) II. ix. 130 A certain divination, which the Greeks call prophecy, that is a presension, and knowledge of future things. *a* **1711** KEN *Hymnotheo* Poet. Wks. 1721 III. 11 Ants have presensions of the Change in Air, And never work Abroad but when 'tis fair. **1836** DK. SOMERSET in Lady G. Ramsden *Corr. Two Brothers* (1906) 328 Major Howard..appeared to have a very decided presension of his untimely death.

presensitiˈzation, *a.* and *sb.* **A.** *adj.* [PRE- B. 2.] Existing or occurring before sensitization.

1964 W. G. SMITH *Allergy & Tissue Metabolism* ii. 28 These responses rapidly returned to pre-sensitisation levels.

B. *sb.* [PRE- A. 2.] Sensitization beforehand.

1977 *Lancet* 27 Aug. 419/1 Data from patients whose serum had been tested for the presence of lymphocytotoxic antibodies before transplantation against a panel of at least 40 random lymphocyte donors were used in analyses of the effect of humoral presensitisation.

So **preˈsensitize** *v. trans.*, to sensitize beforehand; **preˈsensitized** *ppl. a.*

1963 *Lancet* 5 Jan. 45/1 In 2-month-old neonatally thymectomised C_3H mice, an established Ak skin graft broke down within 12 days after the injection of lymphoid cells from C_3H donors presensitised against Ak. **1967** KARCH & BUBER *Offset Processes* vi. 230 Presensitized plates are surface coated by the manufacturer and ready for exposure when removed from the original package. **1977** *Lancet* 27 Aug. 419/1 Recipients whose serum reacted against more than 5% of the panel members were regarded as being presensitised.

present (ˈprɛzənt), *a.* (*adv.*) Also 6 præsent. [a. OF. *present* (11th c. in Littré), in mod.F. *présent* (see PRESENCE):—L. *præsens*, *præsent-em* present, immediate, prompt, properly pres. pple. of *præesse* to be before, to be at hand. In verse often stressed *preˈsent* down to *c* 1500.]

A. *adj.* An adjective of relation; expressing a local or temporal relation to a person or thing which is the point of reference.

I. Senses relating to place, etc.

1. a. Being before, beside, with, or in the same place as the person to whom the word has relation; being in the place considered or mentioned; that is here (or there). Chiefly in predicate. Opp. to ABSENT *a.* 1. ***present company excepted*** (and varr.), phr. used to indicate that a generalization does not apply to the hearers of it; (***to be***) ***among those present***: to be present (at a function, etc.); to be in the vicinity; (orig. used in reports of social gatherings, etc.; hence in jocular use).

1340 *Ayenb.* 10 Huanne he þet me spekþ of ne is naȝt present. **1382** WYCLIF *Deut.* xxix. 15 Ne to ȝow alone..but to alle present & absent. *c* **1385** CHAUCER *L.G.W.* 1769 (*Lucrece*) Ryght so thogh that hir forme were absent The plesaunce of hir forme was present. **1390** GOWER *Conf.* III. 288 Whanne he sih the king present, He preith he moste his dowhter have. *a* **1425** *Cursor M.* 10294 (Trin.) Into wildernes he went þere as his fe was present. **1503** DUNBAR *Thistle & Rose* 85 All present wer in twynkling of ane e. **1552** ABP. HAMILTON *Catech.* (1884) 133 How is it possibil that the precious bodie and blude of our salviour Christ Jesus..may be really and corporally present in the sacrament of the Altar? *Ibid.* 207 That the verai body of our Lord is really and substancially present in the sacrament of the Eucharist. **1570** T. NORTON tr. *Nowel's Catech.* (1853) 165 What is presenter, what nearer, what closer joined than every man's soul to himself? **1611** SHAKS. *Wint. T.* II. ii. 17, I must be present at your Conference. **1697** DRYDEN *Alexander's Feast* ii, A present deity, they shout around; A present deity, the vaulted roofs rebound. **1784** COWPER *Task* VI. 252 Whom..what he views of beautiful or grand In nature..Prompts with remembrance of a present God. **1793** J. O'KEEFFE *London Hermit* I. ii. 25 Sir, you should always except the present company. **1832** *Reg. Deb. Congress U.S.* 14 June 3530 Mr. C[layton] observed that the gentleman ought to remember that the present company is always excepted. **1839** KEIGHTLEY *Hist. Eng.* II. 30 To be present at his burial. **1846** DICKENS *Dombey* (1848) iii. 20 There's a Tartar within a hundred miles of where we're now in conversation, I can tell you, Mrs. Richards, present company always excepted too. **1862** STANLEY *Jew. Ch.* (1877) I. xiii. 258 We are present at the details of the ancient custom. *a* **1909** *Mod.* Were you present, when he made the statement? **1913** F. L. BARCLAY *Broken Halo* vii. 92 'Present company excepted' is always understood, without being expressed, when sweeping generalities are being made. **1925** WODEHOUSE *Carry on, Jeeves!* iv. 84, I hopped out of bed pretty early next morning, so as to be among those present when the old boy should arrive. **1947** —— *Full Moon* vi. 111 There had unquestionably been mosquitoes among those present. **1975** G. MOFFAT *Miss Pink* iii. 54 Women never strike out for themselves... Present company excepted, of course.

b. Existing in the thing, class, or case mentioned or under consideration; not wanting; 'found'. Opp. to ABSENT *a.* 2.

1809–10 COLERIDGE *Friend* (1865) 94 The reason is either lost or not lost, that is, wholly present or wholly absent. **1838** T. THOMSON *Chem. Org. Bodies* 1003 If plants only emit oxygen gas by absorbing and decomposing carbonic acid gas,..unless carbonic acid gas be present, they can emit no oxygen gas. **1877** HUXLEY *Anat. Inv. Anim.* 423 In the Hemiptera..wings may be present or absent.

c. ***present under arms*** (*Mil.*): see quot.

1829 SIR W. NAPIER *Penins. War* VIII. i. II. 266 His own British and German troops, about twenty-six thousand in number; of which the present under arms, including sergeants, amounted to twenty-two thousand. [*Note*] In the British army, when speaking of the number present under arms, the corporals and privates only are understood. In the French army, the present under arms includes every military person.

2. That is actually in hand, being dealt with, written, discussed, or considered: often used in a book or writing to denote that book or writing itself, or the writer himself. (Formerly *this present* (cf. OF. *ceste present chartre*); now usually *the present* is emphatic for 'this').

1382 WYCLIF *2 Pet.* i. 12 And sotheli I wole ȝou wityng and confermid in present treuthe. *c* **1450** *Godstow Reg.* 349 And fro all maner of right and clayme therfro, they to be excluded for evermore by this present writyng. **1526** *Pilgr. Perf.* (W. de W. 1531) 2, I beseche all the reders so to study this present treatyse, that [etc.]. **1592** WEST *1st Pt. Symbol.* §103 A, The said parties to these present Indentures. **1729** LAW *Serious C.* xix. 354 The much greater part of them, are not brought up so well..as in the present instance. **1872** MORLEY *Voltaire* 295 One has some hesitation in adding Hume to the list in the present connection. **1895** J. ADDISON in *Law Times* XCIX. 546/1 The entire subject..cannot be fully considered in such a paper as the present. *Mod.* The present writer has been unable to verify this.

3. Being before or in the mind or thought; of which one is conscious; directly thought of, remembered, or imagined. Usually const. *to.*

1500–20 DUNBAR *Poems* xc. 12 With all thi synnes into thi mynde present. **1634** W. TIRWHYT tr. *Balzac's Lett.* (vol. I.) 344 Though the half of France divide us, yet are you as present to my spirit, as the objects I see. **1741** WATTS *Improv. Mind* I. xvi. §3 The ample mind takes a survey of several objects.., keeps them all within sight and present to the soul. **1739** HUME *Hum. Nat.* I. iii. (1874) I. 317 When any impression has been present with the mind, it again makes its appearance there as an idea. **1875** JOWETT *Plato* (ed. 2) V. 6 The legends of the place are present to the imagination throughout the discourse.

4. Having the mind or thought directed to, intent upon, or engaged with what one is about; attentive (opp. to ABSENT *a.* 4); having presence of mind, collected, self-possessed (in this sense usually *present to oneself*); prompt to perceive or act, ready, quick. Now *rare* or *Obs.*

1451 CAPGRAVE *Life St. Gilbert* (E.E.T.S.) 96 Now wex he absent to seculer þingis and more present to euerlasting desires. **1548** PATTEN *Exp. Scot.* G vj, My lord Marshal & the other, with present mynde & courage, waerely and quikly continued their coorse towarde them [= the enemy]. **1554** HOOPER *Let.* in Foxe *A. & M.* (1583) 1513/2 Oure memorie..be not as present and quicke as theirs be. **1612** T. TAYLOR *Comm. Titus* ii. 14 Shewing in all his answers a present mind and courage. **16..** L'ESTRANGE (J.), 'Tis a high point of philosophy and virtue for a man to be so present to himself, as to be always provided against all accidents. **1754** RICHARDSON *Grandison* III. xv. 114 You must be present to yourself, and put in a word now-and-then. **1864** LOWELL *McClellan's Rep.* Wks. 1890 V. 115 It is the faculty of being a present man, instead of a prospective one; of being ready, instead of getting ready.

5. a. Ready at hand, immediately accessible or available; *esp.* ready with assistance, 'favourably attentive, not neglectful, propitious' (J.). *arch.* (See also 9.)

1539 BIBLE (Great) *Ps.* xlvi. 1 God is our hope & strength: a very present helpe in trouble. **1590** SPENSER *F.Q.* II. i. 46 He oft finds present helpe, who does his griefe impart. **1611** B. JONSON *Catiline* II. Chorus, Be present to her now, as then. **1697** DRYDEN *Virg. Past.* I. 59 Nor cou'd I hope in any place but there, To find a God so present to my Pray'r. **1817** JAS. MILL *Brit. India* II. IV. iv. 133 This sum, could it only be extorted from him, was a large and present resource.

†**b.** ***present money***: money in hand or paid at the time, ready money. *Obs.*

1600 E. BLOUNT tr. *Conestaggio* 249 To whom they graunted many things, as titles,..rents for life, offices, and to some present money. **1671** tr. *Palafox's Conq. China* vii. 138 They..in exchange thereof, receive present Money. **1721** BERKELEY *Prev. Ruin Gt. Brit.* Wks. 1871 III. 200 The temptation of a pistole present money never faileth.

II. Senses relating to *time.*

6. a. Existing at the time of speaking or writing; that is, or that is so, at this time or now; occurring or going on now, current, contemporary; in use or vogue at this time, modern. Opp. to *past* and *future.*

at* (*this*) *present writing: at the time of writing this, as I now write (? *obs.*).

a **1300** *Cursor M.* 3578 (Cott.) He [the old man] praises al thing þat es gon O present thing he praisses non. **1382** WYCLIF *1 Cor.* iii. 22 Eithir thingis present, either thingis to comynge. **1466** in *Archæologia* (1887) L. I. 50 Any other acte or ordynance made or to be made in this present parlement. **1535** COVERDALE *Baruch* i. 19 Sens the daye that he brought oure forefathers out of the londe of Egipte vnto this present daye. **1566** *Eng. Ch. Furniture* (1866) 37 Imprimis the rood mary and Jhon with all other Images of papistry—brokin and defacid in this prissent yere. **1665** MANLEY *Grotius' Low C. Warres* 764 If a remedy should be sought for present and future mischiefs. **1710** HEARNE *Collect.* 24 Feb. (O.H.S.) II. 348 Our present ambidexter Vice-Chancellour. **1751** HARRIS *Hermes* Wks. (1841) 113 [To] help us to a juster estimate both of present men, and present literature. **1860** PUSEY *Min. Proph.* 44 All things, past, present, and to come, are present before God. **1889** GRETTON *Memory's Harkb.* 245 There were three candidates: the present Dean of Exeter..; the present Bishop of Winchester; and William Selwyn.

b. Actually existing, actual (as contrasted with something that may formerly have existed or in other circumstances might exist).

1774 GOLDSM. *Nat. Hist.* (1776) II. 316 In the present state of nature, the means of safety are rather superior to those of offence. **1842** A. COMBE *Physiol. Digestion* (ed. 4) 98 On the present plan, there is ample food and enjoyment for all. *Ibid.*, An immense class of animals, which, with their present constitution, could not otherwise have existed.

c. *Comm.* ***present value*** or ***worth*** of a sum due at a definite future date: that sum which, together with the compound interest upon it for the time from the present until that date, will amount to the sum then due.

1797 J. GRAY *Arith.* 56 As the amount of 100*l.* for the given rate and time: Is to 100:: So is the debt: To the present worth. **1831** *Encycl. Brit.* (ed. 7) III. 210/2 The present value of £1 to be received certainly at the end of any assigned term, is such a sum less as, being improved at compound interest during the term, will just amount to one pound. **1868** MILL *Eng. & Irel.* 36 What annual payment would be an equivalent..for the present value of whatever prospect there may be of an increase.

7. *Gram.* Applied to that tense of a verb which denotes an action now going on or a condition now existing (or one considered generally without limitation to any particular time). Opp. to *past* (or *preterite*) and *future.*

present imperfect: see quot. 1866, and IMPERFECT *a.* 5. ***present perfect***: a name for the tense denoting action that is completed at the present time (usually called simply *perfect*: see PERFECT *a.* 9 b).

1388 WYCLIF *Prol.* 57 A participle of a present tens, either preterit, of actif vois,..mai be resoluid into a verbe of the same tens, and a coniunccioun copulatif. **1530** PALSGR. Introd. 31 His preterit participle and his present infynityve. **1581** FULKE in *Confer.* II. (1584) N iv b, But you did English it before, the doores being shut, which is the *present tempus.* **1669** MILTON *Accedence* Wks. 1851 VI. 448 The Present Tense speaketh of the time that *now is*, as *laudo* I praise. **1845** STODDART in *Encycl. Metrop.* (1847) I. 56/1 As absolute existence is naturally contemplated under the form of a time perpetually present, it is sufficient for us to consider this as one of the uses of the present tense. **1866** MASON *Eng. Gram.* (ed. 7) §206 The Present Imperfect, showing that an action is going on at the present time; as, *I am writing.* **1904** C. T. ONIONS *Advanced Eng. Syntax* §118 In the earlier period of Old English..the Past tense form had the meanings of the Past, Past Imperfect, Present Perfect, and Pluperfect of Latin.

8. Existing or in use at, or belonging to, the particular time under consideration; that was, or that was so, at that time or then. Now *rare.* (Cf. FUTURE A. 3.) † ***near present*** (quot. *c* 1450), near at hand, imminent (*obs.*).

c **1450** *St. Cuthbert* (Surtees) 6559 He saw his dede day nere present. **1563** GOLDING *Cæsar* VII. (1565) 220 The whyche suffysed to obtein libertie for the present time, but littel or nothing auailed, to kepe peace and quietnes in time to come. **1568** GRAFTON *Chron.* II. 343 Other Capteynes of the rebelles affirmed at the present houres of their death, the same to be true. **1622** GATAKER *Spir. Watch* (ed. 2) 90 Such holy meditations, as the present occasion should require. **1788** PRIESTLEY *Lect. Hist.* v. lxii. 497 There was, however, a present advantage in the system, when it was successful. **1868** FREEMAN *Norm. Conq.* II. viii. 196 Roger, the present Lord of Montgomery, was, at the time of Duke Robert's death, in banishment. *Mod.* The present business was to attend to present needs; other things could wait.

†**9. a.** Occurring or used at the very time, without delay; immediate, instant. (In quot. 1616, Needed immediately, urgent, pressing.) *Obs.* (or merged in 6). (Cf. also *present help* in 5.)

1563 B. GOOGE *Cupido* 15 Eglogs, etc. (Arb.) 107 Care.. bad me seeke sume present helpe, for to relyue my wo. **1578** LYTE *Dodoens* III. lxxii. 420 Such as haue eaten therof do seeme to laugh, and so they dye laughing, without some present remedie. **1597** BACON *Ess. Sacr. Medit.* ii. (Arb.) 103 Peter stroke Ananias..with present death. **1616** B. JONSON *Devil an Ass* III. vi, Alas! the vse of it is so present. *a* **1661** FULLER *Worthies, Northampt.* (1662) II. 285 The Queen.. rigorously demanded the present payment of some arrears. **1793** SMEATON *Edystone L.* §241 An accident..which, without some present resolution, might have prevented my seeing the first stone placed. [**1836** *Penny Cycl.* V. 405/1 The attenuation..will depend..upon..whether the beer is for present use or keeping.]

†**b.** Of a remedy or poison: Taking immediate effect, acting speedily; immediate. (So in 16th c. F.)

1555 EDEN *Decades* 123 The sauour of the woodde is presente poyson. **1563** *Homilies* II. *Repentance* III. (1859) 547 Most present and deadly poison. **1576** BAKER *Jewell of Health* 145 If a man happen to be burned in any place with fyre, that the presentest remedie is, to burne the same place agaime. **1615** MARKHAM *Eng. Housew.* II. i. (1668) 13 Wash the eye therewith, and it is a present help. **1694** SALMON *Bate's Dispens.* (1713) 499/2 It is a present Remedy against the Suffocation of the Womb.

10. *Comb.*: chiefly phrases used *attrib.*, as ***present-time***, ***-use***; also ***present-minded*** adj. (cf. sense 4: opp. to *absent-minded*). See also PRESENT-DAY *a.*.

1836 *Penny Cycl.* V. 405/1 A very good criterion is about 2-5ths of the original saccharometric gravity for present-use ale, and 1-3rd for keeping-ale. **1881** J. H. INGRAM *Mem. Poe* in *P.'s Wks.* I. p. xlviii, Cheerful and present-minded at his work. **1902** *Fortn. Rev.* June 1020 The mysterious and elaborate structure which present-time physiology attributes to the ganglions and the nerve cells.

†**B.** as *adv. Obs.*

1. At the present time; immediately, instantly; at present, now: = PRESENTLY *adv.* 2.

c **1381** CHAUCER *Parl. Foules* 423 Or let me deye present in this place. *c* **1386** —— *Knt.'s T.* 880 It am I That loueth so hoote Emelye the brighte That I wol dye present in hir sighte. **1595** *Locrine* V. v, That which Locrine's sword could not perform, This present stream shall present bring to pass (*drowns herself*). **1654** GAYTON *Pleas. Notes* III. iii. 83, I cannot pay you, what I present owe.

2. In or into the presence of some one; in the (or this) very place, there (or here).

a **1425** *Cursor M.* 2404 (Trin.) As þei þiderwarde went þis forwarde made þei þere present. *Ibid.* 3532 His broþer he fonde þat toke tent To diȝte a noble mete present. *c* **1450** LOVELICH *Grail* liv. 322 That he ne schal ful sore Repente, Tyl that A worthy knyht Come presente. **1554** *Lady Jane Grey's Lament.* in Furniv. *Ballads fr. MSS.* I. 427 The lorde Gilforde my housbande, Whiche suffred here presente.

present ('prɛzənt), *sb.*[1] [Elliptical or absolute use of prec. adj.: in most senses already so used in OF. In ME. orig. *pre'sent.*]

I. †**1.** = PRESENCE 1, 2, 2b. *Obs.* Chiefly in phr. ***in present*** (OF. *en present*), whence *to*, *out of* (your, etc.) *present*.

[The OF. *en present* represented 7th c. barbarous L. *in præsenti* or *præsente*, for L. *in re præsenti*, *in rem præsentem*, in, into the place itself, on or to the very spot. Cf. *Lex Baiuwariorum* (Text 1, 7th c.) xiii. §2 tunc iudex iubeat eum in præsente (*v.r.* -ti) venire, et iudicet ei 'then shall the judge order him to come before him and shall judge him'.]

1303 R. BRUNNE *Handl. Synne* 10800 Ȝe men þat are now yn present, þat haue herd me rede þys sacrament. **13..** *Evang. Nicod.* 76 in Herrig's *Archiv* LIII. 393 On knese here kneled he to Ihesu Right in þine awen present [*rimes* tent, went]. *c* **1400** *Ywaine & Gaw.* 1252 Sone unto the kirk thai went, And war wedded in thair present. *c* **1440** *Ipomydon* 1750 And thynke ye shuld haue be shent, Had he be oute of youre present. *c* **1470** *Golagros & Gaw.* 1287 Heir am I cumyn at this tyme to your present.

†**b.** In pl. *presents*: prob. error for *presence*.

a **1578** LINDESAY (Pitscottie) *Chron. Scot.* (S.T.S.) I. 259 In presentis of all his lordis. **1592** KYD *Sol. & Pers.* III. i. 92 To make thee well assurde How well thy speach and presents liketh vs.

II. †**2.** The thing or person that is present; that which is before one, or here; affair in hand; present occasion; *pl.* things present, circumstances.

c **1325** *Lai le Freine* 163 O Lord, he seyd, Jesu Crist,.. Vnderfong this present. *a* **1400–50** *Alexander* 3162 And he ..þus ordans a pistill... 'To Porrus vndire my present, plesance and ioy'. **1588** SHAKS. *L.L.L.* IV. iii. 189 What Present hath thou there?.. Some certaine treason... I beseech your Grace let this Letter be read. **1601** —— *Twel. N.* III. iv. 380 Ile make diuision of my present with you. **1607** —— *Cor.* III. iii. 42 Shall I be charg'd no further then this present? Must all determine heere? **1764** REID *Inquiry* I. i. 29 That immediate knowledge which we have of our presents.

b. ***this present***, more commonly ***these presents***: the present document or writing; these words or statements: used in a document to denote the document itself (cf. PRESENT *a.* 2). (So obs. F. *ces presentes* (sc. *lettres*), 1537 in Godef.) Chiefly, now only, in legal use.

1389 in *Eng. Gilds* (1870) 48 Be it open and knowen..be þeis presentes, þ[t] [etc.]. **1405** *Rolls of Parlt.* III. 605/1 We Henry Percy..has constitut and assigned and by this presentz constitutes and assignes Sir Henry Boynton..our generalls and specialls Attornes and Deputes. **1497** *Cal. Anc. Rec. Dublin* (1889) I. 383 Which is..ordeined and establid, by auctorite of this preseint. **1546** *Reg. Privy Council Scot.* I. 51 The saidis parteis hes subscryvit thir presentis with thair handis. **1634** W. TIRWHYT tr. *Balzac's Lett.* (vol. I.) 235 As I was ready to seale these Presents. **1752** in Cruise *Digest* (1818) VI. 76 Know all men by these presents, that I John Griffin make the aforementioned my last will and testament. **1778** *Art. Confederation* in Bryce *Amer. Commw.* (1888) I. App. 575 Know ye, that we, the undersigned delegates,..do, by these presents..fully and entirely ratify. **1854** THACKERAY *Rose & Ring* xv, [The herald]..began to read:—'O Yes!..know all men by these presents, that we, Giglio, King of Paflagonia' [etc.].

III. 3. The present time, the time that now is (as opposed to *the past* and *the future*).

c **1600** SHAKS. *Sonn.* cxv, When I was certain ore incertainty, Crowning the present, doubting of the rest. **1759** JOHNSON *Rasselas* xxix, To judge rightly of the present we must oppose it to the past. **1850** BLACKIE *Æschylus* II. 151 The present..is everywhere at once the child of the past, and the parent of the future. **1855** BROWNING *Childe Roland* xviii, Better this present than a past like that.

†**b.** With ellipsis of *month* (usually *this present*): = INSTANT *a.* 2b. *Obs.*

1509 in *Mem. Hen. VII* (Rolls) 435 On the tenthe day of thys present y spake wyth the kyng. **1585–6** EARL LEYCESTER *Corr.* (Camden) 444 Your excellences letter dated the 19. of this present. **1660–1** MARVELL *Corr.* Wks. (Grosart) II. 42 Your kind letter of the 8th present.

c. *Gram.* Short for *present tense*: see PRESENT *a.* 7. ***present stem***, the stem of the present tense.

1530 PALSGR. 101 Of the Potentiall Mode. The present tense like the present of the indicative. **1871** ROBY *Lat. Gram.* II. xx. (*heading*), Tenses formed from the present stem. *Ibid.* §605 The verb *sum* and compounds have apparently merely a different form of the present for the future.

4. In phrases with prepositions.

†**a. in present** [= OF. *en present* (10th c.)], (*a*) in or at the present time, now; (*b*) immediately (cf. PRESENT *a.* 9); (*c*) at that time, then. So *in this present* = (*a*). *Obs.*

a **1300** *Cursor M.* 4956 (Cott.) And þat find yee now in present. *c* **1330** *Amis & Amil.* 509 He bileft at hom in present, To kepe al that ther ware. *c* **1440** *York Myst.* xxv. 345 What wolde þou man..in þis present? **1633** G. HERBERT *Temple, Mans Medley* i, Mans joy and pleasure Rather hereafter, then in present, is. **1720** MRS. MANLEY *Power of Love* (1741) 202 Offering a very large Dowry with his Daughter in Present, and the rest of his Estate in Reversion. *a* **1797** H. HOWARD in *3rd Rep. Hist. MSS. Comm.* 434/1 Y[e] father could not afford to part with any thing in present upon the marriage.

b. at present, at the present time, now (formerly † ***at this present***; so † ***at that present***, at that time, then; † ***at the present***, in both senses).

1547 J. HARRISON *Exhort. Scottes* C iv, The ruynes..are to be seen at this present. **1558** in *10th Rep. Hist. MSS. Comm.* App. v. 388 A parcell of our ground, being at thes presentes waste withoute proffit. **1577–87** HOLINSHED *Chron.* III. 1197/1 The duke Daumale was there at that present with the Reingraue. **1647** CLARENDON *Hist. Reb.* VIII. §254 He was not himself without that design at that present. **1652** NEEDHAM tr. *Selden's Mare Cl.* 99 Nations which at this present are in high repute and autoritie. **1709** STEELE *Tatler* No. 26 ¶3 My Reason for troubling you at this present is [etc.]. **1837** WHEWELL in Todhunter *Acc. Writ.* (1876) II. 263, I myself am a busy man at this present.

1647–8 COTTERELL *Davila's Hist. Fr.* (1678) 40 All men believed at the present that he was poisoned. **1672** C. MANNERS in *12th Rep. Hist. MSS. Comm.* App. v. 24 At the present the King and the Duke have put severall things into his hands.

1662 STILLINGFL. *Orig. Sacr.* II. i. §3 This is all we at present desire. **1766** FORDYCE *Serm. Yng. Wom.* (1767) I. iv. 128 Of miraculous interposition I think not at present. **1868** LOCKYER *Elem. Astron.* v. xxxv. (1879) 206 At present we are nearest to the sun about Christmas time.

†**c. of present** [OF. *de present*, 14–15th c.], **on the present**, at present, now. *Obs.*

c **1500** *Melusine* 45 A grete and meruayllous auenture whiche is happed as of present [Fr. *à present*] in the place. **1607** SHAKS. *Timon* I. i. 141 Three Talents on the present; in future, all.

d. for the present [= F. *pour le présent*], (†formerly also, ***for this present***, ***for that present***, ***for present***), for the time; †for that time, just then (*obs.*); in mod. use, for this time, just now.

1548 in Ellis *Orig. Lett.* Ser. III. III. 295 [He] wold not be spoken withall that night, nor this daye untill nine a clock in the morning, so as they departed for that present. **1565** *Reg. Privy Council Scot.* I. 360 Monitionis..necessar for this present. **1585** T. WASHINGTON tr. *Nicholay's Voy.* I. vii. 5 b, To whom, for the present they would giue no eare. **1608** *Great Frost* in Arb. *Garner* I. 91 The wounds that this frost gave the commonwealth were for that present scarce felt. **1643** TRAPP *Comm. Gen.* xxxiv. 26 Jacob gave place, for present, to his sons rage and fury. **1660** F. BROOKE tr. *Le Blanc's Trav.* 2, I..shall satisfie my self for the present to tell you, that..we sailed happily for some few dayes. **1709** ATTERBURY *Serm., Luke* x. 32 (1726) II. 226 They desire to be excus'd from that Duty for the present. **1885** *Bookseller* July 647/1 For the present it [the business] will be continued without change of name.

e. until the present, up to the present [= F. *dès à présent*], until now, up till now. †So formerly ***till, until this*** or ***that present***, up to this or that time (*obs.*).

1600 J. PORY tr. *Leo's Africa* VIII. 304 Inscriptions engrauen in marble, and remaining til this present. **1609** BIBLE (Douay) *Exod.* vii. 16 Until this present thou wouldest not heare. **1652** NEEDHAM tr. *Selden's Mare Cl.* 12 From the Peace of Venice 1522 until that present. **1883** *Manch. Exam.* 27 Nov. 5/2 Up to the present the armies of France and China have not been brought into collision.

present ('prɛzənt), *sb.*[2] Also 3–4 **-ant**, 3–5 **-aunt**, (3 *pl.* **-auns**), 3–6 **-ente**, 4 **-end**, **-aunde**, 4–6 **-and(e**, 5 **-aunte**, **-awnte**, **-ond**, **-ound**, 6 **-aunt**, *Sc.* **praisant**. [a. OF. *present* (10th c. in Hatz.-Darm.) = Pr. *prezens*, It., Sp., Pg. *presente* an offering, a gift. In OF., originating in the phrase *en present* in or into the presence (cf. PRESENT *sb.*[1] 1): *mettre* (une chose) *en present à* (quelqu'un), to put a thing into the presence of or before any one (i.e. to offer or *present* it to him), in which *en present* was in effect = *en don* 'in the form of, or as a gift', making *présent* at length = *don* 'gift'. Cf. PRESENT *v.* 11.]

†**1.** In the expression, ***in*** (***into, intil***), ***to present***, = OF. *en present*: in or into a person's presence, before a person (as an offering); as a gift.

a **1225** *Ancr. R.* 114 Þet þeo ilke þet he bledde uore ne brouhten heo him to presente ne win, ne ale, ne water. *c* **1290** *S. Eng. Leg.* I. 178/22 Gold, and mirre, and An-sens, In presaunt heo him brouȝten. *a* **1300** *Cursor M.* 7588 And broght it þe king to presand. *c* **1320** *Sir Tristr.* 825 Heuedes of wild bare Ichon to presant brouȝt. **1375** BARBOUR *Bruce* XVIII. 170 [Thai] send it [the head] syne in-till Ingland, To Eduard king in-till presand.

2. a. A thing that is offered, presented, or given: = GIFT *sb.* 3. (The ordinary current sense).

a **1225** *Ancr. R.* 152 Þoa uormest heo unwrien þet present þet heo beren. *a* **1300** *Cursor M.* 160 Þe kynges þat him soght thre presandes til him broght. **1470–85** MALORY *Arthur* I. viii. 44 The kyng made grete ioye and sente the kynges and knyghtes grete presentes. **1495** *Trevisa's Barth. De P.R.* VI. xiii. (W. de W.) m viij, To wynne the loue of her that he wowyth wyth yeftes..and wyth dyuers presents. **1585** T. WASHINGTON tr. *Nicholay's Voy.* I. xvii. 19 b, The Ambassadour sent his presents vnto the Bascha. **1611** BIBLE *Gen.* xliii. 25 They made ready the Present against Ioseph came at noone. **1687** A. LOVELL tr. *Thevenot's Trav.* I. 85 The Mules that carried the Presents were..unloaded. **1703** MAUNDRELL *Journ. Jerus.* (1732) 7 We went to visit the Aga with a small Present in our hands. **1861** M. PATTISON *Ess.* (1889) I. 45 Silver and pewter plate,..presents to the Corporation from all parts of the Continent.

transf. **1625** BACON *Ess., Greatn. Kingdoms* (Arb.) 483 Romulus after his death..sent a present to the Romans that [L. *illud civibus suis legavit ut*] above all things they should intend arms.

b. The act or fact of presenting or giving, presentation: = GIFT *sb.* 1. Usually in phr. ***to make a present*** (formerly also ***to make present***): to make a gift or presentation (*to* a person, or with indirect dative obj.); ***to make a present of*** = to present, give, bestow. With indirect passive: ***to be made a present***.

13.. *Coer de L.* 1218 Over the see thenne are they went, For to make the fayr present. *c* **1325** *Spec. Gy Warw.* 1018 Riht to my-selfe,..þu dost þi present euery dele. *c* **1385** CHAUCER *L.G.W.* 1135 (MS. Gg. 4. 27) How that he schulde make The presentis [*other 5 texts* presenting]. *c* **1440** *York Myst.* xv. 110, I am ovir poure to make presande. **1513** DOUGLAS *Æneis* III. ix. 44 My fader Anchises..gaif that ȝoung man hys richt hand, And assuris his spreit with that presand. **1645** WALLER *Apol. having Lov'd* ii, To the first that's faire or kind, Make a present of their heart. **1774** J. BRYANT *Mythol.* II. 379 Pausanias mentions one, which had been made a present to the Deity at Olympia. **1849** MACAULAY *Hist. Eng.* v. I. 667 To purchase the connivance of the agents..by presents of hogsheads of wine, and of gloves stuffed with guineas. **1884** J. T. TROWBRIDGE *Farnell's Folly* xxvi, Marian had made her a present of a new dress.

†**c.** *spec.* A bribe: = GIFT *sb.* 5. *Obs.*

1362 LANGL. *P. Pl.* A. III. 80 Bote Meede þe Mayden þe Meir heo bi-souȝte, Of alle such sullers seluer to taken, Or presentes withouten pons as peces of seluer. *Ibid.* 208 Þe pope and his prelates presentes vnderfongen.

d. An offering to God or a deity: = GIFT *sb.* 4. Now *rare* or *Obs.*

1535 COVERDALE *Ps.* lxxv[i]. 11 Brynge presentes vnto him y[t] ought to be feared. **1606** G. W[OODCOCKE] *Hist. Ivstine* XLIII. 135 Returning from Delphos (whither they had bene sent to carry presents vnto Apollo). **1707** WATTS *Hymn, 'When I survey the wondrous cross'* v, Were the whole realm of nature mine, That were a present far too small.

e. ***a present from*** (***Brighton*** etc.): an inscription on a piece of souvenir pottery etc., bearing the name of the town in which it is sold; hence, a piece of pottery etc. so inscribed, a souvenir.

1852 DICKENS *Bleak Ho.* (1853) iv. 28 We found a mug, with 'A Present from Tunbridge Wells' on it. **1890** KIPLING *Courting of Dinah Shadd* 125 She gave me a drink out of a china mug wi' gold letters—'A Present from Leeds'. **1921** W. DE LA MARE *Mem. Midget* viii. 49 A gay little bumper of milk gilded with the enwreathed letters, 'A Present from Dover'. **1962** N. MITFORD *Water Beetle* 113 The china cabinet will contain Rose Pompadour Sèvres cheek by jowl with A Present from Bexhill. **1964** F. SINCLAIR *Three Slips to Noose* vii. 61 A small square room furnished with..china shepherds and presents from Clacton. **1974** J. STUBBS *Painted Face* i. 32 A small ash-tray..inscribed *A Present from Brighton*.

†**3.** An offer, proposal. *Obs.*

c **1330** R. BRUNNE *Chron.* (1810) 75 Of pes þei mad present, to turne ilkon þer pers Ageyn to Danmark go with his wille & his leue. *Ibid.* 303 To maynten þam in stoure, þei mad him þer present, Scotlond of him to hold.

4. *Comb.*, as ***present-giver, -giving***, etc.

1895 *Daily News* 22 Oct. 6/5 It is an occasion of present-giving ad lib.; the confirmee receiving gifts from all her relatives and friends. **1897** *Westm. Gaz.* 28 Dec. 4/2 A mission steamer made her usual trips present-laden to the lightships of the Thames Estuary. **1901** *Daily Chron.* 20 Aug. 5/1 The procrastinations of a present-giver indefinitely prolong and augment his sufferings.

present (prɪ'zɛnt), *sb.*[3] *Mil.* [f. PRESENT *v.* 9a.] The act of presenting or aiming a weapon, esp. a fire-arm; the position of the weapon when presented, *esp.* the position from which a rifle is fired.

1833 *Regul. Instr. Cavalry* I. 98 Bring the carbine down to the 'Present'. **1846** MARRYAT *Privateersman* xvii, 'Who are you?' said she, with the musket ready for the present. **1847** *Infantry Man.* (1854) 40 *c* The first file comes to the present. **1859** *Musketry Instr.* 42 The most minute attention is to be given to each man's position when at 'the present'. **1902** R. W. CHAMBERS *Maids of Paradise* vii, An Uhlan..stood on guard below the steps, his lance at a 'present'.

present (prɪ'zɛnt), *v.* Also 4–6 **presente**, 5 **presand**, 6–7 **præsent**; *contr. pa. t.* 4 **presende**, 4–7 **present**, 5 **presand**; *pa. pple.* 4–6 **present**. [a. OF. *presenter* (11th c. in Littré, in mod.F. *présenter*):—L. *præsentāre* to place before, exhibit, hold out, exhibit a likeness to, in late and med.L. to present to a person as a gift, lit. to make present, f. *præsent-em* PRESENT *a.*]

I. To make present *to*, bring into the presence of.

1. a. *trans.* To bring or place (a person) before, into the presence of, or under the notice of, another; to introduce, esp. formally or ceremoniously; *spec.* to introduce at court, or before a sovereign or other superior.

c **1290** *Beket* 289 in *S. Eng. Leg.* I. 115 For þe king was in Normandie, I presented he was To henri, is sone, in Engelonde. *c* **1400** *Destr. Troy* 7837 He..went with þo worthy, &..Present hom to Priam, þat was prise lord. **1526** TINDALE *Acts* xxiii. 33 They delivered the pistle to the debite [= deputy], and presented Paul before him. —— *Jude* 24 Vnto hym that is able..to present you fautlesse before the presence off hys glory. **1582** N. T. (Rhem.) *Acts* ix. 41 And when he had called the saincts and the widowes, he presented her aliue. **1612** BOYLE in *Lismore Papers* (1886) I. 13 Sir Thomas Roper presented W[m] my cook and his wyffe into my service. **1670** LADY M. BERTIE in *12th Rep.*

Hist. MSS. Comm. App. v. 21 The Dutchesse..presented mee to kisse the Queene's hand. **1716** LADY M. W. MONTAGU *Let. to Lady X*—— 1 Oct., Whoever pleases may go, without the formality of being presented. **1844** DISRAELI *Coningsby* III. ii, The Duke and Duchess had returned from London..with their daughter, who had been presented this year. **1853** LYTTON *My Novel* v. viii, 'They say he is clever'. 'Present him, my love; I like clever people', said Mrs. M'Catchley. **1903** MCNEILL *Egregious English* 31 Sometimes even Mr. and Mrs. Man-of-Business manage to get presented.

b. To bring before or into the presence of God; to dedicate by so bringing: cf. PRESENTATION 1.

13.. *Cursor M.* 10358 (Gött.) Scho sal be al godd bekende; To him presentyd [*Cott.* offrid: cf. 10581] at thre ȝer ende. **1387** TREVISA *Higden* (Rolls) IV. 269 After [þat] fourty dayes of þe nativite, in a þorsday, þe secounde day of Feverer, Criste was presented in þe temple. *c* **1400** MAUNDEV. (Roxb.) xxv. 114 þe first [feste] es at þat tyme þat þe Grete Caan was borne; þe secund es at þat tyme þat he was presented in to þaire tempill..whare he was circumcised. **1526** TINDALE *Luke* ii. 22 They brought hym to hierusalem, to present hym to the lorde. **1548-9** (Mar.) *Bk. Com. Prayer, Collect Purification*, As thy onelye begotten Sonne was this day presented in the Temple.., so graunte that we maie bee presented unto thee with pure and cleare myndes; By Jesus Christ our Lorde. **1818** BENSON *Comm. Bible* Luke ii. 22-24 Luke himself introduces both the parents as presenting Jesus. **1881** E. A. GREENE *Saints & Symbols*, (1888) 135 When she [Mary B. V.] was three years old she was taken by her parents to be presented in the Temple.

c. A candidate is said to be presented (or to present himself) for examination; one who has passed a university examination, or is honoured with a degree, is presented for the degree; a theatrical manager is said (in recent use) to present an actor, etc. Also *fig*.

1661 WOOD *Life* (O.H.S.) I. 414 Severall noble men [were] created Masters of Art,..who were presented in scarlet robes belonging to Doctors. **1721** AMHERST *Terræ Fil.* No. 24 (1726) 131 The next congregation he was presented to his degree. **1797** *Cambr. Univ. Calendar* 143 [The public orator] His duty is to present noblemen to their degrees [etc.]. **1859** *Lond. Univ. Calendar* 51 On receiving each instalment he shall declare his intention of presenting himself at the Second Examination within two years from the time of his passing the First Examination. **1880** *Plain Hints Needlework* 54 In infant schools, and in others where children are not presented [for examination] in needlework under Article 19c. 1, but only under Article 17f. **1906** J. WELLS *Oxford Degree Ceremony* 11 *note*, The old principle is that no one should be presented except by a member of the University who has a degree as high or higher than that sought. **190.** *Mod. Newspaper* (Advt.) Charles Frohman presents Ellaline Terriss and Seymour Hickes in 'The Gay Gordons'. **1923** *Adelphi* Aug. 236 Osbert is a born impresario... Osbert 'presents' the [Sitwell] family, and does it with originality.

†**d.** To bring (a person) by proxy or in a figure; to offer the salutation or greetings of (one at a distance); to give greeting from, to 'remember' (any one) *to*.

a **1657** R. LOVEDAY *Lett.* (1663) 55 Present me tenderly to my Sisters F. and J. **1774** BURKE *Corr.* (1844) I. 503 Present me cordially to Mrs. Champion. **1792** JEFFERSON *Writ.* (1859) III. 495 Present me affectionately to Mrs. Gilmer.

2. a. *refl. to present oneself*: to come into the presence and sight of another or others, or into a particular place, esp. in a formal manner; to appear, attend. Cf. sense 9b.

c **1375** *Sc. Leg. Saints* l. (*Katerine*) 1001 þane sir purphire ..Has present hyme befor þe king. *c* **1450** HOLLAND *Howlat* 152 How thai apperit to the Pape and present thaim aye Fair farrand and fre. **1585** T. WASHINGTON tr. *Nicholay's Voy.* III. vi. 79 They are bound to present themselues euery morning at his house. **1611** BIBLE *Job* i. 6 Now there was a day, when the sons of God came to present themselues before the Lord. *a* **1792** BP. HORNE *Disc. Purification* Wks. 1818 III. 157 That he who was thus offered in the temple, ..still continues to present himself, to appear in the presence of God for us. **1841** LANE *Arab. Nts.* I. ii. 85 [He] presented himself before the king. **1859** [see 1c]. **1880** [see PRESBYOPE]. **1896** *Law Times* C. 488/1 He presented himself at the museum, and attempted to enter the reading-room.

†**b.** *intr.* in same sense. *Obs.*

c **1380** WYCLIF *Sel. Wks.* III. 357 ȝif two men ben of o date, whoever presentiþ first, shal be avaunsid bifore. **1605** B. JONSON *Volpone* III. v, Has shee presented? **1626** —— *Staple of N.* II. ii, I must correct that ignorance and ouersight, Before I doe present.

3. *trans.* **a.** To name and recommend (a clergyman) to the bishop for institution *to* a benefice. Often *absol.* (Cf. also 12.) Also, to introduce or recommend to a presbytery (a candidate) for licence as a preacher.

[**1278** *Rolls of Parlt.* I. 3/2 Quod idem Abbas permitteret predictum Ricardum presentare idoneam personam ad Ecclesiam de Shire].

1473-5 in *Calr. Proc. Chanc. Q. Eliz.* (1830) II. Pref. 61 To..put youre seid besecher frome hys free nominacion and will of presentyng to the seid church. **1523** FITZHERB. *Surv.* 29 He yt hath right to present to a churche at one tyme. **1595** in *Calr. Laing Charters* (1899) 319 Mr. James..has presentit and proponit him to the presbyterie of Couper..to be tryit. *c* **1650** *Rolls of Parlt.* II. 437/1 The Incumbent.. thereunto presented by the Chancellor of Ireland. **1673** P. HENRY *Diary* (1882) 259 He was praesented to a living by ye lord Ward. **1726** AYLIFFE *Parergon* 415 The Patron may present several Persons to the Bishop, though he can only give Institution to one. **1818** CRUISE *Digest* (ed. 2) III. 26 A lunatic cannot present to a church, nor his committee. For where a lunatic is seised of an advowson, the Lord Chancellor..presents to the living. **1856** FROUDE *Hist. Eng.* (1858) I. iv. 291 The supposed right of the pope to present to English benefices.

b. To nominate to the benefits of any foundation or charitable institution.

1820 LAMB *Elia* Ser. I. *Christ's Hosp. 35 Years Ago*, L.'s governor (so we called the patron who presented us to the foundation) lived in a manner under his paternal roof.

4. a. To put before the eyes of some one; to hold forth to view; to offer to sight or observation; to show, exhibit, display; also (in recent use), To offer (some quality or attribute) to view or notice; to exhibit, be characterized by. Also *refl.*

1500-20 DUNBAR *Poems* lxxi. 30 And thy bidding we trest thay sall ganestand, Without thow cum and present thame thy face. **1563** HYLL *Art Garden*. (1593) 65 If any would put away the red spots of the face, which do present a kinde of leaprie. **1610** SHAKS. *Temp.* v. i. 85, I will discase me, and my selfe present As I was sometime Millaine. **1664** POWER *Exp. Philos.* I. 17 The Glass [microscope] failed in presenting them. **1717** POPE *Eloisa to Abelard* 327 In sacred vestments may'st thou stand,..Present the Cross before my lifted eye. **1823** F. CLISSOLD *Ascent Mt. Blanc* 23 The snow-topped Apennines presented an appearance of low scattered clouds. **1816** KEATINGE *Trav.* (1817) I. 11 *note*, Who would have thought it should have presented the interest it does at the hour, March the 18th, 1814? **1835-6** *Todd's Cycl. Anat.* I. 685/1 The shells of the Balanids present several striking peculiarities of structure. **1853** J. H. NEWMAN *Hist. Sk.* (1873) II. I. ii. 63 Lands, as Asia Minor, which have presented a very different aspect in different ages. **1885** SIR N. LINDLEY in *Law Rep.* 14 *Q. Bench Div.* 714 The few points which present any difficulty.

b. *present arms* (*Mil.*), to hold a fire-arm or other weapon in a position expressing honour and deference, in saluting a person of superior rank.

1759 [W. WINDHAM] *Plan Discipl. Norfolk Militia* 10 *note*, Presenting the arms, being the same position as the rest, needs no further explanation; it is so termed when used as a compliment. **1796-7** *Instr. & Reg. Cavalry* (1813) 244 The men present arms, and the officers salute, so as to drop their swords with the last motion of presented arms. **1798** *Brit. Milit. Jrnl.* Oct., Manual Exercise of Pikes [2nd word of command]..Present Pike. **1837** DICKENS *Pickw.* iv, There was a general clash of muskets, as arms were presented. **1853** STOCQUELER *Milit. Encycl.*, *Present arms!* is the salutation of a sentry, a guard, or an entire line when a superior officer appears, or the 'colours' are saluted. The motion is performed by bringing the firelock in a perpendicular position in front of the body, and at the same time placing the hollow of the right foot against the heel of the left.

c. Of a radio or television producer or broadcaster: to bring (a broadcast item) before the listening or watching audience, to introduce or announce (a programme). Of a performer: to perform (a song etc.).

1933 *Radio Times* 14 Apr. 120/1 Tonight Mr. James Agate 'presents' perhaps the greatest..star of this glittering series. **1961** *N.Y. Times* 30 Jan. 19 Ellie Mao, soprano, and Frederick Fuller, baritone, presented a program of folksongs entitled 'East meets West' in Carnegie Recital Hall last night. **1972** *Listener* 10 Aug. 187/2 The need felt by ..the Presentation Department at Television Centre..to do something more than merely 'present' the evening's programmes. 'Presenting' means seeing that the programmes get on the air tidily and on time, smoothing over or explaining disaster, making announcements and trailing coming events. **1976** *Laurel* (Montana) *Outlook* 9 June 6/3 A solo, presented by Marilyn Parker, was accompanied by Mrs. Markegard.

5. a. To make present to mind or thought, exhibit to mental perception; to offer to notice or consideration; to suggest to the mind; to set forth or describe; to represent (*as* or *to be*); to set forth. Also *absol.*

1579 TOMSON *Calvin's Serm. Tim.* 1001/1 To cut off all the desires which Sathan presenteth vs, to cause vs to loue the world. **1604** SHAKS. *Oth.* I. iii. 124 So iustly to your Graue eares, Ile present How I did thriue in this faire Ladies loue. **1649** JER. TAYLOR *Gt. Exemp.* Pref. §32 Faith which is presented to be an infused grace. **1667** MILTON *P.L.* IX. 213 Hear what to my mind first thoughts present. **1774** GOLDSM. *Nat. Hist.* II. 55 The creature is presented as very shy. **1885** *Manch. Exam.* 21 May 6/1 The arguments on both sides.. were presented with clearness and precision. **1976** *Daily Tel.* 20 July 3/2 How can anyone, any lawyer, present any case that is acceptable in common sense. **1976** *Dallas Morning News* 22 Sept. 10B/5 Learn to read, learn to listen, learn to think, learn to write, learn to present. *Ibid.*, Businesses have botched sales efforts mainly because their people..could not present their information in clear and 'selling' English.

†**b.** To offer (battle or the like); to offer or propse (a toast). *Obs. rare.*

1600 DYMMOK *Ireland* (1843) 40 The lord Lieutenant.. presented a charge to the rebells grosse of horse and foote. *a* **1627** HAYWARD (J.), He was appointed admiral, and presented battle to the French navy, which they refused. **1632** LITHGOW *Trav.* x. 431 To pledge or present his Maiesties health.

6. a. *refl.* (from 4, 5) Of a thing: To offer itself to view or perception; to come before one's sight or notice; to show itself, appear; to suggest itself, come into one's mind; to occur.

1590 SPENSER *F.Q.* III. vii. 19 She went in perill, of each noyse affeard, And of each shade that did it selfe present. **1603** SHAKS. *Meas. for M.* III. i. 204 A remedie presents it selfe. **1638** JUNIUS *Paint. Ancients* 72 Here also presenteth it selfe in the open fields a great and fearfull spectacle. **1746-7** HERVEY *Medit.*, *Tombs* (1818) 73 They look forward, and nothing presents itself but the righteous Judge; the dreadful tribunal. **1860** TYNDALL *Glac.* I. xxv. 191 The terrible possibility of his losing his hands presented itself to me.

b. *intr.* in same senses: cf. *to offer*. Now *rare.*

1697 J. SERGEANT *Solid Philos.* 370 Our First Principles.. govern all our Thoughts as occasion presents. **1759** GOLDSM. *Bee* No. 1 Whichever way I turned, nothing presented but prospects of terror. **1805** EUGENIA DI ACTON *Nuns of Desert* II. 148 The idea of ventriloquism never presented to either of the Gentlemen or the Lady. **1868** *Chambers' Encycl.* V. 252/2 When no other resource presents.

7. a. *trans.* To bring before the mind by means of a symbol, to symbolize; to represent, to be the representative of; to be a sign of, stand for, denote; to be a picture of. *arch.*

c **1400** *Destr. Troy* 2189 Thou shuld..herkon my wille,.. present myn astate; To lede all my legis with likyng in werre. **1578** WHETSTONE *Promos & Cass.* I. i, He absent, I present our Soueraigne styll. **1599** THYNNE *Animadv.* (1875) 36 Whiche venome they call by all names presentinge or signyfyinge poysone, as a toode, a dragon, a Basiliske, a serpente, arsenicke, and suche lyke. **1640** FULLER *Joseph's Coat* (1867) 55 'This is My body.' That is, that which signifies, signs, and presents My body. **1651** HOBBES *Leviath.* II. xviii. 88 The Right to Present the Person of them all, (that is to say, to be their Representative). **1813** SCOTT *Rokeby* I. xx. *note*, A remarkable figure, called Robin of Risingham, or Robin of Reedsdale. It presents a hunter, with his bow raised in one hand, and in the other what seems to be a hare.

b. To represent (a character) on the stage; to act (the character of); to personate, *arch.*

1588 SHAKS. *L.L.L.* v. i. 124 Sir, you shall present before her the Nine Worthies. *Ibid.* v. ii. 537 He presents Hector of Troy. **1598** —— *Merry W.* IV. vi. 20 To-night at Hernes-Oke..Must my sweet Nan present the Faerie Queene. **1824** SCOTT *St. Ronan's* xx. **1826** —— *Woodst.* vii, We saw Mills present Bomby at the Fortune playhouse. **1847** TENNYSON *Princ.* I. 193 Remembering how we three presented Maid Or Nymph, or Goddess,..In masque or pageant.

†**c.** To act (a play, or scene in a play). *Obs.* (? With mixture of sense 4.)

a **1610** HEALEY *Epictetus' Man.* (1636) 50 Now they sound the Trumpets, and presently they present the Tragedies. **1637** MILTON (*title*) A Maske presented at Ludlow Castle, 1634: on Michaelmasse night. **1637** EVELYN *Diary* (1819) I. 7 At Christmas the Gentlemen of Exeter College presented a Comedy to the University.

8. *Law.* To bring or lay before a court, magistrate, or person in authority, for consideration or trial; to make presentment of. **a.** To make a formal statement of; to submit (a fact, or a request, complaint, etc.). Also *absol.*

[**1290** *Rolls of Parlt.* I. 56/2 Presentatum fuit coram eis quod Abbas Sancti Benedicti obstruxit quandam ripariam barrera et catena.]

a **1400** *Pistill of Susan* 206 þus wiþ cauteles qwaynt, Preostes presented þis playnt. **1450** *Rolls of Parlt.* V. 212/2 The seid xii men dar noo-thing say ne present agayns the seid mysdoers. **1546** in *Eng. Gilds* (1870) 202 A house.. whych hath byn always employed, as hit was presented before the kynges Maiestyes Commyssioners there, to the mayntenaunce of one scolemaster ther. **1724** SWIFT *Drapier's Lett.* Wks. 1755 V. II. 104 A sharp censure.. against dissolving grand-juries..while matters are under their consideration and not presented. *Ibid.* 105 Scroggs dissolved the grand-jury of London for fear they should present; but ours in Dublin was dissolved, because they would not present. **1891** MAITLAND & BAILDON *Court Baron* (Selden Soc.) 100 The ale-tasters present that Agneta the widow brewed and sold contrary to the assize.

b. To bring (an offence, or something faulty) formally under the notice of the proper authority, for enquiry or action.

1429 *Rolls of Parlt.* IV. 359 And he yat..presenteth yat offence to ye Tresorer. **1477** *Ibid.* VI. 190/1 Then the same Serchours present such defautes before the Justices of peas. **1555** *Nottingham Rec.* (1889) IV. 108 We presente the common bulle, that he be put a-way, for he ys nothyng worth. **1705** HEARNE *Collect.* 2 Sept. (O.H.S.) I. 40 The Grand Juries..presented 'the Memorial of the Ch. of England'. **1881** *Times* 28 July 9/5 There is not a rural dean in England who would not present St. Margaret's churchyard to his archdeacon at the next Visitation.

c. To bring a formal charge or accusation against (a person), to charge formally; to report or bring up for trial.

1526 TINDALE *Mark* xiii. 11 But when they leade you and present you take no thought. **1588** W. SMITH *Brief Descr. Lond.* (Harl. MS. 6363, lf. 13), They present euery man, at whose dore the street is not well paved. **1603** *Constit. & Canons Eccl.* cxxi. **1701** PRIDEAUX *Direct. Ch.-wardens* 2 The Church-wardens are also to present all such as come not to Church. **1745** *De Foe's Eng. Tradesman* (1841) II. xxxix. 117 A tradesman wrangling in every bargain..should be presented as a public nuisance.

9. To place (a thing) in, or give to (it), a particular direction or position. **a.** To point (a weapon, esp. a fire-arm) at something; to hold (it) out in the position of taking aim, so as to be ready to fire immediately. Also *absol.* (esp. as word of command). (See also 4b.)

1579 *Reg. Privy Council Scot.* III. 227 The said George Hume presentand ane pistolet to him. **1678** SIR G. MACKENZIE *Crim. Laws Scot.* I. xxxi. §3 (1699) 158 William Hamilton pursued for wearing of Pistols, and presenting one to the Provost of Edinburgh. **1719** DE FOE *Crusoe* (1840) I. xvi. 280 He sees me cock and present. **1725** —— *Voy. round World* (1840) 155 He presented his piece, and shot them both flying. **1801** STRUTT *Sports & Past.* III. i. §14 According to Virgil, the Roman youth presented their lances towards their opponents in a menacing position. **1823** SCOTT *Peveril* vii, He ordered his own people to present their pistols and carabines. **1853** STOCQUELER *Milit. Encycl.*, *Present*, to level; to aim; to bring the firelock to an horizontal position, the butt resting against the right shoulder for the purpose of discharging its contents at a given object.

b. *Obstetrics.* Of the fœtus: To direct (a particular part) towards the *os uteri* during labour. Usually *intr.* for *refl.* said of the part so directed, or of the fœtus in relation to its position during labour. Also *Path.* of a tumour or abscess: To be directed, to project. Also more widely in *Med.*: of a condition: to be manifest, to occur. Of a patient: to present himself or appear for an initial medical examination. Cf. sense 2 b above, and quot. 1880 in sense 2 a.

1597 A. M. tr. *Guillemeau's Fr. Chirurg.* 36/1 Followinge the naturall Childebirth, the childe allways præsenteth first his heade. **1722** QUINCY *Lex. Physico-Med.* 163/1 When the Child presents in any other Posture. **1790** R. BLAND in *Med. Commun.* II. 415 The head of the child presented. **1897** *Allbutt's Syst. Med.* III. 377 A periœsophageal abscess frequently presents laterally. **1925** *Boston Med. & Surg. Jrnl.* 23 July 179/1 A rather marked purplish hemorrhagic area presented about the wound. **1960** *Lancet* 16 Jan. 138/2 A patient presenting with an exacerbation of bronchitis was initially assigned by the doctor to one of three categories. **1972** *Nature* 8 Sept. 102/2 These complications may present as hypersensitivity reactions.., but most often they take the form of gastric erosions. **1976** *Lancet* 20 Nov. 1107/2, 73 boys who presented to their general practitioners..with symptoms of urinary-tract infection..were referred to a three-year prospective study. **1977** *Proc. R. Soc. Med.* LXX. 262/1 It is not unusual for patients to present in an eye department with symptoms associated with either poor accommodation or poor convergence.

c. *trans.* To point, direct, or turn (a thing) to face something, or in a specified direction. Also *intr.*

1793 SMEATON *Edystone L.* §225 The first course, consisting of four stones,..which, as they all presented some part of their faces to the sea, were all of Moorstone. **1820** SHELLEY *Œdipus* I. 318 The swine..with bare tusks And wrinkled snouts presented to the foe. **1849** E. B. EASTWICK *Dry Leaves* 128 Occasion was now offering us her forelock: we strove in vain afterwards to catch the close-shorn backhead which she presented to us in her flight.

†**d.** *intr.* for *refl.* Of the wind (*Naut.*): To take a favourable direction; to begin to blow from the right quarter. *Obs.*

1687 *Lond. Gaz.* No. 2306/1 The Wind presenting fair, they were obliged to sail that Evening. **1698** FRYER *Acc. E. India & P.* 2 A rich and numerous Fleet of Merchants,.. designed for their several Places of Traffick, when the Wind should present. **1712** W. ROGERS *Voy.* (1718) 375 In case the wind should present sooner.

10. To bring, introduce, or put (a substance) into the presence of or into close contact with another.

1758 REID tr. *Macquer's Chym.* I. 21 If a pure Alkali be presented to a pure Acid, they rush together with violence. **1807** T. THOMSON *Chem.* (ed. 3) II. 392 When the vapour of alcohol is mixed with oxygen.., the mixture detonates when presented to a lighted taper.

II. To make an offering, present, or gift of; to offer, deliver, give.

11. a. *trans.* To bring or place (a thing) before or into the presence of a person, or to put (it) into his hands, for acceptance; to offer, proffer, deliver, hand over, bestow, give (usually in a formal or ceremonious manner).

With various connotations: as (*a*) to offer or give as a gift (cf. PRESENT *sb.*[2]); (*b*) to offer as an act of worship, as a sacrifice, etc.; = OFFER *v.* 1; (*c*) to offer or hand something in ministration, service, or courtesy; †(*d*) to deliver or hand a letter: formerly used in addressing a letter; see quots.; (*e*) to offer a book or literary work to readers, to put it in their power to buy or read it. In the earliest quots. the things presented are gifts, but it is doubtful whether this was implied in the verb: there is no implication of a gift in F. *présenter* or *présentation*.

(*a*) *c* **1325** *Chron. Eng.* (Ritson) 625 He brohte a riche present,..he presentede him also Other thinges fele mo. **13..** *K. Alis.* 686 (Bodl. MS.) His man him brouȝth by a cheyne A grisely beest, a hugged colte..He presented it to þe kynge. *a* **1400–50** *Alexander* 5138 ȝit sall I send ȝow..a sertan of giftis,..I presand ȝow, of panters full of proud mascles, Foure hundreth fellis. *c* **1430** LYDG. *Min. Poems* (Percy Soc.) 7 Three gostly giftes..Unto the kyng anone they did present. **1508** DUNBAR *Goldyn Targe* 87 Thare saw I Nature present hir a gounn Rich to behald..Off ewiry hew. **1585** T. WASHINGTON tr. *Nicholay's Voy.* I. xv. 15 b, [They] presented vnto him a mulet. **1665** BOYLE *Occas. Refl., Occas. Medit.* IV. iv, The best Trees present us their Blossoms, before they give us their Fruit. **1794** MRS. A. M. BENNETT *Ellen* I. 148 To present Miss Meredith in his name, a very elegant little watch. **1859** TENNYSON *Lancelot & Elaine* 70 With purpose to present them [the diamonds] to the Queen.

(*b*) **1548–9** (Mar.) *Bk. Com. Prayer, Communion*, Here wee offre and present unto thee (O Lorde) oure selfe, oure soules, and bodies, to be a reasonable, holy, and liuely sacrifice unto thee. **1611** BIBLE *Rom.* xii. 1, I beseech you therefore brethren,..that ye present your bodies a liuing sacrifice, holy, acceptable vnto God, which is your reasonable seruice. **1901** BP. GORE *Body of Christ* iii. §3 (1907) 198 The earlier practice..was to present the earthly prayers and sacrifices at the heavenly altar. **1907** *Ibid.* 310 *note*, The Fathers in general teach..that our Lord..is now acting as our great high-priest in heaven;..presenting His sacrifice on our behalf, or presenting our sacrifices for us.

(*c*) *a* **1533** LD. BERNERS *Huon* xlv. 150, I present you this cuppe, that ye shulde drynke therof. **1601** SHAKS. *Jul. C.* III. ii. 101, I thrice presented him a Kingly Crowne, Which he did thrice refuse. **1712–14** POPE *Rape Lock* III. 130 So Ladies in Romance assist their Knight, Present the spear, and arm him for the fight. **1777** W. DALRYMPLE *Trav. Sp. & Port.* xliii, Another nobleman..to hand him his wine and water, which he tastes and presents on his knee.

(*d*) **1536** in M. A. E. Green *Lett. R. & Illust. Ladies* (1846) II. cviii. 266 To the right honourable and my singular good lord, the Lord Privy Seal, this be presented. **1635** N. BACON in *Priv. Corr. Lady J. Cornwallis* (1842) 274 To my deare and loving mother, the Lady Bacon, presente these. **1642** in Ellis *Orig. Lett.* Ser. II. IV. 2 To the hands of the Lady Marie, Princesse of Aurania, these present. **1720** in *Lett. Lit. Men* (Camden) 354 To the Hon[ble] the Lord Harley, present.

(*e*) **1647** CLARENDON *Hist. Reb.* I. §1 To present to the world..a full and clear Narration. **1662** in *Boyle's Spring of Air* Publisher to Rdr., These following answers to Franciscus Linus and Mr. Hobbs are presented in compensation of the delay. **1860** HOOK *Lives Abps.* (1869) I. i. 2 The work now presented to the reader. *Ibid.* v. 267 The document by which it was accomplished shall be presented to the reader.

b. With a person as obj.: To deliver up as a prisoner.

c **1360** *E.E. Allit. P.* B. 1217 Hise gentyle..presented wern as presoneres to the prynce rychest. **1375** BARBOUR *Bruce* xv. 301 Bot weill soyne eftir he wes tane, And presentit wes to the kyng. *c* **1820** LINGARD *Hist. Eng.* (1855) IV. ii. 93/1 They [Queen Margaret and ladies] were.. discovered, and presented as prisoners to the King [Edw. IV].

c. To deliver, convey, give (something non-material, esp. a message, greeting, or the like); to offer (compliments, regards, etc.); †to offer or render (service or assistance).

13.. *Coer de L.* 2179 The messengers told al the dishonour, That them did the emperour;..And the steward's presenting His behest, and his helping. *c* **1385** CHAUCER *L.G.W.* 1297 (*Dido*) And ek mercurye his massage hath presentid. **1398** TREVISA *Barth. De P.R.* III. xvi. (1495) d iv/1 What he [the wyt] take of that he felyth, he presentyth to thynwytt. **1604** E. G[RIMSTONE] *D'Acosta's Hist. Indies* v. xxix. 422 This Service presented, the old man returned. **1611** SHAKS. *Wint. T.* II. i. 17 We shall Present our seruices to a fine new Prince One of these dayes. **1638** R. BAKER tr. *Balzac's Lett.* (vol. II) 19 To present you my complements. **1656** B. HARRIS *Parival's Iron Age* (1659) 43 That..the Hollanders..had presented all kind of help to the Venetians. *Mod.* Mr. A. presents his compliments to Mr. B., and regrets to say [etc.].

d. To deliver formally to the proper quarter (a document, as a written address, petition, order, bill, account, etc.) for acceptance, or to be dealt with according to its tenor. Also *fig.*

1509 HAWES *Past. Pleas.* xxxi. (Percy Soc.) 151 In our court there is a byll presented By Graund Amour. *c* **1655** MILTON *Sonn., On his Blindness* 5 My Soul more bent To serve therewith my Maker, and present My true account. **1742** POPE *Dunc.* IV. 136 Now crowds on crowds around the Goddess press, Each eager to present their first Address. **1771** GOLDSM. *Hist. Eng.* IV. 181 Both houses presented her warm addresses. **1819** SHELLEY *Cenci* II. ii. 59 But you, Orsino, Have the petition: wherefore not present it? **1863** H. COX *Instit.* I. ix. 165 After a bill is prepared and presented, the question is put that it be read a first time. **1900** *Westm. Gaz.* 30 Jan. 9/3 'Present again',..shows that the banker has reason to believe that the cheque will be met.

e. Of things: To offer, furnish, afford, supply.

1604 E. G[RIMSTONE] *D'Acosta's Hist. Indies* III. xxv. 197 Some [fountains] are quite dried vp, according to the force and vigour they have, and the matter that is presented. *a* **1614** DONNE *Βιαθανατος* (1644) 191 If a man when an urgent occasion is presented, expose himselfe to a certaine and assured death. **1817** JAS. MILL *Brit. India* II. IV. iv. 118 An opportunity which good fortune seemed to present. **1863** LYELL *Antiq. Man* ii. 19 [Their] thatched roofs and wooden walls could present but a poor defence.

†**12.** To give, make presentation of (a benefice) *to* a clergyman. *Obs.* (Cf. 3.)

c **1390** *York Manual* (Surtees) 120 All those that maliciously distourbes or lettis the right presentacion of a chirche, the whiche the very patron sholde present. *c* **1425** *MS. Cott. Claud.* A. 2 lf. 124 Alle þoo þat lettuth þe rytheful patron to present his chyrche þat he hath ryte to. **1579** *Reg. Privy Council Scot.* III. 177 Lyke as..all benefices hes bene presentit and collationat sen the begynning of his Hienes regnne. **1796** MRS. M. ROBINSON *Angelina* III. 33, I had, this morning, the happiness of presenting him a living in Herefordshire, (of three hundred pounds annually).

13. To make a presentation or gift to; to give a present or presents to; to bestow something upon; to endow.

[The resultant sense here is as in 11, but the person, who is the dative object in 11, is here the direct object, the thing presented being either introduced by *with*, or (in b) unexpressed. This construction appears to have been of Eng. development, there being nothing similar in OF. or med.L. It is notable that it is represented as early as sense 11.]

a. ***to present*** a person ***with*** a thing = *to present* a thing *to* a person (sense 11). Formerly in the full extent of sense 11; now always implying bestowal of something as a gift to be kept (11 (*a*)). Also *fig.* to furnish or supply *with* something.

a **1300** *Cursor M.* 12318 Iesus..bar it ham als in a ball, And present þan his moder wit-all. *a* **1310** in Wright *Lyric P.* xxxiv. 96 When the kynges come wery, to presente hyre sone With myrre, gold, ant encenz. **13..** *Guy Warw.* (A.) 1039 This present ȝe schullen vnderfong,..And present þer-wiþ..Rohaut, mi kinde lord. *c* **1400** MAUNDEV. (Roxb.) xxv. 116 Efter þaim commez grete barounes and presandez him with sum iowell. *c* **1500** *Melusine* 304 He was.. receyued with grete joye, & presented with gret ryches. **1596** SHAKS. *Tam. Shr.* II. i. 55, I do present you with a man of mine Cunning in Musicke, and the Mathematickes, To instruct her fully in those sciences. **1660** BARROW *Euclid* II. prop. i. Schol., You must take all the Rectangles of the parts, and they will present you with the Rectangle of the wholes. **1676** HALE *Contempl.* I. 65 The knowledge of Christ Jesus presents me with a continual Object of a higher value. **1787** JEFFERSON *Writ.* (1859) II. 103 To present the public with this acceptable present. **1803** J. MORSE in *M. Cutler's Life*, etc. (1888) II. 130 Yesterday week Mrs. Morse presented me with a fine daughter. **1831** SOUTHEY *Lett.* (1856) IV. 247 Mrs. Bray..has desired to present you with a copy of Mary Colling's poem.

†**b.** with personal obj. only; rarely *absol.*

c **1330** R. BRUNNE *Chron. Wace* (Rolls) 3219 Þou scholdest vs presente & gyue, And helpe vs alle in pes to lyue; Bot now þou comest to reue vs our socour. *c* **1400** MAUNDEV. (1839) xxii. 237 Whan þat all men han þus presented the Emperour. **1594** T. BEDINGFIELD tr. *Machiavelli's Florentine Hist.* (1595) 209 [He] was by the King so bountifully presented, and louingly vsed. *a* **1648** LD. HERBERT *Hen. VIII* (1683) 210 Francis not only richly presented him, but conducted him through the Town. **1676** SOUTH *Serm.* (1823) I. 240 In these days men present just as they soil their ground, not that they love the dirt, but that they expect a crop. **1691** tr. *Emilianne's Observ. Journ. Naples* 105 They bestow them [benefices] upon such Seculars as Present them highest. **1712** ARBUTHNOT *John Bull* II. iv, Have I not presented you nobly? Have I not clad your whole family?

presentable (prɪˈzɛntəb(ə)l), *a.* [f. PRESENT *v.* + -ABLE: cf. F. *présentable*.]

1. That can or may be presented; capable of, or suitable for, presentation (to a person, to the mind, as a gift, etc.).

a **1626** A. LAKE *Medit.* (1629) aij b, Faultring words, wandring thoughts, are neither of them presentable to thee. **1756** BURKE *Subl. & B.* v. vii, Here are again two ideas not presentable but by language. **1854** FARADAY *Exp. Res.* lv. 468 Under that form it is easily presentable to the mind. **1868** E. EDWARDS *Ralegh* I. xv. 280 These possibilities of a presentable claim.

2. *Law.* That may or should be presented, or formally brought up or charged, as an offence, an offender, etc.; liable to presentment.

1540 *Act 32 Hen. VIII*, c. 43 Things enquirable presentable or determinable before iusticers of peas. *a* **1701** in Prideaux *Direct. Ch.-wardens* (1701) 11 They will.. present such persons and things as are presentable by the Ecclesiastical Laws. **1739** *N. Bacon's Disc. Govt. Eng.* I. lxvi. 145 *note*, This was originally presentable and punishable in the Leet. **1863** KEBLE *Life Bp. T. Wilson* I. x. 327 It [drunkenness] should be especially enumerated among the presentable offences.

3. *Eccl.* **a.** Of a benefice: To which a clergyman may be presented: = PRESENTATIVE 1. **b.** Of a clergyman: Capable of being presented to a benefice (*rare*$^{-0}$).

1636 PRYNNE *Unbish. Tim.* (1661) 130 Were all Appropriations, and impropriations..made presentable. **1686** PLOT *Staffordsh.* 297 To found such a Church or Chappel, and to ordain that it shall be a donative and not presentable. **1726** AYLIFFE *Parergon* 90 No more..than Incumbents of Churches Presentable can by their sole Act grant the Incumbencies to others. **1882** OGILVIE (Annandale), *Presentable*..3. *Eccles.* (*a*) Capable of being presented to a church living; as, a presentable clerk. [So in later Dicts.]

4. Suitable, by attire or appearance, to be presented or introduced into society or company; in proper trim; of decent appearance, fit to be seen. (Properly of persons; often extended to things.) The usual current sense. Also *fig.*

1800 M. EDGEWORTH *Parent's Assistant* (ed. 3) VI. 147 Do send my *ooman* to me to make me *presentable*. **1801** —— *Belinda* I. iv. 132 Excuse me for showing you the simple truth; well dressed falsehood is a personage much more *presentable*. **1827** SCOTT *Jrnl.* 29 Aug., I am glad..that his friends are so presentable. **1835** WILLIS *Pencillings* II. xlii. 34 A wash in the clean water made him once more a presentable person. **1848** THACKERAY *Van. Fair* xiv, Is he a presentable sort of a person? **1858** HAWTHORNE *Fr. & It. Note-Bks.* I. 170 The pictures being in a more presentable condition than usual. **1887** R. N. CAREY *Uncle Max* v, She ..was quite a presentable young lady. **1898** MRS. CRAWFORD in *Daily News* 12 Dec., This table looks very fine set out for an official dinner, but only the ends are of mahogany and have presentable legs. **1907** J. M. SYNGE *Lett. to Molly* (1971) 172, I will show it to you tomorrow if it is presentable enough. **1925** C. CONNOLLY *Let.* 23 Apr. in *Romantic Friendship* (1975) 72 He [*sc.* Maurice Bowra] is extremely presentable in any society. **1965** F. RAPHAEL *Darling* xix. 87 It was enough to be socially presentable. **1974** *Times* 19 Oct. 6/7 Bowra remarked that he had had his hair cut—'makes one more presentable'. The word 'presentable'..was a very important epithet in the Bowra system of social terminology... Those who had 'unpresentable' pinned on them were remorselessly barred. **1979** A. MORICE *Murder in Outline* ii. 12 A group of more presentable-looking seniors granted the privilege of handing round the apéritifs.

Hence **presentaˈbility**, the quality of being presentable; (*a*) capability of presentation; (*b*) state of being fit to be seen; **preˈsentably** *adv.*, in a presentable manner, so as to have a decent appearance.

1865 MASSON *Rec. Brit. Philos.* 297 The phænomenal presentablility within it..of other and non-native sentiencies, angelic or demonic. **1888** J. MARTINEAU *Stud. Relig.* I. I. iv. 124 We adopt the test of objective presentability (*Anschauung*). **1888** *Pop. Sci. Monthly* Aug. 447 Old boots, which had long passed the season of presentability. **1892** A. E. LEE *Hist. Columbus* (Ohio) I. 252 The Square was enclosed, for the first time presentably, with a fence of cedar posts and white painted palings.

presental (prɪˈzɛntəl). *rare.* [f. as prec. + -AL[1] 5, after *bestowal*, etc.] = PRESENTATION.

1869 *Chicago Advance* 14 Jan. (Cent.), As illustrations of the author's presental of different sides of a subject, we give two extracts.

†**presen'taneous**, *a. Obs.* [f. L. *præsentāneus* operating quickly (Plin.) (f. *præsent-em* PRESENT *a.* + suffix *-āne-us*) + -OUS.] **a.** Acting immediately or speedily: = PRESENT *a.* 9 b. **b.** = PRESENT *a.* 1.

1656 BLOUNT *Glossgr.*, *Presentaneous*, present, ready, speedy, forceable, effectual. **1665** G. HARVEY *Advice agst. Plague* 10 Some [plagues] partaking of such a pernicious degree of malignity, that in the manner of a most presentaneous poyson, they enecate in two or three hours. **1668** HOWE *Bless. Righteous* (1821) 63 But our relation to eternity..will render the same invariable appearance of glory always presentaneous.

†'**presentary**, *a. Obs.* Also 7 præ-. [ad. L. *præsentāri-us* that is at hand, ready, quick, f. *præsent-em*: see PRESENT *a.* and -ARY[1].] = PRESENT *a.* 6, 8.

c **1374** CHAUCER *Boeth.* v. pr. vi. 134 (Camb. MS.) For this ilke infynyt moeuynge of temporel thinges folweth this presentarye estat of lyf vnmoeuable. **1621** T. BEDFORD *Sin unto Death* 67 He alloweth a præsentary lapse. **1657** HAWKE *Killing is M.* 15 These..were the presentary and explicite Testimonies of the peoples general approbations, and congratulations.

presentation (prɛzən'teɪʃən). [ME. a. OF. *presentacion* (13th c. in Littré, mod.F. *présentation*), or ad. late L. *præsentātiōn-em*, n. of action f. *præsentāre* to PRESENT.] The action of presenting, in various senses; *rarely*, something presented.

I. 1. The action of presenting or introducing a person: see PRESENT *v.* 1. **a.** The formal bringing or presenting of a person before God, as a religious act: see PRESENT *v.* 1 b.

Specifically, the ***Presentation of Christ in the Temple***, as recorded in Luke ii. 22–39, and ***Presentation of the Virgin Mary***, as a child, narrated in the Apocryphal Gospels. Also applied to the festivals in which these incidents are celebrated by various branches of the Christian Church, the former on Feb. 2 (see CANDLEMAS, PURIFICATION), the latter, by the Greek and Roman Churches, on Nov. 21. Also, in *Art*, a representation of either of these incidents. ***Order of the Presentation of the Virgin Mary***: a Roman Catholic order of nuns, founded in 1777 in Ireland, and mainly devoted to the education of poor girls.

c **1400** MAUNDEV. (1839) xxii. 232 The firste feste is of his [the grete Chane's] byrthe, þat oþer is of his presentacioun in here temple..where þei maken a manere of circumcisioun. *c* **1450** *Cov. Myst.* ix. (Shaks. Soc.) 89 Lo! sofreynes here ye have seyn, In the temple of oure ladyes presentacion. **14..** in *Tundale's Vis.* (1843) 131 He [Simeon] hath the way nom To the temple with hye devocion To se of Cryst the presentacion. **1662** *Bk. Com. Prayer*, The Presentation of Christ in the Temple, commonly called, The Purification of Saint Mary the Virgin. **1859** MRS. JAMESON *Early Ital. Painters* 250 (*Raphael*) The subjects..were all from the life of Christ, and were as follows:—..4. The Presentation in the Temple. *Ibid.* 297 (*Titian*) The first of his historical compositions..is the Presentation of the Virgin in the Temple. **1879** *Encycl. Brit.* IX. 34/1 (*Farinato*) In the Berlin gallery [is] a Presentation in the Temple. **1880** F. MEYRICK in *Dict. Chr. Antiq.* II. 1140/1 (*Festivals of Mary*) The Greek and Latin churches agree in celebrating the Assumption and the Presentation. *Ibid.* 1144/1 The Festival of the Presentation of St. Mary..did not pass into the West till 1375... Its purpose is to commemorate the presentation of St. Mary as narrated in the Gnostic legend which is embodied in the Protevangelion and the Gospel of the Birth of Mary. **1885** *Cath. Dict.* 691/1 The story of Mary's presentation in the temple when three years old and her sojourn there till her marriage first appears in Apocryphal Gospels. *Ibid.* 691/2 Order of the Presentation of the Blessed Virgin Mary... In 1874 it possessed seventy-three houses, with 1,140 nuns and more than 20,000 pupils.

b. The formal or ceremonious introduction of a person to another, esp. to a superior; *spec.* the presenting of a person at court.

1788 LD. AUCKLAND *Corr.* (1861) II. 62 The presentations of our countrymen are very troublesome when they happen here. **1796** JANE AUSTEN *Pride & Prej.* v, His presentation at St. James's had made him courteous. **1863** MARY HOWITT *F. Bremer's Greece* I. i. 16, I was promised an early presentation to Her Majesty. **1881** LADY HERBERT *Edith* 150 After May there would be no drawing-rooms or presentations.

c. The presenting of a candidate for examination, for admission to a degree, etc.

1683 WOOD *Life* (O.H.S.) III. 57 The duke, after he was presented, took his place on the right of the vicechancellor; the rest, after presentation, on the left. **1864** *Lond. Univ. Cal.* 59 A Certificate..shall be delivered at the Public Presentation for Degrees to each Candidate who has passed. **1883** *Camb. Univ. Reporter* 22 May 732 The Presentation for Doctor's Degrees..conferred *honoris causa*..shall take precedence of all others. **1906** J. WELLS *Oxf. Degree Cerem.* 11 The second part of the ceremony is the presentation of the candidates to the Vice Chancellor and Proctors.

2. *Eccl.* The action, or the right, of presenting a clergyman to a benefice, or to the bishop for institution: see PRESENT *v.* 3.

[**1278** *Rolls of Parlt.* I. 5/1 Diu ante presentacionem factam Radulpho per regem fuit institutus.]

c **1380** WYCLIF *Wks.* (1880) 248 þouȝ pore prestis myȝtten frely geten presentacion of lordis to haue benefices wiþ cure of soulis. **1467–8** *Rolls of Parlt.* V. 599/2 The next Presentation, power and auctorite of presentyng of a..persone to the Parissh Chirche. **1568** GRAFTON *Chron.* II. 55 Concerning the nomination and presentation into benefices, if any controuersie arise betweene the layetie and Clergie: or betweene one spirituall man with another [etc.]. **1607** COWELL *Interpr.*, *Presentation*..is vsed properly for the act of a patron offering his Clerke to the Bishop, to be instituted in a benefice of his gift. **1622** CALLIS *Stat. Sewers* (1647) 107 One who hath the presentation or nomination to a Church as Patron. **1766** [see PRESENTATIVE *a.* 1]. **1818** CRUISE *Digest* (ed. 2) III. 14 A presentation in writing is a kind of letter, not a deed, from the patron to the bishop.., requesting him to admit the person presented to the church. **1852** HOOK *Ch. Dict.* (1871) 607 Presentation..differs from nomination, inasmuch as nomination signifies offering a clerk to the patron in order that he may be presented to the bishop. **1880** FOWLER *Locke* ii. 24 Locke..was made Secretary of Presentations—that is, of the Chancellor's church patronage.

3. *Law.* †**a.** = PRESENTMENT 2. *Obs.* **b.** ***bond of presentation*** (Sc. Law): see quot. 1861.

[**1278** *Rolls of Parlt.* I. 13/1 Certificet de presentacione facta in Itinere suo.]

1604 in *Eng. Gilds* (1870) 436 No presentation of blood drawing or beareing wepons of a childe, shall be presented before hee be twelve years of age. **1610** HOLLAND *Camden's Brit.* (1637) 181 The Clerke of Presentations. *a* **1765** ERSKINE *Inst. Law Scot.* (1773) III. iii. §70 The granter of a bond of presentation who has failed to present the debtor's person in the terms of his obligation. **1861** W. BELL *Dict. Law Scot.*, *Bond of Presentation* is an obligation granted for behoof of a person in custody on a legal warrant, in order to obtain his temporary liberation. The obligant in such a bond becomes bound to present the person so liberated, to the officer holding the warrant, at a particular day and place.

II. 4. a. The action of offering for acceptance, esp. formally or ceremoniously; handing over, delivery; bestowal, gift, offering.

1433 LYDG. *St. Fremund* 814 To the Bysshop off the diocyse Made off his bullis presentacioun. *c* **1550** *Cov. Corp. Chr. Plays* 26 Here make owre presentacion Vnto this kyngis son clensid soo cleyne And to his moder for ovre saluacion. **1597** HOOKER *Eccl. Pol.* v. xlviii. §11 Prayers..are..sometime a presentation of mere desires, as a means of procuring desired effects at the hands of God. **1700** C. NESSE *Antid. Armin.* (1827) 81 The two parts of his priestly office, oblation and presentation, cannot be separated. **1866** CRUMP *Banking* iv. 93 It would seem sufficient that the post of the second day should be the medium of presentation [of a cheque at a bank]. **1883** *Act 46 & 47 Vict.* c. 52 §10 The Court may..after the presentation of a bankruptcy petition stay any action..against..the debtor.

b. Something offered for acceptance; a present, gift, donation; in quot. 1714, an address presented (with allusion to sense 3 a). ? *Obs.*

1619 *Time's Storehouse* II. iv. 154/2 The height or top of an oliue tree..wherof the Doue broght a presentation to the good old man, as a symbol of grace. **1663** GERBIER *Counsel* aiij, This is a kinde of Attome, in comparison of other Presentations. **1714** STEELE *Lover* No. 3 (1715) 16 A Sett of Persons whom they call in their Presentation the Lovers Vagabond.

III. 5. a. The action of presenting to sight or view, or that by which something is so presented; theatrical, pictorial, or symbolic representation; a display, show, exhibition. Also, a display or show (e.g. of slides) used esp. in advertising.

1600 SHAKS. *A.Y.L.* v. iv. 112 He vses his folly like a stalking-horse, and vnder the presentation of that he shoots his wit. **1672** DRYDEN *Ess.*, *Heroic Plays* (ed. Ker) I. 150 These warlike instruments, and even their presentations of fighting on the stage, are no more than necessary to produce the effects of an heroic play. **1858** HAWTHORNE *Fr. & It. Note-Bks.* II. 19 To aim at any other presentation of female beauty. **1898** R. F. HORTON *Commandm. Jesus* v. 78 The plain presentation of it [the Passion] by the peasants of Ober-Ammergau has an overwhelming effect even on careless spectators. **1972** G. BROMLEY *In Absence of Body* i. 13 'We've got the OOO-Frooty presentation tomorrow.'..The presentation was to show the client proposals for a new [advertising] campaign. **1976** *National Observer* (U.S.) 12 June 3/4 Picnic lunches, public speeches, and presentations about Proposition 15 were to be the order of the day. **1976** J. H. SPENCER *Surgenor Campaign* i. 16 Cusack taking him through a slide presentation on their international capability: twenty-seven offices in fourteen countries.

b. An image, likeness, semblance (= PRESENTMENT 5 b); a representation, a symbol.

1594 SHAKS. *Rich. III*, IV. iv. 84, I call'd thee then, poore Shadow, painted Queen, The presentation of but what I was. **1866** J. H. NEWMAN *Gerontius* iii. 32 Thou livest in a world of signs and types, The presentations of most holy truths.

c. In Broadcasting, the action or an instance of presenting a programme; also *ellipt.* for *presentation department* (see sense 10 below).

1941 *B.B.C. Gloss. Broadcasting Terms* 26 *Programme presentation.* (1) Action of presenting a sequence of programmes by means of a framework of microphone announcements... (2) Framework of microphone announcements in a sequence of programmes, its purpose being to supply continuity, to link programmes together, and to attract listeners. **1963** [see NEWSPEAK]. **1968** *Listener* 22 Aug. 252/1 In bad periods of radio..language is usually what they [*sc.* programmes] are about, or, to call it by its new, pompous name, Presentation. **1968** *Radio Times* 28 Nov. 23/3 Television presentation by Nick Hunter. **1974** *Some Technical Terms & Slang* (Granada Television), *Presentation*, the department within Granada responsible for shape and coordination of the daily programme schedule. **1978** *Listener* 7 Dec. 762/4 The business of neat, informative presentation.

6. a. The action of presenting to notice or mental view; a setting forth, a statement.

1597 HOOKER *Eccl. Pol.* v. lxvii. §4 This new presentation of Christ not before their eyes but within their soules. **1674** *Essex Papers* (Camden) I. 283, I have not further to trouble yr Excellcy then wt the presentation of my reall desires to serve you. **1829** I. TAYLOR *Enthus.* x. 302 In the Bible, there are no scientific presentations of the body of divinity. **1907** *Hibbert Jrnl.* July 927 His presentations of the orthodox case are sometimes the merest travesties of what educated opponents really hold.

b. The action of representing to the mind or thought; representation or suggestion to the mind. (Cf. PRESENTIVE.)

1871 EARLE *Philol. Eng. Tongue* (1873) §229 The letter A was once a picture, and it represented a bull's head... It began in presentation and has reached a state of symbolism.

7. *Metaph.* and *Psychol.* (tr. Ger. *Vorstellung.*) All the modification of consciousness directly involved in the knowing or being aware of an object in a single moment of thought. By some authors restricted to perceptual cognition, in order to mark the distinction between it and ideational cognition or *representation*.

1842 ABP. THOMSON *Laws Th.* §46 (1860) 71 The impression which any object makes upon the mind may be called a Presentation. **1864** BOWEN *Logic* 1 Such acts are called Intuitions or Presentations; the former is the more generally received appellation. **1871** FARRAR *Witn. Hist.* ii. 51 *note*, Strauss..shewed how essential were the differences between dogma and speculation, between the presentation and the notion. **1874** LEWES in *Contemp. Rev.* Oct. 691 The specific facts of feeling, perception, desire, will, &c., in so far as they are *known*, may on the whole be called Presentation (*Vorstellung*). **1884** SULLY *Outl. Psychology* vi. 152 The percept involves the immediate assurance of the presence of the whole object. Hence psychologists commonly speak of percepts in their totality as presentations. **1886** J. WARD in *Encycl. Brit.* XX. 41/1 All that variety of mental facts which we speak of as sensations, perceptions, images, intuitions, concepts, notions, have two characteristics in common: (1) they admit of being more or less attended to, and (2) can be reproduced and associated together. It is here proposed to use the term *presentation* to connote such a mental fact, and as the best English equivalent for what Locke meant by idea, and what Kant and Herbart called a Vorstellung.

8. a. The action of placing, or condition of being placed, in a particular direction or position with respect to something else or to an observer; the mode in which a thing is presented or presents itself.

1833 HERSCHEL *Astron.* xi. 349 A presentation of the one planet to the other in conjunction, in a variety of situations, tends to produce compensation. **1866** —— *Fam. Lect. Sc.* 205 Among them occurs every variety..of oblique presentation from a plane passing..edgeways thro' the eye of the spectator to one perpendicular to the visual line. **1881** T. W. WEBB in *Nature* 10 Nov. 38/2 The Earl of Rosse..finds a narrow ray on either side, making..a singular resemblance to Saturn with a very thin presentation of the ring.

b. *Obstetr.* The presenting of a particular part of the fœtus towards the *os uteri* during labour: see PRESENT *v.* 9 b. Often with defining word indicating the part, as ***arm***, ***breech***, ***face***, ***foot***, ***head***, ***shoulder***, ***vertex***, etc.

1754–64 SMELLIE *Midwif.* I. 195 The presentation of the head was always deemed the most natural. **1842** STEPHENS *Bk. Farm* (1849) I. 512/1 The presentation [of lambs, etc.] is sometimes made with the hind-feet foremost. **1851** RAMSBOTHAM *Obstetr. Med.* (ed. 3) 121 Discriminating marks of a Head Presentation.

¶ **9.** Used for *presence* (app. for the sake of rime).

c **1485** *Digby Myst.* (1882) II. 180 Bounde to Ierusalem, with furyous vyolacion, Be-for cesar caypha, and annas presentacion.

IV. 10. *attrib.* in sense 4, as ***presentation binding***, ***bowl***, ***box***, ***clock***, ***copy***, ***cup***, ***drawing***, ***pack***, ***plate***, ***silver***, ***watch***, etc.; in sense 1 b, as ***presentation dress***, ***frock***, ***gown***; (in sense 5 c) ***presentation assistant***, ***studio***, ***suite***; **presentation day**, a day on which a ceremonial presentation is made, e.g. a degree-day in a university: see quots.; **presentation department** (see quot. 1978); **presentation value**, value as a fact presented to mental view or knowledge.

1941 *B.B.C. Gloss. Broadcasting Terms* 24 **Presentation Assistant* (*abbrev.* P.A.), Broadcasting official immediately responsible for the smooth running of a sequence of programmes, and hence for co-ordinating the activities of programme producers, announcers, and engineers directed to that end. **1939–40** *Army & Navy Stores Catal.* 841 Books in *presentation bindings. **1952** J. CARTER *ABC for Bk. Collectors* 139 *Presentation binding*, used variously for *gift binding* or *author's binding*. **1907** *Yesterday's Shopping* (1969) p. li/2 *Presentation bowls. **1973** L. COOPER *Tea on Sunday* ii. 30 Silver, some of it..presentation cups and bowls, shining behind shining glass doors. **1908** *Sears, Roebuck Catal.* 333/2 Alaska metal tableware set in a fancy *presentation box. **1976** *Sunday Mail* (Glasgow) 28 Nov. 31/4 The two bigger boxes have ribbons and bows on them. We know there is a demand for the presentation box. That's why they are dearer. **1935** D. L. SAYERS *Gaudy Night* i. 17 A *Presentation Clock was to be unveiled. **1803** SCOTT *Lett.* (1932) I. 182 Be so good as to disperse the following *presentation copies with 'From the Editor', on each. **1819** LADY MORGAN *Autobiog.* (1859) 337 The others [books] were all presentation copies. **1837** LOCKHART *Scott* lxii. (1839) VII. 406 There are few living authors of whose works presentation copies are not to be found here. **1938** [see CANCELLANDUM]. **1978** A. WAUGH *Best Wine Last* xxiv. 304 There were a great many presentation copies, signed by brother and sister writers. **1973** *Presentation cup [see *presentation bowl*]. **1843** E. P. BELDEN *Sk. Yale Coll.* 131 A short time previous to '*Presentation Day'—the day when the Senior class leaves the Institution. [*Note*] At the middle of the third term..certificates are presented by the Faculty to the Corporation recommending those who have passed a satisfactory examination as worthy of degree. This gave rise to the term 'Presentation Day'. **1866** *Newspr.*, Presentation

Day at the University of London. **1978** *A–Z of BBC* (ed. 2) 163/1 *Presentation Department is editorially responsible for supervising the transmission operation; for promoting programmes on the screen; for network identification..; for programme announcements and public service information, ..; and for running the Television Duty Office. **1975** *Country Life* 20 Feb. 428 Among the drawings there are those, aptly christened by Johannes Wilde '*presentation drawings'. **1896** *Girl's Own Paper* 12 Dec. 161/1, I was borne off to the Court Dressmaker to choose the ..*presentation dresses. **1938** N. MARSH *Death in White Tie* viii. 83 He looked at the two photographs... One was of the Lady Mildred Potter in the presentation dress of her girlhood. **1895** *Westm. Gaz.* 19 Feb. 5/2 *Presentation gown of white duchesse satin. **1976** *Shooting Times & Country Mag.* 9–15 Dec. 11/1 (Advt.), Supplied in *presentation pack with supply of BB shot. **1867** C. L. EASTLAKE in *Queen* 15 June 470/1 If the pieces of '*presentation plate'.. were only entrusted to art-workmen of sound education, we might hope for something better than the everlasting palm trees, camels and equestrian groups. **1967** N. FREELING *Strike Out* 40 Here on shelves was *presentation silver.. for Rob was the best bicycle champion Holland had had. **1960** *B.B.C. Handbk.* 40 It (*sc.* the Television Centre) will provide the service with.. seven major production and two *presentation studios. **1974** *B.B.C. Handbk. 1975* 264/2 The Television Centre houses separate *presentation suites incorporating network control rooms, and studios for announcements and weather forecasts. **1868** STEPHENS *Runic Mon.* I. 296 It must have been a *presentation-sword. **1889** LIDDON in *Pall Mall G.* 22 Apr. 1/2 The death, burial, and resurrection of Jesus had a mystical side and aspect over and above their *presentation value as events in the world's history. **1931** M. ALLINGHAM *Police at Funeral* iv. 51 *Presentation watch... The company gave him this watch.

Hence **presen'tationism**, the doctrine that in perception the mind has an immediate cognition of the object; **presen'tationist**, one who holds this doctrine, a believer in the immediate perception of sensible things (also *attrib.*).

a **1842** SIR W. HAMILTON in *Reid's Wks.* (1846) 820/1 His doctrine of perception is.. one of immediate cognition, under the form of real *presentationism. **1843** *Blackw. Mag.* LIV. 657 If the reader wants a name to characterise this system, he may call it the system of Absolute or Thorough-going presentationism. *a* **1842** SIR W. HAMILTON in *Reid's Wks.* (1846) 816/1 The *presentationists or Intuitionists constitute the object of which we are conscious in perception, into a sole, absolute, or total object; in other words, reduce perception to an act of immediate or intuitive cognition. **1871** FRASER *Life Berkeley* x. 390 He is virtually a representationist as well as a presentationist. **1907** *Athenæum* 6 Apr. 407/1 Let him consider the whole 'Presentationist' controversy.

presentational (prɪzɛn'teɪʃənəl) *a.* [f. PRESENTATION + -AL¹.] Of or pertaining to presentation (orig. in sense 7). Also *absol.*

1886 E. J. HAMILTON *Mental Science* xviii. 131 The whole doctrine is more comprehensive than that of presentational realism, and.. may be designated by the unrestricted term 'presentationalism'. **1907** *Athenæum* 18 May 610/3 The subjective self is.. an inference from certain presentational changes that cannot be ascribed to physical stimuli, and Ward's view is justified. **1928** *Daily Tel.* 19 July 18/3 The intelligent theatres of New York.. show an admirable sympathy both for good European drama and new forms of presentational art. **1929** A. N. WHITEHEAD *Process & Reality* II. iv. 170 Perception which merely, by means of a sensum, rescues from vagueness a contemporary spatial region, in respect to its spatial shape and its spatial perspective from the percipient, will be called 'perception in the mode of presentational immediacy'. **1942** S. K. LANGER *Philos. in New Key* iv. 97 The meanings given through language are successively understood, and gathered into a whole by the process called discourse; the meanings of all other symbolic elements that compose a larger, articulate symbol are understood only through the meaning of the whole... This kind of semantic may be called 'presentational symbolism', to characterize its essential distinction from discursive symbolism, or 'language' proper. **1958** C. H. WHITMAN *Homer & Heroic Tradition* vi. 107 It is by means of the image and the poetic symbol.. that language is made presentational. *Ibid.* 127 If metaphor flags and facts prevail, the presentational is lost, and the poem sinks to prose. **1959** W. A. CHRISTIAN *Interpr. Whitehead's Metaphysics* iii. 54 For occasions of a relatively high grade of complexity, a contemporary region may be given in presentational immediacy. That is, the region may be perceived as the locus of sensa, and as the subject to mathematical relations. **1962** *Listener* 3 May 765/1 A personal style, an effective or original rhetoric, a brilliant presentational technique are cheerfully accepted in lieu of any real human adequacy. **1975** *Nature* 23 Oct. 723/1 An author with the technical knowledge and presentational skill of John Maddox needs no introduction. **1980** *Times* 24 May 14/3 It all was done for 'presentational' reasons.. not merely to make the Americans feel good, but.. to show solidarity.

Hence **presen'tationalism, -alist** (see quots.).

1886 [see PRESENTATIONAL *a.*] **1895** *Funk's Standard Dict.*, *Presentationalism*, the doctrine that man has an immediate perception of all the elemental forms of entity, as space, time, substance, and power; natural realism, in an extended sense. *Ibid.*, Presentationalist.

presen'tationally, *adv.* [f. prec. + -LY².] In a presentational manner; by means of or as regards presentation.

1934 *Mind* XLIII. 390 We have a number of unconscious sensations as elements in wholes in which they do not figure presentationally, but only as ingredients. **1954** *Mind* LXIII. 196 How does this internal occupation of the visual field itself come to occupy that field presentationally? **1958** C. H. WHITMAN *Homer & Heroic Tradition* vi. 105 Yet when we speak of the 'direct appeal' of an image or symbol, we mean that it appeals as an image of painting or sculpture appeals to the mind, that is, presentationally. **1979** *Guardian* 30 June 8/4 Presentationally speaking, as they say in the public relations business.

presentative (prɪ'zɛntətɪv), *a.* [ad. med.L. type **præsentātīvus*: see PRESENT *v.* and -ATIVE. Cf. REPRESENTATIVE.]

1. *Eccl.* Of a benefice: To or for which a patron has the right of presentation: see quot. 1766. Also said of the advowson, the tithes, etc. connected with such a benefice. Opp. to APPROPRIATE, COLLATIVE, DONATIVE, IMPROPRIATE.

1559 in Strype *Ann. Ref.* (1709) I. App. viii. 22 Foundations of free-chappels.. to be donatyve and not presentatyve. **1612** W. TRAVERS *Supplic.* in *Hooker's Wks.* (1888) III. 555 The place of ministry whereunto I was called was not presentative. **1628** COKE *On Litt.* 300b, Parson Impersonee is the Rector that is in possession of the Church Parochiall, be it presentative, or impropriate. **1646** *Spelman's De non Temer. Eccl.* bj, The same remedy both for the presentative and impropriate Tithe. **1648** HEYLIN *Undeceiv. People* 30 The Churches will no longer be *presentative* at the choice of the Patron; but either made *Elective* at the will of the People, or else *Collated* by the Trustees of the severall Counties (succeeding.. in the power of Bishops). **1766** BLACKSTONE *Comm.* II. iii. 22 An advowson presentative is where the patron hath a right of presentation to the bishop or ordinary, and moreover to demand of him to institute his clerk, if he find him canonically qualified: and this is the most usual advowson. **1872** O. SHIPLEY *Gloss. Eccl. Terms* s.v. *Dean*,[This] deanery is not presentative, but donative.

†**2.** Of or pertaining to presentation or bestowal.

1594 *Mirr. Policy* (1599) 189 The manlike hand of the Poet Claudian that hath so well and eloquently set downe the presentatiue Epigram of the said gift.

†**3.** = REPRESENTATIVE *a.* 1, 2. *Obs.*

c **1430** [implied in PRESENTATIVELY]. **1642** *Lett. fr. Gentl. to Friend in Lond.* 4 If the Parliament without the King make the presentative body, the King is the reall head to that body of the kingdome. **1653** H. WHISTLER *Upshot Inf. Baptism* 22 Christ being God the Son, spake in the glory, the Majesty presentative of Christ. *Ibid.* 86 The Angell visionally, presentative Christ our Redeemer.

4. Having the function or power of presenting an idea or notion to the mind.

1855 BRIMLEY *Ess., Tennyson* 37 That phrase, 'a great water',.. is an instance of the intense presentative power of Mr. Tennyson's genius. **1885** STEVENSON in *Contemp. Rev.* Apr. 550 Those arts.. like architecture, music, and the dance, which are self-sufficient and merely presentative.

5. *Metaph.* and *Psychol.* Of, pertaining or relating to, or of the nature of presentation (sense 7); by some authors (e.g. Hamilton and Herbert Spencer) distinguished from *representative*, but now more usually employed as the wider term including this.

a **1842** SIR W. HAMILTON in *Reid's Wks.* (1846) 804 The distinction of Presentative, Intuitive or Immediate, and of Representative or Mediate cognition. *Ibid.* 805/1 An immediate cognition, in as much as the thing known is itself presented to observation, may be called a presentative; and in as much as the thing presented, is, as it were, viewed by the mind face to face, may be called an intuitive, cognition. A mediate cognition, in as much as the thing known is held up or mirrored to the mind in a vicarious representation, may be called a representative cognition... In a presentative or immediate cognition there is one sole object. *Ibid.* 823/1 If then he declare that his own opinion coincides with that of the vulgar, he will, consequently, declare himself a Presentative Realist. **1855** H. SPENCER *Princ. Psychol.* (1872) I. II. iv. 5 Sensations are sometimes called presentative feelings. **1871** FRASER *Life Berkeley* ii. 43 In his account of sense perception, he anticipates the spirit of the presentative psychology of Reid and Hamilton. *a* **1881** A. BARRATT *Phys. Metempiric* (1883) 176 This division of outer and inner seems to correspond with those between impressions and ideas, sensations and thoughts, and primary or presentative or vivid, and secondary or representative or faint states of consciousness.

Hence **pre'sentatively** *adv.* (in quot. *c* 1430, representatively, by representation).

c **1430** *Pilgr. Lyf Manhode* I. lxxxvii. (1869) 49 With inne this bred al the souereyn good is put,.. nouht ymaginatyfliche, nouht presentatyfliche, nouht vertualliche, .. but.. bodiliche and rialliche, presentliche and verreyliche. **1878** S. H. HODGSON *Philos. of Reflection* I. 172, I represent to myself what *I imagine* you to be feeling presentatively.

,present-'day, *a.* [PRESENT *a.* (*adv.*) 10.] Current, contemporary; now in existence or in use; prevalent; living at the present time.

1887 *Pall Mall G.* 23 Aug. 6/1 Replying that this was not a present-day practical question. **1902** in C. W. Cunnington *Eng. Women's Clothing* (1952) ii. 47 Present-day fashions require for the ideal figure an upright poise of the shoulders. **1925** I. A. RICHARDS *Princ. Lit. Crit.* 222 That Dante is neglected is due only indirectly to his present-day obscurity. **1926** D. L. SAYERS *Clouds of Witness* vi. 142 A present-day girl, who rushes about bareheaded in all weathers. **1930** *Times Educ. Suppl.* 31 May 245/3 Much of present-day British India never was under Mogul rule. **1934** *Amer. Speech* IX. 83/1 An invitation from Edward C. Ehrensperger to address the Present-Day English Section of the Modern Language Association of America. **1934** *Discovery* Nov. 309/1 There is a reversal back to negative phototropism, that is, they [*sc.* the termites] revert to the normal conditions of their present-day life. **1946** 'S. RUSSELL' *To Bed with Grand Music* v. 77 A pigskin bag at present-day prices. **1959** *Universities & Left Rev.* Spring 54/1 The passivity of the present-day working-class reader. **1967** E. SHORT *Embroidery & Fabric Collage* iii. 63 In present-day furnishing also there is a feeling for function as well as decoration. **1974** P. ERDMAN *Silver Bears* iii. 35 My family has an obligation not only to present-day Iran, but also to the Persia of the past. **1977** G. W. H. LAMPE *God as Spirit* ii. 51 Saul's sudden possession by the Spirit when he met a group of ecstatics coming down from a high place, preceded, like some of their present-day counterparts, by a musical group.

Hence **present-'dayness**, actuality, contemporaneity.

1963 *Times* 9 Jan. 11/3, 1960 doesn't view the eighteenth century as 1920 did—fashion and social economic state of society affect our attitude to the past, and it's the designer's job to bring out this present-dayness.

presented (prɪ'zɛntɪd), *ppl. a.* [f. PRESENT *v.* + -ED¹.] Brought or placed before one, introduced; offered, bestowed, directed, etc.: see the verb. In quot. 1631 *absol.* = next, 1.

1592 SHAKS. *Ven. & Ad.* 405 Learne of him.. To take aduantage on presented ioy. **1631** WEEVER *Anc. Fun. Mon.* 303 Knowing the presented, to bee a very vnlearned and vnsufficient man. **1732** POPE *Hor. Sat.* II. ii. 51 Avidien, or his Wife.. Sell their presented partridges, and fruits, And humbly live on rabbits and on roots. **1800** *Chron.* in *Asiat. Ann. Reg.* 26/1 His Excellency will enter at the St. George's gate, and be received with presented arms by his Majesty's 51st regiment. **1855** H. SPENCER *Princ. Psychol.* (1872) I. II. vi. 245 Presented feelings hinder the representation of other feelings.

pre'sentedness. *Philos.* [f. PRESENTED *ppl. a.* + -NESS.] (See quot. 1951.)

1925 C. D. BROAD *Mind & its Place* v. 255 The premise.. might be derived from an uncritical jump from 'presentedness' to 'presentness'. **1933** *Mind* XLII. 307 It is part of the notion of a specious present that a certain characteristic, which we will call 'presentedness', has a maximum value at a certain point in it, and tails off to nothing in two opposite directions within it, *viz.* towards the point where the perceived past merges into the remembered past, and towards the point where the anticipated future merges into the perceived future. **1951** *Mind* LX. 162 'Presentedness' seems to be Broad's name for the characteristic Hume called 'force and vivacity'. **1954** *Mind* LXIII. 33 Broad does not explain what he means by 'presentedness' beyond saying 'This is meant to denote a psychological characteristic.'

presentee¹ (prɛzən'tiː). [a. AF. *presentee* a presentee = F. *présenté*, pa. pple. of *présenter* to PRESENT: see -EE.]

1. A person presented.

a. *Eccl.* A clergyman presented (for institution) to a benefice: see PRESENT *v.* 3.

[**1351–2** *Rolls of Parlt.* II. 244/1 Vos Presentees sont a yceux Benefices ensi receuz.] **1498–9** *Plumpton Corr.* (Camden) 132, I have.. shewed to him as your mastership presented in after the deith of the last Incumbent, which presentee was in by the space of iiii or v dayes at the least. **1570–6** LAMBARDE *Peramb. Kent* (1826) 229 King John presented a Clarke to the Churche and commaunded by his writ that his presentee should be admitted. **1639** EARL OF CORK *Diary* in *Lismore Papers* Ser. I. (1886) V. 94 The vickaridge of colligan, fallen voide by the death of Thomas Vyning, my laste presentee. **1753** *Scots Mag.* XV. 86/1 The people of the parish had no colour of an objection to the presentee. **1854** H. MILLER *Sch. & Schm.* ii. (1857) 32 Donald's minister.. died in middle life, and an unpopular presentee was obtruded on the people. **1884** SIR C. E. POLLOCK in *Law Times Rep.* 19 Apr. 239/1 The bishop wrote to the plaintiff that.. he was obliged to refuse to institute his presentee.

b. A person nominated or recommended for any office or position.

1896 *Westm. Gaz.* 14 May 8/1 In one old case the court rejected a nominee as not being duly qualified,.. which led to the passing of an Act, which provided that, even if the presentee is reported not to be qualified, the Crown may nevertheless insist on his admission. Nowadays.. the Lord Probationer is invariably found qualified, and is at once transformed from an 'apprentice' into a regular Senator of the College of Justice.

c. A person presented at court: see PRESENT *v.* 1.

1822 *Blackw. Mag.* XII. 276 In the palace, the presentees were crowded into a mob. **1897** *Daily News* 12 May 9/3 The latest 'presentees' had not all returned from the Drawing Room.

2. A person to whom something is presented; the recipient of a present or gift.

1854 *Tait's Mag.* XXI. 385 The frequency of testimonials does not lessen their effect to the presentee. **1874–7** SIR H. TAYLOR *Autobiog.* (1885) II. xii. 167 Most presentees would rather dispense with the present than have to invent the necessary letters of eulogy and thanks.

presentee² (prɛzən'tiː). *joc.* [f. PRESENT *a.* (*adv.*) in imitation of ABSENTEE.] One who is present. Hence **presen'teeism.**

1892 'MARK TWAIN' *Amer. Claimant* xxi. 211 There was an absentee who ought to be a presentee—a word which she meant to look out in the dictionary. **1931** H. WITHERS *Everybody's Business* ix. 161 Certainly he is an absentee.. —if he adopted the habit of dropping in at the works and making well-meant suggestions.., is it likely that his presenteeism would be helpful? **1943** *Nat. Liquor Rev.* July 4/2 The Kaiser Company's public relation officials discovered that the term 'absenteeism' irked the people who read it... The Kaiser Company.. changed its policy and praised those who were on the job by using the term 'presenteeism'.

pre-'sentence, *sb.* and *a.* **A.** *sb. Linguistics.* [PRE- B. 1.] A construct that precedes or underlies the formation of a sentence.

1940 BRYANT & AIKEN *Psychol. of Eng.* iv. 33 These primitive 'pre-sentences' came to be broken up. **1965**

Language XLI. 459 Let us call these sequences of morphemes presentences when they label nonsurface P-markers.

B. *adj.* [PRE- B. 2.] **a.** That occurs before a judicial sentence.

1957 *Encycl. Brit.* VI. 719/2 Under the federal rules of criminal procedure and the law of a few states, a presentence investigation by the probation service and a report to the trial judge must be made. **1974** *Guidelines to Volunteer Services* (N.Y. State Dept. Correctional Services) 36 *Pre-sentence report*, a background investigation conducted by a probation department following an individual's conviction of a crime. **1979** *Arizona Daily Star* 1 Apr. A8/2 As Raymond said in a pre-sentence interview: 'My closest friends are my mother and my brothers. They're the only people I can trust.'

b. *Linguistics.* That occurs before a spoken or written sentence.

1965 N. CHOMSKY *Aspects of Theory of Syntax* ii. 102 Sentence Adverbials which form a 'pre-Sentence' unit in the underlying structure. *Ibid.* iv. 148 Verbs are strictly subcategorized into Intransitives, Transitives, pre-Adjectival, pre-Sentence, etc.

† **presen'tens.** *Obs. rare.* [a. OF. *present tens* (mod.F. *temps présent*) present time: see PRESENT *a.*, TENSE *sb.*] **a.** Present time. **b.** Present tense.

c **1475** *Partenay* 1439 What be ye? what is your name þis presentens? **1530** PALSGR. 43 We shulde confounde the persons of this tens with the same persons of their presentenses.

presenter (prɪ'zɛntə(r)). [f. PRESENT *v.* + -ER[1]. See also PRESENTOR.] One who presents, in various senses of the verb.

1. One who presents a person to a benefice, or to any position or office, or for a degree; one who formally introduces a person, esp. at court; in quot. 1597, a sponsor. (See also PRESENTOR 1 b.)

1544 *Supplic. to King* (E.E.T.S.) 38 The presenter of the clercke to a benefyce. **1597** HOOKER *Eccl. Pol.* v. lxiv. §5 It is the Church which doth offer them to Baptisme by the Ministery of Presenters. **1706** A. BOYER *Ann. Q. Anne* IV. 254 The prolocutor..chose for his presenter the Dean of Christ Church..who accordingly presented him..with an elegant Latin speech. **1830** GODWIN *Cloudesley* I. xiv. 235 We had been presented to King George the First,..the presenter being Robert earl Danvers. **1903** *Daily Chron.* 26 June 5/1 Lord Kelvin..The first honorary Doctor of Science of London University was described by his presenter on Wednesday as 'a greater philosopher than Democritus, and one in whom are united the qualities of Archimedes and Aristotle'.

2. *Law.* One who makes a presentment (of a fact, or an offence, etc.); = PRESENTOR 1 a. Now *rare.*

1545 BRINKLOW *Compl.* ii. 11 The thyrd [part] to the presenter that can iustyfye the matter. **1561** in Sir J. T. Gilbert *Calr. Anc. Rec. Dublin* (1891) II. 14 The presenter, fynder or spier of thoffence to have thone haulfe. **1656** in *1st Cent. Hist. Springfield, Mass.* (1898) I. 251 John Harman was chosen to ye Office of a Presenter to present breaches of ye Lawes. **1705** HEARNE *Collect.* 2 Sept. (O.H.S.) I. 40 If we consider of w[t] Persons the juries consist, & who are the Presenters. **1891** MAITLAND & BAILDON *Court Baron* (Selden Soc.) 100 The said Benedict complaineth of all the presenters that falsely and maliciously have they indicted him.

3. One who makes a present; a donor, giver.

1548 GEST *Pr. Masse* Ded. to Cheke, Not respectynge so muche the vylenes therof, as the good mynde of the presenter of y[e] same. **1608** WILLET *Hexapla Exod.* Ded., One presented vnto him a booke..the presenter replied. **1699** R. L'ESTRANGE *Erasm. Colloq.* (1711) 37 He tells us the Weight, the Price, and the Presenter of every Piece. **1903** *Motor. Ann.* 184 Mr. Gordon Bennett, the presenter of the Cup, is entitled to a seat on every such Committee.

4. One who 'presents' a part in a play; an actor. *arch.* or *Obs.*

a **1586** SIDNEY *Arcadia* (1622) 247 The deuice did teach the eyes the present miserie of the Presenter himselfe. **1606** HARINGTON in Nichols *Progr. Jas. I* (1828) II. 73 Strange Pageantries..of this sort in our Queen's days I was sometime an humble Presenter and Assistant. **1634** FORD *Perkin Warbeck* III. ii, Are the presenters ready?..[*Stage direct.*] Enter at one door four Scotch Anticks [etc.]. **1824** SCOTT *St. Ronan's* xx, His skill in performing the presenter of Pyramus.

5. One who presents an address, petition, memorial, an order, bill, cheque, etc.

1714 J. MACKY *Journ. thro. Eng.* (1724) I. xi. 213 These Officers..are the Presenters to his Majesty of all Memorials. **1766** W. GORDON *Gen. Counting-ho.* 364 No presenter [of a bill] is obliged to wait longer. **1784** J. BROWN *Hist. Brit. Ch.* (1820) II. iii. 48 To intimidate the presenters of this remonstrance. **1864** *Daily Tel.* 27 Apr., Addresses were presented to Garibaldi this afternoon... The presenters and a large number of other persons had interviews with the General in the library. **1868** *Act 31 & 32 Vict.* c. 101 §64 Any person seeking to obtain a Crown writ shall lodge..in the office of the presenter of signatures a draft of the proposed writ. **1881** *Philad. Record* (U.S.) No. 3473. 6 The rules of the bank required that the presenter of a check should be identified.

6. One who (or that which) presents something to the mind or to notice.

1871 EARLE *Philol. Eng. Tongue* (1873) §232 But if we ask, ..What idea does this word [*thing*] present? we answer, None! There is no creature, no subject of speech or of thought, which can claim the word *thing* as its presenter. **1897** DOWDEN *Fr. Lit.* I. iii. §3. 53 The presenter in literature of this glittering spectacle is the historian Jean Froissart.

7. One who presents or introduces a programme on radio or television.

1967 *Listener* 24 Aug. 249/2 A few words spoken into a camera by a presenter can smooth..an awkward script. **1974** *Radio Times* 16 Feb. 17/3 You and Yours. Presenter Lyn MacDonald. **1976** *Evening Times* (Glasgow) 1 Dec. 6/1 It's the fact that the Nationwide presenter made a quick dash by air from London to Abbotsinch and then on to Paisley.

presential (prɪ'zɛnʃəl), *a.* Now *rare.* Also præ-. [ad. med.L. *præsentiālis* present (Du Cange), f. L. *præsenti-a* presence: see -AL[1].]

1. Of or pertaining to presence; having or implying actual presence with a person or in a place; present.

1635 BRATHWAIT *Five Senses, Contin.* v. 143 To see the presentiall countenance of God with the blessed and Elect. **1647** JER. TAYLOR *Lib. Proph.* xiv. 204 By fiction of Law.. the paines of Hell are made presentiall to him. **1724** R. WELTON *Chr. Faith & Pract.* 34 He has been pleased to exhibit to us a presential communication of Himself. **1833** LAMB *Elia* Ser. II. *Barrenn. Imag. Faculty*, What associating league to the imagination can there be between the seers, and the seers not, of a presential miracle?

2. Mentally present; having presence of mind; attentive to the matter in hand: = PRESENT *a.* 4.

1649 AMBROSE *Media* xi. (1652) 291 One hath quickness of parts,..another is solid, but not so ready and presential. **1815** LAMB *Let. to Wordsw.* in *Final Mem.* vi. 244, I lose all presential memory of what I had intended to say.

3. Pertaining or relating to present time.

1846 MOZLEY *Ess., Carlyle's Cromwell* (1878) I. 232 The two worlds of futurity have a praesential existence as of imagery within the mind.

b. *Gram.* Applied to those tenses of a verb formed on the present stem.

1898 W. M. RAMSAY *Was Christ born in Bethlehem?* vi. 124 Here the presential tenses [ἀπογράφεσθαι and ἐπορεύοντο] are necessitated by the sense; all persons, individually and severally, repaired to their proper cities for their respective enrolment.

Hence † **pre'sentialist** *Obs. nonce-wd.*, a believer in the Real Presence: see PRESENCE 1 c, REAL *a.*[2] 2 b.

a **1655** VINES *Lord's Supp.* iii. (1657) 50 As the Romish Præsentialists and Schoolmen dream.

presentiality (prɪzɛnʃɪ'ælɪtɪ). Now *rare.* [ad. med.L. *præsentiālitās* (of time, Aquinas): see prec. and -ITY. So OF. *presencialité* (in Godef.).] The condition or character of being presential.

a. Presentness (in time).

1624 F. WHITE *Repl. Fisher* 424 This vnion is onely accidentall, and in regard of presentialitie and vbitie. **1652** T. FROYSELL *Gale Opportunity* Ep. Ded. 2 Let Faith give you a presentiality of things to come... Faith gives them a present Existence. **1664** BAXTER *Divine Life* I. v. 28 That terms of priority, presentiality, and posteriority, have not that significancy in or about Eternity as they have with us. **1692** SOUTH *Serm.* (1697) I. 334 Which..makes all futures actually present to him; and it is the Presentiality of the Object which founds the unerring certainty of his knowledge. **1848** HAMPDEN *Bampt. Lect.* (ed. 3) 175 They [events] are fixed and immutable in their 'presentiality' before God, whose eternity admits no change, no succession. **1911** tr. *Aquinas's Summa Theol.* I. xiv. 205 His glance is carried from eternity over all things, as they are in their presentiality. **1969** G. LEFF *Hist. & Social Theory* i. 18 Its presentiality takes precedence over all its other attributes.

b. The fact or quality of being present in place; presence.

1651 BIGGS *New Disp.* §287 It's the significator of the presentiality of heat. **1852** BP. FORBES *Nicene Cr.* 54 Incomprehensibility implies the negation of any limit in substantial presentiality or presence. **1894** FROUDE *Life & Lett. Erasm.* 125 Circumincession is when a thing subsists really in something else which is really distinct, by the mutual assistance of presentiality in the same essence.

pre'sentially, *adv.* Now *rare* or *Obs.* [f. PRESENTIAL + -LY[2]. Cf. med. schol. L. *præsentiāliter*, OF. *presentialment* (Bruno Lat., 13th c.).] In a presential manner; in the way of actual presence; as being present.

1615 T. ADAMS *Leaven* Wks. 1862 II. 72 He reigns in this place..presentially by his grace. **1651** JER. TAYLOR *Clerus Dom.* 28 Himselfe actually and presentially in heaven. **1691** E. TAYLOR *Behmen's Theos. Philos.* 165 How doth Christ himself teach presentially in the Office of Preaching, and yet sitteth at the Right Hand of God?

pre'sentialness. Now *rare* or *Obs.* [f. as prec. + -NESS.] The quality of being presential; = PRESENTIALITY (in quots., presence in space).

1692 NORRIS *Curs. Refl. Ess. Hum. Und.* 20, I account for the Mode of human Understanding..by the Presentialness of the Divine λόγος, or Ideal World to our Souls. **1713** A. COLLIER *Clavis Univ.* I. i. §2 (1836) 36 If..the Presentialness of the Object be necessary to the Act of Vision, the Object perceived cannot possibly be External to ..us.

presentiate (prɪ'zɛnʃɪeɪt), *v.* Now *rare.* [f. L. *præsentia* PRESENCE + -ATE[3]; cf. *differentiate, substantiate.*] *trans.* To make or render present in place or time; to cause to be perceived or realized as present. Hence **pre'sentiated** *ppl. a.*; **presenti'ation**, the act of rendering present.

1659 HAMMOND *On Ps.* v. 7 Paraphr. 32 That place where thou art pleased to præsentiate thy self. **1689** W. TAYLOR in *Manton's Treat. Self-Denial* Ep. Ded., That faith which realiseth the unseen glory, presentiateth our future hopes, looketh beyond time to eternity. **1755** AMORY *Mem.* (1766) II. 252 A realizing, presentiating faith of the unseen things promised by God. **1845–7** P. FAIRBAIRN *Typol. Script.* (1857) I. I. iii. 66 To figure and presentiate to the soul the future realities of the divine Kingdom. **1974** *Southern Calif. Law Rev.* XLVII. 800 If we say that the squirrel is futurizing the present, *i.e.*, preparing for the future, or presentiating the future, *i.e.*, bringing the future into the present, we are expressing an inaccurate anthropomorphism. *Ibid.* 802 The entire credit structure, including the monetary system itself, is founded on presentiation. Virtually no aspect of life in a modern society is left untouched by presentiation related to exchange. *Ibid.* 805 Because trouble is expected in a relation, efforts may be made in advance to deal with it transactionally, i.e., to eliminate it before it occurs through resolving the conflicts in advance, thereby turning what would have been relational into what is simply an allocated (presentiated) cost. **1976** *Jrnl. Econ. Issues* X. 15 Contracts 'presentiate' the future, or bring the future into the present where it is arranged. *Ibid.* 47 The transaction would be fully presentiated.

presentic (prɪ'zɛntɪk), *a. Gram.* [f. PRESENT *a.* (*adv.*) + -IC.] Pertaining to or characteristic of the present tense.

1964 H. S. SØRENSEN in *Eng. Stud.* XLV. (Suppl.) 81 As in the case of the incomplete perfect, grammarians have overlooked the fact that what is 'presentic' about the perfect is the point of reference, and nothing else. **1965** W. WINTER *Evidence for Laryngeals* 210 In B nonpresentic forms with an /a/ suffix were found in one and the same paradigm with presentic forms with an /n/ infix and no /a/ suffix.

presentient (priː'sɛnʃ(ɪ)ənt), *a.* [ad. L. *præsentient-em*, pres. pple. of *præsentīre* to feel or perceive beforehand: see PRE- A. 3 and SENTIENT.] Feeling or perceiving beforehand; having a presentiment; scenting beforehand.

1814 SOUTHEY *Roderick* XVIII. 322 The ravenous fowls of heaven Flock there presentient of their food obscene. **1818** J. H. HUNT tr. *Tasso* XIX. 76 Shrinks then thy heart, presentient of its doom? **1854** PATMORE *Angel in Ho.* I. I. xii. (1879) 133 And, ere we reached her father's gate We paused with one presentient mind. **1888** QUILLER-COUCH *Troy Town* ix, Mrs. Buzza,..presentient of evil, ran downstairs.

† **presen'tific,** *a. Obs. rare.* [f. L. type **præsentific-us*, f. *præsenti-*, stem of *præsens* present: see -FIC.] Making or rendering present. Hence † **presen'tifical** *a.*, † **presen'tificly** *adv. Obs. rare.*

1642 H. MORE *Song of Soul* II. iii. II. xliv, I have already told, and did descry How presentifick circularity Is spread through all. **1653** —— *Conject. Cabbal., Def.* 171 Adam.. notwithstanding that he found no want of any covering to hide himself from that presentifick sense of him. *Ibid.* (R.), The whole evolution of times and ages, from everlasting to everlasting, is collectedly and presentifickly represented to God at once. **1668** —— *Div. Dial.* v. xvii. (1713) 466 Phancy becomes sometimes presentifical, as in Mad-men and those in high Fevers, whose Phantasms seem real external Objects to them.

presentiment (priː'sɛntɪmənt, prɪ'zɛ-). Also 8 **præsentiment.** [a. obs. F. *presentiment* (Cotgr.): see PRE- A. 2 and SENTIMENT.]

1. A mental impression or feeling of a future event; a vague expectation resting on no definite reason, but seeming like a direct perception of something about to happen; an anticipation, foreboding (most commonly of something evil).

1714 MRS. MANLEY *Adv. Rivella* 71 Some Presentiment told me this agreeable Gentleman would certainly succeed. **1736** BUTLER *Anal.* I. vi. 114 God..must have given us this discernment..as a Pre-sentiment of what is to be hereafter. **1761** MRS. F. SHERIDAN *Sidney Bidulph* III. 340 She seemed to have a pre-sentiment of those evils. **1830** WORDSW. *Presentiments* i, Presentiments! they judge not right Who deem that ye from open light Retire in fear of shame. **1884** L. J. JENNINGS *Croker Papers* I. vi. 181 They appear to have had a sad presentiment of the truth.

2. A previously conceived sentiment or opinion; a prepossession. *rare.*

1751 CHESTERF. *Lett.* (1792) III. 109 You would not give people reason to change their favourable prae-sentiments of you. **1872** LIDDON *Elem. Relig.* ii. 49 The idea or presentiment of God, everywhere rooted in the mind of man.

Hence **presenti'mental** *a.*, of the nature of, expressing, or conveying a presentiment.

c **1819** COLERIDGE in *Lit. Rem.* (1836) II. 242 The affecting beauty of the death of Cawdor and the presentimental speech of the King. **1848** THACKERAY *Van. Fair* xiii, Amelia ..thought somehow it was a mysterious and presentimental bell.

presenting (prɪ'zɛntɪŋ), *vbl. sb.* [f. PRESENT *v.* + -ING[1].] The action of the verb PRESENT, in its various senses. Also *attrib.*

c **1380** WYCLIF *Wks.* (1880) 66 Whanne a lord haþ þe gold for his presentynge [to a benefice], þe gold dwelliþ stille in oure lond, but whanne þe pope haþ þe furste fruytes þe gold goþ out & comeþ neuere aȝen. *c* **1410** *Sir Cleges* 401, I thanke the hartyly, seyd the kynge, Of thy yeft and presentynge. **1563** WINȜET *Wks.* (S.T.S.) II. 43 Nocht a fenȝeit, bot a trew persoun; nocht in præsenting, bot in substance. **1639** FULLER *Holy War* v. xiii. (1840) 266 They..as it were scattered their powder in presenting, before they came to discharge. **1720** WHITE *Monit. Clergy Peterb.* I. 29 They [churchwardens] have a general Prejudice to the sworn Duty of Presenting; for fear of offending this or that Neighbour. **1856** KANE *Arct. Expl.* II. vi. 75 Discovered.. out of presenting-distance. **1901** BP. GORE *Body of Christ* iv. §1 (1907) 226 The presenting before God of the one sacrifice.

b. ***presenting term***: in Ireland, the term or date for making legal presentments.

1779–80 *Ir. Act 19 & 20 Geo. III*, c. 19 §1 Any person.. may sue..in the county of Dublin at the next presenting term. **1898** *Act 61 & 62 Vict.* c. 37 §113 (1) The grand jury of..the county of Dublin at the Easter presenting term, next after the passing of this Act, may choose [etc.].

pre'senting, *ppl. a.* [f. as prec. + -ING².] That presents in various senses of the verb; that presents or shows itself. *spec.* in *Med.*: cf. PRESENT *v.* 9b.

1802 *Med. Jrnl.* VIII. 394 The integuments of the presenting arm. **1853** KANE *Grinnell Exp.* xv. (1856) 114, I could see that the dark knoblike protrusions..were the presenting faces of hills. **1872** ANSTIE in *Practitioner* Jan. 62 The presenting part seemed firm. **1911** R. C. CABOT *Differential Diagnosis* 17 A 'presenting symptom', comparable to the 'presenting part' in obstetrics, may turn out to be of minor importance when we have studied the whole case. **1948** MARTIN & HYNES *Clin. Endocrinol.* iv. 96 Increasing weight may be the presenting symptom. **1960** R. D. LAING *Divided Self* vi. 111 All that could not find direct expression and open acknowledgement in her was condensed in her presenting symptom. **1973** *Times* 17 Oct. 14/4 The temptation to shoplift may be a presenting complaint in depressive illness or melancholia.

presentist ('prɛzəntɪst), *sb.* (*a.*) [f. PRESENT *a.* + -IST.] An advocate of the present; in quot. 1878, one who believes that the prophecies of Scripture, esp. of the Apocalypse, are at present in course of fulfilment: opp. to PRETERIST and FUTURIST. Also, one who has a bias towards the present or is influenced by present-day attitudes. Also *attrib.* or as *adj.* Hence **'presentism**.

1878 H. G. GUINNESS *End of Age* (1880) 93 Three distinct classes..denominated Preterist, Futurist and Presentist schemes of interpretation. **1927** [see PASSÉISME]. **1956** *N.Y. Times Bk. Rev.* 8 Jan. 22/3, I think Mr. Nevins' review underscores the danger of 'presentism'; I suggest historians would strengthen their position by applying the chief test of their profession—perspective and caution in contemporary analyses. **1975** *Nature* 24 Apr. 729/3 Such history as is dealt with reads soundly, but it is often drawn from secondary sources and professional historians of science would judge it presentist and Whiggish. **1976** T. STOIANOVICH *French Hist. Method* i. 36 Even the attempt to understand the past in its own terms is 'presentist' to the extent that it is founded on what contemporary science and bias lead us to believe to have been its own terms. **1977** *Times Lit. Suppl.* 27 May 655/1 The author wants to explain how the world got to be the way it is at the start of the last quarter of the twentieth century. 'Presentism' accordingly governs the way he distributes attention.

presentive (prɪ'zɛntɪv), *a.* (*sb.*) [irreg. f. PRESENT *v.* + -IVE; used for distinction from the etymologically regular *presentative*.] Presenting an object or conception directly to the mind (opp. to *symbolic*); also *sb.*, a presentive word. Hence **pre'sentively** *adv.*; **pre'sentiveness**.

1871 EARLE *Philol. Eng. Tongue* (1873) §227 We will call these two classes of words by the names of Presentive and Symbolic. The Presentive are those..which present any conception to the mind. *Ibid.* §230 The numerals I and II and III and IIII are presentive of the ideas of one and two and three and four... The figures 1 and 2 and 3 and 4 are and always were pure symbols. *Ibid.* §232 In Chaucer's Prologue it [the word *thing*] occurs twice presentively. *Ibid.* §235 The word *shall* offers a good example of the movement from presentiveness to symbolism. When it flourished as a presentive word, it signified to *owe*. *Ibid.* §244 A passage with many proper names and titles in it may, however, bring the presentives up to, or even cause them to surpass, the number of the symbolics. *Ibid.* §464 The pronoun *I*..has also a sort of reflected or borrowed presentiveness, which we will call a subpresentive power. **1883** *Q. Rev.* Jan. 187 If, as some philologists maintain, the development of a language is to be estimated by the proportion it shows of 'symbolic' as opposed to 'presentive' words.

presently ('prɛzəntlɪ), *adv.* [f. PRESENT *a.* + -LY².]

†**1.** So as to be, or as being, present; in presence; in the very place, on the spot; in person, personally.

c **1380** WYCLIF *Wks.* (1880) 454 ȝif a man be presently nyȝ his sheep, & fayle not to fede hem & to defende hem.., his bodily presense is skileful to hym to dwelle vpon þes sheep. *c* **1430** [see PRESENTATIVELY]. **1537** POLE *Let. to Hen. VIII* in Strype *Eccl. Mem.* (1721) I. App. lxxxii. 199 Places [in my book] that cannot so vively be perceived by writing as..by conferring..presently with the author. **1565** JEWEL *Def. Apol.* (1611) 199 When God himselfe in his owne person, and presently spake vnto Abel. **1579** W. WILKINSON *Confut. Familye of Loue* B ij, Whereto also the Author presently as a concordable witnes with the same doth onely point and direct us.

2. a. At the present time; at this time, at present, now. *Obs.* (since 17th c.) in lit. Eng. (No certain instance in Shaks.) But in regular use in most Eng. dialects, and common in Sc. writers; revived in U.S. and to some extent in Great Britain in 20th c.

1485 CAXTON *Chas. Gt.* 50 Thou arte not presently in helthe of thy body. **1489** —— *Faytes of A.* I. v. 11 Charles the fyfthe..fader of this that presently regneth. *a* **1533** LD. BERNERS *Gold. Bk. M. Aurel.* (1546) G g ij b, Dedes done presently in our daies. **1637** R. HUMPHREY tr. *St. Ambrose* I. 31 A reward to be rendred hereafter, not presently. **1697** tr. *C'tess D'Aunoy's Trav.* (1706) 191 It is, says he, too long and melancholy a Mischance to relate presently. **1740** TULL *Horse-hoing Husb.* Suppl. 257 Enough to make the Horse hoing common in Time to come, if not presently. **1764** REID *Inquiry* vi. §17 The question presently under consideration. **1826** SCOTT *Provinc. Antiq.* 85 Sir William Rae, Baronet,.. presently Lord Advocate. **1849** RUSKIN *Sev. Lamps* vi. §9. 171 Our presently disputed claims. **1897** GEIKIE *Anc. Volcanoes Brit.* I. I. i. 5 The presently active volcano must be the basis and starting-point of inquiry. **1901** *Leeds Mercury* 4 July, A young man belonging to Rotherham and presently staying with his parents at Bridlington. **1939** *Topeka* (Kansas) *State Jrnl.* 20 Feb. 12/1 Sunner is presently minister of interior and one of the outstanding leaders of the Falangists. **1943** *Time* 20 Sept. 25 They said Mussolini assured them he would return to power and re-establish the Fascist regime, comparing himself presently with Napoleon—the parallel being Napoleon's exile on Elba. **1945** *Richmond* (Virginia) *Times-Dispatch* 21 June 1/3 The one class of cadets presently at the academy. **1949** *Sun* (Baltimore) 9 Apr. 6/1 The members of the presently major coalition can hardly refuse to meet with the Mayor. **1957** G. MARX *Let.* 12 Apr. (1967) 213, I am presently building a house and doing my own show, but sometime within the next two months I'll make it. **1958** *Economist* 9 Aug. 433/1 It is entirely possible that Mr Macmillan..may now be getting greater commendation from the commentators of his generation than he will eventually get from historians; certainly the praise presently being heaped upon him seems to be..a consequence of the recent recovery in the Conservatives' fortunes. **1968** *Globe & Mail* (Toronto) 17 Feb. 52 (Advt.), We want a go-getter who is well established and presently calls on machinery, tool, and equipment supply firms. **1968** B. FOSTER *Changing Eng. Lang.* v. 215 This meaning of 'at present'..is one which once again has been reintroduced from across the Atlantic where it had also lingered on, with the result that it is now in good use in England. 'Warm air is presently moving north-east' reported a B.B.C. weather bulletin (20 May 1963). **1969** *Daily Tel.* (Colour Suppl.) 24 Jan. 8/4 Ivan Cooper, a Protestant and former Unionist,..and presently chairman of the Derry Labour Party, was elected chairman. **1971** *Nature* 2 July 23/1 The Caribbean area is a subplate presently attached to the South American plate. **1978** *N.Y. Times* 30 Mar. D14/5 (Advt.), GTE Sylvania is presently engaged in the research, design, development and production of high energy Lithium Battery power sources for use in highly specialized applications. **1978** *Dumfries Courier* 13 Oct. 2/5 Mr. William O'Brien, solicitor, Dumfries, for the accused, said Mr. Savage was presently unemployed, his last employment being a year ago.

†**b.** For the present; on the present occasion.

1593 FALE *Dialling* A iij, The making of the Horologicall Cylindre..we have presently omitted. **1632** SANDERSON *Serm.* 319 That which hath beene presently delivered.

†**c.** At the time referred to; for the time being; at that time, just then. (In quot. 1597, At the very time, or immediately before; 'just'.) *Obs.*

1577 HOLINSHED *Chron.* II. 573/2 [They] fauoured not yᵉ race of the Kyngs that presently raigned. **1597** GERARDE *Herbal* I. xxxv. §4. 48 Neuer cast any colde water vpon them presently taken out of a well. **1614** RALEIGH *Hist. World* III. (1634) 128 Every one retaining what he presently had. **1696** STILLINGFL. *12 Serm.* iii. 90 Although the people might not presently believe what they said. **1740** tr. *De Mouhy's Fort. Country-Maid* (1741) I. 46 My Illness..being presently attributed to the indifferent Health I had enjoy'd for some Days past.

3. At the very time, without any delay; at once, forthwith; immediately, instantly, directly, speedily, quickly, promptly. *Obs.* or *arch.*

c **1430** LYDG. *London Lackpenny* Min. Poems (Percy Soc.) 105 Then to Westmynster-Gate I presently went When the sonn was at hyghe pryme. **1537** CROMWELL in Merriman *Life & Lett.* (1902) II. 90 Without some reparacion to be presently doon upon it, it canne not be enhabited. **1591** SHAKS. *Two Gent.* IV. iv. 76 Go presently, and take this Ring with thee. **1615** G. SANDYS *Trav.* 110 The Sacrament which they administer in both kinds, and giue it to infants presently after Baptisme. **1692** LOCKE *Educ.* §83 It should not be done presently, lest Passion mingle with it. **1749** FIELDING *Tom Jones* IX. iv, The poor woman,..no sooner looked at the serjeant, than she presently recollected him. **1834** SIR H. TAYLOR *Artevelde* I. xi, The terms are just and merciful indeed! But then they must be offered presently [*ed.* 1877 promptly proffered]. **1869** HT. MARTINEAU *Autobiog.* Pref., Making arrangements for the issue of this Autobiography presently after my decease.

4. In blunted sense (gradually weakened from 3): In the space of time that immediately follows, in a little while, before long, after a short time, soon, shortly. (Cf. ANON 5, BY AND BY 4, and colloq. use of *directly*, *immediately*, and nearly all advbs. of the same kind). Now the ordinary use.

(The growth of this was so imperceptible, that early examples, esp. before *c* 1650, are doubtful.)

a **1566** R. EDWARDES *Damon & Pithias* in Hazl. *Dodsley* IV. 90 For Pithias I bewail, which presently must die. **1598** SHAKS. *Merry W.* IV. ii. 99 Nay, but hee'l be heere presently: let's go dresse him like the witch of Brainford. **1666** PEPYS *Diary* 5 Oct., The Polyglottes and new Bible which he believes will be presently worth 40*l.* a-piece. **1699** LOCKE *Educ.* (ed. 4) §130 Toys..which are presently put out of order. **1721** BRADLEY *Philos. Acc. Wks. Nat.* 10 Others, which are softer in the Quarry, grow hard and firm presently after they are taken out of it. **1766** FORDYCE *Serm. Yng. Wom.* (1767) II. xiii. 230 Pride will be presently brought down. **1829** I. TAYLOR *Enthus.* iv. (1867) 73 But the very same extravagances..when caught up by inferior spirits presently lose their garb..of beauty. **1833** HT. MARTINEAU *Brooke Farm* ii. 20 The elder boys might earn their own shoe-leather presently. **1857** BUCKLE *Civiliz.* I. xi. 647 The struggle, as we shall presently see, lasted two generations. *Colloq.* I cannot attend to it at once; I will do so presently.

†**5.** Immediately (in space or relation); so as to be adjacent or contiguous; directly, closely. *Obs.*

1601 HOLLAND *Pliny* I. 119 Neither the hils Ceraunij, nor yet the region Adiabene, do presently and immedialty confine thereupon: for the country of the Sopheni lyeth between. *a* **1619** FLETCHER, etc. *Knt. Malta* II. i, I have a business Which much concerns you, presently concerns you. **1656** HEYLIN *Surv. France* 102 Presently without the Chappell is the Burse. **1661** LOVELL *Hist. Anim. & Min.* Introd., The stomach is joyned presently to the mouth, and is little.

6. In the way of immediate consequence or inference; as a direct result or conclusion, directly; consequently, thereupon; necessarily, *ipso facto*.

1634 W. TIRWHYT tr. *Balzac's Lett.* (vol. I) 292, I cannot thinke..that it is sufficient onely to slander an honest man, to make him presently wicked. **1659** BP. WALTON *Consid. Considered* 94 We do not infer, nor doth it presently follow, that the present reading is corrupt and false. **1741** WATTS *Improv. Mind* I. ix. §11 Do not presently imagine you shall gain nothing by his Company. **1849** W. FITZGERALD tr. *Whitaker's Disput.* 296 It does not presently follow that all have the Holy Spirit who say they have it. **1859** GANDELL tr. *Lightfoot's Horæ Heb.* II. 45 Nor was he presently to be called an Eremite who dwelt in the wilderness.

†**'presently,** *a. Obs. rare.* [f. as prec. + -LY¹.] = PRESENT *a.* I.

c **1449** PECOCK *Repr.* II. ix. 193 God is lijk presentli euery where, and therfore he is lijk redi for to ȝeue hise gracis and ȝiftis euery where. **1548** GEST *Pr. Masse* I iv b, Though we mought praye vnto yᵉ sayd sainctes as beyng presentlye and conversaunt wyth vs.

presentment (prɪ'zɛntmənt). Also 5 (in sense 2a) **presentamente**; 7 **præsentment**. [a. OF. *presentement* (12th c. in Godef.): see PRESENT *v.* and -MENT.] The act of presenting or fact of being presented, presentation; an instance or embodiment of this: chiefly in technical or special uses.

1. The act of presenting a person to or for any office, esp. a clergyman for institution to a benefice: see PRESENT *v.* 3, PRESENTATION 2. *Obs.* exc. *Hist.*

darrein presentment: see DARREIN.

1303 R. BRUNNE *Handl. Synne* 10944 þe order of þe bysshopes presentement. *c* **1450** *Godstow Reg.* 423 Henry the fyrst..Comandit the busshop of lincolne & hys archydiacon that edwynus the sone of Godgose shold haue in pece & rest hys chyrche of seynt Gylys, and put hys clerke whom he wold by hys presentment. **1494** FABYAN *Chron.* VII. 351 The commons of the cytie of London chase vnto their maire ..Thomas fiz Thomas..and made no presentement of hym vpon the morowe folowynge, nouther to the kynge nor yet to the barons of the kynges excheker, as they of right ought to haue donn. **1531** *Dial. on Laws Eng.* II. xxvi. 58 b, In the lawes of the realme..the right of presentment to a church, is a temporall enheritaunce. **1579** *Expos. Law Terms* 159 *Presentment* is when a man which hath right to geeue a benefice spirituall nameth the person to whome he wil giue it, and maketh a writing to the Bishop for him, that is a presentation or presentment. **1641** *Termes de la Ley* s.v., If divers coheires may not agree in presentment, the presentee of the eldest shall be admitted. [**1760**, **1833** Darrein presentment [see DARREIN]. **1874** STUBBS *Const. Hist.* I. xiii. 617 The great charter of John..retains the three recognitions of Novel disseisin, Mort d'ancester, and Darrein presentment.]

2. *Law.* The act of presenting or laying before a court or person in authority a formal statement of some matter to be legally dealt with (see PRESENT *v.* 8). **a.** A statement on oath by a jury of a fact within their own knowledge. This includes:

(*a*) The statement by a grand jury at assizes or quarter sessions of an indictable offence, or of the existence of a nuisance. †(*b*) The statement by the grand jury, or (later) of a presentment sessions (see d) in Ireland, of the amount due by a county or barony, and the method of its assessment (*obs.*). (*c*) The statement by the jury of a court baron or court leet of matters from which rights accrue to the lord, or in respect of which his jurisdiction is invoked.

[**1308–9** *Rolls of Parlt.* I. 279/1 Le Viscunte fet travayler les gentz des ditz Hundrez a fere presentemenz devant ly en sun turn, des articles avantdiz. *c* **1340** *Modus tenendi Curias* in *Court Baron* (Selden Soc. 1891) 100 Ore doit le seneschal feare lever un douszeyne de fraunk tenauntz qe ount oy ceaux presentementz e serrent chargeez de touz les articles. [*trans.* Then shall the steward cause to be constituted a dozen of free tenants who have heard the presentments, and they shall be charged with all the articles].] **1439** *Rolls of Parlt.* V. 29/2 Presentamentes, Writtes, and al other maner of Recordes. **1447** *Shillingford Lett.* (Camden) 134 No man shuld be putte to answere before the King or his Counseill wᵗout presentment before Justice. **1588** FRAUNCE *Lawiers Logic* I. xii. 53 b, I take a presentment to bee a meere denuntiation of the iurors themselues or of some other officer without any other information. **1615** *Henley-in-Arden Rolls* (1890), Presentments by the aletasters for vitlers: William Kerby shumaker faultie; John Knight Couper faultie; [and 10 others; each fined] xijᵈ. **1630** COKE *On Copyholds* §57 (1668) 159 Of Acts which amount to Forfeiture, some are Forfeits *eo instante* that they are committed, some are not Forfeits till Presentment. *a* **1715** BURNET *Own Time* III. (1823) II. 389 The grand juries made [1683] high presentments against all that were esteemed whigs and nonconformists. **1755** *Irish Act 29 Geo. II*, c. 14 §6 The power given to grand-juries at quarter-sessions, to raise money by presentment for the use of houses of correction hath been frequently abused, and the money so presented misapplied. **1769** BLACKSTONE *Comm.* IV. xxiii. 298 Presentment..is a very comprehensive term; including not only presentments properly so called, but also inquisitions of office, and indictments by a grand jury. A presentment, properly speaking, is the notice taken by a grand jury of any offence from their own knowledge or observation, without any bill of indictment laid before them at the suit of the king. *Ibid.* 301 The presentment of a nuisance, a libel, or the like; upon which the officer of the

Court must afterwards frame an indictment, before the party presented can be put to answer it. **1798** DALLAS *Amer. Law Rep.* I. 237 The bills, or presentments, found by a grand jury are an official accusation, in order to put the party accused upon his trial. **1863** H. COX *Instit.* II. v. 457 The grand jury has also an important constitutional right of presentment of offences from their own knowlege. **1882** *Scriven's Law of Copyholds* (ed. 6) xii. §2. 352 If no presentment was made in the court leet of articles of which that court had cognizance, they were to be presented in the tourn. **1889** MAITLAND *Sel. Pleas Manorial Courts* Introd. 24 [In 16th c.] it is still theoretical law that the jury ought to make presentment concerning all who are not in frankpledge.

†**b.** A similar statement (formerly) made by a magistrate or justice of peace, or by a constable.

1523 FITZHERB. *Surv.* 20 b, I shall true constable be..and true presentment make [etc.]. **1535** CROMWELL in Merriman *Life & Lett.* (1902) I. 437 (Let. to Mayor & Aldermen, etc., of Cambridge), Ye have also refused alonly this yere, to make a certain othe..for..the presentement to the vicechauncelor of vagabundes and others. **1581** LAMBARDE *Eiren.* II. vi. 404 Of like strength also..is the Presentment of the Constables concerning sundrie poinctes contayned in the Statute of Winchester, 13 E. I. **1607** COWELL *Interpr.*, *Presentment*, is a meere denuntiation of the Iurours themselues, or some other officer, as Iustice, Constable, searcher, surueiours &c...of an offence inquirable in the court wherevnto it is presented. **1827** LD. ELDON in Barnewall & Cr. *Reports* VII. 516 The presentment of a justice on his own knowledge has, by statute, in some cases, the force of a presentment by a grand jury. **1827** *Act 7 & 8 Geo. IV*, c. 38 No petty constables shall be required at any petty session or elsewhere to make, nor shall any high constable be required at any gaol delivery, great session, or general or quarter session..to deliver any presentment respecting popish recusants [etc.]. **1828** BARNEWALL & CR. *Reports* VII. 514 R. Hooper, high constable of the hundred of Whitley..signed the following presentment in writing upon paper. **1875** T. S. PRITCHARD *Pract. Quarter Sessions* I. iv. §3. 173 It may fairly be assumed that presentments by constables will be discontinued, and that..indictments will be substituted in the necessary cases.

c. *Eccl.* A formal complaint or report of some offence or fault, made by the churchwardens or other parish authorities to the bishop or archdeacon at his visitation.

1576 GRINDAL *Articles Canterb.* xliv. in *Rem.* (Parker Soc.) 170 Sums..forfeited..since the feast of Easter..until the day of giving up the presentment. *c***1583–4** in Usher *Presbyt. Movemt. in reign Eliz.* (Camden) 86, 89. **1603** *Constit. & Canons Eccl.* cxiii, Every parson..may join in every presentment with the said church-wardens. **1624** CAPT. SMITH *Virginia* 195 The Church-wardens should meet twice a yeere, to haue all their presentments made perfect against the Assises. *a***1715** BURNET *Own Time* (1766) II. 183 The Clergy of the City refused to make presentments. **1720** WHITE *Monit. Clergy Peterb.* I. 28 The due Presentment of Defaults and Offences by the Church-Wardens upon their Oaths. **1901** *Blunt's Bk. Ch. Law* (ed. 9) IV. i, Such presentments are now usually made once a year, at the archdeacon's or the bishop's visitation.

†**d. presentment sessions**, special sessions held in Ireland for the raising of public money for certain purposes, in which certain cess-payers were associated with the Grand Jury. *Obs.*

1836 *Act 6 & 7 Will. IV*, c. 116 (*title*) An Act to consolidate and amend the Laws relating to the Presentment of Public Money by Grand Juries in Ireland. *Ibid.* §4 Such justices are hereby required to assemble..with the cess payers associated with them..to hold a special or presentment sessions for the purposes of this Act. *Ibid.* §5 Grand juries..are hereby required, at each assizes, to appoint..certain places..(one in each barony or half barony) where..presentment sessions shall be..holden previous to the next assizes. **1898** *Act 61 & 62 Vict.* c. 37 §4 (1) The county council..shall..have the powers and duties of the grand jury and the said [county at large] presentment sessions. *Ibid.* §27 There shall be transferred..to the district council of every county district, the business of any baronial presentment sessions so far as respects that district.

3. The act of offering for acceptance or consideration; the dedication of a book; giving, bestowal; handing over, delivery; the presenting of a bill or an account for payment: = PRESENTATION 4, 1 a. Now *rare*.

1607 SHAKS. *Timon* I. i. 27 When comes your Booke forth? *Poet.* Vpon the heeles of my presentment sir. **1608** HEYWOOD *Sallust* Ded., I haue adventured rather to tempt your acceptance in this small presentment. *a***1627** MIDDLETON *Mayor Quinborough* IV. ii, Mark but the least presentment of occasion, As these times yield enough, and then mark me. **1642** MILTON *Apol. Smect.* Wks. 1851 III. 259 To trick up the name of some Esquire..to be his book-patron with the appendant form of a ceremonious presentment. **1646** EARL MONM. tr. *Biondi's Civil Warres* VI. 48 Lord Howard and Lord Stanley..loaded him with the presentment of their services to the King. **1659** H. L'ESTRANGE *Alliance Div. Off.* 244 The presentment of children at the Font, is most properly the Act of the Church. **1665** COLLINS in Rigaud *Corr. Sci. Men* (1841) II. 459 He desires the presentment of his most humble service. **1690** W. WALKER *Idiomat. Anglo-Lat.* Pref. 1 To make presentment of a new book to you. **1769** BURKE *Corr.* (1844) I. 216 To settle matters about the presentment of the petition. **1776** ADAM SMITH *W.N.* II. ii. (1869) I. 327 They promised payment..six months after such presentment. **1882** *Act 45 & 46 Vict.* c. 61 §87 (2), Presentment for payment is necessary in order to render the indorser of a note liable.

†**4.** Ceremonial introduction (of a person): = PRESENTATION 1 b. *Obs. rare.*

1668 HOWE *Bless. Righteous* (1825) 54 An exceeding joy..that shall attend the presentment of saints there. **1754** C'TESS SHAFTESB. in *Lett. Ld. Malmesbury* (1870) I. 81 It was to attend my niece to the ceremony of presentment.

5. The act of presenting to sight (or hearing), or something so presented: = PRESENTATION 5.

a. A theatrical or dramatic representation; the performance of a play or the like. (In quot. 1881 the performance or 'rendering' of a musical work.)

*c***1605** ROWLEY *Birth Merl.* III. i, Earl Cador's marriage, and a masque to grace it, So, so, This night shall make me famous for presentments. **1668** DRYDEN *Ess. Dram. Poesy* Ess. (ed. Ker) I. 83 Three hours and a half, which is no more than is required for the presentment on the stage. **1834** BANCROFT *Hist. U.S.* I. 116 (C.D.) She was an honored guest at the presentment of a burlesque masque. **1841** LONGF. *Childr. Lord's Supp.* 26 The Feast of the Leafy Pavilions Saw we in living presentment. **1881** *Athenæum* 10 Sept. 348/1 Works of Beethoven and Wagner present the greatest facilities for presentment in this way.

b. Representation of an object by a picture, image, or graphic description; delineation; usually quasi-*concr.* a picture, portrait, image, likeness.

1602 SHAKS. *Ham.* III. iv. 54 The counterfet presentment of two Brothers. **1855** BRIMLEY *Ess.*, *Tennyson* 45 A poem which consists of a series of actions admitting of splendid pictorial presentment. **1862** T. A. TROLLOPE *Marietta* I. iv. 62 Pleasing presentment of advanced old age. **1871** M. COLLINS *Mrq. & Merch.* II. i. 3 He could not recognise in his own daughter the feminine presentment of himself. **1882** STUBBS *Med. & Mod. Hist.* xiv. (1900) 368 Oxford dropped the canon law degree altogether; Cambridge, by adopting a more general form, retained a shadowy presentment of the double honour. **1885** E. GARRETT *At any Cost* xvi, Landseer's touching presentment of the faithful dog resting its head on its dead master's coffin.

c. The appearance, aspect, form, or mode in which anything is presented; exhibition, display.

1634 MILTON *Comus* 156 To cheat the eye with blear illusion, And give it false presentments. **1853–8** HAWTHORNE *Eng. Note-Bks.* (1879) II. 247 We did not see Loch Katrine, perhaps, under its best presentment. **1874** BLACKIE *Self-Cult.* 65 In his presentment as a member of society he should take a sacred care to be more than he seems, not to seem more than he is. **1905** *Academy* 4 Feb. 99/2 The stories are naught, for they are a common fund, and, when stripped of the presentment, they are not very numerous.

6. The action of presenting to notice or mental perception; statement, setting forth, description; the form or mode of so presenting or stating.

1611 HEYWOOD *Gold. Age* I. i, The Gods of Greece..Haue giuen old Homer leaue to view the world And make his owne presentment. **1828** SOUTHEY *Ess.* (1832) II. 334 It is in a fair way of putting an end to that particular cause of complaint, which, in all latter presentments of the grievances of Ireland, had been made to hold the most prominent place. **1873** M. ARNOLD *Lit. & Dogma* (1876) 4 The feeling of the chief people in the religious world..seems to be just now..in favour of dogma, of a scientific and exact presentment of religious things, instead of a literary presentment of them. **1875** WHITNEY *Life Lang.* x. 206 Every point is too doubtful to allow of summary presentment. **1881** *Athenæum* 5 Feb. 195 Not less vivid are the presentments of character afforded us.

7. The act of presenting to consciousness, or to the imagination; suggestion; the conception thus given.

1633 T. ADAMS *Exp. 2 Peter* ii. 14 That sin at the first presentment would affright a man, which he juggles on by degrees. **1817** COLERIDGE *Biog. Lit.* I. ix. 144 The writings of these mystics..gave me an indistinct, yet stirring and working presentment. **1856** RUSKIN *Mod. Paint.* III. IV. iv. §9 The continual presentment to the mind of this beautiful and fully realized imagery more and more chilled its power of apprehending the real truth. **1884** H. D. TRAILL in *Macm. Mag.* Oct. 443/1 Vividness of presentment to the imagination is not all that language has to provide for.

b. *Metaph.* and *Psychol.* = PRESENTATION 7.

*a***1842** SIR W. HAMILTON *Dissert.* in *Reid's Wks.* App. 819 Which..supposes that the Idea is an original and absolute presentment, and..constitutes the doctrine of Ideal presentative perception. **1856** FERRIER *Inst. Metaph.* v. 144 The qualities of matter by themselves are, equally with matter itself, an objective presentment without a subject. **1877** E. R. CONDER *Bas. Faith* iv. 153 Such is our knowledge of our own sensations, emotions, and all direct presentments of consciousness apart from memory. *Ibid.* 162 All those immediate judgments which the intellect passes on the presentments of sense, or the representments of memory and imagination. **1882** FARRAR *Early Chr.* II. 382 the Nominalist who regards abstract terms as representing nothing but the generalisations of the mind out of concrete presentments.

presentness ('prɛzəntnɪs). [f. PRESENT *a.* + -NESS.] The quality or condition of being present in place, time, or thought.

†**1.** The state of being in the presence of or close proximity to a person or thing: = PRESENCE 1. *Obs.*

1530 PALSGR. 258/1 Presentnesse, *presence*. **1571** GOLDING *Calvin on Ps.* xxiv. 8 It was a presentnesse of his power and grace. **1609** OVERBURY *Observ. State France* (1626) 28 The presentnesse of danger inflames their courage.

2. The fact of existing at this time, or at the time referred to; present existence or condition.

1616 SURFL. & MARKH. *Country Farme* 131 Not after, but euen in the instant and presentnesse of time. **1660** INGELO *Bentiv. & Ur.* I. (1682) 116, I can see beyond the presentness of this world. **1829** JAS. MILL *Hum. Mind* (1869) II. 119 Time is the equivalent of Pastness, Presentness, and Futureness, combined. **1885–6** SPURGEON *Treas. Dav.* Ps. cxliv. 1 It has also a presentness about it, for Jehovah is now his strength, and is still teaching him.

†**3. a.** Attentiveness, readiness. **b.** *presentness of mind* = presence of mind: see PRESENCE 7. *Obs.*

1647 CLARENDON *Hist. Reb.* VIII. §169 Goring had..a much keener Courage, and presentness of Mind in danger. *a***1653** BINNING *Serm.* (1845) 310 Do you either listen and apply your hearts to a presentness in hearing. **1660** INGELO *Bentiv. & Ur.* II. (1682) 32 He had such an undaunted Presentness of a prepared Mind.

‖**presentoir** (prezɑ̃twar). *Obs.* [In form French, as if:—L. type **præsentōrium*; but not known in French use; apparently of English invention.] (See quot.)

1854 FAIRHOLT *Dict. Terms Art*, *Presentoir* (Fr.), an ornamental cup, very shallow, and having a tall, enriched stem; it was a decorative article of luxury, serving no particular use; but was much fabricated in the sixteenth century, at which period the one engraved was executed. Hence in WEBSTER 1864, *Cent. Dic.*, etc.

presentor (prɪ'zɛntə(r)). [Early mod.E. *presentour*, a. AF. *presentour* = F. *présenteur*, agent-n. f. *présenter* to PRESENT: see -OR.]

†**1. a.** One who makes a presentment: = PRESENTER 2. *Obs.*

[*c* **1340** *Modus tenendi Curias* in *Court Baron* (Selden Soc. 1891) 97 Ore doit le seneschal fere elire xij. fraunkes tenauntz..qe puissent oier le presentement de presentour sil facent nul conseylement.]

1532–3 *Act 24 Hen. VIII*, c. 10 The stewarde with two of the presentours shall assesse..suche amerciament to them shall seeme reasonable. **1592** in *Vicary's Anat.* (1888) App. xv. 277 Thone halfe [of the fine] to the comon chamber, and thother halfe to the presentor. **1614** SELDEN *Titles Hon.* 270 Ouer euery Hundred is written (before the Iurors) *Alder. Iuratorum* with a name prefixt, then *Electores Iuratorum* with two names, and next the Presentors.

b. One who presents to a benefice: = PRESENTER 1. *rare*.

1865 NICHOLS *Britton* II. 193 If..the presentor pending the presentation dies [*orig.* IV. iv. §13 Si..pendaunt le presentement, moerge le presentour]. **1904** A. F. POLLARD *Cranmer* vii. 195 The sale of benefices was to be punished by deprivation of the presentee, and by forfeiture of the presentor's patronage.

2. = PRESENTOIR (? misprint).

1882 *Pall Mall G.* 28 June 10/1 A silver-gilt presentor, formed as an infant Bacchus on a barrel, 9½ in. high, 290 guineas.

pre-separate: see PRE- A. 1.

presepe, obs. form of PRÆCIPE.

‖**presepio** (pre'sepjo). [It., f. L. *præsæpe* enclosure, stall: cf. PRÆSEPE.] A crib; a model of the manger in which Christ was laid.

1759 M. W. MONTAGU *Let.* 19 July (1967) III. 220 The devout people who spend 20 years in making a magnificent presepia [*sic*] at Naples. **1958** *Listener* 25 Dec. 1067/1 Every Italian family has its own *presepio*, as the crib is called. **1969** E. H. PINTO *Treen* 173/2 Presepio or Nativity figure tableaux have been and still are used in most parts of Christendom.

preservable (prɪ'zɜːvəb(ə)l), *a.* [f. PRESERVE *v.* + -ABLE.] Capable of being preserved.

1647 *Eng. Mountebank Casting Sickly Water of State* 5 Meere Notions, and not vindicable, nor preservable by Law. **1832** W. TAYLOR in Robberds *Mem.* II. 537, I have often meditated to collect my preservable works under the denomination Wilhelm Taylor. **1868** RUSKIN *Pol. Econ. Art* Add. 232 No work can be wasted.., provided only the kind of it..be preservable and distributable.

Hence **preserva'bility**.

1889 *Lancet* 27 Apr. 35 Advt., Securing safety, palatability, convenience and preservability of drugs. **1959** *Brno Studies in English* I. 11 This feature [*sc.* the documentary, preservable character of written utterances], which one may perhaps term 'preservability', has been appreciated by men since time immemorial. **1972** *Science* 22 Sept. 1067/1 Some biologic groups show fossil diversities closer to their actual diversities than do other groups because of inherent differences in preservability.

preserval (prɪ'zɜːvəl). *rare.* [f. PRESERVE *v.* + -AL[1].] Preservation.

1640 GLAPTHORNE *Wallenstein* III. ii, To thanke you For this same deare preservall of my life. **1827** SOUTHEY *Hist. Penins. War* II. 237 The preserval of the deposit of the sovereignty entrusted into their hands. **1882** *Med. Temp. Jrnl.* L. 86 Conducive to the preserval of order.

preservation (prɛzə'veɪʃən). [a. F. *préservation* (13–14th c. in Hatz.-Darm.), ad. med.L. *præservātio* (Duns Scotus, *Sentent.* 4. 22. 17), n. of action f. late L. *præservāre* to PRESERVE.]

1. a. The action of preserving or keeping from injury or destruction; the fact of being preserved (esp. with objective genitive, e.g. your preservation = your being preserved).

1472–3 *Rolls of Parlt.* VI. 17/2 Youre seid Suppliaunt shall pray to God for the preservation of youre moost roiall estate. **1472–3**, **1485** [see PRAY *v.* 5 c]. **1555** EDEN *Decades* 103 Thankes geuynge to almyghty god for his delyuery and preseruation from so many imminent perels. **1594** T. B. *La Primaud. Fr. Acad.* II. 233 Remedies meete for the maintenance and preseruation of his bodie. **1641** *More's Rich. III*, Ep. Ded. 1 The great care..observed..for the preservation of antiquities. **1662** *Bk. Com. Prayer, General Thanksgiving*, We bless thee for our creation, preservation, and all the blessings of this life. **1770** *Phil. Trans.* L. 318

Varnished over with the same sort of varnish that is used for the preservation. **1844** LD. BROUGHAM *Brit. Const.* xx. (1862) 387 The preservation of the peace always must be the first interest of all who have property. **1845** R. HUNTER *Landlord & Tenant* (ed. 2) II. 213 Melioration and preservation, or repairs, often admit of little distinction.

b. preservation order, a legal obligation on an owner to preserve a building of historic interest or value.

1947 *Act 10 & 11 Geo. VI* c. 51 §29 If it appears to a local planning authority that it is expedient to make provision for the preservation of any building of special architectural or historic interest in their area, they may for that purpose make an order (in this Act referred to as a 'building preservation order') restricting the demolition, alteration or extension of the building. **1953** *Act 1 & 2 Eliz. II* c. 49 §11 The Minister may.. make an order (in this Act referred to as a 'preservation order') placing under the more lasting protection of the Minister a monument with respect to which an interim preservation notice is in force. **1968** *Guardian* 13 Aug. 5/8 Residents of.. Bridgnorth have won a battle to preserve the Crown Hotel.. from being knocked down... A preservation order on the building has been confirmed by the Minister of Housing and Local Government. **1971** 'J. ASHFORD' *Bent Copper* iv. 27 Parkham Green village was justly famous for its ancient architectural beauty... The whole village was covered by a special preservation order. **1978** N. J. CRISP *London Deal* iv. 83 Those houses are the subject of preservation orders now.

2. The state or condition of being (well or ill) preserved; state of keeping.

1751 J. STUART in *Lett. Lit. Men* (Camden) 386 The outward precinct of an Amphitheatre in excellent preservation. **1816** CHALMERS in Hanna *Mem.* (1849) II. iv. 82 The fox-tails are still in great preservation. **1890** BARKER *Wayfaring in France* 216 The ramparts of Aigues-Mortes.. are in a much better state of preservation.

†**3.** The means of preservation; a preservative.

1584 COGAN (*title*) The Haven of Health... Hereunto is added a Preseruation from the Pestilence. **1597** HOOKER *Eccl. Pol.* v. lv. §2 Measure is likewise the preseruation of all things. **1617** MORYSON *Itin.* II. 166 Hallowed meddals, which they woare as preseruations against death.

†**4.** A thing preserved from decay. *Obs.*

1796 BURNEY *Mem. Metastasio* III. 188 We should.. be in the state of those preservations which.. without salting, become incorruptible when buried under a deep snow.

preservationist (prɛzə'veɪʃənɪst). [f. PRESERVATION + -IST.] An advocate of preservation, *esp.* one who advocates the preservation of historic buildings or antiquities. Also *attrib.* or as *adj.* Hence **preser'vationism**, the practice or advocacy of preservation.

1927 *Blackw. Mag.* Sept. 314/1 The excuses made for her [*sc.* the peregrine falcon] by modern 'Preservationists' are altogether paltry. **1937** *Archit. Rev.* LXXXII. 50/1 We would not.. do more than note in passing Raphael's plea for the preservation of antiquities and his appointment as controller of monuments by Pope Leo X. Distance has dimmed too much for us the true nature of Raphael and his kind as constructive artists, as opposed to the 'preservationists' of today, for us to risk such an appointment. **1957** *Observer* 10 Nov. 3/4 Town planning councils, preservationist maniacs and 'good taste' committees all came in for a drubbing. **1959** *Archit. Rev.* CXXVI. 205/2 Old houses in New Zealand have not yet acquired a period value. Preservationism is completely absent; too much so, one is inclined to say. **1960** *Guardian* 25 Feb. 1/2 A preservationist undergraduate.. threatened to send 'Save Cowley Vicarage' telegrams. **1961** *Architect & Building News* 21 June 815/1, I hope the preservationists will not let up for a minute in their struggle to protect our dwindling countryside. **1973** *Times* 16 Oct. 2/5 In 1964 the London County Council wanted to demolish it, but a public inquiry ended in a victory for preservationists led by Sir John Betjeman. *a* **1974** R. CROSSMAN *Diaries* (1975) I. 623 She regarded it as pure sentimentalism and called it 'preservationism', a word of abuse. **1978** *Courier-Jrnl.* (Louisville, Kentucky) 16 Apr. D-4/1 Announcement of the discovery was delayed until recently.. because the mining concern.. feared there would be a preservationist outcry.

preservative (prɪ'zɜːvətɪv), *a.* and *sb.* Also 5–6 -yve, -if(fe, -yf(e. [ad. F. *préservatif* adj. and sb. (13–14th c. in Hatz.-Darm.), ad. med.L. *præservātīvus* (R. Grosseteste *c* 1225): see PRESERVE *v.* and -ATIVE.]

A. *adj.* Having the quality of preserving; tending to preserve; protective.

1398 TREVISA *Barth. De P.R.* VII. lxix. (Bodl. MS.), He [the physician] techeþ to vse certeyne medicines preseruatyues to [= against] feblenes. *c* **1430** LYDG. *Min. Poems* (Percy Soc.) 91 Demyng theyr odour.. Was to his courage most preservatyve. **1483** CAXTON *Gold. Leg.* 334 b/1 The medecyne preseruatyf is that whiche preserueth fro fallyng. **1578** LYTE *Dodoens* IV. xli. 501 Treacles and Mithridates, and suche lyke preseruatiue medicines. **1644** HUNTON *Vind. Treat. Monarchy* ix. 69 This is the Doctors preservative Doctrine. **1699** SHAFTESB. *Inq. conc. Virtue* I. iii. 78 Virtuous and preservative of virtue. **1827** SIR J. BARRINGTON *Personal Sk.* I. 12 A bad example may sometimes be more preservative against error than a good one. **1899** *Allbutt's Syst. Med.* VIII. 929 A preservative injection for anatomical purposes.

B. *sb.* (absolute use of adj.)

1. a. A medicine that preserves health, protecting from or preventing disease; a safeguard against poison or infection; a prophylactic.

1466 *Manners & Household Expenses* (Roxb.) 369 A lyte boxe of preser[u]atyffe, and a pote of tryakel. *a* **1548** HALL *Chron., Hen. VIII* 176 b, Whiche place was.. purged daily with fyers and other preseruatiues. **1672** *Phil. Trans.* VII. 5063 To swallow a Vipers head was a most certain Preservative and Remedy against the biting of a Viper. **1779** JOHNSON *Let. to Mrs. Thrale* 17 June, I am glad that you have Heberden, and hope his restoratives and his preservatives will both be effectual.

fig. **1534** MORE *Comf. agst. Trib.* I. Wks. 1150/1 Tribulacion is double medicine, bothe a cure of the synne passed, & a preseruatiue fro the syn that is to come. **1611** BIBLE *Transl. Pref.* 3 The Scripture.. is.. a Physicions-shop .. of preseruatiues against poisoned heresies.

b. *gen.* A thing that preserves *from* (or *against*) any danger or injury; a safeguard.

1526 *Pilgr. Perf.* (W. de W. 1531) 113 b, Preseruatyues agaynst enuy & wroth. **1670** WALTON *Lives* IV. 286 Strong preservatives against all disquiet. *a* **1703** BURKITT *On N.T.* Rom. xi. 21 The best preservative from falling, is humility and holy fear. **1775** ADAIR *Amer. Ind.* 175 *note*, An infallible preservative against the legions of evil spirits. **1874** L. STEPHEN *Hours in Library* (1892) I. v. 197 A delicate sense of humour, which is the best preservative against all extravagance.

2. That which preserves, or tends to preserve or protect from decay, loss, or destruction.

1503 HAWES *Examp. Virt.* v. 17 Lete wysedome than be to the comfortyfe That to thy brayn is best preseruatyfe. **1520** WHITINTON *Vulg.* (1527) 5 b, Good dyet, the preseruatyue of helthe. **1575–85** ABP. SANDYS *Serm.* v. (Parker Soc.) 93 Two preservatives and defences of unity and love. **1683** *Brit. Spec.* 68 The main Preservatives of Peace are the Durability and Order of the Government. **1808** MRS. M. T. KEMBLE *Day after Wedding* 22 This preservative of happiness. **1864** BOWEN *Logic* i. 24 But Words are not only signs and preservatives, they are also substitutes, for Thoughts.

3. *spec.* A chemical substance or preparation used to preserve things subject to decomposition, as perishable food-stuffs.

[**1756** C. LUCAS *Ess. Waters* II. 36 Salt is not.. an effectual preservative from putrefaction.] **1875** H. C. WOOD *Therap.* (1879) 440 M. Carville affirms that glucose acts well as a preservative. **1898** *Westm. Gaz.* 23 Feb. 3/2 A question of great difficulty to the public analyst is the introduction of preservatives into articles of food. **1904** *Brit. Med. Jrnl.* 10 Sept. 620 The campaign.. against the use of preservatives in other food-stuffs [than milk].

†**4.** *Photogr.* Formerly used for *fixing solution.*

1878 ABNEY *Photogr.* (1881) 94 The preservative is usually applied by floating it on the surface of the film for about a minute. **1890** *Anthony's Photogr. Bull.* III. 288 The processes at that time known as 'dry' were those where the collodion employed had received an application of so-called preservative.

pre'servatize, *v.* [f. PRESERVAT-IVE *sb.* + -IZE. Cf. *sensitize.*] *trans.* To treat with a preservative.

1901 *Rep. Preservatives Com.* in *Daily Chron.* 27 Nov. 6/7 The imported goods are preservatised to a much greater extent than the home produce. **1904** *Brit. Med. Jrnl.* 10 Sept. 620 Milk has never been much preservatized in Liverpool. **1905** F. L. DODD *Municip. Milk* 3 So long as it is profitable to sell dirty milk as clean, or preservatized butter as fresh, these efforts will produce but scanty fruit.

†**pre'servator, -our.** *Obs.* Also 6 *erron.* -itour. [ad. obs. F. *preservateur* (1514 in Godef. *Compl.*), ad. L. **præservātōr-em*, agent-n. from *præservāre* to PRESERVE.] = PRESERVER.

1540–1 ELYOT *Image Gov.* 115 Which shall sweare by the gods preseruatours of the Citee of Rome. **1579** NORTH *Plutarch* 64 He imagined that his death.. should be as a seale of confirmation of his lawe and the continuall preseruitour of his cittie.

preservatory (prɪ'zɜːvətərɪ), *a.* and *sb. rare.* [ad. L. types **præservātōri-us, -ōri-um*, f. *præservāre* to PRESERVE: see -ORY[1] and [2]: cf. *conservatory, observatory*, etc.]

A. *adj.* Tending to preserve; preservative.

1649 BP. HALL *Cases Consc.* II. iii. 128 The intentions, and indevours must be no other than preservatory. **1701–2** *Narr. Lower Ho. Convocation Vind.* 47 Business not so much Preparatory, as Preservatory.

B. *sb.* (absol. use of adj.)

1. A means of preserving; a preservative.

1654 WHITLOCK *Zootomia* 410 Such vain Preservatories of us, are our Inheritances, even once removed. **1665** G. HARVEY *Advice agst. Plague* 13 Most people that carry those perfumed boxes about with them, imagine them sufficient preservatories, as if the Infection were only taken by inspiration through the Nostrils. **1758** SIR J. FIELDING (*title*) A Plan for a Preservatory and Reformatory, For the Benefit of Deserted Girls, and Penitent Prostitutes.

2. A place for preserving; = PRESERVE *sb.* 4.

1823 D'ISRAELI *Cur. Lit., Secr. Hist. Blenheim*, Atossa.. had driven [her hunted prey] to a spot which she flattered herself would inclose it with the security of a preservatory.

3. *U.S.* An apparatus for preserving substances for food, etc.

1875 in KNIGHT *Dict. Mech.*

†**pre'servatrice.** *Obs. rare*[−1]. [fem., in F. form, of obs. F. *preservateur* (see PRESERVATOR); ad. L. type **præservātrix, -trīcem*.] = next.

1559 BERCHER *Nobylytye Wymen* (Roxb.) 103 Lady nature, the moste sage preservatrice of hyr werkes.

†**preser'vatrix.** *Obs. rare.* [a. mod.L. *præservātrix*: see prec.] A female preserver.

1650 T. BAYLY *Herba Parietis* 15 A fond lover and preservatrix of so great a worthy. **1684** tr. *Agrippa's Van. Arts* lxiii. 190 Rhodope.. the Preservatrix and Bedfellow of Æsop.

preserve (prɪ'zɜːv), *sb.* [f. next.]

†**1. a.** A preserving agent; a preservative. *Obs.*

1552 LYNDESAY *Monarche* 4926 Off Malideis it generis mony mo,—Bot gyf men gett sum Souerane preserue. **1594** GREENE & LODGE *Looking Glass* G.'s Wks. (Rtldg.) 124/1 Fetch balsamo, the kind preserve of life. **1627–77** FELTHAM *Resolves* II. xliii. 242 Plainness and freedom are the preserves of amity. **1839** J. D. HOOKER in L. Huxley *Life J. D. Hooker* (1918) I. 43 That Capt. Ross did *not* intend to treat me thus .. I am sure, from his asking me to tell the quantity of preserves for animals required.

b. Weak spectacles intended to preserve the sight (*Sc.*). **c.** Goggles used to protect the eyes from dust, excess of light, etc.

1808 JAMIESON, *Preserves*, spectacles, which magnify little or nothing. **1883** J. PURVES in *Contemp. Rev.* Sept. 354 He will at a corner throw off his coat.. and be at work stone-breaking with preserves on his eyes. **1887** A. BRUCE in *Encycl. Brit.* XXII. 372/2 Preserves are used to conceal deformities or to protect the eyes in the many conditions where they cannot tolerate bright light. **1893** J. WATSON *Conf. Poacher* 146 We carried about us stone-breakers' hammers, and 'preserves' for the eyes. *Ibid.* 147 The preserves cover the face.

2. A confectionary preparation of fruit or other vegetable products preserved with sugar; jam; often in *pl.* (cf. *conserves*).

1600 SURFLET *Countrie Farme* II. li. 350 There is but very seldome any preserues made of the flowers and leaues of herbes; I vnderstand by this preserue taken properly, the preseruing of things whole and not stampt and beaten into one bodie. **1670** CAPT. J. SMITH *Eng. Improv. Reviv'd* 198 The Syrops, Conserves, and Preserves of the said Berries are of great use in a Family. **1794** MRS. A. M. BENNETT *Ellen* I. 8 A great manager, who.. made the best pastry, pickles and preserves in the Kingdom. **1854** MRS. GASKELL *North & S.* xx, Perhaps, I might take her a little preserve, made of our dear Helstone fruit. **1888** J. C. HARRIS *Free Joe*, etc. 87 My companion had a theory of his own that ginger-preserves and fruit-cake were not good for sick people.

†**3.** A thing preserved. *Obs. rare*[−1].

a **1682** SIR T. BROWNE *Mummies* Wks. 1835 IV. 273 Wonderful indeed are the preserves of time, which openeth unto us mummies from crypts and pyramids.

4. a. A wood or other ground set apart for the protection and rearing of game; a pond or piece of water for fish; a vivarium.

1807 WINDHAM *Sp.* 22 July (1812) III. 32 They secured them as country-gentlemen do the game in those places near their houses, which, by an odd misnomer, are sometimes called 'the preserve', where the game are, indeed, preserved, but only till some circumstance.. shall furnish an occasion for falling upon them with redoubled fury. **1814** COL. HAWKER *Diary* (1893) I. 103 The pheasants from Lord Portsmouth's preserves. **1849** MACAULAY *Hist. Eng.* iii. I. 290 The moats were turned into preserves of carp and pike. **1867** TROLLOPE *Chron. Barset* II. lvii. 135 A husband with broad acres, a big house, and game preserves.

b. *transf.* and *fig.*

1829 MOORE *Mem.* (1854) VI. 44 Taken to the Ancient Music by Lord Essex.. and sat in 'the preserve', as the directors' box is called. **1862** 'SHIRLEY' *Nugæ Crit.* II. 134 A man unendowed with this capacity, when turned loose in a historical preserve, wanders about blindly and aimlessly, committing the most flagrant blunders. **1882** PEBODY *Eng. Journalism* xxi. 155 The expresses of the *Times* and the *Morning Chronicle*.. did a good deal to disturb the quiet preserves of the Provincial Press. **1897** *Daily News* 2 Feb. 5/2 In the Colonies.. we have not so much neutral markets, as preserves.

5. *attrib.* and *Comb.*, as (sense 2) ***preserve-can, -dish, -jar, -pot.***

1882 W. D. HAY *Brighter Britain!* I. v. 138 There were empty preserve-cans, gallipots, and oyster-shells! **1856** M. J. HOLMES *'Lena Rivers* 108 The big preserve dish got broken. **1867** G. W. HARRIS *Sut Lovingood* 92 Preserve jars, vinegar jugs, seed bags, yarb bunches.. all mix'd. **1885** E. P. ROE *Nature's Serial Story* xliii. 307 Racoons.. will uncover preserve-jars.., and with the certainty of a toper uncork a bottle and get drunk on its contents. **1969** R. & D. DE SOLA *Dict. Cooking* 183/2 *Preserve jar*, jar or pot for holding homemade preserves. **1854** THOREAU *Walden* 235 He goes to the mill-pond, she to her preserve-pot.

preserve (prɪ'zɜːv), *v.* [a. F. *préserver* 'to save from an evil that might happen' (14–15th c. in Hatz.-Darm.), ad. late L. *præservāre* (Hilary) to preserve, f. *præ* before + *servāre* to keep, protect.]

1. *trans.* To keep safe from harm or injury; to keep in safety, save, take care of, guard. Const. *from* (†*of, out of*).

1375 BARBOUR *Bruce* I. 608 God of mycht Preserwyt him till hyer hycht, That wald nocht that he swa war dede. **1390** GOWER *Conf.* II. 86 Forto kepe and to preserve The bodi fro siknesses alle. *c* **1430** LYDG. in *Pol. Rel. & L. Poems* (1866) 26 Daniel lay.. preseruyd in prison with lyouns. **1483** CAXTON *Cato* C ij b, Thus was the cytee kept and preserued of the pestylence. **1605** SHAKS. *Lear* II. iii. 6 Whiles I may scape I will preserue myselfe. **1606** G. W[OODCOCKE] *Hist. Ivstine* XXXIX. 125 To preserue her out of captiuity. **1621** T. WILLIAMSON tr. *Goulart's Wise Vieillard* 22 Who braggingly gaue it out, that hee had a receipt would preserue a man from growing old. **1748** *Anson's Voy.* II. ix. 229 Instructions.. to the officers to preserve themselves from being seen from the shore. **1800** ADDISON *Amer. Law Rep.* 142 Perhaps.. reasons which would preserve a presumed innocent man from a second trial would not preserve a presumed guilty man.

b. In invocations. Now esp. *Sc.* (with ellipsis).

1467 *Mann. & Househ. Exp.* (Roxb.) 173 Jesewes.. preserve ȝowe my moste drede soveren lord in his blesed safegard. **1535** in *Lett. Suppress. Monasteries* (Camden) 84 Jhesu preserve yow in helthe with myche honore. **1597** SHAKS. *2 Hen. IV*, II. iv. 315 Oh, the Lord preserue thy good Grace. **1796** R. GALL *Tint Quey* Poems (1819) 28 She cried, 'Preserve us! whare's the cow?' **1885** 'J. STRATHESK' *More Bits* iii. (ed. 2) 42 Preserve me, George, that's liker a 'risp' than a razor! **1899** CROCKETT *Kit Kennedy* iii. 20 Preserve us a' —— we mauna raise a finger against the brat.

2. To keep alive, keep from perishing (*arch.*); to keep in existence, keep from decay, make lasting (a material thing, a name, a memory).

[**1390** GOWER *Conf.* III. 221 If a king the lif preserve Of him which oghte forto dye. *c* **1430** LYDG. *Min. Poems* (Percy Soc.) 62 O welle of swetnes.. That al mankynd preserved hast fro dethe.] **1560** DAUS tr. *Sleidane's Comm.* 130 Peter Wirtemie beyng in daunger amonges the rest, at the request of the Lantgraue, was preserued. **1615** G. SANDYS *Trav.* 82 In these Monasteries many excellent manu-scripts haue bene preserued. **1694** *Acc. Sev. Late Voy.* Introd. 9 They preserved themselves with Geese, Ducks, vast large Muscles..etc. **1738** GRAY *Propertius* III. 100 And the short Marble but preserve a Name. **1839** DE LA BECHE *Rep. Geol. Cornwall*, etc. viii. 235 These sands..have not preserved many of their exuviæ. **1874** GREEN *Short Hist.* ii. §3. 67 A tiny little village preserves the name of the Percy. **1875** JOWETT *Plato* (ed. 2) IV. 238 The bodily frame is preserved by exercise and destroyed by indolence. **1904** W. M. RAMSAY *Lett. Seven Ch.* i. 13 Few private letters older than the imperial time have been preserved.

b. To keep up, maintain (a state of things).

1676–7 MARVELL *Corr.* Wks. (Grosart) II. 529 The Bill from the Lords, for preserving a Protestant clergy..was read. **1810** SOUTHEY in *Edinb. Ann. Reg.* I. I. 92 Other means that would be equally effectual in preserving discipline. **1830** D'ISRAELI *Chas. I*, III. x. 223 Knox..preserved an uninterrupted correspondence with Calvin. **1860** TYNDALL *Glac.* I. vii. 56 To enable the striæ to preserve the same general direction.

c. To keep in one's possession; to retain (a possession, acquisition, property, quality, etc.).

1617 MORYSON *Itin.* III. 176 The Turkish and Greekish women haue most delicate bodyes, and long preserue their beauties. **1687** A. LOVELL tr. *Thevenot's Trav.* III. 46 There are People in Dehly, vastly rich in Jewels, especially the Rajas who preserve their Pretious Stones from Father to Son. **1720** OZELL *Vertot's Rom. Rep.* II. XIV. 330 Cæsar contented himself with preserving the advantage he had gain'd. **1828** D'ISRAELI *Chas. I*, I. vi. 150 In politics they often yield the name while they preserve the thing. **1834** MRS. SOMERVILLE *Connex. Phys. Sc.* xxvi. (1849) 293 The seas preserve a considerable portion of the heat they receive in summer. **1886** WILLIS & CLARK *Cambridge* II. 165 The whole preserves a venerable air of undisturbed antiquity.

3. To keep from physical or chemical change. **a.** To prepare (fruit, meat, etc.) by boiling with sugar, salting, or pickling, so as to prevent its decomposition or fermentation. Also *absol.*

1579 [see PRESERVED 2]. **1584** COGAN *Haven Health* cv. 92 The Damasin Plummes are woont to be dryed and preserued as figges. **1611** SHAKS. *Cymb.* I. v. 13 Hast thou not learn'd me how To make Perfumes? Distill? Preserue? **1663** BOYLE *Usef. Exp. Nat. Philos.* II. ii. 107 A Friend of.. mine..hath a strange way of preserving Fruits, whereby even Goos-berries have been kept for many Moneths, without the addition of Sugar. **1796** C. MARSHALL *Garden.* xii. (1813) 167 The morella cherry is..not wanted till late in the season to preserve. **1870** YEATS *Nat. Hist. Comm.* 286 This art of preserving meat is one of modern times.

b. To keep (organic bodies) from decomposition, by chemical treatment, freezing, etc.

1613 PURCHAS *Pilgrimage* (1614) 540 Little Apes..which they used to preserve with certaine Spices, having flayed off their skinnes,..and sell them. **1677** W. HUBBARD *Narrative* II. 72 The body of Captain Lake, preserven entire and whole and free from putrefaction by the coldness of the long winter. **1727–41** CHAMBERS *Cycl.* s.v. *Timber*, The Dutch preserve their gates, portcullices, draw-bridges, sluices, etc. by coating them over with a mixture of pitch and tar [etc.]. **1893** SELOUS *Trav. S.E. Africa* 44, I shot and preserved a great many fine specimens of..antelopes. **1899** *Allbutt's Syst. Med.* VIII. 929 Those engaged in dissecting bodies preserved with arsenic. *Mod.* Specimens of snakes and other reptiles, locusts, etc. preserved in spirits.

c. *intr.* (for *refl.*) To remain without physical or chemical change; to remain in wholesome condition; to 'keep'; also, to endure or 'stand' preserving.

1585 T. WASHINGTON tr. *Nicholay's Voy.* III. i. 69 b, The snow..preserveth all the whole Sommer in hys accustomed nature and coldnesse without melting. **1748** *Anson's Voy.* I. v. 45 The water..is excellent, and preserves at sea as well as that of the Thames.

4. To keep (game) undisturbed for personal use in hunting, shooting, or fishing; to keep (game runs, fishing rivers, etc.) for private use. Also *absol.*

1612 EARL OF EXETER in *Buccleuch MSS.* (Hist. MSS. Comm.) I. 239 The game was well preserved by his uncle. **1807** [see PRESERVE *sb.* 4]. **1853** LYTTON *My Novel* VIII. v, Squire Thornhill..had taken the liberty to ask permission to shoot over Mr Leslie's land, since Mr Leslie did not preserve. **1867** TROLLOPE *Chron. Barset* I. xxii. 187 A man who preserves is always respected by the poachers. **1886** *Field* 13 Feb. 182/2 There is no better preserved wood throughout the length and breadth of the Hertfordshire country. *Ibid.* 27 Feb. 269/2 Mr. A. H. Longman has foxes strictly preserved.

preserved (prɪˈzɜːvd), *ppl. a.* [f. prec. + -ED[1].]

1. *gen.* Kept safe, protected; kept in existence, maintained, retained, etc.: see prec. 1, 2.

1552 HULOET, Preserued, *præseruatus.* Preserued in health, *sospes.* **1573–80** BARET *Alv.* P 680 Kept, Preserved, ..*ab hostium populatione defensa.* **1861** WHYTE MELVILLE *Mkt. Harb.* iii. 22 A strong odour of preserved tobacco-smoke. **1902** *Westm. Gaz.* 29 Sept. 3/2 Professor Dixon.. described the contents of libraries as the 'preserved verbosity of centuries'.

2. *spec.* **a.** Treated so as to resist putrefaction.

1579 LANGHAM *Gard. Health* (1633) 136 Preserued Cheries and Plummes. **1582** N. LICHEFIELD tr. *Castanheda's Conq. E. Ind.* I. vi. 15 A pot a Dates preserued. **1820** W. IRVING *Sketch-Bk., Leg. Sleepy Hollow* §40 Delectable dishes of preserved plums. **1861** *Times* 27 Sept., Jars of preserved meats which had been brought from England. **1890** SARAH J. DUNCAN *Soc. Depart.* 414 She had never seen anything so utterly horrid as a preserved Capuchin.

b. In combinations used attrib.

1901 *Westm. Gaz.* 1 May 2/2 He had the rations of condemned prisoners handed to him in old preserved-meat cans. **1904** *Ibid.* 12 May 2/3 The development of the marmalade and preserved-fruit industry. **1906** *Daily Chron.* 28 July 5/5 A 'preserved provision' merchant.

c. Kept undisturbed, as game or game-runs.

1881 *Daily News* 1 Sept. 5/3 The Duke of Edinburgh.. fished Lord Dalhousie's preserved water on South Esk, having good sport.

preserver (prɪˈzɜːvə(r)). [f. PRESERVE *v.* + -ER[1].]

1. A person who preserves. **a.** One who keeps safe from destruction or injury; a saviour.

1535 COVERDALE *Job* vii. 20, I haue offended, what shal I do vnto yᵉ, O thou preseruer off men? **1611** SHAKS. *Cymb.* v. v. 2 You, whom the Gods haue made Preseruers of my Throne. **1631** GOUGE *God's Arrows* III. §65. 304 The Church..is a faithful keeper and preserver of the Oracles of God. **1662** *Bk. Com. Prayer, Pr. all Conditions Men*, O God the creator and preserver of all mankind. **1749** FIELDING *Tom Jones* XVII. ii, He hath been the preserver of me and mine. **1806** SURR *Winter in Lond.* (ed. 3) II. 2 Her open and warm expressions of thanks to the preserver of her life.

b. One who preserves the bodies or stuffed skins of animals, etc.; a taxidermist.

1770 KUCKHAN *Pres. of Dead Birds* in *Phil. Trans.* LX. 310 One fault very common with most preservers.

c. One who preserves game, fish, etc., for sport.

1884 *Pall Mall G.* 4 Apr. 4/2 It would be sad..if the efforts of preservers should succeed in reducing our already painfully small stock of native mammals by further extirpating the four or five now menaced species.

2. a. A thing that preserves or keeps safe from harm.

1615 LATHAM *Falconry* (1633) 110 A present and speciall remedie against such inward diseases, and a great preseruer of health and lustinesse. **1750** tr. *Leonardus' Mirr. Stones* 84 Coral is a wonderful preserver. **1844** *Civil Engin. & Arch. Jrnl.* VII. 155/1 Inverted vessels (which the inventor denominates 'preservers') fixed at or near the bottom of the boiler or pan. **1899** *Allbutt's Syst. Med.* VIII. 580 In the form of bandages, and..with large pieces fitting like a 'chest preserver'.

b. *pl.* Spectacles for preserving the sight; 'preserves': see PRESERVE *sb.* 1 b.

1797 MRS. A. M. BENNETT *Beggar Girl* (1813) IV. 53 Miss put on her preservers, and said she was quite a well-grown young woman.

c. = LIFE-PRESERVER 2.

1912 *Chambers's Jrnl.* Aug. 636/1 In the panic which is certain to ensue after a wreck even the handling of this preserver would be awkward in the narrow passages and gangways.

Hence **preˈserveress**, a female preserver. Chiefly *fig.* and *poetic.*

1595 DANIEL *Civ. Wars* (1609) I. vi, And Memorie, preserv'resse of things done, Come thou, vnfold the woundes, the wracke, the waste. **1621** LADY M. WROTH *Urania* 228 The true preseruresse of pure truths. **1863** BARING-GOULD *Iceland* iii. 62 The ancient Finns made.. Antermen, 'the steam of the bath', the preserveress of vigour.

pre-ˈservice, *a.* [PRE- B. 2.] Of or relating to a period before a person or thing is ready for service (*spec.* national service) or use.

1928 [see *in-service* s.v. IN *prep.* 18]. **1944** W. TEMPLE *Church looks Forward* xix. 135 During the war, with the Pre-Service Units of various kinds, still more has to be done. **1948** *News Chron.* 24 Aug. 2/3 Britain's self-supporting Boy Scouts still find it easier to make recruits than do the Treasury-backed pre-Service cadet organisations. **1963** F. F. LAIDLER *Gloss. Home Econ. Educ.* 56 *Preservice training*, training given to a person before he/she enters an occupation. **1967** M. CHANDLER *Ceramics in Mod. World* v. 150 Short-term pre-service protection can be provided by coating such bricks with tar. **1974** H. L. FOSTER *Ribbin'* iv. 164 A few years ago I participated as a guest lecturer in a preservice education program for teacher aides in a large city.

preserving (prɪˈzɜːvɪŋ), *vbl. sb.* [-ING[1].] **a.** The action of the vb. PRESERVE, in various senses.

c **1470** G. ASHBY *Active Policy* 386 Being circumspect, as youre progenitours In suche caas haue bene, to the preseruing Of their Royal estate. **1530** PALSGR. 258/1 Preservyng, kepyng, *conseruation.* *a* **1610** HEALEY *Theophrastus* (1636) 10 Whatsoever belongeth to the womens Academie, as paintings, preservings, needle-workes, and such like. **1691** T. H[ALE] *Acc. New Invent.* 90 Application of Lead to the preserving of Iron-work. **1824** MISS MITFORD *Village* Ser. I. (1863) 221 Oh! the saltings, the picklings, the preservings..over which she presided.

b. *attrib.* esp. designating utensils used in making and keeping preserves, and fruit fitted for being preserved. **preserving sugar**, a coarse kind of sugar used in the preserving of fruits.

1679 MARG. MASON *Tickler Tickl.* 1 Superintendant of her Limbecks, Preserving-Pans, and Washes. **1719** LONDON & WISE *Compl. Gard.* 87 The truly good and fair Cherries, commonly call'd preserving Cherries, are those of Montmorancy. **1861** MRS. BEETON *Bk. Househ. Managem.* xxx. 758 In all the operations for preserve-making, when the preserving-pan is used, it should not be placed on the fire, but on a trivet. **1886** *York Herald* 11 Aug. 1/2 Preserving Jars..in any quantity. **1909** M. LITTLE *Cookery Up-to-Date* xi. 235 Weigh the apricots and to every pound of fruit add three-quarters of a pound of preserving sugar. **1916** *Daily Colonist* (Victoria, B.C.) 13 July 7/1 (Advt.), Preserving Kettles. Best grey enamel, 12 quarts, strong bail handle. **1921** *Ibid.* 30 Oct. 3/1 (Advt.), Preserving Quinces, 2 lbs. for 25¢. **1926** *Ibid.* 13 July 7/5 (Advt.), Preserving Crocks. For butter or eggs; four-gallon size, with cover. **1948** *Good Housek. Cookery Bk.* 667 If you intend to make jams, jellies and marmalades regularly, you would be well advised to invest in a good strong preserving pan. **1949** *Nat. Geogr. Mag.* XLVI. 193/2 [Watermelon] will cross with the so-called preserving melon, or citron, which is simply a hard, white-fleshed watermelon, good only for preserving. **1970** *Canad. Antiques Collector* July–Aug. 23/2 One of the first commercial potteries..to make..preserving jars. **1972** K. STEWART *Times Cookery Bk.* xx. 265 Strawberry Jam... 4 lb strawberries 3½ lb granulated or preserving sugar. **1977** *Western Morning News* 30 Aug. 2/3 Attractive Sale of Furniture and Effects, including:..preserving pan.

preserving (prɪˈzɜːvɪŋ), *ppl. a.* [f. as prec. + -ING[2].] That preserves; preservative.

1581 PETTIE tr. *Guazzo's Civ. Conv.* III. (1586) 130 b, The onelie preseruing remedie against that iealousie. **1594** PLAT *Jewell-ho.* I. 13 Which Niter is a preseruing salt. **1597** A. M. tr. *Guillemeau's Fr. Chirurg.* 15 b/2 The thirde stitchinge we call the conseruatiue or the præseruinge suture, because she præserueth and keepeth the lippes of the wounde. **1849** MACAULAY *Hist. Eng.* x. II. 663 It is because we had a preserving revolution in the seventeenth century that we have not had a destroying revolution in the nineteenth.

preservitor, erron. form of PRESERVATOR.

preses: var. PRÆSES.

†**preˈsession.** *Obs. rare*[−1]. [ad. L. *præsessiōn-em*, n. of action from *præsidēre* to PRESIDE.] The office or function of presiding, presidence.

a **1677** BARROW *Pope's Suprem.* (1680) 292 The Legates of Pope Leo..would not sit down in the Synod, because the præsession was not given to their Holy See [orig. *quod non data fuerit præsessio sanctæ Sedi eorum*].

pre-ˈset, *a.* [PRE- A. 1.] Decided or determined in advance; (of apparatus, etc.) set in advance of its operation.

1934 *Practical Wireless* 10 Mar. 1127/2 (*heading*) Bank of pre-set condensers. **1946** *Jrnl. Inst. Electr. Engin.* XCIII. II. 426/2 Pressure switches..which close circuit on the pressure falling to a pre-set point, may be installed. **1954** *N.Y. Times Mag.* 29 Aug. 49/1 The pre-set missile is not guided; it is fired, like a shell, at a pre-determined trajectory. **1961** G. MILLERSON *Technique Television Production* iii. 23 (*caption*) Height is pre-set and not readily adjusted. **1966** D. G. BRANDON *Mod. Techniques Metallogr.* 102 The specimen stage..will remain in a preset position sufficiently long to permit any area to be photographed with the full resolution of the instrument. **1973** *Country Life* 29 Nov. 1796 (Advt.), This ultramodern..oven..switches off at a pre-set time. **1978** R. V. JONES *Most Secret War* xlv. 447 Graphite rudders that were placed in the main jet so as to deflect the stream of incandescent gases and thus turn the rocket on to a preset trajectory both in bearing and in elevation.

pre-ˈset, *v.* [PRE- A. 1.] *trans.* To set or fix (apparatus) in advance of its operation; to settle or decide beforehand.

1946 *Sun* (Baltimore) 18 July 13/2 A pressure gauge..can be preset to open at an altitude where there is enough oxygen for a man to breathe. **1958** *Engineering* 11 Apr. 468/3 Temperature controllers which can be remotely pre-set from the control room. **1960** [see BIAS *a.*, *sb.*, and *adv.* B. 7]. **1962** D. SLAYTON in *Into Orbit* 68 You could preset the trainer for any kind of mission you wanted to fly. **1962** *Which?* May 148/1 The grinder was pre-set to give a certain particle size. **1977** *Gramophone* Feb. 1343/2 Under a sliding lid..are four similar controls for pre-setting your choice of 'instant' programmes.

presewme, obs. form of PRESUME.

preˈsexual, *a.* [PRE- B. 1.] Preceding or not yet influenced by sexual activity or sexual awareness; pre-pubertal; also *Gram.*, not (yet) differentiated by natural gender.

1919 M. K. BRADBY *Psycho-Anal.* IV. xii. 164 Because our own sexuality is associated with sense of guilt, to us innocence implies a pre-sexual state of mind. **1925** D. H. LAWRENCE *St. Mawr* 204 They [*sc.* pine-trees] hedged one in with the power..of the pre-sexual primeval world. **1927** B. MALINOWSKI *Sex & Repression in Savage Society* I. ix. 77 The development of pre-sexual life at this stage also differs in Europe and Melanesia. **1949** *Archivum Linguisticum* I. 168 A syntactic peculiarity of old Bulgarian declension.. discloses the existence of a presexual division of nouns into animate and inanimate. **1961** R. F. C. HULL tr. *Jung's Coll. Wks.* IV. 118 The necessity for this becomes really urgent when we ask ourselves whether the intense joys and sorrows of a child in the first years of his life, that is, *at the presexual stage*, are conditioned solely by his sexual libido. **1971** G. H. BOURNE *Ape People* xi. 254 Presexual play in humans often involves the nibbling or biting of the earlobes.

pre-shadow: see PRE- A. 2.

preshow: see PRE- B. 2 a.

preˈshrink, *v.* [PRE- A. 1.] *trans.* To shrink (fabric) prior to cutting or (a garment) prior to sale, so as to prevent shrinkage following washing or cleaning.

1936 G. G. DENNY *Fabrics* (ed. 4) I. 104 A process for completely pre-shrinking cotton and linen fabrics. **1963** *Home Dressmaking* (B.B.C.) i. 4 Pre-shrink wool, cotton, silk fabrics, linings, interfacings, tapings, etc., before cutting. **1975** J. LABARTHE *Elements of Textiles* vii. 301 There is no economy to any customer to buy cotton garments..unless these have been preshrink by a dependable process. **1978** *Detroit Free Press* 5 Mar. D 9/1 Preshrink fabric and fringe, or it may shrink and pucker from steam.

Hence **pre'shrunk** *ppl. a.*; also **pre'shrinkage**, the process of preshrinking.

1942 G. G. DENNY *Fabrics* (ed. 5) v. 191 Use of terms 'Full shrunk', 'Preshrunk', 'Shrunk'.. prohibited if there is residual shrinkage left in the goods. **1951** *Good Housek. Home Encycl.* 251/1 All cloth.. should be shrunk before cutting, unless it is guaranteed pre-shrunk. **1960** *Guardian* 9 May 4/6 Pre-shrinkage is one of the things the Irish are rather good about. *a* **1963** L. MACNEICE *Astrol.* (1964) vii. 232 Astrology has been used to sell anything from pre-shrunk shirts to alcoholic drinks. **1975** J. LABARTHE *Elements of Textiles* vii. 301 An.. advantage given by a satisfactory preshrinkage process is that the strength of the fabric has been increased. **1978** *Detroit Free Press* 16 Apr. A14/4 (Advt.), Water-repellent nylon taffeta with pre-shrunk cotton flannel lining.

preside (prɪ'zaɪd), *v.* Also 7 præ-, *Sc.* preceid, -seid. [a. F. *présider* (15th c. in Littré), ad. L. *præsidēre* to sit before, hence, to preside over, to guard, f. *præ*, PRE- + *sedēre* to sit.]

1. a. *intr.* To occupy the chair or seat of authority in any assembly, or at the ordinary meetings of a society or company; to act as chairman or president.

1611 COTGR., *Presider*, to preside. **1638** R. BAKER tr. *Balzac's Lett.* (vol. III.) 152 Nor [do I] suspect the integritie of the Judges that præside there. **1647** CLARENDON *Hist. Reb.* I. §98 By his place, he presided in all Publick Councils. **1682** in *Scott. Antiq.* (1901) July 7 Possessing him selfe in preseiding. *Ibid.* 8 His possessione of preceiding in the meetingis of the facultie as formerlie. **1782** PRIESTLEY *Corrupt. Chr.* I. III. 310 Remi himself presided. **1839** KEIGHTLEY *Hist. Eng.* II. 104 Norfolk presided as lord high Steward.

b. To sit at the head of the table.

1871 R. ELLIS tr. *Catullus* xxvii. 3 So Postumia, queen of healths presiding, Bids. **1900** 'SARAH GRAND' *Babs* xxiv, He led his guests into the dining-room.. 'Will you preside, dear lady?' he said.

c. *transf.* To take the foremost place.

1735 SOMERVILLE *Chase* II. 236 In the rapid Course Alternate they preside, and justling push To guide the dubious Scent.

2. To exercise superintendence, direction, or control. Also *fig.* to sit or reign supreme.

1656 BLOUNT *Glossogr.*, *Preside*, to have authority or rule, to have the protection and tuition of any thing, place or people. **1675** OGILBY *Brit.* Introd. 3 One Alderman to each Ward, over which he Presides. **1726** SWIFT *Gulliver* III. iii, That part of the earth over which the monarch presides. **1728** YOUNG *Love of Fame* I. 201 How comes it then to pass we see preside On both their brows an equal share of pride? **1754** J. WOOLMAN *Wks.* (1840) 198 When self-love presides in our mind our opinions are biased in our own favour. **1796** MORSE *Amer. Geog.* I. 279 In none of their meetings have they [Quakers] a President; as they believe Divine Wisdom alone ought to preside. **1823** DE QUINCEY *Lett. Educ.* ii. Wks. 1860 XIV. 32 The same ideal must have presided. **1849** MACAULAY *Hist. Eng.* vi. II. 14 Others presided over important departments of the civil administration. **1869** TOZER *Highl. Turkey* II. 282 Some law must have presided over their formation.

3. *trans.* To direct, control.

1665 MANLEY *Grotius' Low C. Warres* 649 Some accusing the unskilfulness of those that were to preside the Naval Affairs. **1802–12** BENTHAM *Ration. Judic. Evid.* (1827) II. 119 A trial before a jury, presided by one of the twelve judges. **1837** CARLYLE *Fr. Rev.* I. III. iii, He.. sits there, since he must sit, presiding that Bureau of his. **1967** *Decision & Decision-Makers in Mod. State* (Unesco) 82 The council is presided by the President or the Vice-President. **1974** *Amer. Speech* 1971 XLVI. 113 The meeting was presided.. by Dean Pinero.

4. *intr.* ***to preside at the organ***, or ***piano*** (***harpsichord***, etc.). *orig.* To conduct or be ready to guide the band on the instrument in question; now, in popular use, To have general control of the instrument for the time, to be (or act as) organist or pianist during any social, religious, or musical assembly.

'In former times the chief musician sat at a pianoforte in the orchestra with the score before him; but it does not appear that he beat time continuously, or in any way influenced the band, or did more than put in a few chords now and then when the orchestra was going astray' (Grove in *Dict. Mus.* I. 390).

1799 *Chron.* in *Ann. Reg.* 451 *Preside* is the word now applied—not to the leader of the band, but to some distinguished performer—as, 'Mr. —— will *preside* at the harpsichord'. Dr. Johnson did not live long enough to insert this meaning of the word, or to inquire whether it had any. **1907** *West Cumberld. Times* 4 Dec. 2/6 The hymn 'Rock of ages' was then sung by the congregation, Mr. T. L—— presiding at the organ.

¶ **5.** *catachr. intr.* To preponderate.

1718 J. FOX *Wanderer* 12 These were no sooner in the Scales, but I perceiv'd that [scale] to preside, which held so unhappy a Part of the Female World.

presidence ('prɛzɪdəns, 'prɛs-). [a. F. *présidence* (14th c. in Hatz.-Darm.), ad. med.L. *præsidentia* (see next).]

1. The action or fact of presiding; superintendence, direction.

1595 J. KING *Queens Day Serm.* in *Jonas* (1618) 693 They in the proper and internall offices,.. and he for outward authority and presidence; they as ouer-seers of the flocke of Christ, hee an ouer-seer of ouer-seers. **1603** HOLLAND *Plutarch's Mor.* 1331 The Dæmons ordained for the presidence and superintendance of prophesies and Oracles doe faile. **1722** WOLLASTON *Relig. Nat.* v. §18. 105 By some secret law.. or rather by the presidence and guidance of an unseen governing power. **1865** W. G. PALGRAVE *Arabia* II. 258 Presidence in worship was.. the privilege merely of greater age or of family headship.

2. The office or function of president; = PRESIDENCY 1. Now *rare.*

1606 *Rep. Disc. Supreme Power* 32 The Emperours.. had the primacie, and office of presidence in the eight generall Councels. **1717** L. HOWEL *Desiderius* 40 When you come to be sensible by what Methods I obtain'd the Presidence of this place. **1889** HAMERTON *French & Eng.* 136 The strong popular conservative tendency.. may possibly preserve both the senate and the presidence.

presidence, obs. form of PRECEDENCE.

presidency ('prɛzɪdənsɪ, 'prɛs-). [= med.L. *præsidentia* (1265 in Bonaventura), It. *presidenza*, Sp., Pr. *presidencia*, f. L. *præsidēns*, *-entem*: see PRESIDENT and -ENCY.]

1. The office or function of president; presidentship, chairmanship; superintendence, direction; also, the term during which a president holds office.

1591 PERCIVAL *Sp. Dict.*, *Presidencia*, presidencie, gouernment. **1608** CAPT. SMITH *True Relat.* Wks. (Arb.) 9 With one consent he [Capt. Wingfield] was deposed from his presidencie. **1613** PURCHAS *Pilgrimage* (1614) 768 All which were.. seruiceable in Captaine Smiths presidencie, to the English. **1633** T. STAFFORD *Pac. Hib.* I. i. (1821) 3 The Presidencie of Mounster being voyd, by the unfortunate death of Sir Thomas Norris. *c* **1796** T. TWINING *Trav. Amer.* (1894) 136 General Washington.. remained there till 1789, when the general voice of his country called him from his pastoral pursuits to the Presidency of the Government. **1823** CANNING *Sp. Repeal For. Enlistment Bill* 16 Apr., In the days of the presidency of Washington. **1847** LEWES *Hist. Philos.* (1867) I. 135 Of the fifty Prytanes ten had the presidency every seven days. **1849** MACAULAY *Hist. Eng.* viii. II. 293 The presidency [of Magdalen College] was not vacant: Hough had been duly elected; and all the members of the college were bound by oath to support him in his office. **1884** *Law Times* 13 Sept. 332/2 The Queen's Bench Division, under the presidency of the late Lord Chief Justice, refused to interfere.

fig. **1691** RAY *Creation* I. (1692) 91 Without the Presidency and Guidance of some superior Agent. **1836** J. GILBERT *Chr. Atonem.* iv. (1852) 92 Minds.. perceived in these parts of his glorious works the presidency and the wisdom, as well as the power and majesty, of God.

b. ***First Presidency*** (among the Mormons): the board of presiding officers, consisting of the president of the church and two counsellors.

a **1853** GUNNISON in Gardner *Faiths World* I. 492/2 The hierarchy of the Mormon church has many grades of offices and gifts. The first is the presidency of three persons. **1858** MRS. M. E. V. SMITH *Fifteen Years am. Mormons* 151 The Prophet and his two counsellors.. form that fearful centre of all ecclesiastical and temporal power in the Church known as the First Presidency or simply the 'Presidency'.

2. A district under the administration of a president; *spec.* in India, Each of the three divisions of the East India Company's territory, which were originally governed by the Presidents of the Company's three factories. Loosely, the seat of government of each of these. Also *attrib. Obs.* in official use: see quot. 1872.

[**1698** FRYER *Acc. E. India & P.* Contents p. iv, Relation of the English Presidency at Surat. **1702** in *Charters East Ind. Comp.* 323 (Y.) Under the Presidency of the aforesaid Island Bombay.] **1796** MAJ. J. TAYLOR (*title*) Observations on the Mode proposed by the new arrangement for the distribution of the off-reckoning Fund of the several Presidencies in India. **1839** *Lett. fr. Madras* (1843) 257 Those whose knowledge of India is limited to the Presidency, and whose native acquaintance extends only to a few writers in Government offices. *Ibid.*, It is.. a Presidency prejudice that the natives are averse to being taught from books of our selecting. **1845** STOCQUELER *Handbk. Brit. India* (1854) 63 The enviable possession of a chaplaincy at the presidency. **1848** THACKERAY *Van. Fair* lx, Jos's friends were all from the three presidencies, and his new house was in the comfortable Anglo-Indian district of which Moira Place is the centre. **1859** LANG *Wand. India* 73 The doctor had been appointed a presidency surgeon, and had charge of one of the hospitals in Calcutta. **1872** *Whitaker's Almanack* 246 The term 'Presidency'.. applied to the Provinces or Governments of Bengal, Madras, and Bombay, is no longer applicable to the present condition of things, and in the case of Bengal is positively misleading. It is a relic of the time when the three settlements of Fort William, Fort St. George, and Bombay, each under the authority of a president, may be said to have comprised the whole of the British possessions in India.

†**3.** Superior, foremost, or leading position. *Obs.*

1608 WILLET *Hexapla Exod.* 12 Caietan denieth that there was any such presidencie and superiority among the midwiues. **1647** N. BACON *Disc. Govt. Eng.* I. xx. (1739) 36 The German Priests had a liberty to be present.. and to have some presidency therein.

president ('prɛzɪdənt, 'prɛs-), *sb.* Also 4–5 preci-, precy-, 4–6 prece-, 5–6 presy-, 5–7 prese-, 6 præsi-. [a. F. *président* (1296 in Godef. Compl.), ad. L. *præsidēns*, *-dēnt-em* a president, governor, sb. use of pres. pple. of *præsidēre* to PRESIDE.]

1. a. The appointed governor or lieutenant of a province, or division of a country, a dependency, colony, city, etc. Now, in this sense chiefly *Hist.* (But see also 3 b.)

c **1375** *Sc. Leg. Saints* xliv. (*Lucy*) 192 Befor kingis quhen ȝe sal stand or befor precydentis of þe land. **1382** WYCLIF *Acts* xxiii. 24 Make ȝe redy iumentis, or hors, that thei puttinge Poul vpon, schulden lede him saf to Felix, president. **1413** *Pilgr. Sowle* (Caxton 1483) v. xi. 102 He was bryght before the false precydent Pylate. **1451** CAPGRAVE *Life St. Gilbert* (E.E.T.S.) 89 Þat I schuld take up-on me to be president ouyr þis puple. **1480** CAXTON *Chron. Eng.* IV. (1520) 31 b/1 Vitellus that was Presydent of Fraunce chalenged the Empyre. ? *a* **1500** *Chester Pl.* vi. 265 Warne hym that there is president, that this is fullie myne intent. **1604** E. G[RIMSTONE] *D'Acosta's Hist. Indies* VI. xx. 475 They said Pizarre was afterwards vanquished, taken, and executed by the President Guasca. **1607** COWELL *Interpr.*, *President*.. is vsed in Common law for the kings Lieutenent in any Prouince or function: as President of Wales, of Yorke, of Barwick. President of the Kings Councell. **1683** *Brit. Spec.* 148 They wrote to Ætius, then President of Gallia, this short but lamentable Epistle. **1777** WATSON *Philip II* (1839) 183 When the States found that the governor was equally deaf to the remonstrances of the president as he had been to theirs, they began to dread the effects of his displeasure. **1863** MARY HOWITT *F. Bremer's Greece* I. vi. 190 The presidents are changed, and the advocates of order are often compelled to fly before the power of the lawless.

b. *fig.* A presiding deity, patron, or guardian.

c **1611** CHAPMAN *Iliad* v. 23 The God, great president of fire. **1615** CROOKE *Body of Man* 238 The Nymphes are sayed to bee presedents or dieties of the fountaines. *c* **1650** *Don Bellianis* 216, I do most humbly beseech you (sole president of Divine Excellency..) to let me kiss the wonder of your hands. **1697** POTTER *Antiq. Greece* III. xx. (1715) 153 The Tutelar Deities of the Place, and Presidents of the Sea.

2. The appointed or elected head of a temporary or permanent body of persons, who presides over their meetings and proceedings.

a. In various general senses, now sometimes expressed by other terms.

c **1374** CHAUCER *Troylus* IV. 185 (213) For which was delibered by Parlement... And it pronuncede by þe precident Al-þey þat Ector nay ful ofte preyede. *a* **1400** *Pistill of Susan* 304 Thow hast be president, þe peple to stere, þou dotist in þin olde dayes now in þe dismale. **1538** STARKEY *England* II. ii. 183 Of the wych [council] the kyng schold be hede and presydent. **1560** DAUS tr. *Sleidane's Comm.* 178 b, He would assigne some to be as presidentes of the disputation. **1641** in Rushw. *Hist. Coll.* III. (1692) I. 294 Because all meetings of many must be disorderly,.. unless there be one to guide and to direct the rest, I shall desire, that in every Shire, over every Presbytery, we may establish one President. **1663** JER. TAYLOR *Funeral Serm. Bramhall* 44 He receiv'd publick thanks from the Convocation, of which he was President. **1740–1** in *Johnson's Debates* 4 Mar. (1787) I. 244 The president of the Commons, who always in a Committee takes his seat as another member, rose here, and spoke,.. his honour being pay-master of the navy. **1742** J. GLAS *Lord's Supp.* v. VI. 241 The Elder, who is distinguished.. by the Name President, is he who presided ordinarily in the Assemblies of the Church and had the chief Direction in their Order and Discipline. **1781** GIBBON *Decl. & F.* xvii. II. 35 After the office of Roman consuls had been changed into a vain pageant,.. the præfects.. were soon acknowledged as the ordinary presidents of that venerable assembly. *Mod.* The President of the Wesleyan Conference.

†**b.** The head of a religious house or of a college of priests; also of a hospital. *Obs.*

1387 TREVISA *Higden* (Rolls) VII. 165 Elfworde bisshop of Londoun, and somtyme abbot of Evesham,.. wolde have bene president at Evesham, but þe breþer of þe place denyenge þat.. he went to Ramesey. **1480** in *Bury Wills* (Camden) 65 The maister, precedent, or othir reuler of the colage of preestes newe bildid within the town of Bury. **1513** BRADSHAW *St. Werburge* I. 2508 [She] consyderynge herselfe a lady and presydent, Ordered her monasteryes. **1519** *Mem. Ripon* (Surtees) I. 315 Master Newman, Precedent of the Chapitor of Ripon. **1557** *Order of Hospitalls* C iij b, These xiij persons or vij of them at the leaste, the President being one of the Number. *Ibid.* D iv, The President of euery seuerall Howse shal be taken as chief Ruler.

c. The title often borne by the head of a college in a university, or in U.S. of a university consisting of (or originating in) a single college.

In Great Britain used in four of the Oxford and one of the Cambridge Colleges, also in some University Colleges, as Bristol, Newcastle, and the three Queen's Colleges in Ireland (instead of the more usual title *Principal*); in U.S. the most usual title of the head of a college or university. In Great Britain, also of the heads of the Royal Colleges of Physicians and Surgeons of London, Edinburgh, and Ireland, and of a number of colleges for professional education.

1464 *Rolls of Parlt.* V. 518/1 Felawes and Scolers, President and Felawes of any College, Halle, Hospitall, Hous incorporate, or any other place. **1473** *Ibid.* VI. 74/2. **1530** CROMWELL in Merriman *Life & Lett.* (1902) I. 329 He .. was ons ellect presydent of Maudlen Colledge. **1577** HARRISON *England* II. iii. (1877) I. 81 There is.. in euerie house a maister who hath vnder him a president, and certeine censors or deanes, appointed to looke to the behauour and maners of the students there. **1642** (Sept. 7) *Mass. Colony Recds.* (1853) II. 30 Together with the teaching elders of the sixe next adioyning townes.. and the president of the colledge [Harvard] for the time being. **1725** BERKELEY *Proposal* Wks. 1871 III. 230 Which College is to contain a President and nine Fellows. **1889** BRYCE *Amer. Commonw.* II. ci. 549 A visitor from Europe is struck by the prominence of the president in an American university or college, and the almost monarchical position which he sometimes occupies towards the professors as well as towards the students. **1904** *Oxford Univ. Calendar* 298 The corporate designation of the College is 'The President and Scholars of the College of St. Mary Magdalen in the University of Oxford'.

d. The person elected to preside over the meetings and proceedings of an academy, society, or institution, literary, scientific, artistic, or the like.

1660 in Birch *Hist. Roy. Soc.* (1756) I. 6 That the standing officers of the society be three, a president or director, a treasurer, and a register. **1667** SPRAT *Hist. Roy. Soc.* 93 Their Chief Officer, is the President; to whom it belongs to call, and dissolve their meetings;..to regulate the Proceedings [etc.]. **1725** *Act 11 Geo. I* (*Guy's Hospital*), The President, Treasurer, and one and twenty Committees of the said hereby erected Corporation. **1780** (Mar. 15) *Pennsylv. Acts* (1782), They [the American Philosophical Society] shall have the following officers..one president, three vice-presidents, four secretaries [etc.]. **1842** *Rules Philol. Soc.* iii, The Council..shall consist of the President, the Vice-Presidents, a Treasurer, 1 or 2 Honorary Secretaries, and twenty ordinary members. **1902** (Aug. 8) *Charter of British Academy* §5 There shall be a President and a Council of the Academy. The President and the Council shall be elected by the Fellows from amongst their own number.

e. In U.S. the title of one who presides over the proceedings of a financial, commercial, or industrial company, as a bank, railway, mining company, commercial trust, etc. (In Great Britain usually styled 'chairman'; in the Bank of England and some other banks, 'governor'.)

1781 (Dec. 31) *Jrnls. Congress U.S.*, [To] be a corporation ..by the name and stile of 'The President, Directors and Company of the Bank of North America'. **1790** (Dec. 13) in *Hist. Bank of U.S.* (1832) 31 A general meeting to be called by the President of the Bank. **1798** (Mar. 1) *Mass. Statutes*, The Massachusetts Mutual Fire Insurance Company.. shall have power to choose a President..and fifteen Directors. **1808** (Dec. 15) *S. Carolina Stat.* VIII. 245 President of the South Carolina Homespun Company. **1830** (Mar. 12) *Mass. Stat.*, The said directors [of the Massachusetts Rail-road Corporation] shall elect one of their number to be president of the board, who shall also be president of the corporation. **1883** FREEMAN *Impress. U.S.* xii. 192 In England..we never, I think, give it [the title] to the head of a purely commercial body. But in America we find the President of a railroad and the President of a bank —that is, what we should call by the simpler name of Chairman. **1902** *Revised Laws of Mass.* 964 The directors [of manufacturing corporations] shall choose one of their number as president.

f. The priest or minister who presides at the Eucharist; the celebrant.

[**1867** M. DODS et al. tr. *Writings of Justin Martyr & Athenagoras* 63 There is brought to the president of the brethren bread and a cup of wine mixed with water. (*Note*) This expression may quite legitimately be translated 'to that one of the brethren who was presiding'.] **1945** G. DIX *Shape of Liturgy* v. 111 Justin says: '...Then the bread is 'offered' to the president and a cup of water mingled with wine.' **1971** *Order for Holy Communion* (Alternative Services Series 3) 30 The Breaking of the Bread. The president breaks the consecrated bread, saying [etc.]. *Ibid.* 31 The president and the other communicants receive the holy communion. At the administration the ministers say to each communicant, [etc.]. **1973** in *Mod. Eucharistic Agreement* 63 The eucharistic gathering and its president live their dependence on the one Lord and great High Priest. **1977** *Oxf. Diocesan Mag.* Aug. 17/2 The building now consecrated, the Eucharist began, with the Bishop of Oxford as president, and the Bishop of Reading, the Archdeacon of Berkshire, the Vicar and the Curate..as concelebrants.

g. At some sporting events, a referee, judge, or official in charge.

1961 F. C. AVIS *Sportsman's Gloss.* 285/2 *President*, the senior judge in a group, as required at international show jumping competitions. **1971** L. KOPPETT *N.Y. Times Guide Spectator Sports* xiv. 210 The official in charge of [fencing] competition is called the 'president'. **1975** *New Society* 10 July 81/2 The 'president' (ie, ref) of a fencing match. **1976** *Sunday Tel.* 13 Mar. 36/6 Too few countries trouble to train presidents—officials who take charge of bouts.

3. a. The head or chief of an advisory council, or administrative board or department of government, as, in Great Britain, the (Lord) President of the Council, the President of the Board of Agriculture, of Education, of Trade, etc.; also of certain courts of justice, as the Court of Session in Scotland, the Court of Probate in England, etc.

Lord President of the Council: an officer of the English crown whose duty is to preside at the meetings of the Privy Council, and to report to the King the business transacted there. He takes precedence next after the Lord Chancellor and the First Lord of the Treasury. ***President of the Board of Control***: see CONTROL *sb.* 1.

1530–1 *Act 22 Hen. VIII*, c. 8 §4 Provyded alwaye that the tables..shall fyrst be vieued, examyned and approved by the Chauncellour and Treasorer of England, the presydent of the Kynges Counsell, the Lorde privye Seale [etc.]. **1533** *Acc. Ld. High Treas. Scot.* VI. 154 To my lord of Cambuskenneth, precedent in the sessioune, for his fee. *a* **1548** HALL *Chron., Hen. V* 33 For which offence [striking the Chief Justice] he [Henry] was [*a* 1412]..of his father put out of the preuy counsaill.., and his brother Thomas duke of Clarence elected president of the kynges counsaill. **1560** DAUS tr. *Sleidane's Comm.* 86 Fridericke Palatyne, presydent of the counsell imperiall. **1596** DALRYMPLE tr. *Leslie's Hist. Scot.* I. 126 Ouer the Senat is set a præsident of the Ecclesiastical number, quha obteines the first place to giue out his sentence & to speik his opinione. **1607** [see sense 1]. **1644–5** MILTON *Sonn. to Lady M. Ley*, Daughter to that good Earl, once President Of Englands Counsel, and her Treasury. **1661** (Apr. 3) *Lett. Pat. Merch. Trading with E. Ind.* (Y.), Any Person or Persons, being convicted and sentenced by the President and Council..in the said East Indies, their Factors or Agents there [etc.]. **1669** J. DAVIES tr. *Mandelslo's Trav.* 19 The Commanders of the two Ships treated the [English] President, who afterwards return'd to Suratta. *Ibid.*, I..found company..at the Dutch Presidents, who had his Family there. **1776** J. ADAMS in *Fam. Lett.* (1876) 189 The Congress..have established a board of war and ordnance and made me President of it. **1844** H. H. WILSON *Brit. India* II. II. v. 203 The President of the Board of Control, Mr. Canning. **1845** M. PATTISON *Ess.* (1889) I. 28 The Bishop of Bordeaux, acting as president of the council, addressed the accused. **1863** H. COX *Instit.* 652 Legally, the highest rank in the Council belongs to the President of the Council; but according to modern usage, the chief member of the Council is the First Lord of the Treasury. *Ibid.* 653 In that year [1839]..the Crown appointed the new Board of Education, consisting of the Lord President and certain other privy councillors. **1905** *Whitaker's Almanack* 343 Court of Session—Lord President of the whole Court, Right Hon. Lord Kinross. **1908** *Ibid.* 172 Local Government Board. President, Rt. Hon. John Burns, M.P.

†**b.** Formerly the title of the chief magistrate in some of the British North American colonies, and in the States to which they gave rise.

Such a President was always associated with a Council, by whom he was usually elected, and in early instances is often denominated *President of the Council*. In 1776 the title was in use in Delaware, New Hampshire, Pennsylvania, and South Carolina. Before 1800, it was exchanged in every case for 'Governor'.

1608 CAPT. SMITH *True Relat.* Wks. (Arb.) 8 The President and Captaine Gosnold, with the rest of the Counsell, being for the moste part discontented with one another. **1654** in *United Col. Recds.* (1859) II. 442 [Documt. signed] Roger Williams of Prouidence Colony Presidt. **1681** (Dec. 7) in *Publ. Colon. Soc. Mass.* (1902) V. 168 By Advice of ye Honered President of this Provence [Maine]. **1732** GEO. II *Charter of Georgia* in Poore *State Constit.* (1877) I. 371 And our will and pleasure is, that the first president of the said corporation is and shall be our trusty and well-beloved, the said Lord John Viscount Percival. **1776** *Constit. of Delaware* §7 A President or Chief Magistrate shall be chosen by joint ballot of both Houses. **1776** *Constit. of Pennsylv.* §3 The supreme executive power shall be vested in a president and council. ['Governor' adopted 1790.] **1787** (Apr. 15) FRANKLIN in *Writings* (1906) IX. 559 Having served one year as President of Council. **1792** BELKNAP *Hist. New Hampsh.* III. 268 The President is annually elected by the people. ['Governor' adopted 5 Sept. 1792.] *c* **1796** T. TWINING *Trav. Amer.* (1894) 34 Mr. Bingham, the President of the Pennsylvanian State. *a* **1817** T. DWIGHT *Trav. New Eng.*, etc. (1821) II. 154 His Excellency Josiah Bartlett, some years since President of this State [New-Hampshire].

4. The officer in whom the executive power is vested in a modern republic, the elected head of the government, having during his term of office some of the functions of a constitutional monarch in a monarchical state.

Used first in the United States of America, and subsequently in various republics of Spanish America, etc. In U.S. the name was app. continued from that of the president or presiding officer of the congresses of the separate states, held, from 1774 onward, during the revolutionary struggle (cf. quot. 1783), which belonged rather to sense 2 a. To this also the office of President of the Swiss Confederation (quot. 1840) is more analogous than to that of the President of the U.S. under the Constitution of 1789 and its amendments.

[**1783** in Hildeburn *Cent. of Printing* (1886) 4344 Proclamation. By his Excellency Elias Boudinot, Esquire, President of the United States in Congress assembled.] **1787** A. LEE in *J. Adams's Wks.* (1854) IX. 554 An oligarchy, however, I think, will spring from it [the Constitution of the U.S.] in the persons of the President and Vice-President, who, if they understand one another, will easily govern the two Houses to their will. **1789** *Constitution of U.S.* II. §1 The executive power shall be vested in a President of the United States of America. He shall hold his office during the term of four years. **1789** J. MAY *Jrnl. & Lett.* (1873) 121 His Excellency the President [Washington] is to be sworn into office. **1839** *Penny Cycl.* XV. 165/1 (Mexico) The executive power is vested in a president and vice-president, both elected by the state legislatures for a term of four years. **1840** *Ibid.* XVIII. 10/1 Towards the end of 1826, the Bolivian constitution was adopted [in Peru], according to which a president was to be placed at the head of the government, with the power of naming his successor. [**1840** *Encycl. Brit.* (ed. 7) XXI. 47/2 The [Swiss] diet meets for two successive years by turns, at the capital..of Lucerne, Zürich, and Berne, the burgomaster or avoyer of which acts as president for the turn, with the title of Landmann.] **1863** HAWTHORNE *Our Old Home* (1883) I. 380 In consequence of our proud prerogative of caring no more about our President than for a man of straw. **1889** BRYCE *Amer. Commonw.* I. v. 48 Four Presidents (Harrison, Taylor, Lincoln, Garfield) have died in office, and been succeeded by Vice-Presidents. *Ibid.* I. xxv. 290 Only four years after the power of the executive had reached its highest point in the hands of President Lincoln, it was reduced to its lowest point in those of President Johnson.

5. a. Trade-name of a heavy union fabric, of cotton warp and low woollen, mungo, or shoddy weft, the face resembling that of doeskin or plain dress-face cloth. **b.** A kind of damask of silk, or silk and wool, used for upholstery (U.S.) (*Cent. Dict.*).

1886 *Daily News* 6 Oct. 2/4 Some sellers of pilots and presidents have also had their stocks considerably reduced. *Ibid.* 18 Oct. 2/4 Large orders are still being placed for cheap tweeds, meltons, and low worsteds and presidents at the advanced rates lately obtained. **1894** *Times* 7 May 13/2 For other kinds of woollens suitable for the fall trade such as pilots, presidents, and reversibles, there is a scarcity of orders.

6. *attrib.* and *Comb.*, as ***president-founder***, ***-king***, ***-maker***; **b. president-general**, a president who is over all the minor presidents of a system.

1895 *Westm. Gaz.* 4 July 7/1 The annual convention of the European section of the Theosophical Society.., under the presidency of Colonel H. S. Olcott, the President-Founder. **1899** *Daily News* 30 June 6/4 The President-maker, a man who holds in his hands all the strings of the most complex organization in modern politics. **1905** *Daily Chron.* 4 Oct. 4/6 Prince George of Denmark was elected to the throne of Greece..and on the whole he has been a popular Monarch of a democratic community—a 'President-King'.

b. 1754 in Franklin *Wks.* (1887) II. 355 That the said general government [proposed for the N. Amer. colonies] be administered by a President-General, to be appointed and supported by the crown. **1809** J. ADAMS *Wks.* (1854) IX. 620 At the meeting of the Cincinnati at New York, when they choose Hamilton their President-General. **1876** BANCROFT *Hist. U.S.* IV. xii. 402 Galloway, of Pennsylvania,..with the governor of New Jersey and with Colden of New York, proposed [in 1774] for the government of the colonies a president-general, to be appointed by the king, and a grand council to be chosen once in three years by the general assemblies. **1897** ETHELRED L. TAUNTON *Eng. Bl. Monks St. Benedict* II. 298 The high office of president-general of the whole congregation.

president ('prɛzɪdənt, 'prɛs-), *a.* Now *rare.* [ad. L. *præsidentem*, pr. pple. of *præsidēre* to PRESIDE.] That presides or occupies the chief place; presiding, superintending. (Sometimes hyphened, as if attrib. use of prec.)

c **1400** *Rule St. Benet* 1362 It ordand es, þat a president subpriores Sal non be chosin for no chanch Bot by þe priores puruyanch. **1588** J. UDALL *Demonstr. Discipl.* (Arb.) 44 That there should be one byshop or pastor (at the least) president ouer euery congregation. **1599** HAKLUYT *Voy.* II. 294 The state of Venice..keepe there their Agent, president ouer other Marchants. *a* **1619** FOTHERBY *Atheom.* I. xv. §4 (1622) 159 Not onely present with them, but also president among them. **1664** H. MORE *Myst. Iniq.* 270 Mars the President-Dæmon of the Roman Polity. **1671** MILTON *P.R.* I. 447 Whence hast thou then thy truth, But from him or his Angels President In every Province? **1697** POTTER *Antiq. Greece* III. vii. (1715) 66 Mercury the President God of their Occupation. **1808** PIKE *Sources Mississ.* III. (1810) 208 The village of St. John's,..the residence of the president priest of the province.

president(e, obs. form of PRECEDENT.

'presidentess. [f. PRESIDENT *sb.* + -ESS.]

a. A female president. **b.** The wife of a president.

1782 *Eng. Chron.* 8–10 Jan. 3/3 Beau Monde Intelligence, ..Arranged by the Ton Committees..Lady Ar—— Presidentess. **1786** MME. D'ARBLAY *Diary & Lett.* III. 171, I became by that means the presidentess of the dinner and tea table. **1801** H. C. ROBINSON *Diary*, etc. (1869) I. 91, I.. was introduced to the well-bred, accomplished presidentess, Fräulein Gerstendorf. **1844** *Blackw. Mag.* LV. 294 La Gitana became all but presidentess of the Transatlantic republic. **1891** *Daily News* 23 June 5/4 Cards are out in Madame Carnot's name for a 'Matinée dansante'..the Presidentess alone issues them.

presidential (prɛzɪ'dɛnʃəl, prɛsɪ-), *a.* [ad. med.L. *præsidentiāl-is* (*c* 1120 in Du Cange), f. *præsidentia* PRESIDENCY: see -AL[1]. Cf. F. *présidentiel.*]

1. Of or pertaining to a president or his office.

1603 FLORIO *Montaigne* III. xii. 629 A President of the law ..vanted himselfe, to have hudled vp together two hundred and od strange places in a presidentiall law-case of his. **1656** HEYLIN *Surv. France* 134 Presidentiall Courts. **1668** in *R. Boyle's St. Papers* (1742) I. *Mem.* App. 52 The presidential Court of Munster. *a* **1693** *Urquhart's Rabelais* III. xxxvii. 313 With a Presidential Majesty holding his Bable. **1785** R. H. LEE in *J. Adams's Wks.* (1854) IX. 544 My presidential year being ended, I had left New York for this place. [Lee had been President of Congress.] **1797** MERY WARREN in *Abigail Adams's Fam. Lett.* (1848) 374 My congratulations on Mr. Adams's elevation to the Presidential chair. **1846** N. F. MOORE *Hist. Sk. Columbia Coll.* 75 The professorship which for about three years had been annexed to the presidential office. **1860** LOWELL *Election in Nov.* Prose Wks. 1890 V. 19 The next Presidential Election looms always in advance. **1869** SYMONDS in *Biog.* (1895) II. 53 Some of the presidential addresses [Social Science Association] were mildly interesting. **1906** D. M. FORREST *Authority of Christ* VII. v. 411 The mother Church of Jerusalem where James had held a presidential position.

2. Of the nature of a president; presiding.

1650 R. GELL *Serm.* 8 Aug. 10 He would..govern them.. by a presidentiall Angel. **1659** GAUDEN *Slight Healers* (1660) 105 The order and eminency of presidential Episcopacy. **1676** GLANVILL *Ess.* VI. 26 Thus Origen and others understand, that to be spoken by the Presidential Angels.

3. Of or belonging to one of the (former) East Indian presidencies.

1857 S. WILBERFORCE *Sp. Missions* (1874) 107 The necessity of establishing missions in the presidential and other principal cities [of India]. **1877** OWEN *Wellesley's Desp.* p. xlvi, The Presidential designation of the young civilian should be left to the Governor-General.

Hence **presi'dentially** *adv.*, in a presidential way, in the character or person of a president; **presi'dentialism**, the system or practice of presidential government; **presi'dentialist**, a supporter or advocate of such government.

1882 J. PARKER *Apost. Life* I. 30 She was there not officially, not presidentially. **1884** *Daily News* 24 July 5/2 On each of the six days a new president of the Conference will be elected, so that each of the great Powers will be represented presidentially. **1964** J. E. S. HAYWARD in *Parliamentary Affairs* XVIII. 35 *L'Express* drew the conclusion that the Opposition must accept Presidentialism and find a candidate for the next election. **1965** *Economist* 28 Aug. 787/3 Professor Burns himself is a convinced Presidentialist (and Democrat), and offers some concluding recommendations for reducing the four-party competition to two. **1973** W. G. ANDREWS in *Political Stud.* XXI. 311 The French constitutional structure has undergone radical change from parliamentarism towards presidentialism since 1958. **1974** *Times* 6 Nov. 14/6 If one begins to indulge in presidentialism after the South American pattern, then we shall have changed republics. **1975** *Government &*

Opposition X. 28 The bipolarizing pressures inherent in a system of presidentialism based on election by universal suffrage have led to changes.

† **presi'dentiary**, *a.* and *sb. Obs.* [f. as prec. + -ARY[1].]

A. *adj.* = PRESIDENTIAL 2; presiding.

1668 H. MORE *Div. Dial.* v. x. (1713) 439 They [Angels] are Presidentiary Powers over such in this Terrestrial Region. **1681** —— *Exp. Dan.* v. 144 Michael is the Presidentiary Angel of the Jewish Nation.

B. *sb.* A presidential or presidial officer.

1655 tr. *Com. Hist. Francion* II. 2 You are more eloquent than all the parlaments, presidentiaries, and seneschals, or the subalternate courts of justice in France.

† **presidentress**, bad form for PRESIDENTESS (after words in -TRESS from *-ter*, *-tor*).

1650 FULLER *Pisgah* 340 Huldah's colledge... Perchance a female foundation of women alone, and she the Presidentress thereof. **1810** *Splendid Follies* I. 181 Flouncing on the duchess presidentress's sofa. *Ibid.* II. 41.

'presidentship. [See -SHIP.] The office or function of a president; the period over which this extends.

c **1525** L. STUBBS *to Wolsey* in Ellis *Orig. Lett.* Ser. III. II. 66, I do thank your Grace for my restitucion of the possession of my Presedentship of Magdalen College at Oxford. **1607** SIR J. HARINGTON in *Nugæ Ant.* (1804) II. 253 He went down with the presidentship of Yorke, in the vacancie,.. committed to him. **1619** in *Crt. & Times Jas. I* (1849) II. 161 They confirmed Sir Thomas Smith in his presidentship of the Bermudas, or Summer Islands. **1687** *Lond. Gaz.* No. 2299/2 They ordered him forthwith to depart the College,.. declaring the Presidentship to be Void. **1702** C. MATHER *Magn. Chr.* III. II. xxiii. (1852) 475 In.. the seventeenth year of his presidentship over Harvard-Colledge. **1711** *Lond. Gaz.* No. 4938/1 The Presidentship of the Council of the Finances. **1779** *Hist. Eur.* in *Ann. Reg.* 131/1 The appointment of his brother.. to the government and presidentship of Madras. **1884** LADY VERNEY in *Contemp. Rev.* Oct. 552 A leading politician, who is looking forward to the Presidentship.

presider (prɪ'zaɪdə(r)). [f. PRESIDE *v.* + -ER[1].] One who presides.

1692 *Christ Exalted* 117, I might refer the Bishop again to the Doctrines of the Church, (whereof he is an Honourable Presider). **1729** T. COOKE *Tales, Proposals*, etc. 4 Thou just Presider o'er th' illustrious Train. **1886** *Pall Mall G.* 1 May 2/1 Melpomene, scroll in hand, as the presider over Tragic Poetry.

presidial (prɪ'sɪdɪəl), *a.* and *sb.* Also *rare* præsidial. [a. F. *présidial* (15th c. in Godef. *Compl.*), as sb. a provincial court, as adj. belonging to such a court, ad. late L. *præsidiālis* = *præsidālis*, f. *præses*, *-idem*, the governor of a province, esp. (in 14th c.) of one of the second rank: see PRÆSES and -AL[1]. In sense 4, f. L. *præsidium*, Sp. *presidio* garrison, fort.]

A. *adj.* **I. 1.** *French Hist.* Of or pertaining to a province, provincial. ***presidial court***, a court of justice having jurisdiction within certain limits, formerly established in France in towns or cities not having a *parlement*: see B. So ***presidial seat*** = F. *siège présidial.*

1611 COTGR. s.v. *Presidiaux*, The Offices of a Presidiall Seat, or Court. **1613** in *Crt. & Times Jas. I* (1849) I. 267 To translate, by way of punishment, the presidial seat of justice, which is there [Nismes], to Beaucaire. **1661** CRESSY *Refl. Oathes Suprem. & Alleg.* 66 Fossart.. was sentenced by the presidial Court of Justice in Caen publickly and bare-headed to acknowledge that the said propositions were false. **1706** tr. *Dupin's Eccl. Hist. 16th C.* II. IV. xix. 305 *note*, Presidial Courts are usually held in Cities, in which there are no Parliaments which are what in France they call Sovereign Courts. **1815** *Paris Chit-Chat* II. 158 A man.. who continued to talk of Metz, and of the Presidial Court.

† **2.** Of a Roman province: Under a præses (but sometimes vaguely or incorrectly used). *Obs.*

a **1654** SELDEN *Eng. Epin.* ii. (1683) 6 A good part of the Isle conquered, and into a presidial Province reduced. **1731** *Hist. Litteraria* II. 59 The *Consulares*, *Correctores*, and *Præsides* had the Government of one single Province, which from the quality of its Governour was called *Consular*, *Correctorial*, or *Presidial*. **1771** MACPHERSON *Introd. Hist. Gt. Brit.* 264 They were succeeded in the presidial provinces by new levies of hardy and uncorrupted barbarians.

3. Of or pertaining to a president or the action or function of presiding. *rare.*

[**1598** FLORIO, *Presidiale*, of or pertaining to a president, or presidencie, presidiall, of a garrison.] **1656** BLOUNT *Glossogr.*, *Presidial*, pertaining to a Lieutenant, Vice-Roy, chief Ruler or President. **1685** COTTON tr. *Montaigne* III. 495 Judgment holds in me a presidial seat, at least it carefully endeavours to make it so. **1769** *De Foe's Tour Gt. Brit.* II. 98 The Lord Mayor and Aldermen of London have a Right Presidial in Southwark, and hold frequent Courts at St. Margaret's-hill in the Borough. **1891** *Harper's Mag.* Jan. 215/1 Watching the scene with a suave, presidial gaze, as if he were the patron of the ball. **1918** C. G. ROBERTSON *Bismarck* v. 285 Bismarck persuaded the King of Bavaria to write to the King of Prussia, inviting him.. to take the Imperial Crown and exercise as Emperor his Praesidial rights in the Confederation.

II. 4. † **a.** Of, pertaining to, or occupied by a garrison; fortified; = PRESIDIARY *a.* (*obs.*) **b.** Of or pertaining to a presidio.

[**1598**: see sense 3.] *c* **1645** HOWELL *Lett.* I. xxxix, There are three Presidiall Castles in this Citie. **1650** —— *Giraffi's Rev. Naples* I. Ded., Naples, commanded by a Viceroy, and three præsidiall Castles. **1652** *Ibid.* II. 10 They plac'd presidiall forces of their own there. **1883** *Century Mag.* XXVI. 203 A second class of pueblos, called, in the legal phrase of California's later days, 'Presidial Pueblos', had originated in the settlement of the presidios.

B. *sb. French Hist.* A presidial court of justice in France: see A. 1.

1683 *Apol. Prot. France* ii. 15 He cites them before the Presidial of Nismes. **1756** NUGENT *Gr. Tour, France* IV. 6 Under these supreme courts, there are others for smaller matters, established in all the considerable towns of the kingdom, and distinguished by the name of presidials. **1820** A. RANKEN *Hist. France* VII. III. iii. 339 There shall be.. a presidial in the town of Rhodes.

Hence **pre'sidially** *adv. rare.*

1611 COTGR., *Presidialement*, presidially; within presidiall Iurisdiction, or compasse.

presidiary (prɪ'sɪdɪərɪ), *a.* and *sb.* [ad. L. *præsidiārius* that serves for defence, f. *præsidium* a presiding over, defence, assistance, a garrison, f. *præsidēre* to PRESIDE: see -ARY[1].]

A. *adj.* Of, pertaining to, or serving as a garrison, garrisoning; having a garrison, garrisoned.

1599 HAYWARD *1st Pt. Hen. IV* 57 But the Romane Conquerors kept not their presidiarie Souldiers in idle garrison. **1601** R. JOHNSON *Kingd. & Commw.* (1603) 242 The number of soldiers in all the presidiarie places of Spaine is 8000. **1620** J. DYKE *Counterpoyson* 4 A martiall and presidiary guarding of a mans selfe. **1711** LD. MOLESWORTH tr. *F. Hotman's Franco-Gallia* (1721) 23 Those Germans which were transplanted by the Emperor Frederick the IId, into.. Naples and Sicily, and establish'd there as a presidiary Colony, were called Franks. **1757** J. H. GROSE *Voy. E. Indies* 61 The presidiary force of the island [Bombay]. **1856** MERIVALE *Rom. Emp.* (1865) IV. xxxv. 217 Presidiary cohorts were stationed at every threatened point of attack. **1875** —— *Gen. Hist. Rome* lxxvii, Britain had been nominally recovered, but the presidiary legions had been withdrawn.

B. *sb.* A guard, a protection; in quot. 1745, a relay, a reserve to fall back upon.

1623 BP. HALL *Contempl.*, *O.T.* XIX. ix, Not one of those heavenly Presidiaries strucke a stroke for the Prophet. **1745** tr. *Columella's Husb.* III. xvi, Some cuttings must be planted as presidiaries for the regular vines.

† **pre'sidiate**, *ppl. a. Obs. rare*$^{-1}$. [f. L. *præsidium* garrison + -ATE[2].] Garrisoned.

1543 *St. Papers Hen. VIII*, IX. 472 It is thowght that the Turke wil use his powar ayenst Albaregal, wich is rekenid strong and wel presidiate.

presiding (prɪ'zaɪdɪŋ), *ppl. a.* [f. PRESIDE + -ING[2].] **a.** That presides.

1667 *Phil. Trans.* II. 534 The Specifick Form is often not so much as the Presiding, but only the most eminent. **1707** NORRIS *Treat. Humility* vi. 245 Not the condescending, but the governing and presiding part. **1839** DE QUINCEY *Recoll. Lakes* Wks. 1862 II. 217 Awful solitude.. the natural and presiding sentiment—the '*religio loci*'—that broods for ever over the romantic pass. **1878** BOSW. SMITH *Carthage* 212 It is difficult.. to withdraw the attention even for a moment from its presiding genius.

b. *attrib.* and *Comb.* as ***presiding judge*** (U.S.); **presiding elder**, an elder who has charge of a district in the U.S. Methodist Church; **presiding officer**, an official in charge of a polling-station at an election.

1831 J. M. PECK *Guide for Emigrants* 258 There are three [Methodist] districts, over each of which is a presiding Elder. **1844** I. D. RUPP *He Pasa Ekklesia* 447 A presiding elder, though no higher as to order than an elder, has charge of several circuits and stations, called collectively a district. **1904** G. H. LORIMER *Old Gorgon Graham* ix. 186 The Doc. ..knew more Scripture when he was sixteen than the presiding elder. **1961** W. E. B. DUBOIS *Worlds of Color* ix. 137 He emphasized to the Presiding Elder the plan of giving up the old church and moving across the river. **1802** *Deb. Congress U.S.* 19 Jan. (1851) 117 The constant change of presiding judges.. hung up the business. **1874** 'H. CHURTON' *Toinette* xxiii. 245 Geoffrey's counsel called the attention of His Honor, the Presiding Judge of the Court, to the fact. **1745** *Life & Adventures B.-M. Carew* vii. 86 By this Means no presiding Officer has it in his Power to make one more than two, which sometimes happens in the Elections amongst other Communities. **1872** *Act 35 & 36 Vict.* c. 33 sched. I. §21 The returning officer shall appoint a presiding officer to preside at each station. **1978** D. DEVINE *Sunk without Trace* xviii. 170 Voting papers, to be valid, must have the official stamp embossed on them by the Presiding Officer at the time of issue to the individual voter.

‖ **presidio** (pre'sidio, prɪ'sɪdɪəʊ). [Sp., a garrison, a fort:—L. *præsidium*: see PRESIDY, -DIE.] In Spain and in parts of America originally settled by Spaniards, e.g. the south-western United States: A fort, a fortified settlement, a military station, a garrison town. Also, a Spanish penal settlement in a foreign country.

1808 PIKE *Sources Mississ.* III. (1810) App. 28 The presidio of Rio Grande is situated on that river. **1839** *Penny Cycl.* XV. 158/1 For the protection of the latter [white settlers] the Spaniards erected [in Texas, etc.] presidios; a presidio consists of a wooden wall of a quadrangular form, within which the houses are built, and the gates are shut at sunset. **1843** MARRYAT *M. Violet* xvi, The population rose. .. The presidio was occupied by the insurgents. *c* **1847** IRVING *Span. Papers* (1866) I. 285 A presidio or stronghold of the Moors. **1853** CDL. WISEMAN *Ess.* III. 20 An African *presidio* or prison-fort, where galley-slaves are detained. **1885** *Encycl. Brit.* XIX. 763/1 The bulk of the prison population in Spain is still sent to *presidios*, or convict establishments. **1905** *Whitaker's Almanack* 620/2 Spanish Over-Sea Possessions... In Morocco are several 'Presidios'; Ifni near Cape Non, Tetuan and Ceuta.. opposite Gibraltar [etc.]. **1906** *Daily Chron.* 19 Apr. 5/4 The presidio or fortified settlement of San Francisco was founded by the Spaniards in 1776.

Presidium (prɪ'sɪdɪʌm, -z-). Also **Præsidium.** [Russ. *prezídium*, ad. L. *præsidium*, garrison, f. *præsidēre* (see PRESIDE *v.*).] The presiding body or standing committee in a Communistic organization, esp. in the Supreme Soviet. Also *attrib.*

1924 *Observer* 23 Mar. 13/5 In a second decree the Presidium of the Union C.E.C. decided to replace the sentence of ten years strict isolation passed on the Catholic Archbishop Ciepliak by the All-Russian C.E.C. by expulsion from the territories of the Union of Socialist and Soviet Republics. **1927** *Glasgow Herald* 10 Oct. 11 Mr Arthur Horner (South Wales), a member of the National Executive of the Miners' Federation, presided, and was supported by a presidium of 11. **1930** *Economist* 1 Nov. (Russian Suppl.) 1/2 The Central Executive Committee meets ordinarily about three times a year and, when it is not sitting, is represented by a small elected committee or Presidium, and by the Council of People's Commissaries, which is the executive organ. **1931** G. D. H. COLE in W. Rose *Outl. Mod. Knowl.* 727 The Congress [of Soviets].. is .. an occasional gathering of delegates, represented between sessions by a Præsidium. **1955** *Times* 9 May 10/3 The presidium of the Supreme Soviet yesterday annulled the Anglo-Soviet and Franco-Soviet treaties of alliance. *Ibid.* 14 July 6/6 The Praesidium, known in Stalin's day as the Politburo, is the highest policy-making body in the Soviet Union. **1958** *Spectator* 20 June 791/3 Khrushchev's last execution of a Præsidium member, in 1956, was kept quiet for a month or so. **1960** *Evening Bull.* (Philadelphia) 14 Dec. 13/6 A Russian official who made the mistake of referring to a member of the Presidium (the 14-member body that rules the Soviet Union) as a fool. **1968** *Listener* 1 Aug. 133/3 Dubcek started at the top with his bloodless revolution. First, he infiltrated the Party Praesidium, effectively the Party's ruling body, and excluded Novotny supporters in separate reshuffles. **1974** L. DEIGHTON *Spy Story* xiii. 129 Madame Furtseva, the first woman to reach the Presidium of the Central Committee.

† **'presidy, -die.** *Obs.* [ad. L. *præsidium* a guard, garrison, defence, assistance, aid, etc., f. *præsidēre* to sit in front of, guard: see PRESIDE.]

1. A guard or garrison.

1529 *Let. to Wolsey* (MS. Cott. Vit. B. XI. lf. 14), To treate upon a presidie to be yeven unto the pope. **1544** *St. Papers Hen. VIII*, IX. 732 It semith that the Frenchmen intendith to leve a certaine presidye in Piemont. **1570** FOXE *A. & M.* (ed. 2) 1128/2 The Frenche kyng hath ordeined, that Seignior Renzio shal lie in a presidie, betwene the armye of Naples and the Citie of Rome. **1656** BLOUNT *Glossogr.*, *Presidie*, a Garrison, all manner of aid and defence.

2. Succour, remedy, aid.

1432-50 tr. *Higden* (Rolls) I. 63 That drye grownde thurstethe as with owte presidye. **1657** TOMLINSON *Renou's Disp.* 113 [To] cure this symptom with these presidies.

presie, var. PREZZIE.

presign (priː'saɪn), *v. arch.* [f. PRE- A. 1 + SIGN *v.*; cf. med.L. *præsignāre* (*præsignātor* 1088).] *trans.* To signify or indicate beforehand.

1598 J. DICKENSON *Greene in Conc.* (1878) 121 The day presign'd being come. **1608** ARMIN *Nest Ninn.* (1842) 26 By the fourth taile is presigned the presumption of greatnesse. **1665** SIR T. HERBERT *Trav.* (1677) 93 At the place presigned [he] calls for Assaph-chan and his Son. **1839-48** BAILEY *Festus* xix. 203 Agents of destruction, like the flood, Presign regeneration.

† **presig'nificant**, *a. Obs. rare.* [ad. L. *præsignificānt-em*, pr. pple. of *præsignificāre* to PRESIGNIFY.] Signifying or intimating beforehand. So † **presig'nificance, -ancy**, the fact or quality of presignifying or foreshowing.

1576 FLEMING *Panopl. Epist.* 192 My presignificant speache, and forewarning watchwordes, were counted vnworthy credite. **1685** H. MORE *Paralip. Prophet.* xxi. 191 This Introductory Vision.. may have some more general Presignificances of the state of things in the times it may thus presignifie. *Ibid.*, This Roaring and Thundering has a presignificancy in general of the Calamities and Miseries that will befal that Party.

presignification (priː,sɪgnɪfɪ'keɪʃən). Now *rare.* [ad. L. *præsignificātiōn-em*, n. of action from *præsignificāre* to PRESIGNIFY.] The action of signifying or indicating beforehand; an indication or sign (of what is coming).

1603 HOLLAND *Plutarch's Mor.* 1191 Then is not this a bare guesse.. but a præsignification and denouncing peremptorily of such things as without faile shall be. *a* **1677** BARROW *Wks.* (1686) II. 130 There having scarce happened any considerable revolution.. whereof we do not find mentioned in history some presignification or prediction. **1695** J. EDWARDS *Perfect. Script.* 11 These ceremonies.. were presignifications of.. the evangelical dispensation. **1835** J. P. KENNEDY *Horse Shoe R.* v, R. directed his eye to the presignifications of good cheer that were now before him. **1838** —— *Rob of Bowl* xxv, The broad arrow, the mysterious presignification of mischief.

So **presignificative** (-'sɪgnɪfɪ,keɪtɪv, -sɪg'nɪfɪkətɪv) *a.*, characterized by presignification, giving a forecast; † **presignificator**, one who or that which gives pre-intimation or pre-indication.

1588 J. HARVEY *Disc. Probl.* 79 Looke into the Semeiotical or presignificatiue iudgements of phisitions. **1669** WORLIDGE *Syst. Agric.* (1681) 297 The blowing of the Winds from several Coasts.. are the truest Pre-significators of Thunder.

presignify (priːˈsɪgnɪfaɪ), *v.* [= obs. F. *presignifier* (*presignifié*, in Cotgr.), ad. L. *præsignificāre*, f. *præ*, PRE- A. 1 + *significāre* to SIGNIFY.] *trans.* To signify or intimate beforehand.

1586 FERNE *Blaz. Gentrie* II. 20 Whereby the constancy and fortitude of the bearer is and may be secretly presignified. 1598 J. DICKENSON *Greene in Conc.* (1878) 132 The hottest sommer presignifies the coldest winter. 1646 SIR T. BROWNE *Pseud. Ep.* V. xxi. 264 Owles and Ravens are ominous appearers, and presignifying unlucky events. 1776 R. CHANDLER *Trav. Greece* (1825) II. 163 A long cloud resting on Hymettus in winter presignified a violent storm. 1872 BP. FORBES *Kalendars Scot. Saints* 336 Full of years, he presignified the day of his death.

†**presle**, *sb. Obs. rare.* Also 8 *erron.* prescle. [a. obs. F. *presle* 'small Horse-taile, Tadpipes, naked Shaue-grasse' (Cotgr.), erron. f. *prêle*, *la prêle* being a corruption of *l'asprele* (13th c. in Hatz.-Darm.) = It. *asperella*, dim. f. L. *asper* rough.] The rough horsetail, shavegrass, or Dutch rushes, *Equiestum hyemale*. Hence †**presle** *v.*, *trans.* to polish with this plant.

1661 NEEDHAM in Birch *Hist. Roy. Soc.* (1756) I. 51 Rub it smooth with dried presle, i.e. the herb horse-tail. 1703 T. S. *Art's Improv.* 27 Cleanse it well with Prescle,.. wash over the Wood, and hold it to the Fire until it has done smoaking; when dry, Prescle it again. *Ibid.* 45 Having.. Polish'd it [your Work] with Prescle.

pre-sleep: see PRE- B. 2 a.

presly, variant of PRESSLY, *Obs.*

pre-soak: PRE- A. 1 and 2.

pre-socialist: PRE- B. 1 d.

pre-So'cratic, *a.* and *sb. Philos.* Also **Presocratic, presocratic.** [PRE- B. 1.] **A.** *adj.* Of or relating to the period before Socrates (chiefly the sixth and early fifth centuries B.C.) when, in Greece, systematic enquiry into things and their causes began.

1871 FRASER *Life Berkeley* viii. 293 And shows supposed novelties.. to be as old as the Neoplatonic, or even the Pre-Socratic age. 1892 J. BURNET *Early Greek Philos.* 2 The common practice of treating this younger contemporary of Sokrates [*sc.* Demokritos] along with the 'pre-Socratic philosophers' has obscured the true course of historical development. 1913 P. V. COHN *Nietzsche's Compl. Wks.* (Index) XVIII. 117 The real philosophers of Greece pre-Socratic. 1957 KIRK & RAVEN *Presocratic Philosophers* p. vii, We have limited our scope to the chief Presocratic 'physicists' and their forerunners, whose main preoccupation was with the nature (physis) and coherence of things as a whole. 1964 C. S. LEWIS *Discarded Image* iii. 37 The pre-Socratic philosophers of Greece invented Nature. 1974 *Nature* 8 Nov. 130/2 In the treatment of Greek science emphasis is laid upon the importance of the presocratic belief that causal relationships existed between natural phenomena. 1977 I. MURDOCH *Fire & Sun* 33 Sexual love (Aphrodite) as cosmic power had already appeared in Presocratic thought in the doctrines of Empedocles.

B. *sb.* Any of the Greek philosophers of the sixth and fifth centuries B.C. who preceded Socrates (d. 399 B.C.).

1945 B. RUSSELL *Hist. Western Philos.* (1946) I. xiii. 126 'The Good' dominated his [*sc.* Plato's] thought more than that of the pre-Socratics. 1957 KIRK & RAVEN *Presocratic Philosophers* 1 The Neoplatonist Simplicius,.. who lived a whole millennium after the Presocratics, made long and evidently accurate quotations, in particular from Parmenides, Empedocles, [etc.]. 1972 E. HUSSEY *Presocratics* i. 1 What gives the group of Presocratics such unity as it possesses is.. that all these men were involved in the movement of thought which led to the separation of science and philosophy from one another and from other ways of thinking. 1977 I. MURDOCH *Fire & Sun* 51 Nor is he at all like the cosmic 'gods' of the Presocratics.

presolar: see PRE- B. 1.

pre-sold: PRE-SELL *v.*

†**pre-so'lution.** *Obs. rare*$^{-1}$. In 7 præ-. [f. PRÆ-, PRE- A. 2 + SOLUTION.] A preliminary or prior solution (*of* a difficulty).

1683 E. HOOKER *Pref. Pordage's Mystic Div.* 64 A fair præsolution of som præmised objections.

presome, presompcion, obs. ff. PRESUME, PRESUMPTION.

presomtweste (-té), var. PRESUMPTUOSITY, *Obs.*

preson(e, -oun-e, -own-e, presonar, etc., obs. ff. PRISON, PRISONER, etc.

presond, -ound, obs. ff. PRESENT *sb.*[2]

pre-Soviet: PRE- B. 1 a.

presphenoid (-ˈsfiːnɔɪd). *Anat.* [f. PRE- A. 4 + SPHENOID.] The anterior part of the sphenoid bone of the skull, which forms a separate bone in (human) infancy. Hence **presphenoidal** (ˌpriːsfiːˈnɔɪdəl) *a.*, of or pertaining to the presphenoid.

1854 OWEN *Skel. & Teeth* in *Orr's Circ. Sc.* I. *Org. Nat.* 193 The basisphenoid and presphenoid form a single bone, and the chief keel of the cranial superstructure. *Ibid.* 251 The superior turbinals extend.. below into the presphenoidal sinus. 1855 HOLDEN *Hum. Osteol.* (1878) 85 The front part of the body, termed 'presphenoid', has two centres of its own. 1872 MIVART *Elem. Anat.* 83 The anterior part of the body, or pre-sphenoidal part. 1881 —— *Cat* 60 The occipital, two parietals, two frontals, two temporals, the sphenoid, the presphenoid, the ethmoid—which ten bones compose the cranium, or skull proper.

prespinal, -splenomegalic: see PRE- B. 3. 1.

pre-spiracular: PRE- B. 3.

press (prɛs), *sb.*[1] Forms: α. 3-7 presse, (4 presce), 4- press. β. 3-6 pres (*dative* 3-4 prese, prece), 4-6 prees, prese, prece, 5 preesse, *Sc.* preys, 5-6 preas, preese, *Sc.* preis, 5-7 preace, preasse, 6 *Sc.* preise, preiss, ? prais, 6-7 prease. [Two distinct forms: α. ME. *presse*, a. F. *presse* (11th c. in Littré) = Pr. *pressa*, It. *pressa*, verbal sb. from stem of F. *presser* = It. *pressare*, L. *pressāre*, freq. of *premĕre*, *press-um* to press; or ? Romanic fem. sb. from *press-us*, *-a*, *-um*, pa. pple. of *premĕre*; β. ME. *prês*, *prees*, in 16-17th c. *prese*, *preas(e*, *preace*, found as a parallel form only in early senses. The relation of this to the Fr. and the α-forms presents difficulty. Cf. the two corresponding forms of the verb, *press* and *prese*, *prease*, and see Note below. (The spelling *pres* generally means *prês*, but may be sometimes = *press*. *Press* in Barbour is doubtful, and may have been = *prês*.)]

I. In reference to crowding, pressure of persons, circumstances, affairs, etc.

1. a. The condition of being crowded or thronged; a crowd, a throng, a multitude. *arch.*

α. *a* 1225 *Ancr. R.* 168 Me is loð presse. *a* 1400 *R. Brunne's Chron. Wace* (Rolls) 11255 (Petyt MS.) Grete presse was at the procession. *c* 1400 *R. Gloucester's Chron.* (Rolls) App. XX. 190 Þe king forþ com & out of þe presce [*v.r.* pres] mid strengþe him nom. *c* 1400 *Destr. Troy* 2157 The pepull was depertid & the presse voidet. 1500-20 DUNBAR *Poems* lxxvii. 50 Great was the press of peopill dwelt about. 1557 N. T. (Genev.) *Matt.* viii. 1 Great presse of people folowed him. 1581 W. STAFFORD *Exam. Compl.* iii. (1876) 76 As in a presse going in at a straight, the formost is driuen by him that is nexte hym. 1601 SHAKS. *Jul. C.* I. ii. 15 Who is it in the presse, that calles on me? *a* 1657 SIR J. BALFOUR *Ann. Scotl.* (1824-5) II. 170 The presse so augmented, that the Ducke was forced to returne with speed to his lodgeing. 1741-3 WESLEY *Extract of Jrnl.* (1749) 45 It was some time before I could possibly get out of the press. 1866 WHITTIER *Our Master* xiv, We touch him in life's throng and press, And we are whole again. 1891 C. E. NORTON *Dante's Purgatory* x. 64 Round about him there seemed a press and throng of knights.

β. *c* 1290 *S. Eng. Leg.* I. 101/30 [She] cam ant touchede þe lappe of ore louerdes cloþes ene Ase he eode In grete prece. *c* 1330 R. BRUNNE *Chron. Wace* (Rolls) 11242 So þey ches, ffor to departe þer mykel pres. 13.. *E.E. Allit. P.* B. 880 Þay .. distresed hym wonder strayt, with strenkþe in þe prece. *c* 1386 CHAUCER *Wife's Prol.* 522 Greet prees at Market maketh deere ware. *c* 1390 —— *Truth* 1 Flee fro þe prees. *c* 1440 *Promp. Parv.* 412/2 Prees, or thronge, *pressura*. 1480 CAXTON *Chron. Eng.* cxcviii. 177 Anon doth hym oute of prece [*ed.* 1520 prees]. 1500-20 DUNBAR *Poems* xv. 33 Convenient tyme, lasar, and space, But haist or preiss of grit menȝie. 1526 TINDALE *Mark* v. 27 She cam into the preace [*Great, Rhem.* preasse, *Genev.*, 1611 prease] behynde hym and tewched hys garment. 1558 PHAER *Æneid* III. G ij b, The preas with crooked paws [the Harpies] are out. 1590 SPENSER *F.Q.* I. iii. 3 Far from all peoples preace. 1601 B. JONSON *Poetaster* v. ii, Those whom custome rapteth in her preasse. 1613 SHAKS. *Hen. VIII*, IV. i. 77 Great belly'd women,.. would shake the prease And make 'em reele before 'em. 1700 DRYDEN *Iliad* I. 338 When didst thou thrust amid the mingled preace [*rime* peace]?

b. A throng or crush in battle; the thick of the fight; an affray or mêlée.

†Phr. ***proud in pres***, said of a knight: see PROUD *a.*

α. 1375 BARBOUR *Bruce* II. 430 Thai prikyt then out off the press [*rime* wes]. *c* 1489 CAXTON *Sonnes of Aymon* i. 44 Grete was the presse and the bataylle fyers. *c* 1500 *Lancelot* 867 And in the press so manfully them seruith, His suerd atwo the helmys al to-kerwith. 1610 DONNE *Pseudo-martyr* 264 They.. are seldom drawen to any presse or close fight. *c* 1764 GRAY *Triumphs Owen* 24 There the thundering strokes begin, There the press, and there the din. 1849 MACAULAY *Hist. Eng.* vii. II. 168 He.. fought, sword in hand, in the thickest press.

β. *c* 1330 R. BRUNNE *Chron. Wace* (Rolls) 720 At which bataille þe Troiens lees, & fledde fro þat mykel prees. *c* 1350 *Will. Palerne* 3848 Bliue with his burnes he braide in-to prese. *c* 1400 *Destr. Troy* 1201 Mony perysshet in þe plase er þe prese [*mispr.* prise] endit. *c* 1489 CAXTON *Blanchardyn* li. 194 He brake & departed the grete preesses, so that his enmyes made waye byfore his swerde. *a* 1500 *Sir Beues* 3087 (Pynson) Beuys thoroughe the preas dyd ryde. 1513 DOUGLAS *Æneis* X. xiv. *heading*, Hym to ravenge his lyfe lost in the pres [*ed.* 1555 preis]. 1523 LD. BERNERS *Froiss.* I. cvii. 129 They.. russhed into ye thyckest of the preace. 1550 LYNDESAY *Sqr. Meldrum* 1135 Than Makferland that maid the prais, From time he saw the Squyeris face, Upon his kneis he did him yeild. 1596 SPENSER *F.Q.* IV. iv. 34 Into the thickest of that knightly preasse He thrust.

†**c.** ***in press***: in a crowd, crowded together, in the thick of the fight. *Obs.*

β. 1509 HAWES *Past. Pleas.* xliv. (Percy Soc.) 213, I marveyle muche of the presumption Of the dame Fame so puttyng in ure Thy great prayse, saiyng it shall endure For to be infinite evermore in prease [*rime* cease]. 15.. *Adam Bel* 143 in Hazl. *E.P.P.* II. 144 Among them all he ran, Where the people were most in prece, He smot downe many a man. 1581 MULCASTER *Positions* xvi. (1887) 74 Here will desire throng in prease, though it praise not in parting. 1587 FLEMING *Contn. Holinshed* III. 1986/2 The Scots.. ran sharplie forward.., and without anie mercie, slue the most part of them that abode furthest in prease.

2. The action or fact of pressing together in a crowd; a crowding or thronging together.

α. 1595 SHAKS. *John* V. vii. 19 With many legions of strange fantasies, Which, in their throng and presse to that last hold, Confound themselues. 1617 MORYSON *Itin.* I. 134 There was such a presse to kisse his feet. 1823 BYRON *Juan* XIII. xviii, Give gently way, when there's too great a press. 1833 HT. MARTINEAU *Tale of Tyne* iv, The press of vessels near the port is very awful. 1849 MACAULAY *Hist. Eng.* iii. I. 369 The great press was to get near the chair where John Dryden sate.

β. *c* 1290 *S. Eng. Leg.* I. 15/494 Þat folk him siwede with gret pres. *c* 1375 *Sc. Leg. Saints* ii. (*Paulus*) 87 For to here hym wes sik prese, þat fawt of rowme gret þar wes. *c* 1489 CAXTON *Sonnes of Aymon* xxiv. 504 By the grete prees & stampyng of their horses. 1560 DAUS tr. *Sleidane's Comm.* 24 b, Where was suche prease of the people, that harnessed men had muche a do to kepe them backe. *a* 1643 W. CARTWRIGHT *Lady Errant* II. iv, Our loves what are they But howerly Sacrifices, only wanting The prease and tumult of Solemnity?

†**3.** The condition of being hard pressed; a position of difficulty, trouble, or danger; a critical situation; straits, distress, tribulation. *Obs.* or *arch.*

α. 1375 BARBOUR *Bruce* III. 129 The King wes then in full gret press. *c* 1440 *York Myst.* xlviii. 289 In harde presse when I was stedde, Of my paynes ȝe hadde pitee. 1627-77 FELTHAM *Resolves* I. lxxv. 115 Such Cordials, as frolick the heart, in the press of adversity.

β. *a* 1300 *Cursor M.* 5608 Born in þat sith was moyses þat þe folke was in þat pres [*Trin.* prees]. *c* 1330 R. BRUNNE *Chron.* (1810) 311 In alle þis grete pres praied þe kyng of France, þe Scottis suld haf pes þorgh Edward sufferance. 1523 LD. BERNERS *Froiss.* I. ccclvii. 577 They wolde not medell, nor be in no busynesse nor prease. 1573 J. DAVIDSON *Commend. Vprichtnes* 153 Bot cheifly anis he was put to ane preace, Quhen that the Quene of tressoun did accuse him. 1601 J. MELVILL *Diary* (Wodrow Soc.) 496 But pruff thy preass can nocht be understude.

4. Pressure of affairs; urgency, haste, hurry.

α. 1641 *Vind. Smectymnuus* xi. 111 Poore men cannot have their Presse wayted on, as your greatnesse may. 1836 *Going to Service* vi. 69 Roused to the press of an occasion, as if she acquired double power of diligence. 1883 *Fortn. Rev.* May 734 The eager press of our modern life. 1888 LIGHTHALL *Yng. Seigneur* 52 What.. is your press about going to England?

β. *a* 1400-50 *Alexander* 3382 For no prayer ne preese [*v.r.* pres] ne plesaunce on erth.. rynne shuld he neuer. *c* 1400 *Destr. Troy* 11910 Þan the grekes.. With proses and pres puld vp þere ancres. 1533 BELLENDEN *Livy* II. xxii. (S.T.S.) I. 222 The fray and noyis.. causit þe Veanis to rusche with maist preiss to harnes. *a* 1547 SURREY *Æneid* II. 430 Amid the flame and armes ran I in preasse.

†**5. a.** Phr. ***to put oneself in press***: (?) to exert oneself, use one's endeavour, set oneself, undertake. (Cf. PRESS *v.* 17.) *Obs.*

α. 1540 HYRDE tr. *Vives' Instr. Chr. Wom.* (1541) 135 b, Lest she be to homely, to put her self in presse, in company of her seruauntes, namely if she be yonge.

β. 1387-8 T. USK *Test. Love* Prol., That I.. wil putten me in prees to speke of loue. *c* 1420 LYDG. *Assembly of Gods* 1755 When the Son of Man put hym in prese, Wylfully to suffre dethe for mankynde. *a* 1529 SKELTON *Bowge of Courte* 44 But than I thoughte I wolde not dwell behynde; Amonge all other I put myselfe in prece. 1542 RECORDE *Gr. Artes* Pref. a iij, Yet am I bolde to put my selfe in preasse with suche abilitie as God hathe lente me.. to helpe my countrey men. 1551 BIBLE (Matthew) *Ps.* xxii. 21 *note*, The common people of the Iewes, who cruelly & furiously put them selues in prease agaynst Christe, cryinge, crucifie him, crucifie him. 1560 DAUS tr. *Sleidane's Comm.* 208 We see hym put hymselfe in prease, to occupie a place in thys most noble consistorye.

†**b.** ***to put in preace***: ? to exercise, put in practice. (Perh. a Spenserian misuse.) *Obs. rare.*

β. 1579 SPENSER *Sheph. Cal.* Oct. 69 The vaunting Poets found nought worth a pease, To put in preace emong the learned troupe.

6. *Psychol.* Something in the environment to which (a need in) the organism reacts (see quot. 1938).

1938 H. A. MURRAY *Explorations in Personality* ii. 40 A tendency or 'potency' in the environment may be called a *press*... For example, a press may be nourishing, or coercing, or injuring, or chilling,.. or amusing or belittling to the organism. *Ibid.* 42 The endurance of a certain kind of press in conjunction with a certain kind of need defines the duration of a single episode. 1953 *Jrnl. Abnormal & Social Psychol.* XLVIII. 532/2 So we know *two* things about his narrators: their ambition and their most recent press. That press, as our hypothesis predicts, they projected directly into their.. Tests. 1969 J. W. GETZELS in Lindzey & Aronson *Handbk. Social Psychol.* (ed. 2) V. xlii. 501 There was no evidence that student press influenced the level of aspiration, at least so far as Merit students are concerned. 1973 *Jrnl. Genetic Psychol.* CXXIII. 87 Four slides were used to test for the presence of hostile press.

II. In reference to the physical act or process. (Rarely in β-form.)

7. a. The act of pressing (something); pressure.

1513 DOUGLAS *Æneis* III. i. 73 But eftir that the thrid syon of treis,.. I schupe to haue wprevin with mair preise [*rime* peice]. 1899 E. J. CHAPMAN *Drama Two Lives, Dream's End.* 95 The proud lips meet with icy press. 1903 D. MCDONALD *Garden Comp.* Ser. II. 82 Give it [the bulb] a gentle press sufficient to more than half bury it.

b. In Gymnastics, a raising of the body by continuous muscular effort.

1901 *Health & Strength* Apr. 36/2 (*heading*) One arm body press... Lie flat on the ground.. and with hand beneath centre of chest press the body up to arm's length. **1956** KUNZLE & THOMAS *Freestanding* i. 22 The presses to handstand are one of the best forms of strength training because at the same time the gymnast learns how to fight for and maintain a hand balance when the arms feel extremely tired.

c. *Weight-lifting.* A raising of a weight from the floor to shoulder-height followed by its gradual extension above the head.

1908 *Health & Strength Ann.* 93 Continental lifts differ considerably from those in practice in this country... The Continental 'Press' is a cross between the above [*sc.* the 'Push'] and the English 'Press'... The Continental 'Press' can only be distinguished from our 'Arm Press' by a slight side wriggle. **1914** *Ibid.* 83 Thomas Inch lifted 304½ lbs. (bent press) at Scarborough in December. **1925** F. G. L. FAIRLIE *Official Rep. VIIIth Olympiad, 1924* 255 Middleweights... Two hands, Military Press: Galimberti (Italy), 214½ lb. **1928** *Health & Strength Ann.* 77 Lifters are urged to maintain themselves in a state of readiness on the three Olympic lifts, viz: 'Two Hands Clean and Military Press with Barbell', 'Two Hands Snatch', and the 'Two Hands Clean and Jerk with Barbell'. **1935** *Encycl. Sports* 704/2 There are swings, presses, snatches, jerks, all made with one hand, as well as two-hand and shoulder lifts. **1975** *Oxf. Compan. Sports & Games* 1099/1 At the 1924 Olympic Games the lifts were one hand snatch, opposite one hand jerk, two hands clean and press, two hands snatch, and two hands clean and jerk.

d. The action of pressing clothes.

1932 D. C. MINTER *Mod. Needlecraft* 145/2 Muslin and lawn dresses usually require a final all-over press. **1957** J. OSBORNE *Look Back in Anger* I. 16 I'll give them a press while I've got the iron on. **1962** M. DUFFY *That's how it Was* iii. 33 The girls would.. run up something new.. to wear the same evening with a quick press before they went out. **1975** BYFIELD & TEDESCHI *Solemn High Murder* i. 6 'These things could do with a press if that's possible.' The smell of tropical mildew clung to the rumpled winter-weight clericals he handed the man.

e. In Basketball, any of various forms of close marking by the defending team. Also *transf.*

1961 J. S. SALAK *Dict. Amer. Sports* 341 *Press* (basketball), a maneuver designed to hamper the offensive team's ability to move the ball toward their basket. There are many types of 'presses'. **1971** L. KOPPETT *N.Y. Times Guide Spectator Sports* iii. 86 The press itself creates openings for the offense. **1976** *Honolulu Star-Bull.* 21 Dec. H-1/5 A full-court press enabled Kalani to wipe out a 13-point third quarter lead. **1978** W. SAFIRE *Political Dict.* 248 'Full-court press' became White House lingo in the late sixties... In politics, the term has come to mean a strenuous effort to get legislation passed probably because of its resemblance to 'all-out pressure'. In basketball, however, the phrase is used only to describe a defense.

8. A mark made by pressing; a crease; *fig.* an impression.

1601 SIR W. CORNWALLIS *Ess.* II. xl. (1631) 175 Meditation goeth with so faint a presse in my braine, that it is soon wiped out. *a* **1688** VILLIERS (Dk. Buckhm.) *Restoration* (1775) 95 May their false lights undo 'em, and discover presses, holes, strains and oldness in their stuffs.

9. The action of pressing (forward).

1893 *Daily News* 14 Apr. 2/2 The press forward of the horse against the stress of the blast. **1895** *Ibid.* 16 May 6/3 Russia is beginning to feel uncomfortable from the press forward of Chinese in her Asiatic States.

10. *Naut.* ***press of sail, canvas*** (formerly *press sail, prest sail, pressing sail*): 'as much sail as the state of the wind, etc., will permit a ship to carry' (Smyth *Sailor's Word-bk.*). Cf. CROWD *sb.*[3] 3 b.

The earlier variants *press sail*, etc., leave the origin obscure.

1592 NASHE *Four Lett. Confut.* Wks. (Grosart) II. 240 I my self,.. make my stile carry a presse saile. *a* **1642** SIR W. MONSON *Naval Tracts* III. (1704) 331/2 Keeping the Sea.. with a contrary Wind, foul Weather, and a press Sail. **1693** *Lond. Gaz.* No. 2888/2 All Night we run along the shore with a press Sail. **1710** J. HARRIS *Lex. Techn.* II. s.v. *Prest Sail*, A Ship at Sea is said to carry a Prest Sail, when she carries all that She can possibly Croud. **1772** *Phil. Trans.* LXIV. 129 We.. carried a pressing sail, with hopes of reaching Torbay before dark.

1794 NELSON in Nicolas *Disp.* (1845) I. 372 The gale.. obliged me to carry a press of sail to clear the shore towards Cape Corse. **1806** A. DUNCAN *Nelson* 61 He bore away with a press of sail for Malta. **1836** MARRYAT *Midsh. Easy* xxvi, Foaming in her course, and straining under the press of sail. **1884** H. COLLINGWOOD *Under Meteor Flag* 92, I carried on under a heavy press of sail.

III. An instrument or machine by which pressure is communicated. (Only in form *press*.)

11. a. An instrument used to compress a substance into smaller compass, denser consistency, a flatter shape, or a required form: usually distinguished by prefixing a qualifying word, expressing purpose, as ***baling, coining, copying, packing, rolling, sewing, stamping press***, the name of the thing pressed, as ***bonnet, cheese, clothes, cotton, hay, napkin press***, or the power or mechanical contrivance employed, as ***cam, hydraulic, screw, toggle press***; etc.

1362 LANGL. *P. Pl.* A. v. 127 þenne I drouȝ me a-mong þis drapers,.. Among þis Riche Rayes lernde I a Lessun,.. Putte hem in a pressour [*v.r.* presse (so in B.); C. VII. 219 pressours] and pinnede hem þer-Inne. *c* **1440** *Promp. Parv.* 412/2 Presse, or pyle of clothe, *panniplicium, pressorium.* **1483** *Cath. Angl.* 290/2 A Presse for clathe, *lucunar, panniplicium, vestiplicium.* **1513** *Act 5 Hen. VIII*, c. 4 §1 Divers Strangers.. dry calander Worsteds with Gums, Oils, and Presses. **1532** MORE *Confut. Barnes* VIII. Wks. 797/1 Stretched out as it wer in the presse or tenter hokes of a strong fullar. **1570** LEVINS *Manip.* 84/31 A Presse for backs, *prælium.* **1674** in J. Simon *Irish Coins* (1749) 138 To import such a quantitie of copper blocks or chipps as may possible with two presses, to be coyned by the spring ensueing. **1727–41** CHAMBERS *Cycl.* s.v., *Rolling Press*, is a machine used for the taking off prints from copper-plates. **1776** WITHERING *Brit. Plants* (1796) I. 31 Directions for drying.. Specimens of Plants... First prepare a press, which a workman will make. **1787** M. CUTLER in *Life*, etc. (1888) I. 269 Another great curiosity was a rolling press, for taking the copies of letters or any other writing. **1824** J. JOHNSON *Typogr.* II. xv. 553 Hydraulic Presses.. are now deemed a valuable acquisition to the printing profession. **1846** J. BAXTER *Libr. Pract. Agric.* (ed. 4) II. 77 The wood is fit for ..screws for presses, spokes for wheels, chairs, &c. **1858** SIMMONDS *Dict. Trade, Copying-press, Copying Machine*, a press for taking duplicate or manifold impressions on damped paper from manuscripts by a lever. **1873** E. SPON *Workshop Rec.* Ser. I. 394/1 The necessary tools for small [book-binding] work are:.. a sewing press; a cutting press [etc.].

fig. c **1374** CHAUCER *Troylus* I. 559 And so kan leye oure Iolyte on presse. And bryng oure lusty folk to holyness.

b. The apparatus for inflicting the torture of *peine forte et dure*: see PRESS *v.*[1] 1 b.

a **1734** NORTH *Lives* (1826) I. 287 He would not plead to the country.. till the press was ready; and then he pleaded, and was, at last, hanged. **1839** W. H. AINSWORTH *J. Sheppard* III. xv, The ponderous machine, which resembled a trough, slowly descended upon the prisoner's breast. Marvel, then, took two iron weights, each of a hundred pounds, and placed them in the press.

12. a. An apparatus for expressing or extracting the juice, or the like, out of anything: usually designated by prefixing the name of the substance extracted, as ***wine, oil, cider, sugar press***, etc.

a **1380** *Minor Poems fr. Vernon MS.* lii. 131 Til grapes to þe presse beo set, þer renneþ no red wyn in raþe. **1382** WYCLIF *Isa.* lxiii. 3 The presse I trad alone. **1398** TREVISA *Barth. De P.R.* XVII. cxii. (Bodl. MS.), þe faster oile reneþ oute of þe presse.. þe better it is acounted. **1483** *Cath. Angl.* 291/1 A Presse for wyne, *bachinal, calcatorium* [etc.]. **1530** PALSGR. 258/1 Presse for lycour, *pressover.* **1553** EDEN *Treat. Newe Ind.* (Arb.) 40, 28 . suger presses, to presse ye sugre whiche groweth plentifully in certaine canes or redes of the same countrey. **1616** SURFL. & MARKH. *Country Farme* 430 Put them in a haire cloth or hempen bagge, for to presse in a presse that hath his planke hollow and bending downeward. **1707** MORTIMER *Husb.* (1721) II. 328 After your Apples are ground they should be.. committed to the Press. **1825** J. NICHOLSON *Operat. Mechanic* 291 Presses used for expressing liquors, are of various kinds.

†**b.** ***press of Herophilus*** [Gr. ληνός (Herophilus, in Galen), L. *torcular Herophili*]: the enlarged reservoir at the union of the four sinuses of the dura mater, opposite the tuberosity of the occipital bone. *Obs.*

1578 BANISTER *Hist. Man.* v. 78 The quadruplication of Dura mater.. is called a presse, & lyeth betwene the brayne and Cerebellum. **1594** T. B. *La Primaud. Fr. Acad.* II. 150 [A vessel] which both the Greeke & Latine physicions call by a name that signifieth a presse, because the blood is pressed into it for the nourishing of the braine.

13. In the Jacquard loom, The mechanism which disengages the needles or wires which are not to act from the lifting-bar.

1875 URE *Dict. Arts* (ed. 7) III. 3 The name *press* is given to the assemblage of all the pieces which compose the moveable frame BB.

14. a. A machine for leaving the impression of type upon paper, vellum, or other smooth surface; a machine for printing, a printing-press. Often qualified, as ***Stanhope, Albion, Miehle press***, etc.

[**1507** in Blades *Caxton* Plate vii. (from Ascensius Bk.), Prelum Ascensianum.] **1535** [see d]. **1536** J. RASTELL *Will*, My house in St. Martyns, with my presse, notes and lettres comprised in the same. **1565** COOPER *Thesaurus, Prelum*, a presse that eyther Printers or any other occupation vseth. **1574** *Will of Johane Wolfe*, All the presses, letters, furniture, etc., belonging to the arte of prynting. **1588** *Marprel. Epist.* (Arb.) 22 Waldegraues printing presse and Letters were takken away. **1594** R. ASHLEY tr. *Loys le Roy* 22 Then the gouernour of the Presse taketh these last chasies or fourmes, and laieth them on the marble of his Presse. **1598** STOW *Surv.* 394 Therin [the Ambry,] Islip, Abbet of Westminster, first practized and erected the first Presse of booke Printing that euer was in England, about.. 1471. **1683** MOXON *Mech. Exerc., Printing* ii. ¶1 His Presses have a solid and firm Foundation. **1827** HALLAM *Const. Hist.* (1876) III. xiii. 3 The privilege of keeping presses was limited to the members of the stationers' company. **1853** *N. & Q.* 1st Ser. VIII. 10/1 Charles Earl Stanhope, whose versatility of talent succeeded in abolishing the old wooden printing-press, with its double pulls, and substituting.. the beautiful iron one, called after him the 'Stanhope Press'. **1873** H. SPENCER *Stud. Sociol.* (1882) 126 The last achievement in automatic printing—the Walter-Press. **1896** HOWELLS *Impressions & Exp.* 11 A second-hand Adams press of the earliest pattern and patent.

b. Used as an inclusive name for the place of business of which the printing-press is the centre, in which all the stages and processes of printing are carried on; a printing-house or printing-office. Often used in the names of such printing establishments, e.g. the Clarendon Press, Oxford, the Pitt Press, Cambridge, the Aldine Press, Leadenhall Press, Chiswick Press, etc. Hence, contextually, for the *personnel* of such an establishment, the compositors or printers, printer's readers, etc.

1579 GOSSON *Sch. Abuse* To Rdr. (Arb.) 18 Because you are learned amende the faultes freendly, which escape the Presse. **1589** *Pasquil's Ret.* A iij b, That worke shall come out of the Presse like a bryde from her chamber. **1590** NASHE *Pasquil's Apol.* I. B j, When he carried his coppie to the Presse. **1641** J. JACKSON *True Evang. T.* III. 200 While these Sermons were betweene the Pulpit, and the Presse. **1647** CLARENDON *Hist. Reb.* IV. §104 The Presses swell'd with the most virulent Invectives against them. *a* **1656** BP. HALL *Rem. Wks.* (1660) 82 We should not have such libellous presses. **1670** G. H. *Hist. Cardinals* I. III. 87 There is a Press .. for all Foreign Languages. **1797** *Monthly Mag.* III. 46 An elegant and splendid edition of 'Archimedes', from the Clarendon Press. **1841** MACAULAY *Ess., L. Hunt* (1887) 594 The Athenian Comedies.. have been reprinted at the Pitt Press and the Clarendon Press under the direction of Syndics and delegates. **1849** —— *Hist. Eng.* vii. II. 263 The Dutch arms.. were scarcely so formidable to James as the Dutch presses. **1900** H. HART (*title*) Notes on A Century of Typography at the University Press, Oxford, 1693–1794.

c. The printing-press in operation, the work or function of the press; the art or practice of printing.

1579 FULKE *Confut. Sanders* 661 His report is more to bee credited then the Printers presse. **1641** *More's Rich. III*, Ded., Having for many yeares escaped the presse. **1656** EARL MONM. tr. *Boccalini's Advts. fr. Parnass.* I. xxxv. (1674) 42 Of all Modern inventions.. the precedency ought to be given to the Press..; and that now the Press had.. for ever secured the past and present labours of the Vertuosi. **1663** R. L'ESTRANGE (*title*) Considerations and Proposals in Order to the Regulation of the Press. **1791–1823** D'ISRAELI *Cur. Lit., Licensers Press*, Under.. William III.. the press had obtained its perfect freedom. *c* **1880** TENNYSON *Despair* xvi, These are the new dark ages, you see, of the popular press.

d. In phrases belonging to 14, b, or c, as ***at, in,*** †***under*** (***the***) ***press***, in the process of printing, being printed; ***off the press***, finally printed, issued; † ***out of press***, = prec., also out of print (*obs.*).

1665 BOYLE *Occas. Refl.* Introd. Pref. (1848) 11 Papers.. discovered to have been lost when some of the rest were to be *at the Press. **1823** J. BADCOCK *Dom. Amusem.* p. viii, After the volume has been at press upwards of a year. **1535** JOYE *Apol. Tindale* (Arb.) 21 One bothe to wryte yt and to correcke it *in the presse. **1545** LELAND *New-Year's Gift* (1549) C iv, Part of the exemplaries,.. hath bene emprynted in Germany, and now be in the presses chefely of Frobenius. **1642** CHAS. I in Clarendon *Hist. Reb.* v. §399 A Declaration now in the Press. **1670–1** T. PIERCE in *Lett. H. More* (1694) 43, I have a Book in the Press. **1764** BURKE *Let. to J. Dodsley* 9 Feb. (in *Westm. Gaz.* 12 Jan. (1898) 2/1) I suppose that by this our work is in the press. **1900** *Advertisement*, In the press, and shortly will be published, a new work by [etc.]. **1823** J. BADCOCK *Dom. Amusem.* p. iv, The first intelligence .. of the sheets being in hand, was the announcement that they were also '*off the press'. **1622** PEACHAM *Compl. Gent.* xiii. (1634) 128 His peeces have been long since worne *out of press. **1674** NEWTON in Rigaud *Corr. Sci. Men* (1841) II. 367 Hearing that Mr. Kersey's book is out of press, I desire you would send in the fourth part. **1612** SIR R. NAUNTON in *Buccleuch MSS.* (Hist. MSS. Comm.) I. 113 The great work of his Chrysostome then *under press. **1721** *Lond. Gaz.* No. 5961/2 A Memorial of the Grocers.. said to be under the Press.

e. In many other phrases, in which *press* passes from the literal sense 14 into that of c, as ***to bring, put, commit, send, submit to the press; to carry, see through the press; to come to, pass, undergo the press; to correct the press***, i.e. the printing, or the errors in composing the type; ***to go to press*** (also *fig.*), ***to read for press.***

1582 T. WATSON *Centurie of Loue* Ep. Ded., The world.. called vpon mee, to put it to the presse. **1597** MORLEY *Introd. Mus.* 75 If I had seene it before it came to the presse, it should not have passed so. **1605** *Gunpowder Plot* in *Harl. Misc.* (Malh.) III. 5 Being about to commit them to the press. **1631** MASSINGER *Emperor East* Ded., Such trifles of mine as have passed the press. **1646** EARL MONM. tr. *Biondi's Civil Warres* II. To Rdr., I know not whether they may ever undergoe the Presse. **1649** W. DUGDALE in *Lett. Lit. Men* (Camden) 175 Soe may he correct the presse, which will be an especiall matter. **1691** WOOD *Ath. Oxon.* II. 696 A stop was made for some years of bringing the second [vol.] to the Press. **1715** T. HEARNE *Let.* 2 Feb. (MS.), I find Mr. Urry's Chaucer advertised as being to go to yᵉ Press in a little time. *a* **1764** LLOYD *Author's Apol.* Poet. Wks. 1774 I. 2 But when it comes to press and print You'll find, I fear but little in't. **1800** *Med. Jrnl.* III. 274 It will be submitted to the Press in the course of the ensuing month. **1810** *Irish Mag.* III. 279/2, I shall, therefore.. go immediately to press, be squeezed into the genteelest form I can. **1846** G. DODD *Brit. Manuf.* 6th Ser. 57 To read for press—that is, to search for the minutest errors. **1848** HALLIWELL *Ingelend's Disobed. Child* (Percy Soc.) Pref., It was formerly a very common practice to correct and alter the press whilst the impression was being taken. **1867** E. QUINCY *Life J. Quincy* 477 My father took an active interest in this publication, and corrected the press himself. **1869** SIR J. T. COLERIDGE *Mem. Keble* (ed. 2) 265 A translation.. is now being carried through the press. *a* **1909** *Mod.* In his absence, I am to see the book through the press. **1929** YEATS *Let.* 13 Sept. (1954) 768, I will work at it here and there... I should go to press with it next spring. **1933** [see HOPE *sb.*[1] 4 a]. **1951** [see BED *sb.* 6 c]. **1961** *Financial Times* 11 July 6 At the time of going to press.. it is not possible to determine any very definite trend of trading at the present time.

f. ***freedom*** or ***liberty of the press***: free use of the printing-press; the right to print and publish anything without submitting it to previous official censorship; see LIBERTY 2 b, and quots. So in ***free press, unfettered press***, etc.

[**1644** (*title*) Areopagitica; a Speech of Mr. John Milton for the Liberty of Vnlicenc'd Printing To the Parlament of England.] **1680** R. L'ESTRANGE (*title*) A Seasonable Memorial,.. upon the Liberties of the Presse and Pulpit. **1681** W. DENTON *Jus Cæsaris* ad fin., An Apology for the Liberty of the Press. **1769** BLACKSTONE *Comm.* IV. xi. 151 The liberty of the press is indeed essential to the nature of a free state; but this consists in laying no previous restraints upon publications, and not in freedom from censure for criminal matter when published. **1771** Smollett *Humph. Cl.* 15 July, He said, he should always consider the liberty of the press as a national evil, while it enabled the vilest reptile to soil the lustre of the most shining merit. **1789** *Constit. U.S.* Amendm. i, Congress shall make no law..abridging the freedom of the press. **1827** Hallam *Const. Hist.* (1876) III. xv. 167 The liberty of the press consists, in a strict sense, merely in an exemption from the superintendence of a licenser. **1903** in *Westm. Gaz.* 11 Aug. 8/2 It has been pointed out over and over again,..that the licence of the Press is not the liberty of the Press.

g. (Also ***periodical*** or ***public press, daily press***, etc.) The newspapers, journals, and periodical literature generally; the newspapers and journals of a country, district, party, etc., as the French Press, the London Press, the Conservative Press, the religious press, the secular press, etc. Hence sometimes the title of a newspaper, as *The Press, The Scottish Press, The Aberdeen Free Press*, etc.

This use of the word appears to have originated in phrases such as *the liberty of the press, a servile* or *shackled press, to write for the press*, etc., in which 'press' originally had sense c above, but was gradually taken to mean the products of the printing-press. Quotations before 1820 are mostly transitional, leading gradually up to this sense.

1797 *The Press* (Dublin) No. 1. 1 By some fatality of late, the Press of the harassed country has been either negligent or apostate; it has been a centinel a-sleep on its post... It is now proposed to establish a newspaper, to be solely and unalterably devoted to the people of Ireland and their interests, under the appellation of *The Press*. **1798** *Anti-Jacobin* No. 36. 281 For this purpose, the Press was engaged, and almost monopolized in all its branches: Reviews, Registers, Monthly Magazines, and Morning and Evening Prints sprung forth in abundance. **1807** *Edin. Rev.* X. 115 Unlimited abuse of private characters is another characteristic of the American press. **1817** Cobbett in *Weekly Polit. Reg.* 11 Jan. 53 Silencing the press would not enable them to pay the interest of the debt. **1820** *Lond. Mag.* I. 569 The Manager has thought it his duty to suspend the Free List during the representation, the public press excepted. *Ibid.* 575 The gentlemen-critics of the daily press. **1823** *Edin. Rev.* XXXVIII. 349 (*Article*) The Periodical Press. *Ibid.*, If he had not had the fear of the periodical press before his eyes. *Ibid.* 359 The staple literature of the Periodical Press may be divided into Newspapers, Magazines, and Reviews. *Ibid.* 360 This paper [the *Morning Post*] we have been long used to think the best..that issued from the daily press. **1828** *Lancet* 19 Jan. 595/1 Sir Astley Cooper, in a silly speech at a public dinner, talked of the 'reptile press'. **1840** *Penny Cycl.* XVI. 194/1 The two principal persons..at this time concerned in the newspaper press. *Ibid.* 195/1 Capital to the amount of £500,000 at least is invested in the daily press of London, of which two-thirds ..may be represented by the morning papers. **1843** Ruskin *Arrows of Chace* (1880) I. 3, I seldom, therefore, read..the ordinary animadversions of the press. **1862** Trollope *Orley F.* xiii, There was also a reporter for the press. **1885** Sir C. P. Butt in *Law Times Rep.* LIII. 61/2 After so much discussion..in the public press on this question. *Mod.* The book has been favourably noticed by the press.

h. ***a good press***: see good *a.* 13. Hence ***to have*** (***receive***, etc.) ***a good*** (or ***bad, mixed***, etc.) ***press***: to be favourably (or unfavourably, divergently, etc.) commented on or criticized in current newspapers, journals, etc. Also *transf.*, to receive (favourable, etc.) publicity, to be (favourably, etc.) appraised in conversation or in literature.

1908 [see good *a.* 13]. **1913** R. Fry *Let.* Oct. (1972) II. 373 Has it [*sc.* an exhibition] been a success, and has there been any decent Press on it? **1915** [see good *a.* 13]. **1920** *Sat. Rev.* 10 July 26 Mr Austen Chamberlain has a very bad press. **1928** [see good *a.* 13]. **1932** *Statesman* (Calcutta) 2 Aug., It was the clearest case, for years, of how county cricket should not be conducted. Allom had a lively Press last Wednesday! **1934** H. G. Wells *Exper. Autobiogr.* II. vii. 501, I wish I could hear at times of people still reading these three stories: they got, I think, a rather dull press. **1958** *Listener* 13 Nov. 769/1 Cromwell had rather a mixed press for his great day. **1961** P. Kemp *Alms for Oblivion* i In Britain General Franco had not enjoyed a good Press. **1967** *Observer* 26 Nov. 8/3 The Phoenicians had a largely hostile press from the Bible and from their rivals the Greeks and Romans. **1976** *Women's Report* Sept./Oct. 4/1 Chiswick Women's Aid has had a good press recently because the DHSS has withdrawn some of its grant money. **1977** *Sunday Times* 30 Jan. 38/1 Rape is enjoying a very educative Press from TV dramatists at the moment.

i. Usu. with *the*: used collectively for journalists, esp. reporters; also, of an individual reporter.

1926 in S. Bent *Ballyhoo* (1927) ii. 55 At least a half dozen times since the wedding the unfortunate composer has been badgered by the press until some such statement as 'we are very happy' has been wrung from him. **1949** 'J. Tey' *Brat Farrar* xii. 102 'He says he's a reporter,' Lana said... 'Oh, *no*!' Bee said. 'Not the Press. Not already.' **1951** M. Dickens *My Turn to make Tea* iv. 45 'Here's the Press, Waldo,' his wife told him, 'come to put Marjorie in the *Post*.' *Ibid.* vii. 122 Sister..said that if I was The Press, Matron had deputed her to show me round. **1956** C. Mackenzie *Thin Ice* x. 129 The dinners of the East Indiamen were held once a quarter without excessive formality and, what was more important for the speaker, without the Press. **1973** A. S. Neill *Neill! Neill! Orange Peel!* ii. 235 The Salvation Army damsel..came to a young man sitting alone. 'Are you saved?' 'Press,' he said. 'Oh, I beg your pardon,' and she moved hastily away. **1974** P. N. Walker *Major Incident* viii. 95 As the police were desperately trying to clear the streets, the first of the press were trying to drive in. **1978** M. Butterworth *X marks Spot* ii. i. 73 Arrange for the exhumation forthwith. Seal off Highgate Cemetery... No Press. No television.

IV. 15. A large (usually shelved) cupboard, esp. one placed in a recess in the wall, for holding clothes, books, etc.; in Scotland, also for provisions, victuals, plates, dishes, and other table requisites. Cf. clothes-press 1. Also *attrib.*

c **1386** Chaucer *Miller's T.* 26 His presse ycovered with a faldyng reed. **1398** Trevisa *Barth. De P.R.* xviii. cv. (1495) gg iv/1 Whanne the cloth is to longe in presse & thicke ayre. *a* **1533** Ld. Berners *Huon* cxi. 384 There were presses..in the whiche presses were gownes and robes of fyne golde, and ryche mantelles furryd with sabyls. **1552** in *Bury Wills* (Camden) 142, I gyve her my newe cubbord with the presse in yt and too great books the Bybyll and the New Testament, with the Booke of the Kings Statuts. **1566** *Eng. Ch. Furniture* (1866) 67 One sepulcre—sold to Johnne orson and he haith made a presse therof to laie clothes therein. **1598** Shaks. *Merry W.* iii. iii. 226 In the house, & in the chambers, and in the coffers, and in the presses. **1600** J. Pory tr. *Leo's Africa* iii. 125 Each chamber hath a presse curiously painted and varnished belonging thereunto. **1686** *Inv.* in *Essex Rev.* (1906) XV. 172 Two chayers, one presse cubbord. **1709** Hughes *Tatler* No. 113 ¶9 A Press for Books [with four shelves]. **1753** Smollett *Ct. Fathom* (1784) 35/2 He should..conceal himself in a large press or wardrobe, that stood in one corner of the apartment. **1790** Burns *Tam o' Shanter* 125 Coffins stood round like open presses, That shaw'd the dead in their last dresses. **1802** Findlater *Agric. Peebles* iii. 41 The ambry, or shelved wooden press, in which the cow's milk, and other.. provision are locked up. **1859** Jephson *Brittany* xiii. 221 In a press with glass doors, she showed me some beautiful reliquaries. **1888** Barrie *Auld Licht Idylls* ii. 50 A 'press' or cupboard containing a fair assortment of cooking utensils. **1892** *Pall Mall G.* 16 Jan. 7/3 The Sliding Book-Press at the British Museum. *Ibid.*, The principle of a sliding or hanging press is entirely peculiar to the British Museum, and hardly could have originated elsewhere than in a building possessing..floors and ceilings entirely grated. **1952** J. Gloag *Short Dict. Furnit.* 374 *Press cupboard*, a large cupboard with a superstructure consisting of a shelf with smaller cupboards behind it..introduced during the second half of the 16th century. **1959** L. A. Boger *Compl. Guide Furnit. Styles* xxii. 384 The name *press cupboard* was given in America to a form of cup-board resembling the English hall and parlor cupboard. **1970** *Canad. Antiques Collector* Jan. 29/1 A further kind of cupboard..was called a press, or press-cupboard, and was about the same general size and shape as a modern wardrobe. **1975** *Oxf. Compan. Decorative Arts* 651 *Press cupboard*, a large cupboard, sometimes confused with a court cupboard, which came into use in the latter half of the 16th c. and remained in fashion until the 18th c. It had the upper part recessed with contained cupboards and a shelf running in front of them.

V. *attrib.* and *Comb.*

16. General combinations: **a.** attributive, (*a*) of a press (senses 11, 12), as ***press-bar, -beam, -block, -board, -frame, -plunger, -shop, -table***, etc.; (*b*) of or pertaining to the printing-press, to printing, or to journalism, as ***press advertising, boss, camera, campaign, censor, press-censorship, club, -correspondent, -folk*** (cf. pressman), ***freedom, -girthing, interview, -mohawk, -organ, pass, -people, photo, photograph, photographer, photography, -reader, ticket, -worker***. **b.** [from the vb. stem.] (*a*) Used to press, pressing, as ***press-barrel, -box, -harrow***; (*b*) Operated by pressing, as ***press-cock, switch***; (see also sense 17 d below); also pressbutton *sb.* and *a.*, press-fastener, etc. **c.** objective genitive, as ***press-builder, -building, -haunter, -maker, -mauler***. **d.** instrumental, as ***press-made, -noticed, -ridden*** adjs.

1961 *Travel Topics* June 41/1 When one first thinks of *press advertising, it conjures up the thought of taking space in the national dailies or Sunday papers. **1839** Ure *Dict. Arts* 158 (*Bookbinding*) The *pressbar, or beam, has two holes upon its under surface, for securing it to two pegs standing on the top of the chest. **1794** *Rigging & Seamanship* 55 **Press-barrels* are old tar-barrels filled with clay, and laid on the sledge or drag to add weight when the rope is closing. **1803** *Naval Chron.* X. 477 The [old] tar barrels..are applied to the purpose of serving as a weight in laying..rope, and are called press barrels. **1932** E. Pound *Let.* 18 Feb. (1971) 239 There is no reason why young England shd. pardon the ineffable polluters and saboteurs. What they have done to stifle literature in Eng., tho not so important as the *press-bosses' stifling of economic discussion, is all of piece [*sic*]. **1825** J. Nicholson *Operat. Mechanic* 448 (*Oil-mill*), 16, the first *press-box, (also hollowed out of the block,) in which the grain is squeezed, after it has come for the first time from below the mill-stones. 17, the second press-box, at the other end of the block, for squeezing the grain after it has passed a second time under the pestles. **1890** W. J. Gordon *Foundry* 194 Associated with Smith, he [Richard Hoe's father] had turned his attention to *press building in general. **1896** T. L. De Vinne *Moxon's Mech. Exerc., Printing* 410 Press-building was not a distinct trade in 1683. **1948** A. L. M. Sowerby *Dict. Photogr.* (ed. 17) 89 The typical *Press camera consists of a frame containing the shutter, fitted at the back for plates in dark slides and with the lens carried on a flat panel supported at the four corners by struts and connected with the camera body by bellows. **1964** M. McLuhan *Understanding Media* xx. 200 The press camera contributed to radical changes in the game of football. **1974** *Encycl. Brit. Macropædia* XIV. 330/2 Press cameras are loaded with sheet film..for fast, handheld shooting; they are traditionally of folding-bellows design with a lens standard on an extendable baseboard. **1903** 'Vigilans sed Æquus' *German Ambitions* vi. 86 The German *press campaign against our army in South Africa. **1951** M. McLuhan *Mech. Bride* (1967) 40/1 The working woman was put into adolescent short skirts and told in big press campaigns that the age-old tyranny of man was at an end. **1900** W. S. Churchill *Let.* 1 May in R. S. Churchill *Winston S. Churchill* (1967) I. Compan. ii. 1174 Wolverton is here, one of the *press censors. **1940** L. Durrell *Spirit of Place* (1969) 65 George Seferiades..chief foreign press censor, who is a remarkable poet and person. **1887** *Pall Mall G.* 9 Aug. 5/1 An aggressive and oppressive *press-censorship. **1939** 'G. Orwell' in *New English Weekly* 12 Jan. 203/2 The radio, press-censorship, standardised education and the secret police have altered everything. **1978** 'A. York' *Tallant for Disaster* vi. 93 Even the British have press censorship... What about all those D-notices and things? **1896** *Peterson Mag.* Mar. 311/1 The Pittsburgh Women's *Press Club made a wise choice in selecting for a secretary Miss Marie de Sayles Coyle. **1967** L. T. Braun *Cat who ate Danish Modern* ii. 20 Why don't we meet for drinks at the Press Club? **1932** *Jrnl. R. Aeronaut. Soc.* XXXVI. 854 The ideal starter..was a self-contained unit in which only one simple operation, such as pressing a *press-cock, was required. **1900** *Macm. Mag.* May 36 One of our *press-correspondents at the present day. **1729** Swift *Wks.* (1841) II. 98 Mist..happened to reprint this paper in London, for which his *press-folk were prosecuted. **1825** J. Nicholson *Operat. Mechanic* 448, Fig. 460 is the elevation of the pestle and *press-frame, their furniture, the mortars, and the press-pestles. **1974** *Times* 18 Nov. 15/1 Advertisers threaten *press freedom if they try to use their advertising power as a form of censorship. **1840** J. Buel *Farmer's Comp.* 146 For pulverizing stiff clays, Concklin's *press-harrow is an admirable instrument. **1597** G. Harvey *Trimming Nashe* Wks. (Grosart) III. 67 To all ballet-makers, pamphleters, *presse hanters, boon pot poets, and such like. **1923** *Radio Times* 23 Sept. 18/3 Mr. J. W. Reith, the General Manager of the B.B.C...has managed to avoid..the usual *press interviews. **1976** L. Henderson *Major Enquiry* viii. 47 The report of Shenton's press interview was given great prominence by the *Evening News*. **1886** *Pall Mall G.* 4 Sept. 14/1 The original introducer of *press-made pens. **1900** *Daily News* 11 May 3/2 The..theory that this is a capitalist- and Press-made war. **1705** J. Dunton *Life & Err.* 244 He has been an indefatigable *Press-mauler, for above these Twenty years. **1844** Thackeray *Box of Novels* Wks. 1900 XIII. 399 The nation..looks upon the *press-Mohawks.. as it did upon the gallant young noblemen who used a few years since to break the heads of policemen. **1906** in *Westm. Gaz.* 24 Sept. 4/2 One of the best *Press-noticed books he had ever published. **1895** *Daily Tel.* 27 Aug. 4/7 The pernicious example..was followed by more than one Parisian *press-organ. **1914** *Automobile Topics* 6 June 303/1 Primary cause for protest was the method adopted by the Speedway management of distributing *press passes. **1977** H. Innes *Big Footprints* ii. i. 103 They weren't interested in my press pass or the fact that I was an American TV man. **1964** M. McLuhan *Understanding Media* xx. 200 A *press photo of battered players in a 1905 game. *Ibid.*, The press photo coverage of the lives of the rich. **1980** R. McCrum *In Secret State* xviii. 168 The dashing whizz-kid of the press photos. **1944** M. Laski *Love on Supertax* ii. 31 Suppose you wanted a really flattering *press photograph and I knew someone who'd fake it up. **1974** 'J. Le Carré' *Tinker, Tailor* xxiii. 196, I had with me the American press photographs of the arrest. **1922** M. Arlen *Piracy* 7 Those young women of patrician and careless intelligence, whom it is the pet mistake of bishops, diarists, *press-photographers, and Americans, to take as representing the 'state' of modern society. **1974** 'M. Innes' *Appleby's Other Story* v. 44 One has to think of the reporters and press-photographers. **1922** L. Warren *Journalism* xxi. 230 In a book such as this it is quite out of the question to go into details concerning *press photography. **1980** *Times* 3 Mar. 14/6 *Life*..was press photography for the press photographer at its most splendid. **1884** C. G. W. Lock *Workshop Receipts* Ser. iii. 361/1 The die is easily reached by lifting the chamber *e*, which is done by attaching the same to the *press-plunger and elevating the latter. **1849** Longf. *Kavanagh* xiii. (1857) 228 This country is not priest-ridden, but *press-ridden. **1798** *Times* 28 June 1/3 At the back of the said dwelling-house are also a *press-shop and other conveniences for carrying on the Business of a Merchant. **1958** *Engineering* 11 Apr. 461/1 The current expansion programme, which includes the opening of a new press shop later this year and a new assembly building early in 1959. **1959** *Motor Manual* (ed. 36) i. 8 In the latest press shops, all the presses engaged in the production of one component are arranged in a long line, and are linked by roller conveyors. **1892** E. J. Houston *Dict. Electr. Words* (ed. 2) 424/2 *Pressel*, a *press switch or push connected to the end of a flexible pendant conductor. **1971** *Engineering* Apr. 20/2 Mounting of the equipment on the movable *press-table is also easy. **1851** J. Chapman *Diary* 10 July in G. S. Haight *Geo. Eliot & J. Chapman* (1940) 191 Spencer gave me a ticket for the Opera..and might have had an excellent place but for the vexing regulation that '*press tickets' must be exchanged which destroyed my chance of admittance. **1976** 'D. Fletcher' *Don't whistle 'Macbeth'* 17 Some idiot in the box office had allocated press tickets for the first matinée instead of the first night.

17. Special combs. **a.** from senses 11, 12: **press-cake**, = mill-*cake* (*a*); **press-copy** *sb.*, a copy of a writing made by transfer in a copying-press; hence **press-copy** *v.*; **press-drill**, (*a*) = land-*presser*; (*b*) see quot. 1884; †**press-fat**, a vat used for collecting the produce in an oil- or wine-press; **press-forged** *a.*, forged by pressure; **press-house**, the house or building containing a press; a place where pressing is done; **press-iron**, = pressing-iron; **press-key**, a thumb-screw used to tighten and hold the cords of a sewing-press, in bookbinding; **press-mould** (see quot. 1974); so **press-mould** *v.*, **press-moulding** *vbl. sb.*, **press-moulded** *ppl. a.*; **press-pack** *v.*, *trans.* to pack or compress (something) into small compass by means of a press (Webster 1864); **press-pin**, the lever of a screw-press; **press-plate**, (*a*) in Bramah's press = follower *sb.* 5; (*b*) a plate of metal placed between the press-boards of a standing press;

press-pole, a pole used in pleaching: see quot.; **press-printing**, printing by a press; a method of printing porcelain: see quot.; **press-ware**: see quot.

1839 Ure *Dict. Arts* 629 It comes out in large thin solid cakes, or strata, distinguished by the term *press-cake. **1858** Greener *Gunnery* 43 Two pieces of lignum vitæ..are placed on the broken press-cakes in each sieve. **1796** Gouv. Morris *Let. to Lady Sutherland* 22 Aug., I will fold up in this a *press copy of my last, because the original may have been drowned. **1834** *Penny Cycl.* II. 224/2 In such soils an artificial pan may be formed by the land-presser or *press-drill. **1884** Knight *Dict. Mech.* Suppl., *Press Drill*, a drilling machine largely used in gun and sewing machine work. **1611** Bible *Haggai* ii. 16 When one came to the *press-fatte [**1885** *R.V.* winefat] for to draw out fiftie vessels out of the presse, there were but twentie. **1895** *Daily News* 14 Nov. 6/5 His gun, Captain Jaques explained, would be made of a few hollow, *press-forged, cold-drawn, taper cylinders of alloyed steel. **1744** *N. Jersey Archives* XII. 211 To Be Sold, ..A new Fulling-Mill, *Press-House and Dye-House. **1878** J. Inglis *Sport & W.* iv. 34 The huge lever is strained and pulled at by the press-house coolies. **1900** *Westm. Gaz.* 25 Oct. 7/2 Allowing the populace to enter the press-house of the vine-yard. **1892** Zangwill *Children of Ghetto* I. 45 He taught them how to handle a *press-iron. **1974** Savage & Newman *Illustr. Dict. Ceramics* 233 **Press-mould*, an absorbent mould made of lightly fired clay or plaster of Paris, and into which clay is pressed by hand to make such objects as small ornaments for relief or sprigged decoration. *a* **1977** *Harrison Mayer Ltd. Catal.* 95/2 A range of simple Press Moulds in 5 basic shapes. **1969** Speck & Sutherland *Eng. Antiques* 190/2 *Press-moulded glass. **1971** *Country Life* 27 May 1303/1 The [Staffordshire slipware] dish is press-moulded and is signed 'I.S.'. **1958** H. Wakefield in Edwards & Ramsey *Connoisseur Period Guides: Early Victorian Period* 100/2 It was the period in which the process of *press-moulding was first developed for the production of dishes and other open shapes. **1839** Ure *Dict. Arts* 1031 Upon the top of the ram, the *press-plate or table..rests, which is commonly called the follower, because it follows the ram closely in its descent. **1868** *Report U.S. Commissioner Agric.* (1869) 257 Two men use the *press-pole,..the other uses the pleaching-hook. The pole is thrust through behind each stout vertical sapling, when both men pull gently and equally. Thus bent back a little, the third man cuts it two-thirds through, cutting obliquely downward with the pleaching-hook. **1875** Ure *Dict. Arts* (ed. 7) III. 620 There are two distinct methods of printing in use for china and earthenware; one is transferred on the bisque, and is the method by which the ordinary printed ware is produced,..called '*press-printing'. **1612** Sturtevant *Metallica* 38 *Press-ware or Mould-ware is any thing that can bee made, wrought, or formed of clay and earth,..by Presse and Mould, or by pressing and moulding.

b. (connected with printing and journalism): **press attaché**, a diplomat responsible for the dealings of an embassy with the press; **press baron**, a powerful newspaper owner, a newspaper magnate, esp. one who is a member of the peerage (see baron 2 b); **press-blanket**, a piece of flannel or felt used on a printing-press to equalize the impression of the type; **press boat**, a boat reserved for the use of reporters at a boat race or similar event; **press book**, (*a*) a volume of press cuttings; (*b*) a book printed at a private press, a type of fine book (see fine *a.* 12 d); **press-box**, a shelter for newspaper reporters in the open air, as at a cricket or football match; **press-boy**, a boy employed as messenger in a printing-office; in the United States, a machine-boy; **press card**, a document that authorizes a reporter to practise journalism, or one that gains him admission; **press clipping** orig. *U.S.* = *press cutting*; also *attrib.*; hence ***press-clipper***; **press conference**, a meeting at which journalists and other representatives of the news media are given an opportunity to put questions to a politician, writer, etc.; also (*rare*) (with hyphens) as *v. trans.*; **press corps**, a group of reporters (usu. in a specified place); **press-corrected** *a.*, designating a text of which the proof sheets have been corrected before publication; **press correction**, (*a*) the act or process of correcting errors in a text during preparation for publication; (*b*) an error marked for correction; **press-corrector**, a proof-reader; **Press Council**, a body established in the U.K. in 1953 to raise and maintain professional standards among journalists; **press coverage**, the reporting (of an event) by the press; **press-cutter** = *press cutting agency*; **press cutting**, a paragraph, article, or notice, cut from a newspaper; also *attrib.* as ***press-cutting agency, album, book, bureau, people***; **press day**, (*a*) a day on which journalists are invited to an exhibition, a performance, etc.; (*b*) the day on which a journal goes to press; **press digest**, a digest or summary of press reports; **press-gallery**, a gallery or part of the house at any public meeting, set apart for reporters; esp. that in the House of Commons or other legislative chamber; **press kit**, a dossier prepared for journalists; **press-law**, a law as to the licensing of printing, esp. of the newspaper press; **press notice**, a review in a newspaper or other periodical of a book, play, or the like; **press number**, a number at the foot of the page of an early printed book showing on which press or by which printer the page was printed (see quot. 1961); **press office**, an office within an organization or government department responsible for dealings with the press; **press-proof, -revise**, the last proof examined before printed matter goes to press; **press release**, an official statement offered to newspapers for publication; **press run**, a spell of allowing a printing-press to run; the amount of printed material produced as a result; **press secretary**, a secretary who deals with publicity and public relations; **press show**, a performance given for the press, esp. a film shown to journalists before general release; also *attrib.*; so **press-show** *v. trans.*; **press stand**, a section of the tiered seats for spectators at racing or field events reserved for reporters; also *attrib.*; **press-stone**, the bed of a printing-press; **press table**, a table reserved for journalists esp. in a court of law; **press time**, the time at which a newspaper goes to press; **press-tradition**, handing down in print; **press view**, a viewing of an exhibition by journalists before it is open to the general public. See also press agent.

1938 A. Barmine *Mem. Soviet Diplomat* i. 16 When Krestinsky was at the Berlin Embassy, Stern had served for many years as his *Press Attaché. **1980** 'R. Deacon' *Spy!* iii. 86 She had made a favourable impression with the press attaché. **1958** *Spectator* 20 June 794/3 The history of the rise in the peerage of the *press barons..is one of the shoddiest episodes in the whole story of the press. **1975** *Times* 3 July 14/3 (*caption*) Press barons together; Lord Thomson shares a smile with..Lord Beaverbrook. **1870** D. J. Kirwan *Palace & Hovel* xxiv. 363 By the side of the *Press boat, the Umpire's boat..was anchored, many of the passengers wearing the rival colors. **1901** R. H. Davis in *Scribner's Mag.* Aug. 131/1 The press-boats buried their bows in the waters of the Florida Straits and raced for the cable-station at Port Antonio. **1897** A. Beardsley *Let.* 6 Jan. (1971) 240, I quite forgot to return you the cuttings for your *press book. I enclose them now. **1930** *Publishers' Weekly* 19 Apr. 2116/2 The past five years has seen keen collecting interest in Press books both early and modern. **1976** *Times Lit. Suppl.* 5 Mar. 271/3 There is also a large output of less sumptuous..books..produced by a host of part-time private presses, small publishers who commission fine books, and trade printers who..take time off to print a worthwhile book... It is to cover these books that the term 'press books' has been coined. **1889** *Sporting Life* (Philadelphia) 10 July 5/5 The upper stand..will contain the seats for ladies and their escorts and the private boxes, not forgetting the *press box. **1905** *Westm. Gaz.* 12 Dec. 9/2 A series of scrimmages on that side of the field remote from the press-box. **1976** Dexter & Makins *Testkill* 61 Festing followed me to the Press box and sat..in silence until the end of the game. **1890** *Cent. Dict.*, *Machine-boy*, in the United States known as feeder or *press-boy. **1934** *N.Y. Times* 20 Feb. 18/3 The number of *press cards has been cut by 55 per cent. **1951** 'A. Garve' *Murder in Moscow* iii. 41, I went on to see the head of the Soviet Press Department and collect my press card. **1976** *Times* 27 Feb. 15/2 The use of fake press cards by soldiers in Ulster puts genuine journalists in danger. **1903** *Everybody's Mag.* July 127/1 The *press-clippers caught every reprint. **1903** *Christendom* Apr. p. ii (Advt.), United States *Press Clipping Bureau. **1904** G. B. Shaw *Let.* 6 Apr. (1972) II. 416 PPS I subscribe to an American press clipping agency. **1942** D. Powell *Time to be Born* (1943) i. 20 Julian fussed with some press clippings. **1975** *Language for Life* (Dept. Educ. & Sci.) xv. 232 The same is no less necessary for English, the 'materials' of which are duplicated sheets, press-clippings, files, photographs, and so on. [**1923** A. Cecil in *Cambr. Hist. Brit. Foreign Policy* III. viii. 628 [During the 1914–18 war] Lord Robert Cecil used to hold a kind of weekly reception for American journalists, when they were at liberty to question him on Foreign Affairs.] **1937** *Time* 1 Mar. 9/3 One afternoon Mrs. Roosevelt stole into the President's regular semi-weekly *press conference to say good-by to her husband. **1953** *Manch. Guardian Weekly* 2 Apr. 7/4 Another general was soon to press-conference himself into the Presidency. **1958** *New Statesman* 15 Mar. 332/3 This programme..takes one of two forms: either it is a press-conference in which an eminent person is questioned by journalists in several countries, or it is a straight discussion between those taking part. **1976** *Eastern Even. News* (Norwich) 9 Dec. 1/5 'I don't believe anyone in this industry wants a dispute,' Sir Derek said at a Press conference during a visit to Bedlay Colliery Lanarkshire. **1940** G. Seldes *Witch Hunt* i. 6 He came to Trier and used the American *press corps. **1974** *Sunday Times* 21 July 1/3 A 200-strong international Press corps confined to the hotel by the island's [*sc.* Cyprus's] 24-hour curfew. **1964** F. Bowers *Bibliogr. & Textual Crit.* v. ii. 139 Editors should choose the First Folio *press-corrected reading..instead of the quarto and the uncorrected Folio reading. *Ibid.* I. iii. 19 A brief look at some problems of *press-correction will illustrate with suitably neutral examples. *Ibid.*, *Press-correctors do not deliberately introduce typographical errors in the copy. **1947** *Minutes of Evidence R. Comm. on Press* 12 Nov. 23/2 in *Parl. Papers 1947–8* (Cmd. 7330) XIV. 533 The proposal is that there should be a *Press Council, something..approximating to the General Medical Council.., and that there should be punishments and rewards instituted in order to raise and preserve the standards of professional behaviour within the newspaper profession. **1953** *Times* 5 Nov. 4/2 The new Press Council had proclaimed deep concern at the unwholesome exploitation of sex by certain newspapers and periodicals. **1977** *Evening Post* (Nottingham) 27 Jan. 6/1 If a newspaper were genuinely hostile to the Labour Party and decided, as a result, that in future no reference would be made to it or its troubles and triumphs, there would be an excellent case for reporting the newspaper to the Press Council for failing to do its duty. **1957** J. Mitford *Poison Penmanship* (1979) 34 These examples represent only a very tiny sampling of *press coverage of this part of the case. **1961** C. Willock *Death in Covert* iii. 71 All goes down to advertising. Whynne says we'll get it back twice over in press coverage. **1976** *Times* 27 Feb. 15/1 Documents from army sources critical of press coverage in Northern Ireland. **1901** G. Gissing *Let.* 30 Nov. in *G. Gissing & H. G. Wells* (1961) 200, I have never dared to subscribe to the *press-cutters, for I remember..the day when a press notice meant a sneer which disturbed my work. **1888** *Pall Mall G.* 4 May 11/1 A Visit to a *Press-cutting Agency... For some time an agency has been at work for supplying newspaper references—at so much per hundred cuttings or a yearly subscription. **1898** G. B. Shaw *Let.* 24 Mar. (1972) II. 22 A sheaf of pamphlets & press cuttings. **1899** *Westm. Gaz.* 5 May 2/3 Mr. Chamberlain has recently made a feeling protest against government by Press-cutting agency. **1901** *Cycl. Tour. Club Gaz.* Oct. 389 The press cuttings that lie before us. *a* **1916** 'Saki' *Infernal Parliament* in *Square Egg* (1924) 148 Pasting notices of modern British plays into a huge press-cutting book. **1922** A. E. Housman *Let.* 26 Oct. (1971) 206 The press-cutting agency sends me..more notices than I want to see. **1929** T. S. Eliot *Dante* iii. 63 He, Dante Alighieri, was an important person who kept press-cutting bureaux busy. **1936** 'G. Orwell' *Let.* 26 Aug. in *Coll. Ess.* (1968) I. 228, I don't know what sort of reviews it got in France—I only saw about two..the press-cutting people didn't get them. **1941** V. Nabokov *Real Life S. Knight* xi. 102 A press-cutting agency began to pepper him with samples of praise. **1942** 'M. Innes' *Daffodil Affair* I. 37 He has consulted his colleagues; assistants have been turning over press cuttings. **1967** 'E. Peters' *Black is Colour* iii. 53 Things like the press-cutting book and the photographs get into arrears very easily. **1967** J. B. Priestley *It's an Old Country* vii. 84 Magazines and paperbacks, jigsaw puzzles, photograph and press-cutting albums. **1923** A. Huxley *Antic Hay* vii. 103 It was *Press Day. The critics had begun to arrive. **1956** J. Symons *Paper Chase* xiii. 99 'Press day. Very busy.' He waved the galleys. **1972** C. Fremlin *Appointment with Yesterday* xiv. 113 The Editor ringing up, more and more irate, as press day drew near. **1958** *New Statesman* 20 Sept. 368/3 The *press-digest which the President and Mr Dulles receive from the US embassy in London. **1977** G. Markstein *Chance Awakening* xxv. 76 The press digest was lying on his desk. **1884** Yates *Recoll.* II. vii. 286, I..was in the *press-gallery of the Chamber..on the 24th May. **1897** [see gallery *sb.* 3 d]. **1968** *Globe & Mail* (Toronto) 17 Feb. 1/8 The ad hoc committee of five had already quietly rented space in a downtown Ottawa office building and prepared a slick *press kit. **1977** *New Yorker* 3 Oct. 36/2 Our advance word on this event [*sc.* the publication of a new encyclopaedia] came to us in the form of a fat press kit, stuffed with fact sheets and kind words about the work. **1897** Mrs. E. L. Voynich *Gadfly* ix, A new *press-law was expected. **1888** 'Mark Twain' *Let.* 1 Oct. in C. Clemens *Mark Twain* (1932) iii. 49, I thank you ever so much for not forgetting to remember to send me the *press notice. **1977** J. Aiken *Last Movement* i. 37 'What about your opening?'..'Big success. I'll show you our press notices.' **1895** *Funk's Stand. Dict.*, *Press-number. **1949** *Harvard Library Bull.* III. 11. 198 (*title*) Press numbers as a bibliographical tool. **1961** T. Landau *Encycl. Librarianship* (ed. 2) 283/2 *Press number*, small figures which in books printed between 1680 and *c.* 1823 often appear at the foot of a page, sometimes twice in a gathering. The figures indicate on which press in the printer's workshop the sheet was printed or perhaps the identity of the worker. **1937** L. Hellman *Diary* 17 Oct. in *Unfinished Woman* (1969) viii. 87, I have been to the *Press Office [in Valencia]..and paid a visit to Rubio, the Press Chief. *a* **1974** R. Crossman *Diaries* (1976) II. 269, I must send it straightaway across to the Press Office in Transport House. **1841** W. Savage *Dict. Art of Printing* 597 **Press proof*, a good impression of a sheet of a work, or of a job, to read it carefully by, and to mark the errors, previous to its being put to press. **1972** P. Gaskell *New Introd. Bibliogr.* 115 The third and final stage of proof correction was the press proof, when a forme or sheet was read for residual blemishes..just before the actual printing run was about to begin. **1958** M. H. Saringulian *Eng.-Russ. Dict. Libr. & Bibliogr. Terms* 148/1 *Press release. **1964** W. Markfield *To Early Grave* (1965) ii. 29 He sent out press releases, and the *Brooklyn Eagle* ran a small story. *a* **1974** R. Crossman *Diaries* (1975) I. 67, I therefore gave instructions that for one month all the press releases and all the actual letters to authorities written in my name on planning permissions and compulsory purchase orders should be sent to me. **1976** *Oxf. Diocesan Mag.* July 14/2 There must be the news angle to the press release which, of course, should be factual and not based on rumours or hearsay. **1888** C. T. Jacobi *Printers' Vocab.* 103 **Press revise*, the final proof for press or machine. **1960** G. A. Glaister *Gloss. Bk.* 324/1 *Press revise*, an extra proof from the corrected type when ready for machining. **1958** *New Statesman* 15 Mar. 328/2 Since there is no 'preventive censorship', a paper which incurs the wrath of the government risks losing its entire *press-run, which is simply impounded and placed in the Reuilly Barracks. **1976** M. Ierley *Year that tried Men's Souls* III. 198 (*caption*) At the left is the page as it appeared when Publisher Benjamin Towne began his press run. **1959** J. Ludwig in *Tamarack Rev.* Summer 20 Eisenhower with that puzzled look which meant if his *press secretary didn't say something fast he was a goner. **1967** H. P. Levy *Press Council* p. xiii, Sir Richard Colville, the Press Secretary to Her Majesty the Queen, kindly read the chapter on the Royal Family in typescript. **1976** P. Alexander *Death of Thin-skinned Animal* xv. 150 He..announced himself as the London correspondent of *Paris Match* and said he'd like to speak to Colonel Njala's press secretary. **1958** *Vogue* July 44 American horror films..are never *press-shown and are a disappointment to connoisseurs. **1961** *John o' London's* 15 June 671/1 A hard-boiled press-show audience. **1962** *Ibid.* 2 Aug. 115/1 On my way to the press-show of *The Lion.* **1963** *Movie* Jan. 20/3, I don't think there are any plans for press-showing it. **1972** *Times* 3 July 7/3 In Rome..I started going to press shows. **1914** *Automobile Topics* 6 June 303/1 Incidentally each applicant was put through the third degree in order to establish his complete identity and right to the *press stand privileges. **1915** G. Patten *Courtney of Center Garden* 53 Passing the press stand, Whip caught Chatterton's eye again. **1937** E. Rickman *On & off Racecourse* vi. 137 He would usually watch the racing from the press-stand. **1683** MOXON *Mech. Exerc., Printing* xi. ¶17 The *Press-Stone should be Marble, though sometimes Master Printers make shift with Purbeck. **1922** JOYCE *Ulysses* 454 From the *presstable, coughs and calls. **1974** F. NOLAN *Oshawa Project* i. 1 By the time the speeches started, the general was drunk... Every correspondent at the press table..could see the signs. **1927** S. BENT *Ballyhoo* ix. 240 It may be timely..but the reasons for printing it are that there is a glut of space to be filled in advance of news *press-time, and that it must be filled with bait which will give the paper 'attention value'. **1978** *Rugby World* Apr. 19/1 At press-time, Royal High were level on 14 points with Glasgow Academicals and Madras, each club having two games to play, but with only one of the sides to go up alongside Leith. **1675** J. SMITH *Chr. Relig. Appeal* I. 16 Conveyed down to us in the same way of pen or *press-tradition that other writings are. **1890** G. B. SHAW *London Music 1888–89* (1937) 284 My ticket for the *Press view at the Old Masters on Friday! *Ibid.* 368, I have been at the Royal Academy all day, 'Press-viewing' it. **1929** R. FRY *Let.* 27 Dec. (1972) II. 646, I may be able to wangle you one [ticket] for the Press view on Monday.

c. (sense 7 d) **press cloth**, a piece of cloth placed between the fabric and iron while pressing; **press line**, a crease made by a pressing iron; **press mark**, a mark left on fabric by the impress of an iron; hence **press-mark** *v. trans.*; **press-pad**, a soft pad used in pressing clothes.

1918 M. J. RHOE *Dress you Wear* xi. 127 Nearly all pressing is done over a damp press cloth. **1933** A. M. MIALL *Home Dressmaking* vii. 51 You should have a second wet press-cloth ready, and change to it as soon as the first dries, to avoid scorching. **1964** *McCall's Sewing* viii. 118/1 Always use a press cloth to prevent shine when necessary to press on the right side of the garment. **1979** *Tucson* (Arizona) *Citizen* 20 Sept. 2B/3 A final pressing (with press cloth) from the right side will give your coat (and its hem) a brand-new look. **1947** C. TALBOT *Compl. Bk. Sewing* xxxi. 208/1 Remove the sharp line by moving the seam back and pressing the sleeve under the seam, removing the press lines from the sleeve. **1948** H. HALL *Home Dress-Making Simplified* vii. 64 It is important to press-mark all the side seams of the waist, the shirt, and the sleeves, as these seams will be the fitting lines of the dress. **1948** E. L. TOWERS *Standard Processes in Dressmaking* xvi. 116 If press marks appear on the right side of the garment, hold the fabric in the steam of a kettle to remove them. **1974** J. ROBINSON *Penguin Bk. Sewing* I. ii. 44 If during making a few press marks..do show then remove these by steaming. **1924** W. D. F. VINCENT *Cutters' Pract. Guide Overcoats* 73/1 A good plan when damping fronts, lapels and collar is to damp through a double piece of cloth from the back, the silk being face down on the soft cloth press-pad.

d. From the vb. stem (cf. sense 16 b): **press fit** *Engin.*, an interference fit between two parts in which one is forced under pressure into a slightly smaller hole in the other; cf. *shrink fit* s.v. SHRINK *v.* 17; hence **press-fitted** *a.*; **press-key**, a control or switch similar to a piano key, operated by pressing the end with the finger.

1888 *Lockwood's Dict. Mech. Engin.* 265 *Press fit*, a fitting of contiguous parts slightly tighter than a sliding fit.., to allow of the sliding parts being pressed together with a hydraulic press. **1902** *Internat. Libr. Technol.* III. §22. 33 In a press fit, the internal piece..must be enough larger than the hole to insure the development of enough friction between the two pieces to hold it there securely when pressed home. **1971** B. SCHARF *Engin. & its Language* xi. 111 Considerable effort is required to assemble the parts: this is reflected in the use of terms such as force, drive or press fit. **1970** K. BALL *Fiat 600, 600D Autobook* vi. 53/2 The side bevels embody the axle shaft slip joint cavities, the free bevels being mounted on a shaft press-fitted into the differential casing. **1976** *Gramophone* Dec. 1092/1 Tape transport is controlled by an array of press-keys all fitted with a non-slip tread to prevent finger slip.

[*Note.* The origin of the *β* forms *prês, prees, preas, prese, prease, preace*, is not clear. So far as concerns the lengthened vowel, they go with the similar forms of the verb *prêse-n, preese, prease*, beside the ordinary *press-en*, PRESS *v.*[1] These agree with *cease, lease, decease* from OF. or ME. *cesse, lesse*, ME. *decesse*, also with *beast, feast*, in which original short *e* before *ss, st* is lengthened. (See Note to PRESS *v.*[1]) The special difficulty in the sb. is that ME. *prês* had no final *e* (the 15–16th c. *-e* being only graphical), so that it cannot be identified with OF. and ME. *presse*. Could it be an Eng. derivative from the long-vowel stem of the vb. *prês-e(n*? As a formation, it appears to be distinct from *presse, press*, and might have been treated as a separate word *prease* or *preace*; but being obsolete, and its senses (so far as they went) coinciding with those of *press*, it has for convenience been treated as a parallel form of this word.]

press (prɛs), *sb.*[2] Now *rare*. [An alteration of or substitution for PREST *sb.*[1] 5, as in PRESS *v.*[2], and PRESS-MONEY.]

1. The impressing of men for service in the navy or (less frequently) the army; compulsory enlistment; = IMPRESS *sb.*[2], IMPRESSMENT[2]. Now *Hist.*

[**1592** KYD *Sol. & Pers.* I. v. 27 A common presse of base, superfluous Turkes May soone be leuied. (But this may be PRESS *sb.*[1], crowd.)]

1599 MINSHEU *Sp. Dict., Léva*, a presse or taking vp men for the war. **1601** R. JOHNSON *Kingd. & Commw.* (1603) 99 He giueth his captaines commissions to take vp souldiers through the whole Realme, (not by presse, as with us) but by striking vp the drumm. **1615** *Trade's Incr.* in *Harl. Misc.* (Malh.) III. 304 The general press that was made of men from all the coasts to man the ships. **1667** *Lond. Gaz.* No. 154/2 The Press for Seamen is great, and several Captains are imployed to raise men both in Denmark and Lubec. **1676** I. MATHER *K. Philip's War* (1862) 139 At Boston there is a Press in order to sending forth another Army to pursue the enemy. *a* **1715** BURNET *Own Time* (1766) II. 9 It looked liker a press than a levy. **1761–2** HUME *Hist. Eng.* (1806) III. xlix. 779 An English army of twelve thousand foot and two hundred horse was levied by a general press throughout the kingdom. **1771** *Junius Lett.* lix. (1797) II. 196 With regard to the press for seamen..bounties..have a limit. **1793** NELSON in Nicolas *Disp.* (1845) I. 299, I have only got a few men.., and without a press I have no idea our Fleet can be manned. **1803** *Naval Chron.* IX. 328 There was a very hot press last night throughout Plymouth. **1894** C. N. ROBINSON *Brit. Fleet* 413 The 'Press' does..derive its name ..from the 'prest' or 'imprest' money paid to the man on entry as an earnest of his wages on enlisting in the King's service.

†**b.** A warrant or commission giving authority to impress recruits. *Obs.* exc. *Hist.*

1596 SHAKS. *1 Hen. IV*, IV. ii. 13, I haue mis-vs'd the Kings Presse damnably. I haue got, in exchange of a hundred and fiftie Souldiers, three hundred and odde Pounds. **1667** DRYDEN *Wild Gallant* Epil. 22 They shrink like seamen when a press comes out.

†**c.** = PRESS-MONEY. *Obs.*

1626 *Faithful Friends* I. ii, *Marc.* Hold thee, here's gold; furnish thyself with speed:..These shall along with us too. Receive your press. *Calve.* Oh, good captain, I have a wife, indeed, sir. *Marc.* If she be a striker, I will press her too.

2. *transf.* and *fig.* Impressment into service of any kind; a requisition.

1667 *Decay Chr. Piety* viii. ¶44, 233 'Tis this Fear [of singularity] that engages many in it; and though it hath too many voluntiers, yet sure 'tis this press that helps to make up its numbers. **1670** EACHARD *Cont. Clergy* 119 If men of knowledge, prudence, and wealth, have a phansie against a living of twenty or thirty pounds a year, there is no way to get them into such an undertaking, but by sending out a spiritual press. **1855** W. SARGENT *Braddock's Exped.* 166 To be reminded that such things as a Press of private means for the benefit of the State still existed. **1894** *Daily News* 25 July 5/6 The Central Government [of China] has placed an emergency press upon the fleet of the China Merchants Company to be taken when necessary for transport of troops.

3. *attrib.* and *Comb.*, as ***press-boat, -ketch, -smack, -vessel*** (a vessel employed in pressing seamen). See also PRESS-GANG, PRESS-MONEY, etc.

1688 LUTTRELL *Brief Rel.* (1857) I. 457 The next day the presse boats went down the river to presse seamen. **1696** *Lond. Gaz.* No. 3164/1 On Board any of His Majesty's Ships of War, or Hire-Ships, or on any Press-Vessels, or Tenders. **1702** *Flying Post* Apr. 4/7 Some Press-Ketches in that [Dublin] Harbour have pressed 400 Seamen within a few Days, and..a great many are voluntarily come in. **1745** *Proj. Manning Navy* 6 Those who are daily dragg'd into the Press-Smacks.

†**press**, *a.* *Obs.* [ad. L. *press-us*, of style, compressed, concise, also close, exact, accurate, precise; in origin pa. pple. of *premĕre* to press.] Concise, compendious; close, precise, exact, minute: chiefly of language.

c **1611** CHAPMAN *Iliad* XIV. Comm. 199 Homers maner of writing..is so presse, and puts on with so strong a current, that it farre ouer-runnes the most laborious pursuer. **1615** CROOKE *Body of Man* 432 There is a double acception of the word *Caput* among Physitions, one strickt & presse, another large and ample. **1661** RUST *Origen & Opin.* in *Phnix* (1721) I. 33 They observe not those terms and conditions, being drawn away from a press and careful attendance to them. **1675** R. BURTHOGGE *Causa Dei* 329 Of which persuasion [that the World should have End by Fire]..were all the Stoicks; Seneca is press and full, *At illo tempore, solutis Legibus, fine modo fertur* [etc.].

press (prɛs), *v.*[1] Forms: *α.* 4–5 **press-en, -yn,** 4–7 **presse,** 6– **press** (5 **pres**). *Pa. t.* and *pple.* **pressed**; also 4– **prest** (4 **yprast**). *β.* 4–7 **prese,** 4–5 **prece** (4–7 **praise**), 5–6 **preace,** 5–7 *Sc.* **preis, -ss,** 5–7 (*dial.* 8–9) **prease,** 6–7 **preasse,** 9 *dial.* **preese, -ze.** [Two forms: *α.* ME. *press-en*, a. OF. *press-er* (13th c. in Littré) = It. *pressare*:—L. *pressāre*, freq. of *premĕre, press-um* to press. *β.* ME. *prêse(n, prêce(n*, with lengthened vowel: cf. *prês, prees, prese*, parallel form of PRESS *sb.*[1], and see Note below. The *β* form prevails in branch III, where it appears to be the earlier; it is rare in I and II.]

I. Literal and directly connected senses. Primarily *trans.*

1. a. *trans.* To act upon (a body) with a continuous force directed towards or against it (the body by or through which the force is exerted being in contact with that acted upon); to exert a steady force against (something in contact), e.g. by weight (downwards), or by other physical agency or voluntary effort (in any direction); to subject to pressure. ***to press the button***: see BUTTON *sb.* 4 b and cf. PRESS-BUTTON *sb.* and *a.*

[**13..** *E.E. Allit. P.* B. 1249 Prestes & prelates þay presed to deþe.] *c* **1385** CHAUCER *L.G.W.* 1787 (*Lucrece*) And as she wok hire bed she felte presse. *c* **1440** *Promp. Parv.* 412/2 Pressyn, *premo, comprimo, presso.* *c* **1445** LYDG. *Nightingale* 152 Like hem that pressen quayers of entent In the pressour. **1592** SHAKS. *Rom. & Jul.* III. ii. 60 Thou and Romeo presse one heauie beere. **1656** tr. *Hobbes' Elem. Philos.* (1839) 211 Of two moved bodies one presses the other, when with its endeavour it makes either all or part of the other body to go out of its place. **1820** SHELLEY *Sensit. Pl.* II. 21 Her step seemed to pity the grass it prest. **1839** G. BIRD *Nat. Philos.* 89 The layer of fluid would be submitted to unequal pressure, being in B pressed by the long column, and in A pressed only by the shorter column. *Ibid.* 341 The plane glass against which it is pressed. **1893** W. S. GILBERT *Utopia* I, You only need a button press.

b. *to press* (*to death*): to execute the punishment of *peine forte et dure* upon (a person arraigned for felony who stood mute and would not plead): see PEINE. *Obs.* exc. *Hist.*

1554 *Dial. on Laws Eng.* II. xli. 133 He shalbe pressed to death [see PEINE]. **1604** G. DUGDALE *Disc. Pract. Eliz. Caldwell* B iij. According to the Law, he was adiudged to be prest, receiuing his iudgement on the Saturday, to be executed on Munday following. *Ibid.*, [He] was prest. **1675** *3 Inhumane Murthers* 6 The same day he was pressed, being very willing to dye. **1770** *Chron.* in *Ann. Reg.* 129/2 Conoway at first refused to plead, but being taken down and shewn the apparatus for pressing him to death, if he refused, he relented. **1900** *Daily News* 31 Dec. 6 There can be no doubt that it was in 1736 that the barbarous practice of 'pressing to death' was last resorted to.

c. As a sign of affection or courtesy (with a person, the hand, etc. as object). Hence ***to press the flesh***: to greet by physical contact; *spec.* to shake hands (*U.S. slang*).

1700 DRYDEN *Iliad* VI. 173 She..press'd Th' illustrious infant to her fragrant breast. **1780** COWPER *Doves* 26 'Tis then I feel myself a wife, And press thy wedded side. **1810** SCOTT *Lady of L.* II. xxxvii, The Minstrel's hand he kindly pressed. **1832** TENNYSON *Miller's Daughter* 160 She..rose, and..press'd you heart to heart. **1926** MAINES & GRANT *Wise-Crack Dict.* 8/1 *Press the flesh*, shake hands. **1933** A. E. W. MASON *Sapphire* ii. 16 'Press the flesh,' said I, extending my hand. **1975** W. SAFIRE *Before the Fall* VI. v. 436 The Soviet leader [*sc.* Brezhnev] surprised Kissinger..with his American political habit of 'pressing the flesh'—punching an arm, squeezing, backpatting. **1977** *National Observer* (U.S.) 22 Jan. 14/3 After the assassination of John Kennedy, some said no future President would be able to 'press the flesh'. But both Lyndon Johnson and Gerald Ford felt that personal appearances were integral to campaigning. **1977** *Time* 7 Nov. 31/2 Aides had to coax him into playing fewer tennis matches with celebrities..and spending more time pressing the flesh.

d. *intr.* To exert pressure; to bear with weight or force *on, upon, against.* Also in Gymnastics, with various prepositions.

1815 J. SMITH *Panorama Sc. & Art* I. 76 The column sustained by the bottom of such a vessel..is therefore no more than what would press upon the bottom of a vessel Y. *Ibid.* 232 To make the surfaces intended to be in contact, press against each other simultaneously and uniformly in every part. **1837** W. IRVING *Capt. Bonneville* III. 240 The heavy buffalo..are easily overtaken by the Blackfeet; whose fleet steps press lightly on the surface. **1878** HUXLEY *Physiogr.* 88 Since air possesses weight, it necessarily presses upon any object exposed to its influence. **1956** KUNZLE & THOMAS *Freestanding* i. 25 From prone support jump up to a knee and elbow balance... From there learn to press up to handstand and then lower again. *Ibid.* 26 Use the ankles to bounce the body into the air again, pressing through with the toes to get the maximum impulse. *Ibid.* ii. 32 Straighten out with the knees, press off on to one leg and lower the trunk sideways. **1964** G. C. KUNZLE *Parallel Bars* iii. 83 Do not neglect specific strength training, such as..pressing to handstand against the wall bars.

2. a. *trans.* To cause to move in some direction or into some position by pressure; to push, drive, thrust. (With various advbs. and preps.)

c **1410** *Master of Game* (MS. Digby 182) xxiv, If..þe foote and þe knees haue..ypressede þe grasse a doune. *a* **1425** *Cursor M.* 11829 (Trin.) Þe dropesy so to gider him prest. *c* **1440** *Promp. Parv.* 412/1 Precyn in, *ingero.* *Ibid.* 412/2 Presse downe, *deprimo, reprimo.* **1526** TINDALE *Luke* vi. 38 Good measure, pressed doune, shaken to gedder, and runnynge ouer. **1697** DAMPIER *Voy.* I. xviii. 495 The Wind being on our broad side, prest her down very much. **1824** R. STUART *Hist. Steam Engine* 196 The steam presses the pistons or valves forward in that direction. **1832** R. & J. LANDER *Exped. Niger* I. xi. 84 The weight of his.. ornaments almost pressed him to the ground. **1842** TENNYSON *Locksley Hall* 90 Baby fingers, waxen touches, press me from the mother's breast. **1899** *Allbutt's Syst. Med.* VII. 250 The blood pressed up the vena cava can be aspirated into the right heart.

b. *fig.* (usually with *down*).

a **1340** HAMPOLE *Psalter, Cant.* 497 Noght pressid down in þe luf of þis warld. **1382** WYCLIF *Bible* Pref. Ep. i. 61 Pictagorax..more wilnyng other mennus thingis shamfastli to lernen, than his owne vnshamfastli to prece forth [*sua impudenter ingerere*]. **1576** FLEMING *Panopl. Epist.* 82 We felt the burthen of necessitie pressing downe our shoulders. **1668** R. STEELE *Husbandman's Calling* vii. (1672) 188 The husbandman..hath weights to press him down, and therefore hath need of wings to lift him up.

c. *intr.* In Golf and Tennis. (See quots. 1975, 1977.)

1910 *Encycl. Brit.* XII. 223/2 *Press*, to strive to hit harder than you can hit with accuracy. **1922** WODEHOUSE *Clicking of Cuthbert* vi. 132 Keep the head still..don't press. **1975** *Oxf. Compan. Sports & Games* 423/1 To 'press' is to try to hit the ball too hard, usually with a resultant mis-hit. **1977** *Tennis World* Sept. 17/2 'Pressing' is trying too hard: a player is said to be pressing if his shots are over-eager or impatient.

3. *trans.* To extract by pressure; to express; to squeeze (juice, etc.) *out of* or *from* something.

1388 WYCLIF *Gen.* xl. 11 Therfor Y took the grapis, and presside [*c* 1430–40 *MSS. I. & S.* presside hem] out in to the cuppe which Y helde. *c* **1420** *Liber Cocorum* (1862) 49 Sethe hom in water..; þen take hom up; presse a non þe water of hom. **1526** *Pilgr. Perf.* (W. de W. 1531) 246 b, This ..shall presse out teares of our eyes. **1697** DRYDEN *Virg. Georg.* I. 412 To gather Laurel-berries, and the Spoil Of bloody Myrtles, and to press your Oyl. **1744** BERKELEY *Siris* §212 Wine is pressed from the grape. **1830** M. DONOVAN *Dom. Econ.* I. 13 It is very probable, that it was much the same word as is used..in Gen. ix. 21, viz. [yyn] from [ynh] to press out.

4. a. To subject to pressure so as to reduce to a particular shape, consistence, smoothness, thinness, or bulk, or so as to extract juice, etc. from; to compress, squeeze. *spec.* to smooth or flatten (fabric or clothes) with an iron or clothes press. Also with *out*.

c **1430–40** [see prec., quot. 1388]. **1549** *Act 3 & 4 Edw. VI*, c. 2 §8 That no person shall..put to sale here within the Realme..any cloth being pressed to be..worne here within the Realme of England. **1555** Eden *Decades* 3 They neuer eate *Iucca* excepte it be first sliced & pressed. **1562** J. Heywood *Prov. & Epigr.* (1867) 137 He hath turnd his typpet and prest it so close, That for a turnd typpet it hath a fayre glose. **1659** Leak *Waterwks.* 1 The Aire may be prest, but not the Water. **1715** Desaguliers *Fires Impr.* 45 You have always more dense Air in the Room, it being more press'd. **1764** Harmer *Observ.* x. iv. 155 Into these they put the curds, and binding them up close, press them. **1796** Mrs. Glasse *Cookery* xxi. 339 Press them as long as there is any milk in the almonds. **1844** G. Dodd *Textile Manuf.* iii. 106 'Pressing' it [cloth] between hot iron plates and smooth millboard. **1901** A. H. Rice *Mrs. Wiggs of Cabbage Patch* vi. 92 She pressed out Asia's best dress. **1908** M. H. Morgan *How to dress Doll* viii. 67 Sew the tucks firmly, then press them open. *a* **1911** D. G. Phillips *Susan Lenox* (1917) I. iii. 37 I'm going to wear my white dress with embroidery, and it's got to be pressed. **1928** A. Christie *Mystery of Blue Train* xxiv. 195 He found the imperturbable George pressing trousers. **1949** D. Smith *I capture Castle* xiv. 257 Your frock's quite a bit creased, miss... I could press it, if you like. **1957** C. MacInnes *City of Spades* i. ix. 68 At one time I pressed suits by day and worked in the Post Office by night. **1976** C. Dexter *Last seen Wearing* xvi. 123 The little woman at home cooking a meal for you and probably pressing your pants or something.

b. To dry and flatten (leaves, flowers, etc.) in order to preserve them.

1785 T. Martyn tr. *Rousseau's Lett. Elements Bot.* viii. 82 Your pile of plants and papers thus arranged, must be put into the press, without which your plants will not be flat and even; some are for pressing them more, others less. **1840** C. Fox *Jrnl.* 22 Mar. in *Memories Old Friends* (1882) vi. 75 Clara has been collecting flowers, and they have been together pressing many of them. **1930** R. Macaulay *Staying with Relations* ii. 20 'You see, I press... Do you enjoy pressing, Catherine?' 'Flowers, she means,' Benet explained. 'Isie likes to keep her verbs intransitive.' **1974** W. C. Cartner *Fun with Botany* 23 Plant specimens can be pressed and dried for further study... Lay out the fresh specimens between sheets of newspaper, and press the sandwich between two boards.

c. To make (a gramophone record), to record (a song, etc.). *colloq.*

1918 [see matrix 4 c]. **1929** Wilson & Webb *Mod. Gramophones* xi. 253 The stampers which press records have to be kept at a certain temperature in order that the record material will flow properly. **1954** W. W. Johnson *Gramophone Bk.* 55 By 1929 one record manufacturer alone was pressing records at the rate of a million a week. **1968** P. Oliver *Screening Blues* 5 In the ensuing months more stores carried Race records, specially pressed for the Negro market. **1976** *Sunday Times* 21 Mar. 58/3 Island is coy about how many albums it is pressing.

†**5.** To print: = impress *v.*[1] 4. *Obs.* or *arch.*

1579 Fulke *Confut. Sanders* 691 Howe proue you that this picture was pressed when that leafe came to correction? **1637** Laud *Relat. Confer.* Ep. Ded. (1639) A iij b, The Discourse upon this Conference stayed so long, before it could endure to be pressed. **1857** T. H. Warren *By Severn Sea* 32 He who pressed, He who bound.

II. Figurative senses, denoting actions compared to physical pressure. Usually *trans.*

6. a. *trans.* (*fig.* of 1.) Of an enemy, an attacking force, etc.: To bear heavily on, to assail with much force; to reduce to straits; to beset, harass. Now chiefly in ***hard pressed***.

1375 Barbour *Bruce* x. 316 [He] presyt the folk that thar-in ves, Swa that nocht ane the ȝet durst pas. *c* **1400** *Destr. Troy* 8606 Polidamas, the pert, was presset so fast, þat he was wonen in wer, & away led. **1560** Daus tr. *Sleidane's Comm.* 353 The horsemen pressed him before, and the fotemen gaue the onset at his back. **1607** Topsell *Four-f. Beasts* (1658) 101 All of them being pressed with Dogs or other wilde Beasts, will fly unto a man for succour. **1686** tr. *Chardin's Coronat. Solyman* 94 The Generalissimo ceas'd not to press the Armenians. **1693** *Mem. Cnt. Teckely* ii. 153 The Place was pressed with vigour enough till the 11th of September. **1769** Robertson *Chas. V*, iv. Wks. 1813 V. 405 The castle of Milan was pressed more closely than ever. **1893** Forbes-Mitchell *Remin. Gt. Mutiny* 23 Although hard pressed at first, the force eventually gained a..victory.

†**b.** Of a tyrant, adverse circumstances, etc.: To oppress; to crush, reduce to distress or misery; to load or burden with impositions or restrictions; to distress, afflict. *Obs.*

c **1400** *Destr. Troy* 5093 Non proffer, apon payne, to prese hym no more. *c* **1425** Wyntoun *Cron.* i. 1663 (Cotton MS.) Na man sulde swa hardy be Hym to presse, to tak or sla. **1553** T. Wilson *Rhet.* (1580) 202 Chrisogonus here that moste can doe, will presse vs with his power. **1585** T. Washington tr. *Nicholay's Voy.* iii. xiii. 95 Yet are they pressed wyth a more grieuous tribute. **1609** Bible (Douay) *Hist. Table* II. 1079 The children of Israel were pressed with servitude in Ægypt. **1633** P. Fletcher *Purple Isl.* iii. xix, So when a tyrant raves, his subjects pressing, His gaining is their losse. **1720** Ozell *Vertot's Rom. Rep.* II. x. 153 The People, press'd by Hunger, called loudly for Bread. **1793** Smeaton *Edystone L.* §102, I should not be able to..get out when there pressed with danger.

c. To affect with a feeling (physical or mental) of pressure, constraint, or distress; to weigh down, burden, oppress (the feelings, mind, spirits, etc.).

1604 Shaks. *Oth.* iii. iv. 177, I haue this while with leaden thoughts beene prest. **1656** Ridgley *Pract. Physic* 259 When he ascends a steep place, he is pressed with an unusual difficulty of breathing. **1695** Prior *Ode Queen's Death* vi, If prest by Grief our Monarch stoops. **1738** Wesley *Ps.* lxxxviii. i, These horrid Clouds that press my frighted Soul.

†**d.** Of a difficulty or the like: = beset *v.* 3 b.

1654 Jer. Taylor *Real Pres.* 35 On the other side no inconvenience can presse our interpretation of 'spiritual eating Christ by faith'. **1662** Stillingfl. *Orig. Sacr.* iii. i. §8 The Atheist in denying a Deity, must assert something else instead of it, which is pressed with the same, if not greater difficulties, and proved by far less reason.

e. To put to straits, as by want of time, space, means, etc.: in passive, usually with *for*. (Cf. 8 b.)

1678 Hickes in Ellis *Orig. Lett.* Ser. ii. IV. 47, I..am very sensible how much you press yourself to keep correspondence with me. **1813** Macaulay in *Life & Lett.* (1880) I. 42 Being pressed for room, I will conclude. **1817** Cobbett *Wks.* XXXII. 354 In writing the last Number I was pressed for time. **1845** Disraeli *Sybil* iii. iii, I am pressed for business, but I will wait and watch over him till the crisis is passed. **1861** Craik *Hist. Eng. Lit.* I. 89 He had felt continually pressed by the necessity of economising his paper or parchment. **1866** G. A. Lawrence *Sans Merci* xiv, You can have money sooner, if you are much pressed for it.

7. *intr.* To produce a strong mental or moral impression *upon*; in mod. use usually (*fig.* from 1 d), to bear heavily, weigh *upon* (the mind, etc.).

1561 T. Norton tr. *Calvin's Inst.* i. 5 Least they shoulde in al thinges seme to despise him, whoes maiestie still presseth vpon them. **1802** Mar. Edgeworth *Moral T.* (1816) I. xvii. 144 The reflection that he had wasted his time ..pressed upon his mind. **1838–9** Fr. A. Kemble *Resid. in Georgia* (1863) 131 People in the South, pressed upon by northern opinion.

8. a. *trans.* To urge on, impel or try to impel to action; to constrain, compel, force.

[The frequency of *prese* forms in 8, 9, 9 b, perh. indicates some association with the intr. senses in III.]

α. **1390** Gower *Conf.* I. 217 Sodeinly the jugge he nom.. and hath him pressed, That he the sothe him hath confessed. **1590** Shaks. *Mids. N.* iii. ii. 184 Why should hee stay whom Loue doth presse to go? What loue could presse Lysander from my side? **1611** Bible *Acts* xviii. 5 Paul was pressed in spirit, and testified to the Iewes, that Iesus was Christ. **1758** J. S. *Le Dran's Observ. Surg.* (1771) 164 The Patient being pressed to go backwards, went behind the Tent. **1861** May *Const. Hist.* (1863) I. i. 62 They [the Commons] could withhold the supplies, and press the king with representations against his ministers.

β. **1565** *Reg. Privy Council Scot.* I. 372 Thair Majesteis heirtofoir hes na wayis preissit ony personis in the fre use of thair conscience. **1580** *Ibid.* III. 281 They have nevir persuadit nor preissit his Majestie to this hour. **1586** J. Carmichael *Let.* in *Wodrow Soc. Misc.* (1844) 444 Turncotes..if they were preasit, they wald be readie to cap, and cope, and surpleis. **1623** Pr. Charles *Let.* (in *Athenæum* 24 Feb. (1872) 241/2) Ye euer promised that the King [my] father should be no farder preaced in matters of religion. *a* **1627** Middleton *Mayor of Quinborough* i. (1661) 8 Great Constantine our Noble Father,..therefore prais'd me into this profession.

b. Said of danger, business, etc., or of time. Now only *absol.* or *intr.* To compel haste or dispatch; to be urgent; to be pressing; to demand immediate action. (Cf. 6 e.) So mod.F. *le temps presse*; *le péril presse.*

c **1440** *York Myst.* xl. 192 Here may we notte melle of more at þis tyde, For prossesse of plaies þat precis in plight. **1683** Temple *Mem.* Wks. 1731 I. 396 The Prince wou'd have had me stay, but..I pretended some Letters press'd me, and so went away. **1746** *Col. Rec. Pennsylv.* V. 44 Let it be done with Dispatch, for the time presses. **1823** Scott *Peveril* xxviii, Do you think I will read all these?.. I mean, is there any thing which presses? *Mod.* Time presses: I must go.

c. To impel to rapid movement; to urge on, hasten, drive quickly. *rare.*

1611 Bible *Esther* viii. 14 So the posts..went out, being hastened, and pressed on by the kings commandement. **1856** Kane *Arct. Expl.* II. xx. 198, I..pressed my dogs for the hut.

d. With the movement as obj.: To urge, hasten, execute quickly.

1742 Collins *Oriental Ecl.* iv. 9 Fast as they prest their flight. **1821** Scott *Kenilw.* xiii, Tressilian and his attendants pressed their route with all dispatch. **1968** *Globe & Mail* (Toronto) 3 Feb. 10/1 About 2,000 enemy troops had pressed an attack there since Tuesday against a U.S.-advised Vietnamese garrison of about the same size.

9. a. To urge by words or arguments; to try hard to persuade; to importune, beg, beseech, entreat (a person *to do* something or *for* something).

α. **1593** Bilson *Govt. Christ's Ch.* 273 They be Ieromes owne words that I presse you with. **1596** Shaks. *Merch. V.* iv. i. 425 You press mee farre, and therefore I will yeeld. **1617** Moryson *Itin.* i. 23 Neither they nor any other would take the least reward of mee, though I pressed them to receiue it. **1698** Fryer *Acc. E. India & P.* Pref., More than Four hundred Queries..to which I was pressed for Answers. **1748** *Anson's Voy.* iii. x. 409 He was much pressed to go into a neighbouring apartment. **1800** De Quincey in 'H. A. Page' *Life* (1877) I. iii. 53 To avoid being pressed.. to stay another day. **1875** Jowett *Plato* (ed. 2) I. 15, I will share the enquiry with you, but I will not press you if you would rather not.

β. **1623** Pr. Charles *Let.* (in *Athenæum* 24 Feb. (1872) 241/2) Which the Pope so earnestlie preases to be added.

b. *intr.* or *absol.* To use urgent entreaty; to ask or seek importunately. Const. *for* or *inf.*; formerly also *on, upon* (a person).

β. **1401** *Pol. Poems* (Rolls) II. 33 Freer, what charity is this, to prease upon a rich man, and to intice him to be buried among you from his parish church? **1529** More *Dyaloge* iii. Wks. 214/1 He was in his examinacion sore preaced vpon to tell for what intent he made such a sermon ready. *a* **1699** Lady A. Halkett *Autobiog.* (1875) 43 As much as was fitt to prese for the reason.

α. *a* **1533** Ld. Berners *Huon* clvi. 599 Kynge Arthur hath sore pressed on me to haue my dignyte & realme. **1648** in *Hamilton Papers* (Camden) 220 My Lord Newcastle hes prest mouch for his dispach, and a comision for the North. **1709–10** Addison *Tatler* No. 121 ¶1 There was a Gentlewoman below who..pressed very much to see me. **1766** Goldsm. *Vic. W.* viii, And spread his vegetable store And gaily pressed, and smiled. **1833** Ht. Martineau *Manch. Strike* ix, Don't press for an answer yet. **1895** Lake in *Law Times* XCIX. 468/1, I applied for this on the 9th May, and pressed for it day by day.

10. *trans.* To urge, insist on the doing of (something); to solicit, request (a thing) earnestly. Const. *on, upon* (a person).

1625 Burges *Pers. Tithes* 16 The Apostles peremptory commaund more then once pressed in the Gospel. **1673** *Essex Papers* (Camden) I. 93 The discontented part of ye Citty press, that ye Election last mentiond may be confirm'd. **1710** Prideaux *Orig. Tithes* iii. 143 *note*, St. Ambrose very earnestly presseth the payment of Tithes. *a* **1716** Blackall *Wks.* (1723) I. 294, I suppose, it was not press'd upon such, by the Apostles, as a Duty. *a* **1770** Jortin *Serm.* (1771) I. iv. 65 Such a person might earnestly press the observance of a duty which himself had so well fulfilled. **1834** *Tracts for Times* No. 40. 2 This material part of piety..had not been sufficiently pressed on my people. **1899** *Allbutt's Syst. Med.* VII. 591 Nothing now remained but to press the use of anti-pneumococcic serum.

11. To urge, insist on the belief, admission, or mental acceptance of (something); to impress (a thing) upon the mind, emphasize, inculcate earnestly; to present earnestly, plead with insistence (a claim, etc.). Const. *on, upon* (a person, his attention, etc.).

1625 Burges *Pers. Tithes* 35 It must be pressed..vpon the Magistrate, that he is bound in Conscience to pull down all Churches, once superstitiously prostituted to Popish Idolatry. **1692** Bentley *Boyle Lect.* ix. 303 The Apostle presseth this advice in the text. **1781** Cowper *Conversation* 104 Remember, if you mean to please, To press your point with modesty and ease. **1836** J. Gilbert *Chr. Atonem.* vi. (1852) 174 Thus are we brought again to the conclusion already pressed upon attention. **1875** Jowett *Plato* (ed. 2) I. 379 Crito is but pressing upon him the opinions of the many. **1878** Stubbs *Const. Hist.* III. xviii. §664. 129 Letters..in which he..presses on the potentates of east and west the great opportunity for ecclesiastical union.

12. To urge, thrust (something to be taken or accepted) *upon* a person.

1797 Mrs. Radcliffe *Italian* i, He pressed the offer so repeatedly and respectfully that at length she accepted it. **1815** W. H. Ireland *Scribbleomania* 285 *note*, He..refused the first ecclesiastic dignities, which were unsolicitedly pressed upon him. **1879** M. Pattison *Milton* v. 63 The garden-house in Aldersgate-street had before been found too small for the pupils who were being now pressed upon Milton.

13. To push forward (arguments, views, considerations, positions, etc.).

1665 Sir T. Herbert *Trav.* (1677) 355 Nor am I willing to press these conjectures any further. **1766** Fordyce *Serm. Yng. Wom.* (1767) I. i. 17, I press not any farther an argument so exceedingly plain. **1856** Froude *Hist. Eng.* I. ii. 130 Charles had no desire to press matters to extremities. **1874** Stubbs *Const. Hist.* I. x. 320 Stephen pressed his advantage.

III. Senses connected with the notion of a crowd or throng, or of pushing one's way as in a throng: cf. press *sb.*[1] 1. Primarily *intr.* Here the β forms are usually the earlier, and predominate till *c* 1600.

As L. *premĕre* and *pressāre* and OF. *presser* were only transitive, the intransitive use appears to have been developed in Eng., and perh. in connexion with the notion of pressing or crowding upon each other.

14. a. *intr.* To come closely to or about a person or place; esp. of a number of persons: to come up or gather in a crowd; to crowd, throng. Also *fig.*

β. **13..** *Gaw. & Gr. Knt.* 830 Mony proud mon þer presed, þat prynce to honour. **13..** *Cursor M.* 2796 (Gött.) þe mare þat loth [= Lot] þaim [þus] bisoght, þe mare þai presid [*Trin.* pressed] and sesid noght. *c* **1440** *Bone Flor.* 1082 They presyd abowte syr Sampson all. **1526** Tindale *Luke* vi. 19 All the people preased to touche hym. **1559** *Mirr. Mag., Worcester* xvii, I could not passe, so sore they on me preast. **1569** Stocker tr. *Diod. Sic.* i. xxxii. 38 Commanding them to prease and talke with the Captaynes. **1593** Shaks. *3 Hen. VI*, iii. i. 19 No humble suters prease to speake for right. **1610** Holland *Camden's Brit.* (1637) 175 By reason of the multitude preasing up to him.

α. *c* **1400** *Song Roland* 635 Ingler, and arnold, of the peres, I say, Pressen to the prince in þer palle wedis. *c* **1400** *Destr. Troy* 8227 Then the grekes.. Oppressit hom with pyne, pressit full hard. **1642** H. More *Song Soul* ii. i. ii. lvii, The crosse lines of a Rhomboides That from their meeting to all angles presse. **1648** in *Hamilton Papers* (Camden) 210 The enemy presseth harde upon us. **1776** Gibbon *Decl. & F.* xii. (1869) I. 341 The nations of Germany, who perpetually pressed on the frontiers of the empire. **1833** Ht. Martineau *Manch. Strike* ix, The most thinking men in the crowd pressed towards the waggon. **1876** C. M. Davies *Unorth. Lond.* 106 Consisting..of 'thoughts that had been pressing in upon his own soul'. **1881** Henty *Cornet of Horse* xxvi, All the sailors pressed up, eager to know how the pursuit had been shaken off.

b. *trans.* To crowd upon, throng. *Obs.* or *arch.*

1549–62 Sternhold & H. *Ps.* cxlii. 7 When thou art good to me, the just shall prease me round about. **1582** N. T. (Rhem.) *Luke* viii. 45 Maister, the multitudes throng and presse thee [*Vulg.* te comprimunt et affligunt; Wyclif 1382 thringen and turmentyn thee, 1388 thristen and disesen thee; Tindale, etc. thruste the and vexe the; *Geneva*, thrust thee and treade on thee; 1611 throng thee and preasse thee;

Revised, press thee and crush thee]. *c* **1586** C'TESS PEMBROKE *Ps.* LVI. iv, They presse me neere, my soule in snare to take.

c. *Naut.* ***to press sail*** = to crowd sail: see CROWD *v.*[1] 9, and cf. *press of sail*, PRESS *sb.*[1] 10.

1860 *Merc. Marine Mag.* VII. 98 Press on sail, to see if you can come in.

15. a. *intr.* To push or strain forward, as through a crowd or against obstacles or hindrances; to push one's way, advance with force or eagerness; to hasten onward, urge one's way. Also with *on* (and as *adj. phr.*). Freq. *fig.* and in colloq. phr. ***to press on regardless***, to persevere despite the dangers or difficulties (see REGARDLESS *a.* 1 c).

β. *c* **1330** R. BRUNNE *Chron.* (1810) 112 After þis fest praised Steuen with alle his here, þe castellis he seised, þat he hat neuer ere. *c* **1330** —— *Chron. Wace* (Rolls) 13811 Among þe moste euere he presed, His harde strokes nought ne sesed. *c* **1385** CHAUCER *L.G.W.* 642 (*Cleopatra*) In with the polax presith he & sche. *c* **1400** *Destr. Troy* 5138 So þai past fro þat pales, preset vnto horse. **1526** TINDALE *Phil.* iii. 14, I forget that which is behynde me..and preace vnto the marke apoynted. *a* **1599** SPENSER *F.Q.* VII. vi. 13 The Giantesse.., boldly preacing-on raught forth her hand. **1603** FLORIO *Montaigne* II. x. (1632) 226 Sometimes they prease out thicke and threefold. **1621** BRATHWAIT *Nat. Embassie*, etc. (1877) 257 Two iollie shepheards, that do hither prese.

a. *c* **1400** *Destr. Troy* 2156 And þus pertid þe persons & presset to þere ynnes. *c* **1407** LYDG. *Reson & Sens.* 5129 Ay the more I gan to presse The more my Ioy[e] gan tencresse. **14..** in *Tundale's Vis.* (1843) 158 Efthyr them full fast I prest. **1500–20** DUNBAR *Poems* xxxiii. 49 Vnto no mess pressit this prelat, For sound of sacring bell nor skellat. **1560** DAUS tr. *Sleidane's Comm.* 136 So made way for their fellowes without, which immediately pressed in with a strong power. **1660** BOYLE *New Exp. Phys. Mech.* xvii. 110 Air would..press in at some little Avenue or other. **1738** WESLEY *Ps.* LXXXIX. iv, With Reverence and religious Dread His Servants to his House should press. **1810** SCOTT *Lady of L.* III. xiv, Pressing forward like the wind. **1870** BRYANT *Iliad* I. v. 138 Trojans, great in mastery of steeds, Press on! **1916** JOYCE *Portrait of Artist* (1969) v. 243 And why were you shocked, Cranley pressed on in the same tone, if you feel sure that our religion is false and that Jesus was not the son of God? **1921** G. B. SHAW *Back to Methuselah* v. 266. After passing a million goals they press on to the goal of redemption from the flesh. **1930** *Flight* 23 Oct. 1177/2 Lord Thomson and his gallant crew would still have said press on, instead of crying halt, in airship development. **1948** PARTRIDGE *Dict. Forces' Slang* 147 *Press on, regardless*—or merely *press on*, to act keenly, to be efficiently busy. Hence, *press-on type*, an almost too keen person—applied mostly to 'operational types'. They press on, regardless of fog, flak, fighter opposition. **1950** G. HACKFORTH-JONES *Worst Enemy* iii. 212 Action was needed to stem this tide of defeatism. Head down was the way to progress through the blizzard. 'When in doubt, press on.' A good motto that. **1952** M. TRIPP *Faith is Windsock* xiv. 209 The Vicar was laudatory: 'A magnificent press-on effort, old chap.' **1958** *Times* 18 Dec. 11/4 A few colourful wartime metaphors survive... A third and uncouth example, to press on regardless, stands for a dashing and stoical, if disillusioned, perseverance which continues to find a place in life today just as it did in the early days of the war. **1959** *Listener* 5 Mar. 428/2 While the scientists press on regardless, the humanists go on worrying. **1960** *Times Lit. Suppl.* 18 Mar. 182/1 What vitality the man must have had! And it is this vitality which Mr. Coulter's press-on-regardless manner succeeds very well in conveying. **1961** J. DAWSON *Ha-Ha* i. 7 The other students..used to wave as they passed and cry: 'How goes it?' or 'Press on regardless.' **1968** *Listener* 15 Aug. 203/2 That kind of Irishman—admirable rather than safe: the kind I'd heard junior RAF men in the war refer to as 'a press-on type'. **1977** *Drive* May–June 54/2 Covering 40 miles for every gallon of 4-star fuel (even press-on drivers could manage at least 35 mpg).

†**b.** *refl.* in same sense. *Sc. Obs. rare.*

c **1425** WYNTOUN *Cron.* II. 1310 Qwha wiþe in walde presse hym out, þan hym behuffit to mak entre. *Ibid.* VII. 2570 (Cotton MS.) Wiþe al þe kynge of Inglandis mycht He pressit hym [*Wemyss MS.* He schupe him] to þe cite richt.

16. a. *intr.* To push one's way, thrust oneself, advance into a person's presence, or into a place, boldly, presumptuously, or insistently; to approach venturously, to venture; to push oneself forward, obtrude oneself, intrude. *arch.*

β. **1377** LANGL. *P. Pl.* B. XIV. 212 þere þe pore preseth bifor þe riche with a pakke at his rugge. *c* **1394** *P. Pl. Crede* 749 So of þat beggers brol a bychop schal worþen, Among þe peres of þe lond prese to sitten. *c* **1460** *Urbanitatis* 25 in *Babees Bk.* 13 Amonge þe genteles gode & hende, Prece þou not vp to hyȝ for no þyng. **1535** COVERDALE *Prov.* xxv. 6 Prease not in to yᵉ place of greate men. —— *Ecclus.* xiii. 10 Preasse not thou vnto him, that thou be not shott out. **1587** TURBERV. *Trag. T.* (1837) 14 The peevishe puttocke may not preace in place where Eagles are. **1606** J. CARPENTER *Solomon's Solace* viii. 32 Forbidden to prease forth to do the priests office. **1615** CHAPMAN *Odyss.* IV. 663 Men's knowledges have proper limits set, And should not prease into the mind of God.

a. **1393** LANGL. *P. Pl.* C. XVII. 55 There þe poure presseþ by-fore with a pak at hus rygge. **1599** SANDYS *Europæ Spec.* (1632) 76, I will not here presume to presse in with my determination upon this great difference and question. **1607** DEKKER & WEBSTER *Hist. Sir T. Wyatt* D.'s Wks. 1873 III. 88 Pardon me Madam, that so boldly I presse into your Chamber. **1714** SWIFT *Imit. Horace* II. vi. 89 You ne'er consider whom you shove, But rudely press before a duke. **1885** G. MACDONALD *Diary Old Soul* 16 May, I would go near thee—but I cannot press Into thy presence—it helps not to presume.

†**b.** *refl.* To presume, take upon oneself. *rare.*

1500–20 DUNBAR *Poems* xxxv. 14 Me thocht Deme Fortoun..said on this maneir..preiss the nocht to stryfe aganis my quheill. **1535** STEWART *Cron. Scot.* (Rolls) I. 4 And preis the nocht my purpois till impung.

†**17.** *intr.* To strive, try hard, endeavour, attempt *to do* something (usually with eagerness or haste); to aim at, strive or endeavour after something. Also in weaker sense: To essay, undertake, take in hand. *Obs.* (So F. *presser* in Froissart (Godef.).)

β. *c* **1374** CHAUCER *Troylus* I. 446 To seen here goodly look be gan to prese [*rimes* encrese, cece]. *c* **1380** WYCLIF *Wks.* (1880) 166 Ȝonge childre presen faste to be prestis. *c* **1475** *Rauf Coilȝear* 615 To cum to this Palice he preissis to preif. **1513** DOUGLAS *Æneis* X. xi. 193 Athir way till assay thrys preisyt hes he. **1578** T. PROCTOR *Gorg. Gallery, Lament. Gentilw.*, With Poets pen, I doo not preace to write. **1586** J. CARMICHAEL *Let.* in *Wodrow Soc. Misc.* (1844) 442 To.. prease..to wesh ane Indiane or black-more, whom al the watir in the sea can never mak quhite. *a* **1598** PEELE *David & Bethsabe* Prol., Of this sweet poet, Jove's musician..I prease to sing. **1637–50** ROW *Hist. Kirk* (Wodrow Soc.) 24 The Kirk in this mean tyme preassing to keep their Assemblies, but got little good done. **1642** ROGERS *Naaman* Ep. Ded. 2 We had now need to prease upon more familiar acquaintance with God.

a. **1375** (MS. 1487) BARBOUR *Bruce* XVIII. 105 And thai that pressit mast to stand War slane doune. **1456** SIR G. HAYE *Law Arms* (S.T.S.) 79 Thai movit bataill and weris, pressand quha mycht be lord. *a* **1500** *Ratis Raving* I. 337 Bot that þow pres to do, my sone, Rycht as þow wald to the war done. **1500–20** DUNBAR *Poems* xi. 4 Lang heir to dwell na thing thow press. **1632** LITHGOW *Trav.* III. 100 They had.. sworne, if I pressed to escape, before the rest.., they would throw me..into the sea. **1811** J. LOVE *Let.* 29 Oct. (1840) 349 To press after attaining and communicating to others more of the beginnings and pledges of that glorious life which now we view at a distance.

18. *intr.* To strive, contend, make resistance. *rare.* (Now only as *fig.* from 1 d.)

c **1375** *Sc. Leg. Saints* ii. (*Paulus*) 543 Saule, saule,..is it nocht hard to þe agane þe brod þu for to prese? **1590** SPENSER *F.Q.* I. xii. 19 Ne I against the same can iustly preace [*rimes* peace, release]. **1872** MORLEY *Voltaire* i. (1886) 3 Human nature, happily for us, presses ever against this system or that.

For the verb-stem in Comb., see PRESS *sb.*[1] 16 b.

[*Note.* The *β* forms *prês-en, prêse, prease, preace*, agree in their lengthened vowel with *cease, lease, decease*, compared with F. *cesser, lesser*, and ME. *decesse*; but while in the latter the long-vowel form alone survives (in the simple word), here *press* is the surviving form, *prease, preace*, scarcely appearing in literary Eng. after 1650, though still used in north. Eng. dialects from the Scottish border to Lancashire and Yorkshire, written *preese, prease, preeze, preaze* (priːz). This English lengthening of French short *e* before *ss* and *st* (cf. *beast, feast*) has not been satisfactorily explained; it is discussed (with other lengthenings) by Morsbach in *Festschrift für Wendelin Foerster* (1902) 327. The fact that OF. *presse, cesse, beste, feste*, were in Picard *priesse, ciesse, bieste, fieste*, has suggested that double ME. forms such as *presse, prêse*, might come from two French dialects, *priesse, ciesse*, giving *prêse, cêse*, as *piece* gave ME. *pêce*; but the *e* of *prese, prease*, seems to be the open *ê*, not the close *ē* as in *pêce*.]

press (prɛs), *v.*[2] *Pa. t.* and *pple.* pressed; also 6–8 prest. [Altered from or substituted for PREST *v.*[2], by association with PRESS *v.*[1]: see PRESS-MONEY.

This result may have been facilitated by the fact that the pa. t. and pa. pple *prest* could be the pa. t. and pple. either of *prest* vb. (cf. *cast, cost, thrust*), or of *press* vb. (cf. *drest, past, tost*), so that 'he was prest' could be understood either as 'he was prested' or 'he was pressed'.]

†**1.** *trans.* To engage (men) with earnest-money for service; to enlist by part-payment or 'bounty' in advance; = PREST *v.*[2] 1. *Obs.*

1600 HOLLAND *Livy* XXVI. xxxv. 610 When the Consuls could neither raise men enow, nor yet find monie..for to presse and hire them, and pay their wages withall.

2. a. To force (a man) to serve in the army or navy; = IMPRESS *v.*[2], PREST *v.*[2] 2, with further development of the sense of compulsion.

(Quots. 1543 and 1568, from their early date, may belong to PREST *v.*[2], *prest* being a shortened form of *prested*, as in *cast, thrust*, etc.)

[**1543** BECON *Policy of War* Pref., Wks. 1564 I. 125 b, The men, which wer prest to go vnto the warres, it is almost incredible..what alacryte & quickenes of spirite was in them. **1568** GRAFTON *Chron.* II. 25 Euery Souldiour there prest should pay ten shillynges, and thereupon to be discharged from that voyage.] **1578** *Court Min. Grocers' Comp.* 11 Aug., 15 men which were pressed by this Company to serue in the Quenes Maᵗⁱᵉˢ shipps. **1595** *Locrine* II. ii. D ij, O wife..if I had bene quiet, I had not bene prest. .. But come,..shut vp, for we must to the warres. **1600** FAIRFAX *Tasso* XX. xvi, Men halfe naked, without strength or skill.., Late pressed foorth to warre, against their will. **1627–77** FELTHAM *Resolves* I. xlvii. 74 Like Sons prest from an indulgent Father, they would come for a sad *Vale*. **1697** DRYDEN *Virg. Georg.* I. 681 The peaceful Peasant to the Wars is prest; The Fields lye fallow in inglorious Rest. **1708** MRS. CENTLIVRE *Busie Body* II. ii, Let me catch you no more Puppy-hunting about my doors, lest I have you prest into the Service, Sirrah. **1745** WESLEY *Wks.* (1872) I. 512 The Constables and Churchwardens came to press you for a soldier. **1749** FIELDING *Tom Jones* XVI. viii, To contrive some method of having him [Jones] pressed and sent on board a ship. **1833** MARRYAT *P. Simple* xvi, He replied that he had been pressed out of an American ship, that he was an American born, and that he had never taken the bounty. **1874** GREEN *Short Hist.* viii. §3. 485 Poor men who refused to lend were pressed into the army.

b. *intr.* or *absol.*

a **1625** FLETCHER *Hum. Lieut.* II. iv, Come get your men together..And presse where please you as you march. **1678** MARVELL *Growth Popery* 43 The King is fain to press now. **1819** CRABBE *T. of Hall* v. 174 Gangs came pressing till they swept the shore. **1901** LD. RAGLAN in *Westm. Gaz.* 22 May 2/3 We pressed for the Navy until a time remembered by many present; we pressed for the Army until a much more recent period.

c. *trans.* To take authoritatively for royal or public use; = IMPRESS *v.*[2] b.

1633 T. STAFFORD *Pac. Hib.* II. xxiv. (1821) 450 To presse and take up any the Boats, or Vessels that are or shall bee within the compasse of your command. **1687** A. LOVELL tr. *Thevenot's Trav.* I. 178 Saturday after noon the Cachef of Catie pressed our Camels to fetch wood from the Sea-side. **1698** CROWNE *Caligula* I. Wks. 1874 IV. 369 And all the horses, in, or near the town, You press'd, to bring th' imperial treasure home. **1813** WELLINGTON in Gurw. *Desp.* (1839) X. 393 He was not authorised to press boats, yet he pressed at the British landing place boats which had been in our service two years. **1907** C. B. WINCHESTER in *Let. to Editor*, In British India to this day every executive officer when he moves camp 'presses carts' to obtain means for transporting his tents.

d. *transf.* and *fig.* To seize and force into some service; = IMPRESS *v.*[2] c. Also in phr. ***to press into service***.

1598 B. JONSON *Ev. Man in Hum.* III. ii, Would we were eene prest, to make porters of; and serue out the remnant of our daies, in Thames-street. **1621** BURTON *Anat. Mel.* III. ii. II. i. (1651) 450 They press and muster up wenches as we do soldiers. **1733** POPE *Ess. Man* III. 86 Reason..but serves when prest,..But honest Instinct comes a volunteer. **1824** LAMB *Elia* Ser. II. *Capt. Jackson*, The anecdote was pressed into the account of the family importance. **1871** FREEMAN *Hist. Ess.* Ser. I. iv. 85 In Thierry's well-known History..he is pressed into the service of that writer's peculiar theories. **1883** GILMOUR *Mongols* xxvii. 322 The 'shirt' aforementioned..is pressed to do duty as a towel. **1926** *Discovery* June 191/2 Bait, such as a meal-worm, may be pressed into service [by the bird-photographer] to entice a bird on to some particular twig. **1935** *Yachting* Dec. 82/3 *Press into service*, a reminiscence of the press-gangs which caused the War of 1812 by stopping American merchantmen on the high seas and 'pressing' members of their crews into service in the British navy. **1961** NEW ENG. BIBLE *Mark* xv. 21 Simon, from Cyrene,..was passing by.. and they pressed him into service to carry his cross. **1978** K. J. DOVER *Greek Homosexuality* ii. 97 They masturbate constantly..if no living being with a suitable orifice is available, but prefer horses, mules, or deer..; even the neck of a jar may be pressed into service.

Hence **ˈpressing** *vbl. sb.*, impressment; also *attrib.*

1591 PERCIVALL *Sp. Dict.*, *Maherimiento*, pressing of soldiers, *delectus*. **1640** PYM in Rushw. *Hist. Coll.* III. (1692) I. 23 But now there follows Pressing of men against their Wills, or to find others. **1748** SMOLLETT *Rod. Rand.* xxiv, I was disarmed, taken prisoner, and carried on board a pressing-tender. **1761** HUME *Hist. Eng.* II. App. iii. 510 The power of pressing both for sea and land service..was another prerogative. **1809** J. ADAMS *Wks.* (1854) IX. 327 A few words more on the subject of pressing.

press (of parchment): see PREST *sb.*[2]

press-. The stem of PRESS *v.*[1], used in combination with advbs. to form adjs. designating things that can be pressed *down, in, on*, etc. (See also PRESS *sb.*[1] 16 b (*b*), 17 d.)

1903 *Work* XXV. 218/2 A treacle tin, washed out and dried, with a burner soldered in the press-in lid, will serve quite well if the experiments are conducted outside the house. **1936** A. RANSOME *Pigeon Post* xviii. 189 It was an ordinary tin of paint with a wire handle..and a press-in lid. **1962** L. S. SASIENI *Princ. & Pract. Optical Dispensing* viii. 203 The third type [*sc.* of bridge lining] (press-on or snap-on) is shaped roughly in the form of a half tube which presses on to, and snaps over, the metal bridge. **1963** *Rep. Comm. Inquiry Decimal Currency* viii. 68 in *Parl. Papers 1962–3* (Cmnd. 2145) XI. 195 The two main groups of cash registers are the 'press-in' key type and the 'press-down' key type. **1975** B. WOOD *Killing Gift* (1976) II. i. 48 A vacuum jar with a press-on lid.

pressable (ˈprɛsəb(ə)l), *a.*[1] *rare.* [f. PRESS *v.*[1] + -ABLE. Also in form PRESSIBLE.] That may be pressed: in various senses of the verb.

a **1652** BROME *Eng. Moor* III. iii, Of all ages that are pressable, From sixteen unto sixty. **1667** WATERHOUSE *Fire Lond.* 156 Which,..I think..is pressable upon rich exempted persons now.

ˈpressable, *a.*[2] *rare.* [f. PRESS *v.*[2] + -ABLE.] Liable to be pressed or taken by a press-gang.

1833 M. SCOTT *Tom Cringle* ii. (1859) 37 Pick up all the information you can regarding the haunts of the pressable men at Cove.

press agency. [f. PRESS *sb.*[1] + AGENCY.] = *news agency* (*b*) s.v. NEWS *sb.* (*pl.*) 6 c.

1897 H. MAXWELL *Sixty Years a Queen* VIII. 190 The British Government has no official or semi-official organ in the press. Official pronouncements are communicated..to press agencies, and through them find their way into journals of all shades of politics. **1973** D. MAY *Laughter in Djakarta* ii. 35 He ought to make a further check on the news by going to the Indonesian press agency.

press agent. A man employed in connexion with a theatre or the like to attend to the advertising, and the reporting of the performances. Also, more widely, one employed by any person or organization to handle publicity.

1883 *Railway Age* 25 Jan. 46/3 On general principles..we desire to observe that the associate press agent, or some one who make Wichita conspicuous in the dispatches is an ass. **1902** W. H. CHANTREY *Theatre Accounts* ii. 28 Salaries... Press Agent and Bill Inspector 5-10-0. **1917** WODEHOUSE *Uneasy Money* x. 114 Roscoe Sherriff, her press agent. **1949** *Chicago Tribune* 9 Dec. 18/3 This was the first time that a press agent had hit on a truthful first page story in a month of Sundays. **1964** M. McLuhan *Understanding Media* xxi. 213 Today's press agent regards the newspaper as a ventriloquist does his dummy. **1977** *Time* 10 Oct. 61/1 A former pressagent, Condon, 62, boasts average book sales of 1.3 million.

Hence **ˈpress-agent** *v. trans.*, to advertise in the manner of or by means of press agents; **ˈpress-agented** *ppl. a.*; **press-agenting** *vbl. sb.*; **ˈpress-agentry**, the employment or activities of press agents.

1909 Wodehouse *Swoop* II. ii. 68 Come now, your Grand Grace, is it a deal? Four hundred and fifty chinking o'Goblins a week for one hall a night, and press-agented at eight hundred and seventy-five. **1913** *Writer's Mag.* Nov. 172/1 There is no 'side line' open to the young writer better than press agentry. **1920** W. T. Tilden *Art of Lawn Tennis* 3, I shall be accused of 'press-agenting' my own book by this statement. **1926** *Daily Express* 6 Aug. 3/5 Even the Hohenzollerns know something about Press agentry. **1930** P. W. Slosson *Great Crusade & After* x. 271 The same press-agenting which helped make the reputation of a grand-opera star . . was also at the service of a pugilist. **1933** *Nation* (N.Y.) 11 Jan. 43 He press-agented most of the striking new theories, from those of the Lombrosian criminology . . on down to the neo-Nietzchean doctrines of Elie Faure. **1939** *Sun* (Baltimore) 22 Nov. 13/1 Mr. Frank Murphy, the present highly press-agented Attorney General. **1947** M. Berger in R. de Toledano *Frontiers of Jazz* 100 Bunk indulged in some personal press-agenting. **1948** *Archit. Rev.* CIV. 89 The same press-agentry that ballooned the popularity of other stars in the field of jazz. **1959** *Time* (Atlantic ed.) 24 Aug. 45 A longstanding and well pressagented public 'feud'. **1973** E. Bullins *Theme is Blackness* 9 Whether they will regard Black dramatic criticism seriously and not degenerate into professional press agentry. **1977** *Irish Press* 29 Sept. 10/2 Meanwhile back in Ireland we are faced with the usual problem of press agentry.

press-bed. *Obs.* exc. *dial.* A bed constructed to fold up, when not in use, into a press (press *sb.*[1] 15) closed by a door or doors; sometimes less correctly applied to a box-bed (which does not fold up) shut in by folding doors. Also *attrib.*

1660 Pepys *Diary* 14 May, The Judge and I . . lay in one press bed, there being two more in the same room. **1670** Redway in Bedloe *Popish Plot* (1679) 20 An inclosed Bed (commonly called a Press-Bed). **1708** *Phil. Trans.* XXVI. 39 She removed a Table Press-Bed from the Place where the Hair Trunk stood. **1785** Boswell *Tour Hebrides* 21 Aug. an. 1773, [At Aberdeen] I was to sleep in a little press-bed in Dr. Johnson's room. I had it wheeled out into the dining-room. **1843** Ballantine *Gaberlunzie* i. 21 The press-bed doors, stools, tables, and other furniture.

So †**press-bedstead**.

1683 Tryon *Way to Health* 590 You are to destroy all Press-Bedsteads which stand in Corners of Rooms, being made up with Boards so close, that the Air cannot penetrate or dry up and consume the . . Vapours that are contracted.

ˈpress-board. [f. press *v.*[1] or *sb.*[1] + board *sb.*]

1. An ironing-board; *spec.* (see quot. 1939).

1849 G. G. Foster *New York in Slices* i. 14 The press-board has been placed across the back corner of the shop. **1896** J. C. Harris *Sister Jane* i. 17 I've got this press-board on my lap, or I'd fetch it myself. **1924** W. D. F. Vincent et al. *Cutters' Pract. Guide Body Coats* 33/1 The seam should be placed straight on the press-board in front of you. **1939** M. B. Picken *Lang. Fashion* 116/2 *Press-board*, padded board, a small ironing board, used for pressing fabrics when sewing.

2. *Electr. Engin.* (Written pressboard.) A material consisting of compressed laminations of paper, used as a separator or insulator in electrical equipment; a piece of this.

1910 H. M. Hobart *Dict. Electr. Engin.* II. 415/1 *Pressboard*, sometimes termed *pressed board*, a fibrous material closely resembling press-spahn. **1926** A. P. M. Fleming in J. A. Fleming *Electr. Educator* II. 1354/2 The manufacture of pressboards . . is the same as for paper making so far as the production of pulp. **1952** J. P. Casey *Pulp & Paper* II. xvi. 957 Pressboards made . . in thicknesses ranging from 0·005 to 0·125 in. are used as a spacing and insulating medium. **1973** R. W. Sillars *Electr. Insulating Materials* vii. 123 Pressboard is prepared from cotton rag fibres or from pulp processed like other electrical papers, but instead of drying out as a single layer, a number of wet layers are placed together, pressed in a hydraulic press and dried by heat.

ˈpress-button, *sb.* and *a.* [f. press *v.*[1] or *sb.*[1] + button *sb.*] **A.** *sb.* **a.** = push-button *sb.*

1892 [see pressel]. **1977** *Gramophone* Nov. 959/3 To the right of the main tuning knob . . are two press-buttons.

b. A fastener similar to a press-stud.

1907 *Yesterday's Shopping* (1969) 404/1 Pocket for powder, lined white silk, with puff, and press button fastening. **1917** M. A. Souder *Notion Department* xv. 122 There are two types of snap fasteners: those built upon the principle of the ball and pocket reinforced with a wire spring, properly designated as snap fastener, and those of a flatter and structurally weaker design of a ball and socket without this wire spring, called press buttons. **1933** *Archit. Rev.* LXXIV. 30/1 (*caption*) The upholstery is easily removable on the motor car press-button principle.

B. *adj.* **a.** = push-button *a.* a.

1958 *Oxford Mail* 23 Aug. 3/6 Very neat press-button catches are fitted on all doors. **1965** *Wireless World* July 34/1 (Advt.), Press-button operation.

b. = push-button *a.* b.

1948 *Daily Tel.* 23 Apr. 5/2 Lord Montgomery said although we heard much talk of 'press-button' warfare, scientists had not so far produced any new weapon that could justify the discarding of the present-day technique of land warfare. **1958** *Listener* 12 June 990/3 A press-button world. **1965** M. McIntyre *Place of Quiet Waters* i. 5 All this high-powered, press-button living is wrong. **1971** *Daily Tel.* 30 Jan. 3/4 It was joked about as obsolete and useless in the age of press-button warfare.

‖**presse.** *Obs. rare.* [Fr., ad. Prov. (Gascon) *pressec*:—L. *persic-um*: see peach *sb.*[1]] A clingstone peach.

1604 E. G[rimstone] *D'Acosta's Hist. Indies* IV. xxxi. 294 Peaches, presses and apricockes have greatly multiplied, especially in New Spaine.

presse (of parchment): see prest *sb.*[2]

pressed (prɛst), *ppl. a.*[1] Also † prest. [f. press *v.*[1] + -ed[1].] **1.** Subjected to pressure; forced or squeezed into a smaller volume or denser consistence than the ordinary. Often qualifying articles in the preparation of which pressure is specially used, as ***pressed beef***, ***brick***, ***fuel***, ***glass***, etc. Also with adv. as ***hard-pressed***, ***hot-pressed***, etc.

c **1400** tr. *Secreta Secret., Gov. Lordsh.* 81 Froo a draghte of wyn to þe quantyte of oon pressyd grape. **1594** T. B. *La Primaud. Fr. Acad.* II. 399 Out of pressed milk and cruds as it were. **1594** Lyly *Moth. Bomb.* III. iv, Three damaske prunes in veluet caps and prest satten gownes. **1781** Crabbe *Library* 147 The close-prest leaves, unclosed for many an age. **1850** E. Dobson *Rudimentary Treat. Manuf. Bricks & Tiles* I. iii. 83 Pressed bricks . . are prepared by putting the raw bricks one at a time, when nearly dry, into a metal mould, in which they are forcibly compressed by the action of a powerful lever which forces up the piston forming the bottom of the mould. This gives a very beautiful face to the brick. **1869** *Our Young Folks* V. 86 We are making pressed glass nowadays that is almost as clear and beautiful as blown. **1887** *Pall Mall G.* 22 July 6/2 Extensive purchases of pressed hay have been effected in Holland. **1891** E. Kinglake *Australian at H.* 95 The hard pressed artist is obliged to cut down his price. **1894** *Daily News* 5 June 7/5 The best British pressed glass tumblers . . are made in the North. **1895** *Army & Navy Co-op Soc. Price List* 111/2 Pressed veal & ham (Blanchflower's). **1896** *Daily News* 30 Jan. 3/1 A . . building erected in pressed Leicester facing bricks of dark red. **1912** J. Armstrong *Motor* 266, I expect to see the clutch and flywheel as pressed parts in the near future, while pressed-steel pistons and connecting-rods are most likely to become common. **1926** F. Hurst *Appassionata* I. 10 Two empty pressed-glass perfume-bottles that had stood equidistant on that dressing-table ever since you could remember. **1935** H. C. Bryson *Gramophone Record* ix. 212 As soon as the press is opened, the steam commences to circulate in the dies, so that the operator has to remove the pressed record speedily or it will adhere to the rapidly-warming die. **1955** *Sci. Amer.* Jan. 68/1 One result of these studies has been the discovery of two new kinds of magnetic materials, the ferrites and the pressed-powder magnets. **1955** *Railway Mag.* June 388/2 The floor . . is built up of $1\frac{5}{16}$ in. thick boards . . bolted to dove-tailed galvanised steel sheeting carried on pressed-steel floor members. **1968** *Radio Times* 28 Nov. 20/1 The week's 'Newly Pressed' pop records. **1976** *Country Life* 1 Apr. 814/1 Apart from the addition of a 'bib' spoiler, the Mexico has the normal pressed-steel front of the rest of the range.

2. *U.S. slang.* Well dressed.

1970 H. E. Roberts *Third Ear* 11/1 *Pressed*, to be very well dressed. **1972** T. Kochman *Rappin' & Stylin' Out* 165 Being well dressed is . . expressed kinetically ('pressed'), and . . the term refers to a favoured norm.

pressed, †**prest,** *ppl. a.*[2] [f. press *v.*[2] + -ed[1].] †**1.** Hired, engaged (with earnest-money). *Obs.*

1650 Fuller *Pisgah* II. ii. *Gad* §16. 79 Ahimaaz . . being a messenger volunteer, would confess . . no more news then what he knew would be welcome, whilest Cushi a prest Post must relate the full of his message.

2. Forced to enlist in, or seized for use in, the royal or public service.

1589 *Late Voy. Sp. & Port.* (1881) 51 Our slovenly prest men, whome the Iustices . . have sent us out as the scumme and dregges of their Countrey. **1652** Collinges *Caveat for Prof.* (1653) A iij b, They were all prest men, that ran away presently. **1705** Ld. Seymour in Hearne *Collect.* 31 Oct. (O.H.S.) I. 62, 100 Voluntiers are better than 200 press'd men. **1748** *Anson's Voy.* I. iii. 31 The Spaniards were sensible of the disaffection of their prest hands. **1878** Stubbs *Const. Hist.* III. xviii. 88 A great part of the naval service was still conducted by pressed ships.

pressel (prɛs(ə)l). [f. press *v.*[1]] A press-button switch; orig., one attached to a flexible pendant conductor. Also ***pressel-switch***.

1892 T. O'C. Sloane *Stand. Electr. Dict.* 434 *Pressel*, a press-button often contained in a pear-shaped handle, arranged for attachment to the end of a flexible conductor, so as to hang thereby. **1911** W. P. Maycock *Electr. Wiring* (ed. 4) ii. 159 Instead of a cord pull-switch, one might connect an ordinary or two-plate ceiling-rose to the switch leads . . and hang therefrom a 'pressel' or suspension or pendant switch . . which is a convenient pattern for operating with one hand. **1916** G. Frankau *Guns* 21 And he hears, as he plays with the pressel-switch, the strapped receiver click on his ear that listens, listens. **1971** B. W. Aldiss *Soldier Erect* 79, I handed the microphone to Gor-Blimey. After some frigging about with the pressel-switch until he got things right, he spoke to Blue Spot. **1973** B. Callison *Web of Salvage* ii. 25 He released the pressel switch and the static came back.

presse-pâte (prɛspɑt). [Fr.] The section of a paper-making machine in which superfluous water is extracted from the pulp before it is formed into sheets or rolls. Also *attrib.*

1888 Cross & Bevan *Text-bk. Paper-Making* vi. 96 The presse-pâte system, originally adopted for the treatment of straw, has of late years been extensively applied to esparto. The presse-pâte consists of the wet end of a paper machine, and is furnished with sand-tables and strainers. **1937** E. J. Labarre *Dict. Paper* 194/2 Presse-pâte . . is a machine practically identical with the wet end of the paper-machine. . . It serves to extract 'loose' water from the (wood) pulp, which is allowed to accumulate on a press roll or round an iron rod, until a sheet or roll of wet board of sufficient thickness is obtained. **1963** R. R. A. Higham *Handbk. Papermaking* ii. 62 The pulp may either be concentrated on deckers, or presse-pâtes, or left in slush form.

presser (ˈprɛsə(r)). Also 6 -or. [Partly f. press *v.*[1] + -er[1]; partly from pressour, with change of suffix.]

1. One who presses. Applied to workmen in various trades, often with specification, as ***cloth-presser***, ***cotton-presser***, ***hat-presser***, ***stocking-presser***, ***tailor's presser***, ***trouser-presser***, etc. **a.** One who is employed to press cloth, felt, etc. into shape in tailoring, hat-making, etc. Also, one who presses wool into bales.

1549 *Act 3 & 4 Edw. VI*, c. 2 §10 Clothworkers Dyers and Pressors howses shoppes and other places. **1724** Swift *Drapier's Lett.* Wks. 1755 V. II. 95, I am not richer . . with the sale of all the several stuffs I have contrived: for, I give the whole profit to the dyers and pressers. **1892** *Labour Commission* Gloss., *Pressers*, men engaged in pressing the seams of garments with heated irons. **1902** *Brit. Med. Jrnl.* 15 Feb. 380/1 Blockers, including 'pressers' [hat-manufacture]. **1911** W. H. Koebel *In Maoriland Bush* viii. 122 The 'presser' climbs inside the high, square, wooden structure that rises in the centre of the floor, in readiness to receive the fleeces. **1955** G. Bowen *Wool Away!* vii. 95 Pressing wool is a simple straightforward job, but good pressers work without waste movement and without getting in each other's way. **1965** J. S. Gunn *Terminol. Shearing Industry* II. 9 *Presser*, a skilled man who presses the wool into bales so that they are not 'light on' (short in weight).

b. One who works a press of any kind; †a printer; a wine-presser (*obs.*).

1545 Elyot *Dict.*, *Torcularius*, a presser. **1573–80** Baret *Alv.* P 688 A presser, or he that presseth, *torcularius.* **1614** *Monstr. Serp.* in *Harl. Misc.* (Malh.) III. 228 Pamphleting pressers. **1641** T. Herbert *Repl. Defence Oxford Petition* 4 It is not fit the Presser should the Vine Cut downe.

c. *Pottery.* A workman who makes plates or hollow-ware by pressing the prepared clay into plaster-of-Paris moulds. Distinguished into ***flat pressers***, who make plates; ***hollow-ware pressers***, who make cups, basins, vases, and the like; and ***ornamental pressers***, who make ornamental porcelain, relief work, etc. Also in *Glass-making.*

1770 A. Young *Tour N. Eng.* (1771) III. xx. 255, I had the pleasure of viewing the Staffordshire potteries at Burslem. . . Modellers, . . Pressers, . . Painters, . . Moulders in plaister of Paris. **1898** Binns *Story of Potter* IV. i. 202 The hollow-ware presser uses a whirler, but not a jigger, and does all his work by hand. . . The clay is beaten out into suitable bats, and these are pressed and beaten into the mould until every crevice is properly filled. **1962** *Gloss. Terms Glass Industry* (B.S.I.) 45 *Presser*, a worker who shapes glass by pressing in a mould by hand or by machine.

2. One who urges or strongly inculcates.

1643 J. White *1st Cent. Scand. Malignant Priests* 35 A great practiser and presser of the late illegall Innovations. *a* **1658** J. Durham *Exp. Rev.* II. iii. (1680) 122 That learned author is an eminent batterer down of presumption and a presser of holinesse.

3. a. An instrument, machine, or part of a machine which applies pressure. Often with specification, as ***brawn-presser***, ***drill-presser***, etc.

Among other things, applied to a form of ironing-machine; the *presser-bar* of a knitting-machine, which drives the barb of the needle into the groove of the shank; the foot-piece or *presser-foot* in a sewing-machine which rests upon the cloth to hold it steady; the presser-roller of a drawing-frame; the spring-finger of a bobbin-frame.

1766 *Museum Rust.* VI. 10 The presser, which Mr. Crockatt's chaff-cutter uses. **1799** G. Smith *Laboratory* I. 7 To these sort of saddles are also made pressers, whereby the cases on the roller are pressed down with a heavy hand. **1844** Stephens *Bk. Farm* II. 523 The number of pressers should be increased, or a considerable extent of land be pressed before it is sown. **1852** *Trans. Soc. Arts* LVI. 475, I have made experiments with the drill and drill-presser in the same field. **1853** Ure *Dict. Arts* II. 831 The legs of the flyers carry an arm called a 'presser'. **1873** *Young Englishwoman* Mar. 150/2, I get the stitching as close as the width of space between the needle hole and the edge of presser. **1884** *Health Exhib. Catal.* 110/2 Tobacco and Vegetable Slicers. Brawn, Tongue and Lard Pressers.

b. A cider-press or wine-press.

1570 Levins *Manip.* 73/12 A presser, *pressorium.* **1616** Surfl. & Markh. *Country Farme* 408 The way to breake them [apples] in peeces, is to put them in a presser made round. **1845** Ld. Campbell *Chancellors* (1857) I. xiii. 197 From the vat of the purest presser it passed, dregless, into the vat of our memory.

†**4. a.** A press, a cupboard. *Obs.*

1503 in *Ripon Ch. Acts* (Surtees) 296 Unum magnum le buke presser. **1592** *Knaresborough Wills* (Surtees) I. 188 One presser standinge at my bedd head.

†**b.** A press-bed. *Obs.*

1557 in *Wills & Inv. N.C.* (Surtees) I. 159 In the Chamber ouer the Hall. . . A presser wth a mattres in it vj[s] viij[d].

5. *Comb.*: **presser-bar**, (*a*) the presser in a knitting-machine: see 3; (*b*) the vertical bar in a sewing-machine which bears the presser-foot; **presser-eye** *Spinning*, an aperture or eye through which cotton yarn passes before being wound on the spindle; **presser-flyer** (*Spinning*), a flyer (see FLYER 3 e) having a spring-arm which presses against the bobbin to regulate the tension in winding on the yarn; **presser-foot**, the foot-plate of a sewing-machine which holds the cloth down to the feed-plate; also *attrib.*; **presser-frame**, a spinning-frame furnished with presser-flyers.

1908 *Sears, Roebuck Catal.* 41/2 The presser bar is round and fitted with a presser bar adjuster by which the pressure on the goods is regulated. **1974** J. ROBINSON *Penguin Bk. Sewing* ii. 36/1 Presser Bar.. Stitch Length Regulator. **1892** J. NASMITH *Students' Cotton Spinning* ix. 340 In short, the traveller performs the same function as the flyer eye in the throstle or the presser eye in the roving frame. **1895** *Montgomery Ward Catal.* 262/1 Parts for Old Style Low Arm Singer.. Presser Foot. **1908** *Sears, Roebuck Catal.* 41/1 The presser foot has a very large under surface, which extends on both sides of the needle and holds any weight goods firmly in place over the feed. The forward part of the presser foot nearest the operator is curved upward so that foot will not catch in seams of fleecy materials. **1932** Presser-foot [see HEMMING *vbl. sb.*[1] b]. **1961** *Which?* Nov. 277 (*caption*) Presser-foot screw.. presser-foot lever. **1964** A. BUTLER *Teaching Children Embroidery* 29 Stitches with the presser foot, on..a [sewing] machine with a zigzag attachment.

†**'presserage.** *Obs. rare.* [a. OF. *pressorage* (1296 in Godef.), *-oirage, -ouerage*, etc. (mod.F. *pressurage*), f. *pressoirier* (mod.F. *pressurer*) to press (grapes), f. *pressoir* a wine-press.] ? Pressing, pressure.

c **1430** *Pilgr. Lyf Manhode* IV. xvii. (1869) 184 Wher of men haue seyn wel ofte, bi þe condyt bi which it discendeth, a gret presserage [F. *pressoueraige*] of teres.

press-fastener. [f. PRESS *v.*[1] + FASTENER.] = PRESS-STUD.

1926–7 *Army & Navy Stores Catal.* 664/3 Press fasteners ..in black or white, 1 dozen on card. **1956** *Good Housek. Home Encyl.* (ed. 4) 185/2 One side must be left open.., press fasteners or hooks and eyes being used to close it. **1960** *Mrs. Beeton's Cookery & Househ. Managem.* 145 Hooks and Eyes, Press Fasteners. **1976** J. WAINWRIGHT *Who goes Next?* 95 Racing gloves.. fastened at the back of the wrist, with a good press-fastener.

'pressful. [f. PRESS *sb.*[1] + -FUL.] As much or as many as a press will hold.

1854 H. MILLER *Sch. & Schm.* iii. (1858) 52 He possessed a whole pressful of tattered, hard-working volumes. **1898** *Engineering Mag.* XVI. 128/1 The charge for a press-full is disposed between crates in thin layers, 16 in number.

'press-gang, *sb.* [f. PRESS *sb.*[2] or *v.*[2] + GANG *sb.*[1]]

1. A body of men employed, under the command of an officer, to press men for service in the navy or army. Also *transf.*

1693 in C. N. Robinson *Brit. Fleet* (1894) 424 That all officers who send men to the press shall give them tickets, No. 1 to 15, expressing in their tickets what press-gang they belong to. **1707** *Inquiry Causes Miscarriages* in *Harl. Misc.* I. 566 Being the other day at the water-side, I saw a press-gang hauling and dragging a man, in a most barbarous manner, in order to send him on board a press-ketch. **1739** WESLEY *Wks.* (1872) I. 212 In the middle of the sermon, the press-gang came, and seized on one of the hearers. **1771** C. BURNEY *Present State of Mus. France & Italy* 119 These boys are a kind of *press-gang*, who seize all other boys they can find in their way to the church, in order to be catechised. **1820** W. IRVING *Sketch Bk., Widow & Son* §12 He was entrapped by a press-gang, and carried off to sea. **1969** I. & P. OPIE *Children's Games* i. 18 In some places the press-gang think they will be successful if they demand, 'Join the ring or tell us your sweetheart's name.'

2. *joc.* A group of journalists; the press (PRESS *sb.*[1] 14 g).

1840 *Spirit of Times* 11 Jan. 535/1 In compliment to the 'Press gang' Messr. Prentice and Weissinger.. were invited to occupy seats over the Judge's stand. **1859** L. WILMER *Our Press Gang* xxvi. 353 Our newspapers, in general are the organs of the mob, and.. the Press Gang *itself* is..a mob of the worst kind. **1859** G. H. LEWES *Let.* 20 Apr. in *Geo. Eliot Lett.* (1954) III. 54 Nor have I any relations with the pressgang here..the Edinburgh papers might advantageously be employed in this matter. **1869** 'MARK TWAIN' *Lett. to Publishers* (1967) 27, I will attend to the Buffalo books for the press.. did I tell you that I took dinner with the whole press gang yesterday? **1889** *Pall Mall Gaz.* 21 Oct. 4/3 Ask what you like, my good sir; don't you know I am one of the press gang myself? **1941** F. L. MOTT *Amer. Journalism* xxxv. 603 Many stories are told of the conviviality of the Chicago 'press gang' of the nineties, and from the legends which grew up.. sprang the concept of the romantic sot of the newspaper office. **1975** H. WAUGH *Bride for Hampton House* (1976) i. 1 She.. waved at the press gang when she took the big elevator to the newsroom floor.

Hence **'press-gang** *v., trans.* and *intr.* = PRESS *v.*[2]; **'press-ganged** *ppl. a.*, **'press-ganging** *vbl. sb.*

1863 MRS. GASKELL *Sylvia's L.* vii, There'll be no more press-ganging here awhile. **1882** *Fraser's Mag.* XXV. 756 The surfeit of learning which so unhesitatingly leads the pressganged scholar to accelerate his emancipation from the school or university. **1899** *Westm. Gaz.* 14 Mar. 1/2 Mr. George Harwood,..member for Bolton,..mentioned casually that his grandfather had been 'press-ganged' into the Royal Navy... The grandfather of Mr. Billson, the Radical member for Halifax, had similarly been the victim of 'press-ganging'.

'pressible, *a. rare*[−1]. [f. PRESS *v.*[1], on analogy of COMPRESSIBLE, *repressible, suppressible*.] Capable of being pressed: cf. PRESSABLE.

1865 *Pall Mall G.* 6 Sept. 11/2 No doubt my friend the Italian innkeeper would be more easily pressible,—what we generally call more reasonable,—in his financial arrangements if you could argue out the question of your bed and supper in good Tuscan.

pressie, var. PREZZIE.

'pressing, *vbl. sb.*[1] [f. PRESS *v.*[1] + -ING[1].]

1. The action of PRESS *v.*[1], in various senses.

c **1400** *Rom. Rose* 6436 Withoute presing more on thee, I wol forth, and to him goon. *c* **1440** *Promp. Parv.* 412/2 Pressynge, *compressio*. **1568** GRAFTON *Chron.* II. 297 Then was there great preassing to take the King. **1616** SURFL. & MARKH. *Country Farme* 414 Good housholders doe not loose the drosse of their pressings, but..cast them into vessells, and with..water, make Cider for the houshold. **1674** *Essex Papers* (Camden) I. 265 Without yᵉ extraordinary pressing of friends I cannot remaine in it. **1681** *Trial S. Colledge* 10 The common Judgment of Pressing to Death must not pass upon him, but an Attainder of High-Treason. **1719** DE FOE *Crusoe* I. 207 Those secret Hints, or Pressings of my Mind, to doing, or not doing any Thing that presented. **1838** JAMES *Robber* vi, The madman required no pressing. **1881** *Porcelain Works, Worcester* 21 The manufacture of soup tureens, covered dishes,.. basins, &c. is called Hollow Ware Pressing. *Ibid.*, The manufacture of plates and dishes is called Flat Pressing. *a* **1911** D. G. PHILLIPS *Susan Lenox* in *Hearst's Mag.* (1915) June 538/1 Susan finished her pressing and started to dress. **1960** *Vogue Pattern Bk.* Autumn 61 Careful pressing, at every stage in making clothes, helps to give your work that smooth professional finish. **1969** T. C. THORSTENSEN *Pract. Leather Technol.* xii. 192 This pressing of the oil removes some of the high melting point components and gives the oil a lower cold test. **1976** *Southern Even. Echo* (Southampton) 15 Nov. 15/5 The match was one of two halves, with Basingstoke doing all the pressing in the first.

2. a. That which results from or remains after pressing; the product of the pressing, the juice; in *pl.* also, the solid matter left after expressing juice.

1607 TOPSELL *Four-f. Beasts* (1658) 59 Where is want of such pulse, they may give them pressings of Grapes dryed and cleansed. **1707** MORTIMER *Husb.* (1721) II. 335 Which ..you may put among your pressings for a Water Cyder. **1898** *Rev. Brit. Pharm.* 32 The third pressing is evaporated to such a volume that when added to the first two the whole shall measure 2 pints.

b. An article formed or shaped in a press; *spec.* a gramophone record made by stamping a blank with a matrix.

1922 *Metal Industry* XX. 273/1 Many parts are now being manufactured as pressings which a few years ago would have been thought impossible. **1927** *Gramophone* Sept. 139/1 The new white label pressings arrived just in time for me to take them to Paris. **1952** GODFREY & AMOS *Sound Recording & Reproduction* v. 143 A vinyl pressing is superior to one made in shellac in that it is far less fragile. **1959** *Motor Manual* (ed. 36) 7 A pressing is produced by squeezing the sheet of steel between a die, securely anchored in the base of the press, and the punch which is forced into it at a pressure of 750 tons or more. **1959** *Times Rev. Industry* Nov. 46/2 Quantities of pressings and castings are required by makers of household equipment. **1962** *Times* 5 July 15/6 A master tape of a recent recording of music by Prokofiev and an ordinary commercial pressing of a disc made from it were started simultaneously. **1973** D. WESTHEIMER *Going Public* v. 77 Lee.. turned on the stereo. It was an LP pressing of some old John Kirby RPM singles.

3. *attrib.* and *Comb.* with sense 'used in or for pressing', as ***pressing-bag, -case, cloth, -cylinder, -knife, -machine, pad, -plank, plant, -plate, rag, -roller, room, -shed***, etc.; **pressing board** (*a*) one of a pair of boards used in bookbinding to compress the sheets or volumes, and by botanists in pressing specimens of plants; (*b*) an ironing board. **pressing-fat** = *press-fat*: see PRESS *sb.*[1] 17 a; **pressing-paper** (sense in quot. 1545 uncertain); now, botanical drying-paper.

1875 KNIGHT *Dict. Mech.*, *Pressing-bag, the horsehair cloth bag in which flaxseed or stearic acid is pressed. **1823** G. MARTIN *Bookbinder's Compl. Instr.* 9 *Pressing Boards, are flat boards made of well seasoned beech. **1875** URE *Dict. Arts* (ed. 7) I. 424 (*Bookbinding*) The volumes are carefully laid between pressing-boards with their rounded backs put outside the edges of each pressing-board so as to escape the coming squeeze. **1894** FENN *In Alpine Valley* I. 153 Only let me get my pressing-boards and the alpenstock. **1969** E. H. PINTO *Treen* 151/1 (*heading*) Ironing and Pressing Boards. **1897** MRS. E. L. VOYNICH *Gadfly* (1904) 5/2 He expended half his spare cash on botanical books and *pressing-cases, and started off..for his first Alpine ramble. **1917** E. R. HAMBRIDGE *Simple Dressmaking* iii. 65/2 Wring out the *pressing cloth *very* tightly, and lay it on the fabric. **1974** LIPPMAN & ERSKINE *Dressmaking made Simple* iv. 59 A pressing cloth can be obtained pre-treated. **1810** *Patent Specif.* No. 3385 Having the *pressing cylinder reduced at one side in the well-known form called the D roller (chiefly used by calicoe printers). **1561** DAUS tr. *Bullinger on Apoc.* (1573) 214 There shall the right *pressing-fat be set vp and made readie. **1825** *Austin Papers* (1924) II. 1028 We intend to send a gin and probably a *pressing machine. **1884** *Health Exhib. Catal.* 113/1 Two Cloth Cutting Machines. One Pressing Machine. **1940** *Chambers's Techn. Dict.* 671/2 *Pressing machine*, a machine in which the whole forming operation is carried out by pressing the plastic glass by a plunger forced into a die or mould. The machine may be operated by hand or it may be fully automatic. **1947** C. TALBOT *Compl. Bk. Sewing* xxxi. 208/1 The rounded shaping of armhole and shoulder.. must be protected in pressing. A tailor's cushion, a *pressing pad, or a sleeve board will help. **1974** LIPPMAN & ERSKINE *Dressmaking made Simple* vi. 87 Press..shaped parts over the tailor's pressing cushion/pad. **1545** *Rates of Customs* c ij b, *Pressing papers the C. leues xx d. **1601** HOLLAND *Pliny* I. 488 Make thy *pressing plank..of the black Sapine or Horn-beam tree. **1958** *Manch. Guardian* 21 Jan. 6/6 Oriole Records Ltd. ..has its own *pressing plant and..presses all Mr. Lonsdale's records for him. **1934** A. L. HIRD *Princ. & Pract. Needlework & Dressmaking* iv. 41 *Do not apply water directly* to any materials except wool and wool mixtures, but always by way of *pressing rag or as steam. **1922** O. MITCHELL *Talking Machines* vi. 70 When the discs pass into the *pressing room the steel backing is laid upon a heated table with the mould upwards. **1937** F. STARK *Baghdad Sketches* 36 He was a tailor in his spare time, and he used the roof as a pressing room.

pressing, *vbl. sb.*[2]: see under PRESS *v.*[2]

'pressing, *ppl. a.* [f. PRESS *v.*[1] + -ING[2].] That presses, in various senses of the verb.

1. That presses, or weighs heavily; burdensome.

1591 *Troub. Raigne K. John* i. 14 The heauy yoke Of pressing cares, that hang vpon a Crowne. **1657** AUSTEN *Fruit Trees* II. 15 The sense of his present misery is therefore the more pressing.

2. That presses physically; exerting or causing pressure. ***pressing sail***: see PRESS *sb.*[1] 10.

1656 tr. *Hobbes' Elem. Philos.* (1839) 211 Bodies, whose parts yield more or less to the endeavour which the pressing body makes at the first arrival. **1807** WORDSW. *White Doe* v. 65 Nor wanted 'mid the pressing crowd Deep feeling.

3. Calling for immediate attention; urgent.

1616 J. CHAMBERLAIN in *Crt. & Times Jas. I* (1848) I. 400 Providing for matters most necessary, and discharging the most pressing and crying debts. **1690** LOCKE *Govt.* I. iv. §42 His pressing wants call for it. **1781** GIBBON *Decl. & F.* III. 175 [He] advanced into the provinces of the South, to encounter a more pressing and personal danger. **1807–8** SYD. SMITH *Plymley's Lett.* Wks. 1859 II. 151/2 Pressing evils are not got rid of, because they are not talked of. **1885** *Law Rep.* 29 *Ch. Div.* 459 The real object.. was to enable the directors to pay off pressing liabilities.

b. Of a request, invitation, etc.: Expressed with an earnest desire for compliance; also of the person: persistent in solicitation; importunate.

1705 STANHOPE *Paraphr.* III. 201 They received fresh and more pressing Invitations. **1710** STEELE *Tatler* No. 200 ¶2 My Mother..is very pressing with me to marry. **1790** BURKE *Fr. Rev.* Pref., A new and pressing application for the Author's sentiments. **1845** FORD *Handbk. Spain* I. 29 They are very pressing in their invitations whenever any eating is going on. **1855** MACAULAY *Hist. Eng.* xxi. IV. 662 He had.. come up to town..in consequence of a pressing summons from Porter.

†**'pressing-iron.** *Obs.* An iron implement (= IRON *sb.*[1] 5) used by tailors, dressmakers, laundresses, etc., which is heated, and used to press down seams, smooth cloth, and the like; a smoothing-iron. Also *fig.*

1343 *Reading Abbey Tailor's Compotus* (Add. MS. 19657), In Reparacione vnius pressynge yryn pro Scissore viij.d. **1459** *Maldon, Essex, Court Rolls* Bundle 34. No. 1 b, A pressynge yren, precii ii d. **1577–87** HOLINSHED *Chron.* III. 1064/2 Then Mosbie hauing at his girdle a pressing iron of fourteene pounds weight, stroke him on the hed with the same. **1607** TOPSELL *Four-f. Beasts* (1658) 313 Take a Taylors pressing Iron made hot and rub it up and down upon the cloth. *c* **1637** WOTTON *Let. to Sir R. Baker* in *Reliq.* (1651) 446 Your worldly troubles have been but Pressing-Irons to your heavenly cogitations.

'pressingly, *adv.* [f. PRESSING *ppl. a.* + -LY[2].] In a pressing manner; urgently; importunately.

1642 HOWELL *For. Trav.* (Arb.) 33 The one contracts and enchaines his words, and speakes pressingly and short. *a* **1661** HOLYDAY *Juvenal* 125 First, in respect of the express testimonie of the poet;..secondly, and more pressingly (as I think) because of the absurd consequence. **1760** C. JOHNSTON *Chrysal* (1822) II. 149 My motive for writing to you so pressingly to come to me. **1871** CARLYLE in *Mrs. Carlyle's Lett.* (1883) I. 392 W. E. Forster.. pressingly hospitable, took us home with him.

'pressingness. [f. as prec. + -NESS.] The quality of being pressing; urgency; importunity.

a **1681** ALLESTREE *Serm., Matt.* vi. 22, 23 (1684) II. 258 This consideration alone might apply it self with pressingness upon us. **1684–5** BOYLE *Min. Waters* Advt., Which pressingness of theirs he could not deny to be the more excusable, on this occasion. **1881** P. BROOKS *Candle of Lord* 127 He has been allowing the nearness and pressingness of his own circumstances to delude him.

pression ('prɛʃən). Now *rare.* [a. F. *pression* (16th c. in Hatz.-Darm.), ad. L. *pressiōn-em*, n. of action f. *premĕre*: see PRESS *v.*[1]]

1. The action of pressing; pressure.

1661 BOYLE *Spring of Air* (1682) 110 This is the difference between Pression and Suction, that suction makes such an adhesion and pression doth not. **1674** GREW *Disc. Mixture* iv. §3 Weight it self is but Pression. **1880** *Nature* XXI. 422/2 Under ordinary conditions of pression diamond will withstand a high temperature.

†**2.** In the Cartesian physics: Pressure or impulse communicated to and propagated through a fluid medium. *Obs.*

1672 NEWTON in *Phil. Trans.* VII. 5089 Other Mechanical Hypotheses on which Light is supposed to be caused by any Pression or Motion whatsoever, excited in the aether by the agitated parts of Luminous bodies. **1704** —— *Optics* III. (1721) 336 If Light consisted only in Pression propagated without actual Motion, it would not be able to agitate and heat the Bodies which refract and reflect it. **1756** AMORY

Buncle (1770) I. 187 If the moon..by pression and attraction, was the principal cause of flux and reflux.

3. In massage: 'A method of pressing or compressing the muscles, by means of the whole hand, the tips of the fingers, or the roulette' (*Syd. Soc. Lex.*).

1887 D. MAGUIRE *Art Massage* i. (ed. 4) 15 In the sundry pressions he should not fatigue the patient. *Ibid.* ii. 27, I believe that a soft percussion..might accomplish the same result as massage by pression.

pressiroster (prɛsɪˈrɒstə(r)). *Ornith.* [ad. F. *pressirostre* (Cuvier), ad. mod.L. *pressirostris* adj., f. L. *press-us* pressed + *rostrum* beak, bill.] A bird of the *Pressirostres* of Cuvier, now included in the *Charadriomorphæ* or plover-snipe group. So **pressiˈrostral** *a.*, having the characteristics of the *Pressirostres*; **pressiˈrostrate** *a.*, having a compressed beak (Mayne *Expos. Lex.* 1858).

1842 BRANDE *Dict. Sci.*, etc., *Pressirosters*, a tribe of wading birds, including those which have a flattened or compressed beak. **1847** WEBSTER, *Pressirostral*, having a compressed or flattened beak; applied to certain birds, as the lapwing. *Partington.*

†**ˈpressitant**, *a.* *Obs.* *rare*$^{-1}$. [ad. L. type **pressitānt-em*, pr. pple. of **pressitāre*, iterative of *pressāre* to PRESS: cf. *cursitāre*.] Continuing to press; exerting continuous pressure.

1668 H. MORE *Div. Dial.* I. ix. 34 Neither the Celestial matter of the Vortices nor the Air nor Water are pressitant in their proper places.

pressive (ˈprɛsɪv), *a.* Now *rare.* [ad. obs. F. *pressif, -ive*, pressing, urgent, violent (16th c. in Godef.): see PRESS *v.*[1] and -IVE.]

†**1.** Pressing, urgent. *Obs.*

1619 *Times Storehouse* III. II. iii. 301/1 If the affairs are pressiue..each canton must aduertise his confederates, to be in readinesse for aduising (altogether) on that which is to bee done.

†**2.** Oppressive. *Obs.*

1623 BP. HALL *Contempl.*, *O.T.* XVIII. i, How did he make siluer to be in Ierusalem as stones, if the exactions were so pressiue?

†**3.** Impressive. *Obs.*

1623 tr. *Favine's Theat. Hon.* II. xiii. 213 These are the most pregnant and pressiue passages.

4. a. Characterized by pressure; pressing.

1822–34 *Good's Study Med.* (ed. 4) I. 133 From the pressive violence of the action, it has also been highly beneficial in many cases of obstruction. **1887** D. MAGUIRE *Art Massage* (ed. 4) Introd. 6 Give pressive movements to the several joints.

b. *Psychol.* That pertains or relates to environmental press (see PRESS *sb.*[1] 6).

1938 H. A. MURRAY *Explorations in Personality* ii. 96 In emotional action it is the sudden, close, pressive situation that seems to 'do the work' by releasing energy in the motor centres of the interbrain.

press lord. Also with capital initials. [f. PRESS *sb.*[1] + LORD *sb.*] A powerful newspaper owner, a newspaper magnate, esp. one who is a member of the peerage. Cf. *press baron* s.v. PRESS *sb.*[1] 17 b.

1930 *Economist* 30 Aug. 396/2 At the Labour Party Conference..resolutions will be discussed.. putting forward claims, rather reminiscent of those of the Press Lords, that certain Labour interests should dictate how the Cabinet should be composed. **1932** *Ann. Reg. 1931* 23 The 'press lords', Lord Rothermere and Lord Beaverbrook, who had never abated their hostility to Mr. Baldwin, had once more opened a campaign against him, and in London at any rate they were not without a considerable following. **1947** *Sat. Rev. Lit.* (U.S.) 22 Feb. 15/2 Roy Howard still dresses and acts among the press lords like a police reporter. **1955** T. H. PEAR *Eng. Social Differences* 22 Some Press-lords are wounded..or amused at the suggestion that increased circulation is one of their first aims. **1965** AUDEN *About House* (1966) 15 Only a press lord Could have built San Simeon. **1977** *Time* 17 Jan. 5/2 But the press lord from Down Under is no stranger to *Time* readers—or *Time* staffers.

†**ˈpressly**, *adv.* *Obs.* Also 6 precely, 7 presly. [f. PRESS *a.* + -LY[2]; in sense 1 perh. short for *expressly*.] **1.** ? Expressly.

*a***1518** SKELTON *Magnyf.* 2577 This mater we haue mouyd, you myrthys to make, Precely purposyd vnder pretence of play.

2. Concisely; precisely, exactly.

1636 B. JONSON *Discov.*, *Dominus Verulamius*, No man ever spake more neatly, more presly, more weightily. **1642** H. MORE *Song Soul* II. ii. II. xxviii, Still more presly this point to pursue. *a***1675** LIGHTFOOT *Rem.* (1700) 48 Study them pressly, for they are of infinite sweetness and satisfaction.

ˈpressman[1]. [f. PRESS *sb.*[1] + MAN *sb.*[1]]

1. A man engaged in a wine-press. *rare*$^{-1}$.

*c***1611** CHAPMAN *Iliad* XVIII. 516 One only path to all, by which the pressmen came In time of vintage.

2. A man who operates or manages a printing-press; *esp.* a hand-press printer.

1598 FLORIO, *Battitóre*,..a Printers presse-man. **1683** MOXON *Mech. Exerc.*, *Printing* xxiv. ¶5 When the Press-man Pulls, the Tennants of the Head shall have an equal Horizontal level Check. **1763** W. LEWIS *Comm. Phil.-Techn.* 374 The care and attention of the pressmen in well working the ink on the types with the balls, are very material points. **1866** BRANDE & COX *Dict. Sc.*, etc. III. 74/1 Pressmen, who apply ink to the surface of the form of types, and take off the impressions upon paper. The pressmen who work steam presses are called machine minders. **1894** *Labour Comm. Gloss.*, *Pressmen*, mechanics engaged in printing by the old hand presses (very few now) taking off impressions on paper, whether from type, stone, wood-cuts, or metal plates.

3. One who writes or reports for the daily or weekly press; a reporter, a journalist.

1859 SALA *Tw. round Clock* (1861) 34 This brave old press-man, who,..when there were neither contributors nor compositors to be found at hand, bravely took off his coat, and in his shirt-sleeves first translated, and then.. proceeded to set up in type his own manuscript. **1888** *Pall Mall G.* 13 Sept. 4/2 Our Commissioner..was not the first press man presented to the Japanese Sovereign. **1898** *Daily News* 31 Aug. 6/3 (Institute of Journalists) Sir Edward Russell delivered his presidential address before a large audience of pressmen from various parts of the country.

4. In shoemaking: A workman who stamps out the sole-leather for boots or shoes with a press.

1895 *Daily News* 22 Mar. 7/3 The demand for an increase of wages to clickers and pressmen. **1897** *Ibid.* 17 Mar. 3/2 A minimum wage of 28*s.* per week for clickers and 26*s.* per week for press men.

†**ˈpressman**[2]. [f. PRESS *sb.*[2] or *v.*[2] + MAN *sb.*[1] In sense 1 perh. for *prest-man.*]

1. A man 'pressed' into naval or military service; an impressed man. Also *fig.* Now only *arch.*

1638 EARL OF MANCHESTER in *Buccleuch MSS.* (Hist. MSS. Comm.) I. 282 The soldiers that are to go must now be press men. **1665** PEPYS *Diary* 10 May, To get some soldiers..to go keep pressmen on board our ships. **1978** *Church Times* 17 Feb. 11/4 In religious education there has been a constant battle waged to rise to the challenge of the 1944 Act and ensure that the subject is taught by qualified specialists rather than by willing amateurs or, worse, by reluctant press-men.

†**2.** A member of a press-gang. *Obs.*

1755 JOHNSON, *Pressman*, 1. One who forces another into service; one who forces away. **1775** in ASH. **1828** in WEBSTER; and in mod. Dicts.

ˈpressmanship. [f. PRESSMAN[1] + -SHIP.]

1. Occupation or skill as pressman in a printing-office.

1825 HANSARD *Typographia* 912 Those sheet-anchors of pressmanship called points. **1923** H. A. MADDOX *Printing* ix. 106 Most printing is in the indifferent class and much good typography is marred by careless pressmanship. *Ibid.* x. 125 Printing from three-colour half-tone blocks demands a high standard of pressmanship.

2. Occupation as a writer or reporter for the press.

1882 *Sat. Rev.* 1 Apr. 409/1 During his sixteen years of pressmanship..the passion for truth has solely possessed him.

ˈpress-mark. [PRESS *sb.*[1] 15.] In libraries, a mark or number written or stamped in or on each book (now usually on the inside of the cover), and also given in the library catalogue, specifying the room, book-press, book-case, shelf, etc., where the book is kept. Now chiefly with reference to manuscripts and early books in old libraries. Also *attrib.*

[**1684** E. CHAMBERLAYNE *Pres. St. Eng.* (ed. 12) II. 228 *margin*, The several Marks on the Presses which contain the Records.] **1802** PLANTA *Cat. MSS. Cott. Libr. Br. Mus.* p. xii. *note*, The books were deposited in fourteen presses, over which were placed the busts of the twelve Cæsars and of Cleopatra and Faustina, whence the press-marks given to the volumes in its several catalogues. **1841** HALLIWELL in *Cov. Myst.* Introd. 6 A quarto volume,..now preserved in the Cottonian collection of manuscripts..under the press-mark Vespas. D. viii. **1906** *Edin. Rev.* Jan. 130 The press-mark was always omitted. **1941** N. R. KER *Medieval Libraries* p. xviii, Pressmarks are useful indications of provenance just in so far as they are distinctive. **1952** J. CARTER *ABC for Bk.-Collectors* 141 Seymour de Ricci, in his *English Collectors of Books and Manuscripts*, shows how much can be learned from the study of press-marks by anyone concerned with the provenance of books. **1963** *Times Lit. Suppl.* 1 Mar. 160/3 A stock of the press-mark tickets used by Louis-Henri. **1971** *Eng. Stud.* LII. 351 The press-mark of the Leiden manuscript is not *Voss 106*, but *Voss. 106*, in which *Voss.* is an abbreviation of *Vossianus*.

Hence **press-mark** *v. trans.* and *intr.* (see quots. 1889 and 1895).

1889 *Cent. Dict.*, *Press-mark*.., *v.t.* and *i.* To place a press-mark on; also, to use press-marks. **1895** *Funk's Stand. Dict.*, *Press-mark*,..*vt.* & *vi.* To mark (a book) with characters showing the proper place in a bookcase. **1915** *Trans. Bibliogr. Soc.* XIV. 5 The Society's library..has been rearranged and re-pressmarked.

†**ˈpress-ˌmaster.** *Obs.* [f. PRESS *sb.*[2] + MASTER *sb.*[1]] One who was authorized to impress recruits; the officer in command of a press-gang.

1673 A. WALKER *Leez Lachrymans* 12 He that's taken by this great Press-master, must serve in person. **1690** *Lond. Gaz.* No. 2541/4 These are to desire all Officers, Press-Masters and others whom it may concern, to Press the foresaid Samuel Courtner wherever they shall find him. **1697** *View Penal Laws* 52 Two men for every hundred Tun [collier] Vessel..Press free; and if any Press-master presume to press such then he shall forfeit 10*l.* **1705** *Lond. Gaz.* No. 4087/4 In case he should have been forced from his Duty by..Press Masters by Land or Sea.

ˈpress-ˌmoney, †**ˈprest-ˌmoney.** Now only *Hist.* Also 6 presse-, 7 pressed-. [Orig. *prest-money*, f. PREST *sb.*[1] + MONEY.

The change to *press-money* may have been at first a phonetic simplification, the *t* between two consonants being squeezed out, as in OE. *blóstma*, *blósma*, blossom, *Christmas* (ˈkrɪsməs), *Christ-cross*, *criss-cross*, etc.; this would naturally encourage association with the notion of pressing and pressure, as in PRESS *v.*[2] Cf. the 17th c. spelling *pressed-money*, as if money paid to men when *pressed.* (Some 17th c. etymologists fancifully derived the name from PREST *a.*, and explained it as money paid to men for being 'prepared' or 'ready' for service.)]

1. Money advanced, a loan; esp. to the sovereign in an emergency; = PREST *sb.*[1] 1.

α. **1560–1** *Newcastle Guilds* (Surtees) 89 An act mayd for the payment of the prest [*mispr.* press] money. [Cf. quots. 1560–1 in PREST *sb.*[1] 1 and PREST *v.*[1] 1.]

2. Money paid in advance for work undertaken, or expenses to be incurred; = PREST *sb.*[1] 3.

α. **1445** *Order Queen's Coronation* in Rymer *Fœdera* (1710) XI. 83 That ye Deliver under oure saide Tresorer..in Prest Moneye the some of Five Hundred Pounds. **1539** in *Househ. Ord.* (1790) 228 The said Cofferer shall give prest money beforehand to every of the said Purveyors. **1604** *Ibid.* 309 Item, that the Cofferer doe give Prest-Money before hand to Our Purvayers.

3. Earnest-money paid to a sailor or soldier on his enlistment, the acceptance of which was the legal proof of his engagement; 'the King's (or Queen's) shilling'; = PREST *sb.*[1] 4.

α. **1523** LD. BERNERS *Froiss.* I. cccxc. 667 Then it was ordayned..to gyue all maner of men of warre lycence to go thyder [to Spain]; And the kyng delyuered them their first prest money. **1545** *St. Papers Hen. VIII*, I. 792 Master Hugh Stuycklye..hathe..laid owt certen summes of monye for the conduyt and prest monye of such maryners as he towke up to go to Portesmouthe. **1548** ELYOT *Dict.*, *Authoramentum*,..also earnest money, wages or hyre, preast money. **1555** PHILPOT in Foxe *A. & M.* (1583) 1833/1 They haue taken his prest money a great while, and now let them shew themselues readye to serue hym faythfully. **1600** HOLLAND *Livy* II. xxiv. 59 The comminaltie..encouraged one another not to take prest-monie, or to enter their names in the muster-masters book. **1619** DALTON *Country Just.* cvii. (1630) 280 Souldiers entered of Record and having taken prest Money. **1633** D. R[OGERS] *Treat. Sacram.* I. 170 Baptisme is our prest-mony to bind us to Christ in all estates to be his souldiers. **1666** PEPYS *Diary* 30 June, He had not money to pay the pressed-money to the men. **1710** J. HARRIS *Lex. Techn.* II, *Prest Money*,..is Money given to Soldiers when they are *Prest*: and binds such as receive it to be *ready* at command at all Times appointed.

β. **1585** *Founders' Comp.* (MS.) *Acct. Books*, Imprimis payd the xvjth day of aprill unto them in presse monye..iiij s. *Ibid.*, Itm. payd unto gefferaye voo the xxiiijt of Iuly ffor Presse monye..xij d. **1595** *Locrine* II. ii, *Thra.* My captain and the cobler so hard at it? Sirs, what is your quarrell? *Capt.* Nothing sir, but that he will not take presse-mony. **1649** G. DANIEL *Trinarch.*, *Hen. V*, ccxcix, The Subtle traps Of Pay, or Press-money. *a***1659** BP. BROWNRIG *Serm.* (1674) II. xxiii. 294 'Tis like Press-money, if once thou receivest it, thou art bound to do service. **1689** *Royal Proclam.* 29 Apr. in *Lond. Gaz.* No. 2450/2 Nevertheless His Majesty is informed, that several Mariners,..Press'd for His Service, and having received Press-Money, do neglect to repair to, and desert the said Service. **1714** GAY *What D'ye Call It* II. ii, Here—Peascod, take my pouch—'tis all I own... 'Tis my press money—can this silver fail? *a***1720** SEWEL *Hist. Quakers* (1722) II. 41 The Justices..resolved to press him for a Soldier..and Bennet sent Constables to give him Press-Money.

†**ˈpressness.** *Obs.* *rare*$^{-1}$. [f. PRESS *a.* + -NESS.] Conciseness.

1728 YOUNG *Love Fame* Pref. A iv b, An excellent critick of our own commends Boileau's closeness, or, as he calls it, pressness, particularly.

press officer. Also with capital initials. [f. PRESS *sb.*[1] + OFFICER *sb.*] An official appointed by an individual or institution to handle publicity and public relations.

1919 J. BUCHAN *Mr. Standfast* xx. 366, I was about to make a rush for..one of the Press officers, who would..be in the way of knowing things. **1941** *Whitaker's Almanack* 321/2 Colonial Office... *Press Officer*, A. Ridgway..£800. **1949** H. NICOLSON *Diary* 14 Jan. (1968) 163 One man..had asked Philip Jordan, as Attlee's Press Officer, to describe what the P.M. had had for breakfast that morning. **1959–60** A. BUTLER in *Parliamentary Affairs* XIII. 57 Journalists under great pressure make use of guidance from Press officers in Government departments when handling reports and Bills. **1961** *Times* 25 July 2/2 (Advt.), 'English Electric' require a Press Officer..to..be responsible for all press and public relations functions. **1969** A. G. THOMAS in L. Durrell *Spirit of Place* 57 In 1939 Durrell..moved to Athens working first for the Embassy as an unestablished press officer. **1972** 'H. CARMICHAEL' *Naked to Grave* v. 71 You would get all the information from the press officer which was currently available.

pressor (ˈprɛsə(r)), *a.* *Phys.* [Agent-n. in L. form from *premĕre* to press, used *attrib.*] That presses; stimulating, exciting.

1890 BILLINGS *Med. Dict.*, *Pressor nerves*, nerves whose stimulation increases activity of vaso-motor centres. **1895** *Syd. Soc. Lex.*, *Pressor*, exciting, stimulating. **1899** *Allbutt's Syst. Med.* VII. 258 If the basilar artery be embolised by injections into the vertebral arteries the greatest pressor effects occur. **1904** *Brit. Med. Jrnl.* 10 Sept. 603 The extract ..seems to contain both a pressor and a depressor substance.

pressor, obs. f. PRESSER; var. PRESSOUR.

pressoreceptor (ˈprɛsəʊrɪsɛptə(r)). *Physiol.* Also with hyphen. [f. *presso-*, taken as comb.

form of *pressure* + RECEPTOR.] A proprioceptor which responds to changes in blood pressure.

1941 P. BARD *Macleod's Physiol. in Mod. Med.* xl. 576 (*caption*) Effects of electrical stimulation of nerves from pressoreceptors and chemoreceptors in the dog. **1943** *Physiol. Rev.* XXIII. 244 In man the diastolic pressure has been shown to rise during standing. This is a sign of increasing vasomotor tone. It is compensatory in nature until it encroaches too far upon pulse pressure. The reflexes originating in the vascular presso-receptors are responsible for this control. **1975** *Investigative Urology* XII. 465 We studied the influence of pressoreceptor stimulation on micturition reflex and urethral pressure profile.

†**pre'ssorian**, *a. Obs. rare.* [f. L. *pressōri-us* (see next) + -AN.] Of or pertaining to pressing and moulding in clay: cf. *press-ware* in PRESS *sb.*[1] 17 a.

1612 STURTEVANT *Metallica* xii. 82 Earthen pipes by the Pressorian Art, being well made are as strong to hould and conuey water as leaden pipes or potters pots.

†**pressour**. *Obs.* Also 4–6 -ure, 5 -ur, 6 -or, (4 presour, 5 prassur). [a. OF. *pressor*, *-our*, *-eur*, variants of *pressoir* (12th c. in Littré):—late L. *pressōrium* a press for wine, oil, etc., sb. use of neut. of *pressōrius* adj., f. *press-*, ppl. stem of *premĕre* to press: cf. *pressor*. See also PRESSER.]

1. An apparatus or instrument for pressing or squeezing. **a.** A wine- or oil-press: = PRESS[1] 12 a.

a **1340** HAMPOLE *Psalter* lv. 1 Haly kirke as a grape in þe pressure cries god hafe mercy of me. **1382** WYCLIF *Matt.* xxi. 33 Ther was an husbondman, that plantide a vyne ȝerd, ..and dalue a pressour [*v.r.* pressure, **1388** presour] therynne. *c* **1425** *Voc.* in Wr.-Wülcker 666/14 *Hoc torcular*, prassur. *c* **1430** *Pilgr. Lyf Manhode* IV. xvii. (1869) 184 It is streyned in a pressour [F. *pressouer*]. **1558** WARDE tr. *Alexis' Secr.* (1568) 46 b, Presse them in a faire white linnen cloth in a pressour, vntyll there issue out a very cleare oyle. **1570** LEVINS *Manip.* 192/45 A Préssure, *pressorium*.

b. = PRESS *sb.*[1] 11 a.

1362 [see PRESS *sb.*[1] 11 a]. **1398** TREVISA *Barth. De P.R.* XIX. lxxv. (1495) ll ij/2 Chese eten after meete thurstyth dounwarde þe meete as it were a pressour.

c. *fig.*

1426 LYDG. *De Guil. Pilgr.* 15897 In a pressour off gret peyne They kan ful offte A man dystreyne. *c* **1445** —— *Nightingale* 304 The strong pressour of oure Redempcioun, On whiche the bloode downe be his sides Ranne.

2. A clothes-press, a cupboard: = PRESS *sb.*[1] 15.

1471 in *Ripon Ch. Acts* (Surtees) 154 Unum pressur in alta camera mea. **1551** *Knaresborough Wills* (Surtees) I. 59 My sone to have one pressour. **1564** in *Wills & Inv. N.C.* (Surtees) I. 218, I geue him my pressor, my gownes my surpless, my ij furred amysis..and all other rayments apperteynyng vnto me.

presspahn ('prɛsʃpaːn, 'prɛspaːn). *Electr. Engin.* Also **press-spahn**. [a. G. *preßspahn* (now *-span*) pressboard, orig. pieces of card for pressing clothes f. *preß-* (in comb.) pressed, pressing + *span* shred, splinter.] Pressboard (sense 2).

1904 *Electr. Engineer* 14 Sept. 412/2 Creasing 'fibre, presspahn, etc.,' destroys the glazed surface..and is..likely to reduce its insulating value. **1913** BARR & ARCHIBALD *Design Alternating Current Machinery* ii. 39 Press-spahn, in thin sheets, is largely used for the insulation of low-voltage windings. **1938** W. T. MACCALL *Electr. Engin.* I. iii. 38 Many special forms of paper and cardboard, such as presspahn,..are used for moderate pressures.

'press-,paper. [ad. F. *presse-papier* (in *Dict. Acad.* 1878), f. *presse*, imperative or stem of *presser* to PRESS + *papier* paper.] A plain or ornamental weight with a flat base for pressing or securing loose papers; a paper-weight.

1821 PELLATT *Mem. Glass Manuf.* Expl. Plates 6 A solid square block of glass..to serve as a press paper or chimney ornament. [**1877** D. M. WALLACE *Russia* (ed. 2) I. 383 A library table, with ink-stand, presse-papier, paper-cutters, and other articles in keeping.]

press roll[1]. *Papermaking.* [f. PRESS *sb.*[1] + ROLL *sb.*[1]] (See quot. 1940.)

1881 J. DUNBAR *Pract. Papermaker* (ed. 2) 47 The author has tried a contrivance which effectually prevents the paper breaking at the press rolls. **1937** E. J. LABARRE *Dict. Paper* 195/1 *Press rolls* are pairs of heavy rolls, termed 'first', 'second', and 'third' press rolls according to their order in the paper-machine, serving to press out the water from the web of paper. **1940** *Chambers's Techn. Dict.* 671/1 *Press rolls* .., heavy cylinders of the paper-making machine which press out moisture from the wet web. Before the last pressing, the web is reversed in order to remove felt-marks.

press roll[2]. *Jazz.* [f. PRESS *sb.*[1] + ROLL *sb.*[2]] A drum-roll (see ROLL *sb.*[2] 2) in which the sticks are pressed against the drum-head.

1934 [see DRAG *sb.* 7 i]. **1939** W. HOBSON *Amer. Jazz Music* iii. 53 A 'press roll', one of the many rhythmic patterns which have been used by jazz drummers for years. **1956** S. LONGSTREET *Real Jazz* 148 A press roll is played on snare drums. **1966** *New Yorker* 11 June 153/1 Barbarin, in addition to a marvellous press roll, in which his sticks come at one another low from opposite edges of the snare in fat blurs, like gulls after the same clam, uses a high hat [etc.]. **1977** *Ibid.* 9 May 51/1 He principally used..powerful, accented press rolls on his snare drum.

'press-room[1]. [f. PRESS *sb.*[1] + ROOM *sb.*]

1. The room in a printing-office in which the presses stand, and where the printing is done.

1683 MOXON *Mech. Exerc.*, *Printing* ii. ¶ 1 The Roof and Sides of the Press Room. **1824** J. JOHNSON *Typogr.* II. viii. 222 The press-room should, if possible, be separated from the composing-room. **1882** J. SOUTHWARD *Pract. Printing* (1884) 411 The press-room is generally in the basement.

2. A room in which a press of any kind is kept.

1696 *Lond. Gaz.* No. 3186/4 That none but Persons of Quality, and those concerned in the Coinage, be permitted to enter the Melting-houses, Mill-rooms, Press-rooms. **1839** W. H. AINSWORTH *J. Sheppard* III. ix, The Press Room, a dark close chamber, near Waterman's Hall, obtained its name from an immense wooden machine kept in it, with which such prisoners as refused to plead to their indictments were pressed to death. **1839** URE *Dict. Arts* 863 The press-room at the Royal Mint contains eight machines. **1878** *Rep. Vermont Board Agric.* V. 79 At the end from the road were the press and wash rooms. **1966** P. V. PRICE *France: Food & Wine Guide* 164 Visitors see the pressroom ..and the huge stone container for 13,000 litres of wine.

3. A room reserved for the use of reporters.

1902 *Evening Star* (Washington D.C.) 16 Dec. III. 10/3 The press room at the District building is quite a center of interest. **1941** F. L. MOTT *Amer. Journalism* xxxv. 607 President Theodore Roosevelt..provided a press room and telephones for the reporters. **1943** L. C. WILSON in F. L. Mott *Journalism in Wartime* 99 Merrimann Smith, on the White House,..fills a notebook..and then he literally runs to the United Press telephone booth in the Press Room. **1952** F. L. MOTT *News in Amer.* xiii. 137 The doors were opened, and there was a grand rush for the telephones in the press-room and for taxis and cars. **1973** *Guardian* 19 Apr. 1/6 The President's sudden appearance last night in the White House press rooms. **1976** *National Observer* (U.S.) 31 Jan. 1/1 The press room..is a bit boggling. It is really a complex of rooms, encompassing a Western Union setup, a Sports Comm., Inc., service.., a bank of dictation phones, a wall of releases and handouts, and eight long rows of tables ..stacked with 125 typewriters. **1977** *Cleethorpes News* 6 May 7/2 She spent most of her time in the Press room before leaving through a small but enthusiastic crowd.

†**press-room**[2]. *Obs.* [f. PRESS *sb.*[2] + ROOM.] The cabin or apartment in which newly impressed men were confined.

1812 *Chron.* in *Ann. Reg.* 152/2 The new raised men on board the Neptune tender..broke through the pressroom, and took possession of the vessel.

press sail = *press of sail*: see PRESS *sb.*[1] 10.

press-spahn, var. PRESSPAHN.

press-stud. [f. PRESS *v.*[1] + STUD *sb.*[1]] A fastener made of metal, plastic, etc., used for joining two parts of a garment etc. together and consisting of two components, one with a short shank which is pressed into a corresponding hollow in the other. Also *attrib.*

1917 *Harrods Gen. Catal.* 1425/2 Press Studs, Black and White..2/9 per gross. **1928** *Daily Express* 19 Mar. 5/5 The chalk will leave an impression at exactly the correct place for the other half of the press-stud to be sewn. **1955** *Times* 29 June 12/4 A beautifully tucked skirt, complete even with a pink and white striped nylon petticoat kept in place by press studs attached to the dress. **1966** *Price List* (Olney Amsden & Sons Ltd.) 31 Press stud tape..22/6 doz. yards. **1974** *Drive* Autumn 32/2 Floor coverings used to be fixed by press studs. **1977** *Offshore Engineer* Apr. 74/2 The boot's normal strap and buckle fastening is backed up with a press-stud arrangement which allows the wearer to release it in two seconds.

pressumyt, obs. Sc. form of PRESUMED.

'press-up. [f. PRESS *v.*[1] + UP *adv.*[1]] An exercise in which the body is raised from a prone position by straightening the arms while keeping the hands and feet on the ground and the legs straight; (see also quot. 1961).

1947 J. BERTRAM *Shadow of War* 208 Press-ups are a fairly strenuous exercise at the best of times. **1955** M. E. B. BANKS *Commando Climber* iii. 33 We went through the usual climbing exercises such as press-ups with the finger tips and not the palms of the hands. **1956** KUNZLE & THOMAS *Freestanding* i. 22 Start with the feet on the third or fourth wall bar and do press-ups as before. **1961** J. S. SALAK *Dict. Amer. Sports* 341 *Press Up* (mountain climbing), an upward movement on rock completed by pressing down on the palms of the hands on large flat holds and ledges. **1967** *New Scientist* 28 Dec. 766/1 When we say that an athlete is 'fit', we generally mean that he can perform some arbitrary feat, like 50 press-ups, without getting unduly puffed. **1978** *Rugby World* Apr. 33/3 It's hard on the club coach who has to motivate players with whom he probably played and has to try to get one of his best friends to do another half-a-dozen sprints or extra press-ups.

'pressurage. *rare.* [a. F. *pressurage* the action of pressing, 'also, the fee thats due to th' owner, or giuen for th' vse, of a common wine-presse' (Cotgr. 1611), f. *pressurer* to press: see -AGE 3.] (See quot.)

1858 SIMMONDS *Dict. Trade*, *Pressurage*, the juice of the grape extracted by the press; a fee paid to the owner of a wine-press for its use. Hence in mod. Dicts.

'pressural, *a.* [f. next + -AL[1].] Of, pertaining to, or of the nature of pressure.

1890 in *Cent. Dict.* **1896** *N. Brit. Daily Mail* 17 Feb. 4 Arrangement for obtaining pressural disturbance through a considerable space of air.

pressure ('prɛʃ(j)ʊə(r), 'prɛʃə(r)), *sb.* [a. obs. F. *pressure* (12th c. in Godef.), ad. L. *pressūra*, f. *press-*, ppl. stem of *premĕre* to press: see -URE.]

I. 1. The action or fact of pressing; the fact or condition of being pressed (in the various senses of PRESS *v.*[1]); the exertion of continuous force upon or against a body by some other body in contact with it (the results being various according to the relative positions of the bodies, and the yielding or non-yielding nature of that which is pressed); compression, squeezing, crushing, etc.

1601 ? MARSTON *Pasquil & Kath.* III. 98 The pressure of my haires, or the puncture of my heart, stands at the seruice of your sollide perfections. **1602** —— *Ant. & Mel.* v. Wks. 1856 I. 66 In the soft pressure of a melting kisse. **1656** tr. *Hobbes' Elem. Philos.* (1839) 333 When two bodies having opposite endeavours, press one another, then the endeavour of either of them is that which we call pressure, and is mutual when their pressures are opposite. **1725** N. ROBINSON *Th. Physick* 308 Let every thing be remov'd, that may cause the least Pressure upon his Breast. **1744** BERKELEY *Siris* §46 The juice of olives or grapes issuing by the lightest pressure is best. **1815** SCOTT *Ld. of Isles* v. xix, Verdure meet For pressure of the fairies' feet. **1830** KATER & LARDNER *Mech.* v. 55 If motion be resisted, the effect is converted into pressure. *c* **1860** FARADAY *Forces Nat.* iv. 119 We can obtain heat..by the pressure of air. **1875** WHYTE MELVILLE *Riding Recoll.* xii. (1879) 216 They [blood-hounds] are sad cowards under pressure from a crowd.

2. a. *Physics.* The force exerted by one body on another by its weight, or by the continued application of power, viewed as a measurable quantity, the amount being expressed by the weight upon a unit area.

absolute pressure, the total pressure (of steam, etc.), found by adding the amount of the atmospheric pressure to that indicated by the ordinary steam-gauge (which shows the ***relative pressure***, or pressure above that of the atmosphere). ***pressure of the atmosphere***: see ATMOSPHERIC *pressure*. ***centre of pressure***: see CENTRE. ***high pressure***, ***low pressure***: see 8.

1660 BOYLE *New Exp. Phys. Mech.* xliii. Wks. 1772 I. 115 The conjecture..that perhaps the pressure of the air might have an interest in more phænomena than men have hitherto thought. **1739** LABELYE *Short Acc. Piers Westm. Bridge* 55 Buildings of very considerable Weight and Pressure are found to stand firm on such Foundations. **1774** GOLDSM. *Nat. Hist.* (1776) I. 186 If the vessel filled with water be forty feet high, the bottom of that vessel will sustain such a pressure as would raise the same water forty feet high. **1820** SCORESBY *Acc. Arctic Reg.* I. 191 At great depths, the effect of the pressure of the sea is not a little curious. **1827** N. ARNOTT *Physics* I. 337 In a fluid the pressure is in all directions. **1858** LARDNER *Hand-bk. Nat. Phil.*, etc. 287 Steam produced under a pressure of 35 atmospheres has the temperature of 419°. **1878** HUXLEY *Physiogr.* 91 The weight or pressure of the atmosphere is about 15 lbs. in every square inch. **1890** *Pall Mall G.* 18 Sept. 7/2 A final test ascertains what is called the 'pressure' of the powder—that is to say, its explosive impact upon the breech.

†**b.** In the Cartesian theory: = PRESSION 2. *Obs.*

1710 J. HARRIS *Lex. Techn.* II, *Pressure*, by this word some Philosophers, addicted to the Cartesian Hypothesis, mean a kind of Motion which is impressed upon and propagated through a Fluid Medium.

c. In *Electricity*: see quots. 1907.

1889 *Nature* 24 Oct. 630/2 Currents of high tension are converted into pressures suitable for incandescent lamps by means of transformers. **1907** *Regulations Use Electrical Energy under Factory and Workshop Act 1901* In these Regulations..*Pressure* means the difference of electrical potential between any two conductors, or between a conductor and earth, as read by a hot wire or electrostatic volt-meter. **1907** A. P. TROTTER in *Let.*, *Electrical pressure* is used officially in Acts of Parliament and in Regulations, in preference to *electromotive force* (which is neither electromotive nor force). But the relation between 'electrical pressure' and the ordinary pressure of mechanics or dynamics is nothing more than an analogy; the same may be said of *tension* which some prefer. Strictly speaking, *pressure, tension*, and *force* apply only to matter. In reference to Electricity, all these terms mean 'That which causes or tends to cause an electric current'.

d. ***pressure of canvas, sail*** = press of canvas: see PRESS *sb.*[1] 10.

1823 SCORESBY *Jrnl. Whale Fish.* 3 By carrying a pressure of canvas, we were enabled to weather the Calf of Man.

†**3.** (?) That which is pressed or prepared by pressing: see quots. *Obs.*

1486 *Bk. St. Albans* c vij b, Take pressure made of a lombe that was borne in vntyme..and put it in a gut of a coluer and fede her therwith. **1727** BRADLEY *Fam. Dict.* s.v. *Back-worm*, Take a Pressure made of a Lamb that was slink'd, and make thereof two or three Pieces, which put into the Gut of a Dove or the like Fowl, and feed your Hawk therewith.

†**4.** *fig.* The mark, form, or character impressed; impression, image, stamp. *Obs.*

1602 SHAKS. *Ham.* I. v. 100 Yea, from the Table of my Memory, Ile wipe away..all presures past, That youth and obseruation coppied there. *Ibid.* III. ii. 27 To shew Vertue her owne Feature..and the verie Age and Bodie of the Time, his forme and pressure. **1809** MALKIN *Gil Blas* v. i. ¶ 53 No sooner did I cast my eyes on her face, than I knew ..the very form and pressure of Lucinda.

II. 5. The action of pressing painfully upon the sensations or feelings; the condition of being painfully pressed in body or mind; the weight or burden of pain, grief, trouble, poverty, etc.; affliction, oppression.

(The earliest sense in Eng.; also in 12th c. in OF.)

1382 Wyclif *John* xvi. 21 Whanne sche hath borun a sone, now sche thenkith not on the pressure [*gloss* or charge; Vulg. *pressuræ*], for ioye, for a man is borun in to the world. **1447** Bokenham *Seyntys* (Roxb.) 176 Thorgh thi greth grace and cheryte In alle the pressurs of my chyldyng. **1526** *Pilgr. Perf.* (W. de W. 1531) 57 b, In all perylles, temptacyons, pressures, & necessitees. *c* **1586** C'tess Pembroke *Ps.* cxix. S. ii, In presure and in paine My joyes thy preceptes give. **1662** R. Mathew *Unl. Alch.* p. viii, His Fatherly chastening of pains, sicknesses, and bodily pressures. **1667** *Decay Chr. Piety* viii. ¶ 19 Job, whom we find not so often nor so passionately complaining of any of his pressures, as of the unkind censures of his friends. **1794** Mrs. Radcliffe *Myst. Udolpho* viii, Emily struggled against the pressure of grief. **1889** Gretton *Memory's Harkb.* 97 He said..that the mental pressure and excitement was far the worst; it robbed him of his sleep.

†**6. a.** The action of political or economic burdens; a heavy charge; the state or condition of being weighed down or oppressed by these. *Obs.*

1616 Bullokar *Eng. Expos.*, *Pressure*, an oppression. **1628** Sir H. Martin in Rushw. *Hist. Coll.* (1659) I. 581 The pressures and grievances of the people, with the easie remedies. **1642** *Ibid.* iii. (1692) I. 641 Detaining our Arms, destroying our Trade and Markets, with many more Pressures upon us than we are willing to repeat. **1647** Clarendon *Hist. Reb.* i. §8 A proportion (how contemptible soever in respect of the pressures now every day imposed,) never before heard of in Parliament. *a* **1715** Burnet *Own Time* (1823) II. 422 He [Baillie] thought it was lawful for subjects, being under such pressures, to try how they might be relieved from them. **1719** W. Wood *Surv. Trade* 113 That our Goods were first sent into Holland, Flanders, Italy, &c., and afterwards into France, under the pressures of the high duties.

b. A state of trouble or embarrassment; stress, strain; *pl.* straits, difficulties. In *Finance*, forces (*on* a currency) tending towards a change in its value.

1648 Gage *West. Ind.* 68 The Common-wealth hath soon fallen into heavy pressures and troubles. **1727** Swift *Wonder of Wond.* Wks. 1755 II. ii. 53 In all urgent necessities and pressures he applies himself to these deities. **1817** Jas. Mill *Brit. India* III. vi. i. 47 The finances of the Company were in their usual state of extreme pressure and embarrassment. **1868** M. E. G. Duff *Pol. Surv.* 202 The summer of 1868 is remembered as a period of financial pressure. **1961** *N.Y. Times* 5 July 31 Throughout 'The Making of a President' Mr. White shows wonderfully well how the pressures pile up on candidates. **1964** *Ann. Reg. 1963* 203 Pressure on the peso..became so strong in May that the authorities could no longer resist it. **1976** *Times* 30 Mar. 4/4 Not that they do not want freedom; but it brings pressures and choices with which they find it hard to cope. **1976** *Howard Jrnl.* XV. i. 13 There may also be cases in which a period of detention is necessary as a respite from problems or pressures that will otherwise entrap the offender in greater trouble. **1977** A. Ecclestone *Staircase for Silence* v. 95 As a sensitive man he registered the pressures which were..shaping men to make choices which would carry them to such lengths.

c. Urgency; demand of affairs on one's time or energies.

1812 *Q. Rev.* May 159 At the end of the same session, the third bill, from the pressure of business, was given up without having come to a final hearing. **1845** Disraeli *Sybil* iv. xiii, Another day: I have a great pressure of affairs at present. **1861** Dickens *Lett.* 9 Jan., I write under the pressure of occupation and business. **1885** Austin Dobson *Steele* Introd. 46 Writing hastily and under pressure, his language is frequently involved and careless. **1911** D. H. Lawrence *White Peacock* iii. v. 442 In spite of his pressure of business he had become a County Councillor. **1926** S. Jameson *Three Kingdoms* x. 292 She worked on with an aching heart on the evenings when pressure of business kept her in the office until it was too late even to see Sandy before he was in bed and asleep. **1938** R. C. Hutchinson *Testament* i. vi. 60 They were supposed to undergo examination every week, but that, from the pressure on the doctors' time, was often omitted. **1960** E. Stopp tr. *St. François de Sales's Sel. Lett.* 238, I can see that it is hopeless to wait for a better opportunity, since continual pressure of affairs seems to be my fate.

7. a. The action of moral or mental force, or of anything that influences the mind or will; constraining influence.

1625 Bacon *Ess.*, *Unity in Relig.* (Arb.) 433 It was a notable Obseruation of a wise Father..That those, which held and perswaded pressure of Consciences, were commonly interessed therin. **1656** Earl Monm. tr. *Boccalini's Advts. fr. Parnass.* ii. ii. (1674) 135 Rebelling against their natural Lords, at the pressure of Forrein Princes. **1791** Mrs. Radcliffe *Rom. Forest* i, His virtue, such as it was, could not stand the pressure of occasion. **1792** D. Stewart *Philos. Hum. Mind* I. iv. viii. 270 In every state of society..the multitude has..acted from the immediate impulse of passion, or from the pressure of their wants and necessities. **1860** Warter *Sea-board* II. 8 The pressure from without will be a benefit to outlying clergy. **1949** *Sun* (Baltimore) 7 Feb. 8/2 There is no doubting the fortitude the Norwegians show thus far against Russian pressure. **1964** Gould & Kolb *Dict. Social Sci.* 530/2 [S. E. Finer] reserves the term pressure for those activities..which amount to the 'application or threatened application of a sanction should a demand be refused'. **1966** *Listener* 19 May 713/1 The effects of the sort of social pressures described by Professor Sprott depend largely on the age of the person, the length of time they last, and their intensity. **1976** *Times* 30 Mar. 4/2 The Conservative Party should resist well intentioned pressures to spell out in detail what it would do when it won a general election.

b. *to bring pressure* (*to bear*): to exert influence to a specific end; *to bring* (or *put*) *pressure on* (someone): to urge or press (someone) strongly in order to persuade.

1864 W. Hardman *Let.* 21 Apr. in S. M. Ellis *Lett. & Mem. Sir W. Hardman* (1925) 172 Some pressure had evidently been brought to bear. **1897** Miss Broughton *Dear Faustina* xv, I really have some influence with her..if I put pressure on, I really have a good deal. **1908** A. F. Bentley *Process of Govt.* x. 208 We frequently talk of 'bringing pressure to bear' upon someone, and we can use the word here with but slight extension beyond this common meaning. Pressure, as we shall use it, is always a group phenomenon. **1912** T. Dreiser *Financier* xlv. 489 He thought once of going to Mrs. Cowperwood and having her bring pressure to bear on her husband. **1934** *Amer. Speech* IX. 11/2 *To put on the pressure* is to run the cards of a long suit in an effort to force the discard of cards which might otherwise win tricks. **1937** *Sun* (Baltimore) 22 July 1/5 Republic Steel Corporation officials and leaders of a local back-to-work movement and of a law and order league brought sustained 'pressure' on city officials of an Ohio town, seeking the use of force in reopening strike-bound mills. **1960** L. P. Hartley *Facial Justice* iii. 25 These dissidents brought pressure to bear on their Governments to leave the upper air alone. **1961** *Times-Picayune* (New Orleans) 1 Jan. ii. 3 This might be done to arouse those who have been squeezed out by the trims to exert pressure on the Legislature, so it would be more receptive to a tax proposal later in the year.

III. 8. a. high pressure. orig. A pressure higher than that of the atmosphere, said in reference to steam-engines, but now only a relative term without any absolute limits: esp. in reference to compound engines in which the steam is used at different pressures in the different cylinders; mostly *attrib.*, as in ***high-pressure cylinder, engine, steam***, etc. **b.** *transf.* of speed, work, business, conditions of life, etc., and in *Pathol.*, as a ***high-pressure pulse***. **c.** In *Meteorol.* said of a dense condition of the atmosphere over a certain region, indicated by a high barometer, as in ***high-pressure area, high-p. system*** (of winds). So **low pressure**, of the steam-engine, and in *Pathol.* and *Meteorol.*

1824 R. Stuart *Hist. Steam Engine* 67 To supersede the high-pressure engines. **1833** N. Arnott *Physics* (ed. 5) II. i. 97 In proportion as the fluid is more condensed—high-pressure steam is merely condensed steam, just as high-pressure air is condensed air; and to obtain a double or triple pressure, we must have twice or thrice the quantity of steam under the same volume. *Ibid.* [see low *a.* 20]. **1851** *Illustr. Catal. Gt. Exhib.* 212 High-pressure oscillating steam-engine. *Ibid.* 213 Self-acting..damper, for high and low pressure steam. **1890** Webster s.v. *Compound*, The steam that has been used in a high-pressure cylinder is made to do further service in a larger low-pressure cylinder.

b. 1838 *New Monthly Mag.* LII. 448 The importation of the battu,..by which the slaughter of game is achieved with a high-pressure velocity, is another illustration of the same truth. **1839** Stonehouse *Axholme* p. xi, A small freeholder, who was working under the high pressure of a stiff mortgage. **1862** T. C. Grattan *Beaten Paths* II. 3 The high-pressure engine of refinement is always furnished with a safety-valve against the danger of explosion. **1888** Mrs. H. Ward *R. Elsmere* xx, As for Robert, he, of course, was living at high pressure all round. **1895** *Daily News* 31 Oct. 6/6 There was no high pressure work going on, and no high pressure oratory. **1897** Low-pressure pulse [see low *a.* 20]. **1901** *Daily Chron.* 25 Dec. 5/1 The strain of another high-pressure Session like that of last year.

c. *c* **1891** *Daily News* 9 Feb. 2/7 About the middle of last week a large high-pressure system spread over the United Kingdom from the southward. **1900** *Westm. Gaz.* 27 Aug. 4/2 A high-pressure area lies over our northern regions, but a depression exists over the west of France.

IV. 9. *attrib.* and *Comb.* **a.** of pressure, as ***pressure drop, gradient, height, stage***; **b.** used to indicate or ascertain the amount of pressure exerted, as ***pressure-anemometer, transducer***. **c.** worked by means of pressure, as ***pressure fan, pump, valve***; **d.** caused by pressure, as ***pressure-displacement, -figure, -forging, sensation, -sign, -symptom***; **e.** for pressing, or causing pressure, as ***pressure-ball, -bandage, -bottle, -box, -forceps, -frame, -screw***; **f.** objective and obj. gen., as ***pressure-fixing, -reciprocating, -relieving, -reducing, -retaining*** adjs.; ***pressure-reducer***. **g.** other Combs.: ***pressure-sensitive*** adj.

1898 *Westm. Gaz.* 24 Jan. 7/2 Passing a current of air by means of indiarubber *pressure-balls through a glass bottle full of glass shavings steeped in sulphuric acid. **1897** *Allbutt's Syst. Med.* II. 232 The application of *pressure bandages is very useful. **1899** *Ibid.* VII. 239 In its turn it is attached by a T-tube, to a *pressure bottle. **1882** *Rep. to Ho. Repr. Prec. Met. U.S.* 626 In order to utilize the pressure due to the elevated position..the water is conducted from the ditches into a tank called the '*pressure box'. **1903** Agnes M. Clerke *Astrophysics* 38 *Pressure-displacements and motion-displacements are, in fact, respectively concerned. **1949** O. G. Sutton *Sci. of Flight* i. 14 The solution of practical problems, such as the determination of the *pressure-drop in pipes. **1964** J. C. Catford in D. Abercrombie et al. *Daniel Jones* 31 For normal voice the liminal pressure-drop across the glottis is of the order of 3 cm of water. *c* **1890** W. H. Casmey *Ventilation* 7 The *pressure fan..used where a small volume of air at a high velocity of pressure is required. **1899** *Allbutt's Syst. Med.* VIII. 821 Excision associated with the rapid application of the *pressure forceps. **1875** Knight *Dict. Mech.*, *Printing-frame* (Photography), also known as a *pressure-frame. **1918** *Meteorol. Gloss.* (Met. Office), *Gradient wind*, the flow of air which is necessary to balance the *pressure-gradient. **1968** R. A. Lyttleton *Mysteries Solar Syst.* i. 27 For a heated gas-cloud rotating round the sun, there can be a pressure-gradient perpendicularly away from the general equatorial plane of the distribution. **1899** *Allbutt's Syst. Med.* VII. 253 At a certain *pressure-height the fluid meniscus exhibits maximal pulsations. **1881** *Nature* 15 Dec. 167 The total work done by a fluid *pressure-reciprocating engine. **1889** *Electrical Rev.* XXV. 583 An accumulator is..merely a chemical converter which is unequalled as a *pressure-reducer. **1934** Webster, *Pressure-reducing, adj. **1950** *Sci. News Let.* XV. 79 The liquids are displaced from the tanks by an inert gas. Nitrogen, stored under a high pressure and fed to the tanks through pressure-reducing valves, is commonly used for this purpose. **1971** B. Scharf *Engin. & its Lang.* xii. 177 Pressure control valves may be pressure-reducing valves which maintain reduced pressure on the downstream side (i.e. after the valve), *pressure-retaining valves which maintain the pressure on the upstream side, and indirect pressure control valves to maintain the pressure at a point other than in the line in which the valve is located. **1895** *Amer. Jrnl. Psychol.* VII. 81 *Druckempfindung*, *pressure sensation. **1901** [see contact *sb.* 1 d]. **1932** *Mind* XLI. 363 Whenever I touch anything I have pressure-sensations with a characteristic local sign. **1937** *Jrnl. Exper. Psychol.* XX. 458 There were relatively more *pressure sensitive spots on the dorsal side of the arm than on the ventral side. **1970** *New Yorker* 3 Oct. 108/3 Repair the damage with pressure-sensitive tape. **1880** Barwell *Aneurism* 41 The *pressure symptoms of innominate aneurisms are very variable. **1949** *Jrnl. Sci. Instruments* XXVI. 327/2 (*caption*) Final form of electronic *pressure transducer. **1956** *Nature* 25 Feb. 380/1 The time it takes for the wave to cover a known distance was measured by means of two barium titanate crystal pressure-transducers. **1963** H. K. P. Neubert *Instrument Transducers* iv. 348 Through the year the main application of piezoelectric pressure transducers has been the 'engine indicator' for use with internal-combustion engines, which employs quartz disks or piles of disks. **1897** *Weekly Sun* 19 Sept. 15/2 It is forced down by the tremendous *pressure-valves into a small chamber within the tank.

10. Special Combs.: **pressure arch** *Mining*, a distribution of pressure over an excavation resembling that in a structural arch, caused by increased pressure on the side walls of the excavation, which act as abutments supporting the strata forming the roof; **pressure-bar**, a device in a planing-machine for holding down the material to be planed; **pressure-blower**, a blower for producing a blast in which the air is driven by the pressure of pistons; **pressure-boiler**, a boiler designed to withstand great pressure, for heating liquids above the normal boiling point; **pressure breathing** (see quot. 1965); **pressure broadening** *Physics*, pressure-dependent broadening of spectral lines caused by collisions of emitting molecules with their neighbours in a fluid; so **pressure-broadened** *a.*; **pressure-button**, a 'button' or stud, by pressing which a spring is liberated or an electric bell rung; **pressure cabin**, in an aircraft, an airtight cabin in which the air is maintained at a pressure safe and comfortable for the occupants; **pressure cable** *Electr. Engin.*, a paper-insulated cable that contains gas or oil under pressure within the outer sheath or pipe, in order to counteract the tendency of the oil to move away from the conductors in operating conditions and enable higher voltages to be used; **pressure chamber**, a chamber designed to hold material under pressure, or in which pressure can be applied; **pressure-cylinder**, the cylinder of the pressure-gauge of an engine; **pressure (die-)casting**, die-casting in which the metal is forced into the mould under pressure; a casting so made; so **pressure-cast** *a.*; **pressure drag** *Aeronaut.*, the drag on a moving body which results from the aerodynamic pressure distribution over its surface; form drag; **pressure-engine**, a machine driven by the pressure of a column of water, esp. one in which the piston of a cylinder is driven by water-power; a hydraulic engine; **pressure-filter**, a filter in which the liquid is forced through filtering material by pressure greater than that of its own weight; **pressure-flaker**, a pointed bone tool used for pressure-flaking; **pressure flaking** *Archæol.*, the flaking of flint tools by applying pressure with a hard point; hence **pressure-flaked** *a.*, shaped in this way; **pressure flask**, a flask designed to withstand pressure greater than that of the atmosphere; **pressure-gauge, -gage**, an instrument for showing the pressure of an elastic agent, as steam or gas; also, one for showing the pressure in a cannon or fire-arm at the instant of explosion of the charge; **pressure heater**, an apparatus for heating water, etc., by steam under pressure; **pressure hold** *Mountaineering*, a hold maintained by the exertion of sideways or downward pressure; **pressure hull**, the hull (or part of the hull) of a submarine which is designed to withstand the pressure of the sea when the vessel is submerged; **pressure jump** *Meteorol.*, a mobile zone of atmospheric disturbance, characterized by a steep pressure gradient and usu. marking a discontinuity in the height of an inversion layer; so ***pressure-jump line***; **pressure lamp**, a portable oil or paraffin lamp in which the fuel is forced up into the mantle or burner by the air pressure in an enclosed reservoir, which is increased by pumping with a built-in plunger; **pressure line** = *pressure ridge*; **pressure microphone**, a microphone which responds to the instantaneous pressure of sound waves; **pressure mine**, a mine designed to be activated by the temporary reduction in hydrostatic pressure caused by a passing ship; **pressure-note**, *Mus.* a note marked with a crescendo; **pressure pack, package**, a dispenser containing a substance, freq. an aerosol, under pressure; so **pressure-packaged** *ppl. a.*; **pressure-packaging** *vbl. sb.*; **pressure pad**, a pad designed to transmit or absorb pressure; **pressure paralysis**, paralysis caused by pressure on part of the brain; **pressure pattern**, a pattern of prevailing atmospheric pressures; usu. *attrib.*, as ***pressure-pattern flying***, denoting the use of air routes which enable aircraft to take advantage of the air currents associated with such patterns to economize on fuel or time; **pressure-pipe**, the pipe of the pressure-gauge of a steam-engine; **pressure pouch** = PHARYNGOCELE; **pressure-register**, a recording pressure-gauge, particularly one that records the fluctuations of pressure of air, steam, or gas; **pressure ridge**, a ridge caused by pressure; *esp.* a ridge of ice in the polar seas caused by lateral pressure; **pressure saucepan** = PRESSURE COOKER a; **pressure sore** *Med.*, a sore produced by continued pressure on a part of the body; **pressure-spot** = PRESSURE POINT 1; **pressure stove**, a portable stove supplied with oil or paraffin under pressure; **pressure suit**, a garment that can be made airtight and inflated to protect the wearer against low ambient pressure (as in high-altitude flight); **pressure tank**, a tank in which a fluid, esp. fuel, is held under pressure; **pressure tendency** *Meteorol.* = *barometric tendency*; **pressure-tight** *a.*, (of a joint, container, or the like), tightly enough constructed to prevent the passage of a fluid under pressure; hence **pressure-tightness**; **pressure vessel**, a vessel designed to contain material at high pressures; esp. in a nuclear reactor, a vessel containing the reactor core immersed in the pressurized coolant; **pressure wave**, a wave consisting of a sudden change in pressure propagated through a medium; **pressure welding**, welding in which pressure is applied to the parts to be joined; welding brought about by pressure. Also PRESSURE COOKER, PRESSURE(-)FEED *v.* and *sb.*, etc.

1950 FERRARI & WARDELL in E. Mason *Pract. Coal Mining* I. ix. 145/2 Props and bars, chocks and cutter nogs, all of which can be withdrawn and reset, are used for carrying the weight of stone inside the *pressure arch. **1958** A. NELSON *Methods of Working* iv. 32 A true pressure arch can only exist underground where two side abutments exist, each being strong enough to support its share of the load on the arch and also to provide the lateral thrust necessary for its stability. **1973** L. J. THOMAS *Introd. Mining* viii. 340 The recommendation of the committee was that stalls should be limited to three-quarters of the width of the pressure arch for stability, and that pillar width should be equal to stall width. **1884** KNIGHT *Dict. Mech.* Suppl. s.v., The long suits of the Woodworth and the Woodbury Patents were upon *pressure bars and pressure rollers. **1891** S. P. SADTLER *Hand-bk. Industr. Org. Chem.* v. 179 Three grammes of substance are placed in a small beaker (preferably of metal), which is placed as one of several in a Soxhlet *pressure-boiler, or the test is carried out in the Lintner pressure-flask, —and heated to the temperature of boiling water. **1952** A. HUXLEY *Let.* 20 May (1969) 644, I have had no return of my iritis and, thanks to the newly invented *pressure-breathing treatment,..have practically eliminated the slight chronic bronchitis. **1965** *Gloss. Aeronaut. Terms* (*B.S.I.*) XVII. 3 *Pressure breathing*, a technique in which oxygen is supplied to the lungs at a pressure higher than the ambient barometric pressure. **1936** *Rev. Mod. Physics* VIII. 48/2 These *pressure-broadened lines show the expected larger shifts and half-widths. **1970** A. F. HARVEY *Coherent Light* xxv. 1095 For most atmospheric phenomena the pressure-broadened line is appropriate. **1932** *Physical Rev.* XXXIX. 860 The pressure shift of spectral lines, unexplained by the usual theories of *pressure broadening. **1967** W. R. HINDMARSH *Atomic Spectra* viii. 86 The three main causes of line-broadening are: the natural width of atomic energy levels..; Doppler width..; and collision, or pressure broadening. **1893** *Star* 19 May 1/8 The new electric bells.. the substitution of *pressure buttons for the existing lever pulls. **1935** *Jrnl. R. Aeronaut. Soc.* XXXIX. 1045 *Pressure cabins and/or free oxygen in the cabins are both being experimented with today. **1948** 'N. SHUTE' *No Highway* iv. 109 They..went into the rear fuselage, behind the pressure cabin. **1965** J. D. STORER *Behind Scenes in Aircraft Factory* iii. 33 A door in a normal pressure cabin would have to withstand an outward load of some seven tons. **1931** M. HOCHSTADTER et al. in *Jrnl. R. Soc. Arts* LXXX. 95 The utilisation of an impregnated paper cable..could be greatly increased if it were possible to get rid of the heterogeneity in the dielectric, or to render it harmless so far as the time-voltage curve and stability are concerned... It is possible to do this (a) By the use of a very thin impregnating oil and the provision of channels along the cable... (b) By radial compression of the cable in such a way that the radial 'breathing' is reversible at all temperatures, such vacuous spaces as tend to form being closed by the compression or the pressure in them raised to such an extent that no ionisation takes place. The latter alternative leads to the '*Pressure Cable'. **1966** *IEEE Trans. Power Apparatus & Syst.* LXXXV. 375 (*heading*) A few aspects of the general problem concerning tightness of connections formed by pressure cables. **1973** J. G. TWEEDDALE *Materials Technol.* II. ii. 41 A *pressure-cast material is likely to be..more uniformly consistent in structure than other cast materials. **1979** MILLS & MANSFIELD *Genuine Article* iv. 71 'Beirut Sovereigns.' Untold numbers of these superb pressure cast forgeries now adulterate the market. **1922** *Proc. Inst. Mech. Engin.* I. 27 *Pressure castings in iron though not yet out of the experimental stage, would..tend to eliminate holes due to occluded air or shrinkage. **1933** *Iron Age* 30 Nov. 18/1 Brass pressure castings are subject to porosity in the same manner that zinc and aluminum die castings are subject to porosity. **1973** J. G. TWEEDDALE *Materials Technol.* II. ii. 42 (*caption*) Systems for pressure casting. (a) Gravity pressure. (b) Gas pressure. (c) Mechanical pressure. (d) Centrifugal pressure. (e) Another system for using centrifugal pressure. **1915** *Jrnl. Chem. Soc.* CVIII. II. 820 A press is described.. which by means of a lower cylinder with narrow holes bored vertically in it forces a molten solid out of the *pressure chamber and so causes a sudden drop in pressure. **1934** *Jrnl. Cellular & Compar. Physiol.* V. 335 A pressure chamber was constructed which permits of viscosity measurements by the 'centrifuge method' at high hydrostatic pressures. **1966** *Lancet* 24 Dec. 1406/1 A small brass pressure chamber was constructed of about 20 ml. capacity. **1898** *Westm. Gaz.* 19 Nov. 2/3 Whilst carrying out a speed trial..the *pressure cylinder burst, and the engineer..got badly scalded. **1919** *Bull. Amer. Inst. Mining Engin.* Feb. 240 On fracture, the *pressure die casting will be found to consist of a dense closely grained outer stratum and a porous inner stratum. **1933** *Machinery* XXXIX. 781/1 Pressure die-castings do not have a homogeneous structure, but, upon fracture, exhibit a dense fine-grained exterior and a coarser grained interior. **1973** J. G. TWEEDDALE *Materials Technol.* II. ii. 8 We have..injection moulding technologists concerned only with pressure-die-casting of thermo-plastic polymers. **1950** KUETHE & SCHETZER *Found. Aerodynamics* xii. 212 Two types of drag, form or *pressure drag and skin friction, are evident in the flow of a viscous incompressible fluid past a body. **1959** F. D. ADAMS *Aeronaut. Dict.* 79/1 Inasmuch as pressure drag is a function of form, form drag and pressure drag are sometimes considered synonymous. **1961** H. H. KOELLE *Handbk. Astronaut. Engin.* v. 23 In ideal, inviscid, and incompressible two-dimensional flow there is no pressure drag. The sum of the pressure-force components in the free-stream direction is zero. **1815** *Chron.* in *Ann. Reg.* 91/1 A new steam boiler, worked by what is called a *pressure engine of about six horse power. **1853** GLYNN *Power Water* 96 By the pressure-engine and the turbine, the power of waterfalls of any height..may at once be made available. **1874** KNIGHT *Dict. Mech.*, *Filtering-press*, a *pressure-filter. **1934** *Geogr. Jrnl.* LXXXIII. 302 A knife of neolithic age, *pressure-flaked from tabular chert. **1959** J. D. CLARK *Prehist. S. Afr.* vi. 161 Small pressure-flaked points shaped like equilateral triangles. **1954** S. PIGGOTT *Neolithic Cultures Brit. Isles* ii. 43 The same floor produced three antler tines, and Floor 58..another, associated with a heap of minute flakes, indicating their use as *pressure-flakers. **1927** PEAKE & FLEURE *Hunters & Artists* 49 The new technique..includes a high finish by the process of *pressure-flaking, that is to say the removal of small thin flakes by pressing near the edge with a bone tool rather than by striking with another stone. **1949** K. P. OAKLEY *Man the Tool-Maker* v. 29 Some of the tribes..dress spearheads by pressure-flaking. **1959** J. D. CLARK *Prehist. S. Afr.* vi. 157 The finish is much finer and pressure flaking is frequently used. **1891** *Pressure flask [see *pressure boiler* above]. **1967** *Oceanogr. & Marine Biol.* V. 188 Pressure flask for studying plants under a few atm. **1862** *Catal. Internat. Exhib.* II. XIII. 17 The Deep-Sea *Pressure-Gauge. **1879** *Cassell's Techn. Educ.* IV. 211 Some mode of indicating at any moment the exact pressure which the steam exerts, and this we learn by means of the 'pressure-gauge'. **1896** *Rep. Aerated Bread Co.* 11 The little boiler which is generally termed the *pressure heater. **1941** T. A. H. PEACOCKE *Mountaineering* iv. 46 Sideways *pressureholds, with the palms of the hands pointing down, should be used as much as possible. **1955** J. E. B. WRIGHT *Technique of Mountaineering* Pl. 10 (*caption*) Last man on Kern Knotts Crack using plimsolls for pressure holds for feet. **1975** W. UNSWORTH *Encycl. Mountaineering* 120/1 Pressure holds are holds where there in no grip as such and one relies on the friction of the rock. **1923** *Man. Seamanship* (Admiralty) II. 171 Situated on the *pressure hull..is what is known as the 'diver's connection'. **1966** *McGraw-Hill Encycl. Sci. & Technol.* XIII. 211/2 The pressure hull, comprising all of the inner and part of the outer hull, is the strong hull that resists external sea pressure. **1974** L. DEIGHTON *Spy Story* xx. 210 The crash came like a sledgehammer pounded against the hollow steel of the pressure hull... Obviously some dire damage had been done to the submarine. **1950** M. TEPPER in *Jrnl. Meteorol.* VII. 21 It is proposed that a squall line might be considered as a disturbance generated by accelerations along the cold front and which travels along the warm sector inversion as a gravitational wave. It is recommended that any series of meteorological events similar to this mechanism be called a *Pressure Jump Line. *Ibid.* 23/1 The leading edge of this pressure gradient, which shall be referred to as the pressure jump, is clearly defined on the maps, seems to undulate rather violently, and moves in a non-uniform manner. **1955** *Sci. News Let.* 12 Mar. 170/2 This squall line is also known as a pressure jump line, since a sudden rise in barometric pressure always accompanies it. **1963** E. R. REITER *Jet-Stream Meteorol.* iv. 271 We may.. point out some..research work..which makes a pressure jump that travels as a gravity wave along the inversion between moist and dry air responsible for the formation of squall lines and tornadoes. **1967** *Oceanogr. & Marine Biol.* V. 42 Sudden rises in sea level..have been experienced occasionally at coastal locations with the passage over the sea of a moving squall line or pressure jump. **1939–40** *Army & Navy Stores Catal.* 279 'Tilley' lamps... A '*pressure' lamp. **1958** L. DURRELL *Balthazar* vii. 154 A whole encampment..had sprung up in the darkness, fitfully lit by oil and paraffin stoves, by pressure lamps and braziers. **1974** J. WAINWRIGHT *Hard Hit* 150 The white-hot mantle of the pressure-lamp. **1909** *Daily Chron.* 3 Sept. 1/2 Much of our hard work was lost in circuitous twists around troublesome *pressure lines and high, irregular fields of very old ice. **1934** OLSON & MASSA *Appl. Acoustics* v. 93 If the response corresponds to the variations in pressure of the medium, it is termed a *pressure microphone. **1966** *McGraw-Hill Encycl. Sci. & Technol.* VIII. 360/1 Pressure microphones are inherently nondirectional (omnidirectional), because pressure is a scalar and not a vector quantity. **1949** J. S. COWIE *Mines, Minelayers & Minelaying* viii. 162 The Germans, meanwhile, had played their last card, the 'Oyster' or *pressure mine. **1957** *Encycl. Brit.* XV. 535/1 Since pressure mines are fired by the reduced water pressure produced by a ship passing over them, the best method of sweeping them is to simulate the passage of a ship by towing a large, expendable target over them. **1969** *New Scientist* 28 Aug. 421/2 In fairways that are not more than 100 or 200 feet deep, the pressure mines are a special hazard. **1958** HERZKA & PICKTHALL *Pressurized Packaging* (*Aerosols*) iv. 78 The first *pressure packs marketed in Great Britain were packed in aluminium dispensers which monopolized the British market until the advent of the all-tinplate dispenser in 1955. **1959** *News Chron.* 30 June 6/5 The pressure-pack has no screw-cap and the dispensing valve automatically seals itself after use. **1966** HARRIS & PLATT in A. Herzka *Internat. Encycl. Pressurized Packaging* vi. 81 In the case of the pressure pack..the basic source of energy is provided by the propellant, which may be either compressed or liquefied gas. **1958** *Food Technol.* XII. 331/1 Results of one or both of the above mentioned methods will indicate whether the existing product is applicable to the *pressure package. **1957** *Mod. Packaging* Dec. 156/2 Many foods that are *pressure packaged cannot be subjected to heat without quality loss and thus must be refrigerated. **1959** *News Chron.* 30 June 6/3 A familiar product..is the pressure-packaged insecticide. **1957** *Mod. Packaging* Dec. 156/2 Most foods that have application to *pressure packaging will require some sort of preservation treatment. **1912** *Machinery* 31 Oct. 148/2 The shell stripper..also acts as the spring *pressure pad during the drawing operation. **1941** C. W. HINMAN *Pressworking Metals* vi. 75 The power of compression is adjusted by nuts beneath a pressure pad at the lower end of the casing. **1969** *Times* 7 Mar. 15/1 A group of research workers in California claims to have discovered a way of presenting visual information to blind people through an array of pressure pads which vibrate against the skin of their backs. **1979** B. FREEMANTLE *Charlie Muffin's Uncle Sam* xvi. 146 Battery-operated bells..rang if.. anyone..stepped on one of the pressure pads..around the display cases. **1899** *Allbutt's Syst. Med.* VI. 658 *Pressure paralysis for the most part is rapidly recovered from. **1946** *Sci. News Let.* 2 Nov. 278/2 A new technique, '*pressure pattern flying', is now available to air pilots on the Atlantic route from Europe... This new technique consists in determining the shortest flight-time path to the destination by a series of late accurate reports..which locates pressure areas and enables a pilot to take advantage of the airflow circulating around them. **1954** *N.Y. Times* 6 June II. 31/2 During the past eight years Trans World Airlines pilots flying over the Atlantic..have mastered the techniques of getting maximum range from their planes by flying 'pressure patterns'. **1962** G. D. P. WORTHINGTON *Flight Planning* iv. 53 The study of pressure pattern flying and the increasing knowledge being obtained of jet streams has made it apparent that the shortest route is not always the quickest or most economical. **1889** *Pall Mall G.* 27 Nov. 4/3 During her gun trials the *pressure pipe, which was 8 feet long, burst. No one was hurt. **1897** *Allbutt's Syst. Med.* III. 363 *Pressure pouches, though often called œsophageal, in reality arise from the lower part of the pharynx. **1897** *Nansen's Farthest North* I. vi. 241 The *pressure-ridges.. are apt to run at right angles to the course of the pressure which produced them. **1913** I. COWIE *Company of Adventurers* xv. 264, I..was aroused every now and again by the cracking, rumbling and thunderous resounding of the ice as the cold took a firmer grip on it and upheaved it into pressure ridges. **1951** *Beaver* June 13 The entire ice-cover is criss-crossed by a network of pressure ridges. **1975** E. IGLAUER *Denison's Ice Road* ix. 230 Denison pointed to a *pressure ridge, a wide band of broken ice, several feet high. **1951** *Good Housek. Home Encycl.* 229/1 For cooking a single dish for four or five persons, or a complete meal for one or two, a *pressure saucepan will serve. **1889** *Buck's Handbk. Med. Sci.* VIII. 748/3 (Index), *Pressure-sores. **1905** R. HOWARD *Surg. Nursing* ii. 23 In applying back splints to the leg and foot..the heel itself only rests lightly on the splint, otherwise a pressure-sore may occur. **1977** *Lancet* 10 Sept. 548/1 Chairfast patients consistently had a higher pressure-sore frequency than bedfast patients of a similar degree of helplessness. **1887** G. T. LADD *Physiol. Psychol.* 410 The finest point, when it touches a '*pressure-spot', produces a sensation of pressure, and not one of being pricked. **1914** *Handbk. Amat. Camping Club* 51 The increasing popularity of the paraffin *pressure stove, the best-known form of which is perhaps the 'Primus', is an indication that this form of kitchen range probably best fits the camper's bill. **1956** C. EVANS *On Climbing* viii. 129 For high altitudes, and extreme cold, it is possible to have a pressure-stove made with an extra large cup to hold more priming fuel. **1966** B. KIMENYE *Kalasanda Revisited* 31 The self-pitying thought, 'I might as well be dead', kept recurring in his mind as he pumped his pressure stove to boil a kettle of tea. **1936** *Flight* 1 Oct. 340/2 To enable the pilot to stand the extremely low pressure encountered at about 50,000ft..a special '*pressure-suit' has been produced. **1949** *Startling Stories* Sept. 125/2 The multiple layers of my pressure suit had made movement very difficult. **1962** J. GLENN et al. *Into Orbit* 244 G-suits are not to be confused with pressure suits (or, now, spacesuits) which the Astronaut wears during space flight to maintain atmospheric pressure at high altitudes. **1977** P. WAY *Super-Celeste* 58 The sudden expansion of his pressure suit turned his body into a heavy, rigid block... He was catapulted.. into..the sky. **1862** *Electrician* 10 Jan. 115/2 (*heading*) Mr. Reid's *pressure tank, used in testing cables during manufacture. **1917** 'CONTACT' *Airman's Outings* viii. 225 A small gravity tank for his machine, to be used when the pressure tank is ventilated by a bullet. **1929** F. P. GIBBONS *Red Napoleon* xii. 403 'Pressure tank hit,' Binney shouted. 'I'm dumping her.' **1962** *Sci. Survey* III. 85 Modern machines [*sc.* electrostatic generators] of this type, enclosed in steel pressure-tanks, have produced about 10 MeV. **1939** R. C. SUTCLIFFE *Meteorol. for Aviators* xvii. 218 The closest attention should always be given to the *pressure tendencies. **1946** W. L. Donn *Meteorol.* vii. 118 The pressure tendency is the net change in pressure for the preceding 3 hours. **1970** F. W. Cole *Introd. Meteorol.* xiv. 323 While pressure, as such, is not a useful weather parameter, the change in pressure and the pressure tendency are both helpful in developing a forecast. **1946** *Nature* 21 Dec. 897/2 Pressurization of cabins for high-altitude flying now appears to be essential... This creates a fresh outlook on the body structure, which now has to be a *pressure-tight shell. **1963** R. Hammond *Automatic Welding* ii. 85 Eight spot welds fix the spider to the rim, eliminating rivet holes and ensuring a pressure-tight joint. **1951** H. H. Doehler *Die Casting* xi. 458 (*heading*) Inspecting for *pressure tightness. **1970** tr. *Zoebl's Fund. Hydraulic Circuitry* viii. 156 This type of plant is used for checking the pressure tightness of welded pipes. **1915** Haven & Swett (*title*) The design of steam boilers and *pressure vessels. **1960** *Practical Wireless* XXXVI. 298/1 X-ray photographs of the welds in the pressure vessel of a nuclear power station. **1962** *Newnes Conc. Encycl. Nucl. Energy* 707/2 For safety reasons the reactor is located inside a steel pressure vessel about 70 ft in diameter and 70 ft high. **1975** Bram & Downs *Manuf. Technol.* ii. 60 If the product is a pressure vessel, very high-integrity welds are essential. **1949** O. G. Sutton *Sci. of Flight* vi. 140 (*heading*) *Pressure waves caused by moving bodies. **1956** A. H. Compton *Atomic Quest* iii. 212 The pressure waves in a metal strained far beyond the elastic limit. **1962** A. Nisbett *Technique Sound Studio* xi. 191 The water-tank artificial reverberation machine.., in which the sound is modulated on to a 80-kc/s carrier and fed via a piezo-electric element to produce pressure waves in the water-tank. **1975** T. Allbeury *Special Collection* iv. 18 He could feel the vibration in his ears, the pressure waves of the guns and bombs. **1926** Stoughton & Butts *Engin. Metall.* vii. 137 (*heading*) Electric heating for *pressure welding. **1954** H. Udin et al. *Welding for Engineers* iii. 34 Oxyacetylene pressure welding is accomplished by butting together under pressure the two pieces of metal to be joined and heating the junction by oxyacetylene torches. **1967** A. H. Cottrell *Introd. Metall.* xxii. 435 In extrusion, the great pressure developed between the metal and the die can lead to sticking, due to pressure welding.

'pressure, *v.* orig. *U.S.* [f. the sb.] **1. a.** *trans.* To exert pressure on. Chiefly *fig.*, to urge or impel (someone *to do*, something or *into* a situation or course of action); to drive or force (someone *out of* something). Also *absol.* (const. *for*), to exert pressure, to press. Hence **'pressured** *ppl. a.*, of work, affairs, etc.: urgent, pressing; of people: under pressure.

1939 R. Chandler in *Dime Detective Mag.* Jan. 103/2 I'm not trying to pressure you. **1944** *Sun* (Baltimore) 6 Oct. 7/3 You can't pressure the War Labor Board into action through strikes. **1951** L. Z. Hobson *Celebrity* (1953) x. 140 It's too bad Gregory Johns is so set against public appearances, but even the studio isn't trying to pressure him. **1957** J. F. Horner *Summary of Scientology* i. 10 Finally he was pressured into writing a popular treatise on Scientology. **1960** *Daily Mail* 12 May 10/6 Baldies can be 'pressured' into paying more than £200 for a course of treatment. **1961** S. Raven *Eng. Gentleman* III. iv. 170 Was Rufus trying to pressure him? asked Henry. Certainly not. Just trying to make him see things in a sensible way. **1963** *Economist* 12 Jan. 111/2 Preachers..'were pressured out of the pulpits they held'. **1968** P. Oliver *Screening Blues* vi. 248 The imputation that the singers were pressured by the record companies which is frequently made, though probably having some measure of truth, is probably much overstated. **1971** H. Cheetham *Portrait of Oxford* xiii. 202 The trouble about an Oxford education..is that no-one.. pressures you into working. **1971** C. Bonington *Annapurna South Face* iii. 32, I..was near to exhaustion from weeks of pressured work and worry. **1973** J. Goodfield *Courier to Peking* I. iii. 45 You personally have never pressured for unlimited resources. **1976** *Times* 8 July 2/5 He said the personalities of Joseph Markham and later Clive Mildoon began as fantasies, providing relief for the pressured and overburdened public figure of Mr John Stonehouse.

b. *trans.* To gain by bringing pressure to bear. *U.S.*

1944 *Sun* (Baltimore) 7 May 8/3 He intervened himself and pressured a better settlement for the unions. **1952** *Ibid.* 22 Mar. 6/4 Other strong unions will now immediately pressure comparable or greater gains for their own people.

2. *trans.* = pressurize *v.* 1.

1961 in Webster. **1979** *Daily Tel.* 8 June 2/1 The engine on the right would have continued to pressure the No. 3 [hydraulic] system under normal circumstances.

pressure cooker. [f. pressure *sb.* + cooker.] **a.** An airtight vessel in which food can be cooked in steam under pressure, so that a higher temperature is reached and the food is cooked more quickly.

1915 *Jrnl. Home Econ.* VII. 375 Why should the modern household more than the modern factory reject a tool of value? This question might well be asked concerning pressure cookers. **1919** *Delineator* Nov. 53/1 Of all modern household saving devices on the market to-day..there is no one article which does more toward lessening household burdens..than the pressure cooker. **1937** H. W. Tilman *Ascent of Nanda Devi* x. 111 Weight was saved by the abandonment of two pressure cookers..a cooker that cooks by steam under pressure and in which, I think, even a pair of boots would be made edible. **1950** F. Swinnerton *Flower for Catherine* 57 Probably some tough old sheep, with lambs of her own, that I shall have to tenderize in the pressure cooker. **1951** *Good Housek. Home Encycl.* 229/1 Some pressure cookers have lids which seal internally, fitting under a rim. **1969** *Islander* (Victoria, B.C.) 5 Oct. 5/2, I had brought along my pressure cooker for speed, and soon I had this filled with the tasty ingredients for a stew.

b. *fig.* (freq. *attrib.*).

1954 Koestler *Invis. Writing* iv. 54, I had acquired it [*sc.* Russian]..by the same pressure-cooker method by which I had learnt modern Hebrew. **1958** *Spectator* 13 June 759/1 Strict curfews and a huge concentration of troops restored order, but the valve of the pressure-cooker was seen to be under enormous strain. **1968** Mrs. L. B. Johnson *White House Diary* 18 Dec. (1970) 758 Every day of the last four years it seems to me she [*sc.* Mrs. Hubert Humphrey] has grown..and especially in the pressure cooker of a campaign. **1974** *Spartanburg* (S. Carolina) *Herald* 18 Apr. C4/1 With the season now almost four months old and the pressure cooker of the Masters just behind them, most of the game's top guns are taking a break. **1976** L. Sanders *Hamlet Warning* (1977) iv. 36 Santo Domingo was a pressure cooker, ready to explode. **1976** *National Observer* (U.S.) 25 Dec. 6/5 An auction's pressure cooker atmosphere is no place for split second decisions involving tens of thousands of dollars.

Hence (*lit.* and *fig.*) **pressure-cook** *v. trans.* (also *absol.*), **pressure-cooked** *ppl. a.*, **pressure-cooking** *vbl. sb.*; also **pressure cookery**.

1940 *Sears, Roebuck Catal.* Spring/Summer 612 Your meals will taste better, too, because pressure cooking retains all the delicate flavors. **1950** *Mrs. Beeton's Bk. Househ. Managem.* 1155 (*heading*) Hay-box and pressure cookery. **1951** *Good Housek. Home Encycl.* 616/2 Pressure-cook for 25–30 minutes. *Ibid.* 618/2 Pressure cookery is the only safe method for the home sterilising of bottled and canned vegetables. **1958** *Listener* 2 Jan. 13/2 The Russians..avoid early specialisation or pressure-cooking in education. **1958** *Woman* 27 Sept. 4/3, I pressure-cooked it until the meat left the bone. **1960** *Farmer & Stockbreeder* 9 Feb. (Suppl.) 2/1 Nut and raisin pressure-cooked loaf cake is covered with a double thickness of greased paper. **1968** *Time* 11 Oct. 28 We concocted Chicago from one Bat for peace, Numerous Democratic toads, And a pressure-cooked American flag.

pressure-feed, *v.* and *sb.* [See feed *v.* 7, 8 c and feed *sb.* 5.] **A.** *v. trans.* To supply (material, esp. fuel) by means of applied pressure. **B.** *sb.* Also **pressure feed**. A supply system in which the flow of material is maintained by applied pressure; the supplying of material in this way. So **'pressure-fed** *ppl. a.*, supplied with material in this way; utilizing a pressure feed.

1904 *Autocar* 6 Aug. 164/1 (*heading*) Carburetter. Pressure feed from the exhaust. *Ibid.*, The lubricator..is also pressure fed. **1906** W. W. Beaumont *Motor Vehicles* II. viii. 158 Pressure-fed lubrication is adopted for the engine and for the petrol feed. *Ibid.* xii. 206 Pressure feed is used, obtained by a shunt from the exhaust pipe to a distributing box. **1909** D. Leechman *Carburetters* ix. 66 Petrol is maintained at a certain level..by means of a float and needle valve when the petrol is pressure fed. **1914, 1925** [see gravity(-)feed *sb.*]. **1936** *Discovery* Sept. 299/2 The rocket motor of today with its..complicated system of pressure feeds, safety valves and dual liquid-fuel storage tanks, little resembles the old-style cardboard tube and gunpowder. **1961** H. H. Koelle *Handbk. Astronaut. Engin.* xx. 16 Pump-fed systems are lighter than pressure-fed systems for all but the very shortest-duration requirements.

pressure group. [f. pressure *sb.* + group *sb.*] A group or association of people representing some special interest, who bring concerted pressure to bear on public policy. Also *attrib.* Hence **pressure groupism**, activity characteristic of a pressure group.

1928 P. H. Odegard *Pressure Politics* vii. 202 The character of pressure groups as of individuals can frequently be understood from the manner in which they spend their money. **1934** W. Lippmann *Method of Freedom* iii. 97 We come then to the conclusion that it is not the pressure groups as such which make it impossible for the state to act in the general interest..but pressure groups attached to and reinforced by political machines. **1936** A. Huxley *Eyeless in Gaza* xxii. 316 One joined the Party, one distributed literature, one financed pressure-groups. **1937** B. Zeller *Pressure Politics in N.Y.* viii. 229 The outstanding feature of modern pressure group technique is the widespread use of propaganda channels. *Ibid.* ix. 263 This frequent and flagrant abuse of pressure group politics. **1941** W. Temple *Citizen & Churchman* iii. 56 One American professor opened his reply with the words: 'It is obvious that the Church is a pressure-group.' **1953** Wodehouse *Performing Flea* 154 You can no longer put a negro on the stage unless you make him very dignified. Owing to the activities of the Negro pressure group, comic negro characters are absolutely taboo. **1954** *Encounter* Mar. 58/2 The illusion.. that US opposition to the admission of Communist China to the UN is..an ephemeral, emotional attitude dictated by a nebulous pressure-group called 'The China Lobby'. **1959** *Oxf. Univ. Gaz.* 16 Mar. 795/1 It is an interesting aspect of the workings of pressure-group politics to see that in Australia and New Zealand it is the interests of the manufacturers which prevail, with both political parties, against the general good of those countries, which urgently require greater production and export of farm products. **1960** *Encounter* Jan. 39/2 Those literal-minded pressure-groups which haunt all public organs of opinion. **1966** *New Statesman* 13 May 683/1 Comment on this affair included, not surprisingly, accusations of pressure groupism and intolerance. **1971** P. Gresswell *Environment* 18 In a literate society, such pressure groups [*sc.* amenity societies] are a necessary adjunct to parliamentary democracy. **1978** *Dædalus* Spring 75 Almost equally annoying to scientists is the change in political attitudes; members of Congress now tend to look on them as just another selfish pressure group, and not as the wizards of perpetual progress.

pressure head. [f. pressure *sb.* + head *sb.*] **1.** The pressure exerted by a fluid, expressed as the height of a column of fluid which would produce that pressure by virtue of its weight (cf. head *sb.*[1] 17 a and b).

1907 Woodward & Preston tr. *Sorel's Carbureting & Combustion in Alcohol Engines* viii. 160 Let..*H* = pressure head on the liquid. **1974** J. A. Fox *Introd. Engin. Fluid Mech.* viii. 283 A velocity change of 1 ft/s can generate a pressure head of approximately 125 ft if it occurs rapidly enough.

2. *Aeronaut.* A pitot-static tube.

1930 *Aircraft Engin.* II. 95/2 The standard pressure head ..consists of pressure and static tubes mounted parallel and near to each other. **1964** E. H. J. Pallett *Aircraft Instrument Man.* ii. 11 Pressure heads now in general use are ..electrically heated.

pressure jet. [f. pressure *sb.* + jet *sb.*[3]] **a.** Used *attrib.* with reference to a type of oil burner in which the fuel is burned at a fine nozzle through which it is passed under pressure.

1911 W. H. Booth *Liquid Fuel* xiii. 212 The pressure-jet system will recover from 70 per cent. to 75 per cent. of the theoretical calorific value of the oil fuel used in actual practice. **1920** E. C. Bowden-Smith *Oil Firing* iv. 90 In the pressure-jet burner great care must be taken to maintain a high temperature, or the burner may fail entirely. **1968** J. Slome *Domestic Oil-Fired Central Heating* iii. 61 Pressure jet burners can make quite a considerable amount of noise.

b. A small jet engine mounted at the tip of a helicopter rotor blade and supplied with compressed air through a duct in the blade. Freq. *attrib.*

1950 *Jrnl. Helicopter Assoc. Gt. Brit.* III. 153 The pressure jet helicopter is..suitable for longer ranges. **1958** Lambermont & Pirie *Helicopters & Autogyros* 201 The XV-1 has a reciprocating engine..which acts by feeding air through tubes to small pressure jets at the tips of the three-bladed rotor during vertical flight.

pressure plate. [f. pressure *sb.* + plate *sb.*] **a.** A plate for detecting or receiving pressure, *spec.* in an anemometer. **b.** A plate for applying pressure, *spec.* in a clutch.

1845 *Rep. Brit. Assoc. Adv. Sci. 1844* 24 A contrivance.. is affixed to the pressure plate, by means of which the fluid is deposited at a variable rate, but always depending on the force on the pressure plate at the time. **1856** *Ibid. 1885* 127 The force of the wind is ascertained by means of a circular plate having an area of four square feet, which is kept by the vane at right angles to the current of the wind... To this pressure-plate is attached a wire which communicates with a recording pencil. **1892** *Q. Jrnl. R. Meteorol. Soc.* XVIII. 174 It was not possible to obtain a perfectly distinct line from the pen of the Pressure Plate during a gale unless the paper moved at least 2 inches in each minute. **1921** J. V. Woodworth *Amer. Tool Making* xxvii. 445 The pressure on the foot treadle, which causes the pressure plate to clamp the can and lid against the chuck, also throws in the friction clutch which starts the work. **1958** *Newnes Compl. Amat. Photogr.* iv. 71 In a 35 mm. camera, the pressure plate should be examined carefully. **1963** D. H. McIntosh *Meteorol. Gloss.* (ed. 4) 16 In the pressure-plate anemometer, the deflexion of a flat plate placed in the wind is measured; its use is confined mainly to atmospheric turbulence measurement. **1976** *Horse & Hound* 3 Dec. 66 (Advt.), Superb rebuilt Land-Rovers fitted with..new clutch and pressure plate.

pressure point. [f. pressure *sb.* + point *sb.*[1]] **1. a.** A point where pressure is supposed to stimulate or inhibit convulsions.

1876 tr. *von Ziemssen's Cycl. Med.* XI. 315 It is in this form of spasm that the pressure points which are capable of inhibiting spasm have been recognised. **1885** J. Ross *Handbk. Dis. Nervous Syst.* 167 Pressure points are frequently observed in spasmodic affections. Pressure upon certain points puts a stop at times to the convulsion when present, and consequently these points may be called pressure-arresting points. In other cases the convulsions are brought on by pressure on particular points, and these may ..be called pressure-exciting points. **1896** J. M. Da Costa *Med. Diag.* (ed. 8) ii. 233 There are 'pressure-points' which when acted on will cause the convulsive movements to be arrested. **1910** J. L. Salinger tr. T. Ziehen in A. Church *Dis. Nervous Syst.* 1082 The relation of the pressure-points is also noteworthy. Pressure upon these occasionally increases the severity of the attack, or may produce a new attack [of hysteria].

b. One of numerous small areas on the skin that are specially sensitive to pressure; also, a point at which pain is felt on pressure.

1882 *Amer. Jrnl. Med. Sci.* LXXXIV. 589 Dr. Meyer discovered a painful pressure-point at the upper part of the brachial plexus. **1891** W. Stirling tr. *Landois's Text-bk. Human Physiol.* (ed. 4) II. xiv. 1018 The 'pressure-points'.. lie much closer together, and are more numerous than the temperature-points. **1906** C. P. Flint et al. tr. *Sahli's Diagnostic Methods* 758 The pressure sense is not scattered diffusely in the skin, but..depends upon localized organs. The projections of the latter upon the surface of the skin are called 'pressure points'. **1940** *Jrnl. Exper. Psychol.* XXVI. 516 This parallelism of the two kinds of sensation [*sc.* pressure and vibration] could not be proved for the pressure points. **1958** R. Wartenberg *Neuritis, Sensory Neuritis, Neuralgia* xli. 406 In cases of neuralgia of the last intercostal nerve, typical pressure points, especially on the back, could always be found.

c. A point where an artery can easily be pressed against a bone to inhibit bleeding.

1909 R. Howard in *Sci. & Art of Nursing* III. xxii. 5 (*heading*) The main arteries and their pressure points. **1933** Bailey & Love *Surg. for Nurses* xxix. 308 Pressure points.. are situations in which large arteries are adjacent to bones, and so are easily compressed against the rigid underlying part. **1954** Diehl & Laton *Health & Safety for You* iv. 46/1 (*caption*) Find the pressure point between the wound and the heart; press against the bone. **1973** *Guardian* 11 Apr. 11/4 He..sliced the top off his thumb. But he knew about pressure points.

d. A pressure sore, or a point where one is apt to develop owing to the pressure on it.

1929 E. L. ELIASON et al. *Surg. Nursing* xvi. 389 After the immediate effects of the operation have disappeared, a vigilant watch must be kept for the development of pressure points. **1941** K. D. KEELE *Mod. Home Nursing* iii. 43 Pressure points of the body have to be learnt. They are those parts which, being exposed to the brunt of bearing the weight of the body, get most wear. **1964** M. C. T. MORRISON *Basic Princ. Accident Surg.* xvi. 89 The patient should be nursed on pillows or foam rubber pads to distribute the pressure evenly over the whole of his back or side rather than on his 'pressure points'. **1969** BRAIN & WALTON *Dis. Nervous Syst.* (ed. 7) xiv. 630 The dressing should be well covered with adhesive plaster attached to skin some distance from the pressure points and changed every day.

2. *fig.* A person or thing that can be used by someone as a means of exerting pressure on another.

1975 T. ALLBEURY *Palomino Blonde* xv. 91 The girl..is being used as a pressure point on him to give the details of his discovery to the Soviets. **1977** R. LUDLUM *Chancellor Manuscript* xv. 167 Hoover..will soon control the pressure points of the country. He'll be running it. **1978** *Internat. Relations Dict.* (U.S. Dept. State Library) 25/1 An international political strategy relating two or more issues in negotiations, and then using them as tradeoffs or pressure points, much as in a 'carrots and stick' technique.

pressure-test, *sb.* and *v. trans.* [f. PRESSURE *sb.* + TEST *sb.*[1]] **A.** *sb.* A test for pressure of any kind, or of ability to withstand or sustain pressure. **B.** *v. trans.* To subject to a test of this nature.

[**1882** R. SENNETT *Marine Steam Engine* xxvii. 570 The water-pressure test should be double the working steam pressure, provided that during the examination no indication of weakness is observed.] **1888** W. C. UNWIN *Testing of Materials of Construction* xv. 479 It may be useful to examine if the rate of hardening in pressure tests can be expressed as simply as that in tension tests. **1897** *Allbutt's Syst. Med.* III. 87 The muscles may be so wasted that no pressure-test is available. **1941** WYNDHAM LEWIS *Let.* 17 Oct. (1963) 300 No. 1 doctor said that if the [ocular] pressure-test gave a negative result, that then another cause must be looked for. **1957** *Sun* (Baltimore) 19 June 40/3 They were pressure-testing it with oxygen, after welding it, when the tank exploded. **1977** *Offshore Engineer* June 50/3 We pressure-tested flotation chambers to check water-tightness.

pressure treatment. [f. PRESSURE *sb.* + TREATMENT.] **a.** *Timber.* Impregnation of timber with a preservative fluid, such as creosote, under applied pressure.

1914 MOON & BROWN *Elem. Forestry* xii. 235 The Rueping, Card, Lowry and other more or less important processes are in common use but they are all variations of the same pressure treatment. **1942** H. D. TIEMANN *Wood Technol.* xvii. 258 Wood preservation against decay consists in impregnating wood, either by soakage or by pressure treatment, with antiseptic liquids. **1950** A. J. PANSHIN et al. *Forest Products* iv. 65 Practically all southern pine poles are given a full-length pressure treatment with creosote oil before being placed in service.

b. *Biol.* Subjection (of cells, organisms, etc.) to increased pressure.

1940 *Biol. Bull.* LXXVIII. 106 It is clear that the time relationships between nuclear and cytoplasmic division may be somewhat disturbed by pressure treatment. **1956** *Internat. Rev. Cytol.* V. 215 The cell is rendered incapable of performing the work of cleavage by any combination of temperature and pressure treatments that jointly weakens the gel structure to approximately the same degree. **1970** S. B. & A. M. ZIMMERMAN in A. M. Zimmerman *High Pressure Effects on Cellular Processes* viii. 183 Numerous vacuoles appear in the cell cytoplasm following decompression and may be representative of some damage caused by the pressure treatment.

Hence (as a back-formation) **'pressure-treat** *v. trans.* So **'pressure-treated** *ppl. a.*; **'pressure-treating** *vbl. sb.*

1936 *Jrnl. Cellular & Compar. Physiol.* VIII. 159 The Amoebae are placed in a centrifuge-pressure chamber which is so designed that the control and pressure-treated specimens are simultaneously centrifuged for a suitable period. **1938** HUNT & GARRATT *Wood Preservation* vi. 221 Untreated wood, exposed when pile heads are cut off to grade, may be pressure treated by a method developed by E. F. Hartman. **1950** A. J. PANSHIN et al. *Forest Products* iv. 66 One of the empty-cell processes is usually employed, unless customer specification for total retention of creosote is such that a full-cell pressure-treating process is required. **1960** *Farmer & Stockbreeder* 2 Feb. (Suppl.) 9/1 Concrete stanchions and pressure-treated timber trusses and purlins. **1963** H. R. CLAUSER *Encycl. Engin. Materials* 738/1 Pressure-treating operations must be conducted in plants with considerable equipment. *Ibid.*, Some of the American species are easy to pressure-treat, others are difficult to penetrate with any chemical. **1970** S. B. & A. M. ZIMMERMAN in A. M. Zimmerman *High Pressure Effects on Cellular Processes* viii. 187 The pressure-treated cells revealed a loss of Golgi complex and pinocytotic channels.

pressure tube. [f. PRESSURE *sb.* + TUBE *sb.*] **1.** A tube open at one or more points to a surrounding fluid whose velocity or pressure it is used to measure. Usu. *attrib.* in ***pressure tube anemometer***.

1894 *Q. Jrnl. Meteorol. Soc.* XX. 186 Lately he had spent a good many hours by the side of Mr. Dines's pressure tube anemometer, watching the action of the pen in squalls of wind. **1920** G. TAYLOR *Austral. Meteorol.* viii. 77 The pressure and suction tubes..act together to move the float. **1970** R. W. LONGLEY *Elements Meteorol.* vii. 140 The record ..came from a Dines pressure-tube anemometer which is able to measure rapid fluctuations in the wind.

2. A tube in which pressurized coolant or moderator is passed through the core in certain types of nuclear reactor.

1961 J. K. PICKARD et al. *Power Reactor Technol.* iv. 214 A graphite reflector can be used..which compensates for the loss of neutrons in the pressure tubes. **1968** MOORE & HOLMES in *Steam Generating & Other Heavy Water Reactors* (Brit. Nuclear Energy Soc.) 3/2 One of the important features of a pressure tube reactor is that not only can different materials be used for the moderator and coolant, but the operating conditions of these media can be selected quite independently to suit their functions.

pressurization (prɛʃəraɪ'zeɪʃən). [f. as next + -ATION.] The action or result of pressurizing (*lit.* or *fig.*).

1937 *Jrnl. Aeronaut. Sci.* IV. 99/1 The problems of cabin pressurization will increase rapidly as wall pressure differentials of over 1300 lbs. per sq. ft. will maintain. **1946** *Nature* 21 Dec. 897/2 Pressurization of cabins for high-altitude flying now appears to be essential with the adoption of the gas turbine. **1958** 'P. BRYANT' *Two Hours to Doom* 86 Have the pressurization..set for full. **1963** *Daily Tel.* 26 Apr. 14 A luncheon appointment between a publicity expert and an M.P. to discuss a particular interest appears suspect to Mr. Edelman as 'pressurization'. **1969** *Ibid.* 21 Nov. 2/3 A decompression explosion can also be ruled out as the plane was too low to need pressurisation. **1975** F. R. PALMER in W. F. Bolton *Eng. Lang.* ii. 44 The stop (or plosive) consonants..involve the pressurization of air pushed up from the lungs into the vocal tract. **1979** *Daily Tel.* 2 July 22/2 Cruel and critical but sympathetic pressurisation each day from the organising consultants.

pressurize ('prɛʃəraɪz), *v.* [f. PRESSURE *sb.* + -IZE.] **1.** *trans.* To produce or maintain pressure artificially in (a container, closed space, etc., esp. an aircraft); to apply pressure to.

1944 *Aeronautics* Sept. 56/2 The fuselage will be pressurized so that at all altitudes cabin conditions will be equivalent to a height of 8,000 ft. **1958** *Times* 25 Jan. 9/2 This machine consists of a small electric compressor pump, which pressurizes the container to a pressure of 80 lb. to the square inch. **1958** *Times* 14 Aug. 9/7 This means she [*sc.* an undersea cargo ship] would have an empty space which must either be pressurized to balance the pressure of the sea, or made strong enough to withstand that pressure. **1970** *Nature* 18 Apr. 249/2 Before re-entry, the camera and payload section were sealed and pressurized to two atmospheres. **1972** *Daily Tel.* 11 Dec. 15/6 We returned from our first drive, pressurised the lunar module cabin and took our helmets off. **1975** *Sci. Amer.* July 52/3 The surface of the journal and the surface of the bearing are separated by a film of lubricant when the journal is turning rapidly enough to pressurize the wedge with lubricant.

2. To subject to moral or mental pressure or suasion; to urge or constrain.

1956 *Essays in Crit.* VI. 238 The best poems..have all these qualities together with a strict sense of form that pressurizes the colloquial idiom. **1964** *Listener* 26 Nov. 859/2 This is the move which concedes the initiative, since White is now able to gain space and pressurize the black squares on the king's side. **1970** N. BAWDEN *Birds on Trees* ii. 32 Charlie said we didn't want to pressurize him. **1973** 'M. INNES' *Appleby's Answer* xiii. 116 Perhaps Bulkington has developed a quiet pressurising line on his young charges. **1978** *Guardian Weekly* 30 Apr. 15/3 U.S. officials are pressurising the Saudis to increase production capacity.

Hence **'pressurizing** *vbl. sb.*

1946 *Sun* (Baltimore) 16 May 6/3 Pressurizing enables passengers to enjoy the comfortable flying conditions of 8,000 feet while at a ceiling of 25,000. **1976** J. M. KELLY *Stud. Civil Judicature Roman Republ.* v. 130 The pressurizing of the defendant into surrendering the plaintiff's property.

pressurized ('prɛʃəraɪzd), *ppl. a.* [f. as prec. + -ED[1].] **1.** Containing, or made to contain, fluid under pressure. **a.** Of an aircraft cabin, spacesuit, etc.: designed to maintain an interior air pressure close to normal atmospheric pressure in a low-pressure environment.

1938 *Time* 23 May 33 Without pressurized cabins, planes now fly as high as 14,000 feet. **1945** *Times* 2 Oct. 2/4 It has a pressurized cabin which, up to a height of 20,000 ft., maintains a pressure inside the passengers' cabin equivalent to that at 8,000 ft. **1949** *Archit. Rev.* CV. 237/2 A very highly streamlined low-wing, four-motor monoplane, with tricycle undercarriage and pressurized cabin. **1951** A. C. CLARKE *Across Sea of Stars* (1959) 4 We could live comfortable for a month in our pressurised tractors. **1958** *Times* 28 Aug. 9/4 'Colonists' [on the moon]..unable to quit their pressurized suits for a moment. **1962** F. I. ORDWAY et al. *Basic Astronautics* xiii. 516 (*caption*) First pressurized suit..was developed for Wiley Post and worn by him in 1934. **1975** D. LODGE *Changing Places* i. 3 They were protected from the thin, cold air by the pressurized cabins of two Boeing 707s.

b. Of an aerosol container or spray.

1955 *Industr. & Engin. Chem.* June 1198/1 Aerosol products are pressurized, self-spraying products that at the press of a valve button deliver an active ingredient in a fine spray (insecticides and room deodorants), a heavier spray (paints and enamels), a foam (shave creams), and newest among the applications, a dry powder. **1958** *Times* 24 Nov. 11/5 Helena Rubinstein has a new pressurized scent spray. **1961** *Lancet* 2 Sept. 506/1 It was decided to recommend that the surgical staff should use..a pressurised powder spray of polybactrin. **1976** *Which?* Feb. 37/1 Technically, an aerosol is simply a fine spray. Most people use the word to describe the pressurised can that produces a spray.

2. Of a fluid: increased in pressure; ***pressurized-water reactor***, a nuclear reactor in which the coolant is water at high pressure.

1953 *Chem. & Engin. News* 3 Aug. 3187/3 The AEC is continuing research and development work on the pressurized water reactor. **1957** E. HYAMS *Into Dreams* III. vi. 236 As if the pressurized air contained some poison of the mind. **1958** *Times Rev. Industry* July 32/2 Pressurized fluid is fed to the power valve which..actuates the brake. **1960** *Economist* 22 Oct. 392/2 One important aspect of *Dreadnought* is that it gives British technicians a first experience of a pressurised water reactor. **1966** *McGraw-Hill Encycl. Sci. & Technol.* XI. 363/1 The sodium-cooled reactor originally installed on the submarine USS *Seawolf* has been replaced by a pressurized-water reactor. **1968** M. WOODHOUSE *Rock Baby* xviii. 182 Find out if there's still pressurized gas within the casing. **1977** *Sci. Amer.* June 46/1 The lower piston rests against the dividing plate, supported by a cushion of pressurized nitrogen gas.

3. *fig.* Of a person or situation: subject to pressure; under moral, mental, or social pressure or constraint.

1959 *Times* 30 Nov. 4/1 This age of pressurized competition. **1965** *Punch* 22 Sept. 425/2 This going out of London has made the job very pressurised. Weekends are hectic.

'press-,warrant. Now *Hist.* [f. PRESS *sb.*[2] + WARRANT *sb.*] A warrant giving authority to impress men for the service of the navy or army.

a **1688** VILLIERS (Dk. Buckhm.) *Sea Officers*, And in their Pockets carried their Press-Warrants. **1770** *Chron.* in *Ann. Reg.* 147/2 Press-warrants were sent to Portsmouth, and next morning the press-gangs went on board the merchant ships. **1904** *Daily Chron.* 3 Sept. 3/2 In 1673-4..Colonel Strode, the Governor of Dover Castle, had refused point blank to execute a press warrant till he knew what Parliament would say.

'press-work. [f. PRESS *sb.*[1] + WORK *sb.*] **1.** The work and management of a printing-press; the printing off on paper, etc. of what has been 'composed' or set up in type; the result of this, the work turned out from a press, esp. from the point of view of its quality.

1771 LUCKOMBE *Hist. Print.* 47 His excellent method of disposition, composition, and press-work. *Ibid.* 52 His first works..resemble the press-work of Worde and Pinson. **1832** BABBAGE *Econ. Manuf.* xxi. (ed. 3) 208 The press-work, or printing off, is charged at a price agreed upon for each two hundred and fifty sheets. **1867** BRANDE & COX *Dict. Sc.*, etc. s.v., By *fine presswork* is meant work printed with the best paper and ink, and with the utmost care at a hand press. **1896** T. L. DE VINNE *Moxon's Mech. Exerc., Printing* 412 The new method has..cheapened common presswork.., but it has not bettered the presswork of books.

2. Literary work done for the press; journalistic work.

1888 BARRIE *When a Man's Single* v, His first press-work had been a series of letters he had written when at school, and contributed to a local paper.

3. a. *Pottery.* The making of ware by pressing the clay into moulds.

1839 URE *Dict. Arts* 1012 A great variety of pottery wares ..are made by two different methods, the one called press-work, and the other casting. The press-work is done in moulds made of Paris plaster... All vessels of an oval form, and such as have flat sides, are made in this way.

b. The pressing or drawing of metal into a shaped hollow die; a piece of metal shaped by such means.

1896 O. SMITH *Press-Working of Metals* i. 14 In press-work the metal is sometimes heated as in forging, but in the great majority of cases it is handled cold. **1903** *Engineering* 16 Jan. p. v (Index), Press work for sheet metal. **1904** *Ibid.* 22 Jan. 132/3 We illustrate below a very remarkable specimen of 'press' work... The barrel shown..has been drawn out of a steel-plate $\frac{1}{32}$th of an inch in thickness. **1941** C. W. HINMAN *Pressworking of Metals* i. 1 Today, it is a wonder how the past generation ever produced any satisfactory presswork. **1963** BIRD & HUTTON-STOTT *Veteran Motor Car* 82 This was a most remarkable piece of presswork and comprised a complete chassis..of deep-section side girders, upswept over the rear axle.

4. *Joinery.* (See quot.)

1875 KNIGHT *Dict. Mech.*, *Press-work*.., cabinet work of a number of successive veneers crossing grain, and united by glue, heat, and pressure.

Hence as *v. trans.*, to shape (metal) in this way; usu. as *pres. pple.*; so **'press-working** *vbl. sb.*

1896 O. SMITH (*title*) Press-working of metals. *Ibid.* v. 120 It is taken for granted that the materials employed for press-working..must be to some considerable degree in a malleable or ductile physical condition. **1941** C. W. HINMAN *Pressworking of Metals* vi. 62 (*heading*) Press-working nonmetallic materials. **1949** *Tool Engineers Handbk.* (Amer. Soc. Tool Engineers) lxxiii. 1058 Heated dies are used in the pressworking of brass and magnesium. **1958** EARY & REED (*title*) Techniques of pressworking sheet metal.

'press-yard. *Obs.* exc. *Hist.* [f. PRESS *v.*[1] 1 b + YARD.] Name of a yard or court of old Newgate Prison, in which the torture of *peine forte et dure* (PEINE, PRESS *v.*[1] 1 b) is supposed to have originally been carried out; and from which, at a later period, capitally convicted prisoners started for the place of execution.

1654 GAYTON *Pleas. Notes* III. v. 99 It was as good and all one, as if God had done it with the Country, or else the Presse-yard had ended the quarrell. **1717** (*title*) The History of the Press-Yard: or a Brief Account of the Customs and Occurrences..to be met with in.. His Majesty's Goal of Newgate in London. *Ibid.* 3 The Press-Yard being no part of the Prison, but taken in as a part of the Governor's House ..it is in the Keeper's Breast to refuse any Prisoner a Reception there without a Conditional Premium. *a* **1720** SEWEL *Hist. Quakers* (1722) VII. 374 Bidding the Turnkey bring down the said Prisoners to him in the Press-yard. **1771** *Chron.* in *Ann. Reg.* 161/1 Their wives and children were admitted into the press-yard to take their leave of them before they set out [for the gallows at Tyburn]. **1780**

Newgate Cal. V. 109 Being brought down into the press-yard, his irons were knocked off, and he was put into the cart. **1840** BARHAM *Ingol. Leg.* Ser. I. *Execution*, Round the debtors' door Are gather'd a couple of thousand or more; As many await At the press-yard gate. **1906** *Daily Chron.* 5 Oct. 4/7 The new Old Bailey... There will be no 'peine forte et dure', commemorated in the name Press Yard.

† **'pressyly**, *adv. Obs. rare*⁻¹. [perh. after F. *pressément*, with substitution of English suffix.] Urgently, pressingly.

1491 CAXTON *Vitas Patr.* (W. de W. 1495) I. lxxxii. 122 Lettres.. By the whyche they wrote well pressyly that her sone sholde be delyuerde to her agayne.

† **prest**, *sb.*[1] *Obs.* Also 5 prestte, 5–7 preste, 6 preast(e. [a. OF. *prest* (12th c. in Littré), mod.F. *prêt*, the action of preparing or lending, a loan, purveyance for the king's table, advance pay for soldiers; vbl. sb. f. OF. *prester*, mod.F. *prêter* to afford, lend, PREST *v.*[1] So It. *presto* a loan. (In Eng. hist. documents the L. word is usually *prestitum*, pa. pple. of *præstāre*, PREST *v.*[1])]

1. An advance of money; a loan; *esp.* one made to the sovereign in an emergency; a forced loan; a grant, gift, bequest.

1439 *Rolls of Parlt.* V. 8/2 Ne hadde leen ye gret loones and presttes. **1475** *Bk. Noblesse* (Roxb.) 80 The creditours have not been duelie paide of here lonys and prestis made to highe sovereins. *a* **1512** FABYAN *Chron.* VII. 683 In thys yere [1486] a prest was made to the kynge of .ii. M. li. of the whyche the mercers, grocers, & drapers lent .ix. C. xxxvii. li. and .vi. s. *a* **1529** SKELTON *Col. Cloute* 352 The people mones For prestes and for lones Lent and neuer payd. **1560–1** *Newcastle Guilds* (Surtees) 89 A serteyn some of money beyng granted by waye of loon or prest. **1577–87** HOLINSHED *Chron.* III. 1090/2 The first of September the queene demanded a prest of the citie of London of twentie thousand pounds, to be repaied againe within foureteene daies after Michaelmasse next folowing. **1643** PRYNNE *Sov. Power Parl.* App. 29 For lack of money, he was driven of necessitie to aske a preste of the citizens of Paris.

2. A charge, duty, or impost; a deduction made from or in connexion with any payment. See also quot. 1898.

1472–3 *Rolls of Parlt.* VI. 59/2 The said Maire, Feliship and Merchauntes [of the Staple of Caleys], nor their successours, shall not sett nor put any ymposition, prest or charge, uppon the Wolles or Wollefelles of any persone of the said Feliship. **1491** HEN. VII in Ellis *Orig. Lett.* Ser. II. I. 170 We.. charge you that.. ye content and paye unto theim [for their wages of the half yere ended at Estre last].. the summes aforsaid, withoute any prest or charge setting upon theim.. for the same. *Ibid.* 172, 173. **1548** *Act 2 Edw. VI*, c. 4 §2 [For allowance of sheriffs upon their account] That the same tayles soe hereafter there to be levyed and striken, shalbe delyvered unto everye of the same Sheriffes .. without prest or other chardge to be sett upon them for the same. [**1898** *Encycl. Laws Eng.* X. 327 *Prest*, a duty which sheriffs formerly had to pay on receiving their tallies for the sums standing due from them in the accounts of the Exchequer.]

3. A payment or wages in advance; money paid on account to a person to enable him to proceed with an undertaking; cf. IMPREST *sb.*[1] 1, PRESS-MONEY 2. ***auditor of prests***: see IMPREST *sb.*[1] 1 c.

1495 *Naval Acc. Hen. VII* (1896) 137 Sommes of money by the said Robert.. by way of preste at the Receipte of the Kinges Escheqquier.. hade or receyued. **1515** T. LARKE in Willis & Clark *Cambridge* (1886) I. 499 One hundreth poundes sterling to be delivered unto.. the Kinges Glasier in way of prest towardes the glaising of the great Churche. **1522** *Rutland Papers* (Camden) 76 Prestes to diuers personnes for prouision of vitailles for themperor. *a* **1562** G. CAVENDISH *Wolsey* (1893) 197 Yt was concludyd that he shold have by the way of prest, a thousand marks owt of Wynchester byshopriche, byfore hand of his pencion. **1657** HOWELL *Londinop.* 370 The Auditor of the Prests, whose Office it is to take the Accounts of the Mint.. and of all other impressed or moneys advanc'd before hand.

4. *esp.* Earnest-money paid to a sailor or soldier on enlistment, enlistment-money.

1480 *Howard Househ. Bks.* (Roxb.) 9 [Of this sum] is prest for j. M. j.ᶜiiij.ˣˣ maryners, every of them ij.s. for prest, C. xviij. li. **1491** *Act 7 Hen. VII*, c. 1 §1 Any Souldeour.. which herafter shalbe in Wages and reteyned or take any prest to serve the King uppon the See. **1562** *Royal Letters* 23 July (City of London, Jor. 18 lf. 57), For their prest, coates, and conducte money. **1583** *Exec. for Treason* (1675) 45 As it were an earnest or prest. **1588** *Letter Bk. &c. City Lond.* lf. 200 b, Fraunćys Iohnson who was appoynted to serve as a soldyar .. and receyved her Maiesties prest.

5. An engagement of a person by payment of earnest-money; an enlistment of soldiers or sailors.

1542 *St. Papers Hen. VIII*, IX. 139 We wolde you shuld provyde us of ten good dromes, and as many fifers. For the prest and setting forward of whiche persons you maye receyve, what money you wolle desire, of our servaunt Guidenfingre. **1602** CAREW *Cornwall* 101 This towne furnisheth more able Mariners at euery prest for her Highnesse seruice, then many others of farre greater blaze.

6. ***in prest***: As a 'prest' or loan; in advance; on account; as earnest-money. (Cf. senses 1, 3, 5.)

1486 *Naval Acc. Hen. VII* (1896) 9 Receyued.. by thandes of the said Henry Palmer in prest vpon the said office.. clⁱⁱ. **1550** EDW. VI *Jrnl.* in Froude *Hist. Eng.* xxvii. (1870) IV. 518 For which I should give him 15,000*l.* in prest, and leave to carry 8000*l.* over sea to abase the exchange. **1557** *Order of Hospitalls* F iv, You shall not deliuer any mony in prest to any Officer,.. without the Thresorer will yow the same to doe. **1579** FENTON *Guicciard.* x. (1599) 456 They departed to their houses, hauing receiued in prest only one Florin of the Rhein for a man. **1603** KNOLLES *Hist. Turks* (1621) 999 There was taken up in prest of privat merchants in.. Aleppo only, the summe of three score thousand Cecchini.

7. *attrib.* and *Comb.*: **prest-warrant**, see quot. and cf. PRESS-WARRANT.

1894 C. N. ROBINSON *Brit. Fleet* IV. iv. 413 In Elizabeth's reign there was no great difficulty experienced in obtaining men when wanted by 'prest warrants', or warrants for paying 'prest' money.

† **prest**, *sb.*[2] *Obs.* Also 7–8 press(e. [Of uncertain origin.] A sheet (of parchment or the like).

1405 *Will of Bullok* (Somerset Ho.), My wille as it ys wryten in a prest of parchemyne. **1658** *Practick Part of Law* 232 Fees.. For the transcript of a Record, being a presse, 6*s.* 8*d.* For every presse more 6*s.* 8*d.* **1705** LUTTRELL *Brief Rel.* (1857) V. 520 Yesterday the lords read.. the commons bill for relief of the poor, containing 60 presses of parchment.

† **prest**, *a.* and *adv. Obs.* Also 3–6 preste, 5 preest, (prast), 6 preast, ? *Sc.* priest, (7 *erron.* pressed). [a. OF. *prest* (11th c. in Littré), in mod.F. *prêt* = Pr., Cat. *prest*, It., Sp., Pg. *presto*:—late or pop.L. *præst-us* ready (Inscr. and 5th c. in Salic Law), f. earlier L. *præstō* (*præstū*) adv., near at hand, in readiness, at one's service; supposed to be contr. from **præsitō*, f. *præ* before, in front + abl. or dat. of *situs* placed, situated, lying; or from **præsitū*, f. *præ* + *situ*, abl. of *situs* situation.]

A. *adj.* **1.** Ready for action or use; at hand; prepared, or in proper order.

1297 R. GLOUC. (Rolls) 7217 Nou wole vr louerd ssake is suerd, is bowe is ibend, & prest imad uor to smite men þat beþ mis wend. *c* **1300** *St. Margarete* 302 Nou in mi louerdes name prest ic am þerto. **13..** *K. Alis.* 1187 Ten þousande, al prest & ȝare In to bataile forto fare. **1382** WYCLIF *Bible* Pref. Ep. vii. 68 Prest is the book of Leuy [Vulg. *In promptu est Leviticus liber*]. *c* **1400** *Sowdone Bab.* 1164 To Iuste thai made hem preest. **1513** DOUGLAS *Æneis* II. vi. 10 With eris prest stude thair als still as stone. **1549–62** STERNHOLD & H. *Ps.* xi. 2 Behold the wicked bend their bowes, and make their arrowes prest. **1566** DRANT *Horace, Sat.* ii. B j, Then cums this foxe, this Fusidie, wyth money preste in hande. **1578** WHETSTONE *Promos & Cass.* III. ii, Who styll is preast His lawles love to make his lawful wife. **1635** HEYWOOD *Hierarch.* v. 282 A huge Nauy prest at all Essayes. **1697** DRYDEN *Virg. Georg.* III. 733 The Victim Ox, that was for Altars prest, Trim'd with white Ribbons, and with Garlands drest.

b. Often in association with *ready*, *readily*.

c **1475** *Partenay* 1585 Greffon with swerdes fors was redy and preste. **1489** CAXTON *Faytes of A.* I. xv. 42 To see that althyng be redyly prest at hande. **1526** *Pilgr. Perf.* (W. de W. 1531) 304 All was prest and redy. *a* **1548** HALL *Chron., Edw. IV* 200 b, .xv. thousand men euen ready prest to set on the citie of Yorke. **1600** HOLLAND *Livy* XXXV. XXXV. 909 The Ætolians.. were ready and prest to come to Lacedæmon. **1632** —— *Cyrupædia* 27, I may find them [soldiers] prest and ready for any service. **1675** BROOKS *Gold. Key* Wks. 1867 V. 37 He is ready pressed to break all. *Ibid.* 396 Christ is ready prest for action.

2. Ready in mind, disposition, or will; inclined, disposed, willing; prompt, alert, eager, keen.

c **1290** *Becket* 2073 in *S. Eng. Leg.* I. 166 Þat min heorte prestore nis þene deþ for-to take. *a* **1300** *Cursor M.* 25 To rede and here Ilkon is prest, Þe thynges þat þam likes best. **1362** LANGL. *P. Pl.* A. VI. 41 He is þe presteste payere þat pore men habbeþ. *c* **1475** *Babees Bk.* 78 Take eke noo seete, but to stonde be yee preste. **1560** DAUS tr. *Sleidane's Comm.* 378 This verely should.. make them preste and willing to doe all thinges for your sake. **1600** FAIRFAX *Tasso* I. lxxxii, Each Mind is prest, and open every Ear To hear new Tydings. **1697** DRYDEN *Virg. Georg.* IV. 106 Every Knight is.. Prest for their Country's Honour, and their King's.

b. Alert, active, sprightly, brisk.

a **1400** *Pistill of Susan* 75 Þere were papeiayes prest, Nihtgales vpon nest. *a* **1529** SKELTON *Ph. Sparowe* 264 As prety and as prest As my sparowe was. **1573** TUSSER *Husb.* (1878) 142 More people, more handsome and prest, Where find ye? (go search any coast).

3. Close at hand. (Cf. *handy*.)

c **1500** *Robin Hood & Potter* lxiii. in Child *Ballads* (1888) III. 112 Berdys there sange on bowhes prest. **1589** PUTTENHAM *Eng. Poesie* III. xix. (Arb.) 231 In presence prest of people mad or wise.

B. *adv.* Readily, quickly; = PRESTLY *adv.* 1.

1297 R. GLOUC. (Rolls) 5217 As prest eft sone hii come. *c* **1320** *Sir Tristr.* 3145 He seyd tristrem prest, 'Now it were time to ride'. **1393** LANGL. *P. Pl.* C. XXI. 274 Princes of þis palys prest vndo þe ȝates. *c* **1475** *Rauf Coilȝear* 408 Out of Paris proudly he preikit full prest. *a* **1547** SURREY *Æneid* IV. 789 Shall not my men do on theyr armure prest? **1557–8** *Frere & Boye* 48 in Hazl. *E.P.P.* III. 62 The lytell boye wente on his waye, To the ffellde full prest.

prest, *ppl. a.*: see PRESSED *ppl. a.*[1] and [2].

† **prest**, *v.*[1] *Obs.* [a. OF. *prester* (11th c. in Godef. *Compl.*), mod.F. *prêter* to furnish, place at one's disposal, lend, pay in advance (= It. *prestare*, Pr., Sp., Pg. *prestar*):—L. *præstāre* to stand before; to be superior, excel; to stand for, vouch for, take upon oneself; to perform, show, offer, furnish; in late and med.L. (5th c. Salvianus and Salic Law) to lend; f. *præ* before + *stāre* to stand.]

1. *trans.* To lend (money); to advance on loan.

1543–4 *Act 35 Hen. VIII*, c. 12 Money so aduanced, prested, or lent to hys hyghnes. *a* **1548** HALL *Chron., Rich. III* 41 b, Requirynge hym farther to prest to hym a conveniente some of money. **1560–1** *Newcastle Guilds* (Surtees) 90 Money whyche ys prested, or lent, to the Quens Maiesties [use].

b. To get on loan, to borrow. *rare.*

a **1548** HALL *Chron., Hen. VI* 176 Lest the lordes there should borow of them any money, as they did prest of the marchantes of the staple .xviij. M. l. late before.

2. To advance (money) on account of work to be done or service to be rendered or not yet completed.

1539 in *Vicary's Anat.* (1888) App. ii. 106 Item, prested to Anthony Chobo, the kingis Surgion, in aduauncement of his half yeres wagis beforehande.. xx li. **1586** EARL LEICESTER in Motley *Netherl.* (1860) I. viii. 523 *note*, I myself have prested above 3000*l.* among our men here since I came.

† **prest**, *v.*[2] *Obs.* [f. PREST *sb.*[1]; or perh. an inverted use of PREST *v.*[1]]

1. *trans.* To engage or hire the services of (a person) or the use of (a ship, etc.) by giving part-payment in advance.

1513 *Lett. & Pap. Hen. VIII*, I. No. 3978 (P.R.O.) Shyppys prested for the King in the West Countrey. **1532** CROMWELL in Merriman *Life & Lett.* (1902) I. 351 The kinges messenger.. hathe repayryd.. to Burrye Saynt Edmondes and therabowtt For to haue taken and prestyd masons For the accomplyshment of the kynges sayd woorkes. **1545** *St. Papers Hen. VIII*, III. 542 Suche shippez as were prested in Chestre and Bewmarres. *Ibid.* 544 Your Highnez had byn at so great chardges, both with the presting, and victualing of shippez.

2. *esp.* To engage (men) for military service on land or sea by giving part-payment or earnest-money in advance; to enlist, levy (without reference to method): passing at length into the sense of PRESS *v.*[2] 2. (Cf. IMPREST *v.*[2])

1542 HEN. VIII *Declar. Scots* B ij, In this meane tyme staied a great part of our army alredy prested and in our wages, to go forwarde. **1545** *St. Papers Hen. VIII*, III. 536 Those that be all redy comme nowe demaunde here their wages, which thei say thei be not paide; and here is non that can enforme us, whether thei be paide or not, nor for howe longe tyme thei were prested. **1560** DAUS tr. *Sleidane's Comm.* 395 b, They.. whan this league was made, going into Germany, prested souldioures, and broughte them into France. **1600** HOLLAND *Livy* XXV. v. 548 So many as they thought able men of bodie to beare armes.. to prest them for soldiours. *Ibid.* XXVI. XXXV. 611 One whiles buying them up to the warre, for some small peece of money: otherwhiles levying and presting them to the seas to be gallie-slaues, for a thing of nothing. *Ibid.* XLII. i. 1116 Commaunded they were to prest [*scribere*] fifteene hundred footmen and a hundred horse of Romane citizens.

Hence **'presting** *vbl. sb.*, hiring, enlisting.

1545 [see 1 above]. **1546** *St. Papers Hen. VIII*, I. 874 Wee have also commoned with theym of the Admyraltye, whoo have onely twoo shipps in aredynes,.. wee have geven theym charge to procede, and delyvered theym money for the presting of men for the purpose.

† **prest**, *v.*[3] *Obs. rare.* [? f. PREST *a.*] *refl.* **a.** To make oneself ready. **b.** To make haste, to hasten.

14.. *Lybeaus Disc.* (Ritson) 1738 A morow Lybeaus hym prest [*v.r.* was prest] In armes that wer best, And fressch he was to fyght. **1581** A. HALL tr. *Homer* I. 14 One morning Thetis from the sea to heauen hir selfe doth prest.

prest, obs. ME. form of PRIEST.

'prestable, *a. Sc.* Now *rare.* Also 7 -ible. [a. obs. F. *prestable* (mod.F. *prêtable*) lendable, that may be lent (Cotgr.), also, ready to afford or give (16th c. in Godef.), f. *prester*: see PREST *v.*[1] and -ABLE.] Capable of being paid or advanced; payable; capable of being performed or discharged.

1650 *Acts Sederunt* 29 Jan. (1790) 67 After discussing of the first suspensioun for liquid soumes or deeds presentlie prestable. **1665** J. FRASER *Polichron.* (S.H.S.) 159 Sir Walter ..promised Lord Hugh all the kindness and service prestible by him, south and north. **1715** in *Wodrow Corr.* (1843) II. 54 Seriously to consider this, and fall upon some more prestable methods. **1746–7** *Act 20 Geo. II*, c. 43 §17 Recovery of multures or services payable or prestable to their mills. **1826** SCOTT *Let. to Lockhart* 20 Jan., To offer my fortune so far as it was prestable.., to make good all claims upon Ballantyne & Co. **1868** *Act 31 & 32 Vict.* c. 101 §8 All feu duties or other duties and services or casualties payable or prestable to the superior.

prestance. *rare*⁻¹. [f. as next + -ANCE. Cf. F. *prestance* (prɛstɑ̃s), ad. It. *prestanza*.] = next.

1893 *Nat. Observ.* 21 Jan. 231/2 They.. put their trust in great names and social prestance.

† **'prestancy.** *Obs. rare.* [ad. L. *præstāntia* pre-eminence, f. *præstāre* to excel: see PREST *v.*[1] and -ANCY.] Priority, superiority, pre-eminence.

1615 A. STAFFORD *Heav. Dogge* 39 If then the prestancy of instructing be such; surely Diogenes.. may in name, but not in deed bee a slaue. **1658** J. ROBINSON *Endoxa* iv. 30 In Adam, yet intire, there was a priority and a prestancy, but no soveraignty.

'prestant. *Music.* [a. F. *prestant*, ad. It. *prestante* excellent.] (See quot.)

1876 STAINER & BARRETT *Dict. Mus. Terms*, *Prestant*, the open diapason of an organ, sometimes of 16 feet, sometimes of 8 feet in length.

† **pre'stantious, præ-**, *a. Obs. rare*⁻¹. [f. L. *præstāntia* excellence, PRESTANCY + -OUS.] Characterized by excellence; excellent.

1638 T. WHITAKER *Blood of Grape* 35 This innate [humour] so praestantious, so necessary, as without it mix bodies cannot subsist.

prestate (ˈprɛsteɪt), *v. Rom. Law.* [f. ppl. stem of L. *præstāre* to stand before, to stand good for, vouch for, answer for: see PREST *v.*[1] and -ATE[3].] *trans.* To undertake, take upon oneself, become responsible for; to furnish, manifest.

1880 MUIRHEAD *Gaius* II. §215 All that the heir is bound to prestate in such a case..is sufferance [*damnetur heres patientiam præstare*]. —— *Ulpian* ii. §9. 367 Any person to whose good faith it can be committed to prestate a thing [*ad rem aliquam præstandam*] may also have it committed to his good faith to confer freedom.

prestation (prɛˈsteɪʃən). [a. F. *prestation* (1272 in Godef. *Compl.*) action of lending, tendering, etc., ad. L. *præstātiōn-em*, in late L. a payment, in med.L. esp. a feudal due, n. of action f. *præstāre*: see PREST *v.*[1], PRESTATE.] **a.** The action of paying, in money or service, what is due by law or custom, or in recognition of feudal superiority; a payment or the performance of a service so imposed or exacted; also, the performance of something promised.

1473 *Rolls of Parlt.* VI. 66/1 That no prises, exactions nor prestations, shal be sette upon their persones or goodes. **1607** COWELL *Interpr., Ayde*..in the common lawe, it is applied..sometime to a prestation due from tenents to their Lords, as toward the releife due to the Lord Paramount..or for the making of his sonne knight, or the marying of his daughter. *a* **1670** HACKET *Cent. Serm.* (1675), Not..as if the richer and mightier Church did, or could bind the smaller to the prestation of her customs. *a* **1754** SIR J. STRANGE *Reports* II. 879 The bishop libelled in the spiritual court, suggesting that Dr. Gooche, as arch-deacon of Essex, *tenetur solvere* 10*l.* due to the bishop as a prestation, for the exercise of his exterior jurisdiction. **1788** REID *Active Powers* v. vi. 667 It is obvious that the prestation promised must be understood by both parties. **1818** HALLAM *Mid. Ages* I. ii. II. 144 The military tenant..was subject to no tribute, no prestation, but service in the field. **1868** *Act 31 & 32 Vict.* c. 101 Sched. (y), No. 2 The yearly feu duties and the whole other prestations. **1890** GROSS *Gild Merch.* I. 195 The gild merchant with the right to exact money requisitions or prestations from the brethren as well as from non-gildsmen trading in the town. **1973** *Proc. Gen. Board of Faculties Oxf. Univ.* CXXXIII. 568 The directive also lays down that in the case of provision ('prestation') of services [etc.]... This expression refers to a short visit to another country in order to provide services on a temporary or transient basis.

b. *prestation-money*: see quots.

1536 in Strype *Eccl. Mem.* (1721) I. App. lxxix. 187 The Archdeacons had their acquittance of the Bp. by the name of Prestation-mony. **1607** COWELL *Interpr.* s.v. *Commissarie*, The Bishop taking prestation money of his arch-deacons yearely. *Ibid., Spiritualties of a Bishop*..be those profits which he receiueth, as he is a Bishop, and not as he is a Baron of the Parlament...[e.g.] prestation money, that *subsidium charitatiuum*, which vppon reasonable cause he may require of his Clergie. **1710** J. HARRIS *Lex. Techn.* II, s.v.

c. *Anthrop.* A gift, payment, or service that forms part of some traditional function in a society, given or due either to specific persons or to the group.

1889 W. R. SMITH *Lect. Relig. of Semites* xi. 403 The very idea of an execution implies a public function, and not a private prestation. *Ibid.* 413 Even in the theology of the Rabbins penitence atones only for light offences, all grave offences demanding also a material prestation. **1935** B. MALINOWSKI *Coral Gardens* I. vi. 204 Since the English language has a really unaccountable and intolerable gap, I am deliberately introducing here the word 'prestation' in the French sense, that is, of legally defined services to be tendered by one individual or group to another. **1951** *Jrnl. R. Anthrop. Inst.* LXXXI. 35/2 In Kachin type systems it is an exchange of women for gifts (prestations). *Ibid.* 51/1 The 'prestations'..may not only take on a variety of forms, they may have several quite different structural functions. **1954** I. CUNNISON in *Mauss's Gift* p. xi, There is no convenient English word to translate the French *prestation* so this word itself is used to mean any thing or series of things given freely or obligatorily as a gift or in exchange; and includes services, entertainments, etc., as well as material things. **1957** M. FORTES in R. Firth *Man & Culture* 178 Exogamy is evidently enforced without exception, as we should expect with a jural obligation that..is validated by prestations on both sides. **1967** F. BARTH in R. Firth *Themes in Econ. Anthropol.* 152 The rights of the cultivator as *user* as distinct from *owner* are expressed in the symbolic prestation of one pot of beer to the title holder after each harvest. **1968** R. NEEDHAM et al. tr. *Lévi-Strauss's Elem. Struct. Kinship* (1969) vi. 77 The *ufuapie* exchange prestations which are economic, legal, matrimonial, [etc.]. **1973** *Sci. Amer.* July 74/1 In general anthropologists have argued that the goods are a 'prestation', which has been defined as the act of paying in money or service what is due by law or custom.

Prestel (prɛˈstɛl). The proprietary name of a computerized visual information system operated by British Telecommunications, by which data selected from one or more data bases may be made to appear on a television screen by dialling an appropriate telephone number.

1978 *Times* 28 July 17/7 A Post Office brain-child, originally called Viewdata and now known as Prestel.., is now operating in a test version in preparation for its full public launch. **1978** *Trade Marks Jrnl.* 6 Dec. 2689/1 *Prestel*... Electrical, electronic and electro-mechanical apparatus, instruments and installations; monitoring, control and data storage apparatus and instruments... The Post Office. **1979** *Observer* 11 Feb. 42 (Advt.), Even at this early stage, there are thousands of pages of information available to Prestel subscribers. It's a sign of the way television is moving from being a simple means of entertainment to a much more complex domestic information medium.

prestellar: see PRE- B. 1.

†**ˈprester.** *Obs.* [a. L. *prēstēr*, a. Gr. πρηστήρ a fiery (or scorching) whirlwind, also a kind of venomous serpent, agent-n. f. πιμπρά-ναι, πρή-ειν (root *pra-*) to burn, also to inflate, blow.]

1. A serpent, the bite of which was fabled to cause death by swelling.

1398 TREVISA *Barth. De P.R.* XVIII. x. (Bodl. MS.), Prester is an horrible addre alwei wiþ open mouþe and castinge and schedinge venym as he goþe. **1562** TURNER *Herbal* II. 118 The bramble..is good for the biting of yᵉ serpent called prester. **1608** TOPSELL *Serpents* (1658) 745 The Dipsas killing by thirst, and the Prester by heat, as their very names do signifie. **1627** MAY *Lucan* IX. 828 The Prester too, whose sting distendeth wide The wounded's foamy mouth. **1706** PHILLIPS, *Prester*, a venomous Serpent, whose Sting causes a deadly Thirst. [**1847** EMERSON *Repr. Men, Swedenborg* Wks. (Bohn) I. 328 Philosophers are, therefore, vipers, cockatrices, asps,..presters.]

2. A burning or scorching whirlwind.

1601 HOLLAND *Pliny* I. 25 The same [wind], if it be more hot and catching a fire as it rageth, is named Prester; burning. **1643** HOWELL *Parables on Times* 15 As if it had been that incendiary Prester wind, or rather an Haraucana ..had blowne here. **1655** STANLEY *Hist. Philos.* II. (1701) 61/2 Thunders, Lightnings, Presters, and Whirl-winds are caused by the wind enclosed in a thick Cloud, which.. breaketh forth violently. **1727-41** CHAMBERS *Cycl., Prester*, a meteor, consisting of an exhalation from the clouds downwards with such violence, as that by the collision it is set on fire. **1797** *Monthly Mag.* III. 518/2 (tr. Procl. in Crat.) From him leap forth the implacable thunders, and the prester-capacious bosoms [πρηστηροδόχοι κόλποι] of the all-splendid strength of the father-begotten Hecate.

‖**3.** (See quots.)

1753 CHAMBERS *Cycl. Supp., Prester*, a word used by some to express the external part of the neck, which is usually inflated in anger. **1858** MAYNE *Expos. Lex., Prester, ēris*, formerly used for the white of the eye when inflamed; also, for the veins, when swollen under excitement.

ˈPrester ˈJohn. Forms: α. 4-6 **prestre, -ere**, 6 **preter, -our, prater, prest, priester**, (6-7 **precious**), 6-8 **presbyter**, 7 **priest**, 6- **prester**; 4-6 **Jon, Johan**, 6 **Joan, Jan**, (7 **Jack**), 8 **Jean**, 5- **John**. Also β. 6 **Pretian** (= Pret Ian), 7 **Prete Gianni, Janni, Prestegian, -giane.** [ME. *Prestre Johan*, a. OF. *prestre Jehan* (13th c. in Littré), mod.F. *prêtre-Jean*, med.L. *presbyter Johannes*, 'Priest John', in It. *prete Gianni*, whence OF. *prette-jan* and the β forms above.] The name given in the Middle Ages to an alleged Christian priest and king, originally supposed to reign in the extreme Orient, beyond Persia and Armenia, but from the 15th c. generally identified with the King of Ethiopia or Abyssinia.

(For the history of the subject, see Col. Yule's article in *Encycl. Brit.* (1885) XIX. 715- 718. It is there shown that from the first mention of *Presbyter Johannes* in the twelfth c. European belief placed him in some remote region of the East; but that, after growing knowledge of geography had at once cast doubt upon his existence there, and revealed the existence of a Christian king and kingdom in 'Ethiopia' or Abyssinia, 'Prester John's land' was located by the Portuguese, and after them by other writers, in the latter region. Col. Yule is even inclined to think that the original germ of the legend may have consisted in vague rumours as to the rule of a Christian king in 'Ethiopia', at a time when Ethiopia and India were still vaguely imagined to be conterminous or adjacent regions; although reports of the warlike achievements of Mongol or other Asiatic conquerors may in process of time have been credited to, or associated with, the name of 'Prester John'. As to the origin of this name or title, though numerous conjectures have been offered, there is no historical evidence.)

13.. *K. Alis.* 2589 (Bodl. MS.) Oute of Inde from prestre Johne Hym com kniȝttes manyon. *a* **1400** in *Rel. Ant.* I. 272 The lasse Asia and the lond of Histria; These ben Prestere Johanes londes. *c* **1400** *Three Kings Cologne* 117 He schulde be cleped preester Iohn..for þer is no degre in þis world aboue þe degre of priesthode. *c* **1400** MAUNDEV. (1839) xxii. 246 Prestre Iohan [*Roxb.* xxix. 132 Prestre Iohne] that is Emperour of the high Ynde. **1485** CAXTON *Paris & V.* 69 The londe of Prester Iohan. **1513** DOUGLAS *Æneis* VIII. Prol. 155 To reyd I begane The riotest ane ragment..Of all the mowis in this mold... The horne and the hand staff, Prater John and Port Jaff. **1562** PILKINGTON *Expos. Abdyas* Aa iij, The Souldan, priester Iohn & other Heathen princes. **1582** N. LICHEFIELD tr. *Castanheda's Conq. E. Ind.* I. i. 1 That in the East India were Christians, which were gouerned by a King of great power called Præsbiter Ioan. **1620** MELTON *Astrolog.* 11 As for Prester Jacke, the Great Mogul, the Sophy of Persia, and the Great Turke, I can see them as often as I doe my Boy. **1712** ADDISON *Spect.* No. 495 ⁋5 Not to mention whole Nations bordering on Prester-John's Country. **1788** GIBBON *Decl. & F.* xlvii. IV. 597 The fame of *Prester* or *Presbyter* John has long amused the credulity of Europe.

(*b*) **1532** MORE *Confut. Tindale* 85 Bothe the Latyn chyrch & the Greke chyrche and pretour Iohns Chyrche to. **1554** W. PRAT *Africa* E ij, The kynge of Ethiope whiche we call pretian or prest John. **1555** EDEN *Decades* To Rdr. (Arb.) 51 Preciosus Iohannes, otherwyse cauled Presbyter Iohannes, Emperour of many Chrystian nations in Ethiope. *Ibid.* 374 In the East syde of Afrike beneth the redde sea, dwelleth the greate and myghtye Emperour and Chrystian kynge Prester Iohan, well knowen to the Portugales in theyr vyages to Calicut. **1585** T. WASHINGTON tr. *Nicholay's Voy.* III. x. 86 b, The Prester Ian king of Ethyopia. **1598** W. PHILLIP *Linschoten* I. (Hakl. Soc.) I. 34 The countrey of Prester John, which is called by them the countrey of Abexines. **1600** J. PORY tr. *Leo's Africa* Introd. 21 The emperour Prete Ianni hath two speciall princely names, to wit, Acegue..and Neguz, a king. **1634** SIR T. HERBERT *Trav.* 130 The great Christian of Æthiopia, vulgarly cald Prester, Precious, or Priest-Iohn. **1678** BUTLER *Hud.* III. *Lady's Answ.* 277 Like the mighty Prester John, Whose Person none dares look upon.

b. *transf.* and *fig.* A ruler likened to Prester John; one who is supreme (in a particular sphere).

1598 E. GILPIN *Skial.* (1878) 34 And fooles doe sit, More honored then the Prester Iohn of wit. **1667** DRYDEN *Sir Martin Mar-All* v. i, Your Prester Johns of the East Indies.

c. *Heraldry.* (In the arms of the see of Chichester.)

1688 R. HOLME *Armoury* IV. iv. (Roxb.) 287/1 (Coates of Bishopricks) He beareth Saphire, a Prester John or Presbyter John sitting on a tombstone, haueing in his left hand a Mound, and his right extended..with a sword in his mouth..his is the Sea of Chichester. **1894** *Parker's Gloss. Heraldry* 476 Azure, a Presbyter John hooded sitting on a tombstone.

Hence **Prester-ˈJohnian** *a. nonce-wd.*, of or pertaining to Prester John.

a **1643** W. CARTWRIGHT *Ordinary* I. iv, On them, a lay Of Prester-Johnian whispers.

‖**pre-ˈsternum, præˈsternum.** [f. PRE- A. 4 b + STERNUM.]

1. *Entom.* = PROSTERNUM.

1828 STARK *Elem. Nat. Hist.* II. 279 Pre-sternum dilated at its anterior extremity. **1836** tr. *Cuvier's Anim. Kingd.* IV. 141 The præsternum forms a sort of chin-cloth anteriorly.

2. *Comp. Anat.* The front part of the sternum; the part corresponding to the first segment of the human sternum.

1872 NICHOLSON *Palæont.* 399 The præsternum is the 'manubrium sterni' of human anatomy. **1872** MIVART *Elem. Anat.* 35 The broad upper part to which the first rib is annexed is called the manubrium or pre-sternum.

Hence **pre-ˈsternal** *a.*, of or pertaining to the pre-sternum, as *pre-sternal bone, region*, etc.

1890 in WEBSTER.

presthold, obs. form of PRIESTHOOD.

†**ˈprestial,** *a. Obs. rare*[−1]. [f. ME. *prest*, PRIEST *sb.* + -IAL.] Priestly.

c **1449** PECOCK *Repr.* IV. v. 450 In the lay parti of Goddis peple, and..in the prestial parti of Goddis peple.

prestiˈdigital, *a. nonce-wd.* [f. after next and *digital.*] Light-fingered; practising sleight of hand.

1856 READE *Never Too Late* vi, The two hands he gathered coin with were Meadows and Crawley. The first his honest, hard-working hand—the second his three-fingered Jack, his prestidigital hand.

prestidigitation (ˌprɛstɪdɪdʒɪˈteɪʃən). [a. F. *prestidigitation*, f. as next: see -ATION.] Sleight of hand, legerdemain. Also *fig.*

1859 [see next]. **1862** *Leisure Hour* No. 542. 319 The real fact upon which all prestidigitation or quick finger conjuring depends, is the fact that human hands are quicker than human eyes. **1887** STEVENSON *Mem. & Portraits* xi. 188 This sort of prestidigitation is a piece of tactics among the true drawing-room queens.

prestidigitator (ˌprɛstɪˈdɪdʒɪteɪtə(r)). Also in F. form ‖**prestidigitateur** (prɛstidiʒitatœr). [ad. F. *prestidigitateur* (J. de Rovère, *a* 1830: see quot. 1859), f. *preste* nimble (ad. It. *presto*, L. *præstus*: see PRESTO) + L. *digit-us* a finger + *-ateur*, L. *-ator* agent-suffix: perh. suggested by F. *prestigiateur* PRESTIGIATOR, or due to a perverted derivation of it.] One who practises sleight of hand or legerdemain; a juggler, a conjurer; hence *fig.* a juggler with words, a trickster.

a **1843** in Southey *Comm.-pl. Bk.* IV. 603/1 De M. G. Ferizer the celebrated enchanter..prestidigitateur, and author of several experiments adapted to public amusement. **1859** WRAXALL tr. *R. Houdin* viii. 166-7 Jules de Rovère, the first to employ a title now generally given to fashionable conjurors... One day the pompous title of '*Prestidigitateur*' was visible on an enormous poster, which also condescended to supply the derivation of this breath-stopping word, *presto digiti* (activity of the fingers). *Ibid.*, The learning of the conjuror—I beg pardon, prestidigitator... This word, as well as Prestidigitation, due to the same author, were soon seized upon by Jules de Rovère's rivals. **1870** M. D. CONWAY *Earthw. Pilgr.* xvi. 201 Whether our young men should turn themselves into intellectual prestidigitateurs. **1879** BARING-GOULD *Germany* I. 392 A prestidigitator can work magic with his nimble fingers. **1905** *Contemp. Rev.* June 877 The repeated successes of the prestidigitator who is at the head of its Government.

Hence **prestidigitaˈtorial, prestiˈdigitatory** *adjs.*, of or pertaining to prestidigitation.

1860 *All Year Round* No. 63. 312 Prestidigitatory elements of entertainment were not wanting. **1861** in *Daily Tel.* 22 Oct., He has managed his cards well if he has substituted prestidigitatorial feats for operatic.

prestige (prɛˈstiːʒ, -stiːdʒ; formerly also ˈprɛstɪdʒ). [a. F. *prestige* (16th c. in Littré) an illusion, esp. in pl. 'deceits, impostures, delusions, iugling or cousening tricks' (Cotgr.), in mod.F. illusion, magic, glamour, ad. L. *præstigium* a delusion, illusion, usually in pl. *præstigiæ*, illusions, juggler's tricks, for **præstrigium* f. *præstringĕre* to bind fast (*præstringere oculos* to blindfold, hence, to dazzle the eyes): see PRESTRINGE.]

†**1.** An illusion; a conjuring trick; a deception, an imposture. Usually *pl. Obs.*

1656 BLOUNT *Glossogr.* [from Cotgr.], *Prestiges*.., deceits, impostures, delusions, cousening tricks. **1661** *Justiciary Rec.* (S.H.S.) I. 12 The Dittay does not condescend upon the Sorcery and prestiges whereby the Pannell did effectuat the particulars lybelled. **1753–4** WARBURTON *Princ. Nat. & Rev. Relig.* v. Wks. 1788 V. 92 That faith.. we are told, was founded on a rock, impregnable.. to the sophisms of infidelity, and the prestiges of imposture! [**1870** M. D. CONWAY *Earthw. Pilgr.* vii. 99 Prestige is simply *præstigium*, deceit; and surely that is a dangerous weapon for a true cause to use. **1881** FREEMAN in *Life & Lett.* (1895) II. 228 *Prestige*, you know, I always like to have a pop at; I take it it has never lost its first meaning of conjuring tricks.]

2. *transf.* Blinding or dazzling influence; 'magic', glamour; influence or reputation derived from previous character, achievements, or associations, or esp. from past success. [So in mod.F.]

[**1815** SCOTT *Paul's Lett.* (1839) 58 He [Napoleon] needed.. the dazzling blaze of decisive victory to renew the charm, or *prestige*, as he himself was wont to call it, once attached to his name and fortunes.] **1829** *Westm. Rev.* Oct. 397 The pleasure of these people does not consist in acting upon their maxims of *ton* among themselves, but in the effect of them on the inferior world. Dissipate the *prestige*, and you deprive them of the delight. **1837** FONBLANQUE *Eng. under Seven Administr.* I. Introd. 7 The *prestige* of the perfection of the law was unbroken. **1838** MILL *A. de Vigny* Diss. & Disc. (1859) I. 316 The *prestige* with which he [Napoleon] overawed the world is.. the effect of stage-trick. **1845** FORD *Handbk. Spain* I. 201 Such is the prestige of broad cloth. **1847** EMERSON *Repr. Men, Shaks.* Wks. (Bohn) I. 354 Had the *prestige* which hedges about a modern tragedy existed, nothing could have been done. **1856** KANE *Arct. Expl.* I. xviii. 216 The prestige of the gun with a savage is in his notion of its infallibility. **1859** KINGSLEY *Misc.* I. 11 She [Elizabeth] comes to the throne with such a prestige as never sovereign came since the days when Isaiah sang his pæan over young Hezekiah's accession. **1868** M. PATTISON *Academ. Org.* iv. 66 Balliol.. can set off a prestige of long standing against a deficiency in the stipend. **1871** L. STEPHEN *Playgr. Eur.* iii, In 1861.. the prestige of the mountains was rapidly declining. **1878** GLADSTONE *Prim. Homer* viii. 112 *Aidōs*.. means honour, but never the baseborn thing in these last times called *prestige*. **1898** SIR W. HARCOURT in *Daily News* 9 May 8/6 People talk sometimes of prestige... I am not very fond of the word. What I understand by prestige is the consideration in which nations or individuals are held by their fellows.

3. *attrib.* or quasi-*adj.* (not clearly distinguishable from some of the examples listed in sense 4 below). Cf. PRESTIGEFUL *a.*, PRESTIGIOUS *a.* 2.

1934 R. BENEDICT *Patterns of Culture* (1935) iv. 85 The Dionysian bent in the North American vision quest.. did not usually have to make compromise with prestige groups and their privileges. **1937** *Time* 16 Aug. 34/2 The cinema has a special category for what it calls 'prestige pictures'. **1944** W. S. MAUGHAM *Razor's Edge* vii. 325 Though she didn't much care for them [*sc.* some modern paintings] she thought quite rightly that they would be a prestige item in their future home. **1949** L. P. HARTLEY *Boat* xi. 156 If only they could all put off their company manners and change into their old clothes! But no; this was a prestige occasion. **1953** *Time* 23 Mar. 104/2 A 'prestige production', in broadcasting circles, is a show that abounds in a specific type of intelligence. **1957** *Times Lit. Suppl.* 8 Nov. 674/1 Serious books, normally prestige ware, had overnight changed into consumer goods, so that both conscience and bank-balance slept tight. **1958** M. ARGYLE *Relig. Behaviour* viii. 85 Prestige suggestion, in which people change their opinion after being told that a prestige person holds a different one. **1961** D. JENKINS *Equality & Excellence* viii. 175 Too many expensively educated young women aspire to careers as secretaries or receptionists in 'prestige offices'. **1962** *Rep. Comm. Broadcasting 1960* 92 in *Parl. Papers 1961–2* (Cmnd. 1753) IX. 259 The occasional, highly-advertised prestige programme put on for the occasion of a Christian festival. **1967** *Word Study* Mar. 3/2, I do find it difficult not to blame Miss Prouty at least a little bit.. for rejecting usages so widely current in the prestige dialect that they are sanctioned even by her own textbook. **1968** *Globe & Mail* (Toronto) 13 Jan. 37/2 (Advt.), Accommodation available in Toronto's finest small nursing home, central prestige location, single or double occupancy, with or without private bath. **1969** *Nature* 29 Nov. 840/1 The Soviet Union still.. seems to treat all scientific and technological progress (from sputniks to fish-spotting and from television sets to trans-continental pipelines) as primarily 'prestige' achievements. **1971** E. JONES in J. Spencer *Eng. Lang. W. Afr.* 84 Yams are a kind of prestige crop and item of food in rural West Africa. **1974** *Times* 20 Sept. 1/4 Aston Martin, one of Britain's prestige car companies. **1977** *Irish Times* 8 June 13/6 (Advt.), Superb town residence in prestige location.

4. *Comb.*, as ***prestige-object, -principle, -product, -structure, -value, -word; prestige-hunting, -ranking, -rating*** vbl. sbs.; ***prestige-bearing, -building, -conferring, -conscious, -marking*** adjs.; **prestige advertising**, advertising with the principal aim of furthering the prestige of the advertiser (rather than increasing sales, etc.).

1958 P. SHORE in N. Mackenzie *Conviction* 39 I.C.I. is not alone in this kind of prestige advertising. **1959** *Manch. Guardian* 2 July 6/5, I doubt whether prestige advertising is important in recruiting university graduates. **1972** *Lebende Sprachen* XVII. 46/2 Prestige advertising. **1949** R. K. MERTON *Social Theory* II. v. 201 Pickpockets who.. delight in mastering the prestige-bearing feat of 'beating a left breech'. **1964** R. A. HALL *Introd. Linguistics* 21 Prestige-bearing persons. **1965** *Economist* 13 Nov. 723/1 A very different and very prestige-building new activity. **1961** D. JENKINS *Equality & Excellence* viii. 151 Those prestige-conferring occupations which used to be reserved for those 'of good family'. **1971** *Guardian* 25 Sept. 8/1 Prestige-conscious companies like IBM and Alcan. **1930** M. MEAD *Growing up in New Guinea* iii. 29 But this is neither child labour nor idle prestige hunting on the part of the parents. **1957** M. JOOS *Readings in Linguistics* 376/2 The dialects and idiolects of higher prestige were more advanced in this direction [of phonetic drift], and their speakers carried the drift farther along so as to maintain the prestige-marking difference against their pursuers. **1955** D. CHAPMAN *Home & Social Status* iii. 42 The piano, which was formerly the principal prestige-object. **1939** *Brit. Jrnl. Psychol.* Jan. 220 Concrete manifestations of the 'prestige-principle' at work. **1958** *Observer* 25 May 16/2 To-day 'culture' is being marketed as a prestige-product. **1955** T. H. PEAR *Eng. Social Differences* i. 29 How far does their [*sc.* adolescents'] prestige-ranking of occupations resemble that made by adults? **1957** YOUNG & WILLMOTT in 'C. H. Rolph' *Human Sum* vii. 140 An earlier national study of the prestige-ranking given to occupations by people who were predominantly non-manual workers. **1960** *New Left Rev.* Sept.–Oct. 3/1 The changing patterns of prestige-ranking. **1954** J. A. C. BROWN *Social Psychol. of Industry* v. 140 The worker may be.. upset when he is moved to another job at the same pay, but with a lower prestige-rating. **1949** R. K. MERTON *Patterns of Influence* iv, in Lazarsfeld & Stanton *Communications Res.* II. 198 He begins his climb in the prestige-structure at a relatively high level. **1929** L. D. WHITE (*title*) The prestige value of public employment in Chicago. **1942** *Mind* LI. 170 Mathematics has indeed, a tremendous prestige value. **1958** *Listener* 21 Aug. 283/2 The two- or three-garage house, even the monster car itself, looked like losing its prestige value. **1967** E. SHORT *Embroidery & Fabric Collage* iii. 68 A good patchwork quilt has a prestige value in keeping with the labour that goes into the making of it. **1972** J. L. DILLARD *Black English* vi. 233 The prestige value of more expensive toys, bicycles, and athletic equipment. **1964** C. BARBER *Ling. Change Present-Day Eng.* ii. 25 There are many men of the professional classes who, far from practising the sounds of R[eceived] P[ronunciation] and the prestige-words of R[eceived] S[tandard], are deliberately refusing to do so. **1964** *Eng. Stud.* XLV. (Suppl.) 22 But very often there is a marked difference in tone between the foreign and the native terms, the former being felt as prestige-word, the latter as the plain terms.

prestigeful (prɛˈstiːʒfʊl), *a.* [f. PRESTIGE + -FUL.] = PRESTIGIOUS *a.* 2.

1956 C. W. MILLS *Power Elite* iii. 53 There is.. an appreciation of the new for its own sake: that which is new is prestigeful. **1959** *Encounter* Aug. 71/1 The more or less prestigeful 'pure fields'. **1961** S. R. HERMAN in J. A. Fishman *Readings Sociol. of Lang.* (1968) 507 In the new environment he [*sc.* an immigrant] is often without the prestigeful status he enjoyed in his country of origin and he is very much in need of recognition. **1967** M. ARGYLE *Psychol. Interpersonal Behaviour* v. 93 The experimenter should be prestigeful, an attractive person of the opposite sex, or at any rate compatible. **1971** *Times Lit. Suppl.* 22 Oct. 1310/4 Bateson had his contributions refused publication by the prestigeful periodical *Nature*. **1974** R. A. HALL *External Hist. Romance Lang.* 22 Many scholars.. are inclined to follow the folk-lore of our Western European culture in ascribing the status of 'language' only to those types of speech which manifest the prestigeful features just mentioned.

prestigey (prɛˈstiːʒɪ, prɛˈstiːdʒɪ), *a. colloq.* [f. PRESTIGE + -Y[1].] = PRESTIGIOUS *a.* 2.

1963 *Spectator* 27 Sept. 385 Desires for prestigey bigness. **1968** J. BINGHAM *I love, I Kill* xi. 133 What you want is the serious actor bit. Something more prestigey. **1968** M. RICHLER *Cocksure* vi. 36 We're no more than a bauble.. a prestige-y trinket.

†**preˈstigiate**, *v.* ? *Obs. rare.* Also 8 præ-. [f. late L. *præstigiāre* (f. *præstigium*: see PRESTIGE) + -ATE[3].] *trans.* To deceive by jugglery or as by magic; to delude. Hence †**preˈstigiated** deluded, †**preˈstigiating** deluding, *ppl. adjs.*

1647 WARD *Simp. Cobler* 17 To take Christ as himselfe hath revealed himselfe in his Gospel, and not as the Divell presents him to prestigiated phansies. **1716** M. DAVIES *Athen. Brit.* II. 229 Præstigiating and ensnaring Arians.

prestigiˈation. Now *rare.* Also 7 præ-. [n. of action from L. *præstigiāre*: see prec.] The practice of juggling, sorcery, or magic; deception or delusion by such practice; conjuring.

c **1540** tr. *Pol. Verg. Eng. Hist.* (Camden) I. 83 Least thei might.. bee evegeled with the sorceres and prestigiation of devils. *c* **1645** HOWELL *Lett.* (1650) III. xxiii. 37 Examples.. of fascinations, incantations, prestigiations, of philtres, spells, charmes, sorceries, characters and such like. *a* **1670** HACKET *Cent. Serm.* (1675) 338 If such a thing come to pass by the Devil's mists and devices, then it is præstigiation or delusion. **1885** *St. James' Gaz.* 20 June, At Piccadilly Hall.. To-day. Séances of Prestigiation, Mesmerism, and Thought Transmission.

prestigiator (prɛˈstɪdʒɪeɪtə(r)). Also 8 præ-. [a. L. *præstigiātor*, agent-n. f. *præstigiāre*: see PRESTIGIATE. So F. *prestigiateur* (16th c. in Godef. *Compl.*).] One who practises 'prestigiation'; a juggler, a conjurer; †a cheat.

1614 RALEIGH *Hist. World* II. vi. §7 (1634) 270 Prestigiators are such as dazell men's eyes, and make them seeme to see what they see not. **1660** H. MORE *Myst. Godl.* IV. iii. 105 This cunning Prestigiator took the advantage of so high a place to set off his Representations the more lively. **1784** J. WHITE *Bampton Lect.* iii. 141 Augustus.. had published very rigorous edicts against the whole race of Præstigiators. **1861** MISS BRADDON *Lady Lisle* (1885) 74 The coin which the prestigiator shows is not the first shilling at all.

†**preˈstigiatory**, *a. Obs.* [f. L. *præstigiātor*: see prec. and -ORY[2].] Practising 'prestigiation'; juggling, conjuring; deceptive, delusive.

1588 J. HARVEY *Disc. Probl.* 66 Hypocriticall subornations, in some like prestigiatory, and sophisticall veine. *a* **1677** BARROW *Serm.* (1683) II. xx. 283 Wicked spirits deal onely in petty, low and useless prestigiatory tricks. **1681** GLANVILL *Sadducismus* II. 204 By that κλεψωκια, or Prestigiatory art or faculty of these ludicrous Dæmons.

prestiginous (prɛˈstɪdʒɪnəs), *a. rare*[−1]. [f. PRESTIGE + *-in-* + -OUS, irreg. after *multitudinous*, etc.] = PRESTIGIOUS *a.* 2.

1896 G. B. SHAW *Let.* 16 Mar. (1965) I. 614 A commercial and prestiginous success for Janet.

†**preˈstigion.** *Obs. rare.* [irreg. f. late L. *præstigium* a delusion, illusion, trick (see PRESTIGE) + -ION[1].] = PRESTIGIATION.

1635 HEYWOOD *Hierarch.* IX. Comm. 610 Simon Magus.. after all his cheating, jugling and prestigion (if I may so call it),.. at the prayers of St Peter his spells failed. **1637** —— *London's Mirr.* Wks. 1871 IV. 314 Pride, Arrogance, Sloath, Vanity, Prestigion.

prestigious (prɛˈstɪdʒəs, prɛˈstiːdʒəs), *a.* Also 7 præ-. [ad. late L. *præstigiōsus* full of tricks, deceitful, f. *præstigi-um* PRESTIGE + -OUS. So F. *prestigieux* (16th c. in Hatz.-Darm.) illusive, using charms.] **1.** Practising juggling or legerdemain; of the nature of or characterized by juggling or magic; cheating, deluding, deceitful; deceptive, illusory. Now *rare.*

1546 BALE *Eng. Votaries* I. (1550) 48 b, Ashamed are not these prestygiouse Papystes, to vtter it in their storyes and reade it in their Sayntes legendes. **1607** DEKKER *Whore of Babylon* Wks. 1873 II. 195 That inchantresse.. by prestigious trickes in sorcerie, Has raiz'd a base impostor. *a* **1711** KEN *Edmund* Poet. Wks. 1721 II. 116 As in the Mines prestigious Spirits lurk, And while the Miners sleep, seem hard at work. **1884** SWINBURNE in *19th Cent.* May 771 The prestigious influence which turned the heads and perverted the hearts of the Byrons and the Hazlitts of his day. **1887** T. CHILD in *Contemp. Rev.* May 713 The grandiose language, the ringing rhymes, and the prestigious metaphors. **1957** *Eng. Lang. Teaching* XII. I. 5 Ogden, whose prestigious virtuosity in paraphrase had enabled him to work Basic English out. **1974** *Times Lit. Suppl.* 11 Jan. 32/3 For the period of nearly five years during which he remained as Prime Minister after the war he was.. engaged in promoting policies which were actively disliked, or accepted reluctantly, by a majority of his supporters. This was the essential nature of the prestigious balancing act which he was constantly obliged to perform.

2. Having, showing, or conferring prestige (sense 2).

In this sense many prefer to use PRESTIGEFUL *a.* or some other adjective.

1913 CONRAD *Chance* I. iii. 76 'You have had all these immense sums... What have I had out of them?' It was perfectly true. He had had nothing out of them—nothing of the prestigious or the desirable things of the earth. **1958** *Economist* 25 Oct. (Suppl.) 19/1 But then came a form of competition that the American automobile industry had never envisaged—a competition from other industries for the consumer's dollar spent on prestigious purchases. **1960** *Time & Tide* 8 Oct. 1179/1 The commercial [television] companies agreed—.. to give ITN enough cash for its extremely prestigious and worthy coverage of the United Nations. **1963** *Listener* 18 Apr. 656/2 Once established in these prestigious places men leave only if they have to. **1967** G. STEINER *Lang. & Silence* 72 Recent French linguistic philosophy also assigns a special function and prestigious authority to silence. **1969** *Daily Tel.* (Colour Suppl.) 5 Sept. 32/1 Those hotels such as every prestigious capital needs. **1970** B. M. H. STRANG *Hist. English* 75 Of course, before 1770, not everyone was confined to the English of his town or village unless he hiked or hacked to another; many were exposed to the highly prestigious and influential written form. **1973** *Oxf. Univ. Gaz.* CIII. Suppl. 5. 33 The small but prestigious collection of German drawings in the Department. **1974** *Times* 27 Apr. 15/5 A career in pure science is still more socially prestigious, in Britain, than one in engineering or in applied science. **1975** *Physics Bull.* May 219/3 Halley was already quite distinguished, established as the Savilian Professor of Geometry at Oxford (a prestigious position).

Hence **preˈstigiously** *adv.*; **preˈstigiousness**.

1593 G. HARVEY *Pierce's Super.* 208 He.. that was prestigiously besieged, and inuisibly vndermined with that weapon of weapons. **1646** GAULE *Cases Consc.* 115 There is nothing but præstigiousnesse of Forme, End, Effect. **1664** H. MORE *Myst. Iniq.* 437 Their being able to make a consecrated wafer appear to be the very Body and Person of Christ is such a piece of prestigiousness as has no parellel. **1671** SALMON *Syn. Med.* III. xxv. 459 We cannot be so prestigiously Impudent, as to pretend to the World.. that these our Pills will Cure all diseases. **1962** *Listener* 27 Dec. 1098/1 Art has become a commodity, albeit a highly prestigious one. But it is its very 'prestigiousness' that has brought upon its none too sturdy back the hordes of P.R.O.s and promoters. **1968** J. M. ZIMAN *Public Knowl.* vi. 118 He uses the standard technical words and phrases of the subject, not.. to associate himself prestigiously with his would-be colleagues.

†**ˈprestigy.** *Obs. rare*[−1]. In 7 præstigie. [ad. L. *præstigi-um*: see PRESTIGE.] ? = PRESTIGE I.

1652 GAULE *Magastrom.* 250 They committed it, to nurse, to a prodigious hagge that hight praestigie.

prestimony (ˈprɛstɪmənɪ). *Canon Law.* Also 8 præ-. [ad. F. *prestimonie* (1690 in Hatz.-Darm.), ad. med.L. *præstimōnium* (781 in Du Cange), f.

L. *præstāre* to furnish, etc.: see PRESTATION and -MONY.] (See quot.)

1727–41 CHAMBERS *Cycl.*, *Prestimony, Præstimonia*, in the canon law, a term about which authors are much divided.. Upon the whole, the surest opinion seems to be this, that præstimony is a fund or revenue appropriated by the founder for the subsistence of a priest, without being erected into any title or benefice, chapel, prebend, or priory. **1848** in WHARTON *Law Lex.*; and in mod. Dicts.

Hence **prestimonial** (-'məʊnɪəl) *a.*, of or pertaining to prestimony.

1706 tr. *Dupin's Eccl. Hist. 16th C.* II. IV. xx. 332 Some simple Benefices,..also Donatives, or Prestimonial Portions, as they are called.

prestinate, obs. form of PRISTINATE.

‖**prestissimo** (pres'tissimo), *a.*, *adv.*, *sb. Mus.* [It. *prestissimo*, superl. of *presto* adj. and adv.: see PRESTO.] A musical direction indicating very rapid performance: Very quick, very fast; as *sb.* a very quick piece or movement. Hence *transf.*

1724 *Short Explic. For. Words in Mus. Bks.*, *Prestissimo*, is Extream Fast or Quick. **1841** MARRYAT *Poacher* lxiv, At the report of the pistol, the..choristers struck up prestissimo with their feet. **1882** MISS BRADDON *Mt. Royal* ii, Angus had naturally taken the time of life's march prestissimo. **1904** *Westm. Gaz.* 22 Feb. 3/1 Our opponents' totals of 388 and 351 must seem big enough in England, but out here on these prestissimo wickets they are really nothing like so formidable as they look.

†'**prestly**, *adv. Obs.* Also 4–5 **pristly**, **prystly**, 6 **preastly**. [f. PREST *a.* + -LY[2].]

1. Readily, quickly, promptly, immediately.

1340 *Ayenb.* 140 Þe ournemens of boȝsamnesse byeþ zeuen, þet ys, þet me bouȝe prestliche, gledliche, simpleliche, klenliche, generalliche, zuyftliche, and wiluolliche. *c* **1350** *Will. Palerne* 1146 Boþe partiȝes prestly a-paraylde hem. ? *a* **1400** *Morte Arth.* 2762 He flenges to syr Florent, and prystly he kryes,—'Why flees thow, falls knyghte? Þe fende hafe þi saule!' *c* **1420** *Avow. Arth.* xix, He prekut oute prestely. **15..** *Adam Bel & Clym of Clough* 451 They preced prestly into the hall. **1548** UDALL *Erasm. Par. Luke* xxiv. 189 b, His speciall great strength..was preastly and readily shewed foorth at the houre of his death. *c* **1557** ABP. PARKER *Ps.* ciii. 288 His sauing helth comth prestly on To ryd thy life from peryls all.

2. Eagerly, urgently, earnestly.

c **1400** *Destr. Troy* 230 Yiff þu puttes þe pristly þis point for to do. **1522** *World & Child* in Hazl. *Dodsley* I. 253 Now pray you prestly on every side To God omnipotent. **1642** H. MORE *Song of Soul* II. I. II. x, The heart, the heart-bloud, brains fleet aire, hot fire To be the thing that they so prestly sought, Some have defin'd.

prest-money, earlier form of PRESS-MONEY.

†'**prestness**. *Obs. rare*[−1]. [f. PREST *a.* + -NESS.] Readiness, preparedness.

1582 LD. BURGHLEY in Ellis *Orig. Lett.* Ser. II. III. 100, I was glad to perceaue your prestnes to enter into Scotland.

‖**presto** ('presto, 'prɛstəʊ), *a.*[1], *adv.*[1], *sb.*[1] *Music.* [It. *presto* quick, quickly (*tempo presto* quick time):—late L. *præst-us*, f. earlier *præstō* adv., at hand, ready, in med.L. prompt, quick: see PREST *a.*]

A. *adj.* or *adv.* A direction indicating rapid performance: In quick time; fast. Also *transf.*

1683 PURCELL *Sonnatas in III Parts* Pref., The English Practitioner..will find a few terms of art, perhaps unusual to him, the chief of which are.. *Presto*. **1724** *Short Explic. For. Words in Mus. Bks.*, *Presto Presto*, or *Piu Presto*, very Fast or Quick. *Ibid.*, *Men Presto*, not too Quick; or not quite So Quick. **1752** AVISON *Mus. Expression* 107 The words *Andante, Presto, Allegro*, &c., are differently apply'd in the different kinds of Music. **1876** STAINER & BARRETT *Dict. Mus. T.*, *Presto*, fast. **1952** A. CHRISTIE *They do it with Mirrors* i. 9 Everyone's life has a tempo. Ruth's was *presto* whereas Miss Marple's was..*adagio*. **1976** C. BERMANT *Coming Home* II. vii. 215, I was an andante being in a *presto* setting.

B. as *sb.* A movement or piece in quick time.

1869 *Athenæum* 20 Nov., The final *presto* was a miracle of consentaneousness, the rapidity of the movement never interfering with the distribution of light and shade. **1888** MRS. H. WARD *R. Elsmere* 394 How the presto flew as though all the winds were behind it.

presto ('prɛstəʊ), *adv.*[2], *a.*[2], *sb.*[2] [a. It. *presto* adj. and adv., quick, quickly: the same words as prec., but the two uses are unconnected in Eng.]

A. *adv.* (*interj.*) Quickly, immediately, at once; used by conjurers and jugglers in various phrases of command, esp. ***Presto, be gone, Hey presto, pass***, etc.; hence, = immediately, forthwith, instanter. Also interjectionally: see quots. 1821, 1892.

1598–9 B. JONSON *Case is Altered* I. i, Presto, Go to, a word to the wise; away, fly, vanish! **1622** MABBE tr. *Aleman's Guzman d' Alf.* I. 47 Crying out *Presto*, bee gone,..hee flies away in the ayre. **1656** BLOUNT *Glossogr.*, *Presto*.., a word used by Juglers, in their *Hocus Pocus* tricks. *a* **1683** OLDHAM *Poet. Wks.* (1686) 89 Hey Jingo, Sirs! What's this? 'tis Bread you see; Presto be gone! 'tis now a Deity. **1721** SWIFT *South Sea* Wks. 1755 III. II. 132 Put in your money fairly told; Presto be gone—'Tis here agen. **1821** BYRON *Vis. Judgm.* lxxviii, The moment that you had pronounced him one, Presto! his face changed, and he was another. **1858** LYTTON *What will he do* I. iii, Hey, presto,—quick, while we turn in to wash our hands. **1892** E. REEVES *Homeward Bound* 72 You pressed a bell, the boy appeared with his lift, and, presto! you are in the street again.

B. as *sb.* An exclamation of 'presto!'

1622 FLETCHER *Beggars Bush* III. i. (1647) 83, 1 *B.* Cloakes? looke about ye boys: mine's gone. 2 *B.* A —— juggle 'em! [Pox] o' their Prestoes: mine's gone too. *a* **1677** BARROW *Serm.* (1686) III. xvi. 185 Neither..a spirit, that will be conjured down by a charm, or with a Presto driven away.

C. *adj.* or *attrib.* At hand, in readiness; active, ready, rapid, quick, instantaneous; of the nature of a magical transformation; juggling.

1644 BULWER *Chiron.* 100 Upon the hearing of which watchword they were to be presto and at Hand to execute their dumbe commands. **1767** S. PATERSON *Another Trav.* I. 80 Instantaneously she betook herself to presto-prayer. **1826** H. N. COLERIDGE *West Indies* (1832) 285 There is no hocus pocus.., no presto movements. **1877** *Paperhanger, Painter, Grainer*, etc. 107 The presto system [of graining] is very useful where work is required to be done out of hand, as it may be varnished almost immediately.

Hence '**presto** *v. trans.*, to convey or transfer instantaneously, by or as by magic; to conjure.

1831 *Examiner* 92/2 The man of magic must have 'prestoed' the watch into his own pocket. **1853** *Fraser's Mag.* XLVII. 19 The latter, by a process of etymological conjuring..have sought to presto *thunnus* out of *tannim*.

prestod, obs. form of PRIESTHOOD.

†'**prestolate**, *v. Obs. nonce-wd.* [f. F. *prestoler* (Rabelais), ad. L. *præstōlārī* to stand ready for, wait for: see -ATE[3].] *trans.* To await.

1653 URQUHART *Rabelais* II. vi. 31 We prestolate the coming of the Tabellaries [orig. *prestolans les tabellaires à venir*] from the Penates and patriotick Lares.

‖**prestomium, præ-** (priː'stɒmɪəm). [mod.L., f. PRE- B. 3 + Gr. στόμιον, dim. of στόμα mouth.] The anterior segment of the head of an annelid, bearing the eyes and tentacles. Hence **pre'stomial** *a.*, of or pertaining to the prestomium.

1877 HUXLEY *Anat. Inv. Anim.* v. 232 The peristomium and the praestomium together are ordinarily confounded under the common term of 'head'. *Ibid.*, The praestomial tentacle is similar in structure to an ordinary cirrus.

'**prestress**, *sb.* and *a.* **A.** *sb.* [PRE- A. 2.] Tension applied to an object during manufacture or prior to some other treatment, usu. in order to counteract applied compressive loads (as in prestressed concrete).

1934 *Engineering News-Record* 13 Sept. 345/1 A pre-stress of 8,392 lb. per sq. in. **1940** *Structural Engineer* XVIII. 642/1 (*heading*) Diminution of the preliminary tensile pre-stress in steel by shrinkage and creeping. **1956** *Archit. Rev.* CXIX. 146/3 Strips of shuttering supported on props are necessary under the transverse diaphragms and these also support the precast units before the pre-stress is applied. **1967** *New Scientist* 10 Aug. 295/1 The higher the prestress applied, the higher the fatigue strength of the section. **1977** *Design Engin.* July 64/1 Forces depend on prestress, i.e. initial deflection of spring, as well as direction of motion.

B. *adj.* [PRE- B. 2.] Occurring before a stressed syllable.

1973 *Word 1970* XXVI. 98 In the traditional analysis long vowels occur only under stress... Therefore, no prestress vowel may be long. **1975** *Amer. Speech 1972* XLVII. 171 The sets of intersyllabic consonants and consonant clusters differ remarkably in different slots; for instance prestress / bh bt nk/ (as in *abhór, obtáin, enquíre*).

prestress (priː'strɛs), *v.* [PRE- A. 1.] *trans.* To apply stress to (an object or material) prior to some other treatment; to introduce stress into (an object) during manufacture, so as to enable it more successfully to withstand applied loads; *spec.* with reference to reinforced concrete (cf. PRESTRESSED *ppl. a.*).

1934 *Engineering News-Record* 13 Sept. 345/1 The idea of destroying the bond between steel rods inserted in concrete, and prestressing the rods in tension and the concrete in compression, is not new. **1936** *Structural Engineer* XIV. 252/1 The concreting operation is carried out in the usual manner, the only difference being that the longitudinal rods are pre-stressed. **1940** *Concrete & Constructional Engin.* XXXV. 330/1 Thin piano wires, of a strength of 350,000 lb. to 450,000 lb. per square inch, are prestressed to a stress equivalent to half that of yield point. **1967** *New Scientist* 10 Aug. 295/1 When the concrete is prestressed the steel is dynamically opposed to the applied load. *Ibid.*, Any series of units can be cast separately and then prestressed together to convert them into a monolithic whole. **1971** *Materials & Technol.* II. iv. 113 (*caption*) The vertical outer wall..was prestressed with Freyssinet cables.

So **pre'stressing** *vbl. sb.*

1934 *Engineering News-Record* 13 Sept. 345/1 One advantage of the prestressing is to postpone the formation of cracks. **1940** *Structural Engineer* XVIII. 629 Notwithstanding the cost of the pre-stressing operations, this great saving in materials renders also pre-stressed designs very economical. **1953** *Sci. News Let.* 24 Jan. 63/2 In one phase of the study, it was found that prestressing doubled the ability of one aluminum alloy, used in the aircraft industry, to carry an external load. **1964** C. W. GLOVER *Structural Precast Concrete* xix. 328 The basic idea of pre-stressing is to induce in the unloaded members stresses that are contrary to the stress normally produced by loading. **1974** *Encycl. Brit. Macropædia* IV. 1078/1 The calculation of the initial tensile force required in the prestressing tendons to produce compressive stresses that will counteract the tensile stresses in the concrete.

pre'stressed, *ppl. a.* [f. prec. + -ED[1].] Previously subjected to stressing; into which stress has been deliberately introduced during manufacture; *spec.* of concrete: reinforced by steel rods or wires which have been tensioned while the concrete is setting, so that after setting they tend to compress the concrete and thereby strengthen it.

1936 *Structural Engineer* XIV. 251/1 Two telegraph posts 40 ft. long,..one..in pre-stressed concrete, and the other.. in ordinary reinforced concrete, were subjected to alternate stressing. **1948** *Concrete & Constructional Engin.* XLIII. 260 The resiliency and freedom from cracks of prestressed concrete make the material very suitable for railway sleepers and runways. **1955** *Times* 19 July 4/7 Huge pipes in cast iron, or spun iron, or prestressed concrete. **1963** SIMONDS & CHURCH *Conc. Guide Plastics* (ed. 2) vii. 172 These prestressed laminated structures show strengths three to four times those of the unstressed fabric laminates. **1969** *Jane's Freight Containers 1968–69* 68/1 Crane—18-inch pre-cast, pre-stressed concrete piles; pre-stressed concrete deck. **1973** *Times* 14 Mar. 4/7 As Lancashire County Council's chief assistant in charge of bridges he designed about fifty, including..its first prestressed bridge.

pre-'stretch, *v. Building.* [PRE- A. 1.] = PRE-TENSION *v.* Hence **pre-'stretched** *ppl. a.*; **pre-'stretching** *vbl. sb.*

1936 *Structural Engineer* XIV. 251/1 By inducing tension in the reinforcement one secures..a decrease of the tension produced in the concrete by the shearing process, or even its total suppression if the reinforcement is pre-stretched in two directions. **1941** *Concrete & Constructional Engin.* XXXVI. 93/1 M. Freyssinet's device with pre-stretched wires needs no anchorage for the manufacture of a long row of articles after one stretching operation. **1946** *Ibid.* XLI. 147 With pre-stretching the member has to remain in the mould until the stretching force, produced by tensioning of the reinforcement.., can safely be transmitted to the concrete. **1949** [see POST-STRETCHING *vbl. sb.*]. **1965** E. C. HISCOCK *Cruising under Sail* (ed. 2) v. 79 Terylene..is.. more suitable for halyards and headsail sheets; but for those purposes Marlow Ropes Ltd. make a pre-stretched three-strand rope.

†**pre'striction**. *Obs. rare*[−1]. [ad. late L. *præstrictiōn-em* binding fast, n. of action f. *præstringĕre*: see next.] The binding or tying up of the eyes; blindfolding, blinding.

1641 MILTON *Animadv.* iii. Wks. 1851 III. 213 Boast not of your eyes, 'tis fear'd you have Balaams disease, a pearle in your eye, Mammons Præstriction.

†**pre'stringe**, *v. Obs. rare.* [ad. L. *præstringĕre* to bind fast, also to touch upon, mention, f. *præ*, PRE- A. + *stringĕre* to draw tight, to touch.] *trans.* To touch upon, mention, refer to.

1668 H. MORE *Div. Dial.* IV. iii. (1713) 292 The greatest Wits of the World have been such Persons as you seem so freely to prestringe.

pre-structuralist: see PRE- B. 1.

prest sail = press of sail: see PRESS *sb.*[1] 10.

pre-study: see PRE- A. 1.

prestwoode, obs. form of PRIESTHOOD.

pre-subject: PRE- B. 2 a.

presubsistent, presubterminal: see PRE- A. 3, B. 3.

presuffixal: see PRE- B. 1.

presul ('priːsʊl). *rare.* [a. L. *præsul* a dancer in public, the leader of the *Salii* (dancing priests), hence in late L. a president, in med.L. a prelate, bishop, f. **præsilīre, præsult-um*, to dance before others, f. *præ* before, in front + *salīre* to leap, dance.] A prelate, a bishop. Hence '**presulate**, the tenure of office of a 'presul'.

[**1377** LANGL. *P. Pl.* B. xv. 42 For bisshopes yblessed þei bereth many names, *Presul* and *pontifex* and *metropolitanus*.] **1577** tr. *Bullinger's Decades* (1592) 885 These are called both bishops, chiefe priests, and presuls. **1853** J. STEVENSON *Hist. Wks. Beda* 431 *note*, Upon which day Deusdedit.. commenced the tenth year of his presulate.

‖**pre'sultor**. *Obs. rare*[−1]. In 7 **præ-**. [Late L. *præsultor* one who dances before others, agent-n. f. **præsilīre*: see prec.] One who leads the dance.

1678 CUDWORTH *Intell. Syst.* 397 In the world, God, as the Coryphæus, the Præcentor and Præsultor, beginning the Dance and Musick, the Stars and Heavens move round after him according to those numbers and measures, which he prescribes them, all together making up one most excellent Harmony.

†**pre'sultory**, *a. Obs. nonce-wd.* [f. after DESULTORY: see PRE- A. and prec.] Characterized by leaping forward, presumptuous.

1652 GAULE *Magastrom.* 147 Betwixt the desultory levity of an indifferent casualty and the presultory temerity of an urging and inevitable necessity.

presumable (prɪ'zjuːməb(ə)l), *a.* [f. PRESUME *v.* + -ABLE; so F. *présumable* (16th c. in Godef.).]

1. Capable of being presumed or taken for granted; probable, likely.

1692 LOCKE *Toleration* III. viii. Wks. 1727 II. 380 Which Corruption of Nature, that they may retain..I think is very presumable. **1704** NORRIS *Ideal World* II. i. 5 Supposing myself to consist of soul and body, 'tis fairly presumable that 'tis my soul that thinks. **1868** STANLEY *Westm. Abb.* iii. 145 No other presumable mark of violence was seen.

2. To be expected or counted on beforehand.

1825 LAMB *Let. to Old Gentleman*, Whether a person..of sixty-three..may hope to arrive, within a presumable number of years, at..the character..of a learned man. **1860** ADLER *Fauriel's Prov. Poetry* xix. 435 The abrupt return of Philip Augustus..compromised the presumable results of the third crusade.

pre'sumably, *adv.* [f. as prec. + -LY².]

†**1.** With presumption or taking of things for granted without examination. *Obs. rare*⁻¹.

1646 SIR T. BROWNE *Pseud. Ep.* 34 Authors presumably writing by common places, wherein for many yeares promiscuously amassing all that makes for their subject.

2. Qualifying a statement: As one may presume or reasonably suppose; by presumption or supposition; probably.

1846 POE *Kirkland* Wks. 1864 III. 38 A journal exclusively devoted to foreign concerns, and therefore presumably imbued with something of a cosmopolitan spirit. **1869** BROWNING *Ring & Bk.* VIII. 1257 Where all presumably is peace and joy. **1880** L. STEPHEN *Pope* i. 2 The little household was presumably a very quiet one. **1885** SIR H. COTTON in *Law Times* LXXIX. 195/1 A vendor is presumably aware of the nature of his title.

†**pre'sumant,** *a. Obs. rare.* [a. F. *présumant*, pres. pple. of *présumer* to PRESUME.] Presuming, presumptuous.

1600 W. WATSON *Decacordon* (1602) 318 If his Maiestie permit it to passe currant without due punishment inflicted vpon the presumant scribe [Father Parsons]. **1612** T. JAMES *Jesuit's Downf.* 66 This great auctority, which this presumant Scribe tooke vpon him, made him no little prowd.

Hence †**pre'sumantly** (in MS. *presumatlye*) *adv.*, presumingly, presumptuously.

c **1536** in Furniv. *Ballads fr. MSS.* (1872) I. 411 She spake þes wordes presumatlye, & sayd: 'ye Byrdes, behold & se! Do nat gruge, for þis wyll hyt be; Suche ys my fortune.'

†**pre'sume,** *sb. Obs.* [f. next.] The act of presuming.

1. Anticipation, expectation.

c **1470** HENRYSON *Mor. Fab.* VIII. (*Pr. Sw.*) xxxiii, Thir small birdis..lichtit doun, Bot of the nettis na presume thay had.

2. Presumption, audacity; an instance of this.

1590 T. WATSON *Eglogue Death Sir F. Walsingham* 360 Ah but my Muse..begins to tremble at my great presume. **1610** W. FOLKINGHAM *Art of Survey* Ep. Ded. 2 Praying your gracious Indulgence for my rude Presume. *c* **1611** CHAPMAN *Iliad* XI. 495 When their cur-like presumes More urged the more forborne.

presume (prɪ'zjuːm), *v.* Also 4 -sewme, -sum, *Sc.* pressume, 6 preswme, *Sc.* presome, 7 præsume. [a. F. *présumer* (12–13th c. in Hatz.-Darm.), or ad. L. *præsūm-ĕre* to take before, anticipate, in late L. to take for granted, assume, suppose, dare; f. *præ*, PRE- A. 1 + *sūmĕre* to take.]

†**1.** *trans.* To take possession of without right; to usurp, seize. *Obs. rare.*

c **1380** WYCLIF *Sel. Wks.* III. 363 Þe pope mai not opinlier telle þat he is Anticrist..þan for to putte many mennis lyves for þis office þat he presumeþ. **1432–50** tr. *Higden* (Rolls) II. 157 Kinadius..presumede alle the grownde [orig. *terram omnem usurpavit*].

2. To take upon oneself, undertake without adequate authority or permission; to venture upon.

a. with simple object.

c **1380** WYCLIF *Serm.* Sel. Wks. I. 76 Þei ben contrarie to alle þes newe ordris þat ben presumed aȝens Crist. **14..** *Rule Syon Monast.* liii. in *Collect. Topogr.* (1834) I. 31 If any haue desire to lyghe in her cowle, none schal presume thys, withe oute special licence of the abbes. **1490** CAXTON *How to Die* 7 Late none presume nothynge of hym selfe. **1541** *Act 33 Hen. VIII*, c. 6 Evill disposed persons,..presumynge wilfullye and obstynatlye the violacion and breach of the saide Acte. **1669** LD. CHAWORTH in *12th Rep. Hist. MSS. Comm.* App. v. 13, I had not præsumed so much but that I have heard my Lorde off Rutland say [etc.]. **1780** JOHNSON *Let. to Mrs. Thrale* 10 July, Hopes of excellence which I once presumed, and never have attained. **1784** COWPER *Task* III. 459 One..whose powers, Presuming an attempt not less sublime, Pant [etc.].

b. with *inf.* To be so presumptuous as; to take the liberty; to venture, dare (*to do* something).

1375 BARBOUR *Bruce* I. 572 [The King] swour that he suld wengeance ta Off that brwys, that presumyt swa Aganys him to brawle or rys. *c* **1375** *Sc. Leg. Saints* iii. (*Andreas*) 822 Fore he be-cause of cowatice, pressumyt sik a man to sla. **1460** CAPGRAVE *Chron.* (Rolls) 43 He [Uzziah] presumed to do upon him the prestis stole. **1548–9** (Mar.) *Bk. Com. Prayer, Communion*, We do not presume to come to this thy table (o mercifull lord) trusting in our owne righteousnes, but [etc.]. **1634** W. WOOD *New Eng. Prosp.* To Rdr., Yet dare I presume to present thee with the true relation. **1732** POPE *Ess. Man* II. 1 Know then thyself, presume not God to scan. **1791** MRS. RADCLIFFE *Rom. Forest* v, May I presume to ask what has interested you thus in her favour? **1868** E. EDWARDS *Ralegh* I. xxiii. 517 To his mind, it was..intolerable that historians should presume to sit in judgment on the actions of kings.

†**c.** Also *presume oneself*, *presume upon oneself*, in same sense. *Obs.*

c **1440** *Gesta Rom.* xxiii. 78 (Harl. MS.) O! rybawde, whi hast þou presumyd thi self for to sey that þou were emperour? **1444** *Rolls of Parlt.* V. 108/2 Who so evere presume opon hym or thaime, to accept or occupie the seide Office of Sherreff, by vertue of such Grauntes. **1489** CAXTON *Faytes of A.* IV. xv. 275 Noon ought to presume himself to take eny thinge of the armes of an other.

†**d.** *refl.* To set oneself up, be presumptuous.

c **1340** HAMPOLE *Prose Tr.* 21 Presumynge of thi silfe and veynlikynge of thi silfe of eny thynge that God hath sent the bodili or gostely.

†**3.** *trans.* (with *inf.* or *cl.*) To profess, pretend, make pretension. Also *presume upon oneself* (quot. 1470).

1470–85 MALORY *Arthur* II. i. 76, I wille my self assaye.., not presumynge vpon my self that I am the best knyghte. **1557** NORTH *Gueuara's Diall Pr.* III. xiii. (1568) 22 The prince whiche is vertuous, and presumethe to be a christian, ..oughte to considre what losse or profyte will ensue thereof. *Ibid.* xxxvii. 62 If a man did narowly examin yᵉ vyces of many, which presume to bee very vertuous. **1581** PETTIE *Guazzo's Civ. Conv.* II. (1586) 51 Those who will not presume to bee able to doe anie thing, knowe how to doe most thinges, and those who take upon them to knowe all thinges, are those which commonlie knowe nothing at all. **1652** GAULE *Magastrom.* 279 Although he much presumed to be an astrologer or diviner, himselfe.

†**b.** *intr.* *presume of*: to lay claim to presumptuously, pretend to. *Obs. rare*⁻¹.

1599 THYNNE *Animadv.* 31, I will not presume of muche knowledge in these tounges.

4. *trans.* To assume or take for granted; to presuppose; to anticipate, count upon, expect (in earliest instances with the notion of over-confidence). *spec.* in *Law*: To take as proved until evidence to the contrary is forthcoming.

a. with inf., obj. clause or obj. and compl.

1377 LANGL. *P. Pl.* B. Prol. 108 Þe cardinales atte Courte þat..power presumed in hem a Pope to make. *c* **1386** CHAUCER *Merch. T.* 259 A ful greet fool is any conseillour.. That dar presume, or elles thenken it That his conseil sholde passe his lordes wit. **1456** SIR G. HAYE *Law Arms* (S.T.S.) 227 Fra tyme a man be ressavit in service he is presumyt ay to be servand quhill he be releschit of his service. **1538** STARKEY *England* I. iv. 121 That, by the law ys presupposyd and vtturly presumyd to be truth. **1590** SWINBURNE *Testaments* VI. xiii. 223 Some are of opinion, that euery man is presumed to liue till he be an hundred yeares old. **1628** T. SPENCER *Logick* 304 The proposition presumes, that one of the three must be indured, and no more but one of them. **1759** ROBERTSON *Hist. Scotl.* III. Wks. 1813 I. 236 Elizabeth, we may presume, did not wish that the proposal should be received in any other manner. **1805** E. H. EAST *Reports* VI. 82 At any time beyond the first seven years they might fairly presume him dead. **1879** LUBBOCK *Addr. Pol. & Educ.* i. 20 Cicero in one of his letters to Atticus..presumes that he would not care to have any from Britain.

b. with simple object.

1565 *Reg. Privy Council Scot.* I. 343 Hir Majestie nevir presumit alteratioun of the guid and quiet estait of the commoun weill. **1646** SIR T. BROWNE *Pseud. Ep.* 131 We cannot presume the existence of this animall, nor dare we affirme there is any Phænix in Nature. *a* **1703** BURKITT *On N.T.* Matt. i. 19 Kind and merciful men always presume the best. **1818** CRUISE *Digest* (ed. 2) V. 412 Until a writ of seisin is awarded, executed, and returned, (all which must appear upon record, and cannot be presumed). **1871** SIR W. M. JAMES in *Law Rep. 6 Chanc.* App. 357 Death is presumed from the person not being heard of for seven years.

5. *intr.* To act or proceed on the assumption of right or permission; to be presumptuous, take liberties. Often *presume on, upon* (†*of*): to act presumptuously on the strength of, to rely upon as a pretext for presumption; also in neutral sense, to take advantage of.

c **1430** LYDG. *Min. Poems* (Percy Soc.) 37 To be coupled to so hihe astate, I am unable, I am not apt thereto, So to presume. **1580** LYLY *Euphues* (Arb.) 246 Presume not too much of the curtesies of those. **1600** E. BLOUNT tr. *Conestaggio* 16 The Catholique King knowing the Portugals to presume beyond their strength. **1683** D. A. *Art Converse* 6 If they presume too much upon their nobility. *a* **1708** BEVERIDGE *Thes. Theol.* (1710) II. 250 To take no care, is to presume upon providence. **1797** GOUV. MORRIS in Sparks *Life & Writ.* (1832) III. 106 Ignorance will presume, and its presumption will be chastised. **1877** FREEMAN *Norm. Conq.* (ed. 3) I. App. 785 Lest other strangers should venture to presume on their kindred with Kings. **1885** [see PRESS *v.*¹ 16].

6. *intr.* To press forward presumptuously; to advance or make one's way over-confidently into an unwarranted position or place; to aspire presumptuously; to presume to go. Now *rare* or *Obs.*

c **1430** *Freemasonry* 717 Presume not to hye for nothynge, For thyn hye blod, ny thy comynge. **1565** STAPLETON tr. *Bede's Hist. Ch. Eng.* 159, I straightly chardged him not to presume to that mynisterie which he could not do accordingly. **1667** MILTON *P.L.* VII. 13 Up led by thee, Into the Heaven of Heavens I have presumed, An earthly guest. **1697** DRYDEN *Virg. Past.* VII. 31 If my Wishes have presum'd too high.

7. *presume on, upon,* (†*of*): to rely upon, count upon, take for granted; to form expectations of, look for. Now *rare* or *Obs.*

c **1586** C'TESS PEMBROKE *Ps.* XCI. ii, [Thou shalt] on his truth noe lesse presume, Then most in shield affy. **1597** J. KING *On Jonas* (1618) 46 Some haue presumed, by coniecture, vpon his going to Tarshish, and fleeing from the face of the Lord. **1608** DOD & CLEAVER *Expos. Prov.* ix–x. 125 They presumed of peace and safety, and so their destruction commeth suddenly without resistance. **1664** PEPYS *Diary* 27 July, How uncertain our lives are, and how little to be presumed of. **1688** *Pennsylv. Archives* I. 107 Upon which accounts I shall presume on you. **1766** ENTICK *London* IV. 202 These could not be presumed upon for columns exceeding four feet in diameter. **1803** *Forest of Hohenelbe* I. 9, I was not to presume on any further favours.

presumed (prɪ'zjuːmd), *ppl. a.* [f. prec. + -ED¹.] Assumed before or without proof; taken for granted; anticipated, expected.

1597 HOOKER *Eccl. Pol.* v. lx. §6 As there is in their Christian Parents and in the Church of God a presumed desire that the Sacrament of Baptisme might be given them. **1646** SIR T. BROWNE (*title*) Pseudodoxia Epidemica: or Enquiries into Very many received Tenents, And commonly presumed Truths. **1817** JAS. MILL *Brit. India* II. IV. v. 169 The unpopularity..of Jaffier's administration, and the presumed weakness of his government.

presumedly (prɪ'zjuːmɪdlɪ), *adv.* [f. prec. + -LY².] As is or may be presumed; supposedly.

1869 *Daily News* 11 June, The majority..of presumedly educated people. **1885** J. PAYN *Luck Darrells* ii, The cab was ..presumedly within a few doors of her destination. **1895** SALMOND *Chr. Doctr. Immort.* III. i. 29 Take the synoptical account..as presumedly the earliest.

presumer (prɪ'zjuːmə(r)). [f. PRESUME *v.* + -ER¹.] One who presumes.

1. A presumptuous person.

1509 FISHER *Serm.* Wks. (1876) 270 Of such presumers scante one amonges a thousande cometh vnto this grace. **1645** MILTON *Colast.* Wks. 1851 IV. 345 An illiterat, and arrogant presumer in that which hee understands not. **1791** PAINE *Rights of Man* II. iv. (1792) 55 Mr. Burke is such a bold presumer. **1845** MRS. S. C. HALL *Whiteboy* viii, The broad, vulgar, pompous presumer who dared to tattle of 'his family'.

2. One who assumes or takes something for granted, without proof.

1692 LOCKE *Toleration* iii. Wks. 1727 II. 462 He must pass for an admirable Presumer, who seriously affirms that it is presumable that all those who conform to the National Religion where it is true, do so understand, believe and practice it, as to be in the way of Salvation. **1708** H. DODWELL *Nat. Mort. Hum. Souls* 152 The Question.. whether the Mistakes be such as the Presumer takes them to be.

pre'suming, *vbl. sb.* [f. PRESUME *v.* + -ING¹.] The action of the verb PRESUME; presumption.

1582 BENTLEY *Mon. Matrones* II. 172 By the transgression of Adam, whose haughtie presuming..thought to be as Thy selfe. *a* **1694** TILLOTSON *Serm. Eph. iv.* 29 Wks. 1717 II. 396 An affront to modest Company, and a rude presuming upon their approbation. **1871** R. ELLIS tr. *Catullus* xxiv. 6 Ere you suffer his alien arm's presuming.

pre'suming, *ppl. a.* [f. PRESUME *v.* + -ING².] That presumes; presumptuous, arrogant.

1604 *Supplic. Jas. I* in Southey *Comm.-pl. Bk.* Ser. II. (1849) 50 The Puritan as he increaseth daily above the Protestant in number, so is he of a more presuming.. disposition and zeal. **1676** DRYDEN *Aurengz.* Epil. 42 He more fears (like a presuming Man) Their votes who cannot judge, than theirs who can. **1859** MILL *Liberty* iv. 139 If one person could honestly point out to another that he thinks him in fault, without being considered unmannerly or presuming.

Hence **pre'sumingly** *adv.*, Presumptuously.

1608 HIERON *Wks.* I. 697 Grant that I may not bee presuminglie secure touching mine owne estate. **1852** *Blackw. Mag.* LXXII. 515 And thus may'st thou..meet the Fate thou can'st not see, In hope, but not presumingly.

†**pre'sumpted,** *pa. pple. Obs. rare*⁻¹. [f. L. *præsumpt-us*, pa. pple. of *præsūmĕre* (see next) + -ED¹.] Made or done presumptuously.

1550 BALE *Apol.* 106 b, Neither is it a poynte of infidelyte against God, in them whych hath..dampnably vowed, nor yet a goynge backe from a godly purpose [to break a vow], the vowe beynge presumted, dyssembled, and fayned.

presumption (prɪ'zʌm(p)ʃən). Forms: 3 presumciun, 4 -sumpciun, 4- presumption; also 4–5 -som(p)cion, -sumpsion(e, 4–6 -cio(u)n(e, -cyon, 5 -sumcyoun(e, -sumpscione, 6 *Sc.* -tioun, 7 -sumtion; 7 præ-. [ME. a. OF. *presumpcion* (12–13th c. in Hatz.-Darm.), *presompcion*, mod.F. *présomption* = Sp. *presuncion*, It. *presunzione*, ad. L. *præsumptiōn-em* a taking beforehand, anticipation, in late L. confidence, audacity, n. of action f. *præsūmĕre* to PRESUME.]

†**1.** Seizure and occupation without right; usurpation; presumptuous assumption (*of* an office): cf. PRESUME *v.* 3 b. *Obs. rare.*

[?*a* **1135** *Leges Henrici I*, c. 10 §1 (Schmid 442) Praemeditatus assultus; robaria, stretbreche; praesumptio terrae vel pecuniae regis.] **1432–50** tr. *Higden* (Rolls) II. 147 So that peple, of robbers made inhabitatores, occupiede the northe partes of Briteyne thro presumpcion. *Ibid.* VII. 181 Stigandus..entrede the seete of Wynchestre by presumpcion and supportacion [L. *Wyntoniensem sedem invaserat*]. **1565** HARDING *Confut. Apol.* VI. xix. 333 In their presumption of that office they are not duly called vnto. **1809–10** COLERIDGE *Friend* (1844) I. 34 An office which cannot be procured gratis. The industry, necessary for the due exercise of its functions, is its purchase-money: and the absence..of the same..implies a presumption in the literal ..sense of the word.

2. The taking upon onself of more than is warranted by one's position, right, or (formerly) ability; forward or over-confident opinion or conduct; arrogance, pride, effrontery, assurance.

a **1225** *Ancr. R.* 208 Nis hit þe spece of prude þet ich cleopede presumciun. **1340** *Ayenb.* 17 Þe pridde [boȝ of prede is] ouerweninge þet we clepeþ presumcion. **1395** PURVEY *Remonstr.* (1851) 131 To compel alle cristen men to believe ech determination of the church of Rome is a blinde and open presumption of Lucifer and antichrist. *c* **1440**

Gesta Rom. xxiii. 78 (Add. MS.) Thou shalt go to my lord, and there thou shalt aunswere of thyn presumpscion. **1535** COVERDALE *2 Sam.* vi. 7 God smote him there because of his presumpcion, so that he dyed there besyde the Arke of God. **1601** SHAKS. *All's Well* II. i. 154 But most it is presumption in vs, when The help of heauen we count the act of men. **1789** BELSHAM *Ess.* II. xli. 544 It would be great presumption in me to attempt a reply. **1875** MANNING *Mission H. Ghost* iv. 107 Presumption is a confidence founded upon ourselves.

3. The assuming or taking of something for granted; also, that which is presumed or assumed to be, or to be true, on probable evidence; a belief deduced from facts or experience; assumption, assumed probability, supposition, expectation.

13.. *Cursor M.* 27800 (Cott.) O þis bicums presumpcion, þat es hoping of vnreson. **1362** LANGL. *P. Pl.* A. XI. 42 þei puyteþ forþ presumpciun to preue þe soþe. *c* **1386** CHAUCER *Melib.* ¶440 By certeyne presumpcions and coniectynges I holde and bileeue that God..hath suffred this bityde by Iuste cause resonable. **1533** MORE *Debell. Salem* Wks. 981/1 A man may sometime be so suspecte of felony by reason of sore presumpcions, that though no man saw hym doe it..yet may he be founden giltye of it. **1597** MORLEY *Introd. Mus.* 150 Others haue done the contrary, rather vpon a presumption then any reason which they haue to doe so. **1662** J. DAVIES tr. *Mandelslo's Trav.* 230 They..never order any to be tortured, but upon very great presumptions. **1747** GOULD *Eng. Ants* 53 It will be proper to shew on what Presumptions it is grounded. **1838** DE MORGAN *Ess. Probab.* 91 We do not know the contents of the urn, but only the result of a certain number of drawings, from which we can draw presumptions..about the whole contents. **1846** GROTE *Greece* I. xxi. II. 160 The presumptions are all against it. **1881** WESTCOTT & HORT *Grk. N.T.* Introd. §8 The..presumption that a relatively late text is likely to be a relatively corrupt text.

b. *spec.* in *Law.* ***presumption of fact***: the inference of a fact not certainly known, from known facts. ***presumption of law***: (*a*) the assumption of the truth of anything until the contrary is proved; (*b*) an inference established by the law as universally applicable to certain circumstances.

1596 BACON *Max. & Use Com. Law* I. v. (1636) 25 So great a perturbation of the judgment and reason as in presumption of law mans nature cannot overcome. **1766** BLACKSTONE *Comm.* II. ix. 146 Having sown the land, which is for the good of the public, upon a reasonable presumption, the law will not suffer him to be a loser by it. **1844** GREENLEAF *Law Evid.* I. iv. §14. 75 Presumptions of Law consist of those rules, which, in certain cases, either forbid or dispense with any ulterior inquiry. **1877** WHARTON *Law Evid.* II. §1226. 440 A presumption of fact is a logical argument from a fact to a fact; or..it is an argument which infers a fact otherwise doubtful, from a fact which is proved. **1895** *Pitt-Taylor's Law Evid.* (ed. 9) I. v. 69 Presumptive evidence is usually divided into two branches, namely, *presumptions of law*, and *presumptions of fact*. Presumptions of law consist of those rules, which, in certain cases, either forbid or dispense with any ulterior inquiry. Presumptions of law are sub-divided into two classes, namely, *conclusive* and *disputable*.

4. A ground or reason for presuming or believing; presumptive evidence.

1586 A. DAY *Eng. Secretary* II. (1625) 13 If you will now aske me what presumption I haue then to charge him more then another..I will answere you. **1658** BRAMHALL *Consecr. Bps.* v. 132 If the strongest presumtion in the world may have any place. **1771** *Junius Lett.* xliv. (1820) 239 The presumption is strongly against them. **1838–9** HALLAM *Hist. Lit.* I. I. iv. §81. 323 There seems strong internal presumption against the authenticity of these epistles. **1880** CARPENTER in *19th Cent.* Apr. 614 The presumption is altogether very strong, that these vast masses have originally formed part of a great ice-sheet, formed by the cumulative pressure of successive snow-falls.

†pre'sumptious, *a. Obs.* Also 5 -tius, 5–6 -teous, 6 -tiouse, presumtious. [ME. a. OF. *presoncieus* (14th c. in Godef.), ad. late L. *præsumptiōsus* (5th c.), f. *præsumptiōn-em* PRESUMPTION: see -IOUS; cf. the less regular PRESUMPTUOUS.] = PRESUMPTUOUS *a.* I. (In quot. 1596 as *adv.*)

c **1400** *Destr. Troy* 3847 Machaon the mody kyng was.. Proude & presumptius, prouyt of wille. **1549** *Compl. Scot.* i. 19 Princis..beand ambitius ande presumpteous, throucht grite superfluite of veltht. **1570** LEVINS *Manip.* 227/32 Presumptiouse, *præsumptuosus.* **1596** DALRYMPLE tr. *Leslie's Hist. Scot.* I. (S.T.S.) 71 Mair arrogantlie, presumpteous, and mair proudlie, than was decent. *a* **1607** SIR E. DYER *Writ.* (1872) 39 Presumptious eye, to graze on Phillis face. **1662** R. MATHEW *Unl. Alch.* §81. 108 People desperately presumptious both to abuse themselves and me. **1815** *Zeluca* II. 248 The growth of presumptious hopes.

Hence **†pre'sumptiously** *adv.*; **†pre'sumptiousness**.

1501 DOUGLAS *Pal. Hon.* I. lx, Thou..*Presumpteouslie ..My Lady heir blasphemit in thy rime. **1512** *Act 4 Hen. VIII*, c. 19 *Preamble*, Presumtiously contrary to the lawes of Gode and all holy Churche. *a* **1642** SIR W. MONSON *Naval Tracts* III. (1704) 337/2 That he carry not himself proudly or presumptiously. **1662** R. MATHEW *Unl. Alch.* §87. 122 Some that have used it presumptiously. **1550** VERON *Godly Sayings* (1846) 91 He receiveth..the sacrament..too the condemnatyon of hys *presumptiousnes.

presumptive (prɪ'zʌm(p)tɪv), *a.* [a. F. *présomptif, -ive* (15th c. in Hatz.-Darm.), also obs. *presumptif*, ad. late L. *præsumptīvus* (Priscian), f. *præsumpt-*, ppl. stem of *præsūmĕre* to PRESUME: see -IVE.]

1. = PRESUMPTUOUS I. Now *rare* or *Obs.*

1609 DANIEL *Civ. Wars* VIII. lxvii, To keepe his forwardnes Backe from presumptiue pressing. **16..** BROWN (J.), There being two opinions repugnant to each another, it may not be presumptive or sceptical to doubt of both. **1748** SMOLLETT *Rod. Rand.* (1812) I. 418 Your presumptive emulation in a much more interesting affair. **1816** J. EVANS in *Monthly Mag.* XLI. 124 Having so far proceeded in a strain of dictatorship, that some..may deem altogether presumptive. **1883** SCHAFF *Hist. Ch.* I. IV. xxvi. 254 He protested in presumptive modesty, when Christ would wash his feet.

2. Giving reasonable grounds for presumption or belief; warranting inferences.

1561 *Reg. Privy Council Scot.* I. 174 Quhilk claus is adjectit to mak the mair cleir probatioun presumptive. **1685–6** in Ellis *Orig. Lett.* Ser. II. IV. 87 The evidences against him were very many, and the circumstances very numerous and presumptive. **1766** BLACKSTONE *Comm.* II. xiii. 197 The presumptive evidence of that right is strongly in favour of his antagonist. **1817** W. SELWYN *Law Nisi Prius* (ed. 4) II. 1028 That will be presumptive against him, that he made that return, unless he shews the contrary. **1836–9** DICKENS *Sk. Boz, First of May*, This is strong presumptive evidence, but we have positive proof—the evidence of our own senses. **1895** [see PRESUMPTION 3 b].

3. a. Based on presumption or inference; presumed, inferred. ***heir presumptive***: see HEIR *sb.* 1 b.

1628, 1683, 1875 Presumptive heir, etc. [see HEIR *sb.* 1 b]. **1673** *Essex Papers* (Camden) I. 89 This estate, wherein I have a reall & presumptive, tho' not a present or a certain interest. **1818** SCOTT *Hrt. Midl.* v, The case of Effie..Deans ..is one of those cases of murder presumptive. *a* **1854** H. REED *Lect. Eng. Hist.* ix. (1855) 289 The Duke of York being the heir presumptive. **1858** SEARS *Athan.* II. xii. 249 Immortality is not made presumptive, as a conclusion hanging on the last link of a syllogism, but its giant glories are disclosed. **1874** GREEN *Short Hist.* ix. §4. 635 As the King was childless..Mary was presumptive heiress of the Crown.

b. *Embryol.* Applied to undifferentiated tissue that becomes a specified part in the normal course of development.

1935 *Jrnl. Morphol.* LVIII. 432 Each presumptive mid-gut epithelial nucleus appropriates a portion of the vitellophage cytoplasm and thus are formed the definitive mid-gut epithelial cells. **1950** B. M. PATTEN *Early Embryol. of Chick* iv. 66 The sharpness of the boundaries between different presumptive areas..is an entirely artificial device. **1977** *Sci. Amer.* July 76/3 In the 1910's and 1920's Harrison and his colleagues demonstrated that in amphibian embryos the presumptive limb region (the region that will later produce a leg) behaves in many ways like a typical epimorphic field.

pre'sumptively, *adv.* [f. prec. + -LY[2].] By presumption or inference; presumably.

a **1677** BARROW *Unity of Church* (1680) 14 Presumptively every member of this [society] doth pass for a member of the other. **1771** BURKE *Powers of Juries* Wks. 1812 V. 402 When he who could read and write was presumptively a person in Holy Orders, libels could not be general or dangerous. **1885** LD. SELBORNE in *Law Rep. 14 Q. Bench Div.* 647 The furniture of an hotel is not presumptively the property of the person who is occupying the hotel.

†pre'sumptorily, *adv. Obs. rare*[−1]. [f. late L. *præsumptōriē* adv., from *præsumptōrius* adj. (rare), presumptuous: see -ORY[2] and -LY[2].] = PRESUMPTUOUSLY.

1681 in *Savile Corr.* (Camden) 234, I durst not presumptorily undertake..that whatever stock of that kind [tin at Marseilles] they should carry over should bee safe.

†presumptu'osity. *Obs. rare*[−1]. In 5 presomtweste. [a. obs. F. *presomptuouseté, -osité* (15th c. in Godefroy): see next and -ITY.] Usurpation; = PRESUMPTION I.

c **1450** LOVELICH *Grail* I. 340 But now knowe I wel that thilke same se, That I Inne sat be presomtweste, It Is that same seye to mene Wher as God to his disciples Made his Sene.

presumptuous (prɪ'zʌm(p)tjuːəs), *a.* Also 4 -somptuose, 5 -sumptuose, (-suis), 5–6 -tuouse, -tuows(e. [a. OF. *presuntuex* (12th c. in Hatz.-Darm.), *presumptuoux*, mod.F. *présomptueux*, ad. L. *præsumptuōsus*, late variant of the regular *præsumptiōsus* PRESUMPTIOUS, perh. influenced by *sumptuōsus*, f. *sumptus* (*u*-stem).]

1. Characterized by presumption in opinion or conduct; unduly confident or bold; arrogant, presuming; forward, impertinent.

c **1350** *Medit. de Passione Dom.* in *Hampole's Wks.* (1896) I. 92 Neuere to be presumptuous ne proud of þi ȝiftis. *c* **1440** *Promp. Parv.* 412/2 Presumptuowse, or bolde, or malapert (*P.* ouer bolde), *presumptuosus.* **1456** SIR G. HAYE *Law Arms* (S.T.S.) 84 Suppose a knycht wald be..sa presumptuous that he wald assailȝe ane hundreth knychtis him allane. **1535** COVERDALE *Dan.* vii. 20 A mouth speakynge presumptuous thinges. **1593** SHAKS. *3 Hen. VI*, I. i. 157 'Tis not thy Southerne power..Which makes thee thus presumptuous and prowd. **1635** QUARLES *Embl., Hieroglyph* i, That glorious, that presumptuous thing, call'd man. **1673** O. WALKER *Educ.* (1677) 108 Such persons..if not well regulated become scornful and presumtuous. **1777** ROBERTSON *Hist. Amer.* II. v. 82 Narvaez, no less brave in action than presumptuous in conduct, armed himself in haste. **1810** SCOTT *Lady of L.* I. xi, The tower which builders vain Presumptuous piled on Shinar's plain. **1881** P. BROOKS *Candle of Lord* 299 It is almost as presumptuous to think you can do nothing as to think you can do everything.

†2. = PRESUMPTIVE 2. *Obs. rare.*

a **1639** SPOTTISWOOD *Hist. Ch. Scot.* v. (1677) 226 A number of presumptuous likelihoods and conjectures, to make it appear she was privy to the Murther. **1653** A. WILSON *Jas. I* 285 Suspected of being poisoned; the Symptoms being very presumptuous.

†3. That assumes beforehand; anticipative. *Obs. rare*[−1]. (But referred by Puttenham to sense I.)

1589 PUTTENHAM *Eng. Poesie* III. xix. (Arb.) 239 This figure was called the *presumptuous.* I will also call him the figure of *presupposall* or the *preuenter.* [*Marginal note*: *Procatalepsis*, or the presumptuous, otherwise the figure of Presupposall.]

pre'sumptuously, *adv.* [f. prec. + -LY[2].] In a presumptuous manner; with presumption; with overweening self-confidence or forwardness.

1362 LANGL. *P. Pl.* A. XII. 8 þou woldest konne þat I can and carpen hit after. Presumptuowsly, the parauenture a-pose so manye, That [etc.]. **1413** *Pilgr. Sowle* (Caxton) II. xliii. (1859) 49 Heretykes, and Scysmatikes presumptuously peruertyn hooly Scrypture. *c* **1536** M. NISBET *Tindale's Prol. to Romans* in *N.T. in Scots* (S.T.S.) III. 338 They..ar blynde, and gangis to wryk presumptwslye. **1542** HENRY VIII *Declar. Scots* B iij, All these be ouer presumptuously done agaynste vs. **1622** ROWLANDS *Gd. Newes & Bad* 5 Grosse ignorance presumptuously will prate Of serious matters that concerne a State. *a* **1720** SHEFFIELD (Dk. Buckhm.) *Wks.* (1753) II. 136 Presumptuously to arrogate a Preheminence above all their Brethren.

pre'sumptuousness. [f. as prec. + -NESS.] The quality of being presumptuous; groundless self-confidence; over-bold forwardness.

c **1420** *Chron. Vilod.* 2810 Ny suche presumpsuisnas vpone here take. *c* **1490** *Promp. Parv.* 412/2 (MS. K.) Presumptuowsnes, *presumptuositas.* **1535** COVERDALE *1 Sam.* xvii. 28, I knowe thy presumptuousnesse well ynough, and the wickednesse of thine hert: for thou art come downe to se the battayll. **1688** BUNYAN *Jerus. Sinner Saved* (1700) 98 This presumptuousness is a very heinous thing in the eyes of God. **1802** *Edin. Rev.* I. 201 It seems to be the business of philosophy..to restrain the presumptuousness of the theorist. **1882** A. W. WARD in *Macm. Mag.* XLVI. 425 One thing..may be asserted without presumptuousness.

†presu'ppone, *v. Obs.* Chiefly *Sc.* [In 1400 ad. med.L. *præsuppōnĕre* (Albertus Magnus, *a* 1250), f. *præ*, PRE- A. I + *suppōnĕre* to SUPPOSE; in Sc. perh. f. PRE- A. I + SUPPONE (found *c* 1535).] *trans.* To presuppose; to assume beforehand.

c **1400** *Apol. Loll.* 19 þerfor þow a persoun prescit curse bi autorite of þe [kirk], neuer þe lesse he presupponiþ þe kirk. *a* **1598** ROLLOCK *Serm.* Wks. 1849 I. 480 This presupponeth ..that the church is full of sin so long as it is in this world. **1609** HUME *Admon.* in *Wodrow Soc. Misc.* (1844) 583, I presuppone that theis grave personages wer alyve to behold your proceedingis.

presupposal (priːsə'pəʊzəl). Now *rare.* [f. next + -AL[1]: cf. SUPPOSAL.] A 'supposal' or supposition formed beforehand; a presupposition.

1589 PUTTENHAM *Eng. Poesie* III. xix. (Arb.) 206 If our presupposall be true, that the Poet is of all other the most auncient Orator. *Ibid.* 239 [see PRESUMPTUOUS 3]. **1687** R. L'ESTRANGE *Answ. Diss.* 35 He..Proceeds upon the Presupposal of an Imaginary Breach, and Right. **1847–8** DE QUINCEY *Protestantism* Wks. 1858 VIII. 131 Scriptural truth..is protected by its prodigious iteration, and secret presupposal in all varieties of form.

presuppose (priːsə'pəʊz), *v.* Also 6–7 præ-. [a. F. *présupposer* (14th c. in Littré), after med.L. *præsuppōnĕre* (cf. PRESUPPONE): see PRE- A. I and SUPPOSE *v.*]

1. *trans.* Of a person: To suppose, lay down, or postulate beforehand; hence, to take for granted or assume beforehand or to start with; to presume.

1426 LYDG. *De Guil. Pilgr.* 3043 Pre-supposyd ther be no whyht To whom the offyce sholde of ryht Appertene off duete. **1482** CAXTON *Trevisa's Higden* III. xv, Yf hester had be in his tyme [it] is to presuppose he wolde somwhat haue spoken of hir. **1530** PALSGR. 52 For the declaryng of whiche thyng thre thynges be to be presupposed. **1581** LAMBARDE *Eiren.* II. vii. (1588) 243 The lawe presupposeth that he carieth that malicious mind with him. **1641** BEST *Farm. Bks.* (Surtees) 37 In makinge of a pyke they first frame theire staddle accordinge to the loades of hey that they presuppose shall bee layde in them. **1703** MOXON *Mech. Exerc.* 308 All the Authors I have met with seem to presuppose their Reader to understand Geometry. **1809** SYD. SMITH *Wks.* (1867) I. 179 Pre-supposing such a desire to please. **1875** JOWETT *Plato* (ed. 2) III. 273 You can tell that a song or ode has three parts—..that degree of knowledge I may presuppose.

†b. To suppose or assume the existence of (something) as prior *to* something else. *Obs. rare.*

(Here the *pre-* does not qualify the supposing, but indicates the order of the things supposed.)

1697 G. K. *Disc. Geom. Problems* 7 To presuppose the knowledge of Conick Sections to the knowledge of some necessary Problems in plain Geometry, is greatly incongruous.

2. To suppose beforehand, or *a priori*; to think or believe in advance of actual knowledge or experience.

c **1530** L. COX *Rhet.* (1899) 87 Presupposynge hym nat to be in muche other case. **1555** EDEN *Decades* 321

Presupposynge the thynge to bee impossible they neuer attempted it. **1573** G. HARVEY *Letter-bk.* (Camden) 25 A man wuld have præsupposid that the Masters letters to his præsident miht have dun somewhat with his præsident. **1605** BACON *Adv. Learn.* II. xxi. §9 Men of corrupted minds presuppose that honesty groweth out of simplicity of manners. **1865** DICKENS *Mut. Fr.* I. x, With a pervading air upon him of having presupposed the ceremony to be a funeral.

3. Of a thing: To require as a necessary preceding condition; to involve or imply as an antecedent.

1526 *Pilgr. Perf.* (W. de W. 1531) 22 The holy lyfe of religyon presupposeth grace. **1594** *Mirr. Policy* (1599) 51 Gouernement presupposeth Order, forasmuch as without Order, there can be no due gouernment. **1669** CLARENDON *Ess.* Tracts (1727) 123 Princes..can have few friends, because friendship presupposeth some kind of equality. **1802** PALEY *Nat. Theol.* xxiii. (1819) 369 A law presupposes an agent, for it is only the mode according to which an agent proceeds. **1866** *Cornh. Mag.* Aug. 231 Healthy sleep presupposes a healthy state of brain. **1877** E. R. CONDER *Bas. Faith* vii. 296 An effect presupposes a cause.

4. *passive* (from 1 or 3). To be implied or involved as something previously or already present or in existence. Formerly with *to* (cf. 1 b).

1526 *Pilgr. Perf.* (W. de W. 1531) 155 [This] is necessaryly required to be had, as yᵉ meane directly presupposed, before yᵗ euery persone can attayne to yᵉ perfeccyon of yᵉ contemplatyue lyfe. **1557** EDGEWORTH *Serm.* Repert., Faith, hope, and charitie, be presupposed to the .vii. giftes of the holy gooast. **1597** HOOKER *Eccl. Pol.* v. lviii. §3 Other principles..although not specified in defining, are notwithstanding in nature implied and presupposed. **1653** ASHWELL *Fides Apost.* 142 And Christs descent into Hell, is presupposed to the Article of his Resurrection. *a* **1716** SOUTH *Serm.* (1744) IX. xi. 319 In all rational agents, before every action there is presupposed a knowledge of the thing that is to be produced by that action. **1853** LYNCH *Self-Improv.* iv. 84 In all culture, nature is presupposed.

Hence †**presu'ppose** *sb.*, a presupposition. *Obs.*

1592 R. D. *Hypnerotomachia* 84 Having made thys.. swasive praesuppose..I..determined..to come backe againe to this noble..Nymph.

presupposed (-'pəʊzd), *ppl. a.* [f. prec. + -ED¹.] Supposed, assumed, or implied beforehand.

1577–87 HOLINSHED *Chron.* III. 195/1 All which presupposed plagues concurring. **1643** MILTON *Divorce* II. xvi. Wks. 1851 IV. 103 The efficacie of those [rites] depends upon the presupposed fitnesse of either party. **1794** HOME in *Phil. Trans.* LXXXV. 14 It was a particular satisfaction to have an evidence who had no presupposed opinion, therefore impartial. **1840** THACKERAY *Paris Sk.-bk.*, *Case Peytel* (1872) 194 The dreadful weight of his presupposed guilt.

presupposition (priːsʌpə'zɪʃən). Also 8 præ-. [ad. med.L. *præsuppositiōn-em* (*a* 1308 in Duns Scotus *Rer. Princip.* 5. 21), n. of action from med.L. *præsuppōnĕre*: see PRESUPPONE. So F. *présupposition* (14th c. in Godef.).]

1. The action or an act of presupposing; a supposition antecedent to knowledge; the assumption of the existence or truth of something, as a preliminary to action, argument, etc.

a **1533** LD. BERNERS *Gold. Bk. M. Aurel.* xxx. (1535) 50 To my iugement, these princis are not chosen, that they shulde eate more mete than all other,..but with presupposition, yᵗ they ought to knowe more than all other. **1614** SELDEN *Titles Hon.* 4 That cannot..be conceiued..otherwise than with a presupposition of a Democracie, out of which, as is related, a Monarchie might haue originall. **1701** NORRIS *Ideal World* I. v. 238 That which Suaver calls a priority of præsupposition. **1871** EARLE *Philol. Eng. Tongue* §387 The verb and adjective alike have their very nature based upon the pre-supposition of the substantive.

2. That which is presupposed, assumed, or taken for granted beforehand; a supposition, notion, or idea assumed as a basis of argument, action, etc.; an antecedent supposition, preliminary assumption.

1579–80 NORTH *Plutarch* (1676) 383 As in a Mathematicall Proposition, there were many great conjectures and presuppositions, and many long circumstances to bring the matter to a conclusion. **1660** JER. TAYLOR *Duct. Dubit.* II. ii. rule vi. §1, I will not now examine whether they certainly follow from their premises and presuppositions. **1847** LEWES *Hist. Philos.* (1867) I. iv. 307 The presupposition, absurd as it really is, has been generally entertained. **1882** W. WALLACE in *Academy* 1 Apr. 231/3 He sought to set before those who ignore philosophy,..the consideration that there are a few presuppositions still unanswered and apparently unanswerable by scientific methods. **1895** *Athenæum* 23 Feb. 242/3 Pre-suppositions, axioms, postulates, call them what you will, are discovered by analysis to be a necessary ingredient of knowledge; and their acceptance is an act of faith, which is justified by its results.

3. Comb., as *presupposition-free* adj.

1966 *Jrnl. Philos.* LXIII. 699 (*heading*) Completeness theorems for some presupposition-free logics. **1972** *Jrnl. Symbolic Logic* XXXVII. 424 'Presupposition-free' here refers to the absence of presuppositions that there are individuals in the domain over which individual variables range.

Hence **presuppo'sitionless** *a.*, without presuppositions; **presuppositionlessness**.

1871 DAVIDSON tr. *Trendelenburg* in *Jrnl. Spec. Philos.* V. 358. Presuppositionless. **1885** A. SETH in *Encycl. Brit.* XVIII. 795/1. Presuppositionless. **1906** *Mind* XV. 281 There is no absolutely presuppositionless psychology. **1940** *Philos. Rev.* XLIX. 285 The idea of a presuppositionless philosophy. **1974** *Jrnl. Ecumenical Stud.* XI. 140 Presuppositionless appreciation of..convictions. **1976** *Word 1971* XXVII. 191 A presuppositionless analysis of a child's corpus will not have any theoretical import. **1940** M. FARBER *Philos. Ess. in Memory E. Husserl* 44 The claim of presuppositionlessness has been made at various times.

presuppositional (priːsʌpə'zɪʃənəl), *a.* [f. PRESUPPOSITION + -AL¹.] Of or pertaining to presuppositions.

1909 W. M. URBAN *Valuation* i. 14 The method of psychological worth analysis we may..characterise as the Presuppositional Method. It begins with analysis of presuppositions. **1954** *Mind* LXIII. 154 Banishing all this presuppositional meaning. **1975** R. M. KEMPSON *Presupposition* iv. 74 Anomalies..arise for a presuppositional account with each logical connective. **1978** *Language* LIV. 494 McClaran's paper, 'Presuppositional aspects of Yucatec sentences', investigates the semantic and syntactic properties associated with Yucatec verbs bearing the suffixes *ik*, *Ak*, *il*, and *Al*.

pre-surmise, -suspect: see PRE- A. 1, 2.

presydent, obs. f. PRECEDENT, PRESIDENT.

presyes, -syse, obs. forms of PRECISE *a.*

pre-syllabic, -symptomatic: see PRE- B. 1.

presylvian, -symphysial: see PRE- B. 3.

presy'naptic, *a.* **1.** *Cytology.* [PRE- B. 1.] Prior to meiotic synapsis.

1909 *Ann. Bot.* XXIII. 21 In common with Grégoire ('07), we may adopt, provisionally at least, the following scheme of phases for convenience of clearness in description. The prophases of division naturally fall into two periods, the pre-synaptic and the post-synaptic phases. **1912** [see LEPTOTENE]. **1921** *Ann. Bot.* XXXV. 367 Fig. 5 represents a presynaptic pollen mother-cell.

2. *Physiol.* [PRE- B 3] Of, pertaining to, or designating a neurone that transmits a nerve impulse across a synapse. Opp. POSTSYNAPTIC *a.* 2.

1937 *Proc. R. Soc.* B. CXXII. 113 The response is erratic in that by no means every pre-synaptic stimulus yields a post-synaptic response. **1950** [see HYPERPOLARIZE *v.*]. **1965** G. H. BELL et al. *Textbk. Physiol. & Biochem.* (ed. 6) xxxix. 796 In general the presynaptic fibre divides up into numerous fine branches which then end in greatly expanded terminals, presynaptic knobs, which make intimate contact with part of the membrane of the cell body or dendrites of the postsynaptic cell. **1979** *Internat. Rehabilit. Med.* I. 45/1 New evidence of the blocking of pain specific receptors..by morphine-like substances produced by presynaptic dendrites.

Hence **presy'naptically** *adv.*

1971 *Nature* 12 Nov. 102/1 In the central nervous system, amphetamine releases presynaptically bound NE [*sc.* norepinephrine] or DA [*sc.* dopamine] and blocks their re-uptake. **1976** *Ibid.* 3 June 418/1 The fact that chlorpromazine also blocks α-adrenoceptors, possibly presynaptically located, may also contribute to the enhanced presence of catecholamines at the synaptic cleft.

pre-systematic(ally): see PRE- B. 1.

‖**presystole** (priː'sɪstəliː). *Physiol.* [mod.L., f. PRE- B. 1 + SYSTOLE.] The interval immediately preceding the systole. Also *attrib.*

1884 *Nature* 4 Sept. 460/1 A study of the sphincters of the cardiac and other veins, with remarks on their hermetic occlusion during the presystole state. **1895** *Syd. Soc. Lex.*, *Presystole*, the latter part of the *diastole*, corresponding to the time occupied by the dilatation of the ventricles.

presystolic (priːsɪ'stɒlɪk), *a. Physiol.* [f. as prec. + -IC; so F. *présystolique*.] Preceding the systole; of or belonging to the presystole.

1857 DUNGLISON *Dict. Med.* s.v., Presystolic friction sound. **1876** [see PERIDIASTOLIC]. **1897** *Allbutt's Syst. Med.* III. 58 He has..a well-marked presystolic thrill and a loud presystolic murmur at the cardiac apex.

†**Pret**, *sb. Obs. rare.* [short for It. *Prete Gianni.*] = PRESTER JOHN, applied to the Negus of Abyssinia.

1635 PAGITT *Christianogr.* I. ii. 40 The Abassins reckon a succession of Christian Emperors... The Prets or Emperours dwell in a moveable City of Tents.

†**pret**, *a. Sc. Obs.* [a. mod.F. *prêt* ready: see PREST.] Ready; = PREST *a.*

1535 STEWART *Cron. Scot.* (Rolls) I. 63 Witht laureat language and pret for till prys [= ready for to praise], His orisoun begouth he on this wyss.

pre'tape, *v.* [PRE- A. 1.] *trans.* To prerecord using magnetic tape. So **pre'taped** *ppl. a.*, **pre'taping** *vbl. sb.*

1968 J. PHILIPS *Hot Summer Killing* (1969) III. ii. 151 The networks will be giving up commercial time. Pretaped shows are already prepared. **1972** *Listener* 6 July 3/1 Becton insists on live transmission... 'You are not really trusting people with the airtime if you insist on pre-taping.' **1972** W. P. MCGIVERN *Caprifoil* (1973) viii. 144 He pre-taped a series of television speeches to camouflage his absence. **1973** *Sociometry* XXXVI. 103 Subjects listened to pre-taped instructions. **1976** *National Observer* (U.S.) 16 Oct. 6/2 They were a poor substitute for journalism, pretaped and all but tensionless.

‖**prêt-à-porter** (prɛtapɔrte). [Fr., 'ready to wear'.] Phr. used *attrib.* and *absol.* to denote clothes that are sold in standard sizes ready for wear.

1957 *Punch* 16 Jan. 136/3 Gloves, scarves, jewellery, and *prêt-à-porter* clothes..all the fleeting frivolities..of the passing mode. **1958** M. STEWART *Nine Coaches Waiting* vi. 71 The young and lovely buy dresses *prêtes à porter*... Off the peg. **1959** *Guardian* 4 Dec. 6/3 The prêt-à-porter spring and summer shows are in full swing in Paris. **1967** *Times* 21 Feb. 9/2 As at the Paris prêt-à-porter fair, the Mary Quant stand was jampacked for the parades. **1973** *Sat. Rev. Arts* (U.S.) Jan. 84/3 The last two pieces contain an onslaught of information about the vigorous young designers and the boom of *prêt à porter*. There is worry that the heyday of French couture is over. **1977** *New Yorker* 11 July 79/1 The feverish search on Seventh Avenue for novelty and for sure profits has come to rival the showings of the Paris prêt-à-porter.

pre-taste: see PRE- A. 2.

'pre-tax, *a.* and *adv.* **A.** *adj.* [PRE- B. 2.] Designating gross assets, earnings, funds, or profits considered before the deduction of tax.

1963 *Times* 7 June 17/2 Group pre-tax profit is £124,000, £14,000 more than forecast, and after tax of £64,000 there is available to the holding company nearly £60,000. **1968** *N.Y. Times* 12 Jan. 38 They forecast a sales gain of 8 to 10 per cent but see an almost dramatic improvement in margins as pretax earnings rise 15 to 20 per cent above those of 1967. **1969** *Times* 2 May 28/5 Pre-tax profits are up from £810,000 to £930,000. **1977** *New Yorker* 29 Aug. 47/1 They'd give me five percent of the pretax profit.

B. *adv.* [PRE- B. 2 c.] Before the deduction of tax.

1976 *Daily Tel.* 17 Feb. 19 (*heading*) Lonrho advances 35pc pre-tax. *Ibid.* 16 July 17/1 It is encouraging to see a £4·57 million turnround to interim profits of £3·61 million pre-tax.

†**pre'taxate**, *a. Obs. rare*⁻¹. [f. med.L. *prætaxāre*: see next and -ATE².] Estimated, or fixed as to amount, beforehand. In quot. const. as *pa. pple.* So †**pre'taxed** *pa. pple. Obs.*

c **1520** BARCLAY *Jugurth* li. 72 That suche excused of warr ..shulde pay a certayne somme of money pretaxed to warde the wages of such as laufully were admytted to warre. **1570** FOXE *A. & M.* (ed. 2) 464/2 That no man, vpon payne pretaxate, should helpe, reskew, or relieue the sayd rebells.

pretaxation (priːtæk'seɪʃən). Also præ-. [ad. med.L. **prætaxātiōn-em*, n. of action f. med.L. *prætaxāre* to count, reckon, or estimate beforehand: see PRE- A. and TAXATION. The intermediate sense was app. that of giving a preliminary opinion.] The action of giving a vote before others; prior election: see quots.

1769 ROBERTSON *Chas. V* (1796) I. 358 This privilege of voting first is called by the German lawyers the right of Praetaxation. **1864** BRYCE *Holy Rom. Emp.* xiv. (1866) 251 At the election of Lothar II. A.D. 1125 we find a certain small number of magnates exercising the so-called right of prætaxation; that is to say, choosing alone the future monarch, and then submitting him to the rest for their approval. *Ibid.* 252 The right of prætaxation had ripened into an exclusive privilege of election, vested in a small body. **1878** STUBBS *Const. Hist.* III. xx. 417 A pretaxation was made by the ruling officers of the community.

pre-teach: see PRE- A. 1.

pre'tectal, *a. Anat.* [ad. mod.L. *prætectālis*, f. PRE- B. 3 + TECT(UM + -AL.] Lying in front of the tectum; of or pertaining to the pretectum.

1925 *Jrnl. Compar. Neurol.* XXXIX. 195 (*caption*) Horizontal section through the posterior commissure, showing the pretectal nucleus in relation to the other parts of the thalamus and midbrain. **1959** *Folia Psychiatrica et Neurologica Japonica* XIII. 268 The pretectal region is located between the posterior part of the thalamus and the tectum, equipped with admixture of cells of both thalamic and mesencephalic origin. **1973** *Brain Res.* LXIII. 360 The fact that two or three optic tract volleys were needed to evoke a response in the short ciliary nerve..indicates a low excitability of the pretectal neurones concerned.

Hence (as a back-formation) **pre'tectum**, the pretectal region of the brain.

1961 *Lancet* 9 Sept. 568/2 The disturbances in ocular motility and the radiological findings, led to the diagnosis of a small lesion in the pretectum. **1973** *Nature* 1 June 295/1 The control of pupil size..is known to be mediated by a reflex pathway through the pretectum.

pre-'teen, *a.* orig. *U.S.* [f. PRE- B. 2 + TEEN *sb.*²] Prior to one's teens; denoting the years of a child's life (usu. immediately) before the age of thirteen. Also *absol.* as *sb.* Hence **pre-'teenager**, **pre'teener**, a child (just) before the age of thirteen.

1960 V. PACKARD *Waste Makers* vii. 76 Even pre-teen boys' shoes were slated for obsoleting. They were being designed away from their 'sexless' look to a real 'nervous' look of flashy casualness. **1966** *N.Y. Times* 6 Jan. 33 Darlene [is] mother of two pre-teen children. **1966** *Economist* 10 Dec. 1144/2 One feature of nightlife on the Strip which the casual visitor is most likely to notice are the regular contingents of pre-teenagers, especially young girls of twelve and even less. **1967** *Atlantic Monthly* Jan. 77 The texts of many popular songs are so obviously coital that one wonders how they get on the radio and are sold openly to pre-teens. **1967** *Punch* 15 Mar. 377/2 Close behind the teen-age revolution, the emancipation of the pre-teens is gathering momentum... In North America the female pre-teen is already 'a knacky, switched-on dolly'. **1969** *Punch* 12

Mar. 384/3 By the time that the American child has reached the age of three, he is known as a sub pre-teener. 1970 *Daily Tel.* 8 May 17 The tendency is for children to experiment with cigarettes from as early as eight years old, and pre-teenagers are often regular smokers. 1972 J. L. Dillard *Black English* vi. 260 Twelve- and thirteen-year-old boys revealed the same type of half-funny, half-pathetic misinformation about sex which practically all preteens seem to have. 1972 *N.Y. Times* 3 Nov. 3/5 (Advt.), Both for preteen sizes 6 to 14. 1977 *Maclean's Mag.* 2 May 23/3 A mini crime wave involving gangs of teen-agers and pre-teens. 1978 *Church Times* 25 Aug. 6/2 An imaginative collection of prayers and poems for pre-teenagers.

pre-telegraph, pre-telescopic, -television, etc.: see pre- B. 1 d, 2 a.

pre'temporal (priː-), *a.*[1] (*sb.*) [ad. mod.L. *prætemporālis*: see pre- B. 3 and temporal (belonging to the temple).] Situated in front of the temporal region of the skull: applied to a muscle. Also *ellipt.* as *sb.*

[1866 Owen *Vertebr. Anim.* I. 223 The temporal is represented by two muscles, one of which, the *pretemporalis* ..has its origin extended forward into the orbit from beneath the postfrontal.] *Ibid.*, Its fibres pass vertically external to those of the pretemporal.

pretemporal, *a.*[2]: see pre- B. 1.

pretence, pretense (prɪ'tɛns), *sb.* [= late AF. *pretensse* (*c* 1471 in Godef.), ad. med.L. **prætensa* vbl. sb., f. *prætens-us* for class.L. *prætent-us*, pa. pple. of *prætendĕre*: see pretend. The spelling *pretense* is now usual in the U.S.; cf. *defense*.]

1. a. An assertion of a right or title; the putting forth of a claim; a claim. Now *rare*.

1425 W. Paston in *P. Lett.* I. 19 His pretense of his title to the priourie of Bromholme is adnulled. 1495 *Act 11 Hen. VII*, c. 47 *Preamble*, Youre seid Suppliant [hath] contynually ben seised..therof..hidirto without any pretence or clayme made therto by the seid Duke. 1522 in Ld. Herbert *Hen. VIII* (1649) 127 To prevent ambiguities and quarrels, each Prince before May 1524, shall declare his pretences. 1667 Milton *P.L.* ii. 825 Spirits that in our just pretenses arm'd Fell with us from on high. 1683 Temple *Mem.* Wks. 1731 I. 410 His Highness had a long Pretence depending at Madrid, for about Two hundred thousand Pounds owing to his Family from that Crown. 1707 *Curios. in Husb. & Gard.* 186 No Man has..more Pretence to speak of Nitre, than M. Boyle. 1855 Macaulay *Hist. Eng.* xvi. III. 679 Marlborough calmly and politely showed that the pretence was unreasonable.

b. *Her. in pretence*, borne on an inescutcheon to indicate a pretension or claim, e.g. that of a husband to the estates of his wife. *escutcheon of pretence*, such an inescutcheon.

1562 Leigh *Armorie* 43 If the man haue maried an heyre, he shall beare her cote, none other wise, vntill he haue begotten an heyre of the heyre. Then may he, by the curtesy of armes, beare her armes in an Inscocheon, that is to saye, a scocheon of pretence. 1611 Guillim *Heraldry* ii. vii. (1611) 65 Escocheon of Pretence. 1677, 1823 [see escutcheon 1 c]. 1869 Cussans *Her.* (1882) 231 The only difference between the Arms of William and those of Mary was, that the former bore Nassau in pretence. *Ibid.* 233 From [1801] until the accession of our present Queen, the Royal Arms were: Quarterly of four: 1 and 4. England: 2. Scotland: 3. Ireland: in Pretence, Hanover, ensigned with an Imperial Crown.

2. The putting forth of a claim to merit, dignity, or personal worth; pretension, profession; ostentation, parade, display.

1526 *Pilgr. Perf.* (W. de W. 1531) 81 But for shame she wyll not make suche pretence as to aske them openly. 1567 *Satir. Poems Reform.* iv. 39 My Princelie pretence began to decay. 1649 Jer. Taylor *Gt. Exemp.* Disc. xiv. §26 There are no greater fools in the world then such, whose life conformes not to the pretence of their baptisme and institution. 1729 Butler *Serm.* Wks. 1874 II. 87 Persons.. who yet make great pretences to religion. 1802 Mar. Edgeworth *Moral T.* (1816) I. iv. 20 Fashionable dialect.. destitute of any pretence to wit. 1885 *Manch. Exam.* 20 Mar. 8/6 His bearing had always a kind of stateliness, utterly free from pomp or pretence.

†3. a. An expressed aim, intention, purpose, or design; an intending or purposing; the object aimed at, the end purposed. *Obs.*

1526 *Pilgr. Perf.* (W. de W. 1531) 181 In whome he coude fynde neyther synne nor pretense of synne. 1547 Boorde *Introd. Knowl.* xxxii. (1870) 205, I, knowyng theyr pretence, aduertysed them to returne home to England. 1621 Elsing *Debates Ho. Lords* (Camden) 102 E. Marshall. Wysheth well to the pretence of the byll, but not his vote thereunto as yt is. 1626 W. Vaughan *Direct. Health* vi. viii. (ed. 6) 169 Cause your bed to be heated with a warming pan: vnlesse your pretence be to harden your members. 1648 Milton *Tenure Kings* (1650) 3 Fainting ere their own pretences, though never so just, be half attain'd. 1700 Dryden *Pal & Arcite* 306 But thou, false Arcite, never shalt obtain Thy bad pretence. 1700 Congreve *Way of World* Prol. 33 To please, this time, has been his sole pretence. 1783 Burke *Rep. Affairs India* Wks. 1842 II. 17 It appears, that the subscription, even in idea or pretence, is not for the use of the company.

b. *esp.* A false, feigned, or hypocritical profession or pretension.

1545 Joye *Exp. Dan.* vii. 103 He shall do all his fraudelent featis vnder a meruelouse pretence of holynes innocencye and mekenes. 1596 Spenser *F.Q.* iv. v. 23 With boastfull vaine pretense Stept Braggadochio forth, and as his thrall Her claym'd. *a* 1677 Hale *Prim. Orig. Man.* 145 Manetho, ..with very great pretence hath carried up their Government to an incredible distance before the Creation of Mankind. *a* 1763 Shenstone *Ess.* (1765) 57 How often do we see pretence cultivated in proportion as virtue is neglected. 1872 Morley *Voltaire* i. (1886) 8 A piece of ingeniously reticulated pretence.

4. A profession of purpose; *esp.* a false profession, a merely feigned aim or object, a pretext, a cloak.

In earlier use the falsity is only expressed by the context.

1538 Starkey *England* i. iii. 85 Vnder the pretense and colure therof [the common weal], euery one of them procuryth the pryuate and the syngular wele. *a* 1648 Ld. Herbert *Hen. VIII* (1683) 259 He commanded one Francisco Campana..into England, on pretence to confer with the King and Cardinal, but indeed to charge Campejus to burn the Decretal. 1665 Manley *Grotius' Low C. Warres* 694 That under the pretence of bringing in several prisoners to Gertruydenbergh, he should open the Town to the Enemy. 1712 tr. *Pomet's Hist. Drugs* I. 195 A good Pretence to cover their Knavery. 1845 James *A. Neil* iv, He had some other object—this is all a pretence.

5. a. An assertion, allegation, or statement as to fact; now usually with implication that it is false or misleading.

1608 Topsell *Serpents* 79 [The Drones] suffer punishment..for pretence of idlenesse, gluttony, extortion, and rauenous greedinesse, to which they are too much adicted. 1642 tr. *Perkins' Prof. Bk.* vi. §470. 205 The wife dyeth within one day after the descent, so as the husband could not enter during the coverture for the shortnesse of the time, yet hee shall not bee tenant by the curtesie. And yet according to common pretence there is no default in the husband. *c* 1656 Bramhall *Replic.* ii. 111 How many of the orthodox Clergy without pretence of any other delinquency have been beggered? 1754 Sherlock *Disc.* (1759) I. i. 5 But let us, if you please, examine this Pretence. 1856 Emerson *Eng. Traits, Aristocr.* Wks. (Bohn) II. 79 The pretence is that the noble is of unbroken descent from the Norman... But the fact is otherwise.

b. The action of pretending, as in children's play; make-believe, fiction.

1863 Kingsley *Water-Bab.* ii. 80 Don't you know that this is a fairy tale and all fun and pretence; and that you are not to believe one word of it, even if it is true?

6. The assertion or alleging of a ground, cause, or reason for any action; an alleged ground or reason, a plea; now usually, a trivial, groundless, or fallacious plea or reason, a pretext.

1560 Daus tr. *Sleidane's Comm.* 392 b, Vnder this pretence of the law, he might by little and little tourn both him and his children out of all theyr landes. 1627 Donne *Serm.* v. (1640) 39 Moses having received a commandement from God,..and having excused himselfe by some other modest and pious pretences. 1654 Bramhall *Just Vind.* ii. (1661) 12 Heresie obtruded upon them under the specious pretences of obedience and Charity. 1674 Marvell *Corr.* Wks. (Grosart) II. 422 This new bauke which occasions it, will serve for a just pretense to the variance of our judgements. 1759 Robertson *Hist. Scot.* vi. Wks. 1813 I. 448 A pretence was at hand to justify the most violent proceedings. 1823 J. Gillies tr. *Aristotle's Rhet.* xii. 228 Villany, according to the proverb, wants but a pretence. 1846 Greener *Sc. Gunnery* 166 For what purpose? Under the pretence that the barrels are firmer, and not so liable to become loose. 1880 *Scribner's Mag.* June 284 And ring for the servants on the smallest pretense.

7. *attrib.* (in sense 5), passing into *adj.*, denoting something that is imitative or 'phoney'.

1941 *Punch* 17 Sept. 256/3 That lorry buzzing along High Street has got some pretence bombs and it's going to strew them about and we've got to pretend they have been dropped by the Blen. 1953 *Mind* LXII. 209 If I dream of a snake my dream must contain, if not a snake then an illusory or pretence snake.

†pre'tence, pre'tense, *v. Obs.* [Back-formation from pretenced *ppl. a.*; or f. late L. *prætens-*, ppl. stem of *prætendĕre*: see pretense *a.*]

1. *trans.* To offer, proffer. *rare.*

a 1548 Hall *Chron., Hen. VIII* 82 None ceased till they all that would entre were deliuered of their pretence in chalenge royall pretenced.

2. To cloak, to give a feigned appearance to.

1548 Gest *Pr. Masse* A j b, It is also pretensed & cloked wyth the pretense and vsurped name of the Euangelicall truthe. 1648 J. Goodwin *Right & Might* 36 Much more may the most worthy actions and services of men, bee compelled to pretense the worst and vilest deeds.

3. To pretend, profess, allege, esp. falsely.

1567 *Reg. Privy Council Scot.* I. 525 To mak publicatioun ..that nane pretense ignorance of the same. 1592 Warner *Alb. Eng.* vii. xxxv. (1612) 168 A Priests base Puple, he By his Complottors was pretens'te Duke Clarence sonne to be. 1627 W. Sclater *Exp. 2 Thess.* (1629) 257 That impossibility, or difficulty may not be pretensed. 1691 *Pol. Ballads* (1860) II. 27 The Nations salvation From mal-administration Was then pretenc'd by the Saints, but now 'tis abdication.

4. To intend, purpose, design.

1565 in *Calr. Scott. Papers* (1900) II. 119 The overthrow of religion ys pretensed.

pre'tenced, pre'tensed (-'ɛnst), *ppl. a.* [orig. *pretensed*, f. L. *prætens-us* (see pretense *a.*) + -ed[1] 2.]

1. Put forward in defence or excuse; alleged, asserted, professed, claimed, esp. falsely; feigned, counterfeit, spurious; = pretended 1, 2. *arch.*

1425 *Rolls of Parlt.* IV. 273/1 Y[e] pretensed ryght of my said Lord. 1461 *Ibid.* V. 467/2 Eny Acte made in the pretensed Parlement holden at the Citee of Coventre. 1535 in *Lett. Suppress. Monasteries* (Camden) 77 Vexede without cause or any pretenced occasion motioned of your saide oratours partie. 1591 G. Fletcher *Russe Commw.* (Hakl. Soc.) 35 Upon some pretensed crime objected against them. 1660 R. Coke *Power & Subj.* 225 Such as then had obtained pretenced licences and dispensations from the See of Rome. 1798 B. Washington *Rep.* I. 39 An act against buying pretensed titles. 1883 R. W. Dixon *Mano* i. iv. 11 Through the pretensed commission which they gave.

†2. Intended, purposed, designed. *Obs.*

1513 More *Rich. III* (1641) 2 He set forth openly his pretensed enterprise. *c* 1540 tr. *Pol. Verg. Eng. Hist.* (Camden) I. 207 Thei beganne to goe forwarde with their pretenced jornie. 1543 Grafton *Contn. Harding* 469 His mischeuous imagened & pretenced enterprise. 1577–87 Holinshed *Chron.* (1807–8) IV. 245 That wicked practise missed the pretensed effect. 1596 J. Smyth in *Lett. Lit. Men* (Camden) 92 That I had a pretensed intencion to stirre the soldyers to mutynye.

†b. esp. in *pretenced* or *pretensed malice*, frequent in 15–16th c. for *purpensed*, *prepensed malice* (from similarity of sound and sense). *Obs.*

1483 *Parl. Roll 1 Rich. III.* m. 9 (P.R.O.) Of thair pretenced malices and traitours entent. 1542 Becon *Pathw. Prayer* vii. D vij b, It came to passe accordynge to his pretensed malyce, that he slewe his brother. 1579 Tomson *Calvin's Serm. Tim.* 74/2 He resisted not the Gospell, nor fought against the trueth of God of a pretensed malice.

†3. Seriously intended (as opposed to feigned).

1547 Hooper *Answ. Bp. Winchester's Bk.* E iij, This reason and accompt of fayth yeuen, with a moost ernist, and pretensyd uowe to lyue for euer uerteusly.

Hence **pre'tencedly, pre'tensedly** *adv.*, with pretence, feignedly, pretendedly. *rare.*

1567 Drant *Horace, Epist.* xvi. E viij, In case thou walke pretensedly and thereby hope to gaine. 1607 Bp. Andrewes *Serm.* (1843) V. 191 Let the world be preached..be it sincerely, or be it pretensedly. 1885 R. W. Dixon *Hist. Ch. Eng.* xv. (1893) III. 40 The Parliament saw..their own statute of repeal traversed by these royal, or pretensedly royal edicts.

pre'tenceful, *a. rare.* [f. pretence *sb.* + -ful.] Full of pretence, or of loud pretension.

1841 *Tait's Mag.* VIII. 564 Sounding the trump ecclesiastic with pretenceful blare and fanfare.

pre'tenceless, *a.* [f. as prec. + -less.] Without any pretence of reason; without excuse.

1641 Milton *Reform.* ii. Wks. 1851 III. 41 What Rebellions, and those the basest, and most pretenselesse have they not been chiefe in? 1817 Bentham *Parl. Reform* Introd. 26 Oh! pretenceless and inhuman tyranny! 1818 —— *Ch. Eng.* 352 The number of these pretenceless instances of dereliction of duty is more than half as great again as in either of the two preceding years.

pretend (prɪ'tɛnd), *v.* Also 7 præ-. [ad. L. *prætend-ĕre* to stretch forth, hold before, put forward, allege, pretend, f. *præ*, pre- A. + *tendĕre* to stretch, extend, tend. So F. *prétendre* (15th c. in Littré).]

I. †1. *trans.* To stretch, extend, or hold (something) before, in front of, or over a person or thing (e.g. as a covering or defence). *Obs.*

1596 Spenser *F.Q.* vi. xi. 19 But Pastorella..Was by the Captaine all this while defended, Who..His target alwayes over her pretended. 1658 Evelyn *Fr. Gard.* (1675) 145 They may pretend them [bells of earth over plants] for the night only, and to prevent hail. 1670 H. Stubbe *Plus Ultra* 146 There was an opacous, dark red setling, with an enaeorema of contexed filaments pretended to the top.

†2. To bring or put forward, set forth, hold out, offer for action, consideration, or acceptance; to proffer, present; to bring (a charge, an action at law).

c 1450 tr. *De Imitatione* iii. xlv. 115 Lorde, what may I.. riȝtwesly pretende ayenst þe if þou do not þat I aske? 1563 B. Googe *Eglogs*, etc. (Arb.) 78 Suche towardenes,..Doth sure a hope, of greater thyngs pretende. 1569 *Reg. Privy Council Scot.* II. 30 Without prejudice of the said Gilbertis actioun..that he may have, pretend, or move, aganis the airis. 1594 Carew *Huarte's Exam. Wits* xii. (1596) 198 God ..had pretended a remedie in that behalfe, which was.. Manna. 1616 R. C. *Times' Whistle, Cert. Poems* (E.E.T.S.) 110, I had not thought..to have pretended thus conspicuously in thy sight this rude and indigested chaos of conceites. 1621–3 Middleton & Rowley *Changeling* iv. ii. 91 To that wench I pretend honest love, and she deserves it. 1653 Holcroft *Procopius* ii. 55 Women..offered their breasts; but the child would not take womans milk, neither would the Goat leave it; but importunatly..pretended to it her own. So that the women let it alone, and the Goat nursed it. 1690 Leybourn *Curs. Math.* 345 When there is an Aequation pretended like $aa+ba+ca = -bc$, present judgement may be made.

3. †a. *refl.* To put oneself forward in some character; to profess or claim (with *inf.* or *compl.*).

c 1380 Wyclif *Sel. Wks.* III. 518 Þo þat pretenden hem to ben principal folewers of Cristis steppis. *c* 1412 Hoccleve *De Reg. Princ.* 886 He þat pretendiþ him of most nobley. 1508 Kennedie *Flyting w. Dunbar* 26 Pretendand the to wryte sic skaldit skrowis. 1660 Fuller *Mixt Contempl.* (1841) 252 Poor, petty, pitiful persons, who pretended themselves princes. 1672 in Picton *L'pool Munic. Rec.* (1883) I. 246 A paper or libell..pretending itselfe to be a remonstrance. 1680 H. Dodwell *Two Lett.* (1691) Ep. Ded., None can now pretend themselves unconcerned in the Advice of a Laick, or a private Person.

b. Without reflexive pronoun, in same sense as a; gradually passing into one closely akin to 7: To put forth an assertion or statement (expressed by an *inf.*) about oneself; now usually implying mere pretension without foundation:

to feign *to be* or *do* something. (A leading modern sense.)

1412-20 LYDG. *Chron. Troy* II. x. (1555), She vnto some pretendeth to be trewe. **1526** *Pilgr. Perf.* (W. de W. 1531) 204 Yf he had pretended to suffre payne & had feled no smarte. **1530** PALSGR. 665/2 He pretendith to be my frynde, but he doyth the worst for me that he can. **1535** COVERDALE *Job* xxxv. 8 Of yᵉ sonne of man that is rightuous as thou pretendest to be. **1638** CHILLINGW. *Relig. Prot.* I. i. §10. 37, I may, and doe believe them, as firmely as you pretend to do. **1662** J. DAVIES tr. *Mandelslo's Trav.* 227 He will pretend not to have seen him. **1749** FIELDING *Tom Jones* II. vi, He was ignorant, or at least pretended to be so. **1794** MRS. RADCLIFFE *Myst. Udolpho* xxxi, The people pretend to know nothing about any prisoners. **1847** HELPS *Friends in C.* I. 10 Pretending to agree with the world when you do not. **1866** G. MACDONALD *Ann. Q. Neighb.* xxx, I cannot pretend to feel any of the interest you consider essential.

†**c.** with ellipsis of refl. pron. or inf. *Obs.*

1671 MILTON *Samson* 212 Wisest Men Have err'd, and by bad Women been deceiv'd; And shall again, pretend they ne're so wise.

d. To feign in play; to make believe. (With *inf.* as in b, or *clause* as in 7 a.)

1865 'L. CARROLL' *Alice in Wonderl.* i, This curious child was very fond of pretending to be two people. **1871** —— *Through Looking-gl.* i, 'Let's pretend we're kings and queens.'.. 'Nurse! do let's pretend that I'm a hungry hyæna, and you're a bone!' **1891** E. KINGLAKE *Australian at H.* 20 The boys used to pretend that they were a court of justice, and appoint a judge, jury [etc.].

4. *trans.* To give oneself out as having (something); to profess to have, make profession of, profess (a quality, etc.). Now always in a bad sense: to profess falsely, to feign (some quality).

1401 *Pol. Poems* (Rolls) II. 55 Anticristis menye,.. the which pretenden first mekenesse of herte, and aftir rysyng to arrogaunce, disdeynynge al other. *Ibid.* 102 Thou seist that we pretenden the perfeccioun of apostlis. **1412-20** LYDG. *Chron. Troy* I. v. (MS. Digby 230) lf. 40 b/2 Thouȝ þᵗ þei feith aforn pretende. **1563-4** *Reg. Privy Council Scot.* I. 256 Nane of his liegis pretend ignorance heirin. **1629** MASSINGER *Picture* IV. ii, That comfort which The damned pretend, fellows in misery. **1654** FULLER *Two Serm.* 37 Leastwise they seemingly pretended it [real piety]; and Joshua charitably beleeved it. **1654** WHITLOCK *Zootomia* 203 Good Meanings rather pretended than intended, are ful of Hel, and Mischiefe. **1740** GRENVILLE in *Johnson's Debates* 4 Dec. (1787) I. 79, I do not pretend any other skill in military affairs, than may be gained by casual conversation with soldiers. *c* **1850** *Arab. Nts.* (Rtldg.) 707 The enchantress then related.. how she pretended illness, and thus excited Prince Ahmed's compassion.

†**b.** *esp.* To profess or claim to have (a right, title, power, authority, or the like); to claim. *Obs.*

1427 *Rolls of Parlt.* IV. 326/2 Any right þat he wolde pretende or clayme in the governance. **1469** *Paston Lett.* II. 344 My Lorde of Norffolk pretendeth title to serteyn londys of Sir John Pastons. **1523** FITZHERB. *Surv.* 17 b, Where a man pretendeth a tytle and after releseth in the court. **1658** BRAMHALL *Consecr. Bps.* v. 133 Where the Bishop of London never pretended any Jurisdiction. **1667** in *10th Rep. Hist. MSS. Comm.* App. v. 44 Notwithstanding any priviledge hee may pretend as being our servant. **1784** COWPER *Let. to J. Newton* 11 Dec., Its right being at least so far a good one, that no word in the language could pretend a better.

†**5.** To put forth or lay a claim to (a thing); to assert as a right or possession; to claim. *Obs.*

1495 *Rolls of Parlt.* VI. 489/1 That your said Oratour may have.. the said Manours.. ayenst.. all other persones and their heyres, havyng, claymyng or pretendyng any thing therin. **1622** MABBE tr. *Aleman's Guzman d'Alf.* II. 39 He hath no reason to pretend the Diamond. **1680** MORDEN *Geog. Rect., Japan* (1685) 427 At this day the Hollanders pretend all Trade at Japan. **1693** EVELYN *De la Quint. Compl. Gard.* I. 70 The Peach-tree might well pretend a place there, for the Excellency of its good Fruit. **1755** MAGENS *Insurances* II. 165 Seamen taken and made Slaves shall not pretend any thing for their Ransom, either of the Master, Owners or Freighters.

†**b.** with *inf.* or *clause. Obs.*

c **1500** in I. S. Leadam *Star Chamb. Cases* (1903) 95 [Henry] Erle of Northumberland claymythe and pretendythe to haue the warde and mariage of your saide Oratoure. **1654** tr. *Martini's Conq. China* 129 This Prince pretended that the K. called *Lu.* should yield up his right to him. **1686** F. SPENCE tr. *Varillas' Ho. Medicis* 36 The deputy of the Ruffians pretended to receive the full sum which his accomplices had agreed upon. **1761** HUME *Hist. Eng.* I. ix. 204 As both the archbishops pretended to sit on his right hand, this question of precedency begat a controversy between them.

†**6.** To put forward as a reason or excuse; to use as a pretext; to allege as a ground or reason.

1456 SIR G. HAYE *Law Arms* (S.T.S.) 191 The resoun that thai pretend is this. **1532** TINDALE *Expos. Matt. v-vii.* vi. 67 b, Hyrelinges wil pretende their worke and saye: 'I haue deserued it, I haue done so much and so much and my laboure is worth it'. **1560** DAUS tr. *Sleidane's Comm.* 339 b, Thou canst not hereafter pretend the name of the Turkishe warre. **1600** E. BLOUNT tr. *Conestaggio* 27 At this time the Irishmen rebelled.. pretending the libertie of Religion. **1654** GATAKER *Disc. Apol.* 54 When I pretended mine unfitnes for such a place and imployment. **1658** *Whole Duty Man* xiv. §5 We must.. not pretend conscience for a cloak of stubbornness. *a* **1715** BURNET *Own Time* an. 1684 (1823) II. 423 The only excuse that was ever pretended for this infamous prosecution was [etc.]. **1776** JEFFERSON *Writ.* (1892) I. 47 Speak in honest language and say the minority will be in danger from the majority. And is there an assembly on earth where this danger may not be equally pretended?

7. To put forward as an assertion or statement; to allege; now *esp.* to allege or declare falsely or with intent to deceive. (A leading current sense.)

a. with *clause.*

1610 HOLLAND *Camden's Brit.* (1637) 362 Pretending that he was sickly. **1629** PRYNNE *Ch. Eng.* 87 If they have power to leave their sinnes as they prætend they have, why are their lives so vicious? **1637** HEYLIN *Brief Answ. Burton* 21 It is pretended that.. you were not bound to answer to it. **1693** DRYDEN *Juvenal* 15 Noblemen wou'd cause empty Litters to be carried to the Giver's Door, pretending their Wives were within them. **1703** MOXON *Mech. Exerc.* 257 By this construction he pretends.. that.. this charge, or weight, will be stopped, or stayed by the Inverse Arches. **1765** H. WALPOLE *Vertue's Anecd. Paint.* (ed. 2) III. App., It is pretended that to satisfy their natural impatience, he formed a hasty manner that prejudiced his works and reputation. **1804** *Med. Jrnl.* XII. 537 [This] induced practitioners to suppose, or to pretend, that the small-pox sometimes degenerates into the chicken-pox. **1839** KEIGHTLEY *Hist. Eng.* II. 26 A monk wrote a letter in golden characters which she was to pretend had been given her by Mary Magdalen.

†**b.** *passive* with *inf.* or *compl. Obs.*

(*The work was pretended to be ready* = *it was pretended that the work was ready*; passive of *they pretended that the work was ready*.)

1639 LD. DIGBY, etc. *Lett. conc. Relig.* (1651) 108 The precedency.. is pretended due upon another ground also. **1658** BRAMHALL *Consecr. Bps.* i. 7 He might heare many things.. from the persons prætended to have bene then consecrated. **1690** LOCKE *Hum. Und.* II. xxviii. §10 Vertue and Vice are Names pretended and suppos'd every where to stand for Actions in their own nature right and wrong. **1748** *Anson's Voy.* II. xii. 260 These rocks.. are by the help of a little imagination, pretended to resemble the form of a cross. **1781** S. PETERS *Hist. Connecticut* 22, I will now consider the right they are pretended to have acquired after possession.

c. with *simple obj.* To allege the existence or presence of.

1587 HARRISON *England* II. v. (1877) I. 128 Monie haue a cote and armes bestowed vpon him by heralds (who in the charter of the same doo of custome pretend antiquitie and seruice, and manie gaie things). **1655** FULLER *Ch. Hist.* IX. vii. §2 What ever was pretended to the contrary, England at that time flourished with able Ministers more then ever before. **1668** HALE *Pref. Rolle's Abridgm.* b j b, Men not much acquainted with the study.. pretend two great prejudices and exceptions against the study of the Common-Law. **1710** BERKELEY *Princ. Hum. Knowl.* I. §52 To pretend difficulties and inconsistencies. **1873** H. ROGERS *Orig. Bible* App. (1875) 438 In any 'type' it is only analogical resemblance that is pretended.

d. with infinitive: see 3 b.

†**8.** To intend, purpose, design, plan. *Obs.*

a. with *simple obj.*

c **1470** HARDING *Chron.* CLXXVII. vii, Flakes.. ouer the mosse.. he layde with fagottes, There gate away [= going away] and passage to pretend. **1502** ATKYNSON tr. *De Imitatione* III. lxiv. 258 Thou alonly pretendest and sekest my profyte and helthe eternall. **1551** ROBINSON tr. *More's Utopia* II. (1895) 152 This ende is onlye and chiefely pretended and mynded. **1579** LYLY *Euphues* (Arb.) 110 That women when they be most pleasaunt, pretend most mischiefe. **1587** TURBERV. *Trag. T.* (1837) 75 One that did pretend the spoyle, and slaughter of her sonne. **1633** T. STAFFORD *Pac. Hib.* I. v. (1821) 72 They pretend a journie towards the Countie of Limerick. [**1840** BARHAM *Ingol. Leg.* Ser. I. *Barney Maguire*, And now I've ended, what I pretended, This narration splendid in swate poe-thry.]

b. with *clause.*

c **1477** CAXTON *Jason* 30 Pretending that men shold speke of his faytes and vailliaunces. **1612** DAVIES *Why Ireland*, etc. (1787) 36 To make a perpetual separation and enmity between the English and the Irish, pretending.. that the English should in the end root out the Irish. **1728** MORGAN *Algiers* II. v. 298 We pretend, that this City, already famous for the Defeat of two of your Armadas, shall become far more so by the Disgrace of this your third.

c. with *inf.*

1512 *Helyas* in Thoms *Prose Rom.* (1828) III. 126 Never .. shall I departe fro this regyon where as I pretende to save my soule. **1604** E. G[RIMSTONE] *D'Acosta's Hist. Indies* I. xvii. 58 They shall stray wonderfully in their course, and arrive in another place then where they pretended to go. **1665-6** *Phil. Trans.* I. 99 He pretends to make a visit into England with some of his Pieces. **1728** MORGAN *Algiers* II. iii. 237 The Christians,.. out of whose Hands he pretended to wrest some Place of Strength, wherein to fortify himself.

9. To aspire to; to take upon one, to undertake; to venture, presume; to attempt, endeavour, try. Const. with *inf.*

1482 *Monk of Evesham* (Arb.) 45 The deuyls.. whyche pretendyn by mony weys of reson to haue her to hem. **1550** *Reg. Privy Council Scot.* I. 84 In caise it sal happin ony army to pretend to invaid and persew the said fort. **1604** E. G[RIMSTONE] *D'Acosta's Hist. Indies* I. xiii. 43 Whether King Iosaphats fleete, pretending to go, did suffer shipwracke. **1711** ADDISON *Spect.* No. 128 ¶1 Whether.. there may not be a kind of Sex in the very Soul, I shall not pretend to determine. **1722** DE FOE *Plague* (1756) 142 The people offered to fire at them, if they pretended to go forward. **1855** BAIN *Senses & Int.* II. ii. §10 (1864) 191 How many ultimate nerve fibres are contained in each unit nerve, we cannot pretend to guess. **1869** BROWNING *Ring & Bk.* x. 1781 Dost thou dare pretend to punish me For not descrying sunshine at midnight?

†**10.** To portend, presage, foreshow. *Obs.*

c **1425** *Found. St. Bartholomew's* (E.E.T.S.) 38 All the elementys pretendid to the wrecchid shipmenne deith of nature. **1513** DOUGLAS *Æneis* x. v. 147 The sing Pretendand tyll all mortale folk,.. Contagyus infirmyteis and seyknes. **1513** BRADSHAW *St. Werburge* I. 741 It pretended by all reasone Synguler grace and goodnes to her comynge soone. **1560** DAUS tr. *Sleidane's Comm.* 63 b, The signes and wounders that are seene in all places, doe pretende no good. **1609** HOLLAND *Amm. Marcell.* 218 Which the standers by.. said did pretend some such accident unto the elder of the two Consuls. **1634** R. H. *Salernes Regim.* 16 Overmuch repleation pretendith strangling or suddaine death.

†**11.** To indicate, signify, import, mean. *Obs.*

1526 *Pilgr. Perf.* (W. de W. 1531) 181 That her name pretendeth, in that she is called Maria, that is, the sterre of yᵉ see. **1588** LAMBARDE *Eiren.* IV. iii. 395 These men be not truly Iurors, till they be sworne, as their name pretendeth. **1607** TOPSELL *Four-f. Beasts* 459 Although the curling of his haire be a token of sluggish timidity, yet if the haire bee long and curled at the top onely, it pretendeth generous animosity. **1639** CHAPMAN & SHIRLEY *Ball* III. iii, What pretends this, to dance? there's something in't.

II. *intr.* (from prec. senses.)

†**12.** To stretch or reach forward; to move or go forward; to extend, tend; to direct one's course *to*, to make *for*. *Obs.*

1387-8 T. USK *Test. Love* I. i. (Skeat) I. 110 It maketh me backwarde to meue, whan my steppes by comon course euen forthe pretende. **1481** CAXTON *Myrr.* III. xv. 168 Who pretendeth to god, God attendeth to hym. *c* **1485** *Digby Myst.* (1882) III. 1076, I wyll pretende To stey to my father. *Ibid.* 2073 On-to my sell I woll pretend. [*Stage direct.* Her xall þe prest go to his selle.] **1633** T. ADAMS *Exp. 2 Peter* ii. 20 Though we pretend for heaven, yet still we bear about us a twang of our native country. **1650** W. BROUGH *Sacr. Princ.* (1659) 35 Suffer none.. to pull down Thy throne, whilst they pretend for Thy scepter.

†**b.** *fig.* To tend in action, speech, etc. to an end or point; to extend in time. *Obs.*

c **1374** CHAUCER *Troylus* IV. 894 (922) For to what fyn he wolde a-non pretende þat wot I wel. *c* **1520** BARCLAY *Jugurth* (1557) 67 b, The wordes and counsel of the enchantour and preest whiche helde his sacrifice pretended to the same poynte and conclusion as the desyre of his mynde moued him longe before. **1655** STANLEY *Hist. Philos.* III. (1701) 75/1 None of his arguments pretend beyond Meton's time. **1657** JER. TAYLOR *Collect. Polemical Disc.* (1674) Ep. Ded., I find by experience that we cannot acquire that end which is pretended to by such addresses.

13. *to pretend to.* †**a.** To aspire to, aim at, make pretension to; to be a suitor or candidate for. *Obs.*

1481 CAXTON *Myrr.* I. xiv. 45 Some pretende to hye estates & grete richesses, & other ben content with lytil estate. *c* **1500** *Lancelot* 559 Shir knycht, your lorde wondir hie pretendis, When he to me sic salutatioune sendis. **1583** *Leg. Bp. St. Androis* 132 To heich promotione he pretendit. **1633** G. HERBERT *Temple, Unkindnesse* iv, When that my friend pretendeth to a place, I quit my interest, and leave it free. **1672** SIR C. LYTTELTON in *Hatton Corr.* (Camden) 100 My Lᵈ Fanshaw was disapointed of his desire to goe to Constantinople, having long pretended to it.

b. *spec.* [ad. F. *prétendre à.*] To make suit for, try to win in marriage.

1652 J. WRIGHT tr. *Camus' Nat. Paradox* IV. 82 In this.. the Salvage Podolian had two ends; One, to hinder Liante from pretending to his Daughter. **1723** DE FOE *Col. Jack* (1840) 206 That.. step.. lays her under the foot of the man she pretends to. **1855** THACKERAY *Newcomes* xxiv, He might pretend surely to his kinswoman's hand. **1874** T. HARDY *Madding Crowd* xxix, I am not such a fool as to pretend to you now I am poor, and you have altogether got above me.

c. To lay claim to; to assert a right of ownership to.

1647 CLARENDON *Hist. Reb.* I. §11 The House of Commons never then Pretending to the least part of Judicature. **1683** BURNET tr. *More's Utopia* (1753) 127 Yet they pretended to no Share of the Spoil. **1769** *Junius Lett.* xvi. (1820) 70 The ministry have not yet pretended to such a tyranny over our minds. **1834-43** SOUTHEY *Doctor* cxviii. (1848) 289/1 He was as justly entitled to the appellation of a learned man.. as he was far from pretending to it.

d. To claim or profess to have; to make profession of having; to affect.

1659 HAMMOND *On Ps.* xviii. 20 What is here meant by the cleannesse of David's hands, to which he here pretends. *a* **1674** CLARENDON *Surv. Leviath.* (1676) 320 Lamented by all men living who pretended to Virtue. **1711** STEELE *Spect.* No. 51 ¶2 Persons who cannot pretend to that Delicacy and Modesty, of which she is Mistress. **1734** tr. *Rollin's Anc. Hist.* (1827) V. 223 Each party pretended to the victory. **1836-7** SIR W. HAMILTON *Metaph.* viii. (1870) 147 To determine the shares to which the knowing subject, and the object known, may pretend in the total act of cognition. **1843** MIALL in *Nonconf.* III. 1 A bondage which it becomes all who pretend to intelligence to renounce and abjure. **1868** HELPS *Realmah* viii. (1876) 203 People who pretend to supernatural wisdom.

†**e.** To make pretensions or claims on behalf of, to support the claims of. *Obs.*

1650 T. VAUGHAN *Anthroposophia* 19, I know the Peripateticks pretend to four, and with the help of their Masters Quintessence to a fift Principle. **1659** BP. WALTON *Consid. Considered* 8 Witness a late Pamphlet, pretending to the integrity and purity of the Hebrew and Greek Text. **1670** E. BORLASE *Lathom Spaw* Ep. Ded., I know, Medicinal Springs were never more pretended to than of late.

†**14.** To form designs; to plot (against). *Obs.*

1559-66 *Hist. Estate Scotl.* in *Wodrow Soc. Misc.* (1844) 63 She said, That it wes against her authoritie that they pretended.

15. To make pretence; to make believe; to counterfeit, feign.

1526 *Pilgr. Perf.* (W. de W. 1531) 78 Pretendynge and shewynge outwardly as though it were of very mekenes, but it is of false mekenes. **1560** DAUS tr. *Sleidane's Comm.* 125 b, The byshop nowe pretendeth as though he would calle a counsel. *c* **1640** WALLER *À la Malade* 6 Had the rich gifts, conferred on you So amply thence, the common end Of giving lovers—to pretend? **1733** FIELDING *Quix. in Eng.* III. xv, Pretend madness! Give me leave to tell you, Mr. Brief, I am not to be pretended with. **1780** COWPER *Progr. of Err.* 15 Weak to perform, though mighty to pretend.

b. In imagination or play: *absol.* of 3 d.

let's pretend (*sb. phr.*): see as main entry.

1893 MRS. H. BURNET *One I knew best* xiv, So she wandered about in a dream—'pretending'. That changed it all. The heaps of earth and rubbish were mounds of flowers [etc.].

¶ **16.** = PERTAIN (perh. an error).

1470-85 MALORY *Arthur* I. xviii. 64 They furnysshed hem ..of good men of armes and vytaille and of alle maner of abylement that pretendith to the werre [*ed.* 1529 ordynaunce that belongeth to warre].

pre'tend, *sb.* [f. prec. vb.] †**1.** The act of pretending; a pretension. *Obs. rare.*

1600 W. WATSON *Decacordon* (1602) 15 The honour of Priesthood doth [hinder] the vsurpate pretend of Iesuiticall esteeme. *Ibid.* 314 This platforme doctrine and pretend of the Iesuits.

2. In (imitation of) children's use: the act of pretending in imagination or play (cf. PRETEND *v.* 15 b). Also *attrib.* passing into *adj.*, denoting a thing or action that is imitative or imaginary.

1888 F. H. BURNETT *Sara Crewe* I. 28 One of her 'pretends' was that Emily was a kind of good witch, and could protect her. Poor little Sara! **1911** G. STRATTON-PORTER *Harvester* iii. 48 Not so indifferent after all... That was all 'pretend!' But she waited just a trifle too long. **1928** BARRIE *Peter Pan* II. 70 in *Plays*, Now that they know it is pretend they acclaim her greedily. *Ibid.* IV. 97 It is a pretend meal this evening, with nothing whatever on the table. *a* **1936** KIPLING *Something of Myself* (1937) i. 10, I have learned since from children who play much alone that this rule of 'beginning again in a pretend game' is not uncommon. **1955** J. MASTERS *Coromandel!* 31 It's all pretend, Jason, isn't it? **1959** J. L. AUSTIN *Sense & Sensibilia* (1962) vii. 72 The water in toy beer-bottles is not toy beer, but *pretend* beer. **1960** *Guardian* 3 May 2/1 All 'pretend' space outfits can be dangerous and should be banned. **1962** *Listener* 4 Jan. 20/2 A diminutive, waif-like figure, dressed in rags, with his pretend sword and his pretend gun. **1965** G. MCINNES *Road to Gundagai* iii. 54 'It's only pretend,' she kept on saying. 'You mustn't be afraid of pretend.' **1974** W. REES-MOGG *Reigning Error* 109 Gold is real money and paper is pretend money.

pre'tendable, *a. rare.* [f. PRETEND *v.* + -ABLE.] That may be pretended or professed.

1657 J. SERGEANT *Schism Dispach't* 592 That dwindling, puling puritanical expressions of one flock..&c. equally pretendable (if taken alone) by Quakers, as by them. *Ibid.* 628 Motives to Unity..some of them equally pretendable nay actually pretended by Turks, Hereticks, etc.

pretendant, -ent (prɪ'tɛndənt), *sb.* and *a.* [a. F. *prétendant* (16th c. in Littré), pr. pple. of *prétendre* to PRETEND (also as sb.).]

A. *sb.*

†**1.** One who purposes: = PRETENDER 1. *Obs. rare.*

1598 FLORIO, *Pretendente*, a pretendent, a pretender, an intender, a meaner.

2. A claimant; esp. to any office or honour, e.g. to a throne. Now *rare.*

1600 E. BLOUNT tr. *Conestaggio* 59 The pretendants to the succession. **1618-29** in Rushw. *Hist. Coll.* (1659) I. 382 All the Pretendants were called in upon these proceedings, divers of the Ships and Goods were condemned and divers were released in a legal course. **1652-62** HEYLIN *Cosmogr.* II. (1682) 78 Whether of the two Pretendents had the juster Cause. **1670** G. H. *Hist. Cardinals* III. III. 315 Almost all the pretendants came into the Conclave with an absolute intention to advance every one his own proper interest. **1855** MILMAN *Lat. Chr.* VI. 73 All censures, excommunications, interdicts, issued by the two pretendants, were annulled.

b. A fictitious or fraudulent claimant; a mere pretender.

1826 SOUTHEY *Vind. Eccl. Angl.* 189 They..are always heightened in proportion to the attention which the pretendant, whether knave or fanatic, obtains.

3. A suitor: **a.** at law; **b.** a wooer.

1652 WADSWORTH tr. *Sandoval's Civ. Wars Spain* 30 It is reported that a certain Pretendent or Petitioner..had presented Xeures with a very handsom Mule. **1655** tr. *Com. Hist. Francion* II. 45 By this, and other like subtilties, she screwed..a small summe of Money out of her penurious Pretendant. **1883** HOWELLS *Woman's Reason* (1884) II. 252 The good-natured slight with which husband and wife always talk over the sorrows of unlucky pretendants.

†**B.** *adj.* That claims to be (somebody); of or pertaining to a claimant. *Obs.*

1594 PARSONS *Confer. Success.* II. iv. 58 Richard Earle of Cambridge father to this Richard pretendent duke of Yorke. **1595** DANIEL *Civ. Wars* IV. xxxv, How easie had it beene for thee All the pretendant race t' haue laid full low. **1620** BRENT tr. *Sarpi's Counc. Trent* VII. 681 The Cardinall of Loraine came to the Councell as Head of one of the pretendent parties.

pre'tended, *ppl. a.* [f. PRETEND *v.* + -ED¹.]

†**1.** Put forward for consideration or acceptance.

1646 GATAKER *Mistake Removed* To Rdr. 1 A bush sufficient of itself to invite to such pretious pretended liquor.

2. Alleged, asserted; claimed to be such.

a. Said of a title or designation which the speaker does not admit or allow: Reputed, so-called.

1461 *Rolls of Parlt.* V. 490/2 The pretensed reigne of any of the seid late pretended Kynges. **1640-1** *Kirkcudbr. War-Comm. Min. Bk.* (1855) 4 The woode and bark thairof, quhilk pertaines to the pretendit bischope of Edinburgh. **1683** *Apol. Prot. France* iv. 52 The Edict..allowed the Protestants the free exercise of their Religion, which..was to be called *The Pretended Reformed Religion.* **1688** BURNET *Let.* 25 Dec. in *Eng. Hist. Rev.* July (1886) 535 That this Assembly is to Judge..the birth of the Pretended Prince. **1709-10** STEELE *Tatler* No. 115 ⁋1 One Isaac Bickerstaff, a Pretended Esquire.

b. Applied to things of which the speaker does not admit the existence, reality, or validity.

c **1500** in I. S. Leadam *Star Chamb. Cases* (1903) 96 The saide Erle hathe seased the body of your saide Oratoure by reason of his pretended title. **1564** in *Scott. Antiq.* Oct. (1901) 80 The makyng and compulsit grantyng of the said pretendit infeftment. *a* **1661** FULLER *Worthies, Westmld.* (1662) II. 140 A railing Jesuit wrote a pretended Confutation thereof. **1679** EVELYN *Diary* 23 Nov., Shewing with how little reason the Papists applied those words..to maintaine the pretended infallibility they boast of. **1771** LUCKOMBE *Hist. Print.* 68 Dr. Barnes was prior, who was burnt for pretended heresy. **1849** RUSKIN *Sev. Lamps* v. §17. 153 A stranger instance..of the daring variation of pretended symmetry.

c. Put forward as a pretext, excuse, defence, etc.; professed falsely or insincerely.

1643 MILTON *Divorce* ix. Wks. 1851 IV. 46 The pretended reason of it is as frigid as frigidity it self. **1695** *Enq. Anc. Const. Eng.* Pref. 7 Sacrificing (under the will-worship of a pretended loyalty) the religion, civil Liberties and properties of their country to Cæsar's will. **1873** H. ROGERS *Orig. Bible* i. (1875) 33 They..made the pretended service of God a reason for evading the most sacred obligations.

3. Hence, That professes or is represented to be what it is not; fictitious, counterfeit, feigned.

1727 GAY *Fables* I. xvii. 34 An open foe may prove a curse, But a pretended friend is worse. **1782** MISS BURNEY *Cecilia* III. viii, With a pretended laugh, he hastily left her. **1884** D. HUNTER tr. *Reuss' Hist. Canon* xiii. 264 A pretended Confession of Faith, dated 1120, which is now known to be forged, at least antedated, and to belong at the earliest to the year 1532.

†**4.** Intended, designed, purposed, proposed. *Obs.*

1573 *New Custom* I. i. in Hazl. *Dodsley* III. 13 For the better accomplishing our subtlety pretended, It were expedient that both our names were amended. **1597** A. M. tr. *Guillemeau's Fr. Chirurg.* Author's Pref. 2 Therbye to attayne vnto his pretended intente. **1600** HAKLUYT *Voy.* (1810) III. 86 Two small barks..wherein he intended to complete his pretended voyage. **1691** T. H[ALE] *Acc. New Invent.* p. lxxiii, The suffering Populace, whose pretended Forfeitures were granted before Conviction. **1703** DE FOE *Reas. agst. War w. France* Misc. 194 That we should..be Insulted by the French in the Article of the pretended New King [of Spain].

pre'tendedly, *adv.* [f. prec. + -LY².] In a pretended manner; in or by a pretence; ostensibly, professedly: usually, and in mod. use always, implying feigning or deceit; hence, by false representation, feignedly, fictitiously, not really.

1611 SPEED *Hist. Gt. Brit.* IX. ix. (1623) 638 Pretendedly founded vpon that Charter. **1627** W. SCLATER *Exp. 2 Thess.* (1629) 76 Yet liues his Heresie amongst men pretendedly most Orthodox. **1643** MILTON *Divorce* II. iii. Wks. 1851 IV. 70 If any one be truly, and not pretendedly zealous for Gods honour. **1683** *Apol. Prot. France* i. 7 Those of the said Religion pretendedly Reformed..may not hereafter be overcharged or oppressed with any Imposition..more than the Catholicks. **1716** B. CHURCH *Hist. Philip's War* (1865) I. 98 He and his English Men pretendedly fled, firing on their retreat towards the Indians that pursued them. **1788** BURKE *Sp. agst. W. Hastings* Wks. XIII. 223 Every kind of act done by Mr. Hastings—pretendedly for the Company, but really for himself. **1807** *Monthly Mag.* XXIII. 362 Things are pretendedly explained and classed in unmeaning words. **1851** RUSKIN *Stones Ven.* III. ii. §22. 47 The pretendedly well-informed, but really ignorant, artist.

†**pre'tendence.** *Obs. rare.* [f. PRETEND *v.* + -ENCE.] A pretension, claim.

1603 DANIEL *Panegyric to King* xiv, Their projects, censures, vain pretendences. **1613** SHERLEY *Trav. Persia* 100 There is no possible pretendence from one to the others getting.

pretendent, variant of PRETENDANT.

pretender (prɪ'tɛndə(r)). [f. PRETEND *v.* + -ER¹.] One who pretends.

†**1.** One who intends or purposes. *Obs. rare.*

1591 PERCIVALL *Sp. Dict.*, *Pretensor*, a pretender, he that purposeth. **1598** [see PRETENDANT *sb.* 1].

2. One who puts forth a claim, or who aspires to or aims at something; a claimant, candidate, or aspirant; now, one who makes baseless pretensions.

1622 MABBE tr. *Aleman's Guzman d'Alf.* I. 214 By how straight a Rule..must that Pretender carry himselfe, who is to saile thorow the sea of this world, hoping for a fortune from another mans hand? *a* **1631** DONNE *Serm.* xxxii. (1640) 315 The sinister supplantations of pretenders to places in Court. **1646** H. LAWRENCE *Comm. Angells* 116 Every one is a pretender and a runner; but few carry the prize. **1766** BLACKSTONE *Comm.* II. xiv. 218 The issue of the eldest son excludes all other pretenders, as the son himself (if living) would have done. **1780** JOHNSON *Let. to Mrs. Thrale* 25 May, A candidate for a school at Brewood in Staffordshire; to which, I think, there are seventeen pretenders. **1845** DISRAELI *Sybil* IV. vii, I would sooner gain five thousand pounds by restoring you to your rights, than fifty thousand in establishing any of these pretenders in their base assumptions.

†**b.** One who aspires to the hand of a woman in marriage; a suitor, a wooer. *Obs.*

1612 *Two Noble K.* v. i, He, of the two pretenders, that best loves me. *a* **1699** LADY HALKETT *Autobiog.* (Camden) 17 An Earles daughter,..whose mother not allowing him to come as a pretender shee made apointmentt with him and mett him att her cousin's howse. **1728** ELIZA HEYWOOD *Mme. de Gomez's Belle A.* (1732) II. 235 It is not my design to dispose of Irene to the most noble, but most wealthy of the Pretenders to her Love.

c. A claimant to a throne or the office of a ruler; *orig.* in a neutral sense, but now always applied to a claimant who is held to have no just title. ***the Old*** and ***the Young Pretender*** (Eng. Hist.): the designation of the son and grandson of James II of England, who successively asserted their claim to the British throne against the house of Hanover.

1697 DRYDEN *Virg. Georg.* IV. 93 If intestine Broils allarm the Hive, (For two Pretenders oft for Empire strive). **1708** Q. ANNE *Sp. Ho. Parl.* 11 Mar. in Chandler *Hist. Ho. Comm.* (1742) IV. 92 The French fleet sailed from Dunkirk..with the Pretender on board. *a* **1715** BURNET *Own Time* (1734) II. 503 She [Q. Anne] also fixed a new Designation on the Pretended Prince of Wales, and called him the Pretender; he was so called in a new Set of Addresses..upon this occasion ..made to the Queen. **1745** P. C. WEBB (*title*) Remarks on the Pretender's Son's Second Declaration. **1747** (*title*) Genuine Memoirs of John Murray..Late Secretary to the Young Pretender. **1824** SCOTT *Redgauntlet* ch. xvi. **1827** HALLAM *Const. Hist.* (1876) III. xvi. 223 The pretender.. had friends in the tory government more sincere probably and zealous than [the earl of] Oxford. **1845** S. AUSTIN *Ranke's Hist. Ref.* III. 633 Wullenweber..turned to the nearest protestant pretender, Duke Christian, and offered him his assistance to obtain the crown. **1855** MACAULAY *Hist. Eng.* xiv. III. 442 Every province..had its own Augustus. All these pretenders could not be rightful Emperors.

3. One who pretends or lays claim *to* something; one who makes a profession, show, or assertion, esp. without adequate grounds, falsely, or with intent to deceive; a dissembler, deceiver, charlatan, hypocrite.

1631 MASSINGER *Emperor East* II. i, A pretender To the art, I truly honour..your majesty's opinion. **1631** —— *Believe as You List* II. ii, This false pretender To the correction of the law. **1651** HOBBES *Leviath.* II. xviii. 89 So evident a lye, even in the pretenders own consciences. **1738** SWIFT *Pol. Conversat.* Introd. 45 It is not so easy an Acquirement as a few ignorant Pretenders may imagine. **1784** COWPER *Task* I. 492 That honour has been long The boast of mere pretenders to the name. **1848** MRS. JAMESON *Sacr. & Leg. Art* (1850) 122 Simon, a Samaritan, a pretender to divine authority and supernatural powers. **1871** JOWETT *Plato* I. 28 To distinguish the pretender in medicine from the true physician.

Hence **Pre'tenderism** *Eng. Hist.* = JACOBITISM 1.

1710 G. HICKES *Let.* in *Thoresby's Corr.* (ed. Hunter) II. 278 To purge themselves from all suspicion of Pretenderism (this is a new word) which their adversaries lay to their charge. **1859** W. CHADWICK *De Foe* iv. 239 The Duke..was conquering Toryism, Churchism, and Pretenderism.

pre'tendership. [See -SHIP.] The position or character of a pretender.

1712 SWIFT *Public Spirit of Whigs* ⁋48, I am at a loss how to dispose of the dauphin, if he happen to be king of France before the pretendership to Britain falls to his share. **1848** in *Life A. Fonblanque* (1874) 393 Apart from his pretendership, which has latterly been in abeyance, he is a thoroughly sensible and well-informed man. **1858** BUSHNELL *Nat. & Supernat.* i. (1864) 22 The stolidly physical pretendership of Comte.

pre'tending, *vbl. sb.* [f. PRETEND *v.* + -ING¹.] The action of the verb PRETEND; pretence; *esp.* the making of a profession or false show.

1647 CLARENDON *Contempl. Ps.* Tracts (1727) 405 A pretending to do that which I do not do, or to be that I am not, being..a lie in action. **1665** BOYLE *Occas. Refl.* IV. ii, When the pretending of religion grows to be a thing in request, many betake themselves to a form of religion, who deny the power of it. **1865** DICKENS *Mut. Fr.* II. i, There's no pretending about my sister.

pre'tending, *ppl. a.* [f. PRETEND *v.* + -ING².] That pretends, in various senses of the vb.; *esp.* making mere professions; pretentious. Also (in senses 3 d, 15 b of the vb.), of a thing or action: imitative, imaginary; of a game, etc.: that involves pretence or imitation. Cf. PRETEND *sb.* 2 above.

c **1400** *Apol. Loll.* 20 [The curse] be wilke þe iust man be cursid as contrari to Godds lawe, þat is but only in name or pretendand. **1657** OWEN *Commun. w. God* Wks. 1851 II. 258 The pretending spirit of our day. **1727** DE FOE *Syst. Magic* I. iv. (1840) 105 Things out of the reach of the most pretending of the rest of his fellow-magicians. *c* **1815** FUSELI in *Lect. Paint.* vi. (1848) 489 Correggio's numerous pretending imitators. **1842** J. WILSON *Chr. North* (1857) I. 254 Remembered when more pretending edifices are forgotten. *a* **1901** C. M. YONGE *Autobiogr.* in C. Coleridge *C. M. Yonge* (1903) iii. 95 They were not perfect playmates, for they called all 'pretending games' falsehood. **1960** *Times* 27 Apr. 1/3 Only a proper castle, not an 18th/19th-century Gothic pretending one. **1965** *Vogue* Aug. 64 Pretendin' racoon, pretty as a picture.

Hence **pre'tendingly** *adv.*; †**pre'tendingness.**

1648 J. GOODWIN *Right & Might* 2 Many pretendingly complain of want of conscience. **1697** COLLIER *Ess. Mor. Subj.* I. (1703) 2, I have a particular reason to look a little pretendingly at present. **1701** —— *M. Aurel.* (1726) 135 No man could charge him with vanity, flourish, and pretendingness. **1834** *New Monthly Mag.* XLI. 319 To smile, either really or pretendingly.

†**pre'tendment.** *Obs. rare.* [f. PRETEND *v.* + -MENT.] A pretension, claim.

1640 T. LECHFORD *Plain Dealing* (1867) 146 If the congregations be not united under one Diocesan in fit compasse, they are in a confusion, notwithstanding all their classicall pretendments. **1657** W. MORICE *Coena quasi Κοινή* vi. 62 None should presume to do, but such as can justly make that pretendment.

‖**prétendu** (pretɑ̃dy). ? *Obs.* Also fem. prétendue. [Fr.] An intended husband or wife; a fiancé(e).

1847 THACKERAY *Van. Fair* (1848) xxxiii. 295 In reply to the exhortation of her daughter's *prétendu*, Mr. Pitt Crawley. **1850** —— *Pendennis* II. i. 9 Lady Ann Milton, Mr. Foker's cousin and *prétendue*. *Ibid.* xx. 201 She has her mamma on one side, her *prétendu* on the other.

†**pre'tensary.** *Obs. rare*⁻¹. [f. late L. *prætens-*, ppl. stem of *prætendĕre* to PRETEND + -ARY[1].] One who makes a pretension or claim.

1594 O. B. *Quest. Profit. Concern.* 14b, Within this same writ..the vnsatiate Legates are named Catholicks and pretensaries to reforme religion, through crueltie to be exercised vpon the annointed of God.

†**pre'tense,** *a. Obs.* Also 5 pretence. [ad. late L. *prætens-us* (in Quicherat *Addenda*) for cl. L. *prætent-us*, pa. pple. of *prætendĕre* to stretch forth, PRETEND.] Pretended, alleged, professed; feigned; dissembling, fictitious.

1396-7 in *Eng. Hist. Rev.* (1907) XXII. 302 Manslaute be batayle or pretense lawe of rythwysnesse, for temporal cause or spirituel, with outen special reuelaciun, is expres contrarious to þe newe testament. *c* **1430** LYDG. *Min. Poems* (Percy Soc.) 165 A double hert withe fayre feyned countenaunce, And a pretence face trouble in his daliaunce. **1461** *Rolls of Parlt.* V. 465/1 In a pretence Parlement.. holden at Coventree. **1496** *Dives & Paup.* (W. de W.) ii. 22 Ther is naturell or kyndely lordshyppe. Ther is also cyuyle or seculer lordshyp. And ther is lordshyp pretense.

pretense, *sb.* and *v.*, variant of PRETENCE.

pretension (prɪ'tɛnʃən), *sb.*[1]. Also 7-9 pretention. [app. ad. med.L. *prætensio* (*c* 1150 in Thomas *Thes. Nov. Lat.*), n. of action f. *prætendĕre* to PRETEND, also med.L. *prætentio* (1100 in Du Cange), F. *prétention* (in 16th c. rarely *pretension*, Godef.).] The action of pretending.

1. An allegation or assertion the truth of which is not proved or admitted; often with an implication that it is unfounded or false, or put forth to deceive, or to provide a false excuse or ground; hence, a pretext, pretence.

1609 DANIEL *Civ. Wars* VIII. lxi, And then, with what pretentions he might hide His priuat comming, and his oft resort. **1624** BACON *Consid. War w. Spain* Wks. 1879 I. 538/1 It was afterwards alleged, that the duke of Parma did artificially delay his coming; but this was but an invention and pretension given out by the Spaniards. **1722** DE FOE *Plague* (1754) 11 The same thing..was the strongest Repulse to my Pretensions of losing my Trade and my Goods. **1773** JOHNSON *Let. to Mrs. Thrale* 21 Sept., The only things of which we, or travellers yet more delicate, could find any pretensions to complain. **1791** J. LEARMONT *Poems* 113, I winnae gang For nae pretension or prayer. *a* **1894** STEVENSON *Foreigner at Home* (Cent.), Miss Bird.. declares all the viands of Japan to be uneatable—a staggering pretension.

2. The assertion of a claim as of right; a claim put forth, a demand.

1600 E. BLOUNT tr. *Conestaggio* 60 By reason of his pretention to the Crowne. **1660** R. COKE *Power & Subj.* 221 Nor can there be any question or process about the state or pretensions of the King, but in his Courts. **1700** DRYDEN *Ajax & Ulysses* 550 All these had been my rivals in the shield, And yet all these to my pretensions yield. **1748** CHESTERF. *Lett.* (1774) I. cxxi. 297 The pretensions also of France, and the House of Austria, upon Naples. **1856** STANLEY *Sinai & Pal.* i. (1858) 39 Jebel Mûsa is now the only one [of the peaks] which puts forward any pretensions to be considered as the place. **1877** FROUDE *Short Stud.* (1883) IV. I. x. 108 Ecclesiastical pretensions were still formidable under the Tudors.

b. A rightful or justifiable claim, a title.

1710 STEELE *Tatler* No. 207 ¶3 The Courtier, the Trader, and the Scholar, should all have an equal Pretension to the Denomination of a Gentleman. *a* **1805** PALEY *Serm.* x. (1810) 163 An opinion of merit is discouraged, even in those who had the best pretensions to entertain it; if any pretensions were good. **1822** P. HENRY in *Priv. Corr. H. Clay* (1855) 67 He has pretensions [to the Presidency] in every respect—a man of business..—an elegant scholar.

3. The assertion or claim that one is or has something; profession. Also of things. Const. *to.*

1662 EVELYN *Chalcogr.* 23 Some pretensions to the Invention of Copper-cuts, and their Impressions. **1718** *Freethinker* No. 66 ¶2, I..have little or no Pretensions to Beauty. **1754** RICHARDSON *Grandison* (1781) II. xxxiv. 323 Sir Charles Grandison, without making an ostentatious pretension to religion, is the very Christian in practice. **1877** FREEMAN *Norm. Conq.* (ed. 3) II. viii. 197 A mediæval castle and a house..of no great pretensions. **1884** SWINBURNE *Misc.* (1886) 23 It would be but too easy a task to..prove by the avowal of his own pretentions that he can pretend to the credit of no such imbecility.

b. The unwarranted assumption of a quality, esp. of merit or dignity; pretentiousness, ostentation.

1727 POPE *Epitaph R. Digby* 4 Good without noise, without pretension great. **1837** EMERSON *Addr., Amer. Schol.* Wks. (Bohn) II. 184 The world is his, who can see through its pretension. **1856** —— *Eng. Traits, Manners* ibid. 50 They avoid pretension, and go right to the heart of the thing. **1869** W. P. MACKAY *Grace & Truth* (1875) 95 This day of self-seeking and pretensions!

†**4.** An intention, a design; aim, aspiration.

1620 E. BLOUNT *Horæ Subs.* 155 In seeking a new fortune, lose their old, and so conuert their substance into pretensions, their certainty into nothing. **1714** LADY M. W. MONTAGU *Lett., to W. Montagu* (1887) I. 96 They are always looked upon, either as neglected, or discontented because their pretensions have failed. **1782** MISS BURNEY *Cecilia* II. vi, Acquaint me, then, freely, what are the pretensions of these gentlemen [to Cecilia's hand]?

Hence **pre'tensional,** †**-tional** *a.*, of, pertaining to, or of the nature of pretension; **pre'tensionless** *a.*, without pretensions, unpretending.

1659 HEYLIN *Examen Hist.* II. 98 Hitherto his intents were reall, not pretentionall only. **1828** *Blackw. Mag.* XXIII. 751 It would..be..unjust to throw the slightest slur or stigma on the pretensionless character of a crowd of humble and high individuals. **1831** *Crayons fr. Commons* 10 A steady grave deliberative man, Pretensionless in manner, air, and tone.

pre-tension (priː'tɛnʃən), *sb.*[2] [f. PRE- A. 2 + TENSION *sb.*] Tension in an object applied previously or at an early stage of a process, e.g. that applied to the reinforcing steel in the manufacture of prestressed concrete.

1936 *Structural Engineer* XIV. 251/2 It is necessary to produce the pretension of the steel and to manufacture concrete of high resistance at a cost sufficiently low to allow one to preserve the greater part of the savings effected on the materials. **1941** *Concrete & Constructional Engin.* XXXVI. 74/1 Shrinkage, elastic deformation, and creep under stress reduce the pre-tension by 10 tons to 20 tons per square inch. **1976** G. S. RAMASWAMY *Mod. Prestressed Concrete Design* i. 5 Inexpensive end anchorages are produced at the two ends of the bar to retain the pre-tension.

pre-tension (priː'tɛnʃən), *v.* [f. PRE- A. 1 + TENSION *v.*] *trans.* To apply tension to (an object) prior to some other treatment, esp. incorporation in a structure.

1937 *Rep. Building Res. Board 1936* (Dept. Sci. & Industr. Res.) 99 In connection with some tests on a particular lightweight aggregate, four beams have been tested to determine the effect of pre-tensioning the tension reinforcement. **1949** P. W. ABELES *Princ. & Pract. Prestressed Concrete* ix. 63/2 A special process has been developed for the manufacture of hollow slabs in approximately 100 yd. long production lines, in which the wires are pre-tensioned in order to avoid any sag. **1973** *Sci. Amer.* Apr. 114/1 The output of work per cycle can be increased somewhat by pretensioning the fiber before it is immersed in the brine.

Hence **pre-'tensioned** *ppl. a.*, **pre-'tensioning** *vbl. sb.* (freq. *attrib.*).

1936 *Structural Engineer* XIV. 261/2 Thus, with two different steels, an effect was produced similar to that produced by M. Freyssinet's method of pre-tensioning. **1937** *Rep. Building Res. Board 1936* (Dept. Sci. & Industr. Res.) 98 The pre-tensioning apparatus is left in position until the concrete has hardened sufficiently to take the stresses induced in it. **1949** P. W. ABELES *Princ. & Pract. Prestressed Concrete* ix. 58/2 Precast articles having pre-tensioned steel are mainly applicable to slabs, sleepers, beams, [etc.]..where mass production is possible. **1964** C. W. DUNHAM *Adv. Reinforced Concrete* viii. 400 Pretensioned members can be used for other parts of a structure besides the floors and roof. **1965** *Economist* 5 June 1176/1 The first multi-storey prestressed concrete building in the world combining pretensioned, prestressed roof beams manufactured in the factory with post-tensioning on site using the Magnel system. **1971** J. R. LIBBY *Mod. Prestressed Concrete* xiv. 451 Pre-tensioning benches that can be moved from job site to job site have been used to a limited degree. **1975** KONG & EVANS *Reinforced & Prestressed Concrete* ix. 196 In pre-tensioning, the tendons pass through the mould, or moulds for a number of similar members arranged end to end, and are tensioned between external end anchorages, by which the tension is maintained while the concrete is placed.

pretensious, obs. variant of PRETENTIOUS *a.*

pretensive (prɪ'tɛnsɪv), *a. rare.* Also 7 -cive. [f. late L. *prætens-*, ppl. stem (see PRETENSARY) + -IVE.]

1. Characterized by being asserted or pretended to be true; professed; feigned.

1640 H. PARKER *Case of Ship Money* 17 If danger..be far distant..though it bee certaine, and not pretensive, yet Parliamentary Aid may be speedy enough. **1658** SLINGSBY *Diary* (1836) 213 It has been my fortune to make experience of a pretensive stay, which proved so unsteady, that [etc.]. **1851** KITTO *Bible Illustr.* (ed. Porter) VII. xxx. 112 The name [Magism] covered all that was true, all that was pretensive, and all that was false, in the philosophy of the ancient Orientals.

2. Full of pretense; pretentious, ostentatious.

1876 [implied in PRETENSIVENESS]. **1907** *Blackw. Mag.* Jan. 120/2 Their ornament is hideously heavy and pretensive.

pre'tensively, *adv. rare.* [f. prec. + -LY[2].] In a pretensive manner; professedly; as a pretext.

1607 *Schol. Disc. agst. Antichr.* I. i. 36 A stand against them, who pleade fiue things, against the sentence of abolition, for this grosse Idoll pretenciuely chaunged. **1656** HEYLIN *Surv. France* 262 There passed an Act of Parliament pretensively against the depopulation of Villages, and decay of tillage, but purposedly to inable his subjects for the wars. **1665** MANLEY *Grotius' Low C. Warres* 601 He would not vouchsafe to inquire what might be pretensively said, either from the Antients, or at present for the Austrians against them of Cleves.

pre'tensiveness. *rare.* [f. as prec. + -NESS.] †**a.** Pretension (*obs.*). **b.** Pretentiousness.

1710 C. SHADWELL *Fair Quaker of Deal* III. 35 What Pretensiveness have you to it, Sirrah? **1876** W. M. TAYLOR *Ministry of Word* 56 Guilty of the same pretensiveness.

†**pre'tensory,** *a. Obs. rare*⁻¹. [f. as PRETENSIVE + -ORY[2].] ? = PRETENSIVE 1.

1663 *Flagellum, or O. Cromwell* (1672) 119 With the pretensory advice of his Council of Officers unanimously and readily urged.

†**pre'tent,** *v. Obs.* [? ad. L. *prætentāre, -temptāre* to search out beforehand, hold before oneself, make a pretext of, freq. of *prætendĕre* to PRETEND.] = PRETEND *v.* (in various senses).

1494 FABYAN *Chron.* VII. 401 Willyam Waleys, whiche.. pretentyd the rule & gouernaunce of Scotlande. **1582** N. LICHEFIELD tr. *Castanheda's Conq. E. Ind.* I. ix. 24 As though they were such men inwardlye indeede, as in appearaunce outwardlye they then pretented. **1587** GREENE *Penelope's Web* Wks. (Grosart) V. 182 No intent of treacherie shall so much as in thought bee pretented to the person of our Soueraуne. **1602** T. FITZHERBERT *Apol.* 12 Breach of lawes and treason is pretented, but religion condemned.

†**pre'tentative,** *a. Obs. rare*⁻¹. [f. L. *prætentāre* to search or try before + -ATIVE; or f. PRE- A. 3 + TENTATIVE.] Tentative beforehand.

1620 WOTTON in *Reliq.* (1672) 507 This is but an exploratory, and pretentative purpose between us..about the form whereof, and the matter, we shall consult to morrow.

pretention, obs. form of PRETENSION.

pretentious (prɪ'tɛnʃəs), *a.* [ad. F. *prétentieux* (17th c. in Littré), ad. L. type **prætentiōs-us*, f. *prætentiōn-em* PRETENSION: see -IOUS.]

1. Characterized by, or full of, pretension; professing or making claim to great merit or importance, esp. when unwarranted; making an exaggerated outward show; showy, ostentatious.

1845 LEVER *O'Donoghue* xxxi, An hotel of more pretensious exterior. **1851** J. H. NEWMAN *Cath. in Eng.* 360 Round your pretentious sentences, and discharge your concentrated malignity on the defenceless. **1857** KINGSLEY *Two Y. Ago* xix, As severe as he dared on all Pharisees and pretentious persons whatsoever. **1868** BROWNING *Ring & Bk.* II. 515 Pretentious poverty At its wits' end to keep appearance up. **1907** *Athenæum* 25 May 641/3 His two larger pictures..are as clever, but a little more pretentious.

2. Of the nature of a pretension. *rare*⁻¹.

1886 W. CHAPPELL in *N. & Q.* 7th Ser. II. 4/1 After which [Thomson's death] Mallet put in a pretentious claim [to be the author of 'Rule Britannia'], against all evidence.

pre'tentiously, *adv.* [f. prec. + -LY[2].] In a pretentious manner.

1864 in WEBSTER. **1880** MRS. WHITNEY *Odd or Even?* xiv, While she, really, not pretentiously, threaded in her mind the possible moves. **1882** A. W. WARD *Dickens* iii. 64 Even in his newspaper letters..his impressions are never given pretentiously.

pre'tentiousness. [f. as prec. + -NESS.] The quality or condition of being pretentious.

1863 HOLLAND *Lett. Joneses* xii. 172 A pretentious man is, by token of his pretentiousness, a charlatan always. **1880** *Edin. Rev.* Jan. 50 Whatever may have been the faults or the pretentiousness of his classifications.

pretenture (priː'tɛntjʊə(r)). *Rom. Antiq.* Also præ-. [ad. late L. *prætentūra* (Ammian. Marcell.) a guard on the frontier of a province, also a barricade, f. *prætendĕre*: see PRETEND.]

1. A Roman frontier wall or rampart, esp. one of the two defending Roman Britain from the unsubdued tribes in the north.

1658 W. BURTON *Itin. Anton.* 102 There remain yet two doubts: First, whether this Prætenture, or Wall, was made of Stone, or of Turfs. **1771** MACPHERSON *Introd. Hist. Gt. Brit.* 160 *note*, A stone dug out of the ruins of the Roman pretenture, between the Scottish firths, inscribed to Apollo Grannius. **1796** MORSE *Amer. Geog.* II. 112 The most amazing monument of the Roman power in England, is the praetenture, or wall of Severus.

2. A Roman garrison guarding a frontier.

1807 BRITTON *Beauties Eng., Lincolnshire* 596 Carrying corn, and other commodities, from the Iceni, etc., for the use of the northern prætentures.

†**preter** ('priːtə(r)), *a.* (*sb.*) *Obs.* Also 7 præter. [The contraction *præter* for *præteritum* preterite, in *preterperfect*, etc., prefixed in the same way to *tense*, and at length treated as a separate word.]

a. *Gram.* = PRETERITE, past.

1530 PALSGR. 86 Circumlocutyng of al the pretertenses. **1534** MORE *Treat. Passion* Wks. 1347/2 Which wordes wer ..prophesyed by the verbe of the pretertemps or time passed. **1535** JOYE *Apol. Tindale* (Arb.) 9 He englissheth the verbe of the preter tence for the future. **1546** GARDINER *Declar. Art. Joye* 29b, The pretertens rather declareth a perfection in thacte, then the passing ouer the time in the acte. **1599** NASHE *Lenten Stuffe* 14, I..paralogized on their condition in the present and in the preter tense. **1676** DIXON *Two Test.* 30 So the Saying of God runs in the Præter-Tense, 'Unto thy Seed I have given the Land'. **1711** J. GREENWOOD *Eng. Gram.* 114 In Latin..the Preter Time of the Perfect Action, is commonly called the Preter-pluperfect, that is, the Preter more than Perfect. **1747** JOHNSON *Plan Eng. Dict.* Wks. IX. 178 Our verbs are conjugated by auxiliary words, and are only changed in the preter tense.

b. = PAST.

1578 T. PROCTOR *Gorg. Gallery, Vew Vayn Glory*, Diuers mo, whose preter pathes may learne Our future steps, our vayn unsteady stay.

B. *sb.* **a.** *ellipt.* for *preter tense*: see above. **b.** Past time, the past.

1615 BP. ANDREWES *Serm.* (1841) I. 162 But the other hath neither future nor præter, neither mood nor tense; nay, no verb at all. **1618** M. BARET *Horsemanship* I. 60 Let him observe the three (chiefe) parts of time which is, the preter, the present, the future. **1675** G. R. tr. *Le Grand's Man without Reason* 200 The present..is but an individual point, an instant that separates the praeter from the future.

preter-, præter- ('pri:tə(r)), *prefix.* The L. adv. and prep. *præter* past, by, beyond, above, more than; in addition to, besides; comparative of *præ* before, = further forward, more in front.

1. In Latin *præter* adv. was prefixed only to verbs and their derivative sbs. and adjs., as *prætercurrĕre* to run by or past, *prætergredī* to step or march past, to surpass, *præterīre* to go or pass by, omit, pass over, pass away (in time), *præteriens* passing, *præteritus* past, *præteritio* a passing by or over, *præterlābī* to glide or slip by, *prætermittĕre* to let go by, omit, overlook, *prætermissio* omission, etc. Hence the Eng. *pretergress*, *-gression*, *preterient*, *preterite*, *-ition*, *pretermit*, *-mission*, etc., and the analogous *pretergeneration*, *preteroffice*.

2. In Scholastic Latin, adjectives began to be formed from L. phrases with *præter* prep. + sb., e.g. *præternātūrālis*, from *præter nātūram* (Cic.) beyond or outside nature; Du Cange has of 1451 *præternecessārius*, from *quod præter necessārium est* what is beyond the necessary. Hence French *préternaturel* 15.., Eng. *preternatural a* 1600, followed in the 17th c. by *preternotorious*, *-native*, *-regular*, *-royal*, *-legal*, *-intentional*, *-scriptural*, *-seasonable*, etc.; *preterhuman*, *-nuptial*, *-sensual*, etc. are 19th c. formations. From these adjs., adverbs and nouns of quality, as *preternaturally*, *preternaturalism*, are always possible; *preterplurality* follows this analogy.

All the derivatives from words already in Latin, with the more important adjs., appear in their places as Main words; those of less importance (many only nonce-words) follow here.

preter'canine *a.*, more than canine. **preter-'Christian** *a.*, beyond what is Christian; lying outside Christianity. **preterde'ter-mined** *a.*, more than determined; hence **preterde'terminedly** *adv.* **preterdiplo'matic** *a.*, lying outside of or not within the bounds of diplomacy; hence **preterdiplo'matically** *adv.* **preter'equine** *a.*, more than equine. **preter-ero'gation**, *nonce-wd.* [after SUPEREROGATION], performance beyond or outside of what is demanded or required. **pretere'ssential** *a.*, beyond what is essential. **pretergene'ration**, preternatural generation, monstrous birth. **preterin'tentional** *a.*, beyond or additonal to what is intended. **preter'lethal** *a.*, taking place after death. **preter'native** *a.*, beyond or additional to what is native. **preterno'torious** *a.*, surpassingly notorious. **preter'nuptial** *a.*, lying outside of the nuptial relation. **preter'office**, an action contrary to duty: cf. OFFICE *sb.* 2a. **preterplu'rality**, excessive numerousness or multitude. **preterpo'litical** *a.*, lying outside of what is political or civil. **preter-'regular** *a.*, outside the limits of what is regular. **preter-'royal** *a.*, more than royal privilege warrants. **preter'scriptural** *a.*, beyond what is written. **preter'seasonable** *a.*, beyond what is seasonable. **preter'sensual** *a.*, beyond the domain of the senses; **preter'sensuous** *a.* = *pretersensual* adj.

1847 C. BRONTË *J. Eyre* xii, A great dog..passed me..not staying to look up, with strange *pretercanine eyes, in my face, as I half expected it would. **1873** MORLEY *Rousseau* II. 258 A *præter-christian deism, or the principle of natural religion, was inevitably contained in the legal conception of a natural law. **1892** G. MEREDITH *Empty Purse* Poems 1898 II. 200 Not as Cybele's beast will thy head lash tail So *præter-determinedly thermonous. **1904** *Contemp. Rev.* May 615 *Praeter-diplomatic machinery may be set to work to remove them. *Ibid.* June 806 In praeter-diplomatic ways ..Mr. Chamberlain received excellent grounds for believing that Germany was ripe for an alliance with Great Britain. **1900** *Daily News* 24 Dec. 5/1 The drivers are skilled, and their horses endowed with a *preterequine intelligence. **1617** COLLINS *Def. Bp. Ely* II. ix. 346 It is certaine that Supererogation there can be none, though *praetererogation we should graunt you, howbeit subtererogation were the fitter word. **1664** H. MORE *Myst. Iniq., Synopsis Proph.* 542 Puzzled in some opinions and scrupulosities that are *preteressential. **1640** G. WATTS tr. *Bacon's Adv. Learn.* III. iv. 145 Concret Physique hath the same division which Naturall History hath; so that it is a knowledge either concerning the Heavens;..or concerning the lesser Collegiates, or natures specifique; so likewise concerning *Pretergenerations [L. *prætergenerationes*], and concerning Mechaniques. **1690** BOYLE *Chr. Virtuoso* I. Wks. 1772 V. 528 Sir Francis Bacon..assigns the second of them to what he calls præter-generations, such as monsters, prodigies, and other things. **1663** SIR G. MACKENZIE *Religious Stoic* xi. (1865) 103 Define them to be the *preter-intentional works of nature. **1887** W. M. ROSSETTI *Shelley's Prometh. Unb.* 19 The indefinable possibilities of existence prænatal and *præterlethal—the world of spirit before birth and after death. **1647** M. HUDSON *Div. Right Govt.* II. x. 146 Thus much briefly of the Native Fundamentals and Essentials of Politick Government; the next point to be spoken of is the *Preternative. *a* **1625** FLETCHER, etc. *Fair Maid Inn* IV. ii, I confess myself a more *preternotorious rogue than himself. **1833** CARLYLE *Misc. Ess., Diderot* (1872) V. 21 To whom we owe this present *preternuptial *Correspondance*. **1837** *Ibid., Mirabeau* 243 Nay, poor woman, she by and by, we find, takes up with preternuptial persons. **1656** STANLEY *Hist. Philos.* VIII. (1701) 328/2 *Præter-office is an action, which reason requireth [*pr.* acquireth] that we do not, as, to neglect our Parents, to contemn our Brethren, to disagree with our Friends, to despise our Country. **1647** WARD *Simp. Cobler* 28 It is not easily credible, what may be said of the *preterpluralities of Taylors in London. I have heard..there were numbred between Temple-barre and Charingcrosse, eight thousand of that Trade. **1651** HOBBES *Leviath.* IV. xlvii. 385 The analysis, or resolution,..beginneth with the knot that was last tied; as we may see in the dissolution of the *præterpolitical Church Government in England. **1647** WARD *Simp. Cobler* (1843) 37, I had rather suppose them to powder, than expose them to preregular, much lesse to *preter regular Judgements. *Ibid.* 49 The tongues of Times tell us of ten *Preter-royall Usurpations, to one contra-civill Rebellion. **1672** H. MORE *Brief Reply* viii. 240 The former part..is so without analogy, and the latter so turgid and *preterscriptural. **1686** GOAD *Celest. Bodies* I. xii. 56 When 'tis an Ordinary and Durable, though *Preter-seasonable Constitution, Cold will be sure to be remembred. **1885** tr. *Schultze's Fetichism* vii. §2 He must needs go beyond the domain of sense, and assign causes not apprehensible to the senses, *praetersensual or supersensual. **1963** V. NABOKOV *Gift* iii. 172 If..he had had to answer before some *pretersensuous court..he would scarcely have decided to say that he loved her.

‖**preterea** (pri:'tɛri:ɑ). [L. *præterea* adv., beyond those, besides, f. *præter* beyond + *ea* pl., 'those'. Taken in quot. as a sb. (perh. orig. a heading of items in an account) with pl. *-s*; cf. *et ceteras*, *extras*.] In *pl.* Additional items, extras.

1512 *Northumbld. Househ. Bk.* (1770) 181 Item that the saide Clarks of Brevements entre in the Counting-hous Mounethlie alle the Pretereas in the title of Costs Necessary.

preter'gress, *v. rare.* Also præter-. [f. L. *prætergress-*, ppl. stem of *prætergredī* to walk past, go by, surpass, f. *præter*, PRETER- + *gredī* to step.]

1. *trans.* To go beyond (bounds); to surpass.

1596 BARROUGH *Meth. Physick* v. xxv. 346 It keepeth within the precincts of his libertie, which if it shall once pretergresse..it is no longer to be called melancholie, but some other humour. **1851** NEALE *Med. Hymns* 98 Tree.. Every other pretergressing Both in bloom and bud and flower.

†**2.** To go outside of. *Obs.*

1615 JACKSON *Creed* IV. II. viii. §5 If some sins there be, as Roman Catholics teach, only besides the law, in doing them we do not transgress the law, but rather prætergress or go besides it.

preter'gression. *rare.* [n. of action from prec.: see -ION[1].] **a.** The action of passing by (without notice or performance); failure to follow a path, conform to a law, etc. **b.** The action of going beyond or overstepping bounds.

1615 JACKSON *Creed* IV. II. viii. §5 Seeing the Lawgiver's will was that we should do the law, not only hear it, much less go besides it, there is no pretergression of it but is directly against the Lawgiver's will. **1802–12** BENTHAM *Ration. Judic. Evid.* (1827) V. 251 A motion for a writ of prohibition to be directed to the ecclesiastical court, on the ground of prætergression of jurisdiction. *Ibid.* 617 There would be, at least,..no pretergression of the bounds of official authority.

preterhuman (pri:tə'hju:mən), *a.* [f. PRETER- + HUMAN.] Beyond or outside of what is human: often = *superhuman*, but generally used to avoid the specific connotation of that word.

1811 SHELLEY *St. Irvyne* ii, He..started..as from the emanation of superior and preter-human being. **1854** MILMAN *Lat. Chr.* II. iv. (1864) I. 276 The introduction of praeter-human forms. **1866** LIDDON *Bampt. Lect.* vi. (1875) 298 What is it that gives Christ's human acts and sufferings such preterhuman value? **1871** MORLEY *J. De Maistre* Crit. Misc. Ser. I. (1878) 134 Laboriously building up with preterhuman patience and preterhuman sagacity. **1878** GLADSTONE *Homer* xi. 130 Achilles seems everywhere to tread on the bounds of the preterhuman.

preterient (prɪ'tɪərɪənt), *a. rare.* [f. L. *præteriens*, pres. pple. of *præterīre* to go by, pass (of which, however, the stem of the oblique cases is *prætereunt-*).] Passing or going by: transient. So **pre'terience**, the fact or condition of being passing or transient.

1786 CUMBERLAND *Observer* No. 11 I. 97 Migrating after the death of one body into that of another, with the faculty of remembering all the actions of its præterient states. *c* **1827** COLERIDGE in *Blackw. Mag.* (1882) CXXXI. 120 There seems to me a confusion of *schein* with the præterience or impermanence.

preterim'perfect, *a.* (*sb.*) *Gram.* Now *rare.* [ad. L. *præteritum imperfectum* 'uncompleted past', with contraction: see PRETER, PRETERITE, and IMPERFECT.] Expressing a past action which is not stated as completed but as going on: applied to one of the tenses of the verb in the Indo-European languages, as L. *currēbat*, Eng. *he was running*; = IMPERFECT 5. Also *absol.* as *sb.*

1530 PALSGR. 84 The preter imperfit tens as *je parloye* I dyd speke. **1591** PERCIVALL *Sp. Dict.* Cj, The tences are fiue, the present tence, signifying the time that now is:..the preterimperfectence, the time not perfectly past. **1648** GAGE *West Ind.* 215 There is no preterimperfect tense, nor preterpluperfect tense; but the preterperfect tense standeth for them. **1799** *Monthly Rev.* XXVIII. 411 The Verb must be..in the Preterimperfect Tense, when in English we use the Preterpluperfect.

preterist ('prɛtərɪst), *sb.* (*a.*) Also præ-. [f. PRETER-, short for *preterite* + -IST.]

1. One whose chief interest is in the past; one who regards the past with most pleasure or favour.

1864 in WEBSTER; and in later Dicts. **1962** V. NABOKOV *Pale Fire* 35 A preterist: one who collects cold nests.

2. *Theol.* **a.** One who holds that the prophecies of the Apocalypse have been already (wholly or in great part) fulfilled.

1843 G. S. FABER *Sacr. Calend. Prophecy* (1844) I. p. xviii, To consider certain vituperative prophecies..as already accomplished in the course of the first and second centuries: whence, to commentators of this School, we may fitly apply the name of *Preterists*. **1854** Præterists [see FUTURIST]. **1860** JOWETT in *Ess. & Rev.* 371 The Preterists and Futurists.. may alike claim the authority of the Book of Daniel, or the Revelation.

b. *attrib.* or *adj.* Of or pertaining to preterists.

1878 H. G. GUINNESS *End of Age* (1880) 93 Preterist, Futurist and Presentist schemes of interpretation. **1904** G. SMITH *Short Hist. Chr. Missions* I. iv. 43 A Praeterist, or a Futurist interpretation of its visions.

preterite, -it ('prɛtərɪt), *a.* (*sb.*) Forms: 4–7, 9 preterit, 5 -yte, 8–9 præterit(e, 5– preterite. [= F. *prétérit* (13th c. in Littré), ad. L. *præterit-us* gone by, past, pa. pple. of *præterīre*, f. *præter*, PRETER- + *īre* to go.]

1. Of or pertaining to bygone time; occurring or existing previously; past, bygone, former; = PAST *a.* 2.

1340 *Ayenb.* 59 On is preterit, þet is to zigge, of þinge ypased..þe oþer is of present, þet is to zigge, of nou. **1387–8** T. USK *Test. Love* III. iv. (Skeat) l. 56 In..heven..There is nothing preterit ne passed, there is nothing future ne comming; but al thinges togider in that place ben present everlasting, without any meving. **1490** CAXTON *Eneydos* vi. 26 The swete mayntene and semblaunce of the sayd Sychee, her preteryte husbonde. *c* **1500** KENNEDY *Poems* (Schipper) ii. 10 þroch ignorance and foly youþ My preterit tyme I wald nevir spair. **1657** HAWKE *Killing is M.* 25 Compare the store and cheapnesse of our present Commodities, with the Scarcenesse and dearnesse of the preterit times. *a* **1693** *Urquhart's Rabelais* III. xiii. 102 What is preterit, and gone. **1811** L. M. HAWKINS *C'tess & Gertr.* (1812) I. 266 To return to the preterite gala-days of Lady Luxmore. **1854** LOWELL *Cambridge Thirty Y. Ago* Prose Wks. 1890 I. 52 You shall go back with me thirty years, which will bring you among things and persons as thoroughly preterite as Romulus or Numa.

2. *Gram.* Expressing past action or state; past; as ***preterite tense*** [L. *præteritum tempus* (Quint.)], ***preterite participle***; = PAST *a.* 4.

1388 WYCLIF *Prol.* 57 A participle of a present tens either preterit, of actif vois eithir passif, mai be resolued into a verbe..and a coniunccioun copulatif. **1530** PALSGR. 86 The participle preterit after the tenses of *je ay* remayneth for the most part unchanged. **1562** PILKINGTON *Expos. Abdyas* 42 Al the prophets use to speake by the preterit temps. **1728** POPE *Dunc.* III. 337 *note*, Wks. 1736 IV. 225 In the style of other prophets, [he] hath used the future tense for the preterit. **1865** CARLYLE *Fredk. Gt.* XIX. iii. (1872) VIII. 131 Friedrich finds that Loudon *was* there last night—preterite tense, alas.

b. So ***preterite perfect*** = PRETERPERFECT.

1530 PALSGR. Introd. 42 The preterit parfyte tens of the infynityve mode.

B. *sb.* [ellipt. use of the adj.]

†**1.** Past time, the past (= PAST *sb.* 1); also *pl.* past times or events. *Obs. rare.*

c **1374** CHAUCER *Boeth.* v. pr. vi. 133 (Camb. MS.) It.. procedith fro preteritz in to futuris, þat is to seyn fro tyme passed in to tyme comynge. *Ibid.* 134 Thilke thing..to whom ther nis nawht of þe preterite escapyd nor I-passed. *c* **1400** *Rom. Rose* 5011 She wepeth the tyme that she hath wasted, Compleyning of the preterit.

2. *Gram.* = Preterite tense: see A. 2.

1530 PALSGR. Introd. 37 The preterites and supines of suche verbes. **1661** MILTON *Accedence* Wks. 1738 I. 613 The Preterit speaketh of the time past, and is distinguish'd by three degrees: the Preterimperfect, the Preterperfect, and the Preterpluperfect. **1875** WHITNEY *Life Lang.* ii. 13 It is an era in his education when he first begins to employ preterits and plurals and their like.

3. *Theol.* One who is passed over or not elected by God; cf. PRETERITION 4. *rare*[−1].

1864 *Fraser's Mag.* May 533 The reprobates who are damned because they were always meant to be damned, and the preterites who are damned because they were never meant to be saved.

'preteriteness. Also præ-, preteritness. [f. prec. + -NESS.] The state or condition of being preterite or past; pastness.

1665 J. SERGEANT *Sure Footing* 205 The preteritness of the Thing has so fixt its Existence to its proper time, that 'tis not now obnoxious to variation. **1692** BENTLEY *Boyle Lect.* vi. 23 We cannot conceive a Praeteritness (if I may say so) still backwards *in infinitum*, that never was present. **1854** LOWELL *Jrnl. Italy* Prose Wks. 1890 I. 140 The feeling of preteriteness and extinction. **1866** —— *Lessing* ibid. II. 219 Klopstock..is rather remembered for what he was than what he is—an immortality of preteriteness.

'preterite-'present, *a.* (*sb.*) *Gram.* [ad. mod.L. *præterito-præsens*, neut. pl. *-præsentia*, f. *præteritus* PRETERITE + *præsens* PRESENT.] Applied to verbs of which the tense now used as the present was originally a preterite (or to this tense); esp. to the small group of verbs in the Germanic languages (mostly auxiliaries of predication) represented in English by *can*, *dare*, *dow*, *may*, *must*, *shall*, †*thar*, *will*, *wit*, of which the current present tense is in form and origin a preterite, from which the current past tense is a new weak formation; also applicable to the Latin verbs *cœpi*, *memini*, *novi*, *odi*, the Greek οἶδα, etc. Also PRETERITO-PRESENTIAL.

[**1870** HELFENSTEIN *Compar. Gram. Teut. Lang.* 521 The preterite indicative is always in imitation of the præterito-præsentia *wolta*, rarely *wëlta*, subj. *wolti*.] **1874** MASON *Eng. Gram.* (ed. 19) 78 *note*, These preterite-presents may be compared with οἶδα, *novi*, &c., in Greek and Latin. [**1880** EARLE *Philol. Eng. Tongue* §291 These help-verbs are a very ancient group of so-called praeterito-praesentia.] **1888** *New Eng. Dict.* s.v. *Can.* **1892** SWEET *New Eng. Gram.* §1477 Most of the MnE [= mod.Eng.] verbs that we class as anomalous are old preterite-present verbs. **1892** WRIGHT *Primer Gothic Lang.* §272 *Preterite-Presents.* These verbs have strong preterites with a present meaning..to which new weak preterites have been formed.

preterition (priːtəˈrɪʃən). Also præ-. [= F. *prétérition*, ad. late L. *præteritiōn-em* a passing over, n. of action f. *præterīre*: see PRETERIENT.]

†**1.** Passing by, passage (of time). *Obs. rare.*

1647 H. MORE *Song of Soul* Notes 136/1 The præterition of life is the præterition of time. **1647** TRAPP *Comm. Luke* xix. 42 The time of grace is fitly called a day in regard of..speedy preterition.

2. The action of passing over, or fact of being passed by or over, without notice; omission, disregard, neglect; with *a* and *pl.* an instance of this.

1609 BP. W. BARLOW *Answ. Nameless Cath.* 236 His voluntarie but subtile preter-ition, in leauing out all the other disasters in the Oath. *a* **1631** DONNE *Serm.* xxxvi. (1640) 354 As long as they are but preteritions, not contradictions..they are not worthy of a reproofe. **1654** H. L'ESTRANGE *Chas. I.* 208 A preterition..studiously and deliberatively resolved upon. **1709** LAMPHIRE in Hearne *Collect.* 6 Nov. (O.H.S.) II. 300 'Twould be best to pass by without going in. For..Dr. Barlow loves præterition. **1877** SPARROW *Serm.* iii. 40 It is negative in its nature, and consists in the mere preterition and overlooking of the agency of the invisible God.

3. *Rhet.* A figure by which summary mention is made of a thing, in professing to omit it.

1612 T. TAYLOR *Comm. Titus* i. 9 The Apostle thankfully remembreth their diligent love; and yet..by a wise rhetoricall preterition, exhorteth them vnto it. **1619** W. SCLATER *Exp. 1 Thess.* (1630) 386 Such Ironicall preteritions are something frequent in Scripture. **1657** J. SMITH *Myst. Rhet.* 165. **1727-41** CHAMBERS *Cycl.* s.v., The most artful praises are those given by way of preterition.

4. *Theol.* The passing over of the non-elect; non-election to salvation.

1621 BURTON *Anat. Mel.* III. iv. II. iii, Our indiscreet pastors..speak so much of election, prædestination, reprobation *ab æterno*, subtraction of grace, præterition, voluntary permission, &c. **1654** VILVAIN *Theol. Treat.* ii. 66 The Decree of Reprobation (both in the privativ act of preterition, and positiv of punishment) depends on Gods simple Prescience. **1740** WESLEY *Wks.* (1872) VII. 375 Call it..by whatever name you please, Election, preterition, predestination, or reprobation, it comes in the end to the same thing. **1862** *Evangelical Christendom* Oct. 475 The præterition and consequent perdition of the majority of mankind does no violence to our sense, either of the Divine justice or sovereignty.

5. *Rom. Law.* The omission by a testator to mention in his will one of his children or natural heirs: see quot. 1880.

1722 WOLLASTON *Relig. Nat.* v. xviii. (1738) 104 If it had been foreseen, that L would not so much as ask, and had therefore been left out of the will; this preterition would have been caused by his carriage. **1848** WHARTON *Law Lex.*, *Preterition*, the entire omission of a child's name in the father's will, which rendered it null: exheredation being allowed, but not preterition. **1880** MUIRHEAD *Ulpian* xxviii. §2 *note*, Praeterition of a *suus* invalidated a will. *Ibid.*, *Digest* 573 Praeterition in testaments, omission to mention a person that the law required should be instituted or disinherited. **1887** *Tennant's Notary's Man.* (ed. 5) 29 If a soldier upon a military expedition, in making his will, passed over his children in silence, such preterition was held of equal force with a nominal disinherison, and the will could not be set aside as inofficious.

preteritive (prɪˈtɛrɪtɪv), *a.* [f. L. *præterit-*, ppl. stem of *præterīre*: cf. PRETERITE and -IVE.]

1. *Theol.* Of or pertaining to preterition or non-election. *rare*$^{-1}$.

1836 G. S. FABER *Prim. Doctr. Election* I. ix. 139 Augustine's logically correlative doctrine of Absolute Preteritive Reprobation to eternal death.

2. *Gram.* Used only in the preterite tenses: said of a verb. (Webster 1847.)

Mod. The Latin *memini* is called a preteritive verb.

b. *preteritive present* (adj. and sb.) = PRETERITE-PRESENT (verb or tense).

1885 A. S. COOK tr. *Sievers' O. Eng. Gram.* §417 The Germanic preteritive presents [die verba praeteritopresentia des germanischen] have sprung from strong verbs whose preterits have assumed a present meaning (like Lat. *memini*, *novi*, *coepi*, Gr. οἶδα), while the original presents have disappeared. **1899** W. J. SEDGEFIELD *K. Ælfred's Boeth.* 207 Verbs with preteritive presents..e.g. *mæg*, *deah*.

pre'terito-pre'sential, *a.* (*sb.*) *Gram.* [f. mod.L. *præterito-præsentia* (sc. *verba*) + -AL[1].] = PRETERITE-PRESENT *a.*, as in ***preterito-presential verbs***, called in mod.L. *præterito-præsentia* (pl.).

[**1870**, **1880**: see PRETERITE-PRESENT.] **1875** WHITNEY *Life Lang.* v. 93 Important little class of Germanic verbs called 'preterito-presential', because they have won their present meaning through a 'perfect' one.

preterlabent (priːtəˈleɪbənt), *a. rare.* Also præter-. [ad. L. *præterlābent-em*, pres. pple. of *præterlābī* to glide or flow by, f. *præter*, PRETER- + *lābī* to glide.] Gliding or flowing past.

1670 W. SIMPSON *Hydrol. Ess.* 5 Those differ..according to..the different impregnation of the preterlabent water. **1757** WALKER in *Phil. Trans.* L. 143 The præterlabent streams of water. **1905** H. A. EVANS *Oxf. & Cotswolds* xiii. 314 There is the old garden behind the house, with the stone steps descending thereunto, and the praeterlabent Coln.

preter'lapsed, *ppl. a. rare.* [f. L. *præterlaps-us*, pa. pple. of *præterlābī* (see prec.) + -ED[1].] That has glided by; gone by, past, bygone.

1599 A. M. tr. *Gabelhouer's Bk. Physicke* 226/1 When as now the 12 dayes are præterlapsede, he may as then accompanye..with his wife. **1630** J. TAYLOR (Water P.) *Taylor's Trav.* Ded., Wks. III. 76 In the preterlapsed occurrences there hath beene an Antagonisticall repugnancy betwixt vs. **1661** GLANVILL *Van. Dogm.* 137 We look with a superstitious reverence upon the accounts of præterlapsed ages.

preter'legal, *a. rare.* Also præter-. [f. PRETER- + LEGAL.] Beyond or outside of what is legal; not according to law.

1648 *Eikon Bas.* xi. 91, I expected..some evill customes preterlegall, and abuses personall had been to be removed. *a* **1661** FULLER *Worthies, Cheshire* (1662) I. 178 Sir Randal..openly manifested his dislike of such Preter-legal Courses. **1818** COLERIDGE in *Lit. Rem.* (1838) III. 189 This illegal or praeter-legal and desultory toleration by connivance at particular cases.

pre'term, *a.* and *adv. Obstetrics.* **A.** *adj.* [PRE- B. 2.] Born or occurring after a pregnancy that lasted significantly less than the normal time; *spec.* (see quot. 1977[2]).

1928 A. GESELL *Infancy & Human Growth* xv. 300 The pre-term child is viable even though he may have completed but three-quarters of his allotted uterine life-period. **1933**, **1971** [see POST-TERM *a.*]. **1977** *Lancet* 11 June 1255/1 Cigarette smoking during pregnancy is associated with an increased proportion of pre-term deliveries. *Ibid.* 30 July 246/1 The terms 'prematurity' and 'immaturity', with their vague and multiple meanings, have been replaced by the precise terms 'low birthweight' (under 2500 g) and 'preterm' (less than 37 completed weeks).

B. *adv.* [PRE- B. 2 c.] Before the end of the normal period of pregnancy.

1977 *Lancet* 9 July 87/1 We gave pregnant Sprague-Dawley rats 4 mg/kg indomethacin..and killed the fetuses at cæsarean section shortly pre-term.

†**pre'terminable**, *a. Obs. rare*$^{-1}$. [f. PRE- A. 3 + TERMINABLE, app. in an active sense.

The word may represent a Schol. L. **prætermīnābilis*, f. **prætermināre*, rendering Gr. προορίζειν to determine beforehand, f. ὁρίζειν to bound, ὅροι bounds, *fines*, *termini*. Cf. PREDETERMINE. Mr. C. G. Osgood in his ed. of *Pearl* illustrates the passage, which refers to Ps. lxii. 12 [lxi. 13], by Albertus Magnus's comment on the same passage, 'Primo, divinæ voluntatis ordinatio æterna et perfecta', etc.]

Predetermining, foreordaining.

13.. *E.E. Allit. P.* A. 595 In sauter is sayd a poynt determynable, Thou quytez uchon as hys desserte, Thou hyȝe kyng ay pretermynable [*MS.* pertermynable (Gollancz)].

pre'terminal, *a.* [PRE- B. 1.] Preceding that which is terminal.

1947 *Radiology* XLIX. 311/2 A similar preterminal course..is found with such toxic agents as the nitrogen mustards. **1965** N. CHOMSKY *Aspects of Theory of Syntax* ii. 84 A terminal string is formed from a preterminal string by insertion of a lexical formative. **1976** *Lancet* 4 Dec. 1253/2 Children with severe ketoacidosis in association with viral infections have symptoms and signs in the preterminal stage very similar to those of Reye's syndrome. **1977** *Navy News* June 39 (Advt.), Why not spend your pre-terminal leave with us and be introduced to the company.

†**preter'missed**, *a. Obs. rare*$^{-1}$. [f. L. *prætermiss-us*, pa. pple. of *prætermittĕre* to pass over, omit (see next) + -ED[1].] Pretermitted, omitted.

1640 G. WATTS tr. *Bacon's Adv. Learn.* VI. ii. 271 The cause that many things which referre unto it, and are usefull to be knowne, are pretermiss'd [*prætermissa sunt*].

pretermission (priːtəˈmɪʃən). Also præter-. [ad. L. *prætermissiōn-em*, n. of action f. *prætermittĕre*: see next. So F. *prétermission* (16th c. in Godef. *Compl.*).] The action of pretermitting.

1. The passing over, overlooking, or disregarding of anything; omission of anything from a narrative; omission of, or neglect to do, something.

1583 BABINGTON *Commandm.* i. (1637) 11 The pretermission of thankes for any goodnesse..bestowed by the Lord,..is horrible. **1633** T. ADAMS *Exp. 2 Peter* iii. 18 Any pretermission of the physician may exalt the disease. **1704** SWIFT *T. Tub* iii. (1709) 52, I proceed to refute the objections of those who argue from the silence and pretermission of authors. **1879** FARRAR *St. Paul* II. 211 God's righteousness, which might otherwise have been called in question because of the prætermission of past sins.

2. Ceasing to do something (for a time); leaving off the practice of anything; disuse.

1677 CARY *Chronol.* I. I. I. xii. 45 There was no absolute pretermission of that Reckoning. **1831** TYTLER *Lives Scott. Worthies* I. 113 The detestation and pretermission of vice.

3. *Rhet.* = PRETERITION 3.

1727-41 CHAMBERS *Cycl.*, *Preterition*, or *Pretermission*, in rhetoric, a figure whereby, in pretending to pass over a thing untouched, we make a summary mention thereof. **1828** in WEBSTER. Hence in mod. Dicts.

4. *Rom. Law.* = PRETERITION 5.

1795 WYTHE *Decis. Virginia* 104 Inserting in her will apology for the pretermission of her daughter.

pretermit (priːtəˈmɪt), *v.* Also præter-. [ad. L. *prætermittĕre* to let pass, omit, overlook, f. *præter*, PRETER- + *mittĕre* to let go, send.]

1. *trans.* To leave out of a narrative; not to notice, mention, insert, or include; to omit.

1538 STARKEY *England* II. i. 166 Bycause I see here ys not the place now to dyspute..I wyl thys pretermytt and set apart. **1598** STOW *Surv.* xv. (1603) 123 The recitall whereof I pretermit for breuitie. **1651** HOBBES *Leviath.* (1839) 194 In all kinds of actions by the laws prætermitted, men have the liberty, of doing what their own reasons shall suggest, for the most profitable to themselves. **1745-6** FIELDING *True Patriot* No. 13 The lad..had uttered many wicked things, which I pretermitted in my narrative. **1870** GLADSTONE *Glean.* IV. xliii. 228 Some points of conduct relating to the present war..we advisedly pretermit.

†**b.** *Theol.* To pass over in electing to salvation. Cf. PRETERITION 4. *Obs.*

1608 WILLET *Hexapla Exod.* 812 God doth..of his owne will, as he electeth some so pretermit others.

c. *Rom. Law.* To omit mention of (a descendant or natural heir) in a will. Cf. PRETERITION 5.

1875 POSTE *Gaius* II. Comm. (ed. 2) 229 If a descendant of the testator was..pretermitted (*praeteritus*), i.e. not expressly either instituted successor or disinherited, possession was not granted to the devisees but to the pretermitted descendant. **1887** *Tennant's Notary's Man.* (ed. 5) 28 A father was bound to institute his children as his heirs, and could not disinherit them unless for very weighty reasons; for if a father pretermitted or passed them over in silence, the testament was void.

2. To allow to pass without notice or regard; to overlook intentionally.

1542 HEN. VIII *Declar. Scots* A ij b, [Such] as we ought not with sufferaunce to pretermitte and passe ouer. **1571-2** *Reg. Privy Council Scot.* II. 111 Quhilk..oppressioun gif it be pretermittit unpuneist. **1630** DONNE *Serm.* xxv. (1640) 253 God pretermits many times errours in circumstances. **1821** LAMB *Elia* Ser. I. *New Year's Eve*, The birth of a New Year is of an interest too wide to be pretermitted by king or cobbler.

3. To fail or forbear to do, use, or perform; to leave undone, neglect, omit.

1513 DOUGLAS *Æneis* VI. viii. 66 Na thyng, my deir freynd, did thow pretermyt; All that thow aucht to Deiphobus. **1528** FOX in Pocock *Rec. Ref.* I. 142 We..pretermitted nothing which might in any way conduce to the furtherance thereof. **1609** BIBLE (Douay) *Wisd.* x. 8 For pretermitting wisdom they..did slippe. **1665** MANLEY *Grotius' Low C. Warres* 197 Prince Maurice..pretermitted none of those things which had been used by Antiquity in the Art Military. *a* **1797** H. WALPOLE *Mem. Geo. II* (1822) I. 394 Was the necessary defence of her colonies to be pretermitted? **1836** EMERSON *Nature* 47 A care..pretermitted in no single case.

†**b.** Const. with *infin. Obs.*

1570-6 LAMBARDE *Peramb. Kent* (1826) 160 So yet wil I not pretermit to declare out of other men such notes as I finde. **1665** HOOKE *Microgr.* xiii. 85, I must not pretermit to hint.

4. To neglect to avail oneself or make use of; to allow (time or opportunity) to pass unused or unimproved; to miss, lose. Now *rare.*

1538 STARKEY *England* I. i. 25, I schal neuer pretermyt occasyon nor tyme of helpyng my cuntrey. **1609** SIR E. HOBY *Let. to Mr. T. H.* Pref. 3 Throughly to possesse themselues of your fauour, they will pretermit neither time, nor meanes. **1651** WITTIE tr. *Primrose's Pop. Err.* IV. ii. 205. **1840** J. P. KENNEDY *Quodlibet* i. (1860) 27, I cannot pretermit the opportunity now afforded me to glance..at some striking events.

5. To leave off for the time or for a time; to interrupt; *erroneously*, to leave off, cease.

1828 MISS MITFORD *Village* Ser. III. (1863) 484 For her doth Farmer Brookes's mastiff..pretermit his incessant bark. **1878** STEVENSON *Edinburgh* (1889) 36 Some customs..have been fortunately pretermitted. **1882** B. HARTE *Flip* ii, The monotonous strokes of an axe were suddenly pretermitted.

[¶ The alleged sense 'To render ineffectual', 'to frustrate', in *Cent. Dict.* and *Standard Dict.*, is an error due to misreading the passage cited.]

Hence **preter'mitting** *vbl. sb.* Also **preter-**

'**mitter**, one who pretermits; **preter'mittently** *adv.*, erron. for INTERMITTENTLY.

1566 DRANT *Horace, Sat.* II. iii. Prol. F v b, A sluggarde, and pretermitter of duetifull occasions. **1579–80** *Reg. Privy Council Scot.* III. 259 But pretermitting of ony tyme. **1857** MISS MULOCK *Woman's Th. abt. Wom.* 191 One half the parish resolutely declines 'knowing' the other half—sometimes pretermittently, sometimes permanently.

preter'mitted, *ppl. a.* [f. prec. + -ED[1].] That is passed by or overlooked; omitted.

1651 WELDON *Crt. Chas. I* 196 He hath Pensions out of the pretermitted Customs. *a* **1661** FULLER *Worthies* (1662) I. 184 Cheshire is one of the 12. pretermitted Counties, the Names of whose Gentry were not returned into the Tower, in the 12. year of K. Henry the Sixth. **1727** in *6th Rep. Dep. Kpr.* App. II. 118 The Office of Comptroller of the Petty and of the Pretermitted Customs .. in the Port of London. **1875** POSTE *Gaius* II. Comm. (ed. 2) 224 The existence of a pretermitted *suus heres* .. was alone important.

preternatural (priːtəˈnætjʊərəl, -tʃərəl), *a.* (*sb.*) Also **præter-**. [ad. med.L. *præternātūrālis* (1255 in Albertus Magnus *Metaph.* II. xi) f. L. phr. *præter nātūram*: see PRETER-. So obs. F. *préternaturel* (15.. in Godef.), It. *preternaturale.*] That is out of the ordinary course of nature; beyond, surpassing, or differing from what is natural; non-natural; formerly = abnormal, exceptional, unusual; sometimes = UNNATURAL; see also b.

1580 G. HARVEY *Three Lett.* Wks. (Grosart) I. 59 A preternaturall, or supernaturall ominous worke of God. **1593** R. HARVEY *Philadelphus* 49 Some make themselues barren with preternatural dyet. **1651** WITTIE tr. *Primrose's Pop. Err.* 232 We use them [remedies] that we may reduce the body from a preternaturall to its naturall state againe. **1663** J. SPENCER *Prodigies* (1665) 5 Prodigies Præternatural, such I account all strange Events, which hold of no steady causes, but are to us soly casual and uncertain. **1685** BOYLE *Enq. Notion Nat.* iv. 82 That which thwarts this Order [of Nature] may be said to be Preternatural, or contrary to Nature. **1725** BRADLEY *Fam. Dict., Whitloe*, a preternatural and very troublesome Swelling towards the Fingers ends. **1802** PALEY *Nat. Theol.* iii. (1819) 40 Either in the natural or preternatural state of the organ, the use of the chain of bones is to propagate the impulse. **1866** GEO. ELIOT *F. Holt* ii, Mrs. Transome .. seemed to hear and see what they said and did with preternatural acuteness.

b. Used as = SUPERNATURAL.

1774 J. BRYANT *Mythol.* I. 190 People were determined in the choice of their holy places by those præternatural phænomena. **1829** SOUTHEY *Sir T. More* (1831) I. 11 Preternatural impressions are sometimes communicated to us for wise purposes. **1875** E. WHITE *Life in Christ* v. xxxi. (1878) 533 His coming was heralded by a series of preternatural dispensations.

†**B.** *sb.* (*pl.*) Preternatural attributes or qualities. *Obs. rare.*

1708 H. DODWELL *Nat. Mort. Hum. Souls* 138 If Humane Souls, since their loss of Præternaturals, are in course, subjected to these inferior Dæmons.

Hence ˌ**preternatu'rality**, *nonce-wd.*, **preter'naturalness**, preternatural quality; **preter'nature** *nonce-wd.*, that which is out of the course of nature.

1666 J. SMITH *Old Age* (1676) 133 There is such an intricate mixture of naturality and preternaturality in Age. **1727** BAILEY vol. II, *Preter-naturalness*, quality out of the natural Course. **1860** PUSEY *Min. Proph.* 588 The preternaturalness of the deliverance is pictured by the driving the locust .. into two opposite seas. **1842** POE *Marie Roget* Wks. 1864 I. 260 In my own heart there dwells no faith in praeter-nature.

preter'naturalism. [f. prec. + -ISM.]

1. The character or condition of being preternatural; that which is preternatural; with *a* and *pl.* an instance of this; a preternatural occurrence.

1834 *Fraser's Mag.* Dec. 702/2 Byron's drama partakes both of Hamlet and Macbeth. It is the incest of the one with the preternaturalism of the other. **1837** CARLYLE *Fr. Rev.* III. III. viii, Saturated through every fibre with Preternaturalism of Suspicion. **1858** —— *Fredk. Gt.* VI. ii. II. 10 Among the simple People, arose rumours of omens, preternaturalisms, for and against.

2. A recognition of the preternatural; a system or doctrine of the preternatural.

1864 *Realm* 8 June 7 'Frankenstein' and 'Zanoni' are powerful books, but their præternaturalism seems forced and unreal. **1872** A. B. ALCOTT *Concord Days, Sleep & Dreams* 204 A faith, were such possible, destitute of an element of preternaturalism, or of mysticism. **1882** M. ARNOLD in *19th Cent.* May 695 A religion of preternaturalism is doomed.

So **preter'naturalist**, a believer in the preternatural.

1868 M. COLLINS *Sweet Anne Page* I. 93 The ladies were rather puzzled how to deal with this young præter-naturalist.

preter'naturally, *adv.* [f. as prec. + -LY[2].] In a preternatural manner; more than naturally; abnormally, extraordinarily, unusually.

1626 BACON *Sylva* §30 Simple air, being preternaturally attenuated by heat, will make itself room, and break, and blow up that which resisteth it. **1668** CULPEPPER & COLE *Barthol. Anat.* Introd., Warts and Swellings, with other things which grow upon the living Body præternaturally. **1748** HARTLEY *Observ. Man* I. iii. 402 The Vibrations in the internal Parts of the Brain are preternaturally increased. **1848** LYTTON *Harold* III. ii, With a countenance preternaturally thoughtful for his years. **1881** W. COLLINS *Black Robe* vii, The night was almost preternaturally quiet.

preterperfect (priːtəˈpɜːfɪkt), *a.* (*sb.*) [ad. late L. *præteritum perfectum* 'complete past', with contraction: see PRETER, PRETERITE, and PERFECT.]

1. *Gram.* Past perfect; applied to a tense which indicates a past or completed state or action. Also *ellipt.* as *sb.* Now *rare* or *Obs.*

1534 TINDALE *N.T., Matt.* Prol., The Hebrue phrase, or maner of speach .. Whose preterperfectence and presentence is bothe one, and the futuretence is the optatiue mode also. **1530** PALSGR. 84 The preterperfit tens as *je ay parlé* I have spoken. **1591** PERCIVALL *Sp. Dict.* Cj, The preterperfectence, the time perfectly past. *a* **1658** CLEVELAND *To T.C.* 26 How canst thou then delight the Sense In Beauty's Preterperfect-tence? **1711** J. GREENWOOD *Eng. Gram.* 114 In Latin the Present Time of the Perfect action is commonly called the *Preterperfect* Time. **1775** ADAIR *Amer. Ind.* 38 They .. sometimes use the preterperfect, instead of the present tense of the indicative mood.

2. *nonce-use.* More than perfect, surpassing the point of perfection.

1848 *Blackw. Mag.* LXIV. 559 Dumas is one of those persons who love .. to furnish the most preterperfect of apartments with the most fabulous of furniture.

†ˌ**preterpluparen'thetical,** *a. Obs. humorous nonce-wd.* [f. after next + PARENTHETICAL.] Excessively addicted to parenthesis; cf. PARENTHETICAL *a.* 2.

1650 B. *Discolliminium* 16 Let him understand that Ignorance is the Grand-mother of mistaken Necessity; mistaken Necessity, the Father-in-law of intended iniquity; and that a preterpluparentheticall head hath seldome a clear and orderly judgement.

ˌ**preterplu'perfect,** *a.* (*sb.*) [ad. late L. *præteritum plusquamperfectum* (Priscian *c* 525), with contraction: see PRETER, PRETERITE, and PLUPERFECT.]

1. *Gram.* = PLUPERFECT *a.* 1. Also *ellipt.* as *sb.* Now *rare* or *Obs.*

1530 PALSGR. 84 The preterplusperfit tens, as *javóye parlé* I had spoken. **1591** PERCIVALL *Sp. Dict.* Cj, The preterpluperfectence, the time more then perfectly past. **1612** BRINSLEY *Pos. Parts* (1669) 33 What time speaks the Præterpluperfect Tense of? *A.* Of that which is more than perfectly past, or past a long while since. **1685** H. MORE *Paralip. Prophet.* ix. 53, ἐγεγόνει being the Preterpluperfect tense. **1799** [see PRETERIMPERFECT]. **1862** CARLYLE *Fredk. Gt.* XIII. xiv. (1872) V. 137 Friedrich .. gave him to know .. that coöperation was henceforth a thing of the preterpluperfect tense.

2. *gen.* or *allusively.* More than 'pluperfect'; superlatively perfect. (Chiefly in humorous use.)

1599 MASSINGER, etc. *Old Law* IV. i, Darest thou call my wife strumpet, thou preterpluperfect tense of a woman! **1652** J. TAYLOR (Water P.) (*title*) Newes from Tenebris: or preterpluperfect nocturnall or night Worke. *c* **1817** HOGG *Tales & Sk.* II. 334 Most sanctimonious and preterpluperfect maiden! I abhor myself for once suspecting your impenetrability. **1892** LOUNSBURY *Stud. Chaucer* I. 348 There are men who, neither in language nor in literature, can be satisfied with perfect propriety. They insist upon what may be termed preterpluperfect propriety.

pre-terrestrial: see PRE- B. 1 d.

†**preter'vection.** *Obs. rare.* [ad. L. *prætervectiōn-em*, n. of action from *prætervehĕre* to carry or convey past, f. *præter*, PRETER- + *vehĕre* to carry.] The action of carrying past a place or station.

1697 POTTER *Antiq. Greece* IV. iv. (1715) 189 The Place he produces out of Eunapius to that Purpose [παρακομίζειν] seems rather to denote the Praetervection of the Body by some Place, than its Elation from the House wherein it was prepar'd for Burial.

pre'test, *v.* [PRE- A. 1.] *trans.* To test beforehand; *spec.* in *Psychol.*, to test in advance (the efficacy of questions or the methods of administration for use in a projected test). Hence **pre'tested** *ppl. a.*, **pre'testing** *vbl. sb.*

1949 C. I. HOVLAND et al. *Exper. Mass Communication* ii. 26 Qualitative pretesting consisted of face-to-face interviewing... After the first few interviews .. the items were revised and pretested again. **1949** R. K. MERTON *Social Theory* vi. 163 'Pre-testing' in social affairs is only a rough approximation. **1951** in M. McLuhan *Mech. Bride* (1967) 41/2 Columbia Broadcasting System uses Dr. Flesch's findings to pre-test radio scripts. **1969** N. A. ROSEN *Leadership Change & Work-Group Dynamics* (1970) i. 20 Pre-testing, even on a small number of workers, would have led to communication among them. **1970** I. L. HOROWITZ *Masses in Lat. Amer.* i. 7 It further assumes that the masses have an historical mission and a pre-tested political direction. **1970** D. GOLDRICH et al. in *Ibid.* v. 176 The interview schedule had been pretested in Santiago. **1977** *Sci. Amer.* Apr. 25/1 The requirement does not apply to spherical tanks because they are built under conditions where the welds can be pretested for integrity.

'**pretest,** *sb.* and *a.* **A.** *sb. Psychol.* [PRE- A. 2.] An experimental test designed to assess the efficacy of questions or methods of administration intended for use in a projected test. Also occas., a preliminary or qualifying test. Also *attrib.*

1949 C. I. HOVLAND et al. *Exper. Mass Communication* ii. 26 The purpose of the quantitative pretest was the advance determination of the approximate distribution of answers to each question and the relationship between questions. **1966** J. S. BRUNER *Beyond Information Given* (1974) xviii. 321 The experiment was carried out with six- and seven-year-olds and began with a pretest. **1970** *Jrnl. Gen. Psychol.* LXXXIII. 240 After the pretest, all rats were given Richter-type tests for 30 consecutive days. **1971** *Ibid.* LXXXIV. 99 Gross differences in motor performance .. were reduced by training all *S*s to asymptote during a pretest session. **1972** *Jrnl. Social Psychol.* LXXXVI. 14 The first, a pretest phase, was used to select 'high conformers'. **1973** *Jrnl. Genetic Psychol.* CXXII. 101 Their .. pretest scores dropped significantly. **1976** *Columbus* (Montana) *News* 10 June 1/3 You have to have passed your 15th birthday and a pretest.

B. *adj.* (With hyphen.) [PRE- B. 2.] Existing before a test.

1960 *Farmer & Stockbreeder* 2 Feb. 76/1 The Board explains that daily gain on test has been introduced as a measurement of growth which is not complicated either by pre-test environment or the weekly slaughtering routine.

†**pre'tex,** *v. Obs.* [ad. L. *prætexĕre* to weave before or in front, to border; to place before as a covering, to cloak, disguise, pretend; f. *præ*, PRE- A. 4 + *texĕre* to weave.]

1. *trans.* To put forward as a pretext; to allege as a reason or excuse; to pretend; = PRETEXT *v.*

1545 JOYE *Exp. Dan.* xii. 210 Leste their rasshnes (as thei pretex it) shuld confirme the enimies of the gospell. **1562** in *Ressoning betuix Crosraguell & Knox* B iij b, Thairfore keip your promes, and pretex na ioukrie be my Lorde of Cassillis writing.

2. To cover or shield with a pretext; to cloak.

1548 PATTEN *Exped. Scotl.* L j b, Pretexyng this his great vngodlines .. with coolour of religion. ? *a* **1566** EDWARDS *Sonn.* i. (R.), O neuer let ambition's pride, (Too oft pretexed with our Country's good) .. Or thirst of wealth thee from her banks divide.

pretext (ˈpriːtɛkst), *sb.*[1] [ad. L. *prætextus* (*u*-stem) outward display, show, a pretext, f. ppl. stem of *prætexĕre*: see prec. (or ad. L. *prætext-um* a pretext, orig. pa. pple. neut. of the same). So F. *prétexte* (16th c. in Littré). Formerly (until *c* 1840–50) stressed *pre'text.*]

That which is put forward to cover the real purpose or object; the ostensible reason or motive of action; an excuse, pretence, specious plea.

1513 MORE *Rich. III*, Wks. 58/1 The deuise of some conuenient pretext, for which the peple should be content, to depose the prince. **1591** SPENSER *M. Hubberd* 988 We may coulor it with some pretext. **1651** HOBBES *Leviath.* III. xl. 255 A pretext .. to discharge themselves of their obedience. **1736** BERKELEY *Querist* App. §80 Such cash should not be liable to seizure on any pretext. **1790** BURKE *Fr. Rev.* Wks. V. 159 Publick benefit would soon become the pretext, and perfidy and murder the end. **1810** SCOTT *Lady of L.* II. xxviii, The same pretext of sylvan game. **1842** TENNYSON *Gardener's Daughter* 188 Henceforward squall nor storm Could keep me from that Eden where she dwelt. Light pretexts drew me. **1856** KANE *Arct. Expl.* II. xxiv. 241, I .. sent them to their village under pretext of obtaining birds. **1883** H. DRUMMOND *Nat. Law in Spir. W.* (1884) 89 To sit down on the outermost edge of the Holy Ground on the pretext of taking off their shoes.

†**b.** A claim or pretension asserted. *rare*[−1].

1633 STAFFORD *Pac. Hib.* II. iii. 139 Praying that his life might bee spared, in policie of State; for whilest hee lived, his brother Iohn could not make any pretext to the Earledome.

†**pretext,** *a.* (*sb.*[2]) *Obs. rare.* Also **præ-**. [ad. L. (*toga*) *prætexta* a toga bordered or edged with purple, pa. pple. fem. of *prætexĕre* to edge, border: see PRETEX. So F. *prétexte.*]

1. Woven in front; bordered, edged, fringed (in quots., with purple); *pretext gown* = PRÆTEXTA.

1533 BELLENDEN *Livy* I. iii. (S.T.S.) I. 25 Be exempill of þir Ethruschis þe sadill currill and þe pretext govne, with mony vthir ornamentis .. war brocht vp in rome. *Ibid.* II. xxiii. 224 þe ornamentis consulare, þat is to say, þe axis, the sadill curall, the pretext govne.

2. Of a person: Wearing the PRÆTEXTA.

a **1659** LOVELACE *Poems* (1864) 251 A senator prætext, that knewst to sway The fasces.

B. *sb.* = PRÆTEXTA.

1598 GRENEWEY *Tacitus' Ann.* I. i. (1622) 2 His earnest desire was, they should be called Princes of youth, and chosen Consuls elect, before they had cast of their prætext or infants garments. *Ibid.* XII. ix. 167 Britannicus in his pretext, and Nero in triumphing attire.

Hence †**pre'texted** *ppl. a. Obs. rare*[−1], bordered.

1647 R. STAPYLTON *Juvenal* 154 Æmilius Lepidus .. by decree of senate had a statue in his pretexted purple and golden bulla's (or bubbles) set up in the capitol.

pretext (prɪˈtɛkst), *v.* [a. F. *prétexter* (17th c. in Littré) to take as a pretext, f. *prétexte* PRETEXT *sb.*[1]] *trans.* To use or assign as a pretext; to allege as an excuse; to pretend. Also *absol.*

1606 [see PRETEXTED *ppl. a.*[1]]. *a* **1797** H. WALPOLE *Mem. Geo. II* (1822) I. 378 A decency was observed, and conscience always pretexted. **1849** MISS PARDOE *Francis I*, II. xiv. 377 He retraced his steps to the Rue de Fer; where, pretexting business he entered the shop of the armourer.

1885 C. BLACK in *Eng. Illustr. Mag.* III. 241 Pretexting a sprained wrist as excuse for a strange hand.

†**pretex'tatian**, *a.* *Obs.* In 8 præ-. [f. L. *prætextāt-us* clothed with the *toga prætexta* (see PRETEXT *a.*), in *ætās prætextāta* (Gellius) + -IAN.] Of or pertaining to those who wore the *prætexta* (i.e. to children under seventeen years of age).

1716 M. DAVIES *Athen. Brit.* II. 355 Children, under the said Septennian Age; for, from those Years upwards to the Prætextatian term of fifteen or upwards, the Doctor prescribes [etc.].

pre'textatized, *ppl. a.* *nonce-wd.* [f. L. *prætextāt-us* veiled, disguised, hence (of words) equivocal, unchaste.] Rendered equivocal or obscene.

1853 BADHAM *Halieut.* (1854) 507 Debased and pretextatized as the Imperial city had become in Juvenal's time, no Roman was a match for them.

pre'texted, *ppl. a.*[1] [f. PRETEXT *v.* + -ED[1].] Put forward or used as a pretext; pretended.

1606 FORD *Honor Tri.* (1843) 25 Such these are, who.. import the pretexted glosse of beauties name. **1864** *Realm* 23 Mar. 2 What the real truth is with regard to the pretexted Holy Alliances and retrograde policy of the Austrian Government. **1880** *Cornh. Mag.* Jan. 54 He called most of them by their Christian names on some pretexted fiction of cousinship.

pretexted, *ppl. a.*[2]: see after PRETEXT *a.*

†**pre'textuous**, *a.* *Obs. rare.* Also præ- [f. L. *prætextu-s* (*u*-stem: see PRETEXT *sb.*[1]) + -OUS.] Of the nature of a pretext; specious, plausible.

1647 *Quæres presented to his Majesty's Remembr.* 3 To advance the designe with a pretextuous letter, Au Roy. **1649** in *Proc. Comm. Gen. Assembly* (1896) 249 Envyous vnderminers in a singular and praetextuous way aiming at our ruine.

†**pre'texture.** *Obs. rare*[−1]. [f. L. *prætext-*, ppl. stem of *prætexĕre* (see PRETEX) + -URE.] A disguising or cloaking; a pretext.

1618 T. ADAMS *Love's Copy* Wks. 1862 II. 416 Now we have studied both textures of words and pretextures of manners, to shroud dishonesty.

prethe, pre-thee, prethy, obs. ff. PRITHEE.

pretheatre, -theoretical: see PRE- B. 2 a, 1 d.

prethink: PRE- A. 1.

prethoracic, -tibial: see PRE- B. 3.

prethoughtful: see PRE- A. 3.

†**pretifollie.** *Obs. nonce-wd.* Alteration of *trettifollie*, TRE-TRIFOLIE, after PRETTY and FOLLY.

1591 HARINGTON *Orl. Fur.* XXIX. Notes 239 An herbe ..(suppose it to be trettiefolie or pretiefollie) mingled with elder berryes and rew, (which may signifie sage counsell and repentance).

†**pre'tinct**, *v.* *Obs. rare*[−1]. [f. L. *prætinct-*, ppl. stem of *prætingĕre*: see PRE- A. and TINCT *v.*] *trans.* To tinge or imbue beforehand.

1641 LD. J. DIGBY *Sp. in Ho. Comm.* 21 Apr. 11 The eye if it be pretincted with any colour, is vitiated in its discerning.

pretiosity, -tious, obs. ff. PRECIOSITY, -CIOUS.

pretland, obs. Sc. form of PRATTLING *ppl. a.*

†**pre'toir, -oyr(e**, *sb.* and *a.* *Obs.* [a. OF. *pretoire* sb. and adj., ad. L. *prætōrium*, *prætōrius* adj.: see PRÆTORIUM, PRÆTORIAN.] **A.** *sb.* = PRÆTORIUM. **B.** *adj.* = PRÆTORIAL, PRÆTORIAN.

1390 GOWER *Conf.* III. 181 A Romein, Which Consul was of the Pretoire, Whos name was Carmidotoire. **1430–40** LYDG. *Bochas* VIII. i. (MS. Bodl. 263) 367/1 Whilom a prefect in Rome the Cite Of the pretoire. **1485** CAXTON *Chas. Gt.* II. II. iv. 94 In one of the quarters was a gardyn pretoyre meruayllously fayr wherin floures ne fruytes faylled neuer [Fr. *avoit ung pretoire*, i.e. an enclosed yard or space].

pretoir, obs. Sc. form of PRÆTOR.

pretone ('priːtəʊn). *Phonology.* [f. PRE- B. + TONE.] The syllable or vowel preceding the stressed or accented syllable. So **pretonic** (priː'tɒnɪk) *a.*, coming immediately before the stressed or tonic syllable; also *absol.* as *sb.*, = PRETONE.

1864 WEBSTER, *Pretonic*, before a tone; as, a pretonic sound or note. **1874** DAVIDSON *Hebr. Gram.* (1892) 46, *a* in the pretone, or *a* in the tone, or *a* in both places. **1884** C. H. TOY in *Amer. Jrnl. Philol.* Dec. 499 The pretonic vowel is either heavy or lightest, that is, shᵉwā... The number of occurrences of shᵉwā in pretone is considerable. **1895** W. M. LINDSAY *Short Lat. Gram.* 29 The new law of accentuation ..brought with it the possibility of a new variety, namely, suppression of the syllable preceding the accent, Pretonic syncope. **1953** K. JACKSON *Lang. & Hist. Early Brit.* II. 634 There is also..an *h-* prefixed to vowels; but in Brittonic there was not the same extension of this to pretonics not originally ending in *-s* in British that there was in Pr.I. **1973** *Archivum Linguisticum* IV. 24 This kind of system may be dealt with in the same way as the different pretonics of the individual tones.

Hence **pre'tonically** *adv.*, as regards a pretone.

1953 K. JACKSON *Lang. & Hist. Early Brit.* II. 322 It [*sc.* a Latin pronunciation (ɑu)] is not reduced pretonically to *ŏ*; e.g. *awdur*, *cawlai*.

pretor, -orian, -ory, etc.: see PRÆTOR, etc.

pre-torture, -tour, -tracheal, etc.: see PRE- A. 1, B. 2 a, 3, etc.

pre'training, *vbl. sb.* *Psychol.* [PRE- A. 1.] Training which takes place in advance of an experiment or test; also *attrib.* Hence (as a back-formation) **pre'train** *v. trans.*

1955 *Jrnl. Exper. Psychol.* L. 180 This pretraining has generally consisted of verbal paired-associates learning in which stimuli are the same as, or substitutes for, those of the motor task. **1957** J. S. BRUNER *Beyond Information Given* (1974) i. 35 A subject is first given some pretraining, in one of four pretraining groups. **1959** *Psychol. Abstr.* XXXIII. 764/1 The stability of generalized expectancies (GEs) developed under 2 pretraining conditions and with differing frequencies of past reinforcement. **1971** *Nature* 9 July 124/2 Cats were pre-trained, using classical conditioning. **1973** *Jrnl. Genetic Psychol.* CXXII. 17 Children aged 2-½ to 5-½ were pretrained on two three-choice simple discrimination problems. **1974** *Psychol. Abstr.* LII. 1244/1 In Exp II..the type of response in pretraining..was varied.

pre-transformational: see PRE- B. 1 d.

pre'treat, *v.* [PRE- A. 1.] *trans.* To treat beforehand. Hence **pre'treated** *ppl. a.*

1934 *Jrnl. Physical Chem.* XXXVIII. 795 Comparing the form of the characteristic curve of the normally developed strip S with those of the strips that were pre-treated with the iron citrate solutions..the latter are steeper. **1950** *Nucleonics* Mar. 48/1 It may be necessary to pretreat and purify the water before using it in the pile. **1956** *Nature* 21 Jan. 136/1 A variation of the relative concentrations..may account for the variation..of the shape of light curves observed in differently pretreated algae. **1963** *Mechanical World* CXLIII. 17/1 Of recent years the production of pre-treated metal surfaces has increased enormously. **1975** *Jrnl. Immunol. Methods* VIII. 383 Peritoneal macrophages.. cultivated for 48 hr on glass pretreated with poly-L-lysine.

pre'treatment, *sb.* and *a.* **A.** *sb.* [PRE- A. 2.] Treatment given beforehand. Also *attrib.*

1925 *Jrnl. Forestry* XXIII. 921 Within each pretreatment the seed experienced variations of that treatment. **1946** *Nature* 23 Nov. 748/2 Effective control was measured six weeks after treatment, all plots in this case having received pre-treatment with nitro-chalk seven days in advance of the weed-killer application. **1955** *New Biol.* XVIII. 88 Freshly excised grafts, after pre-treatment with 15 per cent glycerol in Ringer, were sealed off in glass tubes and frozen. **1961** *Times* 12 Apr. 17/6 The coil of steel is passed through chemical pre-treatment baths. **1973** *Times* 29 Oct. 20/7 Liquid wastes from all trade and industrial sources, broadly speaking, drain without pre-treatment in to the River Tees or into Tees Bay. **1978** *Jrnl. R. Soc. Arts* CXXVI. 686/1 The aim of pre-treatments is to increase the action of the adhesive bonding forces by eliminating greases, dirt and the oxides which exist on the surface.

B. *adj.* [PRE- B. 2.] Existing before treatment.

1961 *Lancet* 2 Sept. 499/2 This..gave an opportunity for estimation of the pretreatment level of serum-cholesterol. **1962** *Ibid.* 12 May 989/2 In 1 other patient infected with a proteus strain, organisms isolated during and after treatment were more resistant than the pre-treatment cultures. **1972** *Jrnl. Social Psychol.* LXXXVI. 84 The.. pretreatment mean attitude score for the nine treatments is approximately equal.

pretrial, *sb.* and *a.* **A.** *sb.* (Stressed *'pretrial.*) [PRE- A. 2.] A preliminary hearing before a trial. Also *attrib.* *U.S.*

1938 E. J. ELLISON in *Christian Science Monitor* 15 June (Weekly Mag.) 3/1 Why not have a special judge to clear out the legal underbrush, and call it a 'pre-trial'. *Ibid.* 3/2 Some two weeks before a case is scheduled for trial, the opposing parties appear before a pre-trial judge. **1938** *Daily Progress* (Charlottesville, Va.) 18 Aug. 4/1 The 'pre-trial' system was introduced in Detroit six years ago. **1970** *Daily Colonist* (Victoria, B.C.) 23 Apr. 10/1 Black Panther chairman Bobby Seale was accused at his pre-trial hearing of ordering the death of a Panther suspected of turning informer. **1971** *N.Y. Law Jrnl.* 23 Nov. 17/5 If case cannot be settled the Part I judge will assign the case to a pre-trial examiner, who will, with the aid of the attorneys, prepare the pre-trial order. **1976** *National Observer* (U.S.) 17 Jan. 2/2 The judge had ordered the papers not to print stories about a pretrial hearing for a murder defendant because the judge did not want prospective jurors to be influenced by arguments made at the hearing. **1978** *Chicago* June 116/3 Tom Sullivan sat at the defense table in the Hanrahan case, and he handled pre-trial matters for Kemer's co-defendant.

B. *adj.* (Stressed *pre'trial.*) [PRE- B. 2.] Of or pertaining to the period before a trial or trials.

1948 B. VESEY-FITZGERALD *Bk. Dog* 749 Whereas in pre-trial days the range [of sheepdog] was severely restricted, nowadays, as a result of trials, the scope for selection is nation-wide. **1971** *Times* 20 Mar. 11 Most have already spent more than a year in jail awaiting trial, and pretrial detention will be deducted from their sentences. **1978** *Times* 3 Nov. 17 (*heading*) Barristers' immunity from claims in negligence in pre-trial work narrowed. *Ibid.* 13 Nov. 7/8 Mr. Nazaryan, who has been in pre-trial detention for almost a year, is charged with anti-Soviet agitation and propaganda.

†**pre'trude**, *v.* *Obs. rare.* [f. PRE- A. 4 + L. *trūdĕre* to thrust.] *trans.* To thrust or drive in front or before one.

1693 *Phil. Trans.* XVII. 662 Those..which are not small enough to pass those Straits.., being just admitted, stick there till other appelling Substances give them a farther Comminution, and so pretrude them along.

prette, obs. rare pa. t. of PRIDE *v.*

prettied: see PRETTY *v.*

prettification (ˌprɪtɪfɪ'keɪʃən). [f. PRETTIFY *v.*: see -FICATION.] The fact or process of making pretty; prettifying.

1909 in WEBSTER. **1920** *Times Lit. Suppl.* 23 Sept. 617/1 Such work is..the counterfeit of romance. It gives us, not a celebration of life, but a prettification of it. **1930** A. I. NAZAROFF *Tolstoy* vi. 97 He is described very realistically, without the slightest trace of prettification or sugar-coating. **1966** *New Statesman* 23 Dec. 935/2 The sanctification of emotional impotence. The prettification of stultified tragedy. **1969** *Daily Tel.* 10 July 21/3 This [manner], together with some prettification of the action, deprived the play of the savagery that is surely there. **1978** *Listener* 20 July 76/3 The writer, Georgina Masson..is up in arms over the prettification of the cemetery.

prettify ('prɪtɪfaɪ), *v.* Also **prettyfy**. [f. PRETTY *a.* + -FY] *trans.* To make pretty; to represent prettily in a painting or writing. Also *fig.* Hence **'prettified** *ppl. a.*; **'prettifier**, one who prettifies; **'prettifying** *vbl. sb.*

1850 F. TROLLOPE in F. E. Trollope *Life* (1895) II. xi. 203 Keep your money to prettify your house, dear son. **1855** HAWTHORNE *Eng. Note-Bks.* (1870) I. 237, I rather wonder that people of real taste should help nature out, and beautify her, or perhaps rather *prettify* her so much as they do. **1867** G. DU MAURIER *Let.* in D. du Maurier *Young George du Maurier* (1951) 273 Then D and I walked through the lovely Bois de Boulogne to the Mare d'Auteuil which has been brutally modernised and prettyfied. **1889** *Cent. Dict.*, Prettified. **1890** *Univ. Rev.* 15 June 181 He has prettified his market town, and thereby lost much of its reality. **1902** *Academy* 12 Apr. 379/2 Keats said it [Leigh Hunt's angelic optimism] did him positive injury by its eternal prettyfying of fine things, and he might have added its eternal prettyfying of common things. **1919** B. TARKINGTON *Let.* 14 June in *On Plays* (1959) 13 You know..why all the magazines *haf* to have the prettified girl cover. **1934** *Sun* (Baltimore) 2 Apr. 8/1 (*heading*) Prettifying war. *Ibid.*, These endeavors [to outlaw certain forms of warfare] are based on the assumption that we are making progress if somehow we can manage to prettify war. **1936** L. C. DOUGLAS *White Banners* iii. 63 A man doesn't try to prettify himself very much, or make himself over to look different. He wants to be important for owning something rather than being something. **1955** *Times* 24 Aug. 7/4 To anyone who once heard a chanty at sea, such prettified verses, however musical, will always seem a travesty of their originals. **1960** W. MILLER *Canticle for Leibowitz* xiv. 151 A place of majesty that overawed the would-be prettifiers. **1970** *Daily Tel.* 21 Feb. 8/5 The 19th-century weakness for prettifying the lives of great men. **1971** P. GRESSWELL *Environment* 89 Too much prettyfying is damaging enough but the bleak 'serviceable' attitude to details causes the more widespread damage... For this reason, many housing estates..are depressing. **1973** *Times* 30 Oct. 14/8 The Cubist works are prettified exercises in taste. **1976** *Early Music* Oct. 402/2 The *Dido* gathering should be suave and elegant but not prettified or frivolous.

prettily ('prɪtɪlɪ), *adv.* Forms: see PRETTY. [f. PRETTY *a.* + -LY[2].] In a pretty manner.

†**1.** In a cunning or clever manner; cleverly, ingeniously, skilfully, neatly. *Obs.*

14.. *A.B.C.* 6 in *Pol. Rel. & L. Poems* (1866) 244 A bok hym is browt..Pratylych I-wrout. *c* **1489** CAXTON *Sonnes of Aymon* xi. 282 They shoved theym so prately agenste a pyller of marbell stone that their eyen lepte oute of theyr hedes. *c* **1530** *Crt. Love* 420 Though thow seest a faut right at thyne y, Excuse it blyve, and glose it pretily. **1579–80** NORTH *Plutarch* (1676) 881 They were driven to give ground; and so prettily retired, defending the Consull the best they could. **1589** *Hay any Work* B j, You can shift of an haynous accusation very prettily. **1590** SHAKS. *Mids. N.* II. ii. 53 Lysander riddles very prettily. **1594** —— *Rich. III*, III. i. 134 To mittigate the scorne he giues his Vnckle, He prettily and aptly taunts himselfe. **1667** PEPYS *Diary* 23 Sept., I find how prettily this cunning Lord can be partial and dissemble it in this case.

†**b.** To the point; expressively, aptly, neatly.

1584 COGAN *Haven Health* ii. (1636) 20 When hee [Socrates] was laughed to scorne of Alcibiades, for so doing, he answered him very prettily. **1605** CAMDEN *Rem., Epigr.* 16 Which a Poet..expressed thus very briefly, and for that age pretily. **1625** BACON *Ess., Truth* (Arb.) 501 Mountaigny saith prettily [etc.]. **1776** GIBBON *Decl. & F.* i. (1846) I. 12 It is prettily remarked by an ancient historian who had fought against them, that the effusion of blood was the only circumstance which distinguished a field of battle from a field of exercise.

2. In a way that pleases the eye, ear, or æsthetic sense; beautifully but not grandly; 'nicely'.

In nursery language children were told to *eat, ask, behave prettily.*

1423 JAS. I. *Kingis Q.* cliii, Lytill fischis..In a rout can swym So prattily, and dressit tham to sprede Thaire curall fynnis. **1463** *Plumpton Corr.* (Camden) 8 Your daughter & myn..speaketh prattely & french, & hath near hand learned her sawter. *a* **1500** *Flower & Leaf* 89 Therin a goldfinch leping pretily Fro bough to bough. **1573–80** BARET *Alv.* P 661 Pretilie or pleasantly spoken, *lepide aut facete dictum.* **1653** JER. TAYLOR *Serm. for Year* I. xx. 263 It looks prettily, but rewards the eye, as burning basons do, with intolerable circles of reflected fire. **1703** MOXON *Mech. Exerc.* 246 The Ax stroaks..on the Brick,..if they be streight and parallel one to another, look very prettily. **1754** RICHARDSON

Grandison I. xv. 92 So prettily loth to speak till spoken to. **1800** Mrs. Hervey *Mourtray Fam.* II. 237, I mean to be so prettily behaved, as to become the darling of all the old, sober, stupid folks in the kingdom. **1852** Mrs. Stowe *Uncle Tom's C.* xxvi, Eva said, 'Topsy, you arrange flowers very prettily'. **1857** Wood *Com. Obj. Sea Shore* 27 The body is prettily banded with multitudes of narrow dark markings. **1865** Dickens *Mut. Fr.* i. xvi, Her prettily-insolent eyebrows. **1872** Black *Adv. Phaeton* xxx, If you had only asked me prettily. **1883** 'Annie Thomas' *Mod. Housewife* 70 A prettily-worked holland blouse.

b. Gently, softly, quietly. Now *dial.*

c **1500** *Melusine* 9 The kinge hyed hym, & helped to sette her on horsbak moche prately [*orig.* doulcement]. **1533** More *Apol.* 93 b, Wyth that worde putte the tone pretely backe with his hande, and all to buffet the tother about the face. **1674** Ray *N.C. Words* 37 *Prattily*, softly. **1828** *Craven Gloss.* (ed. 2), *Prattily*, softly, delicately. 'Gang prattily, er thou'lt wacken 't barn'. **1883** *Almondb. & Huddersf. Gloss.* s.v., A tap runs pratly when it lets out only a small stream in proportion to its size.

†**3.** Considerably, fairly, passably, moderately; = pretty *adv.* 1 (but also qualifying vbs.). *Obs.*

1533 More *Answ. Poysoned Bk.* Wks. 1037/2 Tyndal the captain of our Englyshe heretikes..was taken for full pretyly learned to. **1540** Coverdale *Confut. Standish* (1547) I iv, Ye can prately well graunt to a thing in one place, and denie the same in another. **1621** Lady M. Wroth *Urania* 201 Hauing now recouerd his strength pretily well. **1656** Sanderson *Serm.* Pref. (1689) 67 By their Education prettily well principled. **1823** Byron *Juan* xii. lxxv, I..had an ear that served me prettily. **1826** Cobbett *Rur. Rides* (1885) II. 7 The English money used to be spent prettily in that country.

prettiness ('prɪtɪnɪs). [f. pretty *a.* + -ness.] The quality of being pretty.

1. 'Beauty without dignity; neat elegance without elevation' (J.); beauty of a slight, diminutive, dainty, or childish kind, without stateliness.

1530 Palsgr. 257/2 Prattynesse, *mignonnerie.* **1653** H. More *Antid. Ath.* ii. ix. (1712) 65 There being..that Majesty and Stateliness, as in the Lion, the Horse, the Eagle, and Cock; or that grave Awfulness, as in..Mastiffs; or Elegancy and Prettiness, as in your lesser Dogs, and most sorts of Birds; all which are several Modes of Beauty. **1663** Cowley *Ess. in Verse & Prose, Greatness*, If I were ever to fall in love again..it would be, I think, with Prettiness, rather than with Majestical Beauty. **1707** *Reflex. upon Ridicule* 190 Tis vast Impertinence in an Old Woman, to think to set up for Prettiness. **1832** W. Irving *Alhambra* II. 13 A neatness, a grace, and an all-pervading prettiness, that were perfectly fascinating. **1859** Lang *Wand. India* 2 These houses..nothing can exceed in prettiness their aspect as they shine in the sun. **1874** J. Fergusson in *Contemp. Rev.* Oct. 755 The vigour of the crude colouring..of the staircase at Cardiff stands in strange contrast with the feeble prettiness of Worcester Chapel.

†**2.** Pleasantness, agreeableness. *Obs.*

1602 Shaks. *Ham.* iv. v. 189 Thought, and Affliction, Passion, Hell it selfe, She turns to Fauour, and to prettinesse. **1658** Evelyn *Diary* 27 Jan., He [a child] was all life, all prettinesse, far from morose, sullen, or childish in any thing he said or did.

†**b.** Cleverness; amusingness. *Obs.*

1674 R. Godfrey *Inj. & Ab. Physic* 90 But the prettiness of the Knack was that Master Docter who denyed strong-beer to his two Patients..was almost angry with his servant for not quickly bringing up a Cup of the Best-beer to quench his thirst.

3. with *a* and *pl.* That which is pretty; a pretty act, thing, feature, etc.; a pretty ornament.

1649 Jer. Taylor *Gt. Exemp.* Disc. i. §10 Receiving and ministring respectively, perpetual prettinesses of love, and fondnesse. **1686** W. de Britaine *Hum. Prud.* xiv. 64, I ever had a Noble Affection for that excellent Sex, as great Instruments of good, and the prettinesses of Society. **1826** Miss Mitford *Village* Ser. ii. *Copse* 47 All this and a thousand amusing prettinesses..does my beautiful greyhound perform. **1832** *Ibid.* Ser. v. *C. Cleveland* 202 The nuptial prettinesses of cake, and gloves, and silver favours. **1865** Trollope *Belton Est.* i, The prettinesses of Somersetshire are among those which are the least known. **1888** Miss Braddon *Fatal Three* i. i, The room was full of flowers and prettinesses of every kind. **1893** Mrs. C. Praed *Outlaw & Lawm.* I. 62 It was always Elsie who did the prettinesses..whether it was in our ball dresses or our parlour.

4. Affected, trivial, or conceited beauty of expression, style, or execution in literature or art. Also, an instance of this, a prettyism.

1660 H. More *Myst. Godl.* v. xiv. 172 The learned Hugo Grotius..the ingenuities and prettinesses of whose expositions had almost imposed upon my self to a belief that there might be some such sense also of the Revelation as he drives at. **1690** Norris *Beatitudes* (1692) 118 There is more prettiness in the Expression, than truth in the Notion. **1712** Steele *Spect.* No. 474 ¶4 Their distinguishing Mark is certain Prettinesses of Foreign Languages, the Meaning of which they could have better express'd in their own. **1751** Smollett *Per. Pic.* (1779) II. lxvii. 233 He..uttered a thousand prettinesses in the way of compliment. **1794** Mathias *Purs. Lit.* (1798) 56 Before they attempt by prettinesses, glittering words, points, conceits, and forced thoughts, to sacrifice propriety and just imagery to the rage of mere novelty. **1887** *Leeds Mercury* 8 Jan. 10/1 A scholar who delights in the delicacies and prettinesses of scholarship.

pretty ('prɪtɪ), *a.* (*sb.*) Forms: α. 1 prættiȝ; pætiȝ, petiȝ; 5 prati, 5–6 praty, pratie, 5–7 (9 *dial.*) pratty, 6 prayty, pratye, prattie, 8–9 *Sc.* proty, protty. β. 5–7 prety, 6–7 pret(t)ie, 6– pretty. γ. 6 preatie, -ty, prittie, 7 preety, prity, 7–8 (9 *dial.*) pritty (8 pritey). δ. 9 *dial.* **perty, pirty, purty, pooty, putty.** [OE. *prættiȝ*, f. *prætt*, prat *sb.*[1], trick, wile, craft, akin to Icel. *prettugr* tricky, deceitful, f. *prettr* trick; also to EFris. and obs. Du. *prettig* sportive, funny, humorous, f. *pret* joke, sport, fun, pleasure (Doornkaat-Koolman, Franck):—WGer. **pratti-* or **pratta*; also, with metathesis, Flem. *pertig*, MDu. (*ghe*)*pertich* brisk, clever, roguish ('*pertigh* Fland. argutulus, fallax', Kilian), f. MDu. *parte*, early mod.Du. *perte, parte, pratte* trick, deceit, cunning (Kilian), Du. *part* trick, prank.

The history has several points of obscurity. The OE. *prættiȝ* appears to be rare and late; it also varies in an unusual way (but cf. *spræc, spæc* speech) with *pætiȝ, petiȝ* or rather *pǣtiȝ, pétiȝ*. After the OE. period the word is unknown till the 15th c., when it becomes all at once frequent in various senses, none identical with the OE., though derivable from it. The earlier forms *prati, pratty*, etc., also correspond to the OE. *prættiȝ*; but *prety, pretty* have *e*, like the ON. and continental words; while *preaty, preety, pritty* may represent OE. **prǣtiȝ*, **prétiȝ* (whence *pǣtiȝ, pétiȝ*). The current spoken word is *pritty*, but spelt *pretty*. The metathesized *pirty, purty*, etc., agree with the usual treatment of *re, ri*, in s.w. dial. (cf. *urd, burches, Urchet, urn*, for *red, breeches, Richard, run*), and with the Flem. and Du. forms above. (Celtic and Latin derivations sometimes conjectured are unfounded.) The sense-development, 'deceitful, tricky, cunning, clever, skilful, admirable, pleasing, nice, pretty', has parallels, more or less extensive, in *canny, clever, cunning* (cf. mod. U.S. use), *fine, nice*, and other adjectives.]

A. *adj.* **I.** In OE.

†**1.** Cunning, crafty, wily, artful, astute. *Obs.*

c **1000** Ælfric *Colloq.* in Wright *Voc.* 12 Vultis esse versipelles, aut milleformes, in mendaciis vafri, in loquelis astuti? *Gloss*, Wille ȝe beon prættiȝe oþþe þusenthiwe on leasungum lytiȝe on spræcum gleawlice? *c* **1000** —— *Voc.* ibid. 47/2 *Sagax, vel gnarus, vel astutus, vel callidus*, petiȝ, *vel* abered.

II. From 15th century.

2. a. Of persons: Clever, skilful; apt. *Obs.* or *arch.*

The sense in some of the quots. is uncertain.

c **1400** *Destr. Troy* 2622 A praty man of pure wit, protheus he hight. *c* **1440** *York Myst.* xx. 276 He schall (and he haue liff) Proue till a praty swayne. **1570** Levins *Manip.* 112/8 Prétie, *scitus, facetus.* **1577–87** Holinshed *Chron.* II. 44/1 Andrew White a good humanician, a pretie philosopher. **1712** Arbuthnot *John Bull* iii. viii, 'There goes the prettiest fellow in the world..for managing a jury'.

b. Of things: Ingeniously or cleverly made or done; ingenious, artful, clever. *Obs.* or *arch.*

c **1440** *Gesta Rom.* xiv. 46 (Harl. MS.) My son..woll with his praty wordis & pleys make me foryete my anger. *c* **1470** Henry *Wallace* vii. 133 The prety wand, I trow be myn entent, Assignes rewlle and cruell jugement. **1547** *Bk. Marchauntes* fiv, A gallant naminge hym selfe an aulmosiner ..played a prety gewgaw. **1565** Jewel *Def. Apol.* ii. (1609) 151 When the right Key of Knowledge was lost and gone, it was time to deuise some other prety pick-locks to worke the feat. **1589** *Hay any Work* B j, A very pretty way to escape. **1671** tr. *Palafox's Conq. China* vi. 119 The King..at last thought of a very pretty way to suppress him, and this was by a stratagem. **1707** Mortimer *Husb.* (1721) I. 84 They have in Kent a pretty way of saving of Labour in the digging of Chalk.

3. A general epithet of admiration or appreciation corresponding nearly to 'fine' in its vaguest sense, or the modern 'nice': excellent, admirable, commendable; pleasing, satisfactory, agreeable. **a.** Of persons: Having the proper appearance, manners, or qualities of a man, etc.; conventionally applied to soldiers: Brave, gallant, stout, war-like (chiefly *Sc.*). ***pretty fellow***, a fine fellow, a 'swell', a fop: common in 18th century. Now *arch.* exc. in *U.S.*

c **1400** *Destr. Troy* 10815 A prouynse of prise, & praty men in. **1483** *Cath. Angl.* 290/1 Praty, *prestans.* **1519** *Interl. Four Elements* (Percy Soc.) 17 Than hold downe thy hede lyke a prety man, and take my blyssyng. **1570–6** Lambarde *Peramb. Kent* (1826) 217 The Bishop of Rochester stept into the Pulpit, like a pretie man, and gave the Auditorie a clerkly collation, and Preachement. **1649** Bp. Guthrie *Mem.* (1748) 28 If it had not been that the said Francis, with the help of two pretty men that attended him, rescued him out of their barbarous hands. **1660** Pepys *Diary* 11 May, Dr. Clerke, who I found to be a very pretty man and very knowing. **1709** *Tatler* No. 21 ¶4 In Imitation of this agreeable Being, is made that Animal we call a Pretty Fellow; who being just able to find out, that what makes Sophronius acceptable, is a Natural Behaviour; in order to the same Reputation, makes his own an Artificial one. **1728** Fielding *Love in Sev. Masques* i. v, I am afraid, if this Humour continue, it will be as necessary in the Education of a pretty Gentleman to learn to read, as to learn to dance. *a* **1732** Gay *Distress'd Wife* ii, A pretty fellow—that is a fine dress'd man with little sense and a great deal of assurance. **1750** Mrs. Delany in *Life & Corr.* (1861) II. 563 They are pretty people to be with, no ceremony. **1754** Richardson *Grandison* (1781) I. v. 20 By his outward appearance he may pass for one of your pretty fellows, for he dresses very gaily. **1768** Ross *Helenore* iii. 118 Tooming faulds or ca'ing of a glen, Was ever deem'd the deed of protty men. **1814** Scott *Wav.* xvii, He..observed they were pretty men, meaning, not handsome, but stout warlike fellows. **1824** —— *Redgauntlet* Let. xi, He gaed out with other pretty men in the Forty-five. **1844** Thackeray *B. Lyndon* xvii, I was a pretty fellow of the first class. **1878** J. H. Beadle *Western Wilds* xxiv. 387 A half-breed squaw, about as 'pretty' as a wild-cat struck with a club. **1886** Stevenson *Kidnapped* i, A pretty lad like you should get to Cramond..in two days of walk. **1891** 'Mark Twain' tr. *Hoffman's Slovenly Peter* (1935, Ltd. Ed.) 25 'Try how pretty you can be Till I come again,' said she. 'Docile be, and good and mild.' **1938** *Amer. Speech* XIII. 6/2 *Pretty*,.. good; fine; excellent. 'He was a real pretty ball player.'

b. Of things: Fine, pleasing, nice; proper. Freq. in negative contexts. Also in phr. ***to say pretty things***, to speak consolingly or in a condescending manner.

1566 J. Alday tr. *Boaystuau's Theat. World* K v, There is recited a pretie historie of a noble Romane. **1577** B. Googe *Heresbach's Husb.* ii. (1586) 90 Women haue a prettie dish made of Peares. **1599** B. Jonson *Cynthia's Rev.* iii. i, To read them asleep in afternoones vpon some pretty pamphlet. **1660** R. Coke *Power & Subj.* Pref. 1 Man's thoughts of life and living are odd things; pritty antitheses. **1667** Pepys *Diary* 1 Sept., It is pretty to see how strange everybody looks. **1777** Sheridan *Sch. Scand.* i. i, He has a pretty wit. **1811** A. Constable *Let.* 28 Apr. in J. Constable *Corr.* (1962) I. 63 Uncle D.P.W. here for a pretty week. **1811** Jane Austen *Sense & Sens.* II. v. 80 It was not very pretty of him, not to give you the meeting. **1815** —— *Emma* v, Such a pretty height and size. *c* **1850** *Colloq.* (said of one who had said or done something kind or graceful) It was very pretty of him. **1867** F. Francis *Angling* i. (1880) 25 Roach-fishing is very pretty sport. **1894** J. T. Fowler *Adamnan* Introd. 34 There is a very pretty legend, possibly founded on facts, about his 'call'. **1898** G. B. Shaw *Philanderer* iv. 140 *Paramore.* I can only admire you, and feel how pleasant it is to have you here. *Julia*... And pet me, and say pretty things to me! I wonder you dont offer me a saucer of milk at once! **1931** E. O'Neill *The Haunted* iv, in *Mourning becomes Electra* 246 Peter is coming, and I want everything to be pretty and cheerful. **1937** M. Allingham *Dancers in Mourning* iii. 43 Go out and say pretty things... We'll all back you up. **1957** P. Kemp *Mine were of Trouble* ii. 28, I have learnt something of that frantic advance on Toledo and the final battle. It is not a pretty story. **1973** *Black Panther* 8 Sept. 17/1, I slipped back..and observed some of these same officers... Their tactics weren't very pretty.

c. Used ironically: cf. fine *a.* 12 c. (***to come to***) ***a pretty pass***: see pass *sb.*[2] 7 a.

1538 *Lett. Suppress. Monast.* (Camden) 198 Sum beynge plucked from under drabbes beddes;..wythe suche other praty besynes, off the whyche I have to moche. **1550** Bale *Apol.* 74 Forsoth it is a praty Ambrose. *a* **1650** in Furniv. *Percy Folio* I. 115 Ther was no mete cam her before, Butt she ete itt vp, lesse and' more, That praty fowlle dameselle. **1742** A pretty kettle of fish [see kettle 2 b]. **1754** Richardson *Grandison* IV. iv. 31 Expecting us to bear with their pretty perversenesses. **1809** Malkin *Gil Blas* ii. iv. ¶4 We drank hard, and returned to our employers in a pretty pickle. **1837** Macaulay *Ess., Bacon* (1865) I. 404/2 A dray-man in a passion calls out, 'You are a pretty fellow', with-out suspecting that he is uttering irony. **1842** Thackeray *Miss Tickletoby's Lect.* vi, A pretty pass things are come to, when hussies like this are to be..bepitied. **1845** Disraeli *Sybil* vi. iii, 'And the new police', said Nick. 'A pretty go when a fellow in a blue coat fetches you the Devil's own con on your head'. **1873** Black *Pr. of Thule* xxi, 'Well, young lady..and a pretty mess you have got us into!'

4. Having beauty without majesty or stateliness; beautiful in a slight, dainty, or diminutive way, as opposed to *handsome*.

a. Of persons (usually women or children): Of attractive and pleasing countenance or appearance; comely, bonny.

Pretty is somewhat of a condescending term; we grant it: *beauty* is imperious, and commands our acknowledgement.

c **1440** *Alphabet of Tales* 440 A fayr yong man..and he was so pratie & so defte at yong wommen wex evyn fond on hym. *c* **1440** *Promp. Parv.* 411/2 Praty, *elegans, formosus, elegantulus, formulosus.* **1483** Caxton *G. de la Tour* G ij, He made her to understonde she was fayr and praty. **1530** Palsgr. 776/2 You shall se me waxe pratye [*amignonner*] one of this dayes. **1590** Greene *Never too late* (1600) 61 Her Iuorie front, her pretie chin, Were stales that drew me on to sin. **1616** Hieron *Wks.* I. 588 As the saying is, euery thing is pretie when it is young. **1653** H. Cogan tr. *Pinto's Trav.* xviii. 62 Brought upon the deck, together with a woman and two pretty children. *a* **1717** Parnell *Elegy to Old Beauty* 34 And all that's madly wild, or oddly gay, We call it only pretty Fanny's way. **1722** Hearne *Collect.* (O.H.S.) VII. 373 She was a very pretty Woman, and is so still, only too fat. **18..** (*Ballad*) Where are you going, my pretty maid? **1870** Mrs. H. Wood *G. Canterbury's Will* II. i. 9 He is not a fine child, for he is remarkably small; but he is a very pretty one. **1907** *Daily Chron.* 11 Sept. 4/7 We never call a man 'beautiful'. With 'pretty' and 'lovely', that adjective has become the property of women and children alone.

b. Frequently applied in a coaxing or soothing way, esp. to children.

c **1460** *Towneley Myst.* xii. 477 Hayll, so as I can hayll, praty mytyng! *a* **1529** Skelton *Agst. Garnesche* Poems 1843 I. 127 Bas me, buttyng, praty Cys. **1590** Shaks. *Com. Err.* i. i. 73 Pitteous playnings of the prettie babes. **1607** —— *Timon* iii. i. 15 And what hast thou there vnder thy Cloake, pretty Flaminius? **1611** —— *Wint. T.* iv. iv. 595 My prettiest Perdita. **1684** Bunyan *Pilgr.* ii. 66 Then said Mr. Great-heart to the little ones, Come my pretty Boys, how do you do? **1847** Tennyson *Princ.* iii, While my little one, while my pretty one, sleeps.

c. Of things: Pleasing to the eye, the ear, or the æsthetic sense. (Cf. fair *a.* 1 f, g, 2.)

1472 John Paston in *P. Lett* III. 55 Forget not..to get some goodly ryng, pryse of xxs., or som praty flowyr of the same pryse,..to geve to Jane Rodon. *c* **1489** Caxton *Sonnes of Aymon* vi. 150 The place is praty and fayr and I wyll that it be called Montalban. **1538** J. London in *Lett. & Pap. Hen. VIII*, XIII. No. 1342 (P.R.O.), They haue oon fayer orchard and sondry praty gardens and lodginges. *c* **1586** C'tess Pembroke *Ps.* cxlviii. ii, You pretie starrs in robe of night, As spangles twinckling. **1687** A. Lovell tr. *Thevenot's Trav.* i. 35 They sing several pretty Songs in the Turkish and Persian Languages. **1732** Earl of Oxford in *Portland Papers* VI. (Hist. MSS. Comm.) 164 We stopped at..Narford, the seat of Sir Andrew Fountaine. It is a pretty box. **1802–21** Mrs. Wheeler *Westmld. Dial.* iv. (ed. 3) 87 Ah Lord! its fearful pratty, indeed. **1888** Miss Braddon *Fatal Three* i. ii, She can have a prettier room at the Hook.

d. Often conjoined with *little*; sometimes app. merely expletive: see LITTLE *a.* 3.

?*a*1400 Lydg. *Chorle & Byrde* (Roxb.) 4 He purposed to make Within his hows a praty litill cage. 1529 Lytle pretty pecadulians [see PECCADILIAN]. 1532 More *Confut. Tindale* Wks. 381/1 A lytle pretty sorowe and verye shortely done. 1552 Huloet, Pratye lyttle one, *paruulus.* 1601 Holland *Pliny* II. 503 In his left hand he bare somtime..a little pretty coach. 1864 Tennyson *En. Ard.* 195 This pretty, puny, weakly little one. 1883 Ruskin *Art Eng.* 25 The mother sent me a pretty little note.

e. In phrases: (*as*) ***pretty as paint, as a picture*** (cf. PICTURE *sb.* 2h), ***as a speckled pup***, etc.

Most of the phrases are more or less restricted to the U.S.

1906 *Dialect Notes* III. 151 *Pretty as a speckled pup,*.. exceedingly pretty. 1909 *Ibid.* 359 *Pretty as a picture,*.. very pretty: often used of a fine specimen of fruit. 1922 E. V. Lucas *Genevra's Money* xvi. 112 Now, there's that girl—she's as pretty as paint. If I were the kind of feller that does these things I could make a fool of myself over her. 1926 M. J. Atkinson in J. F. Dobie *Rainbow in Morning* (1965) 88 As pretty as a speckled pup under a new-painted buggy; as pretty as a speckled hen; as pretty as a picture. 1927 *Amer. Speech* Dec. 169 To him 'pretty as a heart flush' was the supremely beautiful. 1927 E. O'Neill *Marco Millions* III. i. 141 Here! Let me get a good look at you! Why, you're still as pretty as a picture and you don't look a day older! 1936 N. Streatfeild *Ballet Shoes* vi. 77 Cook said it was as pretty as a picture, and Clara that it put her in mind of something off a Christmas card. 1976 *Time* 27 Sept. 39/2 Girls are variously 'ugly as homemade soap' or 'pretty as a speckled pup'.

5. a. Considerable in number, quantity, or extent, as in ***a pretty deal, while, way***, etc.; also ***a pretty many*** = a good many; = FAIR *a.* 3b; *Sc.* GEY, GAY *a.* 7. Cf. PRETTY *adv.* 1. Now *arch.* or *dial.*

*c*1485 *E.E. Misc.* (Warton Club) 88 Caste in your colours that schalbe rede afore a pretty whyle, and..let hem boyle togedyris. 1486 *Bk. St. Albans* D ij b, Holde vp yowre hande a praty way of from the Malarde. *a*1535 More *Mery Jest*, etc. 73 in Hazl. *E.P.P.* III. 122 First faire and wele a pretie deale He hyd it in a potte. 1538 London in *Lett. Suppress. Monast.* 234 Catell, wherof I founde praty store. 1542 Udall *Erasm. Apoph.* 224b, Antigonus..stood hangyng downe his hedde a preatie space. 1579–80 North *Plutarch* (1676) 14 A place of some pretty heighth. 1599 Hakluyt *Voy.* II. II. 30 Their bowes be short, and of a pretie strength. 1656 Heylin *Surv. France* 8 Swine also they have in pretty number. 1703 Moxon *Mech. Exerc.* 199 With a pretty strength press the middle of one end of your Work. 1738 tr. *Guazzo's Art Conversation* 152 A Person, who lived a pretty way off. 1852 Thackeray *Esmond* III. i, The transfer of his commission, which brought a pretty sum into his pocket. 1860 Darwin *Let. to Lyell* Sept., Which is a pretty deal more than I can say of some. 1861 Tulloch *Eng. Purit.* iv. 415 In the light..of this word he went a pretty while.

b. ***a pretty penny***, a considerable sum, a good deal of money: see PENNY 9e.

1712 Steele *Spect.* No. 444 ¶4 Charles Ingoltson..has made a pretty Penny by that Asseveration. 1768, etc. [see PENNY 9e]. 1848 Mrs. Gaskell *M. Barton* v, This mourning..will cost a pretty penny. 1930 E. B. White *Let.* 4 July (1976) 93 The Pierce, after some brilliant road work, burned out a generator—which will cost me a pretty penny. 1978 L. Block *Burglar in Closet* i. 4 The attaché case..was a slim model in cocoa Ultrasuede that had cost someone a pretty penny.

†**c.** ***pretty and*** (with another adj.), was formerly used as = PRETTY *adv.* 1. Cf. GEY *a.* b. *Obs.*

1596 Nashe *Saffron Walden* 153 It was but pretie and so, for a Latine Poet after others. 1615 Markham *Eng. Housew.* II. ix. (1668) 184 You shall blink it more by much than was the strong Ale, for it must be pretty and sharp. 1633 T. James *Voy.* 75 The weather..was pretty and warme. *Ibid.* 78 It was pretty and cleere.

†**6.** Mean, petty insignificant. (? Error for *petty*.)

1513 Douglas *Æneis* x. Prol. 90 For, mycht thou comprehend be thine engyne The maist excellent maieste devyne, He mycht be reput a pretty God and mene.

B. *sb.* (The adj. used absol.) **a.** A pretty man, woman, or child; a pretty one; in phr. ***my pretty! my pretties!*** used in addressing people, etc. Also as a form of address, with ellipsis of *my*.

1773 Goldsm. *Stoops to Conq.* II. Wks. (Globe) 657/2 Back to back, my pretties. *a*1814 *Father & Son* v. i. in *New Brit. Theatre* III. 399 If you would but comprehend me, my pretty. 1886 Fenn *Master of Cerem.* xvii, Wo-ho, my pretties. 1934 *Amer. Speech* IX. 288/2 *A pretty*, any good-looking girl. 1952 M. Allingham *Tiger in Smoke* xiv. 203 He's all right, pretty. He's all right now. 1972 [see LA, L.A. s.v. L 7].

b. A pretty thing, an ornament.

1736 *Boston News-Let.* 15 Apr. 2/2 (Advt.), Just arrived, and to be sold cheap, a choice variety of Haberdashery,.. Dutch Prettys, Silk Cane and Watch Strings, [etc.]. 1882 *Society* 28 Oct. 23/2 A profusion of..shells..completed this list of 'pretties'. 1895 *Dialect Notes* I. 392 *Pretty*, a picture or similar article; a toy. 1927 W. E. Collinson *Contemp. Eng.* 54, I well remember the disgust we children felt at a lady (an Englishwoman) who..called a fancy cake a pretty! 1952 M. Allingham *Tiger in Smoke* viii. 130, I ought to keep that [miniature]. It must go down among the other pretties in the show table in the drawing-room. 1957 H. Croome *Forgotten Place* xx. 229 Scarves, handkerchiefs, nylons, pretties, were pushed aside, or sent flying. 1977 *Daily Mirror* 10 May 12/5 Perhaps the brisk sales of pretties in the shops now shows which way the wind is beginning to blow. 1977 J. Wambaugh *Black Marble* (1978) x. 225 Probably buying her pretties with what little money the kennel took in.

c. The fluted or ornamented part of a glass or tumbler.

1890 Buckman *Darke's Sojourn* ix. 101 He proceeds to pour into the glass whisky nearly up to the 'pretty'.

d. *ellipt.*, a pretty good sum (of money), a ***pretty penny*** (see sense A. 5b). *U.S.*

1851 G. Thompson *Diary* 28 Jan. in N. E. Eliason *Tarheel Talk* (1956) 138, I would not send her an ugly [valentine] for a pirty. 1909 G. Stratton-Porter *Girl of Limberlost* xxi. 393 I'd give a pretty to know that secret thing you say you don't. 1927 *Amer. Speech* II. 277/1 *I'll bet you a pretty*, I'll bet you a good deal. 1935 H. Davis *Honey in Horn* v. 46 I'll bet you a pretty he ain't got any [money]. 1941 W. C. Handy *Father of Blues* v. 69 I'd give a pretty to the ear that could forget them.

e. *Golf.* The fairway.

1907 *Westm. Gaz.* 13 Sept. 3/1 Often..he will get just as far as if he had been lying on the 'pretty'. 1909 *Ibid.* 11 Sept. 7/2, I happened upon Daniel Lambert..wielding a heavy mashie among the thistles that flourish along the pretty to the tenth. 1927 *Daily Tel.* 12 Feb. 10/5 When the ball went sailing down the pretty, straight and true, what a satisfaction it was to both of them.

C. Used interjectionally.

1666 Pepys *Diary* 1 Oct., But pretty! how I took another pretty woman for her, taking her a clap on the breech, thinking verily it had been her.

D. *Comb.* (of the adj.) **a.** Parasynthetic derivatives, as ***pretty-footed, -humoured, -toned, -witted*** adjs.; ***pretty-girlhood*** (the estate or domain of pretty girls). **b. Pretty-and-Little, Pretty-Betty, Pretty-Betsy, Pretty Nancy**, names of flowers (see quots.); **pretty-by-night** *U.S.* = *marvel of Peru* (MARVEL *sb.* 6); **pretty-dancers**, the northern lights: see DANCER 5; **pretty-face**, (*a*) one who has a pretty face; (*b*) (also ***pretty-face kangaroo, wallaby***), the whip-tailed wallaby, *Macropus parryi*, which is found in southern Queensland and northern New South Wales and has white markings on its head; **pretty please**, an emphatic or affected colloq. form of request.

1882 Friend *Devon. Plant Names*, *Pretty-and-Little, the common Virginia Stock. 1887 *Kentish Gloss.*, *Pretty Betty, flowering Valeriana rubra. 1899 *Church Times* 24 Nov. 622/1 He probably means valerian or Pretty Betsy, common on the chalk of North Kent. 1872 E. Eggleston *End of World* xxv. 169 She planted some *pretty-by-nights in an old tea-pot. 1890 *Harper's Mag.* Jan. 282/1 Hollyhocks and larkspur and pretty-by-nights blossomed in the door-yard. 1911 C. Harris *Eve's Second Husband* 275 The 'pretty-by-nights' under the window..refused to consider the tragedy of Adam's unfaithfulness. 1931 W. N. Clute *Common Names of Plants* 135 The four o'clock..bears the name of pretty-by-night and lives up to it. 1947 M. Henry *Misty of Chincoteague* ix. 92 You kin cut a few of them purty-by-nights and some bouncin' Bess fer a centerpiece. 1808 Jamieson, **Pretty-Dancers*, a name given by the vulgar to the Aurora Borealis. 1741 Richardson *Pamela* (1824) I. xviii. 29 She hugged me to her, and said,..*Prettyface, where gottest thou all thy knowledge? 1887 W. S. S. Tyrwhitt *New Chum in Queensland Bush* viii. 145 The smaller kind [of kangaroo], known as pretty faces or whip tails,..are rather smaller and of a grey colour, with black and white on the face. 1911 W. H. D. Le Souëf *Wild Life Austral.* vii. 215 The most graceful of the Kangaroos..are locally called Pretty-face or Whip-tailed Kangaroos. 1943 C. Barrett *Austral. Animal Bk.* xi. 93 Its [*sc.* the whip-tail wallaby's] southern ally, often called 'pretty-face'..is among the most beautiful of all marsupials, with its slender, graceful body, its very long and slender tail, and white-and-grey face markings. 1970 W. D. L. Ride *Guide Native Mammals Austral.* v. 47 Whiptail, Pretty-face Wallaby... tail very long and slender, very marked white face-stripe. 1612 Selden *Illustr. Drayton's Poly-olb.* ii. 34 *margin*, Wel haired, and *pretty-footed; two speciall commendations, dispersed in Greeke Poets. 1784 R. Bage *Barham Downs* I. 319 The Earl expectant had somehow linked together the ideas of pleasure and *pretty-girl-hood. 1664 Pepys *Diary* 1 Aug., Mrs. Harman is a very *pretty-humoured wretch. 1886 Britten & H. *Plant-n.*, *Pretty Nancy, *Saxifraga umbrosa* [London Pride]. [1891 R. T. Cooke *Huckleberries* 169 Say 'please' now—real pretty.] 1959 A. Sinclair *Breaking of Bumbo* v. 74 She was saying, *Please.* **Pretty please.* 1964 *Time* 28 Feb. 28/3 Can I, pretty please? 1966 'T. Wells' *Matter of Love or Death* xii. 122 'I really can't.' I squeezed her hand. 'Not even if I say pretty please?' 1968 J. D. MacDonald *Pale Grey for Guilt* (1969) xv. 180, I guess you're not going to give it back just because I say pretty please with sugar. 1970 W. Smith *Gold Mine* xxxix. 105 Please, please, pretty please times three. 1973 C. Mason *Hostage* vii. 106 Say...'pretty please, with sugar on it.' 1581 J. Bell *Haddon's Answ. Osor.* 36 The man is *prettie witted enough.

pretty (ˈprɪtɪ), *adv.* Forms: see prec. [The adj. in adverbial use.]

1. a. To a considerable extent, considerably; in a fair or moderate degree, fairly, moderately, tolerably; rather. Sometimes expressing close approximation to *quite*, or by meiosis equivalent to *very*; at other times denoting a much slighter degree. (Qualifying an adj. or adv.)

1565 Cooper *Thesaurus, Audaculus*, a pretie hardie felow: vsed in derision. 1598 Florio *Dict.* Ep. Ded. 3 Boccace is prettie hard, yet understood: Petrarche harder but explaned. 1599 Massinger, etc. *Old Law* v. i, The Dutch what-you-call I swallowed pretty well. 1638 Rouse *Heav. Univ.* (1702) 166 They are of a pretty ancient date. 1677 W. Hubbard *Narrative* 44 By the end of November the coast was pretty clear of them. 1727 A. Hamilton *New Acc. E. Ind.* II. liv. 288 It is pretty like a young Willow. 1749 Fielding *Tom Jones* XVIII. iii, I have discovered a pretty considerable treasure. 1775 Sheridan *St. Patr. Day* II. ii, I'll take pretty good care of you. 1779 —— *Critic* I. i, My power with the managers is pretty notorious. 1806 *Gazetteer Scotl.* (ed. 2) 249 On the S. is a small chapel, pretty entire, dedicated to St. Oran. 1888 Bryce *Amer. Commw.* II. xlvi. 195 Parties..are generally pretty equally balanced. 1896 *Law Q. Rev.* July 201 If such be the law, we are pretty sure it is not the law Parliament intended to make.

b. ***pretty much***, almost, very nearly; approximately.

1806 D. Roe *Diary* 27 May (1904) 30 They got sum horsfish & that was pretty much all. 1861 Hughes *Tom Brown at Oxf.* i, The other men..lived pretty much as they did. 1873 [see ACCOUNT *sb.* 9c]. 1937 E. C. Vivian *Tramp's Evidence* vii. 90 Crandon goes to bed with the dicky-birds, pretty much. 1961 'S. Gillespie' *Neighbour* vi. 93 Her flat was pretty much what he had expected. 1976 *Southern Even. Echo* 13 Nov. 12/7 The defendant..'pretty much on impulse' took the television.

2. a. = PRETTILY. *spec.* in phr. ***to sit*** (or ***be sitting***) ***pretty***, to be comfortably placed or well situated; to be in a fortunate or advantageous position. *colloq.*

1667 Pepys *Diary* 6 Sept., The several states of man's age, to 100 years old, is shewn very pretty and solemne. 1861 Geo. Eliot *Silas M.* xvi, I like Aaron to..behave pretty to you. 1864 Trollope *Can you forgive Her?* I. xxii. 173, I must go down. The Duchess of St. Bungay is here, and Mr. Palliser will be angry if I don't do pretty to her. 1876 in Mordaunt & Verney *Warwick. Hunt* (1896) II. 7 Were halloaed on to a fox from Frog Hall Osiers, and ran him very pretty by Kineton Village. 1891 J. Newman *Scamping Tricks* i. 2 We can talk pretty to each other. *Ibid.* vi. 46, I saw they were started on the road of mutual admiration, and travelling pretty, and that he meant calling again. 1902 *Free Lance* 5 Apr. 8/2 They must be spoken 'pretty' to, caressed, humoured, coaxed. 1921 M. Moore (*title of musical comedy*) Sittin' Pretty. 1924 Bolton & Wodehouse (*title of musical comedy*) Sitting Pretty. 1925 Wodehouse *Sam the Sudden* xv. 106 If you're American, we're sitting pretty, because it's only us Americans that's got real sentiment in them. 1932 —— *Hot Water* i. 32 We're sitting pretty. The thing's in the bag. 1932 S. Gibbons *Cold Comfort Farm* xvi. 223 It was nearly half past two, and everybody seemed sitting pretty for the sunrise. 1937 *Times Lit. Suppl.* 25 Dec. 970/2 This submerged Dickens, who would not 'play pretty' to any orthodoxy old or new, comes nearer to raising his head in the Christmas Books than in his longer works. 1939 'N. Blake' *Smiler with Knife* xviii. 256 I'm sitting pretty for the moment, she thought; but [they]..will go over this district with a fine-tooth comb. 1947 *Times* 18 Nov. 2/3 Did he think the country was 'sitting pretty'? 1957 L. P. Hartley *Hireling* xi. 88, I shouldn't be sitting where I am, sitting pretty, to coin a phrase, if it wasn't for you. 1959 *Listener* 13 Aug. 239/1 At the moment the motor industry is 'sitting pretty'. 1967 O. Wynd *Walk Softly* xi. 182 Toba was still sitting pretty, at the most pausing for reassessment. 1972 *Driving* (Dept. of Environment) (ed. 2) 119 Always try to 'park pretty'; that is, squared up in the middle of the marked space. 1976 *Washington Post* 23 May G2 (*heading*) In some cases, they're sitting pretty.

b. Combined with ppl. adjs., as **pretty-behaved** = prettily-behaved; **pretty-spoken**, spoken or speaking prettily. *colloq.*

1787 *Generous Attachment* IV. 167 He thought her..a very decent pretty-behaved sort of a young woman. 1809 Malkin *Gil Blas* III. viii. ¶5 The lady is a very pretty behaved young lady. On my part, I am a very pretty behaved young gentleman.

pretty (ˈprɪtɪ), *v.* [f. the adj.]

Freq. const. *up.* **a.** *refl.* To make (oneself) pretty; to make or dress (oneself) *up* to look attractive. **b.** *trans.* To make (something or someone) pretty or attractive; also used ironically, to spoil or injure. Also *absol.* Hence **prettied (up)** *ppl. a.*; **prettying (up)** *vbl. sb.*

1916 H. L. Wilson *Somewhere in Red Gap* ii. 70 All I think is that he's trying to pretty himself up for Nettie. 1932 *Sun* (Baltimore) 23 Aug. 4/4 The women [pilots] were sent up a new supply of cold cream today, which enabled them to 'pretty up' for their landing. 1935 M. M. Atwater *Murder in Midsummer* viii. 72 The nurse..thought her patient should have waked up to tears and moans, and here she was fussing about the set of the lavender knitted thing about her thin shoulders. Prettying up for company! 1939 R. Chandler *Big Sleep* xxii. 182 A low-voiced prettied-up rhumba. 1943 —— *Lady in Lake* (1944) viii. 50 She was gone a week and came back all prettied up. 1950 D. D. Paige in *Lett. E. Pound* p. xxv, The general aim has been to present a volume that can be read consecutively with as little eye fatigue as possible. The editor alone is responsible for these prettyings up. 1953 K. Tennant *Joyful Condemned* xxi. 203 They wanted..plenty of time to pretty their hair. 1953 *Here & Now* (N.Z.) Oct. 5/2 Again, isn't it rather a sham to seal the roads along which she will travel and pretty up the buildings lining them. 1959 D. Niland *Big Smoke* II. vii. 160 He took the bottle from the bar and..smashed its end into a jagged, terrible weapon... He said, 'I'll pretty up your face, boy.' 1960 *Farmer & Stockbreeder* 19 Jan. (Suppl.) 1/3 I had made up my mind to marry Sue. The next night was our last night ashore and I had spent an hour and a half readying myself and prettying up. 1961 *John o' London's* 6 July 57/4 Even Jaques Becker..can't resist both tarting and prettying up the Modigliani legend. 1969 *Sears Catal.* Spring/Summer 30 Smocking pretties the yoke and sleeves of this broadcloth dress with its ruffled stand-up collar. 1972 *Times* 29 Aug. 10/2 People pay a great deal of attention..to prettying their houses. 1974 'M. Yorke' *Mortal Remains* v. iii. 154 Elsie's still prettying herself... She's been in the beauty shop all afternoon. 1979 J. Scott *Clutch of Vipers* vi. 91 The Chief Constable came in; looking..bull-shouldered in these prettied surroundings.

pretty-boy (ˈprɪtɪbɔɪ). Also without hyphen. [f. PRETTY *a.* 4 + BOY *sb.*[1]] A foppish or effeminate man; a male homosexual. Also used ironically, a 'tough', a thug. Also *attrib.*

1885 *Daily News* 26 Jan. 3/7 The style termed by irreverent mashers the pretty-boy clip, the style sometimes called the upward drag, and the whim which ranges from a delicate fringe to furze-bush proportions, at first amazed and amused the neat Japanese damsels. **1898** R. HUGHES *Lakerim Athletic Club* 241 Sawed-Off had sniffed scornfully that lawn-tennis was a game fit for nobody but girls and pretty boys. **1931** *Amer. Mercury* Nov. 353/2 *Pretty boys*,.. the circus bouncers; strong-arm men. **1941** BAKER *Dict. Austral. Slang* 57 *Pretty-boy*, an effeminate young man. **1946** G. MILLAR *Horned Pigeon* ix. 117 A pretty boy with wavy, brown hair flowing glossily over his round head... 'Who is it?' 'The *colonnello*'s bum-boy. A shit.' **1955** M. ALLINGHAM *Beckoning Lady* v. 71 The middle-aged pretty-boy face, complete with protuberant blue eyes and corrugated dark brown hair. **1956** 'E. MCBAIN' *Cop Hater* (1958) xix. 157 Scar tissue hooded his eyes. He owned cauliflower ears and hardly any teeth. His name, of course, was 'Pretty-Boy Krajak'. **1968** M. WOODHOUSE *Rock Baby* xi. 111, I walked past pretty-boy... Close up, pretty-boy smelled worse than ever. **1970** E. R. JOHNSON *God Keepers* (1971) iv. 46 A man named Al Brunning, pretty-boy greaseball. **1973** M. AMIS *Rachel Papers* 98 She was referring to the Beatles record (late-middle period—between pretty-boy rock and bleared occult) which had just come to an end. **1974** P. DE VRIES *Glory of Hummingbird* (1975) xi. 153 You're not cross-eyed..and your ears are pasted on straight. Not any pretty-boy, but probably photogenic.

prettyish ('prɪtɪɪʃ), *a. colloq.* [See -ISH¹.] Somewhat pretty, rather pretty.

1741 H. WALPOLE *Lett. to Mann* (1834) I. 19 There was Churchill's daughter, who is prettyish and dances well. **1758** MRS. DELANY in *Life & Corr.* (1861) III. 486 She is prettyish, young, and ignorant. **1852** CLOUGH *Poems*, etc. (1869) I. 183 Walk with Emerson to a wood with prettyish pool. **1880** *Sat. Rev.* 2 Oct. 438/2 His work contains some prettyish, and even pretty, passages.

prettyism ('prɪtɪɪz(ə)m). [See -ISM.] Studied prettiness of style or manner; an instance of this.

1776 T. ANBUREY *Let.* 20 Nov. in *Trav. Interior Parts Amer.* (1789) I. 109 These *Enfant du Diable* [*sc.* skunks] differ from your *Enfant du Diable*, the London beaux, who have all their prettyisms perhaps, but are externally exhaling their pestiferous odours. **1806** W. TAYLOR in *Ann. Rev.* IV. 739 We cannot prefer the vague prettyisms of the mere gentleman to the substantial tuition of the mere pedant. **1812** —— in *Monthly Rev.* LXVII. 388 As full of antithesis and prettyism of style, as any other part of the book. **1862** *Q. Rev.* Apr. 324 Surely the following puerilities and prettyisms are unbearable. **1907** M. G. PEARSE in *Life & Work* Apr. 81/2 The ugliest ism in the world is Pretty-ism, when it does not matter so much what you say as how you say it.

pretty-'prettiness. [f. PRETTY-PRETTY *a.* + -NESS.] The state or quality of being pretty-pretty; excess of prettiness.

1901 M. BEERBOHM in *Sat. Rev.* 20 Apr. 500/2 For prettiness—even pretty-prettiness—in the right place I have as great a taste as anyone else. **1924** 'L. MALET' *Dogs of Want* i. 26 The coquettish little Cities of the Plain..and their cheap pretty-prettiness of countless hotels. **1931** *Observer* 6 Sept. 6/4 The revulsions into Sunday School pretty-prettiness are equally surprising. **1945** E. BOWEN *Ivy Gripped Steps* in *Demon Lover* 130 His elder brother's jibes at his pretty-prettiness. **1960** KOESTLER *Lotus & Robot* II. vi. 165 A culture with a surface polish of utterly refined pretty-prettiness. **1965** *Observer* 17 Jan. 28/1 A yearning for the pretty-prettiness of the days when women were women.

'pretty-'pretty, *a.* (*adv.*) and *sb.* [Reduplicated from PRETTY *a.* (Imitating childish talk.)]

A. *adj.* That overdoes the pretty; in which the aim at prettiness is overdone. Cf. GOODY-GOODY. Also as *adv.*

1877 *Punch* 3 Feb. 47/2 To paint pretty-pretty, to compose namby-pamby, and perpetuate the modish and monstrous. **1897** *Bookman* Jan. 119/1 Save in the over-rated, pretty-pretty 'Harbour of Refuge', he is always interesting. **1907** *Daily Chron.* 1 Apr. 4/4 We can't expect men who have to do unpleasant work to be a select gang of pretty-pretty sentimentalists. **1928** GALSWORTHY *Swan Song* I. xi. 80 Nothing pretty-pretty about that memorial—no angels' wings there! **1937** [see ARTY-AND-CRAFTY *a.*]. **1952** L. T. STANLEY *Woman Golfer* 61 A 'pretty-pretty' swing may look nice, but it doesn't get you far. **1961** [see BITCHY *a.* 1]. **1962** 'K. ORVIS' *Damned & Destroyed* xxi. 157 He just might sing pretty-pretty and tell you exactly what's cooking in Moss's fat head. **1973** *Times* 5 Oct. 13/1, I love the baby dresses and suits which are pretty without being pretty-pretty. **1980** A. ALPERS *Life K. Mansfield* vi. 114 Some flabby fiction, and some pretty-pretty verse.

B. *sb.* (*pl.*) Pretty things; ornaments, knick-knacks. Also *sing.*, in absol. use. (Properly nursery prattle.)

1875 TROLLOPE *Autobiog.* (1883) I. ii. 35 My mother.. had contrived to keep a certain number of pretty-pretties which were dear to her heart. **1888** *Bow Bells Weekly* 15 June 376/3 This room contains a small fortune in pretty-pretties. **1899** [see CHANCE *v.* 4 c]. **1929** W. DEEPING *Roper's Row* xxxv. 401 But that was a monstrous argument to use, mush, the pretty-pretty, a kitten-faced sentimentality. **1934** C. LAMBERT *Music Ho!* v. 327 Prokofieff's third piano concerto..is curiously lacking in any sense of direction, oscillating disturbingly between the pretty-pretty and the ugly-ugly.

pre-tune: see PRE- A. 1.

pretympanic: see PRE- B. 3.

†**pre'type**, *v. Obs.* [PRE- A. 1.] = next.

c **1624** LUSHINGTON *Recant. Serm.* (1659) 85 St. Jerome might have pretyped it by the age of Man in general.

pretypify (priː'tɪpɪfaɪ), *v.* [f. PRE- A. 1 + TYPIFY *v.*] *trans.* To typify beforehand, prefigure, foreshadow.

1659 HAMMOND *On Ps.* lxxii. 17 So shall Christ, pretypified by Solomon. **1659** PEARSON *Creed* iv. 412 Our Jesus..did really undergoe those sufferings, which were pretypified and foretold. **1880** W. S. KENT *Man. Infusoria* I. 103 Paramecium and its allies would appear to pre-typify the Turbellaria.

‖**pretzel** ('prɛtsəl), **bretzel** ('brɛtsəl). *U.S.* [G. *pretzel, bretzel*, in OHG. *brizzilla* = It. *bracciello* (Florio) a cracknel; usually taken as ad. med.L. *bracellus* a bracelet; also a kind of cake or biscuit (Du Cange).] **1.** A crisp biscuit baked in the form of a knot and flavoured with salt; used esp. by Germans as a relish with beer. Also *fig.* and *attrib.*

1856 [see BLUTWURST]. **1857** C. KINGSLEY *Two Yrs. Ago* III. ix. 271 After him came..like in *Struwelpeter*, Caspar, bretzel in hand. **1858** *Harper's Mag.* Aug. 327/1 Eating *pretzels* and drinking what is here called *bière de Bavière*. **1889** *Harper's Mag.* Apr. 692/1 The German beer-houses, with their baskets of 'pretzel', are more frequent as we approach the commercial quarters. **1897** *Outing* (U.S.) XXX. 134/1 She brought me some pretzels and a stein that she said her mother brought from the fatherland. **1915** *Lit. Digest* 12 June 1443/1 Prunella's painting pretzels in Przemysl. **1932** E. WILSON *Devil take Hindmost* vii. 45 The pretzel man with his basket and the roast-chestnut man have come out again. **1933** R. L. SUTTON *Arctic Safari* 24 The booby prize was a string of pretzels at least four feet long. **1933** *Sun* (Baltimore) 15 Aug. 8/7 In the old days your newest reporter would have been sufficiently cultured to know that one doesn't twist pretzels; one bends them. Hence the artisan or craftsman who performs the work is a pretzel bender. **1945** *Finito! Po Valley Campaign* (15th Army Group) 5 The air forces twisted the enemy's rail lines into pretzels of steel. **1961** WODEHOUSE *Ice in Bedroom* xvi. 128 You know as well as I do that Chimp Twist is as crooked as a pretzel. **1968** MRS. L. B. JOHNSON *White House Diary* 7 Feb. (1970) 627 Little round tables with cokes and pizza, peanuts and pretzels. **1973** *Times* 25 June 11/3 Ervin Committee Member Lowell Weicker, dropped in for beer and pretzels. **1975** *New Yorker* 31 Mar. 29/2 She dumps an armful of immense pretzel stick cuttings into the pail. **1976** R. COWPER *Paradise Beach* in *Custodians* 71 He snatched her hands to his lips and set about them as if they were a pair of pretzels.

2. *Mus. slang.* (See quots.) Also *pretzel bender.*

1936 *Metronome* Feb. 61/2 *Pretzel*—French horn. **1936** *Amer. Mercury* May p. x/2 *Pretzel bender*—one who favors the French horn. **1945** L. SHELLY *Jive Talk Dict.* 16 *Pretzel*, French horn. *Ibid.* 31 *Pretzel bender*, French horn player.

†**preu, prew**, *a. Obs.* Also 4 preus, 5 pru, 5–6 prue, 6 prewe. [a. OF. *preu, prou, pru*, nom. *preu-z* (*proz, prous, pruz*, 11th c. in Godef.), in mod.F. *preux* valiant, brave, good:—late L. *prōd-is, prōd-em* (*prōde* neut. in *Itala*): see PROW.] Brave, valiant, doughty, gallant; full of prowess: cf. PREUX.

1340 *Ayenb.* 83 Ine prouesse byeþ þri þinges to-deld, hardyesse, strengþe, an stedeuestnesse. Non ne is aryȝt preus, þet þise þri þinges ne heþ. *c* **1386** CHAUCER *Monk's T.* 177 (Harl. MS.) This king of kinges preu was and elate. *c* **1400** *Laud Troy Bk.* 4888 Ector rode forth In gode vertuus Strong knyȝt, hardy and prus. *c* **1477** CAXTON *Jason* 8 b, The worthy hercules and the noble preu Jason. *c* **1489** —— *Sonnes of Aymon* iii. 79 We ben so pru & so good men of armes. **1512** *Helyas* in Thoms *Prose Rom.* (1828) III. 15 The prue king Oriant. **1523** LD. BERNERS *Froiss.* I. i. 1 Wherby the prewe and hardy may haue ensample to incourage them in theyr wel doyng.

preua-, preue-, preui-: see PREV-.

pre-understand, -union, -unite: see PRE- A. 1, 2.

‖**preux** (prø), *a.* [mod.F. *preux* valiant: see the earlier form PREU.] Brave, valiant, gallant; chiefly in *preux chevalier*, gallant knight.

1771 H. WALPOLE *Lett., to G. Selwyn* 9 Sept., If he is a *preux chevalier*, he will vindicate her character *d'une manière éclatante*. **1803** *Edin. Rev.* Oct. 116 When the adventures of a *preux chevalier* were no longer listened to by starts. **1840** BARHAM *Ingol. Leg.* Ser. I. *Cynotaph*, All *Preux Chevaliers*, in friendly rivalry Who should best bring back the glory of Chi-valry.

preva, prevable, obs. ff. PRIVY, PROVABLE.

pre'vaccinated, *ppl. a.* [PRE- A. 1.] Previously vaccinated.

1903 *Brit. Med. Jrnl.* 21 Mar. 663 Prevaccinated Small-Pox [i.e. occurring in a person previously vaccinated].

†**pre'vade**, *v. rare*⁻¹. [app. ad. L. *prævādĕre* to pass before, to be discharged from, to get rid of (perh. here identified with *ēvādĕre* to escape from).] ? To rid oneself of, to omit; 'to neglect' (Jam.).

1641 R. BAILLIE *Lett., to Ld. Montgom.* 2 June, My man, ..give my letters with him to the Generall-Major Baillie, to Meldrum and Durie; prevade not to obtaine him his pay.

†**'prevagely**, *adv. Obs. rare*⁻¹. Of obscure etymology and meaning; there is no answering word in the L. Possibly some error.

1513 DOUGLAS *Æneis* VI. v. 14 His smotterit habit, our his schulderis lidder, Hang prevagely [*Camb. MS.* and *ed.* 1553 pevagely] knyt with a knot togiddir.

†**prevail**, *sb. Obs. rare.* [f. next.]

1. The fact of prevailing: = PREVALENCE 1.

1420 in Ellis *Orig. Lett.* Ser. I. I. 9 Your gracious preuaile ayenst thentent & malice of your evilwillers. **1586** J. HOOKER *Hist. Irel.* in *Holinshed* II. 143/2 His preuaile was to their reproch.

2. Advantage, benefit: = AVAIL *sb.* 1.

c **1475** *Pol. Poems* (Rolls) II. 285 Yt ys necessary to every clothyer, And the most prevayle to theym that may be fownde, Yf they wylle take hede therto and yt undyrstonde.

prevail (prɪ'veɪl), *v.* Forms: 4–7 prevayle, 5 -vayl(l -vaylle, (*Sc.* -vele), 5–7 -vaile, 6 -vaill, 6–8 -vale, 5– prevail. [ME. *prevaylle, -vaile*, ad. L. *prævalēre* to be very able, have greater power or worth, prevail (see PRE- and VAIL *v*). Cf. F. *prévaloir* (subj. †*prévaille*, now *prévale*), 15–16th c.]

†**1.** *intr.* To become very strong; to gain vigour or force, to increase in strength. *Obs. rare.*

1398 TREVISA *Barth. De P.R.* IV. ix. (Tollem. MS.), By the benefyte of bloudde all the lymmes of the body prevayle and be fedde [*orig.* vigent et nutriuntur]. *a* **1500** *Colkelbie Sow* 654 (Bann. MS.) Into the first orising of it to tell, Or it prevelit planeist and popelus, Quhair now Pareiss citie is situat thus. *a* **1540** BARNES *Wks.* (1573) 332/2 We see that nowe hee is preuayled in mischief. **1697** DRYDEN *Virg. Georg.* II. 681 Teach me..Why flowing Tides prevail upon the Main, And in what dark Recess they shrink again. **1755** YOUNG *Centaur* i. Wks. 1757 IV. 105 Prevails not Infidelity as much as Pleasure? And for-ever they must prevail, or decrease, together.

2. *intr.* To be superior in strength or influence; to have or gain the superiority or advantage; to get the better, gain the mastery or ascendancy; to be victorious. Const. *against, over*, †*of*, †*upon.*

c **1450** *Cov. Myst.* xxiv. (Shaks. Soc.) 237 Whan aȝens the ..he may not prevaylle. **1509** HAWES *Past. Pleas.* xxxii. (Percy Soc.) 161 In tyme of fight.. If you prevayle you shall attayne the fame Of hye honour. **1529** *Supplic. to King* (E.E.T.S.) 43 Hell gates shall not prevayle ageinste them. **1553** BRENDE *Q. Curtius* III. 36 Hys men prevayled of their enemies. **1594** *2nd Rep. Dr. Faustus* xxviii. K ij, So much the Christian preuailed vpon the Turke in three houres and a halfes fight. **1650** HUBBERT *Pill Formality* 46 Great is truth, and it shall prevaile. **1671** MILTON *P.R.* III. 167 So did not Machabeus: he..o're a mighty King so oft prevail'd, That by strong hand his Family obtain'd, Though Priests, the Crown. **1692** W. MARSHALL *Gosp. Myst. Sanctif.* (1764) 328 In Christ God's mercy prevails high above our sins. **1711** ADDISON *Spect.* No. 61 ¶5 As Pedantry and Ignorance shall prevail upon Wit and Sense. **1725** DE FOE *Voy. round World* (1840) 341 Some were for returning and others for staying longer, till the majority prevailed to come back. **1729** BUTLER *Serm.* Wks. 1874 II. 16 Cool self-love is prevailed over by passion and appetite. **1818** CRUISE *Digest* (ed. 2) VI. 377 The intention of the devisor must prevail. **1895** *Law Times* C. 5/2 The title of the assignee was..held to prevail over that of the trustee.

†**b.** *trans.* To prevail over, have superiority over, outstrip. *Sc. Obs. rare.*

1535 STEWART *Cron. Scot.* (Rolls) II. 198 Displesit wes the nobillis of the Britis, That sic ane man of law birth and valour, Sould thame prevaill into so grit honour.

3. *intr.* To be effectual or efficacious; to be successful, to succeed.

1432–50 tr. *Higden* (Rolls) IV. 241 Whiche preuaylenge not, [she] was commaunded to kepenge. **1480** CAXTON *Chron. Eng.* ccxlvii. (1482) 314 So he retorned home ageyne with his meyny and preuayled nothynge. **1526** TINDALE *John* xii. 19 Ye se that we prevayle no thynge: loo all the worlde goth after hym. **1561** T. HOBY tr. *Castiglione's Courtyer* III. (1577) O viij b, [He] proued many remedies, but all preuayled not. **1697** DRYDEN *Virg. Past.* IX. 16 Songs ..Prevail as much..As would a plump of trembling Fowl, that rise Against an Eagle. **1830** TENNYSON *Supposed Confess.* 99 But why Prevailed not thy pure prayers?

†**b.** *to prevail to* (a thing) or *to do* (something): to succeed in doing, attaining, etc. *Obs. rare.*

1473–5 in *Calr. Proc. Chanc. Q. Eliz.* (1830) II. Pref. 57 Seeng that the said Richard..coude not prevaile to his said feyned title. **1561** NORTON & SACKV. *Gorboduc* IV. ii, Oh, cruell wight, shulde any cause prevaile To make the staine thy hands with brothers blod? **1644** BP. HALL *Serm.* 9 *June* Rem. Wks. (1660) 109 Let no Popish Doctor prevail to the abatement of this holy sorrow. **1764** GOLDSM. *Hist. Eng. in Lett.* (1772) II. 81 Neither he, nor his ministers, could prevail to alter the resolutions of his society.

c. *to prevail on, upon* (formerly *with*): to succeed in persuading, inducing, or influencing.

1573–80 BARET *Alv.* P 696 With whom when she could nothing preuaile. **1617** MORYSON *Itin.* I. 25, I so preuailed with him, as he let me haue it. **1656** STANLEY *Hist. Philos.* IV. (1701) 133/1 Enquiring what disputes they were wherewith Socrates prevailed so much upon the young Men. **1708** SWIFT *Death Partridge* Wks. 1755 II. I. 158, I prevailed with myself to go and see him. **1711** BUDGELL *Spect.* No. 277 ¶6, I was prevailed upon by her and her Mother to go last Night to one of his Balls. **1805** EMILY CLARK *Banks of Douro* II. 118 They could not prevail with her to stay. **1844** H. H. WILSON *Brit. India* II. 220 The Peshwa..endeavoured to prevail upon the Resident to grant a longer interval. **1863** W. C. BALDWIN *Afr. Hunting* ix. 396 As hard as ever I could prevail on my nag to go.

†**d.** *trans.* = *prevail upon*; to persuade, induce.

1475 *Bk. Noblesse* (Roxb.) 3 The anguisshes, troubles, and divisions..may not prevaile them to the repairing and wynnyng of any soche manere outrageous losses to this Reaume. **1586** LD. BURGHLEY in Ellis *Orig. Lett.* Ser. I. III. 6 Morgan prevaled hir to renew hir intelligence with Babyngton. **1752** FIELDING *Amelia* I. vii, His partner, who was..afterwards prevailed to dance with him. **1834** *Tracts for Times* No. 40. 2 Those who were most likely to be prevailed to act upon the principles of it.

†**4.** *intr.* To be of advantage or use; to profit: = AVAIL *v.* 2. *Obs.*

c **1500** *Melusine* 209 Syth..þat my presence & long abydyng here with you may nought preuaylle to you. **1534** TINDALE *N.T., Prol. Romans* (1551) 66 b/1 What preuayleth it nowe that y[u] teachest another man not to steale, when y[u] thine own selfe art a thefe in thine hert? **1584** COGAN *Haven Health* (1636) 16 Aristotle..saith that it prevaileth greatly both to the health of the body, and to the study of Philosophy.

†**b.** *trans.* To be of advantage or use to, to benefit: = AVAIL *v.* 3. *Obs.*

1442 *Rolls of Parlt.* V. 56/1 Menes how to prevaile the straungers. **1465** MARG. PASTON in *P. Lett.* II. 241 He seyd ..yf it myght prevayle yow, he woulde with ryght good wylle that it choulde be doo. **1549** LATIMER *2nd Serm. bef. Edw. VI*, To Rdr. (Arb.) 50 There thy money so gleaned and gathered of the and thyne..can not preuayle the. **1593** *Tell-Troth's N.Y. Gift* (1876) 32 Vulcans Ielosy preuailed him nothing.

†**c.** To give (any one) the benefit or advantage *of* (something): = AVAIL *v.* 7. Usually *refl.* to avail oneself of: = AVAIL *v.* 5. [F. *se prévaloir*, *a* 1600.] *Obs.*

1617 MORYSON *Itin.* II. 234, I am againe going..to waste the Countrie of Tyrone, and to preuaile the Garrisons there of some Corne to keepe their horses in the Winter. *a* **1648** LD. HERBERT *Life* (1888) 47 No man hath more dexterously prevailed himself thereof. **1681** DRYDEN *Abs. & Achit.* I. 461 Prevail yourself of what occasion gives.

5. *intr.* To be or become the stronger, more wide-spread, or more frequent usage or feature; to predominate. (A later weakening of sense 2.)

1628 HOBBES *Thucyd.* (1822) 3 These cities..began..to be called Hellenes: and yet could not that name of a long time after prevail upon them all. **1690** LOCKE *Hum. Und.* III. vi. §39 If any one will..to such..complex Ideas, give Names that shall prevail, they will then be new Species to them. **1712** ADDISON *Hymn 'The spacious firmament'* ii, Soon as the Evening Shades prevail, The Moon takes up the wondrous Tale. **1718** *Free-thinker* No. 35 ¶6 The Gilded Signs prevailed over those of any other Colour. **1879** HARLAN *Eyesight* ii. 16 Light eyes prevail among northern nations and dark eyes among the races who live in the glare of a tropical sun.

b. Hence, To be in general use or practice; to be commonly accepted or adopted; to exist, obtain, occur, or be present constantly or widely; to be prevalent or current.

1776 GIBBON *Decl. & F.* vii. (1869) I. 145 A silent consternation prevailed on the assembly. **1790** PALEY *Horæ Paul.* i. 2 Reports and traditions which prevailed in that age. **1840** W. IRVING in *Life & Lett.* (1866) III. 155 Now a snowstorm is prevailing. **1875** JOWETT *Plato* (ed. 2) V. 228 Their way of thinking is far better than any other which now prevails in the world.

†**pre'vailable,** *a. Obs. rare.* [f. prec. + -ABLE. Cf. OF. *prevalable* (*a* 1500 in Godef.).] **a.** Able to prevail; efficacious. **b.** Capable of being beneficially used, available. **c.** That may be prevailed *upon* or influenced.

1624 GEE *Foot out of Snare* 68 The Diuell hath no greater cunning, nor preuaileable art. *a* **1638** MEDE *Wks.* (1672) 3 So prevailable with Almighty God is the power of Consent in Prayer. **1668** M. CASAUBON *Credulity* (1670) 111 Who maintained, that Christ his miracles, without further consideration, were not prevailable to that end, to make faith or evidence of his Deity. **1679** MARG. MASON *Tickler Tickl.* 3 Upon the account of their Religion, or of their Sex, very prevailable upon to speak what often is not true.

prevailance, obs. form of PREVALENCE.

pre'vailer. Now *rare.* [f. PREVAIL *v.* + -ER[1].] One who prevails; one who is successful or gains the mastery.

1618 *Hist. P. Warbeck* in *Select. fr. Harl. Misc.* (1793) 71 That so..they might..be..the better welcomed and entertained with the prevailer. **1670** in Somers *Tracts* I. 14 For want of Discipline, the Prevailers applied themselves to plunder the Baggage. **1721–2** WODROW *Hist. Suff. Ch. Scotl.* (1828) I. I. ii. 200 He was mighty in prayer and a singular prevailer. **1800** A. SWANSTON *Serm. & Lect.* I. 437 It signifies a princely prevailer with God.

pre'vailing, *vbl. sb.* [f. as prec. + -ING[1].] The action of the verb PREVAIL; the having or gaining of the mastery or predominance; prevalence.

1607–12 BACON *Ess., Nat. in Men* (Arb.) 358 A smal proceeder thoughe by often prevaylinges. **1710** STEELE *Tatler* No. 195 ¶2 To hinder the creeping in and prevailing of Quacks and Pretenders. **1872** MORLEY *Voltaire* (1886) 4 The prevailing of the gates of hell.

pre'vailing, *ppl. a.* [f. as prec. + -ING[2].] That prevails, in various senses.

1. That is or proves to be superior in any contest; victorious; ruling; effective, influential.

a **1586** SIDNEY *Ps.* XLIII. ii, Why walk I in woes, While prevayling foes Haue of joyes bereft me? **1667** MILTON *P.L.* IV. 973 Farr heavier load thy self expect to feel From my prevailing arme. **1706** ESTCOURT *Fair Examp.* II. i. 20 Effects of Age, not to be remov'd by Physick, tho' never so prevailing. **1848** R. I. WILBERFORCE *Doctr. Incarnation* ix. (1852) 206 Pleading the merits of His death as the prevailing Intercessor for His brethren.

2. Predominant in extent or amount; most widely occurring or accepted; generally current: = PREVALENT *a.* 3.

1685 in *Academy* 21 Oct. (1876) 408/2 The prevailing report is that the Lord Gray is pardoned. **1711** SHAFTESB. *Charac.* (1737) II. II. II. i. 123 Led by false Religion or prevailing Custom. **1815** ELPHINSTONE *Acc. Caubul* (1842) I. 171 The prevailing wind,..in the region south-west of Hemalleh, is from the south-east. **1849** MACAULAY *Hist. Eng.* ii. I. 230 The prevailing discontent was compounded of many feelings. **1867** H. MACMILLAN *Bible Teach.* vii. (1870) 148 The colours..of leaves are wonderfully diversified, though green is the prevailing hue.

pre'vailingly, *adv.* [f. prec. + -LY[2].] In a prevailing manner or degree.

1. With prevailing effect; effectively, successfully. Now *rare* or *Obs.*

a **1638** MEDE *Wks.* (1672) 366 We by him do that here on earth in a meaner way, which he..doth for us in heaven powerfully and prevailingly. *a* **1683** OLDHAM *Poet. Wks.* 15 Sure were the means, we chose, And wrought prevailingly.

2. In a preponderating degree; predominantly; chiefly, mainly.

1797 W. TAYLOR in *Monthly Rev.* XXII. 248 The literature..and the manners..were prevailingly those of protestant Germany. **1845** H. ROGERS *Ess.* (1860) I. 97 The one is the prevailingly philosophical temperament..the other, the prevailingly poetical. **1878** O. W. HOLMES *Motley* 201 Of the seven United Provinces, two..were prevailingly Arminian.

So **pre'vailingness,** *rare*, the quality or faculty of prevailing.

1880 G. MEREDITH *Tragic Com.* viii, His pride in his prevailingness thrilled her.

†**pre'vailment.** *Obs. rare.* [f. PREVAIL *v.* + -MENT.] The action or fact of prevailing, influencing, or gaining ascendancy.

1590 SHAKS. *Mids. N.* I. i. 35 Messengers Of strong preuailment in vnhardned youth. **1599** R. LINCHE *Anc. Fict.* I ij, That..famoused preuailement which Iupiter so victoriously carried ouer his father. **1633** T. ADAMS *Exp. 2 Peter* ii. 10 If we be sensible of the flesh,..repent of her prevailments;..we shall then sing to his glory.

prevalence ('prɛvələns). Also 6–7 **prevailance.** [a. F. *prévalence* (15–16th c. in Godef.), ad. med.L. *prævalēntia* (Digests) superior force, f. *prævalēre* to PREVAIL: see -ENCE.]

1. a. The fact or action of prevailing; the having or obtaining of predominance or mastery. Now *rare.*

1592 KYD *Sp. Trag.* III. xv, Awake, Reuenge, if loue.. Haue yet the power or preuailance in hell. **1633** BP. HALL *Hard Texts, N.T.* 22 Those sins which we commit..upon.. suddaine and forceable prevalence of a temptation. **1711** in *10th Rep. Hist. MSS. Comm.* App. v. 140 There was a strong probability for their prevalence, considering their advantage in the ground, their numbers.., and their resolution. **1748** HARTLEY *Observ. Man* II. ii. 178 The Prevalence of their own Endeavours..over this Opposition. **1833** CHALMERS *Const. Man* (1835) I. iv. 192 The final prevalence of the good over the evil. **1866** SWINBURNE *Two Dreams* 74 Words and sense Fail through the tune's imperious prevalence.

†**b.** Presence or existence of greater power or strength. *Obs.*

1646 SIR T. BROWNE *Pseud. Ep.* IV. v. 188 Many are right handed whose Livers are weakely constituted, and many use the left [hand], in whom that part is strongest; and we observe in Apes and other animals, whose Liver is in the right, no regular prevalence therein.

2. Effective force or power; influence, weight; efficacy; prevailingness. Now *rare.*

1631 T. POWELL *Tom All Trades* (1876) 149 In Colledges, the letters of great persons..have beene of great prevailance [in getting preferments]; But it is not so now in these dayes. **1642** BP. REYNOLDS *Israel's Petit.* 6 There is a kinde of omnipotencie in prayer, as having an Interest and prevalence with Gods omnipotencie. **1718** *Entertainer* No. 15. 101 Great is the Prevalence of a fashionable Practice. **1802** MRS. E. PARSONS *Myst. Visit* IV. 262 Example has great prevalence, whether good or bad. **1879** G. MEREDITH *Egoist* xvii, A sensitive gentleman, anxious even to prognostic apprehension on behalf of his pride, his comfort and his prevalence.

3. The condition of being prevalent, or of general occurrence or existence; extensive or common practice or acceptance. (The ordinary current sense.)

1713 STEELE *Guardian* No. 1 ¶1 The notion I have of the prevalence of ambition this way. **1750** JOHNSON *Rambler* No. 43 ¶3 This position..perhaps, will never gain much prevalence by a close examination. **1792** BURKE *Corr.* (1844) IV. 2 We were a little uneasy from the steady prevalence of winds in the westerly quarter. **1839** *Ann. Rep. Registrar-Gen. England* 87 The prevalence of a disease..is expressed by the deaths in a given time out of a given number of living. **1844** LD. BROUGHAM *Brit. Const.* v. (1862) 77 The prevalence of bribery is the most difficult subject with which we have to deal. **1857** T. W. GRIMSHAW et al. *Man. Public Health Ireland* xxvii. 298 From statistics [of small-pox]..it appears that its greatest prevalence is observed in May, the cases in that month being 13.7 per cent. of the total cases occurring in the year. **1961** M. SCHORER *Sinclair Lewis* IV. viii. 471 He talked..about the prevalence of American slang in British speech. **1975** *Nature* 20 Mar. 168/3 Any successful preventative measure against leprosy will be shown by a fall in the number of new cases or in the incidence rate: the total number of cases (or 'prevalence' rate) will change much more slowly, because of the inclusion of patients who are already crippled.

prevalency ('prɛvələnsɪ). Now *rare.* [ad. med.L. *prævalēntia*: see prec. and -ENCY.] The quality or fact of being prevalent.

†**1.** Superiority, predominance: = PREVALENCE 1.

1623 COCKERAM, *Preualencie*, excellencie. **1642** CHAS. I *Declar.* 12 Aug., Wks. 1662 II. 152 Concurrence was desperate by reason of the Prevalency of the Bishops and of the Recusant Lords. **1691** *Andros Tracts* II. 241 Where the vice of Covetousness has..got the prevalency over the rest. **1710** PRIDEAUX *Orig. Tithes* v. 235 The corruptions of the Church of Rome through the prevalency of the Papal Power brought some such [prescriptions] afterwards in.

†**b.** The quality of being of greater power or strength; superiority of power: = PREVALENCE 1 b.

1646 SIR T. BROWNE *Pseud. Ep.* IV. v. 187 That there is also in men a naturall prepotency in the right [hand], we cannot with constancy affirme, if we make observation in children;..this prevalency is either uncertainly placed in the laterallity, or custome determines its indifferency. *Ibid.* 189 According to the indifferency or original and native prepotency, there ariseth an equality in both, or prevalency in either side.

2. Prevailing or effective power or influence; prevailingness: = PREVALENCE 2.

1656 JEANES *Fuln. Christ* 333 So the value of his sufferings was an argument of prevalency with his father. **1661** FELTHAM *Resolves* II. vii. (ed. 8) 191 Those that are daily attendant upon great Persons,..have a greater prevalency with them, than those..that live as strangers to them. **1794** PALEY *Evid.* II. ix. (1817) 222 For the express purpose of showing to the emperor the effect and prevalency of the new institution. **1842** J. SHERMAN in H. Allon *Mem.* (1863) 296 Prayer has a wonderful prevalency with God.

3. The quality or condition of being prevalent, or of frequent or general occurrence or acceptance: = PREVALENCE 3.

1651 C. CARTWRIGHT *Cert. Relig.* I. 110 Sometimes through..prevalencie of error, the Church may be so obscured as to be scarcely visible. **1766** COLE in Ellis *Orig. Lett.* Ser. II. IV. 485 Convinced of the great prevalency of Deism in that Kingdom. **1794** S. WILLIAMS *Vermont* 63 The prevalency and extent of the westerly winds. **1882–3** *Schaff's Encycl. Relig. Knowl.* II. 885/2 From Cicero down, stress has been justly laid on the prevalency among all nations of a belief in a superior being.

b. With *a* and *pl.* A prevalent feature.

1806 R. CUMBERLAND *Mem.* (1807) II. 262 To..purify my native language from certain false pedantic prevalencies which were much in fashion when I first became a writer.

prevalent ('prɛvələnt), *a.* (*sb.*) (Also 7 **prevailent.**) [ad. L. *prævalēns*, *-ēnt-em* very strong or powerful, pr. pple. of *prævalēre*: see PREVAIL *v.* (Not in Fr.)] That prevails; prevailing.

1. Having great power or force; effective, powerful; influential, cogent; efficacious, potent. *absol.* or const. *with* (a person). Now *rare* (and chiefly in connexions in which *prevail* is in use).

1576 FLEMING *Panopl. Epist.* 67 Neither these, nor those consolations..ought not to seeme so preualent and effectuall, as the verie state it selfe of our citie. **1624** T. TAYLOR *2 Serm.* II. 23 Lifting up hands, and praiers, which are powerfull and prevalent against Amalek. **1642** *Declar. Lords & Comm.* 3 Aug. 15 Ill-affected persons, who are so prevalent with His Majestie. **1711** W. KING tr. *Naude's Ref. Politics* iii. 106 Love is more prevalent in obtaining what you desire than fear. **1796** BURKE *Let. to C. J. Fox* Wks. 1842 II. 389 He, and those who are much prevalent with him. **1805** HOLCROFT *Bryan Perdue* I. 265 Of all other instruction, that of example is the most prevalent. **1828** A. JOLLY *Sunday Serv.* (1840) 76 Praying in faith..we may humbly hope that our prayers shall be prevalent.

†**b.** Of medicines, etc.: Efficacious. *Obs.*

1615 G. SANDYS *Trav.* 126 A kind of Rue..much in request..esteeming it preualent against hurtfull spirits. **1632** tr. *Bruel's Praxis Med.* 7 Pils are more preualent then electuaries in this disease. **1676** WORLIDGE *Cyder* (1691) 194 Cider..is also prevalent against the stone. **1712** tr. *Pomet's Hist. Drugs* I. 163 A most prevalent Thing against the Green-Sickness.

2. Having the superiority or ascendancy; predominant, victorious. Now *rare.*

1614 RALEIGH *Hist. World* v. iii. §15 II. 511 But the yong Nephew..regarded only the things present; the weakenesse of Rome; the prevalent fortunes of Carthage. **1640** LD. SAY in *Laud's Wks.* (1857) VI. 120 A theological scarecrow, wherewith the potent and prevalent party uses to fright and enforce those who are not of their opinions. **1761** HUME *Hist. Eng.* III. xlv. 12 *note*, The Puritans, though then prevalent, did not think proper to dispute this great constitutional point. **1849** MACAULAY *Hist. Eng.* i. I. 79 The gross injustice, insolence, and cruelty of the party which was prevalent at Dort.

3. Most extensively used or practised; generally or widely accepted; of frequent occurrence; extensively existing; in general use.

1658 SIR T. BROWNE *Hydriot.* Introd. (1736) 3 Which.. from that Time spread, and became the prevalent Practice. **1756** C. LUCAS *Ess. Waters* I. 15 The false notion..so universally, so absurdly prevalent. **1816** SINGER *Hist. Cards* 144 The watermark most prevalent..is found on the paper of books printed by Lucas Brandis de Schass. **1827** ROBERTS *Voy. Centr. Amer.* 32, I shall write the proper names.. according to the most prevalent pronunciation. **1834** MRS. SOMERVILLE *Connex. Phys. Sc.* xv. (1849) 139 The most prevalent winds in Europe are the N.E. and S.W. **1870** ANDERSON *Missions Amer. Bd.* IV. xxxv. 271 The cholera was prevalent in that year.

B. *sb.* (absol. use of adj.) That which is prevalent: see quots. Cf. PREVALENCY 3 b. *rare.*

1867 LATHAM *Black & White* 119 The complaint [ague] is familiarly spoken of as the 'Prevalent'... When the 'Prevalent' is very prevalent, families have to arrange not to have it all at the same time. **1872** LYTTON *Parisians* III. vi, A lively pattern, in which the prevalents were rose-colour and white.

prevalently (ˈprɛvələntlɪ), *adv.* [f. prec. + -LY².] In a prevalent manner or degree.

1. Prevailingly, overpoweringly, victoriously; powerfully, effectively. Now *rare.*

1636 JACKSON *Creed* VIII. xiv. §1 They..prevalently tempt them to cruelty and hatred towards this Holy One. **1737** BOYSE *The Olive* xiii, By long succeeding Trials doom'd to get Strength from her Falls, and rise more prevalently Great! **1858** CARLYLE *Fredk. Gt.* II. vi. (1872) I. 82 They fought much and prevalently.

2. To a prevailing extent; in a great proportion of cases; very frequently, generally, usually.

1709 CHANDLER *Effort agst. Bigotry* 30 Censorious Persons (those that are habitually and prevalently so) do really want that Charity which is essential to Christianity. **1869** F. W. NEWMAN *Misc.* 202 Long steppes,..which..like our sheep-downs, were prevalently round and smooth. **1879** CHR. G. ROSSETTI *Seek & F.* 281 Silence and peace are and ought to be more prevalently characteristic of ordinary Christians.

So **ˈprevalentness**, the quality of being prevalent, prevalency. (Bailey, vol. II, 1727.)

†**prevaˈlescent**, *a. Obs. rare*⁻¹. [ad. L. *prævalēscent-em*, pr. pple. of *prævalēscĕre* to become very strong, inceptive of *prævalēre* to PREVAIL: see -ESCE.] Becoming prevalent; growing to prevail. So †**prevaˈlescence**, growing ascendancy.

1653 J. HALL *Paradoxes* 56 In the primitive times..our reason was not deprav'd with long traditionall customes, nor tinctured by any prevalescent humour. *Ibid.* 118 Livia..had that great prevalescence with him, that he by her means disposed the succession of the Empire upon a son of her womb by a former husband.

†**preˈvalid**, *a. Obs. rare*⁻¹. [ad. L. *prævalid-us* very strong, too strong: see PRE- A. 6 and VALID.] Excessively strong.

1657 HAWKE *Killing is M.* 23 Prevalid bodies are secure from external hurts, yet are they burdned and laden with their own strength.

prevaly, obs. form of PRIVILY.

†**preˈvaricable**, *a. Obs. rare*⁻¹. [f. L. *prævāricārī* to PREVARICATE + -ABLE.] Capable of being 'prevaricated' or deviated from.

1644 DIGBY *Nat. Soul* II. Pref. 353 It will follow euidently out of them, (if they be of necessity and not preuaricable) that some other Principle beyond bodies, is required to be the roote and first ground of motion in them.

†**preˈvaricant**, *a. Obs. rare*⁻¹. [ad. L. *prævāricānt-em*, pres. pple. of *prævāricārī* to PREVARICATE.] Deviating from the proper course or method; irregular, improper.

1644 BULWER *Chiron.* 103 To throw downe the Hand from the Head, with the Fingers formed into a gripe or scratching posture;..or to throw it upwards with the Palme turned up, are actions prevaricant in Rhetorick, and condemned by Quintilian.

†**preˈvaricate**, *a. Obs. rare.* Also præ-. [ad. L. *prævāricāt-us*, pa. pple. of *prævāricārī*: see next.] Perverted; perverse.

1635 BRATHWAIT *Arcad. Pr.* II. 58 In this case (see my prevaricate misery!) would I not either be led or driven by any. **1650** CHARLETON *Paradoxes* Prol. 7 The Divine..met with a cure for the nicety of his Conscience, from a prævaricate Adversary.

prevaricate (prɪˈværɪkeɪt), *v.* Also 7 præ-. [f. L. *prævāric-ārī* to walk crookedly, hence, to deviate from a straight course, hence from the path of duty; spec. of an advocate, to practise collusion; in eccl. L. to transgress, f. *præ*, PRE- A. + *vāricāre* to spread the legs apart, straddle (f. *vāricus* straddling, f. *vārus* bent, knock-kneed + -*icus*, -IC): see -ATE³.]

I. Intransitive senses.

†1. To go aside from the right course, method, or mode of action; to swerve from the proper course; to deviate, go astray, transgress. *Obs.*

1582 N.T. (Rhem.) *Acts* i. 25 Shew..whom thou hast chosen, to take the place of this ministerie and Apostleship, from the which Iudas hath preuaricated. **1610** B. JONSON *Alch.* II. iii, If you..should now preuaricate, And, to your owne particular lusts, employ So great, and catholique a blisse. **1657–83** EVELYN *Hist. Relig.* (1850) II. 305 How widely they differ and prevaricate from the wholesome precepts and doctrine delivered. **1681** WHARTON *Soul World* Wks. (1683) 651 Motion..might easily prevaricate, and wander, unless it were Ruled by the Intellect.

2. To deviate from straightforwardness; to act or speak evasively; to quibble, shuffle, equivocate.

a **1631** DONNE in *Select.* (1840) 257 Follow not these men in their severity,..nor in their facility to disguise and prevaricate in things that are. **1645** PAGITT *Heresiogr.* (1662) 309 Let therefore all men no longer prævaricate with their Conscience (in matters of some inconsiderable scruples). **1749** FIELDING *Tom Jones* XVIII. viii, Do not hesitate nor prevaricate; but answer faithfully and truly to every question I ask. **1841** JAMES *Brigand* xxxii, Perhaps we may put it in such a way as to prevent his prevaricating. **1865** J. H. INGRAHAM *Pillar of Fire* (1872) 392 It is impossible..for me either to conceal or to prevaricate.

†3. *Law.* **a.** To betray the cause of a client by collusion with an opponent. **b.** To undertake a matter falsely and deceitfully in order to defeat the object professed to be promoted. *Obs.*

1646 in Somers *Tracts* I. 33 Nor is it an unusual thing for a Lawyer to be of Council with one Party, and to prevaricate, and be of Confederacy under-hand with the adverse Party. **1656** BLOUNT *Glossogr.* s.v. *Calumniate*, He that undertakes ones sute, and either will not urge reasons in the behalf of his Clyent, or answer the Objections of his adversary, when he is able, is said to *Prevaricate*, i. to play the false Proctor. **1672** *Cowell's Interpr.*, *Prevaricate*, is when a man falsly and deceitfully seems to undertake a thing, *ea intentione* that he may destroy it. *a* **1716** SOUTH *Serm.* (1744) XI. 182 For should a brother prevaricate and prove false, nature itself would seem to..upbraid his unhuman perfidiousness.

†4. In etymological sense: To walk or go crookedly; in quot., to plough crookedly. *Obs.*

1801 RANKEN *Hist. France* I. 424 They were careful not to prevaricate, or make crooked serpentine ridges; but to make straight furrows and ridges.

II. Transitive senses.

†5. To deviate from, transgress (a 'law', etc.).

1596 SPENSER *State Irel.* Wks. (Globe) 610/1 The lawes..are sithence either disanulled, or quite prevaricated through chaunge and alterations of times. **1604** T. WRIGHT *Passions* VI. 297 When the Soule did not prevaricate the Lawe of God, or passe the limittes of Reason.

†6. To turn (anything) from the straight course, application, or meaning; to pervert. *Obs.*

1647 WARD *Simp. Cobler* 2 He will therefore bestirre him to prevaricate Evangelicall Truths, and Ordinances. **1660** JER. TAYLOR *Duct. Dubit.* I. ii. rule viii, He may not prevaricate this duty of a judge. **1682** DRYDEN *Relig. Laici* Pref., Wks. (Globe) 189. **1705** *Sequel* xiv, O! Holy Times —when purity our Youth, And P[riests] prevaricate the Sacred Truth, Desert the Ch[urc]h for meaner ends unknown.

preˈvaricating, *ppl. a.* [f. prec. + -ING².]

1. That prevaricates; swerving from the proper course or from straightforward statement; quibbling.

1641 BRATHWAIT *Merc. Brit.* B j b, Pious bashfulnesse is unusuall to prevaricating transgressors. **1713** ADDISON *Ct. Tariff* 12 The Court found him such a False, Shuffling, Prevaricating Rascal. **1833** J. H. NEWMAN *Arians* IV. iii. (1876) 308 Creeds, which were..intolerable only because the badges of a prevaricating party.

2. Deflecting light so as to show objects crookedly. *rare.*

1870 LOWELL *Study Wind.* 237 Flowers..made of French cambric spangled with dewdrops of prevaricating glass.

prevarication (prɪværɪˈkeɪʃən). Also 7 præ-. [= F. *prévarication* (12th c. in Littré), ad. L. *prævāricātiōn-em*, n. of action f. *prævāricārī* to PREVARICATE.

1601 HOLLAND *Pliny* XVIII. xix. I. 579 The ploughman, unlesse he bend and stoupe forward..must..leave much undone as it ought to be; a fault which in Latine we call Prevarication: and this tearme appropriate unto Husbandrie, is borrowed from thence by Lawyers.]

†1. Divergence from the right course, method, or mode of action. **a.** Deviation from rectitude; violation of moral law; transgression, trespass. *Obs.*

1382 WYCLIF *1 Tim.* ii. 14 Forsoth the womman was disceyued in feith, in preuaricacioun [*gloss* or brekyng of the lawe]. **1483** CAXTON *Gold. Leg.* (1892) 45 He was right couenable by cause of the curyng, the whiche by manere was semblable to the preuaricacion, by lyk and contrarye. **1528** ROY *Rede me* (Arb.) 119 Of all oure detestacions And sinfull prevaricacions Thou alone arte the defender. **1665** WITHER *Lord's Prayer* 122 It was thereby subject to many infirmities, and inclinable to all manner of Prevarications. **1701** tr. *Le Clerc's Prim. Fathers* (1702) 337 That all Men do not die through the Death and Prevarication of Adam.

†**b.** Departure *from* a rule, principle, or normal state; perversion or violation *of* a law, etc.; deviation from truth or correctness, error; breach of rule, irregularity. *Obs.*

1615 CROOKE *Body of Man* 258 So is her body a necessary being, a first and not a second intention of Nature, her proper and absolute worke not her error or preuarication. **1633** PRYNNE *Histrio-Mastix* I. VI. xii. 533 b, On Holi-dayes ..men every where runne to the Ale-house, to Playes, to Enterludes, and dances, to the very derision of Gods Name, and the prevarication of the day. **1671** HOWE *Vanity Man* Wks. 1862 I. 430 It is equally a prevarication from true manhood to be moved with everything and with nothing. **1674** OWEN *Holy Spirit* Wks. 1852 III. 146 It is no small prevarication in some Christians to give countenance to so putid a fiction.

†**c.** *lit.* Divergence from a straight line or course.

[**1601**: see etymology above.] **1672** NEWTON in Rigaud *Corr. Sci. Men* (1841) II. 343 How much those errors..are increased or diminished, is to be estimated by the prevarication of the rays.

†2. Deviation from duty; violation of trust; corrupt action, esp. in a court of law. *Obs.*

1541 PAYNEL *Catiline* vii. 11 b, Catiline (the whiche a fewe dayes before was by preuarication and falsehod quite of petye theft). **1567** *Gude & Godlie B.* (S.T.S.) 180 Sen our Hely, in his office, Is lyke in Preuaricatioun, He sall ressaif sic lyke Justice, Mak he nocht reformatioun. **1662** J. DAVIES tr. *Olearius' Voy. Ambass.* 115 The Inhabitants of Pleskou.. charg'd Puskin with prevarication in his Employment, and perfidiousness towards his Prince. **1727–41** CHAMBERS *Cycl.*, *Prevarication* is also used for a secret abuse committed in the exercise of a public office, or of a commission given by a private person. [Hence in Webster 1828, etc.]

†**b.** *Law.* See PREVARICATE *v.* 3. *Obs.*

1552 HULOET, *Preuarication*..is a collusion done in lawe, ..wherby the one partye suffereth the other to obtayne in suite, to the entent to hurte or endomage some other. **1628** LE GRYS tr. *Barclay's Argenis* 256 If it shall appeare, that they haue forfeited their Faith, or wronged their Client by preuarication. **1710** J. HARRIS *Lex. Techn.* II, *Prevarication*, in the Civil Law, is where an Informer colludes with the Defendant, and so makes only a feigned Prosecution.

3. Avoidance of plain dealing or straightforward statement of the truth; evasion, quibbling, shuffling, equivocation, double-dealing, deception.

a **1655** VINES *Lord's Supp.* (1677) 413, I..shall clearly without any fraud or prevarication declare my opinion. **1673** MARVELL *Reh. Transp.* II. 388 When Doctor Heylin's Divinity shall go for orthodox, or his Prævarications pass for History, you may then..be reputed a Classical Author. **1797** BURKE *Regic. Peace* iii. Wks. VIII. 304 Fraud and prevarication are servile vices. *a* **1862** BUCKLE *Civiliz.* (1871) III. v. 337 Hume..was a man..utterly incapable of falsehood, or of prevarication of any kind. **1862** BURTON *Bk. Hunter* (1863) 132 Mr. Justice Best said he had a great mind to commit the witness for prevarication.

preˈvaricative, *a. rare*⁻¹. [f. L. *prævāricārī* to PREVARICATE: see -IVE.] Characterized by or tending to prevarication.

1657 HAWKE *Killing is M.* 38 The Impostors penalty..for his prevaricative and invective pamphlet.

prevaricator (prɪˈværɪkeɪtə(r)). Also 6–7 -tour, 7–9 præ-. [a. L. *prævāricātor*, agent-n. f. *prævāricārī* to PREVARICATE: see -OR.] One who prevaricates.

†1. One who goes astray, diverges, or deviates from the right course; a transgressor. *Obs.*

1542 BECON *Christmas Banquet* i. C iv b, The fyrst sinner, yᵉ fyrst preuaricatour begat synners bonde to death. **1582** N.T. (Rhem.) *Gal.* ii. 18 For if I build the same things againe which I have destroied, I make myself a prevaricatour [WYCLIF, TINDALE trespassour, 1611 transgressour]. **1697** C. LESLIE *Snake in Grass* (ed. 2) 74 Which neither Fox, nor any of his Followers have done; and therefore are accus'd by them as Prevaricators from their own Principles. **1755** SMOLLETT *Quix.* II. II. xi, Thou prevaricator of all the squirely ordinances of chivalry!

†**b.** One who betrays a cause or violates a trust; a renegade; a traitor. *Obs.*

c **1555** HARPSFIELD *Divorce Hen. VIII* (Camden) 177 The King..licensed Queen Katherine to choose counsellors where she would..whereof some played very honest parts and stood stiffly and fast to her cause, some played the prevaricators, and fled from her to the King's side. *a* **1637** B. JONSON *Underwoods, Epist. to Master Colby*, Where.. loud Boasters, and perjur'd, with the infinite more Prevaricators swarm.

†2. One who diverts something from its proper use; a perverter. *Obs.*

1694 D'URFEY *Quix.* I. IV. i. 40 A plague on thee, thou confounded Prevaricator of Language. **1907** G. G. COULTON in *Contemp. Rev.* June 797 Knowing that such prevaricators of tithes were destined to find their part in hell with Cain.

3. One who acts or speaks so as to evade the strict truth; a quibbler, shuffler, equivocator.

1650 BULWER *Anthropomet.* 21 Who have forced Art (the usual imitator of Nature) to turn prævaricator in humanity. **1656** HOBBES *Six Lessons* Wks. 1845 VII. 334 There was never seen worse reasoning than in that philosophical essay; which..proceeded from a prevaricator. **1741** WARBURTON *Div. Legat.* II. II. App. 46 What is to be done with this Prevaricator? **1760–72** H. BROOKE *Fool of Qual.* (1792) II. 29 The judge cried out, Clerk, hand me up the examination of this prevaricator. **1893** *Columbus* (Ohio) *Dispatch* 6 Sept., The prevaricators, who ever they were, said dogs could not be obtained.

4. At Cambridge University: An orator who made a jocose or satirical speech at Commencement; called also *varier*. (In quot. 1885 applied to the corresponding *terræ filius* at Oxford.) *Obs.* exc. *Hist.*

(Cf. Cicero *De Partit. Orat.* c. 36, §126 Prævaricator significat eum qui in contrariis causis quasi varie esse positus videatur.)

1614 J. CHAMBERLAIN in *Crt. & Times Jas. I* (1848) I. 304 The Bishop of Ely sent the moderator, the answerer, the varier or prevaricator, and one of the repliers, that were all of his house, twenty angels a-piece. **1636** LAUD in Peacock *Stat. Cambridge* (1841) App. A. p. xxv, St. Mary's Church [Cambridge] at every Great Commencement is made a theatre and the prævaricator's stage, wherein he acts and sets forth his profane and scurrilous jests. **1706** PHILLIPS, *Prevaricator*.., also a Master of Arts in the University of Cambridge, chosen..to make an ingenious Satyrical Speech reflecting on the Misdemeanours of the principal Members. **1851** *Coll. Life t. Jas. I* 84 The Praevaricator's gibes were launched forth at all present. **1885** HAZLITT in *Antiquary* Oct. 154/1 Randolph the poet appears to have been the prevaricator for 1632.

†5. *Law.* (See PREVARICATE *v.* 3.) *Obs.*

1638 CHILLINGW. *Relig. Prot.* I. Pref. §21 Do we know the Jesuits no better than so? What, are they turned Prevaricators against their own Faction? Are they likely Men to betray and expose their own Agents and Instruments? **1696** B. KENNETT *Romæ Antiq.* II. III. xviii. 136 The Civilians define a Prevaricator to be one that betrays his Cause to the Adversary, and turns on the Criminal's side whom he ought to prosecute. **1793** MURPHY *Tacitus* (1805) III. 355 All persons concerned either in procuring or conducting for hire a collusive action, were to be treated as public prevaricators.

preˈvaricatory, *a. rare.* [f. as PREVARICATE *v.* + -ORY².] Characterized by prevarication; prevaricating; evasive.

c **1656** BRAMHALL *Replic.* iii. 138 His fellows being examined..either refused to answer, or gave such ambiguous and prevaricatory answers, that some ingenuous Catholicks began to suspect that they fostered some treachery. **1812** W. TAYLOR in *Monthly Mag.* XXXIV. 415 Exhibiting the disgrace of prevaricatory witnesses.

†**pre'varica,trice.** *Obs. rare*⁻¹. [ad. late L. *prævāricātrīc-em* (Augustine) a female transgressor, fem. agent-n.: see PREVARICATOR; perhaps through F. *prévaricatrice* (12th c. in Hatz.-Darm.).] A female 'prevaricator' or transgressor.

c **1450** *Mirour Saluacioun* 1198 Oure ladie..wold be purified to be of the lawe Executrice Yᵗ sho ne shuld noght be demed of the lawe preuaricatrice.

†**pre'vary,** *v. Obs. rare*⁻¹. [prob. a. OF. *prévarier* (12th c. in Hatz.-Darm.), ad. L. *prævāricārī*: see PREVARICATE *v.*] *trans.* To pervert: = PREVARICATE *v.* 6.

1541 R. COPLAND *Guydon's Quest. Chirurg.* Bjb, He ought to knowe the accydentes that chaunce to come in dyseases for often tymes it preuaryeth the same selfe cure of the dyseases as Gaylen declareth [*orig.* totam curam præuaricant et peruertunt].

prevaseil, obs. Sc. f. PRIVY SEAL.

prevate, obs. f. PRIVITY.

prevay, obs. f. PRIVY.

preve, var. PRIVE *v. Obs.*; obs. f. PRIVY, PROOF, PROVE.

†**'preveance.** *Obs. rare*⁻¹. [a. obs. F. *preveance* providence, provision (1617 in Godef.):—late L. type **prævidentia*, in sense of *providentia*: see PREVIDE.] Provision: in quot., the *Provisions of Oxford*, drawn up 1258.

c **1325** *Chron. Eng.* (Ritson) 1003 Bituene the barouns ant the kyng, Wes gret stryvyng For the preveance of Oxneford, That sire Simound de Mountfort Meintenede.

pre-Vedic: see PRE- B. 1 a.

prevei, obs. f. PRIVY.

prevelage, -lege, obs. ff. PRIVILEGE.

prevely, obs. f. PRIVILY.

prevenance ('preɪvɪnəns). [a. F. *prévenance* (prevnɑ̃s) (also in Eng. use), f. *prévenir* to anticipate, prepossess: see PREVENE and -ANCE.] Courteous anticipation of the desires or needs of others; an obliging manner; complaisance.

1823 SCOTT *Quentin D.* Introd., A very conversable pleasing man, with an air of *prévenance* and ready civility of communication. **1848** THACKERAY *Van. Fair* lii, The same good-humour, *prévenances*, merriment [etc.]. **1876** MRS. HOPKINS *Rose Turq.* II. xxvii. 112 She did everything he asked carefully and well, but the sweet prevenance was gone.

†**'prevenancy.** *Obs. rare*⁻¹. [f. as prec.: see -ANCY.] = prec.

1768 STERNE *Sent. Journ.* (1775) I. 52 La Fleur's prevenancy (for there was a passport in his very looks) soon set every servant in the kitchen at ease with him.

prevenant ('prɛvɪnənt), *a.* and *sb. rare.* Also as French **prévenant.** [F., orig. pres. pple. of *prévenir* to predispose, prepossess: see PREVENE.]

A. *adj.*

1. In F. form *prévenant* (prevnɑ̃). Courteously anticipating the needs of others; obliging.

1770 MME. D'ARBLAY *Early Diary* (1889) I. 86 There is something in his manner *prévenant*.

†**2.** = PREVENIENT 2. *Obs. rare*⁻¹.

1790 *Bystander* 386 He made me comprehend..a wide difference between..grace prevenant and grace co-operant.

B. *sb.* Something that precedes; an antecedent.

1876 W. G. WARD *Ess. Philos. Theism* (1884) I. 318 On reflection, we think it will be satisfactory if we use the word 'prevenant' to denote what he calls 'cause'.

prevene (prɪ'viːn), *v.* Chiefly *Sc.* Now *rare* or *Obs.* Also 6 **preuine, -veynne, prævene, prauein(e,** 7 **preveen(e, -w(e)ine.** [ad. L. *prævenīre* to come before, precede, anticipate, hinder, excel, f. *præ*, PRE- A. + *venīre* to come. So F. *prévenir* (1539 in Hatz.-Darm.).]

†**1.** *trans.* To take action before or in anticipation of (a person or thing). **a.** To anticipate, take precautions against (a danger, evil, etc.); hence, to prevent, frustrate, evade. *Obs.*

1456 SIR G. HAYE *Law Arms* (S.T.S.) 270 Na man..suld byde his dede, seand it cum till him; bot he suld prevene it, and he mycht. And sen a man seis his fa cum to geve him mortall woundis..he wald..prevene the strakis. **1533** BELLENDEN *Livy* III. xvi. (S.T.S.) II. 13 Be my calamyte ȝe may eschew or ellis prevene siclike displeseris in tymes cummyng. **1578** *Reg. Privy Council Scot.* III. 12 Gif thair treasonabill interprysis be not..spedilie prevenit. **1650** EARL MONM. tr. *Senault's Man bec. Guilty* 329 His justice doth never through punishments prevene our sins. *a* **1657** BALFOUR *Ann. Scotl.* (1824–5) II. 54 Mischieffe..wiche the Lordes of priuey counsaill wyssly preweined. **1678** SIR G. MACKENZIE *Crim. Laws Scot.* II. xxix. §2 (1699) 276 That the Crime committed, may be punished, to preveen the Errour of others.

†**b.** To act before or more quickly than (a person or thing); hence, to forestall, supplant; also *absol.* to intervene. *Obs.*

1500–20 DUNBAR *Poems* xlvii. 70, I salbe als weill luvit agane, Thair may no jangler me prevene. **1600** JAS. VI in *Lett. Jas. & Eliz.* (Camden) 132 In this office of kyndnes touardis me, ye haue farre praueined all other kings my confederatis. **1650** EARL MONM. tr. *Senault's Man bec. Guilty* 73 When the Pagans were surprized with any danger, and that instinct did in them prevene reasoning, they implor'd the succour of the true God. **1708** J. PHILIPS *Cyder* I. 43 If thy indulgent Care Had not preven'd, among unbody'd Shades I now had wander'd.

†**c.** *Theol.* = PREVENT *v.* 4, 4 b. Used esp. in reference to *prevenient grace*: see PREVENIENT 2.

1588 A. KING tr. *Canisius' Catech.* 220 The beginning of iustification in men of perfect aige mon be tain of the grace of God prævening tham through Iesus Christ. **1600** HAMILTON *Facile Traictise* in *Cath. Tractates* (S.T.S.) 223 Saue our king, o lord, preuine him in the blissings of your sueitnes. [Cf. Ps. xxi. 3.] **1633** W. STRUTHER *True Happines* 47 All these works of the Soul neither breed in us, neither begin at us, but he preveeneth us in them all. **1662** A. PETRIE *Ch. Hist.* I. iii. §2. 28 Our good things are both God's and ours, because he preveeneth us by inspiring that we do will.

†**d.** *Sc. Law.* Of a court or judge: To take from (another) the preferable right of jurisdiction, by exercising the first judicial act. *Obs.*

1678 SIR G. MACKENZIE *Crim. Laws Scot.* II. ii. §5 (1699) 182 Where many Judges are competent, they may preveen one another, and prevention is defyned to be *anticipatio sive præoccupatio usus jurisdictionis*.

†**2.** To take in advance. **a.** To preoccupy, prepossess. *Obs. rare*⁻¹.

1513 DOUGLAS *Æneis* I. xi. 55 Bot he [Cupid]..Can [= gan] her dolf spreit for to prevene and steir, Had bene disvsit fra luif that mony ȝeir.

†**b.** Of death, etc.: To overtake prematurely.

1567 *Gude & Godlie B.* (S.T.S.) 165 Thocht pest, or sword wald vs preuene, Befoir our hour, to slay vs clene. **1596** DALRYMPLE tr. *Leslie's Hist. Scot.* II. 158 Bot this capitane is preueined in Camelodune wᵗ deith in few dayes.

†**c.** To anticipate (a time) by earlier action; to provide beforehand for (a coming event). *Obs.*

1570 *Satir. Poems Reform.* xii. 150 Best wer, I think, mycht we preuene ȝone day. *a* **1578** LINDESAY (Pitscottie) *Chron. Scot.* (S.T.S.) I. 397 The Scottis prevenit the tyme and past fourtht at midnight to the fieldis. **1596** DALRYMPLE tr. *Leslie's Hist. Scot.* IX. 261 He oft vset to preueine materis of waicht with a sad counsell and graue,..preueining the tyme to cum, with Judgement incredible.

3. In lit. sense of the Latin: To come or go before; to precede. *rare.*

1596 DALRYMPLE tr. *Leslie's Hist. Scot.* X. 455 Preueineng al the rest, [he] landis in Scotland the first of Maii. **1869** HOLLAND *Kathrina* II. 107 Till our poor race has passed the tortuous years That lie prevening the millennium.

Hence **pre'vening** *vbl. sb.*, anticipation; *ppl. a.*, prevenient.

1633 W. STRUTHER *True Happines* 28 In Spiritual things we must ascend from gifts to grace, and in grace..from a preveening to an exciting grace. **1662** A. PETRIE *Ch. Hist.* I. iii. §2. 28 By preveening grace and good will following, that which is the gift of God, becomes our work. **1678** SIR G. MACKENZIE *Crim. Laws Scot.* I. xxi. §2 (1699) 111 If it could have been proved that the wrong was done immediatly without any preveening provocation.

pre'venience. *rare.* [f. as next: see -ENCE.] **a.** = PREVENANCE. **b.** The fact or condition of being prevenient.

1859 MRS. STOWE *Minister's Wooing* xxv, Striving by a thousand gentle preveniences, to spare her from fatigue and care. **1864** WEBSTER, *Prevenience*, the act of anticipating, or going before; anticipation. **1872** O. SHIPLEY *Gloss. Eccl. Terms* 417 They [Semi-Pelagians] held freewill and predestination from foreknowledge, denying the prevenience of grace.

prevenient (prɪ'viːnɪənt), *a.* [ad. L. *prævenient-em*, pres. pple. of *prævenīre*: see PREVENE.]

1. Coming before, preceding, previous, antecedent.

1656 BLOUNT *Glossogr.*, *Prevenient*, coming or going before, preventing. **1800** LAMB *Let. to Manning* 3 Nov., Wks. (1865) 54 Which..stupidly stood alone, nothing prevenient or antevenient. **1834** SIR H. TAYLOR *Artevelde* v. *Lay Elena* x, The darker, soberer, sadder green Prevenient to decay. **1859** C. BARKER *Assoc. Princ.* iii. 64 The various predisposing or prevenient agencies existing in Europe. **1895** SALMON *Chr. Doctr. Immort.* v. ii. 518 It could not take effect until two prevenient events had occurred.

b. Hence, anticipatory, expectant. Const. *of.*

1814 CARY *Dante* (Chandos) 286 She, of the time prevenient, on the spray, That overhangs the couch, with wakeful gaze, Expects the sun. **1881** J. SIMON in *Nature* XXIV. 374/1 Unless they be regulated and inspected under a special law in much the same prevenient spirit as if they were prostitutes under the Contagious Diseases Act. **1889** *Macm. Mag.* Aug. 300/2 Prevenient of all disgraceful sickness or waste in the unsullied limbs.

2. Antecedent to human action. ***prevenient grace***, in *Theol.*, the grace of God which precedes repentance and conversion, predisposing the heart to seek God, previously to any desire or motion on the part of the recipient. See PREVENE *v.* 1 c, PREVENT *v.* 4.

a **1607** J. RAYNOLDS *Proph. Haggai* ix. (1649) 100 Gods grace must be both prevenient to go before, and subsequent to follow after us in all things. **1667** MILTON *P.L.* XI. 3 From the Mercie-seat above Prevenient Grace descending had remov'd The stonie from thir hearts, and made new flesh. **1747** MALLET *Amyntor & Theodora* III. 127 Love celestial whose prevenient aid Forbids approaching ill. **1809–10** COLERIDGE *Friend* (1818) III. 85 The articles of prevenient and auxiliary grace. **1849** R. I. WILBERFORCE *Doctr. Bapt.* (1850) 59 Since this action of prevenient grace does not supersede human responsibility, it can only persuade, it cannot coerce. **1904** J. R. ILLINGWORTH *Chr. Charac.* ix. 167 This desire..must come from God, by what is technically called His prevenient or antecedent grace. *Ibid.* 168 There is nothing in this term 'prevenient grace' to favour the Calvinistic doctrine of irresistible and indefectible grace.

Hence **pre'veniently** *adv.*, antecedently, previously.

1633 T. ADAMS *Exp. 2 Peter* ii. 3 This is a course that shall make men either preveniently thankful, or inexcusably desperate. **1880** MRS. WHITNEY *Odd or Even?* xxv, Neatly, and perhaps, preveniently, discharged her conscience. **1974** *Times Lit. Suppl.* 29 Nov. 1343/1 Are they those misconceptions of the nature and role of poetry which this most preveniently resourceful essay in metaphysics would correct? **1977** G. W. H. LAMPE *God as Spirit* iii. 74 God's Spirit works preveniently to bring a person to conversion. **1977** *Theology* LXXX. 192 Whenever and wherever there is response to the divine love, *there* that love is preveniently at work.

†**preve'nire,** erron. for PRÆMUNIRE.

c **1460** *Wisdom* 859 in *Macro Plays* 63 A 'preuenire facias' than haue as tyght, And þou xall hurle hym, so þat he xall haue I-now.

†**pre'vent,** *ppl. a. Obs.* [ad. L. *prævent-us*, pa. pple. of *prævenīre* to PREVENE.] Prevented, in various senses: chiefly as pple.; see the verb.

c **1420** *Pallad. on Husb.* I. 248 And tilyng, whenne hit tyme is hit to do, Is not to rathe yf dayis thryis fyue Hit be preuent. **1432–50** tr. *Higden* (Rolls) IV. 397 The lecches seide the deformite of the childe to be causede in that the dewe tyme of childenge was prevente [L. *debita tempora prævenisset*]. *c* **1450** tr. *De Imitatione* II. viii. 49 But if þou be preuent and norisshid wiþ his grace. **1482** *Monk of Evesham* (Arb.) 46 Ye remembre how a certen..cytson of this place was hastly preuent of dethe and sodenly dyed. **1521** *Bradshaw's St. Werburge, 2nd Balade to Auctour* 23 With deth preuent he myght nothyng replique.

prevent (prɪ'vɛnt), *v.* [f. L. *prævent-*, ppl. stem of *prævenīre*: see PREVENE, and cf. prec.]

I. †**1.** *trans.* To act before, in anticipation of, or in preparation for (a future event, or a point of time, esp. the time fixed for the act); to act as if the event or time had already come. *Obs.*

1432–50 tr. *Higden* (Rolls) VI. 37 The peple prevente that feste by the abstinence of a monethe [L. *jejunio præveniturl*]. **1467–8** *Rolls of Parlt.* V. 623/1 Better it were to prevente the tyme, and occupie the seid Adversary at home, than to suffre hym to entre this Londe. **1535** COVERDALE *Ps.* cxix. 148 Myne eyes preuente yᵉ night watches, yᵗ I myght be occupied in thy wordes. **1601** SHAKS. *Jul. C.* v. i. 105 But I do finde it Cowardly, and vile, For feare of what might fall, so to preuent The time of life. *a* **1626** BACON *New Atl.* (1650) 4 He had prevented the Houre, because we might have the whole day before us, for our Businesse. **1633** G. HERBERT *Temple, Self-condemnation*, Thus we prevent the last great day, And judge our selves. **1694** CONGREVE *Double-Dealer* IV. xv, Who does not prevent the hour of Love out-stays the time. **1752** HUME *Ess. & Treat.* (1777) I. 150 Cælia,..preventing the appointed hour,..chides my tardy steps. **1813** SCOTT *Rokeby* II. iv, Bertram..from the towers, preventing day, With Wilfrid took his early way.

b. To meet beforehand or anticipate (an objection, question, command, desire, want, etc.). *arch.*

a **1533** FRITH *Another Bk. agst. Rastell* Wks. (1829) 217 To these two points I answer, preventing their objection, that they should not despise it, because of my youth. **1553** T. WILSON *Rhet.* 100 Anticipacion is when we preuent those wordes that another would saie, and disproue theim as vntrue, or at least wise answere vnto them. **1588** KYD *Househ. Phil.* Wks. (1901) 240 So that I preuented his desire, and in some sort to satisfie him, said I was neuer till nowe in this Countrey. **1633** in *Verney Mem.* (1892) I. 124 My hopes are that your religious care hath prevented these admonitions. **1667** DRYDEN *Maiden Queen* II. i, Your goodness still prevents my wishes. **1700** in *Col. Rec. Pennsylv.* I. 597, I am glad wee have prevented their Commands in doing it before they came. **1788** *Disinterested Love* I. 5 Thus he prevented all my wants. **1830** WORDSW. *Russian Fugitive* I. v, She led the Lady to a seat..Prevented each desire. **1850** SMEDLEY *F. Fairlegh* xliv, It will be the study of my life to prevent your every wish——..'Prevent' means to forestall in that sense.

†**c.** *intr.* or *absol.* To come, appear, or act before the time or in anticipation. *Obs.*

1542 *St. Papers Hen. VIII*, IX. 190 ThEmperour..fearing the comming of the Turques power this next yere, entendeth to prevente, and also to goo Hym self befor into Italie. **1609** BIBLE (Douay) *1 Macc.* x. 4 Let us prevent to make peace with him, before he make with Alexander against us. **1626** BACON *Sylva* §403 Strawberries watered now and then..with water wherein hath been steeped Sheeps-dung..will prevent and come early.

2. *trans.* To act before or more quickly than (another person or agent); to anticipate in action. Now *rare* and *arch.*

1523 SKELTON *Garl. Laurel* 428 So I am preuentid of my brethern tweyne In rendrynge to you thankkis meritory. **1526** *Pilgr. Perf.* (W. de W. 1531) 106 Our lorde knowynge all thoughtes & wordes, preuented his discyples, & made answere hym selfe. **1556** ROBINSON tr. *More's Utop.* Epist. P. Giles (Arb.) 25, I shoulde preuent him, and take frome him the flower and grace of the noueltie. **1627** HAKEWILL *Apol.* (1630) 6th Advert., I finde my selfe for the maine matter prevented by Stephanus Pannonius in that booke of his. **1675** HOBBES *Odyssey* xv. 146 Whil what to answer he was taking care, Helen prevented him. **1715–16** POPE *Let. to E. Blount* 20 Mar., I know you have prevented me in this thought, as you always will in any thing that's good. **1758**

Blackstone *Comm.* I. Introd. 32 Perhaps..I could now.. suggest a few hints in favour of university learning:—but in these all who hear me, I know, have already prevented me. **1776** Gibbon *Decl. & F.* vi. I. 154 The fortunate soil assisted, and even prevented, the hand of cultivation. **1808** Helen St. Victor *Ruins of Rigonda* I. 6 Foventi wished.. to ask the father's consent to address his daughter, when he was prevented by the baron's asking his advice in point of providing a husband.

b. *Canon Law.* 'To transact or undertake any affair before an inferior, by right of position' (*Cassell's Encycl. Dict.*); = prevene *v.* 1 d. Cf. prevention 2 a.

3. To come, arrive, or appear before, to precede; to outrun, outstrip. Now *rare* and *arch.*

1523 *St. Papers Hen. VIII*, VI. 193 The Frence men.. discendyd with incredible diligence, preventing thestimation off all the Italians. **1538** Cromwell in Merriman *Life & Lett.* (1902) II. 138, I have..sent it vnto hym after the departure of the said Muriell, to thentent he myght prevente thambassadours poste and you have leasure to consulte and advise vpon the same. **1557** N.T. (Genev.) *1 Thess.* iv. 15 We which lyue..shal not preuent them [Wyclif schulen not come before hem; Tindale shall not come yerre they] which slepe. *a* **1586** Sidney *Arcadia* I. (1622) 33 The sunne..could never prevent him with earlinesse. *a* **1648** Ld. Herbert *Life* (1886) 175, I went from Lyons to Geneva, where I found also my fame had prevented my coming. **1655** Fuller *Ch. Hist.* I. i. §15 To prove our Old Style before the New (which prevents our Computation by ten dayes..). *a* **1766** Mrs. F. Sheridan *Sidney Bidulph* V. 6, I am an early riser, yet my lord V—— prevented me the next morning, for I found him in the parlour when I came down stairs.

†**b.** *fig.* To outdo, surpass, excel. *Obs.*

1540 Morysine *Vives' Introd. Wysd.* I iv b, Be not onely euen with them that honour the, but..preuente them whan thou mayste. **1548** Udall, etc. *Erasm. Par. Matt.* ii. 26 Preuenting the Iewes, which were thought to be next vnto God. **1634** Sir T. Herbert *Trav.* 52 Had Vulcan and his Cyclopes beene working there, there noise had beene prevented. **1660** tr. *Amyraldus' Treat. conc. Relig.* II. viii. 270 To prevent and go beyond all the world in respect.

4. *Theol.*, etc. To go before with spiritual guidance and help: said of God, or of his grace anticipating human action or need. *arch.*

1531 Tindale *Exp. 1 John* (1537) 34 In all that we do or thynke well, he preuenteth vs with his grace. **1548–9** (Mar.) *Bk. Com. Prayer, Collect 17th Sund. Trinity*, That thy grace maye alwayes preuente and folowe us. *Ibid.*, *Communion* ad fin., Preuent us, O lorde, in all our doinges, with thy most gracious fauour. **1597** J. T. *Serm. Paules Cr.* 65 The benignitie of God did alwaies prevent me, from many dangers freed me. **1676** Hale *Contempl.* I. 45 The Spirit of Truth and Wisdom, that doth really and truly but secretly prevent and direct them. *a* **1711** Ken *Div. Love* Wks. (1838) 303 O let thy grace..ever prevent, accompany, and follow me. **1841** Trench *Parables, Lost Sheep* (1860) 371 It is in fact only the same truth..that grace must prevent as well as follow us. **1869** Goulburn *Purs. Holiness* ii. 12 God in it prevents us (in the old sense of the word 'prevents'), anticipates us with His Grace.

b. Said of the action of God's grace, held to be given in order to predispose to repentance, faith, and good works. See prevenient 2. *arch.*

1548–9 (Mar.) *Bk. Com. Prayer, Collect Easter Day*, As by thy speciall grace, preuentyng us, thou doest putte in our myndes good desyres. **1562** *Articles of Relig.* x, We haue no power to do good workes..without the grace of God by Christe preuentyng vs, that we may haue a good wyll, & workyng with vs, when we haue that good wyll. **1563** *Homilies* II. *Rogation Week* III. (1859) 485 If any will we have to rise, it is he that preventeth our will, and disposeth us thereto. **1577** *St. Aug. Manual* (Longman) 79 Who is so hard harted that he will not be softened by the love of God preventyng man with so harty good will, that he vouchsafed to become man for mans sake? **1670** *Devout Commun.* (1688) 135 If thy grace prevented us before repentance, that we might return, shall it not much more prevent repenting sinners, that we may not perish? **1842** Manning *Serm.* (1848) II. ii. 19 Baptismal regeneration is the very highest and most perfect form of the doctrine of God's free and sovereign grace, preventing all motions, and excluding all merit on our part.

†**c.** To come in front of, to meet in front; to meet with welcome or succour; to meet with hostility or opposition, to confront. *Obs.*

1535 Coverdale *Ps.* xvii[i]. 18 They preuented me [*R.V.* came upon me] in the tyme of my trouble, but yᵉ Lorde was my defence. **1560** Bible (Genev.) *Job* iii. 12 Why did the knees preuent me? and why did I sucke the breastes? **1611** —— *Amos* ix. 10 All the sinners of my people shall die by the sword, which say: The euill shall not ouertake nor preuent vs.

II. †**5.** To forestall, balk, or baffle by previous or precautionary measures. *Obs.* or merged in 7.

1560 Bible (Genev.) *Wisd.* iv. 7 Thogh the righteous be preuented with death, yet shal he be in rest. **1568** *Hist. Jacob & Esau* v. iv. in Hazl. *Dodsley* II. 250 Thy brother Jacob came to me by subtlety, And brought me venison, and so prevented thee. **1600** J. Pory tr. *Leo's Africa* III. 128 The King was preuented by vntimely and sudden death before he could bring his purpose to effect. **1697** Potter *Antiq. Greece* II. xiv. (1715) 315 Unlucky Omens were..Especially if the Beast prevented the Knife, and dy'd suddenly. **1737** Whiston *Josephus, Antiq.* II. x. §2 Moses prevented the enemies, and..led his army before those enemies were apprized.

6. To cut off beforehand, debar, preclude (a person or other agent) *from*, deprive *of* a purpose, expectation, etc. Now *rare* or merged in 7.

1549 Latimer *1st Serm. bef. Edw. VI* (Arb.) 34 How dyd wycked Iesabell preuente kynge Hachabs herte from god and al godlines, and finally vnto destruction. **1586** Marlowe *1st Pt. Tamburl.* v. ii. 335 As the gods, to end the Trojans' toil Prevented Turnus of Lavinia. **1624** Heywood *Gunaik.* VI. 273 The Consull was prevented of his purpose. **1673** Dryden *Assignation* Ep. Ded., I have declar'd thus much before-hand, to prevent You from Suspicion, that I intend to Interest either your Judgment or your Kindness. **1755** B. Martin *Mag. Arts & Sc.* XV. I. 101, I should scarce regret Death so much on any worldly Account as preventing me of so desirable a Sight. **1813** L. Hunt in *Examiner* 15 Feb. 97/2 A wall prevents me from this sight. **1882** W. E. Forster *Let.* 23 Apr. in *19th Cent.* Oct. (1888) 615 To prevent men from the fulfilment of their contracts, or in any way, by boycotting or otherwise, to intimidate them from the full enjoyment of their rights.

7. To stop, keep, or hinder (a person or other agent) *from* doing something. Often with const. omitted. (The usual word for this sense.)

1663 Wood *Life* 7 July (O.H.S.) I. 480 If not prevented by raine [they] would have rode..before the corps [= corpse] up the street. **1665** Manley *Grotius' Low C. Warres* 604 The Fortifications..were very weak, and the enemy prevented them in perfecting their design. **1674** Ashmole *Diary* (1774) 343 This night Mr. T—— was in danger of being robbed, but most strangely prevented. **1711** Swift *Conduct of Allies* Wks. 1765 IX. 104 So great a number of troops..as should be able to..prevent the enemy from erecting their magazines. **1758** Blackstone *Comm.* I. 24 The intention is evidently this; by preventing private teachers within the walls of the city, to collect all the common lawyers into the one public university, which was newly instituted in the suburbs. **1814** Cary *Dante, Paradise* XXXI. 22 Through the universe..celestial light Glides freely, and no obstacle prevents. **1839** Keightley *Hist. Eng.* II. 33 Henry took due precautions to prevent the bull from getting into his dominions. **1875** Jowett *Plato* (ed. 2) V. 352 There is nothing to prevent us from considering..the subject of law.

b. Const. obj. and gerund.

prevent me going appears to be short for *prevent me from going*, perh. influenced by *prevent my going* (8 b).

1689 *Col. Rec. Pennsylv.* I. 253 Any Expedient..for preventing ffurther heats arriseing vpon such occasions. **1718** J. Fox *Wanderer* 147 A free Confession..easily prevents a little Error growing to a great Evil. **1765** Geo. III *Let. to Gen. Conway* in Ellis *Orig. Lett.* Ser. III. IV. 379 The only method..by which the French can be prevented settling on the coast of Newfoundland. **1768** Sterne *Sent. Journ.* (1778) I. 134 (*Amiens*) She had been prevented telling me her story. **1807** Southey *Let. to N. Lightfoot* 24 Apr., Circumstances have prevented me going to Portugal. **1835** Whewell in Todhunter *Acc. Writ.* (1876) II. 216 Sedgwick is prevented joining you by a misfortune in his family. **1867** Morley *Burke* 92 To prevent this becoming a serious affair. **1874** Dasent *Half a Life* II. 275, I know of no accident that ought to prevent you being in the first class.

8. To provide beforehand against the occurrence of (something); to render (an act or event) impracticable or impossible by anticipatory action; to preclude, stop, hinder. (A chief current sense.)

In the earlier quots. the notion of anticipating or acting previously is generally prominent; in modern use that of frustrating.

1548 Elyot, *Præcidere causam belli*, to preuent and take awaie cleane the occasion of warre. **1624** Laud *Diary* 13 Dec., He prevented his punishment by death. **1669** Sturmy *Mariner's Mag., Penalties & Forfeit.* n ij b, If all concerned had..knowledge of what they should know, they might prevent this loss and damage. **1736** Butler *Anal.* II. v. Wks. 1874 I. 209 Persons may do a great deal themselves towards preventing the bad consequences of their follies. **1818** Cruise *Digest* (ed. 2) I. 489 To place the legal estate in trustees, on purpose to prevent dower. **1836** W. Irving *Astoria* III. 213 Should any thing occur..to prevent his return. **1863** Geo. Eliot *Romola* xxviii, He ..had produced the very impression he had sought to prevent. **1872** Ruskin *Eagle's N.* §61 We cannot prevent the religious education of our children more utterly than by beginning it in lies.

b. Const. gerund (or vbl. sb.); rarely clause.

1704 N. N. tr. *Boccalini's Advts. fr. Parnass.* II. 174 All the Monarchies in the World..consult in a General Diet how to prevent being Oppress'd by'em. **1769** Goldsm. *Hist. Rome* (1786) I. Pref. 6 It was found no easy matter to prevent crowding the facts. **1841** Lane *Arab. Nts.* I. ii. 112 Thou has prevented my sleeping from the commencement of darkness until morning. **1847** Marryat *Childr. N. Forest* xxi, I shall not prevent your going. **1878** Browning *La Saisiaz* 135 What, forsooth, prevents That..I fulfill of her intents One she had the most at heart?

†**9.** To keep (something) from befalling oneself; to escape, evade, or avoid by timely action. *Obs.*

1591 Sylvester *Du Bartas* I. vi. 245 Th'hast not onely lent Prudence to Man, the Perils to prevent, Wherewith these foes threaten his feeble life. **1598** W. Phillip *Linschoten* 168/1 The cloud came with a most horrible storme, and fell vppon them before they coulde preuent it. **1632** Lithgow *Trav.* x. 439 To conclude this Epitome of France, three things I wish the way-faring man to preuent there. **1705** Hickeringill *Priest-cr.* II. Wks. 1716 III. 87 Fox..had the Wit to keep his own Fingers out of the Fire, and prevent the Honour of dying a Martyr. **1710** Shaftesb. *Charac.* (1737) I. III. i. 290 The surest method to prevent good sense, is to set up something in the room of it.

†**10.** To frustrate, defeat, bring to nought, render void or nugatory (an expectation, plan, etc.). *Obs.*

1555 *Lydgate's Chron. Troy* Address to Rdr., To preuent the malice of suche, as shal happlye accompte my trauayle herein rather rashe presumpcyon. **1616** Sir C. Mountagu in *Buccleuch MSS.* (Hist. MSS. Comm.) I. 248 The putting off of the arraignments spent much money and prevented most men's expectations. **1622** Bacon *Hen. VII* 4 Which if it had beene true, had preuented the Title of the Lady Elizabeth. *a* **1652** Brome *Queenes Exchange* IV. i. Wks. 1873 III. 523 All our art, And the Kings policy will be prevented.

†**11.** *intr.* or *absol.* To use preventive measures. Usually with extension, *that..not*, *but that*. *Obs.*

1600 W. Watson *Decacordon* (1602) 303 Doth it not stand her in hand to preuent that the number of catholiks do not increase? **1601** Shaks. *Jul. C.* II. i. 28 So Cæsar may; Then least he may, preuent. **1656** Earl Monm. tr. *Boccalini's Advts. fr. Parnass.* I. xiv. (1674) 17 It was impossible to prevent, but that a pair of shooes..should in process of time become torn. **1723** *Present St. Russia* II. 122 The Design.. was, to prevent that no body might be sent to meet me.

III. †**12.** *causative.* To hasten, bring about or put before the time or prematurely; to anticipate.

1548 Udall, etc. *Erasm. Par. Matt.* xxvi. 116 As preuentyng the honour of his burial. **1553** Brende *Q. Curtius* VIII. 54 Whyche counte it the most gloryous thyng to preuente their awne deathe. **1654** Whitlock *Zootomia* 230 Such as are of this nature, prevent the Worlds Doome, and their own, not staying for the general Conflagration, but beginning it. *a* **1683** Oldham *Sunday Th. in Sickness* Wks. (1686) 59 Fear is like to prevent and do the work of my Distemper.

†**13.** To take possession of or occupy beforehand; *fig.* to employ before another person. *Obs.*

1577–87 Holinshed *Chron.* I. 73/1 Preuenting euerie conuenient place where the barbarous people might lie in wait to doo mischiefe. *Ibid.* 148/1 Thus like a worthie prince and politike guernor, he preuented each way to resist the force of his enimies, and to safegard his subiects.

†**b.** To preoccupy, prejudice (a person's mind).

1551 Robinson tr. *More's Utop.* (1895) 97 Whose myndes be all reddye preuented with cleane contrarye persuasyons. **1654** tr. *Martini's Conq. China* 56 Rather..[not to] accuse the least default in his Sovereign's judgement, though prevented, by very unjust impressions. **1704** Hearne *Duct. Hist.* (1714) I. 143 Without labouring to prevent the Minds of People by a studious Excuse. **1718** J. Chamberlayne *Relig. Philos.* (1730) Ded., Endeavouring to prevent your Lordship in Favour of my Author.

Hence **pre'vented** *ppl. a.*

1605 Bacon *Adv. Learn.* II. xvii. §4 In this same anticipated and prevented knowledge, no man knoweth how he came to the knowledge which he hath obtained.

preventable (prɪ'vɛntəb(ə)l), *a.* [f. prevent *v.* + -able; cf. *acceptable*, *attributable*, *creditable*. See also preventible.] That may be prevented, capable of prevention.

1640 Bp. Reynolds *Passions* xl, The Ignorance of the End is far more preventable..than of the Meanes. **1828** in Webster. **1859** Kingsley *Misc.* (1860) II. 315 Lord Shaftesbury told you just now that there were 100,000 preventable deaths in England every year. **1871** Napheys *Prev. & Cure Dis.* 34 All preventable diseases. **1879** Lubbock *Addr. Pol. & Educ.* viii. 147 This immense loss.. due to preventable causes.

Hence **preventa'bility**.

1860 in Worcester citing *Ec. Rev.* **1883** *Nature* 19 Apr. 574/2 Knowledge of the Causation or Preventability of some important Disease. **1894** W. Walker *Hist. Congregat. Ch. U.S.* 357 His theories regarding the nature and preventability of sin.

preventative (prɪ'vɛntətɪv), *a.* and *sb.* Also 8 erron. **-itive.** [f. prevent *v.* + -ative. See also preventive, the preferable formation.]

A. *adj.* = preventive *a.* 2, 2 b, 2 c.

1654–66 Earl Orrery *Parthen.* (1676) 581 All preventative thoughts of hostility were silenced. **1722** De Foe *Plague* 137 To send a preventative Medicine to the Father of the Child. **1822** A. Ranken *Hist. France* IX. v. 104 This was merely a preventative measure. **1860** Warter *Sea-board* II. 207 No preventative man but knew the name of Coaly! **1884** *Chr. World* 10 July 513/3 Its action has been rather preventative than corrective. **1936** W. H. S. Smith *Let.* 18 July in *Young Man's Country* (1977) ii. 16 My principal occupation was trying 'Bad Livelihood' cases. These are preventative cases for securing the good behaviour of criminals by taking a bond. **1939** *Ann. Reg. 1938* 93 Two new types of prison sentences were proposed. One was called 'corrective training'... The other was called 'preventative detention', and was to be for not less than two and not more than four years for persons over 30, but up to ten years on certain types of offenders with long criminal records. **1968** *Globe & Mail* (Toronto) 5 Feb. 10/8 A Democratic administration had gotten the United States deeply involved in Vietnam..by failing to apply 'preventative diplomacy'. **1973** *Black Panther* 21 July 8/3 The People's Free Health Clinic..provides medical treatment and preventative care on a clinical level. **1976** *Oxf. Mission Q. Paper* July/Sept. 15 Many of the people are illiterate and it takes a lot of patient talking and convincing before they can see the benefits of preventative medicine.

B. *sb.* **a.** = preventive *sb.*

1775 S. J. Pratt *Liberal Opin.* cxv. (1783) IV. 75 Without meeting any new preventative in my way, I at length took by the hand my friend Mr. Green. **1776** Adam Smith *W.N.* IV. v. (1869) II. 116 The most effectual preventative of a famine. **1809** Syd. Smith *Serm.* I. 413 The most effectual preventative against the perils of idle opulence. **1812** Wellington in Gurw. *Desp.* (1838) IX. 462, I shall..not trouble Government..with suggestions of remedies or preventatives. **1829** Lytton *Devereux* III. iv, The only preventative to rebellion is restraint. **1847** Lewes *Hist. Philos.* (1853) 233 A preventative against ill fortune.

b. *Med.* = preventive *sb.* b.

1774 Pennant *Tour Scot. in 1772*, 175 The practice of bleeding—as a preventitive against the pleurisy. **1793** Washington *Writ.* (1892) XII. 395 Wearing flannel next the skin is the best cure for, and preventative of the Rheumatism I ever tried. **1812** Southey *Omniana* II. 265 A preventative for canine madness. **1848** J. H. Newman *Loss & Gain* 163 Dr. Baillie's preventative of the flatulency which tea produces. **1879** MRS. A. E. JAMES *Ind. Househ. Managem.* 24 Essence of Jamaica ginger, which is a very good preventative of sea-sickness.

c. A contraceptive; = PREVENTIVE *sb.* c.

1901 J. A. GODFREY *Science of Sex* II. vi. 257 The checks employed by women are more diverse in mechanical detail. .. Opinions differ greatly as to both the reliability and the physiological harmlessness of these forms of preventative. *Ibid.* 256 So long as the sheath remains whole, it is an absolute preventative. **1918** R. B. ARMITAGE *Private Sex Advice to Women* x. 130 The use of 'contraceptives' or 'preventatives' is considered justified in certain cases. **1934** DYLAN THOMAS *Let.* Oct. (1966) 143 Do you believe in preventatives?

preventer (prɪˈvɛntə(r)). [f. PREVENT *v.* + -ER¹. See also PREVENTOR.] One who prevents.

†**1. a.** One who goes or acts before another, an anticipator. *Obs.*

1624 BACON *War w. Spain* Wks. 1879 I. 540/2 The arch-duke was the assailant, and the preventer, and had the fruit of his diligence and celerity.

†**b.** The rhetorical figure of procatalepsis, by which an opponent's arguments are anticipated.

1589 PUTTENHAM *Eng. Poesie* III. xix. (Arb.) 239, I will also call him the figure of presupposall or the preuenter, for by reason we suppose before what may be said, or perchaunce would be said, by our aduersary, or any other, we do preuent them of their aduantage.

2. A person or thing that hinders, restrains, or keeps something from occurring or being done.

1587 GREENE *Penelopes Web* Wks. (Grosart) V. 150 Consideration, the preuenter of had I wist, tied him .. to the performing of these forenamed premisses. *a* **1684** LEIGHTON *Comm. 1 Pet.* Wks. (1868) 274 Prayer .. that preventer of judgments. **1725** BRADLEY *Fam. Dict.* s.v. *Wind*, The fierce bitter Blasts in the Spring destroying whole Fields; of which nothing is a preventer but Inclosures. *a* **1846** CAR. FRY *Script. Reader's Guide* viii. (1863) 118 The preventers, till their cup of wrath be full, of the Saviour's reign. **1884** *Health Exhib. Catal.* 46/1 The latest improvements of Water-waste Preventers. **1920** *Chambers's Jrnl.* Mar. 208/1 A single set of hydrofoils under the bow, known as a preventer, helps to lift the boat when getting up speed, while checking any tendency to nose-dive.

3. *Naut.* **a.** Orig. ***preventer-rope***, as in quot. 1625; later, applied to any rope used as an additional security to aid other ropes in supporting spars, etc., during a strong gale, or to prevent the mischief caused by their breaking; and at length extended to supplementary parts generally: see quot. 1867.

a **1625** *Nomenclator Navalis* s.v. *Roape* (Harl. MS. 2301) A preuenter-roape (which is a little rope seased crosse ouer the Ties close at the Ramhead that if one parte of the Ties should breake the other should not run through the Ram-head to endanger the Yard). So **1627** CAPT. SMITH *Seaman's Gram.* vi. 28; **1678–1706** in PHILLIPS.

1711 W. SUTHERLAND *Shipbuild. Assist.* 162 *Preventers*, Ropes that have Wale Knots at each End, chiefly used in Sea-fights. For when Rigging is in part shot, such Ropes are apply'd to prevent the damaged Ropes being quite broke off. **1840** R. H. DANA *Bef. Mast* xxxiii, We .. ran out the boom and lashed it fast, and sent down the lower halyards as a preventer. **1859** F. A. GRIFFITHS *Artill. Man.* (1862) 115 Two luff tackles, one preventer rope. **1867** BRANDE & COX *Dict. Sc.*, etc., *Preventer*, on Shipboard [is] a term applied to any rope, chain, bolt, &c., which is placed .. as a deputy or duplicate for another similar instrument. **1868** *Morn. Star* 6 Jan., The main yard was supported from the lowermost head by stay tackles; from the topmost head there was a strengthening tackle, and from the lowermost head to the yard there were preventers.

b. *attrib.* and *Comb.* (*a*) with specification of the rope, as ***preventer-backstay, -brace, -gasket, -guy, sheet, -shroud, -stay, -stopper***; (*b*) denoting various other secondary or additional parts serving to strengthen or take the place of the main ones, as ***preventer-bolt, -plate, -post, -stern-post***: see quots.

1832 MARRYAT *N. Forster* xxvi, The boatswain proposed a *preventer backstay. **1880** *Daily Tel.* 7 Sept., The wind is playing a tune on the preventer backstay as if it were a fiddlestring. **1912** W. I. DOWNIE *Reminisc. Blackwall Midshipman* ii. 22, I expect preventer backstays were practically a permanent part of her equipment during the trip. **1939** H. HUGHES *Through Mighty Seas* x. 264 For the first time I saw preventer back-stays being rigged from the main top-gallant mast. **1815** BURNEY *Falconer's Dict. Marine*, **Preventer-Bolts*, are bolts driven in the lower end of the preventer-plates, to assist the strain of the chain-bolts. **1776** FALCONER *Dict. Marine*, s.v. **Preventer-brace*, .. *Preventer-shrouds*, and *Preventer-stays*. **1840** R. H. DANA *Bef. Mast* xxxiii, Preventer braces were reeved and hauled taut. **1867** G. E. CLARK *Seven Years of Sailor's Life* xx. 203 We had the barque under a close-reefed main-topsail, and with preventer braces on the yard, flew on the waves. **1926** T. M. HEMY *Deep Sea Days* ii. 64 It was 'all hands wear ship'; then up aloft and change the preventer braces from one side to another. **1888** CHURCHWARD *Blackbirding* 138 We then closely furled the sails, putting *preventer gaskets round them all. **1907** M. ROBERTS *Flying Cloud* xxxii. 304 Budd went aloft on the cro' jack-yard and passed a couple of preventer gaskets. **1888** CLARK RUSSELL *Death Ship* I. 41 *Preventer guys were clapped on the swinging-booms. **1923** *Man. Seamanship* (Admiralty) II. xi. 188 In the recent America Cup Races, both craft tried taking a preventer guy out to the weather crosstrees if the wind was light enough. **1815** BURNEY *Falconer's Dict. Marine*, **Preventer-plate*, a broad plate of iron, fixed below the toe-link of the chains to support them against the efforts of the masts and shrouds, having a chain-bolt driven through its upper end, and a preventer-bolt through the lower. **1874** THEARLE *Naval Archit.* 60 The lower bar, which is fitted to give support to the bolt in the lower end of the upper bar, is known as a preventer plate. **1841** R. H. DANA *Seaman's Man.* 77 Lash the upper part of the *preventer post to the upper part of the ship's stern-post. **1867** G. E. CLARK *Seven Years of Sailor's Life* xix. 191 The mainsail was furled, and *preventer sheets put on the fore boom. **1748** *Anson's Voy.* I. v. 56 The other ships .. set up a sufficient number of *preventer shrouds to each mast, to secure them in the most effectual manner. **1776** *Preventer-stay [see *preventer-brace*]. **1794** *Rigging & Seamanship* I. 108 This sail .. is extended on the main-topmast preventer-stay. **1830** N. S. WHEATON *Jrnl.* 515 To construct one .. with a *preventer stern-post, would have required the labour of a fort-night. **1730** CAPT. W. WRIGLESWORTH *MS. Log-bk. of the 'Lyell'* 24 Mar., Wee .. put a *preventer Stoper on the Stranded Shroud and set it up again.

4. In full ***blow-out preventer***. A heavy valve or assembly ('stack') of valves usu. fitted at the top of an oil well during drilling and closed in the event of a blow-out.

1916 A. B. THOMPSON *Oil-Field Devel. & Petroleum Mining* vii. 367 An apparatus which is largely employed with rotaries is what is called a 'Blow-out Preventer'. **1934** *Proc. World Petroleum Congr. 1933* I. 370/2 The main feature is a heavy rubber sleeve packer held in a container which is free to revolve in ball bearings inside the body of the preventer. **1962** *Economist* 15 Sept. 1046/2 The blow-out preventers and the drill bit itself can be lowered. **1972** L. M. HARRIS *Introd. Deepwater Floating Drilling Operations* x. 98 All preventers should have a pressure rating in excess of the maximum that could be expected on the wellhead. **1976** *Offshore Engineer* July 6/4 Shell has recovered, from 130m of water, the blow-out preventer (bop) stack which fell to the seabed while being lowered into position from the rig *Chris Chenery*. **1977** *Daily Tel.* 29 Apr. 2/1 They went to the gang boss and it was decided to rectify it when another driller noticed a small stream of mud running from the preventer's outlet.

†**pre'vential**, *a.* *Obs. rare*⁻¹. [irreg. f. PREVENT.] = PREVENTIONAL b, PREVENTIVE *a.* 2.

1657 *Burton's Diary* (1828) II. 56 A prevential provision is as fit in such cases as in physic.

preventible (prɪˈvɛntɪb(ə)l), *a.* [f. L. *prævent-*, ppl. stem of *prævenīre* (see PREVENE) + -IBLE, on analogy of *contemptible, permissible, susceptible*, etc. The earlier Eng. formation is PREVENTABLE.] That may be prevented, capable of prevention.

1850 DICKENS *Begging Letter Writer* Wks. 1858 VIII. 179 Sacred from preventible diseases, distortions, and pains. **1871** TYNDALL *Fragm. Sc.* (1879) II. xii. 290 This preventible destruction is going on to-day. **1885** *Manch. Exam.* 8 May 4/7 A large loss of life .. which was in a great degree preventible and ought to be prevented.

Hence **preventi'bility**.

1852 *Q. Rev.* (Flügel), The preventibility of disease.

pre'venting, *vbl. sb.* [See -ING¹.] The action of the verb PREVENT. †**a.** Anticipation. *Obs.* **b.** Hindrance, stopping, keeping from action.

1530 PALSGR. 258/1 Preventyng, *prevention.* **1573–80** BARET *Alv.* P 705 Anticipation, preventing, *anticipatio.* **1586** in *10th Rep. Hist. MSS. Comm.* App. v. 440 For avoydinge and preventinge of any other .. unlawfull custome. **1636** SANDERSON *Serm.* II. 56 For the avoiding and preventing both of sin and danger. **1818** COBBETT *Pol. Reg.* XXXIII. 222 As to the preventing of those colonies from becoming free.

pre'venting, *ppl. a.* [See -ING².] That prevents, in various senses of the vb.

†**1.** Going before, preceding, anticipating. *Obs.*

1643 [ANGIER] *Lanc. Vall. Achor* 3 This preventing Petition found this satisfying Answer. **1688** DRYDEN *Brit. Rediviva* 3 Preventing angels met it [the prayer] half the way, And sent us back to praise, who came to pray. *a* **1716** SOUTH *Serm.* (L.), A preventing judgement and goodness, .. able not only to answer but also to anticipate his requests.

b. Of divine grace: That goes before and leads or guides; *spec.* that predisposes to repentance and salvation; = PREVENIENT 2.

1605 SYLVESTER *Du Bartas* II. iii. I. *Vocation* 1431 If thou but turn thy face, And take but from us thy preventing grace. **1699** BURNET 39 *Art.* x. (1700) 120 There is a preventing Grace, by which the Will is first moved and disposed to turn to God. *a* **1711** KEN *Div. Love* Wks. (1838) 243 Out of what motive didst thou suffer, O boundless Benignity, but out of thy own preventing love? **1850** E. H. BROWNE *Expos.* 39 *Articles* x. ii. (1856) 265 The grace of God acts in two ways. First it is preventing grace, giving a good will. Afterwards it is co-operating grace, working in and with us, when we have that good will. **1875** MANNING *Mission H. Ghost* ii. 36 There is what is called preventing grace; that is, God going before us by His operations in every good thing we do.

†**c.** = PREVENANT *a.* 1. *Obs. rare*⁻¹.

1751 *Female Foundling* II. 78 The polite Manners, the preventing Care, and the infinite Complaisance, the Court shewed me.

2. That provides against anything anticipated; that keeps from occurring; precautional, precluding, hindering.

1677 HALE *Contempl.* II. 194 It may be it is Preventing Physick against a greater mischief. **1697** DRYDEN *Æneid* x. 361 He charg'd the Souldiers with preventing Care, Their flags to follow, and their arms prepare. *a* **1716** SOUTH *Serm.* (1717) V. 16 Minds .. seasoned with a strict and virtuous, an early and preventing Education.

b. = PREVENTIVE *a.* 2 c.

1800 COLQUHOUN *Comm. Thames* 177 Superior Officers [of the Customs]. 4 Inspectors, 16 Tide Surveyors, 3 Preventing Officers, 1 Tobacco Inspector [etc.].

pre'ventingly, *adv. rare.* [f. prec. + -LY².] In a preventing manner; so as to prevent, anticipate, keep from occurring, etc.

c **1557** ABP. PARKER *Ps.* cxix. 361 The dawning day preuentingly I cried most earnest than Trust fast I did thy words for why my hope therby I wan. **1619** W. SCLATER *Exp. 1 Thess.* (1630) 206 How necessary comfort and confirmation was for this people, Paul here preuentingly sheweth. **1678** ANTH. WALKER *Lady Warwick* 99 Before I could suggest the reasons, she preventingly replied, she would never give less than the third part.

prevention (prɪˈvɛnʃən). [ad. late L. *præventiōn-em*, n. of action f. *prævenīre*: see PREVENE. So F. *prévention* (14th c. in Godef.).] The action of the verbs PREVENE and PREVENT in various senses.

†**1.** The coming, occurrence, or action of one person or thing before another, or before the due time; previous occurrence, anticipation; in *Theol.* the action of prevenient grace. *Obs.*

1544 *St. Papers Hen. VIII*, X. 179 The prevention of the tyme of the French Quenes retourne. **1621** BRATHWAIT *Nat. Embassie* (1877) 18 His gracious preuention that giueth to each work a happy period. **1626** BACON *Sylva* §210 The greater the distance, the greater is the prevention: as we see in thunder which is far off, where the lightning precedeth the crack a good space. **1651** C. CARTWRIGHT *Cert. Relig.* I. 213 Workes, which none can attaine unto without the prevention of Gods mercy. **1705** STANHOPE *Paraphr.* III. 577 That those Preventions might furnish an opportunity for rendering both his Humility and his Faith exemplary and publick.

2. a. *Canon Law.* The privilege possessed or claimed by an ecclesiastical superior of taking precedence of or forestalling an inferior in the execution of an official act regularly pertaining to the latter.

1528 *St. Papers Hen. VIII*, I. 311 Hys .. desier is, Your sayd Grace, by verteu off your Legantine prerogative and prevention, conferr to hys chapleyn, Mr. Wilson, the vicarege off Thackstedd. *a* **1548** HALL *Chron., Hen. VIII* 184 b, [Wolsey was] called on for an answere .. to the premunire, for geuyng benefices by preuension in disturbance of mennes inheritaunce. **1562** JEWEL *Apol. Ch. Eng.* VI. xxi. Wks. (1579) 726 Peradventure they will saie That Peter .. solde Iubilees, Graces, Liberties, Aduousons, Preuentions. **1706** tr. *Dupin's Eccl. Hist. 16th C.* II. IV. xx. 346 *note*, Preventions are Privileges that a Superior claims over an Inferior; that when he comes first, the Inferior loses his Right for that Time.

b. *Sc. Law.* A similar privilege exercised by a superior judge or civil magistrate: see quot.

1678 SIR G. MACKENZIE *Crim. Laws Scot.* II. ii. §5 (1699) 182 Prevention is, when one Judge interposes his authority, or when a tryal is entered upon by one Judge, before another Judge do exerce any action of Jurisdiction about that subject.

†**3.** Action or occurrence before or in anticipation of the expected, appointed, or normal time; anticipation; in *Rhet.* prolepsis. *Obs.*

1571 GOLDING *Calvin on Ps.* lx. 12 In the way of preuention he proceedeth further, and sayth that he looked for the residew at Gods hand. **1575–85** ABP. SANDYS *Serm.* (Parker Soc.) 284 He answereth that objection by a prevention (so to term it) calling him Lord of all. **1583** *Reg. Privy Council Scot.* III. 619 The effect of the law wes fulfullit be preventioun of the terme. **1658** BP. REYNOLDS *Rich Man's Charge* 4 This Duty is pressed by a very elegant reason, .. as a prolepsis or prevention of what might be objected. **1711** SHAFTESB. *Charac.* (1737) III. VI. v. 376 How particularly our philosophical Historian affects to speak, by way of prevention, of the solitary place where Hercules was retir'd.

4. †**a.** The action of forestalling, of securing an advantage over another person by previous action, or of baffling or stopping another person in the execution of his designs. *Obs.*

1582 N. LICHEFIELD tr. *Castanheda's Conq. E. Ind.* I. vii. 18 b, Appointing also there shoulde be great watch, for preuention of the Moores, least that they should by anye deuice set on fire the ships. **1601** SHAKS. *Jul. C.* III. i. 19 Caska be sodaine, for we feare preuention. **1667** MILTON *P.L.* VI. 129 Half way he met His daring foe, at this prevention more Incens't, and thus securely him defi'd.

†**b.** Action intended to obviate or provide against an anticipated danger or mischief; precaution; a precaution, a defensive measure. *Obs.*

1600 E. BLOUNT tr. *Conestaggio* 93 This preuention was done like a valiant and wise Prince. **1614** RALEIGH *Hist. World* II. (1634) 210 The same prevention Herod long after practised. *a* **1639** T. CAREW *Poems* Wks. (1824) 105 Where our prevention ends, danger begins. **1774** FOOTE *Cozeners* III. Wks. 1799 II. 196, I took the liberty, by way of prevention, to get him secured for the money.

c. The action of keeping from happening or rendering impossible an anticipated event or an intended act. (The chief current use.)

1661 GLANVILL *Van. Dogm.* xii. 110 For the prevention of such inconveniences in meditation, we choose recess and solitude. *c* **1710** PRIOR *Own Monument* 1 Doctors give physic by way of prevention. **1751** N. COTTON *Vis. Verse, Health* 31 Prevention is the better Cure, So says the Proverb, and 'tis sure. **1813** *Gentl. Mag.* LXXXIII. I. 53/2 Lord Erskine's Bill for the Prevention of Cruelty towards Animals. **1861** MRS. OLIPHANT *Last Mortimers* vi, 'Ah! but prevention is better than cure', said the wicked little creature.

†**d.** A means of preventing; a preventive, a safeguard; an obstacle, obstruction. *Obs.*

1589 GREENE *Menaphon* (Arb.) 28 No preuention [prevails] to diuert the decree of the Fates. 1597 HOOKER *Eccl. Pol.* v. lxv. §8 A kinde of barre or preuention to keepe them euen from apostasie. 1641 MILTON *Animadv.* Wks. 1851 III. 203 A better prevention then these Councells have left us against heresie. *a* 1716 SOUTH *Serm.* (1744) X. 349 Those, who, not being hampered with such early preventions, break forth into the most open, and flagitious practices. 1821 CRAIG *Lect. Drawing* viii. 440 They furnish preventions for that lassitude which so often arises.. from want of employment.

†5. A mental anticipation; a presentiment. *Obs.*

a 1601 ? MARSTON *Pasquil & Kath.* I. 32, I could burst At the coniectures, feares, preuentions, And restles tumbling of our tossed braines. 1649 JER. TAYLOR *Gt. Exemp.* I. Ad Sect. iv. 53 These [delights] are the antepasts and preventions of the full feasts.. of Eternity. 1801 CHARLOTTE SMITH *Lett. Solit. Wand.* I. 247 Which I had a strange prevention would be fatal to one of us.

†6. Prepossession, bias, prejudice. *Obs.*

1688 BURNET *Lett. conc. Pres. St. Italy* 16 A man that sees the exteriour of another,.. and is much taken with his face, .. and mien, and thus has a blind prevention in his favour. 1711 SHAFTESB. *Charac.* (1737) III. Misc. II. iii. 108 'Tis a known Prevention against the Gentlemen of this Character, 'That they are generally ill-humour'd'. 1755 J. SHEBBEARE *Lydia* (1769) II. 179 Much assisted by his natural prevention in favour of himself. 1829 LANDOR *Imag. Conv.*, *Chaucer, Boccaccio*, etc. Wks. 1853 I. 403/2 My prevention, in regard to the country about Rome, was almost as great, and almost as unjust to Nature.

pre'ventional, *a. rare.* [f. prec. + -AL[1].]

†a. Precedent, antecedent. *Obs.* b. Preventive. Hence **pre'ventionalist**.

1658 ROWLAND *Moufet's Theat. Ins.* 1097 What concerns preventional means, Hemp-seed, or winter Cherries laid near the bed, or hanged up drive away Wall-lice. 1678 PHILLIPS (ed. 4), *Preventional Full Moon*, that.. which comes before any grand moveable Feast or Planetary Aspect. 1820 BENTHAM *Headings Bk. Fallacies* Wks. 1843 X. 520 Anti-preventionalist's; or, Suffer-first argument. 1831 GEN. P. THOMPSON *Exerc.* (1842) I. 376 The various degrees of preventional infliction, from the fivefold retribution of Moses, to the gallows or the guillotine.

preventionism (prɪ'vɛnʃənɪz(ə)m). [f. PREVENTION + -ISM.] A policy of prevention. So **pre'ventionist**, one who favours such a policy.

1918 A. GRAY tr. *Grelling's Crime* II. ii. 109 All these questions.. must simultaneously be answered in the affirmative, if the preventionists wish to justify their point of view. *Ibid.* 118 When preventionism suits their purpose, they speak of the right and the duty of the anticipated defence against future attack. 1978 D. GRYLLS *Guardians & Angels* ii. 66 The child-cruelty furore.. promoted sympathy for children's sufferings, and preventionists tended to deprecate not only cruelty but strictness.

preventive (prɪ'vɛntɪv), *a.* and *sb.* [f. L. type **præventīv-us*, f. *prævent-*, ppl. stem of *prævenīre*: see PREVENE and -IVE; cf. *inventive*. So mod.F. *préventif*.]

A. *adj.* †1. That comes or goes before something else; antecedent, anticipatory. *Obs.*

1641 MILTON *Ch. Govt.* II. Wks. 1851 III. 142 A preventive fear least the omitting of this duty should be against me when I would store up to my selfe the good provision of peacefull hours. 1678 CUDWORTH *Intell. Syst.* 73 Atoms.. were not then directed by any previous Counsel or preventive Understanding. 1698 NORRIS *Pract. Disc.* IV. 147 The First is previous to our Repentance, and indeed wholely preventive of any thing we can do.

2. a. That anticipates in order to ward against; precautionary; that keeps from coming or taking place; that acts as a hindrance or obstacle; *spec.* ***preventive arrest***, ***detention***, ***maintenance***, ***war***.

1639 FULLER *Holy War* I. ix. (1840) 15 A preventive war, grounded on a just fear of an invasion, is lawful. 1769 BLACKSTONE *Comm.* IV. xviii. 251 This preventive justice consists in obliging those persons, whom there is probable ground to suspect of future misbehaviour, to.. give full assurance to the public, that such offence as is apprehended shall not happen. *a* 1822 C. ELLIS *Clergyman's Assist.* 325 [Chapter heading] Statutes preventive of blasphemy and profaneness. 1828 SOUTHEY in *Q. Rev.* XXXVII. 227 Politics, if it content itself with devising remedies for immediate danger, instead of acting with preventive foresight, ceases to be a science. 1875 JOWETT *Plato* (ed. 2) I. 116 The preventive nature of punishment. 1908 *Act 8 Edw. VII* c. 59 §10 (1) Where a person is convicted on indictment of a crime,.. and subsequently the offender admits that he is or is found by the jury to be a habitual criminal, and the court passes a sentence of penal servitude, .. the court.. may pass a further sentence ordering that on the determination of the sentence of penal servitude he be detained for such period not exceeding ten nor less than five years,.. and such detention is herein-after referred to as preventive detention. 1918 E. POUND *Let.* 15 Nov. (1971) 140 The wholesale preventive arrests surely prevented another rising... Similar preventive arrests would have prevented the Easter rising. 1932 *Rep. Dept. Comm. on Persistent Offenders* iv. 14 in *Parl. Papers 1931–2* (Cmd. 4090) XII. 553 Preventive Detention is a sentence intended for 'professional' criminals or criminals who definitely give themselves up to a career of serious crime. 1945 *Facts on File* 28 Feb. 70/2 Paris reports that the French police have released from 'preventive detention' P. G. Wodehouse, British novelist. 1948 H. NICOLSON *Diary* 29 Nov. (1968) 155 A preventive war is always evil. 1953 B. V. BOWDEN *Faster than Thought* iv. 86 The technique of preventive maintenance.. has considerably reduced the number of valve failures which occur while the machines are running. 1959 *Listener* 16 Apr. 674/1 Southern Rhodesian Government publishes a new preventive detention bill. 1963 *New Statesman* 22 Feb. 260/1 Preventive detention, a relatively humane experiment begun in 1908 and modified 40 years later, has been finally adjudged a failure and abolished. 1966 SCHWARZ & HADIK *Strategic Terminol.* 130 *Preventive war*, war initiated to prevent the enemy from making gains he might be expected to make if he were allowed to initiate the war, or that he might make without resorting to war if not forcibly opposed in good time. 1967 E. DUCKWORTH in Wills & Yearsley *Handbk. Managem. Technol.* vi. 119 *Preventive maintenance*, a scheme for regular overhaul of equipment to prevent unexpected breakdown.

b. *Med.* Having the quality of preventing or keeping off disease; prophylactic. *spec.* ***preventive medicine***.

1646 SIR T. BROWNE *Pseud. Ep.* IV. xiii. 230 Physicke is either curative or preventive. 1722 DE FOE *Plague* 36 Posts of Houses.. were plaster'd over with Doctor's Bills.. set off with such Flourishes as these, (viz.) Infallible preventive Pills against the Plague. [1769 W. BUCHAN *Domestic Med.* II. 531 Dr Mead recommends a preventive medicine.] 1870 *Food Jrnl.* I. I. 22 Preventive medicine received a great impulse by the labours of Coleman in relation to ventilation. 1881 J. SIMON in *Nature* 18 Aug. 372/2 Those parts of pathology which make the foundation of preventive medicine. 1884 *Pall Mall G.* 20 May 7/2 The celebrated scientist hopes.. that the dogs inoculated by him with preventive virus will prove the correctness of his investigations. 1926 *Eng. Rev.* Sept. 315 What preventive medicine can do is illustrated by the clearing up of the infective diseases of Panama. 1957 A. HUXLEY *Let.* 22 Feb. (1969) 818 If we could combine Krishnamurti with old Dr Vittoz's brand of psychotherapy.. and a sensible diet, we would have solved the problem of preventive medicine. 1963 *Lancet* 19 Jan. 145/2 (*heading*) Statistical methods in clinical and preventive medicine.

c. Belonging to that department of the Customs which is concerned with the prevention of smuggling; *spec.* of or belonging to the Coast Guard.

1827 LYTTON *Pelham* vii, After having met.. one officer on the preventive service. 1833 HT. MARTINEAU *Loom & Lugger* I. i, The Preventive Service.. To *prevent* prohibited goods being brought on shore; to *prevent* smugglers' boats from landing. 1873 MRS. H. WOOD *Mast. Greylands* I. 31 The heights were tolerably flat, and.. the preventive men were enabled to pace. 1884 PAE *Eustace* 222 Preventive stations were planted at every harbour or likely landing-place.

3. = PREVENTER 3 b.

1831 J. HOLLAND *Manuf. Metal* I. 110 When the blocks were made secure to the chain, two capstans and also two preventive capstans commenced working. *c* 1860 H. STUART *Seaman's Catech.* 19 What is the use of yard tackles? For hoisting in and out boats and spars,.. and for preventive braces.

B. *sb.* a. A preventive agent or measure; a means of prevention; a hindrance, obstacle, obstruction.

a 1639 WOTTON *Let. to Dr. C.* in *Reliq.* (1651) 487 Though it be a natural preventive to some evils. 1769 BLACKSTONE *Comm.* IV. i. 10 Where the evil to be prevented is not adequate to the violence of the preventive, a sovereign that thinks seriously can never justify such a law to the dictates of conscience and humanity. 1860 MILL *Repr. Govt.* (1865) 126/1 Such a federation is more likely to be a cause than a preventive of internal wars. 1899 *Allbutt's Syst. Med.* VII. 747 These [beverages].. are in most people powerful preventives of sleep.

b. *Med.* A drug or other medical agent for preventing disease; a prophylactic.

1674 R. GODFREY *Inj. & Ab. Physic* 203 Yet would I not have you think there are no Preventives, or means to preserve Health for the future. 1789 W. BUCHAN *Dom. Med.* (1790) 481 When used as a preventive, it will be sufficient to rub daily a drachm of the ointment into the parts about the wound. 1802 *Med. Jrnl.* VIII. 21 If properly conducted, it is a preventive of small-pox, and he has practised it himself with success. 1871 NAPHEYS *Prev. & Cure Dis.* I. viii. 237 A more potent preventive has been found.

c. A contraceptive; = PREVENTATIVE *sb.* c.

1822 F. PLACE *Illustr. & Proofs Princ. Population* v. 150 The proposals of Mr. Malthus, to persuade the poor that they have no right to eat.., as well as Mr. Godwin's infanticide, are.. proposals to commence at the wrong end. The remedy alone can be found in preventives. 1901 E. B. FOOTE *Home Cycl.* IV. vii. 1137 To lessen the 'vicious employment of preventives' outside of marriage. 1911 R. BROOKE *Let.* Mar. (1968) 292 The Church'll declare that God gave every man the Right-not-to-use-Preventives. 1943 R. MALKIN *Marriage, Morals & War* 159 In 1940, when Lieutenant Colonel Gardner of the United States Army Medical Corps gave happy birth to the idea of a pamphlet explaining venereal diseases, which.. would be sold together with a set of preventives and prophylactics. 1961 A. H. NETHERCOT *First Five Lives A. Besant* vii. 117 Before marriage, pure will power and moral determination were to be the only preventives. Physical preventives were .. against the will of God.

Hence **pre'ventiveness**.

1890 in *Cent. Dict.*

pre'ventively, *adv.* [f. prec. + -LY[2].] In a preventive manner; in such a way as to prevent.

†1. Previously, by anticipation. *Obs.*

1646 SIR T. BROWNE *Pseud. Ep.* VII. xiv. 368 To engrosse the messe, he would preventively deliver his nostrils in the dish. 1678 CUDWORTH *Intell. Syst.* I. iii. §36. 146 We shall shew how the Ancient Atomick Atheists did preventively over-throw the foundation of Hylozoism.

2. By way of prevention, precaution, or hindrance; so as to preclude or hinder.

1694 SALMON *Bate's Dispens.* (1713) 680/1 It is chiefly to be done (if used preventively) three days before and after the Full and New Moons. 1796 BURKE *Regic. Peace* i. Wks. VIII. 187 It is preventively, the assertor of its own rights, or remedially, their avenger. 1862 T. A. TROLLOPE *Sent. Journ.* xiv. 216 Many persons of known bad character.. were preventively imprisoned.

†**pre'ventor**. *Obs.* [a. L. *præventor*, agent-n. from *prævenīre*: see PREVENE.] One who goes before or precedes; a predecessor; an anticipator.

1598 FLORIO, *Preuentore*, a preuentor, an ouertaker, an anticipator. 1599 *Broughton's Let.* ii. 8 With Simon Magus your Preuentor,.. you are not contented to be accompted.. a great Diuine.

preventorium (priːvɛn'tɔərɪəm). orig. and chiefly *U.S.* [f. PREVENT *v.*, after SANATORIUM.] An institution where preventive care is given to people at risk from tuberculosis or other diseases.

1907 W. EWART in *Jrnl. Balneol. & Climatol.* XI. 155 The place for the 'Prevention-Sanatorium', or 'Preventorium', is the sea-coast. 1909 *Boston Even. Transcript* 10 Nov. (*heading*) To fight tuberculosis New York will have $700,000 preventorium. 1929 W. B. TOMSON *Prevention of Tuberculosis* vii. 51 The preventorium stands out as the predominating instrument for prophylaxis and early treatment in childhood in America. 1930 *Aberdeen Press & Jrnl.* 21 Oct. 6/1 There are two preventoria in Aberdeen. 1936 *Dict. Amer. Biogr.* XVIII. 130/1 In 1909 he [*sc.* Nathan Straus] established in his cottage in Lakewood, N.J., the pioneer tuberculosis preventorium for children. 1953 H. R. LEAVELL in Leavell & Clark *Textbk. Preventive Med.* xvi. 497 'Preventoriums', where children from families with tuberculosis were sent and cared for.. did not prove useful enough to justify their cost, and they were not taken over by government. 1968 *Awake!* 8 May 12/2 When I was eighteen, I had to spend some months in a preventorium.

preverb, *sb.* and *a. Gram.* A. *sb.* With pronunc. ('priːvɜːb). 1. [PRE- B. 1.] A particle or prefix preceding the stem of the verb.

1930 [see ALFREDIAN *a.*]. 1939 L. H. GRAY *Foundations of Lang.* iii. 62 In English, many compound verbs borrowed from French consisting of a preverb (commonly, but erroneously, called a preposition..) and a base-word, and serving either as a noun.. or as a verb, are distinguished in their use.. by a difference of stress-accent. 1946 L. BLOOMFIELD in C. F. Hockett *Leonard Bloomfield Anthol.* (1970) 460 Certain particles, *preverbs*, freely precede verb stems. 1951 *Archivum Linguisticum* III. 28 The early loss in NGmc of unstressed prefixes (*i.e.* mainly preverbs). 1967 C. J. FILLMORE in *Glossa* I. 91 Many of the syntactic properties of the positive and negative adverbial elements called 'preverbs' have already been discussed.

2. [PRE- A. 2.] A verb which precedes another verb; an auxiliary verb.

1965 F. BEHRE in *Eng. Stud.* XLVI. 91 It is the content of the pre-verb that is qualified by *if* and not the pre-verb (*would, should, could, might*, etc.).

B. *adj.* With pronunc. (priː'vɜːb). [PRE- B. 2.] Occurring before a verb. Also as *adv.*

1976 *Archivum Linguisticum* VII. 33 Essentially, then, medial position means non-initial, pre-verb position. 1976 *Amer. Speech 1974* XLIX. 82 The collocation of *much* with *prefer* applies only when *much* is preverb, as in *I much prefer a dry wine.*

preverbal (priː'vɜːbəl), *a.* [PRE- B. 1.]

1. Preceding the formulation of an utterance; prior to or present before the development of speech.

1931 G. STERN *Meaning & Change of Meaning* v. 115 A pre-verbal phase of 'gedankliche Gliederung' follows on the preliminary adjustment. 1938 I. GOLDBERG *Wonder of Words* ii. 28 Obviously there was what may be called a preverbal intelligence. 1957 C. E. OSGOOD et al. in Saporta & Bastian *Psycholinguistics* (1961) 287/1 The auditory effects of hearing 'hammer' do not produce behavior in any way relevant to *hammer* object in the pre-verbal child. 1978 RUSSELL & DEWEY in P. Moore *Man, Woman, & Priesthood* vii. 93 Mother-figures reign in the pre-verbal layers of personality laid down in infancy. 1979 *Nature* 13 Dec. 724/1 The stimulus comparison task.. appears to have been carried out at a post-perceptual, pre-verbal level.

2. *Gram.* Preceding the verb. Also *absol.* as *sb.*

1948 [see COMPLEMENTATION]. 1958 *Archivum Linguisticum* X. 32 Or a post-verbal, counter to appearances, may vie with a preverbal. 1959 M. A. K. HALLIDAY *Lang. of Chinese 'Secret Hist. Mongols'* vi. 88 The conditional is marked lexico-grammatically, by a system of adverbs; these, designated by position as 'preverbal' and 'final', occur either alone or in combination one with the other. 1972 J. L. DILLARD *Black English* iv. 152 Abram.. is represented as using the pre-verbal durative particle *a* (*Your a gwine*). *Ibid.* v. 220 A preverbal *done* can be found as far back as Dunbar. 1977 *Word 1972* XXVIII. 147 The use of a preverbal particle in sentence initial position has recently become more common in the literary language.

preverbalization, -vernal: see PRE- A. 2, B. 1.

preversion (priː'vɜːʃən). [f. PRE- A. 2 + L. *vertĕre* to turn, after REVERSION.] (See quot.)

1903 MYERS *Human Personality* I. p. xx, *Preversion*, a tendency to characteristics assumed to lie at a further point of the evolutionary progress of a species than has yet been reached; opposed to *reversion*.

†**pre'vert**, *v. Obs. rare*[−1]. [ad. L. *prævertĕre* to outstrip, f. *præ*, PRE- A. 4 c + *vertĕre* to turn.] *trans.* To go beyond, outstrip.

1513 DOUGLAS *Æneis* VII. xiv. 64 And throu the speid of fut in hir rynning The suift windis [to] prevert and bakwart ding [*orig.* cursuque pedum prævertere ventos].

prevertebral, -vesical: see PRE- B. 3.

prevetie, prevey, obs. ff. PRIVITY, PRIVY.

previable (priːˈvaɪəb(ə)l), *a.* [PRE- B. 1.] Before the stage when a fœtus has developed sufficiently to survive outside the womb.

1910 F. J. TAUSSIG *Prevention & Treatm. Abortion* 2 Abortion is the pre-viable expulsion of the human ovum. **1936** —— *Abortion* iv. 81 The previable stage of pregnancy. **1945** *Jrnl. Obstetr. & Gynæcol.* LII. 35/1 The term 'pre-viable' has been proposed for the separate category of liveborn premature infants with a birth-weight of less than 2⅜ pounds. **1972** *Daily Tel.* 24 May 17/4 Research on pre-viable foetuses (those which may show some signs of life, but which have no hope of an independent existence) should be safeguarded further by limiting such work only to foetuses weighing less than 300 grammes (about two-thirds of a pound). **1978** *Church Times* 7 July 12/5 Difficult questions also arise over baptism, when a fully formed but pre-viable foetus is delivered by a legally procured abortion, still living but inevitably destined to die.

†**ˈprevial**, *a.* Also præ-. [f. L. *prævi-us* (see PREVIOUS) + -AL¹.] Going before, previous.

1613 JACKSON *Creed* II. §2 The original causes of their error.. serue as præuiall dispositions, for their Agents to work vpon. **1636** *Ibid.* VIII. v. §3 The previal sinne of omitting this duty. **1662** HIBBERT *Body Div.* II. 45 There are many prævial and antecedent dispositions.

†**ˈpreviant**, *a.* *Obs. rare*⁻¹. [ad. late L. *præviānt-em*, pres. pple. of *præviāre* to go before, f. *præ*, PRE- A. + *viāre* to travel.] = prec.

1601 GILL *Treat. Trinitie* Wks. (1635) 215 It is suddenly framed without any previant knowledge, to faith and obedience.

†**preˈvide**, *v.* *Obs.* Also 8 præ-. [ad. L. *prævidēre* to foresee, anticipate, f. *præ*, PRE- A. 1 + *vidēre* to see; in late L. used for *providēre* to provide.] **a.** *intr.* To provide. **b.** *trans.* To foresee.

c **1420** LYDG. *Assembly of Gods* 946 Whyle Vertu thus preuydyd For hym and hys pepyll the feld for to wynne. **1543** *St. Papers Hen. VIII*, III. 443, I.. perceyve howe your excellent wysdome previdеth your princely affaires to no small comforte of me. *a* **1660** *Contemp. Hist. Irel.* (Ir. Archæol. Soc.) III. 116 Some of the comaunders (.. preuidinge what after hapned). **1784** tr. *Swedenborg's New Jerusalem* §275 It is to be noted that there is providence, and praevidence; good is what is provided by the Lord, but evil is what is praevided.

So †**ˈprevidence** *Obs.* [late L.], foresight.

c **1374** CHAUCER *Boeth.* v. pr. vi. 83 (Sk.) For which it nis nat y-cleped previdence, but it sholde rather ben cleped purviaunce. **1656** BLOUNT *Glossogr.*, *Previdence* (*prævidentia*), fore-seeing, or fore-casting. **1784** [see above].

preview (ˈpriːvjuː), *sb.* [f. PRE- A. 2 + VIEW *sb.*; in sense 2 after REVIEW *sb.*]

1. Previous viewing; foresight, prevision. *rare.*

1855 BAILEY *Mystic* 6 The preview clear of prophet-bard.

2. a. A previous view, inspection, or survey. Also, a foretaste, a preliminary glimpse.

1882 F. RUSSELL in *Chicago Advance* 13 Apr. 227 At the beginning of each quarter a pre-view of the lessons should be given to the Sabbath-schools. **1899** *Lutheran* (Philad.) 6 Apr. 321 The consecutive lessons.. may furnish both review and preview as essential features. **1935** *Sun* (Baltimore) 4 Apr. 1/5 Voting,.. held this week in Michigan, Illinois and Maryland, has left a somewhat mottled political picture as a 'preview' of the important Presidential contest which will take place next year. **1938** *Ibid.* 24 Jan. 6/3 His preview of the budget probabilities for the fiscal year now current. **1946** *War Report* (B.B.C.) 263 They were taking with them into captivity a preview of the wreckage of Hitler's Deutschland. **1956** W. H. WHYTE *Organization Man* i. 10 The best place to get a preview of the direction the Social Ethic is likely to take in the future. **1959** *New Statesman* 31 Jan. 136/3 Mr Dene.. was to be given a pre-view of army life on a special advance visit to Winchester Barracks. **1978** LAROSA & TANENBAUM *Random Factor* xii. 179 The morning of November 18 brought a preview of the winter to come.

b. (Occas. prevue.) *spec.* A showing or presentation of films, books, exhibitions, etc., before they are available to the public. Also *attrib.*

1922 *Opportunities in Motion Picture Industry* (Photoplay Research Soc.) 76 Where the studio employs a number of directors usually all of them sit in on the 'pre-views' that are given a film before it is actually ready for the final release. **1928** L. NORTH *Parasites* 84 He attended a preview of a picture made by a small independent group of players. **1931** *Amer. Speech* VII. 74 Why should the word *trailer* be used to apply to a prevue of a motion picture? **1936** W. DE LA MARE in *J. Freeman's Lett.* p. xvii, That dubious puff, the pre-view, was not as yet in fashion. **1940** *Times* (Weekly ed.) 7 Aug. 17/3 A pre-view and mannequin parade of women's sportswear, coats, and costumes was held in London on Thursday. **1955** *Radio Times* 22 Apr. 42/2 (*heading*) Sport. Today's results and weekend pre-view. **1958** *Photoplay* Oct. 15 The first studio preview of *Stage Struck.* **1961** G. MILLERSON *Technique Television Production* i. 15 Picture monitors. These pre-view screens give a continuous view of what the three or more studio cameras and other video sources are seeing. **1977** *Rolling Stone* 13 Jan. 22/5 They finally came to a preview theater to see the 'Stairway to Heaven' segment.

preview, *v.* [f. PRE- A. 1 + VIEW *v.*]

1. (*preˈview*) *trans.* To view beforehand; to foresee; to behold or get a sight of previously; to look at or examine antecedently. *rare.*

1607 MARSTON *What you will* v. i. H iij b, Preuiew but not preuent No mortall can the miseries of life. **1632** VICARS *Æneid* I. 24 That none preview, and so prevent our skill. **1839–52** BAILEY *Festus* xiv. 164, I cast my spirit sight Into the orient future, to preview The features of thy lifelot. **1902** 'R. CONNOR' *Sky Pilot* xiv, Every act of importance had to be previewed from all possible points.

2. (*ˈpreview*) **a.** *trans.* To show or present (a film, etc.) before its public presentation; to give a preview or foretaste of (something).

1928 L. NORTH *Parasites* v. 66 We pre-view a picture every week. **1939** *Sun* (Baltimore) 26 Sept. 10/3 In some respects it promises to preview the World Series. **1950** BLESH & JANIS *They all played Ragtime* i. 16 Such was the Negro's position in our society that it was inevitable that this rich new vein of music should be previewed for white America in whorehouses. **1951** *Newsweek* 27 Sept. 74/3 Euclid previewed a new line of vehicles which it is counting on to send its sales volume soaring. **1965** *Observer* 31 Jan. 23/5 The BBC did preview 'Culloden', but only on the same day that it was shown. **1966** *Listener* 15 Sept. 397/1 The first edition,.. which previewed the Commonwealth Conference, merits only subdued congratulation. **1968** *Radio Times* 28 Nov. 33/1 William Douglas Home introduces his first television play—and previews his own edgy performance. **1977** *New Yorker* 6 June 108/1 His full-length opera 'The Voyage of Edgar Allan Poe', was 'previewed' in Minneapolis.

b. *intr.* Of a production, performance, etc.: to be previewed.

1978 *Tucson Mag.* Dec. 99/1 On the same afternoon, the TMA League's annual 'Christmas Fair' previews to members only. **1980** *Times* 11 June 9 Yet another massive stage project, now previewing at the Aldwych, where it officially opens on June 19. **1981** *Times* 26 Aug. 9/3 *Two Gentlemen of Verona* and *Titus Andronicus*, which start previewing tonight.

Hence **ˈpreviewer**; **ˈpreviewing** *ppl. a.*

1970 *Guardian* 6 Aug. 8/2 The previewing critics. **1970** *Globe & Mail* (Toronto) 25 Sept. 12/5 Some of the previewers yesterday were the photographer's grandmother, Mrs. Arthur S. King, Mr. and Mrs. J. A. Blackey, [etc.]. **1976** *National Observer* (U.S.) 23 Oct. 22/1 The previewers all have a common goal: to latch on to the money and fame that can be made on the billion-dollar-a-year lecture circuit.

previlege, obs. Sc. form of PRIVILEGE.

previous (ˈpriːvɪəs), *a.* (*adv.*) Also 7 prævious. [f. L. *prævi-us* going before, leading the way (f. *præ*, PRE- A. + *via* way) + -OUS.]

A. *adj.* †**1.** Going before or in front; leading the way. (*fig.* in quots.) *Obs.*

1658 PHILLIPS, *Prævious*, leading the way, or going before. **1660** COWLEY *Ode on His Majesties Restauration* vii, For in the glorious General's previous Ray We saw a new created Day. **1678** H. VAUGHAN *Thalia Rediv.*, *Recovery*, Fair vessell of our daily light, whose proud And previous glories gild that blushing cloud.

2. a. Coming or going before (in time or order); foregoing, preceding, prior, antecedent.

1625 W. PEMBLE *Justification* (1629) 44 Disputes touching præuious, or fore-going dispositions. **1742** YOUNG *Nt. Th.* III. 218 A previous blast foretels the rising storm. **1797** GODWIN *Enquirer* I. v. 34 The mind seems to have acquired a previous obstinacy. **1845** M. PATTISON *Ess.* (1889) I. 23 His oath of the previous evening. **1860** TYNDALL *Glac.* I. xii. 88 A previous inspection of the glacier.. induced us to fix on a place.

b. With *to*: Coming before, preceding, antecedent to. Now *rare*: cf. B.

1702 STEELE *Funeral* IV, I hope my Felicity is previous to yours. **1731** POPE *Ep. Burlington* 42 Something there is more needful than Expense, And something previous ev'n to Taste—'tis Sense. **1808** PIKE *Sources Mississ.* II. (1810) 120 We wish to improve every moment of time previous to its [the river's] entire fall.

c. ***previous question*** (in parliamentary procedure): the question whether a vote shall be taken on the main question or issue, moved before the main question is put.

In the British Parliament, the previous question is moved for the purpose of avoiding the putting of the main question; its original form being 'that this question be now put', and its mover and seconder, with those in favour of shelving the main question, voting in the negative; but since 1888, to avoid frequent misunderstanding, and confusion with the closure motion then introduced, its form has been 'that that question be *not* now put', so that those who wish to shelve vote 'Aye'. In the House of Representatives and many State legislatures in the United States, the previous question retains the original form, but is used in order to close debate and obtain an immediate vote on the main question (its supporters voting in the affirmative): see quot. 1888.

Hatsell *Proc. Ho. Com.* (1746) II. 104 says 'On the 25th of May, 1604, is the first instance I have found of putting the previous question': but the entry in the Journal of Ho. Com. on that occasion is 'The Bill much disputed put to Question, and upon Question, dashed without one Yea'. In 1673, according to Grey's *Debates* (1769) II. 113, Sir T. Littleton said 'Sir Henry Vane was the first that ever proposed putting a Question, "Whether the Question should be now put"'; and Sir R. Howard, who followed, said 'This Question is like the image of the inventor, a perpetual disturbance'. The latter is erroneously quoted by Hatsell as 'This previous question'; but no example of the phrase before 1700 has yet been pointed out.

1700–15 BURNET *Own Time* (1766) I. 544 The previous question being then put whether the main question should be then put or not. [**1710** S. SEWALL *Diary* 3 Nov., After reading papers and debates, at last they who were against the precinct, mov'd that a previous Vote might be put; whether they would vote it now, or no; and the Council was divided, so nothing was done.] **1775** G. MASON in Sparks *Corr. Amer. Rev.* (1853) I. 62 We had.. no other way of preventing improper measures, but by procrastination, urging the previous question, and giving men time to reflect. **1790** *Debate Ho. Com. on Repeal of Corp. & Test Acts* 49 He [Mr. Burke] declared.. he had formed an idea of moving the previous Question. **1817** *Parl. Deb.* 332 The House then divided on the previous question moved by Lord Castlereagh:—Ayes.. 208 | Noes.. 152 – Majority 56. **1844** MAY *Treat. Proc. Parlt.* viii. 173 The previous question is an ingenious method of avoiding a vote upon any question that has been proposed... The words of this motion are, 'That this question be *now* put'. **1888** BRYCE *Amer. Commw.* I. I. xiii. 177 The great remedy against.. obstructive debate is the so-called previous question, which is moved in the form, 'Shall the main question be now put?' and when ordered closes forthwith all debate, and brings the House to a direct vote on that main question. *Ibid.* 181 The 'previous question' is often applied to expedite appropriation bills. **1893** *May's Parl. Proc.* ix. (ed. 10) 269 In the Commons, the words of this motion are, 'That that question be *not now* put'. [*Note*] The Speaker, with the concurrence of the house, first put the previous question in these words, 20th March, 1888.. because the motion 'That the question be now put', is akin to the closure motion.

transf. **1724** T. CHUBB (*title*) The Previous question with regard to Religion. **1725** —— A Supplement to the Previous Question.

d. ***Previous Examination*** (Cambridge University): the first examination for the B.A. degree; colloquially called *Little-go.* (Also ellipt. as *sb.*)

1828 GUNNING *Cerem. Univ. Camb.* 97 Previous Examination of all Persons, who take the Degree of Bachelor of Arts [etc.]. **1885** *Ordinances Univ. Cambr.* 6 By Grace, 4 Apr. 1878, selected Candidates for the Civil Service of India who are Candidates for Honours are excused the Previous Examination. **1905** *Abol. Compulsory Greek* (Cambridge Univ.) 6 As regards the smaller and the local schools it may be pointed out that these are practically unaffected by the requirements of the Previous... In such schools the inclusion or exclusion of Greek in the regular curriculum does not depend on the Previous Examination. **1950** M. MARPLES *University Slang* 81 Soon after this date [*sc.* 1863] *Little-go* died out at Oxford, leaving the field to *Smalls*, and retired to Cambridge, where its official title, corresponding to *Responsions*, is *Previous.* **1979** *Jrnl. R. Soc. Arts* Oct. 706/2 As late as 1861, the subjects were little more than a repetition of the 'Previous' on a slightly larger scale.

e. *ellipt.* as *sb.* Previous convictions. *slang.*

1935 G. INGRAM *Cockney Cavalcade* x. 168 He ain't got no 'previous', so you ought-a get bound over, didn't yer, Jack? **1970** G. F. NEWMAN *Sir, You Bastard* i. 34 'Neither has any previous, Terry,' Burgess said. 'I thought perhaps the fella might have had a little bit,' he shrugged. **1974** E. JONES *Barlow comes to Judgement* 14 Sitting on the benches.. were ten men... Nine of them had previous. The tenth had a clean record. **1977** 'M. UNDERWOOD' *Murder with Malice* v. 56 Anthony Rivings.. five convictions for dishonesty.. three other Rivings.. all with previous.

3. *slang* or *colloq.* (orig. *U.S.*) Done, occurring, acting, etc., before the proper time; coming too soon, hasty, premature. (Usually with *too.*)

1885 *Daily Tel.* 14 Dec. (Farmer *Slang*), He is a little before his time, a trifle previous, as the Americans say. **1890** *Boston* (Mass.) *Jrnl.* 21 June 2/3 The grumbling in this matter has been too previous. **1895** *Boston* (Mass.) *Herald* 11 May 6/6 Summer is too previous. **1902** *Westm. Gaz.* 16 July 9/1 The Stock Exchange has been, in the slang of the Street, a little 'too previous'.

B. as *adv.* = PREVIOUSLY; usually ***previous to*** = before, prior to.

1719 S. SEWALL *Diary* 25 Feb., I.. would have them previous to it, freely confer about it. **1747** W. HORSLEY *Fool* (1748) II. 190 His being brought to Judgment here, previous to his appearing before a most solemn Judicature. **1802** MAR. EDGEWORTH *Moral T.*, *Prussian Vase* (1816) 217 The company, previous to his majesty's arrival, were all assembled. **1843** MILL *Logic* III. v. §3 The event not only exists, but begins to exist immediately previous. **1849** F. W. NEWMAN *Soul* 205 Previous to Ordination, they may be subjected to some literary ordeal.

previously (ˈpriːvɪəslɪ), *adv.* [f. prec. + -LY².] At a previous or preceding time; before, beforehand, antecedently.

1718 PRIOR *Solomon* I. 166 Darting their stings, they previously declare Design'd revenge, and fierce intent of war. **1797–1803** FOSTER in *Life & Corr.* (1846) I. 216 Principles previously known. **1860** TYNDALL *Glac.* I. vi. 45 They were different from any I had previously seen. **1879** *Cassell's Techn. Educ.* III. 176/2 About two years previously.

b. With *to*: = before (some action or event).

1806 SURR *Winter in Lond.* I. 250 The few weeks which were to be passed previously to their entering the metropolis. **1863** H. COX *Instit.* III. viii. 708 Previously to describing the changes then made.

c. Qualifying (and usually hyphened to) a ppl. or other adj. in attrib. relation, forming a kind of compound adj.: cf. *aforesaid*, etc.

1849 D. CAMPBELL *Inorg. Chem.* 37 Introduced into a previously weighed thin small bulb with a long neck. **1849** J. GRAY *Earth's Antiq.* III. 116 A.. previously-existing Earth. **1875** JOWETT *Plato* (ed. 2) III. 285 In accordance with our previously-declared rule.

ˈpreviousness. [f. as prec. + -NESS.] The quality or fact of being previous.

1. Existence or occurrence before something else; antecedence, priority. *rare.*

1677 OWEN *Justification* i. Wks. 1851 V. 77 As to the previousness of the conviction of sin unto faith, they are found in all who sincerely believe. **1731** BAILEY vol. II, *Previousness*, foregoing or introductory quality.

2. *slang* or *colloq.* (See PREVIOUS 3.)

1884 *Boston* (Mass.) *Jrnl.* 4 Mar. 2/1 A Case of Previousness. **1885** *Ibid.* 16 Apr. 2/1 The victim of his own over-confidence and indiscreet previousness. **1892** *N.Y. Law Jrnl.* in *Law Times* XCIII. 413/1 He gets there sooner than the rest. His previousness, however, is not always effective.

previse (prɪˈvaɪz), *v.* [f. L. *prævīs-*, ppl. stem of *prævidēre*: see PREVIDE.]

†**1.** *trans.* To provide, supply, furnish. Const. *of* a thing. *Obs. rare.*

c **1470** HARDING *Chron.* CCXX. vii, She was so wel, within her selfe auysed Of great sadnesse, and womanhede preuised.

2. To foresee; to forecast. Also *absol.*

1597 J. KING *On Jonas* (1618) 287 God had a purpose preuised herein, to worke the glorie of his name. **1622** MABBE tr. *Aleman's Guzman d'Alf.* II. 290 Neither do they previse, and provide for after-claps. **1694** MOTTEUX *Rabelais* V. xxii, Faculties, that do not previse the facility of the operation adequately. **1863** LYTTON *Caxtoniana* I. 51 [They] only through reason discover what through imagination they previse. **1890** J. SKINNER *Diss. Metaph.* 98 He had intelligence to previse the possible future.

3. To advise or inform beforehand. *rare.*

1834 LYTTON *Pompeii* II. i, Who sent to previse thee of it? **1849** —— *Pelham* xv. *note*, Mr. Pelham..has prevised the reader, that Lord Vincent was somewhat addicted to paradox.

Hence **preˈvised** *ppl. a.*, foreseen.

1644 QUARLES *Barnabas & B.* 257 He takes benefit by prevised misery that strives to eschew it. **1890** J. SKINNER *Diss. Metaph.* 98 He had power to accomplish an almost infinite amount of good in that prevised future.

prevision (prɪˈvɪʒən), *sb.* Also 7–9 præ-. [= F. *prévision* (14th c. in Littré), ad. L. type **prævīsiōn-em*, n. of action f. *prævidēre* PREVIDE.] The action or faculty of foreseeing; knowledge of or insight into the future; foresight, foreknowledge.

1612 T. TAYLOR *Comm. Titus* iii. 7 The Apostle by mentioning of grace againe, secludeth all that prevision of workes formerly mentioned, which might be motiues vnto God for the bestowing of his Grace. **1647** TRAPP *Comm. Matt.* xxiv. 25 Prevision is the best means of prevention. **1741** WARBURTON *Div. Legat.* VI. v. II. 623 Such a Relation ..could not possibly come about but by divine Prevision. **1833** MRS. BROWNING *Prometh. Bound* 313, I have known All in prevision!

b. With *a* and *pl.* An instance of this; a prophetic or anticipatory vision or perception.

c **1652** J. SMITH *Sel. Disc.* VI. iii. (1821) 200 'The mind of the universe', which mingling its influence with our minds, begets these προγνώσεις or previsions. **1682** FLAVEL *Fear* 80 We see the benefit of such previsions and provisions for sufferings. **1851** THACKERAY *Eng. Hum.* i. (1858) 51 Stella was quite right in her previsions. She saw from the very first hint what was going to happen. **1866** MRS. GASKELL *Wives & Dau.* l, She had a prevision of what was coming.

Hence **preˈvision** *v. trans.*, (*a*) to endow with prevision; (*b*) to have prevision of, to foresee; **preˈvisional** *a.*, relating to, depending on, characterized by, or exhibiting prevision (whence **preˈvisionally** *adv.*); **preˈvisionary** *a.* = *previsional.*

1891 T. HARDY *Tess* xxxvi, Like all who have been *previsioned by suffering, she could..hear a penal sentence in the fiat, 'You shall be born', particularly if addressed to potential issue of hers. **1901** *Westm. Gaz.* 23 Mar. 2/1 He must have previsioned clearly..that whatever..may be about to befall Empires..cooks, at any rate, will always be in request. **1836** G. S. FABER *Prim. Doctr. Election* II. viii. (1842) 376. *Ibid.* II. ix. (1842) 387 Election, whether absolute and unconditional, or *previsional and conditional, is equally, both on the Calvinistic Scheme and on the Arminian Scheme, An Election of certain individuals, directly and immediately, to eternal life. **1887** *Spectator* 15 Oct. 1394 In a spirit of previsional self-defence. **1836** G. S. FABER *Prim. Doctr. Election* II. ix. (1842) 405 Certain individuals..predestinated either absolutely or *previsionally to eternal life. **1818** —— *Horæ Mosaicæ* II. 261 A special *previsionary regard..to a very remarkable part of our Saviour's history. **1851** —— *Many Mansions* 373 As respects the previsionary mercy of God.

previsive (priːˈvaɪsɪv), *a. rare*⁻¹. [f. as PREVISE + -IVE.] Of, pertaining to, or of the nature of prevision; foreseeing.

1907 C. FRASER in *Hibbert Jrnl.* Jan. 244 Past customary uniformity is apt..to produce blindly in us a previsive habit.

previte, obs. form of PRIVITY.

†**previˈvation.** *Obs. rare*⁻¹. [irreg. f. PRE- A. I. + L. *vīv-ĕre* to live + -ATION.] The fact of living before another; seniority.

a **1650** MAY *Satir. Puppy* (1657) 60 The first (who claims precedencie by previvation) strove to excuse his absurd writing by publishing a worse sort.

prevoˈcalic, *a.* Also (occas.) prae-vocalic. [PRE- B. 1.] Before a vowel; of or pertaining to the position before a vowel. Hence **prevoˈcalically** *adv.*

1909 in WEBSTER. **1934** M. K. POPE *From Latin to Mod. French* II. xvii. 223 In educated speech throughout the sixteenth century final consonants, whether single or supported, were maintained when in prae-vocalic position in the phrase. **1943** A. L. KROEBER in *Univ. Calif. Publ. Linguistics* I. 30 The stops p, t, k are universal and stable. In the Arizona dialects they are less aspirated, prevocalically, than in other languages and have often been written b, d, g. **1949** *Language* XXV. 400 It is..improbable that *l* [in Umbrian] was treated differently before *j* and prevocalic *ī*. **1957** N. FRYE *Sound & Poetry* 114 The two methods are even more sharply contrasted in the line endings of the two poets, where the frequencies of Spenser's prevocalic and Milton's postvocalic clusters are more than doubled. **1964** R. H. ROBINS *Gen. Linguistics* 101 In Scots English, /r/ occurs both prevocalically and postvocalically. **1966** [see *chest register* s.v. CHEST 10b]. **1970** B. M. H. STRANG *Hist. English* I. ii. 51 Dark *l* post-vocalically, and clear *l* pre- or inter-vocalically. **1976** *Archivum Linguisticum* VII. 164 Both to postulate an analogical extension of the pre-vocalic forms, since in the majority of the cases they do not even exist, and to assume lost vowels, is to beg the question.

prevocalized (priːˈvəʊkəlaɪzd), *ppl. a. Philol.* [f. PRE- A. 1 + *vocalized*, f. VOCALIZE.] Preceded (as a consonant) by a vowel.

1876 DOUSE *Grimm's Law* App. E. 205 The close resemblance of certain simple *prævocalized* roots (e.g. *ak-*, *ag-*..) to the simple *post*vocalized roots, exhibiting the same consonant (e.g. *ka*, *ga*...).

pre-volitional: see PRE- B. 1 d.

†**prevost**, ‖**prévôt**. [a. OF. *prevost*, mod.F. *prévôt* (prevo):—L. *præpositus* one appointed over others, PROVOST.] The French equivalent of PROVOST, retained by Caxton in translating from Fr., and used in modern times in reference to France and the Channel Islands.

†**1.** The provost or president of a chapter or collegiate church; = PROVOST 1. *Obs.*

1483 CAXTON *Gold. Leg.* 35 b/1 Whome wilt thou gyue me of thise preuostes that entende not more to empte the purse of his subgettis than [etc.]? **1838** *Penny Cycl.* XI. 90/1 Gassendi was promoted to a canonry in the cathedral of Digne, where he was..appointed prevôt of the church.

‖**2. a.** In France: Formerly, an officer of the king or a feudal seigneur charged in his name to collect imposts and administer justice; also, a provost-marshal; now, the judge of a prevotal court.

†*prevost de l'hostel*, an officer of the French King's household, who had cognizance of criminal cases affecting members of the court.

1644 EVELYN *Diary* 20 Apr., The Prevost Martial, with his assistants, going in persuite. **1670** COTTON *Espernon* III. XI. 538 An Archer belonging to the Prevost de l'Hostel, that the Partners had substituted, for the gathering in of this Impost. *Ibid.* XII. 617 He sent a Prevost to take him, wherein he was also so successful, as to have him forc'd away from his own Country. **1841** JAMES *Brigand* xxv, What he has done requires the chastisement of my prévôt.

b. In Guernsey: The name of the officer corresponding to the High Sheriff of an English county; also, both in Jersey and Guernsey, an estates bailiff or sergeant of a fief.

[**1331** *Precepte d'Assize* (Billet d'Etat, Guernsey 9 May 1906) Ung sergeant appellé le Prevost du Roy. **1580–83** *Approbation des Lois* (1897) 9 Les Seigneurs qui ont prévôts ou meûniers les peuvent faire arrêter par le Prévôt du Roi.] **1682** WARBURTON *Hist. Guernsey* (1822) 55 The King's Prévôt is elected after the same manner as the Jurats are. His office is..to bring all criminals before them [the court]..to see the sentence executed. He executes all arrests. *Ibid.* 68 The private men's fiefs, most commonly the rents are received by prévôts. *Ibid.* [see PRÉVÔTÉ]. **1857** *Order in Council* 21 Feb., That the Prevost is the Executive Officer of Justice in the Island of Guernsey, both in civil and in criminal matters. **1862** ANSTED *Channel Isl.* IV. xxiii. (ed. 2) 525 In Jersey there is an officer called Vicomte, or Viscount, who represents the High Sheriff of an English County. The corresponding officer in Guernsey is called the Prevôt. **1908** A. HILGROVE TURNER in *Let. to Editor*, In ten of the twelve parishes of Jersey there are subordinate officers of the Royal Court called 'The King's Prévôts'. These are furnished in turn by the various proprietors on the Crown fiefs... There are also what de Geyt calls 'les petits Prevosts', i.e. *Prévôts* of 'Fiefs subalternes' or private fiefs.

Hence †**ˈprevostship**, the office, jurisdiction, or district of a prevost; **ˈprevotal** [F. *prévôtal*] *a.*, of or pertaining to a French prévôt; *prevotal court*, a French temporary criminal tribunal, from which there is no appeal; ‖**prévôté** [F., = PROVOSTY], in Jersey and Guernsey, a fief held by a prévôt.

1577 *F. de L'isle's Legendarie* A vj, The seconde [daughter] ..was giuen to Iames Marquise of Baden, with the dowrye of three preuostshipps..besides a good summe of money. **1821** *New Monthly Mag.* I. 303 Military police was established; the ordinary laws suspended; a prevotal tribunal erected at Mayence. **1839** *Blackw. Mag.* XLV. 435 Nine years of agitations, civil war, regicide, insurrections, prevotal courts, states of siege, and then amnesty, order, prosperity, and peace. **1682** WARBURTON *Hist. Guernsey* (1822) 68 There are yet other fiefs where the lord's rent is received by prévotés, which are tenements or lands, parcel of the fief, obliged by their tenure to collect the lord's rents. .. Such as hold by this sort of tenure are, in the old Coutumier, called *prévôts-receveurs.*

pre-vowel: see PRE- B. 2 a.

prevoyance (prɪˈvɔɪəns). *rare.* [a. F. *prévoyance*, f. *prévoir*:—L. *prævidēre* to PROVIDE: see -ANCE.] Foresight. So **preˈvoyant** *a.* [ad. F. *prévoyant*, pres. pple. of *prévoir*], foreseeing.

1820 C. R. MATURIN *Melmoth* (1892) III. xxvii. 93 To whom misfortune had taught an anxious and jealous prevoyance. *Ibid.* xxx. 229 Affectionate and delicate prevoyance. **1862** MRS. OLIPHANT *E. Irving* I. vi. 149 But Nature, prevoyant, tingled into his heart an inarticulate thrill of prophecy. **1883** MRS. LYNN LINTON *Ione* viii, The girl is all obedience and prevoyance, all self-sacrifice and devotion.

prevue, var. PREVIEW *sb.* 2 b.

prevy, prevyledge, obs. ff. PRIVY, PRIVILEGE.

†**prew.** *Obs.* [var. of *preu*, *pru*: cf. PREU *a.*] A parallel ME. form of PROW, advantage, profit, good; *to his prew*, advantageously.

c **1330** R. BRUNNE *Chron. Wace* (Rolls) 12754 Þenne had Marcel a neuew þat was horsed vntil his prew.

prewa (for *preva*), obs. Sc. form of PRIVY.

pre-ˈwar, *a.* and *adv.* **A.** *adj.* [PRE- B. 2.] Pertaining to or characteristic of the period before a war, esp. the wars of 1914–18 and of 1939–45.

1908 *Daily Chron.* 24 Apr. 7/3 The Transvaal Government..are thoroughly honest—a great difference from the pre-war days. **1915** *Political Q.* May 90 The relations of the engineers (employers and workmen) were governed by two separate pre-war agreements. The earlier ..made in 1911,..the second..dated April 1914. **1917** [see FOGGY *a.* 5 b]. **1926** GALSWORTHY *Silver Spoon* III. vii. 277 How stupid and pre-war! Why couldn't he, like her, be free, be supple, take life as it came? **1928** *Publishers' Weekly* 30 June 2617 The government of France has succeeded in stabilizing the franc at 25·52 to the dollar, approximately one-fifth of its pre-war ratio. **1938** *Encycl. Brit. Bk. of Year* 20/1 Tricycle undercarriages familiar in pre-war days, have been re-introduced in modernized form for greater safety in high-speed landings. **1942** E. PAUL *Narrow St.* xxix. 260 What dealt our pre-war world its mortal blow was the supine cowardice and hypocrisy of so-called democrats. **1946** *R.A.F. Jrnl.* May 172 All the women were free..to resume their pre-war occupation... Already they have resumed their pre-war studies. **1958** *Listener* 6 Nov. 719/1 He [*sc.* Lord Montgomery] has severe and deserved strictures on the pre-war governments for their failure to bring the army up to date. **1975** *New Yorker* 28 Apr. 112/2 The Thai Nguyen steelworks now produces only pig iron, but planners hope that in two or three years it will regain its prewar capacity of a hundred and seventy thousand metric tons of steel annually. **1977** *Times* 22 Apr. 2/8 The pre-war, Spanish-style house has..indoor swimming pool.

B. *adv.* [PRE- B. 2 c.] Before a war, esp. the wars of 1914–18 and of 1939–45.

1920 *Econ. Conditions Central Europe* I. 12 Four million tons of coal were imported annually pre-war, mainly to Petrograd and Baltic ports. **1923** *Westm. Gaz.* 25 Aug. 4/5 The new tourist hails from districts and from classes which, pre-war, never dreamed of leaving England. **1928** *Daily Tel.* 4 Sept. 9/6 Some time pre-war there was a large contract out for tender from a foreign Government for water tanks. **1959** *Times Lit. Suppl.* 24 Apr. 288/4 The turnover of land is low, indicating a considerable decrease in distress sales as compared with pre-war. **1974** *Daily Tel.* 17 July 18 Pre-war, the 1933 Wimbledon final..bears a similarity to this last championship.

prewarn (priːˈwɔːn), *v. rare.* [PRE- A. 1.] *trans.* **a.** To give warning of (an event) beforehand. **b.** To warn (a person) beforehand; to forewarn. Hence **preˈwarning** *vbl. sb.*

1603 H. CROSSE *Vertues Commw.* (1878) 31 Deseruing either prewarning in the beginning, or reproofe in the ende. **1612** *Two Noble K.* v. i, [Whose approach] Comets prewarne; whose havocke in vaste feild Unearthed skulls proclaime. **1881** DUFFIELD *Don Quix.* II. xxxvii. 184, I am prewarned..of this my squire that your greatness is overthrown.

pre-wash: see PRE- A. 1, 2.

prewe (*w* = *v*), obs. Sc. f. PRIVY, PROOF, PROVE.

pre-wear: see PRE- A. 1.

prewely, prewete (*w* = *v*), obs. Sc. ff. PRIVILY, PRIVITY.

pre-work, -world: see PRE- B. 2 a.

pre-wrap, -write: see PRE- A. 1.

prews, -e, obs. ff. PRUCE.

prewy, -ledge, obs. Sc. ff. PRIVY, PRIVILEGE.

Prex. U.S. college slang for PRESIDENT (of a college). Also *transf.*

1828 *Yankee* (Portland, Maine) 16 July 232/1 Our Prex says this: You surely miss [etc.]. **1858** *N.Y. Tribune* 16 Oct. 3/2 But the face of the 'Prex' [of Amherst College] appearing, all parties ceased contention. **1862** *Mem. Hamilton Coll.* 154 Prex Backus was a jovial Prex, The roughest, kindest of his sex. **1906** *N.Y. Even. Post* 11 June 6 If the various unpopular 'Prexes' would study the grounds of their unpopularity. **1942** BERREY & VAN DEN BARK *Amer. Thes. Slang* §854/10 Government officials and employees... Prex, Prexy, the President. **1967** H. KEMELMAN *Nine Mile Walk* 150, I was still officially a member of the faculty [of history] and as such was invited to the President's annual Christmas reception for the faculty. I accepted..because of past favours from Prex.

Prexy (ˈprɛksɪ). *U.S. slang.* Also Prexie, p-. [f. prec. + -Y⁶.] = PREX.

1871 L. H. BAGG *4 Years at Yale* 655 The title 'Prex'..is oftener used alone to designate him [*sc.* the President] among the Seniors, the modified form of 'Prexy' is somewhat in vogue, in familiar talk. **1905** *N.Y. Even. Post* 1 Sept. 7 Scores of entering classes are lined up in chapel to listen to good advice from the dean or 'Prexie'. **1909** O. D. VON ENGELN *At Cornell* 58 The avenue is still, for Prexy is delivering his annual address in the Armory. **1929** *Publishers' Weekly* 22 June 2859/1 Professor Charles E. Merriam..has hobnobbed with politicians as well as prexies. **1948** *Variety* 25 Aug. 1/4 Madison Sq. Garden 'prexy' Gen. John Reed Kilpatrick. **1973** *Center City Office Weekly* (Philadelphia) 9 Oct. 3 Dr. Richard N. Harner, prexy of the Epilepsy Foundation, will appear in a taped interview with Frank Ford. **1974** *Cleveland* (Ohio) *Plain*

Dealer 13 Oct. c. 13/1 While the NHL is controlled basically by the board of governors..the silver-haired prexy still wields a powerful stick when it comes to meting out fines and suspensions. **1979** *Honolulu Advertiser* 8 Jan. A. 3/1 Brokers at Stapleton Assoc. think they had more than their share of the breaks in '78. Prexy John Stapleton started things off by busting his leg on a ski trip.

prey (preɪ), *sb.* Forms: 3 **preiȝe**, 3–6 **praie**, 3–7 **preie, preye**, 4 **preȝe**, 4–5 **prai, prei**, 4–7 **pray(e**, 6 *Sc.* **pra, praii**; 4– **prey.** *β.* 5–6 **proye, proie.** [ME. *preye*, a. OF. *preie* (*a* 1140 in Godef.) booty, prey, also a flock, later OF. and mod.F. *proie*, earlier OF. **preide*, Pr., It. *preda*:—L. *præda* booty, spoil, prey; in med.L., also, a flock. Cf. PREDE *sb.* The *β*-form was immed. from 15th c. F.

Now collective: formerly also with *a* and *pl.*]

I. 1. a. That which is taken in war, or by pillage or violence; booty, spoil, plunder. Formerly, often with *pl.* † *in prey*, † *to prey*, as a prey. *arch. rare.*

c **1250** *Gen. & Ex.* 4028 Ðis leun sal oðer folc freten, Lond canaan al preiȝe bi-geten. **1297** R. GLOUC. (Rolls) 6163 þe deneis..wende estward in to kent & robbede þere vaste & hor preye at medeweie in to ssipes caste. **1382** WYCLIF *1 Macc.* i. 33 He toke prayes of the citee [**1388** preies; Vulg. *spolia*] and brente it with fijr. **1475** *Bk. Noblesse* (Roxb.) 31 The men of Gaule had wonne gret praies and good, as horse harneis, vesselle of golde and of silver gret plente. **1535** STEWART *Cron. Scot.* (Rolls) II. 89 To be maid als with oure mortall fa, At thair plesour baith presoner and pra. **1563** GOLDING *Cæsar* VII. (1565) 237 Al the rest of the prysoners he dystrybuted among hys souldiers euery man one in name of a pray. **1580** *Reg. Privy Council Scot.* III. 308 Exponand ..the saidis compliners guidis.., in prey to the enemy. **1584** POWEL *Lloyd's Cambria* 77 Returned to their ships with their praie. **1603** KNOLLES *Hist. Turks* (1621) 127 Great Monarchies destitute of their lawfull heires, had..become rich preyes unto such as could first lay strong hand upon them. **1641** *Declar. to Chas. I* in Rushw. *Hist. Coll.* III. (1692) I. 529 The Prey, or Booty which they take from the English, they mark with the Queen's mark. **1697** DRYDEN *Virg. Georg.* III. 621 Thy faithful Dogs..hold at Bay The Mountain Robbers, rushing to the Prey.

β. **1481** CAXTON *Godeffroy* ccxii. 310 There gadred he many grete proyes, that is to wete, horses, beufes, Kyen and sheep, And ryche prysonners. **1489** —— *Faytes of A.* III. xi. 191 Where as byfore he was a powere knyght he was becom ryche by the proyes that he had goten and taken. **1552** HULOET, Proye, praye, and spoyle.

b. *fig.* (In Scriptural use.) That which one brings away or saves from any contest, etc.

1388 WYCLIF *Jer.* xxi. 9 He that goith out,..schal lyue, and his lijf schal be as a preye to hym. **1535** COVERDALE *Ibid.*, He shal saue his life, and shall wynne his soule for a pray. **1611** BIBLE *Ibid.*, His life shall be unto him for a prey. *Ibid.* xxxviii. 2 He shall have his life for a prey, and shall live. **1642** ROGERS *Naaman* 25 Craving [that] our owne lives may be given us as a prey, if we can speed for no more. **1827** KEBLE *Christian Year, 11th S. aft. Trin.* vii, Too happy if, that dreadful day, Thy life be given thee for a prey.

2. a. An animal hunted or killed, esp. (now only) by carnivorous animals for food; quarry. Also *fig.*

a **1240** *Wohunge* in *Cott. Hom.* 273 Þu band ta helle dogges, and reftes ham hare praie. *a* **1300** *Cursor M.* 833 Þe strang þe weker for to sla, Ilkan to mak of oþer prai. *Ibid.* 4216 Of him has beistes made þair prai. *Ibid.* 22901 An hungre leon mete he son, Vp and dun his prai [*Trin.* prey] sekand. **1390** GOWER *Conf.* III. 258 As the Tigre his time awaiteth In hope forto cacche his preie. **1481** CAXTON *Myrr.* II. xvi. 102 The goshawke and sperhawk taken their prayes by the ryuers. **1577** B. GOOGE *Heresbach's Husb.* IV. (1586) 169 So fall they many times out, and become a pray to Vermine. **1608** TOPSELL *Serpents* (1658) 686 The Crocodiles ..run up and down to seek preys to satisfie their hunger. **1622** R. HAWKINS *Voy. S. Sea* (1847) 70 There doth accompany this fish [shark] divers little fishes, which are callet pilats fishes,..and feede of the scraps and superfluities of his prayes. **1751** JOHNSON *Rambler* No. 153 ¶12 The hungry family flew like vultures on their prey. **1853** J. H. NEWMAN *Hist. Sk.* (1873) II. I. ii. 75 Down they came one after another, like wolves after their prey.

β. **1484** CAXTON *Fables of Æsop* I. xiv, The Egle beganne to flyhe and lete fall his proye.

†**b.** That which is procured or serves for food.

1382 WYCLIF *Prov.* xxxi. 15 Fro the nyȝt she ros, and ȝaf prei [**1388** prey; *marg.* liyflode] to hir homli men. [**1555–8** PHAER *Æneid* I. A iij b, Than all bestyrd them to the praye [*orig.* Illi se praedae accingunt] the bankettes gan beginne.] **1683** *Brit. Spec.* 41 [They] satisfied their Hunger with any sort of Prey, as Venison, Natural Fruits, and Milk, and many times with Roots and Barks of Trees.

3. One who or that which falls or is given into the power of (*a*) a hostile or injurious person, or (*b*) an injurious influence; a victim: esp. in const. *to be* or *become a prey to.*

(*a*) *c* **1325** *Metr. Hom.* 55 Satanas was ful redie, And tok that sawel gredilye, And mad ful gret joi of his prai. *c* **1330** R. BRUNNE *Chron.* (1810) 269 Opon þe þrid day, at a toun hamelet, Thomas was his pray, as he to mete was set. *c* **1400** *Rom. Rose* 5143 But unto Love I was so thral, Which callith over-al his pray. *c* **1430** *Hymns Virg.* 14 Lete me not be þe feendis pray. **1560** DAUS tr. *Sleidane's Comm.* 331 The Emperour setteth forth against them new proclamations, & maketh them a praye vnto all men. **1681** H. MORE *Exp. Dan.* p. lxxviii, Like to make us a prey to the common enemy. **1757** BURKE *Abridgm. Eng. Hist.* vii. Wks. 1842 II. 579 Jerusalem fell an easy prey to his arms. **1849** MACAULAY *Hist. Eng.* vii. II. 194 A man who had hitherto been the prey of gamesters. **1878** SIMPSON *Sch. Shaks.* I. 140 The Cardinal succeeded to the crown, and after a brief reign left it a prey to pretenders.

β. **1413** *Pilgr. Sowle* (Caxton 1483) IV. xxx. 78 The chyuetayns..yeuen weye to their enemyes and made the peple proye to them.

(*b*) **1593** SHAKS. *2 Hen. VI*, II. i. 198, I banish her my bed and company And giue her as a prey to law and shame. **1697** DRYDEN *Virg. Georg.* III. 844 The slow creeping Evil eats his way, Consumes the parching Limbs, and makes the Life his Prey. **1741** WATTS *Improv. Mind* I. i. §15 Given up a Prey to a thousand prejudices. **1750** GRAY *Elegy* xxii, To dumb Forgetfulness a prey. **1770** GOLDSM. *Des. Vill.* 51 Ill fares the land, to hastening ills a prey, Where wealth accumulates, and men decay. **1865** DICKENS *Mut. Fr.* III. iv, An unresisting prey to that inscrutable toothache.

4. a. The action of preying; seizing or taking by force or violence, or (of an animal) in order to devour; depredation, pillage, capture, seizure. Now *rare.*

1523 LD. BERNERS *Froiss.* I. cccxciii. 675 *heading*, Of the great pillage and proyes [*table of contents* proies] done by the Chanone Robirsarde and his company agaynst the kynge of Castyll. **1586** J. HOOKER *Hist. Irel.* in *Holinshed* II. 112/1 Ormond..by the dailie inuasions and preies of Piers Grace was almost wasted and vnhabited. **1651** HOBBES *Leviath.* I. xiv. 65 To expose himselfe to Prey..rather than to dispose himselfe to Peace. **1675** TEMPLE *Let. to Sir J. Williamson* Wks. 1731 II. 350 Both Parties will be out upon Prey. **1721** BRADLEY *Philos. Acc. Wks. Nat.* 116 The Otter..whose Prey is chiefly upon Fish. **1787** JEFFERSON *Writ.* (1859) II. 100 The general prey of the rich on the poor. **1855** TENNYSON *Maud* IV. iv, The whole little wood where I sit is a world of plunder and prey.

b. *bird* (†*fowl*) *of prey*: one that kills and devours other animals; a predatory or rapacious bird, esp. one belonging to the order Falconiformes or Strigiformes. Also *attrib.* and *fig.* Similarly *beast, fish*, etc., *of prey.*

1340 *Ayenb.* 142 Uor þe uoȝeles of praye þet byeþ þe dyeulen. *a* **1398** TREVISA tr. *Bartholomæus Anglicus' De Proprietatibus Rerum* (1975) II. 1288 Most hote briddes of complexioun and colerik, as briddes of pray, haueþ þe vtter partyes ȝelowe. **1485** CAXTON *Chas. Gt.* 107 Fawcons and other byrdes of proye. *c* **1532** DU WES *Introd. Fr.* in *Palsgr.* 910 *heading*, Haukes of pray syxtene kyndes. **1603** SHAKES. *Meas. for M.* II. i. 1 We must not make a scar-crow of the Law, Setting it up to feare the Birds of prey. **1662** STILLINGFL. *Orig. Sacr.* III. iii. §8 Even beasts of prey are not such to those of their own kind. **1721** BRADLEY *Philos. Acc. Wks. Nat.* 51 Subject to the voracious Appetites of the Fish of Prey. **1854** Birds of prey [see RAPTOR 4]. **1899** W. E. H. LECKY *Democracy & Liberty* (ed. 2) I. p. xxii, He [*sc.* W. E. Gladstone] had a wonderful eye—a bird of prey eye—fierce, luminous and restless. **1920** H. E. HOWARD *Territory in Bird Life* vii. 269 A bird of prey would have more difficulty in approaching a flock unawares than it would have in approaching a single individual. **1956** D. A. BANNERMAN *Birds Brit. Isles* V. p. v, It is a sad fact that several of our most noble birds of prey can no longer be studied in what were once their native haunts. **1974** M. BIJLEVELD *Birds of Prey in Europe* i. 1 During the last two hundred years, the European continent has seen a period of intensifying persecution of the diurnal birds of prey.

transf. *a* **1732** GAY *Fables* II. xii. 24 Yet this you do, whene'er you play Among the gentlemen of prey.

II. †**5.** *transf.* A company of men, a troop, an army. *Obs.* [So OF. *proie*, troupeau (*a* 1300 in Godef.), med.L. *præda* (Du Cange).]

a **1300** *K. Horn* 1235 Horn tok his preie And dude him in þe weie. **13..** *K. Alis.* 1991 (Bodl. MS.) Alisaundre þi foo.. Liggeþ now wiþ swiche preye þat he wriȝeþ al þe contreye. *Ibid.* 2595 Of his poeple þe grete praye Lasted twenty milen waye.

III. 6. *attrib.* and *Comb.*, chiefly objective, as *prey-catcher, -devourer, -getter, -seeker, -taker*; **prey bird, fish**, a bird, fish of prey.

1812 BYRON *Ch. Har.* I. lxxxviii, Unworthy of the *prey-bird's maw. **1821** SHELLEY *Hellas* 255 The prey-birds and the wolves are gorged and sleep. **1548** UDALL, etc. *Erasm. Par. John* x. 72 To discerne the true shepeherd from yᵉ thefe or *prayecatcher. **1638** FALKLAND in *Jonsonus Virbius*, The *prey-devourer had our prey been made. **1899** O. PETTERSSON in *19th Cent.* Feb. 295 The numbers of useful fishes devoured by *prey fishes, &c. **1552** HULOET, *Praye getter or seker, *prædator.* **1553** GRIMALDE *Cicero's Offices* (1556) 85 Who with their riches do raunsome men taken by *preyeseekers. **1619** MIDDLETON *Love & Antiq.* Wks. VII. 320 The sturdiest *prey-taker that here assembles.

prey (preɪ), *v.* Forms: 3–4 **prei-e(n**, 4 **prai**, 4–7 **pray**, 5–6 **praie**, 5– **prey.** *β.* 6 **proie.** *Pa. t.* **preyed**; 3 **preide**, 5–6 *Sc.* **prayit**, 6 **preid, prayde.** [ME. a. OF. *preer, preier* (in earlier form, *preder*, *c* 1040 in Godef.):—late L. *prædāre* (Vulgate), collateral form of *prædārī* to plunder, spoil, rob, f. *præda* PREY *sb.* Cf. PREDE *v.*]

†**1.** *trans.* To plunder, pillage, spoil; to rob, ravage (a place, person, etc.). *Obs.*

13.. *Cursor M.* 2503 (Cott.) Siþen þai spred to prai [*Fairf.* spoly; *Gött.* winne] þe land, Al þai tok þai forwit fand. **1375** BARBOUR *Bruce* XV. 330 The nethir end of tevy-daill He prayit doune till him all haill. **1422** tr. *Secreta Secret., Priv. Priv.* 183 The extorcioner rubbyth and Preyeth good men and trew. **1579–80** NORTH *Plutarch* (1676) 925 To prey and spoil the Countrey. **1594** SPENSER *Amoretti* lviii, Devouring tyme and changeful chance have prayd, Her glories pride that none may it repayre. **1654** R. CODRINGTON tr. *Iustine* xxiv. 336 Having plundered the Towns, and preyed the Fields.

β. **1562** J. SHUTE *Cambini's Turk. Wars* 39 The Turckes.. went and spoyled and proied all the contre.

†**b.** To make prey or spoil of; to take possession of as booty. *Obs. rare.*

1596 SPENSER *F.Q.* V. iv. 14 Yet my good lucke he shall not likewise pray. *Ibid.* VI. x. 35 His loves deare spoile, in which his heart was prayde. **1623** BINGHAM *Xenophon* 7 The Cilicians, abundance of whose persons and goods, we haue preid and carrie with vs.

2. *intr.* To take booty; to pillage, plunder; *to prey on, upon*, † *over* = sense 1.

1297 R. GLOUC. (Rolls) 471 Hii wende aboute & preide, hom ne miȝte noȝt atstonde. **1375** BARBOUR *Bruce* XVII. 226 The king gert men of gret nobillay Ryde in-till ynglande, for till pray. *c* **1400** *Destr. Troy* 2643 If Parys with a pepull past into Grese, In purpas to pray or profet to gete. **1576** FLEMING *Panopl. Epist.* 115 Either to aske that which was another mans right, or else to pray vpon that which was none of their owne. **1634** SIR T. HERBERT *Trav.* 71 He gaue.. treasure there, to the Ianizaries and Spaheis to prey ouer. **1840** MACAULAY *Ess., Clive* (1887) 530 Ferocious invaders had descended through the western passes to prey on the defenceless wealth of Hindostan. **1872** YEATS *Growth Comm.* 264 The buccaneers preying upon Spanish commerce were masters of the smaller W. India Islands.

3. *intr.* To seek for or take prey, as an animal; esp. with *on, upon*: To seize and kill as prey; to kill and devour, to feed on. Also *fig.*

a **1340** HAMPOLE *Psalter* xvi. 13 The princes ware like til the leoun, that is the deuel, redy til pray of mannys saule. **1575** TURBERV. *Venerie* 185 They pray also vppon all Pullen. *Ibid.*, After three dayes they [Badgers] haue come out for pure hunger, and gone to praye for meate. **1575** —— *Falconrie* 156 As they feede when they pray of themselues at large. **1580** SIDNEY *Ps.* XVIII. ii, On me the paines of death ..gan to prey. **1587** GOLDING *De Mornay* xxi. (1592) 323 He prepareth foode for the Rauens to pray vpon. **1600** SHAKS. *A.Y.L.* IV. iii. 119 'Tis The royall disposition of that beast To prey on nothing, that doth seeme as dead. **1610** ROWLANDS *Martin Mark-all* 14 Brokers I meane and Vsurers, that like vultures prey vpon the simple. **1647** N. BACON *Disc. Govt. Eng.* I. xxxiv. (1739) 51 Nature taught Beasts to prey for themselves. **1770** LANGHORNE *Plutarch* (1879) I. 142/2 Another fox finds the same fields to prey in. **1841** EMERSON *Lect., Man the Reformer* Wks. (Bohn) II. 240 Every species of property is preyed on by its own enemies, as iron by rust, timber by rot. **1859** MILL *Liberty* i, To prevent the weaker members of the community from being preyed upon.

4. *intr.* To exert a baneful, wasting, or destructive influence *on, upon*; to destroy gradually.

1713 ADDISON *Cato* III. ii, Language is too faint to show His rage of love; it preys upon his life. **1798** FERRIAR *Illustr. Sterne* v. 150 The secret which preyed upon his mind. **1833** WORDSW. *Composed by Sea-Shore* 3 How baffled projects on the spirit prey. **1885** *Law Times* 7 Feb. 270/2 His health was bad, and this had no doubt preyed very much upon his mind.

Hence **'preyed-upon** *ppl. a.*

1888 H. WALLER in *Times* 12 Nov. 13/3 To help the poor, wretched, preyed-upon Africans. **1905** *Westm. Gaz.* 22 Mar. 2/1 The preyers and the preyed-upon.

prey, preye, obs. forms of PRAY.

preyche, preychour, obs. ff. PREACH, -ER.

preyer ('preɪə(r)). [f. PREY *v.* + -ER[1].] One who or that which preys.

1586 J. HOOKER *Hist. Irel.* i. in *Holinshed* II. 1/1 She became and would needs be a preie vnto the preier. **1834** *Fraser's Mag.* X. 535 The heartless preyer will in turn be prey. **1848** *Ibid.* XXXVIII. 398 Useless preyers upon the public revenues.

preyer, -ere, -or, obs. forms of PRAYER.

†**'preyful**, *a. Obs. rare.* [f. PREY *sb.* + -FUL.] Killing much prey or quarry; prone to prey.

1588 SHAKS. *L.L.L.* IV. ii. 58 The prayfull Princesse pearst and prickt a prettie pleasing Pricket. **1624** CHAPMAN *Homer's Hymn to Venus* 115 The Preyfull broode of sauage Beasts.

'preying, *vbl. sb.* [f. PREY *v.* + -ING[1].] The action of the verb PREY; pillaging, plundering.

1588 KYD *Househ. Phil.* Wks. (1901) 276 In the olde time prayeng or robberye was not to be blamed. **1651** HOBBES *Govt. & Soc.* xiii. §14. 203 Preying is nothing else but a warre waged with small forces. **1897** MARY KINGSLEY *W. Africa* App. I. 664, I hate the preying upon emotional sympathy by misrepresentation.

'preying, *ppl. a.* [f. as prec. + -ING[2].] That preys; predatory, predacious; *fig.* wearing, baneful.

1611 FLORIO, *Alita*, a kind of praing bird. **1822–34** *Good's Study Med.* (ed. 4) III. 74 Preying anxiety or lurking discontent.

preyne, obs. f. PREEN.

preynkte, preynte, obs. pa. t. of PRINK *v.*[1]

preynte, preyntyce, obs. ff. PRINT, PRENTICE.

preys, obs. Sc. f. PRICE.

preyse(n, preysse, preyze, obs. ff. PRAISE.

preyst, obs. Sc. f. PRIEST *sb.*

prez[1] (prɛz). Also pres and with capital initial. Colloq. abbrev. of PRESIDENT *sb.*

1892 [see J.C.R. (*J III)]. **1936** *Esquire* Sept. 64/1 Mr. Roosevelt may be Mr. President to statesmen but he's the Prez to *Variety*. So is Harry Cohn, prez of Columbia Picts. **1942** BERREY & VAN DEN BARK *Amer. Thes. Slang* §183/4 *Pres*,..*prez*, president. **1956** *Washington Star* 7 Nov. A. 47 We should give the President our full support... Let's give three rousing cheers for the Pres! **1969** C. BURKE *God is Beautiful, Man* (1970) 88 So this derty rat fink he says to the prez of the gang, Caiaphas, 'What's in it for me?' **1973** *Philadelphia Inquirer* (Today Suppl.) 14 Oct. 29/2 Reuben

Malonado, 'prez' of the Royal Javelins, picked up an easy $150 a week. **1975** *N.Y. Times* 27 Feb. 20/5 'Look, there's the Prez,' one shouted when Mr. Ford came into view.

prez², **pres** (prɛz). Colloq. abbrevs. PRESENT *sb.*²

1922 JOYCE *Ulysses* 270 Accept my little pres. **1967** *She* Dec. 9/2 Perfect tree prez. for the husband of any wife who's fed up with having her best kitchen knives whisked away to the toolshed.

prezygapophysis (priːzɪgəˈpɒfɪsɪs). *Anat.* Pl. -ses (-siːz). [PRE- B. 3.] An anterior zygapophysis; each of the two anterior or superior articular processes of a vertebra.

1866 OWEN *Vertebr. Anim.* II. 37 The neural arch [in birds] has prezygapophyses, very small postzygapophyses. **1875** HUXLEY in *Encycl. Brit.* I. 752/1 The tubercular process is represented by a mere facet placed below the prezygapophysis.

Hence **prezygapophysial** (priːzɪgæpəʊˈfɪzɪəl) *a.*, pertaining to or of the nature of a prezygapophysis.

1890 in *Cent. Dict.* **1895** in *Syd. Soc. Lex.*

prezzie (ˈprɛzɪ). *colloq.* Also **pres(s)ie**, (*rare*) **presee**. [f. PREZ² + -IE.] = PREZ².

1937 E. D. METCALFE *Let.* 27 Jan. in F. Donaldson *Edward VIII* (1974) xxv. 312 The rest of the time will be spent shopping (buying presees for Wallis). **1961** J. ROSE *At Cross* 141 Bella said 'I brought you quite a lot prezzies.' **1967** A. DIMENT *Dolly Dolly Spy* xiv. 184 We'll have the pressies first. **1975** *Australian* 24 Apr. 13 From..endeavours yesterday to discover what presents the Whitlams were taking overseas with them, we can inform you of the following piece of government policy: From this day forth no public announcements will be made about the nature of prime ministerial pressies. **1977** *Harpers & Queen* Dec. 164/2 A presie from Mummy. **1980** *Times* 12 Mar. 21/3 Beswick is chuffed by the reception from the shop floor. He is getting little prezzies from them.

priacanthine (praɪəˈkænθaɪn), *a.* and *sb.* *Ichth.* [f. *Priacanthus*, generic name (Cuvier 1817, f. Gr. πρίων a saw + ἄκανθα thorn) + -INE¹.] **A.** *adj.* Related to the genus *Priacanthus*. **B.** *sb.* A fish of this genus or of the family *Priacanthidæ*.

prial, dial. f. PAIR-ROYAL.

‖**priamel** (priˈaːməl). Also **Priamel**. Pl. **priameln**. [G., ad. L. *praeambulum*: see PREAMBLE *sb.*] A kind of epigrammatic verse cultivated in Germany in the fifteenth and sixteenth centuries; also applied to a similar literary form in ancient Greek poetry.

1950 *Chambers's Encycl.* XI. 838/2 *Rosenplüt, Hans*.., recited epigrammatic poems (in a form known as the Priamel) at public ceremonies in honour of towns, princes or noblemen. [**1953** T. G. ROSENMEYER tr. *Snell's Discovery of Mind* iii. 48 Sappho makes use of the 'preamble', a species of folk poetry emphasizing one thing above the rest.] **1962** R. W. B. BURTON *Pindar's Pythian Odes* viii. 106 The last sentence of the epode..is in the form of a Priamel or *praeambulum*, a series of parallel statements leading by stages to a climax, an extended form of paratactic simile of a type frequent in archaic poetry. **1976** *Oxf. Compan. German Lit.* 683/2 *Priamel*, a minor poetic form, cultivated in the 15th c. and 16th c., in which, after a preparatory cumulative build-up, a comic or witty *pointe* forms the final line... The chief exponent of Priameln is Hans Rosenplüt. **1976** *Classical Q.* XXVI. 194 The first line is a priamel, the three terms of which are all applicable to Peleus, who is to be the subject of the myth that follows.

prian, var. PRYAN.

†ˈ**priape**, *sb.* *Obs. rare.* [a. F. *Priape*, ad. L. *Priāp-us*.] = PRIAPUS. Hence †**priape** *v. intr.* (*nonce-wd.*), to act lasciviously.

1561 T. NORTON *Calvin's Inst.* I. 25 (Hor. *Sat.* I. viii), I was sometime a fig tree log,.. The workeman douted what of me were fittest to be wrought: A fourm to sit vpon, or els a Priap God to be. **1586** WARNER *Alb. Eng.* VI. xxxi, That cowled, celled, he, or she, whoso, or wheresoeuer, Or Uotarie, or Secular, scarce one pryaped neuer. **1598** MARSTON *Sco. Villanie* I. iii, What peece of lustfull flesh Hath Luscus left, his Priape to redresse?

Priapean (praɪəˈpiːən), *a.* Also **-æan**. [ad. F. *priapéen*, f. L. *Priāpēi-us* (a. Gr. Πριάπει-ος adj., f. Πρίᾱπος PRIAPUS) + *-en*, -AN.] **1.** Priapic.

a **1693** *Urquhart's Rabelais* III. xxvii. 224 The Priapæan Prowess of.. Hercules. **1849** LAYARD *Nineveh & Rem.* I. v. I. 128 A broken..vase, on which were represented two Priapean human figures.

2. *Anc. Pros.* Name of a logaœdic metre consisting of a catalectic Glyconic and a Pherecratean, associated with poems to Priapus.

It was used by Anacreon, also by Catullus (xvii), and by the writer of the poem to Priapus in the Appendix Vergiliana, 'Hunc ego o iuvenes locum villulamque palustrem'. See R. Ellis *Comment. on Catullus*, pp. xliii, 62,503; Ramsay *Prosody* 214; Gildersleeve *Lat. Gram.* 805.

Priapian, Priapiform: see s.v. PRIAPUS.

Priapic (praɪˈæpɪk), *a.* (*sb.*) [f. PRIAP-US + -IC. So F. *priapique*.] Of or relating to Priapus or his cult; phallic.

1786 R. P. KNIGHT *Worship of Priapus* (1865) 145 The use of priapic figures as amulets..so common among the Romans, was certainly continued through the middle ages. **1818** —— *Symbolic Lang.* (1876) 30 The key which is still worn, with the Priapic hand, as an amulet, by the women of Italy. **1850** LEITCH tr. *C.O. Müller's Anc. Art* §241 (ed. 2) 247 *note*, Baal-Peor in Moab was probably priapic. **1882** *Q. Rev.* July 50 Priapic and pornographic literature.

B. *sb. pl.* Verses of obscene nature addressed to Priapus. [med.L. *priāpia*.]

1865 SYMONDS in *Life* (1895) I. 324 Unpardonable panderism no less odious than Latin Priapics.

priapism (ˈpraɪəpɪz(ə)m). [= F. *priapisme*, ad. late L. *Priāpism-us*, a. Gr. Πριαπισμ-ός (Galen), n. of action f. Πριαπίζειν to act Priapus, to be lewd: see PRIAPUS and -ISM.]

1. *Path.* Persistent erection of the penis.

[**1590** BARROUGH *Meth. Physick* 179 Priapismus.] *a* **1625** FLETCHER & MASS. *Elder Bro.* IV. iv, Potatoes and Eringoes, and, as I take it, Cantharides—Excellent, a Priapism follows. **1626** BACON *Sylva* §722 Lust causeth a Flagrancy in the Eyes; and Priapisme. **1875** H. C. WOOD *Therap.* (1879) 563 Neither amatory desire nor true priapism is, however, a constant symptom in cantharidal poisoning. **1894** *Lancet* 3 Nov. 1031 There was complete retention of urine, but no priapism.

2. = PRIAPUS 3; also, an obscene mental image.

1662 J. BARGRAVE *Pope Alex. VII* (1867) 117 Two Priapisms, in brass, being votes or offerings to that absurd heathen deity. **1896** C. K. PAUL tr. *Huysman's En Route* II. v. 248 Fluids passed before his face and peopled the space with priapisms.

3. Licentiousness; intentional indecency.

1758 J. CLUBBE *Misc. Tracts, Hist. Wheatfield* (1770) I. 42 The nakedness of the boys and girls..I do not consider as a tincture of Priapism, or want of modesty, but real want of cloathing. **1892** *Nation* (N.Y.) 7 Apr. 262/3 Those proclamations of utter nudity which Emerson called 'priapism', in connection with 'Leaves of Grass'.

4. *fig.* Prostitution to what is low or base.

1856 EMERSON *Eng. Traits* xiv. 254 In the absence of the highest aims..there is the suppression of the imagination, the priapism of the senses and the understanding.

So †ˈ**Priapist**, a votary of Priapus; †ˈ**Priapize** *v.* [ad. Gr. Πριαπίζειν], to act Priapus; to be lewd.

1532 MORE *Confut. Tindale* Wks. 366/1 Priapistes, ydolaters, whoremaisters, and sodomites. *a* **1693** *Urquhart's Rabelais* II. xxvii. 220 If there pass long intervals between the Priapising Feats. **1694** MOTTEUX *Rabelais* V. xl. 189 Priapus full of Priapism had a mind to priapise.

priapulid (praɪˈæpjʊlɪd), *sb.* and *a.* [f. mod.L. name of class or phylum *Priapulida*, f. generic name *Priapulus* (J.B.P.A. de M. de Lamarck *Hist. Nat. Animaux sans Vertèbres* (1816) III. 76), diminutive form of PRIAPUS: see -ID³.] **A.** *sb.* A marine unsegmented worm belonging to the class Priapulida, found in mud at the bottom of cold seas. **B.** *adj.* Of, pertaining to, or designating an animal of this kind.

1906 H. THEEL in *Kungl. Svenska Vetenskapsakad. Handlingar* XL. IV. 5, I am now going to give a summary review of those Priapulids..which pass their life in the northern and arctic seas. **1926** A. HUXLEY *Burning Wheel* 36 Your heaven's so, With a path leading up to it past a row Of votary Priapulids. **1951** L. H. HYMAN *Invertebrates* III. xiii. 184 The priapulids are animals of modest size, up to 8 cm., and drab coloration. *Ibid.* 194 The priapulid larvae live in the bottom muck along with the adults. **1967** *New Scientist* 14 Sept. 547/2 In the case of the priapulids..a plausible explanation for their pentamery is not so hard to furnish. **1979** *Sci. Amer.* July 114/1 The mud supported an active group of burrowing invertebrates, with priapulid worms predominant.

Priapus (praɪˈeɪpəs). [a. L. *Priāpus*, a. Gr. Πρίᾱπος.]

1. The Greek and Roman god of procreation; hence, also, of gardens, vineyards, etc. (in which his statues were placed).

1508 DUNBAR *Gold. Targe* 118 Thare was the god of gardingis, Priapus. **1608** SHAKS. *Per.* IV. vi. 4 Shee's able to freze the god Priapus, and vndoe a whole generation. **1651** STANLEY *Poems* 46 Satyrs Priapusses in mourning weeds. **1870** ROSSETTI *Jenny*, Let offerings nicely plac'd But hide Priapus to the waist, And whoso looks on him shall see An eligible deity.

2. A statue or image of the god Priapus; often placed in gardens to protect them from depredators or as a scarecrow.

1632 SHIRLEY *Ball* IV. i, Thou wot stop a breach in a mudde wall, Or serve for a Priapus in the garden to Fright away crowes. **1633** MARMION *Fine Companion* V. i, *Lack.* How doe I looke..? *Cro.* Very dreadfully: like a Citizen in a fray, as fearefull as Priapus in a garden. **1743** FIELDING *Jos. Andrews* I. ii. **1746** FRANCIS tr. *Horace, Sat.* I. viii. 4 The joiner doubting, or to shape us, Into a stool, or a Priapus, At length resolved, for reasons wise, Into a god to bid us rise. **1756** C. SMART tr. *Horace, Sat.* I. viii. (1826) II. 69.

3. A representation of the male generative organ; a phallus. **b.** A drinking-vessel of phallic shape.

1613 PURCHAS *Pilgrimage* (1614) 79 Two Phalli, or Priapi (huge Images of the priuie part of a man). **1693** TATE in *Dryden's Juvenal* II. 143 Another in a Glass-Priapus swills, While twisted Gold his platted Tresses fills. **1705** ADDISON *Italy, Rome* 324 Urns, Lamps, Lachrymary Vessels, Priapus's.

4. *transf.* **a.** The generative capacity or function. **b.** *Med.* and *Path.* The male genitals; *esp.* the virile organ in a state of erection.

1637 T. MORTON *N. Eng. Canaan* (1883) 205 This beast [Beaver] is of a masculine vertue for the advancement of Priapus. **1727–41** CHAMBERS *Cycl.*, *Priapus*, a term sometimes applied to the genital parts of men. **1811** in HOOPER *Med. Dict.* **1857** in DUNGLISON *Dict. Med.*

†**5.** A kind of holothurian. [F. *priape de mer*.]

1765 *Univ. Mag.* XXXVII. 129/1 They have two holes as the priapuses.

Hence †**Priˈapian** (also as *sb.*), †**Priˈapish** *adjs.*, of, relating or belonging to Priapus, lewd; obscene; **priˈapiform** *a.*, of phallic shape.

1598 MARSTON *Pygmal., Sat., Prayse of precedent Poem*, The Salaminian titillations, Which tickle vp our leud Priapians. **1872** T. G. THOMAS *Dis. Women* (ed. 3) 37 Called priapiform pessaries. **1530** TINDALE *Answ. More* IV. ii. Wks. (1573) 320/1 That filthy priapishe confession which ye spew in the eare.

ˈ**pribble**. Weakened echo of PRABBLE, used along with it in the phr. ***pribble and prabble***, and the reduplicated ***pribble-prabble*** = Petty disputation, paltry discussion, vain chatter.

1598 SHAKS. *Merry W.* I. i. 56 It were a goot motion, if we leaue our pribbles and prabbles, and desire a marriage betweene Master Abraham, and Mistris Anne Page. **1615** *Val. Welshm.* (1663) B iij, Cousin Caradoc, well, in all these pribble-prabbles, how doth our Uncle Cadallan? **1769** *Stratford Jubilee* II. i. 29 Without any balderdash pribble-prabble. **1824** MISS FERRIER *Inher.* xiv, Miss P.'s pribble prabble was, therefore, music to her ear. **1855** THACKERAY *Newcomes* ii, All these squabbles and jokes, and pribbles and prabbles,..may be omitted.

†**pricasour**. *Obs. rare*⁻¹. [Derivative of PRICK *v.*, of unusual form; prob. of Anglo-Fr. origin.] ? A quick rider, (or perh.) a huntsman: cf. PRICKER 2, 3.

c **1386** CHAUCER *Prol.* 189 A Monk ther was..he was a prikasour [*v.rr.* pryk-, pric-, prek-] aright Grehoundes he hadde as swift as fowel in flight Of prikyng and of huntyng for the hare Was al his lust.

pricasse, var. PRIKAZ.

priccatte, obs. Sc. form of PRICKET.

pricche, obs. form of PRITCH *sb.* and *v.*

price (praɪs), *sb.* Main forms: 2–5 **pris**, 4–7 **prise**, 5– **price**: others see below. [ME. a. OF. *pris* (mod.F. *prix*):—earlier **prieis* (= Pr. *pretz*, Sp. *prez*, It. *prezzo*):—late L. *precium*, orig. *pretium* 'price, value, wages, reward'; in OF. also 'honour, praise, prize'. The long *ī* of ME. *prīs* was variously represented by *ii*, *ij*, *iy*, *yi*, *y*, *ie*, and indicated later by final *e*, *prise*; but to avoid the *z* sound of *s* between two vowels (cf. *rise*, *wise*), *prise* was changed to *price* (as in *dice*, *mice*, *twice*). The pl. had, sometimes at least, the *z* sound (cf. *house*, *houses*) and was commonly written *prises*, *prizes* in 16–17th c.; but though (ˈpraɪzɪz) is still common dialectally and with individuals, the standard pronunciation is now (ˈpraɪsɪz) after the sing., *prices* being thus distinguished from *prizes*. ME. *pris* had all the OF. senses 'price, value, honour, prize, praise'; it first threw off the last of these, for which in 15th c. the sb. *preise*, PRAISE, was formed from the cognate vb. *preisen*, PRAISE. During the last 300 years it has also thrown off the fourth sense, for which the by-form PRIZE has been established. The sense 'honour' is obsolete, that of worth or value ('a pearl of great price') obs. or arch., so that *price* now retains only the primitive sense of OF. *pris* and L. *pretium*. See also PRAISE *sb.* and *v.*, PRIZE *sb.* and *v.*]

A. Illustration of Forms.

α. 2–5 **pris** (4 **priis**, **priys**, 4–5 **prijs**, **prys**, **preis**, 5 **pryys**, **priss**, **-e**, **pries**, 5–6 **pryis**, **pryss**).

a **1225**, *c* **1250** pris [see B. 7, 12]. *c* **1250** *Hymn Virgin* 6 in *Trin. Coll. Hom.* App. 255 Of alle wimmen þu hauest þet pris. **1303** R. BRUNNE *Handl. Synne* 6635 A ryche man was sum tyme of prys. **13..** *Guy Warw.* (A.) 712 Þe mantels weren of michel priis. **13..** *Cursor M.* 4613 (Gött.) Þu art sua mekil of prijs. *Ibid.* 16529 'Lo! here þe preis', he said, 'þat i gun for mi lauerd sell'. **13..** *E.E. Allit. P.* A. 754 Quatkyn of priys Berez þe perle so maskellez. **1375** BARBOUR *Bruce* I. 21 Thai suld weill hawe pryss. *c* **1380** WYCLIF *Sel. Wks.* III. 328 Sette more priss bi a wrongful curs. **1382** —— *Ezek.* xxii. 25 Thei deuoureden soule, of the nedi man, and thei token priys. **1388** *Ibid.*, Thei token richesses and prijs [*opes et pretium acceperunt*]. **1387** TREVISA *Higden* (Rolls) V. 31 Paide þe prys [*v.r.* pryys]. *c* **1400** *Ywaine & Gaw.* 2924 Oft-sithes winnes ful litel pries. *c* **1400** *St. Alexius* (Laud) 92 She was..Louelich, & of gret prijs. *a* **1400–50** *Alexander* 4242 Mare passand of prisse þan all þi proude rewmes. *c* **1470** HENRY *Wallace* II. 2 In prys of armys. *c* **1483** CAXTON *Dialogues* 26/20 At pris of viij. pens. *c* **1560** A. SCOTT *Poems* (S.T.S.) vi. 32 Thocht gold gif grittar pryss.

β. 4–7 **prise** (5–6 **pryse**, 6–8 (9 *dial.*) **prize**).

c **1325** *Metr. Hom.* 18 Another an honderet or the prise [*rime* penis]. **13..** *Cursor M.* 6146 (Cott.) Clathes þat was o prise dere. **1340** HAMPOLE *Pr. Consc.* 1143 Worldes riches of grete pryse. **1483** *Cath. Angl.* 291/1 A Pryse of wodde, *lucar.* **1567** *Gude & Godlie B.* (S.T.S.) 91 And all gude men he haldis in to pryse. **1599** T. M[OUFET] *Silkwormes* 75 Your new found stuffe, chaffred at highest prize. **1656** EARL MONM. tr. *Boccalini's Advts. fr. Parnass.* 333 Purchased..at the prise of much blood. **1707** *Reflex. upon Ridicule* 213 Who ..would, at any Prize, have Intimacies with the Great. **1886** ELWORTHY *W. Somerset Word-bk.* s.v., 'I baint gwain to gee no jis prize' [such price]. **1888** *Sheffield Gloss.*, *Prize*, *sb.* the price, as of goods.

γ. (4–7 **pryce**) 5– **price**.

13.. (MS. *a* **1400**) *Coer de L.* 395 To be bolde to wynne the pryce. *c* **1425** *Cursor M.* 10415 (Laud) This lady was of muche price [*earlier MSS.* pris, prise]. **1617** SIR W. MURE *Misc. Poems* xxi. 44 Of highest pryce.

δ. *plural.* 4– prices (4 -is, 6–7 pryces; 6 prises, 6–8 prizes).

1382 WYCLIF *Acts* iv. 34 Thei sellynge brouȝten to the prices [*v.r.* pris; **1388** pricis, *v.r.* priys] of tho thingis that thei solden. **1542** UDALL *Erasm. Apoph.* 17 b, In Athenes the prices of all thynges was veray high. **1599** HAKLUYT *Voy.* II. I. 217 To buy or sell at the prises currant. **1627** HAKEWILL *Apol.* (1630) 145 The high prizes of victuals. **1642** FULLER *Holy & Prof. St.* IV. xi. 292 Thus the prices of Martyrs ashes rise and fall in Smithfield market. **1653** HOLCROFT *Procopius* III. 93 But Bessas..grew rich, hunger and necessity setting the prises for him. **1697** T. BROWN *Dispensary* II. Wks. 1709 III. III. 81 To settle what ought to be the Prizes of our Medicines. **1875** JOWETT *Plato* (ed. 2) V. 3 That the same goods should not be sold at two prices on the same day.

B. Signification.

I. Money, or the like, paid for something.

1. a. The money (or other equivalent) for which anything is bought or sold (or a thing or person ransomed or redeemed); the rate at which this is done or proposed; also, less usually, money paid as the equivalent of labour, wages; rate of wages.

a **1300** *Cursor M.* 15967 (Cott.) Moder, i haf mi maister sald..And in mi purs þe pris i bere. **1382** [see A. δ]. **1388** WYCLIF *Isa.* xlv. 13 He schal delyuere my prisoneris not in prijs. **1433** *Rolls of Parlt.* IV. 477/2 Uch of hem have..yerely XXVI*s.* VIII*d.* and a Robe pris of X*s.* **1461** *Cal. Anc. Rec. Dublin* (1889) I. 308 To syll the whet iiii.*d.* undyr the comyn prys in every peke. **1481** CAXTON *Godeffroy* clxv. 244 To haue vytaylles at resonable prys. *c* **1489** —— *Sonnes of Aymon* xxviii. 577, I wyll not reteyn you for that pryse that I do knaves, for I shall paye you in conscyence after the werke that ye shall doo. **1535** COVERDALE *Zech.* xi. 13 A goodly pryce for me to be valued at of them. **1596** SHAKS. *Merch. V.* III. v. 26 This making of Christians will raise the price of Hogs. **1599** HAKLUYT *Voy.* II. I. 217 When as the Marchant thinketh that he cannot sell his goods at the prise currant. **1687** A. LOVELL tr. *Thevenot's Trav.* I. 32 The common price of the Bagnio, is two Aspres to the Master. **1734** POPE *Ess. Man* IV. 151 Is the reward of Virtue bread? That, Vice may merit, 'tis the price of toil. **1745** *De Foe's Eng. Tradesman* (1841) I. 202 She comes up to his price within half-a-crown a yard. **1828** LD. GRENVILLE *Sink. Fund* 45 The farmer who has sold his wheat at its market price, has obtained for it neither more nor less than a just equivalent. **1885** *Manch. Exam.* 10 Sept. 5/3 He is supplied..at a reduction of 40 per cent. on the trade price.

b. *Pol. Econ.* (See quots.)

1691 LOCKE *Lower. Interest* Wks. 1727 II. 49 The Value or Price of any thing, being only the respective Estimate it bears to some other, which it comes in Competition with. **1757** JOS. HARRIS *Coins* 94 What measures and pays the price of labour will be ultimately the real standard of the nation. **1776** ADAM SMITH *W.N.* I. v. (1869) I. 31 The real price of everything, what everything really costs to the man who wants to acquire it, is the toil and trouble of acquiring it... Labour was the first price, the original purchase-money that was paid for all things. *Ibid.* 34 Labour..is their real price; money is their nominal price only. **1848** MILL *Pol. Econ.* III. i. §2 Exchange value requires to be distinguished from Price... The most accurate modern writers..have employed Price to express the value of a thing in relation to money; the quantity of money for which it will exchange. **1862** RUSKIN *Unto this Last* iv. 136 The price of anything is the quantity of labour given by the person desiring it, in order to obtain possession of it. **1863** FAWCETT *Pol. Econ.* III. i. 307 If the value of a commodity is estimated by comparing it with those precious metals which civilised countries employ as money, then it is said that the price, and not the value of a commodity is ascertained. **1868** ROGERS *Pol. Econ.* iii. (1876) 21 The price of an article..is its estimate in some one uniform measure. **1900** LD. ALDENHAM *Colloquy on Currency* ii. 31 Price..is the ratio..between the money-measure and the purchaseable commodity measured. Price is a Ratio, but it does not follow that a Ratio is always Price.

†**c.** Phr. ***in price with***: in treaty to buy. *Obs.*

1621 J. REYNOLDS *God's Rev. agst. Murder* I. i. 12 Buying a Iewell from her which she was in price with, of a Gold-Smyth at Dijon.

d. Payment of money in purchase of something. *Obs.* exc. in phr. ***without price*** = without payment, gratis, for nothing (*arch.*).

c **1380** WYCLIF *Wks.* (1880) 393 For welle niȝ alle her blessyngis ben sett to sale and to prise. **1611** BIBLE *Isa.* lv. 1 Come, buy wine and milke without money, and without price. **16..** DRYDEN (J.), Wisely make that kind of food thy choice, To which necessity confines thy price. **1745** *Scott. Paraphr.* XXVI. i, Free to the Poor, Life's Waters flow, and bought without a Price. **1781** COWPER *Hope* 496 Here see the encouragement Grace gives to vice, The dire effect of Mercy without price!

e. Reckoning or statement of the value; estimation of value: in such phrases as ***above, beyond, without price*** = so valuable that no definite price can be reckoned or stated; = PRICELESS 1.

1582 N. LICHEFIELD tr. *Castanheda's Conq. E. Ind.* I. xxxii. 79 b, His girdell,..made of Golde and Stone that the same was aboue all price. *a* **1674** TRAHERNE *Innocence* v. Poet. Wks. (1903) 13, I..had a Sight of Innocence, Which was beyond all bound and price. **1781** COWPER *Friendship* 56 But will Sincerity suffice? It is indeed above all price, And must be made the basis. **1859** TENNYSON *Merl. & Vivien* 220 A robe Of samite without price..clung about her lissome limbs.

f. *colloq.* A high price.

1920 'K. MANSFIELD' *Bank Holiday* in *Athenæum* 6 Aug. 166/1 He likes to watch..her puzzled eyes lifted to his: 'Aren't they a *price*!'

2. A sum of money offered for the capture, apprehension, or death of a person. Usually in phr. ***to set*** (or ***put***) ***a price on*** (***the head of***, etc.).

1766 tr. *Beccaria's Ess. Crimes* xxv. (1793) 87 The law..sets a price on the head of the subject. **1842** *Penny Cycl.* XXIII. 159/2 On the 6th of August [1745] a reward of 30,000*l.* was offered..to any person who should secure the eldest son of the Pretender... The prince having heard of the price put upon his person, issued a counter proclamation, offering 30,000*l.* for apprehending the elector of Hanover.

3. *Betting.* = ODDS 5.

1882 *Daily Tel.* 30 Jan., Cyrus..made such light work of the Aintree Hunt Steeplechase in November that several people wanted to know his price. **1882** *Standard* 6 Sept. 2/6 The starting price of Mr. Perkins's horse was 5 to 1. **1895** *Times* 10 Jan. 3/3 The defendants and others made prices on the horses and shouted out the odds as upon a racecourse.

4. The amount of money, or other consideration, by which a man's support or interest may be purchased.

[**13..** *K. Alis.* 1489 (Bodl. MS.) Forto ben of his frenderade. Þe Romeynes hym sendeþ þis prise, And gretyng, and redy to his seruise. **1631** WEEVER *Anc. Fun. Mon.* 254 To procure his fauour for an election, either by petition, or price.] **1780** BENTHAM *Princ. Legisl.* xiv. §8 *note*, It is a well-known adage, though it is to be hoped not a true one, that every man has his price. **1860** WARTER *Sea-board* II. 327 Amongst the lower orders most have their price. **1907** *Daily Chron.* 27 Mar. 6/6 By the time Sir Robert Walpole arrived on the political scene it was possible for him to be credited with the now familiar saying, 'Every man has his price'.

5. *fig.* What it costs to obtain some advantage; that which is given, surrendered, or undergone, for the sake of something else. Freq. in phr. ***at a price***; also ***at any price***: whatever it may cost, whatever loss or disadvantage is or may be entailed.

c **1430** LYDG. *Min. Poems* (Percy Soc.) 169 The sleyghti fox..Takithe to his larder at what price he wold, Of gretter lambren, j., ij., or thre. **1588** SHAKS. *L.L.L.* v. ii. 223 *Rosa.* We can afford no more at such a price. *Kin.* Prise your selues: What buyes your companie? **1613** PURCHAS *Pilgrimage* (1614) 775 They vse smokie fires in their rooms, almost with the price of their eyes sauing their skins. *c* **1647** CLARENDON *Hist. Rebellion* (1703) II. VII. 189 So much enamoured on Peace, that he would have been glad, the King should have bought it at any price. **1653** H. COGAN tr. *Pinto's Trav.* lxxv. 308 He determined to bring his design to pass at any price whatsoever. **1755** YOUNG *Centaur* vi. Wks. 1757 IV. 253 The lowest price of virtue is vigilance, and industry; and if it costs us no more, it comes very cheap. **1849** THACKERAY *Pendennis* I. xiii. 118 He's too young for you..and..poor as Job. Can't have him at no price, can she Mr. Bo? **1859** B. JERROLD *Wit & Opinions D. Jerrold* 155 We love peace, as we abhor pusillanimity; but not peace at any price. **1866** R. W. DALE *Disc. Spec. Occas.* v. 164 We know at how great a price our inheritance of truth has been purchased. **1873** C. M. YONGE *Pillars of House* I. xi. 230 Mr. Froggatt says he would not go at any price. **1923** R. FRY *Let.* 29 Apr. (1972) II. 533 The British public won't have me at any price. **1928** A. CHRISTIE *Mystery of Blue Train* xxi. 172 I'm going to leave you... I can't stand my father-in-law at any price. **1934** G. B. SHAW *On Rocks* Pref. 177, I am not offering you the truth at a price for my own profit. **1961** L. MUMFORD *City in Hist.* xvii. 544 The machines..that would lend themselves to decentralization in a life-centered order, here become either a means to increase congestion or afford some slight temporary palliation—at a price. **1974** J. POPE-HENNESSY *R. L. Stevenson* viii. 151 Louis Stevenson had stipulated..that he would not at any price stay in a hotel..but wished to live in a house. **1978** 'W. HAGGARD' *Poison People* IV. 144 It's..illegal to hold it [*sc.* gold] in quantity. I don't say bullion can't be found at a price.

6. ***what price*** ——?: what is the value or use of ——?, what is the likelihood of ——? Freq. merely an expression of contempt: 'so much for ——'.

1893 P. H. EMERSON *Signor Lippo* xiv. 52 What price you, when you fell off the scaffold? **1895** H. W. NEVINSON *Neighbours of Ours* iii. 73 What price the little backstairs Dook? **1899** R. WHITEING *No. 5 John St.* ix. 94 What price grammar? It don't seem to teach people to keep a civil tongue in their 'ead. **1905** E. NESBIT *Oswald Bastable* 93 Oswald now thought that politeness was satisfied..so he said: 'What price treasures?' **1907** G. B. SHAW *Major Barbara* II. 245 *Bill* (cynically..) Wot prawce Selvytion nah? **1914** C. MACKENZIE *Sinister St.* II. IV. ix. 1114 It's all very nice for you to be so calm. But what price its being my watch that's lost, not yours, old sport? **1920** D. H. LAWRENCE *Women in Love* i. 10 'What price the stockings?' said a voice at the back of Gudrun. **1930** R. LEHMANN *Note in Music* VII. 301 But what price jaunts on Sundays—eh? **1959** M. GILBERT *Blood & Judgement* xvi. 164 Quick work...What price the law's delays. **1973** 'B. GRAEME' *Two & Two make Five* iv. 31 What price himself to replace Perkins, he asked himself with cynical amusement. **1977** *New Scientist* 12 May 336 (*heading*) What price Australian uranium?

II. Value, worth. *Obs.* or *arch.*

7. a. Preciousness, value, worth; the quality or condition of being (much or little) prized, valued, or esteemed. Usually with qualifying adj., as *great, much, dear, high; little; some, no,* etc. (See also 8 a, and cf. 9.) *arch.*

a **1225** *Ancr. R.* 290 Dem þerefter pris, & beo on hire þe deorre. **13..** *Cursor M.* 29040 (Cott. Galba) Fasting es of ful grete prise. **1382** WYCLIF *Luke* xii. 7 ȝe ben of more priys then many sparowis. **1413** *Pilgr. Sowle* (1483) IV. ix. 62 The prys of myn Appel is of suche valewe. **1570–6** LAMBARDE *Peramb. Kent* (1826) 159 The place was at the first of little price. **1611** BIBLE *Matt.* xiii. 46 One pearle of great price [WYCLIF oo preciouse margarite; TINDALE, *Great, Rheims,* one precious pearle]. **1690** LOCKE *Hum. Und.* Ded., Trial and examination must give it [truth] price. **1703** T. N. *City & C. Purchaser* 58 To them Method and Confusion are both of a Price. **1872** BLACKIE *Lays Highl.* 92 Like some old creed Erect, to show what price it had before When men believed it had a power indeed.

†**b.** Personal or social worth; excellency, honourableness. *Obs.* (See also 8 b.)

c **1250** *Gen. & Ex.* 2690 Riche maiden of michel pris. **1297** R. GLOUC. (Rolls) 281 An doȝter..of gret pris noble & god al so. *a* **1300** *Cursor M.* 436 Þai all war fair and wis And sum of less and sum mare pris. ? *c* **1475** *Sqr. lowe Degre* 417 To watche that lady, muche of pryce, And her to kepe fro her enemyes. **1523** LD. BERNERS *Froiss.* I. ccclxxiii. 616 Two barownes of great prise and hardynesse. **1608** BP. HALL *Char. Virtues & V.* I. 47 Those orphans which neuer knew the price of their father; they become the heires of his affection.

†**8.** ***of price*** (adj. phr.): of great value, worth, or excellence. (Often passing into sense 9 or 10: Highly esteemed or regarded; famous, renowned.) *Obs.*

a. Of things: Precious, valuable.

c **1250** *Gen. & Ex.* 2700 He carf in two gummes of pris, Two likenesses so grauen & meten. **1340–70** *Alex. & Dind.* 716 A fair pocok of pris. *c* **1386** CHAUCER *Sir Thopas* 186 Men speken of Romances of prys Of Hornchild and of Ypotys. *c* **1400** *Destr. Troy* 13712 In aparell of prise, on a proud wyse..In his palais of prise prudly he leuyt. **1597** SHAKS. *2 Hen. IV*, v. iii. 100 Happie Newes of price. **1615** G. SANDYS *Trav.* 11 Faire pillars of marble..and other stones of price. **1775** BURKE *Sp. Conc. Amer.* Wks. III. 124 Freedom is..the commodity of price which you have the monopoly.

†**b.** Of persons: Worthy, excellent. *Obs.*

1303 [see A. α]. **1307** *Elegy Edw. I*, iv, With fourscore knyhtes al of pris. **13..** *Guy Warw.* (A.) 168 Kniȝtes to hauen & holden of pris. *c* **1400** *Destr. Troy* 1693 Mykell pepull of prise & proude men of Armys. *c* **1430** *Hymns Virg.* 53 Horible deuelis of helle, Þat sumtyme were aungils of prijs. **1475** *Bk. Noblesse* (Roxb.) 26 Men of price and renomme. *c* **1554** *Interlude of Youth* Bj b, I can spede the of a seruaunte of pryce That wildo the good seruice.

†**9. a.** Sense or estimate of worth; esteem, estimation, regard. Chiefly in phrases: ***to have*** or ***hold in*** (***great,*** etc.) ***price***, ***to set at*** (***light, little***) ***price***, ***to have*** or ***hold*** (***great, little***) ***price of***, ***to set*** or ***tell*** (***much, little, no***) ***price of*** or ***by***, later ***to put*** or ***set*** (***high, little, no***) ***price upon***; also (without defining word) ***to have*** or ***hold in price***, ***to hold*** or ***tell price of***, ***to set price by***: to value or esteem highly. ***in*** (***much, some,*** etc.) ***price***: esteemed, valued (much, somewhat, etc.); also (without defining word) ***in price***: highly esteemed, thought much of. *Obs.*

c **1250** *Gen. & Ex.* 292 He saȝ Adam and eue in mike[l] pris. *c* **1300** *Beket* 150 Ech man tolde of him pris that him miȝte iseo. *c* **1386** CHAUCER *Frankl. T.* 206 Wel biloued and holden in greet prys. **1429** *Rolls of Parlt.* IV. 345/2 Setting no price by your saide Prive Seal. *c* **1440** *Generydes* 35 Shuld sette hyr wurchippe atte so litill prise. **1526** TINDALE *Heb.* xiii. 4 Let wedlocke be had in pryce in all poyntes. **1581** W. STAFFORD *Exam. Compl.* i. (1876) 25 They fall to those sciences that they see in some pryce. **1594** WILLOBIE *Avisa* (1635) 120 Her vertue shall be had in prise. **1601** F. GODWIN *Bps. of Eng.* 444 Perceiuing the monkes onely were now in price, and other cleargy men little esteemed. **1662** H. MORE *Philos. Writ.* Pref. Gen. (1712) 11 Where men have an over-proportion'd Zeal for or against such things in Religion as God puts little or no price upon.

†**b.** Valuation, appraisement. *Obs. rare.*

1606 SHAKS. *Ant. & Cl.* v. ii. 183 Cæsars no Merchant, to make prize with you Of things that Merchants sold. **1611** —— *Cymb.* III. vi. 77 Would..they Had bin my Fathers Sonnes, then had my prize Bin lesse, and so more equall ballasting To thee Posthumus.

III. Leading up to PRAISE. *Obs.* in this form.

†**10.** General recognition of excellence; honour, glory, renown. *Obs.*

a **1225** *Ancr. R.* 66 Heo hunteð efter pris, & kecceð lastunge. ? *a* **1366** CHAUCER *Rom. Rose* 1161 Gret loos hath Largesse, and gret prys. *c* **1380** *Sir Ferumb.* 467 Þoȝ y slowe þe her in fiȝt, what prys were þat for me? Men wolde sayn y were to blame. **1423** JAS. I *Kingis Q.* cxxviii, That wil be to the grete worschip and prise. **1523** LD. BERNERS *Froiss.* I. cciv. 240 Certayne yonge knyghtes and squyers to get prise in armes..iusted one with another. **1600** HOLLAND *Livy* I. xxxvii. 27 In this conflict the horse-men won greatest price and praise [L. *gloria*].

†**11. a.** The verbal expression of one's recognition of worth or excellence; = PRAISE *sb.* 1. *Obs.* (Survived longer in the north.)

a **1240** *Lofsong* in *Cott. Hom.* 205 Prude & wilnunge of pris. *c* **1320** *Sir Tristr.* 1340 Of ysoude þan spekeþ he, Her prise, Hou sche was gent and fre. *c* **1374** CHAUCER *Troylus* II. 1536 (1585) To preisin a man & vp with pris hem reise A þousent fold ȝit heyȝere þan þe sunne. **1390** GOWER *Conf.* III. 225 The king..hem axeth this, What king men tellen that he is..touchende his name, Or be it pris, or be it blame. **1423** JAS. I *Kingis Q.* clxxxviii, Of quhom [the gods], In laud and prise, With thankfull hert I say richt In this wise. **1426** LYDG. *De Guil. Pilgr.* 14922 Whan he herde the prys was more Off Davyd than off hym-sylff, allas! **1567** *Satir. Poems Reform.* v. 3 Gif to that leuing Lord all pryse.

†**b.** ***a price, aprys***: so as to gain praise or approval; laudably. *Obs. rare*$^{-1}$.

c **1400** *Langl.'s P. Pl.* C. xv. 194 + 1 (MS.S) Iob was a paynym & plesede god a prys.

IV. Leading up to PRIZE *sb.*[1] *Obs.* in this form.

†**12.** The position of excelling others; place of honour; first or highest place; pre-eminence. Usually in phr. ***to bear*** or ***have the price***, to have the pre-eminence, to surpass all others. *Obs.*

c **1250** *Gen. & Ex.* 326 A tre..ðat ouer alle oðre bereð pris. **1390** GOWER *Conf.* III. 298 Receive he scholde a certein mede And in the cite bere a pris. *c* **1430** *Syr Tryam.* 1692 A lorde..That beryth the pryce in prees. *c* **1450** LOVELICH *Grail* xliii. 222 Of konnenge hadde he not þe pris. **1470–85** MALORY *Arthur* IX. xix. 366 Of goodely harpynge he bereth the pryce in the world. **1540** Hyrde tr. _Vives' Instr. Chr. Wom._ (1592) B vj, All..by one assent gaue her the price of goodnesse and chastity. **1573** _New Custom_ ii. ii. in Hazl. _Dodsley_ III. 28 All these bear the price.

†**13.** The position of excelling in a match or struggle; superiority, victory. _Obs._

1307 _Elegy Edw. I_, xi, In much bataille thou hadest pris. _c_**1330** R. Brunne _Chron._ (1810) 67 Alle þe day þei fauht, at euen he had þe pris. **1470–85** Malory _Arthur_ v. x. 178, I had leuer to haue ben torn with wylde horses, than ony.. page or pryker shold haue had prys on me. **1494** Fabyan _Chron._ vi. clxix. 162 Fynally the Danys wan the pryce, and slewe bothe the foresayde kynges. **1523** Ld. Berners _Froiss._ I. ccccxv. 726 If y^e flemynges had achyued the prise ouer them. **1542** Udall _Erasm. Apoph._ 160 Tethrippo had gotten the price & chief maisterie at Olympia.

†**14.** The symbol, trophy, or reward of victory or superiority (Fr. _le prix_); = prize _sb._^{1}, which see for examples. _Obs._

V. 15. _attrib._ and _Comb._, as **_price-boom, -boost, control_** (so **_price-controlled_** adj.), **_freeze, hike, -history, -issue, -level, -maintenance_** (so **_price-maintain_** vb. trans., **_-maintained_** ppl. adj.) **_-making_** (make _v._^{1} 13 e), **_raiser, range, -reduction, -regulation, review, rise, -wave; price-conscious, -deciding, -enhancing, -ruling, -sensitive_** adjs.; **price-cutting**, the action of 'cutting down' or lowering prices, esp. in or by way of competition; so **_price-cutter_**; hence (as a back-formation) **_price-cut_** vb. intr. and trans.; also **_price cut_** sb.; **price discrimination**, the action of charging different prices to different customers for the same goods or services; **price-earnings ratio** (see quot. 1965); **price elasticity** (see quot. 1971); hence **_price-elastic_** adj.; **price-fixing**, the action of introducing a fixed or standard price for something esp. by agreement between manufacturers; also _attrib._; hence (as a back-formation) **_price-fix_** vb. trans., **_price-fixed_** ppl. adj.; **price-gouging**, the action of increasing prices by large amounts at once; **price index**, an index showing the variation in the prices of a set of goods, etc., since a chosen base period; also (with hyphen) _attrib._; **price leader** orig. _U.S._, a dominant firm that determines the prices within an industry; hence **_price leadership_**; also **_price-leading_** ppl. adj.; **price-list**, (_a_) a list of the prices of commodities offered for sale; (_b_) a list of the 'prices' or odds in betting; **price-mark**, a mark upon goods indicating the price; **price movement**, a fluctuation in price; **price ring**, an association of traders formed to control certain prices; **price-slashing**, price-cutting by large amounts; so **_price-slasher_**; **price stop**, a ban on price increases; **price support**, assistance in maintaining price levels regardless of supply or demand; **price system** (quot. 1968); **price tab** _U.S._, a bill; **price-tag**, a tag or ticket attached to something and bearing an indication of its price; also _fig._; hence as _v. trans._ and **_price-tagging_** vbl. sb.; **price ticket** = _price-tag_; **price war**, intense competition among traders by price-cutting. Also price-current.

1928 Britain's Industr. Future (Liberal Industr. Inquiry) iv. xx. 268 The rapid industrial slump which followed the *price-boom of 1919–20. **1961** Wall St. Jrnl. 23 Jan. 2/2 A *price-boost might well be delayed until mid-summer. **1974** News & Press (Darlington, S. Carolina) 25 Apr. 8/6 Both business men and consumers are fearful that the lifting of economic controls will set off new waves of price and wage boosts. **1961** Wall St. Jrnl. 4 Oct. 1 Farmers aren't as *price conscious as last year, so we can get more money on a sale. **1963** Economist 20 July 281/1 The price-conscious professional classes. **1974** Country Life 28 Nov. 1662/1 From the price-conscious north I have news of good stocking fillers. **1914** Automobile Topics 12 Dec. 321 (caption) Ford loses *price control suit. **1936** Discovery Apr. 128/1 He waxes..mildly indignant over price-control of new metals by monopolies. **1944** Sun (Baltimore) 6 Oct. 13/5 Price control clinics, manned by officers and enlisted men, to hear reports from GIs on instances of overcharging, were ordered established. **1955** T. H. Pear Eng. Social Differences 184 The freeing of both tea and coffee from price-control. **1974** Listener 3 Oct. 422/3 The attempted price controls..have been far too severe. **1948** Hansard Commons 5 Mar. (Written Answers) 105 Mr. J. Morrison asked..What are the wholesalers' and retailers' margin of profit allowed on..such household goods as are *price controlled. **1976** Sci. Amer. Nov. 138/2 Of its two million citizens more than 12,000 were dead of the flu and its concomitant pneumonia by the middle of November, against a macabre background of military embalmers and a price-controlled quick-coffin industry. **1925** Wireless Dealer I. ii. 259/1 The retailer who is given a big discount must not *price-cut to the public. **1928** Publishers' Weekly 30 June 2596 If turnover is secured by price cuts which decrease the normal profit [etc.]. **1957** Chem. & Engin. News 1 Apr. 28/2 In the chemical industry it is impossible to tell in advance whether a price cut may at some time in the future 'tend substantially to reduce competition'. **1964** Financial Times 31 Jan. 1/2 The..Adsega supermarket chain..has been price-cutting cigarettes. **1965** Mod. Law Rev. XXVIII. v. 554 The assumption of the publishers was that 'best sellers' would be price-cut. **1901** N.Y. Publ. Wkly. in Publ. Circ. 14 Sept. 243/1 This firm..have great difficulty in maintaining their reputation as *price-cutters on net books. **1967** Economist 4 Mar. 845/1 The steady erosion of prices that followed the arrival of the price-cutters. **1969** D. C. Hague Managerial Econ. iv. 89 Even if several firms do follow the price cutter..price cutting may still be attractive. **1899** Pall Mall G. 11 Oct. 5/3 *Price Cutting in the Cycle Trade. **1929** Times 2 Nov. 7/5 That could only be done with the abolition of the suicidal policy of price-cutting and competition. **1962** E. Godfrey Retail Selling & Organization i. 6 Price-cutting and the widespread introduction of supermarkets have made competition very difficult to meet. **1974** 'G. Black' Golden Cockatrice ii. 32 I'll fight a price-cutting war by matched price-cutting. **1784** Cowper Task vi. 291 Oft as the *price-deciding hammer falls. **1957** Clark & Gottfried University Dict. Business & Finance (1967) 276 When the purpose or result of such *price discrimination is to reduce competition or to injure competitors, either of the seller or the buyer, it is illegal under the anti-trust laws. **1969** D. C. Hague Managerial Econ. iv. 83 We were considering a special case of price discrimination... We supposed that the producer was in the most favourable of all situations and could charge a different price to each individual consumer. **1974** News & Courier (Charleston, S. Carolina) 25 Apr. 17-c/2 White failed to show International was guilty of breach of contract and price discrimination. **1961** Dallas Morning News 9 Apr. iv. 1 Foods, which long had been considered 'recession resistant' but hardly dynamic stocks, have been acting like growth stocks, going to higher *price-earnings ratios. **1965** McGraw-Hill Dict. Mod. Econ. 390 Price-earnings ratio, the current market price of a company's stock expressed as a multiple of the company's per-share earnings. It is computed by dividing the annual per-share earnings of a company into the market-value of its stock. For example, if company A's stock is selling at $100 per share and the company earned $5 per share, the price-earnings ratio is 20. **1968** Newsweek 25 Nov. 91/2 Other stocks may continue to show solid earnings growth but then they become overexploited. Investors simply bid too high for them. This shows up in the price-earnings ratio. **1972** Observer 22 Oct. 15/3 A couple of dark clouds... One is the sky-high price-earnings ratio of your stock. **1964** Economist 15 Feb. 620/2 The argument that books are *price-elastic. **1967** Times Rev. Industry Mar. 16/1 This company clearly believes that shoe demand is price elastic. **1976** P. R. White Planning for Public Transport vi. 127 Weekend and day return fares..relate to trips such as shopping and visiting friends, demand for which is more price-elastic. **1952** T. W. Hutchinson tr. Schneider's Pricing & Equilibrium i. 23 We can measure the reaction of the quantity demanded to changes in price, when all other prices and income remain constant, by the *price elasticity. **1971** J. A. Perrow Econ. i. 17 Price elasticity may be defined as the responsiveness of demand for a good to a small change in its price. **1976** P. R. White Planning for Public Transport viii. 157 The non-business market. Here, the time and price elasticities are almost the reverse. c**1760** Hogarth in Hilda Gamlin Romney (1894) 24 Let the picture rust, Perhaps Time's *price-enhancing dust..may mark its worth. **1949** Time 25 July 24/2 In the past, prices had been held down by a combination of price fixing and subsidies. Bread was *price fixed, so were cooking oils [etc.]. **1933** K. T. Langguth Financial Dict.: Eng.-German 186 *Price-fixed. **1949** Consumer Reports Aug. 344/1 Places to buy price-fixed merchandise at less than the established price. **1971** 'E. McBain' Hail, Hail, Gang's all Here ii. 183 That apartment's price-fixed... If he gets out, they can put a new tenant in and legally raise the rent. **1920** Argus (Melbourne) 4 June 6 Competition will reduce prices in time, but *price-fixing..will only arrest the tendency to cheapness. **1930** Economist 15 Feb. 352/2 Rationalisation must also be distinguished from price-fixing associations or cartels. **1965** Spectator 26 Feb. 251/1 The price of whisky and gin was slashed following the end of price-fixing. **1973** Country Life 29 Nov. 1773/3 This 20-year-old price-fixing procedure [for Champagne] comes to an end in 1975. **1958** Times Rev. Industry Feb. 106/2 Those whose task it was to determine relaxations of the *price-freeze. **1978** Ld. Hailsham Dilemma of Democracy xix. 122 Inflation has led to a demand either for a price freeze, or a wage freeze or both. **1967** Guardian 5 Aug. 7 Negro housewives..are the victims of *price-gouging in the neighbourhood shops..owned by whites. **1974** Aiken (S. Carolina) Standard 22 Apr. 1-B/2 Each wage demand that is not balanced against productivity and each incident of price gouging motivated by greed help perpetuate the inflation cycle. **1977** Times 8 Aug. 42/3 This week the agency will open an investigation of alleged price gouging on fuel oil used in home heating; one consumer group is claiming the FEA permitted oil companies to overcharge by $2 billion last year. **1948, 1968** *Price hike [see hike sb. 2]. **1977** Rolling Stone 24 Mar. 16/2 Industry spokespersons tend to cite increased costs on every level when explaining the dollar price-hike. **1900** Westm. Gaz. 4 Jan. 7/3 The *Price History of the Stock. **1902** Ibid. 18 Feb. 11/1 An introduction, a price-history of the market. **1886** *Price index [see index sb. 9 e]. **1930** Economist 5 Apr. 763/1 The Economist price index has fallen during the past two years much more heavily than price indices in certain other countries on the gold standard. **1930** W. K. Hancock Australia ix. 184 The Statistician's price-index numbers. **1954** M. Beresford Lost Villages vi. 183 It cannot be said that our price-indexes are yet near prefection. **1954** E. H. Carr Interregnum 77 A price-index issued by the labour section of the Moscow Soviet for the calculation of wages in Moscow. **1973** Price index [see index sb. 9 e]. **1885** Pall Mall G. 13 May 5/2 Some of the borrowers will..find it necessary to be generous in their *price issue when so many are in the field. **1936** A. R. Burns Decline of Competition iii. 77 The United States Steel Corporation is more frequently classified as a *price leader than any other American corporation. **1962** Economist 13 Jan. 151/2 The International Nickel Company of Canada..is the acknowledged price leader. **1936** A. R. Burns Decline of Competition iii. 76 *Price leadership exists when the price at which most of the units in an industry offer to sell is determined by adopting the price announced by one of their number. **1979** Internat. Jrnl. Sociol. of Law May 133 For price leadership to work, the price leader must have close to the largest share of the market. **1961** New Left Rev. July–Aug. 5/2 In Italy, each of the industrial sectors is dominated by a single, *price-leading firm. **1927** Bowley & Stamp Nat. Income 1924 58 On account of the change in *price-level, we should substitute a comparative level of £9,500, [etc.]. **1940** Economist 13 Jan. 53/1 Voluntary negotiation..can only result in a welter of independent wage decisions in different industries, each bearing a different relation to the general price level. **1972** Accountant 19 Oct. 485/2 Differences between financial statements prepared along the alternative bases of current-value and price-level accounting. **1872** Young Englishwoman Dec. 662/3 Will you be so kind as to send a *price-list of the combs and hair-pins. **1915** W. Owen Let. 8 Jan. (1967) 313 What my friend advised me to do is get price-lists and samples from England immediately. **1973** Sat. Rev. Society (U.S.) May 68/1 A list of catalogs or 'price lists', of items stocked by the Government Printing Office. **1960** Guardian 10 Dec. 9/6 The intending signatories agreed..that they would *price maintain their vehicles. **1964** Financial Times 31 Jan. 1/2 More price-maintained lines would be added to their lists of reductions. **1968** Times 29 Nov. p. iv/4 Since they are still price-maintained it is not possible for retailers to cut prices, though in recent years budget labels have emerged. **1930** Economist 13 Sept. 483/1 The *price-maintenance scheme is ultimately financed by the Reich. **1965** Mod. Law Rev. XXVIII. v. 552 Fifty years have now passed since the head of a well-known department store, in opposing enactment of a general price-maintenance law, told a Congressional Committee [etc.]. **1969** D. C. Hague Managerial Econ. xiv. 297 Is there a well-established (and legal) tradition of price maintenance? **1632** Lithgow Trav. x. 439 [Let him beware] the eating of Victuals, and drinking of Wine without *price making; least (when he hath done).. his charges be redoubled. **1901** Wide World Mag. VI. 491/1 The children left Port Darwin with new boots, and when they returned the *price-marks were not even rubbed off the soles. **1934** Discovery Sept. 245/2 They [sc. the farmers] have the advantage of being able to hear things that should be known at once to them: such as *price movements, weather reports, harvest conditions and prospects. **1948** G. Crowther Outl. Money (rev. ed.) iii. 95 This is one way in which price movements have a direct causal effect on the level of production and employment. **1965** J. Meuvret in Glass & Eversley Population in Hist. xxi. 517 Here again, however, price-movements can afford some illumination. **1906** 'Mark Twain' Autobiogr. (1924) II. 24 That congregation's real estate stands at a low figure. What they are anxious to have now..is a *price-raiser. **1965** Punch 7 July 2/1 George Brown's challenge to price-raisers to justify themselves. **1925** Ladies' Home Jrnl. May 146/2 *Price ranges from 25c to 45c. **1937** M. Hillis Orchids on your Budget (1938) iii. 46 Another good rule is not to attempt to have everything come within the same price range. **1973** D. Westheimer Going Public i. 15 The fact that so much of your business is in the lowest price-range has its positive side... You'll find your bread-and-butter business is in the lower price-range. **1919** J. M. Keynes Econ. Consquences Peace vi. 225 The effect on foreign trade of *price-regulation and profiteer-hunting as cures for inflation is even worse. **1935** Economist 12 Oct. 704/1 This shortage..is largely a consequence of planning and price-regulation. **1959** Chambers's Encycl. XI. 195/2 Price-regulation was in existence in Babylonia as early as the middle of the third millennium B.C. **1960** Farmer & Stockbreeder 22 Mar. 78/3 On Wednesday, representatives of the Branch met seven Conservative M.P.s at the House of Commons..when there was a long and useful discussion about many aspects of the White Paper and the *Price Review. **1969** Times 6 Jan. 7/7 In spite of occasional controversy, especially before annual price reviews, the overall impression one gets of the past 10 years is one of fair stability. **1928** Britain's Industr. Future (Liberal Industr. Inquiry) ii. viii. 97 The majority of cartels and *price rings fall under the category of Trade Associations..and not under that of Public Companies or Corporations. **1957** Observer 1 Dec. 1/4 This is no moment ..for a price ring designed to keep prices up, or restrictive principles to prevent them going down. **1965** M. Hilton tr. J. Meuvret in Glass & Eversley Pop. in Hist. xxi. 511 The *price-rise..can be explained..by bad harvests. **1977** Times 4 Oct. 15/2 Price rises are still at an unacceptable level. **1890** Spectator 23 Aug., Wheat..is still pre-eminently the *price-ruling grain. **1966** Economist 3 Dec. 1046/1 In the *price-sensitive group of semi-manufacturers, the bigger impact was on imports of textiles, paper and, above all, iron and steel. **1976** Scotsman 24 Dec. 3/7 Dunford and Prudential were justified in passing on information of a 'price-sensitive' character to their institutional shareholders, as potential underwriters. **1964** Punch 11 Mar. 377/3 John Bloom..is a notorious *price-slasher. **1930** Publisher's Circular 14 June 793/3 The economic and cultural consequences of reckless *price-slashing. **1940** Economist 28 Dec. 799/1 The 'price-stop order', designed to prevent war-time increases in prices, has been reinforced several times by stricter penalties; but it has not been possible to prevent some rise in prices. **1950** Ann. Reg. 1949 244 A price stop was placed on certain essential commodities. **1949** Sun (Baltimore) 10 Sept. 11/4 Corn from this year's crop is expected to move into Government hands under *price-support programs to join more than 400,000,000 bushels remaining there from the 1948 crop. **1957** M. Swan Brit. Guiana 95 Price support has come in the form of the Commonwealth Sugar Agreement. **1965** J. L. Hanson Dict. Econ. 326/1 Price Support. The U.S. Government's method of giving assistance to farmers. Prices are fixed well above the equilibrium level and so output cannot be completely disposed of on the market, the U.S. Government agreeing to purchase at the fixed prices any surpluses resulting from this policy. **1962** M. McLuhan Gutenberg Galaxy 118 Complex markets, *price-systems, and commercial empires. **1968** P. A. S. Taylor Dict. Econ. Terms (ed. 4) 85 Price system. This is an economic system in which prices are determined by the forces of the market. **1974** Encycl. Brit. Macropædia XIV. 1004/2 A price system weighs the desires of consumers in terms of the prices they are willing to pay for various quantities of each commodity or service. **1949** Sun (Baltimore) 12 Sept. 1/8 A big victory for labor in the board's belief that companies should pick up the *price tab on pensions. **1881** Harper's Mag. Sept. 587/1 Untying a little green *price tag from the handle of the umbrella. **1888** Chautauquan VIII. 422 Accordingly they attached 'etiquettes', or price-tags, to their articles. **1942** D. Powell Time to be Born (1943) iv. 97 Vicky was uncomfortably aware of Miss Finkelstein's eagle eye putting price tags on her suit, her hair, her shoes. **1951** Sport 30 Mar. 7/2 When I remember what a record transfer-fee price-tag did to Bryn Jones.., I can only sympathise with you. **1961** L. van der Post Heart of Hunter ii. viii. 123 Though no price-tag could be put on them [sc. protected animals], we knew our lives would be immeasurably poorer without them. **1971** C. Fick Danziger Transcript (1973) 20 Your uniform smells as though the price tags are still on it. **1972** *Countryman* Winter 61 These faceless experts make an attempt to price-tag the social benefit of forestry. **1974** W. Foley *Child in Forest* II. 159 She price-tagged them by instinct. **1977** *Offshore Engineer* July 14/2 The NEB says that 'the project is likely to incur a 20–30% cost overrun' on the $8,000 million price tag it currently sees as realistic. **1972** *Straits Times* (Malaysian ed.) 23 Nov. 6/5 Encik Khir chaired the meeting which was held to resolve the problems facing shopkeepers over *price-tagging. **1977** *Daily Times* (Lagos) 11 Jan. 17/2 Given the low level of enlightenment in the country, the intransigence of Nigerians to any government directive, price tagging was born with a lot of problems which have so far retarded its success. **1934** *Archit. Rev.* LXXVI. 27/2 A well-lettered *price-ticket, decorative value apart, is more desirable than a label covered with hieroglyphics. **1957** P. Worsley *Trumpet shall Sound* viii. 159 Natives..tore the price-tickets off the goods. **1930** *Economist* 22 Mar. 652/2 Experience shows that this group invariably emerges from a *price-war with a stronger hold on the oil markets than before. **1969** D. C. Hague *Managerial Econ.* iv. 74 A market which is free from the dangers of occasional, or continual, price cutting or even major price wars. **1977** *Times* 6 Aug. 3/1 A tea price war began yesterday as packers ordered cuts after auction prices fell. **1891** G. Clare *Money-Market Primer* 89 At all times some semblance of agreement is traceable between the respective *price-waves.

†**price, prise,** *a. Obs.* Forms: 4–5 pris, (4 priis, prijs, 4–5 prys, 5 pryss); 4–5 price, pryce; pryse; 4–7 prise. [attrib. use of prec. sb., from the phrase *of price*, OF. *de pris*; thus *roi de pris* 'kyng of *pris*' or '*pris* king'.] A general term of appreciation: Worthy, excellent, valiant, eminent, prime, choice.

13.. *Coer de L.* 4300 A mangenel..To the prys tour a ston gan sende. **1340–70** *Alex. & Dind.* 161 As prest as þe pris king sai his pres stinte. **1377** Langl. *P. Pl.* B. xix. 261 Iohan ..þe prys nete of Piers plow. **1387** Trevisa *Higden* (Rolls) II. 79 þis citee [Chester] haþ plente of..pris salmoun [orig. *salmonis optimi*]. ? *a* **1400** *Morte Arth.* 355 Send prekers to þe price toune, and plaunte there my segge. *c* **1400** *Destr. Troy* 6010 And Paris the prise with pepull ynogh. *Ibid.* 9111 There were plenty of pepull, prise men & noble. *c* **1450** *Merlin* II. 220 So dide well thoo prise knyghtes in her companye, and also the knyghtes of the rounde table. **1480** Caxton *Chron. Eng.* ccxxiv, Tho had euery English batayll II winges of pris archiers. **1615** Brathwait *Strappado*, etc. (1878) 292 More prise and richer than those sisters three, Which kept the apples of faire Hespery.

b. *absol.* The most excellent; the chief.

c **1330** *Amis & Amil.* 137 Ouer al the lond than were thai priis. **13..** *E.E. Allit. P.* B. 1614 A prophete of þat prouince & pryce of þe worlde. *c* **1394** *P. Pl. Crede* 256 þe prijs of popes at Rome, And of gretest degre. **1398** Trevisa *Barth. De P.R.* xvi. lxxxvii. (Bodl. MS.), Smaragdus is pris of alle grene preciouse stones. *c* **1400** *Destr. Troy* 8954 Palomydon for prise þe pert kynges toke.

price (praɪs), *v.* Also 6 pryce. [A later variant of the earlier *prise*, of which prize *v.*[1] is the direct modern representative. The regular forms of sb. and vb. after 1400 were *pris* (*prȳs*, *pryce*), *price* sb., and *prise*, *prize* vb. (cf. *device*, *devise*; *advice*, *advise*). In the verb, *price* is a new form, assimilated to the sb., and used in the literal sense, while *prize* has become more or less fig. For the full history see prize *v.*; the following instances illustrate this special form, which hardly appears before the 16th c., and was cited by Johnson in 1773 only in the Spenserian instance in sense 2. In many parts of England *to prize* is still said instead. Cf. also apprise *v.*[2]]

1. a. *trans.* To set the selling price to, to fix the price of (a thing for sale); to state the price of. (Originally *preyse*, praise *v.* 1; then *prise*, prize; finally *price*.)

1382- [see praise *v.* 1]. *c* **1440–1713** [see prize *v.*[1] 1]. *c* **1490** *Promp. Parv.* 413/2 (MS. K.) Pricynge, *P.* prisinge, *licitacio.* **1570** Levins *Manip.* 114/41 To Price, *appreciare, æstimare.* **1620** in *Essex Rev.* (1907) XVI. 206 Item, for peutter, priced vs. **1652** *Boston Rec.* (1877) II. 108 Good-wife Howen hath chosen Elder Coleborne to price and accept of a Cow from the Towne. **1831** *Examiner* 338/2 The next jeweller..will price at 10,000*l.*..the baubles that may sell for 3,500*l.* **1845** J. Saunders *Cab. Pict. Eng. Life, Chaucer* 251 In 1504, London ale was priced 5*s.* a barrel more than that of Kent. **1865** Sala *Amer. in War* I. 136 The decimal monetary system has been legalised in our possessions—though the shopkeepers are given to pricing their wares in shillings and pence.

b. To quote a price for: cf. price *sb.* 3.

1865 *Morn. Star* 1 June, The layers of the odds complaining that nothing but the favourites were backed, not-withstanding their tempting 'pricing' of the outsiders.

c. *fig.* To value relatively, to estimate.

1876 Geo. Eliot *Dan. Der.* xxxix, The girls' doings are always priced low.

d. ***to price out of the market***: to eliminate (oneself or another) from commercial competition through prohibitive prices; to charge a prohibitive price for (goods or services) or to (the customer). Also simply ***to price out***: to charge a prohibitive price to.

1938 *Sun* (Baltimore) 3 Jan. 8/3 Building material dealers and manufacturers, and to a less extent building labor, not only priced themselves out of the market but also priced the country out of an anticipated increase of $2,000,000,000 of national income. **1946** *Ibid.* 10 Aug. 4/1 Our price policies in the past..have had a tendency to price our export commodities out of the world market. **1946** *Your Investments* Sept. 9 Many consumers were being priced right out of the market..by the accelerated rise in living costs. **1947** *Daily Progress* (Charlottesville, Va.) 4 June 1/3 Government support prices for peanuts are so high that 'it forces peanut butter up so far as we are being priced out of the market'. **1949** *Sun* (Baltimore) 28 Jan. 10/1 Earlier support plans have simply priced cotton out of the world market. **1955** *Times* 15 June 3/1 The country should realize that we could be easily priced out of international markets. **1958** *Spectator* 14 Feb. 201/1 As for the story that we should have been 'priced out of our export markets', time has shown that this does not happen so easily as pessimists predict. **1971** *Guardian* 6 Sept. 9/8 Swiss exports may be pricing themselves out of world markets. **1975** *Times* 4 Sept. 2/1 In an effort to price out [football] hooligans..most Saturday concessionary fares are being ended. **1977** *Guernsey Weekly Press* 21 July 1/6 His members were very concerned about the risk of being priced out of the market.

e. ***to price up***: to increase the price of.

1943 *Our Towns* (Women's Group on Public Welfare) ii. 58 The shop then prices up the goods in order to cover..the commission. **1976** N. Roberts *Face of France* xxv. 227 The [champagne] trade started pricing up its wares to restrain demand.

†**2.** To pay the price for, pay for. *Obs.*

1500–20 Dunbar *Poems* xc. 42 And rype thi mynde how every thing befell, The tyme, the place, and how, and in quhat wyis, So that thi confessioun ma thi synnes pryce. **1590** Spenser *F.Q.* I. v. 26 The man that made Sansfoy to fall, Shall with his owne blood price that he hath spilt. *Ibid.* ix. 37 What justice can but judge against thee right, With thine owne blood to price his blood, here shed in sight?

3. To inquire the price of, bargain for; = cheap *v.* 3, cheapen *v.* 1.

a **1845** Barham *Ingol. Leg.* Ser. III. *Ld. Thoulouse* xxi, If you priced such a one in a drawing-room here, And was ask'd fifty pounds, you'd not say it was dear. **1859** Sala *Tw. round Clock* (1861) 94 That glorious avenue of Covent Garden Market, where they price cucumbers at Mrs. Solomon's and bouquets at Mrs. Buck's. **1872** Howells *Wedd. Journ.* (1892) 179 The evening they spent in..pricing many things.

†**4.** To raise the price of, to make dear. *Obs. rare.*

1533 J. Heywood *Play Weather* (1903) 636 And well it is knowen, to the most foole here, How rayne hath pryced corne within this vii. yeare.

†**5.** To value highly; to value; = prize *v.*[1] 3. (Quot. *c* 1375 is a casual instance of the spelling *price* for *prise.*)

[*c* **1375** *Sc. Leg. Saints* xxxvi. (*Baptista*) 145 For-þi suld men hym gretly price, And lowe hym in mony wyse.] **1561** tr. *Calvin's Foure Godlye Serm.* iii. G iij b, It is..suche a special prerogatyue as can not for ye great dignitie therof sufficiently be pryced to remaine and lyue in the churche. **1606** Shaks. *Tr. & Cr.* I. ii. 315 (Qo. 1, 1609) Men price [*Fol.* 1 prize] the thing ungained more then it is. **1643** Burroughes *Exp. Hosea* (1652) 420 We have had a peace a long time and..have not priced that mercy.

price, obs. form of prise, prize *sb.*[1], [2], [3].

price-current. Also *pl.* prices-current (occas. used for the sing.). [= F. *prix courant* in same sense (1769 in Littré): so also Du. *prijs courant*, Ger. *preiskurant.*] A list of current prices of commodities; a price-list.

1696 J. Houghton *Collect. Impr. Husb. & Trade* No. 180 4/1 Mr. Procter's Price Current is published every Friday. .. These are the Prices of most Foreign Merchandizes, with the Customs payable for each. **1706** Phillips, *Price Current*, a weekly Account publish'd in London, of the current Value of most Commodities. **1733** Budgell *Bee* I. 181 Looking in our senseless Pamphlet for the Price Courant. **1815** *Niles' Reg.* IX. 3/2 This account of the *selling prices* of the several stocks mentioned, is taken from the *public prices current* of the two places. **1839** *Southern Lit. Messenger* V. 38/2 There are no daily papers..no prices current—no reports from the stock market. **1848** Mill *Pol. Econ.* II. iv. §3 (1876) 150 There is at each time and place a market price, which can be quoted in a price-current. **1856** *Trans. Mich. Agric. Soc.* VII. 533 A glance at our 'prices current' might suffice to satisfy the most incredulous. **1866** Lowell *Seward-Johnson Reaction* Wks. 1890 V. 293 His own countrymen were also unprovided with a price-current of the latest quotation in phrases. **1908** *Economist* 8 Feb. 308–9 (*Heading*) London Stock Markets, Price Current. **1965** J. L. Hanson *Dict. Econ.* 326/1 *Prices Current*, a price list showing the prices ruling at a certain date.

priced (praɪst), *ppl. a.* [f. price *sb.* or *v.* + -ed.]

1. Having the price fixed or stated; containing a statement of prices.

1552 Huloet, Pryced, *licitatus, taxatus.* **1837** Hallam *Hist. Lit.* I. iii. §147 The priced catalogues of Colinæus and Robert Stephens are extant. **1901** *Westm. Gaz.* 24 July 2/1 Seven priced works have been sold in this gallery.

2. Having a (specified or indicated) price: in parasynthetic combinations, as ***high-priced***, ***low-priced***: see high *a.* 22 b, low *a.* 21.

†'**priceful,** *a. Obs. rare.* In 4 prisful, 5 prycefull. [f. price *sb.* II. + -ful.] Full of 'price' or value; precious, worthy, excellent.

13.. *Cursor M.* 18173 (Cott.) Sua prisful [*Laud MS.* prycefull] quar es þou o pight [*Gött.* Sua prisful quat ert þu of pith]?

priceite ('praɪsaɪt). *Min.* [See quot. and -ite.] 'Hydrous borate of calcium, near colemanite' (Chester).

1873 Silliman in *Amer. Jrnl. Sc.* Ser. III. VI. 130 As it [this borate of lime] appears therefore to be a new species I would propose for it the name priceite, in honour of Mr. Thomas Price, the well known metallurgist of San Francisco.

priceless ('praɪslɪs), *a.* Also 6 prise-, 7 prizelesse, 8 -less. [f. price *sb.* + -less.]

1. a. 'Without price'; having a value beyond all price or equivalent; invaluable, inestimable.

1593 Shaks. *Lucr.* 17 What priselesse wealth the heauens had him lent In the possession of his beauteous mate. **1607** Walkington *Opt. Glass* 13 Crasie barkes,..ballist with prizelesse marchandise. *c* **1616** Fletcher & Mass. *Thierry & Theod.* II. i, His ignorance of the priceless jewel. **1735–6** Thomson *Liberty* II. 227 Tutor of Athens! he in ev'ry street Dealt priceless treasure. **1863** Bright *Sp., Amer.* 3 Feb. (1876) 116 That priceless possession which we have perhaps more clearly established..that of personal freedom.

b. With mixture of literal sense 'having no market price; that cannot be obtained for money'.

1884 *Fortn. Rev.* Jan. 34 Those gifts that cannot be purchased with money, that are priceless. **1888** *Lady* 25 Oct. 374/2 These [stencil-plates]..are priceless, not to be bought in common shops.

2. Having no value; valueless, worthless. *rare.*

1771 *Muse in Min.* 60 Beauty that prizeless pageant of a day. **1847** Webster, *Priceless*...2. Without value; worthless or unsalable. *J. Barlow.*

3. *colloq.* Amusing, absurd, ludicrous; delightful.

1907 *Punch* 23 Jan. 59 Lady Bountiful: Oh, dear Miss Smith, *do* send me some of your priceless little sketches for my rummage sale on the 26th. **1914** D. O. Barnett *Let.* 19 Nov. (1915) 11 There was a priceless 'drunk' here the other day when I was on guard... He made the most magnificent remarks en route and so did the chaps who were carrying him. **1921** G. B. Shaw *Back to Methuselah* II. 87 What a priceless humbug old Lubin is! **1924** D. Moore *Fen's First Term* xii. 127 She had been a 'priceless idiot'. **1925** 'R. Crompton' *Still—William* xi. 201 'I do hope I remember all this when I wake up,' said the Toreador, 'it's too priceless.' **1978** S. Naipaul *North of South* I. i. 29 The European.. burst out laughing... 'Can you imagine how they must have ..rolled their eyes? Absolutely priceless.'

Hence '**pricelessly** *adv.*; '**pricelessness,** inestimable value.

1879 Trollope *Eye for Eye* II. i. 13 There came a day in which the pricelessness of the girl he loved sank to nothing. **1883** *Century Mag.* XXVI. 804 The pricelessness of water in a land where no rain falls during six months. **1910** G. Murray tr. *Euripides' Iphigenia in Tauris* 62 Brother, and home, and sister pricelessly Beloved. **1934** G. B. Shaw *On Rocks* I. 222 You see, what makes your diagnosis so pricelessly funny to me is that as a matter of fact my life has been a completely intellectual life, and my training the finest intellectual training in the world. **1977** J. B. Hilton *Dead-Nettle* vi. 61 Frank, you are pricelessly sweet.

†'**pricely,** *adv. Obs. rare.* In 4 prisely. [f. price *a.* + -ly[2].] Excellently, choicely.

1340–70 *Alisaunder* 733 Hee was ishape as a sheepe shinand bright, I-painted full prisely and precious stones Wer sticked on þat stock, stoute too beholde.

pricement, var. prizement *Obs.*

pricer ('praɪsə(r)). [f. price *v.* + -er[1].] One who prices. (Cf. prizer[1] 1.)

1878 Mackintosh *Hist. Civiliz. Scotl.* I. xi. 454 There were public pricers of flesh in all the burghs.

pricey ('praɪsɪ), *a. colloq.* Also pricy. [f. price *sb.* + -y[1].] Expensive, high-priced. Also *Comb.*

1932 'C. L. Anthony' *Service* III. ii. 101 I've got the day off to-day—been up to a sale to see about a show-case. But I couldn't touch it. It was a very pricey article. **1944** *World's Press News* 31 Aug. p. iii/1 (*heading*) 'Pricy' at second hand. .. The advertiser offered 4s. 6d. for each issue of *Vogue* ten days after publication. The price of *Vogue* is 3s. **1953** D. Whipple *Someone at Distance* xxvii. 243 'Pricey, I know,' continued Mr. Pye. 'But worth it, Madam.' **1957** *Economist* 19 Oct. (Suppl.) 10/1 The 'pricier' models like the Ford Zodiac or the Vauxhall Cresta. **1962** M. Procter *Devil in Moonlight* xi. 114 It's pricey... It might cost you a lot of money. **1971** *Daily Tel.* 19 Aug. 2/5 Meat has become a very pricey business for most households. **1976** W. H. Canaway *Willow-Pattern War* xvii. 174 A pricey-looking transistor radio. **1978** *SLR Camera* Aug. 88/1 It can..be fitted with a motor drive unit, but not with the wide variety of viewing heads and viewing screens available for the more pricy sisters in the catalogue.

prich: see pritch.

pricipe, obs. f. præcipe.

prick (prɪk), *sb.* Forms: 1 pric(c)a, price, (pryce), 2, 5–6 prike (5 pryke); 3–7 pricke, 4– prick (4–6 prikke, prik, 5 prykke, prikk, 5–7 pryck, -e, pryk). [OE. *prica, pricca* m., *price* f. = mod.Du. *prik* m. (†*prick* Kilian) a sharp point or stick, prickle, etc.; LG. *prik* a dot, spot, point, *prik, prikke* a pricking instrument; WFris. *prik*; also Icel. *prik* a dot, a little stick (? from Eng.), Da. *prik*, Norw. *prikk*, Sw. *prick* (fr. LG.) a dot, mark. From same root as prick *v.*, q.v. See also pritch *sb.* (The W. *pric* stick, broach, and Ir. *prioca* sting, are from Eng.)]

I. An impression or mark made by pricking.

1. a. An impression in a surface or body made by pricking or piercing; a puncture: = point *sb.*[1] 1.

(This seems to be etymologically the earliest sense, and is app. the meaning in Ælfric.)

c **1000** Ælfric *Gram.* xxviii. (Z.) 180 *Pungo*, ic pricige ..(of ðam is nama *punctus* prica [*v.r.* pricca]). **13..** *Minor Poems fr. Vernon MS.* lii. 58 In fot and hond bereþ blodi prikke. **1585** T. Washington tr. *Nicholay's Voy.* II. viii.

41 b, They haue firste p[r]icked them, out of which prickes do.. breed certaine.. wormes. **1638** R. BAKER tr. *Balzac's Lett.* (vol. III) 113 The less credulous tooke the pricke of a pinne for a Saintes marke. **1878** BROWNING *Poets Croisic* cxli, No pin's prick The tooth leaves. **1897** *Allbutt's Syst. Med.* II. 1078 The prick may continue to drip for hours.

b. *spec.* in *Farriery.* A puncture or wound in the quick or sole of the foot of a horse.

1607 TOPSELL *Four-f. Beasts* (1658) 322 Of a Prick in the sole of the Foot, by treading on a nail, or any other sharp thing. **1831** YOUATT *Horse* 303 Prick or wound in the sole or crust... The sole is very liable to be wounded by nails, pieces of glass, or even sharp flints, but much more frequently the fleshy little plates are wounded by the nail in shoeing. **1899** *Allbutt's Syst. Med.* VIII. 788 Loosening and detachment of the nail following a 'prick' or crush.

c. The footprint or track of a hare.

1598 FLORIO, *Pedata*, a tracke,.. the print of a foote,.. the prick of a hare. **1741** *Compl. Fam.-Piece* II. i. 301 If it be smooth and plain within,.. so that you may discern the Pricks,.. then endeavour to recover the Hare upon the Trail. **1875** 'STONEHENGE' *Brit. Sports* I. I. i. §5. 8 [The hare] leaves her mark or prick in the soil.

2. a. A minute mark made by slightly pricking or indenting a surface with a pointed tool; formerly also the impression or mark made with the point of a pen or pencil or the like, or a mark having this appearance; a dot, tick, point. Cf. POINT *sb.*[1] 2. Now *rare* or *Obs.*

c **1000** *Sax. Leechd.* I. 188 Heo hæfð on æȝhwylcum leafe twa endebyrdnyssa fæȝerra pricena & þa scinað swa gold. *c* **1391** CHAUCER *Astrol.* II. §5 Set ther a prikke of ynke. *Ibid.* §42, Y sette þer a prikke at my foote; þan goo [y] ner to þe tour,.. & þere y sette a-noþer prikke. **1530** PALSGR. 258/1 Pricke a marke, *marque.* **1607** NORDEN *Surv. Dial.* III. 129 Upon this line I make a pricke, which is the very station where the instrument is supposed to stand. **1676** T. MILLER *Compl. Modellist* 1 Set 1 foot of your Compasses at B, and with the other mark a prick at G. **1766** *Compl. Farmer* s.v. *Surveying*, A point is.. ordinarily expressed with a small prick, like a period at the end of a sentence.

†**b.** Each of the marks by which the circumference of a dial is divided, or the divisions of any scale indicated. *Obs. rare.*

1592 SHAKS. *Rom. & Jul.* II. iv. 119 The bawdy hand of the Dyall is now vpon the pricke of Noone. **1593** —— *3 Hen. VI*, I. iv. 34 Now Phaeton hath tumbled from his Carre, And made an Euening at the Noone-tide Prick.

†**3. a.** A dot or other small mark used in writing or printing; as, a punctuation or metrical mark, a diacritical point, the points in Hebrew or other languages, etc.; = POINT *sb.*[1] 3. *Obs.*

c **1000** ÆLFRIC *Gram.* l. (Z.) 291 Se forma prica on þam ferse is ȝehaten *media distinctio*, þæt is on middan todal. **1530** PALSGR. 11 If they.. be nat part of a diphthong, they shall have ii prickes over theyr heed, thus *ÿ, ϋ.* **1567** SALESBURY *Playne Introd.* E j, The sound of *u*, in French, or *ü*, wyth two prickes ouer the heade in Duch. **1605** WILLET *Hexapla Gen.* 26 This word Iehouah.. borroweth all the prickes from Adonai. **1646** *Topicks in Laws of Eng.* Errata, Some mistakes are in the pricks and commaes. **1693** J. EDWARDS *Author. O. & N. Test.* 53 One tittle.. is meant of those little horns, pricks and dots belonging to the Hebrew letters.

†**b.** A mark or dot used in musical notation; = POINT *sb.*[1] 4. (*a*) In mediæval music, a note. (*b*) In later musical notation, a dot placed after a note or rest for various purposes. Cf. PRICK *v.* 13.

1597 MORLEY *Introd. Mus.* Annot., A pricke is a kinde of Ligature, so that if you would tie a semibrief and a minime together you may set a pricke after the semibrief, and so you shall bind them. *Ibid.* 12 *Phi.* I pray you say what Prickes or poynts signifie in singing. *Ma...* As your rests signified the whole lengthe of the notes in silence, so dothe the pricke the halfe of the note going before to be holden out in voyce.. and this pricke is called a pricke of augmentation. **1659** C. HOOLE *Comenius' Vis. World* xcix. (1672) 203/1 Musique setteth Tunes with Pricks. **1674** PLAYFORD *Skill Mus.* I. viii. 27 This Prick of Perfection or Addition is ever placed on the right side of all Notes, for the prolonging the sound of that Note it follows. **1749** *Numbers in Poet. Comp.* 31 By a proper Use of the Pricks and Pauses it may be so contrived.. as to make no alteration in the Time of the Tune, or manner of beating it.

II. A minute particle.

†**4.** A point of space (or particle of matter) viewed in reference to its minuteness, a mere point.

c **1374** CHAUCER *Boeth.* II. pr. vii. 44 (Camb. MS.) Al the enuyronynge of the erthe abowte ne halt but the resoun of a prikke at regard of the gretnesse of heuene. **1601** HOLLAND *Pliny* I. 33 This little pricke of the world (for surely the earth is nothing else in comparison of the whole). **1606** SHAKS. *Tr. & Cr.* I. iii. 343 In such Indexes, although small prickes To their subsequent Volumes, there is seene The baby figure of the Gyant-masse Of things to come at large. **1616** BOYS *Expos. Proper Ps.* lvii. 102 The earth.. compared vnto the greatnes of the starrie skies circumference, is but a center or little pricke.

†**5.** A minute part or quantity of anything; a jot, whit, particle; = POINT *sb.*[1] 6.

to the prick, to the smallest jot, with minute exactness or precision.

In the first quot. and in quots. 1579, 1645, orig. fig. from 3.

c **1000** *Ags. Gosp.* Matt. v. 18 An i oððe an prica [*Royal MS.* pryce; *c* **1160** *Hatton G.* an prike] ne ȝewit fram þære æ. *a* **1225** *Ancr. R.* 228, & te deouel ne mei nout gon furðer a pricke. *c* **1450** *Mirour Saluacioun* 4270 Alle thire thinges.. wille he weghe streytly thare And to the prikke thaire value tofore alle men declare. **1501** DOUGLAS *Pal. Hon.* II. lii, Of all that rout was neuer a prik disioynt. **1535** STEWART *Cron. Scot.* (Rolls) II. 291 Syne all the lawe remanand wes behind, Rycht equalie,.. Be the leist prick.. Distribute hes amang his men of weir. **1579** FULKE *Heskins's Parl.* 84 Not a iote, or a pricke of the law shall passe, vntill all be fulfilled. **1645** USSHER *Body Div.* (1647) 13 Not one jot or prick of the Law shall perish.

†**6. a.** The smallest portion of time; an instant, moment; = POINT *sb.*[1] 7. *Obs.*

1340 *Ayenb.* 71 Þaȝ he leuede a þousond year þet ne ssolde by bote onlepy prikke to þe zyȝþe of þe oþre lyue þet eure wyþoute ende ssel yleste. **1387–8** T. USK *Test. Love* I. viii. (Skeat) l. 128 That dureth but a pricke, in respecte of the other. **1577** tr. *Bullinger's Decades* (1592) 75 They that shall bee then liuing.. shall in a very prick of time be changed. **1579** TWYNE *Phisicke agst. Fort.* I. xcii. 114 The tyme present is lesse then a pricke, and euermore vnstable.

†**b.** In mediæval measure of time: The fourth or (according to some) the fifth part of an hour; = POINT *sb.*[1] 10. Cf. ATOM *sb.* 7. *Obs.*

c **1000** ÆLFRIC *Hom.* (Th.) I. 102 And swa swa se mona dæghwonlice feower pricon lator arist, swa eac seo sæ symle feower pricum lator fleowð. *c* **1050** *Byrhtferth's Handboc* in *Anglia* VIII. 317 Feower *puncti* æt synt prican, wyrcað ane tid on þære sunnan ryne... Syx and hundniȝontiȝ prican beoð on þam dæȝe.

†**c.** *Astron.* = DIGIT *sb.* 4, POINT *sb.*[1] 11. *Obs.*

1561 EDEN *Arte Nauig.* II. viii. 35 The quantitie of these Eclipses, the Astronomers deuide into .xii. equall partes, as well the Diameter of the Sunne as of the Moone. And these partes they call fyngers, punctes or prickes.

III. A point in reference to position.

†**7.** A point in space; a geometrical point: = POINT *sb.*[1] 18. *Obs.*

[**1387–8** T. USK *Test. Love* I. viii. (Skeat) l. 95 A pricke is wonder little, in respecte of all the cercle.] **1551** RECORDE *Pathw. Knowl.* I. Defin., A Poynt or a Prycke, is named of Geometricians that small and vnsensible shape, whiche hath in it no partes, that is to say: nother length, breadth, nor depth. **1555** EDEN *Decades* 247 Zenith (that is the pricke ouer the head). **1578** BANISTER *Hist. Man* VIII. 103 That which you see in the centre, or middle pricke of the eye is named Pupilla. **1589** IVE *Fortif.* 10 Draw a right line.. which must cut the line C.D. in the pricke E. *a* **1619** FOTHERBY *Atheom.* II. ix. §3 (1622) 296 Hee calleth a Pricke the parent of all magnitude.

†**8.** A point marking a stage in progression; degree, pitch. ***the prick***, the height, highest point, apex, acme. Cf. POINT *sb.*[1] 22. *Obs.*

c **1386** CHAUCER *Man of Law's T.* 21 Alle dayes of poure men been wikke Be war therfore er thou come to that prikke. *a* **1400–50** *Alexander* 45 Þer preued neuer nane his prik for passing of witt, Plato nor Piktagaras ne Prektane him seluen. *c* **1510** MORE *Picus* Wks. 7/1 He was come to that pricke of parfit humilitie. **1548** UDALL, etc. *Erasm. Par. Matt.* iii. 30 Endeuour with all your herte to the hygh prycke of vertue. **1594** PLAT *Jewell-ho.* I. 30 Vntill you haue attayned vnto the verie pricke of proportion. **1606** HOLLAND *Sueton.* 141 Setting the prices.. and enhaunsing the same to such a prick, that some men enforced to buye certaine things at an extreame and exceeding rate.. cut their owne veines and so bled to death.

†**9.** The precise instant of time at which anything happens; the critical moment: = POINT *sb.*[1] 23. ***prick of the day*** (after Fr. *le point du jour*), daybreak. *Obs.*

c **1400** *Laud Troy Bk.* 6639 He was dryuen so ney the prikke, That he myght not his lippis likke. *c* **1422** HOCCLEVE *Learn to Die* 847 Remembre or þat he come to the prikke. *c* **1460** *Towneley Myst.* xxx. 370, I trowd it drew nere the prik. *c* **1532** DU WES *Introd. Fr.* in *Palsgr.* 927 At the prick of the day, *au point du jour.*

IV. In archery.

†**10. a.** The mark aimed at in shooting; the spot in the centre of the target; the bull's-eye; hence, a target, esp. one at a fixed distance, having such a mark in its centre. (Opposed in the latter sense to BUTT *sb.*[4] 2 and ROVER.) *Obs.*

1382 WYCLIF *1 Sam.* xx. 20 And Y shal sende thre arowis biside it, and shal throwe as hauntynge me to a prik [1388 exercisynge me at a signe [*v.r.* marke]]. *c* **1400** *Sowdone Bab.* 2260 Thou kanste welle hit the prikke. **1464** *Mann. & Househ. Exp.* (Roxb.) 269 Item, payd.. for my masterys lossys att the prykkys, viij.*d.* Item, at the buttys, viij.*d.* **1477** EARL RIVERS (Caxton) *Dictes* 89 An archier to faile of the butte is no wonder, but to hytte the pryke is a greet maistrie. **1541** *Act 33 Hen. VIII*, c. 9 §4 No man, vnder the age of .xxiiii. yeres, shall shote at anie standing pricke, excepte it be at a rouer. **1545** ASCHAM *Toxoph.* (Arb.) 113 A bowe of Ewe must be hadde for perfecte shootinge at the prickes. **1577–87** HOLINSHED *Chron.* III. 1208/1 Diuerse of the court.. shot dailie at pricks set vpon the Thames. **1611** MARKHAM *Country Content.* I. i. (1668) 46 The Prick is a Mark of some compasse, yet most certain in the distance. **1845** J. SAUNDERS *Cabinet Pict. Eng. Life, Chaucer* 89 In every village were three kinds of marks set up:.. the prick, a 'mark of compass', requiring strong light arrows, with feathers of moderate size.

†**b.** ***twelve*** (***twenty-four***) ***score prick***: a 'prick' or target placed 240 (or 480) paces distant, the regular distance at which shooting at the prick was practised. *Obs.*

1569 in *Camden's Eliz.* (1717) Pref. 29 The shotinge with the Standerd, the shotinge with the brode arrowe, the shotinge at the twelve skore prick, the shotinge at the Turke. **1602** CAREW *Cornwall* (1811) 194 Their shaft was a cloth yard, their pricks twenty-four score. **1608** *Pennyless Parl.* in *Harl. Misc.* (Malh.) III. 76 A Turk can be hit at twelve score pricks in Finsbury Fields. **1620** MIDDLETON & ROWLEY *World Tost at Tennis* Induct. 67 The bowman's twelve score prick.

†**11.** *fig.* (or in fig. context): That at which one aims; an object, end: = POINT *sb.*[1] 28. *Obs.*

c **1412** HOCCLEVE *De Reg. Princ.* 528 Than myghte siluer walke more thikke Among þe peple þan þat it doþ now; Ther wolde I fayne that were sette the prikke. *a* **1533** LD. BERNERS *Gold. Bk. M. Aurel.* (1546) R j b, They shote at the pricke of the woman's beautie. **1558** MORWYNG *Ben Gorion* (1567) 1 Seyng all the prophetes haue bent and directed their prophesies.. to this pricke, that the kingdome of the house of Dauid should be restored. **1592** TIMME *Ten Eng. Lepers* C ij, What madnes is it then in those men, who because they cannot be in the prick, wil not be in ye but neither.

V. Anything that pricks or pierces; an instrument or organ having a sharp point.

12. a. A small sharp projecting organ or part; a thorn or prickle; a spine on the skin of an animal, or the like. Now *rare* or *Obs.*

a **1300** *Cursor M.* 24084 A crun o thorn his hefd on stod, Þat ilk prick broght vte þe blod. **1390** GOWER *Conf.* I. 283 And thus myn hand ayein the pricke I hurte and have do many day And go so forth as I go may. *c* **1440** *Promp. Parv.* 413/1 Pryke, or pynne, *spintrum*, vel *spinter.* **1519** *Interl. Four Elem.* in Hazl. *Dodsley* I. 14 In comparison.. they be so small, No more than the pricks that be on a gall. **1548** TURNER *Names of Herbes* (1881) 17 It [Asparagus] maye be called in englishe pricky Sperage, because it is all full of pryckes. **1579–80** NORTH *Plutarch* (1676) 998 As pricks be hidden under Roses. **1633** BP. HALL *Occas. Medit.* (1851) 136 [The hedgehog] knows how to roll up itself round within those thorns,.. so as the dog, instead of a beast, finds now nothing but a ball of pricks to wound his jaws. **1688** R. HOLME *Armoury* II. 84/2 The Thorns or pricks, are sharp points growing from the branches of some trees.

†**b.** The sting of a bee, scorpion, or the like.

1382 WYCLIF *Rev.* ix. 10 Thei hadden tayles lijk of scorpiouns, and prickes weren in the tayles of hem. *c* **1386** CHAUCER *Pars. T.* ¶394 Bees, whan they maken hir kyng, they chesen oon that hath no prikke wherwith he may stynge. *c* **1412** HOCCLEVE *De Reg. Princ.* 3378 Othir bees, prikkes han euerichon.

†**c.** *fig.* Something that causes mental irritation, vexation, or torment; a 'thorn', sting. *Obs.*

prick of conscience: see 19.

c **1380** WYCLIF *Serm.* Sel. Wks. II. 264 God ȝaf him [Paul] a prikke of his fleish, an angel of þe fend to tempte him. **1382** —— *1 Cor.* xv. 55 Deeth, wher is thi pricke? Forsoth the pricke of deeth is synne. **1600** HOLLAND *Livy* XXVI. xl. 615 It was never well taken by Hanno, nor joyously accepted, in regard of the person, who was a pricke alwaies in his eie. **1612** T. TAYLOR *Comm. Titus* Ded., That cursed race of the Cananites, who were ever pricks in the sides, and thornes in the eyes of Gods people. **1645** USSHER *Body Div.* (1647) 374 Who will seem to forgive, and yet keep a prick and quarrell in their hearts.

13. a. A goad for oxen. ***to kick*** (†***work, spurn***) ***against the pricks***: said of oxen; now *arch.* and usually *fig.* (after Acts ix. 5): cf. KICK *v.*[1] 1 c.

c **1350** *Nominale Gall.-Angl.* (E.E.T.S.) 862 *Feut et agiloun*, gode and prikke. **1382** [see KICK *v.*[1] 1 c]. **14..** *Cursor M.* 19626 (Fairf.) Hit is to þe ful harde & wik For to wirk a-gaine þe prik. *c* **1440** *Promp. Parv.* 413/1 Pryk, or prykyl (*S.* prykkar), *stimulus, stiga.* **1520** NISBET *N. Test. in Scots, Acts* xxii. 7 It is hard to thee to spurn aganis the prick. **1530** PALSGR. 258/1 Pricke to drive oxen with, *aguillon.* **1679** BLOUNT *Anc. Tenures* 17 Pryk signifies a Goad or Spur. **1775** ROMANS *Florida* App. 56 In that case an attempt to beat up under Cuba will be nothing better than kicking against the pricks. **1904** MARIE CORELLI *God's Good Man* i, For the past ten years he has known what it is to 'kick against the pricks' of legitimate Church authority.

†**b.** *fig.* That which incites or stimulates; a spur, an incentive. *Obs.*

1387 TREVISA *Higden* (Rolls) VII. 397 He feng þe prikkes of þe love of God. *c* **1450** *Mirour Saluacioun* 2421 His prikke specially is a womman gloosyng. **1526** *Pilgr. Perf.* (W. de W. 1531) 240 b, The moost speciall medicyne & prycke agaynst slouth. **1579** GOSSON *Sch. Abuse* (Arb.) 29 Which rather effeminate the minde, as pricks vnto vice, then procure amendement of manners, as spurres to vertue. **1638** JUNIUS *Paint. Ancients* 114 The greatest wits are ever by the prickes of emulation driven forward to greater matters.

14. A slender piece of wood or metal tapering to a sharp point, used to fasten things or parts of a thing together; a skewer; a pin (or in quot. 1721 a thorn) for fastening one's clothes; a thatcher's broach. Also, an early kind of knitting-needle; cf. ***knitting-prick*** (KNITTING *vbl. sb.* 3). See also PUDDING-PRICK. *Obs.* exc. *Hist.*

1377 in Cowell *Interpr.* s.v. *Pryk*, Per servitium inveniendi unum equum, unum saccum & unum *Pryk* in Guerra Walliæ. *c* **1440** *Promp. Parv.* 413/1 Prykke, for pakkys, *broccus. c* **1450** *Two Cookery-bks.* 82 Take a prik, and prik him togidur, And lete him roste. **1530** PALSGR. 258/1 Pricke to pricke meate, *brochette.* **1551** [see PRICK-TREE]. **1578** LYTE *Dodoens* VI. li. 726 The wilde Cornell tree.. Butchers vse it to make prickes of it. *Ibid.* [see PRICK-TIMBER]. **1621** BURTON *Anat. Mel.* III. ii. III. iii. (1651) 477 Set out with bables, as a Butchers meat is with pricks. *c* **1630** *MS. Egerton* 923 lf. 3 Like to a packe without a pricke, Or o-per-se in arithmeticke. **1688** R. HOLME *Armoury* III. xiv. (Roxb.) 19/2 Thatchers Termes... Thatch pricks, and binding pricks. [**1707** *Rec. Convention R. Burghs Scotl.* (1880) I. 431 For the better improvement of stocking manufactures it is thought fitt that for hereafter all prick stockings may be made of three plyed wosten and of due proportione.] **1721** KELLY *Scot. Prov.* 184 It's a bare Moor that you'll go o'er, and no get Prick to your Blanket. *Ibid.* 198 If ever you make a good Pudding, I'll eat the Prick. That is, I am much mistaken if ever you do good. **1838** W. HOWITT *Rural Life Eng.* I. III. iii. 309 They knit with crooked pins called pricks. **1969** E. H. PINTO *Treen* 304 Bow curved needles, made from wire sharpened both ends.. and known as pricks, were commonly used for 'bump' or coarse knitting.

15. A pointed weapon or implement. Applied to †a dagger or pointed sword; †a fish-spear (*obs.*); a pronged eel-spear (*local*: cf. PICK *sb.*[1] 4 d); a small chisel or punch used by stone-workers; etc.

1552 Huloet, *Prycke*, a fyshers instrumente. Loke in Trowte speare. *c* **1590** Greene *Fr. Bacon* xi. 62 I'll set a prick against my breast. **1837** *Civil Eng. & Arch. Jrnl.* I. 33/2 The backs are to be scappled with a prick. **1859** *Kansas Hist. Coll.* (1896) V. 581 Ordnance stores this day turned over to Samuel Medary... 100 cap pouches and pricks, worn. **1882** Day *Fishes Gt. Brit.* II. 246 The prick is constructed of four broad serrated blades or tines spread out like a fan, and the eel becomes wedged between them.

†**16.** An upright tapering spike, spire, or similar object. Applied among other things to: The upright pole of a tent; the spike on which a candle was fixed (see pricket 2); the spike of a prick-measure (see 21); an iron spike set on a building; a spire; a pinnacle; a pointed top of a rock or mountain, an 'aiguille' or 'needle'; the first 'head' of a deer. *Obs.*

1497 *Naval Acc. Hen. VII* (1896) 99 Pavilion of xvj and a prik. *c* **1530** in Gutch *Coll. Cur.* II. 339 Twoo Aulter Candilstickes parcell gilte with prickes. **1563** Winȝet *Wks.* (S.T.S.) II. 66 Than the deuil tuke him..and set him aboue the prik of the temple. **1587** *Sc. Acts Jas. VI* (1814) III. 522/1 þt þair be a prik of Irne.. Ryssing vpricht out of þe centrie or middis of þe bottom of þe firlot and passing throw þe middis of þe said ovir corss bar. *c* **1600** in A. Maxwell *Hist. Old Dundee* (1884) 150 [To erect] ane sufficient prick of fine ashler wark weill hewn, rising with aucht square panes like the old foundation of the wark, in hicht..eleven foots. **1604** E. G[rimstone] *D'Acosta's Hist. Indies* v. xxv. 400 High and stiep rockes, which have prickes or poynts on them, above two hundred fadome high. **1650** [? Sanderson] *Aulicus Coquin.* 34 His head to be set upon a prick of Iron upon the highest part of the Talboth. *a* **1700** B. E. *Dict. Cant. Crew*, *Prick*, the first Head of a Fallow Deer.

17. a. The penis. *coarse slang.*

1592 R. D. *Hypnerotomachia* 42 b, The pissing Boye lift up his pricke. **1598** Florio s.v. *Pisciaruola.* **1599** Minsheu *Sp. Dict.* s.v. *Pica de niño.* **1655** Moufet & Bennet *Health's Impr.* (1746) 267 The Frenchmen call this Fish the Ass's Prick, and Dr. Wotton termeth it grosly the Pintle-fish. **1680** Rochester *Poems* 14 But though St. James has the honor on't, 'Tis consecrate to Prick and Cunt. **1683** Snape *Anat. Horse* III. v. (1686) 114 It [*glandula pinealis*] is also called the Yard or Prick of the Brain. **1744, 1763** [see bollock 1]. **1896** A. Beardsley *Let.* c 3 Dec. (1970) 223 Yes *everything* is phallic shaped except Symons's prick. **1922** Joyce *Ulysses* 424 Trinity medicals... All prick and no pence. **1965** W. Young *Eros Denied* xiv. 132 You know, the young men's pricks seem to be getting bigger and bigger. It must be the Welfare State. **1971** 'A. Burgess' *MF* iii. 39 His nakedness and limp prick..were now properties of the changing room. **1976** 'E. McBain' *Guns* (1977) ii. 38 Jocko had..a very small pecker... Blood on the bulging pectorals, tiny contradictory prick.

†**b.** As a vulgar term of endearment. *Obs.*

1540 [see princock]. **1671** H. M. *Erasm. Colloq.* 547 One word alone hath troubled some, because the immodest maid soothing the young man, calls him her Prick... He who cannot away with this, instead of 'my Prick', let him write 'my Sweetheart'.

c. As a vulgar term of abuse for a man.

1929 *Amer. Speech* IV. 343 *Prick*, one in authority who is abusive or unjust. **1934** H. Miller *Tropic of Cancer* 110 Jesus, what I'd like is to find some rich cunt—like that cute little prick, Carl. **1935** J. T. Farrell *Guillotine Party* 193 That's what I think of you, Merton..you're a p...k! **1937** Partridge *Dict. Slang* 659/1 *Prick*... An offensive or contemptuous term (applied to men only). **1961** P. Kemp *Alms for Oblivion* ii. 40 Winn drafted a bitter reply, concluding with the *cri-de-coeur*: 'Uncomplaining gravest difficulties here but how long oh how long must we continue to kick against the pricks in your office.' **1967** 'E. Trevor' *Freebooters* xi. 124 We don't like bein' pushed around by an incompetent prick of a commanding officer. **1971** B. W. Aldiss *Soldier Erect* 52 Don't you call *me* a cunt, you Midland prick, you, or I'll sort you out! **1973** J. Wainwright *Devil you Don't* 25 John Smith said: 'Some men have big pricks.' 'Some men *are* big pricks.' **1978** M. Puzo *Fools Die* ix. 115 They have good jobs, big futures. And the pricks won't even do their service.

18. A small roll (of tobacco).

1666 J. Davies *Hist. Caribby Isles* 190 The place design'd for making of it [tobacco] up into rolls or pricks. **1704** *Lond. Gaz.* No. 4054/6 Lots..Cont. 4000 Pricks of Tobacco. **1888** Clark Russell *Death Ship* II. 88, I had the remains of what sailors term a prick of tobacco in my pocket. **1975** B. Meyrick *Behind Light* iv. 57 Normally Pa had thirty or so good leaves left to make rolled 'pricks' as a change from pressing into wads. *Ibid.*, Soon our back pantry was full of thick hanging 'pricks' of twisted and rolled tobacco. **1977** *Navy News* Feb. 6/6 The hair on the nape of the neck was bound in yarns..and called a perique. In my days we rolled leaf tobacco in a similar way and called the result a 'prick', just modern spelling of an old word.

VI. 19. a. The act of pricking, or the fact of being pricked; a puncture. (The chief extant sense.) Also *fig.*, esp. in phrase ***prick of conscience***, stinging or tormenting reflection or compunction, remorse; in earlier use, that which pricks the conscience or causes compunction: see 12 c.

13.. *Hampole's Pr. Consc.* (Yates MS.), Here bigynneþ þ e boke whiche is iclepid þe Prick of Conscience. *c* **1425** *Castell Persev.* 1858 in *Macro Plays* 129 It puttyth a man to pouerte, & pullyth hym to peynys prycke. *a* **1548** Hall *Chron., Rich. III*, 53 b, This was no dreame, but a punccion and pricke of hys synfull conscience. **1599** Shaks. *Hen. V*, II. i. 36 Gentlewomen that liue honestly by the pricke of their Needles. **1699** Dampier *Voy.* II. I. 171 Captain Minchin..was like to lose his hand by a prick with a Catfishes Fin. **1867** Smiles *Huguenots Eng.* ix. (1880) 513 Every prick of conscience was succeeded by new resolutions to extirpate heresy. **1884** tr. *Lotze's Metaph.* 504 A stimulus, strictly limited in its local extent—say the prick of a needle.

†**b.** The act of 'pricking the card' or marking a ship's position on the chart: see prick *v.* 16.

c **1595** Capt. Wyatt *R. Dudley's Voy. W. Ind.* (Hakl. Soc.) 21 Wee shall.., if God prosper our proceedings, see land such a daie by the prick of this my carde.

†**20.** Alliterative phrase, ***prick and praise*** (also *prise, price, prize*): the praise of excellence or success; success and its acknowledgement: perh. connected with prick *v.* 15, or ? with the use in archery: see sense 10. *Obs.*

a **1500** Medwall *Nature* (Brandl) II. 324 Now forsoth I gyue the pryk and pryse, Thou art worth the weyght of gold. **1565–73** Cooper *Thesaurus*, *Primas deferre alicui*, to giue to one the chiefe praise; to attribute most vnto one; to giue him the pricke and price. **1586** J. Hooker *Hist. Irel.* in *Holinshed* II. 6/2 In these seruices, as in all other, Robert of Barrie, and Meilerius had the pricke and praise. *c* **1589** *Whip for Ape* in *Lyly's Wks.* (1902) III. 419 For knaue and foole thou maist beare pricke and price. **1600** Holland *Livy* IX. xvi. 324 For in running..he had not his peere, but went away with pricke and prise before all other in those daies. **1657** Thornley tr. *Longus' Daphnis & Chloe* 49 The women gave him prick and praise for beauty. *a* **1700** B. E. *Dict. Cant. Crew*, *The Prick and Praise of our Town*, that bears the Bell..in all Exercises, as Wrestling, Running,..&c.

VII. 21. *attrib.* and *Comb.*, as ***prick-point, -spot, -thorn***; ***prick-protected*** adj.; †**prick-arrow** = prick-shaft; †**prick-candlestick** = pricket 2; †**prick-cast**, ? = *prickshot*; **prick-farrier** *Services' slang*, a medical officer; †**prick-grass**, a prickly weed, petty-whin; †**prickhead**: see quot.; **prick-hedge**, a thorn hedge; **prick-line**, a dotted line; **prick-lugged** *a.*, prick-eared; †**prick measure**, **prick-met** *Sc.*, a measure for grain, having an iron rod of stated length rising erect from the centre of the bottom: see sense 16; †**prick-pear** = prickle-pear, prickly pear; †**prick-penny**, some kind of trick at dice; **prick punch**: see quots.; **prick-shooting**, shooting at the 'prick' or target; **prickshot**, a shot at the 'prick' or target; hence, the distance at which this was usually practised: cf. bowshot; **prick-spur**, a spur having a single point; also used as a heraldic charge; **prick-stitch** (see quots.); so **prick-stitch** *v. trans.* and *intr.*, **prick-stitching** *vbl. sb.*; **prick-sucker** *coarse slang*, a fellator or fellatrix; †**prick-tackle**, ? tackle for catching fish with a 'prick': see sense 15; **prick-teaser** *coarse slang* = *cock-teaser* (cock *sb.*[1] 23); also **prick-tease** *sb.*; hence (as back-formations) **prick-teased**, **prick-teasing** *ppl. adjs.*; **prick-tobacco**, tobacco made up into a small roll: see sense 18; †**prick-wand**: see quot. 1765; **prick-wheel**, a toothed wheel mounted on a handle, used by saddlers for marking places for stitches at regular intervals; also = pattern-*wheel*. See also prick-eared *a.*, prick-song, etc.

1547 in Meyrick *Anc. Armour* (1824) III. 10 Quyver for *pricke arrows for crosse-bowes. **1610** Boys *Expos. Domin. Epist. & Gosp.* Wks. (1622) 170 Her prick-arrowes, as the shafts of Jonathan forwarne David of the great kings displeasure. **1566** in Peacock *Eng. Ch. Furniture* (1866) 50 Item ij *pricke candlestickes—broken and sold to george nyxe. **1578** in Feuillerat *Revels Q. Eliz.* (1908) 300 Pricke Candlestickes vi. **1580** Hollyband *Treas. Fr. Tong*, *Vn coup d'estoc*, a *pricke cast. **1611** Cotgr., *Coup d'estoc*, a thrust, foine, stockado, stab; also, a pricke-cast. **1961** Partridge *Dict. Slang* Suppl. 1232/1 **Prick(-)farrier*, a medical officer: R.A.F. regulars': since ca. 1928. **1971** S. Kerry *Doctor's Cabin* iv. 48 'Meet Doc Kerry, our prick farrier.' They both laughed. 'No offence meant,' said Johnny. 'It's just a vulgar Naval term for a surgeon.' **1616** Surfl. & Markh. *Country Farme* IV. iv. 498 If the gound haue beene much subiect to small whynnes or *prick-grasse, which is a most venimous weed in anie ground. **1688** R. Holme *Armoury* III. 76/1 **Prickhead*, is the first head of a Fallow Deer. **1601** Holland *Pliny* I. 510 This was at first practised with foot sets for a *prick-hedge, namely by pitching down into the earth Elder, Quince-cuttings and brambles. **1611** *Nottingham Rec.* IV. 302 He to sett a prick hedge betwixt the chappell and the dwelling howse. **1854** Miss Baker *Northampt. Gloss.*, *Prick-hedge*.., a dry hedge of thorns, set to protect a newly planted fence. **1653** R. Sanders *Physiogn.* 262 The *prick lines poynt to the back part of the body. **1700** Moxon *Mech. Exerc.* (1703) 261 The black Lines shew a stretching course, and the Prick-Lines an Heading course. **1847–78** Halliwell, **Prick-lugged*, having erect ears. **1641** *Sc. Acts Chas. I* (1817) V. 425/1 Thay ar chairgit to ressave þe *prick measure, conforme to þe act of Parliament. **1647** *Rec. Elgin* (New Spald. Cl. 1903) I. 182 For the lend of the *prick mett of Elgin. **1622** R. Hawkins *Voy. S. Sea* (1847) 87 One other fruit we found.. compassed about with prickles; our people called them *pricke-pears. **1662** J. Wilson *Cheats* IV. i. (1664) 46 Did not I (..) teach you, your Top, your Palm, and your Slur? .. And generally, instructed you from *Prick-penny, to Long Lawrence? **1894** *Outing* (U.S.) XXIV. 22/1 Place one point on the prick spot on the staff, and prick the board for the plank with the other point... Remove the staff, bend a batten to the *prick-points on the plank. **1905** *Longm. Mag.* July 272 The birds resort to its *prick-protected shade. **1677** Moxon *Mech. Exerc.* No. 2. 28 A *Prick-punch, is a piece of temper'd Steel with a round point at one end, to prick a round mark in Cold iron. **1683** *Ibid.*, *Printing* xi. ¶1 Make a small mark with a fine Prick-Punch. **1921** *Daily Colonist* (Victoria, B.C.) 2 Oct. 26/5 A chalk mark is good, but a prick punch makes a mark that will not rub out. **1801** T. Roberts *Eng. Bowman* 241 Of *Prick-shooting..the marks used in this kind of shooting have..consisted either of a small circular piece of white paper, fixed to a post..; or of a target. **1887** W. Butt *Ford's Archery* (rev. ed.) 138 This prick-shooting next became known as the paper-game. **1548** Patten *Exped. Scotl.* E iij b, The tentes..were deuided in to iiii. seuerall orders and rewes liynge east & west and a *prikshot a sunder. **1688** R. Holme *Armoury* III. 325/1 **Prick Spur*, with a Nail or sharp point. **1824** Meyrick *Anc. Armour* I. 12 The..spike of the pryck-spur. **1839** Knight *Pict. Shaks.*, *John* 10 The spur worn [*temp.* K. John] was the goad or pryck spur, without a rowel. **1868** Cussans *Her.* (1882) 122 Spur..may either be..with a revolving rowel, or with a single point. The latter is the most ancient, and is known as the Pryck-spur. **1924** W. D. F. Vincent et al. *Cutters' Pract. Guide Body Coats* 62/1 Hunting Coats are generally finished with plain seams, and have the front edges seamed and *prick-stitched. **1928** A. S. Bridgland *Mod. Tailor* II. xviii. 242 *Prick-stitch.*—This stitch is employed to give either strength or appearance, and consists in alternately passing the needle straight up and down through the material, the stitch itself being either a back or a side-stitch. **1933** J. E. Liberty *Pract. Tailoring* iii. 18 *Prick-stitch.* This is exactly similar to side-stitch but is made by two actions, one upward, the other downward, the stitch actually being pricked alternately through the material which would be too thick for side-stitching. *Ibid.* v. 54 Prick back over the felling and along the seam for not quite ¼ in., then prickstitch parallel to the felling up to the top of the welt and to the same width. *Ibid.* vii. 100 To obtain the desired result, it will need to be prick stitched. **1955** —— *Ibid.* (ed. 2) v. 56 The usual D tack, with a little addition of a short row of prickstitching midway between the flap seam and the top edge of the jetting. **1964** *McCall's Sewing* xiii. 239/2 *Prick stitching.* Take short half-back-stitches in which only two or three threads of the fabric are picked up. Pull each stitch tight. **1968** J. Ironside *Fashion Alphabet* 83 *Glove-stitch*, also known as 'prick' stitch. Stitch used for hand glove-making and sometimes for sewing very heavy materials and leather. The thread is taken through one layer of material and then the other. **1868** *Index Expurgatorius of Martial* 21 Cotilus, the *prick-sucker,..is shown to be the filthiest of men. **1974** *New Direction* IV. iv. 5/4 From then onward she became an ardent prick-sucker. **1464** *Mann. & Househ. Exp.* (Roxb.) 250 To Robart Clerke for a *pryke-takylle for my mastyr, and for botehyre, iij.*d.* **1977** E. J. Trimmer et al. *Visual Dict. Sex* (1978) ii. 31 A girl who works her way through several partners without actually having intercourse will become known as a '**prick-tease*'. **1975** D. Durrant *With my Little Eye* viii. 74 *Prick-teased boys had up for rape. **1961** Partridge *Dict. Slang* Suppl. 1232/1 **Prick-teaser*, a late C. 19–20 variant of *cock-teaser*. **1971** R. Busby *Deadlock* i. 8 He laughed..and pulled her roughly across the seat. 'A prick teaser, are we?' **1978** F. Norman *Dead Butler Caper* v. 32 That Gloria's a right prick teaser. She'll con 'im somethin' rotten. **1967** 'P. Loraine' *W.I.L. One to Curtis* i. 16, I supplied..an empty house..for whatever *prick-teasing kind of a party they wanted to throw. **1972** J. Mann *Mrs. Knox's Profession* iv. 24 He shouted after her: 'Prick-teasing bitch.' **956** in Birch *Cart. Sax.* III. 123 Andlang fura on *pric þorn. **1688** R. Holme *Armoury* III. xxii. (Roxb.) 274/1 *Prick tobacco, thick roll all made vp together without any wreathing. *a* **1650** *Guye of Gisborne* 126 in Furniv. *Percy Folio* II. 233 Robin hoode shott it better then hee, for he cloue the good *pricke wande. **1765** *Percy Reliques* I. Gloss., *Pricke-wand*, a wand set up for a mark. **1875** Knight *Dict. Mech.*, **Prick-wheel* (Saddlery), a tool used to prick off the work for the harness-stitcher.

prick (prɪk), *v.* Forms: see A. below. [Late OE. *prician*, pa. t. **pricode*, ME. *prikie(n*, *prīke*, pa. t. *prikede*: cognate with OE. *prica*, prick *sb.* Cf. Icel. *prika* (1394) to stab slightly, Norw. *prika* (*preeka*); also MLG., LG., EFris., Du. *prikken*, MDu. *prikken, pricken*, WFris. *prykje*, Wang. *prikje*, NFris. *pricken*; also Da. *prikke*, Sw. *pricka*, Norw. *prikka* (from LG.), all pointing to WGer. doublet forms **prikôjan* and **prikkôjan*. Cf. also pritch *v.*, representing an OE. **pricc(e)an* (found in *apriccan*):—WGer. **prikjan*.

Like the sb., the verb appears to belong peculiarly to the Low German domain, being evidenced first in OE., and next in MLG.; it was prob. in OLG., OFris., and ODu. From LG. it seems to have passed into Scandinavian. Perh. from an onomatopœic root *prik*, expressing the action and sound of piercing abruptly stopped. In the later *prikke*, *pricke*, the *kk*, *ck* was perh. merely graphic, to show the short vowel. The form *prēke* appears to be a northern development of *prĭcian*; but the 14–15th c. *prīke*, *pryke* point to an OE. *prīcian*; cf. WFris. *prykje* = *prīkje*. But cf. also *pīke*, *pyke* as parallel form of *pik*, *pikk*, pick *v.* and *sb.*]

A. Illustration of Forms.

α. 1 prician; 2–4 prikie(n, (4 prykie, -kye); 2–5 prike, 4–5 pryke; (5 *pr. pple.* pricande).

c **1000** Prician [see B. 1]. *c* **1000** Ælfric *Gram.* xxviii. (Z.) 174 *Pungo*, ic pricige. —— Priciað [see B. 4]. *a* **1050** *Liber Scintill.* lxi. (1889) 188 Pricigende eaȝe utȝelæt tearas & se þe pricaþ heortan. *c* **1200** *Trin. Coll. Hom.* 205 þornene helm.. him swiþe prikede. **1297** R. Glouc. (Rolls) 9415 þat hor fon toward hom ne come prikie vaste. **13..** *Guy Warw.* (A.) 899 þe douke come prikiand on his stede. *c* **1386** Chaucer *Friar's T.* 296 So priketh [*v.rr.* prykyth, prickeþ] it in my side. **1387** Trevisa *Higden* (Rolls) IV. 211 He was i-priked & i-dryve in idel. *Ibid.* VII. 35 þanne he gan to pryke his hors. *Ibid.* VIII. 251 He hadde leve..to prike a coursere. **1393** Langl. *P. Pl.* C. v. 24 Thenne conscience on hus capel comsed to prykie [*v. r.* prike]. *c* **1400** *Sowdone Bab.* 42 Whan kynde corage begynneth to pryke [*rime* like]. *Ibid.* 1383 He priked forth. *c* **1400** *Laud Troy Bk.* 6631 Theseus..come thedur pricande sone. *c* **1440** *Jacob's Well* 154 Whanne on pryketh an-oþer. *c* **1440** Prike [see B. 19]. **1483** *Cath. Angl.* 291/2 To Pryke.

β. 4–5 prik, pryk; 4 prikke, 5 prykkyn; 4–7 pricke (5–6 prycke(-n)); 6– prick.

13.. *Gaw. & Gr. Knt.* 2049 Hym lyst prik for poynt. *c* **1325** *Poem Times Edw. II* (Percy Soc.) 7 He pricket out on hys contre. *c* **1375** *Sc. Leg. Saints* iv. 299 He gert fele knychtis..pryk efter þame. **1402** Hoccleve *Lett. Cupid* 106 Now prikke on fast. *c* **1470** Henryson *Mor. Fab.* IV. (*Fox's Conf.*) xxii, The fox he prikkit fast vnto the eird. *c* **1470** *Gol. & Gaw.* 539 To..prik in your presence, to purchese his pray. *c* **1490** *Promp. Parv.* 413/1 (MS. H.) Prykkyn, or poynten, *puncto.* **1530** Palsgr. 432/2 This fellowe can bothe flatter and pricke. **1552** Huloet, Prycken, *agito*,..*stimulo*, ..Prycke wrytynges wyth a penne,..*dispungo.* **1562** J.

HEYWOOD *Prov. & Epigr.* (1867) 164 His prouender prickth him. **1579** GOSSON *Sch. Abuse, To Gentlew.* (Arb.) 58 Wanton wil begins to prick. **1597** MORLEY *Introd. Must.* 58 As they are commonly prickt now. **1638** JUNIUS *Paint. Ancients* 103 He did pricke on the other.

γ. 4–6 prek(e; 5–6 preik, 6 preak; 8–9 (*dial.*) preek.

c **1375** *Sc. Leg. Saints* v. (*Johannes*) 430 [He] come prekand in sic degre. **1375** (MS. 1487) BARBOUR *Bruce* XVI. 615 Prek we apon thame hardely. **1387** TREVISA *Higden* (Rolls) VIII. 287 Slow hym so wiþ prekynge and wiþ hunger. *c* **1400** *Melayne* 999 Prekande one a stede. *a* **1400–50** *Alexander* 3483 A powere of þe Persens..On kyng Porrus to preke. *c* **1475** *Rauf Coilȝear* 410 Out of Paris proudly he preikit. **1535** STEWART *Cron. Scot.* (Rolls) I. 362 Thair preikand on the plane. *a* **1572** KNOX *Hist. Ref.* Wks. 1846 I. 86 To provok gready and imprudent men to preak at thame. **1825** JAMIESON, Preek. **1894** [see B. 20].

B. Signification.

I. To pierce, or indent with a sharp point.

1. a. *trans.* To pierce slightly, make a minute hole in (a surface or body) with a fine or sharp point; to puncture; hence, to wound (or hurt) with or as with a pointed instrument or weapon; in *Shooting*, to wound or disable (a game bird) by shooting: PRICKED *ppl. a.* 1 c. Said also of the instrument. Also *fig.*

c **1000** ÆLFRIC *Hom.* (Th.) II. 312 He..het..ðæs papan lima ȝelome prician, oðþæt he swulte ðurh swylcum pinungum. *c* **1200** [see A. a]. **1382** WYCLIF *Rev.* i. 7 Thei that pungeden [*gloss* or prickeden] him. **1426** LYDG. *De Guil. Pilgr.* 14165 Lyk a bladdere..Pryke yt with a poynt, a-noon, And ffarwel, al the wynd ys gon. *c* **1440** *Alphabet of Tales* 446 þai myght not be wakynd with no maner of criyng, nor þai myght fele nothyng sore and þai had bene nevur so prykkid. **1530** PALSGR. 666/1, I pricke with a sharpe nedell, or pynne, or thorne. **1621** QUARLES *Esther* Div. Poems (1717) 45 A bubble full of care, Which (prickt by death) straight enters into Air. **1626** BACON *Sylva* §326 Take an Apple, &c. and pricke it with a Pinne full of Holes, not deepe. **1667** PEPYS *Diary* 18 Aug., I could perceive her to take pins out of her pocket to prick me. **1688** R. HOLME *Armoury* III. iii. 86/1 *Prick the Loafe*, is to make little holes on the top of the Loafe with a Bodkin. **1789** BRAND *Hist. Newcastle* II. 679 By the wetness of the rods they [the borers] know when any feeder of water is pricked. **1888** LADY D. HARDY *Dang. Exper.* II. v. 66 A tall thin church spire pricked the skies. **1900** 'BLAGDON' *Shooting* 89 Too often, when cover is deficient and birds are consequently difficult to approach, there is a tendency to take long shots at birds which are really beyond sporting range, with the result that a large number of birds are 'pricked', or slightly wounded, without being brought to bag. **1916** *Shooting Don'ts* 39 Don't 'brown' into a covey. To be continually killing more than one bird at a shot will make you suspected. It results in a waste of birds, on account of the number that get 'pricked', and die.

b. To make (a hole or mark) by pricking.

[*a* **1023** WULFSTAN *Hom.* xxx. 146 þonne man ænne prican apricce on anum bradum brede.] **1680** MOXON *Mech. Exerc.* No. 12. 214 Prick there an Hole for a mark. *Mod.* Prick a hole in it with a pin.

c. *Farriery.* To pierce the foot of (a horse) to the quick in shoeing, causing lameness.

1591 FLORIO *2nd Fruites* 35, I will goe hyre a horse, for mine was so prickt yesterdaie, that he can not goe. **1592** GREENE *Blacke Booke's Messenger* Wks. (Grosart) XI. 19 His horse..halted right downe:..I wondered at it, and thought he was prickt. **1622** FLETCHER & MASS. *Span. Curate* III. ii, You shall have the tenth horse I prick, to pray for. **1725** BRADLEY *Fam. Dict.* s.v. *Prickt*, By the negligence or unskilfulness of the farrier they are prick'd in driving the nails. **1831** YOUATT *Horse* 304 No one who considers the thinness of the crust..will blame him [the smith] for sometimes pricking the horse.

d. To detect (a witch) by pricking her skin until a spot was discovered which did not bleed. *Hist.*

[Cf. **1627** R. BERNARD *Guide Grand Jurymen* xviii. 219 This [witches' mark] is insensible, and being pricked will not bleede.] **1661** in Pitcairn *Crim. Trials* III. 602 The Magistrat and Minister caused Johne Kinkaid, the comon pricker, to prik hir, and found tuo marks upon hir, which he called the Devill his markis. [Cf. quot. 1895 in 4 b.]

e. To affect with a sensation as of pricking.

1398 TREVISA *Barth. De P.R.* v. xxxviii. (Bodl. MS.), 3if it [evil meat or drink] picceþ and prickeþ þe stommake, it is yp[i]chched and ipricked and compelleþ it to passe oute. *Mod. colloq.* I don't like soda-water; it pricks my mouth.

f. To convert by puncturing *into* something.

1830 TENNYSON *Talking Oak* 69, I swear (and else may insects prick Each leaf into a gall).

2. *fig.* To cause sharp mental pain to; to sting with sorrow or remorse; to grieve, pain, torment, vex. Also *absol.*

a **1050** *Liber Scintill.* xvi. (1889) 79 He nys ȝepricud [*stimulatus*] on unrotnysse gyltes. *a* **1340** HAMPOLE *Psalter* iv. 5 If þai pryk vs in forthynkynge of oure synne. *a* **1400–50** *Alexander* 2628 þe pite of þe Persens him prickis in his saule. **1530** PALSGR. 666/1 As any displeasure pricketh one at the herte. **1694** F. BRAGGE *Disc. Parables* XIII. 445 Let those who find themselves pricked by what is now said take care that their religion be more pure. **1874** L. STEPHEN *Hours in Library* (1892) I. i. 15 His conscience pricks him so much that he cannot rest.

†**3.** To sting or bite, as a serpent, an insect, or the like. Also *absol.* *Obs.*

c **1200** *Trin. Coll. Hom.* 191 Neddre..attreð hwat heo prikeð. **1484** CAXTON *Fables of Æsop* IV. iii, The scorpion.. prycketh sore with his taylle. **1687** A. LOVELL tr. *Thevenot's Trav.* I. 260 There are always swarms of them [insects] buzzing about People, and continually pricking of them.

4. a. *intr.* To perform the action of pricking or piercing; to cause a pricking sensation; also, to have the quality of pricking, to be prickly or sharp.

c **1000** ÆLFRIC *Hom.* (Th.) II. 88 Ðornas priciað. *c* **1200** *Trin. Coll. Hom.* 207 þe þornes swiðe prikeden. *c* **1386** CHAUCER *Merch. T.* 391 Thanne is..no thyng may me displese Saue o thyng priketh in my conscience. **1546** J. HEYWOOD *Prov.* (1867) 77 It pricketh betymes that will be a good thorne. **1625** BACON *Ess., Revenge* (Arb.) 502 It is but like the Thorn, or Bryar, which prick, and scratch, because they can doe no other. **1872** TENNYSON *Gareth & Lyn.* 191 At times the spires and turrets half-way down Prick'd thro' the mist. *Mod.* Give me something to prick with. The leaves are acute, but they do not prick.

b. In various pregnant uses and phrases.

to prick for, to try, choose, or decide for something by pricking (cf. sense 15); also *fig.* ***to prick for a soft plank*** (*Naut.*): see quot. 1867. † ***to prick for witches***, to prick suspected persons with a pin, to find out, by their sensibility or insensibility to the pain, whether they were witches; cf. 1 d. ***to prick (in) the belt, garter, loop***, to play at FAST-AND-LOOSE; cf. GARTER *sb.* 7, LOOP *sb.*[1] 1. † ***to prick in (on, upon) a clout***, to do needlework, to sew. See also phraseological derivatives below.

1584 LYLY *Campaspe* v. iv, The one pricking in cloutes haue nothing els to thinke on. **1594** —— *Moth. Bomb.* I. iii, My daughter..shall prick on a clout till her fingers ake. **1615** CROOKE *Body of Man* 274 Women..liue an idle and sedentarie life, pricking for the most part vppon a clout. **1758** GOLDSM. *Mem. Protestant* (1895) II. 229 Players at Slight of Hand; others who invite the ignorant to prick in the Belt. **1828** *Times* 23 Aug., [A grave-digger] so well acquainted with the ground, crowded as it was, that he could prick for room in little or no time. **1836** DISRAELI *Runnymede Lett.* (1885) 176 To arrange a whitebait dinner at Blackwall, or prick for an excursion to Richmond or Beulah Spa. **1867** SMYTH *Sailor's Word-bk.*, *Pricking for a soft plank*, selecting a place on the deck for sleeping upon. **1895** J. CHAMBERLAIN *Sp. Ho. Comm.* 14 May, There were witch-finders in the Middle Ages who pricked for witches.

5. a. *intr.* To thrust *at* something as if to pierce it, to make a thrust or stab *at*. Also *fig.*

c **1470** HENRY *Wallace* VI. 473 Sum brak a pott, sum pyrlit [*v.r.* prikkit] at his E. **1560** DAUS tr. *Sleidane's Comm.* 257 Who can doubt any longer, but that you pricke at relygion? **1837** CARLYLE *Fr. Rev.* III. II. i, Thus Marat..is, as the Debate goes on, prickt at again by some dextrous Girondin. **1863** MRS. OLIPHANT *Chron. Carl., Salem Ch.* xv. 255 All his own duties pricked at his heart with bitter reminders in that moment.

†**b.** *Archery.* To shoot at a 'prick' or target; hence *fig.* to aim *at*. *Obs.*

1545 ASCHAM *Toxoph.* (Arb.) 106 This prayse belongeth to stronge shootinge and drawinge of mightye bowes, not to prickinge, and nere shootinge. *c* **1555** HARPSFIELD *Divorce Hen. VIII* (Camden) 94 His authors..roved far from the mark they should prick at. **1622** DRAYTON *Poly-olb.* xxvi. 331 With Broad-arrow, or But, or Prick, or Rouing Shaft, At Markes full fortie score, they vs'd to Prick, and Roue.

6. a. *intr.* or *absol.* Of a hare: To make a track in running.

c **1410**, etc. [see PRICKING *vbl. sb.* 2]. **1602** *2nd Pt. Return fr. Parnass.* II. v. 937 By that I knewe that they had the hare, ..and by and by I might see him sore and resore, prick and reprick. **1632** GUILLIM *Heraldry* III. xiv (ed. 2) 176 For when she [a hare]..Beateth the plaine high-waie where you may yet perceiue her footing, it is said she..Pricketh. *a* **1700** B. E. *Dict. Cant. Crew*, *Pricketh*, the Footing of a Hare on the hard Highway, when it can be perceived.

b. *trans.* To look for or find the 'pricks' of (a hare); to trace or track (a hare) by its footprints. Also *absol.* or *intr.*

c **1386**, etc. [see PRICKING *vbl. sb.* 2]. *a* **1673** J. CARYL in Spurgeon *Treas. Dav.* Ps. xvii. 11 Hunters, who go poring upon the ground to prick the hare, or to find the print of the hare's claw. **1678** DRYDEN *Limberham* IV. i, You have been pricking up and down here upon a cold scent. **1756** *Connoisseur* No. 105 ¶7 We were often delayed by trying if we could prick a hare. **1828** *Craven Gloss.* (ed. 2), *Prick*, to trace a hare by its footsteps. **1886** ELWORTHY *W. Somerset Word-bk.* s.v., To examine the mud in a gate-way or road to see if a hare has passed, is to 'prick the hare'.

7. *intr.* To have a sensation of being pricked; to tingle.

1850 TENNYSON *In Mem.* l, When the blood creeps, and the nerves prick And tingle. **1868** BROWNING *Ring & Bk.* III. 55 Her palsied limb 'gan prick and promise life At touch o' the bedclothes merely.

8. *intr.* Of wine, beer, etc.: To become or begin to be sour; to be touched or tainted with acetous fermentation; to be just 'turned': = F. *se piquer.* Cf. PRICKED *ppl. a.* 2.

1594 PLAT *Jewell-ho.* III. 66 If they [wines] pricke a little they haue a decoction of honie. **1651** HOWELL *Venice* 30 By reason of the over delicatnes therof it cannot brook the Sea any long time, but it will prick. **1703** *Art & Myst. Vintners* 67 Draw half your Wine into another Butt; then take your Lags of all sorts that do not prick, and so much Syrup as will not prick.

II. To urge with a sharp point or spur.

9. *trans.* To urge forward (a beast) with a goad (*obs.*); to spur (a horse) (*arch.*).

c **1290** *S. Eng. Leg.* I. 61/249 An Asse..is..I-priked and i-scourget. **13..** *Sir Beues* (A.) 229 þo prikede is stede sire Gii. *a* **1485** *Promp. Parv.* 413/2 (MS.S.) Prikkyn, or punchyn, as men doþ beestis, *pungo*. **1530** PALSGR. 666/1, I pricke an oxe, or any other beest with a gade. **1600** HOLLAND *Livy* IX. xxvii. 334 The Romane horsemen pricked and gallopped their horses to flanke them. **1737** [S. BERINGTON] *G. di Lucca's Mem.* (1738) 76 Short Goads to prick on their Dromedaries. **1753** CHAMBERS *Cycl. Supp.*, *Prick*, or *Pinch*, in the manege, is to give a horse a gentle touch of the spur, without clapping them hard to him. **1893** BARING-GOULD *Cheap-Jack Z.* I. vii. 102 He pricked his horse on, but she held to the bridle and arrested it.

10. *fig.* **a.** To drive or urge as with a spur; to impel, instigate, incite, stimulate, provoke. *arch.*

a **1225–1340** [see PRICKING *vbl. sb.* 4]. *c* **1385** CHAUCER *L.G.W.* 1192 (*Dido*) So prikyth hire this newe iolye wo. *c* **1386** —— *Prol.* 11 So priketh hem nature in hir corages. **1526** *Pilgr. Perf.* (W. de W. 1531) 59 b, Now prycked or stered by the consyderacion of his feruent loue. **1568** *Jacob & Esau* v. iv. in Hazl. *Dodsley* II. 251 Well, nature pricketh me some remorse on thee to have. **1609** HOLLAND *Amm. Marcell.* XIV. i. 2 The Queene ever at his elbow to pricke and proke him forward. **1675** tr. *Camden's Hist. Eliz.* IV. (1688) 622 His perverse Obstinacy..did so prick her forward to use Severity. **1868** LOWELL *Willows* Poet. Wks. (1879) 375 Pricked on by knightly spur of female eyes. **1871** R. ELLIS *Catullus* lxiii. 76 Let a fury, a frenzy prick him to return to the wood again.

†**b.** Phr. ***provender pricks*** (a horse, etc.): abundance of food stimulates and makes high-spirited.

(Cf. Ger. *der hafer sticht ihn* in similar use.)

1546 J. HEYWOOD *Prov.* (1867) 27 When prouander prickt them a little tyne. **1550** CROWLEY *Way to Wealth* B ij b, The paisant knaues be to welthy, prouender pricketh them. **1658** T. WALL *God's Revenge agst. Enemies Ch.* 58 Profit pricks forward zeal, as provender does the Ass. *a* **1688** BUNYAN *Exp. Gen.* Wks. 1861 II. 494/1 When provender pricks us, we are apt to be as the horse or mule, that is without understanding.

11. a. *intr.* To spur or urge a horse on; to ride fast; hence, to ride, advance on horseback. *arch.*

c **1290** *S. Eng. Leg.* I. 415/423 Wel i-Armed þe maister cam prikie and ride fast. **1340–70** *Alisaunder* 382 þei putt þem in perril & prikeden aboute. **1362** LANGL. *P. Pl.* A. II. 164 Soþnesse..prikede on his palfrey and passede hem alle. *c* **1400** MAUNDEV. (1839) xxiii. 249 Als wel on hors bak, prikynge, as on fote rennynge. **1470–85** MALORY *Arthur* XIV. v. 647 Anone the yoman came pryckynge after as fast as euer he myghte. **1590** SPENSER *F.Q.* I. i. 1 A gentle Knight was pricking on the plaine. **1667** MILTON *P.L.* II. 536 Before each Van Pric forth the Aerie Knights, and couch thir spears. **1808** SCOTT *Marm.* I. xix, For here be some have pricked as far On Scottish ground as to Dunbar. **1884** J. PAYNE *Tales fr. Arabic* I. 283 Presently, I espied a horseman pricking after me.

†**b.** *intr.* Also said of a horse; and in allit. phr. ***to prick and prance***, of either rider or horse. *Obs.*

1390 GOWER *Conf.* III. 41 Wherof this man was wonder glad, And goth to prike and prance aboute. *c* **1420** *Pallad. on Husb.* IV. 878 So thewed that..Anoon they [foals] may be stered forto prike. *c* **1440** LYDG. *Hors, Shepe, & G.* 344 The Goos may gagle, the hors may prike & praunce. *c* **1441** *Pol. Poems* (Rolls) II. 208 Now I lyste nother to pryke nor praunce; My pryde ys put to poverté. **1590** NASHE *Pasquil's Apol.* I. E j b, I trust they shall see me pricke it, and praunce it, like a Caualiero.

†**12.** ***to prick fast upon***, to approach closely (a time or age); ***to prick near***, to approach closely in attainment or quality. Cf. PRICK *sb.* 2 b, 9.

1565 T. STAPLETON *Fortr. Faith* 15 b, Euer sence the faith hath ben knowen and preached.., which pricketh nowe fast vpon a thousand yeares. *a* **1566** R. EDWARDES *Damon & Pithias* in Hazl. *Dodsley* IV. 92 It pricketh fast upon noon. **1580** GOLDING in Baret *Alv.* To Rdr. xii, It would pricke neere the learned tungs in strength. **1586** J. HOOKER *Hist. Irel.* in *Holinshed* II. 88/1 You may growe to..that hoary winter, on which you see me your father fast pricking.

III. To mark by or with pricks or dots.

13. a. *trans.* To write or set down (music) by means of 'pricks' or notes (*arch.*); also, to write music in (a book) (*obs.*). Also *absol.* or *intr.*

c **1325** *Song Deo Gratias* 6 in *E.E. Poems* (1862) 124, I seiȝ a clerk a boke forthe brynge, þat prikked was in Mony a plas, Fast he souht what he schulde synge. **1463**, *a* **1509**, *c* **1520**, etc. [see PRICKED *ppl. a.* 3, PRICKING *vbl. sb.* 6]. **1549** *Ludlow Churchw. Acc.* (Camden) 39 For paper to pryk songes in for the churche..ijd. **1598** DALLINGTON *Meth. Trav.* V ij b, The Italian hath a prouerbe:..The French neither pronounce as they write, nor sing as they pricke, nor thinke as they speake. **1623** *Cheque Bk. Chapel Royal* (Camden) 58 For pricking of a sett of bookes..iij li. iij s...for pricking in the bookes iij li. xij s. **1668** PEPYS *Diary* 24 Mar., To my chamber, to prick out my song 'It is Decreed'. **1765** WESLEY *Wks.* (1872) XIV. 330 They [tunes] are pricked true, exactly as I desire all our congregations may sing them. **1826** SCOTT *Woodst.* iii, A book having some airs pricked down in it.

b. To write out bell-changes in figures, thus: 123, 132, 312, 321, 231, 213, etc.

1843 LE FEVRE *Life Trav. Phys.* I. I. viii. 178 Who can prick the peal of bells—the bobs and treble bobs?

†**14.** To write down; to note or jot down; to record in writing. *Obs.*

c **1400** *Destr. Troy* 418 Als put is in poisé and prikkit be Ouyd.

15. To mark or indicate by a 'prick'; *esp.* to mark (a name, or an item) in a list by making a 'prick' through or against it; hence, to mark off or tick off in this way; *spec.* (of the sovereign) to select (persons) for the office of sheriff from a list by this means; whence of other appointments; also, to appoint, choose, pick *out*. Also ***prick down, off***, etc.

1557 RECORDE *Whetst.* K ij, First I set theim downe and pricke theim, as here doeth appeare 18766224. **1577** HARRISON *England* II. iv. (1877) I. 99 The prince.. foorthwith pricketh some such one of them..who herevpon is shiriffe of that shire for one whole year. **1599** B. JONSON *Cynthia's Rev.* v. ii, Why did the ladies pricke out mee? I am sure there were other gallants. **1654** WHITLOCK *Zootomia* 538 Known he is sure, that is pricked down for one of the Judges of the twelve Tribes of Israel. **1788** J. BEVERLEY *Cerem. Univ. Cambr.* 14 Election of the Caput... The Proctors nominate only, unless they prick as

Representatives of their Masters. *Ibid.* 15 Each Person is to prick only one of the three nominated for each Faculty. **1853** JERDAN *Autobiog.* III. vi. 68 My friend was pricked as High Sheriff of the county. **1861** HUGHES *Tom Brown at Oxf.* vii, What do you think of that fellow..offering..the junior servitor..a bribe of ten pounds to prick him in at chapel when he isn't there? **1907** W. TUCKWELL *Remin. Oxford* viii. 107 J. G. Wood..was a Bible clerk of Merton,..who pricked Chapel attendance and said grace.

16. To mark or trace something on (a surface) by pricks or dots; esp. ***to prick the chart*** (†*card, plot*): see quots.; also, to mark or trace (a position, direction, design, etc.) on a surface by pricks or dots (in quot. 1665–76, with pegs). Also ***prick off, out.***

1598 FLORIO *Dict.* To Rdr. bj, I was but one..to sit at sterne, to pricke my carde, to watch vpon the vpper decke. **1627** CAPT. SMITH *Seaman's Gram.* xv. 73 To learne to..know the tides, your Roomes, pricke your Card, say your Compasse. **1665–76** REA *Flora* (ed. 2) 5 Prick down a line eight or ten foot long. **1669** STURMY *Mariner's Mag.* IV. xv. 196 To find the Latitude, Rhomb, and Longitude, and..to prick the same down in a Blank Chart. **1704** J. HARRIS *Lex. Techn.* I. s.v., To prick the Chart or Plot at Sea, signifies to make a Point in their Chart whereabout the Ship is now. **1867** SMYTH *Sailor's Word-bk.*, *Pricking her off*, marking a ship's position upon a chart by the help of a scale and compasses. **1872** *Routledge's Ev. Boy's Ann.* 95/2 The lights of the eyes..must all be pricked out with a fine needle. **1875** SIR T. SEATON *Fret Cutting* 144 With a very fine steel point prick out lightly the whole pattern.

†**17.** To insert the points or stops in (a writing, etc.); to punctuate, point. *Obs. rare*$^{-1}$.

1637 HEYLIN *Answ. to Burton* 161 This is the place at large, so pricked and commade..in the said old booke.

IV. To put into some position or condition by piercing or transfixing.

†**18.** To stick, fix, or impale (anything) *on* the point of an instrument. *Obs.*

c **1420** *Anturs of Arth.* ix. (Irel. MS.), Opon the chefe of hur cholle, A padok prykette [*v.rr.* pikes, pykit] on a polle. *c* **1559** R. HALL *Life Fisher* xii. (1655) 211 The head..was pricked upon a pole and set on high upon London Bridge. **16..** *Childe Maurice* xxviii. in Child *Ballads* IV. (1886) 266/1 Child Maurice head he did cleeue And he pricked itt on his swords poynt. **1615** G. SANDYS *Trav.* 27 The cookes, who..slicing it into little gobbets, prick it on a prog of iron, and hang it in a fornace. **1683** MOXON *Mech. Exerc.*, *Printing* xi. ¶23 They..prick the Oynion fast upon the end of a small long Stick.

†**19.** To secure or fasten with a pin or skewer, or the like; to pin, skewer. *Obs.*

c **1440** *York Myst.* xiii. 303 Gadir..now all oure gere; Slike poure wede as we were, And prike þam in a pak. *c* **1450** *Two Cookery-bks.* 82 Take a prik, and prik him [stuffed pig] togidur, And lete him roste. **1596** SHAKS. *Tam. Shr.* III. ii. 70 An old hat, and the humor of forty fancies prickt in't for a feather. **1647** J. LAWNIND *Putney Projects* 46 To Sit..like so many Plovers pricked down for stales. **1780** FORBES *Dominie* III. 14 The clout about me shou'd be pricked At the kirk-door. **1819** W. TENNANT *Papistry Storm'd* IV. (1827) 133 The warden's trunk-hose to his fecket Wi' gowden corken-priens was pricket.

20. To attire (a person) with clothes and ornaments fastened by pins, bodkins, etc.; to attire elaborately, dress *up*. Now *dial.*

c **1340** [see PRICKING *vbl. sb.* 7]. **1522** *World & Child* in Hazl. *Dodsley* I. 244, I am nat worthily wrapped nor went, But poorly pricked in poverty. *c* **1540** HEYWOOD *Four P.P.* ibid. 351 But prick them [women] and pin them as nice as ye will, And yet will they look for pinning still. **1599** MASSINGER, etc. *Old Law* II. i, Pricked up in clothes, Why should we fear our rising? **1638** BRATHWAIT *Barnabees Jrnl.* I. (1818) 27 On earth she only wished To be painted, pricked, kissed. **1790** D. MORISON *Poems* 81 Ne'er price a weardless, wanton elf, That nought but pricks an' prins herself. **1894** *Northumbld. Gloss.*, *Preek*, to adorn. 'She's a' preeked up wi' ribbons an' laces.'

†**21.** To remove, or bring into some position, by pricking. *Obs.*

1573–80 BARET *Alv.* P 706 *Oculis punctu erutis*, eies pricked out. *Ibid.* 709 To pricke out crowes eies, *configere cornicum oculos.* **1592** SHAKS. *Rom. & Jul.* I. iv. 66 A small ..Gnat, Not halfe so bigge as a round little Worme, Prickt from the Lazie-finger of a man. **1645** HARWOOD *Loyal Subj. Retiring-room* 3 Please you to observe the comfortable lessons I shall prick out of it. **1683** MOXON *Mech. Exerc.*, *Printing* xvii. ¶3 If the Matrice be too thin on the right or left side, or both; They prick up that side,..and so raise a Bur upon that side.

22. To plant (seedlings, etc.) in small holes made by piercing the ground at suitable intervals. Const. †*forth, in, out, off.* Also, ***to prick in*** (manure): see quot. 1847.

1627 tr. *Bacon's Life & Death* (1651) 13 A young Slip or Cions..if it be pricked into the Ground. **1664** EVELYN *Kal. Hort., Mar.* (1729) 194 Prick them forth at distances. *Ibid.*, *Aug.* 215 Prick out your Seedlings. **1712** J. JAMES tr. *Le Blond's Gardening* 179 Make a Hole..at every Foot distance, and throw a Nut or Acorn into it; after which, you fill up the Hole again..; which is called pricking Fruit into the Ground. **1789** *Ann. Agric.* XI. 51 My first parcel [of seeds] was pricked in upon a small garden bed. **1847** MRS. LOUDON *Amateur Gardener* 85/2 Rotten hotbed dung is..merely 'pricked in', as gardeners term it, that is, incorporated only with the top stratum of the soil. **1851** GLENNY *Handbk. Fl. Gard.* 22 The seedlings, when grown enough, may be pricked out into small pots. **1854** *Jrnl. R. Agric. Soc.* XV. II. 408 Cabbage plants are pricked in in March. **1882** *Garden* 21 Jan. 48/3 The most critical time with seedling ferns is when they require pricking off for the first time. **1913** J. WEATHERS *Twentieth-Cent. Gardening* vii. 67 Annuals sown under glass are first of all 'pricked out' into other pots or boxes when large enough to handle. **1935** A. G. L. HELLYER *Pract. Gardening* v. 46 Seeds..should not be very close together unless it is certain that time will be available to 'prick' them out. **1952** C. E. L. PHILLIPS *Small Garden* vi. 55 When the youngsters have developed their first pair of true leaves, prick them off into other boxes or pots. **1977** 'E. PETERS' *Morbid Taste for Bones* i. 8 He was content to help Brother Cadfael prick out early lettuces.

23. ***to prick up*** (in plastering on laths): to scratch or score the surface of the first coat so as to afford a hold for the next; hence, to lay on the first coat which is afterwards so scored.

1778 [see PRICKING *vbl. sb.* 9]. **1823** P. NICHOLSON *Pract. Build.* 373 Pricking-up is similar to laying, but is used as a preliminary to a more perfect kind of work. *Ibid.* 392 *Pricking-up*, in plastering, the first coating of three-coat work upon laths. **1873** E. SPON *Workshop Rec.* Ser. I. 122/1 The wall is first pricked up with a coat of lime and hair.

24. To propel (a punt) by pushing with a pole on the ground under the water; to punt.

1891 *Daily News* 26 May 4/8 A man or woman who cannot run or prick a punt, scull, or handle a Canadian canoe, is regarded as an outsider by his or her friends.

V. To insert or stick as a point.

25. To thrust or stick (a pointed object) *into* something; to set, fix, or insert by the point; to stick *in, on.* Also *fig.* ? *Obs.*

c **1430** *Two Cookery-bks.* 36 Ley .iij. lechys on a dysshe, & on euery leche prycke .iij. Almaundys. *c* **1450** *Mankind* 30 in *Macro Plays* 2 Pryke not yowur felycytes in thyngis transytorye! *c* **1460** *Play Sacram.* 468 *Stage direct.*, Here shalle yᵉ iiij Jewys pryk yᵉʳ daggeris in iiij qua[r]ters þus sayng. **1594** SIR G. CAREY in I. H. Jeayes *Catal. Charters Berkeley Castle* (1892) 335 The findinge of his picteur framed in wax, with one of his owne heares prict directely in the hart therof. **1611** COTGR. s.v. *Passage*, So tender that a pinne pricked into it cannot fetch it vp any height. **1669** WORLIDGE *Syst. Agric.* (1681) 245 Observe also, that you prick small Sticks, in manner of a Hedge, cross-wise, athwart all the other by-passages.

26. To stick (something) *full of*, or set (it) *with* pointed objects or points; hence, to stud, mark, or dot *with* something. ? *Obs.*

1530 PALSGR. 666/1, I pricke full of bowes, as we do a place or a horse whan we go a mayeng, *je rame.* **1584** COGAN *Haven Health* (1636) 141 If it be pricked with cloves it is the better. **1856** MRS. BROWNING *Aur. Leigh* I. 275 Brown hair pricked with gray. **1861** L. L. NOBLE *Icebergs* 139 Belle Isle, a rocky, blue mass, with a wavy out-line, rising from the purple main pricked with icebergs.

VI. To stick up as or in a point.

27. To raise or erect, as the ear of an animal when on the alert or listening; hence, of a person, ***to prick up one's ears***, to become attentive or alert to listen.

1587 TURBERV. *Trag. T.* (1837) 200 And prickt his plumes to please his Ladies eyes. *a* **1591** H. SMITH *Wks.* (1866–7) I. 207 To put a pedlar's shop upon their backs, and colour their faces, and prick their ruffs, and frizzle their hair. *a* **1626** BACON *Ess.*, *Fame* (Arb.) 579 She pricks up so many Ears. **1682** BUNYAN *Holy War* i, At this the town of Mansoul began to prick up its ears. **1697** DRYDEN *Virg. Georg.* III. 132 The fiery Courser, when he hears..the Shouts of War, Pricks up his Ears. **1826** J. W. CROKER *Diary* 26 Oct., I pricked up the ears of curiosity at this exordium. **1858** R. S. SURTEES *Ask Mamma* li, The roused hounds prick their ears.

28. a. *intr.* ***to prick up***, to rise or stand erect with the point directed upward; to point or stick up.

[**1610**, **1614**: see PRICKING *ppl. a.* 4.]
1657 W. MORICE *Coena quasi Κοινή* v. 55 The full ear [of corn] hangs the head, when the empty pricks up. **1763** J. CLUBBE *Misc. Tracts, Physiognomy* (1770) I. 22 Their heads were both under water, but that the tips of their ears just pricked up above it. **1887** BESANT *The World went* xv, His ears..prick up at the sound of a fiddle. **1905** *Blackw. Mag.* Sept. 321/2 The spires of churches are to be seen pricking up through the greenery.

b. ***to prick out***, to come into view as specks or points.

1930 R. MACAULAY *Staying with Relations* xx. 305 By two o'clock a few stars had pricked out, tiny candles shaking between the drifting gloom of clouds.

VII. 29. Phraseological derivatives. ***prick-(in-)the-garter, -the-loop***, sb. phr., one who plays the game of fast-and-loose: see 4b; also, the game itself; ***prick-the-clout*** adj. phr., tailoring. Also PRICKLOUSE.

1763 *Brit. Mag.* IV. 548 *Prick in the Garter,..a knave well known By silly rusticks,—when their money's gone; For near his side, to make the cheat go down, Stands his accomplice, like a simple clown, Who pricks, and ev'ry time is sure to win; But if another pricks—he's taken in. *a* **1861** R. RAE in W. Hunter *Biggar & Ho. Fleming* iii. (1867) 37 To prick-the-garter gaed the law. **1886** WILLOCK *Rosetty Ends* xxi. (1887) 154 The money-sellin' dodge, or the three-card trick, or prick-the-garter, or the pea-an'-thummils. **1891** R. FORD *Thistledown* xvi. 313 *Prick-the-loops, wha are sae familiar wi' the hangman's loop that they've turned the idea into business, and set up wi' their garter. **1824** SCOTT *Redgauntlet* Let. xii, Ye *prick-the-clout loon.

prick (prɪk), *a. rare.* Also 5–6 prik. [Only in reference to ears; app. by resolution of the compound PRICK-EARED.] Pricked up, erect and pointed.

a **1449** W. BOWER in *Fordun's Scotichronicon* (1759) II. XIV. xxxi. 376 Wyth prik 3oukand eeris, as the awsk gleg. **1513** DOUGLAS *Æneis* IV. v. 20 Als mony has scho prik wpstandand eris. **1889** GORDON STABLES *Dog Owners' Kennel Comp.* v. §11. 59 The hard-haired Scotch terrier... Ears very small, prick or half prick, but never drop.

†**pri'ckado.** *Obs. rare*$^{-1}$. [f. PRICK *v.* + -ADO.] A piercing or stab (of the sword).

1592 KYD *Sol. & Pers.* II. ii. 21 With that they drew, and there Ferdinando had the prickado.

†**prickal.** *Obs.* [app. for *prick-aul*; cf. PRITCH-AULE.] See quot.

1688 R. HOLME *Armoury* III. 273/2 (Upholsterer's tools) A Prickal..is a kind of Aul with a great Box or other hard Wooden head.

†**'prickant,** *a. Obs. rare.* [Humorous f. PRICK *v.* + -ANT[1], after heraldic terms in *-ant.*]

1. Pricking or riding; errant.

1611 BEAUM. & FL. *Knt. Burn. Pest.* II. ii, What knight is that,..ask him if he keep The passage bound by love of Lady fair, Or else but prickant.

2. Pricking up or out.

1611 BEAUM. & FL. *Knt. Burn. Pest.* III. ii, Without his door doth hang A copper bason, on a prickant spear. **1633** MARMION *Fine Companion* II. v, They are three asses rampant, with their ears prickant.

prick-bill. [f. PRICK *v.* + BILL *sb.*[3]] At Christ Church, Oxford, One of the junior students to whom was given the task of pricking off on a printed list the names of undergraduates attending chapel.

1825 C. M. WESTMACOTT *Eng. Spy* I. 174 Another visit from the prick bill. **1853** 'L. CARROLL' *Diary* 15 Oct. in *Life & Lett.* (1898) 53 Found I had got the prickbills two hundred lines apiece for not pricking in in the morning. **1879** SIMMONS *Lay Folks Mass Bk.* 371 *note.*

'prick-,ear, prick ear. [app. a back-formation from PRICK-EARED, q.v.]

1. *pl.* The erect pointed ears of some beasts, *spec.* of dogs; ears that are pricked up or stand erect; hence *fig.* those of a person on the alert to hear: cf. PRICK *v.* 27.

1634 T. JOHNSON *Parey's Chirurg.* 1004 Having two hornes, pricke ears, and armes. **1652** GAULE *Magastrom.* 184 *Prick-eares* [presage or note] a medler. **1839** C. KNIGHT *Pict. Shaks., Hen. V.* 340/2 A portrait of the Esquimaux dog, which strikingly exhibits the prick ear. **1853** KINGSLEY *Hypatia* xxi, The faithful Bran, whose lop-ears and heavy jaws, unique in that land of prick-ears and fox-noses, formed the absorbing subject of conversation.

b. The ears of a person when conspicuous by naturally standing out, or by having the hair cut short, as those of a 'Roundhead': cf. sense 2 and PRICK-EARED 2.

1641 BRATHWAIT *Merc. Brit.* IV, How these..round heads with their prick eares doe listen. **1650** BULWER *Anthropomet.* (1653) 158 Wee of this Nation..affect a small Eare, standing close to the Head... Our Eares are naturally extant and looke forward..all which commodities our mickle-wise Mothers defraud us of by their nice dislike of Lugs, and as they call them in reproach, Prick-eares. **1685** CROWNE *Sir C. Nice* II. 16 Hot. Sirrah, if you be a Presbyterian, I'le kick you down Stairs.., woe be to your prickears, Sirrah.

2. A person having prick-ears; one whose ears are conspicuous; †a nickname for a Puritan (see PRICK-EARED 2, and cf. ROUNDHEAD).

1642 *Grand Plutoes Remonstr.* Title-p., How far he differs from Round-head, Rattle-head or Prick-eare.

b. (*prick-ears.*) One of a breed of pigs characterized by erect ears. *dial.*

1830 *Cumbld. Farm Rep.* 57 in *Libr. Usef. Knowl., Husb.* III, What are provincially called the 'prick ears', a well made, short-legged animal of its kind.

prick-eared ('prɪk,ɪəd), *a.* [app. f. PRICK *sb.* (branch V) + EARED: see Note below.]

1. a. Having erect ears: *spec.* of dogs. Also, of corn or wheat.

c **1420** ? LYDG. *Assembly of Gods* 328 And at hys feete lay a prykeryd curre. **1523** FITZHERB. *Husb.* §77 The .ix. propertyes of a foxe. The fyrste is: to be prycke eared, the seconde to be lytell eared. **1599** SHAKS. *Hen. V*, II. i. 44 Pish for thee, Island dogge: thou prickeard cur of Island. **1607** TOPSELL *Four-f. Beasts* (1658) 285 By this..you may make any lave-ear'd Horse, to be as prick-ear'd and comely, as any other Horse whatsoever. **1637** G. DANIEL *Genius Isle* 23 Here the ffawnes And prick-ear'd Satires shall your Groves frequent. *a* **1873** S. WILBERFORCE *Ess.* (1874) I. 45 Any prick-eared tree-inhabiting monkey. **1877** GORDON STABLES *Pract. Kennel Guide* (ed. 3) vii. §3. 81 Dogs both prick-eared and drooping are often found in the same litter. **1922** BLUNDEN *Shepherd* 81 From the young corn the prick-eared leverets stare At strangers come to spy the land. **1940** C. DAY LEWIS tr. *Virgil's Georgics* I. 25 The dangers of showery spring, When the prick-eared harvest already bristles along the plains. **1946** L. B. LYON *Rough Walk Home* 11 Prick-eared, he lurks To leeward, patiently bold.

†**b.** Applied opprobriously (with pun) to prick-song. *Obs.*

1519 *Interl. Four Elem.* (Percy Soc.) 50 For me thynkyth it servyth for no thyng, All suche pevysh prykeryd song! Pes, man, pryksong may not be dispysyd.

c. *fig.* Having the ears pricked or erected in attention; hence, attentive, alert.

1550 BALE *Apol.* 141 b, These prycke eared prynces myghte truste those vowers, as hawkes made to theyr handes. **1608** MIDDLETON *Mad World* III. ii. 181 Jealousy is prick-eared, and will hear the wagging of a hair. **1682** H. MORE *Annot. Glanvill's Lux O.* 184 The prick-eared Acuteness of that trim and smug saying. **1897** S. S. SPRIGGE *T. Wakley* I. 500 A prick-eared public official.

2. Of a man: Having the hair cut short and close, so that the ears are prominent; a nickname applied in the 17th century to the Puritans or 'Roundheads'; whence opprobriously, priggish.

1641 in Rushw. *Hist. Coll.* III. (1692) I. 482 The said Captain Hide said,..that they were a company of prick eared and cropt eared Rascals, and that he would believe a Papist before a Puritan. *a* **1700** B. E. *Dict. Cant. Crew, Prickear'd Fellow*, a Crop, whose Ears are longer than his Hair. **1707** HEARNE *Collect.* 21 Nov. (O.H.S.) II. 74 These Prickear'd, starch, sanctify'd Fellows. **1752** FOOTE *Taste* II. Wks. 1799 I. 21, I adore the simplicity of the antients! How unlike the present, priggish, prick ear'd puppets! **1872** GEO. ELIOT *Middlem.* xvi, Fred Vincy had called Lydgate a prig, and now Mr. Chicheley was inclined to call him prick-eared.

[*Note.* Of *prick-eared*, *prick* adj., *prick-ear(s*, *pricked* or *prickt ear(s*, *to prick the ears*, the first is much the earliest, and is app. to be compared with such formations as *block-headed*, *bow-legged*, *club-footed*, *club-shaped*, and the like, in which the first element is a sb., the sense being 'eared (i.e. having ears) like pricks', in some early sense of PRICK sb., e.g. 12, 13, or 14. Of the other expressions, *prick ear(s* is prob. a back formation from *prick-eared*, on the analogy of *club foot*, *club-footed*, and the like, and *pricked ears*, *to prick the ears* derived from it.]

pricked (prɪkt, 'prɪkɪd), *ppl. a.*

I. [f. PRICK *v.* + -ED^1.] **1. a.** Pierced with pricks or with a prick; punctured; wounded by pricking; *spec.* of a horse: see PRICK *v.* 1 c.

1467 in *Charter of Selby Abbey* (Brit. Mus. Addit. Ch. 45, 861), 1 panem album vocatum Prikkedlof [in ch. of 1324 brochee, 1433 brochet]. **1597** A. M. tr. *Guillemeau's Fr. Chirurg.* 30/2 The wounde of the pricked synnue. **1855** MACAULAY *Hist. Eng.* xx. IV. 503 The money bags shrink like pricked bladders. **1898** P. MANSON *Trop. Diseases* iii. 71 Malarial blood..does not flow freely from the pricked finger.

b. *spec.* In plastering, ***pricked up***: see PRICK *v.* 23.

1825 J. NICHOLSON *Operat. Mechanic* 619 Over the pricked-up coat of lime and hair. **1832** *Encycl. Brit.* (ed. 7) V. 679/2 When the pricked up coat is..dry.., preparations may be made for the floating.

c. Of a game bird or part of a bird: wounded or disabled by shooting. Also *transf.*

1937 *Discovery* Dec. 385/1 Wounded or pricked birds left about the place are numerous. **1940** N. M. SEDGWICK *Young Shot* v. 45 The guns should carefully mark where game falls, ..where..a bird with a pricked wing comes down. **1952** *Chambers's Jrnl.* Apr. 212/1 Thereafter, for days, a salmon was seen constantly to move in the one place, and gradually I became certain that it was one and the same fish that had twice been lost. Never did any of us visit the Island but there it was, rolling up every few minutes as so often a pricked fish will. **1958** R. WADDINGTON *Grouse* ix. 105 Very high grouse mean many pricked birds and the moor in general is the sufferer.

2. Of liquor: Turned or tending to turn sour. (Cf. PRICK *v.* 8.) Also *fig.* [= F. *piqué* (*vin piqué*, 'vin qui tend à se transformer en vinaigre', Littré).]

1678 BUTLER *Hud.* III. i. 696 And turn as eager as prick'd Wine. *a* **1700** B. E. *Dict. Cant. Crew*, *Prickt*, decayed Wine, tending to Sower. **1743** *Lond. & Country Brew.* II. (ed. 2) 108 Which will occasion the Whole [ale] to become sometimes only pricked, or just tainted. **1834** HOOD *Tylney Hall* (1840) 3 Technically speaking her temper was a little pricked. **1845** DISRAELI *Sybil* III. ii, Making the Vicar.. praise a bottle of Burgundy that he knew was pricked. **1886** ELWORTHY *W. Somerset Word-bk.*, *Pricked*, or *Prilled*, turned sour; said of any liquid turning acid.

3. Formed of, traced or written in pricks or dots; dotted; written; *spec.* in *Pottery*, ornamented with designs traced in dots. ***pricked song***: see PRICK-SONG.

1463–1606 [see PRICK-SONG 1 *a*]. *c* **1520** *Bk. Mayd Emlyn* 33 in Hazl. *E.P.P.* IV. 84 We do nought togyder, But prycked balades synge. **1532** MORE *Confut. Tindale* Wks. 405/2 The clergie of the realme haue burned vp their false prycked bookes. **1669** STURMY *Mariner's Mag.* IV. xi. 180 Draw the prickt Line NS. **1748** *Anson's Voy.* II. vi. 192 In the plan..the road..is marked out by a prickt line. **1820** M. EDGEWORTH *Let.* 20 Dec. (1971) 226, I think the pricked map upon the whole better out and have seen the proof sheets and left it out. **1880** in L. Higgin *Handbk. Embroidery* 107 Designs..on pricked paper. **1900** F. JACKSON *Hist. Hand-Made Lace* 216 *Pricked*, the term used in pillow lace-making to denote the special marking out of the pattern upon parchment. **1927** 'R. CROMPTON' *William—in Trouble* v. 119 Half a dozen Italian stamps..turned out..to be 'pricked' and useless for collections. **1933** *Burlington Mag.* Jan. 43/1 There are pricked designs for figures which can be identified on vestments still existing. **1967** *Daily Tel.* 1 Feb. 13/2 Making lace borders, using a pricked parchment pattern, and placing pins in the holes, which control the completed stitches.

4. Produced or obtained by pricking.

1901 *Munsey's Mag.* XXV. 644/1 A pricked drop of blood from a wild animal injected into a healthy tame animal would cause it to fall sick of *nagana*.

5. Erect; pointed upright; set *up*, cocked *up*.

1579 SPENSER *Sheph. Cal.* Feb. 72 So smirke, so smoothe, his pricked eares. **1741** *Compl. Fam.-Piece* II. i. 304 A Kind of Dog..with prickt Ears. **1842** J. WILSON *Chr. North* I. 39 A smallish, reddish-brown, sharp-nosed animal, with pricked-up ears. **1898** *Bk. of Dogs* 62 [The Pomeranian] has sharp features and pricked ears.

6. ***pricked-out***, of seedlings, planted out in a bed after being moved from the trays or boxes in which the seeds were germinated.

1938 G. GREENE *Brighton Rock* IV. 154 The small pricked-out plants irritated him like ignorance. **1975** *Country Life* 13 Feb. 388/3 Space the picked-out seedlings at seven by four.

II. [f. PRICK *sb.* + -ED^2.]

†**7.** Having a prick or point; pointed, tapering; prickly, sharp; bearing prickets; furnished with a sting. *Obs.*

c **1400** MAUNDEV. (Roxb.) ii. 6 Whyte and prikked..as thornes. **1552** HULOET, Prycked or stynged, *aculeatus.* **1584** in Feuillerat *Revels Q. Eliz.* (1908) 368, iii prickt candle-stickes.

†**8.** Furnished with a prick or pricks; dotted.

1665 PEPYS *Diary* 23 Apr., Every barr to end in a pricked crochet and quaver. **1667** C. SIMPSON *Compend. Pract. Mus.* 24 Here you have a Prickt-Crochet (or Crochet with a Prick after it). **1715** *Phil. Trans.* XXIX. 204 Prickt Letters never signify Moments, unless when they are multiplied by the Moment *o* either exprest or understood to make them infinitely little.

pricker ('prɪkə(r)). Also 4–5 prikiere, -yere, prikere, 5–6 preker, *Sc.* -ar. [f. PRICK *v.* (ME. *prikie*) + -ER^1.] One who or that which pricks.

1. a. One who pricks or goads; †*spec.* one who professed to discover if a woman were a witch by sticking pins into her: see PRICK *v.* 1 d. Also *fig.* One who incites, provokes, or stimulates.

1382 WYCLIF *Jer.* xlvi. 20 The prickere fro the north [Vulg. *stimulator ab aquilone*] shal come to hir. **1552** HULOET, Prycker or stynger, *stigator.* **1565** COOPER *Thesaurus*, *Stimulator*..a pricker or stirrer forwarde. **1661** [see PRICK *v.* 1 d]. **1836** SIR W. HAMILTON *Discuss.* (1852) 330 For a few holders of the plough, there are many prickers of the oxen. **1865** GEO. ELIOT *Ess.*, *Infl. Rationalism* (1884) 211 It was the regular profession of men called 'prickers' to thrust long pins into the body of a suspected witch in order to detect the insensible spot which was the infallible sign of her guilt.

b. A northern name for the Basking-shark (BASKING *ppl. a.* 2), from its habit of lying at the surface with its back-fin projecting. Also (*dial.*) applied to some species of dog-fish.

1701 BRAND *Descr. Orkney* i. 4 When before Peterhead we saw the fins of a great Fish, about a yard above the Water, which they call a Pricker. **1890** P. H. EMERSON *Wild Life on Tidal Water* xxiii. 99 All we got out of a mass of weed and mud..[were] two prickers, and an old mussel.

2. One who spurs or rides a horse; a rider, a horseman; hence, a mounted warrior or soldier; *esp.* a light horseman employed as a skirmisher or scout; also, a mounted moss-trooper, a 'rider'. *arch.* and *Hist.*

1362 LANGL. *P. Pl.* A. x. 8 A proud prikere [C. XI. 134 prikyere] of Fraunce, *princeps huius mundi.* **1377** *Ibid.* B. x. 308 Ac now is religioun a ryder..A priker on a palfray. ? *a* **1400** *Morte Arth.* 355 Send prekers to þe price toune, and plaunte there my segge. **1519** HORMAN *Vulg.* 258 The pryckers be gone to spye, what oure ennemyes go aboute. *a* **1572** KNOX *Hist. Ref.* Wks. 1846 I. 210 The Erle of Warwik and the Lord Gray..perceaving the host to be molested with the Scotishe preakaris. *a* **1600** *King & Barker* 30 in Hazl. *E.P.P.* I. 5 A preker abowt..yn maney a contre. *a* **1639** SPOTTISWOOD *Hist. Ch. Scot.* VI. (1655) 401 Iohnston ..after the Border fashion, sent forth some prickers to ride, and make provocation. **1785** GROSE in *Archæologia* (1787) VIII. 113 This sort of spur [having only one very long and very thick point] was worn by a body of light horsemen in the reign of Henry VIII. thence called prickers. **1808** SCOTT *Marm.* v. xvii, Northumbrian prickers wild and rude. **1894** TWEEDIE *Arabian Horse* III. i. 165 What the cleverest collie is to the Cheviot shepherd gives but a faint idea of what his mare is to the desert pricker.

3. *spec.* A mounted attendant at a hunt, a huntsman. Now chiefly in YEOMAN ***pricker***.

1575 TURBERV. *Venerie* 103 If the hart be accompanyed with any other deare, then the pricker on horsebacke must ryde full in the face of him, to trie if he can part them or not. **1586** T. RANDOLPH in Ellis *Orig. Lett.* Ser. II. III. 123 To lend him..a cowple of her Majesties Yeomen prickers and a cowple of the Groomes of the Leese. **1616** BULLOKAR *Eng. Expos.*, *Pricker*, a Huntsman on horse-backe. **1760** R. HEBER *Horse Matches* ix. 23, 50 l. was run for, free only for the Huntsmen, Yeomen Prickers, and Keepers of Windsor Forest. **1837** CARLYLE *Fr. Rev.* I. I. ii, Who is it that the King..now guides? His own huntsmen and prickers. **1891** *Daily News* 12 June 3/1 At Ascot..the Royal procession.. was headed by Lord Coventry, the Master of the Buckhounds, and the whips and yeomen prickers in their picturesque uniform of green and scarlet.

4. a. An instrument or tool for pricking or piercing.

14.. *Nom.* in Wr.-Wülcker 682/37 *Hoc punctorium*, a prykker. **1806** HUTTON *Course Math.* I. 80 With the point of a fine pin or pricker, prick through all the corners of the plan to be copied. **1875** SIR T. SEATON *Fret Cutting* 145 One of the best instruments to use as a pricker is a bit of a knitting needle put into a stout handle, and ground to a fine point.

b. in many specific applications; as

(*a*) An awl; a brad-awl (cf. PRICKAL); in *Sail-making*, a tool for making holes in sails. (*b*) A goad; a spur. (*c*) A priming-iron. (*d*) In *Blasting*, A metal rod which is placed in the drill-hole during the packing of the charge, leaving when it is withdrawn a touch-hole for firing. (*e*) A fork or prong used in handling sugar; also, a two-pronged fork used in handling blubber. (*f*) A surgical instrument. (*g*) A toothed tool or wheel used for marking equidistant holes for stitching leather, etc. (*h*) A climbing-iron. (*i*) A slender iron rod used in sounding bogs, probing for sunken timber, or the like. (*j*) In some organs, A small upright rod beneath the front end of each of the manual keys, which, when the key is pressed down, transmits the motion to other parts of the mechanism so as to open the valve and admit air to the pipe.

1611 FLORIO, *Agúcchia*,..amongst gunners a pricker or [priming] iron. **1649** G. DANIEL *Trinarch.*, *Hen. IV*, cclxxxviii, The Sharpest prickers for his vse, To drive the Restive Lords. **1678** MOXON *Mech. Exerc.* No. 6. 111 *Pricker* is vulgarly called an Awl. **1688** R. HOLME *Armoury* III. xxii. (Roxb.) 280/1 Sugar Boylers Instruments... A Lofe Pricker or a small Pricker. It much resembles the Shoomakers or Sadlers Aule.., being a long slender Iron sharp pointed, set in a wooden round head or haft hooped at the bottom. **1747** HOOSON *Miner's Dict.* s.v., It is best..to put a little Clay on the top of the hole, upon the Raming fast about the Pricker. **1788** W. MARSHALL *Yorksh.* Gloss. (E.D.S.), *Pricker*, a brad-awl. **1794** *Rigging & Seamanship* I. 88 *Pricker*, a small instrument, like a marline-spike.., to make the holes with. **1824** MANDER *Derbyshire Miner's Gloss.* 54 The Pricker is then withdrawn, and a straw filled with gun-powder, is placed in the hole in its stead, which communicates with the powder in the Chamber. **1836** *Uncle Philip's Convers. Whale Fishery* 42 The pricker..is used in packing the blubber in casks. **1842** S. LOVER *Handy Andy* iii, Dick poking the touch-hole of the pistol with a pricker. **1852** SEIDEL *Organ* 64 These prickers are small pieces of wood a few inches long and one third of an inch thick. **1858** SIMMONDS *Dict. Trade*, *Pricker*,..a toothed instrument used by workmen for stabbing or marking leather, paper, &c. **1869** G. LAWSON *Dis. Eye* (1874) 150 If an iridectomy has to be performed, instead of tearing through the lens capsule with the ordinary pricker, a pair of fine iris forceps is introduced through the corneal wound. **1875** KNIGHT *Dict. Mech.*, *Pricker*, 5. (*Saddlery*)...*b.* A tool used to mark stitch-holes so as to render them uniform in distance. *Ibid.*, *Pricker*, 4. a long slender iron rod used for probing or sounding the depth of a bog or quicksand. **18..** *Ann. Philad. & Pennsylv.* II. 20 (Cent.) He had iron prickers to the hands and feet to aid in climbing lofty trees.

c. Phr. ***to get*** (or ***have***) ***the pricker***: to become (or be) angry. *Austral.* and *N.Z. slang.*

1945 BAKER *Austral. Lang.* vi. 121 A man in a temper is said..*to have the dingbats, the pricker* or *the stirks.* **1955** D. NILAND *Shiralee* 102 You've got the pricker properly, eh? You'll knock him into next week, will ya? **1959** G. SLATTER *Gun in my Hand* viii. 91 You'll come a gutzer son I ses... Got the pricker with me.

†**5.** A pricket candlestick: see PRICKET 2. *Obs.* *rare*$^{-1}$.

1552 *Inv. Ch. Surrey* (1869) 89 Item v candilstyckes ij pryckers and ij standardes and one with ij sockes and a pryckett in the myddes.

pricket ('prɪkɪt). Forms: 4–6 prik(k)-, pryk-, prek-, prick-; -et, -ett, -ette, 5– pricket; also (chiefly *Sc.*) 5 pre-, prycate, 6 prekat(te, priccate, (7 ? proket). [app. ad. med. (Anglo-) L. *prikettus* (13th c.), f. Eng. *prike*, PRICK *sb.* + Rom. suffix *-ettus*, *-etto*, -ET^1.]

1. A buck in its second year, having straight unbranched horns. ***pricket's sister***, a female fallow deer in its second year. Cf. BROCKET.

[**1285** *Close Roll 14 Edw. I*, m. 8 (P.R.O.), Capiendo vnam damam et vnum Prikettum de Ceruo... De quibus quidem dama et Priketto iidem Robertus et Johannes indictati sunt.] *c* **1440** *Promp. Parv.* 413/1 Pryket, beest, *capriolus.* **1486** *Bk. St. Albans* E iv, The secunde yere a preket. **1579** SPENSER *Sheph. Cal.* Dec. 27, I..ioyed oft to chace the trembling Pricket. **1657** *Verney Mem.* (1894) III. 409 Non but dows and faunes and prickets and prickets sisters..tuenty shillins a peece for all thees. **1772** R. GRAVES *Spir. Quix.* (1820) II. 209. **1859** *Todd's Cycl.* V. 518/1 At the second year the ..'pricket' puts forth a simple 'dag'.

†**b.** *transf.* A boy. *Obs.*

1582 STANYHURST *Æneis* IV. (Arb.) 97 You with your pricket [orig. *tuque puerque tuus*] purchast loa the victorye famouse. **1782** ELPHINSTON tr. *Martial* IV. I. xxvii. 180 Their industry industrious to deride, The pricket points the bed; but not the side.

c. The straight unbranched horn of a buck or young stag; a dag. *rare.*

1855 SWAINSON *Quadrupeds* 296 The bucks..never bear other than prickets, or single dags on the head.

2. A spike on which to stick a candle; hence, ***pricket candlestick***, a candlestick having one or more of these.

c **1420** *Anturs of Arth.* 451 (Thornton MS.) Preketes [*Douce MS.* torches, *Irel. MS.* troches] and brokettes, and standertis by-twene. *c* **1440** *Promp. Parv.* 413/1 Pryket, of candylstykke, or other lyke, *stiga.* **1534** *Inv. Wardr. Kath. Arragon* 41 in *Camden Misc.* (1855), Syxe candil-styckes.. wherof ij. with prickettes and iiij. withe sockettis. **1552** *Inv. Ch. Surrey* (1869) 24 Item ij small prykett candel-sticks. **1859** JEPHSON *Brittany* xii. 195 The thicker end [of the taper] was hollowed out for the convenience of sticking on the pricket. **1884** A. J. BUTLER *Coptic Ch. Egypt* I. 82 The picture is mounted in a frame: before it is fixed a little beam set with a row of prickets for candles. **1886** MORSE *Jap. Homes* IV. 220 In England the pricket candlestick went out of use a few centuries ago; in Japan it is still retained.

†**3.** A candle or taper (orig. such as was stuck on a pricket candlestick). *Obs.*

a **1331** *MS. Cott. Galba E. iv.* lf. 45 Item parui torticii minores de tribus filis qui vocantur prikettes coram priore in cena...viij. priketti ponderant vnam libram cere. **1398** TREVISA *Barth. De P.R.* VI. xxiv. (Tollem. MS.) Candelis and oþer priketis beþ set on candelstikkis, and chaundelers. **1432** [see PERCHER^2]. **1527** in *Visit. Southwell* (Camden) 129, iij or iiij poundes of prikketts to burne also abowte my herse. **1557–75** *Diurn. Occurr.* (Bannatyne Cl.) 103 All the barronis and gentilmen bure priccattis of waix. *a* **1639** SPOTTISWOOD *Hist. Ch. Scot.* IV. (1655) 197 Walking betwixt two ranks of Barons and Gentlemen..holding every one a proket [? preket] of wax in their hands.

†**4.** A small prick or spike; a thorn, a prickle.

1682 WHELER *Greece* I. 7 Each leaf ended with a Pricket.

†**5.** A pinnacle or spire; a pointed finial. *Obs.*

c **1600** in A. Maxwell *Hist. Old Dundee* (1884) 150 Ane steeple and pricket of ashler wark upon the east neuk and cunyie. **1652** URQUHART *Jewel* Wks. (1834) 196 Outjetting of kernels, erecting of prickets, barbicans, and such like various structures. **1717** *Records of Elgin* (New Spald. Cl.) I. 397 The Contract with the masons for the four vaults of the tolbooth and the pricket was £1000 Sc.

†**6.** A chrysalis. *Obs. rare*$^{-1}$.

1707 MORTIMER *Husb.* (1721) I. 327 To prevent their numerous increase on Trees gather them off in Winter, taking away the Prickets which cleave to the Branches, and burn them.

7. An old name of the Stonecrops, *Sedum acre*, *S. album*, and *S. reflexum*; = PRICK-MADAM.

[? From the awl-shaped leaves, or the biting taste of *S. acre*.]

1611 COTGR. s.v. *Ioubarbe, Petite Ioubarbe*, the male Prickmadame, or Sengreene the lesser; also, Mousetaile, Pricket, Stonehore, little Stonecrop, Wall-pepper, Countrey-pepper, Iacke of the Butterie. **1866** *Treas. Bot.*, Pricket, or Prick-madam, *Sedum acre, album*, and *reflexum*.

pricking ('prɪkɪŋ), *vbl. sb.* [f. PRICK *v.* + -ING[1].] The action of the verb PRICK.

1. a. Piercing, puncturing, wounding: see the verb. With *a* and *pl.*, an instance of this.

1382 WYCLIF *Lev.* xix. 28 Upon the deed ʒe shulen not kitte ʒoure flesh, ne eny . . pryckyngis ʒe shulen make to ʒow. **1607** TOPSELL *Four-f. B.* (1658) 475 By thorns and prickings of bushes. **1762** GOLDSM. *Nash* Wks. (Globe) 545/2 Country men are deceived by gamblers, at a game called Pricking in the Belt, or the old Nob. **1899** *Allbutt's Syst. Med.* VIII. 768 The exudation of sebum after pricking is of importance.

b. The sensation of, or as of, being pricked or wounded; smarting, tingling. Phr. ***pricking of*** (or ***in***) ***one's thumbs***, used in various constructions with allusion to quot. 1605: an intuitive feeling or hunch; a premonition, a foreboding.

c **1175** *Lamb. Hom.* 145 þer scal beon . . [dunge] wið-uten prikunge. **1495** *Trevisa's Barth. De P.R.* XVII. clxxxv. (W. de W.) 726 A dronklew mann feleth and is greuyd with sore pryckynge [*Bodl. MS.* picchinge] and aking in his heed. **1605** SHAKS *Macb.* IV. i. 44 By the pricking of my Thumbes, Something wicked this way comes. **1897** MARY KINGSLEY *W. Africa* 687 Producing terrible pricking and itching. **1935** 'G. ORWELL' *Clergyman's Daughter* i. 43 'I had a feeling I was going to meet you to-day.' 'By the pricking of your thumbs, I presume?' **1946** D. C. PEATTIE *Road of Naturalist* v. 52, I stood then on the back platform of the flying *Overland* with the knowledge that I had got into new terrain, not easily to be mastered, pricking in my thumbs. **1966** E. PALMER *Plains of Camdeboo* vi. 92 There should have been a pricking in our thumbs the morning we went to see the fossils, but we had no warning at all.

c. *fig.* The infliction of mental pain; grief, distress, sorrow; remorse, compunction, regret.

c **1000** ÆLFRIC *Hom.* (Th.) II. 88 Hi ða sawla toterað mid pricungum mislicra ʒeðohta. *c* **1400** *Destr. Troy* 2183 My payne with prickyng in hert. **1526** *Pilgr. Perf.* (W. de W. 1531) 127 Without drede or feare, scruple or pryckynge of conscyence. **1617** HIERON *Wks.* II. 328 To the pricking and astonishing of thy heart. **1815** W. H. IRELAND *Scribbleomania* 205 Those elected to this function Ne'er feel the prickings of compunction.

2. The footprint or track of a hare (rarely of other beasts). Hence, the tracking of a hare by its pricks or footprints; also † ***pricking forth***.

c **1386** CHAUCER *Prol.* 191 Of prikyng and of huntyng for the hare. *c* **1410** *Master of Game* (MS. Digby 182) xxxiv, Till she [a hare] be retreued, or þat . . he fynde her poyntynge, or pryckynge. **1575** TURBERV. *Venerie* 163 If he can finde the footing of the hare (which we call pricking). **1616** SURFL. & MARKH. *Country Farme* 696 By these traces or footsteps, he shall by little and little picke out which way she is gone, and this amongst hunts-men is called the pricking forth of the hare. **1630** BRATHWAIT *Eng. Gentlem.* (1641) 156 The prints and prickings of sundry sorts of beasts might easily be discerned. **1834** MEDWIN *Angler in Wales* I. 262 These tracks were sometimes lost . .; but by careful pricking, they were hit upon again.

3. The souring of wine or liquor.

c **1645** HOWELL *Lett.* (1650) I. 371 The length of the voyage makes them [wines] subject to pricking. **1799** G. SMITH *Laboratory* I. 432 To prevent wine from pricking.

4. The action of spurring or goading onward; instigation, incitement, provocation. Now *rare*.

a **1225** *Ancr. R.* 234 Seinte Powel hefde . . flesches prikiunge. *c* **1230** *Hali Meid.* 3 Wið hare pricunges of fleschliche fulðen. ? **12..** tr. *Charter of Æðelstan* in Birch *Cart. Sax.* II. 452 ʒelad by þe pricingge of ðe Haly Goste. **1340** *Ayenb.* 148 þe poudres efterward and prekiinde of harde wyþniminge. **1422** tr. *Secreta Secret., Priv. Priv.* 205 Ofte Prayer quynchyth the Pryckynges of vices. **1666** BUNYAN *Grace Ab.* 41, I did . . find in my mind a secret pricking forward thereto. **1882** *Daily Tel.* 12 Sept. 2/1 In former times there was a custom called pricking—a sailor got behind a boy and forced him up by digging into him with a sharp marlingspike.

†5. Spurring; galloping; riding. *Obs.*

c **1386** CHAUCER *Knt.'s T.* 1741 The heraudes lefte hir prikyng [*v.r.* prykynge, prikking] vp and doun. *c* **1440** *Promp. Parv.* 413/2 Prykynge, of hors, *cursitacio*. **1549** *Compl. Scot.* xiv. 114 In prikkyng contrar ther enemes. **1560** DAUS tr. *Sleidane's Comm.* 119b, When a benefice or prebende is fallen . . what busie suite, what gadding and prickyng vp and downe.

6. a. Marking or writing by means of pricks, dots, etc.; †chiefly of music: see PRICK *v.* 13 (*obs.*); appointing a sheriff: see PRICK *v.* 15; †in quot. 1532–3, figured ornamentation, embroidery (*obs.*).

a **1509** *Proverbs* in Grose *Antiq. Rep.* (1809) IV. 405 A songe myssoundithe yf the prickynge be not right. **1532–3** *Act 24 Hen. VIII*, c. 13 No manne vnder the degree of a barons soune . . shall weare any maner embrodery, prickyng or printing with golde, siluer, or other sylke. **1621** *Cheque Bk. Chapel Royal* (Camden) 10 For pricking of songes and for a new sett of bookes for the Chappell. **1699** WANLEY in *Lett. Lit. Men* (Camden) 273 The reducing of any Tune in that book to our way of pricking on five lines. **1755** CARTE *Hist. Eng.* IV. 464 It was now the usual time of the year for the Kings pricking of sheriffs. **1811** *Self Instructor* 116 By pricking over the book, is meant an examining every article of the Journal against the Ledger.

b. In *Palæography*, the piercing of a series of holes on a leaf to assist with the ruling of lines; a set of such holes.

1908 E. JOHNSTON *Writing & Illuminating* (ed. 2) vi. 110 The writing line dots are pricked through all the sheets by means of a fine awl or needle. . . See also *methods of ruling without pricking*. **1912** E. M. THOMPSON *Introd. Gk. & Lat. Palaeogr.* 55 In earlier MSS. these prickings are often found near the middle of the leaf. **1971** T. A. M. BISHOP *English Caroline Minuscule* p. xii, In English MSS. written after c. 900 the prickings for horizontal ruling are found only in outer lateral margins. **1973** *Bodl. Libr. Rec.* IX. 12 Prickings with an awl had been made along outer bounding-lines of four bifolia simultaneously with hair-sides up. **1976** *Codicologica* I. 78 Other aspects of the medieval book: the nature of parchment, ink, pricking, and ruling.

7. Fastening with a pin, etc.; dressing up, adornment; = PRINKING.

c **1340** HAMPOLE *Prose Tr.* 21 With in thi herte thynkynge, boostynge, and prikkynge and preysynge of thi silfe. **14..** *Voc.* in Wr.-Wülcker 583/31 *Fixura*, prykkynge or festenynge. **1550** LATIMER *Serm., Luke xii.* 15 (1562) 116b, Women . . haue muche pryckynge when they put on their cap. *Ibid.*, They would not make so muche pryckynge vp of theym selues as they dooe now a dayes.

8. *Hort.* The planting *out* or *off* of seedlings.

1796 C. MARSHALL *Garden.* xiv. (1813) 189 The pricking out the young plants . . when they are three or four days old. **1935** A. G. L. HELLYER *Pract. Gardening* v. 47 Pricking out should be done as soon as it becomes necessary. **1952** C. E. L. PHILLIPS *Small Garden* vi. 53 Pricking out simply means lifting the seedlings from this nursery bed . . and replanting them more widely somewhere else. **1976** *Abingdon Herald* 9 Dec. 5/2 A heating cable will enable you to carry on plants after pricking out.

9. ***pricking up*** (Plastering): see PRICK *v.* 23. Also *attrib.*

1778 LD. MAHON in *Phil. Trans.* LXVIII. 887 Common coarse lime and hair (such as generally serves for the pricking-up-coat in plastering). **1832** *Encycl. Brit.* (ed. 7) V. 678/2 In three-coat plastering on laths . . the first [coat] is called the pricking up. *Ibid.* 679/2 The first, or pricking up, is roughly laid on the laths, the principal object being to make the keying complete.

10. *attrib.* and *Comb.*: † **pricking-hat**, a riding hat; **pricking-iron** *Saddlery* (see quot. 1960); † **pricking-knife**, a carpenter's tool; **pricking-note**, a note of goods for shipment, on which the customs officer pricked each item as it was delivered on board, and on which the captain gave a receipt for the goods; † **pricking-pallet** (PALLET *sb.*[3]), a riding head-piece; **pricking-pole**, a pole with an iron point for propelling a boat; **pricking-up** *Basketry* (see quot. 1912); **pricking-wheel** = *prick-wheel* (see PRICK *sb.* 21).

1438 *Durham Chapter Munim., Misc. Charters* 5603, j *prekynghatt coopertum cum Welwete. **1441** *Plumpton Corr.* (Camden) p. liv, Either a prickinghate or a sallett upon their heads. **1904** P. N. HASLUCK *Saddlery & Harness-Making* (1962) II. i. 18 Fig. 32 shows a tool used in stamping the lines preparatory to stitching. These tools vary in width from three teeth, which are used only for round points and scalloped work, to twenty-four teeth for straight lines. . . (*caption*) Fig. 32.—*Pricking-iron. **1946** N. WYMER *Eng. Country Crafts* v. 47 From the start he was taught to keep his needle-holes as equidistant as possible, the length he must make each stitch being marked off for him on his leather by means of a pricking-iron. **1960** G. E. EVANS *Horse in Furrow* xvi. 206 On the cart-trace *back* decorative sewing . . was the rule. A *pricking iron*—a chisel-shaped implement with points or teeth at regular intervals on the blade—was first used to mark out the pattern and to ensure that the stitches were uniformly placed. **1975** J. H. L. SHIELDS *To handmake a Saddle* x. 42 The end to be stitched is then pricked with a No. 4 pricking iron. *c* **1500** *Debate Carpenter's Tools* in Halliwell *Nugæ Poet.* 15 Than bespake the *prykyng-knyfe, 'He duellys to nyʒe the ale-wyfe'. **1858** SIMMONDS *Dict. Trade*, **Pricking-note*, a form of custom-house order . . delivered by a shipper of goods to the searcher. **1412–20** LYDG. *Chron. Troy* III. xxii. (MS. Digby 230) lf. 102 b/2 His vauntbrace may be cured ner A *prikinge palet of plate þe kever. **1892** P. H. EMERSON *Son of Fens* xv. 153 Carry my *pricking-pole up. **1912** T. OKEY *Introd. Art of Basket-Making* 153 **Pricking up*, turning up the stakes after their insertion in the bottom with the point of the shop-knife to form the framework of the sides of a basket. **1959** D. WRIGHT *Baskets & Basketry* vi. 136 *Pricking-up*: turning up of willow stakes over the point of the knife after they have been inserted into the base. **1960** E. LEGG *Country Baskets* 93 The turning up of the stakes is done rather differently than with cane, the *pricking up* method being adopted.

pricking ('prɪkɪŋ), *ppl. a.* [f. PRICK *v.* + -ING[2].] That pricks, in various senses of the verb.

1. Causing a prick or puncture; piercing, prickly.

a **1225** *Ancr. R.* 134 Nest is herd, of prikinde þornes wiðuten, & wiðinnen nesche & softe. **1535** COVERDALE *Ezek.* xxviii. 24 She shal no more be a prickinge thorne, & an hurtinge brere vnto the house of Israel. **1604** E. G[RIMSTONE] *D'Acosta's Hist. Indies* IV. xxvi. 282 In a huske somewhat bigger, and more pricking than a chesnut. **1608** TOPSELL *Serpents* (1658) 639 With their pricking stings they [bees] grievously wound and torment.

b. *transf.* and *fig.* Producing the sensation of being pricked; having a wounding or paining effect on the feelings or mind; causing a sharp sudden pain; piercing; smarting.

1483 CAXTON *Gold. Leg.* 430/2 Kepyng hymself ryght curyously from the pryckyng sawtes and watche of the world the flesshe and the deuyll. **1528** PAYNEL *Salerne's Regim.* E j, Mylke . . is good agaynst prickynge humours in the entrayles. **1629** T. BROWNE in *Darcie's Ann. Q. Eliz.* II. 371 Marshall Byrone, who with pricking words wounded the Maiesty of the King, was now beheaded. **1656** RIDGLEY *Pract. Physick* 140 There is no pricking cold. **1834** J. FORBES *Laennec's Dis. Chest* (ed. 4) 473 Attended with pricking pains in the right side.

†2. That presses forward; keen, eager. *Obs.*

1575 *Appius & Virginia* in Hazl. *Dodsley* IV. 112 The pert and pricking prime of youth ought chastisement to have.

†3. Goading, stimulating. *Obs.*

1586 A. DAY *Eng. Secretary* I. (1625) 46 The Hortatorie and Dehortatorie are a little more vehement, stirring and pricking then the others.

4. Pointed or arrect, as an ear.

1610 B. JONSON *Masque of Oberon* 73 Stick our pricking ears With the pearl that Tethys wears. **1614** MARKHAM *Cheap Husb.* I. i. (1668) 2 A small thin ear short and pricking.

prickle ('prɪk(ə)l), *sb.*[1] Forms: 1 **pricels, pricel,** *inflected* **-ele, -le,** 4–5 **prykel, -yl,** 5 **-elle,** 5–6 **prikle,** 6 *Sc.* **prickil,** 6–7 **prickel, -ell,** 6– **prickle.** [OE. *pricel*, later form of *pricels*, f. stem *pric-* of *prician* to PRICK + instrumental suffix *-els* from earlier *-isl* = OHG. *-isli*:—WGer. **-islja*. Cf. MDu., MLG. *prickel, prēkel*, Du. *prikkel*, LG. *prickel* a prickle, sting, spur, etc. In later times the suffix was app. sometimes associated with the dim. *-el, -le* from Fr., and a *prickle* viewed as a small prick. See also PRITCHEL.]

†1. A thing to prick with; a goad. *Obs.*

a **1000** in *Aldhelm Gloss.* (Napier) 4228 and 4656 *Stimulis*, pricelsum. *c* **1000** *Ags. Gosp., Luke* Pref., Wið priclom eftdræʒend [L. *contra stimulos recalcitrantem*]. *c* **1330** R. BRUNNE *Chron. Wace* (Rolls) 16218 Penda poyned hym als a prykel. *c* **1400** *Laud Troy Bk.* 6578 Wel ney his flanke his strok he tecles, And strikes him with spere and pricles. *c* **1440** *Promp. Parv.* 413/1 Prykyl . ., *stimulus, aculeus*; idem quod pryk. **1570** LEVINS *Manip.* 121/41 A Prickle, *stimulus*. **1609** BIBLE (Douay) *Ecclus.* xxxviii. 26 That holdeth the plough, and glorieth in the goade, driveth oxen with the prickle, and converseth in their workes.

†2. A pricking or goading sensation. *Obs.*

a **1050** *Liber Scintill.* xviii. (1889) 87 þænne mid oferfylle wamb byð aþened pricelas [L. *aculei*] galnysse beoð awehte. *c* **1050** *Byrhtferth's Handboc* in *Anglia* (1885) VIII. 307 Ac seo ræding pingð þæne scoliere mid scearpum pricele. **1303** R. BRUNNE *Handl. Synne* 8485 Y fele a ful hard prykyl þat my flesshe temptel me mykyl.

†3. A small mark or character in writing; a jot, iota; a minute fraction, part, or particle; = PRICK *sb.* 3, 5. *Obs.* (Only OE.)

c **950** *Lindisf. Gosp.* Matt. v. 18 *Iota unum* [*gloss*] foruord *vel* pricle an *vel* enne, *aut unus apex* enne pricle *vel* stæfes heafod *non præteribit* ne forgæs. —— Luke xii. 59 Đone hlætmesto pricclu [*Rushw.* lætemestu pricla].

†4. The sting of an insect. *Obs.*

c **1412** HOCCLEVE *De Reg. Princ.* 3376 (Royal MS.) Senek seithe how the kyng and the leder Of bees prikles hathe he right none, . . Othir bees prikles han eueryehone.

5. A rigid sharp-pointed process developed from the bark or any part of the epidermis of a plant, consisting of a compound hair.

Botanically, a *prickle* differs from a *thorn* or *spine* in that it may be peeled off with the epidermis and does not grow from the wood of the plant; but popularly a prickle is a smaller or finer kind of prick or thorn, and the prickles of the rose are commonly called *thorns*.

c **1440** [see 1]. **1580** LYLY *Euphues* (Arb.) 388 Nettles . . haue no prickells, yet they sting. **1660** R. COKE *Power & Subj.* 63 No roses without prickles. *a* **1672** STERRY *Freed. Will* (1675) 157 It hath prickels to guard those Roses from rash and rude hands. **1776** WITHERING *Brit. Plants* (1796) II. 188 The prickles at the edge of the leaves . . readily distinguish this from the G[*alium*] *montanum*. **1870** HOOKER *Stud. Flora* 123 *Rosa canina* . . distinguished from *spinosissima* by its hooked prickles.

6. a. A hard-pointed spine or outgrowth of the epidermis of an animal, as in the hedgehog; formerly applied also to the quills of the porcupine.

1567 MAPLET *Gr. Forest* 89 Almost on euerie prickle or brestle he getteth an Apple or Grape. **1577** NORTHBROOKE *Dicing* (1843) 84 Histrix is a little beast with speckled prickles on his back. **1661** LOVELL *Hist. Anim. & Min.* 74 [The Urchin] of the Sea, drunk with the prickles, expelleth the stone. *Ibid.* 102 Porcupine. They have . . on the back and sides diverse coloured prickles. **1840** HOOD *Kilmansegg, Dream* xiv, He lies like a hedgehog roll'd up the wrong way, Tormenting himself with his prickles.

b. One of the minute spines on a prickle-cell.

1875 *Encycl. Brit.* I. 897/1 The cells . . next in order are polygonal, and not unfrequently possess pointed processes or prickles projecting from them, hence the name, *prickle cells*, employed by Schultze. **1899** *Allbutt's Syst. Med.* VIII. 881 The prickle cells in the neighbourhood of the lacunæ, which are found here and there over the papillæ, have lost their prickles.

7. *fig.* Something that pricks the mind or feelings. (Chiefly in *pl.*)

1638 BAKER tr. *Balzac's Lett.* (vol. II.) 128 The wisedome of the Cardinall will strip off all the thorny prickles of passion. **1682** DRYDEN *Medal* 148 The man who laughed but once . . Might laugh again to see a jury chaw The prickles of unpalatable law. **1705** tr. *Cowley's Plants* Wks. 1711 III. 364 The Rose has prickles, so has Love, Though these a little sharper prove.

†8. = FILE-FISH b. *Obs.*

1681 GREW *Musæum* I. v. iii. 113 The Prickle or longest File-Fish . . on the sides hinderly grows a little short Prickle upon the centre of every Scale.

9. *attrib.* and *Comb.*, as ***prickle-edge***; ***prickle-armed, -edged, -nosed, -shaped*** adjs.; † **prickle-apple** = PRICKLED *apple*; **prickle-cell** *Biol.*, a descriptive term applied to the round cells found in the deeper layers of stratified epithelium, bearing fibrils or minute spines; †**prickle-fish**, the stickleback; **prickle-layer**, the lowest layer of epidermis, made up of prickle-cells (Billings *Dict. Med.* 1890); †**prickle-palm** = *prickly palm* (PRICKLY *a.* 3); **prickle-tree**, the Spindle-tree: see EUONYMUS; **prickle-yellow**, prickly yellowwood: see PRICKLY 3.

1681 GREW *Musæum* II. I. ii. 186 Part of a *Prickle-Apple. .. The Fruit is remarkable for the several Tussucks or Bunches of Thorns wherewith it is armed all round about. *c* **1620** T. ROBINSON *Mary Magd.* I. 310 No thistle heere was seen, no *pricle-armed thorne. **1875** *Prickle-cell [see 6 b]. **1899** *Allbutt's Syst. Med.* VIII. 542 The prickle layer is thinned or absent, and the prickle cells flattened horizontally. **1962** BLAKE & TROTT *Periodontology* ii. 17 This epithelium consists of a few layers of prickle cells. **1974** R. M. KIRK et al. *Surgery* v. 72 Histologically the tumour is of the prickle-cell layer, invading the deeper tissues, and later spreading to the regional lymph glands. **1885-8** FAGGE & PYE-SMITH *Princ. Med.* (ed. 2) I. 119 Not infrequently some of the cells [of keratoid carcinoma] have *prickle-edges, exactly as in certain layers of the epidermis. **1857** GOSSE *Creation* 136 Its great *prickle-edged stiff leaves grow in long diagonal rows. **1668** CHARLETON *Onomast.* 144 *Atherina*..the *Prickle-fish. **1681** GREW *Musæum* I. VII. ii. 162 The *Prickle-Nos'd Beetle..hath only a small short Prickle. **1684** tr. *Bucaniers Amer.* 33 Another sort of these Palm-trees is called *Prickle-Palm..by reason it is infinitely full of prickles. **1776** WITHERING *Brit. Plants* (1796) IV. 105 Leaves..edged with *prickle-shaped substances the same as those on the surface. **1607** TOPSELL *Four-f. Beasts* (1658) 190 The *prickle or spindle tree (called also Euonymus).

Hence 'pricklet *nonce-wd.*, a minute prickle; †'**pricklish** *a.*, somewhat prickly.

1878 OGLE tr. *Kerner's Flowers & Unbidden Guests* iv. 76 The under side..being studded..with numerous sharp pricklets. **1698** J. PETIVER in *Phil. Trans.* XX. 328 The.. Leaves stand on a pricklish or rough Footstalk.

prickle ('prɪk(ə)l), *sb.*[2] [Derivation obscure.] A wicker basket, esp. for fruit or flowers. ? *Obs.*

1609 N. F. *Fruiterers Secrets* 17 When your baskets or prickels be ful. **1625** B. JONSON *Pan's Anniversary* 21 Rain roses still,..and fill Your fragrant prickles for a second shower. **1883** SYMONDS *Shaks. Predec.* ix. (1900) 278 Nymphs, carrying prickles, or open wicker baskets.

attrib. **1693** EVELYN *De la Quint. Compl. Gard.* II. 181 The prickle Baskets, and Hand-barrows should at this time be plyed with the greatest vigour and diligence.

b. Also used in specific senses: see quots.

1674 in Strype *Stow's Surv.* (1754) II. v. xxi. 415/1 For each Prickle or Basket, holding not above one Bushel, one Half-penny *per* Day. **1825** BROCKETT *N.C. Gloss., Prickle*, a basket or measure of wicker work among fruiterers. Formerly made of briers. Hence, perhaps, the name. **1851** MAYHEW *Lond. Labour* I. 27/2 The prickle is a brown willow basket, in which walnuts are imported..from the Continent; they are about thirty inches deep, and in bulk rather larger than a gallon measure; they are used only by the vendors of walnuts. **1858** SIMMONDS *Dict. Trade, Prickle*, a sieve of filberts, containing about ½ a cwt.

prickle ('prɪk(ə)l), *v.* [Partly f. PRICKLE *sb.*[1]; = MDu., MLG. *prēkelen*, MDu. *prickelen*, Du. *prikkelen*, LG. *prikkeln*, *prickeln*, whence G. *prickeln* to prickle, sting, prick. Partly dim. of PRICK *v.*]

1. *trans.* (or *absol.*) To prick, as with a goad or other sharp instrument; hence, to goad, instigate.

1513 DOUGLAS *Æneis* XII. Prol. 299 So pryklyng hyr grene curage for to crowd In amorus voce and wowar soundis lowd. **1570** LEVINS *Manip.* 122/3 To Prickle, *stimulare*. **1585** LUPTON *Thous. Notable Th.* (1675) 16 The outward part of the Nettle, doth sting, prickle, or burn. **1693** CONGREVE *Old Bach.* III. x, You have such a beard, and would so prickle one. **1828** *Craven Gloss.* (ed. 2), *Prickle*, to prick. **1876** T. S. EGAN *Heine's Atta Troll*, etc. 222 If that point I shall once unpack, 'Twill prickle and hackle your faces.

b. *transf.* To affect with a prickling sensation.

1855 TENNYSON *Maud* I. xiv. 36, I..Felt a horror over me creep, Prickle my skin and catch my breath.

†**2.** *fig.* To affect with a feeling of pain or compunction. *Obs.* Cf. PRICK *v.* 2.

1500-20 DUNBAR *Poems* xxix. 15 My panefull purss so prikillis me. *Ibid.* 20 So pricliss me. **1533** GAU *Richt Vay* 62 Thay war priklit in thair hartis and said to hime..quhat sal we dw?

3. *intr.* To tingle as if pricked.

1634-5 BRERETON *Trav.* (Chetham Soc.) 42 His finger burned and prickled. **1872** TENNYSON *Gareth & Lyn.* 1361 Sir Gareth's head prickled beneath his helm.

4. *trans.* To sprinkle or cover with minute points; to dot. *rare.*

1888 *Harper's Mag.* Apr. 753 Evening shadowed; the violet deepened and prickled itself with stars.

5. *intr.* To rise or stand up like prickles. Cf. PRICK *v.* 28.

1905 *Blackw. Mag.* Sept. 305/2 The roofs of gray shingles or red tiles prickling up through the mass of greenery.

Hence '**prickling** *vbl. sb.* and *ppl. a.*

1590 SPENSER *F.Q.* II. v. 29 The fragrant Eglantine did spred His prickling armes, entrayld with roses red. **1656** W. D. tr. *Comenius' Gate Lat. Unl.* §258 With very little pricklings, Itching. **1726** MONRO *Anat. Nerves* (1741) 63 The Numness and Prickling we..feel point out the Course of this Nerve. **1853** KANE *Grinnell Exp.* xxxiii. (1856) 289 The wind was like prickling needles.

'**prickle-back.** Also 8 -bag. [f. PRICKLE *sb.*[1] + BACK *sb.*[1]] Name of the three-spined stickleback.

1746 ARDERON in *Phil. Trans.* XLIV. 424 Observations made on the Bansticle, or Pricklebag, alias Prickle-back. **1787** BEST *Angling* (ed. 2) 4 The Common Prickle Back, Sharpling, or Banstickle. **1843** JAMES *Forest Days* i, A little rivulet, full of pricklebacks.

†**prickled** ('prɪk(ə)ld), *a. Obs.* [f. PRICKLE *sb.*[1] + -ED[2].] Furnished or set with prickles; prickly. *prickled apple*: app. the fruit of *Anona muricata*, the sour-sop. *prickled pear* = next.

1598 FLORIO, *Sonco*, an herbe.. whereof be two kindes, the one prickled, the other not prickled. **1607** TOPSELL *Four-f. Beasts* (1658) 546 Within which the beast draweth up his body, as a Hedge-hog doth within his prickled skin. **1610** JOURDAN *Discov. Bermudas* 15 The Country yeeldeth diuers fruits, as prickled peares. **1613-16** W. BROWNE *Brit. Past.* II. iii. 63 The little Redbrest to the prickled thorne Return'd. **1657** R. LIGON *Barbadoes* 70 The Prickled apple ..is shap't like the heart of an Oxe,..a faint green on the outside, with many prickles on it, the tast very like a musty Limon. **1725** BRADLEY *Fam. Dict.* s.v. *Spinach*, Having its Corners very sharp-pointed and prickled.

†'**prickle-pear.** *Obs.* [f. PRICKLE *sb.*[1] + PEAR *sb.*; cf. *prick-pear*.] = PRICKLY PEAR.

1624 CAPT. SMITH *Virginia* v. 170 The Prickell-peare.. growes like a shrub by the ground, with broad thick leaues, all ouer-armed with long and sharpe dangerous thornes. **1697** DAMPIER *Voy. round World* (1699) 222 Here are several sorts of Fruits, as Guavo's, Pine-apples, Melons and Prickle-Pears. *Ibid*, The Prickle-Pear Bush, or Shrub,..3 or 4 foot high. **1792** MAR. RIDDELL *Voy. Madeira* 86 A tribe of the cactus, or prickle-pear species.

prickless ('prɪklɪs), *a.* [f. PRICK *sb.* + -LESS.] Having no pricks; without a sting; thornless.

c **1412** HOCCLEVE *De Reg. Princ.* 3376 (Harl. MS.) Senek seith how þe kyng and þe ledere Of bees is prikkēles. **1601** HOLLAND *Pliny* I. 118 Smooth and prickless plants. *Mod.* A prickless species of thistle.

'**prickliness.** [f. PRICKLY + -NESS.] The quality of being prickly.

1661 J. CHILDREY *Brit. Baconica* 105 The sharp prickliness of its finnes. **1725** BRADLEY *Fam. Dict.* II. s.v. *Presage*, A Thistle..assuming a new Form, and without any prickliness. **1878** A. FORBES in *Daily News* 15 Aug. 6/2 Closer inspection disclosed the furious and impossible prickliness of their surface.

†'**prickling,** *sb. Obs.* [f. PRICK *sb.* + -LING[1].] A name of the stickleback.

1668 CHARLETON *Onomast.* 161 *Pisciculus Aculeatus*..the Banstickle, or Prickling. **1696** *Phil. Trans.* XIX. 348 A small Fish, called..*Stickle-back*, elsewhere *Prickling*.

pricklouse ('prɪklaʊs). Now *dial.* Also 8- prick-the(-a)-louse. A derisive name for a tailor.

1500-20 DUNBAR *Poems* xxvii. 5 Betuix a telȝour and ane sowtar, A pricklouss and ane hobbell clowttar. **1587** *Durham Depos.* (Surtees) 322 Pricklouse that thou arte. **1668** R. L'ESTRANGE *Vis. Quev.* (1708) 151 The poor Prick-Lice were damn'dly startled at that, for fear they should not get in. **1709** O. DYKES *Eng. Prov. & Refl.* (ed. 2) 117 What an ignorant Presumption..for an impudent Prick-lowse to set up for a Lawyer, or a Statesman. *a* **1796** BURNS *Answ. to Tailor* ii, Gae mind your seam, ye prick-the-louse, An' jag-the-flae. **1828** *Craven Gloss.* (ed. 2), *Prick-a-louse*, a contemptuous name for a tailor.

prickly ('prɪklɪ), *a.* [f. PRICKLE *sb.*[1] + -Y.]

1. a. Having, armed with, or full of prickles; aculeate.

1578 LYTE *Dodoens* VI. xxxiv. 700 The leaues of Holly are ..full of sharpe poyntes or prickley corners. *a* **1661** FULLER *Worthies, Middlesex* (1662) II. 182 Mr. John Denley..began to sing a Psalm at the Stake, and Dr. Story..caused a prickley fagot to be hurled in his face, which so hurt him, that he bled therewith. **1774** GOLDSM. *Nat. Hist.* (1776) VI. 315, I examine its fins, whether they be prickly or soft. **1784** COWPER *Task* I. 527 The common, overgrown with fern, and rough With prickly gorse. **1870** HOOKER *Stud. Flora* 120 Rose. Erect sarmentose or climbing shrubs, usually prickly.

b. *fig.* Full of contentious or irritating points; difficult to deal with. Also, of persons: quick to react angrily, touchy.

c **1862** E. DICKINSON *Poems* (1955) II. 490 His pretty estimates Of Prickly Things. **1871** E. F. BURR *Ad Fidem* xi. 217 Prickly Christianity. **1882-3** *Schaff's Encycl. Relig. Knowl.* II. 943/2 The discussion over this extremely complicated and prickly question is not yet closed. **1894** *Idler* Sept. 207 Anxious to try, in his own person, the effect of wedding what one may call the Prickly Young Person. **1935** N. MITCHISON *We have been Warned* IV. 340 Would you mind particularly if the C.P. were involved..? They're a nasty, prickly lot. **1943** A. RANSOME *Picts & Martyrs* i. 11 It's Mother she's getting at, not us... She's prickly with disapproval. **1950** *Listener* 9 Nov. 482/1 Hence the prickly suspicions of the new China's relations with the Western Powers. **1957** R. WATSON-WATT *Three Steps to Victory* cxxiv. 453, I was probably being needlessly prickly. **1975** *N.Y. Times* 2 Apr. 37/2 They were self-conscious gentry, prickly of their privileges and independence. **1980** T. MORGAN *Somerset Maugham* iii. 168 Janet Vale of the *Morning Telegraph* found him prickly.

2. Having a sensation as of many pricking points; smarting, as if full of prickles; tingling.

1836 J. M. GULLY *Magendie's Formul.* 4 The patient complained of a prickly feeling of the limbs. **1902** BUCHAN *Watcher by Threshold* 81 The skin grows hot and prickly.

3. Special collocations: **prickly ash**, any of several North American shrubs or trees whose aromatic bark is used medicinally, including those belonging to the genus *Zanthoxylum*, esp. *Z. americanum*, of the family Rutaceæ, and the angelica tree, *Aralia spinosa*, of the family Araliaceæ; **prickly back**, (*a*) = PRICKLE-BACK; (*b*) see quot. 1890; **prickly box**: see BOX *sb.*[1] 3 c; **prickly broom**, the whin or furze, *Ulex europæus*; **prickly bullhead**, a freshwater fish of the genus *Cottus* (Webster 1864); **prickly cedar**: see CEDAR; also applied to an evergreen shrub of Tasmania and Victoria, *Cyathodes Oxycedrus*; **prickly fern**, rigid species of the genus *Polystichum*; **prickly grass**, any species of *Echinochloa*; **prickly lettuce**, Wild Lettuce, *Lactuca Scariola*; **prickly Moses** *Austral.*, one of several species of *Acacia* bearing prickles, esp. *A. verticillata*, *A. juniperina*, or *A. pulchella*; **prickly palm, pole**, a slender West Indian palm, *Bactris Plumierana*; **prickly poppy**, an annual or perennial herb belonging to the genus *Argemone* of the family Papaveraceæ, native to North or Central America, esp. *Argemone mexicana*, a widespread weed of tropical and subtropical regions; **prickly rat**, any one of the species of *Ctenomys* and allied genera of S. American burrowing rodents, the hair of which is usually intermingled with sharp spines (Webster 1890); **prickly rhubarb** = GUNNERA; **prickly samphire**, the sea-parsnip, *Echinophora spinosa*; **prickly withe**, a cactaceous plant of Jamaica and Mexico, *Cereus triangularis*; **prickly yellowwood** (also *prickle-yellow*), a West Indian tree, *Xanthoxylum caribæum*. See also PRICKLY PEAR. For *prickly* COMFREY, GLASSWORT, TANG, etc., see the sbs.

1709 J. LAWSON *New Voy. Carolina* 101 *Prickly-Ash grows up like a Pole. **1743** J. F. GRONOVIUS *Flora Virginica* II. 150 *Aralia*... Gambriar and Prickly-ash. **1778** J. CARVER *Trav. N.-Amer.* 393 The chief..prepared for him a decoction of the bark of the roots of the prickly Ash. **1805** PIKE *Sources Mississ.* (1810) 31 The whole bottom covered with the prickly ash. **1817** J. BRADBURY *Trav. Amer.* 30 The underwood consisted chiefly of the prickly ash. **1860** M. A. CURTIS *Bot.* 91 Prickly ash. (*Aralia spinosa*)... The berries ..are thought by some to be also a valuable remedy for the bite of a rattlesnake. **1899** M. GOING *Field, Forest, & Wayside Flowers* 74 Prickly-ash, and hackberry..are thus unsystematic in their mode of conducting their affairs. **1931** M. GRIEVE *Mod. Herbal* I. 70/1 The Prickly Ash..is a small North American tree. *Ibid.* 71/2 The name Prickly Ash has also been given to *Aralia spinosa*.., the Prickly Elder, or Angelica Tree. **1938** M. K. RAWLINGS *Yearling* xxix. 379 She..made him a tonic of prickly ash and poke-root and potassium. **1975** M. C. DAVIS *Near Woods* ii. 27 A clumped prickly ash had found a home among sandstone boulders. **1883** *Fisheries Exhib. Catal.* (ed. 4) 174 Tom Cods, ..*Prickly Backs... Dog Fish. Bill Fish. **1890** *Cent. Dict.*, *Pricklyback*, the edible crab, *Callinectes hastatus*, when the new shell is only partially hardened; a shedder (Long Island). **1862** ANSTED *Channel Isl.* II. viii. (ed. 2) 182 The *prickly fern (*Polystichum aculeatum*)..exceedingly abundant in England and Jersey. **1887** *Australian* Apr. 9/3 An expedition was now made into the scrub for fishing rods. .. I cannot recommend 'snap-scrub' for a rod, nor that awful thing which our philosopher called '*prickly moses'. **1965** *Austral. Encycl.* VII. 276/1 Prickly Moses, a corruption of 'prickly mimosa' applied to several species of wattle. **1666** J. DAVIES *Hist. Caribby Isles* 36 If the *Prickly-Palm before described, afford Wine. **1725** SLOANE *Jamaica* II. 121 **Prickly Pole*. The Stem is very small,..and thick beset with large and long prickles round it. **1724** P. MILLER *Gardeners & Florists Dict.* I. s.v. *Argemone*, Argemone is a sort of Poppy, and some call it the *prickly Poppy. **1760** J. LEE *Introd. Bot.* App. 323 Poppy, Prickly, *Argemone*. **1869** *Amer. Naturalist* III. 163 The Prickly Poppy (*Argemone*) looks now like a common thistle. **1898** A. M. DAVIDSON *Calif. Plants* 112 The prickly poppy will send out great white flowers with crumpled petals and a great many yellow stamens. **1977** LEWIS & ELVIN-LEWIS *Med. Bot.* ii. 31/2 Prickly poppies are widely distributed in weedy habitats in temperate and tropic regions. **1895** W. ROBINSON *Eng. Flower Garden* (ed. 4) 501/2 Gunnera (*Prickly Rhubarb). —South American plants remarkable for large and handsome foliage, somewhat resembling that of gigantic Rhubarb. **1900** *Century Bk. Gardening* 98/2 Gunneras are called 'Prickly Rhubarbs', and the big leaves are not unlike those of a large Rhubarb. **1952** A. G. L. HELLYER *Sanders' Encycl. Gardening* (ed. 22) 217 Gunnera (Prickly Rhubarb). .. Hardy herbaceous perennials. First introduced mid-nineteenth century. **1725** SLOANE *Jamaica* II. 155 *Prickly Withe. This plant has several small roots sticking to the bark of trees.

4. *Comb.*, as *prickly-cupped*, *-headed*, *-stemmed*.

1858 HOMANS *Cycl. Comm.* s.v. *Leather*, the acorn cups of *Quercus Ægilops*, or prickly-cupped oak, growing in the Morea. **1871** KINGSLEY *At Last* x, The prickly-stemmed scarlet-flowered Euphorbia. **1872** *Routledge's Ev. Boy's Ann.* June 419/1 The prickly-headed Poppy.

prickly heat. A common name for *Lichen tropicus*, an inflammatory disorder of the sweat glands, prevalent in hot countries, characterized by eruption of small papules or vesicles, accompanied by a sense of pricking or burning.

1736 WESLEY *Wks.* (1830) I. 36, I found she had only the prickly heat, a sort of rash. **1822** J. FLINT *Lett. Amer.* 10 Called the prickly heat, from the pungent feeling that attends it. **1898** P. MANSON *Trop. Diseases* xxxvii. 559. **1899** *Allbutt's Syst. Med.* VIII. 586 'Prickly heat' in which the papules are formed by the blocking of the mouths of the sweat-pores.

prickly pear. The name given to various species of the cactaceous genus *Opuntia*, prickly plants with pear-shaped fleshy edible fruit; also the fruit itself. Formerly also ***prick-pear***, ***prickle-pear***, ***prickled pear***.

1612 W. STRACHEY *Trav. Virginia* (1849) I. x. 119 Here is a cherry-redd fruict both within and without..which wee call the prickle peare;..they beare a broad, thick, spungeous leafe, full of kernells. **1672** W. HUGHES *Amer. Physitian* 38 Most call it the Prickle-Pear Bush, and the fruit the Prickle-Pear. **1725** H. SLOANE *Voy. Jamaica* II. p. vi, Tab. VIII Shews..the sort of Prickly Pear, thought in Jamaica to be that particular kind of Opuntia, whereon feeds the small Worm or Beatle, from whence comes in Cochineel. **1760** J. LEE *Introd. Bot.* App. 322 Prickly Pear, *Cactus*. **1764** GRAINGER *Sugar-Cane* I. 536 On this lay cuttings of the prickly pear; They soon a formidable fence will shoot. **1825** *Gentle. Mag.* XCV. I. 318 The Jack-fruit, sweet sops, sour sops, mannees, prickly pears. **1836** J. HILDRETH *Dragoon Campaigns Rocky Mts.* xvi. 141 It was covered with the prickle-pear. **1870** DISRAELI *Lothair* lxxvi, Gardens enclosed with hedges of prickly pear. **1877** C. GEIKIE *Christ* (1879) 19 He will recognize such fruits as the lime, the banana, the almond, and the prickly pear. **1925** T. S. ELIOT *Poems 1909–1925* 98 Here we go round the prickly pear Prickly pear prickly pear... At five o'clock in the morning. **1956** C. MACKENZIE *Thin Ice* iii. 36 We left Tangier about an hour before sunrise, riding through plantations of prickly pear. **1978** G. D. ROWLEY in V. H. Heywood *Flowering Plants of World* 65/1 Opuntias (prickly pears) are grown commercially in parts of Mexico and California for their large juicy fruits.

attrib. **1672** [see above]. **1739** P. DELEGAL in *Georgia Hist. Soc. Coll.* (1840) I. 188 The islands in Georgia are full of the prickly pear shrubs which feed flies. **1832** J. A. HERAUD *Voy. & Mem. Midshipm.* ix. (1837) 174 An arid plain, with straggling hedges of prickley pear bushes. **1839** *Lett. fr. Madras* (1843) 272 Prickly-pear hedges, enclosing black-looking Palmyra-trees. **1917** *Nature* 20 Sept. 57/2 The prickly pear cactus (*Opuntia tuna*) has become extensively naturalised [in Hawaii]. **1974** V. NABOKOV *Look at Harlequins* (1975) I. iii. 12 We walked round the house, skirting prickly-pear shrubs.

ˈprick-madam. *Herb. Obs.* exc. *Hist.* Also 7 prick-my-dame. [Altered from F. *trique-madame* (1545 in Hatz.-Darm.): see Littré.] An old name of the Stone-crops, esp. *Sedum acre*; also *S. album* and *S. reflexum*.

1545 ELYOT *Dict., Aizoon*,..called..singrene or house-leeke..The lesse..is called in english pricke madame. **1578** LYTE *Dodoens* I. lxxvii. 114 Prickmadame hath small narrow thicke and sharpe poynted leaues. **1688** R. HOLME *Armoury* II. 73/2 Leaves long and slender, and thick, like Prick-my-dame. *Ibid.* 99/1 Prick Madam, or stone Crop... It is termed also Trick Madam. **1883** *Cassell's Fam. Mag.* Oct. 672/2 Sweet country flowers..pansy, rose, lady-smock, prick-madam, &c. **1955** G. GRIGSON *Englishman's Flora* 182 Prick-madam was the name used [for the yellow stonecrop] in the sixteenth and seventeenth centuries. **1978** *Verbatim* May 2/2, I have never grown *stonecrop*; now that I know it as prickmadam I am tempted to try.

ˈprick-mark. [f. PRICK *sb.* 10 + MARK *sb.*[1]]

†**1.** *Archery.* The mark aimed at; the bull's-eye; hence *fig.*, an end, aim, object. *Obs. rare.*

1556 WITHALS *Dict.* (1566) 64a/2 The pricke markes, *dicuntur destinata*. **1563** *Burgh Rec. Edinb.* (1875) III. 168 Within the said space..salbe maid dry buttis and prik merkis. **1588** A. KING tr. *Canisius' Catech.* 29 Baith ye beginning and prikmark of our wil, and of al our doings.

2. A mark made by pricking, a prick on a surface.

1703 MOXON *Mech. Exerc.* 206 With the points of your Compasses..describe a Circle.., by placing one Foot in the prick-mark, and turning about the other Foot. **1875** SIR T. SEATON *Fret Cutting* 144 Pick out lightly the whole pattern. A single line of prickmarks will suffice for the stems.

ˈprick-me-ˈdainty, *sb.* and *a.* Now *Sc.* or *arch.* Also 6 **pryckmedenty, prickmydante**; 9 **prig-, prick-my-dainty, prick ma dainty, -denty.** [f. PRICK *v.* (sense 20) + ME + DAINTY *a.*]

A. *sb.* 'One who dresses in a finical manner, or is ridiculously exact in dress or carriage' (Jam.); one who is affectedly finical; a dandy.

a **1529** SKELTON *El. Rummyng* 582 There was a pryckemedenty, Sat lyke a seynty, And began to paynty, As thoughe she would faynty. **1548** B. OCHYNE *Serm.* A ij, If any prety pryckemydantes shal happen to spy a note in thys godly labour. *a* **1553** UDALL *Royster D.* II. iii. (Arb.) 36 Mary then prickmedaintie come toste me a fig. **1576** NEWTON *Lemnie's Complex.* (1633) 63 As some nice Dames and Prickmedainties..curiously combe and bring their haires into a curled fashion and crisped lockes. **1898** LD. E. HAMILTON *Mawkin* vi. 75 She..took it to be one of her young prick-me-dainties coming a-jinking after her.

B. *adj.* Excessively or affectedly precise in personal adornment; over-nice, finical.

1820 HOGG in *Blackw. Mag.* VI. 392 One can't think the blacksmith had been jealous Of any of these prig-my-dainty fellows. **1824** SCOTT *St. Ronan's* xii, It's an ill world since sic prick-my-dainty doings came in fashion. **1897** L. KEITH *Bonnie Lady* vii. 67 What a high-bendit, prickmadenty lady he had in his mind's eye.

pricknickety, -nikity, *a. Sc.* arbitrary var. of PERNICKETY *a.*

1845–67 *Autobiog. Eliz. Grant* (1898) 311, I was by nature tidy, had all theRaper methodical pricknikity ways.

ˈprick-post. [f. PRICK *sb.* + POST *sb.*[1]] (See quot. 1842–76.)

1587 HARRISON *England* II. xii. (1877) I. 233 In the open ..countries they are inforced for want of stuffe to vse no studs at all, but onlie franke posts, raisins, beames, prickeposts, groundsels,..and such principals. **1663** GERBIER *Counsel* 67 Prick post seven inches one way. **1703** MOXON *Mech. Exerc.* 163 *Prick-Posts*, Posts that are framed into Bressummers, between Principal-Posts, for the strengthning of the Carcass. **1776** G. SEMPLE *Building in Water* 115 The Prick-posts..are designed to shorten the bearing. **1842–76** GWILT *Archit.* Gloss., *Prick Post*, the same as a Queen Post of a roof. Also the posts in a wooden building placed between the principal posts at the corners. Also the posts framed into the breast-summer, between the principal posts, for strengthening the carcass of a house.

ˈprick-seam. [f. PRICK *sb.* or *v.* + SEAM.] A particular stitch used in glove-sewing. Also *attrib.* and *comb.*, as ***prick-seam sewer***, ***sewing***.

1632 B. JONSON *Magn. Lady* IV. i, With your Prick-seam, and through-stitch. **1635** *Roxb. Ballads* VII. 142 If that a Glover marrys me, part of his Trade I know, Whether it plain or prick-seam be, that makes the braver show. **1839** URE *Dict. Arts* 599 Adapted for what are called 'drawn sewing, and prick-seam sewing'. **1884** *Pall Mall G.* 16 May 4/2 Around Torrington, in Devon, for instance, are the best prick-seam sewers in the country.

Hence **ˈprick-seamed** *a.*, sewn with prick-seam.

1624 in *Archæologia* XV. 161 Item for a pare prick seamed gloves o. I. 4. **1635** T. CRANLEY *Amanda* xlv. 31 White prick-seam'd Gloves of Kid, full many a paire.

†**ˈprick-shaft.** *Obs.* An arrow or 'shaft' for shooting at the 'prick' (PRICK *sb.* 10).

1538 in *Priory of Hexham* (Surtees) I. App. p. clxiv, My bowe and my qwyver with prike shaftes. **1541** *Act 33 Hen. VIII*, c. 9 §2 Noe person above the saide age of xxiiij yeres shall shoote at any marke of xj score yardes or under, withe anye prickshafte or fleight. **1551** TURNER *Herbal* I. F v b, Flechers make prykke shaftes of byrche because it is heuier than espe is. **1633** ROWLEY *Match at Midnight* II. i. in Hazl. *Dodsley* XIII. 39 Why, to shoot at butts, when you should use prick-shafts.

prick-song (ˈprɪksɒŋ). *Mus. Obs.* exc. *Hist.* [Shortened from the early form *pricked song*, *prickt song*: cf. PRICK *v.* 13 and *sb.* 3 b.]

1. orig. ***pricked song***: Music sung from notes written or 'pricked', as distinguished from that sung from memory or by ear; written vocal music.

α. *a* **1463** in *Bury Wills* (Camden) 17, I wille y[t] on the day of myn intirment be songge a messe of prikked song at Seynt Marie auter. **1556** *Burgh Rec. Stirling* (1887) 70 The said Sir Johne sall study continualie quhill he be cunnand in prikat sang. **1597** MORLEY *Introd. Mus.* Title-p., The first teacheth to sing with all things necessary for the knowledge of pricktsong. **1606** HOLLAND *Sueton.* 187 Beeing much delighted with the Alexandrines praises in prict song.

β. **1519** *Interl. Four Elem.* (Percy Soc.) 50 Pes, man, pryksong may not be dispysyd. **1522** *Churchw. Acc. St. Giles, Reading* 16 Paid for a boke of priksong iij[s]. **1607** CHAPMAN *Bussy D'Ambois* I. i. Wks. 1873 II. 16, I can sing prickesong, Ladie, at first sight. **1872** ELLACOMBE *Ch. Bells Devon, Bells of Ch.* ix. 457 The staff is of five lines, and the notes are of the lozenge form, usually seen in prick-song of the period.

2. *esp.* A written descant or accompanying melody to a 'plain-song' or simple theme; hence, *gen.* descant or 'counterpoint' accompanying a simple melody (also *fig.*).

1501 DOUGLAS *Pal. Hon.* 500 In modulatioun hard I play and sing Faburdoun, pricksang, discant, countering. **1503** *Mem. Ripon* (Surtees) IV. 276 Nullus diaconus..admittatur nisi scit distincte cantare cantum planum, et eciam fractum, viz. prykesange. **1513** Priket sang; **1545** Priksong [see PLAIN-SONG 1]. **1593** R. BARNES *Parthenophil & P.* Elegy xiv. in Arb. *Garner* V. 425 I'll sing my Plain Song with the turtle dove; And Prick Song, with the nightingale rehearse! *a* **1670** HACKET *Abp. Williams* I. (1692) 91 The unsatisfied that sung so far out of tune, had another ditty to their prick-song. **1776** SIR J. HAWKINS *Gen. Hist. Mus.* II. II. x. 243 From the preference which the old writers give to written descant, which they termed Prick-song, in regard that the harmony was written or pricked down.

3. *attrib.*, as ***prick-song book***, ***lesson***, ***music***, etc.

1518 in *Vicary's Anat.* (1888) App. x. 232 Item to Doctor Fairfax, for a pricksonge boke xx li. **1529–30** *Rec. St. Mary at Hill* 351 Paid to Iohn Northfolke for prykkyd song bokes. *c* **1547** in Strype *Eccl. Mem.* (1721) II. App. A. 15 Which mass [being] solemnely sung in prick song descant, and organ playing. **1598** E. GILPIN *Skial.* (1878) 20 Yee that haue beauty and withall no pitty, Are like a prick-song-lesson without ditty. *a* **1668** LASSELS *Voy. Italy* (1670) I. 34 They sing..without pricksong musick, organs, or other instruments, using only the ancient plain-song. **1691** WOOD *Ath. Oxon.* I. 572 The..Archb. [Warham] left all..the prick-song books belonging to his Chappel, to New coll.

†**b. pricksongwort,** an old name for the herb 'honesty' (*Lunaria*), bearing flat round pods. *Obs.*

1597 GERARDE *Herbal* II. cxvii. 378 We cal this herb in English Pennie flower, or money flower, siluer plate, Prick-songwoort,..& among our women it is called Honestie.

†**ˈprick-timber.** *Obs.* [See PRICK *sb.* 14.]

a. The Spindle-tree: = PRICKWOOD a. **b.** The Dogwood: = PRICKWOOD b; also ***prick-timber tree***.

a. 1578 LYTE *Dodoens* VI. lxxix. 760 This plant..some call ..in Englishe, Spindeltree, and Pricke Timber: bycause the timber of this tree serueth very well to the making both of Prickes and Spindelles. *a* **1697** AUBREY *Nat. Hist. Wilts.* (1847) 56 The butchers doe make skewers of it, because it doth not taint the meate as other wood will doe: from whence it hath the name of prick-timber. **1753** CHAMBERS *Cycl. Supp.* App., *Prick-timber*, a name sometimes given to the *Euonymus*, or spindle-tree.

b. 1578 LYTE *Dodoens* VI. li. 726 The wilde Cornell tree, is called..in Englishe..Dogge berie tree, and the Pricke timber tree, bycause Butchers vse to make prickes of it. **1611** COTGR., *Cornillier femelle*, Hounds-tree, Dog-berrie tree, Prick-tymber tree.

†**ˈprick-tree.** *Obs.* [See PRICK *sb.* 14.] **a.** The Wild Cornel; = next, b. **b.** The Spindle-tree; = next, a. **c.** The Alder Buckthorn, *Rhamnus Frangula*.

1551 TURNER *Herbal* I. M j b, Sume because bucheres vse to make prykkes of it call it [cornel] pryke tree. **1597** GERARDE *Herbal* III. ci. 1286 *Alnus nigra, siue frangula*..is called in English Aller tree, and of diuers Butchers Pricke tree. **1671** SKINNER *Etymol. Ling. Angl., Bot.*, Butchers Prick tree, *Euonymus*.

ˈprickwood. [See PRICK *sb.* 14.] **a.** The Spindle-tree, *Euonymus europæus*. ? *Obs.* **b.** The Wild Cornel or Dogwood, *Cornus sanguinea*. *dial.*

a. 1661 LOVELL *Hist. Anim. & Min.* 115 They [Sheep] are hurt by aconite, nereon, prickwood, savin,..and scortching fennel. **1760** J. LEE *Introd. Bot.* App. 323 Prick Wood, *Euonymus*. **1861** MISS PRATT *Flower. Pl.* II. 64 *Euonymus Europæus* (Common Spindle-tree)..known to the old English herbalists chiefly by the name of Prickwood.

b. 1869 *Hardwicke's Sc. Gossip* 1 Feb. 30/1 The Dog-wood (*Cornus sanguinea*) means dagge-wood, dagge being the old English equivalent for a dagger, and the wood having been used for skewers... In Buckinghamshire it is still called Prickwood and Skewerwood. **1886** BRITTEN & HOLL. cite it from *N. Bucks.*

pricky (ˈprɪkɪ), *a.* Now *dial.* [f. PRICK *sb.* + -Y.] Furnished with pricks or spines; prickly.

1548 Pricky Sperage [see PRICK *sb.* 12]. **1578** LYTE *Dodoens* IV. xxvii. 485 The whiche beareth rough and prickie buttons. **1601** HOLLAND *Pliny* XIX. iii. II. 9 A prickie stalke it [Madder] hath of the owne. *Ibid.* 10 Prickie moreover it [Soap-wort] is like a thorne. [**1684** *Banks' Alb. Queen* Epil., But Nolens-Volens, Pricky must appear.] **1903** *Eng. Dial. Dict.* cites it from Scotland to Kent.

b. Comb. **pricky-back** or **pricky-back urchin, pricky urchin,** *dial.* the hedgehog.

1796 W. MARSHALL *Yorks.* (ed. 2) II. 337 Pricky Urchin; ..the hedge hog. **1855** ROBINSON *Whitby Gloss.*, *Prick-a-back urchin*, the prickly hedge-hog. **1863** ATKINSON *Stanton Grange* (1864) 219 Next I kenned 'twere a prickyback.

pricy, var. PRICEY *a.*

priddy, var. PREDY (*Naut.*) *Obs.*, ready.

pride (praɪd), *sb.*[1] Forms: see A. below. [Late OE. *prýto*, *prýtu* str. fem., *prýte* weak fem.; also (*prýdo*), *prýde*; abstract sb. from *prút*, *prúd*, PROUD; cf. ON. *prýði* gallantry, bravery, ornamentation, f. *prúðr* gallant, brave, stately; both generally held to have been adopted *c* 1000 from OF. *prūt*, *prūd*, mod.F. *preux*. The period of umlaut formations had passed long before 1000; and these quasi-umlaut derivatives in OE. and ON. must app. be explained as analogical, after the numerous original umlaut derivatives existing in the langs., as in OE. *full*, *fyllo*, ON. *fullr*, *fylli*.]

A. Illustration of Forms.

α. (*OE. and Southern ME.*) 1 **prýto, -u, -e,** 3–5 **prute** (= y), **pruyte;** 1 **prýde,** 2 **priede, prudu,** 2–4 **prude** (= y), 3–5 **pruyde, pruyd,** 4–5 **pruide.**

a **1000** *Aldhelm Gloss.* in Napier *O.E. Gloss.* 18 B. *Fastus*, ..pryte. **1014** WULFSTAN *Sermo ad Anglos* in *Hom.* (Napier) 165 ȝelice þam dwæsan, þe for heora prytan lewe nellað beorȝan. *a* **1023** *Ibid.* 178 Se ðe for his prydan gode nele hyran. *c* **1175** *Lamb. Hom.* 7 Ne we ne beoð iboren for to habbene nane prudu ne forðe nane oðre rencas. *Ibid.* 61 þe angles of heouene uolle for heore prude in to helle. *c* **1200** *Vices & Virt.* 89 Of modinesse and priede. *c* **1290** *S. Eng. Leg.* I. 47/16 And pruyte he louede lest. **1297** R. GLOUC. (Rolls) 1252 Such pruyd hym hath ynome [*v.rr.* *a* **1400** pruyd, prude]. *c* **1300** *Beket* 1928 Forto..alegge his prute [*v.r.* pruyte]. **1362** LANGL. *P. Pl.* A. Prol. 23 Summe putten hem to pruide. **1387** TREVISA *Higden* (Rolls) III. 113 For his pride [*MS.* γ pruyde]. *Ibid.* 213 Grete boost of pryde [*MS.* γ pruyte]. *Ibid.* VII. 263 Pride of herte [*MS.* γ prute]. *c* **1400** *Rom. Rose* 3723 Devoyde of pruyde she was.

β. (*Kentish*) 2–4 **prede.**

a **1175** *Cott. Hom.* 221 þe ham ȝearcod was fer hare prede. *c* **1250** *O. Kent. Serm.* in *O.E. Misc.* 33 þurch senne, þurch prede oþer þurch an-vie. **1340** *Ayenb.* 21 þe pridde boȝ of prede is arrogance.

γ. (*midl.* and *north.*) 3– **pride** (3–6 **prid,** 4–5 **priyd,** 4–6 **pryde,** 4–7 **pryd,** 5 **pryte,** 6 **pried**).

c **1300** *Cursor M.* 23751 (Edin.) þe warlaw, swernes, wrepe, and prid [*other MSS.* pride]. *c* **1330** R. BRUNNE *Chron.* (1810) 280 Priue pride in þes es nettille in herbere. **13** .. *E.E. Allit. P.* B. 179 For bobaunce & bost & bolnande priyde. *Ibid.* 1450 Wyth bost & wyth pryde. *c* **1375** *Sc. Leg. Saints* xxvii. (*Machor*) 1048 Thru priyd & awaris gredy. *Ibid.* xxx. (*Theodera*) 215 Na ogart na pryd is þe with-in. **1375** (MS. 1487) BARBOUR *Bruce* I. 408 The King Eduuard, with mekill prid. *c* **1425** Pryd [see B. 5]. **15..** *Sir A. Barton* in *Surtees Misc.* (1888) 68 She is dearelye deighte, and of mickell pried. **1596** DALRYMPLE tr. *Leslie's Hist. Scot.* v. 284 Thair pryd sa now was dantount.

B. Signification. The quality of being proud.

I. 1. a. A high or overweening opinion of one's own qualities, attainments, or estate, which gives rise to a feeling and attitude of superiority over and contempt for others; inordinate self-esteem.

Reckoned the first of the 'seven deadly sins': see DEADLY 5.

c **1000** ÆLFRIC *Hom.* II. 220 Of ydelum ʒylpe bið acenned pryte and æbiliʒnys. *a* **1050** *Instit. Polity* c. 10 *note* in Thorpe *Anc. Laws* II. 318 Ne ʒerisað heom prita ne idele rænca. *a* **1225** *Ancr. R.* 52 Lucifer..leop into prude, & bicom of engel atelich deouel. **1340** HAMPOLE *Pr. Consc.* 3363 Þir er þa hede syns þat er dedely; Pride, hatreden, and envy [etc.]. *c* **1380** WYCLIF *Sel. Wks.* III. 101 By stynkynge pryde holdyng ous self worþyer to God þan oþer trewe men. **1382** —— *Mark* vii. 22 Fro withynne, of the herte of men comen forth yuele thouȝtis..pride, folye. *c* **1440** *Promp. Parv.* 413/1 Pryde, *superbia, fastus, elacio, ambicio.* *c* **1530** LD. BERNERS *Arth. Lyt. Bryt.* (1814) 96 Blessed be God! pryde alwayes ouerthroweth his maister. **1650** JER. TAYLOR *Holy Living* II. iv. iii. ¶8 Spiritual pride is very dangerous, ..because it so frequently creeps upon the spirit of holy persons. **1667** MILTON *P.L.* IV. 809 Vain hopes, vain aimes, inordinate desires Blown up with high conceits ingendring pride. **1783** BLAIR *Lect.* I. x. 197 Pride makes us esteem ourselves; Vanity makes us desire the esteem of others. It is just to say, as Dean Swift has done, that a man is too proud to be vain. **1837** SIR W. HAMILTON *Metaph.* xlvi. (1870) II. 519 Pride, or the overweening sentiment of our own worth. **1872** DARWIN *Emotions* xi. 264 A peacock or a turkey-cock strutting about with puffed-up feathers, is sometimes said to be an emblem of pride.

b. in plural. *rare.*

c **1000** in *Sax. Leechd.* III. 428 Mid ofermettum afylled ne mid woruld-prydum, ne mid nyðum. **1609** BIBLE (Douay) *2 Esdras* xv. 18 Because of their prides the citie shal be trubled. **1878** RUSKIN *Lett. to Faunthorpe* (1895) I. 13 My selfishnesses, prides, insolences, failures.

c. with specification of the cause or subject of pride. (Often passing into 3 or 4.)

[**1768–74** TUCKER *Lt. Nat.* (1834) I. 189 Pride..may be called a habit of dwelling upon the thought of any supposed excellences or advantages men believe themselves possessed of; as well power, birth, wealth, strength of body, or beauty of person as endowments of the mind.] **1797** MRS. RADCLIFFE *Italian* i, His pride of birth was equal to either. **1827** POLLOK *Course T.* IX. 723 Pride of rank And office, thawed into paternal love. **1879** FARRAR *St. Paul* (1883) 133 The pride of system, the pride of nature, the rank pride of the self-styled theologian, the exclusive national Pharisaic pride in which he had been trained—forbade him to examine seriously whether he might not after all be in the wrong.

d. Personified, esp. as the first of the seven deadly sins.

c **1420** LYDG. *Assembly of Gods* 621 Pryde was the furst þat next hym roode, God woote, On a roryng lyon. **1606** DEKKER *Sev. Sinnes* II. (Arb.) 22 Because Pride is the Queene of Sinnes, thou hast chosen her to be thy Concubine. **1870** LONGF. *Tales Wayside Inn* II. *Bell of Atri*, Pride goeth forth on horseback grand and gay, But cometh back on foot, and begs its way.

e. In various proverbs.

1382 WYCLIF *Prov.* xvi. 18 Pride goth befor contricioun; an befor falling the spirit shal ben enhauncid. *c* **1425** *MS. Digby* 230 lf. 223 b, Pees makith Plente Plente makith Pride Pride makith Plee Plee makith Pouert Pouert makith Pees. *c* **1440** *Jacob's Well* 70 Pride goth beforn, & schame folwyth after. **1509** BARCLAY *Shyp of Folys* (1874) II. 159 For it hath be sene is sene, and euer shall That first or last foule pryde wyll haue a fall. **1646** J. WHITAKER *Uzziah* 26 That pride will have a fall, is from common experience grown proverbiall. **1784** JOHNSON *Let.* 2 Aug. in *Boswell*, I am now reduced to think..of the weather. Pride must have a fall.

2. The exhibition of this quality in attitude, bearing, conduct, or treatment of others; arrogance; haughtiness.

c **1205** LAY. 19409 Bruttes hafden muchel mode & vnimete prute. *a* **1300** *Cursor M.* 6224 He [pharaon] went wit mikel prid and bost. *c* **1330** R. BRUNNE *Chron. Wace* (Rolls) 6222 þey preied hym [Constantine] he wolde make defens, & abate þe pruyde of Maxens. **1483** *Cath. Angl.* 291/1 A Pryde, *arrogancia.* **1588** SHAKS. *Tit. A.* I. i. 33 Since first he..chasticed with Armes Our Enemies pride. **1601** —— *Twel. N.* III. i. 163, I loue thee so, that maugre all thy pride, Nor wit, nor reason, can my passion hide. **1764** GOLDSM. *Trav.* 327 Pride in their port, defiance in their eye, I see the lords of human kind pass by. **1859** TENNYSON *Geraint & Enid* 195 Doubling all his master's vice of pride.

3. a. A consciousness or feeling of what is befitting or due to oneself or one's position, which prevents a person from doing what he considers to be beneath him or unworthy of him; esp. as a good quality, legitimate, 'honest', or 'proper pride', self-respect; also as a mistaken or misapplied feeling, 'false pride'.

1297 R. GLOUC. (Rolls) 3393 Vor þe brutons nolde uor prute after þe erl do, Vor he nas noȝt king & þeruore þe worse hom com to. **1570–6** LAMBARDE *Peramb. Kent* (1826) 251 He, which before writing unto the King, refused in his letters for pride to call him his Lord. **1667** MILTON *P.L.* I. 527 But he his wonted pride Soon recollecting, with high words..dispel'd their fears. **1736** GRAY *Statius* I. 25 These conscious shame withheld, and pride of noble line. **1769** *Junius Lett.* ii. (1820) 13 He was trained..to the truest and noblest sort of pride, that of never doing or suffering a mean action. **1802** WORDSW. *Resolution & Indep.* vii, I thought of Chatterton, the marvellous Boy, The sleepless Soul that perished in his pride. **1836** W. IRVING *Astoria* II. 304 This ludicrous affair excited the mirth of the bolder spirits,..and roused the pride of the wavering. **1855** J. R. LEIFCHILD *Cornwall Mines* 296 A man of considerable scientific attainments, who, I believe, has no false pride about him, and who will rejoice to find that his example may be influential to others. **1880** DIXON *Windsor* III. viii. 74 His pride of virtue was as lofty as his pride of birth.

b. Phr. ***pride and prejudice***; occas. ***prejudice and pride.*** Cf. PREJUDICE *sb.* 3.

1610 J. HALL *Sixt Decade of Epistles* v. 42 Lay downe first, all pride and preiudice, and I cannot fear you. **1647** J. TAYLOR *Liberty of Prophesying* xii. 185 Epiphanius makes pride to be the onely cause of heresies..Pride and Prejudice cause them all, the one criminally, the other innocently. **1650** —— *Holy Living* iv. 323 There is in it [*sc.* anger] envy and sorrow, fear and scorn, pride and prejudice, [etc.]. **1758** *Idler* 13 May 41/2 The prejudices and pride of man. **1758** C. LENNOX *Henrietta* II. 48 The triumph of virtue over pride and prejudice. **1769** H. BROOKE *Fool of Quality* IV. 292 Reason, and the workings of nature had begun to get the better of pride, and prejudice, in the peer. **1782** F. BURNEY *Cecilia* V. x. x. 379 The whole of this unfortunate business ..has been the result of Pride and Prejudice. **1782** COWPER *Hope* in *Poems* I. 170 Now truth perform thine office, waft aside The curtain drawn by prejudice and pride. **1796** R. BAGE *Hermsprong* I. xxxi. 204 But the tender interest they had in each other was torn asunder by pride and prejudice; and this pride and this prejudice, she feared, had been infused into the tender mind of Miss Campinet. **1813** JANE AUSTEN (*title*) Pride and prejudice.

4. A feeling of elation, pleasure, or high satisfaction derived from some action or possession; esp. in *to take a pride* (*in*, †*to do* something, etc.).

1597 SHAKS. *2 Hen. IV*, I. ii. 7 Men of all sorts take a pride to gird at mee. **1603** —— *Meas. for M.* II. iv. 10 My Grauitie Wherein..I take pride. **1666** DRYDEN *Ann. Mirab.* cxvi, To rescue one such friend he took more pride, Than to destroy whole thousands of such foes. **1774** GOLDSM. *Nat. Hist.* (1776) V. 156 Her parental pride seems to overpower every other appetite. **1857** RUSKIN *Pol. Econ. Art* i. 13 You will see the good housewife taking pride in her pretty table cloth, and her glittering shelves. **1867** LADY HERBERT *Cradle L.* viii. 225 Achill Aga..produced, with natural pride and pleasure, the watch and pistols given him by the Prince of Wales.

5. a. That of which any person or body of persons is proud; that which causes a feeling of pride in those to whom it belongs; hence, the flower, the best, of a class, country, etc.

1382 WYCLIF *Ezek.* xxiv. 21 Y shal defoule my seyntuarie, the pryde of ȝour empyre, and desyrable thing of ȝour eyen. *c* **1425** *Eng. Conq. Irel.* 32 Her þe pryd of waterford felle; her all hys myght went to noght. **1599** SHAKS. *Hen. V*, I. ii. 112 O Noble English, that could entertaine With halfe their Forces, the full pride of France. **1611** BIBLE *Job* xli. 15 His [leviathan's] scales are his pride. *a* **1721** PRIOR *Garland* i, The pride of every grove I chose,..To deck my charming Cloe's hair. **1742** GRAY *Propertius* II. i. 77 Love and the Fair were of his life the Pride. **1770** GOLDSM. *Des. Vill.* 55 A bold peasantry, their country's pride. **1813** SCOTT *Rokeby* III. xv, See yon pale stripling! when a boy, A mother's pride, a father's joy!

b. In names of plants: **pride of Barbadoes** (see BARBADOS *pride*); **pride-of-California**, a perennial wild pea with pink or violet flowers, *Lathyrus splendens*, native to California; **pride of China, pride of India**, a tree, the AZEDARAC; = MARGOSA, NEEM; **pride of Columbia**, an American species of Phlox, *P. speciosa*; **pride of London** = LONDON PRIDE; **pride of Ohio**, the American cowslip, *Dodecatheon Meadia.*

1629 PARKINSON *Paradisus* 321 Spotted sweet Williams or pride of London. **1683, 1688** [see LONDON PRIDE]. **1756** P. BROWNE *Jamaica* 225 Barbadoes Pride... It grows wild in many parts of Liguanea, and makes a beautiful show when in bloom. **1785** G. WASHINGTON *Diary* 13 June (1925) II. 383 Next 3 rows of the Seed of the Pride of China. **1803** J. DAVIS *Trav. U.S.A.* 79 The mocking-bird..was warbling, close to my window, from a tree called by some the Pride of India. **1834** J. J. AUDUBON *Ornith. Biogr.* II. 191 They.. feed voraciously on..the berries of the pride of India. **1835** J. H. INGRAHAM *South-West* II. 101 The 'pride of China', —the universal shade-tree in the south-west. **1842** DUNGLISON *Med. Lex.*, Pride of China,..p. of India, *Melia azedarach.* **1849** LYELL *2nd Visit U.S.* (1850) II. 60 Before the house stood a row of Pride-of-India trees. **1856** OLMSTED *Slave States* 416 A broad avenue, planted with Pride-of-China trees. **1893** *Harper's Mag.* Apr. 756/2 This causeway broadened into a sandy street under huge pride-of-India trees, whose branches met overhead. **1895** 'F. FRANCESCHI' *Santa Barbara Exotic Flora* 64 *Lathyrus Splendens*, appropriately called 'the pride of California',.. has made its appearance in our gardens quite lately. **1949** *Bull. Hist. & Philos. Soc. Ohio* VII. 71 A tall conical envelope of straw..protected the Pride of China, a tree brought from New Orleans. **1970** W. SMITH *Gold Mine* xxvii. 63 The moonlight came in through the window, playing shadow pictures through the branches of the Pride of India tree onto the wall. **1976** *Hortus Third* (L. H. Bailey Hortorium) 638/2 *Lathyrus*...*splendens* Kellogg. Pride-of-California...somewhat shrubby.

II. 6. a. Magnificence, splendour; pomp, ostentation, display. *poet.* and *rhet.*

c **1205** LAY. 14292 He heo lette scruden mid vnimete prude. **1297** R. GLOUC. (Rolls) 9898 Þe sixte day of Iul he deide and mid gret onour & prute At founte ebraud he was ibured. *c* **1400** *Laud Troy Bk.* 4078 For Theman dyed in that stede And beryed he was with mochel pride. *a* **1450** *Le Morte Arth.* 572 They reseyved hym with grete pride, A Riche soper there was dight. *c* **1460** *How Gd. Wif thaught hir Doughter* 95 in Hazl. *E.P.P.* I. 186 Ouere done pride makythe the nakid syde. **1604** SHAKS. *Oth.* III. iii. 354 Oh fare-well..all Qualitie, Pride, Pompe, and Circumstance of glorious Warre. **1732** POPE *Ess. Man* II. 44 Trace Science then, with Modesty thy guide; First strip off all her equipage of Pride. **1876** MORRIS *Sigurd* IV. 369 Folk looked on his rich adornment, on King Atli's pride they gazed.

†**b.** Love of display or ostentation. *Obs.*

c **1460** *How Gd. Wif thaught hir Doughter* 97 in Hazl. *E.P.P.* I. 186 Mekille schame ben wymmen worthi,..That bryngyn her lordis in mischef for here mekille pride. **1593** SHAKS. *Lucr.* 864 He..leaues it [gold] to be maistred by his yong: Who in their pride do presently abuse it. **1680** OTWAY *Orphan* I. ii. 157 Wealth beyond what Woman's Pride could waste.

c. ***pride of life, pride of the world***, worldly pride or ostentation, vainglory. *arch.*

1340 HAMPOLE *Pr. Consc.* 1129 Al þat in world men tel can, Es outher yhernyng of þe flesshe of man, Or yhernyng of eghe, þ at may luke, Or pride of lyfe, als says þe buke. **1382** WYCLIF *1 John* ii. 16 Coueytise of flesch, and coueytise of iȝen, and pride of lijf [Vulg. *superbia vitæ*, Gr. ἡ ἀλαζονεία τοῦ βίου. So **1611**; *R.V.* vainglory of life]. **1729** LAW *Serious C.* iv. (1732) 49 It is not left to the rich to gratify their passions in the indulgencies and pride of life. *Ibid.* vi. 82 In conforming to those passions and pride of the world.

d. *Her.* ***in his pride***: applied to a peacock when represented with the tail expanded and the wings drooping. See also PEACOCK *sb.* 1 c.

1530 in *Ancestor* XI. (1904) 181 Banester beryth to his crest a pecoke in his pryde. **1721** STRYPE *Eccl. Mem.* II. II. xii. 339 His standard [was] of yellow and blue, with a peacock in pride gold, and pensils with a peacock. **1766** PORNY *Heraldry* Dict. s.v., Peacocks are said to be in their pride when they extend their tails into a circle, and drop their wings. **1864** BOUTELL *Her. Hist. & Pop.* xvii. §2 (ed. 3) 272.

7. Magnificent, splendid, or ostentatious adornment or ornamentation. *arch.*

a **1300** *Cursor M.* 21050 He wroght O grauel bi þe se side Stanes precius o pride. **13..** *Guy Warw.* (A.) 6382 He ȝaf him armes and riche stede, And diȝt him þer alle wiþ prede. **1390** GOWER *Conf.* II. 45 The Sadles were of such a Pride, ..So riche syh sche nevere non. **1590** SPENSER *F.Q.* I. i. 7 Loftie trees, yclad with sommers pride. *c* **1600** SHAKS. *Sonn.* lxxvi, Why is my verse so barren of new pride? So far from variation or quicke change? **1634** SIR T. HERBERT *Trav.* 15 Their armes are loaden with pride, such make the Iron shackles, beades, twigges of trees and brasse Rings. **1697** DRYDEN *Virg. Georg.* III. 663 A Snake..renew'd in all the speckl'd Pride Of pompous Youth. **1725** POPE *Odyss.* VIII. 439 Whose ivory sheath, inwrought with curious pride, Adds graceful terror to the wearer's side. **1767** SIR W. JONES *Sev. Fountains* Poems (1777) 33 Deck'd with fresh garlands, like a rural bride, And with the crimson streamer's waving pride.

†**8. a.** Exalted or proud position or estate. *Obs.*

c **1400** *Laud Troy Bk.* 46 For ther were, In that on side, Sixti kynges and dukes of pride. **1509** HAWES *Past. Pleas.* xxvii. (Percy Soc.) 118 Beholdynge Mars how wonderly he stode, On a whele top with a lady of pryde Haunced aboute. **1729** LAW *Serious C.* xi. (1732) 167 The man of pride has a thousand wants.

†**b.** Honour, glory. *Obs.*

13.. *Guy Warw.* (A.) 970 Þer-fore, on euerich a side, On him was leyd al þe pride. **1591** SHAKS. *1 Hen. VI*, IV. vi. 57 If thou wilt fight, fight by thy Fathers side, And commendable prou'd, let's dye in pride.

9. a. The best, highest, most excellent or flourishing state or condition; the prime; the flower.

c **1420** *Avow. Arth.* lv, Hertis conne thay home bring, And buckes of pride. *c* **1590** MARLOWE *Faust.* xiii. 31 Since we have seen the pride of Nature's works..Let us depart. **1591** SHAKS. *1 Hen. VI*, IV. vii. 16 There di'de My Icarus, my Blossome, in his pride. **1611** SIR W. MURE *Misc. Poems* i. 54 Lyk to a blooming meadou Quhose pryd doth schort remaine. **1615** W. LAWSON *Country Housew. Gard.* (1626) 19 If you remoue them in the pride of sap. **1674** PLAYFORD *Skill Mus.* I. 65 When as May was in her pride. **1688** R. HOLME *Armoury* II. 188/1 Pride of Grease is full Fat and in good liking. **1851** MAYHEW *Lond. Labour* (1861) II. 58/2 Sometimes, in the pride of the season, a bird-catcher engages a costermonger's poney or donkey cart. **1904** *Daily Chron.* 24 May 3/1 But deer are already almost in 'pride of grease'.

†**b.** Exuberance. *Obs.*

1603 OWEN *Pembrokeshire* viii. (1892) 62 One Cropp of oates pulleth downe the pride of good grounde verye lowe. **1613** MARKHAM *Eng. Husbandm.* I. v. 24 The ground hauing his pride abated in the first croppe.

10. Mettle or spirit in a horse.

1592 SHAKS. *Ven. & Ad.* 420 The colt that's backt and burthend being yong, Loseth his pride, and neuer waxeth strong. **1596** —— *1 Hen. IV*, IV. iii. 22 Your Vnckle Worcesters Horse came but to day, And now their pride and mettal is asleepe. **1864** *N. & Q.* 3rd Ser. VI. 495/1 A little pride is good even in a wild horse.

†**11.** Sexual desire, 'heat'; esp. in female animals.

1486 *Bk. St. Albans* E v, The noyes of theyes beestys thus ye shall call For pride of theyre make thay vsen hit all. **1590** COKAINE *Treat. Hunting* B iij b, Your man must be very carefull in the time of the Braches pride. **1604** SHAKS. *Oth.* III. iii. 404 As salt as Wolues in pride.

12. A group of lions forming a social unit.

1486 *Bk. St. Albans* F vi, A Pride of Lionys.

1929 *Times* 30 Sept. 12/6 Owing to the dry weather a pride of 16 lions, including females and cubs, concentrated on the Kajiado road..less than 20 miles from Nairobi. **1940** V. POHL *Bushveld Adventures* x. 218 Presently we distinguished outlines of several other forms beyond the one we now knew to be the leader of the pride. **1964** C. WILLOCK *Enormous Zoo* v. 75 We found the pug-marks of a pride of lion. **1975** *Sci. Amer.* May 54/2 The social unit of the lion —the pride—is a long-lasting entity. *Ibid.* 55 (*caption*) A typical pride usually includes two or three adult males, from five to ten adult females and a number of cubs.

13. *Falconry.* ***pride of place***: see PLACE *sb.* 8 c.

14. ***pride of the morning***, a widely used rural phrase for a morning shower which promises or is expected to usher in a fine day.

1854 in *N. & Q.* 1st Ser. X. 360 (fr. Cornwall). **1867** *Ibid.* 3rd Ser. XI. 529 (fr. Kent). **1877** *Ibid.* 5th Ser. VIII. 129 (fr. Yorksh.). *Ibid.* 275 (fr. Lancash., Shropsh., Berks.).

15. *Comb.*: objective, as ***pride-inspiring*** adj.; instrumental as ***pride-blind, -blinded, -bloated, -inflamed, -ridden, -sick, -swollen*** adjs.; **pride-money**: see quot. 1632.

1598 MARSTON *Scourge of Villanie* x. sig. H3, These pride-swolne dayes. **1599** *Broughton's Let.* xii. 43 A..brainsicke, pride-swolne companion. **1632** BROME *Court Beggar* I. i. Wks. 1873 I. 193, 1 *P.* For every wearer of his first o' th' fashion To pay a groat to th' King... *Gab.* And what may this pride money amount unto Per annum, can you guesse? **1712** M. HENRY *Popery a Spir. Tyranny* Wks. 1853 II. 350/1 Your glory may well be turned into shame if you be pride-ridden, and passion-ridden, and lust-ridden. **1818** MILMAN *Samor* 12 Like the pride-drunken Babylonian king. **1839** BAILEY *Festus* xxxi. (1852) 502 Then she elate, and with pride-blinded soul The towering seat..assumed. *a* **1846** B. R. HAYDON *Autobiogr.* (1927) i. 10 His large, red, pride-swollen, big-featured face. **1884** J. TAIT *Mind in Matter* (1892) 332 A pride-inspiring style of Christianity, leading to a dangerous consciousness of power.

pride (praɪd), *sb.*² *local.* [Etymology obscure. Perh. abbreviated from obs. *lamprid* (17th c.: see LAMPRET; orig. stressed *lam'prid*) = med.L. *lamprēda, lamprīda*, LAMPREY.] The fresh-water or river lamprey; also called *sand-pride*.

a **1490** BOTONER *Itin.* (1778) 291 Homines possunt piscare ..de prides ad similitudinem lampreys. **1538** ELYOT *Dict.* Additions, *Lumbrici*, lytell fyshes taken in small riuers whyche are lyke to lampurnes,..callyd in Wylteshire prides. **1661** WALTON *Angler* xiii. (ed. 3) 192 A very little Lamprey, which some call a Pride.., may..be found many of them in the River Thames. **1677** PLOT *Oxfordsh.* 183 We have a sort in the River Isis, that we call here a Pride, of the long cartilagineous smooth Kind. *a* **1705** RAY *Syn. Method. Piscium* (1713) 35 A Lampern, Pride of the Isis. **1886** SEELEY *Fresh-water Fishes Europe* xii. 427 *Petromyzon branchialis* (Linnæus),..is locally known as the Pride.

b. *Comb.*; ***pride-net.*** (See also PRIDE-GAVEL.)

a **1300** *Liber Custum.* (Rolls) I. 117 Ilia un autre manere de reies, qe len apele 'pridnet'. **1584** in R. Griffiths *Ess. Conserv. Thames* (1746) 63 A pride Net, not to be occupied but by Special Licence of the Water-Bailiff, and not above a Yard in Length.

†**pride**, *sb.*³ *Obs. rare.* [Origin and sense uncertain.] ? The spleen of a deer. (So taken by editor of S.T.S. ed.)

13.. *Sir Tristr.* 475 Tristrem schare þe brest, þe tong sat next þe pride.

pride (praɪd), *v.* Forms: 3 *south.* prude (ü); 4 *Kentish* prede (*pa. t.* prette); 4– pride (5 *north.* prid, 5–7 pryde, 6 *Sc.* pryd). [Early ME. *prüden, prūden*, f. *prūde* PRIDE *sb.*¹; cf. ON. *prýða* to adorn, f. *prýði* an ornament. The pa. t. *prette* in Ayenbite perh. points to a form *prēte* beside *prēde*: cf. PRIDE *sb.*¹]

†**1.** *trans.* To ornament or adorn magnificently or proudly. *Obs.*

a **1225** *Leg. Kath.* 1460 Se prudeliche ischrud & iprud [*v.r.* iprudd] ba wið pel & wið purpre. *a* **1661** HOLYDAY *Juvenal* (1673) 22 One, with his crisping pinne, his eye-brows dies With black: paint too prides-up his lustful eyes.

†**2.** *intr.* To be or become proud. Also *to pride it.*

a **1225** *Ancr. R.* 232 *note*, An is, þet we ne pruden. *a* **1340** HAMPOLE *Psalter* ix. 23 Whils þe wickid prides, kyndeld is þe pore. **1382** WYCLIF *Ecclus.* x. 9 What pridist thou, erthe and asken? [1388 What art thou proude?] *c* **1440** *Promp. Parv.* 413/1 Prydyn, or wax prowde, *superbio.* **1656** S. H. *Gold. Law* 103 If then thou..seest more, or beyond me, pride it not, nor contemn me. *a* **1670** HACKET *Abp. Williams* II. (1692) 203 Neither were the vain-glorious content to pride it upon Success. **1802** H. MARTIN *Helen of Glenross* IV. 50, I pride to feel [etc.].

3. *trans.* To make proud, fill with pride; †to display proudly (quot. 1667). Chiefly in *pass.*, to be made or become proud.

a **1340** HAMPOLE *Psalter* ii. 11 If ȝe doe wele as ȝe aghe at doe, seruys til god in dred that ȝe be noght pridid. *c* **1430** *Pilgr. Lyf Manhode* IV. xx. (1869) 186 þat þe seruantes of Adonai ben so pryded ayens us. *a* **1619** FOTHERBY *Atheom.* II. vii. §4 (1622) 265 Those, that are prided with prosperous Fortune. **1639** EARL OF BARRYMORE in *Lismore Papers* Ser. II. (1888) IV. 39 Titles and commissions..with which they are soe pryded vpp. **1667** WATERHOUSE *Fire Lond.* 159 King Sesostris..forgot himself much, when he caused four captive kings to draw his chariot..when he prided his inconstant Fortune, in the desport of their Vassalage. **1785** BURNS *Holy Fair* xi, Nae wonder that it pride him! **1884** J. SHARMAN *Hist. Swearing* 42 A people who, perhaps unjustly, have been prided for the choiceness of their swearing.

4. a. *refl.* To make or show oneself proud; to take pride, take credit to oneself, congratulate oneself; to plume oneself. Const. *on, upon, in* (†*for, of, about, with*), *that.*

a **1275** *Prov. Ælfred* 686 in *O.E. Misc.* 138 þe luttele mon ..Bute he mote himseluen pruden, he wole maken fule luden. **1340** *Ayenb.* 258 Onder þe uayre robes is þe zaule dyad be zenne, and nameliche ine þan þet ham gledyeþ and predeþ [F. *orgoillissent*]. Yef þe pokoc him prette [F. *orgueillist*, v.r. *orgueillissoit*] uor his uayre tayle, and þe coc uor his kombe, hit ne is no wonder... Ac man oþer wyfman ..he ne ssel him naȝt prede [F. *orgueillir*]. *c* **1386** CHAUCER *Pars. T.* ¶385 For to pride hym in his strengthe of body it is an heigh folye. *Ibid.* ¶387 Eek for to pride hym of his gentrie is a ful greet folie. *c* **1412** HOCCLEVE *De Reg. Princ.* 1063 Prydē þe noght for no prosperitee. **1535** COVERDALE *Ecclus.* x. 9 What prydest thou the, o thou earth and aszshes? **1674** BOYLE *Excell. Theol.* II. ii. 138 The variety of inventions..make us pride ourselves about things, that [etc.]. **1691** tr. *Emilianne's Frauds Rom. Monks* (ed. 3) 361, I know..Reason, why the Priests should pride themselves with this. **1756–7** tr. *Keysler's Trav.* (1760) III. 108 At Mantua, where they pride themselves not a little on account of their city being the birthplace of that great poet. **1806** *Med. Jrnl.* XV. 437, I prided myself that my hands had never been guilty of communicating that disease. **1807–8** W. IRVING *Salmag.* (1824) 35 We pride ourselves upon giving satisfaction in every department of our paper. *a* **1849** H. COLERIDGE *Ess.* (1851) II. 146 The impotence of that which some women pride themselves in. **1850** D. M. CRAIK *Olive* I. v. 71 How Elspie then prided herself for the continual tutoring which had made the image..an image of love. **1882** A. W. WARD *Dickens* iv. 91 He prided himself on his punctuality.

b. *intr.* in same sense. Now *rare.*

c **1470** HENRY *Wallace* XI. 1271 Quha pridys tharin, that laubour is in waist. *a* **1578** LINDESAY (Pitscottie) *Chron. Scot.* (S.T.S.) II. 17 [They] prydit everie ane of thame quho sould be maist gallzeart in thair clething. **1648** tr. *Senault's Paraphr. Job* 326 Hee walkes publikely with lost men, and priding in his sinne. **1659** HOOLE *Comenius' Vis. World* (1672) 43 The gay Peacock prideth in his feathers..*pennis superbit.* **1747** RICHARDSON *Clarissa* (1749) I. xxx. 193 Distinction or quality may be prided in by those to whom distinction or quality are a new thing. **1897** ANNA M. WILSON *Days Mahommad* 39 My brother, I pride in your courage.

Hence **'prided** *ppl. a.*, filled with pride.

[See *a* **1340** in 3 above.] *c* **1400** GOWER *Addr. Hen. IV*, in *Pol. Poems* (Rolls) II. 11 Whan humble pacience is prided. **1883** A. S. HARDY *But yet Woman* 12 Many a stouter heart, whose prided stoicism is often only a strait-jacket.

prideful ('praɪdfʊl), *a.* Chiefly *Sc.* and *N. Amer.* [f. PRIDE *sb.*¹ + -FUL.] **a.** Full of pride; proud, arrogant.

c **1450** *Mirour Saluacioun* 4017 Some man wille he impugne be pridefulle bolnyng. **1533** GAU *Richt Vay* 12 Thay quhilk ar pridful of thair wisdome or science. *a* **1572** KNOX *Hist. Ref.* Wks. 1846 I. 155 The pridefull and scornefull people that stood by, mocked him. **1740** WHITEHEAD *Gymnasiad* II. 36 High disdain sat prideful on his brow. **1817** COLERIDGE *Alice Du Clos* iii, As if in prideful scorn Of flight and fear he stay'd behind. *c* **1843** CARLYLE *Hist. Sk. Jas. I & Chas. I* (1898) 340 Why should not such a man be prideful? **1900** *Century Mag.* Dec. 293 The doctor's stately and prideful wife. **1945** R. HARGREAVES *Enemy at Gate* 64 A prideful, unbending spirit was in no mood to bow a compulsory knee without a fight for it. **1956** B. CHUTE *Greenwillow* v. 64 He's prideful, and that's a sin, but he's been good to me. **1974** G. M. FRASER *McAuslan in Rough* 159 When that veteran has not only learned his political science at Govan Cross but is also a member of an independent and prideful race. **1974** R. HELMS *Tolkien's World* iv. 73 The true heroism in this situation was..the endurance of his men, forced by his prideful act to exhibit their loyalty to the death. **1977** *Time* 28 Feb. 23/1 He also was continuing to have his problems with prickly, prideful Senator Robert Byrd.

b. Full of pride in some fact or achievement; pleased, elated. Also, meriting a feeling of pride.

1841 *Tait's Mag.* VIII. 110/1 The father prideful as the scene reveals, And the fond mother smiling as she feels. **1848** TALFOURD *Final Mem. Lamb* 300, I well remember the flush of prideful pleasure which came over his face. **1897** H. W. STRONG in *Westm. Gaz.* 14 July 2/1 He may, in a prideful moment, declaim Cowper: I am monarch of all I survey; My right there is none to dispute. **1939** *Sun* (Baltimore) 19 Oct. 11/3 She was very prideful of this, and when she finished Bill ..went over and congratulated her. *a* **1967** A. RANSOME *Autobiogr.* (1976) i. 19, I was practising day in day out the simpler conjuring tricks that were to lead me to the prideful moments of a professional magician who, before vast audiences, should produce rabbits out of a hat. **1968** *Globe & Mail* (Toronto) 17 Feb. 28 They find they can now choose from a prideful list for entertaining..or just revel in that greatest joy of all..a leisurely candlelit dinner with fine wines and matching service. **1978** J. CARROLL *Mortal Friends* I. v. 56 Collins was aware of the pleasure, the prideful pleasure, Brady was taking in his words.

Hence **'pridefully** *adv.*, in a prideful manner; with pride; **'pridefulness**, proudness, pride.

16.. *Lindesay* (Pitscottie)'*s Chron. Scot.* (MS. F. 16 b), The king, hearing of this prydfullness [S.T.S. I. 82 prudeness]. *a* **1670** SPALDING *Troub. Chas. I* (1851) II. 256 The toun thocht evill of Haddochis behaveour, to ryde so prydfullie about thair cross. **1820** SCOTT *Monast.* viii, A white kirtle the wench wears..and a blue hood, that might weel be spared, for pridefulness. **1843** CARLYLE *Past & Pr.* II. iii, The man..had walked..humbly and valiantly with God..instead of walking sumptuously and pridefully with Mammon. **1865** RUSKIN *Sesame* 159 Strange that they will complacently and pridefully bind up whatever vice or folly there is in them. **1947** S. J. PERELMAN *Westward Ha!* (1949) x. 123 His new ball-point fountain pen, which he had been exhibiting pridefully all morning. **1977** *Time* 14 Feb. 56/3 A play that will most appeal to people of the sort he has so wickedly satirized—the pridefully literate.

†**pride-gavel.** *Obs. local.* Also prid-. [app. from PRIDE *sb.*² + GAVEL¹ tax; but cf. quot. 1779.] (See quots.)

1663 S. TAYLOR *Hist. Gavelkind* ix. 112 A *Pride-gavel*; which in the Lordship of Rodely in the County of Gloucester is used and paid..as a Rent to the Lord of the Mannour, by certain Tenants..for their Liberty and Privilege of Fishing in the River Severn for Lampraves. **1679** BLOUNT *Anc. Tenures* 18. **1779** RUDDER *Gloucestersh.* 551 Acknowledgements are paid..for fishing in the river Severn, some of which were antiently called *Prid-gavel*, from the word *Gavel* a rent, and *Pride*, the name of a kind of wicker'd putt, or pouchin, which is laid in the water to catch the fish. [No authority is given for this alleged sense of *Pride*: it is unknown to all the archaic and dialect glossaries and dictionaries.]

'prideless, *a.* [f. PRIDE *sb.*¹ + -LESS.] Devoid of pride (either in bad or good sense); having, feeling, or manifesting no pride.

c **1386** CHAUCER *Clerk's T.* 874 Ful of pacient benyngnytee Discreet and pridelees. **1508** DUNBAR *Flyting* 115 Thow lay full prydles in the peise this somer. **1703** TATE *Her Majesty's Pict.* xiii, Behold 'em now, Pacifick and Serene, With Prideless Pomp, possess'd by Britain's Queen! **1817** COLERIDGE *Biog. Lit.* xxii. (1882) 216 This lofty, yet prideless impartiality in poetry. **1889** *Pall Mall G.* 26 Aug. 3/1 The prideless, drunken parent feels no humiliation in going before the managers pleading poverty.

prideling ('praɪdlɪŋ). *nonce-wd.* [f. PRIDE *sb.*¹ + -LING.] A 'child' of pride.

1824 R. C. DALLAS *Corr. Ld. Byron* (1825) I. 22, I think he [Byron] was inoculated by the young pridelings of intellect, with whom he associated at the University.

priderite ('praɪdəraɪt). *Min.* [f. the name of R. T. *Prider*, 20th-c. Australian geologist, who made a study of the suite of rocks from which the first identified sample was taken: see -ITE¹.] A lustrous black titanate of potassium and barium that is optically similar to rutile and occurs as rectangular prisms and plates.

1951 K. NORRISH in *Mineral. Mag.* XXIX. 496 (*heading*) Priderite, a new mineral from the leucite-lamproites of the West Kimberley area, Western Australia. *Ibid.* 500 The formula of priderite is approximately $(K, Ba)_{1.33}(Ti,Fe)_8O_{16}$. **1960** *Jrnl. Geol. Soc. Austral.* VI. 72 Priderite, a potassium titanate.., is the mineral which was earlier referred to as rutile. **1968** *Mineral. Mag.* XXXVI. 869 The priderite bearing rocks are alumina-deficient and alkali-rich but sodium-poor.

pridian ('prɪdɪən), *a. rare.* [ad. L. *prīdiān-us*, f. *prīdiē* adv., on the day before, f. stem *pri-* before + *diēs* a day: see -AN.] Of or pertaining to the previous day.

1656 BLOUNT *Glossogr.*, *Pridian*, of the day before. **1840** THACKERAY *Shabby Genteel Story* ii, Thrice a week..does Gann breakfast in bed—sure sign of pridian intoxication.

pridie, var. PREDY *Obs.* (*Naut.*) ready.

priding ('praɪdɪŋ), *vbl. sb. rare.* [f. PRIDE *v.* + -ING¹.] The action of showing or taking pride.

1594 CAREW *Tasso* (1881) 24 The king of streames on priding set.. Beyond his banckes abroad all wrackfull goes. **1645** TOMBES *Anthropol.* 11 From the Pastours or peoples priding in guifts.

'priding, *ppl. a. rare.* [f. PRIDE *v.* + -ING².] Affecting or displaying pride. Hence **'pridingly** *adv.*, with display of pride.

1592 GREENE *Art Conny Catch.* III. 7 This fellowe in a kinde of priding scorne would vsuallie saye [etc.]. *a* **1677** BARROW *Pope's Suprem.* (1687) 123 He pridingly doth set himself before all others. **1711** in *10th Rep. Hist. MSS. Comm.* App. v. 153 Lett them keep their prideing cavalry to stop bottles with.

'pridy, *a. Obs.* exc. *dial.* Also 5 *Sc.* prydy, 9 *dial.* preedy. [f. PRIDE *sb.*¹ + -Y.] Characterized by pride; proud.

1456 SIR G. HAYE *Law Arms* (S.T.S.) 113 He suld nocht be callit a gude knycht, bot ane orguillous, hychty, and prydy rebelloure unworthy. **1865**, etc. in *Eng. Dial. Dict.*, Pridy, preedy (cited fr. Cornwall).

prie, obs. form of PRY *sb.* and *v.*

‖**prie-dieu** (pridjø). [F., lit. 'pray God'.] **a.** A desk made to support a book or books, and having a foot-piece on which to kneel; a praying-desk, kneeling-desk. **b.** A chair with tall sloping back, for the same purpose; also, a chair of this form for ordinary use. Also ***prie-dieu chair.***

[**1362** LANGL. *P. Pl.* A. v. 163 þe Clerk of þe churche, Sire Pers of pridye, and pernel of Flaundres.] **1760** H. WALPOLE *Let. to G. Montagu* 28 Jan., Before the altar, was an arm-chair for him, with a blue damask cushion, a *prie-Dieu*, and a footstool of black cloth. **1826** [H. BEST] *Four Y. in France* 8 The litanies are..chanted in the middle of the choir, from what I have since learned to call a *prie-Dieu*. **1852** M. ARNOLD *Tristram & Iseult* III. 91 She will fall musing..then rise And at her prie-dieu kneel. **1882** MISS BRADDON *Mt. Royal* III. vi. 123 Miss Bridgeman placed a *prie-dieu* chair in a commanding position for the reciter to lean upon gracefully.

prief(e, obs. Sc. form of PROOF, PROVE.

prier ('praɪə(r)). Also 6 priar, 6– pryer. [f. PRY *v.* + -ER¹.] One who pries.

1552 HULOET, Pryer or loker after some myschiefe, *limax.* **1575** LANEHAM *Let.* (1871) 59 A lystenar, or a priar in at the chinks or at the lokhole. **1674** BOYLE *Excell. Theol.* II. i. 127 Curious priers into nature. **1790** J. BRUCE *Source Nile* II. 577 The monks, the constant pryers into futurity.

pries, obs. form of PRICE *sb.*¹

priest (priːst), *sb.* Forms: 1–4 préost, (1 príost, preast, 2 proest, 3 prost), 1–6 prēst, (3–5 prust, pruest, 4–5 prist, 4–6 pryst, preste, priste), 4–7 preest, -e, (2) 4– priest, (4–6 preist, -e, 5 preyst, 6 preast, pryste). [OE. *préost* = OHG. *prêst, priast*, ON. *prest-r* (Norw. *prest*, Sw. *präst*, Da. *præst*); app. shortened from the form seen in OS. *prêstar*, OHG. *prêstar, priestar* (MDu., Du., MHG., Ger. *priester*), OFris. *prêstere*; ultimately from L. *presbyter* (*-biter*), a. Gr. πρεσβύτερος elder: see PRESBYTER; perh. immediately through a Com. Romanic **prester* (whence OF. *prestre*, F. *prêtre*, Sp. *preste*, It. *prete*). The origin of *éo* in OE. *préost*, and the anterior phonetic history of this and the other monosyllabic forms, are obscure; see Pogatscher *Lehnworte im Altengl.* §142. The ON. may have been from OLG. or OE.]

A. Illustration of Forms.

[**805** *Charter Cuðred of Kent* in *O.E. Texts* 442 Beforan wulfre[de] arcebiscope & æðelhune his mæsseprioste.] *a* **900** (MS. *c* 1120) *Eng. Laws Ælfred* c. 21 ȝif preost oþerne man ofslea.. hine biscop onhadiȝe. [*c* **950** *Lindisf. Gosp.* Matt. ii. 4 *Principes sacerdotum* [gl.] ða aldormenn biscopa *vel* mesapreasta. *c* **1000** ÆLFRIC *Colloquy* in Wr.-Wülcker 100/13 *Sacerdos*, mæsseprest.] *c* **1175** *Lamb. Hom.* 17 Al swa þe proest þe techet. *c* **1200** *Vices & Virtues* 29 Priest oðer munec. *a* **1250** *Owl & Night.* 733 An prostes upe londe singeþ. *a* **1325** *Poem on Consistory Crts.* in *Pol. Songs* (Camden) 159 A pruest proud ase a po, Seþþe weddeþ us bo. **13..** *Cursor M.* 2145 (Cott.) He was king and prest [*Gött.* priest] o salem. *Ibid.* 19136 (Edin.) Þai gaderit oute baþe prince and priste [*v. rr.* prist, prest, preist, preest]. *Ibid.* 28137 (Cott.) Til vncouth pryst. *c* **1380** WYCLIF *Wks.* (1880) 195 Preostes, þat shulden ben lyȝt of heuenly lif. **1387** TREVISA *Higden* VI. xxix. (MS. Cott. Tib.), 'Nay', quaþ Harold, 'hy beþ no prustes, bote a beþ wel stalword knyȝtes. **1426** AUDELAY *Poems* 3 Pristis that bene lewyd in here levyng. *c* **1440** *Promp. Parv.* 412/2 Preeste, *sacerdos, presbiter, capellanus*. *c* **1450** *St. Cuthbert* (Surtees) 6942 A preste sange at ane altere. **1504** LADY MARGARET tr. *De Imitatione* IV. vi. 268 Whan the preyst sayth masse. **1521** *Test. Ebor.* (Surtees) VI. 4 To a preiste to syng for my saull. **1529** Preest, *c* **1540** Pryst [see B. 2 a]. **1548–9** (Mar.) *Bk. Com. Prayer* (passim) Priest. **1551** ROBINSON tr. *More's Utop.* I. (1895) 74 If I were a priest. **1587** Preist [see B. 2 c].

B. Signification.

[Etymologically *priest* represents Gr. πρεσβύτερος, L. *presbyter*, ELDER; but by A.D. 375 or earlier, and thus long before the L. or Romanic word was taken into Eng., the L. word *sacerdos*, originally, like Gr. ἱερεύς, applied to the sacrificing priests of the heathen deities, and also, in the translations of the Scriptures, to the Jewish priests, had come to be applied to the Christian ministers also, and thus to be a synonym of *presbyter*. In OE., L. *presbyter* was usually represented by *préost*; L. *sacerdos*, applied to a heathen or Jewish priest, was usually rendered by *sacerd* (regularly so in Hexateuch, Psalms, and Gospels); sometimes, when applied to a Jewish or Christian priest, by *préost* or more particularly *mæsse-préost* (MASS-PRIEST). But, with the close of the OE. period, *sacerd* became disused, and *préost*, *prēst*, like OF. *prestre*, became the current word alike for *presbyter* and *sacerdos*, and thus an ambiguous term.

1583 FULKE *Defence* i. 15 Which distinction [of ἱερεύς and πρεσβύτερος] seeing the vulgar Latine texte doth alwaies rightly obserue, it is in fauour of your hereticall Sacrificing Priesthoode, that you corruptly translate *Sacerdos* and *Presbyter* alwayes, as though they were all one, a Priest. **1827** WHATELY *Logic* 257 The term 'Ἱερεὺς does seem to have implied the office of offering sacrifice,.. the term Priest is ambiguous, as corresponding to the terms 'Ἱερεὺς and πρεσβύτερος respectively, notwithstanding that there are points in which these two agree. These therefore should be reckoned, not two different kinds of Priests, but Priests in two different senses. **1869** LIGHTFOOT *Phillipians* (ed. 2) 184 The word 'priest' has two different senses. In the one it is a synonyme for presbyter or elder, and designates the minister who presides over and instructs a Christian congregation: in the other it is equivalent to the Latin *sacerdos*, the Greek ἱερεύς, or the Hebrew כהן, the offerer of sacrifices, who also performs other mediatorial offices between God and man. **1897** R. C. MOBERLY *Ministerial Priesthood* vii. §4. 291 The Church of England in her refusal to abandon the title 'priests' (by this time identified verbally with *sacerdotes* and ἱερεῖς).]

I. One whose office is to perform public religious functions; an official minister of religious worship. (See also HIGH PRIEST, PARISH PRIEST.)

†**1.** Used for a PRESBYTER or elder of the early church. *Obs. rare.* (Chiefly in early translations of Gr. πρεσβύτερος, L. *presbyter*, in N. Test.)

1382 WYCLIF *Tit.* i. 5, I lefte thee at Crete, that thou.. ordeyne by cytees prestis [*Vulg.* presbyteros; **1582** (*Rhem.*) shouldest ordaine priestes by cities]. *c* **1400** *Apol. Loll.* (Camden) 30 Bi forn þat presthed was hied,.. ilk prest of Crist was callid indifferently prest and bischop. **1563** MAN *Musculus' Commonpl.* 274 Thei do alleage the place of James [v. 14]: 'Whan any bodie is sicke amongest you, let him brynge in the Priestes [*inducat presbyteros*] of the Churche and let them praie ouer him'.

2. In hierarchial Christian churches: A clergyman in the second of the holy orders (above a deacon and below a bishop), having authority to administer the sacraments and pronounce absolution.

Historically repr. L. *presbyter*, but often including the sense of L. *sacerdos* (see above), and thus that of 4 b.

a. before the Reformation.

? **601–4** (MS. *c* 1120) *Laws of Æthelberht* c. 1 Biscopes feoh xi ȝylde. Preostes feoh ix ȝylde. Diacones feoh vi ȝylde. Cleroces feoh iii ȝylde. **695–6** (MS. *c* 1120) *Laws Wihtræd* c. 6 ȝif priost læfe unriht hæmed oþþe fulwihðe untrumes forsitte,.. sio he stille his þeȝnungæ oþ biscopes dom. *a* **900**, *c* **1175**, etc. [see A.]. *c* **1205** LAY. 1 An preost wes on leoden Laȝamon wes ihoten. *c* **1380** WYCLIF *Sel. Wks.* III. 367 Þei sey þat iche bischop and prest may lawfully leeve hor first dignyte, and after be a frere. **1483** in *Somerset Medieval Wills* (1901) 239, I woll that my executours fynde an honest seculer prest to syng for my soule. **1529** RASTELL *Pastyme, Hist. Rom.* (1811) 29 Preestis Grekes myght haue wyfis which to preestis Latens was forboden. *c* **1540** *Pilgr. T.* 54 in *Thynne's Animadv.* (1865) App. 78 Benet.. was a brother & no pryst. **1670** G. H. *Hist. Cardinals* I. III. 68 And from hence was the original of Bishops, Priests, Deacons, and Cardinals; there being several Titles and Cardinal Churches in Rome, the Priests that were Rectors over them, were call'd Cardinal Priests. **1765** BLACKSTONE *Comm.* I. Introd. iv. 111 Every man was at liberty to contribute his tithes to whatever priest or church he pleased, provided only that he did it to some. **1844** LINGARD *Anglo-Sax. Ch.* (1858) I. iv. 133 These ministers were at first confined to the three orders of bishops, priests, and deacons. *Ibid.* II. i. 15 The seventh order (that of the priesthood) was subdivided into two classes,—of bishops, who possessed it in all its plenitude, and of priests. **1874** STUBBS *Const. Hist.* I. viii. §85. 227 As the kingdom and shire were the natural sphere of the bishop, so was the township of the single priest.

b. in the Church of England since the Reformation. (The specific name of the order; but in common speech usually comprehended under the more general term *clergyman*, except in rural parts of the northern counties, where the parish clergyman is commonly called 'the priest'.) ***priest-in-charge*** (see quot. 1977).

1548–9 (Mar.) *Bk. Comm. Prayer*, The Fourme of Ordering Priestes. *Rubric.* The Bisshoppe with the priestes present, shal lay theyr handes seuerally upon the head of euery one that receiueth orders. **1652** (*title*) A Priest to the Temple; or the Character of a Country Parson. By G. Herbert. **1652** EVELYN *Diary* 14 Mar., It being now a rare thing to find a priest of the Church of England in a parish pulpit. **1706** A. BEDFORD *Temple Mus.* iv. 78 Our not admitting Priests until Four and Twenty Years old, is an Argument. **1833** *Tracts for Times* No. 5. 11 The Priests and Deacons (whom we usually class together under the common name of Clergymen).

1814 WORDSW. *Excursion* VII. 316 You, Sir, know that in a neighbouring vale A priest abides before whose life such doubts Fall to the ground. **1868** ATKINSON *Cleveland Gloss.*, *Priest*, a Church-of-England clergyman: not infrequently called a Church-priest. **1887** 'MABEL WETHERAL' *Two N.-C. Maids* xxiv, Mr. Northcote they called the priest, and a real good gentleman he was.

1941 A. THIRKELL *Northbridge Rectory* iii. 59 At St. Sycorax, where he was priest-in-charge, a title which gave him deep pleasure, he indulged in a perfect orgy of incense and vestments. **1963** *Times* 4 Feb. 12/4 In the summer.. he will become priest-in-charge of Titsey.. in the Southwark diocese. **1976** *Oxf. Diocesan Mag.* July 18/2 Stanford Dingley is not typical of rural parishes, in that, though very small, it has had its own priest, though not actually resident, for the last 20 years—a rector, a curate, and now a priest-in-charge. **1977** MACMORRAN & ELPHINSTONE *Handbk. Churchwardens* (new ed.) vi. 61 The unbeneficed clergy.. fall into two classes: first, ministers in charge of benefices which for the time being lack the services of any incumbent (generally called 'curates-in-charge' or 'priests-in-charge'): and secondly, assistant curates, viz. clergymen appointed to assist incumbents within their parishes. **1979** *Guardian* 31 Oct. 10/7 Actually he isn't even a vicar. He's just a priest in charge who's been there about eighteen months.

c. in *R.C. Ch.* since the Reformation, and in the Eastern Church. (The usual name in common as well as official use.)

1587 *Reg. Privy Council Scot.* IV. 233 Jesuitis or seminarie preistis. **1615** G. SANDYS *Trav.* 164 This place belongeth to the Georgians: whose Priests are poore, and accept of almes. No other nation say Masse on that altar. **1631** *High Commission Cases* (Camden) 197 A petition to the Court in behalf of a Popish priest, a prisoner. **1885** *Catholic Dict.* (ed. 3) 193/1 If a coadjutor is wanted for a parish priest, it is for the bishop of the diocese to nominate one. *Ibid.* 564/2 Missionary priests, such as those in England and Scotland, are mere delegates of the bishop without cure of souls in the strict sense. **1901** *Macm. Mag.* 414/2 In every Catholic parish the priest is at the very heart of things.

3. a. In more general sense: A clergyman, a member of the clerical profession, a minister of religion (in OE. often transl. *clericus*).

'[In Anglo-Saxon use] *priest* is a generic term including all clergymen, from the lowest rank; *mass-priest* specifies one who has received the order of priesthood. The simple clerk is the mass-priest's priest—mæsse-preostes preost.—Thorpe II. 412 No. 15' (Lingard *Anglo-Saxon Ch.* I. iv. (1858) 134).

a **900** tr. *Bæda's Hist.* v. xvii. [xix.] (1890) 454–6 He [Wilfrid] wæs to preoste besceoren fram him [*orig.* attonsus est ab eo]... Þa fyliȝde hine Wilfrið his preost & his hondþeng [*orig.* secutus est Vilfrid clericus illius]... On þa tid.. was Willfrid to mæssepreoste ȝehalȝad [*orig.* presbyter ordinatus est]. *c* **1000** ÆLFRIC *Voc.* in Wr.-Wülcker 155/30 *Sacerdos*, sacerd... *Clericus*, preost. *c* **1450** *Prov.* in *Deutsch. Neuphil.* (1906) 53 Thow shall do as þe preste says, but not as þe preste does. **1483** *Cath. Angl.* 291/1 A Preste, *capellanus, flamen,.. sacerdos, presbiter*. **1560** PILKINGTON *Expos. Aggeus* D j b, They said it was neuer good worlde synce euery shoomaker could tel the priests duty. **1653** HOLCROFT *Procopius, Gothic Wars* I. ii. 6 For let Priests or private men speake as they are perswaded, I can say no other thing concerning God, but that he is absolutely good. **1807** CRABBE *Par. Reg.* I. 777 Each village inn has heard the ruffian boast That never priest believed his doctrines true. **1813** SHELLEY *Q. Mab* IV. 168 War is the statesman's game, the priest's delight. **1847** JAMES *Convict* iv, We are priests of different churches.

b. *fig.* One whose office is likened to that of a priest, as ***a priest of nature, of science***, etc.

1697 DRYDEN *Virg. Georg.* II. 675 Ye sacred Muses.. Whose Priest I am, whose holy Fillets wear. **1803–6** WORDSW. *Intim. Immort.* v, The Youth, who daily farther from the east Must travel, still is Nature's Priest. **1827** HARE *Guesses* (1859) 32 Eschylus and Aristotle, Shakspeare and Bacon, are priests who preach and expound the mysteries of man and the universe. **1850** TENNYSON *In Mem.* xxxvii, This faith has many a purer priest, And many an abler voice than thou.

4. A sacrificing priest, a minister of the altar.

a. In the Jewish church, and other pre-Christian systems (as used in the Bible, rendering Heb. *kōhēn*, Gr. ἱερεύς, L. *sacerdos*).

[*c* **950**: see A. *c* **1000** *Gosp. Nicodemus* x. (Thwaites) Ða cwædon þa ealdras & þa mæssepreostas to Pilate.. he byþ deaþes scyldiȝ.] *c* **1200** ORMIN 293 Aaron wass þe firrste preost Off Issraæle þeode. *Ibid.* 466 He [Zacaryas] wass, alls icc hafe seȝȝd, God prest, & Godd full cweme. *a* **1300** *Cursor M.* 5584 (Cott.) Of [iudas] com kinges.. And of his broþer leui bredd, þe pristes þat þair lagh ledd. **1382** WYCLIF *Gen.* xiv. 18 Melchisadech, the kyng of Salem.. forsothe he was the prest of the heiȝest God. —— *Heb.* vii. 1. **1535** COVERDALE *Exod.* xxxi. 10 The mynistrynge vestimentes of Aaron ye prest. **1597** HOOKER *Eccl. Pol.* v. lxxviii. §2 Because the most eminent part both of Heathenish and Jewish service did consist in sacrifice, when learned men declare what the word Priest doth properly signify according to the mind of the first imposer of that name, their ordinary scholies do well expound it to imply sacrifice. **1611** BIBLE *John* xix. 21 Then said the chiefe Priests [Vulg. *pontifices*, WYCLIF bischops, TINDALE to *Geneva* hye prestis, *Rhem.* cheefe priests] of the Iewes to Pilate, Write not, The king of the Iewes. **1667** MILTON *P.L.* XII. 353 Factious they [Israelites] grow; But first among the Priests dissension springs, Men who attend the Altar. **1860** GARDNER *Faiths World* II. 713 The high-priest and the ordinary priests were chosen exclusively from the family of Aaron. It was the duty of the priests to serve at the altar, preparing the victims for sacrifice, and offering them up on the altar. **1901** *Encycl. Biblica* II. 2052 Before the Exile there were.. differences of rank among the priests; but the chief priest was only *primus inter pares*; even Ezekiel knows no high priest in the sense of the Priestly Code.

b. In specific Christian use, The officiant at the Eucharist and other sacerdotal offices. (Denoting the same ecclesiastical order as in 2, but with a specific connotation.)

695–6 *Laws Wihtræd* c. 18 Preost hine clænsie sylfæs soþe, in his halȝum hræȝle ætforan wiofode.. Swylce diacon hine clænsie. *a* **1225** *Juliana* 44 Hwen þe preost inwið þe messe noteð godes licome. **1466** in *Archæologia* (1887) L. I. 37 A hole sute of vestments.. for prest dekyn and sudekyn. **1548–9** (Mar.) *Bk. Com. Prayer, Communion, Rubric*, At the tyme appoincted for the ministracion of the holy Communion, the Priest that shal execute the holy ministery shall put upon hym the vesture appoincted for that ministracion. *Ibid.*, Here the priest shall turne hym toward those that come to the holy Communion, and shall saye. You that do truly [etc.]. *Ibid.*, Then shall thys generall Confession bee made.. by one of the ministers, or by the prieste himselfe. **1657** SPARROW *Bk. Com. Prayer* (1684) 217 [Of Eucharistic rite in Eastern Ch.] When this Hymn of praise is finished, the Deacons with the Priest, set the holy Bread and Cup of Blessing upon the Altar. *Ibid.* 340 In respect of this Sacrifice of the Eucharist, the Ancients have usually call'd those that offer it up, Priests. **1858** J. H. BLUNT (*title*) The Position of the Priest at the Altar. **1870** —— *Dict. Doctr. & Hist. Theol.* 591 The chief sacerdotal function of the Christian priest is to offer up on behalf of the people the Eucharistic Sacrifice. **1885** *Catholic Dict.* (ed. 3) 691 It is the office of a priest, according to the Pontifical, 'to offer, bless, rule, preach, and baptise'. First, he is empowered to offer that sacrifice of the Mass which is the centre of all the Church's worship... He succeeds the Jewish 'elder' as well as the Jewish priest. Hence he is called ἱερεὺς and *sacerdos*—i.e. 'sacrificing priest', but also *presbyter*—i.e. 'elder'.

c. In a spiritual sense, applied (*a*) to Christ in his sacrificial or mediatorial character. (After Heb. v. 6, vii. 15–21.) (Cf. HIGH PRIEST 1 b.)

c **1200** ORMIN 361, & ec forrþi þatt he [Crist] wass Preost, Hæfedd off alle preostess. *a* **1340** HAMPOLE *Psalter* xix. 1 Þe prophet spekis of crist as of a prest, þat sall offire. **1382** WYCLIF *Heb.* vii. 17 Thou art a prest into withouten ende, vp the ordre of Melchisedech. **1667** MILTON *P.L.* XI. 25 See Father,.. these Sighs And Prayers.. I thy Priest before thee bring. **1681–6** J. SCOTT *Chr. Life* (1747) III. 586 That individual Humanity, which as our Priest be offered up for us on the Cross. **1719** WATTS *Ps.* cx. 17 Jesus our Priest for ever lives To plead for us above. **1901** BP. GORE *Body of Christ* iii. § 3 (1907) 192 This means that all our prayers and offerings have been united to the abiding sacrifice and offered by the Heavenly Priest.

(*b*) to all believers (after Rev. i. 6), and to the Christian Church.

1382 WYCLIF *Rev.* i. 6 The which.. made us a kingdom, and prestes to God and to his fadir. [**1539** BIBLE (Great) *Exod.* xix. 6 Ye shall be vnto me also a kyngdome of prestes & an holy people.] **1626** DONNE *Serm.* iv. (1640) 33 Every man should come to that Altar, as holy as the Priest, for there he is a Priest. **1810** J. BENSON *Bible* I. Exod. xix. 6 Thus all believers are, through Christ, made to our God kings and priests. **1897** R. C. MOBERLY *Ministerial Priesthood* vii. §2. 256 Then the Church is God's priest in the world and for the world. *Ibid.* §3. 279 If the Christian Church is a 'priest', offering 'sacrifice' in the perpetual Eucharist.

5. a. An official minister of a pagan or non-Christian religion; originally implying sacrificial functions, but in later use often applied to the functionaries of any religious system, whether sacrificial or not.

c **1250** *Gen. & Ex.* 3922 Balaac king was for-dred forðan, .. And sente after balaam ðe prest. *a* **1300** *Cursor M.* 5412 (Cott.) Þe landes or þat lede, Þat taght was for þe preiste to fede. **1382** WYCLIF *2 Kings* xi. 18 Mathan.. the prest [**1388** preest] of Baal, thei slewen before the auter. *c* **1400** *Destr. Troy* 10784 In Iono ioly temple.. Therein Paris was put with prestis of þe laghe. **1601** SHAKS. *Jul. C.* II. ii. 5 Go bid the Priests do present Sacrifice. **1615** G. SANDYS *Trav.* 55 The Priest doth sometimes reade vnto them some part of the Alcoran. **1732** POPE *Ess. Man* II. 27 As Eastern priests in giddy circles run, And turn their heads to imitate the Sun. **1796** H. HUNTER tr. *St.-Pierre's Stud. Nat.* (1799) III. 315 He had me educated by the priests of the Temple of Osiris. *a* **1822** E. D. CLARKE *Trav. Russia* (1839) 70/1 A party of the elder Calmucks, headed by their priest. **1835** THIRWALL *Greece* I. vi. 201 The term *priest* always related not only to some particular deity, but to some particular seat of his worship. **1866** TENNYSON *Victim* i, The Priest in horror about his altar To Thor and Odin lifted a hand. **1885** W. R. SMITH in *Encycl. Brit.* XIX. 730/1 Orthodox Islam has never had real priests, doing religious acts on behalf of others.

†**b.** Applied to a PRIESTESS. *Obs. rare.*

1599 NASHE *Lenten Stuffe* Wks. (Grosart) V. 262 She was a pretty pinckany and Venus priest. **1608** SHAKS. *Per.* v. i. 243 *Diana.* My Temple stands in Ephesus.. There when my maiden priests are met together [etc.]. **1614** CHAPMAN *Masque Mid. Temple* ii. A iij b, A little more eleuate, sate Eunomia, the Virgine Priest of the Goddesse Honor.

†**6.** Allusively, ***to be*** (a person's) ***priest***: to kill him. ? *Obs.* (In allusion to the function of a

priest in performing the last offices to the dying.)

(The sense of quot. *c* 1430 is doubtful.)

[*c* **1430** *Syr Gener.* (Roxb.) 3858 The Iren with the hawberk met Right ageyn the self brest; Wel nigh it had ben his prest.] **1592** KYD *Sp. Trag.* III. iii. 37 Who first laies hand on me, ile be his Priest. **1593** SHAKS. *2 Hen. VI*, III. i. 272 And to preserue my Soueraigne from his Foe, Say but the word, and I will be his Priest. ? *a* **1800** in *Cock's Simple Strains* (1810) 135 (Jam.) Syne claught the fellow by the breast, An' wi' an awfu' shak, Swore he wad shortly be his priest.

II. Transferred senses.

7. A mallet or other weapon used to kill a fish when spent. (Chiefly in Ireland.) Cf. 6.

1851 NEWLAND *Erne, Leg. & Fly-Fishing* 284 *note*, *Priest*, a short wooden mallet, whose offices are required when the salmon is *in extremis*. **1900** W. SENIOR *Pike & Perch* xi. 175 The baton, or short cudgel, used to perform the last offices for captured fish is still called the 'priest', the name lingering, perhaps, more in Ireland than in England or Scotland. **1906** *Macm. Mag.* Nov. 28 Lydon.. lifted an iron thole-pin for a 'priest', gave a couple of decisive taps, and then laid it on the boards of the boat.

8. *Angling.* Name for a kind of artificial fly.

1867 F. FRANCIS *Angling* x. (1880) 369 The Priest.. is a good general fly.

9. A fancy breed of pigeons, of various colours.

1904 *Times* 6 Jan. 8/5 Priests, birds rarely seen nowadays at exhibitions.

III. *attrib.* and *Comb.*

10. a. Appositive (= that is a priest), as ***priest-astronomer***, ***-chaplain***, ***-doctor***, ***-hermit***, ***-king***, ***-knight***, ***-monk*** (= HIEROMONACH), ***-noble***, ***-philosopher***, ***-poet***, ***-prince***, ***-ruler***, ***-statesman***, ***-victim***. **b.** Of or pertaining to a priest or priests; priestly, sacerdotal, as ***priest-death***, †***-flock***, ***-kingdom***, †***-linen***, ***-massacre***, ***-trap***. Also PRIESTCRAFT. **c.** Objective, instrumental, etc., as ***priest-baiting***, ***-catcher***, ***-harbouring***, ***-hunter***, ***-taker***; ***priest-catching*** adj. (all in reference to the treatment of R.C. priests under the penal laws); ***priest-striver*** (one who strives or contends with a priest); ***priest-educated***, ***-guarded***, ***-hating***, ***-led***, ***-prompted*** adjs. Also PRIEST-RIDDEN. **d.** Special combs. (often with *priest's*): †**priest's bonnet**, name of some plant (? = *priest's hood*); **priest-cap, priest's cap**, (*a*) *lit.* a cap worn by a priest; (*b*) *Fortif.* an outwork with three salient and two re-entrant angles; †**priest('s) crown**, an old name for the dandelion, from the bald appearance of the receptacle (like a priest's shaven crown) when the pappus is blown off; **priest-fish**, the black rock-fish (*Sebastichthys mystinus*), common along the Pacific coast of N. America; **priest's hole**, a secret chamber or hiding-place for a (Roman Catholic) priest (in times of the penal laws); **priest's hood**, a name for the wild Arum (*A. maculatum*), from the form of the spathe (cf. MONKSHOOD); **priest-ill**, the ague (*dial.*) (Halliw. 1847–78); **priest-in-the-pulpit** = *priest's hood* (the spathe representing the pulpit, and the spadix the priest); **priest('s) pintle**, (*a*) = prec. (from the form of the spadix: cf. CUCKOO-PINT); (*b*) a name for *Orchis mascula* or other species of *Orchis*; **priest-vicar**, in some cathedrals, the name of a vicar choral who is a priest; a minor canon.

1899 *Q. Rev.* Apr. 456 The crowd.. cheerfully joined the sport of *priest-baiting. **1685** J. CHAMBERLAYNE *Coffee, Tea & Choc.* 7 The Berries grow on a tree much like our *Priests Bonnet. **1704** J. HARRIS *Lex. Techn.* I, *Bonnet à Prestre*, or the **Priest's Cap*, in Fortification, is an Out-work having at the Head three Saliant Angles, and two Inwards. **1887** R. B. IRWIN in *Battles & Leaders Civ. War* III. 595 Paine attacked.. at.. the strongest point of the whole work, the priest-cap near the Jackson road. **1899** *Daily News* 14 Sept. 6/4 Rabbi—, attired in white robes, bound by a girdle, and surmounted by the scarf and priest-cap of white silk. **1688** SIR J. KNATCHBULL *Diary* in *N. & Q.* 3rd Ser. (1864) VI. 2/1 We should pay that respect to our *Priest-catchers they expected att our hands. **1886** J. GILLOW *Lit. & Biog. Hist. Eng. Cath.* II. 531 One of those objectionable officials called pursuivants or priest-catchers. **1644** *Mercurius Civicus* 17–25 July 587 He would have nothing to doe with such *priest-catching Knaves. **1654** *Nicholas Papers* (Camden) II. 133 Wee found him besett close with Walter Montague, his *priest chaplaine. **1483** *Cath. Angl.* 291/1 *Preste crowne, *quedam herba vel flos*. **1530** PALSGR. 258/2 Prestes crowne that flyeth about in somer, *barbedieu*. **1598** FLORIO, *Ambrosine*,.. Also Dandelion, Priests crown, Swines snout, Monkshead or Dogs teeth. **1897** HAZLITT *Ourselves* 67 The *Priest-Doctor has, like the Barber-Surgeon, relinquished his double function. *c* **1200** ORMIN 489, & talde laȝhess *prestefloce Comm all off þa twa prestess. **1848** ELIZA COOK *He that is without Sin* i, A simple creed, Whose saving might has no *priest-guarded bound. **1894** FISHWICK *Hist. Lancs.* 222 *Priest-harbouring was soon amongst the most prolific causes of arrest and imprisonment. *c* **1440** *Alphabet of Tales* 128 Þe maister of his felowship went & shrafe hym vnto a *preste hermett. **1660** PEPYS *Diary* 23 May, At a Catholique house, he was fain to lie in the *priest's hole a good while. **1850** E. WARBURTON *R. Hastings* II. 185 This was one of the old places of concealment called Priests Holes. *c* **1516** *Grete Herball* ccxv. Nj b/1 Some call it *prestes hode, for it hath as it were a cape & a tongue in it lyke serpentyne of dragons. **1875** FOLEY *Rec. Eng. Prov. Soc. Jesus* I. i. 493 Mr. Wiseman .. got the *priest-hunters to come there at midnight with their band. **1907** *Daily News* 28 May 11/2 It is known also as Wake-Robin, Cuckoo Pint, and Lords-and-Ladies, but neither of these names describes the plant so well as the quaint *Priest-in-the-Pulpit. **1866–7** BARING-GOULD *Cur. Myths Mid. Ages, Prester John* (1894) 46 The reports.. of the piety and the magnificence of the *Priest-King [Prester John]. **1877** J. E. CARPENTER tr. *Tiele's Hist. Relig.* 55 Lower Egypt throws off the yoke of the priest-Kings of Thebes. **1895** SAYCE *Patriarchal Palestine* iii. 74 [Abram] had restored peace to the country of the priest-king [Melchizedek]. **1898** R. BROWN in R. M. Dorson *Peasant Customs* (1968) I. 168 The majestic figure of the Priest-king of Uru-salim. **1920** H. G. WELLS *Outl. Hist.* III. xix. 124/2 The beginnings of organized war, first as a bickering between villages, and then as a more disciplined struggle between the priest-king and god of one city and those of another [in Mesopotamia]. **1928** A. EVANS *Palace of Minos* II. II. 774 The remains of the remarkable painted relief of the personage wearing a plumed lily crown and collar, in whom we may with good reason recognize one of the actual Priest-Kings of Knossos. **1939** J. D. S. PENDLEBURY *Archaeol. Crete* iv. 249 One [chariot] drawn by winged griffins contains two female figures, one of whom.. has a headdress resembling in some ways that of the Priest King. **1958** *Times Lit. Suppl.* 24 Jan. 42/2 But he [*sc.* Charlemagne] was not a priest-king. **1978** *Listener* 28 Sept. 402/4 Were not priest-kings adored just because they were victims, in the sense that they were sacrifices for the people? **1905** *Expositor* Mar. 185 The character assumed by the Maccabaean *priest-kingdom. **1826** W. E. ANDREWS *Exam. Fox's Cal. Prot. Saints* 47 The cause for which the *priest-knight and the duchess-gentlewoman suffered. **1649** MILTON *Eikon.* xv. Wks. 1851 III. 451 Those *Priest-led Herodians with their blind guides are in the Ditch already. **1871** G. MACDONALD *Sonn. conc. Jesus* xviii, Despised! rejected by the priest-led roar Of multitudes! **1561** *Reg. Privy Council Scot.* I. 175, Thre fardellis *prest lynnyng, allegit schippit be Anthonie Triciane. **1711** SHAFTESB. *Charac.* (1737) I. 86 Much less wou'd you.. have carry'd on this magophony, or *priest-massacre, with such a barbarous zeal. **1881** T. E. BRIDGETT *Hist. Eucharist in Gt. Brit.* II. 167 Regulations regarding the private masses of the *priest-monks. **1872** BAGEHOT *Physics & Pol.* (1876) 38 The policy of the old *priest-nobles of Egypt and India. **1711** SHAFTESB. *Charac.* (1737) III. 76 'Twas satisfaction enough to the *priest-philosopher. **1578** LYTE *Dodoens* II. lvi. 222 The first kinde is called in Greeke ὄρχις, Orchis.. in English.. *Priest pintell. *Ibid.* III. vii. 323 This plant is called.. in Latine Arum:.. in English also it is commonly called Aron, Priestes pyntill, Cockowpintell. **1688** R. HOLME *Armoury* II. 56/1 A Dog-stone flower.. is generally known by the name of Priest-Pintle, or Goat-Stones. **1895** *Pop. Sci. Monthly* Aug. 440 The *priest-poet, appointed eulogizer of the deity he serves, is the first poet. **1877** J. E. CARPENTER tr. *Tiele's Hist. Relig.* 56 The conflict of the Ethiopian *priest-princes.. was in part national. **1839–52** BAILEY *Festus* xix. 271 As guiltless .. As is the oracle of an extinct god Of its *priest-prompted answer. **1920** H. G. WELLS *Outl. Hist.* III. xvi. 94/2 There [in the Euphrates-Tigris valley] flourished the first temples and the first *priest-rulers that we know of among mankind. **1860** PUSEY *Min. Proph.* 27 He says not, they *were* *priest-strivers, but were *like* priest-strivers, persons whose habit it was to strive with those who spoke in God's Name. **1679** BRADLEY in R. Mansel *Narr. Popish Plot* (1680) 49 She heard the said Lawton was a *Priest-taker. **1681** DRYDEN *Spanish Friar* III. iii. 36 A *Priest-trap at their door to lay, For holy Vermin that in houses prey. **1688** *Exped. Prince of Orange* in *Select. fr. Harl. Misc.* (1793) 471 The prince commanded Dr. Burnet to order the *priest-vicars of the cathedral, not to pray for the prince of Wales. **1837–8** *Act 1 & 2 Vict.* c. 106 §39 Any spiritual person, being Prebendary, Canon, Priest Vicar, Vicar Choral, or Minor Canon in any Cathedral or Collegiate Church. **1901** *Crockford's Cler. Direct.* p. lvii, Exeter... Priest-Vicars, a Corporation. **1895** GLADSTONE in *19th Cent.* Dec. 1074 The recovery of this race.. is by a *Priest-Victim foreshadowed in ancient predictions.

priest (priːst), *v.* [f. prec. sb.]

1. *intr.* To exercise the ministry or functions of a priest. Also *to priest it*. ? *Obs.*

c **1400** *Apol. Loll.* 34 Prestis þat prestun wel be þei hade worþi dowble honor. **1509** BARCLAY *Shyp of Folys* (1874) I. 158 Courters become prestes nought knowynge but the dyce; They preste not for god, but for a benefyce. **1642** T. GOODWIN *Christ set forth* 120 Christ had not been an High-Priest, if he had not gone to heaven, and Priested it there too (as I may so speak).

2. *trans.* To make (any one) a priest; to ordain to the priesthood, admit to priest's orders.

1504 *Bury Wills* (Camden) 97 Tyll he be of lawfull age to be prystyd. **1508** KENNEDIE *Flyting w. Dunbar* 309 Thow wes prestyt, and ordanit be Sathan For to be borne to do thy kin defame. **1581** J. BELL *Haddon's Answ. Osor.* 285 One Stephen was made Pope, who.. doth first unpriest, and afterwardes newpriest agayne all such as Const. before him had priested. **1647** TRAPP *Comm. Phil.* i. 1 And yet how eager were our late factours for Rome to have priested us all. **1823** BP. J. JEBB in Forster *Life* App. 721 Deacons seeking to be priested, must exhibit their letters of orders. **1896** J. H. WYLIE *Hist. Eng. Hen. IV*, III. 394 John was only in deacon's orders, but he was priested by Cardinal Brogny.

†**3.** To bless as a priest: see PRIESTED below.

Hence **'priested** *ppl. a.*, (*a*) ordained to the priesthood; †(*b*) blessed by a priest (quot. 1603); **'priesting** *vbl. sb.*, (*a*) the function of a priest, priestly ministration; (*b*) ordination to the priesthood.

1550 CROWLEY *Inform. & Petit.* 2 For lyk causes do our ministers.. applye themselues to priestyng, because they lyke wel the ydelnes of the lyfe. **1603** HARSNET *Pop. Impost.* 80 To have a precious payre of priested gloves.. [such] as they may use against any Sparrow-blasting or Sprite-blasting of the Devil. **1609** BP. W. BARLOW *Answ. Nameless Cath.* 123 Had She not relied too much vpon the Priested sort, her End had not beene so sudden nor vnkinde. **1641** MILTON *Prel. Episc.* 24 Bearing the image of God according to his ruling, and of Christ according to his priesting. **1891** S. MOSTYN *Curatica* ix, It was the anniversary.. of my ordination, and the day of my priesting. **1916** JOYCE *Portrait of Artist* (1969) v. 221 A priested peasant, with a brother a policeman in Dublin and a brother a potboy in Moycullen.

priestal ('priːstəl), *a. rare.* [f. PRIEST *sb.* + -AL[1].] Pertaining to or having the character of a priest or priests; sacerdotal.

1839 J. ROGERS *Antipopopr.* xvii. §2. 340 Apparent priests may be not really priestal. **1848** CHEEVER *Wand. Pilgr.* xxviii. 184 The matter has ended in the establishment of a priestal republican despotism.

priestcraft ('priːstkrɑːft, -æ-).

1. The 'craft' or business of a priest; the exercise of priestly functions. (Now only as an etymological nonce-use.)

1483 *Seill of Caus* Edin. 2 May, MS. (Jam.), To the wpholde of devyne service at the said alter ouklie and daylie, and to the priestcraft at the alter as effeirs. **1900** in *Ch. Times* 9 Mar. 267/2 'Craft' means art, dexterity, skill... Priestcraft in a good sense simply means the diligent and able exercise of priestly functions.

2. Priestly craft, or policy; the arts used by ambitious and worldly priests to impose upon the multitude or further their own interests.

1681 DRYDEN *Abs. & Achit.* I. 1 In pious times ere priest-craft did begin. **1700** TOLAND *Clito* x, Religion's safe, with Priestcraft is the War. **1796** BP. WATSON *Apol. Bible* (ed. 2) 197 The extreme folly, to which credulity and priestcraft can go. **1834** LYTTON *Pompeii* I. viii, I would preserve the delusions of priestcraft, for they are serviceable to the multitude. **1869** L. SCHMITZ in *Smith's Dict. Gr. & Rom. Antiq.* 838/2 Freethinkers and unbelievers looked upon the [Delphic] oracle as a skilful contrivance of priestcraft which had then outgrown itself.

Hence **'priestcrafty** *a.*, characterized by priestcraft.

1846 WORCESTER cites *Ch. Ob.*

priestdom ('priːstdəm). [f. PRIEST *sb.* + -DOM.] †**a.** The office of priest, priesthood. *Obs.* †**b.** With possessive, as a mock title (cf. PRIESTSHIP). *Obs.* **c.** The rule or dominion of priests. *rare.*

1528 TINDALE *Obed. Chr. Man* 135 b, He was cursed and loost the kyngdome and also the prestdome. **1588** *Marprel. Epist.* (Arb.) 26, I woulde praye your priestdomes to tell me which is the better scholler. **1615** SIR E. HOBY *Curry-combe* iii. 130 Your answer puts the nose of your Priestdome clean out of ioynt. **1871** H. B. FORMAN *Living Poets* 372 The people crucified by king-craft and priest-dom. **1895** CROCKETT *Bog Myrtle* I. i. 20 It is a mistaken belief that priestdom died when they spelled it Presbytery.

priesteen ('priː,stiːn). [f. PRIEST *sb.*; see -EEN[2].] Anglo-Irish diminutive of PRIEST *sb.*

1907 J. M. SYNGE *Playboy of Western World* I. 23 'It isn't fitting,' says the priesteen, 'to have his likeness lodging with an orphaned girl.' **1912** JOYCE *Let.* 19 Aug. (1966) II. 304 Can your friend in the sodawater factory or the priesteen write my verses? **1922** —— *Ulysses* 212 The quaker's pate godlily with a priesteen in booktalk.

†**'priesterly**, *a. Obs. rare*[−1]. [app. ad. G. *priesterlich*, f. *priester* PRIEST *sb.* + *-lich*, -LY[1].] = PRIESTLY.

1535 COVERDALE *Exod.* xix. 6 Ye shall be vnto me a presterly kingdome, and an holy people.

†**'priestery**. *Obs. nonce-wd.* [f. PRIEST *sb.* + -ERY.] Priests collectively; a body or company of priests. (*contemptuous.*)

1649 MILTON *Eikon.* i, The King among all his priestery, and all those numberless volumes of their theological distillations, not meeting with one man or book of that coat that could befriend him with a prayer in captivity.

priestess ('priːstɪs, 'priːstɛs). [f. PRIEST *sb.* + -ESS[1], taking the place of the earlier PRIESTRESS.]

1. a. A female priest; a woman who holds the postition and performs the functions of a priest, or (loosely) of a minister of religion.

1693 CREECH in *Dryden's Juvenal* xiii. (1697) 336 He goes to Delphos, humbly begs Advice; And thus the Priestess by Command replies. **1709** J. JOHNSON *Clergym. Vade M.* II. 99 Priestesses or women-presidents are not to be constituted in the church. **1756–7** tr. *Keysler's Trav.* (1760) II. 416 In the next room are the heads of Livia Augusta veiled, and a priestess of Cybele. **1768–74** TUCKER *Lt. Nat.* (1834) II. 451 The gifted priestess among the quakers is known by her green apron. **1884** SIR S. ST. JOHN *Hayti* v. 184 He [Salnave].. made considerable presents to the [Vaudoux] priests and priestesses.

b. *fig.* and *transf.*

1738 POPE *Epil. Sat.* II. 234 Her priestess Muse forbids the Good to die, And opes the temple of Eternity. **1811** L. M. HAWKINS *C'tess & Gertr.* I. 101 If mistresses of families will make their own passions their idols, they can seldom hope for virtuous priestesses to serve the altar. **1817** LADY MORGAN *France* I. (1818) I. 48 Pretty *bouquets* are tossed into the carriage windows.. while the little priestesses of Flora offer their gratuitous prayer of '*bon voyage*'. **1850** TENNYSON *In Mem.* iii, O Sorrow, cruel fellowship, O Priestess in the vaults of Death.

2. A priest's wife. (*colloq.*)

1709 MRS. MANLEY *Secret Mem.* I. 158 The Priestess flounced out of the House, call'd for her Coachman, and bid him put in his Horses, for away would she go. **1778** *Chron.* in *Ann. Reg.* 207/2 The Jew priest of the Hamburgh Synagogue, in Fenchurch-Street, was divorced from his priestess.

3. *Comb.*, as ***priestess-queen*** (after *priest-king*).

1920 H. G. WELLS *Outl. Hist.* III. xix. 114/1 The Sumerians allowed much more freedom and authority to women than the Semites. They had priestess-queens, and one of their great divinities was a goddess, Ishtar.

Hence **'priestesshood**, the office of a priestess; the system of priestesses.

1841 C. E. LESTER *Glory Eng.* II. 139 When one of the six ..happens to die, the remaining five fill up the void; and thus the priesthood, or, rather, priestesshood, lives on in a sort of corporate immortality. **1887** H. R. HAWEIS *Light of Ages* v. 145 The priesthood and priestesshood were as perfectly organised.

†'priesthead. Forms: see PRIEST: also 4–6 **prestede, -hed.** [f. PRIEST *sb.* + -HEAD.] = next.

a **1300** *Cursor M.* 21695 Quen strijf was bute þe preisthede In þaa dais mang þe Iuus lede. *c* **1375** *Sc. Leg. Saints* xxxii. (*Justin*) 62 Of þar prestede he had hade, Bot seruice til ydolis he made. *c* **1400** *Apol. Loll.* 30 Biforn þat presthed was hied. **1533** GAU *Richt Vay* 36 S. Paul writis..of his [Christ's] halie preistheid and sacrifis. **1535** COVERDALE *Mal.* iii. *heading*, Off the abrogacion of the olde leuiticall prestheade. **1556** *Chron. Gr. Friars* (Camden) 96 Thomas Creme some tyme archebyshoppe of Cantorbery..was degradyd..of hys archebyshoppecheppe, & presthed. **1588** A. KING tr. *Canisius' Catech.* 110 The onlie Prince of ye priestheed of God.

priesthood ('pri:sthʊd). Forms: see PRIEST and -HOOD; also 4 **prestod, -hold,** 6 **-woode.** [OE. *prēosthād*, f. *prēost*, PRIEST *sb.* + *-hād*, -HOOD.]

1. The office or function of a priest; the condition of being a priest; the order of priest.

a **900** tr. *Bæda's Hist.* I. vii. (1890) 34 Ða ʒelamp þæt he sumne Godes mann preosthades [*orig.* clericum quendam] ..on gestliðnysse onfeng. *c* **1000** *Aldhelm Gloss.* 3692 in Napier *O.E. Glosses* 98 *Clericatus*, preosthades. *c* **1380** WYCLIF *Wks.* (1880) 58 Who euere comeþ to prestod. *Ibid.* 78 Nowe, whanne presthold stondeþ in peny clerkis. **1387** TREVISA *Higden* (Rolls) IV. 105 Symon..preost of þe temple and bisshop,..bouʒte þe preosthood of Appolinus duke of Phenicia. *Ibid.* 125 He hadde renewed þe principalte and þe preosthode. *c* **1440** *Promp. Parv.* 412/2 Preesthood, *presbiteratus.* **1548–9** (Mar.) *Bk. Com. Prayer, Ordering of Priests*, Reuerende Father in God, I presente unto you, these persones presente, to bee admitted to the ordre of Priesthode. **1662** STILLINGFL. *Orig. Sacr.* II. vii. §12 When an order of Priesthood different from the Aaronicall should be set up. **1729** LAW *Serious C.* x. (1732) 142 He therefore ..is like him that abuses the Priesthood. **1865** R. W. DALE *Jew. Temp.* xiii. (1877) 139 It was these circumstances that made the priesthood of Melchizedek unique.

b. The priestly office of Christ, of his Church, or of believers.

1382 WYCLIF *Heb.* vii. 24 [Christ], for that he dwelle into withouten ende, hath euerelastyng presthod. **1681–6** J. SCOTT *Chr. Life* (1747) III. 130 To explain the Priesthood, and Priestly Acts of our Saviour. **1851** PUSEY *Let. to Bp. London* 25 In His abiding Priesthood after the order of Melchisedech, He pleads, in Heaven, what He has commanded us to plead on earth. **1868** LYNCH *Rivulet* cx. ii, And the pale Victim, in the strife, Eternal priesthood earns. **1897** R. C. MOBERLY *Ministerial Priesthood* iii. 87 The true rationale and the true distinction (within the inclusive priesthood of the Christian Church Body) at once of the priesthood of the Christian layman, and of the priesthood of the Christian minister. *Ibid.* iii. §2. 251 The Church's priesthood being in its inner truth the priesthood of Christ, is a substantial reality.

c. The priestly office personified.

1393 LANGL. *P. Pl.* C. XXII. 334 Grace deuysede A cart, hihte cristendome, to carien home peers sheues;..And made preesthood haiwarde. *c* **1420** ? LYDG. *Assembly of Gods* 839 Preesthood theym folowyd with the Sacramentes, And Sadnesse also with the Commaundementes. *Ibid.* 1426, 1452, etc.

†d. With possessive, as a mock title for a priest.

1593 SHAKS. *2 Hen. VI*, II. i. 23 What, Cardinall? Is your Priest-hood growne peremptorie?

2. The office or order as embodied in or represented by the persons holding it; hence, The system of priests; the or a body of priests.

1377 LANGL. *P. Pl.* B. xv. 93 Riȝt so out of holicherche alle yueles spredeth, There inparfyt presthod is prechoures and techeres. *c* **1400** *Destr. Troy* 11778 The glemyng of gold, þat glottes þere hertis..puttes the pouer of pristhode abake. **1539** BIBLE (Great) *1 Tim.* iv. 14 The layinge on of handes by the auctoryte of presthode. **1678** DRYDEN & LEE *Œdipus* III. i, Oh, why has priesthood privilege to lie, And yet to be believed! **1756–7** tr. *Keysler's Trav.* (1760) I. 415 This severity is easily accounted for from the dignity assumed by the priesthood. **1820** BYRON *Mar. Fal.* I. ii, But the priests —I doubt the priesthood Will not be with us. **1883** GILMOUR *Mongols* xxxi. 361 Sacred books used by the priesthood and laity of Mongolia.

transf. and *fig.* **1382** WYCLIF *1 Pet.* ii. 9 Ȝe ben a kynd chosun, kyngly presthod, holy folk [**1526** TINDALE, a chosen generacion, a royall presthod]. **1805** W. TAYLOR in *Ann. Rev.* III. 257 Schemes of public instruction..may hire the literary priesthood of philosophy, to all the servility which it imputes to the Christian clergy. **1901** BP. GORE in *Daily Chron.* 18 Oct. 6/7 There must be a priesthood of medicine.

priesti'anity. *nonce-wd.* [Humorously f. PRIEST *sb.* after *Christianity.*] A hostile appellation for a priestly system or doctrine.

1720 T. GORDON (*title*) Priestianity, or a View of the Disparity between the Apostles and the Modern Inferior Clergy. **1823** PARR *Let. to R. Odell* Wks. 1828 VIII. 224 He has a larger share of priestianity than of christianity.

†'priestish, *a. Obs.* [f. PRIEST *sb.* + -ISH[1].] Of, belonging to, or characteristic of a priest; priestly, sacerdotal. (Chiefly *contemptuous.*)

1529 *Supplic. to King* (E.E.T.S.) 45 No neade of longe, prystishe prayers. **1553** BECON *Reliques of Rome* (1563) 26 b, Pope Siricius ordayned yt priestishe orders should not be geuen altogether at one time, but at sundrye tymes. **1569** E. HAKE *Newes Powles Churchyarde* F vij, Much lesse that I depraued haue all Preachers so attyrde In Priestish weedes, as Popelings were.

priestism ('pri:stɪz(ə)m). [f. PRIEST *sb.* + -ISM.] The system, spirit, methods, or practices of priests; sacerdotalism. (In hostile use.)

1842 MIALL in *Nonconf.* II. 145 Priestism, the first-born child of worldliness and hypocrisy. **1887** J. PARKER in *Chr. World* 4 Aug. 589 All priestism is bad, whether in the Establishment or in Nonconformist churches.

priestless ('pri:stlɪs), *a.* [f. PRIEST *sb.* + -LESS.] Without a priest; not having, or not attended by, a priest.

1297 R. GLOUC. (Rolls) 11301 Euere lokede þis burgeis wan hii were vorþ idriue, Prestles hom was wel wo þat hii nere issriue. **1879** BARING-GOULD *Germany* II. 145 In these priestless parish churches, at the hour of mass the congregation assembles. **1885** FAIRBAIRN *Catholicism Rom. & Angl.* iv. (1899) 169 It stood among the ancient faiths as a strange and extraordinary thing—a priestless religion.

priestlet ('pri:stlɪt). [f. as prec. + -LET.] = PRIESTLING 1. (Contemptuous.)

1880 VERN. LEE *Stud. Italy* 157 Dapper literary priestlets redolent of bergamot and sonnets. **1883** *Cornh. Mag.* 568 The priestlets in the train of a bishop.

priestlike ('pri:stlaɪk), *a.* (*adv.*) [f. as prec. + -LIKE.] Like, or like that of, a priest; resembling, pertaining or proper to, characteristic of, or befitting a priest; priestly, sacerdotal.

c **1470** HENRY *Wallace* IV. 702 Than Wallace..Arayit him weill in till a preistlik goun. **1559** AYLMER *Harborowe* O iv b, Let your portion be priestlike and not princelike. **1600** W. WATSON *Decacordon* (1602) 345 A very learned, religious, and priestlike apology. **1607** SHAKS. *Cor.* v. i. 56 We haue suppler Soules Then in our Priest-like Fasts. *a* **1821** KEATS *Last Sonn.*, The moving waters at their priestlike task Of pure ablution round earth's human shores. **1831** CARLYLE *Misc.* (1857) II. 189 There is something priest-like in that Life of his.

B. *adv.* Like a priest; in the character or manner of a priest.

1565 T. STAPLETON *Fortr. Faith* 152 Hazard their liuinges rather then go priestlike. **1611** SHAKS. *Wint. T.* I. ii. 237, I haue trusted thee..With all the neerest things to my heart, as well My Chamber-Councels, wherein (Priest-like) thou Hast cleans'd my Bosome.

priestliness ('pri:stlɪnɪs). [f. PRIESTLY *a.* + -NESS.] Priestly quality or character.

1681 *Whole Duty Nations* 22 Cloath'd with that Denomination of Priestliness, use hath appropriated to it. **1870** DISRAELI *Lothair* xliv, The Bishop..had now..to restrain his exuberant priestliness. **1897** R. C. MOBERLY *Ministerial Priesthood* vii. §3. 263 The true priestliness necessarily carries with it the pastoral character: the real pastoral character is but an expression, in outward life, of priestliness.

priestling ('pri:stlɪŋ). [f. PRIEST *sb.* + -LING[1].]

1. A little, young, petty, or insignificant priest. (Usually contemptuous.)

1629 MAXWELL tr. *Herodian* (1635) 286 This brave young priestling as he sacrificed, and caperd about the Altars,.. was curiously eyed of all. **1648** MILTON *Observ. Art. Peace* Wks. 1851 IV. 570 The Rebellion which was even then design'd in the close purpose of these unhallow'd Priestlings. **1816** SOUTHEY in *Q. Rev.* XIV. 352 For the purpose of conciliating the good will of the prelates and priestlings. **1866** J. H. NEWMAN *Gerontius* iv. 29 Such fudge, As priestlings prate, Is his guerdon.

2. A person weakly or servilely devoted to a priesthood or priestly system. *rare.* (Cf. *worldling.*)

1720 GORDON & TRENCHARD *Independ. Whig* (1728) 179 It is no Wonder that weak People now a-days should believe in Priests, and not in Christ; should be Priestlings, and not Christians. **1907** *19th Cent.* Mar. 464 The priestlings of the Centre exclaimed that the finger of God had done it.

priestly ('pri:stlɪ), *a.* [f. PRIEST *sb.* + -LY[1]: in OE. *prēostlic.*]

1. Of or pertaining to a priest or priests; sacerdotal; †in OE., canonical (*obs.*).

c **1000** *Corp. Chr. Coll. Camb. MS.* 191, 150 Eac ic minȝie þæt hi ȝemunon þæs preostlican reȝoles. **1535** COVERDALE *1 Esdras* viii. 55, I weied them the golde & the syluer & all the prestly ornamentes of the house of oure God. **1561** T. NORTON *Calvin's Inst.* II. vii. (1634) 156 They are all endued both with Priestly and Kingly honour. **1641** *Impeachm. Wren* in Rushw. *Hist. Coll.* III. (1692) I. 354 Some of which he did against his Priestly Word given to the said Patrons, or their Friends, *in verbo Sacerdotis*, not to do the same. **1782** PRIESTLEY *Corrupt. Chr.* I. II. 224 Lactantius said little..of Christ's priestly office. **1838** THIRLWALL *Greece* xi. II. 6 The tribe which has been taken for a priestly caste. **1891** MARQ. SALISBURY in *Daily News* 22 Jan. 6/1 Priestly rule is the great vice of the religious organization..; it is the attempt to use the influence gained by teachers of religion, by virtue of their holy mission, in the furtherance of secular ends. **1901** BP. GORE *Body of Christ* iv. §4 (1907) 255 The fathers..clearly see that the priestly action of Christ is now in heaven.

b. ***priestly code***, in O.T. criticism: A name given to one of the constituent elements which recent criticism finds in the Hexateuch, and holds to constitute the framework of the whole in its existing form. Also called ***priests' code, priestly writing***; so ***priestly writer***, the writer of this.

[**1891** DRIVER *Introd. Lit. O. Test.* 9 By Ewald it was termed the 'Book of Origins'; by Tuch and Nöldeke, from the fact that it seemed to form the groundwork of our Hexateuch, the 'Grundschrift'; more recently, by Wellhausen, Kuenen, and Delitzsch, it has been styled the 'Priests' Code'. This last designation is in strictness applicable only to the ceremonial sections in Ex.—Nu... It may be represented conveniently, for the sake of brevity, by the letter P.] **1899** F. H. WOODS in *Hastings' Dict. Bible* II. 365/2 Thus we find three distinct codes—the Covenant code (C), the Deuteronomic (D), the Levitical or Priestly (P). *Ibid.* 368/2, P. The Priestly Book. The most striking general characteristics of P. **1900** CARPENTER & HARFORD-BATTERSBY *Hexateuch* I. xiii. 121 The Priestly Code. The large extent and the complicated character of this great collection raise many problems. **1901** *Encycl. Biblica* II. 2050 The characteristic feature in the hypothesis of Graf is that the Priestly Code is placed later than Deuteronomy, so that the order is no longer Priestly Code, Yahwist (JE), Deuteronomy, but Jehovist (JE), Deuteronomy, Priestly Code. **1905** *Expositor* Jan. 68 The district..is termed by the Priestly Writer the 'Steppes of Moab'.

2. Befitting or characteristic of a priest; like that of a priest.

1504–5 in Brand *Hist. Newcastle* (1789) I. 641 Such.. honest conversation..as..shalbe thought convenient and prestly. **1608** SHAKS. *Per.* III. i. 70 Hie thee whiles I say A priestly farewell to her. **1905** A. C. BENSON *Upton Lett.* (1906) 25 He [Newman] had little of the priestly hunger to save souls.

3. Having the character or aspect of a priest; such as a priest is or should be; like a priest.

1465 MARG. PASTON in *P. Lett.* II. 242 A prystly man and vertusly dysposyd. **1832** CARLYLE *Remin.* (1881) I. 51 John Johnston, the priestliest man I ever under any ecclesiastical guise was privileged to look upon.

4. Holding the office of a priest; that is a priest. ***priestly writer***, in O.T. criticism: see 1 b.

1817 SHELLEY *Rev. Islam* XII. ix, Scared by the faith they feigned, each priestly slave Knelt for his mercy whom they served with blood.

'priestly, *adv. rare.* [f. PRIEST *sb.* + -LY[2].] In the character of, or in a way befitting, a priest.

c **1400** *Apol. Loll.* 59 þat þey be þolid to minister prestly oþer sacrements. **1493** *Festivall* (W. de W. 1515) 170 b, How blessyd ben preestes sayth he [S. Bernard] yf they preestly lyue. **1511** COLET *Serm. Conf. & Ref.* B iv b, Pristes, nat lyuynge pristly but secularly, to the vtter and miserable distruction of the churche. **1755** J. SHEBBEARE *Lydia* (1769) II. 78 His peruke was priestly smart.

†'priestress. *Obs. rare.* [Late ME. *prestresse*, a. OF. *prestresse* (mod. *prêtresse*), f. OF. *prestre* PRIEST + *-esse*, -ESS[1].] = PRIESTESS.

1480 CAXTON *Ovid's Met.* XI. ii, There serued grete plente of prestis and priesteresses. **1490** —— *Eneydos* xvii. 66 Thyas ye grete prestresse. **1603** HOLLAND *Plutarch's Mor.* 866 The priestresse of Minerva in Athens. *Ibid.* 1301.

priest-ridden ('pri:st,rɪd(ə)n), *ppl. a.* Also **-rid** (*obs.* or *arch.*). [f. PRIEST *sb.* + RIDDEN *ppl. a.*] 'Ridden', i.e. managed or controlled by a priest or priests; held in subjection by priestly authority.

α. **1653** WATERHOUSE *Apol. Learn.* 82 That pusillanimity ..which by many in our Age scornfully is called Priest-riddenness as I may so say, their term being Priest-ridden when they express a man addicted to the Clergie. **1681** DRYDEN *Spanish Friar* II. iii, Was ever man thus priest-ridden? **1705** HICKERINGILL *Priest-cr.* II. viii. 80 Nothing but the Redemption of the Priest-ridden Laiety from Priest-craft Slavery and Tyranny could have perswaded me to this ungrateful..Toil. **1818** SCOTT *Hrt. Midl.* xi, I have been abroad, and know better than to be priest-ridden. **1849** [see *press-ridden*: PRESS *sb.*[1] 16]. **1864** BURTON *Scot Abr.* I. v. 290 *note*, The Scots are called a priest-ridden people, yet their most esteemed jests are against the clergy.

β. **1664** H. MORE *Myst. Iniq.* 411 Which..they endeavoured to keep as ignorant as they could, that the People might be the more patiently Priest-rid. **1714** MANDEVILLE *Fab. Bees* (1733) I. 260 Men [may] be.. religious tho' they refus'd to be priest-rid. **1860** READE *Cloister & H.* (1861) II. 28 Not the first fool that has been priest-rid, and monk-bit.

Hence **'priest-,riddenness**, the condition of being priest-ridden. So (*nonce-wds.*) **'priest-,riding**, the domination or tyranny of priests; **'priest-ride** *v. trans.* (*rare*), to control as a priest.

1653 Priest-riddenness [see above]. **1705** in W. S. Perry *Hist. Coll. Amer. Col. Ch.* I. 156 Common aversion against Priest-riding. **1733** *Revolution Politicks* III. 59 'Tis well if they don't priest-ride you.

priestship ('pri:st-ʃɪp). Now *rare.* [f. as prec. + -SHIP.] The office of priest; also as a mock title: = PRIESTHOOD 1, 1 d.

1642 SIR E. DERING *Sp. on Relig.* 96 The Kingship and Priestship of every particular man. **1648** MILTON *Observ. Art. Peace* Wks. 1851 IV. 572 We know your classic Priestship is too gripple, for ye are always begging. **1868** BROWNING *Ring & Bk.* VI. 1442 My salutation to your priestship! **1896** GODDARD in *Mission. Herald* Jan. 27/1 The priestship for this temple descends from father to son.

priest-shire. *Hist. rare.* [repr. OE. *prēostscīr*, f. *prēost*, PRIEST *sb.* + *scīr*, SHIRE.] A district to which a priest ministered: a term equivalent to 'parish'.

c **1000** *Eccles. Inst.* c. 14 in Thorpe *Anc. Laws* II. 410 Ne spane nan mæsse-preost nanne mon of oðre cyrcean hyrnysse to his cyrcan, ne of oðre preost-scyre lære, þæt mon hys cyrcan ȝesece. **1844** LINGARD *Anglo-Sax. Ch.* (1858) I. iv. 144 *note*, These districts allotted to priests were called priestshires.

† **prie'stybulous**, *a. Obs. rare*$^{-1}$. A pun on PROSTIBULOUS, meretricious (also in Bale).

1550 BALE *Image Both Ch.* xiii. H iij, Their more then Iewish ceremonies, their priestybulous priesthoode, theyr vowing to haue no wiues.

prieue, prieve, obs. f. PROOF and PROVE.

prife, var. PRIVE *v. Obs.*

priffe, obs. f. PRIVY *a.*

† **prig**, *sb.*^{1} *Obs.* Also 5–6 prigg, pryg(ge (7 prydg). [App. another form of SPRIG *sb.* (nail). Cf. PRAG *sb.*^{1}] (?) = SPRIG, brad (usually collective).

1410 in Rogers *Agric. & Prices* (1882) III. 447 (Wye) Tileprig 6200 @ *m*/10. **1411** *Ibid.*, Wogh prig nails... Tyle prig. **1415** *Ibid.*, (Charles & Rowhill) Prignail. **1420** *Ibid.* 448 (Lullington) Prigg. **1460** *Ibid.* 453 Prigs. **1490** *Churchw. Acc. St. Dunstan's, Canterb.* (1885) 12 Item payde for prygge and lathe iiij*d*. **1548** *Hawkhurst Ch. Acc.* in *Archæol. Cant.* V. 61 Payde.. for prygge and nayls iiij^s iiij^d. **1611** *MS. Acc. St. John's Hosp., Canterb.*, For a thousand of prydgs xviij d.

Comb. **1540** *MS. Acc. St. John's Hosp., Canterb.*, Payd for a pryg hammer ij d.

prig (prɪg), *sb.*^{2} Now *dial.* Also 6 pryg, *pl.* prygges. [Origin unascertained. Cf. PIG *sb.*^{2}] A small pan of brass or tin; see also quot. 1674.

1511 *Pleadings Duchy Lancaster* (1896) XXXII. 53, v brasse pottes, iij pannes, iij prigges. **1573** *Lanc. Wills* (Chetham Soc.) III. 60 Ffyve pannes and twoo prygges or lyttel pannes. **1636** *Farington Papers* (Chetham Soc.) 15 Apperteyninge to the Kitchen. 2 Priggs. **1674–91** RAY *S. & E.C. Words* 110 A *Prigge*, a small Pitcher: this is I suppose, a general word in the South Country. **1703** THORESBY *Let. to Ray* Gloss. (E.D.S.), *Prigge*, a little brass skellet. **1896** *Leeds Merc. Suppl.* 16 May (E.D.D.), Put t' prig on t' fire.

prig (prɪg), *sb.*^{3} (*a.*) Also 6 prygg, 7–8 prigg. [In branch I originally Rogues' Cant, of obscure origin: cf. the cognate vb. PRIG *v.*^{1} It is not clear whether the other senses (which appear more than a century later) arose out of 1, or represent, as is possible, a different word; in either case, the history of their sense-development is uncertain; they are here arranged chronologically. (If there should prove to be two separate words, the derivatives PRIGGISH, PRIGGISM, PRIGSTER, will also consist each of two distinct words.)

In the following passage Baxter plays on this word as agreeing with the initial letters of PRoud IGnorance, in which, and the want of Christian Love, he sees the cause of excommunication, persecution, and schism.

1684 BAXTER *Twelve Argts.* §16. 29 The worldly PR. IGs. and the unruly PR. IGs. by Persecution, and by causeless Separation and Alienation, have done the hurt.]

I. † **1.** *Rogues' Cant.* A tinker. *Obs.*

1567 HARMAN *Caveat* (1869) 59 These dronken Tynckers, called also Prygges, be beastly people.

2. *slang.* A thief. Now usually a petty thief.

1610 ROWLANDS *Martin Markall* (Hunter. Cl.) 42 That did the prigg good that binged in the kisome. **1611** SHAKS. *Wint. T.* IV. iii. 108 Hee.. married a Tinkers wife.. and (hauing flowne ouer many knauish professions) he setled onely in Rogue: some call him *Autolicus*. *Clowne.* Out vpon him: Prig, for my life Prig: he haunts Wakes, Faires, and Beare-baitings. **1651** J. SHIRLEY (*title*) An Excellent Comedy, Called, The Prince of Priggs Revels, or, The Practices of that grand Thief Captain James Hind. **1743** FIELDING *J. Wild* I. v, The same endowments have often composed the statesman and the Prig: for so we call what the vulgar name a Thief. **1831** *Lincoln Her.* 28 Jan., Serenely thieved the nightly prigs. **1838** DICKENS *O. Twist* xliii, Why didn't he rob some rich old gentleman.., and go out as a gentleman, and not like a common prig, without no honour nor glory! **1842** MIALL in *Nonconf.* II. 66, I am a prig, Sir: I lives by prigging whatever I can get. **1874** W. S. GILBERT *Charity* II, D'you sit at quarter-sessions.. and sentence poor prigs?

II. *slang* and *colloq.*

† **3.** A spruce fellow, a dandy, a fop; a coxcomb.

1676 ETHEREDGE *Man of Mode* III. iii, What spruce prig is that? **1688** SHADWELL *Sqr. Alsatia* I. i, Thou shalt shine and be as gay as any Spruce Prigg that ever walk'd the Street. **1709** STEELE *Tatler* No. 77 ¶1 A Cane is Part of the Dress of a Prig, and always worn upon a Button. **1788** V. KNOX *Winter Even.* I. III. iv. 264 The dealers in silks and sattins might adopt some good hints from prigs in pulpits. **1835** [see PRIGGISH *a.* 2].

† **4.** A vague term of dislike or disrespect. *Obs.*

(But perh. closely allied to 6, as a censorious and didactic person who made himself disliked.)

1679 SHADWELL *True Widow* Ded. A ij b, A sensless, noisie Prig. **1695** CONGREVE *Love for L.* v. vi, What does the old Prig mean? I'll banter him, and laugh at him, and leave him. **1700** T. BROWN *Amusem. Ser. & Com.* 135 There's that Old Prig my Father,.. as sound as a Roach still. **1712** ADDISON *Spect.* No. 403 ¶5 Well, Jack, the old Prig [Louis XIV of France] is dead at last. ? **1730** *Royal Remarks* 21 They said.. Doctor Puzzlepate [was] an Old Put, and my self an Old Prigg. **1749** CHESTERF. *Lett.* (1792) II. 218 What does the old prig threaten then?

† **5.** In late 17th and early 18th c.: Applied to a puritanical person, a precisian in religion, *esp.* a nonconformist minister. *Obs.*

In quot. 1693, 'Young Mr. Prig' may have been so called in sense 3, from his self-adornment. But Jeremy Collier treats him as a Dissenting minister: see his *Short View Immor. Stage* iii. (1698) 102 and *Defence* (1699) 65.

[**1693** CONGREVE *Old Bach.* IV. ii, Young Mr. Prig.. he is a wanton young Levite, and pampereth himself up with Dainties, that he may look lovely in the Eyes of Women;.. while her good Husband is deluded by his godly Appearance.] *a* **1704** T. BROWN *Sat. French King* Wks. 1730 I. 59 In thy old age to dwindle to a Whig, By heaven, I see, thou'rt in thy heart a prig. **1720–1** *Lett. fr. Mist's Jrnl.* (1722) II. 212 He may be as subtile as a young Prig, who held forth for two long Hours.. against Episcopacy. **1744** Z. GREY *Notes Butler's Hudibras* I. i. 10, I have heard of.. a Precisian.., who after the Restoration, rebuking an orthodox clergyman for the length of his hair;.. he [the clergyman] replied, 'Old Prig, I promise you to cut my hair up to my ears, provided you will cut your ears up to your hair'. **1752** *Adventurer* No. 12 ¶11 A formal prig, of whom he knew nothing but that he went every morning and evening to prayers. **1752** A. MURPHY *Gray's Inn Jrnl.* No. 8 The Sectaries, who are in Possession of this Place, are entitled Prigs.

6. A precisian in speech or manners; one who cultivates or affects a propriety of culture, learning, or morals, which offends or bores others; a conceited or self-important and didactic person. (Only in later use including women.)

1753 SMOLLETT *Ct. Fathom* (1784) 57/1 The templar is, generally speaking, a prig; so is the abbé: both are distinguished by an air of petulance and self-conceit, which holds a middle rank betwixt the insolence of a first-rate buck, and the learned pride of a supercilious pedant. *a* **1771** GRAY *Lett. Alphabet* Wks. 1843 V. 220 Now a pert Prig, he perks upon your face, Now peers, pores, ponders, with profound grimace. **1778** JOHNSON 7 Apr. in *Boswell*, Harris, however, is a prig, and a bad prig... (Boswell) He says things in a formal and abstract way to be sure. *a* **1805** A. CARLYLE *Autobiog.* 441 The clergy.. are in general.. divided into bucks and prigs... The prigs are truly not to be endured, for they are but half learned, are ignorant of the world, narrow-minded, pedantic, and overbearing. **1824** W. IRVING *T. Trav.* I. 256 The school was kept by a conscientious prig of the ancient system. **1828** *Blackw. Mag.* XXIII. 372 The peculiar impudence ingrained into the natural disposition of the prig. **1872** GEO. ELIOT *Middlem.* xi, A prig is a fellow who is always making you a present of his opinions. **1877** MRS. FORRESTER *Mignon* I. 39 The ideal woman is a prig. **1879** TROLLOPE *Thackeray* v. 129 The virtues are all there with Henry Esmond, and the flesh and blood also... But still there is left a flavour of the character which Thackeray himself tasted when he called his hero a prig. **1897** *Academy* Suppl. 20 Nov. 111/1 A prig may repent of his or her ways and yet not be able to turn from them, and so at last we find her confirmed in her priggishness.

b. *fig.* Applied to a thing considered priggish.

1873 BROWNING *Red Cott. Nt.-cap* 49 Only, I could endure a transfer.. just Of Joyeux church, exchanged for yonder prig, Our brand-new stone cream-coloured masterpiece.

7. *attrib.* or *Comb.* in sense 6. **a.** = 'of a prig or prigs', as ***prig-manufactory***; **b.** appositive = 'that is a prig', as ***prig-parson***, ***-preacher***, ***-puppy***, ***-scoundrel***; **c.** **prig-napper** (*Rogues' Cant*): see quot. *a* 1700.

a **1700** B.E. *Dict. Cant. Crew*, *Prig-napper*, a Horse-Stealer; also a Thief-taker. [So **1725** *New Cant. Dict.*] **1728** SWIFT *Let. Publ. Dublin Wkly. Jrnl.* 14 Sept., To laugh at all the prig puppies that could not speak Spanish. **1785** TRUSLER *Mod. Times* I. 139 A smart prig preacher of twenty-five. **1824–9** LANDOR *Imag. Conv.* xiii. Wks. 1846 I. 80/2 Cowper.. possessed a rich vein of ridicule,.. opening it on prig parsons, and graver and worse impostors. **1889** *Sat. Rev.* 16 Feb. 184/2 The subtle and fatal influences of the prig-manufactory. **1904** A. LANG *Tennyson* viii. 187 He is that venomous thing, the prig-scoundrel.

B. *adj.* (from attrib. use in 7) = priggish, precise, proper, exact. *rare.*

1775 S. J. PRATT *Liberal Opin.* lxxxv. (1783) III. 129 Stockings.. and buckles.. of so modest.. a pattern, that they utterly discarded all the vagaries of the mode; yet were they.. prig, prim, prue, and parsonly. **1872** H. W. BEECHER in *Chr. World Pulpit* II. 341 That.. which is contained in our system of trig and prig theology.

Hence (from 6) **'prigdom**, **'prighood**, the state or condition of a prig or prigs; **'priggess** *rare*, a female prig.

1878 BESANT & RICE *Monks Thelema* iv, So you really think.. that my son.. will drop the livery of prigdom, and talk.. like other people. **1884** J. HAWTHORNE *N. Hawthorne & Wife* I. 120 He steered equally clear of the Scylla of prigdom, and the Charybdis of recklessness. **1890** *Longm. Mag.* Mar. 532 Unwholesome little pragmatical prigesses. **1906** *Daily Chron.* 31 Aug. 3/2 George Washington's heroism has always hovered uncomfortably near the region of prighood.

prig (prɪg), *v.*^{1} [In sense 1, goes with PRIG *sb.*^{3} 2, both being orig. Rogues' Cant. Branch II may be a different and even earlier word (in which case the derivatives PRIGGING, etc. will also consist of two words); but nothing has been ascertained as to the origin in either sense.

(Some compare sense 4 with It. *preg-are* to pray, beg.)]

I. 1. *trans.* To steal. (*Thieves' Cant.*) Now, usually said of petty theft.

(In early instances often in reference to horse-stealing.)

1561 [implied in PRIGGER^1 and PRIGMAN]. **1567** HARMAN *Caveat* (1869) 42 A Prigger of Prauncers be horse stealers; for to prigge signifieth in their language to steale. **1591** GREENE *Conny Catching* II. Wks. (Grosart) X. 78 He bestrides the horse which he priggeth, and saddles and bridles him as orderly as if he were his own. **1616** BULLOKAR *Eng. Exp.*, *Prigge*, to filch, to steale. **16..** *Tom O'Bedlam's Song* (L.), The palsie plague these pounces When I prig your pigs or pullen. **1812** *Sporting Mag.* XXXIX. 210 It was Billy's boast, that he had not for many years worn a single article of dress that had not been prigged. **1840** BARHAM *Ingol. Leg.* Ser. I. *Jackd. Rheims*, And the Abbot declared that, 'when nobody twigg'd it, Some rascal or other had popp'd in, and prigg'd it!' **1891** E. ROPER *By Track & Trail* xxvi. 387 Anecdotes.. 'prigged' from comic papers. *Mod. Schoolboy slang*, Who has prigged my pencil?

2. ? To plunder, to cheat.

1819 *Sporting Mag.* III. 213 The President.. shook hands with me, and trusted I should soon prig the London cockneys.

II. 3. *intr.* To chaffer, to higgle or haggle about the price of anything. *Sc.* and *north. dial.*

1513 [implied in PRIG-PENNY]. *c* **1620** Z. BOYD *Zion's Flowers* (1855) 54, I will not prigge, I will not you deceive. **1632** RUTHERFORD *Lett.* (1671) 447 As the frank buyer who cometh near to what the seller seeketh, useth at last to refer the difference to his will, and so cutteth off the course of mutual prigging. Madam, do not prigge with your frank-hearted.. Lord. **1681** COLVIL *Whigs Supplic.* (1710) 78 The love of Pelf.. makes them prigg for Milk and Eggs, Put in their Broth, Cocks-halfs, and Legs. **1755** RAMSAY *Ep. J. Clerk* 16 In comes a customer, looks big, Looks generous, and scorns to prig. **1786** BURNS *Brigs of Ayr* 186 Men wha grew wise priggin owre hops an' raisins. **1824** MACTAGGART *Gallovid. Encycl.* 387 Some merchants alter not the price of their goods, let the buyer prigg as he may. **1825** BROCKETT *N.C. Gloss.*, *Prig*, to plead hard in a bargain, to higgle in price.

b. *fig.* To haggle about terms, to try to drive a hard bargain.

1632 [see prec.]. *a* **1688** J. RENWICK *Serm.*, etc. (1887) 431 O come and lay all down at his feet and prigg not with Him. **1692** *Scot. Presbyt. Eloquence* (1738) 106, I see Christ will not prigg with me. **1703** D. WILLIAMSON *Serm. bef. Gen. Assemb. Edin.* 59, I pray that none of Nobility or Gentry prigg with God in this matter.

c. *trans.* ***to prig down***, to try to beat down (the ***price*** demanded, or the ***person*** who demands it).

1853 in *Eng. Dial. Dict.* s.v., [He'l] ettle sair to prig you doun. **1903** *Ibid.*, He's be sure to prig doon yer price.

4. *intr.* To make entreaty, beg, importune.

1714 WODROW *Corr.* (1843) I. 553 Many think it was very great imprudence.. to prigg so with the Assembly from the throne upon this head. **1755** R. FORBES *Ajax* 25 (*Poems Buchan*) Fat gars you then, mischievous tyke! For this propine to prig? **1818** SCOTT *Hrt. Midl.* xxiv, To tell us that the poor lassie behoved to die, when Mr John Kirk, as civil a gentleman as is within the ports of the town, took the pains to prigg for her himsell. **1901** G. DOUGLAS *Ho. w. Green Shutters* 297 He prigged and prayed for a dose o' the whiskey.

† **5.** *intr.* (Sense uncertain: quot. not Sc.). *Obs.*

1623 WEBSTER *Devil's Law-Case* I. ii, Let none of these come at her.. Nor Deuce-ace, the wafer woman, that prigs abroad With musk-melons, and malakatoones.

Hence **'priggable** *a.*, that may be pilfered.

1900 'MAUD MARYON' *How Garden grew* 103 Lay aside, from hedgerows, corners of field or other prigable parts, some rolls of turf.

† **prig**, *v.*^{2} *Obs.* or *dial.* [Origin obscure; perh. variant of PRICK *v.* Cf. Sc. *prig-me-dainty* = PRICK-ME-DAINTY, *prigga trout* a stickleback.]

1. *intr. slang.* To ride; = PRICK *v.* 11.

1567 HARMAN *Caveat* (1869) 84 *To prygge*, to ride. **1609** DEKKER *Lanthorne & Candle-light* C ij. **1611** L. BARRY *Ram-Alley* I. B iv, Some of our clients will go prig to hell Before our selues. *a* **1700** B. E. *Dict. Cant. Crew*, *Prigging*, Riding.

2. *U.S.* To dress *up*, adorn: cf. PRICK *v.* 20, PRINK *v.*^{2} 2.

1845 S. JUDD *Margaret* I. iv, He's no more use than yer prigged-up creepers [vines].

'prigger^1. *slang.* Also 6 -ar. [f. PRIG *v.*^{1} + -ER^1.] One who prigs; a thief.

1561 AWDELAY *Frat. Vacab.* (1869) 4 A Stealer of Horses, which they terme a Priggar of Paulfreys. **1567** HARMAN *Caveat* (1869) 43 A Gentleman.. espying a Pryggar,.. charging this prity prigginge person to walke his horse well... This peltynge Priggar.. walkethe his horse vp and downe tyll he sawe the Gentleman out of sighte, and leapes him into the saddell, and awaye he goeth a mayne. **1591** GREENE *Conny Catch.* II. (1592) 3 The Priggar is he that steales the horse. **1673** [see CACKLER]. *a* **1700** B. E. *Dict. Cant. Crew*, *Priggers*, Thieves. **1712** J. SHIRLEY *Tri. Wit, Black Profess.*, A Prigger of Cacklers.. steals.. the Poultry.

† **prigger^2**. *Obs. rare.* [? f. PRIG *v.*^{2}] A rider; *spec.* A mounted highwayman.

c **1600** DAY *Begg. Bednall Gr.* I. iii. (1881) 21 He wo'd be your prigger, your prancer, your high-lawyer.

priggery ('prɪgərɪ). [f. PRIG *sb.*^{3} + -ERY.] The action or conduct of a prig (PRIG *sb.*^{3} 6).

1823 J. WILSON in *Blackw. Mag.* XIV. 501 This particular piece of priggery. **1886** *Sat. Rev.* 10 Apr. 518/2 The Bayard of India did enough good work to make all right-minded men ready to forget his self-righteousness and (to use plain language) his priggery. **1886** D. HANNAY *Adm. Blake* i. (1888) 9 There was hypocrisy and spite and acrid priggery on the side of the Parliament.

'prigging, *vbl. sb. slang.* [f. PRIG *v.*^{1} + -ING^1.] The action of PRIG *v.*^{1}; **a.** (*Thieves' Cant.*) Stealing; in *mod. slang*, petty thieving, pilfering. ***prigging law*** or ***lay***, thieves' trade or way.

1591 GREENE *Conny Catch.* II. (1592) 3 This base villany of Prigging, or horse-stealing. **1627** E. F. *Hist. Edw. II.* (1680) 82 The Scots, that love not rest, delight in prigging. **1799** in *Spirit Pub. Jrnls.* III. 353 Three boys brought in for prigging of wipes [pocket handkerchiefs]. **1859** *Autobiog. Beggar Boy* 99 He had tried the prigging, and had been nabbed four times, and had been twice on the mill.

Comb. **1591** GREENE *Conny Catch.* II. Wks. (Grosart) X. 75 The discovery of the Prigging Law or nature of horse stealing. *Ibid.* 87 In Prigging Law. The towling place, *All-hallowes.* **1829** *Blackw. Mag.* XXVI. 131 As from ken to ken I was going, Doing a bit on the prigging lay.

b. Higgling or haggling about price or terms; hard bargaining.

1632 [see PRIG *v.*[1] 3]. **1654** A. GRAY *Gt. Salvation* (1755) 129 Take it and have it, and there shall be no more prigging. **1821** *Joseph the Book-Man* 81 The prigging o'er,—the penny down Admitted, beef is bought anon. **1889** BARRIE *Window in Thrums* xviii. 169, I wondered at her want o' pride in priggin' wi' him.

'prigging, *ppl. a.* [f. PRIG *v.*[1] + -ING[2].] That prigs. **a.** Thieving; **b.** haggling.

1567 [see PRIGGER[1]]. **1599** SANDYS *Europæ Spec.* (1632) 119 Sundry of their prigging and loose Friers..have robbed their Convents of their Church-plate and Repositories. *c* **1620** Z. BOYD *Zion's Flowers* (1855) 55 Wee merchands are, wee are not prigging men. **1668** ROLLE *Abridgm.* I. 73 Thou art a prigging, pilfering Merchant, and hast pilfered away my Corn and my Goods. **1886** J. R. REES *Divers. Bk.-worm* iv. 136 The works of the prigging author of *Tristram*.

†**c.** ? Connected with PRIGGISH 2. *Obs.*

a **1625** FLETCHER *Nice Valour* IV. i, Was ever such a prigging coxcombe seen! One might have beat him dumb now in this humour, And he'd ha' grinn'd it out still.

priggish ('prɪgɪʃ), *a.* [f. PRIG *sb.*[3] + -ISH.] Having the character of a prig (in various senses).

†**1.** Dishonest, thievish. *Obs. Cant.*

a **1700** B. E. *Dict. Cant. Crew, Priggish*, Thievish.

†**2.** ? Dandyish, dandified; coxcombical. *Obs.*

1702 STEELE *Funeral* IV. (1723) 62 Major General Trim, no, Pox Trim sounds so very short and Priggish—that my Name should be a Monosyllable! **1755** J. SHEBBEARE *Lydia* (1769) II. 116 The priggish affection of yon thin old coxcomb, the earl, is so insipid and irksome, that it is intolerable. **1835** BOOTH *Analyt. Dict. Eng. Lang.* 59 In common language a Prig is a young Coxcomb, and has the adjective and adverb Priggish and Priggishly.

3. Precise, particular, conceited, pragmatical.

1752 FOOTE *Taste* II. Wks. 1799 I. 21, I adore the simplicity of the antients! How unlike the present, priggish, prick ear'd puppets! **1816** SCOTT *Fam. Let.* 22 Nov., The forehead..has not a narrow, peaked, and priggish look.. which strongly marks all the ordinary portraits [of Shakspere]. **1836–9** DICKENS *Sk. Boz, Mr. Minns*, He was always exceedingly clean, precise, and tidy; perhaps somewhat priggish. **1869** *Pall Mall G.* 7 Jan. 12 There is..no moralizing of that offensively priggish kind which the instinct of boys teaches them to despise and mistrust. **1898** SIR E. MONSON in *Times* 7 Dec. 5/2 At the risk of being branded by that terrible epithet 'priggish', which is, I suppose, held in some quarters to be the antithesis of 'frank'.

Hence **'priggishly** *adv.*, **'priggishness.**

1834 *Tait's Mag.* I. 56/1 For the 'compliment extern' of Cockney priggishness and petty intellectual pretension, look at..Lord S——. **1835** [see PRIGGISH *a.* 2]. **1847** MRS. GORE *Castles in Air* v, 'It is with great regret', said I, as priggishly and consequentially as became an Esquire. **1873** SYMONDS *Grk. Poets* viii. 262 The priggishness of upstart science had to Aristophanes the air of insolent irreligion. **1876** BANCROFT *Hist. U.S.* V. lvii. 171 A good secondary officer, priggishly exact in the mechanism of a regiment, but unfit to plan a campaign or lead an army. **1898** *Spectator* 19 Feb. 268 Priggishness is narrow mindedness, with a turned up nose.

priggism ('prɪgɪz(ə)m). [f. PRIG *sb.*[3] + -ISM.]

†**1.** Professional thievery or roguery. *Obs.*

1743 FIELDING *J. Wild* I. iii, An undeniable testimony of the great antiquity of Priggism. *Ibid.* IV. iii, While one hath a roguery (a Priggism they here call it) to commit, and another a roguery to defend.

†**2.** (Sense obscure.) *Obs.*

1754 A. MURPHY *Gray's-Inn Jrnl.* No. 86 At a Board of Priggism held here, it was pretty warmly debated..whether a Gentleman acquires more Honour by whoring than by gaming?

3. Priggishness.

a **1805** A. CARLYLE *Autobiog.* 481 The minister,..an old bachelor,..who had such a mixture of odd qualities in his composition, such as priggism and pendantry, with the affectation of being a finished gentleman. **1857** HUGHES *Tom Brown* I. ii, That your great Mechanics' Institutes end in intellectual priggism. **1891** *Times* 14 Oct. 13/6 The priggism of intellectual pretension is the one unpardonable sin.

prighte, priȝte, obs. pa. t. of PRITCH *v.*

†**'prigman.** *Obs.* In 6 pryg-, pridgeman. [f. PRIG *v.*[1] 1 + MAN *sb.*[1]] A thief; = PRIG *sb.*[3] 2.

1561 AWDELAY *Frat. Vacab.* (1869) 3 A Prygman goeth with a stycke in hys hand like an idle person. His propertye is to steale cloathes of the hedge..or els filch Poultry. **1567** DRANT *Horace Epist.* II. ii. Hij, A pridgeman from him pryuilie his money did purloyne.

†**'prignet.** *Obs. rare*[−1]. [app. an irreg. dim. of PRIG *sb.*[2], perh. after POSNET.] A small prig or brass vessel.

1570 *Richmond Wills* (Surtees) 228, 17 April ..One spittell. ij prignetts xij[s].

†**'prig-penny.** *Sc. Obs.* [f. PRIG *v.*[1] 3 + PENNY.] One who prigs or haggles for pence; a hard bargainer.

1513 DOUGLAS *Æneis* VIII. Prol. 98 Sum prig penny, sum pyk thank wyth privy promyt.

†**'prigster.** *Obs.* [f. PRIG *v.*[1] + -STER.]

1. = PRIG *sb.*[3] 4 or 6.

1688 SHADWELL *Sqr. Alsatia* III. 38 If you meet either your Father, or Brother, or any from those Prigsters, stick up thy Countenance. **1714** C. JOHNSON *Country Lasses* v. i, Hah! Thou art a very pretty metaphorical prigster.

2. A thief, a pilferer; = PRIGGER[1].

a **1807** G. S. CAREY *Song 'Every man his Mode'* v, The Player's a Prigster of every kind.

priis, prijs, obs. ff. PRICE, PRYS.

‖**prikaz** (prji'kaz). Also pricasse, prikas. Pl. **prikazy.** [Russ.] In Russia: an office or a department, esp. in the central administration (now only *Hist.*); an order or a command.

a **1725** C. WHITWORTH *Acct. Russia* (1758) 61 The Court ..was very numerous and magnificent, being filled on solemn occasions by the *Bojars*, or privy Counsellors, with all the officers of each Pricasse. **1854** R. G. LATHAM *Native Races Russ. Empire* xii. 165 The *Prikas* is a kind of *Divan* or *Council*, consisting of two Kirghiz and two Russian assessors. **1886** *Encycl. Brit.* XXI. 105/1 He [*sc.* Kotoshikhin] served in the ambassador's office (*posolski prikaz*), and when called upon to give information against his colleagues fled to Poland about 1664. **1905** *Contemp. Rev.* Feb. 155 No law, ukaz, prikaz, can be decided upon except on the report of a Minister. **1917** [see COLLEGIUM]. **1952** S. HARCAVE *Russia* iv. 58 Administrative offices (*prikazy*) were set up as new problems arose. **1963** N. V. RIASANOVSKY *Hist. Russia* xviii. 212 The authority of a prikaz extended over a certain type of affairs, such as foreign policy in the case of the ambassadorial prikaz. **1971** J. S. RESHETAR *Soviet Polity* vi. 217 Collegium decisions can be carried out only by an order (*prikaz*) issued by the minister because the collegium as such has no authority.

priket(e, prikkett, prikle, obs. ff. PRICKET, PRICKLE.

†**prill,** *sb.*[1] *Obs.* [app. related to It. *pirla*, *pirlo* 'a childes top, a gig, or twirle' (Florio) (cf. PIROUETTE), and prob. to PIRL *v.*] A whirligig, or top that one spins.

c **1440** *Promp. Parv.* 413/2 Prylle, or whyrlegygge, as chylderys pley (or spylkok,..*K.* prille of chyldrys pleyynge, *S.* whyrgyg), *giraculum.* [*a* **1500** *Medulla Gram.* in *Promp. Parv.* 413 *note*, *Giraculum*, a pirlle.]

prill (prɪl), *sb.*[2] Now *local.* [A phonetic variant of *pirle*, PURL, a small rill. Cf. PRILL *v.*] A small stream of running water; a rill.

1603 J. DAVIES *Microcosm.* (Grosart) 12/2 Each siluer Prill gliding on golden Sand. **1614** —— *Eclogue* 150 By some prill, that 'mong the Pibbles plods. **1610** R. VAUGHAN (*title*) Most Approved And Long experienced Water-Workes. Containing The manner of Winter and Summer-drowning of Medow and Pasture, by the aduantage of the least Riuer, Brooke, Fount or Water-prill adiacent. **1862** *Temple Bar Mag.* VI. 464 Tints of orange-brown..coloured the prill of water running on the wayside. **1879** MISS JACKSON *Shropsh. Word-bk.*, *Prill*, a streamlet of clear water, a rill; a runnel from a spring. [**1903** in *Eng. Dial. Dict.* from Worc., Shrop., Heref., Radnor, Glouc.]

†**prill,** *sb.*[3] *Obs. rare.* [Origin doubtful; perh. a generalized use of the proper name *Prill*, short for *Priscilla*, which according to Elworthy is very common in West Somerset. Cf. GILL *sb.*[4]] A girl, a lass.

1587 M. GROVE *Pelops & Hipp.* (1878) 78 The change of dames within the court: For Countrey prilles. *Ibid.* 83 Though that she be a countrey prill, no weight thereof doth stand: Thinke you that some those Courtly dames are not of countrey land?

prill, *sb.*[4] *Mining.* [A local term in Cornwall.]

1. In Cornish copper-mining: The rich copper ore which remains after cobbing and separating the inferior pieces.

1778 PRYCE *Min. Cornub.* 263 The reduced Copper, or as it is more usually called by the Cornish assayers, the Prill, will be found beneath the slagg. *Ibid.*, The refining the prill is a very nice operation. **1839** DE LA BECHE *Rep. Geol. Cornwall*, etc. xv. 594 At present the copper-ores..are broken or spalled as before, and divided into pieces of good ore, commonly termed prills. **1875** *Ure's Dict. Arts* II. 80 Detaching from each piece the inferior portions, and thus forming prill or best dradge ore.

2. Hence, A button or globule of metal obtained by assaying a specimen of ore in the cupel. *U.S.* and *Colonial.*

1864 in WEBSTER. **1880** J. PERCY *Metallurgy, Silver & Gold* I. 249 Examination of the Silver 'Prills' for Gold... One or more of the 'prills' are flattened out by hammering, and heated with dilute nitric acid [etc.].

†**prill,** *sb.*[5], obs. variant of BRILL *sb.*[1]

1668 CHARLETON *Onomast.* 145 *Rhombus squammosus*.. Turbut, Bret-cock, Bret, or Prill.

†**prill,** *v. Obs. rare.* [app. a variant of *pirl*, PURL *v.*: see PRILL *sb.*[2]] *intr.* To flow, spirt, purl.

1603 STOW *Surv.* xxx. (ed. 2) 269 An Image..of Diana, and water conuayd from the Thames prilling from her naked breast for a time.

[**prill, prile,** in *Rom. Rose* 1058, app. a scribal error; ? for *brill* or *prick.*]

'prillion. *Mining. dial.* [? Related to PRILL *sb.*[4], or to *prill* vb. dial. (Cornwall), to mix.] An inferior tin extracted from the slag.

[**1778** PRYCE *Min. Cornub.* 263 The pillion (for so all Tin recovered out of the slags is called). See PILLION *sb.* [3].] **1825** HAMILTON *Dict. Terms of Art*, *Prillion*, in Metallurgy, tin extracted from the slag of the furnace is thus named in Cornwall. **1839** URE *Dict. Arts* 1249 The scoriæ..are stamped in the mill, and washed, to concentrate the tin grains; and from this rich mixture, called *prillion*, smelted by itself, a tin is procured of very inferior quality. **1892** *Black's Guide Cornwall* 53 The slag is pounded, stamped, and washed, and the tin, or *prillion*, extracted from it is again smelted.

†**prim,** *sb.*[1] *Obs.* Also 6 prym(me. [Origin obscure; the sense and date are against connexion with PRIM *a.*] A pretty girl or young woman; a paramour.

1509 BARCLAY *Shyp of Folys* (1874) I. 250 Than must he have another prymme or twayne. **1514** —— *Cyt. & Uplondyshm.* (Percy Soc.) 2 Aboute all London there was no propre prym But long tyme had ben famylyer with hym. *c* **1520** *Bk. Mayd Emlyn* 42 in Hazl. *E.P.P.* IV. 84 With suche wordes douse Thys lytell prety mouse The yonge lusty prymme She coude byte and whyne. *c* **1530** *Hickscorner* in Hazl. *Dodsley* I. 181, I would that hell were full of such prims, As Jane, Kate, Bess, and Sybil. **1573** G. HARVEY *Letter-bk.* (Camden) 102 So pretty a prim of every limme. [**1847–78** HALLIWELL, *Prim*, (2) a neat pretty girl. *Yorksh.* (*Obs.*, *Eng. Dial. Dict.*)]

prim, *sb.*[2] Now *local.* [app., like PRIMP, short for PRIM-PRINT.] A name of the privet.

1573 TUSSER *Husb.* (1878) 33 Set priuie or prim, set boxe like him. **1610** G. FLETCHER *Christ's Vict.* II. xliv, How her watchman, arm'd with boughie crest, A wall of prim hid in his bushes bears. **1629** PARKINSON *Paradisus* 445 *Ligustrum* —Primme or Priuet. **1828** *Craven Gloss.* (ed. 2), *Prim*, privet, spindle tree, *Ligustrum vulgare.* **1845–50** MRS. LINCOLN *Lect. Bot.* 137 The prim or privet..is found growing wild in some parts of New England.

prim, *sb.*[3] *Obs.* or *dial.* [orig. app. a slang or cant word. Related to PRIM *a.* and PRIM *v.*, q.v.] A formal, precise, or 'stuck-up' person.

a **1700** B. E. *Dict. Cant. Crew*, *Prim*, a silly empty starcht Fellow. **1876** BLACKMORE *Cripps* III. xii. 192 A prude, or a prim, she would never wish to be.

prim, *sb.*[4] *rare.* [f. PRIM *v.*] The act of primming or screwing up the mouth.

a **1825** MRS. SHERWOOD in *Houlston Tracts* II. No. 31. 11 When..a peculiar prim of the mouth was observed in the good housekeeper, the subject which had excited these symptoms was never pursued any further.

prim, *sb.*[5] *dial.* (See quot.)

a **1825** FORBY *Voc. E. Anglia*, *Prim*, very small smelts. So called at Lynn, where the smelts are remarkably fine.

prim, *a.* [Goes with PRIM *sb.*[3] and *v.*: see the latter.] **a.** Of persons, their manner, speech, etc.: Consciously or affectedly strict or precise; formal, stiff, demure.

1709 STEELE & SWIFT *Tatler* No. 66 ¶4 A spruce Mercer is farther off the Air of a Fine Gentleman, than a downright Clown... I indeed proposed to flux him; but Greenhat answer'd, That if he recovered, he'd be as prim and feat as ever he was. **1727** GAY *Begg. Op.* II. iv, As prim and demure as ever! **178.** SHERIDAN *Sch. Scand.*, *Portrait*, Tell me, ye prim adepts in Scandal's school. **1806–7** J. BERESFORD *Miseries Hum. Life* (1826) XVIII. viii. 148 The next figure is that of a prim Miss of 12 or 13. **1833** HT. MARTINEAU *T. Tyne* i. 10 Setting his lips in a prim form. **1838** MRS. CARLYLE *Lett.* (1883) I. 91 Pretty fairish for a prim Quakeress. **1885** BLACK *White Heather* i, His costume was somewhat prim and precise.

b. Of things: Formal, regular, stiff.

1771 H. WALPOLE *Vertue's Anecd. Paint.* IV. vii. 137 The garden in its turn was to be set free from its prim regularity, that it might assort with the wilder country without. **1796** MORSE *Amer. Geog.* I. 399 In many places, their forest trees have more the appearance of a prim hedge, than of timber. **1865** TROLLOPE *Belton Est.* vii, A square prim garden, arranged in parallelograms.

c. *Comb.*, as ***prim-lipped***, ***-mouthed***, ***-seeming***, ***-set*** adjs.

1735 *Prompter* 21 Jan. 2/2 Will she give Room to the prim-seeming Wife, or the less-cautious Widow? **1899** *Westm. Gaz.* 12 June 1/3 Then Force scarce hid, with a prim-set lip, the length of its eager tooth. **1926** J. MASEFIELD *Odtaa* xix. 318 A prim-lipped man, with the look of a 'spoiled priest',..seemed to be in charge of the guard. **1953** E. S. GRENFELL in C. K. Stead *N.Z. Short Stories* (1966) 74 The old man turned a..prim-lipped face to the parson.

prim, *v.* [*Prim* vb., *prim* sb.[3], and *prim* adj., appear to have come into use in the end of the 17th and beginning of the 18th c., the vb. being evidenced in 1684, the sb. *a* 1700, and the adj. in 1709. The sb. appears first as a cant word, and in this capacity it may have been used before the vb. But the latter is the first of the group to appear in Dictionaries: see quots. 1706 and 1721. Johnson knew the vb. (in sense 2 b), and the adjective. (He thought the vb. derived from the adj., and the adj. a contraction of *primitive.*)]

1. *intr.* (also *to prim it*). To assume a formal, precise, or demure look or air; 'to set the mouth conceitedly'; ***to prim up***, to bridle up, set the face or mouth firmly, as if to repel familiarities.

1684 OTWAY *Atheist* 111, A vain, pert, empty rogue, That can prim, dance, lisp, or lie very much. **1703** *Rules Civility* 206 A Lady will Prim it, or bridle it up, or pull off her Glove to shew a fine Hand. **1706** PHILLIPS, *To Prim*, to be full of affected Ways, to be much conceited. **1721** BAILEY, *Prim*, to set the Mouth conceitedly, to be full of affected ways. **1748** RICHARDSON *Clarissa* IV. 99, I therefore wink'd at her. She primm'd; nodded, to shew she took me. **1781** MME. D'ARBLAY *Lett.* 22 Sept., Tell dear Kitty not to prim up as if we had never met before. **1893** G. MEREDITH *Ld. Ormont* i, They mince and prim and pout, and are sigh-away and dying-ducky.

2. *trans.* To form (the face or mouth) into an expression of affected preciseness or demureness; to close (the lips) primly.

1706 E. Ward *Wooden World Diss.* (1708) 44 The Choicest Looking-Glass in Christendom for a Country Corridon to prim his Phiz by. **1748** Richardson *Clarissa* (1810) III. 350 She prims up her horse-mouth. **1809** Malkin *Gil Blas* II. vii. ¶22 Primming up her mouth into a smile, [she] promulgated this comfortable doctrine. **1816** Scott *Old Mort.* vii, Her arms were folded, her mouth primmed into an expression of respect mingled with obstinacy. **1837** Carlyle *Fr. Rev.* I. IV. iv, Mark also the Abbé Maury: his broad bold face; mouth accurately primmed; full eyes. **1876** G. Meredith *Beauch. Career* III. viii. 138 Rosamund primmed her lips at the success of her probing touch.

b. 'To deck up precisely, to form into an affected nicety' (J.); chiefly with *up*, *out*. In later use, to make prim.

1721 Ramsay *Tartana* 344 May she.. Be ridicul'd while primm'd up in her scarf. **1748** Richardson *Clarissa* (1810) III. iv. 36 When she was primmed out, down she came to him. **1860** Holme Lee *Leg. fr. Fairy Land* 5 So Idle primmed herself up.. and went out in the finest intentions. **1863** —— *Annie Warleigh's Fort.* III. 229 My Gypsy.. trimmed and pruned and primmed in the likeness of a wee quakeress, the picture of precision and demure obedience. **1875** Ruskin *Fors Clav.* lii. 95 This [church] has been duly patched.. and primmed up.

Hence '**primming** *vbl. sb.* and *ppl. a.*

1690 D'Urfey *Collin's Walk thro. Lond.* I. 36 Where primming Sister, Aunt, or Coz, Tune their warm zeal with Hum and Buz. **1822** W. Irving *Braceb. Hall* (1845) 368 Mrs. Hannah,.. with much primming of the mouth, and many maidenly hesitations, requested leave to stay behind.

‖**prima**[1] ('praɪmə). *Typogr.* [a. L. *prima* (? *pagīna*) first (page).] The page of printer's copy on which a new sheet begins and on which the first word of the sheet is marked.

1880 Jacobi *Printers' Vocab.* 104 In reading [the proofs of] a work sheet by sheet, the first word of the ensuing signature is marked by the reader as 'the prima'.

‖**prima**[2] ('pri:mə). It. fem. of *primo* first, used in some phrases, chiefly musical (or relating to cards) as PRIMA DONNA; also **prima buffa**, chief comic singer or actress; **prima viola**, first viola; **prima volta**, first time or turn, denoting that the passage so marked is to be played the first time the section is played, but omitted when it is repeated, its place being taken by that marked *seconda volta*. See also PRIMA VISTA.

b. Short for PRIMA BALLERINA, PRIMA DONNA.

1930 T. Karsavina *Theatre St.* xiv. 183 From a group in the first wing, a sanctum reserved only for primas, an infuriated figure rushed up to me. **1951** Green & Laurie *Show Biz* 561/1 *Prima*, prima donna. **1968** J. M. White *Nightclimber* xv. 97 Her voice lacked the sheer power needed to make a real impression in the bigger opera-houses. In central and eastern Europe, nevertheless, she always enjoyed the reputation of an undisputed prima.

‖**prima**, in L. phrases: see PRIMA FACIE.

‖**prima ballerina** ('pri:mə balə'ri:nə, bælər-). Pl. **prime ballerine, prima ballerinas.** [It., lit. = first female dancer.] **1. a.** A ballerina of the highest rank; the leading ballerina of a ballet company. Cf. BALLERINA, PREMIÈRE DANSEUSE.

1900 J. T. Grein in *Sunday Special* 23 Sept. 2/2 Curiously enough for many years the London public has failed to do justice to the prima ballerina. **1912** J. E. C. Flitch *Mod. Dancing & Dancers* iv. 62 At the Alhambra.. the dancing of the *prime ballerine*, almost all of whom were foreign, left little to be desired. **1918** D. H. Lawrence *Let.* 12 Jan. (1962) I. 536, I dreamed you were a sort of *prima ballerina*—which is the translation of a cinema star, I suppose. **1921** *Dancing Times* June 709 Lydia Lopokova has made a welcome re-appearance.. as prima ballerina of the Diaghileff Company. **1955** *Times* 19 May 3/7 The transformation of Mephistopheles into the *prima ballerina* Mephistophela is thoroughly Heinesque. **1958** *Times* 13 Sept. 10/5 Her Giselle was a fragile, vulnerable creature, excessively shy, and bearing no mark of the *prima ballerina*. **1976** P. Harcourt *Dance for Diplomats* iii. 30 He paid homage to his *prima ballerina* and the *corps de ballet*.

b. prima ballerina assoluta [It., lit. = absolute], a prima ballerina of outstanding excellence.

1870 T. A. Brown *Hist. Amer. Stage* 33/2 She made her *debut* as prima ballerina assoluta in the Teatro Regio in Ancona. **1904** A. Bennett *Great Man* xvii. 181 The glimpse which Henry had of the *prima ballerina assoluta* in her final pose.. caused him to turn.. to Geraldine to see whether she was not shocked. **1915** M. E. Perugini *Art of Ballet* xxxii. 272 With Signorina Maria Bordin.. as *prima ballerina assoluta*.. the production achieved instant success. **1928** *New Statesman* 31 Mar. 793/1 Tilly Losch (*prima ballerina assoluta* of the Vienna Opera-house). **1957** G. B. L. Wilson *Dict. Ballet* 37 Only twice in the history of the Imperial Th. was the additional title of 'prima ballerina assoluta' bestowed—on Pierina Legnani and on Mathilde Kschessinska. **1975** *New Yorker* 26 May 31/1 She.. said that the Bolshoi's former prima ballerina assoluta, Galina Ulanova, was now one of its most valued teachers. **1978** Ld. Drogheda *Double Harness* xxi. 300 She would inherit the position of *prima ballerina assoluta*, with her name standing alone at the top of the list of dancers.

2. *transf.* and *fig. spec.* an important or self-important person; something which has leading status in its particular field.

1954 *Economist* 11 Sept. 1/1 A prolonged attack of stage fright has repeatedly postponed the entrance of the new fighters.. into squadron service with the RAF and the new *prima ballerina*, the supersonic P.1 fighter, has not turned up this week at rehearsals. **1964** M. Clive *Day of Reckoning* viii. 71 Any old lady.. could turn.. her daily round into a sort of sacred ballet, herself the prima ballerina. **1975** N. Luard *Robespierre Serial* xvi. 146 I'm right with you however our prima ballerina responds. But what the hell are you going to tell him?

Primacord ('praɪməkɔ:d). *Mil.* Also **primacord.** [f. PRIMER *sb.*[2] + CORD *sb.*[1]] A proprietary name in the U.S. for a type of detonating fuse consisting of a core of high explosive in a textile and plastic sheath.

1937 *Official Gaz.* (U.S. Patent Office) 23 Feb. 699/2 The Ensign-Bickford Co., Simsbury, Conn... *Primacord.* For detonating fuse. Claims use since Dec. 11, 1936. **1950** [see CORDTEX]. **1959** *N.Y. Times Mag.* 31 May 38/2 One crew has its primacord all set to blow a big obstacle. **1972** *Daily Colonist* (Victoria, B.C.) 27 Feb. 30/1 Police.. warned parents.. that 1,000 feet of primacord—an explosive detonating cord used to trigger dynamite—had gone missing.

primacy ('praɪməsɪ). Also 6 **-tie.** [a. OF. *primacie* (14th c. in Godef. *Compl.*), in mod.F. *primatie* (pron. *-sie*), ad. med.L. *prīmātia* (1174 in Hoveden) for earlier *prīmātus* (*u*-stem): see PRIMATE *sb.*[2]]

1. a. The state or position of being 'prime' or first in order, rank, importance, or authority; the first or chief place; pre-eminence, precedence, superiority.

1382 Wyclif *Col.* i. 18 The firste bigetun of deede men, that he be holdinge primacie [*gloss* or the firste dignyte] in alle thingis. —— *3 John* 9 This Diotropis, that loueth for to bere primacye [Vulg. *primatum*] in hem, receyueth not us. **1483** Caxton *Gold. Leg.* 249/2 The blessid laurence is he that after Saynt Stephen ought to holde the prymacye. **1583** Stubbes *Anat. Abus.* II. (1882) 71, I grant the prince to haue the soueraigntie and primacie ouer the church of God, within his dominions. **1614** Raleigh *Hist. World* II. (1634) 282 In after times Tyre contended with Zidon for Primacie. *a* **1677** Barrow *Pope's Suprem.* (1687) 30 There are several kinds of Primacy,.. 1. A Primacy of Worth or Personal Excellency. 2. A Primacy of Reputation and Esteem. 3. A Primacy of Order, or bare Dignity and Precedence. 4. A Primacy of Power or Jurisdiction. **1796** Burney *Mem. Metastasio* I. 341 All this theatrical primacy.. is your work. **1817** Coleridge *Biog. Lit.* 160 The earlier appearance and established primacy of the Tuscan poets. **1885** *Manch. Exam.* 7 Apr. 4/4 The position of primacy which England sustains among the commercial communities of the world.

b. *Psychol.* The predominance of certain impressions, esp. first impressions, over subsequent or derived ones, in the mind or memory; also *attrib.*, as ***primacy effect, principle.***

1896 M. W. Calkins in *Psychol. Rev. Monogr. Suppl.* I. II. 35 Ordinary self-observation has.. enumerated frequency, recency, vividness.., and primacy (the earliest position in a definite series of events) as the factors of interest. **1913** C. E. Seashore *Psychol. in Daily Life* v. 151 Familiar illustrations of the secondary or quantitative laws are (1) the law of primacy: other things being equal, the first impression will be the most effective. **1926** R. M. Ogden *Psychol. & Educ.* xii. 199 Primacy is popularly expressed by the statement that 'first impressions are lasting'. **1931** *Psychol. Rev.* XXXVIII. 217 The law of primacy has also been suggested on the basis of experimentation, and this has been contrasted with recency. **1953** C. I. Hovland et al. *Communication & Persuasion* iv. 117 Experimental psychology for a long time postulated a Law of Primacy and a Law of Recency. **1959** Lambert & Fillenbaum in Saporta & Bastian *Psycholinguistics* (1961) 457/1 The European cases in most instances fail to support either a primacy or a habit strength principle. **1971** *Sci. Amer.* Aug. 85/1 The increased probability of recall for the first few words in the list is called the primacy effect.

2. *Eccl.* **a.** The first place or leadership in spiritual matters (sometimes identified with, but properly distinguished from, *supremacy*); the office, dignity, or authority of a primate; *spec.* the chief dignity in an ecclesiastical province: cf. PRIMATE *sb.*[1] 2.

[**1174** in *Roger of Hoveden's Chron.* (Rolls) II. 59 Consecrato pallium.. dedit, et.. primatiam addidit.] *c* **1470** Harding *Chron.* CII. v, To depriue Lambert of Caunterbury, Of primacy. **1529** *Supplic. to King* (E.E.T.S.) 36 Bokes which write agaynste the Popes prymacie. **1534** More *Let. to Cromwell* in Strype *Eccl. Mem.* (1721) I. App. xlviii. 134 As touching.. the primatie of the Pope, I nothing meddle in the matter. **1552** Abp. Hamilton *Catech.* (1884) 3 The office of ane Archbischop and general primacie of this kirk of Scotland. **1635** Pagitt *Christianogr.* I. iii. (1636) 174 They yeild a Primacie to the Pope, if he be Orthodox, but no Supremacie. **1641** 'Smectymnuus' *Answ.* (1653) Post. 87 The Archbishop.. spends the rest of his dayes in a long contention.. with York about Primacie. *a* **1715** Burnet *Own Time* (1766) II. 229 They declared themselves for abolishing the Papal authority and for reducing the Pope to the old Primacy again. **1746** Berkeley *Let. to T. Prior* 12 Sept., Wks. 1871 IV. 311 The Primacy or Archbishopric of Dublin, if offered, might have tempted me. **1833** *Tracts for Times* No. 15. 5 Rome has ever had what is called the primacy of the Christian Churches. **1867** Freeman *Norm. Conq.* I. v. 304 The primacy fell to the lot of Sigeric, Bishop of Ramsbury. **1907** *Q. Rev.* Oct. 366 Perhaps about the time [*c* 250 B.C.] began the hereditary primacy of Taoism in the Chang family.

b. The ecclesiastical province or see of a primate.

1552 Abp. Hamilton *Catech.* (1884) 3 Within the boundis of al our hail primacie of Scotland. **1807** G. Chalmers *Caledonia* I. III. viii. 428 The church of Dunkeld appears to have formed the primacy of Dunkeld.

‖**prima donna** ('pri:mə, 'praɪmə 'dɒnə). Pl. **prime donne, (prima donnas).** [It. ('prima 'donna) 'first lady'.] **1.** The first or principal female singer in an opera. Also **prima donna assoluta** [It., lit. = absolute], a *prima donna* of outstanding excellence.

[**1768** [W. Donaldson] *Life Sir B. Sapskull* II. viii. 53 So great is the infatuation of playing, and the secret satisfaction of being the prima of a Company so prevalent, that [etc.].] **1782** W. Beckford *Let.* 5 Apr. in J. W. Oliver *Life William Beckford* (1932) v. 110 Our Prima Donna, Miss Fawkener.. has real talent. **1812** Southey *Lett., to Miss Barker* 3 May, An author, like a *prima donna*, has a sort of dignity from appearing sometimes *incog.*, when, in reality, everybody knows him. **1842** Longf. in *Life* (1891) I. 433 The prima donna of the Düsseldorf theatre. **1855** Geo. Eliot in *Fraser's Mag.* LII. 50/2 He will.. interpolate no *cantata* to show off the powers of a *prima donna assoluta*. **1880** W. S. Rockstro in Grove *Dict. Mus.* II. 509/1 [In an Opera] the First Woman (*Prima donna*) was always a high Soprano. **1887** J. A. F. Maitland in *Dict. Nat. Biog.* XII. 274/1 In managing recalcitrant *prime donne* and other mutinous persons. **1938** *Oxf. Compan. Mus.* 749/2 The term *Prima Donna Assoluta* ('absolute first lady') is sometimes used to make perfectly clear the position of the *very* most important woman member of an opera company. **1958** *Listener* 14 Aug. 250/2 A singer who is hailed as a *prima donna assoluta*. **1976** S. Galatopoulos (*title*) Callas: prima donna assoluta.

2. *transf.* and *fig.* A person of the highest standing in a particular field or activity; one who behaves in a self-important or temperamental manner.

1834 [see ANGRIAN *a.*]. **1846** *Swell's Night Guide* 36 Here also hang out some of the prima donnas of the flags and curbs, some of the small fry of 80, Quadrant. **1861** B. Hemying in H. Mayhew *London Labour* (1862) Extra vol. 215/1 Two classes of prostitutes come under this denomination—first, kept mistresses, and secondly, prima donnas or those who live in a superior style. **1877** A. Macmillan *Let.* in C. Morgan *House of Macmillan* (1943) vii. 117 It is clear that our *Prima Donna* must be paid on a different scale from the others. **1936** *Amer. Mercury* May p. x/2 *Prima donna*, the first-class gripe artist; a temperamental [jazz] musician. **1938** *Times Lit. Suppl.* 639/3 We see her [*sc.* Madame de Stael].. as the 'prima donna', exacting, torrential and exasperating. **1943** *Sun* (Baltimore) 24 Sept. 14/2 A willingness to merge his identity with that of the journal of which he was a part. He was no prima donna. **1948** D. Cecil *Two Quiet Lives* II. 146 The most trivial points.. were enough to produce a violent explosion of prima donna temperament. **1970** S. Ellin *Bind* iv. 22 You've been putting on a prima donna act for the last hour. What's it all about? **1973** C. Bonington *Next Horizon* ix. 140 He had invited Royal Robbins.. to be chief [climbing] instructor, and the two men, both prima donnas in their own right, could not have offered a greater contrast. **1976** Botham & Donnelly *Valentino* iv. 34 Di Valentina was rapidly becoming the prima donna of the Manhattan cabaret set. **1978** *Jrnl. R. Soc. Arts* CXXVI. 537/2 The industrial designer tends often to adopt the rôle of catalyst rather than that of a prima-donna in his relationship with his colleagues in the development team.

Hence as *v. intr.*; also **prima 'donna-ish** *a.*, **prima 'donnaism, prima-'donnaship.**

1889 *Scottish Art Rev.* II. 114 Miss Macintyre.. is still too young and amateurish to make it possible to predict whether she will be.. spoiled by her early prima-donnaship. **1940** E. Hemingway *For whom Bell Tolls* xiv. 181 Stop prima-donnaing and accept the fact. **1961** A. Wilson *Old Men at Zoo* i. 25 It.. served to increase my dislike for their unusual touchy, prima donna-ish relationship. **1969** P. Dickinson *Pride of Heroes* I. 16 Pibble had taken a prima-donna-ish dislike to the stationmaster. **1970** 'B. Mather' *Break in Line* ix. 117, I felt no resentment... It was going to be hairy enough without any prima-donnaing on my part. **1970** C. F. Hockett *Leonard Bloomfield Anthol.* p. xiv, We can still know.. his reaction to the pettishness, the prima-donnaism, the neglect of already accumulated experience, and the antiscientific bias that have all too often characterized our discussions. **1973** 'B. Mather' *Snowline* vi. 73 He is apt to get prima donna-ish when he is out of temper. **1980** *Daily Tel.* 14 Jan. 12 We hope that he will go on being equally modest and lazy, cocking a snook at the prima-donna-ish antics of some chess masters while continuing from strength to strength.

primætiall, obs. erron. form of PRIMITIAL.

primæval, etc.: see PRIMEVAL, etc.

‖**prima facie** ('praɪmə 'feɪʃɪi:), *adv.* and *adj. phr.* (*sb.*) [L. *prīmā faciē* at first sight (M. Seneca), *faciē*, ablative of *faciēs* face. Formerly anglicized, after F. *de prime face*, 'at' or 'of prime face': see PRIME *a.* 9 c.]

A. *adv.* At first sight; on the face of it; as appears at first without investigation.

c **1420** (?) Lydg. *Assembly of Gods* 157 Here, prima facie, to vs he doth apere That he hath offendyd—no man can sey nay. **1586** A. Day *Eng. Secretary* II. (1625) 55 A Phisiognomer by chance.. was demanded what (*Prima facie*) he thought of Socrates. **1624** Bedell *Lett.* vii. 115 And indeed, *prima facie* they haue reason. **1766** Blackstone *Comm.* II. xiii. 196 Such actual possession is, *prima facie*, evidence of a legal title in the possessor. *a* **1676**, **1797** [see DOLI CAPAX]. **1883** *Law Rep.* *11 Q.B. Div.* 597 The plaintiff has been defamed, and has primâ facie a cause of action. **1900** [see EN BLOC]. **1955** *Times* 5 May 4/1 If the right given to the tenant was an asset, it was something which *prima facie* would on his death pass to his personal representative. **1971** *Mod. Law Rev.* XXXIV. 693 The recommendation was prima facie *unlawful*.

B. *adj.* Arising at first sight; based or founded on the first impression. Also *ellipt.* as *sb.*

prima facie case (*Law*), a case resting on *prima facie* evidence.

1800 J. Adams *Wks.* (1854) IX. 50 This Gazette is said by lawyers and judges to be *primâ facie* evidence in courts of justice, of matters of State and of public acts of the government. **1864** *Spectator* 16 Apr. 440/2 Doubtless.. there is a *primâ facie* reason for his suggestion. **1870** J. H. NEWMAN *Gram. Assent* II. vi. 174 A *primâ facie* assent is an assent to an antecedent probability of a fact, not to the fact itself. **1895** L. J. KAY in *Law Times Rep.* LXXIII. 624/1 It lies upon the plaintiff to make out a *primâ facie* case. **1916** G. B. SHAW *Androcles & Lion* p. lx, An objection from an average stockbroker constitutes in itself a *prima facie* case for any social reform. **1955** *Times* 1 July 6/5 The Magistrate.. said that on the girl's evidence there was plainly a *prima facie* case. **1978** P. LOVESEY *Waxwork* 153 If anyone can supply the *prima facie* evidence that her husband was involved, it's her. **1980** N. FREELING *Castang's City* xxv. 169 You've nothing for a *prima facie*... Any lawyer could knock it down.

So ‖**prima fronte** (ˈpraɪmə ˈfrɒntiː) *adv. phr.* [L. (Quintil.); *fronte*, ablative of *frons, frontem*, forehead, front], at first appearance, on the face of it.

1790 BURKE *Fr. Rev.* Wks. V. 299 To make a revolution is a measure which, *prima fronte*, requires an apology.

primage[1] (ˈpraɪmɪdʒ). [Known first in med. (Anglo-)L. form *primāgium* (see -AGE); of obscure origin: cf. PRIMEGILT. Hence mod.F. *primage* (1771 in *Dict. Trévoux*).]

1. A customary allowance formerly made by the shipper to the master and crew of a vessel for the loading and care of the cargo; also called *hat-money*; subsequently merely a percentage addition to the freight, paid to the owners or freighters of the vessel.

[**1297** *Boston Customs Acc.* Customs, K.R. Bd. 5 No. 5 *dorso* (P.R.O.), In frectagio pro .lij. saccis et .xx. petris lane ..et in touwagio dictarum lanarum et in loadesmanagio .lxxj.s... Item in primagio .ij.s.] **1540** *Act 32 Hen. VIII*, c. 14 A piece of flemmishe mony called an Englyshe for lodemanage and for primage of euery fardell of wollen clothe. **1598** W. PHILLIP *Linschoten* I. iii. 4/2 And receaue before hand, each man twenty foure millreyes,..as also primage, & certaine tunnes fraught. **1661** MARVELL *Corr.* Wks. (Grosart) II. 68, I haue spoke with Mr. Porter, who assures me he hath giuen order to stop the Primage, loadage [etc.]. **1755** MAGENS *Insurances* I. 73 In Lieu of all.. petty Port charges, it is usual at some Places to pay 5 per Cent calculated on the Freight, and 5 per Cent more for Primage to the Captain. **1809** R. LANGFORD *Introd. Trade* 134 *Primage*, an allowance to masters of vessels for the use of cables and ropes, and to mariners for their assistance in loading and unloading cargoes. **1882** BITHELL *Counting-ho. Dict.* (1893), *Primage*, a small contribution, usually about one-tenth the amount of the freight, formerly paid to the captain of a vessel for taking care of the cargo: but which is now regularly charged as an addition to the freight, and applied to the shipowner's benefit.

2. A small duty formerly paid to a local society of pilots, as at Newcastle-on-Tyne. Also *attrib.*

1606 *Mariners' Charter* in Brand *Hist. Newcastle* (1789) II. 700 An ancient duetie heretofore..paid to the Companie, Misterie, Brotherhood, and Society [the Maister, Pilotts, and Seamen of the Trinitie House of Newcastle upon Tyne], called Primage, that is to say, 2*d.* of everie tunn of wine, oile, and other goods.. rated.. by the tunn [etc.]. **1789** BRAND *ibid.* 714 Primage is still paid to this society [of Pilots] at two-pence per ton. *Ibid.* 31 *note*, The primage book of the Trinity-House of Newcastle. [Abolished on the Tyne in 1865, on formation of the 'Pilotage Board'.]

ˈ**primage**[2]. *Engineering.* [f. PRIME *v.*[1] 6.] The amount of water carried off suspended in the steam from a boiler.

1881 J. HILL in *Metal World* 8 Oct. 342 Experience shows that steam always carries a certain percentage of water in suspension as it rises from the body of water of which it is formed... The water so suspended in the steam is known as water entrained or as primage. **1890** *Cent. Dict.* s.v., It is estimated.. usually as a percentage..as, a primage of three per cent.

primal (ˈpraɪməl), *a.* [ad. med.L. *prīmāl-is* (1485 in Du Cange), f. L. *prīmus* first: see -AL[1].]

1. a. Belonging to the first age or earliest stage; original, pristine; primitive, primeval.

1602 SHAKS. *Ham.* III. iii. 37 Oh my offence is ranke, it smels to heauen, It hath the primall eldest curse vpon 't, A Brothers murther. **1606** —— *Ant. & Cl.* I. iv. 41. **1615** *Marr. & Wiving* iii. in *Harl. Misc.* (Malh.) III. 258 The primal blessing, Increase and multiply. **1784** COWPER *Task* I. 364 See him sweating o'er his bread Before he eats it.—'Tis the primal curse, But soften'd into mercy. **1817** MOORE *Lalla R.* (1824) 15 And bring its primal glories back again. **1879** HUXLEY *Hume* ii. 63 He.. falls into the primal and perennial error of philosophical speculators.

b. *Psychol.* Relating or pertaining to such needs, fears, behaviour, etc., as form the origins of emotional life, esp. as in Freud's theory that, in the hypothesized murder of the dominant father who possesses the females in a primal horde, lies the unconscious origin of the Oedipus complex and the begining of conscious emotions.

1918 A. A. BRILL tr. *Freud's Totem & Taboo* iv. 218 If the totem animal is the father, then the two main commandments of totemism.. agree in content with the two crimes of Oedipus..and also with the child's two primal wishes whose insufficient repression..forms the nucleus of perhaps all neuroses. **1934** R. MONEY-KYRLE tr. *Róheim's Riddle of Sphinx* i. 81 All this forms a 'religion' in which the infantile primal fantasies recur in a projected form. **1950** J. STRACHEY tr. *Freud's Coll. Papers* V. 229 Parricide, according to a well-known view, is the principal and primal crime of humanity. **1961** R. FLIESS *Ego & Body Ego* III. v. 301 (*heading*) Primal hate against the eldest brother. **1968** M. HARRIS *Rise of Anthropol. Theory* xvi. 425 In this fashion, the primal patricide, helped along by hereditary memory traces in the 'racial unconscious', gave rise to the Oedipus complex, nuclear family, incest taboo, [etc.]. **1969** P. A. ROBINSON *Freudian Left* 109 Freud had in fact asserted that the primal-crime hypothesis was not to be understood as a simple statement of fact. **1970** A. JANOV *Primal Scream* v. 55 It is when we force the neurotic patient to feel, rather than act out his primal fears that we can help him understand the feelings that are terrorizing him. **1973** D. NICHOLSON-SMITH tr. *Laplanche & Pontalis's Lang. of Psycho-Anal.* 332 If we consider the themes which can be recognised in primal phantasies..the striking thing is that they all have one trait in common: they are all related to origins. *Ibid.* 334 This anticathexis..is unlikely to derive from the super-ego, whose formation is subsequent to primal repression. **1976** N. THORNBURG *Cutter & Bone* i. 7 He was..indistinguishable from the evangelists and fire-worshippers, the pornographers and primal screamers. **1977** *Undercurrents* June–July 16/1 Another group is that at Atlantis near Burtonport, Co. Donegal, who practice self-sufficiency and primal therapy. *Ibid.* 26/1 Tim Eiloart discusses the development of the treatment, its basic methods, and the attitude of primal therapists to other forms of psychiatric treatment. **1978** *Listener* 19 Oct. 499/1 In America, one of the best-known of the therapies which claim to help you relive those early traumas is primal therapy.

c. Special collocations (sense 1 b): ***primal father***, the dominant male, possessing all the females, assumed to have existed by some theories of the origins of social life; ***primal horde***, a conjectured original form of human group; ***primal law***, the conjectured law of nature whereby human beings originally lived, esp. under the dominance of the male; ***primal scene***, a Freudian term for the first time that a child is emotionally aware of his parents copulating.

1918 A. A. BRILL tr. *Freud's Totem & Taboo* iv. 245 An ideal could arise having as a content the fullness of power and the freedom from restriction of the conquered primal father, as well as the willingness to subject themselves to him. **1934** R. MONEY-KYRLE tr. *Róheim's Riddle of Sphinx* iv. 179 All human institutions are regarded as foundations of the primal father. **1918** A. A. BRILL tr. *Freud's Totem & Taboo* iv. 246 The family was a reconstruction of the former primal horde and also restored a great part of their former rights to the fathers. **1934** R. MONEY-KYRLE tr. *Róheim's Riddle of Sphinx* iii. 171 What is the relation between the ontogenic conception of culture and the primal horde theory. **1969** P. A. ROBINSON *Freudian Left* 98 Verbal communication is the only vehicle of traditional continuity we know of; but, *ex hypothesi*, the primal-horde epoch must have been over before the development of speech. **1903** J. J. ATKINSON (*title*) Primal law. *Ibid.* i. 210 The following thesis, however, on the genesis of primal law in human marriage, treats of a *conjectural* series of events in the ascent of man. **1925** J. STRACHEY tr. *Freud's Infantile Neurosis* in *Coll. Papers* III. v. 510 We will proceed with the study of the relations between this 'primal scene' and the patient's dream. **1955** M. KLEIN et al. *New Directions in Psychoanal.* xiii. 327 When, in this emotional state, he covers his eyes with his hand he is, I think, reviving the young infant's wish never to have seen and taken in the primal scene. **1957** M. MCCARTHY *Memories Catholic Girlhood* viii. 204, I conceived an aversion to apricots..from having watched her with them, just as though I had witnessed what Freud calls the primal scene. **1973** D. NICHOLSON-SMITH tr. *Laplanche & Pontalis's Lang. of Psycho-Anal.* 335 Should we look upon the primal scene as the memory of an actually experienced event or as a pure phantasy? **1977** A. SHERIDAN tr. *Lacan's Écrits* iii. 96 The Wolf Man never managed..to integrate his recollection of his primal scene into his history.

2. Of first rank, standing, or importance; chief, principal; fundamental, essential.

1812 BYRON *Ch. Har.* II. xlvii, He..left the primal city of the land. **1814** WORDSW. *Excurs.* IX. 244 The primal duties shine aloft—like stars. **1878** GLADSTONE *Glean.* (1879) I. 201 The great questions of policy which appeal to the primal truths and laws of our nature.

†**3.** = PRIMATIAL 1. Cf. PRIMALTY. *Obs. rare*[−1].

1543 *Harding's Chron.* CII. v, Whiche the byshop Adrian, anone hastely Graunted him then, by bulles written papal, Lambert depriuyng of his sea primal.

4. *Geol.* The name given by H. D. Rogers to the earliest or lowest member of the palæozoic strata of the Appalachian chain, and to the period at which this was deposited.

1858 H. D. ROGERS *Geol. Pennsylv.* II. II. 749 These periods..are the Primal, Auroral, Matinal, Levant, Surgent [etc.]. **1859** in PAGE *Handbk. Geol. Terms.*

5. *Biol.* Pertaining to the *Primalia*, a third kingdom of organized beings, comprising those least specialized, not recognized as being distinctly either animal or vegetable (proposed by T. B. Wilson and J. Cassin, 1863); cf. PROTISTA.

[**1863** T. B. WILSON & J. CASSIN in *Proc. Acad. Nat. Sc. Philad.* 116, 1. The Reproductive Organs are first specialized in the kingdom *Primalia*.] **1890** *Cent. Dict.*, Primal.

6. *Comb.*, as ***primal-born*** adj., firstborn.

1874 T. HARPER *Peace through Truth* Ser. II. I. 60 The physical light of heaven, primal-born of all the things of creation.

primalism (ˈpraɪməlɪz(ə)m). *rare.* = PRIMALITY.

1904 CHESTERTON *G. F. Watts* 145 This indescribable primalism, which we have noted as coming out in the designs, in the titles and in Watts' very oil-colours.

primality (praɪˈmælɪtɪ). [In sense 1, f. PRIMAL + -ITY: cf. PRIMALTY; in sense 2, f. PRIME *a.* + -AL + -ITY.] **1.** The quality or condition of being primal; with *pl.* that which is primal. *rare.*

1670 BAXTER *Cure Ch. Div.* 234 As Campenella saith, The abuse of the Potestative Primality is Tyranny, the abuse of the Intellective Primality is Heresie, and the abuse of the Volitive Primality is Hypocrisie. **1846** T. W. JENKYN *Baxter's Wks.* Pref. Ess. 51 The perspicacity necessary for detecting the trinal 'primalities' as they develope themselves in the phenomena of the Universe.

2. *Math.* The property of being a prime number.

1919 L. E. DICKSON *Hist. Theory Numbers* I. xvii. 397 A test for the primality of $2^n \pm 1$. **1958** *Computer Jrnl.* I. 101/1 It proved possible to test for primality a series of numbers of the form $2^k - 1$. **1975** *Nature* 16 Oct. 544/1 They added that A. Ferrier, using a desk machine, had just demonstrated the primality of another large number.

ˈ**primally**, *adv.* [f. PRIMAL + -LY[2].] Originally, primitively; first in order.

1875 RUSKIN *Fors Clav.* lviii. 296 The carrying out of the primally accepted laws of Obedience and Economy. **1887** E. P. POWELL *Heredity fr. God* 146 Primally, Adam was perfect, morally and physically.

†ˈ**primalty.** *Obs. rare.* In 4 primalte, -aute. [a. OF. *primalte, primaute*, ad. L. type **prīmālitāt-em*: see PRIMAL and -TY.] = PRIMACY 2.

c **1330** R. BRUNNE *Chron.* (1810) 138 þe kirke of Scotland to Canterbirie ore se Obliged þam & band, as to þer primalte [Fr. *cum al primalté*]. *Ibid.* 283 Forto gyue ansuere Roberd of Wynchelse Studied how he mot were alle his primaute [Fr. *primacye*].

‖**prima materia** (ˈpraɪmə məˈtɪərɪə). [L., = first matter. Cf. Gr. ἡ πρώτη ὕλη.] = MATERIA PRIMA.

1906 W. B. YEATS *Poems, 1899–1905* p. xii, I know I have been busy with the Great Work, no lesser thing than that, although it may be the Athanor has burned too fiercely, or too faintly and fitfully, or that the *prima materia* has been ill-chosen. **1919** D. H. LAWRENCE *Phoenix II* (1968) 232 From the conjunction of fire and water within the living plasm arose the first matter, the Prima Materia of a living body, which, in its dead state, is the alchemistic Earth. **1954** R. F. C. HULL tr. *Jung's Coll. Wks.* XVI. II. iii. 189 The refining of the *prima materia*, the unconscious content, demands endless patience, perseverance..and ability on the part of the doctor. **1969** K. MINOGUE in Ionescu & Gellner *Populism* 209 Nationalism has supplied them with a vocabulary suitable to their self-assertion expressing their claim to be unique and valuable, rather than simply indistinguishable *prima materia* fit for the inevitable process of industrialization.

primaquine (ˈpraɪmə-, ˈpriːməkwiːn). *Pharm.* [f. PRIMA[2] + QUIN(OLIN)E.] A synthetic quinoline derivative which is used (in the form of an orange-red crystalline phosphate) in the treatment of malaria; 8-(4-amino-1-methylbutylamino)-6-methoxyquinoline, $C_{15}H_{21}N_3O$.

1949 *Jrnl. Amer. Med. Assoc.* 3 Sept. 26/2 The Malaria Study Section, Laboratory of Tropical Disease, National Institutes of Health..suggested the term 'primaquine', to distinguish the compound from 'pentaquine' and 'isopentaquine'. **1960** *Times* 11 Nov. 17/1 Primaquine, one of the newer and most efficient drugs for the treatment of malaria. **1962** *Lancet* 1 Dec. 1133/1 An erythrocyte defect similar to that found in primaquine sensitivity. **1965** *New Scientist* 19 Aug. 440/1 Medical officers at the Walter Reed Army Research Institute in Washington..report that the anti-malarial drugs, chloroquine and primaquine..are proving less and less effective. **1973** B. J. WILLIAMS *Evolution & Human Origins* iv. 65/2 Such hemolytic reactions also occur in persons with G6PD deficiency ion response to certain drugs, including some antimalarials (receiving the terms 'primaquine sensitivity', etc.). **1974** M. C. GERALD *Pharmacol.* iv. 77 Of the 15,000 compounds.. screened as substitute antimalarials, only two, chloroquine and primaquine, were found to be superior to quinine. **1978** *Nature* 22 June 627/1 The antimalarial drugs selected for the WHO list are chloroquine, primaquine, pyrimethamine and quinine.

†ˈ**primar**, *sb. Sc. Obs.* (exc. *Hist.*). Also 7 -er. [ad. L. *prīmārius*, f. *prīmus* first.] The principal of a college or university.

(In the Scottish colleges, as in Germany, *primarius* occurs in early Latin documents in the sense of *principal*. In a document of 7 Feb. 1539, the first head of St. Mary's College, St. Andrews, is designated by Archbp. Beaton *Primarius*, but in one three days later is styled *Principalis*. After the re-foundation of the college in 1554, the titles used were *Principalis, Præpositus*, and *Præfectus*, esp. the last. The Principal of this college is now 'Primarius Professor of Divinity'. In St. Leonard's College, *Primarius* is frequent in the 17th c.; and at Edinburgh in the 17th c. this appears to have been the regular Latin form: see the extracts from the Register of 1664 and later, in Append. II and III to Alex. Bower's *Hist. of the University*, 1817.)

1620 *Aberdeen Regr.* (1848) II. 370 Be the erection and foundation of the said college, the primar is appoyntit to teache divinitie. **1649** BP. GUTHRIE *Mem.* (1702) 54 As for the College of Edinburgh,..Mr. John Adamson, primer thereof, was furious enough in their Cause. **1646–62** T. CRAUFURD *Hist. Univ. Edin.* (1808) 91 The Primar's charge, who before had been Rector and Professor of Divinity, was divided; the Council and Ministers chuseing Mr Andrew Ramsay, Minister, to be Rector of the University and Professor of Theology, and Mr Patrick Sands, Primar of the Philosophy College. **1693** SLEZER *Theatrum Scotiæ* 28 In it [Aberdeen Univ.] there is a Primar or Principal, a Professor of Theology, a Professor of the Civil Law. [**1830** *Rep. of Commission St. Andrews*, The Principal of St. Mary's College is Primarius Professor of Divinity.] **1907** C. G. MCCRIE *Confess. Ch. Scot.* iii. 83 In one of his lectures when Primar of the University of Edinburgh.

So †**pri'mariat** *Obs.*, the office of principal.

1646–62 T. CRAUFURD *Hist. Univ. Edin.* (1808) 97 The Citie-Council.. unanimouslie set their eyes upon Mr. John Adamson.. to succeed to Mr. Robert Boyd in the Primariat.

†**'primar**, *a. Sc. Obs.* [f. L. *prīmāri-us*, f. *prīmus* first: see -AR[2].] First; = PRIMARY *a.* 1, PRIMER *a.* 1, PRIMITIVE *a.* 1.

1721 RAMSAY *To Music Club* 7 The primar speech with notes harmonious clear.

primare, obs. esp. Sc. form of PRIMER *sb.*[1]

primarian (praɪ'mɛərɪən). *U.S. rare.* [f. as PRIMARY *a.* + -AN.] A pupil in a primary school; a member of the primary class.

1883 *Education* (U.S.) III. 637 As important for a primarian to develop a keen perception.

primarily ('praɪmərɪlɪ; also increasingly, following Amer. usage, praɪ'mɛərɪlɪ), *adv.* [f. PRIMARY *a.* + -LY[2].]

1. a. In the first order in time or temporal sequence; at first, in the first instance, firstly; originally.

1631 GOUGE *God's Arrows* III. §2. 182 Amalek, the man.. from whom the name was primarily taken. **1852** ROBERTSON *Serm.* Ser. III. xiv. 170 Which originated primarily in the oriental schools of philosophy. **1897** MARY KINGSLEY *W. Africa* 657 These men, although primarily Africans, had by their deportation from Africa in the course, in some cases, of only one generation, lost the power of resistance to the deadly malarial climate their forefathers possessed.

†**b.** In its primary or original sense or first meaning; as first used, in its first intention. *rare.*

1617 DONNE *Serm., Ps.* lv. 19 (1661) III. 99 Elohim.. a name primarily rooted in power and strength. **1640** J. STOUGHTON *Def. & Distrib. Divinity* i. 8 Signifying primarily habits of the understanding. **1724** A. COLLINS *Gr. Chr. Relig.* 42 Literally, obviously, and primarily understood. *Ibid.* 265 In interpreting the celebrated prophecy of Isaiah [he] refers it primarily to the Prophet's own Son.

2. With reference to other than temporal order: In the first place, first of all, pre-eminently, chiefly, principally; essentially.

1620 T. GRANGER *Div. Logike* 66 Because it issueth immediately, and primarily from the forme, or essence. *a* **1638** MEDE *Wks.* (1672) 880 The Apocalyps is properly and primarily the Gentiles Prophecy,.. and of the Jews but by accident and coincidence only. **1664** POWER *Exp. Philos.* III. 162 The World was not made Primarily, nor Solely for the use of Man. **1719** WATERLAND *Vind. Christ's Div.* 183 The Father is primarily, and the Son secondarily, or immediately, Author of the World. **1825** MACAULAY *Ess., Milton* (1887) 17 Their hostility was primarily not to popery but to tyranny. **1859** MILL *Liberty* iii. (1865) 33/1 It is desirable, in short, that in things which do not primarily concern others, individuality should assert itself.

primariness ('praɪmərɪnɪs). [f. PRIMARY *a.* + -NESS.] The quality of being primary.

1687 NORRIS *Coll. Misc.* (1699) 353 That.. which is peculiar and discriminative must be taken from the Primariness and Secondariness of the Perception. **1854** RUSKIN *Lect. Archit.* Add. 121 From a confusion of the idea of essentialness or primariness with the idea of nobleness.

primarize ('praɪməraɪz), *v. rare*[−1]. [f. PRIMARY *a.* + -IZE.] *trans.* To make primary; in quot. to convert into primary (crystalline) rocks.

1834–5 J. PHILLIPS in *Encycl. Metrop.* VI. 555/1 Have many repetitions of igneous action primarized, to use Mr. Conybeare's remarkable expression, strata of all ages, secondary and tertiary, which happened to be the lowest at the points of action?

primary ('praɪmərɪ), *a.* and *sb.* [ad. L. *prīmāri-us* of the first rank, chief, principal, f. *prīmus* first: see PRIME *a.* and -ARY[1].]

A. *adj.* **I.** General senses.

1. Of the first order in time or temporal sequence; earliest, primitive, original.

1471 RIPLEY *Comp. Alch.* IX. v. in Ashm. *Theat. Chem. Brit.* (1652) 174 Fyrst thou them Putrefye Her prymary qualytes destroying utterly. **1646** SIR T. BROWNE *Pseud. Ep.* 357 Besides this originall, and primary foundation, divers others have made impressions according unto different ages and persons. **1651** C. CARTWRIGHT *Cert. Relig.* I. 107 So we grant that primary antiquity is a sure note of truth. **1840** CARLYLE *Heroes* i. (1872) 3 Let us look.. at the Hero as Divinity, the oldest primary form of Heroism. **1855** H. SPENCER *Princ. Psychol.* II. xvi. 273 In the order of constructive thought, the sensation of muscular tension is primary, and that of pressure secondary.

2. Of the first or highest rank or importance; that claims the first consideration; principal, chief.

1565 BULLINGER *Let. to Bps.* 3 May in Strype *Ann. Ref.* (1709) I. xlii. 428 We would do nothing.. without the privity of you, the primary ministers. *a* **1631** DONNE *Serm.* xxvii. (1640) 270, I meane of a primary necessity, of a necessity to be beleeved *De fide.* **1769** ROBERTSON *Chas. V*, VI. Wks. 1813 VI. 106 The primary object of almost all the monastic orders is to separate men from the world. **1850** ROBERTSON *Serm.* Ser. III. ii. (1872) Introd. 16 Every apostle, in his way, assigns to faith a primary importance. **1883** H. SPENCER in *Contemp. Rev.* XLIII. 11 The primary use of work is that of supplying the materials and aids to living completely.

3. Of the first order in any series, sequence, or process, esp. of derivation or causation: with various shades of meaning. **a.** Not subordinate to or derived from something else; original; independent; often with the connotation Having something else derived from, or dependent on, it; fundamental, radical. (Cf. PRIMITIVE *a.* 3.)

a **1631** DONNE *Serm.* xi. (1640) 102 Their faith.. was not the principle and primary cause of his mercy. **1656** tr. *Hobbes's Elem. Philos.* (1839) 81 That order of speech which begins from primary or most universal propositions, which are manifest of themselves, and proceeds by a.. composition of propositions into syllogisms. **1762** KAMES *Elem. Crit.* ii. §5 (1833) 43 The emotions produced.. may.. be termed secondary, being occasioned either by antecedent emotions or antecedent passions, which in that respect may be termed primary. **1766** BLACKSTONE *Comm.* II. xx. 309 Original, or primary conveyances.. are those by means whereof the benefit or estate is created or first arises. **1789** W. BUCHAN *Dom. Med.* xxv. (1790) 249 Sometimes it is a primary disease, and at other times only a symptom of some other malady. **1826** SYD. SMITH *Wks.* (1859) II. 95/1 Words, in their origin, have a natural or primary sense. The accidental associations.. afterwards give to that word a great number of secondary meanings. **1868** LOCKYER *Elem. Astron.* v. xxxiii. (1879) 190 The Sun.. gives us the primary division of time into day and night. **1874** DAVIDSON *Hebr. Gram.* (1892) 3 The first line exhibits the three primary vowel sounds *a i u.* **1899** MIDDLETON & CHADWICK *Treat. Surveying* I. v. 170 The methods.. are not so complicated, or so minutely accurate, as those employed in dividing up a 'grand' or primary triangulation. **1920** W. N. THOMAS *Surveying* xiii. 382 On the Ordnance Survey the first framework of triangles set out over the country constituted the 'Principal' or 'Primary' triangulation. **1923** GLAZEBROOK *Dict. Appl. Physics* III. 571/2 For precision of definition, it is essential that there shall be one, and only one, material standard to represent each of the fundamental units. This is called the primary standard, and is preserved under the strictest conditions of custody, used only at very rare intervals, and then solely for purposes of comparison with the corresponding secondary standards. **1945** R. A. KNOX *God & Atom* iii. 41 St. Thomas.. distinguished God as the Primary Cause from those secondary causes to which we attribute this or that effect in our daily experience, and taught that the influence of the Primary Cause was present everywhere, conspiring with the secondary cause to produce the effect. **1966** *McGraw-Hill Encycl. Sci. & Technol.* XIV. 441/1 In 1907, the International Union for Cooperation in Solar Research adopted the value 6438·4696 Å as the primary standard for the wavelength of red radiation from cadmium measured relative to the meter. **1973** *Nature* 12 Jan. 146/3 The time interval between publication in a primary journal and the appearance of the corresponding abstract. **1973** *Sci. Amer.* Dec. 65/2 The tangle that springs up where the forest has been felled is the first stage in the growth of a 'substitute forest'. In more formal terms it is an early stage in the development of a 'secondary forest', which will replace the cleared 'primary forest'. **1975** J. B. HARLEY *O.S. Maps* ii. 18 A succession of local central meridians were as a result brought into use before the associated tertiary triangulations could be adjusted to the primary triangulation of Great Britain.

b. Not involving intermediate agency; direct, immediate, first-hand.

1621 T. WILLIAMSON tr. *Goulart's Wise Vieillard* 193 We call them immortall..: first by reason of their essence, which is spirituall and originarie, or primarie from God the giuer of it. *a* **1655** VINES *Lord's Supp.* (1677) 279 The schoolmen distinguish between the primary and *per se* effects.. and these that are *per accidens.* **1831** BREWSTER *Nat. Magic* ix. (1833) 222 The direct or primary echoes from each reflecting surface reach the ear in succession. **1849** NOAD *Electricity* (ed. 3) 211 When a substance yields uncombined and unaltered at the electrodes, those bodies which have been separated by the electric current, then the results may be considered as primary. **1901** *Daily Chron.* 9 Dec. 3/3 Poverty, due to absolute deficiency of money income, is called 'primary', and comprises nearly ten per cent. of the population.

c. Belonging to the first in a series of successive divisions or branchings; constituting the main undivided body, or its first divisions or branches.

1804 ABERNETHY *Surg. Obs.* 207 The large primary branches of the carotid artery. **1835** HENSLOW *Princ. Bot.* I. I. iii. 63 The primary nerves branch off from it on either side, throughout its whole length. **1868** OWEN *Vertebr. Anim.* III. 119 The primary cerebral convolutions in the hoofed Mammals have a general disposition. **1877** F. HEATH *Fern W.* 21 In compound fronds.. the mid-rib of the frond, is called the primary rachis.

d. Belonging to the first stage in a process of compounding or combination; constituting the ultimate or simpler constituents of which a more complex whole is made up; elementary.

1807 T. THOMSON *Chem.* (ed. 3) II. 2 Compound bodies are of two kinds. Some of them are formed by the combination of two or more simple substances with each other... Others are formed by the combination of two or more compound bodies with each other... The first of these kinds of compounds I call Primary Compounds; to the second I give the name of Secondary Compounds. **1813** SIR H. DAVY *Agric. Chem.* (1814) 123 To ascertain the primary elements of the different vegetable principles, and the proportions in which they are combined. **1855** *Orr's Circ. Sc., Chem.* 2 When two atoms of different kinds unite to form a third or compound atom,.. they may be called elementary or primary atoms. **1869** J. MARTINEAU *Ess.* II. 100 He descends into the primary elements of human knowledge.

II. Special and technical senses.

4. Connected with sense 1.

a. *Geol.* Of the first or earliest formation; formerly applied to crystalline rocks, as having been formed before the appearance of life on the earth (= PRIMITIVE *a.* 7); now, of or pertaining to the lowest series of strata, including all the sedimentary formations up to the Permian (= PALÆOZOIC).

1813 SIR H. DAVY *Agric. Chem.* (1814) 192 Rocks are generally divided by geologists into two grand divisions, distinguished by the names of primary and secondary... The primary rocks are composed of pure crystalline matter, and contain no fragments of other rocks. **1829** BAKEWELL in *Glover's Hist. Derby* I. 44 [Lehman] inferred that the lower rocks were formed prior to the creation of animals, and he gave them the name of *primitive* or *primary*, and distinguished the upper by the name of *secondary.* **1845** J. PHILLIPS in *Encycl. Metrop.* VI. 560/2 In England.. gneiss and mica schist, and primary limestone, and quartz rocks, are almost unknown. **1854** BREWSTER *More Worlds* iii. 44 The Primary formations consist of granite rocks, trap, syenite, and porphyry. **1871** LYELL *Student's Elem. Geol.* viii. (1884) 105 Tabular view of the Fossiliferous Strata.. Post-Tertiary.. Tertiary or Cainozoic.. Secondary or Mesozoic.. Primary or Palæozoic [containing the formations] 19 Permian [to] 30 Lower Laurentian. *Ibid.* xxiii. 344 It has at length been made clear that the.. Permian rocks are more connected with the Primary or Palæozoic than with the Secondary or Mesozoic strata.

b. *Biol.* Belonging to or directly derived from the first stage of development or growth, and (often) forming the foundation of the subsequent structure (cf. 3 a). Cf. PRIMITIVE *a.* 8 a.

1848 CARPENTER *Anim. Phys.* 34 This membrane is termed the basement or primary membrane. **1854** OWEN *Skel. & Teeth* in *Orr's Circ. Sc.* I. *Org. Nat.* 165 In no system of the skeleton are bones a primary formation of the animal: they are the result of transmutations of pre-existing tissues. **1873** DAWSON *Dawn of Life* iv. (1875) 63 The original skeleton or primary cell-wall. **1875** BENNETT & DYER *Sachs' Bot.* 78 Originally the whole mass consists of.. a uniform tissue, out of which by diverse development of its layers these tissue-systems have their origin; this tissue.. which is not yet differentiated may be termed.. Primary Tissue. *Ibid.* 117 This tissue is termed Primary Meristem.. because it presents the primary condition of the tissue, out of which the different forms of the permanent tissue are successively formed. **1885** GOODALE *Physiol. Bot.* (1892) 119 The primary cortex consists essentially of parenchyma in which isolated cells of a peculiar character may often be found. **1914** M. DRUMMOND tr. *Haberlandt's Physiol. Plant Anat.* i. 61 More often.. it [*sc.* the middle lamella] also comprises the primary thickening layers. **1943** *Bot. Rev.* IX. 125 Current concepts of the origin of primary vascular tissues.. are much confused. *Ibid.* 129 'Procambium' has come to mean specifically the vascular meristem from which primary xylem and phloem are derived. **1953** K. ESAU *Plant Anat.* iii. 39 The primary walls have primary pit fields. *Ibid.* iv. 77 If these cells [that give origin to the meristem] are the direct descendants of the embryonic cells.. the meristems are called primary. **1971** F. C. FORD-ROBERTSON *Terminol. Forest Sci.* 41/1 The primary (cell) wall.. is the wall of the meristematic cell modified during differentiation.

c. ***primary amputation*** (*Surg.*), amputation performed before inflammation supervenes.

1879 *St. George's Hosp. Rep.* IX. 289 Primary amputation 2 inches below elbow. **1895** *Syd. Soc. Lex., Primary amputation*, amputation performed within the first twenty-four hours after an accident, before inflammation has had time to supervene.

d. ***primary education***, that which begins with the rudiments or elements of knowledge: used as an inclusive designation of that provided for the children liable to compulsory attendance; now formally applied in Great Britain to the education of children between the ages of five and eleven years; also ***primary instruction***. ***primary school***, one at which such instruction is given; so ***primary scholar***. ***primary age***, used *attrib.* of children receiving or ready to receive primary education; also *ellipt.* as ***primary***.

1802 *Times* 27 Apr., The Paris journals.. are full of a plan, brought forward by Fourcroy, for the establishment of primary schools, which is not interesting to an English reader. **1828** WEBSTER, *Primary*... 3. Elemental; intended to teach youth the first rudiments; as, *primary* schools. **1861** M. ARNOLD *Pop. Educ. France* 2 M. Magin, now Inspector-General of primary instruction, and formerly Rector of the Academy of Nancy. **1868** ROGERS *Pol. Econ.* xx. (1876) 264 The German emigrants.., most of whom are fairly possessed of primary education, are much more handy than those who come from states where equal care is not taken. **1877** HUXLEY *Physiogr.* Pref. 6 The boys and girls who pass through an ordinary primary school. **1908** A. RUHL *Other Americans* x. 173 In the gymnasium four little primary girls were imitating.. the gestures of the elocution teacher. **1944** *Act 7 & 8 Geo. VI* c. 31 §8 It shall be the duty of every local education authority to secure that there shall be available for their area sufficient schools—(*a*) for providing primary education, that is to say, full-time education suitable to the requirements of junior pupils. *Ibid.* §7 The statutory system of public education shall be organised in three progressive stages to be known as primary education, secondary education, and further education. *Ibid.* §9 For the purpose of fulfilling their duties under this Act, a local education authority shall have power to establish primary and secondary schools. **1956** H. M. POLLARD *Pioneers Popular Educ. 1760–1850* xxi. 265 Kay-Shuttleworth recommended that particular attention be paid to the large primary schools which had grown up.. in The Hague [etc.]. **1958** K. LOVELL *Educ. Psychol. & Children* xvi. 198 The primary school child like the pre-school child has his fears and anxieties. **1963** BARNARD & LAUWERYS *Handbk. Brit. Educ. Terms* 151 *Primary education*,.. comprises full-time education suitable to the requirements of junior pupils (*i.e.* pupils under twelve). **1964** CURTIS & BOULTWOOD *Introd. Hist. Eng. Educ.* (ed. 3) viii. 184 All normal children.. may be transferred at the age of 'eleven plus' from the primary or preparatory school to one type or another of secondary school. **1964** D. HOLBROOK *Eng. for Rejected* 54 How inefficient of the primary school to suppose that Joan has 'no imagination'. **1972** *Jrnl. Social Psychol.* LXXXVI. 167 The first study cited presents highly similar results for black and white primary-age subjects. **1976** *Times* 27 Apr. 14/7 It is impossible to generalize about English primary schools: some are progressive, informal, unauthoritarian, while others are strictly traditional. **1978** *Nagel's Encycl.-Guide: China* 316 *Primary Schools* take children from 7 to 13. For these six years, they learn little more than Chinese and arithmetic.

e. ***primary assembly*** or ***meeting***, a gathering at which a preliminary selection of candidates for election, or of delegates, is effected; *spec.* in *U.S.*, a general meeting of the voters belonging to a party in an election district, for these purposes; so ***primary election***, an election at a primary meeting; also ***primary caucus***. See B. 6.

1792 *Ann. Reg. 1789* [214/2] The primary elections had for some days been carried on in the different districts of Paris. *Ibid.* [215/1] The inhabitants of every district in France, preparatory to the election of delegates, hold what is called a primary assembly, where they choose a prescribed number of electors who are to act for the whole in the choice of a representative. **1801** *Spirit of Farmers' Museum* 61 The Editor of the Gazette of the United States..notices the 'Primary Assemblies' of our towns. **1821** *Massachusetts Spy* 11 Apr. 3/3 This was all the *hocus-pocus* of a primary caucus. **1829** *Niles' Reg.* XXXVI. 363/2 The battle is in reality fought in the primary meetings, and not on the day appointed by law for the election. **1833** ALISON *Hist. Europe* (1847) V. xviii. 117 The privilege of electing members for the legislature was taken away from the great body of the people, and confined to the colleges of delegates. Their meetings were called the Primary Assemblies. **1835** C. P. BRADLEY *Biogr. Isaac Hill* 54 The freemen of the State were called upon to give at their primary elections, an expression of their opinion. *a* **1850** T. FORD *Hist. Illinois* (1854) 88 Personal politics..were carried from the primary elections into the legislature. **1885** *Century Mag.* Apr. 825 Nine out of ten of our wealthy and educated men..are really ignorant of the nature of a caucus, or a primary meeting, and never attend either. **1905** *Westm. Gaz.* 8 Nov. 1/3 All the party voters in a district assemble at a 'primary' meeting to vote for delegates to attend a 'nominating convention'. The business of this nominating convention is to decide on the party candidates. **1961** *Atlanta Constitution* 4 Nov. 1 An investigation of Atlanta's recent primary election produced 'no evidence' that any irregularities took place. **1974** *Hartsville* (S. Carolina) *Messenger* 22 Apr. 6-A/1 This is the first time in the state's history that the Republican Party decided to nominate its candidates in a primary election, rather than by the convention method.

f. ***primary spermatocyte*** (Zool.), a spermatocyte which will undergo meiosis to yield further spermatocytes.

1896 E. B. WILSON *Cell* iii. 122 The primary spermatocyte first divides to form two daughter-cells known as spermatocytes of the second order or sperm-mother-cells. Each of these divides again..to form two spermatids or sperm-cells. **1927** *Jrnl. Exper. Zool.* XLIX. 463 The darkly colored pycnotic primary spermatocytes..are the most conspicuous cells in the germinal epithelium. **1960** W. B. CROW *Synopsis of Biol.* viii. 40 In the grasshopper each primordial germ cell divides eight times producing $2^8 = 256$ cells... The cells finally formed by such division are called primary spermatocytes; they undergo the reduction division.

g. ***primary endosperm nucleus*** (Bot.), the (usu. diploid) nucleus formed in an ovule by fusion of the two polar nuclei; also, the (usu. triploid) nucleus formed by fusion of a sperm nucleus with these nuclei.

1899 *Bot. Gaz.* XXVII. 58 The polar nuclei may fuse to form the primary endosperm nucleus. **1950** ROBBINS & WEIER *Bot.* ix. 205/2 The nucleus resulting from this triple fusion is called the primary endosperm nucleus. **1960** W. B. CROW *Synopsis of Biol.* viii. 42 The immotile male nuclei..are carried to the embryo-sac wherein one fertilizes the ovum... The other nucleus usually in angiosperms fuses with the primary endosperm nucleus, itself the product of fusion of two polar nuclei, so that triple fusion occurs, the triploid nucleus provided dividing up to form the nuclei of the endosperm. **1974** G. W. BURNS *Plant Kingdom* xx. 487/1 One sperm passes to the egg, uniting with it to form the zygote, and the other combines with the two polars, producing the primary endosperm nucleus.

h. Designating an earthquake P wave (see P III. 3).

[**1912** *Nature* 5 Sept. 4/2 The usual seismographic record shows three chief groups of disturbances, due respectively to the longitudinal and transverse waves through the core..and to the superficial waves round the crust. These..are complicated and supplemented by reflections of the deep waves at the surface, and sometimes by twin earthquakes caused by the primary.] **1919** *Proc. R. Soc. Edin.* XXXIX. 161 Tables familiar to all seismologists, in which times of transit of the primary and secondary waves are expressed in terms of the arcual distances of the stations of observation from the..epicentre. **1955** *Sci. Amer.* Sept. 56/3 In 1897 R. D. Oldham of England identified on seismograms three main types of seismic waves: (1) primary (P) waves, which are compression-and-expansion waves like those of sound; (2) secondary (S) waves, which vibrate at right angles to the direction of travel, as light waves do; (3) surface waves, which appear in the upper 20 miles or so near the earth's surface. **1968** R. A. LYTTLETON *Mysteries Solar Syst.* ii. 56 The velocity of the primary waves..is always essentially faster than that of the secondary waves.

i. ***primary road*** = *main road* s.v. MAIN *a.* 8 b.

1956 R. BRADDON *Nancy Wake* xviii. 215 They had frequently to cross primary roads. **1974** *State* (Columbia, S. Carolina) 27 Feb. 18-A/1 There are roads (even primary roads) which look impressive on a map but which fade away into mystery on the ground.

5. Connected with sense 2. ***primary feather***, one of the large flight-feathers of a bird's wing, growing from the manus. †***primary humours*** (*obs.*), the 'cardinal humours': see HUMOUR *sb.* 2 b. ***primary wings*** (of an insect): see quot. 1826.

1621 BURTON *Anat. Mel.* I. i. II. ii. 21 To maintaine those foure first primary Humors. **1803** *Med. Jrnl.* IX. 556 We cannot admit..that the hypothesis of four primary humours..was already established in the writings of Hippocrates. **1826** KIRBY & SP. *Entomol.* III. 374 External anatomy of insects... *Alæ superiores vel primariæ* (the upper or primary wings). **1845** DARWIN *Voy. Nat.* I. vii. (1852) 137 When these birds [Scissor-beaks] are fishing, the advantage of the long primary feathers..in keeping them dry, is very evident.

6. Connected with sense 3. **a.** ***primary colours***: see COLOUR *sb.* 2.

1612 PEACHAM *Gentl. Exerc.* I. xxiii. 79 Blacke, white, and yealow according to Aristotle are the foure primary or principall colours. **1672** NEWTON in *Phil. Trans.* VII. 5095 That Colour is Primary or Original, which cannot by any Art be changed, and whose Rays are alike refrangible. **1822** IMISON *Sc. & Art* (ed. Webster) I. 248 The separation of the primary colours of light. **1848** WORNUM in *Lect. Paint.* 211 *note*, Although there are but three primitive colours, painters have nine. These are—yellow, red, blue, which are primary; orange, purple, green, which are secondary, being compounds of the primaries [etc.]. **1876** BERNSTEIN *Five Senses* 109 These three colours, red, green, and violet, are now received as primary colours, because they are the only three pure colours in the spectrum which, when combined, produce a nearly perfect white. **1879** *Cassell's Techn. Educ.* III. 178 The primary or simple, and the secondary or mixed colours.

b. ***primary qualities*** (in *Philos.*): see quots.

1656 STANLEY *Hist. Philos.* v. (1701) 181/1 In Sensibles, some are Primary, as qualities, colour, whiteness, others by accident, as white coloured, and that which is concrete, as fire. **1690** LOCKE *Hum. Und.* II. viii. §9 These I call original or primary Qualities of Body, which I think we may observe to produce simple Ideas in us, viz. Solidity, Extension, Figure, Motion, or Rest, and Number. **1810** D. STEWART *Philos. Ess.* I. II. ii. 95 The line which I would draw between primary and secondary qualities is this; that the former necessarily involve the notion of extension, and consequently of externality or outness; whereas the latter are only conceived as the unknown causes of known sensations. **1856** FERRIER *Inst. Metaph.* v. v. (ed. 2) 148 It is through our perceptions, and not through our sensations, that we are made acquainted with the primary qualities of matter—that is with the extension, the figure, and the solidity of external objects.

c. ***primary planets***, those planets which revolve directly around the sun as centre, as distinguished from the secondary planets or satellites, which revolve around primary ones. †See also quot. 1704.

1664 [see PLANET *sb.*[1] 2.]. **1704** J. HARRIS *Lex. Techn.* I, *Primary Planets* (according to some) are the Three Superior Planets, *viz.* Saturn, Jupiter, and Mars; but more properly a *Primary Planet* is one that moves round the Sun, as its Centre; whereas a *Secondary Planet* moves round some other Planet. **1816** PLAYFAIR *Nat. Phil.* II. 339 The elliptical motions of the planets, both primary and secondary.

d. ***primary rainbow***, the rainbow produced by the simplest series of refractions and reflexions; the inner and usually brighter when two are seen.

1793 STURGES in *Phil. Trans.* LXXXIII. 1 In this shower two primary rainbows appeared. **1815** J. SMITH *Panorama Sc. & Art* I. 444 In the true or primary bow, the rays of light arrive at the spectator's eye after two refractions and one reflection. **1831** BREWSTER *Optics* xxxii. 265 The primary or inner rainbow, which is commonly seen alone, is part of a circle whose radius is 41°.

e. *Cryst.* = PRIMITIVE *a.* 5 b.

1823 H. J. BROOKE *Introd. Crystallogr.* 75 These secondary molecules would consist of certain numbers of primary ones arranged in the same order as they would be in the production of the entire secondary crystals. **1851** RICHARDSON *Geol.* v. (1855) 85 We can invariably, by a careful dissection of the crystal, extract from it a nucleus which has constantly the same form in the same mineral species... Such a nucleus is called a primary form.

f. *Chem.* (i) Orig. applied to compounds regarded as being derived from any of four molecules (water, ammonia, hydrogen chloride, and hydrogen, by replacement of one hydrogen atom by an organic radical. This sense survives in mod. use with respect to ammonia derivatives, *spec.* amides (but see quots. 1965), amines, and ammonium salts, and is extended to analogous derivatives of other elements, esp. phosphorus. [The sense is due to Gerhardt & Chiozza, who used F. *primaire* (*Compt. Rend.* (1853) XXXVII. 88).]

1854 *Q. Jrnl. Chem. Soc.* VI. 195 The amides thus produced, which we shall call primary amides, represent a molecule of ammonia in which 1 atom of hydrogen is replaced by the negative radicals. **1888** BLOXAM *Chem.* (ed. 6) 586 The amides, like the amines..may be primary, secondary, or tertiary accordingly as one, two, or three atoms of H in the NH_3 group has been replaced. **1889** G. M'GOWAN tr. *Bernthsen's Text-bk. Org. Chem.* 119 Just as amines are derived from ammonia, so from phosphuretted hydrogen, PH_3, are derived primary, secondary, and tertiary phosphines by the exchange of hydrogen for alcoholic radicals. **1938** G. H. RICHTER *Textbk. Org. Chem.* xiv. 230 The reduction of compounds that contain a $> C = N -$ linkage also produces primary amines. **1962** COTTON & WILKINSON *Adv. Inorg. Chem.* xx. 392 The phosphines are less basic than amines of the same type, but for phosphines the order is tertiary > secondary > primary, whereas for amines it is commonly irregular but usually with primary > tertiary. **1965** *Nomencl. Org. Chem.* (I.U.P.A.C.) C. 176 The generic name 'amine' is applied to compounds NH_2R, NHR^1R^2, and $NR^1R^2R^3$, which are called primary, secondary, and tertiary amines, respectively. *Ibid.* 188 Compounds containing one, two, or three acyl groups attached to nitrogen bear the generic name 'amide'. When only one acyl group is attached to a nitrogen atom, the generic name 'primary amide' may be used; when two acyl groups are so attached, the generic name 'secondary amide' may be used; and when three acyl groups are so attached, the generic name 'tertiary amide' may be used. *Ibid.* 190 *N*-substituted primary amides $R^1-CO-NHR^2$ and $R^1-CO-NR^2R^3$. [*Note*] These compounds have been called, respectively, secondary and tertiary amides, but this usage is not recommended.

(ii) Subsequently applied to organic compounds (except amines, etc.: see (i) above) in which the characteristic functional group is located on a saturated carbon atom which is itself bonded to not more than one other carbon atom. [Applied orig. to alcohols by H. Kolbe, who used G. *primär* (*Ann. d. Chem. u. Pharm.* (1864) CXXXII. 102).]

1864 *Chem. News* 26 Nov. 260/1 Primary alcohol. **1888** MORLEY & MUIR *Watts's Dict. Chem.* (rev. ed.) I. 100/1 In the primary alcohols the carbon-atom joined to the hydroxyl is connected immediately with only one other carbon atom. **1929** L. A. COLES *Introd. Mod. Org. Chem.* xii. 140 Methyl and ethyl alcohol are the two most important members of the primary alcohol series. **1968** J. MARCH *Adv. Org. Chem.* ix. 866 Primary alcohols or aldehydes can be converted directly to nitriles by air oxidation in the presence of ammonia, a strong base..and a copper complex.

(iii) Applied to a saturated carbon atom which is bonded to only one other carbon atom; also, bonded to or involving a primary carbon atom. Of an ion or a free radical: having (respectively) the electric charge or the unpaired electron located on a primary carbon atom.

1903 WALKER & MOTT tr. *Holleman's Text-bk. Org. Chem.* I. 46 A carbon atom which is only linked to one other carbon atom is called primary. **1926** H. G. RULE tr. *J. Schmidt's Text-bk. Org. Chem.* 70 When a carbon atom is combined in such a manner that only one of its four valencies is satisfied by carbon, it is termed a primary carbon atom. **1951** I. L. FINAR *Org. Chem.* iii. 31 A primary carbon atom is one that is joined to one other carbon atom. **1968** J. MARCH *Adv. Org. Chem.* ix. 866 Primary amines at a primary carbon can be dehydrogenated to nitriles. **1972** DEPUY & CHAPMAN *Molec. Reactions & Photochem.* iv. 46, 2,2-Dimethylcyclohexanone..cleaves to give the tertiary alkyl radical rather than the primary alkyl radical. **1972** NORMAN & WADDINGTON *Mod. Org. Chem.* ix. 116 A tertiary carbonium ion is a relatively more stable species than a primary carbonium ion..and is formed much faster. **1972** S. J. WEININGER *Contemp. Org. Chem.* v. 106 The secondary ($-CH_2-$) carbon-hydrogen bonds..of propane are more easily broken than the primary ($-CH_3$) carbon-hydrogen bonds of ethane.

g. *Electr.* (i) Orig. of an electric current: supplied directly by a cell or battery, as opposed to an induced current. Now, with reference to any device utilizing electromagnetic induction, esp. a transformer: of, pertaining to, or carrying the input electrical power.

1837 M. FARADAY in *Ann. Electr., Magn., & Chem.* I. 176 The conducting power of the connecting system A B D was sufficient to carry all the primary current. *Ibid.* 177 These experiments establishing..a distinction between the primary or generating current and the extra current, led me to conclude that the latter was identical with the induced current described..in the first series of these researches. **1862** *Electrician* 21 Feb. 183/2 In the primary wire of the induction coil, the 'return' or 'extra' current is an effect which is equally objectionable. *c* **1865** J. WYLDE in *Circ. Sc.* I. 253/2 When we employ the term *primary* to a wire, we mean that which *conveys* the current of electricity from the battery; and the *secondary* wire, is that in which a current is *induced* by its proximity to the primary one. **1893** G. KAPP *Dynamos* xvii. 435 Such an apparatus is known as a transformer, the coil through which we send the alternating current being called the primary or driving coil. **1896** F. BEDELL *Princ. Transformer* i. 3 The primary electromotive force..is equal to the product of the number of primary turns, and the rate at which the magnetic flux in the magnetic circuit is changing. **1929** A. T. DOVER *Electr. Traction* (ed. 2) x. 281 The primary winding..has tappings to give 1000, 800, and 220 volts. **1938** KERCHNER & CORCORAN *Alternating-Current Circuits* vii. 193 The primary current could thus be made to lead or lag the primary voltage by adjusting the degree of coupling between the two transformer windings. **1963** WILLIAMS & PRIGMORE *Electr. Engin.* x. 333 In the open-circuit test..the rated voltage..is applied to the primary terminals of the transformer. **1971** H. A. ROMANOWITZ *Introd. Electr. Circuits* xxii. 491 When a transformer is used to deliver energy at a higher voltage than that at which it is received, the primary winding is the one with the small number of turns and the larger wire in its coils.

(ii) Of a cell or battery: in which the chemical reaction that generates the current is irreversible, and which therefore cannot store electrical energy applied to it.

1882 *Engineer* 19 May 365/2 The distinction between a primary and a secondary battery is in no sense an important one when we are considering either as the producer of a current. **1886** R. WORMELL *Electr. in Service of Man* 427 The primary battery gives out a current of electricity, and the secondary acquires a condition which gives it also in turn the power of producing an electric current. **1922** GLAZEBROOK *Dict. Appl. Physics* II. 59/2 Polarisation is one of the difficulties encountered in all primary cells. **1971** H. A. ROMANOWITZ *Introd. Electr. Circuits* ii. 36 The wet cells and dry cells just described, which are not rechargeable, are classified as primary cells.

h. Applied to the testes and ovaries as sexual characters essential to reproduction and determined directly by the genetic sex, without hormonal intervention; sometimes the sexual ducts and organs are included, as essential to reproduction though developing as a result of hormonal influence (these are otherwise classed as either accessory or secondary characters). Cf. SECONDARY *a*.

1871 DARWIN *Descent of Man* I. viii. 253 With animals which have their sexes separated, the males necessarily differ from the females in their organs of reproduction; and these are the primary sexual characters. *Ibid.* 254 Unless.. we confine the term 'primary' to the reproductive glands, it is scarcely possible to decide which ought to be called primary and which secondary. **1894** H. ELLIS *Man & Woman* ii. 18 When we are dealing with Man it is perhaps most convenient to set aside as primary the sexual glands.. and the organs for emission and reception in immediate connection with these glands. **1926** J. R. BAKER *Sex in Man & Animals* ii. 26 The primary sexual characters are..the testes and ovaries. The accessory sexual characters are the obviously useful sex characters other than the testes and ovaries, such as the vas deferens..and the vagina... The secondary sexual characters are those which seem not to be directly concerned in reproduction, such as beards, antlers, and crests. **1948** C. D. TURNER *Gen. Endocrinol.* viii. 263 The primary sex characters are the gonads... Ducts and glands involved in the transmission of gametes or developing zygotes are known as the sex accessories. **1960** B. I. BALINSKY *Human Embryol.* xvi. 432 The primary sex characters distinguishing a male from a female animal are the sex glands—the testis and the ovary, respectively. By secondary sex characters are meant the distinctions between the sexes other than the presence of sex glands. These..fall into two groups: the organs which are essentially necessary for reproduction,..and organs or characters..such as the spurs and comb in the cock, the beard in man, [etc.]. **1977** E. J. TRIMMER et al. *Visual Dict. Sex* (1978) xxii. 262/1 A boy castrated before puberty will fail to develop the primary and secondary sexual characteristics of a normal male that would otherwise be stimulated by hormones produced by the testes.

i. *Geol.* Of a mineral: that is an original constituent of the rock. Of a rock: whose constituents have undergone no alteration since formation. Usu. applied *spec.* to minerals and rocks that have crystallized from magma.

1886 J. GEIKIE *Outl. Geol.* xiii. 151 It is the primary or original constituents of a rock which ought to determine its species, but these are often replaced by secondary minerals, and thus it is not in all cases possible to say what were the primary minerals. **1905** —— *Struct. & Field Geol.* iii. 37 Those rock-constituents which crystallised out from the magma are termed primary or original, to distinguish them from another group of minerals which are of later origin than the rocks in which they occur. **1914** J. PARK *Text-bk. Geol.* xii. 191 A primary mineral or rock constituent is one that is developed during the cooling of the molten magma, or, in the case of sedimentary rock, that appeared among the original constituents. **1921** *Trans. Geol. Soc. S. Afr.* XXIV. 116 In some varieties..a titaniferous lime-iron garnet comes in, together with primary calcite. **1931** A. JOHANNSEN *Descr. Petrogr. Igneous Rocks* I. ii. 28 The primary minerals of the igneous rocks are comparatively few in number... The feldspars, the pyriboles, the micas, quartz, olivine, and the feldspathoids are practically all. **1966** READ & WATSON *Beginning Geol.* xii. 147/1 In this environment, the primary minerals..are no longer stable, and they give place to new minerals and fabrics more in harmony with the new conditions. **1971** B. W. SPARKS *Rocks & Relief* iv. 132 A relatively small class of primary calcareous rocks, known as carbonatites, are [*sic*] associated in some areas with alkaline igneous rocks.

j. *Sociol.* Esp. as ***primary group***: a term for the sort of direct and informal relationships that an individual forms by reason of family or environmental associations which are considered basic to social life and culture (see esp. quots. 1933 and 1971).

1894 SMALL & VINCENT *Introd. Study of Society* III. ii. 183 (*heading*) The primary social group: the family. **1909** C. H. COOLEY *Social Organization* iii. 23 By primary groups I mean those characterized by intimate face-to-face association and coöperation... They are primary.. chiefly in that they are fundamental in forming the social nature and ideals of the individual. **1933** —— et al. *Introd. Sociol.* iv. 55 If human nature belongs, then, to men in association what kind or degree of association is required to develop it?.. Are there simple forms of association..? It appears that there are, and we shall call them *primary groups*. *Ibid.*, A primary group may be defined as a group of from two to possibly fifty or sixty people..who are in relatively face-to-face association for no single purpose, but merely as persons rather than as specialized functionaries. **1950** E. A. SHILS in Merton & Lazarsfeld *Continuities in Social Res.* 25 The primary group, they say, 'served two principal functions in combat motivation: it set and emphasized group standards of behavior and it supported and sustained the individual in stresses he would not otherwise have been able to withstand.' **1971** Z. BARBU *Society, Culture & Personality* ii. 34 E. Farris rejects the criterion of face-to-face association and specifies that intimate relationships, together with group consciousness, *esprit de corps*, and the feeling of 'we' constitute the main characteristics of a primary group. On the other hand E. A. Shils considers primary groups as identical with what other writers call informal groups, i.e. more or less spontaneous gatherings based on some kind of mental affinity.

k. *Physics* and *Astr.* Of, pertaining to, or designating radiation that is not produced by other radiation but may itself produce other (secondary) radiation; of cosmic rays: originating outside the earth's atmosphere.

1900 J. S. TOWNSEND in *Proc. Cambr. Philos. Soc.* X. 218 The apparatus shown..was used to determine the relative intensities of the secondary radiations given out by different bodies, and the intensity of the secondary radiation compared with that of the primary radiation which excites it. **1921** J. SCOTT-TAGGART *Thermionic Tubes* i. 23 When the primary or original electron attains a velocity sufficiently high to break off electrons from the gas molecule, it will leave the latter positively charged. **1938** R. W. LAWSON tr. *Hevesy & Paneth's Man. Radioactivity* (ed. 2) v. 61 The number of secondary electrons corresponding to each incident primary electron depends on the velocity of the primary electron. **1944** *Ann. Reg. 1943* 361 Results which they regarded as..confirming that the main part of the primary cosmic ray radiation does not consist of electrons. **1946** *Electronic Engin.* XVIII. 75/1 An electrode will emit primary electrons when its temperature is raised sufficiently to overcome the work function of the material of which it is made. **1959** K. HENNEY *Radio Engin. Handbk.* (ed. 5) vii. 15 Secondary emission may be obtained by electron bombardment of pure metals... In this case a part of the energy of the bombarding or primary electron is transferred to one or several conduction electrons of the solid. **1973** SMITH & JACOBS *Introd. Astron. & Astrophysics* xviii. 459 The fact that positrons..are only one-tenth as numerous indicates that these electrons are primary particles, and not secondaries like the light nuclei. This conclusion is based on the fact that more positrons than electrons are produced when primary cosmic rays collide with interstellar atoms.

l. ***primary poverty***, lack of means to buy the basic necessities of life.

1901 B. S. ROWNTREE *Poverty* p. viii, Families whose total earnings are insufficient to obtain the minimum necessaries. .. Poverty falling under this head I have described as 'primary' poverty. **1909** M. F. DAVIES *Life in Eng. Village* II. xii. 140 An estimate has been made of the minimum cost at which food, fuel, dress, household sundries, and house-room..can be obtained.. and it has then been seen how many families were below this standard, or in primary poverty. **1936** R. C. K. ENSOR *England 1870–1914* xiv. 515 The number of people found by Rowntree in 'primary' poverty in 1901 was 15·46 per cent. of the wage-earning class in York. **1960** *Guardian* 25 Feb. 3/6 Primary poverty was uncommon..although 130 fathers were out of work. **1964** M. LASKI in S. Nowell-Smith *Edwardian England* iv. 173 Primary poverty, that is to say,..conditions where the family income..is insufficient to maintain health and working efficiency.

m. ***primary succession*** (Ecol.) = PRISERE.

1905 F. E. CLEMENTS *Res. Methods Ecol.* iv. 241 Primary successions..arise on newly formed soils, or upon surfaces exposed for the first time, which have in consequence never borne vegetation before. **1932** FULLER & CONARD tr. *Braun-Blanquet's Plant Sociol.* xiii. 235 The Anglo-American school distinguishes between primary successions or sequences of communities which originate independently of men and secondary successions. **1952** P. W. RICHARDS *Trop. Rain Forest* xii. 269 The successions or seres leading to the establishment of stable climax Rain forest are classified.. into primary successions or priseres starting on soil not previously occupied by plants..and secondary successions or subseres. **1961** HANSON & CHURCHILL *Plant Community* v. 151 (*caption*) Primary succession on sand and gravel. **1973** P. A. COLINVAUX *Introd. Ecol.* vi. 77 The successions so far discussed are all primary successions, that is to say they are supposed to proceed by pioneering new sites.

n. ***primary industry, production***, the husbandry or use of raw materials, as in agriculture, forestry, fishing, mining, etc.; ***primary produce, products***, the fruits of these activities; ***primary producer***, one engaged in such industries; ***primary-producing*** adj., that produces or is the source of raw materials.

1930 *Economist* 8 Feb. 290/1 Our exporting manufacturers will be faced with lessened purchasing power in the hands of primary producers overseas. **1935** *Ibid.* 12 Jan. 57/2 Our own index of the dollar prices of primary products shows a rise of fully 20 per cent. **1941** BAKER *N.Z. Slang* v. 38 We were gaining [1880–1900] a footing in world markets for our primary produce. *Ibid.* vii. 60 [The] social and economic existence [of Australia and New Zealand] is largely dependent upon primary production—upon the soil. **1950** *N.Z. Jrnl. Agric.* Jan. 3/1 The basis of New Zealand's economic standards is the country's primary industries. There has been an inclination to overlook the fact that in the economic structure of New Zealand agriculture must always be the cornerstone. *Ibid.* Aug. 99/1 It has been a particularly interesting experience to attend in my capacity as Minister of Agriculture..and to see in action the machinery of the several bodies that administer the interests of different sections of primary producers. **1956** T. BALOGH in A. Pryce-Jones *New Outl. Mod. Knowl.* IV. 506 Political influence in primary-producing countries was secured by concluding bulk-buying agreements. **1959** A. H. MCLINTOCK *Descr. Atlas N.Z.* 44 In common with other exporters of primary products, New Zealand representatives have, at international conferences, drawn attention to the serious effects produced by protective barriers established at unrealistically high levels. **1965** S. T. OLLIVIER *Petticoat Farm* xi. 160 The primary produce from New Zealand went to feed other countries. **1966** G. W. TURNER *Eng. Lang. Austral. & N.Z.* iv. 85 In both Australia and New Zealand, a land naturally infertile by English standards has been made to yield products which have made the term 'primary industry' synonymous with farming, by the application of scientific agriculture. **1974** M. B. BROWN *Econ. of Imperialism* iv. 94 The extraction by the United States and by other developed countries of minerals and primary products from the whole world would not be regarded by classical economists as any sort of plunder. **1974** *Globe & Mail* (Toronto) 12 Oct. 8/3, 37 per cent of Quebec's labor force is employed in primary industry (mining, forestry, etc.) and manufacturing. **1975** *Listener* 11 Sept. 322/3 Indexing of the export prices of primary-producing countries against the rise in prices of the goods *they* need to import. **1976** *Oxford Times* 12 Mar. 11/1 The role of a University Department of Agricultural Science is..to provide graduates who can..become leaders in the field of primary production. **1977** *Herald* (Melbourne) 18 Jan. 4/1 On the talks so far, the Primary Industry Minister, Mr. Sinclair, probably sums up best by saying that he is 'relatively happy'.

o. ***primary air***, air admitted to the fuel in a furnace or burner at or before the earliest stage in its burning.

1931 *Engineering* 9 Jan. 39/3 The primary air and coal enter at the side of the burner through a long, narrow port. **1932** *Discovery* Aug. 248/1 The 'primary air' or 'bottom air' entering from beneath the fuel bed..meets the incandescent coke, and immediately the oxygen disappears and is converted into carbon dioxide. **1971** E. R. NORSTER *Combustion & Heat Transfer in Gas Turbine Syst.* 91 The earlier Python engine had a 'vaporizing' tubular-type chamber, the fuel being pre-mixed with some primary air before being fed tangentially into a swirl chamber.

p. ***primary constriction*** (Cytology), a chromosomal constriction associated with the centromere.

1932 C. D. DARLINGTON *Rec. Adv. Cytol.* 495 *Primary* or *attachment constriction*, that always associated with the spindle attachment. **1937** *Ibid.* (ed. 2) 575 *Primary* or *centric constriction*, that always associated with the centromere. **1957** C. P. SWANSON *Cytol. & Cytogenetics* v. 112 The localized centromere produces the primary constriction. **1969** BROWN & BERTKE *Textbk. Cytol.* xviii. 344/1 This 'constriction' associated with the centromere is often loosely called the centromere, or kinetochore, but more exactly it is the primary constriction.

q. *Ecol.* Forming part of the lowest trophic level in a community, either as a producer or as a consumer that feeds on a producer; of or pertaining to a producer.

[**1893** W. K. BROOKS in *Mem. Biol. Lab. Johns Hopkins Univ.* II. 148 A few forms are so predominant that..we may regard the great primary food-supply as made up of two simple protozoa, Globigerina and the Radiolarians, and some five or six unicellular plants.] **1934** *Q. Rev. Biol.* IX. 163/1 In connection with..his phrase ('primary food supply') which I have undertaken to use, Brooks gives..a meaning somewhat more comprehensive than that which I prefer... It suits my purpose better to confine the usage to the microscopic plants equipped with chlorophyll and capable of manufacturing carbohydrates from raw materials. **1940** *Ibid.* XV. 48/2 The various primary animals (phytophages) of a formation are often independent of each other. **1953** E. P. ODUM *Fund. Ecol.* iv. 82 In speaking of productivity, it is important to distinguish between the basic or primary productivity..and consumer or secondary productivity. **1956** *Limnology & Oceanogr.* I. 116/1 The diagram shows how some streams may be fertile in having high total respiratory metabolism and yet possess little primary productivity. **1969** B. K. SLADEN in Sladen & Bang *Biol. of Populations* vii. 92 The knapweed plants were the producers, and nine animal species were primary consumers eating the knapweed plant. *Ibid.* 93 The productivity of the producers, the photosynthetic plants, must be greater than that of the primary consumers. **1971** M. ALEXANDER *Microbial Ecol.* xvi. 410 Aquatic algae are typically primary organisms in that their energy is obtained from sunlight. **1976** S. B. CHAPMAN in *Methods in Plant Ecol.* iv. 161 Primary production is the production of organic matter by photosynthesis. *Ibid.*, Gross primary production, the total amount of organic matter produced (including that lost in respiration) over a given period of time. *Ibid.*, Net primary production, the amount of organic matter incorporated by a plant or an area of vegetation (gross primary production minus the loss due to respiration) over a given period of time.

r. *Psychol.* Relating to abilities or traits which, through factor analysis, appear basic to other aspects of intelligence or personality.

1938 L. L. THURSTONE *Primary Mental Abilities* p. vi, These subsequent studies have had the advantage of some orientation about the first seven primary factors as landmarks... It is probably better to find the principal landmarks in the cognitive and conative primary traits by means of group procedures. *Ibid.* vi. 92 The tests will be improved by making them relatively pure measures of the primary abilities. **1958** K. LOVELL *Educ. Psychol. & Children* iii. 58 Thurstone has termed these primary mental abilities and claims that they are found both in very young children and in adults. **1965** R. B. CATTELL *Sci. Analysis of Personality* iii. 60 Several 'primary abilities' were also involved, such as numerical, spatial, verbal, and logical abilities. **1969** H. J. & S. B. EYSENCK *Personality Struct. & Measurement* 328 We have seen that while primary factors emerge in considerable profusion, these seldom if ever agree precisely with those postulated by Cattell and Guilford. **1970** L. J. BISCHOF *Interpreting Personality Theories* (ed. 2) VI. xii. 464 In his current work, Cattell calls the source traits Primary Personality Factors. With few exceptions, the Primary Personality Factors are bipolar or dichotomized. **1972** *Jrnl. Social Psychol.* LXXXVI. 187 Disputes about the number and nature of primary personality factors in questionnaire data are still rife.

s. ***primary structure*** (Aeronaut.), those parts of an aircraft whose failure would seriously endanger safety.

1939 *Aircraft Engin.* Feb. 66/1 The primary structure of the main plane is erected in a wall jig. **1959** F. D. ADAMS *Aeronaut. Dict.* 132/1 Elements not a part of the primary structure include cowlings, fairings, windshields, etc. **1964** J. E. D. WILLIAMS *Operation of Airliners* ix. 133 To ensure that throughout the operational life of the aircraft the possibility of disastrous fatigue failure is remote, the primary structure must either have an extremely long probable life or be designed to fail safely.

t. Of radar: transmitting radiation for targets to reflect, not requiring any generation of signals by targets.

1945 R. WATSON-WATT in *Nature* 15 Sept. 323/2 Primary radar is that form of radar which 'does not require the co-operation of the object to be located'. **1960** T. J. MORGAN *Radar* xii. 137 The measurement of the wind direction and velocity was carried out by means of direction finding stations, then later by primary radar. **1963** R. S. H. BOULDING *Princ. & Pract. Radar* (ed. 7) xxii. 470 In secondary radar as distinct from normal (or primary) radar, the target plays an active part in the operation of ranging and position finding.

u. ***primary stress***, the principal stress in a word (see STRESS *sb.* 9). Also *attrib.* So ***primary-stressed*** adj., (of a word or syllable) carrying a primary stress.

1951 TRAGER & SMITH *Outl. Eng. Struct.* i. 36 There must be a stress phoneme whose characteristic is maximum normal loudness, which we may call *primary stress.* **1964** G. L. TRAGER in D. Abercrombie et al. *Daniel Jones* 267 When a clause begins with the primary-stressed syllabic, there are only two pitches. **1968** CHOMSKY & HALLE *Sound Pattern Eng.* 34 We note that primary stress falls on the prefix if the stem is monosyllabic. *Ibid.* 114 The other..vowels..have never received primary stress at any stage of their derivation. **1971** *Eng. Stud.* LII. 349 From recorded readings we know that the unnatural stress-patterns which result can be emended by a prolongation of the first of two primary-stressed syllables. **1972** *Language* XLVIII. 328 In simple declarative sentences ending in a predicate, primary stress is often most naturally placed on the subject. *Ibid.* 331 Surface structure alone is insufficient to determine primary-stress placement.

v. ***primary structure*** (Biochem.), the sequence of amino-acids forming the chain structure of a protein or polypeptide, as opposed to the three-dimensional configuration and arrangement of the chains.

1952 K. U. LINDERSTRØM-LANG *Proteins & Enzymes* 58 The presence of intrahelix as well as interhelix bonds may justify a classification into secondary (intrahelix) and tertiary (interhelix) structures, as distinct from the primary structure of the simple β-chain. **1964** G. H. HAGGIS et al. *Introd. Molecular Biol.* iii. 48 The peptide chains coil up, and fold back on themselves, to form a complex three-dimensional molecular structure, and..the determination of sequence, or primary structure, is only the beginning of a description of the protein molecule. **1970** R. W. MCGILVERY *Biochem.* viii. 150 Any disruption of protein structure that does not involve the primary structure ought to be self-healing once the cause of the disruption is removed. **1974** *Nature* 29 Nov. 351/2 Let us now discuss the effect of natural selection on secondary or tertiary structure, as natural selection acts through these higher order structures and not on primary structure.

B. *sb.* [elliptical use of adj. Mostly in *pl.*]

1. That which (or one who) is first in order, rank, or importance; anything from which something else arises or is derived. Usually *pl.* = primary things or ones; first principles.

1760–72 H. BROOKE *Fool of Qual.* (1809) III. 52 Where any secondary agents attempt to defeat the power of their primaries. **1846** G. S. FABER *Lett. Tractar. Secess.* 248 Though there may be occasional disagreement in subordinates, there is a very singular and a very striking agreement in primaries. **1856** DOVE *Logic Chr. Faith* Introd. §5. 13 Every science..begins with primaries or with ultimates.

2. Short for *primary planet*: see PLANET *sb.*[1] 2.

a **1721** KEILL *Maupertuis' Diss.* (1734) 33 We see that the Sun attracting the Planets, is the Cause why they move round him, as the attraction of the Primaries confines their Secondaries. **1868** LOCKYER *Elem. Astron.* III. x. (1879) 58 The only satellite which takes a longer time to revolve round its primary than our Moon, is Iapetus, the eighth satellite of Saturn.

3. A primary feather: see A. 5. Usually in *pl.*

1776 PENNANT *Zool.* II. 441 Primaries and tail black. **1834** R. MUDIE *Feathered Tribes Brit. Isles* (1841) I. 9 The primaries or principal quills. **1883** MARTIN & MOALE *Vertebr. Dissect.* II. 99 The primaries are ten in number and are inserted upon the manus.

4. Short for *primary colour*: see A. 6.

1848 [see A. 6]. **1884** A. F. OAKEY in *Harper's Mag.* Mar. 586/2 The eye supplies the absent primary, blue. **1967** E. SHORT *Embroidery & Fabric Collage* i. 14 If the three primaries are placed on a white background the reverse will happen. **1972** *House & Garden* Feb. 70/2 The most successful rooms are those using vivid primaries. **1979** *Guardian* 13 June 12/5 Cellular cotton shirts come in all pastels and primaries.

5. *Electr.* Short for *primary coil* or *wire*: see A. 6 g. Also, a primary circuit, current, etc.

1837 M. FARADAY in *Ann. Electr., Magn., & Chem.* I. 200 The renitency encountered in the conductors will necessarily exercise a due influence in lessening the force of secondary currents, but cannot be made available as a cause of the comparative atony which these currents, by the initial impulses of the primary, invariably display. **1849** NOAD *Electricity* (ed. 3) 490 The coil of thick wire is called the primary. **1869** *Eng. Mech.* 17 Dec. 335/2 The core and primary are enclosed in an ebonite cylinder. **1896** F. BEDELL *Princ. Transformer* i. 2 The alternating current transformer ..consists simply of two independent circuits, a primary and a secondary, wound independently upon a common core of laminated soft iron. **1931** B. BROWN *Talking Pictures* iii. 36 Modulation of the voltage is accomplished through a transformer, the primary of which is supplied with the speech recording curent coming from the microphone, via the amplifiers. **1938** KERCHNER & CORCORAN *Alternating-Current Circuits* vii. 182 Circuit 1, energized by means of an alternating potential difference, is called the primary. **1967** M. F. BUCHAN *Electr. Supply* vi. 156 Consider now what happens if the secondaries are connected in delta, whilst the primaries are star-connected to a 3-wire supply.

6. Short for *primary meeting* or *assembly*, a caucus: see A. 4 e; now usu. = *primary election*, one at which candidates for political office in the U.S.A. are chosen. *U.S.*

a **1861** T. WINTHROP *Life in Open Air* (1863) 147 'Boys,' said he,..'when I accepted the office of Orator of the Day at our primary and promised to bring forward our resolutions in honor of Mr. Wade.' **1868** *All Year Round* 19 Sept. 351/2 He is 'powerful' in 'primaries', where he votes early and often for his favourite candidates. **1880** E. KIRKE *Garfield* 31 The clergy..and many of the leading business men..never attend the township caucus, the city primaries, or the county convention. **1888** BRYCE *Amer. Commw.* II. lx. 421 If the district is not subdivided, i.e. does not contain any lesser districts, its meeting is called a *primary.* A primary has two duties. One is to select the candidates for its own local district offices... The other duty is to elect delegates to the nominating meetings of larger areas. **1896** *Harper's Mag.* XCIII. 147/2 He knew the primaries and the value of pulls and colonizations. **1900** B. C. CLARK in *Mod. Eloquence* X. p. xvii, Those of you who remember as I do the times that tried men's souls will not, I hope, forget their humble servant when the primaries shall be held. **1908** *Contemp. Rev.* Apr. 404 Other Western States have passed similar laws for direct primaries. **1930** *Economist* 7 June 1267/1 They have nominated Mr. Franklin Fort, a 'dry' Congressman, as his opponent in the Republican 'primaries'. **1966** *Listener* 25 Aug. 289/3 He could be freed from this bondage either by a system of primaries in which the field of choice were extended to others beyond the narrow range of committed party workers or through the introduction of the alternative vote. **1967** *Boston Herald* 1 Apr. 1/1 George C. Wallace, Jr., said Friday that he was thinking of entering the New Hampshire presidential preferential primary next March 12. **1976** *Times* 26 Feb. 15/2 Sitting Presidents need to do far more than escape disaster in the primaries, which are popularity contests among their own party's voters.

7. Short for *primary scholar*: see A. 4 d.

1908 ROBINS *Come & Find Me* 36 'Serves her right' said Primarys, Academics and Collegiates all with one voice.

8. *Physics* and *Astr.* A primary ray or particle, esp. a primary cosmic ray.

1923 *Physical Rev.* XXII. 243 The emission is comprised in part of electrons whose speeds are not appreciably less than that of the primaries. **1932** *Ibid.* XLI. 545 The average number of secondaries per primary is about 100 in iron and 230 in lead. **1942** J. D. STRANATHAN *'Particles' of Mod. Physics* xii. 488 Many of the primaries and many of the large number of secondaries formed high in the atmosphere are unable to penetrate the entire atmosphere. **1956** *Spaceflight* Oct. 27/1 The charged cosmic ray primaries..consist of approximately 80 per cent. protons, 18 or 19 per cent. alpha particles, and the remainder heavier nuclei. **1959** K. HENNEY *Radio Engin. Handbk.* (ed. 5) vii. 15 If all the energy brought into the body by the bombarding primary could be transformed into the energy required for the emission of secondary electrons, the ratio δ would be very high. **1974** *Encycl. Brit. Macropædia* V. 203/1 The discovery in meteoritic crystals of particle tracks produced by primaries heavier than iron.

9. *Gram.* In Jespersen's terminology, a word or group of words (normally a noun or a noun-phrase) of primary importance in a phrase or sentence. Cf. ADJUNCT *sb.* 5 b, SUBJUNCT.

1924 O. JESPERSEN *Philos. Gram.* vii. 97 We may, of course, have two or more coordinate adjuncts to the same primary: thus, in *a nice young lady*, the words *a*, *nice*, and *young* equally define *lady.* **1928** —— *Internat. Lang.* II. 97 When adjectives are made into primaries, we have the endings already considered. **1928** *Mod. Lang. Rev.* XXIII. 143 After a chapter on clauses as 'primaries', about 150 pages are devoted to a thorough survey of relative clauses. **1935** [see *noun-equivalent*]. **1940** *Eng. Stud.* XXII. 88 *Primary, secondary* and *tertiary*, intended to connote ..*headwords, attributes* and *adjuncts*, the terms representing their relative importance or ranks within the sentence, headwords coming first. **1959** M. SCHLAUCH *Eng. Lang. in Mod. Times* viii. 221 In this system [of Otto Jespersen's] a leading term, for instance a noun subject, is a primary.

pri'matal, *a.* (*sb.*) *Zool. rare.* [f. L. PRIMATES + -AL[1].] Of or pertaining to the order *Primates.* Also as *sb.*, An animal of this order.

1870 COBBOLD in *Athenæum* 8 Oct. 468/2 It was..held that either of these groups, as we now know them, might have been separately evolved from more generalized primatal types... The assumedly missing tertiary primatals constituted a great and natural bar to the popular acceptance of the theory of descent by natural selection.

primate ('praɪmət), *sb.*[1] (*a.*) Forms: 3–7 **primat,** 4–5 **prymat(e,** 5 **premate,** 4– **primate.** [= F. *primat* (12th c. in Littré), ad. late L. *prīmās, -ātem* adj. (Apul.), of the first rank, chief, excellent, in med.L. sb. a primate; f. *prīmus* first.]

A. *sb.* **1.** One who is first in rank or importance; a chief, head, superior, leader. Now *rare.*

13.. *E.E. Allit. P.* B. 1570 He schal be prymate & prynce of pure clergye. **1382** WYCLIF *Micah* v. 5 We shuln reyse on hym seuen sheperdis, and eiȝt primatis [*gloss* or first men in dignyte]. **1387** TREVISA *Higden* (Rolls) II. 325 þis preost was primat [L. *sacerdos iste primas fuit*] in þat lond of Madyan. **1513** BRADSHAW *St. Werburge* I. 21 Byrdes besely syngynge ..Praysynge theyr prymate all that they may. **1548** UDALL, etc. *Erasm. Par. Mark* v. 32 Although he were a ruler of the Synagoge, that is, a primate among stately felowes. **1581** MULCASTER *Positions* xxxix. (1887) 197 The prince which is the primate and pearle of nobilitie. **1683** *Brit. Spec.* 30 They [Druids] were subject to two Primates; one of which..had his Residence in the Isle of Man; the other..in Anglesey. **1866** *Reader* 28 July 676 Man is a primate in his particular locality—that of intelligence and thought; but fish and birds are equally primates in their peculiar stations.

2. *Eccl.* An archbishop, or formerly sometimes a bishop, holding the first place among the bishops of a province; also applied to a patriarch or exarch of the Eastern Church.

In England both the archbishops are primates, the archbishop of Canterbury being entitled 'primate of all England', and the archbishop of York 'primate of England'; so, the archbishop of Armagh is 'primate of all Ireland', the archbishop of Dublin 'primate of Ireland'; before the Reformation, the archbishop of St. Andrews was (from 1487) primate of Scotland; but on the continent, there are primates having archbishops under them; in France there were formerly three primates, the archbishops of Lyons, Bourges, and Rouen.

c **1205** LAY. 29736 He [Austin] was icleopped legat, of þissen londe he wæs primat. *c* **1330** R. BRUNNE *Chron.* (1810) 73 þe archbissop Stigand, of Inglond primate, þat tyme was suspended, þe pape reft him þe state. **1387** TREVISA *Higden* (Rolls) II. 115 But now beeþ but tweie primates in al Engelond, of Caunterbury, and of ȝork. **1427** *Rolls of Parlt.* IV. 322/2 The Archebisshopp of Canterbury and Primat of al this land. **1451** CAPGRAVE *Life St. Aug.* 43 This bischop of Cartage was premate þorw all Affrik, þan was þere anoþir bischop premate of al Numidie. *c* **1460** *Oseney Reg.* 98 Walter, By þe grace of god Archiebisshop of ȝorke, a primat of Ingelonde. **1552** ABP. HAMILTON *Catech.* (1884) 1 Legatnait and primat of the kirk of Scotland. **1601** R. JOHNSON *Kingd. & Commw.* (1603) 23 It hath one primate, and two Archbishopricks, Armach and Cassels. **1709** J. JOHNSON *Clergym. Vade M.* II. 160 (African Code, A.D. 418) Let not any number of Bishops presume to ordain another without the leave of the Primate. **1726** AYLIFFE *Parergon* 90 Tho' an Archbishop be superiour to all the Bishops of his Province; yet, according to the Canon Law he is inferiour to a Primate. **1756** NUGENT *Gr. Tour, France* IV. 158 The archbishop [of Lyons] is primate of Gaul, and has 48,000 livres a year. **1756–7** tr. *Keysler's Trav.* (1760) IV. 62 He [Archbp. of Venice] is primate of Dalmatia, metropolitan of the archbishops of Candia and Corfu, as also of the bishops of Chiozza and Tercello. **1833** *Tracts for Times* No. 15. 6 These Patriarchs..were the Primates or Head Bishops of their respective Patriarchates. **1889** *Whitaker's Alm.* 239 Colonial Bishops... Sydney. Alf. Barry, D.D. Primate of Australia and Metropolitan New South Wales. **1896** *Dict. Nat. Biog.* LVI. 281/2 On 22 Feb. 1354..the pope.. directed that York should be styled primate of England, and Canterbury primate of All England.

3. Name of a variety of pear. ? *Obs.*

1664 EVELYN *Kal. Hort., July* 70 Pears. The Primat, Russet-pears, Summer-pears [etc.]. **1707** MORTIMER *Husb.* (1721) II. 375.

4. *Zool.* (Usually with pronunciation ('praɪmeɪt).) A mammal belonging to the order Primates, which includes man, apes, monkeys, and several groups of prosimians. Also *attrib.*

1898 *Westm. Gaz.* 26 Aug. 8/2 It was a fixed fact that man is a member of the primate order. **1899** J. FISKE *Through Nat. to God* II. v. 83 Forthwith..she [natural selection] invested all her capital in the psychical variations of this favoured primate. **1906** E. INGERSOLL *Life of Animals* 7 The higher the Primate in the scale of organization the more perfectly are its fore limbs and hands adapted to seizing and handling objects. **1929** R. M. & A. W. YERKES *Great Apes* i. 2/1 No infrahuman primate, least of all the great ape, has been thoroughly domesticated. **1967** J. R. & P. H. NAPIER *Handbk. Living Primates* p. v, Animal behaviour, ecology and genetic biology..today dominate basic research trends in primate biology. **1977** RAINIER III & BOURNE *Primate Conservation* p. xviii, All authors of this book agreed that the royalties earned should be used to further primate conservation.

†**B.** *adj.* First, earliest. *Obs. rare.*

1554–9 *Songs & Ball.* (1860) 5 The gates infernall, Wheryn ower primat parent had closyd us. **1580** HOLLYBAND *Treas. Fr. Tong, Premier*, first or primate.

†**primate,** *sb.*[2] *Obs.* [= OF. *primat* (15th c. in Godef.), ad. L. *prīmātus* (*u*-stem) the first place, preference, pre-eminence, primacy.]

1. Chief place, primacy.

a **1340** HAMPOLE *Psalter* xxiii. 6 þat god gif þaim þe primate in blisse. **1432–50** tr. *Higden* (Rolls) II. 273 After that..Cesares, emperoures, and men callede Augusti holdede the primate and chiefe place [L. *primatum tenuerunt*].

2. A first or chief point or article. *rare*[−1].

1592 WARNER *Alb. Eng.* IX. lii. (1612) 235 Gods Cou'nant with the Patriarchs..is a Primate of our Creede.

‖**Primates** (praɪ'meɪtiːz, 'praɪmeɪts), *sb. pl.* *Zool.* Sing. **primas** ('praɪmæs), also anglicized PRIMATE. [L. *prīmātēs*, pl. of *prīmās* PRIMATE *sb.*[1], in mod.L. (Linn.) name of an order.] The highest order of the *Mammalia*, including man, monkeys, and lemurs, and, in the Linnæan order, bats.

1774 GOLDSM. *Nat. Hist.* IV. v. 138 This was a sufficient motive for Linnæus to give it the title of a Primas, to rank it in the same order with mankind. **1826** GOOD *Bk. Nat.* (1834) II. 47 The 1st order, Primates or Chieftains, is distinguished by the possession of four cutting teeth in each jaw. **1863** LYELL *Antiq. Man* xxiv. 474 All modern naturalists, who retain the order Primates, agree to exclude from it the bats or cheiroptera. **1871** DARWIN *Desc. Man* I. i. 24 Man differs conspicuously from all the other Primates in being almost naked.

'primateship. [f. PRIMATE *sb.*[1] + -SHIP.] The office or position of primate.

1631 WEEVER *Anc. Fun. Mon.* 253 Thence remoued to this Primatship of Canterbury. **1799** *Chron.* in *Ann. Reg.* 67/1 The primateship will remain vacant for two years.

primatial (praɪ'meɪʃəl), *a.* [a. F. *primatial* (16th c. in Littré), f. L. *prīmātia* PRIMACY: see -AL[1].]

1. Of, pertaining to, or having ecclesiastical primacy; pertaining to a primate.

1623 tr. *Favine's Theat. Hon.* II. xiii. 249 Toledo, which he made Primatiall of all Spaine. **1725** tr. *Dupin's Eccl. Hist. 17th C.* I. v. 119 People were commonly perswaded, that the Church of Lyons was Primatial. **1750** CARTE *Hist. Eng.* II. 613 The consequences of his being advanced to the primatial see of Canterbury. **1876** FREEMAN *Norm. Conq.* V. xxiii. 317 Henry of Winchester pleaded hard..that the ancient capital should be raised to primatial rank, as the metropolitan see of Wessex. **1904** POLLARD *Cranmer* iv. 95 Another attempt..against his primatial dignity.

b. *gen.* Of pre-eminence or superiority.

1892 GLADSTONE in *Daily News* 5 Dec. 3/5 The claims of Bristol to what I may call the primatial position in British commerce.

2. *Zool.* Of or pertaining to the mammalian order *Primates*: more properly PRIMATAL.

1864 *Spectator* 4 June 650/2 The lemurine—and consequently quadrumane (Professor Huxley would call them *primatial*)—affinities of the *Chiromys*.

primatic (praɪˈmætɪk), *a.* [f. PRIMATE *sb.*[1] + -IC: cf. OF. *prematic* (1491 in Godef.).]

1. Of or pertaining to ecclesiastical primacy; = PRIMATIAL *a.* 1. ? *Obs.*

1687 S. HILL *Cath. Balance* 76 The Bishopric of Jerusalem, the Metropolis of all the Jews of the World, and therefore the primatic See of all the Jewish Christians. *Ibid.*, The three great primatic Bishoprics of the Gentiles, Antioch, Rome, and Alexandria. **1826** G. S. FABER *Diffic. Romanism* (1853) 218 They submitted, not to Peter's primatic mandate, but to the very ample reason which he gave for his conduct.

2. Of or pertaining to the *Primates*; = PRIMATAL.

a **1890** HUXLEY cited in *Cent. Dict.*

So, in sense 1, **priˈmatical** *a.*

a **1677** BARROW *Pope's Suprem.* (1687) 171 The original and growth of Metropolitical, Primatical, and Patriarchal Jurisdiction. **1747** CARTE *Hist. Eng.* I. 356 Stigand, the canonicalness of whose primatical dignity was not as yet called in question. **1872** O. SHIPLEY *Gloss. Eccl. Terms* s.v. *Exarch*, A bishop of primatical rank, having under him metropolitans.

primatife, -ive, etc., obs. forms of PRIMITIVE.

primatology (praɪməˈtɒlədʒɪ). [f. PRIMATE *sb.*[1] 4 + -OLOGY.] The study of primates.

1941 J. F. FULTON in T. C. Ruch *Bibliographia Primatologica* I. p. xi, Dr. Ruch has followed Linnaeus in adopting the term 'primate', and in the title of his bibliography he has introduced a new and useful derivative 'Primatology'. **1942** RUCH & FULTON in *Science* 9 Jan. 47/1 It is only within the past decade or two that the study of the primates as a distinct zoological group has come into sufficient stature to warrant separate designation—'primate biology' or if you will, 'primatology'. **1956** *Nature* 17 Mar. 505/2 Duckworth had very wide interests in anatomy, teratology, primatology, anthropology, archaeology and general natural history. **1967** *Guardian* 20 Oct. 6/3 With the growth of primatology we are increasingly aware how unusual are man's problems in dealing with his fellows. **1973** *Sci. Amer.* Jan. 11/1 Geza Teleki ('The Omnivorous Chimpanzee') is completing work for his Ph.D. in primatology at the University of Georgia. **1976** *Primate Eye* VII. 1 In this issue of Primate Eye, we are including a number of reviews of books in the field of primatology.

Hence **primatoˈlogical** *a.*, of or pertaining to primatology; **primaˈtologist**, one who studies primates.

1945 M. F. A. MONTAGU *Introd. Physical Anthropol.* ii. 11 Dead primates enable the primatologist to make detailed studies of their anatomy. **1949** *Antiquity* XXIII. 126 One of the few technical treatises on man's embryology that is anthropological and primatological in its orientation. **1957** L. EISELEY *Immense Journey* 105 Primatologists may therefore be forgiven their fumblings over great gaps of millions of years from which we do not possess a single complete monkey skeleton. **1973** *Nature* 18 May 175/2 A general section on the radiation of the placental mammals, placing primate evolution in its proper perspective—a perspective which is far too readily forgotten in many modern primatological studies. **1977** *Ibid.* 20 Oct. 654/3 He launched an attack on primatologists..for the way they have generally discussed the adaptive significance of social behaviour.

‖**primavera** (priːməˈvɛərə). [Sp. *primavera*, lit. spring; so called from its early flowering, the flowers appearing at the top like a bright yellow cloud, usually before the leaves.] A tall tree, *Tabebuia Donnell-Smithii*, a native of Mexico and Central America, the wood of which, also known as *white mahogany*, has been since *c* 1885 much used in cabinet-making in U.S.A.

1892 in *Coulter's Botanical Gaz.* XVII. 418. **1953** R. CHANDLER *Long Good-Bye* xv. 95 The table of polished primavera.

primaveral (ˌpraɪməˈvɪərəl), *a. rare.* [f. Prov. or It. (= Sp., Pg.) *primavera* springtime (:—L. *prīma vēra*, pl. of *prīmum vēr* 'first or earliest spring', used as a fem. sing.) + -AL[1].] Of or pertaining to the earliest springtime. Also *fig.*

1824 T. FORSTER *Perennial Cal.* 106 The Primaveral Flora ..comprehends the Snowdrop, the Crocus [etc.]. **1887** *Daily Tel.* 30 Apr. 3/2 An aspect of morning brightness and primaveral gaiety.

‖**prima vista** (ˈprima ˈvista). [It., lit. 'first sight': see PRIMA[2].]

†**1.** (Also *corruptly* **6 primo visto, 7 primuiste, primivist(e, -ta, -efisto, -ofistula**). An old game at cards (by some identified with PRIMERO). *Obs.*

1591 GREENE *Disc. Coosnage* Wks. (Grosart) X. 25 What will you play at, at Primero, Primo visto, Sant, one and thirtie, new cut, or what shall be the game? **1598** FLORIO, *Prima*,..a game at cardes called Prime, Primero, or Primauista. **1617** MINSHEU *Ductor*, *Primero*, and *Primavista*, two games at cardes..*primum, & primum visum*, that is first and first seene, because hee that can shew such an order of cardes, first winnes the game. **1621** J. TAYLOR (Water P.) *Motto* Wks. (1630) E e iv b/2 At Primefisto, Post and payre, Primero, Maw, Whip-her-ginny, he's a lib'rall Hero. **1628** EARLE *Microcosm.*, *Reserved Man* (Arb.) 35 His words are like the cards at Primuiste, where 6. is 18. and 7. 21, for they neuer signifie what they sound. **1632** HAUSTED *Rival Friends* Pref. A iij b, A set at Maw or Primivista. *a* **1652** BROME *New Acad.* III. i, Gleek and Primero, Gresco, sant, primofistula, I know all by hear-say.

2. *Music.* At first sight; as, to play or sing *prima vista*.

1845 [see TRANSPOSE *v.* 7]. **1974** *Listener* 14 Feb. 218/2 The London Symphony Orchestra..is still full of excellent players who can read almost everything *prima vista*.

primcock, obs. form of PRINCOCK.

prime (praɪm), *sb.*[1] [OE. *prîm*, ad. L. *prīma*, from *prīma hōra* the first hour (in Roman reckoning): see PRIME *a.* Reinforced after the 11th c. by F. *prime* (:—L. *prīma*), from which the non-ecclesiastical senses were prob. mainly taken.]

I. In the ecclesiastical and connected senses.

1. One of the Day Hours of the Western Church: a Canonical Hour of the Divine Office, appointed for the first hour of the day (beginning originally at 6 A.M., but sometimes at sunrise); = *prime-song* (see 11); also, the hour or time of this office.

Prime is one of the *horæ parvæ* or 'Little Hours' (*prime, tierce, sext, none,* and *compline*) as distinguished from the 'Greater Hours' (*lauds* and *vespers*), and is said to be of later origin than the others, having been, according to Cassian (born *c* 350), added in his boyhood at the monastery of Bethlehem.

Etymologically and historically in Latin, the sense 'first hour of the day' is earlier than the ecclesiastical use; but, in English, as in French, *prime* was app. introduced as the name of the office, and came only secondarily to be applied to its time.

c **961** ÆTHELWOLD *Rule St. Benet* xvi. (Schröer) 40 On þisum tidum we herian urne scyppend..on dægred, on prim, on undern, on middæᵹ, on non, on æfen, on nihtsange [þat is compli]. *c* **1000** ÆLFRIC *Colloq.* in Wr.-Wülcker 101 We sungon..æfter þysum prim and seofon seolmas mid letanian and capitol mæssan. *c* **1200** *Vices & Virt.* 19 Ðar hwile ðe h(i)e singeð lofsang at prime. *c* **1290** *St. Brendan* 224 in *S. Eng. Leg.* I. 225, & of þe sauter seide þe uers, & siþþe also prime, & vnderne siþþe, & middai, & after-wardes non. *c* **1386** CHAUCER *Pard. T.* 334 Thise Riotours thre..Longe erst er prime rong of any belle Were set hem in a Tauerne to drynke. **1450–1530** *Myrr. our Ladye* 138 As mattyns longe to the nyghte, & Laudes to the morow tyde, so Pryme longeth to the fyrst houre of the day after sonne rysynge. **1526** *Pilgr. Perf.* (W. de W. 1531) 164 b, In..the.. houres canonicall,..that is to saye, in matyns, pryme, tierce, sext, none, euensonge, & complyn. **1547** in Cardwell *Doc. Ann.* (1839) I. 20 Item when any sermon or homily shall be had, the prime and hours shall be omitted. **1647** CRASHAW *Poems*, *Hour of Prime* 7 The early prime blushes to say She could not rise so soon as they Call'd Pilate up. **1660** F. BROOKE tr. *Le Blanc's Trav.* 254 So omit they not to sing the Prime, the third, the sixt, and other Canonical houres. **1706** tr. *Dupin's Eccl. Hist. 16th C.* II. v. 43 Cassander is much perplexed about the Office of Prime, how to reconcile it with the ancient Lauds, which he would not have been had he known that the Office had not been so ancient. **1843** [see LAUD *sb.*[1] 2]. **1854** MILMAN *Lat. Chr.* III. vi. (1864) II. 89 From prime to noon..was devoted to labour. **1877** J. D. CHAMBERS *Div. Worship* 129 Prime succeeded Lauds at an interval.

2. Hence, in general use, The first hour of the day, beginning either at six o'clock throughout the year, or at the varying time of sunrise; also sometimes used for the period between the first hour and tierce, the end of which period (about nine o'clock) is believed to have been ***high prime***, or ***prime large***.

(See Skeat's notes to P. Pl. p. 162, also Astrolabe p. lxi. Cf. the expressions *ad tertiam plenam*, etc. in Benedictine Rule xlviii.)

c **1290** *St. Michael* 461 in *S. Eng. Leg.* I. 313 And for þe sonne is feor a-boue riȝt at-fore þe prime, bi-neoþen hire þe Mone is euene. **1362** LANGL. *P. Pl.* A. VII. 105 At heiȝ prime perkyn lette þe plouȝ stonde. *c* **1374** CHAUCER *Troylus* II. 943 (992) Al so syker as þow lyst here by me, And god toforn I wole be þere at pryme. *c* **1400** MAUNDEV. (1839) xxx. 301 From pryme of the day in to noon. *c* **1400** *Song Roland* 776 Be that it was prym, the prese wex ille. **1412–20** LYDG. *Chron. Troy* (E.E.T.S.) 2968 My lady it is tyme þat we arise, for sone it wil be pryme: ȝe may se wel þe day begynneth springe. *c* **1430** —— *Min. Poems* (Percy Soc.) 105 Then to Westmynster-Gate I presently went, When the sonn was at hyghe pryme. **1493** *Festivall* (W. de W. 1515) 7 An husbonde man wente in to his gardyn or vyneyerde at pryme. **1513** BRADSHAW *St. Werburge* I. 1054 Vnto huntynge..was his resorte Euery day in the morowe longe afore pryme. **1656** BLOUNT *Glossogr.*, *Prime*..the first hour of the day, in Summer at four aclock, in Winter at eight. **1746–7** HERVEY *Refl. Fl.-Gard.* Wks. 1767 I. 114 How charming to rove abroad, at this sweet Hour of Prime! **1814** SCOTT *Ld. of Isles* VI. i, Early and late, at evening and at prime. **1814** CARY *Dante's Inf.* I. 35 The hour was morning's prime, and on his way Aloft the sun ascended. **1870** BRYANT *Iliad* I. I. 30 At early prime She sat before thee and embraced thy knees.

†**3.** The general meeting of a guild; also, the hour of its assembling. *Obs.*

1389 in *Eng. Gilds* (1870) 79 (*St. John Bapt., Bps. Lynn*) Also, qwat broþere or sistere þat cometȝ aftere prime be smeten, he shal pay j.d. to þe lytȝ; and prime shall be smet[en] ij. howres aftere noon. *Ibid.* 94 (*St. Edmund*) And if he come after prime be thriis smeten, he schal paie j.d. **1431** *Ibid.* 275 (*St. Clement, Camb.*) Who-so comyth aftir prime be smette, he schal payen ij. denar. And yᵉ oure prime is clepyd the secounde oure aftyr noone. **1812** tr. *Rules & Ordin. Gild of Holy Trin. Kings Lynn* in Richards *Hist. Lynn* I. 456–7, 11. If any one is called and cited at a prime (or general meeting) and does not come before the issue of the first consult, he is to pay 1*d.* by order of the dean... 14. If any servant of the brethren comes at the drinking, or the prime, he is to lay down the cap and cloak [etc.].

II. The beginning of a period or cycle.

4. The Golden Number: see GOLDEN 6. *arch.*

1338 R. BRUNNE *Chron.* (1810) 341 Þe day is for to witen, Idus þat is of May left I to write þis ryme, D. letter & Friday bi ix þat ȝere ȝede prime. **1387** TREVISA *Higden* (Rolls) III. 135 Whanne prime gooþ by oon, þanne falleþ the prime þe þre and twenty day of Ianyuer, and þe next ȝere after it schal falle..enleuene dayes raþer. *c* **1430** LYDG. *Min. Poems* (Percy Soc.) 24 The aureat noumbre in kalenders set for prime. **1546** LANGLEY *Pol. Verg. De Invent.* II. iv. 42 The Prime, whereby we fynde the coniunction of the mone and al moueable feastes as Lent, Easter..was inuented by the greate Clarcke S. Barnarde. **1574** BOURNE *Regiment for Sea* ii. (1577) 9 b, The cause..it is called the Prime, was for that it was the first order that the Moones course was known by. **1604** *Bk. Com. Prayer*, *To find Easter for ever*, When ye haue found the Sunday letter..guide your eye downe-ward from the same, till ye come right ouer against the Prime. **1752** *Ibid.*, *Table to find Easter-Day*, To find the Golden Number, or Prime, add one to the Year of our Lord, and then divide by 19; the remainder, if any, is the Golden Number.

¶**b.** Confusedly explained as the lunar cycle of 19 years. *Obs.*

1574 BOURNE *Regiment for Sea* ii. (1577) 10 The Prime or Golden Number, is the tyme of 19 yeares, in the which tyme the Moone maketh all her chaunges or coniunctions with the Sunne. **1594** J. DAVIS *Seaman's Secr.* (1607) 6 The Prime is the space of 19 yeres, in which time the Moone performeth al the varieties of her motion with the Sunne. **1669** STURMY *Mariner's Mag.* I. ii. 9.

†**c.** *transf.* in reference to a cycle of weather. *Obs. rare.*

1625 BACON *Ess.*, *Vicissitude of Things* (Arb.) 571 They say, it is obserued, in the Low Countries..that Euery Fiue and Thirtie years, The same Kinde and Sute of Years and Weathers, comes about agaïne: As Great Frosts, Great Wet, Great Droughts, Warme Winters, Summers with little Heat, and the like: And they call it the Prime.

†**5.** The beginning or first appearance of the new moon. *Obs.*

1387 TREVISA *Higden* (Rolls) III. 133 Þe ȝere of þe mone is from prime in a monþe of þe ȝere to þe firste prime in þe same monþe anoþer ȝere. *Ibid.* 135 [see 4]. *c* **1450** *St. Cuthbert* (Surtees) 6569 Þat day was of þe mone pryme. **1562** LEIGH *Armorie* 102 Yᵉ moone in her prime, which is yᵉ thyrd day after the coniunction, or, as we commonly cal it, the newe moone. **1587** MASCALL *Govt. Cattle, Oxen* (1627) 49 Take no calfe that is calued within the prime, which is counted the fiue dayes after the change. **1607** TOPSELL *Four-f. Beasts* (1658) 162 When the Moon is changed untill her prime and appearance, these beasts..take boughs,..and then look upon the Moon. **1635** QUARLES *Embl.* III. i. (1718) 129 Falls have their risings, wainings have their primes. **1704** J. HARRIS *Lex. Techn.* I, *Prime of the Moon*, signifies the New Moon, at her first Appearing, or about Three Days after the Change, at which time she is said to be primed.

6. *fig.* The beginning or first age of anything.

1430–40 LYDG. *Bochas* I. i. (MS. Bodl. 263) lf. 11/1 It was off chaunge to hem a newe pryme For to beholde a thing disnaturalle. *c* **1440** CAPGRAVE *St. Kath.* IV. 1698 The maister princypal..Of hir doctryne was ful Ioyeful and gladde; For god had poynted in hym a newe pryme. **1594** HOOKER *Eccl. Pol.* II. iv. §6 Let them cast backe their eies.. and marke what was done in the prime of the World. **1631** CHAPMAN *Cæsar & Pompey* IV. Plays 1873 III. 176 Betwixt the ends of those things and their primes. **1657** THORNLEY tr. *Longus' Daphnis & Chloe* 124 The Daffodil, the Primrose, with the other primes and dawnings of the Spring. **1865** MOZLEY *Mirac.* viii. 303 *note*, In the first conversion of the Franks, or in the prime of that church.

b. The beginning or first age of the world.

1616 J. TAYLOR (Water P.) *Seiges Jerus.* i, Who in the Prime, when all things first began, Made all for Man, and for him-selfe made Man. **1814** WORDSW. *Wh. Doe* VII. 360 Thou, thou art not a Child of Time, But Daughter of the Eternal Prime. **1850** TENNYSON *In Mem.* lvi, Dragons of the prime, That tare each other in their slime.

7. The first season of the year (when this began at the vernal equinox); spring. (So OF. *prime*.)

1541 *St. Papers Hen. VIII*, VIII. 641 This prime the French King entendith to work great maisteries against th' Empereur in sundry places. **1591** SYLVESTER *Du Bartas* I. v. 615 A thousand Winters, and a thousand Primes. *c* **1600** SHAKS. *Sonn.* xcvii, The teeming Autumne big with ritch increase, Bearing the wanton burthen of the prime. **1725** POPE *Odyss.* IV. 770 The fields are florid with unfading prime. **1885** BURTON *Arab. Nts.* (1887) III. 82 Winter had gone..and Prime had come to it with his roses and orange blossoms.

8. The 'springtime' of human life; the time of early manhood or womanhood, from about 21 to 28 years of age. (Sometimes distinguished from sense 9 as the ***prime of youth***.) Now *rare*.

1592 KYD *Sp. Trag.* I. i. 8 My discent..inferiour far To gratious fortunes of my tender youth: For there in prime and pride of all my yeeres..In secret I possest a worthy dame. **1594** SHAKS. *Rich. III*, I. ii. 248 And will she yet abase her eyes on me, That cropt the Golden prime of this sweet Prince? **1603** KNOLLES *Hist. Turks* (1638) 158 But when he was out of his childhood, and grown to be a lusty youth,.. and in the prime of his youth. **1632** LITHGOW *Trav.* III. 106 Whereof in the prime of my adolescency..I had the full proofe. **1645** MILTON *Sonn.* ix, Lady that in the prime of earliest youth, Wisely hath shun'd the broad way and the green. **1712** STEELE *Spect.* No. 282 ¶3 They had by this time passed their Prime, and got on the wrong side of Thirty. **1726** SWIFT *Gulliver* I. ii, He was then past his prime, being twenty-eight years and three quarters old. **1770** *Junius Lett.* xxxvi. (1820) 171 The vices operate like age..and in the prime of youth leave the character broken and exhausted. **1838** PRESCOTT *Ferd. & Is.* (1846) III. xvi. 160 She followed to the grave..her only son, the heir and hope of the Monarchy, just entering on his prime. **1877** BLACK *Green Past.* xxii, There was he, in the prime of youthful manhood.

III. That which is first in quality or character.

9. Of human life: The period or state of greatest perfection or vigour, before strength begins to decay. (Sometimes distinguished from sense 8 as ***prime of age***, or ***of middle age***.)

1615 CROOKE *Body of Man* 385 In yonger men it is faster, in the prime of our age more rare and hollow. **1697** COLLIER *Ess. Mor. Subj.* II. (1703) 180 When he is past his prime, his vigour is perpetually wearing off. *c* **1718** PRIOR *Ladle* 80 The honest farmer and his wife, To years declin'd from prime of life. **1728** YOUNG *Love Fame* v. 498 Nought treads so silent as the foot of time; Hence we mistake our autumn for our prime. **1802** WORDSW. *Sailor's Mother*, A Woman on the road I met, Not old, though something past her prime. **1838** LYTTON *Calderon* i, The king was yet in the prime of middle age. **1863** GEO. ELIOT *Romola* xxxix, He was still in the prime of life, not more than four-and-forty. **1875** JOWETT *Plato* (ed. 2) III. 342 Those years are the prime of physical as well as of intellectual vigour. **1887** JESSOPP *Arcady* ii. 30 When a man has arrived at the prime of life..he is apt to become sensitive on the subject of his age.

b. Of things, material or immaterial: The best or most flourishing stage or state; the state of full perfection.

prime of grease: cf. *pride of grease*, PRIDE *sb.*[1] 9, quot. 1688.

c **1536** in Furniv. *Ballads fr. MSS.* (1872) I. 410 Plesantly I am plyghte in the prime of my fortune! *c* **1590** GREENE *Fr. Bacon* vi. 34 As Greece affoorded in her chiefest prime. **1601** R. JOHNSON *Kingd. & Commw.* (1603) 105 They are onely for the owners pastime in the prime of sommer. **1621** T. WILLIAMSON tr. *Goulart's Wise Vieillard* 11 It may be said, that the world was then in his prime and best dayes. **1664** EVELYN *Kal. Hort.* (1729) 202 *April*... Flowers in Prime or yet lasting, Anemonies,..Cyclamen, Bell-flower, Dens Caninus. **1688** R. HOLME *Armoury* II. 188/1 Prime of his Grease [is] a term used to a Boar when he is full Fat. **1794** BLAKE *Songs Exper., Little Girl Lost* iii, Where the summer's prime Never fades away. **1800** MAR. EDGEWORTH *Will* i. (1832) 91 The second week in November is the time when the rabbits are usually killed, as the skins are then in full prime. **1823** P. NICHOLSON *Pract. Build.* 259 Those trees which have been cut before they had reached their prime. **1830** TENNYSON *Recoll. Arab. Nts.* ii, A goodly time, For it was in the golden prime Of good Haroun Alraschid. **1849** RUSKIN *Sev. Lamps* vi. §16. 178 A building cannot be considered as in its prime until four or five centuries have passed over it.

10. The choicest, principal, or chief member or members of a company or number of persons or things. (The later examples may be absolute uses of PRIME *a.*)

1579 TWYNE *Phisicke agst. Fort.* II. iv. 166 The father of Phisitions, and the primes of Keruers and painters, namely, Hippocrates, and Phidias and Apelles. **1599** B. R. in Wordsw. *Eccl. Biog.* (1818) II. 57 The red rose..of all hearbes and flowers the prime and soveraigne. **1608** MIDDLETON *Mad World my Masters* I. i. 96 A fellow whose only glory is to be prime of the company. **1671** MILTON *P.R.* I. 413 Among the Prime in Splendour. **1725** POPE *Odyss.* IV. 432 Prime of the flock, and choicest of the stall. **1804** WORDSW. *Afflict. Margaret* iii, He was among the prime in worth. **1844** KEBLE *Lyra Innoc.* (1873) 19 Hard it is, 'mid gifts so sweet Choosing out the prime.

b. The best, choicest, most attractive or desirable part of anything.

1635 R. BOLTON *Comf. Affl. Consc.* (ed. 2) 343 He now gives up the flower and prime of all his abilities to the highest Majesty. **1782** MISS BURNEY *Cecilia* VI. i, [He] always chused to have the prime of everything. **1873** E. SMITH *Foods* 63 The 'prime' of three shoulders and other joints.

IV. 11. *attrib.* and *Comb.*: †**prime day**: see quots.; **prime-song** *Hist.* [repr. OE. *primsang*], the office or service of prime (= sense 1).

1574 W. BOURNE *Regiment for Sea* iii. (1577) 12 b, The Sea men do imagin a *prime day, which is the halfe quarter of the Moone. **1594** BLUNDEVIL *Exerc.* VII. l. (1636) 739 When the Moone is three daies and 18 houres, which is the halfe quarter of the Moone, the Sea-men doe call that time the Prime day, because the Moone is then 4 points to the Eastward of the Sunne. *c* **961** ÆTHELWOLD *Rule St. Benet* xvi. (Schröer) 40 Ðæt seofonfealde ȝetæl..dæȝredsang, *primsang, undernsang, middæȝsang [etc.]. **1844** LINGARD *Anglo-Sax. Ch.* (1858) I. vii. 272. **1853** ROCK *Ch. of Fathers* III. II. 126 At the end of prime-song, all the clergy went in procession from the choir to the chapter-house.

prime (praɪm), *sb.*[2] [Absolute use of PRIME *a.*, or of its Lat., Fr., or other equivalent. (Senses 10 and 11 may be different words.)]

I. 1. a. *Arith.* A prime number: see PRIME *a.* 7.

1594 BLUNDEVIL *Exerc.* I. vii. (1636) 25 But such [numbers] as cannot bee divided but that there will remaine some odde unite, those are called Primes. **1709–29** V. MANDEY *Syst. Math., Arith.* 22 Numbers are Primes between them-selves, all which Unity only measures, as 5, 7, 9: also 3, 11, 13. **1806** HUTTON *Course Math.* I. 54 If a number cannot be divided by some quantity less than the square root of the same, that number is a prime, or cannot be divided by any number whatever. **1875** TODHUNTER *Algebra* (ed. 7) lii. §705 Thus *p'* is divisible by *p*, and is therefore not a prime.

b. *Linguistics.* A simple, indivisible linguistic unit.

1959 F. W. HOUSEHOLDER in *Word* XV. 231 (*title*) On linguistic primes. **1961** —— in Saporta & Bastian *Psycholinguistics* 19/1 We must recognize at least two kinds of linguistic units: (1) *ultimate units*, or *primes*, out of which other more complex units may be constructed. **1963** J. LYONS *Structural Semantics* ii. 11 The lexeme is a formal unit of grammatical analysis, established distributionally. It may or may not be a 'prime',..though it frequently is for Greek. **1964** E. BACH *Introd. Transformational Gram.* v. 58 Each *level* of a linguistic theory comprises..a set of *primes* (i.e., atoms or indivisible elements). **1965** N. CHOMSKY *Aspects of Theory of Syntax* 222 Each level *L* is a system based on a set of primes (minimal elements—i.e. an alphabet). **1975** —— *Logical Struct. Linguistic Theory* iii. 105 If *a* and *b* are (not necessarily distinct) primes of L, we can form a⌢b and b⌢a as new elements of L.

2. a. A subdivision of any standard measure or dimension, which is itself subdivided in the same ratio into seconds, and so on; e.g. $\frac{1}{60}$ of a degree, a minute ($\frac{1}{60}$ of which is in its turn a *second*); the twelfth part of a foot, an inch; or, with some, $\frac{1}{12}$ of an inch; in Scottish Troy weight for gold and silver, $\frac{1}{24}$ of a grain, itself consisting of 24 seconds, etc. [So obs. F. *prime*.]

Primes, seconds, etc., were formerly used instead of decimals.

1604 in Moryson *Itinerary* I. (1617) 282 (Table of Scottish Weights of Coins) [1 denier] 24 Graines; [1 grain] 24 Primes; [1 prime] 24 Seconds [etc.]. *Ibid.*, xx. s. [sterling] = 06 pennyweights, 10 graines, 16 mites, 18 droits, 10 periots, English Weight; 07 deniers, 21 graines, 07 primes, 01 seconds, 09 thirds, 19 fourths, Scottish Weight. **1641** in R. W. Cochran-Patrick *Rec. Coinage Scotl.* (1876) I. Introd. 32 The pund Troy English consisting of 12 oz..is equall to 12 oz 5 drs 9 gr 18 pr Scots or 169,002 primes Scots. **1695** W. LOWNDES *Amendm. Silv. Coin* 66 And one other Piece which may be called the Prime, which shall be equal to..a present standard peny. **1703** T. N. *City & C. Purchaser* 123 Inches by Inches, produce Primes, or (12th) Parts (of an Inch); Inches by (12th) Parts, produce Seconds, or 12th Parts of the 12th Part of an Inch. **1727–41** CHAMBERS *Cycl.* s.v. *Degree*, Thus, a Degree, as being the integer or unite, is denoted by °, a first minute or prime by ′, a second by 2 or ″, a third by 3 or ‴, etc. Accordingly 3 Degrees, 25 minutes, 16 thirds, are written 3°. 25′. 0″. 16‴. **18..** B. GREENLEAF (Webster 1890), 12 seconds (″) make 1 inch or prime. 12 inches or primes (′) make one foot.

b. In decimal fractions: see quots. Now *Obs.* or *rare*.

1608 R. NORTON tr. *Stevin's Disme* C ij, Each tenth part of the vnity of the Comencement, wee call the Prime, whose signe is thus (1)..3(1) 7(2) 5(3) 9(4) [= 0·3759], that is to say 3 Primes, 7 Seconds, 5 Thirds, 9 Fourths..of valeu. **1610** W. FOLKINGHAM *Art of Survey* II. iv. 52 Deuide each foote of the Rule..into decimals or Tenths, and each Tenth or Prime of the Rule into Seconds. **1695** E. HATTON *Merch. Mag.* 83 That place in a Decimal Fraction next the prick is called Primes, being so many Tenth parts. **1806** HUTTON *Course Math.* I. 66 The 1st place of decimals, counted from the left-hand towards the right, is called the place of primes, or 10ths; the 2d is the place of seconds, or 100ths.

c. *Surveying.* A linear measure of $\frac{1}{10}$ or ·1 of a pole or perch.

1658 PHILLIPS, *Prime*, is in Surveying, an exact part containing 19 inches and four fift parts of an inch.

d. *Printing.* The symbol ′ or ′, written above and to the right of a letter or figure, to denote primes, or merely to distinguish it from another not so marked. [So F. *prime* in Algebra.]

1875 KNIGHT *Dict. Mech., Prime*, (*Printing*) a mark over a reference letter (*a′*, *b″*, etc.) to distinguish it from letters (*a*, *b*, etc.) not so marked. [Usually read '*a* dash', etc.] **1917** D. W. PAYNE *Founder's Man.* p. xi, The prime mark ′ above a number means minutes or linear feet. **1964** *Amer. Jrnl. Physics* XXXII. 264/2 The prime (′) here indicates ordinary differentiation of a function of a single variable. **1973** A. H. SOMMERSTEIN *Sound Pattern Anc. Greek* iii. 91 A Roman numeral followed by a prime indicates that the convention in question is intended to *replace* the Chomsky-Halle convention of the same number. **1976** *Physics Bull.* May 191/2 We would like to draw the attention of readers to the equation $(B_0)_i = B_0 - D'M$ (our prime) appearing in the last column.

3. *Chem.* A single atom as a unit in combination; a combining equivalent.

1839 URE *Dict. Arts* 627 The nitre contains five primes of oxygen, of which three, combining with the three of charcoal, will furnish three of carbonic oxide gas, while the remaining two will convert the one prime of sulphur into sulphurous acid gas. The single prime of nitrogen is, therefore, in this view, disengaged alone.

4. *Music.* **a.** Short for *prime tone* (PRIME *a.* 10): The fundamental note or generator, as distinguished from the harmonics or partial tones. **b.** The 'interval' of a unison; ***superfluous prime***, a chromatic semitone. **c.** 'The lowest note of any two notes forming an interval' (Stainer & Barrett).

1788 CAVALLO in *Phil. Trans.* LXXVIII. 239 If a string stretched between two fixed points..be struck, it will produce a sound called the prime, first or key-note. **1866** ENGEL *Nat. Mus.* ii. 25 It must..be remembered that a semitone is called small when it consists of a superfluous prime, as C—C♯, A♭—A♮; and that it is called large when it consists of a minor second, as C—D♭, F♯—G. **1881** BROADHOUSE *Mus. Acoustics* 135 The fundamental or prime partial tone, or simply the *prime*. **1884** SIR G. A. MACFARREN in *Encycl. Brit.* XVII. 93/2 Thus, E over C, the fourth and fifth harmonic, produce C, the prime or generator, at the interval of two octaves under the lower of those two notes.

5. *Fencing.* †**a.** The lower half of a sword. *Obs.*

1688 R. HOLME *Armoury* III. xix. (Roxb.) 159/2 The sword is diuided into two parts, namely into the Prime and the Secunde. The Prime is measured from the hilt to the Midle of the Rapier. **1692** SIR W. HOPE *Fencing-Master* (ed. 2) 3 The Strong, Fort, or Prime of the Blade is from the Shell to the middle of the Blade.

b. (Also *preem.*) A position in fencing: the first of the eight parries or guards in sword-play, used to protect the head; also, a thrust in such a position. [F. *prime.*]

1710 PALMER *Proverbs* 203 Which they wou'd find of more satisfaction and use in the conduct of life, than tierce and cart, prime and second, dancing and dress. **1730** *Gentl. Tutor for Small Sword* 8 Some teach upon a Preem with the Edge upwards. *Ibid.* 13 The Third [Parry] is, turning your Hand in Preem, You may parry and thrust him at the same time. **1889** *Badminton Libr., Fencing* ii. 44 *Prime*, the hand in pronation opposite the left shoulder; the arm bent, the elbow lowered somewhat, the point low and a little outside the lower line.

6. Colloq. abbrev. of PRIME MINISTER (sense 3). Cf. PRIME *sb.*[1] 10.

1916 A. HUXLEY *Let.* May (1969) 99 The Prime received suddenly one morning a letter..'Dear Mr. A[squith]'. **1924** GALSWORTHY *White Monkey* I. ii. 14 Didn't he think that the cubic called 'Still Life'—of the Government, too frightfully funny—especially the 'old bean' representing the Prime?

7. *Cycling.* An especially difficult stage in a long-distance cycle race.

1959 *Observer* 31 May 32/4 Weatherlaw was the first 'prime'—a specially marked stretch of hilly road which gives the first three men to the summit a bonus of money and time. **1961** *Times* 7 June 5/6 Pewter tankards being offered as prizes at the town primes along the route. **1975** *Oxf. Compan. Sports & Games* 235/1 On mountainous stretches certain summits are designated as *primes*.

8. Short for *prime rate.*

1973 *Business Week* 10 Feb. 19 The all-out struggle over the prime. **1977** *Offshore Engineer* July 19/3 Citibank's current prime is 6¾%. **1978** *Daily Tel.* 25 Nov. 19/2 At 11·5 p.c., the prime now stands at its highest level since October 1974.

II. Related to PRIMA VISTA, PRIMERO.

†**9.** *Cards.* A hand in primero consisting of a card from each of the four suits. Also, an old game of cards, by some identified with primero. *Obs.*

1598 FLORIO, *Prima*,..also a game at cardes called Prime, Primero, or Primauista. **1599** MINSHEU *Span. Dial.* 26 *M.* I was a small prime. *L.* I am flush... *O.* I made fiue and fiftie, with which I win his prime [*mato su primera*]. **1606** *Choice, Chance*, etc. (1881) 45 He that wil not pluck a card, is not worthy of a prime, but..he that can be flush, may better carrie the rest. *a* **1612** HARINGTON *Epigr.* II. xcix. *Marcus at Primero*, For either Faustus prime is with three knaves, Or Marcus never can encounter right. **1616** B. JONSON *Epigr.* cxii. 22 There's no vexation, that can make thee prime. **1798** *Sporting Mag.* XII. 142 The prime is four cards of different suits. **1816** SINGER *Hist. Cards* 245 He who holds the prime (primero), that is, a sequence of the best cards, and a good trump, is sure to be successful over his adversary, and hence the game has its denomination. *Ibid.* 246 The varieties which daily occur at Primero, as the greater and lesser flush, the great and little Prime.

III. Of uncertain origin and position.

10. *Basket-making.* A kind of stout conical bodkin.

1894 *Parker's Gloss. Her.* 46 The four implements, viz. prime, iron, cutting-knife, and out-sticker, used in basket-making are represented on the insignia of the Basket-makers' Company.

11. The footstep of a deer; cf. PRICK *sb.* 1 c.

1847–78 in HALLIWELL.

prime, *sb.*[3] [f. PRIME *v.*[1]]

†**1.** The priming of a gun. In quot. 1655, perhaps the pan for the priming. *Obs.*

1655 MRQ. WORCESTER *Cent. Inv.* §44 A perfect Pistol.. with Prime, Powder and Fire-lock. **1706** PHILLIPS, *Prime of a Gun*, the Powder that is put in the Pan, or Touch-hole. **1738** WESLEY *Wks.* (1830) I. 164 He went and got fresh prime, beat the flint with his key and..shot himself through the head. **1769** FALCONER *Dict. Marine* (1789), The.. priming-iron..serves to clear the inside of the touch hole, and render it fit to receive the prime. **1823** W. FAUX *Mem. Days in Amer.* 48 The colonel..then attempted to shoot himself, but had no prime.

attrib. **1753** CHAMBERS *Cycl. Supp.* s.v. *Priming*, That so they may put in the prime-powder, or touch-powder, to fire off the piece.

†**2.** A first coat of paint; priming. *Obs.*

1658 W. SANDERSON *Graphice* 58 Lay your ground or Prime therein of Flesh-Colour. **1669** STURMY *Mariner's Mag.* VII. xxxiv. 49 The Prime is made thus. **1735** *Dict. Polygraph.* s.v. *Face*, You ought to cover rather too much than too little of your ground with this prime.

prime (praɪm), *a.* (*adv.*) [= F. *prime* adj. (now only in certain phrases), ad. L. *prīm-us* first.]

A. *adj.* **1.** First in order of time or occurrence; early, young, youthful; primitive, primary.

1399 LANGL. *Rich. Redeles* III. 34 And myȝte nat passe þe poynte of her prime age. *c* **1450** *Mirour Saluacioun* 4587 In the houre of pryme dayes thyne hoege luf shewed thow me. *c* **1489** CAXTON *Sonnes of Aymon* viii. 191 Yonge men of pryme berde. **1553** BRENDE *Q. Curtius* R vj, He was in the prime floure of his youth. **1587** GOLDING *De Mornay* xxvi. (1617) 441 It befell in the prime time of the world. **1639** LAUD *Wks.* (1849) II. 93 If the speech be of the prime Christian Church. **1707** MORTIMER *Husb.* (1721) I. 273 If the prime Swarm be broken, the second will both cast and swarm the sooner. **1850** S. DOBELL *Roman* vii, The men of whom I speak Lived by the prime tradition.

2. Of persons: First in rank, dignity, influence, authority, or importance; highest in degree; principal, chief, foremost.

1610 SHAKS. *Temp.* I. ii. 72 Prospero, the prime Duke, being so reputed In dignity. **1613** —— *Hen. VIII*, III. ii. 162 Haue I not made you The prime man of the State? **1630** *R. Johnson's Kingd. & Commw.* 206 These are chosen..out of the Nobilitie and primest Magistrates, both of the Provinces and Citizens. **1691** WOOD *Ath. Oxon.* I. 301 Rich. Smith.. had been prime Mourner at his Brother's Funeral. **1707** E. CHAMBERLAYNE *Pres. St. Eng.* III. xi. (ed. 22) 357 [The Lord Mayor] upon the Death of the King, is said to be prime Person of England. **1761** HUME *Hist. Eng.* III. liii. 155 The nobility and prime gentry of the nation. **1862** GOULBURN *Pers. Relig.* III. ix. (1873) 232 He was God's prime agent in the spread of the Gospel.

3. a. First in importance, excellence, or value; principal, chief, main; of primary importance.

1610 SHAKS. *Temp.* I. ii. 425 My prime request (Which I do last pronounce) is..If you be Mayd, or no? **1613** —— *Hen. VIII*, II. iv. 229 To come, with her, (Katherine our Queene) before the primest Creature That's Parragon'd o' th' World. **1620** VENNER *Via Recta* iv. 80 It might..be numbred among the fishes of primest note. **1717** PRIOR *Alma* II. 364 That prime ill, a talking wife. **1776** G. SEMPLE *Building in Water* 110 Waterford and Wexford..have constantly enjoyed a prime Place in my Mind. **1814** WORDSW. *Sonn.*, '*From the dark chambers of dejection freed*', A soaring spirit is their prime delight. **1874** H. R. REYNOLDS *John Bapt.* VI. i. 359 The prime intention of each Evangelist is to establish the same sublime position.

b. *Broadcasting.* Pertaining to or associated with the largest audience of the day. See also PRIME-TIME 3.

1959 *Times Lit. Suppl.* 6 Nov. p. xxxi/5 John Fischer, the editor of *Harpers*,..asks for an autonomous authority empowered to produce programmes of exceptional merit, financed by a levy on the income of the broadcasters, who will also be under an obligation to transmit these programmes in the cherished prime-viewing hours. **1961** WEBSTER s.v., Prime television time. **1976** *Broadcast* Dec. 15/3 We have to go through the routine again slap in the middle of prime listening time on a Saturday morning. **1977** *Times* 7 Dec. 19/1 It is seldom that anyone gets handed such a quantity of prime television time to do what he likes with.

4. a. 'First-class', 'first-rate'; of the best quality; now used esp. of cattle and provisions.

prime fish, the more valuable kinds of fish caught for food: opposed to OFFAL sense 3, q.v. ***prime rib***, best rib of beef, i.e. one of the first two ribs in the forequarter; also *attrib.*

1628 DIGBY *Voy. Medit.* (Camden) 37 Shee was a shippe of a 100 tonnes, a prime sayler. **1663** COWLEY *Disc. Govt. Cromwell* Verses & Ess. (1669) 75 This Son of fortune, Cromwell (who was himself one of the primest of her Jests). **1743** BULKELEY & CUMMINS *Voy. S. Seas* 1 The Ships were all in prime Order, all lately rebuilt. **1805** R. W. DICKSON *Pract. Agric.* II. 1032 Removing the lambs from the ewes.. in order to complete them on young clover or other sorts of 'prime keep'. **1833** HT. MARTINEAU *T. Tyne* ii. 28 Coal enough—and no little of a prime quality,—was destroyed at the pit-mouth. **1884** *Brit. Alm. & Comp.* 29 Soles, turbots, and brills, which are technically termed 'prime' fish. **1892** E. REEVES *Homeward Bound* 285 The butcher won't cut prime joints off a bullock. **1960** E. DAVID *French Provincial Cooking* 335 To satisfy customers, butchers bone, trim and tie up secondary cuts of meat..and sell them at a small amount less than, say, sirloin or prime ribs. **1973** D. BARNES *See the Woman* (1974) II. 195 I'll buy us a prime-rib dinner. **1973** *Listener* 19 Apr. 501/1 A landscape of luscious rib roasts, lamb chops, shell steaks, T-bone steaks, sirloin steaks, fillet mignon, prime ribs, veal piccata and so on. **1978** *Chicago Tribune Mag.* 2 Oct. 8/2 The 25-cent hot beef special is now a $2.75 prime rib sandwich, served with salad and potato.

b. *spec.* used of land, the position of real estate, etc.

1634 *Relat. Ld. Baltimore's Plantation* (1865) 12 As good, (if not much better) than the primest parcell of English ground. **1850** *Househ. Words* 3 Aug. 433/1 Sir Roger Rockville..was the last of a very long line... His first known ancestor came over with William, and must have been a man of some mark,..for he obtained what the Americans would call a prime location. **1961** J. D. ADAMS in *Webster* s.v., Prime farming land. **1976** *Western Mail* (Cardiff) 27 Nov. 17/2 (Advt.), A charming detached Freehold four-bedroom residence built in 1935,..in a prime residential area. **1977** *Grimsby Even. Tel.* 24 May 4/9 (Advt.), A thriving newsagents, tobacconist, sweets and general business situated in a prime position in a growing village close to Grimsby. **1978** *Church Times* 1 Sept. 4/1 It may still occupy a prime site on a busy thoroughfare.

5. Sexually excited, ruttish.

1604 SHAKS. *Oth.* III. iii. 403 Were they as prime as Goates, as hot as Monkeyes, As salt as Wolues in pride.

6. First in order of existence or development; primary, original, fundamental; from which others are derived, or on which they depend.

prime feathers, primary feathers: see PRIMARY *a.* 5.

1639 LAUD *Wks.* (1849) II. 152 Excommunication on their part was not the prime cause of this division. **1657** W. COLES *Adam in Eden* lix, The prime root shooteth down-wards like a Cinquefoile. **1742** *Lond. & Country Brew.* I. (ed. 4) 17 The prime Cause of our British Malady the Scurvy. **1769** E. BANCROFT *Guiana* 156 The prime middle feathers on the tail are red. **1871** BLACKIE *Four Phases* i. 51 According to the prime postulate not of the philosophy of Socrates only, but of Plato and Aristotle also. **1878** ABNEY *Photogr.* (1881) 8 What the prime form of these undulations may be we cannot tell.

7. *Arith.* **a.** Of a number: Having no integral factors except itself and unity. So ***prime divisor, factor, quotient***, etc. **b.** Of two or more numbers in relation to each other: Having no common measure except unity.

1570 BILLINGSLEY *Euclid* VII. def. xii. 186 A prime (or first) number is that, which onely vnitie doth measure. **1660** BARROW *Euclid* VII. xxiii. (1714) 156 Numbers prime the one to the other,..are the least of all numbers that have the same proportion with them. **1674** JEAKE *Arith.* (1696) 5 Six.. though it may be made by Addition of Five and One, yet shall it not be Prime. **1722** HORSLEY in *Phil. Trans.* LXII. 327 Two or more numbers, which have no common integral devisor, besides unity, are said to be Prime with respect to one another. **1795** HUTTON *Math. Dict.* II. 276 Prime Numbers are..otherwise called Simple, or Incomposite numbers. *Ibid.* 279 The whole number, whether it be Prime or composite. **1829** *Nat. Philos.* I. *Mechanics* II. vii. 30 (Usef. Knowl. Soc.) Making the number of teeth and the number of leaves prime to each other, that is, such that no integer divides both exactly. **1875** TODHUNTER *Algebra* (ed. 7) lii. §703 If *a* and *b* be each of them prime to *c*, then *ab* is prime to *c*. *Ibid.* §708 A number can be resolved into prime factors in only one way. *Ibid.* §713 If *n* be a prime number, and *N* prime to *n*, then $N^{n-1} - 1$ is a multiple of *n*. (Fermat's Theorem.) *Ibid.* §717 If *n* be a prime number, $1 + |n - 1$ is divisible by *n*. (Wilson's Theorem.)

8. First in numerical order, as in ***prime meridian***, the first meridian (of any system of reckoning).

1878 HUXLEY *Physiogr.* xix. 330 The meridian from which the reckoning begins is called the prime meridian.

9. *Astronautics.* Originally designated to take part or be used in a space mission, esp. in ***prime crew***, the original person or persons selected to man a spacecraft.

1965 *Life* 3 Dec. 48 Pete Conrad, who spent a week in space, is the prime crew. **1970** N. ARMSTRONG et al. *First on Moon* iii. 63 At 4:30 A.M. the transfer vans arrived—one prime, one backup. **1970** R. TURNILL *Language of Space* 13 Every manned space flight, American or Russian, has a back-up crew, to replace the prime crew in the event of illness or death.

10. Special collocations and phrases: **a. prime cost**, the direct cost of something, not including discounts, expenses involved, etc.; **prime dun**, an artificial fly in angling: cf. DUN *sb.*[1] 3; **prime entry**, an entry of two thirds of a ship's cargo liable to duty, made before discharge (on which an estimate of the duty is paid): cf. POST ENTRY 2a (Bithell *Counting-ho. Dict.* 1882); **prime figure**: see quot.; **prime function** (*Eccl.*): see quot.; **prime (interest, lending) rate**, the lowest rate of interest offered on bank loans at a given time and place; †**prime number**, the Golden Number = PRIME *sb.*[1] 4; see also 7; **prime tint**: see quot.; **prime tone** (*Music*), the fundamental note of a compound tone. Also ***prime*** CONDUCTOR, COST, MOVER, SERJEANT, VIZIER, WARDEN: see the sbs.

1718 C. HITCHIN *Receivers & Thief-Takers* 11 For instance, suppose you steal Goods to the value of twenty Pounds *prime Cost. **1732** R. JOHNSON *Let.* 6 Oct. in *Cal. State Papers, Amer. & W. Indies* (1939) 231, I have examined what dutys are payd in this Province on English European ships or goods, and there is only 2½ *p.c.* our currency upon the prime cost of goods from Europe in general. **1775** in *15th Rep. R. Comm. Hist. Manuscripts* App. VI. 297 in *Parl. Papers 1897* (C. 8551) LI. 1 Vessels have come from Hispaniola, and sold gunpowder to the Provincials at prime cost. **1890** A. MARSHALL *Princ. Econ.* I. VI. vi. 519 This is the Prime cost which a manufacturer has commonly in view when, trade being slack, he is calculating the lowest price at which it would be worth his while to accept an order. **1925** S. E. THOMAS *Elem. Econ.* xiii. 168 The excess is 'dumped' on foreign markets at a price just sufficient to cover prime cost, or even below prime cost. **1938** BOWERS & ROWNTREE *Econ. for Engineers* (ed. 2) xiii. 258 Prime costs, according to accounting procedure, are direct labor and materials expenses alone... Many economists, however, define prime costs as all *avoidable* costs, so that a plant shutdown would eliminate all prime costs. **1944** A. CAIRNCROSS *Introd. Econ.* xvi. 199 Normally, some surplus over prime or variable costs will be earned. **1953** STONIER & HAGUE *Textbk. Econ. Theory* v. 110 'Variable', 'prime' and 'direct' costs represent all those costs which can be altered in the short run as output alters. **1962** S. STRAND *Marketing Dict.* 573 *Prime cost*, the cost of a product involving labor and all the parts that go into making it. **1978** J. KELLOCK *Elements of Accounting* x. 175 The value of rejected materials or by-products will be credited to the cost of raw materials purchased or deleted from the prime cost. **1799** G. SMITH *Laboratory* II. 309 *Prime-dun. Wings, of the feather got from the quill of a starling's wing. **1696** PHILLIPS (ed. 5), **Prime Figure.* **1704** J. HARRIS *Lex. Techn.* I, *Prime Figure*, is that which cannot be divided into any other Figures more simple than it self; as a Triangle in Planes, the Pyramid in Solids: For all Planes are made of the First, all Bodies or Solids compounded of the Second. **1866** *Direct. Angl.* (ed. 3) 258 **Prime Function.* From the Credo inclusive to the end of the Office. **1669** STURMY *Mariner's Mag.* I. ii. 9 In what year you would know what is the *Prime Number, add 1 to the date thereof, and then divide it by 19, and that which remaineth upon the Division..is the Number required. **1958** *Wall St. Jrnl.* 29 Dec. 8/3 The '*prime' rate was thus brought back to within a half percentage point of the 4½% rate which was in effect from August, 1957... The 'prime' rate is the interest banks charge their biggest borrowers with the best credit status. **1970** *Daily Tel.* 4 Mar. 19 Several reductions in 'prime lending rate' by small American banks, are not likely to lead to cuts by major American banks for at least a fortnight. **1972** *Bankers Mag.* (Boston, Mass.) Winter 45/1 Many bankers have turned critical on the concept of a prime rate. **1973** *N.Y. Law Jrnl.* 26 July 3/3 Better-quality construction loans with a takeout were being made at the beginning of the year at a spread of about three points over the prime rate. **1978** S. BRILL *Teamsters* vi. 252 Glick's Las Vegas loans were given at a time when he was far from being a candidate for a prime rate. **1753** HOGARTH *Anal. Beauty* xii. 96 The first we shall call *prime tints, by which is meant any colour or colours on the surfaces of objects. **1881** BROADHOUSE *Mus. Acoustics* vii. 130 The *prime tone is always the sound which is called by the name which the note bears, as C, B, A, or any other note. This tone is called the prime tone because ..it is always much louder than any of the constituent parts of the sound.

b. prime vertical: (*a*) in full ***prime vertical circle***, a great circle of the heavens passing through the east and west points of the horizon, and through the zenith, where it cuts the meridian at right angles; (*b*) short for ***prime vertical dial***, a dial the plane of which lies in that of the prime vertical circle, a north and south dial. ***prime vertical transit instrument***, a transit instrument the telescope of which revolves in the plane of the prime vertical, for observing the transit of stars over this circle.

1669 STURMY *Mariner's Mag.* VII. xiv. 21 If a Plane shall decline from the Prime Vertical, and incline to the Horizon. **1704** J. HARRIS *Lex. Techn.* I, *Prime Verticals*, or *Direct Erect North or South Dyals*, are those whose Planes lie parallel to the Prime Vertical Circle. **1761** DUNN in *Phil. Trans.* LII. 185 In taking altitudes, I always observe, when the sun, or other celestial body, is as near the prime vertical, or east and west azimuth, as possible. **1868** LOCKYER *Elem. Astron.* IV. xxvi. (1879) 147.

†**c.** ***at, of prime face*** [F. *de prime face*], at first sight, PRIMA FACIE. *Obs.*

c **1374** CHAUCER *Troylus* III. 870 (919) This accident so petous was to here And ek so lyk a soth at pryme face. **1387–8** T. USK *Test. Love* I. vi. (Skeat) l. 57 At the prime face, me semed them noble and glorious to all the people. **1426** LYDG. *De Guil. Pilgr.* 10173 But thow make resistence Be tymes & at prime face. **1490** CAXTON *Eneydos* xv. 56 It appiered of prymeface, that the heuens were broken and parted a sondre.

d. ***prime ratio***: the initial limiting ratio between two variable quantities which simultaneously recede from definite fixed values or limits. (Correl. to ***ultimate ratio***.)

The ***method of prime and ultimate ratios*** is essentially the same as the ***method of limits*** in the differential and integral calculus (see LIMIT *sb.* 2b).

B. as *adv.* In prime order, excellently. *colloq.*

1648 GAGE *West Ind.* 148 If the Indians bring that which is not prime good, they shall surely be lashed. **1785** BURNS *To James Smith* iv, My barmie noddle's working prime. **1886** C. SCOTT *Sheep-farming* 96 The hoggets will be prime fat by Christmas.

prime (praɪm), *v.*[1] [Origin uncertain.

If sense 1 was the source of PRIMAGE, PRIMEGILT, it must be older than the quotations show. The fact that, in most of the senses, 'priming' is a *first* operation preliminary to something else, suggests connexion with L. *primus*.]

1. *trans.* To fill, charge, load. Now chiefly *dial.*

1513 DOUGLAS *Æneis* III. vi. 213 Our kervalis howis ladis and prymys he With huge charge of siluir in quantite. **1606** G. W[ODCOCKE] *Hist. Ivstine* Pref., To read as birds skip from bow to bough, more to prime their bils, then benefit their bodies. **1791** LEARMONT *Poems* 199 Her bottle prim'd came last night frae the town. **1805** MᶜINDOE *Poems* 149 John calmly prim'd his nose. **1883** G. MᶜMICHAEL *Way thr. Ayrshire* 126 The injector for priming the steam boiler.

2. a. To supply (a fire-arm of old-fashioned type, or more strictly its pan) with gunpowder for communicating fire to a charge; also, to lay a train of powder to (any charge, a mine, etc.); cf. PRIMING *vbl. sb.*[1] 1, 2. Also *intr.* or *absol.*

1598 BARRET *Theor. Warres* II. i. 17 He ought to haue his peece readie charged and primed. *Ibid.* III. i. 35 Then to prime his pan with touch powder. **1660** BOYLE *New Exp. Phys. Mech.* xiv. 88 We took a Pistol.., and..prim'd it with well dry'd Gun-powder. **1748** SMOLLETT *Rod. Rand.* ix, Before he had time to prime again. **1796** *Instr. & Reg. Cavalry* (1813) 251 The commanding officer orders the battalion to prime and load. **1873** E. SPON *Workshop Receipts* Ser. I. 127/2 Rockets are primed with mealed powder and spirits of wine. **1895** G. MEREDITH *Amazing Marriage* I. viii, Midway on the lake he perceived his boatman about to prime a pistol.

†**b.** To put (powder) in the touch-pan. *Obs.*

1610 B. JONSON *Alch.* V. v, An old Hargubuzier..Could prime his poulder, and giue fire, and hit, All in a twinckling.

3. *fig.* and *transf.* **a.** To charge, fill, or fully furnish (a person) beforehand *with* information which he may subsequently give forth or otherwise use.

1791 CUMBERLAND *Observer* No. 130. V. 44, I primed my lips with such a ready charge of flattery, that [etc.]. **1800** WELLINGTON in Gurw. *Desp.* (1837) I. 254 All that I can say is that I am ready primed, and that if all matters suit, I shall go off with a dreadful explosion. **1876** T. HARDY *Ethelberta* (1890) 234 Primed with their morning's knowledge as they appeared to be. **1884** *Manch. Exam.* 20 Sept. 5/3 Every man present..is primed with a speech which he is not satisfied till he has delivered.

b. To fill with liquor.

1823 *Hints for Oxford* 73 A determination when they sit down to table to have a row as soon as they are primed, and often before they rise they commence the work of destruction on glasses and plates and decanters. **1854** WHYTE MELVILLE *Gen. Bounce* viii, A fat little man, primed with port.

4. a. ***to prime a pump***: see quots., and cf. FANG *v.*[2] 2, FETCH *v.* 2c. (= F. *charger la pompe*.) Also *fig.*

a **1840–** [In common use in south of Scotland]. **1882** OGILVIE (Annandale), *To prime a pump*, to pour water down the tube with the view of saturating the sucker, so causing it to swell, and act effectually in bringing up water. **1894** *Northumbld. Gloss.*, *Prime*, to pour water into a pump bucket to make it lift. When a pump bucket becomes dry and leaky and fails to induce suction, it is said to have lost its *primin.* [Known in South Yorksh.] **1930** *Engineering* 11 Apr. 473/1 Special arrangements for priming the pumps are not required, as the latter themselves exhaust all the air automatically during the first few revolutions, when the engine is being started on compressed air. **1973** L. RUSSELL *Everyday Life Colonial Canada* v. 64 The..shaft had a piston with a leather diaphragm, which had to be wetted ('primed') by pouring a little water into the pump. **1977** T. SHARPE *Gt. Pursuit* xiii. 124 Significance is all... Prime the pump with meaningful hogwash.

b. *Aeronaut.* To inject fuel into (the cylinders of an aircraft engine) to facilitate starting. Also *intr.*, or with the engine as *obj.*

1915 G. A. BURLS *Aero Engines* i. 20 L is a cock, or tap, communicating with the 'combustion chamber'..and may be used to 'prime' the chamber with a few drops of petrol. **1927** V. W. PAGÉ *Mod. Aircraft* (1928) xiv. 571 Prime engine by injecting a small quantity..of gasoline through each priming cock. **1931** M. M. FARLEIGH *Princ. & Probl. Aircraft Engines* x. 166 The cylinders should then be primed with fresh gasoline in the case of extreme sub-zero climatic conditions. **1939** *Aero Engines* II. 256 Do not prime excesively,..one stroke of the priming pump usually being found sufficient for a hot engine. **1941** A. W. JUDGE *Aircraft Engines* II. xi. 395 If the engine had been properly primed with mixture it was possible to start it by means of the starter magneto alone. **1977** D. BEATY *Excellency* vi. 80 He primed the engines, pressed the starter button, heard the propeller creak round.

c. *fig.* Cf. PUMP-PRIMING *vbl. sb.*

1959 *Conferences & Exhibitions* Mar. 23/2 The aim is to introduce a trade to a fair in which it has not exhibited before by 'priming the pump'. **1963** *Times* 26 Jan. 12/1 He was understandably slow to prime the pump when a quick success in the Brussels negotiations might have given enough extra, uncontrollable impetus to start an inflation.

5. a. To cover (a surface of wood, canvas, etc.) with a ground or first colour or coat of paint, or with size, oil, etc. to prevent the paint from being absorbed: cf. PRIMING *vbl. sb.*[1] 3, 4.

1609 *MS. Acc. St. John's Hosp., Canterb.*, Rec. for primyng wood ijs. **1669** STURMY *Mariner's Mag.* VII. xxxiv. 49 To Paint them, you must first Prime them. **1762–71** H. WALPOLE *Vertue's Anecd. Paint.* (1786) II. 182 His..works are chiefly..on a fine linen cloth, smoothly primed with a proper tone to help the harmony of his shadows. **1801** FUSELI in *Lect. Paint.* i. (1848) 350 A plane or tablet primed with white. **1859** GULLICK & TIMBS *Paint.* 220 The intention of priming the ground with size or oil is to prevent the very rapid absorption of the colours.

†**b.** *transf.* To 'make up' (the face, etc.) with cosmetics. *Obs.*

1609 [see *priming colour*, PRIMING *vbl. sb.*[1] 10]. *a* **1683** OLDHAM *Sat. Poetry* Poet. Wks. (1686) 172 Commend her Beauty, and bely her Glass, By which she every morning primes her face. **1771** SMOLLETT *Humph. Cl.* II. 18 July Let. i, Her face was primed and patched from the chin up to the eyes. **1782** J. TRUMBULL *McFingal* 56 Your gay sparks.. With wampom'd blankets hid their laces, And like their sweethearts, primed their faces.

6. *intr. Engineering.* Of an engine boiler: To let water pass to the cylinder in the form of spray along with the steam.

1832 *Edin. Rev.* LVI. 139 The steam..is charged with water suspended in it in minute subdivision—an effect called by engineers *priming*. **1839** *Civil Eng. & Arch. Jrnl.* II. 456/2 The carrying over of water with the steam... There are moments when this effect is so violent, that it manifests itself externally in the form of an abundant fall of rain from the top of the funnel. The engine is then said to prime; and this takes place especially when the boiler is too full. **1849** *Proc. Inst. Civ. Eng.* VIII. 182 When a steam-vessel came from sea and entered the Thames, she began to prime at the moment of passing from salt to fresh water. **1881** THWAITE *Factories & Workshops*, etc. (1882) 138 If a boiler foams or primes, it is because it has insufficient steam room or because the feed water is dirty.

7. *trans. Biol.* and *Med.* To treat (an animal or tissue) so as to induce a desired susceptibility or proclivity.

1943 *Jrnl. Endocrinol.* III. 273 Excellent results were obtained with rabbits..primed by five daily injections of 2 mg. of AP61B or AP118B. *Ibid.*, Of eleven rabbits primed with five daily doses of 1 mg. only four accepted the buck. **1963** *Rec. Progress Hormone Res.* XIX. 674 In the latter effect, the body is in a true sense 'primed' for new biological activity. **1967** *Science* 17 Nov. 939/3 The 30 mice anesthetized with ether were exposed for 30 seconds to atmosphere containing 5 ml of ether per 1 liter of air; half of these were acoustically primed 10 seconds later. **1971** *Nature* 24 Dec. 456/1 In guinea-pigs primed with DNP-OA, injection of allogeneic lymphoid cells stimulates synthesis of antibodies to both hapten and carrier. **1975** *Jrnl. Compar. & Physiol. Psychol.* LXXXIX. 214/2 At 16 days postnatally, 18..mice were acoustically primed by a 30-sec exposure to the sound produced by an electric bell.

Hence **'primed** *ppl. a.*, (*a*) prepared to receive paint; (*b*) *Biol.* and *Med.*, rendered susceptible; prepared; (cf. sense 7 above).

1725 BRADLEY *Fam. Dict.* s.v. *Painting*, The Primed Cloth, which is usually good Canvas made smooth, sized over with a little Honey, and when dry'd, whited over with Size and Whiting..upon which you paint. **1799** G. SMITH *Laboratory* II. 64 Having first made a rough sketch upon your primed cloth with white chalk. **1943** *Jrnl. Endocrinol.* III. 273 In considering the question of inducing superovulation from the primed ovary, the first question arising is whether the ovulation-producing act of mating is sufficient to cause ovulation in a greater than normal number of follicles. **1960** *Proc. Soc. Exper. Biol. & Med.* CIV. 589/2 The primed mechanism responds to the second stimulus of the protein, but the resulting antibody is apparently specific for certain particular loci on the protein surface. **1967** *Science* 17 Nov. 940/1 Biochemical examinations of primed and nonprimed mice may reveal whether differences in oxidative phosphorylation..are associated with changes in audiogenic seizure susceptibility. **1975** *Behavior Genetics* V. 328 In an attempt to determine the increase in susceptibility due exclusively to acoustic priming, the seizure severity scores from the nonprimed.. mice of a concurrently run study..were subtracted from the severity scores of the primed, non-cross-fostered mice of the present study.

prime (praɪm), *v.*[2] [f. PRIME *a.* or *sb.*[1] With sense 2 cf. F. *primer* to take the first place, lead, anticipate, outstrip, f. *prime* PRIME *a.*]

†**1.** *intr.* Of the moon: To enter on the first phase; to become new, appear first after the change.

1549–62 STERNHOLD & H. *Ps.* LXXII. vii, Vntill the Moone shall leaue to prime, waste, chaunge, and to encrease. **1647** J. HEYDON *Discov. Fairfax* 6 So long as the Sun shall shine, or the Moon prime.

2. To be first; to domineer; to lord it. So *to prime it.* ? *Obs.*

1756 F. GREVILLE *Maxims, Charac. & Refl.* 78 Whether men like best to prime over others, or to have others prime over them. **1805** W. TAYLOR *Hist. Surv. Germ. Poetry* (1830) I. 332 Lessing loved to prime, and was adapted for it. **1821** JEFFERSON *Writ.* (1830) IV. 340 Harvard will still prime it over us with her twenty Professors.

3. Of a tide: To come at a shorter interval: usually in PRIMING *vbl. sb.*[2] (So F. *primer.*)

1890 C. A. YOUNG *Elem. Astron.* viii. §267 At the time of the spring tides, the interval between the corresponding tides of successive days is less than the average, being only about 24 hours 38 minutes (instead of 24 hours 51 minutes), and then the tides are said to prime. At the neap tides, the interval is greater than the mean—about 25 hours 6 minutes, and the tide lags.

prime (praɪm), *v.*[3] [Origin obscure. ? Related to *proyne*, PRUNE.] **1.** *trans.* To prune or trim (trees). Also *fig.*

1565 T. STAPLETON *Fortr. Faith* 86 b, The vine being.. primed multiplieth the more. **1601** R. JOHNSON *Kingd. & Commw.* (1603) 114 They..prime and draw such woods as grow too thick and obscure. **1613** BEAUM. & FL. *Coxcomb* IV. ii, Two-edged winds that prime The maiden blossoms. **1631** *MS. Acc. St. John's Hosp., Canterb.*, To Newton for priming our trees iiijs. **1790** CULLUM *Hist. Hawsted* iii. Gloss. 172 *Priming* a tree, is pruning it. **1823** E. MOOR *Suffolk Words, Priming*, pruning the lower, or washboughs of a tree. *a* **1825** FORBY *Voc. E. Anglia, Prime*, to trim up the stems of trees; to give them the first dressing or training. **1884** *American* VII. 350 All he needs is to prime down extravagances and modify excesses in voice and expression.

2. *U.S.* To pull off the lower leaves of tobacco plants.

1792 J. POPE *Tour S. & W. Terr. U.S.* 63 [The Creeks] scarcely ever weed, hill, prime, top or succour their Tobacco. **1963** H. GARNER *Best Stories* 167 Taking suckers first make [*sic*] it better to prime after. *Ibid.* 168, I thought of the rows upon rows still to be primed of sand leaves, the lowest leaves on the plant.

prime (praɪm), *v.*[4] [Origin unascertained.] *intr.* Of a fish: To leap or 'rise'.

1787 BEST *Angling* (ed. 2) 41 In fine sunshiny days, carps will often *prime* about noon and swim about the edges of a pond to catch such flies as fall upon the surface of the water. *Ibid.* 168 *Prime*, fish are said to prime when they leap out of the water. **1867** F. FRANCIS *Angling* iii. (1880) 76 When the angler notes a bubble or two..left after the priming of large fish. **1883** G. C. DAVIES *Norfolk Broads* xii. (1884) 93 The bream are 'priming' in shoals on the top of the water.

primecocks, obs. form of PRINCOX.

primed (praɪmd), *a.* [f. PRIME *sb.*[2] + -ED[2].] Having the symbol ′ as a superscript.

1927 *Proc. R. Soc.* A. CXIII. 630 We shall make it a rule always to use..primed or multiply primed letters such as ξ' and a'' to denote parameters, representing matrix rows and columns. **1944** C. PALACHE et al. *Dana's Syst. Min.* (ed. 7) I. 13 Projection values are primed, and polar values unprimed. **1968** *Amer. Jrnl. Physics* XXXVI. 1105/1 He obtained $F' = l^2(1, \gamma, \gamma)F$ and $a' = l(\gamma^3, \gamma^2, \gamma^2)a$, for the force and acceleration transformed to the instantaneous (primed) rest frame of the electron.

†**'primeful**, *a. Obs. nonce-wd.* [f. PRIME *sb.*[1] + -FUL.] Characterized by being in the prime.

1606 WARNER *Alb. Eng.* XIV. lxxxix. (1612) 361 A paire of Loues, fresh in their primefull dayes.

†**'primegilt.** *Sc. Obs.* In 6–7 pryme-, prym-. [? from PRIME *v.*[1] 1 + *gilt* = *gelt*, GELD, payment.] = PRIMAGE 1.

1518–19 *Burgh Rec. Edinb.* (1869) I. 187 To be furit to the port of Deip in France for the fraucht of xxvjs. and xvjs. the most chairge frie of all vther chairges except pryme gilt. **1576** *Ibid.* (1882) IV. 54 The pryme-giltt, quhilk was gevin be the liberaltie of merchantis, hes bene in all tymes past vplifted and spent be the marinaris in vane and wicked vses. **1621** *Sc. Acts Jas. VI.* (1816) IV. 668/2 þe prymgilt To be vplifted for sustentatioun Of the pure and decayit Marineris wtin The said toun of leith. **1633** *Sc. Acts Chas. I.* (1817) V. 93/2 Grantit..the indraucht thairof and prymegilt of all shipes coming to the said port.

primely ('praɪmlɪ), *adv.* [f. PRIME *a.* + -LY[2].]

1. In the first place, in the highest degree; firstly, primarily, originally. Now *rare* or *Obs.*

1613 W. BROWNE *Sheph. Pipe* II. (1614) Dj, The Nightingale records againe What thou dost primely sing. **1649** JER. TAYLOR *Gt. Exemp.* Pref. §13 Some parts of it [natural law] are primely necessary, others by supposition and accident. **1698** NORRIS *Pract. Disc.* (1707) IV. Pref., The application..made to men's Reason and Understanding (as the part primely affected).

2. Exceedingly well; excellently. *colloq.*

c **1746** COLLIER (Tim Bobbin) *View Lanc. Dial.* Wks. (1862) 40 Theaw looks primely. **1755–73** JOHNSON, *Primely* ..2. Excellently, supremely well. A low sense. **1873** A. G. MURDOCH *Doric Lyre* 26 He who this night dares the road, Should have his good steed primely shod. **1900** A. LANG in *Blackw. Mag.* Mar. 367/1 It was primely witty to half-poison somebody with a surreptitious dose of medicine.

'prime 'minister. Also Prime Minister, esp. in specific uses. [PRIME *a.* 2, MINISTER *sb.* 2, 3.]

†**1.** *generally.* Used in the ordinary sense of the two words: A principal or chief minister, servant, or agent. Often in *pl. Obs.*

1646 BP. MAXWELL *Burd. Issach.* 11 To effectuate his private Designes, he made much of some few prime leading Ministers. **1647** CLARENDON *Hist. Reb.* VII. §337 He [Charles I] received advice and information from some of his prime ministers of that kingdom [Ireland]. **1694** LUTTRELL *Brief Rel.* (1857) III. 355 The emperor of China and several of his prime ministers are turnd Christians. **1713** M. HENRY *Meekness & Quietn. Spirit* (1822) 143 The apostles, those prime ministers of state in Christ's kingdom. **1906** *Westm. Gaz.* 9 May 2/3 Those who were jealous of too much personal power being placed in the hands of a single statesman were accustomed to describe all the leading members of the Administration as 'the Prime Ministers of State' in order to prevent the title being arrogated by one among them.

2. The first or principal minister or servant of any sovereign, ruler, or state, or more vaguely of any person of rank or position; = *premier minister*, PREMIER *a.* 1 b. *sb.* a.

Applied descriptively to the chief minister of some foreign rulers, before it became usual in sense 3; but in the 19th c. largely extended from the English use.

1655 LD. NORWICH in *Nicholas Papers* (Camden) III. 144 He bein in close treaty with the Pr. of Condés prime minister. *a* **1678** MARVELL in *Casquet of Lit.* (1873) I. 310/1 Time, the prime minister of death, There's nought can bribe his honest will. **1678** EVELYN *Diary* 8 Feb., I had a long discourse with the Conte de Castel Mellor, lately Prime Minister in Portugal. **1730** T. BOSTON *View Covt. Grace* (1771) 212 The prime Minister of the Kingdom of Egypt. **1790** BEATSON *Nav. & Mil. Mem.* I. 168 Cardinal Tencin, who, on the death of Cardinal Fleury, assumed the lead in the French councils, was now regarded as Prime Minister. **1815** ELPHINSTONE *Acc. Caubul* (1842) I. 248 The Moollah ..had charge of the prime minister's son (a boy of sixteen when I saw him). **1882** *Whitaker's Alm.* 333 Japan..Prime Minister, Sanjô Saneyoshi. **1889** *Ibid.* 516 Sweden..Prime Minister, Baron Bildt. **1884** JESSOPP in *19th Cent.* Jan. 110 The prior was the abbot's prime minister.

3. In Great Britain (in early use, *prime minister of state*): A descriptive designation, which has gradually grown to be the official title of the First Minister of State or leader of the administration.

Originally merely descriptive and unofficial; in the early 18th c. (perh. from its prior application in sense 2 to the sole minister of a despotic ruler) odious (see quot. 1733); applied opprobriously to Walpole, and disowned by him, as later by Lord North. Little used in later part of 18th c., *premier* being often substituted, also *first minister*; became usual by the middle of the 19th c., and began to creep into official use from 1878. In 1905 fully recognized, and the precedence of the Prime Minister defined by King Edward VII. For fuller history, see A. F. Robbins in *N. & Q.* 8th s. XI. 69, and onward to 10th s. IX. 425; also Morley *Walpole* vii.

1694 GIBSON in *Lett. Lit. Men* (Camden) 231 My Lord Keeper, who is..(what my Lord Burleigh..was) Prime-Minister of State. **1698** EVELYN in *Thoresby's Corr.* (ed. Hunter) I. 345 The Earl of Leicester, prime minister of State to Queen Elizabeth. **1704** ST. WEST *Let. to Harley* 29 Aug. in *Portland Papers* IV. (Hist. MSS. Comm.) 119, I have heard of people's talk, that..if the Court had appointed my Lord Rochester, or any other person to be the Prime Minister, it would have been the same thing to you, and that your aim is in time to be the Prime Minister yourself. **1733** *Fog's Jrnl.* 28 Apr., In Countries where Royal Prerogative is limited by Laws, the Name of prime Minister has been always odious. **1734–5** C. D'ANVERS *Craftsman* No. 446 ¶3 The late Earl of Oxford stands charged, in the Impeachment against Him, with being the Prime, if not the sole Minister, and engrossing to Himself the absolute Management and Direction of all Affairs. **1741** LD. HARDWICK in *Gentl. Mag.* XI. 405 It has not been yet pretended that he [Walpole] assumes the Title of Prime Minister, or indeed, that it is aplied to him by any but his Enemies. **1741** WALPOLE *Sp. Ho. Comm.* in Doran *Lond. in Jacob. T.* (1877) II. 89 Having invested me with a kind of mock dignity, and styled me a *Prime Minister*, they impute to me an unpardonable abuse of that chimerical authority, which only they created and conferred. **1747** *Biog. Brit.* I. 379 Yet he [Bacon] behaved..towards the Earl of Salisbury, who was now become Lord Treasurer and Prime-Minister, with submission and respect. **1849** MACAULAY *Hist. Eng.* ii. I. 254 When there was a lord treasurer, that great officer was generally prime minister: but..it was not till the time of Walpole that the first lord of the Treasury was considered as the head of the executive government. **1878** (July 13) *Treaty of Berlin*, The Earl of Beaconsfield, First Lord of the Treasury and Prime Minister of Her Britannic Majesty. **1894** *Times* 5 Mar. 10/4 The Queen has summoned the Earl of Rosebery, K.G...and offered him the post of Prime Minister vacated by the Right Hon. W. E. Gladstone, M.P. **1899** LD. ROSEBERY in *Anglo-Saxon Rev.* June 105 The Prime Minister, as he is now called, is technically and practically the Chairman of an Executive Committee of the Privy Council, or rather, perhaps, of Privy Councillors, the influential foreman of an executive jury. **1905** *King's Warrant* 2 Dec., Whereas We taking it into Our Royal consideration that the precedence of Our Prime Minister has not been declared or defined by due authority..We do hereby declare Our Royal Will and Pleasure that..the Prime Minister of Us, Our Heirs and Successors shall have place and precedence next after the Archbishop of York.

b. Formerly also the official designation of the leader of the administration in some of the self-governing British colonies and 'dominions beyond the sea'. Now *Hist.*

During the colonial period, the usual title of the chief of the ministry in the colonies was PREMIER; in Canada and in Australia this was retained in most cases for the chief minister of each constituent colony, while *prime minister* was used for the first minister of the whole Dominion and of the Commonwealth; it was also the title in the Dominion of New Zealand, and in the colonies of Transvaal and Natal. The modern states of Australia, Canada, and New Zealand all retain the title in sense 3 a above for the leader of the government; in the Republic of S. Africa, the offices of President and Prime Minister are combined in a single person.

1901 *Whitaker's Alm.* 520 New Zealand . . Prime Minister, Colonial Treasurer, etc. Rt. Hon. Richd. J. Seddon. **1902** *Ibid.* 529 The Commonwealth of Australia . . Prime Minister and Minister of State for External Affairs, Rt. Hon. Edmund Barton. **1906** *Ibid.* 513 Dominion of Canada . . Prime Minister and President of Privy Council, Rt. Hon. Sir Wilfrid Laurier.

Hence **prime-minister** *v.*, *nonce-wd.*, *intr.* to act as a prime minister; **'prime-mini'sterial** *a.*, of or pertaining to a prime minister; **'prime-'ministership**, †**'prime 'ministry**, the office or position of a prime minister.

1742 FIELDING *J. Andrews* II. i, There are certain Mysteries or Secrets in all Trades . ., from that of *Prime Ministring to this of Authoring. **1897** *Westm. Gaz.* 9 Dec. 10/1 What may be regarded as Mr. Gladstone's *Prime Ministerial youth was very vigorous. **1905** *Sat. Rev.* 8 Apr. 439 Sir Alexander—chief reporter on the Priministerial staff. **1867** *Athenæum* 23 Nov. 679/2 He won . . the *Prime Ministership. **1887** *Spectator* 6 Aug., If . . Lord Salisbury should find the combined burden of the Foreign Office and the Prime Minister-ship too much for his health. **1730** T. BOSTON *View Covt. Grace* (1771) 141 God . . exalted him to the *prime ministry of heaven.

prime 'mover. [f. PRIME *a.* (*adv.*) + MOVER^1.]

1. = *first mover* s.v. MOVER^1 3.

1674 *Essex Papers* (1890) I. 191 Four or five men . . have made it their whole business . . to incite the Citizens to these disturbances . ., which prime movers are men of small Estates. **1867** FREEMAN *Norm. Conq.* (1877) I. iv. 197 The prime mover in the whole matter was Hugh the Great. **1972** *Science* 26 May 892/3 Jamie L. Whitten, . . a prime mover in the passage 18 years ago of Public Law 566. **1973** *Amer. Speech 1969* XLIV. 293 Concerning the origin of the jargon, Adams . . relies on the theories of his informants. . . Their views focus on the probable ages of the originators: teenagers or adults or an intermediate group of 'prime movers'. **1973** *Nature* 17 Aug. 467/1 Both of them have been prime movers, in the period of forty years covered, in securing the establishment of ethology as a separate, respectable and inevitable branch of animal biology. **1977** *Jrnl. R. Soc. Arts* CXXVI. 40/2 Maria Grey, 'prime mover' of this enterprise, would have been the first to wish to have associated with her the men and women who helped in the work.

2. = *first mover* s.v. MOVER^1 2 b.

1809 *Edin. Rev.* XV. 146 Suppose a delicate magnetic bar were made the prime-mover of a watch. **1859** RANKINE (*title*) A manual of the Steam engine and other Prime movers. *Ibid.* 13 Prime Movers . . are machines for driving other machines. **1869** *Eng. Mech.* 31 Dec. 378/1 Until recently (and even now for convenience) such machines as windmills, water-wheels, and steam-engines, were called 'prime movers'. **1870** YEATS *Nat. Hist. Comm.* 30 Previous to the employment of steam as a motive force, water was the prime mover. **1884** HIGGS *Mag. Dyn.-Electr. Mach.* Pref. 6 Steam and other prime movers. **1967** R. WHITEHEAD in Wills & Yearsley *Handbk. Managem. Technol.* iv. 55 Up to almost the present time engineering has been concerned with the study of prime movers—heat converted into usable energy. **1971** *Sci. Amer.* Sept. 37/3 By the 16th century the waterwheel was by far the most important prime mover. *Ibid.* 152/3 The piston engines in the nation's more than 100 million motor vehicles have a rated capacity in excess of 17 billion horsepower, or more than 95 percent of the capacity of all prime movers (defined as engines for converting fuel to mechanical energy). **1974** *Petroleum Rev.* XXVIII. 783/2 Primary production equipment, comprising gas/oil separators and forwarding pumps with gas turbine prime

3. A towing vehicle; *spec.* (see quot. 1963).

1938 T. J. HAYES *Elem. Ordnance* xix. 677 Artillery prime movers are used to tow artillery. **1945** *Finito! Po Valley Campaign* (15th Army Group) 51 A German convoy of two 170 mm cannon pulled by prime movers. **1962** *Exhib. Brit. Military Vehicles* 128 This vehicle is a development of the tractor 30 ton 6 × 4 G.S. . . for semi-trailer F.V. 12002 which it will replace in the service as prime mover for the 50 and 60-ton semi-trailer tank transporters. **1963** *Dict. U.S. Mil. Terms* (U.S. Dept. Defense) 171 *Prime mover*, a vehicle, including heavy construction equipment, possessing military characteristics, designed primarily for towing heavy, wheeled weapons and frequently providing facilities for the transportation of the crew of, and ammunition for, the weapon. **1969** *Age* (Melbourne) 24 May 61/9 (Advt.), Commer semi trailer outfit complete, 61 mod., petrol motor, prime mover and 34 ft. semi trailer. . . $2000. **1976** *Daily Times* (Lagos) 22 Sept. 15/1 Those above eight tonnes but not articulated prime movers i.e. with trailers now cost ₦35. **1977** 'D. RUTHERFORD' *Return Load* ii. 28 He had . . invested a legacy . . in a Leyland prime mover. . . Like most owner-drivers he made a practice of hiring the semi-trailers which, when hitched to the tractor, made up the complete articulated vehicle.

primeness ('praɪmnɪs). [f. PRIME *a.* + -NESS.] The quality of being prime; †primitiveness, earliness (*obs.*); first quality, excellence.

1611 COTGR., *Primeur*, . . primenesse, perfection, excellencie. **1624** R. B. in F. White *Repl. Fisher* App. 12 Euerie thing Fundamentall is not of a like neerenesse to the Foundation, nor of equall Primenesse in the Faith. **1628** GAULE *Pract. The. Panegyr.* 25 As they of their Emperour, for primenesse and eminence. **1837** DICKENS *Pickw.* xl, 'All fun, ain't it?' 'Prime!' said the young gentleman. . . The young gentleman, notwithstanding his primeness and his spirit, . . reclined his head upon the table, and howled dismally. **1842** THACKERAY *Fitz-Boodle Prof.* ii. Wks. 1898 IV. 360 He . . is able at a glance to recognise the age of mutton, the primeness of beef. **1892** *Daily News* 13 Dec. 6/5 Sheep that for neatness of form and primeness of quality have never been surpassed.

primer ('prɪmə(r), 'praɪmə(r)), *sb.*^{1} Forms: α. 4- primer; also 4–6 **prymer**, 5 **prymar**, **-mere**, **premere**, 6 **primare**, 7 **primere**, **-mier**. β. 5–6 **prymmer**, 6–8 **primmer**. [In 15th c. = med.L. *prīmārius*, *-ārium*, f. L. *prīm-us* first, or (?) *prīma* PRIME *sb.*^{1}: see -ARIUM and cf. PRIMER *a.*

(The actual reason for the name does not appear; the sense 'first or primary book', which suits sense 2, is less suitable to sense 1, which some would connect, as a book of *Hours*, with PRIME *sb.*^{1})]

1. A name for prayer-books or devotional manuals for the use of the laity, used in England before, and for some time after, the Reformation.

The mediæval *Primarium* or *Primer* was mainly a copy, or (in English) a translation, of different parts of the Breviary and Manual. For its origin and structure, see the Introduction to 'the Prymer or Lay Folks' Prayer Book', edited by H. Littlehales, E.E.T.S. 1895–7. In the 14th and 15th centuries, in its simplest form, it contained the Hours of the Blessed Virgin, the 7 Penitential and 15 Gradual Psalms, the Litany, the Office for the Dead (Placebo and Dirige), and the Commendations; to which however various additions were often made. In the early 16th c., the printed editions of this in English (examples known from 1527) are often called on the title-page *Prymer*, and in the colophon, *Horæ Beatæ Mariæ*, or the like. The name was also given in 16th c. to books similar in character and purpose, partly based upon the *Sarum Horæ*, whether put out by private persons (e.g. Marshall's Primer, 1534), or with some sort of authority (e.g. Bp. Hilsey's Primer, 1539), or by royal authority, as the King's Primer of 1545 and the successive recensions issued in the reigns of Hen. VIII, Edw. VI, and Elizabeth; also to 'the Uniform and Catholyke Prymer in Latin and English', appointed for general use by Queen Mary's Letters Patent in 1555. The title was also used for several English or Latin and English editions of *Horæ* according to the Roman use, published in 1599 and later.

After the Reformation, *Primer* was also applied to books in which the offices for daily prayers were based upon the orders contained in the Book of Common Prayer. These are described in the Privilege to William Seres, the printer of the first of them in 1553 (see quot.) as 'books of private prayers, called and usually taken and reported for Primers . . set forth agreeable and according to the Book of common prayers'. Later forms of this, under the title 'The Primer or Catechism set forth agreeable to the Book of Common Prayer', were issued under Chas. II, Jas. II, Geo. II, and Geo. III, the latest app. in 1783.

[**1323** *Will Eliz. Bacon* (cf. transl. in A. Gibbons *Early Lincoln Wills* 4) Domino Johanni la Ware fratri meo unum primarium quod fuit Margr' sororis mee . . Item Margarete sorori mee . . unum tressour cum primario meo.]

1393 LANGL. *P. Pl.* C. VI. 46 The lomes þat ich laboure with and lyflode deserue Ys pater-noster and my prymer placebo and dirige. **1434** *E.E. Wills* (1882) 102 Also a prymmer for to serve god with. ? **1460** *Paston Lett.* I. 539 My Maister Fastolf . . by his othe made on his primer ther, grauntted and promitted to me to have the maner of Gunton. *c* **1475** *Pict. Voc.* in Wr.-Wülcker 755/13 *Hoc primarium*, a premere. **1511** FABYAN *Will* in *Chron.* (1811) Pref. 7 W^t my great masse booke, and also the great prymar, whiche before daies I gave to my wif. **1530** PALSGR. 183 *Vnes hevres*, a primer or a mattyns boke. **1534** (*title*) A Prymer in Englyshe, with certeyn prayers and godly meditations, very necessary for all people that vnderstonde not the Latyne Tongue. (Marshall's.) **1539** J. HILSEY *The Manuall of Prayers, or the Prymer in Englyshe* Prol., Called the prymer, because (I suppose) that it is the fyrste boke that the tender youth was instructed in. **1545** (*title*) The Primer, set foorth by the Kynges maiestie and his Clergie, to be taught, lerned, and read: and none other to be vsed throughout all his dominions. **1553** BECON *Reliques of Rome* (1563) 159 b, Reade we not these wordes in their Popish primare. **1553** (*title*) A Prymmer or boke of priuate prayer nedeful to be vsed of al faythfull Christianes. (Seres.) **1605** *Gunpowder Plot* in *Harl. Misc.* (Malh.) III. 25 Having, upon a primer, given each other the oath of secrecy. **1651** N. BACON *Disc. Govt. Eng.* II. xxx. (1739) 139 This was the Clergy's Primmer, wherein they imployed their study. **1669** (*title*) The Primer, or Three Offices of the B. Virgin Mary, in Latin and English [by Thomas Fitz Simon]. (Rouen.) **1686** EVELYN *Diary* 12 Mar., One Hall, who styl'd himselfe his Majesty's printer . . for the printing Missalls, Offices, Lives of Saints, Portals, Primers, &c., books expressly forbidden to be printed or sold, by divers Acts of Parliament. **1716** M. DAVIES *Athen. Brit.* II. 116 All Prayers to Saints were to be struck out of the Primmers, publish'd by the late King. **1846** MASKELL *Mon. Rit.* II. p. xxxii, xliii.

2. a. An elementary school-book for teaching children to read; formerly, 'a little book, which children are first taught to read and to pray by' (Phillips 1706); 'a small prayer-book in which children are taught to read' (Johnson 1755–73).

This sense gradually disengaged itself from the preceding, from which in early use it cannot be separated. The books included under sense 1 appear to have been also used in teaching to read and as first reading-books; and there may have been from early times forms of them specially intended for this purpose; such was perhaps the primer of quot. *c* 1386. In the 16th c., printed books of this kind became common; that mentioned in quot. *c* 1537 has a section containing the A. B. C., followed by the Pater Noster, Ave Maria, Creed, Decalogue, forms of Grace before and after meat, and certain prayers. Recensions of Marshall's and Hilsey's Primers (quot. 1539), also began with the A. B. C. Smaller works containing the part for children only, began to be officially published in 1545, under the title of 'The A B C'. Primers for children, issued under Edward VI and Elizabeth, contained also the Church Catechism; and after 1600 the main purpose of the Primer appears to have been educational; as known to Dr. Johnson, it contained, besides the alphabetic matter, 'godly prayers and graces, very meet and necessary for the instruction of youth'. In Scotland, 'the A B C with the Shorter Catechism', containing also the Lord's Prayer, the Creed, Graces before and after meat, etc., was used as the first reading-book down to *c* 1800, and was until 1872 published as the official form of the Shorter Catechism. The use of the Primer, thus variously transformed, as a book in which children learned to read, at length so overshadowed its original purpose that, when all the devotional parts were eliminated, popular usage still continued to apply the ancient name to the Abecedarium pure and simple.

c **1386** CHAUCER *Prioress' T.* 65 This litel child his litel book lernynge As he sat in the scole at his prymer He Alma redemptoris herde synge As children lerned hire Antiphoner. *c* **1500** *Regr. Moone* lf. 29 b (Somerset Ho.), The prymmer that she lernyth vppon. *c* **1537** (*title*) The Primer in English for children, after the vse of Sarum. **1539** (*title*) The Primer in English most necessary for the education of children. *a* **1617** BAYNE *On Coloss.* (1634) 82 It is a good primmer for us to spell in. **1639** in *Bury Wills* (Camden) 176 For the buyeing and provideing of horne bookes and primers to be giuen to poore children of the said parish of St Maries. **1727** POPE, etc. *Art Sinking* 89 But for which . . the substance of many a fair volume, might be reduced to the size of a primmer. **1810** CRABBE *Borough* xxiv, Where humming students gilded primers read. *a* **1839** PRAED *Poems* (1864) II. 105 The treasured primer's lettered rows.

b. By extension, a small introductory book on any subject.

1807 T. BURGESS (*title*) A Hebrew Primer. **1846** (*title*) Primer of the Irish Language. **1875** (*title of Series*) Science Primers, edited by Professors Huxley, Roscoe, and Balfour Stewart. **1889** (*title*) Primer of the History of the Catholic Church in Ireland. **1895** E. CLODD (*title*) Primer of Evolution.

c. *fig.* That which serves as a first means of instruction.

1640 QUARLES *Enchirid.* IV. xcix, Keepe him from vaine . . and amorous Pamphlets as the Primmers of all Vice. **1658** J. ROBINSON *Endoxa* i. 4 Thus did Adam, Noah, . . teach their Families, by the primmer of divine Traditions. **1871** B. TAYLOR *Faust* (1875) II. III. 201 Spell in lovers' primers sweetly. **1901** *Munsey's Mag.* XXV. 672/1 In China, . . learning is the first primer of power.

d. *N.Z.* With pronunc. ('prɪmə(r)). One of the primer classes, covering the first years of instruction in a primary school; also, a child in a primer class.

1928 *Syllabus of Instruction for Primary Schools* (N.Z. Dept. Educ.) 55 In all schools teachers of Primer classes will use 'Physical Exercises and Games for Infants'. *Ibid.*, Where there are three teachers: Primers do infant work; Squad I, Tables 1–36; [etc.]. **1947** 'A. P. GASKELL' *Big Game* 92 There was Micky, her [*sc.* the teacher's] smallest primer, a little wizened creature with sad eyes. **1957** J. FRAME *Owls do Cry* xxviii. 125 He is in primer three at school. **1963** N. HILLIARD *Piece of Land* 191 It seemed no time since he'd been in the primers. **1963** B. PEARSON *Coal Flat* i. 8 She had taught in the primers of his school when he was in Standard six.

3. *Typogr.* **a.** ***Great Primer***, a size of type between Paragon and English, of 51 ems to a foot. **b.** ***Long Primer***, a size between Small Pica and Bourgeois, of 89 ems to a foot. ***Two-Line Long Primer*** = PARAGON (type).

1598 *Ord. Stationers' Co.* in T. B. Reed *Hist. Lett. Foundries* (1887) 129 Those in brevier and long primer letters at a penny for one sheet and a half. **1612** STURTEVANT *Metallica* xiii. 89 The Long-primer, the Pica, the Italica. **1629** C. BUTLER *Oratoria* A iv b, Genera literarum . . corporum proceritate distinguuntur: Primier, Pique, English: & supra hæc, Great Primier, Double Pique, Double English. **1683** MOXON *Mech. Exerc.*, *Printing* ii. ¶ 2 Most Printing-Houses have . . Pearl, Nomparel, Brevier, Long-Primmer, Pica, English, Great-Primmer, Double-Pica, Two-Lin'd-English. **1771** LUCKOMBE *Hist. Print.* 135 Two Lines Great Primer. **1771** FRANKLIN *Autobiog.* Wks. 1887 I. 144 It was a folio, pro patria size in pica, with long primer notes. **1882** *Clar. Press List New Bks.* 44 The Book of Common Prayer. Long Primer, 24mo.

†**4.** The first one. *Obs.*

1597 WARNER *Alb. Eng.* IX. Ded. 210 Such as that Henrie (Primer of you Hunsdon Barons) bee Your Lordshippe, to your Countrie. **1625** F. MARKHAM *Bk. Hon.* I. x. § 1 When I looke . . into the great Antiquitie of your Noble House (being in descent the Primere of our Nation).

†**5.** A student of the first grade at the university of St. Andrews. *Obs.*

1684 A. SKEINE *Let.* in *Scottish Antiq.* XI. 19 If his sone be a primer his expence will be as foloueth.

6. *attrib.* and *Comb.*, as **primer-school**, an elementary school; **primer-state**, elementary state.

1545 *Primer Hen. VIII* Injunction, For the auoydyng of the dyuersytie of primer bookes that are nowe abroade . . whiche minister occasion of contentions. *a* **1680** CHARNOCK *Attrib. God* (1834) I. 257 The law . . could no more spiritualize the heart, than the teachings in a primer-school can enable the mind, and make it fit for affairs of state. **1903** *Critic* XLIII. 368/1, I have passed this primer-state of religious emotion.

primer ('praɪmə(r)), *sb.*^{2} [f. PRIME *v.*^{1} + -ER^1.]

1. A priming-wire: see PRIMING *vbl. sb.*^{1} 10.

1497 *Naval Acc. Hen. VII* (1896) 100 Wire for prymers. **1627** CAPT. SMITH *Seaman's Gram.* xiv. 68 His Primer is a small long peece of iron, sharpe at the small end to pierce the Cartrage thorow the toutch hole. **1826** SCOTT *Woodst.* viii, Poise your musket—Rest your musket—Cock your musket—Handle your primers—and many other forgotten words of discipline.

2. a. A cap, wafer, cylinder, etc., containing fulminating powder or other compound, in communication with the powder of a cartridge, blasting charge, etc., which it ignites when exploded by percussion or otherwise.

1819 *Sporting Mag.* IV. 185 The flash of fire from the end of the primer communicates fire, by the touch-hole, to the gunpowder contained in the barrel. **1838** COL. HAWKER *Diary* (1893) II. 138 Had not my primer missed fire, [I] should have had about 30 geese at another shot. **1869** *Pall Mall G.* 8 Oct. 3 Unless purposely arranged to explode, or purposely ignited with a detonating primer, it [gun-cotton] is not an explosive at all. **1890** W. J. GORDON *Foundry* 21 In the large turret-guns the primer is fired by electricity, entirely under command of the officer on duty.

b. *Biochem.* A molecule that serves as a starting material for a polymerization (see quot. 1976). Freq. *attrib.*

1954 CANTAROW & SCHEPARTZ *Biochem.* xvii. 391 A 'primer' of branched polysaccharide, the main linkages of which are α-1,4, is essential for the action of animal phosphorylase. **1963** *Proc. Nat. Acad. Sci.* XLIX. 533 *(heading)* Formation of DNA-RNA hybrids with single-stranded DNA as primer. **1965** M. W. NEIL *Vertebr. Biochem.* (ed. 2) xii. 182 Polysaccharide synthesis involving the addition of uridine diphosphate-bound units to a primer chain is widespread in nature, and is the mechanism whereby such macromolecules as cellulose, chitin, starch and the mucopolysaccharides, in addition to glycogen, are elaborated. **1976** CONN & STUMPF *Outl. Biochem.* (ed. 4) xviii. 507 Primer, in biochemistry, refers to the initial terminus of a molecule onto which additional units are added to produce the final product. **1977** D. E. METZLER *Biochem.* xv. 903/2 The enzyme displays many of the properties expected of a DNA-synthesizing enzyme. It requires a template strand of DNA as well as a shorter primer strand.

c. *Physiol.* (See quots. 1963, 1975.) Freq. *attrib.*

1963 WILSON & BOSSERT in *Recent Progress Hormone Res.* XIX. 674 We propose to distinguish the releaser effect, involving the classical stimulus-response mediated wholly by the central nervous system, from the primer effect, in which the endocrine and reproductive..systems are altered physiologically. *Ibid. (caption)* The pheromone may be the primary stimulus causing a quick behavioral response (releaser effect), or it may act more slowly and indirectly by altering the physiology and 'priming' the animal for a different behavioral repertory (primer effect). **1971** *Nature* 16 Apr. 432/2 Pheromonal primer effects are near-universal in social mammals, including primates. **1975** *Ibid.* 20 Nov. 194/2 The action of pheromones is commonly divided into two classes..: chemical 'releasers' of specific acts of behaviour, and 'primers' which seem to act initially on the endocrine system.

3. = PRIMING *vbl. sb.*^{1} 4 a.

1688 R. HOLME *Armoury* III. 369/2 By this Instrument [the Priming Knife] are all sorts of Cloths laid over with their first colour, which is called Primer. **1703** T. N. *City & C. Purchaser* 215 Spanish-brown, Spanish-white, and Red-lead,..ground with Linseed-oyl, will make excellent Primer. **1937** *Times* 13 Apr. (Brit. Motor Suppl.) p. xiii/1 Before colour can be applied the body undergoes a number of preparatory stages, being thoroughly washed down with an acid cleaner and afterwards with hot and cold water, and dried off in preparation for the first coat of primer. **1958** *Listener* 14 Aug. 251/2 If the patches are touched in with primer and undercoat you will not run into any trouble. **1969** W. R. R. PARK *Plastics Film Technol.* vi. 156 An effective primer works better with a thick coating. **1976** *Southern Even. Echo* (Southampton) 11 Nov. 8/3 These were then given a 'primer' coat of lime plaster—almost like white-wash—and the geometrical designs painted on.

4. A person who primes. **a.** One who loads or charges detonators.

1890 *Pall Mall G.* 18 Sept. 7/2 When compounded, it has still to be packed into the detonator cases by the primer. The primer's work is done upon a copper-plate, perforated like a cullender.

b. One who prepares canvas, etc. for a painter.

1896 *Daily News* 15 Feb. 10/4 Canvas Primer Wanted. Must be thoroughly experienced in preparing all kinds of Artist's Canvas.

5. *Aeronaut.* = *priming pump* s.v. PRIMING *vbl. sb.*^{1} 8.

1923 *Gloss. Aeronaut. Terms* (Brit. Engin. Standards Assoc.) 48 *Engine primer*, a device for supplying fuel to the induction pipe or combustion chambers to facilitate starting. **1932** CHATFIELD & TAYLOR *Airplane & Engine* (ed. 2) x. 225 In automobiles this temporary excess of fuel for starting is supplied by means of the choke but for airplane engines a primer is usually used. **1939** *Aero Engines* II. 256 Always turn off the primer after use.

primer ('praɪmə(r)), *sb.*^{3} *rare.* [f. PRIME *v.*^{3} + -ER^1.] One who prunes trees, etc.

1611 COTGR., *Arborateur*, a planter, primer, dresser, breeder of trees.

primer ('prɪmə(r), 'praɪmə(r)), *a.* [a. AF. *primer* = OF. *primer* (*a* 1000 in Godef. *Compl.*), also *premer*, mod.F. *premier*, Pr. *primer*, Sp. *primero*, Pg. *primeiro*, It. *primiero*:—L. *prīmāri-us* PRIMARY: see PREMIER.] (Now only in phrases in sense 3.)

†**1.** First in time; early; primitive. *Obs.*

[**1343** *Rolls of Parlt.* II. 144/1 Aussi bien des Beneficz come des primers Fruitz.] **1448** HEN. VI in Willis & Clark *Cambridge* (1886) I. 353 The prymer notable werk purposed by me. **1525** LD. BERNERS *Froiss.* II. xx. 40 They to enioye them as in their primer state. *c* **1557** ABP. PARKER *Ps.* lxxviii. 225 He stroyd theyr fruites..Their prymer fruts. **1581** J. BELL *Haddon's Answ. Osor.* 255 All thynges may be referred to this, as to the primer cause efficient. **1622** DRAYTON *Poly-olb.* xxiv. 123 Sᵗ Lucius (call'd of us) the primer christen'd King.

†**2.** First in position, rank, or importance; chief, leading, foremost, premier. *Obs.*

1589 WARNER *Alb. Eng.* VI. xxix. (1612) 143 These primer Yorkests. **1602** *Ibid.* XIII. lxxvi. 316 The Primer Mouers violence. **1610** GUILLIM *Heraldry* IV. vii. (1660) 293 The..Mercers being the primer Company of the City of London. **1637** W. CROWNE *True Relation*, etc. (title-p.), Lord Howard, Earle of Arundell and Surrey, Primer Earle, and Earle Marshall of England. **1747** *Mem. Nutrebian Crt.* II. 212 The contemptible pity of the primer sort.

3. a. primer fine, in *Feudal Law* [lit. 'first fine': see FINE *sb.*^{1} 7 a], the sum, usually about one-tenth of the annual value of the land sued for, paid to the crown by a plaintiff who sued for the recovery of lands by a writ of covenant; = PRE-FINE. Now only *Hist.*

a **1634** COKE *2nd Pt. Inst.* (1642) 511 A Writ of covenant is brought to levy a fine of land, of the yearly value of v. marks, there is vi.s. viij.d. due presently [i.e. at once] for the primer fine, or fine in the Hamper. **1766** BLACKSTONE *Comm.* II. xxi. 350 On this writ there is due to the king, by antient prerogative, a primer fine, or a noble for every five marks of land sued for; that is, one tenth of the annual value.

b. primer seisin, in *Feudal Law* [lit. 'first seisin'], a feudal right of the English Crown to receive from the heir of a tenant *in capite* who died seised of a knight's fee, such heir being of age, the profits of his estate for the first year; abolished in 1660. Now only *Hist.*

1488 *Rolls of Parlt.* VI. 415/2 Savyng to the King and his Heires, the avantage of his primer cession of thos Landes. **1495** *Act 11 Hen. VII*, c. 39 §5 Thissues and profites for the Premer season of the same Honours Manoris londes. **1540** *Act 32 Hen. VIII*, c. 1 Saving alway and reserving to the King..all his right title and interest of prymer season and reliefis, and..all other rightes and dueties. *a* **1625** SIR H. FINCH *Law* (1636) 148 Tenure by Socage in chiefe giueth the King primer seisin, or the value of that land by a yeere, if the heire be of the age of 14, at his ancestors death. **1648** *Articles Peace* vii. in *Milton's Wks.* (1851) II, Profit by Wardship, Liveries, Primer-seisins, Measne Rates, Ousterlemains or Fines of Alienations without Licence. **1660** *Act 12 Chas. II*, c. 24 §1 It is hereby Enacted That..all Wardships Liveries Primer-Seizins and Ouster-le-mains ..be taken away. **1672** *Cowell's Interpr.* s.v., All the charges arising by Primer seisins are taken away by the Stat. made 12 *Car.* 2. ca. 24.

‖**primeras** (pri'meras). [Sp., pl. of *primera*: see next.] A term in Ombre: see quot.

1878 H. H. GIBBS *Ombre* 35 *Primeras.* If the Ombre win the first five tricks before either of the adversaries has won one.

‖**primero** (pri'mero). Also 6 -row, priemeero, 7 primera. [Altered from Sp. *primera* (= It. *primiera*), fem. of *primero* first:—L. *prīmāri-us*: see PRIMER *a.*] A gambling card-game, very fashionable from about 1530 to about 1640, in which four cards were dealt to each player, each card having thrice its ordinary value.

(See a long description in Sir J. Harington's Epigram, '*The Story of Marcus's Life at Primero*'.)

[**1526** (*Italian title*) Capitolo del Gioco della Primiera col commento di Messer Pietropaulo da San Chirico.]

1533 ELYOT *Knowledge* Pref. A vj b, It is soone lerned, in good faythe sooner thanne Primero or Gleeke. **1545** *Acts Privy Council* (1890) I. 289 A fraye..whiche grewe apon certaine wourdes..for a questyon of playeng at Primero at Domyngo's howse. *c* **1550** *Dice-Play* (Percy Soc.) 12 Some kept the goodman company at the hazard, some matched themselves at a new game called primero. **1589** *Pappe w. Hatchet* (1844) 27 If you had the foddring of the sheep, you would make the Church like Primero, foure religions in it, and neere one like another. **1589** *Hay any Work* A iij b, Our brother Westchester had as liue playe twentie nobles in a night, at Priemeero on the cards. **1648** GAGE *West Ind.* 26 They challenged us..to a Primera. **1658** PHILLIPS, *Primero*, and *Primavista*, two games at Cards formerly much in use. **1762** STERNE *Tr. Shandy* V. xvi, How the holy man managed the affair, unless he spent the greatest part of his time in combing his whiskers, or playing at primero. **1816** SINGER *Hist. Cards* 27, 248. **1887** *All Year Round* 5 Feb. 66 Primero ..was probably introduced to the English Court in the suite of Catherine of Arragon.

fig. **1641** MILTON *Animadv.* Postscr. 73 At that primero of piety, the pope and cardinals are the better gamesters, and will cog a die into heaven before you.

†'**primerole.** *Herb. Obs.* Forms: 4-5 primerole, 5 -erolle, prymrol, 5-6 -erol(le. [ME. a. OF. *primerole* (13-15th c. in Godef.), dim. of OF. *prime* first (cf. *féverole*, *pommerole*, etc.), and thus rendering or corresponding to med.L. *prīmula*, dim. of *prīma* first.] A name given to one or more early spring flowers, esp. to the cowslip (? including the primrose) and the field daisy. **b.** *fig.* A pretty young woman.

The early literary uses in OF. and ME. are not sufficient to identify the plant meant. The Great Herbal, Fr. ed. of *c* 1475, Eng. of *c* 1516, identifies it with the Cowslip, St. Peter's wort, or Palsywort, *Primula veris*; in mod. Norman dialect *primerole* (*plumerole*, *pomerole*) is a popular name of the Primrose, and this may have been the case in England also: see PRIMROSE, PRIMULA. But *Alphita*, *c* 1450, distinctly identifies it with the field daisy, *Bellis perennis*.

a **1310** in Wright *Lyric P.* v. 26 The primerole he [= she] passeth, the parvenke of pris. *a* **1350** *Song* in *Anglia* (1907) XXX. 175 Wat was hire mete The primerole ant the violet. *c* **1386** CHAUCER *Miller's T.* 82 Hir shoes were laced on hir legges hye She was a prymerole, a piggesnye. **1390** GOWER *Conf.* III. 125 The frosti colde Janever,..of his dole He yifth the ferste Primerole. *Ibid.* 130 Canis minor..His Ston and herbe, as seith the Scole, Ben Achates and Primerole. *c* **1420** *Liber Cocorum* (1862) 42 Þo prymrol, violet, þou take þerto Town cresses, and cresses þat growene in flode,..Alle þese erbs þou noȝt forsake, But lest of prymrol þou shalle take. *c* **1430** LYDG. *Min. Poems* (Percy Soc.) 242 The honysoucle, the freisshe prymerollys, Ther levys splaye at Phebus up-rysyng. **14..** *Noble Bk. Cookry* (1882) 57 Strawe ther on flour of prymerolle. *c* **1450** *ME. Med. Bk.* (Heinrich) 224 Drynke ofte þe jus of calamynte, or drynke pouder of primerole. *c* **1450** *Alphita* (Anecd. Oxon.) 146 *Primula ueris, prima rosa*, gallice et anglice primerole. Respice in consolida minor. [*Consolida minor, primula ueris* idem, ossa fracta consolidat, gallice, le petite consoude, angl. dayseghe [*MS.* waysegle] uel bonwort, uel brosewort. Respice in uenti minor. *Venti minor*, consolida minor idem, an. Bonwrt, a. dayesegh.] *c* **1516** *Grete Herball* cccl. T v, Primula veris is called prymerolles. Some call it saynt peterworte. Other paralisie. It is called prymerolle or primula of pryme tyme, because it beareth the fyrst floure in pryme tyme. [*Fr.* Est appellee primerole ou primule de ver ou de printemps pour ce qu'elle pourte la premiere fleur en printemps.]

'**prime-sign, 'primsign,** *v.* Now only *Hist.* Also 3 (Orm.) primmseȝȝnenn, 4 primsene, *pa. pple.* yprimisined, 5 primsein(e. [ME. *primseȝnen*, ad. ON. *prim-signa*, f. eccl. L. **prīmum signāre*, implied in *prīma signātio* 'the first signing', the signing of a person with the cross as a preliminary to baptism: see PRIME *a.* and SIGN *v.* The ME. form *primse(i)n(e* was perh. ad. OF. *prim-*, *prinseign(i)er* (*c* 1170 in Godef.), which was perh. from ON. OF. *preseign(i)er* (:—L. *præsignāre* to mark before or in front) was also used in the same sense.] *trans.* To mark (a person) with the sign of the cross before baptism; to make a catechumen.

c **1200** ORMIN 16560 Þatt tu ne mahht nohht husledd ben ..þohh þatt tu be primmseȝȝnedd rihht, ȝiff þatt tu narrt nohht fullhtnedd. *c* **1315** SHOREHAM *Poems* i. 331 Þe children atte cherche dore So beþ yprimisined. **1340** *Ayenb.* 188 Martin yet nou y-primsened me heþ yssred mid þise cloþe. *c* **1425** *Eng. Conq. Irel.* 64 That the chyldren, at þe chyrche dorre shullen ben I-primseined [*catechizentur*] of the prestes hond, & yn þe holy fantstones yn har moder chyrches to be I-fulled. [**1874** VIGFUSSON *Icelandic-Eng. Dict.* 479/1 *Primsigndra messa*, the mass for the 'prime-signed'... These 'prime-signed' men, returning to their native land, brought with them the first notions of Christianity into the heathen Northern countries. **1893** S. O. ADDY *Hall of Waltheof* 218 They were also admitted to a special part of the mass, known as the mass of the prime-signed.]

[**primet**, erroneously stated by Prior to occur in the *Grete Herball* as a name of the primrose, and used by him and others to suggest an etymology for *privet*. No such word is there found.]

†'**prime-temps.** *Obs.* Also 5 prime-tens, pryme temps, prymtemps (prymsauns, ? for -tauns). [ad. OF. *prin(s) tans*, mod.F. *printemps* spring, lit. 'first time'; with PRIME *a.* for OF. *prin*, *prim*: see TENSE *sb.*] Springtime, spring.

c **1400** *Rom. Rose* 3373 How he is feers of his chere, At prime temps, Love to manace. *Ibid.* 4747 Pryme temps, ful of frostes whyte. *c* **1400** *Sowdone Bab.* 965 In the prymsauns of grene vere, Whan floures spryngyn and bygynne. *c* **1430** *Pilgr. Lyf Manhode* I. xli. (1869) 24 The earthe is of my robes and in prime temps alwey j clothe it. *c* **1445** LYDG. *Nightingale* 11 Fresschly encoragyt, as galantes in prime-tens [*rime* presence]. **1484** CAXTON *Æsop* IV. vii, The byrdes ..Ioyeful and gladde as the prymtemps came.

†'**primetide, 'prime-tide.** *Obs.* [f. PRIME *a.* or *sb.* + TIDE; in sense 2 prob. after prec.]

1. The time of prime; early morning.

a **1300** *K. Horn* 849 Riȝt at prime tide Hi gunnen vt ride.

2. Springtime, spring; also *fig.* the 'springtime' of life, or of any movement.

1549 CHALONER *Erasm. on Folly* A j, Whan, after a sharpe stormie wynter, the new primetyde flourisheth. **1553** T. WILSON *Rhet.* 8 b, Beyng in their primetide and spryng of their age. **1593** BILSON *Govt. Christ's Ch.* 306 At the Prime tide of the Gospell.

prime-time. [f. PRIME *a.* + TIME, in senses 1, 2 prob. after F. *printemps*: cf. prec.]

†**1.** Springtime, spring. *Obs.*

1503 *Kalender of Sheph.* a iij, iiij. sayssons the qwych ar:.. Prymtym, sommer, autom, & wynter. *Ibid.* a iij b, The saysons..of the qwych ewyrych oon has iii. moneth. Prymtym as fewryer, mars, awryl. *c* **1516** [see PRIMEROLE]. *a* **1533** LD. BERNERS *Gold. Bk. M. Aurel.* xiv. (1534) G vij b, If a tree beareth not in Primetime his flowers, we hope not to haue the fruite in haruest ripe. *a* **1548** HALL *Chron.*, *Hen. VII* 4 b, In yᵉ pryme tyme of the yere he toke his iorney towardes Yorke. **1609** BIBLE (Douay) *Jer.* xxiv. 2 Good figges: as the figges of the prime time are wont to be.

†**2.** The early age (of the world, etc.). *Obs.*

1587 GOLDING *De Mornay* xxvi. (1592) 402 It befel in the primetime of the worlde.

3. *Broadcasting.* (Except in *attrib.* use usu. as **prime time.**) The time of day when an audience is expected to be at its largest; a peak listening- or viewing-period. Also *attrib.* and *absol.*, prime-time television. Also *transf.*

1964 *Variety* 2 Dec. 31/3 For the first time in years, WNBC-TV has copped the number one rating position in prime time, in the highly competitive N.Y. market. **1966** [see *E.S.T.* s.v. E. III]. **1971** *Daily Tel.* 13 Feb. 15/7 A 2p coin will buy three minutes time for local calls in prime time and six minutes at night and weekends. *Ibid.* 17 Apr. 19/3 The average [commercial local radio] station should aim to sell some 17,500 minutes of prime time in an average year at an average rate of £10 per minute. **1973** R. STOUT *Please pass Guilt* (1974) xiv. 143 That ad would have made a wonderful five-minute spot... She would have been glad to pay for prime time—say ten o'clock. **1976** *Billings* (Montana) *Gaz.* 18 June 12-D Jaclyn Smith is one of the gals who's huckstered in TV commercials a committee studied along with prime-time programs to determine the image given women on the small screen. **1977** *New Yorker* 10 Oct. 124/2 The Grand Central Racquet Club..charges the highest fee I know of for renting either of its two courts—forty-five dollars an hour in prime time. **1978** G. VIDAL

Kalki vii. 179 Wasn't Kalki blown to bits before our very eyes on prime-time?

‖**primeur** (primœr). [Fr., the quality or condition of being quite new; anything that is quite new; f. *prime* PRIME *a.* + *-eur*, -OUR.]

a. Anything new or early; *esp.* fruit before its ordinary season; an early piece of news; first-fruits, firstlings. (A word affected by newspaper writers.) **b.** New wine.

1885 W. L. MACGREGOR in *Pall Mall G.* 15 June 2 If I desire to send some flowers or primeurs in the shape of early asparagus or fruits to friends in Germany. **1897** *Daily News* 26 May 3/2 She had the *primeur* both of the Rand and of the 'women and children' letter—and both plums she allowed Mr. Chamberlain to share with 'The Times'. **1907** *Daily Chron.* 21 Aug. 4/7 Joy..over anything that is out of season, provided that it be before its time, a true primeur. **1913** E. WHARTON *Custom of Country* II. xii. 172 A bill burdened by Undine's reckless choice of *primeurs.* **1924** R. FRY *Let.* 2 July (1972) II. 555 They raise three crops a year of *primeurs.* **1937** W. FORTESCUE *Sunset House* vi. 118 She prides herself upon her *primeurs*, being a scientific gardener. **1950** *Vogue* Aug. 100/4 Intellectuals..spend a lot on:..Exotic food (but not *primeurs*). **1968** A. & G. SAINSBURY *France & her People* i. 19 In Brittany are places..with a mild climate which has made them famous for the production of *primeurs*, the early fruit and vegetables. **1973** *Times* 15 Dec. 11/3 A wine can be called 'Primeur' if it is offered for drinking before the date when the wines made in the normal way and bearing a vintage date are put on the market. **1975** *Harpers & Queen* May 34/2 Beaujolais is the success of the century,..even the new *primeur*..now brought over to be tasted at two months old. **1978** *Chicago* June 206/2 The Wassermans discuss the continuing tendency to produce Rhône reds—wines to be aged for as long as 30 years—in the *primeur* fashion.

primeval, primæval (praɪˈmiːvəl), *a.* (*sb.*) [f. L. *primæv-us* (see PRIMEVE) + -AL[1].] Of or pertaining to the first age of the world or of anything ancient; primitive.

a. [**1653** URQUHART *Rabelais* II. vi. 33 The primeval origin of my aves and ataves, was indigenarie of the Lemonick regions, where requiesceth the corpor of the hagiotat St. Martial.] **1775** DE LOLME *Eng. Const.* I. i. (1784) 25 The principle of primeval equality. **1830** LYELL *Princ. Geol.* (1875) I. I. viii. 140 A primeval state of the globe. **1847** LONGF. *Ev.* Prel. 1, This is the forest primeval.

β. **1662** H. MORE *Philos. Writ.* Pref. Gen. 24 It is very plain that the primæval Ages of the Church had no ill conceit of the opinion of the Soul's Præexistence. **1728** POPE *Dunc.* III. 338 With Night primæval, and with Chaos old. *Ibid.* IV. 630. **1868** FREEMAN *Norm Conq.* II. vii. 145 *note*, These two remarkable monuments of primæval times.

b. as *sb.* in *pl.* Primeval men.

a **1845** HOOD *Recipe for Civiliz.* 115 But, the naked truth is, stark primevals, That said their prayers to timber devils.

Hence **priˈmevalism, priˈmevalness**, the quality of being primeval; primitiveness; **priˈmevally** *adv.*, in the first age of the world; also, in a primeval manner or degree.

a **1711** KEN *Urania* Poet. Wks. 1721 IV. 475 Sweet Poetry ..From God primevally it streams. **1727** BAILEY vol. II, Primevalness. **1839** LADY LYTTON *Cheveley* iii, How gloriously, how primevally beautiful, is just this one favoured spot! **1899** F. R. STOCKTON *Associate Hermits* 22, I had visions of forests and wilds..and a general air of primevalism. **1971** D. CRYSTAL *Linguistics* ii. 49 What evidence there was about language-history..militated against acceptance of even the most basic assumptions used in the arguments about primevalness.

†**priˈmeve, priˈmæve**, *a. Obs.* [ad. L. *primæv-us* in the first period of life, f. *prīm-us* first (see PRIME *a.*) + *æv-um* age.] = PRIMEVAL *a.*

1626 W. FENNER *Hidden Manna* (1652) 77 A power of beleefe was included in their primæve innocency, as *minus in majori.* **1693** J. EDWARDS *Author. O. & N. Test.* 104 Footsteps of the old and primeve state of man.

†**priˈmevity, priˈmævity.** *Obs. rare.* [f. as prec. + -ITY; cf. L. *primævitās* youth.] The quality of being primeval; primitiveness.

1756 AMORY *Buncle* (1770) I. 38 My father..says we must ascribe primævity and sacred prerogatives to this language [Hebrew]. **1772** L. D. NELME *Ess. Lang.* Pref. 9 Without considering that simplicity as a proof of its primævity. **1786** GLASS in *Archæologia* (1787) VIII. 84 Argument in favour of the primævity of the Hebrew language.

†**priˈmevous, priˈmævous**, *a. Obs.* [f. as PRIMEVE + -OUS.] Primeval, primitive.

1656 BLOUNT *Glossogr.*, *Primevous*, the elder, or of the first age. **1658** PHILLIPS, *Primævous*, of a former age, elder. **1728** MORGAN *Algiers* I. i. 11 Those primevous Phœnicians, or Canaanites. **1875** H. MILLER *Test. Rocks* ix. 358 Sufferings to which they had been subjected in a primevous state.

Hence †**priˈmevousness.**

1727 in BAILEY vol. II.

ˈprim-gap. *Derbysh. Lead-mining.* [app. comb. of GAP *sb.*; first element uncertain.] See quot. 1851.

1653 MANLOVE *Lead Mines* 60 (E.D.S.) Perchance the Farmers may a Prim-gapp get. *Ibid.* 264 Starting of oar, Smilting, and driving drifts, Primgaps, Roof-works, Flat-works, Pipe-works, Shifts. **1747** HOOSON *Miner's Dict.* I ij b, All odd Yards of Ground under half a Mear intervening between them is the Lords, and we call it a Primgap. **1851** TAPPING *Gloss. to Manlove, Primgap*.., a portion of metalliferous rock less than half a meer, lying between different titles or different jurisdictions. By custom such portion belonged to the lord or farmer.

†**primicere.** *Obs. rare*[−1]. [ME. *prymycere*, a. obs. F. *premicere*, mod.F. *primicier*, *princier*), ad. late L. *prīmicēri-us* the first among those holding a similar office (lit. the first of those whose names are inscribed on the wax-coated tablets, f. *prīmus* first + *cēra* wax), in med.L. a precentor; also explained as 'the first candle-bearer before a bishop' (Du Cange).] Applied *fig.* to Lucifer, the morning star.

[**1398** TREVISA *Barth. De P.R.* XIX. lxi. (1495) 898 They that serue in chyrches of wexe candyls ben callyd *Ceroferarii*: as he that seruyth in halles of kynges and of bysshops ben callyd *Primecerii*.] ? *a* **1412** LYDG. *Two Merch.* 685 Eek Lucifer, at morowhil prymycere, By nyht hym hidith vndir our empeere.

†**ˈprimices**, *sb. pl. Obs.* Also 4 **prymysies, primyssis, primycies**, 6 **premities**, 7 **premices**. [a. OF. *pri-*, *premices* (12th c. in Littré, mod.F. *prémices*):—L. *prīmitiæ*, *-iciæ* first-fruits, f. *prīmus* first.] First-fruits.

c **1250** *Gen. & Ex.* 921 Abel primices first bi-gan. **1382** WYCLIF *Ezek.* xx. 40 There I shal seche ȝour prymysies [*gloss* or first fruytis]. **1382** —— *Rev.* xiv. 4 Primycies [*gl.* or firste fruytis] to God, and to the lomb. **1595** GOODWINE *Blanchardine* II. Ded., And as these (my Premities, patronized by you) shall seeme pleasing; so wil I alwaies be most readie..to offer it vp in all dutie at your shrine. **1603** HOLLAND *Plutarch's Mor.* 683 The primices and first gatherings of those herbs and roots. **1693** DRYDEN *Disc. Orig. & Prog. Satire* Ess. (ed. Ker) II. 54 Fruits offered to the gods at their festivals, as the *premices*, or first gatherings.

primidone (ˈprɪmɪdəʊn). *Pharm.* [f. P(Y)RIMID(INE + -DI)ONE.] A white, crystalline pyrimidine derivative, $C_{12}H_{14}N_2O_2$, which is an anticonvulsant used esp. to treat *grand mal* and psychomotor epilepsy. Cf. MYSOLINE.

1953 *Brit. Med. Jrnl.* 5 Sept. 540/1 The introduction of primidone ('mysoline'; 5-phenyl-5-ethylhexahydro-pyrimidine-4:6-dione) as an anticonvulsant drug some two years ago. **1958** [see MYSOLINE]. **1961** *Lancet* 9 Sept. 569/1 He was treated with primidone..and benzhexol hydrochloride..with striking reduction in the frequency of the seizures. *Ibid.* 569/2 He was discharged on primidone therapy. **1974** M. C. GERALD *Pharmacol.* xi. 214 Among the safest and most effective drugs are..primidone (Mysoline) and diphenylhydantoin for psychomotor seizures.

primier, obs. form of PREMIER.

†**ˈprimifeste.** *Obs. nonce-wd.* [ad. mod.L. *primifest-us* adj. (More), f. L. *prīm-us* first + *fest-um* a feast.] (See quot.)

1551 ROBINSON tr. *More's Utop.* II. (1895) 289 The whyche woordes maye be interpreted primifeste and finifest; or els, in our speache, first feast and last feast.

†**priˈmifluous**, *a. Obs. rare*[−1]. [f. L. type **prīmiflu-us* (f. *prīm-us* first + *flu-ĕre* to flow) + -OUS.] That flows first (after incision).

1657 TOMLINSON *Renou's Disp.* 377* Primifluous Rosine by negligent collection, contracts, and retains sand [etc.].

†**primigenal** (praɪˈmɪdʒɪnəl), *a. Nat. Hist. Obs.* [f. L. *prīmigen-us* (= *prīmigenius*: see PRIMIGENIAL) + -AL[1].] Belonging to or constituting the *regnum primigenum*, a kingdom of nature proposed to include the lowest or most primitive forms of animals and plants (corresponding to Wilson's *Primalia* or Haeckel's *Protista*).

1860 J. HOGG in *Edinb. New Phil. Jrnl.* XII. 223, I here suggest a fourth or an additional kingdom, under the title of the Primigenal kingdom. *Ibid.*, The Primigenal kingdom might be placed either the fourth and last, or between the vegetable and the animal kingdoms.

primigene (ˈpraɪmɪdʒiːn), *a. rare.* [ad. L. *prīmigen-us*, *prīmigenius*: see next.] = next.

1623 COCKERAM, *Primigene*, that commeth naturally of itself, with-out father or mother. **1661** EVELYN *Fumifugium* Misc. Writ. (1809) 215 The benefit which we derive from it [the air]..for the use of the spirits and primigene humours. **1884** *Athenæum* 13 Sept. 343/2 Bones of the primigene ox, arrow-heads, and other flint implements.

primigenial (praɪmɪˈdʒiːnɪəl), *a.* Now *rare.* Also *erron.* **primogenial, -geneal.** [f. L. *prīmigeni-us*, also *prīmigen-us* first of its kind, original (f. *prīmi-*, comb. form of *prīm-us* first + *genus* kind, or *gen-*, stem of *gignĕre* to beget, produce) + -AL[1]. Often erroneously spelt *primogenial* (*-geneal*), by confusion with derivatives of L. *primo genitus*.]

†**1.** First generated or produced; earliest formed; belonging to the earliest stage of existence of anything; original, primitive, primary. *Obs.*

1602 FULBECKE *2nd Pt. Parall.* 1, I am verie desirous..to know the first and primigeniall existence of Tythes. **1662** J. CHANDLER *Van Helmont's Oriat.* 48, I call these two Elements Primigeniall, or first-born, in respect of the Earth. **1707** FLOYER *Physic. Pulse-Watch* 343 The two Causes of the Pulse, the Spirits from the primigenial Heat, or the Spirits of the radical Moisture.

β. **1627** HAKEWILL *Apol.* I. i. 5 The radicall moisture, and primogeniall heat naturally ingrafted in us wastes alwayes by degrees. **1680** BOYLE *Scept. Chem.* II. 162 It will follow that Salt and Sulphur are not Primogeneal Bodies. **1753** JOHNSON *Adventurer* No. 95 ¶ 13 It has been discovered by Sir Isaac Newton, that the distinct and primogenial colours are only seven. **1822** T. TAYLOR *Apuleius* 264 The primogenial Phrygians call me [Cybele] Pessinuntica.

2. *Zool.* Applied to species belonging to a primitive type (rendering the specific name *primigenius*, as in *Bos primigenius*, *Elephas primigenius*).

1868 OWEN *Vertebr. Anim.* III. xxxv. 618 This is seen in the Musk-bubale, and was the case with the primigenial Elephant and Rhinoceros.

β. **1851** D. WILSON *Preh. Ann.* (1863) II. III. vi. 153 The Primogenial or slender-legged horses. **1867** W. T. THORNTON in *Fortn. Rev.* Nov. 593 Neither could Cain do the like with respect to a primogenial zebra which his father fancied as much as himself.

Hence †**primiˈgenialness.**

1731 BAILEY vol. II, Primigenialness, Primigeniousness.

primiˈgenian, *a. rare.* Also 7 *erron.* **primo-**. [f. as prec. + -AN.] = prec.

1650 ASHMOLE *Chym. Collect.* 55 Even as the heat of Animals [is hidden] in the Primogenian moisture. **1847** WHEWELL *Hist. Induct. Sc.* (ed. 2) III. 694 The primigenian elephant or mammoth.

†**primigenie**, *a. Obs. rare.* [ad. L. *prīmigeni-us* (see above); or error for *primigene*.] = prec.

1615 CROOKE *Body of Man* 199 The exhaustion or expence of the Primigenie moysture by the Elementary heat.

†**primigenious** (praɪmɪˈdʒiːnɪəs), *a. Obs.* Also *erron.* **primogenious, -eous.** [f. L. *prīmigeni-us* (see PRIMIGENIAL) + -OUS. Often erroneously *primogenious* (*-eous*): see above.] = PRIMIGENIAL.

1620 BP. HALL *Hon. Mar. Clergy* I. xxv. 134 The Primigenious [*Wks.* 1628 primogenious] Antiquitie (which proceeded from the ancient of Dayes). *a* **1646** J. GREGORY *Assyrian Mon.* Posthuma (1650) 211 The greatest Alchimist in Historie can scarce extract one dram of the pure and primigenious metal. **1693** J. BEAUMONT *On Burnet's Th. Earth* I. 68 In the primigenious Mass the Earth must have held the lower place.

β. **1628** [see 1620 above]. **1634** T. JOHNSON tr. *Parey's Chirurg.* (1678) IX. ix. 221 The inbred and primogenious humidity of the Nerves is wasted. **1712** *H. More's Antid. Ath.* II. ix. §10 *Schol.* 157 This he determines primogenious moisture. **1765** *Museum Rust.* IV. ii. 7 In poor lands it opposes the most active primogeneous agents. **1799** *Trans. Soc. Arts* XVII. 268 Allow me to call the first tree primogeneous or stock.

Hence **primiˈgeniousness.**

1727 BAILEY vol. II, *Primigeniousness*, originalness, the being the first of the kind.

†**priˈmigenous**, *a. Obs. rare.* [f. L. *prīmigen-us*, PRIMIGENAL + -OUS: cf. *indigenous*.] = prec.

1677 GALE *Crt. Gentiles* II. IV. 166 This Discourse reteining the vestigia of the primigenous Truth.

‖**primigravida** (praɪmɪˈgrævɪdə). Pl. **-æ**. [mod.L., prop. fem. adj., f. *prīm-us* first + *gravidus* GRAVID; after PRIMIPARA.] (See quot. 1890.)

1890 BILLINGS *Med. Dict.*, *Primigravida*, one pregnant for the first time. **1899** *Allbutt's Syst. Med.* VII. 818 The disease affects chiefly primigravidæ.

priminary, obs. and dial. form of PRÆMUNIRE.

primine (ˈpraɪmɪn). *Bot.* [= F. *primine* (Mirbel 1828), f. L. *prīm-us* first + -INE[1].] The first of the two coats or integuments of an ovule; i.e. **a.** (originally), the outer one; but subsequently **b.** applied to the inner, as being formed first. Opp. to *secundine*.

a. 1832 *Encycl. Brit.* (ed. 7) V. 52 *note*, The extensible side of the secundine, and even of the tercine or nucleus, soon ceases to increase with the corresponding side of the primine. **1835** LINDLEY *Introd. Bot.* (1848) I. 395 The outermost of the sacs is called the primine. **1858** MAYNE *Expos. Lex.*, *Primina, Bot.*, name given by Mirbel to the more exterior of the two membranes which envelope the nucleus of the ovule when the latter has assumed a certain degree of increase: the primine.

b. 1875 BENNETT & DYER *Sachs' Bot.* 501 When there are two or three integuments, the innermost (the *Primine*..) is always formed first, then the outer one (the *Secundine*), and finally..the Aril. **1875** HUXLEY & MARTIN *Elem. Biol.* (1883) 83 Its two coats, an inner (*primine*) and outer (*secundine*). **1885** GOODALE *Physiol. Bot.* (1892) 178 The integuments of the seed answer morphologically to the primine and secundine of the ovule.

priming (ˈpraɪmɪŋ), *vbl. sb.*[1] [f. PRIME *v.*[1] + -ING[1].] The action of PRIME *v.*[1]

[In the following quot., the sense is, from the date, uncertain (? 3):

1427–8 *Rec. St. Mary at Hill* 67 Also for primyng of þe haly water stop, viij[d].]

1. The putting of gunpowder in the pan of an old-fashioned fire-arm.

1598, etc. [see *priming-iron*, etc. in 10]. **1655** MRQ. WORCESTER *Cent. Inv.* §58 To make a Pistol discharge a dozen times with one loading, and without so much as once new Priming requisite. **1816** *Sporting Mag.* XLVIII. 174 Any of the compounds or matters to be used in priming. **1851** LAYARD *Pop. Acc. Discov. Nineveh* ix. 238 This..led to the drawing of sabres and priming of matchlocks.

2. a. *concr.* The gunpowder which was placed in the pan of a fire-arm and to which the match or spark was applied; also, the train of powder connecting a fuse with a charge in blasting, etc.

1625, etc. [see *priming-horn*, etc. in 10]. **1781** THOMPSON in *Phil. Trans.* LXXI. 260 The sailors bruise the priming after they have put it to their guns, as they find it very difficult, without this precaution, to fire them off with a match. **1799** G. SMITH *Laboratory* I. 19 Make a little receptacle for the priming. **1870** LOWELL *Study Wind.* 143 The man who pronounced the Nibelungen Lied not worth a pinch of priming.

b. *fig.* (in quot. applied to liquor).

1833 MARRYAT *P. Simple* xxxv, 'Well, Mr. Simple, so I will; but I require a little priming, or I shall never go off.' 'Will you have your glass of grog before or after?' 'Before, by all means.'

3. The preparing of (a surface) for painting, by coating it with a body colour, etc. Also *transf.*

1609 [see *priming colour* in 10]. **1676** C. HATTON in *H. Corr.* (Camden) 139 Yᵉ priming of yᵉ cloath is very good. **1796** MORSE *Amer. Geog.* I. 410 Ruddle, or a red earth.. used as a ground colour for priming, instead of Spanish brown. **1825** J. NICHOLSON *Operat. Mechanic* 641 There can be no better mode adopted for priming, or laying on the first coat on stucco. **1847** SMEATON *Builder's Man.* 97 Priming has also the advantage of preventing the knots from being seen through the paint.

4. *concr.* **a.** The substance or mixture used by painters for the preparatory coat. **b.** A coat or layer of the substance. Also *fig.*

1625 *Nomenclator Navalis* s.v. *Pryming* (Harl. MS. 2301) The first grounde or cullor wᶜʰ is laid on for others to rome over it in Painting the Shippe is called Priming. **1661** FELTHAM *Resolves* II. lix. (ed. 8) 310 Prayer..t'is the priming of the Soul, that laying us in the Oyl of Grace preserves us from the Worm and Wether. **1741** *Compl. Fam.-Piece* III. 524 Grind your Red-Lead with Linseed Oil, and use it very thin for the first Colouring or Priming. **1825** J. NICHOLSON *Operat. Mechanic* 722 When the priming is quite dry, a thin coat of gold-size must be laid on. **1873** E. SPON *Workshop Receipts* Ser. I. 76/1 The priming or undercoat makes a saving in the quantity of varnish used.

5. (See quot. 1896.)

1896 *Westm. Gaz.* 16 Mar. 3/2 The use of 'priming'—which is a preparation of sugar, added after brewing, to give the beer 'body' and make it more palatable. *Ibid.*, In addition to permitting 'priming' we have specially allowed the use of adjuncts for the preparation of water for brewing purposes, and for fining and colouring the beer.

6. *fig.* The hasty and imperfect imparting of knowledge; cramming.

1859 G. MEREDITH *R. Feverel* xxvii, Tom also received his priming. **1894** E. C. SELWYN in *Westm. Gaz.* 23 July 2/3 He was primed for the occasion, and such priming deserves the name of pot-hunting.

7. *Engineering.* (See PRIME *v.*¹ 6.)

1841 *Civil Eng. & Arch. Jrnl.* IV. 15/2 The total loss both by the safety-valve and by priming. **1869** E. A. PARKES *Pract. Hygiene* (ed. 3) 24 Salt water is sometimes mixed with it [distilled water] from the priming of the boilers. **1901** *Feilden's Mag.* IV. 413/1 The first point to aim at is to have the steam and any water of priming or condensation flowing in the same direction.

8. In the sense of PRIME *v.*¹ 4. Cf. PUMP PRIMING *vbl. sb.*

1888 *Lockwood's Dict. Mech. Engin.* 266 *Priming*,..(2) the priming of a force pump is the expulsion of the air from the water space, in order that the water shall enter into the partial vacuum thus produced... (3) The fetching of a lift pump by pouring liquid into the bucket in order to produce sufficient vacuum to enable it to draw. **1928** A. L. DYKE *Aircraft Engine Instructor* 217 The idling system also contains an air bleed which serves the..purpose of.. contributing to the operation of the priming device. **1931** M. M. FARLEIGH *Princ. & Probl. Aircraft Engines* x. 166 When..continued priming of the cylinders fails to bring about any combustion, the ignition should be checked carefully both for quality of spark and the time of its occurrence. **1969** W. T. INGRAM et al. *Gloss. Water & Wastewater Control Engin.* 247 *Priming*,..the action of starting the flow in a pump or siphon.

9. *Biol.* and *Med.* (See PRIME *v.*¹ 7.)

1943 *Jrnl. Endocrinol.* III. 270 Pituitary extracts were administered by a series of subcutaneous injections for the purpose of stimulating the follicles ('priming'). **1963** *Recent Progress Hormone Res.* XIX. 673 New external stimuli following the priming are required to release the altered behavior patterns. **1967** *Science* 17 Nov. 939/2 Acoustic priming appears to be ineffective before the age of 14 days, corresponding to the normal onset of hearing in mice. **1975** *Behavior Genetics* V. 324 This failure of the 17-day-old albino mice to exhibit as great a change in seizure severity as a result of acoustic priming might have been due to their innately elevated auditory thresholds. **1978** *Nature* 5 Jan. 10/1 Production of interferon can also be modulated in other ways; pretreatment of cells with small amounts of homologous interferon before addition of an interferon inducer often increases the yield, a phenomenon termed 'priming'.

10. *attrib.* and *Comb.*, as *priming colour*, *position*; **priming-box**, a box carried at the waist containing priming for cannon, etc.; **priming-hole**, the touch-hole of a gun or the vent in blasting; **priming-horn**, (*a*) a horn containing priming-powder formerly carried by gunners; (*b*) the powder-horn carried by miners and quarry-men; **priming-iron** = *priming wire*; **priming-machine**, a machine for putting the priming in cartridge-shells or percussion-caps; **priming-pan**, a small plate in a match-lock or flint-lock gun, for holding the priming; = PAN *sb.*¹ 4 b; **priming-powder**, = sense 2; detonating or fulminating powder; **priming pump** *Aeronaut.*, a small pump in an aircraft for priming its engine; **priming-tube**, a tube containing fulminating powder or some inflammable composition for firing the charge of a cannon; **priming-valve**, a valve connected with a steam cylinder, to allow water carried over by priming to escape; **priming-wire**, a sharp pointed wire used in gunnery and blasting to ascertain whether the touch-hole or vent is free and to pierce the cartridge.

1829 MARRYAT *F. Mildmay* iii, The captains of guns, with their *priming-boxes buckled round their waists. **1609** B. JONSON *Silent Wom.* II. vi, One o' their faces has not the *priming color laid on yet, nor the other her smocke sleek'd. **1665** *Phil. Trans.* I. 84 The round side, where the *Priming-hole is, being uppermost. **1838** *Civil Eng. & Arch. Jrnl.* I. 292/1 If the firing did not succeed, a fresh priming-hole was bored in the tamping. **1625** *Nomenclator Navalis* s.v. *Pryming* (Harl. MS. 2301) The Gunner hath it [powder] in a greate horne at his girdle in fighte wᶜʰ horne he calls his *priming horne. **1759** [W. WINDHAM] *Plan Discipl. Norfolk Militia* Introd. 9 They had..a priming horn hanging by their side. **1598** BARRET *Theor. Warres* III. i. 34 To be prouided of a *priming iron or wyer. **1622** F. MARKHAM *Bk. War* I. ix. 34 His priming-yron, being a small artificiall wiar, with which he shall clense and keepe open the touch-hole of his peece. **1769** FALCONER *Dict. Marine* (1789), *Dégorgeoir*, the bit or priming-iron of a cannon. **1650** R. STAPYLTON *Strada's Low C. Warres* IX. 56 With the flash firing the *priming pans of the muskets that lay on heaps. **1833** *Regul. Instr. Cavalry* I. 103 Place the carbine in the *priming position. **1613** FLETCHER, etc. *Captain* IV. iii, Now could I grind him into *priming powder. **1869** BOUTELL *Arms & Arm.* (1874) 246 By this contrivance fire is conveyed to the priming-powder by a gun-cock, which holds in its grasp the flint. **1932** R. MAHACHEK *Airplane Pilot's Man.* vi. 49 On large engines the choke is replaced by a *priming pump which injects fuel directly into the intake system. **1942** D. M. CROOK *Spitfire Pilot* 79, I..gave the priming pump a couple of strokes, and pressed the starter button. **1598** *Priming wyer [see *priming iron*]. **1709** *Conn. Col. Rec.* (1890) XV. 565 With a good fire lock, a cartouch box, priming-wire and horn, worm, 3 flints. *c* **1860** H. STUART *Seaman's Catech.* 4 What is the use of a priming wire? To ascertain if the vent is clear, and the cartridge home.

priming ('praɪmɪŋ), *vbl. sb.*² [f. PRIME *v.*² 3 + -ING¹.] ***priming of the tides***: the acceleration of the tides, or shortening of the interval between corresponding states of the tide, taking place from the neap to the spring tides; opposed to *lagging*.

1833 HERSCHEL *Astron.* xi. 337 Another effect of the combination of the solar and lunar tides is what is called the priming and lagging of the tides. **1867** DENISON *Astron. without Math.* 122 The tide of any place is not regularly 49 minutes later every day, as if it obeyed the moon solely, but sometimes..an hour later and sometimes only 38 minutes. This is called the priming and lagging of the tides.

priming ('praɪmɪŋ), *vbl. sb.*³ *U.S.* [f. PRIME *v.*³ + -ING¹.] The action of removing the lowest leaves, or other layers of leaves, from a tobacco plant; also, the leaves removed.

1899 M. L. FLOYD *Cultivation of Cigar-Leaf Tobacco* 14 The first priming, which means the first four leaves taken from the stalk, also the last priming, which means the last four or six leaves taken from the top of the stalk, are kept separate. **1904** E. GLASGOW *Deliverance* 166 The very primings ought to be as good as some top leaves. **1938** *Daily Progress* (Charlottesville, Va.) 21 Oct. 5/1 Following the change from 'stalk cutting' to 'priming' (cutting of separate leaves for curing in bundles), less heat was required.

priming ('praɪmɪŋ), *ppl. a. Biol.* and *Med.* [f. PRIME *v.*¹ + -ING².] That primes (see PRIME *v.*¹ 7).

1930 *Amer. Jrnl. Physiol.* XCII. 129 The first test consisted of 'priming' injections of two rat units of purified extract into all animals. **1940** *Anat. Rec.* LXXVII. 1 Four to 6 month old rabbit does of medium-sized strains were injected subcutaneously..with a priming dose of the gonadotropic material. **1975** *Behavior Genetics* V. 324, 24 hr after the priming exposure the pigmented mice show an identically large increase in audiogenic seizures, whereas the albino mice have a lesser increase.

‖**primipara** (praɪ'mɪpərə). [L., f. *prīm-us* first + *-parus*, from *parĕre* to bring forth.] A female that brings forth for the first time.

1842 DUNGLISON *Med. Lex.*, *Primipara*..a name given to females who bring forth for the first time. **1880** *Med. Temp. Jrnl.* July 152, I was called..by a midwife to Mrs. T. aged 28, primipara.

Hence **primiparous** (praɪ'mɪpərəs) *a.*, bearing a child (or young) for the first time; **primiparity** (praɪmɪ'pærɪtɪ), the condition of being primiparous.

1857 BULLOCK *Cazeaux' Midwif.* 128 This line may generally be regarded, especially in a primiparous female, as a certain sign of pregnancy. **1860** TANNER *Pregnancy* ix. 320 Multipara..are probably more liable to attacks of insanity during pregnancy, than primiparous young females. **1890** *Cent. Dict.*, Primiparity. **1895** in *Syd. Soc. Lex.*

primipilar (praɪmɪ'paɪlə(r)), *a. Rom. Antiq.* [ad. L. *prīmipīlār-is* adj. and sb., f. *prīmipīl-us*: see PRIMIPILE.] Belonging to, or that is, a *primipilus* or primipile.

1600 HOLLAND *Livy* VII. xiii. 257 This Tullius now had been seuen times alreadie a primipilar or principall Centurion. *a* **1677** BARROW *Pope's Suprem.* I. III. v. Wks. 1831 VII. 150 A primacy of order; such a one..as the primipilar centurion had in the legion. **1782** ELPHINSTON tr. *Martial* I. xxxi. 39 Soon as the brave centurion shall attain The primipilar honours. **1891** FARRAR *Darkness & Dawn* xl. (1893) 339 He had risen to the rank of a primipilar centurion.

So †**primi'pilary** *a. Obs. rare*⁻¹, 'first-class'.

a **1693** *Urquhart's Rabelais* III. xxxviii. 316 Primipilary [Fr. *primipile*] fool.

primipile ('praɪmɪpaɪl). Also in L. form **-pilus**. [= F. *primipile*, ad. L. *prīmipīlus* the chief centurion of the *triarii* or third rank in a legion, for *prīmī pīlī centurio* centurion of the *primus pīlus* (*prīmus* first, *pīlus* a body of pikemen, f. *pīlum* a pike, javelin).] In *Rom. Antiq.*, The first centurion of the first maniple of the *triarii* in a legion. Also *fig.*

[**1600** HOLLAND *Livy* VIII. viii. 287 Two *Primipili* or chiefe Centurions there were amongst the Triarij in the one armie & the other.] **1856** MERIVALE *Rom. Emp.* (1865) V. xlii. 161 All its officers, from the imperator to the centurion and primipile. **1898** *Daily News* 14 Feb. 6/5 Mr. William O'Brien, a primipilus in the Parnell movement.

pri'mipotent, *a. rare.* [ad. L. *primipotens, -potentem*, f. *prīmus* first + *potens* powerful.] 'Of chief power' (Blount *Glossogr.* 1656).

primite ('praɪmaɪt). *Zool.* [f. L. *prīm-us* first (see PRIME *a.*) + -ITE¹ 3.] The first member of a catenated series of gregarines.

1898 SEDGWICK *Text Bk. Zool.* I. 57 The anterior individual of an association is called the *primite*, the rest the *satellites*. **1901** G. N. CALKINS *Protozoa* v. 156 Catenoid colonies, where the protomerite of one [individual] (*satellite*) becomes attached to the deutomerite of another (*primite*).

‖**primitiæ** (praɪ'mɪʃiː), *sb. pl.* [L. *prīmitiæ*, *-ciæ* the first things of their kind, firstlings, first-fruits, f. *prīm-us* first: cf. PRIMICES.]

1. First fruits or produce; *spec.* = ANNATES 1.

1591 SPENSER *M. Hubberd* 518 The Courtier needes must recompenced bee With a Benevolence, or have in gage The Primitias of your Parsonage. **1657** THORNLEY tr. *Longus' Daphnis & Chloe* 92 They offerd too the *Primitiæ*, or the first carvings of the flesh. **1672** *Cowell's Interpr.*, *Primitiæ*, First-Fruits..in our Law, are the profits after avoidance of every spiritual Living for one year.

2. *Obstetrics.* (See quot.)

1858 MAYNE *Expos. Lex.*, *Primitiæ*. **1895** *Syd. Soc. Lex.*, *Primitiæ*...term applied to the *amniotic fluid*, whose discharge precedes the expulsion of the fœtus.

primitial (praɪ'mɪʃəl), *a.* Now *rare.* Also 7 erron. **-ætiall**. [= obs. F. *primicial* (Cotgr.), ad. med.L. *prīmitiāl-is* (Du Cange): see prec. and -AL¹.]

1. Of, pertaining to, or of the nature of, first-fruits.

1645 HARWOOD *Loyal Subj. Retiring-room* Ep. Ded., So doe they now most gratefully present their Primætiall offering. **1658** J. ROBINSON *Endoxa* Pref. 1 He that hath not had a primitiall tast and prelibation of them here below.

2. *loosely.* First, primitive, original.

1736 AINSWORTH, Primitial, *primitius*. **1814** SOUTHEY *Roderick* XVIII. 346 Thou Covadonga with the tainted stream Of Deva, and this now rejoicing vale, Soon its primitial triumphs wilt behold! **1839** BAILEY *Festus* xix. (1852) 290 But ah! from that primitial world to this, From Eden to Chaldæa, what a change.

†'**primitist**. *nonce-wd. Obs.* [contr. for *primitivist*, f. next + -IST.] An advocate or adherent of primitive practices or beliefs.

1818 R. P. KNIGHT *Symbol. Lang.* §92. 69 The Persians.. were the primitists, or puritans of Heathenism.

primitive ('prɪmɪtɪv), *a.* and *sb.* Forms: α. 5 primitif, prymytiff, 6 primityve, (premetive), 6– primitive. β. (5 premative, 6 -yve), 6 primatife, -yve, prymatyfe, -ive, 5–7 primative. [ME. *primitif*, a. F. *primitif* (14th c. in Hatz.-Darm.), ad. L. *prīmitīv-us* first or earliest of its kind, f. *prīmus* first, PRIME *a.*: cf. PRIMITIÆ. The β-forms were app. influenced by PRIMATE *sb.*]

A. *adj.* **I.** General senses.

1. a. Of or belonging to the first age, period, or stage; pertaining to early times; earliest, original; early, ancient. ***Primitive Church***, the Christian Church in its earliest and (by implication) purest times.

α. **1526** *Pilgr. Perf.* (W. de W. 1531) 27 No religyon is founded hytherto, yᵗ so nere representeth yᵉ primityue chirche of Chryst. *c* **1540** tr. *Pol. Verg. Eng. Hist.* (Camden) I. IV. 178 Which good primitive successe purchased him muche quietnes. **1548–9** (Mar.) *Bk. Com. Prayer, Commination*, In the prymitiue churche there was a godlye disciplyne, that at the begynnyng of lente suche persones as were notorious synners were put to open penaunce. **1581** J. HAMILTON *Cath. Traictise* in *Cath. Tractates* (S.T.S.) 76 According to the ancient estait of the premetiue kirk. **1603** HOLLAND *Plutarch's Mor.* 671 The primitive generation came first and immediatly from the earth, but afterwards.. they breed their yoong. **1669** FLAMSTEED in Rigaud *Corr. Sci. Men* (1841) II. 77 That illustrious body [the Royal Society], of which you have stood a primitive member. **1795** BURKE *Corr.* (1844) IV. 285, I wish very much to see..an image of a primitive Christian Church. **1858** LONGF. *M. Standish* IX. 89 Like a picture it seemed of the primitive, pastoral ages, Fresh with the youth of the world, and recalling Rebecca and Isaac. *a* **1878** SIR G. G. SCOTT *Lect. Archit.* (1879) I. 5 The great valleys of Egypt and Mesopotamia..were the cradles of primitive art.

β. **1486** *Hen. VII at York* in *Surtees Misc.* (1888) 54 This rigalitie, Whos primative patrone I peyre to your presence, Ebrauk of Britane. **1534** MORE *Treat. Passion* Wks. 1346/2 It was knowen..unto the primatiue churche or congregacion of chrysten people. **1589** COOPER *Admon.* 217

The practise of the primatiue Church. **1630** PRYNNE *Anti-Armin.* 119 Adam in his primatiue estate.

b. Applied to behaviour or mental processes that apparently originate in unconscious needs or desires and have not been affected by objective logical reasoning.

1910 *Amer. Jrnl. Psychol.* XXI. 115 The following investigation of children's spontaneous constructions and primitive activities is made in the hope..that a clearer, saner insight into the child's nature and needs may follow. **1919** M. K. BRADBY *Psycho-Anal.* iii. 28 The mind is unevenly developed, and what is relatively primitive co-exists with what is advanced without completely harmonising with it. **1923** L. A. CLARE tr. *Lévy-Bruhl's Primitive Mentality* 32 If then, primitive mentality avoids and ignores logical thought, if it refrains from reasoning and reflecting, it is not from incapacity to surmount what is evident to sense. **1924** *Brit. Jrnl. Med. Psychol.* IV. 32 Synthetic or intuitional conceptions of the unconscious, based on analogies with primitive notions and behaviour. **1962** M. GABAIN tr. *Piaget's Moral Judgment of Child* ii. 189 It is not nearly so natural as one would think for primitive thought to take intentions into account.

2. a. Having the quality or style of that which is early or ancient. In first quot. = Conformed to the pattern of the early church (see 1 a). Also, Simple, rude, or rough like that of early times; old-fashioned. (With implication of either commendation or the reverse.)

1685 EVELYN *Diary* 2 Oct., The Church of England..is certainely, of all the Christian professions on the earth, the most primitive, apostolical and excellent. *Ibid.* 26 Oct., A maiden of primitive life,..who..has for many years refus'd marriage, or to receive any assistance from the parish. **1752** H. WALPOLE *Lett.* (1846) II. 459 A poor good primitive creature. **1822** W. IRVING *Braceb. Hall* iii, Her manners are simple and primitive. **1838** LYTTON *Alice* II. ii, At her very primitive wardrobe. **1889** G. FINDLAY *Eng. Railway* 9 The engines employed [in 1830] were of an extremely primitive character.

Comb. **1847** HOOK *Eccl. Biog.* III. 546 (*Chad*) Struck by the worth of this primitive-mannered christian. **1865** *Cornh. Mag.* July 40 To..hear such primitive-sounding words as ..'overtune' for the burden of a song.

b. *Anthrop.* That relates to a group, or to persons comprising such groups, whose culture, through isolation, has remained at a simple level of social and economic organization.

[**1781** GIBBON *Decl. & F.* III. xxxviii. 638 From this abject condition, perhaps the primitive and universal state of man.] **1903** C. S. MYERS in *Rep. Cambr. Anthropol. Exped. Torres Straits* II. II. 143 Stories which travellers relate about the remarkable capacity possessed by primitive peoples for distinguishing faint sounds amid familiar surroundings, cannot be accepted as evidence of an unusually acute hearing. **1920** R. H. LOWIE *Primitive Society* (1921) i. 12 The knowledge of primitive society has an educational value that should recommend its study. **1938** R. BUNZEL in F. Boas *Gen. Anthropol.* 333 There are.. certain primitive societies where the accumulation of wealth is considered undesirable. **1954** R. FIRTH in *Inst. Primitive Society* ii. 15 As I (and I think most of my colleagues) use it, 'primitive' is little more than a technological index—a shorthand term for a type of economic life in which the tool system and level of material achievement is fairly simple: little use of metals; no complex mechanical apparatus; no indigenous system of writing. **1963** *Brit. Jrnl. Sociol.* XIV. 21 Many books by social anthropologists have titles which include the word *primitive*. When we use this word..we refer to a low level of technology which limits social relationships to a narrow range. **1976** J. FRIEDL *Cultural Anthropol.* viii. 316 The primitive economy is one that is controlled exclusively by the local community.

3. Original as opposed to derivative; primary as opposed to secondary; *esp.* said of that from which something else is derived; radical. (Cf. PRIMARY *a.* 3 a.)

c **1400** *Lanfranc's Cirurg.* 65 (Add. MS.) þere beþ oþere causes þat beþ clepyd causes prymytiff. **1543** TRAHERON *Vigo's Chirurg.* 26/2 It commeth of the cause primitiue thoroughe brusynge or breakyng. **1581** MULCASTER (*title*) Positions wherin those Primitive Circumstances be Examined, which are Necessarie for the Training vp of Children. *a* **1628** PRESTON *New Covt.* (1634) 27 God is the primitive, he is the originall, he is the first, the universal cause. **1678** CUDWORTH *Intell. Syst.* 854 Life and Understanding, Soul and Mind are to them, no Simple and Primitive Natures, but Secondary and Derivative. **1812** BRACKENRIDGE *Views Louisiana* (1814) 38 This valley is confined by what may be termed, as distinguished from the alluvions, primitive ground. **1846** GROTE *Greece* I. xv. (1862) I. 238 The primitive ancestor of the Trojan line of kings is Dardanus.

II. Special and technical senses.

4. a. *Gram.* and *Philol.* Of a word or language: Original, radical: opposed, or correlative to *derivative*.

1530 PALSGR. Introd. 29 Of pronownes there be thre chefe sortes, primityves, derivatyves, and demonstratyves. *Ibid.*, Pronownes primityves be fyve, *je, tu, se, nous, vous.* **1612** BRINSLEY *Lud. Lit.* viii. (1627) 123 The primitiue word whereof they come, or some words neere vnto them. **1687** A. LOVELL tr. *Thevenot's Trav.* I. 36 The Turkish Language is a primitive and original Language, that's to say, not derived from any of the Oriental or Occidental Tongues that we have any knowledge of. **1706** PHILLIPS s.v., Primitive Word (in Grammar) an original Word, from which others of the kind are derived. **1824** L. MURRAY *Eng. Gram.* (ed. 5) I. iii. 55 A primitive word is that which cannot be reduced to any simpler word in the language: as, man, good, content. **1856** R. A. VAUGHAN *Mystics* (1860) I. 18 To have a distinction in the primitive and not in the derivative word is always confusing.

b. *Philol.* Applied to a parent language at an early, unrecorded, or reconstructed stage of its development into a group of dialects or languages.

1878 T. L. K. OLIPHANT *Old & Middle Eng.* i. 13 The Primitive Aryan *katvar* changes to the Gothic *fidwor* (our *four*). **1895** KELLNER & BRADLEY *Morris's Hist. Outl. Eng. Accidence* (rev. ed.) iii. 30 The Teutonic languages differ much more from Primitive Aryan in the consonants than in the vowels. **1898** Primitive Germanic [used s.v. GERMANIC *a.* 2]. **1914** H. C. WYLD *Short Hist. Eng.* ii. 32 Parent, or Primitive Germanic, was divided into three great branches. **1920** *Trans. Philol. Soc. 1916–20* 129 (*heading*) Primitive Slavonic. **1933** L. BLOOMFIELD *Language* i. 13 If a language is spoken over a large area,..the result will be a set of related languages... We infer that..the Germanic (or the Slavic or the Celtic)..have arisen in the same way; it is only an accident of history that for these groups we have no written records of the language, as it was spoken before the differentiation set in. To these unrecorded parent languages we give names like *Primitive Germanic* (*Primitive Slavic, Primitive Celtic*, and so on). [*Note*] The word *primitive* is here poorly chosen, since it is intended to mean only that we happen to have no written records of the language. German scholars have a better device in their prefix *ur-* 'primeval'. **1972** M. L. SAMUELS *Linguistic Evol.* 2. The alternation corresponding to *stand-stood* was regular in the Indo-European system, and so with that corresponding to *seek-sought* in Primitive Germanic.

5. a. *Math.*, etc. Applied to a line or figure from which some construction or reckoning begins; or to a curve, surface, magnitude, equation, operation, etc., from which another is in some way derived, or which is not itself derived from another.

primitive circle or ***plane***, the circle or plane upon which projection is made. ***primitive radii***, in geared wheels, = PROPORTIONAL *radii*.

1690 LEYBOURN *Curs. Math.* 668 b, The Meridian passing through L is the Primitive Circle. **1727–41** CHAMBERS *Cycl.* s.v. *Number*, *Primitive* or *prime Number*, is that which is only divisible by unity. **1831** BREWSTER *Optics* xxi. 185 The plane *R r s*, or the plane in which the light is polarised, is called the plane of primitive polarisation. **1864** WEBSTER s.v., *Primitive axes of co-ordinates*, that system of axes to which the points of a magnitude are first referred with reference to a second set or system, to which they are afterward referred. **1878** GURNEY *Crystallogr.* 34 The great circle is called the primitive. **1895** STORY-MASKELYNE *Crystallogr.* ii. 25 The plane of projection thus bounded by a great circle of the sphere is represented by the plane of the paper on which the circle is drawn, which latter will be termed the circle of projection or primitive circle.

b. *Cryst.* Applied to a fundamental crystalline form from which all the other forms may be derived by geometrical processes; the form obtained by cleaving the crystal, inferred to be that of the nucleus from which the crystal grew. ***primitive cell***, the smallest unit cell of any particular lattice, having lattice points at each of its eight corners only; ***primitive lattice***, a lattice generated by the repeated translation of a primitive cell.

1805–17 R. JAMESON *Char. Min.* (ed. 3) 136 This new regular form is by Hauy named the Primitive nucleus; and the crystal whose form is the same the Primitive form. **1807** T. THOMSON *Chem.* (ed. 3) II. 536 The primitive form of muriate of barytes is, according to Hauy, a four-sided prism, whose bases are squares. **1831** BREWSTER *Optics* xxv. 214 This mineral,..called cubizite, has been regarded by mineralogists as having the cube for its primitive form. **1931** *Zeitschr. f. Kristallogr.* LXXIX. 501 The cell chosen is..not necessarily the primitive, i.e. smallest cell, as such a cell would often demand a description in oblique and inconvenient axes. But it is always either the primitive cell or a one- or three-face-centred or a body-centred cell. **1932** *Ann. Rep. Progr. Chem.* XXVIII. 263 *P* stands for primitive lattice. *Ibid.*, The rhombohedral lattice is designated by *R*, and the hexagonal by *C* or *H* according as the crystallographic axes coincide with or are perpendicular to the primitive translations of the lattice. **1945** C. W. BUNN *Chem. Crystallogr.* vii. 223 In a set of symbols characterizing a space-group, the first is always a capital letter which indicates whether the lattice is simple (*P* for primitive), body-centred (*I* for inner), side-centred (*A, B*, or *C*), or centred on all faces (*F*). **1966** *McGraw-Hill Encycl. Sci. & Technol.* III. 595/1 The three primitive cells of the cubic lattices are, respectively, a cube, a rhombohedron with a plane angle of 109° 28′, and a rhombohedron with an angle of 60°. The two rhombohedra are extremely inconvenient to handle; consequently, the body-centered and face-centered cubes are adopted in their stead. **1974** D. M. ADAMS *Inorg. Solids* ii. 12 In general it is convenient to work with the cell of highest symmetry and this is not necessarily primitive.

c. Applied to any root of an integer *n* such that the least power to which the root can be raised to yield unity modulo *n* is the totient of *n*.

1837 J. HYMERS *Treat. Theory Algebraical Equations* x. 193 If *r* be one of the roots and *a* be a primitive root of the prime number *n*..it is proved..that all the roots of this equation may be represented by r, r^a, [etc.]. **1916** G. A. MILLER et al. *Theory & Applic. Finite Groups* xv. 308 For any prime *p*, it is shown in the theory of numbers that there exists a primitive root *g* of *p* such that $1, g, g^2, \ldots, g^{p-2}$, when divided by *p*, give in some order the remainders $1, 2, 3, \ldots, p-1$. **1972** J. E. & M. W. MAXFIELD *Discovering Number Theory* viii. 65 A primitive root (mod *m*) exists for $m = 2, 4, p^a$, and $2p^a$, where *p* is an odd prime and *a* is a positive integer. There is no primitive root for other values of *m*.

d. *Group Theory.* [tr. G. *primitiv* (S. Lie *Theorie der Transformationsgruppen* (1888) I. xiii. 221).] Applied to a substitution group whose letters cannot be partitioned into disjoint proper subsets in a way that is preserved by every element of the group.

1888 *Amer. Jrnl. Math.* X. 300 A group in the plane is primitive when with each ordinary point which we hold, no invariant direction is connected. **1897** W. BURNSIDE *Theory of Groups of Finite Order* ix. 177 A simple group can always be represented in primitive form. **1933** L. P. EISENHART *Continuous Groups of Transformations* ii. 80 The group of motions in the euclidean plane is primitive. **1968** D. PASSMAN *Permutation Groups* i. 14 Let G be a transitive permutation group of prime degree. Then G is primitive.

e. *Logic* and *Math.* [tr. It. *primitive* (G. Peano 1897, in *Atti della R. Accad. delle Sci. di Torino* XXXII. 568).] Applied to concepts and propositions that serve as the basis of a deductive system and are not further defined or demonstrated; ***primitive recursive*** (see RECURSIVE *a.* 2 a).

1903 B. RUSSELL *Princ. Math.* p. xi (*heading*) Two indefinables and ten primitive propositions in this calculus. **1910** WHITEHEAD & RUSSELL *Principia Math.* I. I. i. 95 Following Peano, we shall call the undefined ideas and the undemonstrated propositions primitive ideas and primitive propositions respectively. **1922** tr. *Wittgenstein's Tractatus* 121 The possibility of crosswise definition of the logical 'primitive signs' of Frege and Russell shows by itself that these are not primitive signs and that they signify no relations. **1932** LEWIS & LANGFORD *Symbolic Logic* i. 23 Thus it is proved that these primitive ideas and postulates for logic are the only assumptions required for the whole of mathematics. **1952** P. GEACH tr. *Frege's Philos. Writings* 161 The same happens for the formula $a = b$. In some cases its meaning can be assumed as a primitive idea, in others it is defined. **1959** M. BUNGE *Causality* ix. 233 Neither Aristotle nor his followers seem to have been aware of the *logical* necessity of admitting..a set of unexplained or primitive concepts and ideas in order to avoid reasoning in a circle. **1970** E. DUCKWORTH tr. *Piaget's Genetic Epistemol.* 7 Simultaneity, then, is not a primitive intuition; it is an intellectual construction.

f. Applied to those *n*th roots of unity of which the *n*th power, but no lower power, is unity.

1916 G. A. MILLER et al. *Theory & Applic. Finite Groups* xvii. 325 For $p^3 = 9$, the six primitive ninth roots of unity are $\rho, \rho^2, \rho^4, \rho^5, \rho^7, \rho^8$ and are the roots of $x^6 + x^3 + 1 = 0$. **1971** E. C. DADE in Powell & Higman *Finite Simple Groups* viii. 274 We conclude that *F* contains a primitive *e*th root of unity.

6. Of colours: = PRIMARY *a.* 6 a.

1759 SYMMER in *Phil. Trans.* LI. 368 He ranged a number of ribbands, of all the primitive colours. **1822** IMISON *Sc. & Art* I. 247 As a ray of the sun may be separated into these seven primitive colours. **1867** J. HOGG *Microsc.* I. ii. 27 The primitive rays—red, yellow, and blue—of which a colourless ray of light is composed.

7. *Geol.* Belonging (or supposed to belong) to the earliest geological period; applied to those rocks or formations held to be older than any fossiliferous strata, or of which the contained fossils have been obliterated by metamorphism; = PRIMARY *a.* 4 a (in its obs. sense).

1777 HAMILTON in *Phil. Trans.* LXVIII. 106 Most of the mountains which are called primitive..are of this texture. **1813** BAKEWELL *Introd. Geol.* (1815) 446 Those rocks which are called primitive, in reality the original coat of the nucleus of our planet. **1842** BRANDE *Dict. Sc.*, etc. s.v. *Geology*, The crystalline, massive, and unstratified rocks, which seem to form the bases or foundations upon which the others have been deposited..have therefore been called primary or primitive rocks. **1863** A. C. RAMSAY *Phys. Geog.* iv. (1878) 45 The term *Primitive*, as applied to gneiss, is no longer tenable.

8. *Biol.*, *Anat.*, etc. **a.** Applied to a part or structure in the first or a very early stage of formation or growth (whether temporary and subsequently disappearing, or developing into the fully formed structure); rudimentary, primordial. ***primitive streak*** or ***trace***, the faint streak which constitutes the earliest trace of the embryo in the fertilized ovum; ***primitive groove***, (*a*) = *primitive streak*; (*b*) a groove or furrow which appears (in vertebrates) in the upper surface of the primitive streak, and marks the beginning of the vertebral column. **b.** Applied to the minute or ultimate elements of a structure, or to some part connected with these: as the ***primitive fibrillæ*** of a nerve; the ***primitive sheath*** investing each of these (also called *neurilemma*). **c.** Rarely applied to a structure from which secondary structures arise by branching, as the ***primitive carotid artery***: see quot. 1895.

1857 DUNGLISON *Dict. Med.* 435/2 *Primitive Groove, Primitive streak* or *trace*.., a bright streak in the long axis of the pellucid part of the area germinativa, after it presents a central pellucid and a peripheral opake part. **1879** tr. *Haeckel's Evol. Man* I. 299 In the centre of the primitive streak an even, dark line, the so-called primitive groove, becomes defined. **1884** BOWER & SCOTT *De Bary's Phaner.* 345 These are called by Dippel bast-fibres, and by Russow protophloem, because they appear as the primitive elements of the phloem. **1888** ROLLESTON & JACKSON *Anim. Life* Introd. 29 The cells [of the mesoblast] arise..from the primitive streak behind the blastopore in *Peripatus*. **1895** *Syd. Soc. Lex.*, *Primitive carotid artery*..the common carotid artery... *P. iliac artery*,..the common iliac artery. **1899** *Allbutt's Syst. Med.* VIII. 547 It [i.e. pityriasis rosea] usually begins as a solitary patch situated in the neck, trunk, abdomen, or arms,—the 'primitive patch' of Brocq.

9. *Mus.* Applied to a chord in its original or direct form, not inverted.

1811 BUSBY *Dict. Mus.* s.v., *Primitive Chord*, that chord the lowest note of which is of the same literal denomination as the fundamental bass of the harmony. The chord taken in any other way, as when its lowest note is the third, or the fifth of the fundamental bass, is called a *derivative*.

10. ***Primitive Methodist Connexion*** (subsequently ***Church***): a society of Methodists founded by Hugh Bourne in 1810 by secession from the main body; so called as adhering to the original methods of preaching, etc., practised by the Wesleys and Whitefield. ***Primitive Methodist***: a member or adherent of this society. ***Primitive Methodism***: the principles of this society, or adherence to it. Also ***Primitive Baptist***: in the U.S.A., a member of a loosely organized secession of conservative character from the Baptist Church; also *attrib.*

The *Primitive Methodist Connexion* (after 1902 known as *Primitive Methodist Church*) united in 1932 with the United Methodists and Wesleyan Methodists to form the Methodist Church. The *Primitive Methodist Church, U.S.A.*, remains however a separate denomination.

1812 H. BOURNE *Jrnl.* in J. Gardner *Faiths World* II. 426 Thursday, February 13, 1812, we called a meeting, made plans for the next quarter, and made some other regulations; in particular, we took the name of the Primitive Methodist Connexion. **1851** T. A. BURKE *Polly Peablossom's Wedding* 143 Brethren Crump and Noel were both members of the Primitive Baptist Church. **1856** in N. E. Eliason *Tarheel Talk* (1956) 288 Was recived by examinytion on the primitive baptis faith. **1860** J. GARDNER *Faiths World* II. 428/1 Open-air worship is frequently practised by the Primitive Methodists. **1872** Z. N. MORRELL *Flowers & Fruits* vi. 72 There was also an organization calling themselves 'Primitive Baptists', on the Colorado River. **1933** *Sun* (Baltimore) 24 Aug. 6/4 Elder A. J. Harrison.. was elected head of the Ketockin Association, Old School, Primitive Baptists. **1948** *Daily Ardmoreite* (Ardmore, Okla.) 15 July 14/1 The Washita Valley Primitive Baptist association will meet at the Primitive Baptist church here, July 22. **1972** J. S. HALL *Sayings from Old Smoky* 144 Dave Reagan said of the Primitive Baptists, 'They are just like yellow jackets. They'd 'cruit [recruit] up in summer, and in winter they'd all die out.'.

11. *Art.* **a.** Applied to the art and artists of pre-Renaissance western Europe.

[**1843** A. DE MONTOR (*title*) Peintres primitifs.] **1847** LD. LINDSAY *Sk. Hist. Christian Art* II. ii. 93, I strongly suspect an ancestral relation between them [*sc.* the frescoes of the Baptistery at Parma] and the primitive and interesting school of Bologna. **1857** G. SCHARF *Handbk. Paintings by Anc. Masters* (Art Treasures Exhib., Manchester) 5 Ottley, .. an earnest student of the earlier periods of Italian art, had formed a small, but very authentic, collection of primitive works. **1923** J. GORDON *Mod. French Painters* ix. 94 In the early Italian primitive painters, and, indeed, in primitives of every order, we find beneath the artists' learning the foundations laid upon what may be called folk painting. **1927** R. FRY *Flemish Art* i. 24 This realization of space implies a sense of colour as a plastic function which is also almost entirely absent in primitive Flemish art. **1932** KONODY & LATHOM *Introd. French Painters* i. 3 What is known as primitive French painting is a hybrid art, composed of Italian, French, Spanish and German elements in varying proportions. **1970** *Oxf. Compan. Art* 925/1 Within the European context art historians and connoisseurs have used the term 'primitive' for early phases within the historical development of painting or sculpture in the various European countries.

b. Executed by one who has not been trained in a formal manner. Also, imitative of an early style suggesting lack of formal training. Of an artist: without formal training. Cf. NAÏF *a.* 1 b, NAÏVE *a.* 1 c.

1942 J. LIPMAN *Amer. Primitive Painting* 5 The critic.. has come.. to evaluate primitive art positively rather than negatively. *Ibid.* 7 The primitive artist typically allowed himself free rein in depicting pose, gesture.. and background. **1952** M. MCCARTHY *Groves of Academe* (1953) viii. 148 On the walls were dark paintings of the first presidents, clergymen and theologians, a primitive engraving showing William Penn and the Indians. **1957** Primitive painting [see NAÏVE *a.* 1 c]. **1962** W. GAUNT *Everyman's Dict. Pictorial Art* I. 12 A native development [in U.S.A.] of great interest in the eighteenth and nineteenth centuries was that of a 'primitive' or folk art, practised by sign painters and other craftsmen and amateurs. **1964** J. SUMMERSON *Classical Lang. Archit.* v. 39 Laugier's primitivism.. certainly appealed to him [*sc.* Sir John Soane] but he was prepared to go much further than Laugier in.. inventing a 'primitive' order of his own. **1967** Primitive portrait [see *mourning-piece* s.v. MOURNING *vbl. sb.*[1] 5]. **1976** *Sunday Times* (Colour Suppl.) 8 Feb. 7/3 Beryl Cook, seaside landlady and primitive painter, talks to Allen Saddler. **1978** I. MURDOCH *Sea* 126 Hartley and Fitch were sitting stiff and upright, like a married pair rendered by a primitive painter.

12. ***primitive accumulation*** (Econ.): in Marxist theory, the original accumulation of capital, supposedly derived from the expropriation of small producers or smallholders, from which capitalist production was able to start; hence ***primitive socialist accumulation***: the accumulation of capital which would be needed to start socialist production, also to be derived from the expropriation of small producers, smallholders, or peasants.

1887 MOORE & AVELING tr. *Marx's Capital* II. VIII. xxvi. 736 The whole movement.. seems to turn in a vicious circle, out of which we can only get by supposing a primitive accumulation.. preceding capitalistic accumulation. *Ibid.*, This primitive accumulation plays in Political Economy about the same part as original sin in theology. *Ibid.* 738 The so-called primitive accumulation.. is nothing else than the historical process of divorcing the producer from the means of production. **1935** E. BURNS *Handbk. Marxism* xvi. 258 The so-called primitive accumulation of capital consisted in this case in the expropriation of these immediate producers. **1950** A. ERLICH in *Q. Jrnl. Econ.* LXIV. 69 This formative period of modern capitalism.. had now to find its counterpart in 'primitive socialist accumulation' which was assumed to serve as midwife in the same way for the socialist society of the future. **1959** *Listener* 29 Oct. 726/1 Trotsky proposed to carry through this Draconian programme, of what he called 'primitive socialist accumulation' without Stalin's terrible methods. **1965** B. PEARCE tr. *Preobrazhensky's New Econ.* 67 If we partly exclude the operation of the law of value.. we must accordingly replace its regulatory action by another law, inherent in planned economy at its present stage of development—the law of primitive socialist accumulation. **1967** I. DEUTSCHER *Marxism in our Time* (1972) 242 It was out of the question that a country like this should be able to achieve socialism in such circumstances. It had to devote all its energies to 'primitive accumulation', that is, to the creation under state ownership of the most essential economic preliminaries to any genuine building of socialism.

B. *sb.* **I.** Senses related to A. 1.

1. An original or early member of a society or body. †**a.** A primitive Christian; a member of the early Church. *Obs.*

1600 W. WATSON *Decacordon* (1602) Pref. A iij b, Did not then the primitiues of the East Church amongst the Christians carry away the auriflambe of all religious Zeale? **1651–3** JER. TAYLOR *Serm. for Year* I. xiii. 173 The fervors of the Apostles, and other holy primitives. **1686** EVELYN *Diary* 7 Mar., The severall afflictions of the Church of Christ from the primitives to this day.

b. An original inhabitant, an aboriginal; a man of primitive (esp. prehistoric) times. Also *transf.*, someone uncivilized, uncultured.

1779 FORREST *Voy. N. Guinea* 273 The Haraforas, who seem to be the primitives of the island. **1895** *Daily News* 13 May 6/3 The effects sought here relate to the 'primitives' of the Irish heroic age. **1924** *Brit. Jrnl. Med. Psychol.* IV. 35 The primitive has in many ways a contact with his environment of a refinement and subtlety that is more than a match for civilized brains. **1926** L. A. CLARE tr. *Lévy-Bruhl's How Natives Think* 13 Primitives... By this term, an incorrect one, yet rendered almost indispensable through common usage, we simply mean members of the most elementary social aggregates with which we are acquainted. *a* **1936** KIPLING *Something of Myself* (1937) vii. 184 Out of the woods.. came two dark and mysterious Primitives. **1967** [see CHARLEY, CHARLIE 8]. **1972** *Buenos Aires Herald* 2 Feb. 7/1 The primitives fight for their territories and economic planners insist that the vast region must be opened. **1977** M. COHEN *Sensible Words* iii. 122 The newly emphasized methods of linguistic analysis include studying the language of children and 'primitives'.

†**2.** *pl.* The primitive or earliest stage; the 'beginnings'. *Obs. rare.*

1600 W. WATSON *Decacordon* (1602) 52 Probably.. in the primitiues of their institutions they had better, lowlier, and more religious spirits then now they haue. **1609** BIBLE (Douay) *Exod.* xxix. 28 They are the primitives and beginninges of their pacifique victimes which they offer to the Lord.

3. Short for *Primitive Methodist*: see A. 10.

1855 J. R. LEIFCHILD *Cornwall Mines* 303 Those worthy though singular people, the Primitives of Redruth. **1906** *Essex Rev.* XV. 135 The 'Primitives' in their little thatched and clay-lump chapel.

4. In art criticism: **a.** A painter of the early period, i.e. before the Renaissance; also *transf.* a modern painter who imitates the style of these. More recently, a naïve painter; also *transf.* of artists working in another medium. **b.** A picture painted by any of these. Also *attrib.*, and *transf.* of other art forms.

1892 *Spectator* 30 Jan. 168/1 O impressionist, do I find you among the primitives? **1892** *Athenæum* 13 Feb. 220/3 In Italy artists we call 'primitives', such as Crivelli.. still adhered to the early manner while Titian was in his glory. **1895** *Westm. Gaz.* 7 Feb. 3/3 On the left as you enter the room are some notable examples of what may be considered 'primitives'. **1907** *Edin. Rev.* July 237 Among the work of the Italian 'primitives' towns are pretty common in the background. **1907** R. FRY *Let.* 5 Mar. (1972) I. 282 A great Ferrarese altarpiece... The effect will be fine in our Primitive room. **1910** E. SINGLETON *Art of Belgian Galleries* i. 17 The Last Supper is one of the most profound and best-painted works of the Fifteenth Century; and if one were to make a list of five or six supreme masterpieces of the Flemish Primitives, this would have to be included. **1922** C. BELL *Since Cézanne* 51 One definitely artistic gift.. many children do possess.. is a sense of the decorative possibilities of their medium. This gift they have in common with the Primitives; and this the *douanier* possessed in an extraordinary degree. **1923** [see PRIMITIVE *a.* 11 a]. **1932** F. F. SHERMAN *Early Amer. Painting* p. xv, Numerous dealers in antiques.. offer them for sale.. as 'primitives'. Primitives they certainly are not... They are worthless as works of art or of antiquity. **1934** *Musical Q.* Apr. 214 The Primitives stem from Moussorgsky, through Debussy and the *Sacre*. **1947** G. GREENE *19 Stories* 155 The first season of 'primitives' [*sc.* films] was announced (a high-brow phrase). **1951** R. FIRTH *Elem. Social Organiz.* v. 163 When we talk.. of the Italian primitives.. we are referring.. to art that is distinguished primarily by being earlier in time, though it.. also bears the character of lack of sophistication. **1952** O. KALLIR in A. M. Moses *Grandma Moses* p. xv, Grandma Moses is called a 'primitive'. Each of her pictures shows plainly that its author has had no art training. **1958** *Listener* 21 Aug. 269/2 The school of the 'primitives', represented by John Osborne, Sheelagh Delaney, and.. Bernard Kops. **1959** E. POUND *Thrones* ci. 78 *Hs'uan Tsung*, 1389 natus, painted kittens, and Joey said, 'are they for real' before primitives in the Mellon Gallery. **1964** MRS. L. B. JOHNSON *White House Diary* 20 Jan. (1970) 56 There was also a little American Primitive—just made you merry to look at it. **1974** P. DE VRIES *Glory of Hummingbird* (1975) iii. 39 We respected the artist's [*sc.* a writer's] reluctance to show portions of work not in sufficiently polished form because we felt.. that here was a true primitive. **1976** *Sunday Times* (Colour Suppl.) 8 Feb. 22/1 Most of all, her paintings are funny. You can't say that about many primitives. **1977** *Jrnl. R. Soc. Arts* CXXVI. 35/2 The Flemish Primitives.. would superimpose the dark colours and leave the pale colours transparent.

II. Senses related to A. 3.

5. An original ancestor or progenitor (of humans or animals). ? *Obs.*

1486 *Hen. VII at York* in *Surtees Misc.* (1888) 54, I [Ebrauk] am premative of your progenie. **1530** LYNDESAY *Test. Papyngo* 771 ȝe bene, all, Degenerit frome ȝour holy prematyuis. *a* **1677** HALE *Prim. Orig. Man.* II. vii. 201 The various kinds of Dogs.. might in their Primitives be of one Species.

6. *Gram.* A word from which another or others are derived; a root-word. Opp. to *derivative*. Also, = PHONETIC *sb.*

1565 COOPER *Thesaurus* *iv, Whether the worde be a Primitiue, or Deriuatiue deduced of some other. **1657–8** EVELYN *Diary* 27 Jan., He.. got by heart almost the entire vocabularie of Latine and French primitives. **1755** JOHNSON *Dict.* Pref. B j b, Of thieflike or coachdriver no notice was needed, because the primitives contain the meaning of the compounds. **1759** ADAM SMITH *Orig. Lang.* (1790) 451 All the words in the Greek Language are derived from about 300 primitives. **1814** J. MARSHMAN *Elem. Chinese Gram.* 36 If we then add the 214 elements to the 1689 primitives, we shall have one thousand nine hundred and three characters producing nearly the whole language. **1820** *Q. Rev.* Jan. 314 The absence of all distinction between primitives and derivatives. **1874, 1907** [see PHONETIC *sb.*]. **1909–10** L. BLOOMFIELD in C. F. Hockett *Leonard Bloomfield Anthol.* (1970) 1 Derivative nouns and verbs also stand.. in a definite ablaut relation to their primitives. **1975** *Language* LI. 969 It. *bozz-ello*.. is an authentic derivative from *bozza*; while *bosel, bossel, bozel* in Renaissance French is a cluster of completely isolated forms lacking a primitive—a situation which reflects on the grammatical status of *-el*.

7. Anything from which something else is derived; in quot. 1784, a primitive or primary colour.

1628 T. SPENCER *Logick* 139 These arguments haue the same force to argue, that the primitiues haue, from which they are derived. **1784** J. BARRY in *Lect. Paint.* vi. (1848) 211 Yellow, red, and blue... These three uncompounded primitives.

8. *Math.* Any algebraical or geometrical form in relation to another derived from it; as, the original expression or function of which another is the derivative; the original equation from which a differential equation, etc. is obtained; the original curve of which another is the polar, inverse, evolute, etc. *spec.* a complete primitive. (Short for *primitive expression, equation, curve*, etc.: see A. 5.)

complete primitive: a primitive equation containing the requisite number of constants to furnish the solution of the derived equation.

1885 A. R. FORSYTH *Treat. Differential Equations* i. 8 The relation, which exists between the variables themselves without their differential coefficients and which is the most general one possible, is called sometimes the general solution, and sometimes the primitive, of the differential equation. **1929** T. C. FRY *Elem. Differential Equations* ii. 27 This relation includes every possible solution of the differential equation. It is called the general solution or primitive. **1969** B. SPAIN *Ordinary Differential Equations* i. 9 Obtain the differential equations corresponding to the primitives.. $y = c \log x$.. [etc.].

9. *Logic* and *Math.* A primitive concept or proposition (see A. 5 e). Also in extended use.

1950 *Jrnl. Symbolic Logic* XV. 130 Hence ϕ and μ as defined above will suffice as the sole primitives for the arithmetic of positive integers. **1960** G. BERGMAN *Meaning & Existence* ii. 44 It is not required that an improved language be interpreted by interpreting separately all, or even any, of its primitives. **1964** M. BLACK *Compan. Wittgenstein's Tractatus* 25 We find Wittgenstein.. constantly returning to the theme of the 'logical indefinables' or the 'logical primitives'. **1964** R. H. ROBINS *Gen. Linguistics* iv. 133 Many linguists are prepared to accept these terms [sc. *contrast* and *distinctive*] as primitives, i.e. as requiring no further definition within linguistics. **1975** *Language* LI. 621 We are not yet in a position to characterize seriously the semantic representation of roots. My guess is that we are not yet aware of the majority of semantic primitives. **1975** M. A. SLOTE *Metaphysics & Essence* iii. 41 This notion of (an) experience, like the other notions we have been using as primitives, is not just an arbitrary primitive with which to attempt the definition of the concepts we wish to define. **1976** J. S. GRUBER *Lexical Struct. Syntax & Semantics* II. i. 260 Interpretive semantics is valuable only for those functions which a logical calculus entails, and for this it must operate on trees of semantic primitives.

primitively ('prɪmɪtɪvlɪ), *adv.* [f. prec. adj. + -LY[2].] In the primitive way, manner, or order.

1. In the earliest age or time; at the beginning; anciently; originally in time, at first.

1607 TOPSELL *Four-f. Beasts* (1658) 580 That rare concord and agreement which was primitively ordained by God to be betwixt man and beast. *a* **1677** HALE *Prim. Orig. Man.* II. vii. 201 So possibly might the Sheep of Peru,.. be primitively Sheep, but differenced by their long abode.. in Peru. **1704** in Collier *Dissuasive fr. Play Ho.* 30 Whether this Primitive Church of his was primitively pure, or originally Profane. **1893** SIR R. BALL *Story of Sun* 126 A beam of light which was primitively white.. becomes sensibly red.

2. Originally, as opposed to *derivatively*, or as giving origin to something else; radically, fundamentally; primarily.

1646 SIR T. BROWNE *Pseud. Ep.* 59 This direction proceeds not primitively from themselves, but is derivative and contracted from the magneticall effluxions of the earth. **1827** Carlyle *Misc.* (1857) I. 61 This is the Absolute the Primitively True.

b. Originally; in origin or derivation.

1589 Puttenham *Eng. Poesie* II. xi. (Arb.) 121 One other pretie conceit..also borrowed primitiuely of the Poet, or courtly maker. **1659** T. Philipott *Vill. Cant.* 227 The Medway, from whence it [Maidstone] primitively borrowed its Name. **1869** Huxley *Phys.* xii. (ed. 3) 314 That inverted portion of the integument, from which the whole anterior character of the eye and the lens are primitively formed.

3. In a primitive style; with the purity, simplicity, or rudeness of early times.

1672–5 Comber *Comp. Temple* (1702) 106 Ordinances, which are purely and primitively administred there. *a* **1716** South *Serm.* (1717) VI. 129 The purest, and most primitively ordered Church in the world. **1902** *Words Eyewitness* 72 The most primitively manly race on earth. *Mod.* The concern was very primitively put together.

primitiveness ('prɪmɪtɪvnɪs). [f. as prec. + -ness.] The quality, character, or condition of being primitive (in any sense of the adj.).

1668 Wilkins *Real Char.* II. i. §4. 35 Transcendental Relations of Quality at large... 1. Primitiveness, Root, original, simple, underived. **1684** *Def. Resol. Case of Consc. conc. Symbolizing w. Ch. Rome* 30 Replying to those few lines that follow against the Primitiveness of our Episcopacy. **1856** Miss Mulock *J. Halifax* xxvii, The folk in our valley, out of their very primitiveness, had more faith in the master. **1881** Westcott & Hort *Grk. N.T.* II. 281 These gradations of primitiveness in corruption.

primitivism ('prɪmɪtɪvɪz(ə)m). [See -ism.]

1. Adherence to or practice of that which is primitive. Also, a belief in the desirability of a 'return to nature'; an exaltation of simplicity or of irrationalism; the practice of primitive art.

1861 Neale *Notes on Dalmatia, Croatia*, etc. 137 Had he not provocation enough,..to confirm him in his primitivism. **1896** *Westm. Gaz.* 14 May 3/1 This country, in which primitivism—if I may be permitted the expression—and progressivism are sometimes so oddly mixed. **1934** A. Huxley *Beyond Mexique Bay* 257 To introduce a salutary element of primitivism into our civilized and industrialized way of life. **1938** *Burlington Mag.* June 302/2 Far more primitivism has been attributed to him [*sc.* Rousseau] than is actually justified. **1939** J. Charlot *Art from Mayans to Disney* xi. 86 Political cartoons reminiscent of Monnier and Grandville, which are not flavoured at all by the 'primitivism' of his [*sc.* Posada's] later work. **1947** A. Einstein *Mus. Romantic Era* ix. 95 What formal primitivism, after Beethoven! **1950** E. H. Gombrich *Story of Art* xxvii. 440 This Primitivism advocated by Gauguin became perhaps an even more lasting influence on modern art than either Van Gogh's Expressionism or Cézanne's way to Cubism. **1951** *Essays in Crit.* I. 97 The term 'Back to Nature' covers the many and varied forms of primitivism. **1952** J. Summerson *Sir John Soane* 17 Soane's 'primitivism'..is formalized at Bentley Priory (1798). **1958** H. R. Hitchcock *Archit. in 19th & 20th Cent.* 450/2 'Primitivism' in painting and sculpture has been of recurrent importance since the days of the Fauves and the Expressionists; a comparable primitivism in architecture has been much rarer, except for Gaudí. **1969** *Daily Tel.* 10 Feb. 10/4 He [*sc.* Thomas Mann] puts the German character on the operating table..: the loneliness, the smug provincialism, the Wagnerian primitivism, the eroticism. **1976** *Survey* Summer-Autumn 107 Khrushchev was only comprehensible if one began by accepting his Marxist primitivism.

2. Short for *Primitive Methodism*: see primitive A. 10, and cf. B. 3.

1907 *Daily News* 28 May 8 Closing Day of Primitive Methodist Centenary... The Rev. Jabez Bell described 'Primitivism' as neither painfully poor nor rascally rich.

primitivist ('prɪmɪtɪvɪst), *sb.* and *a.* [f. primitive *a.* + -ist.] A. *sb.* A believer in primitivism (sense 1); an advocate of the superiority of primitive customs or of primitive art; a person who uses obsolete methods or techniques. B. *adj.* Of or pertaining to primitivism or to the primitive, esp. in art; irrational, opposing scientific development.

1926 W. R. Inge *Lay Thoughts* 204 So the Utopians are usually primitivists. They glorify the noble savage, who runs wild in woods. **1934** *Musical Q.* Apr. 213 Three currents are left in the wake of the Modern Movement—Primitivist, Classicist, Popularist. **1949** B. Willey in *Ideas & Beliefs of Victorians* (B.B.C.) 43 Perhaps as Rousseau and other primitivists had urged, civilisation was a monstrous aberration, and men were happier and better when fresh from the hands of God or Nature in some primeval Eden. **1952** J. Summerson *Sir John Soane* 33, I mentioned earlier the 'primitivist' element which is so important a factor in the Soane style. **1961** *Times* 7 June 17/3 All the rather flashy vitality and 'primitivist' imagery of his old manner have been discarded. **1975** *Nature* 20 Mar. 219/1 Attacked by the new school of linguistics and cognitive epistemology as an ignorant primitivist, Skinner not only maintains his position but makes it more dogmatic. **1977** *Times Lit. Suppl.* 15 July 874/3 Nothing but primitive commonplaces: without laws, private property or rulers, the Indians 'live according to nature'. It is a primitivists' fantasy world characterised by the observance of natural moral practices. **1977** D. Watkin *Morality & Archit.* I. ii. 25 He [*sc.* Viollet-le-Duc] has..a related 'primitivist' notion that Roman and Renaissance architecture lost contact with the pure fount of Greek truth, and is thus morally and stylistically in questionable taste.

Hence **primiti'vistic** *a.*

1943 [see isolationistic *a.*]. **1948** L. Spitzer *Linguistics & Lit. Hist.* 210 Claudel can sing..not only 'Georgica', as did Vergil in a primitivistic mood. **1958** H. R. Hitchcock *Archit. 19th & 20th Cent.* iv. 60 Soane's Dulwich Gallery of 1811–14, outside London, is likewise built of common brick and has similarly primitivistic detailing. **1959** *Encounter* Nov. 76/1 A kind of atavism, an inability to think..in any but primitivistic terms. **1972** M. Bradbury in Cox & Dyson *20th-Cent. Mind* III. xii. 343 Golding's universe is normally a-social or perhaps pre-social, primitivistic at its core and yet also conscious that it is only through *knowing* our primitivism that we will find our innocence.

primitivity (prɪmɪ'tɪvɪtɪ). [f. primitive *a.* + -ity. Cf. F. *primitivité*.] = primitiveness.

1759 H. Walpole *Lett. to Mann* 8 Aug., The age of George the Second is likely to be celebrated for more primitivity than the disinterestedness of Mr. Deard. **1890** *Cent. Dict.* s.v., In mathematics we speak of the primitivity of a form. **1891** L. Rivington in *Dublin Rev.* Apr. 372 They have added to the notes of the Church that of 'Primitivity'.

primitivize ('prɪmɪtɪvaɪz), *v.* [f. primitive *a.* + -ize.] *trans.* and *intr.* To render primitive; to impute primitiveness to; to simplify; to return to an earlier stage. So **primitivi'zation**, **'primitivizing** *vbl. sb.* and *ppl. a.*

1942 Primitivisation [see overinclusion]. **1955** *Times* 18 May 8/6 It does not bring about a primitivizing or animalizing of the human, but rather it celebrates man at his human best. **1959** *Encounter* May 50/2 Mr. Logue is a primitivizing poet. **1968** D. Lawton *Social Class, Lang. & Educ.* iii. 23 'Cultural deprivation' or absence of external stimulation resulted in a 'primitivization' of an individual's behaviour. **1969** D. Daube *Roman Law* iii. 168 A common failing of modern research into ancient law is the inclination to primitivize the sources, to press the naive side of any statement or custom and overlook the element of sophistication which is often quite strong. **1971** *Jrnl. Gen. Psychol.* LXXXIV. 208 In psychology the term 'regression' refers to a primitivization of behavior, a 'going back' to a less mature way of behaving which the individual has 'outgrown'. **1976** T. Stoianovich *French Hist. Method* 146 Since the impairment of an existing superstructure provokes economic primitivization, staunch support develops in favor of a viable new superstructure.

†**'primity.** *Obs.* [f. L. *prīm-us* (prime *a.*) + -ity; = obs. F. *primité* (16th c. in Godef.) and med.L. *prīmitās* firstness in time (*a* 1308 Duns Scotus, *De primo principio* 2. 2).]

1. The fact or position of being first in rank or order; first or chief place, priority, supremacy.

1659 Pearson *Creed* i. 40 This primity God requires to be attributed to himself. **1660** R. Sheringham *King's Suprem. Asserted* viii. (1682) 70 He grants him a primity of share in the supreme power. *Ibid.* 94 Where a transcendent interest, or primity of state, is in one man, it is sufficient to constitute a Monarchy.

2. The first part, the beginning. *rare*[−1].

1684 H. More *Answer* xiv. 103 Which being not a final or total Ruine of Babylon, but, as it were, the Primity thereof.

'primly, *adv.* [f. prim *a.* + -ly[2].] In a prim or precise manner, with primness.

1837 Mrs. Carlyle *Lett.* (1883) I. 66 She primly promulgates her opinion that influenza is masculine. **1853–8** Hawthorne *Eng. Note-Bks.* (1879) II. 207 The grounds..had not the appearance of being very primly kept. **1897** *Bookman* Jan. 122/2 She was not quite so primly decorous as the young persons of her epoch.

primmer, obs. spelling of primer *sb.*[1]

primmy ('prɪmɪ), *a. rare.* [f. prim *a.* + -y[1].] Tending to primness.

1879 [see governessy *a.*].

'primness. [f. prim *a.* + -ness.] The quality of being prim; formal or affected preciseness.

1713 Steele *Guard.* No. 29 ¶11 Her lips are composed with a primness peculiar to her character. **1758** Gray *Let.* Poems (1775) 265 Primness and affectation of style..has turned to hoydening and rude familiarity. **1858** Hawthorne *Fr. & It. Note-Bks.* II. 98 A primness of eternal virginity about the mouth. **1894** Doyle *Mem. S. Holmes* 99 He affected a certain quiet primness of dress.

‖**primo** ('primo), *a.* and *sb.* [It., = first: cf. prima[2].] A. *adj.* Used in some phrases, chiefly musical, as **primo basso**, chief bass singer (also *fig.*); **primo buffo**, chief male comic singer or actor; **primo tenore (assoluto)**, chief tenor singer (of outstanding ability); **primo uomo**, singer of the chief male part; (see also quots.).

1740 J. Grassineau *Mus. Dict.* 183 *Primo*, the first; this word is often abridg'd, P°, I°..and added to other words, as *Primo canto,—the first treble.* **1801** Busby *Dict. Mus., Primo* (Ital.). First: as *Primo Violono* [sic], first violin; *Primo Flauto*, first flute. **1826** M. Kelly *Reminisc.* I. 48 The celebrated Genaro Luzzio was the primo buffo, and the principal female, La Coltellini, was delightful, both as a comic actress and singer. **1848** Geo. Eliot *Let.* 8 June (1954) I. 266 Dear Quartett of Friends—I may still say so, though I fear your primo basso has departed. **1855** —— in *Fraser's Mag.* July 50/2 He will write no *part* to suit a *primo tenore.* **1876** Stainer & Barrett *Dict. Mus. Terms* 366/1 *Primo, (It.)* First (masc.), as *tempo primo*, at the original pace or time; *violino primo*, first fiddle; *primo buffo*, chief comic actor or singer; *primo musico* and *primo uomo*, principal male singer in the opera. **1880** Grove *Dict. Mus.* II. 509/1 It was *de rigueur* that the First Man (*Primo uomo*) should be an artificial Soprano. *Ibid.* 514/1 The chief, or *Buffo* group, consisted of two Female Performers..and three Men, distinguished as the *Primo Buffo*, [etc.]. **1889** G. B. Shaw *London Music 1888–89* (1937) 166 His dignity as *primo tenore assoluto.* **1938** *Times Lit. Suppl.* 28 May 370/3 What the *primo uomo* was to the eighteenth-century opera..the man with the stick is to the symphony concerts. **1955** E. Dent in H. Van Thal *Fanfare for E. Newman* 86 The first half of the nineteenth century..was the triumph of the *prima donna* over the *primo uomo*, the *castrato* hero of the eighteenth century, though she soon had to face her rival in the *primo tenore.*

B. as *sb.* 1. *Mus.* In a pianoforte duet, the upper part; the pianist who plays this part.

1792 J. A. K. Colizzi *Three Duets for Two Performers on the Harpsichord or Piano Forté* 3 Primo. **1883** Grove *Dict. Mus.* III. 30/2 In pianoforte duets, *Primo* or 1mo is generally put over the right-hand page, and then means the part taken by the 'treble' player. **1954** K. Dale *19th-Cent. Piano Mus.* xii. 284 Swirling cadenzas of scales in demisemiquavers for performance by *primo. Ibid.* 286 The playing of six quavers in a bar by *primo* against four by *secondo* throughout the whole of the trio section cannot have been altogether easy for the young performer. **1964** G. Read *Mus. Notation* xviii. 298 For four-hand music on one instrument, the two parts are placed on facing pages..the first player (*primo*; top part) reads from the right-hand page. **1965** *Listener* 1 July 33/3 Britten's rhythmic control as *secondo* balancing and counteracting Richter's natural genius as *primo.*

2. (With capital initial.) A title given to an official of the Royal Antediluvian Order of Buffaloes.

1879 *Buffalo* 16 Jan. 3/3 Yours fraternally, Primo James Dewsbury. *Ibid.* 5/1 Primos who..have been elevated to the position of Knights of the Order of Merit. **1928** *Daily Express* 2 Aug. 9/5 Mr. J. C. E. Cartwright.., Grand Primo of England, inaugurated the Croydon and District Provincial Grand Lodge... The Grand Primo of the new lodge is Mr. L. R. N. Percy. **1966** *R.A.O.B. Centenary, South Yorkshire, 1866–1966* (Royal Antediluvian Order of Buffaloes), Of the 17 Provincial Grand Primos..only two have been taken from us by the call of the reaper.

primogenial, -genian, -genious (-geneous), erroneous forms of primigenial, -genian, -genious; app. in imitation of *primogenit, -geniture*, etc., in which the first element is L. *prīmō*.

†**primo'genit,** *a.* and *sb. Obs.* [ad. L. *prīmōgenit-us*, properly two words, *prīmō genitus*, first born, f. *prīmō* adv., first + *genit-us*, pa. pple. of *gignĕre* to bring forth, bear. (Hence, not a compound of *prīmus*, like *primigene*, etc.) So OF. *primogenit* (13th c. in Godef.).] First-born.

[**1160–80** *Laws Henry I*, c. 70 §21 Primo patris feodum primogenitus filius habeat; emptiones vers, vel deinceps acquisitiones suas, det cui magis velit. *a* **1190** Glanvil *Tract. de Leg.* vii. iii, Tunc secundum ius regni Anglie primogenitus filius patri succedit in totum. *a* **1635** Naunton *Fragm. Reg.* (1641) 11 Our Common Law..did ever of old provide aydes for the *primo-genitus*, and the eldest Daughter.]

c **1450** *Mirour Saluacioun* 3435 Crist the Primogenit of the dede rose tofore. **1609** A. Craig *Poet. Recreat.* To Rdr., They are my children, you haue them as they were borne: And so the Primo-genit must haue the prioritie at the Presse. **1619** Sir J. Sempil *Sacrilege Handled* App. 39 Sem could beget (and did) diuers Primogenit Priests.

primogenital (praɪməʊ'dʒɛnɪtəl), *a.* [ad. late L. *prīmōgenitāl-is* (Tertull.), f. *prīmōgenit-us* (taken as sb.): see prec. and -al[1].] Of or pertaining to the first-born or to primogeniture.

1657–83 Evelyn *Hist. Relig.* (1850) II. 21 Those garments Rebecca put on Jacob, his sacerdotal vestment; but it was still the primogenital right, till a family separated. **1859** G. Meredith *R. Feverel* iv, The primogenital cellars were not niggard of their stores. **1888** *Science* 14 Sept. 124/1 Genesis..considered under some of its subordinate phases, as heredity, physiological selection, sexual selection, primogenital selection, sexual differentiation,..hybridity, &c.

primogenitary (praɪməʊ'dʒɛnɪtərɪ), *a.* [f. L. *prīmōgenit-us* (see above) + -ary[1].] = prec.

1827 Hallam *Const. Hist.* (1876) I. vi. 294 The consciousness of this defect in his parliamentary title put James on magnifying..the inherent rights of primogenitary succession. **1838–9** —— *Hist. Lit.* III. iii. iv. §47. 160 Derived by some one..through primogenitary descent. **1867** W. L. Newman in *Quest. Reformed Parl.* 83 It is sufficient to say of this law, that it adheres more strictly to Primogeniture than the practise of the Primogenitary class.

primogenitive (praɪməʊ'dʒɛnɪtɪv), *a.* and *sb. rare.* [f. as prec. + -ive.] A. *adj.* = prec. B. † *sb.* = primogeniture 2. *Obs.*

1606 Shaks. *Tr. & Cr.* i. iii. 106 How could Communities, Degrees in Schooles, and Brother-hoods in Cities,..The primogenitiue, and due of Byrth, Prerogatiue of Age,..(But by Degree) stand in Authentique place? **1842** Mrs. F. Trollope *Vis. to Italy* II. iv. 87 She had a sort of primogenitive right to..a red cap and tricoloured banner.

primogenitor (praɪməʊ'dʒɛnɪtə(r)). [a. med.L. *prīmōgenitor* (1361 in Du Cange), f. L. *prīmō* adv., at first, first + *genitor* begetter, genitor, after L. *prīmōgenitus*; so OF. *primogeniteur* (1340 in Godef.).] First parent, earliest ancestor; *loosely*, ancestor, forefather, progenitor.

1654 Gayton *Pleas. Notes* iv. 181 If your primogenitors be not belied, the generall smutch you have, was once of a deeper black, when they came from Mauritania into Spain. **1768–74** Tucker *Lt. Nat.* (1834) II. 211 The supposition of our being punished for the offence of our primogenitor. **1824** *Mirror* III. 402/2 The male descendants of our great primogenitor. **1888** Hasluck *Model Engin. Handybk.* (1900) 2 A model of this, the primogenitor of the modern steam-engine, can be bought..for one penny.

Hence **primo'genitrix**, a first female ancestor.

1875 M. Collins *Fr. Midnight to Midn.* III. xii. 202 Fluent as that 'affable archangel' who delighted our primogenitrix.

primogeniture (praɪməʊˈdʒɛnɪtjʊə(r)). [ad. med.L. *prīmōgenitūra*, f. L. *prīmō* adv., first + *genitūra* GENITURE; after *prīmōgenitus*. So F. *primogéniture* (13–14th c. in Hatz.-Darm.).]

1. The fact or condition of being the first-born of the children of the same parents.

[*c* **1225** WILLIAM BRITTO *Philipis* IV. 2 Lege patrum veteri Richardum, patre sepulto, Efficit Anglorum primogenitura monarcham. **1594** PARSONS *Confer. Success* I. vi. 128 That *primogenitura* or eldership of birth.. was greatly respected by God.] **1605** BACON *Adv. Learn.* I. v. §7 These were the Arts which had a kinde of *Primo geniture* with them seuerally. **1626** T. H. *Caussin's Holy Crt.* 121 Al those, say with Esau:..To what vse, will this goodly prerogatiue of primogeniture serue me? *a* **1715** BURNET *Own Time* (1766) II. 238 If primogeniture from Noah was the ground settled by God for monarchy, then all the Princes now in the world were Usurpers. **1867** FREEMAN *Norm. Conq.* I. v. 291 Though primogeniture gave no positive right.

b. *esp.* in ***right of primogeniture*** (also †***primogeniture-right***), the right (of succession, etc.) of the first-born: see 2.

1602 FULBECKE *Pandectes* 16 The right of Primogeniture, or elder-brothership is fenced, supported, and defended against this last decree of the Millanasses, and that first of the Persians. **1612** SELDEN *Illustr. Drayton's Poly-olb.* xvii. 269 Claiming his Primogeniture-right, & therby the kingdom. **1683** *Brit. Spec.* 162 That his present Majesty of Great Britain is by Right of Primogeniture the next and undoubted Heir to Cadwalladar, will manifestly appear. **1766** BLACKSTONE *Comm.* II. i. 13 In the division of personal estates, the females of equal degree are admitted together with the males, and no right of primogeniture is allowed. **1865** KINGSLEY *Herew.* ix, The rights of primogeniture.. were not respected.

2. The right of succession or inheritance belonging to the first-born; the principle, custom, or law by which the property or title descends to the eldest son (or eldest child); *spec.* the feudal rule of inheritance by which the whole of the real estate of an intestate passes to the eldest son. (Introduced into England at the Norman Conquest, and still prevailing in most places in a modified form: but cf. BOROUGH-ENGLISH, GAVELKIND.) Also *fig.*

a **1631** DONNE *Serm.* xxxiv. (1640) 340 Heires of heaven, which is not a Gavel-kinde, every Son, every man alike: but it is an universall primogeniture, every man full, so full, as that every man hath all. **1726** DE FOE *Hist. Devil* I. ix. (1840) 108 Abel had broken the laws of primogeniture. **1788** GIBBON *Decl. & F.* (1869) II. xliv. 654 The insolent prerogative of primogeniture was unknown. **1875** MAINE *Hist. Inst.* vii. 199 When the Teutonic races spread over Western Europe they did not bring with them Primogeniture as their ordinary rule of succession. **1876** FREEMAN *Norm. Conq.* V. xxiv. 491 Under the working of the new feudal doctrines, the custom of primogeniture gradually supplanted the Old-English custom of equal partition of lands.

primoˈgenitureship. Now *rare.* [f. prec. + -SHIP.] = prec. 2.

1622 MABBE tr. *Aleman's Guzman d'Alf.* II. 59 It is likely to proue.. an immortall kinde of businesse, like vnto that of your Mayorasgos or Primo-genitureship, which your fathers settle vpon their eldest sonnes. **1762** tr. *Busching's Syst. Geog.* IV. 156 The Emperor Frederick I..introduced into the house of Austria the right of primogenitureship. **1822** J. FLINT *Lett. Amer.* 177 Local attachments are much weakened by the open prospects of an extensive country, by the abolition of primogenitureship, and by the introduction of laws that promote family justice. **1830** *Examiner* 259/1 A younger brother, corrupted at heart with envy by the injustice of primogenitureship.

primoˈgeniturist. *rare.* [f. PRIMOGENITURE + -IST.] One who believes that the right of succession or inheritance belongs to the first-born.

1976 I. MURDOCH *Henry & Cato* I. 7 His father, a rigid primogeniturist, had left everything to..the elder son.

†**primo-prime**, *a. Obs.* [f. L. *prīmō* adv., first + PRIME *a.*] First of all; the very first; absolutely primary. So †**primo-ˈprimitive** *a.*, earliest of the primitive.

1673 O. WALKER *Educ.* v. 46 As if not taken at the first moment, as it were, the primo-prime acts. **1679** ALSOP *Melius Inquirend.* I. i. 48 It would be a severe charge upon all the Primo-primitive Fathers that they were Arians. **1693** BEVERLEY *True St. Gosp. Truth* 9 This is the Primo-prime, as may be said, Foundation of Holiness, and Happiness; To Know and Enjoy the only True God. **1715** M. DAVIES *Athen. Brit.* I. Pref. 87 The Secular Ignorance and Candid Simplicity of the Primo-Primitive Christians.

ˌprimo-ˈrational. *Math. rare*⁻¹. [f. as prec. + RATIONAL, as derivative of *prime ratio*: see -O *suff.*[1] 1 and cf. *politico-economic.*] A quantity expressing a prime ratio: see PRIME *a.* 10 d.

1862 DE MORGAN in Graves *Life Sir W. Hamilton* (1889) III. 576, I would rather use primo-rationals than differentials.

primordial (praɪˈmɔːdɪəl), *a.* (*sb.*) Also 5, 8 *erron.* pre-. [ad. late L. *prīmordiāl-is* that is first of all, original, f. PRIMORDIUM: see -AL[1]. So F. *primordial* (1480 in Hatz.-Darm.).]

A. *adj.* **1. a.** Of, pertaining to, or existing at (or from) the very beginning; first in time, earliest, original, primitive, primeval.

1398 TREVISA *Barth. De P.R.* VIII. i. (Tollem. MS.), The virtu of God made primordial mater, in þe whiche as it were in massy þinge þe foure elementis were vertually, and nouȝt distinguid. **1486** *Reception Hen. VII at York* in *Surtees Misc.* (1888) 55 Theiz premordiall princes of this principalitie. *a* **1626** BP. ANDREWES *Serm.* (1856) I. 385 Abstinence is a virtue..Sure I am the 'primordiale peccatum', the primordial sin was not abstaining. **1687** T. K. *Veritas Evang.* 98 There would have remained illustrious Memory thereof, at least in some of the primordial Churches. **1844** DISRAELI *Coningsby* II. i, To recur to the primordial tenets of the Tory party. **1875** POSTE *Gaius* I. Introd. (ed. 2) 6 The portion of primary rights that..we shall call Primordial rights (right to life, health, liberty, reputation, etc.) are never so much as mentioned by Gaius.

b. ***primordial soup***: see SOUP *sb.*

2. Constituting the beginning or starting-point; from which something else is derived or developed, or on which something else depends; original (as opposed or correlated to derivative); fundamental, radical; elementary.

a **1529** SKELTON *Agst. Garnesche* IV. 104 It plesyth that noble prince roialle Me as hys master for to calle In hys lernyng primordialle. **1666** BOYLE *Orig. Formes & Qual.* 388 Primordial Textures (if I may so call them). **1678** CUDWORTH *Intell. Syst.* 837 Being no Simple Primitive and Primordial thing, but Secondary, Compounded and Derivative. **1799** KIRWAN *Geol. Ess.* 327 The primordial chaotic fluid, in whose bosom most stones were formed. **1856** DOVE *Logic Chr. Faith* v. ii. 323 Space and time are the primordial necessaries of thought. **1893** TRAILL *Soc. Eng.* I. Introd. 53 A primordial instinct of human nature insures this concurrence and maintains it.

3. *Anat.* and *Zool.* Applied to parts or structures in their earliest or rudimentary stage, or to those formed at first, and afterwards replaced by others: = PRIMITIVE *a.* 8 a.

1786 *Phil. Trans.* LXXVI. 448 New ones are formed above, under, or at the sides of the primordial or temporary teeth, but in different sockets. **1870** ROLLESTON *Anim. Life* p. xxxv, In all Vertebrata above the Amphibia, a primordial as well as a secondary kidney is developed. *Ibid.* 38 Two fused primordial vertebrae. **1905** *Brit. Med. Jrnl.* 1 July 18 Final or dictyate condition of the primordial ovum.

4. *Bot.* **a.** First or earliest formed in the course of growth: said of leaves, fruit, or other parts. ***primordial meristem*** = ***promeristem*** (PRO-[2] 1).

1785 MARTYN *Rousseau's Bot.* xxviii. (1794) 443 The Scotch Pine..has two leaves in a sheath; and the primordial ones, solitary and smooth. **1830** LINDLEY *Nat. Syst. Bot.* 247 When fascicled, the primordial leaf to which they are then axillary is membranous, and enwraps them like a sheath. **1870** HOOKER *Stud. Flora* 220 Leaves broadly obovate obtuse toothed, primordial orbicular. **1925** EAMES & MACDANIELS *Introd. Plant Anat.* iii. 41 The youngest cells in a region of growing plant body in which the formation of new organs or parts of organs is taking place constitute a promeristem, or primordial meristem. **1943** *Bot. Rev.* IX. 142 The limits between primordial meristem cells at the apex and procambium cells below are vague.

b. Applied to tissues, etc., in their simplest or rudimentary stage or condition: as ***primordial cortex, epidermis.***

primordial cell, a cell in its simplest form, consisting merely of a mass of protoplasm, without cell-wall, cell-sap, etc. ***primordial utricle***, name for the layer of denser protoplasm lining the wall of a vacuolate cell, and forming a sac inclosing the thinner protoplasm and cell-sap.

1849 E. LANKESTER *Schleiden's Princ. Bot.* 569 Mohl asserts that the primordial utricle is the forerunner of the formation of the cellulose cell-wall. **1875** BENNETT & DYER tr. *Sachs' Bot.* 5 It has hence become usual even to consider a protoplasmic body of this kind as a cell, and to designate it as a naked membraneless cell or Primordial Cell. *Ibid.* 126 The outermost layer of the primary meristem which covers the *punctum vegetationis* together with its apex is the immediate continuation of the epidermis of the older part which lies further backwards; it may therefore be termed the Primordial Epidermis.

fig. **1893** BARROWS *Parl. Relig.* II. 1481 The primordial cell of organic Methodism is the class-meeting.

5. *Geol.* and *Palæont.* †**a.** = PRIMITIVE *a.* 7. *Obs.* **b.** Applied by Barrande (1846) to a series or 'zone' of strata in Bohemia, containing the earliest fossil remains there found; hence extended to the corresponding strata in other parts of the world, forming part of the Cambrian system; also applied to fossils found in these strata.

1796 KIRWAN *Elem. Min.* (ed. 2) I. 285 In the primordial stones of Vesuvius. **1802** PLAYFAIR *Illustr. Hutton. The.* 161 De Luc..applies the term primordial to the rocks in question and considers them as neither stratified nor formed by water. **1885** LYELL *Elem. Geol.* xxviii. (ed. 4) 454 M. Barrande found in Étage C, in Bohemia, Trilobites of the genera *Paradoxides, Conocoryphe* [etc.]... These primordial Trilobites have a peculiar facies of their own. **1894** *Geol. Mag.* Oct. 445 M. Barrande..then recognised the 'Lingula Flag' of Sedgwick as the exact equivalent of his primordial stratum (Etage C).

¶ **6.** App. misused (as if f. L. *ordo, ordin-* order) for: Of the first order or rank.

1849 *Fraser's Mag.* XXXIX. 383 From the time of Bossuet..no primordial champion of Catholicism arose in France.

B. *sb.* **1.** Something primordial, original, or fundamental; beginning, origin; a first principle, an element. *rare.*

1522 SKELTON *Why not to Court* 486 The primordyall Of his wretched originall. **1610** MARCELLINI *Triumphs Jas. I* 85 It consisteth of 3. Letters..as the primordials and Radicall Letters of the Hæbrewes. **1668** H. MORE *Div. Dial.* I. 37 The Primordialls of the World are not Mechanicall, but Spermaticall or Vital. **1813** T. BUSBY *Lucretius* I. *Dissert.* p. iv, Like his own primordials, they are not only indestructible, but unassailable.

†**2.** Name for an early variety of plum. *Obs.*

1664 EVELYN *Kal. Hort., July* 70 Plums, etc. Primordial, Myrobalan, the red, blew, and amber Violet. **1707** MORTIMER *Husb.* (1721) II. 376.

Hence **priˈmordialism**, primordial nature or condition; **primordiˈality**, the quality of being primordial; something characterized by this quality.

1874 W. WALLACE tr. *Hegel's Logic* 297 The cause therefore appears as passing into its correlative, and to be losing its primordiality in the latter. **1879** H. SPENCER *Princ. Sociol.* IV. §343 Yet another indication of primordialism may be named... Even between intimates greetings signifying continuance of respect, begin each renewal of intercourse. **1889** H. F. WOOD *Englishm. of Rue Caïn* xiv. 206 There be those that have construed simple grandeurs, grand simplicities, from idyllic gold-fields, to mean primordialities which, elsewhere, receive much precious time and space from the assize court and the gaol. **1977** J. A. FISHMAN in H. Giles *Lang., Ethnicity & Intergroup Relations* i. 17 Primordiality denotes both primacy, in the sense of a presumably original essence, as well as primitivism or irreducibility.

priˈmordially, *adv.* [f. PRIMORDIAL *a.* + -LY[2].] In a primordial way. **a.** At or from the very beginning; in the earliest stage; at first, originally, primitively. **b.** In relation to the beginning or starting-point; radically, fundamentally.

1856 FERRIER *Inst. Metaph.* III. xviii. 120 Everything which I, or any intelligence, can apprehend, is steeped primordially in me. **1871** DARWIN *Desc. Man* viii. (1874) 228 We have no grounds for supposing that male bees primordially collected pollen. **1875** LYELL *Princ. Geol.* (ed. 12) II. III. xxxvii. 324 His dogma of the immutability of primordially created species.

†**priˈmordian.** *Obs.* [f. L. *prīmordi-us* (see PRIMORDIUM) + -AN.] = PRIMORDIAL *sb.* 2.

1731–3 MILLER *Gard. Dict.* s.v. *Prunus*, The Jean-Native, or White Primordian. This is a small white Plum, of a clear yellow Colour,..and for its coming very early, deserves a Place in every good Garden of Fruit. **1755** in JOHNSON, whence in many mod. Dicts.

†**priˈmordiate**, *a. Obs. rare.* [f. L. *prīmordi-us* (see next) + -ATE[2].] = PRIMORDIAL *a.*

1599 NASHE *Lenten Stuffe* 15 Farewel the Baylies of the Cynque ports whose primordiat Getheneliaca was also dropping out of my inckhorne. **1680** BOYLE *Scept. Chem.* VI. 356 'Tis not every Thing Chymists will call Salt, Sulphur, or Spirit, that needs alwaies be a Primordiate and Ingenerable body.

‖**primordium** (praɪˈmɔːdɪəm). Pl. -ia. [L. *prīmordium* sb., orig. neut. of *prīmordius* adj., original, f. *prīmus* first + *ordīrī* to begin.]

a. The very beginning, the earliest stage; opening part, introduction; primitive source, origin.

1671 HOWE *Wks.* (1834) 199/1 (Stanf.) The mere preludes of this glory, the *primordia*, the beginnings of it. **1677** —— *Work Holy Spirit* vi. Wks. 1832 I. 66 They..want the radical, fundamental preparation; the *primordia*, or first principles by which they are to be adopted to that kingdom. **1704** SWIFT *T. Tub* viii. §3 Those Beings must be of chief Excellence wherein that Primordium appears most prominently to abound. **1846** R. GARNETT in *Proc. Philol. Soc.* II. 212 It would seem more probable that those roots are in many cases the real primordia of the ostensible *d'hatoos* or verbal roots. **1847** LYTTON *Lucretia* I. i, This is the primordium,—now comes the confession.

b. *Biol.* The first rudiment or germ of an organ or structure. In *Embryol.* = ANLAGE.

1875 BENNETT & DYER tr. *Sachs's Text-bk. Bot.* II. 531 In Primulaceæ..five protuberances (primordia) appear on the receptacle above the calyx, each of which grows up into a stamen. **1898** A. WILLEY in *Nature* 25 Aug. 390/1 The word that commends itself to me [for the German 'Anlage'].. is primordium. **1908** F. R. LILLIE *Devel. of Chick* 8 The ovum is the primordium of the individual, the ectoderm the primordium of all ectodermal structures,..the first thickening of the ectoderm over the optic cup the primordium of the lens, etc. **1935** *Jrnl. Morphol.* LVIII. 425 The primitive mesenteron..consists of a single layer of squamous epithelium dorsal to the attachments of the cardiac primordia, and two layers ventral to them. **1965** BELL & COOMBE tr. *Strasburger's Textbk. Bot.* 115 The primordia of the leaves arise at the apex from the outer layers of cells. **1978** M. J. T. FITZGERALD *Human Embryol.* ix. 75 At the end of the fifth week the primordia of the hands and feet are already apparent.

†**priˈmore.** *Obs. rare*⁻¹. [ad. It. *primore* (priˈmore), L. *prīmōr-is* first, foremost, chief, L. pl. *prīmōrēs*, as *sb.* the front rank in battle, deriv. of *prīm-us* first.] A chief man.

1625 T. GODWIN *Moses & Aaron* (1641) 18 The Patriarke of Constantinople and his Primore termed Protosyncellus, and amongst the Romans, the Centurion and his Optio. [**1856** J. BROWN in Cairns *Mem.* x. (1860) 325 My earlier friends among the *primores* of the Synod..have most of them long ago departed.]

Hence †**priˈmority**, foremost place or importance.

1727 *Philip Quarll* 142 Sally,..seeing the Primority of Marriage so much pleaded for, thought it may be worth her while to claim it.

†**pri'mortive**, *a. Obs. rare*⁻¹. [f. L. *prīm-us* first + ORTIVE.] Arising from that which is prime, primary, or primitive; derivative.

1620 T. GRANGER *Div. Logike* 12 Artificiall Argument is either prime, or primortiue [margin, *Primum, vel a primo ortum*].

†**primosity** (praɪˈmɒsɪtɪ). *Obs. humorous nonce-wd.* [f. PRIM *a.* + -OSITY.] Primness.

a **1839** LADY H. STANHOPE *Mem.* xi. (1845) II. 27, I should really like to know what excuse Lord A. could offer for his primosity to us, when he was riding with such a Jezebel as Lady ——.

†**pri'movable.** *Obs. rare*⁻¹. [f. PRIME *a.* + MOVABLE, after *primum mobile.*] = PRIMUM MOBILE. Also †**pri'movant** [cf. F. *prime, mouvant* moving].

1570 DEE *Math. Pref.* b iij, As the Heauen, is, by the Primouant, caried about in 24. æquall Houres. *Ibid.* d ij b, A ..way..of hauing the motion of the Primouant (or first æquinoctiall motion) by Nature and Arte, Imitated. **1625** LISLE *Du Bartas, Noe* 162 This power hath the Moone by motion of the Primouable; which maketh her rise and set, as the Sunne and other Starres doe, in the space of a day.

primp (prɪmp), *sb.* Now only *dial.* Also 7 **prympe.** [app. like PRIM *sb.*², short for PRIMPRINT.] The privet; = PRIM *sb.*²

1616 SURFL. & MARKH. *Country Farme* 156 The Garden of Pleasure is to be set about with Arbors, couered with Iesamin,..Bay trees, Woodbind, Vines,..Prympe, sweet Bryer, and other rare things. **1658** R. FRANCK *North. Mem.* (1821) 140 A beautiful arbour adorned with primp hedges. **1877** *N.W. Linc. Gloss.*, *Primp*, privet. **1886** *S.W. Linc. Gloss.*, *Primp*, the shrub Privet.

primp (prɪmp), *v.* orig. *dial.* [Related to PRIM *v.*]

1. *trans.* To make prim; to dress (*up*) or deck neatly or showily; to dispose or arrange primly. Also *refl.*

1801 W. BEATTIE *Parings* (1873) 14 (E.D.D.) Just i' the newest fashion primped. *a* **1860** in Bartlett *Dict. Amer.* s.v., Arter marm and Aunt Jane had primped up an' fixed my har an' creevat, I was reddy. **1880** J. E. WATT *Poet. Sk.* 73 (E.D.D.) Ye lassies,..A' primpit up an' dressed like leddies. **1914** R. FROST *North of Boston* 103 Lord, if I were to dream of everyone Whose shoes I primped to dance in! **1945** J. STEINBECK *Cannery Row* viii. 47 A Lee cousin primped up slightly wilted heads of lettuce the way a girl primps a loose finger wave. **1959** *Numbers* Feb. 30 Primping yourself up like a damned quean. **1965** F. KNEBEL *Night of Camp David* xiv. 232 She came willingly enough, after primping her hair and smoothing her charcoal linen dress. **1974** 'A. HAIG' *Peruvian Printout* 45 When Heinrich..came back..Shirley even forgot to primp herself.

b. *intr.* (for *refl.*) To make oneself smart; to prink. Also const. *up*.

1887 *Harper's Mag.* Mar. 544/1 When you was primping so, I thought all the time it was for Mrs. Rainwater. **1901** W. N. HARBEN *Westerfelt* iv. 49 Ef you want to primp up a little an' bresh that hoss-hair off'n yore pants, go in yore room. **1903** *Review of Rev.* Apr. p. xix. (*Cartoons*) The world is beginning to primp for the big show at St. Louis in 1904. **1937** *Daily Tel.* 31 Aug. 12/4 It [*sc.* the women's dressing-room of an American flying-boat] is described as containing 'mirrors and leather-covered stools for primping'—which I take to mean such running repairs as passengers find necessary. **1939** N. COWARD *Words & Music* in *Play Parade* II. 120 In tropical heat Nobody who's sweet, survives We powder and primp And try to be sympathetic. **1977** *Daily News* (Perth, Austral.) 19 Jan. 6/4 (*caption*) Dorothy Hamill, 1976 Olympic figure skating champion, primps before making her New York debut with the Ice Capades at Madison Square Garden.

c. *intr.* To make tidying or smoothing movements. *rare.*

1881 I. M. RITTENHOUSE *Maud* (1939) 1 Eva..pulled down her basque, 'primped' at her hair,..and looked expectantly towards the door.

2. *intr.* To behave primly; to put on affected airs.

1804 [see below]. **1875** W. WELSH *Poet. & Prose Wks.* 39 Pridefu' like she primpit Wi puckered neck and glancin' cheek And ruffles neatly crimpit.

3. *trans.* and *intr.* To move (oneself or another person) fussily or mincingly.

1951 W. SANSOM *Face of Innocence* xiii. 184 She primped us over to Roddy with all the posturing, like a dove stamping out its love-dance, of one person meeting another. **1953** J. MASTERS *Lotus & Wind* vii. 89 She opened the door..and primped along the passage. The skirt clung so tightly around her thighs that she had to hobble. **1977** *N.Z. Listener* 15 Jan. 46/4 The comedians pranced and primped with Ronnie Corbett.

Hence **primped**, *Sc.* **'primpit**, *ppl. a. dial.*, affected, prudish; of the mouth, closed primly, pursed up (*Sc.*); also **primped-up**; **'primping** *vbl. sb.*, preparing, dressing up; *ppl. a.*, demure, prudish (*Sc.*).

c **1739** J. SKINNER *Christmas Ba'ing* iv, The tanner was a primpit [*Gloss.* 'delicate, nice'] bit, As flimsy as a feather. **1804** TARRAS *Poems* 72 Young primpin Jean, wi' cuttie speen, Sings dum' to bake the bannocks. **1853** CADENHEAD *Bon-Accord* 199 (E.D.D.) Lady Ladles—primpit dame. *Ibid.* 169 Some wi' primpit mou', And upturn'd e'en. **1888** *Amer. Ann. Deaf* Apr. 100 Helen has a great notion of 'primping'. Nothing pleases her better than to be dressed in her best clothes. **1894** ELIZ. L. BANKS *Campaigns Curiosity* 40 Annie insisted that I wasted too much time in 'primping'. **1899** WINSTON CHURCHILL *R. Carvel* x, You are content to see Richard without primping. **1935** Z. N. HURSTON *Mules & Men* (1970) I. vi. 126 Tain't no use in you gittin' yo' mouf all primped up for no hoein' and rakin' out of me, Bertha. Call yo' grandson and let him do it. **1959** *News Chron.* 11 Aug. 6/4 Adolescence..is early enough to begin real primping. **1963** *Listener* 28 Mar. 570/1 One had the primped-up stage, gorgeous to the eye. **1977** *New Yorker* 16 May 108/2 When the course is closed to play and the green-keeping staff is giving it a final primping for the opening round.

primp (prɪmp), *a.* [f. the vb.] Smart, neat, prim.

1835 *Fraser's Mag.* July 17 Your primp wizand faces. **1903** *N.Y. Times* 26 Sept. 4 (Advt.), All-weather coats they are—just as primp, good-fitting and handsome as a man could wish to wear. **1931** *Aberdeen Press & Jrnl.* 19 Feb., Scotia's leed has mony a kin', Tae fit baith primp an' pliskie. **1966** J. S. COX *Illustr. Dict. Hairdressing* 122/1 *Primp*, smart, neat.

†**'prim-print.** *Obs.* Also 6 **prymprynt**, 6–8 **prime(-)print.** [Derivation unknown.

Appears too early to be connected with PRIM *a.* The first element has been conjectured to be F. *prime*, L. *prīm-us* first, and the second short for F. *printemps* spring; but for this there is no confirmatory evidence, nor is the sense probable. (The statement in Prior's *Pop. Names of Plants* that *prim-print* was orig. the primrose, and that the name was transferred from the herb to the shrub, is erroneous, and arises from the fact that *ligustrum*, in Pliny the privet, has been supposed by some to be in Virgil and Ovid the name of some white-flowered herb.)]

An early name of the Privet.

1548 TURNER *Names of Herbes* E j b, Ligustrum is called in greke Cypros, in englishe Prim print or priuet, though Eliote more boldely then lernedly, defended the contrary [cf. quot. 1542 s.v. PRIVET¹ 1]. **1562** —— *Herbal* II. 36 b, The herbe which is called..prymprynt or pryuet. **1578** LYTE *Dodoens* VI. xxv. 690 This plant is called in..English, Priuet, or Primprint, in Frenche, *Troesne.* **1598** FLORIO, *Ligustro*, the priuet or prime print tree vsed in gardens for hedges. Also a kind of white floure. **1674–5** in Willis & Clark *Cambridge* (1886) II. 642 Two thousand two hundred of Quicksetts and Prim-print. **1749** J. MARTYN tr. *Virg. Bucol.* II. 18 *note*, If the *Ligustrum* of Pliny was that..by us called privet or primprint.

primrose ('prɪmrəʊz), *sb.* (*a.*) Forms: 5 **prymrose, prima rose,** 5–6 **prymerose, prime rose,** 5–7 **primerose,** 6 **pryme rose, (prymer rose, primorose,)** *Sc.* **prymross,** 7 **prim rose, prim-rose, prime-rose,** 6– **primrose.** [Late ME. *primerose* (1413: see (*c*) below; not used by Chaucer or Gower; occurring in several glossaries and vocabularies *a* 1450, but not in *Sinon. Barthol.* or *Alphita*); corresp. in form to early OF. *primerose* (12–13th c.), and to med.L. *prima rosa*, lit. 'first' or 'earliest rose', in Eng.-Lat. vocabularies of 15th c.: the latter in *Alphita* a synonym of *primula veris* (see PRIMULA), and F. and Eng. *primerole*; by Palsgr. *primerolle* is given as Fr. for *primorose*, and is still so used dialectally in parts of Normandy. In It., Florio 1598 has '*Prima rosa* the flowre called the primrose or cowslip'. *Primrose* is not in the *Great Herbal* 1516–29, but is in Turner's *Libellus* 1538, and *Names of Herbs* 1548, also in Lyte and later Herbals. See Note below.]

A. *sb.* **1. a.** A well-known plant (*Primula veris* var. *acaulis* Linn., *P. vulgaris* Huds., *P. acaulis* Jacq., *P. grandiflora* Lam.), bearing pale yellowish flowers in early spring, growing wild in woods and hedges and on banks, esp. on clayey soil, and cultivated in many varieties as a garden plant. Also, the flower of this plant. Sometimes extended to include other species of the genus PRIMULA.

(*a*) in glossaries and vocabularies.

14.. *Voc.* in Wr.-Wülcker 592/41 *Ligustrum*, a primerose. **14..** *Nominale* ibid. 712/18 *Hoc ligustrum*, a primerose. [*Ibid.* 713/11 *Hoc ligustrum*, a cowslowpe.] *c* **1440** *Promp. Parv.* 413/2 Prymerose, *primula, calendula, ligustrum.* *a* **1450** *Stockh. Med. MS.* 196 Prymrose, *ligustrum.* *c* **1475** *Pict. Voc.* in Wr.-Wülcker 786/24 *Hoc ligustrum*, a prymrose. *Hoc ligustrum*, a cowyslepe. **1483** *Cath. Angl.* 291/2 A Prymerose, *primarosa, primula veris.* **1530** PALSGR. 56 b/2 Primorose a flour, *primerolle.* **1538** ELYOT, *Verbascum*, an herbe wherof be ii. kindes: of which one is supposed to be Molin or long wort, the other is supposed to be that whiche is callyd primerose. **1573–80** BARET *Alv.* P 715 A Primerose, or cowslip, *verbascum, vel verbasculum minus. Primula veris.* Dodon.

(*b*) in herbals, botanical works, etc.

1538 TURNER *Libellus* A ij b, *Arthritica* officinis est primula veris quæ ab anglis dicitur a prymerose. **1548** —— *Names of Herbes* G vij, There are .iij. Verbascula... The fyrste is called in barbarus latin Arthritica, and in englishe a Primerose. **1578** LYTE *Dodoens* V. lxxxiii. 122 Of Petie Mulleyn or the kindes of Primeroses... The smaller sorte.. we call Primerose, is of diuers kindes, as yellow and greene, single and dubble. *Ibid.* 123 [Figure of] Verbasculum minus, Prymerose. **1597** GERARDE *Herbal* II. cclx. 637 The common white fielde Primrose needeth no description. **1626** BACON *Sylva* § 512 There is a Greenish Prime-Rose, but it is Pale, and scarce a Greene. **1629** PARKINSON *Paradisus* 242, I know, that the name of *Primula veris* or Primrose, is indifferently conferred vpon those that I distinguish for *Paralyses* or Cowslips. I doe therefore..call those onely Primroses that carry but one flower vpon a stalke... And those Cowslips, that beare many flowers vpon a stalke together constantly. **1688** R. HOLME *Armoury* II. 70/1 Primroses are also double of variable colours. **1856** DELAMER *Fl. Gard.* (1861) 101 Double Primroses delight in the same soil and situation as Polyanthuses, but are somewhat less robust.

(*c*) in literature.

1413 *Pilgr. Sowle* (Caxton) v. ii. (1859) 75 One [world] is corowned with faire rede rosys,..and the thyrd with lusty prymerosys and lylyes entermellyd, and graciously arrayed. **1486** *Bk. St. Albans* B vij, Take alisawndre and the Roote of prima rose. **1508** DUNBAR *Flyting* 192 Powderit with prymross, sawrand all with clowiss. *c* **1530** *Crt. of Love* 1437 Eke eche at other threw the floures bright, The prymerose, the violet, the gold. **1576** FLEMING *Panopl. Epist.* 352 What man..euer sawe the Spring tide without Marche Violettes, Primeroses, and other pleasant floures? **1612** DRAYTON *Poly-olb.* xv. 150 The Primrose placing first, because that in the Spring It is the first appeares, then onely florishing. **1621** QUARLES *Esther* (1638) 117 Now plucks a Vi'let from her purple bed And then a Prim rose (the yeares Maidenhead). **1637** MILTON *Lycidas* 142 The rathe Primrose that forsaken dies. **1772** FOOTE *Nabob* II. Wks. 1799 II. 303 The poor fellow's face is as pale as a primrose. **1798** WORDSW. *P. Bell* I. xii, A primrose by a river's brim A yellow primrose was to him, And it was nothing more. **1899** *Daily News* 19 Apr. 6/4 Blue primroses, that came into vogue a few years ago, were of course not wanting.

b. Formerly applied to the Daisy, *Bellis perennis*; and now in *U.S.* to a kind of wild rose (? *Rosa setigera*).

1585 LUPTON *Thous. Notable Th.* v. § 94 (1675) 133 The Primroses (which some take to be Dasies). **1864** LOWELL *Fireside Trav.* 108 A kind of wild rose (called by the country folk the primrose).

2. With qualifying words, applied to **a.** Other species of the genus *Primula*: as **bird's-eye primrose**, *P. farinosa*, a mountain plant, bearing compact umbels of light purple flowers with yellow centres; **Chinese primrose**, *P. sinensis*, a Chinese species bearing white or lilac flowers in umbels, familiar as a greenhouse and room plant in winter and early spring; **fairy primrose**, *P. minima*, a small plant of Southern Europe, bearing large white or rose flowers (Nicholson 1887); **Himalayan primrose**, *P. sikkimensis*; **Scotch primrose**, *P. scotica*, a native of the north of Scotland, bearing umbels of purple yellow-eyed flowers; sometimes applied to *P. farinosa*.

1796 WITHERING *Brit. Plants* (ed. 3) II. 235 *Primula farinosa*..*Birds-eye Primrose. Marshes and bogs on mountains in the north. **1867** BABINGTON *Man. Brit. Bot.* (ed. 6) 277 *P*[*rimula*] *farinosa*... North of England and South of Scotland... Bird's-eye Primrose. **1858** HOGG *Veg. Kingd.* 595 The *Chinese Primrose. **1887** *Nicholson's Dict. Gard.* s.v. *Primula*, Perhaps the best-known Primula is that which is very generally cultivated for greenhouse and room decoration.., namely, the Chinese Primrose (*P. sinensis*).

b. Some other plants having flowers resembling those of the common primrose; as **Cape primrose**, a plant of the genus *Streptocarpus*, of S. Africa, etc., bearing showy pale purple, blue, or red flowers; **evening (night, †nightly) primrose**, the genus *Œnothera*: see EVENING *sb.*¹ 5 b; **peerless primrose** = PRIMROSE PEERLESS 2; **tree primrose** = *evening primrose*.

1884 MILLER *Plant-n.* 253/2 *Streptocarpus*, *Cape Primrose. **1902** *Westm. Gaz.* 28 May 6/3 On entering the first tent, the visitor is face to face with..a wonderful bed of Cape primroses, creamy-white, mauve, and in many shades. **1866** *Treas. Bot.* 927 *Evening or Night Primrose, *Œnothera.* **1760** J. LEE *Introd. Bot.* App. 323 *Night Primrose. **1849** [see NIGHT *sb.* 13 e]. **1884** MILLER *Plant-n.*, *Narcissus biflorus*, *Peerless Primrose or Primrose Peerless, Two-flowered Daffodil. **1629** PARKINSON *Paradisus* 264 The *tree Primrose of Virginia. **1785** MARTYN *Rousseau's Bot.* xix. (1794) 256 Tree Primrose, a Virginian plant... The corolla is a fine yellow, shut during the day, but expanding in the evening; whence some call it Nightly Primrose.

†**3.** *fig.* **a.** The first or best; the finest, or a fine, example; the 'flower', 'pearl' (cf. *pink of perfection*); also, a person in the flower of youth. *Obs.*

c **1425** in *Leg. Rood* 212 My swete sone..þou art þe flour, My primerose, my paramour. *c* **1425** *Cast. Persev.* 2024 in *Macro Plays* 134 A! Meknesse, Charyte & Pacyens,.. prymrose pleyeth parlasent. *c* **1450** *Cov. Myst.* xvi. (Shaks. Soc.) 158 Heyle, perle peerles, prime rose of prise! **1523** SKELTON *Garland of Laurel* 912 Ye be, as I deuyne, The praty primrose, The goodly Columbyne. *a* **1568** ASCHAM *Scholem.* I. (Arb.) 66 Two noble Primeroses of Nobilitie, the yong Duke of Suffolke, and Lord H. Matreuers. **1579** SPENSER *Sheph. Cal.* Feb. 166 Was not I planted of thine owne hand, To be the primrose of all thy land? **1664** COTTON *Scarron.* I. 86 O Dido Primrose of Perfection, Who only grantest kind Protection To wandring Trojans.

†**b.** Prime; first bloom; first-fruits. *Obs.*

1611 BRATHWAIT *Golden Fleece* II. *Sonn.* IV. iii, For she [Rosamond] poore wench did flourish for a while Cropt in the primrose of her wantonnesse. **1647** TRAPP *Comm. Rom.* xvi. 5 Gods soul hath desired such first ripe fruits, *Mic.* 7. 1, such primroses. **1650** —— *Comm. Lev.* ii. 14 God should bee served with the first-fruits of our age, the primrose of our childe-hood.

†**4.** In ancient cookery, A 'pottage' in which the flowers of this plant were a principal ingredient.

c **1430** *Two Cookery-bks.* 25 Prymerose. Take oþer half-pound of Flowre of Rys, .iij. pound of Almaundys, half an vnce of hony & Safroune, & take þe flowre of þe Prymerose, & grynd hem, and temper hem vppe with Mylke of þe Almaundys [etc.].

5. *Her.* A conventionalized figure of this flower as a charge; in quot. 1562 said to have four petals.

1562 LEIGH *Armorie* 64 Quater foyles, otherwise called, prime Roses. **1894** *Parker's Gloss. Her.* 477 *Primrose*, this flower occurs in some few instances. Though the colour varies, the shape of the natural flower should be retained.

6. a. Elliptical for *primrose colour*: A pale greenish yellow or lemon colour.

1882 *Garden* 21 Oct. 355/3 Take, for instance.. Narcisse, primrose, tipped with white.

b. A commercial soap of a yellowish colour. In full, *primrose soap*.

1907 *Yesterday's Shopping* (1969) 39/2 *Soaps (Plain)*. Pale Primrose (Army & Navy) bar about 3 lb. 0/9. The Royal Primrose (J. Knight's) bar about 3 lb. 0/9½. **1909** H. G. WELLS *Tono-Bungay* III. i. 265 We had added to the original Moggs' Primrose several varieties of scented and superfatted. *c* **1938** *Fortnum & Mason Catal.* 56/2 *Soaps, Household*.. Primrose Royal.. per bar 1/3.

7. *attrib.* and *Comb.*, as, in sense 'of primroses', 'of the primrose', ***primrose bank, bed, breath, bud, chaplet, colour, drop*** (DROP *sb.* 10 g), ***-peep, -picker, season, star, -tide, yellow***; instrumental and parasynthetic, as ***primrose-coloured, -decked, -haunted, -scented, -spangled, -starred, -sweet, -tinted, -vested*** adjs.; †**primrose cowslip**, Parkinson's name for the hybrid OXLIP; **primrose path, way**, a path abounding in primroses; *fig.* the path of pleasure; **primrose soap**: see sense 6 b above; **primrose-time**, *fig.* the time of early youth; **primrose tree** = *tree primrose*: see 2 b.

1592 SHAKS. *Ven. & Ad.* 151 This *Primrose banke whereon I lie. **1834** MRS. HEMANS *Sonn., Happy Hour* 8 The wandering *primrose-breath of May. **1777** WARTON *Ode Friend leaving Hampsh.* 56 His *primrose-chaplet rudely torn. **1629** PARKINSON *Paradisus* 244 Of the very same *Primrose colour that the former is of. **1796** WITHERING *Brit. Plants* (ed. 3) IV. 238 Gills primrose-colour. **1788** *Gazetteer* 12 May 2/3 The train was a *primrose coloured goffree'd crape spotted with blue crape in relief. **1830** *Withering's Brit. Plants* (ed. 7) IV. 216 *Agaricus Primula* (Primrose-coloured Agaric). **1888** *Times* 2 Jan. 7/4 The young.. Lady Mansfield in her primrose-coloured dress. **1629** PARKINSON *Paradisus* 244 *Paralysis altera odorata flore pallido polyanthos*. The *Primrose Cowslip. **1625** B. JONSON *Pan's Anniv.*, The *primrose drop, the Spring's own spouse! **1835** MRS. HEMANS *Remembr. Nat.* 3 Feeding my thoughts in *primrose-haunted nooks. **1567** GOLDING *Ovid* XIII. 929 More whyght thou art then *primrose leaf [*folio nivei ligustri*]. **1602** SHAKS. *Ham.* I. iii. 50 Doe not as some vngracious Pastors doe, Shew me the steepe and thorny way to Heauen; Whilst like a puft and recklesse Libertine, Himselfe the *Primrose path of dalliance treads. **1820** HAZLITT *Lect. Dram. Lit.* 80 To tread the primrose path of pleasure. **1882** FROUDE *Carlyle* I. xix. 355 Never to sell his soul by travelling the primrose path to wealth and distinction. **1831** E. FITZGERALD *Lett.* (1889) I. 8 So winter passeth Like a long sleep From falling autumn To *primrose-peep. **1796** WITHERING *Brit. Plants* (ed. 3) II. 398 *Hypopithys*.. *Primrose scented Birds-nest. **1634** MILTON *Comus* 671 Brisk as the April buds in *Primrose-season. **1796** M. EDGEWORTH *Parent's Assistant* (ed. 2) II. 127 A fresh assortment of.. *Primrose Soap. **1648** HERRICK *Hesper.*, *Epitaph upon a Child*, Virgins promis'd when I dy'd, That they wo'd each *primrose-tide, Duely morne and ev'ning, come, And with flowers dresse my tomb. **1606** *Wily Beguiled* in Hazl. *Dodsley* IX. 231 I'll prank myself with flowers of the prime; And thus I'll spend away my *primrose-time. **1741** *Compl. Fam.-Piece* II. iii. 357 Towards the End of this Month, sow Pinks,.. Sweet Williams, *Primrose-trees. **1760** J. LEE *Introd. Bot.* App. 324 Primrose-tree, *Oenothera*. **1922** JOYCE *Ulysses* 195 *Primrosevested he greeted gaily with his doffed Panama as with a bauble. **1605** SHAKS. *Macb.* II. iii. 21 Some of all Professions, that goe the *Primrose way to th' euerlasting Bonfire. **1817** SCOTT *Harold* v. xiv, Chief they lay Their snares beside the primrose way. **1882** *Garden* 2 Dec. 481/1 A large.. flower of a soft *primrose-yellow. **1907** *Yesterday's Shopping* (1969) 478/2 Oil Colours.. Primrose yellow.. Raw sienna. **1954** T. S. ELIOT *Confid. Clerk* I. 32, I thought a primrose yellow would be cheerful. **1978** *Vogue* 1 Mar. 128 Shirtdress.. primrose yellow with Peter Pan collar.

8. From the association of the flower with the memory of Benjamin Disraeli, Earl of Beaconsfield, who died 19th April, 1881: **Primrose Day**, the anniversary of that event; **Primrose League**, a political association formed in 1883, in memory of Lord Beaconsfield and in support of the principles of Conservatism as represented by him; so **Primrose Leaguer**. Hence, in sense 'of the Primrose League', ***Primrose dame, habitation, knight***: see the sbs.; so ***Primrose associate, banner, circle, lady, literature***, etc.

1883 (*title*) Primrose League. **1884** E. W. HAMILTON *Diary* 21 Mar. (1972) II. 581 Mrs. G... carried a splendid bouquet of primroses,.. to show that the 'Primrose Leaguers' have no title to appropriate the flower to themselves. *Ibid.* 19 Apr. 597 'Primrose Day'. Were I an admirer of Lord Beaconsfield, I should be furious that his memory should be so ridiculed. **1886** SIR A. BORTHWICK in *19th Cent.* July 39 The badges are.. an absolute introduction into all Primrose Circles. **1890** (*title*) A Little Primrose Knight, a story of the autumn of 1885, by a Primrose Dame. **1891** *Pall Mall G.* 2 Dec. 6/2 In the accompanying cartoon a Primrose dame is depicted fastening a primrose posy into Mr. Chamberlain's buttonhole. **1898** *Westm. Gaz.* 9 Dec. 8/1 Although Sir George Birdwood has never publicly claimed any credit in that direction, we are, we believe, not very wide of the mark in suggesting that he was the originator of 'Primrose Day'. **1912** CHESTERTON *Manalive* II. ii. 240, I have faced many a political crisis in the old Primrose League days at Herne Bay. **1923** J. M. MURRY *Pencillings* 146 Disraeli.. was a far more remarkable man than the most enthusiastic Primrose Leaguer has ever imagined. **1959** B. & R. NORTH tr. *Duverger's Pol. Parties* (ed. 2) I. i. 66 The Primrose League, an organization distinct from the party proper, aimed at social mixing. **1975** R. TAYLOR *Lord Salisbury* viii. 134 He told the Primrose League in a memorable speech: 'You may roughly divide the nations of the world as the living and the dying.'

B. as *adj.* Of primrose colour.

1788 *Gazetteer* 12 May 2/3 An immense panache of white, blue and primrose feathers. **1815** in R. W. Chapman *Jane Austen's Pride and Prejudice* (1923) 398 Primrose sandals, and white kid gloves. **1844** WILLIS *Lady Jane* II. 366 Serene in faultless boots and primrose glove. **1851** G. MEREDITH *Love in Valley* xxv, Soft new beech-leaves, up to beamy April Spreading bough on bough a primrose mountain. **1931** [see JUMPER *sb.*[2] 3 c]. **1976** *S. Wales Echo* 25 Nov. 27/4 (Advt.), Bathroom/w.c., half-tiled in Primrose, matching Primrose suite.

[*Note.* The history of this word and its original application are obscure. The designation 'first' or 'earliest rose' is not very applicable to the flower, which in no respect resembles a rose in colour, form, or habit of growth. And if 'rose' be taken as vaguely synonymous with 'flower', the primrose is not manifestly the 'first flower' of spring. The same holds good of the F. *primevère* or cowslip, which flowers still later than the primrose. The L. *prima rosa* is not known before *c* 1450 (in *Alphita*: see PRIMULA), which is later than the Eng. word. The It. *prima rosa*, in Florio, is of uncertain age. In OF., *primerose* is cited only from some MSS. of the *Geste des Lohérains*, and from *Perceval*, both of 12th c. The meaning is uncertain; though, as other MSS. of the *Lohérains* have the variant *primevoire* (mod.F. *primevère* cowslip), the flower meant may possibly have been the cowslip or the primrose. According to Bouillet *Dict. des Sciences* 1862–3, and Littré 1863–72, *primerose* is a synonym of *passe-rose*, popularly or locally applied to the Hollyhock, and to the Rose Campion (*Lychnis Coronaria*); but *primerose* is not recognized as an existing name of any flower in *La Flore des Jardins et du Champ* of Le Maoulet & Decaisse, 1855. Historical connexion between the OF. and the 15th c. Eng. word is thus uncertain. The original application in Eng. is obscure; the 15th c. vocabularies and glossaries use it to gloss *ligustrum*, a plant noted in Roman poets for its *white* flowers (now identified as the PRIVET, but by early glossists taken to be a herb); but as *ligustrum* is also glossed by *cowslepe, cowslope*, and one explanation of *prymrose* in Promp. Parv. is *primula* (and in Cath. Angl. *primula veris*), it is fairly certain that by the middle of the 15th c. *primrose* was applied to one or both species of *Primula*. By Palsgrave it is, like *prima rosa* in *Alphita*, identified with PRIMEROLE, which in parts of Normandy is now a name of the primrose. In Turner's *Libellus* and *Names of Herbes*, *primrose* is certainly a *Primula* and prob. the primrose; in Lyte, 1578, it is figured and is there clearly the primrose (though the 'cowslippe, oxelippe, and prymerose' are all included as 'kindes of Primeroses'). See also *Note* to PRIMULA.]

'primrose, *v.* [f. prec.: cf. BLACKBERRYING *vbl. sb.* and NUT *v.* 1.] **a.** *intr.* To look for, or gather, primroses; esp. in phr. ***to go (a) primrosing***. **b.** *humorously* (see prec. 8), to speak at or take part in Primrose League gatherings.

1830 MISS MITFORD in L'Estrange *Life* (1870) II. 301, I.. had gone to a copse primrosing. **1887** *Pall Mall G.* 9 Sept. 4/2 Co-operative farming is a good deal better than 'primrosing'. **1888** *Manchester Courier* 19 Apr. 5/7 One section of the Unionist party went primrosing with Mr. Smith. **1928** *Daily Express* 10 Mar. 5/3 There are few of the many who enjoy the country who will be able to resist primrosing. **1941** E. BOWEN *Look at Roses* 122 This afternoon.. we'll go primrosing. **1967** 'L. BRUCE' *Death of Commuter* viii. 82 'I'm going to take her primrosing tomorrow,' he told Carolus. 'In Langley Wood'. **1973** J. THOMSON *Death Cap* vi. 88 To go bird's-nesting, or blackberrying or primrosing.

primrosed ('prɪmrəʊzd), *a.* [f. PRIMROSE *sb.* + -ED[2].] Abounding in primroses; covered or adorned with primroses.

1655 H. VAUGHAN *Silex Scint.* I. *Regeneration*, It was high-spring, and all the way Primrosed, and hung with shade. **1777** WARTON *Hamlet* 35 Or through the primros'd coppice stray. **1835** *Blackw. Mag.* XXXVII. 714 On primrosed bank and brae.

'primrose 'peerless. [See the two words.]

†**1.** Originally used in the senses of the two words: A peerless or unrivalled primrose; usually *fig.*: see PRIMROSE *sb.* 3. *Obs. rare.*

1523 SKELTON *Garl. Laurel* 1447 This ieloffer ientyll, this rose, this lylly flowre, This primerose pereles. **1542** BALE *Myst. Iniq.* (1545) D iv, Holye Thomas Becket wold sumtyme for his pleasure make a iournaye of pylgrymage to the prymerose peerlesse of Stafforde. [*c* **1580** JEFFERIE *Bugbears* I. ii. 31 in *Archiv Stud. Neu. Spr.* (1897) XCVIII. 307 Old Brancatio hath a passing pereles primrose to his daughter.]

2. A name formerly given to the species of Narcissus, including the wild daffodil; now spec. to *Narcissus biflorus*, the two-flowered narcissus.

1578 LYTE *Dodoens* II. l. 211 These pleasant flowers are called.. in Latine, *Narcissus*.. in Englishe, Narcissus, white Daffodill, and Primerose pierelesse. **1597** GERARDE *Herbal* I. lxxv. §15. 114 Generally all the kindes are comprehended vnder this name *Narcissus*, called.. in English Daffodilly, Daffodowndilly, and Primerose peerelesse. **1599** —— *Catal. Arb.*, *Narcissus Pisanus*, Italian Daffodill, or Primerose peerelesse. **1629** PARKINSON *Paradisus* 74 Bearing.. flowers .. of a pale whitish Creame colour,.. (which hath caused our Countrey Gentlewomen, I thinke, to entitle it Primrose Peerlesse). **1861** MISS PRATT *Flower. Pl.* V. 237 This beautiful species, the Primrose-peerless of old writers. **1866** *Treas. Bot.*, Primrose peerless, *Narcissus biflorus*.

primroser ('prɪmrəʊzə(r)). [f. PRIMROSE *sb.* + -ER[1].] **a.** One who seeks or gathers primroses. **b.** (With capital initial.) *Political slang.* An adherent of the Primrose League. So **'Primrosery, 'Primrosism**, the principles and practice of the Primrose League.

1885 *Pall Mall G.* 6 May 3/2 What in Dawson's day was figurative only has by the Primrosers been made literally true. **1886** *Sat. Rev.* 20 Nov. 683/2 The 'Liberal League for the Association of Men and Women' in fighting Primrosism. **1897** *Westm. Gaz.* 20 Apr. 2/2 Primrosery is not so much a reasoned faith as a social cult.

primrosy ('prɪmrəʊzɪ), *a.* [f. PRIMROSE *sb.* + -Y.] **a.** Abounding in or characterized by primroses; resembling a primrose, primrose-coloured.

1826 MISS MITFORD *Village* Ser. II. 47 (*Copse*) Primrosy is the epithet which this year will retain in my recollection. **1880** J. HATTON *Three Recruits* III. vi, April surely used to be a gayer, brighter, and more primrosy month.. than it is now. **1882** MARG. VELEY *Damocles* III. 39 A trifle pale... Almost primrosy, isn't it?

b. (With capital initial.) *humorous.* Of, pertaining to, or having the character of the Primrose League.

1890 *Daily News* 9 Sept. 6/5 Salvation will no more come to him by class legislation than it has reached him by doles ecclesiastical or Primrosy. **1904** *Sat. Rev.* 16 July 66 The meeting was distinctly Primrosey in its enthusiasm and adornments.

c. *fig.* (Cf. *primrose path* s.v. PRIMROSE *sb.* (*a.*) 7.)

1908 E. V. LUCAS *Over Bemerton's* xx. 202 His duty always lies along the primrosiest path.

primsie ('prɪmzɪ), *a.* *Sc. rare.* [f. PRIM *a.*] Demure, formal, precise.

1785 BURNS *Halloween* ix, Poor Willie, wi his bow-kail runt, Was brunt wi' primsie Mallie.

†**primstaff.** *Obs.* Also 9 **primestaff**; *pl.* 7– **primstaves.** [Sw. *primstaf*, Norw. and Da. *primstav*, Icel. *prímstafr* (in text of *c* 1200), f. *prím* PRIME *sb.*[1] + *staf-r* stave, letter.] The Icelandic and Scandinavian name of a clog almanack. (Partly in Eng. form in Evelyn and Plot, and in mod. Dicts., but never in Eng. use.)

1662 EVELYN *Chalcogr.* (1769) 38 Runic writings, or engraven letters, as in their *rimstoc* or *primstaff*. **1686** PLOT *Staffordsh.* 419 By the Norwegians.. [wooden Almanacks] are call'd Primstaves,.. the principall.. thing inscribed on them, being the Prime or golden number. *Ibid.* 420 The Primstaf of the Norwegians.

primula ('prɪmjʊlə). *Bot.* [a. med.L. *prīmula*, fem. of *prīmul-us*, dim. of *prīm-us* first; originally in the name *prīmula vēris* 'little firstling of spring', applied by 1101 app. to the Cowslip, but at an early date also to the Field Daisy, perh. as an earlier spring flower, or because both plants were from their supposed virtues known as *herba paralysis*. Matthioli in 1565 confined *Primula veris* to the Cowslip; Linnæus adopted *Primula* as a generic name, and made *Primula veris* a species, including three subspecies, *P. veris officinalis* the Cowslip, *P. v. elatior* the (true) Oxlip, *P. v. acaulis* the Primrose; but these are now generally considered as three species. See Note below.]

A genus of herbaceous, mostly hardy, perennial plants, of low growing habit, having radical leaves, and yellow, white, pink, or purple flowers mostly borne in umbels; chiefly natives of Europe and Asia, and cultivated in many varieties.

1753 CHAMBERS *Cycl. Supp.* s.v., The species of primula enumerated by Mr. Tournefort, are these [etc.]. **1834** MRS. SOMERVILLE *Connex. Phys. Sc.* xxvii. (1849) 303 On the lofty range of the Himalaya the primula, the convallaria, and the veronica blossom. **1841** *Penny Cycl.* XIX. 3/1 The Primula, Anagallis, [etc.],.. are the gayest of the genera, some of whose species are found in almost all gardens. **1882** *Garden* 18 Feb. 121/3 One of the finest varieties of the Chinese Primula yet produced.. was shown.

[Note. *Primula veris* occurs *c* 1101 in *Regimen Sanitatis Salerni*, app. in a list of plants supposed to cure paralysis: 'Salvia, Castoriumque, Lavendula, Primula veris, Nasturtium, Armoracia, hæc sanant paralytica membra', in which *Primula veris* appears to mean the Cowslip, often called *Herba Paralysis*. But both names appear also to have been applied to other plants. Thus the *Sinonoma Bartholomei a* 1387 (*Anecd. Oxon.* 1882) has, p. 23, '*Herba paralisis*, i. couslop, alia est a primula veris'; also, '*Herba Sancti Petri*, primula veris idem'; and, p. 35, '*Primula veris*, herba Sti. Petri idem, solsequium idem, alia est ab herba paralisi'. *Alphita a* 1450 (*Anecd. Oxon.* 1887) identifies *Primula veris* with the common Field Daisy: thus (p. 146) '*Primula ueris*, prima rosa idem, gall. et angl. primerole. Respice in *consolida minor*. (p. 45) *Consolida minor*, primula ueris idem, ossa fracta consolidat, gallice, le petite consoude, angl. dayseghe [*MS.* waysegle] uel bonwort uel brosewort. Respice in *uenti minor*. (p. 190) *Venti minor*, consolida minor idem, an. Bonwrt, a. dayesegh.' The difference of opinion is also hinted by Simon Januensis, *Clavis Sanationis* (*a* 1400, ed. Venice 1486) '*Passerella*, primula veris, herba paralisis idem, ut volunt quidam'. *Primula veris* was identified with the daisy in the *Ortus Sanitatis* (Augsb. 1486), and by the 16th c. botanists Brunsfels, Lonicerus, Tragus, and Fuchs, several of whom figure the plant. Parkinson *Theat. Bot.* 531 gives the name to both the daisy and the primrose. Hieronymus of Brunschwygk, 1531, says that there were three plants called *Herba paralysis*, of which *H. paralysis minor* was the Daisy, and *H. paralysis major* was *Primula veris*. Matthioli 1565 has 'Eas vulgaris notitiæ plantas, quæ quibusdam *Bractea cuculi* [cf. F. *coucou* cowslip], officinis *Primula veris*, Germanis *Claves Sancti Petri*, nonnullis *herba paralysis* appellantur', and figures the Cowslip as *Primula veris*. The names *Claves Sti. Petri, Herba Sti. Petri, St. Peter's wort*, and Ger. *Schlüsselblume*, are due to the resemblance of a cowslip head to a bunch of keys.]

Hence **primu'laceous** *a.*, belonging to the natural order *Primulaceæ*, of which *Primula* is the typical genus; **'primulin** *Chem.* [-IN [1]] (see quots.).

1841 *Penny Cycl.* XIX. 3/1 The *Primulaceous order consists of herbaceous plants inhabiting the temperate parts of the world, in moist situations. **1851** GLENNY *Handbk. Fl. Gard.* 46 Pretty little plants of the primulaceous order. **1837** R. D. THOMSON in *Brit. Ann.* 352 **Primulin.*—When the roots of the *primula veris* or cowslip are digested in water or spirit a bitter tincture is obtained—the spirituous solution deposits after a considerable time by spontaneous evaporation many small prismatic crystals—these are primulin mixed with some vegetable matter. **1897** *Naturalist* 45 An acrid principle called primulin.

primuline ('prɪmjuːliːn). *Chem.* Also Primuline. [f. PRIMUL(A + -INE[5].] A synthetic yellow dyestuff which is the sodium salt of the sulphonic acid derivative of primuline base (see below) and is used in the dyeing of cotton.

The dye may also contain other analogous salts.

1887 *Dyer & Calico Printer* VII. 101/1 A new series of colours..are just now being brought out by Brooke, Simpson, & Spiller (Limited). These colours, the discovery of Mr. A. G. Green, promise to compete successfully with the direct cotton colours at present in the market. The basis of the series is a compound, to which the name of primuline has been given. **1919** E. DE B. BARNETT *Coal Tar Dyes* 108 Primuline dyes cotton in bright yellow shades, but these are too fugitive to be of any value. **1950** *Thorpe's Dict. Appl. Chem.* (ed. 4) X. 215/1 The sodium salts of the sulphonic acids of the higher thionated *p*-toluidines (primuline bases) were first manufactured..in 1887 under the name of 'Primuline' and employed for the production of so-called 'ingrain colours' by..diazotising and developing upon the fibre. **1968** E. N. ABRAHART *Dyes* v. 135 Among the direct dyes C.I. Direct Red 70..employs Primuline as diazo component and Schäffer's acid as coupling component.

2. Special Combs.: **primuline base**, a yellow thiazole derivative, $C_{21}H_{15}N_3S_2$, which is obtained when *p*-toluidine is heated with sulphur and is an intermediate in dye manufacture; *loosely*, any of the related compounds also formed by this process; **primuline red**, a red dyestuff obtained from primuline base by diazotization followed by coupling with β-naphthol.

1889 *Jrnl. Chem. Soc.* LV. 228 The product is not homogeneous, but consists of about 50 per cent. of a base, $C_{14}H_{12}N_2S$,..40 per cent. of primuline-base, and 10 per cent. of unaltered paratoluidine. **1913** *Thorpe's Dict. Appl. Chem.* (ed. 2) IV. 385/1 These more condensed bases ('primuline bases') were obtained in larger amount by increasing the proportion of sulphur to 4½–5 atoms to 1 mol. amine. **1961** COCKETT & HILTON *Dyeing of Cellulosic Fibres* v. 156 Primuline Base may be sulphonated to give the monosulphonic acid, the sodium salt of which is the yellow dye Primuline, a direct dye for cellulosic fibres. **1968** E. N. ABRAHART *Dyes* v. 135 The sulphurization products of *p*-toluidine, primuline base and dehydrothio-*p*-toluidine are used..in the manufacture of some valuable cotton dyes. **1900** *Jrnl. Soc. Chem. Industry* 30 Apr. 345/1 Primuline Red is obtained by dyeing with Primuline, diazotising, and developing with β-naphthol. **1917** *Jrnl. Soc. Dyers & Colourists* XXXIII. 140/1, I replied by pointing out the greater fastness of Primuline Red compared to Benzopurpurine.

‖**primum frigidum** ('praɪməm 'frɪdʒɪdəm). *Obs.* [L., first cold.] Absolute or pure cold, which Parmenides (*c* 450 B.C.) accounted an elementary substance; the origin or source of cold.

1626 BACON *Sylva* §69 The Earth being (as hath beene noted by some) *Primum Frigidum*. **1665** BOYLE *Exp. Hist. Cold* xvii. §2, I think, that, before men had so hotly disputed, which is the *Primum Frigidum*, they would have done well to inquire, whether there be any such thing or no.

‖**primum mobile** ('praɪməm 'məʊbɪliː). [med.L., lit. 'first moving thing', L. *prīm-us* first, *mōbilis* movable: see PRIME *a.* and MOBILE *sb.*[1] and *a.*

Primum mobile (also *primus motus, primus motor*) was an 11–12th c. rendering of the Arabic *al-muḥarrik al-awwal*, the first mover or moving (thing), cited from Avicenna (*a* 1037) by Shahrastānī (*a* 1153). The L. occurs in Thomas Aquinas *Comment. in Aristot. De Cœlo* II. ix. §1, xv. §7; also in John of Holywood (de Sacrobosco) 1256.]

1. The supposed outermost sphere (at first reckoned the ninth, later the tenth), added in the Middle Ages to the Ptolemaic system of astronomy, and supposed to revolve round the earth from east to west in twenty-four hours, carrying with it the (eight or nine) contained spheres. Cf. MOBILE *sb.*[1] 1, and MOVABLE *sb.* 1.

[**1256** JOH. DE SACROBOSCO *Sphæra Mundi* (Paris *c* 1500) A ij, Sphera diuiditur..secundum substantiam in spheras novem, sc. Spheram nonam que primus motus siue primum mobile dicitur, et in spheram stellarum fixarum que firmamentum nuncupatur, et in septem spheras septem planetarum. *c* **1391** CHAUCER *Astrolabe* I. §17 This equinoxial is cleped the gyrdelle of the firste Moeuyng, or elles of the *angulus primi motus vel primi mobilis*.] **1460–70** *Bk. Quintessence* (1889) 26 Philosofirs puttyn 9 speris vndirewritten; but Diuinis putten þe tenþe spere, where is heuyn empire,..in þe whiche is crist..and also owre lady, & seyntis þat arosen with criste. þe first spere of þe 9 is clepid 'primum mobile', þe first mevabil thyng. **1559** W. CUNNINGHAM *Cosmogr. Glasse* 10 The .x. heauen or Primum mobile, comprehendeth the .ix. heauen callid also Cristalline. *Ibid.* 12 And that, which you call the eight heauen, they name primum mobile. **1669** STURMY *Mariner's Mag.* I. ii. 13 The Motion of the Moon is..caused by the diurnal swiftness of the Primum Mobile. **1686** J. DUNTON *Lett. fr. New-Eng.* (1867) 18 He is always looking upwards; yet dares believe nothing above Primum Mobile, for 'tis out of the reach of his Jacob's Staff. **1690** LEYBOURN *Curs. Math.* 451 Others are of Opinion that they [comets] are fiery Meteors, generated of copious exhalations from the Earth and Sea,..elevated to the Supreme Region of the Air, and hurried about by the swift Motion of the *Primum Mobile*. **1733** P. SHAW tr. *Bacon's Nov. Org.* I. lx, Of the former kind [i.e. Names of Things that have no Existence] are such as Fortune, the *Primum Mobile*, the Orbs of the Planets, the Element of Fire, and the like Figments; which arise from imaginary false Theories. **1847** LD. LINDSAY *Sk. Chr. Art* I. p. xxxii, Beyond the region of fire..succeeded the spheres of the seven planets;..the firmament, or eighth heaven;..the crystalline, or ninth heaven;..and the *primum mobile*, a void;—the whole continually revolving round the earth, and encompassed in their turn by the empyrean.

2. *transf.* and *fig.* A prime source of motion or action; an original cause or spring of activity; a prime mover, mainspring. Cf. PRIME MOVER 1, 2.

1612 G. CALVERT in *Crt. & Times Jas. I* (1848) I. 191 You know the *primum mobile* of our court, by whose motion all the other spheres must move, or else stand still. **1655** MRQ. WORCESTER *Cent. Inv.* §98 An Engine so contrived that working the *Primum mobile* forward or backward, upward or downward, circularly or corner-wise, to and fro, streight, upright or downright, yet the pretended Operation continueth, and advanceth. **1673** KIRKMAN *Unlucky Citizen* 207 My Son, keep thou ready Money in thy Pocket: this is the *primum Mobile* of all their Science of thriving. **1753** HANWAY *Trav.* (1762) II. IX. ii. 216 Their religion, which the Mahommedans consider as the basis and primum mobile of political government. **1768–74** TUCKER *Lt. Nat.* (1834) II. 670 Each man's own satisfaction, interest, or happiness, is the primum mobile or the first spring of all his schemes and all his actions. **1802–12** BENTHAM *Ration. Judic. Evid.* (1827) III. 285 Modified by the other known primum mobiles, or causes of motion and rest. **1864** BRYCE *Holy Rom. Emp.* xv. (1889) 255 There must, in every system of forces, be a 'primum mobile'.

‖**primus** ('praɪməs), *a.* and *sb.* [L. *prīmus* first: see PRIME *a.*]

A. *adj.* First (in time, age, order, or importance); original, earliest; chief, principal.

1. In Latin phrases, as ***primus inter pares***, first among equals; also fem. ***prima inter pares***; ***primus motor***, prime mover, the original source of motion or action; †***primus secundus*** (lit. 'first second'), some game.

1813 J. ADAMS *Let. to Jefferson* 12 Nov., Mr. Dickinson was **primus inter pares*, the bellwether, the leader of the aristocratical flock. **1887** *Athenæum* 16 Apr. 507/1 The sovereign, relatively, was but *primus inter pares*, closely connected by origin and intermarriage with a turbulent feudal nobility. **1909** WEBSTER, Prima inter pares. **1919** M. BEER *Hist. Brit. Socialism* I. II. v. 162 He could be their self-sacrificing father and teacher, their authoritative adviser and leader, but never the *primus inter pares*. **1961** *Times* 12 Oct. 18/1 But this is a ballet in which Dame Margot is but *prima inter pares*. **1973** *Times* 20 Oct. 13/5 Herr Schneiderhan did not attempt to stand out as a virtuoso but attacked his solos as *primus inter pares*, playing with and to his accompanying strings. **1979** *Guardian* 5 May 21/3 Mrs Thatcher.. becomes..*primus inter pares* in that quaint and English system known as Cabinet Government. *c* **1592** MARLOWE *Jew of Malta* I. ii. Wks. (Rtldg.) 150/1 The plagues of Egypt, and the curse of heaven..Inflict upon them, thou great *Primus Motor! **1617** J. CHAMBERLAIN in *Crt. & Times Jas. I* (1848) II. 9 Now the *primus motor* of this feasting, Mr. Comptroller, is taking his leave of this town. *a* **1670** HACKET *Abp. Williams* II. (1693) 11 You have said somewhat.. concerning the last Parliament, somewhat of the *Primus motor*, and Divine Intelligence which enliv'd the same. **1584** R. SCOT *Discov. Witchcr.* XI. x. (1886) 159 It [lottery] is a childish and ridiculous toie, and like unto childrens plaie at **Primus secundus*, or the game called The philosophers table.

2. In some boys' schools, appended to the surname to distinguish the eldest (or the one who has been longest in the school) of those having the same surname. Cf. MAJOR *a.* 7c.

1796 T. ROBBINS *Diary* (1886) I. 6 My classmate Romeyn *primus*, was, I hear, quite unwell. **1826** DISRAELI *Viv. Grey* I. iii, 'Mammy-sick', growled Barlow *primus*.

B. *sb.* **1.** In the Scottish Episcopal Church: The presiding bishop, who is chosen by the other bishops, and has certain ceremonial privileges, but no metropolitan authority. Hence **'primus-ship**, the position or dignity of the primus.

1860 J. GARDNER *Faiths World* II. 830/2 Scottish Episcopal Church... One of the bishops is elected primus or chief bishop during pleasure, there having been no archbishops in Scotland since the Revolution. **1899** J. WORDSWORTH *Episcopate C. Wordsw.* v. 178, I wrote to the Primus, Bishop Gleig. *Ibid.* 156 The second [year] was the beginning of the reign of King George III, and of the Primus-ship of Bishop William Falconar.

2. Also **Primus.** The proprietary name of a make of pressure stove or lamp, usu. burning paraffin; *loosely*, any pressure stove. Freq. *attrib.*

1904 *Outing* Mar. 698/1 At last we found and packed with rucksacks, small kerosene cans, Primus stove, etc. **1904** *Railway Mag.* XIV. 45/1 A ¾ in. scale locomotive is more expensive to construct, and needs a 'Primus' burner. **1907** *Athenæum* 12 Oct. 436/2 Robinson with great efforts made the 'Primus' work, and then burnt the stew with it. **1910** *Trade Marks Jrnl.* 22 June 989 Primus... Stoves. Aktiebolaget B. A. Hjorth & Co..., Stockholm, Sweden; manufacturers. **1910** *Official Gaz.* (U.S. Patent Office) 5 July 246/2 Aktiebolaget B. A. Hjorth & Co., Stockholm... *Primus*. **1933** E. A. ROBERTSON *Ordinary Families* iii. 53 It was asking too much of anyone's stomach to expect primus cookery. **1944** M. LASKI *Love on Supertax* i. 11 Have you ever tried..to light a primus stove?.. The methylated spirits flare up... You must frantically pump paraffin through to the burner. **1951** G. MILLAR *White Boat from England* ii. 16 We had several gadgets for the primus, including a pyramidal toaster. **1973** J. STRANGER *Walk Lonely Road* xiv. 108 Coffee, thick and strong and sweet, brewed over a Primus. **1974** O. MANNING *Rain Forest* III. i. 254 Simon folded back the flaps of a large, square tent... A primus lamp hung from the roof.

'primwort. *Bot.* [f. *prim-rose* or *prīm-ula* + WORT.] In *pl.* Lindley's name for the Natural Order, *Primulaceæ*.

1846 LINDLEY *Veg. Kingd.* 644 The Order of Primworts. *Ibid.* 645 Primworts are uncommon within the tropics. **1866** in *Treas. Bot.* 927/2.

¶Incorrectly stated by some to be an old name of the Privet or Primprint.

primy ('praɪmɪ), *a. rare.* [f. PRIME *sb.* + -Y.] That is in its prime.

1602 SHAKS. *Ham.* I. iii. 7 A Violet in the youth of Primy Nature; Forward, not permanent; sweet not lasting. **1828** *Blackw. Mag.* XXIII. 536 Sent forth..by those of powerful and primy manhood. [**1842** *Fraser's Mag.* XXVI. 142 The youth of primy nature is gone by.]

†**prin.** *Sc. Obs. rare*[−1]. [Origin unknown.] Some appliance for catching fish.

1469 *Sc. Acts Jas. III* (1814) II. 96/2 Fisch..ar distroyit be cowpis narow massis nettis prinnis set in to Reueris that has course to þe sey or set within þe flude merk of þe Seye. [**1892** COCHRAN-PATRICK *Mediæval Scot.* vi. 70 The act of 1469 prohibiting the use of 'coups', narrow mesh nets, and prins in rivers running into the sea.]

prin, obs. or dial. var. PREEN *sb.*, *v.*[1] and [2].

†**pri'nado.** *Obs. slang* [Origin obscure. In form it might be a corruption of Sp. *preñada* 'pregnant woman'; but the sense does not favour this.]

? Some kind of female sharper or impostor.

1620 DEKKER *Dreame* (1860) 38 Base heapes tumbled together, who all yell'd Like bandogs tyed in kennels: high-way-standers, Foists, nips, and tylts, prinadoes, bawdes, pimpes, panders. **1631** BRATHWAIT *Whimzies* 12 You shall see him guarded with a Ianizarie of Costermongers, and Countrey Gooselings: while his Nipps, Ints, Bungs and Prinado's, of whom he holds in fee, ofttimes prevent the Lawyer by diving too deepe into his Clients pocket. **1658** —— *Honest Ghost, Chym. Ape* 231 Flankt were my troups with bolts, bands, punks, and panders, Pimps, nips and ints, Prinado's.

prince (prɪns), *sb.* Also 3–6 prynce, 4 princs, pryns, prines, preins, 4–6 prins(e, 6 prynse, *Sc.* prence. [a. F. *prince* (12th c. in Littré) = Pr. *prince*, ad. L. *princeps, -cip-em* adj., first; as sb. the first or principal person, a chief, leader, sovereign, prince; f. *prīm-us* first, PRIME *a.* + *-cip-*, from *capĕre, -cipĕre* to take.

As applied in sense 1, it prob. came down from Roman usage under the principate and empire: see PRINCEPS, and cf. Hor. C. I. 2. 50, Ovid P. I. 2. 23, Tac. A. I. 1.]

I. In primary general sense.

1. a. A sovereign ruler; a monarch, king. Now *arch.* or *rhetorical*.

a **1225** *St. Marher.* 2 Of þat heðene folc patriarke ant prince. *a* **1225** *Leg. Kath.* 578 Ða onswerede þe an swiðe prudeliche, þus, to þe prude prince. *c* **1290** *S. Eng. Leg.* I. 20/32 He dude him sone bringue To þe prince of Engelond Aþelston þe kyngue. **1340–70** *Alex. & Dind.* 811 God by-secheþ to saue þe soueraine prinse. *c* **1380** WYCLIF *Wks.* (1880) 375 Seculer lordis, pryncis of þe worlde. *c* **1400** *Destr. Troy* 7371 Then partid the prinsis, and the prise dukes. *c* **1440** *York Myst.* xv. 7 Preued þat a prins withouten pere. **1536** *Cal. Anc. Rec. Dublin* (1889) I. 498 We most umbly desyre youre grase to be oure solester to oure prynse. **1552** *Bk. Com. Prayer, Communion, Prayer Ch. Mil.*, We beseche thee also to saue and defende all Christian Kynges, Princes, and Gouernoures. *a* **1555** LYNDESAY *Tragedy* 344 Imprudent Prencis but discretioun, Hauyng in erth power Imperiall. **1607–12** BACON *Ess., Empire* (Arb.) 308 Princes are like the heavenly bodyes which cause good, or evill tymes, and which have much veneration, but noe rest. **1774** GOLDSM. *Nat. Hist.* (1776) II. 398 These animals are often sent as presents to the princes of the east. **1861** THACKERAY *Four Georges* I. (1904) 29 In the good old times..noblemen passed from Court to Court, seeking service with one prince or another. **1885** *Encycl. Brit.* XIX. 738/1 The emperor of Russia, the queen of England, and the king of the Belgians are equally princes or monarchs, and the consorts of emperors or kings are princesses.

†**b.** Applied to a female sovereign. *Obs.*

1560 GESTE *Serm.* in H. G. Dugdale *Life* (1840) App. I. 191 Let us low our prince [Q. Eliz.],..nothing thinking sayeng or doyng that may turne to hyr dyshonor, prayeng all way for hyr long and prosperus reigne. **1562** *Act 5 Eliz.* c. 13 *Preamble*, The Reigns of the late Princes King Philip and Queen Mary. **1581** W. STAFFORD *Exam. Compl.* i. (1876) 29 Yea, the Prince,..as she hath most of yearely Reuenewes,.. so should shee haue most losse by this dearth. **1594** WILLOBIE *Avisa* (1880) 29 Cleopatra, prince of Nile. **1610** HOLLAND *Camden's Brit.* (1637) 511 Another most mighty Prince Mary Queene of Scots. **1650** STAPYLTON *Strada's*

Low C. Warres II. 37 They had now been governed by female Princes for forty years together.

c. In phrases and proverbs: see quots.

1589 GREENE *Spanish Masquerado* Wks. (Grosart) V. 266 The iolly fellowes that once in England liued like Princes in their Abbeies and Frieries. 1660 PEPYS *Diary* 1 Nov., We came to Sir W. Batten's, where he lives like a prince. 1804 *Europ. Mag.* Jan. 33/2 If I..would send..a pound of good tobacco, I should make her husband as happy as a Prince. 1868 YATES *Rock Ahead* III. iii, 'Princes and women must not be contradicted', says the proverb.

†2. a. One who has the chief authority; a ruler, commander, governor, president; also, the head man, chief, or leader of a tribe: cf. DUKE 1 c. *Obs.*

prince of priests, chief priest, high priest.

a1225 *Ancr. R.* 54 Hire ueader & hire breðren, se noble princes alse heo weren, vtlawes imakede. a1300 *Cursor M.* 16903 þe prince o preistes o þair lagh went to þat monument. 1377 LANGL. *P. Pl.* B. XIX. 218 And pryde shal be pope, prynce of holycherche. 1382 WYCLIF *Matt.* ii. 6 Thou, Bethlem,..thou art nat the leste in the princis of Juda. 1382 —— *Acts* iv. 23 The princes [1388 the princis of preestis] and eldere men seiden to hem. *Ibid.* xviii. 8 Crispe..prince of the synagoge, bileuyde to the Lord. a1450 *Knt. de la Tour* (1906) 106 Whiche Iacob hadde .xij. sones that were the princes of .xij. lynages. 1535 COVERDALE *Gen.* xxxvi. 40 Thus are the princes of Esau called in their kynreds, places & names. 16.. in *Longfellow's M. Standish* App., It is incredible how many wounds these two prinses, Pecksuot and Wattawamat, received before they died.

†b. A literal rendering of *princeps* in the Vulgate (Gr. ἀρχή) where the English Authorized and Revised Versions have 'principality'. *Obs.*

1382 WYCLIF *Ephes.* vi. 12 For stryuynge is not to vs aȝens fleisch and blood, but aȝens the princes [L. *principes*, Gr. ἀρχαί] and potestatis, aȝens gouernours of the world of thes derknessis. [TINDALE, CRANMER, etc. rule; *Geneva* rulers; *Rheims* Princes, 1611 principalities.]

3. a. One who or that which is first or pre-eminent in a specified class or sphere; the chief, the greatest. Cf. KING *sb.* 6.

c1275 *Serving Christ* 39 in *O.E. Misc.* 91 Seynte peter wes prynce and pyned is on rode. c1315 SHOREHAM *Poems* iv. 306 þat oþer feend of onde [envy] Hys pryns and cheuetayn. 13.. *Cursor M.* 28071 (Cott.), I will first at pride be-gin, þat prince es of all oþer sin. 1484 CAXTON *Fables of Poge* v, One named Hugh prynce of the medycyns sawe a catte whiche had two hedes. 1583 FULKE *Defence* x. Wks. (Parker Soc.) 381 As though you were prince of the *Critici* or *Areopagitae*. a1658 CLEVELAND *Elegy B. Jonson* 1 Poet of Princes, Prince of Poets (we, If to Apollo, well may pray to thee). 1698 FRYER *Acc. E. India & P.* 373 Des Cartes, the Prince of Philosophy in this Age. 1753 HOGARTH *Anal. Beauty* viii. 47 Sir Christopher Wren,..the prince of architects. 1799 C. WINTER *Let.* in W. Jay *Mem.* (1843) 28 Mr. Toplady called him [Whitefield] the prince of preachers. 1891 *Speaker* 2 May 527/2 Gray is a prince of letter-writers. 1896 *Westm. Gaz.* 31 Jan. 2/1 The prince of Australian reptiles is the black snake.

b. A person with power or influence; a magnate. *U.S.*

1841 J. S. BUCKINGHAM *America* III. 427 Capitalists and merchants [of Boston]..are here called 'princes'. 1884 *Century Mag.* Sept. 796 At a shady end of the veranda, are seen the railroad king,..the bonanza mine owner, the Texas rancher, and the Pennsylvania iron prince. 1904 [see BARON 2 b]. 1976 T. GIFFORD *Cavanaugh Quest* (1977) viii. 137 He was a perfect reflection of the typical Minneapolis power broker, though somewhat better dressed than the grain barons and the department store princes and computer tycoons.

c. An admirable or generous person. *colloq.* (chiefly *U.S.*).

1911 H. B. WRIGHT *Winning of Barbara Worth* xvi. 252 Yes sir, gents, I'm here to tell you that that there man, Jefferson Worth, is a prince—a prince. Let me tell you what he done for me. 1939 I. BAIRD *Waste Heritage* v. 69 Hep ain't like other guys, he's a prince. 1951 J. D. SALINGER *Catcher in Rye* iii. 31 He's crazy about *you*. He told me he thinks you're a goddam prince. 1966 J. CLEARY *High Commissioner* viii. 164 'You have a lot of time for him, haven't you?' 'They don't come any better. He's a prince, you know?'

4. a. Applied to Christ, esp. in the phrase ***Prince of Peace***. b. Applied to an angel or celestial being of high rank; sometimes (in *pl.*) = PRINCIPALITY 5. (Cf. 2 b, above.) c. Applied to Satan in the phrases ***prince of the air, darkness, evil, fiends, the world***, etc.

a1300 *Cursor M.* 9317 'Princs o pees' sal man him call. 1340 HAMPOLE *Pr. Consc.* 1084 þarfor God him [the devil] prince of þe world calles. 1382 WYCLIF *Isa.* ix. 6 Fadir of the world to come, Prince of Pes. —— *Dan.* x. 13 Mychael, oon of the first princis, came in to myn help. *Ibid.* 21 No man is myn helper in alle these thingis, no bot Miȝhel, your prince. —— *John* xii. 31 Now is dom of the world, now the prince of this world schal be cast out. c1440 *Alphabet of Tales* 295 So his sawle was broght vnto þe prince of Hell syttand opon þe pytt bra. 1573 L. LLOYD *Marrow of Hist.* (1653) 3 That..Princes should be so misguided by the Prince of the ayr. 1599 SHAKS. *Hen. V*, III. iii. 16 Impious Warre, Arrayed in flames like to the Prince of Fiends. 1601 —— *All's Well* IV. v. 44 The blacke prince sir, alias the prince of darkenesse, alias the diuell. c1800 COLERIDGE *Christmas Carol*, Peace, Peace on Earth! the Prince of Peace is born. 1854 FABER *Oratory Hymns, St. Michael*, Hail, bright Archangel! Prince of Heaven! 1861 R. M. BENSON *Hymn, 'Praise to God Who reigns above'*, Thrones, Dominions, Princes, Powers, Marshall'd Might that never cowers.

II. Specific uses.

5. *spec.* The ruler of a principality or small state actually, nominally, or originally, a feudatory of a king or emperor.

In origin, app. a use of sense 2, describing a ruler who had no recognized title such as duke, count, etc. First used of Italian and Welsh, subseq. of German and other rulers of petty states. The rulers of Wales, or its divisions, down to the 11th c., bore the title of 'king' (*brenhin, rex*); then the title sank to 'prince' (*tywysog, princeps*).

1297 R. GLOUC. (Rolls) 11484 Lewelin prince of walis robbede mid is route. 1387 TREVISA *Higden* (Rolls) VIII. 187 Kyng John mariede his baast douȝter to Lewelyn prince of Wales. 1432-50 tr. *Higden, Harl. Contin.* (Rolls) VIII. 438 A soore batelle was hade..betwene Edward prince of Aquitanny and Henricus Bastarde occupyenge the crowne of Speyne. 1560 DAUS tr. *Sleidane's Comm.* Pref., How he [Luther]..pleaded his own cause, before themperour and counsell of princes. *Ibid.* 54 b, The Princes that were of the confederacie and league of Swekland..were these, Cesar as Prince of Austriche [etc.]. 1617 MORYSON *Itin.* III. 193 Not onely the Emperour, but also many Princes of Germany..haue Kingly power in their owne Dominions, and these absolute Princes are so many in number, as a passenger in each dayes iourney, shall obserue one or two changes of Prince, Money and Religion. 1727-41 CHAMBERS *Cycl.*, *Prince* is also used for a person who is sovereign in his own territory; yet holds from some other, as his superior or lord, and pays homage or tribute to him. Thus all the princes of Germany are feudatories of the Emperor. 1845 S. AUSTIN *Ranke's Hist. Ref.* I. 371 The hostility of the most able and prudent of all the princes of the empire was provoked. 1885 *Encycl. Brit.* XIX. 738/2 Princes regarded as the political chiefs of states are inferior to emperors and kings, and not necessarily superior to reigning grand-dukes or dukes. 1885 *Whitaker's Alm.* 314/2 Bulgaria. Prince, Alexander (of the House of Hesse)... The Principality of Bulgaria is under the suzerainty of Turkey. 1890 *Ibid.* 511/1 Waldeck. Prince, George Victor, Prince of Waldeck-Pyrmont. 1900 *Ibid.* 456/1 Native States of India... The States are governed by their native Princes, Ministers, or Councils, with the help and under the advice of a political officer of the Supreme Government. 1905 *Ibid.* 595/1 Lippe, Principality of. Reigning Prince, Charles Alexander.

6. A male member of a royal family; *esp.* in Great Britain, a son or grandson of a king or queen. Also called ***prince of the blood (royal)*** (BLOOD *sb.* 9). ***Prince Consort***, the husband of a reigning female sovereign being himself a prince.

In this sense originating in the title *Prince of Wales*, which, in the first instance, was simply a continuation of sense 5, as title of the deposed native Welsh princes; but being, from the reign of Edward III, customarily conferred upon the eldest surviving son of the King or Queen of England, came to be associated with this relationship. The Prince of Wales was at first the only 'prince' in England (see quot. 1577); but in the reign of James I 'prince' was extended to all the sons of the sovereign, and under Victoria (with 'princess') to all the grandchildren, being children of sons (quot. 1885). After the example of England, the equivalent of 'prince' has been given, with some addition, to the heir-apparent to the throne in various countries, as *crown-prince* in Germany, Sweden, Denmark, and Japan, *prince imperial* in the French Empire of 1852-70, *Prince of Asturias* in Spain, *Prince of Piedmont* in Italy, etc. In most of these countries the title of prince has also been given to male members of the reigning family. (This sense may have been partly influenced by Roman usage under the empire, in which the title *princeps juventutis* 'chief' or 'prince of the youth', which was bestowed by the Equites upon the two grandsons of Augustus, was afterwards customarily conferred upon the probable successor to the throne on his first entry into public life.)

c1305 *Flem. Insurr.* in *Pol. Songs* (Camden) 194 Ȝe[f] the Prince of Walis his lyf habbe mote. 1455 E. CLERE in *Four C. Eng. Lett.* (1880) 5 The Queen..brought my Lord Prynce [of Wales] with her. c1475 *Harl. Contin. Higden* (Rolls) VIII. 433 Edwarde sonne of kynge Edwarde, prince of Wales, saylede to Caleys. a1548 HALL *Chron., Hen. IV* 32 b, The prince his sonne..entered into the chamber and toke away the crowne. *Ibid.*, Leuyng behind him by the lady Marie..Henry prince of Wales, Thomas duke of Clarence [etc.]. *Ibid., Hen. VIII* 9 On Newyeres daye, the first day of Ianuary, the Quene was deliuered of a Prince. 1563, etc. [see BLACK PRINCE]. 1577 HARRISON *England* II. v. (1877) I. 106 The title of prince dooth peculiarlie belong to the kings eldest sonne... The kings yoonger sonnes be but gentlemen by birth (till they haue receiued creation of higher estate, to be either visconts, earles, or dukes) and called after their names, as lord Henrie, or lord Edward. 1597 SHAKS. *2 Hen. IV*, IV. iv. 83 Health to my Soueraigne,..Prince Iohn, your Sonne, doth kisse your Graces Hand. 1610 —— *Temp.* III. i. 60, I am, in my condition A Prince (Miranda), I do thinke a King. 1611 —— *Wint. T.* IV. iii. 13, I haue seru'd Prince Florizell,..but now I am out of seruice. 1614 SELDEN *Titles Hon.* 178 After the Conquest, no speciall title more then *Primogenitus filius Regis* was for the Prince, vntill the name of Prince of Wales came to him. 1624 MASSINGER *Parl. Love* I. iv, Next unto the princes of the blood, The eyes of all are fixed on you. 1707 CHAMBERLAYNE *Pres. St. Eng.* II. vii. 102 Prince George, Hereditary Prince of Denmark and Norway. *Ibid.* 103 By the Articles of Marriage, he is declared to be received as one of the Princes of the Blood-Royal of England. 1725 WATTS *Logic* I. iv. §4 When we speak of the Prince, we intend his Royal Highness George Prince of Wales. 1839 *Encycl. Brit.* (ed. 7) XIX. 513/2 The husband of a queen regnant, as Prince George of Denmark was to Queen Anne, is her subject. 1885 *Encycl. Brit.* XIX. 738/2 In England..it was considered necessary only about a quarter of a century ago to make express provision by royal authority that the titles of 'prince' and 'princess' should be enjoyed by the children of the sons as well as by the sons and daughters of any sovereign of the United Kingdom. 1901 *Daily Chron.* 9 Nov. 3/1 Dukes of Cornwall, like poets, are born; but the King alone can make a Prince of Wales.

7. a. The English rendering of a title of nobility in some foreign countries, which, in Germany (when representing *Fürst*), France, Italy, Belgium, Holland, in the early 20th c. ranked next below *duke*: see quot. 1885.

1727-41 CHAMBERS *Cycl.* s.v., The moment a pope is elected, all his relations become princes. 1819 SHELLEY *Cenci* I. iii. 2 Welcome, ye Princes and Cardinals, pillars of the church. 1831 SIR J. SINCLAIR *Corr.* II. 275 Prince Gabriel de Gagarin. This Prince held a high office at Moscow,—that of 'Procureur de Senat'. 1885 *Whitaker's Alm.* 322/1 The German Empire...Chancellor, Otto, Prince Bismarck. 1885 *Encycl. Brit.* XIX. 739/1-2 In Germany and Austria the title of 'prince' is represented by 'Prinz' when it appertains to the members of imperial and royal families..and by 'Fürst' when it appertains to the members of..noble families... According to its identification with 'Prinz' or 'Fürst' it is a higher or lower dignity than 'Herzog' (duke). *Ibid.*, In Spain and Portugal we are not aware that the title of 'prince' has ever been conferred on a subject outside of the royal family except in the well-known case of Godoy, Prince of the Peace.

b. Applied as a title of courtesy in certain connexions to a duke, marquis, or earl.

1707 CHAMBERLAYNE *Pres. St. Eng.* III. iii. 273 *Duke*... His Title is Grace; and being written unto may be Stiled, Most High, Potent and Noble Prince... *Marquis*... His Title is Most Noble, Most Honourable, and Potent Prince. 1851 *Burke's Peerage* Introd. 12 He [an earl or marquis] bears also, upon some occasions, the title of 'Most Noble and Puissant Prince'. 1898 *Whitaker's Titled Persons* Introd. 10 A Duke is styled 'Most Noble', or more commonly 'Your Grace'; but in very formal language he can be spoken of as 'The Most High, Potent, and Noble Prince'. *Ibid.* 11 The style of a Marquess is 'Most Honourable', not 'Most Noble', though it is stated that in some formal descriptions both he and an Earl may be termed 'Most Noble and Puissant Prince'.

c. ***Prince of the (Holy Roman) Church***, a title applied to a Cardinal.

[1782 PRIESTLEY *Corrupt. Chr.* II. x. 251 Cardinals..have the rank of princes in the Church.] 1901 WALKER & BURROW *Cdl. Newman* x. 145 His body was laid in state with the insignia of a Prince of the Holy Roman Church.

III. Transferred applications.

†8. Applied to a queen-bee. *Obs. rare*$^{-1}$.

1609 C. BUTLER *Fem. Mon.* v. (1623) N ij, I obserued once, that the Prince being scarce ready, fell downe from the stoole vnable to recouer hir wings, whereupon the swarme returned. She being put into the Hiue, the next day the swarme rose againe and setled.

†9. *Chess.* = BISHOP *sb.* 5. *Obs. rare.*

1562 ROWBOTHUM *Play Cheasts* A iv, The Bishoppes some name Alphins, some fooles, and some name them Princes. *Ibid.* A vj, Of the Bishop or Archer... The Spaniardes named him prince..for he is nerer vnto the King and the Quene then any other of the Cheastmen.

IV. *attrib.* and *Comb.*

10. a. appositive, 'that is a prince': as ***prince-abbot, -angel, -duke, -god, -infanta, -poet, -pope, -priest, -primate, -teacher***. See also PRINCE-BISHOP, -ELECTOR, PRINCE REGENT.

1650 R. STAPYLTON *Strada's Low C. Warres* x. 19 Whether the King would allow him place, as a Prince-Infanta within the Cloth of State. 1656 EARL MONM. tr. *Boccalini's Advts. fr. Parnass.* I. lix. (1674) 76 Apollo..created him Prince-Poet, and..gave him the Royal Ensigns used to be given to Poets-Laureat. 1679 C. NESSE *Antid. agst. Popery* 92 That Prince-fowl of the air, the Devil. 1865 T. F. KNOX tr. *Life H. Suso* 28 As if he were a prince-angel. 1866-7 BARING-GOULD *Cur. Myths Mid. Ages, Prester John* (1894) 47 The papal epistle..assures the Eastern Prince-Pope that his Christian professions are worthless, unless he submits to the successor of Peter. 1897 Prince-abbot [see PRINCE-BISHOP]. 1908 H. A. L. FISHER *Bonapartism* iii. 54 'Monsieur L'Abbé', said Napoleon to Dalberg, the subservient prince-primate.

b. simple attributive, 'of a prince, princely', as ***prince-dish, -humour***; objective and obj. genitive, etc., as ***prince-killer, -pleaser, -queller, †-treacher, -worship***; ***prince-killing*** adj.; instrumental, etc., as ***prince-fit, -graced, -loyal, -protected, -proud, -ridden, -trodden*** adjs.

a1618 SYLVESTER *Wood-man's Bear* xxxvii, In the Crofte so faire and pleasant, Harbour of the *Prince-dish Pheasant. 1614 —— *Bethulia's Rescue* IV. 197 From Powdred Tresses, from forc't Apish Graces, From *Prince-fit Pompe. 1591 —— *Du Bartas* I. vi. 655 Through Newbery, and *Prince-grac't Aldermaston. 1602 FITZHERB. *Apol.* 39 For manquellars and *princekillers, traytours, and homicides. 1595 *Polimanteia* (1881) 57 A Queene..more valiant then *prince-killing Judith. a1618 SYLVESTER *Miracle of Peace* xxxiv, Th'yerst most *Prince-loyal people..Are now Prince-treachers. 1589 PUTTENHAM *Eng. Poesie* I. viii. (Arb.) 32 Poesie was a delicate arte, and the Poets them selues cunning *Princepleasers. a1548 HALL *Chron., Hen. VI* 135 b, The people..found out the *princequellers, and theim brought to straight prisone. *Ibid.* [see REGICIDE[1] 1]. a1618 *Prince-treacher [see *prince-loyal*]. 1652 *Persuasive to Compliance* 16 His poor *prince-trodden people.

11. Combinations with *prince's*; ***prince's cord***, ? a fabric resembling corduroy; ***prince's mixture***, a kind of snuff: see quot. 1858; ***prince's pine***, (*a*) the Grey Pine, *Pinus Banksiana*; (*b*) = PIPSISSEWA; ***prince's stuff***, a corded textile material, ? = *prince's cord*. Also PRINCE'S FEATHER, METAL.

1810 *Sporting Mag.* XXXVI. 240 White *Prince's-cord breeches. 1836 *Backwoods of Canada* 124 A little rappee or *prince's mixture added by way of Sauce. 1858 SIMMONDS *Dict. Trade*, *Prince's-mixture*, a dark kind of snuff so called, which is scented with otto of roses. 1807 F. PURSH *Jrnl. Bot. Excursion* (1869) 15 Pyrola umbellata calld here *Princess [*sic*] pine. 1818 A. EATON *Man. Bot.* (ed. 2) 203 *Chimaphila ..umbellata*, (prince's pine, bitter wintergreen). 1884 [see PIPSISSEWA]. 1891 *Lancet* 3 Oct. 772/1 Liquor kava kava..composition, kava kava.., prince's pine.., golden seal.., tag alder.., and uva ursi. 1954 C. J. HYLANDER *Macmillan Wild Flower Bk.* 280 Pipsissewa... Also known as Prince's Pine, this is a trailing and somewhat woody perennial. 1814 *Hist. Univ. Oxford* II. 261 The gown of Bachelor of Arts is made of *prince's stuff, with a full sleeve. 1825 in *Hone's*

Every-day Bk. I. 1334 The lord mayor of London..the household now all wear black gowns,..made of prince's stuff faced with velvet.

12. Phraseological combinations: ***Prince of Wales check***, a large check pattern; ***Prince of Wales('s) feathers***: (*a*) see FEATHER *sb.* 8; also *ellipt.* and *fig.*; (*b*) = *crape-fern* (CRAPE *sb.* 3 b); ***Prince of Wales knot*** (see also quot. 1978); ***Prince Rupert's drop***: see DROP *sb.* 10 h; also *fig.*; ***Prince Rupert's*** (erron. ***Robert's***) ***metal*** = PRINCE'S METAL.

1958 P. MORTIMER *Daddy's gone a-Hunting* vii. 35 A tall, thin man in *Prince of Wales check. **1959** *Sunday Express* 21 June 14/3 Prince of Wales check trousers. **1960** *News Chron.* 11 July 6/5 The Prince of Wales check Sudan cotton in grey and black. **1972** *Vogue* Feb. 73 Prince of Wales check wool tent coat. **1882** T. H. POTTS *Out in Open* 108 *T[odea] superba*, 'the glory of the west'. How great the impression made by its marvellous beauty, may be assumed from the number of familiar names..bestowed upon it, as the Royal fern, the King's fern, *Prince of Wales' feather. **1919** T. WRIGHT *Romance of Lace Pillow* ix. 82 Other patterns were the *Prince of Wales's Feathers*. **1933** *Flight* 29 June 626/2 And a final break-up in a 'Prince of Wales Feathers', were other manoeuvres which held the spectators literally spell-bound. **1944, 1951** [see *crape-fern*]. **1958** C. FREEMAN *Pillow Lace in E. Midlands* 46 The names given to the various patterns often refer to some element of the design... Other favourites were..Prince of Wales's Feathers [etc.]. **1966** H. SHEPPARD *Dict. Railway Slang* (ed. 2) 9 *Prince of Wales*, blowing off steam by engine. **1971** D. J. SMITH *Discovering Railwayana* x. 58 *Prince of Wales*, short for Prince of Wales' feathers, a plume-like emission of steam. **1977** BINNEY & BURMAN *Change & Decay* 143/2 (*caption*) Lea, Wiltshire; St. Giles. Bell of 1622, with Prince of Wales feathers. **1977** *R.A.F. News* 22 June–5 July 1/1 The manœuvre takes the nine Gnats up into a Prince of Wales feathers, with eight aircraft trailing white smoke and the leader trailing red. **1897** *Sears, Roebuck Catal.* 222/2 Illustration No. 2205 shows the De Joinnile [necktie] as worn with an ordinary finger ring. No. 2206 shows it tied in a *Prince of Wales knot. **1971** *Guardian* 3 Aug. 9/3 Broad kipper ties..tied in loose Prince of Wales knots, were featured by many Paris houses. **1978** 'K. BLAKE' *Professionals 1: Where Jungle Ends* iii. 39 His Prince of Wales knotted tie in rich brown. **1695** *Lond. Gaz.* No. 3121/4 The Drops known by the name of *Prince Rupert's Drops. **1849** DANA *Geol.* iii. (1850) 180 Nearly as brittle as a Prince Rupert's drop. **1862** RUSKIN *Unto this Last* iv. 145 Nay, boiled bulbs they might have been—glass bulbs—Prince Rupert's drops, consummated in powder..for any end or meaning. **1878** EMERSON *Misc. Papers, Fort. Rep.* Wks. (Bohn) III. 395 In Mr. Webster's imagination the American Union was a huge Prince Rupert's drop..which will snap into atoms if so much as the smallest end be shivered off. **1698** *Phil. Trans.* XX. 170 The Buttons we wear..said to be made of *Prince Robert's Mettal. **1789** *Chambers' Cycl.* s.v. *Zinc*, Compositions or alloys called tombac, similor, pinchbeck, and Prince's metal... The English..called their invention Prince's metal, or Prince Rupert's metal. **1875** KNIGHT *Dict. Mech.*, *Prince Rupert's Metal*, an alloy for cheap jewelry,..composed of copper, 75; zinc 25.

prince (prɪns), *v.* ? *Obs.* [f. prec. sb.] *intr.* with *it*: To play the prince, carry oneself as a prince. Also *refl.*

c **1590** GREENE *Fr. Bacon* i. 103 I'll to the court, and I'll prince it out. **1611** SHAKS. *Cymb.* III. iii. 85 Nature prompts them In simple and lowe things, to Prince it, much Beyond the tricke of others. **1656** S. H. *Gold. Law* 100 Whose Principles are to Prince themselves, and precipitate al sorts. **1658** J. HARRINGTON *Pop. Govt.* II. v, A Metropolitan..with whom nothing will agree but Princeing of it in the Senat.

princeage ('prɪnsɪdʒ). *rare.* [f. PRINCE *sb.* + -AGE.] Princes collectively.

1846 WORCESTER cites *Month. Rev.*

Prince Albert. 1. The name of Prince Albert Edward, afterwards King Edward VII, used *attrib.* and *absol.* to designate a kind of frock coat or suit made fashionable by him. orig. *U.S.*

1884 I. M. RITTENHOUSE *Maud* (1939) 270, I ran out and ushered Mr Lyons in, gotten up to kill in his Prince Albert coat. **1890** [see JIMSWINGER]. **1895** *Montgomery Ward Catal.* 273/1 Prince Albert Suits. **1897** KIPLING *Day's Work* (1898) 221 A man in a black Prince Albert, without a collar, came up. **1903** S. CLAPIN *New Dict. Amer.* p. viii, If a Londoner is fortunate enough to cross the Atlantic,..but is unfortunate enough to have to buy a frock-coat..he must call it a 'Prince Albert'. **1919** *Ladies' Home Jrnl.* July 19/2 Instinctively I looked about him for revolvers. There were none, not even the slightest bulge at the hips of the Prince Albert coat he wore. **1927** *Scribner's Mag.* Feb. 164/1 Antone was dressed for a call, having donned a shiny Prince Albert coat over his collarless shirt. **1941** W. C. HANDY *Father of Blues* vii. 91 Glittering young devils in silk toppers and Prince Alberts. **1967** C. O. SKINNER *Madame Sarah* viii. 147 Amid the..city coats, Prince Alberts and pin-striped trousers, Sarah looked vainly for a single woman. **1972** H. KEMELMAN *Monday the Rabbi took Off* xv. 103 Others [*sc.* Chassidim]..favored a Prince Albert, which because it was warm, they kept open.

2. The name of Prince Albert, the Prince Consort, used in *pl.* to designate foot- or toe-wraps worn by tramps, sailors, etc., inside boots; the boots themselves. *Austral.*

1893 K. MACKAY *Out Back* (ed. 2) II. v. 191 With bent shoulders..they 'mouched' along,..showing glimpses of brown, unwashed skin above the frayed edges of their 'Prince Alberts', the toes of their bluchers gaping wide. **1903** 'T. COLLINS' *Such is Life* (1937) i. 52 Unlapping from his feet the inexpensive substitute for socks known as 'prince-alberts'. **1924** *Truth* (Sydney) 27 Apr. 6 *Prince Alberts*, rags or bandages used by a swagman or sun-downer around his feet in place of socks. **1945** BAKER *Austral. Lang.* 105 *Prince Alfreds* or *Prince Alberts* as synonyms for *toe-rags*. These terms developed from the malign suggestion that the Prince Consort was so poor when he came to England to marry Queen Victoria that he wore toe-rags instead of socks. *Ibid.*, Rough lace-up boots were also known as *Prince Alberts* in Queensland in the closing years of last century. **1958** J. BISSET *Sail Ho!* v. 48 These foot-wraps were known in British ships as 'Prince Alberts'.

'prince-'bishop. A bishop who is also a prince (sense 5); also one who (as in certain cases in Germany) enjoyed the temporal possessions and authority of a bishopric, with princely rank (= Ger. *Fürst-bischof*: see PRINCE *sb.* 7).

1867 FREEMAN *Norm. Conq.* I. v. §3. 321 Durham..with its highest point crowned not only by the minster, but by the vast castle of the Prince-Bishop. **1879** *Whitaker's Alm.* 63 Family of Geo. III...2. Frederick, born 16th Aug., 1763, was at the age of six months declared Prince-bishop of Osnaburgh. **1879** *Encycl. Brit.* X. 469/2 Breslau (where the archbishop has the title of prince-bishop). **1883** H. A. WEBSTER *ibid.* XVI. 781/2 (*Montenegro*) The people chose their bishop as their chief. Prince-bishops or vladykas, elected by the people, continued to lead them..till 1697. **1886** C. E. PASCOE *London of To-day* v. (ed. 3) 69 The Prince-Bishops and other small German potentates. **1897** FLÜGEL, etc. *Eng. & Germ. Dict.*, *Fürst-abt, -bischof*.. prince-abbot, prince-bishop, sovereign bishop (of princely rank, and bearing the title of prince).

Prince Charming. [Partial tr. F. *Roi Charmant*, the name of the hero of the Comtesse d'Aulnoy's *L'Oiseau Bleu* (1697). In English the name first appears as that of the hero of Planché's *King Charming* or *Prince Charming*, and was later adopted for the hero of various fairy-tale pantomimes, *esp.* the *Sleeping Beauty* and *Cinderella*.] A fairy-tale hero; the lover every girl dreams of; a perfect young man.

[**1850** *Times* 27 Dec. 5/2 Lyceum... Then followed the principal attraction of the evening, in the shape of a new and original fairy extravaganza, in two acts, entitled *King Charming; or, the Blue Bird of Paradise*. *Ibid.*, We would particularly notice..the final scene of the restoration of King Charming.] **1855** *N.Y. Daily Times* 25 Dec. 4/3 The burlesque of 'King Charming'..The legend is taken from the Countess D'Aulnoy's fairy tale of 'L'Oiseau Bleu', and relates to the adventures of the wonderful *Prince Charming*, an immortal monarch, gifted with perpetual youth. *Ibid.* 4/4 Mrs. H. C. Watson as *Prince Charming* scarcely did herself justice. **1862** *Welcome Guest* 4 Jan. 152/3 They tell me I am good looking, but I don't believe it; although the young ladies of my acquaintance, who are too bold for me, call me 'Prince Charming'. **1913** W. J. LOCKE *Stella Maris* xv. 205 Love she had heard of, the love of Prince Charming for Princess Rose. **1920** [see BACKFISCH]. **1929** E. WILSON *I thought of Daisy* v. 286 When Prince Charming comes along, he's always just a great, big, strong, clean-limbed American. **1931** G. C. D. ODELL *Ann. N.Y. Stage* VI. 427 A holiday frippery, Planché's King Charming, or, the Blue Bird of Paradise, ushered in, on Christmas Eve [1855], a success that lasted, without interruption, until January 12th. *Ibid.* 450 [Laura Keene] hired the unlucky Metropolitan theatre ..and advertised the opening for December 24th, with Two Can Play at that Game and Prince Charming... The Broadway Theatre on the same evening produced King Charming, as it called Planché 's extravaganza... Prince Charming was not played at Miss Keene's..some miscreant had so slashed the chief scene of Prince Charming that the play could not be given. **1936** R. C. K. ENSOR *England 1870–1914* vii. 215 He [*sc.* Rosebery] had come to the front as the Prince Charming of politics—young, handsome, rich, eloquent, candid, and popular. **1939** J. CURTIS *What Immortal Hand* iii. 36 She had not the slightest wish to marry anybody from Lowdham Street... No, she wanted some kind of Prince Charming like they had in the pictures. **1939** WODEHOUSE *Uncle Fred in Springtime* xv. 225 There was a look in her eyes that made me think right away that she was feeling he was her Prince Charming. **1945** G. ENDORE *Methinks the Lady* (1947) ii. 27 And your Prince Charming? You met him at Mona's? **1960** E. ELIOT *They all married Well* xiii. 201 Virginia Bonynge was too pretty..to be forever scorned by *all* the Prince Charmings who abounded in London. **1961** *Guardian* 17 May 6/1 Like most other English schoolgirls, I spent many an hour dreaming... Prince Charmings used to come and carry me off on white chargers. **1975** *Radio Times* 9 Jan. 43/2 They are destined to find their Prince Charmings at a commercial fair in Rochefort. **1976** *Daily Mail* 25 Mar. 22/1 We all know..the story of Cinderella... Our hero is a progressive Prince Charming who doesn't mind the privilege and protocol provided he can marry the girl of his choice. *Ibid.*, Way back in the days of Dr Kildare, Richard Chamberlain must have been every girl's idea of Prince Charming. **1977** *Christian* IV. 124 The beast has by the kiss of love become the Prince Charming who, far from having to be shut away, is now the very life and soul of what I am.

prince consort: see CONSORT *sb.*[1] 3, PRINCE *sb.* 6.

'prince-craft. *rare.* [f. PRINCE *sb.* + CRAFT, after *priestcraft*.] The skill or art of a prince or ruler. Chiefly *dyslogistic*.

1741 WARBURTON *Div. Legat.* II. 3 Princecraft or Priest-craft. **1862** MCDUFF *Sunsets Heb. Mount.* 105 By consummate art, or rather by unprincipled princecraft, he had undermined his father's throne.

princedom ('prɪnsdəm). [f. as prec. + -DOM.]

1. The state or country ruled over by a prince; a principality.

1560 WHITEHORNE *Arte Warre* 39 He that shall consider the partes of Europe, shall finde it to haue bean full of common weales, and of princedomes,..constrained to kepe liuely the warlike orders. **1599** SANDYS *Europæ Spec.* (1632) 49 [They] are likely also to draw in the Princedome of Transilvania. **1611** CORYAT *Crudities* 573 Those frontier parts of their Princedomes. **1800** COLERIDGE *Piccolom.* III. i, To me he portions forth the princedoms, Glatz And Sagan. **1876** L. TOLLEMACHE in *Fortn. Rev.* Jan. 119 About as populous as the princedom of Monaco.

2. The position, rank, or dignity of a prince; princehood; princely power or sovereignty.

1560 WHITEHORNE *Arte Warre* 108 b, He then that despiseth these studies, if he be a Prince, despiseth his Princedome. **1590** SPENSER *F.Q.* II. x. 44 Next Archigald, who for his proud disdayne Deposed was from princedome soverayne. **1610** BP. CARLETON *Jurisd.* 11 The princedome and double portion are generally acknowledged to belong to the birthright. **1854** MILMAN *Lat. Chr.* VII. vi. (1864) IV. 197 Some of all ranks up to princedoms. **1871** *Echo* 13 Dec., The abeyance of the Princedom of Wales.

b. The personality of a prince. *rare.*

1828 SCOTT *F.M. Perth* xvi, So please your princedom, I have yet far to go. **1832** *Fraser's Mag.* V. 542 A gigantic carter..challenged his princedom to box.

3. = PRINCIPALITY 5.

1667 MILTON *P.L.* III. 320 Under thee as Head Supream Thrones, Princedoms, Powers, Dominions I reduce. **1814** CARY *Dante* (Chandos) 239 In one orb we roll, One motion, one impulse, with those who rule Princedoms in heaven. **1844** MRS. BROWNING *Drama of Exile* Poems 1850 I. 18 The angelic hosts, the archangelic pomps, Thrones, dominations, princedoms, rank on rank. **1899** C. E. CLEMENT *Angels in Art* 26 The Princedoms and Powers of Heaven are represented by rows and groups of angels.

'prince-e'lector. [= Ger. *Kurfürst*.] One of the princes who elected the Holy Roman (German) Emperor; = ELECTOR 3. Hence **'prince-e'lectorship**, the office or dignity of a prince-elector.

1560 DAUS tr. *Sleidane's Comm.* Pref., To the most excellent Prince Augustus, Prince Electour, Duke of Saxon [etc.]. **1606** G. W[OODCOCKE] *Lives Emperors in Hist. Ivstine* Llv, Ferdinandus brother of Charles, was consecrate Emper. in the towne of Francfort, by the Princes electors. **1624** *Aphorisms of State* in *Harl. Misc.* (1810) V. 511 Maximilian, the Duke of Bavaria, for the establishing the state of his prince-electorship, hath sought unto the authority of the apostolical seat. **1692** WASHINGTON tr. *Milton's Def. Pop.* M.'s Wks. (1847) 352/2 The emperour of Germany never was summoned to appear before one of the prince electors. **1845** S. AUSTIN *Ranke's Hist. Ref.* I. 57 When the prince-electors proceeded to the vote, they swore that 'according to the best of their understanding, they would choose the temporal head of all Christian people, *i.e.* a Roman king and future emperor'.

†'princehead. *Obs.* [f. PRINCE *sb.* + -HEAD.] **a.** = PRINCEHOOD 1. **b.** = PRINCEDOM 2 b.

1382 WYCLIF *Prov.* xxix. 2 Whan vnpitous men han taken princehed [1388 prinshod] the puple shal weilen. **1382** —— 1 *Cor.* xv. 24 He schal auoyde al princehede, and power, and vertu. **1456** SIR G. HAYE *Law Arms* (S.T.S.) 4 The prophecyes..maist worthy be verifyit in 3our maist noble and worthy princehede. **1483** *Cath. Angl.* 291/2 A Prynse-hede, *archia, principatus*. **1535** STEWART *Cron. Scot.* (Rolls) I. 1 Ane nobill buke his princeheid for to pleis.

princehood ('prɪnshʊd). [f. as prec. + -HOOD.]

1. The condition, dignity, or dominion of a prince or ruler. Now *rare.*

1382 WYCLIF 1 *Macc.* xi. 27 The kyng..ordeynide to hym princehod [**1388** prinshod] of presthod. **1422** tr. *Secreta Secret., Priv. Priv.* 132 But Sum Pryncis ther bene, that..by colour of har Pryncehode and coloured defense of the commyn Pepill, takyn atte har talent trew men goodis. *a* **1548** HALL *Chron., Hen. VI* 98 b, Promisyng and behightyng, by the faith of his body and worde of his prince-hode. **1617** COLLINS *Def. Bp. Ely* I. iii. 142 Their chiefdom or princehood ought to stand in the loue of such as are vnder them. **1907** *Daily Chron.* 23 Sept. 3/6 The feeling used to prevail that the Princehood should be limited to the great historical families.

†b. = PRINCEDOM 1. *Obs. rare*[−1].

1565 JEWEL *Def. Apol.* IV. (1567) 405 Pipinus..gaue the Pope the Exarchate, or Princehoode of Rauenna.

†2. a. An order of angels or other spiritual beings: = PRINCIPALITY 5. **b.** Each of the three celestial hierarchies: = HIERARCHY 1. *Obs. rare.*

1388 WYCLIF *Col.* i. 16 Ether trones, ether dominaciouns, ether princehodes, ethir poweris. **1450–1530** *Myrr. our Ladye* 119 So are the nyne orders of aungels departed in thre pryncehoodes, as in thre hoostes.

Princeite ('prɪnsaɪt). Name of a small religious sect: see quots.

1874 in J. H. BLUNT *Dict. Sects.* **1902** *Daily Chron.* 9 Sept. 5/2 The Princeites, in whose Ark of the Covenant at Clapton on Sunday evening the Second Coming of Christ was claimed to be realised, are the disciples of the late Rev. Henry James Prince. *Ibid.*, The..tenets of the Princeites and the rumoured life of the Agapemone were severely criticised by Hepworth Dixon in his 'Spiritual Wives', in 1868.

princekin ('prɪnskɪn). [f. PRINCE *sb.* + -KIN.] A little, young, or diminutive prince. (Usually jocose or belittling.)

1855 THACKERAY *Newcomes* liii, Every one of us..can point to the Princekins of private life who are flattered and worshipped. **1858** CARLYLE *Fredk. Gt.* I. ii. I. 25 There have already been two little Princekins, who are both dead. **1894** DU MAURIER *Trilby* II. 141 This genial, dainty, benevolent little princekin.

'princeless, *a. rare.* [f. PRINCE *sb.* + -LESS.] Without a prince; having no prince.

a **1661** FULLER *Worthies, Rutland* (1662) II. 347 This County is Princeless, I mean affords no Royal Nativities.

princelet ('prɪnslɪt). [f. PRINCE *sb.* + -LET.] A little or petty prince; the ruler of a small principality.

1682 T. FLATMAN *Heraclitus Ridens* No. 73 (1713) II. 196 The Princelet..employ'd his Emissaries to enjoyn all his Dependents to make their whole strength against the Lovers of the King and Government. **1850** KINGSLEY *Alt. Locke* xxxii, German princelets might sell their country piecemeal to French or Russian! **1870** LOWELL *Among my Bks.* Ser. I. (1873) 325 Lessing..was librarian of one of those petty princelets who sold their subjects to be shot at in America. **1882** *Athenæum* 9 Dec. 767/2 Negotiations..with single Italian princelets like Sigismondo Malatesta.

†'**princelihood.** *Obs. rare.* [f. PRINCELY *a.* + -HOOD.] Princely condition or state.

1597 J. KING *On Jonas* (1618) 479 Whatsoeuer he had, making for honour and princelihood, that hee forsooke.

princelike ('prɪnslaɪk), *a.* (*adv.*) [f. PRINCE *sb.* + -LIKE.] **A.** *adj.* Like or resembling a prince; characteristic of or suitable to a prince; princely, royal.

1532 HERVET *Xenophon's Househ.* (1768) 56 He that can make them maisters, can make them princelyke, and able to be kinges. **1553** EDEN *Treat. Newe Ind.* (Arb.) 33 They interteined their gestes after a barbaros and beastly maner, which..semed to them princelike. **1560** DAUS tr. *Sleidane's Comm.* 434 b, Crafts and policies, neither commendable nor princelike. **1625** BACON *Char. Jas. I* in Rushw. *Hist. Coll.* (1659) I. 158 Your Majestie's manner of Speech is indeed Prince-like. **1726** POPE *Odyss.* XVII. 498 Thou dost not seem the worst Of all the Greeks, but Prince-like and the first. **1826** SCOTT *Woodst.* ii, I have outlived the kindest and most princelike of masters.

†**B.** *adv.* In a princely manner; like a prince.

1567 DRANT *Horace Epist.* xix. F vij, I euer set my fotestepps fre princelike where none had gone. **1660–1** PEPYS *Diary* 12 Jan., I went home with Mr. Davis, storekeeper.. and was there most prince-like lodged. **1859** TENNYSON *Geraint & Enid* 545 Thro' these Princelike his bearing shone.

princeliness ('prɪnslɪnɪs). [f. PRINCELY *a.* + -NESS.] The quality of being princely.

1571 GOLDING *Calvin on Ps.* xlv. 17 The princeleynesse.. consisteth not in the persons of men, but is referred to the head. **1637** BASTWICK *Litany* I. 5 By his princlynesse and royall munificence they haue such power. **1813** L. HUNT in *Examiner* 1 Feb. 65/2 You have a certain indescribable air of Princeliness. **1872** HOWELLS *Wedd. Journ.* (1892) 66 The ridiculous princeliness of their state-room.

princeling ('prɪnslɪŋ). [f. PRINCE *sb.* + -LING[1].]

1. A little or young prince.

a **1618** SYLVESTER *Panaretus* 4 To see our Princeling with a name indewed. **1745** YOUNG *Refl. Public Situation Kingd.* 161 Shall a pope-bred princeling crawl ashore, Replete with venom? **1862** H. MARRYAT *Year in Sweden* I. 367 No new born princeling ever came into the world at so ill-omened a period for royalty.

2. A petty prince; the ruler of an insignificant principality.

1794 COLERIDGE *Relig. Musings* 179 Leagued with these Each petty German princeling, nursed in gore! **1874** FARRAR *Christ* lx. II. 372 Herod Antipas..this petty princeling drowned in debauchery and blood. **1876** GREEN *Stray Stud.* 64 His army reminds one of the famous war establishment of the older German princelings.

princely ('prɪnslɪ), *a.* [f. PRINCE *sb.* + -LY[1].]

1. a. Of, pertaining, or belonging to a prince or princes (in various senses); held or exercised by a prince; royal, regal, kingly.

1503 DUNBAR *Thistle & Rose* 118 He did thame ressaif with princely laitis. **1513** MORE *Rich. III*, Wks. 59/1 She said also y^t it was not princely to mary hys owne subiect. **1611** SHAKS. *Wint. T.* IV. ii. 37 The Prince..is lesse frequent to his Princely exercises then formerly he hath appeared. **1774** J. BRYANT *Mythol.* II. 439 The Bull's head was esteemed a princely hieroglyphic. **1845** S. AUSTIN *Ranke's Hist. Ref.* II. III. iv. 119 To destroy the Council of Regency, which Hutten looked upon as the representative of the princely power. **1869** FREEMAN *Norm. Conq.* III. xii. 177 Among the princely houses of Western Europe.

b. *princely states*, the states of India that were ruled by native princes before the Indian Independence Act of 1947. Also (*rare*) in *sing.*

1952 *Columbia Lippincott Gazetteer of World* 835/2 By Jan. 26, 1950, when India became a sovereign republic, all acceding princely states had been brought within the constitutional framework. **1959** *Listener* 19 Mar. 497/2 The Princely States..have disappeared. **1967** SINGHA & MASSEY *Indian Dances* iv. 59 Both the South Indian Princely States and the Madras High Court recognized their rights and status. **1975** *Times* 29 Aug. 12/1 The map of India..was redrawn to incorporate the former princely states. **1980** H. R. F. KEATING *Murder of Maharajah* xviii. 225 Here is a simple District Superintendent of Police..invited to a princely state because a murder has been committed.

2. That is a prince; of princely descent or royal rank; royal, kingly.

1582 STANYHURST *Æneis* I. (Arb.) 19 Too this princelye regent [Æolus] her suit ladie Iuno thus opned. **1594** *1st Pt. Contention* (1843) 5 We thank you all for this great favour done In entertainment to my Princely Queen. **1769** GRAY *Installation Ode* 42 Princely Clare, And Anjou's heroine. **1828** SCOTT *F.M. Perth* xxiii, The Constable's lodgings received the owner and his princely guest. **1867** FREEMAN *Norm. Conq.* I. v. §3. 321 The sovereign powers enjoyed by the princely churchmen of the Empire.

3. Like a prince, princelike; having the appearance, manner, or qualities of a prince; dignified, stately, noble.

1500–20 DUNBAR *Poems* lxxxviii. 49 Thy famous Maire, by pryncely governaunce,..the rulith prudently. **1561** T. NORTON *Calvin's Inst.* II. iii. (1634) 128 God..furnisheth those with a Princely nature whom he appointeth to beare governement. **1588** *Copy of Letter*, etc. in *Harl. Misc.* (Malh.) II. 75 Praising her for her stately person and princely behaviour. **1793** BURKE *Rem. Policy Allies* Wks. VII. 149 His conversation is open,..his manners gracious and princely. **1810** SCOTT *Lady of L.* II. xxxii, I see him yet, the princely boy! **1871** M. COLLINS *Mrq. & Merch.* II. i. 3 A merchant might be princelier than he.

transf. **1850** R. G. CUMMING *Hunter's Life S. Afr.* (ed. 2) I. 188 He was a princely old stag, carrying splendid horns and a beautiful coat of new hair.

4. Like that of a prince; befitting or fit for a prince; sumptuous, magnificent, munificent.

1539 *Act 31 Hen. VIII*, c. 5 A goodly sumptuous beautifull and princely manour, decent & convenient for a king. **1555** EDEN *Decades* To Rdr. (Arb.) 49 Yet gaue he a greate parte of his glory to that princely buyldynge. **1614** LATHAM (*title*) Falconry or The Faulcons Lure and Cure: in two bookes,..published for the delight of noble mindes, and instruction of young Faulconers in things pertaining to this Princely Art. **1677** EVELYN *Diary* 10 Sept., My Lord..is given to no expensive vice but building, and to have all things rich, polite, and princely. **1688** R. HOLME *Armoury* III. 372/1 The Jacobs Staff..is a Princely Instrument being set forth in its Perfection. **1838** JAMES *Robber* ii, The estates are princely. **1866** NEALE *Sequences & Hymns* 183 Princeliest galleys bedropped the main, bound outward or inward. **1889** *Pall Mall G.* 21 Nov. 6/1, I am told in the newspapers that Sir E—— G——'s gift of £250,000 is 'princely'.

5. *Comb.*, as ***princely-loyal***, ***-proud***.

1605 SYLVESTER *Du Bartas* II. iii. IV. *Captains* 1268 O Peers, Princely-loyall Paladines. **1872** TENNYSON *Gareth & Lyn.* 158 Her own true Gareth was too princely-proud To pass thereby.

'**princely**, *adv.* Now *rare.* [f. as prec. + -LY[2].] In the manner of or befitting a prince; royally.

a **1548** HALL *Chron.*, *Edw. IV* 234 The kyng..answered to hys wordes so soberly, so grauelye, and so princely, that the Frenchmen their at not a littell mused. **1573** L. LLOYD *Marrow of Hist.* (1653) 25 Thou shalt live princely, thou shalt injoy pleasures. **1668** H. MORE *Div. Dial.* II. xxi. (1713) 154 Some Vertuous and Beautiful Virgin, Royally descended and Princely attired. **1807** E. S. BARRETT *Rising Sun* I. 104 Georgy did go it till he got (according to the vulgar idiom) princely drunk. **1885** HOWELLS *Silas Lapham* I. 169 She would have gone to Rome..and lived princely there for less than it took to live respectably in Boston.

‖**princeps** ('prɪnsɛps), *a.* and *sb.* Pl. 'principes (-sɪpiːz). [L. *princeps* adj., first, chief; as sb. first man, first person, head man, chief, prince; f. *prīm-us* first + *-cep-s*, *-cip-* f. *capĕre* to take.]

A. *adj.* First, original; *spec.* of a book, from L. phrase ***editio princeps*** original edition.

1809 FERRIAR *Bibliomania* 6 The Princeps-copy, clad in blue and gold. **1815** *Chron.* in *Ann. Reg.* 80/2 No editio princeps of any classic. **1889** JACOBS *Aesop* 20 Eight complete editions appeared within a year of the *princeps*.

b. Also frequent in L. phr. ***facile princeps*** (Cicero), indisputably the first or chief.

B. *sb.*

1. The title under which Augustus Cæsar and his successors exercised supreme authority in the Roman Empire: now generally used by historians instead of *emperor* (which, in its L. form *imperator*, originally denoted military command) to describe the constitutional position of the head of the state.

Formerly supposed to be for *princeps senatus* first man of the senate; now generally held to be for *princeps civitatis* first person of the city or state.

1837 *Penny Cycl.* IX. 382/2 The term Princeps was adopted by Augustus as the least invidious title of dignity, and was applied to his successors. **1893** BURY *Hist. Roman Emp.* ii. 15 A word was wanted, which without emphasizing any special side of the Emperor's power, should indicate his supreme authority in the republic. Augustus chose the name *princeps* to do this informal duty. *Ibid.* 17 The position of the new Princeps was fully established when he was acknowledged by both the senate and the army. *Ibid.* 26.

2. The name applied by Tacitus and by some mediæval Latin chroniclers and writers, and, after these, by some modern historians, to the head man or chief of a *pagus*, tribe, or small community in early Teutonic times. He corresponded generally to the Old English *ealdor* or *ealdorman* (by which words the L. *princeps* was often rendered).

See Tacitus *Germ.* xiii, xiv; Hucbald *Vita S. Lebuini* in Stubbs *Const. Hist.* I. iii. §22, 44 note, etc.

[*c* **825** *Vesp. Ps.* lxvii. 28 (O.E.T.) *Principes* (*gl.* aldermen) *Iuda..principes* (aldermen) *Zabulon. Ibid.* lxxxii. 12 *Omnes principes eorum* (*gl.* alle aldermen heora). *a* **1000** *Psalms* lxvii. 25 (Thorpe) *Principes Iuda..principes Zabulon* (*tr.* ealdormenn eac of Iudan..and ealdras eac of Zabulone). *c* **1000** *Ælfric's Voc.* in Wr.-Wülcker 155/18 *Princeps, uel comes*, ealdorman. *a* **1200** *Ibid.* 538/19 *Princeps*, aldermon.]

1874 STUBBS *Const. Hist.* (1875) I. ii. §14. 24 Outside of his official authority, the chief or only privilege of the *princeps* was the right of entertaining a *comitatus*... The *princeps* provided for them horses, arms, and such rough equipment as they wanted. *Ibid.* §16. 29. *Ibid.* iii. §22. 44 Over each of their [the heathen Saxons'] local divisions or *pagi*..a single *princeps* or chieftain presides.

3. *ellipt.* for *editio princeps*: see A.

'**Prince** '**Regent.** [PRINCE 10 a, and REGENT.] A prince who is regent of a country, during a minority, or in the absence or disability of the sovereign. Particularly, in Eng. Hist., the title commonly given to George Prince of Wales (afterwards Geo. IV) during the mental incapacity of George III, 1811–20.

His official title in the Act of 1811 (51 Geo. III, c. 1) was 'Regent of the United Kingdom of Great Britain and Ireland', but as he was 'the Prince' (of Wales), the word 'Prince' was, in non-official language, commonly prefixed to 'Regent', even by speakers in Parliament; he was also empowered by the Act to sign documents George P.R. or G.P.R., instead of his initials G.P. as Prince of Wales. 'Prince Regent' had also been casually applied to him in January 1789, in course of the Regency resolutions on the occasion of the King's first illness, which came to nothing because of his recovery.

1789 LD. THURLOW *Sp. in Ho. Lords* 22 Jan. (Cobbett *Parl. Hist.* XXVII. 1072), That the patronage of the royal household was not likely to be exercised by the exalted personage, in whose hands the resolutions went to place it, to the disadvantage of the Prince Regent, her son. **1811** WHITBREAD *Sp. in Ho. Com.* 1 Jan. (Hansard XVIII. 594), Is it fit that the Prince Regent should have only an ephemeral evanescent establishment? **1811** SHERIDAN 18 Jan. (Ibid. 906), The recommendation which that right hon. gent. gave himself, in order to fill the Prince Regent with the idea that he was the best minister he could have. **1812** SCOTT *Let. Ld. Byron* 3 July, I dare say our worthy bibliopolist overcoloured his report of your Lordship's conversation with the Prince Regent.

prince royal. Also prince-royal. [a. F. *prince royal* 'royal prince': see PRINCE *sb.* and ROYAL.] The eldest son of a reigning monarch; *spec.* of the king of Prussia.

1702 *Lond. Gaz.* No. 3879/2 The Prince Royal of Prussia intends to accompany the Queen his Mother to Hanover. **1710** *Ibid.* No. 4731/1 The Prince-Royal sent his Majesty the first News of it.

fig. **1845** G. MURRAY *Islaford* 143 That scape-grace, Prince-royal of a comet.

b. A variety of cherry. ? *Obs.*

1664 EVELYN *Kal. Hort.* (1729) 233/2 Cherries.. Carnation, Hartlib..Morocco, Prince Royal [etc.].

Prince's feather. A popular name of several plants. **a.** London Pride (*Saxifraga umbrosa*). Now *dial.*

1629 PARKINSON *Paradisus* 234 Some of our English Gentlewomen have called it, The Princes Feather. **1688** R. HOLME *Armoury* II. 91/2 Princes Feather hath the leaves invecked, the Flowers grow in branches. **1899** *Daily News* 30 Oct. 8/3 The..London girl is looked upon with suspicion and dislike by the rustics. She is nick-named 'Princess [*sic*] Feather', the local name for the flower known as 'London Pride'.

b. A tall handsome garden plant, *Amaranthus hypochondriacus*, bearing feathery spikes of small red flowers; also *A. speciosus*, a larger species.

1712 J. MORTIMER *Whole Art Husb.* II. 166 Amaranth Flowers gentle, or Princes Feathers, are of great Variety; but the principal are, 1. The great purple Flower with a thick tall Stalk, and many Branches, large green Leaves [etc.]. **1857** HENFREY *Bot.* §533 The species of *Amaranthus*, such as *A. candatus*, Love-lies-bleeding, and *A. hypochondriacus*, Prince's-feathers. **1883** W. ROBINSON *Eng. Flower Garden* 14/1 Prince's Feather, Love-lies-bleeding... Among annuals none are more in want of judicious use and appreciation than these. **1925** E. GLASGOW *Barren Ground* I. xi. 134 A narrow path led between rows of log cabins, each with its patchwork square of garden, and its clump of gaudy prince's feather or coxcomb by the doorstep. **1974** M. ALLAN *Plants that changed our Gardens* i. 41 Prince's Feather ..grows up to 5 ft tall and has flower plumes of deep crimson.

c. Locally applied to other plants: see quots.

1853 G. JOHNSTON *Nat. Hist. E. Bord.* I. 164 *Prunella vulgaris*... In the Merse called Heart-o-the-Yearth and Prince's-Feathers. **1866** *Treas. Bot.*, Prince's feather,..also an American name for *Polygonum orientale*. **1886** BRITTEN & HOLLAND *Eng. Plant-n.*, Prince's Feather..(4) *Syringa vulgaris*..Dev[on], Rutl[and].., pronounced Princy Feather.

princeship ('prɪnsʃɪp). [f. PRINCE *sb.* + -SHIP.] The position, dignity, or rank of a prince; the period of his being prince.

1570 LEVINS *Manip.* 140/39 A Princeship, *principatus*. **1599** NASHE *Lenten Stuffe* Wks. (Grosart) V. 275 In the Princeship or nonage of Cerdicke Sandes. **1868** FREEMAN *Norm. Conq.* II. vii. 16 Within the circle of ordinary continental princeship. **1896** A. DOBSON in *Longm. Mag.* Sept. 453 Some, especially in the princeship of the second George..were also accomplished and sensible.

b. With poss., as humorous title for a prince.

1664 KILLIGREW *Pandora* I. 5, I wish your Prince-ship had all the Ladies you desire.

Prince's metal. [From Prince Rupert of the Rhine, who invented it.] An alloy of about three parts of copper and one of zinc, in colour resembling gold; now chiefly used for cheap jewellery. Also (*Prince*) *Rupert's metal* (PRINCE *sb.* 12).

1682 *Lond. Gaz.* No. 1779/4 A Tall Man,..having a Cane with a Crooked Head, of the Princes Mettal. **1691** *Ibid.* No. 2650/3 A dark coloured Cloth Coat with Princes-Metal Buttons. **1758** REID tr. *Macquer's Chym.* I. 94 The composition will prove but a Tombac or Prince's Metal having very little malleability. **1842** FRANCIS *Dict. Arts* s.v. *Alloy*, The chief alloys are brass, tombac, pinchbeck, prince's metal, bell metal, type metal, gun metal..etc.

princess ('prɪnsɛs, prɪn'sɛs), *sb.* Also 5 prinses, *Sc.* prynsace, 5–7 princes. [ME. *prin'cesse*, a. F. *princesse* (15th c. in Littré), fem. of *prince*: see

-ESS[1]. So med.L. *principissa* (1338 in Du Cange), It. *principessa.*

The *e* in the second syllable is usually pronounced clear when unstressed, and by some with secondary or primary stress, to avoid confusion with *prince's, princes.*]

I. 1. A female sovereign or ruler; a queen. *arch.*

c **1400** MAUNDEV. (Roxb.) xv. 70 He wedded þe princesse, whilk was called Cadrige. *c* **1470** HENRY *Wallace* VIII. 1381 Ingland sen syn has boucht it der enewch, Thocht scho had beyn a queyn or a prynsace. **1483** *Cath. Angl.* 291/2 A Pryncesse, *principissa.* **1526** *Pilgr. Perf.* (W. de W. 1531) 262b, I wolde..moue them to folowe the example of yᵉ noble princesse saynt Edithe. **1562** A. SCOTT *Poems, To Q. Mary* 7 Welcum! oure plesand princes, maist of pryce. **1613** SHAKS. *Hen. VIII*, v. v. 58 She shall be to the happinesse of England, An aged Princesse. **1709** SWIFT *Adv. Relig.* ⁋14 So excellent a princess, as the present queen. **1842** MACAULAY *Ess., Fredk. Gt.* (1865) II. 271/1 The Empress Queen took a very different course. Though the haughtiest of princesses,..she forgot in her thirst for revenge..the dignity of her race.

2. The wife of a prince. ***princess dowager***: see DOWAGER.

c **1400** *Destr. Troy* 8473 Therat Ector was angry,.. Repreuet the prinses with a pale face: With his worshipful wife wrathit hym þen. **1447** BOKENHAM *Seyntys* (Roxb.) 8 Whan Olibrius hyr profryd his wyf to be And that she shuld be clepyd a pryncesse. **1568** GRAFTON *Chron.* II. 319 The Prince and princes his wife, with their yong sonne Richard ..entered into their Shippes. **1613** SHAKS. *Hen. VIII*, III. ii. 70 Katherine no more Shall be call'd Queene, but Princesse Dowager, And Widdow to Prince Arthur. **1834** JAMES *J. M. Hall* xxi, The princess dowager..is every day presenting some new petition. **1885** [see PRINCE 1].

3. The daughter or grand-daughter of a sovereign; a female member of a royal or princely family: see PRINCE 6. ***princess of the blood***: see BLOOD *sb.* 9. ***Princess royal***, (a title that may be conferred upon) the eldest daughter of the sovereign in Great Britain; also formerly in Prussia.

1508 FISHER *Seven Penit. Ps.* title-p., Compyled..at the exhortacion..of the moost excellent Princesse Margarete Countesse of Rychemount and Derby. **1556** *Chron. Gr. Friars* (Camden) 32 The second of Lent [1525], the kynge, qwene, and princes [Mary], with all other stattes both spirituall and temporall, came to Powlles. **1594** SHAKS. *Rich. III*, IV. iv. 211 Wrong not her Byrth, she is a Royall Princesse. **1626** MASSINGER *Rom. Actor* III. i, She..esteems herself Neglected when the princesses of the blood On every coarse employment are not ready To stoop to her commands. **1646–7** *Cal. St. Papers, Dom.* 525 The Princess Royal has been very well received, the King [of France] says he never saw a more handsome princess. **1650** CHAS. II in *Nicholas Papers* (Camden) I. 211 If you finde our deere brother att the Hague, you shall entreat our sister the Princesse Royall to use her best endeavours to perswade his returne into Fraunce. **1708** *Lond. Gaz.* No. 4494/2 (At Berlin) Their Majesties, the Prince and Princess-Royal.. performed the usual Ceremony. **1756–7** tr. *Keysler's Trav.* (1760) I. 267 Soon after the birth of the prince of Piedmont, the princess of Carignan being at court, a celebrated female singer..began *Son finite le Speranze.* **1765** BLACKSTONE *Comm.* I. iii. 216 The princess Sophia dying before queen Anne, the inheritance thus limited descended on her son and heir king George the first. **1819** *Times* 25 May, Her Royal Highness the Duchess of Kent was safely delivered yesterday morning, at Kensington-palace, of a Princess, at a quarter past four o'clock. **1879** *Whitaker's Alm.* 67 Princess Louise (Marchioness of Lorne). **1905** *Lond. Gaz.* 9 Nov. 7495 The King has been graciously pleased to declare that His Majesty's eldest Daughter, Her Royal Highness Princess Louise Victoria Alexandra Dagmar (Duchess of Fife) shall henceforth bear the style and title of Princess Royal.

4. Princess Regent. a. A princess who is regent during the minority or the absence of the nominal sovereign (in quot. 1714 applied to the Princess Ulrike Eleonore, sister of Charles XII of Sweden, who was Regent during his absence). **b.** The wife of the Prince Regent.

1714 *Lond. Gaz.* No. 5210/1 It has been proposed in the Assembly of the States to enter into a Treaty with the Allies of the North during the King's Absence... But the Princess-Regent has declared that she cannot consent to any Negotiations of Peace without Instructions from his Majesty. **1812** *Chron.* in *Examiner* 4 May 282/2 The Princess Regent..should go before the Prince Regent.

II. 5. a. Applied to a female, or anything personified as feminine, that is likened to a princess in pre-eminence or authority; formerly often to the Virgin Mary, also to female deities, etc.

a **1380** *Minor Poems fr. Vernon MS.* xxviii. 45 Heil puyred princesse of paramour, Heil Blosme of Brere, Brihtest of ble. *c* **1407** LYDG. *Reson & Sens.* 2234 With the cheff princesse of kynde, Which that called ys nature. **1423** JAS. I *Kingis Q.* xcix, Pitouse princes, and planet merciable! **1609** BIBLE (Douay) *1 Kings* xv. 13 He [Asa] removed also Maaca his mother, that she should not be princess in the sacrifices of Priapus. **1645–52** BOATE *Irel. Nat. Hist.* 64 The Liffie is the princess of the Irish-Rivers. **1678** *Yng. Man's Call.* 73 This is the day of his Saviours resurrection, the flower of time, a princess amongst all other daies. **1898** *Westm. Gaz.* 23 Feb. 4/3 The princess of milliners and dress-maker to the Princess of Wales.

b. Used as a form of address to a woman or girl. *colloq.*

1924 J. BUCHAN *Three Hostages* xviii. 254, I have waked you from sleep, my princess. Therefore so far it is good. **1968** J. SYMONS *Man whose Dreams came True* I. v. 42 'This is celebration night, Princess.' He had called her Princess the whole evening. **1969** A. LASKI *Dominant Fifth* iii. 120 Ah come on, princess, you're being morbid. **1970** J. AIKEN *Embroidered Sunset* i. 7 It was one of Uncle Wilbie's pleasantries to address Lucy as Princess. **1972** R. LUDLUM *Osterman Weekend* i. 12 Hey, Princess—get your brothers out and help your mother with the smaller bags.

6. A size of roofing slate, 24 inches by 14.

1878 D. C. DAVIES *Slate & Slate Quarry.* 136 Princesses ..Duchesses..Marchionesses..Countesses.

7. *attrib.* and *Comb.* (chiefly appositive), as ***princess-nun, -president, -priest, -queen; princess ring, (tele)phone, -worship.***

1594 MARLOWE & NASHE *Dido* I, Till that a Princesse priest conceau'd by Mars, Shall yeeld to dignitie a dubble birth. **1809** MALKIN *Gil Blas* IV. iv. ⁋4 Your subjects..may ask of you a princess-queen, descended from a long line of kings. **1865** RUSKIN *Sesame* ii. §61 (1907) 69 [The] simple princess-life of happy Nausicaa. **1880** *Archæologia Cant.* XIII. 89 Mary, daughter of Edward I, and princess-nun of Amesbury. **1962** M. & G. GORDON *Journey with Stranger* (1963) iii. 28 If you want a good bargain in princess rings, go down New Road in Bangkok. **1966** B. GLEMSER *Dear Hungarian Friend* viii. 139 She..picked up the azure blue Princess telephone, and said, 'Hello?' **1969** D. E. WESTLAKE *Up your Banners* (1970) xxxi. 210 We had to go next door and use Mrs. Lupowitz' Princess phone, a skittering pink beast that traveled all over its waxed table..whenever anybody tried to dial it. **1972** G. BAXT *Burning Sappho* ii. 42 He'd been watching Pat circling her gold princess phone for ten minutes. **1973** M. & G. GORDON *Informant* iii. 13 She was..constantly twisting a princess ring from Thailand. **1973** *Sat. Rev. Society* (U.S.) Mar. 70/1 Colored phones and such models as the lighter and smaller 'Princess' and the 'Trimline' (with the dial mechanism in the handset). **1976** M. MACHLIN *Pipeline* ii. 29 Brandon opened the chest and removed a brown princess telephone from it.

8. princess (or **princesse**) **dress**, a lady's robe of which the lengths of the bodice and skirt are cut in one piece; also applied to modifications of this shape; so ***princess cut, frock, line, polonaise, robe, -shape, skirt, tunic***, etc.; also ***princess-shaped*** adj., and ***princess*** adj. or ellipt. = princess-shaped.

1867 in A. Adburgham *Shops & Shopping* (1964) xi. 119 Princess breakfast dress. **1872** *Young Englishwoman* Oct. 541/1 A long princess-tunic. *Ibid.* 546/1 A lovely Princess dress, with cape. **1877** in A. Adburgham *Shops & Shopping* (1964) xvi. 178 The Princess cut. **1879** WEBSTER Suppl., *Princesse, a.*,..a term applied to a ladies' costume, made with a train flowing from the shoulders. **1879** MRS. A. E. JAMES *Ind. Househ. Managem.* 14 Half a dozen white morning wrappers made Princesse shape. **1883** *Pall Mall G.* 31 Dec. 6/1 A princesse dress of severe simplicity. **1887** *Daily News* 14 Oct. 6/1 The dress is princess-shaped at the back. **1898** *Ibid.* 15 Oct. 6/4 Some gowns are plain, others princess, others double-skirted. **1899** *Ibid.* 15 July 7/4 The princess dress is rarely seen, but the long princess tunic, or polonaise, has come to stay. **1900** *Bladud* 17 Oct. 6/2 A Princess skirt sounds an anomaly, but it..is nothing more or less than an abbreviated robe; it comes up more or less deeply towards the bust and is met by the ubiquitous bolero. **1960** C. W. CUNNINGTON et al. *Dict. Eng. Costume* 172/1 *Princess dress*,..a style popularly associated with the Princess of Wales when *c.* 1878–80 it was very fashionable. **1964** *McCall's Sewing* i. 5/1 A narrow centre panel, often seen in a princess-line dress, will add height. **1968** J. IRONSIDE *Fashion Alphabet* 25 *Princess*, a line which follows the curves of the body..darted for shape but with no seam at the waistline. **1973** *Times* 15 Nov. 1/3 The wedding dress was in pure white silk in the traditional *Princess* line.

Hence †**'princess** *v. Cookery, trans.* to dress (meat) in a certain way: see quot. *Obs.*

1769 J. SKEAT *Art Cookery* 8 Sweetbreads Princess'd... Inlay them with the lean of ham, and carrot cut thin, three rows in each sweetbread. These must be done in an oven, and a good ragout sauce in the dish, with parsley chopt fine. A Leg of Lamb Princes'd. Take a fine white leg, and inlay it with ham, carrot, and chopt parsley [etc.].

'princessdom. [f. prec. sb. + -DOM.] The position, dignity, or territory of a princess.

1883 M. BETHAM-EDWARDS *Exchange no Robbery* I. 33 It had seemed probable at one time that she would lose her princessdom altogether. **1900** CROCKETT *Black Douglas* 469, I have many castles there, and, they tell me, a princessdom of mine own.

‖**princesse lointaine** (prɛ̃sɛs lwɛ̃tɛn). [Fr., lit. 'distant princess', title of a play by E. Rostand (1868–1918), based on a theme of the poetry of the 12th-cent. troubadour Jaufré Rudel.] An ideal but unattainable woman. Also as *attrib. phr.*, aloof, unapproachable.

1921 W. J. LOCKE *Mountebank* viii. 96 The woman who could satisfy all his romantic imaginings was the Princesse Lointaine. **1934** A. THIRKELL *Wild Strawberries* xi. 238 Pierre had sat with Agnes, feeling like Geoffroy Rudel with the Princesse Lointaine. **1940** A. CHRISTIE *Sad Cypress* I. i. 17 That little air of yours—aloof—untouchable—*la Princesse Lointaine.* **1949** R. HARVEY *Curtain Time* 127 Papa was the romantic and the mystic, following the gleam of the fiercer bass, the more golden wall-eyed pike, and sailing in search of a muskelunge, as if for some *princesse lointaine.* **1957** L. DURRELL *Bitter Lemons* 97, I had seen her..driving about the hills with the same *princesse lointaine* expression. **1962** I. MURDOCH *Unofficial Rose* xxxiii. 314 He had loved Lindsay as the enticing but untouchable *princesse lointaine.* **1969** M. DRABBLE *Waterfall* 42 She lay there, the unachievable *princesse lointaine.* **1976** P. QUENNELL *Marble Foot* iv. 162 Constant's *princesse lointaine* was the Chinese film-actress Anna May Wong.

princessly ('prɪnsɛslɪ), *a.* [f. PRINCESS + -LY[1].] That is a princess or like a princess; befitting or appropriate to a princess.

1747 RICHARDSON *Clarissa* (1810) I. xxxi. 216 To engage her (for example-sake to her princessly daughter) to join in their cause. **1813** LD. BYRON in *Ld. R. Gower's Rec. & Remin.* (1903) 33 She is handsome..and her manners are princessely [*sic*]. **1899** JUDGE PARRY *Gold. Jujube* ii. in *Scarlet Herring*, etc. 88 Imprinting a kingly kiss upon her princessly cheek, [the king] rushed from the room.

princess-ship ('prɪnsɛsʃɪp). [f. PRINCESS + -SHIP.] The condition or fact of being a princess; with possessive as title for a princess.

1733 FIELDING *Quixote* I. vi, If your princess-ship could but prevail on my master. **1884** LUCY B. WALFORD *Nan*, etc. (1885) I. 13 Her days of princess-ship are over.

Princeton-First-Year. Applied to a form of male homosexual activity in which partners achieve orgasm by intercrural friction.

1969, 1971 [see *plain sewing* s.v. PLAIN *a.*[1] and *adv.* C. c. **1980** *Times Lit. Suppl.* 21 Mar. 324/5 'Princeton-First-Year' is a more condescending version of the term 'Princeton Rub'; that is, *coitus contra ventrem.*

Princetonian (ˌprɪn'stəʊnɪən), *sb.* and *a.* [f. *Princeton* (see below) + -IAN.] **A.** *sb.* A student or graduate of Princeton University, New Jersey, U.S.A. **B.** *adj.* Of or pertaining to Princeton University.

1876 (*title of newspaper*) The Princetonian. **1896** J. BARNES (*title*) A Princetonian. A Story of undergraduate life at the College of New Jersey. **1898** J. W. ALEXANDER *Princeton* 5 These two renowned and useful organizations ..[are] exclusively Princetonian. *Ibid.* 26 Some cynical Princetonian has said that nothing less than two armies and a revolution could drive a son of Old Nassau to a New England college. **1928** [see *old-line* s.v. OLD E. 3]. **1949** *Cavalier Daily* (Univ. of Virginia) 22 Oct. 4/2 Staffers of the Daily Pennsylvanian visited the Princetonian offices following the Penn-Princeton football game. **1971** M. MCCARTHY *Birds of Amer.* 192 The languid voice of a Princetonian major in government studies. *Ibid.* 193 The ultra-WASP Princetonian, who bore the curious name of Silvanus Platt. **1977** *New Yorker* 23 May 88/1 Thus ringingly begins an 'Alumni Primer' that is distributed to each Princetonian during the summer following his.. graduation from that hallowed institution.

†**Prin'cetta, -ette.** Trade name of a fabric.

1844 G. DODD *Textile Manuf.* iv. 114 The trade-list of a large worsted-factory..contains the following enumeration, ..Merino, Say Plainback,..Says,..Princettes. *c* **1850** in Rachel J. Lowe *Farm & Inhab.* (1883) 84 [On ordinary days she wore a thick camlet, which was called] 'Princetta stuff'. **1858** SIMMONDS *Dict. Trade*, *Princettas*, a worsted fabric, which is sometimes made with a cotton warp.

prince-wood. Also prince's wood. A dark-coloured and light-veined timber produced by two W. Indian trees, *Cordia gerascanthoides* and *Hamelia ventricosa*; also called *Spanish elm.*

1686 *Lond. Gaz.* No. 2183/4 Stolen.., a strong Box of Princes Wood Varnished. **1707** SLOANE *Jamaica* I. p. lv, The goods..exported from the island are Sugars, Indico, Cotton-wool,..Prince-wood. **1756** P. BROWNE *Jamaica* 170 Spanish Elm or Prince-wood..is generally esteemed as one of the best timber woods in the island. **1858** SIMMONDS *Dict. Trade*, *Prince's-wood*, a light-veined brown wood, the produce of *Cordia Gerascanthus*, obtained in Jamaica, and principally used for turning. **1866** *Treas. Bot.*, Princewood.

†**'prince-worthy,** *a. Obs.* [f. PRINCE *sb.* + WORTHY *a.*] Worthy of or befitting a prince.

1574 *Life Abp. Parker* To Rdr. C iv b, His commendable and Princeworthy thyrste off knowledge had excused his ignorance. **1593–5** *Norden's Spec. Brit., M'sex* II. Pref., Prince-worthy touch. **1632** J. HAYWARD tr. *Biondi's Eromena* 58 To this her sound judgement shee hath conjoyned a Prince-worthy erudition.

†**princhе,** *v. Obs.* App. a by-form of PINCH *v.*

1390 GOWER *Conf.* II. 290 Ther was with him non other fare, But forto prinche and forto spare, Of worldes muk to gete encress.

princify ('prɪnsɪfaɪ), *v. rare.* [f. PRINCE *sb.* + -(I)FY.] *trans.* To make into a prince; to make princely. Hence **'princified** *ppl. a.*, princelike, stately, majestic. So **princifi'cation.** (*nonce-wds.*)

1847 THACKERAY *Lords & Liv.* i, Napoleon princified him. **1859** —— *Virgin.* v, The English girls..laughed at the princified airs which she gave herself. **1865** *Daily Tel.* 8 Nov. 5/2 The Emperor..has been persuaded to do injudicious things—witness the princification of the Iturbides.

principal ('prɪnsɪpəl), *a.* and *sb.* (*adv.*) Also 3–6 **princy-, prynci-, pryncy-**; 3–6 **-pale**, 4–7 **-pall(e**, 5 *Sc.* **-paill**; 5 **prinsipall, -sepall, prynsipall, prencipall, -ale.** [a. F. *principal* (11th c. in Hatz.-Darm.), ad. L. *principāl-is* first, chief, original, primitive; princely, imperial; as sb. in late L. an overseer, a chief; f. *princeps, princip-em*: see PRINCE *sb.* and -AL[1]. In early use the adj. was often in plural *principal(e)s* (after F.) esp. when following the sb.]

A. *adj.* **I.** General senses.

1. First or highest in rank or importance; that is at the head of all the rest; of the greatest account or value; foremost: = CHIEF *a.* 3.

a. of persons.

1297 R. GLOUC. (Rolls) 9154, & þe bissop roger of salesbury after him suor anon..& þo was þe principal þe sacringe vor to do & vor ensample of hom oþere encentede þer to. **1390** GOWER *Conf.* III. 144 As a king in special Above all othre is principal Of his pouer. *c* **1400** MAUNDEV. (1839) xxiii. 248 Of his iij wyfes, the firste and the princypalle þat was Prestre Iohnes doughter. **1535**

COVERDALE *Esther* (Apocr.) xvi. 11 He was..had in hye honoure of euery man, as the next and pryncipall vnto the kynge. **1578** in I. H. Jeayes *Catal. Charters Berkeley Castle* (1892) 324 Robert Commendatar of Dunfermelenge owre principall Secretar and Ambassador. **1662** J. DAVIES tr. *Olearius' Voy. Ambass.* 3 The principal Minister, who among the Lutherans is look'd upon as a Bishop. **1795** *Gentl. Mag.* July 544/2 He was the principal projector of the fund for decayed musicians.

(*b*) *spec.* as ***principal boy***, the leading male role in a pantomime, usu. played by a woman; ***principal girl***, the leading female role in a pantomime.

1893 H. E. MCLELLAND *Jack & Beanstalk* 11 She's Jill, our 'principal girl', the gallery's joy. *Ibid.*, So it's only natural, as I'm the principal boy! **1897** G. B. SHAW *Our Theatres in Nineties* (1932) III. 24 Why..is the 'principal boy' expected to be more vulgar than the principal girl? **1900** *London Lett.* 26 Jan. 133/1 In the part of principal girl [in a pantomime] Miss L. L... dances and sings delightfully, ..Miss F. L. as principal boy has no equal. **1901** R. J. BROADBENT *Hist. Pantomime* xxi. 224 Towards the close of the 'fifties..the character of Harlequin began to be played by women, the origin of what is now known as the 'principal boy'. **1910** BARONESS ORCZY *Lady Molly* ix. 236 The little actress looked ready to cry... 'I am principal boy at the Grand,' she explained. **1925** M. W. DISHER *Clowns & Pantomimes* xvii. 317 This obsession with barbaric splendour was shown in Harris's choice of 'principal boys'. **1932** D. L. SAYERS *Have his Carcase* xv. 201 Airy-fairy-Lilian they used to call me when I was principal boy in old Rosenbaum's shows. **1962** *Oxford Mail* 24 Dec. 6/6 In 1947 he met his wife in pantomime at Lincoln. 'She was the principal girl, Maid Marion. I was just one of the bad robbers.' **1969** *Listener* 2 Jan. 18/1 Gone are the good days when principal boys were girls. **1971** *Petticoat* 17 July 28/1 He..was wearing a pink voile shirt with principal-boy sleeves. **1975** *Times* 2 May 11/3 The greatest of pantomime principal boys, Dorothy Ward.

b. of things.

c **1386** CHAUCER *Pars. T.* ¶441 The remedie agayns the foule synne of Enuye First is the louynge of god principal and louyng of his neighebor as hym self. *c* **1400** MAUNDEV. (Roxb.) v. 14 þe principale citee of Cypre es Famagost. **1413** *Pilgr. Sowle* (Caxton) v. i. (1859) 71 This hows is chyef and pryncipalle of alle other howses. **1526** *Pilgr. Perf.* (W. de W. 1531) 1 The princypall purpose of our entent. **1611** BIBLE *Prov.* iv. 7 Wisedome is the principall thing, therefore get wisedome. **1697** tr. *Burgersdicius his Logic* I. xvii. 62 Cause Efficient is divided into Principal and less Principal. **1799** G. SMITH *Laboratory* I. 121 Your first or principal matter for enamel colours. **1860** TYNDALL *Glac.* I. xv. 100 The glacier which had filled the principal valley. **1875** JOWETT *Plato* (ed. 2) III. 27 Their principal food is flour and meal.

2. Less definitely: Belonging to the first or highest group in rank or importance; of the first order; main, prominent, leading: = CHIEF *a.* 4. In this sense formerly sometimes with comparative *principaller* (or *more principal*), often with superlative *principallest* (or *most principal*); otherwise referring usually to a number of individuals.

a. of things.

c **1290** *S. Eng. Leg.* I. 345/15 Bote þreo wateres principales of alle ne beoth, i-wis: þat on is homber, þat oþur seuerne, and temes þe þridde is. **1340** HAMPOLE *Pr. Consc.* 7299 Yhit es over þase a payne generalle, þat of alle other es mast principalle. *c* **1391** CHAUCER *Astrol.* I. §5 The 4 quarters of thin astrelabie, deuyded after the 4 principals plages or quarters of the firmament. **1483** CAXTON *Cato* Bj b, The scoler which wyl lerne ought to haue thre pryncipalle condycions. **1533** *Test. Ebor.* (Surtees) VI. 36 The fyve pryncypall woundes of our Lord. **1577** B. GOOGE *Heresbach's Husb.* (1586) 10 Water is one of the principalest things to be cared for. **1665** BOYLE *Occas. Refl.* v. i, A further and more principal Consideration. **1690** in Locke *Govt.* I. vi. §62 He..has the Sovereignty over the Woman, as being the nobler and principaller Agent in Generation. **1723** *Present St. Russia* I. 305 Among the Drugs which Russia produces, Rhubarb is one of the most principal. **1874** J. SULLY *Sensation & Intuition* xi. 298 Character is but one, though a principal, source of interest among several that are employed by the drama.

b. of persons.

c **1400** MAUNDEV. (1839) xxii. 242 It hath xii princypalle kynges in xii prouynces. *c* **1430** LYDG. *Min. Poems* (Percy Soc.) 4 Alle clad in white, and the most principalle Afforne in reed, with thaire mayre ryding. **1523** LD. BERNERS *Froiss.* I. clxi. 196 The frenche kynge wolde nat agree without he myght haue foure of the princypallest of the englysshmen at his pleasure. **1598** GRENEWEY *Tacitus' Ann.* I. vii. (1622) 11 Certaine of the Principallest Gentlemen of the citie. **1648** GAGE *West Ind.* 133 A principall family of Indians, who are said to descend from the ancient Kings. **1771** FRANKLIN *Autobiog.* Wks. 1840 I. 73, I made acquaintance with many principal people of the province. **1808** ELEANOR SLEATH *Bristol Heiress* III. 263 Attended by some of the principal of the nobility.

3. Specially great (in comparison with things of the kind generally); of high degree or importance; special, eminent. Now *rare* or *Obs.*

1417 *Let. to Hen. V* in Ellis *Orig. Lett.* Ser. II. I. 55 The same beinge soe gracious and joyous newes as any can imagine or thinke to the principall comforte and especiall consolation of us and all your faythfull subjectes. **1424** in *Calr. Pat. Rolls, 8 Hen. VI* 30 The xxiiij aldermen..xal.. supporten the mair..walkyng with hym on principal dayes and in procession. **1576** FLEMING *Panopl. Epist.* 353 Some beastes..as they are vnto man principall benefites, so to themselues and to their kind, they are most louing and tender. **1611** BIBLE *Transl. Pref.* 3 The Pen-men [of the Scripture being such as were] endewed with a principall portion of Gods spirit. **1748** HARTLEY *Observ. Man* II. iii. 213 That which is prior in the Order of Nature is always less perfect and principal, than that which is posterior. **1868** BUSHNELL *Serm. Living Subj.* 252 Which is understood to be the manner to a principal degree of a certain immense trading house.

†**4.** Of special quality; excellent, goodly, choice; first-class, first-rate. *Obs.*

c **1430** *Hymns Virg.* 1 In þi palijs so principal I pleyde priuyli wiþoute mys. **1535** COVERDALE *Song Sol.* v. 13 His lippes droppe as the floures of the most principall Myrre. *a* **1552** LELAND *Itin.* IV. 44 From Kiddey Mouth..to the Mouthe of Thawän a 3 Miles by very principal good Corn Ground. **1589** NASHE *Pasquil & Marforius* B iij b, A great Nosegay in his hande, of the principalest flowers I could gather. **1609** BIBLE (Douay) *Ezek.* xxvii. 17 Juda and the land of Israel they were thy merchants in the principal corne [Vulg. *in frumento primo*].

†**5.** Of, belonging to, or befitting a prince; princely, royal. *Obs.*

13.. *E.E. Allit. P.* B. 1581 Fyrst knew hit þe kyng & alle þe cort after In þe palays pryncipale. **1382** WYCLIF *Esther* ii. 18 He ȝaf reste to alle prouyncis, and grauntide large ȝiftis aftir principal gret doing [1388 the worschipful doyng of a prynce; *Vulg.* magnificentiam principalem]. —— *Ps.* l. 14 [li. 12] With the spirit principal conferme thou me [*Vulg.* spiritu principali confirma me, LXX πνεύματι ἡγεμονικῷ στήριξόν με; COVERDALE, etc. with thy free spirit]. **1578** *Chr. Prayers* in *Priv. Prayers* (Parker Soc.) 499 Give me the comfort of thy saving help again, and strengthen me with a principal Spirit. **1582** BENTLEY *Mon. Matrones* Ep. Ded., Hauing the principal and heroicall spirit of your holie father good King Dauid. **1591** SPENSER *Muiopotmos* 380 But walkt at will, and wandred to and fro, In the pride of his freedome principall.

II. Special and technical senses.

6. Of money: Constituting the primary or original sum; that is the main or capital sum invested or lent, and yielding interest or income; capital, capitalized. (Cf. B. 9.)

† ***principal cost, money***, original or prime cost.

1340 *Ayenb.* 35 Hi..makeþ ofte of þe gauel principale dette. **1494** FABYAN *Chron.* VII. 496 It was ordeyned yᵗ the sayd..dettours to the sayd vsurers shuld paye the pryncipall dette vnto the kynge at theyr dayes of payment. **1540–1** ELYOT *Image Gov.* 121 He desired theym..to take for that time their principall summe that was borowed, and clerely to remette the residue. *c* **1677** in Marvell *Growth Popery* 62 The parties..swore the Principal Costs of their Goods was to the Value of 3902*l.* *a* **1687** PETTY *Pol. Arith.* Pref. (1690) a iij, Actions [shares] in the East-India Company are near double the principal Money. **1731** GAY *Let. to Swift* 20 Mar., At the same time tell me what I shall do with the principal sum. **1852** BRIGHT *Let. to Dr. Gray* 25 Oct. in *Speeches* (1876) 549/2, 500,000*l.* per annum..or a principal sum, at twenty years' purchase, of 10,000,000*l.* **1864** *Will* in *Law Rep.* (1871) 11 Eq. 232, I declare that the income arising from my principal money shall be paid [etc.]. [MALINS *Ibid.* 234 In using the words 'principal money' I think he intended to signify all his capital.]

7. *Law.* **a.** That is the chief person concerned in some action or proceeding; *esp.* that is the actual perpetrator of, or directly responsible for, a crime: cf. B. 2 b. ? *Obs.* **b.** ***principal challenge***: a challenge against a jury, or against a particular juror, alleging a fact such as, if proved, would disqualify such jury or juror as a matter of law.

1448 *Paston Lett.* I. 74 Before the coroner of Coventre, up on the sygth of the bodyes, ther ben endited, as prynsipall for the deth of Richard Stafford, Syr Robert Harcourt and the ij. men that ben dede. And for the ij. men of Harcourts that ben dede, ther ben endited ij. men of Syr Umfrey as prynsipall. **1486** *Act 3 Hen. VII*, c. 2 Such Mis-doers, Takers,..and Receitors..[shall] be..judged as principal Felons. **1553** BRENDE *Q. Curtius* VI. 112 b, The residue of the counsail were of opinion that Philotas woulde neuer haue conseiled this conspiracie, excepte he had bene either principall or priuye therunto. **1607–72** Challenge principal [see CHALLENGE *sb.* 3]. **1768** BLACKSTONE *Comm.* III. xxiii. 363 A principal challenge is such, where the cause assigned carries with it *prima facie* evident marks of suspicion, either of malice or favour. **1863** H. COX *Instit.* II. iii. 354 Where there are manifest reasons of suspecting partiality..in which case the challenge is called a principal challenge.

†**8.** Of a document: Original (as opposed to a copy): cf. B. 5. *Obs.*

1567 in *6th Rep. Hist. MSS. Comm.* 642/1 This is the autentik and iust copy of the principall lettir aboue mentionat... And the same originall and principall extant to schaw will testifie.

9. *Gram.* Said of a sentence or clause, or of a word (esp. a verb), in relation to another which is auxiliary to or dependent upon it: opp. to *subordinate* or *dependent*. ***principal parts*** of a verb: see PART *sb.* 19 b.

1590 STOCKWOOD *Rules Construct.* 2 After the nominatiue case commeth the principall verbe... First of all, the principall verbe must be sought out. **1824** L. MURRAY *Eng. Gram.* (ed. 5) I. 272 This rule refers to principal, not to auxiliary verbs..the principal and its auxiliary form but one verb. **1871** ROBY *Lat. Gram.* IV. iii. §1024 A compound sentence contains two or more single sentences... If they are not independent of each other, one will be principal and the others subordinate. *Ibid.* §1032 A subordinate sentence may itself be principal to a third sentence. **1876** MASON *Eng. Gram.* (ed. 21) §400 A Complex Sentence is one which, besides a principal subject and predicate, contains one or more subordinate clauses, which have subjects and predicates of their own. *Ibid.* §403 A Substantive Clause.. may be either the subject or the object of the verb in the principal clause.

10. *Building.* Applied to the main rafters, posts, or braces in the wooden framework of a building, which support the chief strain. Cf. B. 7.

1594 PLAT *Jewell-ho.* I. 10 The principall postes, the Rafters, and the beames of any house. **1663** GERBIER *Counsel* 45 Beams of the Roof for the principal Rafters to stand on. **1703** MOXON *Mech. Exerc.* 163 Principal-Posts, the corner Posts of a Carcass. **1710** J. HARRIS *Lex. Techn.* II, *Principal Posts*, in any wooden Building, are the Corner Posts. **1860** WEALE *Dict. Terms Archit.*, *Principal brace*, a brace immediately under the principal rafters or parallel to them, in a state of compression, assisting with the principals to support the timbers of a roof.

11. *Math.*, etc. ***principal axis***: (*a*) of a conic, that axis which passes through the foci, the transverse axis (opp. to *conjugate axis*); (*b*) each of three lines in a body or system used as the chief lines of reference in relation to forces operating upon it; as ***principal axes of inertia, of stress*** (see quots.); ***principal component***, one of the components of a set of statistical data (regarded as points in a multi-dimensional space) which contribute most strongly to its variance; freq. *attrib.* (in *sing.* or *pl.*), designating a method of analysis which involves finding the principal component and removing the variance due to it, and repeating this successively; ***principal focus*** of a lens or concave mirror, the focus of rays that impinge upon it parallel to its axis; ***principal ideal***, an ideal whose elements can be generated by multiplying some particular member of the ring by each member (including itself) in turn; ***principal plane***, (*a*) of a symmetrical body: an imaginary plane of symmetry, as, in an oblate or prolate spheroid, the plane passing through the centre at right angles to the axis of revolution; in an ellipsoid there are three principal planes at right angles to each other, two of which pass through the longest axis, and the third through the centre of both the others; (*b*) ***of stress***: see quot. 1883; ***principal point***: in *Perspective*, the point where the *principal ray* meets the plane of delineation; ***principal points*** of a lens or combination of lenses (tr. Ger. *Hauptpunkte*, Gauss), two points on the optical axis such that the straight line between the first of these and any point of the object is parallel to that between the second and the corresponding point of the image; ***principal quantum number*** (Physics), the quantum number symbolized by *n* (see N I. 4 b); ***principal ray***: in *Perspective*, the straight line from the point of sight perpendicular to the plane of delineation; ***principal section*** of a crystal, any section passing through the optical axis; ***principal stress***, each of the three purely tensile or compressive stresses acting in mutually perpendicular directions into which any combination of stresses acting at a point can be resolved; ***principal value***, the one real value of a function which has also several imaginary values.

1879 THOMSON & TAIT *Nat. Philos.* I. I. 262 Any axis is called a *principal axis of a body's inertia, or simply a principal axis of the body, if when the body rotates round it the centrifugal forces either balance or are reducible to a single force. **1882** ROUTH *Dynamics Rigid Bodies* (ed. 4) 99 The existence of principal axes was first established by Segner in the work *Specimen Theoriæ Turbinum.* **1883** THOMSON & TAIT *Nat. Philos.* I. II. 207 For any stress.. there are three determinate planes at right angles to one another such that the force acting in the solid across each of them is precisely perpendicular to it. These planes are called the principal or normal planes of the stress; the forces upon them, per unit area,—its principal or normal tractions; and the lines perpendicular to them,—its principal or normal axes. **1933** H. HOTELLING in *Jrnl. Educ. Psychol.* XXIV. 421 We..determine the components, not exceeding *n* in number, and perhaps neglecting those whose contributions to the total variance are small. This we shall call the method of *principal components. **1963** SOKAL & SNEATH *Princ. Numerical Taxon.* vii. 195 Two different methods of factor analysis are customarily practiced: the principal components method is largely employed by British factor analysts. **1968** *Brit. Med. Bull.* XXIV. 236/2 Examples of the use of the older established techniques of principal components analysis..and factor analysis..rather than taxonomic analysis, predominate in the literature. **1969** A. P. DEMPSTER *Elem. Contin. Multivariate Anal.* vii. 136 The principal component analysis of a given sample relative to a given reference inner product over variable-space consists of finding the eigenvalues and eigenvectors of the sample covariance inner product relative to the reference inner product. The eigenvalues found in this way will be called sample principal components of total variance relative to the chosen reference inner product or, more briefly, principal components. **1831** BREWSTER *Optics* i. 9 When the rays which the mirror collects are parallel, as in the present case, the point F is called its **principal focus*, or its focus for parallel rays. **1937** A. A. ALBERT *Mod. Higher Algebra* (1938) xi. 255 Every two quantities of a *principal ideal ring have a greatest common divisor. **1965** J. J. ROTMAN *Theory of Groups* iv. 66 A principal ideal domain is a domain in which every ideal is a principal ideal. **1970** D. M. BURTON *First Course in Rings & Ideals* ii. 19 An ideal (*a*) generated by just one ring element is termed a principal ideal. **1862** SALMON *Analytic Geom. Three Dimens.* iv. 45 A diametral plane is said to be principal if it be perpendicular to the chords to which it is conjugate... Hence a quadric has in general three *principal diametral planes, the three diameters perpendicular to which are called the axes of the surface. **1704** J. HARRIS *Lex. Techn.* I, **Principal Point*, which some Writers call the *Centre of the Picture*, and the *Point of Concurrence.* **1922**, etc. *Principal quantum number [see N I. 4 b]. **1973** J. G. TWEEDDALE *Materials Technol.* I.

ii. 23 A specific maximum possible number of orientations of orbital pattern, each pattern being completely occupied if two electrons are in it, is possible for each mode, the number being determined by the relevant Principal Quantum Number. **1704** J. HARRIS *Lex. Techn.* I, **Principal Ray*, in Perspective. **1831** BREWSTER *Optics* xvii. 151 Every plane passing through the axis is called a **principal section* of the crystal. **1858** W. J. M. RANKINE *Man. Appl. Mech.* I. v. 94 The three conjugate normal stresses are called *principal stresses, and their directions, principal axes of stress. **1922** GLAZEBROOK *Dict. Appl. Physics* I. 803/2 The intensity of greatest shearing stress at any point is equal.. to one-half the algebraic difference of the greatest and least principal stresses. **1944** A. HOLMES *Princ. Physical Geol.* vi. 78 The various types of faults depend on the relationships between the three principal stresses.., assuming of course, that.. the stress difference is sufficient to bring about fracture and movement. **1971** I. G. GASS et al. *Understanding Earth* xix. 272/1 Making certain other reasonable assumptions about the shear fracture character of the fault, it is possible to derive.. the direction of the maximum principal stress.

12. *Surveying.* = PRIMARY *a.* 3 a.

1790 *Phil. Trans. R. Soc.* LXXX. 248 The first set [of Secondary triangles] consists of thirty-five, whereby the relative distances of so many points have been determined from certain stations of the principal series. **1795** *Ibid.* LXXXV. 490 (*heading*) Of the selection of the angles constituting the principal triangles, and the manner of reducing them for computation. **1847** W. YOLLAND *Acct. Measurement of Lough Foyle Base* VII. 113 From the commencement of the Irish Survey, in 1825, secondary objects required for breaking up the principal triangulation into a smaller network.. were regularly observed at the same time as observations were made of the principal stations. **1920** [see PRIMARY *a.* 3 a].

13. *Seismology.* Applied to the most intense shock or earthquake occurring in a sequence.

1899 C. DAVISON *Hereford Earthquake Dec. 17, 1896* iv. 199 The principal shock was also registered by magnetographs at Kew. *Ibid.* 200 The principal earthquake was felt by several persons in the Isle of Wight. **1902** *Q. Jrnl. Geol. Soc.* LVIII. 374 The focus of this shock was evidently close to the northern end of the focus of the first and principal shock. **1938** L. D. LEET *Pract. Seismol.* ix. 295 Davison has cited several well-studied cases.. where the range of audibility of after-shocks increased progressively and systematically, giving evidence of decreasing depth of foci following the principal shock. **1965** A. HOLMES *Princ. Physical Geol.* (ed. 2) xxv. 893 The principal shock, which generally lasts only a few seconds, or at most, and rarely, a few minutes, may be preceded by fore-shocks and is invariably followed by a series of after-shocks.

B. *sb.*

I. 1. a. A chief or head man or woman; a chief, head, ruler, commander, superior; a governor, a presiding officer, as the head of a religious or educational institution, the manager of a house of business, an employer, etc.; †the master or mistress of a household (*obs.*).

1390 GOWER *Conf.* II. 345 Criseide,.. Which was.. Of thilke temple principal, Wher Phebus hadde his sacrifice. *c* **1400** *Rule St. Benet* 2211 Þe Priores als principall Es 'lady' & leder of þam all. *c* **1440** *Alphabet of Tales* 219 Sho.. went vnto ane abbay.. And when þer principall was dead, sho was made principall. **1489** CAXTON *Faytes of A.* III. ii. 170 The Emperoure of Rome.. is the pryncypall of the worlde. **1608** SHAKS. *Per.* IV. vi. 89 Why, hath your principall made knowne vnto you who I am? **1754** RICHARDSON *Grandison* (1781) III. vii. 48 The servants throughout the house adore you: And I am sure their principals do. **1805** SURR *Winter in Lond.* (1806) I. 43 [He] attended the banking-house in the capacity of a pupil, who was hereafter to become a principal in the concern. **1827** S. RODMAN in B. Swan *New Bedford in 1827* (1935) 3/2, I visited the High School, Wm. Johnson, principal. **1833** *Century Mag.* XXX. 780/1, I am, sir.. permitted to be the Principal of the Canterbury, (Conn.) Female Boarding School. **1836** SIR H. TAYLOR *Statesman* xxiii. 167 A minister's private secretary has the care and management, under his principal's direction, of all affairs relating to the disposal of offices and employments. **1949** *Lubbock* (Texas) *Morning Avalanche* 23 Feb. I. 10/6 Price was named to the position of principal of the new school. **1973** *N.Y. Law Jrnl.* 30 July 13/7 Petitioner, a probationary assistant principal in James Wilson Young High School, resigned in writing on Feb. 13, 1973 (effective June 29, 1973) after being pressed to do so by both the District Principal (Mr. Covell) and the Assistant District Principal (Mr. Pecorale) of the School District. **1974** *Hartsville* (S. Carolina) *Messenger* 22 Apr. 1-A/4 Dr. Black pointed out that students who presented certificates to their principals in September, 1973 will not need another one.

b. *fig.* or *transf.* Of a thing.

1390 GOWER *Conf.* I. 322 Thi will is thi principal, And hath the lordschipe of thi witt. *Ibid.* III. 101 So is the herte principal, To whom reson in special Is yove as for the governance. *c* **1420** *26 Pol. Poems* xv. 14 Þe brayn is pryncypal Chef of counseil ymagenyng.

c. In Great Britain, the most usual designation of the head of a COLLEGE in senses 4 c, d, e; sometimes also in senses 4 a, b, and often in 4 f; also of the head of a HALL (sense 4 b). (Cf. PRESIDENT 2 c.)

In Oxford, used to designate the heads of a number of colleges and private halls (the others being variously called president, master, provost, warden, rector, and dean); in Cambridge, used only of the heads of Newnham and Homerton Colleges.

1438 *Early Chan. Proc.* (P. R. O.) 75/11 One Roger Grey, Clerk, principalle of Brasenose in Oxynforde. **1563** *Act 27 Hen. VIII*, c. 42 §1 The Deanes, Wardeynes, Provostes, Maisters, Presidentes, Rectours, Principalles,.. Scolers and Studentes.. within the said Universities. **1569** *Reg. Privy Council Scot.* I. 675 Maister Alexander Andirsoun principall, Maister Andro Galloway sub-principall,.. of the College of Auld Abirdene. **1582** *Reg. Privy Council Scot.* III. 490 Maister Thomas Smetoun, principall of the College of Glasgow. **1691** [see PRINCIPALITY 6]. **1706** PHILLIPS s.v., The chief person in some of the Inns of Chancery is also called Principal of the House. **1899** *Oxford Univ. Cal.* 511 The King's Hall and College of Brasenose... The foundation was for a Principal and twelve fellows. **1900** *Oxford Directory* 104 Mansfield College, founded here in October 1886 by the Congregationalists as a Faculty of Theology. Principal, Rev. A. M. Fairbairn, M.A., D.D. *Ibid.* 106 Lady Margaret Hall, founded in 1879 for the higher education of women. Lady Principal, Miss Elizabeth Wordsworth. **1908** *Camb. Univ. Calendar* 785 A student of.. Newnham College may present.. a certificate signed by the Principal of her College.

†**d.** *pl.* Principal or chief men; leading or prominent persons; nobles, notables. *Obs.*

1388 WYCLIF *Jer.* xxv. 34 Ȝelle, ȝe scheepherdis, and crye, and ȝe princypals of the floc. **1460** CAPGRAVE *Chron.* (Rolls) 160 Ther the kyng tok the principalis of London, and sette hem in prison at Wyndsore. **1576** FLEMING *Panopl. Epist.* A ij, The principalls of ech Prouince, stayed themselues vpon his determination. **1588** PARKE tr. *Mendoza's Hist. China* 20 The garments which the nobles and principals do vse, bee of silke. **1622** BACON *Hen. VII* 11 To attaint by Parliament the Heads and Principals of his Enemies.

e. A rank in the Civil Service.

1890 A. E. HOUSMAN *Let.* 9 Oct. (1971) 27 The Administrative Principal, Mr Webb, has to-day taken up the comparison of Trade Mark applications. *Ibid.* 28 The position as Principal held by Mr Webb would give him a status not justified.. by length of service. **1915** F. G. HEATH *Brit. Civil Service* xxii. 230 The salaries are as under: Twelve Analysts (Second Class), £160 by £15 annually to £350;.. one Deputy Principal, £700 by £25 to £800; and one Principal Chemist, £1200, and after five years.., £1500 per annum. **1951** T. A. CRITCHLEY *Civil Service Today* ii. 38 Under these high officials.. are the assistant secretaries, in charge of divisions, and principals, in charge of sections. **1951** *Posts in Civil Service for University Graduates* 9 The Principal's day to day work is not confined to his desk. **1967** *Times Rev. Industry* Feb. 100/2 The full time staff is small... Of these five are 'principals'—as the Civil Service calls executives.

f. A fully-qualified practitioner or partner in a professional business.

1968 *Economist* 13 Apr. 41/1 A young man can.. become a principal in general practice.. after four to five years' training.. plus a year's pre-registration service—in hospital. **1972** *Accountant* 26 Oct. 502 (Advt.), Principals with the responsibility for training newly articled clerks should ensure that the best course of action for their newly articled clerks is to enrol with the Metropolitan College. **1975** *Law* (Employment Service Agency: Careers and Occupational Information Centre) 8 The principal with whom he has served his articles or apprenticeship may offer him an opening.

2. a. A chief actor or doer; the chief person engaged in some transaction or function, esp. in relation to one employed by or acting for him (*deputy*, *agent*, etc.); the person for whom and by whose authority another acts.

1625 BACON *Ess.*, *Faction* (Arb.) 81 Those that are Seconds in Factions, doe many times.. proue Principals. *c* **1645** HOWELL *Lett.* (1650) I. 58 Their factors live in better equipage, and in a more splendid manner than in all Italy besides, than their masters and principals in London. **1654** PELL *Let. to Secr. Thurloe* 29 July in Vaughan *Protectorate O. Cromwell* (1838) I. 35 He will say, 'I shall report this your answer to my principals', that is to those that sent me... It is a form of speaking not yet in fashion in England. **1707** *Lond. Gaz.* No. 4368/2 The Deputy was dismissed with no other Reply than, That they would send an Answer to his Principals in due Time. **1732** POPE *Ess. Man* I. 57 So man, who here seems principal alone Perhaps acts second to some sphere unknown. **17..** SWIFT (J.), We were not principals, but auxiliaries in the war. **1788** JEFFERSON *Writ.* (1859) II. 496 The functions of the vice-consul would become dormant during the presence of his principal. **1848** WHARTON *Law Lex.* s.v., He who being competent and *sui juris* to do any act for his own benefit or on his own account, employs another person to do it, is called the principal, constituent, or employer, and he who is thus employed is called the agent, attorney, proxy, or delegate. **1962** H. O. BEECHENO *Introd. Business Stud.* xiii. 117 Whereas an agent is not normally allowed to relend his principal's money at interest.. a bank is allowed to do this. **1976** *Times* 22 Apr. (Baltic Exchange Suppl.) p. i/9 The Baltic is unusual in being open both to middle men and principals.

b. A person directly responsible for a crime, either as the actual perpetrator (***principal in the first degree***), or as present, aiding and abetting, at the commission of it (***principal in the second degree***). Opp. to ACCESSARY. (Cf. A. 7 a.)

1594 NASHE *Unfort. Trav.* 40 To prison was I sent as principal, and my master as accessarie. **1596** SPENSER *State Irel.* Wks. (Globe) 620/1 By the Common Lawe, the accessoryes cannot be proceeded agaynst, till the principall receave his tryall. **1769** BLACKSTONE *Comm.* IV. iii. 34 A man may be principal in an offence in two degrees. **1771** *Junius Lett.* xlix. (1820) 257 In murder you are both principals. **1849** MACAULAY *Hist. Eng.* v. (1871) I. 312 In cases of felony, a distinction.. is made between the principal and the accessory after the fact.

c. A person for whom another is surety; one who is primarily liable for a debt.

1576 *Reg. Privy Council Scot.* II. 545 We Alexander Arbuthnot merchand, and Thomas Bassinden imprentair.. bindis and oblissis us, conjunctlie and severalie as principallis; David Guthrie [etc.] as souirteis conjunctlie and severalie. **1652** Z. BOYD in *Zion's Flowers* (1855) App. 24/2 The foirsaids persones principallis and catiounaris. **1789** W. BROWN *Cases Chancery* II. 581 The defendant.. insisted upon the benefit of the said plaintiff's bond, and that he was to be deemed a principal and not a surety. **1802** LD. ELDON in *Vesey's Rep.* VI. 734 But the surety is a guarantee; and it is his business to see, whether the principal pays, and not that of the creditor. **1848** WHARTON *Law Lex.* s.v. *Guaranty*, A surety or guarantor who has paid the debt of his principal, is entitled to a reimbursement therefor... *Story on Contracts*, chap. v.

d. Each of the actual or intending combatants in a duel, as distinguished from their *seconds*.

1709 STEELE *Tatler* No. 39 ¶24 The Principals put on their Pumps. **1824** SCOTT *St. Ronan's* xxix, Your principal, I presume, is Sir Bingo Binks?.. I have not forgotten that there is an unfortunate affair between us. **1837** DICKENS *Pickw.* ii, 'We may place our men, then, I think', observed the officer, with as much indifference as if the principals were chess-men, and the seconds players. **1848** W. H. KELLY tr. *L. Blanc's Hist. Ten Y.* II. 232 The principals were placed at forty paces from each other, and were to fire as they advanced.

e. Each of the solo or leading performers at a concert, as distinguished from the members of the band or chorus.

1881 W. H. STONE in Grove *Dict. Mus.* III. 32/1 Principals, in modern musical language, are the solo singers or players in a concert.

f. A leading performer in a drama or entertainment.

1936 N. STREATFIELD *Ballet Shoes* xiv. 212 The production was on a very large scale... The principals became unduly important. **1961** *Times* 20 June 16 The three principals are admirable: as Danila, Mr. Yuri Soloviev gives a tremendous performance; he has a prodigious technique in leaps and turns. **1971** *Morning Star* 28 June 4 Steve Hodson and Gillian Blake, the two principals in Yorkshire TV's new children's series. **1976** *National Observer* (U.S.) 8 May 20/3 To add to my discomfort, I found the voices of the principals, Michael Cristofer and Tyne Daly, distinctly unpleasant.

II. 3. a. The chief, main, or most important thing, part, point, or element. ? *Obs.*

In early quots. perh. the adj.

1396–7 in *Eng. Hist. Rev.* (1907) XXII. 298 Fals beleue, þe whiche is þe principal of þe deuelis craft. *c* **1400** tr. *Secreta Secret., Gov. Lordsh.* 85 Þys ys þe þrydde medicyne, his properte ys to efforce þe pryue, and namly þe pryncypales. **1523** LD. BERNERS *Froiss.* I. ccccxxvi. 748 They shulde take downe the leaues of the gates of the foure princypals of the cytie. **1596** SPENSER *F.Q.* v. x. 2 That Vertue.. Which.. to preserve inviolated right Oft spilles the principall to save the part. **1611** W. SCLATER *Key* (1629) 35, I meane not to prosecute every particular at large, but to cull out the principals. **1726** AYLIFFE *Parergon* 21 A Quality is said to be an Accessory unto a Fact or Crime, which is the Principal. **1845** STODDART *Gram.* in *Encycl. Metrop.* (1847) I. 16/1 The words which are necessary for communicating the thought.. may well be called principals, and those which only help to make out the thought more fully and distinctly may be called accessories.

†**b.** ***in principal***: principally, chiefly. *Obs.*

1390 GOWER *Conf.* III. 85 As of thre pointz in principal. Wherof the ferste in special Is Theorique. **1470–85** MALORY *Arthur* VI. xi. 198 That wylle I refuse in pryncypal for drede of god. **1815** SOUTHEY *Lett.* (1856) II. 410 Thanks to my friends, and to you in principal.

†**c.** A primary or fundamental point of a subject, upon which the rest depend; a PRINCIPLE (in most or all cases app. identified with that word, or perhaps an erroneous spelling of it). *Obs.*

1545 JOYE *Exp. Dan.* Argt. 5 b, Let euery diligent reder knowe hymselfe miche to haue profited, if he but the cheif principalls vnderstand, although it be but meanly. **1578** *Cat.* in *Maitl. Cl. Misc.* (1840) I. 11 The principallis of astronomie. **1663** *Flagellum or O. Cromwell* (ed. 2) 4 His Father.. sent him to School to learn the Elements of Language and principals of Religion. **1784** J. BARRY in *Lect. Paint.* iv. (1848) 158 A centre and a great uniting principal which associates all parts of the composition. **1816** ACCUM *Chem. Tests* (1818) 51 The test combines with some principal of the body.

†**4.** The head, top. *Obs. rare*$^{-1}$.

a **1533** LD. BERNERS *Gold. Bk. M. Aurel.* xlviii. (1535) 93 In the principall of the sayd table was pictured a Bulle.

†**5. a.** The original document, drawing, painting, etc., from which a copy is made; an original. *Obs.* (Cf. A. 8.)

1560 DAUS tr. *Sleidane's Comm.* 78 He shewed him the copie of the confederacie, promysing hym also the principall. **1646** CRASHAW *Delights Muses, Upon Dk. York's Birth* 48 Thou art of all This well-wrought copy the fair principal. **1660** PEPYS *Diary* 19 May, Another pretty piece of painting I saw, on which there was a great wager laid by young Pinkney and me whether it was a principal or a copy.

†**b.** Origin, source. Cf. PRINCIPLE *sb.* 2. *Obs.*

1555 W. WATREMAN *Fardle Facions* I. i. 27 To Jupiter also thei Sacrificed, and did honour as to ye principall of life. **1616** R. C. *Times' Whistle* I. 18 For heresie, Scisme, Puritanisme, Brownisme, papistrie,.. Proceed from thee, thou art the principall.

†**6.** The best beast or other chattel of any kind bequeathed, or passing by custom. *Obs.* exc. *Hist.*

[**1367** (Trinity term) *Coram Rege Roll* 41 Edw. III. ro. 21 Consuetudo hundredi de Stretford in com. Oxon., talis est quod heredes terrarum et tenementorum.. post mortem antecessorum suorum habebunt.. principalia, videlicet de quocumque genere catallorum, utensilium et necessariorum domorum et culturarum melius catallum illius generis, videlicet optimum plaustrum optima caruca et optimum ciphum, et sic de aliis instrumentis [etc.].] **1420** *E.E. Wills* (1882) 47, I bequeth my body to be beryed yn the chapele.. and my beste best in the name off principale. **1424** *Ibid.* 57 After my principal is taken, I wul my wyf haf my best ambeler. **1511** in *10th Rep. Hist. MSS. Comm.* App. v. 325 Forasmuch as taking of such principales is not by commene lawe, butt only by custume and usage. **1512** in *Southwell Visit.* (Camden) 115 Item I bequeth my best horse for my principall. **1534** *Ibid.* 138, I gyffe and bequethe unto the vicar for my principall accordynge to the acte of parliament. **1670** BLOUNT *Law Dict.*, *Principal*,.. an Heir-lome. **1895** POLLOCK & MAITLAND *Eng. Law* II. II. vi. §4. 361 There are many traces of local customs which under the name of 'principals' or 'heirlooms', will give him [the heir-at-law] various chattels, not merely his ancestor's sword and hauberk, but the best chattel of every different kind, the best horse (if the church does not take it) and the best ox, the best chair and the best table, the best pan and the best pot.

7. *Building.* A principal rafter (see A. 10); any one of the rafters upon which rest the purlins which support the common rafters. Also applied to a main iron girder.

1448–9 in Willis & Clark *Cambridge* (1886) II. 10 The principalles shalbe..x inch thik with a purlyn in the Middes from one principall to a nother. **1579** *Ibid.* I. 310 Braces to the principals eche of them xij foote longe. **1624** A. WOTTON *Runne fr. Rome* 4 To trie how every tenant and mortuis is fitted each to other, what principals are too weake, which peeces are too long. **1778** *Phil. Surv. S. Irel.* 146 The remainder they lay parallel to the principals. **1860** [see A. 10]. **1898** *Westm. Gaz.* 25 Mar. 7/2 Four massive iron principals (or girders) of a building in course of erection.. fell yesterday afternoon.

†**8.** An upright pillar or stem having branches to bear tapers; formerly used on a 'hearse'. *Obs.*

a **1548** HALL *Chron. Hen. VIII* 1 b, A curious herse made of .ix. principalles, full of lightes. **1594** in *Coll. Top. & Gen.* (1837) IV. 286 This..Bishope of Norwiche was buried with a hearse of foure pryncypales or vprightes. **1849** ROCK *Ch. of Fathers* vii. II. 496 These uprights [of a hearse of lights], technically called 'principals'.

9. The original sum of money dealt with in any transaction, as distinguished from any later accretions; the sum lent or invested upon which interest is paid; the capital sum as distinguished from the interest; also, capital as distinguished from income. (Cf. A. 6).

c **1390** EARL OF MARCH *Let.* in *Rec. Priory Coldingham* (Surtees) 65 We wylle garre rayse till us alle the fermes and the profittes of Coldynghame, quylle we be assethit als wele for owr scathes and of our costages as of owr principale. **1502** *Ord. Crysten Men* (W. de W. 1506) IV. xxi. T viij b, And the other it receyue ouer the pryncypall for to kepe hym, & to recompense hym the domage. **1571** *Act 13 Eliz.* c. 8 §4 So muche as shal be reserved by way of Usurie above the Principall for any Money so to be lent. **1572** T. WILSON *Disc. Vsurye* 85. **1693** DRYDEN *Persius* vi. 159 Put out thy Principal..: Live of the Use. **1728** T. SHERIDAN *Persius* vi. (1739) 93 But you have broke in upon the Principal. That I did for my own Use. **1827** HUTTON *Course Math.* I. 129 The sum of the principal and its interest added together, is called the Amount. **1856** *Settlement* in *Law Rep.* (1908) 1 Ch. 523 To hold as well the capital or principal of the said trust funds as the dividends, interest and annual income thereof upon the usual trusts for the children of the marriage. **1868** M. E. G. DUFF *Pol. Surv.* 14 It will facilitate the reduction of the principal of the National Debt.

fig. **1818** BYRON *Juan* I. ccxiii. I have spent my life, both interest and principal. **1874** T. HARDY *Far fr. Madding Cr.* xli, 'You'll never see Fanny Robin no more—use nor principal—ma'am'. 'Why?' 'Because she's dead in the Union'.

10. *Falconry.* Each of the two principal feathers in each wing (the two outermost primaries).

1575 TURBERV. *Falconrie* 120 Then cutte off some part of hir two principalles in each wing. **1579** E. K. in *Spenser's Sheph. Cal.* Ep. Ded., So finally flyeth this our new Poete, as a bird, whose principals be scarce growen out. **1677** N. COX *Gentl. Recreat.* (ed. 2) 186.

11. *Mus.* †**a.** The subject of a fugue or other contrapuntal piece, as distinguished from the answer or 'reply'. *Obs.*

1597 MORLEY *Introd. Mus.* 105 The first [sort of double descant] is, when the principall (that is the thing as it is firste made) and the replie..are sung changing the partes. **1898** STAINER & BARRETT *Dict. Mus. Terms, Principal* (Old Eng.), the subject of a fugue, the answer being termed the Reply.

b. An organ-stop of the same quality as the Open Diapason, but an octave higher in pitch. †***small principal*** (obs.), a similar stop two octaves higher than the open diapason; now called *fifteenth*. Also, with qualification, applied to other stops an octave higher than the ordinary pitch, as ***dulciana principal*** (also called DULCET).

In German, *Prinzipal* is applied to the Open Diapason, and (with qualifications) to all stops of the same quality, of any pitch higher or lower.

1613 *Organ Specif. Worcester Cathedral*, The particulars of the great organ, 2 principals of mettal, 1 twelfth of mettal. *Ibid.*, In the chaire organ, 1 principal of mettal, 1 flute of wood, 1 smal principal or fiftenth of mettal. **1776** HAWKINS *Hist. Mus.* IV. i. §10. 46 The simple stops are the..Principal ..and some others. **1789** *Organ Specif. Greenwich Hosp.* in Grove *Dict. Mus.* II. 598/1 Swell Organ. Open Diapason. Stopped Diapason. Dulciana. Principal. Dulciana Principal. **1881** BROADHOUSE *Mus. Acoustics* 219 The principal is a stop of four feet in length.

†**c.** A kind of trumpet used in the orchestra in the time of Handel: see quots. *Obs.*

1881 W. H. STONE in Grove *Dict. Mus.* III. 32/1 *Principal* or *Prinzipale*, a term employed in many of Handel's scores for the third trumpet part.... It is obvious that whereas the tromba..represented the old small-bored instrument now obsolete,..the Principal..more nearly resembled the modern large-bored military trumpet. **1898** STAINER & BARRETT *Dict. Mus. Terms, Principal*, the name given by Handel to the third trumpet in the Dettingen 'Te Deum'.

†**C.** *adv.* Principally, chiefly; in the chief place.

c **1400** *Destr. Troy* 2895 And prinsipall of Parys the pepull dessiret, Of þat comly to Ken. **1456** in *Coventry Leet Bk.* (E.E.T.S.) 288 Prince Edwarde, my gostly chylde, whom I love principall. **1480** *Newcastle Merch. Vent.* (Surtees) I. 5 Maires, shereffs, and aldermen..shall go princypall in the sayd solemp procession.

principality (prɪnsɪˈpælɪtɪ). Forms: α. 4–5 **principalte**, (4 **pry-**, 5 **-tee**). β. 4–6 **principalite**, etc. (with *y* for *i*; also 5 **-ete**), 5–7 **-allitie**, 6–7 **-alitie**, (6 **-ye**), 6– **principality**. [ME. *principalite*, *principalte*, a. OF. *principalite* (*c* 1170 in Godef.) dominion, power (in mod.F. *principalité* headship of a college); also *principaltee* (1362 in Godef. *Compl.* and in AF.), in mod.F. *principauté* territory of a prince; both ad. late L. *principālitāt-em* the first place, superiority, in med.L. also the authority or territory of a prince, f. *principāl-is* PRINCIPAL *a.*: see -ITY.]

1. The quality, condition, or fact of being principal; chief place or rank; pre-eminence. Now *rare*.

α. **1387–8** T. USK *Test. Love* II. iii. (Skeat) l. 12 For right as man halte the principalte of al thing vnder his beinge, in the masculyne gender. *c* **1400** *Lanfranc's Cirurg.* 85 Þo lymes þat han principalte in mannes body.

β. *c* **1380** WYCLIF *Wks.* (1880) 327 As wille haþ principalite to-fore witt of mannes soule. **1483** CAXTON *Gold. Leg.* 202/2 He was sayd chief by reson of the pryncipalyte in prelacyon. **1576** BAKER *Jewell of Health* 160 b, For the recovering of memory, defnesse, and the crampe, this obtaineth principalitie. **1631** GOUGE *God's Arrows* III. §5. 191 The word..signifieth to obtaine principality, or to prevaile. *a* **1677** MANTON *Christ's Eternal Exist.* vi. Wks. 1870 I. 468 Christ hath the primacy of order and the principality of influence. **1884** RUSKIN *St. Mark's Rest* x. §196 The heavenly look on the face of St. Stephen is not set off with raised light, or opposed shade, or principality of place.

†**b.** That which is principal; the chief point or part. *Obs.*

1567 MAPLET *Gr. Forest* 29 b, But now let vs heare in eche Plant his principalitie. *a* **1619** FOTHERBY *Atheom.* I. xi. §5 (1622) 121 The Atheist, giuing the principalitie of his loue and seruice, onely to himselfe.

2. The position, dignity, or dominion of a prince or chief ruler; sovereignty; supreme authority.

α. **13..** *E.E. Allit. P.* B. 1672 Now is alle þy pryncipalte past at ones. **1387** TREVISA *Higden* (Rolls) IV. 225 He brouȝte al þe worlde into oon principalte and lordschippe.

β. *a* **1400–50** *Alexander* 2311 In a wrath þe wale kyng swyth Him of his principalete priued. ? *a* **1500** *Chester Pl.* xii. 2 Now by my soverayntie I sweare and principalitie that I beare. **1560** BIBLE (Genev.) *Tit.* iii. 1 Pvt them in remembrance that they be subiect to the Principalities [1881 *R.V.* rulers] & powers. **1589** COOPER *Admon.* 157 At the beginning.., all men were alike, there was no principalitie. **1643** PRYNNE *Sov. Power Parl.* I. (ed. 2) 92 If a Royall Principality be thus instituted, as it is in the proper pleasure and power of the people to ordaine. **1692** WASHINGTON tr. *Milton's Def. Pop.* ii. M.'s Wks. 1851 VIII. 65 Josephus.. calls the Commonwealth of the Hebrews a Theocracy, because the principality was in God only. **1737** WHISTON *Josephus, Antiq.* XIII. viii. §2 The first year of the principality of Hyrcanus. **1878–83** VILLARI *Life & Times Machiavelli* (1892) II. II. iv. 180 He then goes on to treat of the civil principality.

b. With possessive, as a title. *nonce-use.*

1828 SCOTT *F.M. Perth* xvi, May it please your honour —I mean your principality.

c. Princely action or behaviour. *nonce-use.*

1819 BYRON *Let. to Murray* Wks. (1846) 572/1 It was a very noble piece of principality.

3. The sovereignty, rule, or government of the prince of a small or dependent state.

1459 *Rolls of Parlt.* V. 363/1 Offices, perteynyng to the said Principaltee and Duchie [of Cornwall]. **1485** *Ibid.* VI. 350/1 Auditour of the Principalite of Northwales. **1584** POWEL *Lloyd's Cambria* C j, The beginning of the Principalitie..of Wales. *a* **1727** NEWTON *Chronol. Amended* i. (1728) 119 Caranus and Perdiccas..erected small principalities in Macedonia. **1853** J. H. NEWMAN *Hist. Sk.* (1873) II. I. iv. 176 China was for many centuries the seat of a number of petty principalities. **1897** *Daily News* 25 Mar. 5/4 The proposed Principality of Crete under Prince George.

4. A region or state ruled by a prince. ***the Principality***, a familiar designation of Wales.

a **1400–50** *Alexander* 1737 Þe prouynce & principalte [*v.r.* principalite] of Persye la graunt. **1592** WYRLEY *Armorie, Chandos* 60 He safely went his way The principalitie through I him conuay. **1617** MORYSON *Itin.* I. 275 Vpon the confines of Italy, and the seuerall principalities thereof. **1705** ADDISON *Italy* 8 On the Promontory..was formerly the Temple of Hercules Monœcus, which still gives the Name to this small Principality [Monaco]. **1838** *Murray's Handbk. N. Germ.* 331 Paderborn..formerly capital of an ecclesiastical principality, and seat of a University. **1889** GRETTON *Memory's Harkb.* 189 Of your fashionable sea-bathing resorts, the Principality boasts a pair—Tenby and Aberystwith. **1905** *Whitaker's Alm.* 617 Samos... A principality of the Ottoman Empire, more or less independent.

5. A spiritual being (good or evil) of a high order; *spec.* in *pl.*, in mediæval angelology, one of the nine orders of angels (see ORDER *sb.* 5), which has been variously reckoned as the seventh, fifth, or fourth. (Representing L. *principātūs*, Gr. ἀρχαί. In the Dionysian hierarchy, ἀρχαί were the seventh order.)

This use is founded mainly on passages in the Pauline epistles, in which ἀρχή 'rule, ruler', has been taken to refer to a spiritual power. (In the Bible of 1611, *principality* renders ἀρχή seven times; in five of these the Vulgate has *principātus*, in two (Eph. vi. 12, Tit. iii. 1) *principes* 'princes'. The Revised version has in Eph. i. 21, *rule*; in Tit. iii. 1, *rulers*: cf. 1560 in sense 2.)

[**1560** BIBLE (Genev.) *Eph.* vi. 12 For we wrestle not against flesh and blood, but against principalities [1557 Rulers], against powers, and against the worldlie gouernours. —— *Col.* i. 16 By him were all things created, which are in heauen, and which are in earth..whether they be Thrones, or Dominions, or Principalities, or Powers [1534 TINDALE to 1557 *Geneva*, maieste or lordshippe, ether rule or power].] **1621** BURTON *Anat. Mel.* I. ii. I. ii. (1651) 45 Plato..made nine kindes of [spirits], first God, secondly Ideæ, 3 Intelligences, 4 Arch-Angels, 5 Angels, 6 Devils, 7 Heroes, 8 Principalities, 9 Princes. **1667** MILTON *P.L.* VI. 447 In th' assembly next upstood Nisroc, of Principalities the prime. **1756** A. BUTLER *Lives Saints* 8 May II. 317 The fathers from the sacred oracles distinguish nine Orders of these holy spirits, namely the Seraphims, Cherubims and Thrones; Dominations, Principalities and Powers; Virtues, Arch-angels, and Angels. **1839** CHARLOTTE ELLIOTT *Hymn, 'Christian, seek not yet repose'* ii, Principalities and Powers, Mustering their unseen array, Wait for thine unguarded hours.

6. The office of principal of a college, university, etc.; principalship. Now *rare.* (In quot. 1641 applied to the lordship or presidency of a colony.)

[**1423** *Act 2 Hen. VI*, c. 8 §1 Qils ne preignent sur eux la principalte dascun Sale ou Hostell.] **1641** in E. Hazard *Hist. Coll.* (1792) I. 474 Sir Ferdinando Gorges Knight Lord of the Province of Maine..in the second yeare of my Principallity in Newe England. **1660** WOOD *Life* Dec. (O.H.S.) I. 363 First, the principality of Jesus; then, the presidentship of Trinity College. **1691** —— *Ath. Oxon.* I. 148 In 1546 he was made Principal of St. Maries Hall,..in 1550 he resign'd his Principality. **1712** HEARNE *Collect.* (O.H.S.) III. 460 No body to have two Principalities at the same time. **1855** G. HILL (*title*) The Right of Appointment to the Principality of St. Edmund's Hall. *a* **1882** SIR R. CHRISTISON *Life* (1885) I. 428 The principality of a small University like that of St. Andrews.

principally (ˈprɪnsɪpəlɪ), *adv.* [f. PRINCIPAL *a.* + -LY².]

1. In the chief place; as the chief thing concerned; chiefly, mainly, above all.

1340 *Ayenb.* 26 Þo byeþ fole ypocrites, þet..doþ manie penonces,..principalliche, uor þe los [= fame] of þe wordle. **1398** TREVISA *Barth. De P.R.* III. xxi. (1495) d vij/2 His wytte [*sc.* of gropyng]..is pryncypally in þe palme of þe hondes and in soles of þe fete. *c* **1440** *Gesta Rom.* li. 229 (Add. MS.) Pryncipally and before all thyng he oweth to take a way toward his owne countre. **1580** HOLLYBAND *Treas. Fr. Tong, Principalement*, chiefly, especially, principally. **1624** DK. BUCKHM. in Ellis *Orig. Lett.* Ser. I. III. 180 For manie waightie considerations, but principally this. **1677** DRYDEN *Apol. Heroic Poetry & Ess.* (Ker) I. 179 They wholly mistake the nature of criticism, who think its business is principally to find fault. *a* **1745** SWIFT (J.), What I principally insist on, is due execution. **1872** RUSKIN *Eagle's N.* iii. §41 My steady habit of always looking for the subject principally, and for the art only as the means of expressing it.

†**b.** In the way of main division; primarily. *Obs.*

1340 *Ayenb.* 50 Þeruore him to-delþ þe ilke zenne in tuo deles principalliche. **1340** HAMPOLE *Pr. Consc.* 433 Alle mans lyfe casten may be, Principaly, in þis partes thre.. Bygynnyng, midward, and endyng.

†**c.** In the first place; in the first instance; originally, primarily, fundamentally; at first. *Obs.*

c **1380** WYCLIF *Sel. Wks.* II. 91 His lore is not his, for it is not principali his, but it is Goddis þat sent him. *c* **1425** *Cursor M.* 880 (Trin.) Of þis gult here Is she to wite þat is my fere..For principaly she bed hit me. *a* **1552** LELAND *Itin.* I. 8 Ruines of a very large Hermitage and principally well buildid but a late discoverid and suppressid.

†**2.** In a special or marked degree; above or beyond the rest, above all; especially. *Obs.*

1377 LANGL. *P. Pl.* B. XIV. 194 Of pompe and of pruyde þe parchemyn decorreth, And principaliche of alle peple but þei be pore of herte. *c* **1400** *Lanfranc's Cirurg.* 184 If þou wolt worche more stronglich.., and principaly if he be a riche man. *c* **1489** CAXTON *Sonnes of Aymon* iv. 121 Whan she sawe theym so blacke and soo hidous, and pryncypally Reynawde. **1560** tr. *Fisher's Godlye Treat. Prayer* D vj b, There be three sortes of fruites principallye growyng vnto man by prayer. **1647** SALTMARSH *Sparkles Glory* (1847) 89 To administer Peace and Judgment to the world..and more principally to his people in the flesh.

3. For the most part; in most cases; in the main; mostly.

1832 DE LA BECHE *Geol. Man.* (ed. 2) 331 Camerated shells..have been principally discovered in these rocks of central Italy. **1845** MᶜCULLOCH *Taxation* II. xii. (1852) 388 Those who subsist wholly or principally on incomes derived from the state or from taxes. **1868** LOCKYER *Elem. Astron.* vii. (1870) 268 The astronomer, to make observations on his sphere of observation merely, makes use principally either of a sextant or an altazimuth.

ˈ**principalness.** *rare.* [f. PRINCIPAL *a.* + -NESS.] The quality of being principal.

1530 PALSGR. 258/2 Principalnesse, *principalité*. **1668** WILKINS *Real Char.* 35 Degrees of Being or Causality, whether superior and before all others, or inferior, and after some others. Principalness. **1856** RUSKIN *Mod. Paint.* III. IV. xiv. §15 Principalness of delight in human beauty.

principalship (ˈprɪnsɪpəlʃɪp). [f. PRINCIPAL *sb.* + -SHIP.] The office of principal, the headship (of a college, etc.).

1593 NASHE *Christ's T.* (1613) 161 A great office is not so gainful, as the principalship of a Colledge of Curtizans. **1707** HEARNE *Collect.* 12 July (O.H.S.) II. 25 Dr. Hudson's chances of the Principalship are small. **1865** *Pall Mall G.* No. 208. 6/1 The principalship of the Theological College.

principate (ˈprɪnsɪpət), *sb.* Also 4–6 with *y* for *i*; β. 4–7 **-at**. [ad. L. *principāt-us* the first place, pre-eminence, esp. in the army or state, the post of commander-in-chief, rule, sovereignty; in eccl. L. the hosts of angels, good or bad, f. *princeps, princip-*: see PRINCE *sb.* and -ATE[1]. With the obs. form *principat*, cf. F. *principat* (13th c. in Godef. *Compl.*).]

1. The office or dignity of, or as of, a prince or ruler; supreme position or power; supremacy, primacy, headship, pre-eminence: = PRINCIPALITY 1, 2. Now *rare*.

a **1340** HAMPOLE *Psalter* xlvi. 3 He made folke suget til vs ..þis principate has nane bot haly men. **1382** WYCLIF *Eph.* i. 21 Aboue ech principat [*gloss* or power of princes], and potestate, and vertu and lordschiping. **1387** TREVISA *Higden* (Rolls) II. 317 Oon schulde be i-bore of þe Hebrewes þat schulde bere adoun þe principat of Egypt, and arere þe kynde of Israel. *Ibid.* VIII. 291 Kyng Edward ȝaf his sone Edward þe principate of Wales and þe erldom of Chestre. **1398** —— *Barth. De P.R.* v. ii. (Tollem. MS.), Amonge all þe uttir membris of þe body..þe heed haþ þe beste principate [orig. *obtinens principatum*]. **1483** CAXTON *Gold. Leg.* 233/2 The cyte the whiche helde the pryncipate of the other citees in Italye. **1555** EDEN *Decades* 286 They proudely denye that the Romane churche obteyneth the principate and preeminent autoritie of all other. **1606** WARNER *Alb. Eng.* XVI. ci. (1612) 399 And Rees thus slaine the Principate of South-Wales so was done. *a* **1641** BP. MOUNTAGU *Acts & Mon.* iv. (1642) 255 Thus ended..the Dukedome, or Principate of the Maccabees. *a* **1677** BARROW *Pope's Suprem.* i. (1687) 59 That under two metaphors the principate of the whole Church was promised. **1904** W. M. RAMSAY in *Expositor* Apr. 246 As yet Ephesus had no principate in the Church except what it derived from its own character and conduct.

b. *Rom. Hist.* The rule of the PRINCEPS; the imperial power of Augustus and his successors, while some of the republican forms were still retained; the period of rule of a princeps.

(The L. *Principatus* is applied by Pliny to the reign of Tiberius and of Nero; and is also used by Tacitus and Suetonius.) Quot. 1862 shows the earlier opinion that the title stood for *princeps senatus*: see Note to PRINCEPS.

1862 MERIVALE *Rom. Emp.* (1865) VI. liv. 466 In the emperor's principate or first place in the senate they fully acquiesced. **1875** —— *Gen. Hist. Rome* lviii. (1877) 464 The principate of Claudius had been, on the whole, a period of general prosperity. **1893** BURY *Hist. Rom. Emp.* ii. 15 The Empire as constituted by Augustus is often called the Principate, as opposed to the absolute monarchy into which it developed at a later stage... §3 According to constitutional theory, the state was still governed under the Principate by the senate and people. **1900** T. HODGKIN in *Pilot* 7 July 9/1 The 'Principate' as it is now usual to style the supreme power held by Augustus and Tiberius.

†**2.** = PRINCIPALITY 5. *Obs.*

[**1382** WYCLIF *Rom.* viii. 38 Nether angels, nether pryncipatis, nether virtutes, nether potestatis,..may departe vs fro the charite of God.] **1483** CAXTON *Gold. Leg.* 255 b/2 The Angels were glad, tharchangels enioyed, The Thrones songen, The domynacyons maden melodye, The pryncypates armonysed, The potestates harped, Cherubyn and Seraphyn songen louynges and preysynges. **1566** *Pasquine in a Traunce* 73 Euen as a man woulde saye Angels, Arch-angels, Thrones, Dominations, Principates. **1635** HEYWOOD *Hierarch.* IV. 194 In the third order Principates are plac't; Next them, Arch-Angels.

†**3.** A person having the chief position or pre-eminence; a chief, a prince. *Obs.*

1413 *Pilgr. Sowle* (Caxton 1483) v. iii. 93 Seynt Powle claymed by the deth that he suffred the Aureole of martirs, ..he must also as one chyef and pryncipate were also the aureole of prechours. **1596** FITZ-GEFFRAY *Sir F. Drake* (1881) 28 Fettring with golden chaines their principates, And leading captive Spaines chief potentates. **1651** BIGGS *New Disp.* §31 His ambition to be Principate in Physick.

4. A state, territory, or community ruled by a prince or petty king: = PRINCIPALITY 4.

1494 FABYAN *Chron.* v. xci. 67 This Hengiste and all the other Saxons whiche ruled the .vii. pryncipates of Brytayne ..are called of moste wryters Reguli. **1529** RASTELL *Pastyme, Hist. Brit.* (1811) 112 [They] rulyd ioyntly the princypat of West Saxons. *c* **1570** SIR H. GILBERT *Q. Eliz. Achad.* (E.E.T.S.) 3 All monarchies and best knowen Common weales or principates that both haue bene and are. **1652–62** HEYLIN *Cosmogr.* II. (1682) 9 There is reckoned one Principate, 10 Earldoms, 12 Peerdoms or Pairries. **1884** J. REIN *Japan* i. 7 The Riukiu..constituted until lately a separate principate or Han.

†**'principate**, *v. Obs. rare.* Erroneous variant of PRINCIPIATE *v.*

c **1650** *Don Bellianis* 47 Is it possible..that Don Bellianis should with such glory principate his haughty deeds of Chivalry? *a* **1677** HALE *Prim. Orig. Man.* IV. vi. 344 The Things or Effects principated or effected by this intelligent active Principle.

†**principatie**. *Obs. rare.* [f. L. *principāt-us* PRINCIPATE *sb.* + -Y; perh. error for *principacy*: see -ACY 3.] = PRINCIPALITY, PRINCIPATE.

1677 GALE *Crt. Gentiles* II. IV. 187 Arche, a Prince, Principatie or Governement... Rom. 8. 38. ἀρχαὶ is taken for Principaties.

†**principe**. *Obs.* [a. F. *principe* (14th c. in Hatz.-Darm.), or ad. L. *principi-um* a beginning.] = PRINCIPLE *sb.* 7, 3.

1649 JER. TAYLOR *Apol. Liturgy* §99 Such as must be one in the *principe*, and diffused in the execution. **1669** GALE *Crt. Gentiles* I. I. i. 2 God..being the first principe, and last end of al things. *Ibid.* 4 The effective, productive principe of al that wisdome, and truth.

‖**principessa** (printʃi'pɛssa). [It., f. med.L. *principissa* (see PRINCESS *sb.*)] An Italian princess. Also *attrib.*

1823 LADY BLESSINGTON *Jrnl.* 27 July in E. Clay *Lady Blessington at Naples* (1979) 38 The Principessa Partanno is ..no longer in her *première jeunesse*. **1861** C. M. YONGE *Young Step-Mother* xxiii. 333 He should go and marry the Principessa Bianca, a foreigner and Papist. **1945** E. WAUGH *Brideshead Revisited* I. ii. 50 The Principessa Fogliere gave a ball and Lord Malton was not asked. **1963** *Times Lit. Suppl.* 11 Jan. 21/3 The increasingly angular principessa who adores him. **1967** P. E. H. DURSTON *Mortissimo* (1968) iii. 27 The most elegant little *principessa* in the Villa Borghese. **1973** 'D. JORDAN' *Nile Green* xxxiii. 159 The princess..smiled, a weary principessa smile. **1979** N. SLATER *Falcon* i. 22 The pretty principessas would be storming the Embassy gates.

‖**principia**, L. pl. of PRINCIPIUM.

†**prin'cipial**, *a. Obs. rare.* [f. L. *principi-um* a beginning + -AL[1]: cf. L. *principiāl-is* existing from the beginning, original.] Standing at the beginning; initial.

1625 BACON *Ess., Prophecies* (Arb.) 537 The Princes.. which had the Principiall Letters, of that Word Hempe (which were Henry, Edward, Mary, Philip, Elizabeth). **1626** —— *Sylva* §251 There are Letters, that an Eccho will hardly expresse; as S, for one; Especially being Principiall in a Word.

principiant (prɪn'sɪpɪənt), *a.* and *sb.* [a. obs. F. *principiant*, pr. pple. (also used as sb.) of *principier* (1464 in Godef.), ad. late L. *principiāre*: see PRINCIPIATE *v.* and -ANT.]

†**A.** *adj.* Constituting the beginning or source of something; originating; primary. *Obs.*

a **1615** DONNE *Ess.* (1651) 109 It consists not of the chief and principiant parts. **1660** JER. TAYLOR *Duct. Dubit.* (L.), There are some principiant and mother sins pregnant with mischief of a progressive nature. **1675** R. BURTHOGGE *Causa Dei* 244 A Paternal is a Generative or Principiant Monad, and so is this, for he begetteth or Principleth the Number next in Nature, and that is Two.

B. *sb.* †**1.** A beginner, a novice. *Obs.* [Cf. It. *principiante.*]

1629 SHIRLEY *Grateful S.* III. iv, Do you think that I have not wit to distinguish a principiant in vice from a graduate?

2. *Math.* (See quot.)

1887 SYLVESTER in *Amer. Jrnl. Math.* IX. 20 Instead of the cumbrous terms Projective Reciprocants or Differential Invariants, it is better to use the single word Principiants to denominate that crowning class or order of Reciprocants which remain to a factor *près*, unaltered for any homographic substitutions impressed on the variables.

†**prin'cipiate**, *a.* and *sb. Obs. rare.* [ad. late L. *principiātus*, pa. pple. of *principiāre*: see next.]

a. *adj.* Properly, Originated, initiated; but in quot. 1661 used as = Constituting the beginning, origin, or source; original. **b.** *sb.* See quot. 1694.

1661 GLANVILL *Van. Dogm.* iv. 27 Our eyes, that see other things, see not themselves: And those principiate foundations of knowledge are themselvs unknown. **1694** R. BURTHOGGE *Reason* 101 Of Substances some are Principles, some Principiates... By Principiates (give me leave to make an English word of one not very good Latin) I mean substances that are caused or composed of Principles. Principles make, Principiates are made to be.

†**prin'cipiate**, *v. Obs.* [f. late L. *principiāre* to begin (f. *principi-um* a beginning) + -ATE[3].] *trans.* To cause to begin; to originate, initiate.

1613 SHERLEY *Trav. Persia* 4 Some parts might have bene found fit for the Indian Nauigation, then principiated in Holland, and muttered of in England. **1697** J. SERGEANT *Solid Philos.* 218 The Soul, by reason of her Potential State here, cannot principiate any Bodily Action.

principiation (prɪnsɪpɪ'eɪʃən). *rare.* [ad. med.L. *principiātio* (*a* 1250 Albertus Magnus *De Prædic.* 4. 1), n. of action f. *principiāre*: see prec.]

†**1.** Reduction to 'principles' or elements; decomposition or analysis of a substance. *Obs.*

a **1626** BACON *Phys. Rem.* Wks. 1879 I. 244/1 The third is, the separating of any metal into its original or materia prima, or element,..which work we will call principiation.

2. *Logic.* The process of deriving a general principle, as by induction.

1895 in *Funk's Stand. Dict.*

†**prin'cipiative**, *a. Obs. rare.* [f. late L. *principiāt-*, ppl. stem of *principiāre* (see PRINCIPIATE *v.*) + -IVE.] Having the quality of 'principiating'; originative, initiative.

1651 BIGGES *New Disp.* §160 Its grand principiative fundamina. **1662** STANLEY *Hist. Philos., Chaldaic* (1701) 18/2 They..assert a Principiative Son from the Solar Fountain, and Archangelical, and the Fountain of Sense. **1662** J. CHANDLER *Van Helmont's Oriat.* 40 To know by a Syllogisme, cannot be an intellectual essentiall, as neither a principiative thing, or from a former cause.

‖**principium** (prɪn'sɪpɪəm). Pl. prin'cipia. [L. *principium* beginning, origin, source, first place; in pl. front (of an army), staff, general's quarters, also foundations, elements; f. *princeps, princip-em* first in time or order: see PRINCE.]

1. a. Beginning, commencement; origin, source; first principle, element; fundamental truth, etc.: = PRINCIPLE *sb.* in various senses.

1600 W. WATSON *Decacordon* (1602) 138 The doctrine of the Catholike Church, consists of three speciall *principia* or causes. **1628** T. SPENCER *Logick* 43 The matter is the *principium* of individuation, saith Thomas. [See INDIVIDUATION 1.] *Ibid.* 281 The principium of a demonstration is an immediate proposition, *viz.* that hath none before it. *a* **1635** NAUNTON *Fragm. Reg.* (Arb.) 34, I have noted the causes or *principia* of the Warres following. *a* **1679** T. GOODWIN *Christ Mediator* II. vi, God is the *principium* of subsistence to all. **1693** tr. *Blancard's Phys. Dict.* (ed. 2), *Elementa*, or *Principia*, are the Simplest Bodies that can be... There are Five Elements, Spirit, Salt, Sulphur, Water and Earth. **1796** Z. MACAULAY in *Life & Lett.* vi. (1900) 173 Useful productions, containing the principia of religious knowledge. *a* **1871** GROTE *Eth. Fragm.* v. (1876) 130 Not able to imbibe even the *principia* of ethical reasoning.

b. *pl. Principia*: The common abbreviation of the title of a famous work of Sir Isaac Newton, setting forth the principles of natural philosophy or physics.

[**1687** NEWTON (*title*) Philosophiæ Naturalis Principia Mathematica.] **1727** CHAMBERS *Cycl.* s.v. *Projectile*, Sir Isaac Newton, shews, in his *principia*, that [etc.]. **1878** HARE *Walks in Lond.* II. ii. 76 The 'Principia', which occupies the same position to philosophy as the Bible does to religion.

c. ***principium individuationis***: the principle through which an entity is differentiated from matter, or being from non-being. (Cf. INDIVIDUATION 1 *note*.)

1694 LOCKE *Essay Hum. Und.* (ed. 2) II. xxvii. 179 'Tis easie to discover, what is so much enquired after, the *principium Individuationis*, and that 'tis plain is Existence it self, which determines any sort of Being to a particular time and place incommunicable to two Beings of the same kind. **1739** HUME *Treat. Hum. Nature* I. IV. 349 In order to justify this system, there are four things requisite. *First*, To explain the *principium individuationis*. **1883** F. H. BRADLEY *Princ. Logic* 265 It was shown above..that space and time-relations are no *principium individuationis*; for they fall within the *what*, and do not make the *this*. **1947** *Horizon* Feb. 150 But above this layer of all-embracing 'identification' Sorge reappears as *principium individuationis*, isolating a person and stimulating his intellect into the frightful awareness of his nakedness and his fate. **1965** *Listener* 2 Sept. 344/1 Something..must divide us from other people, there must be some kind of *principium individuationis*.

2. In the mediæval University, **a.** A public lecture or disputation by which a Bachelor in any faculty, who had received the Chancellor's licence, entered upon his functions, and became an actual Master or Doctor, with certain ceremonies. **b.** Also applied at Paris and elsewhere, in the Theological Faculty, to the disputation by which a student became a Bachelor of Divinity, and to the discourse upon some theological problem which the B.D. at a later stage, as a Sententiarius, was required to deliver before beginning his course of lectures on each of the four books of the *Sententiæ* of Peter the Lombard.

In sense a, also called *Inception*; the day on which this took place is still called at Cambridge and in some American universities 'the Commencement' (at Oxford 'the Act').

1895 RASHDALL *Univers. Europe Middle Ages* I. 150, 229, 465, 466.

3. *Rom. Antiq.* (*pl.*) The general's quarters in a camp.

1581 SAVILE *Tacitus, Hist.* III. xiii. (1591) 121 They only of the conspiracie might assemble themselues in the Principia. **1600** HOLLAND *Livy* VII. 257 In the verie *Principia*, yea and within the quarter of the L. Generall his pavilion, were heard confused speeches.

principle ('prɪnsɪp(ə)l), *sb.* Also 4–6 with *y* for *i*; 6 pryncypull. [ad. F. *principe* (Oresme *c* 1380), or f. L. *principium* (see above); formed on the analogy of *manciple, participle*, L. *mancipium, participium*, there being app. in this case no OF. form in *-ple*.] In various senses often emphasized by prefixing *first*.

I. Origin, source; source of action.

†**1.** Beginning, rise, commencement; fountainhead; original or initial state. (Also in *pl.*)

c **1430** LYDG. *Min. Poems* (Percy Soc.) 209 Knyghthood in Grece and Troye the Cité Took hys principlys, and next in Rome toun. **1432–50** tr. *Higden* (Rolls) I. 105 The begynnenges of that water callede Tiberiades, and of the water off Iordan, whiche haue their originalle principle at the foote of the mownte callede Libanus. **1553** EDEN *Treat. Newe Ind.* (Arb.) 9 Reason vsing sense, taketh his principles and fyrst sedes of thinges sensyble. **1596** SPENSER *F.Q.* v. xi. 2 Doubting sad end of principle unsound. **1674** EVELYN *Navig. & Commerce* §20. 46 From how small a principle she had spread. *Ibid.* §21. 47 Richlieu..by..Improving their Ports and Magazines, has..given Principle to no inconsiderable Navy.

†**2.** That from which something takes its rise, originates, or is derived; a source; the root (of a word). *Obs.* (exc. as in 3).

1382 WYCLIF *Job* xxviii. 1 Siluer hath the principlis [1388 bigynnyngis; Vulg. *principia*] of his veynes. **1628** COKE *On Litt.* 294 b, *En Attaint. Attincta*, is a Writ that lyeth where a false Verdict in Court of Record vpon an Issue ioyned by the parties is giuen... And is deriued of the principle *Tinctus*, or *Attinctus*, for that if the petty Iury be attainted of a false Oath, they are stained with periury. **1649** JER. TAYLOR *Gt. Exemp.* II. Disc. vi. 14 Jesus.. is the principle, and he is the promoter, he begins our faith in revelations, and perfects it in commandments. **1697** DRYDEN *Virg. Georg.* II. 17 With Osiers thus the Banks of Brooks abound, Sprung from the watry Genius of the Ground: From the same Principles grey Willows come.

3. In generalized sense: A fundamental source from which something proceeds; a primary element, force, or law which produces or determines particular results; the ultimate basis upon which the existence of something depends; cause, in the widest sense.

1413 *Pilgr. Sowle* (Caxton 1483) IV. xxviii. 74 Nothyng cometh of nouȝt, that is to seye, withoute a begynner, but a cause and pryncyple ther must nedes be. **1526** *Pilgr. Perf.* (W. de W. 1531) 12 Certeynly grace is in man ye chefe principle of meryte. *a* **1620** J. DYKE *Worthy Commun.* To Rdr., Man in his first estate had in himselfe a principle of life. **1701** GREW *Cosm. Sacra* II. i. 35 For the performance of this Work, a Vital or Directive Principle seemeth.. to be assistant to the Corporeal. **1704** SWIFT *Mech. Operat. Spirit* ii. ¶ 1 Those Idolaters adore two Principles; the Principle of Good, and that of Evil. **1780** BENTHAM *Princ. Legisl.* i. §2 *note*, The word principle.. is applied to any thing which is conceived to serve as a foundation or beginning to any series of operations. **1849** NOAD *Electricity* (ed. 3) 134 Electricity .. for a time, reigned as the vital principle, by which 'the decrees of the understanding, and the dictates of the will were conveyed from the organs of the brain to the obedient member of the body'. **1871** BLACKIE *Four Phases* i. 20 Thales said that the first principle of all things was water.

4. An original or native tendency or faculty; a natural or innate disposition; a fundamental quality which constitutes the source of action.

c **1386** CHAUCER *Sqr.'s T.* 479 Of verray wommanly benignytee That nature in youre principles hath yset. **1642** ROGERS *Naaman* 136 A man.. who hath no inward principle of skill to enable him, in comparison of a skilfull workman. **1669** STURMY *Mariner's Mag., Penalties & Forfeit.* n ij, Out of a Principle of good will I have to you. **1711** BUDGELL *Spect.* No. 116 ¶ 1 Every Man has such an active Principle in him, that he will find out something to employ himself upon. **1732** POPE *Ess. Man* II. 53 Two Principles in human nature reign; Self-love, to urge, and Reason, to restrain. **1796** MORSE *Amer. Geog.* I. 201 They, from a principle of instinct, affix themselves to her teats. **1823** SCORESBY *Jrnl. Whale Fish.* 75 Several of them followed the ship, and seemed to be attracted by a principle of curiosity. **1875** JOWETT *Plato* (ed. 2) IV. 229 The comparison of sensations with one another implies a principle which is above sensation.

II. Fundamental truth, law, or motive force.

5. a. A fundamental truth or proposition, on which many others depend; a primary truth comprehending, or forming the basis of, various subordinate truths; a general statement or tenet forming the (or a) ground of, or held to be essential to, a system of thought or belief; a fundamental assumption forming the basis of a chain of reasoning.

† ***craving of the principle*** (quot. 1587): begging of the question, *petitio principii*.

c **1380** WYCLIF *Wks.* (1880) 290 The þridde manere of errour þat fallip in mannes iugement is falceheed of here pryncipe þat þei grounden hem on. **1387** TREVISA *Higden* (Rolls) III. 251 Plato afterward made þat art [of logic] more, and fonde þerynne meny principles and rules. **1538** STARKEY *England* I. i. 16 Thys law ys the ground and end of the other, to the wych hyt must euer be referryd, non other wyse then the conclusyonys of artys mathematical are euer referryd to theyr pryncypullys. **1587** GOLDING *De Mornay* ix. (1617) 132 Is not this a setting downe of that thing for a ground, which.. resteth to be prooued, and (to speake after his owne maner) a crauing of the principle? **1664** POWER *Exp. Philos.* Pref. cj, Hence wil unavoidable follow some other Principles of the ever-to-be-admired DesCartes. **1732** BERKELEY *Alciphr.* III. §1 Principles at other times are supposed to be certain fundamental Theorems in Arts and Sciences, in Religion and Politics. **1825** MCCULLOCH *Pol. Econ.* 61 (*heading*) Principles of political economy. **1875** JOWETT *Plato* (ed. 2) I. 488 First principles, even if they appear certain, should be carefully considered.

b. *Physics*, etc. A highly general or inclusive theorem or 'law', admitting of very numerous special applications, or exemplified in a multitude of cases.

Often named after the discoverer, as the ***Archimedean principle*** and ***D'Alembert's p.*** (in mechanics), ***Carnot's p.*** (in heat), ***Doppler's p.*** and ***Helmholtz's p.*** (in acoustics and optics), ***Huyghens's p.*** (in wave-motion), ***Pascal's p.*** (in hydrostatics). Cf. LAW *sb.*[1] 17c.

1710 J. CLARKE *Rohault's Nat. Phil.* (1729) I. 85 From this Principle [that of the parallelogram of forces], the Method of explaining the Forces of the Mechanick Powers.. may excellently well be deduced. **1838** DE MORGAN *Ess. Probab.* 49 Principle II. The probability of any number of independent events all happening together, is the product of their several probabilities.

c. ***first principle***: a primary proposition, considered self-evident, upon which further reasoning or belief is based; freq. in *pl.*

In some quots. influenced by sense 3.

1638 [see sense 10 a]. **1690** LOCKE *Essay Hum. Und.* I. ii. 10 Those (as they are called) first Principles. **1701** J. NORRIS *Ideal World* I. ii. 75 As much above the Possibility as the Necessity of Demonstration, in one Word, a very first Principle. **1785** REID *Intell. Powers* VI. vi, There are also first principles in morals. **1817** COLERIDGE *Biog. Lit.* I. xii. 253 Philosophy in its first principles must have a practical or moral as well as a theoretical or speculative side. *Ibid.* 260 Those original and innate prejudices.. which to all but the philosopher are the first principles of knowledge. **1871** B. JOWETT tr. *Plato's Dialogues* I. 711 And this is the reason why every man should expend his chief thought and attention on the consideration of his first principles:—are they or are they not rightly laid down? **1934** *Times Lit. Suppl.* 19 July 497/2 It is to Coleridge's search for first principles in literature that appeal is made. **1961** *Cambr. Daily News* 10 Feb. 7 Once you have absorbed the first principles in art.

6. A fundamental quality or attribute which determines the nature of something; essential characteristic or character; essence.

1662 GERBIER *Princ.* 1 The three chief Principles of Magnificent Building, viz. Solidity, Conveniency, and Ornament. **1706** PHILLIPS s.v., The Epicurean Principles, are Magnitude, Figure, and Weight. **1817** JAS. MILL *Brit. India* II. v. iii. 388 This was the principle and essence of his plan. **1862** MAURICE *Mor. & Met. Philos.* IV. v. §35. 163 [This] indeed must involve the very principle and meaning of the subject with which he is occupied.

7. a. A general law or rule adopted or professed as a guide to action; a settled ground or basis of conduct or practice; a fundamental motive or reason of action, esp. one consciously recognized and followed. (Often partly coinciding with sense 5.)

c **1532** DU WES *Introd. Fr.* in *Palsgr.* 895 To teche and instruct by the principles and reules made by divers well expertz auctours. **1590** GREENE *Never too late* (1600) 61 You keepe the prouerbe for a principle, to bed with the Bee and vp with the Lark. **1656** EVELYN *Diary* 8 July, Some Quakers ..; a new phanatic sect, of dangerous principles, who shew no respect to any man, magistrate or other. **1762–71** H. WALPOLE *Vertue's Anecd. Paint.* (1786) III. 68 He painted the great staircase, and as ill, as if he had spoiled it out of principle. **1763** JOHNSON 1 July in *Boswell*, This shews that he has good principles. **1844** DISRAELI *Coningsby* VIII. iii, Before I support Conservative principles, .. I merely wish to be informed what those principles aim to conserve. **1853** J. H. NEWMAN *Hist. Sk.* (1873) II. I. iv. 183 The barbarian lives without principle and without aim.

b. Used *absol.* for *good*, *right*, or *moral principle*: An inward or personal law of right action; personal devotion to right; rectitude, uprightness, honourable character. (Also in *pl.*)

1653 CROMWELL *Speech* 4 July in *Carlyle*, If I were to choose any servant.. I would choose a godly man that hath principles... Because I know where to *have* a man that hath principles. **1697** COLLIER *Immor. Stage* (1698) 287 The management of the Stage.. strikes at the Root of Principle, draws off the Inclinations from Virtue, and spoils good Education. **1704** J. HARRIS *Lex. Techn.* I. s.v., We say, a Person is *a Man of Principles*, when he always acts according to the Eternal Rules of Morality, Virtue and Religion. **1721** DE FOE *Moll Flanders* (Bohn) 45 Thus my pride, not my principle.. kept me honest. **1874** BANCROFT *Footpr. Time* i. 87 He had brilliant powers, but little principle. **1894** F. WATSON *Genesis a true Hist.* v. 103 The religion of the prophets.. the religion of principle rather than of law, and of morality rather than of ritual. *Mod.* A man of high principle.

c. Phr. ***on principle*** (usually in sense b): as a matter of (moral) principle; on the ground of fixed rule or obligation; from a settled (conscientious) motive. Also ***on general principles***, freq. in weakened sense: in general, for no specified reason, from a settled motive.

[Cf. quot. 1762–71 in 7.]

1824 LANDOR *Imag. Conv.* xxxii. II. 267 Principles do not much influence the unprincipled, nor mainly the principled. We talk on principle, but we act on interest. **1835** J. H. NEWMAN *Par. Serm.* (1837) I. i. 10 Outward acts, done on principle create inward habits. **1871** LOWELL *Pope* Prose Wks. 1890 IV. 26 There was a time when I could not read Pope, but disliked him on principle. **1894** *Westm. Gaz.* 3 May 5/3 He was acting as counsel for an insurance company, and they told him that they were defending on principle. **1894** SOMERVILLE & 'ROSS' *Real Charlotte* II. xxi. 90 She had no particular dislike for Francie.. but on general principles she was pleased that discomfiture had come to Miss Fitzpatrick. **1898** R. HUGHES *Lakerim Athletic Club* 246 Pretty wanted to punch his head on general principles, but decided it would be better to beat him at tennis. **1914** *New Republic* 26 Dec. 15/1 In one Spanish village he was locked up on general principles, because the King happened to be passing through town that day. **1930** J. C. RANSOM *God without Thunder* II. viii. 173 It is like the flattery of the man who flatters us on general principles. **1938** 'G. GRAHAM' *Swiss Sonata* 87 Vicky will be held responsible for it just on general principles, and that will be that.

d. Phr. ***in principle***: theoretically; in general but not necessarily in individual cases.

1820 G. CANNING in C'tess of Airlie *Lady Palmerston* (1922) I. vi. 102 So objectionable does it appear to them in principle as well as in practice. **1859** PALMERSTON in P. Guedalla *Palmerston Papers* (1928) 117 The First Method would evidently be the best in Principle. **1874** GEO. ELIOT *Let.* 15 July (1956) VI. 67, I am thoroughly opposed in principle (quite apart from any personal reference to myself) to the system of *contemporary* biography. **1932** *Ann. Reg. 1931* 295 These [proposals] were rejected by Washington, but the latter made a counter-proposal: that France accept the scheme 'in principle', and leave to a conference of technical experts those practical modifications which she desired. **1951** J. CORNISH *Provincials* 102 Still, we were loggers; we had won in principle. **1963** RICHARDSON & TOYNBEE *Thanatos* 87 When we say that we know a thing it involves us in saying that it is, at least in principle, verifiable by the senses.

8. a. A general fact or law of nature by virtue of which a machine or instrument operates; a natural law which furnishes the basis of the construction, or is exemplified in the working, of an artificial contrivance; hence, the general mode of construction or operation of a machine, etc. (Cf. 5 b.)

1802 PALEY *Nat. Theol.* iii. §2 (1819) 24 Constructed upon strict optical principles; the self-same principles upon which we ourselves construct optical instruments. **1829** *Nat. Philos.* I. ii. 8 (Usef. Knowl. Soc.) The principle of the Archimedian Screw is occasionally adopted in the wheel-form. **1838** W. BELL *Dict. Law Scot.* s.v. *Patents*, The subject of a patent must be something vendible. A mere principle or method would not be sufficient; but if the patent were actually for a process or thing produced, it would not be a valid objection that the specification described it as a method. *a* **1842** in Meeson & Welsby *Reports* VIII. 806 *note*, In this specification the plaintiff did not claim a patent for a mere principle, but for a mode of applying a well-known principle, viz. the heating of air, by means of a mechanical apparatus, to fires and furnaces. **1858** LARDNER *Handbk. Nat. Phil.* 255 This thermometer is sometimes varied in its form and arrangement, but the principle remains the same.

b. A general fact which forms the basis of any artificial device (e.g. of a system of measurement).

1821 J. Q. ADAMS in C. Davies *Metr. Syst.* III. (1871) 121 The real original connection between the cubic foot and the English bushel was not formed by avoirdupois weights and water, but by the easterling pound of twelve and fifteen ounces and Gascoign wine. It was the principle of the quadrantal and congius of the Romans, applied to the foot and the nummulary pound of the Greeks. *Ibid.* 179 Thus the gallon of wheat and the gallon of wine, though of different dimensions, balance each other as weights... This observation applies, however only to the original principle of the English system.

†**9.** A motive force or appliance, as in a machine.

1631 MILTON *Univ. Carrier* II. 10 And like an Engin mov'd with wheel and waight, His principles being ceast, he ended strait. **1830** *Chron.* in *Ann. Reg.* 84/1 Much attention was excited in the neighbourhood of Portland-place, by the appearance of a steam-carriage, which made its way through a crowded passage, without any perceptible impulse..; one gentleman directed the moving principle, and another appeared to sit unconcerned behind.

III. Rudiment, element.

†**10. a.** *pl.* The earliest or elementary parts of a subject of study; elements, rudiments. *Obs.* or merged in 5.

1534 ELYOT *Doctr. Princes* 7 These be the principles and chiefe introduction to the right.. gouernance of a publike weale. **1638** JUNIUS *Paint. Ancients* 10 The first principles.. of these Arts of imitation. **1706** PHILLIPS s.v., Principles are the first Grounds and Rules.., otherwise call'd Elements and Rudiments; as the Principles of Geometry, Algebra, Astronomy, &c.

†**b.** *concr.* A rudiment of a natural structure; a germ, embryo, bud. *Obs.*

1721 BRADLEY *Philos. Acc. Wks. Nat.* 109 All the Trunk of a Tree.. is fill'd with Principles or little Embrio's of Branches. **1732** BERKELEY *Alciphr.* III. §1 Sometimes by Principle we mean a small particular seed, the growth or gradual unfolding of which doth produce an Organized Body, animal or vegetable.

†**11. a.** A component part, ingredient, constituent, element. *Obs.* (exc. as in c).

PROXIMATE *principle*, ULTIMATE *principle*: see these words.

1615 CROOKE *Body of Man* 33 There are two materiall principles, the Crassament or substance of the seede.. and Bloud. **1644** *Bury Wills* (Camden) 187 My body I committ to the earth whereof it was framed, knowing it must returne to its first principles. **1655** FULLER *Hist. Camb.* (1840) 101 Within few years hither came a confluence of buyers, sellers, and lookers-on, which are the three principles of a fair. **1732** BERKELEY *Alciphr.* II. §1 Sometimes by Principles we mean the parts of which a whole is composed, and into which it may be resolved. Thus the Elements are said to be principles of compound bodies. And thus words, syllables, and letters are the principles of Speech.

†**b.** *Old Chem.* Chiefly in *pl.*: The five supposed simple substances or elements of which all bodies were believed to be composed; classed into three ***active principles*** (or HYPOSTATICAL *principles*), by which the sensible properties of the body were supposed to be determined, called respectively *spirit* (or *mercury*), *oil* (or *sulphur*), and *salt*; and two ***passive principles***, called *water* (or *phlegm*), and *earth* (or *caput mortuum*). *Obs.*

1650 T. VAUGHAN *Anthroposophia* 22, I speak not of Kitchin-stuffe, those three Pot-Principles Water, Oyle and Earth, or as some Colliers call them Mercury Sulphur and Salt. **1658** SIR T. BROWNE *Hydriot.* iii. 44 When the heavy Principle of Salt is fired out, and the Earth almost only remaineth [in burnt bones]. **1661–1706** Hypostatical Principles [see HYPOSTATICAL 2]. **1727–41** CHAMBERS *Cycl.* s.v. **1799** G. SMITH *Laboratory* I. 334 In this manner are extracted from roses the three principles, spirit, oil, and salt.

c. In later chemical use: One of the constituents of a substance as obtained by chemical analysis; usually restricted to a constituent which gives rise to some characteristic quality, or to which some special action or effect is due, as in ***active***, ***bitter***, ***colouring***, ***neutral principle***.

Of these, *bitter principle*, is almost the only one commonly used; for the rest *constituent* or *matter* is preferred.

1732 ARBUTHNOT *Rules of Diet* in *Aliments*, etc. (1736) 265 By which Principles they [spices] are heating, and act strongly. **1769** E. BANCROFT *Guiana* 299 It is but seldom that either Animal or Vegetable Poisons derive their deleterious properties from either of these principles. **1799** [see NARCOTIC *a.* 1]. **1813** SIR H. DAVY *Agric. Chem.* iii. (1814) 94 The narcotic principle is found abundantly in opium. *Ibid.*, The bitter principle is very extensively diffused in the vegetable kingdom. *Ibid.* 123 When any vegetable principle is acted on by a strong red heat, its elements become newly arranged. **1831** T. P. JONES *Convers. Chem.* xxviii. 282 Those distinct compounds which exist ready formed in a plant, are called its *proximate*, or *immediate principles*..sugar, starch, and gum are proximate principles, and these we obtain by proximate analysis. **1842** PARNELL *Chem. Anal.* (1845) 284 To coagulate various animal principles which may be present. **1874** GARROD & BAXTER *Mat. Med.* (1880) 98 The increase of the colouring matter and other principles of the bile in the evacuations from the bowels. **1875** H. C. WOOD *Therap.* (1879) 26 The active principle of the vegetable astringents is tannic acid,.. it is almost their sole therapeutic principle. **1879** *Chemical Society, Instr. to Abstractors* ¶ 16 Basic substances should invariably be indicated by names ending in *-ine*, as aniline.. the termination *-in* being restricted to certain neutral compounds, viz. glycerides, glucosides, bitter principles, and proteids, such as palmitin, amygdalin, albumin.

†**principle**, *v. Obs.* [f. prec. sb.]

1. *trans.* To ground (any one) in the principles or elements of a subject; to impress with principles of action; to instruct, teach, train, indoctrinate; to influence by instruction. (See also PRINCIPLED 1 a.)

1608 D. T[UVIL] *Ess. Pol. & Mor.* 124 b, Simplicitie hath principled her selfe with stronger Axiomes then heeretofore. **1651** *Fuller's Abel Rediv., Regius* (1867) I. 152 Urbanus Regius was born.. of honest parents, who principled him in the rudiments of learning. *a* **1661** FULLER *Worthies, Durham* (1662) I. 300 Pious and orthodox Professors to have Principled and Elemented the Members therein with Learning and Religion. **1690** LOCKE *Hum. Und.* I. iii. §22 Such, who are careful (as they call it) to principle Children well. **1760** STERNE *Serm.* vi. (1773) 73 He had been so principled and instructed as to observe a scrupulous nicety ..in the lesser matters of his religion.

b. To act upon or influence (one) as a principle; to dispose to some course of action.

1712 M. HENRY *Serm. Death R. Stretton* Wks. 1853 II. 392/2 O that grace might..principle you with a concern for their spiritual lives. *a* **1716** SOUTH *Serm.* (1744) XI. 305 It is not the mere interest of his own salvation, but of God's honour, that principles and moves him in the whole course of his actions.

2. To be the principle, source, or basis of; to give rise to, originate.

1650 T. VAUGHAN *Anima Magica* 2 They would ground Nature on Reasons fram'd and principl'd by their own Conceptions. **1668** OWEN *Nat. & Power Indwell. Sin* xv. 259 All neglect of private duties is principled by a weariness of God. **1675** R. BURTHOGGE *Causa Dei* 242 Not conceiving how any lower Being should be able to inspire and principle it [world].

Hence **'principling** *vbl. sb.*

1649 in *Perfect Diurnall* 26 Mar., Public Schools for the better education and principling of youth in virtue and justice. **1692** LOCKE *Educ.* §70 If the foundation of it be not laid in the Education and Principling of the Youth, all other Endeavours will be in vain.

principled ('prɪnsɪp(ə)ld), *ppl. a.* [f. prec. + -ED[1], but in later use as if f. PRINCIPLE *sb.* + -ED[2].]

1. Imbued with or established in principles; trained or instructed in certain principles of action; holding or habitually actuated by particular principles; that is so or such on principle. Often in parasynthetic combs., as ***high-, honest-, right-principled.*** **a.** In predicate, or following its noun.

1642 MILTON *Apol. Smect.* Wks. 1851 III. 277 He shall be to me so as I finde him principl'd. **1657** TITUS *Killing no Murder* 12 What are the people in Generall but Knaues, Fooles, and Cowards; principled for Ease, vice, and Slavery? **1700** T. BROWN *Amusem. Ser. & Com.* 126 Poets are better Principled than to hoard up Trash. **1712** BERKELEY *Passive Obedience* To Rdr., Take care they go into the world well principled. **1799** WASHINGTON *Lett.* Writ. 1893 XIV. 196, I am principled against this kind of traffic in the human species. **1886** RUSKIN *Præterita* I. 423 She was firm, and fiery, and high principled.

b. In attributive relation, preceding its noun.

1655 *Nicholas Papers* (Camden) II. 279, I think him..a very honest, right principled man in the mayne. *a* **1744** POPE (J.), He seems a settled and principled philosopher, thanking fortune for the tranquillity he has by her aversion. **1774** tr. *Helvetius' Child of Nature* II. 224 A Knave, Fanny, is a principled impostor, who, guided by self-interest,.. acts in defiance to the Law. **1846** URWICK *J. Howe* 29 Though a principled Nonconformist, he was on intimate terms with Tillotson.

2. Having good or right principles; actuated by moral considerations; devoted to rectitude; upright, honourable. (The opposite of *unprincipled*.)

1697 C. LESLIE *Snake in Grass* (ed. 2) 224 Now let any honest-Hearted People judge, whether these be found Principled Men, that can Turn, Conform, and Transform to every Change according to the Times. **1785** G. A. BELLAMY *Apology*, etc. IV. 63 He was the most principled man I ever was acquainted with. **1856** BAGEHOT *Biog. Stud.* 36 To expect..a principled statesman from such a position, would be expecting German from a Parisian or plainness from a diplomatist.

3. Founded on or involving a principle; instilled into or settled in the mind as a principle.

1784 J. BARRY in *Lect. Paint.* (1848) I. 73 A loose mechanical abridgment..of the other more entire, principled, and more perfect art. **1824** SOUTHEY *Bk. of Ch.* (1841) 526 A steady and principled resistance. **1865** BUSHNELL *Vicar. Sacr.* II. iii. 127 That the love is a principled love, grounded in immovable convictions of right.

4. Based on or guided by (technical) principles or rules; not arbitrary or *ad hoc*.

1968 P. M. POSTAL *Aspects Phonol. Theory* iii. 47 The one principled way to make such a choice independently of the grammar..is to pick one of the several representations which eliminate *all* phonetically predictable features. **1970** *Canad. Jrnl. Linguistics* XVI. I. 3 Both factions agree on what constitutes the natural domain of linguistics:..the principled explanation of sound-meaning relations in languages. **1972** *Language* XLVIII. 301 It is interesting that there is a principled basis for choosing, in certain types of circumstances, a rule with a global environment over a corresponding non-global rule plus an ordering statement. **1978** *Ibid.* LIV. 410 As there is no principled way to prevent base rules from generating intransitive prepositions in any PP position, 5c could be base-generated, given E's base rules.

princke, obs. form of PRINK.

†**'princock, -cox.** *Obs.* exc. *dial.* Forms: α. 6 pryn-, 6–7 (9) princox; also 6 -coxe, -cockes, -cocks, -kox, -kockes (7 primecocks). β. 6–7 princock, (prime-cocke, primcock), 9 (*dial.*) princy-cock. [Etymol. and original form obscure; the form *-cocks*, *-cox* appears earlier than *-cock*. See Note below.]

A pert, forward, saucy boy or youth; a conceited young fellow; a coxcomb. *humorous* or *contemptuous*.

α. **1540** PALSGR. *Acolastus* R ij b, *Aco.* Wylt thou gold .i. any pieces of golde? *Lais.* This chayne my lyttell prycke .i. I wolde fayne haue this chayne (of golde) my pretye pryncockes, or my ballocke stones. *a* **1553** ? INGELEND *Nice Wanton* (1560) A iv b, What ye pryncockes, begin ye to raue? **1568** *Hist. Jacob & Esau* v. x. in Hazl. *Dodsley* II. 260 It is your dainty darling, your prinkox, your golpol. **1592** NASHE *P. Penilesse* (ed. 2) 23 A Caualier of the first feather, a princockes that was but a Page the other day in the Court. **1592** SHAKS. *Rom. & Jul.* I. v. 88. **1602** *2nd Pt. Return fr. Parnass.* III. ii. 1197 Your proud uniuersity princox thinkes he is a man of such merit the world cannot sufficiently endow him with preferment. **1606** WARNER *Alb. Eng.* XVI. cv. (1612) 410 And dares the Prime-cocks interrupt me in my loue, quoth she? **1636** HEYWOOD *Loves Mistr.* II. i. Wks. 1874 V. 113 Who doe you thinke maintaines this princox in his *Pontificalibus*? **1821** SCOTT *Kenilw.* vii, Well-a-day—God save us from all such mis-proud princoxes! **1825** BROCKETT *N.C. Gloss.*, *Princox*, a pert or forward fellow.

β. **1562** PHAER *Æneid* IX. D d ij, Euryalus,..Fyne princock fresh of face furst vttring youth by buds vnshorne. **1570** LEVINS *Manip.* 159/1 A Princocke, *precox, lasciuus.* **1589** *Mar Martine* A iij, Siker, thous bot a pruid princock thus reking of thy swinke. **1598** FLORIO, *Pinchino*, a pillicock, a primcock, a prick, a prettie lad, a gull, a noddie. **1611** *Ibid.*, *Pinchino*, a prime-cocke, a pillicocke, a darlin, a beloued lad. **1617** MINSHEU *Ductor*, A Princocke, a ripe headed yong boy. **1674** RAY *N.C. Words* 37 *A Princock*, a pert, forward Fellow. **1719** *Gloss. Angl. Nova*, *Princock*, a forward Youth, a brisk Spark. **1828** *Craven Gloss.* (ed. 2), *Princy-cock*, a term used here in addressing a young person. **1869** *Lonsdale Gloss.*, *Princy-cock*, a dandified, conceited young fellow.

b. *attrib.* or as *adj.*; esp. in ***princock-boy***.

1595 *Locrine* II. iv, Naught reck I of thy threats, thou princox boy. **1598** FLORIO, *Herba da buoi*..vsed for a princock boy [**1611** a prime-cock-boy], a fresh man, a milke sop, a nouice, or fresh water souldier. **1611** CORYAT *Crudities* 414 Proud princocke scholars that are puffed vp with the opinion of their learning. **1621** BP. MOUNTAGU *Diatribæ* 367 Such vpstart princox Youths as you. **1634** CANNE *Necess. Separ.* (1849) 25 They shall be called asses, geese, fools, dolts, princock boys, beardless boys,..new come out of the shell, &c. *a* **1668** DAVENANT *Play-house to let* v. i, Proud Princock-Cæsar hardly seems to mind him.

[*Note.* One suggestion is that the first element is *prime*, but though *primecock* is used by Florio, this looks rather like an etymological manipulation; other early writers held it for an alteration of L. *præcox* 'early, precocious'. Apparently the word was originally of slang or low use, perh. somewhat obscene or equivocal; cf. quot. 1540, and the synonyms in Florio.]

princod, a pincushion: see PREEN *sb.* 4.

†**'princum.** *Obs. colloq.* [? Mock-latin f. PRINK *v.*[2]] Nicety of dress, behaviour, etc.

1690 D'URFEY *Collin's Walk thro. Lond.* I. 41 An aukward fear..That my behaviour may not yoke With the nice Princums of that Folk.

princum-prancum: see PRINKUM-PRANKUM.

†**prine.** *Obs. rare.* [ad. late L. *prīn-us* (Vulg.), a. Gr. πρῖν-ος holm oak, ilex. Cf. OF. *prin* (Godef.).] Also ***prine tree***: The holm or evergreen oak; ilex.

a **1400** *Pistill of Susan* 342 (Vern. MS.) Þat roþly cherl.. seide bifore þe prophet: þei pleied bi a prine [*MS. Phil.* pryne; *MSS. Ing., Cott.* pyne; Vulg. (Dan. xiii. 58) *sub prino*]. **1609** BIBLE (Douay) *Susanna* i. 58 Tel me, under what tree thou tookest them speaking one to an other. Who said: Under a prine tree [**1611** a holme tree].

prine, obs. form of PREEN, pin, brooch.

pring (prɪŋ), *sb.* [Echoic.] The sound made by a bell.

c **1921** D. H. LAWRENCE *Phoenix II* (1968) 183 She heard a loud prrring-prrring of a bicycle-bell.

pring (prɪŋ), *v.* [Echoic.] *intr.* To make a sound like a bell.

1927 *Scots Observer* 30 Apr. 10/4 The bell of no. 13 was pringing lustily.

†**'pringle**, *sb. Obs. dial.* Also **prindle**. [Origin unascertained: perh. from the surname *Pringle*.] A silver coin: see quots.

1683 G. MERITON *Yorks. Dial.* 183 Here's good Tobacco, Wife, it cost a Pringle [*v.r.* prindle]. [**1697** (ed. 3) *Gloss.*, *Pringle*, a little silver Scotch Coin about the bigness of a penny, with two xx. on it.]

pringle, *v.* [Alteration of PRINKLE *v.* (app. influenced by *tingle*).] *intr.* To have a prickly and tingling sensation.

1889 DOYLE *Micah Clarke* xxi, You must be still pringling from the first [hand-grip]. *Ibid.* xxxii, My eyes ached and my lips pringled with the smack of the powder. **1894** —— *Round Red Lamp* xii. 230 There was something in this sudden, uncontrollable shriek of horror which chilled his blood and pringled in his skin.

pringling ('prɪŋglɪŋ), *ppl. a.* [f. PRINGLE *v.* + -ING[2].] That pringles, or causes a prickly sensation.

1896 A. CONAN DOYLE *Uncle Bernac* i. 7, I..pressed my lips upon the wet and pringling gravel. **1923** C. MORLEY *Where Blue Begins* i. 5 In the golden light and pringling air he felt excitable and high-strung.

'pringling, *vbl. sb.* [f. the vb.] A prickly and tingling sensation.

1956 P. WENTWORTH *Silent Pool* xli. 214 Young Watson felt a pringling at the back of his neck.

†**prink**, *v.*[1] *Obs.* exc. *dial.* Pa. t. in 4 (? 5) **preynte, preynkte, prengte, prent, prentede, prynkid**; 9 *dial.* **prenk'd, prinked.** [app. connected with OE. *princ* (or *prince*) a blink, a wink, a twinkle of the eye (Defensor *Lib. Scint.* ix. (1889) 43).]

1. *intr.* To wink, to give a wink.

1377 LANGL. *P. Pl.* B. XIII. 112 Þann conscience curteisliche a contenaunce he made, And preynte [*v.rr.* prentede, prynkid]; 1393 C. XVI. 121 preynte, prengte] vpon Pacience to preie me to be stille. *Ibid.* XVIII. 21 'Is Piers in þis place?' quod I, and he preynte [*v.rr.* twynclid, prent; 1393 C. XXI. 19 preynkte] on me. *c* **1380** *Sir Ferumb.* 1238, & þan sche preynte with hure eȝe oppon hur chamberere þar sche stod. ? *a* **1800** in W. Walker *Bards Bon-Accord* (1887) 634 The dear, the lovely blinkin' o't [an eye]..plagues me wi' the prinkin' o't. **1873** *St. Paul's Mag.* Mar. 259 Professedly prudish..they..nod, osculate, prink, quiz.

2. *trans.* ***to prink the eye***: to wink.

c **1380** *Sir Ferumb.* 4507 With þat Richard preynte ys eȝe, Oppon ys feleschip þat was him neȝe. *a* **1900** in *Eng. Dial. Dict.* s.v., He never prinked his eyes for the night. 'Evvent prenk'd an eye far tha neight.

¶ The following are perh. incorrect uses, which may have arisen from confusing this with PRINK *v.*[2] 2 b.

1776 ANSTEY *Election Ball* I. 241 How she simpers and prinks while the glass is before her. **1841** C. H. HARTSHORNE *Salopia Antiq.* Gloss. 536 *Prink*, to look at, gaze upon, as a girl does at herself in a glass.

prink (prɪŋk), *v.*[2] Also 6 princke. [Known from *c* 1570; evidently related to PRANK *v.*[4], in similar senses (occurring 1546): see Note below.]

†**1.** *trans.* with *up*: (?) To set up, exalt; to display ostentatiously, show off. *Obs.*

1573 TWYNE *Æneid* XI. Hh iv b, Fortune whom she did disgrace Oft times agayne doth rayse and prinkes him up in prouder place. **1581** J. BELL *Haddon's Answ. Osor.* 407 He so chaufeth and moyleth in sturryng the coales in princkyng upp the glory of this whotthouse.

†**b.** *intr.* (?) To make ostentatious display; also ***to prink it***. *Obs.*

1573 *New Custom* I. i. in Hazl. *Dodsley* III. 6 See how these new-fangled prattling elves Prink up so pertly of late in every place. **1576** GASCOIGNE *Philomene* xxi, To get more grace by crummes of cost And princke it out hir parte. **1600** J. LANE *Tom Tel-troth* 254 Some princk and pranck it.

2. *trans.* To make spruce or smart; to deck or dress *up* with many petty adornments; esp. *refl.* to deck oneself out, dress oneself *up*. *colloq.*

1576 GASCOIGNE *Steele Gl.* Ep. Ded., Now I stand prinking me in the glasse. **1579–80** NORTH *Plutarch* (1595) 1010 When he [Demetrius] was to make any preparation for warre, he had not then..his helmet perfumed, nor came not out of the Ladies closets, picked and princt to go to battell. **1600** BRETON *Pasquill's Mad-Cappe* (1626) B j, Who hath not seene a logger headed Asse..Prinking himselfe before a Looking-glasse? **1705** tr. *Bosman's Guinea* 142 The Women prink up themselves in a particular manner. **1775** in F. Moore *Songs & Ball. Amer. Rev.* (1856) 100 All prinked up in full bag-wig. **1784** COWPER *Task* VI. 303 To gather king-cups in the yellow mead, And prink their hair with daisies. **1808** SOUTHEY *Chron. Cid* 246 Since midnight they had done nothing but prink and prank themselves. **1828** *Craven Gloss.* (ed. 2), *Prenk, Prink, Pronk*, to decorate, to dress in a showy, affected manner. **1871** B. TAYLOR *Faust* (1875) II. I. ii. 8 Adorned and prinked with wondrous art, Yet so grotesque that all men start.

transf. **1876** BLACKIE *Songs Relig. & Life* 95 Nor, where flowers prink the mead with diverse hue. **1877** —— *Wise Men* 63 My Ctesibias, who not with gold And silver only prinks his princely hall. **1899** CROCKETT *Kit Kennedy* i, The flowers which have slept,..prink themselves again, and give forth a good smell.

b. *intr.* (for *refl.*) To dress or deck oneself up, make oneself look smart. *colloq.*

1709 D'URFEY *Pills* (1719) I. 177, I hate a Fop that at his Glass Stands prinking half the Day. **1753** MISS COLLIER *Art Torment.* I. ii. 59 She was every day longer prinking in the glass than you was. **1858** O. W. HOLMES *Aut. Breakf.-t.* ii. (1865) 15 Ironing out crumpled paragraphs, starching limp ones, and crimping and plaiting a little; it is as natural as prinking at the looking-glass. **1898** *Daily News* 8 Aug. 5/4

The young man, after an appropriate time spent in his room, prinking, appears in all the glory of starch and perfumery.

3. *trans.* Of a bird: To trim (the feathers); to preen. Also **b.** *intr.*

1575 GASCOIGNE *Weeds, Farew. Mischief* vi, But marke his plumes, The whiche to princke he dayes and nights consumes. **1820** SCOTT *Monast.* xxiv, Meantime he went on with his dalliance with his feathered favourite,..'Ay, prune thy feathers, and prink thyself gay—much thou wilt make of it now'. **1878** B. TAYLOR *Deukalion* I. i. 21 Yonder bird Prinks with deliberate bill his ruffled plumes.

b. 1877 LANIER *Mocking Bird* 11 This bird..perched, prinked, and to his art again.

4. *intr.* To be pert or forward. *dial.*

1828 *Craven Gloss.* (ed. 2), *Prenk, Prink, Pronk,* to be forward or pert. *Ibid., Prenkin,* pert, forward. **1863** MRS. TOOGOOD *Yorks. Dial.*, She's a prenkin, forward, lass.

Hence **prinked** (prıŋkt) *ppl. a.*, **'prinking** *vbl. sb.*; also **prink** *sb.*, the act of prinking or making spruce; **'prinker**, one who dresses up with minute care. (All *colloq.*)

1579–80 NORTH *Plutarch* (1676) 579 To apparel himself so sumptuously, and to be more fine and prinked then became a private man. **1699** FARQUHAR *Constant Couple* v. ii, I knew, sir, what your powdering, your prinking, Your dancing, and your frisking, would come to. *a* **1700** B. E. *Dict. Cant. Crew, Prinkt up,* set up on the Cupboards-head in their Best Cloaths, or in State. Stiff-starched. **1783** tr. *Rollin's Belles Lettres* (ed. 10) I. II. 49 He compares this florid prinked eloquence to young people curled out and powdered. **1864** WEBSTER, *Prinker,* one who prinks; one who dresses with much care. **1883** HOWELLS *Register* ii, That just gives me time to do the necessary prinking. **1895** *Westm. Gaz.* 6 Aug. 3/1 Most..of the present Bench..have had a full-dress 'prink' in front of the large looking-glass..before venturing to make their first appearance in court.

[*Note.* The late appearance of PRANK *v.*[4] and PRINK *v.*[2] makes it difficult to refer them to an ablaut stem *prink, prank, prunk,* or to suppose *prink* to represent an earlier *prenk,* an umlaut deriv. of *prank.* It seems more likely that *prink* was formed from *prank,* with the thinner vowel sound, to express a more slight or petty action, or perhaps in the reduplicated formation *prink-prank, prink* and *prank,* as in *clink-clank, crinkle-crankle, jingle-jangle,* etc. It may have also been associated with or influenced by PRICK *v.* 20: cf. PRINKLE. There is no decisive evidence.]

prink, *v.*[3] *dial.* [app. related to PRANK *v.*[3]] ? To walk jauntily or affectedly. Also, to walk daintily or with precise movements. Hence **'prinking** *vbl. sb.*

1697 C. LESLIE *Snake in Grass* (ed. 2) 41 Thou, and thy Godfather Fox can know a Saint from a Devil, without speaking, but not without a little Mincing and Prinking. **1803** MARY CHARLTON *Wife & Mistress* II. 28 'Oh', says she, mincing and prinking, 'I find, Mrs. Maunder, that you have been so unlucky as to affront Boden'. **1880** *W. Cornwall Gloss., Prink,* to walk jauntily. **1962** M. BALDWIN *Death on Live Wire & On stepping from Sixth Storey Window* 11 Uncle Cyclops Had one eye To bulge at ankles prinking past. **1962** J. ONSLOW *Bowler-Hatted Cowboy* xiii. 124 In the morning a doe with her twin fawns had passed us, stopping to nibble at the willow bushes as she prinked down the hill.

prinkle ('prıŋk(ə)l), *sb. Sc.* [Origin obscure.] A young coal-fish, *Pollachius virens.*

1832 P. BUCHAN *Secret Songs of Silence* (MS.) 177 The laddie and the lassie, Gaed out to gather prinkle, O. **1903** G. SIM *Vertebrate Fauna of 'Dee'* 238 In the young stages, the names of 'Prinkle', 'Gerrick', 'Poodlie', are given [to the coal fish]. **1943** W. S. FORSYTH *Guff o' Waur* 54 Wupp it weel wi' curly 'oo', The prinkles to confoun'. **1972** *Which?* May 135/1 Saithe..may be called coal fish, coley, and a whole host of local names from codfish to prinkle.

prinkle ('prıŋk(ə)l), *v. Sc.* [Origin obscure; in sense 1, perh. a modification of PRICKLE *v.*; in sense 2, perh. dim. or frequent. of PRINK *v.*[1] See PRINGLE *v.*]

1. *intr.* To have a thrilling sensation, such as the feeling of 'pins and needles'; to tingle, prickle. Hence **'prinkling** *vbl. sb.*

1721 KELLY *Sc. Prov.* 396 I'll gar your Daup [*note* Backside] dirle [prinkle, smart]. **1807** HOGG *Song, 'Sing on, sing on'* i, My blude ran prinklin' through my veins, My hair begoud to steer, O. **1818** —— *Brownie of B.* I. xii. 270 Are ye an angel o' light..that ye gar my heart prinkle sae wi' a joy that it never thought again to taste? **1819** W. TENNANT *Papistry Storm'd* 175 The dulefu' dart, That sent a prinklin' to his heart Mair fierce than burr or nettle.

2. *intr.* To twinkle, scintillate, sparkle.

1724 RAMSAY *Vision* xvii, Starrie gleims..prinkled, and twinkled. **1851** MAYNE REID *Rifle Rangers* xi, His rays, prinkling over the waves, caused them to dance and sparkle with a metallic brightness. *Ibid.* xii, The humming-birds.. prinkled over the parterre like straying sunbeams.

† **'prinkum-'prankum.** *Obs.* Also princum-prancum. [In sense 1, reduplication of *prankum,* PRANCOME, related to PRANK *sb.*[1]; in sense 3 related to PRANK *a.* and *v.*[4]: cf. also Du. *pronckeprincken, pronckepinken* to glitter in a fine dress (Oudemans).]

1. A prank, freak, frolic, trick.

1596 NASHE *Saffron Walden* Wks. (Grosart) III. 191, I wil not present into the Arches, or Commissaries Court, what prinkum prankums Gentlemen (his nere neighbors) haue whispred to me of his Sister.

2. = CUSHION-DANCE.

a **1635** RANDOLPH *Muses' Looking-Gl.* v. i, No wanton jig, I hope: no dance is lawful But prinkum-prankum! *a* **1668** DAVENANT *Playhouse to Let* v. i, Call in the Fidlers..Yet let 'em play us but princum and prancum, And we'll pay at last, or els we'll thank 'um. **1698** *Dancing Master* 7 Then he lays down the Cushion before a Woman, on which she kneels and he kisses her, singing, 'Welcom, Joan Sanderson, welcom, welcom'. Then she rises, takes up the Cushion, and both dance, singing, 'Prinkum-prank'um is a fine Dance, and shall we go dance it once again.., and shall we go dance it once again?'

3. Fine attire, fine clothes and adornments: cf. PRINCUM. See also quot. 1725.

1715 tr. *C'tess D'Aunoy's Wks.* 408 Yonder she hides her self, because she was not dress'd up in her Princum Prancums. **1725** *New Cant. Dict., Mistress Princum-Prancum,* such a stiff, over-nice, precise Madam.

'prinky, *a.* [f. PRINK *v.*[2]; cf. PRANKY.] Prinked up, decked out; spruce-looking; precise.

1834 *New Monthly Mag.* XLII. 442 Nothing can be more at variance than the aristocratic-looking houses half buried in gloom..in May Fair, and those prinky green and white dwellings, where city folks enjoy themselves. **1895** *Chicago Advance* 18 Apr. 1025/3 The idea may suggest itself that prinky, medieval, despised China has been making a resistance which amounts to something.

Prins (prıns). *Chem.* The name of H. J. *Prins* (1889–1958), Dutch chemist, used *attrib.* to designate the condensation of an olefin with formaldehyde or other aliphatic aldehydes in the presence of a dilute mineral acid.

1944 *Jrnl. Chem. Soc.* 296 Under the conditions of the Prins reaction, a normal, acid-catalysed addition to the olefinic linking occurs. **1970** *Tetrahedron Lett.* I. 37 (*heading*) The isolation and synthesis of a novel tetracyclic ether from East Indian sandalwood oil. A facile intramolecular Prins reaction.

print (prınt), *sb.* Forms: 4 prient(e, pryente, preynte, 4–5 preent(e, 4–6 prente, printe, prynte, 4–7 preinte, 5 preynt, (prend), 4–6 (7– *Sc.*) prent, 5– print. [ME. (= obs. Du. *printe* (Kilian), Du., Da. *prent,* MLG., LG. *prente* print, impression), a. OF. *priente* (1317 in Godef.), *preinte* impression of a seal, etc., f. *prient, preint,* pa. pple. of *preind-re, priemb-re* to press, stamp:—L. *prem-ĕre* PRESS *v.*[1]]

A. Illustration of Forms.

a **1300** *Cursor M.* 557 (Cott.) Als prient [*Gött.* preinte, *F.* prent] of seel in wax es thrist. **13..** *Sir Beues* (A.) 1244 To schewe þe prente of me sele! *a* **1340** HAMPOLE *Psalter* iv. 7 Þe prynt we bere of þ[t] light. **1340** *Ayenb.* 81 His ryȝte pryente, þet is þe ymage of his sseppere. *c* **1380** WYCLIF *Serm.* Sel. Wks. I. 92 Sum..fordiden soone Cristis prente. **1390** GOWER *Conf.* I. 60 My lady therupon Hath such a priente of love grave. **1393** LANGL. *P. Pl.* C. XVIII. 73 A badde peny with a good preynte [*v.rr.* preente, prente]. *a* **1400–50** *Alexander* 3162 To Porrus vnder my print. *c* **1400** *Three Kings Cologne* 101 Þe same preent is made, boþe in gold and in copyr. *c* **1440** *Promp. Parv.* 412/1 Preente (*K.* prend, *S.* preynt), *effigies, impressio.* **1512** *Act 4 Hen. VIII,* c. 19 §14 Pennys..havynge the prente of the Coigne of this realme. **1555** EDEN *Decades* 219 The printe of his feete. **1583** *Reg. Privy Council Scot.* III. 583 Libellis bayth in write and prent. *a* **1660** *Contemp. Hist. Irel.* (Ir. Archæol. Soc.) I. 203 They issued a declaration in preinte. **1785** BURNS *To J. Smith* vii, To try my fate in guid black prent.

B. Signification.

I. General non-typographical senses.

* *An impression or impress.*

1. a. The impress made in a plastic material by a stamp, seal, die, or the like; a distinctive stamped or printed mark or design, as on a coin.

a **1300** [see A.]. *c* **1315** SHOREHAM *Poems* i. 1205 Caracter, þet is prente ycliped, Nys non of eliinge. **1382** WYCLIF *1 Macc.* xv. 6 Y suffre the for to make smytyng [*gloss* or printe; **1388** prynte] of thin own money in thi regyoun. *c* **1450** *Godstow Reg.* 295 He strengthed hit with the prynte of his seale. **1463–4** *Rolls of Parlt.* V. 501/2 Sealed with a double prynt of Leede at the ende therof. **1523** *Act 14 & 15 Hen. VIII,* c. 12 All suche farthinges..shall haue vppon the one side therof the printe of the port collice. **1548–9** (Mar.) *Bk. Com. Prayer, Communion* Rubric, That the breade..for the Communion bee made..without all maner of printe, and somethyng more larger and thicker than it was. **1599** DAVIES *Immort. Soul* x. ii, As the Wax retains the Print in it. **1660** F. BROOKE tr. *Le Blanc's Trav.* 69 That famous Idol made of the tooth of a Monkey... The King of Pegu..sent yearely Ambassadours thither, to take the print of it upon Amber.

† **b.** A symbolic mark, a character; a badge.

1382 WYCLIF *1 Sam.* Prol., Samarytans also the fyue bokis of Moyses wryten in as feele lettris, oonli in figuris and printis dyuersynge. **1387** TREVISA *Higden* (Rolls) III. 11 [Solomon] fond vp figures and prentis to be grave in precious stones. **1399** LANGL. *Rich. Redeles* II. 108 Þat comounes of contre..Sholde knowe be hir quentise þat þe kyng loued hem Ffor her priuy prynte passinge anoþer. **1546** LANGLEY *Pol. Verg. De Invent.* I. vi. 13 b, Afore that time [of Esdras] the Hebrues and Samarites vsed all one carecters and print of their letters.

c. See quot. (A doubtful sense.)

1840 PARKER *Gloss. Archit.* (ed. 3) 169 *Print, Prynt,* a plaister cast of an ornament, or an ornament formed of plaister from a mould. The term is used in the record of St. Stephen's chapel. [Founded upon instances of *prynts, preynts,* in accounts cited in J. T. Smith *Antiq. of Westminster* (1807) pp. 203, 217, 219–21, of uncertain meaning but prob. belonging to sense 1. Hence, with modifications, in recent Dicts.]

2. *fig.* **a.** An image or character stamped upon the mind or soul, *esp.* the Divine likeness (in allusion to Gen. i. 27); a mental impression. Now *rare.*

c **1315** SHOREHAM *Poems* i. 450 For wanne me takeþ þis sacrement, His soule prente takeþ. **1413** *Pilgr. Sowle* (Caxton) I. xiii. (1859) 10 Deformynge in hym self the prent and the figure, that god hath set in hym. **1583** BABINGTON *Commandm.* vii. (1622) 58 Which needeth no proofe besides ..that print which in his conscience euerie one carrieth about. **1642** R. CARPENTER *Experience* II. viii. 196 To lay him low, and make him supple to take the print of Humility. **1855** TENNYSON *Maud* I. i. 8 Sooner or later I too may passively take the print Of the golden age.

b. An image or likeness of anything.

1388 WYCLIF *Ezek.* xxviii. 12 Thou a preente of licnesse, ful of wisdom, perfit in fairnesse, were in delicis of paradijs of God. *c* **1470** HENRYSON *Mor. Fab.* VII. (*Lion & Mouse*) xix, It bair the prent of my persoun. **1513** MORE *Rich. III* Wks. 61/1 This is quod he, y[e] fathers owne figure, this is his own countenance, y[e] very prent of his visage.

† **c.** Form, appearance. *Sc. Obs. rare.*

c **1450** HOLLAND *Howlat* 854 The pure Howlatis appele completly was planyt,..He besocht..That thai wald pray Natur his prent to renewe. **1535** STEWART *Cron. Scot.* (Rolls) III. 415 Hir plesand prent, hir perfit portrature, Exceidit far all vther creatuir.

3. a. *gen.* Any indentation in a surface, preserving the form left by the pressure of some body, as the print of a foot in the ground; *esp.* = *finger-print* s.v. FINGER *sb.* 15; also, by extension, a mark, spot, or stain produced on any surface by another substance.

c **1400** MAUNDEV. (Roxb.) xi. 47 Ȝet may men see in þe roche þe prynte of oure Lorde hend. **1474** CAXTON *Chesse* 116 The prynte of the hors shoo and nayles abode euer in his vysage. **1546** PHAER *Bk. Childr.* (1553) Q viij, The swellyng or puffyng vp..pressed wyth the finger, there remaineth a print. **1601** HOLLAND *Pliny* II. 141 A faire medicine to cure ..the black prints remaining after strokes. **1712** ARBUTHNOT *John Bull* III. i, He would pinch the children..so hard that he left the print of his forefingers and thumb in black and blue. **1853** KANE *Grinnell Exp.* xxix. (1856) 239 Returning ..we saw the recent prints of a bear and two cubs. **1867** MURCHISON *Siluria* ii. (ed. 4) 29 Smaller ripples..together with apparent rain-prints [in stratified rocks]. **1902** *Westm. Gaz.* 25 Sept. 5/1 Informed that the Finger-print Office had stated that the finger-prints..were identical with those of a convicted person. **1924** P. MACDONALD *Rasp* vi. 88 But how to explain the finger-prints? And Deacon did not know of those prints. **1929** 'G. DAVIOT' *Man in Queue* ii. 18 Attached ..was a report from the finger-print department. There was no trace of these prints in their records. **1936** A. CHRISTIE *Cards on Table* xxii. 215 Handled it with gloves,..and..the last prints would be those of Mrs. Benson herself. **1938** N. MARSH *Artists in Crime* v. 66 If you come across any keys, try them for prints. **1952** E. GRIERSON *Reputation for Song* xxi. 170 They *will* take his prints. **1957** F. & R. LOCKRIDGE *Tangled Cord* (1959) xiii. 170 Harry here gets to thinking maybe he touched something and left prints. **1975** J. MCCLURE *Snake* viii. 113 The drinking vessels had been cleaned of any prints, and the wash basin..given a thorough rub-over. **1980** P. G. WINSLOW *Counsellor Heart* ii. 32 While the print man was working Capricorn had a few words with..the Divisional Surgeon.

† **b.** A vestige, trace, indication. *Obs.*

a **1548** HALL *Chron., Edw. IV* 223 b, That no print or shadowe should remain of the adverse faccion, in his realme. **1615** G. SANDYS *Trav.* 228 The inhabitants..yet retaine some print of the Punicke language. *a* **1668** LASSELS *Voy. Italy* (1670) II. 160 Hard by it appeare some prints of the Temple of Venus and Cupid. *a* **1715** BURNET *Own Time* (1766) I. 247 Scarce any prints of what he had been remained.

** *An instrument for impressing.*

4. a. An instrument or apparatus which produces a mark or figure by pressing; a stamp or die; a mould. Also *fig.*

c **1470** HENRY *Wallace* v. 606 The prent off luff him punȝeit at the last So asprely. **1586** in *Wills & Inv. N.C.* (Surtees) II. 139, v printes for gingbreade 12[d]. **1594** *Ibid.* 245, vj printes for printinge jens-breade, 3/4[d]. **1660** STANLEY *Hist. Philos.* IX. (1701) 419/2 Matter is the print, mother, nurse, and productrix of the third essence. **1789** O'BRIEN *Calico Printing* E viij, Some treacle and lamp-black may be mixed and diffused with a pad..over the face of the print [i.e. the 'block' used in block-printing of calicoes]. **1847–78** HALLIWELL, *Print,* a mould for coin, &c.

b. *Cutlery.* (See quot.)

1839 URE *Dict. Arts* 379 In order to make the bolster of a given size, and to give it..shape and neatness, it is introduced into a die, and a swage placed upon it; the swage has a few smart blows given it by the striker. This die and swage are, by the workman, called prints.

c. *Founding.* A support for the core of a casting.

1864 WEBSTER s.v., *Core print,* a projection on a pattern, forming a mortise in the mold made from it, to receive a portion of the core that does not appear in the casting, for the purpose of holding the core in place. **1884** *Spon's Mechanic's Own Bk.* (1893) 37 Prints are extensions of the cores, which project through the casting and into the sides of the mould, to be held by the sand or flask.

*** *A thing impressed.*

5. A pat of butter, moulded to a shape. Also *attrib.*

1768 STERNE *Sent. Journ.* (1778) II. 128 He had brought the little print of butter upon a currant leaf. **1777** in J. Hancock *His Bk.* (1898) 216 Mrs. Smith sent up..a print of Butter. **1877** *Cornh. Mag.* Feb. 175 Saucers of cream and prints of butter were to be found upon the dresser. **1909** [see CREAMERY 1 b]. **1955** J. G. DAVIS *Dict. Dairying* (ed. 2) 153 The cream..goes through either a box moulder for packing into 56 lb. boxes or a pat moulder for wrapping 1 lb. and ½ lb. prints. **1963** M. MCCARTHY *Group* ix. 194 Libby was scandalized by the amount of fresh print butter Polly mixed in..*plus* brandy and sherry. **1972** E. WIGGINTON *Foxfire Bk.* 188 When it [*sc.* a mould] is filled, push down on the handle of the mold, which acts like a piston, thus releasing the 'print' of butter.

6. A printed cotton fabric; a piece of printed cotton cloth. Also, a pattern printed on fabric. Often *attrib.*

1756 E. Holyoke in G. F. Dow *Holyoke Diaries* (1911) 16 Put Prints out to whiten. 1825 E. Weeton *Let.* 22 Apr. in *Jrnl. of Governess* (1969) II. 352 When you open the parcel ..you will find the print which I have procured for you: there are two patterns, a yard each. 1837 Marryat *Dog-fiend* xl, Shrouding herself..in her cotton print cloak. 1852 Hawthorne *Blithedale Rom.* iii. I. 31 She was dressed as simply as possible, in an American print. 1858 Lytton *What will he do* I. xiv, In a coloured print, of a pattern familiar to his observant eye in the windows of many a shop. 1883 Stevenson *Silverado Sq.* 133 He chose the print stuff for his wife's dresses. 1891 T. Hardy *Tess* xvii, Mrs. Crick ..wore a hot stuff gown in warm weather because the dairymaids wore prints. 1893 J. Ashby Sterry *Naughty Girl* vi, Their print frocks..were gone. 1899 *Prospect. Calico Printers' Assoc.*, Certain markets are closed to English prints owing to hostile tariffs. 1917 *Harrods Gen. Catal.* 1409/2 Best English Prints, for Servants' Dresses. 1957 M. B. Picken *Fashion Dict.* 264/1 *Print*, fabric stamped with design by means of paste dyes used on engraved rollers, wood blocks or screens. 1964 *McCall's Sewing* i. 7/1 Like stripes, prints also can be used to create desirable effects. *Ibid.* vii. 108/1 First check to see if the print has a regular directional pattern. 1972 *Vogue* June 94 Mandarin coat and slit dress of matching print. 1976 *Times* 25 Mar. 11/3 Made in pure silk chiffon, it was chosen from a range of evening dresses in many prints and colours. 1976 *Guardian* 2 Apr. 4/1 Detail from Nympheus: a hand blocked print on linen copied from an 11th century Chinese painted silk, now in the British Museum.

II. Typographical uses.

7. The state of being printed, printed form: chiefly in phrases. **a.** ***in print.*** (*a*) In a printed state, in printed form. Cf. also sense 15. So ***into*** (†***unto***) ***print.***

1482 J. Paston in *P. Lett.* III. 300 A Boke in preente off the Pleye off the Chess. *c* 1493 in *Christ Church Canterbury Lett.* (Camden) 59, I can nat thynke yt lykely that ther shall come ony moo of them yn prentys, as be that I her off them that selle such bokys. 1529 More *Dyaloge* III. Wks. 245/2 The worke..by theyr authorities so put vnto prent, as all the copies should come whole vnto the bysshoppes hande. 1533 *Test. Ebor.* (Surtees) VI. 38 A antiphonar in prynt. 1563 Winȝet *Four Scoir Thre Quest.* To Rdr., Wks. 1888 I. 60 To put furth our mynd in prent at hame. 1606 *Choice, Chance, etc.* (1881) 45 My Mistris was saluted by a spruse companion that lookt like a letter in print. [Cf. sense 14.] 1617 Moryson *Itin.* II. 71 A certaine dangerous seditious Pamphlet was of late put forth into print. 1712 Steele *Spect.* No. 509 ¶1 My present Correspondent, I believe, was never in Print before. 1816 Byron *Eng. Bards & Sc. Rev.* 51 'Tis pleasant, sure, to see one's name in print; A book's a book, although there's nothing in't. *a* 1839 Praed *Poems* (1864) II. 6 Rush like a hero into print.

(*b*) Of a book or edition: On sale at the publisher's, not yet sold out.

1880 (*title*) The American Catalogue... Author and Title Entries of Books in Print and for Sale... July 1, 1876.

b. ***out of print*** (of a book or edition): no longer to be bought at the publisher's, sold out.

1674 Boyle *Excell. Theol.* I. v. 194 Divers excellent little Tracts, which..are already out of print. 1895 *Prospectus of E.E.T.S.* 6 Half the Publications for 1866..are out of print, but will be gradually reprinted.

c. In other constructions.

1932 E. V. Lucas *Reading, Writing & Remembering* iii. 69, I have no recollection that the article ever reached print. *Ibid.* vi. 121, I publish it here for the first time—it has waited only forty-five years for print. 1934 H. G. Wells *Exper. Autobiogr.* I. vi. 356 This success whetted my appetite for print and I sent Harris a further article..which he packed off to the printers at once. 1950 *Science News* XV. 7 There is one fundamental reason why freelance articles so rarely see print. 1970 G. F. Newman *Sir, You Bastard* viii. 204 He knew that the fray with James would make some print. 1977 *Time* 14 Mar. 31/1 Nor is it likely that a British version of the Pentagon papers or the Watergate scandals would ever have seen the light of print.

8. *concr.* Language embodied in a printed form; printed lettering; typography; esp. with reference to size, form, or style, as ***small print, clear print.***

1623 Massinger *Dk. Milan* I. i, And if you meet An officer preaching of sobriety, Unless he read it in Geneva print Lay him by the heels. 1657 T. Atkin in Fuller *Worthies* (1662) II. 309 Forty years since he could not read the biggest Print without Spectacles, and now there is no Print so small,..but he can read it without them. 1773 Johnson *Let. to Boswell* 5 July in *Life*, I can now write without trouble, and can read large prints. 1856 Emerson *Eng. Traits, Voy. Eng.* Wks. (Bohn) II. 12 The sea-fire shines in her wake... Near the equator, you can read small print by it.

b. *fig.* (Cf. also 1623 in a.)

1623 Wither in *C. Butler's Fem. Mon.* Ad Author. 28 An Abstract of that Wisdome, Power, and Loue, Which is imprinted on the Heav'ns aboue In larger volumes, for their eies to see That in such little prints behold not thee. 1637 Suckling *Aglaura* I. i, Well, Ile away first, for the print's too big If we be seene together. 1844 Dickens *Mart. Chuz.* xxvi, All the wickedness of the world is Print to him.

9. †**a.** A printing-press (with its accessories). Hence, the work of the press, the process of printing. *Obs.* Cf. press *sb.*[1] 14.

1507 Jas. IV in *Dict. Nat. Biog.* (1887) X. 187/1 To furnis and bring home ane prent, with all stuff belangand tharto, and expert men to use the samyne for imprenting..of the bukis of our lawis. 1538 Coverdale *Prol. N.T.* Wks. (Parker Soc.) II. 36 The turning of a letter is a fault soon committed in the print. 1549 Coverdale, etc. *Erasm. Par. Eph.* Prol., Neither translated ready to the Prynte nor yet appointed certaynle to be translated. 1691 Wood *Ath. Oxon.* I. 134 Mr. Doctor Stevens..espyed certain false allegations in his Masters book, whilst it was under the print in London.

b. ***in the print,*** in the printing trade.

1973 L. Heren *Growing up Poor in London* ii. 39 For our mother, only a minimum of education was required to ensure a good safe job in the print. *Ibid.* viii. 193 For her [*sc.* his mother] a good job in the print and a house in Bromley or Beckenham meant security, respectability and keeping yourself to yourself.

10. An impression of a work printed at one time; an edition.

1535 Joye *Apol. Tindale* (Arb.) 20 When these two pryntes (there were of them bothe aboute v thousand bokis printed) were al soulde..the dewch men prynted it agen.. in a small volume lyke their firste prynt. 1623 T. James in *Ussher's Lett.* (1686) 304 To compare old Prints with the new. 1634 *Raynold's Byrth Mankynde* Pref. 1 In the other prints, there lacked matter necessary to the opening and declaration of the Figures. 1887 *Daily News* 11 July 3/2 Notwithstanding an immense 'print', the papers rapidly reached a premium of, in some cases, 300 per cent.

11. a. A printed publication; *esp.* a printed sheet, news sheet, newspaper; ***the prints*** = the press. Now chiefly *U.S.*

1570 Dee *Math. Pref.* A ij, Will they prouoke him, by worde and Print. 1651 Cleveland *King's Disguise* 44 A Psalm of mercy in a miscreant print. 1654 *Nicholas Papers* (Camden) II. 108 The English letters came not till last evning and soe late as I could not see the prints, but heare they conteyne little. 1696 H. Sampson in *Thoresby's Corr.* (ed. Hunter) I. 246 Manuscripts, if lost, can never be made good, as prints may. 1727 Swift *Imit. Horace* II. vi. 115 Inform us, will the emp'ror treat? Or, do the prints and papers lye? 1777 J. Adams in *Fam. Lett.* (1876) 234 The particulars you will have..in the public prints. 1779 Sheridan *Critic* I. ii, I believe, Mr. Puff, I have often admired your talents in the daily prints. 1871 Morley *Crit. Misc.* Ser. I. *Condorcet* (1878) 52 The freedom of the press, the multitude of the public prints, were all so many insurmountable barriers against a French Cromwell. 1892 *Nation* (N.Y.) 22 Dec. 470/3 Of course, the Government prints take in each case the opposite view. 1942 D. Powell *Time to be Born.* (1943) iv. 80 A few names, if sufficiently in the public prints, naturally did stick. 1961 R. M. Williams in D. N. Barrett *Values in America* iii. 74 The criticisms levelled against higher education in the public prints. 1973 *Daily Tel.* (Colour Suppl.) 30 Nov. 7/2 The popular prints are interested in Parliament only when something dramatic blows up, or when an MP, possibly overworked, makes an ass of himself.

b. A printed copy (of a bill in parliament). Also in general use.

1828 in Picton *L'pool Munic. Rec.* (1886) II. 329 That the intended Bill..be read.., and Prints of the Bill circulated. 1831 *Ibid.* 331 Laid before the Council a Print of the Bill. 1928 *Daily Mail* 25 July 18/5 Prints of the Memorandum and Articles of Association can be inspected at any time.

12. A picture or design printed from a block or plate; an impression from an engraved or otherwise prepared plate. Hence ***in print,*** quot. 1662.

In a general sense, including impressions from a raised surface as in wood-engravings, and from sunken lines as in copperplate and steel engravings; also from a flat surface as in lithographs; but sometimes excluding lithographs and etchings, and otherwise variously restricted.

1662 Evelyn *Chalcogr.* iii. 38 With eight more Prints [i.e. woodcuts by Dürer] of this subject. *Ibid.* iv. 45 After Raphaels death, did Julio Romano publish some of his own designes in print. *Ibid.* 48 Diogenes..a very rare print [i.e. a chiaroscuro]. *Ibid.* v. 129 Copies are in Prints much more easily detected, then in paintings. *Ibid.* 141 An Universal, and choice Collection of prints and cuts. 1703 Maundrell *Journ. Jerus.* (1732) 7 Were fastned to the Wall two or three old Prints. 1710 J. Harris *Lex. Techn.* II. s.v., Prints or Cutts, as we sometimes call them. *a* 1745 Jon. Richardson *Ess. Prints* Wks. (1792) 262 He hath etched several valuable prints. 1755–73 Johnson s.v., It is usual to say wooden prints and copper plates. 1762–71 H. Walpole *Vertue's Anecd. Paint.* (1786) II. 206 There is a print of him, painted by John Lyvyus, and engraved by Vosterman. 1774 Goldsm. *Nat. Hist.* (1776) II. 307 In such a case..there is no other substitute but a good print of the animal to give an idea of its figure. 1815 J. Smith *Panorama Sc. & Art* II. 752 This combination of the two modes of colouring prints has a good effect. 1821 Craig *Lect. Drawing* vii. 384 The earliest specimen that we have of it is in a print, by Albert Durer. 1898 Pennell *Lithography* 54 From 1817 onwards the great lithographic houses issued their prints by 'hundreds and thousands'. 1901 *Blackw. Mag.* Nov. 663/1 Garish coloured prints and execrable oleographs.

13. *Photogr.* A picture produced from a negative: see print *v.* 15. In mod. use applied to (*a*) a (usu. positive) photographic picture produced on an opaque medium for direct viewing (as opposed to a transparency); (*b*) a positive copy of a motion picture (on a transparent medium).

1853 R. Hunt *Man. Photogr.* 22 Attempts are being made, at this time, to fix the images produced by the Daguerreotype—perfect prints, it is true, but which are as light as the vapour from which they are produced. 1855 Hardwich *Man. Photogr. Chem.* 293 Some advise that on removal from the colouring Bath the print should be soaked in new Hypo for ten minutes. 1879 *Cassell's Techn. Educ.* III. 207 A good print may be obtained by a person who is unskilled in making a negative. 1893 *Photogr. Ann.* 50 Rough paper for prints in silver is now on the market, and certainly gives most pleasing results.

(*a*) 1915 [see *colour transparency* s.v. colour *sb.*[1] 18 b]. 1939 Mack & Martin *Photogr. Process* ix. 304 It is the final objective of the photographic process to produce a positive image (either a transparency or a paper print). 1958 C. L. Thomson *Colour Films* 39 Transparencies as a basis for prints have the advantage that the printer knows in advance that the colour photograph is a successful one, and will therefore produce an acceptable print. 1970 C. B. Neblette *Fund. Photogr.* xxi. 299 Ektachrome paper is designed for making color prints from transparencies on Ektachrome and Kodachrome film. 1978 *Sci. Amer.* Apr. 110 (*caption*) In this negative print made with the 48-inch Schmidt telescope on Palomar Mountain the nebulas appear black.

(*b*) 1912 F. A. Talbot *Moving Pictures* viii. 87 The majority of cinematograph manufacturing establishments undertake to develop negatives, and to supply positive prints ready for projection. 1914 J. B. Rathbun *Motion Picture Making* ii. 29 The light of the projector passes through the transparent positive print and traces the image on the screen. 1942 *Sun* (Baltimore) 23 Feb. 10/7 Lou Fonseca, director of the American League's motion picture, 'The Ninth Innings', said today that a number of prints of the film are now available for clubs, schools and other organizations. 1973 H. Gruppe *Truxton Cipher* (1974) xiv. 141 The movie was a..bad Western... The print was on its sixth tour through the Atlantic Fleet, and..the worse for wear. 1978 R. Hill *Pinch of Snuff* xii. 125 They made a film I'm interested in... I'd like to find out how many prints there were.

14. A signal on magnetic tape produced by print-through.

1950–1 *B.B.C. Quarterly* V. 250/2 On playback..the comparatively high-level prints resulting from storage are replayed at their initial level. 1958 H. G. M. Spratt *Magn. Tape Recording* iii. 110 The strength of the print rises rapidly immediately the reel has been wound up and then, with the rate of increase falling, tends towards an ultimate limiting value. 1962 A. Nisbett *Technique Sound Studio* iv. 84 The erasure is more marked on the small printed signal than on the main body of the recording (the print being reduced by perhaps 16 dB, as against 3 dB off the main signal).

III. Transferred uses, of uncertain origin.

By Nares and others derived from the typographical sense, 'from the exact regularity and truth of the art of printing, which was at first deemed almost miraculous'. But printing was not new in 1576 and in various respects this explanation seems doubtful, though Shakspere plays on the two senses of 'in print' in *Two Gent.* II. i. 175, *A.Y.L.* v. iv. 94, and the phrase may sometimes have been so taken: cf. quot. 1881, and 1606 in sense 7. The use in reference to the ruff, 14 b, may yet prove to be the earlier, though not evidenced in the quots.

15. a. In phrase ***in print:*** In a precise and perfect way or manner; in exact order, with exactness or preciseness; to a nicety. Now *dial.*

1576 Fleming *Panopl. Epist.* 357 Considering that what soeuer is vttered in such mennes hearing, must bee done in printe, as wee say in oure common Prouerbe. 1580 Lyly *Euphues* (Arb.) 407 Concerning the body, as there is no Gentlewoman so curious to haue him in print, so is there no one so careles to haue him a wretch, onlye his right shape to shew him a man. 1583 Greene *Mamillia* II. Wks. (Rtldg.) 316/1 Dames now-a-days..Pac'd in print, brave lofty looks, not us'd with the vestals. 1588 Shaks. *L.L.L.* III. i. 173, I will doe it sir in print. 1591 —— *Two Gent. Verona* II. i. 175 All this I speak in print, for in print I found it. 1621 Burton *Anat. Mel.* III. ii. IV. i. (1676) 328/1 A young lover..must.. speak in Print, walk in Print, eat and drink in Print, and that which is all in all, he must be mad in Print. 1658 Gurnall *Chr. in Arm.* verse 14. xi. § 1 (1669) 97/2 If his heart be on his Garden, O how neatly it is kept! it shall lie, as we say, in print. 1692 Locke *Educ.* § 22 Not design'de to lie always in my young Master's Bed at home, and to have his Maid lay all Things in print, and tuck him in warm. *a* 1700 B. E. *Dict. Cant. Crew* s.v., *To set in Print*, with Mouth skrew'd up and Neck Stretcht out. 1854 Miss Baker *Northants. Gloss.* s.v., She's always in print, and so is her house. 1881 *Leicestersh. Gloss.* s.v., 'The house is as neat as print'... 'Shay kips all 'er plazes in print', is high praise for a servant who keeps her own part of the house neat and clean.

†**b.** With a sb.: ***a man, fool*** (etc.), ***in print,*** a perfect or thorough man, fool, etc. *Obs.*

1604 Dekker *Honest Whore* I. Wks. 1873 II. 10, I am sure my husband is a man in print, for all things else, save only in this. 1611 Cotgr. s.v. *Bosse, Sot en bosse et platte peinture*, a foole in print, asse in graine, compleat coxcombe, absolute hoydon. 1633 Massinger *Guardian* II. i, Is he not, madam A monsieur in print? What a garb was there!

†**c.** Applied, *a* 1600 to *c* 1630, to the exact crimping, goffering, or set of the plaits or pleats of the ruffs then worn. Nearly always in the phrases ***to set the ruff in print,*** or ***the ruff stands in print.*** See also print *a.* 1, printed 1 b. Said also of *clothes. Obs.*

Quot. 1628 appears to mean a ruff of the size or pattern worn by Puritans: cf. 1614 in printed 1 b. There may also be a reference to the small print of Geneva Bibles: cf. 1623 in sense 8.

1598 E. Gilpin *Skial.* (1878) 58 Neat as a Merchants ruffe, that's set in print. 1602 Middleton *Blurt, Master Constable* III. iii. 105 Your ruff must stand in print; and for that purpose, get poking-sticks. 1615 *Band, Ruffe, & C.* (Halliw.) 5 The presse Ruffe Cuffe and Band (what reason's in't) And yet desire they still should stand in print. 1616 J. Lane *Contn. Sqr.'s T.* XI. 363 Yet these mote sett their ruffes and clothes in print, Yea, keepe them so: elles dames will looke a squint. 1625 B. Jonson *Staple of N.* I. i, Put on my girdle, rascal: fits my ruff well? *Lin.* In print. 1628 Earle *Microcosm., Shee Precise Hypocr.* (Arb.) 63 Shee is a Non-conformist in a close Stomacher and Ruffle of Geneua Print, and her puritie consists much in her Linen. *a* 1641 Suckling *To Ld. Lepington* Poems (1648) 18 It is so rare.. to see Ought that belongs to young Nobility In print (but their own clothes) that we must praise.

d. Said of the beard or hair. So also ***out of print,*** out of proper order, in disorder. *Obs.* or *dial.*

1605 Chapman *All Fools* v. i. H iv b, Tis such a picked fellow, not a haire About his whole Bulke, but it stands in print. 1629 Gaule *Holy Madn.* 91 His [a proper squire's] Beuer cocks, Feather waggs, Locks houer, and Beard stands in print. 1851 *N. & Q.* 1st Ser. IV. 12/1 An old Somersetshire servant..used to say..'Take care, Sir, you'll put your hair out of print'.

IV. 16. *attrib.* and *Comb.*, in sense 1, as ***print-mark;*** in sense 6, as ***print-broker;*** in sense 7, as ***print-blurred*** adj.; in sense 12, as ***print-collector, -pedlar;*** **print chain**, an endless chain of printing types in some printers; **print-cutter,** (*a*) a person occupied in cutting prints; (*b*) a knife for cutting photographic prints; **print hand,** handwriting imitating or resembling print: so **print letters; printhead,** the part of a printer in which characters are held or assembled immediately before printing, and from which their images are transferred to the printing medium; cf. HEAD *sb.*[1] 11 g; **print-holder,** (*a*) a small frame for holding a photograph or engraving; (*b*) a device for holding a photographic print flat or in a desired position (*Cent. Dict.*); **print letters** see *print-hand*; **print-maker, -making** (as sense 12); **print order,** an order for a certain number (of an issue of a book, paper, etc.) to be printed; **print-room,** a room in a museum or the like, containing a collection of prints; **print run** = RUN *sb.*[1] 20 d; **print-script,** a style of handwriting that imitates typography; **print-state,** state or condition of an engraving, resulting from the number of impressions that have been previously printed; **print train** = *print chain* above; **print-trimmer** = *print-cutter* (*b*); **print-washer,** an apparatus for washing photographic prints after fixing. See also PRINT-SELLER, -SHOP; **print wheel,** a disc having printing types round its rim that can be brought into position by rotation of the disc.

1905 *Academy* 30 Dec. 1362/1 They have done duty so often, that they are now like battered wood-blocks, and only *print-blurred. **1851** MAYHEW *Lond. Labour* I. 374/1 The '*print-brokers', who sell 'gown-pieces' to the hawkers or street-traders. **1967** R. BREGZIS in Cox & Grose *Organiz. Bibliogr. Rec. by Computer* V. 119 The cards are printed out by an IBM 1401 computer using a *print chain with an expanded set of 101 characters. **1972** *Computers & Humanities* VII. 97 High quality printout, suitable for publication purposes and from an extended print chain with a large character set, is highly desirable. **1880** WARREN *Book-plates* xii. 126 A *print-collector, an ex-librist, and a herald. **1851** in *Illustr. Lond. News* 5 Aug. (1854) 119/3 (Occupations of People) *Print colourer, *print cutter, print mounter. **1773** GOLDSM. *Stoops to Conq.* IV. Wks. (Globe) 668/2, I can read your *print hand very well. **1826** MISS MITFORD *Village* Ser. II. 250 (*My Godfather*) The letter in print-hand, proper to the damsel of six years old. **1968** *Computer Design* July 56/2 The page printer consists of the *print head, paper drive, character select and print head advance mechanisms. **1978** *Sci. Amer.* June 116/2 (Advt.), A rare combination of design characteristics—bidirectional drive, high positioning accuracy, penless and inkless thermal printhead, and a 200-foot roll of paper—rounds out its capability to operate unattended. **1980** *Nature* 11 Dec. p. xxii/3 The printhead is a..solid-state thermal device that eliminates the need for conventional pen-and-ink systems. **1985** *Personal Computer World* Feb. 99 (Advt.), What other printer could offer you a printhead guaranteed for over 200 million characters—each one as clear and precise as the last? **1837** DICKENS *Pickw.* lii, It ain't my father's writin', 'cept this here signatur in *print letters. **1928** M. DOBSON *Block-Cutting & Print-Making by Hand* xx. 176 He who would be his own *print-maker will really find no great obstacle in the way. **1961** *Times* 18 May 17/5 The work of 27 Soviet print-makers..and..almost our first view of current artistic activity in Russia. **1928** M. DOBSON *Block-Cutting & Print-Making by Hand* ii. 4 There are..many terms peculiar to the craft of *print-making. **1965** ZIGROSSER & GAEHDE *Guide to Collecting Orig. Prints* i. 4 Printmaking is a democratic form of art, for it enables not one but many persons to own and enjoy the same work of art... Every medium has both utilitarian and aesthetic functions. This is especially true of printmaking. **1977** J. TREVALYAN in S. Turner *Handbk. Printmaking Supplies* 8 Today printmaking has grown into a vast and profitable business... When several printmakers meet together their talk is almost always where can this or that be bought. **1701** *Lond. Gaz.* No. 3694/4 A bright-bay Gelding near 16 hands,..a *Print-Mark pretty high on the near Buttock. **1953** POHL & KORNBLUTH *Space Merchants* (1955) ii. 13 The first issue comes out in the fall, with a *print order of twenty million. **1971** M. RUSSELL *Deadline* vii. 75 There's a 15,000 extra print order. Some newsagents sold out by ten yesterday. **1979** J. SHERWOOD *Hour of Hyenas* iii. 32 The only subject discussed was the money value of various contracts and the size of the resulting print order. **1804** *Europ. Mag.* XLV. 360/1 An open saloon, where are petty book-stalls and *print-pedlars. **1849** *Index to Add. MSS. Brit. Mus. 1783–1835* p. iv, A certain number also of manuscripts..have long since been transferred to the *Print Room. **1862** GEO. ELIOT *Let.* 17 May (1956) IV. 34 We..went to the Printroom of the British Musuem to see Italian portraits of 15th cent. **1901** A. WHITMAN *Print-Collector's Handbk.* x. 132 Six officials have presided over the destinies of the Print Room. **1921** E. J. SULLIVAN *Art of Illustration* xxxvii. 252 Push past the unpretentious and silent swing door to the Print Room. **1956** HAYDEN & BUNT *Old Prints* p. viii, He will pass from our modest book to the masterpieces in the Print Rooms of the British and the Victoria and Albert Museums. **1970** B. ALLEN *Print Collecting* vi. 97 The little blue card..entitles him to be a regular visitor to the Print Room. **1975** *Language for Life* (Dept. Educ. & Sci.) xxi. 311 These books..cannot always command the large *print runs of text books. **1979** *Bookseller* 23 June 2836/1 This compilation..sold out of its first print-run rapidly. **1979** *Times* 19 Dec. 12/4 Increasingly..books with a strong American end are being entirely printed in the United States, with a proportion of the print run bought for the United Kingdom. **1922** *Print Script* (Board of Educ.) 5 During the last few years the movement in favour of '*print-script' has spread so widely in the schools of this country that a wish has been expressed that the experience of the Board's Inspectors should be made available to the general public. **1932** A. J. FAIRBANK *Handwriting Man.* Introd., Of the problems arising in the schools today.., one..is how to adapt the handwriting which has been named 'print-script'..so that there may remain in the revised model nothing to hinder the tempo at which an adult writes. **1955** P. RUDLAND *From Scribble to Script* 6 A comparatively recent innovation in the teaching of handwriting is what is known as *print-script*... Print-script originated from an address on penmanship given by Edward Johnston at the Annual Conference of Teachers in 1913. **1959** J. C. GAGG *Beginning Three R's* xii. 82 It would seem that print-script is..the most useful first style for slower children. **1975** *Language for Life* (Dept. Educ. & Sci.) xi. 185 Some teachers believe that a print-script should be used. **1902** *Blackw. Mag.* Nov. 616/2 Had '*print-states' been numbered consecutively by the old publishers, we should now have graduated prices. **1970** *Computers & Humanities* IV. 247 Lest one despair of limitation in the number of possible escape codes, it should be pointed out that the standard IBM *print train for the 360 line of computers permits 240 characters and to date (August 1969) only 174 are used on the extended set now planned by the Library of Congress for catalog card printing in all Roman alphabets. **1892** *Photogr. Ann.* II. 57 If a circular *print-trimmer is used, the print, if albumen, can be cut while damp. **1889** E. J. WALL *Dict. Photogr.* 261 [Advt.] 'Optimus' rocking *print-washer. **1892** *Photogr. Ann.* 480 Combined Tank and Print Washer..will accommodate any plate rack up to half-plate size. **1941** T. J. RHODES *Industr. Instruments for Measurement & Control* iv. 144 The multiple-point recording potentiometer is achieved by substituting a *print wheel for the recording pen and by equipping the potentiometer with a motor-driven selector switch synchronized with the print wheel. **1961** L. W. HEIN *Introd. Electronic Data Processing* xiii. 255 Print wheel 1 will be used to print the first letter of the name, and wheel 120 will be used for the cents position of the net pay figures on the stub. **1970** A. CAMERON et al. *Computers & Old Eng. Concordances* 39 We had print wheels made; we never even got to fitting them on the machine.

b. print journalism, writing, reporting or writing for newspapers (as opp. television); so ***print journalist*; print medium** (usu. pl., **media**), newspapers (as opp. broadcasting); **print union,** a trade union for printers (also *printing union* s.v. PRINTING *vbl. sb.* e).

1975 *Listener* 1 May 578/3 Michael Barratt can be taken to task for unwittingly imposing the techniques of popular print journalism on television reportage. **1977** *Listener* 1 Dec. 708/1 Eric Sevareid..has done for television what Walter Lippman did..for print journalism. **1971** *Ibid.* 25 Nov. 711/3 Some other print journalists—the editor of the *Evening Standard* is one—have chosen to break the solidarity of press and television to suggest that television's standards have been lower. **1973** *Times* 25 June 15/3 It will be the print journalists' and historians' task to review and criticize. **1975** *Listener* 10 Apr. 463/3 The camera simply recorded..the cycle of a diplomatic issue in a way no print journalist could ever hope to describe. **1968** *Globe & Mail* (Toronto) 13 Feb. B3/1 The message..is accentuated in print media advertising. **1972** *Guardian* 29 Jan. 11/5 The print media..claim..that they are being discriminated against. **1978** *Verbatim* Feb. 1/1 Part of the responsibility for our bent language rests with the print media. **1959** *Daily Tel.* 22 July 1/5 Print unions reject hours and pay offer. **1975** *Times* 7 Aug. 1/4 (*heading*) Print unions' ultimatum to 'Observer'. **1980** *Times* 13 Aug. 1/7 The unexpectedly strong reaction among other print unions brings a new dimension into the dispute over machine managers' pay. **1976** *New Yorker* 13 Sept. 103/3 (Advt.), Print writing is tougher than television writing.

print, *a.* Now only *dial.* Also *Sc.* **prent.** [In sense 1 perh. pa. pple. of PRINT *v.*; cf. quot. 1513 in sense 2 b, also MDu. *geprent*; but possibly sometimes attrib. or adj. use of PRINT *sb.*]

1. Printed.

1475 *Bk. Noblesse* (Roxb.) 84 Late us..bring forthe..the golde and silver of coyne and print money that every of us senatours and statis haven. **1542** in *Archæologia* (1887) L. I. 46 Item a prynte masse boke. **1816** SCOTT *Antiq.* xxvi, She can speak like a prent buke. **1864** MRS. LLOYD *Ladies Polc.* 103, I can't spake like print books—never could. **1865** J. YOUNG *Pictures* 64 (E.D.D.) Thou com'st wi' some prent scrap in han'.

b. Of a ruff: cf. PRINT *sb.* 15 c, PRINTED 1 b. ***new print,*** ? newly printed, pressed, or goffered.

1600 ROWLANDS *Lett. Humours Blood* (Hunter. Cl.) 52 [They] are foorth comming sir, and safe enough Sayes good-man Broker, in his new print ruffe.

2. *dial.* Clear, bright (of moonlight, etc.).

1736 PEGGE *Kenticisms* s.v. (E.D.S.), The moon shines print. **1787** GROSE *Provinc. Gloss.* s.v., Print star, or moon-light. **1875** *Sussex Gloss.*, *Print-moonlight*,..very clear moonlight. **1887** *Kent Gloss.* s.v., The night is print;..The moonlight is very print.

print (prɪnt), *v.* Forms: 4 **prente,** 4–5 (6– *Sc.*) **prent,** 4–6 **prynt(e,** 5 **preent(e,** 5–6 **printe,** 6– **print.** *Pa. pple.* **printed:** *Sc.* 6 **prent,** 6– **prentit.** [ME. *prente-n*, *printe*, known from *c* 1350, app. f. the earlier *prente*, *printe*, PRINT *sb.*, like OF. *emprienter*, *empreinter*, f. *empriente*, *empreinte*, IMPRINT *sb.* The vb. corresponds to MDu., Du. *prenten*, WFris. *printjen*; MLG., LG. *prenten* (whence Da. *prente*, Sw. *prenta*), also app. f. the corresp. sb., MDu. *prente*, *printe*, Du. *prent*, MLG. *prente*, a. OF. *priente*, *preinte*. Cf. also obs. F. *printer* to coin or stamp money (1544, Liège, in Godef.).]

I. General senses.

1. a. *trans.* To impress or stamp (a surface) with a seal, die, or the like; to mark with any figure or pattern, impressed or coloured; to brand. Said also of footsteps upon soft or yielding ground.

1340–70 *Alex. & Dind.* 256 Whan we sihen þi sonde wiþ þi sel prented, We kenden þi couaitise. *c* **1400** MAUNDEV. (Roxb.) xxv. 117 Þis monee es prynted on bathe þe sydes. *c* **1466** SIR J. PASTON in *P. Lett.* II. 294 The other ij. pottys be prentyd with that merchauntys marke. **1637** G. DANIEL *Genius this Isle* 26 The Naiades..the willing Sand shall print. **1697** DRYDEN *Virg. Georg.* III. 308 He..treads so light, he scarcely prints the Plains. **1708** *Lond. Gaz.* No. 4421/8 Stoln.., a black Mare.., printed in the near Hip. **1750** GRAY *Elegy* 116 + 4 Little footsteps lightly print the ground. **1820** W. IRVING *Sketch Bk.* I. 194 A spot that has been printed by the footsteps of departed beauty. **1879** *Cassell's Techn. Educ.* IV. 246/2 The butter is then salted.. and then moulded and printed.

†**b.** *fig.* To stamp, brand, stain. *Obs.*

c **1380** WYCLIF *Wks.* (1880) 473 Crist..forfendide hem to prynte þer soulis to myche wiþ erþly godis. *c* **1440** *York Myst.* xxxvi. 111 Sette þat he saide.., As he þat was prente full of pride, 'Jewes kyng am I', comely to knawe, Full playne. **1598** E. GILPIN *Skial.* (1878) 21 It is Cornelius that braue gallant youth, Who is new printed to this fangled age.

†**c.** To coin (money). *Obs.*

1393 LANGL. *P. Pl.* C. XVIII. 80 God coueiteþ nat þe coygne þat crist hym-self prentede. **1432–50** tr. *Higden* (Rolls) VIII. 265 He caused halpenys and ferthynges to be printed and made rownde. **1533** BELLENDEN *Livy* IV. xxiii. (S.T.S.) II. 135 Becaus na siluer was as ȝit prentit in rome, thay cunȝeit grete sovmes of brasin money. **1567** *Sc. Acts Jas. VI* (1814) III. 29/1 That our Souerane Lord..may cause prent, and cunȝe gold and siluer of sic fynes as vtheris cuntreis dois.

2. a. To impress or stamp (a form, figure, mark, etc.) in or on a yielding substance; also, by extension, to set or trace (a mark, figure, etc.) on any surface, by carving, writing, or otherwise.

c **1400** MAUNDEV. (1839) v. 62 And in that roche is prented the forme of his body. **1494** in *Somerset Med. Wills* (1901) 318 A basyn and lavor of siluer, myne armes printed thereon. **1494** FABYAN *Chron.* 3 Lyke the Prentyse that hewyth the rowgth stone, And bryngeth it to square,..That the mayster after may..prynte therin his fygures and his story. **1536** BELLENDEN *Cron. Scot.* (1821) I. 195 On the ta side of this money was prentit ane croce, and his face on the tothir. **1611** BIBLE *Lev.* xix. 28 Ye shall not make any cuttings in your flesh for the dead, nor print any markes vpon you. **1658** A. FOX *Würtz' Surg.* II. xxv. 158 The plaisters..growing hard there, would print a hole into the flesh. **1789** E. DARWIN *Bot. Gard.* II. 90 Thrice round the grave Circaea prints her tread. **1812** J. WILSON *Isle of Palms* III. 834 The child prints many a playful kiss Upon their hands. **1890** 'R. BOLDREWOOD' *Col. Reformer* (1891) 156 If you'd only had those patterns printed out slowly and indelibly.., you'd have known it was no joke [to be tattooed].

b. *fig.* To impress (an image, thought, saying, etc.) upon the heart, mind, or memory; to fix in the mind.

c **1374** CHAUCER *Troylus* II. 851 (900) Euery word þat sche of hire herde Sche gan to prentin in h[i]re herte faste. *c* **1420** ? LYDG. *Assembly of Gods* 1784 Remembre hit well and prynte hit in thy mynde. **1513** DOUGLAS *Æneis* IV. i. 8 Deip in hir breist so wes his figur prent. **1563** *Homilies* II. *Matrimony* (1859) 505 This sentence is very meet for women to print in their remembrance. **1678** CUDWORTH *Intell. Syst.* 681 Contrived by a Perfect Understanding Being or Mind.. which hath every where Printed the Signatures of its own Wisdom upon the Matter. *a* **1704** T. BROWN *Imit. 1st Sat. Persius* Wks. 1730 I. 53 Then will grey hairs on all thou say'st print awe. **1850** TENNYSON *In Mem.* lxxix, And hill and wood and field did print The same sweet forms in either mind.

3. a. To press (anything hard) into or upon a yielding substance, so as to leave an indentation or imprint. Also with *in.*

1382 WYCLIF *Jer.* xxxii. 44 Prented in shal be the sel. **1530** PALSGR. 666/2 Let me printe your seale in a pece of waxe, me thynketh it is antique. *a* **1541** H. S. in *Wyatt's Penit. Ps.* Prelim. Sonn. 15 In princes' hearts God's scourge y-printed deep, Ought them awake out of their sinful sleep. **1599** SHAKS. *Hen. V*, Prol. 27 Horses..Printing their prowd Hoofes i' th' receiuing Earth. **1697** DRYDEN *Virg. Georg.* I. 101 If the Soil be barren, only scar The Surface, and but lightly print the Share. **1884** TENNYSON *Becket* II. ii, Only the golden Leopard printed in it Such hold-fast claws.

†**b.** *fig.* To fix in or on (something). *Obs. rare.*

1398 TREVISA *Barth. De P.R.* VIII. xiv. (Tollem. MS.), þe sonne entrynge in to þat parti of þe signe prenteþ in his bemis more scharpely [orig. *acriter radios imprimit*] þan he dooþ in þe ende. **1513** DOUGLAS *Æneis* VII. v. 132 His sycht vnmovyt to the erd dyd he prent.

c. *Founding.* To make an impression of in a mould with a core-print or with a pattern.

1895 in *Funk's Standard Dict.*

†**4.** To commit (anything) to writing; to express in written words; to inscribe. *Obs.*

c **1400** *Destr. Troy* 11772 This poynt is not prynted in proces þat are now. *c* **1430** *Hymns Virg.* 114 The hiȝest lessoun þat man may lere.. Yf þou haue grace to holde & heere, Is playnli printid in poulis booke. *c* **1440** *York Myst.* xxvi. 76 Loo! sir, þis is a periurye To prente vndir penne. **1588** SHAKS. *Tit. A.* IV. i. 75 Heauen guide thy pen to print thy sorrowes plaine.

†**5.** To form in a mould; to cast, shape. *Obs. rare.*

1530 PALSGR. 157 A moulde, to moulde or print a thyng in. **1558** WARDE tr. *Alexis' Secr.* (1568) 110 b, Thinges that remain in the fire without melting, wherein men print very well all maner of metall. *Ibid.* 114 b, Untill that turninge downwarde the mouldes, they come out. And if in case they be not wel printed,..you may put them in agayne.

II. Senses relating to typography.

6. a. To make or produce (a book, picture, etc.) by the application to paper, vellum, or any similar substance, in a press or machine, of inked types, blocks, or plates, bearing characters or designs. (In printing for the blind, embossed characters, without ink, are produced.)

In this sense *enprynte, emprynte*, is found earlier, and was app. at first more in use: see IMPRINT *v.*

[**1474** CAXTON *Chesse* Pref., By cause thys sayd book is ful of holsom wysedom.. I haue purposed to enprynte it.] **1511** *Pilton Churchw. Acc.* (Som. Rec. Soc.) 62 Item for a new processionary printed..xvj[d]. **1533** *Gau's Richt Vay* 109 (Colophon) Prentit in Malmw Be me Ihone Hochstraten the xvi day of October Anno MD xxxiii. **1560** DAUS tr. *Sleidane's Comm.* 160 Englishe Bibles were printed at Paris. **1603** JAS. I in Ellis *Orig. Lett.* Ser. I. III. 78, I sende you herewith my booke latelie prentid: studdie and profite in it. **1633** PRYNNE *Histriomastix* To Rdr., They are now new-printed in farre better paper than most Octavo or Quarto Bibles. **1639** GENTILIS *Servita's Inquis.* (1676) 882 Things of importance ought equally to be handled, as well in those that are Printed, as in those that are to Print. **1660** F. BROOKE tr. *Le Blanc's Trav.* 22 He procured me the Mappe of Babylon, or Bagdet, printed upon a Cotton. **1711** ABP. KING in *Swift's Lett.* (1767) III. 239 The *Spectators* are likewise printing in a larger and a smaller volume. **1712** HEARNE *Collect.* (O.H.S.) III. 426 'Tis about half printed off. **1720** *Lond. Gaz.* No. 5850/3 His Majesty's Picture, printed in natural Colours. **1839** URE *Dict. Arts* 217 The copper-plate printing of calico is almost exactly the same as that used for printing engravings on paper from flat plates. **1887** *Chicago Advance* 19 May 306/1 She..prints it herself with the cyclostyle. **1906** L. GILES *Musings Chinese Mystic* 31 The philosopher's works, in Kuo Hsiang's standard edition, were printed for the first time in the year 1005 A.D.

b. ***to print out***: to produce in or as a print-out.

See also 15 c below.

a **1884** KNIGHT *Dict. Mech.* Suppl. 722/1 The sending operator prints out his message in plain letters at the distant end of the line, whether the receiving operator is at the instrument or not. **1953** *IRE Trans. Instrumentation* June 68 This Binary Outscriber indicated that it would adequately perform its required task: that of rapidly printing-out the memory contents. **1955** *IRE Trans. Electronic Computers* IV. 2/2 The typewriter can operate directly upon information received from the accumulator and alphanumeric translator and print out a completely general format. **1957** *IRE Trans. Instrumentation* Sept. 194/1 A Flexowriter prints out the character that was stored in the interim flip-flop storage registers. **1969** *Listener* 10 July 44/3 In the case of the two computers, of course, the actual difference could be shown by printing out their programmes. **1977** *Sci. Amer.* Sept. 23/1 (Advt.), Results are displayed to hospital personnel and printed out as reports.

7. Said of an author or editor, not of the actual printer: **a.** To cause (a manuscript, book, etc.) to be printed; to give to the press.

1530 PALSGR. 666/1 Whan wyll you printe your booke, *quant voulez vous faire imprimer vostre liure?* **1669** STURMY *Mariner's Mag.* VII. Aaaa ij b, Being desired by some Friends ..to Print it,..I have so done. **1678** BUNYAN *Pilgr.* I. Author's Apol., Some said, John, print it; others said, Not so;..At last I thought, Since you are thus divided, I print it will; and so the case decided. **1789** BURNS *Capt. Grose's Peregrin.* i, A chield 's amang you taking notes, And, faith, he'll prent it. **1897** J. W. CLARK *Barnwell* Introd. 9 My first idea was to print the Latin text alone.

b. To express or publish in print (ideas, etc.).

1638 BAKER tr. *Balzac's Lett.* (vol. II) 23 They thinke it not enough to do me wrongs unlesse they print them too. **1672** VILLIERS (Dk. Buckhm.) *Rehearsal* v. (Arb.) 133 I'l be reveng'd on them too: I will both Lampoon and print 'em too, I gad. **1751** LABELYE *Westm. Br.* 107 My Intention, in Printing and distributing this Plan..is..to ease the Minds of many Persons. **1874** BLACKIE *Self-Cult.* 17 Young men of course may..have opinions on many subjects, but there is no reason why they should print them.

†**c.** To designate in a printed statement, describe in print as. *Obs. rare.*

1611 BEAUM. & FL. *King & no King* III. ii, My safest way were to print myself a coward. *c* **1646** MILTON *New Forcers Consc.* 11 Men whose Life, Learning, Faith and pure intent Would have been held in high esteem with Paul, Must now be nam'd and printed Hereticks.

8. *intr.* or *absol.* **a.** Of a person (in senses 6, 7): To exercise the vocation of a printer; to employ the press in printing. †***print upon***, to print an edition of a book immediately after that published by (the author or editor), in order to appropriate some of the profits (*obs.*).

1699 BENTLEY *Phal.* Pref. 5 Before they ventur'd to Print, which is a Sword in the Hand of a Child. **1716** HEARNE *Collect.* (O.H.S.) V. 324 There may be danger they may print upon you, unless you print more Copies. **1733** POPE *Hor. Sat.* II. i. 100 In durance, exile, Bedlam or the Mint, —Like Lee or Budgel, I will rhyme and print. **1771** LUCKOMBE *Hist. Print.* 25 [Caxton] printed likewise for.. Henry VIIth. **1802** SYD. SMITH *Wks.* (1859) I. 13/2 Every man who prints, imagines he gives to the world something which they had not before, either in matter or style.

b. Of type, a block, a plate: To yield an impression on paper, etc. **c.** Of a manuscript or of literary matter: To run *up* or amount in type (to so much). *rare.*

1886 TUPPER *My Life as Author* 282, I wish there was space here to say more about all this; but the great book before me would print up into several volumes. **1904** *19th Cent.* Apr. 672 Here scarcely a line has been added: but the plate 'prints', and the plate began by *not* printing. **1912** *Englishwoman* July 73 The line block will print well on paper on which the delicate shades of the half-tone would be lost. **1971** D. POTTER *Brit. Eliz. Stamps* ix. 95 On rare occasions the embossed stamp appears albino, when the colour has failed to print through lack of ink. **1979** *SLR Camera* June 41/1 For the other cases which will not print on these medium grade papers you'll have to use harder or softer grades to produce a result that even approaches the satisfactory.

d. With pass. force: to appear in print; to be printed.

1775 JOHNSON in Boswell *Life* 10 Oct., Maps were printing in one of the rooms. **1930** *Sat. Rev. Lit.* (U.S.) 2 Aug. 21/2 The *Return* began printing in *Collier's*. **1953** *Northampton Dioc. Mag.* Autumn 11 The spoken word rarely prints satisfactorily. **1973** M. RUSSELL *Double Hit* xviii. 132 The newsvendors' stands stood untended: the first editions were still printing.

9. *trans.* To mark (paper, etc.) with printed characters or designs.

1727–41 CHAMBERS *Cycl.* s.v. *Printing*, The wetting of the paper ought to be done two or three days before printing it.

10. To take an impression from (a forme of type, a plate, block, etc.); to use in printing.

1727–41 CHAMBERS *Cycl.* s.v. *Printing*, Engraving several plates of Sandro Boticello's design, and printing them off this new way. **1839** *Encycl. Brit.* (ed. 7) XVIII. 572/1 These machines, however, are better adapted to printing stereotype plates, to which a curved form could be given. **1875** KNIGHT *Dict. Mech.* 1335/2 The stone is then etched, washed out, and printed.

11. To write in imitation of typography; to form (letters) in the style of printed letters; also *absol.*

1837 DICKENS *Pickw.* xxxvii, 'Mr. Weller..here's a letter for you'... 'It can't be from the gov'ner', said Sam, looking at the direction..'He always prints, I know, 'cos he learnt writin' from the large bills in the bookin' offices'. *Mod.* A little boy, who cannot write yet, has *printed* me a letter.

12. Of magnetic tape or a recorded signal: to give rise to print-through. Also *trans.*, to transfer (a signal) as a result of print-through.

1950–1 *B.B.C. Quarterly* V. 245/2 After a certain time,.. measure the level of the signal printed on to the erased slip. **1952** *Appl. Electronics Ann.* *1951* 43/2 Trouble..occurs sometimes with the programme 'printing' from one layer to another of the reel. **1958** J. TALL *Techniques Magn. Recording* iii. 33 Homogeneous tape was..favored until a few years ago in some parts of Europe and is still used occasionally there. It is subject to one major fault..: it 'prints' excessively.

III. Technical senses analogous to II.

13. a. *trans.* To stamp or mark (a textile fabric, as cotton or oilcloth), by hand or machinery, with a pattern or decorative design in one or more colours. Also *absol.*

1588 HICKOCK tr. *Frederick's Voy.* 7b, Goods and marchandize that come out of the kingdom of Cambaia, as cloth of Bumbast white, painted, printed, great quantitie of Indico [etc.]. **1600** in Nichols *Progr. Q. Eliz.* (1823) III. 505 One coveringe for a Frenche gowne of lawne, embrodered all over with fountaines, snaikes,..and other devises, upon silver chamblet prented. **1700** *Act 11 & 12 Will. III*, c. 10 All Calicoes, painted, dyed, printed or stamped there [in E. Indies] shall not be worn or otherwise used within the Kingdom of England. **1712** *Act 10 Anne* c. 19 There shall be..Paid for and upon..all Callicoes to be so Printed, Stained, Painted or Dyed..the Sum of Three Pence for every yard in length. **1758** FRANKLIN *Lett.* Wks. 1887 III. 7 There are also fifty-six yards of cotton, printed curiously from copper plates. **1839** URE *Dict. Arts* 214 The manufacturer..can print at whatever hour he may receive an order... Under the patronage of parliament, it was easy ..to buy printed calicoes.

b. ***print on*** (in *Calico-printing*): to apply (the colouring matter of the design) upon the surface by printing.

1839 URE *Dict. Arts* 215 Four different methods are in use for imprinting figures upon calicoes..the fourth is by a system of copper cylinders..by which two, three, four, or even five colours may be printed on in rapid succession. *Ibid.* 222 Some mordants..liquefy in the course of a few days; and being apt to run in the printing-on make blotted work. *Ibid.* 241 Print-on the resist to preserve the white.

14. *Pottery.* To transfer to the unglazed surface a decorative design in colour from paper, or in oil from a gelatine sheet or bat, the colour in the latter case being dusted on afterwards. With the pottery, or the design, as obj.

1839 URE *Dict. Arts* 1017 The old plan of passing the biscuit into the muffle after it had been printed... The [glue] cake..is..transferred to the surface of the glazed ware which it is intended to print. *Ibid.* 1029 M. Saint Amans..says the English surpass all other nations in manufacturing a peculiar stoneware..as also in printing blue figures upon it.

15. *Photogr.* **a.** To produce (a positive picture) by the transmission of light through a negative placed immediately upon the sensitized surface, or, in an enlarging camera, before it; to produce (a print) of a motion picture or from a transparency. Also with *off*, *out*.

1851 HUNT *Photogr.* 80 The Printing Process... It is..a negative picture,..a matrix which is capable of yielding a vast number of beautiful impressions. I have had as many as fifty printed from one, and I have no doubt that as many more might be obtained from it. **1851** TALBOT in *Athenæum* 6 Dec. 1286/2. **1852** *Chemist* III. 222/1 The positive pictures are..printed off, and fixed. **1855** HARDWICH *Man. Photogr. Chem.* 173 It is always necessary to print the picture some shades darker than it is intended to remain. **1893** *Photogr. Ann.* 49 These papers are somewhat quicker in printing, but the surface will not bear the rough treatment which coagulated albumen would stand. **1915** J. B. RATHBUN *Motion Picture Making* ii. 36 In printing the positive film from the negative, the teeth of the sprockets in the printing machine pass through both films, holding them in perfect register. **1931** B. BROWN *Talking Pictures* x. 229 The usual method in printing is to mask the sound track space on the unexposed film and then print off the picture. *Ibid.* 243 While printing cinema films is similar in principle to ordinary photographic work, it is carried out on entirely different lines, due to the enormous length of the negative. **1974** *Encycl. Brit. Macropædia* XII. 549/2 From this optical negative the sound track can be printed photographically on the exhibition release prints. Sometimes the release prints are printed as positives directly from the final magnetic track, rather than from a negative made from this track.

b. *intr.* Of a negative (with a qualifying adv.): To produce a photograph (*well*, *badly*, etc.).

1852 *Chemist* III. 221/2 [A negative] which will, as the phrase goes, print well. **1855** HARDWICH *Man. Photogr. Chem.* 290 As a general rule, the best Negatives print slowly. **1929** R. H. GOODSALL *Beginner's Guide Photogr.* vii. 37 A piece of printing paper is placed in contact with the negative and the light allowed to pass through the latter... Where there is little or no deposit on the negative it prints dark.

c. ***to print out*** (intr.): to produce an image (or, of an image, to appear) without chemical development. Also *trans.*, to print without development.

See also 6 b above.

1882 *Rep. Brit. Assoc. Adv. Sci. 1881* 595 The author has 'printed out' the spectrum on chloride of silver. **1902** *Encycl. Brit.* XXXI. 703/2 Considerable use is also made of ready-prepared platinotype paper, sensitized with salts of platinum and iron, which can be printed out entirely or only partly printed and developed with potassic oxalate. **1906** R. C. BAYLEY *Compl. Photographer* xiv. 175 In order that P.O.P. may be sufficiently sensitive to be usable at all, and give a rich image by printing out, it is not sufficient that it should contain silver chloride only. **1913** HIND & RANDLES *Handbk. Photomicrogr.* xiv. 230 The paper is printed-out in daylight until all detail is visible, then developed in potassium oxalate solution. **1948** *Rep. Progress Physics* XI. 255 When exposures are increased by a factor of 10^7 to 10^8 the photographic material 'prints out'; it darkens visibly due to a process of reduction of the emulsion grains. **1953** *Phil. Mag.* XLIV. 223 This [exposure to radiation] caused silver to print-out internally both in strained crystals and in crystals which had been annealed. **1963** JOHN & FIELD *Textbk. Photogr. Chem.* ii. 26 Emulsions of this type..were coated on paper, to give 'printing-out papers', so called because the image printed out directly. **1965** *Photogr. Jrnl.* CV. 285/2 A positive image is 'printed out', that is, it becomes visible without chemical development.

d. *trans.* To produce a positive print from (a negative or transparency).

1913 F. A. TALBOT *Pract. Cinematogr.* vii. 93 An enterprising amateur who had an excellent negative handed it over to a topical-film firm to print and circulate. **1929** R. H. GOODSALL *Beginner's Guide Photogr.* vii. 37 When the negative has been developed, washed and dried..it is ready to be printed. **1940** G. G. QUARLES *Elem. Photogr.* x. 133 When a number of negatives are to be printed at one time, it is well to sort them into piles according to contrast. **1974** C. SWEDLUND *Photogr.* ix. 221/2 Contact printing was the original method of printing negatives, and it remains the process most typically used for negatives of such size..that their images do not require enlargement.

e. ***to print down*** (trans.): to transfer a photographic image from (a negative) to a printing plate.

1923 F. T. COCKETT *Photo-Litho. & Offset Printing* 30 The seccotined worsted will adhere to the base glass and to the cut edges of the negatives so that the whole series can be printed-down in one operation. **1944** J. C. TARR *Printing To-day* ix. 106 The negatives are printed down on to the metal vacuum frames. **1967** E. CHAMBERS *Photolitho-Offset* iv. 48 Further treatment would result in a grey dot formation which would prove unsatisfactory for printing-down to metal.

f. ***to print in*** (trans.): to transfer (an image on a negative) to another negative that has already been exposed once; to produce an additional image on (an exposed negative); also *absol.*

1929 R. H. GOODSALL *Beginner's Guide Photogr.* viii. 51 This is one method by which clouds may be printed-in. The foreground negative is exposed first, partially developed, and then returned to the easel and the sky portion printed in from another negative while the foreground is screened by a card. **1956** *Focal Encycl. Photogr.* 910/2 To print in large areas, such as a sky, a plain card is used to shade the remainder of the image. **1958** *Newnes Compl. Amat. Photogr.* 1 The man who spends joyful evenings printing in clouds. **1976** M. J. ROSEN *Introd. Photogr.* vi. 119/2 For printing in small areas of the print, the typical tool is an opaque mask of light cardboard or plastic with a small hole in it. To print in, the print first is given its normal exposure.

16. See NATURE-PRINTING.

17. [f. PRINT *sb.* 3.] **a.** *trans.* To test (an object) for finger-prints.

1938 N. MARSH *Death in White Tie* xv. 163 We'd better print the brandy-glass. **1951** A. HOCKING *Death disturbs Mr. Jefferson* ii. 24 Austen said to the policeman: 'Print all the rest of the stuff, will you?' **1967** 'D. SHANNON' *Rain with Violence* (1969) iii. 39 The lab men had printed the patent leather tote bag. **1971** 'L. EGAN' *Malicious Mischief* (1972) i. 9 Dick Hunter, who had just been made Detective again.. was printing the kitchen door.

b. To record the finger-prints of (a person).

1952 J. STEINBECK *East of Eden* I. 484 Ever been mugged or printed? **1955** D. W. MAURER in *Publ. Amer. Dial. Soc.* xxiv. 147 He is *printed* (his fingerprints taken) and *mugged* (photographed). **1957** C. MACINNES *City of Spades* II. xiii. 192 The screws can print you in the nick at Brixton. **1970** G. F. NEWMAN *Sir, You Bastard* viii. 232 He had been charged, printed, and provisionally questioned.

18. To make (a printed circuit or component).

1946 *Business Week* 23 Feb. 19/2 (*caption*) Developed for proximity fuses, radio circuits 'printed' on ceramic plates are space savers adaptable to miniature pocket receivers. **1946** *Wireless World* Oct. 349/1 The connections are printed on the panels, the 'ink' being a solution of silver, which is dried, baked on and finally varnished over. *Ibid.*, Even the resistors are printed by the use of appropriate solutions.

1956 *Appl. Electronics Ann. 1955–56* 46/1 It is now possible to print a complete piece of electronic equipment except for the larger components. **1958** *Daily Mail* 8 Sept. 8/2 Using modern techniques of etching and engraving, a wiring circuit is actually 'printed' on to a flat base. **1966** *McGraw-Hill Encycl. Sci. & Technol.* X. 596/1 Resistive inks are composed of various forms of carbon with a resin binder.. and a solvent vehicle. This mixture is applied through a stencil to form a rectangular pattern..and then baked... Resistive elements printed in this manner have wide tolerance limits. **1973** DOKTER & STEINHAUER *Digital Electronics* vi. 227 What is printed is not generally the whole circuit but merely the wiring connections.

19. *Combs.*, in which **print-** is used attrib. in the sense of PRINTING *vbl. sb.*, as **print-cloth**, cotton cloth of the kind suitable for printing; **print-ground** = PRINT-FIELD. Also **print-out paper** *Photogr.* = *printing out paper*: see PRINTING *vbl. sb.* e. See also PRINT-FIELD, -HOUSE, etc.

1839 URE *Dict. Arts* 213 Calico-printing..was unknown as an English art till 1696, when a small print-ground was formed upon the banks of the Thames, near Richmond. **1886** *Pop. Sci. Monthly* Feb. 480 A yard of cotton cloth of the kind called print-cloth. **1893** *Photogr. Ann.* 444 A new toning agent..said to be superior to any yet introduced for the toning of albumen or gelatine print-out papers.

printability (ˌprɪntəˈbɪlɪtɪ). [f. PRINTABLE *a.* + -ITY.] **a.** Of type, a block, a plate, etc.: capacity to produce print. **b.** Of paper: capacity to take print. **c.** Of language, statements, etc.: suitability or fitness to be printed. Also *attrib.*

1967 E. CHAMBERS *Photolitho-Offset* iv. 43 The positives are printed-down by the deep-etch method of plate-making which creates a plate with firm hand dot fringes of good printability, sharpness and long press-life. **1969** *R. & E. Coordinator* (Res. & Engin. Council Graphic Arts Industry) Apr. 8/1 A meter and a modified IGT Printability Tester are used to measure the drying time..of quick drying inks into paper. **1971** *Scholarly Publishing* II. 361 The first experimental paper, both sized and unsized, substantially exceeded the minimum specifications..and was found to have good printability as well. **1979** M. RUSSELL *Touchdown* i. 18 His only difficulty would be to stay within the limits of printability.

printable (ˈprɪntəb(ə)l), *a.* [f. PRINT *v.* + -ABLE.] Capable of being printed; fit to be printed.

1837 CARLYLE *Fr. Rev.* III. IV. iv, Such ground-scheme, ..still legible and printable, we shall now..present to the reader. **1862** *Temple Bar Mag.* V. 293 Lemaire..called him names not printable in these prim days. **1891** J. D. CAMPBELL in *Athenæum* 31 Oct. 583/3 Talfourd had printed ..all in the letters that was printable in 1837 and 1848.

b. Capable of being printed from. *rare.*

1885 *Manch. Exam.* 22 June 5/7 Of all the modern methods of producing printable plates, heliogravure stands undoubtedly pre-eminent.

‖**printanier** (prɛ̃tanje), *a.* (*sb.*) Also **printanière**. [F. *printanier*, lit. 'of springtime' (*printemps*), f. L. *primus* first + *tempus* time.] Made from or garnished with spring vegetables. Also as *sb.*

1861 MRS. BEETON *Bk. Househ. Managem.* 78 (*heading*) Potage printanier, or spring soup. **1867** TROLLOPE *Claverings* I. xix. 237 There's just a little soup, printanière; yes, they can make soup here. **1897** *Sears, Roebuck Catal.* 15/1 Soups..French Bouillon, Julienne, Printanier, Vegetable [etc.]. **1907** *Yesterday's Shopping* (1969) 19/1 *Soups*..Printanière—½ lb. tin 0/5½. *c* **1938** *Fortnum & Mason Price List* 57/1 *Soups*..Printanier—per tin 1/-. **1965** *House & Garden* Dec. 84/2 *Printanier*, neatly..diced very young vegetables, sometimes cooked in with the dish, but mainly used for garnishing.

printed (ˈprɪntɪd), *ppl. a.* [f. PRINT *v.* + -ED[1].]

1. a. Impressed, stamped, marked, †moulded.

c **1483** CAXTON *Dialogues* 12 Of mylke soden with the flour Men make printed cakes. **1616** SURFL. & MARKH. *Country Farme* 683 Their dung is printed, grosse, long, and knottie. **1742** COLLINS *Oriental Ecl.* II. 52 Oft in the dust I view his printed feet.

b. Said of a ruff: In print (PRINT *sb.* 15 c); ? with the pleats properly pressed or goffered; cf. PRINT *a.* 1 b.

1611 B. JONSON in *Coryat's Crudities* a iij b, He [Coryat] will shortly be reputed a Knowing proper, and well traueld scholer, as by his starchd beard, and printed ruffe may be as properly insinuated. **1614** —— *Barth. Fair* III. ii, *Mooncalf.* [Of a party of Puritans.] A body may read that i' their small printed ruffes [i.e. ruffs in small or Geneva print].

2. a. Produced or prepared by typography; bearing printed characters; expressed or published in print.

1509 HAWES *Past. Pleas.* xiv. (Percy Soc.) 53 Whose godly name In printed bokes doth remayne in fame. **1553** EDEN *Treat. Newe Ind.* (Arb.) 5 A shiete of printed paper. **1665** *Orders of Ld. Mayor Lond.* in De Foe *Plague* (Rtldg.) 62 With these usual printed Words,..'Lord have Mercy upon us'. **1709** LADY M. W. MONTAGU *Let. to Miss A. Wortley* 21 Aug., I don't see any violent necessity of printed rules. **1841** D'ISRAELI *Amen. Lit.* (1867) 215 The first printed book in the English language was not printed in England.

b. Used of a writer.

1893 W. G. COLLINGWOOD *Life & Work J. Ruskin* I. v. 56 He was quite an artist; and a printed poet!

c. ***printed matter, paper***, leaflets, papers, cards, circulars, etc., that are printed, not written. So ***printed-matter mail***, a cheaper rate of postage than that for ordinary mail.

1876 in *Jrnl. R. Soc. Arts* (1976) May 343/1, I am directed by the Council of this Society respectfully to draw your Lordship's attention to the anomaly which exists with reference to the conveyance of printed matter by the post, owing to the distinction which the Post-office makes between the book post and the newspaper post. **1897** *Post Office Guide* July 375 The Articles which are entitled to be sent at the rate applicable to *Printed Papers* are mostly impressions or copies obtained upon paper, parchment, or cardboard, by means of printing, lithography, engraving, photography, or any other mechanical process easy to recognize... Besides these articles, there are some others which are admitted, though not really printed matter, as, for instance, manuscripts intended for the press (when sent with the proofs of the same), papers impressed for the use of the blind, and cardboard drawing models stamped in relief. **1918** *Ibid.* July 9 The expression 'Printed Paper' means a packet not exceeding 2 oz. in weight which consists of or contains one or more of the following articles or documents, that is to say:—..Books..Sketches..Maps..[etc.]. **1929** H. CRANE *Let.* 6 Sept. (1965) 345 My old landlady..had thought they were 'printed matter' and had failed to forward them. **1929** D. H. LAWRENCE *Let.* 9 July (1962) II. 1163, I will address them..by registered printed-matter mail. **1957** C. BROOKE-ROSE *Languages of Love* 32 Two newspapers and three letters for her lay on the hall table. One was only printed matter, and one an unsealed invitation. **1959** *Spectator* 14 Aug. 181/1 Printed matter is not much read by the non-Communists or the uncommitted. **1967** *Economist* 15 July 238/3 With the inevitable rise in the price of newspapers..and the probable ending of resale price maintenance on confectionery and even tobacco, newsagents will be keener than before to sell printed matter.

3. Coloured or figured by a process of printing, as cotton goods, carpets, pottery, etc.

1588 [see PRINT *v.* 13]. **1633** WOTTON *Let. to Sir E. Bacon* 3 June in *Reliq.* (1672) 464, I send you herewith two printed Caps... The Caps is a pretty fresh invention of a very easie rate;..which may come to some pretty perfection in the ornament of Curtains and Valances of Beds, or in some fine historified Table-cloth for a Banquet. **1758** FRANKLIN *Lett.* Wks. 1887 III. 7 Seven yards of printed cloth. **1791** HAMILTON *Berthollet's Dyeing* I. Introd. 2 A mode..we use for colouring printed linens. **1839** URE *Dict. Arts* 1028 The blue printed ware of England has been hitherto a hopeless object of emulation in France. **1888** BLACK *In Far Lochaber* viii, I've bought each o' them a printed cotton gown. **1900** *Daily News* 24 Feb. 6/5 Printed in the medley of colours and the designs so long associated with cashmere shawls.

4. Reproduced by nature-printing, photographic printing, etc. Also ***printed-out*** (see PRINT *v.* 15 c).

1856 T. MOORE (*title*) Nature-Printed British Ferns. **1859** [see NATURE-PRINTED]. **1907** *Westm. Gaz.* 9 Nov. 18/2 The development of a partially printed-out image. **1934** *Jrnl. Optical Soc. Amer.* XXIV. 316/1 Weigert found that if shorter exposures than were required to produce a printed-out image were given..the image rendered visible by suitable development was dichroic. **1976** K. I. & R. E. JACOBSON *Imaging Syst.* ii. 55 The colour of the printed out silver is usually reddish purple.

5. ***printed circuit***, an electric circuit in the form of a flat sheet of insulating material bearing thin conducting strips and components, usu. mass-produced by a method that involves printing the circuit design on the sheet using a stencil or photograph of it; so ***printed circuitry, wiring***; also applied to individual components made by such processes.

1946 *Business Week* 23 Feb. 19/2 On the back of the plate are solder spots that connect through holes in the plate with the 'printed' circuit. **1946** *Sci. News Let.* 2 Mar. 133 'Printed wire', the new development that reduces wiring radio circuits to a two-dimensional lithographic process. **1946** *Wireless World* Oct. 349/1 (*heading*) Printed 'wiring'. **1952** *Electronic Engin.* XXIV. 129/1 A major disadvantage of printed circuits has been the difficulty of incorporating satisfactory resistors. **1956** *Mod. Plastics* XXXIII. 223/2 Use of printed circuitry in 1955..increased in electronic computers, industrial control units, servo-mechanisms, and similar equipment. **1958** *Daily Mail* 8 Sept. 8/2 Research men working with printed circuits have evolved a way of reducing the thickness of the copper foil which carries the current from five-thousandths of an inch..to half a thousandth of an inch. **1966** *McGraw-Hill Encycl. Sci. & Technol.* X. 596/2 Printed capacitors are fabricated as part of the conductor circuit pattern when a high dielectric constant ceramic..is used as the circuit base material. Conductive patterns are screened on opposite sides of the circuit base to form the capacitor. **1970** J. EARL *Tuners & Amplifiers* vi. 141 The vast majority of tuner-amplifiers are now transistored, the designs being based on printed circuit boards..and sometimes integrated circuits. **1971** *Engineering* Apr. 30/1 The introduction of solid-state electronics and printed circuitry to vending machinery has minimized the number of separate electrical relays required. **1977** *Gramophone* Nov. 960/3 Normally these would flex the board during transit, with the possibility of cracking the printed wiring.

6. Produced by print-through (sense 1).

1950–1 *B.B.C. Quarterly* V. 245/1 In an investigation of accidental printing, one of the main difficulties is in measuring printed signals which are more than 50 db lower in level than the recorded signal, but are closely spaced about it on the tape. **1962** A. NISBETT *Technique Sound Studio* iv. 84 (*caption*) Wavelength of original and printed signal.

printeis, obs. Sc. form of PRENTICE.

printer (ˈprɪntə(r)). Also 6 prent-; 6 -or, -our, *Sc.* -ar. [f. PRINT *v.* + -ER[1]. So MDu. and early mod.Du. *prenter, printer*.]

1. a. A person who prints, in any sense of the word; one engaged in impressing or stamping marks or designs upon a surface, as a calico-printer, and (formerly) a coiner.

1567 *Reg. Privy Council Scot.* I. 556 All Meltaris, Forgearis and Prentaris within the said cunyehous. **1570–1** *Ibid.* XIV. 89 The generall maister cunzeour, warrandis,..sinkar, meltaris,..and prentaris of the cunze hous. **1704** *Collect. Voy.* (Churchill) III. 803/2, 100 Printers of Callicoes. **1839** URE *Dict. Arts* 214 The great disadvantage under which the French printers labour is the higher price they pay for cotton fabrics, above that paid by the English printers. **1853** DICKENS *Let.* in *Daily News* 12 Jan. (1899) 5/2, I hope we shall never terminate our business engagements until that printer in stone, who will have to be employed at last, shall set 'Finis' over our last binding in boards! **1966** J. & P. DIXON *Photography* i. 18 A good printer is of tremendous value to a studio. Without seeing the original subject he can take the negative and produce prints of superb quality.

b. *spec.* One whose business is the printing of books, etc.; the owner of a printing business (formerly usually identical with a publisher); a workman employed in a printing-office.

1504 *Statuta in Parliamento* (Colophon), Emprented at London..by me Rycharde Pynson, Squyer and Prenter unto the Kynges noble grace. **1509** *Hawes' Conv. Swearers* 90 (Colophon) Enprynted at London..by Wynkyn de Worde, prynter vnto the moost excellent pryncesse my lady the kynges graundame. *a* **1520** DUNBAR *Poems* lxiii. 220 Pryntouris, payntouris, and potingaris. **1532** MORE *Confut. Tindale* Wks. 499/1 Of that writing that remayneth, some corrupted bi writers, some by prenters. **1570** LEVINS *Manip. Vocabul.* 77/17 A Printer, *chalcographus*. **1596** DALRYMPLE tr. *Leslie's Hist. Scot.* x. (S.T.S.) 468 Thay consult to hinder his labour, to tak Mr. Ninian, to punise the prenter. **1613** PURCHAS *Pilgrimage* (1614) 14 Wee can no more ascribe these things to chance, than a Printers Case of letters could by chance fall into the right composition of the Bible which he printeth, or of Homers Iliads. **1770** *Junius Lett.* i. 1 To the Printer of the Public Advertiser. **1867** BRANDE & COX *Dict. Sc.*, etc. III. 69/2 Caxton's types, as well as those of most of the early printers, were the Gothic, or black letter characters.

2. An instrument or appliance used for printing.

a. A telegraphic printing instrument; now usu. short for TELEPRINTER; **b.** a photographic negative in its printing capacity; **c.** ***mechanical printer***, a name for a typewriter. (U.S.)

1859 T. P. SHAFFNER *Telegr. Manual* xviii. 273 The apparatus comprises two essential mechanisms, the 'Transmitter' or 'Compositor', and the 'Receiver' or 'Printer'. **1890** *Harper's Mag.* Feb. 432/1 Edison's various devices in his old stock printer have formed the basis of all later variations on that sort of instrument. **1890** *Cent. Dict.* s.v. *Motor, Motor printer*, a printing telegraph in which the mechanism is moved by electric, steam, or other motive power. **1905** *Westm. Gaz.* 11 Mar. 14/2 It is not always the negative which looks best which is the best printer. **1928** A. WILLIAMS *Telegraphy & Telephony* ii. 36 (*caption*) A specimen of the printing done with the Creed printer. **1960** I. FLEMING *For your Eyes Only* 26 Anything you have to say I'll put straight on the printer to London. **1972** R. BUSBY *Reasonable Man* xviii. 161 Williams flicked the telex message... 'When this came up on the printer it jogged my memory.'

d. *Photogr.* and *Cinemat.* An apparatus for producing positive prints from negatives.

1912 F. A. TALBOT *Moving Pictures* viii. 82 This is the Williamson printer. **1940** G. G. QUARLES *Elem. Photogr.* x. 135 The actual darkroom technique of making the exposure will depend upon the type of printer available. The simplest ..is the simple hinged-back printing frame. **1951** R. SPOTTISWOODE *Film & its Techniques* viii. 196 The step printer (whether of the contact or optical type) is much like a camera or projector. The printing and printed films are pulled down one frame at a time..and held in front of a frame-sized aperture while exposure takes place. **1974** L. LIPTON *Independent Filmmaking* ix. 371 The highest quality masters are made with optical and contact step printers, although continuous contact machines are also used.

e. *Computers.* A device which produces a printed record of the input or output of a computer of which it is part or to which it is connected.

1946 *Math. Tables & Other Aids to Computation* II. 103 The static outputs of a total of 80 decade counters and 16 PM counters are connected to the printer. **1949** E. C. BERKELEY *Giant Brains* viii. 137 The recorder consists of a printer, a reperforator, and a tape transmitter... The printer is a regular teletypewriter connected to the machine. **1962** *Communications Assoc. Computing Machinery* V. 477/2 Routines intended for line-at-a-time printers do not yield optimal output for typewriters. **1974** 'A. HAIG' *Peruvian Printout* 37 The high-speed printer in the New York computer room was still for a moment... Howard and Sam walked round the backs of the printers lifting the boxes of printout on to a rubber-wheeled trolley. **1975** T. ALLBEURY *Special Collection* xix. 135 Their addresses were typed up on the fast printer in 3·4 seconds.

3. *Trade.* A cotton cloth made to be printed on; printing-cloth.

1864 J. S. BUCKLE *Manuf. Compend.* p. ix, 36 inches wide Cambric Printer, 50 yards long. **1883** *Daily News* 25 June 2/7 Cotton Goods... Mexicans, T-cloths, and printers are generally dull, with occasional sales at a slight decline.

4. *attrib.* and *Comb.* chiefly appositive, 'that is a printer' (sense 1 b), as ***printer-author, -journalist***; **printer-slotter**, a machine used for printing on cardboard or other packaging materials.

1663 GERBIER *Counsel* 105 Printer setters will commit faults, as appears by the Errataes at the end of books. **1888** *Pall Mall G.* 13 Sept. 5/2 Caxton and Wynkyn de Worde command large sums,..and so..of many other printer-authors who combined both professions in those primitive times when labour was undivided. **1906** *Athenæum* 25 Aug. 209/3 In 1618 the Community of Printer-Booksellers was sanctioned by the king [of France]. **1954** *TAPPI* Feb. 144A/1 Another..development which appears very near is a printer-slotter arranged to handle aniline inks. **1957** *Ibid.* Nov. 190A/2 A completely new design Langston printer-slotter is currently available in three sizes... This machine is of a split or opening construction so arranged that a two-color press can be easily converted..into a press of three, four, or even more stations. **1968** *Globe & Mail* (Toronto) 13 Jan. 48/2 (Advt.), Corrugated box printer-slotter operator. Call Mr. Cherry.

b. With *printer's*: as **printer's devil** = DEVIL 5 a; **printer's flower** = FLOWER *sb.* 5 c; **printer's imprint** = IMPRINT *sb.* 3; **printer's mark,** a monogram or other device used by a printer as a trade-mark. **c.** With *printers'*, as ***printers' fat*** (= FAT *sb.*² 5 b), ***ink*** (see INK *sb.*¹ 1), ***pie*** (see PIE *sb.*⁴), ***ream*** (see REAM *sb.*³), ***roller, varnish***; **printers' bible** (see quot.); **printers' gauge** = GAUGE *sb.* 12.

1898 *Home Mag.* 31 Dec. 378/2 The so-called '*Printers'' Bible, which contains..the..misreading..'Printers have persecuted me without a cause' (Psalm cxix. 161), 'printers' being substituted for 'princes'. **1763** H. ROSE in *Fam. Rose Kilravock* (Spald. Club) 438 Harassed every morning by the *printer's devil. **1782** MME. D'ARBLAY *Let. to Mrs. Thrale* 24 Apr., I think I could submit to be printer's devil, to get a sight of the next volume. **1873** H. SPENCER *Stud. Sociol.* (1882) 127 The hand implements used by 'printer's-devils' fifty years ago. **1898** *N. & Q.* 9th Ser. II. 33/1 Type.. occupying exactly three-sevenths of the open page, the remaining four-sevenths being '*printer's-fat'. **1820** URE *Dict. Chem.* (1823) 506/2 Good *printers' ink is a black paint, smooth and uniform in its composition. **1838** *Penny Cycl.* XII. 478/1 Printers' ink may be considered as a black paint, writing ink..as a black dye.

Hence **'printerdom,** the 'world' of printers.

1903 *Brit. & Col. Printer* 19 Nov. 4/1 The list of present entrants is being spread abroad through printerdom. **1904** *Ibid.* 10 Mar. 15/3 There are enough titled men in printerdom to give a little point to a story [etc.].

printergram ('prɪntəgræm). [f. TELE)PRINTER + TELE)GRAM.] A telegram transmitted by telex.

1932 *Telegraph & Telephone Jrnl.* Oct. 2/2 Printer-grams are charged for at the same rate as phonograms. **1942** CROOKS & DAWSON *Dict. Typewriting* (ed. 4) 268 Telex subscribers..have the advantage of being able to send and receive inland or overseas telegrams directly to and from the Post Office and/or the cable companies who are also on Telex. Telegrams handled in this manner are known as 'Printergrams'. **1976** [see PHONOGRAM 3].

printery ('prɪntərɪ). Chiefly *U.S.*; also *Austral.* and *Afr.* [f. PRINTER: see -ERY. Cf. *imprimery.*]

1. A printing-office.

1638 H. PETERS in *4 Mass. Hist. Coll.* VI. 99 Wee have a printery here. **1657** W. RAND tr. *Gassendi's Life Peiresc* II. 28 He would cause the Vatican Printery to be set on work again. **1864** WEBSTER, *Printery*,..also, sometimes, a printing-office. **1894** *N. Brit. Daily Mail* 7 Sept. 2 The American Government,..and some of our colonies, had established Government printeries. **1921** MENCKEN *Amer. Lang.* (rev. ed.) 187 *Printery*..appeared very early, and..has been reinforced by many analogues, e.g., beanery, bootery [etc.]. **1943** K. TENNANT *Ride on Stranger* x. 102 The Order owned ..a share in a printery. **1969** *Sydney Morning Herald* 24 May 1/7 Mr Newton..watched the search for several minutes before announcing: 'I'm bored with this. I'm off to the factory (a printery he operates in Canberra).' **1973** *New Journalist* (Austral.) July–Aug. 6/2 The licence of 3KZ is owned by Industrial Printing and Publicity Co. Ltd. This began as a Labor printery. **1975** B. GARFIELD *Hopscotch* xxii. 226 An *Evening Standard* van..returning to the printery from its last delivery. **1979** V. S. NAIPAUL *Bend in River* xiv. 229 We didn't have many printeries in the town.

2. A cotton-printing factory; = PRINT-WORK 1.

1846 in WORCESTER citing PITKIN. **1903** *Fabian News* XIII. 34/2 [He] was head of a big calico printery.

†**'print-field.** *Obs.* [f. PRINT *v.* + FIELD *sb.*] An establishment for printing and bleaching calicoes; = PRINT-WORK 1.

1799 J. ROBERTSON *Agric. Perth* 380 Printfields for staining cotton cloth have been established at Cromwell-haugh, Huntingtower, Stormont-field and Tulloch. **1806** *Gazetteer Scotl.* (ed. 2) 138/1 The banks of the Leven..are covered with numerous bleachfields, printfields, and cotton-works. **1839** URE *Dict. Arts* 214 One of his foremen.. worked for a year in a print-field in Lancashire.

†**print-house.** *Obs.* [f. PRINT *v.* + HOUSE *sb.*]

1. = PRINTING-HOUSE.

1629 WADSWORTH *Pilgr.* iii. 13 Father Wilson, ouerseer of the Print-house. **1668–9** WOOD *Life* (O.H.S.) IV. 81 Mr. Delgardno, who lived in the house now the little print-house. **1711** HEARNE *Collect.* (O.H.S.) III. 221 They are about pulling down our Print-House.

2. *print house.* †**a.** A cotton-printing factory. **b.** A house of business selling prints (PRINT *sb.* 6).

1839 URE *Dict. Arts* 242 Filters for the colour shop of a print house are best made of wool.

printing ('prɪntɪŋ), *vbl. sb.* [f. PRINT *v.* + -ING¹.] **a.** The action of the verb PRINT, in various senses; an instance of this.

1398 TREVISA *Barth. De P.R.* v. iii. (Tollem. MS.), In comparison to þe formest party [of the brain] he be menely harde, þat þe prentynge of shappis [orig. *formæ impressio*] and of liknesse be þerinne þe longer holde. *Ibid.* XIV. ii. (Bodl. MS.), þe printinge of þe sonne bemes is strenger in lowe places þanne in hiȝe. *c* **1450** *Godstow Reg.* 542 She strengthed hit with the pryntyng of her seale. **1532–3** *Act 24 Hen. VIII*, c. 13 No manne vnder the degree of a barons sonne..shall weare any maner embrodery, prickyng or printing with golde, siluer, or sylke. **1728** DE FOE *Plan Eng. Commerce* 296 It is but a few Years ago since no such thing as painting or printing of Linen or Callicoe was known in England. **1835** E. BAINES *Hist. Cotton Manuf.* 257 In some parts [of the East] block printing is wholly unknown. **1839** URE *Dict. Arts* 1029 Unsized paper fit for printing upon stoneware. **1904** *Daily Chron.* 22 Oct. 4/4 Finger-printing, first suggested and practically applied by Sir William Herschel, of the Indian Civil Service. **1966** *Listener* 1 Sept. 301/2 In the United States they have far greater fingerprinting output than we have..though they have not quite universal printing. **1970** O. DOPPING *Computers & Data Processing* xv. 234 In programming editing operations for printing, it is essential to consider how the form will look to the user.

b. In *Typography*. (See PRINT *v.* 6.) Also, the total number of copies (of a book) printed at one time; an impression.

1530 PALSGR. 258/2 Printyng of bokes, *impression.* *a* **1548** HALL *Chron., Hen. VI* 170 b, In which season [*c* 1457] the craft of Printyng was first inuented in the citie of Mens in Germanie. **1613** PURCHAS *Pilgrimage* (1614) 438 Their printing is not by composing the letters as with vs; but.. they make for euery leafe a Table or boord, with characters on both sides. **1771** LUCKOMBE *Hist. Print.* 30 Caxton distinguished the books of his printing by the following particular device. **1837** HALLAM *Hist. Lit.* (1843) I. iii. §19. 148 The invention of printing..from moveable letters, has been referred by most to Gutenberg, a native of Mentz. **1928** *Publishers' Weekly* 26 May 2117 A best selling novel... Four large printings were necessary before publication. **1933** *Morning Post* 7 July 14/7 (Advt.), 7 printings in 5 weeks. *Peter Abelard.*

c. In *Photography*. (See PRINT *v.* 15.) Also ***printing out***: the production of an image without chemical development (cf. PRINT *v.* 15 c); ***printing-out paper*** (abbrev. P.O.P.), a printing paper capable of being used for this.

1853 *Family Herald* 3 Dec. 510/2 The printing of positives will take from three or four minutes to one hour and a half, according to the sun. **1855** HARDWICH *Man. Photogr. Chem.* 289 Photographic Printing... A. The exposure to light, or printing, properly so called.—B. The fixing and colouring [etc.]. **1891** W. E. WOODBURY *Gelatino-Chloride of Silver Printing-Out Process* ii. 6 One of the principal advantages of the chloride emulsion paper is its ability to give good prints from weak negatives—superior, in fact, to any that could be obtained by other printing-out processes. **1893** *Photogr. Ann.* 49 These papers are somewhat quicker in printing. **1902** *Encycl. Brit.* XXXI. 703/2 The most notable change in recent years is the supersession of albuminized papers by papers coated by machinery with emulsions of silver haloids in gelatine, the chloride being used for most of the printing-out papers,..while the bromide forms the basis of most of the developable papers. **1904** *Daily Chron.* 28 Apr. 8/4 The sensitive paper—ordinary gelatino-chloride printing-out paper answers well. **1918** J. R. ROEBUCK *Sci. & Pract. of Photogr.* vi. 127 Photographers generally still rank prints on printing out paper ahead of prints on developing paper, but the former requires more time and labor, so that they have gone largely out of general use. **1939** [see *printing paper* (sense e below)]. **1968** H. ASHER *Photogr. Princ. & Pract.* (1970) viii. 230 Printing-out papers are not normally stocked by dealers but they are still obtainable. **1976** K. I. & R. E. JACOBSON *Imaging Syst.* ii. 54 One of the oldest systems.. uses printing out papers which produce visible images of good photographic quality directly on exposure to a strong light source..without the need for development or any other amplification process. *Ibid.* 55 Exposure to light of lower intensity for longer periods..causes these internal latent images to act as centres for the printing out of silver.

d. = PRINT-THROUGH 1.

1949 S. J. BEGUN *Magn. Recording* v. 98 Impregnated mediums exhibit 'printing' to an objectionable extent. **1950–1** *B.B.C. Quarterly* V. 248 (*caption*) Records of printing at various frequencies. **1962** A. NISBETT *Technique Sound Studio* iv. 84 (*caption*) Printing depends on the thickness of the tape base layer, as well as temperature and physical shock.

e. *attrib.* and *Comb.*, as ***printing-hammer, -industry, -material, -pad, -process, -roller, -works***; in Typogr., as ***printing-letter, -plate, -room, -tool, -type***; in cotton-printing, as ***printing-shop***; in pottery-printing, as ***printing-colour***; in Photogr., as ***printing light, negative***; **printing-body**: see quot.; **printing-cloth,** cotton cloth made specially for printing; **printing-cylinder,** in some printing-machines, the cylinder by which the paper is pressed on the flat forme of type, the impression cylinder; **printing-drum,** a revolving drum in a printing-machine serving to guide the paper; **printing-frame** (*Photogr.*): see quot. 1875; †**printing-irons,** implements for coining; **printing-machine,** a printing-press of the kind used for printing rapidly and on a large scale, generally one in which mechanical power is employed; †**printing-mould,** ? a set of matrices for type: see MOULD *sb.*³ 2, MATRIX *sb.* 4; **printing paper,** (*a*) paper used for printing on; (*b*) in *Photogr.* sensitized paper on which pictures are printed (also *printing-out paper* sense c); **printing union** = *print union* s.v. PRINT *sb.* 16 b; **printing-wheel**: see quot.

1839 URE *Dict. Arts* 1015 Three kinds of glazes are used in Staffordshire; one..for the finer pipe-clay ware to receive impressions, called *printing body. **1883** *Daily News* 22 Oct. 7/1 Cotton goods... *Printing cloth quiet, and rather unsteady. **1839** URE *Dict. Arts* 1015 As to the stoneware.. it is covered with a glaze composed of 13 parts of the *printing-colour frit. **1790** *Patent Specif.* No. 1748, A is the *printing cylinder covered with woollen cloth. **1839** URE *Dict. Arts* 1036 The paper is thus conducted from the first printing cylinder F, to the second cylinder G. *Ibid.* 1037 Then encompassing the left-hand side and under portion of the *printing drum..it passes in contact with the..rollers. **1855** HARDWICH *Man. Photogr. Chem.* 159 With sensitive paper..the picture will look well on its first removal from the *printing-frame. **1858** Printing-frame [see ACCELERATOR b]. **1875** KNIGHT *Dict. Mech.*, *Printing-frame*,..a quadrangular shallow box in which sensitized paper is placed beneath a negative and exposed to the direct rays of the sky or of the sun. *Ibid.* 1801/1 The type-wheel is continuously rotated by an independent motor, the circuit of the *printing-hammer being closed when the letter is opposed to the printing-pad. **1976** *Times* 23 Mar. 1/5 The union said in a letter to the *printing industries committee that the question had not arisen because of the dispute at Barnsley. **1531** *Acc. Ld. High Treas. Scotl.* VI. 49 For bering of the kist with the *prenting irnis to the abbay. **1538** ELYOT *Dict.*, *Tudicula*, a ladell, a pryntynge yron, wherwith vessell is marked. **1771** LUCKOMBE *Hist. Print.* 227 The Sizes of *Printing Letter would not perhaps have been carried lower than Brevier. **1889** *Anthony's Photogr. Bull.* II. 267 Good *printing light. **1858** SIMMONDS *Dict. Trade* 302/2 Hand-presses are now for the most part superseded in large establishments by steam-presses, generally called *printing-machines. **1664** ATKYNS *Orig. Printing* 4 Thomas Bourchier, Arch-Bishop of Canterbury, moved the then king (Hen. the 6th) to use all possible means for procuring a *Printing-Mold..to be brought into this Kingdom. **1856** *Pract. Chem.* in *Orr's Circ. Sci.* 206 For the production of a *printing negative. **1875** *Printing-pad [see *printing-hammer*]. **1806** R. SUTCLIFF *Trav. N. Amer.* (1811) xiv. 258 The mill..is..employed in making writing and *printing paper. **1828** WEBSTER, **Printing-paper*, paper to be used in the printing of books, pamphlets, &c. **1892** *Bothamley's Ilford Man. Photogr.* App. 164 The printing paper of the future. **1905** *Westm. Gaz.* 11 Mar. 14/2 Close contact between negative and printing-paper. **1939** MACK & MARTIN *Photogr. Process* ix. 313 Silver halide printing papers may be divided roughly into two classes, *viz.*: printing-out papers ('P.O.P') in which the reduction of the halide to metallic silver is completed by the action of the light, no development being required; and developing-out papers ('D.O.P.') in which the latent image formed by exposure is subsequently developed. **1968** G. L. WAKEFIELD *Introd. Photogr.* viii. 146 A printing paper is coated with a sensitive emulsion similar to that on a film but much slower and generally sensitive only to blue light. **1976** M. J. ROSEN *Introd. Photogr.* v. 117/1 Photographic printing papers are manufactured in a variety of contrast grades. **1772** *Patent Specif.* No. 1007 The top *printing roller and iron levers must then be raised. **1890** W. J. GORDON *Foundry* 168 Printing a Cotton Gown... The inner roller revolves in the colour, and distributes it over the printing roller, which in its turn presses against the gliding cloth. **1839** URE *Dict. Arts* 215 The *printing shop is an oblong apartment. **1683** *Printing Tools [see PRINTING-HOUSE]. **1976** *Times* 23 Mar. 1/5 The union asked other *printing unions to follow its example and refuse to take part in joint meetings or federated chapels (office branches) where the institute was represented. **1875** KNIGHT *Dict. Mech.*, **Printing-wheel*, one used in paging or numbering machines or in ticket-printing machines.

'printing, *ppl. a.* [f. PRINT *v.* + -ING².] That prints, in various senses of the vb.

1841 WRIGHT & BAIN *Brit. Pat. 9204* In Sheet 3 we exhibit a side view,..of an electro-magnetic printing telegraph. **1849** *Rep. Brit. Assoc. Adv. Sci.* Notices & Abstr. 133 A colloquial and also a printing telegraph are used. **1856** MRS. BROWNING *Aur. Leigh* v. 805 'Ah', Said I, 'my dear Lord Howe, you shall not speak To a printing woman who has lost her place..compliments, As if she were a woman'. **1875** KNIGHT *Dict. Mech.*, *Printing-telegraph*, an electro-magnetic telegraph which automatically records transmitted messages. The term is, however, generally applied only to those which record in the common alphabet. **1929** *Bell Syst. Techn. Jrnl.* VIII. 267 Commercial telegraph operation..is carried on almost exclusively by two well known methods, manual morse and printing telegraph. **1940** *Chambers's Techn. Dict.* 674/2 *Printing telegraph*, a telegraph system in which the received signals are translated and operate a printing machine, giving a readable message. **1968** *Gloss. Terms Offset Lithogr. Printing* (*B.S.I.*) 28 *Printing pressure*, the pressure applied at the point of contact between two printing surfaces to transfer ink from one surface to the other. **1971** *Gloss. Electrotechnical, Power Terms* (*B.S.I.*) III. iii. 7 *Printing telegraphy*, any method of telegraph operation in which the received signals are automatically recorded as printed characters.

'printing-house. A building in which printing is carried on, a printing-office.

Printing House Square, a small square in London, the former site of the office of the *Times* newspaper; hence *transf.* and in allusive use.

1576–7 *Reg. Privy Council Scot.* II. 583 The prenting hous and necessaris appertening thairto. **1594** T. B. *La Primaud. Fr. Acad.* II. 337 Euery one abideth in his owne office..as.. is to bee seene in the printing house. **1683** MOXON *Mech. Exerc., Printing* ii. ⁋1 They say, Such a One has set up a Printing-House,..thereby they mean he has furnish'd a House with Printing Tools. **1721** AMHERST *Terræ Fil.* No. 11 (1754) 51 Of all the sumptuous edifices which of late years have shot up in Oxford, and adorn'd the habitation of the muses, the new printing-house..strikes me with particular pleasure and veneration. **1856** EMERSON *Eng. Traits, Times* Wks. (Bohn) II. 117 The perfect organization in its printing-house. **1861** B. MORAN *Jrnl.* 3 Dec. (1949) II. 917 *The Times*, is filled with such slatternly abuse of us and ours, that it is fair to conclude that all the Fishwives of Billingsgate have been transferred to Printing House Square. *a* **1910** 'MARK TWAIN' *Autobiogr.* (1924) II. 285 Orion severed his connection with the printing-house in St. Louis. **1938** H. NICOLSON *Diary* 9 Sept. (1966) 358 Colin Coote..says that *The Times* leader urging the Czechs to surrender their fringes was written by Leo Kennedy and merely glanced at by Geoffrey Dawson. He is appalled by the lack of responsible guidance in Printing House Square. **1951** S. JENNETT *Making of Bks.* iii. 48 In some printing houses one of the boxes in the case is set aside for the reception of defective or battered types. **1956** C. COCKBURN *In Time of Trouble* vi. 88 *Is, indeed, anyone, anywhere, truly worthy of* The Times? This was the awfully solemn thought which..sometimes oppressed Printing House Square. **1964** F. BOWERS *Bibliogr. & Textual Crit.* III. i. 64 McKerrow.. once remarked that some contradictory pieces of evidence could be reconciled most easily by the hypothesis that the entire printing-house had adjourned to the nearest pub and got drunk. **1978** *Times* 18 Apr. 17/7 Surely you cannot be so short-sighted in Printing House Square as to..believe..as you grandly state in a recent leading article. **1979** *N.Y. Rev. Bks.* 25 Oct. 44/4 The great printing houses became nodal points in a semi-secret network of cultural communications.

ˈprinting-ink. The ink used in printing, printers' ink; *fig.* printed matter, print.

1676 MARVELL *Mr. Smirke* 9 Such [books] as are writ to take out the Blots of Printing-Inke. **1765** *Dict. Arts & Sc.* s.v. *Ink*, Black printing Ink for engraving on Copper. **1875** URE *Dict. Arts* II. 916 Printing Ink..is essentially a combination of lamp-black..with oil. **1904** *Athenæum* 21 May 657/3 Amid all this flood of printing-ink English students have had to wait till now for any connected and detailed account of this new branch of physics.

Comb. **1823** J. BADCOCK *Dom. Am.* 27 Printing-ink-makers.

ˈprinting-office. An establishment in which the printing of books, newspapers, etc. is carried on.

1733 B. FRANKLIN *Poor Richard* (title-page), Printed and sold by B. Franklin, at the New Printing-Office. **1802** *Monthly Mag.* XIV. 347/2 This portrait is done by the letter-engraver who executed in wood for the printing-office of Fust. **1827** *Oxford Guide* 79 The Clarendon Printing Office. **1864** A. MCKAY *Hist. Kilmarnock* 159 His printing-office, in which the poems of Burns were first put into type.

ˈprinting-press. An instrument or machine for printing on paper, etc., from types, blocks, or plates: = PRESS *sb.*[1] 14; sometimes restricted to a hand-press, as distinguished from a *printing-machine*, worked by machinery, with cylinders.

1588 [see PRESS *sb.*[1] 14]. **1655** CULPEPPER *Riverius* Advt., At his Shop at the sign of the Printing-Press in Cornhil, neer the Exchange. **1714** MANDEVILLE *Fab. Bees* (1725) I. 258 Would you..break down the Printing-Presses, melt the Founds, and burn all the Books in the Island? **1861** MUSGRAVE *By-roads* 127 It is only because chroniclers were scarce, and printing-presses unknown, in those times.

attrib. **1683** MOXON *Mech. Exerc.*, *Printing* xi. ¶1 The Worms for Printing-Press Spindles.

printiz, obs. form of PRENTICE.

printless (ˈprɪntlɪs), *a.* (*adv.*) [See -LESS.]

1. Making or leaving no print or trace.

1610 SHAKS. *Temp.* v. i. 34 Ye, that on the sands with printlesse foote Doe chase the ebbing-Neptune, and doe flie him When he comes backe. **1634** MILTON *Comus* 897 Whilst from off the waters fleet Thus I set my printless feet O're the Cowslips Velvet head. **1855** O. W. HOLMES *Poems* 79, I heard the spirits' printless tread, And voices not of earthly sound.

2. That has received, or that retains, no print.

a **1797** MARY WOLLSTONECR. *Posth. Wks.* (1798) IV. 160 Pacing over the printless grass. **1809** SYD. SMITH *Serm.* II. 333 We leave his infant body to the winds, and engrave upon his printless heart, in the first morning of life the feeling of pain. **1874** B. TAYLOR *Prophet* II. iv, Wandering birds.. Strike their way across the printless air.

B. as *adv.* Without leaving, or without receiving, a print.

1792 WOLCOTT (P. Pindar) *Odes to Kien Long* III. vii, Let the widow's and the orphan's tear Fall printless on thy heart as on a stone. **1818** MILMAN *Samor* 198 The moss springs printless up beneath her feet.

ˈprint-out. [f. vbl. phr. *to print out* (PRINT *v.* 15 c, 6 b).] **1.** *Photogr.* Used *attrib.*, = *printing out* (PRINTING *vbl. sb.* c).

1899 P. N. HASLUCK *Bk. Photogr.* 184/1 Something may be done in the development of print-out papers. **1929** *Proc. 7th Internat. Congr. Photogr. 1928* 23 (*heading*) Parallelism between photo-electric conductivity effects and direct print-out effects. **1930** O. WHEELER *Photogr. Printing Processes* iii. 28 While daylight is still commonly employed for exposure in print-out processes, artificial light..is often used commercially. **1939** MACK & MARTIN *Photogr. Process* v. 175 If an emulsion receives a very great exposure, the halide is reduced directly by the light without the aid of a developer. This print-out effect was the only means of producing a photograph in the very earliest days of photography. **1965** *Photogr. Jrnl.* CV. 285/2 A special kind of print-out paper has been in use for data recording for some years. **1973** W. THOMAS *SPSE Handbk. Photogr. Sci. & Engin.* vi. 407 Sufficient exposure of an emulsion to light causes visible darkening without development (a print-out image).

2. (A sheet or strip of) printed matter produced by a computer or other automatic apparatus; the production of such matter. Also *fig.*

1953 *IRE Trans. Instrumentation* June 68 An hour's operation includes some 40 print-outs of the complete memory. **1957** *Ibid.* Sept. 193/2 The reading system consists of a film reader, control and decoding section, and print-out equipment. *Ibid.* 194/1 A stepping switch is caused to step to the next position at the end of each character print-out. **1961** *Aeroplane* CI. 573/2 In addition to the automatic print-out unit for the recording of positional information, an optional addition to the data presentation unit is a computer to convert the slant range and elevation co-ordinates into ground range and height data. **1966** 'C. E. MAINE' *B.E.A.S.T.* vi. 79 Synøve and..Wetherby..were standing by one of the print-out machines, reading a long sheet of paper as it emerged. **1969** *New Scientist* 1 May 238/2 Everyone should be entitled to a print-out of the information in the data bank in regard to him. **1971** K. GOTTSCHALK in B. de Ferranti *Living with Computer* iv. 31 The drafting and print-out of leases, wills and forms used in lawyers' offices to eliminate repetitive work. **1974** *Ellery Queen's Mystery Mag.* Nov. 148/1 We could use computers at this end too, to run through possible letter combinations and produce the necessary printouts almost at once. **1979** M. BABSON *Twelve Deaths of Christmas* xvii. 87 Sod your computers, *I'm* getting the printout from the marrow of my bones.

ˈprint-ˌseller. A person who sells prints (PRINT *sb.* 12) or engravings.

1710 *Lond. Gaz.* No. 4685/4 Sold by C. Browne, Print and Map-Seller. **1818** COBBETT *Pol. Reg.* XXXIII. 688 He connived at a print-seller's carrying away a great many valuable prints. **1857** RUSKIN *Elem. Drawing* ii. 139 Any printsellers who have folios..of old drawings, or facsimiles of them.

ˈprint-shop. **1.** A print-seller's shop.

a **1697** AUBREY *Lives* (1898) I. 407 To take viewes, land-skapes, buildings, etc...which wee see now at the print shopps. **1778** *English Mag.* Feb. 59/1 Notwithstanding the many satirical exhibitions at the print-shops, of grown gentle-men learning to dance..there are many arguments that may be used in defence of this genteel exercise. **1780** T. DAVIES *Garrick* II. xlii. 186 An engraving of her..is still to be seen in the print-shops. **1859** JEPHSON *Brittany* xix. 310 Circular frames, which revolved after the manner of those in the print-shops. **1897** A. BEARDSLEY *Let.* 13 Apr. (1970) 302 The book and print shops [in Paris] are an evergreen joy to me.

2. *U.S.* A printing-office or printery.

1921 *Amer. Printer* 5 Nov. (*heading*) Visit to an old Oxford printshop. **1961** R. L. DUNCAN *Voice of Strangers* IV. iii. 246 He went into the print shop, where Fletcher had just finished cleaning the press. **1970** *Eng. Stud.* LI. 164 His quarrel with Sir John Cheke.., the exegetic controversy with Edward Lee, the question of Henry VIII's divorce were all reflected in the books pouring out of Basle's printshops. **1977** C. MCCARRY *Secret Lovers* xiii. 170 Each afternoon he sent Joëlle to collect the typescript from the printer; she took it back to the print shop every morning.

print-through (ˈprɪntθruː). Also **print through.** [f. vbl. phr. *to print through.*] **1.** The accidental transfer of recorded signals to adjacent layers in a reel of magnetic tape. Freq. *attrib.*

1956 R. E. B. HICKMAN *Magn. Recording Handbk.* ii. 24 The print-through is..dependent upon the output level of the original signal. **1958** H. G. M. SPRATT *Magn. Tape Recording* iii. 110 The ratio of the level of the original signal to that of the last echo before and the first echo after that signal is termed the print-through or transfer ratio. **1962** *Times* 5 July 15/7 Dangers to tape..arise from prolonged storage without rewinding, which can cause 'print-through' (detectable as pre-echo on some discs). **1975** *Hi-Fi Answers* Feb. 76/2 To be sure no print through is occurring it would be a good idea if you were to rewind each tape in your collection at least once in six months to redistribute the tape in the reel and minimise any print through effect.

2. *Printing.* (See quot. 1961.)

1961 R. F. BOWLES *Printing Ink Manual* xi. 349 Another factor which has a marked effect on the quality of the print is the degree of 'print through' which is visible. 'Print through' is the degree to which the print is visible on the reverse side of the sheet, and is the combination of 'show-through' and 'strike-through'. **1973** L. C. YOUNG *Materials in Printing Processes* ix. 121 When the printing on one side of a paper can be seen through the paper, this print-through may either be due to show-through or strike-through... Normally the vehicle only penetrates a short distance into the sheet, but even this will have the effect of reducing the printing opacity, so making print-through more likely.

ˈprint-work. [f. PRINT *sb.* + WORK *sb.*]

1. (Now usually *printworks*, often const. as *sing.*) A factory in which cotton fabrics are printed.

1835 URE *Philos. Manuf.* 400 Employed in the drying-room of a calico print-work. **1844** G. DODD *Textile Manuf.* ii. 54 A large print-work..consists of several distinct departments, such as the mechanical department, the chemical department, the artistic or designing department, the printing department, &c. **1885** *Manch. Exam.* 10 Sept. 5/1 Manager of the calico printworks.

2. Lettering imitating printed characters. *rare.*

1824 MISS MITFORD *Village* Ser. I. 68 (*Lucy*) But never was MS. so illegible..as the print-work of that sampler.

printyce, obs. form of PRENTICE.

priodont (ˈpraɪədɒnt), *a.* *Zool.* [f. mod.L. *Priodōn*, *-ont-em* (Cuvier), generic name, f. Gr. πρί-ειν to saw + ὀδούς, ὀδοντ- a tooth, later altered to *Prionodon*, f. πρίων, πριον- a saw, whence PRIONODONT.] Saw-toothed. **a.** Belonging to the genus *Priodon* (*Priodontes*, *Prionodon*), or the subfamily *Prionodontinæ*, of armadillos (the kabalassous), characterized by very numerous teeth set closely like the teeth of a saw. **b.** Applied to a form of the mandibles in stag-beetles, having the projections or teeth small and closely set.

1854 OWEN *Skel. & Teeth* in *Orr's Circ. Sc.* I. *Org. Nat.* 278 The priodont armadillo..has ninety-eight teeth. **1883** *Athenæum* 29 Dec. 870/3 Four very distinct phases of development in their mandibles, which the author proposed to term 'priodont', 'amphiodont', 'mesodont', and 'telodont'. **1899** *Cambr. Nat. Hist.* VI. 193 In each species [of *Lucanidæ* (stag-beetles)] these variations [of the mandibles] fall..into distinct states, so that entomologists describe them as 'forms', the largest developments being called teleodont, the smallest priodont.

† **priol,** obs. form of PAIR-ROYAL.

1776 MRS. HARRIS in *Priv. Lett. Ld. Malmesbury* (1870) I. 341 If the highest has a priol of aces all the company give five guineas each.

‖ **prion** (ˈpraɪən). *Ornith.* [mod.L. (Comte B. G. E. de la V. Lacépède *Tableaux Méthodiques des Mammifères et des Oiseaux* (1799) 14), a. Gr. πρίων a saw.] A small saw-billed petrel belonging to the genus once so called, now included in the genus *Pachyptila* of the family Procellariidæ and found in southern seas.

1848 J. GOULD *Birds Austral.* VII. 54 (*heading*) Dove-like Prion. **1862** *Proc. Zool. Soc.* 125 In form and colouring it is precisely similar to the other *Priones.* **1901** A. J. CAMPBELL *Nests & Eggs Austral. Birds* II. 917 Mr Travers frequently found these Prions caught in the branches of scrubby trees. **1937** *Discovery* May 141/2 The prion is a ghost. A fluttering thing of pale grey-blue and white. **1959** *New Biol.* XXIX. 112 Some small bird species such as the prions owe their survival to the fact that they are only active at night, thereby avoiding the skuas' attack. **1972** K. SIMPSON *Birds in Bass Strait* 71/2 The Dove or Antarctic Prion is perhaps one of the most numerous of all southern seabirds.

prionodont (praɪˈɒnəʊdɒnt), *a.* (*sb.*) *Zool.* [f. mod.L. *Prionodon*, or f. Gr. πρίων, πριον- a saw + ὀδούς a tooth: see PRIODONT.] Having teeth serrated or resembling the teeth of a saw.

a. Of an armadillo: = PRIODONT a; as *sb.* a prionodont armadillo, a kabalassou. **b.** Of a civet-cat: Belonging to the genus *Prionodon* or subfamily *Prionodontinæ* (the linsangs), having only one tubercular molar on each side in each jaw; as *sb.* a prionodont civet-cat, a linsang. **c.** Transversely plicated, as the hinge of the bivalve shells of the group *Prionodesmacea*.

1890 in *Cent. Dict.*

prior (ˈpraɪə(r)), *sb.* Forms: 1–3 **prior**, 4–6 **priour**, **-e**, **pryour**, (5 **priowr**, **pryo(u)r**, **pryowre**, **prier**), 6– **prior.** [Late OE. *prior*, a. L. *prior*, *-ōr-em* former, superior (see next), in med.L. as sb. the superior or chief officer of a society, spec. a prior; in ME. reinforced by OF. *priur* (12th c. in Hatz.-Darm.), *priour* (mod.F. *prieur*), whence the ME. form *priour*, etc. In sense 2 b ad. It. *priore.*]

1. A superior officer of a religious house or order.

a. In an abbey, the officer next under the abbot, appointed by him to exercise certain authority, maintain discipline, and preside over the monastery in his absence (***prior claustral***); in a smaller or daughter monastery the resident superior (***prior conventual***). In monastic cathedrals, in which the Bishop took the place of Abbot, the Prior was the actual working head of the abbey. In some large foreign abbeys, e.g. Cluny and Fécamp, there were several priors, the chief of whom was called ***Grand Prior***. **b.** The superior or head of a house of Canons Regular (Augustinians, Arroasians, and originally Premonstratensians). **c.** Also the superior of a house of Friars.

Grand Prior, the commander of a priory of the Knights of St. John of Jerusalem, or of Malta.

1093 *Charter of Wulfstan* in Thorpe *Dipl. Angl. Aev. Sax.* (1865) 445 Hine God ȝeferade þæt he wearð prior & fæder þæs bufan cweðenan mynstres. *a* **1123** *O.E. Chron.* an. 1107 Ernulf þe ær wæs prior on Cantwarbyrig. *a* **1131** *Ibid.* an. 1129 þa priores, muneces and canonias þa wæron on ealle þa cellas on Engla land. *c* **1290** *S. Eng. Leg.* I. 219/642 And þe prior with procession to þe ȝate comez. *c* **1330** R. BRUNNE *Chron. Wace* 7065 He asked leue atte priour To speke wyþ Constant. *c* **1380** WYCLIF *Sel. Wks.* III. 350 Þer [friars] ordre lettiþ þes, but ȝif þei han þer priours leeve. **1455** *Cal. Anc. Rec. Dublin* (1889) I. 287 The Priowrys of the fowre Orderys of Freyerys. *c* **1475** *Pict. Voc.* in Wr.-Wülcker 780/20 *Hic prior, -ris*, a prier. **1533** MORE *Confut. Tindale* II. 532 In the same house whereof I was master and pryour. **1570–6** LAMBARDE *Peramb. Kent* (1826) 270 Laurence his successor, brought Monks into the house, the head whereof was called a Prior, which woorde..was in deede but the name of a seconde officer, bicause the Bishop himselfe was accompted the very Abbat. **1703** *Lond. Gaz.* No. 3918/1 The Grand Prior is at present with the Duke of Vendosme, his Brother. **1706** PHILLIPS, *Priors Aliens*, were certain Priors born in France, that had the Government of Monasteries founded for outlandish Men in England. **1706** tr. *Dupin's Eccl. Hist. 16th C.* II. IV. xxi. 379 The general Chapters, or the Visitors of the same Orders, shall appoint Priors-claustral, or Sub-Priors, in the Priories in which there is a Convent, to exercise Corrections and Spiritual Government. **1727–41** CHAMBERS *Cycl.* s.v., In the monastery of St. Denys, there were anciently five priors; the first whereof was called the grand prior... There are also grand priors in the military orders. **1901** J. T. FOWLER in *Durham Acc. Rolls* (Surtees) III. Introd. 3 In Durham, as in Winchester, Ely, and other monastic Cathedrals, the Bishop was the honorary and titular head, while the true head of the house was the Prior.

2. a. In foreign countries, the title of the elected head of a guild of merchants or craftsmen. **b.** The title of a chief magistrate in some of the former Italian republics, e.g. Florence: cf. PRIORATE 1 b. *Obs.* exc. *Hist.*

1604 *Merch. New-Royall Exchange* B ij b, The Merchants [at Rouen]..shall chuse out of the said number three officers, viz. A Prior and two Consulls, to remaine in their authoritie for one yeare. *c* **1618** MORYSON *Itin.* IV. vi. (1903) 93 Still the cittizens had theire wonted Magistrate called Gonfaloniere, and theire Priour of Justice. **1748** *Earthquake of Peru* i. 60 The Court of Commerce is the Consulship, where a Prior and two Consuls preside. [**1832** tr. *Sismondi's Ital. Rep.* x. 224 His son Cosmo, born in 1389, was priore in 1416.] **1878–83** VILLARI *Life & Times Machiavelli* (1898) II. xiv. 398 The working-classes placed the Priors of the Guilds at the head of the Government.

† **3.** A superior. (After L. *prior* in *Vulg.* John i. 15.)

c **1380** WYCLIF *Serm.* Sel. Wks. I. 75 He is to come after Joon, al if he be Joonis pryour. Ffor he was not made bifore Ioon in tyme..for Ioon spekiþ of forþerhede of manhede of Crist bifore Ioon in grace, and also in worþynes. *Ibid.* 77 After me is to comen a man, þe whiche is made bifore me, for he was anoon my priour [cf. *Vulg.* John i. 15 quia prior me erat].

†**4.** The first or greatest; the chief. *Obs.*

1644 BULWER *Chiron.* 127 Plato, the Prior of all ancient Philosophers.

5. *Commerce.* The head of a firm. Now *rare.*

1853 MILLHOUSE *Dizion. Ingl.-Ital., Prior* (com.), socio principale, direttore. **1865** (Jan. 2) *Circular of Messrs. A. Gibbs & Sons,* We beg leave to inform you that we have this day admitted as partner in our House Mr. George Louis Monck Gibbs, nephew of our prior. **1908** *Morning Post* 1 Jan., Messrs. Antony Gibbs and Sons announce that they have admitted into partnership the Hon. Gerald Gibbs, son of their prior, Lord Aldenham.

Hence **'prioracy**, the office of prior: = PRIORATE 1; **'prioral** *a.*, of or pertaining to a prior.

1895 E. MARG. THOMPSON *Hist. Somerset Carthusians* 71 St. Hugh's immediate successor in the prioracy was Bovo. **1882** *Athenæum* 30 Sept. 427/3 The Abbot of Bath, who thereto had at once erected a prioral cell.

prior ('praɪə(r)), *a.* (*adv.*) [a. L. *prior* former, earlier, elder, anterior, superior, more important, f. OL. prep. *pri* before.] **A.** *adj.* Preceding (in time or order); earlier, former, anterior, antecedent.

1714 R. FIDDES *Pract. Disc.* ii. 38 Whether we become partakers of it by a prior or an after-consent. **1754** EDWARDS *Freed. Will* II. ii. (1762) 39 That is what is meant by a Thing's being prior in the Order of Nature, that it is some Way the Cause or Reason of the Thing, with Respect to which it is said to be prior. **1765** BLACKSTONE *Comm.* I. xv. 436 The first of these legal disabilities is a prior marriage. **1791** WASHINGTON *Let. Writ.* 1892 XII. 17 The necessity of a prior attention to those duties. **1856** MISS MULOCK *J. Halifax* xi, I was fully acquainted with all the prior history of her inmates. **1865** H. PHILLIPS *Amer. Paper Curr.* II. 12 The meeting in the prior year was under different circumstances.

b. Const. *to.*

1714 R. FIDDES *Pract. Disc.* ii. 37 The sin is prior to and ..independent of the action. **1739** HUME *Hum. Nat.* I. ii. (1874) I. 316 Our simple impressions are prior to their correspondent ideas. **1774** J. BRYANT *Mythol.* II. 263 These rites are said to have been..far prior to the foundation of Rome. **1907** H. JONES in *Hibbert Jrnl.* July 747 They come in obedience to a necessity prior to their own will.

c. *Statistics.* Applied to the result of a calculation made in ignorance of, or previously to, some observation(s); ***prior probability***, the probability that a hypothesis is true calculated without reference to certain relevant observations. Opp. POSTERIOR *a.* 1 b.

1921, etc. [see POSTERIOR *a.* 1 b]. **1977** *Sci. Amer.* May 126/3 With this valuable extra information, which statisticians call a 'prior distribution,' it is possible to construct a superior estimate of each player's true batting ability.

d. ***prior charge***, in *Finance*: see quots. 1968, 1974; also (with hyphens) as *attrib. phr.*

1877 *Encycl. Brit.* VII. 15/1 The Companies Clauses Act, 1863, part iii., which makes debenture stock a prior charge on the undertaking, and gives the interest thereon priority of payment over all dividends or interest on any shares or stock of the company. **1930** *Economist* 22 Mar. 653/1 Foreign bonds, industrial prior-charge stocks and even industrial preference shares shared in the general tendency, though to a less conspicuous extent. *Ibid.* 29 Mar. 695/2 Gilt-edged stocks and well-secured industrial debentures and prior charges. **1968** JOHANNSEN & ROBERTSON *Managem. Gloss.* 105 *Prior charges*, all types of debentures, preference shares and other stocks ranking for payment of interest or dividend in precedence to the ordinary shares. **1974** *Terminol. Managem. & Financial Accountancy* (Inst. Cost & Managem. Accountants) 62 *Prior charge capital*, those classes of share and loan capital, the holders of which have a claim on the profits and assets of a business before the ordinary shareholders.

B. as *adv.* with *to*: Previously to, before.

1736 BUTLER *Anal.* Introd., Wks. 1874 I. 6 There is no presumption against this prior to the proof of it. **1766** MRS. S. PENNINGTON *Lett.* I. 127 It existed prior to the formation of these bodies. **1826** G. S. FABER *Diffic. Romanism* (1853) 116 Prior to the year 1215, a man..might be perfectly orthodox, who denied Transubstantiation, if he held Consubstantiation. **1875** SCRIVENER *Lect. Text N. Test.* 6 [It] seems, prior to experience, very improbable.

priorate ('praɪərət). [ad. late L. *priōrāt-us* (Tertull.) priority, preference, in med.L. the office of prior, a priory, f. *prior* PRIOR *a.*: see -ATE[1].]

1. The office and dignity of a prior; also, the term of office of a prior: **a.** of an ecclesiastical prior or prioress.

c **1400** *Apol. Loll.* 51 Wat euer clerk takiþ priorate, religioun, bischophed, or dignite of þe kirk. **1737** M. JOHNSON in *Bibl. Topogr. Brit.* (1790) III. 68 Sir John Weston, in whose priorate this exchange was made or confirmed. **1775** WARTON *Hist. Eng. Poetry* xxiv. II. 112 Benoit's successour in the priorate of saint Genevieve was not equally attentive to the discipline and piety of his monks. **1854** MILMAN *Lat. Chr.* III. 363 That ascending ladder of ecclesiastical honours, the priorate, the abbacy, the bishopric, the metropolitanate. **1925** C. S. DURRANT *Link betw. Flemish Mystics & Eng. Martyrs* I. x. 150 The Priorate of Mother Salome has ever been looked back to as a time when [etc.].

b. The dignity of prior in the Florentine republic: see PRIOR *sb.* 2 b.

1818 COLERIDGE in *Lit. Rem.* (1836) I. 86 Members of this family [the Pulci] were five times elected to the Priorate, one of the highest honours of the republic. **1872** LOWELL *Dante* Prose Wks. 1890 IV. 130 Just before his assumption of the priorate, however, a new complication had arisen. **1874** M. CREIGHTON *Hist. Ess.* i. (1902) 16 This priorate Dante calls the source of all his woes.

2. A priory; also, the inmates as a community.

1749 *Hist. Windsor* viii. 107 The Manour, or Priorate of Munclane, in the County of Hereford..with all and singular its appurtenances. **1762** tr. *Busching's Syst. Geog.* IV. 264 Bethleem, a priorate, or college of regular canons of the order of St. Augustine. **1829** SOUTHEY in *Q. Rev.* XLI. 211 An address from the priorate of the order of Malta to the prince of Brazil, spoken by one of their *Commendadores.* **1844** S. R. MAITLAND *Dark Ages* 323 On his return he found that his uncle was dead, and that the see of Frisingen, as well as his own priorate, was filled by a successor.

priore, obs. variant of PRIORY.

prioress ('praɪərɪs). [ME. a. OF. *prioresse, prieuresse* (13th c. in Godef.) = med.L. *priōrissa* (*c* 1135 in Abelard): see PRIOR *sb.* and -ESS[1].] A nun holding a position under an abbess similar to a claustral prior; also, one governing her own house like a conventual prior: see PRIOR *sb.* 1.

c **1290** *St. Edmund* 161 in *S. Eng. Leg.* I. 436 Boþe his sustren..Nounnes he made þere..þe eldore was sethþe prioresse of þe lauedies ech-on. **1303** R. BRUNNE *Handl. Synne* 7808 Þyr com to hym, for hys godenesse, A nunne, y wene a pryores. *c* **1386** CHAUCER *Prol.* 118 Ther was..a Nonne a Prioresse That of hir smylyng was ful symple and coy. *c* **1440** *Promp. Parv.* 413/2 Pryowresse, *priorissa.* **1535** in *Lett. Suppress. Monasteries* (Camden) 91 The two prioresses wolde not confesse this,..nor none of the nunnes. **1603** SHAKS. *Meas. for M.* I. iv. 11 When you haue vowd, you must not speake with men, But in the presence of the Prioresse. **1759** JOHNSON *Rasselas* xlix, [She] wished only to fill it with pious maidens, and to be made prioress of the order. **1808** SCOTT *Marmion* II. xix, Tynemouth's haughty Prioress. **1861** CRAIK *Hist. Eng. Lit.* I. 301 With how genuine a courtesy..he first addresses himself to the modest Clerk, and the gentle Lady Prioress, and the Knight.

†**'prioressy.** *Sc. Obs.* [f. prec. + -Y.] A nunnery or convent presided over by a prioress.

1575 in McCrie *Life A. Melville* (1819) I. 150 *note*, His hienes chalmerlan and factor to the said priorissie of the Senis. **1633** *Sc. Acts Chas. I* (1817) V. 164/1 It is fund.. That the richt of superioritie Off all lands..perteining to quhatsumever abbacies pryories pryoressis [etc.] pertenis to his Majestie.

†**'priorhede.** *Obs. rare*$^{-1}$. [f. PRIOR *sb.* + *-hede*, -HEAD.] Priorship; priorate.

c **1425** *Found. St. Bartholomew's* (E.E.T.S.) 14 Rayer optenynge cure and office of the priorhede.

priori, *a.*: see *high priori* (HIGH *a.* 17 g).

1762 *Gentl. Mag.* 546 Most of you take the priori highroad. **1823** J. GILLIES *Aristotle's Rhet.* II. 79 The schoolmen audaciously followed the priori road.

prioric (praɪ'ɒrɪk), *a. rare.* [f. A PRIORI + -IC.] Of *a priori* character.

1895 *Athenæum* 7 Dec. 796/1 If we consider that the *posterius* of one inference becomes the *prius* of the next, so that a conclusion may be prioric though drawn from premises obtained posteriorically, the prioric and posterioric seem to have no connexion with Kant's *à priori, à posteriori. Ibid.* [see POSTERIORIC].

priorily, erron. var. of PRIORLY *adv.*

prio'ristic, *a.* [f. PRIOR *a.* + -ISTIC.] Of or belonging to Aristotle's *Prior Analytics*: opposed to POSTERIORISTIC. Hence **prio'ristically** *adv.*

c **1600** *Timon* IV. iii. (Shaks. Soc.) 67 Thou art moved formally, prioristically in the thing considered, not posterioristically in the manner of considering. **1890** *Cent. Dict.*, Prioristic. **1902** *Baldwin's Dict. Philos. & Psych.* II. 740/1 *Prioristic dictum de omni* and *Prioristic universal*: universal predication as defined by Aristotle at the end of the first chapter of the first book of the *Prior Analytics*:..We say that anything, P, is predicated universally (*dictum de omni*) when nothing can be subsumed under the subject of which P is not intended to be predicated.

priorite ('praɪəraɪt). *Min.* [ad. G. *priorit* (W. C. Brögger 1906, in *Skr. udgivne af Vidensk.-Selsk. i Christiania* (*Mat.-Nat. Kl.*) I. VI. 111), f. the name of G. T. *Prior* (1862–1936), British mineralogist: see -ITE[1].] A mixed oxide, chiefly of niobium, titanium, and yttrium, with traces of several other elements, which occurs as black or dark brown orthorhombic crystals.

1907 *Jrnl. Chem. Soc.* XCII. II. 886 Another mineral of this series is one from Swaziland, South Africa, analysed by G. T. Prior..; for this, the name *priorite* is proposed. Blomstrandine and priorite are isomorphous and are respectively dimorphous with polycrase and euxenite. **1944** C. PALACHE et al. *Dana's Syst. Min.* (ed. 7) I. 796 Priorite was found originally at Urstad on the island of Hitterö in southwest Norway. **1966** *Amer. Mineralogist* LI. 156 Only two well-established Ce-Y rare-earth mineral series are known for which names have been assigned to the end members: 3. aeschynite-priorite series [;] 4. britholite-abukumalite series. **1968** I. KOSTOV *Mineral.* 254 Euxenite group... The chief members of the group are euxenite.., priorite $((Y, Th)(Nb, Ti)_2O_6)$.

prioritize (praɪ'ɒrɪtaɪz), *v.* orig. *U.S.* [f. PRIORITY + -IZE.] **a.** *trans.* To designate as worthy of prior attention, to give priority to (in the sense of PRIORITY 2). **b.** *trans.* To determine the order in which (items) are to be dealt with, to establish priorities for (a set of items). Also *absol.*

A word that at present sits uneasily in the language.— R.W.B.

1973 T. H. WHITE *Making of President 1972* xii. 325 The storefront operators in the counties that Malek had 'prioritized' had identified independents, wavering Democrats and 'don't knows'. **1975** R. BURNS *Alvarez Jrnl.* 47 But in the meantime I've got to prioritize the operations, and the priority standard is the probability of conviction. **1977** *Time* 14 Mar. 28/2 From then on toward midnight, he tries, in his own words, 'to prioritize'. **1977** *Daily Colonist* (Victoria, B.C.) 15 May 33/5 A special committee had been struck..to prioritize their recommendations and to report. **1981** *Times* 3 Feb. 13/6 In the Nato headquarters..we are well used to prioritizing our targets.

Hence **pri,oriti'zation; pri'oritized, pri'oritizing** *ppl. adjs.*

1977 *Financial Times* 24 Dec. 3/6 It has two meanings, depending on whether one is doing the prioritization, or having it thrust upon one. **1977** *Time* 14 Mar. 28/2 Prioritizing takes him into the Oval Office to talk each day with the President and to drop in on..Vice President Mondale. **1978** *Verbatim* Feb. 1/2 A teacher in Mill Valley has drawn up a 'prioritized list of all components of the school program'.

priority (praɪ'ɒrɪtɪ). Also 5 priorte. [ME. a. F. *priorité* (14th c., Hatz.-Darm.), ad. med.L. *priōritās*, f. L. *prior*, *-ōrem*: see PRIOR *a.* and -ITY.]

1. a. The condition or quality of being earlier or previous in time, or of preceding something else.

1387–8 T. USK *Test. Love* III. iv. (Skeat) I. 166 In diuers times, and in diuers places temporel, without posteriorite or priorite. **1432–50** tr. *Higden* (Rolls) VII. 273 The seetes of Cawnterbery and of Yorke not to be subiecte in eny wise to other after the constitucion of Gregory, excepte that the oon is moore then that other for the priorite of tyme. **1597** HOOKER *Eccl. Pol.* v. lxxxi. §16 The preeminence of prioritie in birth. **1662** STILLINGFL. *Orig. Sacr.* III. ii. §7 Though there might bee some priority in order of causes between them, yet there was none in order of time or duration. **1879** H. GEORGE *Progr. & Pov.* VII. i. (1881) 309 No priority of appropriation can give a right which will bar these equal rights of others.

b. *Taxonomy.* The claim of the first validly published Latin name to be taken as the correct one for any given organism.

1842 *Rep. Brit. Assoc. Adv. Sci.* 109 We have no hesitation in adopting as our fundamental maxim, the 'law of priority', viz... The name originally given by the founder of a group or the describer of a species should be permanently retained. **1928** D. B. SWINGLE *Textbk. Systematic Bot.* vii. 68 By agreement botanists do not go back of Linnaeus' 'Species Plantarum' (1753) to establish priority in the publication of names. **1953** E. MAYR et al. *Methods & Princ. Systematic Zool.* xi. 213 It would be unfair..to blame all name changes on the law of priority. **1963** DAVIS & HEYWOOD *Princ. Angiosperm Taxon.* viii. 291 Enough information should be given to indicate why a name has not been adopted if it appears to have priority over the accepted name.

2. Precedence in order, rank, or dignity. Also, the right to precede others or to receive attention, supplies, etc., before others. Hence *transf.*, an interest having a prior claim to consideration; often in *pl.* or preceded by a qualifying word, as *first, high, top priority.*

c **1400** *Cursor M.* 27562 (Cott. Galba) Pride..riueliest.. For werldes hap,..Erthly honowre, or priorte, Welth, or lordschip, or pouste. *c* **1440** *Alphabet of Tales* 248 Þer it is semand þat þe fathur suffer þe son to hafe a prioritie. **1534–1704** [see POSTERIORITY 2]. **1606** SHAKS. *Tr. & Cr.* I. iii. 86 The Heauens themselues, the Planets, and this Center, Obserue degree, priority, and place. **1803** STUART in Gurw. *Wellington's Desp.* (1837) II. 190 *note*, The priority of his rank to that of Major General Wellesley would render his presence to the northward of the Kistna incompatible with a due exercise of the powers..delegated to the latter officer. **1861** *Sat. Rev.* 14 Dec. 608 The courtesy of the American dockyard officers would probably grant to a British man-of-war priority over several merchantmen which were in need of similar accommodation. **1917** *Times* 10 Mar. 6/4 The Minister of Munitions..has issued an important Order under the Defence of the Realm Act as to priority of war work... During the last 12 months the Ministry of Munitions has been administering a scheme which ensured for war work and for work of national importance priority over all other work in regard to labour and materials. **1922** *Encycl. Brit.* XXXII. 147/1 The Priorities Committee undertook whenever necessary to administer priorities in the production of all raw materials and finished products. *Ibid.* 835/1 The labour needs of employers in war industries were graded as entitled to 'Super-Priority', 'First' or 'Second Class Priority', or as not deserving special treatment. **1940** *Economist* 18 May 893/1 How far can we tap reserves of skill for war work by the full mobilisation of this class of man power and its allocation, according to an infrangible schedule of priorities, exclusively to war and export manufacture? *Ibid.* 24 Aug. 236/2 There was no priority at all until June of this year, and since then there has only been a general Priority of Production Direction which went no further than to notify to industry two short lists of very broad categories of munitions. **1941** *New Statesman* 26 Apr. 429/2 First priority is being given to dairy cattle. **1944** *Daily Tel.* 23 Sept. 2/2 The obvious remedy for that would be to make civil aviation priority No. 1 at the Ministry. **1948** 'N. SHUTE' *No Highway* ii. 49, I think this trip to Canada is top priority of anything that's going on at Farnborough today. **1949** G. COTTERELL *Randle in Springtime* IV. iii. 213 I'm going into furnishing, see. Anything you've got to have dockets and priorities for. Lino, stair carpets. **1958** *Listener* 11 Sept. 368/1 The Minister had to explain that their area did not have early priority. **1960** M. SPARK *Ballad of Peckham Rye* iii. 42 She came up with an estimate and said 'priority'... I said, 'Excuse me, Miss Coverdale, but I've got two priorities already.' **1968** *Highway Code* 37 (*caption*) Give priority to vehicles from opposite direction. **1969** *Morning Star* 29 Jan. 1/1 Improvements..are much less than could be achieved if the Government got its priorities right. **1970** G. F. NEWMAN *Sir, You Bastard* iv. 122 There was a priority on at the Yard, all detectives were being called back. **1972** A. ULAM *Fall of Amer. Univ.* v. 211 He would couple this frankness with a plea to the young not to give up, to work within the system, for with reordered priorities this country might still be saved and might even be worth saving. **1977** *Listener* 26 May 682/2 There will be questions of social priorities involved.

3. *Law.* †**a.** See quot. 1607. *Obs.* **b.** A precedence among claims, or a preference in order of payment.

1523 FITZHERB. *Surv.* 23 b, The lorde that the tenaunt holdeth of by priorite shall haue the warde of the body, be it heyre male or heyre female. **1607** COWELL *Interpr.* s.v. *Posteriority*, A man holding lands or tenements of two lords, holdeth of his auncienter Lord by prioritie, and of his later Lord by posterioritie. **1766** BLACKSTONE *Comm.* II. xxxii. 511 In payment of debts he must observe the rules of priority; otherwise, on deficiency of assets, if he pays those of a lower degree first, he must answer those of a higher out of his own estate. **1869** *Act 32 & 33 Vict.* c. 46 §1 In the administration of the estate of every person who shall die.. after [1 Jan. 1870] no debt or liability..shall be entitled to any priority or preference by reason merely that the same is secured by or arises under a bond, deed, or other instrument under seal, or is otherwise made or constituted a specialty debt. **1884** SIR J. PEARSON in *Law Rep. 28 Ch. Div.* 178 At that time the law of Ireland gave judgment creditors priority over simple contract creditors.

4. = 'Apriority' (*Cent. Dict.*).

5. *attrib.*, passing into *adj.*: **priority-bond** = preference bond (PREFERENCE 8).

1849 DARWIN in *Life & Lett.* (1887) I. 368 If I, a priority man called a species C. D. **1884** *Pall Mall G.* 7 Apr. 5/1 New issues of Turkish Tobacco and Priority bonds, of Spanish, and even of Russian bonds. **1897** *Westm. Gaz.* 29 Nov. 2/2 [He] insisted on the importance and significance of the 'priority pledge', which he asserts is always given by Liberal candidates. **1917** *Times* 10 Mar. 6/4 (*heading*) National work. Important priority scheme. **1922** *Encycl. Brit.* XXX. 818/2 Trades specified in a priority list drawn up with reference to the relative urgency of the industrial requirements of the country. **1934** T. E. LAWRENCE *Let.* 8 Apr. (1938) 795 She..has no one aboard now to get her priority treatment. **1942** *Times* (Weekly ed.) 2 Dec. 15 Various priority and freight rationing schemes are in operation. **1946** K. TENNANT *Lost Haven* (1947) xvi. 248 Young Len's working for the mill, ain't he? And that's a priority job. **1960** O. MANNING *Great Fortune* xiii. 153 This young man might have been granted a priority flight over Europe. **1967** *Guardian* 10 Jan. 4/4 Measures should be taken to increase the ratio of teachers to children in educational priority areas. **1976** *Broadcast* Dec. 1/3 The achievement of a shorter working week for weekly paid staff is a priority objective.

'priorly, *a. nonce-wd.* [f. PRIOR *sb.* + -LY[1].] Proper to or befitting a prior.

1838 *Fraser's Mag.* XVII. 62 Blandly he patteth his priorly paunch.

'priorly, *adv.* [f. PRIOR *a.* + -LY[2].] As a prior step; previously, antecedently.

1779 R. BAKER *Remarks Eng. Lang.* (ed. 2) 94 It seems a wonder that we have no such word as *priorly*. It would be naturally formed from *prior*, and would be very useful. **1792** GEDDES *Transl. Bible* I. Pref. 2 Whether, priorly to that æra, it had ever been inhabited..is a question which it would be rash to decide. **1839** J. ROGERS *Antipopopr.* XVI. iii. 332 Thus people may neither marry nor unmarry without priorly obtaining permission from the priesthood. **1965** *Amer. Psychologist* XX. 1007/2 After a certain point in human evolution, the only means whereby man could fill his evolutionary niche was through the cultural transmission of the skills necessary for the use of priorly invented techniques, implements, and devices. **1970** *Jrnl. Gen. Psychol.* LXXXII. 207 It states that organisms respond to discrepancies between contemporaneous stimuli and some internalized average of other imputs, experienced priorly or as context.

'priorship. [f. PRIOR *sb.* + -SHIP.] The office or dignity of a prior.

1553 BECON *Reliques of Rome* (1563) 22 b, Those byshops which sell..priorships, or any other ecclesiasticall dignityes ..should be adiudged Simoniakes. **1626** *MS. Acc. St. John's Hosp., Canterb.*, Rec. for my whole wages dureing my Pryorshipp the some of vjs viijd. **1671** WOODHEAD *St. Teresa* II. xviii. 120 Father Antonio quitted his Priorship with great willingness. **1762** tr. *Busching's Syst. Geog.* IV. 66 The order of St. John has likewise a priorship or grand priorship in Bohemia. **1840** CARLYLE *Heroes* iii. (1872) 82 In Dante's Priorship, the Guelf-Ghibelline, Bianchi-Neri, or some other confused disturbances rose to such a height, that Dante..was with his friends cast unexpectedly forth into banishment. **1900** GASQUET *Eve of Reformation* ii. 24 Election to the Priorship at Canterbury.

priorte, obs. form of PRIORITY.

†**Pri'orums,** *sb. pl. Obs.* [L. *priōrum*, as in the usual Latin title in 15th c., *Analyticorum priorum libri duo*, the two books of the Prior Analytics (of Aristotle): with Eng. pl. suffix -*s*.] Aristotle's Prior Analytics, or questions taken from them.

1596 HARINGTON *Metam. Ajax* (1814) 4 That he had before in his priorums. **1665** J. BUCK in Peacock *Stat. Cambridge* (1841) App. B. p. lxviii, All the Quæstionists between the time of their Admission and Ash Wednesday are to enter their Priorums.

priory ('praɪərɪ). Also 3–6 priorie; β. 5–6 pryoure, priore. [ME. *priorie*, a. Anglo-F. *priorie* (*a* 1240), med.L. *priōria*: see PRIOR *sb.* and -Y. The form might also arise from OF. *prioré*, mod.F. *prieuré*:—L. *priōrātus*; but in Eng. *priouré*, *prioré* is of late occurrence.]

1. A monastery or nunnery governed by a prior or prioress; generally an offshoot of an abbey on which it was more or less dependent; also, a house of Canons Regular. ***alien priory***: see ALIEN *a.* 2.

Sometimes the name of a dwelling-house on the site of a priory.

c **1290** *S. Eng. Leg.* I. 71/10 In þe priorie of wiricestre. **1297** R. GLOUC. (Rolls) 5599, & þoru [h]is conseil chirchen wide he let rere & abbeys & prioryes aboute her & þere. **1432–50** tr. *Higden* (Rolls) VII. 475 The priory of Norton in the province of Chestre was founded this tyme by William sonne of Nigellus. *a* **1552** LELAND *Itin.* III. 50 Here was a Priorie of Nunnes lately suppressed. **1726** AYLIFFE *Parergon* 6 The Churches which are given to them [priors] *in Titulum*, or by way of Title, are called Priories. **1806** *Gazetteer Scotl.* (ed. 2) 96/1 Coldstream..was anciently the seat of a priory or abbacy of the Cistertian order. **1845** ELIZ. M. SEWELL *Gertrude* i, The modern Priory..had no connection with the old religious house except that of bearing the same designation. **1889** JESSOPP *Coming of Friars* iii. 136 A priory was a monastery which in theory or in fact was subject to an abbey.

β. *c* **1500** *Melusine* 210 Ye muste doo founde a Pryoure of twelue monkes, & the pryour, in suche place there as my lady shal ordeyne. **1530** PALSGR. 258 Priore, *prioré*.

attrib. **1470–85** MALORY *Arthur* XIV. i. 642, I wel ought to knowe you.., al though I be in a pryory place.

b. ***grand priory***, a province, next below a 'language', of the order of the Knights of St. John or of Malta, under the rule of a Grand Prior.

Cf. PRIORATE 2, quot. 1829, and PRIORSHIP, quot. 1762. **1885** *Cath. Dict.* 413/2 The Hospitallers..After the order had attained its full development, it was divided into eight languages... Each language was divided into grand priories and bailiwicks, which again were subdivided into commanderies.

2. = PRIORATE 1, PRIORSHIP.

1387 TREVISA *Higden* (Rolls) VII. 443 After þe fifteenþe ȝere of his priourie Herlewyn abbot of Becco deide, and Anselme was i-made abbot in his stede. **1879** tr. *Montalembert's Monks of West* VII. 161 *note*, During the fifteen years of his priory.

¶**3.** = PRIORITY. *Obs. rare.*

1600 *Sc. Acts Jas. VI* (1816) IV. 246/2 Anent þe priorie in places and voting ffor removeing of all sic occasionis of controverseis.

pris, obs. form of PRICE *sb.*[1], PRIZE *v.*[1]

prisable ('praɪzəb(ə)l), *a.* Also **prizable.** [a. AF. *prisable*, f. *prise* PRISE *sb.*[1]: see -ABLE; cf. *dutiable*.] Liable to the custom of prisage.

[**1392–3** *Rolls of Parlt.* III. 307/1 Paiant pur chescun tonell de Vyns prisables Vynt deners.] **1882** HUB. HALL in *Antiquary* VI. 231/1 The primary meaning of the term prizage—viz. that the Crown took prizable wines at its own price. **1885** —— *Hist. Customs* II. 106 An equivalent of the Custom of 2s. paid by aliens, namely, 20d. for every prisable pipe, and 10d. for every other pipe.

prisage[1] ('praɪzədʒ). Now *Hist.* Also 7 pry-, prisadge, 7–9 prizage. [f. as prec. + -AGE.

Spelman mentions a med. (Anglo-) L. *prisāgium* 'jus prisas capiendi vel ipse actus', which may have been the immediate source.]

1. An ancient custom levied upon imported wine; in later times correlated to and often identified with BUTLERAGE 1. (Abolished 1809 by 49 Geo. III. c. 98 §35.)

For the nature of the impost, its changes, and its relation to BUTLERAGE, see Hubert Hall *Hist. Customs* (1885) II. 90 et seq. 'The "Butlerage" was..the commutation of the prizage into a petty custom, and was paid by aliens alone, who consequently paid no prizage. Prizage was the ancient toll in kind retained for choice by natives, who therefore paid no butlerage, as it was afterwards called' (H. Hall in *Antiquary* (1882) VI. 230/2).

1505 in *Facsimiles Nat. MSS.* I. (1865) 71 Rec. of William Spencer for buttlerage & prisage of the porte of Ippyswiche Cxij s. vj d. **1588–9** *Act 31 Eliz.* c. 5 §4 Any Offence.. committed..for the concealinge or defraudinge the Quenes Majestie..of any Custome Tonnage Pondage Subsidie Ymposte or Prisage. **1655** *Cal. State Papers, Domestic* (1882) 46 Your late Declaration reviving the Act for Prizage of Wines will ruin us unless suspended. **1682** LUTTRELL *Brief Rel.* (1857) I. 230 They have a right by prescription to appoint and alter markets in the said citty [London], and to ascertain tolls and prisages therein. **1736** CARTE *Ormonde* II. 219 The Marquis [of Ormond] did not esteem any part of his revenue so much as he did that which arose from the prisage of wines. **1757** BURKE *Abridgm. Eng. Hist.* III. ii. Wks. X. 400 The last general head of his [the king's] revenue were the customs, prisages, and other impositions upon trade. **1812** J. SMYTH *Pract. of Customs* (1821) 278 Wine entered for prisage; of the Cape of Good Hope; in a British-built Ship, the tun 12 19 0; in a Foreign Ship, the tun 14 0 0. **1832** *Act 2 & 3 Will. IV*, c. 84 §40 For..Surrender of the Estate, Right, Title, and Interest..in the..Duties of Prisage and Butlerage within the said County Palatine [Lancashire]. **1882** [see prec.].

†**b.** Short for *prisage wine*: see c. *Obs.*

?*c* **1525** in *10th Rep. Hist. MSS. Comm.* App. v. 292 The commene wyne callid prisage.

c. *attrib.* and *Comb.*, as ***prisage fund, lease, wine.***

1586 J. HOOKER *Hist. Irel.* in *Holinshed* II. 139/1 Also that they haue the prisage wines and the iurisdiction of the admeraltie, within the limits of the said riuer. **1601** F. TATE *Househ. Ord. Edw. II.* §66 (1876) 47 Let him presently cause the prisage wines & the wines he hath bought, presentli to be caried & lodged. **1619** in *N. Eng. Hist. & Gen. Reg.* XLVII. 128, I give unto my daughter..one sixteenth part of the 'prysadge' lease and unto my son..the other sixteenth part of the same prysadge lease I now hold, which prysadge lease I did put my husband..to buy for me. **1902** *Daily Chron.* 25 Oct. 7/5 The Prisage Fund is, I believe, now represented by real estate—about 3,020 acres, producing a present gross rental of £2,597 per annum, the net rental being £2,126.

¶**2.** (See quots.)

1607 COWELL *Interpr.*, *Prisage*, seemeth to be that custome or share, that belongeth to the King out of such merchandize, as are taken at sea, by way of lawfull prize, anno 31 Eliz. cap. 5. **1670** BLOUNT *Law Dict.*, *Prisage*, is that Custom or Share, that belongs to the King, or Lord Admiral, out of such Merchandises as are taken at Sea, by way of lawfull Prize, which is usually a Tenth part. **1848–83** in WHARTON *Law Lex.*

(But this seems to be merely a conjecture of Cowell, accepted as fact by his successors and handed down in the law dictionaries. Act 31 Eliz. c. 5, referred to by Cowell, contains nothing about prizes taken at sea, but mentions prisage, app. in sense 1: see quot. 1588–9 there.)

†**prisage**[2]. *Obs. rare*$^{-0}$. [a. obs. F. *prisage*, f. *priser* to prise, reckon, value: see PRIZE *v.* and -AGE.] Valuation, appraisement. (Perh. only a misuse of the word by Cotgr.)

1611 COTGR., *Prisage*, a prisage, prising, praising, rating, valuing.

†**'prisal, 'prizal.** *Obs.* Also 7 prisel. [a. AF. *prisel*, f. F. *prise* seizure, taking, PRISE *sb.*[1], PRIZE *sb.*[3]: see -AL[1], and cf. REPRISAL.]

1. The taking or seizure of a thing as by legal right or custom.

[*a* **1481** LITTLETON *Tenures* §693 (1557) 158 Si tiel prisel de estate ne soit par fait endent.] **1628** COKE *On Litt.* 311 Hee shall auow the prisel to bee good and rightfull, as in lands or Tenements so charged with his distresse, &c. **1647** N. BACON *Disc. Govt. Eng.* I. lxiv. (1739) 135 But the Statute in his [Edw. I's] 28th year had a sting in the tail that was as ill as his saving of ancient aids and prisals.

2. The taking of anything (a ship, etc.) as a prize of war. With *a* and *pl.* an act of such capture; also *concr.* an article so acquired.

1590 SIR R. SIDNEY in Motley *Netherl.* (1867) III. 174 *note*, They complain of two ships taken on the coast of Portugal... They of Zeland did send unto Holl[d] to let them know of these prisals. **1594** DANIEL *Cleopatra* III. ii, The greatest Trophy that my Travels gain, Is to bring Home a Prizal of such Worth. *a* **1643** SIR J. SPELMAN *Alfred Gt.* (1709) 62 Of what Credit soever the Omination of the [Raven] Standard was in itself, the Prisal of it [from the Danes] by the Christians was of no little Consequence. **1651** HOWELL *Venice* 67 But the Venetians freed the Town from the siege..with great slaughter of the enemy, and prizall of many rich booties.

prisar, obs. form of PRIZER[1].

'priscal, *a. rare*$^{-1}$. [f. as next + -AL[1].] = next.

1831 *Examiner* 181/1 Priscal manners, undebased by corruption.

priscan ('prɪskən), *a. rare.* [f. L. *prisc-us* old + -AN.] Ancient, primitive, of early times.

1877 ROLLESTON *Brit. Barrows* 742 A pack of wild dogs co-operating with priscan men in driving a herd of wild cattle..along a track in which a pitfall had been dug. **1880** DAWKINS *Early Man* vi. 173 The wide area occupied by this priscan population. **1881** *Smithsonian Rep.* 506 We seem to hear..the echoes of our own priscan history.

Priscian ('prɪʃ(ɪ)ən). [ad. L. *Prisciān-us.*] Name of a celebrated Roman grammarian, *c* 500–530: used esp. in the phrase ***to break*** (***knock***) ***Priscian's head*** (***pate***), to violate the rules of grammar (L. *diminuere Prisciani caput*).

c **1525** SKELTON *Sp. Parrot* 176 Prisians hed broken now handy dandy, And *Inter didascolos* is rekened for a fole. *c* **1533** R. LIST in Ellis *Orig. Lett.* Ser. III. II. 252 Many a tyme when he [Father Forest] hath preched..I have harde hym soo often breke Master Precyens hede. **1588** SHAKS. *L.L.L.* v. i. 31. **1606** *Sir G. Goosecappe* I. iv. in Bullen *O. Pl.* III. 26 Will speake false Latine, and breake Priscians head. **1633** GERARD *Descr. Somerset* (1900) 224 Knocking poore Priscian's pate soe familiarly as in most ancient evidence they doe. **1664** BUTLER *Hud.* II. ii. 224 [They] hold no sin so deeply red, As that of breaking Priscian's Head. **1728** POPE *Dunc.* III. 162 Some free from rhyme or reason, rule or check, Break Priscian's head, and Pegasus's neck. *a* **1849** H. COLERIDGE *Ess.* (1851) II. 124 If he has not broken Priscian's head, he has at least boxed his ears.

†**b.** *transf.* A grammarian. So **'Priscianist.**

1598 MARSTON *Pygmal.* IV. 64 But thus it is when pitty Priscians Will needs step vp to be Censorians. **1611** CORYAT *Crudities* 64 He had a little beggarly and course latin, so much as a Priscianist may have.

Priscillianist (prɪ'sɪlɪənɪst), *sb.* and *a.* [= F. *Priscillianiste*, ad. med.L. *Priscillianista*, f. *Priscilliān-us* Priscillian: see -IST.]

A. *sb.* **1.** A disciple of Priscillian, bishop of Avila, in Spain, in the 4th c., who taught doctrines alleged to be Gnostic or Manichæan.

1594 T. B. *La Primaud. Fr. Acad.* II. 506 Manie.. amongst the Christians haue imagined that the soules of men are the substance of God. I omit to speake of the heretikes, as the Priscilianists, & some others that haue been of this opinion. **1680** BAXTER *Answ. Stillingfl.* lxxiv. 95 Our Quakers are much like the Priscillianists. **1834** *Penny Cycl.* II. 528/2 The doctrine of astrology was among the errors imputed to the Priscillianists.

2. A name sometimes given to the MONTANISTS, from Priscilla, the name of one of the two women associated with Montanus.

1874 in J. H. BLUNT *Dict. Sects.*

B. *adj.* Of or pertaining to the Priscillianists or their doctrines.

1887 *Dict. Chr. Biog.* IV. 476/2 A specimen of the Priscillianist allegorical treatment of the Christian Scriptures. **1900** *Contemp. Rev.* Sept. 354 The smaller Priscillianist movement in Spain. **1902** *Ibid.* Apr. 504 He has succeeded in tracing the interpolation to a Priscillianist and therefore heretical source.

So **Pri'scillian**, **Pri'scillianite** = A. 1; **Pri'scillianism**, the doctrines or principles of Priscillian.

1680 BAXTER *Answ. Stillingfl.* lxxiv. 95 Those Bishops.. suspecting men that Fasted and Prayed much, to be *Priscillians. **1620** BP. HALL *Hon. Mar. Clergy* I. ix, He, being suspected of *Priscillianisme, wrote affectly against that heresie. **1882** *Dict. Chr. Biog.* III. 841/2 Priscillianism is usually.. considered as a phase of Gnosticism. **1585–7** T. ROGERS *39 Art.* xxxix. (Parker Soc.) 357 The ..*Priscillianites,.. who for ease, and to avoid troubles and persecution, dread not to swear and forswear themselves. **1676** W. HUBBARD *Happiness of People* 40 The success of capital punishment inflicted on the Priscillianites.

Priscol ('prɪskɒl). *Pharm.* Also **priscol**. A proprietary name for TOLAZOLINE.

The trade-mark registration in the U.S. is no longer active (see next, quot. 1949).

1938 *Trade Marks Jrnl.* 18 May 604/2 Priscol... All goods included in class 3 [*i.e.* chemical substances prepared for use in medicine and pharmacy]. Society of Chemical Industry in Basle.., Basle, Switzerland; manufacturers and merchants. **1938** *Official Gaz.* (U.S. Patent Office) 14 June 247/2 Society of Chemical Industry in Basle... *Priscol* for preparation having an action on the circulation of the blood. Claims use since May 6, 1936. **1945** *Federation Proc.* IV. 114/1 Although priscol, 15 mgm., was adrenolytic in relation to blood pressure, it was not adrenolytic or sympatholytic in respect to the cervical sympathetic functions studied. **1956** LD. AMULREE in A. Pryce-Jones *New Outl. Mod. Knowl.* 222 On the theory that the confusion [in senile dementia] is increased by a shortage of oxygen within the brain, priscol and other vaso-dilators have been used without any definite improvement in the patient's condition. **1968** W. C. BOWMAN et al. *Textbk. Pharmacol.* xxix. 763 Tolazoline (Priscol) exhibits a wide range of pharmacological activity in addition to its antiadrenaline action.

Priscoline ('prɪskəliːn). *Pharm.* Also **priscoline**. [f. PRISCOL + -INE[5].] A proprietary name in the U.S. for TOLAZOLINE.

1949 *Jrnl. Amer. Med. Assoc.* 21 May 272/2 Since this paper was written, the name priscol has been changed to priscoline. **1950** *Official Gaz.* (U.S. Patent Office) 22 Aug. 996/2 Ciba Pharmaceutical Products, Inc., Summit, N.J... *Priscoline*... For preparations having an action on the circulation of the blood. Claims use since Mar. 15, 1949. **1966** W. F. BARKER *Peripheral Arterial Dis.* vi. 85 Priscoline is perhaps one of the most widely used drugs in peripheral vascular occlusions.

prise (praɪz, ‖priz), *sb.*[1] *Obs.* or *Hist.* Also 5 pryse, 6 prese, 6–7 prize. [a. F. *prise* a taking, seizure, capture, sb. fem. from pa. pple. *pris*, *prise* of *prendre* to take; in med.L. *prīsa* (Du Cange). The original form of the word now spelt *prize* (PRIZE *sb.*[3]), which has been retained in some early uses (senses 1, 2) now historical or archaic, and is the only spelling found in other senses now obsolete. For the specific sense in hunting, see PRYSE.]

1. The taking or seizing of anything by a lord for his own use from his feudal tenants or dependants; a requisition; a thing seized or requisitioned for the king's use by his officers or purveyors, or for the use of the garrisons in his castles; the right of such seizure. *Obs.* exc. *Hist.*

[**1170** GERVASE (in Du Cange), Et de omnibus prisis inquirant causam et testimonium. **1274–5** *Act 3 Edw. I*, c. 7 (Stat. Westm.) Purveu est que nul Conestable ne Chasteleyne desoremes nule manere de prise [*transl.* 1543 pryse] ne face dautre houme.. qui de la Vile ou son Chastel est assis. *Ibid.*, Si ceo ne seit auncìene prise due au Rey ou al Chastel ou al Seygnur del Chastel.] **1297** R. GLOUC. (Rolls) 10742 Sir hubert de boru.. Acused was to þe King of mani luþer prise. *c* **1400** *Brut* ccxviii. 257 þe Quene Isabel and þe Mortymer had a grete manie of her retenue, þat folwede euermore þe Kyngus courte, and went and tok þe Kyngus prises for her penyworthes at gode chepe. **1502** ARNOLDE *Chron.* 31 Y[t] the Constable of the tour of London make no preses by londe ne by water of vytayle or any other thinges what so euer thei ben of men of ye forsaid cite. **1621** BOLTON *Stat. Irel.* 1 (Act 3 Edw. II) Forasmuch as merchants and the common people of this land are much impoverished and oppressed by the prises of great Lords. *Ibid.*, That no such prises be henceforth made without ready payment. **1750** CARTE *Hist. Eng.* II. 319 That the king might live of his own without taking unusual prises. **1771** *Antiq. Sarisb.* 53 The former used to make captures upon the latter of hay, corn, beer, and other things under divers denominations, to wit, Pryse, Tyne of Castle, forrage, &c. Thus the Constable of Dover Castle and the Soldiers, were accustomed to take from the Kentish-men, straw, hay, vetches, peas, beans, corn, and other things. **1866** ROGERS *Agric. & Prices* I. ix. 155 All tallages, fifteenths, and prises levied.. in the county.

2. *pl.* (rarely *sing.*) The king's customs; that is, portions taken by him from goods brought into the realm, or duties levied in lieu thereof. Cf. PRISAGE[1]. *Obs.* (or only *Hist.*)

[**1290** *Rolls of Parlt.* I. 27/1 Cum Dominus Rex capiat.. per Vicecomitem.. Prisas suas et Custumas debitas ad Portum.. videlicet, de qualibet nave vini duo dolia ante et retro electa, quodlibet dolium pro viginti solidis.] **1455** *Rolls of Parlt.* V. 293/2 Delyvered to the said Prynce.. the said Duchie of Cornewayll, and all.. Wayfes, Strayes, Forfaitures, wrekkes of the See, prises of Wyne, Custumes Havenary, Tolles, Cunage of Tynne, Stannaries [etc.]. **1467–8** *Ibid.* 585/1 A Tonne of Wyne, to be takyn of oure Pryse within our Port of Bristowe. **1577–87** HOLINSHED *Chron.* III. 1240/2 Peter de Oriall,.. gardian of all the forrest of England, of all the escheats, of all the ports of the sea, and of all the prises of England and Ireland. **1607** COWELL, *Prise*,.. signifieth also a custome due to the King.

†**3.** *Her.* Anything assumed; a bearing. *Obs.*

1572 BOSSEWELL *Armorie* II. 116 b, Thus those prises in coates armoures, which are of many called Fusils, that is to saye Spyndles, may aptly be taken for pillers.

†**4.** A small piece of gold or silver coin taken for the assay at the Mint. (= F. *prise d'essai*, 'morceau de monnaie pour essayer' Littré.) *Obs.*

1469 in *Archæologia* XV. 170 Whenn the seid prises of gold and syluer be made and putte in a box to make the assaies.

†**5.** The quantity of medicine to be taken at once; a dose, a pinch. (Cf. F. *une prise de tabac.*) *Obs.*

1683 SALMON *Doron Med.* Pref., They are to be found, together with their certain prizes by the Ounce.

6. *attrib.*: (sense 1) **prise ale** (see quot. *a* 1600); (sense 2) **prise wine**, wine taken as prisage.

[**1300** *Wardrobe Acc. Edw. I* (1787) 14 Vinis de prisa.] **1530** MORE *Let. to Wolsey* 10 July in P. H. Hore *Hist. Wexford* (1900) 234 Disturbing the citie of Waterford in the use of a certayn graunt of prize wynys, made and confermed unto theym, as they allegge, by the Kyngs progenitors. **1550** *Fiat* 18 Nov. in *8th Rep. Dep. Kpr. Irel.* 91 The prise wines of Waterford, Rosse, Lymerick, Dublin, Drogheda and Dundalk. ? *a* **1600** G. OWEN *Baronia* (1861) 45 *Prise ale* is certen monye payed by custome used within the said baronye [of Kemeys], of all those that sell ale within the said baronye, burghe or manors aforesaid, vz., vd. for every brewinge, which is due to the lorde there by custome used time out of mynde.

†**prise**, *sb.*[2] *Obs.* [Origin obscure.

Known only in the work cited (in which the number of alliterations in *p-* and *pr-* is extraordinary). The only conjecture offered is that *prise* was a shortening of F. *reprise*, ppl. sb. of *reprendre* 'to reprehend, blame, check, reprove, rebuke, find fault with, carp at'; but examples of the sb. in the appropriate sense are app. unknown even in OF.]

? Reprehension, reproof, rebuke, angry check; utterance of angry disapproval or rejection.

c **1400** *Destr. Troy* 2032–4 The proude wordis & þe prise of Pelleus the kyng; The tene and the torfor of Telamon after; The Reprofe and prise of Pollux & Castor; The noy and þe new grem of Nestor the Duke. *Ibid.* 2042 That his message was manast o þo men all, And reproued with prise in þere proude yre. *Ibid.* 5114 With presumpcoun & prise of his proude hert.

prise, *sb.*[3] and *v.*: see PRIZE *sb.*[4] and *v.*[3]

[**prise**, a frequent misreading of *prese*, *preese*, PRESS *sb.*[1], senses 2–5, PRESS *v.*[1] 16, 17, in E.E.T.S. ed. (1869–74) of *Destruction of Troy* (*c* 1400).

c **1400** *Destr. Troy* 1201 Mony perysshet in þe plase er þe prise [*MS.* prese] endit. *Ibid.* 1331 Ercules.. Pricket furthe into prise [*MS.* prese] and full playne made... Bere the batell a-bake, mony buerne qwellid [cf. 8317 Past furth into prese, paynet hym ther-for]. *Ibid.* 12048 Eneas egerly.. Put hym in prise & profferit to say.]

prise, obs. f. PRICE, PRIZE, PRYSE.

prisel, variant of PRISAL. *Obs.*

priser, obs. form of PRIZER[1] and [2].

prisere ('praɪsɪə(r)). *Ecol.* [f. PRI(MARY *a.* + SERE *sb.*[2]] A sere that began on an area not previously occupied.

1916 F. E. CLEMENTS *Plant Succession* ix. 182 Within the same climax, seres are classified as primary and secondary, i.e., as priseres and subseres. **1926** TANSLEY & CHIPP *Study of Vegetation* ii. 19 We distinguish a sere beginning on bare soil.. as a primary sere, or prisere. **1939** A. G. TANSLEY *Brit. Islands & their Vegetation* x. 218 Any concrete example of succession, i.e. any definite series of communities leading to a climax, is called a sere, and the complete succession from bare habitat to climatic climax is a primary sere or prisere. **1960** N. POLUNIN *Introd. Plant. Geogr.* xi. 324 The complete sere just indicated is a primary sere (prisere), beginning on a bare substratum without organic material. **1977** A. S. COLLINSON *Introd. World Vegetation* vi. 103 Where plants begin their succession on virgin territory.. the process is termed a primary succession or prisere.

†'**prishede**. *Obs. rare*[−1]. [f. PRICE, PRISE *a.* + *-hede*, -HEAD.] Worthiness, excellence, valour.

c **1400** *Destr. Troy* 2907 The prishede of parys was praisit so mekyll.

‖**prisiadka** (prji'sjatkə). Also **prisjádka**, **prisyadka**. [Russ.] A dance-step in which the male dancer squats on his heels and kicks out each leg alternately to the front. Also used for the dance itself. Cf. KAZACHOC.

1938 B. SCHÖNBERG tr. *Sachs' World Hist. of Dance* i. 28 Wilder still are the Bavarian *Schuhplattler* and the Ukrainian *prisjádka* with their heel stamping. *Ibid.* 30 The squat-fling dance is still the possession of many European peoples... In the Ukraine it is known by the term *prisjádka*. **1972** *Daily Tel.* 14 Aug. 6/9 They.. burst out into wild Ukrainian dancing with every possible variation of the squatting step 'prisyadka'. **1977** J. WAMBAUGH *Black Marble* (1978) xii. 292 'I don't care if I'm six feet tall,' Valnikov said, squatting on his haunches, trying some prisiadka kicks that put him temporarily on his ass.

†**prisk**, *a.* *Sc. Obs. rare.* [ad. L. *prisc-us* old, primitive, old-fashioned.] Ancient, primitive.

1533 BELLENDEN *Livy* I. xiii. (S.T.S.) I. 75 þe fader patrat of prisk latynis. *Ibid.* 76 Or ellis þe prisk latyne men, has faleȝit or done Iniuris aganis þe quirites & romane pepil.

prism (prɪz(ə)m). Also 8 *erron.* prysm. [ad. late L. *prisma* (Martianus Capella), a. Gr. πρίσμα a thing sawn, a prism (Euclid), f. πρίζειν to saw. So F. *prisme* (1680 in Hatz.-Darm.).]

1. *Geom.* A solid figure of which the two ends are similar, equal, and parallel rectilineal figures, and the sides parallelograms.

1570 BILLINGSLEY *Euclid* XI. xl. 355 Euery parallelipipedon may be resolued into two like, and equal Prismes. **1706** PHILLIPS s.v., *Triangular Prism*, a kind of Prism whose two opposite Bases are Triangles alike, parallel and equal. **1806** HUTTON *Course Math.* I. 331 A Prism takes particular names according to the figure of its base or ends, whether triangular, square, rectangular, pentagonal, hexagonal, &c. A Right or Upright Prism.. has the planes of the sides perpendicular to the planes of the ends or base. **1847** SMEATON *Builder's Man.* 177 To find the Solidity of a Prism.

2. Any body or object of this form.

1661 J. CHILDREY *Brit. Baconica* 81 In little Columnes, or Prismes an inch long or more. **1758** REID tr. *Macquer's Chem.* I. 191 An iron grate, the bars of which are quadrangular prysms of half an inch square. **1800** tr. *Lagrange's Chem.* II. 105 The salt deposits itself in compressed prisms of great length. **1836** MACGILLIVRAY tr. *Humboldt's Trav.* xvii. 232 A granitic prism, terminated by a flat surface covered with a tuft of trees, rises to the height of 213 feet. **1862** RAWLINSON *Anc. Mon.* I. v. 329 Hexagonal or octagonal prisms made in extremely fine and thin Terra Cotta.

3. *Optics.* A transparent body of this form, usually a triangular geometrical prism, of which the refracting surfaces are at an acute angle with each other. ***Nicol('s) prism*** = NICOL[2].

1612 PEACHAM *Gentl. Exerc.* III. 150 A most pleasant and delightfull experiment.. in a three square cristal prisme, wherin you shal perceiue the blew to be outmost next to that the red. **1656** W. D. tr. *Comenius' Gate Lat. Unl.* §480. 139 Prismes (called fools paradises) which transform the colours of things into a thousand shapes. **1728–46** THOMSON *Spring* 208 Here, awful Newton, the dissolving clouds Form, fronting on the sun, thy showery prism. *a* **1743** LD. HERVEY *Monimia to Philocles* Poet. Wks. (1808) 48 So in a prism to the deluded eye Each pictur'd trifle takes a rainbow dye. **1847** DE MORGAN *Formal Logic* ii. 35 Wollaston and Fraunhofer have discovered black lines which always exist in the spectrum of solar colours given by a glass prism, in the same relative places. **1873** J. P. COOKE *New Chem.* 57, I have a prism.. made of Icelandspar, and called a Nicol prism.

b. *fig.*

1820 W. IRVING *Sketch Bk.* II. 207, I had surveyed the landscape through the prism of poetry, which tinged every object with the hues of the rainbow. **1847** L. HUNT *Men, Women, & B.* I. viii. 140 A bit of health is a fine prism to see fancies by. **1874** SAYCE *Compar. Philol.* i. 35 Thought and its expression are but the two sides of the same prism.

c. Loosely used for a spectrum produced by refraction through a prism; *pl.* prismatic colours.

c **1840** MRS. OPIE in Miss Brightwell *Mem.* xxii. (1854) 334 Oh! the exquisite beauty of the prisms on my ceiling just now. **1842** TENNYSON *Day-Dream, Sleeping Pal.* v, The beams, that thro' the Oriel shine, Make prisms in every carven glass, And beaker brimm'd with noble wine. **1866** *Cornh. Mag.* Sept. 358 A glass drop chandelier, quaint and old-fashioned, reflected it [the light] in bright prisms.

4. *Cryst.* A 'form' consisting of three or more planes parallel to the vertical axis of the crystal. (Cf. DOME *sb.* 5 b.)

1878 GURNEY *Crystallogr.* 51 A group of tautozonal faces is in some cases called a prism. **1895** STORY-MASKELYNE *Crystallogr.* v. §108 The prismatic forms.. are constituted each of four planes, the first form being technically termed a prism.

5. *Engineering.* A length of cutting or embankment, treated roughly as a prismoid or a parallelepiped, of which the content is calculated by the *prismoidal formula*.

1906 *Rep. Board Consulting Engineers Panama Canal* 25 Very accurate cross sections of the Canal Prism included between Obispo and Paraiso, seven miles and a half, were obtained. *Ibid.* 49 There is much rock to be removed from the Canal prism at Obispo.

†**6.** Sawdust. *Obs. rare*[−0].

1656 BLOUNT *Glossogr.*, *Prism*,.. the powder or dust of those things that are cut with a Saw. *a* **1700** B. E. *Dict. Cant. Crew*, *Prisme*,.. Saw-dust.

7. *attrib.* and *Comb.*, as ***prism-form***, ***-glass***, ***-maker***; ***prism-hued***, ***-like***, ***-shaped*** adjs.; **prism-battery**, an electric battery in which the materials forming the positive pole are compressed into a prism or block (Knight *Dict. Mech.* Suppl. 1884); **prism-binocular(s)**, binoculars containing two pairs of triangular prisms, introduced so as to shorten the apparatus and improve the stereoscopic effect; **prism-train**, a combined series of prisms used with the spectroscope to give increased dispersion.

1666 BOYLE *Orig. Formes & Qual.* Wks. 1772 III. 56 These crystals.. would shoot into prism-like figures, as roched petre. **1688** R. HOLME *Armoury* III. 375/1 Prismes Glasses.. represent things of diverse colours, as red, green, yellow, like a Rain-Bow. **1760** J. LEE *Introd. Bot.* III. xxii. (1765) 229 The Pericarpium is..prismatic, Prism-shaped. **1839** BAILEY *Festus* vi. (1852) 68 Joyous feelings, prism-hued. **1859** R. F. BURTON *Centr. Afr.* in *Jrnl. Geog. Soc.* XXIX. 134 The prism-shaped ceiling is composed of thin poles extending from the long walls to the centre. **1895** STORY-MASKELYNE *Crystallogr.* vii. §328 One of these varieties [of prismatids] includes the vertical or ortho-prism ..usually distinguished as the prism-form, the faces of which lie in the zone. **1901** *Brit. Optical Jrnl.* Sept. p. iv (Advt.), Busch's Prism Binoculars... The lightest and most portable Prism Binocular on the market. **1919** *Jane's Fighting Ships* 59 adv., Bausch & Lomb Optical Co... Field Glasses (Stereo Prism Binocular). **1957** *Encycl. Brit.* III. 583/2 Ernst Abbe took the matter up *de novo* in 1893 when he designed prism binoculars and telescopes. His constructions were the forerunners of the modern prism binocular.

prismal (ˈprɪzməl), *a.* [f. PRISM + -AL[1].] Of, pertaining to, or produced by a prism; prismatic.

1850 ALLINGHAM *Poems, Bubble* vii, Prismal life outgoing, Welling without sound. **1855** B. TAYLOR *Poems of Orient, L'Envoi* 23 Gathering from every land the prismal beams. **1862** LYTTON *Str. Story* lxxxvii, Coruscations of all prismal hues.

prismated (ˈprɪzmeɪtɪd), *a. rare.* [f. L. ppl. type **prismāt-us* + -ED[1]; after F. *prismé* (Haüy).] Formed as a prism; see quot. So ˈ**prismate** *a.* in same sense.

1805–17 R. JAMESON *Char. Min.* (ed. 3) 197 A crystal is named..Prismated.., when the primitive form is composed of two pyramids, joined base to base, and the pyramids separated by a prism. **1858** MAYNE *Expos. Lex., Prismatus* ...presenting a prism between two pyramids..as prismate felspar.

prismatic (prɪzˈmætɪk), *a.* [f. Gr. πρισματ-, stem of πρίσμα PRISM + -IC. So F. *prismatique* (1690 in Hatz.-Darm.).]

1. Of or pertaining to a prism; having the form of a prism or prisms; prism-like.

prismatic powder: a gunpowder the grains of which are hexagonal prisms.

1709 POPE *Ess. Crit.* 311 False Eloquence, like the prismatic glass, Its gaudy colours spreads on ev'ry place. **1812** SIR H. DAVY *Chem. Philos.* 73 Certain saline solutions likewise that shoot into prismatic crystals. **1843** PORTLOCK *Geol.* 146 The truly prismatic basalt is confined to narrow limits. **1880** *Times* 27 Dec. 9/2 Prismatic powder was exclusively used during the gunnery trials on board.

b. *absol.* Short for *prismatic powder*.

1894 SIR A. NOBLE in *Nature* 26 July 310/2 The erosive effect of cordite..is very slightly greater than that of brown prismatic, but very much higher effects can, if it be so desired, be obtained with cordite.

2. Of or pertaining to the optical prism; formed, effected, separated, or distributed by or as by a transparent prism; hence, of varied colours, bright-coloured, brilliant. Also *fig.*

prismatic colours, the seven colours into which a ray of white light is separated by a prism. ***prismatic compass***, a surveying compass so arranged that by means of a prism the angle of position of the object sighted can be read at the same time as the object itself is seen.

1728 PEMBERTON *Newton's Philos.* 332 The result..of mixing together all the prismatic colours. **1788** V. KNOX *Winter Even.* I. iii. 27 All the hues of the prismatic spectrum. **1820** HAZLITT *Lect. Dram. Lit.* 308 [Jeremy Taylor's] style is prismatic. It unfolds the colours of the rainbow. **1859** F. A. GRIFFITHS *Artil. Man.* (1862) 371 The traversing may be performed..with the Prismatic compass. **1868** LOCKYER *Guillemin's Heavens* (ed. 3) 429 The light of this Nebula, unlike any other ex-terrestrial light which had yet been subjected to prismatic analysis, was not composed of light of different refrangibilities.

3. *Cryst.* = ORTHORHOMBIC *a.*

1858 MAYNE *Expos. Lex., Prismatic System*...that derived from the great number and variety of the prisms it contains. **1868** DANA *Min.* Introd. (ed. 5) 25 Orthorhombic system. (Also called Rectangular, Prismatic, Trimetric.) **1878** GURNEY *Crystallogr.* 37 There may be three planes of symmetry at right angles. Such crystals..belong to the Prismatic..System.

4. *Comb.* **prismatic-cellular**, of prismatic cells.

1854 WOODWARD *Mollusca* II. 292 The shell structure is prismatic-cellular, as first pointed out by Sowerby... In Cardium the outer layer is only corrugated or obscurely prismatic-cellular.

prisˈmatical, *a.* Now *rare.* [f. as prec. + -AL[1].] = PRISMATIC *a.* 1.

1654 T. WHITE *Daillé's Arts Discov.* in *Apol.* etc. 181 Prismatical glasses, in which we are pleased to know our selvs delightfully cosen'd. **1672** *Phil. Trans.* VII. 4096 The exquisite uniformity of shape, so admired in Gems (especially the Prismatical one in Crystal). **1794** SIR W. HAMILTON *ibid.* LXXXV. 88 The prismatical form of basalt columns. **1845** LINDLEY *Sch. Bot.* i. (1858) 13 *Prismatical*, when, being tubular, it [the calyx] is also regularly angular. **1866** *Treas. Bot., Prismenchyma*, prismatical cellular tissue.

prisˈmatically, *adv.* [f. prec. + -LY[2].] In a prismatic manner; like a prism; with, or as if with, prismatic colours.

1680 BOYLE *Scept. Chem.* v. Wks. 1772 I. 556, I might.. demand, what addition or decrement..befalls the body of the glass by being prismatically figured. **1824** MEDWIN *Convers. Byron* I. 212 His colour changed almost prismatically. **1897** HOWELLS *Landl. Lion's Head* 11 The colossal forms of the Lion's Head were prismatically outlined against the speckless sky.

prisˈmatico-, combining form of PRISMATIC, as in **prisˈmatico-ˈclavate** *a.*, *Nat. Hist.*, club-shaped with polygonal section like a prism.

1856–8 W. CLARK *Van der Hoeven's Zool.* I. 404 Crepuscularia.—Antennæ prismatico-clavate or fusiform.

prismatid (ˈprɪzmətɪd), *a.* (*sb.*) *Cryst. rare.* [f. Gr. πρισματ-, stem of πρίσμα PRISM + -ID[2].] Applied to a crystalline form consisting of faces parallel to an axis and thus constituting the sides of a geometrical prism. **b.** *sb.* A prismatid form.

1895 STORY-MASKELYNE *Crystallogr.* vii. §302 The designations of..the horizontal prismatid forms as domes, the vertical one as a prism, have already been given in article 109. *Ibid.* §328 Among the varieties of prismatids, of which the poles always lie in a zone perpendicular to the zone-circle of symmetry, two are especially noticeable.

prismatize (ˈprɪzmətaɪz), *v.* [f. as prec. + -IZE.] *trans.* To make or render prismatic; to cause to consist of prismatic crystals. Hence **prismatiˈzation**, the process of rendering prismatic.

1834–5 PHILLIPS *Man. Geol.* (1855) 189 Dikes of greenstone..producing upon the coal the effect of charring and partial prismatization. *Ibid.* 260 The prismatizing of shale by the action of basalt. **1869** —— *Vesuv.* iii. 63 The lava is rather earthy in texture, except at the end, where it is compact and prismatized.

ˈ**prismato-**, repr. Gr. πρισματο-, combining form of πρίσμα PRISM, as in ˈ**prismato-rhomˈboidal** *a.*, having the form of a rhomboidal prism.

1821 R. JAMESON *Man. Mineral.* 190 Emerald... Cleavage prismato-rhomboidal, or prismatoidal.

prismatoid (ˈprɪzmətɔɪd), *a.* and *sb.* [ad. Gr. πρισματοειδής prism-shaped, f. πρισματο-: see prec. and -OID. So mod.F. *prismatoïde.*]

A. *adj. Cryst.* Applied to any plane, in a crystallographic system, parallel to one of the three axes of co-ordinates and intersecting the other two; so called because a group of eight such planes would form a prism. Opposed to *octahedrid* and *pinakoid*.

1858 MAYNE *Expos. Lex., Prismatoides.., Mineral.*, resembling a prism; applied to a single cleavage face that is parallel to the axis: prismatoid; also erroneously translated prismatoidal. **1895** STORY-MASKELYNE *Crystallogr.* ii. §18.

B. *sb. Geom.* A solid figure having parallel polygonal ends connected by triangular sides.

1890 in *Cent. Dict.*

prismaˈtoidal, *a.* [f. as prec. + -AL[1].]

a. Resembling a prism. **b.** 'In the form of or connected with a prismatoid' (*Cent. Dict.*). **c.** = PRISMOIDAL.

1821 URE *Dict. Chem.* s.v. *Zeolite*, Prismatoidal zeolite, or stilbite. **1821** [see PRISMATO-]. **1858** [see prec.]. **1876** *Catal. Sci. App. S. Kens. Mus.* §10 *Estimator.* A sliding rule, by which the volume of prismatoidal bodies (embankments, ditches, cuttings, &c., occurring in the construction of railroads, canals, fortifications, &c.) is calculated mechanically.

prismatory, erron. form of PRESBYTERY.

prismed (ˈprɪz(ə)md), *a.* [f. PRISM *sb.* + -ED[2].] Produced by refraction in a prism; having prismatic colours, bright-coloured.

1820 C. PHILLIPS *Queen's Case Stated* 13 Too soon life's wintry whirlwind must come to sweep the prismed vapour into nothing. **1876** MRS. HOPKINS *Rose Turq.* I. iv. 72 The sunbeams came and made prismed glories in her hair.

prismenchyma (prɪzˈmɛŋkɪmə). *Bot.* [f. as PRISM + Gr. ἔγχυμα infusion, after PARENCHYMA.] Vegetable tissue consisting of prismatic cells.

1866 [see PRISMATICAL]. **1895** in *Syd. Soc. Lex.*

ˈ**prismic**, *a. rare*[−1]. [f. PRISM + -IC.] Of or pertaining to a prism; PRISMATIC *a.* 2.

1884 W. C. SMITH *Kildrostan* I. i. 41 Broken prismic lights.

prisˈmodic, *a. rare*[−1]. [f. PRISM, after *spasmodic.*] Like that of a (transparent) prism.

1854 W. WATERWORTH *Eng. & Rome* 126 Prejudice, which distorts and multiplies with prismodic power every object subjected to its action.

prismoid (ˈprɪzmɔɪd), *sb.* (*a.*) [= F. *prismoïde*, f. *prisme* PRISM: see -OID.]

1. A body approaching in form to a prism, with similar but unequal parallel polygonal bases.

1704 J. HARRIS *Lex. Techn.* I, *Prismoid*, is a solid Figure, contained under several Planes whose Bases are rectangular Parallelograms, parallel and alike situate. **1743** EMERSON *Fluxions* 208 Let *BF* be a Prismoid, whose Bases are right angled Parallelograms, though not similar. **1837** W. IRVING *Capt. Bonneville* (1849) 317 In this neighborhood, he saw.. several prismoids of basaltes, rising to the height of fifty or sixty feet. **1870** TRACY in *Eng. Mech.* 28 Jan. 489/1 The greater end of a prismoid measures 12 in. by 8.

2. (See quot.)

1895 *Syd. Soc. Lex., Liquid prismoid*, J. Thompson's name for the refracting watery fluid found in the corneal reflexion of the conjunctiva of the eye. [Also called] *watery prismoid.*

B. *adj. rare.* = next.

1840 E. WILSON *Anat. Vade M.* (1842) 1 The shaft is cylindrical or prismoid in form. *Ibid.* 64 The shaft of the bone is prismoid at its upper part, and flattened from before backwards below.

prismoidal (prɪzˈmɔɪdəl), *a.* [f. prec. + -AL[1].] Of the form of, or pertaining to, a prismoid.

prismoidal formula, a formula for the measurement of railway cuttings or the like, based on the consideration of a solid body as being composed of prismoids. ***prismoidal railway***, a railway in which the wheels run on a single central prism-shaped rail mounted on posts; a mono-railway.

1826 KIRBY & SP. *Entomol.* IV. xlvi. 266 *Prismoidal*.., having more than four sides and whose horizontal section is a polygon. **1872** E. MORRIS (*title*) Easy Rules for the Measurement of Earthworks by means of Prismoidal Formulæ. **1874** P. SMYTH *Our Inher.* ii. 16 After chipping off the prismoidal angles and edges. **1884** KNIGHT *Dict. Mech., Suppl., Prismoidal Railway*, a wooden or iron beam is supported on posts, the cars are mounted saddle-fashion; the engine grips the rail. Used in South Africa.

prismy (ˈprɪzmɪ), *a.* [f. PRISM + -Y.] Like those of a prism; prismatic; refracted; refracting.

1799 H. GURNEY tr. *Apuleius' Cupid & Psyche* viii. 14 Round lustres wreaths of diamonds fix'd, Their prismy rays profusely pour. **1811** W. R. SPENCER *Poems* 149 As still those sunbeams brightest shine Which light the diamond's prismy fires! **1824** *Blackw. Mag.* XVI. 230 Light wings of prismy gossamer.

prison (ˈprɪz(ə)n), *sb.* Forms: 2–5 **prisun** (dat. 2–4 **-une**), 4–5 **-une**; 3– **prison** (dat. 3–4 **-one**), 4–6 **prisone**; 3–6 **-oun** (5 **-oune**), 4–5 **-own**; 4–6 **pryson, -one, -oun, -own** (5 **-yn**); 6 **prissoun.** *β.* 4–5 **presun** (4 **pressone**), 4–7 **preson(e, -oun(e,** 5 **-own,** 6 **preassoun.** [Early ME. *prisun, -on*, a. OF. *prisun* (11th c. in Littré), *prison*, the action of taking, imprisonment, captivity, a prison; a prisoner; altered (prob. by assimilation to the pa. pple. *pris* taken) from earlier OF. *preson*:—L. *prensiōn-em*, contr. from *prehensiōn-em* a seizing, apprehending, n. of action f. *prehendĕre, prendĕre* to seize. So Pr. *preiso-s*, It. *prigione*, Sp. *prision*, Pg. *prisão*. Sense 2, which existed also in OF., It., Sp., and med.L., appears to have arisen from a person taken (in war) and held as a captive, being considered as a capture, prise, or PRIZE.]

1. *orig.* The condition of being kept in captivity or confinement; forcible deprivation of personal liberty; imprisonment; hence, a place in which such confinement is ensured; *spec.* such a place properly arranged and equipped for the reception of persons who by legal process are committed to it for safe custody while awaiting trial or for punishment; a jail.

a. without article. Here the primary sense is that of the condition, though the notion of a definite place of confinement is now more or less present. Often with certain verbs, as ***to break prison*** (BREAK *v.* 19); ***to cast*** (CAST *v.* 32), † ***do, put, set in prison; to keep, lay, lie in prison.***

a **1123** *O.E. Chron.* an. 1112 Rotbert de Bælesme he let niman and on prisune don. **1154** *Ibid.* an. 1137 Þa namen hi þa men..& diden heom in prisun. *c* **1175** *Lamb. Hom.* 13 Ȝe beoð iseald eower feonde to prisune. *c* **1250** *Gen. & Ex.* 2070 Ðre daies ben ȝet for to cumen, Ðu salt ben ut of prisun numen. **1297** R. GLOUC. (Rolls) 875 Þe quene hor aunte in bataile hii nome & in stronge prison broȝte [*v.rr.* dude, putte]. *a* **1300** *Cursor M.* 9556 Til his aun fa felun Was he be-taght for to prisun [*v.rr.* presoun, preson, prisoun]. *c* **1400** MAUNDEV. (Roxb.) x. 40 A place whare oure Lord was done in prisoun. *c* **1430** LYDG. *Min. Poems* (Percy Soc.) 183 Songe and prison have noon accordaunce, Trowest thou I wolle syng in prisoun? **1448** *Paston Lett.* I. 74 Sum be in pryson in the jayll at Coventre. *a* **1500** in Arnolde *Chron.* (1811) 264 Yf ony thing in this lettre be vntrue, I am contente that your Grace giue vnto me therfore perpetuell prison. **1535** COVERDALE *Ps.* cxlv[i]. 7 The Lorde lowseth men out of preson. **1559** *Mirr. Mag., Dk. of Suffolk* xx, And caused me in prison to be thralled. **1581** MARBECK *Bk. of Notes* 665 The King caused him to be clapt in prison, but he brake prison. **1621** *Execution at Prague* in *Harl. Misc.* (Malh.) III. 411 Remain in perpetual prison. **1700** DRYDEN *Pal. & Arc.* I. 461 While I Must languish in despair, in prison die. **1897** *Daily News* 30 Aug. 5/1 Prison for lads should be the last, and not the first, resort.

b. with *a, the*, or a possessive, or in plural, referring more distinctly to a material structure.

State prison: (*a*) a prison for the confinement of political offenders; (*b*) *U.S.* a prison under the control of the authorities of a State.

c **1175** *Lamb. Hom.* 33 Þe mon Þe leie xii. moneð in ane prisune. *c* **1200** *Trin. Coll. Hom.* 131 Seint iohan baptiste was bihaueded in herodes prisone. *a* **1300** *Cursor M.* 13068 Iohn..Þou sal in mi presun lii. **13..** *E.E. Allit. P.* C. 79, I com wyth Þose typynges, Þay tame bylyue, Pynez me in a prysoun, put me in stokkes. **1382** WYCLIF *Acts* v. 23 We founden the prisoun schit with al diligence, and the keperis stondinge at the ȝatis. *c* **1400** *Destr. Troy* 3518 The kyng Þen comaund to..fetur hir fast in a fre prisoune,—A stithe house of stone. **1490** CAXTON *Eneydos* xxxii. 120 Thus eschaped dedalus oute of the pryson of Mynos kynge of Crete. **1530** PALSGR. 258/2 Prison a dongyon, *chartre*. *a* **1572** KNOX *Hist. Ref.* Wks. 1846 I. 383 The uthir [was] in vyle preassoun cassin. **1600** J. PORY tr. *Leo's Africa* 33 There are no prisons in al his empire: for..iustice is executed out of hand. **1637** *Documents agst. Prynne* (Camden) 91 The order to send Doctor Bastwicke, Mr. Burton, and Mr. Prin to their severall remote prisons. **1649** LOVELACE *To Althea from*

Prison iv, Stone Walls doe not a Prison make, Nor Iron bars a Cage. **1777** Howard (*title*) The State of the Prisons in England and Wales, with Preliminary Observations, and an account of some foreign Prisons. **1795** *Jemima* II. 77 Gave the air of a state prison to the apartment. **1823** *Act 4 Geo. IV*, c. 64 §76 Nothing in this Act contained shall extend to the.. Prison of Bridewell, nor to the Fleet Prison, or to the Prison of the Marshalsea. **1885** Major Griffiths in *Encycl. Brit.* XIX. 747/2 The atrocities perpetrated [*c* 1730] by the keepers of the chief debtors' prisons in London. *Ibid.* 755/2 Where the sentence passes beyond two years..the prisoner becomes a convict, and undergoes his penalty in one or more of the convict prisons. **189.** Sir G. Kekewich in *Westm. Gaz.* 20 Mar. (1900), 10/1 Every time I hear of a new school being opened, I say to myself 'There goes another prison'.

c. *transf.* and *fig.* (from a and b.)

a **1225** *Ancr. R.* 54 Eue..leop..vrom þes eorðe to helle, þer heo lei ine prisune uour þusend ȝer & moare. **1377** Langl. *P. Pl.* B. xi. 128 Resoun shal..casten hym in arrerage, And putten hym after in a prisone in purgatorie to brenne. **1382** Wyclif *1 Pet.* iii. 19 To hem that weren closid to gydere in prisoun he comynge in spirit prechide [1611 He went and preached vnto the spirits in prison]. **1387** Trevisa *Higden* (Rolls) VI. 377 Aluredus..ladde uncerteyn and unesy lyf in þe wode contrayes of Somersete..Aluredus com out of prison. **1509** Hawes *Past. Pleas.* xxxii. (Percy Soc.) 157 This False Reporte hath broken pryson, With his subtyl crafte and evyl treason. **1526** *Pilgr. Perf.* (W. de W. 1531) 75b, The Cite is to me a pryson, and the wyldernes a paradyse. **1602** Shaks. *Ham.* ii. ii. 246–9. **1606** Bp. Hall *Medit. & Vows* ii. §5. 132, I may not breake prison, till I bee loosed by death. **1719** De Foe *Crusoe* i. 113 The Island was certainly a Prison to me. **1835** Sir J. Ross *Narr. 2nd Voy.* xxxiii. 473 Our winter prison was before us. **1880** E. H. Plumptre in *Dict. Chr. Biog.* II. 196/1 So Cyril of Jerusalem..speaks of Christ as descending to Hades... The souls that had been long in prison were set free.

d. In *Roulette* and related board-games: a position on the board where bets are held in abeyance until the next round of play; *spec.* in phr. *to put* (a stake) *in prison*.

1867 *Bohn's Hand-Bk. Games* 346 The punters may..have their stake moved into the middle semicircles of the colour they then choose, called 'la première prison', the first prison, to be determined by the next event, whether they lose all or are set at liberty. **1940** Wodehouse *Eggs, Beans & Crumpets* 32 When Zero turns up..stakes on the even chances aren't scooped up—they are what is called put in prison. **1977** P. Arnold *Encycl. Gambling* 247/1 *Prison*, a convention whereby a stake on the even-money chances at roulette is left on the table, or 'put in prison' when zero appears, to be either retained by the bettor or lost according to the next spin.

e. ***prison-without-bars*** (colloq.): an open prison (open *a.* 2c).

1948 *Manch. Even. News* 10 Nov., The former governor of Britain's 'prison-without-bars' at Loudham Grange. **1952** 'J. Henry' *Who lie in Gaol* v. 69, I heard a great deal of the many advantages I would enjoy at the prison-without-bars at York; in fact it was looked upon as a form of heaven by most of the prisoners [at Holloway]. **1959** 'H. Carmichael' *Stranglehold* vi. 58 A solicitor who was doing time at the prison-without-bars.

†**2.** A person held in prison; a prisoner. *Obs.*

[**1195** *Charter Rich. I* in Rymer *Fœdera* I. 92/2 Hiis omnibus per actis Comes Leicestriæ, et omnes Prisones, et hostagii Prisonum..liberabuntur.] *a* **1225** *Ancr. R.* 32 þe pine þet prisuns þolieð; þet heo liggeð mid iren heuie iveotered. [**1292** Britton i. xii. §2 Et si le prisoun qi si avera eschapé.] *a* **1300** *Cursor M.* 4436 (Cott.) All þe prisuns [*v.rr.* presunes, prisouns] þat þar was, þat oþer in prisun war or band. **13..** *Evang. Nicod.* 521 in Herrig's *Archiv* LIII. 401 A pryson þai had hight Barabas. **1377** Langl. *P. Pl.* B. xviii. 58 Pitousliche and pale as a prisoun þat deyeth. **1438** *Bk. Alexander Grt.* (Bann.) 4 Thay tuik na tent to tak presounis. **1494** Fabyan *Chron.* vii. 530 They..toke with them all seyntwary men, & the prysons of Newgate, Ludgate, & of bothe Counters.

3. *attrib.* and *Comb.* **a.** attributive: (*a*) of or pertaining to a prison or prisons, as *prison-accommodation, -boat, -buildings, -cell, chaplain, -clock, Commission* (commission 6), *-discipline, -dream, -dress, -garment, -ground, guard, -hour, -industry, -labour, -library, officer, -official, pallor, -piety, reform, -rime, -roof, -sister, -thrall, -torture, -wall* (also *fig.*), *warder, yard*; (*b*) confined in a prison, as *prison-author, -slave, woman*; (*c*) serving as a prison or place of confinement, as *prison camp, chamber, farm, fort, fortress, hold, hospital, island, isle, pit, place, room, ship, tower*. **b.** objective and object. gen., as *prison-cleaner, -keeper, -making, visitor*; *prison-visiting* sb.; *prison-bursting, -escaping, fancying* adjs. **c.** instrumental, locative, etc., as *prison-born, -bound, -caused, -flavoured, -grey, -made, -taught*; also *prison-free, -like* adjs. **d.** Special comb.: **prison-bird**, one who has been often or long in prison for felonies: cf. jail-bird; **prison-breach, -breaking**, a breaking out of a lawfully confined person from prison: cf. *to break prison*: see 1a and break *v.* 19; so *prison-breaker*; **prison-crop**, hair cut very short, 'county-crop': cf. crop *sb.* 13; so *prison-cropped* adj.; **prison editor**, an editor (of a newspaper) who takes the legal responsibility for what appears in the paper, and serves the terms of imprisonment that conviction may entail; **prison-fever** = jail-fever; **prison haircut** = *prison-crop*; **prison-van**, a close carriage for the conveyance of prisoners. Also prison-bar, -door, etc.

1907 *Westm. Gaz.* 23 Oct. 16/2 Mrs. Price..had many distinguished predecessors as *prison-authors. It was in Newgate that Defoe wrote his 'Jure Divino' [etc.]. **1632** Massinger *City Madam* i. i, I sent the *prison-bird this morning for them. **1898** Besant *Orange Girl* Prol., 'I venture to ask who you are.' 'A prison bird, madam. Nothing more.' *c* **1820** S. Rogers *Italy, St. Mark's Place* 114 Most nights arrived The *prison-boat. **1660** Fuller *Mixt Contempl.* (1841) 173, I lack..many things which thou, being *prison-born, neither art nor can be sensible of. **1853** Kane *Grinnell Exp.* xxix. (1856) 240 Us, poor *prison-bound vagrants. **1903** Ld. W. N[eville] *Penal Servitude* vi. 63 A most irregular proceeding,..calculated to lead to conspiracy, *prison-breach. **1725** (*title*) The *Prison-Breaker; or, the Adventures of John Sheppard. *a* **1849** J. C. Mangan *Poems* (1859) 455 *Prison-bursting Death! Welcome be thy blow! **1925** *Scribner's Mag.* Oct. 386/1 The scene is a Turkish *prison-camp during the recent war. **1978** *Lancashire Life* Nov. 150/1 (Advt.), Mr. P——, a Pole who arrived in England in 1947 after..escaping from a German prison camp. **1902** Major Griffiths in *Encycl. Brit.* XXXII. 7/1 The *prison cell, which in effect typifies the modern system. **1797** Mrs. Radcliffe *Italian* xii, The passage..probably led to the *prison-chamber which Olivia had described. *a* **1902** S. Butler *Way of All Flesh* (1903) lxv. 293 He might experimentalise advantageously upon the viler soul of the *prison chaplain. **1910** *Encycl. Brit.* V. 851/2 Prison chaplains are appointed by the home secretary. **1972** N. Marsh *Tied up in Tinsel* iii. 78 The prison chaplain gave a short, civilized sermon. **1898** O. Wilde *Ballad of Reading Gaol* 18 The *prison-clock Smote on the shivering air. **1898** *Westm. Gaz.* 18 May 9/2 Down till after 1801 'a *prison crop' was unknown in the services—officers and men wore their hair in queue. **1894** A. Robertson *Nuggets* 13 You'll find he's *prison cropped. **1818** T. F. Buxton *Inquiry Prison Discipline* 137 Having..described two..opposite modes of *prison discipline, I would suggest.., that a comparison of these is the most certain criterion of their respective merits. **1834** J. S. Mill in *Monthly Repos.* VIII. 590 Has not a notion grown up within a few years, (we believe a very false one), that the increased mildness of prison-discipline has made our gaols..places where the prisoner is actually too comfortable, and too well off? **1857** Ruskin *Pol. Econ. Art* i. §2. 56 Without..pushing our calculations quite to this prison-discipline extreme. **1885** Major Griffiths in *Encycl. Brit.* XIX. 749/1 Stimulated..by the success achieved by Mrs. Fry, the Prison Discipline Society continued its useful labours. **1869** W. P. Mackay *Grace & Truth* (1875) 26 The *prison-dress that you have on. **1896** *Daily News* 14 Nov. 6/7 A writer in the 'Pretoria Press' says, in connection with the Coercion Act recently passed: 'Should the Press Law come into force, it will be necessary for some of our papers to become possessed of a '*Prison Editor'. **1905** *Daily Chron.* 28 Sept. 4/6 In France..most of the important political articles are signed, and the name of an editor is generally printed on the main page. But it is sometimes merely that of the 'prison editor'. **1961** *Atlanta Constitution* 4 Nov. 1 The jury praised the administration and operation of the Atlanta Police Department, the Fulton Tax Commissioner's Office, the Bellwood and Alpharetta *prison farms, [etc.]. **1968** *Listener* 15 Feb. 210/1 As remarkable..is the improvement he has brought about in his year in charge of the smaller prison farm, Tucker. **1975** C. Weston *Susannah Screaming* (1976) iii. 39 Delgado made a break from the prison farm where he had been sent after a period of good behavior in a federal cellblock. **1853** Cdl. Wiseman *Ess.* III. 20 An African..*prison-fort, where galley-slaves are detained. **18..** *Lang Johnny Moir* xlix. in Child *Ballads* viii. (1892) 400/1 They've taen the lady by the hand And set her *prison-free. **1560** Bible (Genev.) *Jer.* lii. 33 Euil-merodach..broght him out of prison,..And changed his *prison garments [Coverd. clothes of his preson]. **1956** 'H. MacDiarmid' *Stony Limits & Scots Unbound* 90 A flash of sun in a country all *prison-grey. **14..** *Sir Beues* 1311 (MS. M) Whan he was down in *preson grund Beues handis they on-bound. **1961** W. T. Ballard *Night Riders* i. 15 Two wore the uniform of *prison guards, three the striped suits of convicts. **1970** G. Jackson *Let.* 10 June in *Soledad Brother* (1971) 40, I am being tried in court right now..for the alleged slaying of a prison guard. **1977** *Time* 12 Dec. 47/3 With only good time remaining as a route to early release, the potential for abuse by prison guards would be heightened as well. **1974** *Times* 17 Aug. 7/1 A snotty little nervous kid with a *prison haircut. **1837** Chalmers *Lect. Rom.* I. iv. 68 They chain it, as it were, in the *prison-hold of their own corruptions. **1933** J. Buchan *Prince of Captivity* ii. i. 178 You would spend some weeks in a *prison hospital till they patched you up. **1943** F. Thompson *Candleford Green* ix. 142 Such a journey..and a prison hospital..at the end of it. **1978** P. G. Winslow *Coppergold* 48 He fell a victim to influenza..was taken to the prison hospital. **1727–46** Thomson *Summer* 1507 Raleigh..with his *prison-hours enrich'd the world. **1855** Dickens *Dorrit* (1857) i. i. 4 The *prison-keeper appeared carrying..a basket. **1881** W. W. Newton *Serm. Boys & Girls* 2 Order the prison-keepers to let me go. **1967** H. Pinter *Night School* in *Tea Party & Other Plays* 101, I was running the *prison library. **1979** K. Bonfiglioli *After You with Pistol* vi. 31 He gets a nice job in the prison library but *horrid* things happen to him in the showers. **1839** E. A. Poe in *Burton's Gentleman's Mag.* Oct. 206 This *prison-like rampart formed the limits of our domain. **1847** Smeaton *Builder's Man.* 198 Far superior to the bald and prison-like structures which haunt the metropolis. **1916** D. H. Lawrence *Amores* 77 The town Glimmers with subtle ghosts Going up and down In a common, prison-like dress. **1944** A. L. Rowse *Eng. Spirit* xxxv. 244 That sepulchral, prison-like building. **1970** P. Dickinson *Seals* ii. 53 Many criminals..are really only happy..when..their day is shaped by a prison-like discipline. **1895** *Westm. Gaz.* 21 Feb. 3/3 Legislation..effectual in keeping out of this country *prison-made goods. **1905** *Daily Chron.* 20 May 3/1 The prison-made workman is liable to be spotted in an outside factory. **1907** B. Thomson *Story of Dartmoor Prison* xxi. 260 The better class of men came to realize that *prison officers were their friends rather than their enemies. **1961** *Observer* 9 Apr. 22/8 He refers to prison officers as prison warders, a title abandoned something like thirty years ago. **1978** P. Lovesey *Waxwork* 79 It is quite impossible to conduct a conversation through an iron grille with two prison officers at my client's shoulder. **1935** A. J. Cronin *Stars look Down* ii. xx. 446 He sat there with his *prison pallor upon him. **1977** *New Yorker* 24 Oct. 141/1 He squints into the unaccustomed sunlight..and..suffers from a case of prison pallor. **1891** *Daily News* 22 Jan. 7/2 [An] officer of the Mendicity Society produced a *prison photograph of prisoner. **1677** (*title*) *Prison-Pietie: or, Meditations Divine and Moral. Digested into Poetical Heads..By Samuel Speed, Prisoner in Ludgate. **1646** P. Bulkeley *Gospel Covt.* i. 21 To see the children of our father in the dungeon, and *prison-pit. **1890** W. Booth *In Darkest Eng.* i. ix. 74 Once the work of *Prison Reform is taken in hand by men..who are in full sympathy with the class for whose benefit they labour. **1972** A. Roudybush *Sybaritic Death* (1974) vii. 67 His original project had been to devote his activities to the cause of prison reform. **1810** Scott *Lady of L.* vi. xii, 'Twas a *prison-room Of stern security and gloom. **1795** Nelson in Nicolas *Disp.* (1845) II. 47, I am not Captain of the Ça Ira. At present she is a *Prison-ship. **1553** Brende *Q. Curtius* v. 83 Shall our chyldren, shall our brethren acknowledge vs, beyng *prison slaues? **1866** J. H. Newman *Gerontius* i. 12 Rescue..the two Apostles from their *prison-thrall. **1835** L. E. Landon *Misc. Poems* 23 When she left her *prison-tower..It was to seek the sea-beat strand. **1858** Simmonds *Dict. Trade*, *Prison-van, a police carriage for conveying prisoners to and from a court of justice. **1880** G. R. Sims *Three Brass Balls* xvii, The time when 'Black Maria', the prison van, stands waiting at the door. **1838** H. Martineau *Retrospect of Western Travel* I. 224, I trust that the practice of *prison-visiting will gain ground. **1973** L. Cooper *Tea on Sunday* i. 21 Barry Slater, the unfortunate legacy of Alberta's spell of prison visiting. **1837** H. Martineau *Society in Amer.* II. iii. iv. 285 Every *prison visitor has been conscious, on first conversing privately with a criminal, of a feeling of surprise at finding him so human. **1975** N. Freeling *What are Bugles blowing For?* xv. 88 Vera made a good prison visitor. **1593** Shaks. *Rich. II*, v. v. 21 The Flinty ribbes Of this hard world, my ragged *prison walles. **1706** Watts *Horæ Lyr.* i. *Happy Frailty* xii, Devotion breaks the prison-walls, And speeds my last remove. **1855** Trollope *Warden* xvi. 248 No convict, slipping down from a prison wall, ever feared to see the gaoler more entirely than Mr. Harding did to see his son-in-law. **1898** O. Wilde *Ballad of Reading Gaol* 16 The weeping prison-wall. **1951** M. Kennedy *Lucy Carmichael* i. vii. 62 Rickie peeped for a moment over the prison walls of his own depression. *a* **1902** S. Butler *Way of All Flesh* (1903) lxiv. 286 The *prison warder..sent for the doctor. **1914** *Prison Officers Mag.* Nov. 450/2 For the past four years the majority of the Irish Prison Warders have favoured us with their confidence and support. **1928** [see wardering *vbl. sb.*]. **1961** [see *prison officer* above]. **1978** M. Butterworth *X marks Spot* 179 With two escorting prison warders as witnesses. **1655** (*title*) The Oppressed Close Prisoner In Windsor-Castle, his Defiance to The Father of Lyes. By Chr. Feake, in his *Prison-Watch-tower. **1898** *Daily News* 19 Nov. 6/3 It took half a dozen of these poor nerveless *prison women to do what one ordinary energetic laundry woman would accomplish. **1642** in *Rec. Early Hist. Boston* (1877) II. 70 The Constables are appointed..to take care for the building a salt peter howse in the *prison yarde. **1776** *Jrnls. Continental Congress U.S.* (1906) IV. 121 Resolved, That the said J. Connolly be allowed..to walk in the prison yard or hall. **1851** J. J. Lancaster in *Rep. Sel. Comm. Passengers' Act* 142 in *Parl. Papers* XIX. 1 Those in Millbank [*sc.* a London military hospital] are drawn up in the prison-yard or wards. **1856** Dickens *Dorrit* (1857) ii. vi. 383 They prowled about..in the old, dreary, prison-yard manner. **1963** N. Marsh *Dead Water* (1964) v. 126 She..walked aimlessly..as if the garden were a prison yard.

prison ('prɪz(ə)n), *v.* Forms: see the sb. [f. prison *sb.*] *trans.* To put in prison, make a prisoner of; to incarcerate; to keep in a prison or other place of confinement; to detain in custody. Now *poet.* or *rhet.*, and *north. dial.* (the usual word for the literal sense being imprison).

[**1292** Britton i. xii. §6 Mes les prisounez pur felounie en nule manere voloms suffrer de nul homme enpleder.] *a* **1300** *Cursor M.* 4484 (Gött.) First men stal me [Joseph] fra mi thede And presuned [*v.rr.* prisund, prisoned] me, sacles of dede. *c* **1330** R. Brunne *Chron.* (1810) 101 Sir William Crispyn with þe duke was led, Togider prisoned. *c* **1380** Wyclif *Wks.* (1880) 79 So trewe prestis schullen be cursed & prisoned. **1387** Trevisa *Higden* (Rolls) IV. 181 His felawes were..i-prisoned to her lyves ende. **1432–50** tr. *Higden* (Rolls) III. 39 Cordeilla the doȝter of kynge Leir,..whom Morganus and Cunedagius prisonede at the laste. **1526** Tindale *Acts* xxii. 19, I presoned and bett in euery sinagoge them that beleued on the. **1542** Brinklow *Compl.* xii. 29 Many tymes thei preson men for their fryndes pleasure. **1608** Sylvester *Du Bartas* ii. iv. iv. *Decay* 1104 Even as a Lion pris'ned in his grate,..Roars hideously. **1813** Byron *Corsair* ii. xi, A chief on land—an outlaw on the deep—Destroying—saving—prison'd—and asleep! [**1903** in *Eng. Dial. Dict.* instanced from Shetland Is. to Mid Yorksh.]

b. *transf.* and *fig.* To restrain from liberty of movement; to confine; = imprison 1b and 2.

1413 *Pilgr. Sowle* (Caxton) iv. xxxviii. (1859) 67 Here myght thou see the meschyef of vntrewe counceylle, that made this gentil Lyberalite prisond. **1450–1530** *Myrr. our Ladye* 11 Whyle our soulles ar prysoned in these dedly bodyes. **1593** Shaks. *Lucr.* 642 His true respect will prison false desire. **1633** Bp. Hall *Hard Texts, N.T.* 358 Whose spirits are now fast prisoned in Hell. **1742** Young *Nt. Th.* iii. 524 From winds, and waves, and central night, Tho' prison'd there, my dust too I reclaim. **1847** C. Brontë *J. Eyre* xxxvii, I arrested his wandering hand, and prisoned it in both mine. **1878** Browning *Poets Croisic* xxv, Why prison his career while Christendom Lay open to reward acknowledged worth?

Hence 'prisoned *ppl. a.*, confined in or as in a prison; imprisoned.

a **1327** in *Pol. Poems* (Camden) 202 The lafful man ssal be i-bund,..And i-holdin fast prisund. *c* **1375** *Lay Folks Mass Bk.* (MS. B.) 378, I pray þe, lord..To hom þat are..seke or prisonde, or o-pon þo see..til alle hom, þou sende socoure. **1598** Sylvester *Du Bartas* ii. i. iii. *Furies* 462 W[th] prisoned winds the wringling Colick pains them. **1790** Cowper *Stanzas* 2 Where the prison'd lark is hung. **1811** Scott *Don Roderick* xxxii, The groans of prisoned victims mar the lays. *a* **1881** Rossetti *House of Life* iii, Thine eyes Draw up my prisoned spirit to thy Soul.

'prison-'bar. a. *pl.* The iron bars by which a prison, its door, windows, etc., are made fast; bars which imprison. b. ***prison-bars***, a game: see PRISONERS' BARS.

1844 WELBY *Poems* (1867) 86 Yet from my prison-bars A narrow strip of sky is all I see. **1860** EMERSON *Cond. Life, Worship* Wks. (Bohn) II. 393 He to captivity was sold, But him no prison-bars would hold.

'prison-'door. The door of a prison. *lit.* or *fig.*

a **1300** *Cursor M.* 19305 þe angel..þe prisun dors lefte als he fand. *a* **1450** MYRC *Festial* 81 He openyd þe pryson-dyrre, and bade hym go. **1684** T. BURNET *Th. Earth* II. 67 The particles of fire, that are shut up in several bodies, will easily flie abroad, when by a further degree of relaxation you shake off their chains, and open the prison-doors. **1869** W. P. MACKAY *Grace & Truth* (1875) 26 The man that was condemned walks out free through the opened prison-doors.

'prisoner[1]. *Obs.* exc. *dial.* [f. PRISON *sb.* or *v.* + -ER[1]: cf. *jail-er*; also med.L. *prœsonerius* (1285 in Const. K. James of Sicily, Du Cange), and Anglo-L. *prisonātor* (*c* 1290 in *Fleta* I. xx. §9).] The keeper of a prison; a jailer.

c **1250** *Gen. & Ex.* 2042 So gan him [iosep] luuen ðe prisuner, And him ðe chartre haueð bi-taȝt, Wið ðo prisunes to liuen in haȝt. [Still sometimes so used dialectally. It was familiar to me in childhood. J.A.H.M.]

prisoner[2] ('prɪz(ə)nə(r)). Forms: see PRISON *sb.*; also 6 priesoner. [ME. a. F. *prisonnier* (*prisonier*, 12–13th c. in Hatz.-Darm.) = med.L. *pris(i)ōnāri-us* (14th c. in Du Cange): see PRISON *sb.* and -ER[2] 2.]

1. a. One who is kept in prison or in custody; *spec.* one who is in custody as the result of a legal process, either as having been condemned to imprisonment as a punishment, or as awaiting trial for some offence.

prisoner at the bar: a person in custody upon a criminal charge, and on trial in a court of justice. ***prisoner of conscience***, one who is detained or imprisoned because of his or her political or religious beliefs. ***prisoner of state, state prisoner***, one confined for political or state reasons.

13.. *Coer de L.* 754 To the jayler thanne sayd he: 'Thy presoners let me see!' **1377** LANGL. *P. Pl.* B. III. 136 She leteth passe prisoneres and payeth for hem ofte. *c* **1425** *Cursor M.* 9598 (Laud) She was algate abowte For to haue this presonar [*earlier MSS.* prisun, etc.] owt. **1552** LYNDESAY *Monarche* 4107 The rest in Egypt thay did sende, Presonaris to thare lyuis ende. **1637** *Documents agst. Prynne* (Camden) 68 A letter..for the removing of William Prinne from the Goale or Castle of Carnarvon,..to one of the two Castles of the Isle of Jersey,..to be there kept close prisoner. **1644** MILTON *Areop.* (Arb.) 60 A prisner to the Inquisition. **1660** *Trial Regic.* 32 The Court being Assembled, the Keeper was commanded to set the Prisoners to the Bar. **1670** *Act 22 & 23 Chas. II*, c. 20 §13 That it shall not be lawful hereafter.., to put, keep or lodge Prisoners for Debt and Felons together in one Room. **1769** BLACKSTONE *Comm.* IV. xxii. 296 The justice, before whom such prisoner is brought, is bound immediately to examine the circumstances of the crime alleged. **1807** (*title*) Case of St. John Mason, who was confined as a state-prisoner, in Kilmainham. **1824** *Act 5 Geo. IV*, c. 85 §26 If there be indorsed upon such Pass..the Words 'Pass of a discharged Prisoner'. **1834** *Tait's Mag.* I. 416/2 When a convict or prisoner (for that is the colonial phrase) becomes free, either by serving out the period of his sentence of transportation or by obtaining a pardon. **1848** W. H. KELLY tr. *L. Blanc's Hist. Ten Y.* II. 75 Standing in a firm and graceful attitude, at the end of the prisoner's bench, he gazed deliberately upon the audience. *c* **1900** *What of the Night?* (Ch. Army Press) 20 The Church Army has been officially appointed by the Home Office a 'Discharged Prisoners' Aid Society'. **1961** *Amnesty* 11 July 2/1 What are the facts we need? There are thousands of them and each one is a human being, a prisoner of conscience behind bars because of his political views or religious beliefs. **1962** *Time to keep Silence* (Amnesty International), Prisoners of Conscience are of two distinct sorts—those prepared to suffer persecution because they have the courage of their convictions, and those who are prisoners of their own conscience because they lack the courage of their convictions. When the latter become the former, all of us will be free. **1970** *Times* 20 Apr. 6/5 A great many prisoners of conscience, it claims, are sent with or without trial 'to the so-called special psychiatric hospitals'. **1977** *Guernsey Weekly Press* 21 July 6/6 A prisoner of conscience is a person who is detained because of his political, racial or religious beliefs.

b. prisoner's dilemma (see quot. 1957); **prisoner's friend** *Armed services*, an officer who represents a defendant at a court martial.

1957 LUCE & RAIFFA *Games & Decisions* v. 95 We turn now to a different example of a non-zero-sum game. This one is attributed to A. W. Tucker... The following interpretation, known as the prisoner's dilemma is popular: Two suspects are taken into custody and separated. The district attorney is certain that they are guilty of a specific crime, but he does not have adequate evidence to convict them at a trial. He points out to each prisoner that each has two alternatives: to confess to the crime the police are sure they have done, or not to confess. If they both do not confess ..he will book them on some very minor trumped-up charge..and they will both receive minor punishment; if they both confess they will be prosecuted, but he will recommend less than the most severe sentence; but if one confesses and the other does not, then the confessor will receive lenient treatment for turning state's evidence whereas the latter will get 'the book' slapped at him. **1963** *Jrnl. Abnormal Psychol.* LXVI. 308/2 Trust of the other person plays a critical role in determining choices made in Prisoner's Dilemma games. **1977** A. W. TUCKER *MS. letter* (*copy in O.E.D. files*), The Prisoner's Dilemma is my brain child. I concocted it at Stanford in early 1950 as a catchy example to enliven a semi-popular talk on Game Theory... My example became known by the 'grapevine', but I did not publish it. **1900** *Westm. Gaz.* 24 Nov. 10/1 Lieutenant —— ..was assigned as advocate for the prisoner, or 'prisoner's friend', as the term stands in the military system of jurisprudence. **1914** 'BARTIMEUS' *Naval Occasions* xxi. 198 The Prisoner's Friend then gave evidence. **1972** J. POTTER *Going West* 191 He was prisoner's friend to you in that spot of unpleasantness during the war.

2. a. One who has been captured in war; one who has fallen into the hands of or surrendered to an opponent; a captive. ***to take*** (a person) ***prisoner***, to seize and hold as a prisoner, esp. in war. Now often more fully ***prisoner of war*** (freq. abbrev. *P.O.W.*, *POW* (see P II)). Also *attrib.*, esp. in ***prisoner(s) of war camp***. Hence ***prisoner-of-wardom*** nonce-word.

c **1350** *Will. Palerne* 1267 þan william..Profered him þat prisoner prestely at his wille To do þan wiþ þe duk what him dere þouȝt. **13..** *E.E. Allit. P.* B. 1297 Presented him þe prisoneres in pray þat þay token. *c* **1420** *Avow. Arth.* xxxiii, He toke him there to presunnere. *c* **1450** *Merlin* 412 Whan thei hadde chaced hem to the nyght, thei returned with grete plente of prisoners. **1460** *Lybeaus Disc.* 412 For prisoner i mot me yeld, As overcome yn feld. *c* **1460** FORTESCUE *Abs. & Lim. Mon.* ix. (1885) 130 The Erlis of Lecestir and Glocestre..rose ayenest thair kynge Herre the iij[de], and toke hym and his sonne prisoners in the ffelde. **1553** EDEN *Treat. Newe Ind.* (Arb.) 13 The gouernour..so by crafte circumuented him, that he toke him priesoner, and commaunded him to be hanged on the sayle yarde of the shyp. **1596** SHAKS. *1 Hen. IV*, v. iii. 10 This Sword hath ended him, so shall it thee, Vnlesse thou yeeld thee as a Prisoner. **1601** —— *Jul. C.* v. iii. 37 In Parthia did I take thee Prisoner, And then I swore thee, sauing of thy life, That whatsoeuer I did bid thee do, Thou should'st attempt it. **1665** MANLEY *Grotius' Low C. Warres* 305 To make Exchange of Prisoners. **1678** BUTLER *Hud.* III. iii. 113 Ralph himself, your trusty Squire Wh[o]..though a Prisoner of War, Have brought you safe, where now you are. *Ibid.* 120 The Infernal Conjurer Pursu'd and took me Prisoner. **1864** BURTON *Scot Abr.* I. i. 20 Baliol, being then a prisoner of war. **1902** BARCLAY in *Encycl. Brit.* XXXIII. 753/2 Prisoners of war are in the power of the hostile government, but not in that of the individuals or corps who captured them. **1922** C. E. MONTAGUE *Disenchantment* x. 146 To 'take it out of' German prisoners of war. **1922** *Encycl. Brit.* XXXII. 163/1 The inspection of prisoners-of-war camps by the accredited representatives of the protecting State. **1944** [see KRIEGIE]. **1946** *Encycl. Brit. Bk. of Yr.* 605/1 (*caption*) Japanese inmates of a prisoner of war camp on Guam. **1961** *Times* 7 June 17/1 A Union prisoner-of-war camp. **1974** *Times* 4 Mar. 9/4 (*heading*) Prisoner-of-wardom. **1974** [see OFLAG].

b. A captive at the game of prisoners' bars.

1801 STRUTT *Sports & Past.* II. ii. §12 If the person sent to relieve his confederate be touched by an antagonist before he reaches him, he also becomes a prisoner, and stands in equal need of deliverance.

3. *transf.* and *fig.* One who or that which is confined to a place or position.

c **1380** WYCLIF *Wks.* (1880) 323 Siche bildyngis makyn pride, and not comfort of goddis prisounneris. **1526** *Pilgr. Perf.* (W. de W. 1531) 100 This worlde is the pryson, & we be the prysoners. *c* **1586** C'TESS PEMBROKE *Ps.* XLIX. iii, Death his prisoner never will forgoe. **1613** SHAKS. *Hen. VIII*, I. i. 5 An vntimely Ague Staid me a Prisoner in my Chamber. **1717** POPE *Elegy Unfort. Lady* 18 Most souls, 'tis true, but peep out once an age Dull sullen pris'ners in the body's cage. **1867** LATHAM *Black & White* 115 Here we remain, still prisoners at Fortress Monro..the steamboat never came to take passengers to Norfolk. **1878** RUSKIN *Hortus Inclusus* (1887) 53, I came to see Prince Leopold, who has been a prisoner to his sofa lately. *Mod.* He made her hand a prisoner.

4. *attrib.* Of or pertaining to a prisoner; that is a prisoner.

1846 C. G. PROWETT *Prometh. Bound* 8 Thou com'st to find A prisoner-God. **1855** LONGF. *Hiaw.* XIII. 153 With his prisoner-string he bound him. **1878** W. PATER *Wks.* (1901) VIII. 196 On one of those two prisoner days when Lewis was sick. **1896** *Daily News* 21 Nov. 8/2 His medical attendant..remained with the prisoner-patient throughout a considerable part of the night. **1904** A. GRIFFITHS *Fifty Years Public Service* xix. 277 He cut off remorselessly the prisoner gardeners and the prisoner stable-man.

Hence **'prisonership**, the condition of a prisoner.

1906 tr. *Fogazzaro's Saint* Introd. 14 That other fiction, the Pope's prisonership in the Vatican.

prisoners' 'bars, 'base. Forms: α. 7– prison-bars (8 bar); β. prison-base (7 prison bace, 8 bass); γ. 9 prisoner's, -ers' bars; δ. 9 prisoner's, -ers' base. [See PRISONER[2] and BAR *sb.*[1] 17, BASE *sb.*[2] The earlier forms were *prison-bars* and *prison-base*, the former app. the original: cf. the Fr. name of the game *les barres*; also the Fr. and earlier Eng. pronunciation of *base* (bɑːs, bɑːz).

1331–2 *Rolls of Parlt.* II. 65/1 Qe nul enfaunt ne autres jue en ul lieu du Paleys de Westmonstre, durant le Parlement.. a bares ne a autres jues. **1530** PALSGR. 196/1 Bace playe, *jeu aux barres*.]

A game played in a variety of ways, chiefly by boys; the players are divided into two parties, who occupy distinct demarcations, 'bases', 'homes', or 'dens', the aim of each side being to make prisoner by touching any player of the opposite side who runs out from his enclosure.

α. **1611** COTGR., *Barres*, the play at Bace; or, Prison Bars. **1706** FARQUHAR *Recruiting Officer* II. i, Our Army did nothing but play at Prison Bars, and hide and seek with the Enemy. **1755–73** JOHNSON, *Prisonbase*, a kind of rural play, commonly called *prisonbars*. **1768–74** TUCKER *Lt. Nat.* (1834) II. 624 Whether cricket or prison-bar, shuttle-cock or trap-ball be the better amusement? *a* **1795** [see BAR *sb.*[1] 17]. **1883** BURNE *Shropsh. Folk-lore* 524 Men-servants, in the last century, were wont to ask a day's holiday to join or witness a game of prison-bars, arranged beforehand as a cricket-match might be.

β. **1598** DRAYTON *Heroic. Ep.* xxi. 200 Where light-foot Fayries sport at Prison-Base. **1630** —— *Muses Elizium* I. 27 Whilst the Nimphes..Disposed were to play At Barly-breake and Prison-base. **1707** E. CHAMBERLAYNE *Pres. St. Eng.* I. v. (ed. 22) 51 They will go in the Evening to Football, ..Cricket, Prison-base, Wrestling. **1796** MORSE *Amer. Geog.* I. 342 Jumping, hopping, foot races, and prison bass.

γ. **1801** STRUTT *Sports & Past.* II. ii. §12 There is a rustic game called Base or Bars..and in some places Prisoners' Bars. **1864** CAPERN *Devon Provinc.*, *Prisoner's-Bars* or *bonds*, a very ancient game. **1872** *Punch* 6 Apr. 141/2 Prisoner's-bars. **1901** *Pall Mall Mag.* Sept. 38 He was never too busy to..be umpire at 'tig' or prisoners' bars.

δ. **1855** THACKERAY *Newcomes* ii, Playing at cricket, hockey, prisoner's base, and football, according to the season. **1861** *Fun* 12 Oct. 42 An unextinguishable affection for 'prisoners' base'. **1876** GRANT *Burgh Sch. Scotl.* II. v. 180 A game less known, though a most admirable one, is ..'prisoner's base'. **1880** Prisoners' base [see BASE *sb.*[2]].

†**'prison-,fellow.** *Obs.* A companion in prison; a fellow-prisoner.

1526 TINDALE *Col.* iv. 10 Aristarchus my preson felowe [1582 (Rhem.) fellow-prisoner] saluteth you. **1577–87** HOLINSHED *Chron.* III. 1110/2 The lord Thomas Greie being my prison-felow. **1721** STRYPE *Eccl. Mem.* III. xxxiii. 259 Bishop Barlow, who was prison-fellow with him.

'prisonful. [-FUL.] As much or as many as a prison will hold.

1911 G. B. SHAW *Getting Married* 173 If a prisonful of thieves were asked what induced them to take to thieving, [etc.]. **1922** A. BENNETT *Lilian* II. ii. 66 Only the malice of a prisonful of women could have seriously asserted her to be older than Felix.

'prison-'gate. The gate or entrance of a prison. Also *attrib.*, esp. in reference to the rescue and reclamation work for discharged prisoners on leaving the prison.

1590 SHAKS. *Mids. N.* I. ii. 36 Shiuering shocks shall break the locks of prison gates. **1794** HEL. M. WILLIAMS *Lett. on France* (1795) I. 44 He used through the lonely day to count the hours till the prison-gates were closed. **1900** *Westm. Gaz.* 8 Jan. 5/3 As a leading member of the Army's 'Prison Gate' branch, Archie was in his element, and many an old gaol-bird was brought to a better frame of mind..by Archie's judicious ministrations. **1901** *Ibid.* 28 Aug. 8/2 The Salvation Army never turns a deaf ear to any appeal of the kind, and the applicant is now in the prison-gate home.

'prison-house. A house of imprisonment; a building that is or serves as a prison. Often *fig.*

c **1475** *Pict. Voc.* in Wr.-Wülcker 804/6 *Hic carcer*, a presunhowse. **1579–80** NORTH *Plutarch* (1595) 850 So [he] put them both into the prison-house, and made the dores be shut after them. **1602** SHAKS. *Ham.* I. v. 15, I am forbid To tell the secrets of my Prison-House. **1784** COWPER *Task* II. 661 So fare we in this prison-house, the world. **1803–6** WORDSW. *Intim. Immort.* 68 Heaven lies about us in our infancy! Shades of the prison-house begin to close Upon the growing boy. **1864** A. MCKAY *Hist. Kilmarnock* 39 In the old prison-house of the town. **1902** *Daily Chron.* 25 Apr. 6/5 To escape from the prison-house of London streets and factories into the 'great spaces of nature'.

prisoning ('prɪz(ə)nɪŋ), *vbl. sb.* Now *rare.* [f. PRISON *v.* + -ING[1].] The action of the verb PRISON; imprisonment, confinement.

a **1300** *Cursor M.* 21259 Siþen efter prisuning, His saul he yeld to heuen king. *c* **1380** WYCLIF *Serm.* Sel. Wks. II. 376 Boþe þes two prisounyngis..in Moises tyme and Jeremyes. **1561** T. NORTON *Calvin's Inst.* I. xvii. 65 b, I speake not of prysonninges, treasons, robberies, open violence. **1907** *Dublin Rev.* Jan. 30 Feet..Too wayward for the straight path's prisoning.

'prisoning, *ppl. a.* [f. PRISON *v.* + -ING[2].] That prisons or imprisons; imprisoning, confining. Usually *fig.*

1652 BENLOWES *Theoph.* I. i, Souls..Enfranchis'd from their pris'ning clay. **1868** NETTLESHIP *Browning* 243 Spring, which has freed the mountain from its prisoning breastplate of snow. *a* **1892** J. HYSLOP in *Pall Mall G.* 26 Apr. (1892) 6/1 My soul..When that has passed beyond life's prisoning bars.

prisonize ('prɪz(ə)naɪz), *v.* [f. PRISON *sb.* + -IZE.] *trans.* To cause (a person) to adapt himself to prison life. Chiefly in *pass.*: to adapt to the attitudes and social behaviour of prison life, esp. at the expense of one's 'normal' personality. Hence **,prisoni'zation**, the fact or process of becoming adapted to prison life and unfitted for the outside world.

1940 D. CLEMMER *Prison Community* xii. 299 As we use the term Americanization to describe a greater or less degree of the immigrant's integration into the American scheme of life, we may use the term *prisonization* to indicate the taking on in greater or less degree of the folk-ways, mores, customs, and general culture of the penitentiary. *Ibid.* 300 First offenders..'wise up', as the inmates say, or in other words, by association they become prisonized. **1963** T. & P. MORRIS *Pentonville* vii. 169 Prisonization may be defined as the continuous and systematic destruction of the psyche in consequence of the experience of imprisonment, and the adoption of new attitudes and ways of behaving..which may frequently make it impossible for the individual to act successfully in any normal social role. *Ibid.* 170 While the majority of inmates become 'prisonized' in some aspects, few are wholly prisonized. *Ibid.*, A certain type of prisonized man whose behaviour forms the hard core of inmate subculture. **1972** E. HEFFERNAN *Making it in Prison* i. 7 The 'outlaw' has been found to be the most highly 'prisonized' in terms of loyalty to the inmate code. *Ibid.* ii. 32 If any category may be considered 'new' to prisonization, it is the professional, with shorter sentence length..and fewer total years in an institutional atmosphere. **1973** CULL & HARDY *Fund. Criminal Behavior & Correctional Syst.* viii. 147 He found that those inmates who were farthest from release.. were the most prisonized. **1975** D. DUFFEE *Correctional Policy & Prison Organization* iii. 35 The counter-suggestion was made that prisonization is just an institutional form of deprivation felt by the lower class, uneducated, and black offenders most of their lives.

'prisonment. Now *rare.* [f. PRISON *v.* + -MENT; cf. IMPRISONMENT and obs. F. *prisonnement* (? 16th c. in Godef.).] The action of imprisoning, or fact or condition of being imprisoned; detention in a prison or place of confinement; = IMPRISONMENT. Also *fig.*

1387-8 T. USK *Test. Love* II. xi. (Skeat) I. 54 For prisonment or any other disese, [if] he take it paciently, discomfiteth he not, the tiraunte ouer his soule no power maie haue. **1468** *Maldon, Essex, Liber B.* lf. 12 b, Nat.. wythout licence of the Baillies, vpon xl. dayes prisonement and a grete fyn. **1526** TINDALE *2 Cor.* vi. 5 In anguysshe, in strypes, in presonment, in stryfe, in labour. **1607** J. CARPENTER *Plaine Mans Plough* 188 Mockings, scourgings, bands, prisonments, stonings. **1641** J. TRAPPE *Theol. Theol.* vii. 286 The taking away of..thy good Ministers by exile, prisonment, and death. **1893** *Columbus* (Ohio) *Dispatch* 17 Aug., The transformation from prisonment to thrilling liberty is so inexpressibly complete.

b. An imprisoning or confining condition.

1900 CROCKETT *Black Douglas* 6 If he may not sometimes ..lay aside his heavy prisonment of armour and don such a suit as this.

'prisonous, *a. nonce-wd.* [f. PRISON *sb.* + -OUS, after *poisonous*, etc.] Characteristic of a prison.

1855 DICKENS *Dorrit* I. vi, His son began..to be of the prison prisonous and of the street streety. **1888** J. ASHBY STERRY in *Eng. Illustr. Mag.* 109 Horsemonger Lane Gaol.. has an impressive façade..distinctly prisonous in every line and ornamentation.

'prisonry. *nonce-wd.* [f. PRISON *sb.* + -RY.] State or place of imprisonment.

1830 W. TAYLOR *Hist. Surv. Germ. Poetry* II. 389 For worse than death awaited me In this sepulchral prisonry.

prisoptometer (praɪzɒp'tɒmɪtə(r)). [Arbitrarily f. Gr. πρίσ-ις sawing (allied to *prism*) + ὀπτ-ός seen + -(O)METER.] An optical instrument: see quots.

1894 A. L. ADAMS in *27th Bienn. Rep. Illinois Instit. Deaf & Dumb* 62, I found Culbertson's Prisoptometer invaluable as a means of diagnosing the amount and various kinds of astigmatism. **1895** *Syd. Soc. Lex.*, *Prisoptometer*.., an instrument designed for the estimation of varying degrees of ametropia of the eye, by means of two prisms fixed together at their bases.

prisor, obs. f. PRIZER[1].

priss (prɪs). *U.S. colloq.* [Back-formation from PRISSY *a.*] One who is prissy; a prim girl; an effeminate man, a 'pansy'.

1923 G. MCKNIGHT *Eng. Words* iv. 61 Youthful impatience with anything or anybody that interferes with a good time is expressed by such names as *kill-joy*, *frost*, *wet-blanket*... To these may be added, from the language of girls,..*poor potato*,..*cuckoo*, *old priss*, *old Jane*. *Ibid.* 62 If she [*sc.* a girl] is unpopular, she is..a *priss*, a *tomato*, a *chunk of lead*, a *drag*. **1942** BERREY & VAN DEN BARK *Amer. Thes. Slang* §825/32 *Priss*, a girl who objects to 'necking'. **1975** A. BERGMAN *Hollywood & LeVine* (1976) ii. 23, I..was led to my room by an elderly priss named Roy. He told me I looked the rugged type. **1976** *National Observer* (U.S.) 16 Oct. 10/3 Randall..is television's consummate comedy priss, his overelocution and self-righteousness maddeningly funny.

priss(e, obs. f. PRICE *sb.*[1], PRIZE *v.*[1]

prissy ('prɪsɪ), *a.* (and *sb.*) *colloq.* (orig. *U.S.*). [Perh. blend of PRIM *a.* and SISSY.] Precise and over-particular; prim, priggish, or prudish, esp. in a supposedly effeminate way. Also *Comb.* and as *sb.*

1895 J. C. HARRIS *Mr. Rabbit at Home* iv. 40 Once, when I was courting, I spoke of a sitting hen, but the young lady said I was too prissy for anything. **1905** *Dialect Notes* III. 91 *Prissy, adj.* Precise, nice, over-particular. 'She's awful prissy.' Rare. **1925** A. WOOLLCOTT in 'L. Carroll' *Alice's Adventures in Wonderland* p. viii, The extraordinary contrast between the cautious, prissy pace of the man and the mad, gay gait of the tale he told. **1927** *Amer. Speech* II. 362/1 *Prissey*.., a boy who acts like a girl. 'Don't be such a prissey, Jim.' **1927** D. MARQUIS *Archy & Mehitabel* xxiv. 107 Some strait laced prune faced bunch of prissy mouthed sisters of uncharity. **1929** W. FAULKNER *Sound & Fury* 49 He don't like that prissy dress. **1932** E. HEMINGWAY *Death in Afternoon* xvii. 205 He should redeem..the prissy exhibitionistic, aunt-like, withered old maid moral arrogance of a Gide. **1948** M. GILBERT *They never looked Inside* xii. 177 She reminded him instantly of one of Walt Disney's prissy little rabbits. **1952** A. WILSON *Hemlock & After* I. ii. 36 He was disgusted at the precise, prissy tones in which he heard himself saying, 'It's lovely to be in the country.' **1957** *Listener* 2 May 722/1 His work is haunted by a disagreeable, sickly, prissy *art nouveau* rhythm. **1963** *Guardian* 28 Mar. 1/3 The rather prissy manner in which Dr Beeching has chosen to announce his determination to make us turn into a new economic man. **1968** *Times Lit. Suppl.* 28 Nov. 1327/1 The prissy, petit-bourgeois level of Robespierre. **1973** B. BROADFOOT *Ten Lost Years* xxi. 244 We weren't quite as prissy as this New Generation thinks we were. **1975** L. GILLEN *Return to Deepwater* viii. 140 Good grief, you little prissy, you've been kissed before, certainly!

Hence **'prissified** *a.*, **'prissily** *adv.*; **'prissiness.**

1934 WEBSTER, Prissily,..*adv.*—prissiness, *n.* **1957** *Observer* 15 Sept. 13/2 When it aspires to epigram, the dialogue falls into a quaint, soggy prissiness. **1958** *Spectator* 22 Aug. 246/2 Little girls prissily painted a still-life of oranges. **1963** P. M. HUBBARD in *Mag. of Fantasy & Sci. Fiction* Jan. 8/1 He had a slightly prissified voice. **1976** *Listener* 15 July 58/1 The blackcurrant eyes, the prissily pursed mouth. **1976** 'J. Ross' *I know what it's like to Die* xxvi. 161 An accountant's clerk of terrifying prissiness.

prist, -e, obs. pa. pple. of PRIZE *v.*

‖**'pristaf.** Also 7 -affe, 9 -av (-aw); 7 prestave. [Russ. *'pristavъ* an inspector, commissioner, bedell, lit. one appointed or commissioned, a prefect; f. *pri-* before + *'stavitʹ* to set up, place, post.] A commissioner, police officer, overseer.

1662 J. DAVIES tr. *Olearius' Voy. Ambass.* 178 To his knowledge, the Pristaf was a person of honour. **1671** CROWNE *Juliana* I. Dram. Wks. 1873 I. 27 A Russian, sir! a pristaffe's son of Archangelo. *a* **1674** MILTON *Hist. Mosc.* v. Wks. 1851 VIII. 516 The Prestaves or Gentlemen assign'd to have the care of his entertainment. **1837** DE QUINCEY *Revolt of Tartars* Wks. 1890 VII. 386 He was styled the Grand Pristaw, or Great Commissioner, and was universally known amongst the Tartar tribes by this title. **1889** G. KENNAN in *Century Mag.* Apr. 893/1 The original report of a Russian police pristav, written upon a printed form.

pristane ('prɪsteɪn). *Chem.* [ad. G. *pristan* (Y. Toyama 1923, in *Chem. Umschau auf d. Gebiete d. Fette, Oele, Wachse u. Harze* XXX. 186/1), f. L. *prist-is*, Gr. πρίστ-ις saw-fish, (*loosely*) shark; see -ANE.] A saturated hydrocarbon, now known to be 2,6,10,14-tetramethyl pentadecane, $C_{19}H_{40}$, which occurs in the liver oils of certain sharks and related species and is a colourless oil solidifying below about 30°C.

1923 *Jrnl. Chem. Soc.* CXXIV. I. 890 The pure hydrocarbon, which is named pristane, has the following characters:..b.p. 158°/10 mm.,..296°/760 mm., without decomposition. **1963** *Nature* 20 July 284/1 It is estimated that pristane constitutes about 1·1 per cent of the total paraffin fraction of crude wool wax. **1965, 1971** [see PHYTANE]. **1975** *Sci. Amer.* June 94/3 Pristane is also found in some marine organisms, whereas phytane almost never appears except in organisms that have been contaminated by petroleum.

†**'pristinary,** *a. Obs. rare*[−1]. [f. L. *pristin-us* PRISTINE + -ARY[1].] = PRISTINE.

1652 URQUHART *Jewel* Wks. (1834) 199 If there hath been no new thing under the sun, according to the..sense of those pristinary lobcocks.

†**'pristinate,** *a.* (*sb.*) *Obs.* [f. L. *pristin-us* PRISTINE + -ATE[2].] = PRISTINE.

1531 ELYOT *Gov.* I. ii, The pristinate authorite and maiestie of a kyng. *Ibid.*, Kynge Edgar..reduced the monarch to his pristinate astate and figure. **1602** FULBECKE *1st Pt. Parall.* 5 The pristinate wildenes and sauagenesse of nature. **1630** *R. Johnson's Kingd. & Commw.* 356 To this day they could never recover their pristinat fortunes.

B. *sb.* The first or original state. *rare*[−1].

1598-9 B. JONSON *Case is Altered* I. ii, Slid, I am no changeling, I am Juniper still, I keep the pristinate.

pristine ('prɪstiːn, 'prɪstɪn), *a.* Also 6-7 pristin. [ad. L. *pristin-us* former, previous, early, original, primitive (f. stem *pris-*, as in *prisc-us*, *pri(s)m-us*: for suffix cf. *cras-tinus*, *diu-tin-us*). So OF. *pristin.*]

1. Of or pertaining to the earliest period or state; original, former; primitive, ancient. (Now usually commendatory.)

1534 Q. ANNE BOLEYN in Ellis *Orig. Lett.* Ser. I. II. 46 Restored to his pristine fredome. **1569** *Reg. Privy Council Scot.* II. 10 To reduce the saidis partiis to thair pristine amytie. **1625** PURCHAS *Pilgrims* II. 1213 An expedition..for recoverie of their pristine possession. **1696** PRIOR *To King, Disc. Conspir.* 75 Hence then, close Ambush and perfidious War, Down to your pristin Seats of Night repair. **1760-72** H. BROOKE *Fool of Qual.* (1809) IV. 31 You speak and prophesy like a sage of some pristine æra. **1782** PRIESTLEY *Corrupt. Chr.* I. I. 151 To restore it to its pristine purity. **1841** D'ISRAELI *Amen. Lit.* (1867) 126 The translators.. have happily preserved for us the pristine simplicity of our Saxon-English. **1849** MURCHISON *Siluria* xx. 500 The extent of pristine shores. **1873** SYMONDS *Grk. Poets* ii. 53 Empedocles believed in a pristine state of happiness.

2. In various *transf.* and extended senses: having its original condition; unmarred, unspoilt. Of a natural object, physical feature, or the like: unspoilt by human interference, untouched; virginal, pure. Of a manufactured object: spotless, pure in colour; fresh, good as new. Hence, in weakened sense: brand-new, newly-made. orig. *U.S.*

These transferred uses, though now increasingly common, are regarded with disfavour by many educated speakers.

1923 W. STEVENS *Harmonium* 59 The responsive man, Planting his pristine cores in Florida, Should prick thereof. **1940** W. FAULKNER *Hamlet* III. i. 180 The furious cold rain ..galloped on in tearful and golden laughter across the glittering and pristine earth. *Ibid.* IV. i. 298 This time the Justice raised one hand, in its enormous pristine cuff, toward her. **1942** —— *Go down, Moses* 166 He felt the old lift of the heart, as pristine as ever, as on the first day. **1951** *Everywoman* May 68/2 (Advt.), Has a slim waist, full skirt and a pristine white detachable collar. **1955** *Bull. Atomic Sci.* Apr. 119/2 The endeavor to retain the pristine secrecy of atomic energy information. **1967** S. ATTANASIO tr. *Hohendorf's Life & Times of Goethe* 44 Christiane was a short, attractive brunette, with a pristine mouth and round cheeks. **1974** *BP Shield Internat.* Oct. 28/4 The value of Lake Sibaya as a pristine system cannot be overemphasised. **1975** *Times* 11 Aug. 4/5 Gone the cluttered spike, the chatter of teleprinters; his habitat now is the pristine, air-conditioned new building on the Barbican promenade of Lazard Brothers. **1976** *Milton Keynes Express* 25 June 44/1 (Advt.), The quality of the coachwork can only be described as in pristine condition. **1977** *Gramophone* May 1725/2 (Advt.), All records and tapes obtained through DLR, including budget labels, are factory fresh, unconditionally guaranteed, pristine products.

Hence **'pristinely** *adv.*

1899 *Westm. Gaz.* 16 May 2/3 This indignant Tory thinks that what would be pristinely beautiful as Dollis Hill would be newly ugly as Gladstone Park. **1972** *Bookseller* 3 June 2456/2 Roughly half the books mentioned are not published within that week. It is only the populars who insist on having something pristinely fresh, published that day. **1975** F. KING *Needle* ix. 48 A Bentley like that one, though it would be a shame to damage and stain something so pristinely beautiful.

pristly, variant of PRESTLY *adv. Obs.*

‖**Prisunic** (prizynik). [Fr., lit. 'sole price'.] One of a chain of multiple stores (in France) in which a cheap class of goods is sold (orig. all at the same price).

1965 R. POSTGATE *Plain Man's Guide to Wine* (ed. 2) ii. 39 The '*Prisunic*' and other French shops which sell every-day wines. **1967** J. PORTER *Chinks in Curtain* ii. 23 A few messy looking shops. A Prisunic. Oh dear! I plodded on. **1970** *Guardian* 19 Dec. 3/5 The old couple set up house in the doorway of the prisunic down the road. **1971** *Ibid.* 30 Oct. 3/7 The..grocer says he is still feeling the draught from the *prisunic* and..may decide to go.

prisyadka, var. PRISIADKA.

pritch (prɪtʃ), *sb. Obs.* exc. *dial.* Also 3 pricche, 5 prytch, 7-9 prich. [app. a by-form of PRICK *sb.*, with palatalized *c*; perh. a southern repr. of OE. *price* from *prick* (cf. *miche*, *much*, from *mice(l*, *quitch* from *cwice*), or possibly assimilated to PRITCH *v.*]

I. †**1.** A prick, goad, or spur; an incentive. *Obs.* Cf. PRICK *sb.* 13.

a **1225** *Ancr. R.* 60 Eien beoð þe earewen & te ereste armes of lecheries pricches.

2. In local dialects, the name of various sharp-pointed tools or implements. Cf. PRICK *sb.* 15.

1800-25 FORBY *Voc. E. Anglia*, *Pritch*,..1. A fold-pritch is that with which holes are made in the ground to receive fold-stakes... 2. An eel-pritch is a spear for taking eels. **1823** E. MOOR *Suffolk Words.* **1863** MORTON *Cycl. Agric.* Gloss (E.D.S.), *Pritch*.., a heavy pointed iron for making holes for stakes. In Worc. a stick, iron shod, hanging at the tail of a cart, and acting as a prop when resting on a steep road. **1879** MISS JACKSON *Shropsh. Word-bk.*, *Pritch*, a long pole furnished with an iron fork at one end, used by Severn boatmen for propelling their boats,—a river term. **1886** ELWORTHY *W. Somerset Word-bk.*, *Perch*,..the iron-pointed stave often fixed by a joint to the axletree of carts and wagons, to prevent their running back when the horse stops on an ascent. The word no doubt is *pritch* or point.

II. †**3.** A grudge, spite, offence taken (*against* any one). *Obs.*

1571 GOLDING *Calvin on Ps.* xii. 1 All of them with one consent taking pritch against a good cace. *Ibid.* xxxix. 5 Hee taketh prytch, that hee is not delte with more meeldly. **1601** DENT *Pathw. Heaven* 371 If a Noblemans Secretarie be cast out of fauour with his Lord, so that he taketh a pritch against him, it is a matter of great sorrow. **1642** ROGERS *Naaman* 270 Oh!..the least conceit taken, or pritch,..is enough to make sutes. *Ibid.* 274 The finer Selfe is spunne, the more she will take pritch if she be defeated.

III. 4. Small or poor beer; perh. originally soured beer: cf. PRICK *v.* 8, PRICKED *ppl. a.* 2. *dial.*

1688 R. HOLME *Armoury* III. 104/2 Wort of the last drawing..is..of some called put up drink, shower-trough, or penny prich. *Ibid.* 105/1 Pritch Drink,..drinks sweet and sower, through a taint that it hath taken through the foulness of the Vessels. **1691** RAY *N.C. Words* (E.D.S.), *Prich*, thin drink. **1828** *Craven Gloss.*, *Prich*, small beer, thin drink.

pritch, *v. Obs.* exc. *dial.* Also 5 pricche. [A by-form of PRICK *v.* with palatalized *c*, partly at least representing OE. **priccan*, **priccean* (in *apriccan*), from WGer. **prikjan*: see PRICK *v.* Pa. t. in 3-4 *priȝte*, *prighte*:—OE. **prihte*.]

1. *trans.* To prick; to affect with a pricking sensation. *Obs.* exc. *dial.*

c **1250** *Hymn Virg.* 53 in *Trin. Coll. Hom.* App. 257 Þe ne stiȝte, ne þe ne priȝte, in side, in lende, ne elles where. *c* **1386** CHAUCER *Sqr.'s T.* 410 And with hir beek hir seluen so she prighte. **1450-80** tr. *Secreta Secret.* 31 If seeknes come therin thus shalle thou knowe, þi tunge shalle be pricchid, þi mouth shalle be bittir. **1562** J. HEYWOOD *Prov. & Epigr.* (1867) 103 His nostrils so pritcht. **1823** E. MOOR *Suffolk Words* s.v. *Bullock*, I ha got sitch a lamentaable push,..an at night ta itch an ta pritch, an ta gaa-alva. **1903** *Eng. Dial. Dict.* s.v., (Worcester) I've got sharp pritching pains.

†**2.** (See quot.) *Obs.*

1688 R. HOLME *Armoury* III. 259/1 (Goldsmith's Work) *Pritching*, is to find the center of the Plate to be worked.

3. To prick or punch holes in. *dial.*

1746 [see 5]. **1778** *Exmoor Scolding* Gloss. (E.D.S.), *To Pritch*, to prick Holes in; to make Holes for the Wires in the Leathers of Wool-Cards. **1886** ELWORTHY *W. Somerset Word-bk.*, *Perch v.t.*, to punch or prick holes in anything, chiefly in horses' shoes, with a pritchil or purchil.

4. To catch (eels) with an eel-pritch or PRICK (*sb.* 15); also *intr.* to use a pritch. *dial.*

1894 E. CLODD *Fitzgerald's Grave* 8 Ditches whence delicious eels are pritched.

5. *pritch thee!* an imprecation. *dial.*

1746 *Exmoor Scolding* 193 Whan the young Zaunder Vursdon and thee stey'd up oll tha Neert a roasting o' Taties, pritch tha vor me! *Ibid.* 244 Tha art a Beagle, Chun, pritch tha! vor anether Trick. [**1746** *Gloss.* in *Gentl. Mag.* XVI. 407/2 *To Pritch*, to check, or withstand. *Note.* A term for making holes in the leathers of cards to admit the wire.]

† **'pritch-aule.** *Obs. rare*⁻¹. ? Comb. of PRITCH *v.* and AWL, or false spelling of PRITCHEL.

1594 NASHE *Unfort. Trav.* 87, I..solde pritch-aule, spunge, blacking tub, and punching yron.

pritchel ('prɪtʃ(ə)l), *sb. dial.* Also prichell, pritchil, purchil. [A southern parallel form of PRICKLE *sb.*¹, repr. the uncontracted forms of OE. *pricel.*] A sharp-pointed instrument or tool of various kinds for prodding, cutting, making holes, etc.; **b.** esp. for punching the nail-holes in horse-shoes.

14.. *Voc.* in Wr.-Wülcker 605/20 *Promotorium*, a prychel. **1833** J. HOLLAND *Manuf. Metal* II. 337 The orifice [in wire-drawing plate] is..brought to the proper size by the introduction of what the workman calls a *pritchel*, or long taper needle. **1847–78** HALLIWELL, *Pritchel*, an iron share fixed on a thick staff for making holes in the ground. *Kent.* **1895** *E. Anglian Gloss.*, *Pritchel*, a kind of hard chisel for millstones. *c* **1900** *Price List of Millstone Tools*, Pritchels and Chisels for cutting Burrs, letting in driving irons, etc.

b. **1820** BRACY CLARK *Descr. New Horse Shoe* 14 Nor was there so much trouble in reducing them [the pritchel bumps on the outside of the shoe]..with the pritchel remaining in the hole to prevent its closing. **1875** KNIGHT *Dict. Mech.*, *Pritchel* (*Forging*), the punch employed by horse-shoers for punching out or enlarging the nail-holes in a horse-shoe. **1886** ELWORTHY *W. Somerset Word-bk.*, *Purchil*, or *Pritchil*, the square point used..to punch the nail-holes in a horse-shoe. [So in *Hartland Gloss.*] **1896** *Farriers' Price List*, A Smith can easily, with his stamp and pritchel, make a hole.

Hence **'pritchel** *v. dial.*, to goad (a beast).

1875– Gloucestersh. etc. in *Eng. Dial. Dict.*

prithee ('prɪðiː), *int. phr. arch.* Forms: 6 preythe, pree-the(e, prethe, 6–7 pre-thee, 6–9 prythee, 7 pree thee, prethee, prethy, 8 pr'ythee, prithy, pri'thee, 8– prithee. Archaic colloquialism for '(I) pray thee'. (Cf. PRAY *v.* 8 b.)

[? *c* **1522** *Inscription* in *Almondbury & Huddersf. Gloss.* p. xxv, Quarfor pray the thy Sweryng lay by.] **1577** G. HARVEY *Letter-bk.* (Camden) 57 But preythe see where Withipolls cum. *a* **1591** H. SMITH *Wks.* (1867) II. 481 Oh deign, I prythee, then, with speed, To help thy servant now at need. **1602** MARSTON *Ant. & Mel.* III. Wks. 1856 I. 30 Pree the observe the custome of the world. **1610** SHAKS. *Temp.* II. i. 171 Pre-thee no more: thou dost talke nothing to me. **1689** *Trial Pritchard v. Papillon* 6 Nov. 4 *L. Ch. Just.* Ay, prethy tell us. **1711** ADDISON *Spect.* No. 131 ¶9 Pr'ythee don't send us up any more Stories of a Cock and a Bull. **1728** T. SHERIDAN *Persius* i. (1739) 15 Prithy tell me the Truth. **1807** CRABBE *Parish Reg.* III. 780, I hunger, fellow; prithee give me food! **1831** MISS MITFORD in L'Estrange *Life* (1870) II. xiv. 319 Come, I prythee! come again! **1875** JOWETT *Plato* (ed. 2) III. 214 Prithee, friend, be obliging and exhibit your wisdom.

prittle, *v.*: see PRITTLE-PRATTLE *v.*

prittle-prattle ('prɪt(ə)l,præt(ə)l), *sb.* Now *rare.* [Reduplicated extension of PRATTLE *sb.*] Trivial, worthless, or idle talk; also, light, easy, familiar conversation, small talk; chatter, tittle-tattle; childish prattle. Also *attrib.*

1556 OLDE *Antichrist* 9 b, I could easily contemne their prittle prattle talking. *Ibid.* 30 To make much prittle prattle of Salomons temple. **1579–80** NORTH *Plutarch* (1676) 546 Every man's mouth was full of prittle prattle and seditious words. **1698** VANBRUGH *Prov. Wife* III. i, Our prittle-prattle will cure your spleen. **1714** MANDEVILLE *Fab. Bees* (1725) I. 287 We took delight in the..Prittle-Prattle of the innocent Babe. **1755** *Gentl. Mag.* XXV. 419 Nor bear a part in prittle-prattle Of rumour-loving tittle-tattle. **1774** *Westm. Mag.* II. 453 He is sure to be a prittle-prattle fellow. **1838** MISS MITFORD in L'Estrange *Life* (1870) III. vi. 85 French, being the very language of chit-chat and prittle-prattle, is one reason why I like so much the 'mémoires' and letters of that gossiping nation.

b. A silly chatterer, a gossip.

[**1602** F. HERING *Anat.* 12 Being in high Credit..with my Gossip Prittle Prattle.] **1725** BAILEY *Erasm. Colloq.* 35 Don't be a prittle prattle, nor prate apace.

† **'prittle-'prattle,** *v. Obs.* [Reduplicated from PRATTLE *v.*] *intr.* To chatter, prate, talk idly. Hence † **'prittle-'prattling** *ppl. a.*

1552 LATIMER *Serm.*, *John ii.* 1 (1584) 306 b, As our Papistes doe, which prittle prattle a whole day vppon theyr Beades, saying our Ladies Psalter. [**1583** Prittle and prattle [see PRATTLE *v.* 2].] **1602** F. HERING *Anat.* 4 Iuglers, Pedlers, prittle-pratling Barbers. **1611** J. DAVIS in Coryat *Crudities* Panegyr. Verses, For, he as t'were his mother's twittle-twattle (That's Mother-tongue) the Greeke can prittle-prattle. [**1634** HEYWOOD *Roy. King* I. Wks. 1874 VI. 9 *Welchman.* Awe man, you prittle and prattle nothing but leasings and untruths. *a* **1800** *Outlandish Knight* xv. in Child *Ballads* I. (1882) 59/2 Don't prittle nor prattle, my pretty parrot, Nor tell no tales of me.]

prlueable, bad form of *prevable*, PROVABLE.

‖**prius** ('praɪəs). [L., neut. of *prior* former, earlier, also adv. before. See also NISI PRIUS.]

a. That which takes precedence; the superior, first, chief. **b.** That which is prior, *esp.* that which is a necessary prior condition.

1891 H. JONES *Browning* 220 That final perfection which ..is first in order of potency,—the *prius* of all things. **1892** E. CAIRD *Ess. Lit. & Philos.* II. 404 Thought is not set up as an absolute prius, but as the prius of experience.

privacy ('praɪvəsɪ, 'prɪvəsɪ). [f. PRIVATE *a.*: see -CY.] The state or quality of being private.

1. a. The state or condition of being withdrawn from the society of others, or from public interest; seclusion.

c **1450** *St. Cuthbert* (Surtees) 611 To kepe þaim in priuace. **1606** SHAKS. *Tr. & Cr.* III. iii. 190 *Achil.* Of this my priuacie, I haue strong reasons. *Vlis.* But 'gainst your priuacie The reasons are more potent and heroycall. **1652** HEYLIN *Cosmogr.* To Rdr. A iij, Some time to spare; some privacies and retreats from business; some breathing fits from the affairs of our Vocations. **1659** T. PECKE *Parnassi Puerp.* 168 Vespasian during his Privacie, Led such a Life, as was Exemplary. **1759** JOHNSON *Idler* No. 51 ¶1 Those that surround them in their domestic privacies. **1832** LYTTON *Eugene A.* II. iv, Your privacy will never be disturbed. **1856** EMERSON *Eng. Traits, Manners* Wks. (Bohn) II. 48 The motive and end..is to guard the independence and privacy of their homes.

b. The state or condition of being alone, undisturbed, or free from public attention, as a matter of choice or right; freedom from interference or intrusion. Also *attrib.*, designating that which affords a privacy of this kind.

1814 J. CAMPBELL *Rep. Cases King's Bench* III. 81 Though the defendant might not object to a small window looking into his yard, a larger one might be very inconvenient to him, by disturbing his privacy, and enabling people to come through to trespass upon his property. **1890** WARREN & BRANDEIS in *Harvard Law Rev.* IV. 193 (*title*) The right to privacy. *Ibid.* 196 The question whether our law will recognize and protect the right to privacy..must soon come before our courts for consideration. **1901** G. B. SHAW *Capt. Brassbound's Conversion* II. 252 Well, I am afraid I want a little privacy, and, if you will allow me to say so, a little civility. **1933** *Post Office Electr. Engineers' Jrnl.* XXVI. 224/1 Overseas radio telephone services operated by the Post Office are provided with privacy equipment on all channels where the necessary deciphering equipment is provided at the distant end. **1940** *Chambers's Techn. Dict.* 752/2 *Secrecy* (or *privacy*) *system*, modification of speech-frequencies within the speech-band, so that during transmission from a radio transmitter to a receiver the signal is unintelligible and cannot be tapped. *a* **1953** E. O'NEILL *More Stately Mansions* (1964) II. iii. 130 Can I never have a moment's privacy in my own home? **1965** [see PRIVATE *a.* (*sb.*) 2 f (*a*)]. **1970** R. K. KENT *Lang. Journalism* 106 *Privacy, right of*, the right of a citizen not to have details of his life explored in the press... The right of privacy also prevents the use of a person's name or picture in an advertisement without his permission. **1975** R. H. RIMMER *Premar Experiments* III. 233 In the meantime, you can live in one of Premar's privacy rooms. **1976** *Billings* (Montana) *Gaz.* 27 June 5-D/5 (Advt.), There's also a large patio with privacy fence and a double attached garage, all on a nicely landscaped half acre. **1977** *Chicago Tribune* 2 Oct. XII. 21/1 (Advt.), Huge patio deck with privacy fence and decorator touches. **1978** I. MURDOCH *Sea* 375 When Titus appeared I decided to go outside to avoid interruption and ensure privacy.

2. a. *pl.* Private or retired places; private apartments; places of retreat. Now *rare.*

1678 R. L'ESTRANGE *Seneca's Mor.* (1776) 343 It soars aloft, and enters into the privacies of Nature. **1749** FIELDING *Tom Jones* XVI. vii, Do you think yourself at Liberty to invade the Privacies of Women of Condition, without the least Decency or Notice? **1878** LANIER *Poems* (1884) 14 Beautiful glooms..Wildwood privacies, closets of lone desire.

† **b.** A secret place, a place of concealment. *Obs.*

1686 PLOT *Staffordsh.* 307 Having rested at Boscobel two days, one in the Oak; the Night in a privacy behind the Chimney in one of the Chambers.

3. a. Absence or avoidance of publicity or display; a condition approaching to secrecy or concealment.

1598 SHAKS. *Merry W.* IV. v. 24 Let her descend: my Chambers are honourable: Fie, priuacy? Fie. **1641** WILKINS (*title*) Mercury: or the Secret and Swift Messenger. Shewing how a Man may with Privacy and Speed communicate his Thoughts to a Friend at any Distance. **1647** CLARENDON *Hist. Reb.* I. §81 The Duke..took a resolution once more to make a Visit to that great Lady, which he believed he might do with great privacy. **1700** *Pennsylv. Archives* I. 129, I caused this Town to be searched but with some Privacy. **1809** WELLINGTON in Gurw. *Desp.* (1838) V. 167, I have also to observe that privacy is inconsistent with every just notion of punishment. **1855** MACAULAY *Hist. Eng.* xiv. III. 403 The emaciated corpse was laid, with all privacy, next to the corpse of Monmouth in the chapel of the Tower. **1876** J. SAUNDERS *Lion in Path* i, A marriage..was solemnised with strict privacy in the chapel of Leigh Court, Yorkshire. **1879** R. K. DOUGLAS *Confucianism* iii. 77 No darkness conceals from its view, and no privacy hides from its knowledge.

† **b.** Keeping of a secret, reticence. *Obs.*

1736 AINSWORTH *Eng.-Lat. Dict.*, Privacy, or keeping of counsel, *taciturnitas*, 3. *silentium*, 2.

4. a. A private matter, a secret; *pl.* private or personal matters or relations. Now *rare.*

1591 HORSEY *Trav.* (Hakl. Soc.) 236 Som other privacies comitted to my charge had ben so whispered owt. **1649** MILTON *Eikon.* vii. Wks. (1847) 293/1 What concerns it us to hear a husband divulge his household privacies, extolling to others the virtues of his wife? **1702** *Eng. Theophrast.* 46 A blab, and one that shall make a privacy as public as a proclamation. **1759** JOHNSON *Rasselas* xi, If he descend to the privacies of life, their habitations are more commodious, and their possessions are more secure.

† **b.** *pl.* The private parts. *Obs.*

1656 EARL MONM. tr. *Boccalini's Advts. fr. P.* I. xxxv, Plucking up her cloaths, and shewing them her privacies.

† **5.** Intimacy, confidential relations. *Obs.*

1638 BAKER tr. *Balzac's Lett.* (vol. II.) 20 At that time.. you gave me leave to boast of your friendship, I dare not now use the privacie of such tearmes. **1653** *Nicholas Papers* (Camden) II. 17 He..observed that there was great intimacy and privacy between that Col. and Sʳ John Henderson. **1683** A. D. *Art Converse* 42 Those that are our equals or have made us such by their privacy or intimate friendship.

6. The state of being privy to some act; = PRIVITY. *rare.*

1719 YOUNG *Revenge* II. i, And now I come a mutual friend to both, Without his privacy, to let you know it. **1888** *Pall Mall G.* 23 July 1/2 The amendment leaves the whole question as to the privacy to crime alleged against Mr. Parnell and his fellow members before the Commission.

‖**privado** (pri'vado). *Obs.* [Sp., private, particular, familiar, a favourite.] An intimate private friend, a confidant; the favourite of a ruler.

1584 *Leicester's Commw.* (1641) 49 The good Earle answered his Servant and deare Privado curteously. **1637** HEYLIN *Antid. Lincoln.* i. 20 The papers were not sent unto the Vicar, but to some one or other of your Privados about those parts. **1679** *Hist. Jetzer* 3 The Friers, who were their Confidents, and Privadoes in the Plott. **1704** STEELE *Lying Lover* ii, *Lat.* May I desire one Favour? *Y. Book.* What can I deny thee, my Privado? **1748** RICHARDSON *Clarissa* (1810) VII. lxxxiii. 347 He beareth a very profligate character..and is Mr. Lovelace's more especial *privado.* **1828** SCOTT *F.M. Perth* xii, A courtly knight..and privado, as they say, to the young prince.

¶ An alleged sense 'a private soldier or inferior (non-commissioned) officer' in some recent Dicts. is founded on a misreading of 'lantz prisadoes' [in Harl. MS. 4031 lf. 244]. see LANCE-PRISADO.

† **'privancy.** *Obs. rare*⁻¹. [f. obs. F. *privance* familiarity: see -ANCY.] Intimacy: = PRIVACY 5.

1622 MABBE tr. *Aleman's Guzman d'Alf.* I. 80 A kinde of friendship was begun betweene them (if any such thing may bee found betweene master and man:)..it is commonly called by the name of Privancie or Inwardnesse.

privant ('praɪvənt), *sb.* and *a. rare.* [ad. L. *prīvāntem*, pres. pple. of *prīvāre* to deprive.]

† **a.** *sb.* A privative (quality). *Obs.* **b.** *adj.* Indicating a privative opposite.

1586 BRIGHT *Melanch.* xii. 57 An absence of one quality is not..an inferring of the other: but only in privants wherof the one is a meere absence. **1890** *Cent. Dict.*, *Privant*, noting privative opposites.

‖**privat-docent, -dozent** (pri'vaːtdo'tsɛnt). [Ger., a private teacher or lecturer: see PRIVATE *a.* and DOCENT B.] In German and some other universities: A private teacher or lecturer recognized by the university but not on the salaried staff.

1881 J. RAE in *Contemp. Rev.* June 925 He meant to habilitate as a *privat docent* when he returned. **1892** *Pall Mall G.* 20 June 6/1 The Queen found the then privatdozent ..busy at a chemical experiment. **1899** J. STALKER *Christol. Jesus* ii. 72 One of those tours de force by which the German Privatdocent seeks to attract public attention.

private ('praɪvət), *a.* (*sb.*) Also 4–6 pryvat, -e, 4–7 privat, 6 privit, -att, pryvatte, *Sc.* prevat, 6–7 privet. [ad. L. *prīvāt-us* withdrawn from public life, deprived of office, peculiar to oneself, private; as sb. a man in private life; prop. pa. pple. of *prīv-āre* to bereave, deprive: see PRIVE *v.*] **A.** *adj.* In general, the opposite of *public.*

† **1.** ? Withdrawn or separated from the public body: by Wyclif applied to the orders of the friars. *Obs.*

c **1380** WYCLIF *Serm.* Sel. Wks. I. 67 Þis asse and hir fole ben comen to þes pryvat ordris, but not to alle Cristene men. *c* **1380** —— *De Ecclesia* v. ibid. III. 350 Comunly þes pryvat priours letten þer felowes here to go out.

2. a. Of a person: Not holding public office or official position.

1432–50 tr. *Higden* (Rolls) IV. 63 A crye was made..that priuate persones [orig. *privatæ personæ*] scholde brynge theire goodes to the place of treasure. *Ibid.* I. 91 [see PRIVY *a.* 4]. *c* **1460** FORTESCUE *Abs. & Lim. Mon.* vii. (1885) 125 He lyved..in more subgeccion than doth a priuate person. **1548–9** (Mar.) *Bk. Com. Prayer, Ceremonies*, The appoyntmente..pertayneth not to pryuate menne. **1579** J. STUBBES *Gaping Gulf* B vij, Whereas mariage is the moste important matter euen to the privatest person that hee can doe all his life long. **1644** MILTON *Areop.* (Arb.) 49 No Poet should so much as read to any privat man, what he had writt'n. **1673** J. RAY *Observations Journey Low-Countries* 305 When the Gallies are at home those [slaves] that belong to private persons are permitted to lodge in their Masters houses. **1712** STEELE *Spect.* No. 429 ¶8 A Woman of Quality; married to a private Gentleman. **1817** J. EVANS *Excurs. Windsor*, etc. 72 It was a most uncommon thing for a private man, and a commoner, to be honoured with so long an audience. **1885** *List of Subscribers, Classified* (United Telephone Co.) (ed. 6) 233 (Advt.), The Birkbeck Bank opens Drawing Accounts with trading firms and private individuals. **1898** *Westm. Gaz.* 16 Mar. 2/3 As for the usurer who advertises himself as a private gentleman, Mr. Justice Hawkins grimly said that he would make him a 'private gentleman' for some time. **1930** G. B. Shaw *Apple Cart* p. xviii, Socialists have said to me that they were converted by seeing that the nation had to choose, not between governmental control of industry and control by separate private individuals [etc.]. *Ibid.* p. xix, We cannot do this as private persons. It must be done by the Government or not at all. **1931** M. Allingham *Look to Lady* xiv. 150 When publicity is fatal.. then the private individual has to get busy on his own account. **1960** N. Mitford *Don't tell Alfred* iii. 41 If my husband were a private person, none of this would matter. **1975** N. Freeling *What are Bugles blowing For?* xi. 67, I find it miserable. Everyone so callous... But I'm just a private individual. **1978** *Verbatim* Sept. 1/1 In certain circles, it has become popular to the point of irritation to characterize every eremitical, dyspeptic, close-mouthed selfish crank as a *private person*.

b. ***private soldier***: an ordinary soldier without rank or distinction of any kind; also †***private man***. Cf. *common soldier* (common *a.* 12 b).

1579 Digges *Stratiot.* 152 They can doe no more than Privat Souldiors. **1597** Shaks. *2 Hen. IV*, iii. ii. 177, I cannot put him to a priuate souldier, that is the Leader of so many thousands. **1691** *Lond. Gaz.* No. 2629/2 We lost 6 private Men, and had 15 wounded. **1698** Ludlow *Mem.* I. 192 Pretending.. to keep the private soldiers, for they would no longer be called common soldiers, from running into greater extravagancies and disorders. **1796** Pegge *Anonym.* (1809) 164 Application.. on behalf of a private man that had deserted from an independent company just as they were embarking for North America. **1844** *Regul. & Ord. Army* 176 All the Officers, Non-commissioned Officers, Drummers, and Private Men, who may be at Home, are to be accounted for. **1898** E. J. Hardy in *United Service Mag.* Mar. 646 Another expression, which is far more objectionable [than the name 'Tommy Atkins'], is to speak of a 'common soldier' instead of a private soldier.

c. ***private member***, a member of the House of Commons who is not a member of the Ministry. Hence ***private member's bill***, a bill introduced in Parliament by a private member.

In quot. 1606 *private member* means 'not a member of the Privy Council'.

1606 *House of Commons Jrnl.* 13 May I. 308/2 Petitions heretofore delivered by the Privy Council:... 28 *et* 43 *Eliz.* .. Last Session, by Mr. Hare, a private Member. **1835** *Mirror of Parliament* 25 Feb. 69/2 In the last Session, Wednesday was usually devoted to Bills brought in by private Members of Parliament... The Chancellor of the Exchequer.—Nobody is more sensible than I am of the extent to which the country is often indebted to private Members, who undertake the management of public Bills. **1852** Disraeli *Ld. George Bentinck* xxvii. 580 Instead of experiencing the usual and almost inevitable doom of private members of parliament and having his statements shattered by official information, Lord George Bentinck on the contrary was the assailant and the successful assailant of an adminstration on these very heads. **1863** H. Cox *Instit.* i. ix. 138 The portion of each session allotted to measures promoted by private members is.. limited. **1883** *Stubbs' Merc. Circular* 26 Sept. 862/1 It is almost hopeless for a private member to get an opportunity of bringing on a Bill before half-past twelve. **1908** J. Redlich *Procedure House of Commons* I. ii. iii. 173 This, it was complained, was done systematically, and the result had been to destroy all chance of private members' bills being carried. **1930** *Daily Express* 6 Nov. 19/2 It was a private members' day, on which neither Government policy nor the fate of the Government came up for discussion. **1939** W. I. Jennings *Parliament* vii. 180 Many private members' Bills are 'inspired' by interests outside. **1950** *Erskine May's Law of Parl.* (ed. 15) xiv. 287 Private Members' *bills* have precedence on Friday up to the Friday before Good Friday. **1964** Abraham & Hawtrey *Parl. Dict.* (ed. 2) 31 *Private member's bill*, a public bill introduced by a private member... It must be carefully distinguished from a private bill. **1969** *Listener* 10 July 37/2 Seldom is a government prepared to offend many of its supporters in Parliament and the country by making itself responsible for contentious reforming measures. Private members' legislation is therefore a necessity. **1976** H. Wilson *Governance of Britain* x. 171 Any Private Member's Bill, such as those which under Standing Orders can be introduced for a limited period of the year under a procedure of balloting for priority, must if a penny of public expenditure is involved carry with it the cachet of 'Queen's recommendation signified'.

d. ***private trader***, one who trades on his own account, as distinguished from an agent of a public company. Also ***private trade, trading***.

1616 in W. Foster *Lett. E. Ind. Co.* (1901) V. 119 With the intelligence concerning the private traders of Captain Downton's merchants. **1671** in *Publ. Hudson's Bay Rec. Soc.* (1942) V. 5 That Capta. Guillam & all others.. bee examined what private trade hath bin by them. **1821** G. Simpson *Jrnl.* 8 Jan. in *Ibid.* (1938) I. 212 Chastellan & Lamallice.. are renewing their old practice of carrying on Private Trade with the Indians. **1929** *Times* 26 Feb. 17/5 He courageously scrapped his own Bolshevist economic theories in 1921 and reinaugurated private trading. **1965** B. Pearce tr. *Preobrazhensky's New Econ.* 97 At the present moment the State Bank hardly grants any credits to private trade and industry. **1979** *Guardian* 12 Nov. 7/1 Most trading skills, shops and trucks remain in the hands of private traders. Private trading is not illegal.

†**e.** Of a city or town: That is not a seat of government. *Obs. rare.*

1632 Lithgow *Trav.* vii. 334 This Citty.. was once the Capitall seat of the Kingdom, though now.. it is onely become a priuate place.

f. ***private detective, investigator***, a detective who is engaged privately and is not a member of an official police force. Also (orig. *U.S.*) in *colloq.* and *slang* collocations, as ***private dick*** (dick *sb.*[6]); ***private eye*** (eye *sb.*[1] 3 d); also (with hyphen) *attrib.*; hence as vb. intr. and ***private-eyeing*** vbl. sb.

(*a*) **1868** Trollope *He knew he was Right* (1869) I. xix. 150 'The man was a policeman once.' 'What we call a private detective.' **1873** G. Lening *Dark Side N.Y. Life* 59 A jealous wife engages a private detective to watch her husband. **1898** F. Remington *Crooked Trails* i. 19 He rode a Spanish pony.. and arrested Polk, his guide, and two private detectives, whom Polk had bribed to set him over the Rio Grande. **1905** Chesterton *Club of Queer Trades* i. 40 Though only a private detective myself, I will take the responsibility. **1936** A. Christie *ABC Murders* v. 38 'Then you're not—anything to do with the police, sir?' 'I am a private detective.' **1940** R. Chandler *Farewell, my Lovely* iii. 21 Philip Marlowe, Private Investigator. One of those guys, huh? **1965** D. Francis *Odds Against* v. 71 The one thing people want when they employ private investigators is privacy. **1974** V. Gielgud *In Such a Night* ii. 17 Giacomo told me of your reputation as a private investigator. **1975** J. Wainwright *Square Dance* 173 You'd be surprised how professional.. some of the better provincial private detective agencies are.

(*b*) **1912** A. H. Lewis *Apaches N.Y.* vi. 128 But w'at wit' th' stores full of private dicks a booster can't do much. **1938** R. Chandler in *Dime Detective* June 23/1 We don't use any private eyes in here. So sorry. **1939** —— *Big Sleep* xviii. 127 Ohls pulled a chair up and sat down and said: 'Evening, Cronjager. Meet Phil Marlowe, a private eye who's in a jam.' **1946** E. O'Neill *Iceman Cometh* i. 14 Yuh remember dey used to send down a private dick to give him the rush to a cure, but de lawyer tells Harry nix, de old lady's off of Willie for keeps dis time and he can go to hell. **1952** Wodehouse *Pigs have Wings* i. 20 'You mean she's a sleuth? ..' 'Substantially that, miss. I gather that she leaves the rougher work to her subordinates.' 'Still she's a genuine private eye.' **1962** [see *gum-shoe* s.v. gum *sb.*[2] 9]. **1964** Wodehouse *Frozen Assets* vi. 119, I imagine private-eye-ing is one of those things where you've either got the knack or you haven't. **1971** B. Malamud *Tenants* 25 He felt in the house,.. a presence other than himself. Nothing new but who now? Private eye snooping for one cause or another? **1974** E. Ambler *Dr. Frigo* ii. 98 Isn't all research private-eye work, Doctor? **1975** J. Hone *Sixth Directorate* iv. v. 176 That's not what I'm here for—to carry on your private eyeing for you. **1979** G. Swarthout *Skeletons* 231 She had offered to marry me again.. if I would private-eye for her.

g. ***private army***, an army not recruited by the State; a mercenary force. Also *transf.* and *fig.*

1941 W. Temple *Citizen & Churchman* ii. 25 Anything like a 'private army' is a contradiction of the civilized state. **1950** V. Peniakoff *Private Army* Part iv (*title*) Popski's private army. **1959** M. Gilbert *Blood & Judgement* ix. 95 The police were a private army. **1964** Gould & Kolb *Dict. Social Sci.* 482/2 *Factions, cliques.. private armies, lobbies, pressure groups*.. are terms which, like *party*, denote voluntary associations to influence government. **1968** *N.Y. Times* 23 July 41 (*heading*) Norman Mailer enlists his private army to act in film. **1968** 'J. Welcome' *Hell is where you find It* i. 15 The security and secret services, so called, had recently.. been shaken up and amalgamated... We were an off-shoot, a semi-amateur show, a private army. **1969** D. Bagley *Spoilers* v. 60 'Some of my patients had been cutting up ructions at the Howard Club. Johnny didn't like it.' 'And you had to take your own private army to back you up?' **1979** J. Rathbone *Euro-Killers* ii. 27 Their riot sticks.. infuriated him—he hated private armies.

h. ***private developer*** (see developer f).

1961 *Kentish Times* 28 July 10 There is little land left in the urban district, with its Green Belt setting, for either Council or private developer. **1965** *New Society* 26 Aug. 6/1 A modern civic centre to be built by a private developer under council guidance. **1970** *Guardian* 17 Aug. 5/2 The private developer is in a better position to judge the demands for development than the planner. **1972** *Country Life* 25 May 1330/1 Berkshire has given planning permission for some 18,000 houses, of which private developers build less than 3,000 new houses a year. **1975** *Times* 30 Aug. 13/5 How many private developers are interested in urban renewal?

3. a. Kept or removed from public view or knowledge; not within the cognizance of people generally; concealed, secret.

1472–3 *Rolls of Parlt.* VI. 29/2 After that dyvers of the Lordes and Knyghtes of the Shires were departed, by mervelous pryvat labour, a Bille signed by the Kyng was brought to the seid Commens.. conteignyng an Ordynaunce to be made. **1593** Shaks. *2 Hen. VI*, ii. ii. 60 In this priuate Plot be we the first, That shall salute our rightfull Soueraigne. **1615** Brathwait *Strappado* (1878) 120 Which he suspecting, lay in private wait, To catch the knaue. **1669** R. Mountagu in *Buccleuch MSS.* (Hist. MSS. Comm.) I. 441 She desired.. to send it over in my name, because that way it would be privater. ?**1677** Lady Eliz. Berkeley in *Hatton Corr.* (Camden) 143 They have not acquainted you wth Lady Alethea's privet wedding. **1700** Tyrrell *Hist. Eng.* II. 842 He lay private, till his Peace was made with the King. **1726** Leoni *Alberti's Archit.* I. 52/1 If the sound comes to you dead, and flat, it is a sign of some private [It. *interna*] infirmity. **1890** *Lippincott's Mag.* Jan. 13, It should be kept private for a time.

b. ***private parts***, the external organs of sex, the pudenda. Also *transf.* and *fig.*

[**1634** Sir T. Herbert *Trav.* 41 A cloth which should couer those parts, made to be priuate.] **1785** Grose *Dict. Vulgar T.*, *Commodity*, a woman's commodity; the private parts of a modest woman, and the public parts of a prostitute. **1853** *Law Jrnl. Rep.* XXXI. iii. 123/1 What do you mean in law by exposing his *person*? The indictment should have been for exposing his *private parts*. **1885–8** Fagge & Pye-Smith *Princ. Med.* (ed. 2) I. 188 She mentioned.. that she had severe pain in micturition, and that her private parts were swollen. *a* **1930** D. H. Lawrence *Last Poems* (1932) 157 The reddened limbs.. and the half-hidden private parts. **1959** I. & P. Opie *Lore & Lang. Schoolch.* vi. 96 It may be a verse in which the private parts are mentioned, as in the baby-washing songs of Tiny Tim. **1969** *Listener* 27 Feb. 282/1 He has an objection to 'showing his private parts' to the reader; and to this modesty, as much as to his dreadful loquacity, must, alas, be ascribed his failure to produce the great autobiography that one might have expected from him. **1971** *Farmer & Stockbreeder* 23 Feb. 30/1 Major Ogilvie recalls some mothers feeling embarrassed at having to see the 'private parts' of an animal's body—like teats and udders—being handled by a man.

4. a. Of a thing: Not open to the public; restricted or intended only for the use or enjoyment of particular and privileged persons. Also, as a sign or notice indicating that a room or the like is private.

1398 Trevisa *Barth. De P.R.* xix. cxxix. (Add. MSS.) Þe priuate wey longiþ to nyȝe towne and is schort and nyȝ and ofte y growe wiþ gras. **1477** *Rolls of Parlt.* VI. 185/2 In pryvat and pryvileged places. **1535** Stewart *Cron. Scot.* (Rolls) II. 63 Quhair he wes bureit in ane prevat place. **1613** Shaks. *Hen. VIII*, iii. i. 28 May it please you Noble Madam, to withdraw Into your priuate Chamber. **1638** Brathwait *Barnabees Jrnl.* (1818) 187 This place it is private. **1817** W. Selwyn *Law Nisi Prius* (ed. 4) II. 1242 A person having a private way over the land of another, cannot, when the way is become impassable by the overflowing of a river, justify going on the adjoining land. **1838** Lytton *Alice* ii. ii, A private staircase conducted into the gardens. **1849** Macaulay *Hist. Eng.* vi. II. 142 News which reached him through private channels. *a* **1911** D. G. Phillips *Susan Lenox* (1917) II. xi. 285 The frosted glass door marked 'Private'. **1973** 'D. Craig' *Bolthole* i. 15 He saw a wide staircase with a tasselled rope across it and a Private sign. **1973** G. Mitchell *Murder of Busy Lizzie* xv. 177 My sitting-room is the one marked private.

†**b.** ***private (play) house***: see quot. 1891. *Obs.*

a **1625** Fletcher *Nice Valour* iv. i, I hope To save my hundred gentlemen a-month by it; Which will be very good for the private house. **1637** Shirley (*title*) The Gamester. As it was presented by her Majesties Servants At the private House in Drury-Lane. **1891** R. W. Lowe *T. Betterton* iii. 60 The Cockpit in Drury Lane.. a small theatre, one of those which, before the Civil War, were called 'Private Houses'. In these the performances took place by candlelight, whereas the larger, or public playhouses, being partly open to the weather, were used only in daylight.

c. In many connexions *private* is used to distinguish something that is not open to the public, or not publicly done or performed, from a thing of the same kind that is 'public', esp. when the normal or usual condition is that of publicity, or when both conditions are common. In this distinctive use, the sense may also be 5, 6, or 7, or may include some notion of 3. Such are ***private assembly, function, meeting***, etc.; ***private baptism, communion, education, funeral, marriage, mass***; ***private boarding-house, brougham, carriage, chapel, hotel, play, theatre, theatricals*** (also *attrib.* or as *adj.*), etc.; see the sbs. **private bar** = *lounge bar* s.v. lounge *sb.* 4; also *ellipt.*; **private bath(room)**, a bath(room) set aside for private use, usu. one attached to a room in a hotel or guest house; **private beach**, a beach that is privately owned, esp. by a hotel for the use of guests; **private box** (see box *sb.*[2] 8); **private business** *Eton College slang*, extra tuition; **private collection**, a collection (of paintings or the like) in private possession; **private development**, development (sense 3 d) undertaken by a private individual or company; **private hotel**, a residential hotel or boarding house which receives guests only by private arrangement; **private inquiry**, work undertaken by a private detective (see sense 2 f above); hence **private inquiry agency, agent**; **private joke**, a joke understood only by oneself or a privileged few; **private motoring**, motoring in a privately owned vehicle; so **private motorist**; **private view** (e.g. of an exhibition of pictures or the like), whence ***private viewer, viewing***.

1794 Malone *Wks. Sir J. Reynolds* in *Life* (1797) p. lv, When not engaged.. in some publick or private assembly, or at the theatre. **1662** *Bk. Com. Prayer*, The Ministration of Private Baptism of Children in houses. **1909** G. B. Shaw in *Nation* 28 Aug. 787/2 Mr. Chesterton.. sees in every public-house a temple... He enters ostentatiously, throws down all the shields and partitions that make the private bar furtive. **1910** H. G. Wells *Hist. Mr. Polly* viii. 259 The policeman... put his head inside the Private Bar, to the horror of every one there. **1953** K. Tennant *Joyful Condemned* xxxiv. 340 The gossip of the Private Bar. **1963** N. Marsh *Dead Water* (1964) i. 15 There was only one other woman in the private beside Jenny. *Ibid.* ii. 55 'I want another drink. Anyone join me?'.. He made towards the old private bar. **1972** M. Gilbert *Body of Girl* xii. 107 She was in here.. just after we opened. She came into the private bar. **1975** A. Hunter *Gently with Love* xxxiii. 132 Come into the private—I would not have you leave without a crack. **1825** E. Weeton *Jrnl.* 14 June (1969) II. 384, I like to bathe alone, and a private bath is just to my taste. **1906** 'O. Henry' *Four Million* 47 The double front room with private bath. **1910** *Bradshaw's Railway Guide* Apr. 1148 Bedrooms with private bath and telephone. **1974** *Country Life* 21 Mar. 692/3 (Advt.), My bedroom, with its own tv and private bath. **1910** *Bradshaw's Railway Guide* Apr. 1148 Suites of rooms with private Bathrooms. **1961** *Sphere* 6 May 212 A new 1st-class hotel, the Hibiscus, with private beach, opens this summer. **1975** S. Brett *Cast* iii. 24 Marius's got a villa down the South... It's a lovely place. Private beach. **1632**, etc. Private box [see box *sb.*[2] 8]. **1829** [see family *sb.* 9 c]. **1897** Kipling *Let.* 1 June in C. E. Carrington *Rudyard Kipling* (1955) x. 254 We went to the Lyceum... Irving put a private box at our disposal. **1979** *Country Life* 9 Aug. 393/2 The top floor will contain 30 private boxes. **1900** J. S. Farmer *Public School Word-Bk.* 158 *Private-business*,..

extra work with the tutor. **1979** D. Newsome *On Edge of Paradise* ii. 87 Half-an-hour's preparation for his Private Business lecture on Napoleon. **1899** R. Fry *Let.* Oct. (1972) I. 174 He took me to an amazing private collection, full of marvellous drawings and sculptures all looking far better for being in a private place. **1979** R. Cox *Auction* i. 24 There were several Memlings in Austrian private collections. Stefan Zweig owned one. **1961** *Recreation* Dec. 531/1 Areas should..have room around the edges to protect the values of the area from encroachment by private developments. **1971** 'D. Halliday' *Dolly & Doctor Bird* ii. 19 Coral Harbour is a private development in one of the moneyed quarters of New Providence Island. **1975** *Times* 30 Aug. 13/5 Impressions of the results of the last boom period for private development are still..fresh. **1581** Mulcaster *Positions* xxxix. (*heading*) Of priuate and publike education, with their generall goods and illes. **1699** Locke *Educ.* (ed. 4) §70 The Faults of a Privater Education. **1857** G. H. Lewes *Jrnl.* 11–18 May in *Geo. Eliot Lett.* (1954) II. 326 We went to *Dingley's Private Hotel*—very comfortable. **1910** *Bradshaw's Railway Guide* Apr. 1012/2 Cullen's private hotel and family boarding house. **1936** [see catch v. 40]. **1960** L. Davidson *Night of Wenceslas* i. 8, I had really borrowed the money from old Imre, who lived in the same private hotel. **1962** Bull & Richardson *Hotel & Catering Law* (rev. ed.) iii. 37 This chapter is concerned with premises which are not conducted as 'inns', that is with private premises as distinct from public premises. It is convenient to refer to such premises as 'private hotels', this term also including guest houses, boarding-houses, apartment houses, and similar places. *Ibid.*, The private hotel proprietor reserves to himself the right to pick and choose his guests, and does not hold himself out as willing to receive anyone who calls. He makes a separate contract, either written or verbal, with his guests. **1970** C. Whitman *Death out of Focus* x. 153 It was a typical private hotel bedroom. **1972** *Times* 1 Apr. 14/1 The very words 'boarding house' are out. Now it is 'guest house' at the very least, and possibly even 'private hotel'. **1874** M. Clarke *His Natural Life* iii. xxii. 331, I dabbled a little in the Private Inquiry line of business. **1892** Private inquiry agency [see inquiry, enquiry 4]. **1897** A. Morrison *Dorrington Deed-Box* ii. 98 Your respectable talents will be devoted to the service of Dorrington & Hicks, private inquiry agents. **1922** Private inquiry agent [see inquiry, enquiry 4]. **1948** 'J. Tey' *Franchise Affair* x. 106 We cannot expect you to turn yourself into a private inquiry agent on our behalf. **1973** R. Lewis *Of Singular Purpose* v. 113 All solicitors use private enquiry agents... They are often ex-policemen. **1974** 'M. Innes' *Appleby's Other Story* xxiii. 181 Miss Kentwell works for a private enquiry agency..of the highest repute. **1949** E. Coxhead *Wind in West* i. 19 She answered it [*sc.* an advertisement]..for a sort of private joke. **1978** J. McNeil *Consultant* v. 68 Susan had learned..not to ask for explanations of Webb's private jokes. **1560** Private mass [see mass sb.[1] 3]. **1885** *Catholic Dict.* 565/2 In all private Masses the priest must have at least a server to represent the body of the faithful. **1816** Galt *Benj. West* 51 A private meeting of the Friends [i.e. Quakers] was appointed to be holden at his father's house. **1974** *Country Life* 2 May 1050/1 The restrictions on private motoring caused by the higher cost of petrol. **1976** *Times* 3 Aug. 2/1 Between 1964 and 1974 passenger traffic increased by 40 per cent, private motoring growing by nearly 65 per cent, rail staying level and bus traffic declining. **1926** *Daily Chron.* 13 May 4 (*caption*) Private motorists made themselves popular by giving lifts to people who would otherwise have had to walk long distances. **1975** *Times* 18 June 4/5 The Egon Ronay *Guide to Transport Cafés*..should also be of help to the economy-minded private motorist. **1970** F. Reynolds *Dramatist* i. 12 Whence arises the pleasure at an Opera, a private Play, or a Speech in Parliament? **1794** C. Mathews *Let.* 3 Aug. in A. Mathews *Mem. Charles Mathews* (1838) I. 100, I left England without calling on Wayte, to whom I am indebted for a few articles; among which are the dresses for the private play. **1868** P. Fitzgerald *Life David Garrick* I. vi. 158 It was once determined to get up a private play..and the parts were cast in a moment. **1784** W. Hayley (*title*) Plays of three acts written for a private theatre. **1807** E. Weeton *Let.* 18 Nov. (1969) 50 She..was never outshone in elegance of movement at a Ball, out-performed at a private Theatre. **1787** J. Powell (*title*) The narcotic & private theatricals. **1818** Keats *Let.* 23 Jan. (1931) I. 96, I began an account of a private theatrical—Well it was of the lowest order, all greasy and oily. **1831** D. E. Williams *Sir T. Lawrence* I. 50 Nor did he ever take part in any private theatricals. **1914** G. B. Shaw *Fanny's First Play* 153 The end of a saloon in an old-fashioned country house..has been curtained off to form a stage for a private theatrical performance. **1836–9** Dickens *Sk. Boz, Scenes* xiii, Private Theatres. **1837** Dickens *Pickw.* xxviii. 289 A select two or three,..were being honoured with a private view of the bride and bridesmaids, up stairs. **1840** —— *Old C. Shop* xxix. 254 Miss Monflathers,..at the head of the head Boarding and Day Establishment..condescended to take a Private View with eight chosen young ladies. **1847** E. Gray *Let.* 28 Apr. in M. Lutyens *Ruskins & Grays* (1972) iv. 33 John [Ruskin] is going to a private view of the Royal Academy. **1852** *Times* 1 May 8/2 (*heading*) Exhibition of the Royal Academy (Private View). **1862** W. Sandby *Hist. Roy. Academy* II. 239 It had..been the custom to regard the anniversary dinner as one of a private nature—a gathering of the members of the Royal Academy and of the friends and patrons of art. *Ibid.* 240 The art-critics for the newspapers, etc., were admitted to the private view of the exhibition. **1884** *World* 3 Dec. 13/1 There were no fewer than five 'private views' on Saturday last. **1887** Ruskin *Præterita* II. i. 27 The private view day of the Old Water Colour came. **1897** *Daily News* 28 Apr. 6/6 The galleries..soon to be refilled by the critics, the private viewers, and the outside crowd. **1898** *Westm. Gaz.* 28 Apr. 5/3 On the whole the private viewing ladies have had the excellent taste of coming in the morning in morning dress.

d. Used with reference to medical treatment and facilities for which fees are charged to the patient instead of being provided by the state or a public body; from 1946 in the United Kingdom *spec.* of treatment and facilities outside the *National Health Service* (see national a. 5), as ***private bed, nursing, patient***, etc. Also *ellipt.*

1754 W. Smellie *Midwifery* II. xxvi. 437, I attended a private patient. **1801** *Med. Jrnl.* V. 7 Those to whom I have communicated the infection out of the Hospital, or among my private patients. **1843** R. J. Graves *Syst. Clin. Med.* ix. 99 In private practice the physician is called at an early period of the disease. **1860** F. Nightingale *Notes on Nursing* vi. 38, I have often seen the private nurse go on dusting..while the patient is eating... The above remarks apply much more to private nursing than to hospitals. *Ibid.* 39 Generally, the only rule of the private patient's diet is what the nurse has to give. **1914** A. Bennett *Price of Love* xii. 256 In those days of State health insurance all doctors were too busy..to be of assistance to private patients. **1934** P. Bottome *Private Worlds* xii. 114 They stood in a small private room off the ward, and looked down at the moaning woman on the bed. **1935** D. L. Sayers *Gaudy Night* ix. 191 He's in a private ward, so you can get in any time. **1942** M. Dickens *One Pair of Feet* vii. 110 Sister Adams..told me that I was to..go on day duty on the Private wards. *Ibid.* 115, I went on cutting bread savagely and the Private Nurse stirred milk with pursed lips. **1942** [see dog's body 2]. **1943** G. Greene *Ministry of Fear* ii. ii. 150 It's a very charming nursing-home and I'm a private patient. **1946** *Act 9 & 10 Geo. VI* c. 81 §5 The Minister may allow any medical practitioner..on the staff of a hospital providing hospital and specialist services to make arrangements for the treatment of his private patients either at their hospital or at any other such hospital. **1946** P. Bottome *Lifeline* ii. 33 Ours is not a state-run affair..but a private hospital. **1956** P. Scott *Male Child* i. i. 26, I spent most of April in a private nursing home. **1960** C. Watson *Bump in Night* i. 15 He lay in a small private ward of Chalmsbury General Hospital. **1961** *Ann. Reg. 1960* 9 There had been a demand that 'private patients' who relieved the finances of the health service by paying their own doctor should get free access to N.H.S. drugs. **1967** M. Sharman *Face of Danger* i. 7 They ..walked out of the private wing of the hospital. **1967** P. Willmott *Consumer's Guide Brit. Social Services* vi. 158 Private beds amount to little over one per cent of the total number of beds in use. *Ibid.*, Financial help towards the cost of private treatment is provided by several provident associations. **1969** B. Turner *Circle of Squares* iv. 27 Poor Flisch had a private room. **1971** *Guardian* 1 July 6/5 Hospital laboratory technicians..will refuse to carry out tests on private patients. **1972** P. Johnson *Offshore Islanders* vi. 400 Labour ministers lacked the will to impose a salaried service on the medical profession... Private practice, private beds in hospitals, private health insurance were permitted. **1976** W. J. Burley *Wycliffe & Schoolgirls* iii. 67 She was a staff nurse..and chucked up her job to go into private nursing. **1976** N. Leigh-Taylor *Doctors & Law* iv. 35 The Government has announced that it intends..to abolish private treatment in N.H.S. hospitals.

e. *Teleph.* and *Telegr.* (i) applied to (*a*) a line that is permanently for the exclusive use of the subscriber or is not connected to the public network; (*b*) a number that is ex-directory; (*c*) a number at a private address rather than business premises.

1878 *Telegr. Jrnl.* VI. 51/1 The regulations concerning the despatch and receipt of telegrams, the tariffs for the same, and for the renting of private wires. **1885** *List of Subscribers* (United Telephone Co.) p. vii, The Charge for Private Lines is at a fixed annual rental, payable in advance, varying with the situation and the distance apart of the points connected. **1911** W. Aitken *Man. Telephone* xxiii. 476 Private Lines..are lines not having exchange service. **1924** J. Buchan *Three Hostages* xvi. 235 This must be a private telephone..of which only his special friends knew the number. **1933** D. L. Sayers *Murder must Advertise* viii. 129 He was not in the telephone-book, but his private number would doubtless be on the telephone-clerk's desk. **1940** *War Illustr.* 16 Feb. p. ii/1 Taking the final proof of his commentary on the foreign news of the day to the 'private wire' room, to be telegraphed or telephoned to Manchester. **1942** A. Christie *Body in Library* vi. 59, I had a private line put in connecting my bedroom with my office. **1969** N. Freeling *Tsing-Boum* xiii. 95 Good morning. Police Judiciaire!.. I'm at a private number in Marseilles; will you ..clear me a direct line. **1972** L. Moir tr. *Simenon's Maigret & Flea* ii. 34 You'll know where to find me. My private number's in the book. **1974** *Encycl. Brit. Macropædia* XVIII. 95/1 Private-line systems for data communications have come into widespread use in the past decade. **1974** D. Gray *Dead Give Away* vii. 72 Cyril decided on a nap in his study, where he had a private line, on which he could ring Nina. **1976** H. MacInnes *Agent in Place* xxiii. 241 Tony.. dialled Bill's number—not his private line, just the ordinary one. **1976** T. H. Flowers *Introd. Exchange Syst.* i. 11 Picture telegraphy..is possible over the telephone service lines but difficulties discourage small users and encourage large users of such services to rent private circuits not subject to switching.

(ii) *spec.* of an exchange: serving private lines; ***private branch exchange***, an exchange on private premises by which private lines may be connected to the public network.

1891 J. Poole *Pract. Telephone Handbk.* vii. 124 Fig. 102 represents a type of switch-board which was designed by the writer in 1881 for the use of private telephone exchanges. **1905** *Ann. Rep. Amer. Telephone & Telegr. Co. 1904* 6 There is an enormous increase in the number of private branch exchanges in hotels. **1911** W. Aitken *Man. Telephone* xxi. 416 No hotel or warehouse of any standing is now considered complete without a private branch exchange connected to the 'Central' by a number of circuits. **1943** A. L. Albert *Fund. Telephony* viii. 170 A private branch exchange or *PBX* in a large store, hotel, manufacturing plant, or to serve a college campus. **1974** *Encycl. Brit. Macropædia* XVIII. 94/1 Typical automatic switching systems in operation include the step-by-step system, used ..for local exchanges and private branch exchanges.

(iii) Describing components in a telephone exchange which belong to a circuit whose potential indicates the condition of a particular subscriber's line and enables its condition to be ascertained without interfering with calls in progress; esp. in ***private wire*** (see quot. 1969).

1906 J. Poole *Pract. Telephone Handbk.* (ed. 3) xxx. 486 When a current is started and stopped through the 'private' magnet, the end of the side-switch arm slips under the outer tooth. **1919** R. Mordin *Strowger Automatic Telephone Exchange* i. 23 The whole arrangement of fixed contacts is called the connector bank; the upper half the private bank, and the lower the line bank. The moveable contacts are termed respectively the private wiper and the line wiper. **1927** C. W. Wilman *Man. Automatic Telephony* vi. 55 This wire is comparable with the test wire in a manual system inasmuch as it indicates whether a particular line is free or busy... It is..known as the private line (because it prevents intrusion on a busy trunk). **1969** S. F. Smith *Telephony & Telegr. A* vi. 153 A third wire is therefore provided on all connexions through the exchange, the potential of which indicates the condition of the circuit. This avoids intrusion on calls in progress and is called the private wire, usually abbreviated to '*P-wire*'.

5. a. That belongs to, or is the property of a particular individual; belonging to oneself, one's own.

1502 Atkynson tr. *De Imitatione* iii. 221 The xxxi. chapiter, the loue of pryuate thynges & of mannys selfe letteth the perfyte goodnes of mannys soule. **1530** Palsgr. 321/1 Private, belongyng to a persons owne selfe, *priuat.* **1560** Daus tr. *Sleidane's Comm.* 127 They teache howe it is not lawfull for the christians..to haue any thynge priuate, y[t] al things ought to be common. **1601** Shaks. *Jul. C.* iii. ii. 253 He hath left you all his Walkes, His priuate Arbors,.. On this side Tyber. **1638** Junius *Paint. Ancients* 147 As for private Libraries, Martial teacheth us, That in them the Images of such Writers as were as yet surviving, might bee admitted. **1845** R. Jebb in *Encycl. Metrop.* (1847) II. 703/1 The divine purpose of the institution of private property is, in general, very inadequately represented. **1899** *Westm. Gaz.* 21 Sept. 4/1 He hoped it would not go forth from the Conference that they wanted to stamp out all private venture schools. **1904** J. T. Fowler *Durham Univ.* 5 His private goods were all seized by his creditors.

b. ***private bank*** (see bank sb.[3] 7 a); hence ***private banker, banking***; ***private car***, (*a*) *U.S.*, a privately owned and used railway carriage; (*b*) a motor car owned and used privately, as distinct from a commercial vehicle; ***private family***, the family occupying a private house; ***private house***, the dwelling-house of a private person, or of a person in his private capacity; with implied or expressed distinction from a public-house or inn, a shop or office, which are open to the public on business, and, in modern use, from a public building or official residence; ***private income***, an income derived from private sources, as investments, property, etc.; an unearned income; ***private man of war***: see privateer sb.; ***private means***, income derived from private sources (cf. *private income* above); ***private press***, a printing and publishing house of limited resources and output, often operated for the owner's personal satisfaction rather than profit, and usually issuing small editions of books designed to meet higher standards of production than those of commercial publishers; ***private residence*** = ***private house***; ***private room***, a room in a club, hotel, etc., that may be hired for private use (see also sense 5 d below); ***private school***, a school owned and carried on by a person or persons for their own profit, as opposed to a *public school*, founded and carried on primarily in the public interest; also, a school that is independent of a State system of education (see independent a. 5 d); often with mixture of other senses; so ***private schoolmaster***; ***private service***, domestic service in a private house.

1714 in A. McF. Davis *Tracts Currency Massachusetts Bay* (1902) 115 Which does most of all import them, the Publick or the Private Bank? **1802** M. Edgeworth *Let.* 1 Dec. (1979) 43 Private banks never issue any notes. **1978** M. Birmingham *Sleep in Ditch* 120 My mother wanted me to be a banker..in one of the small, distinguished private banks. **1837** in W. L. Mackenzie *Life & Times M. Van Buren* (1846) 178 The Bills of the banks of this State only shall be circulated as Money by private bankers. **1978** P. Noyes *Who is Simon Warwick?* viii. 104 A house which only a private banker could possibly have described as a cottage. **1836** in W. L. Mackenzie *Life & Times M. Van Buren* (1846) 176 If the fetters are knocked off by the repeal of the Restraining Law, private banking associations may be formed. **1954** *Econ. Hist. Rev.* VII. 167 A tentative sketch of some developments in London private banking is offered. **1585** T. Washington tr. *Nicholay's Voy.* ii. xiii. 48 Buildings.. aswel publike as priuat. **1897** Kipling *Capt. Cour.* ix. 186 Send 'Constance', private car, here, and arrange for special [train]. **1926** *Brit. Gaz.* 12 May 1/3 There were few private cars on the roads and nearly every vehicle was labelled 'Food only'. **1938** E. Ambler *Cause for Alarm* xiv. 232 We had to wait for a private car and a van to pass. **1979** B. Peterson *Peripheral Spy* ii. 34 It really must be important when Col. Petrovich waited for you with his private car. **1849** Macaulay *Hist. Eng.* iii. (1871) I. 144 By the Petition of Right, it had been declared unlawful to quarter soldiers on private families. **1542** in *10th Rep. Hist. MSS. Comm.* App. v. 410 If [they]..carry anny such wares to pryvat housses shoppis or sellers and not to the costome housse. **1548–9** (Mar.) *Bk. Com. Prayer, Communion*, When the holy Communion is celebrate..in priuate howses. **1657** Evelyn *Diary* 3 Aug., Dr. Wild preach'd in a private house in Fleete Streete. **1781** Gibbon *Decl. & F.* xix. II. 131 The private houses of Antioch, and the places of public resort. **1848** Dickens *Dombey* vii, There was another private house besides Miss Tox's in Princess's Place. **1873** C. M. Yonge

Pillars of House IV. xlix. 385 Between his private income and the endowment he would be able to keep up..a staff of Curates. **1910** A. Bennett *Clayhanger* IV. ii. 470 It's a good thing she has a private income of her own. **1923** J. M. Murry *Pencillings* 86 No one really pays much attention now to the subtle problems which tormented Henry James, simply because no one would earn any gratitude by solving them. Even the attempt to solve them calls for a private income. **1941** 'G. Orwell' in *Partisan Rev.* VIII. 496 Nearly all [Home Guard] commands are held by retired colonels, people with 'private' incomes or, at best, wealthy business men. **1952** M. Laski *Village* iii. 65 Because she's got a private income no one ever expected her to go out and take a job. **1971** G. Household *Doom's Caravan* ii. 53 He was a bachelor with a private income. **1862** Mrs. J. B. Speid *Our Last Years in India* vi. 149 In the case of married military men, under the grade of field officer, I cannot see, unless they have private means..how they can escape involvement. **1976** C. Bermant *Coming Home* II. ii. 131, I was without connections and without private means. **1834** J. Martin *Bibliogr. Catal. Bks. Privately Printed* p. v, The second portion of the work, consisting of an account of the publications from literary clubs, and private presses. **1900** *Library* I. 407 Since the days when Horace Walpole started as a master-printer at Strawberry Hill quite a number of book-lovers have amused themselves with the management, and occasionally with the actual working, of a private press. **1922** D. B. Updike *Printing Types* II. xxii. 215 The types of the Kelmscott, Doves, and other English private presses were from his [*sc.* E. P. Prince's] hand. **1934** H. Waddell *Let.* in M. Blackett *Mark of Maker* (1973) xii. 112 The man who is secretary of the Pilgrim Trust (Tom Jones)..runs a very luxurious private press, for which he wants me to do a translation. **1955** S. H. Steinberg *Five Hundred Years of Printing* iii. 217 It was pleasure in fine printing, or at least in printing according to personal taste, rather than commercial success that made kings and nobles set up private presses in the seventeenth and eighteenth centuries. **1968** *Times* 30 Jan. 13/3 (Advt.), First editions and private press books, including the Shakespeare Head Press *Homer*, 1930–31. **1978** *Times Lit. Suppl.* 15 Sept. 1024/1 Some private presses eventually extended their operations so much that their work is more properly described as commercial. **1885** *List of Subscribers, Classified* (United Telephone Co.) (ed. 6) 8 Any Subscriber who pays £20 a year for an Exchange connection can..have his Private Residence joined up with the system. **1974** P. Lovesey *Invitation to Dynamite Party* iii. 34 'There was a second explosion..at Sir Watkin Wynn's residence.' 'A private residence? What have they got against Sir Watkin Wynn?' **1824** Scott *Redgauntlet* III. vii. 197 Walking into the inn, [he] demanded from the landlord breakfast and a private room. **1847** C. Brontë *Jane Eyre* I. xi. 172 When I asked a waiter if any one had been to inquire after a Miss Eyre, I was answered in the negative; so I had no recourse but to request to be shown into a private room. **1879** Trollope *John Caldigate* II. xviii. 251 'I suppose I can have a private room here, at noon tomorrow?' asked Caldigate, turning to the woman at the bar. **1920** 'Sapper' *Bull-Dog Drummond* 7 Have we ever had staying in the hotel a man called le Comte de Guy?.. Has he ever fed here, or taken a private room? **1974** J. Gardner *Return of Moriarty* 87 A private room had been booked for Moriarty and his guest,.. at the Café Royal. **1857** Hughes *Tom Brown* I. iii, A private school, where he went when he was nine years old. **1875** Trollope *Prime Minister* (1876) I. i. 6 He had been at a good English private school. **1914** C. Mackenzie *Sinister St.* II. III. iii. 547, I don't think it is snobbishness... It's a throw back to primitive life in a private school. **1944** Private school [see independent *a.* 5 d]. **1945** *Guide to Educ. Syst. Eng. & Wales* (Min. of Educ.: Pamphlet No. 2) 59 *Private school*, independent school owned by a private individual or group of individuals. **1969** T. Jenkins *We came to Australia* I. iii. 41 There are both State and private schools. **1976** C. Bermant *Coming Home* II. iii. 154, I was a teacher in one of those private schools, which was basically a very expensive ..crammer for the sons of oil sheiks. **1857** Hughes *Tom Brown* I. iii, Were I a private schoolmaster. **1934** D. L. Sayers *Nine Tailors* 139 Deacon was a waiter in some club. .. He wanted to try private service. **1953** A. Christie *Pocket Full of Rye* v. 36 She'd been in private service first and after that in various cafés. **1978** M. & N. Ward *Home in Twenties & Thirties* 38/1 There was..an inexorable reduction in the number of people engaged in private service.

c. ***private judgement***: see judgement 7 c.

1565 T. Stapleton *Fortr. Faith* 6 He interpreteth it after his owne liking and priuat judgement.

6. a. Of or pertaining to a person in a non-official capacity.

1613 Purchas *Pilgrimage* (1614) 286 In a priuate habit he visited the Markets, and hanged vp the hoorders of coine. **1713** Berkeley *Guardian* No. 69 ¶2 The private letters of great men are the best pictures of their souls. **1797** Godwin *Enquirer* I. vii. 59 A private pupil is too much of a man. **1830** *Chron.* in *Ann. Reg.* 259/1 The eldest of three sons of the grand-duke Charles-Frederick, by his *morganique*, or private-marriage, with Louisa-Caroline, countess of Hochberg. **1859** Kingsley *Lett.* (1878) II. 83 Private correspondence, private conversation, private example may do what no legislation can do. **1859** Sala *Tw. round Clock* 108 While the brass bandsmen at once subside into private life. **1864** (*on a Presentation*), A tribute to private worth and public usefulness.

b. ***private account***, a bank account relating to one's personal (as opposed to business) assets; ***private call***, a personal telephone call to or from one's place of work; ***private life***, a person's domestic or personal (way of) life, as distinct from that relating to employment, official position, etc. (freq. with a notion of sense 3).

1924 'Sapper' *Third Round* i. 34 [The cheque] is drawn on my private account. **1973** A. Behrend *Samarai Affair* viii. 84 He compiled a list of every individual connected with the case... Thus:..Bank Manager, Hartley's private account. **1942** E. Waugh *Put out More Flags* i. 52 There's a ridiculous woman on the line saying is this a private call? **1974** 'J. Le Carré' *Tinker, Tailor* xi. 84 The misuse of unlisted Circus telephones for private calls. **1526** R. Whytford *Martiloge* f. cxxxiv, He resygned his crowne, & lyued a holy pryuate lyfe. **1843** Dickens *Mart. Chuzz.* (1844) xvi. 193 A full account of the Ball..with the Server's own particulars of the private lives of all the ladies that was there! **1886** Kipling *Departmental Ditties* (ed. 2) 22 He heliographed his wife Some interesting details of the general's private life. **1943** J. B. Priestley *Daylight on Saturday* xxii. 169 Her own private life, now in ruins, insisted upon claiming her attention, and she could not pretend to herself that it was less important than the private lives of all the other women in the factory. **1973** A. Behrend *Samarai Affair* viii. 81, I was speaking of Mr. Gosling as a pilot of course... I know next to nothing of Mr. Gosling's private life.

7. a. Of, pertaining or relating to, or affecting a person, or a small intimate body or group of persons apart from the general community; individual, personal.

1526 *Pilgr. Perf.* (W. de W. 1531) 33 Onely for theyr pryuate profyte. **1560** Daus tr. *Sleidane's Comm.* 34 b, Certen priuate dyspleasures did growe betwixte hym & the Frenche kynge. **1601** Shaks. *Jul. C.* II. ii. 73 For your priuate satisfaction..I will let you know. **1651** Hobbes *Leviath.* II. xxii. 122 He, whose private interest is to be debated. **1838** Thirlwall *Greece* II. xv. 260 In reality they had only consulted their own private ambition. **1858** Ld. St. Leonards *Handy-Bk. Prop. Law* iv. 22 If you employ an agent to sell an estate by public auction, a sale by private contract is not within his authority. **1883** *Law Rep. 11 Q.B. Div.* 597 That the censure had been made injuriously and from motives of private malice.

b. ***private bill, act***: a parliamentary bill or act affecting the interests of a particular individual or corporation only: see bill *sb.*³ 3; hence ***Private Bill Office***. ***private notice question*** (see quot. 1964).

1678 Butler *Hud.* III. ii. 901 Who..Can..Lay Publick Bills aside, for Private, And make 'em one another drive out. **1818** Cruise *Digest* (ed. 2) V. 527 An estate tail, granted by Richard III. to the Derby family..which by a private act of 4 Jac. I. was limited to the heirs male of the family in a different manner from that in which it had been limited by the letters patent. **1844** May *Treat. Law*, etc. *Parl.* 302 The functions of Parliament in passing private bills, have always retained the mixed judicial and legislative character of ancient times. **1850** in Jos. Irving *Ann. Our Time* 30 Nov. (1872) 315/1 Plans for about 104 new schemes were deposited to-day in the Private Bill Office. **1863** H. Cox *Instit.* I. ix. 173 In order to the first reading of a private bill in the House of Commons, a petition for leave to bring it in is first presented, by being deposited at the Private Bill Office. A certain interval of time is required to elapse between the first and second readings, during which the bill remains in the custody of the Private Bill Office. **1871** *Hansard Commons* 27 Feb. 941, I wish to ask some questions of the Prime Minister, of which circumstances prevented me from giving any other than a private Notice to him. **1913** *Ibid.* 21 Jan. 225 Private notice question... May I ask the Chancellor of the Exchequer a question of which I have given him private notice. **1929** G. F. M. Campion *Introd. Procedure of House of Commons* iv. 126 Private Notice Questions are of two kinds: (a) those of an urgent character, and (b) non-urgent. **1931** *Daily Express* 13 Oct. 12/2 A private notice question can cause more flutter in the Civil Service than any other of the few instruments of torture left in the hands of back-bench members. **1964** Abraham & Hawtrey *Parl. Dict.* (ed. 2) 168 On specially urgent matters, 'private notice questions' may be asked after the end of the time allotted by the standing orders to questions for oral answer. A member who wishes to avail himself of this privilege must give notice of the terms of his question to the minister and to the Speaker not later than twelve o'clock on the day on which he is to ask it. **1976** S. Lloyd *Mr. Speaker, Sir* iii. 88 The Speaker also has power under the Standing Orders to allow what are called Private Notice Questions (I will refer to them from now on as P.N.Q.s), ones which in his opinion are of an urgent character and relate either to matters of public importance or to the arrangement of business.

c. ***private secretary***: see secretary *sb.*¹ 2; ***private secretaryship***, the office or post of private secretary.

1773 R. Jephson *Let.* 2 Mar. in D. Garrick *Private Corr.* (1831) I. 530 Our friend Tighe is much engaged in his office of Private Secretary to the Lord Lieutenant, but is getting better health and more strength every day. **1814** Jane Austen *Mansf. Park* II. xvii. 155, I would rather find him private secretary to the first Lord than any thing else. **1869** Trollope *Phineas Finn* II. lxv. 232 The Duke of St. Bungay was at work as a Private Secretary when he was three-and-twenty. **1880** E. W. Hamilton *Diary* 25 Apr. (1972) I. 3 Horace Seymour and Henry Primrose are the two between whom the other private secretaryship lies. **1891** W. Fraser *Disraeli & his Day* (ed. 2) 42 Mr Algernon Greville became, some years afterwards, Private Secretary to the Duke. **1930** J. B. Priestley *Angel Pavement* v. 207, I can't bear those private secretary jobs. Yours is one of them, isn't it? **1954** K. Amis *Lucky Jim* iv. 48 Our influencial friend will shortly be declaring his private secretaryship vacant. **1974** R. Ingram *Yoris* i. 1 You'll be this chap's private secretary, so you'll get to know everything.

d. ***private law*** (see quot. 1923).

1773 J. Erskine *Inst. of Law of Scotl.* I. 9 Public law is that which hath more immediately in view the public weal... Private is that which is chiefly intended for ascertaining the civil rights of individuals. The private law of Scotland is to be the proper subject of this treatise. **1923** W. J. Byrne *Dict. Eng. Law* 519/2 Private or civil law deals with those relations between individuals with which the State is not directly concerned; as in the relations between husband and wife, parent and child,..contracts, torts, trusts, legacies. **1932** H. F. Jolowicz *Hist. Introd. Roman Law* i. 5 The change from republic to empire did not make any immediate difference to private law. **1969** D. Daube *Roman Law* iii. 152 The basic structure..is still largely dominated by the criminal trial; but the cases discussed have shifted to lesser crimes and even near to private law. **1973** I. M. Sinclair *Vienna Convention on Law of Treaties* iv. 86 The potentially misleading nature of private law analogies.

e. ***private international law*** (see quots.)

1834 J. Story *Commentaries Conflict of Laws* i. 9 The jurisprudence, then, arising from the conflict of the laws of different nations, in their actual application to modern commerce and intercourse, is a most interesting and important branch of public law... This branch of public law may be fitly denominated private international law, since it is chiefly seen and felt in its application to the common business of private persons. **1861** R. Phillimore *Commentaries Internat. Law* IV. p. iii, This volume is devoted to the consideration of *Jus Gentium—Private International Law, or Comity*: that is, strictly speaking, the law which ought to govern the legal relations of individuals not being the subject of the State which administers the law. **1938** G. C. Cheshire *Private Internat. Law* (ed. 2) i. 22 The expression 'Private International Law', coined by Story in 1834,..and used on the Continent by Foelix in 1838,..has been adopted by Westlake and Foote and most French authors. The chief criticism directed against its use is its implication that the subject forms a branch of International Law. There is, of course, no affinity between Private and Public International Law. The latter comprises those universally accepted customs which are recognized by States in their public relations with each other; the former consists of rules which the Courts of each territorial jurisdiction follow when a dispute containing some foreign element arises between private persons. **1962** J. F. McMahon in *Brit. Year Bk. Internat. Law 1961* 326 The European Economic Community Treaty..devotes two of its articles to what it calls 'approximation of laws'... This gradual approximation of law, however, will have to take place both in the field of legislation and in the jurisprudence of the courts. The Court of the European Communities is not itself concerned with private international law and that question has only been invoked on one occasion before the Court.

f. ***private treaty*** (see quot. 1973).

1858 *Estates Gaz.* 16 Aug. 16/1 (Advt.), To be sold, by private treaty, a substantial and well-built house. **1922** V. Sackville-West *Heir* i. 19 Are we to try for auction or private treaty? Personally I think the house at any rate will go by private treaty. **1957** D. H. D. Alexander in *Auctioneers & Estate Agents* (Chartered Auctioneers' & Estate Agents' Inst.) 99 Almost all general urban practices depend..upon the commissions earned on the sale of houses and properties whether such sales are by private treaty or auction. **1973** Westland & Rodway *Place of your Own* i. 11/2 In Scotland..houses are more often sold 'by private treaty'. This way, the owner places a reserve, or 'upset' price on the property and invites those interested to make offers, in writing, by a specified date. On that date, the offers are examined, and the property will usually go to the highest bidder. An offer made this way is binding by law, unless you withdraw it before it is formally accepted... Some properties in England and Wales are offered for sale on these terms. **1979** *Irish Times* 28 Sept. 23/1 One of the very few [houses] that well justifies its private treaty price tag of over three-quarters of a million pounds.

g. ***private war***: a war fought by a restricted number of participants from personal or private motives. Also *transf.*

1866 C. M. Yonge *Dove in Eagle's Nest* I. p. vi, An offended nobleman, having sent a *Fehdebrief* to his adversary, was thenceforward at liberty to revenge himself by a private war. **1894** Kipling *Jungle Bk.* 85 A wolf who obeyed the orders of this boy who had private wars with man-eating tigers was not a common animal. **1948** G. V. Galwey *Lift & Drop* vii. 196 Operating a war of his own against the gang and the Law. **1973** J. R. L. Anderson *Death on Rocks* x. 175 If there's a senior police officer on the spot..it will help... You and Simon may feel that you have a private war against Potterton, but this is more than a private war. **1974** 'G. Black' *Golden Cockatrice* xi. 194 A killing that was one incident in the continuing private war the Russians and the Chinese have been waging against each other.

h. ***private company***: a company whose membership and transfer of shares are limited by law.

1908 *Act 8 Edw. VII* c. 69 §121 For the purposes of this Act the expression 'private company' means a company which by its articles—(*a*) Restricts the right to transfer its shares; and (*b*) Limits the number of its members..to fifty; and (*c*) Prohibits any invitation to the public to subscribe for any shares or debentures of the company. **1928** *Act 18 & 19 Geo. V* c. 45 §55 If any company, being a private company, alters its articles in such manner that they no longer include the provisions which..are required to be included in the articles of a company in order to constitute it a private company..the company shall, as on the date of the alteration, cease to be a private company. **1928** *Britain's Industr. Future* (Liberal Industr. Inquiry) II. vii. 84 The most important existing legal distinction is between Public Companies..and Private Companies, limited to not more than 50 shareholders. **1948** *Act 11 & 12 Geo. VI* c. 38 §31 If at any time the number of members of a company is reduced, in the case of a private company, below two,..and it carries on business for more than six months while the number is so reduced, every person who is a member of the company during the time that it so carries on business.. shall be severally liable for the payment of the whole debts of the company contracted during that time. **1961** T. E Utley *Occasion for Ombudsman* ii. 18 The recent case of the Esso Petroleum Bill, when a private company sought powers of compulsory purchase.

i. ***private world***: a private 'realm' within which one moves or lives; = world *sb.* 10.

1921 A. Huxley *Crome Yellow* xiii. 128 He determined to retire absolutely from it [*sc.* the great world] and to create.. at Crome a private world of his own. **1958** *Listener* 19 June 1024/1 Never has the private world of the thwarted male been so shamelessly exposed to view. **1976** S. Hynes *Auden Generation* ix. 296 The private world of love is threatened by public violence.

j. ***private sector***: that part of an economy, industry, etc., which is free from direct state control. Usu. with *the*.

1952 T. Surányi-Unger *Compar. Econ. Syst.* iii. 59 Coordination of freedom and planning obviously influences the formation of private and public sectors within the whole economic structure... The compromising countries still reveal larger private than public sectors. Their *private sectors* are relatively much larger than those of the countries under Eastern planning. **1965** J. L. HANSON *Dict. Econ.* 327/2 *Private sector*, that part of the economy which is left to private enterprise. **1971** *Guardian* 22 July 11/3 Sooner or later there will develop a new set of ideas about the private sector in education. **1980** *Illustr. London News* Mar. 19/1 The extension of the steel strike into the private sector.

k. ***private language***: a language which can be understood by the speaker only, esp. in *Logic* involving the query whether such a concept can have meaning. Also *loosely*, a language shared by a privileged few.

1953 G. E. M. ANSCOMBE tr. *Wittgenstein's Philos. Investigations* I. 94 Sounds which no one else understands but which I '*appear to understand*' might be called a 'private language'. **1955** L. P. HARTLEY *Perfect Woman* xiii. 121 Why should you understand my private language? **1964** *Amer. Philos. Q.* I. 20/1 A private language is one of which it is not merely the case that it is not understood by anyone other than the speaker, but more that it is logically impossible that it should be understood by anyone other than the speaker. **1979** D. FRANCIS *Whip Hand* xiv. 173 The reins felt alive, carrying messages... A private language, shared, understood.

l. ***private-label***: used *attrib.* to denote a product manufactured by a particular company for sale through its own retail markets; cf. *own-label* s.v. OWN *a.* 4a.

1961 *Economist* 11 Mar. 984/1 There are the usual 'private-label' teas, flour, butter, and dried cereals, fruit and pulses; besides these, private label jams and biscuits are quite common and several companies market their own canned peas, soups, canned fruit and canned vegetables; there is even a private-label pine essence. **1971** *Guardian* 9 June 13/2 Supermarkets' private label brands were selling at around 1s. 10d., while the major manufacturers were sometimes cutting their prices by as much as 1s.

†**8.** Peculiar to a particular person or body of persons, a people, etc.; particular, special. *Obs.*

1526 TINDALE *2 Pet.* i. 20 So that ye fyrst knowe this, that no prophesy in the scripture hath eny private interpretacion [WYCLIF ech prophecie..is not maad bi propre interpretacioun; COVERD. no prophecie..is done of eny priuate interpretacion; *Geneva* is of any priuate motion; *Rhem.* is made by priuate interpretation; 1611 is of any priuate interpretation.] **1555** EDEN *Decades* 296 [They] haue a priuate language differyng from the Moscouites. **1559** in Strype *Ann. Ref.* (1709) I. App. viii. 20 The realm of Englande hath been alwaies governyd by private lawes and customes. **1593** BILSON *Govt. Christ's Ch.* vii. 86 Neither was this priuate to Timothie, but..it was vsuall in the Apostles times. **1651** C. CARTWRIGHT *Cert. Relig.* I. 120 How can any man assume to himselfe a freedome from Erring by the assistance of a private Spirit?

9. By one's self, alone; without the presence of any one else.

1592 SHAKS. *Rom. & Jul.* I. i. 144 Away from light steales home my heauy Sonne, And priuate in his Chamber pennes himselfe. **1613** —— *Hen. VIII*, II. ii. 15, I left him priuate, Full of sad thoughts and troubles. **1752** FOOTE *Taste* I. Wks. 1799 I. 8 Let us be private.

10. †**a.** Intimate, confidential (*with* a person). *Obs.*

1574 HELLOWES *Gueuara's Fam. Epist.* (1584) 175 The Court is not but for men that be private and in favor, that can gather the fruit thereof. **1641** W. MOUNTAGU in *Buccleuch MSS.* (Hist. MSS. Comm.) I. 286 The King is often very private with Digby and Bristow. **1648** GAGE *West Ind.* 205 A great Politician, and very familiar, private, and secret with the Archbishop of Canterbury.

b. Of a conversation, communication, etc.: Intended only for or confined to the person or persons directly concerned; confidential.

1560 DAUS tr. *Sleidane's Comm.* 113b, The byshoppes hauynge priuate talke with the Quene. **1650** W. BROUGH *Sacr. Princ.* (1659) 334 Private Confession is retained in the reformed churches. **1734** BP. STERNE *Let. to Swift* 25 June, I shall put off my defence till I have the pleasure of half an hour's private conversation with you. **1857** TROLLOPE *Barchester T.* xlvii, He received a letter, in an official cover, marked 'private'. **1859** GEO. ELIOT *Let.* 10 Apr. (1954) III. 43 The letter is marked 'private'. *a* **1908** *Mod.* May I have some private conversation with you? **1971** A. PRICE *Alamut Ambush* x. 125 The letter?.. He said it'd be a bit much to open it because it was marked 'private'.

†**11.** = PRIVY *a.* 4; having secret, unacknowledged, or confidential cognizance. Const. *to*, *with*. *Obs.*

1599 B. JONSON *Cynthia's Rev.* I. ii, Had Eccho beene but private with thy faults. **1621** QUARLES *Argalus & P.* (1678) 69 Not making any private to her flight, She quits the house, and steals away by night. **1742** *Cervantes' Novels, Lady C. Bentivoglio* 92 That Maid-servant of mine, who was private [*ed.* 1640 privie] to my Actions.

12. Of a place: Retired, unfrequented, secluded.

1494 FABYAN *Chron.* VI. clix. 149 Ye sayd bysshoppes were depryued of theyr dignyties, and put into pryuate houses of relygyon. **1662** RAY *Three Itin.* II. 162 We went to Shap,.. where we saw the ruins of the abbey, very pleasantly situate in a private valley. **1817** J. EVANS *Excurs. Windsor*, etc. 192, I scarce go out of my own house, and then only to two or three very private places, where I see nobody that really knows anything.

13. Of persons, etc.: Retiring; retired; secluded.

1585 PARSONS *Chr. Exerc.* II. i. 191 S. Antony..a little before had professed a priuate and a solitarie life in Egypt. **1594** DRAYTON *Idea* 142 O God from You, that I could private be. **1630** *R. Johnson's Kingd. & Commw.* 58 Their women are very private, fearefull to offend. **1759** FRANKLIN *Ess.* Wks. 1840 III. 530 Gentlemen, it is true, but so very private, that in the herd of gentry they are hardly to be found. **1850** L. HUNT *Autobiog.* xvii. 267 The privatest of all public men found himself complimented.

†**14.** Of a person: Secretive, reticent. *Obs.*

a **1627** FLETCHER *Wife for Month* I. i, You know I am private as your secret wishes, Ready to fling my soul upon your service. **1660** MARVELL *Corr.* Wks. (Grosart) II. 34 We hope you will be private in these things, communicated to you out of faithfulness to your interest.

†**15.** ***private seal*** = PRIVY SEAL. *Obs.*

1531 in *Sel. Cases Crt. Requests* (1898) 33 To graunte vnto your seid Orator your most dredd wrytte of pryuatte seale to be dyrected vnto the seid abbot.

16. quasi-*adv.* Privately, secretly.

1590 GREENE *Orl. Fur.* Wks. (Grosart) XIII. 195 Ne're had my Lord falne into these extreames, Which we will parley priuate to ourselves. **1659–60** PEPYS *Diary* 6 Mar., Every body now drink the King's health..whereas before, it was very private that a man dare do it. **1704** J. TRAPP *Abra-Mulé* I. i. 117, I came private, and unattended. **1876** 'MARK TWAIN' *Tom Sawyer* xxxv. 272 I'll smoke private and cuss private. **1883** —— *Life on Mississippi* iii. 54 They all drunk more than usual—not together, but each man sidled off and took it private, by himself. **1905** [see CASE *sb.*[2] 6c].

17. *Comb.*, as ***private-humoured***, ***-spirited***.

1602 FULBECKE *Pandectes* 58 Secreat meetinges of male-contents, phantasticall, and priuate humored persons. **1655** J. SERGEANT *Schism Disarm'd* 19 The Doctors private-spirited opinion. **1895** *Spectator* 21 Sept. 368 Unpatriotic and..private-spirited reason.

B. *sb.* **I.** Of a person.

†**1. a.** A private person; one who does not hold any public office or position. *Obs.*

1483 *Cath. Angl.* 291/2 A Priuate, *priuatus*. **1599** SHAKS. *Hen. V*, IV. i. 255 And what haue Kings, that Priuates haue not too, Saue Ceremonie, saue generall Ceremonie? **1671** MILTON *Samson* 1211, I was no private but a person rais'd With..command from Heav'n To free my Countrey.

b. ***the private***: private people, opposed to *the public*. *Obs.*

1716 POPE *Let. to Jervas* 29 Nov., You have already done enough for the private; do something for the public. *a* **1734** NORTH *Lives* (1826) III. 274 Who hath neither inclination nor temptation to court the public, or flatter the private.

†**2.** An intimate, a favourite. *Obs.*

1602 SHAKS. *Ham.* II. ii. 238 In the middle of her fauour ..her priuates, we. [With play on sense 7.]

3. A private soldier: see 2b above.

1781 JUSTAMOND *Priv. Life Lewis XV*, III. 375 This party ..consisted of a Colonel, four Captains,..and 360 private. **1810** WELLINGTON in Gurw. *Desp.* (1838) VI. 45 One officer, four serjeants and fifty privates of the 23rd light dragoons. **1849** MACAULAY *Hist. Eng.* iii. I. 294 Even the privates were designated as gentlemen of the guard. **1868** *Regul. & Ord. Army* §845 The Wives and Children of Non-Commissioned Officers and privates are entitled to medical attendance.

II. Of things or affairs.

†**4. a.** A private or personal matter, business, or interest; *pl.* private affairs. *Obs.*

1549 RIDLEY *Let. to Somerset* in *Liber Cantab.* (1855) 245 [Letters] to signifye..the privits of my hart and consciance. **1592** UNTON *Corr.* (Roxb.) 289, I will no longer hold your Lordship with this my privatt. **1606** WARNER *Alb. Eng.* xv. xcvi. 383 Phocas for his Priuats Rome the Supreame Sea promoted. **1611** B. JONSON *Catiline* III. ii, Nor must I be unmindful of my private. **1642** J. M[ARSH] *Argt. conc. Militia* 7 When it concerns any mans private.

b. Private opinion, one's own mind or thought. *Obs.*

1586 A. DAY *Eng. Secretary* I. (1625) 145 Yet may you vouchsafe in your owne priuate to reckon mee with the greatest in willingnesse.

†**5.** A private or confidential communication.

1595 SHAKS. *John* IV. iii. 16 The Count Meloone,..Whose priuate with me of the Dolphines loue, Is much more generall, then these lines import.

†**6. a.** Retirement, privacy. *Obs.*

1601 SHAKS. *Twel. N.* III. iv. 100 Go off, I discard you: let me enioy my priuate. *a* **1639** WEBSTER *App. & Virg.* II. i, I see there's nothing in such private done, But you must inquire after. *a* **1653** G. DANIEL *Idyll* i. 58 Perhaps I have To my owne Private, had reflects, as grave On my Condition.

b. ***in*** (†***on***) ***private***: privately, not publicly; in private company; in private life.

1581 MULCASTER *Positions* xxxix. (1887) 187 Doth not that deserue to be liked on in priuate, which is thoroughly tryed being showed forth in common? **1582** STANYHURST *Æneis* I. (Arb.) 28 Hee walcks on priuat with noane but faythful Achates. **1615** G. SANDYS *Trav.* 171 Confesse they do, but not greatly in priuate. **1615** BRATHWAIT *Strappado* (1878) 108 Laugh and spare not So't be in priuate, burst thy sides with laughter. **1832** HT. MARTINEAU *Life in Wilds* vi, Let each family eat in private. **1859** G. MEREDITH *R. Feverel* i, Her opinion, founded on observation of him in public and private, was, that..his ordinary course of life would be resumed.

7. *pl.* The privy or private parts. (See 2.)

1940 C. MCCULLERS *Heart is Lonely Hunter* II. iv. 155 He's so fat he hasn't seen his privates for twenty years. **1955** P. BOWLES tr. *Beckett's Molloy* 77 She..thrust her stick between my legs and began to titillate my privates. **1979** 'E. MCBAIN' *Calypso* v. 49 The dancer..wiped the black man's glasses over what the Vice Squad would have called her 'privates'.

†**8.** = PRIVY *sb.* 3. *Obs.*

1600 HAMILTON *Fac. Traictise* in *Cath. Tractates* (S.T.S.) 235 Young wemen..casting thair new borne babes in filthie priuets, vthers in colpots, and in vther secret places.

9. Short for *private school*.

1925 C. CONNOLLY *Let.* 6 Apr. in *Romantic Friendship* (1975) 64, I met quite a nice small boy who is at my private. **1932** N. MITFORD *Christmas Pudding* v. 81 At my private.. we had a most handy little cemetery for the fathers, just behind the cricket pav. **1940** —— *Pigeon Pie* iv. 80 It is exactly like one's private here. **1965** *Listener* 22 July 128/1 What private were you at?

†'**private**, *ppl. a.* *Obs.* [ad. L. *prīvāt-us* deprived, pa. pple. of *prīvāre*: see next.] Deprived, bereft, dispossessed. Commonly used as pa. pple. of PRIVE *v.* *Obs.* = PRIVATED.

1492 RYMAN *Poems* xx. 2 in *Archiv Stud. Neu. Spr.* LXXXIX. 188 Of her crowne priuat she is. **1509** BARCLAY *Shyp of Folys* (1874) I. 1 Thou shewest by euydence Thy selfe of Rethoryke pryuate and barayne. *a* **1541** WYATT *Absent Lover* v, All worldly felicity now am I private, And left in desart most solitarily. **1552** ABP. HAMILTON *Catech.* (1884) 16 Quha ar private the communioun of sanctis. **1573** J. TYRIE *Refut.* in *Cath. Tractates* (S.T.S.) 22 It is easier the sone to be priuat and destitute of licht, nor the kirk to be ony wais obscurit.

private, *v.* [Originally and chiefly in pa. pple. *privated* (prob. *prī̆vated*), f. L. *prīvāt-us*, pa. pple. of *prīvāre* to deprive (PRIVE *v.*) + -ED[1]: cf. prec. The finite parts of the vb. are later and rare. In II (? '*private*) app. f. PRIVATE *a.*; in III ('praɪvət) f. PRIVATE *sb.* 3.]

I. †**1.** *trans.* To deprive or dispossess (a person) *of*, to cut off *from* something. *Obs.*

c **1425** *Found. St. Bartholomew's* (E.E.T.S.) 45 Both the shippe of her marchauntyse And they of ther lyif are priuatid. **1491** CAXTON *Vitas Patr.* (W. de W. 1495) I. xlvii. 89 We shall be pryuated fro her gracyous syghte corporall. *a* **1533** LD. BERNERS *Gold. Bk. M. Aurel.* (1546) Ii ij b, They wolde be pryuated fro the company of so noble barons. *a* **1548** HALL *Chron.*, *Rich. III* 41b, Promisynge faythefully ..that they would..be priuated of their lyues and worldely felicitee, rather then to suffre Kynge Richarde..to rule and reigne ouer them.

II. †**2.** To keep private; to seclude. *Obs.*

1490 CAXTON *Eneydos* xxiii. 85 The soules pryuated & lowe, that be descended in-to helle. **1581** MULCASTER *Positions* xxxix. (1887) 187 Content to be pent vp within private dores, though it mislike the cloistering, in priuating the person. **1612** W. PARKES *Curtaine-Dr.* (1876) 20 Their vnlawfull and lustfull recreations must be priuated and couered with the Curtaine of Secresie.

III. 3. To furnish (an army) with privates; cf. *to officer*, *to man*. *nonce-use.*

1884 *Sat. Rev.* 15 Nov. 626/1 Between a league of this sort and an army privated by persons like the Three Witnesses, chaplained by Mr. Rogers, and officered by Mr. Wren, there ought to be a very pretty battle, which also may in its time figure in the Chamberlainiad.

Hence † **privated** *ppl. a.*, deprived, robbed.

1656 S. H. *Gold. Law* 58 They hang not,..but reserve their Delinquents for useful service, private or publike, yet to give the privated satisfaction, which done, they return to themselves, and are their own men again.

private enterprise. [PRIVATE *a.* (*sb.*) 4c, 5.] A business or other commerical activity that is privately owned and free of direct state control; such concerns collectively. Also *attrib.*

1844 H. H. WILSON *Brit. India* III. 310 That portion of the trade..which the Company relinquished to private enterprise. **1859** MILL *On Liberty* v. 191 When private enterprise, in a shape fitted for undertaking great works of industry, does not exist in the country. **1888** E. BELLAMY *Looking Backward* xxii. 331 Credit..was the only means you had for concentrating and directing it [*sc.* capital] upon industrial enterprises. It was in this way a most potent means for exaggerating the chief peril of the private enterprise system of industry by enabling particular industries to absorb disproportionate amounts of.. disposable capital. **1905** H. G. WELLS *Kipps* I. ii. 32 The same national bias towards private enterprise and leaving bad alone..now indentured him firmly into the hands of Mr. Shalford of the Folkestone Drapery Bazaar. **1927** *Melody Maker* Sept. 931/1 The present massacre of private enterprise on the exhibiting side of the [cinema] trade. **1930** *Economist* 5 July 14/2, 53,983 houses were built by private enterprise. **1935** *Discovery* Mar. 63/1 In these days, when even established private enterprise meets with official disapproval, it was hardly to be expected that so universal a service as television could escape semi-official monopoly. **1948** 'J. TEY' *Franchise Affair* xiv. 149 The Larborough firm had..replaced the windows... But they, of course, were Private Enterprise. **1958** *New Statesman* 1 Nov. 577/2 The man who at last can get a mortgage may not care if public money is being doled out to him through private-enterprise building societies. **1961** J. HELLER *Catch-22* (1962) xxi. 210 Bombing his own men and planes had therefore really been a commendable and very lucrative blow on the side of private enterprise. **1973** 'D. JORDAN' *Nile Green* xxviii. 126 He must be offering the Egyptians a sort of gadget—on the side, a private-enterprise extra. **1975** *N.Y. Times* 17 Oct. 4/2 Despite three decades of Communist rule, pockets of private enterprise in Poland have not only survived but are also showing signs of a modest renaissance.

So **private enterpriser**, an advocate of or participant in private enterprise.

1896 G. B. SHAW in *London Leader* 19 Dec. 443/2 The public bodies under Socialism could watch the results of private enterprise... Under the present system we pay the successful private enterpriser too well. **1904** —— *Common Sense of Municipal Trading* vii. 57 Free competition between private enterprisers. **1952** *N.Y. Times Mag.* 20 July 13/2 From the days of Jefferson and Jackson..it [*sc.* the Democratic Party] has drawn to its ranks..the immigrant and the private enterpriser in conflict with the 'money interests'. **1956** 'A. GILBERT' *Riddle of Lady* iii. 43 A nice chap, thought Crook, a private enterpriser. **1965** *Economist* 5 June 1163/2 An old-fashioned bureaucracy more afraid of the change that the planners may bring than even the private enterpriser.

privateer (praɪvə'tɪə(r)), *sb.* [f. PRIVATE *a.* + -EER[1], prob. after *volunteer*; in sense 1, app. orig. colloq. for *private man of war*, the name in earlier use. (*Privateer*, used in the Calendars of

State Papers from 1651, does not occur in the original papers before *c* 1664.)

1646 (Oct. 29) *MS. Orders & Instruct.* (Adm. Libr.) 22 Instruccions and a fiat in the usuall form were this day signed for Capt. Wm. Davies employing of the ship the 3 kings of dover being of 250 tons and 17 guns as a private man of warre in her way of merchandize. **1651–2** *State Papers Dom.* I. 32 p. 29 That Warrant be issued to the Judges of the Admiraltie to grant letters for a Private Man of Warr to John Mole. *Ibid.* I. 131 p. 64 Commissions for Private Men of Warre or letters of reprezall. **1665** *Cal. St. P. Dom.* (1863) 182 Obligation..entered into by private men-of-war furnished with letters of reprisal against the Dutch.]

1. An armed vessel owned and officered by private persons, and holding a commission from the government, called 'letters of marque', authorizing the owners to use it against a hostile nation, and especially in the capture of merchant shipping. (See MARQUE[1] 2.)

(The first quotation may belong to sense 2.)

1664 COL. T. LYNCH in *Cal. State Pap., Colon.* (1880) 211 The calling in of the privateers will be but a remote and hazardous expedient... What compliance can be expected from men..that have no other element but the sea, or trade but privateering. **1665** PEPYS *Diary* 17 Apr., How three Dutch *privateers* are taken, in one whereof Everson's son is captaine. **1667** *Ibid.* 20 Feb. **1687** B. RANDOLPH *Archipelago* 46 There are several other ports and creeks, which are often haunted by the privateers. **1702** *Royal Declar.* June in *Lond. Gaz.* No. 3815/3 Her Majesty having Impowered the Lord High Admiral of England to grant Letters of Marque, or Commissions for Privateers. **1748** *Anson's Voy.* II. xiv. 279 Men of war are much better provided with all conveniences than privateers. **1813** WELLINGTON in Gurw. *Desp.* (1839) XI. 143 The capture of a Mediterranean packet by an American privateer.

2. The commander, or *pl.* the crew, of such a vessel.

a **1674** CLARENDON *Life* (1842) 1127/2 It was resolved [1665] that all possible encouragement should be given to privateers. **1687** *Royal Proclam.* 18 Sept. in *Lond. Gaz.* No. 2279/3 His Majesty will..grant unto such Pirat or Pirats, Privateer or Privateers, a full Pardon for all Piracies or Robberies. **1748** *Anson's Voy.* II. i. 120 The usual haunt of the buccaneers and privateers. **1850** GROTE *Greece* II. lxv. VIII. 297 Lysander sent off the Milesian privateer Theopompus to proclaim it [the victory] at Sparta. **1883** S. C. HALL *Retrospect* I. 86 Privateers were little scrupulous as to what kind of victim they pounced upon.

fig. **1692** *Wicked Contriv. S. Blackhead* in *Select. fr. Harl. Misc.* (1793) 530 To give notice of him, that there was such a privateer abroad, and to obviate..the evil practices of so vile a man. **1698** FARQUHAR *Love & Bottle* I. Wks. 1892 I. 13 We masks are the purest privateers! **1836** DICKENS *Let.* 1 Nov. (1965) I. 188, I perceive that 'Bells Life'—'The Carlton Chronicle', and some other Weekly papers, are in the habit of re-publishing my sketches from the Chronicle verbatim... Some remonstrance in the paper might have the effect of inducing the Privateers at all events to acknowledge the source from which they derive the Articles.

†**3.** A volunteer soldier, a free-lance, a guerilla.

1676 I. MATHER *K. Philip's War* (1862) 58 Hearing many profane oaths among some of our Souldiers (namely those Privateers, who were also Volunteers). **1677** W. HUBBARD *Narrative* 18 Our Horsemen with the whole body of the Privateers under Captain Moseley..ran violently down upon them.

4. An advocate or exponent of private enterprise.

1940 *Amer. Guardian* 5 Apr. 4/3 It is the general policy of the privateers never to reduce their rate unless forced to do so by public competition in the shape of municipally or federally owned [electric power] plants. **1965** *Spectator* 19 Feb. 223/1 These two engaging privateers..are concerned not so much with steel as with the general pattern of British politics. **1979** *Arizona Daily Star* 22 July C 10/1 As a privateer, Serrano drove himself to the races and for the last half of the series even served as his own mechanic.

5. *attrib.*, as ***privateer brig, captain, schooner***, *etc.*

1675 *Cal. State Pap., Colon.* (1893) 263 What is due to the Lord Admiral from the privateer captains and their companies that sail under his commission. **1695** LUTTRELL *Brief Rel.* (1857) III. 552 Their King, the nobility and gentry [of France], have subscribed to a new bank (which they call the privateer bank), designing to fit out yearly a certain number of privateers to disturb the trade of the allies. **1743** BULKELEY & CUMMINS *Voy. S. Seas* 3 The Commodore sent out a Privateer Sloop. **1798** *Times* 28 June 2/2 A French privateer brig of 14 guns.

privateer (praɪvəˈtɪə(r)), *v. rare.* [f. prec. Chiefly used in the vbl. sb. and ppl. adj. *privateering* (see next): cf. *mountaineer, parliamenteer*, etc.] *intr.* To play the privateer, to practise privateering.

1691 *Commission of Jas. II*, 29 June (Admiralty Prize Pap., bundle 90, P.R.O.), We..give leave permit and suffer you..to privateer and seaze the ships of all persons whatsoever onely excepted [etc.]. **1696** LUTTRELL *Brief Rel.* (1857) IV. 58 To perswade the [French] King..to fit out all the frigats he has, and to privateer this summer.

privaˈteering, *vbl. sb.* [f. prec. sb. or vb. + -ING[1].] The occupation or practice of a privateer. Often *attrib.*, as ***privateering trade, practices***.

1664 [see PRIVATEER *sb.* 1]. **1698** C. DAVENANT *Disc.* II. 115 The Profits and Advantages they have gain'd..by Privateering. **1715** *Lond. Gaz.* No. 5317/1 Commissions for Privateering are much demanded. **1850** GROTE *Greece* II. lvi. VII. 140 To grant what we may call letters of marque, to any one, for privateering against Athenian commerce. **1863** H. COX *Instit.* III. ii. 598 At the conference at Paris, in 1856,..it was declared that, as to those Powers..'privateering is and remains abolished'.

b. esp. in phr. ***a-privateering***: see A *prep.*

1701 LUTTRELL *Brief Rel.* (1857) V. 82 Several vessells are fitting out..to goe a privateering with his imperial majesties commission. **1760** *N. Jersey Archives* XX. 505 They have both been a Privateering. **1851** CARLYLE *Sterling* I. x. (1872) 61 That they should..sail a-privateering 'to the Eastern Archipelago'.

c. *fig.*

1668 DRYDEN *Evening's Love* IV. iii, When our loves are veering, We'll make no words, but fall to privateering. **1673** MARVELL *Reh. Transp.* II. 30 It is a prædatory course of life, and indeed but a privateering upon reputation. **1890** 'R. BOLDREWOOD' *Miner's Right* x. I. 250 In all privateering on gold-fields..the initiated are aware that the alliance of capital with labour is indispensable. **1891** T. HARDY *Tess* xxii, Mr. Clare..stepped out of line, and began privateering about for the weed.

privaˈteering, *ppl. a.* [f. as prec. + -ING[2].] Following the occupation of a privateer.

1703 C'TESS WINCHELSEA *Pindar. Poem Hurricane* 262 The Wealth..of diff'rent Shores..destroy'd by generous Fight, Or Privateering Foes. **1868** *Digby's Voy. Medit.* Pref. (Camden) 31 The design was that of a general privateering voyage.

privaˈteerism. [f. PRIVATEER *sb.* + -ISM.] 'Disorderly conduct, or anything out of man-of-war rules' (Smyth *Sailor's Word-bk.* 1867).

privaˈteersman. *U.S.* [f. genitive of PRIVATEER *sb.* + MAN *sb.*[1] Cf. *landsman*, etc.] An officer or seaman of a privateer.

1824 W. IRVING *T. Trav.* II. 241 There is but a slight step from the privateersman to the pirate; both fight for the love of plunder. **1876** BANCROFT *Hist. U.S.* V. xviii. 546 An act which described American privateersmen as pirates. **1883** *American* VI. 361 He tells..of the life of a merchant captain and privateersman between 1775 and 1783.

privately (ˈpraɪvətlɪ), *adv.* [f. PRIVATE *a.* + -LY[2].] In a private manner, way, or capacity.

1. In a private capacity; unofficially.

1550 CROWLEY *Epigr.* 1141 (*heading*) Priests that vse theyr Tithes priuatly. **1590** J. SMYTHE in *Lett. Lit. Men* (Camden) 64, I, beeinge pryvatly many yeares beeyond the seas. **1613** PURCHAS *Pilgrimage* (1614) 424 Hee went priuatly to Constantinople, and had sight of the Citie, with all kindnesse from the Emperour. **1877** FROUDE *Short Stud.* (1883) IV. I. iii. 34 Several..prelates wrote privately to the pope to entreat him to interfere.

2. Without publicity; without the participation, presence, or cognizance of the public, in private; in a retired or quiet manner, quietly; secretly.

1548 UDALL *Erasm. Par. Luke* iii. 35 He had priuatelye had testimonie geuen him of Aungels, of Elizabeth, of Simeon, of Anna, of yᵉ Magians. **1552** *Bk. Com. Prayer* Pref., All Priestes and Deacons shalbe bounde to say dayly the Mornynge and Euenyng prayer, either priuatly or openly. **1580** *Reg. Privy Council Scot.* III. 281 Gif he depairtit privatlie from this..place. **1611** SHAKS. *Wint. T.* v. ii. 114 Shee hath priuately, twice or thrice a day, euer since the death of Hermione, visited that remoued House. **1611** BIBLE *Matt.* xxiv. 3. **1617** MORYSON *Itin.* I. 210 All falling on our knees,..praying euery man priuately and silently to himselfe. **1648** *Bury Wills* (Camden) 201 To be buried in the night privately. **1651** HOBBES *Leviath.* III. xlii. 277 If thy Brother offend thee, tell it him privately. **1712** ADDISON *Spect.* No. 475 ¶1 She had been privately married to him above a Fortnight. **1804** *Med. Jrnl.* XII. 463 Having been requested, both publicly and privately, to give my opinion of the preparation of the *Lichen Islandicus*. **1853** MRS. CARLYLE *Lett.* (1883) II. 231 Leaving [Scotland] that morning, privately minded never to return. **1875** JOWETT *Plato* I. 52 Lysis..whispered privately in my ear, so that Menexenus should not hear.

3. In a manner affecting an individual; individually, personally.

1560 DAUS tr. *Sleidane's Comm.* 18 If the head do ake, it greueth the rest of the membres, taking the same to apperteine priuatly to euery of them. **1568** GRAFTON *Chron.* II. 50 He..so louyngly spake vnto them both generally and priuately, that euery man conceyued thereby great hope of his good gouernment to come. **1828** WEBSTER s.v., He is not privately benefited.

4. *Comb.*, as ***privately-minded, -owned.***

1899 *Daily News* 26 Oct. 7/1 The mischiefs of the privately-owned railways. **1905** *Daily Chron.* 8 Aug. 2/7 The one person who is a drag upon progress towards a..happier social life, is the privately-minded person.

ˈprivateness. [f. as prec. + -NESS.] The quality or condition of being private, in various senses; privacy, the opposite of publicity; withdrawal from society, seclusion; †secrecy; †the pursuit of private ends; †the quality of being a private person or of living privately; †confidential intercourse, intimacy.

1585–7 [see OWEDNESS]. *a* **1586** SIDNEY *Arcadia* (1622) 389 All churlish words, shrewd answers, crabbed lookes, All priuatenesse, selfe-seeking, inward spite. **1604** BACON *Apol.* Wks. 1879 I. 435 This difference in two points so main and material, bred in process of time a discontinuance of privateness. **1607–12** —— *Ess., Great Place* (Arb.) 280 Nay, retire men cannott when they would,..but are impatient of privatenes, even in age and sicknes. **1642** ROGERS *Naaman* 245 To attempt the defacing of them in an open manner, where our privatenesse cannot extend. **1667** ANNE WYNDHAM *King's Concealm.* (1681) 76 Into the highest chambers, where Privateness recompensed the meanness of the Accommodation. **1676** TOWERSON *Decalogue* 441 Differenc'd..by the publickness or privateness of the things. **1922** E. R EDDISON *Worm Ouroboros* xv. 212 I'll walk apart, madam,..if thou wouldst have privateness to deliver thy mind. **1939** 'G. ORWELL' *Coming up for Air* IV. vi. 276 The privateness of all those lives! **1941** —— *Lion & Unicorn* 15 What it does link up with..is the addiction to hobbies and spare-time occupations, the *privateness* of English life. **1941** E. R. EDDISON *Fish Dinner* vi. 92 He let go her hands and stood..as if withdrawn for the moment into some inside privateness of deliberation.

privation (praɪˈveɪʃən). [= F. *privation* (14th c. in Littré), ad. L. *prīvātiōn-em* a taking away, deprivation, n. of action from *prīv-āre* to bereave, deprive: see PRIVE.]

1. The action of depriving or taking away; the fact or condition of being deprived *of* or †cut off *from* something; deprivation. Now *rare*.

1340 HAMPOLE *Pr. Consc.* 1806 Þis may be calde..a privacion of þe life, When it partes fra þe body in strife. **1483** CAXTON *Cato* I iv, A man ought to suffer for a vertuous friend priuacion of all worldly goodes. *a* **1548** HALL *Chron., Rich. III* 39 King Richard had bene in greate ieopardie either of priuacion of his realme or losse of his life or both. **1686** tr. *Chardin's Coronat. Solyman* 15 Necessity..constrained them to prefer..the younger, and to fix him in the Throne, tho to the Privation of his elder Brother. **1756** BURKE *Subl. & B.* II. vi, All general privations are great because they are all terrible; Vacuity, Darkness, Solitude, and Silence. **1803** *Man in Moon* (1804) 47 His mind is in a state of privation from the greatest solace of religious hope. **1858** LYTTON *What will he do?* VII. x, Condemned to the painful choice between his society and that of nobody else, or that of anybody else with the rigid privation of his. **1897** *Allbutt's Syst. Med.* III. 130 Rickets may be produced artificially in animals by absolute privation of lime.

b. *Law.* The action of depriving of office or position; = DEPRIVATION 2; in *R.C. Ch.* = SUSPENSION. Now *rare* or *Obs.*

c **1425** WYNTOUN *Cron.* VIII. 1701 Þis Kynge Edwarde gaf sentens And dome of his prywacioun For his hie rebellioun. *a* **1539** in *Archæologia* XLVII. 59, I chardge and commaunde you undre payne of priuacion that ye [etc.]. **1544** tr. *Littleton's Tenures* (1574) 116 b, This warrantise is expired by his [the Abbot's] privasion or by his death. **1628** COKE *On Litt.* 329. **1670** BLOUNT *Law Dict.*, *Privation*,..most commonly applied to a Bishop, or Rector of a Church; when by Death, or other act, they are deprived of their Bishoprick or Benefice. **1885** *Cath. Dict.*, Privation. See *Suspension*.

2. *Logic.* The condition of being deprived of or being without some attribute formerly or properly possessed; the loss, or (loosely) the mere absence of a quality, a negative quality.

Often called the negative or negation of the eighth Aristotelian category, ἔχειν, *habitus*, the fact of having.

1398 TREVISA *Barth. De P.R.* x. i. (Tollem. MS.), Privacion of matter and forme is nouȝt ellis but destruccion of all þinge. **1555** EDEN *Decades* 87 To gyue substance to priuation, (that is) beinge to noo beinge. **1588** FRAUNCE *Lawiers Log.* I. xi. 49 b, The affirmatiue is called the habite, [i.e. *habitus*, ἕξειν] the negatiue the priuation thereof. **1620** T. GRANGER *Div. Logike* 107 Habite signifieth disposition, power, and act, to which priuation is opposite. **1654** Z. COKE *Logick* 95 Privative Opposition, is the fighting betwixt habit and privation. **1685** BOYLE *Enq. Notion Nat.* 22 This Death, which is said to do so many and such wonderful things, is neither a Substance, nor a Positive Entity, but a meer Privation. **1838** EMERSON *Address, Camb., Mass.* Wks. (Bohn) II. 192 Evil is merely privative, not absolute: it is like cold, which is the privation of heat.

3. Want of the usual comforts, or especially of some of the necessaries of life.

1790 CATH. GRAHAM *Lett. Educ.* 67 When you reflect on the many privations which people who cannot help themselves suffer when any of their attendants are out of the way. **1838** LYTTON *Alice* III. vii, 'It can be a privation only to me',..said Maltravers. **1845** S. AUSTIN *Ranke's Hist. Ref.* IV. i. II. 351 A needy band of mercenaries, urged by hunger and privation. **1853** J. H. NEWMAN *Hist. Sk.* (1873) II. I. iv. 219 Prepared by penury and hard fare for the privations of a military life.

privatism (ˈpraɪvətɪz(ə)m). [f. PRIVATE *a.* + -ISM.] An inclination or tendency to be private (in various senses); the use or advocacy of personal or private ideas, institutions, etc. Hence **privaˈtistic** *a.*, **privaˈtistically** *adv.*

1948 C. S. LEWIS in Williams & Lewis *Arthurian Torso* II. vi. 188 'Privatism.' This occurs when the poet writes what the reader, however sensitive and generally cultivated he may be, could not possibly understand unless the poet chose to tell him something more than he has told. **1970** *Time* 28 Dec. 6 Few observers of the U.S. scene foresaw that political passions on the campuses would become muted in a new emphasis on 'privatism'. **1970** C. A. REICH *Greening of Amer.* x. 284 'Human nature' was not necessarily always privatistic, grasping, competitive, materialistic. **1971** J. J. SHAPIRO tr. *Habermas's Toward Rational Society* vi. 121 Student activists are less privatistically oriented to professional careers and future families than other students. **1971** *Atlantic Monthly* Nov. 119, I cannot say in blanket fashion whether this Mao myth is 'good or bad'... The 'privatistic' alternative, anyway, in a country with *per capita* income perhaps one twentieth of America's, is not a glittering one. **1977** *Times Lit. Suppl.* 2 Sept. 1054/2 Self-interest—what Dr. Kammen euphemistically calls 'privatism'—and secularism were strong. **1978** T. HONORÉ *Tribonian* 37 They were trained largely in private law..and imperial constitutions, let alone criminal and public law, had little part to play in legal education. The privatistic outlook of these men is likely to be reflected in the output of constitutions.

privative (ˈprɪvətɪv), *a.* (*sb.*) [ad. L. *prīvātīv-us* denoting privation, in *Gram.* privative, negative, f. ppl. stem of *prīvāre* (see PRIVE *v.* and

-IVE). So F. *privatif*, *-ive* (16th c. in Hatz.-Darm.).]

1. Having the quality of depriving; tending to take away; †having power to prevent (*obs. rare*).

a **1600** HOOKER *Eccl. Pol.* v. App. i. §26 We may add that negative or privative will also, whereby he withholdeth his graces from some, and so is said to cast them asleep whom he maketh not vigilant. *a* **1639** WOTTON *Elect. Dk. Venice* in *Reliq.* (1651) 186 No one of them had voices enough to exclude the other three from making a Duke: for to this Privative Power are required seventeen Bals at least. **1646** S. BOLTON *Arraignm. Err.* 283 The power of a Synod as I told you, is not privative, but cumulative. **1650** R. HOLLINGWORTH *Exerc. Usurped Powers* 45 If the thing sworn should become privative of, or opposite to, the publick good. **1875** POSTE *Gaius* I. Introd. (ed. 2) 3 Title.. is any fact Collative or Privative of a Right and Impositive or Exonerative of an Obligation.

2. Consisting in or characterized by the taking away or removal of something, or by the loss or want of some quality or attribute normally or presumably present; also, in looser sense, by the simple absence of some quality, negative.

(In quot. 1398, *privative* is the Latin adv., after the preceding L. *positive* in the L. and Eng. texts, though both words were mistaken for English in the printed ed. of 1495.)

[**1398** TREVISA *Barth. De P.R.* XIX. xxxviii. (Bodl. MS.), Fumosite.. þat declareþ not þe complection of stone positiue [1495 -yf] & bi presens of odoure, but priuatiue [-yf] & bi absens of odoure (*non positiue, sed per priuationem et absentiam*).]

1598 BACON *Sacr. Medit.* xi. Ess. (Arb.) 127 They.. bring in against God a principle negatiue and priuatiue, that is a cause of not being and subsisting. **1644** VICARS *God in Mount* 185 Remarkable mercies both by Sea and Land, both privative and positive. **1651** JER. TAYLOR *Serm. for Year* I. xii. 151 The very privative blessings, the blessings of immunity, safeguard, and integrity, which we all enjoy. **1651** BAXTER *Inf. Bapt.* 48 Their unbelief which was but negative, was not privative. *a* **1659** Z. BOGAN in Spurgeon *Treas. Dav.* Ps. xxiii. 1 Only privative defects discommend a thing, and not those that are negative. **1805** *Monthly Mag.* XX. 137 As we deprive a body of part or all of its natural share of fluid to produce what is called *negative* electricity, whether the words *privative* electricity would not be more proper? **1838** [see PRIVATION 2]. **1866** T. HARPER *Peace thro' Truth* 309 *note*, We mean by it [aversion].. something which is not positive, but privative,—not an act, but a state.

3. Of terms: Denoting or predicating privation, or (loosely) absence of a quality or attribute.

1646 SIR T. BROWNE *Pseud. Ep.* 152 Although they had neither eyes nor sight, yet could they not be termed blind; for blindenesse being a privative terme unto sight, this appellation is not admittible in propriety of speech. **1656** tr. *Hobbes' Elem. Philos.* (1839) 18 The first distinction of names is, that some are positive, or affirmative, others negative, which are also called privative and indefinite. **1690** LOCKE *Hum. Und.* III. i. §4 All which negative or privative Words cannot be said.. to.. signify no Ideas.. but .. relate to positive Ideas, and signify their Absence. **1829** JAS. MILL *Hum. Mind* (1869) II. xiv. 105 Privative terms are marks for objects, as not present or not existent. [*Note* by J. S. Mill: 'It is usual to reserve the term Privative for names which signify not simple absence, but the absence of something usually present, or of which the presence might have been expected'.] **1871** MORLEY *Crit. Misc.* Ser. I. *Carlyle* (1878) 162 The addition of a crowd of privative or negative epithets at discretion.

4. *Gram.* Expressing privation or negation; esp. applied to a particle or affix.

1590 HUTCHINSON in Greenwood *Collect. Sclaund. Art.* D iv b, Know you what *a* is here, it is *a* priuatiue. **1706** PHILLIPS s.v., A Privative Particle in Grammar. **1837** G. PHILLIPS *Syriac Gram.* 116 The particle.. placed before adjectives assigns a privative signification to them. **1846** *Proc. Philol. Soc.* II. 184 Bopp's theory of the Greek past tenses.. being formed by the addition of the particle called *a* privative.

B. *sb.* A privative attribute, quality, proposition, word, or particle.

1588 FRAUNCE *Lawiers Log.* I. xi. 49 b, Priuatiues they call those whereof one denieth onely in that subiect where-vnto the affirmatiue agreeth by nature. **1627** DONNE *Serm.* v. (1640) 46 Man hath more privatives, then positives in him. *a* **1683** OLDHAM *Poet. Wks.* (1686) 109 In them sin is but a meer privative of good, The frailty, and defect of flesh and blood. **1697** tr. *Burgersdicius his Logic* II. xviii. 83 Of Privatives, The one must of Necessity be in the Capacious Subject, the other not. As, He is blind; and therefore does not see. **1864** BOWEN *Logic* vi. 152 One is merely the Contradictory or the privative of the other.

'privatively, *adv.* [f. prec. + -LY².]

1. In a privative manner; by the taking away or absence of something; negatively.

1659 H. MORE *Immort. Soul* I. xi. §7. 81 This Indifferency of the Matter to Motion or Rest may be understood two wayes: Either privatively, that is to say, That it has not any reall or active propension to Rest, more then to Motion, or *vice versâ*. **1684** tr. *Bonet's Merc. Compit.* VIII. 312 In this Disease.. the Stomach is affected privatively, not positively. **1687** NORRIS *Coll. Misc.* (1699) 301 To be in pain, is not Privatively, but contrarily opposed to being happy. **1707** —— *Treat. Humility* iii. 87 The man who is a sinner is not only negatively, but privatively imperfect. **1710** WHITBY *Disc.* IV. i. §5 (1735) 312 The Devils.. being determined to do Evil in the General, and that only privatively for want of Motive or Inducement to do otherwise.

†**2.** To the deprivation or exclusion of others; exclusively. *Obs.*

1611 SPEED *Theat. Gt. Brit.* xxix. (1614) 57/2 The power of coynage then.. not being so privatively in the King, but borowes, bishops and earles enjoyed it. **1634** W. TIRWHYT tr. *Balzac's Lett.* (vol. I) 267 Assuring yourself there is no one man in the world worthy to enjoy you privatively.

So **'privativeness** *rare*, the quality or condition of being privative.

1668 WILKINS *Real Char.* II. i. §3. 28 Privativeness. **1682** H. MORE *Annot. Glanvill's Lux O.* 211 Indiscerpibility.. of an Atom.. from imperfection and privativeness. **1727** BAILEY vol. II, *Privativeness*, depriving Quality, or Faculty of taking away.

privatization (ˌpraɪvətaɪˈzeɪʃən). [f. PRIVATE *a.* + -IZATION.] **1.** The policy or process of making private as opposed to public, *spec.* the advocacy or exploitation by the State of PRIVATE ENTERPRISE; = DENATIONALIZATION 2.

1959 *News Chron.* 28 July 2/6 Erhard selected the rich Preussag mining concern for his first experiment in privatisation. **1960** *Ibid.* 22 Apr. 11/5 Complete privatisation was opposed by the Socialists.. because they feared.. the little man selling out his shares to the big capitalists. **1970** *Observer* 25 Jan. 1/6 He foresaw 'privatisation' of many sectors of industry now in public ownership. **1970** J. COTLER in I. L. Horowitz *Masses in Lat. Amer.* xii. 440 If rural marginality allows for the.. privatization of State power, the political sphere demands.. a new line of social integration. **1976** *National Observer* (U.S.) 1 May B6/3 The contrast between then and now measures the tendency toward privatization and withdrawal of our commitments from the open, public arena that has occurred during the course of the Twentieth Century. **1976** *Globe & Mail* (Toronto) 12 Dec. 5/7 Privatization in the handing over of elements of the public service to the private sector is threatening the livelihoods of thousands of public servants. **1977** *Ibid.* 20 Jan. 6/1 The Government published a working paper.. which set out some possibilities.. including this: 'The possibility of the private sector providing goods or services that are now provided through government enterprise and programs.' The government, it seemed was toying with the idea of 'privatization'. **1979** *New Statesman* 6 July 14/3 This political formula of controlled privatisation depends on not too many people finding the stringent limits on expression spiritually intolerable.

2. The act or process of regarding as personal or separate, *spec.* the concept of an institution, activity, discipline, etc., seen in terms of its relation to the individual rather than to society generally or to a part of society.

1968 *Listener* 6 June 720/1 On these two points, the privatisation of death, and the loss of any sense of an appropriate length of life, I have contrasted contemporary English society with alien cultures—Celtic or African. **1969** J. H. GOLDTHORPE et al. *Affluent Worker in Class Struct.* iv. 96 Our findings would indicate as the most probable concomitant of these workers' orientation to work and of their present type of employment what we have earlier referred to as *privatisation*—a process, that is, manifested in a pattern of social life which is centred on, and indeed largely restricted to, the home and the conjugal family. **1972** *Clergy Rev.* Mar. 209 Despite our privatization of God, we are all sharers in spiritual matters. **1973** *Times Lit. Suppl.* 26 Oct. 1307/2 To buy things like that secondhand car which initiates the simultaneous privatization and social extension of their life-style. **1974** J. I. M. STEWART *Gaudy* iii. 40 He had carried with him all the privatization of experience that characterizes bourgeois life. **1975** *Amer. Anthropologist* LXXVII. 260 While the stress on language and on inter-subjectivity is fine, the privatization of anthropology, its ultimate inability to issue in a set of explanatory propositions, is disastrous. **1976** NICHOLS & ARMSTRONG *Workers Divided* 20 We also seek to indicate.. what is sometimes called 'privatization'..: a nuclear family-based separation from community. **1976** *Jrnl. Church & State* XVIII. 209 (*title*) Does Church-State separation necessarily mean the privatization of religion? **1978** *Times Lit. Suppl.* 17 Feb. 194/4 The modern 'privatization' of religion owes more to constitutional developments than to Christianity having become 'controversial'. **1979** E. NORMAN *Christianity & World Order* vi. 80 To regard Christianity as being.. concerned primarily with the relationship of the soul to eternity, is these days denounced within Christian opinion as a 'privatization' of religion.

privatize (ˈpraɪvətaɪz), *v.* [f. PRIVATE *a.* + -IZE.]

1. *trans.* To regard as personal or separate, *spec.* in the sense of PRIVATIZATION 2.

1969 W. GLEN-DOEPEL tr. *Metz's Theol. of World* v. 109 The societal dimension of the Christian message was not given its proper importance but, implicitly or explicitly, treated as a secondary matter. In short, the message was 'privatized' and the practice of faith reduced to the timeless decision of the person. *Ibid.* 114 It is impossible to privatize the eschatological promises of biblical tradition: liberty, peace, justice, reconciliation. Again and again they force us to assume our responsibilities towards society. **1972** *Biblical Theol. Bull.* Feb. 47 Because of their transcendental, existentialistic, personalistic drift these theologies have privatized and presentialized the Christian message. **1977** *Times Lit. Suppl.* 8 Apr. 441/4 Few of his dockers were 'privatized' in the sense in which that term was used by Goldthorpe and his colleagues in their Luton study. **1979** E. NORMAN *Christianity & World Order* vi. 80 The modern politicized Christians also 'privatize' religion.

2. To make private as opposed to public, *spec.* of the State, to assign (services, industries, etc.) to PRIVATE ENTERPRISE; = DENATIONALIZE *v.* 2 b.

1970 *New Society* 5 Feb. 222/3 Is the Office of Health Economics trying to hint that the best place to start totally privatising the National Health Service is at eye level? **1972** *Daily Tel.* 10 Feb. 16 Some local government services (water, refuse collection, fire-fighting, sea-side amenities, art galleries, museums) could be 'privatised', as well as national health services and State schools. **1976** *Globe & Mail* (Toronto) 12 Dec. 7/2 The House might want to address itself to the question whether we want the Crown corporations to continue to be involved in business or whether they should all be privatized. **1979** *Ibid.* 24 May 7/5 Mr. Clark intends to proceed with his promise to 'privatize' Petro Canada.

Hence **'privatized** *ppl. a.*

1968 *Brit. Universities Ann.* 95 Until recently, the values of the entertainment industry, and the demand for purely 'privatised' standards of morality gave the young little to act collectively about. **1969** R. BLACKBURN in Cockburn & Blackburn *Student Power* 195 Condemned to a trapped existence in anonymous private or public bureaucracies, 'industrial' man is promised the domestic joys of a 'privatized' existence. **1971** J. J. SHAPIRO tr. *Habermas's Toward Rational Society* ii. 13 The adult role anticipated at the university.. is therefore unsuited for supporting a privatized orientation bound to career and advancement. **1973** GOLDTHORPE & LOCKWOOD in *Sociol. Rev.* II. 154 At this point we may return to our earlier distinction between the 'privatised' and the 'socially aspiring' worker. **1976** *Spare Rib* Dec. 4/3 As long as most people live in nuclear family-type set-ups.. baby-sitting will remain a 'privatised', individual act. **1978** A. BRITTAN (*title*) The privatised world. *Ibid.* v. 121 The 'privatised self' is explicable in terms of developments in the class structures of western societies.

†**pri'vator.** *Obs. rare*⁻¹. [a. L. type **prīvātor*, agent-n. f. *prīvāre*: see PRIVE *v.*] One who or that which deprives or takes away.

1630 J. LANE *Cont. Sqr.'s T.* (Chaucer Soc.) 33 *note*, All thinges demolish, as hates dire privator, In spite off (yet suffred by) their creator.

†**prive**, *v. Obs.* Also 4 preve, *Sc.* priwe, 4–6 pryve. [a. F. *priv-er* (1307 in Godef. *Compl.*), ad. L. *prīv-āre* to bereave, deprive, rob, deliver, perh. orig. to isolate, make solitary, f. *prīv-us* single, individual, private, peculiar, deprived.]

1. *trans.* To deprive, strip, bereave. Const. *of*, also with double obj.

13.. *Evang. Nicod.* 1440 in Herrig's *Archiv* LIII. 418þou has vs schamely schent And pryued vs of our pray. **1340** HAMPOLE *Pr. Consc.* 110 When he had done mys, And thurgh syn was prived of blys. *c* **1400** *Apol. Loll.* 67 þat he priue himsilf power of bynding and lowsing. *c* **1450** tr. *De Imitatione* III. xxxi. 100 þat may.. pryue þe þin inward liberte. *a* **1548** HALL *Chron., Edw. IV* 195 By this mariage were kyng Edwardes .ii. sonnes declared bastardes, & in conclusion pried of their lifes. **1654–66** EARL ORRERY *Parthen.* (1676) 182 He prives me of my hope.

b. *spec.* To strip or divest of office or dignity; to depose.

c **1330** R. BRUNNE *Chron.* (1810) 73 Abbot & prioure, men of Religion,.. Wer priued of þar office. **1390** GOWER *Conf.* III. 202 Leoncius Was to thempire of Rome arrived, Fro which he hath with strengthe prived The pietous Justinian. **1399** *Rolls of Parlt.* III. 424/1 Adjugged ȝowe for to be deposed and pryved, and in dede deposed ȝowe and pryved ȝowe of the astate of Kyng. **1413** *Pilgr. Sowle* (Caxton 1483) III. i. 50 Vpon that condicion that I myght priuen hym his power. **1426** *Paston Lett.* I. 25 By this acceptacion of this bysshopriche, he hath pryved hym self of the title that he claymed in Bromholm. **1559** *Mirr. Mag., Northumbld.* xi, To pryue the king, and part the realme in thre. **1634** S. R. *Noble Soldier* I. ii. in Bullen *O. Pl.* I. 272 To prive thy sonne, .. Spaines heire Apparant.

2. To take away, withdraw, cut off *from*.

c **1375** *Sc. Leg. Saints* I. (*Katerine*) 932, I dout þat sum cristine has now fra oure goddis priwit þe. **1382** WYCLIF *Prol.* i. 3 Pride and couetise of clerkis.. priueth hem fro verrey vndirstondyng of holy writ. **1387** TREVISA *Higden* (Rolls) VII. 335 þe pope.. restored his felowes bisshoppes .. crosses and rynges þat were to forehonde i-preved [*v.r.* ypriued, L. *privatos*]. *c* **1400** *Apol. Loll.* 14 Nor þe kirk may not iustli priue þe comyning of cristun men, nor taking of þe sacraments. **1629** N. CARPENTER *Achitophel* II. (1640) 95 Some inchanted Relicke to prive him safe from danger.

Hence †**'priving** *vbl. sb.*, depriving, privation.

c **1380** WYCLIF *Wks.* (1880) 267 Assentynge to hem.. summe for drede of curs, priuynge of beneficis & sclaundre & prisonynge & brennynge. *c* **1422** HOCCLEVE *Learn to Die* 35 What may profyte the lore of dyynge, Syn deeth noon hauynge is but a pryuynge? *c* **1440** *Promp. Parv.* 414/2 Privynge, *privacio*. *c* **1460** G. ASHBY *Dicta Philos.* 586 Ner in a man errynge, peine deseruing, Ner in hym that hathe be of goode pryuyng.

prive, obs. dial. form of *preve*, PROVE.

privet¹ (ˈprɪvɪt). Also 6–7 -ett(e, 7 -ate; β. 6 privy, -ie. [Instanced from 16th c.: origin unknown; cf. the synonyms *prim-print*, *primp*, and *prim*. See Note below.]

1. A bushy evergreen shrub, *Ligustrum vulgare* (N.O. *Oleaceæ*), a native of Europe, having elliptic-lanceolate smooth dark-green leaves, and clusters of small white flowers, succeeded by small shining black berries; much used for garden hedges.

1542 ELYOT, *Ligustrum*.. this tree dothe growe in watry places, as wyllowes and salowes do, and bearith a blacke fruite lyke to an elder tree; they whiche doo take it for the bushe callyd Priuet, be moche deceyued. **1548** TURNER *Names of Herbes* E j b, Ligustrum is called in.. englishe Prim print or priuet, though Eliote more boldely than lernedly, defended the contrary. **1578** LYTE *Dodoens* VI. xxv. 689 Priuet is a base plante, very seldome growing vpright. **1634–5** BRERETON *Trav.* (Chetham Soc.) 45 Cornowlee makes an hedge like privett. **1779** MASON *Eng. Gard.* III. 114 The hardy Thorn, Holly, or Box, Privet, or Pyracanth. **1842** TENNYSON *Walking to Mail* 48 A skin As clean and white as privet when it flowers. **1859** W. S. COLEMAN *Woodlands* (1862) 132 The clustered white flowers of the Privet appear about midsummer, and are very ornamental.

β. **1573** TUSSER *Husb.* (1878) 33 Set priuie or prim, Set boxe like him. **1591** in *Lyly's Wks.* (1902) I. 433 The 3. and last was a Snayl mount [spiral ascent], rising to foure circles of greene priuie hedges. **1593** BRETON *Daffodils & Primroses* 3/2 The borders round about, are set with priuie sweete.

2. In southern U.S. = *swamp privet*: see 3.

1890 in *Cent. Dict.*

3. With distinctive prefix, applied to other species of *Ligustrum*; also, to other shrubs, chiefly evergreens, in some respect resembling the true Privet; as **barren privet**, *Rhamnus Alaternus*, an evergreen shrub of S. Europe; **California, Japan,** or **Japanese privet**, *Ligustrum japonicum*; **Egyptian privet**, the HENNA of the East, bearing panicles of small white sweet-scented flowers; **evergreen privet**, any evergreen species of the genus *Rhamnus*; **mock privet**, the evergreen genus PHILLYREA, N.O. *Oleaceæ*; Jasmine Box; **swamp privet**, *Adelia* (*Forestiera*) *acuminata*, N.O. *Oleaceæ*, a small evergreen tree of the southern United States, of the same order as the Common Privet, and closely resembling it in general appearance.

1597 GERARDE *Herbal* III. liv. 1209 Of mocke Priuet. 1 *Phillyrea angustifolia.* **1611** COTGR., *Alaterne*, fruitlesse, or barren Priuet. **1629** PARKINSON *Paradisus* 603 *Alaternus.* The euer greene Priuet. **1678** PHILLIPS (ed. 4) s.v., There is also a sort called *Mock-privet*, in Latin *Philyrea.* **1760** J. LEE *Introd. Bot.* App. 324 Evergreen Privet, *Rhamnus.* **1866** *Treas. Bot.* 928/2 Privet, Barren, *Rhamnus Alaternus.* ——, Egyptian, *Lawsonia alba. Ibid.* 665/2 Henna is the Persian name..in England it is often called Egyptian Privet. **1868** *Rep. U.S. Commissioner Agric.* (1869) 197 For..easy propagation, and ample foliage of shining deep-green color, there is no plant superior to the Japan privet (*Ligustrum Japonicum*). **1887** *Nicholson's Dict. Gard., Phillyrea*,.. Jasmine Box; Mock Privet. **1901** MOHR *Plant Life Alabama* (*Contrib. fr. U.S. National Herbarium* VI.) 667 Swamp Privet.

4. *attrib.* and *Comb.*, as ***privet berry, blossom, bush, flower, hedge, leaf***; ***privet-like, -scented*** adjs.; †**privet-fly**, an old name of a Plume-moth, *Pterophorus*; **privet hawk (-moth)**, a large species of hawk-moth which deposits its eggs on the privet; so ***privet-hawk caterpillar***.

1688 R. HOLME *Armoury* II. 81/2 *Privet Berries grow in bunches, and are all black. **1870** MORRIS *Earthly Par.* I. I. 356 And there she stood apart,..pale as *privet blossom is in June. **1650** T. BAYLY *Herba Parietis* 125 If all yonder regiments were but so many *private bushes. **1572** in Feuillerat *Revels Q. Eliz.* (1908) 165 Pinkes and *privett fflowers. **1749** J. MARTYN tr. *Virg., Buc.* II. 18 The white privet flowers drop on the ground [orig. *alba ligustra cadunt*]. **1753** CHAMBERS *Cycl. Supp.*, **Privet-fly*, in natural history, the name of a species of fly very common on the shrub from whence it has its name. It is called the *erinopterus.* **1826** KIRBY & SP. *Entomol.* III. xxxi. 266 *Privet-hawkmoth (*Sphinx Ligustri*). **1859** W. S. COLEMAN *Woodlands* (1862) 133 The Privet..being the chief food of the caterpillar of that very beautiful insect the Privet Hawk Moth. **1591** *Priuie hedges [see 1 β]. **1856** MRS. BROWNING *Aur. Leigh* I. 568 As green as any privet-hedge a bird Might choose to build in. **1831** LANDOR *Misc.* Wks. 1846 II. 633 Thro' the pale-glimmering *privet-scented lane.

[*Note.* *Privet* has been suggested to be a corruption of **primet*, a word erroneously said in Prior's *Names of Plants* to occur in the *Grete Herbal* as a name of the primrose; no such word occurs there. Another suggestion is that *privett*(*e*, *privie*, are the same as *private, privy*, and applied to this shrub from its use in making hedges to cut off a private part of a garden, to conceal dung-heaps, etc.; but of this there is no evidence. *Privet* or *Privett* occurs more than once as a place-name in Hampshire, and the name *Pryfetes floda*, app. in that county, is found in the O.E. Chron.; but no connexion of this with the shrub is known. *Prevet* also occurs in a 13th c. deed, where it is doubtful whether it is a proper name: **1256** June 8 *Ancient Deed* P.R.O.A. 8635, In omnibus mariscis qui pertinent ad villam de Farlingetone [Farlington, Havant, Hants] excepto..parco et excepto cooperto de preuet et Crofta que fuit Rogeri le Lung, que est contra portam curie. If we had other evidence of the name of the shrub in ME., it would be tempting to render this 'covert of privet' (as is done in *Catal. Anc. Deeds* 1902, IV. 338).]

†**privet**[2]. *Obs.* Also 6 provet. [Corruption of *provet*, from F. *éprouvette*, in 16th c. *esprouvette*, f. *é-, esprouver* to try, search out.] A surgical instrument for searching a wound; a probe.

1597 A. M. tr. *Guillemeau's Fr. Chirurg.* b ij b/2 The Provet, or soundinge irone..we sounde the depthe of the fistle with this sounding irone. *Ibid.* b iv b/2 The Privet, or Needle to religate the fistles. *Ibid.* 6/2 The bullet may be felt with the privet or searchinge iron.

privet, obs. form of PRIVATE.

†**privign.** [ad. L. *prīvign-us*.] A stepson.

[**1605-6** B. JONSON *Masque Hymen* Wks. (1616) 917 *note*, A Step-mother insulting on the spoyles of her two *Priuigni*, Bacchus and Hercules.] **1654** R. CODRINGTON tr. *Iustine* xxxvi. 426 To be constituted by the people to be the guardian of Antiochus, the privign of Demetrius.

privilege ('prɪvɪlɪdʒ), *sb.* Forms: α. 2-4 privi-, 4 privy-, pryve-, prevylegie. β. 3- privilege; also 4-5 pryve-, 4-6 preve-, previ-, prevy-, privy-, pryvi-, pryvy-, 4-8 prive-, 5 preva-, priva-, pryva-; 4 -liche, -lag, -leg, -legge, 4-5 -lage, 5-8 -ledge, 6 -lidge, 7 -ledg. [In form *privilegie* (only ME.), ad. L. *prīvilēgi-um* a bill or law in favour of or against an individual; later, a privilege, prerogative, f. *prīv-us* private, peculiar + *lex, lēgem* law; in form *privilege*, a. F. *privilège, -lége* (12th c. in Littré), ad. L. *prīvilēgium*.]

A. Forms: α. **privilegie**, etc.

α. [**701** in Birch *Cart. Sax.* I. 156 Ic Ealdhelm brohte to Ine Wessexena kyncge and to Æþelræde Myrcena kyncge þas *privilegia*.] *a* **1154** *O.E. Chron.* an. 1137 (Laud MS.) Martin abbot..for to Rome..and begæt thare priuilegies. *a* **1327** *Sat. Consist. Courts* in *Pol. Songs* (Camden) 157 Ant suggen he hath privilegie proud of the pope. *c* **1380** WYCLIF *Sel. Wks.* I. 132 Crist apperide to þes holy wommen, fer to graunt a privylegie to wommans kynde. *Ibid.* II. 281 Dignities and pryvelegies þat ben now grauntid bi þe pope.

β. **privilege**, etc.: see B.

B. Signification.

1. *Rom. Antiq.* A special ordinance having reference to an individual.

(Late in English; in Roman Law or Hist., or etymological.)

1483 *Cath. Angl.* 292/1 A Pryvalege, *priuilegium, quasi priuatus legem.* **1548** ELYOT *Dict., Priuilegium*,..a lawe concernyng priuate persons, also a priuate or speciall lawe, a priuilege. **1741** MIDDLETON *Cicero* I. v. 339 It was not properly a law, but what they called a privilege; or an act, to inflict penalties on a particular Citizen by name, without any previous trial. **1799** MACKINTOSH *Stud. Law Nat.* 50 *note*, *Privilege*, in Roman jurisprudence, means the exemption of one individual from the operation of a law.

2. a. A right, advantage, or immunity granted to or enjoyed by a person, or a body or class of persons, beyond the common advantages of others; an exemption in a particular case from certain burdens or liabilities.

a **1154**, etc. [see A.]. **14..** *Customs of Malton* in *Surtees Misc.* (1888) 60 And aske þe prevalege of þe Burgage. **1508** DUNBAR *Tua Mariit Wemen* 207 Hed I that plesand prevelege to part quhen me likit. **1526** *Pilgr. Perf.* (1531) 42 To suche other as he hath graunted suche specyall preuylege. **1644** MILTON *Areop.* (Arb.) 56 The priviledge and dignity of Learning. **1776** GIBBON *Decl. & F.* xiv. I. 407 The privileges which had exalted Italy above the rank of the provinces, were no longer regarded. **1844** WHITTIER *Bridal of Pennac.* Prol. 167 Pastures, wood-lots, mill-sites, with the privileges..and appurtenances. **1879** FROUDE *Cæsar* iii. 26 A monopoly of privileges is always invidious. **1968** *Globe & Mail* (Toronto) 13 Feb. 32/7 (Advt.), Kennedy Rd.—Steeles, home privileges, parking, 1-2 girls. *Ibid.*, $20. wk. Gentlemen 18-25. Good meals, lunches, privileges. Nova Scotian family. **1972** *New Yorker* 22 July 48/1 Hillside homesites..with ocean beach privileges. **1976** J. LEE *Ninth Man* 57 Thirty dollars a week... But you get icebox privileges. All my tenants get icebox privileges.

b. In extended sense: A special advantage or benefit; with reference to divine dispensations, natural advantages, gifts of fortune, etc.

c **1230** *Hali Meid.* 23 þus feole priuileges scheaweð ful sutelliche hwucche beon þe meidnes & sundreð ham fram þe oðre. **1340** *Ayenb.* 15 In erþe ne ys zuo holi man þet moȝe parfitliche be-uly alle þe maneres of zenne..wyþ-oute special priuilege of grace. *c* **1380** [see A.]. **1754** SHERLOCK *Disc.* I. viii. 227 To be the Children of God is the greatest privilege under the Gospel. **1781** GIBBON *Decl. & F.* xxvii. III. 31 The privileges of Christianity, temporal as well as spiritual, were confined to the true believers. **1849** MACAULAY *Hist. Eng.* vi. II. 69 To sit near him at the theatre, and to hear his criticisms on a new play, was regarded as a privilege. **1862** STANLEY *Jew. Ch.* (1877) I. xix. 370 All the greater Prophets claimed, and most of them enjoyed, the privilege of married life.

†**c.** A special distinction; a speciality. *Obs.*

c **1375** *Sc. Leg. Saints* xxii. (*Laurentius*) 790 Ymang al otheris als had he specialis prewylege thre. **1398** TREVISA *Barth. De P.R.* IX. xxxi. (Bodl. MS.), The preuyleges of þis daie [Good Friday] were offringe of criste, spoillinge of helle, and eke ouercomynge of deþe. *Ibid.* XIII. ix, þis ryuer [Jordan] haþ manye priuyleges for it departeþ þe contrey of riȝt beleued men fro þe contrey of mysbileued men, for he departeþ Jewry and Arabia.

†**d.** An advantage yielded, superiority, pre-eminence. *Obs.*

1591 SHAKS. *1 Hen. VI*, III. i. 121, I would see his heart out, ere the Priest Should euer get that priuiledge of me.

e. See *water privilege* (WATER *sb.* 29).

3. A privileged position; the possession of an advantage over others or another.

1390 GOWER *Conf.* III. 152 Largesse it is, whos privilegge Ther mai non Avarice abregge. *c* **1400** *Destr. Troy* 140 Lest he put hym from priuelage & his place toke. *c* **1450** *Pistill of Susan* 33 (Ingilby MS.) Prestes hye of priuylage were praysed saune pere. **1561** T. NORTON *Calvin's Inst.* IV. 28 b, Abbaties and priories are geuen to very boyes, by privilege, that is to say, by common and vsuall custome. *c* **1586** C'TESS PEMBROKE *Ps.* LXXXIX. xv, From this necessity [death]..No priviledge exemptes. **1647** COWLEY *Mistr.*, *Bathing in River* v, As in the Ocean Thou No priviledge dost know Above th' impurest streams that thither flow. **1754** RICHARDSON *Grandison* IV. xx. 150 A..man, who wants to assume airs of privilege, and thinks he has a right to be impertinent. **1861** MILL *Utilit.* iii. 48 Inequalities of legal privilege between individuals or classes.

4. a. The special right or immunity attaching to some office, rank, or station; prerogative.

the privilege, the royal prerogative. ***privilege of clergy*** = *benefit of clergy*: see CLERGY 6. ***privilege of Parliament***, the immunities enjoyed by either House of Parliament, or by individual members, as such; as freedom of speech, freedom from arrest in civil matters, the power of committing persons to prison; similarly of other legislative assemblies; so ***privilege of peerage, of peers***.

a **1225** *Ancr. R.* 160 In onliche stude he biȝet þeos þreo biȝeaten, priuilege of prechur, merit of martirdom, & meidenes mede. *a* **1340** HAMPOLE *Psalter* xix. 6 þat is þe pryuelege of criste godis sune. **1390** GOWER *Conf.* I. 7 The privilege of regalie Was sauf. *c* **1450** *Godstow Reg.* 29 All these yftys kynge Stephyn by the priuilege of hys regal power haþe strenghyd & confermid. **1513** MORE *Rich. III*, Wks. 49/1 Muche of this mischiefe..myghte bee amended, with greate thank of god and no breache of the priueledge. **1588** LAMBARDE *Eiren.* IV. xiv. 561 In all other cases..the prisoner may enjoy the priuiledge of Clergie. **1641** *Protestation of Parlt.* 3 & 4 May (Long Parliament), I A. B. do..promise, vow, and protest, to maintain and defend..the power and privileges of Parliament. **1642** in Whitelocke *Mem.* (1732) 53/1 The House [of Commons] was in a great disorder, crying aloud many of them together, *Privilege, Privilege.* **1642** in Clarendon *Hist. Reb.* IV. §157 In his [the King's] passage through the city, the rude people..crying out, 'Privilege of parliament, privilege of parliament'. **1642** LAUD *Diary* 4 Jan., His Majesty went into the House of Commons, and demanded the persons of [five members].. great stir was made about this breach of the privileges of Parliament. **1663** *Flagellum or O. Cromwell* (1672) 29 Secured from an Imprisonment by his priviledge as a Member. **1689** *Tryal Bps.* 14 It is the Priviledge of the Peers of England. **1765** BLACKSTONE *Comm.* I. 163 An observation, that the principal privilege of parliament consisted in this, that it's privileges were not certainly known to any but the parliament itself. **1827** HALLAM *Const. Hist.* (1876) III. xiii. 23 The commons voted Skinner into custody for a breach of privilege. **1840** RICHARDSON *Dict.* Suppl. s.v., Privilege is in common speech applied in contradistinction to Prerogative. As the Privileges of the Commons, the Prerogative of the Crown. **1863** H. COX *Instit.* I. ix. 204 A peer is, by the privilege of peerage, always exempt from such arrest. **1883** *Chambers' Encycl.* s.v. *Peer*, The House of Lords, on the report of a Committee of Privileges, held that he [Baron Wensleydale] was not entitled to sit and vote in parliament.

fig. **1840** LONGF. *Sp. Stud.* I. i, *Lara...* I think the girl extremely beautiful. *Don C.* Almost beyond the privilege of woman!

b. ***bill of privilege***, a petition of a peer demanding to be tried by his peers. ***writ of privilege***, a writ to deliver a privileged person from custody when arrested in a civil suit.

1453 *Cal. Anc. Rec. Dublin* (1889) I. 277 Gyff any men within the seid cittie will sywe eny wryttis of privelage. **1607** COWELL *Interpr.* s.v. *Writ*, A writ of priuiledge is that which a priuiledged person bringeth to the court, for his exemption, by reason of some priuiledge. **1727-41** CHAMBERS *Cycl.* s.v., A person belonging to the court of chancery cannot be sued in any other court, certain cases excepted; and if he be, he may remove it by writ of privilege. **1763** CHURCHILL *Author* 149 Who would a bill of privilege prefer, And treat a Poet, like a Creditor.

5. a. *R.C. Ch.* A special ordinance issued by the pope, granting exemption in the case of all such acts as are necessary for the purpose for which it is obtained; cf. DISPENSATION 8.

c **1394** *P. Pl. Crede* 467 [The friars] purchaseþ hem pryuylege of popes at Rome. *c* **1400** *Apol. Loll.* 12 þei þat persuen for indulgencs, exempcouns, & priueylegs, sey how þei geyt nowt wiþ out bying. *c* **1425** *Eng. Conq. Irel.* 90 The forme of thay preuyleges, as thay wer endyted yn the Court of Rome a latyne, ne myght I nat comly setten yn Englyshe. **1885** *Cath. Dict.* s.v., A private enactment, granting some special benefit or favour, against or outside the law... A privilege may be granted by word of mouth as well as by deed.

b. *transf.* A licence, permission.

1715 POPE *Iliad* I. 385 Has foul reproach a privilege from Heaven?

6. a. A grant to an individual, corporation, community, or place, of special rights or immunities, sometimes to the prejudice of the general right; a franchise, monopoly, patent; †*spec.* the sole right of printing or publishing a book or the like (formerly often signified by the Latin phr. *cum privilegio imprimendi solum*).

1387 TREVISA *Higden* (Rolls) II. 45 (MS. α) Belinus þe kyng..made foure hiȝe kyng weies i-priueleged wiþ al privilege. **1530** *Rolls of Parlt.* in Palsgr. 10 The Kynges Graces Pryvilege. Here foloweth the copy of the Kynges Graces pryvilege, graunted unto the authour for the space of sevyn yeres... Our favorable letters of privilege. **1540** COVERDALE *Confut. Standish* To Rdr. (1547) a ij b, The shame is it of all Englande, that vnder his [the king's] priuilege anye erroneous, contentious, or slaunderous boke or papyre sholde by prynted. **1579** *Expos. Terms Law* 161/1 *Priuiledges* are lyberties and fraunchises graunted to an Office, place, towne, or mannour, by the Queenes great charter, letters patentes, or acte of Parliament. **1592** NASHE *P. Penilesse* 19 b, The Printer..wer best to get a priuilege betimes, *Ad imprimendum solum.* **1598** in D'Israeli *Cur. Lit.* (1866) 331/1 Of the antiquitie, etimologie, and priviledges of parishes in Englande. **1607** COWELL *Interpr.* s.v., A personall priuiledge is that, which is graunted to any person, either against, or beside the course of the common law:..A priuiledge reall is that, which is graunted to a place, as to the Vniuersities, that none of either may be called to Westm. hall, vpon any contract made within their owne precincts. **1685** PETTY *Last Will* in *Tracts* (1769) p. vii, The copper-plates for the maps of Ireland with the king's privilege, which I rate at 100 l. per ann. **1753** N. TORRIANO *Gangr. Sore Throat* 116 The French Book was also published by Privilege of the King of France. **1890** FISKE *Civ. Govt. U.S.* vi. 150 The charter of Maryland conferred upon Lord Baltimore the most extensive privileges ever bestowed by the British crown upon any subject.

b. A document or deed by which this is granted.

1818 HALLAM *Mid. Ages* I. v. 467 In the famous privilege of Austria granted by Frederic I in 1156.

†**7.** The right of affording security from arrest, attached to certain places; the right of asylum or sanctuary. *Obs.*

1387 TREVISA *Higden* (Rolls) III. 247 þis is he þat ȝaf prisueliche and fredom [orig. *immunitate insignivit*] to temples. **1485** *Rolls of Parlt.* VI. 291/2 He was faine..to take tuition and privilledge of the Seinctuarie of Glouc'. **1513** MORE *Rich. III*, Wks. 46/1 It would bee..to the.. hyghe dyspleasure of Godde, yf the prisueledge of that holye place should nowe bee broken. **1594** SHAKS. *Rich. III*, III. i. 41 God forbid We should infringe the holy Priuiledge Of blessed Sanctuarie. **1648** GAGE *West Ind.* Table, The priviledge of a great river, called Lempa, dividing the Countrey of St. Salvador, and Nicaragua. (Cf. PRIVILEGED *ppl. a.* c.) **1683** *Brit. Spec.* 24 That the Wayes leading to the Temples, and the Roads of Great Cities, should have like Priviledges.

8. *attrib.* and *Comb.*, as ***privilege debate*** (sense 4 above), ***leave*** (LEAVE *sb.*[1] 1 e), ***paper*** (PAPER *sb.* 7 d), ***-pass*** (PASS *sb.*[2] 8 d), ***system***, ***ticket***; †**privilege book**, a book issued with the royal privilege; **privilege cab**, a cab admitted to stand for hire in some private place (esp. a railway station) from which other cabs are excluded; also ***privilege cab-driver***.

1607 in Plomer *Abstr. Wills Eng. Printers* (1903) 42 The *priviledge books quiers and bindings at the price I paid for them. **1906** *Westm. Gaz.* 3 Aug. 4/3 All are agreed..that the *privilege-cab system ought to be abolished. **1896** *Daily News* 22 Dec. 7/3 Many of the *privilege cabdrivers..had preferred to throw up their privilege and cast in their lot with the Union of their trade. **1899** *Westm. Gaz.* 2 Sept. 4/3 It was decided in a *privilege debate in the House of Commons in 1830 that a solicitor in Parliamentary practice cannot occupy a seat in the House. **1883** KIPLING *Let.* 14 Aug. in C. E. Carrington *Rudyard Kipling* (1955) iv. 53 *Privilege leave..gives you the pleasant duty of enjoying yourself in a cool climate for thirty days and being paid £20 for that duty. **1902** *Westm. Gaz.* 12 July 2/1 She was marrying an officer, home on privilege leave, and they had to be back in India by a given date. **1980** J. DITTON *Copley's Hunch* II. ii. 138 Anybody who escapes from enemy hands is entitled to leave—over and above the ordinary ration of privilege leave. **1825** *Gentl. Mag.* XCV. I. 6 A free person of colour is *now* entitled to give evidence against a white, in any Court of Justice, upon producing his *privilege papers. **1897** *Westm. Gaz.* 15 Feb. 5/3 The *privilege ticket system, by which the employés of every railway company were enabled to travel over all parts of the Kingdom, or at any rate over all the leading lines, at..one-half of a single third-class fare for the double journey.

privilege (ˈprɪvɪlɪdʒ), *v.* [ad. F. *privilégier* (13th c. in Littré), ad. med.L. *prīvilēgi-āre* (1190–3 in Hoveden), f. *prīvilēgium*: see prec.]

1. a. *trans.* To invest with a privilege or privileges; to grant a particular right or immunity to; to benefit or favour specially; to invest (a thing) with special honourable distinctions.

[*a* **1193** in *Roger of Hoveden's Chron.* (Rolls) III. 74 Summus pontifex privilegiavit Hugonem Dunelmensem episcopum.] **13..** [see PRIVILEGING below]. *c* **1386** CHAUCER *Pars. T.* ¶965 Certes it [the pater noster] is priuyleged of thre thynges in his dignytee, for which it is moore digne than any oother preyere. **1387** [see PRIVILEGE *sb.* 6]. **1483** *Cath. Angl.* 292/1 To Privalege (*A.* Pryuelege), *priuilegiare.* **1547** *Reg. Privy Council Scot.* I. 78 Oure Soverane Lady privelegis and grantis to thaim that thai may enter within thre termes. **1597** BEARD *Theatre God's Judgem.* (1612) 374 How infamous a thing it is..to priuiledge and allow publike places for adulteries. **1688** BUNYAN *Jerus. Sinner Saved* (1886) 18 He [Christ] had a mind..to privilege the worst of sinners with the first offer of mercy. **1769** BLACKSTONE *Comm.* IV. ii. 22 The law of England does in some cases privilege an infant, under the age of twenty-one, as to common misdemesnors. **1795** SOUTHEY *Joan of Arc* VI. 240 Let this woman who believes her name May privilege her herald, see the fire Consume him. **1885** *Pall Mall G.* 16 May 2/1 They are certainly privileged institutions, and if the country wants universities at all it must 'privilege' them. **1896** *Daily News* 24 Sept. 7/5 (*heading*) Privileged cabs. *Ibid.*, We do not privilege any vehicle unless it is a good one and the driver a steady and respectable man.

†**b.** *refl.* To avail oneself of a privilege (in quot., to take sanctuary). *Obs. rare.*

1602 WARNER *Alb. Eng.* Epit. (1612) 396 He allured out of Sanctuarie his fiue Neeces..who with the Queene-Mother ..had of long time priuiledged themselues there.

c. *trans.* *R.C. Ch.* To make (an altar) privileged.

1844 *Orthodox Jrnl.* 6 Jan. 3/2 The high altar was privileged by Gregory XIII.

d. In *pa. pple.* Entitled *to* (a special right).

1856 MRS. B. G. FERRIS *Mormons at Home* xii. 199 A few who call themselves physicians..are privileged to a seat in this important assemblage.

2. To authorize, license (what is otherwise forbidden or wrong); to justify, excuse.

1592 DANIEL *Compl. Rosamond* ci, Kings cannot privilege what God forbade. **1605** *Lond. Prodigal* I. i, His youth may priuiledge his wantonnesse. *a* **1668** DAVENANT *News fr. Plimouth* IV. i, This Priviledges cowardize, to wrong true valour. **1769** BLACKSTONE *Comm.* IV. ii. 26 The law of England..will not suffer any man thus to privilege one crime by another [i.e. by pleading drunkenness].

3. To give (a person, etc.) special freedom or immunity *from* some liability or burden to which others are subject; to exempt.

1542 UDALL *Erasm. Apoph.* 255 b, He was exempted..or priuileged from bearyng almaner offices of charge. **1597–8** BACON *Ess., Discourse* (Arb.) 16 Some thinges are priuiledged from iest. *a* **1614** P. LILIE *Two Serm.* (1619) 34 Though women be priviledged from bearing of armes. **1718** LADY M. W. MONTAGU *Let. to C'tess Mar* 10 Mar., She represented to him..that she was privileged from this misfortune. **1796** MORSE *Amer. Geog.* I. 431 Representatives are privileged from arrests or mesne process. **1848** WHARTON *Law Lex.* s.v., Barristers are privileged from arrest *eundo, morando et redeundo*, going to, coming from, and abiding in court..: so clergymen as to divine service.

Hence ˈ**privileging** *vbl. sb.*; also ˈ**privileger**, one who grants a privilege or privileges.

13.. *Cursor M.* 25044 (Cott.) Cros it beres o mani thing, O cristen men þe priueleging. **1587** HARRISON *England* I. xii. 65/2 in *Holinshed*, King Athelstane is taken here for the chiefe priuileger of the towne.

privileged (ˈprɪvɪlɪdʒd), *ppl. a.* [f. prec. vb. or sb. + -ED.] Invested with or enjoying certain privileges or immunities. **a.** Of things.

privileged altar, in *R.C. Ch.*: see quot. 1885. ***privileged communication***, in *Law*, (*a*) a communication which a witness cannot be legally compelled to divulge; (*b*) a communication made between such persons and in such circumstances that it is not actionable, unless made with malice. ***privileged cab***: see PRIVILEGE *sb.* 8. ***privileged debt***, a debt having a prior claim to satisfaction. ***privileged deed***, in *Sc. Law*, a deed which is valid without witnesses' signatures, as a holograph deed. ***privileged share***, ***stock***, preference stock: cf. quot. 1842 s.v. PREFERENCE 8. ***privileged summons***: see quot. 1838. ***privileged villeinage***, a form of villeinage in which the service was defined, as distinguished from ***pure villeinage***.

1398 TREVISA *Barth De Propr. Rerum* XVII. lxxxvii. (Tollem. MS.), These herbes were preuelegid, þat þe liknesse of hem were worþi to be set in tokenynge and figure in þe crowne and mytoure of þe chef preste. **1477** *Rolls of Parlt.* VI. 185/2 In pryvat and pryvileged places. **1588** *Marprel. Epist.* (Arb.) 41 In other priuiledged English translations it is, And they [etc.]. **1590** SWINBURNE *Testaments* 24 b, Priuileged testamentes are those, which are enriched with some speciall freedome or benefit, contrarie to the common course of law. *Ibid.* 25 Of priuiledged testamentes there are three sortes,..a testament made by a Souldier, a testament made by a father amongest his children, and a testament made for good and godly vses. **1727–41** CHAMBERS *Cycl.* s.v. *Debt, Privileged Debt*, is that which must be satisfied before all others; as, the king's tax, &c. **1838** W. BELL *Dict. Law Scot.*, *Privileged Debts* are those which humanity has rendered preferable on the funds of a deceased person, and which an executor may pay without decree; as, 1. Sickbed and funeral expenses... 2. Mournings for the widow [etc.]. 3. A year's rent of the house, and servants' wages since the last term. *Ibid.*, *Privileged Deeds.* A legal deed requires certain statutory solemnities; but, from this rule, exceptions have been made in favour of certain deeds and writings on grounds of necessity or expediency. *Ibid.*, *Privileged Summonses*,..a class of summonses in which, from the nature of the cause of action, the ordinary *induciæ*..are shortened. **1843** R. J. GRAVES *Syst. Clin. Med.* Introd. Lect. 2 *note*, The Meath Hospital became for several years a privileged hospital. **1884** *St. James' Gaz.* 22 Aug. 7/2 Guaranteed, privileged, and debenture stocks were less strong than of late. **1885** *Cath. Dict.*, *Privileged altar*, (1) An altar..by visiting which certain indulgences may be gained. (2) An altar at which Votive Masses may be said even on certain feasts which are doubles... (3) Altars with a plenary indulgence for one soul in purgatory attached to all Masses said at them for the dead. **1896** Privileged cab [see PRIVILEGE *v.* 1].

b. Of persons.

1435 MISYN *Fire of Love* I. xxiii. 50, I of men priuelegid speek, for Ioy of godis lufe in to gostly songis or heuenly sound behaldandly for to be takyn. *a* **1548** HALL *Chron.*, *Edw. V* 10 He nether is nor can bee a sanctuarye or priuileged man. **1768** BLACKSTONE *Comm.* III. 33 Where a scholar or privileged person is one of the parties. **1833** ALISON *Hist. Europe* (1849) I. i. §16. 62 The descendants of the freemen in one age become the privileged order in the next. **1888** BURGON *Lives 12 Gd. Men* I. I. 78 He was scarcely ever seen except by a privileged few.

c. Having the privilege of sanctuary attached to it. ? *Obs.*

1601 HOLLAND *Pliny* I. 108 A prieuledged place for all fugitiues. **1648** GAGE *West Ind.* xxi. 184 This River is privileged in this manner, that if a man commit any hainous crime or murther on [either] side..if hee can flie to get over this River, he is free as long as hee liveth on the other side.

d. *Eccl.* Applied to days in the Church's calendar which are placed in the highest category of importance, or one of the higher categories (e.g. as regards the precedence they take when two feasts or observances coincide).

1877 J. D. CHAMBERS *Divine Worship in Eng.* v. 85 Sundays..are distinguished..into Principal Privileged, Greater Privileged, Minor Privileged, Inferior Semi-privileged or ordinary Sundays. *Ibid.* 87 The Privileged Sundays, according to the present Anglican Rite, appear, beside the Principal Double Festivals and their Octaves, to be the First Sunday in Advent, Passion Sunday and Palm Sunday, and Sunday within the Octave of the Ascension. The Privileged Ferials: Ash Wednesday, the Four Days before Easter, the Vigils, Fasts and days of Abstinence above enumerated. **1953** *Anglican Services* v. 56 Ordinary (or lesser) Sundays..give way..to feasts or the privileged Octave days of feasts of Our Lord. *Ibid.* 57 Ferias are of three classes, Privileged, greater, and ordinary. *Ibid.* 61 Octaves are of three kinds, privileged, common, and simple.

†ˈ**privilegement.** *Obs. rare.* [f. PRIVILEGE *v.* + -MENT.] The granting of (ecclesiastical) privilege.

c **1470** HARDING *Chron.* CXLII. x, Thus stode this lande.. Hole enterdite from all holy sacramentes, That none was done, without priuelegementes.

†**priviˈlegiate**, *ppl. a.* and *sb.* *Obs. rare.* Also 7 **-at.** [ad. med.L. *prīvilēgiāt-us*, pa. pple. of *prīvilēgiāre*: see PRIVILEGE *v.*] **A.** *ppl. a.* Privileged. **B.** *sb.* A privileged person. So †**priviˈlegiate** *v.*, to privilege.

c **1555** HARPSFIELD *Divorce Hen. VIII* (Camden) 229 The see apostolic of Rome..is ever in such matters excepted and privilegiated. **1640** BASTWICK *Lord Bps.* vii. E iv b, As if they had the Spirit of Infallibility, and were..the onely Privilegiats not to erre. **1658** MANTON *Exp. Jude* 3 Wks. 1871 V. 95 None have a special privilegiate call from heaven.

†**priviˈlegious**, *a.* *Obs.* *rare*$^{-1}$. [f. L. *prīvilēgium* PRIVILEGE + -OUS.] Having privilege (in quot., of sanctuary); privileged.

1599 R. LINCHE *Anc. Fict.* B iv, Whatsoeuer..had fled to these priuelegious places, had ben freed from any pursuing danger.

privily (ˈprɪvɪlɪ), *adv.* Now *arch.* or *literary.* Forms as in PRIVY (also 4–6 **priva-**, **preva-**, 5 **pryva-**, 6 *Sc.* **preeve-**, *Sc.* **prefa-**); with 3–4 **-liche**, 4–5 **-lich**; 4–5 *north.* **-lik**, **-like**; 4– **-ly** (4 **-li**, **-le**, 4–6 **-lie**). [f. PRIVY *a.* + -LY[2].]

1. In a privy manner; not openly or publicly; secretly, privately; stealthily; craftily.

c **1290** *Beket* 25 in *S. Eng. Leg.* I. 107 Priueliche heo dude for Gilebert Auantages manie and fele. *a* **1300** *Cursor M.* 11152 (Cott.) He..tok his redd al for to fle Priuelik [*v.rr.* preuili, previly] and latt hir be. **13..** *Rule St. Benet* 20 Priuelike man sal amoneste þam, þat tay amende þaim. *c* **1386** CHAUCER *Frankl. T.* 388 His brother weepe and wayled pryuely [*v.rr.* pryuyly, priuyly, prively, priuely]. *c* **1460** *Towneley Myst.* xx. 737 Wold ye thus preualy morder a man? **1480** CAXTON *Chron. Eng.* ii. 5 Preuelich he went hym from the kynges court. **1526** TINDALE *John* vii. 10 Then went he also vppe vnto the feast, nott openly: but as it were preuely [WYCLIF in pryuei, 1611 in secret]. **1535** STEWART *Cron. Scot.* (Rolls) I. 179 ȝit prefalie on ȝow tha wan the feild. **1539** BIBLE (Gr.) *Matt.* i. 19 He was mynded preuely to departe from her [TINDALE to put her awaye secretly, 1611 priuily]. **1560** DAUS tr. *Sleidane's Comm.* 45 That nothing of Luthers..be taught priuely or openly. **1582** STANYHURST *Æneis* III. (Arb.) 72 This Polydor..Preeuelye by Priamus..Too king Treicius was sent. **1688** EVELYN *Mem.* 2 Dec., The Prince of Wales and greate treasure sent privily to Portsmouth. **1869** FREEMAN *Norm. Conq.* III. xiii. 257 He took him aside, and told him the news privily and briefly. **1884** TENNYSON *Falcon* I. i. 41, I left it privily At Florence, in her palace.

†**b.** Closely, so as to conceal. *Obs.* *rare*$^{-1}$.

c **1440** *Alphabet of Tales* 150 He..putt þaim in small boystis, & selid þaim privalie & gaff þaim; and þai tuke þaim.

†**2.** In a private station or rank. *Obs. rare.*

1387 TREVISA *Higden* (Rolls) III. 139 Þan þe kyng..ȝaf his douȝter to a symple knyȝt þat was priueleche i-bore.

†ˈ**priviment**, *adv.* *Obs.* Also 3 **privee-**, 4 **prive-**, **privie-**, 6 **pryvy-**. [ME. *priveement*, a. OF. *priveëment* (Rom. type **privatamente*), mod.F. *privément*, adv. f. *privé* PRIVY *a.*] = PRIVILY *adv.* 1. ***priviment enseint***: see ENCEINTE *a.*

a **1225** *Ancr. R.* 146 Þi gode werc þet tu hefdest idon priueement. *Ibid.* 154 Þeo þet beoð priuiment ham one. *c* **1380** *St. Augustine* 590 in Horstm. *Altengl. Leg.* (1878) 71 He..him isent To a place, to bi hud priuement. **1546** *Test. Ebor.* (Surtees) VI. 247 Also yf dame Marie, my wif, be previment incent. **1559** *Will of G. Taylard* (Somerset Ho.), Yf my wife be pryvyment insentid w[t] a man childe. *a* **1625** SIR H. FINCH *Law* (1636) 34 A man hath issue a daughter, and leaueth his wife priuiment inseint.

†**privisant**, *a.* *Obs.* *rare*$^{-1}$. Also 5 **pryuisant**. (Form and meaning obscure: perh. erron.)

c **1425** *Eng. Conq. Irel.* 80 Þe crye arose, & Reymond (as man that euer was formost redy) went aftyr, with one priuisant [*Rawl. MS.* pryuisant] man an hors wyth hym [Giraldus *satellite quodam comitatus equestri*].

privit, obs. form of PRIVATE.

†**privitate.** *Sc.* *Obs.* *rare.* [app. ad. L. type **prīvitātem*: see next.] = next, 1 b.

1549 *Compl. Scot.* xiii. 111 Cause that the counsel of ingland gettis sa haisty aduertessing of the priuitate that is amang the lordis of scotland.

privity (ˈprɪvɪtɪ). Now chiefly *techn.* (in Law, etc.). Forms: 3–5 **privete**, **-vite** (also 4–6 **pre-**; 3–5 **-vy-**, 4–5 **-ve-**, **-va-**; **-tee**); 5–7 **privitie**, 6– **privity**. [ME. *privete*, *-ite*, a. OF. *priveté*, *privité* (*a* 1200 in Godef.) privacy, a secret, etc., ad. L. type **prīvitās*, *-ātem*, abstr. n. f. *prīv-us* private, peculiar: see -ITY.]

†**1.** A thing that is kept hidden or secret. **a.** A divine or heavenly mystery; a secret of nature. ***the book of privity*** (***privities***), the Apocalypse. *Obs.*

a **1225** *Ancr. R.* 154, I boðe me ivint þet God his derne runes, & his heouenliche priuitez scheawede his leoue freond. *a* **1300** *Cursor M.* 23193 Als sais þe bok in priuete [*v.r.* of priuate], þat to sant Iohn was scaud to se. *c* **1380** WYCLIF *Wks.* (1880) 309 Jon euaungelist spak..in his book of priuetees. **1382** —— *Matt.* xiii. 11 To ȝou it is ȝouen for to knowe the mysterie, or priuyte, of the kyngdam of heuenes. *c* **1400** MAUNDEV. (Roxb.) xiv. 61 In spirit he was rauischt intill heuen, whare he sawe heuenly priuetez. **1470** *Bk. Quintess.* 5 Þis is a passyng souereyn priuytee.

†**b.** A secret matter, design, purpose, or plan; a secret. *Obs.*

a **1300** *Cursor M.* 7228 (Cott.) Þe wijf..For noiþer for luue, dredes, ne au, Dos man his priuetes to scau. **1375** BARBOUR *Bruce* x. 161 [He] schew till sum his preuate. **1382** WYCLIF *Prov.* xx. 19 To hym that openeth priuetes, and goth gilendeli, and spredeth abrod his lippis. **1558** in Feuillerat *Revels Q. Eliz.* (1908) 8 *marg.*, A Privitie to be amongest the officers. **1567** GOLDING *Ovid's Met.* VII. 157 O trustie time of night Most faithfull unto privities. **1625** K. LONG tr. *Barclay's Argenis* 268, I..did willingly scorn the danger which that hope and privity might afford.

†**c.** One's private thought or counsel; private business; personal affairs. *Obs.*

c **1290** *S. Eng. Leg.* I. 22/116 Whon he him schewede þere so muche of his priuyte. *a* **1300** *Cursor M.* 2738 (Cott.) Fra þe wil i noght helle mi priueté. **1375** BARBOUR *Bruce* v. 572 The king..richt towart thair cowert gais..For till do thar his preuate. *c* **1430** LYDG. *Min. Poems* (Percy Soc.) 166 He is a foole, whiche to every wight Tellithe his counsail and his privité. **1596** SPENSER *F.Q.* IV. ix. 19 Yet neither shewed to other their hearts privity.

†**2.** The condition of being private; privacy, seclusion, retirement; concealment, secrecy;

chiefly in phr. ***in privity***, in privacy, in private. *Obs.*

a **1225** *Ancr. R.* 146 Riht hond is god werc & bosum is priuite. *Ibid.* 152 Niht, ich cleopie priuite. *c* **1290** *S. Eng. Leg.* I. 65/409 Ase Moyses opon synay was bi olde dawe Fourti daiȝes in priuete. *a* **1300** *Cursor M.* 16271 (Cott.) Noght als in priueti [*v. rr.* priuite, priuete, previte] i sai, Bot in yur aller sight. *c* **1400** MAUNDEV. (Roxb.) xv. 69 He wald speke with me in priuetee betwene vs twa. **1528** ROY *Rede me* II. (Arb.) 101 Happely they do it in prevete. *a* **1661** FULLER *Worthies, Oxford.* (1662) II. 338 Being ambitious of Privity and Concealment.

†**3.** Private or secret fellowship; intimacy, familiarity. *Obs.*

a **1240** *Ureisun* in *Cott. Hom.* 185 Ich nabbe no mong, ne felawscipe, ne priuete, wiþ þe world. **1390** GOWER *Conf.* III. 289 The question..toucheth al the privete Betwen thin oghne child and thee. *a* **1450** *Knt. de la Tour* (1906) 119 And bare hem more fauour and priuete thanne vnto her owne frendes. **1485** CAXTON *Paris & V.* 37 The pryuete and promesse that he had wyth vyenne.

4. The private parts. Chiefly in *pl.* Now *rare.*

c **1375** *Sc. Leg. Saints* ii. (*Paul*) 712 Ay as men war hyr scherand þai prewetes. *c* **1386** CHAUCER *Monk's T.* 724 His Mantel ouer hise hypes caste he For no man sholde seen his priuetee. *c* **1450** *Cov. Myst.* ii. (Shaks. Soc.) 27 Oure pore prevytés ffor to hede, Summe ffygge levys fayn wolde I fynde. **1555** W. WATREMAN *Fardle Facions* I. iv. 41 The moste part of them..go naked; couering their priuities with shiepes tayles. **1713** HEARNE *Collect.* (O.H.S.) IV. 217 One Hand she holds up, namely yᵉ right one, the left upon her Privities. **1822–34** *Good's Study Med.* (ed. 4) II. 405 The inflammations that are stated to have fallen upon the privities.

transf. **1604** T. M. *Black Bk.* in *Middleton's Wks.* (Bullen) VIII. 24 The bare privities of the stone-walls were hid with two pieces of painted cloth.

5. The fact of being privy to something; participation in the knowledge of something private or secret, usually implying concurrence or consent; private knowledge or cognizance.

1560 DAUS tr. *Sleidane's Comm.* 103 And by the Emperours priuitie, moue a reconciliation & to treate with hym of fyue thynges. **1587** FLEMING *Contn. Holinshed* III. 1374/1 He vnderstood matters were determined in France without his priuitie. *a* **1693** LD. DELAMER *Wks.* (1694) 75 That which makes a Man guilty of Treason or any other Crime is his Privity or Consent to it. **1790** PALEY *Horæ Paul.* i. 2 Without any direct privity or communication with each other. **1850** MERIVALE *Rom. Emp.* (1865) I. iii. 113 Antonius was suspected of privity to their designs. **1877** T. D. WOOLSEY *Pol. Science* §114. I. 358 Mere privity..without active concurrence in some offences is a crime.

6. *Law.* Any relation between two parties recognized by law, e.g. that of blood, covenant, tenure, lease, service, etc.; mutual interest in any transaction or thing.

1523 FITZHERB. *Surv.* 25 Bytwene the lorde and hym that dyed there was no maner of priuyte of bargayn or couynaunt. **1531** *Dial. on Laws Eng.* II. xlix. (1638) 154 Though the Law for the privity of blood that is between them suffer him to have a disadvantage. **1544** tr. *Littleton's Tenures* (1574) 106 The release shalbe voide, for this that there no priuity was betwene me & the tenant for terme of yeres. **1670** BLOUNT *Law Dict.* s.v., If there be a Lord and Tenant, and the Tenant holds of the Lord by certain services, there is a privity between them in respect of the tenure. **1766** BLACKSTONE *Comm.* II. xx. 325 In both these cases there must be a privity of estate between the relessor and relessee. **1818** CRUISE *Digest* (ed. 2) V. 185 The privity must be both in blood and estate, for privity in blood only will not be sufficient [to make a fine bar an estate tail]. **1844** WILLIAMS *Real Prop.* (1877) 407 Between him [the lessor] and the underlessee, no privity is said to exist.

7. *Comb.*, as †**privity-walk**, a private walk.

1600 *Look About You* xxviii. in Hazl. *Dodsley* VII. 471 My lady gentlewoman is even here in her privity-walk.

privy (ˈprɪvɪ), *a.*, *sb.* (*adv.*) *arch.* or *techn.* (in *Law*, etc.). Forms: 3- pri-, 4–6 pry-, pre-; 3–6 (7) -ve (4 *Sc.* -we); 4 -vei, -veie, 4–5 -vee, -vay (5 *Sc.* -way), 4–6 -vey, -veye (5 -veyȝe, *Sc.* -wey), 5–7 -vie; 4- privy (4 previ, 4–6 pry-, prevy; 5 *Sc.* prewy, 5–6 preva; 6 pri-, pre-, pryvye; 7 privi). [ME. *prive*, *privy*, etc., a. F. *privé* (12th c. in Littré) private, tame; as sb. in OF. a familiar friend, a private place:—L. *privātus*: see PRIVATE, a later doublet of the same word, directly from L.; but in sense-development the two words do not run parallel.]

A. *adj.*

I. †**1.** That is of one's own private circle or companionship; intimate, familiar; = PRIVATE *a.* 10. In later quots. with admixture of sense 4. *Obs.*

a **1225** *Ancr. R.* 168 Hwui ȝe habbeð þene world ivlowen ..þet is, uorte beon priue mid ure Louerde. *c* **1290** *S. Eng. Leg.* I. 97/180 Sire porfirie, þat was hire priue knyȝt. **1303** R. BRUNNE *Handl. Synne* 467 Þey þat beyn with god pryue. **13**.. *E.E. Allit. P.* B. 1748 As to þe prynce pryuyest preued þe þrydde. **1375** BARBOUR *Bruce* IX. 227 Sum of his preue men. **1450** *Impeachm. Dk. Suffolk* vi. (Rolls of Parlt. V. 179/1), The seid Duke..seid..that he..coude remeve fro the seid Frenssh Kyng the pryvyest man of his Counseill, yf he wold. **1485** CAXTON *Paris & V.* 4 Hyr damoysel and prevy felowe. **1535** CRANMER in Ellis *Orig. Lett.* Ser. II. II. 66 Servant unto the Cardinall..& more privy with him of all Secrets than any other about him. **1644** MILTON *Jdgm. Bucer* xxxvii. Wks. 1851 IV. 327 If she be privie with those that plot against the State. *a* **1645** FEATLY in Fuller *Abel Rediv.*, *Jewel* (1867) I. 358 Zuinglius, Peter Martyr,..Lavater, Gesner, and other privy pastors of the Reformed churches beyond the seas.

†**b.** Of an animal: Familiar with man; domesticated, tame. *Obs. rare.*

1340 *Ayenb.* 230 Þe priue cat bezengþ ofte his scin. *c* **1410** *Master of Game* (MS. Digby 182) vi, Nor neuer shall he be so pryue..but he shall loke hider and þeder forto looke if he may doo any harme. **1422** tr. *Secreta Secret.*, *Priv. Priv.* 212 Pryue and tame as a culuere.

†**c.** Sexually intimate. *Obs. rare*⁻¹.

c **1400** *Rom. Rose* 5964 So dyvers and so many ther be That with my modir [Venus] have be privee.

†**2.** Of or pertaining exclusively to a particular person or persons; one's own; = PRIVATE *a.* 5; of an attendant, etc., personal. *Obs.* exc. in PRIVY CHAMBER, COUNCIL, COUNSELLOR, SEAL.

a **1300** *Cursor M.* 10432 Sco had a maiden hight vtaine, þat was hir priue [*v.r.* preue] chambur-laine. *c* **1305** *St. Dunstan* 60 in *E.E.P.* (1862) 36 Seint Dunstan..nolde bi his wille no tyme idel beo A priuei smyþþe bi his celle he gan him biseo. **13**.. *K. Alis* 4497 (Bodl. MS.) Weleaway & allas For Archelaus, and Salome, And for his oþer pryue meignee. *c* **1400** MAUNDEV. (1839) xxvii. 274 Whan he [Prester John] hath no werre, but rideth with a pryuy meynee. **1558–9** *Act 1 Eliz.* c. 2 (Act of Uniformity) Either in Common Churches or pryvye Chappelles or Oratories. **1585** T. WASHINGTON tr. *Nicholay's Voy.* III. x. 90 Ordained for the priuy kitchin of the great Lord, & the other for the common sort. **1647** LILLY *Chr. Astrol.* cxv. 561 Neither very much augmenting his prive fortune, or..diminishing his Patrimony. **1670** L. STUCLEY *Gospel-Glass* x. 86 We would count it a favour, if a Prince would give us a privy Key, to come to him when we please. **1694** MOTTEUX *Rabelais* IV. lxiii. (1737) 260 The King..took him into his Privy-garden.

†**b.** Peculiar to or characteristic of an individual or a race. Of language: idiomatic. *Obs. rare.*

1387–8 T. USK *Test. Love* Prol. (Skeat) I. 32 The vnderstandyng of Englishmen woll not stretche to the priuye termes in Frenche, what so euer wee bosten of straunge langage. *Ibid.* II. ix. l. 33, I canne it not otherwise nempne, for wanting of priuie wordes. **1650** FULLER *Pisgah* IV. vii. 128 What art their Priests did use, to keep up the breed, and preserve succession of Cattell with such γνωρίσματα or privy marks, I list not to enquire.

†**3.** Of or pertaining to a person in his private or personal capacity; not public or official; = PRIVATE *a.* 6. *Obs.*

1387 TREVISA *Higden* (Rolls) I. 91 Þey gooþ to priue [1432–50 private] offis [*orig.* officia privata adeunt] and to comyn feestes, but þey techiþ besiliche here children to ride and to schete. **1450–1530** *Myrr. our Ladye* 328 Before the preface, the preste sayeth preuy prayers by hymselfe. *c* **1532** DU WES *Introd. Fr.* in *Palsgr.* 1044 Her Grace beynge with a priuy family in the parke of Theukesbery. **1567** in *Churchyard's Chippes* (1817) 174 Her previe letters written halelie with her awn hand, and sent by her to James, earl Bothwell.

4. Participating in the knowledge of something secret or private; in the secret; privately cognizant or aware; intimately acquainted with or accessory to some secret transaction; = PRIVATE *a.* 11 Const. *to*, †*of*, or †with clause.

1390 GOWER *Conf.* II. 282 Which art prive to tho doinges. *c* **1420** *Chron. Vilod.* 1862 And also þat preueyȝe of his conselle þo was. **1484** *Surtees Misc.* (1888) 42 Ne noon of theim wer nevere prevey to ye sealing of ye forsaid forged and untrue testimonyall. **1537** STARKEY in Strype *Eccl. Mem.* (1721) I. App. lxxxi. 194 Few among al your lovers and friends, which are privy of your judgment. **1548** UDALL, etc. *Erasm. Par.* Pref. 18 Being ferther priuie to myne owne vnwurthynes. **1560** DAUS tr. *Sleidane's Comm.* 115 The Maior makynge his frendes priuie what he would doe. **1573** STOW *Ann.* (1605) 776 It is necessarie to consider what persons we shall first make priuy of this politike conclusion. **1596** J. SMYTH in *Lett. Lit. Men* (Camden) 94, I did..make her Majestie privy to the whole state of Spayne. **1787** JEFFERSON *Writ.* (1859) II. 154 Those who may have supposed me privy to this proposition. *a* **1862** BUCKLE *Civiliz.* (1869) III. iv. 211 The clergy believed that they alone were privy to the counsels of the Almighty.

†**b.** Possessing esoteric knowledge *of*; versed or skilled (in some subject). *Obs. rare.*

1390 GOWER *Conf.* III. 88 To this science [theology] ben prive The clerkes of divinite. **1433** *Rolls of Parlt.* IV. 449/2 Brocours aliens, yat been nowe so prive and expert of merchandises.

II. 5. Withdrawn from public sight, knowledge, or use; kept secret or concealed; hidden; secluded. *arch.* **a.** Of material things.

c **1290** *St. Brendan* 23 in *S. Eng. Leg.* I. 220 To wende in-to a priue stude and stille, þare he miȝte beo al one to a-serui godes wille. *a* **1300** *Cursor M.* 16920 Þai..grofe þaim thre [crosses] for cristen men, wit-in a priue sted. **1382** WYCLIF *Isa.* xlv. 3, I shal ȝyuen to thee..the priue thingus of priuytees, that thou wite. *c* **1440** *Ipomydon* 1855 In at a preuy posterne gate, By night she stale. **1470–85** MALORY *Arthur* I. xiv. 53, I wold that kynge Ban and kynge Bors.. were put in a wood here besyde in an embusshement and kepe them preuy. **1525** LD. BERNERS *Froiss.* II. cxxxiii. 373 Go thou the moost preuyest wayes thou canste (thou knowest all the preuy wayes of the countrey). **1526** TINDALE *Luke* xi. 33 Noo man lighteth a candell and putteth it in a preve place. **1598** BARRET *Theor. Warres* v. i. 128 Round about the ditch there should be another like vault or priuie way. **1613** PURCHAS *Pilgrimage* (1614) 194 He goeth to stoole in some priuie place. **1719** D'URFEY *Pills* IV. 140 The Place did begin to grow privy. **1855** THACKERAY *Newcomes* xxxix, A poet must retire to privy places and meditate his rhymes in secret.

Comb. *a* **1593** MARLOWE *Ovid's Eleg.* II. xiv, And their own privy-weapon'd hands destroy them.

b. Of immaterial things. (Often opposed to *apert*, *pert*: see APERT *a.* 1, PERT *a.* 1.)

c **1300** *Beket* 290 And to al his privei consail Seint Thomas he nom. **1340** HAMPOLE *Pr. Consc.* 2410 Ne swa prive es nathyng þat touches man, þat sal noght be knawen þan. *c* **1384** CHAUCER *H. Fame* II. 209 What so euer..Is spoken either prevy or aperte. *c* **1400** *Apol. Loll.* 33 Hauing þe priuey witt of þe feiþ in a pure consciens. *c* **1450** *Merlin* 47, I knowe alle the prevy wordes that haue ben be-twene hem two. **1512** *Act 4 Hen. VIII*, c. 20 *Preamble*, John Tayler.. having pryve knowlege of the commyng of your seid Beseecher. **1581** J. BELL *Haddon's Answ. Osor.* 269 b, Nor ever obliged themselves by any promise privy or aperte, that they would accomplishe the same. **1660** in J. Simon *Ess. Irish Coins* (1749) 125 Tokens..with a privy marke..in order to discover the counterfeiting of any such like tokens.

6. Acting or done in secret or by stealth; secret, clandestine, furtive, surreptitious, sly. (Often opposed to *apert*, *pert.*) *arch.*

a **1300** *Cursor M.* 7234 Als traitur dern and priue theif. *Ibid.* 11852 To þe barnage tit he sent, To mak a priue parlement. *c* **1374** CHAUCER *Boeth.* IV. pr. iii. 94 (Camb. MS.) Yif he be a preuey awaytor I-hidd and reioyseth hym to Rauysse by whiles þou shalt seyn hym. **1433** *Rolls of Parlt.* IV. 447/1 By murdererys, and prive roberyes. **1535** COVERDALE *Ecclus.* v. 14 He that is a preuy accuser of other men, shalbe hated envyed and confounded. **1548–9** (Mar.) *Bk. Com. Prayer, Litany*, From all sedicion and priuye conspiracie..Good lorde deliuer us. **1560** DAUS tr. *Sleidane's Comm.* 169 The Turke..by priuie espiall, knewe the determination of the Senate longe before. **1563–87** FOXE *A. & M.* (1684) II. 4/1 A certain Image of the Virgin so artificially wrought, that the Friars by privy gins made it to stir, and to make gestures. **1589** PUTTENHAM *Eng. Poesie* III. xviii. (Arb.) 201 When ye giue a mocke vnder smooth and lowly wordes..the Greeks call it (*charientismus*) we may call it the priuy nippe, or a myld and appeasing mockery. **1637** MILTON *Lycidas* 128 Besides what the grim Woolf with privy paw Daily devours apace. **1864** SWINBURNE *Atalanta* 1636 Fallen by war Or by the nets and knives of privy death.

†**7.** Of which the presence or existence is not known or not recognized; that is not outwardly evident; of which no indication is visible; hidden.

a **1548** HALL *Chron.*, *Edw. IV* 192 b, Whether it wer for a priuie sickenes, or an open impediment,..this mocion vanished. **1563** B. GOOGE *Eglogs*, etc. (Arb.) 83 To shun The priuy lurkyng hookes. **1579** GOSSON *Sch. Abuse* (Arb.) 38 The Marriner is more indaungered by priuie shelues, then knowen Rockes. **1654** TRAPP *Comm. Ps.* xi. 2 The privie armour of proof, that the Saints have about their breasts.

III. In specific collocations with sbs.

8. privy evil (*Falconry*), a disease of the hawk: see quot. **privy tithe**, the 'small' or vicarial tithe. **privy verdict**, a verdict given to the judge out of court.

1688 R. HOLME *Armoury* II. 238/1 (Diseases in Hawks) The *Privy, or hidden Evil, is a glottonous Stomack, a greedinesss in eating, and devouring. **1530** *Proper Dyaloge* in Roy *Rede me*, etc. (Arb.) 138 Payenge of tythes open and *preuy. **1765** BLACKSTONE *Comm.* I. xi. 388 A particular share of the tithes..called *privy, small, or vicarial, tithes. **1628** COKE *On Litt.* 227 b, After they be agreed they may,.. if the Court be risen, giue a *priuie verdict before any of the Judges.

†**b. privy coat**, a coat of mail worn under the ordinary dress. *Obs.*

1532 *Will of J. Baynham* (Somerset Ho.), A pryvye coat. **1538** J. BEAUMONT in *Lett. Suppress. Monasteries* (Camden) 252, I have secret warnyng by one off hys counsell to weyre a prevy cote. **1599** BACON *Let.* in Spalding *Life & Lett.* (1862) II. 161, I have the privy coat of a good conscience. *a* **1649** WEBSTER *Cure for Cuckold* III. i, I wear a privy coat.

†**c. privy house** (also 5 **privehouse**) = B. 3. So †***privy stool***, a close-stool. *Obs.*

c **1460** J. RUSSELL *Bk. Nurture* 931 Se þe privehouse for esement be fayre, soote, & clene. **1528** *Test. Ebor.* (Surtees) V. 254 In his owne chambre..A prevey stole, iiij*d.* **1660** WOOD *Life* (O.H.S.) I. 358 A common privy house belonging to Peckwater Quadrangle. **1679** *Ibid.* 30 Jan. II. 435 He throw'd it in the privy house.

d. ***privy members***, ***privy parts***, the external organs of sex; the private parts. *Obs.* or *arch.*

So formerly *privy chose* (of a female), *limbs*, etc.

1297 R. GLOUC. (Rolls) 11731 Hii ne bileuede nouȝt þis, þat [h]is priue membres hii ne corue of iwis. **1387** TREVISA *Higden* (Rolls) VI. 475 Here body..al i-roted..out-take þe thombe and here wombe wiþ þe prive chose byneþe. **1398** —— *Barth. De P.R.* III. xxiii. (1495) ej/1 To assaye the pals ..it were vnsemely & shamly to vnhele þe preuy lymmes. *Ibid.* v. xlviii. (Bodl. MS.), The preuey stones of foules bene smale after þe tyme þat is yordeyned to ham to gendre. *Ibid.* XVIII. xcvi, Þe female ape is like to a womman in þe priuy chose. **1482** *Rolls of Parlt.* VI. 221/2 That no maner of persone..were..any Gowne or Cloke, but if it be of such lengh, as hit..shall cover his prevey membres and buttokks. **1556** W. TOWRSON in Hakluyt *Voy.* (1589) 101 They goe all naked except some thing before their priuie partes, which is like a clout. **1563–87** FOXE *A. & M.* (1596) 89/2 Then in his privie yard had a sharpe reed thrust in with horrible paine. **1607** TOPSELL *Four-f. Beasts* (1658) 500 Of a Dog..the gut of the privy place sodden in Oyl, is a very good and soveraign remedy. **1681** *Trial S. Colledge* 140 *L.C.J.*..Your Privy-members shall be cut off, and your Bowels taken out and burnt before your face.

9. privy purse. a. The allowance from the public revenue for the private expenses of the monarch. **b.** (With capital initial.) Short for ***Keeper of the Privy Purse***, an officer of the royal household charged with the payment of the private expenses of the sovereign.

1664 PEPYS *Diary* 15 Dec., When the King would have him to be Privy Purse. **1765** BLACKSTONE *Comm.* I. viii. 332 The king's private expences, or privy purse; and other very numerous outgoings, as secret service money, pensions, and other bounties. **1837** *Penny Cycl.* VII. 224/1 The civil list.. amounted, during the reign of William III.,..to the annual sum of about 680,000*l.* Out of this sum were paid the expenses of the royal household, of the privy purse [etc.]. **1848** W. H. KELLY tr. *L. Blanc's Hist. Ten Y.* I. 292 He

[Louis Philippe] placed at Lafayette's disposal a hundred thousand francs out of the privy purse to aid the enterprises of the Spanish revolutionists. **1852** DICKENS *Bleak Ho.* i, Maces, or petty-bags, or privy-purses..all yawning. **1908** *Whitaker's Almanack* 85 His Majesty's Household... Keeper of His Majesty's Privy Purse.

10. privy signet: see SIGNET.

See also PRIVY CHAMBER, PRIVY COUNCIL, PRIVY COUNSELLOR, PRIVY SEAL.

B. *sb.* [Absolute or elliptical uses of the adj. Cf. OF. *privé, privée*, in various subst. uses.]

I. Of persons.

†**1.** An intimate, confidential, or trusted friend or counsellor; a confidant, an intimate. Cf. A. 1.

1297 R. GLOUC. (Rolls) 8647 He nom on of is prives þat het water tirel. *a* **1300** *Cursor M.* 8342 For-þi hir enterd bersabe þe quen, his spuse, and his priue. **1377** LANGL. *P. Pl.* B. II. 177 Paulynes pryues for pleyntes in þe consistorie, Shul serue my-self. *c* **1380** *Sir Ferumb.* 2480 Þe kyng of Comble, Sir Sortybraunt & othre of his pryueez. *c* **1450** *Merlin* 377 That he wolde..be oon of his privees.

2. *Law.* One who is a partaker or has any part or interest in any action, matter, or thing: including the parties entering into a contract, and also any one that is bound or has an interest under a contract or conveyance to which he himself is not a party. Cf. A. 6. Opposed to STRANGER.

[**1292** BRITTON III. vi. §15 Pur ceo qe ceste assise ne tient poynt lu par entre privez del saunc. (*tr.* Whereas this assize does not lie between privies of blood.) **1321–2** *Rolls of Parlt.* I. 411/2 Lesquexs demorunt & sount aloynes par les prives a la talye.] **1483** *Act 1 Rich. III*, c. 7 §3 The seid fyne to be fynall ende, and conclude aswell prives as estraunges to the same. **1579** *Expos. Terms Law* 159b/2 Priuie..wher a lease is made to holde at will, for yeres, for life, or a feffement in fee..because of thys that hath passed betweene these parties, they are called priuies, in respect of straungers betwene whom no such dealings, or conueiances hath ben. *Ibid.* 160/1 Priuies are in diuers sorts, as namely priuies in estate, priuies in deede, priuies in law, priuies in right, and priuies in bloode. **1607** COWELL *Interpr.*, *Priuie*..signifieth ..him that is partaker, or hath an interest in any action, or thing: as, *priuies of bloud*..be those that be linked in consanguinitie. Euery heire in tayle is priuy to recouer the land intayled. **1766** BLACKSTONE *Comm.* II. xxi. 355 Privies to a fine are such as are any way related to the parties who levy the fine, and claim under them by any right of blood or other right of representation. **1818** COLEBROOKE *Obligations* 229 His representatives and universal successors, or privies in blood, as heirs, and privies in representation, as executors and administrators, may at the death of a person of non-sane memory avoid his deeds. **1818** CRUISE *Digest* (ed. 2) IV. 308 Privies in blood, as the heir; privies in estate, as the feoffee, lessee, &c.; privies in law, as lord by escheat, tenant by the curtesy, tenants in dower, and others that come in by act of law, or in the *post*; shall be bound, and take advantage of estoppels. **1882** SWEET *Law Dict.* s.v., In the law of fines, the heirs and successors of the parties to a fine were said to be privies to it, and were bound by it as if they had been parties, as opposed to strangers, that is, persons who were neither parties nor privies.

†**b.** One who participates in the knowledge of something private or secret; a confidant; one privy to a plot or crime: see A. 4. *Obs.*

a **1548** HALL *Chron., Hen. VI* 164b, The citezens glad of his commynge, made not the French capitayns, which had the gouernaunce of the towne, either parties or priuies of their entent. **1647** N. BACON *Disc. Govt. Eng.* I. liii. (1739) 94 Mainperners are not to be punished as Principals, unless they be parties or privies to the failing of the Principal.

†**c.** One who belongs to a country or place; a native or denizen, as opposed to a stranger or foreigner. *Obs.*

1565 in W. H. Turner *Select. Rec. Oxford* (1880) 312 Right ye shall doe to every person as well to ye stranger as to ye pryvye. **1641** W. HAKEWIL *Libertie of Subject* 101 (tr. Act 2 Edw. III, c. 9) All Merchants, Strangers and Privies [*touz marchantz aliens & priveez*], may goe and come with their merchandizes into England after the tenure of the Great Charter.

II. Of things.

3. A private place of ease, a latrine, a necessary: see A. 8c.

1375 BARBOUR *Bruce* v. 556 The king had in custum ay For to riss airly euirilk day, And pas weill fer fra his menȝe, Quhen he vald pas to the preue. *c* **1400** *Lanfranc's Cirurg.* 273 Whanne he sittiþ at priuy he schal not streyne him-silf to harde. **1423** *Coventry Leet Bk.* 59 Allso þai orden þat..all þe pryves & swynesties þeron be done away. **1530** *Nottingham Rec.* III. 364 A prevye comyng out of the Kynges Jayle in to the hie-wey, vnto the grett noysance of alle the inhabytantes. **1650** HOWELL *Giraffi's Rev. Naples* I. (1664) 104 They pried into the very privies and jakes. **1704** SWIFT *Mech. Operat. Spirit* §2 Misc. (1711) 303 As if a Traveller should go about to describe a Palace, when he had seen nothing but the Privy. **1869** E. A. PARKES *Pract. Hygiene* (ed. 3) 107 The clearing out of a privy produced in twenty-three children violent vomiting.

attrib. *a* **1225** *Ancr. R.* 276 Ne berest tu two þurles, ase þauh hit weren two priue þurles? **1483** *Cath. Angl.* 292/1 A Pryvay scowrare..*cloacarius*. **1897** *Allbutt's Syst. Med.* II. 413 The bad privy accommodation. **1898** P. MANSON *Trop. Diseases* xi. 194 A peculiar mawkish, privy odour.

†**4.** Short for *privy member* (see A. 8d). *rare.*

c **1400** tr. *Secreta Secret., Gov. Lordsh.* 85 Þys ys þe prydde medicyne, his properte ys to efforce þe pryue, and namly þe pryncypales.

†**5.** That which is secret, secrecy; in phr. ***in privy***, in secret, in private, covertly. ***in privy or apert, in privy or in plain***, covertly or openly.

1388 WYCLIF *Matt.* vi. 18 Þi fadir þat seeþ in privye shal ȝelde to þee. **1390** GOWER *Conf.* I. 182 Alle tho that hadden be Or in apert or in prive Of conseil to the mariage, Sche slowh hem. **1460** *Rolls of Parlt.* V. 378/2 Directely or indirectely, in prive or appert. **1535** STEWART *Cron. Scot.* (Rolls) II. 173 To grant him self in Britane to remane, Quhair plesis ȝow in previe or in plane. **1567** *Satir. Poems Reform.* vii. 3 Twa leirnit men in priuie I hard talk. **1569** *Reg. Privy Council Scot.* I. 652 Nor yit sall we tryist or haif intelligence with thame in previe or apart.

†**C.** *adv.* = PRIVILY *adv.*; privately, secretly, in secret. *Obs.*

Frequent in *privy or (a)pert* (contracted from *in privy or apert*: see B. 5), secretly or openly, privately or publicly.

13.. *Cursor M.* 27180 Preist sal..knau..þe pligth..Queþ er it be priue don, or hid. *c* **1330** R. BRUNNE *Chron. Wace* (Rolls) 3393 Brenne bad þem ber ham [al] pryue, Wiþ-oute noyse. **1485** in *10th Rep. Hist. MSS. Comm.* App. v. 321 That..will goo among them prevy or peart for his propre besynes. **1508** DUNBAR *Tua Mariit Wemen* 273, I hatit him like a hund, thought I it hid preue.

privy (priuie), obs. var. PRIVET[1].

ˌprivy ˈchamber. Now *Hist.* [PRIVY *a.* 2.]

1. In a general sense: A room reserved for the private or exclusive use of a particular person or persons; a private room, in which one is not liable to interruption or disturbance. *Obs.* or *arch.*

c **1400** *Destr. Troy* 2972 Thou dissyret full depely, dame Elan, þi seluon, To pas fro þi palis & þi priuey chamber. *c* **1440** *Promp. Parv.* 414/1 Pryvy chawmyr (*S.* chambyr), *conclave*. *c* **1450** *Merlin* 19 Brynge thy moder in to a prevy chamber. **1581** PETTIE tr. *Guazzo's Civ. Conv.* I. (1586) 13 Those which couet to get learning, seeke it not in publike places..but in their studies and priuie chambers.

fig. **1615** CROOKE *Body of Man* 432 All these indiuiduall formes receiued by the senses, are..resigned vp in token of fœalty to the Common sense or priuy chamber of the soule. **1645** G. DANIEL *Odes* xlvi. Wks. (Grosart) II. 96 Nor can Man in this Motley, meerlie man, Stand in the privie Chamber of his heart.

2. *spec.* A private apartment in a royal residence.

Gentlemen of the Privy Chamber: see quots. 1681, 1727–41.

1540 CROMWELL in Merriman *Life & Lett.* (1902) II. 270 Your Magestye avauncyd toward the galerye owt of your pryvey Chambre. **1681** BURNET *Hist. Ref.* II. 10 Those who attended on him [Edw. VI] in his bedchamber during his sickness, though they were called gentlemen of the privy-chamber; for the service of the gentlemen of the bed-chamber was not then set up. **1727–41** CHAMBERS *Cycl.* s.v. *Chamber*, Gentlemen of the Privy-Chamber are servants of the king, who are to wait and attend on him and the queen at court, in their diversions, progresses, &c... Their number is forty-eight. Their institution is owing to king Henry VII. **1828** TYTLER *Hist. Scot.* (1864) I. 39 The King of England summoned Baliol..into his privy chamber at Newcastle. **1849** JAMES *Woodman* ii, You seem to be of his privy-chamber, goodman Boyd.

Hence **privy-ˈchamberer**, a frequenter of the Privy Chamber.

1640 HABINGTON *Queen of Arragon* I, Who hath art To judge of my confession; must have had At least a Privie Chamberer to his Father.

ˌprivy ˈcouncil. [ME. *prive counseil* (PRIVY *a.* 2 and COUNSEL *sb.*) = OF. *privé conseil* (1276 in Du Cange), mod.F. *conseil privé*, med.L. *consilium privatum*. For the change (17th c.) of COUNSEL to COUNCIL, see these words.]

†**1.** In general sense: A private consultation or assembly for consultation. *Obs.*

In later use usually transferred from sense 2.

c **1300** [see PRIVY *a.* 5b]. *c* **1450** *Merlin* 251 Dodynell.. tolde to his prevy counseile that he wolde go to court. *c* **1530** *Hickscorner* in Hazl. *Dodsley* I. 157 Into lords' favours I can get me soon, And be of their privy council. [**1634** FORD *Perkin Warbeck* II. iii, How the counsel-privy Of this young Phaeton do screw their faces Into a gravity.] **1749** FIELDING *Tom Jones* xv. ix, Jones, by the advice of his privy-council [i.e. Nightingale], replied. **1773** GOLDSM. *Stoops to Conq.* II. i, Then I beg they'll admit me as one of their privy council. **1825** FOSBROKE *Encycl. Antiq.* (1843) II. 591/2 Our nobles had also their privy councils, composed of gentlemen of family and fortune.

2. (With capital initials.) The private counsellors of the sovereign; *spec.* in Great Britain a body of advisers selected by the sovereign, together with certain persons who are members by usage, as the princes of the blood, the archbishops, and the chief officers of the present and past ministers of state.

Its original function of advising the crown in matters of state and administration is now mainly discharged by the Cabinet (CABINET *sb.* 7b), a select body of ministers drawn from the Privy Council; and much of its business is carried on by committees, as the Board of Trade (originally the Committee of Council for Trade and Foreign Plantations, now the Department of Trade and Industry), the Judicial Committee of the Privy Council, etc. Hence, to be 'sworn of His Majesty's Privy Council' is now mainly a personal dignity, conferred chiefly in recognition of eminent public services.

[**1375** BARBOUR *Bruce* I. 603 And forouth hys consaile priue, The lord the bruce thar callyt he [Edward I].] **1450** *Rolls of Parlt.* V. 178/1 Beyng oon of your grete and pryve Counseill, and with you best trusted. **1547–8** *Orare of Communion* 3 And other of our priuey Counsaill. **1555** BRADFORD in Strype *Eccl. Mem.* (1721) III. App. xlv. 130, I was chamberlayn to one of the priuie counsayll. **1613** SHAKS. *Hen. VIII*, IV. i. 112 The King ha's made him [Thomas Cromwell] Master o' th' Iewell House, And one already of the Priuy Councell. **1667** DUCHESS OF NEWCASTLE *Life Dk. N.* (1886) 9 King Charles the First..made him withal a member of the Lords of his Majesty's most honourable Privy Council. **1765** BLACKSTONE *Comm.* I. v. 229 The principal council belonging to the king is his privy council. **1827** HALLAM *Const. Hist.* (1876) III. xv. 185 During the reign of William [III] this distinction of the cabinet from the privy council..became more fully established. **1844** H. H. WILSON *Brit. India* III. 287 The petition of Sir John Grant to the Privy Council. **1863** H. COX *Instit.* III. v. 647 The highest administrative department under the Crown is the Privy Council.

b. Applied (by English writers) to a council of state in a foreign country, or to the council of an ancient king or ruler.

c **1450** LOVELICH *Merlin* 4713 Thanne answerid his [K. Uter's] prevy cownseyl ageyn: 'what wil ȝe þat we do, telle vs now pleyn'. *c* **1450** *Merlin* 372 Than spake the kynge Arthur, and seide..I will that..ye be..of my prive counseile and lordes of my court. *c* **1460** *Towneley Myst.* xvi. 196, I haue maters to mell with my preuey counsell. *a* **1533** LD. BERNERS *Huon* lxxxviii. 278 Thus duke Raoull retournyd to the cyte of Vyen..and sent for his preuey counsell. **1650** *Nicholas Papers* (Camden) I. 184 These foure are noble men and all of his [Russian] Maties Privy Councell. **1769** ROBERTSON *Chas. V* (1783) I. 265 Ferdinand empowered a committee of his privy-Council..to hear the deputies sent from Hispaniola. **1808** *Edin. Rev.* XII. 389 By these, and by other means, the College of Savi, or Privy Council, as it may be termed, had acquired so much power. **1845** S. AUSTIN *Ranke's Hist. Ref.* III. 243 The affair had often been discussed in his [the emperor's] privy-council.

c. A similar body formed to assist the Lord Lieutenant of Ireland, and the governors of some (former) British colonies or dominions. ***Scottish Privy Council***: see COUNCIL *sb.* 7.

1765 BLACKSTONE *Comm.* I. 102 In that shape they [bills] are offered to the consideration of the lord lieutenant and privy council [of Ireland]. **1889** *Whitaker's Almanack* 436/2 Dominion of Canada..The Executive Government and authority is vested in the Queen, and exercised in her name by the Governor-General, aided by a Privy Council.

d. *fig.*

a **1657** LOVELACE *Poems* (1864) 226 Thou art of privy council to the gods! *a* **1708** BEVERIDGE *Thes. Theol.* (1711) III. 329 Who are His [Christ's] Privy-Council? God the Father, the godly His children.

privy-councilship. [-SHIP.] = PRIVY-COUNSELLORSHIP.

1910 *Blackw. Mag.* Sept. 422/1 Even Privy Councilship does not turn nonsense into sound argument.

ˌprivy ˈcounsellor, ˈcouncillor. [ME. *prive counseiller*: see PRIVY *a.* 2 and COUNSELLOR; from 17th c. occasionally, and in 19th c. often spelt *councillor* after PRIVY COUNCIL; but *counsellor* is the official as well as historical form.]

1. A private or confidential adviser.

(Often with allusion to sense 2.)

[**13..** *Cursor M.* 3005 (Fairf.) Þe kinge [Abimelech] made him [Abraham] his counsalour priue [*earlier texts* made him his prive]. *c* **1380** *Sir Ferumb.* 2052 Charlis consailer am y pryue y-sent on his message.] **1390** GOWER *Conf.* III. 292 He hadde a feloun bacheler, Which was his prive consailer. **1422** tr. *Secreta Secret., Priv. Priv.* 167 The kynge Of the Cite..sende for the Philosofre, and makyd hym his prywey consailloure. **1719** DE FOE *Crusoe* I. xx. (1840) 363 My principal guide and privy counsellor, was my good ancient widow. **1837** W. IRVING *Capt. Bonneville* II. xxxii. 256 The old chief and his privy counsellor, the guide, had another mysterious colloquy.

2. (With capital initials.) *spec.* in Great Britain: One of the private counsellors of the sovereign; a member of the Privy Council.

Indicated by the addition to his name of P.C., and styled *Right Honourable*. See note to prec., sense 2.

1647 CLARENDON *Hist. Reb.* I. §42 Having..married a near ally of the Dukes, with wonderfull expedition was made a Privy-Councellour. **1659** RUSHW. *Hist. Coll.* I. 165 The Privy-Counsellors to the late King, with all the Lords Spiritual and Temporal then about London, were in the Council Chamber at Whitehall by Eight of the Clock in the morning. **1765** BLACKSTONE *Comm.* I. v. 232 The privileges of privy counsellors, as such, consist principally in the security which the law has given them against attempts and conspiracies to destroy their lives. **1814** [J. HUNTER] *Who wrote Cavendish's Wolsey?* 22 He left it, at about the age of fifty, a knight, a privy counsellor, and the owner of estates. **1818** CRUISE *Digest* (ed. 2) IV. 277 A deed executed in the presence of four privy councillors. **1891** J. CHAMBERLAIN in *Times* 28 Nov. 12/3 There are those who sit upon the front bench who, by reason of not being Privy Councillors, have no right to sit there. **1907** *Whitaker's Peerage* 49 In the official list the members are termed Privy Counsellors, which is correct, in view of the counsel they are supposed to give; but they are equally Councillors as being members of a Council.

fig. **1657** *North's Plutarch, Add. Lives* (1676) 10 Some.. rashly do fancy to themselves, that they are the Almighties Privy-Counsellours. **1711** ADDISON *Spect.* No. 55 ¶4 Avarice..had likewise a Privy-Counsellor who was always at his Elbow, and whispering something or other in his Ear: The Name of this Privy-Counsellor was Poverty.

Hence **ˌprivy-ˈcounsellorship, -ˈcouncillorship** [see -SHIP].

1880 DISRAELI *Endym.* iii, He retired with the solace of a sinecure, a pension, and a privy-councillorship.

ˌprivy ˈseal. Forms: see PRIVY and SEAL. [PRIVY *a.* 2: lit. private seal.]

1. The seal affixed to documents that are afterwards to pass the Great Seal; also to documents of less importance which do not require the Great Seal. In Scotland, A seal which authenticates a royal grant of personal or assignable rights.

†*clerk of the privy seal* (*obs.*), the Keeper of the Privy Seal; also, one of the four clerks formerly employed in the

office of the privy seal. *Keeper of the Privy Seal*: see KEEPER *sb.* 1 c.

[**1230** in E. Déprez *Etudes de Diplom. anglaise* (1908) 10 Teste me ipso apud Hamsted 11 die decembris Has litteras privato sigillo nostro fecimus sigillari. **1295** *Rolls of Parlt.* I. 133/1 Done desuz nostre prive seal, a Rughemor. **1347–8** *Ibid.* II. 206/2 Notre Seignour le Roi ad mande ces Lettres desouth son Privie Seal a son Chanceller.]

1425 *Rolls of Parlt.* IV. 297/1 Keper of ye Kyngs Prive Seal. *a* **1434** in *Exch. Rolls Scotl.* IV. 572 *note*, Gevin under oure prive sele at Edynburch. **1497** in *Lett. & Papers Rich. III & Hen. VII* (Rolls) I. 104 The Bisshop of Duresme, keper of our pryveseall. **1543** tr. *Act 12 Rich. II*, c. 11 To saye or tell any false newes..of the chauncelar, tresorer, clerke of the pryuye seale [*orig.* Clerc du Prive Seal]. **1607** COWELL *Interpr., Priuie seale*..is a seale that the King vseth some time for a warrant, whereby things passed the priuy signet and brought to it, are sent farder to be confirmed by the great seale of England. *a* **1660** HAMMOND *Serm.* ii. Wks. 1684 IV. 569 That Privy Seal of his annexed to the Patent. **1827** HALLAM *Const. Hist.* (1876) I. vii. 381 He [Chas. I] had issued letters of privy seal..to those in every county whose names had been returned by the lord lieutenant as most capable, mentioning the sum they were required to lend.

2. A document to which the privy seal is affixed; *spec.* a warrant, under the privy seal, demanding a loan; hence *transf.* a forced loan, a benevolence. Now only *Hist.*

1419 in *Proc. Privy Council* (1834) II. 247 We have.. comynd togidder..for þe exploit of the pryve seals þat were ysent to us by..þe lordys of þe Conseil. **1449** *Rolls of Parlt.* V. 167/1 That your seid besecher may have..als mony Writts and Prive Seals, as shall be behovefull. **1530** PALSGR. 258/1 Prevy seale, *mandement du roy.* **1585** *Act 27 Eliz.* c. 3 §6 A Priuy Seale, commanding the same heire to make personall appearance in the Court. **1657** J. WATTS *Vind. Ch. Eng.* 78 May they send out their privie Seals, or Troops, to fetch in money or cattle. **1827** HALLAM *Const. Hist.* (1876) I. v. 244 She [Q. Eliz.] did not abstain from the ancient practice of sending privy-seals to borrow money of the wealthy.

fig. **1660** T. WATSON in Spurgeon *Treas. Dav.* Ps. lxxxiv. 10 In the sacrament God..gives them a smile of his face, and a privy-seal of his love.

3. (With capital initials.) **a.** The Keeper of the Privy Seal; now called ***Lord Privy Seal.***

c **1420** *Brut* (E.E.T.S.) 539 Maistre Symond Islepe, Privey Seal, with xvij men of Armes, and xij Archers on horsebakke. **1425** *Rolls of Parlt.* IV. 297/2 Decreed..by ye said Archebysshop, Ducs, Bisshops, Erle, Prive Seel, and Lord Cromwell. **1556** *Chron. Gr. Friars* (Camden) 61 The lorde Rosselle that was then lorde privisele. **1682** *Lond. Gaz.* No. 1768/3 His Majesty has been pleased to confer the Office of Lord Privy-Seal upon the Right Honourable the Marquiss of Hallifax. **1794** G. ROSE *Diaries* (1860) I. 193 Lord Spencer is to be the Privy Seal. **1874** *Chambers's Encycl.* VII. 775/1 The Lord Privy-Seal is now the fifth great officer of state, and has generally a seat in the cabinet. His office is conferred under the Great Seal during pleasure.

†**b.** The office in which documents were prepared and the privy seal affixed to them. *Obs.*

c **1412** HOCCLEVE *De Reg. Princ.* 1464 So longe as þou, sone, in þe priuē sel Dwelt hast.

c. *ellipt.* The office of Keeper of the Privy Seal.

1771 *Junius Lett.* xlix. (1820) 257 The privy-seal was intended for him.

‖**Prix de Rome** (pri də rɔm). [Fr., = prize of Rome.] In full ***Grand Prix de Rome.*** One of a group of prizes awarded annually by the French Government, established by Louis XIV in 1666 for competition by young painters and sculptors, extended in 1720 to include architects, and in 1803 to include musicians and engravers. The winner of the first prize in each category is entitled to a period of study in Rome; also, the winner of a *prix de Rome.*

1879 GROVE *Dict. Mus.* I. 233/2 In 1828 he [*sc.* Berlioz] took the second, and at last, in 1830,..the first prize—the 'Prix de Rome'. **1884** R. & E. HOLMES tr. *Berlioz' Autobiogr.* I. xxii. 113 The intention of the Government, in establishing the Prix de Rome, was, first, to bring forward year by year the most promising among the young French composers; secondly, to enable them, by means of a pension, to devote themselves entirely for five years to the study of music. **1889** F. F. BUFFEN *Musical Celebrities* 53 At the age of nineteen Gounod succeeded in gaining the second 'Prix de Rome' for his cantata, 'Marie Stuart et Rizzio', and in 1839 took the 'Grand Prix' with his composition of 'Fernand'. **1905** J. WEBSTER *Wheat Princess* i. 10 Allow me to present Monsieur Benoit, the last *Prix de Rome*—he is the man to paint your ghost. **1906** W. J. LOCKE *Beloved Vagabond* (1907) xvi. 204 'You a *Prix de Rome*, Master?' 'Yes, my son, in Architecture.' He was clothed in a new and sudden radiance. To a Paris art student a *Prix de Rome* is what a Field Marshal is to a private soldier. **1957** *Observer* 29 Dec. 11/5 The Master had trained as an architect, won the Prix de Rome. **1968** 'S. JAY' *Sleepers can Kill* xv. 153 Oh, well, there goes the Prix de Rome. He put the charcoal down. **1972** *Guardian* 22 July 9/6 John Skeaping..was living in Rome, having won the Prix de Rome for sculpture.

‖**prix fixe** (pri fiks). [Fr., lit. = fixed price.] A meal served in a hotel or restaurant at a fixed price, a table d'hôte meal (cf. À LA CARTE); the menu offered at such a meal. Also *attrib.*

1883 R. L. STEVENSON in *Magazine of Art* VI. 274/2 You taste the food of all nations in the various restaurants; passing from a French *prix-fixe*, where every one is French, to a roaring German ordinary where every one is German. **1930** A BENNETT *Imperial Palace* xiv. 82 Prevent customers who prefer the *prix-fixe* from choosing more expensive things than the price will stand. **1933** 'G. ORWELL' *Down & Out* vii. 59 A *prix fixe* restaurant where we went for dinner. **1966** P. V. PRICE *France: Food & Wine Guide* 33 In the majority of restaurants there will be at least one *prix fixe*, a fixed price menu, offering several courses. **1973** *Guardian* 28 May 3/4 In Chantilly..there is *crème chantilly* with everything. But..you wouldn't believe how the *prix fixe* can expand. **1975** *Times* 20 Dec. 10/7 The *prix-fixe* menus.. averaged now 25 francs.

priys, obs. form of PRICE *sb.*, PRIZE *sb.*[1]

prizable, prizeable (ˈpraɪzəb(ə)l), *a.*[1] Now chiefly *dial.* Also 7 **priseable.** [f. PRIZE *v.*[1] + -ABLE.] Capable of being, or worthy to be, prized; valuable.

1603 FLORIO *Montaigne* III. xiii. (1632) 628, I..finde it [life] to be both priseable and commodious. **1634** W. TIRWHYT tr. *Balzac's Lett.* (vol. I.) 203 The very ravings of my fever are sometimes more prizeable than Philosophical Meditations. **1686** GOAD *Celest. Bodies* To Rdr. 2, I hope this our Principle is so much the more prizable, that it [etc.]. **1816** KEATINGE *Trav.* I. 108 Clothed with that delicate.. short grass so prizable for the flock and the dairy. **1862** SIR H. TAYLOR *St. Clement's Eve* I. i, A prizeable possession.

†**b.** Comparable in value (*with*). *Obs. rare*$^{-1}$.

1644 QUARLES *Barnabas & B.* 99 Is a poor clod of earth (we call inheritance) prizeable with his greatness?

ˈ**prizable,** *a.*[2] *Chess.* [f. PRIZE *sb.*[3] = F. *prise* capture + -ABLE.] That can be taken or made a prize; exposed to capture.

1808 *Stud. Chess* II. 202 In case you touch a piece not prizable, you..must play your king if you can.

†ˈ**prizal**[1]. *Obs.* [f. PRIZE *v.*[1] + -AL[1].] Estimate of worth; appraisement; valuation.

1610 W. FOLKINGHAM *Art of Survey* I. x. 29 With us Pidgens dung..carries chief preheminence for due prizall of worth. *Ibid.* IV. i. 79 The Valuation of Possessions consists in the due Estimate and Prizall of all Parts and Particulars Essentially and Accidentally thereunto belonging.

prizal[2], late form of PRISAL *sb.*, taking.

prize (praɪz), *sb.*[1] For earlier forms (pris, prys, prise, price, etc.) see PRICE *sb.* [A differentiated variant of ME. *prīs, prise*, now PRICE *sb.* The latter was formerly, and in some dialects is still, *prise, prize* (praɪz), and its plural in 16–18th c. was very commonly *prises, prizes.* The corresp. verb is also *prise*, PRIZE *v.*[1] Cf. also the forms of PRIZE *sb.*[3], *v.*[2]]

1. a. A reward, trophy, or symbol of victory or superiority in any contest or competition.

consolation prize, a prize won in a consolation match: see CONSOLATION 3 b.

α. *a* **1300** *Cursor M.* 25364 (Cott.) For oft þe men þat er rightwis Thoru faanding win þai to þair pris [so *Gött.*; *F.* prise]. **1382** WYCLIF *1 Cor.* ix. 24 Thei that rennen in a furlong, alle forsoth rennen, but oon takith the priys. **1390** GOWER *Conf.* III. 15 So that the heiere hond he [Bacchus] hadde And victoire of his enemys, And torneth homward with his pris. *c* **1460** *Launfal* 487 So the prys of that turnay Was delyvered to Lanfaul that day. **1617** MORYSON *Itin.* III. 196 Shooting for wagers..and for like rewards and prises.

β. **1523** LD. BERNERS *Froiss.* I. clxviii. 205 All..ar playnly acorded..to gyue you the price and chapelette. **1627** HAKEWILL *Apol.* (1630) 239 The onely man to whom the price was of right to be adjudged. **1675** *Phil. Trans.* X. 549 Certain *brabiums* or prices for such as shall do best.

γ. **1596** SHAKS. *Merch. V.* II. ix. 60 (Qo. 1600) Did I deserue no more then a fooles head, Is that my prize, are my deserts no better? **1600** —— *A.Y.L.* I. i. 168 If euer hee goe alone againe, Ile neuer wrastle for prize more. **1668** DRYDEN *Ess. Dram. Poesy* Ess. (ed. Ker) I. 37 They had judges ordained to decide their merit, and prizes to reward it. **1752** HUME *Ess. & Treat.* (1777) I. 193 We overvalue the prize for which we contend. **1802** MAR. EDGEWORTH *Moral T.* (1816) I. 250 A week before the prize was decided by the king. **1899** *Scribner's Mag.* XXV. 7/1, I should have missed the Santiago campaign, and might not even have had the consolation prize of going to Porto Rico.

b. In colleges, schools, etc.: A reward in the form of money, books, or the like, given to the pupil who excels in attainments, usually as tested by a competitive examination. Formerly PREMIUM.

1752 *Cambr. Univ. Notice* 11 Dec., Mr. Finch and..Mr. Townsend having proposed..to give Two Prizes of Fifteen Guineas each to two Senior Batchelors of Arts..who shall compose the best Exercises in Latin Prose. **1768** M. HOWARD *Conqt. Quebec*, Honoured with the Prize given by the..Chancellor of the University of Oxford, for the best English Verses on this Subject. **1769** SIR J. REYNOLDS (*title*) A Discourse, delivered to the Students of the Royal Academy, on the distribution of the prizes. **1784** COWPER *Tiroc.* 473 The prize of beauty in a woman's eyes Not brighter than in theirs the scholar's prize. **1791** (*Circular*) Clarke's..School, Liverpool. *Præmia.* Names of the Young Ladies and Gentlemen to whom the Annual Prizes were publicly adjudged. **1800** *Cambr. Univ. Cal.* 9 University Prizes. Two gold medals, value 15 guineas each, are given annually by the Chancellor of this University. **1847** TENNYSON *Princ.* III. 283 You love The metaphysics! read and earn our prize, A golden broach.

c. A premium offered to the person who exhibits the best specimens of natural productions, works of art, or manufactures, at a competition designed to promote the study, cultivation, or production of such objects, or at an exhibition or 'show' arranged for the instruction or amusement of visitors.

1775 *Orig. Ipswich Jrnl.* 6 May (in *N. & Q.* 29 Feb. 1908), There will be a shew of Tulips... Every person's flower shall be his own actual property and of his own blowing, or they will not be entitled to either of the prizes. **1793** (June 4) *Musical Entertainmt. at Sadler's Wells Th.*, The Prize of Industry. Taken from a Fete given in Oxfordshire for the encouragement of industry amongst the Villagers; and introducing the Spinning for the Prize Medal. **1824** [see 4 a]. **1845** *Florist's Jrnl.* 209 The first prize for 12 Ranunculuses (amateurs' class) was awarded [etc.]. *Mod.* The infant to whom the first prize was awarded at the baby show.

2. A sum of money or a thing of value, offered for competition by chance or hazard, as by trying who shall throw the highest or other specified number at dice, or draw a particular ticket from among a large number to which no advantage attaches, called *blanks.* Often *fig.*

1567 *Lottery Chart* Aug., A very rich Lotterie generall, without any Blanckes, contayning a great number of good Prices. **1711** STEELE *Spect.* No. 242 ¶2 A Ticket in the Lottery, and..'tis come up this Morning a Five hundred Pound Prize. **1728** YOUNG *Love Fame* III. 264 A beauteous sister, or convenient wife, Are prizes in the lottery of life. **1842** MISS MITFORD in L'Estrange *Life* (1870) III. ix. 153 A twenty thousand prize in the lottery. **1883** W. C. SMITH in *Encycl. Brit.* XV. 11/1 The word lottery..may be applied to any process of determining prizes by lot.

3. *fig.* **a.** Anything striven for or worth striving for; a thing of value won by or inspiring effort.

1606 SHAKS. *Tr. & Cr.* III. iii. 83 (Qo. 1609) Place, ritches, and fauour, Prizes of accident as oft as merit. **1610** —— *Temp.* I. ii. 452 But this swift busines I must vneasie make, least too light winning Make the prize light. **1712–14** POPE *Rape Lock* V. 111 The Lock..In ev'ry place is sought, but sought in vain: With such a prize no mortal must be blest. **1838** LYTTON *Alice* x, What a prize to any younger sons in the Merton family. **1849** MACAULAY *Hist. Eng.* iii. I. 326 There were still indeed prizes in the Church: but they were few. **1856** GRINDON *Life* xxii. (1875) 273 Life has a prize for every one who will open his heart to receive it.

b. An advantage, privilege; something prized or highly valued.

1593 SHAKS. *3 Hen. VI*, I. iv. 59 (Qo. 1595) Tis warres prise to take all aduantages. *Ibid.* II. i. 20 (Fol. 1623) Me thinkes 'tis prize [1595 pride] enough to be his Sonne. **1638** WALTON in L. Roberts *Merch. Mapp* Commend. Verses 11 If thou would'st be a Merchant, buy this Booke: For 'tis a prize worth gold.

c. ***glittering prizes.***

1875 F. ARNOLD *Our Bishops & Deans* I. v. 286 There are certain glittering prizes which are the great attractions to these. **1923** LD. BIRKENHEAD in *Times* 8 Nov. 7/4 The world continues to offer glittering prizes to those who have stout hearts and sharp swords. **1976** F. RAPHAEL (*title*) Glittering prizes. **1977** A. CLARKE *Let. from Dead* ix. 104 Just keep your trap shut..and remember the glittering prizes. **1978** *Broadcast* 3 Apr. 9/3 Party political broadcasts are not the glittering prizes that once they seemed to be... The public are bored by them.

4. *attrib.* and *Comb.* **a.** *attrib.* (*a*) That gains a prize; for which a prize is awarded in a competition or exhibition; also *fig.* such as would or might gain a prize; supremely excellent of its kind, first-class; now also *fig.* (as adj.) describing undesirable qualities: outstanding, unrivalled, complete, utter. (*b*) That is offered or gained as a prize. (Often hyphened.)

1803 D. WILSON (*title*) Common Sense: A Prize Essay, recited in the Theatre, Oxford, June 15, 1803. **1807** (*title*) Oxford Prize Poems: being a Collection of such English Poems as have at various times obtained Prizes in the University of Oxford. **1812** *Sporting Mag.* XL. 270 Jemmy Hill claimed his prize-pig, but his competitors disputed his right. **1824** BYRON *Juan* XVI. lx, There was a prize ox, a prize pig, and ploughman, For Henry was a sort of Sabine showman. **1831** *Edin. Rev.* LIII. 556 The world..is pretty well agreed in thinking that the shorter a prize-poem is, the better. **1856** C. M. YONGE *Daisy Chain* II. xviii. 548 He.. had written the best prize poem ever heard at Oxford. **1857** GEO. ELIOT *Let.* 22 May (1954) II. 329 Meditations about a new book..when the Prize Essay has reached a second edition. **1881** JOWETT *Thucyd.* I. 15 My history is an everlasting possession, not a prize composition which is heard and forgotten. **1897** *Daily News* 28 Jan. 3/1 Look at the prize gussets, the prize hemmings, the prize buttonholes, the prize darnings, the prize stitchings.. suspended by innumerable tin tacks to the wall. **1933** BLUNDEN *Charles Lamb* 21 George Richards, whose Oxford prize-poem delighted Byron. **1952** E. O'NEILL *Moon for Misbegotten* I. 63 *Hogan.* All prize pigs, too! I was offered two hundred dollars apiece for them. **1956** K. TILLOTSON *Matthew Arnold & Carlyle* 139 Arnold opens non-committally, using a techinque of evasion common in prize-poems. **1976** *Southern Even. Echo* (Southampton) 13 Nov. (Suppl.) 5/3 The final episode finds Katy..accused of writing to a young man regarded as a prize flirt. **1978** M. TRIPP *Wife-Smuggler* v. 58 I've been made a fool, a prize bloody fool. **1980** E. G. WILSON *John Clarkson* iv. 46 A Cambridge prize essay was bound to have a good circulation.

b. *Comb.*, as *prize-giver, -giving, -holder, -loser, -seeker, -taker, -winner; prize-taking, -winning, -worthy* adjs.; **prize-book**, a book gained as a prize; **prize-fellowship**, a fellowship in a college given as a reward for eminence in an examination, as distinct from an official fellowship; hence **prize-fellow**, one who holds such a fellowship; **prize-list**, a list of the winners of prizes in any competition; **prize-medal**, a medal offered or gained as a prize; **prize-question**, a question or subject for the answer to or discussion of which a prize is offered; **prize-roll**, a roll or list of prize-winners.

1839 C. SINCLAIR *Holiday House* xii. 274 Being the best scholar there [*sc.* at school], he might..receive a whole library of *prize-books. **1858** LYTTON *What will he do* VII. ix, The poor relics of her innocent happy girlhood,..—the prize-books, the lute, the costly work-box. *c* **1909** D. H. LAWRENCE *Collier's Friday Night* (1934) i. 4 Then on the next shelf prize-books in calf and gold. **1897** *Westm. Gaz.* 27 Apr. 2/1 A *prize-fellow in his seventh year is one of the most dolorous sights in the world. These *prize-fellowships ought to be abolished, and the money devoted.. to relieving the intolerable strain on the University chest. **1900** G. C. BRODRICK *Mem. & Impress.* 170 'Prize fellows' as they are ungracefully called, elected for seven years only. **1865** *Daily Tel.* 5 Dec. 7/1 Zealous and more determined *prize-givers and prize-seekers overruled Mr. Wright and his supporters. **1905** E. M. FORSTER *Where Angels fear to Tread* v. 124 Fortunately the school *prize-giving was at hand. **1955** E. BLISHEN *Roaring Boys* II. 100 Prize-giving.. didn't flow naturally out of what had gone before, as it does in a grammar school. **1973** R. PARKES *Guardians* vii. 124 There they all were, droning away.. as though at some Kafkaesque prize-giving. **1864** BURTON *Scot Abr.* I. i. 54 They were naturally the *prizeholders. **1890** *Cent. Dict.*, **Prize-list.* 1. A detailed list of the winners in any competition for prizes, as a school examination or a flower-show. **1793** *Prize Medal [see 1 c]. **1862** *Catal. Internat. Exhib., Brit.* II. No. 3524 Patent and prize-medal artificial eyes,.. &c. **1808** *Edin. Rev.* XI. 268 The subject of the tides was proposed as the *prize-question by the Academy of Sciences in the year 1740. **1912** *Chambers's Jrnl.* May 329/1 A medal can be verified occasionally if the *prize-roll or some other collateral document is extant. **1893** *Outing* (U.S.) XXII. 146/1 The cockpit in the *prize winners is only large enough to contain the feet of the skipper. **1635** J. HAYWARD tr. *Biondi's Banish'd Virg.* 5 Endowments but handmaides to others farre more *prize-worthy.

†**prize**, *sb.*[2] *Obs.* Forms: α. 6 **pryse**, 6–7 **prise, price**; β. 6–8 **prize**. [Of uncertain origin: possibly the same word as the prec. in a transferred use: cf. Gr. ἆθλον, 'the prize of contest, a prize', also 'a contest, hence conflict, struggle'. The forms are the same as the contemporary ones of PRIZE *sb.*[1]; but, not being found before the last third of the 16th century, this has not the earlier *pris*, *prys*.

In Amyot's Fr. transl., 1559, of *Plutarch's Lives*, Pericles c. x., the Gr. μουσικῆς ἀγῶνα, τοὺς μουσικοὺς ἀγῶνας, lit. 'contest of music', 'the musical contests', are rendered *jeux de prix de (la) musique*, lit. 'prize-plays of music'; for this North, 1579, has not 'prizes' but 'games for musicke'.]

A contest, a match; a public athletic contest; *pl.* the public games of the Greeks and Romans; in late use, a prize-fight. Also *fig.*

α. **1577** NORTHBROOKE *Dicing* (1843) 106, I meane not to condemne such publicke games or prices, as are appointed by the magistrate. **1596** SPENSER *F.Q.* VI. viii. 25 His leg, through his late luckelesse prise, Was crackt in twaine.

β. **1596** SHAKS. *Merch. V.* III. ii. 142 (Qo. 1600) Like one of two contending in a prize That thinks he hath done well in peoples eyes. **1597** BEARD *Theatre God's Judgem.* (1612) 349 The people being gathered together to behold the Fencers prizes were fiftie thousand of them hurt and maimed.. by the Amphitheatre that fell vpon them. **1651** N. BACON *Disc. Govt. Eng.* II. vi. (1739) 34 The Prize was now well begun concerning the Pope's power in England. **1663** PEPYS *Diary* 1 June, Here I saw the first prize I ever saw in my life: and it was between one Mathews, who did beat at all weapons, and one Westwicke. **1669** *Ibid.* 12 Apr., Here we saw a prize fought between a soldier and a country fellow.

b. esp. in phrase ***to play a prize***, to engage in a contest or match, esp. a fencing-match; also *fig.* ***to play one's prize***, to play one's 'game', play one's part.

α. **1592** GREENE *Upst. Courtier* Biij b, Ieatting vp and downe like the Usher of a Fense-schoole about to playe his Pryse. **1597** TOFTE *Laura* I. iii, Like to the blacksome night I may compare My Mistres gowne, when darknes playes his prise. **1605** B. JONSON *Volpone* v. ii, Thou 'hast playd thy prise, my precious Mosca.

β. **1588** SHAKS. *Tit. A.* I. i. 399 (Qo. 1600) So Bascianus, you haue plaid your prize, God giue you ioy sir of your gallant Bride. **1620** *Swetnam Arraign'd* (1880) 55 Cupid, the little Fencer playd his Prize At seuerall weapons in Atlanta's eyes. **1640** BROME *Antipodes* IV. iii, A Woman Fencer, that has plaid a Prize, It seemes, with Losse of blood. *a* **1670** HACKET *Abp. Williams* II. (1692) 147 Attributed to the Chairman's dexterity, who could play his prize in all weapons.

c. in *pl.* ***to play prizes*** (= b); ***to fight prizes***, to fight as gladiators; to engage in a prize-fight, or practise prize-fighting; ***to run prizes***, to run races. Also *fig.*

α. **1565** CALFHILL *Answ. Treat. Crosse* Fij b, When y[e] masters of defence came to play their prises, he [Nero] would beholde them in his ring. **1600** HOLLAND *Livy* VIII. xx. 295 That yeare were erected in the great race called Circus, the Barriers, from whence the horses and their chariots are let forth, when they run their prices. **1642** ROGERS *Naaman* 197 This base carnality plaies her prises one way or other, and dares act her part upon Gods stage.

β. **1596** NASHE *Saffron Walden* Ep. Ded., Wks. (Grosart) III. 6 Dick of the Cow.. who plaied his prizes with the lord Iockey so brauely. **1599** —— *Lenten Stuff* ibid. V. 235 Another.playes his prizes in print. **1607** TOPSELL *Four-f. Beasts* 206 When the Prizes of Germanicus Cæsar were played; there were many Elephantes which acted strange feates or partes. **1663** PEPYS *Diary* 1 June, The New Theatre, which.. is this day begun to be employed by the fencers to play prizes at. *a* **1694** TILLOTSON *Serm.* ix. (1743) I. 222 He does not, like some of the cruel Roman emperors, take pleasure.. to see them play bloody prizes before him. **1702** W. J. *Bruyn's Voy. Levant* vii. 8 A Circus or Amphitheatre, wherein Prizes were anciently Fought. **1712** ARBUTHNOT *John Bull* I. iv, He.. went about through all the country fairs, challenging people to fight prizes, wrestling, and cudgel-play. **1715** LEONI *Palladio's Archit.* (1742) I. 77 The whole People came there together, to see the Athletes (or Fencers and Wrestlers) play their prizes.

d. *Comb.* **prize-playing**, the playing of a prize or prizes; acting as an athlete or gladiator; in quot. *attrib.* = won in athletic contests. See also PRIZE-FIGHT, -FIGHTER.

1647 R. STAPYLTON *Juvenal* 36 Our nointed clowne prize-playing ornaments Or a poore basket-scrambling gown contents [*L.* Rusticus ille tuus sumit trechedipna, Quirine, Et aromatico fert niceteria collo.]

prize (praɪz), *sb.*[3] Forms: α. 4–7 **prise**, 5–7 **price**, 6–7 **pryse**. β. 6–7 **pryze**, 6– **prize**. [a. F. *prise* the action of taking, capture, esp. the capture of a ship, the booty taken, a captured ship or cargo = Pr., Sp., It. *presa*:—early Rom. *prēsa*:—*prensa*, L. *præhensa*, fem. sb. from pa. pple. of L. *præhendĕre* to seize: see PREHEND. (In origin, a special sense of PRISE *sb.*[1], which late in 16th c. began to be phonetically spelt *prize*, and thus to be identified with PRIZE *sb.*[1])]

†**1.** The action of taking; capture, seizure. *Obs.*

[**1414** *Act 2 Hen. V*, Stat. I. c. 6 Quils.. facent plein enformacion.. a le conservatour de le port.. de la dite prise et de la quantite dicelle.]

c **1475** *Harl. Contin. Higden* (Rolls) VIII. 576 The cyte of Constantynople.. was taken by the Turke.. by whiche pryse Cristen feyth perysshed in Grece. **1481** CAXTON *Godeffroy* lxxxii. 130 By the prise of this cyte. *Ibid.* clxxxv. 271 *heading*, Of the pryse and takynge of Iherusalem. **1611** CHAPMAN *Iliad* IV. 332 Age, that all men overcomes, hath made his prise on thee. **1648** J. RAYMOND *Voy. Italy* 77 Opposite to this is the Arch of Titus Vespasian, erected to him for his prise of Jerusalem. *a* **1649** WINTHROP *New Eng.* (1853) II. 74 He said he got them by trade, but it was suspected he got them by prize. **1721** DE FOE *Moll Flanders* (1854) 167 This [stealing of a bundle of plate, jewellery, &c.] was the greatest and the worst prize that ever I was concerned in.

2. †**a.** Anything seized or captured by force, especially in war; booty, plunder, prey; a captive of war. *Obs.* exc. as in b.

α. *c* **1386** CHAUCER *Pars. T.* ¶281, I wol departe my prise or my praye by deliberacion. **1390** GOWER *Conf.* I. 246 Gret pris upon the werre he hadde. *c* **1430** *Hymns Virg.* (1867) 53, I haue brouȝt hidir manye a greet price Hidir into helle of al kinde of man. *c* **1450** *Merlin* II. 240 Thei hadden gete the richest prise thut euer was sein in her comynge. *a* **1578** LINDESAY (Pitscottie) *Chron. Scot.* (S.T.S.) II. 72 Returnit hame againe witht great pryce of men and goodis. *c* **1611** CHAPMAN *Iliad* I. 135 Woulst thou maintaine in sure abode Thine owne prise, and sleight me of mine? **1693** *Mem. Cnt. Teckely* I. 40 To shelter the Prises which the Croats had taken from the Turks. *a* **1734** NORTH *Exam.* I. iii. §154 (1740) 222 His Neighbour's Pigs and Hens used to be his Prise, when he could catch them.

β. **1596** SPENSER *F.Q.* IV. iv. 8 His owne prize, Whom formerly he had in battell wonne. **1608** D. T[UVIL] *Ess. Pol. & Mor.* 69 Many have had the victory snatcht.. and themselves become the dishonourable pryze of whome they had earst most honourably surpryz'd. *a* **1735** ARBUTHNOT *Most Wonderful Wonder* Misc. Wks. 1751 I. 195 He took Shipping afterwards with his Prize, and safely landed at Tower-Wharf. **1865** EARL OF DERBY *Iliad* I 220 Ev'n from thy tent, myself, to bear thy prize, The fair Briseis.

b. *esp.* A ship or property captured at sea in virtue of the rights of war; a legal capture at sea.

α. **1512** in Rymer *Foedera* XIII. 328/2 One Shippe Royall .. with the Ordinance and Apparell of every such Prise that shall fortune to be taken by theym. **1588** GREENE *Perimedes* 9 Carrying away, both vessell and marriners as a pryse. **1634** SIR T. HERBERT *Trav.* 188 Calicut, a great Citie ten leagues whence we tooke our price [(1638) 302 prize]. **1672** C. MANNERS in *12th Rep. Hist. MSS. Comm.* App. v. 24 Wee take every day some considerable pryses, which may pay for the warr.

fig. **1593** SHAKS. *Lucr.* 279 Desire my Pilot is, Beautie my prise.

β. **1608** SHAKS. *Per.* IV. i. 93 *Pira.* 2. A prize, a prize. **1613** PURCHAS *Pilgrimage* (1614) 549 They took a prize of nine hundred tunnes. **1615** G. SANDYS *Trav.* 51 The gallies.. towing at their sternes three or foure little vessels no bigger then fisher boats. A ridiculous glory, and a prize to be ashamed of. **1697** DAMPIER *Voy. round World* (1699) 174 We were now 6 Sail, 2 Men of War, 2 Tenders, a Fire-ship and the Prize. **1748** *Anson's Voy.* II. iv. 164 The Commodore ordered.. his first Lieutenant, to take possession of the prize. **1879** LUBBOCK *Addr. Pol. & Educ.* vii. 137 Steamers .. would be the real prizes—if prizes are to be made at all.

c. without *a* or *pl.* Property seized as in war; esp. in the phr. ***to make prize***. Also *fig.*

[In this and the following, *prize* seems to hover between sense 1 'capture, seizure', and the concrete sense 2.]

1594 SHAKS. *Rich. III*, III. vii. 187 (Qo. 1597) A beauty-waining and distressed widow.. Made prise and purchase of his lustfull eye. **1601** J. WHEELER *Treat. Comm.* 68 Diuerse ships.. had beene taken at sea, and the goods therein made prize, and confiscate. **1725** DE FOE *Voy. round World* (1840) 9 We resolved to make prize of it, as in a time of war. **1755** MAGENS *Insurances* I. 496 Prize or not Prize, must be determined by Courts of Admiralty, belonging to the Power whose Subjects make the Capture. **1798** FERRIAR *Illustr. Sterne* vi. 182 He made prize of all the good thoughts that came in his way. **1845** STEPHEN *Comm. Laws Eng.* (1874) II. 18 It is.. necessary that the vessel should have been condemned as prize, by legal sentence. **1885** RIGBY in *Law Rep. 29 Ch. Div.* 286 On matters of prize the judgment could be looked to.

d. In ***good, fair, free, just, lawful prize***, with reference to the legality of the seizure. Also *fig.*

1550 *Reg. Privy Council Scot.* I. 102 The samin schip and gudis.. in caise scho wer nocht fund just prise. **1561** *Ibid.* 162 Decernyng the schippis and gudis.. to be lauchfull pryse. **1610** B. JONSON *Alch.* III. iii, How now? Good prize? **1634** SIR T. HERBERT *Trav.* 185 [The junk] was a good prize and worth the keeping. *a* **1680** BUTLER *Rem.* (1759) I. 168 Plagiary Privateers, That all Mens Sense and Fancy seize, And make free Prize of what they please? **1747** GRAY *Cat* 41 Not all that tempts.. your heedless hearts is lawful prize. **1836** ALISON *Hist. Europe* xlii. §52 (1847) IX. 362 The English Admiralty courts.. declared good prize neutral vessels carrying colonial produce from the enemy's colonies to the mother state. **1854** J. S. C. ABBOTT *Napoleon* (1855) I. xxii. 353 If the command was unheeded, a broadside followed, and the peaceful merchantman became lawful prize.

3. *attrib.* and *Comb.*, as ***prize brandy, cause, goods, property, ship***; **prize agent**, an agent appointed for the sale of prizes taken in maritime war; so ***prize agency***; **prize court**, a department of the admiralty court, which adjudicates concerning prizes; **prize crew**, a crew of seamen placed on board a prize ship to bring her into port; **prize-list**, a list of persons entitled to receive prize-money on the capture of a ship; **prize-master**, an officer appointed to command a prize ship; **prize-office** (see quot. 1706). See also PRIZE-MONEY.

1806 A. DUNCAN *Nelson* 215 The abuses of *prize agency. **1802** NELSON *Parl. Sp.* 21 Dec. *ibid.* 213 Transactions.. with any of the boards or *prize agents. **1867** SMYTH *Sailor's Word-bk.* s.v. *Agent, Prize agent*, one appointed for the sale of prizes, and nominated in equal numbers by the commander, the officers, and the ship's company. **1905** *Whitaker's Almanack* 211 Navy and Prize Agents. **1667** DRYDEN & DAVENANT *Tempest* II. i, This is *prize brandy. **1747** *(title)* Observations on the Course of Proceeding in Admiralty Courts in *Prize Causes. **1810** J. F. POTT *(title)* Observations on Matters of Prize, and the Practice of the Admiralty *Prize Courts. **1830** MARRYAT *King's Own* xxxiv, The *prize crew of the Aspasia. **1625** *Impeachm. Dk. Buckhm.* (Camden) 32 To hasten the raising of monies by sales of *prise goods here. **1711** *Act 10 Anne* c. 22 Preamble, Several considerable Quantities of Prize-Cocoa, Sugars, Indigo, and other Prize-Goods. **1826** KENT *Comm.* (1873) I. xvii. 357, I know of no other definition of prize goods.. than that they are goods taken on high seas *jure belli*, out of the hands of the enemy. **1794** NELSON in Nicolas *Disp.* (1845) I. 417 You want a *Prize-List for one vessel taken by Tartar and myself. **1867** SMYTH *Sailor's Word-bk.*, *Prize-list*, a return of all the persons on board.. at the time a capture is made; those who may be absent on duty are included. **1760** in *Essex Inst. Hist. Coll.* (1911) XLVII. 125 He put a *Prize Master (as he called him) and three more of his Hands on board the Sloop. **1800** *Suppl. to Chron.* in *Asiat. Ann. Reg.* 144/1 The prize-master informed the unfortunate people who were sent on board the Arab, that there was abundance of provisions and water. **1893** *Dict. Nat. Biog.* XXXIV. 152/1 Louis was appointed prize-master of the Phœnix. **1916** in *Outlook* (N.Y.) 9 Aug. 823/2 Prizes cannot be brought into the waters of the United States for the purpose of laying up by a prize master. **1931** *Times Lit. Suppl.* 16 July 555/3 For his conduct as a prizemaster in the captured Genéreux.. he was advanced to commander. **1937** C. S. FORESTER *Happy Return* I. vii. 80 Gerard, whom he had left on board as prizemaster, had served in a Liverpool slaver. **1664** PEPYS *Diary* 22 Nov., To speak with my lord about our *Prise Office business. **1706** PHILLIPS, *Prize-Office*, an Office appointed for the Sale of Ships taken from an Enemy as lawful Prize. **1710** *Boston News-Let.* 26 June 2/2 On the said day arrived Her Majesties Ship the Feversham.. with Col. Hunter, our Governour, and with him a *Prize ship of 300 Tons. *a* **1722** FOUNTAINHALL *Decisions* (1759) I. 333 The oft debated cause of the Capers of the two prize Danish ships. **1863** DICEY *Federal St.* I. 87 The officer in command of the 'Erie' when sent as a prize-ship to New York. **1799** NELSON in Nicolas *Disp.* (1845) IV. 92, I send you a cask of sugar, such as I think you mean by saying *prize-sugar.

prize, prise (praɪz), *sb.*[4] Also 6 **pryse**. [ME. *prise*, a. F. *prise* a taking hold, grasp: see prec.]

1. An instrument used for prizing (see PRIZE *v.*[3]); a lever. Now *dial.*

13.. *St. Erkenwolde* in Horstm. *Altengl. Leg.* (1881) 267 Wyȝt werkemen.. Putten prises þer to, pinchid one vnder, Kaghtene by þe corners w[t] crowes of yrne. **1541** *Aberdeen Regr.* (1844) I. 176 Item, ane pryse, with ane turning staf. *a* **1825** FORBY *Voc. E. Anglia*, *Prise*, a lever used for the purpose of forcing. This instrument is sometimes called a pry. **1825** JAMIESON, *Prise, Prize*, a lever. **1895** T. PINNOCK *Black Co. Ann.* (E.D.D.), Run, fetch a prise, quick to lift on.

2. The act of prizing; leverage, purchase.

1835 KIRBY *Hab. & Inst. Anim.* II. xvii. 150 Those plumes which so ornament the wings of birds, and give them as it were more prise upon the air. **1842** J. AITON *Domest. Econ.* (1857) 166 This spade is.. rounded considerably in the back, to afford the better prize. **1893** F. ADAMS *New Egypt* 88 Is it fanciful to ascribe this curious upward movement of a river-course to the prise given by it, in its enormous stretch in a straight line from north to south, to the diurnal whirl of the earth from west to east?

3. *Comb.*, as **prize-beam**, a beam used in packing tobacco; **prize-bolt**: see quot.

1800 W. TATHAM *Hist. & Pract. Ess. Tobacco* 52 As all tobacco must be in due case when it is put into the hogs-head, so must the prize-beam retain its depressed position until two distinct ends are attained, to wit, that of giving a compact consistency to the cake [etc.]. **1875** KNIGHT *Dict. Mech.*, *Prise-bolts*, the projecting bolts at the rear of a mortar-bed or garrison gun-carriage under which the handspikes are inserted for training and maneuvering the piece.

prize (praɪz), *v.*[1] Forms: α. 4–7 **prise**, 4–6 (*Sc.* -8) **pryse** (also *Sc.* 4 **priss, pryss**, 4–5 **pris, prys**, 6 **pryis(s), prysse**. β. 6– **prize**. γ. See PRICE *v.* [ME. a. OF. *prisier*, F. *priser*, levelled form of OF. *preisier*, PRAISE *v.* (under which see the origin and form-history). In Sc., from the 14th century, *prise* was preferred to *praise* in all its senses (see sense 4 below); but English at length differentiated *praise* and *prise*, retaining *praise* in the sense of F. *louer*, L. *laudare*, and appropriating *prise* to senses connected with the sbs. *pris, prise, price*, and *prize*. In these senses it has received further differentiation, becoming PRICE in the commercial sense of 'set a price to', and remaining as *prize* only in sense 3 below. (But this last differentiation has hardly yet been completed, for in dialect, local, and individual use, *to prise* or *prize* is often said instead of *to price*, even when the latter is written: cf. the distinction of sb. and vb. in *advice, to advise, house, to house, use, to use*.)]

I. †**1.** *trans.* To value, to estimate the (relative) value of; to estimate, esteem, account as worth (so much); to account, reckon. *Obs.* (or *arch.*)

α. **1375** (MS. 1487) BARBOUR *Bruce* VI. 505 He wald nocht priss his liff a stra, With-thi he vengeans on hym mycht ta. **1500–20** DUNBAR *Poems* xix. 44 A prodigall man I am so prysit. *a* **1574** EARL GLENCAIRN *Ep. fr. Hermit of Alareit* 11 Our stait hypocrisie they prysse.. Sayand, That we are heretikes. **1586** A. DAY *Eng. Secretary* I. (1625) 146, I prise your worthinesse at farre greater value. **1599** SHAKS. *Much Ado* III. i. 90 Hauing so swift and excellent a wit As she is prisde to haue. *c* **1611** CHAPMAN *Iliad* VII. 38, I am thy brother, and thy life, with mine is euenly prisde. **1724** RAMSAY *Vision* vii, Devysing, and prysing, Freidom at ony rate.

β. **1596** *Edw. III*, II. i, If on my beauty, take it if thou canst; Though little, I do prize it ten times less. **1633** P. FLETCHER *Purple Isl.* IX. xiv, He in himself priz'd things as mean and base, Which yet in others great and glorious seem'd. **1642** FULLER *Holy & Prof. St.* III. xxv. 230 Oh that their profession were but as highly prized, as their estate is valued.

†**2.** To estimate or fix the money value of; to value, appraise; to fix the price of (a thing for sale). *Obs.* in literary use: see APPRAISE *v.*, PRICE *v.*

α. *c* **1440** *Promp. Parv.* 414/1 Prysyn, or settyn a pryce, *taxo,.. licitor.* **1445** *Aberdeen Regr.* (1844) I. 14 They sal sell na flesche quhill it be prisit be the sworne prisaris. *c* **1475** *Rauf Coilȝear* 254 Thair may thow sell.. als deir as thow will prys. **1530** PALSGR. 666/2, I prise ware, I sette a price of a thyng what it is worthe, *je aprise.* **1535** COVERDALE *Zech.* xi. 12 So they wayed downe xxx. syluer pens, yᵉ value that I was prysed at. **1611** BIBLE *ibid.* 13 A goodly price, that I was prised at. **1625** PURCHAS *Pilgrims* II. x. iv. 1709 *margin*, There Pearles are prised according to the Caracts which they weigh. **1713** S. SEWALL *Diary* 2 June, Owen took a Cow of Veisy pris'd at £4. 0. 0.

β. **1599** H. BUTTES *Dyets drie Dinner* M iv, The Romanes prized this fish at a wonderfull high rate. **1623** WHITBOURNE *Newfoundland* 59 [They] were there prized to be worth two shillings sixepence apiece. **1698** *Phil. Trans.* XX. 442, I will procure you one of the Catalogues of Manuscripts, which is prized by the Delegates of our Press, at One Pound Two Shillings. **1709** HUGHES *Tatler* No. 113 ¶26 The Whole [goods] are to be set up and prized by Charles Bubbleboy, who is to open the Auction with a Speech. **1755** JOHNSON, *Prize*, to rate; to value at a certain price.

†**b.** To be the price of; to equal in value. *Obs. rare.*

1596 SPENSER *Hymn Heav. Love* 175 How can we thee requite for all this good? Or what can prize that thy most precious blood?

†**c.** To offer as the price, to stake. **d.** To offer a price for, bid for. *Obs. rare.*

c **1590** GREENE *Fr. Bacon* xiii. 41 Thou'rt worthy of the title of a squire, That durst, for proof, of thy affection And for thy mistress' favour, prize thy blood. **1590** C'TESS PEMBROKE *Antonie* 264 But terror here and horror, naught is seene: And present death prizing our life each hower [*orig.* Et la presente mort nous marchande à tous coups].

3. To value or esteem highly, to think much of. (The current sense.)

α. **1375** BARBOUR *Bruce* I. 239 And suld think fredome mar to pryss Than all the gold in warld that Is. *c* **1470** *Gol. & Gaw.* 1207, I aught as prynce him to prise for his prouese. *c* **1615** SIR W. MURE *Sonn.* ix, In bewty, (loue's sueit object), ravischt sight Doth some peculiar perfectioun pryse [*rime* lyes]. **1665** BOYLE *Occas. Refl.* VI. iii, That we.. prise many [customs] of our own onely because we never consider'd them.

β. *c* **1586** C'TESS PEMBROKE *Ps.* CXXXIX. x, My God, how I these studies prize, That doe thy hidden workings show! **1618** E. ELTON *Exp. Rom. vii.* (1622) 136 A blessing that cannot be sufficiently prized. **1681** FLAVEL *Meth. Grace* xxxv. 583 When we would express the value of a thing, we say, we prize it as our eyes. **1715** POPE *Iliad* I. 237, I.. prize at equal rate Thy short-liv'd friendship, and thy groundless hate. *a* **1720** SEWEL *Hist. Quakers* (1795) I. 53 Prize your time now, while you have it. **1891** *Speaker* 11 July 36/2 The Swiss seem more and more to prize.. the Referendum and the Initiative.

γ. **1375–1643** [see PRICE *v.* 5].

†**b.** With negative: Not to value at all, to think nothing of, care nothing for. *Obs.*

c **1600** SHAKS. *Sonn.* cxliii, Not prizing her poore infants discontent. **1611** —— *Wint. T.* IV. iv. 386 Had [I] force and knowledge More then was euer mans, I would not prize them Without her Loue.

II. †**4.** To commend or extol the worth, excellence, or merit of; = PRAISE *v.* 3. *Obs. northern.*

α. **1375** BARBOUR *Bruce* x. 776 Of this deid,.. The Erll wes prisit gretumly. **1456** SIR G. HAYE *Law Arms* (S.T.S.) 11 Ilke man did sum thing, that was mekle to lowe and to pris. **1500–20** DUNBAR *Poems* xliii. 45 Sic ladyis wyiss, Thay ar to pryis. **1567** *Satir. Poems Reform.* v. 16 Gif him all thankis.. And pryse his name with all ȝour micht.

prize, prise, *v.*² Forms: α. 6 pryse, 6–7 prise; β. 7– prize. [f. PRIZE *sb.*³] *trans.* To seize, take, capture; to seize as forfeited, to confiscate. *Obs.* exc. as in b.

α. **1535** COVERDALE *Dan.* iii. 29 All people.. which speake eny blasphemy agaynst the God of Sydrac, Misac and Abdenago, shal dye, and their houses shalbe prysed. **1581** LAMBARDE *Eiren.* II. iv. (1588) 177 If any bee afterward found offending,.. their armour and weapon shall be prised,.. to the use of the Queenes Maiestie. *c* **1611** CHAPMAN *Iliad* XI. 385 To kill the five Hippasides And prise their arms.

β. **1602** WARNER *Alb. Eng.* x. lv. (1612) 245 The Queene of Scots from Ours almost her Crowne and life had prizde.

b. *spec.* To make a prize or seizure of; to seize (a ship or her cargo) as a prize of war.

α. **1568** C. WATSON *Polyb.* 60 b, The Romans being both more in number and valianter men, prised her [the Rhodians' ship] without labour and toke the Rhodian. **1600** HAKLUYT *Voy.* (1810) III. 236 The one [ship].. being prised near Silley by a ship of which I am part owner. **1622** MALYNES *Anc. Law-Merch.* 145 If it happen a Ship to be prised for debt or otherwise to bee forfeited, yet the Mariners hire is to be payed.

β. **1886** *American* XII. 67 It was explained that the *David J. Adams* was prized for concealing her name and her sailing-port.

prize, prise (praɪz), *v.*³ [f. PRIZE *sb.*⁴]

1. *trans.* To raise or move by force of leverage; to force up; *esp.* to force open in this way.

1686 PLOT *Staffordsh.* 344 They easily prize up bushes, furses, or broom by the very roots. **1688** R. HOLME *Armoury* III. xx. (Roxb.) 246/1 The Forked end is strucken deep in the ground each side the root and so drawn or prised vp. **1808** JAMIESON, *To prize up*, to force open, to press up a lock or door. **1818** SCOTT *Hrt. Midl.* vi, The door was.. assailed with sledge-hammers, iron crows [etc.].. with which they prized, heaved and battered for some time with little effect. **1822** —— *Pirate* vii, There stands yonder a chest, from which the lid has been just prized off. **1840** DICKENS *Barn. Rudge* lxiv, Many men.. were seen.. striving to prize it [the jail door] down with crowbars. **1897** *Pall Mall Mag.* June 254 The lock was broken, and the lid bore signs of having been prised.

fig. **1824** PRIOR *Burke* (1854) 232 Thus this famous measure.. became the lever by which to prize its authors out of office.

2. a. To compress (cured tobacco) in a hogshead or box. *Southern U.S.*

1724 H. JONES *Present State Virginia* 40 [They] by Degrees *prize* or press with proper Engines into great Hogsheads. **1867** SMYTH *Sailor's Word-bk., Prizing*,.. also, the act of pressing or squeezing an article into its package, so that its size may be reduced in stowage. **1889** BRUCE *Plant. Negro* 183 To the moment that the leaf is prized in the hogshead. **1902** *U.S. Dept. Agric. Farmers' Bull.* No. 60. 17 The leaves.. are tied into hands and bulked down for a short time, after which they are 'prized' into hogs-heads.

b. To pack (persons) into a narrow space.

1799 W. BECKFORD *Let.* 16 Aug. in J. W. Oliver *Life W. Beckford* (1932) x. 269 Assure Lady Heard that she shall not be worn to death with seeing Sights,.. nor prysed into rumbling Carriages.

Hence **prizing, prising** *vbl. sb.*; also *attrib.*

1867 [see 2]. **1890** *Daily News* 14 July 2/8 This pad prevented the splintering of wood, although the prising power would be the same. **1891** ATKINSON *Last of Giant-Killers* 166 More hammering and more prising with the gavelocks and crowbars.

prizeable: see PRIZABLE.

prized (praɪzd), *ppl. a.* [f. PRIZE *v.*¹ + -ED¹.]

1. Greatly valued; highly esteemed.

1538 in *Lett. Suppress. Monasteries* (Camden) 209 The prysed memoryes and perpetuall renowned factes of the famouse princes of Israel. **1856** KANE *Arct. Expl.* II. xvii. 180 Two of our most prized comrades. **1873** EMERSON *Let.* 3 May in *Westm. Gaz.* 7 Aug. (1906) 3/3, I am glad you have seen my prized friend, your Uncle George.

†**2.** = PRICED. In quot. 1642, High-priced, expensive. *Obs.* or *dial.*

1642 HARCOURT in *Macm. Mag.* XLV. 289/2 Some prittee small laces, but not prized ones; for I will spare your pursse as much as may be. **1682** FLAVEL *Fear* 44 'Tis a low priz'd commodity in my eyes. **1710** HEARNE *Collect.* 19 Mar. (O.H.S.) II. 362 The priz'd Catalogue wᶜʰ I have seen. (*Priced* is still so pronounced by some.)

prize-fight (ˈpraɪzˌfaɪt). [app. a late back-formation from next.] A public contest between prize-fighters; a boxing-match for money.

1824 W. N. BLANE *Excursion* 508 There had just been a 'prize fight' well attended by noblemen and gentlemen. **1857** HUGHES *Tom Brown* II. v, The stories he had heard of men being killed in prize-fights rose up horribly before him. **1898** *Daily News* 18 Nov. 4/5 Sir John Bridge said this contest was not, in his opinion, a sparring match, but a prize-fight. He held that fighting for money was a prize-fight, and that was illegal.

prize-fighter (ˈpraɪzˌfaɪtə(r)). [orig. f. PRIZE *sb.*² + FIGHTER, from the phr. 'to fight a prize' or 'prizes'; in later use associated with PRIZE *sb.*¹]

†**a.** *orig.* One who 'fought a prize' (see PRIZE *sb.*²); one who engaged in a public fighting-match or contest. *Obs.* **b.** In mod. use, A professional pugilist or boxer, who fights publicly for a prize or stake; 'one that fights publicly for a reward' (J.).

1703 LUTTRELL *Brief Rel.* (1857) V. 316 Yesterday, one Cook, a prize fighter, was condemned at the Old Baily for killing a constable last May fair was twelve month. **1725** *St. Mary le Bow, Durham, Par. Reg.*, Jane, daughter of Thomas Barrett, Prize fighter, bap. 28 April. **1727** POPE, etc. *Art Sinking* 122 It is proposed.. that Mr. Figg with his prize-fighters, and Violante with the rope-dancers, be admitted in partnership. **1753** SMOLLETT *Ct. Fathom* (1784) 117/2 The sword.. he brandished over the chevalier's head, with the dexterity of an old prize-fighter. **1796** MORSE *Amer. Geog.* II. 104 The encouragement given to prize-fighters and boxers. **1828** SCOTT *F.M. Perth* xiv. **1861** *Sat. Rev.* 7 Dec. 587 He.. had the wit and luck to bring over that bulky prizefighter [Heenan] to make a sensation in England.

fig. **1829** CARLYLE *Misc.* (1857) II. 17 Not that we would say Voltaire was a mere prize-fighter.

So ˈ**prize-ˌfighting** *sb.* and *a.*

1720 SWIFT *T. Tub, Hist. Martin* §2 Hence the origine of that genteel custom of Prize-fighting. *a* **1763** BYROM *Verses Figg & Sutton* i, Long was the great Figg, by the prize Fighting Swains, Sole Monarch acknowledg'd of Marybone Plains. **1796** MORSE *Amer. Geog.* II. 108 The barbarous diversions of boxing and prize-fighting. **1878** *N. Amer. Rev.* CXXVII. 289 Countries that have not been civilized by prize-fighting. **1890** *Review of Rev.* II. 510/2 Prize-fighting in the ordinary sense of the term—i.e., a fight for money with fists, fought out to the bitter end—is absolutely illegal.

prizeless (ˈpraɪzlɪs), *a.* [f. PRIZE *sb.*¹ + -LESS.] Without a prize; not having gained a prize.

1897 *Westm. Gaz.* 11 Feb. 3/2 The kind old lady who went about consoling the prizeless dogs at Cruft's. **1899** *Ibid.* 3 Aug. 2/3 On the return of Harry and Robert home from school; Robert laden with prizes, Harry prizeless.

prizeless, obs. form of PRICELESS.

prize-list: see PRIZE *sb.*¹ 4 b, *sb.*³ 3.

prizeman (ˈpraɪzmən). [f. PRIZE *sb.*¹ + MAN *sb.*¹] A man who wins a prize (esp. for excelling in learning or art). Hence ˈ**prizewoman**.

1800 *Cambr. Univ. Cal.* Title-p., A list of the.. Medallists and Prize-men. *Ibid.* 15 Members' Prizemen. *Ibid.* 22 Seatonian Prizemen. **1834** *Edin. Rev.* LIX. 133 The mere prize-man is often dismissed in a few lines. **1856** LEVER *Martins of Cro' M.* xiv, He's more than that.. he is the great prize man of the year in Trinity. **1896** *Current Hist.* (Buffalo) VI. 463 In his third year he [Lord Kelvin] came out as second wrangler and Smith's prizeman. **1940** *Horizon* Jan. 61 Miss Pitter, a Hawthornden prizewoman.

†ˈ**prizement.** *Obs.* Also 6 prisement, 7 pricement. [f. PRIZE *v.*¹ + -MENT.] The act of 'prizing' or valuing; valuation, appraisement.

1566 *Richmond Wills* (Surtees) 189 All theis to remayne at the house thare withoute prisement so longe as any of the Phillipson name shall dwell at the said house. **1631** WEEVER *Anc. Fun. Mon.* 274 According to the pricement at the suppression. *a* **1700** in Keble *Life Bp. Wilson* vi. (1863) 203 When sufficient men are sworn to prize children's goods.. the executors.. must take all things according to the prizement.

ˈ**prize-ˌmoney.** **a.** [f. PRIZE *sb.*³] Money realized by the sale of a prize (esp. one taken in maritime war), and distributed among the captors.

1748 *Anson's Voy.* III. i. 299 It was.. with.. difficulty that the prize money, which the *Gloucester* had taken.., was secured, and.. the prize goods.. were entirely lost. **1749** *New Hampsh. Probate Rec.* (1916) III. 733, I give to Doctor Robert Ratsey all my Waidges, Prize money, [etc.]. **1757** J. LIND *Lett. Navy* i. 23 All ships are equally entitled to their share of prize-money. **1800** J. WEBBE in Gurw. *Wellington's Desp.* (1837) I. 128 Likely to obtain neither fame nor prize money. **1887** BESANT *The World went* xxiv, The prize-money.. amounted to a very pretty sum.

b. [f. PRIZE *sb.*¹] Money awarded as a prize or as prizes.

1934 in WEBSTER. **1961** *N.Y. Times* 24 Jan. 23 He won the Masters, the United States Open and a record $80,738 in prize money. **1973** M. AMIS *Rachel Papers* 194, I was entering a national under-21 short-story competition, sponsored by one of the colour magazines. With the prize-money we might just have a few days in Paris ourselves.

prizer¹ (ˈpraɪzə(r)). Now *rare*. Forms: 5 pryzer, 5–6 prysar(e, 6 prisar, pryser, -or, 6–7 priser, 7 prisor, prizor, 7– prizer. [f. PRIZE *v.*¹ + -ER¹.] One who prizes.

†**1.** One who estimates the value, or determines the price, of something; an appraiser. *Obs.*

1427 in *Trans. Stirling Nat. Hist. & Archæol. Soc.* (1902) 57 The pain of the Pryzer, if he be negligent & punish not. *c* **1440** *Promp. Parv.* 413/2 Prysare, or settar at price, yn a merket, or oþer placys. **1505** *Berwick Reg.* in *Hist. MSS. Comm., Var. Collect.* I. 7 No bowcher.. shall breke nor cut out any flysh to sell exsept the said prysers be ther present. **1549** *Records of Elgin* (New Spald. Cl.) I. 97 Alexander Wynchester [and five others] electit prisers of flesche. **1552** in Picton *L'pool Munic. Rec.* (1883) I. 59 Assessors and Prysors. *a* **1625** SIR H. FINCH *Law* (1636) 472 The prisors to take them of the price if they prise too high. **1654** H. L'ESTRANGE *Chas. I* (1655) 194 Charges of driving to be set by a priser of the forrage.

2. †**a.** One who values or esteems something at a specified (high, low, etc.) rate. *Obs.* **b.** One who values or esteems something highly.

c **1611** CHAPMAN *Iliad* XVI. 762 Too much prizer of thyself. **1657** *Mrs. Hobson's Brass in Chancel of Clewer Ch.*, A despiser of yᵉ world and a high Prizer of yᵉ Lord Christ. **1691** NORRIS *Pract. Disc.* 33 But now, are the Children of Light such Prizers of Time?

ˈ**prizer**². *arch.* Also 6 priser. **a.** [f. PRIZE *sb.*² + -ER¹.] One who engages in a 'prize' or contest; a prize-fighter.

1599 B. JONSON *Cynthia's Rev.* IV. v, I haue a plot vpon these prizers. **1600** SHAKS. *A.Y.L.* II. iii. 8 Why would you be so fond to ouercome The bonnie priser of the humorous Duke? **1679** MRS. BEHN *Feign'd Curtizan* v, And fought like prizers, not as angry rivals. **1823** SCOTT *Quentin D.* xxxv,

You shall be fought for in real *mêlée*. Only..the successful prizer shall be a gentleman. **1845** BROWNING *Luria* I. 52 The brace of prizers fairly matched Poleaxe with poleaxe.

b. [PRIZE *sb.*[1]] A prize-winner.

1846 E. COPLESTON *Let.* 9 Dec. in W. J. Copleston *Mem. E. Copleston* (1851) 188 My delight was not a little heightened, by seeing my horned countrymen of North Devon among the 'prizers'.

prize-ring (ˈpraɪz,rɪŋ). [f. after PRIZE-FIGHT: see RING *sb.*[1] 14.] A ring or enclosed space (now a square area enclosed by poles and ropes) for prize-fighting; hence *transf.* the practice of prize-fighting (cf. *the turf* = horse-racing); also *attrib.* belonging to prize-fighting, characteristic of prize-fighters.

1822 *Sunday Times* 20 Oct. 4/2 Bill Cropley, one of the heroes of the prize-ring, but now a hard-working coal-heaver. **1840** BLAINE *Encycl. Rur. Sports* §4020 Two of the members of 'the ancient prize-ring' in actual combat. **1848** THACKERAY *Van. Fair* lxiv, Captain Rook with his horse-jockey jokes and prize-ring slang. **1861** J. CRAWFURD in *Trans. Ethnol. Soc.* I. 367 One of this race had nearly carried off the championship of England in the prize-ring. **1884** *Times* (weekly ed.) 17 Oct. 2/2 Better..not to introduce into political controversy the language of the prize-ring.

prizewoman: see PRIZEMAN.

prizing (ˈpraɪzɪŋ), *vbl. sb.*[1] Forms: see PRIZE *v.*[1] [f. PRIZE *v.*[1] + -ING[1].] The action of PRIZE *v.*[1]; †determination of price or value, appraising; valuing, estimation (*obs.*); high estimation.

c **1440** *Promp. Parv.* 414/1 Prysynge, *li(ci)tatio.* **1499** *Exch. Rolls Scotl.* XI. 436 The prising of the said landis. **1552** HULOET, Prisynge or settynge pryce, *licitatio.* **1678–9** LUTTRELL *Brief Rel.* (1857) I. 6 The latter end of this month came out his majesties proclamation for prizeing of wines. [The proclamation has 'to set the Prices of all kinds of Wines'.] **1907** *Daily Chron.* 9 Oct. 6/4 It was a fit prize for a feat that stood above all prizing.

prizing, *vbl. sb.*[2], [3]: see PRIZE *v.*[2], [3].

‖**pro** (prəʊ), *sb.*, *prep.*, and *a.* The L. preposition *prō* before (of place), in front of, for, on behalf of, instead of, in return for, on account of, etc. [Cognate with Gr. πρό forward, before, in front of, earlier than, Skr. *prá* before; more remotely related to OTeut. *for, fora*, Eng. *for, fore.*]

A. as *prep.* in various Latin phrases, more or less used in Eng. (See also PRO AND CON.)

1. pro ˈaris et ˈfocis, for altars and hearths; for the sake of, or on behalf of, religion and home.

1621 BURTON *Anat. Mel.* III. iv. I. iii. (1676) 398/1 When I see two superstitious Orders contend *pro aris & focis*, with such have and hold, *de lana caprina.* **1741** HUME *Ess.* iv. 48, I wou'd only perswade Men not to contend, as if they were fighting *pro aris & focis.* **1859** LOWELL *Biglow P.* 12 They serve cheerfully in the great army which fights even unto death *pro aris et focis.*

2. pro ˈbono ˈpublico, for the public good. Now freq. used as a signature to an open letter (as to a newspaper).

a **1726** GILBERT *Cases in Law & Equity* (1760) 113 It is *pro bono publico*, in which they are included. **1914** 'I. HAY' *Lighter Side School Life* vii. 194 Fiery old gentlemen write.. to say that in their young days boys were boys and not molly-coddles. Old friends like *Materfamilias, Pro Bono Publico*,.. rush into the fray... There is quite a riot of pseudonyms. **1922** JOYCE *Ulysses* 306 Someone..ought to write a letter *pro bono publico* to the papers about the muzzling order for a dog the like of that. **1973** G. BEARE *Snake on Grave* viii. 40 He would..write a letter to *The Times* which he would sign 'Pro Bono Publico'. **1977** *New Yorker* 12 Sept. 133/1 A politician who speaks for an important industry is considered very much pro bono publico.

3. pro conˈfesso, for or as confessed or admitted: chiefly in *Law*.

1631 in *Crt. & Times Chas. I* (1848) II. 141 As if they had taken it *pro confesso* that he is living. **1776** *Claim of Roy Rada Churn* 17/1 in *Trial J. Fowke*, etc., The Court..had informed them, if they did not [support their case by affidavit], the negative of the question put would be taken *pro confesso.*

4. pro ˈforma (-â) (also with hyphen, and as one word), for form's sake; as a matter of form; in the way of formality. Also *attrib.*, ***pro-forma invoice***, an invoice sent to a purchaser in advance of the ordered goods, so that formalities may be completed (see also quot. 1965); also *absol.* as *sb.*, an official form for completion; a pro-forma invoice.

1573–80 G. HARVEY *Letter-bk.* (Camden) 77 To give the choyce of a thousand thankes for every gewegawe; and sumtymes tooe for very meere Nifilles as it were only *pro forma tantum.* **1623** J. CHAMBERLAIN in *Crt. & Times Jas. I* (1848) II. 425 Which is thought to be done rather *pro formâ* than *ex animo.* **1788** *Gentl. Mag.* LVIII. 73/1 The cession of the Crimea by the Porte was contrary to the Alcoran, and was therefore admitted merely *pro forma.* **1827** W. BOLLING in *Virginia Mag. Hist. & Biogr.* (1935) XLIII. 240 Then called proforma at Mr. Robertson's to see my sister. **1858** P. L. SIMMONDS *Dict. Trade Products* 303/2 *Pro-forma-account*, a model or sketch account; a pattern bill of particulars. **1882** BITHELL *Counting-ho. Dict.* (1893) s.v., When a document is drawn up or a process gone through after a prescribed model, and with the special object of complying with some legal requirement it is said to be done *pro formâ.* **1895** *Funk's Stand. Dict., Pro forma*,...as a matter of form; as, a *pro forma* invoice. **1928** BLUNDEN *Undertones of War* ii. 19 He rejoiced in inventing new Army Forms, which he called 'pro forma's'... Some of them were such that one's best information could not find a heading in them. **1930** M. CLARK *Home Trade* 100 An order may be received from an unknown person or firm... In such cases a pro forma invoice may be dispatched. **1945** *Ann. Trop. Med. & Parasitol.* XXXIX. 226 A senior member of the nursing staff..checked that the patient took the tablet and recorded each dose given and taken on a *pro-forma.* **1959** *Punch* 27 May 705/1, I do not know in precisely what form the Department of Meteorology of the Imperial College of Science is asking for information about hail, but at the very least there should be a 'proforma' with columns headed. **1965** J. L. HANSON *Dict. Econ.* 329/2 *Pro-forma invoice*, a commercial document with three main uses: (i) A polite request for payment when a supplier is unwilling to allow his customer credit; (ii) With goods sent on approval, becoming an ordinary invoice if the goods are retained; (iii) When goods are sent to an agent to be sold; (iv) In foreign trade when goods are exported on consignment, informing the importer of the expected prices of the goods. **1977** *Wandsworth Borough News* 16 Sept. 2/2 A pro-forma for all organisations..should contain a sentence encouraging applicants to think of any aspect of their work which might not be covered by the form. **1978** *Jrnl. R. Soc. Med.* LXXI. 413 Details of the illness were recorded on a proforma.

5. pro hac vice, for this turn or occasion (only).

1653 in Rashdall & Rait *Neu College* (1901) 178 Wee therefore shall *pro hac vice* nominate the 13 Seniors and Officers for the carryinge on the government of the said Colledge. **1715** S. SEWALL *Diary* 29 Mar., Made Mr. Little Clark *pro hac vice*, Mr. Cooke being sick of the Gout. **1873** *Oxford Univ. Gazette* 18 Nov. 312 The following gentlemen have been nominated by the Vice-Chancellor and Proctors to examine *pro hac vice* this Term.

6. pro indiˈviso (*Law*), 'as undivided': applied to a right shared by two or more persons without division: see quot.

1607 COWELL *Interpr., Pro Indiuiso*, is a possession, and occupation of lands, or tenements belonging vnto two or more persons, whereof none knoweth his seuerall portion, as Coparceners before partition.

7. pro ˈrata (-â) [= 'for the rate': RATE *sb.*[1] 2], in proportion to the value or extent (of his interest), proportionally. Also *attrib.* or as *adj.*, proportional.

[**1354** *Rolls of Parlt.* II. 260/1 Les Eschetours sont chargez ..a respoundre des parcelles des ditz rentes et fermes Pro rata temporis.] **1575** *Reg. Privy Council Scot.* II. 468 To mak payment of thair part of the said taxatioun pro rata. **1642** tr. *Perkins' Prof. Bk.* v. §310 (1657) 118 His wife shall not have dower of that which the other copercener had *pro rata.* **1877** L. W. M. LOCKHART *Mine is Thine* xv. (1879) 134 I'll take my *pro ratâ* allotment. **1901** *Daily Tel.* 9 Mar. 9/7 The Preference issue will be offered *pro rata* to shareholders at 115.

8. a. pro re ˈnata (-â), 'for the affair born, i.e. arisen'; for some contingency arising unexpectedly or without being provided for; for an occasion as it arises. Also *attrib.*

1578 in Spottiswood *Hist. Ch. Scot.* VI. (1677) 295 It is in the power of the Eldership to send out qualified persons to visit *pro re nata.* **1765** BLACKSTONE *Comm.* I. ii. 174 It was formerly left to the crown to summon, *pro re nata*, the most flourishing towns to send representatives to parliament. **1885** A. P. PETER in *Law Times* 10 Jan. 185/1 Such orders are only granted *pro re natâ*, and must be renewed on each fresh occasion arising. *Mod.* At a *pro re nata* meeting of the Town Council, it was resolved, etc.

†**b.** So **pro-re-nascent** *a.* (*obs. nonce-wd.*), arising unexpectedly.

1647 WARD *Simp. Cobler* 50 In pro-re-nascent occurrences, which cannot be foreseen.

9. pro ˈtanto, 'for so much', so far, to such an extent. Also *attrib.*

1780 BENTHAM *Princ. Legisl.* ii. §4 Any one who reprobates any the least particle of pleasure as such..is *pro tanto* a partizan of the principle of asceticism. **1882** *Macm. Mag.* XLVI. 437 Anything which reduces the amount of payments to be made out of the country *pro tanto* reduces the loss. **1885** *Law Times* LXXVIII. 387/1 The land tax was redeemed and *pro tanto* personal estate converted into real estate.

10. pro ˈtempore, for the time, temporarily; *attrib.* or as *adj.* temporary. (Abbrev. ***pro tem.***)

1468 *Paston Lett.* II. 325 The tythandes did goode *pro tempore.* **1625–6** J. CHAMBERLAIN in *Crt. & Times Chas. I* (1848) I. 73 The Lord Chamberlain is like to be Lord Steward this parliament, *pro tempore.* **1748** J. LIND *Lett. Navy* ii. (1757) 70 Another might be appointed *pro tempore* to command his ship. **1759** E. W. MONTAGU, jr. *Anc. Republics* 353 The *pro tempore* Dictator soon came to be perpetual. **1828** *Reg. Deb. Congr.* IV. 787 President Pro Tempore... The Senate proceeded to the election of a President pro tem. **1835** DICKENS *Let.* ? 30 Oct. (1965) I. 85 Through the stupidity of Frisby who was in attendance pro: tem: Frank Ross 'dropped in' to my writing room. **1846** H. GREVILLE *Diary* (1883) 159 Called to-day upon Craven.. who is *pro tem.* private secretary to Normanby. **1886** [see GADGET]. **1913** *Sat. Even. Post* 4 Oct. 47 It was proper that Sergeant Bagby, in his capacity as host *pro tem.* should do the..explaining. **1955** *Times* 12 May 11/6 One feels that this in only a capital *pro tem.*, making do until the kingdom reaches some new turning-point in its fortunes. **1974** 'E. LATHEN' *Sweet & Low* xv. 146 Would you be willing to take charge of our cocoa trading—on a pro-tem basis?

B. *sb.* **1. a.** An argument for or in favour of something, as opposed to one against it. (Now usually in PRO AND CON, q.v.) **b.** A person who sides or votes in favour of some proposal.

c **1400** *Beryn* 2577 That I may the bet perseyve al inconvenience, Dout, pro, contra, and ambiguite, Thurh yeur declaracioune. **1509** HAWES *Past. Pleas.* vi. (Percy Soc.) 26 Provyng the pro well from the contrary. **1784** GEO. III in *G. Rose's Diaries* (1860) I. 61 Mr. Pultney..should have stood amongst the Pros. **1790** M. CUTLER in *Life*, etc. (1888) I. 462 The pros are afraid to bring it forward until the return of several members on their side of the question. **1835** E. FITZGERALD *Let.* July in *FitzGerald to his Friends* (1979) 18 But then I get a settled home, a good companion, and the other usual pro's that desperate people talk of. **1969** V. E. FRANKL in Koestler & Smythies *Beyond Reductionism* 419 All the protesters are actually anti-testers, they have no 'pro', no positive alternative to offer, but they are fighting against, rather than struggling for something.

2. ***tally of pro:*** see TALLY *sb.*

C. *prep.* For, in favour of. **D.** *adj.* or quasi-*adj.*

a. Favourable, positive, supportive; favourably disposed.

1837 H. MARTINEAU *Diary* in *Autobiogr.* (1877) II. iv. 109 In the morning I am *pro*, and at night..*con* the scheme. **1961** *Dallas Morning News* 17 Feb. I. 5 We're getting more 'pro' letters than 'con' on horse race betting. **1966** 'W. COOPER' *Mem. New Man* I. iv. 49 'In touch' was a phrase everybody used... They used it in a pro sense; being in touch was most desirable. **1974** R. HARRIS *Double Snare* v. 32 It's nice of you to be so pro the idea—*I* don't feel pro or against.

b. ***pro-attitude*** (Philos.), an attitude such as approval, pleasure, satisfaction, etc., which is the normal reaction to all things considered ethically good.

1935 C. A. CAMPBELL in *Mind* XLIV. 298 All usages of the term 'good' signify at least this common feature in that to which goodness is attributed, *viz.*, that it is the object of what may perhaps least misleadingly be called a *pro*-attitude. **1939** W. D. ROSS *Foundations of Ethics* xi. 284 This attractive character, or..the fact that we have a pro-attitude towards them, seems to be all that is common to these three kinds of thing that are habitually called good. **1947** A. C. EWING *Def. of Good* ii. 68 A slightly different view would be that to call anything 'good' is to say that it is the object of some 'pro attitude' on the part of most people. .. I use 'pro attitude' to cover desiring, liking, seeking, choosing, approving, admiring, etc. **1949** *Mind* LVIII. 90 The *ground* of a pro-attitude lies..in the concrete factual characteristics of what we pronounce good. **1964** A. EDEL in I. L. Horowitz *New Sociol.* 224 We may omit here the internal operation of general values, in the sense of obligations and pro-attitudes not peculiar to social science —regard for truth, objectivity and impartiality, [etc.]. **1967** G. R. GRICE *Grounds of Moral Judgement* i. 9 Wanting, for Nowell-Smith is one of many pro-attitudes, and..it is fair to say that his use of the term 'pro-attitude' conceals distinctions of importance.

pro, pro., *abbrev.* A familiar abbreviation of various wds., as *proproctor* and other combs. of PRO- *pref.*[1] 4, also *professional.*

1. Abbrev. of PRO-PROCTOR.

1848 J. H. NEWMAN *Loss & Gain* iii. 17 When he came to Oxford..he reverenced even the velvet of the Pro. **1861** H. KINGSLEY *Ravenshoe* xiv, He had past the Pro's at Magdalen turnpike, and they never thought of stopping him... Both the Proctors were down at Coldharbour turnpike. *a* **1884** M. PATTISON *Mem.* (1885) 229, I had acted as proproctor to Green, the other pro being Kay.

2. a. Abbrev. of PROFESSIONAL *sb.* 2.

1866 *Sporting Life* 17 Oct. 4/4 County matches..are also the true source of our supply of professionals of ability, for you rarely hear of a good 'pro' until he has played for his county. **1885** J. K. JEROME *On the Stage* 86 The poor players helped each other as well as they could, but provincial Pros. are—or, at least, were—not a wealthy class. **1887** *Scott. Leader* 19 Dec. 4/1 A match..between six professional golfers and six amateurs resulted in favour of the 'pros.' by three holes. **1890** *Daily News* 18 Sept. 5/3 'Master or Pro.' ..the burning question of whether school cricket should be under the dominion of the schoolmaster or the professional cricketer. **1902** C. J. C. HYNE *Mr. Horrocks, Purser* 124 'I tell you the man's not a theatrical.'.. 'Never knew any pro. yet bring either honour or profit to any boat,' said the Purser. **1903** *19th Cent.* Sept. 464 Taverns frequented by 'pros', as music-hall artistes are popularly called. **1932** *John o' London's* 25 June 426/1, I spent all my holidays practising in tournaments and having coaching from a pro. **1951** 'J. TEY' *Daughter of Time* xvii. 209 One wouldn't expect an amateur to walk into the Yard and solve a case that had defeated the pro's. **1960** [see GOY]. **1965** *New Statesman* 7 May 712/1 Randall is essentially a pro in the tradition of technician editors, able, almost apolitical. **1975** J. SYMONS *Three Pipe Problem* xvi. 158 They're not pros, how long do you think they'll stand up under questioning?

b. *attrib.* or as *adj.* in the sense of PROFESSIONAL *a.* 4, esp. in sporting uses.

1932 A. J. MORRISON *New Way to Better Golf* ii. 25 The pupil..did not recognize me as the handy man of the pro shop and a former caddy. **1949** *Times Digest* (Richmond, Va.) 26 Nov. 10/4 Riggs was enthusiastic about the crowds which his pro tennis stars have been drawing. **1961** *Boxing News* 20 Oct. 10 Next live pro item will be the Maurice Cullen-Guy Gracia bout from Newcastle on November 13. **1970** *Washington Post* 20 Sept. D1/1 Baseball needs such finishes in order to provide some counter-interest to college and pro football, already moving into high gear. **1975** C. JAMES *Fate of Felicity Fark* II. 20 These *Krauts* are all pro athletes in disguise. **1978** S. BRILL *Teamsters* vi. 236 Three former pro football players were partners. **1978** *Rugby World* Apr. 51/3 New Zealander Ken Bousfield, a Sydney player, rejected a league offer of over £17,000 for three years at the end of last season. But this year, he has turned pro with Penrith.

c. pro('s) shop, a (work)shop run by the resident professional at a golf club.

[**1905** H. VARDON *Compl. Golfer* iv. 39 The proper place for him [*sc.* the beginner] to go is the professional's shop which is attached to the club of which he has become a member. Nearly all clubs have their own professionals, who are makers and sellers of clubs.] **1932** [see sense 2 b above]. **1937** H. LONGHURST *Golf* 3 An extremely high standard of business morality obtains among professional golfers. A novice may enter a pro's shop [to buy clubs], a chicken ready for the plucking, and yet come out with all his feathers on. **1953** J. TURNESA *Low Score Golf* ii. 13 Let's leave the pro shop and go over to the lesson tee. **1964** D. LANGDON *How* *to play Golf & stay Happy* iii. 27 Palmer..rushed back to the pro's shop after a disastrous round of 76, slammed his driver into the vice and filed away the club face. **1976** T. GIFFORD *Cavanaugh Quest* ii. 31 The members' golf committee had allowed Billy to live in the room over the pro shop.

3. Abbrev. of (*professional*) *prostitute*. Cf. PROFESSIONAL *sb.* 2 b.

1937 in PARTRIDGE *Dict. Slang*. **1941** B. SCHULBERG *What makes Sammy Run?* ix. 247 He treats all women like pros. **1950** [see BAG *sb.* 17]. **1968** H. C. RAE *Few Small Bones* II. i. 79 She's a semi-pro actually... She works in a garage.. during the day, but at night she...entertains. **1976** 'E. MCBAIN' *Guns* iv. 95 Benny already had himself two girls.. experienced pros who were bringing in enough cash every week to keep him living pretty good.

pro-, *prefix*[1]. The Latin adv. and prep. (see above), used in combination with verbs and their derivatives, and sometimes with other words not of verbal derivation.

(Unlike the Gr. πρo-, the L. was originally and usually *prō-*; but in some compounds it was occasionally and in others usually or always shortened to *prŏ-*.)

A large number of Latin words so formed were retained in popular use in French (as in the other Romanic langs.); many others were taken into French in earlier or later times as learned words, and were thence taken into English. In later times words of this kind have been adopted or adapted in English directly from Latin, or have been formed immediately from Latin elements.

In OF. the prefix had often the popular form *por-*, *pur-*, *pour-* (see PUR-); but this, in many words, was subseq. changed back to the Latin form in *pro-*.

I. As an etymological element. The following are the principal uses in Latin and English. (All words of this class appear as Main words.)

1. a. Forward, to or towards the front, from a position in the rear, forth, out, into a public position; as *prōclāmāre* to call out, PROCLAIM, *prōdūcĕre* to lead forth, PRODUCE, *prōfundĕre* to pour forth (PROFUSE), *prōjicĕre* to throw forth, PROJECT, *prōminēre* jut out (PROMINENT), *prōnuntiāre* to speak out, PRONOUNCE, *prōpōnĕre* to put forth, PROPONE, PROPOSE, *prōtrūdĕre* to thrust forth, PROTRUDE.

b. To the front of, down before (the face of), forward and down; as *prōcidĕre* to fall forward or down (PROCIDENCE), *prōclīvis* sloping downward, PROCLIVE, *prōculcāre* to trample down, PROCULCATE, *prōcumbĕre* to fall down forwards (PROCUMBENT), *prōflīgāre* to dash down (PROFLIGATE), *prōlābī*, *prōlaps-* to slip down forwards (PROLAPSE), *prōsternĕre*, *prōstrāt-* to strew or lay flat before one, to PROSTRATE.

c. Forth from its place, away; as *prōdĕre* to give away, betray (PRODITION), *prōdigāre* to drive away, dissipate (PRODIGAL), *profugĕre* to flee away (PROFUGATE).

d. Forward, onward, in a course or in time; as *prōcēdĕre* to PROCEED, *prōcessus* PROCESS, *prōcrastināre* to defer till the morrow, PROCRASTINATE, *prōgredī* to step forward, PROGRESS, *prōmināre* to drive onward (PROMENADE), *prōmovēre*, *prōmōt-* to move onward, PROMOVE, PROMOTE, *prōpellĕre* to drive forward, PROPEL.

e. Out, with outward extension; as *prōductilis* able to be drawn out, PRODUCTILE, *prōlixus* PROLIX, *prōpāgāre* to plant out, PROPAGATE, *prōtrahĕre*, *prōtract-* to drag out, PROTRACT.

f. Before in place, in front of; as *prohibēre* to hold in front, hold back, PROHIBIT, *prōscrībĕre* to write in front, PROSCRIBE, *prōtegĕre* to cover in front, PROTECT.

g. Before in time, in anticipation of, in provision for; as *prōdigium* PRODIGY, *prōloquī* to speak before (PROLOCUTION), *prōvidēre* to foresee, PROVIDE.

h. For, in preparation for, on behalf of; as *prōcinctus* girt for, PROCINCT, *prōcūrāre* to take care for, PROCURE, *prosperus* wished for, PROSPEROUS, *prōficĕre* to do service to, PROFIT.

i. With worn-down or obscure force; as *prōcērus* tall, PROCEROUS, *profānus* PROFANE, *profundus* deep, PROFOUND, *prōlēs* offspring (PROLETAIRE), *prōmerēre* to deserve, PROMERIT, *prōmiscuus* mixed, PROMISCUOUS, *prōverbium* PROVERB, *prōvincia* PROVINCE.

2. Frequently prefixed in Latin to names of relationship, answering to Eng. 'great' or 'grand', F. *grand* and *petit*; as *avus* grandfather, *pro-avus* great-grandfather, *amita* aunt, father's sister, *pro-amita* great-aunt, grandfather's sister, *gener* son-in-law, *prōgener* grandson-in-law, granddaughter's husband. So *pronepos* great-grandson, great-nephew, PRONEPHEW, PRONEPOT, *proneptis* great-grand-daughter, great-niece, PRONIECE, PRONEPT.

3. pro- for PRÆ-, PRE-. In late and mediæval Lat. *pro-* was sometimes substituted for *præ-*, *prē-*, partly through confusion of sense, partly perhaps under the influence of words from Greek, such as *prologus*, *prophēta*, *proscænium*. Examples of this are frequent in ME., where, however, as in med.L. MSS., it is often difficult to say whether *pro-* was intended, or was merely a scribal or copyist's error, due to confusion of the written *e* and *o*. Examples will be found among the cross-references.

II. As a living prefix.

4. In Latin *prō-* in the sense 'for', 'instead of', 'in place of', was prefixed to a sb., app. originally in prepositional construction, as *prō consule* (one acting) for a consul, afterwards combined with the sb., as *prōconsul* = deputy-consul; so *prōdictātor*, *prōflāmen*, *prōgubernātor*, *prōlēgātus*, *prōmagister*, *prōpræfectus*, *prōprætor*; also in a few names of things, as *prōnōmen* PRONOUN, *prōtūtēla* deputy-guardianship.

English has examples of *pro-* prefixed: **a.** to names of persons (officials or functionaries), 'acting as deputy', as ***'pro-Grand 'Master***, ***'pro-'guardian***, ***pro-legate***, ***pro-provincial***, ***pro-provost***, ***pro-regent***, ***pro-seneschal***, ***pro-tetrarch***, ***pro-treasurer***, ***pro-tribune***, ***pro-warden***, etc.; also PROCONSUL, PROPROCTOR, PRORECTOR, etc. **b.** to names of things, as ***pro-element***, ***pro-infinitive***, ***pro-name***, ***ˌpro-re'ality*** (something serving the purpose of a reality), ***pro-sentence***, ***'pro-ˌskin***, ***pro-syllable***, ***'pro-ˌverb*** [after *pronoun*], etc.; also PRO-CATHEDRAL, PRO-LEG, ***pro-vicariate***, ***pro-word***, etc.; **pro-form** *Linguistics*, a pronoun or other lexical unit substituted for a longer expression. **c.** to an adj., as **'pro-'ethical**, serving as a substitute for what is ethical; **'pro-'substantive** (see quot.); hence ***pro-substantively*** adv; ***pro-infinitival***, ***pro-syllabic*** adjs.

1975 N. CHOMSKY *Logical Struct. Linguistic Theory* x. 560 'So' is introduced as a *pro-element standing for the verb phrase in such sentences as 'John saw him and so did I'. **1892** H. SPENCER *Princ. Ethics* I. II. ii. §123. 337 We must class them as forming a body of thought and feeling which may be called *pro-ethical; and which, with the mass of mankind, stands in place of the ethical properly so called. **1902** R. R. MARETT in *Personal Idealism* 250 Religion..as often as it happens to take the side of salutary practice..is probably [a] more effectual 'pro-ethical sanction' [than law]. **1964** KATZ & POSTAL *Integrated Theory Ling. Descr.* iv. 83 We stipulate in the general theory of linguistic descriptions that the dictionary entry of every *pro-form (i.e., every form dominated by the constituent Pro) must contain the semantic marker (Selector). **1969** *Canad. Jrnl. Linguistics* XIV. 49 In this structure the head noun is a pro-form which is of the *du* class. **1976** *Analysis* XXXVI. 80 Proforms and modified proforms, upon given occasions of their use, get their semantic content from their antecedents. **1898** *Daily Chron.* 21 Nov. 5/1 Having served with pre-eminent distinction the office of Deputy Grand Master, he was in 1891 elected *Pro-Grand Master, a distinction which can only be understood when it is recalled that the Prince of Wales himself is Grand Master. **1868** *Digby's Voy. Medit.* Pref. 17 Digby's *pro-guardian was a man of considerable celebrity. **1934** J. J. HOGAN *Outl. Eng. Philol.* III. xiv. 136 The modern '*pro-infinitival' *to*, as in *I want to*. **1905** O. JESPERSEN *Growth & Struct. Eng. Lang.* viii. 208 Another recent innovation is the use of *to* as what might be called a *pro-infinitive instead of the clumsy *to do so*: 'Will you play?' 'Yes, I intend to.' 'I am going to.' **1940** —— *S.P.E. Tract* LIV. 153 This leads to the possibility of using an isolated *to* as a 'pro-infinitive': Will he sing? Yes, he wants to. **1964** *Eng. Stud.* XLV. 88 *To* here stands..for *to tell me*, or *to do so*, for which reason Jespersen calls it a 'pro-infinitive'. **1656** BLOUNT *Glossogr.*, A *Prolegate,..a Deputy Legat, or one that stands for a Legat. **1765** J. ELPHINSTON *Princ. Eng. Lang. Digested* II. viii. 184 Instead of a name or noun repeated, a *pro-name or pronoun. **1902** *Westm. Gaz.* 25 Jan. 4/2 In the name of the Trinity, Thomas, *Pro-Provincial of Canterbury, Joseph, Provincial of York, Laurence, Provincial of Caerled, deplore the evil state of the Established Church. **1858** in *Stat. Univ. Oxford* (1863) 158 *Pro-Provost. **1877** E. R. CONDER *Bas. Faith.* iv. 185 This kind of idealised symbol or concept serves as a *pro-reality, which we can reason about as though it were real. **1798** HELEN M. WILLIAMS *Tour Switzerland* I. 238 (Jod.) Don Amatori Solani *proregent, professor extraordinary, and enjoying numerous other titles. **1657** W. RAND tr. *Gassendi's Life Peiresc* II. 84 Cadafalcius *Pro-senescal of Digne. **1972** *Language* XLVIII. 461 To answer the question *Did he do it?*, one requires an element that will affirm or deny. It may appear alone, and in that case will carry the sentence intonation, accent and all. Such a single answer-word might be *Unquestionably*. It may also appear at the end of a *pro-sentence, e.g. *He did it unquestionably*. **1976** *Analysis* XXXVI. 83 The antecedent of the modified prosentence 'it is false', is the quoted sentence together with the quotes. **1886** H. SPENCER in *19th Cent.* May 763 There is produced a new skin, or rather a *pro-skin. **1794** E. BANCROFT *Res. Perm. Colours* I. 176 Such compositions..assume the form of substantive colours, without being such in reality;..I beg leave..to call them **pro-substantive topical colours*. *Ibid.* 390 Of the Uses of Quercitron Bark, in producing Topical Yellow and other Colours, *pro-substantively, upon Cotton and Linen. **1948** J. R. FIRTH in E. P. Hamp et al. *Readings in Linguistics II* (1966) 185 In certain of its prosodic functions the neutral vowel might be described temporarily as a *pro-syllable. However obscure or neutral or unstressed, it is essential in *a bitter for me* to distinguish it from *a bit for me*. In contemporary Southern English many 'sounds' may be *pro-syllabic. **1956** *Archivum Linguisticum* VIII. 123 Structurally the difference [between ij and ₑr] is that of a vocalic phoneme followed by a junctional prosody and a consonantal phoneme preceded by a prosyllabic prosody. **1647** TRAPP *Comm. Luke* viii. 3 His vicar-general, or *protetrach. **1645** WOOD *Life* Jan. (O.H.S.) I. 115 For the space of three yeares he was a *protribune [*mispr.* protobune] of horse under Charles Lewis elector Palatine. In 1641 he was sent into Ireland..where he served in the quality of a tribune for two yeares. **1907** J. M. GRAINGER *Studies K. Jas. Bible* 19 *Do* is sometimes used as a *pro-verb, to avoid repetition of an antecedent verb. **1924** O. JESPERSEN *Philos. Gram.* vi. 83 We should get a class of substitute words which might be divided into pro-nouns, pro-adjectives, pro-adverbs, pro-infinitives, pro-verbs..but it could hardly be called a real grammatical class. **1976** J. S. GRUBER *Lexical Struct. Syntax & Semantics* II. i. 267 For the other occurrences of pro-verbs, the nature of the semantic category common to both the pro-verbs and the verbs embedded in them is more obscure. **1861** NEALE *Notes Dalmatia*, etc. 169 *Pro-Vicar of the Bishop in the southern part of his diocese. **1881** *Dublin Rev.* July 173 The districts of Lake Tanganyika, and the Victoria Nyanza have already been created *Pro-Vicariates Apostolic. **1857** in *Stat. Univ. Oxford* (1863) 83 *Pro-Warden. **1965** *Language* XLI. 393 We can define a set of *proword substitutions which are similar to various types of zeroing.

5. In sense 'for, in favour of, on the side of'.

This use is entirely modern, and has no precedent or analogy in Latin. It appears to have arisen from the use of *pro* in PRO B. 1 b, or in PRO AND CON. To a certain extent, combinations with *pro-* take the place of those with PHILO-, as *philo-Turk*, *philo-publican*. They appear to have begun *c* 1825, but to have been comparatively rare up to 1896, since which date they have swarmed in the journalistic press, usually in antithesis to formations in *anti-* expressed or understood. *Pro-Boer* and *anti-British* were terms of opprobrium during the South African War, 1899–1902.

a. Prefixed to a sb., sb. phr., or adj., forming adjs. with sense 'favouring or siding with (what is indicated by the second element)'; as ***pro-abortion***, ***-abortionist***, ***-alien***, ***-Allied***, ***-Ally***, ***-American***, ***-annexation***, ***-Arab***, ***-Asiatic***, ***-Axis***, ***-Boche***, ***-Boer***, ***-British***, ***-business***, ***-Catholic***, ***-Chinese***, ***-clerical***, ***-Communist***, ***-educational***, ***-English***, ***-Fascist***, ***-foreign***, ***-French***, ***-German***, ***-Irish***, ***-Israeli***, ***-Japanese***, ***-moral***, ***-Nazi***, ***-Negro***, ***-opium***, ***-papist***, ***-patronage***, ***-popery***, ***-rebel***, ***-Russian***, ***-slavery***, ***-Soviet***, ***-tariff reform***, ***-transubstantiation***, ***-Turk***, ***-Turkish***, ***-war***, ***-West***, ***-Western***, ***-Zionist***, etc. Where the form of the second element permits, as in ***pro-Boer***, ***pro-Catholic***, ***pro-negro***, ***pro-papist***, ***pro-Turk***, these are also used as sbs. = 'one who is on the side of, or favours..., a partisan or adherent of...'; **pro-'knock** *a.* and *sb.*, (a substance) tending to cause knocking when present in the fuel burnt in an internal-combustion engine; **pro-'life** *a.*, in favour of the maintenance of life; *spec.* against inducing abortion; hence **pro-'lifer**, someone with these views. **b.** In comb. with a sb. (or verb-stem) + -ER, -EER or -ITE, forming a nonce-sb. = 'one who favours or sides with...'; as ***pro-Boarder*** (one in favour of a School Board), ***-breecher*** (a partisan of breeches), ***-flogger*** (one who favours flogging), ***-slaver*** (a pro-slavery man); ***pro-liquorite*** (one in favour of the unrestricted sale of alcoholic drinks); ***pro-Britisher***, ***-marketeer*** [MARKETEER 3]. **c.** In comb. with a sb. or adj. (or directly from those in a.) + -ISM, forming abstract sbs. = 'the principle or character of being in favour of...', as ***pro-alcoholism***, ***-Arabism***, ***-Boerism***, ***-capitalism***, ***-clericalism***, ***-Germanism***, ***-Russianism***, ***-Semitism***, ***-slaveryism***, ***-Sovietism***. Many of these are of opprobrious or hostile use.

1976 *Pro-abortionist [see *pro-lifer* below]. **1976** *National Observer* (U.S.) 31 Jan. 5/3 If Carter can appeal successfully to both proabortion and right-to-life Democrats, we might as well hand him the nomination now. **1977** *Lancet* 2 July 48/2 Pro-abortionists are left, therefore, with familiar Parliamentary tactics of filibustering to try to prevent progress. **1919** W. S. CHURCHILL in M. Gilbert *Winston S. Churchill* (1977) IV. Compan. I. 536 None of the *pro-Allied Russian Governments would meet them. **1915** H. MUENSTERBERG in *Fatherland* 22 Dec. 347/1 The psychological equation of his personality makes him a pro-German in all that is best in him, and only his temper and his perpetual desire to be with the masses made him a *pro-Ally. **1916** *Lit. Digest* (N.Y.) 1 Jan. 3/2 He has been trapt into the nets of those who wove the pro-Ally newspaper opinion in this country. **1916** MRS. BELLOC LOWNDES *Let.* 29 May (1971) 72 In America it has been rejected by one set of publishers as pro-German—by another as pro-Ally. **1971** D. E. WESTLAKE *I gave at the Office* (1972) 159 They were revolutionaries who were pro-American, which is very rare in the world today. **1898** *Westm. Gaz.* 27 Apr. 6/3 Owing to the *pro-American tone of the English Press. **1899** FITZPATRICK *Transvaal* 21 In demolition of Sir T. Shepstone's *pro-annexation arguments. **1920** G. BELL *Let.* 12 Sept. (1927) II. xviii. 499 It is only quite recently that I have realized how prominent a place I have occupied in the public mind here as the *pro-Arab member of the administration. **1973** 'D. RUTHERFORD' *Kick Start* ix. 186 The Russians..are openly pro-Arab. **1959** *Daily Tel.* 2 Nov. 10/2 Traditional *pro-Arabism influenced us. **1938** *New Statesman* 25 June 1054/1 After he [*sc.* M. Imrédy] had made a speech to this effect, M. de Kánya hastened to deliver his *pro-Axis speech of June 1st. **1942** *Times Rev. Year 1941* 3 Jan. p. i/2 One result of their [*sc.* the Germans'] intrigues was a *coup d'état* in Iraq, where on April 3 Raschid Ali and a group of military malcontents expelled the Regent and set up a pro-Axis government. **1902** *Daily Chron.* 7 May 4/7 The *pro-Boarders were out-voted. **1915** *National Rev.* Apr. 169 A *pro-Boche Government would have been bundled out 'neck and crop' last August. **1923** KIPLING *Irish Guards in Gt. War.* II. 160 Some pro-Boche agent in the far-off lands where it was purchased. **1896** *Pro-Boer [see *pro-British* below]. **1899** *Westm. Gaz.* 23 May 1/3 Liberals need not trouble to be more pro-Boer than the Boers themselves. **1901** J. CHAMBERLAIN *Sp. Ho. Comm.* 18 Feb., We have had six pro-Boers speaking in this debate.. and not one Liberal Imperialist. **1900** *Dundee Advertiser* 23 Aug. 4 Lord Rosslyn brings the novel charge of *pro-Boerism against us. **1896** *Daily News* 22 Apr. 5/1 If it were indeed a necessity of the situation to be pro-Boer or *pro-British..then as Britons we should be for the British, we admit. **1927** H. DOBBS in *Lett. Gertrude Bell* II. 543 The so-called pro-British sections of the populations. **1980** P. VAN GREENAWAY *Dissident* vii. 148 A man, if he is anti-Soviet, must therefore be pro-British..and *vice versa*. **1927** *Leader* 31 Dec. 517/1 That was unexpected talk to what in Ireland is called a Chamber of Commerce—Chambers whose members are mostly *pro-Britishers and Shoneens.

1975 HUNT & SHERMAN *Econ.* (ed. 2) xii. 155 A large amount of *probusiness propaganda. 1978 *New York* 3 Apr. 34/3 It might also provide Kennedy with a pro-business image for a presidential campaign. 1901 *Daily News* 28 June 3/4 This trumpet blare of Triumphant Democracy..almost unnerves us into *pro-capitalism. 1831 SOUTHEY in *Q. Rev.* XLIV. 284 The Roman Catholics and the *pro-Catholics, and their infidel allies, had incessantly employed the periodical press in aid of their cause. 1950 *New Yorker* 6 May 96/2 The *pro-Communist *Lettres Françaises* is the best literary weekly in Paris. 1976 'M. BARAK' *Secret List H. Roehm* iii. 35 The establishment of a pro-communist spy ring. 1839 *Morn. Herald* 22 Oct., The opinions of the *pro-educational and anti-slavery parties throughout the country. 1898 M. DAVITT in *Westm. Gaz.* 14 July 2/1 The *pro-English minority in the United States..are attempting a very hazardous enterprise for the future peace of the Republic. 1937 DUCHESS OF ATHOLL in Koestler *Spanish Testament* 6 A so-called 'Radical Government', reinforced later by members of Señor Robles' *pro-Fascist party. 1940 'G. ORWELL' in *World Rev.* (1950) June 28 The government ..are subjectively pro-Fascist. 1903 *Daily Chron.* 30 June 3/7 The *pro-floggers in the United States are constantly appealing to the condition of Delaware in proof of the efficacy of flogging. 1914 R. BROOKE *Let.* 3 Sept. (1968) 613 The intellectuals..are mostly pacifists and *pro-Germans. 1915 KIPLING *Let.* 12 Aug. in C. E. Carrington *Rudyard Kipling* (1955) xvii. 433 Munthe..tells me of all his grief.. to find that Sweden is so—not pro-German but afraid of Russia. 1938 E. PHIPPS *Let.* 9 Jan. in M. Gilbert *Winston S. Churchill* (1976) V. xliv. 894 Van's displacement..would be represented as a victory for the pro-Germans in England. 1964 *Times Lit. Suppl.* 12 Nov. 1018 He [*sc.* Frank Harris] spent the 1914–18 War in the United States, where he wrote pro-German propaganda. 1914 W. B. YEATS *Tribute to Thomas Davis* (1947) 12, I am not more vehemently opposed to the Unionism of Professor Mahaffy than I am to the *pro-Germanism of Mr. Pearse. 1940 *Tablet* 4 May 421/1 The pro-Germanism of expedience which was once practised by certain politicians. 1897 *Westm. Gaz.* 8 Apr. 2/2 If Russia can arrange a *pro-Greek settlement, do not let us denounce her. 1904 *Daily Chron.* 2 Dec. 4/3 Some of the pro-Greeks [those in favour of retaining Greek in the Previous Examination] at Cambridge would be ready to vote for an anti-Greek motion on the Oxford lines. 1897 *Daily News* 22 Feb. 9/3 The *pro-Hellenic manifestations in the streets.. have..produced an unfavourable impression among business men. 1901 *Daily Chron.* 28 Oct. 4/3 Mr. Chamberlain..described Sir Henry Campbell-Bannerman as the leader of the pro-Boer and Little Englander and *pro-Irish party. 1975 J. CROSBY *Affair of Strangers* iv. 33 French policy..is far more pro-Arab than the French people are. The French people..would be *pro-Israeli. 1896 *Daily News* 7 Mar. 5/7 Kim-Hong-Tsu, the Premier [of Corea], and seven other *pro-Japanese Ministers were beheaded and their corpses dragged through the streets. 1927 *Jrnl. Inst. Petroleum Technologists* XIII. 301 Amyl nitrate and nitrite..according to Midgley are *pro-knock. 1928 *Ibid.* XIV. 188 They might have some indications..as to how the pro-knock worked as against the anti-knock in that particular type of flame propagation. 1953 E. M. GOODYER *Petroleum & Performance in Internal Combustion Engines* viii. 189 Ignition accelerating materials are those which act as pro-knocks in spark-ignition engine fuels, and include organic peroxides, nitrates, nitrites, and various sulphur compounds. 1973 K. OWEN in Hobson & Pohl *Mod. Petroleum Technol.* (ed. 4) xv. 596 Monomethylaniline..acts as an anti-knock agent in its undecomposed form but..if it is decomposed too early in the combustion cycle it can even have a pro-knock effect. 1896 M. DAVITT in *Westm. Gaz.* 15 Dec. 4/2 If the Irish Land Commission were not a practically packed *pro-landlord tribunal. 1961 G. SMITH *Business of Loving* xvii. 284 Benny divides people into..the life-enhancers and the life-diminishers; he is a believer in the first, a leader of the *pro-life party. 1978 *Dædalus* Spring 155 Its eleven members include only five scientists, one of whom was known for his prolife position. 1979 *Time* 30 July 6 As the oldest of eleven children (all married), I'd like to point out our combined family numbers more than 100 who vote only for pro-life candidates. 1976 *National Observer* (U.S.) 31 Jan. 5/2 Carter..had misled proabortionists and *prolifers. 1976 *Observer* 24 Oct. 9/1 Anti-abortion forces have been organising to overturn the decision [of the U.S. Supreme Court]... The pro-lifers, as they prefer to call themselves, can no longer be written off as a lunatic fringe. 1979 *Time* 30 July 6 Pro-lifers have children, pro-choicers do not. 1895 *Voice* (N.Y.) 19 Sept. 3/4 It has even been admitted by *pro-liquorites that the voters of New Jersey would under the Initiative and Referendum adopt county, municipal, and township local option. 1961 *Economist* 2 Dec. 877/1 Mr. Heath's speech may legitimately be criticised by *pro-marketeers. 1976 H. WILSON *Governance of Britain* 10, I had to be aware of..the balance between committed pro-marketeers and committed anti-marketeers. 1895 *Pop. Sci. Monthly* Sept. 649 It may be well to call the ..tendencies favorable to virtue, *pro-moral. 1936 *New Yorker* 29 Feb. 24/3 Ernst Röhm, who in 1928 had written a *pro-Nazi autobiography. 1974 G. JENKINS *Bridge of Magpies* vii. 113 Her husband was the boss of the pro-Nazi underground movement. 1892 *Pall Mall G.* 20 Apr. 6/1 Mr. Malins headed the *pro-negro party when the secession ..took place. 1839 *Conservative Jrnl.* 26 Jan., The interests of..a *pro-papist popularity-hunting viceroy. 1841 J. ROBERTSON in Charteris *Life* v. (1863) 125 The anti-patronage men and the *pro-patronage Non-intrusionists split among themselves. 1828 SYD. SMITH in Lady Holland *Mem.* (1855) I. 217 A deputation of *pro-Popery papers waited on me today to print, but I declined. 1829 WHEWELL in *Life* (1881) 127 He is supported by the pro-popery Ministry. 1897 *Daily News* 25 Jan. 5/7 The *pro-Rhodes feeling in Capetown..is strong to unreason. 1890 *Columbus* (Ohio) *Dispatch* 29 Aug., The so-called United Brethren known as liberals or *pro-secretists. 1856 in L. W. SPRING *Kansas* (1885) 48, I tell you I'm *pro-slave. 1858 *N. York Tribune* 29 Dec. 6/4 The *Pro-Slavers all went home without any action. 1843 WHITTIER *What is Slavery?* Prose Wks. 1889 III. 106 In the midst of grossest *pro-slavery action, they are full of anti-slavery sentiment. 1856 G. D. BREWERTON *War in Kansas* 124 'The hour and the man' of Free-State-ism, or *Pro-Slavery-ism, for we can scarce say which, is yet to come. 1950 L. FISCHER in Koestler et al. *God that Failed* 225 This I did not understand in the years when I was *pro-Soviet. 1977 *Listener* 21 Apr. 499/3 Mao's pro-Soviet opponents. 1950 L. FISCHER in Koestler et al. *God that Failed* 224 My years of *pro-Sovietism have taught me that no one who loves people and peace should favour a dictatorship. 1952 *Sun* (Baltimore) 6 Feb. 1/5 The Soviet claims..treated such 'neutralism' on the part of United Nations members as pro-Sovietism. 1839 J. ROGERS *Antipopopr.* VI. ii. 222 One sense tells that a *pro-transubstantiation passage is in the Bible. 1896 *Daily News* 3 Apr. 4/7 The curious anomaly that some of our strongest anti-Turk politicians on the Armenian question should at the same time be in favour of a *pro-Turk policy in Egypt. 1899 *Ibid.* 6 Mar. 8/5 The *pro-vaccinist statisticians. 1958 'A. BRIDGE' *Portuguese Escape* iii. 44 One of the real stars is *pro-West, and arranged with our man in Hungary to bring him along. 1976 *Billings* (Montana) *Gaz.* 17 June 2-G/1 Kenya, the only pro-West nation on the East African coast. 1934 WEBSTER, *Pro-Western. 1965 H. KAHN *On Escalation* i. 24 It [*sc.* the United States] could have invaded Iraq in 1958 to restore a pro-Western government. 1980 P. VAN GREENAWAY *Dissident* v. 123 Is it possible for a man to be pro-Western *without* being anti-Soviet? 1949 KOESTLER *Promise & Fulfilment* I. ii. 13 'Somehow we like the Arabs' ..confessed a sincere and *pro-Zionist Englishman. 1971 D. MEIRING *Wall of Glass* viii. 65 The idea that Jew could kill Jew in Palestine for political reasons was the more intolerable the more pro-Zionist you were.

pro- (prəʊ), *prefix*[2]. Repr. the Gr. preposition πρό, meaning 'before' (of time, position, preference, priority, etc.), forming in Greek many compounds—verbs, substantives, and adjectives. Of the sbs. and their derivatives more than 60 were adopted in late Latin as technical terms of rhetoric, philosophy, natural history, art, and Jewish or Christian religion (e.g. *problēma*, *proboscis*, *prodromus*, *prolēpsis*, *prologus*, *prophēta* (*prophētia*, *prophēticus*, *prophētizāre*), *propolis*, *proscænium*, *prostylus*, *protasis*). With the revival of learning many more Greek terms were latinized. Many of these latinized forms of both periods have been adopted or adapted in the modern languages generally, and have subsequently served as models for the formation of new combinations from Greek (less commonly from Latin) elements, in the nomenclature of modern science and philosophy. The older and more important of the English words so derived appear in their alphabetical order as Main words. Those in which *pro-* is more obviously a prefix to a word itself used in English, or which are merely technical terms, follow here.

1. In sense 'Before in time': forming (*a*) sbs., chiefly scientific terms denominating the earlier, or (supposed) primitive type of an animal, plant, organ, or structure (with derived adjs.); (*b*) adjs. meaning 'previous to or preceding that which is expressed by the second element'.

proaccelerin (-æk'sɛlərɪn) *Biochem.*, a relatively labile procoagulant present in the blood; **pro'activator** *Biochem.*, a precursor of the activator of a compound; **pro-agonic** (-ə'gɒnɪk) *a.*, *Path.*, preceding a paroxysm; **pro-'amnion**, the primitive amnion in the embryonic stage of some animals; hence **pro-amni'otic** *a.*, pertaining to the pro-amnion; ‖**pro-amphibia** (-æm'fɪbɪə) *sb. pl.* *Zool.*, the (hypothetical) primitive or ancestral amphibious animals; **pro-angiosperm** (-'ændʒɪəʊspɜːm) *Bot.*, a primitive or ancestral angiosperm, from which the existing angiosperms are supposed to have been developed; hence **pro-angio'spermic** *a.*; **pro-bap'tismal** *a.*, preceding or preparatory to baptism; **proba'sidium** *Bot.* [ad. F. *probaside* (P. Van Tieghem 1893, in *Jrnl. de Bot.* VII. 80)], in some fungi, a part of a basidium, or an early stage in its development, in which nuclear fusion takes place; **probi'otic** *a.* = PREBIOLOGICAL, PREBIOTIC *adjs.*; **pro'carcinogen**, a substance that is not directly carcinogenic itself but is converted in the body into one that is; so **pro,carcino'genic** *a.*; **prochorion** (-'kɔərɪən) *Embryol.*, the vitelline membrane or integument of the ovum, which develops into the chorion; **proco'agulant** *sb.* and *a. Biochem.*, (of or pertaining to) any substance that promotes the conversion of the inactive prothrombin to the clotting enzyme thrombin; **procon'vertin** *Biochem.* [CONVERT *v.*], a relatively stable procoagulant present in the blood; **pro-'dialogue** (*nonce-wd.*), an introductory dialogue; **prodissoconch** (-'dɪsəʊkɒŋk), *Zool.* [Gr. δισσό-ς double + CONCH], a name suggested for the early shell of the oyster; **proe'rythroblast** *Med.* [ad. It. *proeritroblasti* (A. Ferrata *Morfologia del Sangue* (1912) v. 232)], the earliest recognizable precursor of the red-cell series, characterized by a large nucleus with nucleoli and by basophilic cytoplasm; **proestrus**, var. *proœstrum* below; **,profibrino'lysin** *Biochem.* = PLASMINOGEN; **progametange** (-'gæmiːtændʒ), **-game'tangium** *Biol.*, 'an immature or resting gametangium' (*Cent. Dict.*); †**pro'gamete** *Biol.*, a structure able to give rise to one or more gametes; **proganoid** (-'gænɔɪd) *Ichthyol.*, *a.* of or belonging to the primitive (fossil) ganoid fishes; *sb.* a primitive ganoid; **proganosaur** (-'gænəʊsɔə(r)) *Palæont.* [Gr. γάνος brightness + σαῦρος lizard], *sb.* a member of the order *Proganosauria* of extinct reptiles; *adj.* belonging to this order; **pro'gymnosperm**, *Bot.*, a primitive or ancestral gymnosperm, from which the existing gymnosperms are supposed to have been developed; hence **progymno'spermic** *a.*; **pro'heterocyst** *Biol.*, an incipient heterocyst; **pro'hormone** *Physiol.*, a natural precursor of a hormone; **proinsulin** (prəʊ'ɪn-) *Biochem.*, the natural precursor of insulin; **pro'kosmial** *a.*, *nonce-wd.* [Gr. κόσμος world: see COSMOS], existing before the cosmos or universe; **pro'mammal** *Zool.*, one of the (hypothetical) *Promammalia* or primitive mammals; so **proma'mmalian** *a.*; **pro'meristem** *Bot.*, primary meristem, protomeristem; **,promito'chondrion** *Cytology*, an inactive form of mitochondrion; **pro'myelocyte** *Med.*, a cell intermediate in development between a myeloblast and a mature myelocyte; so **pro'myelocytic** *a.*; **pronymph** ('prəʊnɪmf), *Entom.* [see NYMPH *sb.* 3], a stage in the development of some dipterous insects, intervening between the larval and pupal stages (cf. *propupa* below); hence **pro'nymphal** *a.*; ‖**pro-œstrum** (-'iːstrəm, -'ɛs-) (**proestrus**, **proœstrus**) *Zool.*, the period immediately preceding that of the œstrum or sexual excitement in animals; so **pro-'œstrous** *a.*, preceding the œstrum; belonging to the pro-œstrum; **pro'peptone** (see quot. 1895); ‖**properistoma** (-pə'rɪstəmə), **properistome** (-'pɛrɪstəʊm) *Embryol.* [cf. PERISTOME], the lip of the primitive mouth of a gastrula; hence **properi'stomal** *a.*; **pro'plastid** *Cytology*, a small unspecialized plastid, able to differentiate into a plastid of any type characteristic of the species; ‖**propupa** (-'pjuːpə) *Entom.*, a stage in the development of some insects, as the cochineal-insect, intervening between the larval and pupal stages (cf. *pronymph* above); **prorenal** (-'riːnəl) *a. Embryol.* [see RENAL], belonging to the primitive kidney or segmental body; ‖**proscolex** (-'skəʊlɛks), *Zool.*, pl. **proscolices** (-'skəʊlɪsiːz) [Gr. σκώληξ worm], the first embryonic stage of a cestode or tape-worm, from which the scolex is developed by budding; hence **proscolecine** (-'skəʊlɪsaɪn) *a.*, pertaining to a proscolex; **prose'cretin** *Physiol.*, a supposed precursor of secretin; ‖**prospo'rangium** *Bot.* (pl. **-ia**) = *prozoosporange*; **pro'theca** [THECA], in Foraminifera, the primary wall; **pro'trichocyst** *Zool.* [ad. G. *protrichocyste* (B. M. Klein 1928, in *Arch. f. Protistenkunde* LXII. 210)], an undeveloped trichocyst; **protrypsin** (-'trɪpsɪn) *Phys. Chem.*, a substance formed in the pancreas, and afterwards converted into trypsin; also called *trypsinogen*; **prozoosporange** (-,zəʊəʊspɒ'rændʒ) *Bot.*, a stage in the development of certain fungi, which produces a thin-walled process into which the protoplasm passes and divides into zoospores.

1951 P. A. OWREN in *Proc. 3rd Internat. Congr. Internat. Soc. Hematol.* 379, I wish to propose the terms *proaccelerin and accelerin instead of Factor V and Factor VI, because.. these factors constitute the system which is responsible for the acceleration of thrombin formation. 1966 *McGraw-Hill Encycl. Sci. & Technol.* II. 266/1 The interreactions of tissue thromboplastin, calcium ions, and several proteins of plasma, including proaccelerin..and proconvertin, result in the conversion of prothrombin into a proteolytic enzyme, thrombin. 1956 T. ASTRUP in *Blood* XI. 783 In blood, human milk, tears, and in other body fluids enzymatically acting activators of plasminogen are also found, or can be produced. The production of activating agents in these cases is caused by the transformation of a precursor (a *proactivator). 1973 *Jrnl. Clin. Invest.* LII. 2591/2 Conversion of highly purified plasminogen proactivator to plasminogen activator was shown to result in the generation of chemotactic activity. 1876 tr. *Wagner's Gen. Pathol.* 621 The termination is doubtful, and transition into the *pro-agonic stage not rare. 1890 BILLINGS *Med. Dict.*, **Pro-amnion*, term applied by van Beneden and Julin to an area around the head of the very young embryo in which there is no mesoderm, the ectoderm and endoderm being in direct contact, and which is soon obliterated by the ingrowth of mesoderm. 1889 *Q. Jrnl. Microsc. Sc.* Dec. 290 Long after the true amnion has been quite completed the head gradually emerges from this *pro-amniotic pit. 1901 *Nature* 14 Mar. 462/2 Connected through a series of hypothetical *Proamphibia or Protetrapoda with equally hypothetical Selachian-like animals. 1886 *Ibid.* 25 Feb. 389/1 The ancestral '*pro-angiosperms' are supposed to have borne leaves such as are found diminished or masked in so many of their existing descendants. *Ibid.* 389/2 Such was the nature of plants in their '*pro-angiospermic' stage. **1840** G. S. Faber *Christ's Disc. Capernaum* viii. 230 *note*, Cyril has devoted to his painful *probaptismal instruction no fewer than eighteen Lectures. **1928** C. W. Dodge tr. *Gäumann's Compar. Morphol. Fungi* xxv. 415 This enlarged hyphal cell which..forms the first stage of the basidium..is called [the] *probasidium. **1979** I. K. Ross *Biol. Fungi* vi. 156 In the spring, each cell of the teliospore [in *Puccinia graminis*] functions as a probasidium and produces a thin-walled metabasidium. **1954** *New Biol.* XVI. 44 We have as yet no basis for confidence about the *probiotic state. **1971** J. Z. Young *Introd. Study Man* xxvi. 372 A probiotic soup of amino-acids, ribose, four purine and pyrimidine bases, and a source of high-energy phosphate. **1963** *Clin. Pharmacol. & Therapeutics* IV. 111/1 A compound requiring metabolic activation is one which when administered to animals is very likely not carcinogenic by itself ('*procarcinogen') but requires transformation in the host to become a 'proximate' carcinogen—a sort of lethal synthesis. **1975** *Pharmacol. Basis of Cancer Chemotherapy* 129 (*heading*) Procarcinogens and their bioactivation. **1944** *Jrnl. Exper. Med.* LXXX. 121 The papers dealing with the 'cocarcinogens' show clearly that the substances thus designated do not cause neoplastic changes but act either by enabling the real carcinogens to reach susceptible cells or by promoting the formation of growths. They are in other words *procarcinogenic. **1976** *New Scientist* 9 Dec. 586/2 Cigarette smoke..contains procarcinogenic polynuclear aromatic hydrocarbons which are broken down by enzymes in the lungs. **1879** tr. *Haeckel's Evol. Man* II. xix. 157 This *prochorion very soon disappears, and is replaced by the permanent outer egg-membrane, the chorion. **1958** Landaburu & Seegers in *Amer. Jrnl. Physiol.* CXCIII. 178/1 Other factors support the production and enzyme function of thrombin, and these we call *procoagulants. **1960** *Nature* 26 Mar. 930/2 The control of prothrombin activation is by a group of anticoagulants and procoagulants functioning in dynamic equilibrium. **1962** W. H. Seegers *Prothrombin* ix. 202 There is a procoagulant effect noticeable in whole blood or plasma following the alimentary intake of certain kinds of fats. **1971** R. S. Shepard *Human Physiol.* xiv. 243/2 (*caption*) Intermediates of prothrombin activation may result in the formation of a number of other procoagulants as well as anticoagulants. **1976** *Nature* 22 Apr. 711/2 It has been shown that human fibroblasts contain a potent procoagulant activity called 'tissue factor' (TF). **1951** P. A. Owren in *Proc. 3rd Internat. Congr. Internat. Soc. Hematol.* 383 This substance acts as the limiting factor for prothrombin conversion and I have thus chosen to give it the name *proconvertin. **1976** *Nature* 17 June 621/2 The coagulation of blood is envisaged as a complex but ordered succession of processes, and at least four of the many factors (prothrombin, proconvertin, Christmas factor and Stuart factor) are known to be dependent on vitamin K. **1884** *Athenæum* 12 July 41/1 In the *pro-dialogue to the 'Isle of Gulls' one of the characters says, 'I cannot see it out.' **1888** Jackson in *Proc. Boston Soc. Nat. Hist.* XXIII. 543 In the oyster..this shell is not single but double-valved, and..as it precedes the dissoconch or true shell, I suggest the name *prodissoconch, or early double shell. **1927** A. Piney *Rec. Adv. Hæmatol.* ii. 29 It is obvious that the adherents of the monophyletic school will be of opinion that the red corpuscle is derived from the primitive stem cell (hæmocytoblast). They contend that all sorts of transitions can be found between large non-hæmoglobiniferous cells (*pro-erythroblasts) and the mature, fully hæmoglobiniferous corpuscle. **1962** *Lancet* 27 Jan. 208/2 A continuous morphological spectrum of cells was evident, indicating many transitional forms between what appeared to be typical small lymphocytes and myeloblasts or proerythroblasts. **1969** Hayhoe & Flemans *Atlas Haematol. Cytol.* (1970) i. 7 The proerythroblast is not itself the functional stem cell serving as a self-maintaining progenitor of the normoblast series. **1947** E. C. Loomis et al. in *Arch. Biochem.* XII. 1 We suggest the following names for the compounds: 1). Fibrinolysin... 2). *Profibrinolysin—the inactive form or precursor of fibrinolysin. This compound is the proenzyme form from serum or plasma activated by streptokinase, organic solvents and other enzyme activators. **1958** *Observer* 14 Dec. 4/3 A precursor, profibrinolysin, is present in the blood and is changed to fibrinolysin by natural agents released when needed. **1968** A. White et al. *Princ. Biochem.* (ed. 4) xxxi. 733 The proteolytic enzyme, plasmin (fibrinolysin), ordinarily exists in plasma as the inactive precursor..plasminogen (profibrinolysin). **1892** *Q. Jrnl. Microsc. Sci.* XXXIII. 6 In my terminology I have used the word[s]..gametogonium and *progamete to express, from slightly different points of view, a cell which divides to form gametes, or (rarely) passes into the state of a gamete. *Ibid.* 54 In most cases of so-called 'parthenogenesis' of Metazoa only one polar body is formed, and the ovum, rather a progamete than an oosphere, segments and develops directly. **1904** *Proc. Amer. Acad. Arts & Sci.* XL. 231 The zygospores are abundant between the gills of the host, and the progametes arise at times from branches of the same hypha. **1889** Nicholson & Lydekker *Palæont.* II. xlix. 959 *Proganoid Series. *Ibid.* 965 The last group of the Proganoids. **1900** Osborn in *Amer. Naturalist* Oct. 797 More probable than that the avian phylum should have originated quite independently from a quadrupedal *proganosaur. **1886** *Nature* 25 Feb. 389/2 In the remote past ..the cambium layer may have existed in an irregular or fugitive manner in the 'pro-angiospermic', as it did in the '*pro-gymnospermic' stem. **1970** *Nature* 14 Nov. 686/1 A close pattern of heterocysts and presumptive heterocysts ('*proheterocysts') is apparent. **1973** *Jrnl. Cell Sci.* XIII. 641 In the presence of ammonia, heterocyst development is affected, so that a pattern consisting largely of proheterocysts, rather than mature heterocysts, is formed. **1935** *Amer. Jrnl. Physiol.* CXII. 511 Many of the published opinions concerning the *prohormone have been made from incidental observations, rather than from directed experiments planned to give information concerning its existence or properties. **1970** *Proc. Nat. Acad. Sci.* LXVII. 1637 Unlike the islet cell, which stores hormone primarily in the form of insulin, the parathyroid may store its hormone as the prohormone, with conversion taking place when the gland is stimulated. **1977** *Lancet* 25 June 1341/2 Vitamin D is a pro-hormone which only becomes active on transformation to its 25-hydroxy derivative, a process that is subject to pronounced but poorly understood constraints. **1916** E. A. Schäfer *Endocrine Organs* xvii. 128 Provisionally, it will be convenient to refer to this hypothetical autacoid as *insuline*. It must, however, be stated that it has yet to be determined whether the active substance is present as such in the pancreas or whether it exists there as **pro-insuline*, which becomes elsewhere converted into the active autacoid. **1967** D. F. Steiner et al. in *Science* 26 Apr. 700/2 The labeling data reported here support our earlier interpretation that component *b* is a precursor in the biosynthesis of insulin. It might be less cumbersome, therefore, to designate this material 'proinsulin'. **1969** *Nature* 15 Nov. 696/1 Proinsulin has little or no biological activity, but is present in the circulation and produces insulin-like effects when injected into normal animals. **1970** *Jrnl. Clin. Investigation* XLIX. 506/2 At present data concerning the biological activity of human proinsulin are not available. **1855** Bailey *Mystic* (ed. 2) 36 Where the *pro-kosmial forms of thought abide. **1889** *Proc. Zool. Soc.* 262 If not the '*Promammal' of Haeckel, it may perhaps have been a near relative of some such transitional form. **1876** tr. *Haeckel's Hist. Creat.* xxi. II. 235 The unknown, extinct Primary Mammals, or *Promammalia.. probably possessed a very highly developed jaw. **1898** tr. *Strasburger's Bot.* I. 90 The tissues..are distinguished as primary and secondary, according as they are derived from the *promeristem or secondary meristem. **1925** Eames & MacDaniels *Introd. Plant Anat.* iii. 41 Promeristems gradually become differentiated. **1953** K. Esau *Plant Anat.* iv. 78 The initiating cells and their most recent derivatives are often distinguished, under the name of promeristem. **1976** Bell & Coombe tr. *Strasburger's Textbk. Bot.* (rev. ed.) 89 Primary embryonic tissues are those which are derived ontogenetically directly from the tissue of the embryo, and they are referred to as primordia or promeristems. **1969** Criddle & Schatz in *Biochem.* VIII. 323/2 Since the term 'proplastid' is well established.., the mitochondria-like particles from anaerobic yeast cells were correspondingly termed '*promitochondria'. **1974** *Nature* 15 Mar. 258/2 Such mitochondria as yeast promitochondria do not contain all the carriers of the respiratory chain and possess an enhanced resistance to anaerobiosis. **1925** Strong & Elwyn *Bailey's Textbk. Histol.* (ed.7) vi. 142 The myelocytes are the most abundant developmental forms of marrow... The most immature are known as *promyelocytes, the fully matured as metamyelocytes. **1957** L. K. Hillestad in *Acta Medica Scand.* CLIX. 189 This paper deals with three cases of a special type of acute myelogenous leukemia... The white blood cell picture in the peripheral blood resembles that of the more chronic forms of leukemia, as it is dominated by promyelocytes and myelocytes with very few myeloblasts. A logical name for this type of leukemia is *acute promyelocytic leukemia*. **1973** *Brit. Jrnl. Haematol.* XXIV. 255 Acute promyelocytic leukaemia..is now recognized as a distinct clinical and pathological entity, classically characterized by..replacement of bone marrow by abnormal myeloblasts and promyelocytes. **1977** *Lancet* 15 Oct. 806/2 Cytoplasmic vacuolation, similar to that in erythroblasts, occurs in promyelocytes in the bone-marrow of alcoholics. **1895** D. Sharp in *Camb. Nat. Hist.* V. 164 The process of forming the various organs goes on in the *pronymph, till the 'nymph' has completed its development. *Ibid.*, The *pronymphal state may be looked upon as being to a great extent a return of the animal to the condition of an egg. **1900** W. Heape in *Q. Jrnl. Microsc. Sc.* Nov. 6 **Pro-œstrum* or the **Pro-œstrous* Period..I have adopted to describe the first phases of generative activity in the female mammal at the beginning of a sexual season. **1901** *Brit. Med. Jrnl.* No. 2097. 593 There is the 'pro-œstrum' ('the coming in season')..characterised by..a pro-œstrous discharge..most usually of mucus. **1923** *Amer. Jrnl. Anat.* XXXII. 306 Through its action on *prooestrus and ovulation the corpus luteum indirectly inhibits those growth processes which are initiated by the maturing follicles. **1923** Proestrus [see metœstrus]. **1937** *Nature* 4 Dec. 950/1 It can no longer be affirmed that the proœstrus of the lower mammal corresponds simply to the menstrual flow of the human female. **1966**, **1973** Proestrus, prooestrus [see metœstrus]. **1976** *Sci. Amer.* July 52/2 In the normal estrous cycle of the rat the pituitary secretes large amounts of luteinizing hormone..in the afternoon of proestrus, approximately 30 hours after the initial increase in estradiol secretion by the ovaries. **1895** *Syd. Soc. Lex.*, **Propeptone*, also termed *Hemialbumose*, one of the intermediate products formed during the conversion of albumins into peptones in gastric digestion. **1897** *Allbutt's Syst. Med.* III. 292 The action of the gastric juice upon the albuminous constituents of the food is indicated by the presence of syntonin, propeptone and peptone. **1879** tr. *Haeckel's Evol. Man* I. viii. 220 At the thickened edges of the gastrula, the primitive mouth-edge (**properistoma*), the endoderm, and the exoderm pass into each other. **1922** L. F. Randolph in *Bot. Gaz.* LXXIII. 345 Since these bodies have been found to occur as a constant feature of the cytoplasm of meristematic cells in maize, and inasmuch as they have been found to be definitely concerned with the formation of chloroplasts, the term '*proplastid' will be used for such bodies. **1934** L. W. Sharp *Introd. Cytol.* (ed. 3) iv. 69 The differentiated plastids seen in mature tissues may be traced back to plastid primordia, or proplastids in the young cells of the meristem or embryo. **1967** Kirk & Tilney-Bassett *Plastids* xiv. 497 It may be generally true that whenever a chloroplast-containing plant cell has to start dividing, the chloroplasts revert to proplastids to facilitate the plastid division that must take place if plastid numbers in the cell are to be maintained. **1895** *Syd. Soc. Lex.*, **Propupa*, that stage in insect development immediately preceding the *pupa*. **1898** Packard *Textbk. Entomol.* III. 627 It passes into what Riley terms the pro-pupa, in which the wing-pads are present. **1888** Huxley & Martin *Elem. Biol.* 169 The *pro-renal (segmental) duct; a conspicuous thick-walled tube seen, on either side, lying within the somatic mesoblast. **1895** *Syd. Soc. Lex.*, **Proscolecine*, belonging to a *Proscolex*. **1870** Rolleston *Anim. Life* 250 Embryo or *proscolex of an ordinary Taenia, armed..with six spines. **1888** Rolleston & Jackson *Anim. Life* 233 That the proscolex may develope in an alimentary canal is proved by P. J. Van Beneden's discovery of proscolices with scolices in all stages of growth in the intestine of the Lump-fish. **1902** Bayliss & Starling in *Jrnl. Physiol.* XXVIII. 331 The distribution of '*prosecretin', as we have proposed to call the mother-substance, corresponds..precisely with the region from which acid introduced into the lumen excites secretion from the pancreas. **1935** *Amer. Jrnl. Physiol.* CXII. 511 In this study we have..attempted to obtain concrete evidence concerning the existence of prosecretin. **1962** R. A. Gregory *Secretory Mech. Gastro-Intestinal Tract* xii. 157 Bayliss & Starling originally supposed that it [*sc.* secretin] might exist in the form of an active precursor 'prosecretin' from which secretin was liberated by acid hydrolysis. This view was later abandoned. **1887** tr. *De Bary's Fungi* 163 When it [*Polyphagus Euglenæ*] has reached a certain size,.. it shows itself in many specimens to be a sporangium, or, if the term is preferred, a *prosporangium. *Ibid.* Explan. Terms 498 *Prosporangium*, in Chytridieæ: vesicular cell the protoplasm of which passes into an outgrowth of itself, the sporangium, and becomes divided into swarm-spores. **1945** M. F. Glaessner *Princ. Micropalaeont.* v. 108 The *protheca or primary wall consists of a layer of clear transparent calcite (diaphanotheca), and a thin dark outer rind-like film (tectum). **1963** K. A. Allen tr. *Pokorny's Princ. Zool. Micropalaeont.* I. vi. 236 In some of these forms [of Foraminifera] there is only a single undifferentiated layer, the protheca. **1933** G. N. Calkins *Biol. Protozoa* (ed. 2) iv. 135 The trichocysts at rest are capsules filled with a densely staining..substance... They appear to be connected with the silver line system and..are here represented by granules when the trichocysts are undeveloped. In such granular form they are sometimes called '*protrichocysts'. **1965** *Jrnl. Cell Biol.* XXVII. 67 The structures containing the amorphous material are variously referred to as protrichocysts, mucoid trichocysts, mucigenic bodies, or secretory ampules. **1972** M. S. Gardiner *Biol. Invertebrates* xix. 850/2 Electron micrographs reveal that the stripes contain refringent granules, considered protrichocysts, which are..blue in *S[tentor] coeruleus*, giving this species its beautiful color. **1900** *Lancet* 27 Oct. 1187/1 The pancreatic zymogen, trypsinogen or *protrypsin.

2. Of local position: forming sbs. and adjs., chiefly anatomical and zoological terms (often correlated with words in meta-[1] and meso-); (*a*) in adjectival relation to the second element, denoting either 'an anterior or front (thing of the kind)', or 'an anterior or front part (of the thing)'; (*b*) in prepositional relation to the second element = 'lying before or in front of (the thing)'.

pro-'atlas, *Zool.* [Atlas *sb.*[1] 2] (see quots.); ‖**procerebrum** (-'sɛrɪbrəm), *Anat.*, the front part of the cerebrum or brain; the fore-brain, prosencephalon; hence **pro'cerebral** *a.*; **procnemial** (-'kniːmɪəl) *a.*, *Anat.* [Gr. κνήμη leg, tibia], situated in front of the tibia; **pro'delta** *a.* and *sb. Geol.*, (the part of a delta) lying underneath and beyond the sloping front of a delta; so **prodel'taic** *a.*; ‖**pro-epimeron** (-ɛpɪ'mɪərən) *Entom.*, the epimeron of the prothorax of an insect, the second sclerite of either propleuron; hence **pro-epi'meral** *a.*; ‖**pro-epi'sternum**, *Entom.*, the episternum of the prothorax, the anterior sclerite of either propleuron; hence **pro-epi'sternal** *a.*; **pro'filmic** *a. Semiotics* [ad. F. *profilmique*: cf. E. Souriau in *Revue Internationale de Filmologie* (1951) II. vii–viii], happening or situated in front of a camera; **pro'neural** *a.*, of the first bone in a turtle's carapace, situated in front of the neural bones; also *absol.*; ‖**pro-'osteon**, *Ornith.* [Gr. ὀστέον bone], an ossification in each anterior lateral process of the sternum in certain birds; ‖**propa'rapteron** *Entom.*, the parapteron of the prothorax; hence **propa'rapteral** *a.*; ‖**pro'plexus** (also anglicized **'proplex**) *Anat.*, (*a*) Wilder's term for the choroid plexus of either of the lateral ventricles of the brain; (*b*) 'the analogue in the Vertebrata generally of the brachial plexus in man' (*Syd. Soc. Lex.*); ‖**pro-postscu'tellum**, ‖**pro-præ'scutum** *Entom.*, the postscutellum and præscutum (respectively) of the prothorax of an insect; hence **pro-postscu'tellar**, **pro-præ'scutal** *adjs.*; ‖**propygidium** (-paɪ'dʒɪdɪəm) *Entom.*, the segment immediately in front of the pygidium in certain beetles; ‖**proscapula** (-'skæpjʊlə) *Ichth.*, the outer bone of the scapular arch, usually passing forwards and articulating with its fellow of the opposite side, and supporting the cartilage or bone which bears the pectoral fin; hence **pro'scapular** *a.*; ‖**proscutellum** (-skjuː'tɛləm), ‖**proscutum** (-'skjuːtəm) *Entom.*, the scutellum and scutum (respectively) of the prothorax; hence **proscu'tellar**, **pro'scutal** *adjs.*; ‖**prozyga'pophysis** = prezygapophysis.

1886 Günther in *Encycl. Brit.* XX. 447/2 The first two vertebræ are differentiated as axis and atlas, and in front of the latter there may be [in Reptiles] a rudiment of another vertebra, which has been distinguished as the *proatlas. **1889** Nicholson & Lydekker *Palæont.* II. xlv. 897 It has been suggested that certain bony splints overlying the arch of the atlas in Crocodiles represent a vertebra intercalated between the latter and the cranium, for which the name *proatlas* has been proposed. It is, however, by no means proved that these splints do not belong to the atlas vertebra. **1895** *Syd. Soc. Lex.*, **Procerebral*, belonging to the *Procerebrum*. **1890** Billings *Med. Dict.*, **Procerebrum*, Prosencephalon. **1854** Owen *Skel. & Teeth* (1855) 64 The proximal end of the tibia..: two ridges are extended from its upper and anterior surface: the strongest of these is the '*procnemial' ridge. **1940** E. S. Hills *Outl. Structural Geol.*

i. 4 The bottom-sets or *prodelta clays represent the finer detritus spread out over the floor of the sea or lake in which the delta was formed. **1963** D. W. & E. E. HUMPHRIES tr. *Termier's Erosion & Sedimentation* xi. 227 This bed is, perhaps, comparable to that formed on a prodelta. **1969** BENNISON & WRIGHT *Geol. Hist. Brit. Isles* xiv. 319 The high percentage of silt in the clays has led to a comparison with some modern pro-delta sediments. **1975** HOBSON & TIRATSOO *Introd. Petroleum Geol.* ii. 32 The sediments of the delta front, pro-delta and continental shelf are organically fairly rich. **1968** MURCHISON & WESTOLL *Coal* v. 89 The seaward advance of delta-fronts and *prodeltaic muds, silts and sands. **1974** *Nature* 8 Feb. 344/2 Interbedded sheets and lenses of moderately well sorted prodeltaic and littoral sands. **1895** *Syd. Soc. Lex.*, *Proëpimeral, *Proëpimeron, *Proëpisternal, *Proëpisternum. **1973** P. WILLEMEN in *Screen* Spring/Summer 13 *Profilmic events should be divided into signifying reality and into non-signifying reality (eg on one level, a city is a signifying reality, a mountain range is not). *Ibid.*, In the cinema one 'sections' the profilmic reality. **1974** M. TAYLOR tr. *Metz's Film Lang.* iii. 33 That great artist . . manages to have beauty, which has been pitilessly rejected from every 'profilmic' occasion. **1952** A. CARR *Handbk. Turtles* I. 36 Along the mid-line twelve of the bones of the carapace are arranged in a row. In front is the *proneural bone (usually known as the nuchal). **1967** P. C. H. PRITCHARD *Living Turtles of World* 10 The foremost bone in the turtle shell . . is large; it is called the proneural or nuchal bone. Behind the proneural comes a midline row of eleven or fewer bones, called neurals. **1868** W. K. PARKER *Shoulder-Girdle Vertebr.* (Ray Soc.) 144 In the genus *Rhea* . . there is, on each side, an osseous centre in front of the first rib: it ossifies the costal process, and, projecting forwards as a wing in front of the sternal ribs, may be called the '*pro-osteon'. **1896** NEWTON *Dict. Birds* 910 Thus in *Rhea*, *Gallinæ*, *Turnix*, *Lestris* and the *Passeres*, each anterior lateral process has its *pro-osteon* . ., but in many other forms . . these processes possess no special centre of ossification. **1882** WILDER & GAGE *Anat. Techn.* 485 *Proplexus. **1899** D. SHARP in *Camb. Nat. Hist.* VI. 187 A similar plate anterior to the pygidium is called *propygidium. **1833** F. WALKER in *Entomol. Mag.* I. 21 The semihyaline spots on the *proscutellum are much larger in this species. **1872** MIVART *Elem. Anat.* 46 But in some Chameleons, a prominence is developed from each *prozygapophysis, which may be a metapophysis.

proa ('prəʊə), ‖**prahu** ('prɑːuː). Forms: 6–7 **parao, paroe,** 7 **paro,** 7–8 **paroo;** 7–9 **prau, praw,** (7 **prawe**); 7–9 **prow,** (7 **provoe, proe**); 9 **praoe,** 8– **proa,** (9 **proah**); 9 **prahu,** 20 **perahu.** [ad. Malay *p(ă)rā(h)ū* a boat, a rowing or sailing vessel; in Pg. *parao*, Du. *prauw*, F. *prao*, *pro*. The forms *prow* and *proa* are assimilated to the Eng. PROW (*sb.*[2]) and its Pg. equivalent *proa*.]

A Malay boat propelled by sails or by oars; *spec.* a sailing boat of a particular type used in the Malay Archipelago.

It is about thirty feet long (now often more: see quot. 1977), has both stem and stern sharp, adapting it to sail equally well in either direction; one side is curved as in other vessels, the other is flat and straight and acts as a lee-board; to steady the boat a small canoe or the like is rigged parallel to it in the manner of an outrigger (see OUTRIGGER 2).

1582 N. LICHEFIELD tr. *Castanheda's Conq. E. Ind.* I. xxv. 62 b, The next day . . there came in two little Paraos, to the number of twelue men. **1599** HAKLUYT *Voy.* II. I. 258 We left our boats or Paroes. **1606** MIDDLETON *Voy.* C iij b, An howre after . . came a prawe or a canow from Bantam. **1623** *St. Papers, Col.* 188 Others violently kept their men from entering Limco's prau. **1625** PURCHAS *Pilgrims* I. III. x. §1. 239 The King sent a small Prow. **1653** H. COGAN tr. *Pinto's Trav.* ii. 35 She imbarqued herself in sixteen . . fishermens Paroos. **1698** FRYER *Acc. E. India & P.* 20 They are Owners of several small Provoes . . and Canooses. **1700** S. L. tr. *Fryke's Voy. E. Ind.* 50 They were carried off in little Praw's, or small Boats, on Board the Men of War. **1726** SHELVOCKE *Voy. round World* 437 We saw several flying prows, but none came near us. **1745** P. THOMAS *Jrnl. Anson's Voy.* 150 The Pinnace . . brought with her an Indian Paroo, which you may see very well described by Capt. Cooke. **1785** FRANKLIN *Lett.* Wks. 1840 VI. 477 We have no sailing boats equal to the flying proas of the South Seas. **1821** J. LEYDEN tr. *Malay Annals* 148 Tun Talani and the mantri Jana Petra returned to their prahus. **1831** TRELAWNEY *Adv. Younger Son* I. 220 They are called by Europeans, owing to the wonderful rapidity with which they sail, flying prows. **1850** W. STANTON in *Merc. Marine Mag.* (1860) VII. 107 Prahus frequently anchor here. **1883** R. A. PROCTOR in *Contemp. Rev.* Oct. 571 At Bima every proa and boat was forced from its anchorage and flung on the coast. **1923** [see BALLAHOU, BALLAHOO]. **1932** W. S. MAUGHAM *Narrow Corner* xv. 114 The harbour was far from crowded: there were only two junks, three or four large prahus, a motor-boat and a derelict schooner. **1939** A. KEITH *Land below Wind* III. xi. 186 The river travel would be accomplished in small native canoes known as *perahus*. **1957** P. WORSLEY *Trumpet shall Sound* vii. 133 The officer . . stayed put, only to see the prophet himself arrive in a beflagged prau. **1958** J. SLIMMING *Temiar Jungle* ii. 19 The kit was . . stowed away in the boat —a thirty-five-foot *perahu* with a thirty-horse-power engine. **1964** K. G. TREGONNING *Hist. Mod. Malaya* 104 They each gave up all right to levy dues upon *prahus* and other local craft. **1965** R. MCKIE *Company of Animals* i. 1 The Malay perahu . . was thirty feet long with a four-foot beam, a thin slice with a stern flattened just enough to hold an outboard motor, and a bow so sharp that it parted the river like a comb. **1966** *Festival Malaysia 1966: Calendar of Events* 6/2 The intricate carvings that decorate the racing perahu can be seen. **1968** *Punch* 4 Dec. 802/2 A fishing *prahu* picked me up. **1971** *Walkabout* (Austral.) Nov. 55/1 On Groote Island . . there are many cave paintings. Some depict Indonesian praus from Macassar. **1973** *Daily Tel.* 2 Oct. 19/6 Cento II, a 31ft proa with a 15ft outrigger and carrying 250 sq. ft of sail was also being repaired. **1977** *Borneo Bull.* 7 May 4/1 The healthy state of the regatta was illustrated this year by the number of racing prahus taking part. **1977** *Austral. Sailing* Jan. 26 For your reporter and for the new Crossbow II, described as a twin masted proa 73 ft overall, this was the highpoint of the fifth annual week of sailing speed trials.

attrib. and *Comb.* **1699** DAMPIER *Voy.* II. I. 111 The Dutch . . do often buy Proe-bottoms for a small matter of the Malagans . . and convert them into Sloops. **1904** *World Mag.* Apr. 21/1 Six lusty proa-men paddled her along.

pro-abortion(ist): see PRO-[1] 5 a.

pro-accelerin, -activator: see PRO-[2] 1.

†**proach, proche,** *v.* *Obs.* [= AF. *proscher* (Britton).] Aphetic form of APPROACH *v.*

[**1292** BRITTON III. xxiv. §2 Sauvement gardez qe nul ne les prosche jekes autaunt qe il eynt respoundu.] **1426** LYDG. *De Guil. Pilgr.* 18761 ȝeue thow be hardy and bolde For to proche to hir presence. *c* **1470** HENRY *Wallace* v. 987 The day was downe, and prochand wes the nycht. **1563** SACKVILLE *Mirr. Mag.*, *Induct.* i, The wrathful winter prochinge on a pace. **1600** FAIRFAX *Tasso* VI. xxxix, To make their forces greater, proaching nire.

pro'active, *a.*[1] *Psychol.* [f. PRO-[2] 1 + ACTIVE *a.* 2.] Of a mental effect from a previous situation which is active in a subsequent activity, esp. in learning theory, as ***proactive inhibition, interference***, the inhibition of or interference with learning caused by effects that remain active from conditions preceding that learning.

1933 WHITELEY & BLANKFORT in *Jrnl. Exper. Psychol.* XVI. 852 Objective results . . indicate . . a somewhat inhibitive influence of the various sets upon learning, and under similar conditions of prior and later learning, they suggest what might be called a *proactive inhibition*. However, perhaps the term *proactive inhibition* might better be reserved to designate the detrimental influence of a condition introduced prior to learning upon a subsequent recall, thus differentiating it from . . retroactive inhibition. **1940** *Amer. Jrnl. Psychol.* LIII. 174 By proactive inhibition is meant either (a) the retardation of the learning of an activity when some other activity has occurred as a prior condition (sometimes called negative transfer), or (b) the fact of poorer retention of an activity when some other activity has occurred as a prior condition to the original learning of that activity, than when a period of comparative rest preceded the original learning. **1943** *Mind* LII. 360 Then we find that remembering is functionally dependent on . . what happens *before* learning (proactive inhibition). **1951** *Brit. Jrnl. Psychol.* Mar.–May 39 It seems unlikely that proactive inhibition would have no permanent effect on the learning of the interpolated series . . retroactive and pro-active processes are essentially interactive processes. **1967** HILGARD & ATKINSON *Introd. Psychol.* (ed. 4) xii. 324/2 Proactive inhibition plays a very important role when 'experienced' subjects are used in an experiment. **1971** E. SALTZ *Cognitive Bases of Human Learning* vi. 204 Most studies of interference are some variation of one of the following three experimental paradigms: (*a*) proactive interference, (*b*) proactive inhibition, or (*c*) retroactive inhibition.

pro'active, *a.*[2] [f. PRO-[1] + RE)ACTIVE *a.*] Of a person, policy, etc.: that creates or controls a situation by taking the initiative or by anticipating events (as opp. to responding to them); also *loosely*, innovative, tending to make things happen. (Freq. in management or business contexts.)

1971 A. J. R. REISS *Police & Public* ii. 64 Citizens usually bring matters to police attention . . . The police department deals with such requests as a *reactive organization* . . . The police also acquire information by intervening in the lives of citizens on their own initiative. In this capacity, they serve as a *proactive organization*. **1977** D. M. SMITH *Human Geogr.* xi. 327 By comparing conditions before and after the change in the five reactive, control, and proactive [*sc.* police] beats, the effectiveness of this strategy could be judged. **1980** W. SAFIRE in *N.Y. Times Mag.* 2 Mar. 9/2 Webster says he has been forced to choose between 'reactive' law enforcement—responding after a bank has been robbed—and 'pro-active' enforcement, in which his men are in on the planning stages of a crime. **1984** *Financial Times* 10 Feb. 26 A new kind of management able to take risks, . . manage change, and be more proactive. **1985** *Globe & Mail* (Toronto) 10 Oct. B20/1 (Advt.), If you are the proactive and innovative individual we are looking for . . we invite you to submit a resume in confidence.

Hence **pro'actively** *adv.*; **pro'action, proac'tivity**, proactive behaviour or practice. Also [as back-formation] **pro'act** *v. intr.*, to take proactive measures; to act in advance, to anticipate.

1978 J. ALDERSON *Communal Policing* p. i, The education of a community and a police force in joint pro-activity was seen as the only way to reduce morbidity of crime levels. **1980** *Times* 3 Nov. 16/3 We anticipate, we plan, we pro-act rather than react to change. **1984** *N.Y. Times* 14 Oct. XI. 30/5 Determinate sentencing, as an alternative to parole, forces the system to wait for the smoking gun, rather than proactively intervene before another terrible tragedy. **1985** R. C. A. WHITE *Admin. of Justice* IV. xiv. 256 A distinction which separates the practice of law in law centres from that in private practice is that between *reactivity* and *proactivity*. **1986** *Mag. Bank Admin.* June 41/1 Aggressiveness, proaction or other performance criteria are paramount. **1986** *Industry Week* 23 June 52/1 This versatility is allowing us to proact rather than react to changing market conditions.

†**proa'djutor.** *Obs. rare*[−0]. [f. PRO-[1] + L. *adjūtor* helper, aider.] (See quot.)

1623 COCKERAM II, A chiefe Author, *proadiutor*.

‖**pro'æresis, -'airesis.** [a. Gr. *προαίρεσις* a choosing one thing before another, f. *προαιρεῖσθαι* to choose before.] A deliberate choice, a resolution.

1644 MILTON *Educ.* Wks. 1851 IV. 387 That act of reason which in Ethics is called Proairesis.

pro-agonic: see PRO-[2] 1.

proague, proak, obs. ff. PROG *sb.*[2], PROKE.

proal ('prəʊəl), *a. Physiol.* [f. Gr. *πρό* before + -AL[1].] Having a forward direction or motion: said of the lower jaw in mastication.

1888 COPE in *Amer. Nat.* Jan. 7 *note*, The propalinal mastication is to be distinguished into the proal, from behind forwards, . . and the palinal, from before backwards.

†'**proalizer.** *Obs. rare*[−1]. [f. **proalize* (ad. Gr. *προαλίζ-ειν* to collect before) + -ER[1].] An empiric, a herb doctor.

1577 B. GOOGE *Heresbach's Husb.* IV. (1586) 191 *Cardus Benedictus*, or blessed Thistle, which the Empirickes, or common Proalisers, doe commend for sundrie . . Vertues.

pro-Allied, -Ally: see PRO-[1] 5 a.

pro-am, *a.* (*sb.*) [f. PRO *abbrev.* + AM(ATEUR 2.] Of a sport or other activity: practised by or open to both professionals and amateurs (see also quot. 1951). Also *ellipt.* as *sb.*, one who takes part in such activities; a pro-am event.

[**1931** *N.Y. Times* 26 May 34/2 (*heading*) Kinder-Hevener . . lead the Pro-Amateurs with 71.] **1949** *Sun* (Baltimore) 12 Mar. 22/1 In the pro-am division, Cross teamed with Al Jamison, professional from Quantico, Va., for one of the 63's. **1951** GREEN & LAURIE *Show Biz* 571/1 *Pro ams*, professional amateurs, those pseudo-tyros who constantly appeared on so-called amateur radio and vaudeville programs. **1968** *N.Y. Times* 11 July 46 They send helicopters to take me from one pro-am to another. **1970** *Times* 13 Feb. 13/3 Since turning professional in 1968 Oosterhuis has won only . . one pro-am event. **1976** *Billings* (Montana) *Gaz.* 24 June 1-D/7 Pate . . practiced Tuesday in light rain and played in a proam Wednesday.

pro-amnion to **-amphibia:** see PRO-[2] 1.

pro-anaphoral (prəʊə'næfərəl), *a.* [f. PRO-[2] + Gr. *ἀναφορά* offering + -AL[1].] Applied to that part of the Eucharistic service (esp. in the Greek rite) which precedes the *anaphora* or more solemn part (the consecration, great oblation, communion).

1850 NEALE *East. Ch.* I. III. i. §8. 319 In every Liturgical family there is one Liturgy, (or at most two,) which supplies the former or proanaphoral portion to all the others. **1866** BLUNT *Annot. Bk. C.P.* 148. **1878** C. E. HAMMOND *Ant. Liturgies* p. xxxi, Another division of the service is into the Anaphora and the Pro-anaphoral part.

pro and con. Forms: 5–7 **pro et contra, pro and contra,** 7 **pro et con,** 6– **pro and con.** [Abbreviation of L. *pro et contra* for and against. The *and* instead of *et* probably originated as an English reading of the character &.]

A. *adv.* (and *adj.*) *phr.* **a.** For and against; in favour and in opposition; on both sides. So ***pro or con.***

1426 LYDG. *De Guil. Pilgr.* 5663, I tauhtë folkys to argue Pro & contra, yong & olde. **1480** CAXTON *Chron. Eng.* ccliii, Wherof aroose a grete Altercacion . . pro and contra. **1572** R. H. tr. *Lavaterus' Ghostes* To Rdr. (1596) A ij, The matter throughly handled *Pro* and *Con.* **1577** DEE *Gen. & Rare Mem.* 10 Much . . may be here sayd, *Pro, et Contra.* **1636** JACKSON *Creed* VIII. iii. §6, I will not determine *pro* or *con*, that [etc.]. **1710** ADDISON *Tatler* No. 224 ¶3 The whole Argument pro and con in the Case of the Morning-Gowns. **1819** BYRON *Let. to Murray* 25 Jan., The rest . . has never yet affected any human production 'pro or con'. **1863** READE *Hard Cash* xxxvii, I have no objection to collect the evidence pro and con.

b. *attrib.* or as *adj.* Also in form ***pro-or-con.***

1715 M. DAVIES *Athen. Brit.* I. Pref. 25 Several Pro and Con-Pamphlets. **1964** A. EDEL in I. L. Horowitz *New Sociol.* 236 At what point do we find science passing into an internal influence in having purposes or pro-*and*-con attitudes? *Ibid.*, The role of social science parameters in having purposes and pro-or-con attitudes can best be grasped by focusing on the very concepts of having a purpose and holding an attitude.

B. *sb. phr.* (now usu. in pl., ***pros and cons.***) Reasons for and against; reasonings, arguments, statements, or votes on both sides of a question. (In quot. 1809, favourable and adverse fortunes.)

[*c* **1400**, **1509**: see PRO B. 1.] **1589** R. HARVEY *Pl. Perc.* 20 Such a quoile about *pro* and *con*, such vrging of *Ergoes.* **1591** *Troub. Raigne K. John* i. 405 Why stand I to expostulate the crime With *pro & contra*? **1640** BROME *Antip.* III. iv, The pro's and contras in the windings, workings And carriage of the cause. **1704** SWIFT *T. Tub* i. §24 A Quill worn to the Pith in the Service of the State, in *Pro's and Con's* upon Popish Plots. **1713** *Humble Plead. for Gd. Old Way* 259 Seeing the *pros and cons* did run equal so that the determination depended on the moderator's casting vote. **1809** MALKIN *Gil Blas* VII. vi. ¶14 A . . true narrative of all my pros and cons, my ins and outs, since that . . separation of ours. **1880** HUXLEY in *Life* (1900) II. ii. 21, I felt justified in stating all the pros and cons of the case. **1923** GALSWORTHY *Captures* 59 The house rocked with pro and con.

C. as *vb.* To weigh the arguments for and against; to debate both sides of a question.

1694 CONGREVE *Double-Dealer* Ded., When a man in soliloquy reasons with himself, and *pro's* and *con's*, and weighs all his designs, we ought not to imagine that this man either talks to us or to himself. **1762** STERNE *Tr. Shandy* VI. xvi, My father's resolution of putting me into breeches.. had..been *pro'd* and *con'd*, and judicially talked over betwixt him and my mother about a month before. **1818** KEATS *Lett.* Wks. 1889 III. 158 The topic was the Duke of Wellington—very amusingly pro-and-con'd. **1835** SOUTHEY *Doctor* cv. III. 324 He was no shillishallier, nor ever wasted a precious minute in pro-and-conning.

D. Used as *prep. phr.*

1895 W. STEVENS *Let.* 4 Aug. (1967) 6 Nor have I any suggestions pro and con anything in particular.

proane, proaness, obs. ff. PRONE *a.*, PRONENESS.

pro-angiosperm, -atlas: see PRO-² 1, 2.

pro-Arab, -Arabism: see PRO-¹ 5 a, c.

pro aris et focis: see PRO 1.

proase, obs. form of PROSE.

proat (prəʊt), *v. dial.* Also prote. [Origin obscure: cf. POTE *v.* and PROD *v.*] To poke. Hence **proter** *dial.*, a poker.

1654 FULLER *Comm. Ruth* (1868) 141 Like sullen chickens ..proating under an old wood-pile. *a* **1825** FORBY *Voc. E. Anglia, Proter*, a poker. **1888** *Sheffield Gloss., Prote*, to poke.

pro-attitude: PRO *Latin prep.* D. 1 b.

†**pro'auctor.** *Obs. rare*⁻⁰. [a. L. *proauctor* remote ancestor, founder: see PRO-¹ 2.]

1623 COCKERAM, *Proauctor*, the chiefe author.

‖**proaulion** (prəʊ'ɔːlɪən). *Archæol.* [a. Gr. προαύλιον a vestibule, f. πρό, PRO-² + αὐλή a court, with dim. ending -ιον.] A portico or colonnade outside a church or temple, opening into the narthex.

1842 BRANDE *Dict. Sci.* etc., *Proaulion*, in Architecture, the same as vestibule. **1850** NEALE *East. Ch.* I. II. ii. §48. 215 The *Proaulion*, or porch, is..sometimes a lean-to against the west end of the narthex. **1869** TOZER *Highl. Turkey* I. 78 The *proaulion*, or porch, a corridor supported on the outside by light pillars. *Ibid.*, Passing onwards from the *Proaulion*, we enter the narthex.

proavis (prəʊ'eɪvɪs). Pl. **-aves** (-'eɪviːz). [f. PRO-² + L. *avis* bird.] A hypothetical animal forming an evolutionary link between fossil reptiles and fossil birds. So **pro'avian** *a.*, of or pertaining to an animal of this kind; also as *sb.*

1907 F. NOPCSA in *Proc. Zool. Soc.* I. 235 An effort to condense these hypothetical changes into a drawing is given in text-fig. 82, which might..be called a 'Pro-Avis'. **1910** W. P. PYCRAFT *Hist. Birds* ii. 37 It is to the earlier Jurassic formations..that we must look for traces of the pro-avian types. *Ibid.* 38 What these 'pro-aves' were like we can only dimly surmise. **1926** G. HEILMANN *Orig. Birds* IV. 191 The term Proavian or Proavis covers a form intermediate between reptile and bird. *Ibid.* 192 Before starting to reconstruct the proavian skeleton, we must try to gain a clear understanding of the particular peculiarities..that would lead on to the bird. **1962** J. C. WELTY *Life of Birds* xxiii. 481/2 Heilmann attempted the reconstruction of a hypothetical, missing-link 'proavian'. **1974** I. C. J. GALBRAITH tr. *Dorst's Life of Birds* I. xvi. 301 An intermediate hypothetical being [between reptiles and birds] has had to be erected and named *Proavis*. *Ibid.* 301 It is really more appropriate to imagine a series of proaves.

pro-Axis: see PRO-¹ 5 a.

prob, dial. variant of PROBE *v.*

probabilify (prɒbə'bɪlɪfaɪ), *v.* [f. L. *probābil-is* PROBABLE *a.* + -IFY.] *trans.* To give probability to; to give (some proposition) reasonable grounds for being true. So **probabilifi'cation**, the action or process of rendering probable; hence **probabili'fiable, probabilifi'catory** *adjs.*

1936 H. H. PRICE *Truth & Corrigibility* 9 It is probabilification which will chiefly concern us. *Ibid.* 16 Some parts of the total body of evidence either imply or probabilify other parts. *Ibid.* 18 A system where the mutual support..is only of the probabilificatory kind. **1949** W. KNEALE *Probability & Induction* I. 11 Some conjunctions containing *A* would not probabilify *B* to the same degree or even at all. *Ibid.*, Admittedly the notion of probabilification requires further elucidation. **1953** *Mind* LXII. 455 Probabilifiable by sense-perception. **1966** A. FLEW *God & Philos.* vii. 148 A traveller's tale not probabilified by any promising theory. **1973** J. L. MACKIE *Truth, Probability & Paradox* v. 213 Equivalent contraposition does not hold even for probabilification between propositions.

probabiliorism (prɒbə'bɪlɪərɪz(ə)m). [f. as next + -ISM.] The doctrine of the probabiliorists; according to which, in opposition to probabilism, it is claimed that that side on which the evidence preponderates is more probably right and therefore ought to be followed.

1845 GLADSTONE *Glean.* (1879) VII. 192 Probabilism is by no means the universal or compulsory doctrine of the Roman theologians... It is confronted by a system called Probabiliorism: which teaches that, when in doubt among several alternatives of conduct, we are bound to choose that which has the greatest likelihood of being right. **1882–3** *Schaff's Encycl. Relig. Knowl.* III. 1931 Probabiliorism.. demands that the more probable opinion shall always be chosen. **1885** *Catholic Dict.* s.v. *Moral Theology*.

probabiliorist (prɒbə'bɪlɪərɪst). [= F. *probabilioriste*, mod.L. *probābiliōrista*, f. L. *probābilior* more probable, compar. of *probābilis*: see -IST.] One who holds the doctrine of probabiliorism.

1727–41 CHAMBERS *Cycl.* s.v. *Probabilists*, Those who oppose this doctrine [of the Probabilists], and assert, that we are obliged, on pain of sinning, always to take the more probable side, are called probabiliorists. The Jansenists, and particularly the Port-royalists, are probabiliorists. **1768** J. BARETTI *Acc. Mann. & Cust. Italy* II. 49 The vain disputes between the..Probabilists and the Probabiliorists, have long divided our friars into nearly equal parties. **1885** *Catholic Dict.* 602/2 The Probabiliorists put no restraint on liberty, where a man was convinced on solid grounds that the balance of evidence was decidedly in favour of his liberty.

probabilism ('prɒbəbɪlɪz(ə)m). [= F. *probabilisme*, f. as next: see -ISM.]

1. *R.C. Casuistry.* The doctrine, orig. propounded by Molina, a Spanish Dominican, in the 16th century, that in matters of conscience on which there is some disagreement among authorities, it is lawful to follow any course in support of which the authority of a recognized doctor of the Church can be cited.

1842 in BRANDE *Dict. Sci.*, etc. **1844** W. G. WARD *Ideal Chr. Ch.* (ed. 2) 326 The very interesting controversies of the last and previous centuries on probabilism. **1845** [see PROBABILIORISM]. **1872** JERVIS *Gallican Ch.* II. v. 164 The doctrine of Probabilism..popularly identified with the Jesuits, did not strictly speaking, originate with this body. **1886** SIDGWICK *Hist. Ethics* iii. 151.

2. *Philos.* The theory that there is no absolutely certain knowledge, but that there may be grounds of belief sufficient for practical life.

1902 BALDWIN *Dict. Philos.* II. 344 The term probabilism is also used to describe the theory which mediates between a sceptical view regarding knowledge, and the needs of practical life.

3. The name given to theories in various fields, freq. contrasted with deterministic or possibilistic theories, which claim that the governing laws are not invariant, but state only probabilities or tendencies.

1952 O. H. K. SPATE in *Geogr. Jrnl.* CXVIII. 419 It does not seem certain that 'possibilism' as often understood..is the automatic alternative to a vigorous environmentalism. There may be a middle term, which one might call 'probabilism'. **1955** *Psychol. Rev.* LXII. 209/2 As Mises has pointed out in dismissing probabilism in physics, macrolaws have their origin in differential equations. **1956** E. BRUNSWIK in K. R. Hammond *Psychol. E. Brunswik* (1966) xvii. 509 The statistical mechanics and quantum theory, being of a microscopic character, has little to do with the probabilism of functional psychology. **1965** H. & M. SPROUT *Ecol. Perspective* vi. 107 A familiar version of behavioral model, derived largely, one suspects, from classical economics, might be called 'common-sense probabilism'. **1970** L. J. COHEN *Implications of Induction* i. 17 Some of Popper's arguments against Carnap are examples of anti-probabilism at this level. **1970** *Jrnl. Gen. Psychol.* LXXXIII. 108 Heider..focused on this region and his assumptions are similar to Brunswik's with regard to probabilism, multiple mediation, and vicarious functioning.

probabilist ('prɒbəbɪlɪst), *sb.* and *a.* Also 7 probablist. [= F. *probabiliste* (17th c.), ad. mod.L. *probābilist-a*, f. L. *probābil-is* PROBABLE: see -IST.]

A. *sb.* **1.** One who holds the casuistic doctrine of probabilism.

1657 J. SERGEANT *Schism Dispach't* 93 Then indeed I shall not refuse to..rank them [men who call us Papists] in Dr. H's Predicament of Probablists. **1727–41** CHAMBERS *Cycl.*, *Probabilists*, a sect, or division, among the Romanists,.. holding, that a man is not always obliged to take the more probable side, but may take the less probable, if it be but barely probable. **1882–3** *Schaff's Encycl. Relig. Knowl.* III. 1931 In 1665 Alexander VII felt compelled to disavow a number of the propositions of the Probabilists.

2. *Philos.* One who holds the philosophical theory of probabilism. More generally, one who holds any theory of probabilism (cf. PROBABILISM 3).

1847 WEBSTER, *Probabilist*. 1. A term applied to those who maintain that certainty is impossible, and that probability alone is to govern our faith and actions. **1965** H. & M. SPROUT *Ecol. Perspective* vi. 107 The common-sense probabilist assumes that the individual applies his environmental knowledge rationally to the choice of ends achievable.

3. An expert or specialist in probability theory.

1973 *Nature* 1 June p. i/1 (Advt.), Forty-six leading probabilists are represented.

B. *adj.* = PROBABILISTIC *a.* 2.

1960 E. DELAVENAY *Introd. Machine Transl.* vi. 93 Linguists who become automatic translation programmers will have to be trained on probabilist methods. **1970** L. J. COHEN *Implications of Induction* i. 29 The attack mounted here against probabilist theories of inductive syntax.

probabilistic (prɒbəbə'lɪstɪk), *a.* [f. PROBABILIST: see -ISTIC.]

1. Pertaining to probabilists or probabilism.

1864 *Chambers's Encycl.* VI. 131/1 In that [R.C.] church his [Liguori's] moral theology,..a modification of the so-called 'probabilistic system' of the age immediately before his own, is largely used in the direction of consciences.

2. Pertaining to or expressing probability; subject to or involving chance variations or uncertainties.

1951 *Philos. of Sci.* XVIII. 216 The recognition of the probabilistic character of environmental cue-object and means-end relationships through replacement of the traditional absolute right-wrong alternatives..by cues or means of lower statistical validity. **1957** N. CHOMSKY *Syntactic Struct.* ii. 17 The development of probabilistic models for the use of language (as distinct from the syntactic structure of language) can be quite rewarding. **1965** C. H. SPRINGER et al. *Adv. Methods & Models* i. 11 Models which are based on the mathematics of statistics and probability, into which we introduce the uncertainties which usually accompany our observations of real events, are called probabilistic models. **1966** C. G. HEMPEL *Philos. Nat. Sci.* v. 65 Many important laws and theoretical principles in the natural sciences are of probabilistic character. **1972** *Computers & Humanities* VII. 17 His lengthier treatment of two stochastic models notes that probabilistic stylistics is somewhat more advanced than deterministic approaches. **1978** *Sci. Amer.* Feb. 131/3 The strict determinism of classical mechanics is abandoned in the quantum theory and is replaced by a probabilistic interpretation of measurements at the microscopic level.

Hence **probabi'listically** *adv.*, in a probabilistic manner; in terms of probabilities.

1955 *Science* 11 Nov. 910/1 Not only perception but also thinking and valuing are fruitfully conceived as only in some degree probabilistically valid achievements. **1965** *Language* XLI. 201 Between the total workings of such a determinate system..and the sound a speaker produces there is a layer of indeterminacy that can only be handled probabilistically. **1975** *Nature* 17 July 166/2 Equations such as (2) and (3) can provide very simple examples of fully deterministic systems whose dynamics are best described probabilistically. **1978** *Sci. Amer.* June 99/2 The processes that govern the placing of telephone calls are so complicated that it is more fruitful to view them probabilistically than to do so deterministically.

probability (prɒbə'bɪlɪtɪ). [ad. F. *probabilité* (14th c. in Littré), ad. L. *probābilitātem*, f. *probābil-is* PROBABLE: see -ITY.]

1. a. The quality or fact of being probable; the appearance of truth, or likelihood of being realized, which any statement or event bears in the light of present evidence; likelihood.

1551 T. WILSON *Logike* (1580) 30 b, In..gatheryng of coniectures that are doubtfull, when probabilitie onely and no assured knowledge, boulteth out the truthe of a matter. **1623** J. MEADE in Ellis *Orig. Lett.* Ser. I. III. 150 Other reports there are, but without any probability of truth, and therefore I will not mention them. **1736** BUTLER *Anal.* Introd. 3 Probability is the very Guide of Life. **1823** J. GILLIES tr. *Aristotle's Rhet.* II. xxiii. 348 Truth and probability are the causes of assent. **1881** FROUDE *Short Stud.* (1883) IV. II. iii. 197 The soundest arguments..went no farther than to establish a probability.

b. *in*, †*by probability*: probably; considering what is probable. (Now always with *all*.)

a **1602** W. PERKINS *Cases Consc.* (1619) 140 In probabilitie they could not bee either many or great. **1615** W. LAWSON *Country Housew. Gard.* (1626) 23 The compasse and roomth that each tree by probabilitie will take and fill. **1617** MORYSON *Itin.* II. 62 The Lord Deputies going into the field,..in all probability could not be for some two moneths after. **1697** LUTTRELL *Brief Rel.* (1857) IV. 202 Otherwise in probability they had fallen into the hands of the French. **1835** DICKENS *Let.* 14 Dec. (1965) I. 105, I shall not in all human probability be home before Wednesday Week. **1880** HAUGHTON *Phys. Geog.* ii. 50 These cliffs corresponding in all probability to ancient lines of faults.

2. a. An instance of the fact or condition described in 1; a probable event, circumstance, belief, etc.; something which, judged by present evidence, is likely to be true, to exist, or to happen.

1576 FLEMING *Panopl. Epist.* 375 Hee beginneth..with the infancie of Alexander..which ministred manifest and manifold probabilities of things which came afterwards to passe. **1620** T. GRANGER *Div. Logike* 80 Many probabilities concurring preuaile much. **1769** *Junius Lett.* xvi. (1820) 71 Arguments..have been drawn from inferences and probabilities. **1856** FROUDE *Hist. Eng.* I. ii. 152 Wolsey's return to power was discussed openly as a probability. **1866** GEO. ELIOT *F. Holt* xl, You must not strain probabilities in that way.

b. *pl.* Probabilities of the weather; weather forecasts. *U.S.*

Old Probabilities, a humorous name for the chief signal-officer of the U.S. Signal Service Bureau.

1875 O. W. HOLMES *Old Vol. Life, Crime & Automatism* (1891) 327 No priest or soothsayer that ever lived could hold his own against Old Probabilities. **1886** *Pop. Sci. Monthly* Aug. 546 The official publications embrace the 'probabilities' and the so-called 'weather-maps'.

3. *Math.* As a measurable quantity: The amount of antecedent likelihood of a particular event as measured by the relative frequency of occurrence of events of the same kind in the whole course of experience; estimated by the ratio of the number of successful cases to the whole number of possible cases. Also, used of quantities which are derived logically by inferential or inductive reasoning, when mathematical concepts may be inapplicable or insufficient.

1718 De Moivre (*title*) The Doctrine of Chances: or, a Method of Calculating the Probability of Events in Play. **1764** T. Bayes in *Phil. Trans. R. Soc.* LIII. 376 The probability of any event is the ratio between the value at which an expectation depending on the happening of the event ought to be computed, and the value of the thing expected upon it's [*sic*] happening. **1788** Rees *Chambers' Cycl.*, *Probability* of an event, in the Doctrine of Chances, is greater or less according to the number of chances by which it may happen, compared with the whole number of chances by which it may either happen or fail. **1838** De Morgan *Ess. Probab.* Pref., At the end of the seventeenth century, the theory of probabilities was contained in a few isolated problems, which had been solved by Pascal, Huyghens, James Bernoulli, and others. **1884** tr. *Lotze's Logic* II. ix. 369 For each draw the probability of a white ball being drawn would = 7/30, so that the probability of two whites being drawn in succession would = 7/30·7/30 = 49/900. **1892** H. Goodwin in *Contemp. Rev.* Jan. 60 To speak of a certain possible event as having a probability of three to one..is to use language in a strictly defined sense. **1939** *Internat. Encycl. Unified Sci.* I. vi. vi. 48 (*heading*) Probability as a unique logical relation. **1949** Hutten & Reichenbach tr. *H. Reichenbach's Theory of Probability* p. v, Philosophical analysis was the starting point for a new mathematical construction of the calculus of probability. **1951** S. S. Stevens *Handbk. Exper. Psychol.* 44/2 Russell once told his lecture audience that 'probability is the most important concept in modern science, especially as nobody has the slightest notion what it means'. **1975** A. R. White *Modal Thinking* iv. 68 The common philosophical confusion of probability with estimates of probability.

4. *attrib.* and *Comb.*, as ***probability amplitude, calculus, field, function, generating function, judgement, measure, proposition, relation(ship), statement, value, wave***; **probability curve**, a graph of a probability distribution; **probability density**, a probability distribution that is a continuous function; **probability distribution**, a function whose integral over any interval is the probability that the variate specified by it will lie within that interval; **probability paper** (see quot. 1933); **probability sample**, a sample whose members are chosen randomly; **probability space**, a space each point of which is an outcome and has a probability associated with it; **probability theory**, a branch of mathematics that deals with quantities having random distributions.

1936 *Physical Rev.* XLIX. 520/2 Let a_s denote the probability amplitudes of states in which the neutron is free and in a state *s*. **1944** H. Reichenbach *Philos. Found. Quantum Mech.* xvii. 84 Since the probabilities are derived always as the squares of complex functions, these latter functions are sometimes called probability amplitudes. **1970** I. E. McCarthy *Nuclear Reactions* I. iii. 74 The probability amplitude description of a quantum process is a very simple one. **1940** *Mind* XLIX. 265 While scientists apply the probability-calculus with great success to, *e.g.*, microphysics, biology and vital statistics, philosophers are still not unanimous as to the right interpretation and 'meaning' of probability. **1971** *Times Lit. Suppl.* 1 Oct. 1180/4 The mathematics of Xenakis's highly sophisticated techniques derived from the probability calculus are no more discernible by the human ear than are the mathematics of the rudimentary chance operations favoured by John Cage. **1893** Probability curve [see normal *a.* 2 e]. **1914** [see *probability paper* below]. **1964** M. McLuhan *Understanding Media* v. 52 Some computer that translates our least gesture into a new probability curve. **1939** H. Jeffreys *Theory of Probability* i. 24 We shall usually write this briefly $P(dx|p) = f'(x)dx$, dx on the left meaning the proposition that x lies in a *particular* range dx. $f'(x)$ is called the probability density. **1961** Powell & Crasemann *Quantum Mech.* ii. 59 The fundamental postulate..states that the quantity $\psi^*\psi = |\psi|^2$ is to be interpreted as a probability density for a particle in the state ψ. More precisely,..in a measurement of the position of the particle, the probability $P(\mathbf{r})d\tau$ of finding it in a volume element $d\tau = dxdydz$ at a point $\mathbf{r}$ is proportional to $|\psi(\mathbf{r})|^2 d\tau$. **1968** P. A. P. Moran *Introd. Probability Theory* ii. 68 When $f(t)$ is continuous, $f(t)dt$ can be regarded as the probability that X lies in the range $(x, x + dt)$ when dt becomes small. $f(t)$ is then known as the probability density of the distribution. **1937** H. Cramé r *Random Variables & Probability Distributions* ii. 11 The use here made of the terms *probability function* and *distribution function* corresponds to the terminology of Kolmogoroff. **1944** H. Reichenbach *Philos. Found. Quantum Mech.* xxiv. 111. The specification of these values is therefore replaced by the statement of their probability distributions. **1970** G. A. & A. G. Theodorson *Mod. Dict. Sociol.* 314 A probability distribution gives the probable frequency of occurrence of each category or class interval..of a given variable. **1940** *Mind* XLIX. 272 The definition of randomness as 'Nachwirkungsfreiheit' is wholly inadequate for the purpose of characterising a probability-field. **1965** R. C. Jeffrey *Logic of Decision* vii. 103 A probability field is a collection of propositions which contains the denial of any proposition that it contains, and which contains the conjunction and the disjunction of any pair of propositions that it contains. **1906** *Acta Univ. Lundensis* I. v. 8 The values of the probability function $\phi(x)$ are most conveniently tabulated by Sheppard. **1974** H. Frank *Introd. Probability & Statistics* ii. 40 A probability function is defined as a function $Y = f(X)$ such that X is a random variable and Y is the set of probabilities associated with X. **1949** *Jrnl. R. Statistical Soc.* B. XI. 217 The recurrence relation for the probability-generating function $\Pi_{r+1}(z)$ for the entire population in the $r + 1^{\text{th}}$ generation is obtained by substituting $G(z)$ for z in $\Pi_r(z)$. **1968** P. A. P. Moran *Introd. Probability Theory* ii. 79 We consider the probability generating function obtained by multiplying (2.62) by z^k and summing over the possible values. **1914** C. D. Broad *Perception* ii. 150 The correct probability is always that relative to the knowledge of the person who makes the probability-judgment. **1934** *Philos. Rev.* XLIII. 133 The given experience of the moment of knowing is the basis of a probability-judgment concerning the experience. **1954** L. J. Savage *Found. Statistics* iii. 33 Let me say precisely what is meant..by a probability measure. **1971** *Sci. Amer.* Aug. 95/1 Mathematical probability is based on a special function that assigns to each subset A of a given set Ω a positive real number that represents the probability that a point selected 'at random' from the set Ω will actually be in A. This function is called a 'probability measure' on the set Ω, and we shall denote it by m. **1914** A. Hazen in *Trans. Amer. Soc. Civil Engineers* LXXVII. 1549 Probability Paper.—The practical difficulty with the plotting of Fig. 1 is the great curvature of the lines showing the required storage. This difficulty is so great as to make the method unsatisfactory in most cases; but it has been removed by using paper ruled with lines spaced in accordance with a probability curve, or, as it is otherwise called, the normal law of error. **1933** *Med. Res. Council Special Rep. Ser.* No. 183. 9 A special form of graph paper known as 'probability paper' has been prepared, on which the ordinates represent a scale of percentages so spaced that the actual distances on the paper are proportional to the corresponding values of the normal equivalent deviation. On 'logarithmic probability paper' the scale of ordinates is identical with that on ordinary probability paper, but the scale of abscissae is logarithmic. **1958** E. J. Gumbel *Statistics of Extremes* i. 29 If the theory holds, the observations plotted on probability paper ought to be scattered closely about the straight line. **1914** C. D. Broad *Perception* ii. 150 This is not as much objectivity as is wanted for probability-propositions. **1922** tr. *Wittgenstein's Tractatus* 111 There is no special object peculiar to probability propositions. **1921** J. M. Keynes *Treat. Probability* i. 4 If a knowledge of *h* justifies a rational belief in *a* of degree α, we say that there is a probability-relation of degree α between *a* and *h*. **1965** P. Caws *Philos. of Sci.* xxxiv. 261 If premise and conclusion are both known, some probability relation may be established between them. **1955** O. Klein in W. Pauli *Niels Bohr* 102 The basic ideas of quantum theory, where the causal relationship between events is replaced by a probability relationship. **1955** F. C. Mills *Statistical Methods* (ed. 3) xix. 659 A probability sample is one for which the inclusion or exclusion of any individual element of the population depends on the application of probability methods, not on personal judgment, and which is so designed and drawn that the probability of inclusion of any individual element is known. **1972** *Jrnl. Social Psychol.* LXXXVIII. 208 Field interviewers..administered the Rokeach Value Survey to a national probability sample of 1489 American adults. **1968** J. B. Johnston et al. *Sets, Functions, & Probability* v. 163 We shall now describe how a probability space can be associated with certain chance phenomena in the real world. **1975** I. Stewart *Concepts Mod. Math.* xvii. 247 Axiomatic probability theory works entirely in terms of probability spaces. **1930** J. Laird *Knowl., Belief & Opinion* xvii. 376 According to this view, probability-statements are statements of proportions in very large series. **1939** E. Nagel *Princ. Theory of Probability* iv. 23 Probability statements are on a par with statements which specify the density of a substance; they are not formulations of the degree of our ignorance or uncertainty. **1941** *Mind* L. 48, I shall here refer to the contrast between two very well-known types of probability-theory. **1962** *Listener* 15 Nov. 793/1 In psychological research, too, probability theory plays an essential part because many of the variables can be measured only approximately. **1974** P. Erdman *Silver Bears* ii. 16 At M.I.T...he had become fascinated with the probability theories of..John von Neumann and Oskar Morganstern [*sic*]. **1922** W. E. Johnson *Logic* II. xi. 251 Mill's position is paradoxical, since he apparently attributes a higher probability-value to a law, merely on the ground of its width. **1940** *Mind* XLIX. 267 From a purely mathematical point of view there would be no obstacle to the choice of series of the above kind as fields of measurement for probability-values. **1942** *Electronic Engin.* XV. 149/1 The term wave is commonly used in a very wide sense, to cover almost everything from a heat wave to the probability waves of modern physics. **1956** E. H. Hutten *Lang. Mod. Physics* v. 186 Physicists have sometimes spoken of the 'probability wave'; but this phrase must not be taken literally.

probabilize (ˈprɒbəbɪlaɪz), *v.* [f. L. *probābil-is* probable + -ize.] *trans.* To render probable or likely.

1802–12 Bentham *Ration. Judic. Evid.* (1827) III. 13 By means of it the fact is probabilized: rendered, in a greater or less degree, probable. *a* **1832** —— *Deontol.* iv. (1834) II. 210 The considerations which tend to probabilize success. **1846** S. R. Maitland *Ess. Reform. Eng.* (1849) 314 That he may take his turn at probableizing [the story], and pass it on.

probable (ˈprɒbəb(ə)l), *a.* and *sb.* [a. F. *probable* (14th c. in Littré), or ad. L. *probābil-is* that may be proved, probable, credible, f. *prob-āre* to try, test, approve, make good: f. *prob-us* good: see -able.]

A. *adj.* **1.** Capable of being proved; demonstrable, provable. Now *rare*.

1485 *Surtees Misc.* (1888) 43 Which..duly examined by hym..and no thing probable object ayenst the same, the..Maire..decreed and finally determyned [etc.]. *a* **1548** Hall *Chron., Hen. VII* 33 It is probable by an inuincible reason and an argument infallible. **1659** Milton *Civ. Power* Wks. 1851 V. 312 No man in religion is properly a heretic,..but he who maintains traditions or opinions not probable by scripture. **1678** Sir G. Mackenzie *Crim. Laws Scot.* II. xiii. §2 (1699) 209 Executions by a Barrons Officer are valid, though not given in Writ, and that the same are probable by Witnesses. **1865** Grote *Plato* I. xix. 536 Neither proved nor probable.

†**2. a.** Such as to approve or commend itself to the mind; worthy of acceptance or belief; rarely in bad sense, plausible, specious, colourable. (Now merged in the modern sense 3.)

1387 Trevisa *Higden* (Rolls) I. 339 It is more probable and more skilful [= reasonable], þat þis lond was from þe bygynnynge alwey ful wiþ oute suche wormes. **1467–8** *Rolls of Parlt.* V. 622/2 As it appereth by probabill persuacions of Philosofers. **1538** Starkey *England* I. iv. 139, I can not wel tel what I schal say, your resonys are so probabyl. **1593** Shaks. *2 Hen. VI*, III. ii. 178 It cannot be but he was murdred heere, The least of all these signes were probable. **1639** S. Du Verger tr. *Camus' Admir. Events* 129 One of his most probable excuses was to frame some journeyes out of towne. *a* **1715** Burnet *Own Time* (1823) I. II. 401 His schemes were probable. **1780** Jefferson *Corr.* Wks. 1859 I. 280 He assigns the most probable reasons for that opinion. **1872** Jervis *Gallican Ch.* II. v. 165 It was proclaimed that an opinion was probable, and might therefore be safely followed in practice, which had the sanction of any single theologian of established reputation.

b. Of a person: Worthy of approval, reliable. *Obs.*

1597 Beard *Theatre God's Judgem.* (1612) 213 There is not one example here mentioned, but it hath a credible or probable Author for the auoucher of it. **1682** G. Topham *Rome's Trad.* 223 If this be but the single opinion of a probable Doctor, we may have the same asserted by an Infallible one.

3. a. Having an appearance of truth; that may in view of present evidence be reasonably expected to happen, or to prove true; likely.

1606 Shaks. *Ant. & Cl.* v. ii. 356 Most probable That so she dyed. **1620** T. Granger *Div. Logike* 142 The birds neither sow, reape, &c. as you doe, *Ergo* tis lesse probable that they should be fed. **1651** Hobbes *Leviath.* II. xxv. 134 The necessary or probable consequences of the action. **1736** Welsted *Wks.* (1787) 469 This were a probable opinion, though not warranted by holy writ. **1809** Roland *Fencing* 67 Is it probable that a man will thrust if he expects that he will be parried? **1814** D. Stewart *Philos. Hum. Mind* II. II. iv. §4. 240 In our anticipations of astronomical phenomena..philosophers are accustomed to speak of the event as only *probable*; although our confidence in its happening is not less complete, than if it rested on the basis of mathematical demonstration. **1879** Thomson & Tait *Nat. Phil.* I. I. §392 The Probable Error of an observation is a numerical quantity such that the error of the observation is as likely to exceed as to fall short of it in magnitude. **1891** E. Peacock *N. Brendon* II. 317 This was the more probable solution.

†**b.** with infinitive as complement: Likely *to be* or *to do* something. *Obs.*

1653 Gauden *Hierasp.* 114 These rustick and rash undertakers..are only probable to shipwrack themselves. **1662** Stillingfl. *Orig. Sacr.* III. iv. §10 None is conceived so probable to have first peopled Greece, as he whose name was preserved..with very little alteration. *a* **1680** Butler *Rem.* (1759) I. 223 'Tis probable to be the truest test.

c. Relating to or indicating probability.

1736 Butler *Anal.* Introd. 1 Probable Evidence is essentially distinguished from demonstrative by this, that it admits of Degrees.

d. Likely to be (something specified).

1890 'R. Boldrewood' *Col. Reformer* (1891) 215 He essayed to make choice of a probable companion.

e. Now chiefly *U.S. Law.* ***probable cause***, reasonable cause or grounds (for making a search or preferring a charge).

a **1676** M. Hale *Historia Placitorum Coronæ* (1736) II. xviii. 150 They are not to be granted without oath made before the justice of a felony committed, and that the party complaining hath probable cause to suspect they are in such a house or place, and do shew his reasons of such suspicion. And therefore I do take it, that a general warrant to search in all suspected places is not good, but only to search in such particular places, where the party assigns before the justice his suspicion and the probable cause thereof, for these warrants are judicial acts, and must be granted upon examination of the fact. **1789** J. Madison in *Congress. Reg.* I. 428 The rights of the people to be secured in their persons, their houses, their papers, and their other property from all unreasonable searches and seizures, shall not be violated by warrants issued without probable cause, supported by oath or affirmation, or not particularly describing the places to be searched, or the persons or things to be seized. **1811** *U.S. Circuit Court Rep.* (1827) 37 What, then, is the meaning of the term 'probable cause'? We answer, a reasonable ground of suspicion, supported by circumstances sufficiently strong in themselves to warrant a cautious man in the belief, that the person accused is guilty of the offence with which he is charged. **1850** *Calif. Sup. Court* I. 11 The offence which..there is probable cause to suppose he has committed. **1878** *U.S. Rep.* XCVII. 646 If there was probable cause of seizure, there was a reasonable cause. If there was a reasonable cause of seizure, there was a probable cause. **1927** *Ibid.* CCLXXV. 106 The liquor was obtained by a search and seizure instituted without warrant or probable cause. **1937** N. B. Lasson in *Johns Hopkins Stud. Hist. & Pol. Sci.* LV. II. iv. 125 In the searching of automobiles..no warrant but only the existence of probable cause is necessary to constitute the search a reasonable one. **1954** *Fed. Reporter* (1955) CCXXII. 556/1 An 'anonymous tip' to officers..was not 'probable cause' for arrest without warrant. **1976** *Washinton Post* 14 Dec. A18/2 Why should the United States, without even a whisper of probable cause, be bugging a dependent ward that had been formally delivered into its care by the United Nations?

f. ***probable error***: the difference between the mean of a distribution and the first or third quartiles, i.e. an error of such a magnitude that larger and smaller errors are equally likely.

It has now been largely superseded as a measure of accuracy or consistency by the standard error.

1812 *Phil. Mag.* XXXIX. 241 All that can be gained is, that the errors are as trifling as possible—that they are equally distributed—and that none of them exceed the probable errors of the observation. **1854** *Amer. Jrnl. Sci. & Arts* XVII. 396, I have calculated..the amount of probable error in the determinations of many of the atomic weights. **1872** Thomson & Tait *Elem. Nat. Philos.* I. iii. 113 The probable error of the sum or difference of two quantities, affected by independent errors, is the square root of the sum of the squares of their separate probable errors. **1886** *Proc. R. Soc.* XL. 66 Throughout this discussion the technical term 'probable error' has been used; it may in every instance be replaced by Mr. Galton's very apt name 'quartile'. **1889**

F. GALTON *Natural Inheritance* v. 58 The term Probable Error is absurd when applied to the subjects now in hand, such as Stature, Eye-colour, Artistic Faculty, or Disease. I shall therefore usually speak of Prob. Deviation. **1903** *Biometrika* II. 273 Unfortunately custom has not taken this standard deviation as the measure of the goodness of the sample, but the whole theory having developed from the normal curve, the probable error instead of the standard deviation has been chosen, i.e. ·67449 × standard deviation. **1938** D. C. BARTON in A. E. Dunstan et al. *Sci. of Petroleum* I. VIII. 369/2 Determinations of relative gravity with a probable error of ± 10 or even ± 5 tenth milligal are of value in geophysical prospecting. **1968** R. A. LYTTLETON *Mysteries Solar Syst.* iii. 104 The value of approximately 0·08 × 10^{12} dyn cm^{-2}..suggests a radius as large as 2770 km, which exceeds the quoted observed value by a little more than twice the probable error.

B. *sb.* †**a.** Something probable; a probable event or circumstance; a probability. *Obs.*

1647 JER. TAYLOR *Lib. Proph.* vi. §8. 117 These probables are buskins to serve every foot. **1652** GAULE *Magastrom.* 27 What talk ye of some immediate and imminent probables, such as even sense may ghesse at? **1692** SOUTH *Serm.* (1697) I. 114 If a thing in it self be doubtfull, let it make for interest and it shall be raised at least into a Probable; and if a truth be certain, and thwart interest, it will quickly fetch it down to but a Probability.

b. One who will probably, though not certainly, be successful; a likely candidate, competitor, etc.; *spec.* a member of the supposedly stronger team in a trial match (opp. to POSSIBLE *sb.* 1 d).

1906 *Pall Mall Gaz.* 23 Jan. 2 The last two 'probables' are untried men as far as Parliament is concerned. **1909** *Westm. Gaz.* 28 May 12/3 All probables ran. **1976** *West Lancs. Evening Gaz.* 8 Dec. 18/1 Fylde lock Bill Beaumont is one of four Lancashire players included in the Probables team for the first England trial at Twickenham on December 18. **1977** R. LUDLUM *Chancellor Manuscript* xxxii. 349 'What have you found out about our four candidates?'..'One..I'd say a probable.'

c. *Mil.* An aircraft recorded as probably shot down. Also, a submarine probably destroyed.

1940 in *Winged Words* (1941) 27 They were the new Heinkel 113s... We got..three or four of what we call 'probables'. **1940** W. S. CHURCHILL in D. McLachlan *Room 39* (1968) vi. 131 At least 5 probables [*sc.* submarines] have occured since the beginning of new year. **1944** *Sat. Even. Post* 22 July 73/3, I chalked him up with only a probable, because I did not see it crash. **1955** C. S. FORESTER *Good Shepherd* II. 278 Out of his escort force he had lost a destroyer... But he had sunk two probables and a possible. **1977** L. DEIGHTON *Fighter* v. 278 The RAF announced that ..584 aircraft 'were probably destroyed'... One assumes that half the probables were downed.

ˈprobableness. [f. prec. + -NESS.] The quality or fact of being probable; probability, likelihood; plausibility.

c **1449** PECOCK *Repr.* II. i. 133 If a treuthe be knowun oonli bi probabilnes and likelihode, and not sureli. **1561** DAUS tr. *Bullinger on Apoc.* (1573) 122 b, He seemeth to reason probably..but this probablenes is of vncleane fleshe, not of God. **1650** *Vind. Dr. Hammond's Addr.* §12. 4 Nor shall I.. fear the probablenesse of his unprov'd groundlesse supposition. **1951** J. S. BRUNER in Blake & Ramsey *Perception* v. 128 The higher the 'probableness' or likeness to English of our nonsense words, the less the amount of stimulus information (in terms of length of exposure) necessary for recognizing them correctly.

probably (ˈprɒbəblɪ), *adv.* [f. as prec. + -LY².] In a probable manner or degree; with probability.

1. In a way that approves itself to one's reason for acceptance or belief; plausibly; in a way that seems likely to prove true; with likelihood (though not with certainty). Now *rare*.

1535 STARKEY *Let.* in *England* (1871) p. xxx, You wrote so probably that hyt put me in a feare of daungerys to come. **1551** T. WILSON *Logike* (1580) I j b, Logike is an Art to reason probablie on both partes, of all matters that be putte forthe, so ferre as the nature of euery thing can beare. **1572** J. JONES *Bathes of Bath* Ep. Ded. 3 The first of these bookes probablie proueth the discent of Bladud. **1678** HOBBES *Decam.* viii. 100 This your Hypothesis..by which you have so probably salved the Problem of Gravity. *a* **1774** GOLDSM. *Hist. Greece* I. 342 With a party of thirty men only, as Nepos says; but, as Xenophon more probably says, of near seventy. **1823** J. BADCOCK *Dom. Amusem.* 28 More than he could probably hope to make by any transaction in the Alley.

2. As a qualification of the whole statement: As is likely; so far as evidence goes; in all probability; most likely. Now the ordinary use.

1613 SHERLEY *Trav. Persia* 101 Now that we haue iudged of all, we must resolue..of that which is probabliest best. **1647** CLARENDON *Hist. Reb.* I. §6 A source, from whence those waters of bitterness..have..probably flowed. **1692** O. WALKER *Grk. & Rom. Hist.* 86 *Secespita*, an Hatchet, probabilier a Knife, to kill the Beast. **1774** PENNANT *Tour Scot. in 1772*, 251 The present stones were probably substituted in place of these [= It is probable that the present stones were substituted]. **1860** MAURY *Phys. Geog. Sea* (Low) xii. §551 The River Tigris is probably evaporated from the upper half of this sea by these winds. **1882** *Med. Temp. Jrnl.* I. 101 Probably both causes operate to account for the failure to perceive the difference.

†**ˈprobacy.** *Obs. rare*⁻¹. [f. L. *probātio*, with suffix-substitution: see -ACY.] ? Probation, evidence; 'affirmative proof' (editor's margin in loc. cit.).

c **1400** *Beryn* 2595 The lawes of þe Cete [Falsetown] stont in probacy; They vsen noon enquestis, þe wrongis for to try.

†**ˈprobal,** *a. Obs. nonce-wd.* [? Alteration of PROBABLE.] Such as approves itself to reason or acceptance; 'calculated to bias the judgment, satisfactory' (Schmidt).

1604 SHAKS. *Oth.* II. iii. 344 When this aduise is free I giue, and honest, Proball to thinking, and indeed the course To win the Moore againe.

probality, error for PROBABILITY.

proband (ˈprəʊbənd). [ad. L. *proband-us*, gerundive of *probāre* to test, examine.] An individual chosen as a propositus because of the presence of some trait whose inheritance is to be studied. Also *attrib.*, as ***proband method, test***.

1929 *Resumptio Genetica* IV. 296/1 (Index), Proband. **1931** E. & C. PAUL tr. *Baur's Human Heredity* xi. 501 A graphic representation of the parent's, grandparents, great-grandparents, etc., of the individual from whom an investigation starts (such a person is called a proband) is known as that person's ancestral table. *Ibid.* 508 The proband method is wrongly supposed to be difficult to apply. **1940** HINSIE & SHATZKY *Psychiatric Dict.* 431/2 The practicable statistical method of probands in the study of selective population groups..is called the proband method. **1962** *Lancet* 29 Dec. 1341/2 Seven probands had a first-degree relative who had been treated with an antidepressant drug while under hospital care for a depressive illness. **1967** *Economist* 9 Dec. 1065/4 It is said that the Proband test effectively screens disease carriers in an endemic herd, and that once foreign buyers got used to it they would still want British pedigree animals. **1977** *Jrnl. Med. Genetics* XIV. 125/2 The same balanced translocation was found in the proband's sister, in 5 of 6 sibs of the mother and in 2 children of one of them.

probang (ˈprəʊbæŋ). Also 7 **provang(g, (provango).** [The name given by the inventor was *provang*, of unknown origin (but cf. *provet* = PRIVET²), subsequently altered, prob. after PROBE *sb.*] A surgical instrument, consisting of a long slender strip of flexible material with a sponge, ball, button, or other attachment at the end, for introducing into the throat to apply a remedy or remove a foreign body. Also, a larger form of this employed in the case of choking cattle.

1657 HOWELL in W. Rumsey *Organon Salutis* a viij, To.. Judge Rumsey, upon his Provang, or rare pectorall Instrument. *Ibid.* b iv, Touching your Provang, or Whale-bone Instrument..it hath purchased much repute abroad among Forreiners. **1661** BLOUNT *Glossogr.* (ed. 2), *Provango*, an instrument made of Whalebone, to cleanse the stomack. **1691** WOOD *Ath. Oxon.* II. 166 Walter Rumsey..was the first that invented the Provangg, or Whalebone instrument to cleanse the throat and stomach. **1809** B. PARR *Lond. Med. Dict.*, *Probang*, a flexible piece of whalebone, with spunge fixed to the end. **1843** R. J. GRAVES *Syst. Clin. Med.* xxv. 311 An inflamed state of the œsophagus, caused by a clumsy probang roughly passed. **1849** STEPHENS *Bk. Farm* (ed. 2) I. 296/2 The probang is 5 feet 1 inch in length, three quarters of an inch in diameter, with pewter cup and ball ends 1½ diameter. **1872** O. W. HOLMES *Poet Breakf.-t.* iii. (1885) 63 There were..Probes and Probangs.

probant (ˈprəʊbənt), *a. rare.* [ad. L. *probānt-em*, pr. pple. of *probāre* to prove: see -ANT.] Proving, demonstrating.

1908 *Month* Jan. 103 The true probant force of interior experience regarding the existence of God.

Pro-Banthine (prəʊˈbænθiːn). *Pharm.* Also **Probanthine, probanthine.** [f. PRO(PYL + *Banthine*, a proprietary name for methantheline bromide, a related compound (see quot. 1954).] A proprietary name for PROPANTHELINE.

1953 *Official Gaz.* (U.S. Patent Office) 17 Mar. 571/1 G. S. Searle & Co., Skokie, Ill... *Pro-Banthine*... For medicinal agent for the treatment of abnormal conditions of the gastro-intestinal system in tablet and ampoule form. Claims use since July 31, 1952. **1953** *Trade Marks Jrnl.* 29 Apr. 358/2 Pro-Banthine... Pharmaceutical preparations in the form of tablets or ampoules for the treatment of gastro-intestinal disorders. G. D. Searle & Co..., Village of Skokie, State of Illinois, United States of America; manufacturers. **1954** [see PROPANTHELINE]. **1955** *Radiology* LXIV. 331/1 Probanthine (15 mg.) should be given intramuscularly one hour before the examination to reduce pancreatic secretion to a minimum and to lower the concentration of enzymes in the juice. **1958** J. H. BURN *Lect. Notes Pharmacol.* (ed. 5) 28 Methantheline (Banthine) and propantheline (Probanthine) are used to relieve the pain of gastric and duodenal ulcers. **1967** H. BECKMAN *Dilemmas in Drug Therapy* 300 In Pro-Banthine you have pure anticholinergic action and in Donnatal there is this action plus the sedative effect of the contained phenobarbital. **1969** I. KEMP *Brit. G.I. in Vietnam* vii. 154, I was told I had a 'pyloric spasm'—in the upper intestine—and given tablets of probanthine, which at last eased the pain.

probaptismal, -basidium: see PRO-² 1.

probate (ˈprəʊbeɪt, -ət), *sb.* Also 5–8 **-bat**. [ad. L. *probāt-um* a thing proved, subst. use of pa. pple. neut. of *probāre* to PROVE: see next.]

†**1.** The act of proving or fact of being proved; that which proves; proof, demonstration; evidence, testimony. *Obs.*

1534 *Cov. Corp. Chr. Plays* ii. 109 Whatt maner a wey They haue made probate of this profece. **1610** BOYS *Exp. Dom. Epist. & Gosp.* Wks. (1629) 80 Abraham assuredly beleeued God before, but his offering vp of Isaac was a greater probate of his faith. **1711** in *10th Rep. Hist. MSS. Comm.* App. v. 187 There are innumerable proofs of this position..among them our late monarch stands a monumental probat. **1842** G. S. FABER *Prov. Lett.* (1844) I. 150 Here, then,..we have another probate of the object of the Tract-School.

†**b.** A putting to the test, experiment. *Obs. rare.*

a **1643** J. SHUTE *Judgem. & Mercy* (1645) 9 As I would not incourage you upon the long-suffering of God, to make a probate, and triall of his patience.

2. *Law.* The official proving of a will; also, the officially verified copy of the will together with the certificate of its having been proved, which are delivered to the executors.

1463 *Bury Wills* (Camden) 43, I wil it be wretyn..in the rolle that my testement and last wil is in, aftir the probat be maad. **1530** TINDALE *Pract. Prelates* K ij b, The hypocrites ..made a reformacyon of mortuaries and probates of testamentes. **1590** SWINBURNE *Testaments* 224 The iudge doth therupon..annex his probate and seale to the testament, whereby the same is confirmed. **1660** R. COKE *Power & Subj.* 118 The Probate of Wills, and letters of Administration are determinable by the Civil Law. **1768** BLACKSTONE *Comm.* III. vii. 96 We find it..asserted..that it is but of late years that the church hath had the probate of wills. **1846** MCCULLOCH *Acc. Brit. Empire* (1854) II. 303 The Lordship of Newry; the proprietor of which holds his spiritual court, and grants marriage licenses and probates of wills, under the seal of the religious house to which the lordship belonged before the Reformation. **1872** *Beeton's Everybody's Lawyer* 472 An executor, upon obtaining probate, is not required to enter into a bond.

b. *attrib.* **Probate Act**, an English statute passed in 1857 (20 & 21 Vict. c. 77), by which the jurisdiction of matters of probate and administration was removed from ecclesiastical and other courts and transferred to a new Court of Probate. **probate bond**, a bond in which an administrator other than an executor gives a guarantee that he will administer the estate in accordance with the will or with the law of intestate succession. **probate court**, a court having jurisdiction of probate and administration. **probate duty**, 'a tax upon the gross value of the personal property of a deceased testator' (Wharton *Law Lex.*): since 1894 merged in the *estate duty*. **probate judge**, a judge having jurisdiction in probate and testamentary causes; hence ***probate judgeship***. †**probate law**, the law of the ecclesiastical probate court (*obs.*).

c **1400** *Beryn* 2069 They were grete Sevilliouns, & vsid probate law; Wher, evir-more affirmatyff shuld preve his owne sawe. **1845** MCCULLOCH *Taxation* II. vi. §3 (1852) 305 The holders of personal property are..entitled to require, either that the probate and legacy duties should be abolished, or that they should be extended to real property also. **1863** W. PHILLIPS *Speeches* vii. 154 Probate judges are the guardians of widows and orphans. **1872** *Beeton's Everybody's Lawyer* 473 A non-executor is required to enter into a probate bond. **1898** *Whitaker's Alm.* 430/2 Estate Duty: In the case of every person dying after 1st August, 1894 (prior to which date Probate, Affidavit, or Inventory Duty is payable). **1901** *Ann. Rep. Incorp. Law Soc.* 24 Probate engrossments as well as the probate piece were to be on paper.

†**probate,** *ppl. a. Obs. rare.* [ad. L. *probāt-us* tried, proved, pa. pple. of *probāre* to PROVE.] Proved, demonstrated. Also (quot. 1513) of a person: Having received proof; confirmed or established in a belief; convinced.

c **1500** *Joseph Armathy* (W. de W.) 2 The veray true and probate assercyons of hystoryal men touchynge and concernynge thantyquytes of..Glastenburye. **1513** BRADSHAW *St. Werburge* I. 1114 Vulfade, conforted and in the fayth probate, Fell downe to his fete. **1621** T. WILLIAMSON tr. *Goulart's Wise Vieillard* 84 If daily experience did not make it manifest and probat vnto vs.

probate (ˈprəʊbeɪt), *v.* [f. ppl. stem of L. *probāre* to prove: see prec.]

†**1.** *trans.* (*pro'bate*) To prove. *Obs. rare*⁻⁰.

1570 LEVINS *Manip.* 39/38 To Probate, *probare.*

2. To obtain probate of, to prove (a will). Chiefly *U.S.* Hence **ˈprobating** *vbl. sb.*

1792 CHIPMAN *Amer. Law Rep.* (1871) 52 C's will has never been probated. **1837** DICKENS *Pickw.* lv, 'Vy not!' exclaimed Sam,—''cos it must be proved, and probated, and swore to, and all manner o' formalities.' **1889** *Proc. N. Eng. Hist. Geneal. Soc.* 2 Jan. 20 Wills..probated as early as 1373. **1892** *Blackw. Mag.* CLI. 622 The contests over the probating of wills reveal too often the unscrupulous, blackhearted ingratitude of children.

3. *U.S.* To place (a convicted person) on probation. Hence **ˈprobated** *ppl. a.*, of or pertaining to a sentence of probation.

1961 in WEBSTER. **1972** *N.Y. Times* 3 Nov. 42/1 [He] was given a 10-year probated sentence. **1977** *Time* 19 Sept. 38/2 That was when he announced that 'whether women like it or not, they are sex objects' as he set free on a probated sentence a 15-year-old youth who had raped a 16-year-old coed in a high school stairwell.

†**proˈbatic,** *a. Obs. rare.* [ad. late L. *probatic-us* (in Vulgate), a. Gr. προβατικός belonging to sheep, f. πρόβατον a sheep. So F. *probatique.*] Of or pertaining to sheep: in ***probatic piscine, probatic pond***, rendering L. *probatica piscina* of

the Vulgate in John v. 2. Also †**pro'batical** *a. Obs.*

c **1430** LYDG. *Commend. Our Lady* 134 Thow misty arke, probatik piscyne. [**1582** N. T. (Rhem.) *John* v. 2 There is at Hierusalem vpon Probatica a pond.] **1656** BLOUNT *Glossogr.*, *Probatick Pond*.., a Pond at Jerusalem, where those sheep were washed, that were by the Law to be sacrificed. **1818** J. MILNER *End Relig. Controv.* II. (1819) 72 *note*, The probatical pond was endowed by an Angel with a miraculous power of healing.

probation (prəʊ'beɪʃən), *sb.* [ME. *probacion*, a. OF. *probacion* (14th c. in Hatz.-Darm.), mod.F. *-ation*, ad. L. *probātiōn-em*, n. of action f. *probāre* to prove, test.]

I. †**1. a.** The action or process of testing or putting to the proof; trial, experiment; investigation, examination. *Obs.* (exc. as in 2).

c **1412** HOCCLEVE *De Reg. Princ.* 376, I þanke it god, non inclinacioun Haue I to labour in probacioun Of his hy knowleche & his myghty werkys. *c* **1440** *Gesta Rom.* xix. 66 (Harl. MS.) What is þe depnesse of the See?.. If I were a ston, I shuld discende to þe grounde of þe see, & telle you the soth by probacion. **1559** FECKNAM in Strype *Ann. Ref.* (1709) I. App. ix. 24 Towchinge the second rule..of.. probation, whether of bothe these religions is the better. **1682** BUNYAN *Holy War* xii, Thy lying flatteries we have had and made sufficient probation of. **1736** NEAL *Hist. Purit.* III. 495 It was published by way of probation, that they might learn the sense of the nation. **1865** MOZLEY *Mirac.* viii. 181 We see a broad distinction, arising..from..the character of the witnesses, the probation of the testimony.

†**b.** *Surg.* Examination by or as by means of a probe; the use of a probe. *Obs.*

1612 WOODALL *Surg. Mate* Wks. (1653) 17 The Probe.. there is much abuse of this instrument oftentimes by making probation (as the phrase is). **1685** COOKE *Marrow Chirurg.* I. i. 3 Probation, made either by hand, Instrument, or both.

†**c.** Trial by ordeal. *Obs. rare.*

1693 I. MATHER *Cases of Consc.* (1862) 273 The *Vulgar Probation* by casting into the Water practised upon Persons accused with other Crimes as well as that of Witchcraft. *Ibid.* 274 When they were brought to their *vulgar Probation*, [they] sunk down under the Water like other Persons.

d. The examining of students as a test of proficiency; a school or college examination. Now only in U.S.

1706 PHILLIPS, *Probation*,..the Tryal of a Student, who is about to take his Degrees in an University. **1766** ENTICK *London* IV. 157 There is an order appointed for the probation of the school. **1895** *Funk's Stand. Dict.*, *Probation*... Specifically: (1) In universities, examination of a student for degrees.

2. The testing or trial of a person's conduct, character, or moral qualifications; a proceeding designed to ascertain these: esp. in reference to the period or state of trial. **a.** Of a candidate for membership in a religious body, order, or society, for holy orders, for fellowship in a college, etc. (Cf. PROBATIONER.)

1432-50 tr. *Higden* (Rolls) IV. 327 This peple [Essenes].. not takenge eny man to theire secte withowte probacion by the space of a yere. **1597** HOOKER *Eccl. Pol.* v. lxviii. §8 They first set no time howe long this supposed probation must continue. **1603** SHAKS. *Meas. for M.* v. i. 72. **1611** BEAUM. & FL. *Philaster* II. ii, She that hath snow enough about her heart,..May be a nun without probation. **1872** O. SHIPLEY *Gloss. Eccl. Terms* s.v. *Monks*, They were subjected to a probation, but did not take solemn vows.

b. In theological and religious use: Moral trial or discipline; the divinely appointed or managed testing and determination of character and principle, esp. as taking place in this life in view of a future state of rewards and punishments.

future probation, a similar moral trial after death, which some believe will be granted to those who have not accepted, or have not had the offer of, the Gospel in this life, or to those who depart this life insufficiently purified.

1526 *Pilgr. Perf.* (W. de W. 1531) 5 b, To saue them in theyr probacyon in deserte. **1529** MORE *Suppl. Soulys* Wks. 315/1 [*margin*] The probacion of purgatorye. **1547** BOORDE *Brev. Health* xcix. 38 b, If aduersitie do come, it is either sent to punysse man for synne, or els probacion. **1563** WINȜET *Wks.* (S.T.S.) II. 36 The prouidence of God sufferis that thing to be for our probatioun. **1703** NELSON *Fest. & Fasts* ii. (1705) 29 At the end of the World. When the state of our Trial and Probation shall be finish'd, 'twill be a proper Season for the distribution of publick Justice. *a* **1805** PALEY *Serm.* xxxiii. (1810) 491 Of the various views under which human life has been considered, no one seems so reasonable as that which regards it as a state of probation. **1907** H. BUCKLE (*title*) The After Life: A Help to a Reasonable Belief in the Probation Life to Come.

c. In general use.

1616 *Cheque Bk. Chapel Royal* (Camden) 8 For a yeare of probacion of his manners and good behavior. **1754** RICHARDSON *Grandison* V. xlii. 262 The creature..who would have lived with you on terms of probation. **1833** CHALMERS in Hanna *Mem.* (1851) III. xviii. 356 After the probation of eighteen years, we have the Second Book of Discipline 1578. **1860** WHYTE MELVILLE *Holmby House* (new ed.) 287 Are they places of probation, of reward, of punishment? **1871** R. ELLIS *Catullus* xxviii. 5 Enough of empty masters, Frost and famine, a lingering probation.

3. In criminal jurisdiction: A system of dealing (chiefly) with young persons found guilty of crimes of lesser gravity, and esp. with first offenders, wherein these, instead of being sent to prison or otherwise punished, are released on suspended sentence during good behaviour, and placed under the supervision of a *probation officer*, who acts as a friend and adviser, but who, in case of the failure of the probationer to fulfil the terms of his probation, can report him back to the court for the execution of the sentence originally imposed. Used in the U.K. by Criminal Courts for certain adult offenders.

The term has been in use in parts of U.S., as Massachusetts, since 1878.

1897 *Resol. Comm. Howard Assoc.* June, Either an industrial discipline in special institutions, or, better still, a system of conditional liberty under the supervision of probation officers. **1906** J. G. LEGGE *Rep. Reform. & Industr. Schools*, There is much discussion at present of the advantages of a probation system and of probation officers. Infinite good will undoubtedly be achieved by an effective probation system. **1907** *Westm. Gaz.* 21 Mar. 2/3 In America the probation-officer, who makes every possible inquiry into the circumstances of the offence and advises the judge, has long been an institution. **1907** *Let. of Secr. N.Y. State Probation Commission* 7 Oct., Since the year 1878 in Massachusetts, and now in most of the commonwealths of the United States, persons found guilty of crimes (usually of the rank of misdemeanors..) have instead of being sent to a penal institution, been placed on probation... The term of probation varies from a few weeks to over a year. Probation officers are either salaried by public authorities or serve as volunteers so far as their official status is concerned... The term ordinarily employed in this country is 'to place on' or 'under probation', 'to put on' or 'under probation'. *Ibid.*, The expression 'probation-law' is coming into usage. The State of New York has recently established a 'Probation Commission'. **1921** E. RUGGLES-BRISE *Eng. Prison Syst.* ix. 108 The principle of conditional conviction is common to most penal codes... It may take the form..of judicial reprimand, or of being bound over to be of good behaviour, or of probation. **1969** F. FINLAY *Boy in Blue Jeans* xix. 218 I'm amazed to hear you got probation. *Ibid.* 219 Within weeks of being put on probation Christopher left the hostel and he was sacked from his job. **1971** R. CROSS *Punishment, Prison & Public* i. 20 Probation is essentially the suspension of punishment conditional on there being no further offence for a period during which the offender is placed under personal supervision. *Ibid.* iii. 110 It leads one to wonder whether magistrates might not make more use of probation and less of imprisonment. **1973** *Howard Jrnl.* XIII. 346 He applies crisis theory to probation, and rightly suggests that there is scope for short-term probation.

II. 4. a. The action of proving, or showing to be true; proof, demonstration; an instance of this, a proof, a demonstration. Now *rare* or *Obs.* exc. *Sc.*

c **1475** *Harl. Contin. Higden* (Rolls) VIII. 468 The seide man..faylenge in the probacion of his accusacion was.. hongede. **1500-20** DUNBAR *Poems* lxv. 9 The curious probatioun logicall. *a* **1533** FRITH *Answ. More* (1548) A v b, The seconde parte..nedeth no probacion. **1558** KNOX *First Blast* (Arb.) 35 In probation whereof, because the matter is more than euident, I will vse fewe wordes. **1598** DRAYTON *Heroic. Ep., Edw. IV to Mrs. Shore* 126 Poore plodding Schoole-men they are farre too lowe, Which by probations, rules, and axiomes goe. **1676** TOWERSON *Decalogue* 35, I will not..attempt the probation of it. **1836** SIR W. HAMILTON *Discuss.* (1852) 308 The cogency of strict probation. **1889** STEVENSON *Master of B.* x, It was clear, even to probation, the pamphlets had some share in this revolution.

†**b.** Something that proves or demonstrates; that which constitutes the ground of proof; proof, demonstrative evidence. Chiefly *Sc. Obs.*

1432-50 tr. *Higden* (Rolls) I. 367 An argumente and a probacion of this thynge dothe appere in that the fischer.. may see in the bryȝhte daies of somer vnder the waters hye towres and rownde of chirches. **1526** *Pilgr. Perf.* (W. de W. 1531) 199 That is a great probacyon of the trewth therof. **1535** STEWART *Cron. Scot.* (Rolls) III. 392 The quhilk wedding wes lauchfull probatioun Of his barnis legitimatioun. **1678** SIR G. MACKENZIE *Crim. Laws Scot.* II. xxiv. §1 (1699) 256 Probation is defined to be, that whereby the Judge is convinced of what is asserted. **1752** W. MILLER in *Scots Mag.* (1753) May 235/2 His..confession would be no probation of his having committed the crime.

†**c.** The proving of a will: = PROBATE *sb.* 2.

1529 *Act 21 Hen. VIII*, c. 5 Dyvers ordynaries take for the probacion of testamentes..sometyme .xl.s. *Passim.* **1571** *Wills & Inv. N.C.* (Surtees) I. 353, I require..James Cole to trauell with my said doughter about the probacion of this my will. **1590** SWINBURNE *Testaments* 224 Formes of prouing testaments..which are referred to that kinde of probation which is called *publicatio testamenti*.

III. 5. *attrib.* and *Comb.*, as (sense 1) ***probation-dish***; (sense 2 a) ***probation sermon***, ***-weed*** (= garment); (sense 2 b) ***probation-space***, ***-state***; (sense 3) ***probation commission***, ***law***, ***officer***, ***system***; also ***probation class***, ***station***, for convicts in convict settlements; **probation order**, a court order committing an offender to a period of probation; **probation report**, a probation officer's report on an accused person submitted to a court before sentence is passed, a social inquiry report; **probation service**, probation and after-care service, a function which carries responsibility for the oversight of probationers and the care of accused persons and discharged prisoners.

1899 *Westm. Gaz.* 31 Oct. 8/3 All prisoners..remain there three months, but if they show docile spirit at the end of that time they are transferred into the *probation class. **1625** B. JONSON *Staple of N.* IV. Interm., Let Master Doctor dissect him, haue him open'd, and his tripes translated to Lickfinger, to make a *probation dish of. **1906** *Rep. N.Y. Probation Comm.* i. 8 The duties of the *probation officer were to inquire into the previous history of any defendant when so directed by the court. **1909** *Westm. Gaz.* 1 Apr. 2/1 Section 107 of the Act contains a most useful conspectus of the substitutes for imprisonment which are at the disposal of the Court. They are..discharging the offender and placing him under the supervision of a probation officer. **1922** H. H. GODDARD *Juvenile Delinquency* 78 Finally she was brought to the Bureau [in Ohio] September 1918, by the probation officer to see if we could give any advice. **1930** *Morning Post* 8 Aug. 10 The Home Secretary has decided to introduce an experimental scheme for training full-time probation officers. **1975** *Howard Jrnl.* XIV. II. 28 Such work should also be familiar to the reporting probation officer if he is to be of real value to the sentencing court. **1921** E. RUGGLES-BRISE *Eng. Prison Syst.* ix. 109 The extent to which *Probation Orders are applied varies to a great extent in different parts of the country. **1948** *Act 11 & 12 Geo. VI* c. 58 §3 Where a court by or before which a person is convicted of an offence..is of opinion that having regard to the circumstances, including the nature of the offence and the character of the offender, it is expedient to do so, the court may, instead of sentencing him, make a probation order, that is to say, an order requiring him to be under the supervision of a probation officer for a period to be specified in the order of not less than one year nor more than three years. **1969** *Listener* 26 June 908/3 Each probation officer has around 60 cases at a time (most in Wales and fewest in London; women probation officers, dealing with female offenders, have a smaller case-load). Out of these, he can expect about six or seven to be so successful that the probation order can be cut short. **1978** J. B. HILTON *Some run Crooked* ix. 91 The Bench..made a probation order: and Harbutt listened like a model penitent. **1973** J. PATRICK *Glasgow Gang Observed* iv. 39 The *probation report offered this summary of Dick at the age of fourteen. **1977** *Wandsworth Borough News* 16 Sept. 17/2 [He] was remanded in custody for probation reports. **1662** PEPYS *Diary* 4 May, The church being full..to hear a Doctor who is to preach a *probacion sermon. **1813** A. BRUCE *Life A. Morus* ii. 37 He heard the probation sermons of the students of divinity. **1958** *New Statesman* 11 Oct. 479/3 It is fair to say..that even if the *probation service can ever carry this added burden, it is likely to be found..that the rehabilitative part of the work calls for welfare workers with a special kind of training not hitherto given to probation officers in this country. **1972** *Times* 19 Dec. 3/6 For the first time since the probation service was set up in 1907, officers in inner London yesterday went on strike. **1878** BROWNING *La Saisiaz* 270 Assuming earth to be a pupil's place, And life, time,—with all their chances, changes,—just *probation-space. **1736** BUTLER *Anal.* I. v. 79 The Consideration of our being in a *Probation-state. **1852** MUNDY *Our Antipodes* (1857) 211 Darlington had been a *Probation Station containing some four hundred prisoners. *Ibid.*, It was resumed when the *Probation System was introduced, and has since again been vacated as a Government station. *a* **1619** FLETCHER, etc. *Knt. Malta* v. i, I must or deliver in..my *probation-weed, Or take the cloke.

Hence **pro'bation** *v. trans.*, to place (an offender) under or on probation (sense 3); whence **pro'bationed** *ppl. a.*

1889 *Charity Organis. Rev.* Nov. 439 The probationed element is admitted in dealing with both. **1907** *Let. of Secr. N.Y. Probation Comm.* 7 Oct., In Indianapolis..the word 'probation' is used as a verb, as for instance 'I probation you'.

probational (prəʊ'beɪʃənəl), *a.* [f. prec. + -AL[1].]

1. = next, 1.

1650 TRAPP *Comm. Exod.* ix. 9 Job's boils were rather probational then penal. **1720** WHEATLEY *Comm. Prayer* vi. §11 (ed. 3) 279* A State of Purgation; which they imagin'd to consist of a probational Fire. **1887** H. S. HOLLAND *Christ or Eccles.* (1888) 121 It is impossible to speak on the probational significance of human life.

†**2.** Performed for the sake of testing or trial; experimental. *Obs.*

1670 MAYNWARING *Physician's Repos.* 14 Medicines..the result of practice and frequent probational experiments in the Laboratory.

probationary (prəʊ'beɪʃənərɪ), *a.* (*sb.*) [f. as prec. + -ARY[1].]

A. *adj.* **1.** Of, pertaining or relating to, or serving for probation; made, performed, or observed in the way of probation; belonging to the testing or trial of character or qualifications.

1664 H. MORE *Myst. Iniq., Apol.* 482 All the Philosophy that I give but so much as a Probationary countenance to. **1693** W. FREKE *Sel. Ess.* xxxiv. 216 The present State of our Nature and Sences is Probationary. **1751** JOHNSON *Rambler* No. 178 ¶1 Pythagoras is reported to have required from those whom he instructed in philosophy a probationary silence of five years. **1856** W. COLLINS *Rogue's Life* v, After a short probationary experience..I was advanced. **1867** *Edin. Med. Jrnl.* Dec. 552 Admitted into the probationary ward of the poorhouse. **1922** *Act 10 & 11 Geo. V* c. 30 §40 Such of those persons as..are serving a probationary period preliminary to establishment. **1963** T. & P. MORRIS *Pentonville* iv. 78 Once he has successfully completed his one-year period of probationary service, the prison officer is in effect a prison officer for life. **1964** A. SWINSON *Six Minutes to Sunset* iv. 54 He passed the Indian Civil Service examinations from Wren's and like most of his class spent two probationary years at Balliol and a third to get his degree. **1971** *Guardian* 8 Feb. 7/7 Introduction of a probationary licence for a period of one year after passing the test.

2. Undergoing probation; that is a probationer; consisting of probationers.

1818 SCOTT *Lett.* 10 May, A probationary piper is exercising a new..pair of bagpipes. **1884** W. J. COURTHOPE *Addison* ii. 30 The College elected him probationary Fellow in 1697, and actual Fellow the year after. **1886** MRS. OLIPHANT in *Blackw. Mag.* Apr. 417 He entered the probationary order of the Scottish ministry. **1926** *N.Z. Educ. Gaz.* 1 Dec. 202/2 Teachers selected for service as probationary assistants must understand they are still under training. **1963** B. PEARSON *Coal Flat* iii. 47 There was her routine of school, and her relations..with Miss James the probationary assistant. **1964** M. BANTON *Policeman in*

Community ii. 17 On the Friday he has instructed a number of new recruits (probationary constables) to parade at the station at 6 a.m.

B. *sb.* = PROBATIONER. *rare.*

1748 RICHARDSON *Clarissa* (1811) VIII. lxxiii. 353, I think I ought to pass some time as a probationary.

pro'bationatory, *a. Obs. rare*$^{-1}$. [f. as prec. + *-atory*, as in *accus-atory*, etc.] Connected with trial or investigation.

1677 GALE *Crt. Gentiles* II. III. 17 The λόγος πειραστικός, the probationatory, or problematic disputes in the old Academie begun by Socrates and Plato.

probationer (prəʊ'beɪʃənə(r)). [f. as prec. + -ER[1].] **a.** A person on probation or trial; one who is qualifying, or giving proof of qualification, for some position or office; a candidate; a novice.

(A term recognized, or in common use, in connexion with many offices or positions: see also b and d.)

1603 FLORIO *Montaigne* III. ii. (1632) 451 He is still a Prentise and a probationer. **1691** SHADWELL *Scowrers* v, You must be at least a year's probationer. **1729** SWIFT *Modest Proposal* §6 They learn the rudiments much earlier; during which time they can however be properly looked upon only as probationers. **1836** SIR H. TAYLOR *Statesman* xxiii. 174 A twelvemonths' probation, at the end of which the probationer is pronounced to be either fit or unfit for admission on the establishment. **1896** *Allbutt's Syst. Med.* I. 423 While probationers are being thus educated they are also instructed in the special branches of the work.

b. *spec.* (*a*) A candidate for a scholarship or fellowship in a college, admitted on probation. (*b*) A novice in a religious house or order, or in a nursing sisterhood. (*c*) A candidate for the ministry of a church, etc.; one licensed to preach but not yet ordained (esp. in Presbyterian and Methodist churches). (*d*) In criminal jurisdiction an offender under probation (see PROBATION 3). (*e*) ***Lord Probationer***, a newly appointed Scottish judge before he undergoes his trial and takes the oath. *Obs.* (*f*) *N.Z.* A teacher during his first year in a school after training at a teachers' training college.

a. 1609 B. JONSON *Sil. Wom.* I. i, And euery day, gaine to their Colledge some new probationer. **1846** MCCULLOCH *Acc. Brit. Empire* (1854) II. 335 It is customary in some colleges for individuals elected to fellowships to pass a year as probationers, during which they receive no income, and are considered as holding their appointment merely at will.

b. 1629 WADSWORTH *Pilgr.* viii. 81 Before they enter their ..Religious Houses, to be Probationers. **1892** 'H. S. MERRIMAN' *Slave of Lamp* xxi, He was in the dress of a Probationer of the Society of Jesus.

c. 1645 MILTON *Colast.* Wks. 1851 IV. 347 A stripling Divine or two of those newly fledge Probationers, that usually come scouting from the University. **1694** *Act Gen. Assembly* c. 10. 12 The General Assembly hereby Appoints, That when such persons are first Licensed to be Probationers, They shall oblidge themselvs to Preach only within the bounds, or by the Direction of that Presbytry, which did License them. **1730** BOSTON *Mem.* iv. (1908) 36, I past two years and three months in the character of a probationer. **1904** R. SMALL *Hist. U.P. Congregat.* II. 428 The presentee was Mr. David Duncan, probationer.

d. 1907 *Let. of Secr. N.Y. Probation Comm.* 7 Oct., In case of failure of the probationer to live up to the terms of his probation, [the probation officer] can report the probationer back to the court for commitment to an institution or for the execution of whatever other sentence may have been originally imposed and then suspended.

e. 1799 *Edin. Weekly Jrnl.* 22 May, William Macleod Bannatyne, Esq. having gone through his trials as Lord Probationer, took the oaths and his seat on the Bench by the title of *Lord Bannatyne*. **1838** W. BELL *Dict. Law Scotl.* 176 The form of trial [for new judges]..consists in the presentee, or Lord Probationer as he is called, hearing and reporting, and delivering an opinion on certain of the causes depending in court. **1910** *Pall Mall Gaz.* 26 Apr. 3/5 He appears again in the First Division, and the junior judge reports to the judges of that court the judgments the Lord Probationer has pronounced.

f. 1921 *N.Z. Educ. Gaz.* 1 Dec. 21/1 Central classes for the instruction of pupil-teachers, probationers, and uncertificated teachers in science and in drawing and handwork may..be established by an Education Board. **1922** *Ibid.* 1 June 62/2 Pupil-teachers and probationers may not attend any classes in hygiene established for uncertificated teachers. **1963** B. PEARSON *Coal Flat* i. 8 You were here [*sc.* at this school] before, as probationer, weren't you?

c. *transf.* and *fig.*

1642 MILTON *Apol. Smect.* §1 Wks. 1851 III. 306 To make my selfe a canting Probationer of orisons. **1689** SHERLOCK *Death* i. §1 (1731) 20 Adam..was but a Probationer for Immortality. **1754** RICHARDSON *Grandison* (1781) V. xxxiii. 211 The brevity and vanity of this life, in which we are but probationers. **1844** EMERSON *Ess.* Ser. II. vi. (1876) 148 The animal is the novice and probationer of a more advanced order.

d. *attrib.*: chiefly *appositive* = that is a probationer; one on probation or trial (for the position indicated by the second element).

1649 FULLER *Just Man's Funeral* 17 What the Probationer-Disciple said to our Saviour. **1674** HICKMAN *Hist. Quinquart.* (ed. 2) 20 It is but a probationer attribute. **1679** WOOD *Life* 24 Aug. (O.H.S.) II. 461 Tom Wood chose probationer fellow of New Coll. *a* **1715** BURNET *Own Time* an. 1666 (1766) I. II. 332 One Maccail, that was only a probationer preacher. **1899** *Westm. Gaz.* 15 Mar. 5/1 A special class of the Naval Reserve, to be called the 'probationer class'. **1905** *Daily Chron.* 14 Oct. 9/1 A probationer nurse at Poplar Hospital.

Hence **pro'bationerhood, pro'bationership,** the position or condition of a probationer.

1845 J. CAIRNS *Let.* in *Life* x. (1895) 234 This knight errant of *probationerhood. *a* **1652** J. SMITH *Sel. Disc.* VII. vi. (1821) 366 Saving faith..is not patient of being an expectant in a *probationership for it [salvation] until this earthly body resigns up all its worldly interest. **1690** LOCKE *Hum. Und.* IV. xiv. §2 That State of Mediocrity and Probationership, He has been pleased to place us in here. **1880** A. SOMERVILLE *Autobiog.* 97 Ten months of what is significantly called 'Probationership'.

pro'bationism. *Theol. rare.* [f. as prec. + -ISM.] The, or a, doctrine of future probation (see PROBATION 2 b).

1886 *Relig. Herald* 15 July (Cent. Dict.).

pro'bationist. *rare.* [f. as prec. + -IST.]

1. = PROBATIONER.

1885 *Congregationalist* 14 May (Cent.), What portion of the probationists uniting with the M[ethodist] E[piscopal] church become full members?

2. One who holds the doctrine of probationism.

1893 E. S. CARR in *N. Western Congregationalist* 14 Apr., I am satisfied the probationists among us are an extremely small minority.

pro'bationship. *rare.* [f. as prec. + -SHIP; cf. *relationship*.] A state or condition of probation; a term or period of probation; novitiate.

1626 tr. *Boccalini's New-Found Politick* III. xi. 202 Before the end of these Ladies probationship and their matriculation, his Maiestie charged the Cathedrall Doctors to dismisse them out of the Vniuersitie. **1691** WOOD *Ath. Oxon.* I. 181 After he had served his probationship, he went into Ireland. **1822** *New Monthly Mag.* IV. 323 Her face covered with the white veil of probationship. **1884** *Weekly Register* 18 Oct. 504/2 At the end of a two year's probationship.

probative ('prəʊbətɪv), *a.* [ad. L. *probātīv-us* belonging to proof: see PROBATE *ppl. a.* and -IVE.]

1. Having the quality or function of testing; serving or designed for trial or probation; probationary. Now *rare.*

1453 in *Epist. Acad. Oxon.* (O.H.S.) I. 320 We assignyd to them a terme probatiffe. **1624** F. WHITE *Repl. Fisher* 559 The second are exemplarie, purgatiue, probatiue, or for the edifying of the Church. **1730** WATERLAND *Script. Vind.* I. 79 A much better Argument against human Sacrifices, than a probative Command, not executed, could be for it. **1816** BENTHAM *Chrestom.* II. 18 On the constancy of the application made of the correspondent probative exercise, by which a lesson is said, depends all the use derivable from any mathetic exercise.

2. Having the quality or function of proving or demonstrating; affording proof or evidence; demonstrative, evidential.

1681 *Sc. Acts Chas. II* (1820) VIII. 242/2 Act concerning probative witnesses in writs & Executions. *Ibid.* 243/1 None but subscryving witnesses shall be probative in Executions of Messingers [etc.]. **1802–12** BENTHAM *Ration. Judic. Evid.* (1827) I. 18 The principal fact may, in a more expressive way, be termed the fact proved: the evidentiary, the probative fact. **1868** *Act 31 & 32 Vict.* c. 10 §142 Which [certificates] shall..be probative of such registration. **1875** POSTE *Gaius* III. Comm. (ed. 2) 412 *Cautio*..signified a probative or evidentiary document, as opposed to a literal contract. **1971** *Jrnl. Gen. Psychol.* LXXXIV. 222 A theorem deducible only from the conjunction of axioms as their only implicate is, therefore, most probative of the theory that contains them. **1972** *Mod. Law Rev.* XXXV. I. 73 The views of the majority have been treated as the most probative, if not the dispositive, factor. **1975** *Sci. Amer.* May 118/1 A new argument for credibility seemed to have emerged when one of the troubled men underwent a polygraph test, which at best is hardly fully probative.

Hence **'probatively** *adv.*, in a probative manner; in the way of probation, or of proof; **'probativeness,** the quality of affording proof.

1869 BROWNING *Ring & Bk.* x. 1415 'Tis even as man grew probatively Initiated in Godship. **1971** *Jrnl. Gen. Psychol.* LXXXIV. 222 Theorems differ in their degree of probativeness of a theory. **1973** *N.Y. Law Jrnl.* 20 July 2/2 Movant has failed to probatively demonstrate that respondent has willfully failed and refused to comply with the judgment of the court.

‖**pro'bator.** *Obs. rare.* [L. *probātor* an examiner, approver, agent-n. f. *probāre* to PROVE.]

1. = APPROVER[1] 1, APPELLANT *sb.* 1.

[*c* **1290** FLETA II. lii. §44 Illi autem qui a probatoribus ipsis mortuis fuerint appellati [etc.].] **1701** *Cowell's Interpr.*, *Probator*, an Accuser, or Approver, or one who undertakes to prove a crime charg'd upon another.

2. An examiner.

1691 MAYDMAN *Naval Spec.* 182 Some nominated, and appointed for Probators.

†**'probatory,** *sb. Obs. rare.* [ad. med.L. *probātōri-um*, neut. sb. from *probātōrius*: see next.]

1. A house for probationers or novices.

1610 HOLLAND *Camden's Brit.* II. 151 In the same yeere Christian, Bishop of Lismore..and Pope Eugenius a venerable man, with whom hee was in the Probatory at Clarevall,..departed to Christ.

2. (See quot.) *rare*$^{-0}$.

1670 BLOUNT *Glossogr.* (ed. 3), *Probatory*, (from *probo*) the place where proof or trial is made of any thing, or the Instrument that tries it.

probatory ('prəʊbətərɪ), *a.* [ad. med.L. *probātōri-us* belonging to trial or proof, f. ppl. stem of L. *probāre* to prove: see -ORY[2]. Cf. F. *probatoire* (1762 in Dict. Acad.).]

1. = PROBATIVE 1; testing. Now *rare.*

1625 USSHER *Answ. Jesuit* 172 Although it be a probatory, and not a purgatory fire that the Apostle there treateth of. **1662** HIBBERT *Body Div.* I. 130 Those tribulations..were onely probatory, to trie his strength. **1799** *Usef. Proj.* in *Ann. Reg.* 411/1 Preparation of the new probatory Liquor [= testing liquid]. **1874** BUSHNELL *Forgiveness & Law* II. 139 In a scheme of probatory discipline. **1970** *Internat. Jrnl. Cancer* V. 311/1 Samples of tumours or normal tissue were obtained by probatory excision.

†**2.** = PROBATIVE 2; proving. *Obs. rare.*

1593 G. HARVEY *Pierce's Super.* Wks. (Grosart) II. 325, I am content to referre Incredulity, to the visible, and palpable evidence of the Terme Probatory. **1638** FEATLY *Transubst.* 179 That [these words] are not argumentative or probatorie. **1656** *Artif. Handsom.* 126 His other heap of arguments are only assertory, not probatory.

3. (See quot.)

1924 P. S. ALLEN in *Library* Mar. 255 The manuscripts are identified in the catalogue by the first words of the second leaf, the 'probatory words'.

‖**probatum** (prəʊ'beɪtəm). ? *Obs.* [L. *probātum* a thing proved: see PROBATE *sb.*]

1. a. A thing proved; a demonstrated conclusion or fact; *esp.* a means or remedy that has been tried and found efficacious; an approved remedy.

1594 NASHE *Terrors of Nt.* Wks. (Grosart) III. 251 He is a mettle-bruing Paracelsian, hauing not past one or two Probatums for al diseases. **1607** WALKINGTON *Opt. Glass* 44 To giue vsuall probatums to trie conclusions. **1654** GAYTON *Pleas. Notes* IV. viii. 219 The very Probatum for a Lethargv. [**1800** COLERIDGE *Wallenst.* IV. ii. 130 That's probatum, Nothing can stand 'gainst that.]

†**b.** A proof or demonstration.

1613 JACKSON *Creed* I. xxxi. §7 His people might have a *probatum* of it either in themselves or others. **1627** SANDERSON *Serm.* I. 275 A good *probatum* of that observation of Solomon, 'When a mans ways please the Lord, He maketh even his enemies to be at peace with him.'

†**c.** Short for *probatum est*: see 2. *Obs.*

1634 MASSINGER *Very Woman* III. i, Feed him with fogs; *probatum.* **1709** O. DYKES *Eng. Prov. & Refl.* (ed. 2) 203 It has every one's Probatum to't. **1741** WATTS *Improv. Mind* I. xvii. §4 He..recommended it to all his friends, since he could set his probatum to it for seventeen years.

†**2.** *Phr.* **probatum est** [L.] 'it has been proved or tested', a phrase used in recipes or prescriptions; also in general sense. Hence as *sb. Obs.*

1573–80 G. HARVEY *Letter-bk.* (Camden) 138 By y[e] masse, all, all is nawght, Probatum est; I teach as I am tawght. **1693** C. MATHER *Wond. Invis. World* N ij b, [The devil] has had the Encouragement of a *Probatum est*, upon these horrid Methods. *a* **1721** PRIOR *Epigram to Dk. de Noalles* iii, Lend him but fifty louis-d'or; And you shall never see him more; Take my advice, probatum est. **1757** *Hist. 2 Mod. Advent.* I. A v, To the above Nostrum, I can subscribe my *Probatum est*, from its powerful effect upon myself. **1831** M. EDGEWORTH *Let.* 20 Jan. (1971) 474 Mother in law gave Fanny..the best receipt for a poultice that ever was (probatum est). **1884** G. MEREDITH *Let.* 17 Sept. (1970) II. 745 All material conquest follows self-conquest... *Probatum est.*

probe (prəʊb), *sb.* [ad. late L. *proba* a proof, in med.L. also an examination, f. *prob-āre* to try, test, PROVE. Cf. Cat. *proba*, Pr. *prova* a probe, a sounding line; also med.L. *tenta*, Sp. *tienta*, f. *tentāre* to try (see TENT).]

1. A surgical instrument, commonly of metal, with a blunt end, for exploring the direction and depth of wounds and sinuses.

1580 HOLLYBAND *Treas. Fr. Tong*, *Vne petite Esprouvette*, a small instrument wherewith Surgeons do search wounds, a probe. **1611, 1656** [see PROOF *sb.* 15 a]. **1612** WOODALL *Surg. Mate* Wks. (1653) 8 Some use the longer sort of Probes, with eyes like needles. **1706–7** FARQUHAR *Beaux Strat.* v. iii, Do, do, Daughter—while I get the Lint and the Probe and the Plaister ready. **1807–26** S. COOPER *First Lines Surg.* (ed. 5) 413 The course of many narrow stabs cannot be easily followed by a probe. **1813** J. THOMSON *Lect. Inflam.* 405 When I passed my probe into it, I did not feel the bone bare, but only its resistance.

fig. **1871** BLACKIE *Four Phases* i. 66 Those whom he submitted to the operation of his ethical probe. **1876** LOWELL *Ode 4th July* IV. iii, We, who believe Life's bases rest Beyond the probe of chemic test.

2. *transf.* **a.** The proboscis of an insect. **b.** *Angling.* A baiting-needle.

1664 POWER *Exp. Philos.* I. 2 At his [the flea's] snout is fixed a Proboscis, or hollow trunk or probe. *Ibid.* 8 The Butter-Fly... The Probe (which you see lyes in her mouth in spiral contorsions). **1681** CHETHAM *Angler's Vade-m.* xxxvii. §9 (1689) 237 Others use the Probe to draw the Arming Wire under the Skin only. [Cf. **1653** WALTON *Angler* vii. 150 The better to avoid hurting the fish, some have a kind of probe to open the way, for the more easie entrance and passage of your wyer or arming.]

c. Any small device, esp. an electrode, which can penetrate or be placed in or on something for the purpose of obtaining and relaying information or measurements about it, or of exciting radiation in it.

1924 *Physical Rev.* XXIV. 597 Potential distribution and ion concentration were investigated by Langmuir's modified probe method. **1938** *Proc. IRE* XXVI. 1534 The electric field intensity was measured by a small probe with a crystal detector, followed by an audio-frequency amplifier and a copper-oxide meter. **1943** F. E. Terman *Radio Engineer's Handbk.* iii. 260 Just as waves can be set up in space by straight wires and loops, so can the wave-guide modes be excited by electric probes and loops. **1965** *Wireless World* July 31 (Advt.), A completely new transducer.. utilizes the variation in capacitance between its probe and the object under investigation to provide an electrical signal. **1971** *Sci. Amer.* Dec. 76/1 W. L. Bretz in our laboratory designed and built a small probe that could record the direction of airflow at strategic points in the respiratory system of ducks. **1972** *Physics Bull.* Jan. 23/3 In its basic form the pulse echo apparatus..comprises a heavily damped piezoelectric transducer source, often called a probe, which is placed on the surface of the sample under test. **1977** *Sci. Amer.* Aug. 63/1 [On the ocean floor] temperature gradients are determined by plunging a long cylindrical probe several meters into the soft sediment and measuring the temperature at one-metre intervals with fixed thermistors.

d. *Aeronaut.* and *Astronautics.* (i) A tube fitted to the nose or wing of an aircraft in order to fit into a drogue towed by another and convey fuel from it in aerial refuelling.

1949 *Flight* 11 Aug. 178/2 Either the tanker or the aircraft to be refuelled..could be fitted with the 'probe'. **1950** C. H. Latimer-Needham *Refuelling in Flight* 186 On the nose of the fighter aircraft, a horizontal tubular member, or probe, approximately 4 ft. in length, is fitted, and this is aimed by the pilot at the trailing drogue so that as the fighter closes with the tanker the probe enters the drogue and thus makes contact. **1966** [see drogue 3]. **1978** *Aeroplane Monthly* Jan. 35/1 This sub-variant incorporated the necessary 'plumbing' to permit in-flight refuelling, achieved with the aid of a probe of gigantic proportions.

(ii) A projecting device on a spacecraft designed to engage with the drogue of another craft during docking.

1969 *Times* 23 May 1/3 Ground control told the astronauts that it suspected that the ring, which serves as a mount for the docking probe, had slipped by about three degrees. **1970** N. Armstrong et al. *First on Moon* iv. 80 The command module had at its top a 'probe', a triangularly shaped assembly with a pencil-like point. **1970** R. Turnill *Lang. of Space* 34 Three tiny capture latches on the nose of the probe provide the first steadying link, and then the command module crewman fires a gas bottle which thrusts the two together so that 12 docking latches snap shut to complete the process.

e. A small, usu. unmanned, exploratory spacecraft (other than an earth satellite) for transmitting information about its environment; also, a rocket or an instrument capsule for obtaining measurements in the upper atmosphere.

1953 *Jrnl. Brit. Interplanetary Soc.* XII. 73 The probe will arrive at Mars nine months after opposition. **1958** *Observer* 17 Aug. 1/6 From then on the probe will be on its own for about 59 hours, coasting through space, gradually slowing down under the pull of the earth's gravity. **1959** F. D. Adams *Aeronaut. Dict.* 132/1 *Probe*,..3. An instrumented research rocket, or its payload, for penetrating the upper atmosphere or beyond. **1967** *Technol. Week* 23 Jan. 2/2 (Advt.), Motorola command receivers are ready to prove themselves again and again..in high altitude probes..and in a multitude of new tactical applications. **1968** *Times* 15 Nov. 8/5 The Russian probe was not able to measure the lower 25 kilometres of the Venusian atmosphere. **1970** R. Turnill *Lang. of Space* 122 A second spacecraft..is intended to go into orbit around Saturn, and drop off at least one probe. **1977** *Nature* 8 Sept. 98/3 The 11 instruments on board include television cameras, infrared and ultraviolet spectrometers, charged particle detectors, magnetometer and plasma wave detectors and, for the first time on an interplanetary probe, radio wave detectors.

†**3.** A printer's proof. *Obs. rare*$^{-1}$.

Perhaps an error for *prove*, proof *sb.*

1563 Grindal *Let. to Sir W. Cecil* 21 Jan., The thanksgiving for the queen's majesty's preservation..ye shall see in the probe of the print, and after judge.

4. a. [f. probe *v.*] An act of probing; a piercing or boring, a prod.

1890 *Athenæum* 10 May 613/3 As the Agora was gradually working itself out we tried probes to the west in the adjoining fields. **1894** *Outing* (U.S.) XXIV. 108/2 The fish felt a probe in the ribs. **1907** *Daily News* 11 Nov. 6/1 A probe with a pin is needed to unfold it.

b. *fig.* A penetrating investigation. Also in other transferred senses of the vb.

1903 *Christendom* 9 May 151/1 Few words are commoner in newspaper headlines than 'probe', which is newspaper English for an investigation of alleged abuses. **1930** *Amer. Speech* VI. 119 Probe started in junk yard blaze. **1945** *Ann. Reg. 1944* 307 With an obbligato of court injunctions, Congressional 'probes', Gallup polls,..the case dragged on. **1948** I. Brown *No Idle Words* 99, I have just seen an inquiry into a fatal explosion in a factory described as a Blast Probe. **1959** *Listener* 31 Dec. 1140/2 Such conventional forces should be capable of performing all the functions for which the troops of Nato are at present organized: to deal with frontier incidents, to distinguish between local probes and deliberate sustained attack. **1962** A. Huxley *Island* xi. 177 Slanting down through chinks in the green vaulting overhead, the long probes of sunlight picked out here a row of black and yellow water jars, there a silver bracelet. **1962** *Listener* 15 Mar. 477/3 The results of the so-called Berlin probe—the recent meetings between Mr Gromyko and the American Ambassador in Moscow—have been 'no wickets and no runs'. **1971** J. B. Carroll et al. *Word Frequency Bk.* p. vii, The AHI Corpus is..a highly informative probe of what might be called the American school lexicon. **1980** R. McCrum *In Secret State* iv. 26 Would Hayter start an internal probe into the background to the Lister business?

5. *fig. spec.* in *Nuclear Physics*, applied to a particle which can be used to penetrate nuclei, atoms, etc., and reveal their internal structure.

1955 C. G. Darwin in W. Pauli *Niels Bohr* i. 5 The α-particle was always Rutherford's favourite. He could see that its great mass and its great energy made it the most effective of all probes to show what was in the atom. **1971** S. Kaufman in L. C. L. Yuan *Elem. Particles* iv. 160 Extremely high-energy..projectiles are required to produce the mass equivalent of these strange particles and to provide probes of short enough wavelength to 'see' any internal structure. **1972** DePuy & Chapman *Molec. Reactions & Photochem.* v. 78 Quenching is another useful probe for determination of mechanism. **1974** I. E. McCarthy *Nuclear Reactions* i. 6 The invention of accelerating machines promised new probes, for example protons, deuterons, and even heavier ions. **1975** Spiro & Loehr in Clark & Hester *Adv. Infrared & Raman Spectroscopy* I. iii. 135 To manipulate the composition of the sample, Oseroff and Callender employed a 'pump' laser beam, to establish the photo-stationary state, coaxial with a 'probe' beam, which produced the Raman spectrum. **1975** *Nature* 5 June 459/1 This effect in α-phenylethylamine was first noticed by Hug *et al.*, who realised that it originated in the two degenerate asymmetric deformations of the methyl group and could function as a new probe of chirality.

6. *attrib.* and *Comb.*, as ***probe-end***, ***-point***; **probe-and-drogue**, used *attrib.* with reference to (i) a method of aerial refuelling (see 2 d (i) above), or (ii) a method of docking spacecraft (see 2 d (ii) above); **probe microphone** (see quot. 1955); also (*colloq.*) **probe mike**; **probe-needle**, a needle used in the manner of a probe (cf. *probe-scissors*); **probe-pointed** *a.*, having a blunt point, like that of a probe; **probe-scissors**, scissors used for opening wounds, having a button on the point of the blade.

1951 *Engineering* 27 Apr. 491/1 In the *probe-and-drogue system, the tanker trails a hose..to the end of which is attached a conical metal drogue..with the open end facing rearward. **1959** *Times* 8 Sept. 4/2 The range of the Vulcan V bomber will be increased significantly by the use of the probe and drogue aerial refuelling system. **1970** R. Turnill *Lang. of Space* 34 *Docking tunnel*... So called because it contains the interlocking probe and drogue system for linking up the two craft in space. **1863–76** Curling *Dis. Rectum* (ed. 4) 105 Using the *probe end of the director as a guide, the surgeon may make an external artificial opening. **1955** *Gloss. Acoustical Terms* (*B.S.I.*) 24 **Probe microphone*, a microphone or device incorporating a microphone for measuring sound pressure at a point in a sound field without significantly altering by its presence the sound field in the neighbourhood of the point. **1976** K. Benton *Single Monstrous Act* iii. 37 'What is it?.. A *probe mike?' 'That's it... It's shaped like a spike.' **1979** 'J. Le Carré' *Smiley's People* (1980) xxi. 257 They'd like to run a couple of probe mikes into the ground floor. **1676** Wiseman *Chirurg. Treat.* iii. v. 231, I prepared a Ligature, and with a *Probe-needle passed it up into the Gut. **1879** *St. George's Hosp. Rep.* IX. 787 The puncture is visible,..*probe-point inserted into it. **1783** Pott *Chirurg. Wks.* II. 155 The extremity of the *probe-pointed knife. **1869** G. Lawson *Dis. Eye* (1874) 59 Into this opening I insert a pair of small probe-pointed scissors. **1676** Wiseman *Chirurg. Treat.* vi. iv. 418 The sinus ..may be..snipt open by a pair of *Probe-scissors. **1783** Pott *Chirurg. Wks.* II. 155 The probe-scissors..is in this case particularly hazardous and improper.

probe (prəʊb), *v.* Also 7 proab. [f. probe *sb.*: in some uses perh. influenced by L. *probāre* to try, test: see prove *v.*]

1. *trans.* To examine or explore (a wound or other cavity of the body) with a probe. Also with the person as *obj.*

1687 Dryden *Hind & P.* iii. 80 Yet durst she not too deeply probe the wound, As hoping still the nobler parts were sound. **1758** J. S. *Le Dran's Observ. Surg.* (1771) 266, I probed him carefully, and found no Stone. **1828** Scott *F.M. Perth* xxii, The leech,..when the body was found, was commanded by the magistrates to probe the wound with his instruments.

2. *fig.* **a.** To search into, so as thoroughly to explore, or to discover or ascertain something; to try, prove, sound; to interrogate closely. Cf. probe *sb.* 4 b.

1649 Lovelace *Poems* 28 She proabed it [*sc.* my heart] with her constancie, And found no Rancor nigh it. **1732** Berkeley *Alciphr.* i. §5 Stand firm, while I probe your prejudices. **1804** Wellington in Gurw. *Desp.* (1837) II. 667, I was anxious to find out to what countries they had claims, and probed them particularly upon that point. **1818** Scott *Rob Roy* viii, A rascally calumny, which I was determined to probe to the bottom. **1875** Helps *Soc. Press.* iii. 53 If they were probed as to their motives. **1884** *N.Y. Weekly Tribune* 12 Mar. 1/2 The Senate Committee did not probe the Public Works Department in vain. **1915** C. Mackenzie *Guy & Pauline* 228 If he could only probe by some remark a generous impulse. **1953** *Manch. Guardian Weekly* 5 Mar. 3/1 The press exhaustively probed the unpublished agenda and was then kept..firmly out of earshot. **1977** F. Branston *Up & Coming Man* xiv. 150 Headlines were mostly variations of 'CID probe M-Way Rolls death mystery'.

b. To ask or inquire probingly. *rare.*

1839 Lady Lytton *Cheveley* (ed. 2) II. x. 334 'Anything about Denham in it?' probed Herbert.

c. To find *out* by probing or similar action. *rare.*

1699 Wanley in *Lett. Lit. Men* (Camden) 284 But I made shift to probe out a few of them myself.

3. *transf.* **a.** To pierce or penetrate with something sharp, esp. in order to test or explore.

1789 G. White *Selborne* vi. (1853) 25 Which the owners assured me they procured..by probing the soil with spits. **1841** Emerson *Addr., Meth. Nat.* Wks. (Bohn) II. 222 As soon as he probes the crust, behold gimlet, plumb-line, and philosopher take a lateral direction. **1863** Lyell *Antiq. Man* ii. 31 The bog or peat was ascertained, on probing it with an instrument, to be at least fifteen feet thick. **1904** *Brit. Med. Jrnl.* 17 Sept. 660, I counted thirty-eight [tsetse flies] probing the body of a large monitor I had shot.

b. To thrust (a piercing instrument) for the purpose of examination or exploration. *rare.*

1889 Gretton *Memory's Harkb.* 109 One of the soldiers probed his bayonet between the logs under which he was lying, and just pricked him.

4. *intr.* To perform the action of piercing with or as with a probe; to penetrate, as a probe.

1835–6 *Todd's Cycl. Anat.* I. 311/2 Which [birds] have occasion to probe for their food in muddy or sandy soils. **1878** Geo. Eliot *Coll. Breakf. P.* 201 Your question..has probed right through To the pith of our belief. **1887** M. Corelli *Thelma* II. iv. 66 Lady Winsleigh..had..the cleverness to probe into Thelma's nature and find out how translucently clear and pure it was. **1906** G. Meredith *Let.* 5 Apr. in *Amer. N. & Q.* (1973) XI. 69/2 'Beauchamp's Career' does not probe so deeply, but is better work on the surface. **1923** *Times Lit. Suppl.* 4 Jan. 9/3 The only instrument by which his *fin-de-siècle* soul..could probe to something solid to live by. **1959** *Listener* 14 May 827/1 If an aggressor were to try a probing action it's just as likely that he would probe on the sea, or even under the sea, as on land or in the air. **1962** *Ibid.* 5 July 3 (*heading*) Anthony Crosland and Donald MacRae probe into the state of the nation.

Hence **ˈprobing** *vbl. sb.*; also **ˈprober**, one who or that which probes.

1680 Otway *Orphan* iv. vi. 1540 Every probing pains me to the heart. **1890** *Pall Mall G.* 27 Nov. 3/1 That greatest prober of the secrets of science, the microscope. **1894** *Athenæum* 12 May 624/2 Probers of feminine hearts. **1948** I. Brown *No Idle Words* 99 They [*sc.* sub-editors] are probers to a man. **1954** L. MacNeice *Autumn Sequel* 75 The probing mind begins to fail the prober. **1958** *Listener* 20 Nov. 822/2 If the probing [of the moon] is carried out recklessly..then the extra-terrestrial bodies will be contaminated. **1970** *Times* 26 Feb. 4/6 Rescue workers today delved with probing rods into a mass of snow. **1974** *State* (Columbia, S. Carolina) 15 Feb. 1-A/4 (*heading*) White House refuses material for probers.

[**probend**, in Wright *Vocab.* 201, Wr.-Wülcker 664/10, error for provend.]

probenecid (prəʊˈbɛnɪsɪd). *Pharm.* [f. pro(pyl + ben(zoic *a.* + -*e*- + a)cid *a.* and *sb.*] A white, crystalline, bitter-tasting powder which is a uricosuric agent used esp. to treat gout; *p*-(di-*n*-propylsulphamoyl)benzoic acid, $(C_3H_7)_2NSO_2{\cdot}C_6H_4COOH$.

1950 *Ann. Internal Med.* XXXIII. 18 Benemid. [*Note*] Sharp and Dohme's trademark for p-(di-n-propylsulfamyl)-benzoic acid. This drug has been tentatively given the generic designation 'probenecid'. **1953** *Proc. Soc. Exper. Biol. & Med.* LXXXII. 604/1 Probenecid has been shown to inhibit reversibly the renal tubular secretion of a number of organic acids, such as penicillin.., phenolsulfonphthalein.., and para-aminohippuric acid. **1963** *Lancet* 5 Jan. 54/2 People with these vague aches associated with uric-acid blood-level elevation have responded well to colchicine intravenously as initial treatment and probenecid daily. **1974** A. Henry in R. M. Kirk et al. *Surgery* xv. 305 Acute attacks [of gout] are controlled by colchicine or phenylbutazone, while uricosuric agents such as probenecid keep the plasma uric level down and must be continued throughout life.

probertite (ˈprəʊbətaɪt). *Min.* [f. the name of Frank H. *Probert* (1876–1940), U.S. mining engineer + -ite[1].] A hydrated borate of sodium and calcium, $NaCaB_5O_9.5H_2O$, which is found as colourless, monoclinic crystals at a number of locations in California.

1929 A. S. Eakle in *Amer. Mineralogist* XIV. 427 The new borate..occurs as one of the minerals of the kernite deposit in the Kramer District, Kern County, California, and the name 'probertite' is proposed for the mineral, in honor of Frank H. Probert, Dean of the Mining College, University of California, to whom the writer is indebted for specimens, photos and notes of its occurrence. **1949** *Amer. Mineralogist* XXXIV. 19 Probertite..is monoclinic, has a radiating prismatic habit, perfect (110) cleavage and specific gravity of 2·141. **1964** Nies & Campbell in R. M. Adams *Boron, Metallo-boron Compounds & Boranes* iii. 93 Hot concentrated borax liquors can be prepared in which the calcium content frequently is manyfold its equilibrium value, and when it finally deposits from these hot solutions it is usually in the form of probertite, $NaCaB_5O_9{\cdot}5H_2O$.

probing (ˈprəʊbɪŋ), *ppl. a.* [f. probe *v.* + -ing[2].] That probes; piercing so as to try. Hence **ˈprobingly** *adv.*, **ˈprobingness**.

1795 Southey *Joan of Arc* iv. 265 Conscious of guilt The Monarch sate, nor could endure to face His bosom-probing frown. **1800** W. Taylor in *Monthly Mag.* X. 320 There is often a tenderness yet a probingness in the pathos. **1868** Browning *Ring & Bk.* vi. 1288 She feels The probing spear o' the huntsman. **1876** Geo. Eliot *Dan. Der.* xl, He could have no conception what that demand was to the hearer—how probingly it touched the hidden sensibility. **1909** *Daily Chron.* 10 Aug. 7/2 He answered probing, keenly-put questions with dogged determination not to betray himself. **1962** F. I. Ordway et al. *Basic Astronautics* v. 187 Contact devices..either require direct contact with the surface in making the measurements or are located in a probing craft on, or in the atmosphere of, the world under examination. **1962** *Daily Tel.* 11 June 12/5 The probing talks between Russia and the United States on Berlin. **1972** *Jrnl. Social Psychol.* LXXXVI. 158 His reasoning is assessed by a series of predetermined probing questions that are administered with each situation.

probiotic: see PRO-² I.

probit ('prəʊbɪt). *Statistics.* [f. PROB(ABILITY + UN)IT.] The unit which forms the scale into which percentages may be transformed so that data evenly distributed between 0 and 100 per cent become normally distributed with a standard deviation of one probit.

1934 C. I. BLISS in *Science* 12 Jan. 38/1 These arbitrary probability units have been called 'probits'. **1947** D. J. FINNEY *Probit Analysis* iii. 20 The probit of the proportion *P* is defined as the abscissa which corresponds to a probability *P* in a normal distribution with mean 5 and variance 1. **1967** J. M. RENDEL *Canalisation & Gene Control* ii. 27 This distance from the mean measured in standard deviations is called a 'probit'.

b. *attrib.*, as ***probit line, unit***; **probit analysis**, the technique of using probits in statistical analysis.

1947 D. J. FINNEY *Probit Analysis* i. 6 The statistical treatment of quantal assay data has been much aided by the development of probit analysis. **1956** *Nature* 25 Feb. 356/2 In general, high resistance is associated with flat probit/regression lines. The probit lines for resistant strains are nearly always flatter than for normal strains. **1958** *Immunology* I. 225 On transforming the per cent haemolysis into probit units and plotting these results against the reciprocal of the corresponding serum dilution, a linear relationship was obtained. **1968** *Brit. Med. Bull.* XXIV. 248/1 An analysis of variance is given, from which it can be seen, for instance, whether a fit by a set of parallel probit lines is justified. **1975** *Jrnl. R. Statistical Soc.* C. XXIV. 259 Probit analysis of dose-response curves and surfaces.

probity ('prɒbɪtɪ). [ad. L. *probitās, -ātem* goodness, honesty, modesty, f. *prob-us* good, honest: see -ITY. So. F. *probité* (1570 in Hatz.-Darm.).] Moral excellence, integrity, rectitude, uprightness; conscientiousness, honesty, sincerity.

1514 BARCLAY *Cyt. & Uplondyshm.* (Percy Soc.) 23 What is..more repugnynge to faythe & probyte? **1570** LEVINS *Manip.* 110/20 Probitie, *probitas, atis.* **1647** CLARENDON *Hist. Reb.* II. §129 Of much reputation for probity and integrity of life. **1752** HUME *Ess. & Treat.* (1777) I. 548 Probity and superstition, or even probity and fanaticism are not..incompatible. **1856** EMERSON *Eng. Traits, Wealth* Wks. (Bohn) II. 75 'Tis not, I suppose, want of probity, so much as the tyranny of trade, which necessitates a perpetual competition of underselling. **1877** A. B. EDWARDS *Up Nile* xxi. 603 The Governor,..a man of strict probity.

problem ('prɒbləm). Forms: 4–7 **probleme**, 5– **problem**. [ME. *probleme*, a. F. *problème* (14th c. in Hatz.-Darm.), ad. L. *problēma*, a. Gr. πρόβλημα, -ματ-, lit. a thing thrown or put forward; hence, a question propounded for solution, a set task, a problem, f. προβάλλειν to throw out, to put forth, f. πρό, PRO-² + βάλλειν to throw.]

†**1.** A difficult or puzzling question proposed for solution; a riddle; an enigmatic statement. *Obs.*

1382 WYCLIF *Judg.* xiv. 15 Faage to thi man [1388 glose thin hosebonde], and meue hym, that he shewe to thee what bitokeneth the probleme. *c* **1386** CHAUCER *Sompn. T.* 511 How hadde the cherl this ymaginacioun To shewe swich a probleme to the frere. *c* **1430** LYDG. *Min. Poems* (Percy Soc.) 179 Problemys of olde likenese and figures, Whiche proved been fructuous of sentence. *c* **1440** *Promp. Parv.* 414/2 Probleme, or rydel, *problema, enigma.* *a* **1548** HALL *Chron., Edw. IV* 199 b, The erle of Warwicke..thought firste to proue hym a farr of, as it wer in a probleme, and after to open to him..the secret imaginations of his stomake. *a* **1562** P. MARTYR *Comm. Judges* xiv. (1564) 218 b, Graue men wer wont to put forth ridles or problemes, omitting dangerous talke. **1602** WARNER *Alb. Eng.* XIII. lxxvii. (1612) 319 Howsoere those Oracles of men were vnderstood, Double construction euer makes their Prothean Problemes good.

2. a. A question proposed for academic discussion or scholastic disputation. *Obs.* exc. *Hist.*

a **1529** SKELTON *Sp. Parrot* 167 *In Academia* Parrot dare no probleme kepe; For *Græce fari* so occupyeth the chayre, That *Latinum fari* may fall to rest and slepe. **1573** G. HARVEY *Letter-bk.* (Camden) 11 Semli for masters problems to dispute uppon. *c* **1590** MARLOWE *Faust.* i. 113, I, that have with concise syllogisms Gravell'd the pastors of the German church, And made the flowering pride of Wittenberg Swarm to my problems. **1603** HOLLAND *Plutarch* Explan. Words, *Problemes*, Questions propounded for to be discussed. **1624** BP. MOUNTAGU *Immed. Addr.* 206 It is..not of force to conclude a Diuinity probleme. **1646** SIR T. BROWNE *Pseud. Ep.* 21 Hereof there want not many examples in Aristotle, through all his booke of animals; we shall instance onely in three of his Problemes. **1851** *College Life t. Jas. I* 65 He attended the common-place, and the problem, which were Latin dissertations read in the chapel by the graduates.

b. *Logic.* The question (expressed, or, more usually, only implied) involved in a syllogism, and of which the conclusion is the solution or answer. (In quot. 1656 restricted to one form of this.)

1656 STANLEY *Hist. Philos.* VI. vi. (1701) 247/1 All Disputation is of things controverted, either by Problem or Proposition. A Problem questions both parts, as *a living Creature, is it the Genus of Man or not?* A Proposition questions but one part, as, *is not living Creature the genus of Man?* **1727–41** CHAMBERS *Cycl.* s.v., A logical or dialectical problem, say the schoolmen, consists of two parts; a subject, or subject matter, about which the doubt is raised; and a predicate or attribute, which is the thing doubted whether it be true of the subject or not. **1837–8** HAMILTON *Logic* xv. (1860) I. 280 (transl. Esser) There are to every syllogism three..requisites..1°, A doubt,—which of two contradictory predicates must be affirmed of a certain subject,—the problem or question, (*problema, quæsitum*); 2°, The application of a decisive general rule to the doubt; and, 3°, The general rule itself. *Ibid.* 282 The Conclusion is the Problem, (*problema*), Question, (*quæstio, quæsitum*), which was originally asked, stated now as a decision. The Problem is usually omitted in the expression of a syllogism; but is one of its essential parts.

3. a. A doubtful or difficult question; a matter of inquiry, discussion, or thought; a question that exercises the mind.

1594 CAREW *Huarte's Exam. Wits* (1616) 126 It is a probleme often demaunded,..For what cause a Diuine being a great man in the Schooles,..and in writing and lecturing of rare learning; yet getting vp into the Pulpit, cannot skill of preaching. **1621** BURTON *Anat. Mel.* I. iii. III. (1651) 207 Why melancholy men are witty..is a problem much controverted. **1795** BURKE *Th. Scarcity* Wks. VII. 416 It is one of the finest problems in legislation,..'What the state ought to take upon itself to direct..and what it ought to leave, with as little interference as possible, to individual discretion.' **1841–4** EMERSON *Ess., Friendship* Wks. (Bohn) I. 85 Not one step has man taken toward the solution of the problem of his destiny. **1854** MILMAN *Lat. Chr.* (1864) II. 173 Mohammed remains..an historic problem: his character, his motives, his designs, are all equally obscure. **1874** GREEN *Short Hist.* vii. §5. 384 Elizabeth..had hardly mounted the throne..when she faced the problem of social discontent.

†**b.** Problematic quality; difficulty of solution. *Obs. rare*⁻¹.

1641 J. JACKSON *True Evang. T.* II. 142 Is it not enigmaticall and full of Probleme, to wash white in bloud?

c. As the second element in various Combs. and collocations describing: (*a*) a supposedly insoluble quandary affecting a specified group of people or a nation; (*b*) a real or imagined chronic personal difficulty, as ***credibility, drink, health, weight problem***.

1950 M. HAY *Foot of Pride* vi. 161 The ship struck a mine ..and all on board, save one, were drowned. A senior official of the British Immigration Office..impulsively expressed his relief that this particular Jewish problem had been solved. **1957** [see JEWISH *a.* 1]. **1965** L. HUGHES in *Negro Digest* Sept. 57/1, I know I am The Negro Problem. **1969** 'J. MORRIS' *Fever Grass* iv. 44 She had the body of a ballet dancer with a weight problem. **1970** D. BAGLEY *Running Blind* iv. 83 He had a drinking problem at one time and decided to cut it out. **1971** 'A. GARVE' *Late Bill Smith* i. 15 'Sugar?' 'No, thanks. I've a waistline problem.' **1974** E. AMBLER *Dr. Frigo* I. 41 If Villegas had a health problem which could be helped by a change of climate [etc.]. **1977** *Grimsby Even. Tel.* 24 May 7/1 [He] told the court he had a drink problem and asked to be given a chance. **1978** S. BRILL *Teamsters* ii. 48 As a convicted bank robber, the inmate has a credibility problem.

d. In various colloq. phrases, as ***no problem***, simple, easy, 'the question does not arise'; ***that's your*** (***his***, etc.) ***problem***, used to disclaim responsibility or connection.

1963 *Amer. Speech* XXXVIII. 271 *No sweat* means 'no problem'. **1967** M. KENYON *Whole Hog* xxii. 217 'Don't you think he just might bring out the acid and the humane killer again? For me?' 'That's your problem.' **1973** M. AMIS *Rachel Papers* 117 Finally, every time I emptied my glass, he took it, put more whisky in it, and gave it back to me, saying 'No problem' again through his nose. **1976** L. SANDERS *Hamlet Warning* (1977) xxiii. 207 'Shouldn't we tell the hotel people what to do with the debris?'..'That's their problem.' **1977** C. FORBES *Avalanche Express* xi. 116 'If I catch you fooling around I'll break your arm.' 'No problem,' John assured him easily.

4. *Geom.* A proposition in which something is required to be done: opposed to *theorem*.

1570 BILLINGSLEY *Euclid* I. Introd. 8 A Probleme, is a proposition which requireth some action or doing. **1658** SIR T. BROWNE *Gard. Cyrus* iii. 53 Which..is become a point of art, and makes two Problemes in Euclide. **1704** J. HARRIS *Lex. Techn.* I, *Problem*, is a Proposition which relates to Practice; or which proposes something to be done; As to make a Circle passe through three given Points not lying in a Right Line. **1885** LEUDESDORF *Cremona's Proj. Geom.* 135 The solution of the problem, To construct by means of its tangents the parabola which is determined by four given tangents.

5. *Physics* and *Math.* A question or inquiry which starting from some given conditions investigates some fact, result, or law.

Many problems in Physics and Mathematics are named after the persons who propounded or solved them: e.g. ***Apollonius's, Kepler's, Pappus's, Viviani's problem***; others by a specification, as ***the problem of duplication of the cube, of quadrature of the circle, of inscription of the heptagon*** (in a circle), ***of three bodies*** (quot. 1812–16), etc.

1570 BILLINGSLEY *Euclid* XI. xxxvi. 353 Consider how near this creepeth to the famous Probleme of doubling the Cube. *a* **1721** KEILL tr. *Maupertuis' Diss.* (1734) 41 It is seen that the solution of these Problems must give the true Figures the cœlestial Bodies may be of, by fixing the Law according to which Gravity increases and decreases proportionably to the distance from the Center. **1798** HUTTON *Course Math.* (1810) I. 2 *A Problem* is a proposition or a question requiring something to be done; either to investigate some truth or property, or to perform some operation. As, to find out the quantity or sum of all the three angles of any triangle... *A Limited Problem* is that which has but one answer or solution. *An Unlimited Problem* is that which has innumerable answers. And a *Determinate Problem* is that which has a certain number of answers. **1812–16** PLAYFAIR *Nat. Phil.* (1819) I. 279 The great problem in gunnery, viz. having given the weight, the magnitude, the direction, and the velocity of a projectile, to determine its path through the air..is very difficult. *Ibid.* II. 244 If there are three bodies, the action of any one on the other two, changes the nature of their orbits, so that the determination of their motions becomes a problem of great difficulty, distinguished by the name of the Problem of the three bodies. **1885** WATSON & BURBURY *Math. Th. Electr. & Magn.* I. 91 The actual solution of this problem consists in the determination of a function *V*, the potential of the system, to satisfy the [following] conditions (1) *V* is constant over *C*; [etc.].

6. *Chess.* An arrangement of pieces upon the chessboard for play in accordance with the rules of the game or other prescribed conditions, in which the player is challenged to discover the method of accomplishing a specified result. Formerly called 'jeopardy', 'situation', 'position'. See quots. 1890, 1894.

1817 MONTIGNY *Stratagems of Chess* iv, These situations are in reality so many problems, the solution of which is required to be found. **1827** W. LEWIS (*title*) Chess Problems. Being a selection of original positions. **1890** RAYNER *Chess Problems* 5 A chess problem is an idea, or combination of ideas, expressed upon the board in accordance with a number of generally accepted principles of construction. **1894** R. F. GREEN *Chess* 21 Problems have come to be a study almost entirely distinct from that of the game proper... Their composition is regulated by elaborate rules.

7. *attrib.* and *Comb.*, as ***problem analysis, -game, -monger, paper, -programmer, -situation, skin, -solution, spot, -tackler***; ***problem-free, -ridden*** adjs.; ***problem-wise*** adv.; (*b*) 'in which a problem is treated or discussed', as ***problem book, column, drama, letter, novel, page, picture, play, poem, story***; (*c*) in sense 6, as ***problem-composer, composition, editor, tourney***; (*d*) 'in which problems of a personal or social character are manifested', as ***problem case*** (CASE *sb.*¹ 8), ***child, family, parent***; **problem-oriented** *a. Computers*, (of a computer language) devised in the light of the requirements of a certain class of problem; **problem-solver**, one who finds solutions to difficult or perplexing questions or situations; hence **problem-solving** *sb.*, the action of finding solutions to such problems; also as *adj.*, applied to behaviour, mental processes, equipment, etc., involved in or related to this activity; **problem tape** *Computers*, a magnetic tape containing the numerical information for a problem.

1969 J. ARGENTI *Managem. Techniques* 200 (*heading*) Problem analysis. **1931** F. M. FORD *Let.* 14 Mar. (1965) 200 It might have an enormous sale as a problem book. **1937** 'L. Q. ROSS' *Educ. Hyman Kaplan* 2 Here was a student who might, unchecked, develop into a 'problem case'. **1949** KOESTLER *Promise & Fulfilment* III. iv. 328 A large number of the immigrants of recent years are psychological problem cases. **1920** J. TAFT in *Proc. Nat. Conf. Social Work* 63 The placing and replacing of a problematic child..is also costly. .. The problem child is such a costly, nagging, persistent proposition that.. we are forced to bring intelligence to bear upon his case. **1944** H. G. WELLS *'42 to '44* 83 What can one forecast from America, the great problem-child of humanity? **1964** M. ARGYLE *Psychol. & Social Probl.* ix. 123 Another group, which includes problem children and psychopathic delinquents, have had discipline that was too strict and harsh. **1977** D. BEATY *Excellency* iv. 50 We're the bankrupt problem child of the E.E.C. **1974** M. CECIL *Heroines in Love* ix. 213 The problem columns of all the new magazines. **1890** RAYNER *Chess Problems* 6 The history of problem composition. **1895** A. W. PINERO in *Daily News* 27 Nov. 3/4 The problem drama is, after all, earnest drama. **1898** *Westm. Gaz.* 6 June 9/3 In 1887 he became problem editor of the *British Chess Magazine*, and that occupied, with his work as judge in problem tourneys, most of his time of late. **1937** W. DE B. HUBERT in C. P. Blacker *Social Problem Group?* vi. 122 It is not at present known with certainty what proportion of families showing *both* mental defect and social problems..contribute to the total number of problem families. **1958** *Sunday Times* 26 Jan. 18/6 The number of hospital admissions is six times greater in the case of children from problem families. **1977** P. JOHNSON *Enemies of Society* xiv. 191 It means more 'problem families' and so more crime. **1964** P. WORSLEY in I. L. Horowitz *New Sociol.* 385 There is no 'problem-free' solution. **1921** H. E. PALMER *Princ. Language-Study* xiii. 145 Many types of puzzles and problem-games are practically identical with mathematical problems. **1970** O. NORTON *Dead on Prediction* i. 7 Whenever a man picks up a woman's magazine he *always* turns to the problem letters. **1900** *Daily News* 17 Sept. 6/1 The healthy, virile English intellect..is naturally suspicious of morbid problem-mongers. **1961** *Computer Jrnl.* IV. 217/1 In most if not all of the current computer program languages—called 'problem-oriented languages'—the programmer must be concerned in some degree with how his program will be handled either on a specific computer or on a class of computers with specific characteristics. **1967, 1970** [see *machine-oriented* adj. s.v. MACHINE *sb.* 10]. **1973** C. W. GEAR *Introd. Computer Sci.* viii. 319 These statements are part of what we call a Problem Oriented Language because they provide a language in which the problem can be described, but in which the method of solution is not described. **1974** M. CECIL *Heroines in Love* viii. 192 The problem page ('Why when I have this beautiful home..do I feel the need for something more?'). **1919** *Granta* 1 May 4/2 The solutions of the problem paper in the Mathematical Tripos. **1961** *Economist* 2 Dec. 909/3 Short 'problem papers' on points of specific difficulty may be either inspired by the staff or requested by a government office or an outside group. **1932** A. S. NEILL (*title*) The problem parent. *Ibid.* i. 9 There is never a problem child; there is only a problem parent. **1956** A. G. MCRAE *Hill called Grazing* x. 104 Problem children, if you like, though I prefer to think of them as the offspring of Problem Parents. **1962** *Listener* 7 June 976/2 The issue of the problem-parent and the uncomprehending home. **1910** *Punch* 30 Mar. 219 (*caption*) The problem picture. **1979** G. MacDonald *Camera* xiii. 180/2 As the [nineteenth] century advanced social realism in Britain did not mature... Instead middle-class dilemmas were explored in 'problem pictures' with titles like 'The Confession',..'The Prodigal Daughter', etc. **1894** *Westm. Gaz.* 16 July 1/2 Who invented the term 'problem play'?.. The phrase is new,..the thing itself dates from twenty years, to go no further back. **1904** *Westm. Gaz.* 13 July 2/1 A problem play,..a piece supposed to prove some particular proposition. **1941** G. Heyer *Envious Casca* iv. 53 A problem-play, is it? **1957** V. Brittain *Testament of Experience* (1979) iii. 96 My chief passion was for work..and my fourth for intellectual drama and 'problem' plays. **1970** R. E. C. Houghton *Shakespeare's Measure for Measure* 5 The very term 'problem plays' is loose and ambiguous—were they problems to their author, or are they only problems to the modern critic?.. The most intelligible use of the term would be for a play primarily concerned to present a moral problem. **1897** *Daily News* 9 Dec. 8/2 He has..given a fuller expression of himself in powerful 'problem' poems. **1970** O. Dopping *Computers & Data Processing* xix. 305 Those who design programming systems..are sometimes called system programmers. In contrast, the user's normal programmers are sometimes called problem programmers or application programmers. **1924** R. Graves *Mock Beggar Hall* 59 A disturbing problem-ridden affair demanding the comments of a moralist. **1950** *Mind* LIX. 385 The problem-situation involving rational argument and discussion. **1978** J. Dunn in Hookway & Pettit *Action & Interpretation* 169 There is no doubt much redundancy and not a little error of one kind and another in agents' characterisations of their problem situations. **1970** *Cape Times* 28 Oct. 3/2 (Advt.), A daily cleanser for problem skins. **1956** J. Klein *Study of Groups* 192 (*heading*) Cooperative versus solitary problem-solution. **1899** J. Milne *Romance of Pro-Consul* xvi. 173 He [*sc.* Sir George Grey] was the problem-solver called in late. **1929** R. Frost *Let.* 6 Jan. (1964) 194, I don't believe in myself as a problem-solver. **1974** *Times* 31 Aug. 4/6 Practical problem-solvers can contribute much to education. **1979** *Dædalus* Summer 148 Pragmatism..is a fairy tale of energies magically released..into what Dewey called the 'situation', jointly apprehended by the problem-solvers involved. **1931** *Psychol. Rev.* XXXVIII. 337 Problem-solving by insight is regarded..as qualitatively different from problem-solving on the basis of trial and error. **1964** *Language* XL. 237 Most problem-solving situations involve concept evocation rather than the formation of new concepts. **1966** A. Battersby *Math. in Managem.* i. 15 A computer is said to have applied a problem-solving programme to the proposition that the base angles of an isosceles triangle are equal. **1978** *Amer. Poetry Rev.* July/Aug. 38/4 Every once in a while the problem-solving yields to an almost basking, sunny Calvinism. **1979** *Yale* Apr. 4/2 Man is a problem-solving animal. **1908** *Daily Chron.* 15 Jan. 3/2 The problem spot in Africa now is the Congo. **1963** *Times* 29 Jan. 9/4 Contributing to a Forum, colliding politely at a Meeting Point, joining in the domestic Parliament of a Woman's Hour, onward the problem-tacklers go. **1948** *Math. Tables & Other Aids to Computation* III. 9 It was intended that the routine tapes should contain all the orders, the table tapes should contain numerical information of a general nature, comparable to function tables used in manual computing, and the problem tape should contain numerical information specific to the problem being solved. **1956** G. A. Montgomerie *Digital Calculating Machines* x. 213 The input tapes are of three kinds. First the problem tape containing the numerical information for a set of data and also, usually, some instructions. **1901** S. S. Blackburne (*title*) Problem Terms and Characteristics. *a* **1859** De Quincey *Posth. Wks.* (1891) I. 37 An idea sketched problem-wise.

Hence † '**probleming**, academical or scholastic discussion: see 2; '**problemize** *v. intr.* to discuss problems, theorize, speculate.

1657 J. Watts *Vind. Ch. Eng.* 96, I fell to Common placing and probleming (as it is called in the Colledge). **1884** Clark Russell *Jack's Courtship* xxxii, To drop all this problemizing for the plain truth. **1890** —— *Ocean Trag.* II. xvii. 88 It was a thing to set me problemising.

† **pro'blematary.** *Obs. rare*$^{-1}$. [f. Gr. πρόβλημα, -ατ-, L. *problēma*, problem + -ary[1].] = problematist.

1581 Mulcaster *Positions* xxxv. (1887) 129 All naturall problemataries, dipnosophistes, symposiakes,..and such as deale with any particular occurence of exercise.

problematic (prɒblɪ'mætɪk), *a.* and *sb.* Also 7 -ique. [a. F. *problématique* (15th c. in Hatz.-Darm.), ad. late L. *problēmatic-us*, a. Gr. προβληματικ-ός, f. πρόβλημα: see problem and -atic.]

A. *adj.* **1.** Of the nature of a problem; constituting or presenting a problem; difficult of solution or decision; doubtful, uncertain, questionable.

1609 *Ev. Woman in Hum.* ii. i. in Bullen *O. Pl.* IV, All which to me are problematique mines, Obscurde inigmaes. **1768** H. Walpole *Hist. Doubts* 73 Were that imputation true, which is very problematic. **1807** Coleridge in *Lit. Rem.* (1836) I. 263 The very existence of any such individual [Homer].., is more than problematic. **1875** H. C. Wood *Therap.* (1879) 522 The value of true expectorants in pneumonia..is exceedingly problematic.

2. *Logic.* Enunciating or supporting what is possible but not necessarily true.

1610 Healey *St. Aug. Citie of God* 260 A problematique form of argument. **1677** [see probationatory]. **1837–8** Sir W. Hamilton *Logic* xiv. (1866) I. 260 A proposition is called..Problematic, when it enounces what is known as possible. **1863** E. V. Neale *Anal. Th. & Nat.* 242 The judgment 'If this house has stone floors it will be fire proof' is as much a problematic judgment as 'the house considered from this point of view is good'. **1884** tr. *Lotze's Logic* i. ii. 51 The ambiguity of the ordinary theory of modality is still more striking in the case of problematic judgments. *Ibid.*, What it [a proposition] states is not a real occurrence, but the possibility of an unreal or only conceived one, and this is enough according to traditional usage to give it the name of problematic.

3. *Chess.* Of or relating to problems.

1890 Rayner *Chess Problems* 5 Aspirants to problematic fame. **1905** A. F. Mackenzie *Chess Lyrics* lii, Three or four-move themes..well worthy of illustration and preservation in problematic form.

B. *sb. Sociol.* Something that constitutes a problem, or an area of difficulty in a particular field of study.

1957 R. K. Merton *Social Theory* (rev. ed.) ii. 127 Working out its problematics, i.e., the principal problems (conceptual, substantive and procedural). **1969** R. Blackburn in Cockburn & Blackburn *Student Power* 194 The dialectical approach to the same problematic adopted by such writers as Isaac Deutscher and Herbert Marcuse enabled them to obtain a more lasting insight into the dynamic of Soviet society. **1971** *Catholic Q.* XXXIII. 439 Essays..sharing the common problematic of attempting to situate the language of faith within language as a whole along the lines indicated by modern linguistic analysis. **1977** R. H. Brown in Douglas & Johnson *Existential Sociol.* ii. 77 A humanistic sociology investigates the problematics of feeling and meaning.

problematical (prɒblɪ'mætɪkəl), *a.* [f. as problematic *a.* + -al[1].]

† **1.** Of the nature of a problem (problem 4). *Obs.*

1570 Billingsley *Euclid* xi. xxxiii. 347 Methods, and engines.. whereby to execute thys Problematicall Lemma. **1696** Phillips (ed. 5), *Problematical*, belonging to a Problem, which is opposed to a Theoreme.

2. Of which the solution, realization, or truth is uncertain; disputable; doubtful; = problematic 1.

1611 Cotgr., *Problematique*, Problematicall, belonging to a Probleme. **1621** Bp. Mountagu *Diatribæ* 293 Those men who propound..their priuate, probable and problematical opinions,..of the Number of the Beast. **1624** Donne *Devot.* 297 His happinesse is but disputable and problematicall. **1628** —— *Serm.* vi. (1640) 61 Problematical points, of which, either side may be true,..should not extinguish particular charity towards one another. **1793** Smeaton *Edystone L.* §253 It appeared to me very problematical whether we might be able..to get another course finished this Season. **1815** W. H. Ireland *Scribbleomania* 69 *note*, Which is..to my mind a very problematical assertion. **1891** *Law Times* XCI. 2/1 No one can help sympathising with the effort.., though its success may be problematical.

b. Involving or giving rise to problems or questions; of which the nature is unsettled.

1770 C. Jenner *Placid Man* I. iii. viii. 206 His lordship's conduct had been a little problematical. **1799** *Monthly Rev.* XXX. 572 We recommend them to the candid attention of future writers on this curious and very problematical branch of natural philosophy. **1830** Lyell *Princ. Geol.* I. 346 Aware of the many problematical appearances which igneous rocks of the most modern origin assume, especially after decomposition. **1875** Whitney *Life Lang.* x. 186 A dialect of peculiar and problematical character.

3. = problematic *a.* 2. *problematical question*, a question put forth merely for discussion, but not of any practical bearing; an academic question.

1588 [implied in problematically]. **1621** Bp. Mountagu *Diatribæ* 140 To follow coniecturall probabilities, or to proue by arguments problematicall, did not stand with the nature or notion of a professed History. **1651** Biggs *New Disp.* §60 Subtile problematicall disputing upon every proposition. **1660** Blount *Boscobel* 36 His Majesty..was pleased merrily to propose it, as a Problematical Question, Whether Himself or the Col. were the Master-cook at Boscobel and the supremacy was of right adjudg'd to His Majesty. **1662** J. Davies tr. *Olearius' Voy. Ambass.* 124 Lutherane Doctours in Sueden and Livonia, who have made it a problematical question, whether the Muscovites were Christians or not? **1842** Abp. Thomson *Laws Th.* §118 (1860) 242 The problematical judgment is neither subjectively nor objectively true: that is, it is neither held with entire certainty by the thinking subject, nor can we show that it truly represents the object about which we judge.

4. *Chess.* = problematic *a.* 3.

1895 B. G. Laws in *Brit. Chess Mag.* 61 On a superficial grasp of the problematical positions.

proble'matically, *adv.* [f. prec. + -ly[2].] In a problematical manner; in the form of, or as, a problem; as an open question; doubtfully.

1588 J. Harvey *Disc. Probl.* 7 Neither dare I peremptorily, or affirmatiuely auow euery part of the premisses, but onely assay problematically, and as our schoolemen tearme it, disputatiuely, what may therin appeare most probable. **1609** Bp. Hall *No Peace w. Rome* iii. Wks. (1624) 650 If they had onely doubtfully and problematically commended their Purgatory to the Church, we might easily haue fauoured them with a conniuence. **1751** *Affecting Narr. of Wager* 5, I have expressed myself problematically, leaving the Determination of the Point to others. **1876** Mrs. Whitney *Sights & Ins.* vii. 90 'If a woman can be a Queen, why can't she be a President?' she said, problematically.

problematist ('prɒblɪmətɪst). [f. Gr. πρόβλημα, -ατ- problem + -ist.] One who occupies himself with problems; a problemist.

1668 Evelyn *Let. to Dr. Beale*, This learned Problematist was brother to him who, preaching at St. Maries, Oxford, tooke [as] his text..'Am I not thine Asse?' **1866** *Chess Player's Mag.* 133 Mr. Healey, long known to the chess world as one of the most skilful living problematists. **1890** Rayner *Chess Problems* 9 The multi-theme or multi-form problem..is the one now composed by the German and British schools of problematists.

† '**problematize**, *v. Obs. rare*$^{-1}$. [f. as prec. + -ize.] *intr.* To propound problems.

1630 B. Jonson *New Inn* ii. ii, Hear him problematize... Or syllogize, elenchize.

problemist ('prɒblɪmɪst). [f. problem + -ist.] One who devotes himself to, studies, or composes problems; *esp.* a composer of chess problems. Hence **proble'mistic** *a.*, of, belonging to, or that is a problemist.

a **1615** Donne *Ess.* (1651) 173 The same Problemist observes this wonder, that every man took a like proportion, and all were alike satisfied, though all could not be of a like appetite and digestion. **1875** J. H. Blackburne in *City Lond. Chess Mag.* II. Aug. 200 Some young and aspiring problemist persisting in showing you a position which he is pleased to call a problem. **1892** in *Brit. Chess Mag.* 457 Our distinguished problemistic confrere Mr. A. F. Mackenzie. **1901** *Daily Chron.* 13 July 9/5 A problemist who has done some good things in both stroke settings and analytical end-games.

'**problemless**, *a.* [f. problem + -less.] Devoid of or unaffected by problems; presenting no problems.

1924 *Public Opinion* 3 Oct. 320/1 Jowett went serenely on his way—apparently problemless. **1967** *Lingua* XVII. 55 As far as word classes are concerned, problemless or 'regular' hypotheses about little-known languages are always very suspicious! *a* **1970** E. Starkie in J. Richardson *Enid Starkie* (1973) iv. x. 80 The advantages... The problemless life. It was sacrificing nothing.

pro-Boche: see pro-[1] 5 a.

‖ **probole** ('prɒbəli:). [a. Gr. προβολή a projection, a bump (of the skull) (Hippocrates), etc., f. πρό, pro-[2] + βολή throwing; cf. προβάλλειν: see problem.] A bony projection or process.

1693 tr. *Blancard's Phys. Dict.* (ed. 2) s.v. *Apophysis*, *Probole*,..is a part of a Bone that is..Continuous with the Bone, and stretching it self beyond a plain Surface. **1874** Dawkins *Cave Hunt.* vi. 193 The occipital tuberosity, or probole, is the most prominent feature. **1880** —— *Early Man* ix. 316 The skulls are broad or round, the supraoccipital tuberosity or probole prominent.

probo'listic, *a. nonce-wd.* [Arbitrary f. Gr. προβολή (see prec.) or προβάλλειν to throw forward, send forth.] ? Of the nature of a forward throw.

1876 Blackmore *Cripps* xlix, He brought his fettered heels, like a double-headed hammer, as hard as his probolistic swing could whirl, against the very thickest-crowded cells of bygone domicile.

pro bono publico: see pro A. 2.

proboscic (prəʊ'bɒsɪk), *a. rare.* [irreg. f. probosc-is + -ic.] = proboscidean *a.* 2.

1835–6 *Todd's Cycl. Anat.* I. 36/2 *Pulmograda*..4. Proboscic.

proboscidal (prəʊ'bɒsɪdəl), *a. rare.* [f. L. *proboscid-em* proboscis + -al[1].] Of the nature or appearance of a proboscis. Also *fig.*

18.. Shuckard (Cent. Dict.), A proboscidal prolongation of the oral organs. **1884** *Edin. Rev.* July 170 Their exuberant hair..depends in proboscidal excrescences. **1922** Joyce *Ulysses* 456 He assumes the avine head, foxy moustache and proboscidal eloquence of Seymour Bushe.

proboscidate (prəʊ'bɒsɪdət), *a. Entom.* [f. as prec. + -ate[2]: cf. F. *proboscidé*.] Furnished with a proboscis; formed as a proboscis.

1826 Kirby & Sp. *Entomol.* IV. xlvii. 382 Diptera... Mouth proboscidate.

† '**proboscide.** *Her. Obs.* [a. F. *proboscide* (16th c. in Hatz.-Darm.), ad. L. *proboscid-em* proboscis.] An elephant's trunk used as a bearing.

1610 Guillim *Heraldry* iii. xiii. (1611) 125 Idomenes.. the son of Deucalion did beare Gules a Proboscide of an Elephant after this manner argent. **1688** R. Holme *Armoury* ii. 132/2 An Elephant his Nose or Snout, is called, a Proboside, or Trunk. **1722** Nisbet *Her.* I. 339 The Elephant's Probicide, as an armorial Figure, flexed and reflexed in Form of an S. is to be seen in the English Herauld-Books.

‖ **Proboscidea** (prɒbə'sɪdi:ə), *sb. pl. Zool.* [mod.L. neut. pl., f. *proboscid-em* proboscis: cf. *lact-eus*, *lign-eus*.] An order of mammalia containing the elephant and its extinct allies; characterized by having a long flexible proboscis and the incisors developed into long tusks.

1836 *Encycl. Brit.* (ed. 7) XIV. 146/2 Mammalia..Order VI. Pachydermata..Family 1st. Proboscidea. **1875** C. C. Blake *Zool.* 43 The order Proboscidea commenced at the beginning of the Miocene period.

proboscidean, -ian (prɒbə'sɪdi:ən, -ɪən), *a.* and *sb.* [f. prec. + -an, or f. L. *proboscid-em* + -ian: cf. F. *proboscidien*.]

A. *adj.* **1.** Of or belonging to the *Proboscidea*.

1839–47 *Todd's Cycl. Anat.* III. 875/2 The nasal prolongation of the Proboscidian Pachyderms is able to move in every needful direction. **1893** *Edin. Rev.* Oct. 354 Then was the culminating epoch of the proboscidean family.

2. Of animals of any kind: Having a proboscis.

1836–9 *Todd's Cycl. Anat.* II. 385/2 In most of the proboscidian species the tongue is short. **1868** OWEN *Vertebr. Anim.* III. 337 In the great proboscidian and hooded Seals. **1901** *Brit. Med. Jrnl.* No. 2101. 842 Marsh fevers are produced by the bites of proboscidian insects.

3. Of, pertaining to, or resembling a proboscis.

1875 C. C. BLAKE *Zool.* 58 The snout of the Hedgehog is elongated, and the nose proboscidean. **1898** F. LEES tr. *Margueritte's Disaster* 72 Du Breuil noticed the proboscidian gravity with which a Captain of Gendarmerie, ..with an enormous nose, carried a *petit-verre* to his mouth.

B. *sb.* A mammal of the order *Proboscidea.*

1835 KIRBY *Hab. & Inst. Anim.* II. xvii. 199 In the Proboscidians of Cuvier, including the elephant and Mastodon, or fossil elephant, there are five toes. **1842** C. H. SMITH *Mammalia* 269 In the next group we have the true Proboscideans. **1863** LYELL *Antiq. Man* xii. 226 Before the growth of the ancient forest, the *Mastodon arvernensis*, a large proboscidian, .. appears to have died out.

proboscideous (prɒbəˈsɪdiːəs), *a.* [f. L. *proboscid-em* PROBOSCIS + -EOUS.] Having a proboscis or something likened to one.

1866 *Treas. Bot.*, *Proboscideous*, having a hard terminal horn, as the fruit of *Martynia*.

probo'scidial, *a.* [irreg. for PROBOSCIDAL.] = PROBOSCIDEAN *a.*

1864 in WEBSTER.

proboscidiferous (prəʊbɒsɪˈdɪfərəs), *a.* [f. L. *proboscid-em* PROBOSCIS + -(I)FEROUS.] Bearing or having a proboscis; *spec.* in *Conch.*, belonging to a division of pectinibranchiate gastropods (*Proboscidifera*) characterized by a long retractile snout.

1828 STARK *Elem. Nat. Hist.* II. 10 The Proboscidiferous Mollusca are carnivorous, making use of the organ for perforating the shells of other animals. **1878** E. R. LANKESTER in *Encycl. Brit.* XVI. 652/1 The modification in the form of the snout upon which the mouth is placed, leading to the distinction of 'proboscidiferous' and 'rostriferous' Gastropods.

proboscidiform (prɒbɒˈsɪdɪfɔːm), *a.* [f. as prec. + -(I)FORM.] Having the form or shape of a proboscis; proboscis-like.

1837 *Penny Cycl.* IX. 452/1 Melanopsis. Animal furnished with a proboscidiform muzzle. **1877** HUXLEY *Anat. Inv. Anim.* iv. 178 With a second hollow muscular proboscidiform organ, which may be termed the frontal proboscis.

probosciformed (prəʊˈbɒsɪfɔːmd), *a.* [f. PROBOSCIS + *formed.*] Proboscis-shaped.

1851 DARWIN *Cirripedia* I. 176 The surface of the probosciformed mouth. **1859** —— *Orig. Spec.* xiii. (1860) 440 The larvæ in the first stage have .. a very simple single eye, and a probosciformed mouth.

proboscigerous (prɒbəˈsɪdʒərəs), *a. Zool.* [f. as prec. + L. *-ger* bearing + -OUS.] Bearing a proboscis.

1890 in *Cent. Dict.*

proboscis (prəʊˈbɒsɪs). *Pl.* **pro'boscides** (-ɪdiːz), **pro'boscises** (-ɪsɪz); *erron.* **probosces.** [a. L. *proboscis, -cidem* (Plin.), a. Gr. προβοσκίς, -κιδ- an elephant's trunk, lit. 'a means of providing food' (Liddell & Scott), f. πρό, PRO-[2] + βόσκειν to feed.]

1. An elephant's trunk; also applied to the long flexible snout of some other mammals, as the tapir and proboscis-monkey.

[**1576** EDEN tr. *Vertomannus' Voy.* IV. ix, The trunke or snoute of the elephant (which of the Latines is called Promuscis or Proboscis). **1601** HOLLAND *Pliny* I. 195.] **1609** BP. W. BARLOW *Answ. Nameless Cath.* 312 As the Elephant vseth her proboscis or trunke. *a* **1631** DONNE *Progr. Soul* 390 Like an unbent bowe carelesly His sinewy Proboscis did remisly lie. **1667** MILTON *P.L.* IV. 347 Th'unwieldy Elephant To make them mirth us'd all his might, and wreathd His Lithe Proboscis. **1694** MOTTEUX *Rabelais* V. xxx. (1737) 138 With their Snouts or *Proboscis's*.. they draw up Water. **1700** S. L. tr. *Fryke's Voy. E. Ind.* 328 At last he lifted up his Proboses, and made a horrid noise. **1803** NICOLLS in Gurw. *Wellington's Desp.* (1837) II. 586 *note*, To each pair of iron 12 pounders, an elephant is attached, which assists them in their draught.. they apply their proboscis.. to the muzzle. **1872** MIVART *Elem. Anat.* xi. (1873) 435 The upper lip may unite with the nose to form an elongated proboscis, as in the Elephant.

2. *humorous.* The human nose.

1630 B. JONSON *New Inn* II. ii, No flattery for't, No lickfoot, pain of losing your proboscis. **1705** *Dyet of Poland* I The World's Proboscis near the Globe's Extreme. **1833** M. SCOTT *Tom Cringle* i, A fair enough proboscis as noses go.

3. *Entom.* Applied to various elongated, often tubular and flexible, parts of the mouth of insects.

a. The beak or rostrum of the *Rhynchophora* or snout-beetles. b. The long coiled *haustellum, antlia*, or sucker of the *Lepidoptera.* c. The buccal apparatus of the *Hymenoptera.* d. The sucking mouth of a fly.

1645 EVELYN *Diary* 18 Jan., Three jettos of water gushing out of the mouthes or proboscis of bees (the armes of the late Pope). **1661** LOVELL *Hist. Anim. & Min.* Introd., Some have a proboscis like flies. **1664** [see PROBE *sb.* 2]. **1792** J. HUNTER in *Phil. Trans.* LXXXII. 173 The male of the humble bee, which collects its own food, has as long a proboscis, or tongue, as the female. **1828** [see PROMUSCIS 2]. **1847** CARPENTER *Zool.* §615 Amongst.. the Bugs.. the mouth is armed with a tubular and cylindrical proboscis, directed downwards and backwards. *Ibid.* §616 Amongst the Flies.. the proboscis.. represents the under lip, and often bears palpi at its base... Sometimes this proboscis acquires an enormous length; sometimes on the contrary it is hardly visible. **1863** BATES *Nat. Amazon* vii. (1864) 173 Their habit is to attach themselves to the skin by plunging their proboscides into it.

4. An extensible tubular structure of varying function in other invertebrates, *esp.* a sucking organ in various worms, and the tongue of some mollusks.

1796 BELL in Southey *Life* (1844) II. 27 These spawns.. dart about in all directions... Some of the largest have proboscises. **1830** R. KNOX *Cloquet's Anat.* 381 *Entozoa*.. the head furnished with fossulæ, suckers, and one or more naked or armed proboscides. **1872** NICHOLSON *Palæont.* 119 The aperture of the anus.. is usually placed excentrically in one of the spaces between the arms, and.. generally.. carried at the end of a longer or shorter tubular eminence or process.. called the 'proboscis'.

5. Short for *proboscis-monkey.*

1882 DE WINDT *Equator* 105 Excitement as to whether the 'moniet' was but a common proboscis or wa-wa.

6. *attrib.* and *Comb.*, as *proboscis-like* adj.; **proboscis-monkey**, a large semnopithecine ape, *Nasalis larvatus*: = KAHAU; **proboscis-rat** = ELEPHANT *shrew* (*Cent. Dict.* 1890).

1849 *Sk. Nat. Hist., Mammalia* III. 58 The Indian tapir .. has no mane, and the snout is longer and more *proboscis-like. **1793** PENNANT *Quadrupeds* (ed. 3) II. 322 *Proboscis Monkey.. the nose projecting very far beyond the mouth.. in the profile it exactly resembles a long proboscis. **1885** HORNADAY *2 Yrs. in Jungle* xxxiii. 395 The proboscis monkey.. is found only in Borneo.

Hence **proboscised** (prəʊˈbɒsɪst) *a.*, furnished with a proboscis.

1883 THOMPSON tr. *Müller's Fert. Flowers* 579 Long-proboscised varieties of insects.

proboscoid (prəʊˈbɒskɔɪd), *a.* [irreg. f. PROBOSC-IS + -OID.] = PROBOSCIDIFORM *a.*

1847–9 *Todd's Cycl. Anat.* IV. 407/1 By means of their proboscoid mouth.. they grasp.. the object on which they are placed.

†**pro'boss.** *Obs. humorous nonce-wd.* [= **proboscе*, shortened from PROBOSCIS.]

1659 T. PECKE *Parnassi Puerp.* 129 Dreaming thus, an Elephant to toss; He was strook Dead, by the flinty Proboss.

probou'leutic, *a. Gr. Hist.* [f. Gr. πρό, PRO-[2] + βουλευτικός belonging to the βουλή or council, deliberative: cf. προβουλεύειν to pass a preliminary decree.] That deliberates preliminarily; *spec.* applied to the Athenian senate, which discussed measures before they were submitted to the Assembly.

1847 GROTE *Greece* II. xi. III. 161 He [Solon] created the pro-bouleutic or preconsidering senate. **1879** W. F. ALLEN in *Penn. Monthly* Feb. 124 (Cent.) A probouleutic body, like that of Athens, which prepared business for the Assembly. **1904** A. LANG *Hist. Scot.* III. iii. 69 Nobles, barons, and burghs should all elect their own representatives on the 'probouleutic' board.

†**'probre.** *Obs. rare.* [ad. L. *probrum* reproach, disgrace.] A reproach, an insult.

c **1460** *Oseney Regr.* 205 Vppon summe despites or probris, harmys, violences, and oþer moony wronges.

pro-Britisher, -business: see PRO-[1] 5 b, a.

proby, probie (ˈprəʊbɪ). *colloq.* [f. PROB(ATIONER + -Y[6], -IE.] A probationer; *spec.* U.S., a fireman undergoing probation.

1899 L. BECKE *Old Convict Days* ii. 42 For a proby (probationer) you're a plucky one. I won't report you. **1946** *Richmond* (Va.) *News Leader* 25 Jan. 11/4 There are times when the 'probies' (students at the probationary firemen's school) must think [etc.]. **1969** *Publ. Amer. Dial. Soc.* LII. 30 *Proby*, a man on probation because he is new on the force [*sc.* the Denver Fire Department]... 'John is still a proby.'

†**proc, prock.** *Obs. U.S.* Abbreviation of *proclamation money*: see PROCLAMATION *sb.* 5.

1755 J. MURRAY *Lett.* (1901) 78 The Money I get since the Presidents Currency came out is all proc. **1768** *N. Carolina Col. Rec.* VII. 775 To the amount of Five Pounds Prock. **1776** *N. Jersey Arch.* Ser. II. I. 80 At 30s. proc. the season. *Ibid.* 94 Joseph Archer.. has this day obtained of me.. a Note of Hand for Twelve Pounds proc. money.

‖**procaccio** (proˈkattʃo). *Obs.* Also 8 -cia, **procace.** [It. *procaccio*, prop. purveying, provision, procuring, diligence: hence obs. F. *procace* 'the Post, or Carrier that goeth weekely betweene Rome and Naples' (Cotgr.).] A regular provision for the conveyance of passengers or goods in Italy; a transit agency.

1645 EVELYN *Diary* 29 Jan., The hast of our Procaccio did not suffer us to dwell so long on these objects,.. as we desired. *a* **1743** OZELL tr. *Brantome's Spanish Rhodomont.* (1744) 167, I was going, one Day, to Naples with the Procace. **1787** BECKFORD *Lett. Italy* (1805) I. xlii. 411 A procaccia sets out every day at twelve o'clock. **1824** W. IRVING *T. Trav.* III. i. (1848) 200 The procaccio and its convoy; a kind of caravan.. for the transportation of merchandize, with an escort of soldiery to protect it from the robbers.

procacious (prəʊˈkeɪʃəs), *a.* Now *rare.* [f. L. *procāx*, stem *-cāci-* (see next) + -OUS.] Forward, insolent, saucy, pert. Hence **pro'caciously** *adv.*

1660 BAXTER *Self-Denial* xliv. 237 The temptations of women, and procacious youth. **1685** —— *Paraphr. N.T.* 1 Pet. iii. 3 A vain, proud, procacious, tempting mind. **1772** NUGENT tr. *Hist. Fr. Gerund* I. 535 Denying procaciously what he wishes to confer. **1869** J. BROWN *Lett.* (1907) 197, I stuck in M. Arnold's brilliant and procacious lecture.

procacity (prəʊˈkæsɪtɪ). Now *rare.* [ad. F. *procacité* (15th c. in Godef.), ad. L. *procācitās, -ātem* impudence, f. *procāx, -ācem* forward, bold, petulent, insolent, f. *proc-āre, -ārī* to ask, demand.] Forwardness, petulance; sauciness, pertness.

1621 BP. MOUNTAGU *Diatribæ* 453 Let Scaliger pay for his malapert procacity against Paulus, concerning ignorance. **1621** BURTON *Anat. Mel.* III. ii. VI. i. (1676) 333/1 In vain are all your flatteries,.. Delights, deceits, procacities, Sighs, kisses, and conspiracies. *a* **1677** BARROW *Pope's Suprem.* I. xv. (1680) 76 Porphyrius with good colour of reason might have objected procacity to S. Paul in taxing his betters. **1859** J. BROWN *Horæ Subs.* Ser. II. *Myst.* (1861) 360 That mouth, ..arch and kind, with a beautiful procacity or petulance about it. **1865** J. H. STIRLING *Secret Hegel* I. 122 Precipitate procacity and pretentious levity.

†**'procacy, -ie.** *Obs. rare*[−1]. [ad. late L. *procācia* insolence.] = prec.

a **1619** FOTHERBY *Atheom.* I. xvi. §4 (1622) 169 Not libertie or audacitie, but petulancie and procacie.

procainamide (prəʊˈkeɪnəmaɪd). *Pharm.* Also **procaineamide.** [f. *procaine amide.*] An amide, $NH_2C_6H_4{\cdot}CONH{\cdot}CH_2CH_2N(C_2H_5)_2$, which is formally derived from procaine (an ester), and is used in cardiac therapy (esp. to control arrhythmia) in the form of a hydrochloride, a white hygroscopic solid.

1954 *Lancet* 8 May 957/1 It is now established that procainamide is superior to quinidine in the treatment of ventricular tachycardia. **1954** *Brit. Pharmaceut. Codex* 610 Procainamide Hydrochloride is *p*-amino-N-(2-diethylaminoethyl)-benzamide hydrochloride and may be prepared by treating the NN-diethylethylenediamine with *p*-nitrobenzoyl chloride, and reducing the nitro-compound obtained. **1971** L. SCHAMROTH *Disorders Cardiac Rhythm* lvii. 326/2 Follow-up therapy may be carried out with oral procaineamide: 250 to 500 mgm 4 to 6-hourly. **1979** *Sci. Amer.* Dec. 52/1 Procainamide, which is administered to counteract irregular rhythms of the heart, must be given to most patients every three hours in order to provide blood levels near the therapeutic range.

procaine (ˈprəʊkeɪn). *Pharm.* Also **procain.** [f. PRO-[1] + CO)CAINE.] The synthetic compound 2-diethylaminoethyl *p*-aminobenzoate, $NH_2C_6H_4{\cdot}COO{\cdot}CH_2CH_2N(C_2H_5)_2$, which is used as a local anæsthetic, usu. in the form of its hydrochloride, a white, crystalline solid. Cf. NOVOCAIN.

1918 *Jrnl. Amer. Med. Assoc.* 23 Feb. 537/2 Procaine is the official name of the product introduced as novocaine. **1919** *Ibid.* 6 Sept. 757/2 Procain is employed largely in infiltration anesthesia. **1940** H. A. MCGUIGAN *Appl. Pharmacol.* 536 The activity of procaine is increased by the addition of 0·25 per cent sodium bicarbonate or 0·50 per cent potassium sulfate to the solution injected. **1951** A. GROLLMAN *Pharmacol. & Therapeutics* xvii. 324 Procaine is relatively non-toxic, being destroyed rapidly by the liver. **1958** *Daily Mail* 24 July 5/7 He thought it contained procaine to help her fibrositis. **1962** H. HEATH in A. Pirie *Lens Metabolism Rel. Cataract* 364 The actions of some drugs, e.g. zoxazolamine, pentobarbital and procaine, are potentiated in the scorbutic state. **1976** H. FERGUSON *Confessions of Long Distance Acid Head* 7 Apart from cannabis, I have used barbiturates,.. morphine, cocaine, procaine, ritalin, even apomorphine once.

b. Special Combs.: **procaine amide** = PROCAINAMIDE; **procaine penicillin**, an in-soluble salt of procaine and benzylpenicillin, which is an antibiotic used in the form of a suspension in oil and which releases penicillin slowly after intramuscular injection.

1950 *Jrnl. Pharmacol. & Exper. Therapeutics* XCVIII. 21/2 (*heading*) The action of procaine amide.. on ventricular arrhythmias. **1963** V. SCHRIRE *Clinical Cardiol.* xix. 348 Procaine amide should be used in preference to intravenous quinidine. **1968** I. L. RUBIN et al. *Treatm. Heart Dis. in Adult* x. 240 Procaine amide is administered intravenously as the drug of choice in the treatment of ventricular tachycardia. **1947** *Proc. Staff Meetings Mayo Clinic* XXII. 567 The preparation is a procaine salt of penicillin G (duracillin) which was prepared in the research laboratories of Eli Lilly and Company. Procaine penicillin G is a crystalline, nonpyrogenic substance which is prepared by combining one molecule of procaine base.. with a molecule of penicillin. **1949** FLOREY & JENNINGS in H. W. Florey et al. *Antibiotics* II. xxxvii. 1220 The first accounts of trials with procaine penicillin in man all mentioned the freedom of patients from local or general toxic effects. **1961** *Times* 27 Mar. 5/4 The fungicidal activity of the antibiotic procain penicillin. **1967** *Martindale's Extra Pharmacopœia* (ed. 25) 1007/2 Procaine penicillin is administered by intramuscular injection to create a depot from which penicillin is slowly liberated.

procaineamide: see PROCAINAMIDE.

‖**procambium** (prəʊˈkæmbɪəm). *Bot.* [mod.L.: see PRO-[2] 1 and CAMBIUM.] The young tissue of a fibrovascular bundle, before its differentiation into permanent cells of wood, bast, etc. Also *attrib.* Hence **proˈcambial** *a.*, of or pertaining to procambium.

1875 BENNETT & DYER tr. *Sachs' Bot.* 93 This form of tissue of the young bundle, which has not yet undergone differentiation, may be termed *Procambium*. *Ibid.*, As soon as a procambium bundle has become transformed into a closed fibro-vascular bundle, all further growth ceases. **1876** J. H. BALFOUR in *Encycl. Brit.* IV. 105/2 A procambial bundle being first formed, which differentiates.. into xylem and phloëm layers.

procarbazine (prəʊˈkɑːbəziːn). *Pharm.* [f. PRO(PYL + CARB(AMIC *a.* + HYDR)AZINE, formative elements of the systematic name.] A hydrazine derivative whose hydrochloride is used in the treatment of some neoplastic diseases, esp. Hodgkin's disease; *N-p*-isopropylcarbamoylbenzyl-*N'*-methylhydrazine, $C_{12}H_{19}N_3O$.

1965 *Brit. Med. Jrnl.* 18 Dec. 1473/1 (*heading*) Natulan (procarbazine) combined with radiotherapy in management of inoperable malignant melanoma. **1974** R. M. KIRK et al. *Surgery* iv. 58 Hodgkin's disease (Lymphadenoma)... Generalized disease responds to chemotherapy, usually with a combination of vincristine, mustine, procarbazine and prednisone in pulsed doses. **1977** *Lancet* 14 May 1041/2 Of all cytotoxic drugs the teratogenicity of the alkylating agents is particularly well-documented; these, and procarbazine too, are best avoided at all stages of pregnancy if possible.

procarcinogen(ic): see PRO-[2] 1.

procarp (ˈprəʊkɑːp). *Bot.* [ad. mod.L. *procarpium*, f. Gr. πρό, PRO-[2] 1 + καρπός fruit, dim. κάρπιον.] The female organ of some algæ and fungi, which when fertilized develops into a sporocarp.

1887 tr. *De Bary's Fungi* 121 In the Florideae it is the procarpium (procarp), which consists of a single cell or a small cell-group. **1892** *Chambers' Encycl.* IX. 289/1 The female organ is a procarp, whose structure varies in complexity in the different orders of Rhodophyceæ.

procaryon, etc., varr. PROKARYON, etc.

procatalectic (prəʊkætəˈlɛktɪk), *a. Pros. rare.* [f. PRO-[2] + CATALECTIC.] Of a verse: Catalectic in its former colon.

1843 T. F. BARHAM tr. *Hephæstion* 195.

‖**procatalepsis** (prəʊkætəˈlɛpsɪs). *Rhet.* [med.L., a. Gr. προκατάληψις anticipation, n. of action f. προκαταλαμβάνειν to take up beforehand, anticipate.] A rhetorical figure by which an opponent's objections are anticipated and answered.

1586 A. DAY *Eng. Secretary* II. (1625) 96 *Procatalepsis* or *Præoccupatio*, when wee doe anticipate vnto our selues that we know will be obiected, as thus, what doe you obiect vnto me the times passed, those seasons and ours are vtterly vnlike? **1589** PUTTENHAM *Eng. Poesie* III. xix. (Arb.) 239 *margin*, Procatalepsis, or the presumptuous, otherwise the figure of Presupposall.

†**procaˈtarctic**, *a.* (*sb.*) *Obs.* [= F. *procatarctique* (16th c. in Littré), ad. mod.L. *procatarctic-us*, a. Gr. προκαταρκτικ-ός antecedent, f. προκατάρχειν to begin first.] *Med.* Applied to an external cause which is the immediate occasion of a disease. Also applied *gen.* to the immediate or exciting cause of any effect, as distinguished from its predisposing cause or ground. (Opposed to PROEGUMENAL.)

1603 HOLLAND *Plutarch* Explan. Words, *Procatarcticke causes of sicknesse*, be such as are evident and comming from without, which yeeld occasion of disease, but do not mainteine the same: as the heat of the Sunne, causing headach or the ague. **1627** W. SCLATER *Exp. 2 Thess.* (1629) 185, I can but wonder at Arminius and others, seeking in the vessels of Mercy, the Procatarcticke Cause of Election. **1666** G. HARVEY *Morb. Angl.* xii. 132 The procatarctick or external causes of Pulmonique Consumptions. **1717** J. KEILL *Anim. Oecon.* (1738) 234 No procatarctic Cause appears of so great a Perspiration in the Night. **1822–34** *Good's Study Med.* (ed. 4) I. 559 In early times the causes of diseases chiefly contemplated were proegumenal or predisponent and procatarctic or occasional. Thus an hereditary taint.. may be regarded as a proëgumenal cause of gout, and catching cold.. may form its procatarctic cause.

¶**b.** By some applied to the primary cause.

1658 PHILLIPS s.v., *Procatarctick cause*, that cause which foregoeth or beginneth another cause [1696 (ed. 5) adds—and cooperates with others which are subsequent]. **1681** tr. *Willis' Rem. Med. Wks.* Vocab., *Procatarctic*, remote, not next cause of a disease. **1689** AUBREY *Lives, Lucius Cary* (1898) I. 152 It so broke and weakned the king's army, that 'twas the procatarctique cause of his ruine. **1695** TRYON *Dreams & Vis.* App. 256 Pride may justly be said to be the chief Procatarctick, or remote original cause of Madness. **1714** MANDEVILLE *Fab. Bees* (1725) I. 311 Whoever would accuse Ignorance, Stupidity, and Dastardness, as the first, and what Physicians call the Procatarctic Cause, let him examine into the Lives.. and Actions of ordinary Rogues and our common Felons, and he will find the reverse to be true.

B. as *sb.* (ellipt. for *procatarctic cause*).

1694 WESTMACOTT *Script. Herb.* 212 It is a procatarctic of the scurvy.

†**procaˈtarctical**, *a. Obs.* [f. as prec. + -AL[1].] = prec.

1601 BP. W. BARLOW *Defence* 92 The procatarcticall, or first moouing cause. **1643** T. GOODWIN *Childe of Light* 168 God often useth even the guilt of that very sinne to terrifie thee;.. it is both the procatarcticall cause and the executioner of it. **1654** WARREN *Unbelievers* 46 His death was.. looked upon.. as the procatarctical, or outward moving cause of the transient act of God in justification. **1697** tr. *Burgersdicius his Logic* I. xvii. 63 Procatarctical, is that which Extrinsically excites the principal Cause to Action. The Proëgumenal, which inwardly disposes, or also excites the principal Cause to Action.

‖**procaˈtarxis**. *Obs.* [mod.L., a. Gr. προκάταρξις a first beginning: see PROCATARCTIC.] A 'procatarctic' or exciting cause, or its operation.

1693 tr. *Blancard's Phys. Dict.* (ed. 2), *Procatarctica*, the pre-existent Cause of a Disease, which co-operates with others that are subsequent; whether it be external or internal, as Anger, or Heat in the Air, which beget ill Juice in the Blood, and cause a Fever. *Procatarxis*, the same. **1699** 'MISAURUS' *Honour of Gout* 24 And remove the Procatarxis of the Gout. **1719–26** QUINCY *Lex. Physico-Med.*, *Procatarxis*.. is the pre-existent Cause of a Disease.

pro-cathedral (prəʊkəˈθiːdrəl), *a.* and *sb.* [f. PRO-[1] 4 + CATHEDRAL *sb.*] **A.** *adj.* Used as the substitute for a cathedral. **B.** *sb.* A church used instead of, or as a substitute for a cathedral church.

1868 A. K. H. BOYD *Less. Mid. Age* 134 The ancient parish church of the Holy Trinity was ranked as pro-cathedral when episcopacy was restored for a while under the Stuarts. **1874** *Catholic Calendar* [R.C.] 36 Pro-Cathedral of Westminster.—Our Lady of Victories,.. opened 2nd July, 1869. *Ibid.* 52 Diocese of Beverley,.. York.. Pro-Cathedral of S. Wilfred. **1884** *L'pool Mercury* 22 Oct. 5/1 The Bishop of Liverpool held his triennial visitation in the pro-Cathedral. **1905** *Westm. Gaz.* 2 Mar. 7/2 At a few minutes before twelve the Bishop of Birmingham knocked three times at the south-west door of the Pro-Cathedral, and on its being opened he was received by the Archdeacon of Birmingham and the rector.

†**proˈcation**. *Obs. rare*[−1]. [ad. late L. *procātiōn-em* suing, wooing, n. of action f. *procāre* to demand.] An asking in marriage, wooing, suit.

1650 BP. HALL *Cases Consc.*, *Add.* iii. (ed. 2) 416 She ought to have made him sensible of so odious a procation.

procatour, obs. form of PROCURATOR, PROCTOR[1].

proccy, obs. form of PROXY.

‖**procédé** (prɔsede), *sb.* [Fr.] Manner of proceeding; method, procedure, process.

1872 GEO. ELIOT *Let.* 14 Mar. (1956) V. 256, I altogether abominate that *procédé* of M. Forgues and others who undertake to trim and abridge. **1935** *Scrutiny* IV. III. 285 The characteristic *procédé* may be seen in this extract from the second section of his [*sc.* Santayana's] essay on Russell. **1962** *Listener* 15 Nov. 832/3 All the familiar *procédés* of opera have vanished, whether set numbers or Wagnerian leading-motives.

‖**procedendo** (prəʊsiːˈdɛndəʊ). *Law.* [L. *prōcēdendo* (*ad judicium*), 'of proceeding (to judgement)': see PROCEED *v.*] (In full (*de*) ***procedendo ad judicium***.) A writ which formerly issued out of the common law jurisdiction of the Court of Chancery, commanding a subordinate court to proceed to judgement, either when judgement had been wrongfully delayed, or when the action had been removed to a superior court by *certiorari* or other writ on insufficient grounds.

1593 PEELE *Chron. Edw. I*, Wks. (Rtldg.) 382/1 Here's a *certiorari* for your *procedendo*. [Attacks them with his staff.] **1630** J. TAYLOR (Water P.) *Trav.* Wks. III. 84/1 Quirks, Quiddits, Demurs, Habeas Corposes, Sursararaes, Procedendoes. **1641** *Termes de la Ley* 225 Then the plaintife shall have this writ of Procedendo, for to send againe the matter unto the first base court, & there to be determined. **1768** BLACKSTONE *Comm.* III. vii. 109 A writ of *procedendo ad judicium* issues out of the court of chancery, where judges of any subordinate court do delay the parties; for that they will not give judgment, either on the one side or the other, when they ought so to do.

procedural (prəʊˈsiːdjʊərəl), *a.* [PROCEDURE + -AL[1].] Of or pertaining to procedure. Hence **proˈcedurally** *adv.*

1889 F. W. MAITLAND in *Pol. Sci. Q.* IV. 506 Our collections include a few documents which bear no legislative authority, namely.. a few procedual [*sic*] formulas. **1908** R. POUND in *Illinois Law Rev.* Nov. 232 The necessity of patient cutting away by the courts of an *abatis* of procedural obstacles in order to attack the substantive points before them. **1919** H. A. L. FISHER *Stud. Hist. & Politics* 52 It includes a reform of the civil, penal, and procedural codes. **1938** *Mind* XLVII. 529 Prof. Schilpp is capable of lapsing into revolting phrases like 'procedurally formal'; but this gives no proper indication of his style, which is on the whole vigorous and beautifully clear. **1947** *Daily Tel.* 13 Dec. 1/1 Mr. Marshall, although sure that M. Molotov's words were 'not seriously designed for consumption here, but for another audience', said that such procedural methods 'do not inspire respect for the Soviet Government'. **1963** J. PRESCOTT *Case for Hearing* vi. 89 We'll make the girl a ward of court... Any quick and procedurally easy application to the magistrates' court for permission to marry would be out. **1968** *Brit. Med. Bull.* XXIV. 252/2 A computer can be used to take procedural decisions during the test itself. **1978** *Nature* 13 July 104/3 Now at least it seems as if the commission is leaning over backwards to be procedurally fair.

procedure (prəʊˈsiːdjʊə(r)). Also 7 procedour, -or, 8–9 proceedure. [a. F. *procédure* (1197 in Godef. *Compl.*), f. *procéder* to PROCEED: see -URE.]

1. a. The fact or manner of proceeding with any action, or in any circumstance or situation; a system of proceeding; proceeding, in reference to its mode or method; conduct, behaviour.

1611 COTGR., *Procedure*, a procedure; a course, or proceeding. **1660** SHARROCK *Vegetables* 21 The best husbandry.. has been in Staffordshire, where this procedure is general. **1671** R. MACWARD *True Nonconf.* 406 Their summare manner of procedor. **1774** M. MACKENZIE *Maritime Surv.* II. 65 Of the Procedure and Operations in surveying Sea-coasts, according to their various Circumstances. **1828** WHATELY *Rhet.* in *Encycl. Metrop.* I. 293/1 This is precisely the procedure which, in Elocution, we deprecate. **1850** GROTE *Greece* II. lxii. VIII. 3 Tasting the difference between Spartan and Athenian procedure.

b. With *a* and *pl.* A particular action or course of action, a proceeding; a particular mode of action.

a **1677** HALE *Prim. Orig. Man.* I. i. 28 Many times the distinction of these several procedures of the Soul do not always appear distinct. **1686** COTTON tr. *Montaigne* (1877) I. 25 This was, indeed, a procedure truly Roman. *a* **1770** JORTIN *Serm.* (1771) V. ii. 30 *note*, Cicero justifies such procedures. **1812** WOODHOUSE *Astron.* xxix. 290 We may adopt a contrary procedure. **1872** GEO. ELIOT *Middlem.* lxxi, He won his fortune by dishonest procedures.

c. *spec.* Legal action or proceeding; the steps taken in a legal action, collectively; the mode or form of conducting judicial proceedings (as distinguished from those branches of the law which define rights or prescribe penalties).

1676 TOWERSON *Decalogue* 486 The manner of the Jews procedure in their several courts of judicature. **1687** *Royal Let. to Privy Counc. Scot.* 12 Feb. in *Lond. Gaz.* No. 2221/2 If any shall be so bold as to shew any dislike of this Our Procedour. **1728** LARDNER *Wks.* (1838) I. 67 The treatment of Paul in Judea, so far as there is any appearance of a legal procedure. **1817** JAS. MILL *Brit. India* I. III. v. 641 The system of procedure; or the round of operations through which the judicial services—inquiry, sentence, and enforcement—are rendered. **1860** *Sat. Rev.* IX. 189/1 The blending of native consuetudinary law and English civil and criminal procedure in the administration of justice.

d. The mode of conducting business in Parliament.

1839 CARLYLE *Chartism* i. (1858) 5 To a remote observer of Parliamentary procedure it seems surprising.. to see what space this question occupies in the Debates of the Nation. **1863** H. COX *Instit.* I. ix. 136 The Standing Orders are rules and forms of procedure which have been adopted as they were found necessary from time to time. **1878** STUBBS *Const. Hist.* III. xx. 375 The rules and forms of parliamentary procedure.

e. *Computers.* A set of instructions for performing a specific task.

1946 *Ann. Computation Lab. Harvard Univ.* I. iv. 98 There are many coding routines.. which occur so frequently as to make standard coding procedures of real value. This chapter includes.. certain of the longer procedures. **1954** *IRE Trans. Electronic Computers* III. 15/1 Specialized procedures, formed from combinations of basic procedures,.. are needed to achieve higher speeds of operation for special purposes. **1965** *Data Processor* Oct. 22/3 A procedure is a block of instructions designed to perform a specific function such as the calculation of overtime pay in a payroll application... Procedures share common elements with different programs. Seldom-used procedures can be held in auxiliary storage and called into the main storage only when required. **1970** O. DOPPING *Computers & Data Processing* xix. 315 Sub-routines are called procedures in Algol. A number of standard functions are obligatory among these procedures,.. but in addition to these the programmer may write his own procedures.

†**2. a.** The going on or continuance of an action or process; progress, course. *Obs.*

1644 [HOWELL] *Merc. Hibernicus* 1 Whether one cast his eyes upon the beginning and procedure of the warre.. or upon the late Cessation. **1703** MOXON *Mech. Exerc.* 253 The hindrance of the Procedure of the Work. *a* **1716** SOUTH *Serm.* (1717) VI. 427 The Confidence reposed by Men in their own Hearts will in the Procedure of this Discourse appear to be inexcusably foolish.

b. The action of proceeding or going on *to* something. *Obs. rare.*

1663 OWEN *Vind. Animadv.* Wks. 1851 XIV. 426 Your next procedure is to your discourse of figures or images and my animadversions upon it.

3. a. The fact of proceeding or issuing *from* a source; origination. *rare.*

1651 C. CARTWRIGHT *Cert. Relig.* I. 37 You will say, your Religion is as ancient as ours; having its procedure from Christ. **1865** GINSBURG in *L'pool Lit. & Philos. Soc. Proc.* XIX. 185 The procedure of multifariousness from an absolute unity.

†**b.** *concr.* Something that proceeds, issues, or is derived from something else; proceeds, produce. *Obs.*

1614 T. GENTLEMAN *Way to Wealth* 6 They.. returne for the procedure of fish and herrings, the fore-named commodities. **1626** BACON *Sylva* §550 There is not any known Substance, but Earth, and the Procedure of Earth (as Tile, Stone, &c.) that yeeldeth any Moss or Herby Substance.

proceed ('prəusi:d), *sb.* Also 7 procede. [f. next.]

†**1.** The action, or manner, of proceeding or going on; proceeding, procedure; course. *Obs.*

1628 in *Crt. & Times Chas. I* (1848) I. 344 He now looks for a present proceed in his affairs, laying by all unnecessary delays. **1653** R. SANDERS *Physiogn.* 1 For one more orderly proceed into the body of this Work. **1674** OWEN *Vind. Doctr. Communion* Wks. 1851 II. 297 His proceed in the same page is to except against that revelation of the wisdom of God which I affirm to have been made.

2. That which proceeds, is derived, or results from something; that which is obtained or gained by any transaction; produce, outcome, profit. Now almost always in *pl.* **proceeds**.

sing. **1643** *Declar. Commons, Reb. Irel.* 48 Saint Mallo in France, where the Hides were sold, and the proceed returned unto him in the said Ship. *c* **1645** HOWELL *Lett.* (1650) I. I. xxix. 47 The only procede (that I may use the mercantile term) you can expect is thanks. *Ibid.* II. 105 The procede of this exchange wil come far short of any Gentlemans expectations. **1767** S. PATERSON *Another Trav.* I. 256 The neat proceed of the same sum, expended in the same given time..will amount only to [etc.]. **1891** STEVENSON *Valima Lett.* viii. (1895) 74 Dust and not flour is the proceed.

pl. **1665** PEPYS *Diary* 11 Dec., About £350,000 sterling was coined out of the French money, the proceeds of Dunkirke. **1706** PHILLIPS, *Proceed*, that which arises from a thing; as The Neat Proceeds among Merchants. **1849** MACAULAY *Hist. Eng.* iii. I. 287 The net proceeds of the customs amounted in the same year to five hundred and thirty thousand pounds. **1885** SIR W. B. BRETT in *Law Rep.* 14 *Q.B. Div.* 877 Handing over the proceeds of sale to the execution creditor.

proceed (prəʊ'si:d), *v.* Forms: 4–8 procede, 5–7 -ceede, 6 -ceade, *Sc.* -ceid(e, (-sede, prossed), 6– proceed. [ME. *procede-n*, a. F. *procéder* (13–14th c. in Hatz.-Darm.), a. L. *prōcēd-ĕre* to go forward, advance, go on: see PRO-[1] and CEDE.]

1. *intr.* To go, move, or travel forward; to make one's way onward; *esp.* to move onward after interruption or stoppage, or after reaching a certain point; to continue one's movement or travel.

c **1430** LYDG. *Min. Poems* (Percy Soc.) 12 The kyng procedyng forthe upon his way, Kome to the Condyte made in cercle wise. **1526** *Pilgr. Perf.* (W. de W. 1531) 26 Before we procede on our iourney. *a* **1550** *Sir A. Barton* in *Surtees Misc.* (1888) 72 But up in haist he did prossed. **1613** PURCHAS *Pilgrimage* III. vi. 224 Then proceeding on their way, they finde an Arch. **1743** J. MORRIS *Serm.* vii. 183 Elisha..did not procede on his intended journey. **1768** *Woman of Honor* III. 87 This intention of her's, to proceed for Lancashire. **1860** TYNDALL *Glac.* I. ii. 18 Accompanied by our guide, we proceeded to the glacier.

2. *intr.* To 'go on' with or carry on an action or series of actions, a discourse, an investigation, etc.; esp. with reference to the manner or order observed. Also with indirect passive.

c **1400** *Apol. Loll.* 13 To þe worschip of our Lord Jhesu Crist, & due ordre procedand up þe gospel. *c* **1400** *Destr. Troy* 5159 To holde A counsell in the case,..And procede on hor purpos, as prise men of wer. **1447** BOKENHAM *Seyntys* Introd. (Roxb.) 1 Two thyngys..To advertysyn begynnyng a werk If he procedyn wyl ordeneely. **1560** DAUS tr. *Sleidane's Comm.* 364 The cause, why the Emperor proceded on thys wise against them. *a* **1586** SIDNEY *Ps.* xv, Who thus proceeds, for aye in sacred mount shall raign. **1647** N. BACON *Disc. Govt. Eng.* I. xx. 59 Matters also of private regard were there proceeded upon. **1718** *Free-thinker* No. 27 ¶1 The true Philosopher must always proceed with a sober Pace. **1884** F. TEMPLE *Relat. Relig. & Sc.* vii. (1885) 210 Science proceeds in far the majority of cases by trial of some theory as a working hypothesis.

†**b.** To carry on an argument, to argue, debate. *it is proceeded* = it is argued. *Obs. rare.*

c **1449** PECOCK *Repr.* 208 As for answere and assoiling to the firste argument, y procede thus. *Ibid.* 565 Aȝens al this blamyng..it is procedid in othere placis of my writingis. **1724** A. COLLINS *Gr. Chr. Relig.* 120 Who proceeds with them on the supposition of a lost New Testament.

c. To deal *with*; to treat, act (in some way, esp. judicially) with regard to. (With indirect passive.)

c **1430** LYDG. *Min. Poems* (Percy Soc.) 141 Ye to be juge, and lyk as ye proceede. We shal obeye to your ordynaunce. **1656** EARL MONM. tr. *Boccalini's Advts. fr. Parnass.* II. xiv. (1674) 157 These men..ought not to be proceeded with, with such rigour. **1667** MILTON *P.L.* XI. 69, I will not hide My judgments, how with Mankind I proceed. **1737** POPE *Hor. Epist.* II. ii. 157 But how severely with themselves proceed The men, who write such Verse as we can read? **1831** in Picton *L'pool Munic. Rec.* (1886) II. 330 The party offending should not only be disfranchised, but otherwise proceeded with to the utmost rigour of the law.

d. *spec.* To institute and carry on a legal action or process; to take legal proceedings, go to law (*against*, †*upon* a person). With indirect (formerly impersonal) passive.

c **1440** *Gesta Rom.* iv. 10 (Harl. MS.) Þerfore we aske of you, þat it be procedid aȝenst him, as owith to be don aȝen a breker of þe lawe. *a* **1533** LD. BERNERS *Huon* lxxxii. 255 Yf ye wyll procede vpon Huon by iustyce. **1596** SHAKS. *Merch. V.* IV. i. 179 In such rule, that the Venetian Law Cannot impugne you as you do proceed. **1607** —— *Cor.* III. i. 314 Proceed by Processe, Least parties..breake out. **1647** CLARENDON *Hist. Reb.* I. §148 Direction in what manner he should proceed against such as refused.

3. *intr.* With stress on the progress or continuance of the action: To go on, advance, to continue acting, speaking, etc.: in various shades of meaning. **a.** To go on with or continue what one has begun; to advance from the point already reached, go further, pursue one's course; to go on after interruption, renew or resume action or speech.

1390 GOWER *Conf.* I. Prol. 38 Ther wist non what other mente. So that thei myhten noght procede. **1413** *Pilgr. Sowle* (Caxton 1483) v. xi. 103 Procedeth now forth in youre mater. *c* **1430** LYDG. *Min. Poems* (Percy Soc.) 8 Thou schalt have strenghte, and myghte, Forth to procede in long felicite. **1535** COVERDALE *1 Sam.* xix. 2 And Ionathas proceaded further, and sware vnto Dauid (he loued him so well). **1560** DAUS tr. *Sleidane's Comm.* 16 b, Exhorting him to procede as he hath begonne. **1665** HOOKE *Microgr.* x. 74, I proceeded on with my trial. **1769** GOLDSM. *Hist. Rome* (1786) II. 378 In this manner Perennius proceeded sacrificing numbers of the Senate. **1856** FROUDE *Hist. Eng.* I. v. 350 Henry..was determined to proceed with the divorce. **1874** GREEN *Short Hist.* viii. §3. 484 The Commons ..refused to proceed with public business till their members were restored.

b. To go on *to do* something; to advance *to* another action, subject, etc.; to pass on from one point to another in a series or sequence of any kind (said also of the series, or of its terms or items).

1390 GOWER *Conf.* III. 105, I wol procede To speke upon Mathematique. **1480** CAXTON *Chron. Eng.* I. (1520) 6/2 Of thes men is lytel wryten in scrypture and therfore I procede to other. **1552** *Bk. Com. Prayer, Ordering Deacons*, Then shal the Bisshop procede to the Communion. **1590** SIR J. SMYTH *Disc. Weapons* 2, I will begin with one of their toyes, and so proceed to greater matters. **1674** T. CAMPION *Art of Descant* 41 The one part proceeding by degree, the other by leap. **1690** LOCKE *Hum. Und.* I. i. §8 Before I proceed on to what I have thought on this Subject. **1743** EMERSON *Fluxions* 35 The Terms in the horizontal Row must be placed to proceed from the greater Indices to the lesser. **1774** WARTON *Hist. Eng. Poetry* Sect. iii. (1840) I. 116, I therefore proceed to observe, that [etc.]. **1825** THIRLWALL *Crit. Ess.* 168 The narrative proceeds from one incident to another, by the slightest connecting phrases. **1854** BREWSTER *More Worlds* xv. 221 From the globular clusters of stars our author proceeds to the binary systems.

c. *absol.* To continue or pursue one's discourse (in speech or writing); to go on to say.

1509 HAWES *Past. Pleas.* xiii. (Percy Soc.) 52, I must procede, and shew of Arismetrik With divers nombres which I must reporte. **1570** *Henry's Wallace* VI. 72 + 6 Heirof as now I will na mair proceid. **1588** SHAKS. *L.L.L.* v. ii. 570 The Conqueror is dismaid: Proceede good Alexander. **1660** F. BROOKE tr. *Le Blanc's Trav.* 280 To proceed, the land of Egypt is highly renowned. **1697** DRYDEN *Virg. Past.* VI. 19 Proceed, my Muse: Two Satyrs, on the Ground Stretch'd at his Ease, their Sire Silenus found. **1814** SCOTT *Wav.* xxxiii, He paused, and then proceeded; 'I do not intrude myself on your confidence [etc.]'. **1868** MILMAN *St. Paul's* 37 The Holy Sacraments, he proceeds, were frightfully profaned.

d. To carry on an action or discourse to a particular point or stage; to advance (so far), make some progress. Now *rare* or merged in sense a.

1560 DAUS tr. *Sleidane's Comm.* 24 b, When he had a litle proceded, he demaundeth of him in Latin, whether he wil kepe the Catholicke faith. **1643** in *10th Rep. Hist. MSS. Comm.* App. v. 492 The..rampier.., begun and considerablie proceeded in in ould time.., was this yeare recontinued. **1660** *Trial Regic.* 105 The treaty was so far proceeded in that it was near a perfection. **1793** SMEATON *Edystone L.* §132 We again proceeded towards mooring the sloop.

†**e.** In emphatic sense: To make progress, advance, get on; to prosper. *Obs.*

c **1592** MARLOWE *Jew of Malta* IV. iii, This is the hour wherein I shall proceed; Oh, happy hour, wherein I shall convert An infidel. **1611** B. JONSON *Catiline* III. i, These things, when they proceed not, they go backward. **1706** *Lond. Gaz.* No. 4191/1 The French proceed but very slowly in the Siege of the Castle. **1777** JOHNSON *Let. to Mrs. Thrale* 18 Sept., Invite Mr. Levet to dinner, and make enquiry what family he has, and how they proceed.

4. *intr.* To advance, in one's university course, from graduation as B.A. to some higher degree, as master or doctor. In the Inns of Court, to advance or be admitted to the status of a barrister.

One is said to graduate B.A., to proceed M.A., B.D., etc. (in U.S. also to proceed B.A.).

1479 W. PASTON in *P. Lett.* III. 246, I supposed..that the Qwenys broder schold have procedyd at Mydsomer. **1536** *Act 28 Hen. VIII*, c. 13 §5 Any person..which shal resorte to any of the sayde vniuersities to procede doctours in diuinitie. *a* **1548** HALL *Chron., Hen. V* 37 b, Althoughe I.. haue not proceded to degre in the Vniuersitie. **1563** FOXE *A. & M.* 1297/1 He proceaded Bachelour of Diuinitye in the sayde Vniuersitye of Cambridge. **1611** RICH *Honest. Age* (Percy Soc.) 41, I am a scholler, and I haue proceeded maister in the seauen Liberall Sciences. **1640** YORKE *Union Hon.* 131 After hee became student in the Temple, where he proceeded Barrester. **1702** C. MATHER *Magn. Chr.* II. ix. (1852) 154 His eldest son he maintained at the Colledge until he proceeded master of arts. **1828** H. GUNNING *Ceremonies Univ. Camb.* (new ed.) 168 Between the two Congregations he [a B.A. of 3 yrs. standing] visits the Vice-Chancellor ..(*Note.* The practice of visiting is now discontinued. The Candidates for degrees ask the Vice-Chancellor leave to proceed as he is quitting the Senate-House.) **1833** B. PEIRCE *Hist. Harvard Univ.* 52 In 1656 he proceeded Bachelor of Arts. **1879** M. PATTISON *Milton* i. 8 In 1632, when he proceeded to his M.A. degree, Milton was twenty-four. **1893** *Daily News* 24 Mar. 5/3 The new Archdeacon was educated at St. John's College, Oxford, graduated B.A...in 1847, and proceeded M.A. in 1851, B.D. in 1856, and D.D. in 1860. **1899** *Oxf. Univ. Cal.* 74 A Bachelor of Arts can proceed to the degree of Master in the twenty-seventh Term from his Matriculation, provided [etc.].

b. *transf.* and *fig.* To advance to some status or function; to grow or develop into; to become.

1579 LYLY *Euphues* (Arb.) 159 That as you haue proued learned Philosophers, you will also proceede excellent diuines. **1598** B. JONSON *Ev. Man in Hum.* Prol., To make a child now swadled, to proceed Man. **1647** FULLER *Good Th. in Worse T.* (1841) 152 Shall a plant take a new degree and proceed sensible? **1697** DRYDEN *Virg. Georg.* IV. 440 Shooting out with Legs, and imp'd with Wings, The Grubs proceed to Bees with pointed Stings. **1704** HEARNE *Duct. Hist.* (1714) I. 224 After they were become Masters in the Law, they proceeded Rabbi or Doctor.

5. *intr.* Of an action, process, etc.

a. To go on, be carried on, take place; to take effect. (Cf. 2.)

c **1440** *Alphabet of Tales* 28 If þe law procede for me, be þe sentance of þe law I sall aw þe no thyng, for I ouercom þe. **1521** *Maldon, Essex, Town clerk's oath of office* Liber B. lf. 57 b, Ye shall truly write all siche procese as shall procede this yere betwix party and party. **1601** SHAKS. *Jul. C.* I. ii. 181 He will..tell you What hath proceeded worthy note to day. **1697** DRYDEN *Virg. Georg.* IV. 244 With Diligence the fragrant Work proceeds. **1726** AYLIFFE *Parergon* 352 This Rule..proceeds and takes place when the Ambiguity thereof consists in some Points of Law alone. **1878** BROWNING *La Saisiaz* 85 Forth I fared:..Saw proceed the transmutation—Jura's black to one gold glow.

b. To go on or advance to a certain point; to be carried on further, to continue. (Cf. 3.)

1670 MARVELL *Corr.* Wks. (Grosart) II. 319 The two Bills are both yet proceeded no further then to a commitment. **1734** tr. *Rollin's Anc. Hist.* (1827) I. 122 To what a pitch.. the depravity of the poet had proceeded. **1885** *Law Times Rep.* LIII. 466/2 The jury was discharged by consent, and the case proceeded before the judge alone. **1892** 'F. ANSTEY' *Voces Pop.* Ser. II. 156 The Pantomime proceeds without further disturbance.

†**6.** *trans.* To proceed with, or cause to proceed; to carry on; in *passive*, of legal proceedings. *Obs.*

1433 *Rolls of Parlt.* IV. 441/2 John Duc of Norffolk.. besekes..yat in yis matier nothing be proceded, nor putte in execution, to his disheritance.., duryng his noun age. **1525** LD. BERNERS *Froiss.* II. cxiv. [cx.] 327 Then I began to wake, to procede this historye more than I dyd before. **1585** *Reg. Privy Council Scot.* IV. 9 That nathing suld be procedit aganis hir be vertew thairof. **1792** MARY WOLLSTONECR. *Rights Wom.* ii. 36 So that the man may only have to proceed, not to begin, the important task of learning to think and reason.

7. *intr.* To go or come forth; to issue.

a. lit. *from* (†*of*), *out of* a material thing or place; and in directly derived uses. In quot. 1703, of position or direction, to arise or spring *from*.

1382 WYCLIF *John* xv. 26 A spirit of treuthe, the whiche procedith [*gloss* or cometh forth] of the fadir, he schal bere witnessing of me. **1420** ? LYDG. *Assembly of Gods* 1609 Oute of whos byll procedyd a gret leme..lyke a son beme. **1500–20** DUNBAR *Poems* xxi. 41 Fra everilk mowth fair wirdis proceidis. **1526** TINDALE *Matt.* iv. 4 Every worde that proceadeth out off the mouth off God. **1548–9** (Mar.) *Bk. Com. Prayer, Communion, Nicene Creed*, I beleue in the holy ghost, the Lorde and geuer of life, who procedeth from the father and the sonne. **1582** N. LICHEFIELD tr. *Castanheda's Conq. E. Ind.* I xiii. 33 (*margin*) Laker is a kinde of gum that procedeth of the Ant. **1604** E. G[RIMSTONE] *D'Acosta's Hist. Indies* III. xvi. 170 There are many other Lakes in the high mountains, whence proceede brookes and rivers. **1703** MOXON *Mech. Exerc.* 30 It is fixed ..by two small Shanks proceeding from that Edge of the Spring. **1813** *Sk. Charac.* (ed. 2) I. 125 Soft sobs were heard proceeding from Catherine's bed. **1889** JESSOPP *Coming of Friars* vi. 264 The most sumptuous work that has ever proceeded from the Cambridge Press.

b. *spec.* To be the issue or descendant *of*; to be descended, spring *from* (a parent, ancestor, or stock). Now *rare* or *Obs.*

1480 CAXTON *Chron. Eng.* III. (1520) 27/2 Maria Cleophe the whiche was wedded to Alphe of whome proceded James the lesse. **1578** T. N. tr. *Conq. W. India* 1 They were both of good birth, and proceeded of foure principal houses. **1667** MILTON *P.L.* XII. 381 Virgin Mother, Haile, High in the love of Heav'n, yet from my Loynes Thou shalt proceed, and from thy Womb the Son Of God most High. **1768–74** TUCKER *Lt. Nat.* (1834) II. 195 We all proceed from the loins of Adam.

c. *fig.* and *gen.* To issue, spring, arise, originate, emanate, result, be derived (*from*, †*of* a source or cause). Formerly also with other constructions: To arise, come into being, come to pass, happen.

c **1393** CHAUCER *Scogan* 6 Allas from whens may þis þyng procede. **1484** CAXTON *Fables of Poge* iv, Wherof procedeth to me grete solas and playsyre. **1514** BARCLAY *Cyt. & Uplondyshm.* (Percy Soc.) 24 Yf by your labour procedeth more rychesse. **1561** T. HOBY tr. *Castiglione's Courtyer* I. (1577) cj b, Whereby somtime it proceedeth that.. customes..which at sometyme haue beene in price, become not regarded. **1697** DRYDEN *Virg. Georg.* II. 680 Teach me the various Labours of the Moon, And whence proceed th' Eclipses of the Sun. **1791** *Gentl. Mag.* 22/2 Where deafness proceeds from an obstruction of the auditory duct, by wax. **1850** McCOSH *Div. Govt.* III. iii. (1874) 425 One-half of man's exertions, and more than one-half of his happiness proceeds from hope.

proceeder (prəʊ'si:də(r)). Also 6 procedar. [f. prec. vb. + -ER[1].] One who proceeds.

1. One who carries on some action, or acts in some particular way; an agent, doer.

1555 H. PENDILTON in Bonner *Homilies* 38 b, The impudente procedars haue taughte the zely people that euery man shoulde and may be a iudge of controuersyes. **1638** *Penit. Conf.* (1657) 344 Which the Devil seeing, thought it seasonable to trip up the proceeders heels.

b. One who carries on a legal process.

a **1618** RALEIGH *Rem.* (1664) 257 Be thou [Christ] my speaker, taintless Pleader, Unblotted Lawyer, true Proceeder.

2. One who is proceeding to a university degree. ? *Obs.* (Cf. INCEPTOR 1.)

1581 MULCASTER *Positions* xli. (1887) 241 Are not the proceeders to reade in any of those sciences? **1625** BP. MOUNTAGU *App. Caesar* II. v. 144 To tender unto Proceeders this Proposition, 'The Pope Is Antichrist'. **1744** TANNER *Notitia Monast.* Pref. 41 A little before the Reformation the greatest part of the proceeders in divinity at Oxford were monks and Regular canons.

3. One who advances or makes progress.

(In 1596 transf. from 2.)

1596 SHAKS. *Tam. Shr.* IV. ii. 11 *Bian.* And may you proue sir Master of your Art. *Luc.* While you sweet deere proue Mistresse of my heart. *Hor.* Quiecke proceeders, marry. **1607–12** BACON *Ess.*, *Nat. in Men* (Arb.) 159 The second will make him a smale proceeder thoughe by often prevaylinges.

proceeding (prəʊˈsiːdɪŋ), *vbl. sb.* [f. as prec. + -ING[1].] The action of the verb PROCEED.

1. The action of going onward; advance, onward movement or course.

1517 TORKINGTON *Pilgr.* (1884) 41 At the procedyng owt of the.. Chapell.., They Shewyd on to vs.. &c. **1526** *Pilgr. Perf.* (W. de W. 1531) 198 b, There is no suche mouynge or outwarde procedynge, as this example sheweth. **1612** BREREWOOD *Lang. & Relig.* xiii. (1614) 114 Plinie, in the deriuation of water, requireth one cubit of declining, in 240 foot of proceeding. **1627** CAPT. SMITH *Seaman's Gram.* x. 50 In the proceeding of 200. foot forward, there should bee allowed one foot of descending. **1832** LONGF. *Brook* 7 To me thy clear proceeding brighter seems, Than golden sands.

†**b.** A company of people marching along in regular order on a festive occasion; a procession.

1660 *England's Joy* in Somers *Tracts* 4th Collect. (1751) II. 142 From this Tent the Proceeding was thus ordered, *viz.* First, The City Marshal.. Next the Sheriffs Trumpets; then the Sheriffs Men in Scarlet Cloaks [etc.]. **1714** *Lond. Gaz.* No. 5270/6 Those who formed the first part of the Proceeding,.. came down in Solemn Procession. **1727** *Acc. Ceremonies Coronations* 13 About 12 of the Clock the Proceeding begins to move.

2. The carrying on of an action or series of actions; action, course of action; conduct, behaviour: = PROCEDURE 1.

1553 BRENDE *Q. Curtius* iv. 39 The Tyrians were as diligent to inuent all such thinges as might giue impediment to their proceding. **1603** DRAYTON *Bar. Wars* I. lvii, For who observes strict Policies true Lawes, Shifts his Proceeding to the varying Cause. **1702** PEPYS *Let. to Kneller* in *Diary*, etc. (1879) VI. 238 My surprise, at the manner of my friend's proceeding with me. **1756** BURKE *Subl. & B.* Pref., We must make use of a cautious, I had almost said, a timorous, method of proceeding. **1816** A. C. HUTCHISON *Pract. Obs. Surg.* (1826) 192 This line of proceeding.. will soon clear the list of such persons, of the description we are adverting to, as have any soul or feeling.

b. A particular action or course of action; a piece of conduct or behaviour; a transaction: = PROCEDURE 1 b. Most usually in *pl.*: Doings, actions, transactions.

1553 BRENDE *Q. Curtius* VII. 140 b, The continuall felicitie he was wont to haue, in all his procedinges. **1641** (*title*) The Diurnall Occurrences, or Dayly Proceedings of Both Houses, in this Great and Happy Parliament, From the third of November 1640, to the third of November 1641. **17..** SWIFT (J.), From the earliest ages of christianity, there never was a precedent of such a proceeding. **1802** MAR. EDGEWORTH *Moral T.* (1816) I. ix. 70, I.. shall inform myself.. of all your proceedings. **1856** FROUDE *Hist. Eng.* I. i. 27 The law.. stepped in to prevent a proceeding which it regarded as petty treason to the commonwealth.

c. *pl.* A record or account of the doings of a society; sometimes *spec.* a record of the business done, with abstracts or reports of the less important papers not included in the *Transactions*.

1830 (*title*) Proceedings of the Royal Society. **1843** (*title*) Proceedings of the Philological Society for 1842–43. **1904** (*title*) Proceedings of the British Academy (vol. I.) 1903–04.

3. *spec.* The instituting or carrying on of an action at law; a legal action or process; any act done by authority of a court of law; any step taken in a cause by either party.

1546 *Reg. Privy Council Scot.* I. 66 Dischargis the.. officiaris, of all arresting, attecting, unlawing, calling or proceding aganis the said George. **1591** GREENE *Disc. Coosnage* (1592) 11 Think you some lawyers could be such purchasers, if al their pleas were short, and their proceedinges iustice and conscience? **1643** *Declar. Commons, Reb. Irel.* 5 Proceedings were begun against the Papists, upon the Statute of 2 Eliz. **1830** J. H. MONK *Life R. Bentley* (1833) II. 279 Having already as much law proceedings on his hands as he could manage. **1849** MACAULAY *Hist. Eng.* ii. I. 268 With these criminal proceedings were joined civil proceedings scarcely less formidable.

4. The action of going on with something already begun; continuance of action; advance, progress; advancement. Now *rare*.

1551 ROBINSON tr. *More's Utop.* II. (1895) 267 To hym allone thy attrybute the begynnynges, the encreasynges, the procedynges, the chaunges, and the endes of all thynges. **1563** *Homilies* II. *Idolatry* III. (1859) 213 The beginning, proceeding, and successe of idolatry. **1660** MILTON *Pres. Means* Wks. 1851 V. 457 When they shall see the beginnings and proceedings of these Constitutions propos'd.

b. The taking of a university degree; graduation.

1479 W. PASTON in *P. Lett.* III. 246, I understod that my moder and yow wold know what the costes of my procedyng schold be.

5. The action of coming forth or issuing from a place or source; egress; emanation.

1587 GOLDING *De Mornay* v. (1592) 61 Then let them be inquisitiue.. for the proceeding of the holy Ghost. **1877** W. BRUCE *Comm. Rev.* 97 Divine Truth in its going forth or proceeding bears witness to Divine Truth in its origin and Essence.

proˈceeding, *ppl. a.* [f. as prec. + -ING[2].] That proceeds; in quot., progressing, advancing.

1847 EMERSON in *Atlantic Monthly* (1892) June 742 The proceeding effects of electric telegraph will give a new importance to such arrangements.

proceleusmatic (prɒsɪljuːsˈmætɪk), *a.* (*sb.*) [ad. late L. *proceleusmatic-us*, a. Gr. προκελευσματικός, f. προκέλευσμα incitement, f. προκελεύειν to rouse to action beforehand.]

1. Serving for incitement; animating, inspiriting.

1773 JOHNSON *West. Isl.*, *Raasay*, The ancient proceleusmatick song by which the rowers of galleys were animated. **1818** C. MILLS *Crusades* (1822) I. 55 *note*, In an army.. there were as many proceleusmatick words as there were banners. **1866** ENGEL *Nat. Mus.* iii. 115 The oar-song of the Hebridians, which resembles the proceleusmatic verse by which the rowers of Grecian galleys were animated.

2. *Pros.* **a.** *adj.* Epithet of a metrical foot of four short syllables; pertaining to or consisting of such feet. **b.** *sb.* A proceleusmatic foot.

[**1706** PHILLIPS, *Proceleusmaticus Pes*, (in Grammar) a Foot consisting of four short Syllables; as *Pelagius*.] **1751** WESLEY *Wks.* (1872) XIV. 74 A Proceleusmatic, which is four short. **1818** HALLAM *Mid. Ages* ix. (1868) 589 The proceleusmatic foot, or four short syllables, instead of the dactyl. **1837** C. P. BROWN *Sanscrit Prosody* 13 One long being equal to two shorts, the admissible feet are the spondee, dactyl, amphibrach, anapæst and proceleusmatic. **1900** H. W. SMYTH *Gk. Melic Poets* 344 Mar[ius] Vic[torinus] says that proceleusmatics were used in Satyric plays, whereas they are alien to sober compositions in anapaests.

procellarian (prɒsɛˈlɛərɪən), *a.* and *sb. Ornith.* [f. mod.L. *Procellāria* (f. *procella* storm) + -AN.] **A.** *adj.* Belonging to or resembling the genus *Procellaria* or family *Procellariidæ* of seabirds. **B.** *sb.* A bird of this genus or family, a petrel. So **proceˈllarid**, a bird of the family *Procellariidæ*; **proceˈllariine** (-ɪaɪn) (erron. **procellarine**), *a.* belonging to the subfamily *Procellariinæ*; *sb.* a bird of this subfamily.

1853 KANE *Grinnell Exp.* (1856) 548 The great families of ducks, Auks, and procellarine birds.. throng the seas and passages of the far north. **1864** WEBSTER, *Procellarian*, one of a family of oceanic birds.. the petrel. **1879** H. N. MOSELEY *Notes Nat. Challenger* 207 Beside the Prion, there is the 'mutton-bird' of the whalers (*Æstrelata Lessoni*), a large Procellarid, as big as a pigeon.

†**proˈcelle.** *Obs. rare*[−1]. [a. OF. *procelle* (15th c. in Godef.), ad. L. *procella*.] A storm.

1426 LYDG. *De Guil. Pilgr.* 16995 Lych vnto a procelle which dryveth all sodeynly a Shyppe vn-to goode aryvaylle.

procello (prəʊˈsɛləʊ). *Glass-making.* ? *Obs.* Also 9 procellos (? *pl.*), **procellas** (*erron.* **pucellas**, **priscillas**). [a. It. *procello*: cf. PROCER.] A tool used for modifying the form of a glass vessel or object while being rotated on the end of the punty (e.g. for pinching in the neck of a bottle).

[**1699** *Blancourt's Making Glass*, The instruments marked E serve to finish the work, which the Italians call Ponteglo, Passago, Procello, Spiei, and also Borsello.] **1788** REES *Chambers' Cycl.* s.v. *Glass*, The aperture, opened thereby, they further augment, and widen with the procello. **1832** G. R. PORTER *Porcelain & Gl.* 172 Taking in his right hand an iron instrument, called a procello, the blades of which are connected together by an elastic bow in the manner of a pair of sugar tongs. **1849** PELLATT *Glass Making* 81 The 'pucellas' is somewhat like a pair of sugar-tongs, the prongs resembling the cutting part of shears, but blunt. **1869** J. LEICESTER in *Eng. Mech.* 3 Dec. 282/1, 3rd, the procellos, exactly like a pair of sheepshears. **1875** KNIGHT *Dict. Mech.*, *Procellas*, (*Glass-making*). *Ibid.*, *Pucellas*,.. a pair of tongs whose flat jaws rub upon the exterior surface of an object to reduce its diameter while it is being rotated. *Ibid.*, *Priscillas*.

†**proˈcellous,** *a. Obs.* [= obs. F. *procelleux* (15th c. in Godef.), ad. L. *procellōs-us* stormy: see PROCELLE and -OUS.] Stormy.

1650 B. *Discolliminium* 22 It is ill building of Steeples in an earth-quake, or setting up weather-cocks in procellous windes. **1772** NUGENT tr. *Hist. Fr. Gerund* II. 265 An happy voyage over the procellous ocean of your funeral parentation.

procephalic (prəʊsɪˈfælɪk), *a.* [f. Gr. πρό, PRO-[2] + κεφαλή head + -IC. In sense 2, f. Gr. προκέφαλος 'long-headed', also in Prosody.]

1. *Zool.* Belonging to the fore part of the head; applied to certain lobes or processes in Crustacea and other Arthropoda: see quots.

1874 LUBBOCK *Orig. & Met. Ins.* iii. 45 This portion is divided by a median fissure into two lobes, which.. will be termed the 'procephalic lobes'. **1877** HUXLEY *Anat. Inv. Anim.* vi. 251 The neural face of the embryo is fashioned first, and its anterior end terminates in two rounded expansions—the procephalic lobes. **1880** —— *Crayfish* iv. 160 Two flat calcified plates, which appear to lie in the anterior of the head (though they are really situated in its upper and front wall).. called the *procephalic processes*.

2. *Anc. Pros.* Having a syllable too many at the beginning; applied to a dactylic hexameter having a syllable in excess in the first foot. [So προκέφαλος in Hephæstion, A.D. 150.]

1890 in *Cent. Dict.*

[**proception**, error in J., whence repeated in later Dicts., for *præreption* (in *Eikon Basilike*): see PREREPTION.]

†**ˈprocer.** *Glass-making. Obs.* [app. of It. origin: cf. PROCELLO.] (See quot.)

1662 MERRETT tr. *Neri's Art of Glass* 363 *Procers* are Irons hooked at the extremity to settle the Pots in their places. **1670** BLOUNT *Glossogr.* (ed. 3), *Procers*, [adds. to prec.] used by makers of Green-glass.

†**proˈcere,** *a. Obs.* [ad. L. *procēr-us* high, tall. Cf. *sincere*.] Tall, lofty, high; long.

a **1560** BECON *Pleas. New Nosegay* Wks. I. 105 It shall cause you to delyght but lytyll in your body, be it neur so strong,.. pleasaunt in aspect, procere and taull. *a* **1652** BROME *Love-sick Court* IV. ii, A perpetual spring of more procere And bigger-bladed grass. **1664** EVELYN *Sylva* (1776) 3 By Trees here, I consider.. such lignous and woody plants, as are hard of Substance, procere of Stature. **1697** —— *Numism.* ix. 314 What is large, procere, goodly, and beautiful to look on.

procerebrum: see PRO-[2] 2.

‖**proceres** (ˈprɒsəriːz), *sb. pl.* [L. *procerēs* (rare sing. *procer*), leading men, chiefs, nobles.] Chief men, nobles, magnates.

1848 LYTTON *Harold* III. ii, In that chamber met the thegns and proceres of his realm. **1875** STUBBS *Const. Hist.* xvii. §294. II. 602 In 1328 it was with the counsel and consent of the prelates and 'proceres', earls, barons, and commons, that Edward resigned his claims on Scotland.

procerite (ˈprɒsəraɪt). *Zool.* [f. Gr. πρό, PRO-[2] + κέρας horn + -ITE[1] 3.] The many-jointed terminal segment (forming nearly the whole length) of the antenna in certain Crustacea, as lobsters. Hence **proceritic** (prɒsəˈrɪtɪk) *a.*, pertaining to the procerite.

1877 HUXLEY *Anat. Inv. Anim.* vi. 314 The last segment, or procerite consists of a long multi-articulate filament.

procerity (prəʊˈsɛrɪtɪ). Now *rare.* [ad. obs. F. *procerité* (15th c. in Godef.) or ad. L. *prōcēritātem* height, tallness: f. *prōcēr-us*: see PROCERE and -ITY.] Tallness, loftiness, height; length.

1550 LATIMER *Last Serm. bef. Edw. VI* (1562) 112 b, They were Gyantes for theyr cruelty.. and not in stature or procerity of body. **1604** TOOKER *Fabrique of Ch.* 13 All trees are not of one growth or procerītie. **1646** J. HALL *Poems* I. 36 [Thou] Com'st as near a Wit, as doth a Rat Match in procerity Mount Ararat. *a* **1677** HALE *Prim. Orig. Man.* II. vi. 173 At 5 Years of age in an ordinary growth the procerity is half of that which will be attained at full age. **1756** JOHNSON *Life King of Prussia* Wks. IV. 532 When he met a tall woman, he immediately commanded one of his Titanian retinue to marry her, that they might propagate procerity. **1864** SIR F. PALGRAVE *Norm. & Eng.* IV. 448 A cubit taller than any of his companions, and rendered even more remarkable by his beauty than his procerity.

†**procerous** (prəʊˈsɪərəs), *a. Obs.* [f. L. *prōcēr-us* (see PROCERE) + -OUS.] **1.** = PROCERE.

1599 NASHE *Lenten Stuffe* 14 The procerous stature of it.. twentie foot and sixe inches. **1657** TOMLINSON *Renou's Disp.* 243 Three sorts, the sharp, the smooth, and the procerous.

2. *Ornith.* Belonging to the order *Procerēs* or *Prōcēri*, the name given by Illiger 1811 to the *Ratitæ*, comprising the ostriches and allied birds.

process (ˈprɒsɛs, ˈprəʊsɛs), *sb.* Forms: 4–7 proces (also *pl.*), -cesse, (5 procese, -ceis, -ses, -seys, -sis(se, -ssesse, 5–6 prosses), 5– process. [ME. *proces*, a. F. *procès* (13th c. in Godef.), ad. L. *prōcess-us* (*u*-stem) advance, progress, process, lapse of time, f. ppl. stem of *prōcēd-ēre* to PROCEED. Orig. stressed *proˈcess*, still used by Milton and others in 17–18th c.; but ˈ*process* already in Chaucer: see ACCESS, and cf. *reˈcess*, *sucˈcess*. In F. the pl. is also *procès*; so sometimes *proces*, *proses*, *prosses* in ME.: see sense 4.]

1. a. The fact of going on or being carried on, as an action, or a series of actions or events; progress, course. Now chiefly in phr. ***in process*** = going on, being done; ***in process of*** (***construction***, etc.) = in course of; being (constructed, etc.).

c **1330** R. BRUNNE *Chron.* (1810) 216 þei teld him þe processe of alle þer comon sawe. *c* **1386** CHAUCER *Frankl. T.* 617 It is agayns the proces [*v.rr.* prosses, processe, process] of nature. *c* **1400** *Lanfranc's Cirurg.* 96 Loke aftirward þe prosis of þi worchinge seiþ þis boke. *c* **1440** *York Myst.* ii. 86 So multeply ȝe sall Ay furth in fayre processe. **1549** COVERDALE, etc. *Erasm. Par. 2 Pet.* 16 Confirmed nowe by longe processe of godlynes in the acquainted knowledge of the trueth. *a* **1619** FOTHERBY *Atheom.* II. iii. §3 (1622) 217 What then, in Causes can there be an infinite processe; And can no End bee found? **1697** DRYDEN *Æneid* VII. 790

Saturnian Juno, now, with double care, Attends the fatal process of the war. **1779–81** JOHNSON *L.P.*, *Addison* Wks. III. 89 The whole drama is..engaging in its process and pleasing in its conclusion. **1858** HAWTHORNE *Fr. & It. Note-bks.* II. 270 New edifices..are in process of erection. **1906** E. F. SCOTT *4th Gosp.* i. 18 A judgment is in process and we follow it stage by stage to the great climax.

†**b.** ***by process***, ***in process***: in the course of events; in course of time; in the sequel, at length, in due course. *Obs.* (Cf. 2.)

c **1385** CHAUCER *L.G.W.* 1553 (*Hypsipyle & Medea*) As wolde god I leyser hadde & tyme By proces al his wowyng for to ryme. *c* **1420** ? LYDG. *Assembly of Gods* 1213 Whyche shall to Vertu bryng yow by processe. **1523** LD. BERNERS *Froiss.* I. xc. 112 So he went forthe, and in processe retourned agayne. **1523** FITZHERB. *Husb.* §127 The sappe wyll nat renne into the toppe kyndely, but by proces the toppe wyll dye. *a* **1641** BP. MOUNTAGU *Acts & Mon.* i. §12 (1642) 8 All Man-kind succeeding..afterward in processe to be derived from him. **1736** WELSTED *Wks.* (1787) 450 That the same thing would, in process, have happened of itself.

c. Used in *Philos.*, esp. in and with reference to the work of A. N. Whitehead (1861–1947), to designate the course of becoming rather than being.

1926 A. N. WHITEHEAD *Relig. in Making* iii. 114 In this fusion of ground with consequent, the creative process brings together something which is actual and something which, at its entry into that process, is not actual. The process is the achievement of actuality by the ideal consequent, in virtue of its union with the actual ground. In the phrase of Aristotle, the process is the fusion of being with not-being. **1949** O. LEE *Existence & Inquiry* 11 Because the world seen as process was very different from what it had been before, a new theory of inquiry was needed to deal with it. Dialectic was the answer first proposed—a logic of process. **1964** E. E. HARRIS *Found. of Metaphysics in Sci.* xxii. 451 Samuel Alexander, J. C. Smuts, Lloyd Morgan and Henri Bergson..expounded theories of process and evolutionary pluralism. Whitehead..like Hegel, attempted to reconcile pluralism with monism and process with holism. **1977** *Theology* LXXX. 187 The world is a dynamic totality of events..hence it is a process, *from* the given past *through* the present..and *towards* a future.

2. Course, lapse (of time). Chiefly in ***in*** (†***by***) ***process of time***, in course of time, as time goes on.

c **1340** HAMPOLE *Prose Tr.* 20 Therfor we muste abide and wirke be processe of tyme. *c* **1400** MAUNDEV. (Roxb.) xi. 49 Of þaire kynredyn by processe of tyme come oure Lady saynt Mary. **1489** CAXTON *Faytes of A.* I. xxiii. 70 That is by long proces of tyme chaunged. *c* **1600** SHAKS. *Sonn.* civ, Three beautious springs to yellow Autumne turn'd In processe of the seasons haue I seene. **1654** R. CODRINGTON tr. *Iustine* xviii. 267 After the process of many yeers..they took shipping again. **1667** MILTON *P.L.* II. 297 To found this nether Empire, which might rise By pollicy, and long process of time. **1711** STEELE *Spect.* No. 154 ¶2 In due Process of Time I was a pretty Rake among the Men. **1838** ARNOLD *Hist. Rome* I. 31 The city of the Palatine Hill grew in process of time, so as to become a city of seven hills. **1842** TENNYSON *Locksley Hall* 138 The thoughts of men are widen'd with the process of the suns.

†**3.** Course (of a narrative, treatise, argument, etc.); drift, tenor, gist. *Obs.*

[*c* **1330**: see sense 1.] *c* **1380** WYCLIF *Sel. Wks.* III. 518 As it is knowun by alle þe processe of þe gospel. **1456** SIR G. HAYE *Law Arms* (S.T.S.) 1 The rubryis..be the quhilkis men may better knaw the process of the said buke and of every chapter. **1563** MAN *Musculus' Commonpl.* 35 This is the processe of the Decalogus [orig. *Hic est contextus Decalogi*]. **1615** G. SANDYS *Trav.* 236 We shall haue occasion to treate of [these] in the processe of our Iournall. **1643** SIR T. BROWNE *Relig. Med.* I. §22 No man will be able to prove it, when, from the process of the Text, I can manifest it may be otherwise.

†**4. a.** A narration, narrative; relation, story, tale; a discourse or treatise; an argument or discussion.

1340–70 *Alisaunder* 171 To profre þis process prestly too here, I karp of a kid king Arisba was hote. **1390** GOWER *Conf.* III. 284 Wherof a tale in remembrance, Which is a long process to hiere. *c* **1400** *Destr. Troy* 247 When Pelleus his proses hade puplishit on highe,..Iason was Ioly of his Iuste wordes. —— 11772 This poynt is not prynted in proces þat are now. —— 13774 Here the prosses of Pyrrus I put to an end. **1486** *Bk. St. Albans* d iij, Here endyth the proceis of hawkyng. **1523** LD. BERNERS *Froiss.* I. i. 1 Who so this proces redeth, or hereth, may take..ensample. **1533** MORE *Apol.* 12 b, They preache some tyme a longe processe to very lytle purpose. **1602** SHAKS. *Ham.* I. v. 37 So the whole eare of Denmarke, Is by a forged processe of my death Rankly abus'd. **1671** J. WEBSTER *Metallogr.* xviii. 251 The way of doing which may be found in many authors,..in Manuscripts, and written Processes. **1753** *Scots Mag.* Oct. 522/2 A verbal process of this day's transactions. [Repr. F. *procès verbal.*] **1784** R. BAGE *Barham Downs* I. 296 Kitty, having heard these dialogues and processes repeated by Molly's mother, who had an excellent knack at this kind of rehearsals.

b. A passage of a discourse. *Obs.*

1388 WYCLIF *Prol.* iii. 4 This proces of Genesis shulde stire cristen men to be feithful. *c* **1449** PECOCK *Repr.* I. xi. 55 Eny proces or parti writen in Holi Writt. **1535** CRANMER *Let.* in *Misc. Writ.* (Parker Soc.) II. 308 Ye take for your purpose some processes of scripture. **1555** J. HARPESFELD in Bonner *Homilies* 44 b, This processe of Scripture hath in it many circumstaunces to be noted.

5. a. Something that goes on or is carried on; a continuous action, or series of actions or events; a course or method of action, proceeding, procedure.

1340 HAMPOLE *Pr. Consc.* 235 Þe bygynnyng of alle þis proces Ryght knawyng of a man self es. *a* **1400** *Pistill of Susan* 294, I schal be proces apert disproue þis a-pele. **1513** MORE *Rich. III* Wks. 50/1 Troweth the protector..that I parceiue not whereunto his painted processe draweth. **1602** SHAKS. *Ham.* III. iii. 29 Behinde the Arras I'le conuey my selfe To heare the Processe. **1691** RAY *Creation* I. (1692) 54 Ignorance of the true Process of Nature. **1760–72** H. BROOKE *Fool of Qual.* (1809) IV. 65, I wished, after the process of my divine Master, to be despised and rejected of men. **1838–9** FR. A. KEMBLE *Resid. Georgia* (1863) 26 The shutting of a door is a process of extremely rare occurrence. **1897** MARY KINGSLEY *W. Africa* 610, I gladly accepted this generous offer and proceeded to wait for the Nachtigal, and a very pleasant process this was.

b. *Social Sciences.* The continuing interaction of human groups and institutions, esp. as observed and studied through its effects in social, political, cultural, etc., life, with the aim of finding underlying patterns of behaviour in the data available, freq. contrasted with the study of such aspects of society through its structures. Also *attrib.*

1887 MOORE & AVELING tr. *Marx's Capital* I. I. i. 12 The different proportions in which different sorts of labour are reduced to unskilled labour as their standard, are established by a social process that goes on behind the backs of the producers, and, consequently, appear to be fixed by custom. **1898** E. A. ROSS in *Amer. Jrnl. Sociol.* III. 860 Everything that is being done to bring to light the processes of socialization and control contradicts the easy-going theory that actual society is a spontaneous product due to the social instincts of man. **1902** L. F. WARD in *Ibid.* VII. 761 Ratzenhofer shows the precise *modus operandi* of the whole process of social assimilation. **1928** [see EDUCATIONAL *a.* 2]. **1939** *Jrnl. Psychol.* VIII. 389 The question may be raised whether any light upon this situation can be obtained by examining the *process* of personality development for leads to..more satisfactory methods and procedures. **1951** R. F. BALES *Interaction Process Anal.* p. iii, An attempt to formulate some of the basic structural characteristics and dynamic processes one would expect to find in small groups. **1954** *Amer. Anthropologist* LVI. 398 In *synchronic* studies of national character, we are discussing not the origins of the culture or the society, but the process of learning of identifiable human beings living within that society at a given period. **1958** *Pol. Stud.* VI. 243 The term 'process' seems to enter social and political discourse today in two different ways: it can be used widely or it can be used more specifically. *Ibid.* 248 Here I think we probably find a plausible separate use for this process notion—to refer to an isolable complex of interactions between procedural rules.. and the internal and external relations of various kinds of social groups. **1960** *Amer. Anthropologist* LXII. 18 The recent advances in the structural-functional approach are impressive..compared to the lag and the disagreements over how to conceptualize cultural processes. **1969** K. CAUTHEN *Science, Secularization & God* v. 165, I have already declared myself in favor of a metaphysical philosophy based on the process model argued so persuasively by Whitehead and Hartshorne. **1971** R. F. MURPHY *Dialectics of Social Life* i. 31 The study of 'process' and 'dynamics' is thus not as processual and dynamic as we would like to believe, for it commonly approximates a seriation of structures through time.

6. A continuous and regular action or succession of actions, taking place or carried on in a definite manner, and leading to the accomplishment of some result; a continuous operation or series of operations. (The chief current sense.)

a. A natural or involuntary operation; a series of changes or movements taking place.

1627 tr. *Bacon's Life & Death* (1651) 57 There are four Processes of the Spirit; To Arefaction; To Colliquation; To Putrefaction; To Generation of bodies. **1733** P. SHAW tr. *Bacon's Phys. Fables* viii. Expl., Philos. Wks. 1733 I. 568 He who knows the Properties, the Changes, and the Processes of Matter. **1871** B. STEWART *Heat* (ed. 2) §91 Ice is not instantly converted into water but the process is gradual. **1875** BENNETT & DYER *Sachs' Bot.* 174 In order to obtain.. a deeper insight into the processes of growth..it is necessary to follow up the history of development.

b. An artificial or voluntary operation; a course or method of operation; a systematic series of actions, physical or mental, directed to some end.

1665 GLANVILL *Def. Vanity Dogm.* 39 Little can be collected from the Chymical Processes he speaks of. *a* **1715** BURNET *Own Time* an. 1681 (1766) II. III. 142, I diverted my self with many processes in Chymistry. **1800** tr. *Lagrange's Chem.* I. 296 These explanations induce us to prefer the process of Fourcroy and Vauquelin. **1807** T. THOMSON *Chem.* (ed. 3) II. 126 Such are the different processes for procuring carbonic oxide. **1860** TYNDALL *Glac.* I. iii. 25 Explained to me the process of making cheese. **1875** J. P. HOPPS *Princ. Relig.* xiv. (1878) 45 Salvation, like education, is a process, not an immediate act.

c. (*a*) A particular method of operation in any manufacture, or in printing, photography, sanitation, etc.: often named from the inventor, as ***Bessemer p.***, ***Fox-Talbot p.***, ***Pattinson p.***, etc., or from the substance or means used, as ***collodion p.***, ***gelatine p.***; ***dry p.***, ***heliotype p.***, ***wet p.***, etc.: q.v. (*b*) In *Patent Law*, applied to any method of obtaining a useful result by other than mechanical (e.g. by chemical) action. (*c*) In 19th-c. use *spec.* applied to methods other than simple engraving by hand (e.g. chemical or photographic) of producing blocks for printing from; *ellipt.* a print from such a block.

1839 URE *Dict. Arts* 1133 The patent process [for separating silver from lead] lately introduced by Mr. Pattinson. **1839** SIR J. HERSCHELL in *Proc. Roy. Soc.* IV. 131 M. Daguerre's concealed photographic process. **1842** *Blackwood Mag.* LI. 388 Having their portraits taken by the photogenic process. **1856** [see BESSEMER]. **1856** *Chambers' Encycl.* VII. 511/1 Photo-Glyphography..a process invented by Mr. Fox Talbot. **1859** *Sat. Rev.* 22 Jan. 98/1 Various processes of photoglyphy and phototypy. **1881** [see PATTINSONIZE]. **1886** *Daily News* 9 Dec. 5/2 There were no photogravures then, nor hideous scratchy and seamy 'processes'. **1886** *Sci. Amer.* 24 July 49/3 They produce by a new process colored prints, so-called photo-chromotypes. **1898** *Daily Chron.* 8 Oct. 3/4 In the Dibdin process..the sewage is pumped on to a coarse ballast filter. **1907** *New Eng. Dict.* (See the articles *Photogravure*, *Photolithography*, *Photomechanical*, *Phototype*, *Phototypography*, *Photozincography*, etc.)

(*d*) A method of straightening and styling the hair by chemical means; *transf.* hair thus treated; the chemicals which effect this. *U.S. Blacks.*

1964 L. HAIRSTON in J. H. Clarke *Harlem* 288 Sonny rubbed the process in so thick with his rubber gloves, it started stingin' a little t'rough the heavy layer of grease he packed in my scalp. *Ibid.* 293 By Friday my process'd need retouchin'. **1967** *Trans-Action* Apr. 8/1 Time may pick up when a familiar car cruises by and a few dudes drive down to Johnny's for a 'process' (hair straightening and styling). **1970** E. OFARI in *Black Scholar* Oct. 49/2 Draper apparently has never heard of cadillacs, processes, chitterlings, the blues. **1972** B. G. COOKE in T. Kochman *Rappin' & Stylin' Out* 64 The 'process' of hair straightening is now considered demeaning; most black brothers have abandoned it.

d. A linguistic operation or change.

1954, etc. [see ITEM *sb.* 2 d]. **1964** R. H. ROBINS *Gen. Linguistics* v. 212 Different forms of the paradigms are then described as the result of processes, vowel change..etc. applied to the root form. (*Process* in this use is a descriptive term; it has nothing to do with historical processes in time or with changes in the forms of the language through the years.) **1974** R. QUIRK *Linguist & Eng. Lang.* v. 92 Educated opinion here is well-informed about the 'existing processes' of English.

7. *Law.* **a.** The whole of the proceedings in any action at law; the course or method of carrying on an action; an action, suit. **b.** *spec.* The formal commencement of any action at law; the mandate, summons, or writ by which a person or thing is brought into court for litigation.

a. *c* **1325** *Poem Times Edw. II* (Percy Soc.) xlvi, That have drive truth out of londe Without process of law. **1414** *Rolls of Parlt.* IV. 57/1 The processe of myn outelawery was unlawefully made. **1560** DAUS tr. *Sleidane's Comm.* 108 All suytes & proces in the law, commenced for Religion, shal in the meane tyme be let falle & suspended. **1627** *Lisander & Cal.* VII. 122 It was a little before the feast of Christmas after which time Calista's processe was to be judged. **1640** YORKE *Union Hon.* 124 He..without processe, was executed at Bridgewater. **1701** SWIFT *Contests Nobles & Comm.* Wks. 1755 II. I. 17 The power of judging certain processes by appeal. **1781** J. MOORE *View Soc. It.* (1790) I. xv. 180 They may..search his papers, make his process and in conclusion, put him to death. **1862** MERIVALE *Rom. Emp.* (1865) VI. lii. 294 He was allowed to..turn the charge against himself into a process against his accuser.

b. **1433** *Rolls of Parlt.* IV. 447 The said John was endited ..and proces made out upon the same enditement. **1467** in *Eng. Gilds* (1870) 391 Yf the seid pleintif require eny seriaunt to serue the seid processe accordynge to the lawe. **1482** *Rolls of Parlt.* VI. 208/1 Power..to awarde processe by Capias, and to make other such processes into every Countie of Englond. **1577** in W. H. Turner *Select. Rec. Oxford* (1880) 390 They of the Towne had servid proces upon him. **1768** BLACKSTONE *Comm.* III. xix. 279 The next step for carrying on the suit, after suing out the original, is called the process; being the means of compelling the defendant to appear in court. **1827** HALLAM *Const. Hist.* (1876) I. vi. 344 The chancellor..had a court of his own,..out of which process to compel appearance of parties might..emanate. **1883** *Law Rep. 11 Q. B. Div.* 545 An attachment granted to enforce compliance with the order of court is process of a punitive and disciplinary character.

†**8.** Onward movement in space; procession; progress, progression. *Obs.*

c **1400** *Destr. Troy* 8793 Fro thethen the lycour..past so by proces to his prise armys. *Ibid.* 11910 Þan the grekes.. With proses and pres puld vp þere ancres. *c* **1440** *Partonope* 3669 Eche Bysschope made hys processe To the dore of hys chambre be sermoun. **1642** H. MORE *Song of Soul* II. ii. II. vi, A point the line doth manfully retrude From infinite processe. **1875** H. JAMES, jr. *Pass. Pilgrim* 41 The whole.. surrounding prospect lay answering in a myriad fleeting shades the cloudy process of the tremendous sky.

9. *fig.* **a.** Of action, time, etc.: Progress, progression, advance; development. Now *rare.*

1638 ROUSE *Heav. Univ.* ix. (1702) 136 Daily to make a Process in his Learning. **1664** POWER *Exp. Philos.* II. 131 But presently our Glass-tube..began to leak, and let in Ayr; so we could make no further process in the Experiment. **1747** GOULD *Eng. Ants* 40 The process of Ant Vermicles is remarkable and worth Observation. **1813** T. BUSBY *Lucretius* I. I. Comm. p. xxvi, Virgil..most admirably describes the gradual process of the fire. **1850** TENNYSON *In Mem.* lxxxii, Eternal process moving on, From state to state the spirit walks.

†**b.** Degree of progress or advance. *Obs. rare.*

1654 H. L'ESTRANGE *Chas. I* (1655) 137 Nor was this a Schisme of an ordinary assise, but grew to that processe, to that degree, as..Altar was erected against Altar. **1774** tr. *Helvetius' Child of Nature* II. 171 That great man.. calculated the process and degree, at which our effeminacy would be followed by a contempt of liberty, and a surrender of the invaluable rights we have inherited from our ancestors.

c. *Logic.* The act of proceeding from a term in one of the premisses to the corresponding term in the conclusion; only in ILLICIT *process* (q.v.).

[**1692** ALDRICH *Artis Logicæ Rudimenta* (ed. Mansel 1852) 69 Processus ab extremo non distributo in præmissis, ad idem distributum in conclusione, vitiosus est. *Ibid.* 77 Quælibet Figura excludit adhuc sex modos. Nempe 1. Propter Medium non distributum... 2. Propter processum majoris illicitum... 3. Propter processum minoris illicitum.]

1827 [see ILLICIT c]. **1864** BOWEN *Logic* vii. 198 The violation of this last Rule, in respect to the Major Term, is called illicit process of the Major.

10. The act of proceeding or coming forth from a source: = PROCESSION *sb.* 4. *rare.*

1537 ABP. LEE in Strype *Eccl. Mem.* (1721) I. App. lxxxviii. 229 The proces of grace in this sacrament cometh from him by whose authority it is institute. *a* **1641** BP. MOUNTAGU *Acts & Mon.* (1642) 552 Beginning with the processe of our Saviour's Fore-runner, John the Baptist. **1877** E. CAIRD *Philos. Kant* ii. 18 The process of the infinite out of itself into the finite.

†**11.** A formal command, mandate, or edict, proceeding from a person in authority. Cf. 7 b.

1602 SHAKS. *Ham.* IV. iii. 65 And England, if my loue thou holdst at ought,.. thou maist not coldly set Our Soueraigne Processe, which imports at full.. The present death of Hamlet. **1606** —— *Ant. & Cl.* I. i. 28 Where's Fuluias Processe? (Cæsars I would say) both?

12. A projection from the main body of something; esp. a natural appendage, extension, or outgrowth; a projection, prominence, protuberance.

a. *Anat.*, *Zool.*, and *Bot.* Orig. and chiefly, of a bone (= APOPHYSIS 1). **b.** *Bot.* In mosses, one of the main divisions or segments of the inner peristome.

1578 BANISTER *Hist. Man* I. 26 These bones are endewed with two notable productions or Processes. **1598** FLORIO, *Corona*,.. a thicke and pointing processe of bones much like to the snagge of a Hartshorne. **1615** CROOKE *Body of Man* 79 In woemen two processes or productions passe from the wombe to the vpper part of the neck of the same. **1682** T. GIBSON *Anat.* (1697) 20 It has two remarkable Processes in men placed before, by the os pubis, on each side one. **1719–22** QUINCY *Lex. Physico-Med.*, *Acromium*.. is the upper Process of the Shoulder Blade. **1862** DARWIN *Fertil. Orchids* ii. 81 [The stigmas] from two protuberant, almost horn-shaped processes on each side of the mouth of the nectary. **1893**, etc. [see DENDRON]. **1977** *Sci. Amer.* Aug. 108/2 In the nervous system a network of nerve cells with elongated processes communicate with one another by secreting neurotransmitters, which traverse the tiny gap between two nerve cells.

c. *gen.* and *fig.*

1775 JOHNSON *Tax. no Tyr.* 23 Mere extensions or processes of empire. **1839** DE QUINCEY *Recoll. Lakes* Wks. 1862 II. 217 Mighty fells, immediate dependencies and processes of the still more mighty Helvellyn. **1873** BURTON *Hist. Scot.* V. liii. 35 The assailants turned the cannon upon the lower processes of the fortress.

13. a. *attrib.* and *Comb.* as (sense 1 c) ***process motif, theism, -thinker, thought, view***; (sense 6 c) ***process block*** (a block to print from, produced by some process other than simple engraving by hand), ***cut, department, embossing, -engraver, engraving, lens, -maker, -owner, photography, picture, plate, print, -printer, reproduction, work***; also with reference to a kind of colour printing in which a continuous and wide range of colours is produced by superimposing half-tones in each of three or four different colours, as ***process colour, ink, printing***; with reference to industrial processes, esp. continuous ones, as ***process cost, engineer, engineering, industry, operation, plant, sheet, work; process-type*** attrib.; (sense 6 d) ***process approach, model, morphophonemic***; **b. process annealing** *Metallurgy*, heat treatment applied to an alloy after cold working to prepare it for further cold working; **process black**, a black ink suitable for use in process work; **process butter** (see quots. 1902, 1906); **process camera**, a camera specially designed for taking photographs for use in process work; **process chart**, a diagram showing the sequence and sometimes the time and place of the different stages in an industrial or commercial process, or the different activities performed by an employee; **process cheese**, cheese made by melting and blending (and often emulsifying) other cheeses; also *fig.*; cf. *processed cheese*; **process control**, the regulation and control of the physical aspects of an industrial process, esp. automatically by instruments; freq. *attrib.*; hence **process controller**; **process heat**, heat supplied or required for an industrial process; so **process heating** *vbl. sb.*; **process philosophy**, philosophy based on the theory of process (sense 1 c); **process projection** *Cinemat.*, projection on to the back of a translucent screen, the other side of which is used as a background for ordinary filming; **process schizophrenia**, endogenous schizophrenia that does not seem connected with environmental causes; hence **process schizophrenic**; **process-server**, a sheriff's officer who serves processes or summonses (sense 7 b): = BAILIFF 2; so **process-serving**; **process shot** *Cinemat.* (see quot. 1973); **process steam**, steam supplied or required for an industrial process other than power generation; **process theology**, theological theory based on the concept of process (sense 1 c); hence **process theologian**; **process water**, water used in an industrial process; **process worker**, one who works in process printing or in an industrial process.

1936 *Metals Handbk.* (Amer. Soc. Metals) 211 *Process annealing*, heating iron base alloys to a temperature below or close to the lower limit of the critical temperature range followed by cooling as desired. **1977** R. B. ROSS *Handbk. Metal Treatm.* 322 The purpose of Process annealing is to remove work hardening prior to further cold work. **1972** W. P. LEHMANN in *Language* XLVIII. 266 Recent grammatical study has led to a preference for a process approach in linguistic analysis. **1907** *Yesterday's Shopping* (1969) 471/1 *Process black*.. for use in drawings intended for process reproduction. **1964** E. CHAMBERS *Camera & Process Work* xv. 208 The ink manufacturers make inks suitable for proofing, these are usually sold under such names as half-tone black, process black or press black. **1888** C. T. JACOBI *Printers' Vocab.* 104 *Process blocks*, illustrations in relief produced by any mechanical process. **1890** W. J. GORDON *Foundry* xi. 216 The lines in the process-block can be thickened in three ways—either by the final planing or by the dusting on of the rosin or by the coarse grain of the zinc. **1925** Process block [see LETTER-PRESS 1]. **1899** *Jrnl. Franklin Inst.* CXLVII. 94 (*heading*) Renovated or process butter. **1902** LEFFMANN & BEAM *Select Methods of Food Analysis* 370 So-called 'process' or 'renovated' butter, made by rendering old or inferior samples, purifying the fat, coloring, salting, and molding it, is now a familiar commercial article. **1906** L. L. VAN SLYKE *Mod. Methods of testing Milk & Milk Products* i. 18 Renovated or process butter is the product made by melting butter and reworking, without the addition or use of chemicals or any substances except milk, cream or salt. **1911** SIMMONS & MITCHELL *Edible Fats & Oils* iv. 44 The preparation of 'process' butter from stale or unsaleable genuine butter. **1895** *Photogr. Jrnl.* XIX. 313 In the construction of a process camera rigidity and parallelism and ability to stand wear and tear have to be carefully studied. **1967** KARCH & BUBER *Offset Processes* v. 141 The lithographic plate is usually produced from a negative which is made with the process camera. **1974** J. CRAIG *Production for Graphic Designer* 72 The first step in making a printing plate is to photograph the copy.. using a special camera, called a process camera. **1941** COLVIN & STANLEY *Running Machine Shop* vi. 256 Process charts can also be made to follow the operator instead of the part or product. **1968** B. YUILL *Supervision Princ. & Techniques* xxi. 240 The layout must be carefully planned by using such techniques as materials and man process charts, which show the proposed courses of materials and the movement of manpower through the plant. **1977** P. E. HICKS *Introd. Industr. Engin. & Managem. Sci.* iv. 63 Whereas analysis was restricted only to operations and inspections in using the operation process chart, the flow process chart includes additional consideration of moves, delays, and storages. **1926** T. R. PIRTLE *Hist. Dairy Industry* i. 110 The development of the process or packaging cheese business is one of the outstanding accomplishments of the cheese industry in recent years. **1951** M. MCLUHAN *Mech. Bride* (1967) 24/1 These wondrous totalitarian techniques for making the public into process cheese. **1972** *Federal Register* XXXVII. 11722/3 The amendments.. will have the effect of providing for optional use of buttermilk in pasteurized process cheese food. **1926** F. B. WIBORG *Printing Ink* xx. 241 *Process color inks.* These inks are made exclusively for the purpose of printing pictorial subjects... Special process inks are made for this class of printing. **1951** R. G. RADFORD *Letterpress Machine Work* II. xii. 134 The majority of experienced process colour printers prefer the Miehle two-revolution machine. **1968** *Heidelberg News* Sept. 4/3 Only use process colour when it is justified. Four colour work is seen at its best, has most impact, alongside black and white. **1931** *Electronics* Oct. 144 (*heading*) Electronic oscillators for industrial process control. **1945** D. P. ECKMAN *Princ. Industr. Process Control* x. 202 Many simple controllers serve in industrial process control as safety devices to protect process equipment from overloads of temperature or pressure. **1967** *Economist* 8 Apr. 162/2 It would make a great difference to the market for, and the cost of, industrial process control if engineers could make headway in designing standardised sections of process control instruments, etc., that could be assembled, building-block fashion, at the client's plant. **1977** *Sci. Amer.* Sept. 122/3 A small process-control computer monitors the temperature, directs the insertion and withdrawal of the wafers and controls the internal environment of the furnace. **1951** *Proc. Inst. Electr. Engineers* XCVIII. II. 609/1 The output signal of the process controller is transmitted to the regulating unit, which adjusts the physical quantity upon which the controlled quantity depends in order to restore it to the desired value. **1955** *Automatic Control* (1957) II. 26 Process controllers supervise the manufacture of plastics, synthetic fibers, drugs, the whole range of products of the chemical industry. **1926** S. I. LEVY *Introd. Industrial Chem.* ii. 47 The process cost sheets reveal clearly the great importance of chemical efficiency. **1974** *Terminol. Managem. & Financial Accountancy* (Inst. Cost and Managem. Accountants) 21 *Process cost centre*, a cost centre in which a specific process or a continuous sequence of operations is carried out. **1967** *Times* 18 Jan. 16/4 There are restrictive practices in the industry, particularly in the machine room and process department. *Ibid.* 16/7 *Process department*, prepares photographs and line drawings as plates. **1968** *Guardian* 29 Feb. 11/2 Joe Balfour's work wasn't good enough for process department, so he was transferred to assembly. **1931** R. R. KARCH *Printing & Allied Trades* xvii. 166 Thermography is known as 'raised letter' printing, and 'process embossing'. **1948** —— *Graphic Arts Procedure* i. 7 Imitation engraving is known by several names, among which are *raised-letter printing*, *process embossing*. **1935** *Proc. Inst. Production Engineers* XIV. 158 Process and rate department (under chief process engineer). **1948** W. H. SCHUTT *Process Engin.* i. 1 The process engineer must visualize exactly how the article should be made and what equipment, tools, and floor space are required. **1960** *McGraw-Hill Encycl. Sci. & Technol.* X. 642/2 Process specifications are set by process engineers (as distinguished from product engineers) and cover just how processes are to be controlled. **1948** W. H. SCHUTT (*title*) Process engineering. **1980** *Jrnl. R. Soc. Arts* May 326/2 'Design for Production' is a discipline which involves both product and process engineering. **1923** H. A. MADDOX *Printing* x. 126 Process engravers usually adapt their filters to certain ink standards. **1951** R. G. RADFORD *Letterpress Machine Work* II. xii. 127 Discoveries.. have made it possible for the process engraver to make a set of three- or four-colour half-tone plates by photo-mechanical means. **1894** *Amer. Dict. Printing & Bookmaking* 464/1 *Process printing or engraving*, a method by which engravings are made by the aid of photography. **1965** *Listener* 23 Sept. 462/3 The year was 1872, when.. *Punch's* tentative introduction of process engraving first heralded the disappearance of the laborious procedure of reproducing line drawings by wood engraving. **1933** E. MOLLOY *Newnes Engin. Pract.* III. 794/2 The faster the machine.. ran, the greater the amount of steam that would be available for process heat. **1947** O. LYLE *Efficient Use of Steam* xx. 597 The two principal uses of process heat are for the heating of water or watery solutions and for the evaporation of water. **1971** *Materials & Technol.* II. xii. 751 Steam generators which raise steam for process heat operate from 15 to about 150 p.s.i. **1926** S. I. LEVY *Introd. Industr. Chem.* iii. 65 (*heading*) Process heating by steam. **1971** *Materials & Technol.* II. xii. 751 Steam has found considerable employment as a heat carrier for process heating. It can easily be ducted from a boiler to the vessel or column wherein the processes take place. **1951** *Industr. & Engin. Chem.* Dec. 2695 (*heading*) Quality control in the process industries. **1926** Process ink [see *process colour* above]. **1974** J. CRAIG *Production for Graphic Designer* 109 Because process inks are transparent, it is the light reflected from the paper's surface that supplies the light to the ink. **1890** W. J. GORDON *Foundry* xi. 215 Half tints have been the difficulty of all process inventors. **1902** *Encycl. Brit.* XXVI. 558/1 A portable process kettle has made canning possible on the farm. **1902** *Encycl. Brit.* XXXI. 696/2 In the 'Process' lens, Series V. *f*/8, the combination is adjusted to secure identical size and sharpness of each colour-image in three-colour process work. **1961** Process lens [see *colour correction* s.v. COLOUR *sb.*[1] 19]. **1900** *Fortn. Rev.* Jan. 65 Engraving.. as a profession, and as a means of obtaining fame, has entirely died out; the engraver nowadays is a process-maker. **1972** W. P. LEHMANN in *Language* XLVIII. 267, I should like to propose that support for a process model of language has been provided by recent typological studies. *Ibid.* 269 In a process-model grammar of language, nominal modifiers are introduced by embedding. **1977** *Trans. Philol. Soc.* 1975 23 The earliest generative ('process morphophonemic') solution I know of to this problem is that of Bloomfield (1933, §13.9). **1967** C. MICHALSON *Worldly Theol.* i. 19 Daniel Day Williams.. was the first theologian to bring the process motifs into combination with other theological traditions. **1958** *IRE Trans. Industr. Electronics* VII. 23/1 Process operations are characterized by the continuous and cyclic handling of large liquid, gas, and bulk flow streams. **1877** RAYMOND *Statist. Mines & Mining* 3 Both parties.. are.. interested in a favorable result: the ore-owner, because it may lend new value to some hitherto refractory and unprofitable material; the process-owner, because it may enlarge the field of his operations. **1941** W. M. URBAN in P. A. Schilpp *Philos. Whitehead* 319 The general group of modern philosophies which are called process philosophies, philosophies, which, in Bergson's terms, find more of reality in becoming than in that which becomes. **1949** B. M. LOOMER in D. Brown et al. *Process Philos. & Christian Thought* (1971) 76 The second criticism .. runs to the effect that process philosophy, being a kind of naturalism and consequently predisposed in favour of continuity of explanation, neglects the discontinuous qualities of existence. **1960** *Times Lit. Suppl.* 15 Apr. p. xv/2 Dr. Pittenger's Christology seems to be the product of a combination of panentheism, process philosophy, and Christian existentialism. **1971** D. BROWN et al. *Process Philos. & Christian Thought* p. v, In recent years, however, process philosophy has come to mean especially, though not exclusively, the philosophy of Alfred North Whitehead and his intellectual descendants, most notably Charles Hartshorne. **1940** *Jrnl. Soc. Motion Picture Engineers* XXXIV. 252 The origination of a combination of projectors superimposing identical prints of the same background on the screen simultaneously compounded the light delivery of a single machine and therefore greatly expanded the scope of background process photography. **1970** C. C. AMMONDS *Printing: Basic Sci.* x. 158 Correction for two colours in the achromatic lens is adequate for the simpler forms of color photography, but for process photography.. much greater correction is necessary. **1928** C. S. DARLING *Exhaust Steam Engin.* ix. 188 It is.. possible in a process plant to obtain useful heat from the condenser of a turbine. **1894** *Amer. Dict. Printing & Bookmaking* 460/2 A number of photographers and printers.. hope that they can print direct from process plates. **1931** R. R. KARCH *Printing & Allied Trades* xvi. 162 Four-color process plates are used in printing most of the magazine advertisements in color. **1965** ZIGROSSER & GAEHDE *Guide to Collecting Orig. Prints* iv. 71 All prints made by photomechanical methods are called process prints. **1901** *Edin. Rev.* Apr. 551 A few.. were found ready to submit their work to the uncertainties and vagaries of the process-printer. **1931** R. R. KARCH *Printing & Allied Trades* xvi. 161 *Process printing.* By the use of three transparent colors, red, yellow, and blue, illustrations may be printed that contain all the colours of the rainbow. **1962** L. M. LARSEN *Industr. Printing Inks* ii. 33 With the coming of process printing.. it has been necessary to use high color strength inks. **1974** J. CRAIG *Production for Graphic Designer* 105 Four-color process printing is the method used to reproduce full-color continuous-tone copy. **1939** *Jrnl. Soc. Motion Picture Engineers* XXXII. 589 Developments in process projection equipment and technology. **1951** A. CORNWELL-CLYNE *Colour Cinematogr.* (ed. 3) vii. 583 Process projection, called in Britain 'background projection', a somewhat more precise description, assumed great importance economically in ratio to the continuous rise in the cost of film production. *Ibid.*, Process projection, as a technique, was evolved for the purpose of dispensing with the necessity of location photography. **1977** *Times Lit. Suppl.* 29 Apr. 525/3 There are eight steel engravings after Turner, reproduced absolutely facsimile—line for line. This is close to the edge of possibility in process reproduction. **1962** *Psychol. Bull.* LIX. 329/1 Process schizophrenia involves a long-term progressive deterioration.. with little chance of recovery. **1967** HILGARD & ATKINSON *Introd. Psychol.* (ed. 4) xxi. 536/2 They hypothesized that process schizophrenia.. might be caused by some sort of brain damage..; consequently process schizophrenics might respond..in a manner similar to patients with diagnosed brain damage. **1611** SHAKS. *Wint. T.* IV. iii. 102, I know this man well, he hath bene since an Ape-bearer, then a Processe-seruer (a Bayliffe), then [etc.]. **1842** S. C. HALL *Ireland* II. 96 The pioneers of the law, called 'Process-servers'. **1856** LEVER *Martins of Cro' M.* xxxix, Is it rack-renting, process-serving, exterminating, would make them popular? **1935** *Proc. Inst. Production Engineers* XIV. 165 Process sheets are drawn up showing the operations to be performed on each component in their correct sequence. **1953** J. J. ROSE *Amer. Cinematographer Hand-bk. & Ref. Guide* (ed. 8) 150 Process shots have been the means of saving studios considerable production time and expense in filming scenes for pictures having a foreign locale. **1960** K. AMIS *New Maps of Hell* ii. 61 Slow-motion process shots of newts. **1973** D. A. SPENCER *Focal Dict. Photographic Technol.* 492 *Process shot*, studio film shot in which a still or moving background is rear projected on to a translucent screen in front of which the action takes place—also called transparency process. **1924** *Power Engineer* XIX. 454/2 In view of the scattered nature of the works, it is not advantageous to attempt to collect condensed process steam. **1954** E. MOLLOY *Power & Process-Steam Plant* i. 4 Breweries require large amounts of process steam. **1963** A. JAGANMOHAN tr. *Shlyakhin's Steam Turbines* xi. 160/1 Back-pressure turbines are used..where both electrical energy and process steam are required at the same time. **1972** D. A. PAILIN in Cox & Dyson *20th-Cent. Mind* III. iv. 130 Process theism cannot deal adequately with the nature of God's actuality. **1974** M. WILES *Remaking of Christian Doctrine* vi. 110 For the process theologian there is no essential problem about the transcendent God's activity in the world. **1977** *Theology* LXXX. 187 The North American process theologians would say..the world is a dynamic totality of events..and not of things. **1971** D. BROWN et al. *Process Philos. & Christian Thought* p. vi, When process theology is talked about in American (and to some extent British) theological schools today, Bergson, Berdyaev and Teilhard may be in the background, but the work of Whitehead, Hartshorne, Ogden and Cobb is primarily in mind. **1975** *Times Lit. Suppl.* 15 Aug. 926/2 Process theology, in which God is in a state of *becoming*, has been shown to be anything but Christian. **1977** F. YOUNG in J. Hick *Myth of God Incarnate* ii. 42 Evolutionary theology and process theology are not foreign to the Christian tradition. **1977** *Theology* LXXX. 189 There is, in Whitehead, Hartshorne, and other process thinkers, a full recognition of the reality of natural evil as well as of moral evil and man's sinfulness. **1972** D. A. PAILIN in Cox & Dyson *20th-Cent. Mind* III. iv. 123 Charles Hartshorne..has been the leading exponent of the 'process' view of God... Whitehead is the father of process thought. **1966** *McGraw-Hill Encycl. Sci. & Technol.* X. 642/1 Processes have..been classified into continuous or process-type operations, as in an oil refinery, and intermittent (or repetitive) or manufacturing-type operations. **1972** Process view [see *process thought* above]. **1928** *Rep. Water Pollution Res. Board 1927–8* 9 In some factories..alternative methods are employed by which the production of process water is avoided. **1949** G. E. H. LEWIS *Factory Steam Plant* iii. 46 Where process water heating is not feasible the air preheater merits consideration. **1978** *Environmental Conservation: Chemicals* (Shell Internat. Petroleum Co.) 2 This has been achieved mainly by segregating contaminated process water from the usually much larger volume of uncontaminated storm and cooling water, and..by re-using and recycling process water. **1898** *Westm. Gaz.* 2 July 4/2 Printers of fine etchings.., and workers in what is known in the trade as 'process work'. **1924** C. A. SUCKAN *Supervision & Maintenance of Steam-Raising Plant* v. 77 Where steam is used for process work such as boiling. **1908** C. T. JACOBI *Printing* (ed. 4) xxiv. 251 The process worker will have arranged his screens at..angular distances for the respective colours. **1974** *Nature* 15 Feb. 421/1 In England the death of a 71 year-old former process worker at ICI is being investigated in order to establish whether or not it was caused by long exposure to the fumes of the monomer.

ˈprocess (see prec.), *v.*[1] [In sense 1, a. OF. *processer* to prosecute (1240 in Godef.), f. *procès*; in senses 2, 3, f. PROCESS *sb.*]

1. *trans.* To institute a process or action against, to proceed against by law, to sue, prosecute; to obtain a process or summons against (a person); to serve a process on. orig. *Sc.*

1532 *Acc. Ld. High Treas. Scotl.* VI. 111 That sche wald be processit for non payment of hir taxt. **1573** *Reg. Privy Council Scot.* II. 284 Being processit and put to the horne thairfore. **1637–50** ROW *Hist. Kirk* (Wodrow Soc.) 95 John Durie made a large narration how and for what he had bene processed before the King and his Councill. *a* **1674** CLARENDON *Hist. Reb.* x. §65 The Chancellor of Scotland told him..that all England would join against him as one man to process and depose him. **1804** MAR. EDGEWORTH *Ennui* viii, He was at the quarter sessions processing his brother. **1883** V. STUART *Egypt* 137 The debt for which they were processed was made up entirely of interest at most usurious rates.

2. *intr.* To go on, take place: = PROCEED *v.* 5 a. *rare*$^{-1}$.

1835 *Blackw. Mag.* XXXVII. 883 The hollow murmur of the earth in the spring season, which some take to be the sound of vegetation, in its multitudinous forms, processing on her surface.

3. a. *trans.* To subject to or treat by a special process (see prec. 6 c); e.g. to reproduce (a drawing, etc.) by a mechanical or photographic process; to prepare by an artificial or special process; to preserve fruit, fish, flesh, etc., by some process; to operate on (data) (cf. *data processing* s.v. DATUM 3). Also *fig.*

1884 *New York Even. Post* 28 Jan. (Cent.), Every cut in Mr. Pyle's admirable book was processed—to use a new verb invented to fit a new thing. **1889** *Athenæum* 14 Dec. 826/3 The illustrations..appear to have been 'processed' very unskilfully. **1896** *Westm. Gaz.* 24 July 3/3 It is often not made on the premises, but is brewer's yeast imported from England, then processed, and sent back to England. **1902** *Encycl. Brit.* XXVI. 558/1 As a general rule fruits and vegetables are only processed once, meats and fish twice. **1948** A. TOYNBEE *Civilization on Trial* 84 The form in which this culture has been 'processed' for export. **1957** *B.B.C. Handbk.* 47 The News Bureau..selects and processes news and other items of urgent information for transmission by teleprinter to the news departments. **1958** *Newnes Compl. Amat. Photogr.* 283 Pakolor film can be processed by the user. **1959** *Times Lit. Suppl.* 27 Feb. 109/3 Mr. Morgan presents a deliberately narrowed vision of life, where every detail is 'processed' to fit. **1960** E. DELAVENAY *Introd. Machine Translation* 122 Language data are indeed processed not only with translation in mind but with the aim of obtaining the widest and deepest penetration of such facts as the relationships between words. **1968** *Brit. Med. Bull.* XXIV. 189/2 Only data which can be explicitly formulated ..can be processed by a computer. **1968** *Listener* 4 July 17/3 Rock music is the most efficient medium of creative expression. A song can be composed, processed and broadcast round the world in a week. **1970** *Daily Tel.* 20 May 2/4 The heart of the system is a computer which processes radio signals and continually plots the airliner's position on a moving chart. **1971** *Nature* 11 June 344/1 It may take two months for this volume of vaccine to be processed. **1972** *Language* XLVIII. 271 The right hemisphere of the human brain can also process oral symbols for concrete nouns. But only the hemisphere with a specialized speech center can process verbs. **1976** P. HILL *Hunters* v. 43 We're processing the statements that have already been taken.

b. To subject (a person) to a process, as of registration, examination, or analysis. orig. *U.S.*

1935 *Sun* (Baltimore) 16 Apr. 4/1, 900 applicants were put through medical examinations and transported to army camps to be 'processed'. **1945** H. L. MENCKEN *Amer. Lang.* Suppl. I. 417 *To process*, now threatens to take its place in the language alongside *to contact*... The New Dealers gave it a much wider range..widening it to include human beings among its objects. It has since been adopted..both in its older sense of doing something to inanimate materials and in its new sense of mauling and manipulating God's creatures. **1948** D. SOIBELMAN *Therapeutic & Industr. Uses of Music* vi. 132 One physician has reported that, since installing music in his waiting room, he has found the average time taken to process a patient reduced by..one-half. **1954** *Manch. Guardian Weekly* 23 Dec. 15/3 All Chinese students.. including those whose cases are still being processed, are completely free to travel anywhere in the United States. **1959** *Times Lit. Suppl.* 27 Mar. 173/2 Maupassant, Lautrec, Gauguin—one by one the wild boys are being expertly processed, attractively jacketed, to emerge as items suitable for ticking off on library lists. **1977** *Detroit Free Press* 11 Dec. 21-A/2 Officials at the center said 12 victims were processed there.

Hence **ˈprocessed** *ppl. a.* (in sense 3); ***processed cheese*** = *process cheese* s.v. PROCESS *sb.* 13 b; **ˈprocessing** *vbl. sb.*[1] (in senses 1 and 3); also *attrib.*

1606 WOTTON *Lett.* (1907) I. 354 They have there [Rome] newly proposed..the processing of the Duke by way of Inquisition. **1676** W. ROW *Contn. Blair's Autobiog.* xii. (1848) 478 Their processing and deposing of Mr. John Forrest. **1888** *Daily News* 10 Dec. 5/2 This business of processing is killing woodcutting, which will soon probably be a lost art. **1899** *Ibid.* 13 Feb. 5/5 The charges..that 'embalmed' and 'processed' beef had been furnished to the troops in the field in the recent war. **1901** *Nation* (N.Y.) 3 Jan. 2/2 The renovating and processing of butter is carried on all over our country. **1912** *U.S. Dept. Agric. Yearbk. 1911* 387 Processing consists in heating the cans to a sufficiently high temperature to insure the preservation of their contents. **1918** THOM & FISK *Bk. Cheese* vi. 84 *Processed cheeses.* Cheese of any group may be run through mixing and molding machines and re-packaged in very different form from that characteristic of the variety... The possible variations are numerous. **1933** *Sun* (Baltimore) 15 July 1/6 He accordingly proclaimed August 1 as..the date upon which the processing tax should become operative. **1936** *Discovery* May 157/1 A well-prepared wood or esparto paper can be more permanent than a carelessly processed rag paper. **1958** *Newnes Compl. Amat. Photogr.* 280 Use a film for which processing kits are available. **1958** *Times Lit. Suppl.* 29 Aug. 478/4 It is instructive, if unedifying, to follow the tergiversations and admire the polemical acrobatics of various practitioners of the art of literary processing, notably of that arch-processor V. Yermilov. **1960** Processed pea [see *garden-pea* s.v. GARDEN *sb.* 6]. **1964** L. DEIGHTON *Funeral in Berlin* xxxviii. 231 His processed cheese sandwiches. **1966** A. YOUNG in *Spero* I. II. 19 He sat behind me in Homeroom, sportshirt, creased pants, shiny black pointy-toed stetsons, jacket, processed hair. **1972** *Daily Tel.* 29 Apr. 12/1 The fully-automated, processed tourist rarely visits Genoa. **1977** B. PYM *Quartet in Autumn* vii. 63 Fresh vegetables..would be better than processed peas. **1977** J. HEDGECOE *Photographer's Handbk.* 70 (*caption*) Various types of processing drum are made for color prints. **1979** *SLR Camera* Jan. 43/1 The catalogue almost swells at the seams with such goodies as processing drums, colour analysers, printing filters, [etc.].

process (prəʊˈsɛs), *v.*[2] [A colloquial or humorous back-formation from PROCESSION *sb.*, after *progress*, *transgress*, etc.] **1.** *intr.* To go, walk, or march in procession.

1814 J. TRAIN *Mountain Muse* 83 As venerably as when they Process on Dedication day. **1824** LADY GRANVILLE *Lett.* 1 Jan. (1894) I. 243 On Christmas Day we processed into the chapel. **1888** MRS. H. WARD *R. Elsmere* xxxviii, The cassocked monk-like clergy might preach and 'process' in the open air as much as they pleased. **1897** 'IAN MACLAREN' in *British Weekly* 1 Apr. 422/3 So sure of themselves that they do not need to protest nor process, but carry their flag in their heart. **1902** *To-Day* 20 Aug. 113/1 Neither Barnum nor the new Lord Mayor will be able to process this year. **1912** A. HUXLEY *Let.* 23 June (1969) 46 On the Bismarck Tower a bonfire was lighted and 1000 odd students processed from the tower to the University. **1953** H. NICOLSON *Diary* 4 July (1968) 242 We process in robes to the City Hall where there are many graduands. **1962** G. MOORE *Am I too Loud?* xxxiii. 254 The vision of our young and beautiful Queen processing slowly up the aisle in her gorgeous robes is never to be forgotten. **1971** K. THOMAS *Relig. & Decline of Magic* iii. 63 They also involved processing across the field with cross, banners and bells to drive away evil spirits and bless the crops.

2. *trans.* To lead or carry (a person, etc.) in procession; to traverse (an area) in procession.

1959 *Times* 10 Dec. 14/7 The Lord of Miracles is solemnly processed all round the city. **1968** D. M. SMITH *Mod. Sicily* lii. 484 The flagellants then processed the streets as they had done in 1647 and 1773. **1974** D. AVERY *Not on Queen Victoria's Birthday* vii. 117 Most of the families left their feasting to attend the sermon in the church under the impression that the saint was to be processed afterwards.

Hence **proˈcessing** *vbl. sb.*[2] and *ppl. a.*

1920 *Blackw. Mag.* Dec. 712/2 The bowings and curtseyings and processings and workings of the Puddispor congregation could have told anybody *that!* **1959** *Antiquity* XXXIII. 19 A single row of processing animals. **1977** *Gramophone* May 1724/2 So we must be prepared for..the shuffling of processing feet, the coughing and the tramping of the congregation.

processable (ˈprəʊsɪsəb(ə)l), *a.* [f. PROCESS *v.*[1] + -ABLE.] That can be processed. Hence **ˌprocessaˈbility**, the capacity to be processed.

1956 *Industr. & Engin. Chem.* May 930/1 Processing studies of Adiprene B urethane rubber have resulted in an understanding of a number of the factors required for processability. *Ibid.* 932/1 They become progressively tougher and more viscous while remaining 'processable' even in an advanced state of scorch. **1965** J. R. SCOTT *Physical Testing of Rubbers* ii. 45 Examples of this empirical approach to the problems of measuring processability are the procedures developed in the U.S.A. for the wartime synthetic rubber program. **1967** COX & GROSE *Organiz. Bibliogr. Rec. by Computer* VII. 183 This may help us in problems of transmission of machine processable cataloguing data. **1971** P. M. HUBBARD *High Tide* ii. 24, I was a sort of raw material, which had not proved as processable as they had hoped.

proˈcessal, *a. rare.* [f. PROCESS *sb.* + -AL[1]. Cf. PROCESSUAL.] Pertaining to a legal process.

c **1645** HOWELL *Lett.* (1650) I. 124 All sorts of damages, and processal charges, come to about 250,000 crowns. **1892** J. JACOBS *Howell's Lett.* I. p. xxxiv, Counting principal and interest and processal charges.

†**ˈprocessar**. *Obs. rare*$^{-1}$. [f. PROCESS *v.*[2] + -AR[3].] ? A process-server.

1534 in *Hist. Fortescues* (1869) II. 204 Item, gevyn to the processar, to stay all the accions *v.li.*

processer, var. PROCESSOR.

procession (prəʊˈsɛʃən), *sb.* Also 2–4 -iun, (4 -iune), 3–5 -ioun, (4–5 -ioune), 3–6 -yon, 4–6 -ione, 5 -yone, -youn, -iowne; 4 procesioun, -sesioun, -scession, -sessyoun, (5 -yon, 6 -ion), 5 -cescion, 6 -ssession. [Early ME. a. F. *procession* (11th c. in Hatz.-Darm.), ad. L. *prōcessiōnem* a marching onwards, advance, in late and med.L. a religious procession, n. of action f. *prōcēdĕre* to PROCEED.] The action of proceeding.

1. a. The action of a body of persons going or marching along in orderly succession, in a formal or ceremonial way; esp. as a religious ceremony, or on a festive occasion.

1103–23 *O.E. Chron.* an. 1103, Æfter sancte Michaeles mæssan on .xii. Kal. Nov' he wæs mid procession under fangan to abbote. **1154** *Ibid.* an. 1154, Was under fangen mid micel wurtscipe at Burch mid micel processiun. *c* **1200** *Trin. Coll. Hom.* 91 Nime was þenne ȝeme ȝif ure procession bi maked after ure helendes procession. *c* **1290** *S. Eng. Leg.* I. 15/471 A-doun of þe hulle wende þe Aumperour with fair processioun. **1297** R. GLOUC. (Rolls) 8368 Massen & processions hii made monion. **13..** *Sir Beues* (A.) 2732 And brouȝte Beues in to þe toun Wiþ a faire prosesioun. **1568** GRAFTON *Chron.* II. 387 The King [Rich. II]..forbad streyghtly all Bishoppes and Prelates that such Processions shoulde be no more vsed. **1613** PURCHAS *Pilgrimage* (1614) 62 When they would haue raine, ten Virgins clothed in hallowed garments of red colour, danced a procession. **1704** NELSON *Fest. & Fasts* vi. (1739) 515 At the Reformation, when all Processions were abolished. **1871** R. ELLIS *Catullus* xvii. 6 Passive under a Salian god's most lusty procession. **1904** W. M. RAMSAY *Lett. to Seven Ch.* xiii. 160 After the analogy of a religious procession on the occasion of a festival.

b. Phr. *to go, walk* (etc.) *in procession*; †formerly also *on, to, with procession*; *to go* (*a*) *procession*.

c **1175** *Lamb. Hom.* 5 Al þat folc eode þar forð to processiun to munte oliueti. *c* **1200** *Trin. Coll. Hom.* 89 Dominica Palmarum. It is custume þat ech chirchsocne goð þis dai a procession. **1389** in *Eng. Gilds* (1870) 19 For to gone with processioun wt her candel. **14..** in *Hist. Coll. Citizen London* (Camden) 162 The kyng and the quene..wentt on processyon through London. **1466** in *Archæologia* (1887) L. I. 49 Also he [the sexton] shall bere the crosse on procession. **1560** DAUS tr. *Sleidane's Comm.* 415 The French men..go a procession about all the Churches in Metz. **1582** N. LICHEFIELD tr. *Castanheda's Conq. E. Ind.* I. ii. 5 All the religious men..went in Procession bare footed, and in their cowles with waxe Candles in their hands. **1662** *Virginia Stat.* (1823) II. 102 Within twelve months after this act, all the inhabitants of every neck and tract of land adjoining shall goe in procession and see the marked trees of every mans land..to be renewed. **1693** DRYDEN *Juvenal* xvi. Notes (1697) 391 As we go once a Year in Procession, about the Bounds of Parishes, and renew them. **1849** MACAULAY *Hist. Eng.* vi. II. 29 The Commons went in procession to Whitehall with their address on the subject of the test.

c. *transf.* Of boats, barges, etc. (See also quot. 1937.)

(At Oxford, 'a Procession of Boats' over the rowing course on the Thames formerly took place annually in Commemoration Week. Described, but not under this name, in *Jackson's Oxf. Jrnl.* of 15 June 1839.)

1843 *Jackson's Oxford Jrnl.* 1 July 3/1 In the evening [of Tuesday 27 June] thousands of persons were congregated on the banks of the river to witness the procession of the racing boats. *Ibid.*, After the procession had ceased a splendid display of fireworks took place. **1893** *President's Bk. Oxf. Univ. Boat-Cl.*, The Procession of Boats took place on Monday June 19. **1893** *Secretary's Bk.* ibid. Oct., The Procession of Boats was abolished unanimously. **1900** W. E. SHERWOOD *Oxford Rowing* xi. 98. **1902** *Daily Chron.* 10 July 5/2 At the half-mile London were leading by fully three lengths, and from Fawley it was simply a procession, the London pair winning anyhow. **1937** PARTRIDGE *Dict. Slang* 661/1 *Procession*, as applied to a race, esp. a boat-race (above all, one in which there are only two crews), implies 'an ignominious defeat'. **1958** *Times* 22 Sept. 14/2 Although she [*sc.* the British yacht] made up half a minute..it was obvious that..it could not now be anything more than a procession.

d. *Cricket.* A rapid succession of batsmen; a batting collapse.

1891 W. G. GRACE *Cricket* iii. 76 West Gloucestershire [scored] 6 only. Only nine overs were bowled, and it was a most inglorious procession. **1927** M. A. NOBLE *Those 'Ashes'* 210 The Civil Service first innings was almost a procession. They were able to make only 59. **1977** *Times* 17 Jan. 7/1 The Australian procession started when Turner was caught by Majid off Sarfraz for 11.

2. *concr.* **a.** A body of persons marching in this way.

13.. *E.E. Allit. P.* A. 1095 Sodanly on a wonder wyse, I watz war of a prosessyoun. **1451** CAPGRAVE *Life St. Gilbert* (E.E.T.S.) 105 In þis mene-while þe procession went fro þe hous. **1696** TATE & BRADY *Ps.* lxviii. 27 Zebulon..And Nephthali..(The grand Procession to compleat) Sent up their Tribes, a Princely Host. **1705** ADDISON *Italy* 195 (*Naples*) My First Days at Naples were taken up with the Sight of Processions. **1866** NEALE *Seq. & Hymns* 131 Again shall long processions sweep through Lincoln's Minster pile.

b. *transf.* and *fig.* A regular series, sequence, row, or succession of things, such as suggests an orderly march.

1688 R. HOLME *Armoury* III. viii. (Contents), In the second plate of this chapter is..a further Procession of Tradesmens Tools. **1878** BOSW. SMITH *Carthage* 13 The majestic procession of stately aqueducts which no barbarism has been able to destroy.

3. *transf.* **a.** A litany, form of prayer, or office, said or sung in a religious procession. *Obs.* exc. *Hist.*

1543 in Strype *Eccl. Mem.* (1721) I. I. 384 Being resolved to have continually..general processions..said and sung with such devotion & reverence as appertaineth. **1560** DAUS tr. *Sleidane's Comm.* 433 By the kyng her fathers commaundement procession was sayde in the vulgare tongue. **1594** *1st Pt. Contention* (Shaks. Soc.) 62 Come let vs hast to London now with speed, That solemne prosessions may be sung. **1616** *Marlowe's Faust.* III. i. Wks. (Rtldg.) 119/1 (*Stage Direct.*) Monks and Friars, singing their procession. **1904** A. F. POLLARD *Cranmer* vi. 172 *note*, The use of litanies had early grown up in the Western Church and from the fact that they were sung in procession they were often themselves called processions.

†**b.** A book of such offices; a processional.

1540 *Knaresborough Wills* I. 34 To by a processione and other ornamentes to ye said church necessaries iijs. iiijd.

4. The action of proceeding, issuing, or coming forth from a source; emanation. Chiefly *Theol.* in reference to the Holy Spirit (cf. FILIOQUE).

1398 TREVISA *Barth. De P.R.* XIX. cxviii. (Add. MS.), By procession þe holy gost comeþ of þe fader and of þe sone. *c* **1440** CAPGRAVE *Life St. Kath.* IV. 2299 After thei had spoken..of the hooly goost and his procession. **1605** A. WOTTON *Answ. Pop. Articles* 56 It is absolutely taketh away the nature of a sonne, and consequently the admirable procession of the second person. **1639** FULLER *Holy War* IV. v. (1840) 183 The Greeks..maintain the procession of the Holy Spirit from the Father alone. **1699** BURNET 39 *Art.* viii. (1700) 106 The Article of the Procession of the Holy Ghost, and all that follows it, is not in the Nicene Creed. **1725** tr. *Dupin's Eccl. Hist. 17th C.* I. VI. v. 253 The Procession and Mission of the Holy Spirit are nothing, according to him [Servetus], but the Action of God, by which he acts on his Creatures. **1865** PUSEY *Truth Eng. Ch.* 263 As the Council of Florence states, the Greek and Latin Fathers, though using different language, meant the same as to the Procession of God the Holy Ghost. **1907** J. R. ILLINGWORTH *Doctr. Trinity* i. 16 The doctrine of the Trinity..confessedly underwent development,..by the adoption..of such terms as substance,..circuminsession, double procession.

5. The action of proceeding, going on, or advancing; onward movement, progress, progression, advance.

a. *lit.* ? *Obs.* or merged in 1.

1607 WALKINGTON *Opt. Glass* 102 There is a double procession or way of choler. **1615** G. SANDYS *Trav.* 245 The women in large Carosses, being drawne with the slowest procession. *a* **1763** SHENSTONE *Elegies* xxiv. 72 And hail the bright procession of the sun.

b. *fig.* Now *rare.*

1585 T. WASHINGTON tr. *Nicholay's Voy.* I. x. 12 b, Of the further procession of our Nauigation. **1663** COWLEY *Pindar. Odes, Isa. xxxiv.* Notes, The motion of the Spirit of God, for it is a Procession of his will to an outward Effect. **1795–1814** WORDSW. *Excursion* IV. 13 An assured belief That the procession of our fate..is ordered by a Being Of infinite benevolence and power. **1875** LEWES *Probl. Life & Mind* I. ii. 393 The flash is antecedent to the sound of the explosion, but the flash is not the cause of the sound; it has no procession in the sound.

6. *attrib.* and *Comb.*, as ***procession-aisle, -gadding, -man, -pace, -road, -way***; ***procession-wise*** adv.; **procession caterpillar, moth** (PROCESSIONARY *a.* 2); **procession-day**, a day on which a procession is made; *spec.* (*pl.*) the Rogation days (= GANG-DAYS); **procession-flower**, a name for the common milkwort (*Polygala vulgaris*), from its blossoming about Rogation week and being worn by persons taking part in the processions (cf. GANG-FLOWER); **Procession-week**, a name for Rogation week, from the processions then made (= GANG-WEEK).

1856 *Ecclesiologist* XVII. 89 The choir-screens facing the *procession-aisle are beautifully treated. **1850** *Chamb. Jrnl.* 25 May 327/1 Interesting communications..concerning the *procession-caterpillar (*Bombyx processionea*, Linn.). **1660** R. COKE *Power & Subj.* 157 If a man accuse another of any crime, let him make him recompence, unless he did it upon *Procession-days. **1668** PEPYS *Diary* 30 Apr., To the Dolphin tavern, there to meet our neighbours,..this being Procession-day. **1633** *Gerarde's Herbal* II. clxix. 564 Milkewort is called by Dodonæus, *Flos Ambarualis*; so called because it doth especially flourish in the Crosse or Gang weeke, or Rogation weeke; of which floures the maidens which vse in the countries to walke the Procession doe make themselues garlands and nosegaies: in English we may call it Crosse-floure, *Procession-floure, Gang-floure, Rogation-floure, and Milkewort. *a* **1555** G. MARSH in Foxe *A. & M.* (1583) 1565/1 Holy water casting, *procession gadding, Mattins mumbling. **1837** DICKENS *Pickw.* iii, What a host of shabby, poverty-stricken men hang about the stage of a large establishment—not regularly engaged actors, but ballet people, *procession men, tumblers, and so forth. **1816** KIRBY & SP. *Entomol.* iv. (1818) I. 131 The *procession moth (*B. processionea*, L.) of which Reaumur has given so interesting an account. *Ibid.* xvi. II. 8 The larvæ..live in society and emigrate in files, like the caterpillar of the procession-moth. **1652** EVELYN *Diary* 23 June, Within three miles of Bromley, at a place call'd the *Procession Oake. **1755** SMOLLETT *Quix.* (1803) IV. 4 The twelve duennas and their lady advanced at a *procession-pace, their faces covered with white veils. **1466** in *Archæologia* (1887) L. I. 51 Thei shal..suffer no grave nor pitte to be made in the *procession way. **1546–7** in Swayne *Sarum Churchw. Acc.* (1896) 274 Payed in the *procession weke to the baner bearers and bell ryngers. **1570** B. GOOGE *Popish Kingd.* IV. (1880) 53 (*margin*) Procession weeke. Bounds are beaten. **1599** HAKLUYT *Voy.* II. I. 56 A great company of virgins go *procession-wise two and two in a rank singing before him.

pro'cession, *v.* [f. prec. sb. So med.L. *prōcessiōnāre* (Du Cange).]

1. *trans.* To honour or celebrate by a procession; to carry in procession.

1546 BALE *Eng. Votaries* I. (1550) 72 b, Whan theyr feastfull dayes come, they [saints] are yet in the papystyck churches of Englande, with no small solempnite mattensed, massed, candeled, lyghted, processyoned..and worshypped. **1837** CARLYLE *Fr. Rev.* II. III. vii, Jean Jacques too.. must be dug up from Ermenonville, and processioned, with pomp,..to the Pantheon of the Fatherland.

2. *intr.* To make a procession, religious or other; to go in procession. (See also PROCESSIONING.)

1691 tr. *Emilianne's Frauds Rom. Monks* (ed. 3) 362 To go a Processioning with great Crosses of Wood upon their Shoulders. **1802** MRS. RADCLIFFE *Gaston de Blondeville* Posth. Wks. 1826 I. 89 As he turned out of the gate, he met the Prior..and a long train processioning, all in full ceremony, bearing precious reliques, to welcome his Highness. **1859** TROLLOPE *West Indies* xviii. (1860) 268 The whole town was processioning from morning..till evening.

b. *spec.* To perambulate the bounds.

1671 WOOD *Life* (O.H.S.) II. 223 June 1. Holy thursday, St. Peter's [in the East] parishioners came a processioning and took in half Alban hall. **1723–4** *Bristol* (*Virginia*) *Parish Vestry Bk.* (1898) 15 It is ordered that Godfry Fowler Junr and Mark Moon procession from Nooning Creek to the Extent of the Parish.

3. *trans.* To go round (something) in procession; *spec.* in some of the N. American colonies (and still in the states of N. Carolina and Tennessee), to make a procession around a piece of land in order formally to determine its bounds (with the land, or bounds, as obj.): = PERAMBULATE *v.* 2 b. Also to walk along (a street, etc.) in procession.

1710 *Acts Assembly Virginia* (1759) 292 The bounds of every persons land shall be processioned or gone round, and the landmarks renewed..such processioning shall be made in every precinct. **1727** *Bristol* (*Virginia*) *Parish Vestry Bk.* (1898) 34 To procession lands on the South Side Bristoll parrish. **1883** E. INGLE in *Johns Hopkins Hist. Studies* Ser. III. II. (1885) 64 Once in every four years the vestry, by order of the county court, divided the parish into precincts, and appointed two persons in each precinct to 'procession' the lands. **1887** *Pall Mall G.* 25 Oct. 4/1 Meetings of the unemployed were held yesterday in Trafalgar-square, and certain streets of the West-end were processioned by the crowd, with a red flag at their head.

†**processio'nade.** *Obs. rare.* [f. PROCESSION *sb.* + -ADE.] **a.** An epic of a procession. *nonce-use.* **b.** A ceremonial procession.

1745 (*title*) The Processionade, in Panegyri-Satiri-Serio-Comi-Baladical Versicles, by Porcupinus Pelagius. **1762** CHURCHILL *Ghost* III. 1179 Proclaim a Grand Processionade—Be all the City Pomp display'd. **1809** in *Spirit Pub. Jrnls.* XIII. 183 If you could transpose Hamlet into a comic opera, with an oriental processionade.

processional (prəʊˈsɛʃənəl), *sb.* [= F. *processional* (1563 in Hatz.-Darm.), ad. med.L. *prōcessiōnāle*, neut. of *prōcessiōnālis* adj.: see next.]

1. *Eccl.* An office-book containing litanies, hymns, etc., for use in religious processions.

14.. *Voc.* in Wr.-Wülcker 605/8 *Processionale*, a processional. **1537** in Glasscock *Rec. St. Michael's Bp. Stortford* (1882) 127 Item v processionals in paper and ij parchement masbooks. **1549** *Act 3 & 4 Edw. VI*, c. 10 § 1 All Books called..Grailes, Processionals,..Pies..shall be..abolished. **1571** GRINDAL *Injunctions* B iv, That the Churchwardens and Minister shall see, that..Processionals ..be vtterly defaced, rent, and abolished. *a* **1646** J. GREGORY *Posthuma* (1650) 96 A Circumstance of the Chapter directed mee to their Processional. **1846** MASKELL *Mon. Rit.* I. p. cxiii, The printed Processionals of Sarum or York Use would, in one important respect, vary from the earlier MSS.

b. A processional hymn: see the adj.

1884 *Pall Mall G.* 24 June, The 48th Psalm was sung as a processional. **1896** H. HOUSMAN *John Ellerton* iv. 71 It was for this book that Mr. Ellerton wrote his spirited processional: 'Onward, brothers, onward!' **1898** *Westm. Gaz.* 8 Mar. 6/2 The processional was 'Blessed City, Heavenly Salem'.

¶**2.** (*erron.*) A procession.

1882–3 *Schaff's Encycl. Relig. Knowl.* II. 1324 Pelagius I. in 555, after the litany was said in a certain church in Rome, had a processional from there to St. Peter's. **1902** *Munsey's Mag.* XXVI. 621 By some strange chance I stood where streams The long processional of dreams.

pro'cessional, *a.* [= OF. *processional* (1472 in Godef. *Compl.*, mod.F. *-ionnel*), ad. med.L. *prōcessiōnāl-is* (*p. crux*, Ademar *a* 1030): see PROCESSION *sb.* and -AL[1].] **a.** Of, pertaining to, or of the nature of a procession; characterized by processions. Of a hymn, psalm, litany, etc.: sung or recited in procession, e.g. by the clergy and choir in proceeding from the vestry to the chancel at the opening of a service: cf. RECESSIONAL.

1611 COTGR., *Processional*, processionall; belonging to, seruing for, a procession. **1656** BLOUNT *Glossogr.*, *Processional*, pertaining to process or proceeding. **1686** J. S[ERGEANT] *Hist. Monast. Convent.* 184 This done, he was carried in the usual processional manner, to the Benediction Hall. **1827** *Gentl. Mag.* XCVII. II. 14 His immediate successor, Cardinal Henry, had the same processional taste. **1830** CHALMERS in Hanna *Mem.* (1851) III. xiv. 280 We entered in processional order. **1877** A. B. EDWARDS *Up Nile* vii. 186 The ceremonial of Egyptian worship was essentially processional.

b. Used or carried in processions. Also, traversed by a procession or processions.

1846 LANDOR *Imag. Conv., Alfieri & Salomon* Wks. I. 191/1 The Cristo Bianco and Cristo Nero of the Neapolitan rabble..two processional idols,..which are regularly carried home with broken heads. **1859** JEPHSON *Brittany* xvi. 271 After Vespers the choir, preceded by a processional cross, walked down the nave. **1895** MRS. B. M. CROKER *Village Tales* (1896) 80 The great processional elephant..had a superb cloth-of-gold canopy. **1906** H. BEGBIE *Priest* viii. 124 The sound of a heavy step approaching from the processional aisle on the south caught her ear. **1942** *Country Life* 9 Oct. 695/1 (*caption*) Processional way to Buckingham Palace from Victoria Station. **1973** *Times* 15 Oct. 4 Thieves broke into St Albans Abbey, Hertfordshire, on Saturday night and stole..the silver gilt top of a processional cross.

c. Walking or going in procession; forming a procession (*lit.* and *fig.*); *humorously*, forming a long series or 'string' (e.g. of words). ***processional caterpillar***: see PROCESSIONARY *a.* 2.

1855 BROWNING *Fra Lippo* 118 Which gentleman processional and fine, Holding a candle to the Sacrament, Will wink and let him lift a plate and catch The droppings of the wax to sell again. **1861** L. L. NOBLE *Icebergs* 175 Long processional lines of broken ice. **1891** *Pall Mall G.* 28 Dec. 6/1 Processional caterpillars, ants of various sizes and sorts, mantises, mason bees, carpenter bees, and such small fry. **1905** J. ORR *Problem O.T.* vii. 206 These processional Js and Es, however, should not be scoffed at as arbitrary.

pro'cessionalist. *nonce-wd.* [f. prec. + -IST.] = PROCESSIONIST.

1780 T. DAVIES *Mem. Garrick* (1781) I. xxix. 337 The stage..amidst the parading of dukes, dutchesses, archbishops, peeresses, heralds, &c., was covered with a thick fog from the smoke of the fire, which served to hide the tawdry dresses of the processionalists.

processionally (prəʊˈsɛʃənəlɪ), *adv.* [f. as prec. + -LY[2]: in ME. directly after med.L. adv.] In a processional manner; in procession.

1432–50 tr. *Higden* (Rolls) VII. 203 That person, whom he mette in a certeyne place of the cite commynge processionally [*orig.* processionaliter] in the ny3hte. **1447** BOKENHAM *Seyntys* (Roxb.) 293 The bisshope & she wyth a grett cumpany Them ageynys wentyn processyonelly. **1651** *Life Father Sarpi* (1676) 100 Processionally the Father Prior accompanied with all the rest (with Torches in their hands) brought him the holy Sacrament. **1728** NORTH *Mem. Music* (1846) 54 In times of calamity the Letanys were sung processionally about the streets of great citty's in divers choruses. **1837** CARLYLE *Fr. Rev.* I. III. ix, Necker's Portrait ..is borne processionally, aloft on a perch, with huzzas. **1851** G. B. PAGANI *Life of Rev. A. Gentili* III. ix. 190 Father Gentili commenced the custom of going processionally on Sundays and singing the Litany of the Holy Name of Jesus, from the chapel at Gracedieu all the way to Osgothorpe. **1895** 'MARK TWAIN' in *N. Amer. Rev.* July 10 There were now three bullets in that one hole—three bullets imbedded processionally. **1936** G. B. SHAW *Simpleton* II. 59 (*stage *directions)* Kanchin and Janga enter processionally, reading newspapers. **1960** R. W. Marks *Dymaxion World of B. Fuller* 8/1 In Fuller's special argot, however, 'regenerative' means 'multi-orbital, cyclic, processionally concentric'—a definition which itself requires definition.

processionary (prəʊˈsɛʃənərɪ), *sb.* [ad. med.L. *prōcessiōnāri-um*, orig. neut. of **prōcessiōnāri-us* adj.: see next. So OF. *proucessionnaire* (1328).]

†**1.** = processional *sb.* 1. *Obs.*

1466 in *Archæologia* (1887) L. I. 37 Item j processionary wryttyn in þe ij^de lefe, Exorsiso te. **1483** *Cath. Angl.* 292/1 A Processionary, *processeonarium, processionale.* c **1544** in *Shropsh. Parish Documents* (1903) 53 Item, bookes in the Church: j mass books, j portehowse, j manuell, j processionaries.

2. *U.S.* = processioner 4. (*Cent. Dict.*)

pro'cessionary, *a.* [f. med.L. type **prōcessiōnāri-us*: see procession *sb.* and -ary[1]. So F. *processionnaire* (16–17th c. in Hatz.-Darm.).]

1. = processional *a.* ? *Obs.* exc. as in 2.

1597 Hooker *Eccl. Pol.* v. xli. §2 Decreed, that the whole Church should bestow yeerely at the feast of Pentecost three dayes in that kind of processionarie seruice. **1664** H. More *Myst. Iniq.* 333 The Pagans in their superstitious and idolatrous Processionary pomps carried the Images of their Gods. **1703** Maundrell *Journ. Jerus.* (1721) 71 With Tapers and Crucifixes, and other processionary solemnities.

2. *Entom.* Applied to caterpillars which go in procession; esp. those of the moth *Cnethocampa processionea*; hence, ***processionary moth*** applied to this species.

1765 *Projects* in *Ann. Reg.* 140/2 M. de Reaumur ranks this species of caterpillars amongst those which are called processionary, from their marching from one place to another, in large bodies..and in great order. **1816** Kirby & Sp. *Entomol.* xvi. (1818) II. 23 A still more singular and pleasing spectacle, when their regiments march out to forage, is exhibited by the Processionary Bombyx. **1861** Hulme tr. *Moquin-Tandon* II. iv. i. 234 Studying the habits of the Processionary Moth.

processioner (prəʊˈsɛʃənə(r)). Also 5 **-yonar(e.** [f. procession + -er; so OF. *processionnier* (book, c 1469 in Godef.).]

1. A person going in procession. ? *Obs.*

1426 Lydg. *De Guil. Pilgr.* 17914 Wherfore, befull [it] is to frerys, sythe they be no processionerys, to get theyr lyvelode wher they may. **1612** Shelton *Quix.* iv. xxv. (1896) II. 279 The Processioners returning into their former order, did prosecute their way. a **1739** Jarvis *Quix.* iv. xxv, The processioners seeing them running towards them.

†**2. a.** *Eccl.* An office-book used in processions: = processional *sb.* 1. *Obs.*

14.. *Nom.* in Wr.-Wülcker 720/1 *Hoc processionale,* a processyonar. c **1440** *Promp. Parv.* 414/2 Processyonal, or pr[oc]essyonare. **1542** in *Archæologia* (1887) L. I. 46 Item v. processioners written and iij prynted. **1558** in *Sussex Archæol. Coll.* XLI. 41, ij masse bokes, one pressessyner. **1566** in Peacock *Eng. Ch. Furniture* (1866) 32 The mass bookes, the processioners, the manuell, and all such peltrei of the popes sinfull service.

b. A processional (candlestick). *Obs.*

1466 *Will of Mortymer* (Somerset Ho.), Par candelabrorum de laton vocat. le precessionars.

3. A processionary caterpillar.

1743 Zollman in *Phil. Trans.* XLII. 458 They may be ranked among the Processioners, or those that follow one another.

4. *U.S.* (See quots., and cf. procession *v.* 3.)

1731 *Bristol Parish* (Va.) *Vestry Bk.* (1898) 59 Order'd that George Tucker be Prosessioner in the Stead of Robert Tucker junr who is Lame and cannott Officiate as prosessioner. **1795** in L. P. Summers *Ann. Southwest Va.* (1929) 463 The said Processioners to examine their business the first day of February next. **1828** W. Bolling in *Va. Mag. Hist. & Biogr.* (1938) XLVI. 321 Attended the processioners around my lines..to the upper line between Dr. Watkins and myself. **1860** Bartlett *Dict. Amer.*, *Processioner*, an officer in Kentucky, and possibly in other States, whose duty it is to determine and mark out the bounds of lands. **1864** Webster, *Processioner*..2. An officer appointed to procession lands. (*Local in North Carolina and Tennessee.*) *Burrill.* **1890** in *Cent. Dict.*

processioning (prəʊˈsɛʃənɪŋ), *vbl. sb.* [f. procession *sb.* or *v.* + -ing[1].] The action of going in procession.

1593 Nashe *Christ's T.* (1613) 57 You Pilgrims..weare the plants of your feete,..by bare-legd processioning..to the Sepulchre. **1769** Colman *Man & Wife* i. Dram. Wks. 1787 II. 240 There is eating and drinking, and processioning, and masquerading, and horse-racing, and fire-works—So gay—and as merry as the day is long. **1837** Carlyle *Fr. Rev.* III. iv. iv, Next are processionings along the Boulevards. **1884** *Manch. Exam.* 18 June 4/6 No harm in allowing cyclists to pass through Victoria Park,..on condition that they did not there engage in racing or processioning.

b. *spec.* = perambulation 3; esp. in N. America: see procession *v.* 3.

1710 [see procession *v.* 3]. **1893** Blomfield *Hist. Fritwell* 21 The ceremony of perambulating the boundaries of a parish ('processioning', as it was commonly called in later times) is an extremely old one. **1896** P. A. Bruce *Econ. Hist. Virginia* I. 544 In case an altercation arose between two neighbors in the course of the processioning, as to the boundaries of their estates, the two surveyors..were required..to draw again the lines in dispute.

attrib. **1663** Wood *Life* (O.H.S.) I. 510 The parishioners ..made their processioning cross [upon a wall].

processionist (prəʊˈsɛʃənɪst). [f. procession *sb.* + -ist.] One who goes in a procession.

1824 *Blackw. Mag.* XV. 682 The most blushless of the processionists, the most fawning of the addressers. **1854** H. Miller *Sch. & Schm.* xxiv. (1857) 535 The processionists had a noble dinner in the head inn. **1889** *Sat. Rev.* 16 Mar. 305/2 Mr. Booth's processionists and preachers.

pro'cessionize, *v.* [f. as prec. + -ize.] *intr.* To go in procession.

1774 *Westm. Mag.* II. 489 Triumphant carrs shall roll, and minstrels play; We can processionize as well as they. **1862** *Sat. Rev.* 6 Sept. 277 Eighteen of the incorporated companies processionized in all their bravery. **1884** *Ibid.* 30 Aug. 270/1 The liberty of processionizing is not..as sacred as the liberty of prophesying.

processive (prəʊˈsɛsɪv), *a. rare.* [In sense 1, ad. F. *processif, -ive* litigious. In sense 2, f. L. *prōcess-*, ppl. stem of *prōcēdĕre* to proceed: cf. med.L. *processīv-us* (a 1250 in Albertus Magnus).]

†**1.** Of the nature of a process or summons (see process *sb.* 7 b); serving to initiate legal proceedings. *Obs.*

1622 Mabbe tr. *Aleman's Guzman d'Alf* ii. 242 They fell to Law about it, whose bills, and answers, together with other writings, processiue, justificatiue..and infinite other the like..came to [etc.].

2. Having the quality of proceeding or going forward; progressive.

1819 Coleridge in *Lit. Rem.* (1836) II. 378 There can be no galaxy in poetry, because it is language, ergo processive —ergo every the smallest star must be seen singly. **1850** Mrs. Browning *Seraphim* ii. 499 His own Processive harmony..Is sweeping in a choral triumph by. **1866** *Reader* 20 Oct. 880 Recognise in its processive and changing phases the varied animal forms, rising higher and still higher in the complexity of their structure up to the advent of Man himself.

processor (ˈprəʊsɛsə(r), *U.S.* ˈprɒs-). Also **processer.** [f. process *sb.* + -or.] **a.** A person who performs a process. **b.** A machine or system which performs a process. Cf. *microprocessor* s.v. micro- 1.

1909 M. B. Saunders *Litany Lane* ii. 10 Her tragic face.. was already being 'blocked' for the night's press in many a rushing 'processor's' den. **1934** *Planning* I. xx. 5 Various industries handling agricultural products between the first processor and the consumer have recently been turned over to the N R A. **1948** *Times* 2 Mar. 2/3 [The] film processor ..was sentenced to 21 months' imprisonment. **1959** *Times* 9 Mar. (Britain's Food Suppl.) p. xviii/1 Processors of Vegetable Oils for the Biscuit and Margarine Industries. **1960** *Farmer & Stockbreeder* 5 Jan. 53/2 It would provide the foundation on which producers and processers could develop quality and reduce costs. **1962** *Times* 9 Oct. (Uganda Suppl.) p. v/4 African processers have invested considerable sums in permanent salting vats. **1977** *New Yorker* 29 Aug. 62/2 Any program that runs on the system can access any information physically accessible to the (central) processor. **1978** *Homes & Gardens* Oct. 140/1 Food processors, or kitchen machines..are food choppers and slicers with some abilities at mixing.

processual (prəʊˈsɛsjuːəl), *a.* [ad. L. type **prōcessuāl-is*, f. *prōcessu-s* (*u*-stem) process *sb.*: see -al[1].] **a.** *Roman Law.* Pertaining to a legal process.

1875 Poste *Gaius* iii. Comm. (ed. 2) 401 The principal function of the Adstipulator..seems to have been processual agency. **1880** Muirhead *Gaius* iii. §180 *note*, These two pars. deal with what has been called necessary or processual novation, in contradistinction to the voluntary or conventional novation described in those immediately preceding.

b. Pertaining to a social or linguistic process.

1957 R. K. Merton *Social Theory* (rev. ed.) ix. 316 An instructive processual analysis of the formation of sub-groups. **1958** Willey & Phillips *Method & Theory in Amer. Anthropol.* 5 In the context of archaeology, processual interpretation is the study of the nature of what is vaguely referred to as the culture-historical process... It implies an attempt to discover regularities in the relationships given by the methods of culture-historical integration. **1960** *Amer. Anthropologist* LXII. 19 How processual analysis might be more systematically related to structural analysis. **1970** *Antiquity* XLIV. 28/1 In both these works..historical activities tend to be viewed as being essentially descriptive, while the ultimate aims of archaeology are characterized as being processual, that is to say, concerned with the formulation of general rules of cultural behaviour. **1971** [see process *sb.* 5 b]. **1977** *Word* 1972 XXVIII. 295 Since understanding sentences, and generating others, in the language described implies constant switches from process to system and from system to process..he will have to find the most reasonable compromise between the requirements of systematic and processual simplicity.

‖**processus** (prəʊˈsɛsəs). [L. *prōcessus* a going forward, advance, also a projection, process.]

1. *Anat.* = process *sb.* 12. *Obs.* exc. as mod.L.

1653 H. More *Antid. Ath.* ii. xii. §3 (1712) 80 The *Tunica Arachnoides*..by virtue of its *Processus Ciliares* can thrust forward or draw back that part of the Eye. **1664** Evelyn tr. *Freart's Archit.* 126 Like the *processus* of a bone in a mans leg.

2. = process *sb.* 5 or 6. *rare.*

1891 tr. *Sabatier's Paul* iv. iii. 256 A logical and inevitable processus.

‖**procès verbal** (prɔsɛ vɛrbal). Pl. **procès verbaux** (-bo). Sometimes anglicized as **process verbal.** [F.: see process and verbal.] A detailed written report of proceedings; minutes; in *Fr. Law*, an authenticated written statement of facts in support of a criminal or other charge.

1635 (*title*) A Relation of the Devill Balams Departure out of the Body of the Mother Prioresse of the Ursuline Nuns of Loudun,..with the Extract of the proces verball, touching the Exorcismes wrought at Loudun. [**1753** Verbal process: see process *sb.* 4.] **1804** *Edin. Rev.* Jan. 390 All this was attested in a *procès-verbal*, signed by the magistrates of the municipality. **1807** Southey *Espriella's Lett.* III. 283 The process-verbal of the conference has been printed. **1815** Scott *Guy M.* x, [To] make up the written report, *procès verbal*, or precognition, as it is technically called. **1906** *Athenæum* 23 June 772/1 Mr. Somers Clarke wishes that the honorary members..could receive the *procès-verbaux* in time to communicate their views as to important decisions before these are irrevocably carried into effect.

prochain, *a.* (*sb.*) Also 5– **-ein,** 6 **-ane, -yn.** [a. F. *prochain* (prɔʃɛ̃), *prucein* (12th c. in Hatz.-Darm.), f. *proche* near:—L. *propius* adv., compar. of *prope* near.]

†**1.** Neighbouring, nearest, next. *Obs.*

1549 *Compl. Scot.* Epist. 4 Godefroid of billon..deffendit his..subiectis of loran, fra his prochane enemeis that lyis contigue about his cuntre. **1555** *Inst. Gentleman* I ij, As wel against our prochane and nere enemis, as also in foren wars. **1592** Wyrley *Armorie* 116 All the prochaine ground We rifled, and toth' siege brought what we found.

‖**2.** ***prochain ami.*** [F. = 'near friend': see ami.] In *Law*: The next friend (next *a.* 3 b), one who is entitled to sue on behalf of an infant or a person of unsound mind.

[**1285** *Early Stat. Irel.* (1907) 82 Si ele seit recoueree al prochein ami a ki le heritage ne purra decendre pur apruer.] **1473–5** in *Calr. Proc. Chanc. Q. Eliz.* (1830) II. Pref. 59 The replicacion of Johan Saunder, by William Cooke, per prochein amy, to the answer and title of John Saunder. **1607** Cowell *Interpr.*, *Prochein Amy*..is vsed in our common lawe, for him that is next of kin to a childe in his nonage, and is in that respect allowed by lawe, to deale for him in the managing of his affaires. **1715** M. Davies *Athen. Brit.* I. 320 For ought I know Fox's Heirs, per Descent, or even his *Prochain-amis*, might bring their Assize for that Disseisin, and so re-enter. **1809** *Q. Rev.* Feb. 103 Had such a *tirade* been delivered in Westminster Hall..the learned Counsel would have been recommended to the care of his *prochein ami.*

3. ***prochain avoidance*** [lit. next voidance], a power to appoint a minister to a church when next it becomes vacant.

1744 in Jacob *Law Dict.*

B. *sb.* One near of kin.

c **1520** *Wyse Chylde & Emp. Adrian* (1860) 15 That they heden then leue to loue theyr prochyns and nereste of blode.

†**proche,** *v. Obs.* [app. either a palatalized form akin to proke *v.*, or due to assimilation of *proke* and *broche*, broach *v.* in a similar sense.] *trans.* and *intr.* To prick, pierce, spur.

(The first quot. is obscure, and the word may be different.)

a **1400–50** *Alexander* 1926 For now he proches [*Dublin MS.* prokes] for pride & propurly he wedis, For-þi him bose to be bett as a barne fallis. **1515** *Scot. Field* 325 in *Percy Folio* I. 228 They proched vs with speares & put many over that they blood out brast at there broken harnish. **1523** Ld. Berners *Froiss.* I. ccclxiii. 591 The englysshe-men and gascoyns proched their horses with their spurres.

prochein, var. form of prochain.

prochlorite (prəʊˈklɔːraɪt). *Min.* [f. pro-[2] + chlorite[1], on account of 'its being the earliest crystallized kind recognized' (Dana 1868, 502).] A species of chlorite, occurring in foliated or granular masses of a green colour, translucent or opaque; a hydrous silicate of alumina, iron, and magnesia, crystallizing in the monoclinic system. Allied to ripidolite, and so called in Brit. Mus. Cat.

1867 *Amer. Jrnl. Sc.* Ser. ii. XLIV. 258 It is accordingly designated..Prochlorite. **1900** *Rosenbusche's Mic. Phys.* 285 Prochlorite is crystallographically and optically like clinochlore.

prochlorperazine (ˌprəʊklɔːˈpɛrəziːn). *Pharm.* [f. pro(pyl- + chlor- + pi)perazine.] A pale yellow viscous liquid which is used, usu. in the form of one of its salts, as a tranquillizer; 2-chloro-10-[3-(4-methylpiperazin-1-yl)-propyl]phenothiazine, $C_{20}H_{24}ClN_3S$.

1958 *Psychiatric Res. Rep.* IX. 23 Proc[h]lorperazine treatment of psychotic patients was begun at Longview Hospital in November, 1955. **1959** *Jrnl. Amer. Med. Assoc.* 16 May 361/1 Caffeine and sodium benzoate seems to be an effective and rapidly acting antagonist to the toxic manifestations of prochlorperazine. **1977** *Lancet* 9 July 94/2 Dizziness and vomiting can be avoided by intravenous prochlorperazine 12·5 mg given 5 min before the mexiletine injection.

‖**prochoos** (ˈprəʊkəʊɒs). *Gr. Antiq.* [a. Gr. πρόχοος, Attic πρόχους a jug, pitcher, f. προχεῖν to pour forth.] A jug of elegant shape, used for pouring water over the hands before meals.

1850 Leitch tr. *C. O. Müller's Anc. Art* §365 (ed. 2) 457 The Delian Artemis..with phial and prochus, stands beside Apollo. **1857** Birch *Anc. Pottery* (1858) II. 94 Another jug was the *prochoos*, with an oval body, tall neck and round mouth, but without a handle.

prochordal (prəʊˈkɔːdəl), *a. Embryol.* [f. PRO-² + CHORD *sb.*¹ + -AL¹.] Anterior to the notochord.
1881 *Academy* 23 Apr. 303 The prochordal part of the trabeculae is segmented off from the parachordal part.

prochorion: see PRO-² 1.

prochromosome (prəʊˈkrəʊməsəʊm). *Cytology.* Also with hyphen. [ad. G. *prochromosom* (J. B. Overton 1905, in *Jahrb. f. wissensch. Bot.* XLII. 126): see PRO-² and CHROMOSOME.] One of the densely staining heterochromatic masses seen in certain interphase nuclei, frequently associated with centromeres; = CHROMOCENTRE.
1906 *Proc. R. Soc.* B. LXXVII. 557 These bodies correspond in fact exactly to what in 1904 we have already described as the Anlagen of the premaiotic chromosomes in the corresponding cells in the testes of Periplaneta, and there can be no doubt that they represent also the structures subsequently alluded to as prochromosomes by Overton, Miyake, and Strasburger in the same stage in certain mono- and dicotyledonous plants. **1907** *Ann. Bot.* XXI. 335 In certain plants there is a tendency of the chromatin to form lumps or masses in the resting condition, in which there is often a general uniformity in size, and when the number of such lumps approaches the number of somatic chromosomes, each mass has been looked upon by some as representing a prochromosome, or the centre of organization of a chromosome. **1934** [see EUCHROMOCENTRE]. **1965** A. K. & A. SHARMA *Chromosome Techniques* viii. 205 The number of prochromosomes may be equal to, or if fused, less than, the number of chromosomes in the complement. **1969** BROWN & BERTKE *Textbk. Cytol.* i. 8/2 Flemming (1882) illustrated stained nodes in the nuclear network... Overton named them *prochromosomes* in 1905 and 3 years later Baccarini called them *chromocenters*; both names are still in use.

prochronic (prəʊˈkrɒnɪk), *a. rare.* [f. PRO-² + Gr. χρόνος time + -IC, after *chronic.*] Pertaining to a period before time began. Hence **proˈchronically** *adv.*, before the beginning of time.
1857 GOSSE *Creation* 87 The two creations—..the prochronic and the diachronic—here unite. *Ibid.* 173 It has been educed..prochronically, by the omnipotent fiat of the Creator.

prochronism (ˈprəʊkrənɪz(ə)m). [f. PRO-² 1 + Gr. χρόνος time + -ISM: cf. ANACHRONISM. So F. *prochronisme* (1762 in Acad.).] The referring of an event, etc., to an earlier date than the true one. A particular case of ANACHRONISM, q.v.
a **1646** J. GREGORY *Posthuma* (1649) 174 An error..herein is called Anachronism:..either saith too much, and that is a Prochronism; or too little, and that is a Metachronism. **1677** CARY *Chronology* II. I. i. v. 105 Which seems to be a Prochronism of 25 Years. **1838** *Archæologia* XXVII. 252 The prochronisms in these [Towneley] Mysteries are very remarkable... Caiaphas sings mass. **1899** J. A. GIBBS *Cotswold Village* (ed. 2) 156 It is a prochronism to talk of the May-fly; for, as a matter of fact, the first ten days of June usually constitute the may-fly season.

procidence (prəʊ-, ˈprɒsɪdəns). *Path.* Now usu. as mod.L. **procidentia.** [a. F. *procidence* 'a falling downe of a thing out of its place', or ad. L. *prōcidentia* (Cels.) in Path. prolapse, f. *prōcidĕre* to fall forward. Often used in L. form.] The slipping of an organ or structure from its normal position; prolapsus. Freq. distinguished from *prolapse* or restricted to the more severe kinds (see later quots.).
1601 HOLLAND *Pliny* XXI. xix, Violets have a peculiar vertue..to help the procidence or falling downe both of tuill and matrice, and to reduce them again into their places. **1607** TOPSELL *Four-f. Beasts* 388 Another disease called *Procidentia ani*, that is to say, the falling out of the fundament. **1640** E. CHILMEAD tr. *Ferrand's Erotique Melanch.* ii. 15 These women were troubled with the Procidence of the Matrix. **1822–34** *Good's Study Med.* (ed. 4) IV. 112 This [prolapse of the vagina]..may..be a relaxation, procidence, prolapse or complete inversion of the organ. **1829** S. COOPER *Good's Study of Med.* (ed. 3) V. 146 If the descent [of the uterus] be only to the middle of the vagina, it is called *relaxatio uteri*; if to the labiæ, *procidentia*; if lower than the labiæ, *prolapsus*. The distinction is of trifling importance. **1888** A. H. N. LEWERS *Pract. Text-bk. Dis. Women* viii. 113 When the uterus has partly, or wholly passed the orifice of the vulva, the case is called one of 'procidentia'. *Ibid.* 114 In extreme cases of procidentia the whole uterus lies outside. **1903** J. P. TUTTLE *Treat. Dis. Anus* xvii. 667 Procidentia..is practically always applied to those cases in which all the coats of the bowel descend. **1956** H. E. BACON et al. *Proctology* xviii. 215 The difference between prolapse and procidentia lies in the coats of the bowel involved. *Ibid.* 218 Protruding through the anal orifice, procidentia is diagnosed from a series of circular folds irregularly placed. **1974** PASSMORE & ROBSON *Compan. Med. Stud.* III. xxviii. 62/2 In third degree prolapse (procidentia) the whole uterus lies outside the introitus.
So **ˈprocident** *a.*, falling forward; prolapsed.
1889 J. M. DUNCAN *Lect. Dis. Women* ii. (ed. 4) 7 On her side, a woman can easily press out a replaced procident uterus. *Ibid.* l. 417 When the patient came to us, the womb was not procident.

procidentia: see prec.

†**proˈciduous,** *a. Obs.* [f. L. *prōcidu-us* fallen or falling forward or down, f. *prōcidĕre*: see PROCIDENCE and -OUS, and cf. *deciduous.*] Falling down or forward from the proper place.
1656 BLOUNT *Glossogr.*, *Prociduous*, that falls down out of his right place. **1657** TOMLINSON *Renou's Disp.* 395 It [gum-arabick] represses prociduous eyes.

†**ˈprocinct,** *sb.*¹ *Obs.* [ad. med.L. *procinct-us, -a* (Du Cange), for L. *præcinctus* PRECINCT: see PRO-¹ 3. So OF. *procincte, proceinte* (13th c.), variants of *pourceinte*: see PURCINCT.] = PRECINCT *sb.*
1432–50 tr. *Higden* (Rolls) I. 401 In whiche procincte [L. *In hoc precinctu Walliæ*] were wonte to be thre courtes. **1448** in Willis & Clark *Cambridge* (1886) I. 355 Aboute the gardynes and alle the procincte of the place. **1491** *Act 7 Hen. VII*, c. 11 §1 Within the seid Towne of Grete Yernemuth and procincte therof. **1583** in Willis & Clark *Cambridge* (1886) II. 688 The scite, circuit, ambulance, and procinct of the late Priory. **1616** *Manif. Abp. of Spalato's Motives* 34 A Prelacie thou hast here..of large procinct, and faire reuenue. **1822** T. TAYLOR *Apuleius* XI. 265 For the priest..shall bear a rosy crown in his right hand, adhering to the rattle, in the very procinct of the pomp.

†**proˈcinct,** *sb.*² *Obs.* [ad. L. *prōcinctus*, vbl. sb. f. *prōcingĕre* to gird up, equip, in phr. *in prōcinctu* in readiness for action.] The condition of being prepared or equipped; readiness for action; only in ***in procinct***, ready, prepared.
c **1611** CHAPMAN *Iliad* XII. 89 And gaue vp each chariot and steed To their directors to be kept, in all procinct of warre, There, and on that side of the dike. *a* **1639** WOTTON *Let.* in *Reliq.* (1651) 453 Being then in procinct of his travels. **1667** MILTON *P.L.* VI. 19 Warr he perceav'd, warr in procinct, and found Already known what he for news had thought To have reported. **1763** C. JOHNSTON *Reverie* II. 128 War! War in procinct! The comforts of Greatness. **1839** *Blackw. Mag.* XLVI. 815 In short, all Rome, and at all times was 'in procinct'.

†**proˈcinct,** *a. Obs.* Also 7 procint. [ad. L. *prōcinctus*, pa. pple. of *prōcingĕre* to gird up, equip (PRO-¹ 1 h): cf. *succinct.*] Ready, prepared.
1618 M. BARET *Horsemanship* I. xxxiii. 98 Many things are now become nocent and hurtfull to man, which at the first was procint and seruiceable to him. **1623** COCKERAM, *Procint*, readie. **1773** J. ROSS *Fratricide* III. 21 (MS.) And from a bubbling fount, procinct and pure, Takes proper portion and dilutes the draught.

procinctive (prəʊˈsɪŋktɪv), *a. rare.* [f. L. *procinct-*, ppl. stem of *prōcingĕre*: see PROCINCT *a.*] ? That girds itself for action.
1841 *Blackw. Mag.* XLIX. 152 To neither of these does the procinctive future belong.

Procion (ˈprəʊsɪən). A proprietary name for any of a large class of reactive dyestuffs based on 1,3,5-triazine and covering a wide range of colours. Usu. *attrib.*
1956 *Trade Marks Jrnl.* 23 May 424/1 *Procion*... Dyes, dyestuffs and colouring matters, none being for laundry or toilet purposes. Imperial Chemical Industries Limited,.. London, S.W.1; Manufacturers and Merchants—10th February 1956. **1957** *Listener* 18 July 73 (Advt.), Polythene, for instance,.. bright and fast new dyes like the 'Procion' range... They're all I.C.I. discoveries, you know. **1957** *Official Gaz.* (U.S. Patent Office) 23 July TM 129/1 *Procion.* .. For dyes, dyestuffs, and colouring matters. **1971** R. L. M. ALLEN *Colour Chem.* xiii. 205 Procion dyes provide a complete range of shades in both the M and H series. **1974** *Sci. Amer.* Jan. 41/1 The branching patterns of a cell can be traced by injecting the fluorescent dye Procion yellow or by stimulating and then recording from its axons in roots and connectives. **1976** *Nature* 25 Mar. 338/2 Procion dye was injected intracellularly by iontophoresis to determine axonal morphology of one or two cells in a particular brain.

†**proˈcision.** *Obs.* [ad. L. *prōcīsiōn-em*, n. of action from *prōcīdĕre* to cut short in front, f. PRO-¹ 1 f + *cædĕre* to cut.] A cutting short in front.
1650 BULWER *Anthropomet.* 213 The shortnesse of the Prepuce,..whether it be original, or adscititious by an artificial procision of it.

prock: see PROC.

prockesy, obs. f. PROXY.

†**proˈclaim,** *sb. Obs. rare.* [f. PROCLAIM *v.* So F. *proclame*, med.L. *prōclāma* a proclamation.] The action of proclaiming; proclamation.
1535 STEWART *Cron. Scot.* (Rolls) II. 12 Quhen the herald had maid his proclame, He tuke his leif, & syne he sped him hame. **1788** T. TAYLOR *Proclus* I. Dissert. 62 Axioms derive all their authority from intrinsic approbation, and not from public proclaim. **1820** KEATS *Hyperion* I. 130 Voices of soft proclaim, and silver stir Of strings in hollow shells.

proclaim (prəʊˈkleɪm), *v.* [ME. *proclame*, ad. L. *prōclām-āre* to cry out (esp. before a judge, in one's defence): see PRO-¹ and CLAIM *v.* (whence altered to the present spelling). Cf. F. *proclamer* (1549 in Hatz.-Darm.).]

1. *trans.* To make official announcement of (something), by word of mouth in some public place; also, to cause this to be done by officers or agents. The object may be a sb. or clause.
c **1400** MAUNDEV. (1839) Prol. 2 He wil make it to ben cryed & pronounced in the myddel place of a town; so þat the thing þat is proclamed..may euenly strecche to alle parties. *c* **1450** *Merlin* 577 The pardon that the legat hadde graunted and proclaymed thourgh all cristindom. **1535** COVERDALE *2 Chron.* xxxvi. 22 He caused it be proclamed thorow out all his empyre. **1596** DALRYMPLE tr. *Leslie's Hist. Scot.* v. 290 In haist the Nobilitie proclames a conuentioune in Skune, to sett another in his place. **1667** MILTON *P.L.* I. 754 The winged Haralds..with..Trumpets sound..proclaim A solemn Councel forthwith to be held At Pandæmonium. **1722** WOLLASTON *Relig. Nat.* vi. 143 A lie is as much a lie, when it is whispered, as when it is proclaimed at the market-cross. **1853** J. H. NEWMAN *Hist. Sk.* (1873) II. I. ii. 92 His titles were proclaimed by the voice of heralds and the applause of the Moslem. **1859** TENNYSON *Enid* 552 Then Yniol's nephew, after trumpet blown,.. proclaim'd, 'Advance and take, as fairest of the fair..The prize of beauty'.

b. ***to proclaim war***: to make public declaration of war *against* another power (formerly also with *between, to*); to declare war. So ***to proclaim peace.***
1496–7 *Act 12 Hen. VII*, c. 12 §6 Yf Warre be reared levyed and proclaymed betwene the seid realmes. **1560** DAUS tr. *Sleidane's Comm.* 269 Sebastian..proclameth warre to the Duke of Saxons people. **1606** G. W[ODCOCKE] *Hist. Ivstine* II. 11 Sodainly they proclaimed open Warres against the Megarenses. **1617** MORYSON *Itin.* I. 185 A French Gentleman..the same day had there proclaimed Peace. **1771** *Junius Lett.* lxiv. (1820) 326 The executive power proclaims war and peace. **1862** LD. BROUGHAM *Brit. Const.* App. ii. 411 The King in England can proclaim war, but without the sanction of Parliament his proclamation must immediately be retracted.

c. To publish (the banns of marriage); also (Sc.) ***to proclaim the parties***: cf. 2 c.
1588 in R. M. Fergusson *Alex. Hume* (1899) 182 Johnne ..and Margaret..desyrit me..to proclame the said persones in this paroche kirk according to the order. **1596** SHAKS. *Tam. Shr.* III. ii. 16 Hee'll wooe a thousand, point the day of marriage..and proclaime the banes. **1773** ERSKINE *Inst. Law Scot.* I. vi. §10. 88 The council of Trent ..ordained bans to be proclaimed on three successive holidays, in the parish church or churches of the persons contracting; and this canon was adopted by our first Reformers, and hath been ever since observed by our church. **1893** *New Eng. Dict.* s.v. *Cry* vb. 5 d, To proclaim the marriage banns of. **1898** *Tit-Bits* 1 Oct. 1/1 The minister, after proclaiming the banns of matrimony between a young couple [etc.].

†**d.** *Law.* ***to proclaim a fine***: to read a fine in open court in order to make it more public and less liable to be levied by fraud or covin: see FINE *sb.*¹ 6.
1483–4 *Act 1 Rich. III*, c. 7 §1 þe Iustices of Assisez..do rede & proclayme the seid fyne openly and solemply in euery their Cession of Assises to be holde the same yere. **1489** *Act 4 Hen. VII*, c. 24. **1588–9** *Act 31 Eliz.* c. 2. **1766** BLACKSTONE *Comm.* II. xxi. 352.

2. To make official announcement of or concerning (a person or thing).

a. With complement.
1494 FABYAN *Chron.* IV. lxxii. 50 For this victory his knyghtes proclaymed hym Emperour. *Ibid.* VI. clxxv. 172 They..conueyed the sayd .ii. children vnto the cytie of Ferrer, and there crowned and proclaymed theym for kynges. **1512** *Act 4 Hen. VIII*, c. 20 *Preamble*, One Archbold Armestrong wich was proclaymed a Rebell to the Kyng and Realme of Englonde. *a* **1548** HALL *Chron., Hen. VIII* 245 At this Parliament the kyng was Proclaymed kyng of Irelande, whiche name his predecessors neuer had. **1741** MIDDLETON *Cicero* I. II. 145 [They] loudly and universally proclamed Cicero the first Consul. **1858** FROUDE *Hist. Eng.* III. xiv. 204 When he found himself proclaimed a traitor.

b. Without complement: Short for 'to proclaim (a person) as a rebel or outlaw'. Also non-officially: To denounce (a person or thing).
1500–20 DUNBAR *Poems* lxxxii. 67 And gar ȝour merchandis be discreit, That na extortiounes be, proclaime All fraud and schame. **1603** SHAKS. *Meas. for M.* II. iv. 151, I will proclaime thee Angelo,.. Ile tell the world aloud What man thou art. **1605** —— *Lear* II. iii. 1, I heard my selfe proclaim'd, And by the happy hollow of a Tree, Escap'd the hunt. **1797** MRS. RADCLIFFE *Italian* ix, I know and will proclaim you to the world.

†**c.** To give public notice of (something) as lost or found; to give public notice of a marriage between (parties): see 1 c. *Obs.*
1531 *Dial. on Laws Eng.* II. li. (1638) 157 Where beasts stray away.., and they be taken up and proclaimed.

d. To proclaim the accession of (a sovereign).
1714 LADY M. W. MONTAGU *Let. to W. Montagu* 9 Aug., I went..to-day to see the King proclaimed. **1849** MACAULAY *Hist. Eng.* v. I. 588 On the morning of the twentieth of June he was proclaimed in the market place of Taunton. **1874** GREEN *Short Hist.* vii. §2. 354 The new sovereign was proclaimed on Edward's death.

e. To place (a district, country, etc.) under legal restrictions by proclamation: *spec.* under the provisions of the various Peace Preservation (Ireland) Acts of 1881 and following years.
1881 [see PROCLAIMED 2]. **1885** *Daily Tel.* 29 Oct. 5/2 In the interest of trade we stamp out other diseases of animals, not scrupling to 'proclaim' whole counties, and put the community to serious inconvenience for the general good. **1887** *Times* 28 July 8 Every part of Ireland is proclaimed.

f. To denounce or prohibit by proclamation; to forbid publicly or openly.
1888 *Sat. Rev.* 14 Apr. 444/2 O, meet me by moonlight alone, Since our meetings by day are proclaimed.

3. *transf.* To declare publicly; to make known aloud or openly; to publish. Const. as in 1, 2 a.
1390 GOWER *Conf.* III. 179 Whanne he made a governour ..He wolde ferst enquere his name, And let it openly proclaime What man he were, or evel or good. **1560** DAUS tr. *Sleidane's Comm.* 337 b, They haue openly proclaimed that nothing be said a misse against him. **1577** HANMER *Anc. Eccl. Hist.* (1619) 203, It shall be expedient that these our

writings be euerie where proclaimed. **1665** BOYLE *Occas. Refl., Disc.* (1848) 61 If.. the Man is happy whose sins God is pleas'd to cover; what may that Man be accounted whose Graces he vouchsafes to proclaim? **1764** GOLDSM. *Trav.* 66 The shudd'ring tenant of the frigid zone Boldly proclaims that happiest spot his own. **1784** COWPER *Task* v. 857 In vain thy creatures testify of thee, Till Thou proclaim thyself. **1867** J. MARTINEAU *Ess.* II. 3 Sir John Herschel.. proclaims the need of a better logic. **1874** GREEN *Short Hist.* v. §5. 250 He proclaims a righteous life to be better than a host of indulgences. **1875** JOWETT *Plato* (ed. 2) I. 164 You proclaim in the face of Hellas that you are a Sophist.

4. *fig.* Of things: To make known or manifest; to intimate, prove.

1597 HOOKER *Eccl. Pol.* v. liii. §2 The true beliefe which maketh a man happie proclaymeth iointly God and man. **1602** SHAKS. *Ham.* I. iii. 72 The Apparell oft proclaimes the man. **1611** —— *Wint. T.* v. ii. 42 Many other Euidences, proclayme her,.. to be the Kings Daughter. *a* **1678** MARVELL *Bermudas* 28 He.. makes the hollow seas, that roar, Proclaim the ambergris on shoar. *c* **1704** PRIOR *Henry & Emma* 242 His steps proclaim no lover's haste. **1757** GRAY *Bard* III. ii, Her eye proclaims her of the Briton-Line. **1813** SCOTT *Rokeby* I. vii, Then did his silence long proclaim A struggle between fear and shame.

5. *intr.* To make proclamation or public announcement. *lit.* and *fig.*

1470–85 MALORY *Arthur* VIII. xxxix. 334 He proclamed in al Cornewaile of alle the aduentures of these two knyghtes; so was his openly knowen. **1603** SHAKS. *Meas. for M.* IV. iv. 27 But that her tender shame Will not proclaime against her maiden losse, How might she tongue me?

Hence **pro'claiming** *vbl. sb.* and *ppl. a.* Whence **pro'claimingly** *adv.*, in a way that proclaims or announces.

1588–9 *Act 31 Eliz.* c. 2 Scarclye one daye in euerie Terme can be spared for the proclaymynge of Fynes. *a* **1716** SOUTH *Serm.* (1727) VI. xi. 372 Is not the Piety and Obedience of our Lives a proclaiming of God to be our King? **1880** G. MEREDITH *Tragic Com.* iv. (1892) 49 Not the less were they proclaimingly alight and in full blaze.

pro'claimant. *rare*⁻¹. [f. PROCLAIM *v.* + -ANT: cf. *claimant.*] A proclaimer.

1847 E. BRONTE *Wuthering Heights* xii, I was spared the pain of being the first proclaimant of her flight.

proclaimed (prəʊ'kleɪmd), *ppl. a.* [-ED[1].]

1. Publicly and officially announced; publicly declared; designated in a proclamation.

1603 DEKKER *Wonderfull Yeare* C j, The holesome receipt of a proclaymed King. **1681** E. MURPHY *State Ireland* §7 Bryan Micardle, a proclaimed Tory. **1826** SOUTHEY *Vind. Eccl. Angl.* 526 Trained up in such a principle of proclaimed intolerance.

2. Of a district: Placed by proclamation under special legal restrictions; of a meeting, etc.: Prohibited by proclamation. See PROCLAIM *v.* 2 e, f.

1881 *Act 44 & 45 Vict.* c. 5 §1 In a proclaimed district a person shall not carry or have any arms or ammunition save as authorised by the conditions set forth in the proclamation herein-after mentioned. **1882** *Ann. Reg.* 65 The bill proposed that in proclaimed districts the police should have power to search for implements of crime.

proclaimer (prəʊ'kleɪmə(r)). [f. as prec. + -ER[1].] One who proclaims or publicly announces.

1548 UDALL *Erasm. Par. Luke* iii. 29 The kyngdome of heauen.. wherof Jhon the soonne of Zacharie was chosen and specially appuincted to bee an open preacher, and proclamer. **1579** FULKE *Heskins's Parl.* 27 Hee chargeth the proclamer with slaundering their Churche. **1604** HIERON *Wks.* I. 522 Spreaders abroad and proclaimers of Gods truth. **1671** MILTON *P.R.* I. 18 Now had the great Proclaimer with a voice More awful then the sound of Trumpet, cri'd Repentance. **1879** MACLEAR *St. Mark* xiv. 158 The Celebrant or Proclaimer of the Feast.

b. *spec.* The official who proclaims the number drawn in a lottery.

1775 in Hone *Every-day Bk.* (1827) II. 1464 The proclaimer is not to suffer [the boy who draws the tickets].. to leave the wheel without being first examined by the manager.

proclamation (prɒklə'meɪʃən). [a. F. *proclamation*, OF. *-acion* (1370 in Godefroy *Compl.*), ad. L. *prōclāmātiōn-em*, n. of action from *prōclāmāre* to PROCLAIM.]

1. The action of proclaiming; the official giving of public notice.

[**1383** *Act 7 Rich. II*, c. 6 Que chescun Viscont Dengleterre soite tenuz decy en avant en propre persone de faire proclamacion de mesme lestatut quatre foitz lan.] *c* **1420** ? LYDG. *Assembly of Gods* 43 Then was there made a proclamasion, In Plutoys name commaundyd silence.. That Diana and Neptunus myght haue audience. **1532** CROMWELL in Merriman *Life & Lett.* (1902) I. 349 It hathe not ben seen nor herd that any Subiecte.. sholde presume to make proclamacion within this your realme but onelie in your graces Name. **1596** SHAKS. *Merch. V.* IV. i. 436 The dearest ring in Venice will I giue you, And finde it out by proclamation. *a* **1651** CALDERWOOD *Hist. Kirk* (1843) II. 348 An edict was published by open proclamatioun, that no man sett furth, or read anie of these libells. **1769** BURKE *Pres. St. Nat.* Wks. II. 139 The writs are issued... A proper space must be given for proclamation and for the election. **1797** *Encycl. Brit.* (ed. 3) IX. 655/1 To prevent bigamy and incestuous marriages, the church has introduced proclamation of banns. **1864** BRYCE *Holy Rom. Emp.* ix. (1875) 151 Intestine feuds were repressed by the proclamation of a public peace.

b. *spec.* The public and formal announcement of the accession of a king or ruler; the fact of being proclaimed king.

1593 SHAKS. *3 Hen. VI*, IV. vii. 70 Sound Trumpet, Edward shal be here proclaim'd: Come, fellow Souldior, make thou proclamation. **1840** THIRLWALL *Greece* VII. lix. 329 Plutarch says that his troops received his rival's proclamation with shouts of applause.

c. The action of denouncing by a public notice, or of declaring a person to be outlawed, a thing to be illegal, a district to be under legal restriction, etc.; the fact of being so proclaimed; proscription.

1561 T. NORTON *Calvin's Inst.* I. 18 The miraculous working, that God preserued the tables of his couenant from the bloody proclamations of Antiochus. **1605** SHAKS. *Lear* v. iii. 183 The bloody proclamation to escape That follow'd me so neere.. taught me to shift Into a mad-mans rags. **1881** *Act 44 & 45 Vict.* c. 5 §2 Any such proclamation [of a county or district] may set forth the conditions and regulations under which the carrying or having of arms or ammunition is authorised. **1887** *Spectator* 27 Aug. 1138 The proclamation of the League by the Government under the Crimes Act.

2. That which is proclaimed, either as to its substance or its form; a formal order or intimation issued by the sovereign or other legal authority, and made public either by being announced by a herald, or by being posted up in public places.

In *Eng. Hist.* applied esp. to decrees issued by the sovereign, in the 16th and 17th centuries, by which it was sought to legislate without the assent of Parliament.

1415 EARL OF CAMBR. in Ellis *Orig. Lett.* Ser. II. I. 45 As for ye forme of a proclamacyon wych schulde hadde bene cryde in ye Erle name, as [t]he heyre to the Corowne of Ynglond ageyns 3ow, my lege lord. **1494** FABYAN *Chron.* VI. ccxvii. 235 The duke.. made his proclamacyons & cryes, that no man shulde.. do any force to the people. **1545** *Reg. Privy Council Scot.* I. 12 Ordourit and furnest eftir the forme and tenour of the proclamatiounis direct herupon. **1613** SHAKS. *Hen. VIII*, I. iii. 17, I heare of none but the new Proclamation, That's clapt vpon the Court Gate. **1671** LADY M. BERTIE in *12th Rep. Hist. MSS. Comm.* App. v. 23 They say the King hath put out a Proclamation to forbid maskerades. **1726** SWIFT *Gulliver* I. i, A proclamation was soon issued to forbid it, upon pain of death. **1832** MACAULAY *Ess., Burghley* (1887) 241 She [Elizabeth] assumed the power of legislating by means of proclamations. **1863** H. Cox *Instit.* I. v. 27 Proclamations.. are usually issued in pursuance of Orders in Council. **1875** TASWELL LANGMEAD *Eng. Const. Hist.* (1890) 398 The King [Henry VIII] then appealed to Parliament to give to his Proclamations the force of statutes. *Ibid.* 580 [Under Chas. I] In lieu of Acts of Parliament, Royal Proclamations.. were issued from time to time and declared to have the force of laws. **1881** [see PROCLAIMED 2].

†**3.** *Law.* **a.** *proclamation of a fine*: see quot. 1607 and PROCLAIM *v.* 1 d. *Obs.*

1483–4 *Act 1 Rich. III*, c. 7 §2 The Iustices of Peas.. do make open and solempe proclamacion of the seid fyne in iiij generall Cessions of Peas to be holden the same yere. **1489** *Act 4 Hen. VII*, c. 24. **1588–9** *Act 31 Eliz.* c. 2. **1607** COWELL *Interpr., Proclamation of a Fine*, is a notice openly, and solemnly giuen at all the Assises that shall be holden in the Countie within one yeare after the ingrossing of the fine,.. and these proclamations be made vpon transcripts of the fine, sent by the Iustices of the Common plees, to the Iustices of Assise, and the Iustices of peace. **1766** BLACKSTONE *Comm.* II. App. 16.

†**b.** *proclamation of rebellion*: see quots. *Obs.*

1607 COWELL *Interpr., Proclamation of rebellion*, is a publike notice giuen by the officer, that a man not appearing vpon a *Sub pœna*, nor an attachment in the Starre Chamber or Chauncerie, shalbe reputed a rebell, except he render himselfe by a day assigned. **1670** BLOUNT *Law Dict.* s.v., *Proclamation of Rebellion* is a Writ so called, whereby publick notice is given, where a Man, not appearing [etc., as above].

†**4.** *transf.* Open declaration; manifestation; favourable or unfavourable notice. *Obs.*

1574 HELLOWES *Gueuara's Fam. Ep.* (1577) 153 Vpon that day, that the gentleman doth begin to hourde vp money, from thence foorth, he putteth his fame in proclamation. **1601** SHAKS. *All's Well* I. iii. 180 Inuention is asham'd Against the proclamation of thy passion To say thou doost not [love]. **1607** TOURNEUR *Rev. Trag.* II. ii, Here a Dame, Cunning, nayles lether-hindges to a dore To auoide proclamation.

5. *Comb.*: †**proclamation-horn**, a horn blown to call public attention before making proclamation; **proclamation hour**, an hour fixed by proclamation for some specified purpose; e.g. for retiring within doors; **proclamation money** (in N.Amer. Colonies), coin valued according to a table prescribed in a proclamation of Q. Anne on 18 June, 1704, in which the Spanish dollar of 17½ dwt. was to be rated at six shillings in all the colonies; **proclamation-print**, the type used in a printed proclamation; **proclamation writ**, a writ directing a proclamation to be made.

1868 G. STEPHENS *Runic Mon.* I. 321 Neither of these Cornucopiæ, or.. Drinking or *Proclamation-Horns, or Horns of Ceremony now exist. **1900** *Westm. Gaz.* 18 Aug. 5/3 Duplessis acknowledged that he had been in the company of Gano and Cordua at night after *proclamation hours. **1735** *N. Jersey Archives* XI. 432, I do hereby promise to Pay to the said Discoverer the Sum of Thirty Pounds, *Proclamation Money. **1748** *N. Hampshire Prov. Papers* (1871) V. 905 His Majesty has recommended that my salary should be fixed and Paid in Sterling or Proclamation money. **1772** *Chron.* in *Ann. Reg.* 86/1 The general assembly.. hath passed a bill for emitting 60,000*l.* proclamation money, in paper bills of credit. **1775** GOUV. MORRIS in Sparks *Life & Writ.* (1832) I. 72, 40 shillings each per day, Proclamation money. **1896** HOR. WHITE *Money & Banking* 15–16 Six shillings was considered by the home government a fair average of the various colonial valuations of the Spanish dollar. This valuation came to be known by the term proclamation money, or proc. money. **1592** NASHE *P. Penilesse* Wks. (Grosart) II. 25 The Kitchin.. was no bigger than the Cooks roome in a ship, with a little court chimney, about the compasse of a Parenthesis in *proclamation-print. **1863** H. COX *Instit.* I. iv. 17 The tenor of them [the Acts] was affixed to *proclamation writs, and directed by the sheriffs to be proclaimed as law in their counties.

Hence **procla'mation** *v. trans. nonce-wd.*, to force or coerce by proclamations.

1864 *Athenæum* 8 Oct. 459/2 If religious disputants had been 'proclamationed' into silence.

†**'procla,mator.** *Obs.* [a. L. *prōclāmātor* one who cries out or proclaims, agent-n. f. *prōclāmāre* to PROCLAIM.] One who proclaims or makes a public announcement; *spec.* an officer of the Court of Common Pleas.

1650 HUBBERT *Pill Formality* 64 Ministers.. were.. proclamators of new engagements. **1658** *Practick Part of Law* 3 The Proclamator of the Court; the Keeper of the Court. **1684** E. CHAMBERLAYNE *Pres. St. Eng.* II. (ed. 15) 101 He is also by inheritance Proclamator of the Court of Common Pleas. **1712** ARBUTHNOT *John Bull* I. xi, Fees to Judges, *puisne* Judges, Clerks,.. Under Clerks, Proclamators [etc.].

proclamatory (prəʊ'klæmətərɪ), *a.* [f. L. *prōclāmātor*: see prec. and -ORY.]

1. That proclaims or makes public announcement.

1636 JACKSON *Creed* VIII. xii. §11 Hee uttered it, *voce magnâ*, with a proclamatory voice. **1830** *Westm. Rev.* Oct. 452 The honourable.. gentleman would of course make a speech declaratory and proclamatory of his disinterestedness. **1884** *St. James' Gaz.* 1 May 8/1 The thunder of the proclamatory cannon.

2. Of, pertaining to, like, or of the nature of a proclamation.

1853 G. J. CAYLEY *Las Alforjas* I. 90, I wrote.. a short notice in the fly-leaf of my pocket-book, setting forth, in proclamatory style, 'who I was, and what was to be done with my body, in case it should be found'. **1882** T. HARDY *Two on Tower* III. iv. 55 To make due preparation for a wedding of ordinary publicity.. with.. a bonfire, and other of those proclamatory accessories.

Proclian ('prɒklɪən), *a.* Also **'Procline** (-laɪn). Of or relating to Proclus (A.D. ? 410–85), a neo-Platonist philosopher and head of the Athenian school after Plutarch and Syrianus, his views, or works.

1912 F. VON HÜGEL *Eternal Life* vii. 118 We find in Eckhart a.. scientific, still predominantly Proclian, thirst for intellectual utter simplicity and clearness. **1951** *Mind* LX. 417 The Proclian *Liber de causis*. **1967** I. P. SHELDON-WILLIAMS in A. H. Armstrong *Cambr. Hist. Later Greek & Early Med. Philos.* 477 The Procline Neoplatonism had worked out those implications. *Ibid.*, The enemies were.. the Procline theology based on polytheism, and the Procline theurgy deriving from the belief in a supernatural power inherent in the phenomenal world.

pro'climax. *Ecol.* [f. PRO-[2] I + CLIMAX *sb.* 4 b.] (See quot. 1938.) Also *attrib.*

1934 F. E. CLEMENTS in *Jrnl. Ecol.* XXII. 45 For those cases in which the community is modified and held for a more or less indefinite period in some other condition, the term 'proclimax' is suggested. **1938** WEAVER & CLEMENTS *Plant Ecol.* (ed. 2) xviii. 480 Proclimax is a general term which includes all the communities that simulate the climax to some extent.. but lack the proper sanction of the existing climate. It thus includes subclimax, preclimax, and postclimax, as well as disclimax. **1951** *Jrnl. Ecol.* XXXIX. 81 The pro-climax communities of Mediterranean cliffs.. develop directly from the crustose-lichen stage. **1975** R. H. WHITTAKER *Communities & Ecosystems* (ed. 2) iv. 182 These may be termed 'subclimaxes', or 'proclimaxes' of various sorts, in Clements' treatment.

pro'cline, *v. rare.* [ad. L. *prōclīnā-re* to lean forward, f. *pro*, PRO-[1] + *-clīnāre*, = Gr. κλίν-ειν to bend.] *intr.* To lean forward; in *Dialling* = INCLINE *v.* 10 b.

1877 *Encycl. Brit.* VII. 155/1 Inclining dials.. were further distinguished as reclining when leaning backwards from an observer, proclining when leaning forwards.

Procline: see PROCLIAN *a.*

proclisis ('prəʊklɪsɪs). *Gram.* [mod.L., f. Gr. πρό forward + κλίσις, f. κλίνειν to lean.] Pronunciation as a proclitic; the transference of stress to a following word.

1893 J. CLARK *Man. Linguistics* vi. 158 The existence of proclisis, which naturally is lifted in emphatic positions, οὐ freeing itself at the end of a sentence. **1955** *Archivum Linguisticum* VII. II. 135 The facts of enclisis and proclisis in Polish are generally on the same lines as in Czech. **1964** *Language* XL. 276 Since he objects to the application of the idea of proclisis as well as enclisis, he keeps to the terms 'anteposition' and 'postposition' in referring to the placing of the pronoun with respect to the verb.

proclitic (prəʊ'klɪtɪk), *a.* and *sb. Gram.* [ad. mod.L. *procliticus* (Hermann, 1801), f. Gr. *προκλιτικός, f. προκλίνειν, f. πρό, PRO-[2] + κλίνειν (see PROCLINE *v.*), after Gr. ἐγκλιτικός ENCLITIC. So F. *proclitique.*]

A. *adj.* In *Greek Gram.*, used of a monosyllabic word that is so closely attached in pronunciation to the following word as to have no accent of its own; hence, generally, used of a word in any language, which in pronunciation is attached to the following stressed word, as in *an 'ounce, as 'soon, at 'home, for 'nobody, to ˌcompre'hend.*

1846 KEY *Lat. Gram.* p. ix, The term *proclitic* is adopted from Hermann's treatise: 'De emendanda ratione Graecae Grammaticae'. **1973** A. H. SOMMERSTEIN *Sound Pattern Anc. Greek* ii. 11 Prepositions, being proclitic, are separated from the following word by a single # boundary.

B. *sb.* A proclitic word.

The proclitics in Greek are certain forms of the article, viz. ὁ, ἡ, οἱ, αἱ; and certain adverbs, prepositions, and conjunctions, viz. ἐκ, ἐν, εἰς, εἰ, οὐ (οὐκ), ὡς.

1864 in WEBSTER. **1874** KEY *Language* v. 72, ἐκ and οὐκ are not in themselves words but always attached as proclitics to that which follows. **1893** SONNENSCHEIN in *Class. Rev.* Mar. 135/2 Why? ∵ the preposition is a *proclitic*... Hence he finds himself compelled to say that mŏdo ĕ Dāuo is equivalent to a single word like rĕcŭbare.

pro'clive, *a. Obs.* or *arch.* [a. obs. F. *proclive* (16th c. in Littré), or ad. L. *prōclīv-is* (also *-us*) sloping, descending, inclined, prone, f. *prō*, PRO-[1] 1 b + *clīvus* a slope.]

† **1.** Sloping steeply forwards and downwards. *Obs.*

1524 PACE *Let. to Hen. VIII* in Strype *Eccl. Mem.* (1721) I. App. xi. 20 The Montens [were] so proclive in descence. **1606** G. W[OODCOCKE] *Hist. Ivstine* XXIV. 90 The temple.. is scituat vpon the Mount Parnassus, on the top of a cliffe from euery side and procliue steep down.

2. a. Of persons: Inclined, prone, disposed; having a proclivity or inclination *to* or *towards* any course or action.

1536 BELLENDEN *Cron. Scot.* (1821) II. 120 The ingine of man is mair proclive and reddy to evil werkis than to gud. **1549** LATIMER *1st Serm. bef. Edw. VI* (Arb.) 34 A woman is frayll and procliue vnto all euels. **1601** B. JONSON *Ev. Man in Hum.* (Qo. 1) II. ii, As that land or nation best doth thriue, Which to smooth-fronted peace is most procliue. **1611** SPEED *Hist. Gt. Brit.* IX. viii. §44 They incensed the Pope (too procliue of himselfe to set forth his owne greatnesse). **1706** BAYNARD in Sir J. Floyer *Hot & Cold Bath.* II. (1709) 234 People were generally Faint, and proclive to Sweat.

b. Of things: Leading or tending towards some course or action (usually one considered bad).

1563 FOXE *A. & M.* 55/1 Howe muche more prone and procliue I sawe the waye to hurt. **1653** GATAKER *Vind. Annot. Jer.* 96 Astrologie.. doth pave a plain and proclive path to Idolatry.

3. Headlong, hasty, forward.

1609 B. JONSON *Case is Altered* I. iv, A foolish fellow, some-what proclive and hasty. **1856** MRS. BROWNING *Aur. Leigh* III. 756 In measure to the proclive weight and rush Of His inner nature.

Hence † **pro'cliveness**, proclivity.

1623 T. SCOT *Highw. God* 73, I speake not of them, which may pretend their excuse from the fraylty of our natures, and our procliuenes to sin. **1638** *Penit. Conf.* (1657) 298 The procliveness of mans nature to plunge into former sins.

pro'clivitous, *a. rare.* [f. next + -OUS: cf. *calamitous.*] Steep.

1859 R. F. BURTON *Centr. Afr.* in *Jrnl. Geog. Soc.* XXIX. 104 Many of the ascents and descents are so proclivitous that donkeys must be relieved of their loads.

proclivity (prəʊ'klɪvɪtɪ). [ad. L. *prōclīvitās* a tendency, propensity, f. *prōclīvis*: see PROCLIVE and -ITY, and cf. F. *proclivité* (1603 in Godef.).]

1. A condition of being inclined to something; an instance of such condition; inclination, predisposition, tendency, leaning, propensity.

a. Const. *to* or *towards* some action, habit, or thing; also *to do* something; esp. said of what is evil.

a **1591** H. SMITH *Wks.* (1867) II. 421 He hath no proclivity or willingness of himself to come. **1594** R. ASHLEY tr. *Loys le Roy* 77 b, Iniquitie of nature, and procliuitie vnto vice. *a* **1639** WOTTON *Life Dk. Buckhm.* in *Reliq.* (1651) 76 To which lessons he had such a dextrous proclivity, as his teachers were fain to restrain his forwardness. **1651** HOBBES *Govt. & Soc.* i. §12. 13 This naturall proclivity of men, to hurt each other. **1721** R. KEITH tr. *T. à Kempis' Solil. Soul* xiii. 202 Known unto thee it is, how great a Proclivity there is in my Nature to fall. **1813** SYD. SMITH *Wks.* (1850) 218 Persons.. found with such a proclivity to servitude. **1864** H. SPENCER *Princ. Biol.* II. iv. §65. 181 The vitalized molecules composing the tissues, show their proclivity towards a particular arrangement. **1876** BRISTOWE *The. & Pract. Med.* (1878) 142 A proclivity to catch cold.

b. *absol.*

1649 JER. TAYLOR *Gt. Exemp.* Disc. iii. §15 The mastering of their first Appetites.. lessening the proclivity of habits. **1656** HOBBES *Lib. Necess. & Chance* (1841) 308 That which he calls a necessity, is no more but a proclivity. **1708** in Fowler *Hist. C.C.C.* (O.H.S.) 263 Persons with Jacobite proclivities. **1879** M. PATTISON *Milton* i. 6 The tutor to whom the young Milton was consigned was specially noted for Arminian proclivities. **1899** *Allbutt's Syst. Med.* VIII. 770 The family proclivity is only.. a local tissue proclivity.

† **2.** A steep slope; an acclivity. *Obs.*

1645 EVELYN *Mem.* 7 Feb., We alighted, crawling up the rest of the proclivity with great difficulty.

proclivous (prəʊ'klaɪvəs), *a.* [f. L. *proclīv-us* (see PROCLIVE) + -OUS.]

1. Inclining downwards. *rare.*

1727 in BAILEY vol. II.

2. Inclined or sloping forward: applied to teeth inclined nearly in the line of the axis of the jaw, as the inferior canine teeth of the hippopotamus.

[**1858** MAYNE *Expos. Lex.*, *Proclivus* [Lat.]; so in *Syd. Soc. Lex.*] **1890** *Cent. Dict.*, *Proclivous.*

Hence **pro'clivousness**, proclivity. *rare.*

1727 BAILEY vol. II, *Proclivousness*, inclination downwards, propensity.

Procne: see PROGNE.

procnemial, -coagulant: see PRO-[2] 2, 1.

‖ **procœlia** (prəʊ'siːlɪə). *Anat.* Pl. **-iæ.** [mod.L. (Wilder), f. Gr. πρό, PRO-[2] + κοιλία a hollow: cf. CŒLIAC.] A prosencephalic ventricle; either of the lateral ventricles of the brain.

1882 WILDER & GAGE *Anat. Techn.* 485 *Procœlia*.. the lateral cavity of the prosencephalon, communicating through the porta with the aula and thus with the platetrope, and with the mesal series of cœliæ. **1895** in *Syd. Soc. Lex.*

procœlian (prəʊ'siːlɪən), *a.* (*sb.*) [In sense 1, f. mod.L. *Procœlia* (f. Gr. πρό, PRO-[2] + κοῖλ-ος hollow) + -AN; in sense 2, f. prec. + -AN.]

1. *Anat.* and *Zool.* **a.** = PROCŒLOUS. **b.** Having procœlous vertebræ; pertaining to the *Procœlia*, a suborder of *Crocodilia* including all the extant and recent crocodiles; also as *sb.* a crocodile of this suborder.

1854 R. OWEN *Skel. & Teeth* in *Orr's Circ. Sc.* I. *Org. Nat.* 196 The vertebræ are 'procœlian'. *Ibid.* 199 The vertebræ of the trunk have the same procœlian character, *i.e.* with the cup anterior and the ball behind.

2. *Anat.* Of or pertaining to the procœliæ or prosencephalic ventricles.

1890 in *Cent. Dict.*

procœlous (prəʊ'siːləs), *a. Comp. Anat.* [f. PRO-[2] + Gr. κοῖλ-ος hollow + -OUS: see prec.] Concave or cupped in front: applied to vertebræ; distinguished from *opisthocœlous* and *amphicœlous.*

1870 ROLLESTON *Anim. Life* Introd. 50 The anterior surfaces of these centra have the procoelous appearance. **1872** NICHOLSON *Palæont.* 347 The dorsal vertebræ are 'procœlous' or concave in front. **1872** MIVART *Elem. Anat.* 39 The ball may be post-axial in each vertebral body, a structure termed procœlous, and found in existing crocodiles.

pro-Communist: see PRO-[1] 5 a.

‖ **pro confesso:** see PRO.

proconsul (prəʊ'kɒnsəl). [a. L. *prōconsul*, from the earlier phrase *prō consule* '(one acting) for the consul': see PRO-[1] 4 and CONSUL.]

1. a. *Rom. Hist.* An officer who acting as governor or military commander in a Roman province discharged the duties and had most of the authority of a consul; in the later republic the office was almost always held by an ex-consul; under the emperors, the governor of a senatorial province.

1382 WYCLIF *Acts* xiii. 7 A fals prophete, Jew,.. that was with the proconsul Sergius Poul, prudent man. **1432–50** tr. *Higden* (Rolls) IV. 173 They were deuicte after that in Apulea by Marchus the proconsul of Rome. **1531** ELYOT *Gov.* I. ix, He [Marcus Antoninus] aduanced hym [Proculus] to be proconsul. **1611** SHAKS. *Cymb.* III. vii. 8 He creates Lucius Pro-Consull. **1652** NEEDHAM *Selden's Mare Cl.* 83 The spatious province of the Proconsul of Asia. **1781** GIBBON *Decl. & F.* xvii. II. 36 The proconsuls of Asia, Achaia, and Africa, claimed a pre-eminence, which was yielded to the remembrance of their ancient dignity. **1844** THIRLWALL *Greece* VIII. lxiv. 275 The proconsul, P. Sempronius.. endeavoured to rouse the adjacent Illyrian tribes against Macedonia. **1904** RAMSAY *Lett. to Seven Ch.* ix. 97 The provincial administration exercised the full authority of the Roman Empire, delegated to the Proconsul for his year of office.

fig. **1583** STUBBES *Anat. Abus.* I. (1879) 61 Our Proconsul, and chief Prouost, Christ Iesus.

b. *transf.* Applied rhetorically to a governor of a modern dependency, colony, or conquered province.

In the earlier period of the French Revolution the title was borne by certain commissioners who accompanied the revolutionary armies in insurgent departments, etc.

1827 SCOTT *Napoleon* Introd., Wks. 1870 IX. 277 Another Jacobin proconsul. **1841** MACAULAY *Ess.*, *W. Hastings* (1887) 684 Such was the aspect with which the great Proconsul presented himself to his judges. **1864** TREVELYAN *Compet. Wallah* (1866) 125 It is a fine thing to see a homely old pro-consul retiring from the government of a region as large as France and Austria together, with a clear conscience and a sound digestion. **1893** MCCARTHY *Red Diamonds* I. 2 The poets and proconsuls who made the Hanoverian rule illustrious.

2. (*pro-consul.*) A deputy consul (CONSUL 8).

1804 NELSON in Nicolas *Disp.* (1846) VI. 87 Had the Dey yielded this point.. I should have had no difficulty in placing a Pro-Consul at Algiers... I should have appointed Mr. McDonough Consul *pro tempore.*

3. (See quot.)

1939 *Sunday Times* 8 Jan. 13/1 A pro-Consul.. is a resident member of a British trading community abroad, generally a shipping agent or merchant of repute.

4. Usu. with initial capital. [A. T. Hopwood 1933, in *Ann. Mag. Nat. Hist.* 10th Ser. XI. 98.] An extinct ape belonging to the genus so called, known from Miocene fossil remains discovered in East Africa by Louis Leakey (1903–72) in 1932.

1933 *Jrnl. Linn. Soc.: Zool.* XXXVIII. 457 It would seem that the dentition of *Proconsul* is more primitive than that of the chimpanzee. **1954** *New Biol.* XVII. 12 The remains of fossil apes are especially abundant [on Rusinga Island in Lake Victoria],.. of which the most famous has been *Proconsul.* **1962** *Listener* 5 Apr. 589/1 This animal, which has been named Proconsul, existed approximately 25,000,000 years ago. **1973** J. BRONOWSKI *Ascent of Man* i. 38 A classical find made by Louis Leakey goes by the dignified name of *Proconsul*... (The name *Proconsul*.. was coined to suggest he was an ancestor of a famous chimpanzee at the London Zoo in 1931 whose nickname was Consul.) **1977** A. HALLAM *Planet Earth* 284 Proconsul, an animal about the size of a small baboon, is known from a good skull, jaws and some limb bones.

proconsular (prəʊ'kɒnsjʊlə(r)), *a.* [ad. L. *prōconsulār-is*: see prec. and -AR[1].]

1. Of or pertaining to a Roman proconsul.

1685 H. MORE *Paralip. Prophet.* xii. 89 He was invested with Proconsular Authority for the more contentfully peracting this Tax. **1778** *Eng. Gazetteer* (ed. 2) s.v. *Tilbury*, The 4 proconsular ways made in Britain by the Romans crossed each other in this town. **1852** CONYBEARE & H. *St. Paul* (1862) I. xii. 391 Gallio is seated on that proconsular chair from which judicial sentences were pronounced by the Roman magistrates. **1904** W. M. RAMSAY *Lett. to Seven Ch.* xxii. 297 The Christians were tried in the proconsular courts.

b. *transf.* Of or pertaining to a mediæval or modern provincial governor.

1798 HEL. M. WILLIAMS *Switzerland* I. xiv. 200 Stung into disobedience by some act of proconsular tyranny, they took up arms against their sovereign.

2. Of a province: Under the administration of a Roman proconsul.

proconsular Asia, the Roman province of Asia, including the districts of Mysia, Lydia, Caria, and Phrygia, the western part of Asia Minor; the 'Asia' of the New Testament.

1685 BAXTER *Paraphr. N.T.* Acts xix. 10 The Gospel was spread through all Asia proconsular. **1832–4** DE QUINCEY *Cæsars* Wks. 1859 X. 228 *note*, Throughout the senatorian or proconsular provinces, all taxes were immediately paid into the *ærarium*, or treasury of the state. **1840** A. JOLLY *Sunday Serv.* 310 Abitina, a city in the proconsular province of Africa. **1885** T. M. LINDSAY *Acts* II. 44 Later [Cyprus] became imperial and still later again proconsular. Luke is strictly accurate.

Hence **pro'consularship**, the position of a proconsular province.

1882–3 *Schaff's Encycl. Relig. Knowl.* I. 301/1 Augustus raised it [Bithynia] into a proconsularship B.C. 27.

† **pro'consulary,** *a. Obs. rare.* [f. as prec.: see -ARY[2].] = prec.

1598 GRENEWEY *Tacitus' Ann.* I. v. (1622) 8 He [Tiberius] entreated.. that proconsularie authority might be giuen Germanicus Cæsar. *a* **1656** USSHER *Ann.* VII. (1658) 809 Hadrian.. was made Colleague with his father in the Proconsulary power. **1728** MORGAN *Algiers* I. ii. 17 To inform our-selves of the State the Roman Proconsulary Province was in.

proconsulate (prəʊ'kɒnsjʊlət). [= F. *proconsulat* (1552 in Hatz.-Darm.), ad. L. *prōconsulāt-us*: see PROCONSUL and -ATE[1].]

a. The office of an ancient Roman proconsul; the district under the government of a proconsul.

a **1656** USSHER *Ann.* VI. (1658) 609 He governed the proconsulate of Asia little to his credit. **1856** MERIVALE *Rom. Emp.* IV. xxxiv. 140 The proconsulate of Syria became the object of every inordinate ambition. **1875** LIGHTFOOT *Comm. Col.* 413 The Proconsulate of Paullus.

b. *transf.* Cf. PROCONSUL 1 b.

1796 BURKE *Regic. Peace* i. Wks. VIII. 113 Citizen Barthelemi had been established.. at Basle; where, with his proconsulate of Switzerland and the adjacent parts of Germany, he was appointed as a sort of factor to deal in the degradation of the crowned heads of Europe. **1933** G. ARTHUR *Septuagenarian's Scrap Bk.* 243 The soldier whose proconsulate was extended for over two years and who was then wistfully asked if he would not come back again.

pro'consulship. [f. PROCONSUL + -SHIP.] The office or position of a proconsul.

1581 SAVILE *Tacitus, Agricola* (1622) 200 Now the yeere was at hand, when as the Proconsulship of Asia or Africke should be alotted vnto him. **1631** MASSINGER *Believe as You List* IV. i, And, shoulde shee begge your procunsulship, yf you heard her, 'Twere her's, upon my life. **1741** MIDDLETON *Cicero* (L.), This.. is shewn by the letters [of Cicero] during his proconsulship. **1807** *Europ. Mag.* LII. 443/2 One of the .. coadjutors of the sanguinary Collot d'Herbois, during the dreadful period of his proconsulship at Lyons. **1976** *Church Times* 25 June 11/4 The only absolutely firm date in the whole of the New Testament is the proconsulship of Gallio, shown by an inscription to have begun in the early summer of 51.

proconvertin: see PRO-[2] 1.

procrastinate (prəʊ'kræstɪneɪt), *v.* [f. L. *prōcrastin-āre* to put off till the morrow, to defer,

f. L. *prō*, PRO-[1] 1 d + *crastin-us* belonging to tomorrow (f. *crās* to-morrow): see -ATE[3].]

1. *trans.* To postpone till another day; to put off from day to day; to defer, delay. Now *rare*.

1588 J. HARVEY *Disc. Probl.* 114 The significations of this Coniunction happening in the watrie Trigon, are procrastinated or prolonged untill after sixe Coniunctions immediately insuing. **1603** HOLLAND *Plutarch's Mor.* 1216 The shortnes of time, which allowed us no leasure..to procrastinate the matter. **1624** CAPT. SMITH *Virginia* IV. 158 Many such deuices they fained to procrastinate the time. **1775** *Sterne's Sent. Journ. Contin.* IV. 246, I blush to take a view of myself, and would procrastinate a scrutiny which harrows me at reflection. **1871** BROWNING *Balaust.* 2385 It was the crowning grace of that great heart, To keep back joy; procrastinate the truth.

2. *intr.* To defer action, delay; to be dilatory.

1638 SIR T. HERBERT *Trav.* (ed. 2) 93 Bacherchan having commission to persecute Curroon, procrastinates not. **1647** WARD *Simp. Cobler* 37 To procrastinate in matters clear.. may be dangerous. **1746–7** HERVEY *Medit.* (1818) 225 While we procrastinate, a fatal stroke may intervene. **1850** MCCOSH *Div. Govt.* I. ii. (1874) 45 He hesitates and procrastinates till the time for action is over.

Hence **pro'crastinated** *ppl. a.*, **pro'crastinating** *vbl. sb.* and *ppl. a.*; **pro'crastinatingly** *adv.*

1624 CAPT. SMITH *Virginia* III. 73 The President seeing the procrastinating of time was no course to liue. **1633** EARL MANCH. *Al Mondo* (1636) 124 There is no safetie in procrastinating. **1665** MANLEY *Grotius' Low C. Warres* 686 Great Winds and Rain..caused a procrastinating Delay in the Transacting of many Affairs. **1774** BURKE *Amer. Tax.* Wks. II. 402 A timid, unsystematick, procrastinating ministry. **1789** M. MADAN tr. *Persius* (1795) 130 *note*, Procrastinated time will always fly on. **1893** HUXLEY in *Life* (1900) II. xxi. 364, I was too procrastinatingly lazy to expend even that amount of energy.

procrastination (prəʊkræstɪ'neɪʃən). [ad. L. *prōcrastinātiōn-em*, n. of action f. *prōcrastināre*: see prec., and cf. F. *procrastination* (16th c. in Godef., now rare).] The action or habit of procrastinating, or putting off; delay, dilatoriness.

a **1548** HALL *Chron.*, *Hen. VI* 165 Without longer procrastinacion, he assembled togither .viii. C. horsemen. **1603** KNOLLES *Hist. Turks* (1621) 1293 Most weightie businesse.., and such as could suffer no procrastination or delay. **1742** YOUNG *Nt. Th.* I. 393 Procrastination is the thief of time; Year after year it steals, till all are fled. **1877** FARRAR *Days of Youth* xiv. 133 They branded prudent caution as mean procrastination.

b. The putting off or deferring *of* something.

1632 LITHGOW *Trav.* VII. 304 That benefite of the procrastination of my Life. **1800** *Proc. E. Ind. Ho.* in *Asiat. Ann. Reg.* 68/2 Whether he would consent to the procrastination of his motion or not.

procrastinative (prəʊ'kræstɪnətɪv), *a.* [f. L. *prōcrastināt-*, ppl. stem of *prōcrastin-āre* to PROCRASTINATE + -IVE.] That tends to procrastinate or put off action. Hence **pro'crastinativeness.**

1824 *Examiner* 289/2 The number of merely procrastinative suits..swells the number of cases decided. **1858** CARLYLE *Fredk. Gt.* VI. ix. (1872) II. 224 Whatever the answer..Negative, procrastinative, affirmative, to me it shall be zero. **1896** A. TRUMBLE *In Jail w. C. Dickens* iii. 105 An Act of Parliament..contested with the usual ponderous procrastinativeness.

procrastinator (prəʊ'kræstɪneɪtə(r)). [agent-n. in L. form from PROCRASTINATE *v.*: see -OR 2 c.] One who procrastinates or defers action to another day or some future time; one who habitually delays or puts off attending to matters.

1607 WALKINGTON *Opt. Glass* 154 So is he no procrastinatour. **1711** SWIFT *Jrnl. to Stella* 2 Nov., Lord Treasurer..is the greatest procrastinator in the world. **1865** T. WRIGHT *Hist. Caricature* xiii. 219 The procrastinator is pictured by another fool, with a parrot perched on his head, and a magpie on each hand, all repeating *cras, cras, cras*.

procrastinatory (prəʊ'kræstɪnətərɪ), *a.* [f. as prec.: see -ORY[2].] Given to or implying procrastination; dilatory.

1846 WORCESTER, *Procrastinatory*, implying procrastination. *Ec. Rev.* **1892** *Black & White* 6 Feb. 175/2 A procrastinatory belief in the protection of Providence.

†**pro'crastine,** *v. Obs. rare*[−1]. [ad. L. *prōcrastin-āre* to PROCRASTINATE, or a. obs. F. *procrastine-r* (15–18th c. in Godefroy).] = PROCRASTINATE.

a **1548** HALL *Chron.*, *Hen. VII* 7 Thinkyng that if that pardon were any lenger space procrastened or prolonged, that..Sir Thomas Broughton..should sodeynly moue a newe insurreccion against him.

procreant ('prəʊkriːənt), *a.* (*sb.*) [ad. L. *prōcreānt-em*, pr. pple. of *prōcre-āre*: see next. So F. *procréant*, pres. pple. of *procréer*.]

1. That procreates or begets; producing young; generating; producing, as in ***procreant cause***.

1588 FRAUNCE *Lawiers Log.* I. iii. 18 b, The procreant and conseruant cause. **1654** TRAPP *Comm. Ps.* cvii. 11 Sin is at the bottome of all mens miseries, as the procreant cause thereof. **1679** [see CONSERVANT]. **1802** PALEY *Nat. Theol.* xviii. 344 But the loss of liberty is not the whole of what the procreant bird suffers. **1849** CLOUGH *Dipsychus* II. iii. 23 The procreant heat and fervour of our youth Escapes, in puff, in smoke.

2. Of, pertaining or subservient to procreation.

1605 SHAKS. *Macb.* I. vi. 8 No Iutty frieze, Buttrice, nor Coigne of Vantage, but this Bird Hath made his pendant Bed, and procreant Cradle. **1767** G. WHITE *Selborne* xii, This wonderful 'procreant cradle' [a harvest-mouse's nest]. **1817** WORDSW. *Vernal Ode* iii, Her procreant vigils Nature keeps Amid the unfathomable deeps. **1824** W. IRVING *T. Trav.* I. 200 The swarms of children nestled and cradled in every procreant chamber of this hive.

†**B.** as *sb.* One who or that which procreates; a generator. *Obs.*

1604 SHAKS. *Oth.* IV. ii. 28 Leaue Procreants alone, and shut the doore. **1620** T. GRANGER *Div. Logike* 16 God the Father, Sonne, and holy Ghost, are Procreants and Conseruants of the world. **1641** MILTON *Animadv.* xiii. Wks. 1851 III. 235 Putrid creatures that receive a crawling life from those two most unlike procreants, the Sun and mudde.

†**'procreate,** *ppl. a.* (*sb.*) *Obs.* Also **-at.** [ad. L. *prōcreāt-us*, pa. pple. of *prōcre-āre* to bring forth or beget, produce, cause, f. *prō*, PRO-[1] 1 a + *creāre* to create.] Procreated, begotten. (Usually construed as *pa. pple.*)

1432–50 tr. *Higden* (Rolls) I. 381 Diuerse kyndes of bestes whiche be procreate of commixtion. *c* **1475** *Songs & Carols* (Percy Soc.) 64 Syns that Eve was procreat owt of Adams syde. **1533–4** *Act 25 Hen. VIII*, c. 22 §4 All the issue hade and procreate, or hereafter to be had and procreate bytwene your Highnes and..Quene Anne. **1609** SKENE *Reg. Maj.* I. 121 b, Gif ane Burges..hes procreat bairnes with ilke ane of his wifes. **1632** LITHGOW *Trav.* IV. 170 Some of these Kings, dying without procreate Heires.

B. *sb.* The produce of money; interest.

1674 JEAKE *Arith.* (1696) 578 If the Paiment be half Yearly or Quarterly,..let the Log. of the Yearly Procreat be multiplied accordingly by ½ or ¼.

procreate ('prəʊkriːeɪt), *v.* [f. L. *prōcreāt-*, ppl. stem of *prōcreāre*: see prec.] *trans.* To beget, engender, generate (offspring).

1536 *Act 28 Hen. VIII*, c. 7 § 5 That the issue borne and procreated under the same vnlawfull mariage..betwene your Highnes, and the said Lady Katheryne, shall be taken demed and accepted illegittimate to all ententes and purposes. **1579** FENTON *Guicciard.* XVI. (1599) 747 Their.. hope to procreate children. **1693** EVELYN *De la Quint. Compl. Gard.* 74 Animals..do not Procreate their Like, but when they are in their Vigor. **1730** T. BOSTON *Mem.* i. 5 Four brothers and three sisters, procreated betwixt John Boston and Alison Trotter, a woman prudent and virtuous. **1859** DARWIN *Orig. Spec.* iv. (1872) 71 A pair of animals, producing..two hundred offspring, of which..only two on an average survive to procreate their kind.

b. *absol.* or *intr.* To produce offspring.

1646 SIR T. BROWNE *Pseud. Ep.* 94 If that be..female which procreates in it selfe;..all plants are female. **1792** A. YOUNG *Trav. France* 408 Couples marry and procreate on the idea, not the reality, of a maintenance; they increase beyond the demand of towns and manufactures.

c. *trans.* (*transf.* and *fig.*) To bring into existence, produce; to give rise to, occasion. Now *rare*.

1546 LANGLEY *Pol. Verg. De Invent.* I. iii. 5 The Riuer Nilus, whiche for the lustye fatnesse of the slime, doeth procreat diuerse kyndes of beastes. **1588** FRAUNCE *Lawiers Log.* I. iii. 11 b, That cause efficient..doth either procreate or bring forth that which was not before, as God the worlde. **1634** SIR T. HERBERT *Trav.* 46 Ormus..procreates nothing note-worthy, Salt excepted. **1674** JEAKE *Arith.* (1696) 305 The sides of Homogeneal Surdes multiplyed procreateth sides of Homogeneal Surdes. **1777** ROBERTSON *Hist. Amer.* (1778) II. v. 41 The offspring of the sun, procreated..in the regions of the east.

Hence **'procreated, 'procreating** *ppl. adjs.*

1552 HULOET, Procreated, *procreatus*. **1653** MANTON *Exp. James* I. 14 Wks. 1871 IV. 93 The true procreating cause of sin is in every man's soul. **1857–69** HEAVYSEGE *Saul* (ed. 3) 135 That procreated race, Which holds 'twixt us and brutes the place. **1864** R. A. ARNOLD *Cotton Fam.* 10 An urgent demand for labour will increase the procreated supply.

procreation (prəʊkriː'eɪʃən). [ME. a. OF. *procreacion* (14th c. in Littré), mod.F. *procréation*, ad. L. *prōcreātiōn-em*, n. of action f. *prōcre-āre*: see above.]

1. The action of procreating or begetting; generation, propagation of species; the fact of being begotten.

c **1386** CHAUCER *Merch. T.* 204 Take hym a wyf..By cause of leueful procreacion Of children. *c* **1412** HOCCLEVE *De Reg. Princ.* 1576 Procreacioun Of children is, vn-to goddes honour. **1494** FABYAN *Chron.* VI. ccvii. 220 Of this Wyllyams procreacion, it is wytnessed of Vyncent Hystoryall & other. **1548–9** (Mar.) *Bk. Com. Prayer*, *Matrimony*, The causes for the whiche matrimonie was ordeined. One cause was the procreacion of children. **1607** SHAKS. *Timon* IV. iii. 4 Twin'd Brothers..Whose procreation, residence, and birth, Scarse is diuidant. **1682** T. GIBSON *Anat.* 22 The parts..minister either to nutrition, for the conservation of the Individual; or to Procreation, for the conservation of the Species. **1766** BLACKSTONE *Comm.* II. vii. 114 As the word *heirs* is necessary to create a fee, so ..the word *body*, or some other words of procreation, are necessary to make it a fee-tail. *a* **1874** SUCKLEY in Coues *Birds N.W.* 11 The indispensable union of a pair for the purpose of procreation.

†**2.** That which is procreated; offspring, progeny.

1533–4 *Act 25 Hen. VIII*, c. 12 To the intente that his maiestie..might haue issue and procreation for the..suretie of this his realme. **1610** GUILLIM *Heraldry* III. xxvi. (1611) 183 No lesse monstrous then those deformed procreations and naturally deformed animals. **1651** HOBBES *Leviath.* II. xxiv. 131 The Procreation, or Children of a Common-wealth, are those we call Plantations, or Colonies.

3. *transf.* and *fig.* Origination, production, natural formation.

1578 BANISTER *Hist. Man* I. 7 For the procreation of Sutures. **1599** NASHE *Lenten Stuffe* Title-p., The Description and first Procreation and Increase of the Towne of Great Yarmouth in Norffolke. **1642** FULLER *Holy & Prof. St.* II. xix. 127 The procreation of peace..is the end of warre. **1671** J. WEBSTER *Metallogr.* iv. 74 In the procreation of Metals some Sulphureous matter doth intervene. **1871** B. TAYLOR *Faust* (1875) II. II. ii. 95 This procreation is most rare; Of the old senseless way we're now well ridden.

procreative ('prəʊkriːeɪtɪv), *a.* [f. L. type **prōcreātīv-us*: see PROCREATE *ppl. a.* and -IVE. So OF. *procreative* (14th c. in Godef.).] Pertaining to procreation; having the power or function of producing offspring. Also *fig.*

1634 T. JOHNSON *Parey's Chirurg.* XXIV. xxxix. (1678) 568 The..procreative faculty ceaseth in some sooner, in some later. **1642** FULLER *Holy & Prof. St.* V. xii. 406 Having made one lye he is fain to make more to maintain it... Not one amongst them shall be barren, but miraculously procreative to beget others. **1815** W. H. IRELAND *Scribbleomania* 252 *note*, The procreative soil will expand the ripening germs, and in the end produce a plenteous harvest. **1850** BLACKIE *Æschylus* II. 153 The irregular gratification of the procreative instinct.

Hence **'procreativeness.**

1655 FULLER *Ch. Hist.* II. iii. §32 The Procreativeness of those Nations presently stinted and abated. **1667** *Decay Chr. Piety* ix. ¶14 To have reconcil'd the procreativeness of corporeal, with the duration of incorporeal substances.

'procreˌator. *rare.* [a. L. *prōcreātor*, agent-n. f. *prōcre-āre* to PROCREATE. So F. *procréateur* adj. (1547 in Hatz.-Darm.).] One who or that which procreates or begets; a parent.

a **1548** HALL *Chron.*, *Edw. IV* 203 b, He is vnkynd and vnnaturall, that will not cherishe hys natural parentes and procreators. **1593** NASHE *Christ's T.* (1613) 185 They.. neuer mention our sinnes, which are his chiefe procreatours. **1975** *Way* Suppl. xxv. 12 In the sexual union, man and woman under God become procreators.

†**'procreatory,** *a. Obs.* [f. as prec.: see -ORY[2].] Of or tending to procreation; procreative.

1576 NEWTON *Lemnie's Complex.* (1633) 32 Thus the wonderfull Creator of Nature..put into all things that were created a power procreatory, and the order of their encreasing, and propagation.

'procreˌatress. *rare.* [f. PROCREATOR + -ESS[1].] A female procreator or parent.

1597 MIDDLETON *Wisd. Solomon* xiv. 26 O idol-worshipping, thou mother art, she-procreatress of a he-offence. **1623** WODROEPHE *Marrow Fr. Tongue* 528/2 The most liberall Mother and Procreatresse of all Things, the Earth.

†**procre'atrix.** *Obs. rare.* [a. L. *prōcreātrix*, fem. of *prōcreātor* PROCREATOR.] = prec.

1592 STUBBES *Motive Gd. Workes* (1593) 18 b, The earth, the mother and procreatrix of all things. **1611** COTGR., *Procreatrice*, a procreatrix; a mother, or damme.

Procrustean (prəʊ'krʌstiːən), *a.* [f. PROCRUSTES + -AN: cf. *Herculean*.] Of or pertaining to Procrustes: aiming or tending to produce uniformity by violent and arbitrary methods.

a **1846** *Christian Observer* (cited in Worcester). **1848** MRS. GASKELL *M. Barton* xv, To..tie them down to their own Procrustean bed. **1857** TOULMIN SMITH *Parish* 118 For which they have cut and dried procrustean remedies ready to hand. **1875** JOWETT *Plato* (ed. 2) II. 271 Neither must we attempt to confine the Platonic dialogue on the Procrustean bed of a single idea. **1876** MOZLEY *Univ. Serm.* vii. (1877) 156 Not to be submitted to any Procrustean process, even of disciplinary moulding.

Hence **Pro'crusteanism,** a Procrustean method or principle; **Pro'crusteanize** *v.*, to render Procrustean; to treat by Procrustean methods.

1864 *Edin. Rev.* July 168 The repulsive *Procrusteanism of the course of instruction. *a* **1846** *Christian Obs.* (cited in Worcester), *Procrusteanize. **1899** *Speaker* 30 Dec. 338/2 The girls sat daily in a horrible machine constructed to Procrusteanize a long and graceful neck by drawing up the head and chin.

Procrustes (prəʊ'krʌstiːz). [a. Gr. *Προκρούστης*, personal name, lit. 'one that stretches', f. *προκρούειν* to beat or hammer out, to stretch out.] The name of a fabulous robber of Attica who is said to have stretched or mutilated his victims to conform them to the length of his bed. Hence allusively. Also *attrib.*

1583 FULKE *Defence* i. (Parker Soc.) 97 You play manifestly with us the lewd part of Procrustes, the thievish host, which would make his guests' stature equal with his bed's, either by stretching them out if they were too short, or by cutting off their legs if they were too long. **1637** T. MORTON *New Eng. Canaan* (1883) 335 This passage is like to the Procrustes of Roome, mee thinks. **1790** HAN. MORE *Relig. Fash. World* (1791) 35 We may rejoice that the tyranny of the spiritual Procrustes is so far annihilated. **1837** SYD. SMITH *1st Let. Archd. Singleton* Wks. 1859 II. 259/2 It is quite absurd to see how all the Cathedrals are to be trimmed to an exact Procrustes pattern. **1870** W. GRAHAM *Lect. Ephesians* v. 129 It became the procrustes bed on which the faith and hope of the nation were offered up.

procry, obs. Sc. form of PROCURACY.

procrypsis (prəʊˈkrɪpsɪs). *Zool.* [f. PRO- (cf. PROCRYPTIC *a.*) + Gr. κρύψις concealment.] Protective colouring in animals.

1920 G. D. H. CARPENTER *Naturalist on L. Victoria* 196 Procryptic colouring conceals its wearer from danger, causing it to resemble either the general surroundings or some particular part thereof (Special Procrypsis). **1933** *Discovery* Nov. 357/2 The resemblance of creatures to their environment.. technically termed Procrypsis. **1946** *Nature* 24 Aug. 278/1 Is resemblance to part of a dead ant to be sharply separated from resemblance to a whole, living ant? To a Darwinian, one is an example of special procrypsis, while the other is pseudoaposematic. **1977** M. TWEEDIE *Insect Life* ii. 74 We see among them [*sc.* insects] the first stages of the type of adaptation commonly known as camouflage, but among biologists as cryptic adaptation or procrypsis.

procryptic (prəʊˈkrɪptɪk), *a.* *Zool.* [f. PRO-[1] or [2] + Gr. κρυπτικός fit for concealing, f. κρύπτειν to hide, conceal: cf. CRYPTIC. (App. formed after *protective.*)] Having the function of protectively concealing: applied to the protective mimicry of colour and form, observed in insects (esp. butterflies and moths and their caterpillars), and some other animals. Hence **proˈcryptically** *adv.*

1891 E. B. POULTON in *Proc. Zool. Soc.* 463 A palatable insect.. which defended itself, like the great majority of its allies, by Protective Resemblance (Procryptic Colouring). **1900** *Nature* 13 Dec. 157/2 These animals are known to be procryptically coloured.

procto- (ˈprɒktəʊ), before a vowel **proct-**, combining form of Gr. πρωκτός anus; used to form modern scientific terms, chiefly medical and surgical, rarely zoological. ‖**procˈtagra** [Gr. ἄγρα seizure], = next (Dunglison 1853). ‖**procˈtalgia** [Gr. ἄλγος pain], pain in the anus; so **procˈtalgy**. ‖**proctaˈtresia** [Gr. ἀτρησία imperforation], imperforation of the anus (Dunglison 1842); so **ˈproctatresy**. **procˈtectomy** [Gr. ἐκτομή excision], excision of the rectum (*Syd. Soc. Lex.*). **procˈtitis** [-ITIS], inflammation of the rectum and anus. **ˈproctocele** (-siːl) [Gr. κήλη tumour], prolapse of the mucous membrane of the rectum through the anus (Dunglison 1842). **ˌproctocyˈstotomy**, cystotomy performed through the anterior wall of the rectum; so **proctoˈcystotome**, an instrument designed for this operation (Mayne *Expos. Lex.* 1858). ‖**proctoˈdæum** *Embryol.* [Gr. ὁδαῖος that is on or by the road], the posterior portion of the digestive tract, beginning as an invagination of the epiblast; hence **proctoˈdæal** *a.* ‖**proctoˈdynia** [Gr. ὀδύνη pain] = *proctalgia* (Dunglison 1857). ‖**procˈtoncus** [Gr. ὄγκος swelling], a swelling of or near the anus (Dunglison 1853). **ˌproctopaˈralysis**, paralysis of the muscles of the rectum (Dunglison 1853). **ˈproctoplasty** [-PLASTY], plastic surgery of the anal region; so **proctoˈplastic** *a.* (*Syd. Soc. Lex.*). **ˌproctoˈpolypus** [POLYPUS 2], anal polypus (Mayne 1858). ‖**proctoˈptoma** [Gr. πτῶμα fall], = *proctocele* (Dunglison 1857). ‖**proctopˈtosis** [Gr. πτῶσις a falling] = prec. ‖**proctoˈrrhagia** [see HÆMORRHAGY], hæmorrhage from the anus (Dunglison 1853). **procˈtorrhaphy** [Gr. ῥαφή suture], suture of the rectum close to the anus (Billings 1890). ‖**proctoˈrrhœa** [Gr. ῥοία flux], a morbid discharge from the anus (Hooper *Med. Dict.* 1811). **ˈproctoscope** [-SCOPE], a rectal speculum; **procˈtoscopy**, use of, or examination with, a proctoscope; hence **proctoˈscopic** *a.* **procˈtotomy** [Gr. τομή cutting], incision of the rectum (Mayne 1858); so **ˈproctotome**, an instrument for this operation (Billings 1890). **ˈproctotrete** [Gr. τρητός perforated], a S. American iguanoid lizard of the genus *Proctotrētus* (*Cent. Dict.* 1890). **procˈtuchous** *a.* [Gr. ἔχειν to have], having an anus; applied to one division of turbellarians, the *Proctūcha*, as distinguished from the *Aprocta* (*Cent. Dict.* 1890).

1811 HOOPER *Med. Dict.*, **Proctalgia*,.. a violent pain at the anus. It is mostly symptomatic of some disease, as piles, ..&c. **1858** MAYNE *Expos. Lex.*, *Proctalgia*.., *proctalgy. *Ibid.*, *Proctatresia*.., *proctatresy. **1811** HOOPER *Med. Dict.*, **Proctitis*,.. inflammation of.. the lower part of the rectum. **1866** A. FLINT *Princ. Med.* (1880) 431 Proctitis occurs from the action of local causes, and may simulate dysentery. **1888** F. E. BEDDARD in *Encycl. Brit.* XXIV. 680/1 The terminal section of the intestine is formed by the *proctodæal invagination. **1878** BELL *Gegenbaur's Comp. Anat.* p. xiv, The corresponding passage leading from the anus I.. propose to call the '*proctodæum'. **1904** *Brit. Med. Jrnl.* 17 Dec. 1632/2 Both cavities—the postanal gut and the proctodeum—are actively growing. **1896** *Mathews' Med. Q.* III. 203 A little practice in Kelly's method teaches the operator how to carry the end of the *proctoscope away from the prostate. **1902** *Brit. Med. Jrnl.* 19 July 170/2 A few days later I examined with the proctoscope. **1904** *Brit. Med. Jrnl.* 3 Dec. 1505/2 The electric proctoscope enables the lower bowel to be examined by the eye without difficulty to a height of 30 centimetres. **1896** *Mathews' Med. Q.* III. 208 The *proctoscopic mirror faces the operator. **1902** *Brit. Med. Jrnl.* 19 July 170/2 Proctoscopic examination. **1896** *Mathews' Med. Q.* III. 332 A central aperture, which.. escaped my own digital perception.. and was not discovered until subsequently revealed by *proctoscopy. **1977** *Lancet* 21 May 1085/1 The diagnosis of inflammatory bowel disease was.. confirmed at proctoscopy.

proctology (prɒkˈtɒlədʒɪ). [f. PROCTO- + -LOGY.] The branch of medicine concerned with the anus and rectum or (with some writers) with the anus and the whole colon.

1899 *Trans. Ohio State Med. Soc.* 257 Thos. Chas. Martin M.D. Cleveland. Teacher of Proctology in the Cleveland College of Physicians and Surgeons; Proctologist to the Cleveland General Hospital. **1929** W. E. MINOR *Clin. Proctology* iv. 37 Some years ago I adopted a terminology which recognizes only one type of hemorrhoid. I find this solution very acceptable and helpful to the student of proctology. **1956** H. E. BACON et al. *Proctology* p. ix, The late Joseph M. Mathews defined proctology as the science that treats of surgical diseases of colon, rectum and anal canal. **1959** K. ZIMMERMAN in R. Turell *Dis. Colon & Anorectum* II. lviii. 1195 The practice of 'office proctology', or 'ambulant proctology', was for many years in the hands of charlatans. **1976** *Times* 29 Apr. 18/4 The section of proctology of the Royal Society of Medicine held their annual dinner at 1 Wimpole Street, yesterday evening.

Hence **proctoˈlogic**, **proctoˈlogical** *adjs.*; **procˈtologist**, an expert or specialist in proctology.

1899 *Trans. Amer. Proctologic Soc.* I. p. v, Article I. The name of this Association shall be the *American Proctologic Society*. Article II. Its object shall be the cultivation and promotion of knowledge in whatever relates to Disease of the Rectum and colon. **1899** *Ohio State Jrnl.* 8 June 3/1 A new national medical association to be known as the American Proctological society was organized yesterday. **1899** Proctologist [see above]. **1907** *Proctologist* I. 1 No medical work.. is complete, today, that does not deal fully and explicitly with proctological diseases. **1926** L. J. HIRSCHMAN *Handbk. Dis. Rectum* (ed. 4) 7 As efficient diagnostic and therapeutic service should be rendered to the proctologic patient as to any other. **1950** J. P. NESSELROD *Proctology* ii. 54 Proctologists are not yet in full accord.. with regard to the extent of their field. **1959** K. ZIMMERMAN in R. Turell *Dis. Colon & Anorectum* II. lviii. 1195 Many.. proctologic conditions may be treated in the office. **1964** *Punch* 26 Aug. 307/2 Proctologists, who are admired as working in a gold mine. **1971** *Dis. Colon & Rectum* XIV. 8/2 Barium-enema examination and proctologic evaluation were requested. **1979** *Guardian* 9 Jan. 8/5 Mr Carter's own proctological history. **1980** S. STEIN *Resort* i. 14 Politicians are assholes attended by proctologists.

proctor (ˈprɒktə(r)), *sb.*[1] [A syncopated form of *procuraˈtour*, PROCURATOR, through *procutour*, *procketour*, *proctour*, etc. Cf. PROXY = PROCURACY, also the ME. weakening of PROCURE *v.* to *proker*.]

A. Illustration of Forms.

α. 3–7 **procuratour** (5–6 **-oure**, 6 *Sc.* **-ure**), 5 **prokeratour**, 3– **procurator**. See PROCURATOR.

β. 5–6 **procutour**, 5–8 **-or** (5 **-oure**, **-ur**, **procatour(e**, **proketowre**, **procketur**), 6–7 **procutar**, 9 **prokitor**. After *c* 1500 only *Sc.*

c **1386** CHAUCER *Friar's T.* 298 May I nat.. answere there by my procutour? [*v.rr.* procatour(e; *Harl.* 7334 procuratour]. **14..** *Cursor M.* 16023 (Gött.) Pilate pair prucketur [*v.r.* procuratur]. *c* **1440** *Promp. Parv.* 414/2 Proketowre (*K.* prokeratour), *procurator*. *c* **1450** *Godstow Reg.* 649 The procutur of the mynchons. **1459** *Paston Lett.* I. 454 The wardeyn and the procutoris.. of the parishe chirche. **1641** *Sc. Acts Chas. I* (1817) V. 413/2 The humble supplication of Mr. Archibald Johnstoun procutor for the Kirk. ? *a* **1700** *Truth's Trav.* in *Pennecuik's Poems* (1715) 106 The Procutars bad him be stout, Care not for Conscience a Leek. **1818** SCOTT *Hrt. Midl.* xvi, Great preferment for poor Madge.. to speak wi' provosts, and bailies, and town-clerks, and prokitors.

γ. 4–7 **proctour**, (5–6 **proktur(e**, 6 **proctoure**, 6–7 **procter**), 5– **proctor**.

c **1380** WYCLIF *Sel. Wks.* I. 412 Many ben traitours to God, and proctours to þe fend. **1432–50** Proctor [see B. 1, 4]. **1483** *Cath. Angl.* 292/2 A Prokture, *accurator*, *procurator*. *a* **1548** HALL *Chron.*, *Rich. III* 44 b, Affiances made and taken by procters and deputies. **1613** R. CAWDREY *Table Alph.* (ed. 3), *Proctour*, a factour or solicitor. *c* **1618** Procter [see B. 2 c].

B. Signification.

†**1.** *Rom. Hist.* = PROCURATOR 1. *Obs.*

14.. [see A. β]. **1432–50** tr. *Higden* (Rolls) IV. 391 Felix was.. made the proctor of the Iewes. **1480** CAXTON *Chron. Eng.* IV. (1520) 28/2 Pontius Pilate was Judge and proctour in the Jury under the Emperoure.

2. A person employed to manage the affairs of another; an agent, deputy, proxy, attorney: = PROCURATOR 2. *Obs.* or *arch.* exc. in technical use.

c **1449** PECOCK *Repr.* III. xvii. 396 Thei schulden be punyschid.. in her procutour or attorney occupiyng.. in her names. *a* **1450** MYRC 22 All þat consenten thereto in hermyng of the person or of þe vicary or her proketours. **1494** FABYAN *Chron.* VII. ccxxxvii. 274 Yᵉ kyng sent ouer bysshoppis & proctours to complayn vpon hym to yᵉ pope. **1560** DAUS tr. *Sleidane's Comm.* 365 Others.. whan they had obtained license, sente theyr Proctours. **1643** PRYNNE *Sov. Power Parl.* App. 206 But he neither vouchsafed to appeare, nor yet to send any one to us in the name of a Proctor.

†**b.** A steward: = PROCURATOR 2 b. *Obs.*

c **1380** WYCLIF *Wks.* (1880) 279 Alle þes goodis ben pore mennus goodis, & clerkis ben not lordis of hem but proctours. **1382** —— *Gen.* xv. 2 The sone of the proctour [1388 procuratour] of myn hows, this Damask of Elyzar. *c* **1449** PECOCK *Repr.* III. xvii. 389 The Lorde of the Vyner.. seide to his procutour thus 'Clepe thou the werkmen and ȝeelde to hem her meede'. **1538** LONDON in *Lett. Suppress. Monasteries* (Camden) 215 We founde the prior of the Charterhowse in hys shortt gowen and velvytt cappe.. and the proctor of that howse in lyke apparell. **1565–78** COOPER *Thesaurus*, *Castaldius*, a proctor: a steward: a baily.

c. An agent for the collection of tithes and other church dues; a tithe-farmer. In full ***tithe-proctor***.

1607 COWELL *Interpr.*, *Procurator*, is vsed for him that gathereth the fruites of a benefice for another man... They are at this day in the West parts called Proctors. *c* **1618** MORYSON *Itin.* IV. III. vi. (1903) 288 Both Ministers and Bishops non resident sent to theire remote liuings only Procters to gather theire tythes and profitts. **1780** A. YOUNG *Tour Irel.* I. 217 Tythes.. were a real grievance; the proctors let the first, and perhaps the second year with them run by bond. **1807** VANCOUVER *Agric. Devon* (1813) 102 Tyranny and extortion.. exercised by the tithe-proctors, or other persons renting the great tithes from the church of Exeter. **1898** MACDONAGH *Irish Life* xiii. 229 The tithe-proctors —the men who collected the impost, or, in default of payment, seized the stock of the Catholic peasants—were objects of intense popular hatred.

3. In a University, one of two or more officers periodically elected by the members of the University or one of its constituent sections, whose duties have varied at different times and in different places. The primary function of the office seems to have been representative, esp. in law-suits, and in the administration of corporate funds.

a. In reference to mediæval (and Scottish) universities, an occasional anglicized form of the L. term *procurator* actually used: see PROCURATOR 3.

1895 RASHDALL *Univ. Europe in Middle Ages* I. 315 (Paris) The first document in which the Rector and Proctors are clearly distinguished from one another is a Statute of the Faculty of Arts in 1245. *Ibid.* II. 121 [At Montpellier] as at Oxford, the Masters are more directly represented by two Proctors, the office circulating among them. The functions of these Proctors were primarily financial, as originally were those of the Proctors of Paris and Oxford. *Ibid.* 298 [At St. Andrews] The Masters and students—divided into the Four Nations of Fife, Lothian, Angus, and Britain, each with its Proctor— elected the Rector. *Ibid.* 306 [At Glasgow] Only on occasions of the Rectorial elections was the organization of Nations and student Proctors called into actual existence —for which purpose it has lasted down to the present day.

b. In modern use, as at Oxford and Cambridge, each of two officers appointed annually to discharge various functions in connexion with the meetings of the University and its various Boards, the examinations and conferment of degrees, and the like; they are also charged with the discipline of all persons *in statu pupillari*, and the summary punishment of minor offences.

In the old English Universities, they were formerly called ***Northern*** and ***Southern Proctor*** respectively (see PROCURATOR 3); they are now distinguished as ***Senior*** and ***Junior Proctor***, in accordance with their university seniority. They are appointed or elected by the various colleges in rotation. At Oxford they are the representatives of the body of Masters of Arts, and, as such, are assessors to the Chancellor or Vice-Chancellor, and ex-officio members of the Hebdomadal Council and of almost all University Boards and Delegacies; they exercise a joint veto upon the proceedings and decrees of Congregation and Convocation, ask graces for degrees in the Ancient House of Convocation, nominate delegates not otherwise specially appointed, supervise the examiners and examinations conjointly with the Vice-Chancellor, and concur with him in the conferring of all degrees. At Cambridge their powers and functions are similar, but less extensive. Proctors also exist with certain functions at Dublin and at Durham.

proctors' dogs or ***bulldogs*** (*Univ. slang*), the sworn constables whose original function was to accompany the proctors in their nightly perambulation of the streets for the purpose of preventing disorder.

[(For the sake of historical continuity earlier examples in the Latin form *procurator* are also given here.) **1248** *Rot. Claus.* 33 *Hen. III*, m. 15 *dorso* (in Rashdall II. 369 *note*), Presentibus apud Woodstocke tam procuratoribus scolarium universitatis quam Burgensibus Oxon. *c* **1250** in *Mun. Acad. Oxon* (Rolls) 12 De assensu Cancellarii et Procuratorum Universitatis. **1257** *Ibid.* 30 Faciant Procuratores congregationem fieri, quæ ultra triduum non differatur. **1314–15** *Rolls of Parlt.* I. 327/1 Quotiens.. per Cancellarium & Procuratores Universitatis fuerint premuniti. **1407** in *Mun. Acad. Oxon.* (Rolls) 237 Magister Ricardus Flemmyng, Canonicus ecclesiæ cathedralis Eboracensis, et Procurator borealis Universitatis Oxoniæ. **1411–12** *Rolls of Parlt.* III. 651/2 Visitatio Cancellarii ac Procuratorum dicte Universitatis.. necnon omnium Doctorum, Magistrorum, regentium et non regentium, ac Scolarium ejusdem Universitatis.]

1536 *Rem. Sedition* 16 In Oxford.. the name of the northern, and southerne proctour, hath been the cause, that many men haue ben slayne. **1536** in W. H. Turner *Select. Rec. Oxford* (1880) 136 Yᵉ Proctor did thrust his pole-axe at him. **1573** G. HARVEY *Letter-bk.* 7 M. Alin, then and now senior proctor. **1574** M. STOKYS in Peacock *Stat. Cambr.* (1841) App. A. p. ix, Then shall the Proctours apoynt them [Determiners] their Senioritie. *a* **1613** OVERBURY *Charact.*, *Meere Scholer* Wks. (1856) 88 University jests are his universall discourse, and his newes the demeanor of the proctors. **1663** WOOD *Life* 24 Sept. (O.H.S.) I. 495, 16 Masters in proctors' gownes. **1797** *Cambr. Univ. Cal.* 140 Proctors are two officers chosen annually from the regent masters of arts on the 10th of October: they are called proctors, from their managing (*procurandis*) the affairs and business of the university, and also rectors from their superintending or governing (*regendis*) the schools. **1828** GUNNING *Ceremonies Cambr.* 3 Cycle for the nomination of proctors. **1841** PEACOCK *Stat. Cambr.* 24 The two proctors, ..after the chancellor or vice-chancellor were the most important administrative officers in the university. They were chosen annually by the regents. **1847** TENNYSON *Princ.* Prol. 113 We, unworthier told Of college: he had climbed across the spikes..And he had breath'd the Proctor's dogs. *Ibid.* 141 Pretty were the sight If our old halls could change their sex, and flaunt With prudes for proctors, dowagers for deans, And sweet girl-graduates in their golden hair. **1863** 'OUIDA' *Held in Bondage* (1870) 39, I had been shown up before the proctor on no less than six separate occasions. **1899** *Oxf. Univ. Cal.* p. xxiii, Cycle for the nomination of proctors... 1899. Trinity, Jesus. 1900. Merton, Lincoln [etc.].

fig. *a* **1667** COWLEY *Elegy J. Littleton* 37 He..might find A little Academy in his mind; Where..Reason, and Holy Fear the Proctors were, To apprehend those words, those Thoughts that err.

4. *Law.* One whose profession is to manage the causes of others in a court administering civil or canon law; corresponding to an attorney or solicitor in courts of equity and common law. (Now in England retained only in courts of ecclesiastical and Oxford university jurisdiction.)

King's (Queen's) Proctor, an official of the Probate, Divorce, and Admiralty Division of the High Court of Justice, who has the right to intervene in probate, divorce, and nullity cases, when collusion between the parties or suppression of material facts is alleged. (The title is a survival from the time when these cases belonged to the ecclesiastical courts.)

1432-50 tr. *Higden* (Rolls) III. 201 Promisenge to hym a grete summe of moneye in that day he scholde be a proctor a fore a iuge and haue þe victory in his causes. **1538** STARKEY *England* I. iii. 83 Prokturys and brokarys of both lawys..are to many. **1546** LANGLEY *Pol. Verg. De Invent.* VIII. ii. 145 Pius the II..instituted the new College of Solicitors & Proctors by whose Counsaill and aduise all bulles and grauntes wer made. **1603** *Const. & Canons Eccl.* §133 The loud and confused cries and clamours of proctors in the courts of the archbishop are..troublesome and offensive to the judges and advocates. **1605-6** *Act 3 Jas. I*, c. 5 §6 No Recusant convict shall..practise the Common Lawe..as a Councellor, Clerke, Attourney, or Sollicitor..nor shall practise the Civill Lawe as Advocate or Proctor. **1693** CONGREVE *Double Dealer* IV. x, I've a cousin who is a proctor in the Commons. **1849** DICKENS *Dav. Copp.* xxiii, 'What is a proctor, Steerforth?' said I. 'Why, he is a sort of monkish attorney... He is, to some faded courts held in Doctors' Commons..what solicitors are to the courts of law and equity'. **1860** *Act 23 & 24 Vict.* c. 144 §5 In every case of a petition for a dissolution of marriage it shall be lawful for the Court..to direct all necessary papers in the matter to be sent to Her Majesty's Proctor, who shall..instruct counsel to argue before the Court any question in relation to such matter. **1899** *Oxf. Univ. Cal.* 21 Proctors in the Vice-Chancellor's Court. William Henry Walsh [etc.], Solicitors. **1908** *Whitaker's Alm.* 181/2 Treasury..Department of Solicitor to the Treasury, Director of Public Prosecutions and King's Proctor.

†**5.** An advocate, patron, defender, guardian: = PROCURATOR 5. *Obs.*

a **1413** in Hall *Chron., Hen. IV* (1548) 21 Henry Percy our eldest sonne..and Thomas Percy erle of Worcester beyng proctours and protectours of the comon wealth. *c* **1420** *Chron. Vilod.* 591-2 Swythelyne, þat was bysshop þo, Was made cheffe procutour of þat place; And so he was procutour and gret helper þerto, For a fully holy mone forsothe he was. *c* **1450** tr. *De Imitatione* II. i. 40 He shal be þi prouisour, þy true procutour in all þinges. **1548** GEST *Pr. Masse* in H. G. Dugdale *Life* (1840) App. I. 74 Whether he bee an hartie hearer or proctour of the sayd masse. **1553** BECON *Reliques of Rome* (1563) 85 The firste promoters & chiefe proctors to haue Images in churches. **1594** SOUTHWELL *M. Magd. Fun. Teares* (1823) 171 Thy teares were the procters for thy brother's life. **1608** TOPSELL *Serpents* 252 Imputing that to the Patron and Proctor some-times of Musick, which ought rather to be attributed to Musicke it selfe. **1653** H. COGAN tr. *Pinto's Trav.* xxvii. (1663) 106 This hard proceeding much astonished these two Proctors for the poor.

6. A deputy elected to represent the chapter of a cathedral or collegiate church, or the clergy of a diocese or archdeaconry (*proctor of the clergy*), in the Lower House of Convocation of either province.

1586 J. HOOKER *Hist. Irel.* in *Holinshed* II. 122/1 The bishop ought..to summon and warne all deanes and archdeacons within his diocesse to appeere in proper person at the parlement, vnlesse they haue some sufficient and reasonable cause of absence, in which case he may appeere by his proctor, hauing a warrant or proxie for the same. **1607** COWELL *Interpr., Procters of the clergie*.., are those which are chosen and appointed to appeare for cathedrall, or other Collegiat churches, as also for the common clergie of euery Dioces, at the Parlament, whose choice is in this sort [etc.]. **1823** LINGARD *Hist. Eng.* VI. 421 To elude the opposition of the clergy, their proctors, who had hitherto voted in the Irish parliaments, were by a declaratory act pronounced to be nothing more than assistants, whose advice might be received, but whose assent was not required. **1875** STUBBS *Const. Hist.* II. xiv. 129 The archbishops and bishops are to bring [to Parliament] one proctor for the clergy of each cathedral, and two for the clergy of each diocese. **1878** *Ibid.* III. xx. 447 On the occasions on which the clerical proctors are known to have attended, their action is insignificant, and those occasions are very few. **1888** LD. COLERIDGE in *Law Rep. 20 Q.B.D.* 744 In the Northern Convocation the parochial clergy are and have been for centuries represented by two proctors from each archdeaconry within the province of York.

†**7.** One who collected alms on behalf of lepers or others who were debarred from begging for themselves; *esp.* one having a patent or license to collect alms for the occupants of a 'spital-house'. (Held in evil repute from the abuse of the system.)

1529 MORE *Suppl. Soulys* Wks. 292/1 And they be also our proctoures & begge in our name, and in our name receiue your money. **1538** FITZHERB. *Just. Peas* 102 b, Al proctours and pardoners goinge about without sufficient auctorite.. shalbe punyshed by whyppynge. **1561** AWDELAY *Frat. Vacab.* (1869) 14 Proctour is he, that will tary long, and bring a lye, when his Maister sendeth him on his errand. **1567** HARMAN *Caveat* (1869) 46 Proctors and Factores all of Spyttell houses. **1577** HARRISON *England* II. x. (1877) I. 220 Among roges and idle persons..we find to be comprised all proctors that go vp and downe with counterfeit licences. **1608** DEKKER *2nd Pt. Hon. Whore* Wks. 1873 II. 149 Y'are best get a clap-dish, and say y'are Proctor to some Spittle-house.

Hence **'proctorage**, management by a proctor; **'proctoral**, **'proctorly** *adjs.* = PROCTORIAL; **'proctorling**, a petty or subordinate proctor.

1641 MILTON *Reform.* II. Wks. 1851 III. 65 As for the fogging *proctorage of money, with such an eye as strooke.. Simon Magus with a curse, so does she looke. **1573** G. HARVEY *Letter-bk.* (Camden) 47 Saiing in his Proctors vois that I shuld read no lecture there; as he bi his *Proctoral autoriti had suspendid me before. **1738** GRAY *Let. to R. West* in W. Mason *Mem.* (1807) I. 171 The University has ..created half a dozen new little *procterlings to see its orders executed. **1601** DEACON & WALKER *Spirits & Divels* 64 Howsoeuer your selfe may haply stand in some neede of a *proctorly bribe: my cause, it standes in no neede of bribe-pursing.

Proctor ('prɒktə(r)), *sb.*[2] The name of Robert George Collier *Proctor* (1863-1903), English bibliographer, used *attrib.* or in the possessive in **Proctor method** = *Proctor('s) order*; **Proctor number**, the number assigned to an early printed book in Proctor's *Index*; **Proctor('s) order**, a system of classifying early printed books geographically and chronologically, first used in the *Index to the Early Printed Books in the British Museum* (1898-1938) begun by Proctor.

[**1903** *Library* IV. 195 Proctor's 'Index'..is arranged under towns and countries in chronological order.] **1904** A. W. POLLARD in *Library* V. 22, I think it was Baer of Frankfurt who first gave the author the pleasure of seeing a 'Proctor number' quoted side by side with that of Hain. **1931** M. R. STILWELL *Incunabula & Americana* 22 In the majority of instances, it will be found that Proctor's order prevails in whatever place-entry bibliography one may wish to consult. **1934** A. ESDAILE *National Libraries of World* I. 18 Incunabula..gathered by Robert Proctor into one room.. and arranged by order of countries, towns, presses, and date, an arrangement now often called 'Proctor order'. **1952** J. CARTER *ABC for Bk.-Collectors* 143 *Proctor's order*, the classification of early printed books, on scientific typographical principles, by country, town and printer. **1955** *N. & Q.* May 229/1 Henry Bradshaw..arranged the books in what he called his natural history method in bibliography; it meant the arrangement and classification of them as natural objects are classified. This arrangement is now popularly known as the Proctor method. **1961** T. LANDAU *Encycl. Librarianship* (ed. 2) 291/1 *Proctor order*, system of classification of incunabula named after the arrangement in R. G. C. Proctor's Index of early printed books in the British Museum. **1967** COX & GROSE *Organiz. & Handling Bibliogr. Rec. by Computer* 137 Since the end of the last century it has been customary to catalogue incunables in 'Proctor Order'.

'proctor, *v.* [f. prec. sb.]

1. *intr.* To officiate as a university proctor.

1676 MARVELL *Mr. Smirke* 37 If a man went out by night on Tranelling, or Bat-fowling, or Proctoring, he might catch these Exposers by Dozens.

2. *intr.* (See quots., and cf. prec. 7.)

c **1730** *Dorsets. Voc.* (MS. in *N. & Q.* 6th Ser. VIII. 45/1), *To proctor*, to scold or lord it. *a* **1825** FORBY *Voc. E. Anglia*, *Proctor*, to hector, swagger, bully... The Proctors connected with this verb were..sturdy beggars.

¶Warburton in his ed. of Shakspere, 1747, substituted 'procter' for 'project' in *Ant. & Cl.* v. ii. 121, remarking '*Project* signifies to *invent* a cause, not to *plead* it; which is the sense here required. It is plain then we should read, "I cannot procter [etc.]." The technical term, to plead by an advocate'. But no example of *proctor* in this sense has been found, while *project* is abundantly supported: see PROJECT *v.* 3.

proctorial (prɒk'tɔərɪəl), *a.* [f. PROCTOR *sb.*[1] + -IAL; cf. *procuratorial.*] Of or pertaining to a proctor (**a.** at the universities, **b.** in the ecclesiastical courts).

proctorial cycle, the order in which the various colleges elect proctors; *proctorial veto*, the power of the two proctors conjointly to veto any decree of Convocation at Oxford; *proctorial year*, the annual period for which the university proctors are elected.

a. **1864** TREVELYAN *Compet. Wallah* (1866) 58 The condition of Oxford or Cambridge on the night of a grand Proctorial raid! **1881** *Nature* XXIII. 377/2 He..shall have proctorial authority over members of the University. **1882** *Standard* 13 Apr. 3/8 The outgoing Senior Proctor.. summarised the events of the past proctorial year. *a* **1893** W. L. COURTNEY in *Jowett's Life* (1897) II. viii. 232 The traditional policeman..was represented by the Senior Proctorial bull-dog.

b. **1883** *Law Times* 13 Oct. 398/2 The two items are inserted in the proctorial charges as 'Probate under seal and court fee'.

So †**proctorical** (-'tɒrɪkəl) *a.*, in same sense.

1715 PRIDEAUX in *Life* (1748) 231 Every Tutor, for the better discharging of his duty, shall have Proctorical authority over his Pupils.

proc'torially, *adv.* [f. PROCTORIAL *a.* + -LY[2].] In a proctorial capacity; in the manner of a proctor.

1883 H. S. HOLLAND in S. Paget *H. S. Holland* (1921) III. iv. 290 You speak of a deeper sense of the power of evil—I have felt it proctorially. **1971** F. R. LEAVIS in *Human World* Aug. 5 As for myself and Cambridge, I haven't to complain that I suffered..proctorially enforced oppression.

proctorize ('prɒktəraɪz), *v.* [f. as PROCTOR *sb.*[1] + -IZE.] *trans.* Of a university proctor: To exercise the proctorial authority on (an undergraduate, etc.); to arrest, summon, and reprimand, fine, or punish (an offender). Hence *transf.*

1833 CHURCH *Let.* 2 June, I have only been proctorised once, for not having my gown on. **1861** HUGHES *Tom Brown at Oxf.* xii, One don't like to go in while there's any chance of a real row..and so gets proctorized in one's old age for one's patriotism. *a* **1884** M. PATTISON in *Mem.* (1885) 18 He took him to task for the colour of his great-coat—proctorised him, my father said.

b. *intr.* To officiate as proctor. *rare.*

1882 'F. ANSTEY' *Vice Versa* v, Somehow he never would proctorise any more—it spoilt his nerve.

Hence **proctori'zation**, the act of proctorizing or fact of being proctorized.

1883 in Whibley *In Cap & Gown* (1890) 136 Did you break the lamps, and hope to escape..Proctorization? **1905** *Athenæum* 17 June 741/2 The proctorization of Jacobson the well-beloved.

proctorrhagia to **proctuchous**: see PROCTO-.

proctorship ('prɒktəʃɪp). [f. PROCTOR *sb.*[1] + -SHIP.] The office, position, or function of a proctor, in various senses of the word.

1535 (13 Oct.) in Weaver *Wells Wills* (1890) 178 To Thos [my son] I leve my parte in the bargyn for the proctor-sheype of the Auterlaege [i.e. altarage] of Upton. **1590** SWINBURNE *Testaments* 246 If the names be artificiall, not naturall, as to vse proctorship, for curatorship. *a* **1656** USSHER *Ann.* vi. (1658) 620 He..was forced..to undertake there the Proctorship and Stewardship for the King. **1706** HEARNE *Collect.* 21 Apr. (O.H.S.) I. 230 [He] was a little after his Proctership preferr'd. **1762** [see PROCURACY 1]. **1886** *Pop. Sci. Monthly* XXVIII. 615 The proctorship for science, justly assumed for matters within his province as a student, is rather hastily extended to matters which he himself declares to be beyond it.

proctotrupid (prɒktəʊ'tru:pɪd), *a.* and *sb. Ent.* Also Procto-, -trypid. [f. mod.L. family name *Proctotrupidæ*, f. generic name *Proctotrupes* (P. A. Latreille *Précis des Caractères génériques des Insectes* (1796) 108), f. PROCTO- + Gr. τρυπ-ᾶν to bore: see -ID[3].] **A.** *adj.* Of, pertaining to, or designating a proctotrupid. **B.** *sb.* A small wasp belonging to the family Proctotrupidæ or the superfamily Proctotrupoidea, which include parasitoids of insects and spiders.

1869 PACKARD *Guide Stud. Insects* (1872) 131 *note*, An exceedingly minute Proctotrupid fly, supposed to be parasitic on *Anthophorabia megachilis*. **1891** [see CHALCID *a.* and *sb.*]. **1932** RILEY & JOHANNSEN *Med. Entomol.* xxiv. 422 In California a little proctotrupid..invades houses in numbers in the fall. **1932** E. STEP *Bees, Wasps, Ants Brit. Isles* 184 The wings are much simpler..in the Chalcids and Proctotrypids. **1972** L. E. CHADWICK tr. *Linsenmaier's Insects of World* 300/2 Equally small and also at home in the water are a few proctotrupids.

proctotrupoid (prɒktəʊ'tru:pɔɪd). *Ent.* [f. mod.L. name of superfamily *Proctotrupoidea*: see prec. and -OID.] = PROCTOTRUPID *sb.*

1954 BORROR & DELONG *Introd. Study of Insects* xxix. 716 The proctotrupoids are not as common as the chalcids or ichneumons. **1971** R. R. ASKEW *Parasitic Insects* viii. 155 The great majority of proctotrupoids are endoparasites.

'proctress. *rare*[−1]. [f. as PROCTOR *sb.* + -ESS[1].] A female proctor.

1628 WITHER *Brit. Rememb.* I. 1025 [Justice speaking to Mercy] Thou hast Proctresse bin For Ieroboam..That hand recuring which he did extend, The Messenger of God, to apprehend.

†**pro'culcate**, *v. Obs. rare.* [f. L. *prōculcāre* (f. *prō*, PRO-[1] 1 b + *calcāre* to tread) + -ATE[3].] *trans.* To tread or trample down; *fig.* to despise, spurn. Hence †**procul'cation** *Obs.* [ad. L. *prōculcātiōn-em*], a treading or trampling.

1623 COCKERAM, *Proculcate*, to tread vnder foot. **1641** J. JACKSON *True Evang. T.* III. 195 Wee should have proculcated and trampled under foote most faire hopes of immortality unto glory. **1656** BLOUNT *Glossogr.*, *Proculcation*, a treading or trampling under foot. **1668** H. MORE *Div. Dial.* IV. xxv. 121 The Proculcation of the outward Court by the Gentiles for 42 months.

†**'proculstant.** *Obs. nonce-wd.* [f. L. *procul* afar + *stānt-em*, pr. pple. of *stāre* to stand, as a pun on *Protestant*.]

1589 *Protestatyon Martin Marprelat* 27 Both [Dr. Andrew Perne and Dean Bridges] old standards, both proculstants, both catercaps, both priests [etc.].

pro'cumb, *v. nonce-wd.* [ad. L. *prōcumb-ĕre*: see next.] *intr.* To prostrate oneself.

a **1784** *Mock Ode* in Boswell *Johnson* (1816) IV. 428 Opin'st thou this gigantic frame, Procumbing at thy shrine; Shall..be thine?

procumbent (prəʊˈkʌmbənt), *a.* [ad. L. *prōcumbent-em*, pr. pple. of *prōcumb-ĕre* to fall forwards, bend down, f. *prō*, PRO-¹ 1 b + **cumb-ĕre* to lay oneself: see CUMBENT.]

1. Lying on the face, prone; prostrate.

1721 BAILEY, *Procumbent*, lying along. **1755** JOHNSON, *Procumbent*, lying down, prone. **1791** COWPER *Odyss.* IX. 580 Procumbent, each obey'd. **1822–34** *Good's Study Med.* (ed. 4) II. 449 It [bleeding] will cease upon bending the head forward, or lying procumbent. **1884** BOWER & SCOTT *De Bary's Phaner.* 486 Medullary rays with procumbent cells are..easy to distinguish from parenchyma of the bundles.

2. *Bot.* Of a plant or stem: Lying flat on the ground without throwing out roots; growing along the ground; having a prostrate or trailing stem.

1668 WILKINS *Real Char.* II. iv. §4. 82 Week procumbent stalks, full of joynts. **1756** *Phil. Trans.* XLIX. 835 The common Tormentil is..very frequently found in a procumbent state. **1851** T. MOORE *Brit. Ferns* 195 *Lycopodium selaginoides*..has a slender, procumbent, often branched stem.

3. *Zool.* Of a tooth: lying along the jaw.

1874 T. C. JERDON *Mammals of India* 62 Upper middle incisors distant; lower ones procumbent. **1902** *Encycl. Brit.* XXX. 506/1 In the lower jaw there is a single pair of procumbent incisors, followed by several small teeth representing the canine and early premolars. **1977** ROONWAL & MOHNOT *Primates S. Asia* 41 It holds small fruit in both hands while chewing, and larger food, such as an unpeeled banana, is chipped with its procumbent lower incisors. **1978** *Nature* 17 Aug. 663/1 Diplodocids had elongated tapering snouts with delicate, procumbent teeth for selecting smaller plant parts.

procurable (prəʊˈkjʊərəb(ə)l), *a.* [f. PROCURE *v.* + -ABLE.] That can be procured or obtained.

1611 COTGR., *Recouvrable*..also gettable, procurable. *a* **1664** BARROW in Rigaud *Corr. Sci. Men* (1841) II. 33 His treatise..I..would gladly see and have it to myself, if procurable. **1754** LEWIS in *Phil. Trans.* XLVIII. 645 It is not to be brought into fusion by the greatest degree of fire procurable in the ordinary furnaces. **1877** LADY BRASSEY *Voy. Sunbeam* xv. (1878) 265 No wine or spirits being procurable on the premises.

ˈ**procuracy** (prəʊˈkjʊərəsɪ). Also 3–6 -acie, 3–4 -asie, 5 -acye, -ase, -esy, (3 procracie, 6 *Sc.* procry): see also PROXY. [ad. med.L. *prōcūrātia* (1245 in Du Cange), for cl. L. *prōcūrātio* PROCURATION. So obs. It. *procurazía*, *procuratía* 'a proctorship, also a procuration' (Florio).]

1. a. The office or action of a procurator; management or action for another. ***letters of procuracy***: = 2.

[**1315** *Rolls of Parlt.* I. 357/2 En les Letres de Procuracie q'il porterent ovesqe eux souz le Seal le dit Count.] *c* **1380** WYCLIF *Sel. Wks.* II. 155 Such procuracie is synful and yvele takun. **1482** in Rymer *Foedera* (1711) XII. 173/1 Lettres of Commission and Procuracye under the Grete Seale. **1565** *Satir. Poems Reform.* i. 134, I sawe..howe the faythfull was enforst with procry to procede. **1631** WEEVER *Anc. Fun. Mon.* 670 Letters of procuracie signed, and sealed by the King his master to redemand diuers great summes of money. **1762** tr. *Busching's Syst. Geog.* IV. 530 The procuracy or proctorship of Lorsch. **1978** *Jrnl. R. Soc. Arts* CXXVI. 672/2 The rôle, function and powers of public security organs, the procuracy and the courts are more closely defined.

†**b.** A deputy, proxy, legate. *rare*⁻¹. *Obs.*

1460 CAPGRAVE *Chron.* (Rolls) 301 Whan this procuracie was come to the Kyng, these articules were offered of the lordis.

†**2.** A document empowering a person to act as the representative of another; a proxy, a letter of attorney. *Obs.*

1425 *Paston Lett.* I. 20, I have, by advys of counseill, in makyng a procuracie *ad agendum, defendendum, provocandum, et appellandum* to yow..; the whiche procuracie..I shal sende to yowr persone. *a* **1548** HALL *Chron., Hen. VIII* 211 b, He sayd he would sende thither a sufficient procuracie and conuenient proctors, & desired to see the Orators commission. **1607** COWELL *Interpr.* s.v. *Procurator*, Procuracy is vsed for the specialitie, whereby he is authorized. [**1845** LD. CAMPBELL *Chancellors* (1857) I. xii. 180, I, William Trussel, procurator of the prelates, earls, and barons, and other people in my procuracy named, having, &c.]

†**3.** *Eccl.* The provision of entertainment for the bishop or visitor by the parson or religious house visited; hence, a sum paid in commutation of this; = PROCURATION 3, PROXY 5. (= Anglo-L. *procuratia*, Matt. Paris, med.L. *procuratio*.) *Obs.*

c **1290** *St. Edmund Conf.* 333 in *S. Eng. Leg.* I. 440 Procracies [*Harl. MS.* 2277 procuracies] huy ȝeuen him also ..Of persones to nime largeliche. *c* **1380** WYCLIF *Wks.* (1880) 249 Whanne bischopis & here officeris comen & feynen to visite,..wrecchid curatis ben nedid to festen hem richely & ȝeue procuracie & synage. *c* **1440** *Jacob's Well* 129 Prelatys of holy cherch,..puttyn here sugettys to outrageous cost,..in vysityng, & in raisynge of procuracyes vnleffully. *c* **1450** *Godstow Reg.* 87 They shold paye..to the Archidekon of Bokyngham, procuracy.

†**4.** The office or official residence of a Venetian procurator (= It. *procuratía*). *Obs.*

1691 tr. *Emilianne's Frauds Rom. Monks* (ed. 3) 253 He.. went up to the Procuracies of S. Mark. [**1715** LEONI *Palladio's Archit.* (1742) I. Pref. 6 In Venice..the new Palace of Procuracy.]

procural (prəʊˈkjʊərəl). [f. PROCURE *v.* + -AL¹.] The action or process of procuring; obtaining.

1861 OWEN in *Athenæum* 27 July 118/1 Alexander the Great devoted large sums of money to the procural of objects of Natural History. **1883** *Gd. Words* 186 Their chief object is the procural of food.

procurance (prəʊˈkjʊərəns). [f. PROCURE *v.* + -ANCE.] The action of procuring; the action by which something is attained or brought about; agency. So also †**proˈcurancy** *Obs. rare*⁻¹, agency, advocacy.

1533 EDW. VI *Let. Bp. Ridley* 9 June in Strype *Eccl. Mem.* (1721) II. xxii. 421 We will and command you, that neither you nor any for you, or by your procurancie..shall admit him. **1559** *Mir. Mag.* (1563) G vij, He thought it best by polytyke procurance, To prive the kyng and so restore hys frend. **1844** G. S. FABER *Eight Dissert.* (1845) II. 101 A knowledge of the Hebrew Law was brought into China during the Seventy Years Captivity, either by the procurance of Laou-sze himself, or in consequence of the emigration of this very Colony. **1887** J. C. ROBINSON *Let. Sir J. Donnelly* 7 Apr. (*Daily News* (1897) 26 Oct. 3/2), Acquisitions..which by procurance have..enriched the South Kensington Museum.

†ˈ**procurate**, *v. Obs. rare.* [f. L. *prōcūrāt-*, ppl. stem of *prōcūrāre*: see PROCURE *v.* and -ATE³.] *trans.* To do (something) as agent *for* another; to do, perform, etc., by or through an agent. Hence †ˈ**procurated** *ppl. a.*, †ˈ**procurating** *vbl. sb.*

1659 H. L'ESTRANGE *Alliance Div. Off.* 262 The principles of Christianity..require from them, no procurated, but a personal, and actual faith, repentance, obedience. **1701** BEVERLEY *Apoc. Quest.* 26 There is Another Beast, spoken of, that was Zealously Concern'd in Procurating all for the Papal Beast.

procuration (prɒkjʊəˈreɪʃən). [ME. *procuracio(u)n*, a. F. *procuration* (13th c. in Littré, also OF. -*cion*), ad. L. *prōcūrātiōn-em*, n. of action f. *prōcūrāre* to PROCURE: see -ATION.]

†**1.** The action of taking care of, looking after, or managing; management, superintendence, administration, agency; attention, care. *Obs.*

c **1420** *Pallad. on Husb.* XII. 193 Ek plauntis han this procuracioun Vnto their gret multiplicacioun. **1460** CAPGRAVE *Chron.* (Rolls) 199 Be procuracion of the qween, Roger Mortimere was mad erl of Kent. **1483** CAXTON *Gold. Leg.* 287/2 Theophyle was receyued into the grace of the Bisshop by the procuracion of the deuyll. *a* **1552** LELAND *Itin.* III. 114 The 2 Towers in the Haven Mouth were begon in King Edwarde the 4 Tyme... Kyng Henry the vij endyd them at the Procuration of Fox Bisshop of Winchester. **1609** SKENE *Reg. Maj., Stat. Dav. II* 39 All they quha are destitute,..salbe vnder the Kings procuration, and protection within his Realme. *a* **1677** HALE *Pomponius Atticus* 24 He avoided the procuration of the Commonwealth, not for sloth, but in judgment.

†**b.** Management for another; stewardship; procuratorship. *Obs.*

1484 CAXTON *Fables of Æsop* 3 b, To thende that my lord depose me not of my procuracion. **1596** DALRYMPLE tr. *Leslie's Hist. Scot.* IV. (S.T.S.) 207 Maximian..eftirward committing the procuratione of Britannie til Dionethie, passid in ffrance. **1689** tr. *Buchanan's De Jure Regni apud Scotos* 35 [They] think that a Kingdom is not a procuration concredited to them by God, but rather a prey put into their hands.

2. The appointment of a procurator or attorney; the authority or power thus delegated; also, the authorized action of one's agent; the function of an attorney or representative. ***letters of procuration*** = b. ***by procuration***, by attorney or proxy.

(The person so appointed signs *p.p.*, or *per proc.*, = *per procurationem*: see PER I. 7.)

1489 CAXTON *Faytes of A.* IV. ii. 232 Yf a man gyueth a procuracyon to another for to doo and execute certeyn thinges of his owne it is not therfore to be vndrestande that he gyueth him a generall procuracyon. **1568** GRAFTON *Chron.* II. 221 The mariage was foorthwith made, and solempnized by procuration from the king of England. **1574** *Reg. Privy Council Scot.* II. 404 Be thair letters of procuratioun under the seill of the same toun. **1682** SCARLETT *Exchanges* 155 When any one doth by the Order, full Power and Authority of another, which is called among Merchants Procuration. **1796** BURKE *Regic. Peace* iii. Wks. VIII. 323 Without a letter of attorney, or any other act of procuration. **1844** LD. BROUGHAM *Brit. Const.* iii. (1862) 43 [He] could, if absent himself from just cause, appear by his procuration or proxy. **1870** *Daily News* 14 Dec., They clamour for sorties, vow to die for their country, and then wish to do it by procuration.

b. A formal document whereby a person gives legal authority to another to act for him; a letter or power of attorney. Now *rare*.

1426 W. PASTON in *P. Lett.* I. 25, I make this day a newe apelle and a new procuracion. *c* **1430** *Pilgr. Lyf Manhode* IV. xlvi. (1869) 198 But þat hire procuracioun be seled with deuocioun. **1523** LD. BERNERS *Froiss.* I. xix. 27 There this princesse was maryed, by a sufficient procuration, brought fro the kyng of Inglande. **1622** MALYNES *Anc. Law-Merch.* 96 For that purpose he hath a Letter of Atturny, called a Procuration. **1719** DE FOE *Crusoe* (1840) I. xix. 342, I caused a procuration to be drawn, empowering him to be my receiver. **1889** W. LOCKHART *Ch. Scot. in 13th C.* 40 They ..sent on their procurations by some ecclesiastic to Rome.

3. *Eccl.* The provision of necessary entertainment for the bishop, archdeacon, or other visitor, by the incumbent, parish, or religious house visited; subsequently commuted to a payment in money (but see quot. 1895).

c **1450** HOLLAND *Howlat* 220 The Ravyne..Was dene rurale..At vicaris and personnis, For the procuraciounis, Cryand full crowss. **1555** in Strype *Eccl. Mem.* (1721) III. App. xlvi. 140 Letted by the said Bisshope from gathering of procurations. **1654** GATAKER *Disc. Apol.* 48 The Annual payments of Tenths and Subsidies to the King, the Procurations to the Bishop and Arch-deacon, the Assessments for the poor. **1661** J. STEPHENS (*title*) Historical Discourse on Procurations. **1726** AYLIFFE *Parergon* 429 Procurations..are certain Sums of Money which Parish-Priests pay yearly to the Bishop or Archdeacon *ratione Visitationis*. **1862** *C.B. Rep.* (N.S.) XII. 416 At the..visitation..the churchwardens..attend the registrar..[and] pay the 'procurations and synodals' claimed as due from the clergy to the archdeacon. **1895** PHILLIMORE *Eccl. Law* (ed. 2) IV. xi. §2. 1051 It seems..that where the estates of bishops have vested in the ecclesiastical commissioners under 23 and 24 Vict. c. 124, these procurations have become payable to the commissioners, who have, however, abandoned their collection.

4. The action of procuring, obtaining, or getting; procurement.

1533–4 *Act 25 Hen. VIII*, c. 20 §2 Somes of money..payd at the seid See of Rome for procuracion or expedicion of any suche bulles breves or palles. *c* **1555** HARPSFIELD *Divorce Hen. VIII* (Camden) 153 He wickedly did let the procuration of children. **1651** WALTON *Life Wotton* in *Reliq.* c iv, His procuration of Priviledges and courtesies with the German Princes, and the Republick of Venice for the English Merchants. **1695** WOODWARD *Nat. Hist. Earth* (1723) 25 Procuration of..Shells from several Parts of this Island. **1828** *Blackw. Mag.* XXIII. 594 Such irrational.. beings..regard the difficulty of procuration as one of the most estimable qualities. **1882** *Standard* 26 Dec. 3/2 Those [coals] used in the procuration of steam power.

b. *spec.* The obtaining or negotiating of a loan for a client; also, the fee for this.

1678 R. L'ESTRANGE *Seneca's Mor.* (1702) 183 As to Judgments and Statutes, Procuration, and Continuance-Mony, these are only..the Dreams of Avarice. **1679** PRANCE *True Narr. Pop. Plot* 32 He would not let 40 or 50*l.* out for six Months, but he would have 40*s.* for Procuration,..and yet the full Legal Interest to run on. **1881** *Times* 18 May 6/5 The action..was one brought by the plaintiffs to recover £120 their commission of 1 per cent for the procuration of a loan of £12,000.

c. The action of a procurer or procuress; pimping.

1696 PHILLIPS (ed. 5) s.v., Procuration is also taken in an Ill sence, for the Act of a Baud or Pander. **1891** [see 5].

5. *attrib.* **procuration fee, money**: see quots.

1706 PHILLIPS, *Procuration*, or *Procuration-Money*, a Duty which Parish-Priests pay yearly to the Bishop or Arch-Deacon, upon account of Visitation. **1769** BLACKSTONE *Comm.* IV. xii. 157 If any scrivener or broker takes more than five shillings *per cent.* procuration-money, or more than twelve-pence for making a bond, he shall forfeit 20*l.* with costs. **1848** WHARTON *Law Lex.*, *Procuration fee*, a sum of money taken by scriveners on effecting loans of money. **1884** *Law Rep.* 25 *Ch. Div.* 280 He agreed to find the money for a lump sum as a procuration fee. **1891** *Pall Mall G.* 17 Oct. 6/3 The Chertsey procuration case... A servant..was charged with procuring her daughter.., aged fifteen years.

Hence **procuˈrational** *a.*, of or pertaining to procuration: see sense 2 above.

c **1702** *Case of Præmunientes Considered* 13 Now, when there is no such Return made, and..seldom distinct Procurational Letters upon the Choice to Parliament.

procurative (prəʊˈkjʊərətɪv), *a.* [f. PROCURE *v.* + -ATIVE.] Having the quality of procuring; tending to procure or obtain.

1633 T. ADAMS *Exp. 2 Peter* ii. 10 There is a procurative uncleanness; that..helps forward the damnation of men. **1657** TOMLINSON *Renou's Disp.* 554 Cassia..is thought procurative of flatulency. **1816–30** BENTHAM *Offic. Apt. Maximized, Extract Const. Code* (1830) 52 Those..by whom..are exercised the several functions, procurative, custoditive, applicative, reparative, and eliminative.

procurator¹ (ˈprɒkjʊəreɪtə(r)). Also 3–7 -our (5–6 -oure, 6 *Sc.* -ure, 5 prokeratour): see also PROCTOR¹ *sb.* A. [a. OF. *procuratour* (13th c. in Hatz.-Darm., mod.F. -*eur*), or ad. L. *prōcūrātōr-em* manager, agent, deputy, collector in a province, attorney, agent-n. f. *prōcūrāre* to PROCURE.]

1. *Rom. Hist.* An officer who collected the taxes, paid the troops, and attended to the interests of the imperial treasury, in an imperial province; sometimes he had the administration of part of a province, as in the case of the Procurator of Judæa, which was part of the province of Syria.

a **1300** *Cursor M.* 16023 All þai gadird o þe tun,..And sent to pilate þair procuratur [*Gött.* procketur], And did him þider bring. *c* **1425** WYNTOUN *Orig. Cron.* V. xiii. 4319 Hade he callyt Lucyus procuratoure, Qwhar þat he callit hym emperoure. **1581** SAVILE *Tacitus, Agricola* (1622) 190 Whereas in former times they had onely one king, now were there two thrust vpon them, the Lieutenant to sucke their bloud, the Procuratour their substance. **1593** G. HARVEY *Pierce's Super.* 81 As Paul demeaned himselfe..before the twoo Romane Procuratours of that Prouince, Felix, and Festus. **1737** WHISTON *Josephus, Antiq.* XIV. viii. 441 [Caesar] made him [Antipater] procurator of Judea. **1877** C. GEIKIE *Christ* lx. (1879) 735 Herod's palace had been taken ..as the residence of the procurators.

2. One who manages the affairs of another; one who is duly authorized to act in behalf of another in any business; an agent, an attorney.

a. (In earliest use) The official agent of a church or religious house. *Obs.* exc. *Hist.* †**b.** The steward or manager of a household, estate, or the like; an overseer, a bailiff. *Obs.* **c.** The agent, deputy, proxy, or representative of a non-ecclesiastical person or body; one who has a power of attorney for another, to sign for him *per procurationem* (see PROCURATION 2). ***procurator general***, an agent-general. †***procurator of parliament***, an early name of the Speaker of the House of Commons.

a. *c* **1290** *St. Brandan* 356 in *S. Eng. Leg.* I. 229 þis procuratour heom cam aȝein and welcomede heom a-non, And custe seint brendanes fet and þe Monekes echon. [**1306** *Rolls of Parlt.* I. 220/1 Mestre William Testa, & les autres clercs & procuratours l'apostoill. **1326–7** *Ibid.* II. 9/2 Qe nul Provisour alien, ne Procuratour de par eux..n'entre la Terre.] *c* **1400** *Plowman's T.* 733 [Secular canons] have a gedering procuratour That can the pore people enplede, And robben hem as a ravinour. *c* **1450** *Godstow Regr.* 492 Hit shold be wele lawfull to the forsaid abbesse and Couent and to ther successours or to ther procuratour to distreyne. **1645** EVELYN *Diary* 26 Mar., The Procurator of the Carmelites preaching on our Savior's feeding the multitude. **1897** ADDIS & ARNOLD *Cath. Dict.* (ed. 5) 761/2 The procurators or official agents of monasteries of nuns should not hold office more than three years. **1909** B. WARD *Dawn Cath. Revival* I. 55 The procurator [at Douay] was Rev. Gregory Stapleton, who had held that office since 1773. **1931** J. CLAYTON *St. Hugh of Lincoln* v. 35 The procurator was guest master... Other visitors to the Grande Chartreuse claimed the procurator's time... They loved him, Hugh the procurator, for the gracious speech and courteous treatment.

b. *c* **1375** *Sc. Leg. Saints* xii. (*Mathias*) 241 He made hyme [Judas] his procuratore, þo he wyste he suld be traytore. **1377** LANGL. *P. Pl.* B. xix. 253, I make pieres þe plowman my procuratour & my reve. **1382** WYCLIF *Matt.* xx. 8 Whenne euenynge was maad, the lord of the vyne ȝerd seith to his procuratour, Clepe the workmen, and ȝelde to hem her hijre. **1451** CAPGRAVE *Life St. Gilbert* (E.E.T.S.) 91 Nowt as a gouernour of his owne, but as a procuratour and a seruaunt of oþer mennes ricchesse. **1555** EDEN *Decades* 72 Alphonsus Nunnez..who also was lyke to haue byn chosen procuratoure of this vyage.

c. **1399** *Rolls of Parlt.* III. 424/1 The States..made thes same Persones that ben comen here to ȝowe nowe her Procuratours, and gafen hem full auctorite. **1494** FABYAN *Chron.* VII. 431, I Wyllyam Trussel, in the name of all men of this lande of Englande, & procuratour of this parlyament, resygne to y[e] Edwarde y[e] homage that was made to y[e] some tyme. *a* **1548** HALL *Chron., Hen. VI* 148 The Marques of Suffolke, as procurator to Kyng Henry, espoused the said Ladie, in the churche of sainct Martyns. **1561** *Reg. Privy Council Scot.* I. 179 At the instance of Johne Baptista de Sambitore, procuratour generall for the Spanische natioun. **1602** FULBECKE *1st Pt. Parall.* 30 Actions doe not passe, but the grauntor if he will haue the grauntees to take any benefit by the graunt, must make the grauntees or one of them his procurators to sue in his name, and to recouer to their owne vse. **1682** SCARLETT *Exchanges* 156 A prudent Merchant.. will advise all his Correspondents (on whom his Procurator shall have occasion to draw, &c.)..that he hath granted to such and such a one such a full Power to draw in his Name Bills of Exchange. **1777** ROBERTSON *Hist. Amer.* II. VI. 236 They elected him procurator general of the Spanish nation in Peru. **1874** STUBBS *Const. Hist.* I. xiii. 634 The early representative members..were frequently..invested with the character or procurators or proxies.

3. In the mediæval universities, one of two or more representative officers, of whom one was elected by each of the 'nations' into which the students and Regent Masters were divided, having financial, electoral, and disciplinary functions. Hence, at Aberdeen (and formerly at other Scottish universities), the name of the student representatives, elected, one by each 'nation' of the whole body of students, to preside over the election of a Rector. See also PROCTOR[1], the modern form of this word in the English universities, under which (sense 3) its later history is given.

At Paris and Cambridge, and prob. also originally at Oxford, they were called indifferently *procurators* (proctors) and *regents*. At Paris there were four 'nations' and four procurators, at the English Universities two, called *Procurator australis* and *Procurator borealis*, the Southern and the Northern Procurator or Proctor.

[**1219** in Bulaeus *Hist. Univ. Paris* (1666) III. 94 Quod super hoc a suis Procuratoribus contingeret ordinari. **1237** *Bull* in Rashdall *Univ. Europe* (1895) I. 314 *note* (Paris), Ut nullus contra universitatem magistrorum vel scholarium seu rectorem vel procuratorem eorum ad quemquam alium pro Universitatis vel facto vel occasione [etc.]. **1244** *Statute of Faculty of Arts, Paris* in Bulaeus III. 195 Quo vsque pro qualitate et quantitate delicti vel transgressionis Mandati Vniuersitatis Rectori et Procuratori pro Vniuersitate fuerit ad plenum et pro ipsorum voluntate satisfactum. **1453** in *Munim. Univ. Glasg.* (Maitland) I. 6 Rectores.., decanos, procuratores nacionum, regentes, magistros et scolares.] **1574** M. STOKYS in Peacock *Stat. Cambr.* (1841) App. A. p. x, Then shall folowe..nexte the Father the two Procuratours. **1664** in *Fasti Acad. Aberdeen* (1898) II. 11 The colledge being fullie conveened and divided in four nationes..did..nominat..procurators for electing of ane Rector. **1831** SIR W. HAMILTON *Discuss.* (1852) 412 In Paris, each of the Four Nations elected its own Procurator. **1885** *Pall Mall G.* 12 May 2/1 In the universities of the Middle Ages the Chancellor had little power; the Rector, elected by Procurators of the Nations, exercised authority in his own right, or more commonly along with the Procurators, and, subsequently, with the Deans of Faculties... In Scotland all these elements of mediæval organization are still existent and active. **1896** *Daily News* 16 Nov. 7/3 The students at Aberdeen do not give a direct vote for the Rectorial candidates. They vote for a student who represents them, called the Procurator. After the recording of the votes..the 'Procurators' meet in another room, and the successful candidate is he who has a majority of Nations. If the Nations are equally divided the winner is he who has the numerical majority of votes.

4. *Law* **a.** An agent in a court of law: = PROCTOR[1] 4; used in countries retaining the Roman Civil Law (cf. also PROCUREUR), and in England in the ecclesiastical courts; *spec.* in Scotland, a law-agent practising before the inferior courts, an attorney. (Now *rare.*)

c **1386** CHAUCER *Friar's T.* 298 (Harl. 7334) May I nat aske a lybel sir Sompnour, And answer þer by my procuratour To suche þing as men wol oppose me? **1456** SIR G. HAYE *Law Arms* (S.T.S.) 109 My procuratour, that I mak on myn awin cost to defend me. **1586** T. B. *La Primaud. Fr. Acad.* I. (1594) 647 There is one procurator for the king, and two advocats, to looke to the kings prerogatives. **1587** *Sc. Acts Jas. VI* (1814) III. 460/2 All and quhatsumeuir lieges of þis realme accusit of tressoun..salhaif þair aduocattis and procuratoris to vse all þe lauchfull defenses. **1702** *Lond. Gaz.* No. 3818/4 Her Majesty has been pleased to appoint.. Thomas Smith Esq.; Her Majesties Procurator in all Causes, Maritime, Foreign, Ecclesiastical and Civil. **1752** LOUTHIAN *Form of Process* (ed. 2) 95 His Majesty's Advocate, or other Advocates, or Procurators for the Pannel, were ordained to debate the Relevancy *viva voce.* **1766** ENTICK *London* IV. 33 The *proctors*, otherwise *procurators*, exhibit their proxies for their clients. **1791** BOSWELL *Johnson* 4 June an. 1781, The Society of Procurators, or Attornies, entitled to practise in the inferior courts at Edinburgh..had taken care to have their ancient designation of Procurators changed into that of Solicitors, from a notion, as they supposed, that it was more genteel. **1845** S. AUSTIN *Ranke's Hist. Ref.* I. 275 That the evil did not arise from his good lords and friends the bishops, but from the judges, officials, and procurators, who sought.. only their own profit.

b. Short for PROCURATOR-FISCAL.

1899 *Daily News* 6 May 2/1 Four pleaded guilty of rioting only. The plea was accepted by the Procurator, and the men were sentenced to thirty days' each with the alternative of a £5 fine.

†**5.** An advocate, defender, or supporter of the cause of any person, system, tenet, proposal, etc.

c **1380** WYCLIF *Wks.* (1880) 139 þei wolen not paie for pore men, not wiþstondinge þat þei ben procuratouris of pore men. **1484** CAXTON *Fables of Alfonce* iii, He went to a philosophre which was the procuratour of the poure peple and prayd hym for charyte that he wold gyue to hym good counceylle of his grete nede. **1528** LYNDESAY *Dream* 1049 Tyll dame Fortune thow nedis no procurature; For scho hes lairglie kyithit on the hir cure. **1609** DANIEL *Civ. Wars* IV. xxvii, To confirm and seal Their vndertaking, with their dearest bloud, As Procurators for the Common-weale.

†**6. a.** One who or that which brings or helps to bring something about; = PROCURER 2; in quot. 1647, a producer, generator.

1486 *Act 3 Hen. VII*, c. 2 Such Mys-doers, takers, and procuratours to the same, and receytours,..[shall] be.. juged as principall felons. **1642** W. BIRD *Mag. Honor* 44 Charge him with..fellony, or to be a procurator thereof, or accessory thereunto. **1647** LILLY *Chr. Astrol.* xliv. 270 [The planet Mars] being a very sharpe heater and procurator of blood.

†**b.** The procurer of a loan: cf. PROCURATION 4 b. *Obs. rare.*

1677 YARRANTON *Eng. Improv.* 8 The Gentleman gets.. Friends..to be bound for his Covenants, whom if they [the lenders] accept, then the Procurator and Continuator have their Game to play.

7. a. (repr. It. *procuratore*, †*-adore.*) In some Italian cities, A public administrator or magistrate; also repr. F. *procureur* (see PROCUREUR). ***Procurator of St. Mark***, a senator, afterwards each of two senators, of the Venetian Republic, charged with high administrative functions.

c **1618** MORYSON *Itin.* IV. vii. (1903) 115 These Procurators, namely the old Dukes chosen for life, and the old Gouernors chosen for two yeares, haue care of the Treasure, and other publique affayrs, and are of great reputation. **1645** EVELYN *Diary* June, The Doge's vest is of crimson velvet, the Procurator's, &c. of damasc. **1656** BLOUNT *Glossogr.* s.v., In the Republique of Venice the Procurator is the second man in dignity. **1727–41** CHAMBERS *Cycl.*, *Procurator* is also a kind of magistrate in several cities of Italy, who takes care of the public interests. **1794** BURKE *Pref. to Brissot's Addr.* Wks. VII. 304 The treacherous Manuel was procurator of the Common-hall. **1832** tr. *Sismondi's Ital. Rep.* ix. 204 Two senators, distinguished by the title of procurators of St. Mark, were charged to attend in the camp. **1865** MAFFEI *Brigand Life* II. 159 The elaborate requisition presented by the royal procurator.. contains some passages which are worth preserving.

b. *attrib.*, as ***procurator treasurer.***

1709 *Lond Gaz.* No. 4545/1 He was there [at Venice] crowned by the Procurator-Treasurer.

pro-curator[2] (prəʊ'kjʊərətə(r)). *Sc. Law.* [f. PRO-[1] 4 + CURATOR I.] One who performs the duties of a curator though not legally appointed as such: see CURATOR I.

1681 STAIR *Instit. Law Scot.* I. vi. §12 Whosoever.. medled with Pupils Means or Minors, as Pro-tutors, or Pro-curators, should be lyable..as Tutors or Curators, for intromission and omission. **1773** ERSKINE *Inst. Law Scot.* I. vii. §28 Pro-tutors and pro-curators. By these are understood persons who act as tutors or curators without having a legal title to the office. **1838** W. BELL *Dict. Law Scot.* 798 The same principle regulates the claims of a pro-tutor or pro-curator against the minor for reimbursement of money expended for the minor.

'procurator-'fiscal, [f. PROCURATOR[1].] In Scotland, the public prosecutor of a shire or other local district, appointed by the sheriff or magistrates. He initiates the prosecution of crimes, and takes the precognitions, also performing some of the functions of a coroner.

The term appears to have originally designated the official who had to collect and administer the fines, fees, and other payments accruing to the criminal, civil, and ecclesiastical courts: he was the *procurator* (in sense 2) who had to do with the *fiscal* or revenue matters of the court. (Cf. PROCURER *fiscal* 1 e.) For history of the office see the *Journal of Jurisprudence* Vol. XXI. (1877) pp. 24–, 67–, 140–, etc., Vol. XXII. (1878) pp. 24–, 69–.

1583–4 *Decree-arbitral of Jas. VI* in *Jrnl. Jurispr.* XXI. 141 Mr. Johnne Skene, procurator fiscall. **1584** in Littlejohn *Aberd. Sheriff Court* (1904) Introd. 44 Actioun..at the instance off our Souerane Lord and Mr. George Barclay his M. Procuratour Phiscall. **1606** *Act Secret Council* 4 Feb. (*Jrnl. Jur.* XXI. 69), Pryces set down to the Procurators-Fiscal, to be taken hereafter for forming of Testaments. **1678** SIR G. MACKENZIE *Crim. Laws Scot.* II. xii. §4 (1699) 207 The way of Procedure before the Sheriff, is by an Assize, and the Procurator-Fiskal is Pursuer in place of his Majesties Advocat. **1752** J. LOUTHIAN *Form of Process* (ed. 2) 254 Application shall be made to the Sheriff by Petition, signed by the private Party complaining, or by the Procurator-fiscal, setting forth the Nature of the Crime. **1818** *Report of Commissioners* in *Jrnl. Jurispr.* XXI. 26 The Procurator-Fiscal likewise receives a certain proportion or share of the fines levied in the Sheriff's Court according to ancient usuage. **1818** SCOTT *Hrt. Midl.* xvi, The city's procurator-fiscal, upon whom the duties of superintendent of police devolved. **1875** W. MCILWRAITH *Guide Wigtownshire* 95 On the ground floor is the office of the Procurator-Fiscal.

procuratorial (prɒkjʊərə'tɔərɪəl), *a.* [f. late L. *prōcūrātōri-us* PROCURATORY (f. *prōcūrātōr-em* PROCURATOR[1]) + -AL[1]. Cf. F. *procuratorial.*]

1. Of or pertaining to a procurator or proctor, in various senses; proctorial.

1726 AYLIFFE *Parergon* 254 A Procuratorial Exception is Twofold, viz. First, that A. is not a lawful Proctor: and, Secondly, That he cannot be a Proctor. **1738** NEAL *Hist. Purit.* IV. 339 Who..sent proxies with procuratorial letters. **1874** *Queen's Printers' Bible-Aids* 81 A procuratorial coinage circulated in Judea from A.D. 6–59. **1874** STUBBS *Const. Hist.* I. xiii. 635 The ecclesiastical practice of which such procuratorial representation was a familiar part. **1899** W. M. RAMSAY in *Expositor* Jan. 46 Pamphylia was a distinct procuratorial province.

2. Of or pertaining to university proctors.

1663 WOOD *Life* 22 Sept. (O.H.S.) I. 492 To be proproctors and exercise procuratorial power. **1845** MOZLEY *Laud* Ess. (1878) I. 198 The procuratorial cycle was his remedy for the disorders then attending the public election of the proctors. **1894** LIDDON, etc. *Pusey* I. xvi. 378 Keble.. dryly observed on hearing the procuratorial veto, that 'others too might play at that game'.

procuratorship ('prɒkjʊəreɪtəʃɪp). [f. PROCURATOR[1] + -SHIP.] The office, function, or period of office of a procurator.

1577 HANMER *Anc. Eccl. Hist.* (1663) 13 The fourth [year] of the Procuratorship of Pontius Pilate. **1762** tr. *Busching's Syst. Geog.* V. 244 The abbey..holds also the procuratorship of Altorf as a mortgage from the Empire. **1836** *Penny Cycl.* V. 235/2 In Nero's time, and during the procuratorship of Catus Decianus.

procuratory ('prɒkjʊərətərɪ), *a.* and *sb.* [ad. late L. *prōcūrātōri-us* belonging to an agent or manager: see PROCURATOR[1] and -ORY[2]; hence med.L. *prōcūrātōrium* sb., whence B.]

A. *adj.* Of or pertaining to a procurator or procurators, or to procuration. Now *rare* or *Obs.*

1459 *Rolls of Parlt.* V. 365/2 The Procuratorie Hous or Priorie of Ware. **1570** FOXE *A. & M.* (ed. 2) 770/1 Apte to receaue of God thys power procuratorye. **1571** WALSINGHAM in Digges *Compl. Ambass.* (1655) 183 He was no longer a Proctor then he kept himself within the limits procuratory of the letter procuratory.

B. *sb.* †**1.** = PROCURATION 2 (= med.L. *procuratorium*). *Obs. rare*[−1].

c **1380** WYCLIF *Sel. Wks.* III. 440 Worldliche excusacioun shal not þenne assoyne, ne onswer by procuratorye, ne suttilte of werkis.

2. *Civil* and *Sc. Law.* Authorization of one person to act for another; an instrument or clause in an instrument giving such power; esp. in ***letters of procuratory***. ***procuratory of resignation***, a deed granted by a vassal authorizing his procurator to return his fee to the superior, either to be retained by him, or to be given out to a new vassal, etc.

1540 *Acc. Ld. H. Treas. Sc.* VII. 281 For making of ane procuratorie to resing the ballierie of Totternes in the Kingis hand. **1565** *Reg. Privy Council Scot.* I. 373 As procuratour..be thair lettres of procuratorie..lauchfullie constitute. **1569** *Ibid.* II. 8 [He] producit ane procuratorie subscrivit be the Quene. *a* **1639** SPOTTISWOOD *Hist. Ch. Scot.* VI. (1677) 444 A number of persons..presented a Procuratory under the Seal of the Town, and the Subscription of the Clerks thereof. **1704** J. HARRIS *Lex. Techn.* I, *Procuratory*, is the Instrument by which any Person or Community did constitute or delegate their Proctor or Proctors to represent them in any Judicial Court of Cause. **1746–7** *Act 20 Geo. II*, c. 50 §12 A..conveyance, containing a procuratory of resignation in favour of such purchaser or disponee. **1874** *Act 37 & 38 Vict.* c. 94 §26 It shall not be necessary to insert in any such conveyances a procuratory or clause of resignation. **1880** MUIRHEAD *Gaius* Digest 578 Under the system of the *legis actiones* procuratory was incompetent except *pro populo*, *pro libertate*, or *pro tutela*.

3. = PROCURACY 4.

1840 STANLEY in *Life & Corr.* (1893) I. viii. 265 The long array of the ancient library, procuratory, and Ducal Palace [at Venice].

procuratrix (prɒkjʊəˈreɪtrɪks). [a. L. *prōcūrātrix*, fem. agent-n. corresponding to *prōcūrātor* PROCURATOR[1].] The inmate who attends to the temporal concerns of a nunnery: cf. PROCURATOR[1] 2a.

1851 ULLATHORNE *Plea Rights & Lib. Relig. Wom.* 11 The second superioress, the procuratrix, who manages the temporalities. 1889 J. G. ALGER *Eng. in Fr. Rev.* 325 The procuratrix produced the little paper money she had.

†**procuraty.** *Obs. rare*[-1]. [ad. It. *procuratia*: see PROCURACY 4.] The official residence of a procurator in Venice: see PROCURATOR[1] 7.

1696 tr. *Du Mont's Voy. Levant* xxvii. 365 The Front of each Procuraty is supported by a large Portico.

†**proˈcure**, *sb. Obs. rare.* Also 6 *Sc.* procuire. [a. OF. *procure* (13th c. in Godef.) procuration, agency, f. *procurer* to PROCURE. So med.L. *prōcūra* (1389 in Du Cange).] = PROCUREMENT 1.

1432-50 tr. *Higden* (Rolls) V. 37 This Comodus..was sleyne..thro the procure and cause of his wife. 1567 *Satir. Poems Reform.* iv. 147 Off Ancus Martius we reid the greit mischance,..Slaine be Lucinio at Tanaquillis procuire.

procure (prəʊˈkjʊə(r)), *v.* Forms: α. 3-5 procure-n (3 -curi), 4- procure (4 -cury, 5 -kure, 6 *Sc.* -cuir). β. 4 procre, -core, 4-5 procur, 5 procour, proker. [a. F. *procurer* (13th c. in Littré), ad. L. *prōcūrāre* to take for, take care of, attend to, manage, to act as procurator: see PRO-[1] and CURE *v.* In ME. usually stressed on the first syllable, ˈ*procure* (from F. inf. *procuˈrer*); hence the weakened β-forms ˈ*procur*, etc., here illustrated:

13.. *Cursor M.* 28201 (Cott.), I wald he ware vn-fere or ded. And bath i procurd þam wit red. c1330 Procore [see 5]. 1340-70 Procre [see 6]. 1375 BARBOUR *Bruce* IV. 531 And mankynd biddis vs that we To procur vengeans besy be. 1387 TREVISA *Higden* (Rolls) VII. 235 (MS. Cott. Tib.) On Aluredus [he] hadde yprocred his deþ. c1400 *Destr. Troy* 9226 He shuld procour the prinse, & the prise grekes, To pas fro þat prouyns, payre hom nomore. *Ibid.* 11555 Sho prayet hym pourly..to..proker hir pes with his prise wordes. a1450 MYRC 689 Al them that..prokeren wher thorgh holy church is peyred. c1470 HENRY *Wallace* VI. 863 To procur pes be ony maner off cace.]

I. †1. *trans.* To care for, take care of, attend to, look after. [So in L., and OF.] *Obs. rare.*

c1425 WYNTOUN *Cron.* VI. iv. 357 (Cott. MS.) Bot þe possessoure to procure [*Wemyss MS.* trete]..wiþe honoure, And habundance of reches. *Ibid.* VIII. xxiv. 3648 Our Kynge Dauid was sende in Frawns, Qwhar he..was..procuryt [*v.r.* tretit] in al esse ilk deil.

†2. *intr.* To put forth or employ care or effort; to do one's best; to endeavour, labour; to use means, take measures. Const. *inf.* with *to* (*for to*); *for*, *to*, *unto* a thing. *Obs.*

c1330 R. BRUNNE *Chron. Wace* (Rolls) 7462 þus þey þrete wyþ manace, & ful yuel þey procure & purchace. c1380 *Antecrist* in Todd *Three Treat. Wyclif* (1851) 127 Crist fleed from seculer lordschip & office; þei procuren fast to have it. c1380 *Sir Ferumb.* 5825 Thar-for ert þow mys-byþoȝte, To procury hym to slee. c1400 *Brut* 249 þai were his enemys.. and procurede forto make debate and contak bituene him and his sone. c1430 *Syr Gener.* (Roxb.) 9220 Vnto his delieuraunce he procured. 1509 *Parl. Devylles* ad fin., Who that wyll for heuen procure, Kepe hym fro the deuylles combrement. 1548 UDALL *Erasm. Par.* Pref. 3 To procure for the commodities and welth of Englande. 1561 T. HOBY tr. *Castiglione's Courtyer* I. (1577) D iv b, Such a countenaunce as this is,..and not so softe and womanish as many procure to haue. 1582 N. LICHEFIELD tr. *Castanheda's Conq. E. Ind.* I. i. 3 Hee gaue them charge..that they shoulde procure to atteine to the sight of Presbiter Ioan. 1608 R. JOHNSON *Seven Champions* II. I iv b, Rosana..did procure to defend her selfe and offend hir enemie.

†3. *trans.* To contrive or devise with care (an action or proceeding); to endeavour to cause or bring about (mostly something evil) *to* or *for* a person. *Obs.*

c1290 *Beket* 1258 in *S. Eng. Leg.* I. 142 A-morewe comen þis bischopes and þe eorles also, To procuri seint thomas al þat vuel þat heo miȝten do. 13.. *Seuyn Sag.* (W.) 1201 He the procureth, night and dai, Al the sschame that he mai. 13.. *Coer de L.* 1730, I pray thee, Sir Tanker king, Procure me none evil thing. 1484 CAXTON *Fables of Alfonce* v, Ofte..the euyll whiche is procured to other cometh to hym whiche procureth it. 1530 PALSGR. 667/1, I procure, I cause a thyng to be done, or I devyse meanes to bringe a thynge to passe, *je procure.* 1573-80 BARET *Alv.* P 740 To procure hatred, or euill will to men, *struere odium in aliquos.* 1620 J. WILKINSON *Courts Leet* 136 Yee shall reasonably and honestly procure the profit of the corporation of this Towne.

†b. ? To care for; ? to endeavour to get or do.

1574 HELLOWES *Gueuara's Fam. Ep.* (1577) 308 For women be of such quality, that they procure nothing [*que ninguna cosa tanto procuran*] so much as that which is most forbidden them.

II. 4. To bring about by care or pains; also (more vaguely) to bring about, cause, effect, produce. a. with simple object. Now *rare.*

c1340 HAMPOLE *Prose Tr.* 11 All maner of wilfull pollusyone procurede one any maner agaynes kyndly oys. 1387 TREVISA *Higden* (Rolls) V. 215 þe emperesse Eudoxia had i-procured þe out puttynge [*procuravit ejectionem*] of Iohn. *Ibid.* VI. 243 He sente Alcuinus..for to procure pees. 1554 BRADFORD in Strype *Eccl. Mem.* (1721) III. App. xxx. 84 It is we..that have sinned and procured thy grievous wrath upon us. 1615 G. SANDYS *Trav.* I. 66 A drinke called Coffa..which helpeth..digestion, and procureth alacrity. 1677 W. HARRIS tr. *Lemery's Chym.* (1686) 536 It is good to procure sweat. 1748 SMOLLETT *Rod. Rand.* xii, This second sneer procured another laugh against him. 1861 O'CURRY *Lect. MS. Materials* 252 His uncle Cobhthach soon procured his death by means of a poisoned drink.

b. with subordinate clause. *arch.*

a1340 HAMPOLE *Psalter* lxviii. 12 Sum procurd þat .i. sould dye. 1551 ROBINSON tr. *More's Utop.* Ep. P. Giles (1895) 8 He is mynded to procure that he maye be sent thether. 1654 tr. *Martini's Conq. China* 226, I will procure all Europe shall understand the Issue of these prodigious revolutions. 1711 *Medley* No. 40 They procur'd that Mony shou'd be lent at 5 per Cent. 1894 R. BRIDGES *Feast of B.* I. 301 Could you procure that I should speak with her?

†c. with *inf.* To manage (*to do* something). *Obs.*

1559 *Mirr. Mag.* (1563) H v b, Eyther I must procure to see them dead, Or for contempt as a traytour lose my head. 1587 FLEMING *Contn. Holinshed* III. 1378/2 Sir Roger Manwood..procured to pas another act of parlement,.. wherein is further prouision made for the said bridge. 1678 R. BARCLAY *Apol. Quakers* II. iii. 25 Men..have procured to be esteemed as Masters of Christianity, by certain Artificial Tricks.

d. with *obj.* and *inf. passive.* To cause or get (a person or thing) *to be* treated in some way; to get something done to (a person). Now *rare.*

a1450 MYRC 696 All that vnrightfully defameth eny person or prokereth to be famed. 1577 B. GOOGE *Heresbach's Husb.* I. (1586) 7 b, Procuring him to be sent in embassage. a1626 BACON *Civ. Char. Jul. Cæsar* Ess. (1696) 161 He procured to be enacted no wholsome Laws. 1724 A. COLLINS *Gr. Chr. Relig.* 34 They procur'd him to be crucify'd. 1794 PALEY *Evid.* II. ix. (1817) 216 [Nero] procured the Christians to be accused. 1866 HOWELLS *Venet. Life* v. 68 An ingenious lover procured his..rival to be arrested for lunacy.

5. To obtain by care or effort; to gain, win, get possession of, acquire. (Now the leading sense.) In early use, to gain the help of, to win over (a person) to one's side.

1297 R. GLOUC. (Rolls) 11483 Sir Ion..turnde aȝe sir simond & procurede oþer mo. c1330 R. BRUNNE *Chron.* (1810) 119 Mald in Bristow lettres fast sendes, Bi messengers trow, forto procore frendes.

1387 TREVISA *Higden* (Rolls) VI. 355 He was þe firste þat ordeyned comyn scole at Oxenforde.., and procrede fredom and priveleges in many articles to þat citee. 1451 CAPGRAVE *Life St. Aug.* 50 The first þat he schuld neuyr procur no wyf to no man. 1538 STARKEY *England* I. i. 7 Hyt ys bettur..for a man being in gret pouerty, rather to procure some ryches then hye phylosophy. 1596 DALRYMPLE tr. *Leslie's Hist. Scot.* IV. 256 To him selfe he procuiret the fame of all æquitie. 1611 BIBLE *Transl. Pref.* 2 This..procured to him great obloquie. 1718 LADY M. W. MONTAGU *Let. to Abbé Conti* 19 May, Things that 'tis very easy to procure lists of. 1776 *Carlisle Mag.* 7 Sept. 143 She endeavoured to procure employment as a needle-woman. 1874 GREEN *Short Hist.* iii. §4. 134 Books were difficult and sometimes even impossible to procure. *Mod.* Could you procure me specimens?

b. To obtain (women) for the gratification of lust. Usually *absol.* or *intr.* To act as a procurer (sense 4) or procuress.

1603 SHAKS. *Meas. for M.* III. ii. 68 How doth my deere Morsell, thy Mistris? Procures she still? 1706 PHILLIPS, *Procure*,..is also taken in an ill Sense, for to act as a Pimp or Bawd. 1745 CHESTERF. *Lett.* (1792) I. 282 Juno..offers to procure for Aeolus, by way of bribe. 1891 *Daily News* 26 Jan. 7/2 Charged..at the Lambeth Police-court, on Saturday, with that he did by false pretences procure E. A. H.

6. To prevail upon, induce, persuade, get (a person) *to do* something. *Obs.* or *arch.*

1340-70 *Alex. & Dind.* 347 Ne we agayn hem to do [*ed.* go] nol no gome procre. c1380 WYCLIF *Sel. Wks.* III. 342 Hou þat Clement left his office and procuride oþir to helpe him. 1401 *Pol. Poems* (Rolls) II. 25 Why procurest thou men to yeve the their almes? 1568 GRAFTON *Chron.* II. 184 Pope Boniface being informed and procured by the Scottes, sent his letters vnto the king of England. 1579 FENTON *Guicciard.* II. (1599) 75 The newes of the reuolt of Nouaro, procured the King..to make way. 1667 EVELYN *Diary* 19 Sept., I procur'd him to bestow them [the Arundelian Marbles] on the University of Oxford. 1736 *Hale's Placit. Coron.* I. 615 An accessory before is he, that being absent at the time of the felony committed doth yet procure, counsel, command, or abet another to commit a felony. 1756 C. LUCAS *Ess. Waters* II. 144 The writer is influenced or procured to write for the one, against the other. 1828 S. TURNER *Anglo-Sax.* (ed. 5) I. III. x. 245 Charlemagne communicates to him [Offa]..his success in procuring the continental Saxons to adopt Christianity.

†b. *spec. Law.* To induce privately, to suborn, to bribe (a witness, juryman, etc.). *Obs.*

[1292 BRITTON I. ii. §11 Et si defendoms a touz Corouners ..qe nul face ses enquestes..par amis procurez.] 1433 *Rolls of Parlt.* IV. 476/1 Whether they..be procured to chese eny persone..to eny maner Office..and yf eny persone..be founde procured, that then he or thei be remeved. 1573-80 BARET *Alv.* P 741 A witnes procured with monie, or bribes, *conflatus pecuniâ testis.* 1620 J. WILKINSON *Coroners & Sherifes* 44 Ye shall..make your pannels your selfe of such persons, as bee..not suspect, nor procured.

†c. With adv. of place: To induce or prevail upon (a person) to come; to bring, lead. *Obs.*

1586 J. HOOKER *Hist. Irel.* in *Holinshed* II. 130/2 [They] agreed to cause Tirlough Lennough to procure in the Scots. 1592 SHAKS. *Rom. & Jul.* III. v. 68 What vnaccustom'd cause procures her hither? a1604 HANMER *Chron. Irel.* (1633) 128 Neither were we procured hither to be idle, or live deliciously. 1625 SHIRLEY *Love Tricks* IV. ii, Yonder is a pleasant arbour, procure him thither.

†7. To try to induce; to urge, press. *Obs.*

1551 EDW. VI *Let. Sir B. Fitz-Patrick* 20 Dec. in *Lit. Rem.* (Roxb.) I. 69 If yow be vehemently procured yow may goe as waiting on the king. 1581 J. BELL *Haddon's Answ. Osor.* 219 b, Where did he euer shake of the obedience of due allegeaunce? or procured any Subjectes to rebellion agaynst their Gouernours? 1590 SPENSER *F.Q.* III. i. 1 The famous Briton Prince and Faery Knight,..Of the faire Alma greatly were procur'd To make there lenger soiourne and abode.

III. †8. *intr.* To act as a procurator or legal agent; to solicit. (In quot. 1401, To act by a proctor or attorney.) *Obs.*

c1380 WYCLIF *Serm.* Sel. Wks. I. 383 Many trewe men, boþe aprentis and avocatis, wolen not procure in a cause bifore þat þei heeren it. 1401 *Pol. Poems* (Rolls) II. 34 You wend or send or procure to the court of Rome, to be made cardinals or bishops of the popes chaplens. 1528 WOLSEY in *St. Papers Hen. VIII*, I. 291 What promysse I demaunded of the said Emperours Ambassadour, who said he wolde procure for restitution. 1536 in Strype *Cranmer* II. (1694) 36 There should be as many..admitted to procure there as shuld be seen convenient to my said Lord of Canterbury. 1539 *Sc. Acts Jas. V* (1814) II. 353/2 Ane writing subscriuit be þe kingis grace..chargeing him & certane vþeris his collegis to procure for þe said James.

†b. *fig.* To plead, make supplication. *Obs.*

1563 WINȜET *Four Scoir Thre Quest.* To Rdr., Wks. I. 57 For in defence of that thing only procuir I, quhilk..the haill Kirk of God..maist clerlie appeiris. a1568 R. NORVALL *O most eternall King* 91 in *Bannatyne MS.* 51 Thairfoir to God for grace procure: He that wold leif most lerne to dy. a1578 LINDESAY (Pitscottie) *Chron. Scot.* II. xxiii. (S.T.S.) I. 351 The king..procurit for his lyfe at the bischopis handis. a1615 *Brieue Cron. Erlis of Ross* (1850) 13 He procurit to him, by nature inclynit to follow such counsel, to mak war in his favour.

IV. †9. *intr.* ? To proceed, advance. *Obs. rare.*

(Sense and sematology obscure.)

1490 CAXTON *Eneydos* xiii. 47 In her thoughte the wounde of ambycyouse desyre..is so procured that she can not hyde it noo lenger. 1573 TUSSER *Husb.* (1878) 146 His hatred procureth from naughtie to wurse, His friendship like Iudas that carried the purse.

procurement (prəʊˈkjʊəmənt). Forms: see PROCURE; also 5 prokyr-. [a. OF. *procurement* (13th c. in Godef.), f. *procurer* to PROCURE: see -MENT. (In ME. orig. ˈ*procur*-.)]

1. a. The action of causing, compassing, accomplishing, or bringing about, esp. through the instrumentality of an agent; management, arrangement; authorization, instigation; prompting, contrivance.

1303 R. BRUNNE *Handl. Synne* 5953 Ȝyf þou hyre one out of seruyse þurgh ȝyft or þurgh procurment, þou synnest gretly yn swych atent. c1400 *Chaucer's Pars. T.* ¶710 (Harl. 7334) He þat bieth þinges espirituelеs..be it by procurement [*six texts* procurynge] or by fleisshly prayere of his frendes. c1440 *Promp. Parv.* 414/2 Prokyrment, *procuracio.* 1534 MORE *Treat. Passion* Wks. 1281/1 By the procurement of the dyuel. 1551 ROBINSON tr. *More's Utop.* Title-p., Translated into Englyshe..at the procurement, and earnest request of George Tadlowe. 1615 G. SANDYS *Trav.* 46 He was poisoned..at the procurement of..his sonne. a1662 HEYLIN *Laud* I. 181 Laud himself, by whose procurement his Majesties Declaration had been published. 1710 HEARNE *Collect.* (O.H.S.) III. 80 The old Testament was translated into Irish at y[e] Procurement of Bp. Bedel. 1767 WESLEY *Wks.* (1872) III. 298 The bells began to ring, by the procurement of a neighbouring gentleman. 1845 STEPHEN *Comm. Laws Eng.* (1874) II. 62 An act to be performed on his part or by his procurement. 1886 STEVENSON *Kidnapped* xxvii. 279 It was by his means and the procurement of my uncle, that I was kidnapped.

†b. An agent or instrument; a means. *Obs.*

1601 WEEVER *Mirr. Mart.* E ij, Sir Roger Acton, in the priests despleasure, Of my escape was thought the chiefe procurement.

2. a. The action or process of obtaining by care or effort; acquisition, attainment, getting, gaining.

1612 T. TAYLOR *Comm. Titus* i. 9 By all good meanes they labour the procurement and presence of it. 1629 SYMMER *Spir. Posie* Ep. A ij b, The witty industry of man about the procurement of artificial smels. 1702 S. PARKER tr. *Cicero's De Finibus* I. 23 Frequently..Pain and Labour prove a necessary Means towards the procurement of Exquisite Pleasures. 1847-8 H. MILLER *First Impr.* viii. (1857) 122 Luxuries of difficult procurement. 1882 H. W. BEECHER in *Chr. World* 20 Apr. 251/3 Within proper bounds, the procurement of riches is training in morality.

†b. A thing procured or obtained; an acquisition.

1753 N. TORRIANO *Midwifry* 4 Nor is there now for Man any Pleasure or Procurement whatsoever without Labour to be had.

3. *Mil.* The action or process of procuring equipment and supplies. Freq. *attrib.*

1957 [see LOGISTICAL *a.* 4]. 1958 *Times Rev. Industry* Mar. 9/2 Strategic materials on the active stockpiling list had reached their procurement priority levels by the middle of last year. 1966 *Amer. Speech* XLI. 300 It receives the plans and decisions of the Secretary of Defense and Secretary of the Air Force, and its own Chief of Staff, and translates them into training, logistic, and procurement programs. 1966 *Electronics* 17 Oct. 103 It is this growth in avionics complexity that is making military procurement officers insist on built-in test capability. 1977 *R.A.F. News* 30 Mar.-12 Apr. 10/4 It is then the task of the operational requirements staff to define the parameters in a detailed operational requirement which..is passed to the Procurement Executive who put it to industry to see how it can best be met.

procurer (prəʊˈkjʊərə(r)). Forms: α. 4–7 procurour, 5–7 -or, (4 *Sc.* -ur, 5 -oure, 6 *Sc.* prokerrour). β. 5– procurer. [ME. and AF. *procuˈrour*, = OF. *procurëur*, *-eeur* (13th c. in Hatz.-Darm., mod.F. *procureur*):—L. *prōcūrātōr-em* PROCURATOR¹. In later ME. ˈ*procurour*; in 15th and 16th c. changed to *proˈcurer*, esp. in senses arising from or naturally associated with the vb. PROCURE: see -ER¹.]

I. † **1.** = PROCURATOR¹, in various uses. **a.** *Rom. Hist.* An imperial procurator. **b.** A steward, a manager. **c.** An attorney; an advocate, a defender. **d.** A deputy, commissioner, representative.

a. α. **1470–85** MALORY *Arthur* v. i. 160 The Emperour Lucyus whiche was called at that tyme Dictatour or procurour of the publyke wele of Rome. **1483** CAXTON *Gold. Leg.* 412 b/1 Accusyng hym that he had synned wyth the doughter of the procurour. **1596** DALRYMPLE tr. *Leslie's Hist. Scot.* III. 187 Ffel in this field Quintine Bassian legat, Hircie the Emperouris Prokerrour in Britannie [etc.].

b. α. c **1375** *Sc. Leg. Saints* xvi. (*Magdalena*) 157 He mad hyr his familiare, & procurur in-to þe way he wald hyr hafe. **1477** EARL RIVERS (Caxton) *Dictes* 100 Make him thy procurour and receyvour of thy money. **1489** CAXTON *Faytes of A.* III. ii. 171 It were a grete oultrage that the procuroure sholde be ageynst the mayster.

c. α. **1390** GOWER *Conf.* II. 224 Thei make here prive procurours, To telle hou [etc.]. **1456** SIR G. HAYE *Law Arms* (S.T.S.) 109 The Emperour suld be procuroure to defend haly kirk. **1598** DALLINGTON *Meth. Trav.* F iv, Two other Lawyers, the one an Aduocate, the other a Procuror.

β. a **1658** CLEVELAND *Rustic Rampant* Wks. (1687) 413 The Places and Houses of Advocates, and Procurers.

d. α. a **1533** LD. BERNERS *Gold. Bk. M. Aurel.* (1546) I iij, He wente to the colledge, where as al the procurours and ambassadours of all prouinces were.

β. **1560** DAUS tr. *Sleidane's Comm.* 32 He by his procurers sheweth causes why he coulde not come. *Ibid.* 425 The Emperour, and kyng Ferdinando,.. appointed their procurers with large and ample commission, whiche should treate and followe the cause, in their names, at Rome.

† **e.** = F. *procureur* or its equivalents in cognate langs.: see PROCUREUR. ***procurer fiscal*** = F. *procureur fiscal*: cf. PROCURATOR-FISCAL. *Obs.*

α. **1575** GASCOIGNE *Pr. Pleas. Kenilw.* (1821) 74, I haue beene by the Procuror generall, twise seuerally summoned to appeare before the great Gods in their Councel chamber. **1647–8** COTTERELL *Davila's Hist. Fr.* (1678) 37 Procuror Fiscal to the King.

β. **1560** DAUS tr. *Sleidane's Comm.* 366 Both the kinges procurer, and also the university of Paris,.. resisted with a stout courage. **1604** E. G[RIMSTONE] *D'Acosta's Hist. Indies* IV. xi. 240 He was in surte against the Procurer fiscal. **1721** STRYPE tr. *Jernegan's Let. to Wolsey* (1515) in *Eccl. Mem.* (1721) I. i. 13 Eloy de la Rice, high procurer of this City [Tournay]. **1762** H. WALPOLE *Vertue's Anecd. Paint.* (1765) III. i. 63 He married.. Mary Van Gamaren, daughter of a procurer at Utrecht.

II. 2. One who or that which brings about, effects, or induces something; *esp.* one who causes something to be done by the agency of another or others; a promoter, prime mover, instigator, contriver, ultimate author. Now *rare* or *Obs.*

β. **1451** *Rolls of Parlt.* V. 225/1 Which shall not be partie to eny such offence, ne Procurer, Councellour, nor Abbettour to the doyng therof. a **1548** HALL *Chron., Hen. VI* 157 Affirmyng him to be.. the chief procurer of the death of the good duke of Gloucester. **1580–1** *Act 23 Eliz.* c. 8 §1 The said Melter Myngler or Corrupter Causer or Procurer thereof, shall forfeyte for everye pounde, Two Shillinges. a **1639** WOTTON in Walton *Angler* i. (1653) 33 Angling.. was .. a procurer of contentedness. a **1651** CALDERWOOD *Hist. Kirk* (1843) II. 346 He was neere of kin to the king, and the cheefe procurer of the matche. **1769** *Chron.* in *Ann. Reg.* 68/2 Mr. Recorder.. hoped that the fate of these two unhappy persons would be a warning to all rioters.. and that the procurers.. as well as the procured, were not exempt, by our laws, from this catastrophe. **1776** ABIGAIL ADAMS in *Fam. Lett.* (1876) 137 How shall the miserable wretches who have been the procurers of this dreadful scene.. lie down with the load of guilt upon their souls? **1822** LAMB *Elia Ser.* II. *Confess. Drunkard*, To be set on to provoke mirth which procures the procurer hatred.

3. One who procures or obtains.

1538 STARKEY *England* I. iii. 81 Al such yl-occupyd personys as be procurarys only of the vayn plesure of man. **1573–80** BARET *Alv.* P 741 A reconciler, or procurer of fauour, *conciliator, ris.* **1882–3** *Schaff's Encycl. Relig. Knowl.* I. 610 Having been one of the procurers of the patent for Massachusetts Colony (1628).. he finally set sail thither.

4. One who procures women for the gratification of lust; a pander. Often feminine = PROCURESS 2.

1632 MASSINGER *City Madam* IV. ii, Thy procurer Shall be sheathed in velvet, and a reverend veil Pass her for a grave matron. **1698** CROWNE *Caligula* II. 23 Shall I.. Provoke the proud adulterer to my couch, And be Procurer to my own reproach? a **1716** SOUTH *Serm.* (1727) II. 182 Strumpets in their Youth turn Procurers in their Age. **1880** MUIRHEAD *Ulpian* xiii. §2 Other persons of free-birth are forbidden to marry.. a freedwoman manumitted by a procurer or procuress,.. or one that has been an actress.

procuress (prəʊˈkjʊərɪs). [ME. *procuˈresse*, syncopated from OF. *procureˈresse* (14th c.), fem. of *procureur* PROCURER: cf. *governess*.]

† **1.** A female advocate or defender. *Obs. rare.*

1413 *Compl. Soul* 169 in *Hoccleve's Wks.* (E.E.T.S.) III. p. lvi, As aduocate for man, & procuresse.. Now be myne helpe o blisful qwene. c **1430** *Pilgr. Lyf Manhode* IV. xlvi, She hath wynges.. for to soone doo hire message bifore god for mankynde, and is procuress whan time is to see him.

2. A woman who makes it her trade to procure women for the gratification of lust; a bawd.

1712 STEELE *Spect.* No. 266 ¶4 Who should I see there but the most artful Procuress in the Town. **1758** J. GRAINGER tr. *Tibullus' Elegies* I. vi. 85 From you my Ruin, curst Procuress, rose. **1850** TENNYSON *In Mem.* liii, For fear divine Philosophy Should push beyond her mark, and be Procuress to the Lords of Hell. **1880** [see PROCURER 4].

‖**procureur** (prɔkyrœr). [F., agent-n. from *procurer* to PROCURE:—OF. *procureeur*, *-ëur*, *-ëor*:—L. *prōcūrātōr-em* PROCURATOR¹.]

a. A procurator (esp. in sense 4); an attorney, agent, or legal representative. ***procureur du roi*** or ***de la république***, in France, a public prosecutor; ***procureur général***, the legal agent of the state, in a court of appeal or court of cassation.

1598 DALLINGTON *Meth. Trav.* 23 There bee of this Court, of Presidents, Councillors, Procureurs, Aduocates. **1682** WARBURTON *Hist. Guernsey* (1822) 11 The then bishop of Coûtance.., sent his procureur, or agent. *Ibid.* 56 The King's Procureur... He is properly the King's Attorney. **1751** CHESTERF. *Lett. to Son* 18 Mar., Not the hand of a *procureur*, or a writing-master. **1763** SMOLLETT *Trav.* ii. (1766) I. 20 To have my books examined on the spot, by the ..*procureur du roy*, or the subdelegate of the intendance. **1804** *Edinb. Rev.* Apr. 112 Bougon, procureur-general of the department of Calvados. **1884** *Pall Mall G.* 1 Aug. 3/2 Sir E. Baring.. goes on to say that he would.. have preferred making the Mudir a magistrate to having the procureur system. **1905** GUNTER *Conscience King* i. 8 A *procureur* attached to the local courts of Rouen.

b. = PROCURATOR¹ 2 a.

1907 *Daily Chron.* 9 July 3/5 The monks.. of La Grande Chartreuse.. were governed by priors and procureurs... the latter [looked] after the temporalities, or revenues and supplies.

c. = PROCURER 4.

1910 *Times* 29 Apr. 14/1 The procureurs (the cant name is 'ponce') at work in this country are mostly foreigners. **1979** W. J. FISHMAN *Streets East London* 52/2 Lodging houses infested by thieves, *procureurs* and prostitutes.

‖**procureuse** (prɔkyrøz). [Fr.] = PROCURESS 2.

1930 E. WAUGH *Vile Bodies* vi. 105 What a coarse face.. she looks like a *procureuse*. **1968** C. COOPER *Thunder & Lightning Man* iv. 52 Does she condone it?.. Is she just an old *procureuse*? **1977** 'R. PLAYER' *Month of Mangled Models* vii. 123 She's only a common procureuse dressed like a duchess.

procuring (prəʊˈkjʊərɪŋ), *vbl. sb.* Also 5 ˈprokering. [f. PROCURE *v.* + -ING¹: in ME. ˈ*procuring*.] The action of the verb PROCURE.

† **1.** Doing one's best, labouring, striving. *Obs.*

1548 UDALL *Erasm. Par.* Pref. 5 Spendyng his lyfe in procuring for owr wealth.

2. The action of causing or contriving to bring about; the fact of being the prime agent; = PROCUREMENT 1. Now *rare*.

1340 *Ayenb.* 39 Greate prelas, þet.. robbeþ hire onderlinges be to moche procuringe. **1387** TREVISA *Higden* (Rolls) II. 35 þat was at erle Harolde his procurynge. c **1400** *Destr. Troy* 13766 Thurgh his prokuryng prestly all the pure Troiens... Were deliuert yche lede, & lause at hor willne. c **1440** *York Myst.* xl. 82 Thurgh prokering of princes. a **1548** HALL *Chron., Hen. VI* 99 He was there by myne excitacion and procuryng to haue slain the fore-saied Prince there in his bedde. **1639** FULLER *Holy War* III. xi. (1840) 133 Henry.. was chosen King of Jerusalem, by the especial procuring of King Richard his uncle.

3. The getting or obtaining (of anything) by effort; = PROCUREMENT 2.

1608 HIERON *Wks* I. 753 We may euen deuote our selues to the procuring of the present and eternall good one of another. **1663** GERBIER *Counsel* 108 The procuring of precious Wood. **1748** *Anson's Voy.* II. ii. 135 The procuring of refreshments. **1885** *Weekly Notes* 72/1 The maliciously procuring a bankruptcy is not actionable unless the adjudication is set aside.

4. The action of a procurer or procuress.

a **1758** RAMSAY *Address of Thanks* xvii, Your procuring Is now sae far frae being a crime.

procuring (prəʊˈkjʊərɪŋ), *ppl. a.* [f. as prec. + -ING².] That procures, in various senses; causing, producing; obtaining, winning; pandering, pimping.

c **1618** MORYSON *Itin.* (1903) 427 If any man, by himselfe or by any frend, makes meanes to be chosen Rectour, he must pay 50 Lyers, and his procuring frend 30. **1672** CAVE *Prim. Chr.* I. iii. (1673) 52 The procuring cause of all those mischiefs and calamities. **1693** DRYDEN *Juvenal* i. 86 With what Impatience must the Muse behold The Wife by her procuring Husband sold? **1761** *Chron.* in *Ann. Reg.* 94/1 To prevent their clergy from.. declaiming on the procuring cause of earthquakes. **1837** RUSSELL in Liddon, etc. *Life Pusey* (1893) I. xvii. 407 Newman strongly insisted,.. that the Atonement alone was the grand procuring and meritorious cause of our pardon.

† **proˈcurish**, *a. Obs. nonce-wd.* [f. PROCUR-ESS + -ISH¹.] Like a procuress.

1687 SEDLEY *Bellamira* III. i, She.. begins to look something procurish.

procuror, -our: see PROCURER.

procurrent (prəʊˈkʌrənt), *a. Ichthyol.* [ad. L. *procurrent-*, *procurrens*, pres. pple. of *procurrere* to run forward.] Of a fish's fin: having rays that are almost parallel.

1902 JORDAN & EVERMANN *Amer. Food & Game Fishes* 538 Procurrent (fin). With the lower rays inserted progressively further forward. **1931** J. R. NORMAN *Hist. Fishes* iii. 72 True spines are never developed in this [caudal] fin, but rudimentary or procurrent rays resembling spines may be found at the base of the lobes.

procursive (prəʊˈkɜːsɪv), *a.* [f. L. *prōcurs-*, ppl. stem of *prōcurrĕre* to run forward + -IVE.] Characterized by running forward; *spec.* applied to a kind of epilepsy in which the fits are marked by an aimless running forward.

1890 in *Cent. Dict.* **1894** *Pop. Sci. Monthly* June 283 Running or 'procursive epilepsy'.

procurˈvation. [n. of action from L. *prōcurvāre* to bend or curve forward.] A curving or bending forward; forward curvature (as of the spine).

1822–34 *Good's Study Med.* (ed. 4) III. 262 This species offers us the four following varieties:—*a.* Anticus, Tetanic procurvation [etc.]. *Ibid.* IV. 249 Lordosis.., imported procurvation of the head and shoulders, or anterior crookedness.

procurvature. [f. PRO-² + CURVATURE.] = PROCURVATION.

1903 R. I. POCOCK in *Ann. & Mag. Nat. Hist.* XI. 411 The species described by Keyserling as *Trechona pantherina* appears to me to be the female of *auromitens*, in spite of a less procurvature of the anterior line of eyes.

proˈcurved, *a.* [f. PRO-¹ + CURVED: cf. PROCURVATION.] Curved in a forward direction.

1898 *Proc. Zool. Soc.* 894 Anterior row strongly procurved, laterals slightly larger than centrals.

procusie, obs. form of PROXY.

procuticle (prəʊˈkjuːtɪk(ə)l). [f. PRO-² + CUTICLE.] The inner, thicker layer of the cuticle of an arthropod, situated below the epicuticle and comprising the exocuticle (if present) and the endocuticle.

1951 A. G. RICHARDS *Integument of Arthropods* xvi. 148 The term procuticle is proposed for the embryologically original (parent) chitin-protein fraction. *Ibid.* 149 The procuticle may remain seemingly unchanged in soft transparent cuticle and soft areas.., in which case the fully formed cuticle is said to consist of epicuticle and endocuticle... Or the outer portion of the procuticle may become hardened and darkened by sclerotization, giving an outer dark exocuticle and an inner transparent endocuticle. **1959** W. ANDREW *Textbk. Compar. Histol.* iii. 91 It [*sc.* the cuticle of arthropods] presents a great diversity of structure but in general may be divided into an outer part without chitin, the 'epicuticle', and an inner part with chitin, the 'procuticle' or 'endocuticle'. **1962** GORDON & LAVOIPIERRE *Entomol.* ix. 53 The procuticle confers on the integument amongst other properties those of hardness and strength and is the real skeletal support of the body of the insect. **1967** [see EXOCUTICLE a]. **1976** C. P. FRIEDLANDER *Biol. Insects* i. 16 When first secreted the entire procuticle is in the endocuticle condition; subsequently a large proportion of it is hardened.. to form the exocuticle.

Procyon (ˈprəʊsɪɒn). [a. L. *Procyōn*, a. Gr. Προκύων (in sense 1), f. πρό before + κύων dog: so called as rising a little before the dog-star Sirius.]

1. The principal star in the constellation of *Canis Minor*; also formerly the constellation itself.

1658 PHILLIPS, *Procyon*, the lesser Dog-Star. **1842** [see DOG-STAR 1]. **1868** LOCKYER *Guillemin's Heavens* (ed. 3) 324 Betelgeuse, Sirius, and Procyon form a triangle.

2. *Zool.* A genus of plantigrade carnivorous mammals, inhabiting N. and S. America, including the racoons, typical of the family *Procyonidæ*.

1843 *Penny Cycl.* XXVI. 57/1 Procyon. **1849** CRAIG, *Procyon*, the Racoon, a genus of quadrupeds, placed by naturalists immediately after the Bears.

Hence **procyˈoniform** *a.*, resembling the racoons in form, racoon-like (*Cent. Dict.* 1890); ˈ**procyonoid** *a.* = *procyoniform*; also as *sb.*

procyonid (ˈprəʊsɪɒnɪd), *sb.* and *a.* [f. mod.L. family name *Procyonidæ*, f. generic name *Procyon* (G. C. C. Storr *Prodomus Methodi Mammalium* (1780) 35): see PROCYON.] A mammal belonging to the family Procyonidæ, which includes racoons and pandas. Also as *adj.*, of, pertaining to, or resembling an animal of this kind.

1909 in *N.E.D.* **1910** H. F. OSBORN *Age of Mammals* iv. 288 This [*sc.* the Lower Miocene] is the first geological appearance of the characteristically American family of raccoons, or procyonids. **1921** *Proc. Zool. Soc.* 419 The genus [*Ailuropoda*] is neither Ursid nor Procyonid. **1941** *Geol. Ser. Field Mus. Nat. Hist.* VIII. 33 (*title*) A new procyonid from the Miocene of Nebraska. **1964** E. P. WALKER *Mammals of World* II. 1179/2 Most procyonids travel in pairs or family groups. **1973** *Nature* 28 Sept. 218/2 Its [*sc.* the giant panda's] closest affinities are with the ursids (bears) or procyonids (raccoons). **1978** T. A. VAUGHAN *Mammalogy* (ed. 2) xii. 217/1 Procyonids are of modest size, weighing from less than a kilogram to about 20 kg.

procyonine ('prəʊsɪəʊniːn), *a.* [f. mod.L. subfamily name *Procyoninæ*: see prec.] Of or pertaining to the subfamily *Procyoninæ*, containing only the racoons.

1869 [see ARCTOID *a.* (*sb.*)]. **1883** W. H. FLOWER in *Encycl. Brit.* XV. 441/1 This name [Bassaricyon] has recently (1876) been given to a distinct modification of the Procyonine type. **1921** *Proc. Zool. Soc.* 418 If the tooth in *Ailuropoda* is not Ailurine or Procyonine, it is certainly not Ursine.

prod (prɒd), *sb.*[1] [f. PROD *v.*]

1. a. An act of prodding; a thrust with some pointed instrument; a poke, a stab.

1802 R. ANDERSON *Cumberld. Ball.* 42 Come, Jobby, gi'e the fire a prod, Then steek the entry duir. **1822** HOGG *Perils of Man* I. x. 247 Ane may ward a blow at the breast, but a prod at the back's no fair. **1849** *Sidonia Sorc.* II. 47 Giving many of them a sharp prod on the shoulder. **1864** *Daily Tel.* 6 Aug., The prisoner..made what he called a 'prod' (thrust) at him with his bayonet. **1886** HALL CAINE *Son of Hagar* I. vii, Prompted by sundry prods from the elbow of a little damsel by his side.

b. *on the prod*: looking out for something to prod; on the attack, on the offensive. *N. Amer. colloq.*

a **1904** A. ADAMS *Log Cowboy* ix, When he [a man] came near enough to us, we could see that he was angry and on the prod. *Ibid.* xi, Several steers showed fight, and when released went on the prod for the first thing in sight. **1910** B. EDWARDS in H. A. Dempsey *Best of Bob Edwards* (1975) v. 96 The old man was on the prod. **1947** B. A. DE VOTO *Across Wide Missouri* 26 Not only the Arikaras but the Blackfeet were on the prod. **1962** [see ORNERY].

2. a. A name given to various pointed instruments, as a goad, a skewer, a brad, a thatcher's pin, etc.

1787 GROSE *Provinc. Gloss.*, *Prod*, an awl. **1808** JAMIESON, *Prod*, a pin of wood. *Ibid.*, *Prod*, *Craw-prod*, a pin fixed in the top of a gable, to which the ropes, fastening the roof of a cottage, were tied. **1825** BROCKETT *N.C. Gloss.*, *Prod*, a prick, a skewer. **1828** *Craven Gloss.* (ed. 2), *Prod*, a goad. *Ibid.*, *Prod*, an iron pin fixed in pattens. *Ibid.*, *Prod*, a short stake driven in the ground. **1855** ROBINSON *Whitby Gloss.*, *Prod*, an iron point at the end of a stick. 'An ox prod', an ox goad. **1873** DIXON *Two Queens* I. II. iv. 92 To drive more soldiers to his camp, he wanted sharper spurs and stronger prods.

b. *Founding.* Any of a number of pointed projections, intended to hold the loam, on the flat metal base used for preparing a loam mould.

1888 *Lockwood's Dict. Mech. Engin.* 267 The pyramidal or conical points cast on loam and core plates for the retention of the loam are termed prods. **1889** J. G. HORNER *Pract. Iron Founding* viii. 103 A plate..is cast, studded over with 'prods' to hold the loam which is swept over its face. **1923** —— *Mod. Ironfoundry* vii. 65 Prods are cast on many loam mould plates. Generally, they occur on one side only, and the pattern prods are mounted in a strip of wood, provided with a handle.

prod, *sb.*[2] *slang.* [app. a variant of PRAD.] An (old) horse.

1891 E. KINGLAKE *Australian at H.* 119 The contemptuous terms..have led Mr. Newcome to suppose that his mount is most likely the quietest old 'prod' on the place. **1900** G. ELSON in *Academy* 4 Aug. 91/1 The horse was a prod, the cart a drag.

Prod (prɒd), *sb.*[3] and *a.* Also prod. An Anglo-Irish colloq. abbrev. of PROTESTANT *sb.* 2 a and *a.* 1. Cf. PROT *sb.* and *a.*

1942 E. BOWEN *Seven Winters* 51 She spoke of 'Prods' (or, extreme, unctuous Protestants) with a flighty detachment that might have offended many. **1961** *Spectator* 28 Apr. 599 He was a 'Mick', I was a 'Prod' but we found no difficulty in being friends although we differed in faith. **1970** M. KENYON *100,000 Welcomes* ii. 14 A long-hair student, or a Prod, or similar riff-raff. **1974** *Irish Democrat* Dec. 7/2 This is..about O'Brienism, which is based on the fearful symmetry that taig is taig and prod is prod and never the twain shall meet. **1977** P. CARTER *Under Goliath* iii. 15 Most of the kids were in tough Prod gangs, like the Tartans... They always seemed to..tell if you were as hard-line Prod as they were.

prod (prɒd), *v.* [Known from 1535; there is no related word in the cognate langs. Perh. of onomatopœic origin, related on one side to *prog*, *proke*, *prick*, and on the other to *brod* (all of which express piercing or stabbing action of some kind).

The word has been thought to enter into the OE. comb. *prod-bore*, *prot-bore* (dative), in Rushworth Gospels, Matt. xi. 16, xx. 3, as the gloss on *foro* 'in the market-place', but which has been conjectured to mean 'auger' or 'boring-tool' (cf. OE. *bor* borer, gimlet), the L. having been erroneously connected by the glossator with L. *foro* I bore.]

1. *trans.* To thrust or stab; to poke with a pointed instrument, or with the end of a stick.

1535 COVERDALE *Ecclus.* xxxviii. 25 He that holdeth yͤ plough, & hath pleasure in proddynge & dryuynge yͤ oxen. *c* **1712** in Hogg *Jacobite Relics* (1819) I. 70 Ane proddit her in the lisk, Anither aneath the tail. **1828** *Craven Gloss.* (ed. 2), *Prod*, *Proddle*, to goad. **1854** THACKERAY *Rose & Ring* xvii, With his fairy sword..his Majesty kept poking and prodding Padella in the back. **1855** —— *Newcomes* xlvii, A physiologist..prods down this butterfly with a pin. **1861** RAMSAY *Remin.* Ser. II. 59 Please tak a brog and prod him weel and let the wind out o' him. **1887** HUXLEY in *Life* (1900) II. xi. 184, I..have vitality enough to kick..when prodded.

b. *fig.* To goad mentally; to stir up, instigate, incite; to irritate.

1871 J. R. GREEN *Lett.* III. (1901) 295 The excitement of trying..to prod them into action. **1890** *Spectator* 4 Oct. 429/2 You complain of Italy,—well, leave off prodding her. **1899** *Daily News* 6 June 2/2 Poor little things!.. I felt it was cruelty to even prod them with my few questions.

2. *intr.* To thrust, to poke. Const. *in*, *into*, *at*.

1696 *Money masters all Things* (1698) 94 The stinking Gold-finder with his white Rod, In common or in private Jakes will prod. **1859** *Sat. Rev.* 10 Dec. 705/2 To prod into the fat sides of the Hereford ox or Devon heifer. **1866** FITZPATRICK *Sham Sqr.* 112 Assailed by them all, and in stepping back, fell; they prodding at him.

3. *trans.* To make by prodding.

1865 DICKENS *Mut. Fr.* I. x, The lady has prodded little spirting holes in the damp sand..with her parasol.

Hence **'prodded** *ppl. a.*, **'prodding** *vbl. sb.*

1879 G. MEREDITH *Egoist* xlvii, Neat as a prodded eel on a pair of prongs. **1883** E. INGERSOLL in *Harper's Mag.* Jan. 206/1 Under resounding thwacks and proddings of an iron-tipped goad, the..cattle snake the log endwise down the hill. **1898** L. STEPHEN *Stud. Biogr.* II. iv. 157 You were subject to a vigorous course of prodding and rousing.

prodatary (prəʊ'deɪtərɪ). [ad. mod.L. *prōdatāri-us*: see PRO-[1] 4 and DATARY[1].] The title given to the presiding official of the datary office at Rome, when a cardinal.

1880 *Libr. Univ. Knowl.* (N.Y.) VIII. 808 Pope Leo [XIII] appointed..Cardinal Sacconi prodatary.

prodder ('prɒdə(r)). [f. PROD *v.* + -ER[1].] One who or that which prods.

1894 *Pall Mall G.* 5 Dec. 2/1 For coarse work Macdonald uses electric needles, which he calls 'prodders'... The largest number of needles which his prodders contain is eighteen. **1902** *Daily Chron.* 14 May 3/2 He prods him in the eyes..The sailor is blinded..the prodder gets his money, and runs off. **1907** *Ibid.* 24 Dec. 4/4 The punchers and prodders are small boys..from eight to twelve.

prodder, proddest, obs. comp. and sup. of PROUD.

Proddy ('prɒdɪ), *a. colloq.* (chiefly *Anglo-Irish*). Also proddy. [f. PROD *sb.*[3] and *a.* + -Y[6].] Protestant. Also *Comb.*, as (children's slang) ***Proddy-hopper***, ***-woddy***; **Proddy Dog** (opp. *Cat*: Catholic).

1954 W. K. HANCOCK *Country & Calling* i. 50 And they would sing: *Proddy Dog, Proddy Dog, Sitting on a well, Up comes the Devil And pulls him down to hell.* Then we and the Catholic boys would pelt each other with cowdung. **1958** I. CROSS *God Boy* 165 Proddy-hopper, proddy-hopper, go to hell. **1959** I. & P. OPIE *Lore & Lang. Schoolch.* xvi. 344 In Ireland, both north and south, Catholics are 'Cathies' and Protestants 'Proddy-woddys'. *Ibid.*, In Staines..R.C. children call the Protestants 'Old Proddy Dogs'... They still call them 'Proddy Dogs' at Ilford. **1961** *Spectator* 28 Apr. 603 In other streets Papist and Proddy schoolboys could pass in peace. **1968** T. PARKER *People of Sheets* 60 We always divided up into the same two sides, The Cats and The Proddy Dogs. **1975** G. SEYMOUR *Harry's Game* v. 76 Nice safe little billet..in a nice Proddy area... I'm not going ..to sit on my arse in Proddyland.

prode, obs. f. PROUD.

prodegate, prodege: see PRODIGATE *ppl. a.*, PRODIGE *v.*

prodelision (prəʊdɪ'lɪʒən). *Prosody.* [f. L. *prōd*, older form of *prō*, PRO-[1], used before vowels + ELISION.] Elision of an initial vowel.

1906 *Academy* 17 Mar. 257/1 Creaking Ionic scazons disfigured..by prodelision and synizesis and crasis. **1933** *Trans. Philol. Soc. 1931–32* 32 They would point to the patent phenomena of adaptation or assimilation of the two sounds to one another..and also to the facts of elision, prodelision, and crasis (in the case of vowels), that is, of coalescence. **1968** W. S. ALLEN *Vox Graeca* iv. 96 Much rarer than elision is the process of 'prodelision' in which it is the short initial vowel of the second word that is lost after a final long vowel or diphthong.

prodelta(ic), -dialogue: see PRO-[2] 2, 1.

†**'prodig, 'prodigue**, *a.* (*sb.*) *Obs.* Also 5 prodyge. [a. F. *prodigue* (13th c. in Littré), ad. L. *prōdig-us* wasteful, lavish, f. *prōdig-ĕre*: see PRODIGE *v.* Perh. in part direct from L.]

A. *adj.* Prodigal.

[*c* **1450** LYDG. *Secrees* 942 Whoo is nat mesurable In his Rychesse, but disordinat, Is Callyd prodigus.] **1491** CAXTON *Vitas Patr.* (W. de W. 1495) I. clxiv. 173 A woman ryche & noble..she was prodyge & lecherous. **1598** SYLVESTER *Du Bartas* II. i. I. *Eden* 543 Where prodig' Nature sets abroad her booth Of richest beauties.

B. *sb.* A prodigal.

a **1600** MONTGOMERIE *Devot. Poems* iv. 4, I am not worthy to be cald thy chylde,..Not lyk thy sone, bot lyk the prodigue wyld.

prodigal ('prɒdɪgəl), *a.* and *sb.* (*adv.*) [a. obs. F. *prodigal* (16th c. in Godef.), ad. late L. **prōdigāl-is* (*prōdigāliter*, Ambrose, *prōdigālitās*, Boeth.), f. *prōdig-us*: see prec. and -AL[1].]

A. *adj.* **1.** Given to extravagant expenditure; recklessly wasteful of one's property or means.

1500–20 DUNBAR *Poems* xix. 44 Gif I be nobill, gentill and fre, A prodigall man I am so prysit. **1538** STARKEY *England* I. iv. 107 Yf the sone be prodygal and gyuen to al vyce and foly. **1601** R. JOHNSON *Kingd. & Commw.* (1603) 136 The nobility is very gallant, prodigall in expenses, spending more than their reuenues in diet and apparell. **1641** J. JACKSON *True Evang. T.* II. 95 The elder and thrifty brother [represents] the Jew; the younger and prodigall, the Gentile. *a* **1716** SOUTH *Serm.* (1727) IV. x. 428 It is hard, if not impossible, for a prodigal person to be guilty of no other Vice, but Prodigality. **1870** DISRAELI *Lothair* vii, Lothair was profuse, but he was not prodigal.

b. with *of*. (Often passing into 3 b.)

1665 MANLEY *Grotius' Low C. Warres* 149 Too late they pleased to be prodigal, both of Wealth and Life. **1773** *Observ. State Poor* 134 Perhaps no nation on earth is so prodigal of life as the English. **1864** KINGSLEY *Rom. & Teut.* i. 15 Nature is prodigal of human life.

c. ***prodigal son, child***: in reference or allusion to the parable, in Luke xv. 11–32: cf. B. 2.

c **1450** [see PRODIGATE (perh. error for *prodigale*)]. **1508** FISHER 7 *Penit. Ps.* cxlii. Wks. (1876) 265 The comynge agayne of this prodygall chylde whiche hath spent his substance. [**1523** *Vulgate*, Luke xv. *marginal note*, parabola de filio prodigo.] **1551** BIBLE (Matthew) *Luke* xv. *heading*, The parables of the loste shepe, of the groat that was loste, and of the prodigall sonne. **1611** SHAKS. *Wint. T.* IV. iii. 103 Then hee compast a Motion of the Prodigall sonne, and married a Tinkers wife. **1662** J. DAVIES tr. *Olearius' Voy. Ambass.* 16 A Clock, on which was represented, in painting, the Parable of the Prodigal Child.

2. Of things or actions: Wastefully lavish.

(In Shakspere sometimes by a kind of hypallage attributed to another noun in the sentence.)

1500–20 DUNBAR *Poems* ix. 124 Prodigall spending, but rewth of peure folkis neiding. **1530** PALSGR. 361 Some by fyre, some by prodigall expences. **1588** SHAKS. *L.L.L.* v. ii. 64 How I would make him..spend his prodigall wits in booteles rimes. **1607** —— *Timon* II. ii. 174 How many prodigall bits haue Slaues and Pezants This night englutted. **1672** CAVE *Prim. Chr.* II. iv. (1673) 78 Our little suppers they traduce as prodigal. **1683** EVELYN *Diary* 4 Oct., This woman's apartment, now twice or thrice pull'd down and rebuilt to satisfie her prodigal and expensive pleasures. **1855** MACAULAY *Hist. Eng.* xix. IV. 327 Under the energetic and prodigal administration of the first William Pitt, the debt rapidly swelled to a hundred and forty millions.

3. Lavish in the bestowal or disposal of things.

1595 DANIEL *Civ. Wars* I. xxv, Too prodigall was nature thus to doe, To spend in one age, what should serue for two. **1613** SHAKS. *Hen. VIII*, v. v. 13 My Noble Gossips, y'haue beene too Prodigall; I thanke ye heartily. **1652–62** HEYLIN *Cosmogr.* III. (1682) 18 Inriched with prodigal veins of Gold and Silver. **1838–9** HALLAM *Hist. Lit.* II. II. i. §3. 4 A more prodigal accumulation of quotations. **1859** KINGSLEY *Misc.*, *Tennyson* I. 228 The prodigal fulness of thought and imagery.

b. with *of*: lavish *of*; also with *in* (*rare*).

1588 SHAKS. *L.L.L.* II. i. 9 Be now as prodigall of all deare grace, As Nature was in making Graces deare. **1681** NEVILE *Plato Rediv.* 25 Of these things I shall be very prodigal in my discourse. **1745** *N. Jersey Archives* XII. 275 Run away..a Servant Man,..appears a weildy young Man, prodigal in his Walk, and much so in his Speech. **1778** HAN. MORE *Florio* I. 183 When..May is prodigal of flowers. **1832** TENNYSON *Palace of Art* xx, Realms of upland, prodigal in oil, And hoary to the wind. **1856** FROUDE *Hist. Eng.* I. ii. 157 Nature had been prodigal to him of her rarest gifts.

¶**4.** 'Proud' (Halliw. *Dict. Arch.* 1847). (? error.)

B. *sb.*

1. One who spends his money extravagantly and wastefully; a spendthrift, waster.

1596 SHAKS. *Merch. V.* III. i. 47 A bankrout, a prodigall, who dare scarce shew his head on the Ryalto. **1620** T. GRANGER *Div. Logike* 171 To play the dingthrift, or prodigall. **1776** ADAM SMITH *W.N.* II. iv. (1869) I. 360 The greater part of the money..would be lent to prodigals and projectors. **1881** BESANT & RICE *Chapl. Fleet* I. 143 Formerly, I was rich and a prodigal.

b. with *of*.

1655 FULLER *Hist. Camb.* (1840) 127 No wonder for those ..who were prodigals of their own persons. **1885–94** R. BRIDGES *Eros & Psyche* Mar. xv, The prodigal of an immortal day For ever spending, and yet never spent.

2. In pregnant sense, with reference or allusion to the career of 'the Prodigal son': see A. 1 c.

1596 SHAKS. *Merch. V.* II. vi. 14, 16. **1601** B. JONSON *Ev. Man in Hum.* (Qo. 1) v. i. 360 Where is he?..the picture of the prodigal, go to, ile haue the calfe drest for you at my charges. **1719** DE FOE *Crusoe* I. 9, I would, like a true repenting Prodigal, go home to my Father. **1751** *Transl. & Paraphr. Ch. Scot.* XL. v, The grieving prodigal bewail'd the follies he had done. **1828** SCOTT *F.M. Perth* x, Should not I be permitted, like him, to reclaim my poor prodigal by affection as well as severity? **1885** S. COX *Expositions* III. 30 Though a prodigal, he was still a son.

3. ***to play the prodigal***: to act prodigally, be wasteful or lavish; to act like 'the prodigal son'.

1602 MARSTON *Ant. & Mel.* I. Wks. 1856 I. 12 Let vollies of the great artillery From of our gallies banks play prodigall. *c* **1820** S. ROGERS *Italy*, *Fountain* 7 The water.. o'erflowed; Then dashed away, playing the prodigal, And soon was lost.

C. as *adv.* Prodigally, lavishly.

1602 SHAKS. *Ham.* I. iii. 116, I doe know When the Bloud burnes, how Prodigall the Soule Giues the tongue vowes.

Hence †**'prodigal** *v. trans.*, to expend wastefully, extravagantly, or lavishly; **'prodigalish** *a.*, that is somewhat of a prodigal; **'prodigalism**, the condition and action of a prodigal; a course of life like that of 'the Prodigal son'.

1628 FELTHAM *Resolves* II. [I.] xx. 67 Hee prodigals a Mine of Excellencie, that lauishes a terse Oration to an approued Auditory. **1654** WHITLOCK *Zootomia* 4 'Nemo se sibi vindicat, sed Alius in Alium consumitur' (saith..Seneca) No man Husbandeth himselfe, but vainly..Prodigalls Himselfe out on others. **1857** HUGHES *Tom Brown* I. ii, He should like to cross a stick wi' the prodigalish young chap. **1896** *Chicago Advance* 1 Oct. 429 Infatuation is the bad element in prodigalism.

† **prodi'galeous,** *a.* *Obs.* *rare*⁻¹. [Erroneous form for **prodigalious*, f. med.L. **prōdigāli-s*: cf. *audaci-ous, bili-ous*.] Of the nature of a prodigal.

c **1400** tr. *Secreta Secret., Gov. Lordsh.* 52 He is a wastour of his goodys,..& he ys callyd a prodegaleous man þat is ffole large.

prodigality (prɒdɪ'gælɪtɪ). [ME. *prodigalite*, a. F. *prodigalité* (13th c. in Littré), ad. med.L. *prōdigālitās* (Boeth.), f. **prōdigālis*: see PRODIGAL.] The quality of being prodigal.

1. Reckless extravagance in expenditure, wastefulness: **a.** of material things, especially of money.

1340 *Ayenb.* 21 Fol niminge of greate spendinge, þet me clepeþ prodigalité. *c* **1412** HOCCLEVE *De Reg. Princ.* 4592 By whiche he cured is of þe seekenesse Of prodigalitee, or fool largesse. **1494** FABYAN *Chron.* VI. ccix. 222 This kyng..was of suche prodegalytie, that his bourdes & tabylles of his courte were spred .iiii. tymes in the day. **1548** UDALL, etc. *Erasm. Par. Mark* xiv. 84 The losse of this oyntment greued them so muche, that they made a great murmuryng agaynst the godly prodigalitie of the woman. **1622** MALYNES *Anc. Law Merch.* 481 Cæsar notwithstanding all his prodigalities, brought to the treasurie fortie millions of Crownes. *a* **1716** [see PRODIGAL *a.* 1]. **1841** ELPHINSTONE *Hist. Ind.* II. x. iii. 433 Sháh Jehán..The most striking instance of his pomp and prodigality was his construction of the famous peacock throne.

b. of immaterial things.

1751 JOHNSON *Rambler* No. 89 ⁋4 This invisible riot of the mind, this secret prodigality of being. **1846** TRENCH *Mirac.* Introd. iv. (1862) 48 There is..an entire absence of prodigality in the use of miracles. **1860–2** MILMAN in *Proc. Roy. Soc.* XI. p. xx, In other departments of poetry he [Macaulay] might have been endangered by his affluence and prodigality.

2. Lavishness, profuseness; lavish display, profuse supply.

1594 SHAKS. *Rich. III*, I. ii. 244 A sweeter, and a louelier Gentleman, Fram'd in the prodigallity of Nature..The spacious World cannot againe affoord. **1658** SIR T. BROWNE *Hydriot.* iii. 45 To drink of the ashes of dead relations [seems] a passionate prodigality. **1832** LYTTON *Eugene A.* I. xi, Merry fellows..; you must take care of the prodigality of their wine. **1890** 'R. BOLDREWOOD' *Col. Reformer* (1891) 144 That wondrous wealth and prodigality of perfect weather.

prodigalize ('prɒdɪgəlaɪz), *v.* [f. PRODIGAL *sb.* + -IZE: cf. obs. F. *prodigaliser* (1605 in Godef.), perh. the immediate source.]

† **1.** *intr.* *to prodigalize it*, to be lavish. *Obs.*

1611 COTGR., *Despendre trop*, to prodigalize it, lauish, or lash out.

2. *trans.* To spend profusely or lavishly.

1611 COTGR., *Prodigalisé*, prodigalized, lauished,.. squandered away. **1650** [? W. SAUNDERSON] *Aul. Coquin.* 68 This Lord..did most vainely prodigallize, what he often begg'd. **1836** LYTTON *Athens* II. iii, [Crœsus] prodigalized fresh presents on the Delphians. **1849** —— *Caxtons* XVII. i, Major MacBlarney prodigalizes his offers of service in every conceivable department of life.

prodigally ('prɒdɪgəlɪ), *adv.* [f. PRODIGAL + -LY².] In a prodigal manner.

1. With reckless extravagance; extravagantly, wastefully.

1530 PALSGR. 841/1 Prodygally, *prodiguement*. *a* **1533** LD. BERNERS *Gold. Bk. M. Aurel.* xlv. (1535) 87b, Some prodigally spende and wast all their goodes. **1682** NORRIS *Hierocles* Pref. 19 That neither spends his goods prodigally & like a fool. **1697** DRYDEN *Æneid* VI. 587 The next, in place and punishment, are they Who prodigally throw their souls away.

2. With lavish abundance; lavishly; profusely.

1590 GREENE *Mourn. Garm.* (1616) 1 Fortune..prodigally had wrapt him in the vestment of her riches. **1613** PURCHAS *Pilgrimage* (1614) 795 The King will not suffer them to haue Oyle or Wine there growing, although the earth would prodigally repay them, that they may still haue neede of Spaine. **1821** BYRON *Juan* V. lxv, The moveables were prodigally rich. *a* **1853** ROBERTSON *Lect.* (1858) 285 We know how prodigally the tongue vows.

† **'prodigate,** *ppl. a.* *Obs.* *rare*⁻¹. In 5 prodegate. [If not an error for *prodigale*, may represent a med.L. **prōdigātus*, pa. pple. of **prōdigāre* = It. *prodigare* to play the prodigal or spendthrift, F. *prodiguer* to spend lavishly.] Prodigal.

c **1450** *Mirour Saluacioun* 1647 This prodegate [*gloss* folelarge] son may wele a synnere signifie.

† **'prodige,** *sb.* *Obs.* *rare.* [a. F. *prodige* (14th c. in Littré), ad. L. *prōdigi-um* PRODIGY; cf. *vestige*.] A prodigy.

c **1470** *Brut* 530 Which was take for A prodige or token þat þe reign of King Henry was ended. **1618** T. ADAMS *Fire Contention* Wks. (1629) 797 Signs and prodiges of a fearefull conflict to come.

† **'prodige,** *v.* *Obs.* *rare.* In 6 prodege. [prob. ad. L. *prōdig-ĕre* to drive forth, squander, f. *prōd*, form of *prō*, PRO-¹ before a vowel + *ag-ĕre* (-*igĕre*) to drive. Cf. F. *prodiguer*, It. *prodigare*, on L. type **prōdigāre*.] *trans.* To squander.

1538 *St. Papers Hen. VIII*, III. 10 All religious incombentes here do not onelie leve theire demaynes,..in maner as waste.., but also dothe contynuallie prodege theire moveables unto them belonging.

† **'prodigence.** *Obs.* *rare.* [ad. L. *prōdigentia*, f. *prōdigent-em*, pr. pple. of *prōdig-ĕre*: see prec. and -ENCE.] Extravagance; waste; prodigality.

1634 BP. HALL *Contempl., N.T.* IV. iv, There is no proportion in this remuneration; this is not bountie, it is prodigence. **1656** BLOUNT *Glossogr.*, *Prodigence*, prodigality, wastefulness, riot, unthriftiness.

† **pro'digial,** *a.* *Obs.* *rare.* [ad. L. *prōdigiāl-is*, f. *prōdigium* PRODIGY: see -AL¹.] Relating to prodigies or portents.

1609 HOLLAND *Amm. Marcell.* 280 Events whereof, such as were skilfull in prodigial learning foretold and prophesied.

prodigiosin (prəʊdɪdʒɪ'əʊsɪn). *Biochem.* [a. G. *prodigiosin* (E. Kraft *Beiträge zur Biol. des B. Prodigiosus* (Dissertation, Würzburg, 1902) 37, following suggestion by K. B. Lehmann), f. mod.L. *prōdigiōs-us* marvellous, PRODIGIOUS (former specific epithet of the bacterium now called *Serratia marcescens*): see -IN¹.] A dark red crystalline pigment with antibiotic properties which is produced by certain bacteria of the genus *serratia* and has a molecule ($C_{20}H_{25}N_3O$) consisting essentially of three pyrrole rings linked to a central carbon atom.

1914 *Chem. Abstr.* VIII. 2894 Prodigiosin, the pigment of *B[acillus] prodigiosus*, is more sol. in alc. than in water. **1950** A. H. CORWIN in R. C. Elderfield *Heterocyclic Compounds* I. vi. 320 Tripyrrylmethanes are also of some interest because of the fact that they are leuco bases of tripyrrylmethane dyes, one of which, prodigiosin, has been isolated from a natural source. **1968** A. ALBERT *Heterocyclic Chem.* (ed. 2) v. 234 Pyrroles are well represented in Nature. Apart from the many porphins and related tetrapyrroles.., there is the bacterial pigment prodigiosin, and the antibiotic netropsin. **1971** *Jrnl. Antibiotics* XXIV. 636 Prodigiosin..is the bright red pigment of *Serratia marcescens* and was probably responsible for many medieval 'miracles' involving the appearance of blood stains on the Holy Host.

prodigiosity (prəʊdɪdʒɪ'ɒsɪtɪ). [f. L. *prōdigiōs-us* PRODIGIOUS + -ITY.] **1.** A person or thing of enormous size; a monster.

1895 G. MEREDITH *Amazing Marriage* II. xxxvi. 407 We're none of us 'fifty feet high, with phosphorous heads', as your friend..says of the prodigiosities.

2. A marvellous quality or performance.

1910 W. J. LOCKE *Simon* vi. 77 He had fallen in love with her when she had first taken Marseilles captive with the prodigiosities of her horse Sultan.

prodigious (prəʊ'dɪdʒəs), *a.* (*adv.*) [ad. L. *prōdigiōs-us* marvellous, prodigious: see PRODIGY and -OUS. Cf. F. *prodigieux* (R. Estienne 1549).]

† **1.** Of the nature of a prodigy; ominous, portentous. *Obs.*

1552 HULOET, Prodigious, *prodigiosus*. **1590** SHAKS. *Mids. N.* V. i. 419 Neuer mole, harelip, nor scarre, Nor marke prodigious,..Shall vpon their children be. **1601** HOLLAND *Pliny* I. 224 It was alwaies taken for a monstrous and prodigious signe. **1663** J. SPENCER *Prodigies* (1665) 204 They carry a fair aspect toward the Prodigious Appearance in Heaven. **1705** STANHOPE *Paraphr.* I. 64 Many dreadful Signs of his Approach, prodigious Darkness and frightful Sights in the Heavens.

2. Having the appearance of a prodigy; unnatural, abnormal.

1579 LYLY *Euphues* (Arb.) 119 As ther hath ben a prodigious Pasiphae, so there hath bene a godly Theocrita. **1667** MILTON *P.L.* II. 625 Nature breeds, Perverse, all monstrous, all prodigious things... Gorgons and Hydra's, and Chimera's dire. **1697** DE LA PRYME *Diary* (Surtees) 10 It rained wheat..several granes of which were sent as miraculous and prodigious presents to several gentlemen about us. **1728** MORGAN *Algiers* I. vi. 190 The Arch-Angel Gabriel assuming a prodigious Form, descended. **1819** SHELLEY *Cenci* III. i. 52 Prodigious mixtures, and confusions strange Of good and ill.

3. Causing wonder or amazement; marvellous, amazing; (in a bad sense) monstrous.

1568 GRAFTON *Chron.* II. 390 He by his euill counsaile and prodigious suggestions, craftilye circumuented the king. **1600** E. BLOUNT tr. *Conestaggio* 25 The gentlemen after a new prodigious manner attired themselues like vnto the Castillians. **1652** NEEDHAM tr. *Selden's Mare Cl.* Ep. Ded., And with a drawn Sword declare prodigious Principles of Enmitie against the Rights and Liberties of England. **1734** tr. *Rollin's Anc. Hist.* (1827) I. 82 It was thought prodigious..to run 1140 Stadia..in the space of two days. **1789** MRS. PIOZZI *Journ. France* II. 374 The spirit of composition, the manner of grouping and colouring, the general effect of the whole, [is] prodigious! **1871** TYLOR *Prim. Cult.* I. viii. 249 Why..are the gods and giants and monsters no longer seen to lead their prodigious lives on earth?

4. Of extraordinarily large size, extent, power, or amount; vast, enormous. (Often hyperbolical.)

1601 HOLLAND *Pliny* II. 368 A fruit..answerable to the mightie, huge, and prodigious tree that beareth it. *a* **1661** FULLER *Worthies*, *Suffolk* (1662) II. 71 He left five thousand Marks, a prodigious sum in that age, to charitable uses. **1667** MILTON *P.L.* VI. 247 Satan, who that day Prodigious power had shewn. **1695** WOODWARD *Nat. Hist. Earth* III. i. (1723) 172 The Andes, that prodigious Chain of Mountains in South America. **1722** HEARNE *Collect.* (O.H.S.) VII. 381 The other Bones are of a prodigious Size. **1734** tr. *Rollin's Anc. Hist.* (1827) III. VII. 414 The prodigious regard which was shown to the Greek physicians. **1846** DICKENS *Lett.* (1880) I. 167 They were in prodigious spirits and delight. **1868** LYELL *Princ. Geol.* (ed. 10) II. II. xxxiii. 214 The prodigious volume of atmospheric water which must be absorbed into the interior. **1878** HUXLEY *Physiogr.* 200 At great depths, the pressure must be prodigious.

b. As an exclamation: 'Monstrous', 'astounding'.

1730 FIELDING *Coffee Ho. Polit.* III. v, *Constant.*—'Prodigious!'..'What in the Devil's Name hath brought thee to the Constable's?' **1735** POPE *Donne Sat.* IV. 255 Let but the Ladies smile, and they are blest: Prodigious! how the things protest, protest. **1815** SCOTT *Guy M.* viii, The good Dominie bore all his disasters with gravity and serenity equally imperturbable. 'Pro-di-gi-ous!' was the only ejaculation they ever extorted from the much-enduring man.

B. quasi-*adv.* = PRODIGIOUSLY; amazingly; wonderfully; exceedingly; 'mightily'. Now *vulgar*.

1676 WOOD *Jrnl.* in *Acc. Sev. Late Voy.* I. (1694) 190 The Sea running prodigious high. **1717** MRS. CENTLIVRE *Bold Stroke for Wife* II. i, This snuff is extremely good,—and the box prodigious fine. **1768–74** TUCKER *Lt. Nat.* (1834) II. 596 Contradictions become elegance and propriety of language; for a thing may be..vastly little, monstrous pretty,..prodigious natural, or devilish godly. **1804** EUGENIA DE ACTON *Tale without Title* I. 51 A prodigious high hill fronting the western tower.

prodigiously (prəʊ'dɪdʒəslɪ), *adv.* [f. prec. + -LY².] In a prodigious manner.

† **1.** Portentously, ominously. *Obs.*

1595 SHAKS. *John* III. i. 91 Pray that their burthens may not fall this day, Lest that their hopes prodigiously be crost. **1605** DRAYTON *Man in Moon* 278 Twice every month, th'eclipses of our light Poor mortals should prodigiously affright. **1663** COWLEY *Verses Sev. Occas.*, *Ode on His Maj. Restaurat.* ii, Auspicious Star again arise,..Again all Heaven prodigiously adorn.

2. Wonderfully, astonishingly; in colloquial use (hyperbolically), Exceedingly, immensely.

1664 POWER *Exp. Philos.* I. 17 Such prodigiously little spindle-shank'd leggs. *a* **1679** GURNALL in Spurgeon *Treas. Dav.* Ps. ci. 6 Among those who were as prodigiously wicked as any there. **1710–11** SWIFT *Jrnl. to Stella* 22 Feb., It snowed all this morning prodigiously. **1778** MISS BURNEY *Evelina* (1791) II. xxxvii. 244 You are prodigiously kind! **1825** MCCULLOCH *Pol. Econ.* II. ii. 85 The wealth and comforts of all classes are, in consequence, prodigiously augmented. **1848** THACKERAY *Van. Fair* lvi, A prodigiously well-informed man.

prodigiousness (prəʊ'dɪdʒəsnɪs). [f. as prec. + -NESS.] The quality or condition of being prodigious; the quality of exciting amazement; enormousness; hugeness; monstrousness.

1631 BP. HALL *Rem. Wks.* (1660) 289 The corporal receiving of Christ hath in it a further prodigiousness and horrour. **1649** JER. TAYLOR *Gt. Exemp.* III. Sect. xv. ⁋13 The Disciples..wondering at the prodigiousnesse of the woman's Religion. **1723** MATHER *Vind. Bible* 309 The prodigiousness and irregularity of the punctuation of some words. **1832** L. HUNT *Sir R. Esher* (1850) 126 The.. neatness of their operations, contrasted with the prodigiousness of their fists.

† **pro'digity.** *Obs.* [ad. L. *prōdigitās* extravagance, prodigality, f. *prōdig-us*: see PRODIG *a.* and -ITY.]

1623 COCKERAM, *Prodigitie*, wilfulnesse. [Ridiculed in *Vindex Anglicus* (1644) 6.]

† **'prodigous,** *a.* *Obs.* *rare*⁻¹. [ad. OF. *prodigueux* (15th c. in Godef.), f. L. type **prōdigōs-us*, f. *prōdig-us*: see -OUS.] Prodigal, lavish.

c **1477** CAXTON *Jason* 5 Be not ydelle ne prodigous of thy tonge, take hede, beholde and see and saye litel.

prodigue: see PRODIG.

prodigy ('prɒdɪdʒɪ). [ad. L. *prōdigi-um*, f. *prōd-*, early form of *prō*, PRO-¹, retained before a vowel + (?) prim.L. **agiom* a thing said: cf. L. *āio* I affirm, also *adagium* ADAGE.]

1. Something extraordinary from which omens are drawn; an omen, a portent. Now *rare*.

1494 FABYAN *Chron.* VII. ccxxv. 252 Many wonderfull prodygyes & tokyns were shewed in Englonde, as yᵉ swellyng or rysyng of the water of Thamys. **1560** DAUS tr. *Sleidane's Comm.* 285 A prodigie [*printed* perdigie] of the Sunne. **1610** HOLLAND *Camden's Brit.* (1637) 448 This slaughter was foretold by many Prodigies. *a* **1658** CLEVELAND *Rustick Ramp.* Wks. (1687) 478 The Insolency of injust Men is a Prodigy of their Ruin. **1741** MIDDLETON *Cicero* II. xii. 553 The province of interpreting prodigies, and inspecting the entrails, belonged to the Haruspices. **1758** JOHNSON *Idler* No. 11 ⁋8 Omens and prodigies have lost their terrors. *a* **1816** JOYCE *Sci. Dial.*, *Astron.* xxiv, Were not comets formerly dreaded, as awful prodigies intended to alarm the world? **1882** FARRAR *Early Chr.* I. 73 The air was full of prodigies. There were terrible storms; the plague wrought fearful ravages.

2. An amazing or marvellous thing; *esp.* something out of the ordinary course of nature; something abnormal or monstrous.

1626 MIDDLETON *Women Beware Wom.* IV. ii. 61 He's a villain As monstrous as a prodigy and as dreadful. **1653** GATAKER *Vind. Annot. Jer.* 52 What is a prodigie, but some thing that comes to passe besides, beyond, above, or against the cours of nature? **1677** W. HARRIS *Lemery's Chym.* (1686) 154 Quicksilver is a prodigy among Metals. **1748** *Anson's Voy.* II. vi. 189 A climate, where rain is considered as a prodigy, and is not seen in many years. **1852** MISS YONGE *Cameos* (1877) I. xxviii. 236 Did not our innate generosity restrain us, I would confound him, and make him a prodigy to all the world!

†**b.** Of a person: in bad sense, A monster. *Obs.*

1594 *2nd Pt. Contention* (1843) 130 Or where is that valiant Crookbackt prodegie? **1656** *Petition to Chas. II* in Clarendon *Hist. Reb.* xv. §113 That prodigy of nature, that opprobrium of mankind,.. who now calls himself our Protector.

3. Anything that causes wonder, astonishment, or surprise; a wonder, a marvel.

[*a* **1638** MEDE *Wks.* (1672) 757, I cannot but think it a *prodigium* that any man should think otherwise.] **1660** SHARROCK *Vegetables* Ep. Ded., A multitude of monstrous untruths, and prodigies of lies. **1680** H. MORE *Apocal. Apoc.* 341 It is a most incredible prodigy.. that he should so rashly reject what he had so devotionally received. **1722** MACKY *Journ. Eng.* II. 30 It's a Prodigy, how so wise a People as the English can be gulled by such Pick-Pockets. **1874** H. R. REYNOLDS *John Bapt.* v. i. 303 The hand and breath of one Ecclesiastic is made to convey to another the power to perform invisible and undemonstrable prodigies.

b. A wonderful example *of* (some quality).

1646 EVELYN *Diary* Apr.–June, Julius Cæsar Scaliger, that prodigie of learning. **1689–90** TEMPLE *Ess. Heroic Virt.* Wks. 1731 I. 194 Alexander was a Prodigy of Valour. **1774** GOLDSM. *Nat. Hist.* (1776) V. 277 This bird, he asserts,.. is a prodigy of understanding. **1844** W. SMITH *Dict. Gr. & Rom. Biog.* (1867) III. 193/2 Pericles.. performed prodigies of valour. **1867** LADY HERBERT *Cradle L.* iii. 104 The knights.. by prodigies of valour, maintained their position. **1874** DEUTSCH *Rem.* 208 If Christianity is a prodigy of sanctity, Hellenism is a prodigy of beauty.

c. A person endowed with some quality which excites wonder; *esp.* a child of precocious genius.

1658 EVELEYN *Diary* 27 Jan., Died my deare son Richard, ..5 yeares and 3 days old onely, but at that tender age a prodigy for witt and understanding. **1794** SHERIDAN *Duenna* II. i, Aye, but her beauty will affect you—she is, tho' I say it, who am her father, a very prodigy. **1824** W. IRVING *T. Trav.* I. 204 The juvenile prodigy, the poetical youth, the great genius. **1831** D. E. WILLIAMS *Life Sir T. Lawrence* I. 51 This infant prodigy had excited so much attention that his likeness was taken, and engraved by Sherwin. *a* **1862** BUCKLE *Civiliz.* (1869) III. v. 453 Whose almost incredible achievements entitle them to be termed the prodigies of the human race.

4. *attrib.* (chiefly appositive).

1889 *Daily News* 29 Jan. 6/6 The 'prodigy' season.. began yesterday, when Master O—— H—— made his rentrée in London. **1891** *Ibid.* 8 Jan. 5/4 The deceased.. made his début at the age of thirteen as a prodigy pianist. **1900** *Ibid.* 19 June 4/7 He was a 'prodigy' violinist at the age of eight.

prodissoconch: see PRO-[2] 1.

†'**prodited,** *pa. pple. Obs. rare*$^{-0}$. [f. L. *prodit-us* betrayed + -ED[1].]

1623 COCKERAM, *Prodited*, betrayed.

prodition (prəʊ'dɪʃən). Now *rare*. [ME. *prodycyon*, a. OF. *prodicion* (14th c. in Godef.), ad. L. *prōditiōn-em*, n. of action f. *prōd-ĕre* to betray, f. *prō*, PRO-[1] + *dăre* to give.] Betrayal, treason, treachery.

1412–20 LYDG. *Chron. Troy* IV. xxxiv. (1555), Of doubilnesse and of false treason Undermyninge with prodycyon. **1500–20** DUNBAR *Poems* xlix. 4 Thocht he remissioun Haif for prodissioun. **1549** *Compl. Scot.* viii. 72 The proditione of ane realme succedis to the hurt of the public veil. **1597** BP. HALL *Guistard & Sismond* II. xv, A traytor guiltie of false prodicion. **1610** ROWLANDS *Martin Mark-all* 21 They are likely to decrease.. through the proditions and betrayings of the people which are contrary to them. **1669** *Addr. Hopeful Yng. Gentry Eng.* 55 The Lanthorn of Judas.. lighted the Traitor to the prodition of our Blessed Saviour. **1794** T. TAYLOR *Pausanias* II. 194 All those who were charged with prodition. **1887** W. DE G. BIRCH *Domesday Bk.* ix. 123 Waltheof does not appear to have entered upon this perilous path of prodition with any intention of acting upon it.

†**pro'ditious,** *a. Obs. rare*$^{-1}$. [f. L. type **proditiōs-us*, f. L. *proditiōn-em*: see prec. and -OUS.] Treasonable, traitorous.

1635 HEYWOOD *Hierarch.* IV. Comm. 260 By the proditious insinuations of the Deuill.

ˌ**prodito-'mania.** *rare*. [Arbitrary f. L. *prodit-*, ppl. stem of *prodĕre* to betray + -MANIA.]

1898 *Contemp. Rev.* Mar. 309 The concomitant proditomania. [*Footnote.* A morbid belief in the ubiquity and omnipotence of traitors.]

†'**proditor.** *Obs.* [ME. and AF. *proditour*, = OF. *proditeur*, ad. L. *prōditōrem*, agent-n. f. *prōd-ĕre* to betray.] A betrayer; a traitor.

1436 *Rolls of Parlt.* IV. 500/2 In resistence of youre Proditours Rebelles and Adversaries. **1546** *St. Papers Hen. VIII*, XI. 95 As manifest ennemy and proditour to the Cristen state. **1591** SHAKS. *1 Hen. VI*, I. iii. 31, I doe, thou most vsurping Proditor, And not Protector of the King or Realme. **1657** HAWKE *Killing is M.* 54 [He] was betrayed by his Servant,.. whom.. they.. as a Proditor precipitated from the Tarpeian stone. **1678** SIR G. MACKENZIE *Crim. Laws Scot.* I. xi. §16 (1699) 67 The Betrayer or Proditor.

prodi'torious, *a. Obs.* or *arch.* [f. prec. + -IOUS, as if from L. type **prōditōri-us*.] Traitorous, perfidious.

c **1475** *Harl. Contin. Higden* (Rolls) VIII. 501 By usurpacion of that proditorious commission. **1577–87** HOLINSHED *Chron.* (1807) II. 487 This reward reaped he for his proditorious attempts. **1641** PRYNNE *Antip.* Ep. 1 The Capitalnesse of such a Concealement in these proditorious times.

b. *fig.* Apt to betray or reveal what is hidden or in the mind.

a **1639** WOTTON *Surv. Educ.* in *Reliq.* (1651) 329, I will now hasten to those more solid and conclusive Characters, which.. are emergent from the Minde; and which oftentimes do start out of Children when themselves least think of it: For let me tell you, Nature is Proditorious. **1709** *Brit. Apollo* II. No. 74. 3/1 Blind to Events, however they might prove, Or Proditorious or Exitious. **1824** SOUTHEY *Colloquies on Soc.* (1887) 140 The eye, then, Sir Thomas, is proditorious, and I will not gainsay its honest testimony. **1828** —— in *Corr. w. C. Bowles* (1881) 144 A strong brow, A proditorious eye, for no dislike Can lurk dissembled there.

†**prodi'toriously,** *adv. Obs.* [f. prec. + -LY[2].] In a perfidious or treacherous manner.

c **1475** *Harl. Contin. Higden* (Rolls) VIII. 501 That thei did slee proditoriously Iames Brueis and Symon Burle. **1599** NASHE *Lenten Stuffe* 57 Thus nefariously and proditoriously prophaning & penetrating our holy fathers nostrils. **1619** *Time's Storehouse* x. vii. 935/1 They.. fell to killing one an other,.. proditoriously massacring their very best friends.

†'**proditory,** *a. Obs.* [f. PRODITOR (see -ORY[2]): as if repr. a L. **prōditōrius*.] Traitorous, treacherous.

1615 SIR E. HOBY *Curry-combe* v. 238 The suspition.. of all proditory or trecherous entendments. **1649** MILTON *Eikon.* ii. Wks. 1851 III. 353 That proditory Aid sent to Rochel and Religion abroad.

prodnose ('prɒdnəʊz), *sb.* [f. PROD *v.* + NOSE *sb.*] An inquisitive person, a nosey-parker; *spec.* a detective.

1934 DYLAN THOMAS *Let.* 11 May (1966) 126 Singing as loudly as Beachcomber in a world rid of Prodnose. **1965** *Spectator* 12 Feb. 213/2, I shall be greatly disappointed if some prodnose does not get a PhD thesis out of these pages in 2065. **1968** V. C. CLINTON-BADDELEY *My Foe Outstretch'd* vi. 103 He was sensitive about his reputation as an amateur prodnose. **1973** D. ROBINSON *Rotten with Honour* 97 I'll tell you why, you squalid prodnose. **1976** *Listener* 5 Aug. 135/2 Were the other lonely prodnoses with clipboards, operating in the dark, copying me? Or was I, daunting thought, the only pollster operating in the entire nation?

prodnose ('prɒdnəʊz), *v.* [f. prec.] *intr.* To pry; to be inquisitive. So '**prodnosing** *vbl. sb.*

1958 *Spectator* 3 Oct. 430/1 At this time [*sc.* the 1940s] the social virtue of prodnosing.. was still at a fairly harmless stage of development. **1969** *Daily Tel.* (Colour Suppl.) 31 Oct. 20/1 It is perhaps high time that the industrial psychologists who are encouraged to prodnose into most things got to work on the Press.

‖**prodroma** ('prɒdrəʊmə), *sb. Path.* Usu. in *pl.* **prodromata** (prəʊ'drɒmətə). [mod.L., an erroneous formation, app. in imitation of such etymological forms as *carci'noma*, *-'nomata*, *sar'coma*, *-'comata*, etc.; possibly originating in a L. *prodroma*, sing. for Gr. προδρομή a running forward, or in mistaking the neuter pl. πρόδρομα (see next) for a sing.] = PRODROME 3, PRODROMUS 3.

1859 SEMPLE *Diphtheria* 317 In young children, I have always met with the following prodromata. **1870** MAUDSLEY *Body & Mind* 89 The uniformity of the prodromata and of the symptoms of the attack. **1882** *Med. Temp. Jrnl.* No. 52. 170 The inebriety.. coming from physical causes was marked by a long prodroma before the trance state appeared.

‖'**prodroma,** *sb. pl.* [mod.L., = Gr. πρόδρομα, neut. pl. of πρόδρομος, -ον adj.: see PRODROMUS.] Premonitory symptoms.

1880 J. W. LEGG *Bile* 546 Yellow fever usually begins very suddenly, with slight prodroma. **1899** *Allbutt's Syst. Med.* VII. 466 He insisted on its prodroma [i.e. those of tuberculous meningitis].

prodromal (prəʊ'drəʊməl, 'prɒd-), *a.* [f. PRODROM-US + -AL[1].]

1. Of or pertaining to a prodromus; forerunning; introductory, preliminary.

1716 M. DAVIES *Athen. Brit.* II. 366 Their Works and Writings were the Prodromal Copies and Consonant Originals to the Nicen Creed. *c* **1720** *Ibid.* VI. *Diss. Physick* 7 That Learned prodromal Protestant of the 12th Christian Century, Rupertus Tuitiensis.

2. *Path.* Precursory or premonitory (of disease).

1861 BUMSTEAD *Ven. Dis.* (1879) 652 Vertigo is a prominent prodromal symptom. **1885–8** FAGGE & PYE-SMITH *Princ. Med.* (ed. 2) I. 170 If.. the patient has been unwell for a few days previously, the disease is said to have had a prodromal stage. **1899** *Allbutt's Syst. Med.* VIII. 463 The more extensive prodromal erythema seen in small-pox.

prodro'matic, *a.* [f. the erroneous PRODROMA, pl. *-omata*: see -IC.] = PRODROMAL. So **prodro'matically** *adv.*, as a preliminary or introductory step.

1871 HAMMOND *Dis. Nerv. Syst.* 34 Impossible to predict with accuracy, from the symptoms of this *prodromatic stage. **1716** M. DAVIES *Athen. Brit.* II. 319 Both together [High and Low Church] should *Prodromatically [*misprinted* -dram-] advance with Carismatical-Emulation. *Ibid.* 429 So happily lucky as to lead Prognostically and Prodromatically to the Metropolitan Crosier.

prodrome ('prɒdrəm), *sb.* (*a.*) Better **prodrom**: cf. *anadrom*, *atom*. [a. F. *prodrome* (*a* 1584 in Godef. *Compl.*), ad. mod.L. PRODROMUS.]

†**1.** Something that is a forerunner; a precursor.

1643 *Sober Sadness* 45 These.. may.. prove the Prodromes.. to the ruine of our Monarchy. **1651** H. MORE *Second Lash* xi. in *Enthus. Tri.*, etc. (1656) 280 Sober Morality.. is like morning light reflected from the higher Clouds, and a certain Prodrome of the Sunne of Righteousnesse it self.

2. An introductory or preliminary treatise or book; a prodromus.

1866 COUES (*title*) Prodrome of a Work on the Ornithology of Arizona Territory. **18..** *Proc. Boston Soc. Nat. Hist.* 243 (Cassell *Suppl.*) Mr. Scudder discussed and reviewed Brongniart's recent prodrome of palæozoic insects. **1903** *Academy* 17 Jan. 71/1 What is 'Donovan' to 'We Two'? Prelude, prodrome, proem or introduction might be used.

3. *Path.* A prodromal or premonitory symptom.

1822–34 *Good's Study Med.* (ed. 4) I. 648 The symptoms of invasion or accession, the prodromes of M. Deveze. **1864** THOMAS *Med. Dict.*, Vertigo is sometimes said to be a prodrome or precursor of apoplexy.

B. *adj.* = PRODROMOUS.

1682 H. MORE *Annot. Glanvill's Lux O.* xiii. 119 The first Predelineations and prodrome Irradiations into the matter [*transl.* προδρόμους ἐλλάμψεις ὕλην].

prodromic (prəʊ'drɒmɪk), *a.* [f. as next + -IC: so F. *prodromique*.] = PRODROMAL.

1866 *Pall Mall G.* 3 Aug. 10 The medical treatment of cholera is successful chiefly as it is directed to the prodromic symptoms. **1891** H. F. STEWART *Boethius* p. vii, An essay of this kind can never be more than prodromic and tentative. **1899** *Allbutt's Syst. Med.* VIII. 492.

†'**prodromist.** *Obs.* [f. as next + -IST.] A precursor, forerunner.

1716 M. DAVIES *Athen. Brit.* II. 228 There were several other Prodromists or Precursors of Arianism in that third Century. *Ibid.* 374 The Popish Clergy made those honest Prodromists of the Reformation to pass for Hereticks.

'**prodromous,** *a. rare.* [f. Gr. πρόδρομ-ος (see next) + -OUS.] Introductory, prodromal.

1652 *Lex Exlex* Title-p., A Prodromous Discourse to a subsequent Tract. **1846** in WORCESTER.

‖**prodromus** ('prɒdrəʊməs). Pl. '**prodromi**. [mod.L., a. Gr. πρόδρομος adj., running before, as sb. a precursor, f. πρό, PRO-[2] + δραμεῖν to run, δρόμος running, race, course.]

1. A forerunner, a precursor, a premonitory event.

1645 in Rushw. *Hist. Coll.* IV. I. 135 Beeston Castle.. a while before the taking of Chester.. as a *Prodromus* of its neighbouring Cities fate was yielded to the Parliament. **1660** T. M. *Cl. Walker's Hist. Independ.* IV. 95 The *Prodromi* of whose miserable end might be these and the like. **1698** FRYER *Acc. E. India & P.* 76 The *Prodromi* of the ensuing Rains. **1708** T. WARD *Eng. Ref.* (1716) 58 As *Prodromus* to its Intrusion.

2. A book or treatise which is introductory or preliminary to some larger work.

1672 JACOMB *Serm. Rom. viii.* Pref. §7 This Volume.. I publish as a *prodromus* to what is yet to come. **1756** *Gentl. Mag.* XXVI. 415 The next year Linnæus published his *Fundamenta Botanica*, which may be considered as the *prodromus* to many of his succeeding works. **1864** HALDEMAN *Bibliogr. Chess Knt.'s Tour* Pref., This Prodromus is offered with the hope that it will be expanded and completed by some one who has more bibliographic facilities.

3. *Path.* A premonitory symptom of disease; = PRODROME 3.

1693 tr. *Blancard's Phys. Dict.* (ed. 2), *Prodromus*, a Disease that comes before a greater, as the straitness of the Breast predicts a Consumption. **1822–34** *Good's Study Med.* (ed. 4) II. 289 The fit [of gout] is often preceded by certain prodromi.

†'**prodromy.** *Obs.* [? ad. Gr. προδρομία a sudden attack, f. πρόδρομ-ος adj.: see prec.] = prec. 1.

1647 WARD *Simple Cobler* (1843) 30 They are.. the certain prodromies of assured judgement.

produce ('prɒdjuːs), *sb.* [f. PRODUCE *v.* (Formerly stressed *pro'duce*, like the vb.)]

1. The fact of producing; production. *rare.*

1769 E. HARGROVE *Hist. Knaresb.* VI. (1798) 246 This place is remarkable for the produce of a delicious apple. **1849** COBDEN *Speeches* 64 They say they cannot compete with the foreigners in the produce of grain.

2. The amount produced, yielded, or derived; the proceeds; the return, yield. Now chiefly in the assay of ore.

1707 MORTIMER *Husb.* 78 They sow it with Barly, allowing 3 Bushels of Seed to an Acre: Its common produce is 30 Bushel. **1716** ADDISON *Freeholder* No. 20 ¶4 This Tax has already been so often tried, that we know the exact Produce of it. **1818** CRUISE *Digest* (ed. 2) VI. 263 Not only the interest but the produce of the real and personal estate was to be applied by such trustees. **1831** *Examiner* 141/1 They had sold their shoes,.. and were getting lushy with the produce. **1871** J. S. PHILLIPS *Explorer's Comp.* 299 A weight of 400 grains [in assaying ores].. is divided into hundredths and again into eighths of one unit of such percentages to represent the market 'produce'. **1881** RAYMOND *Mining Gloss.*, *Produce*,.. the amount of fine copper in one hundred parts of ore.

3. a. The thing (or things collectively) produced, either as a natural growth or as a result of action or effort; product, fruit. Also *fig.*

1699 DRYDEN *Epist. to J. Driden* 118 You hoard not health for your own private use, But on the publick spend the rich produce. 1719 DE FOE *Crusoe* I. 33 Two Pieces of dry Flesh and some Corn, such as is the Produce of their Country. 1771 *Junius Lett.* liv. (1820) 287 They are the produce of his invention.

b. More generally: Result, effect, consequence.

1730 CHUBB *Collection of Tracts* 377 If the actions of men are not the produce of a free choice or election. 1754 EDWARDS *Freed. Will* II. x. (1762) 95 If it were..possible..that every free Act of Choice were the Produce or Effect of a free Act of Choice; yet even then..no one Act of Choice would be free, but every one necessary. 1818 COBBETT *Pol. Reg.* XXXIII. 498 It was the produce of an honest heart, a clear conscience, and a manly mind. 1873 BROWNING *Red Cott. Nt.-cap* IV. 198 Such the days of faith, And such their produce to encourage mine!

c. Offspring, progeny. *rare.*

1845 YOUATT *Dog* iv. (1858) 104 The Artois dog..is a produce of the shock-dog and the pug. 1862 CARLYLE *Fredk. Gt.* XIII. vii. (1872) V. 76 Comte de Saxe..was..the produce of the fair Aurora von Königsmark.

4. Agricultural and natural products collectively, as distinguished from manufactured goods. Also ***raw produce***.

1745 *De Foe's Eng. Tradesman* Introd. (1841) I. 3 The..British product,..whether we mean its produce as the growth of the country, or its manufactures as the labour of her people. 1832 HT. MARTINEAU *Demerara* ii. 15 The cry for higher bounties on West India produce. 1861 M. PATTISON *Ess.* (1889) I. 47 The export trade..consisted chiefly in raw produce, wool and hides, corn, beer, and cheese. 1865 H. PHILLIPS *Amer. Paper Curr.* II. 84 The payments..tempted the farmers to sell to them their produce.

5. *techn.* Materials produced from breaking up ordnance or other military or naval stores: chiefly in phrase ***brought to produce***, i.e. broken up, and the material assorted into various kinds or classes, which may be separately disposed of.

1904 COL. C. F. HADDEN *Let. to Editor*, A gun carriage brought to produce is broken up, and steel, brass, etc., separated, and disposed of as so much metal.

6. *attrib.* and *Comb.* (all from sense 4), as ***produce broker, business, market, merchant, trade***.

1851 C. CIST *Sk. Cincinnati in 1851* 143 Forwarding and Commission merchants and Produce brokers. 1858 SIMMONDS *Dict. Trade, Produce Market*, Fenchurch-street, Mincing-lane, Tower-street, and their immediate localities, where the offices of the principal produce-brokers are situate. 1872 *Rep. Vermont Board Agric.* I. 161 B. F. Rugg, who was then engaged in the produce trade,..undertook to carry out a plan for controlling the Boston butter market. 1887 *Pall Mall G.* 14 Oct. 6/2 Instead of the £500 being paid money down, it should be £500 of tithe money, or rather £500 of produce money, so that it should represent very much the same quantity of stuff. 1892 *Ibid.* 8 Aug. 7/1 The total produce trade for 1891 is estimated at 102 millions sterling..the principal feature being the large increase in the receipts and shipments of wheat. 1899 *Scribner's Mag.* XXV. 55/2 A Missourian, in the produce business.

produce (prəʊˈdjuːs), *v.* [ad. L. *prōdūc-ĕre* to lead or bring forth, extend, promote, produce, f. *prō*, PRO-[1] + *dūc-ĕre* to lead.]

1. a. *trans.* To bring forward, bring forth or out; to bring into view, to present to view or notice; to offer for inspection or consideration, exhibit. Often used of bringing forward witnesses, as well as evidence, or vouchers, in a court of law.

1499 *Exch. Rolls Scotl.* XI. 435 To comper..to produce his takkis and rychtes of the kingis landis of Murray gif he ony has. 1530 PALSGR. 667/1, I produce wytnesses, *je produys tesmoyngs*. 1582 N. LICHEFIELD tr. *Castanheda's Conq. E. Ind.* I. vi. 16 They also produced to sight and viewe of him certaine harnesses or armours, whereat he also meruailed much. 1601 SHAKS. *Jul. C.* III. i. 228, I..am moreouer sutor, that I may Produce his body to the Market-place. 1611 —— *Cymb.* v. v. 363 In a most curious Mantle, wrought by th' hand Of his Queene Mother, which for more probation I can with ease produce. 1611 BIBLE *Isa.* xli. 21 Produce [*marg.* cause to come neere] your cause, saith the Lord, bring foorth your strong reasons. 1624 BP. MOUNTAGU *Immed. Addr.* 130 To make this good, Saint Augustine is produced. 1662 STILLINGFL. *Orig. Sacr.* I. v. §5 Joseph Scaliger who first..produced them into the light out of Georgius Syncellus. 1697 DRYDEN *Virg. Georg.* I. 69 Produce the Plough, and yoke the sturdy Steer. 1776 *Trial of Nundocomar* 16/1 The books must be produced, as we cannot receive parole evidence of their contents. 1828 SCOTT *F.M. Perth* viii, So saying, he produced, from the hawking pouch already mentioned, the stiffened hand. 1877 *Act 40 & 41 Vict.* c. 60 §5 Any person..may, on producing..a copy of his authorisation..enter by day such canal boat.

b. To introduce; now *spec.*, to bring (a performer or performance) before the public; to administer and supervise the production of (a film or broadcast programme). *refl.*, to come forward, come 'out'. Also *absol.*

1585 T. WASHINGTON tr. *Nicholay's Voy.* IV. xxxv. 158 Orpheus was he which produced and celebrated the first sacrifices vnto Liber Pater. 1686 tr. *Chardin's Trav. Persia* 214 They had an extraordinary desire to produce me. 1709 STEELE *Tatler* No. 84 ¶4 My Design of producing obscure Merit into publick View. 1709 SWIFT *Adv. Relig.* ¶6 The pert..demeanour of several young stagers in divinity upon their first producing themselves into the world. 1734 tr. *Rollin's Anc. Hist.* V. 99 Plato..sought every occasion of producing him to the public. 1750 JOHNSON *Rambler* No. 27 ¶8 Hilarius received me with an appearance of great satisfaction, produced me to all his friends. 1766 SMOLLETT *Trav.* vi, I wish they had antigallican spirit enough to produce themselves in their own genuine English dress. 1808 HAN. MORE *Cœlebs* I. 71 They [girls] were always ready to sing and play, but did not take the pains to produce themselves in conversation. 1836 DICKENS *Let.* 25 Aug. (1965) I. 171 A farce in two acts..to be produced at the Saint James's Theatre on the first of October. 1864 *Standard* 31 Dec. 6/3 There is a stringent competition going forward amidst musical managers as to who shall produce her [a singer]. 1897 G. B. SHAW in *Sat. Rev.* 13 Feb. 170/1 Like all plays under Mr. Barrett's management, 'The Daughter of Babylon' is excellently produced. 1912 F. A. TALBOT *Moving Pictures* 329 The Hepworth Manufacturing Company..recently has produced several powerful and excellent film-plays. 1923 *Radio Times* 28 Sept. 23/3 The whole production produced and directed by Mr. R. E. Jeffrey, who has adapted this well-known play for wireless transmission. 1935 E. F. DYER *Producing School Plays* ii. 24 If he [*sc.* the producer] finds no inner meaning there is either something wrong with him or with the play which he has chosen to present; either he is not a suitable person to produce the play, or the play is unworthy of production. 1937 'M. INNES' *Hamlet, Revenge!* I. i. 17 I'm producing. And I've built a sort of Elizabethan stage. 1940 C. P. PURDOM *Producing Plays* i. 2 Any one who knew anything of the theatre could recognize a play produced by Mr. Granville-Barker. 1966 *Listener* 6 Oct. 515/2, I think it was over-ambitious of Mr Wheeler to produce and write the script, yet one cannot belittle his success in presenting very clearly the broad scope of his subject. 1971 N. K. PARROTT in J. R. BROWN *Drama & Theatre* iv. 87 *Othello* got produced, mainly because somebody wanted to do it and convinced enough other people to join him in presenting it.

†**c.** To bring (to a specified condition); to advance, promote. *Obs.*

*a*1618 SYLVESTER *Panaretus* 1351 Till with advantage gracious Heav'ns produce Their Wished Counsails into act and use. 1626 B. JONSON *Staple of N.* III. ii, The Art..Is by the Brotherhood of the Rosie Crosse, Produc'd vnto perfection. 1741 MIDDLETON *Cicero* II. viii. 233 Trebonius..was wholly a new man and the creature of Caesar's power, who produced him through all the honors of the State, to his late consulship of three months.

2. a. *Geom.* To extend (a line) in length; to continue; hence *gen.* to lengthen (anything) out; to extend, enlarge, or develop longitudinally.

1570 BILLINGSLEY *Euclid* I. 5b, To produce a right line finite, straight forth continually. 1669 STURMY *Mariner's Mag.* I. ii. 27 Parallel Lines..produced infinitely on both sides, do never..concur. 1676 GREW *Anat. Flowers* App. §11 The Bottom, is either Reduced towards the Top, as in Ground-Ivy; or Produced upon the Stalk, as in Poplar, Bay, &c. 1827 HUTTON *Course Math.* I. 290 When one side of a triangle is produced, the outward angle is greater than either of the two inward opposite angles. 1869 TYNDALL *Notes Lect. Light* 16 The reflected rays are here divergent; but on being produced backwards, they intersect at the principal focus behind the mirror. 1877 DARWIN *Fertil. Orchids* vi. (ed. 2) 169 An insect with the extremity of its abdomen produced into a sharp point alights on the flower. 1881 MIVART in *Nature* XXIV. 337/1 Each eyebrow is produced into a flexible horn-like prominence.

†**b.** To extend, stretch out. *Obs. rare*$^{-1}$.

1599 B. JONSON *Cynthia's Rev.* v. ii, *Hed.* O, his leg was too much produced. *Ana.* And his hat was carried scurvily.

†**c.** To extend in duration; to prolong, lengthen, spin out. *Obs.*

1603 B. JONSON *Sejanus* III. iii, Perhaps our stay will be Beyond our will produced. 1609 C. BUTLER *Fem. Mon.* Printer to Rdr., The E silent.., serveth onely to produce the vowel precedent. 1643 SIR T. BROWNE *Relig. Med.* I. §43 There goes a great deal of providence to produce a mans life unto threescore.

3. To bring forth, bring into being or existence. **a.** *generally.* To bring (a thing) into existence from its raw materials or elements, or as the result of a process; to give rise to, bring about, effect, cause, make (an action, condition, etc.).

1513 [implied in PRODUCER 1]. 1587 GOLDING *De Mornay* vi. (1592) 81 The One is the Producer or yeelder foorth, the Vnder-standing is the thing produced or yeelded foorth. 1621 FITZ-GEFFRAY *Elisha's Lament.* (1622) 14 Double affection..produceth doubled lamentation. 1651 HOBBES *Leviath.* II. xxvii. 155 There are few Crimes that may not be produced by Anger. 1697 DRYDEN *Virg. Georg.* IV. 57 Nor Birdlime, or Idean Pitch, produce A more tenacious Mass of clammy Juice. 1710 BERKELEY *Princ. Hum. Knowl.* §94 That Eternal Invisible Mind which produces and sustains all things. 1748 HUME *Ess.* xviii. (ed. 3) 193 Art may make a Suit of Clothes. But Nature must produce a Man. 1792 MARY WOLLSTONECR. *Rights Wom.* iv. 129 To use an apt French turn of expression, she is going to produce a sensation. 1868 LOCKYER *Elem. Astron.* II. ix. (1879) 52 Steam is produced by heating water by coal. 1879 LUBBOCK *Sci. Lect.* iii. 87 Certain..insects produce a noise by rubbing one of their abdominal rings against another. 1891 *Law Rep., Weekly Notes* 136/2 The coal was cut in large blocks..the small coal was produced by the friction of the blocks.

b. Of an animal or plant: To generate, bring forth, give birth to, bear, yield (offspring, seed, fruit, etc.). Also *absol.*

1526 *Pilgr. Perf.* (W. de W. 1531) 215b, He may not be sayd to be the holy goost, whiche is produced of yͤ father & the sone. 1650 BULWER *Anthropomet.* 125 Eunuchs..are smooth, and produce not a Beard. 1667 MILTON *P.L.* XI. 687 Who..by imprudence mixt, Produce prodigious Births of bodie or mind. 1715 DE FOE *Fam. Instruct.* I. i. (1841) I. 6 Every creature is produced by its own kind. 1774 GOLDSM. *Nat. Hist.* (1776) III. 54 The goat produces but two at a time. 1857 HENFREY *Elem. Bot.* §22 Flowers..capable of producing seeds. *Ibid.* §28 The anthers..produce pollen, and the carpels..produce ovules. *Ibid.* §452 The Vine..where the temperature is..too high..runs away to leaf and does not produce fruit. 1902 D. MCDONALD *Garden Comp.* (Ser. I) 38 It is these early blooms that..produce the finest pods. 1976 'A. GARVE' *Home to Roost* ii. 26 She had naturally expected to start a family... There was no apparent physical reason why we shouldn't produce.

c. Of a country, region, river, mine, process, etc.: To give forth, yield, furnish, supply; in quot. 1664 to grow, raise (plants); in quot. 1827, to yield or bring in as profit. Also *absol.*

1585 T. WASHINGTON tr. *Nicholay's Voy.* II. x. 44b, A great countrey of vines producing great aboundance of good wines. 1664 EVELYN *Sylva* (1776) 11 To Produce them immediately of the seed is the better way. 1673 *Essex Papers* (Camden) I. 128 Considering yͤ severall Countrys wᶜʰ produce wooll. 1732 BERKELEY *Alciphr.* II. §1 England hath of late produced great philosophers. 1827 ROBERTS *Voy. Centr. Amer.* 244 The other goods produced me about one hundred dollars. 1836 YARRELL *Brit. Fishes* (1859) I. 379 Near London, the Thames..produces Barbel in great quantities. 1879 TOURGEE *Fool's Err.* xlvi. 348 The earth produces in an abundance unknown to other regions.

d. To compose or bring out by mental or physical labour (a work of literature or art); to work up from raw material, fabricate, make, manufacture (material objects); in *Pol. Econ.* often blending with sense c.

1638 JUNIUS *Paint. Ancients* A ij, I had produced..my observations of the manner of painting in use among the ancients. *a*1719 ADDISON *To Sir G. Kneller* 78 This wonder of the sculptor's hand Produced, his art was at a stand. *a*1771 GRAY *Hoel* 17 Nectar that the bees produce. 1793 SMEATON *Edystone L.* §122 When the solid is produced from the drawing by the artist's own hand. 1856 FROUDE *Hist. Eng.* (1858) II. vi. 32 Such volumes..were here multiplied as fast as the press could produce them. 1874 GREEN *Short Hist.* vi. §4. 297 Not a single book of any real value,..was produced north of the Alps during the fifteenth century. 1878 JEVONS *Prim. Pol. Econ.* ii. §10. 18 However much we manage to produce, there are still many other things which we want to acquire. 1901 *Westm. Gaz.* 6 Sept. 9/1 The true principle is to produce for one's self what one can best produce, and with the product buy elsewhere that which others can best produce.

e. *absol.* To produce the goods, money, results. *slang.*

1970 G. F. NEWMAN *Sir, You Bastard* viii. 226 Ring me. And you'd better produce. 1977 *New Yorker* 24 Oct. 64/3 One queen's 'husband' asked her to 'produce' for four of his friends and stabbed her when she declined.

Hence **proˈduced** *ppl. a.*; whence **proˈducedness**, the condition of being produced.

1644 BULWER *Chiron.* 71 The same gesture, but a little more produced and certaine. 1827 [see PRODUCING *ppl. a.*]. 1840 LARDNER *Geom.* xxii. 311 Producing the line *OB* above the directrix till the produced part is equal to the parameter. 1862 F. HALL *Hindu Philos. Syst.* 65 Not from the mere fact of its being uttered by a person, can one say there is producedness of a thing by that person.

produceable: see PRODUCIBLE.

†**proˈducement.** *Obs.* [f. PRODUCE *v.* + -MENT.] The fact of producing, or the condition of being produced; production.

1614 W. B. *Philosopher's Banquet* (ed. 2) 12 The producement of so excellent a creature. 1642 MILTON *Apol. Smect.* Wks. 1851 III. 301 The producement of such glorious effects and consequences in the Church. 1645 —— *Tetrach.* ibid. IV. 157, I am taxt of novelties and strange producements.

producent (prəʊˈdjuːsənt), *a.* and *sb.* [ad. L. *prōdūcens, -entem*, pr. pple. of *prōdūcĕre* to PRODUCE.]

A. *adj.* That produces; in *Eccl. Law*, that brings forward a witness or document. Now *rare*.

1604 *Supplic. Masse Priests* Answ. to §12 Witnesses..that either speake nothing..or els contrary to the party producents intention. 1651 J. GOODWIN *Redempt. Redeemed* IV. §9 God him-self the..producent cause of all men. 1825 COLERIDGE *Aids Refl.* (1861) 138, *b*, *c* being the two products, and *A*, *X*, the producent causes.

B. *sb.* One who or that which produces; a producer; the party producing a witness or document under the old system of the Ecclesiastical Courts. Now *rare*.

1622 MALYNES *Anc. Law-Merch.* 470 That they bee sworne, and the producent payeth his charges. *a*1677 HALE *Prim. Orig. Man.* I. v. 116 Such a production cannot by any possibility be as ancient as the producents. 1726 AYLIFFE *Parergon* 307 If an Instrument be produc'd with a Protestation in respect of these Parts of it which make in Favour of the Producent. *a*1834 COLERIDGE in *Lit. Rem.* (1839) IV. 52 A product divisible from the producent as a snake from its skin. 1835 in Curteis *Rep. Eccl. Cas.* (1840) I. 403 The producent and the deceased did not stand in any other relation to each other, than solicitor and client.

producer (prəʊˈdjuːsə(r)). [f. PRODUCE *v.* + -ER[1].]

1. a. One who or that which produces; in various senses: see the verb.

1513 DOUGLAS *Æneis* XII. xiii. 92 Jupiter the..producer of men and euery thing [*orig.* hominum rerumque repertor]. 1587 [see PRODUCE *v.* 3]. 1676 TOWERSON *Decalogue* 359 Hatred is not murther..yet it is..at least the producer of it. 1752 J. GILL *Trinity* vi. 113 The first parent, bringer forth, or producer of every creature. 1844 *Jrnl. R. Agric. Soc.* V. I. 60 Pearl [wheat].—Very white, compact ear, and great producer. 1881 M. ARNOLD in *Macm. Mag.* Mar. 368/2 The producer of such poems could not but publish them. 1903 *Daily Chron.* 15 Apr. 5/2 Mexico, the greatest silver producer in the world.

b. The person who produces a dramatic performance, film, or broadcast programme.

1891 SCOTT & HOWARD *Life E. L. Blanchard* I. 213 Though he was a clever actor, he rose to greater fame as what we should now call a stage-manager or producer of plays. **1896** G. B. SHAW in *Labour Leader* 19 Dec. 443/4 Our extraordinary clever producer of Ibsen would get enormously rich. **1909** *Westm. Gaz.* 30 Apr. 5/2 Mr. Louis Calvert's appointment as stage manager, or, according to the more modern term, 'producer' of the so-called Millionaires' Theatre in New York, may be reckoned a high compliment. **1911** D. S. HULFISH *Cycl. Motion-Picture Work* II. 95 The producer is in charge of the studio. **1912** F. A. TALBOT *Moving Pictures* 329 There is every indication that the British producers are making up headway. **1915** *Times* 26 Nov. 11/4 The English film-producers of all branches are rapidly proving that..the hustle of the American 'producer', and the mobile features..of the foreign actor are not essential. **1925** *Scribner's Mag.* Sept. 283/2 The great Delando, most resourceful of the Broadway producers, put down the last act of 'The Republic'. **1933** *Radio Times* 14 Apr. 72/2 It will be interesting to see how the producers handle a 'spectacular' show of this kind. **1938**, **1944** [see DIRECTOR 1 g]. **1949** A. HUXLEY *Ape & Essence* 24 Titles, credits and finally..the name of the *producer*. **1961** G. MILLERSON *Technique Television Production* 190 The producer may be the business-head of the programme, responsible for organization, finance, policy, etc., while his director is concerned with interpretation, staging and directing its production. **1973** *Radio Times* 26 July 55/1 The producer [in TV] has overall charge of the production..and it is he who marshals the resources of the BBC to make sure the production is appropriate to the play and to the series of which the play is part. **1976** M. MAGUIRE *Scratchproof* iv. 51 Sam Goldwyn used to say that a producer shouldn't get ulcers, he should give them.

c. ***producer-in-chief.***

1939 M. SPRING RICE *Working-Class Wives* i. 13 Men.. are the recognised producers-in-chief. **1976** *S. Wales Echo* 23 Nov. 6/6 He is also producer-in-chief of a series of plays for Granada which will be shown in Britain.

2. *Pol. Econ.* One who produces (grows, digs, or manufactures) an article of consumption. Opposed to *consumer*.

1784 ADAM SMITH *Wealth of Nations* (ed. 3) II. IV. viii. 515 The interest of the consumer is almost constantly sacrificed to that of the producer. **1790** BURKE *Fr. Rev.* Wks. V. 290 In every prosperous community something more is produced than goes to the immediate support of the producer. **1832** HT. MARTINEAU *Hill & Valley* iii. 40 How many classes of producers do you reckon? **1864** H. SPENCER *Princ. Biol.* III. v. I. 373 He ceases to be a producer, and becomes simply a channel through which the produce of others is conveyed to the public. **1878** HUXLEY *Physiogr.* 227 The pigeon is a consumer, not a producer. **1879** ROGERS in *Cassell's Techn. Educ.* IV. 67/2 The means for bringing producer and consumer together.

3. Short for *gas producer*, a furnace for producing fuel gas by passing a current of air and usually steam through hot solid fuel so that incomplete combustion occurs; ***producer gas***, gas so produced, used as a low-grade but inexpensive fuel and consisting chiefly of nitrogen and carbon monoxide with smaller amounts of hydrogen and carbon dioxide.

1881 RAYMOND *Mining Gloss.*, *Producer*, see *Gas-producer*. **1890** W. J. GORDON *Foundry* 13 Here are the half-dozen producers, to give the gas for the two Siemens's furnaces. **1895** *Daily News* 22 Oct. 9/1 The motive power..supplied by a large Crossley gas engine worked by producer gas and three 20 horse power dynamos. **1902** *Encycl. Brit.* XXVIII. 595/1 In all the attempts to make water gas up to that date the incandescence of the fuel had been obtained by 'blowing' so deep a bed of fuel that carbon monoxide and the residual nitrogen of the air formed the chief products, this mixture being known as 'producer' gas. **1939** *Times* 28 Mar. 11/2 Fuel costs favoured the producer gas engine compared with the oil or petrol engine. **1941** *Thorpe's Dict. Appl. Chem.* (ed. 4) V. 368/1 In the Thwaite cupola producer.., where a dry-air blast..is employed, it is usual to add a certain proportion of limestone to the fuel charge in order to form a liquid slag with the ashes. **1967** M. CHANDLER *Ceramics in Mod. World* ii. 81 If producer gas or heavy oils are used..it is necessary to have a muffle throughout the length of a kiln.

4. *Ecol.* Any organism or part of an organism that produces the organic compounds it needs from simple substances such as water, carbon dioxide, or nitrogen. Freq. *attrib.*

1941 *Q. Rev. Biol.* XVI. 395/1 In the marine plankton the plant type of life is sometimes called 'producer' and the animal type 'consumer' plankton. *Ibid.* 397/1 Certain important groups of producer plankton.. were absent from the neighbourhood of the poles. *Ibid.*, The hotter regions.. favor the more catabolic types of metabolism among the producers by a general increase of vital velocities. **1942** *Ecology* XXIII. 400/2 In the language of community economics introduced by Thienemann ('26), autotrophic plants are producer organisms, employing the energy obtained by photosynthesis to synthesize complex organic substances from simple inorganic substances. **1953** E. P. ODUM *Fund. Ecol.* ix. 223 Considering the fresh-water environment as a whole, the algae are the most important producers. **1976** T. C. EMMEL *Population Biol.* i. 21 The first trophic level in ecosystems is represented by green plants and comprises the producers (or autotrophs). **1978** *Sci. Amer.* Mar. 102/2 These rodents derive energy directly from the primary producers (leaves, shoots, seeds and buds), from other consumers (invertebrates in the forest litter and occasionally birds' eggs and young) and from decomposers (fungi).

5. *attrib.* and *Comb.*, as ***producer-exhibitor***, ***-novelist***, ***-retailer***; **producer goods** (see quot. 1956); **producer-oriented** *a.*, interested in or favouring the producer of goods rather than the consumer.

1920 *Stage Year Bk.* 52 It became increasingly certain, however, that the main body of exhibitors was opposed to the producer-exhibitor. **1951** *Manch. Guardian* 14 May 4/2 It is, of course, extremely difficult to give a coherent picture when you are showing objects..that include producer goods, consumer goods, and transport. **1956** J. C. SWAYNE *Conc. Gloss Geogr. Terms* 114 *Producer goods*, goods used to make other goods. **1969** *Listener* 13 Feb. 219/2 The producer-novelist David Thomson gave us a good example in *From Oblivion to Obscurity* (Third Programme), by another novelist, with previous radio successes, F. C. Ball. **1962** *Times* 18 Oct. (Walter Thompson Suppl.) p. ii/3 Monopolists and critics of advertising..are fundamentally producer-oriented. **1964** M. MCLUHAN *Understanding Media* (1967) II. xxxi. 333 Nearly all of our technologies since Gutenberg have been..not producer-oriented, but consumer-oriented. **1938** *Daily Tel.* 16 Feb. 14/6 Finally, it is said that compulsory pasteurisation would threaten the economic existence of the small producer-retailer. **1960** *Farmer & Stockbreeder* 5 Jan. 87/2 Producer-retailers with over 50 head of poultry will again be required to contribute ½d per dozen.

pro'ducership. [f. PRODUCER + -SHIP.] The position or function of a producer.

?**1924** G. B. SHAW *To a Young Actress* (1960) 65 You are not within five years hard work of being good enough for Comisarjevsky, whose producership I have made a condition of my consent to the Parisian Pygmalion. **1926** *Spectator* 1 May 796/1 By a judicious system of African producership and land ownership peace has prevailed. **1933** V. A. DEMANT *God & Man & Society* iii. 70 The only unassailable standard of producership is the fulfilment of the real demands of the whole body of consumers. **1960** *Times* 16 Mar. 10/4 By 1944 [Dr. Rennert] had risen to the chief producership of the Berlin Städtische Oper.

producibility (prəudjuːsɪ'bɪlɪtɪ). [f. late L. *prōdūcibil-is* PRODUCIBLE + -ITY; cf. med.L. *prōdūcibilitās* (*c* 1300 in Duns Scotus).] The capability of being produced.

1656 HOBBES *Lib., Necess., & Chance* (1841) 387 They imply not the actual production, but the producibility of the effect. **1842** *Blackw. Mag.* LII. 730 The scale passes over, of necessity, from the relative producibilities of things to their relative useabilities.

producible (prəu'djuːsɪb(ə)l), *a.* Also -eable. [In form *producible*, ad. late L. *prōdūcibil-is* (Jerome), f. *prōdūcĕre* to PRODUCE: see -IBLE; in form *produceable* from PRODUCE *v.* + -ABLE.]

1. Capable of being produced, brought forward, or presented to the eye or mind; adducible; procurable, obtainable, available.

a **1641** BP. MOUNTAGU *Acts & Mon.* iii. (1642) 214 There were copies produceable, which were elder, and written before the Incarnation. **1704** NORRIS *Ideal World* II. viii. 381 They are not in themselves of a producible nature. **1809** PINKNEY *Trav. France* 91 They are considered as public records, and are only producible in the courts of justice. **1834** *Oxf. Univ. Mag.* I. 289 The greatest amount of produceable knowledge. **1888** BURGON *Lives 12 Gd. Men* I. IV. 407 No producible recollections remain of that early period.

2. Fit to be produced or introduced; presentable.

1802 SYD. SMITH *Dr. Parr* Wks. 1867 I. 5 The courtly phrase was, that Dr. Parr was not a producible man. **1817** EARL OF DUDLEY *Lett.* 24 Dec., He will never be able to turn him out a producible Emperor. **1894** *Westm. Gaz.* 11 Dec. 5/1 'The Vote Catchers' was written by the plaintiff, and if this had been producible nothing would have been heard about the non-production of the burlesque.

3. That can be produced or extended in length.

a **1696** SCARBURGH *Euclid* (1705) 31 They are producible infinitely both ways.

4. That may be caused or brought about; capable of being brought into being, generated, or made.

1660 JER. TAYLOR *Duct. Dubit.* I. ii, To suppose it producible or possible to be effected. **1677** GILPIN *Demonol.* (1867) 31 Such as are in themselves produceable by nature, but not in such an order. **1794** G. ADAMS *Nat. & Exp. Philos.* I. xi. 431 Mr. Boyle..became solicitous to know whether a fluid of so great importance [air] was not producible by art. **1828** *Examiner* 44/2 Tears..produceable by the pathetics of Mrs. West. **1890** *Spectator* 10 May, There will be no labour millennium, wealth being no more producible without painful toil than any other crop is.

pro'ducibleness. [f. prec. + -NESS.] The quality or fact of being producible.

1666 BOYLE *Orig. Formes & Qual.* II. v, The producibleness of an Alkaly out of Bodies of another nature. **1680** —— *Produc. Chem. Princ.* III. 116 That part of these Notes, that treats of the producibleness of Vinous Spirits.

pro'ducing, *vbl. sb.* [f. PRODUCE *v.* + -ING¹.] The action of the verb PRODUCE; production.

1627 RAWLEY in *Bacon's Sylva* To Rdr., The producing of many noble works and effects. **1691** LOCKE *Lower. Interest* (1692) 16 Trade then is necessary to the producing of Riches, and Money necessary to the carrying on of Trade. **1707** *Curios. in Husb. & Gard.* 35 Generation is but the Producing and Manifestation of an Animal..form'd a few days after the Creation of the Sun.

pro'ducing, *ppl. a.* [f. as prec. + -ING².] That produces; productive.

1827 HUTTON *Course Math.* I. 50 Multiply the producing terms of one line, and the produced terms of the other line, continually, and take the result for a dividend. *a* **1871** GROTE *Eth. Fragm.* i. (1876) 26 The producing cause of pleasures or of pains. **1884** *U.S. Tenth Census* X. 13 'Shale oil' was found at a depth of 751 feet, and in November, 1871, producing sand was struck at 1,110 feet. **1907** *Q. Rev.* July 208 Hordes of mendicants live upon the producing classes. **1920** *Stage Year Bk.* 51 One or two of the bigger and better producing firms had begun to look higher. **1927** *Petroleum Devel. & Technol. in 1926* (A.I.M.E. Petroleum Div.) 202 Where it occurs, naturally no complete travel from the injection well to the producing wells is had. **1932** *New Yorker* 23 July 2/2 (Advt.), Rockland Producing Company 'Death Takes a Holiday': Fri., July 22. **1976** *Daily Tel.* 3 Dec. 5/5 So far.. most of Mexico's producing wells have been on land or in the relatively calm and shallow waters of the Gulf of Mexico.

product ('prɒdəkt, -dʌkt), *sb.*¹ [ad. L. *prōduct-um* a thing produced or brought forth, sb. use of pa. pple. neut. of *prōdūcĕre* to PRODUCE; in sense 1 in Albertus Magnus *Metaph.* V. III. vi.]

1. *Math.* The quantity obtained by multiplying two or more quantities together. Also, more widely, applied to other mathematical entities (as events, matrices, permutations, sets, tensors, vectors, etc.) obtained by certain defined processes of combination of two or more entities, the processes not necessarily being commutative and the entities combined not necessarily being of the same kind (cf. SUM *sb.*¹). Cf. *inner product* s.v. INNER *a.* (*sb.*²) 1 k, *outer product* s.v. OUTER *a.* (*sb.*¹) 3.

c **1430** *Art of Nombryng* 8 In multiplicacioun .2. nombres pryncipally ben necessary,..the nombre multiplying and the nombre to be multipliede... Also..the .3. nombre, the whiche is clepide product or pervenient. **1571** DIGGES *Pantom.* I. viii. D j b, Multiplye the length..by 12. and the producte diuide by the partes in whiche you founde the threade. **1614** T. BEDWELL *Nat. Geom. Numbers* ii. 25 The products of 12 by 2, and of 6 by 4, are equall. **1827** HUTTON *Course Math.* I. 4 A Compound Number is one which is the product of two or more numbers. **1892** F. N. COLE tr. *Netto's Theory of Substitutions* ii. 23 The substitution which results from the successive application of two or more substitutions we call their product. **1913** C. E. CULLIS *Matrices & Determinoids* vi. 158 If *A* and *B* are any two matrices, the product AB is defined below to be a certain third matrix which is completely known when *A* and *B* are known. **1941** COURANT & ROBBINS *What is Math.?* ii. 110 By the 'intersection' or 'logical product' of *A* and *B* we mean the set consisting only of those elements which are in *both A* and *B*. **1962** B. D. SECKLER tr. *Gnedenko's Theory of Probability* i. 22 The event consisting in the simultaneous occurrence of *A* and *B* will be called the product, or intersection, of the events *A* and *B* and will be denoted by *AB*. **1965** BIRKHOFF & MACLANE *Survey Mod. Algebra* (ed. 3) vii. 188 Show that tensor products are distributive on direct sums. **1965** PATTERSON & RUTHERFORD *Elem. Abstract Algebra* ii. 35 Defining the product of two permutations in this way, we obtain a binary operation in the set of all permutations... It is not commutative. **1972** A. G. HOWSON *Handbk. Terms Algebra & Anal.* ii. 11 The Cartesian product, $A \times B$, of two sets *A* and *B* is defined to be the set of all ordered pairs (*a*, *b*) of elements from *A* and *B* respectively. *Ibid.* xxxiv. 172 The vector product is *not* associative.

b. ***product of inertia*** of a body or system of bodies, with respect to two given planes at right angles to each other, or to the two axes perpendicular to such planes: the sum of the elements of mass each multiplied by the product of its distances from the two given planes.

1873 MAXWELL *Electr. & Magn.* (1881) II. 194 We may call the coefficients of the form 2.11 Moments of Mobility, and those of the form 2.12 Products of Mobility. **1877** B. WILLIAMSON *Integral Calculus* (ed. 2) x. §195 *Σxydm*, *Σzxdm*, *Σyzdm* are called the *products of inertia* relative to the same system of co-ordinate axes.

2. a. A thing produced by nature or a natural process; also in collective sense, = produce, fruit.

1653 H. MORE *Antid. Ath.* I. II. iii. (1712) 48 He [man] is the flower and chief of all the products of Nature upon this Globe of the Earth. **1667** MILTON *P.L.* XI. 683 These are the product Of those ill-mated Marriages thou saw'st; Where good with bad were matcht, who of themselves Abhor to joyn. **1690** LOCKE *Govt.* II. v. §48 Land..where he had no Hopes of Commerce..to draw Money to him by the Sale of the Product. **1719** W. WOOD *Surv. Trade* 7 The Exportation of our own Product is, indeed, the Foundation of all our Trade. **1725** POPE *Odyss.* IV. 64 The purest product of the chrystal springs. **1751** JOHNSON *Rambler* No. 153 ⁋5 Enquiries after the products of distant countries. **1813** BAKEWELL *Introd. Geol.* (1815) 337 Among the products of volcanoes there are only three combustible at a moderate temperature. **1892** WESTCOTT *Gospel of Life* 10 The product of any particular seed is fixed within the limits of a type.

b. *fig.*

1682 DRYDEN *Religio Laici* 66 These truths are not the product of thy mind. **1693** *Humours Town* A v, The unpremeditated Products of my Fancy. **1862** H. SPENCER *First Princ.* I. iv. §22 By analyzing either the product of thought, or the process of thought. **1894** H. DRUMMOND *Ascent Man* 171 Intellectual products common to both Animal and Man.

†**c.** A quantity produced or obtained; a supply, provision, stock. *Obs. rare.*

1647 N. BACON *Disc. Govt. Eng.* I. xvi. (1739) 32 A yearly product of Victuals or other service was reserved and allowed to the Saxon Kings by the people. **1762** tr. *Busching's Syst. Geog.* V. 438 Having down all along the Mayn also a good product of wine.

3. a. That which is produced by any action, operation, or work; a production; the result. Now freq. that which is produced commercially for sale. Also *collect.*, merchandise, esp. gramophone records.

1575 *Recorde's Ground Artes* H vj, If you had subtracted the uppermost from the product or totall summe, then the residue thereof woulde bee equall to that middle-moste number. **1646** SIR T. BROWNE *Pseud. Ep.* VI. i. 277 If unto that summe [5509] be added 1645. the product will be 7154. **1656** EARL MONM. tr. *Boccalini's Advts. fr. Parnass.* I. lxxviii. (1674) 105 Whether he brought news of any gallant Italian Product, or of any taking Piece lately Printed? **1657** CROMWELL *Speech* 8 May in *Carlyle*, The things are very honourable and honest, and the product worthy of a Parliament. **1700** DRYDEN *Pythagorean Philos.* 197 The fruit and product of his labours past. **1890** GROSS *Gild Merch.* I. 107 He..sold the products of his handiwork in his shop. **1897** *Pop. Sci. Monthly* Nov. 133 The product of the flaking operations was a leaf-shaped blade. **1903** G. MATHESON *Repr. Men Bible* Ser. II. xiii. 269 Shall a literary product reveal the spirit of its age and be silent as to the spirit of its author! **1928** S. R. HALL *Mail-Order & Direct Mail Selling* xx. 373 To build up a successful mail-order business, one must first have or create the article or products that have mail-order possibilities. **1950** A. TACK *Sell your Way to Success* viii. 113 Work out the sales points around your product. **1976** *Street Life* 7–20 Feb. 22/3 Some records can be sold like soapflakes, but the majority are not purely 'product'. **1977** *Time* 12 Dec. 68/2 More product, to borrow the record-company jargon, from the pianist who burst out of Russia two years ago and has been a one-man industry ever since.

b. The value of goods produced, esp. ***gross national*** (or ***total annual***) ***product*** (see GROSS *a.* 6 c).

1888 E. BELLAMY *Looking Backward* xxii. 314 The total annual product of the nation..would not have come to more than three or four hundred dollars per head. **1962** *Listener* 29 Mar. 548/1 There is a fixed proportion of the gross national product which can be spent on defence. **1966** *Ibid.* 17 Mar. 374/1 [We could] keep our defence expenditure between five and six per cent of gross national product.

4. That which results from the operation of a cause; a consequence, effect.

1651 BAXTER *Inf. Bapt.* 218 Dueness of Reward or Punishment is the immediate Product of Promise or Threatening. **1843** GROVE *Corr. Phys. Forces* (1846) 39 Heat is an immediate product of chemical affinity. **1874** GREEN *Short Hist.* v. § 1. 214 The long French romances were the product of an age of wealth and ease.

5. *Chem.* A compound not previously existing in a body, but formed during its decomposition. See also BY-PRODUCT. Opposed to EDUCT *sb.*

1805 HATCHETT in *Phil. Trans.* XCV. 299 In the first experiment it was obtained as a product, and not as an educt. **1807** T. THOMSON *Chem.* (ed. 3) II. 434 The products of the combustion, besides the soot, are water and carbonic acid. **1845** G. E. DAY tr. *Simon's Anim. Chem.* I. 160 Products of the metamorphosis of a substance of an invariably uniform composition.

6. *attrib.* and *Comb.*: (in sense 1) ***product event, integral, measure, space***; (senses 2–4) ***product design, division, group, launch, line, mix, morpheme, nucleus***.

1959 *Listener* 21 May 885/1 A blackboard in the product design section. **1980** *Jrnl. R. Soc. Arts* May 335/2 There is no doubt that the four companies..have put a lot of effort into product design. **1970** *Financial Times* 13 Apr. 14/3 The new structure of the British Steel Corporation consisting of product divisions is generally considered to be one of two logical management systems for a modern business of international proportions. **1968** P. A. P. MORAN *Introd. Probability Theory* i. 2 Given any two events, A_1 and A_2, we define a 'product' event denoted by A_1A_2 which occurs if any events E_i occur which belong to both A_1 and A_2. **1957** *Which?* Autumn 2 In the United States and the Scandinavian countries, there are independent organisations that issue reports, regularly or occasionally, each dealing with the brands widely available in one product-group. **1962** E. GODFREY *Retail Selling & Organization* i. 7 The Nielsen Survey.. showed that in three product groups—coffees, soft drinks and toilet soaps—50 per cent of all grocery shops offered one or more items below list price. **1968** P. A. P. MORAN *Introd. Probability Theory* vi. 290 Expressions such as (6.40) are known as 'product integrals'. This is a mathematical concept which is related to a product of a number of factors in the same way that an integral is related to a sum. **1976** *Times* 22 Apr. 11/4 They were for use in explaining to salesmen, dealers and executives a product launch, a new marketing philosophy or some new twist in internal communications. **1969** *Time* 17 Jan. 52 The company has greatly broadened its product line, introducing seven new models in the past two years. **1980** *Jrnl. R. Soc. Arts* May 325/2 It has over 400 product lines and thousands of variants. **1950** W. FELLER *Introd. Probability Theory* I. v. 91 Independence of trials means product measure. **1968** P. A. P. MORAN *Introd. Probability Theory* iv. 194 ϕ is the 'product measure' generated by the separate measures on the n one-dimensional spaces. **1953** F. G. MOORE *Manuf. Managem.* v. 85 Valid comparisons of over-all figures sometimes become almost meaningless because variations in the 'product mix'—the quantities of different items produced—occur continually. **1965** H. I. ANSOFF *Corporate Strategy* (1968) i. 18 Strategic decisions are..concerned..specifically with selection of the product-mix which the firm will produce. **1970** O. DOPPING *Computers & Data Processing* xxii. 365 Product mix is an economically important problem which can in many cases be handled by computer. **1965** *Language* XLI. 365 The sentences would have no string structure at all if transformations combined morphemes from separate elementary sentences into novel product-morphemes (portmanteau blends). **1931** G. GAMOW *Constitution of Atomic Nuclei* iii. 63 The particle (α or β) ejected from the nucleus No. 1 may leave the product-nucleus No. 2 in an excited state. **1963** Product nucleus [see *delayed neutron*]. **1968** E. T. COPSON *Metric Spaces* viii. 134 The product space $X \times T$ is an $(m+n)$ dimensional Euclidean space. **1968** P. A. P. MORAN *Introd. Probability Theory* i. 10 The space of all such events is known as the product space of the two spaces.

7. Special Combs.: **product champion**, a person entrusted with the promotion of a product or idea; **products liability**, a manufacturer's legal responsibility to the consumer for his product or products; **product moment**, of a set of pairs of statistical data, the sum of the products of the elements of each pair; freq. *attrib.* (with hyphen), designating a correlation coefficient (symbol *r*) calculated from this, equal to the covariance divided by the geometric mean of the variance; cf. PEARSON b, CORRELATION 1 c.

1969 *Observer* 2 Nov. 12/7 'Product champions' are appointed to help push new ideas through the natural opposition within a big company. **1976** *Jrnl. R. Soc. Arts* CXXIV. 725/1 We welcome ideas from serious-minded enthusiasts or 'product champions'. **1972** *Guardian* 12 Aug. 10/5 American judges and legislators have created..a completely new set of rights known as product liability law. The dramatic effect of this is to make the manufacturer.. strictly liable to the ultimate consumer. **1976** *National Observer* (U.S.) 23 Oct. 11/2 Kerry Choi, head of product-liability research for the Association of Trial Lawyers of America..says most of the cases he handles for member attorneys involve inadequate warnings. **1978** *Rep. R. Comm. Civil Liability & Compensation for Personal Injury* I. v. xxii. 255 Products liability must be considered in the context of public concern to protect the interests of the consumer. **1904** *Drapers' Company Res. Mem.* (Biometric Ser.) I. 32 We shall obtain by the method of mean square contingency satisfactory results, *i.e.*, values close to the coefficient of correlation as found by product moment or four-fold division methods. **1904** *Amer. Jrnl. Psychol.* XV. 78 The method of 'product moments' is valid, whether or not the distribution follow the normal law of frequency, so long as the 'regression' is linear. **1918** *Biometrika* XII. 87 We are now in a position to set down the algebraical values of the product-moment coefficients. **1925** R. A. FISHER *Statistical Methods* vi. 146 Such an estimate is called the correlation coefficient, or the product moment correlation, the latter term referring to the summation of the product terms, *xy*, in the last equation. **1930** M. EZEKIEL *Methods Correlation Anal.* viii. 127 The value $\Sigma(xy)$ is sometimes called the product moment. **1951** PADEN & LINDQUIST *Statistics for Econ. & Business* xiv. 231 The use of the mean x/σ_x, y/σ_y product for this purpose was first proposed by the English statistician Karl Pearson and is therefore called the Pearson product-moment coefficient of correlation. **1972** *Jrnl. Social Psychol.* LXXXVII. 33 Pearson product-moment correlations were calculated between fear ratings and intensity of escape attempts. **1972** E. LUKACS *Probability & Math. Statistics* iv. 90 In the bivariate case one also has a mixed moment (product-moment) of second order.

† **product**, *sb.*[2], app. a corrupt form of PRATIQUE.

1720 *Lond. Gaz.* No. 5888/2, I..have..appointed a Product-Boat to lie..off Europa-Point, to stop all Vessels. **1722** DE FOE *Plague* (1756) 246 Four Ships..being denied Product, as they call it, went on to Turkey, and were freely admitted. **1725** —— *Voy. round World* (1840) 109 The governor presently gave us product, as we call it, and leave to buy what provisions we wanted.

† **pro'duct**, *ppl. a. Obs. rare.* [ad. L. *prōdūct-us*, pa. pple. of *prōdūcĕre* to PRODUCE.] Produced: construed as pa. pple.

1398 TREVISA *Barth. De P.R.* VIII. xxviii. (1495) 340 In an instant oo poynt that is product fillyth all the world of lyghte and shinyng. **1534** WHITINTON *Tullyes Offices* III. (1540) 144 Lawe ciuyle producte out of the law of nature..dothe chalynge malyce and fraud.

product (prəʊ'dʌkt), *v. Obs.* or *rare.* [f. L. *prōduct-*, ppl. stem of *prōdūcĕre* to PRODUCE: cf. *conduct*, *deduct*, *induct*, etc., and the prec. ppl. adj.]

† **1.** *trans.* To bring forward: = PRODUCE *v.* 1.

c **1555** HARPSFIELD *Divorce Hen. VIII* (Camden) 212 Many reasons are producted in the said dialogue. **1563** FOXE *A. & M.* 1093/1 More then the articles whereupon they were producted doth contain. *Ibid.* 1466/2 Beyng producted to his last examinatyon before the sayde byshop.

† **2.** To bring forth, beget: = PRODUCE *v.* 3. *Obs.*

1577 HARRISON *England* I. viii. in *Holinshed* I. 18/2 In these Isles also is great plenty of fine Amber to be had, which is produced by the working of the sea, vpon those coastes. **1610** MARCELLINE *Triumphs Jas. I* 66 Our Great King, who hath producted the most Noble Prince Henry..for the greater height of his good fortune. **1683** E. HOOKER *Pref. Pordage's Mystic Div.* 105 All other Essences, Globes, Worlds, producted, educted, or brought forth out of the Womb of pure Nature.

3. To extend, lengthen out, prolong: = PRODUCE *v.* 2, 2 c. In later use chiefly *Zool. Obs.* or *rare.*

a **1670** HACKET *Abp. Williams* (1693) 89 He that doth much in a short life products his mortality. **1756** P. BROWNE *Jamaica* 405 The shells are producted to a sharp point at both ends. **1826** KIRBY & SP. *Entomol.* III. xxxv. 538 In many of the species..the prothorax is producted posteriorly into a long scutelliform horizontal horn.

Hence **pro'ducted** *ppl. a.*; whence † **pro'ductedness** *Obs.*; † **pro'ducting** *vbl. sb.* and *ppl. a. Obs.*

1623 tr. *Favine's Theat. Hon.* I. i. 3 For the producting of Elementarie bodies. **1628** FELTHAM *Resolves* II. [I.] xxx. 95 For conception, and fostering the producted birth. **1635** HEYWOOD *Hierarch.* III. 142 Time is the sole producting instrument. **1664** H. MORE *Myst. Iniq.* 302 The present Tense may intimate a productedness of the Action as being *in fieri*. **1826** KIRBY & SP. *Entomol.* IV. 328 Prothorax.. Producted... When behind it terminates in a long scutelliform process.

pro'ductible, *a. rare.* [f. L. *prōdūct-*, ppl. stem of *prōdūcĕre* to PRODUCE + -IBLE.] = PRODUCIBLE.

1830 in MAUNDER *Dict.*

Hence **pro,ducti'bility**, the quality or fact of being producible.

1832 S. TURNER *Sacr. Hist.* (1836) I. iv. 127 There are demonstrations of the latent and indefinite productibility of vegetable nature. **1849** *Sk. Nat. Hist., Mammalia* III. 80 The test of excellence is productibility, a readiness to become fat, small bone, and the quality of the whole animal when converted into bacon. **1862** RUSKIN *Unto this Last* ii. 53 *note*, No produce ever maintains a consistent rate of productibility.

pro'ductile, *a. rare.* [ad. late L. *prōductil-is*, f. as prec.: see -ILE.] Capable of being drawn out or produced.

1727 BAILEY (vol. II), *Productile*, drawn out at length. **1755** JOHNSON, *Productile*, which may be produced. **1795** tr. *Mercier's Fragm. Pol. & Hist.* II. 411 Prior to the existence of a line, there was a law which, supposing a line, rendered it productile. **1900** LEWIS & SHORT *Lat. Dict.*, *Prōductilis* adj., that may be drawn out, ductile, productile.

production (prəʊ'dʌkʃən). Also 5–6 -ccion. [Late ME. a. F. *production* (13th c. in Littré), ad. L. *prōductiōn-em* a lengthening, n. of action f. *prōdūcĕre* to PRODUCE.]

I. 1. a. The action of producing, bringing forth, making, or causing; the fact or condition of being produced; with *a* and *pl.*, an act of producing.

1483 CAXTON *Cato* A ij b, God is the unyuersel commaundour of all our production. **1529** MORE *Dyaloge* I. Wks. 129/2 By generacion & produccion did the doers work both willingly & naturally. **1604** E. G[RIMSTONE] *D'Acosta's Hist. Indies* IV. i. 203 Mettals are (as plants,) hidden and buried in the bowels of the earth, which have some conformitie in themselves, in the forme and maner of their production. **1651** BAXTER *Inf. Bapt.* 100 What alteration was in the Deed at the production of the effect? **1660** BOYLE *New Exp. Phys. Mech., Digress.* 346 The Production and Modulation of the Voice by the Elision of the Air, the Larynx, &c. **1776** ADAM SMITH *W.N.* I. viii. (1869) I. 84 The demand for men..necessarily regulates the production of men. **1823** H. J. BROOKE *Introd. Crystallogr.* 95 The manner in which those molecules are aggregated in the production of crystals. **1900** *Jrnl. Soc. Dyers* XVI. 6 The production of delicate and bright shades of pink.

b. *Pol. Econ.* (See quots.)

1784 ADAM SMITH *Wealth of Nations* (ed. 3) II. IV. viii. 515 Consumption is the sole end and purpose of production. .. The mercantile system..seems to consider production and not consumption, as the ultimate end and object of all industry and commerce. **1817** D. RICARDO *Princ. Pol. Econ.* xx. 444 The cost of production, and therefore the prices of various manufactured commodities, are raised to the consumer by one error in legislation. **1825** MCCULLOCH *Pol. Econ.* II. i. 61 By production, in the science of Political Economy, we are not to understand the production of matter,..but the production of utility, and consequently of exchangeable value, by appropriating and modifying matter already in existence. **1863** FAWCETT *Pol. Econ.* I. iv. (1876) 26 Capital is wealth which has been appropriated to assist future production. **1879** H. GEORGE *Progr. & Pov.* I. iii. (1881) 50 Production is always the mother of wages. **1887** MOORE & AVELING tr. *Marx's Capital* I. II. vi. 147 In order that a man may be able to sell commodities other than labour-power, he must of course have the means of production, as raw material, implements, &c. **1933** S. HOOK *Towards Understanding K. Marx* xi. 120 For Marx it is the relations of production, not the forces of production and not the conditions of production, which are the basis of the cultural superstructure. **1964** S. M. MILLER in I. L. Horowitz *New Sociol.* 300 We need sustained economic growth, high production, and high employment in order to solve many of the problems of the unemployed and the poor today in America. **1977** *Undercurrents* June–July 23/1 First, to infiltrate the key institutions, including 'the means of production' (The People's Warehouse).

2. a. That which is produced; a thing that results from any action, process, or effort; a product. In quots. 1695 and 1885 *collective*, = produce.

c **1430** *Art of Nombryng* 9 Whan the digit multipliethe a nombre componede,..afterwarde Ioyne the produccioun, and þere wol be the some totalle. **1624** MASSINGER *Renegado* III. v, Nature, the great queen and mother Of all productions. **1638** CHILLINGW. *Relig. Prot.* I. iii. § 67. 170 A mountain may travail, and the production may be a mouse. **1695** *Pennsylv. Archives* I. 117 Any of the Production or Manufacture of Europe not Legally Imported in the said Province. **1748** HUME *Ess.* xviii. (ed. 3) 193 His utmost Art and Industry can never equal the meanest of Nature's Productions, either for Beauty or Value. **1870** JEVONS *Elem. Logic* iii. 22 We constantly talk of the productions of a country meaning the products. **1885** *Manch. Exam.* 3 June 5/3 The market is reported to be glutted, and the production has of late been largely going into stock.

b. A product of human activity or effort; *spec.* a literary or artistic work. Chiefly in *pl.*

1651 HOBBES *Govt. & Soc.* Ep. Ded., We lay a partiall estimate upon our own productions. **1705** ADDISON *Italy* Pref., It is the great School of Musick and Painting, and contains in it all the noblest Productions of Statuary and Architecture. *a* **1828** H. NEELE *Lit. Rem.* (1829) 48 Chapman's Homer is a production of great value and interest. **1839** YEOWELL *Anc. Brit. Ch.* ix. (1847) 91 Two short writings..deemed by the ablest critics to be the genuine productions of the apostle. **1879** FROUDE *Cæsar* ix. 100 The finest productions of Praxiteles or Zeuxis.

† **c.** An effect; = PRODUCT *sb.* 4. *Obs. rare.*

a **1610** HEALEY *Epictetus' Man.* (1636) 58 To follow..the causes and productions of all that seemeth usefull. **1677**

SEDLEY *Ant. & Cl.* Wks. 1722 I. 155 They're Cleopatra's Subjects: let that be A full Production in our Victory.

d. The total yield, produce, or proceeds *of* (something); = PRODUCE *sb.* 2. *rare.*

1878 SEELEY *Stein* I. 142 The one financial procedure was to increase the production of the royal domains.

II. 3. a. The action of bringing forward or exhibiting; in *Law*, the exhibiting of a document in court. ***to satisfy production*** (*Sc. Law*), to produce and submit a document called for by a court of law (and thereby to admit the title of the pursuer and competence of the court).

1562 *Reg. Privy Council Scot.* I. 224 Eftir the productioun quhairof the personis undirwrittin .. absentit thame selffiis. **1566** *Ibid.* 443 Summondis of errour for productioun and reductioun of the said declaratioun of the assyisis. **1818** in Picton *L'pool Munic. Rec.* (1886) II. 364 That the Surveyor do furnish the Mayor for production at the next Council with a plan. **1828** *Act of Sederunt* 11 July §36 If the defender is to object to the title of the pursuer .. or to state any other action against satisfying the production, he shall return defences confined to these points. **1838** W. BELL *Dict. Law Scot.* 790 Production of articles at criminal trials. *Ibid.* 830 If he [the defender] mean to defend the action on its merits .. he merely returns the summons, which implies that he means to satisfy the production, as it is expressed; *i.e.*, to produce the document called for, and to contest the reasons of the reduction. **1878** E. ROBERTSON in *Encycl. Brit.* VIII. 742/1 Public documents in general must be proved either by the production of the original or by the official copies. **1883** SIR N. LINDLEY *Law Rep. 23 Chanc. Div.* 49 There is a broad distinction between a general application for discovery of documents .. and an application for production of documents referred to in the pleadings. *Mod.* I shall call for the production of that document.

b. *Sc. Law.* A document produced in an action.

1838 W. BELL *Dict. Law. Scot.* s.v., In judicial proceedings, written documents produced in process, *in modum probationis* .. are technically called productions. So also in an action of reduction, the writ, or deed, or decree, called for .., is called the production.

c. The action or process of producing a stage play, film, or other performance. Also, the performance itself.

1894 *Westm. Gaz.* 4 Dec. 2/1 The great event of the past week has been the production of the Greek play. **1925** *Scribner's Mag.* July 7/1 Jesse Lynch Williams has been .. preparing a play for production in New York in the fall. **1928** BARRIE *Peter Pan* p. viii, I remember writing the story of *Peter and Wendy* many years after the production of the play. **1932** *New Yorker* 11 June 52/2 Wherever she appears .., as a telephone operator in some big, showy production —a breath of humanity sweeps over the screen. **1937** *Printers' Ink Monthly* May 40/2 *Production*, the building, organizing and presenting of a radio program. **1942** *N. & Q.* 12 Sept. 161/1 'Business of the Stage' denotes the movements, groupings, vocal inflections, etc., of the players, which are settled at rehearsal. The modern term is 'Production'. **1949** *Radio Times* 15 July 15/2 '*The Dilettanti*' by Thomas Love Peacock. Adapted for broadcasting... Production by Noel Iliff. **1952** GRANVILLE *Dict. Theatr. Terms* 101 *In production* (of a play), in rehearsal and general preparation for *production*. A *dark* theatre sometimes has a notice stating that 'this theatre is closed; a new play is *in production*'. **1962** A. NISBETT *Technique Sound Studio* 267 *Production*, compilation, and studio direction, etc., of a programme. **1976** M. MAGUIRE *Scratchproof* ii. 30 Loose talk .. can ruin a production before it even gets off the ground.

d. *fig.* An unnecessarily elaborate performance; a fuss, commotion, drama. Freq. in phr. ***to make a production*** (***of, out of***, etc., something).

1941 B. SCHULBERG *What makes Sammy Run?* vii. 128 Something tells me that when our blast comes, it will really be a production. **1959** R. CONDON *Manchurian Candidate* (1960) ix. 131 You make a production out of it like I was involved somehow in your life. **1962** M. & G. GORDON *Journey with Stranger* (1963) xi. 74 The simplest tasks at home became productions when travelling. **1967** S. WOODS *Case is Altered* ix. 107 You've made rather a production of this, Inspector. **1974** R. BUTLER *Buffalo Hook* ii. 15 Why should there be this big production over a cargo .. that's covered by insurance anyway.

III. †4. Leading or carrying forth. *rare*⁻¹.

1631 WEEVER *Anc. Fun. Mon.* 11 Men of meaner ranke .. were not allowed this princely kinde of production to their graues.

IV. 5. Drawing out, extending, or lengthening in †time (*obs.*) or space; prolongation, extension.

1536 BELLENDEN *Cron. Scot.* (1821) II. 189 To that fine, that King Gregorius army, be production of lang time, suld laik vittalis. **1653** R. SANDERS *Physiogn.* b ij, Animals long-liv'd, being fed upon, conduce much to the production of life. **1658** PHILLIPS, *Production*, .. also a lengthening, or making longer. **1840** LARDNER *Geom.* 280 Hence a tangent may be drawn to a parabola from any point T, in the production of its axis.

†6. *Anat.* An extension of or projection from a bone or other part; = PROCESS *sb.* 12. *Obs.*

1578 BANISTER *Hist. Man* I. 26 These bones are endewed with three notable productions, or Processes. **1615** CROOKE *Body of Man* 485 Through these passages & productions aire and vapors attracted or drawn in respiration through the nosthrils .. are carried vn to the braine. **1725** SLOANE *Jamaica* II. 284 There being no such production on the upper chap. **1858** MAYNE *Expos. Lex.*, *Productio*, .. a prolongation; a production.

V. 7. *attrib.* and *Comb.* **a.**

1895 W. SMART *Stud. Economics* 8 Production goods .. may be shortly described as .. all the forms of land, capital, and labour that go, proximately or remotely, to provide and produce the consumption goods and services. **1897** LD. MASHAM in *Westm. Gaz.* 29 Jan. 3/2 When capital ceases to be invested in our production industries. **1898** *Engineering Mag.* XVI. 40 This is used either for production order or for sales order. **1929** T. H. BURNHAM *Engin. Econ.* xv. 192 Production control necessitates a system of records and charts which indicate at a glance whether the planned production is being adhered to, or if departure therefrom is occurring, at what stage the divergence is arising. **1938** E. AMBLER *Cause for Alarm* i. 17 He's afraid of the production figures falling off. **1941** B. SCHULBERG *What makes Sammy Run?* xi. 283 Production costs have been too high. **1943** J. B. PRIESTLEY *Daylight on Saturday* viii. 52 If our lads was fightin' like 'ell .. yer'd see them production figures take a high jump. **1951** R. FIRTH *Elem. Social Organization* iv. 136 The organization of production tends to be based not merely on a system of cash rewards... A production relationship is often only one facet of a social relationship. **1957** *Technology* Mar. 8/1 Then he goes into the production shops, where he gains experience of the many aspects of aircraft construction. **1958** J. F. MAGEE *Production Planning & Inventory Control* i. 1 A manager necessarily thinks of problems in production planning in terms of people and their responsibilities. **1962** A. BATTERSBY *Guide to Stock Control* x. 89 In striving for the shop-floor efficiency associated with long manufacturing runs, the Production Manager will always be tending to drive stock levels upwards. **1966** *New Statesman* 20 May 753/1 (Advt.), Book Publishers invite applications .. for the post of production controller to supervise the production of a section of their Home Education list, from manuscript to bound copy. **1970** O. DOPPING *Computers & Data Processing* xxii. 364 The most common problem in production planning in a workshop is to determine the sequence in which different operations, pertaining to different orders, should be placed in the different machine groups. **1975** *North Sea Background Notes* (Brit. Petroleum Co.) 7 Production licences .. give the licensee exclusive rights over a specific area to explore for and produce hydrocarbons. **1975** *Petroleum Economist* Aug. 309/1 The Hamilton Brothers facility involved developing a production riser as a technical innovation. **1976** *Scotsman* 24 Dec. 13/7 (Advt.), Experience of production control within a high volume fabrication and pressing shop would be a distinct advantage. **1977** *Observer* 24 Apr. 1/6 The rig crew was about to install a safety valve on the top of a production pipe. **1978** P. SUTCLIFFE *Oxf. Univ. Press* iv. x. 166 Frowde .. acquired great expertise and used it to good effect in producing his own books. He was his own production manager, firm and clear in his instructions to Hart.

b. In *Broadcasting* and *Cinemat.* (sense 3 c), ***production assistant, clerk, director, editor, manager, staff, team***; also ***production control, control room.***

1960 D. DAVIS *Gram. Television Production* 77 *Production Assistant* (*P.A.*), the director's personal assistant on a programme. **1969** W. RUTHERFORD *Gallows Set* i. 18 In one group were the members of the film crew. In the other .. were .. the most senior director .. [and] Anne, his production assistant. **1972** *Listener* 21 Dec. 852/1 Sequence of calls before a shot. Production Assistant: 'Quiet. Going for a take. Standing by'. Director: 'Right'. **1963** *Movie* Apr. 11/1 Production clerk at R.K.O., then second assistant director. **1961** G. MILLERSON *Technique Television Production* i. 15 Some networks prefer to have separate rooms for production control. *Ibid.*, Through the window of the production control room we can see the studio below. **1937** *Printers' Ink Monthly* May 40/2 *Production director*, individual in charge of the radio studio programs. **1961** G. MILLERSON *Technique Television Production* i. 15 Facing these monitors sit the production director and his assistant. **1972** Production editor [see *make-up editor* s.v. MAKE-UP 6]. **1938** *Times* 7 Jan. 13/6 Beside him [*sc.* the producer] sits the production manager, whose functions are similar to those of a stage manager in a theatre. **1959** W. S. SHARPS *Dict. Cinematogr.* 121/1 *Production manager*, in filming this post is often held by the Assistant Director and he is responsible for ensuring that everything and every person concerned in production is available at the right place at the right time. **1973** *Listener* 22 Nov. 727/1 In .. the film-within-the-film, the wife of the production manager .. sits sourly knitting on set. **1962** A. NISBETT *Technique Sound Studio* 246 *Control cubicle* (*BBC*), the soundproof room equipped with control desk .. which is occupied by production and operational staff. *Ibid.* 10 Although each member of the production team is concentrating on his own job, this is geared to that of the team as a whole. **1974** *Listener* 27 June 820/2 My wanting to make this series of documentaries .. aided by my production team's talents as film makers.

c. Special Combs.: **production brigade**, in communist countries, a unit within a commune required to meet specified agricultural production figures; **production engineering**, the planning and control of the manufacturing processes, plant, and equipment involved in the production of any manufactured product; so **production engineer**; **production line**, a line (LINE *sb.*² 19 c) along which things undergo successive stages of production; **production number**, a spectacular song or dance in a musical show or revue; **production platform**, a platform (sense 8 d) used in the production of oil or gas from the sea bed; **production reactor**, a nuclear reactor designed to produce fissile material; **production relations**, in Marxist theory the social relations arising from and essential to the process of production, as those between the controllers of the means of production (raw materials, land, machinery, etc.) and the labour force; **production run**, a run (RUN *sb.*¹ 19 c) for the purpose of the routine production of a product; **production-sharing** (see quot. 1963); **production testing**, testing under the conditions that would prevail during production; hence **production-test** *v. trans.*; **production well**, a well from which oil or gas is actively being produced.

1962 E. SNOW *Red China Today* (1963) lix. 453 About management? It is in the hands of the production brigade. **1978** HUA KUO-FENG in *Peking Rev.* 10 Mar. 22/1 In some cases the cadres arbitrarily demand grain and money from the commune, production brigade, production team or commune members or even requisition labour power. **1920** *Engin. Production* Mar. 128/3 As a production engineer it has frequently been necessary for me to select machines suitable for the intensive manufacture of various components. **1921–2** (*title*) Proceedings of the Institution of Production Engineers. **1940** E. J. H. JONES *Production Engin.* i. 3 From the schedules thus compiled, it is possible for the production engineer to ascertain whether sufficient plant will be available for the work in hand. **1946** G. GALLE in *Philips Resistance Welding Handbk.* ii. 41 Production engineers should be careful to watch that the seam welder is not overloaded. **1966** S. BEER *Decision & Control* i. 7 Tests have been run in the works to see whether one kind of machine tool is better than another. The purchasing department says that *A* is better than *B* because it is cheaper to buy. The production engineers say that *B* is better than *A* because it produces a better job. **1920** *Engin. Production* Nov. 467/2, I look forward to the time when the curriculum of our universities shall include lectures on production engineering. **1921–2** *Proc. Inst. Production Engineers* I. 39 The name calls up visions of conveyors, elevators, and all such gear, which is by no means the only part of production engineering. **1956** *Nature* 4 Feb. 200/1 The art of precasting concrete has given rise to an established industry producing staple things like blocks, tiles, floor beams and parts for small structures, where problems are in the nature of factory production-engineering. **1966** *McGraw-Hill Encycl. Sci. & Technol.* X. 640/1 Production engineering as a planning activity takes place between product design and the planning of the over-all manufacturing process. **1978** R. V. JONES *Most Secret War* xl. 377 The superiority of American production engineering was often a powerful—even vital—aid. **1935** T. H. BURNHAM *Engin. Econ.* (ed. 3) II. viii. 245 Many nice problems arise as to when it is economic to break up a group system and lay down a special production line. **1943** J. S. HUXLEY *TVA* xii. 112 One, two, and three bedroom houses were built on outdoor production lines and distributed to various communities. **1958** *Listener* 27 Nov. 903/1, I suggest one of those 'production-line' chickens, which is big enough for four. **1964** M. ARGYLE *Psychol. & Social Probl.* viii. 107 A production line must go at the speed of the slowest man. **1971** *Daily Tel.* 14 Aug. 7/4 The nauseating 'production line' feeling experienced in so many crematoria. **1975** *N.Y. Times* 8 Oct. 3/1 The new telescope is to be a production-line 25-meter model .. and has been chosen to keep costs to a minimum. **1936** *Metronome* Feb. 61/2 *Production number*, show tune. **1959** *Listener* 12 Nov. 845/3 One production number, danced in silhouette against a changing background, marked an exciting advance in presentation. **1967** WODEHOUSE *Company for Henry* v. 98 One of those big production numbers so popular in revue, where the whole strength of the company let themselves go in uninhibited dance. **1964** *Oil & Gas Jrnl.* 12 Oct. 104/1 Offshore Louisiana suffered its worst battering in history from Hurricane Hilda... The industry must decide what to do about multiwell production platforms that have been sheared off and sunk. **1976** *Scotsman* 27 Dec. 6/1 The order from Brazil for a production platform from the McDermott yard at Ardersier. **1956** Production reactor [see CONVERTER 3 f]. **1966** *McGraw-Hill Encycl. Sci. & Technol.* XI. 359/1 Water is used as a coolant in the United States production reactors, whereas in the United Kingdom gas cooling has been the basis for most designs. **1950** T. H. MARSHALL *Citizenship & Social Class* ii. 108 The essential factor in this theory is the conception of these production-relations as forces determining the life-situation of individuals. **1973** C. D. KERNIG *Marxism, Communism & Western Society* VII. 36/1 In the historico-materialist view of history .. it is assumed that revolutions arise out of a state of conflict between production and production relations. **1979** G. A. COHEN *Karl Marx's Theory of Hist.* ii. 31 A production relation binds at least one person(s)-term and at most one productive force(s)-term, and no other type of term. **1967** D. GOCH in Wills & Yearsley *Handbk. Managem. Technol.* 146 Compared with the standard usage of 3 lb of moulding powder per unit, the production run required an additional 30 lb. **1973** J. LEASOR *Host of Extras* i. 22 Many people think that the Ford Model T had the longest production run of any car—eighteen years. Rolls beat them on this .. by being in production with the Silver Ghost for nineteen consecutive years. **1963** *Economist* 8 June 1046/1 The concept that the Indonesians prefer is one of 'production-sharing', under which the contractor takes over existing or potential development, brings in his capital equipment to carry it out, and has as his reward a share of what is produced, processed and sold. **1975** *Petroleum Economist* Sept. 348/1 The Lebanese government has invited bids from interested oil companies for offshore acreage on a production-sharing basis. **1960** *Farmer & Stockbreeder* 19 Jan. Suppl. 41/1 It should provide a means of production-testing individual hens. **1975** *Petroleum Economist* Aug. 286/1 An exploratory well was production tested in June last year at rates of 4 200 b/d of condensate and 23 million cubic feet per day of gas. **1975** *Offshore* Sept. 75/2 While the well was not production tested, Shell indicates it could be a major discovery and Amoco calls it 'potentially significant'. **1934** *Proc. World Petroleum Congr. 1933* I. 359/1 (*heading*) The tubing of production wells under pressure. **1976** *Offshore Engineer* Mar. 6/4 At present only one production well is operating; depending on final assessment of reserves, from four to six wells will be used.

d. Designating a vehicle or appliance made in the ordinary course of production, as opposed to one made for testing or other special purposes.

1961 *Motor Sport* Dec. 1002 This talented designer has shown quite outstanding genius in placing another production B.M.C. engine across the front of his Mini. **1971** 'D. RUTHERFORD' *Clear the Fast Lane* 39 The usual changes needed before a production car is ready for rallying. **1972** *Lebende Sprachen* XVII. 136/2 Six Jet-stream prototypes are to be built before production aircraft begin to emerge within the next few months. **1974** *Encycl. Brit. Macropædia* XII. 567/2 Stock-car racing, limited to American production-model passenger cars with suitable modifications, began at Langhorne, Pennsylvania, on July 4, 1939. **1974** *Guardian* 26 Mar. 32/4 Disabled drivers' tricycles should be replaced with modified production cars. **1978** *Gramophone* Mar. 1642/2 A raffle for the first ever production model Quad Electrostatic loudspeaker.

Hence **pro'ductionist**, as in ***co-operative productionist***, one who believes in or advocates cooperative production.

1888 *Co-operative News* 22 Sept. 958 The ideal co-operative productionist begins by ignoring or defying the existence of competition.

productional (prəʊ'dʌkʃənəl), *a.* [f. PRODUCTION + -AL.] Of, pertaining to, or resulting from production.

1931 *Economist* 7 Feb. 285/2 In comparison with its 'productional' programme the Government's 'distributional' programme has been very modest. **1961** G. MILLERSON *Technique Television Production* 11 You will find here..several controversial hypotheses, for which the author must be held responsible (dynamic composition; aural composition; productional rhetoric). **1961** E. WILSON *Shaw on Shakespeare* 255 Shaw denounced script cuts and productional schemes which distorted the plays and destroyed their integrity.

productionism (prəʊ'dʌkʃənɪz(ə)m). [f. PRODUCTION + -ISM.] A doctrine based upon the importance of production.

1930 *Times Lit. Suppl.* 23 Oct. 858/1 They [*sc.* some plays] may be unreadable..because the author was obsessed by the theory of 'productionism' and..contributed nothing of substance or of design but only a few wisps of straw. **1963** J. S. HUXLEY in *New Scientist* 27 June 713/2 In the USSR we have an analogous situation that may be called 'productionism' largely to keep up with and beat the USA in industrial efficiency.

productionize (prəʊ'dʌkʃənaɪz), *v.* [f. PRODUCTION + -IZE.] *trans.* To produce for general use; to put into production. So **pro'ductionized** *ppl. a.*; **pro'ductionizing** *vbl. sb.*

1937 *R. Air Force Q.* VIII. 102 Generally, an experimental military aircraft..attains speeds on tests which are not equalled by the subsequent '*productionized*' craft in the service. **1939** *Neuphilol. Mitt.* 137 Productionize, vb. **1957** *Times Survey Brit. Aviation* Sept. 15/7 There may well be less chance of reducing costs by 'productionizing'. **1961** *Flight* LXXX. 431/2 Ferranti are 'productionizing' the MoA moving-map display. **1970** *Sci. Jrnl.* May 37/2 A parallel programme inside the factory was devoted to productionizing the equipment.

productive (prəʊ'dʌktɪv), *a.* (*sb.*) [ad. F. *productif, -ive* (16th c. in Hatz.-Darm.), or (its source) med.L. *prōductīv-us*: see PRODUCT *ppl. a.* and -IVE.]

A. *adj.* **1. a.** Having the quality of producing or bringing forth; tending to produce; creative, generative.

1612 R. SHELDON *Serm. St. Martin's* 35 What new existencies are made of one Christ, by your productiue, creatiue, and factiue consecrations in your massing fiue words? **1754** EDWARDS *Freed. Will* II. iii. 41 There are many Things which have no such positive productive Influence. **1830** R. KNOX *Béclard's Anat.* 163 These alterations of the hairs..have all their origin and cause in the productive parts. **1870** LOWELL *Among my Bks.* Ser. I. (1873) 168 A writer so busy as Shakespeare must have been during his productive period.

b. Const. *of* the thing produced.

1678 CUDWORTH *Intell. Syst.* I. iv. § 17. 302 That essence, that is generative or productive of all things. **1767** COWPER *Let. to J. Hill* 16 June, This part of the world is not productive of much news. **1870** YEATS *Nat. Hist. Comm.* 81 Oak trees..productive of gall nuts.

c. *Med.* Of a cough: that raises mucus or sputum.

1923 *Radiology* I. 168/2 At the time of examination..she had a persistent and slightly productive cough. **1965** *Brit. Jrnl. Industr. Med.* XXII. 194/1 Those who smoked, and more particularly those who had a productive cough, had lower ventilatory capacities and lower forced expiratory ratios than the remainder.

2. That causes or brings about, that results in; causative. Always with *of*.

1647 CLARENDON *Hist. Reb.* I. §70 His single Misfortune ..(which..was productive of many greater). **1748** *Anson's Voy.* II. ii. 136 Salted cod..was..as productive of the scurvy, as any other kind of salt provisions. **1806** *Med. Jrnl.* XV. 457 It may be productive..of incalculable good. **1886** *Act 49 & 50 Vict.* c. 50 *Preamble*, Such want of uniformity is productive of great inconvenience.

3. *Pol. Econ.* That produces or increases wealth or value; engaged in the production of commodities of exchangeable value; esp. in ***productive labour, labourer, classes***. Also, esp. in Marxist theory, as ***productive forces***.

1776 ADAM SMITH *W.N.* II. iii. (1869) I. 332 There is one sort of labour that adds to the value of the subject upon which it is bestowed: there is another which has no such effect. The former, as it produces a value, may be called productive. **1792** A. YOUNG *Trav. France* 438 A government ..that struck a palsy into all the lower and productive classes to favour those whose only merit is consumption. **1832** HT. MARTINEAU *Life in Wilds* iv. 51, I have been accustomed.. to think productive labourers more valuable than unproductive. **1848** MILL *Pol. Econ.* I. ii. §3 Precious stones ..are to some small extent employed in the productive arts. **1878** JEVONS *Prim. Pol. Econ.* iii. 28 The great object must be to make labour as productive as possible, that is, to get as much wealth as we can with a reasonable amount of labour. **1907** L. BOUDIN *Theoretical System K. Marx* ii. 26 The basis of the structure [of society] is a given state of the development of the productive forces of society. **1909** E. UNTERMANN tr. *Marx's Capital* III. xv. 293 The means, this unconditional development of the productive forces of society, comes continually into conflict with the limited end, the self-expansion of the existing capital. **1927** E. & C. PAUL tr. Lenin in D. Ryazanoff *Karl Marx* 123 At a certain stage of development, the material productive forces of society come into conflict with the..property relationships within which they have hitherto moved. **1973** C. D. KERNIG *Marxism, Communism & Western Society* VII. 36/1 The concept 'productive forces' is very important for the Marxist interpretation of revolution... Designated as 'productive forces' are working people, means of production ..developed and employed by people and, in addition, the means of labour (raw materials, natural resources) that are consumed.

4. That produces readily or abundantly; fertile; prolific.

[**1706** PHILLIPS (ed. 6), *Productive*, apt to produce, or bring forth. **1722** POPE *Chorus Brutus, Youths & Virgins* 24 Chaste as cold Cynthia's virgin light, Productive as the Sun.] **1846** MCCULLOCH *Acc. Brit. Empire* (1854) I. 615 The mine of Ecton..was one of the most productive in the kingdom. **1874** FAWCETT *Pol. Econ.* II. v. (ed. 4) 175 An abundance of productive land.

†**B.** *sb.* That which produces or tends to produce. *Obs.*

1642 R. WATSON *Serm. Schisme* 29 That last productive of Schisme, Inordinate zeal. **1686** GOAD *Celest. Bodies* I. ii, Warmth is the instrumental Productive of Cloud and Rain.

pro'ductively, *adv.* [f. prec. + -LY[2].] In a productive way or manner.

†**1.** By production, as a production. *Obs. rare.*

1602 WARNER *Alb. Eng.* XIII. lxxviii. (1612) 322 Not that yll, productiuely, from Nature firstly springs. **1678** CUDWORTH *Intell. Syst.* I. iv. §36. 582 All things animally; that is, self-moveably, actively, and productively.

2. In a way that produces or increases wealth; profitably.

a **1832** BENTHAM *Man. Pol. Econ.* Wks. 1843 III. 54 The capital..will be applied as productively to other undertakings. **1868** ROGERS *Pol. Econ.* vi. (1876) 55 Capital is invested productively in the enclosure, drainage, and other improvements of land.

productiveness (prəʊ'dʌktɪvnɪs). [f. as prec. + -NESS.] The quality of being productive; capacity of producing; prolificacy; fertility, fruitfulness; abundance or richness in output.

1727 BAILEY vol. II, *Productiveness*, aptness to produce. **1795** W. TAYLOR in *Monthly Rev.* XVIII. 543 Circirello would be preferred to every other on account of its productiveness. **1819** W. LAWRENCE *Nat. Hist. Man* II. i. 265 Indeed, we know no difference in productiveness between such unions and those of the same race. **1825** MCCULLOCH *Pol. Econ.* III. iv. 254 A gold mine..of equal productiveness with the silver mines. **1847** GROTE *Greece* II. xviii. III. 365 The extreme productiveness of the southern region of Spain. *a* **1850** ROSSETTI *Dante & Circ.* II. (1874) 263 Francesco da Barberino shows by far the most sustained productiveness among the poets who preceded Dante. **1878** JEVONS *Prim. Pol. Econ.* vii. 54 To increase the productiveness of labour is really the important thing for everybody.

productivity (prəʊdʌk'tɪvɪtɪ, prɒd-). [f. L. *prōductīv-us* PRODUCTIVE + -ITY. So F. *productivité*.]

1. a. The quality or fact of being productive; capacity to produce; = PRODUCTIVENESS.

1809–10 COLERIDGE *Friend* (1818) III. 202 Its own productivity would have remained for ever hidden from itself. **1840** J. H. GREEN *Vital Dynamics* 30 This is the first character of all life, Productivity. **1865** LECKY *Ration.* (1878) II. 347 A sign of the limited productivity of the soil. **1898** L. STEPHEN *Stud. Biog.* II. i. 29 A publisher..doing all in his power to stimulate the productivity of an author.

b. *Ecol.* The rate of production of biomass.

1908 J. JOHNSTONE *Conditions of Life in Sea* ix. 179 It is much more difficult to attempt..estimations of the productivity of a sea area, than merely to attempt to ascertain the mass of life at one particular time. **1934** *Q. Rev. Biol.* IX. 175/2 Along the Southern California coast the greatest productivity is..within fifty miles of shore. **1953** E. P. ODUM *Fund. Ecol.* iv. 82 It is important to distinguish between the basic or primary productivity on the one hand and consumer or secondary productivity on the other. **1960** N. POLUNIN *Introd. Plant Geogr.* xv. 478 There is insufficient data as yet to compare the vegetational productivity of different climatic zones. Thus although some tropical inland waters may be more prolific as producers of plant or animal life than some extra-tropical ones, others are practically barren. *Ibid.* xvi. 520 The average productivity of similar land and ocean *areas* appear to be roughly comparable over the year, being said to be of the order of three tons of dry material per acre. **1970** W. D. RUSSELL-HUNTER *Aquatic Productivity* xii. 226 This primary productivity of the oceans..amounts to considerably more than half of the primary productivity of the entire world.

c. *Econ.* The rate of output per unit of input, used esp. in measuring capital growth, and in assessing the effective use of labour, materials, and equipment. Also *transf.*

1899 J. B. CLARK *Distrib. Wealth* iv. 49 We have said that the *specific* productivity of labor fixes wages... In like manner, the *specific* productivity of capital fixes interest. **1930** *Economist* 18 Jan. 107/2 Still, if productivity has risen high, profits have not followed suit. **1936** J. M. KEYNES *Gen. Theory Employment* xi. 138 Many discussions of this subject seem to be mainly concerned with the physical productivity of capital in some sense. **1947** *Amer. Econ. Rev.* May 402 We must try to distinguish as sharply as possible between increase and decrease of productivity caused by larger or smaller output volume—volume productivity increase—and the increase and decrease of productivity caused by real improvement of production or organization—real productivity increase. **1955** *Sci. Amer.* July 35/1 Machinery prices being similar for the managements of all the plants, productivity was a direct function of the average hourly earnings of production workers. **1957** *Introd. Work Study* (Internat. Labour Office) i. 5 *Productivity*..is..the arithmetical ratio between the amount produced and the amount of the resources used in the course of production. **1962** *Daily Tel.* 15 Nov. 1/4 The pace at which our productivity is increasing is too slow, and we hope this National Productivity Year will ginger things up a bit. **1965** H. WILSON in *Oxf. Times* 3 Dec. 16/2, I think I may claim the responsibility for introducing the word 'productivity' to Whitehall, and I'm not proud of it. **1970** *Physics Bull.* July 291/1 The 'productivity' of the Council has also edged up, with the subject boards considering more courses at fewer meetings. **1976** A. W. A. PETERSON in T. S. Barker *Econ. Struct. & Policy* v. 107 The model of production..assumes that industrial investment brings about higher labour productivity as a result of the introduction of more modern equipment.

2. *attrib.* and *Comb.*, as (sense 1 c) ***productivity agreement, deal, measure, team***.

1978 *Cornish Guardian* 27 Apr. 12/7 An active participant in the introduction of the Company Productivity Agreements. **1970** G. GREER *Female Eunuch* 243 By playing upon..discontent with wage freezes and productivity deals, an adroit Tory can convert the working class to the most arrant conservatism. **1977** *Navy News* Dec. 18/1 The opinion that in industry some 'spurious productivity deals' are now being drawn up has been voiced in a letter received from a PO. **1959** J. W. KENDRICK *Wages, Prices, Profits & Productivity* (Amer. Assembly, Columbia Univ.) ii. 39 The most commonly used productivity measure is 'output per man-hour'. **1953** *Britannica Bk. of Year* 638/2 A team of experts appointed to study methods of increasing production assumed the title of Productivity Team.

productor (prəʊ'dʌktə(r)). [Agent-n. in L. form (used in late L.) of *prōducĕre* to PRODUCE: see -OR. Cf. F. *producteur* (*a* 1504 in Hatz.-Darm.).] One who or that which produces; a producer.

1624 HEYWOOD *Gunaik.* I. 2 A divine thought was the producter of all things whatsoever. **1631** —— *Eng. Eliz.* (1641) A j, Diligence is the breeder and productour of arts. **1813** T. BUSBY *Lucretius* I. I. *Comm.* p. xxxiii, Every theory of creation that excludes the operation of Mind as the productive cause of being,..makes inanimate matter the productor of mind. **1887** L. PARKS *Star in East* ii. 51 The universal agent is the productor, the generator of beings.

pro'ductress. [f. prec.: see -ESS.] A female productor or producer. Chiefly *fig.*

1751 HARRIS *Hermes* Wks. (1841) 131 The ocean,..the container and productress of so many vegetables and animals. **1796** BURNEY *Mem. Metastasio* II. 419 Magna Græcia, the enviable productress of men of such vigourous and universal genius.

So †**pro'ductrice**, †**pro'ductrix** [from the F. and L. forms].

1585 T. WASHINGTON tr. *Nicholay's Voy.* IV. xxix. 150 The natiue countrie of Hercules..was the productrice of.. Epimanondas. **1630** PRYNNE *Anti-Armin.* 125 You make this vniuersall grace the productrix of sauing grace. **1660** STANLEY *Hist. Philos.* IX. (1701) 419/2 Matter is the print, mother, nurse, and productrix of the third essence.

‖**produit net** (prɔdɥi nɛt). [Fr., lit. 'net product'.] In the politico-economical doctrine of the physiocrats, the amount of the excess of the value of agricultural products over the cost of their production. (Cf. PHYSIOCRAT.)

1792 A. YOUNG *Trav. France* I. xxii. 559 By pursuing the jargon of the *produit net*, and making it variable, instead of fixed, every species of inconvenience and uncertainty has arisen. **1885** *Encycl. Brit.* XIX. 360/1 The real annual addition to the wealth of the community consists of the excess of the mass of agricultural products (including.. metals) over their cost of production. On the amount of this 'produit net' depends the wellbeing of the community. **1931** M. DOBB in W. Rose *Outl. Mod. Knowl.* xvi. 598 The essential definition of 'productive' as creative of surplus or *produit net*. **1965** SELDON & PENNANCE *Everyman's Dict. Econ.* 53 Cantillon's contention that only agricultural enterprises yield a surplus over the costs of production gave rise to the Physiocrats' concept of 'produit net'.

proe, obs. f. PROW *sb.*[2]; var. PROA (Malay boat).

†**proegumenal** (prəʊɪ'gjuːmɪnəl), *a. Obs.* [f. Gr. προηγούμεν-ος, pr. pple. of προηγεῖσθαι to lead, precede (see PRO-[2] and HEGUMEN) + -AL[1].] Preceding, predisposing; applied to an inward predisposing cause, as distinguished from the immediate or exciting cause. So †**proe'gumene**, †**proegu'menic**, †**proegu'menical**, †**proe'gumenous** *adjs.*, in same sense.

1638 MAYNE *Lucian* (1664) 389 Do you not understand that some of these things are proeg[u]menicall, others not proeg[u]menicall? **1654** Z. COKE *Logick* 51 The cause Proëgumene is Gods good will and love. **1656** JEANES *Fuln. Christ* 361 The inward, or proegumenall moving causes of the glory of believers come next to be considered, 1. Gods love of Christ, 2. Gods righteousnesse. **1697** Proegumenal [see PROCATARCTICAL]. **1711** tr. *Werenfels' Logomachys* 90 Aristotle, says he, divides..the Efficient Cause into the Procatarctick, Proegumenick, and Instrumental. **1822–34** Proegumenal [see PROCATARCTIC]. **1858** MAYNE *Expos. Lex.* 1020/1 Proegumenal: proegumenous.

pro-element: see PRO-[1] 4 b.

proem ('prəʊɪm), *sb.* Forms: 4–6 proheme, 5 -heim, 6 proëme, 6–7 prœme, 6–9 proeme, 7–8 proëm, 7–9 procœm, 6– proem. See also PROEMY, PROŒMIUM. [ME. *proheme*, a. OF. *pro(h)eme*

(14th c. in Godef. *Compl.*), mod.F. *proême*, ad. L. *prooemi-um* (Cic.), ad. Gr. προοίμιον an opening, prelude, f. πρό, PRO-² + οἶμος way, road, or ? οἴμη song, lay.]

An introductory discourse at the beginning of a book or other writing; a preface, preamble.

c **1386** CHAUCER *Clerk's Prol.* 43 (Harl. MS.) He first with heigh stile enditith..A proheme [*v.rr.* prohemye, -ie, prochem, procheyn] in the which descriuith he The mounde [*v.r.* Pemonde] and of Saluces þe contre. *c* **1475** *Partenay* 29 In the proheim off hys notabile boke. **1542** UDALL *Erasm. Apoph.* 64 As testifieth Cicero in the proheme of the offices. **1594** CAREW *Huarte's Exam. Wits* ix. (1596) 123 That doctrine of S. Hierome, which is found in his proem vpon Essay and Hierimie. **1655** STANLEY *Hist. Philos.* III. (1701) 120/2 Seven Books; each of which..hath a Procem, the whole none. **1731** SWIFT *On his Death* 71 Thus much may serve by way of proem; Proceed we therefore to our poem. **1765** BLACKSTONE *Comm.* I. Introd. ii. 60 The proeme, or preamble, is often called in to help the construction of an act of parliament. *a* **1861** MRS. BROWNING *Summing up in Italy* ix, I began too far off in my proem. **1882** FARRAR *Early Chr.* II. 404 The procem of the Gospel declared that 'the Word became flesh'.

b. The prefatory part of a speech or discourse; the preliminary remarks; an exordium.

1541 PAYNELL *Catiline* xii. 16 b, M. Cicero..called a great counsayle. He began with a proeme farre fetched, to declare the vengeable dryftes & mischeuous imaginations of Catiline. **1548** UDALL, etc. *Erasm. Par. Mark* x. 70 With this proheme Jesus discouraged the yong man. **1667** MILTON *P.L.* IX. 549 So gloz'd the Tempter, and his Proem tun'd. **1748** GEDDES *Comp. Antients* 84 The proem is the first part of an oration. **1865** GROTE *Plato* I. iii. 130 *note*, He sometimes..opened the debate by a procem or prefatory address in his own person.

c. *fig.* A commencement, beginning, prelude.

1641 M. FRANK *Serm., St. Paul's Day* (1672) 216 These yet are but the Proems of his mercy. **1788** H. WALPOLE *Remin.* Lett. 1857 I. p. xcii, The reign of George I was little more than the proem to the history of England under the House of Brunswick. **1874** H. R. REYNOLDS *John Bapt.* ii. 67 It then becomes part of a record which..does not shrink from the supernatural, the proem of a unique life.

†proem, -eme, *v. Obs. rare*⁻¹. [f. prec. sb.; cf. L. *prooemi-ārī* to make an introduction.] *trans.* To preface, introduce.

1658 SOUTH *Serm.* (1744) VIII. xiii. 367 Moses might.. very well proœme the repetition of the covenant with this upbraiding reprehension.

proembryo (prəʊ'ɛmbrɪəʊ). *Bot.* [a. G. (M. J. Schleiden *Grundzüge der Wissenschaftlichen Botanik* (1843) II. III. 52), f. PRO-² I + EMBRYO; so F. *proembryon.*] A term which has been applied to various structures of plants: e.g. to the *prothallus* of the Pteridophyta (Ferns, etc.); but more especially to embryonic structures, such as the *protonema* of Bryophyta (Mosses, etc.), and the embryos of certain Algae (e.g. *Chara, Batrachospermum*). In seed plants, the group of cells formed by the early divisions of the zygote after fertilization; also, a young embryo. Also *attrib.*

1849 LANKESTER tr. *Schleiden's Princ. Sci. Bot.* 174 (Mosses) The spore-cell expands, emerges from its torn outer coat, and, new cells being developed at the free end, forms for itself a filamentous tissue, composed of linear cylindrical cells ranged end to end (the *proembryo*). *Ibid.* 198. **1862** F. CURREY tr. *Hofmeister's On Germination of Higher Cryptogamia & Fructification of Coniferæ* xvi. 441 The breaking up of the pro-embryo of the Coniferæ into a number of independent suspensors is a phenomenon of the most peculiar kind. **1863** M. J. BERKELEY *Brit. Mosses* Gloss. 312 *Proembryo*, the same with cotyledonoids. (*Cotylenoid* = a term applied to the germinating threads of mosses.) **1875** BENNETT & DYER *Sachs's Bot.* 311 Mosses. The spore produces a conferva-like thallus, the Pro-embryo or Protonema. *Ibid.* 312. **1882** VINES *Sachs's Bot.* 292 *Characeæ.* As a consequence of fertilisation the large cell of the carpogonium becomes a resting spore, producing, by its germination, a pro-embryo from which the sexual plant springs as a lateral shoot. **1919** F. O. BOWER *Bot. Living Plant* xvii. 274 The very first division of the zygote stamps the polarity of the pro-embryo. **1950** D. A. JOHANSEN *Plant Embryol.* xii. 76 The young pro-embryo completely fills the archegonium in *Torreya taxifolia.* **1964** H. J. DITTMER *Phylogeny & Form in Plant Kingdom* xxiv. 587 Embryonic development in this plant [*sc.* tansy mustard] begins with a series of transverse divisions of the zygote forming a chain of proembryo cells. **1978** *Nature* 2 Feb. 441/1 Frequently only two seedlings germinate from a single seed and this suggests that only a small proportion of proembryos reach maturity.

Hence **proembry'onic** *a.*, of, pertaining to, or having the character of a proembryo.

1875 BENNETT & DYER *Sachs's Bot.* 282 (Characeæ) The Pro-embryonic Branches..have a similar structure to the pro-embryos which proceed from the spores... They have only been observed in *Chara fragilis.* **1888** HENSLOW *Orig. Floral Str.* 281 Even after fertilization the embryo cannot grow to maturity, but remains in the arrested proembryonic condition. **1957** H. C. BOLD *Morphol. Plants* xxvii. 522 All of the proembryonic cells descended from the zygote may begin to develop into embryos.

proemial (prəʊ'iːmɪəl), *a.* Also procemial. [f. L. *prooemi-um* PROEM + -AL¹.] Of, pertaining to, or of the nature of a proem; prefatory, introductory.

1447 BOKENHAM *Seyntys* (Roxb.) 136 Thine erys inclyne To prohemyal preyer wych I the made to. **1597** J. KING *On Jonas* (1618) 457 In this procemiall sentence. **1659** H. L'ESTRANGE *Alliance Div. Off.* 240 Baptism was never afforded to persons adult without Repentance, proemial and preparatory to it. **1750** JOHNSON *Rambler* No. 1 ¶3 The epick writers have found the proemial part of the poem such an addition to their undertaking. **1838–9** HALLAM *Hist. Lit.* IV. IV. iii. §15. 69 The Logic is introduced by two procemial books. **1841** *Blackw. Mag.* L. 629 Introduced by the chanter with a proemial address to some deity.

Hence **pro'emially** *adv.*, by way of introduction.

1898 F. DAVIS *Rom.-Brit. City Silchester* 29 A building not less interesting, and proemially far more potent.

†pro'emiate, *v. Obs. rare*⁻¹. In 6 **-hemiate.** [f. ppl. stem of L. *prooemiārī* to make a *prooemium* or PROEM.] *intr.* To write or compose a proem.

1568 H. CHARTERIS *Lyndesay's Wks.* Pref., It is the.. maner..of all thame quhilk dois prohemiate vpon ony vther mannis wark, cheiflie to trauel about twa pointis.

‖**proemptosis** (prəʊɛm(p)'təʊsɪs). *Chronol.* [mod.L., f. PRO-² + ἔμπτωσις a falling in or on: cf. προεμπίπτειν to fall on before: cf. METEMPTOSIS.] An anticipation or occurrence of a natural event earlier than the time given by a rule; esp. the occurrence of the new moon earlier than the Metonic cycle or 19 years' period would make it; also, loosely applied to the lunar equation or correction necessary to bring the calendar into agreement with the actual new moon.

The name *proemptosis* had reference to the Julian Calendar, according to which the actual new moon occurred ·06 day earlier than the 19-year cycle provided; in 19 tropical years and their approximation in the Gregorian Calendar the new moon occurs ·09 day later than provided for by the cycle.

1727–41 CHAMBERS *Cycl.*, *Proemptosis*, in astronomy, that which makes the new moons appear a day later, by means of the lunar equation, than they would do without that equation.

†proemy. *Obs.* In 4–5 **prohemy(e, -ie.** [ad. L. *prooemi-um* PROEM.] = PROEM *sb.*

1382 WYCLIF *Esther* (Apocr.) xii. 6 gloss., Hider to the prohemy [**1388** prohemye]; thoo thingus, that folewen, in that place weren put, wher is write in the volume [etc.]. *c* **1386** CHAUCER *Clerk's Prol.* 43 (Ellesmere) First..he enditeth..A prohemye [*Hengwrt* prohemie]. **1484** CAXTON *Fables of Æsop* ii, The prohemye of the second book of fables.

proenzyme (prəʊ'ɛnzaɪm). *Biochem.* [f. PRO-² I + ENZYME.] The inactive precursor of an enzyme; = ZYMOGEN.

1900 in DORLAND *Med. Dict.* **1902** C. A. HERTER *Lect. Chem. Path.* viii. 254 The glandular cells from which they [*sc.* enzymes] come apparently do not hold them in any considerable quantity, but contain substances called proënzymes, from which they are produced. *Ibid.*, These proënzymes, pepsinagen and rennet zymogen. **1976** *Nature* 22 Jan. 235/2 Plasminogen is the plasma proenzyme which, on conversion to its active form, plasmin, is considered responsible for lysis of fibrin deposits resulting from physiological or pathological activation of the coagulation cascade.

pro-epimeral to **pro-episternum:** see PRO-².

proer, obs. f. PRORE *sb.*, prow.

proerythroblast: see PRO-² I.

proes, -esse, obs. ff. PROWESS.

proese, obs. f. PROSE.

proestasy, erron. f. PROSTASY.

pro-estrus, var. *pro-œstrum* s.v. PRO-² I.

pro-'ethnic, *a.* [PRO-¹ and ².] **1.** *Philol.* Anterior to the division of the primitive Aryans into separate nations or peoples, or of any people or race into separate tribes.

1864 MAX MÜLLER *Sc. Lang.* (1868) 383 Ser. II. viii. Deriving both from a common Aryan or pro-ethnic source. **1887** R. S. CONWAY *Verner's Law in Italy* §5 Medial s between vowels..became voiced (z) in pro-ethnic Italic. **1906** J. H. MOULTON *Gram. N.T. Gk.* I. ix. 221 The Greek participle..represents the proëthnic participle. **1935** G. K. ZIPF *Psycho-Biol. of Lang.* iv. 162 The shift in accent which took place in almost every Indo-European dialect after the pro-ethnic parent language broke up into its dialects.

2. Favouring the Gentiles, as opp. to the Jews. *rare.*

1920 R. HARRIS *Testimonies* II. ii. 13 Propagating by testimonies a Gospel which is at once pro-ethnic and anti-Judaic.

Hence **pro-'ethnically** *adv.*

1920 R. HARRIS *Testimonies* II. ii. 16 As it is written: Father of many nations (ἐθνῶν) have I set thee... The extract from Genesis turns on the use of the word ἐθνῶν, and the words are used pro-ethnically.

proette (prəʊ'ɛt). [f. PRO *abbrev.* + -ETTE.] A female professional golfer.

1968 *Maclean's Mag.* Sept. 39 For obvious reasons, the LPGA objects to its members being called 'pro' golfers, and is trying to popularize the description 'proettes'. **1969** *Sunday Times* 5 Oct. 20 Even a lady 'proette' has lost the US Women's Open through signing for a correct total but a 5 and a 4 when she meant a 4 and a 5. **1971** *Time* 28 June 41 And while no proette has ever topped $50,000 for a season, Jack Nicklaus for one has picked up that much in a single tournament. **1975** *Auckland* (N.Z.) *Star* 18 Jan. 35 Two Australian proettes started the second round of the Benson & Hedges $7000 women's golf classic..today in fine style... New Zealand proette Marilyn Smith..turned in 37.

ˌpro-Euro'pean, *sb.* and *a.* [PRO-¹ 5 a.]

A. *sb.* One who favours or supports Europe or other European countries; *spec.*, a supporter of (British membership of) the European Economic Community. **B.** *adj.* Favouring or supporting Europe or other European countries; *spec.*, supporting (British membership of) the European Economic Community.

1944 *Sun* (Baltimore) 8 July 6/4 An even more rhetorical appeal was issued on the same day by the *PPF*..('pro-European'). **1962** *Guardian* 10 July 18/7 The Liberals alone have a consistently pro-European tradition. **1963** *Ann. Reg. 1962* 35 The pro-Europeans in the country were a majority of the under-45s, of the over-£25 a week men.., and of those educated past the age of 16. **1969** *Time* 4 July 23 Maurice Schumann, 58, Minister of Foreign Affairs, combines impeccable Gaullist credentials with a pro-European outlook. **1970** *Manch. Guardian Weekly* 4 Apr. 8 A strongly pro-European speech from Mr Roy Hattersley, the Minister of Defence. **1971** *New Yorker* 3 July 64 The highly uncertain future if Britain does not go into Europe has not yet been adequately explained or understood, according to some anxious pro-Europeans. **1979** *Guardian* 28 Apr. 32/2 A tougher line on Europe may upset the more pro-European wing of her party.

proeve, obs. f. PROVE *v.*

prof (prɒf). Also †*U.S.* proff. (Colloq.) abbrev. of PROFESSOR 4. Also *attrib.*

1838 *Yale Lit. Mag.* Feb. 144 For Proffs and Tutors too, Who steer our big canoe, Prepare their lays. **1859** G. H. LEWES *Jrnl.* 14 July in *Geo. Eliot Lett.* (1954) III. 116 At Berne I called on Prof. Schiff. **1888** *Athenæum* 30 June 830/3 Prof. Bell exhibited..a specimen of a tube-forming actonian ..in its tube. **1916** H. L. WILSON *Somewhere in Red Gap* ii. 74, I bet Wilbur thinks the prof is awful old-fashioned, playing with his fingers that way. **1933** AUDEN *Dance of Death* 8 With profs. from Germany. **1949** H. WADMAN *Life Sentence* 16 Prof, how are you? You don't look a day older. **1967** O. WYND *Walk Softly* iv. 42 It's certainly not the local practice at prof level. Heads of departments come near to be living gods. **1975** C. FREMLIN *Long Shadow* x. 79 You were at the reception desk, phoning up to the Prof.'s room. **1979** L. MEYNELL *Hooky & Villainous Chauffeur* xi. 150 Don't call me *Prof*; it's an abbreviation I find particularly distasteful.

prof, obs. f. PROOF, PROVE.

†pro'face, *int.* and *sb. Obs.* [a. obs. F. *prou fasse!* in full *bon prou vous fasse!* (also as sb. *prouface*, 1588 in Godef.) 'may it do you good'; f. *prou* PROW¹ + *fasse* (3rd pers. sing. pres. subj. of *faire* to do):—L. *faciat*; cf. PROFICIAT.]

A. *int.* or *phrase.* A formula of welcome or good wishes at a dinner or other meal, equivalent to 'may it do you good', 'may it be to your advantage'.

1515 BARCLAY *Egloges* iii. (1570) C iij/1 A naturall foole of reason dull and rude, Proface Coridon, thus do I here conclude. **1575** LANEHAM *Let.* (1871) 5 Thus proface ye with the Preface. **1580** STOW *Chron.* 955 Before the second course, the Cardinall came in booted and spurred, all sodainely amongest them, and bade them *Proface.* **1597** SHAKS. *2 Hen. IV*, v. iii. 30 Master Page, good M. Page, sit: Proface. **1630** J. TAYLOR (Water P.) *Praise Hempseed* Wks. III. 61 Proface my Masters, if your stomackes serue. **1638** HEYWOOD *Wise Woman* IV. i. Wks. 1874 V. 335 The dinner's halfe done, and before I say Grace, and bid the old Knight and his guest proface.

B. *sb.* A salutation or good wish in drinking, a toast drunk to a person's health. *rare.*

1586 B. YOUNG *Guazzo's Civ. Conv.* IV. 195 This speech makes me think..yᵗ we haue ended our taske, and are now come to the last Proface.

pro'fanable, *a. rare.* [f. PROFANE *v.* + -ABLE.] Liable to be profaned.

1891 *Longm. Mag.* Apr. 623 Something..that was profanable by publicity.

†'profanate, *v. Obs.* Also proph-. [f. ppl. stem of L. *profānāre* to PROFANE: see -ATE³. For *proph-* see PROFANE *a.*] *trans.* To profane.

1526 TONSTALL *Proclam.* 23 Oct., in Foxe *A. & M.* (1576) 990/2 By their wicked and peruerse interpretations, to prophanate the maiestye of the Scripture. *a* **1560** BECON *Humble Supplic.* Wks. II. 19 The wycked Papistes prophanate and vnhallowe these two aforesayde holy Sacramentes. **1570** FOXE *A. & M.* (ed. 2) 555 There..[he] hath in contempt of yᵉ keyes, presumed of his own rashnes to celebrate, nay rather to prophanate.

†profa'natic, *a. Obs. nonce-wd.* [app. f. PROFANE, with word-play on FANATIC.] Infatuated with profanity.

1689 T. PLUNKET *Char. Gd. Commander* 53 What a strange Prophanatick Age is this, When Truth is scorn'd, and falshood courted is?

profanation (prɒfə'neɪʃən). Also 6–8 proph-. [Early mod.E. a. OF. *prophanation* (15th c. in Hatz.-Darm., mod.F. *prof-*), or ad. late L. *profānātiō n-em* (Tert.), n. of action f. *profān-āre* to PROFANE.]

The action of profaning; desecration or violation of that which is sacred; defilement, pollution.

1552 *Bk. Com. Prayer, Communion,* That the Communicants knelyng shoulde receyue the holye Communion..to auoyde the prophanacion and dysordre which..myght els ensue. **1685** BAXTER *Paraphr. N.T.* 1 Cor. xi. 34 Lest your prophanation of so holy a thing bring down God's Judgments on you. **1790** BURKE *Fr. Rev.* 136 To preserve the structure from prophanation and ruin. **1803** R. HALL *Wks.* (1833) I. 176 In no nation..has the profanation of sacred terms been so prevalent. **1877** FROUDE *Short Stud.* (1883) IV. I. xi. 131 A wall was built round the tomb to protect it from profanation.

b. By extension: The degradation or vulgarization of anything worthy of being held in reverence or respect; cheapening by familiarity.

1588 *Marprel. Epist.* (Arb.) 49 You haue ioyned the prophanation of the magistracie, to the corruption of the ministerie. *a***1631** DONNE *Poems* (1650) 41 'Twere prophanation of our joyes To tell the layitie our love. **1780** COWPER *Table-t.* 758 [Poetry] Distorted from its use and just design, To make the pitiful possessor shine,..Is profanation of the basest kind. **1825** COLERIDGE *Aids Refl.* 54 About this time too the profanation of the word, Love, rose to its height. **1862** BURTON *Bk. Hunter* (1863) 225 This morbid terror of the profanation of the treasures committed to their charge.

profanatory (prəʊˈfænətərɪ), *a.* [f. as PROFANATE + -ORY.] That tends to profane; profaning.

1853 C. BRONTE *Villette* xxv, Every one now had tasted the wassail-cup, except Paulina, whose *pas de fée ou de fantasie* nobody thought of interrupting to offer so profanatory a draught.

profane (prəʊˈfeɪn), *a.* (*sb.*) Also 6 prophan, 6–7 -phain(e, 6–8 -phane. [a. obs. F. *prophane* (1228 in Godef. *Compl.*), mod.F. *profane*, ad. L. *profān-us*, in med.L. also *prophān-us*, lit. 'before (i.e. outside) the temple', hence 'not sacred, common'; also, 'impious': see PRO-[1] and FANE[2].

The spelling *proph-* (in med.L., Fr., and Eng.), evidently due to erroneous imitation of such words from Gr. as *prophēta*, *phantasia* (see note under PH), occurs as early as 1025 in *prophānāre* (Du Cange). *Prophane* was the ordinary spelling in Eng. down to 1750, and occurs as late as 1795. So the derivatives, *prophaneness*, *prophanity*, etc.]

1. Not pertaining or devoted to what is sacred or biblical, esp. in ***profane history***, ***literature***; unconsecrated, secular, lay, common; civil, as distinguished from ecclesiastical.

1483 *Rolls of Parlt.* VI. 241/1 The said..Mariage was made privaly and secretely,..in a private Chamber, a prophane place. **1549** *Latimer's 2nd Serm. bef. Edw. VI* To Rdr. (Arb.) 49 We myghte as well spende that tyme in reading of prophane hystories, of cantorburye tales, or a fit of Roben Hode. **1570** FOXE *A. & M.* (ed. 2) 555 In a certeyne chappell not hallowed, or rather in a prophane cotage. **1581** W. STAFFORD *Exam. Compl.* i. (1876) 26 Scholers that came to learne his prophane sciences. **1609** SKENE *Reg. Maj.*, *Forme of Proces* 109 b, All civill actions, that hes not *fidei*, *vel juramenti interpositionem*, are civill, and profane: and therefore perteines not to the Ecclesiasticall jurisdiction. **1614** RALEIGH *Hist. World* II. (1634) 268 If there be any truth in prophaine antiquitie. **1718** *Free-thinker* No. 6 ¶3 The most celebrated Examples of an Heroical Death in Prophane Story, are, Socrates amongst the Greeks [etc.]. **1678** BUNYAN *Pilg. Prog.* I. 104 What you will; I will talk of..things Sacred, or things Prophane. **1726** LEONI *Alberti's Archit.* 83/1 Things sacred..appertain to the public worship:..things profane..regard the welfare and good of the Society. **1788** PRIESTLEY *Lect. Hist.* II. xii. 100 The best guide to the knowledge of prophane history. **1875** SCRIVENER *Lect. Text N. Test.* 4 Not of the Bible only, but of those precious remains of profane literature.

b. Of persons: *orig.* Not initiated into the religious rites or sacred mysteries; *transf.* not participating in or admitted to some esoteric knowledge; uninitiated, 'lay', Philistine.

1616 B. JONSON *Hymenæi* Wks. (Rtldg.) 553/1 Bid all profane away; None here may stay To view our mysteries. *a***1667** COWLEY tr. *Horace's Odes* III. i. Hence, ye Prophane; I hate ye all; Both the Great Vulgar, and the Small. **1697** DRYDEN *Æneid* VI. 368 Far hence be souls profane (The Sibyl cried). **1764** FOOTE *Patron* II. Wks. 1799 I. 350 The ignorant, the profane (by much the majority), will be apt to think it an occupation ill suited to my time of life. **1866** HOWELLS *Venet. Life* 147 No one profane to the profession of artist ever acquired a just notion of any picture by reading. **1875** JOWETT *Plato* (ed. 2) II. 69 Let the attendants and other profane persons close the doors of their ears.

2. Applied to persons or things regarded as unholy or as desecrating what is holy or sacred: unhallowed; ritually unclean or polluted; esp. said of the rites of an alien religion: heathen, pagan.

1500–20 DUNBAR *Poems* lxvi. 35 The ayr infectit and prophane [*v.r.* profane]. **1560** BIBLE (Genev.) *Heb.* xii. 16 Let there be no fornicator, or prophane persone as Esau, which for a portion of meat solde his byrth right. **1596** DALRYMPLE tr. *Leslie's Hist. Scot.* II. 135 *margin*, Tempilis ..to prophane Godis. *Ibid.* III. 188 Prophane rites of the Ethnikis. **1606** CHAPMAN *Monsieur D'Olive* II. Plays 1873 I. 215 Said [of tobacco] 'twas a pagan plant, a prophane weede And a most sinful smoke. **1609** BIBLE (Douay) *Isa.* lxv. 4 A people..that eate swines flesh, and profane pottage in their vessels. **1632** SANDERSON *Serm.* 16 Hypocrites, and vnsanctified and prophane, and such as are in the state of damnation. **1697** DRYDEN *Virg. Georg.* II. 670 Nor are the Gods ador'd with Rights prophane. **1738** WESLEY *Ps.* XLV. ix, Nothing profane can dwell with Thee. **1878** MACLEAR *Celts* ix. 147 [He] was rewarded by seeing many won from their profane rites.

3. Characterized by disregard or contempt of sacred things, esp., in later use, by the taking of God's name in vain; irreverent, blasphemous, ribald; impious, irreligious, wicked.

*c***1560** A. SCOTT *Poems* (S.T.S.) xxxiv. 47 3oʳ prettikes ar profane, Puir ladeis to supplant. **1666** JER. TAYLOR *Serm.*, *Whole Duty Clergy* ii. 202 He is a prophane person who neglects the exterior part of Religion: and this is so vile a crime, that hypocrisie while it is undiscovered is not so much mischievous as open prophaneness, or a neglect and contempt of external Religion. **1666–7** MARVELL *Corr.* Wks. (Grosart) II. 210 The Bill against Atheism and prophane Swearing we have sent up to the Lords. **1722** DE FOE *Relig. Courtsh.* I. i. (1840) 28 We need no profane husbands to keep us back: a loose, irreligious husband, is a dreadful snare. **1755** JOHNSON, *Profane*, irreverent to sacred names or things. **1841** W. SPALDING *Italy & It. Isl.* III. 271 The Testament of this personage, which may usually be purchased at any stall,..is a very profane production.

B. *absol.* or as *sb.* One who is profane.

(The first example may be the pl. of the adj. as in Fr.; the last is a Gallicism.)

*a***1529** SKELTON *Col. Cloute* 208 Howe some of you do eate In Lenton season fleshe mete,..Men call you therfor prophanes. **1596** HARINGTON *Metam. Ajax* (1814) 6 Who can stand against such an army of emperors, kings, magistrates, prophets, all-hallows, all-prophanes,..as are by him brought for enobling his arguments? **1891** M. O'RELL *Frenchm. in Amer.* 294 They will declare you a profane, unworthy to live.

profane (prəʊˈfeɪn), *v.* Also 4–8 prophane. [ME. *prophane* = OF. *prophaner* (1486 in Godef. *Compl.*), mod.F. *profaner*, ad. L. *profānāre*, in med.L. *prophānāre* to render unholy, desecrate, violate, disclose, f. *profān-us* PROFANE *a.*]

1. *trans.* To treat (what is sacred) with irreverence, contempt, or disregard; to desecrate, violate.

1382 WYCLIF *Ezek.* xxiii. 38 Thei prophaneden [*gloss* or maden vnhoolī] my sabotis. **1545** JOYE *Exp. Dan.* iii. 35 He commandeth..to prophane their places and tabernacles euen to make them lothely and abominable. **1611** BIBLE *Lev.* xix. 12 Ye shall not sweare by my Name falsly, neither shalt thou prophane the Name of thy God: I am the Lord. **1623** COCKERAM, *Profane*, to put holy things to a common vse. **1715** DE FOE *Fam. Instruct.* I. v. (1841) I. 97 You have been guilty of profaning the Lord's day. **1795** *Gentl. Mag.* July 542/1 [In France] where licentiousness, prophaning the sacred name of liberty, has gloried in the destruction of order. **1854** MILMAN *Lat. Chr.* IV. viii. (1864) II. 379 Feasts and revels profaned the most hallowed sanctuaries. **1875** JOWETT *Plato* (ed. 2) V. 487 It is an excellent rule not lightly to profane the names of the Gods.

b. To misuse, abuse (what ought to be held in reverence or respect); to violate, defile, pollute.

1563 WINȜET *Wks.* (S.T.S.) II. 21 Mariit women defilit, wedowis spulȝeit, virginis prophanit. **1597** SHAKS. *2 Hen. IV*, II. iv. 391, I feele me much to blame, So idly to prophane the precious time. **1685** *Pennsylv. Archives* I. 94 Least men prophain Government by an unhallowed use of it. **1716** GAY *Trivia* I. 75 Imprudent Men Heav'ns choicest Gifts prophane. **1844** DISRAELI *Coningsby* VII. v, There was no malicious gossip, no callous chatter to profane his ear. **1871** R. ELLIS *Catullus* lxii. 55 (46) Once her body profan'd, her flow'r of chastity blighted.

†**c.** To make (anything of value) the property of the vulgar crowd; to vulgarize. *Obs. rare*$^{-1}$.

1643 SIR T. BROWNE *Relig. Med.* II. §4 Well understanding that wisdome is not prophan'd unto the World, and 'tis the priviledge of a few to be Vertuous.

2. *absol.* or *intr.* To act or speak profanely; to blaspheme. *rare.*

1690 PENN *Rise & Progr. Quakers* i. (1694) 27 They grew very troublesome to the better sort of People, and furnished the looser with an occasion to Profane.

Hence **proˈfaned** *ppl. a.*, **proˈfaning** *vbl. sb.* and *ppl. a.*

*c***1440** *Pallad. on Husb.* I. 847 Myn auctour eek,..Seith this prophaned thyng may nought auaile. **1548** RECORDE *Urin. Physick* Pref. (1651) 7 It is a profaining of learning, and a meanes to bring it into contempt. **1839–52** BAILEY *Festus* 205 Scenes..Of senseless and profaning mirth. **1871** R. ELLIS *Catullus* xv. 14 But should impious heat or humour headstrong Drive thee wilfully, wretch, to such profaning. **1884** BLACK *Jud. Shaks.* iii, The profaning of sacred places will bring a punishment.

†**proˈfaneling, proph-.** *Obs. rare*$^{-1}$. [f. PROFANE *a.* + -LING.] One given to profanity.

*a***1640** W. FENNER *Spir. Man's Direct.* (1649) 55 As if drunkards, and whore-masters, and Atheists, and prophanelings, were holyer than they.

profanely (prəʊˈfeɪnlɪ), *adv.* Also 6–8 proph-. [f. PROFANE *a.* + -LY[2].] In a profane manner; by profanation; irreverently, impiously.

1577 tr. *Bullinger's Decades* (1592) 367 Sacrifices to be made..with holy fire, and not with strange fire, or fire profanely kindled. *c***1586** C'TESS PEMBROKE *Ps.* LXXIX. i, Thy temple..is now prophanely stained. **1653** LAMONT *Diary* (Bann.) 56 He was cast of for profainlie taking the name of the diuill in his mouthe twyse, especiallie vpon the last Sabath the communion was given in Largo. **1712** STEELE *Spect.* No. 298 ¶3 What they profanely term Conjugal Liberty of Conscience. **1728** YOUNG *Love Fame* I. 179 The bailiffs come (rude men, prophanely bold!) **1855** PRESCOTT *Philip II*, I. II. xii. 276 The holy oil was profanely used to anoint their shoes and sandals.

proˈfanement. *rare.* [f. PROFANE *v.* + -MENT.] = PROFANATION.

1815 MOORE *Let. to Lady Donegal* 3 July in *Mem.* (1856) VIII. 197, I rather think you would burn it to the ground after such profanement.

profaneness (prəʊˈfeɪnɪs). Also 6–8 proph-; 6–7 prophanness(e; *β.* 6–8 proph-, profaness. [f. PROFANE *a.* + -NESS. For the *β* form see note under -NESS.] The quality or fact of being profane or unholy, or of openly violating what is sacred; profanity; profane conduct or speech. With *a* and *pl.*, an instance of this. (Now somewhat *rare.*)

1594 T. B. *La Primaud. Fr. Acad.* II. To Rdr., Seeing the generall prophannesse of mens liues almost euery where. **1611** SHAKS. *Wint. T.* III. ii. 155 Apollo pardon My great prophanenesse 'gainst thine Oracle. **1650** TRAPP *Comm. Lev.* xix. 19 All the prodigious errors, lies,..and prophanenesses in the world. **1736** BUTLER *Anal.* II. vi. 224 Profaneness and avowed Disregard to all Religion. **1884** *Law Times Rep.* 19 Apr. 239/1 It seemed almost a profaneness to administer the oath of canonical obedience in the sense in which he was prepared to take it.

β. **1597** BEARD *Theatre God's Judgem.* (1612) 205 To be thus vsed for his vile prophanesse and abusing his holie things. **1633** PRYNNE *Histriomastix* 520 Stage-playes are the Lectures, the Marts, the common treasuries of all ribaldry, scurrility, prophanesse. **1649** FULLER *Just Man's Funeral* 26 Wicked men, persisting in their profaness. *c***1710** EDWARDS in *Camb. Antiq. Soc. Commun.* III. 133 Which at an other time is reckoned to be Prophaness.

profaner (prəʊˈfeɪnə(r)). [f. PROFANE *v.* + -ER[1].] One who profanes; a desecrator, violator, defiler.

*a***1572** KNOX *Hist. Ref.* III. (1586) 462 Prophaners of thy holy name. **1670** G. H. *Hist. Cardinals* III. I. 239 These were such as declar'd him a Heretick,..a Profaner, and so forth. *a***1861** W. CUNNINGHAM *Hist. Theol.* I. viii. 238 Intruders into the sacred office and profaners of sacred things.

proˈfanish, *a. rare.* [f. PROFANE *a.* + -ISH[1].] Somewhat profane. Hence **proˈfanishness.**

1675 T. DUFFETT *Mock Tempest* V. i, He is sweetly in his Scourge-stick of Prophanishness.

†**ˈprofanism, proph-.** *Obs. rare*$^{-1}$. [f. L. *profān-us* PROFANE + -ISM, or f. OF. *prophaniser* to PROFANIZE.] Profaneness, profanity.

1607 MARSTON *What you will* IV. i, Bee it spoken without prophanisme, hee hath more in this traine.

profanity (prəʊˈfænɪtɪ). [ad. late L. *profānitās* (Tertull.): see PROFANE *a.* and -ITY; so OF. *prophanite* (a single instance of 1492 in Godef.).

App. in no Eng. dictionary before the 19th c.; not in Todd's Johnson 1818; added by Jodrell 1820, citing quot. 1813. In Webster 1828. Smart 1836–49 says 'Little authorized'; referring to which, Worcester 1846 says 'It is in common use in America and in Scotland, and it is also used by respectable English authors'. But examples occur both in Eng. and Sc. writers from 1607, though *profaneness* was the usual word with the former down to 1800.]

The quality or condition of being profane; profaneness; profane conduct or speech; in *pl.* profane words or acts.

1607 J. CARPENTER *Plaine Mans Plough* iii. 24 Iniustice, the generall voyce of all malice,..profanity, impiety, naughtinesse and vice. **1621** BP. MOUNTAGU *Diatribæ* 13 Comparison..betwixt these ridiculous prophanities, and your so much admired History. **1637–50** ROW *Hist. Kirk* (Wodrow Soc.) 174 The people perish in ignorance, atheisme, and profanitie. **1699** *Proper Project for Scot.* 28 The avowed and open Profanity..overspreading the whole land. **1763** MRS. HARRIS in *Priv. Lett. Ld. Malmesbury* (1870) I. 101 Lord Temple..could not justify his [Wilkes's] profanity, but thought the seizing of his papers a wrong thing. **1805** *Spirit Pub. Jrnls.* IX. 267 This very seasonable exertion of the law against profanity. **1813** *Edin. Rev.* July 283 There is a tone of blackguardism—(we really can find no other word)—both in his indecency and his profanity. *a***1849** H. COLERIDGE *Ess.* (1851) II. 63 The sacrilegious profanity of his adulation. **1853** MISS YONGE *Heir of Redclyffe* xxxix, He felt it a sort of profanity to disturb her. **1875** GLADSTONE *Glean.* (1879) VI. xliv. 132 Indecency in public worship is acted profanity and is grossly irreligious in its effects.

profanize (ˈprɒfənaɪz), *v. rare*$^{-1}$. [f. PROFANE *a.* + -IZE: cf. OF. *prophaniser* (Godef.).] *trans.* = PROFANE *v.*

*c***1873** J. ADDIS *Elizabethan Echoes* (1879) 92 How he put poison in the Sacred Chalice, And profanized the Holy Mysteries.

So †**proˈfanizate** *v.*, in same sense. *Obs. rare*$^{-1}$.

1578 FLORIO *1st Fruites* 73 The ende of warre is this.. churches are profanizated and sacrileged.

pro-Fascist: see PRO-[1] 5 a.

profe, obs. f. PROOF, PROVE.

profecie, obs. f. PROPHESY *v.*

profect, obs. by-form of PROFIT *sb.*

profection (prəʊˈfɛkʃən). Now *rare.* [Partly a. F. *profection* a progression, in Astrol. (1510 in Godef.), f. L. *prōfect-*, ppl. stem of *prōfic-ĕre* to put forward, go forward, advance, progress; partly ad. L. *profectiōn-em* a setting out, n. of action f. *proficisci* to set out, start.]

I. 1. The action or fact of going forward; progression, advance. *Obs.* exc. *Astrol.*

1597 J. KING *On Jonas* (1618) 225 The great vessell of election..confesseth his profection and going forward; I endeauour my selfe to that which is before. **1609** W. SCLATER *Threefold Preserv.* (1610) B iv b, In the state of this mortal life, there is no meane betwixt profection and defection. **1646** Sir T. Browne *Pseud. Ep.* iv. xii. (1650) 187 Which together with other Planets, and profection of the Horoscope, unto the seventh house, or opposite signes every seventh year, oppresseth living natures. **1652** Wharton *Rothman's Chirom.* Wks. (1683) 638 The Profection, or Revolution of the Sun, comes to the Opposition of Mars, in the year 1600. about the 20 of November. **1819** J. Wilson *Compl. Dict. Astrol.* 326 *Profection*, the progression.

†**b.** The degree of advancement attained; proficiency. *Obs.*

1605 Bacon *Adv. Learn.* i. Ded. to King §2 There seemeth to be no lesse contention betweene the excellencie of your Maiesties gifts of Nature and the universalitie and profection of your learning. **1615** T. Adams *White Devill* Ep. Ded., Your affection to divine knowledge, good profection in it, and much time spent towards the perfection of it. **1631** Heywood *London's Jus Hon.* Wks. 1874 IV. 278 If Kings arrive to my profection Tis by Succession, or Election.

†**2.** A setting forward in process or rank; furtherance, advancement. *Obs.*

a **1540** Cromwell in Burnet *Hist. Ref.* (1681) II. 191 Their said Promotions or Profections into the same [Bishoprics]. **1657** J. Watts *Dipper Sprinkled* 83 The better propagation and profection of the Divine truth.

II. †**3.** A setting out, setting forth, starting. *Obs.*

1598 Hakluyt *Voy.* I. 288 The time of the yeere hasting the profection and departure of the Ambassador. **1652** Gaule *Magastrom.* 303 In his profection into Africa, as he went out of the ship, he chanced to fall flat upon the ground.

Hence † **pro'fectional** *a.*, *Astrol.*, of or relating to 'profection' or progression.

1647 Lilly *Chr. Astrol.* clvii. 655 To consider with which of them, the Profectionall Figure, or of the Revolution, doth agree. **1647** Wharton *Merlini Angl. Errata* Wks. (1683) 297, I have considered the Profectional Figure of the last Conjunction of Saturn and Jupiter.

profec'titious, *a. Rom. Law.* Also -icious. [f. late L. *profectīci-us, -ītius* that proceeds from some one (f. *profect-*, ppl. stem of *proficīscī*: see prec.) + -ous.] That proceeds or is derived from a parent or ancestor. Opposed to *adventitious*.

1656 in Blount *Glossogr.* **1788** Gibbon *Decl. & F.* xliv. IV. 372 The threefold distinction of profectitious, adventitious, and professional, was ascertained. **1880** Muirhead *Ulpian* vi. §3 A dowry is either profecticious, given by the woman's father, or adventicious, given by some other person.

pro'fective, *a. Rom. Law.* [a. F. *profectif, -ive* (legal), f. L. *profect-*: see prec. and -ive.] = prec.

1795 tr. *Mercier's Fragm. Pol. & Hist.* I. 163 We have our distinctions of goods moveable, immoveable, profective.

pro'fer, *v.*[1] *Obs.* or *rare arch.* Also 4 profre, 4–7 'profer, 6 proferre. [app. a. F. *proférer* (13th c. in Brunet Lat.), recorded in sense 'utter, pronounce, *dire tout haut*' (see sense 3 here), = Pr. *proferre*, Cat. *proferer*, It. *profferire* (†*proferire*, Florio) to utter, pronounce, speak, ad. L. *profer-re* to bring forth, produce, utter, bring forward, adduce, also (rarely) to offer, proffer. From the interchange of *f* and *ff*, often confused in form, and sometimes app. in sense, with *proffer*, to which sense 1 may even belong. It is only in later examples that *profer* distinctly appears.]

†**1.** *trans.* To put forth, extend; in first quot. *intr.* for *refl.* to project. *Obs.*

13.. *E.E. Allit. P.* B. 1463 Pinnacles pyȝt þer apert þat profert bitwene. **1377** Langl. *P. Pl.* B. xvii. 141 Þe paume is purely þe hande and profreth forth þe fyngres To mynystre and to make. **1578** Banister *Hist. Man* vii. 97 This inferiour trunke..out of his hynder part profereth Arteries to the spaces of the ribbes.

†**2.** To bring forth, produce, yield. *Obs.*

c **1425** *Found. St. Bartholomew's* (E.E.T.S.) 42 Neyr the tyme that the fruyt shulde be proferid forthe. **1450–1530** *Myrr. our Ladye* 232 The fruyteful moder hathe profered a byrthe. **1600** Hakluyt *Voy.* (1810) III. 249 The said Islands..seem to proffer..plenty of all kinde of our graine.

3. To bring out (words), utter, pronounce. Now *rare*.

c **1400** *Destr. Troy* 1096 When the peopull were pesit, he proffert þes wordes. **1483** Caxton *Gold. Leg.* 432/1 He comyng to the last houre,..and profferyng the laste wordes I commend my sowle in to thyn handes deyed. *c* **1489** —— *Blanchardyn* xxxiv. 125 After many wordes proferred & sayde. *a* **1500** in *Arnolde's Chron.* (1811) 273 Whether priestis can proferre [*printed* proforre] the wordis off the canon and baptym. **1580** Hollyband *Treas. Fr. Tong, Prolation*, pronouncing or profering of wordes. **1830** W. Taylor *Hist. Surv. Germ. Poetry* I. 129 Not a word Had either of us yet proferr'd.

†**4.** To bring or put near or into contact with something; to present. *Obs.*

1523 Fitzherb. *Husb.* §138 Than proferre thy graffe in-to the stocke. **1698** Ballard in *Phil. Trans.* XX. 418, I took my Knife,..and profering it to the Needle, it drew the North Pole.

†**pro'fer, -'ferre**, *v.*[2] *Obs.* [? a. OF. *proferer* = *préferer* (Godef. *Compl.*).] A by-form of (or ? error for) prefer *v.* (see pro-[1] 3); to promote, advance. Hence † **pro'ferring** *vbl. sb.*

1462 J. Paston in *P. Lett.* II. 114 For good will that the seid Sir John Fastolff had to the proferryng of your seid besecher. *a* **1500** in *Arnolde's Chron.* Tiv, Euery trew counceler..ought..to..promote encrece proferre and auaunce the wele and prosperyte of his lorde.

profer, -ere, -erre, obs. forms of proffer.

‖**proferens** (prəʊ'fɛrɛnz). *Law.* Pl. proferentes (prəʊfɛ'rɛntiːz). [L., pres. pple. of *proferre* to offer, adduce.] The party which proposes or adduces a contract or a condition in a contract. Also in phr. ***contra proferentem***, or *-es*, used of legal decisions made 'against the proposer(s)', with reference to the maxim *verba cartarum fortius accipiuntur contra proferentem*, 'the words of contracts should be interpreted most forcibly against him who adduces them'.

[*a* **1626** Bacon *Elem. Common Lawes Eng.* (1630) i. 11 *Verba fortius accipiuntur contra proferentem.* This rule that a mans deedes and his words shall be taken strongliest against himselfe,..is..a rule drawn out of the depth of reason. **1766** Blackstone *Comm.* II. xxiii. 380 That the deed be taken most strongly against him that is the agent or contractor, and in favour of the other party. '*Verba fortius accipiuntur contra proferentem.*'] **1927** *Times Law Reports* 3 June 528/2 At the least the expression was ambiguous and must be construed *contra proferentem.* **1935** *Lloyd's List Law Rep.* 9 May 306/1 In this case the underwriters were not the *proferentes.* **1947** J. Charlesworth *Law of Negligence* (ed. 2) xxix. 617 The Court of Appeal held that the word..was ambiguous and must be construed *contra proferentem.* **1971** R. A. Percy *Charlesworth on Negligence* (ed. 5) xvi. 670 On the first point, Mackinnon J. and the Court of Appeal held that the word 'indemnify' was inapt to exclude a claim by the plaintiffs, and at least was ambiguous and must be construed *contra proferentes.* **1974** E. R. H. Ivamy *Marine Insurance* (ed. 2) xxiii. 349 He saw no reason for coming to the conclusion that the insurers were the *proferentes.*

profert ('prəʊfət). *Law. Obs.* exc. *Hist.* [f. L. *prōfert* (*in cūriā*) 'he produces (in court)', 3rd sing. pres. of *prō fer-re* to bring forward.] The production or exhibition of a deed in court.

1719 Lilly *Pract. Regr.* II. 382 Where the Plaintiff declares upon a Deed, or the Defendant pleads a Deed, he must do it with a *Profert in Curia* to the end that the other Party may at his own Charges have a Copy of it. **1769** Gibbon *Law Evid.* 189 (Jod.) Upon every contract with solemnity there is a profert made of it to the courts, so that it appears to be the same on the declaration and in the evidence. **1852** *Act 15 & 16 Vict.* c. 76 §55 It shall not be necessary to make Profert of any Deed or other Document mentioned or relied on in any Pleading. **1884** Sir H. C. Lopes in *Law Times Rep.* L. 366/2 A plaintiff suing as executor could not maintain his action without making profert of the probate. **1885** L. O. Pike *Yearbks. 12 & 13 Edw. III*, Introd. 61 Profert of a deed had been made by the defendant, and..the deed had been denied by the plaintiff.

profesh (prəʊ'fɛʃ). *slang.* Abbrev. of profession 6; applied *spec.* to the theatrical profession. Also *U.S.*, the body of professional tramps.

1901 J. London *Let.* 6 Dec. (1966) 126 Wyckoff is not a tramp authority... Wyckoff only knows the working-man. .. The profesh are unknown to him. **1907** —— *Road* 236 The profesh are the aristocracy of The Road. **1914** E. Pugh *Cockney at Home* 192 'Mr. Alexander,..being a hartist in his profesh, which there's only one thing as keeps him off the London stage at this present moment, and that is—' 'Eggs!' **1936** Wodehouse *Laughing Gas* xviii. 192 We're most of us in the profesh downstairs.

†**pro'fess**, *sb. Obs.* In 5 professe (prouese). [Late ME. *professe*, either from profess *v.* or from L. *professus* sb., profession of faith, or a Romanic **professa* fem.: cf. obs. F. *professe* in same sense (1610 in Godef.).] The declaration made by one entering a religious order; = profession 1; the document containing this. Also *attrib.*

c **1400** *Rule St. Benet* lviii. 38 When sho sall make hir professe, In þe Kirke bi-fore þame alle sal sho haite stabilnes and buxumnes, by-fore god and alle his haliȝes. *Ibid.* 39 Þe bref of hir professe sal sho noht haue, bot in þe kirke sal be gete. **14..** *Vespasian Ritual* ibid. 145 Att þe bygynnyng of þe mese þe madyn þat salbe mayde nun sal sit in þe quere a-pon a stole be-for þe priores stayle with hir prouese in hir hand. *Ibid.*, Scho with hir professe-boke in hir hand. *Ibid.* 147 When scho hase red hir professe.

†**pro'fess**, *a. Obs.* Also 3–4 profes, 4 -esse. [ME. a. F. *profès, professe* = Pr. *profes*, Sp. *profeso*, Pg., It. *professo*, 'that has taken the vows of a religious order', ad. L. *professus* 'having professed or declared publicly', pa. pple. of *profitērī* to profess.] Professed, that has made a profession, that has taken vows of religion. In early use const. also as pa. pple. Also *absol.*

1297 R. Glouc. (Rolls) 8944, & uor to be siker of ire stat þe abit of nonne heo tok, Ac me nolde hire profes noȝt make a none wise. *c* **1315** Shoreham *Poems* i. 1782 Monek, muneche, ne no frere, Ne no man of religion, Profes ȝef þat he were. **1340** *Ayenb.* 238 Þet neuremor hi ne moȝe by spoused, zeþþe hi byeþ profes. **13..** *Metr. Hom.* (Vernon MS.) in Herrig's *Archiv* LVII. 276 Þis ilke Monk wiþ oute les Was Monk of Cleruaus profes. **1387–8** T. Usk *Test. Love* iii. i. (Skeat) l. 130 Vnder whiche lawe (and vnworthy) bothe professe & reguler am obedien cer am bounden to this Margarit perle, & by knotte of loues statutes. [**1896** *Blackw. Mag.* Aug. 169 Young Fathers are, but do not seem [holy]; Profess Fathers both seem and are.]

profess (prəʊ'fɛs), *v.* [f. L. *profess-*, ppl. stem of *profit-ērī* to profess, f. pro-[1] + *fatērī, fass-* to confess, own, acknowledge: cf. confess, also It. *professare* (Florio 1598), Sp. *profesar*, Pr. *professar*, mod.F. *professer* (1680 in Hatz.-Darm.). Before 1500 only in religious sense (see below), the earliest part occurring being the pa. pple. *professed* (answering to earlier *profes(s)*, L. *professus*, F. *profès, -fesse*: see prec.).]

I. 1. *trans.* **a.** Orig. in passive form, ***to be professed*** (cf. profess *a.*, professed *ppl. a.*), to have made one's profession of religion; to make one's profession, to take the vows of some religious order, *esp.* to become a monk or nun (= c); afterwards app. viewed as passive in sense, whence, in 15th c., **b.** the active voice ***to profess***, to receive the profession of (a person), to receive or admit into a religious order.

[The form *to be professed* app. either arose directly out of *to be profess* (see profess *a.*), F. *être profès*, or was due to rendering the L. deponent *professus est* as a passive.]

c **1315** Shoreham *Poems* i. 1792 Relessed Schel hym nauȝt be religioun, þaȝ he be nauȝt professed. **1390** Gower *Conf.* III. 337 His wif,..Which was professed in the place, As sche that was Abbesse there. *c* **1400** *Lansdowne Ritual* in *Rule St. Benet*, etc. 143 Efter þe gospell on þe day þat sho sall be profeste, hir maistres sall cum til hir & lede hir til þe gree. And þare sho sall rede hir professiun. **1494** Fabyan *Chron.* v. cxiv. 88 Than he sent his sone vnto Paris..and there causyd him to be professed in an howse of relygyon. **1523** Fitzherb. *Surv.* 32 They be all onely p[ro]fessed to god to be his men and women and to none other. **1600** Holland *Livy* xxxix. xii. 1030 When she was a very young wench.. shee, togither with her mistresse, was there professed and consecrated. **1672** Dryden *Assignation* ii. i, A House of Benedictines, call'd the Torre di Specchi, where only Ladies of the best Quality are profess'd. **1797** Mrs. Radcliffe *Italian* xi, Vivaldi was told that a nun was going to be professed. **1939** A. Clarke *Sister Eucharia* i. 8 The day she was professed a year Ago. **1975** *Anglo-Saxon Eng.* IV. 140 If the manuscript was a gift to William of St Calais around 1083 when the first monks were professed at Durham, it is written in a script..that would have been familiar to the new bishop.

fig. *c* **1407** Lydg. *Reson & Sens.* 3683 Folkys that ben amerous, Professed in Venus covent. **1560** Ingelend *Disob. Child* (Percy Soc.) 25, I am profest for losse or gayne, To be thyne owne assuredlye.

b. *c* **1430** W. Paston in *P. Lett.* I. 30 To graunte..to the priour of Thetford..autorite and power as your..depute to professe in dwe forme the seyd monkes of Bromholm unprofessed. **1568** Grafton *Chron.* II. 36 In the .ix. yere of his reigne, the Archbishop Anselme professed Gerard Archebishop of Yorke to the yoke of obedience. **1886** Monahan *Rec. Dioceses Ardagh & Clonmacnoise* 6 The Bollandists hold that St. Mel professed St. Bridget in his own church at Ardagh.

c. *refl.* and *intr.* To make one's profession; to take the vows of a religious order.

c **1510** More *Picus* Wks. 8/2 He chaunged that purpose, and appointed to professe him self in the order of freres prechours. **1533** Cranmer *Let. to Archd. Hawkyns* in *Misc. Writ.* (Parker Soc.) II. 273 She had a commandment from God..as she said, to profess herself a nun. **1745** Pococke *Descr. East* II. ii. i. i. 4 They [Calamarians] cannot profess before they are twenty-five years old. **1829** Southey in *Q. Rev.* XXXIX. 394 The young man went back to France, and professed there in some religious order.

II. 2. *trans.* To declare openly, announce, affirm; to avow, acknowledge, confess: **a.** *oneself to be* (or *do*) *something* (often with omission of either refl. pron. or inf., or sometimes of both). In later use often coloured by 3.

1526 *Pilgr. Perf.* (W. de W. 1531) 9 And professeth them selfe to be pilgrymes in this worlde. **1594** T. B. *La Primaud. Fr. Acad.* ii. 5 Many professe themselues better Philosophers then good Christians. **1596** Spenser *F.Q.* vi. vi. 10 Yet did her face and former parts professe A faire young Mayden, full of comely glee. **1605** Shaks. *Lear* i. i. 74, I professe My selfe an enemy to all other ioyes. **1627** W. Sclater *Exp. 2 Thess.* (1629) 114 Saint Paul is too nice, and professeth Puritane, when hee reckons Fornicators, Adulterers..among the damned crue. **1662** *Bk. Com. Prayer, Pr. for all Conditions of Men*, That all who profess and call them-selves Christians may be led into the way of truth. **1678** Walton *Life Sanderson* 23 They shut up their shops, professing not to open them till justice was executed. **1774** J. Adams *Wks.* (1854) IX. 337 Your plan of a newspaper to profess itself a general channel of American intelligence. **1794** Paley *Evid.* (1825) II. 320 He probably was what he professes himself to be. **1838–9** Fr. A. Kemble *Resid. in Georgia* (1863) 63 She professed herself much relieved. **1890** 'R. Boldrewood' *Col. Reformer* (1891) 220 He..professed himself to be snugly lodged.

b. with object clause.

1557 N.T. (Genev.) *Matt.* vii. 23 And then wil I professe to them, I neuer knewe you. **1619** Visct. Doncaster in *Eng. & Germ.* (Camden) 101, I must professe the cheare was royall. **1670** H. Stubbe *Plus Ultra* 38 Galileo professeth that in the moon there is no rain. **1716** Addison *Freeholder* No. 50 ¶1 He profess'd it was his Design to save Men by the Sword. **1826** Scott *Woodstock* xxv, 'I profess I thought I was doing you pleasure...' 'O ay!..profess—profess. Ay, that is the new phrase of asseveration, instead of the profane adjuration of courtiers and Cavaliers. Oh, sir, *profess* less and *practise* more.' **1869** F. W. Newman *Misc.* 43 It is professed that Mathematical science is demonstrative. **1875** Jowett *Plato* (ed. 2) II. 77 Who professes that he will not leave him.

c. with simple object.

1603 Shaks. *Meas. for M.* iv. ii. 103 Lord Angelo hath to the publike eare Profest the contrarie. **1626** Massinger *Rom. Actor* Ded., I were most unworthy of such noble friends, if I should not..profess and own them. **1709** Steele *Tatler* No. 5 ¶8 [He] took all Opportunities..to strike his Rival, and profess the Spite..which moved him to it. **1853** J. H. Newman *Hist. Sk.* (1873) II. i. iii. 146 They one by one professed their faith in Christ, and were beheaded in the Sultan's presence.

3. a. To make profession of, to lay claim to (some quality, feeling, etc.); often implying insincerity, as 'to profess and not practise'; to make protestation of; to pretend to. With *simple obj.* or *inf.*

1530 PALSGR. 667/1 Wolde to God every man that professeth chastyte coude kepe it well. **1553** EDEN *Treat. Newe Ind.* (Arb.) 5 If a man woulde professe to wryte of Englande. **1604** BACON *Apol.* Wks. 1879 I. 436, I profess not to be a poet. **1644** MILTON *Areop.* (Arb.) 34 That love of truth which ye eminently professe. **1775** JOHNSON *Tax. no Tyr.* 40 The right which their ancestors professed. **1784** COWPER *Tiroc.* 194 Whose only care..Is not to find what they profess to seek. **1826** [see 2 b]. **1842** MACAULAY *Ess., Fredk. Gt.* (1877) 658 It professes, indeed, to be no more than a compilation. **1869** FREEMAN *Norm. Conq.* III. xiii. 269 William professed, and in many respects honestly practised, a devotion to religion beyond that of other men. **1884** *Manch. Exam.* 3 May 6/1 Mr. Raikes..professed extreme regret at being compelled as an act of public duty to make these painful disclosures.

b. *refl.* and *intr.* To make a profession or professions; *esp.* to profess friendship or attachment.

1601 SHAKS. *Jul. C.* I. ii. 77 If you know, That I professe my selfe in Banquetting To all the Rout, then hold me dangerous. **1611** —— *Wint. T.* I. ii. 456 He is dishonor'd by a man, which euer Profess'd to him. **1775** SHERIDAN *Duenna* III. iii, In religion, as in friendship, they who profess most are ever the least sincere.

4. a. *trans.* To affirm or declare one's faith in or allegiance to; to acknowledge or formally recognize as an object of faith or belief (a religion, principle, rule of action; God, Christ, a saint, etc.).

1560 DAUS tr. *Sleidane's Comm.* 20 b, John Phefercorne a Jewe that professed Christianitie. **1565** *Reg. Privy Council Scot.* I. 372 The securitie of thame professing the said religioun. **1603** SHAKS. *Meas. for M.* IV. ii. 192 By the Saint whom I professe, I will plead against it with my life. **1610** HOLLAND *Camden's Brit.* (1637) 395 Who professed the rule of S. Augustine. **1611** BIBLE *Transl. Pref.* 2 The first..that openly professed the faith himselfe. **1631** GOUGE *God's Arrows* III. §2. 185 The Amalekites had forsaken the God..whom Israel still professed. **1755** YOUNG *Centaur* i. Wks. 1757 IV. 122 They, that profess deism for the credit of superior understanding. **1867** R. PALMER *Life P. Howard* 137 In this year F. Vincent Torre professed two Religions.

b. *absol.* or *intr.*

1640 LAUD in Neal *Hist. Purit.* (1733) II. 383 As if he should profess with the Church of England, and have his heart at Rome.

5. *trans.* To make profession of, or claim to have knowledge of or skill in (some art or science); to declare oneself expert or proficient in; to make (a thing) one's profession or business. In quot. 1613 *absol.* or *intr.*

1577 B. GOOGE *Heresbach's Husb.* I. (1586) 6 Ozias as we reade professed husbandry. **1596** SHAKS. *1 Hen. IV*, V. ii. 92, I thanke him, that he cuts me from my tale: For I professe not talking. **1611** BIBLE *Titus* iii. 14 Let ours also learne to maintaine good workes [*marg.* professe honest trades]. **1613** PURCHAS *Pilgrimage* (1614) 827 They..beginne to professe in practise of Physick and Diuination. **1651** HOBBES *Leviath.* II. xxvi. 142 The advice of one that professeth the study of the Law. **1776** GIBBON *Decl. & F.* xiii. (1869) I. 268 War was the only art which he professed. **1818** in Lady Morgan *Autobiog.* (1859) 147 Playing on the harp and piano, which instruments she professes. **1882–3** *Schaff's Encycl. Relig. Knowl.* II. 936/1 When passing his examination, he [Sir W. Hamilton] professed the whole works of Aristotle.

6. a. To teach (some subject) as a professor.

1560 DAUS tr. *Sleidane's Comm.* 1 The same time was Martin Luther an Augustine Frere, & professed diuinitie in the Vniuersitie of Wittemberge. **1611** CORYAT *Crudities* 62 The seuerall Schooles wherein the seuen liberall sciences are professed. **1638** ROUSE *Heav. Univ.* Advt. (1702) 2 That common learning which is profess'd and taught in our Universities. **1871** C. J. MUNRO in *Life Clerk Maxwell* xii. (1882) 379, I hope it is true that you are to profess experimental physics at Cambridge. **1906** SIR O. LODGE in *St. George* IX. 6 Several friends..professing different subjects at the University College in Liverpool.

b. *intr.* To perform the duties of a professor.

1610 *Camden's Brit.* 533 No student in Oxford should publickly professe or reade at Stanford. **1706** tr. *Dupin's Eccl. Hist. 16th C.* II. IV. xi. 457 The University..demanded, Who they were? and by what Right they undertook to Profess? **1850** BROWNING *Christmas Eve* xvi, Down to you, the man of men, Professing here in Göttingen. **1867** LOWELL *Lett.* (1894) I. iv. 427 If I live this life much longer I shall do nothing but profess and review.

pro'fessable, *a. rare.* [f. prec. + -ABLE.] Capable of being professed (in quot., of being publicly taught or lectured on by a professor).

1897 tr. *Balzac's Cousin Pons* 129 We are founding chairs of Mantchu and Slav, and literatures so little professable (to coin a word) as the literatures of the North.

†**pro'fessant**, *a.* and *sb. Obs.* [f. as prec. + -ANT, or immed. a. F. *professant* pres. pple.]

A. *adj.* Professing (to believe in or worship).

1621 AINSWORTH *Annot. Pentat., Gen.* vi. 3 These also..are my peculiar professant people. **1643** TRAPP *Comm. Gen.* vi. 2 His peculiar professant people, called sons of Jehovah.

B. *sb.* One who professes (in various senses).

1615 BRATHWAIT *Strappado* (1878) 24 But of professants, which compose their song To a strange detract! this Ile say they wrong Flowrie Parnassus. **1635** —— *Arcad. Pr.* 157 Presents..are moving objects to mercenary professants. **1665** —— *Comment Two Tales* 27 One trick..wherein none of all his fellow-consorts or Astronomical Professants can ever come near him.

professed (prəʊ'fɛst, prəʊ'fɛsɪd), *ppl. a.* Also 5–8 **profest**. [f. PROFESS *v.* + -ED[1]: see also PROFESS *a.*, in earlier use.]

1. That has taken the vows of a religious order. Also *absol.* as *sb.* (= med.L. *professus*, PROFESS *a.*)

c **1394** *P. Pl. Crede* 348 A prechour y-professed haþ pliȝt me his trewþe. *c* **1440** *Alphabet of Tales* 289 A profeste of þe ordur of Permonstracence;..þis profeste stoppid his hors & haylsid hur honestelie. *c* **1450** *Life St. Cuthbert* (Surtees) 7963 þe bischop bad þaim be profest Monkys, or ga and do þair best. **1554** T. MARTIN (*title*) A Traictise..plainly prouyng, that the pretensed marriage of Priestes and professed persones, is no mariage, but altogether vnlawful. **1588** ALLEN *Admon.* 14 She hathe suppressed all the religious houses..dispersed the professed of the same. **1626** L. OWEN *Spec. Jesuit.* (1629) 58 These professed Iesuites are imployed in hearing Confessions, saying of Masses, Preaching, and Writing. **1766** BLACKSTONE *Comm.* II. xv. 257 One who entered into religion and became a monk professed was incapable of inheriting lands. **1870** FREEMAN *Norm. Conq.* I. v. 265 A natural daughter of Eadgar and already a professed nun.

b. *transf.* Of or pertaining to professed persons.

1526 *Pilgr. Perf.* (W. de W. 1531) 21 b, All though she were not in the professed habyte of religyon. **1662** J. DAVIES tr. *Mandelslo's Trav.* 99 We dined at the Profess'd House of the Jesuits. **1706** tr. *Dupin's Eccl. Hist. 16th C.* II. IV. xi. 455 They [the Jesuits] have Profess'd Houses for their Profess'd Members, and their Coadjutors.

2. Self-acknowledged; openly declared or avowed by oneself; sometimes with an implication of 'not real', and so = Alleged, ostensible, pretended. (Of persons or things.)

a **1569** KINGESMYLL *Confl. Satan* (1578) 15 A professed Satan to all the children of God. **1592** SHAKS. *Rom. & Jul.* III. iii. 50 My Friend profest. **1605** —— *Lear* I. i. 275 Loue well our Father: To your professed bosomes I commit him. **1621** BRATHWAIT *Nat. Embassie* (1877) 42 What I haue giuen thee, I would haue bestowed on my professedst enemy. **1703** ROWE *Fair Penit.* I. i. 278 He bears the noble Altamont Profest and deadly hatred. **1711** STEELE *Spect.* No. 33 ¶1 The Profess'd Beauties, who are a People almost as unsufferable as the Profess'd Wits. **1841** CATLIN *N. Amer. Ind.* II. xlvii. 103 A professed, and I think, sincere Christian.

3. Followed as a profession or vocation.

1598 STOW *Surv. Lond.* (1603) 240 In those dayes euery man liued by his professed trade, no..one interrupting an other.

4. That professes to be duly qualified; professional (as opposed to *amateur*).

1675 R. BURTHOGGE *Causa Dei* 111 Though he were not a Profest Divine. **1712** STEELE *Spect.* No. 473 ¶2 You profess'd Authors are a little severe upon us, who write like Gentlemen. **1796** MRS. GLASSE *Cookery* iii. 16, I do not pretend to teach professed cooks, but my design is to instruct the ignorant and unlearned. **1874** CARPENTER *Ment. Phys.* I. i. §20 (1879) 20 The professed Anatomist would be unable..to determine what is the precise state of each of the muscles concerned.

professedly (prəʊ'fɛsɪdlɪ), *adv.* Also 7 **profestly**. [f. prec. + -LY[2].]

1. By or according to profession or declaration; avowedly.

1570 FOXE *A. & M.* (ed. 2) 831/2 He whiche wrote professedly against the superstitions of the people. **1641** MILTON *Ch. Govt.* Pref., Wks. 1851 III. 97 The reasons thereof are not formally and profestly set downe. **1647** WARD *Simp. Cobler* (1842) 17, I should..suspect..that faith that can professedly live with two or three sordid sins. **1667** PEPYS *Diary* 9 Jan., The Commons do it professedly to prevent the King's dispensing with it. **1693** DRYDEN *Juvenal* (1697) p. xiii, Only Virgil, whom he profestly imitated, has surpass'd him, among the Romans; and only Mʳ Waller among the English. **1751** JOHNSON *Rambler* No. 175 ¶13 Many there are, who openly and almost professedly regulate all their conduct by their love of money. **1884** *Law Times* LXXVII. 382/2 Professedly written,..not for the lawyer, but for the commercial world.

2. Ostensibly, under mere profession or pretence: opposed, implicitly or explicitly, to 'actually' or 'really'.

1831 MACKINTOSH *Hist. Eng.* II. ii. 51 Buckingham..hastened with a body of adherents, professedly to join the king. **1856** FROUDE *Hist. Eng.* I. ii. 181 Her portraits, though all professedly by Holbein,..are singularly unlike each other. **1892** *Law Times* XCIII. 551/1 The process of the court had been used by the solicitor professedly for one purpose, to levy a debt, but really for another purpose.

professing (prəʊ'fɛsɪŋ), *vbl. sb.* [f. PROFESS *v.* + -ING[1].] The action of the vb. PROFESS.

a. = PROFESSION I. **b.** Avowing, acknowledging.

a. 1502 *Privy Purse Exp. Eliz. of York* (1830) 47 The professing of a nonne of Elstowe. **1669** WOODHEAD *Monast. Discalced Nuns* 8 For the professing them, a very great diligence is requisite.

b. 1560 DAUS tr. *Sleidane's Comm.* 449 For the true professing of the Gospell they be expulsed. *a* **1683** OWEN *Posth. Serm.* Wks. 1851 IX. 178 This is a professing that brings conviction.

pro'fessing, *ppl. a.* [f. as prec. + -ING[2].] That professes; that professes to be such.

1675 OWEN *Serm.* Wks. 1851 IX. 311 Believers shall be saved and a professing church shall be preserved. **1822** J. MACDONALD *Mem. J. Benson* 136 He censures himself for things which too many in the professing world would look upon as so many innocent infirmities. **1842** MANNING *Serm., Myst. Sin* (1848) I. 16 What a prodigy in God's world is a professing atheist! **1906** D. S. CAIRNS *Chr. Mod. World* iv. 212 The Church is the visible community of professing Christians founded by our Lord for the propaganda of the Kingdom.

profession (prəʊ'fɛʃən). [ME. a. F. *profession* (12th c. in Hatz.-Darm.), ad. L. *professiōn-em* a public declaration; a business or profession that one publicly avows, n. of action f. *profitērī* to PROFESS.] The action or fact of professing; that which is professed.

I. 1. a. The declaration, promise, or vow made by one entering a religious order; hence, the action of entering such an order; the fact of being professed in a religious order.

a **1225** *Ancr. R.* 6 Non ancre..ne schal makien professiun, þet is, bihoten ase hest, bute þreo þinges, þet is, obedience, chastete, & studestaþeluestnesse. *c* **1300** *Beket* 1407 Ac mi professioun ich habbe to Jesu Crist ido. **1340** *Ayenb.* 225 Huanne þe beheste is solempne ase be hand of prelat oþer be profession of religion. *c* **1386** CHAUCER *Shipman's T.* 155 Nay quod this Monk by god and by seint Martyn..This swere I yow on my profession. *c* **1400** *Lansdowne Ritual* in *Rule St. Benet*, etc. 143 Sho sall rede hir professiun..& þe nouyce sal make a crosse on þe buke of hir profession. **1451** CAPGRAVE *Life St. Gilbert* (E.E.T.S.) 72 Of þis same mannes handes took Gilbert þe habite of profession. **1603** HOLLAND *Plutarch's Mor.* 1288 The searching after such science, is as it were a profession and entrance into religion. **1671** WOODHEAD *St. Teresa* I. iv. 13 When I consider the manner of my Profession, and the great resolution and gust wherewith I made it. **1691** WOOD *Ath. Oxon.* I. 181 He was called to Rome to take upon him the profession of the four vows. **1771** *Chron.* in *Ann. Reg.* 151/1 Madame Louisa of France took the veil of professions at the convent of the Carmelites. **1797** MRS. RADCLIFFE *Italian* xi, The novice kneeling before him made her profession. **1871** FREEMAN *Norm. Conq.* IV. xvii. 89 He had received the second profession of Maurilius, the Primate who still for a short time longer filled the metropolitan throne of Rouen. **1885** *Catholic Dict.* s.v., A religious or regular profession is 'a promise freely made and lawfully accepted, whereby a person of the full age required, after the completion of a year of probation, binds him- (or her-) self to a particular religious institute approved by the Church'.

b. Any solemn declaration, promise, or vow.

1362 LANGL. *P. Pl.* A. I. 98 Dauid..Dubbede knihtes, Dude hem swere on heor swerd to serue treuþe euere. þat is þe perte profession þat a-pendeþ to knihtes. [**1393** C. II. 97 Trewely to take and treweliche to fyȝte, Ys þe profession and þe pure ordre þat apendeþ to knyȝtes.] **1387** TREVISA *Higden* (Rolls) II. 115 þe bisshop of Meneuia was i-sacred of þe bisshoppes of Wales.., and made non professioun noþe subiection to non oþer chirche. **1494** FABYAN *Chron.* VII. ccxxviii. 257 Thurston was choshen archebysshop of Yorke; the which withsayd his professyon of obedyence yᵗ he shuld owe to the See of Caunterbury.

†**2. a.** A particular order of monks, nuns, or other professed persons. *Obs.*

c **1386** CHAUCER *Sompn. T.* 217 So forth al the gospel may ye seen Wher it be likker oure professioun Or hirs that swymmen in possessioun. **1390** GOWER *Conf.* I. 239 If thou er this Hast ben of such professioun, Discovere thi confessioun. **1451** CAPGRAVE *Life St. Aug.* (E.E.T.S.) 1 A gentill woman desired of me..to translate hir treuly oute of latyn, þe lif of Seynt Augustin, grete doctour of þe cherch. Sche desired þis þing of me rather þan of a-noþer man because þat I am of his profession.

†**b.** *transf.* ***Christ's profession***, the order instituted by Christ; Christianity. *Obs.*

c **1375** *Sc. Leg. Saints* xxxiii. (*George*) 696 George wes þe trewest knycht To crist ymang al þat lyf mycht, þat vndir knychtly habit kyd Cristis professione had vnhyde. *c* **1380** *Antecrist* in Todd *Three Treat. Wyclif* (1851) 117 Iche man þat liueþ not after þe reule of Cristis professioun.

†**3.** Special character, nature, or kind. *rare*[−1].

c **1440** *Pallad. on Husb.* III. 64 (E.E.T.S.) And shortte to sai,—se the profession Of every vyne, and wherin thai myscheve As counter it by goode discrecion.

II. 4. a. The action of declaring, acknowledging, or avowing an opinion, belief, intention, practice, etc.; declaration, avowal. In later use often with implied contrast to practice or fact: cf. PROFESS *v.* 3, PROFESSED 2.

1526 *Pilgr. Perf.* (W. de W. 1531) 9 Eyther by his owne fayth & professyon, or els in the fayth of theyr spirituall parentes. **1565** *Reg. Privy Council Scot.* I. 370 Thai mak plane professioun that the establissing of religioun will nocht content thame. **1617** MORYSON *Itin.* I. 142 Having made profession of my great respect to him. **1662** H. MORE *Philos. Writ.* Pref. Gen. (1712) 26 That I may not seem injurious to my self, nor give scandal unto others by this so free profession. **1692** DRYDEN *St. Euremont's Ess.* 353 There are Friends of Profession, that take a pride in following our Party at random, and upon all Occasions. **1750** JOHNSON *Rambler* No. 1 ¶10 That..some should endeavour to gain favour..by a daring profession of their own deserts. **1796** BURKE *Regic. Peace* i. Wks. VIII. 118 In this unity and indivisibility of profession are sunk ten immense and wealthy provinces. **1817** JAS. MILL *Brit. India* III. VI. i. 50 Here, too, profession was at variance with fact. **1868** FREEMAN *Norm. Conq.* II. viii. 218 Such a man was already a saint in practice, if not in profession. **1871** BROWNING *Balaust.* 1442 Nor she, who makes profession of my birth And styles herself my mother, neither she Bore me.

b. with *a* and *pl.* An act of professing; a declaration (true or false).

1674 *Essex Papers* (Camden) I. 236 Of all persons, I need make you the least professions. **1740–1** BUTLER *Serm. Ho. Lords* 30 Jan., Wks. 1874 II. 256 These false professions of virtue..must have been originally taken up in order to deceive. **1755** YOUNG *Centaur* iii. Wks. 1757 IV. 173 Greater professions of friendship can no man make, than this arch-promiser: greater proofs of the contrary can no man give. **1782** MISS BURNEY *Cecilia* V. v, Cecilia..found little difficulty in returning her friendly professions. *Mod.* I believe his professions of regard to be perfectly sincere.

5. *spec.* **a.** The profession of religion; the declaration of belief in and obedience to religion, or of acceptance of and conformity to the faith and principles of any religious community; hence, the faith or religion which one professes.

1526 Tindale *Heb.* iii. 1 Consyder the embasseatour and hye prest of ourre profession Christ Jesus. **1531** —— *Exp. 1 John* (1537) 2 To haue thys profession wrytten in thyne harte, is to consente vnto yͤ law that it is ryghteous. **1548–9** (Mar.) *Bk. Com. Prayer, Collect 3rd Sunday after Easter*, Graunt unto all..that they maye exchew those thinges that be contrary to their profession, and folow all such things as be agreable to the same. **1601** W. Parry *Trav. Sir A. Sherley* 5 Certaine Persians..Pagans by profession. **16..** Hales *Gold. Rem.* I. (1673) 36 True profession without honest conversation, not onely saves not, but increases our weight of punishment. **1689** Popple tr. *Locke's 1st Let. Toleration* L.'s Wks. 1714 II. 243 It is in vain for an Unbeliever to take up the outward shew of another Man's Profession. **1728** Eliza Heywood *Mme. de Gomez's Belle A.* (1732) II. 15 Several who made profession of the Protestant Religion. **1876** Mozley *Univ. Serm.* ii. 40 As the standard of goodness rises the standard of profession must rise too.

b. A religious system, communion, or body.

1600 J. Pory tr. *Leo's Africa* vii. 293 They embrace no religion at all, being neither Christians, Mahumetans, nor Iewes, nor of any other profession. *a* **1646** J. Gregory *Notes & Obs.* (1650) 20 Whatsoever the moderne practice is, the ancient must be to bury towards Ierusalem..for all professions buryed towards the place they worshipped. **1839** J. Martineau *Stud. Chr.* (1858) 131 How think himself safe in a profession, which was without temple, without priest, without altar, without victim? **1904** R. Small *Hist. U.P. Congregat.* i. 72 At the close of his Arts course, he 'left his profession' and joined the Relief.

III. 6. The occupation which one professes to be skilled in and to follow. **a.** A vocation in which a professed knowledge of some department of learning or science is used in its application to the affairs of others or in the practice of an art founded upon it. Applied *spec.* to the three learned professions of divinity, law, and medicine; also to the military profession.

1541 R. Copland *Galyen's Terap.* 2 A j b, The parties of the art of Medycyne.. can not be seperated one from the other without the dommage and great detryment of all the medicynall professyon. **1581** Pettie *Guazzo's Civ. Conv.* I. (1586) A v b, Such as I am, (whose profession should chiefelie bee armes). **1605** Bacon *Adv. Learn.* II. Ded. §8 Amongst so many great foundations of colleges in Europe, I find strange that they are all dedicated to professions, and none left free to Arts and Sciences at large. **1682** Dryden *Relig. Laici* Pref., Wks. (Globe) 185 Speculations which belong to the profession of Divinity. **1687** A. Lovell tr. *Thevenot's Trav.* I. 107 They know not what Physicians, Chirurgeons, Apothecaries, and men of that profession are. **1711** Addison *Spect.* No. 21 ¶1 The three great Professions of Divinity, Law, and Physick. **1727** Gay *Begg. Op.* I. viii, The Captain looks upon himself in the military capacity as a gentleman by profession. **1788** Gibbon *Decl. & F.* xliv. (1846) IV. 186 Arms, eloquence, and the study of the civil law, promoted a citizen to the honours of the Roman state; and the three professions were sometimes more conspicuous by their union in the same character. **1839** Maurice *Lect. Educ. Mid. Classes* 186 Profession in our country..is expressly that kind of business which deals primarily with men as men, and is thus distinguished from a Trade, which provides for the external wants or occasions of men. **1850** *Rep. Oxf. Univ. Commission* 94 A professorship would then ..become a recognised profession. **1870** L. Oliphant *Piccadilly* II. 46 The Church..compared with other professions..holds out no inducements for young men of family. **1888** Besant *50 Years Ago* xix. 262 New professions have come into existence, and the old professions are more esteemed. It was formerly a poor and beggarly thing to belong to any other than the three learned professions.

b. In wider sense: Any calling or occupation by which a person habitually earns his living.

Now usually applied to an occupation considered to be socially superior to a trade or handicraft; but formerly, and still in vulgar (or humorous) use, including these.

1576 Fleming *Panopl. Epist.* 386 Why do not you apply your selfe, to some one kinde of profession, or other, wherin there is certaintie and stay of liuing? **1577** B. Googe *Heresbach's Husb.* I. (1586) 5 b, Princes..delighted with yͤ profession of husbandry. **1600** J. Pory tr. *Leo's Africa* App. 364 Their profession is to robbe and steale from their neighbours, and to make them slaues. **1601** Shaks. *Jul. C.* I. i. 5 (Being Mechanicall) you ought not walke Vpon a labouring day, without the signe Of your Profession. Speake, what Trade art thou? **1616** *Shirburn Ballads* (1907) 71 The Professions of these persons, so vnfortunately drowned, were:—1, a Haberdasher; 2, a Taylor; 3, a Sadler; 4, a Barber; 5, a Waterman. **1665** Boyle *Occas. Refl.* v. vii, This Gard'ner..inherits..of Adam..that primitive profession that imploy'd and recompenc'd his Innocence. **1688** R. Holme *Armoury* III. 326/1 A Graver..is also used for many uses about the Plummers Profession. **1733** Gent *Rippon* 49 Joseph her Spouse, by Profession a Carpenter. **1739** Cibber *Apol.* (1756) I. 175 The different conduct of these rival actors may be of use to others of the same profession. **1762** H. Walpole *Vertue's Anecd. Paint.* (1765) I. iv. 62 Another serjeant-painter in this reign was John Brown, who, if he threw no great lustre on his profession, was at least a benefactor to it's professors. **1828** Scott *F.M. Perth* ii, The forehead of Henry Gow, or Smith, (for..both words equally indicated his profession,) was high and noble. **1828** P. Cunningham *N.S. Wales* (ed. 3) II. 221 The veteran thief assumes the same sort of lofty port and high-toned consequence over the juniors of the profession, that the veteran warrior..does. **1898** *Westm. Gaz.* 17 Nov. 7/3 He is doing a very nice trade in the muffin 'profession'.

c. By extension: ***by profession*** = professed, professional.

1806–7 J. Beresford *Miseries Hum. Life* VII. x, The raillery of some wag by profession.

d. The body of persons engaged in a calling.

the profession, in theatrical use, actors as a body; public performers generally.

1610 Willet *Hexapla Dan.* 52 To take reuenge of the whole profession, and so to punish one for an others offence. **1678** Butler *Hud.* III. iii. 488 Lawyers are too wise a Nation, T' expose their Trade to Disputation:..In which whoever wins the day, The whole Profession's sure to pay. **1700** T. Brown *Amusem. Ser. & Com.* 67 A Company of the Common Profession in Dishabilie. **1840** *Civil Eng. & Arch. Jrnl.* III. 30/2 [Specifications] ought at all times..to accompany the drawings, as they at once convey to the profession the minutiæ of the construction. **1899** *Westm. Gaz.* 25 Nov. 2/1 A heavy tragedian and his leading lady.. confronting a provincial landlady. 'Do you let apartments to —ah—the profession?'

e. Applied allusively and *euphem.* to prostitution 1.

1888 Kipling *In Black & White* 78 Lalun is a member of the most ancient profession in the world. **1914** C. Mackenzie *Sinister St.* IV. ii. 862 There's only Miss Carlyle who's in the profession and comes in sometimes a little late. **1922** A. Woollcott *Shouts & Murmurs* ii. 57 The Actor and the Streetwalker... The two oldest professions in the world—ruined by amateurs. **1936** *Times Lit. Suppl.* 18 Apr. 338/4 Blackham has attempted a comprehensive survey of the activities of womankind from 'the oldest profession' to the magistracy.

IV. †**7.** The function or office of a professor in a university or college; = professorship, professorate; public teaching by a professor. *Obs.*

1580 Lyly *Euphues* (Arb.) 436 There are..in this Islande two famous Vniversities, the one Oxforde, the other Cambridge, both for the profession of al sciences. **1656** Hobbes *Six Lessons* Wks. 1845 VII. 345 There will need but one house, and the endowment of a few professions. **1708** J. Chamberlayne *St. Gt. Brit.* II. III. x. (1737) 443 There is a new Profession erected in the University of Edinburgh, for the Law of Nature and Nations. **1712** Hearne *Collect.* (O.H.S.) III. 391 His Entrance upon the Profession of the Greek tongue.

8. *Rom. Ant.* The public registration of persons and property [literal rendering of L. *professio*].

1856 Merivale *Rom. Emp.* (1865) IV. xxxix. 405 The provincial *Profession*, as it was designated, extended wherever the land tax was exacted.

9. *attrib.* and *Comb.*, as (sense 1) ***profession-book***, ***-ring***; ***profession-making***; ***profession-like*** adj.

14.. *Vespasian Ritual* in *Rule St. Benet*, etc. 147 Scho sal ..lay hir *profession-boke a-pon þe auter, & þe ryng with-al. **1857** G. Oliver *Coll. Cath. Relig. Cornwall* 313 From the profession-book of Lambspring Abbey, I learn that he was born at Ramsbury. **1677** Gilpin *Demonol.* (1867) 97 That under a smoother and *profession-like behaviour, when they are stirred up to persecute, the rigour might seem just. **1654** Owen *Doctr. Saints' Persev.* Wks. 1853 XI. 600 Such an one may forsake the external profession of Christianity, or cease *profession-making. *c* **1420** *Chron. Vilod.* 3217 þe ladyes..tokon seynt Wultrude *profession-rynge, And abouȝt his nekke þey hongedone hit þo. **1489** *Will of Marg. Darcy* (Som. Ho.), My profession Ryng.

professional (prəʊˈfɛʃənəl), *a.* (*sb.*) [f. prec. + -al¹. Cf. mod.F. *professionnel*.]

A. *adj.* **I.** †**1.** Pertaining to or marking entrance into a religious order. *Obs. rare*⁻¹.

c **1420** *St. Etheldred* 797 in Horstm. *Altengl. Leg.* (1881) 300 Hit was hurre professhennalle rynge. [Cf. *profession-ring* in Profession 9.]

II. 2. Pertaining to, proper to, or connected with a or one's profession or calling.

1747–8 Richardson *Clarissa* (J.), Professional, as well as national, reflections are to be avoided. **1809** Malkin *Gil Blas* II. iii. ¶2 He had got into reputation with the public by a certain professional slang. **1838** Dickens *Nich. Nick.* xiv, I dislike doing anything professional in private parties. **1849** Macaulay *Hist. Eng.* iii. I. 332 It was in these rustic priests, ..who had not the smallest chance of ever attaining high professional honours, that the professional spirit was strongest. **1870** Lowell *Study Wind.* 408 As perfectly professional as the mourning of an undertaker. **1890** *Cent. Dict.* s.v. *Education*, Special or professional [education].. aims to fit one for the particular vocation or profession in which he is to engage. **1907** *Scott. Ch. & Univ. Almanac* 266 (Aberdeen Univ.) Every candidate for the degrees of Bachelor of Medicine and..of Surgery must undergo four professional examinations.

3. Engaged in one of the learned or skilled professions, or in a calling considered socially superior to a trade or handicraft. ***professional (middle) class***, members of the learned and skilled professions regarded collectively. Freq. (with hyphen) *attrib.*

1793 Smeaton *Edystone L.* §73 Called upon, not only as a professional man, but as a man of veracity. **1805** *Med. Jrnl.* XIV. 381 The College invites all professional men, who had an opportunity of treating the yellow fever, to communicate their observations. **1871** Miss Braddon *Zoophyte's Rev.* iii, Sometimes there was a party, consisting of professional people..with a sprinkling of the smaller county gentry. **1888** Besant *50 Years Ago* xix. 262 There has been a great upward movement of the professional class. **1919** G. B. Shaw *Heartbreak House* p. viii, Just as Ibsen's intensely Norwegian plays exactly fitted every middle and professional class suburb in Europe. **1960** C. Day Lewis *Buried Day* 131 The professional-class families. **1965** M. Morse *Unattached* ii. 74 Social class (professional-middle to lower working class). **1979** G. St. Aubyn *Edward VII* i. 29 Gibbs had been brought up as a member of the professional Middle Class.

4. a. That follows an occupation as his (or her) profession, life-work, or means of livelihood, as a *professional soldier*, *musician*, or *lecturer*; *spec.* applied to one who follows, by way of profession or business, an occupation generally engaged in as a pastime; hence used in contrast with *amateur*, as *professional cricketer*. Disparagingly applied to one who 'makes a trade' of anything that is properly pursued from higher motives, as a *professional politician*.

professional beauty, humorously applied to a lady with the implication that she makes it her business to be a beauty, or to be known as such.

1798 in *Deb. Congress U.S.* (1852) 10th Congress 1 Sess., App. 2741 The solemn air and dictatorial manner of a professional schoolmaster. **1805** Surr *Winter in Lond.* (1806) II. 223 Professional and amateur singers. **1836** *New Sporting Mag.* July 198 On this point I heard a remark from one of the professional [cricket] players. **1844** *Mem. Babylonian P'cess* II. 30 Professional dancers and singers are usually engaged upon these festive occasions. **1850** 'Bat' *Cricket. Man.* 49 The way to ensure good practice is by engaging a professional bowler. **1882** H. Spencer *Princ. Sociol.* V. xii. §520 The growth of a revenue which serves to pay professional soldiers. **1883** J. Hawthorne *Dust* I. 2 More to fear from young bloods..than from professional thieves and blacklegs. **1883** W. James *Let.* 13 Jan. in R. B. Perry *Tht. & Char. W. James* (1935) I. 611 [S. H.] Hodgson is..a *gentleman* to his finger tips and a professional philosopher as well. **1887** *Pall Mall G.* 11 Feb. 4/2 Ladies raised..to the now extinct position of 'professional beauty'. **1888** Bryce *Amer. Commw.* I. vii. 90 Professional politicians ..conduct what is called a 'campaign'. *a* **1909** *Mod.* He is a professional agitator. **1946** *Mind* LV. 149 But is this work to bear fruit only in the narrow and specialised fields that professional philosophers inhabit? **1968** P. McKellar *Experience & Behav.* xi. 277 Such a person might..be a professional philosopher who gets on well with other people in parties and other social situations.

b. Of play, sports, etc.: Undertaken or engaged in for money, or as a means of subsistence; engaged in by professionals (as distinct from amateurs).

1851 J. Pycroft *Cricket Field* iv. 56 The chief patronage ..was..in London. There the play was nearly all professional: even the gentlemen made a profession of it. **1884** *Cyclist* 13 Feb. 247/2 A rule prohibiting the holding of professional events at amateur athletic meetings.

c. Disparagingly applied to one who pursues relentlessly an activity or belief that is regarded with disfavour; inveterate, habitual, ruthless.

1879 *Cornh. Mag.* Oct. 414 It is one of the misfortunes of the professional Don Juan that his honour forbids him to refuse battle. **1937** *Time* 18 Jan. 75/2 Chekhov was a strong supporter of Zola and the Dreyfusards, Suvorin was a professional anti-Semite. **1978** J. Krantz *Scruples* vi. 167 The 'extra man' invited to sit next to her at dinner was either a homosexual or a professional leech who dined out every night by mere virtue of being unmarried and mildly presentable.

d. Reaching a standard or having the quality expected of a professional person or his work; competent in the manner of a professional.

1926 C. Connolly *Let.* 8 May in *Romantic Friendship* (1975) 124, I think one must be pretty professional to succeed [as a writer]. **1945** 'A. Gilbert' *Black Stage* iv. 56 'This chap's got his head screwed on all right,' exclaimed Goodier. 'Looks like the professional touch to me.' **1969** M. Butterworth *Vanishing Act* xi. 124 The old and tried method of bulk-carrying—by crew members of ships and aircraft who do it on a regular, professional basis, and know all the angles—is safest and best. **1973** D. Francis *Slay-Ride* ix. 100 The cutting edges had been sharpened like razors and the point would have been good as a needle. A professional job: no amateur could have produced that result with a few passes over a carborundum. **1979** *Daily Mail* 31 Jan. 9/6 The average [career] adviser in schools was strictly an amateur... But those responsible for guiding university students into the right jobs were highly professional.

e. Of technical equipment: of a type or standard used by professionals.

1955 *Brit. Communications & Electronics* II. 48/2 Professional recording equipment ranges from the fixed studio equipment, through mobile apparatus, down to portable machines. **1965** *Wireless World* Sept. 460/1 An important thing to check, especially in professional audio amplifiers, is the stability margin. **1971** *Hi-Fi Sound* Feb. 67/2 A professional pickup—a studio or lab component—may well be robust and dependable, but not a candidate for top hi-fi systems, in which tracking weights are at their lowest. **1975** G. J. King *Audio Handbk.* x. 222 Professional machines operating at 38 or 76 cm/s may adopt essentially constant-current recording over the primary bandwidth.

5. That is trained and skilled in the theoretic or scientific parts of a trade or occupation, as distinct from its merely mechanical parts; that raises his trade to the dignity of a learned profession.

1860 Tyndall *Glac.* II. ix. 271 Having constructed, by a professional engineer, a map of the entire glacier. **1898** *Westm. Gaz.* 18 Jan. 10/2 A witness described himself as a professional gardener... 'There is a vast difference between professional and ordinary gardeners. I am competent to give a lecture on botany and horticulture.'

†**6.** = professorial. *Obs. rare.*

1799 *Med. Jrnl.* I. 418 Etmuller filled a professional chair at Leipsig. **1865** Dickens *Lett.* 16 Aug., The Scotch professional chair left vacant by Aytoun's death.

B. *sb.* **1.** One who belongs to one of the learned or skilled professions; a professional man.

1848 Dickens *Dombey* i, The family practitioner opening the room door for that distinguished professional. **1901** *Westm. Gaz.* 19 Mar. 2/2 Some of the speeches of the returned Generals make us glad to think that the 'professionals' (as Lord Salisbury says) are not the politicians.

2. a. One who makes a profession or business of any occupation, art, or sport, otherwise usually or often engaged in by amateurs, esp. as a pastime: see the adj., sense 4.

1811 JANE AUSTEN *Lett.* (1884) II. 86 There is to be some very good music—five professionals,..besides amateurs. **1850** 'BAT' *Cricket. Man.* 63 Averages of Batters—Professionals. **1859** LANG *Wand. India* 318 In nearly all these cases, the witnesses are professionals; that is to say, men who are accustomed to sell their oaths, and who thoroughly understand their business. **1882** *Boy's Own Paper* IV. 807 Our amateurs are improving, and the interval between them and the professionals is growing beautifully less.

b. *spec.* A prostitute. Cf. PROFESSION 6 e.

1861 [see AMATEUR 2]. **1973** 'D. JORDAN' *Nile Green* xxvii. 121 'I'm not a professional,' she said, too coolly, 'and he's not precisely my type.' **1977** *Listener* 17 Feb. 215/1 The girl he offers a client in order to clinch a deal..is already a professional.

3. *Univ. slang.* Short for *professional examination*.

In the Scottish Universities, the four necessary examinations for the degree of M.B.C.M. are commonly known as First, Second, and Third Professional, and Final. **1908** in *Scott. Med. & Surg. Jrnl.* XXII. 528 Those who have failed in one or more of the subjects of the Second Professional.

C. *Comb.*, as ***professional-looking*** adj.

1936 A. HUXLEY *Eyeless in Gaza* vi. 64 She [*sc.* a model ship] was so professional-looking. **1980** J. CARTWRIGHT *Horse of Darius* v. 67 Dieter had..prepared a very professional-looking salad.

pro'fessionalism. [f. prec. + -ISM.]

1. Professional quality, character, method, or conduct; the stamp of a particular profession.

1856 J. GROTE in *Cambr. Ess.* 88 The question of professionalism, or specialism, in education is closely connected with..that..of the suitable ages for different parts of education. **1863** *Sat Rev.* 440 Professionalism stamps its mark more deeply upon the ecclesiastical mind than upon the followers of the non-clerical, but liberal, occupations. **1893** *Athenæum* 14 Oct. 519/1 The bloodthirsty professionalism..[is] decidedly characteristic of the Napoleonic warrior. **1895** *Educat. Rev.* Sept. 169 The ..student should not lose sight of general cultivation and fall into stark professionalism.

2. The position or practice of a professional as distinguished from an amateur; the class of professionals: cf. PROFESSIONAL *a.* 4, *sb.* 2.

1884 *Elocutionist* Aug. 2/1 Local talent..may be very good, but in the majority of cases it fades before proper professionalism. **1886** *Referee* 14 Feb. 1 But Amateurism has a fringe just the same as professionalism. **1894** *Aspects Mod. Oxford* 31 The modern tendency to professionalism in athletics. **1894** [See PROFESSOR *sb.* 5].

pro'fessionalist. [-IST.] One who follows an occupation as a profession; a professional man; a representative of professionalism.

1825 FOSBROKE *Encycl. Antiq.* I. 90* Crockets, as called by Mr. Hawkins ('History of Gothic Architecture'), by professionalists termed 'scroll creepers'. **1840** *Fraser's Mag.* XXII. 363 There certainly are two sets of prejudices—those of professionalists, and those of anti-professionalists. **1856** J. GROTE in *Cambr. Ess.* 90 Against those, then, whom we may call professionalists.

professio'nality. [f. as prec. + -ITY.] Professional quality or character; professionalism.

1861 *Economist* 27 Apr. 456/1 The pungency is given..by that additional flavour of professionality. **1886** *Century Mag.* Jan. 399/2 There is one characteristic in which it is well for every country to imitate France: that is, the honesty and 'professionality', if I may invent such a word, of its work. **1904** COL. L. HALE *People's War* 56 How the 'professionality' of these men is in subjection to their exceeding 'human-ness'.

pro'fessionalize, *v.* [f. as prec. + -IZE.]

1. *trans.* To render or make professional.

1856 J. GROTE in *Cambr. Ess.* 89 The mere professionalizing the education will not better the matter. **1886** *Bicycling News* 22 Jan. 290/1 We do not think that any number of the present offenders will professionalise themselves at once. **1890** *Illustr. Lond. News* 7 June 728/2 Perhaps it is the fate of every form of recreation that it should become more or less 'professionalised'—if I may coin a word—and degraded from its original pure health-giving aim. **1947** *Mind* LVI. 393 In the third period..philosophy has been professionalized. **1954** [see LUBRITORIUM]. **1974** *Nature* 11 Jan. 122/3 Steeds 'professionalises' the subject so that a research student with the aid of this book should be able to make intelligent use of anisotropic elasticity.

2. *intr.* To become professional; to proceed in a professional manner.

1890 in *Cent. Dict.*

Hence **pro'fessionalized** *ppl. a.*, **pro'fessionalizing** *vbl. sb.* and *ppl. a.*; also **pro,fessionali'zation,** the action of making or fact of becoming professionalized.

1899 *Speaker* 2 Sept. 224/2 It will be interesting to see if its popularity will survive the professionalising of warfare. **1901** *Sat. Rev.* 24 Aug. 233/1 Batting has..greatly risen.. due in part to..the process which we may perhaps be allowed to call by the clumsy name of professionalisation. **1907** *Edin. Rev.* Oct. 411 The professionalising of religion. **1923** G. B. SHAW *Perfect Wagnerite* (ed. 4) 152 Wagner was not only the highly professionalized royal conductor of Dresden..: he was also the author of the saying that music is kept alive..on the cottage piano of the amateur. **1958** *Oxford Mag.* 20 Feb. 290/1 The increased professionalisation of sport. **1959** B. WOOTTON *Social Sci. & Social Path.* ix. 287 The history of this rapid growth of professionalization, and of the splintering of generalized welfare work into numerous highly specialized professions, is an interesting story. **1969** H. PERKIN *Key Profession* i. 20 The professionalization of university teaching..turned even more on the reform of Oxford and Cambridge. **1972** *Science* 12 May 645/1 The professionalizing of forestry created a community of interest between private and public policy makers. **1973** L. HOLCOMBE *Victorian Ladies at Work* i. 19 There was a raising of the status of the workers in teaching and nursing, this 'professionalization' being.. distinctive..of the period. **1975** *Language for Life* (Dept. Educ. & Sci.) xxiii. 341 Language should become a well-established option in Dip. H.E. courses and..institutions selecting for a professionalising year should look upon it as an important qualification for acceptance. **1977** *N.Y. Rev. Bks.* 14 Apr. 38/3 The bar became increasingly professionalized—which meant that lawyers and judges were drawn from higher social classes. **1977** R. HOLLAND *Self & Social Context* ix. 265 The relation between sociology and psychology in the United States and Britain, both as disciplines and as *professionalising* disciplines. **1979** *Dædalus* Spring 15 They also believe in the 'professionalization' of sociology.

professionally (prəʊˈfɛʃənəlɪ), *adv.* [f. as prec. + -LY².] In a professional manner; with regard to or by way of one's profession.

1784 COWPER *Tiroc.* 658 Art thou a man professionally tied? **1794** MATHIAS *Purs. Lit.* (1798) 169 Yet do I not speak professionally. **1879** MISS BRADDON *Clov. Foot* II. xiv. 262 Do you wish to consult me professionally? **1901** *Daily Chron.* 21 Dec. 3/2 For German officers, the best professionally trained officers in the world, no preliminary specialisation is required.

†pro'fessionary, *a. Obs.* [f. PROFESSION + -ARY¹.] Of or pertaining to a profession; that is such by profession; = PROFESSIONAL *a.* 2, 4.

a **1734** NORTH *Lives* (1826) III. 277 He resigned himself entirely to the order of his parents, and particularly in their professionary disposition of him. *a* **1764** LLOYD *Genius, Envy & Time* 1 In all professionary skill, There never was, nor ever will Be excellence, or exhibition, But fools are up in opposition. *a* **1813** A. F. TYTLER *Univ. Hist.* (1850) I. III. vi. 347 The great advantage which Rome had gained by her system of professionary soldiers.

†pro'fessionate, *a. Obs. rare*⁻⁰. [f. as prec. + -ATE².] = PROFESSIONAL. Hence **†pro'fessionately** *adv.*, professionally, in the exercise of a profession.

1660 *Trial Regicides* 182, *Cook.* I say it was professionately. *L. Ch. B...* The profession of a Lawyer will not excuse them..from Treason.

†pro'fessionist. *Obs.* [f. PROFESSION + -IST, after G. *professionist* an artizan, tradesman.] A person of a particular profession or trade.

1804 EUGENIA DE ACTON *Tale without Title* II. 278 There is seldom more than a stated number of respective professionists in such a district. **1805** W. TAYLOR in *Ann. Rev.* III. 244 The accumulation of successful professionists is intercepted by them. **1834** in *Rep. Poor Law Comm.* App. F. 482 In Dresden, professionists [N. W. Senior's comment p. xxxix: by which word artizans are probably meant] may not marry until they become masters in their trade.

pro'fessionize, *v. rare.* [f. as prec. + -IZE.]

1. *intr.* To follow or exercise a profession.

1858 W. JOHNSON *Ionica* 63 Professionizing moral men Thenceforth admire what pleased them then.

2. *trans.* To turn (an activity) into a profession.

1920 *Christian World* 23 Sept. 14/1 They professionized the study and diverted literature from its true and best purpose.

pro'fessionless, *a.* [f. as prec. + -LESS.] Without a profession; having learned no profession.

1798 *Hull Advertiser* 15 Sept. 2/3 An unfortunate and professionless gentleman. **1833** *Fraser's Mag.* VII. 65 The harassed parent of half-a-dozen portionless girls and as many professionless boys. **1881** H. JAMES *Portr. Lady* xx, A fresh-looking, professionless gentleman, whose leisured state..was a decided advantage.

†pro'fessively, *adv. Obs. rare*⁻⁰.

1611 COTGR., *Professoirement*, professiuely, or by profession.

†pro'fessly, *adv. Obs.* [f. PROFESS *a.* + -LY².] Avowedly, expressly; = PROFESSEDLY 1.

1652 GAULE *Magastrom.* 56 [To] make a voluminous collection of testimonies and authorities profesly against their arts. **1662** J. CHANDLER *Van Helmont's Oriat.* 185 A disease, which I will at sometime profesly touch at in a Book.

professor (prəʊˈfɛsə(r)), *sb.* Also 5 -oure, 5–8 -our; 6 -er. [a. L. *professor*, agent-n. f. *profitēri* to declare publicly, to PROFESS.]

I. †1. *Eccl.* One who has made profession; a professed member of a religious order. *Obs.*

c **1420** ? LYDG. *Assembly of Gods* 914 Chanons, & nonnes, feythfull professoures. **1761** *Chron.* in *Ann. Reg.* 172/2 In France in the year 1710, there were..612 jesuits colleges.. and 24 professors houses of that society.

†2. One who proclaims or publicly declares. *Obs. rare.*

1387 TREVISA *Higden* (Rolls) I. 7 Storie is wytnesse of tyme,..story weldeþ passyng doynges, storie putteþ forþ hire professoures [orig. *suosque prærogat professores*]. Dedes þat wolde be lost storie ruleþ.

3. a. One who makes open declaration of his sentiments or beliefs, or of his allegiance to some principle; one who professes (sometimes opposed, implicitly or explicitly, to one who practises).

1538 STARKEY *England* I. iv. 135 Professorys of Chrystys name and doctryne. **1554** KNOX (*title*) A Faythfull admonition..vnto the professours of Gods truthe in England. **1580** *Reg. Privy Council Scot.* III. 277 Mantineris and professouris of papistrie. **1625** PURCHAS *Pilgrims* II. 1610 Those Turkes which are professors of Humilitie and Devotion. **1678** WANLEY *Wond. Lit. World* v. i. §98. 468/1 In the treaty of Passaw was granted Liberty of Conscience to the Professors of the Augustane Confession. **1690** LOCKE *Hum. Und.* IV. xix. §17 There is no Error to be named, which has not had its Professors. **1710** ADDISON *Whig Exam.* No. 5 ¶8 If the Professors of Non-resistance and Passive Obedience would stand to their Principle. *a* **1862** BUCKLE *Civiliz.* (1869) III. v. 294 The professors of one creed would stigmatize the professors of other creeds as idolatrous.

b. *spec.* One who makes open profession of religion; a professing Christian. Now chiefly *Sc.* and *U.S.*

[Cf. **391** AUGUST. *Utilit. Cred.* 15 Cuiuspiam religionis.. professores.]

1597 BEARD *Theatre God's Judgem.* (1612) 93 Both two hauing bin professors in time past. **1634** RUTHERFORD *Lett.* (1671) 470 Ye know many honourable friends and worthy professors will see your Ladyship, and that the Son of God is with you. **1684** BUNYAN *Pilgr.* II. 151 Then the Name of a Professor was odious; now specially in some parts of our Town..Religion is counted Honourable. **1714** S. SEWALL *Letter-Bk.* 17 Aug., Give warning to professors, that they beware of worldlymindedness. **1814** SCOTT *Wav.* xxx, An excellent blacksmith: 'but as he was a professor, he would drive a nail for no man on the Sabbath'. **1852** MRS. STOWE *Uncle Tom's C.* xvi, Not a professor, as your town folks have it; and what is worse, I'm afraid, not a practiser, either. **1894** CROCKETT *Raiders* 137 He had never rebuked me as a strict professor would have done.

II. 4. a. A public teacher or instructor of the highest rank in a specific faculty or branch of learning; *spec.* one who holds an endowed or established 'chair' in a university or one of its colleges. Also frequently applied to the tutors or lecturers on the staff of theological and other professional or technical colleges, academies, and seminaries.

In the mediæval European Universities, at first simply a synonym of *Magister* or *Doctor* (degrees being originally qualifications to teach); but in this use not common as an English word. The right originally possessed by any Master or Doctor to teach publicly in the schools of his Faculty was gradually restricted to an inner circle of teachers, and the term *Professor* came eventually to be confined to the holders of salaried or endowed teaching offices, or to the highest class of these, such appellations as *Reader*, *Lecturer*, *Instructor*, being given to teachers of lower rank. In the old English Universities the ancient usage survives in the letters S.T.P. (*Sacræ Theologiæ Professor*) for D.D.; the modern use is largely due to the creation of five *Regius* or *King's Professors* by Henry VIII (a number in recent times increased to seven). The endowed teachers of some other subjects were at first called *prælectors*, but this has gradually been superseded by *professor*. See Rashdall *Univ. Europe Mid. Ages* I. 21, etc.

c **1380** WYCLIF *Sel. Wks.* III. 123 But men þat schulden be professoures of science of God synnen many weies aboute þis science. [**1517** *Statutes Corpus Chr. Coll. Oxford*, Quorum trium unus sit Latinae linguae seminator et plantator, qui Lector seu Professor artium humanitatis appellatur.] **1540–1** ELYOT *Image Gov.* 2 b, By his commandement, the professours of those sciences purposed openly questions. **1599** *Broughton's Let.* vii. 21 [They] amounted him to bee the Chiefe professor in Diuinitie. **1601** R. JOHNSON *Kingd. & Commw.* (1603) 89 Geneua..the professor in diuinity..the professor in law..the professor of philosophy..the professor in Ebrew. **1621** BURTON *Anat. Mel.* To Rdr. (1676) 9/2 Our Regius Professour of physick. **1655** FULLER *Ch. Hist.* IX. i. §65 Dr. Richard Smith kings professour of Divinity in Oxford. *a* **1658** CLEVELAND *Commencement* iv, How bravely the Marg'ret-Professor Disputed. **1812** SIR H. DAVY *Chem. Philos.* 18 The magistrates of Basle established a professor's chair for their Countryman [Paracelsus]. **1831** SIR W. HAMILTON *Discuss.* (1853) 407 It was to the salaried graduates that the title of *Professors*, in academical language, was at last peculiarly attributed. *a* **1878** SIR G. G. SCOTT *Lect. Archit.* I. Pref., Only half of the following Lectures were delivered by me, as the Professor of Architecture, at the Royal Academy. **1895** RASHDALL *Univ. Europe Mid. Ages* I. 21 The three titles, Master, Doctor, Professor, were in the Middle Ages absolutely synonymous.

b. Prefixed as title to the name (sometimes abbrev. *Prof*: see PROF), and used in addressing the person.

1706 BENTLEY *Corr.* I. 231 Pray tell Professor Cotes that the book..is presented by Sir Isaac Newton. *Ibid.* 232 (address) To Mr. Professor Sike, at Trinity College, in Cambridge. **1726** S. SEWALL *Letter-Bk.* 3 Feb., You may.. comunicate this to Mr. Professour. **1735** *St. Andrews University Minutes* 10 June, Sederunt: The Rector, Provost Young, Principal Drew, Professor Tullideph, Masters John Craigie, Henry Ramsay [etc.]. **1787** BURNS *Let. to Clarinda* 21 Dec., If you know anything of Professor Gregory, you will neither doubt of his abilities nor his sincerity. **1790** COWPER *Let. to Mrs. King* 5 Oct., I..do not find among them the name of Mr. Professor Martyn. **1825** *Minutes King's Coll. Aberdeen* 3 May, Professors Paul, Tulloch, and Scott. **1858** O. W. HOLMES *Aut. Breakf.-t.* vii, Stand in the light of the window, Professor, said I.—The Professor took up the desired position.

c. Loosely applied to a professor-like person.

1856 EMERSON *Eng. Traits, Truth* Wks. (Bohn) II. 54 They hate the French, as frivolous;..they hate the Germans, as professors. **1865** MAURICE in *Reader* 8 Apr. 392/3 The sophists, whom Mr. Grote perhaps more rightly calls the professors of Greece, who might bear the name of Critics more properly than either.

d. A schoolmaster, a personal tutor; *spec.* a secondary school headmaster. Chiefly *U.S.*

1903 *Dialect Notes* II. v. 326 *Professor*, a male teacher. This abuse of the word 'professor' seems to have grown up in the country districts recently. It is now applied indiscriminately to any schoolmaster. **1940** W. FAULKNER *Hamlet* I. iii. 65 He's going to be the new school professor next year... Or so they claim. **1972** *Buenos Aires Herald* 4 Feb. 13/5 (Advt.), Spanish. Perfect accent, very clear pronunciation with experienced professor.

5. a. One who makes a profession of any art or science; a professional man. Also, in modern use, a 'professional' as opposed to an 'amateur' in any form of sport.

1563 T. GALE *Inst. Chirurg.* 10 b, It woulde come to estimation, and be a worshipfull lyuynge to the professer. **1577** G. GOOGE *Heresbach's Husb.* I. (1586) 16 b, A greater shame is it for a professor of husbandry, to be vnskilful in the ground whereon his whole trade lyeth. **1581** PETTIE *Guazzo's Civ. Conv.* I. (1586) 41 b, This fault is peculiar to certaine schoolemaisters, and other professours of learning. **1609** HOLLAND *Amm. Marcell.* 327 Asbolius, a professor of wrestling. **1647** CLARENDON *Hist. Reb.* I. §156 The Lawyers ..should more carefully have preserved their Profession and its Professours from being profaned by those Services. **1816** *Sussex Weekly Advertiser* 22 July, Mr. Lambert, professor of Cricket, has published the whole art of playing. **1819** MOORE *Tom Crib* 13 *note*, Mr. Jackson..forms that useful link between the amateurs and the professors of pugilism. **1894** *Westm. Gaz.* 3 Nov. 7/2, I think that professionalism in Rugby football in the North of England is inevitable, and that it will bring with it a rupture between the North and South is no less certain... In this case..there will be no international cups for the professors and no North v. South match. **1954** F. C. AVIS *Boxing Ref. Dict.* 87 *Professor*, a familiar name for a boxing coach.

b. Assumed as a grandiose title by professional teachers and exponents of various popular arts and sciences, as dancing, juggling, phrenology, etc.

1774 in C. S. R. Hildeburn *Century of Printing* (1886) II. 182 Catalogue of New and Old Books, to be sold by Auction, by Robert Bell, Bookseller and Professor of Book-Auctioneering, on Monday, the Seventh of February, 1774. **1848** W. C. MACREADY *Diary* 9 Dec. (1912) II. 415 At James's Hotel, where I dined, the landlord introduced me to *Professor* (!) *Risley*—the balancer and posture-master; *of course* I shook hands with him, etc.! **1864** BURTON *Scot Abr.* IV. v. 255 The word Professor—now so desecrated in its use that we are most familiar with it in connection with dancing-schools, jugglers' booths, and veterinary surgeries. **1893** *Daily News* 22 Mar. 4/3 Professor T. B. (the World's Champion High Diver). **1896** C. H. SHINN *Story of Mine* 56 They were never out of sight of pilgrims—Irishmen with wheelbarrows,..'professors' with divining rods and electric 'silver detectors'. **1927** *Amer. Speech* III. 27 Most of those who insist on being given the title 'professor' are quacks or fakers of some kind... The title 'Professor' is now applied more often jocularly than seriously. **1972** *Times* 30 May 2/8 Their [*sc.* performing fleas] trainer, 'Professor' Len Tomlin, was 'too upset' last night to speak about the tragedy which had struck his troupe of 15 performers.

6. *Comb.*, as ***professor-like*** adj.

1806 W. TAYLOR in *Ann. Rev.* IV. 253 The letter.. displays more understanding..than all the professor-like verbiage of Sir James Steuart.

Hence **pro'fessordom**, the domain or sphere of professors; professors collectively; **pro'fessorling** [see -LING 2], a petty or embryo professor.

1870 *Contemp. Rev.* XVI. 21 Its long combat with German Professordom. **1892** *Cath. News* 23 Jan. 3/3 The tyranny of professordom and tyranny of the state. **1903** H. G. WELLS in *T.P.'s Weekly* 13 Nov. 761/2 A provincial professorling in the very act of budding.

professor (prəʊ'fɛsə(r)), *v.* Also with initial capital. [f. the sb.] *trans.* To address (a person) as 'professor'.

1893 W. JAMES *Let.* 8 July (1920) I. 345 Both you and Angell, being now colleagues and not students, had better stop Mistering or Professoring me. **1901** —— *Let.* 16 June (1920) II. 148, I professor-ed you because I had read your name printed with that title in a newspaper letter. **1908** —— *Let.* 28 July (1920) II. 308 Dear Bergson,—(can't we cease 'Professor'-ing each other?)

professorate (prəʊ'fɛsərət). [f. PROFESSOR *sb.* + -ATE[1]; so F. *professorat* (Dict. Acad. 1835).]

1. The office of professor; professorship.

1860 KINGSLEY *Limits Exact Science* 1 The whole of such small powers as I possess will be devoted to this Professorate. **1875** M. PATTISON *Casaubon* 60 He will do better things in time—that is the cry of these years of the Genevan professorate. **1882-3** *Schaff's Encycl. Relig. Knowl.* II. 1448 Calls to other charges and to theological professorates.

2. A body of professors; = PROFESSORIATE 1.

1872 W. CORY *Lett. & Jrnls.* (1897) 282 Enter Oriel or Corpus, and learn lessons of your great Professorate. **1880** *Encycl. Brit.* XI. 64/1 A complex organization for the higher education, with a regular professorate.

professoress (prəʊ'fɛsərɪs). [f. PROFESSOR *sb.* + -ESS[1].] A female professor.

(Also used for Ger. *Professorin*, wife of a professor.)

1740-87 *Lett. Miss Talbot*, etc. (1808) 34 Nor can [I] be so happy as to have any assistance from the professoress in fine speeches. **1845** *Athenæum* Feb. 204 A Symphony by a Parisian professoress, Madame Farrenc, was performed. **1848** SARA COLERIDGE in *Q. Rev.* Mar. 440 Descriptions are given of the College, and some lecturing of one of the professoresses is reported. **1850** KINGSLEY *Misc.* I. *Tennyson* 228 The female college, with its professoresses, and hostleresses, and other Utopian monsters. **1886** W. J. TUCKER *E. Europe* 352 The worshipful Mr. Professor Zachariah, and..his wife, the worshipful Mrs. Professoress Zachariah.

professorial (prəʊfɛ'sɔːrɪəl, prɒf-), *a.* [f. L. *professōri-us* belonging to a public teacher (see PROFESSOR *sb.*) + -AL[1]. So obs. F. *professorial* (18th c. in Littré).] Of or pertaining to a professor; characteristic of a professor or body of professors; pedagogic, dogmatic.

1713 BENTLEY *Rem. Disc. Freethink.* §43 Those persons, for their Professorial interest, and to keep the Pagan System in some countenance against the objections of Christians, had quite alter'd the old Schemes of Philosophy. **1732** *Hist. Litteraria* III. 384 Too much of the Professorial or Sophistical Spirit. **1818** BYRON *Ch. Har.* IV. lvii. *note*, They endowed a professorial chair for the expounding of his verses. **1886** F. POLLARD in *Antiquary* Feb. 53/2 Causing.. professorial and tutorial duties to be entirely suspended.

Hence **profe'ssorialism**, the professorial system, constitution, or practice; **profe'ssorially** *adv.*, in a professorial manner; in the manner of a professor.

a **1846** *Ec. Rev.* (cited in Worcester), Professorialism. **1864** WEBSTER, *Professorialism*, the character, manners, or habits of a professor. **1901** *Athenæum* 17 Aug. 214/1 An.. invasion of the solemn precincts of professorialism by a petulant Junker. **1884** *Daily News* 27 June (in Cassell's *Encycl. Dict.*), Merely lecturing professorially.

professoriat (prɒfɛ'sɔːrɪət). [f. L. *professōrius* belonging to a public teacher (see PROFESSOR) + -AT.] **a.** = PROFESSORIATE 1. **b.** = PROFESSORIATE 2. Also *fig.*

1860 READE *8th Commandm.* 24 So he dismissed himself from the professariat, and became what we call at our Universities 'a private tutor'. **1933** *Sun* (Baltimore) 19 Dec. 1/2 Privately, they express complete distaste for the program, contempt for the 'professoriat'. **1978** *Encounter* Feb. 62/1 In this essay Davie's learning, verbal intelligence, scrupulousness, and his sense of how a poet actually works, combine to do credit to a text and, incidentally, to the Professoriat.

professoriate (prəʊfɛ'sɔːrɪət). [f. PROFESSOR + -ATE[1]; cf. PROFESSORIAT.]

1. A body of professors; the professorial staff of a university.

1858 W. M. CAMPION in *Cambr. Ess.* 167 The revivification of a teaching professoriate. **1862** MERIVALE *Rom. Emp.* VIII. lxiv. 281 Even the extensive professoriate of the Flavian and later emperors comprised no chairs for the teaching of mathematics. **1895** RASHDALL *Univ. Europe Mid. Ages* II. 276 The Universities [in Germany] were thus provided with a permanent Professoriate, and this Professoriate succeeded in time in ousting the unendowed Regent Masters from all real academic power.

2. The office of professor; a professorship.

1885 *Times* 3 Feb. 9/3 Young men who were studying for the priesthood or for the professoriate.

professorship (prəʊ'fɛsəʃɪp). [f. PROFESSOR *sb.* + -SHIP.]

1. The office or function of a professor.

1641 HEYLIN *Hist. Episc.* II. (1657) 385 After his returne, he tooke upon him the Professour-ship in the Schoole afore said. **1678** WALTON *Sanderson* b 5, Dr. Pridiaux succeeded him in the Professorship, in which he continued till the year 1642,..and then our now Proctor Mr. Sanderson succeeded him in the Regius Professorship. **1706** HEARNE *Collect* 23 Apr. (O.H.S.) I. 233 The Regis Professorship of Divinity. **1854** R. WILLIS in Willis & Clark *Cambridge* (1886) III. 167 The private room and laboratory of the Professorship are placed on the ground floor.

b. with possessive, as a humorous title.

1656 HOBBES *Six Lessons* Wks. 1845 VII. 297 Your professorships could not forbear to take occasion thereby, to commend your zeal against *Leviathan* to your doctorships of divinity. **1721** AMHERST *Terræ Fil.* No. 5 (1754) 25 'Indeed', quoth his professorship upon this, 'yes, really, I have heard of strange doings there'.

2. The position of a professor of religion. *rare.*

1869 W. ARNOT *Life J. Hamilton* iv. (1870) 180 The cozy self-coddling ways of modern professorship.

†**pro'fessory**, *a.* *Obs.* *rare*[−1]. [ad. L. *professōrius*: see PROFESSORIAL and -ORY[2].] Of or pertaining to professors; professorial.

1605 BACON *Adv. Learn.* II. Ded. to King §8 This dedicating of Foundations and Dotations to professory Learning hath..had a Maligne..influence vpon the growth of Scyences.

profet, -ett, -ette, obs. ff. PROFIT, PROPHET.

proff(e, obs. forms of PROOF.

proffer ('prɒfə(r)), *sb.* Forms: 4-6 profre, 4-8 profer, 5 profire, -ure, -yre, etc.: see the vb. [ME. *profre*, a. AF. *profre* (*a* 1240 in Godef.), OF. *poroffe*, **poroffre*, vbl. sb. f. *poroffrir*: see next.] An act of proffering; an offer.

1. The act of offering or presenting something for acceptance, or of proposing to do something; an offer; a proposal. Now chiefly *literary*.

c **1350** *Will. Palerne* 4413 Of þe quenes profer þe puple hadde reuþe. **1390** GOWER *Conf.* I. 346 Thei profren hem to his servise; And he hem thonketh of here profre And seith himself he wol gon offre. *c* **1400** MAUNDEV. (Roxb.) xxvi. 123 Þai behete þaim þat er enseged so faire proffers. *c* **1440** LYDG. *Chron.* in *Harvard Studies* (1897) V. 210 The kynge ..Gret profres made..of golde & tresoure. **1544** tr. *Littleton's Tenures* (1574) 70 b, Hee refused the money when lawful profer was made of it. **1652** T. WHITFIELD *Doctr. Armin.* 58 Though the proferre of Salvation be conditionall. **1796** BURKE *Regic. Peace* i. Wks. VIII. 93 Hoping that the enemy..would make a proffer of peace. **1870** DISRAELI *Lothair* xxxii, Accepting the proffer with a delicate white hand.

†**2.** An act or movement as in beginning or attempting to do something, or as if one were about to do something; a show of intention to do something; an essay, attempt, endeavour, trial.

(The alleged sense 'a rabbit-burrow' (in Halliwell, and thence in recent Dicts.) appears to be founded on a misunderstanding of the use of quot. 1577.)

? *a* **1400** *Morte Arth.* 2857 We salle blenke theire boste for alle theire bolde profire. *a* **1425** *Cursor M.* 8819 (Trin.) For no profur þat þei dude [þe tre] wolde not þere stonde in stude. **1456** in *Cov. Corp. Chr. Plays* App. iii. 116 That no fals treitour, ne cruell tirrant, Shall in eny wyse make profer to your lande. **1532** in More *Confut. Tindale* Wks. 389/2 The priest..playeth out the reste vnder silence with signes and profers, with nodding, becking, and mowing. **1577** HARRISON *England* II. xxiv. (1877) I. 358 Conies in making profers and holes to breed in, haue scraped them [coins] out of the ground. **1577-87** HOLINSHED *Chron.* III. 1094/2 After some resistance..and profer of onset made by their horssemen, they were put to flight. **1626** BACON *Sylva* §236 It is done..by little and little and with many Essays and Proffers. **1668** DRYDEN *Ess. Dram. Poesy* Ess. (ed. Ker) I. 32 You may observe..how many proffers they make to dip. **1703** MOXON *Mech. Exerc.* 206 With your Compasses find the Center on the backside of the Round Board (with several proffers if need require).

†**b.** In extended or loose use: An indication of something about to happen; a very slight manifestation of some quality; a sign, a trace. *Obs.*

1548 UDALL *Erasm. Par. Luke* xxi. 167 Y[e] foresaied signes & profres towardes y[e] chaunge of y[e] worlde. **1739** CIBBER *Apol.* (1756) I. 163 The characters I have nam'd..cannot have the least cast or profer of the amiable in them.

3. *Law.* A provisional payment of estimated dues into the Exchequer by a sheriff or other officer at certain appointed times.

(Inaccurately explained in Cowell and later dicts. as the time of such payments, etc.)

[**1290** *Rolls of Parlt.* I. 58/1 Quod non venerunt ad profrum..etiam quia non venerunt super compotum Vicecomitis tempestive.] **1450** *Ibid.* V. 175/2 Shirreffs, Eschetours, or eny other persones that shall make their profres betwene the Feste of Ester, and the first day of Juyll. **1540** *Act 32 Hen. VIII*, c. 21 §2 The said terme..shall.. begynne the Monday next aftre Trinitie Sonday..for the keping of thessoygnes profers retornes and other ceremonies. [**1607** COWELL *Interpr.*, Profer (*profrum vel proferum*), is the time appointed for the acompts of Shyreeues, and other officers in the Exchequer, which is twice in the yeare, *anno* 51 *H.* 3. *stat. quint.*] **1620** J. WILKINSON *Coroners & Sherifes* 45 He hath entred Recognisance for his proffers. **1701** *Cowell's Interpr.* s.v. *Profre Vice-comitis*, Altho' these Proffers are paid, yet if upon conclusion of the Sheriffs Accompts,..it appears that ..he is charged with more than indeed he could receive, he hath his Proffers paid or allowed to him again. **1874** STUBBS *Const. Hist.* I. xi. 379 Each of these magistrates..paid in to the Exchequer such an instalment or *proffer* as he could afford.

proffer ('prɒfə(r)), *v.* Forms: 3-5 profre, (4 profry, proofre), 4-5 proffre, 4-7 profere, proferre, 4-8 profer, (5 profir, -yr, prouffer, prouffre, peroffer, propher, 5-6 profor(re, profur), 5- proffer. [ME. *profr-en, proffre*, a. AF. *proffrir*, *-er*, late OF. *proffrir* = OF. *purofrir* (*c* 1080 in Godef.), *poroffrir*, f. OF. *pur*, *por* (F. *pour*):—L. *prō*, PRO-[1] + *offrir*:—Romanic type **offerēre* or **offerīre*:—L. *offerre* to OFFER. From the interchange of *f* and *ff*, the early forms are often identical with those of PROFER *v.*; and in certain senses (L. *prōferre* having sometimes the sense 'proffer', and It. *profferire* combining 'proffer' and 'profer') the two verbs are difficult to distinguish: see also PROFER.]

1. *trans.* To bring or put before a person for acceptance; to offer, present, tender. Now *literary* and usually in PROFFERED *ppl. a.* 1.

Const. with direct and indirect (dative) obj., the latter with or without *to*. With direct or indirect passive.

13.. *Cursor M.* 4358 (Gött.) Scho..proferd him hir muth to kiss. *c* **1375** *Lay Folks Mass Bk.* (MS. B.) 254 Oure offrandes þat we offer, And oure praieres þat we profer. **1390** GOWER *Conf.* III. 74 To hire he profreth his servise. *c* **1430** LYDG. *Min. Poems* (Percy Soc.) 105 Cookes..proferred me bread, with ale and wyne. **1456** SIR G. HAYE *Law Arms* (S.T.S.) 174 And he peroffer resonable ransoun. **1526** TINDALE *Matt.* vii. 9 Ys there eny man among you which wolde proffer his sonne a stone if he axed him breed? **1615** G. SANDYS *Trav.* 18 He shall be proffered in marriage the best..virgin of their Iland. **1671** CROWNE *Juliana* I. Dram. Wks. 1873 I. 26 Five thousand crowns are proferr'd To any one that will discover him. **1837** DICKENS *Pickw.* ii, Mr. Winkle seized the wicker bottle which his friend proffered. **1877** BLACK *Green Past.* xxi, Before proffering him this promised help.

b. *refl.* To offer or present oneself (or itself).

Const. *to* with simple obj. or inf., or *that* with clause.

c **1290** *S. Eng. Leg.* I. 84/26 Seinte Fey..profrede hire to þe tormentores. *a* **1330** *Otuel* 1265 Þere-fore he profreþ him to fiȝt. *c* **1400** MAUNDEV. (Roxb.) xxi. 96 Ane of þe grettest meruailes..þat fischez..schall..come þider and profre þam self to þe deed. **1484** CAXTON *Fables of Alfonce* xi, Yet shalle I profere me to hym. **1602** FULBECKE *2nd Pt. Parall.* 30 Others, as executors profered themselues. **1711** ATTERBURY *Serm.*, *1 Cor.* x. 13 (1734) I. 99 The Followers of his Fortune proffered themselves to be the ready Ministers of his

Revenge. **1809** Bawdwen *Domesday Bk.* 411 The Priest.. proffers himself that he will prove.. that it is not as they have given in their verdict.

c. *absol.* or with indirect obj. only: To make an offer. ? *Obs.*

1393 Langl. *P. Pl.* C. v. 67 On men of lawe Wrong lokede and largelich hem profrede. **1423** *Rolls of Parlt.* IV. 258/1 If any man will come and profre as it is supposed. *c* **1435** *Torr. Portugal* 417 The kyng of Gales proferd hym feyer: 'Wed my dowghttyr and myn Eyer'. **1575** R. B. *Appius & Virg.* in Hazl. *Dodsley* IV. 152, I proffer you fair: You shall be my full executor and heir.

2. with *inf.* To make a proposal or offer, propose (to do something): = offer *v.* 4. Rarely with clause (quot. *c* 1350), or simple obj. *Obs.* or *arch.*

1303 R. Brunne *Handl. Synne* 3908 That God almyȝty,.. Profrede hym to kesse so louely. *c* **1350** *Will. Palerne* 2489 þe prouost dede pertli profer.. What man.. miȝt þe beres take, He schuld gete of gold garissoun. **1428** *Surtees Misc.* (1888) 2 John Bower proferd to selle hym a laste of osmundes. *c* **1450** *Merlin* 50 Sende to hem.. that thei yelde yow the castell.. and profer hem to go saf with their lyves. **1648** Boyle *Seraph. Love* Ep. Ded. (1660) 2 A necessitous person.. proffer'd to sell the Copy. **1667** Milton *P.L.* II. 425 None.. So hardie as to proffer or accept Alone the dreadful voyage. **1701** W. Wotton *Hist. Rome, Commodus* i. 191 They proffer'd to submit upon his own terms. **1823** Lamb *Elia* Ser. II. *Poor Relations*, He proffereth to go for a coach and lets the servant go.

†**3.** with *inf.* To make an attempt, to essay: = offer *v.* 5 b. Also *refl.* with *inf.* (quot. *c* 1475). *Obs.*

c **1330** R. Brunne *Chron.* (1810) 326 An engyn had þei þer in, & profred for to kast. *c* **1400** *Destr. Troy* 12048 Eneas.. Put hym in prise & profferit to say. *c* **1475** *Rauf Coilȝear* 149 The King profferit him to gang, and maid ane strange fair. *a* **1548** Hall *Chron., Hen. VIII* 122 When the Frenchemen profered to enter, the Englishmen bet them of with bylles. **1655** Fuller *Ch. Hist.* vi. ii. §9 This priviledge was profered afterwards by some Saxon Kings to be restored; which Turketill would never consent unto.

†**b.** *absol.* or *intr.* To make a movement as if about to do something; to begin to act or move, and then stop or turn back: *spec.* of a stag; see quots., and cf. proffer *sb.* 2 and reproffer. *Obs.*

c **1450** *Brut* (E.E.T.S.) 424 There they lay two dayes and two nyghtis, and no pepull proferid oute to hem. **1486** *Bk. St. Albans* E vij, The hert.. He proferith.. and so ye shall say For he wot not hym selfe yit how he will a way. **1575** Turberv. *Venerie* 100 When he [an hart] leapeth into the water and commeth out againe the same way, then he proffereth. **1602** *2nd Pt. Return fr. Parnass.* II. v. 907 The Hart.. being in the water, proferd, and reproferd, and proferd againe. *a* **1650** Crashaw *Carmen Deo Nostro* Wks. (1904) 213 To play the amorous spies, And peep and proffer at thy sparkling Throne. [**1847–78** Halliwell, *Proffer*, to dodge any one. *Devon.* (Not now known, E.D.D.)]

†**4.** *trans.* To offer (battle, injury, etc.); to attempt to inflict: = offer *v.* 3 f, 5. *Obs.*

1471 *Pol. Poems* (Rolls) II. 273 Dayly he prophered batayle his enmys durst not fyghte. *c* **1489** Caxton *Sonnes of Aymon* xxiv. 507 Ye prouffer me owterage. *a* **1548** Hall *Chron., Hen. VIII* 36 b, The citezens.. manfully profered to skyrmish, but thei wᵗ archers were sone driuen backe. **1579** Lyly *Euphues* (Arb.) 89 Which of them hath profferred me the greatest villany.

Hence ˈ**profferable** *a.*, that can be proffered.

1822 G. Darley *Errors of Ecstasie* 38 Didst thou not quit.. No proferable cause asserted why, The track?

proffered (ˈprɒfəd), *ppl. a.* [f. prec. + -ed¹.]

1. Offered for acceptance.

c **1386** Chaucer *Can. Yeom. Prol. & T.* 513 Swich profred seruyse Stynketh, as witnessen thise olde wyse. **1539** Taverner *Erasm. Prov.* (1552) 27 Profered ware stynketh. Seruyce yᵗ is wyllyngly offered is for moost parte to be suspected. *a* **1591** H. Smith *Wks.* (1867) II. 75 The very best worthy do refuse proffered promotion. **1597** A. M. tr. *Guillemeau's Fr. Chirurg.* 4/2 Most commonly, proferede witnesse is reprehendable. **1687** Dryden *Hind & P.* III. 766 Methinks such terms of proffer'd peace you bring, As once Æneas to th' Italian king. **1777** Watson *Philip II* (1793) II. XIII. II. 155 The conditions annexed to the proffered indemnity. **1868** E. Edwards *Ralegh* I. xxi. 464 The Dean refused the proffered mitre.

†**2.** Attempted; offered, as an injury. *Obs.*

1576 Fleming *Panopl. Epist.* 322 Through the proferred iniuries of naughtie people.

profferer (ˈprɒfərə(r)). [f. as prec. + -er¹.] One who proffers; one who makes an offer.

1515 Barclay *Egloges* II. (1570) B ij, So many woers, baudes and brokers, Flatterers, liers, and hastie proferers. **1591** Shaks. *Two Gent.* I. ii. 56 Maides, in modesty, say no, to that, Which they would haue the profferer construe, I. **1697** Collier *Ess.* II. (1703) 58 He who always refuses taxes the proferer with indiscretion. **1723** *Postmaster* 31 May 4 The best Profferer [at a Sale] shall have a Reasonable Price.

ˈ**proffering,** *vbl. sb.* Now *rare* exc. as gerund. [See -ing¹.] The action of the verb proffer.

1. The action of offering for acceptance or sale; an offer; a proposal: = proffer *sb.* 1.

1388 Wyclif *Gen.* xxxiv. 18 The profryng [1382 profre] of hem pleside Emor and Sichem. **1472–3** *Rolls of Parlt.* VI. 59/1 Such [wools] as shal be opened at Caleys at the sale or proferyng of sale by theym. **1647** in W. M. Williams *Ann. Founders' Co.* (1867) 103 That no person free of this Society .. beare about the Streets.. any Ware made of Brasse or Copper, by the way of Hawking or Proffering.

†**2.** = proffer *sb.* 2. *Obs.*

1546 J. Heywood *Prov.* (1867) 80 In such signes and proffring Many prety tales.. had they.

profibrinolysin: see pro-² 1.

†**profiˈcacious,** *a. Obs. rare*⁻¹. [? f. L. *prōficĕre* to make progress, profit + -acious. Cf. *efficacious.*] Advantageous, profitable.

a **1660** *Contemp. Hist. Irel.* (Ir. Archæol. Soc.) I. 204 It would proue somewhat proficacious, if the Councell did send Gerrolt Fennell.. to advise phisically that potator Generall to forgoe distempers and surfeites.

†**proˈficiary.** *Obs. rare*⁻¹. [app. f. med.L. *prōficium*, var. of *prōficuum* profit, subst. use of neuter of late L. *prōficu-us* beneficial, advantageous (for **prōficivus*), f. *prōficĕre* to be advantageous, to profit.] One who profits.

1621 Bp. Mountagu *Diatribæ* 122 Being ignorant what your practice is, and how you thriue thereby, commonly the best argument of a good Proficiary in that trade.

‖**proficiat** (prəʊˈfɪsɪæt). *Obs.* [obs. F. *proficiat* (16th c. in Littré), a. L. *prōficiat* 'may it profit', 3rd pers. pres. subj. of *prōfic-ĕre* to be advantageous, to profit.] A friendly greeting when meeting; payment to ensure a friendly welcome: cf. proface, footing *vbl. sb.* 9, handsel *sb.* 2.

[**1611** Cotgr., *Proficiat*, a fee, or beneuolence bestowed on Bishops, in manner of a welcome, immediately after their installments.] **1653** Urquhart *Rabelais* I. xvii, These buzzards wil have me to pay them here my welcom hither, and my *Proficiat*. *Ibid.* xxxiv, For my *Proficiat* I drink to all good fellowes. *Ibid.* II. xxx.

†**proˈficience.** *Obs.* [f. proficient: see -ence.] Movement onward, progress, advance, improvement; hence, the degree of advancement attained; skill, proficiency.

1605 (*title*) The Twoo Bookes of Francis Bacon. Of the proficience and aduauncement of Learning, diuine and humane. *a* **1610** Healey *Epictetus* (1636) 91 The tokens of proficience in goodnesse. **1673** Milton *True Relig.* 14 Implicit faith, ever learning and never taught, much hearing and small proficience. **1713** Steele *Guard.* No. 43 ¶8 Bat Pigeon.. has attained to great proficience in his art. **1783** Johnson *Let. to Miss Thrale* 24 July, Your proficience in arithmetick is not only to be commended but admired.

proficiency (prəʊˈfɪʃənsɪ). [f. as prec. + -ency.]

†**1.** Progress or advance towards completeness or perfection; improvement in skill or knowledge, as distinguished from perfection.

1544 Coverdale *Let. to C. Hubert* Wks. (Parker Soc.) II. 517 John Dodman,.. I trust, has by this time made such proficiency in the German language, that I doubt not of his being able to discharge the duties of his office to the benefit of the church. **1624** Donne *Lett.* (1651) 7 Heaven is not a place of a proficiency, but of present perfection. *a* **1662** Heylin *Laud* (1668) 317 The Hebrew and Chaldaick Tongues.. became to be so generally embraced, and so chearfully studied, that it received a wonderful proficiency. **1690** Norris *Beatitudes* (1694) I. 118 We are now in a State of Proficiency, not of Perfection. **1849** Macaulay *Hist. Eng.* vii. II. 164 Meanwhile he made little proficiency in fashionable or literary accomplishments. **1855** Prescott *Philip II*, I. I. ii. 13 In sculpture and painting he also made some proficiency.

2. a. The state or degree of improvement attained; an advanced condition; the quality or fact of being proficient; adeptness, expertness, skill.

a **1639** Wotton *Aphorisms Educ.* in *Reliq.* (1672) 91 Pleasing themselves more in opinion of some proficiency, in terms of hunting or horsemanship. **1699** Bentley *Phal.* Pref. 64 He has shown his Proficiency in the noble Science of Detraction. **1726** Swift *Gulliver* III. ii, A tolerable proficiency in their language. **1758** Blackstone *Comm.* I. Introd. i. 17 The clergy in particular.. were peculiarly remarkable for their proficiency in the study of the law. **1859** C. Barker *Assoc. Princ.* II. 56 A proficiency in the use of these weapons being acquired.. by.. athletic games. **1907** *Daily Chron.* 23 Feb. 4/3 Men of over two years' service will be eligible for this proficiency pay (threepence or sixpence extra a day) by the attainment of a defined standard of skill in musketry, signalling, or some other branch.

b. (With *a* and *pl.*) Progress made or adeptness attained in a particular subject. *rare.*

a **1662** Heylin *Laud* I. (1668) 49 Partly by his own proficiencies, and partly by the good esteem which was had of his Father, he was nominated.. unto a Scholars place in that House. *a* **1729** J. Rogers *Serm., 1 Cor.* x. 12 (1735) 104 Reflecting with too much Satisfaction on their own Proficiencies.

3. *attrib.* and *Comb.*, as ***proficiency certificate***, ***level***, ***test***; **proficiency badge** *Scouting and Guiding*, a badge worn to mark achievement in a given test of skill or endurance; **proficiency pay** *Mil.*, increased pay given in respect of proficiency.

1921 *Daily Colonist* (Victoria, B.C.) 10 Apr. 9/4 It is proposed to further consider the proficiency badges which a Two Star Wolf Cub can obtain. **1970** *Policy, Organisation & Rules of Scout Assoc.* II. 25 The Cub Scout proficiency badges are designed to give advanced training in the twelve areas referred to. **1970** G. F. Newman *Sir, You Bastard* 259 Sneed still held the proficiency certificate for using people. **1977** P. Strevens *New Orientations Teaching of English* viii. 91 *Proficiency level*, particularly the distinction between *beginners* and *non-beginners*. **1909** *Westm. Gaz.* 24 Apr. 2/3 £450,000 is the charge for the service or proficiency pay of British soldiers. **1918** E. S. Farrow *Dict. Mil. Terms* 473 *Proficiency pay*, in the British service, extra pay, varying from 3d. to 6d. daily, issuable to soldiers of cavalry, artillery, infantry and school of musketry, according to conditions laid down in the Royal Warrant. **1960** D. D. Eisenhower in *Public Papers of Presidents of U.S. 1960–1961* 49 Additional longevity pay of career personnel,.. an increased number of men drawing proficiency pay. **1918** E. S. Farrow *Dict. Mil. Terms* 473 *Proficiency test*, in target practice, the annual test conducted to determine the proficiency of organizations in collective marksmanship.

proficient (prəʊˈfɪʃənt), *a.* and *sb.* [ad. L. *prōficiens, -ent-em*, pres. pple. of *prōficĕre* to advance, make progress, profit, be useful, f. *prō*, pro-¹ + *facĕre, -ficĕre* to do, make. So OF. *proficient* (15th c. in Godef.) productive.]

A. *adj.* †**1.** Going forward or advancing towards perfection; making progress, improving: opposed to *perfect*. *Obs. rare.*

1615 W. Hull *Mirr. Maiestie* 126 He is all-sufficient; neither deficient, nor proficient, because he is perfect and all sufficient. **1658** Phillips, *Proficient*, helping forward, or profiting.

2. Advanced in the acquirement of some kind of skill; skilled; adept, expert.

c **1590** Marlowe *Faust.* iii. 28 Who would not be proficient in this art? **1784** Cowper *Task* IV. 145 No powder'd pert, proficient in the art Of sounding an alarm. **1801** Southey *Let. to C. W. W. Wynn* 21 Feb. in *Life* (1805) II. 132 The art.. in which they were so proficient, may now be turned successfully against them. **1878** Holbrook *Hyg. Brain* 41 There are some subjects none can become proficient in. **1892** Greener *Breech-Loader* 189 To become proficient in the use of the gun.

B. *sb.* †**1.** A learner who makes progress in something: opposed to one who is perfect. *Obs.*

1596 Shaks. *1 Hen. IV*, II. iv. 19, I am so good a proficient in one quarter of an houre, that I can drinke with any Tinker in his owne Language. **1678** R. L'Estrange *Seneca's Mor.* (1776) 334 These.. are but proficients, and not yet arrived at the state of wisdom. **1721** R. Keith tr. *T. à Kempis' Solil. Soul* xii. 194 He is the Way to Beginners, the Truth to Proficients, and Life to the more Perfect. **1742** Young *Nt. Th.* v. 165 The world's a school Of wrong, and what proficients swarm around We must or imitate, or disapprove.

2. One who has made good progress in some art or branch of learning; an advanced pupil or scholar; an expert, an adept.

1610 Healey *St. Aug. City of God* x. xxvii. 396 The great proficients of righteousnesse. **1616** Bullokar *Eng. Expos.*, *Proficient*, one that hath well profited. **1651** *Life Father Sarpi* (1676) 6 Who.. became in short time so great a proficient, that he was capable of the more solid Arts. **1661** E. Barker *Fun. Serm. Lady E. Capell* 4 Every pious man is an humble modest man, and never reckons himself a perfect proficient. **1711** Shaftesb. *Charac.* (1737) III. Misc. v. i. 238 A Man of reading, and advanc'd in Letters, like a Proficient in the kind. **1816** W. Hollar *Dance of Death* 67 He.. became so distinguished a proficient in polite learning, that he opened a school in his monastery for teaching the sons of the nobility the.. elegancies of composition. **1868** Freeman *Norm. Conq.* II. x. 438 The architect, painter, and general proficient in the arts.

†**3.** A thing that helps or conduces to progress.

1602 Heywood *Wom. Kilde* Wks. 1874 II. 102, I am studied in all Arts; The riches of my thoughts, and of my time, Haue beene a good proficient.

Hence **proˈficiently** *adv.*, with proficiency; with some skill; skilfully.

1835 Beckford *Recoll.* 104 Twanging away most proficiently. **1843** Hardy in *Proc. Berw. Nat. Club* II. No. 11. 65 *note*, They could not proficiently tint their woollen cloth.

†**proficuous,** *a. Obs.* [f. late L. *prōficu-us* (Cassiodorus) beneficial (f. *prōfic-ĕre*: see prec.) + -ous.] Profitable, advantageous, beneficial, useful.

1622 Callis *Stat. Sewers* (1647) 107 The Law intends the immediate possession of such Tenements which be proficuous. **1665** G. Harvey *Advice agst. Plague* 28 You may now believe nothing more proficuous against the Plague.. than Phlebotomy. **1708** J. Philips *Cyder* I. 38 He for ever blest With like Examples, and to future Times Proficuous.

profight, occasional scribal error for *perfight*, obs. f. perfect.

profile (ˈprəʊfaɪl, -fiːl, -fɪl), *sb.* Also 8 profil. See also purfle. [ad. obs. It. *profilo*, now *proffilo*, a border, a limning or drawing of any figure, sb. f. *profilare*, now *proffilare* to profile; from It. also mod.F. *profil*, formerly *porfil, pourfil* (1539–*c* 1700), profile, section, contour, from which some of the Eng. senses may have been directly taken.]

1. a. A drawing or other representation of the outline of anything; esp. of the human face, outlined by the median line.

1656 Blount *Glossogr.*, *Profile* (Ital. *profilo*), that design that shews the side with the rising or falling of any work; As a place drawn sideways, that is so as onely one side or moyety of it may be seen, is called the *Profile*; and is a term in painting. **1704** J. Harris *Lex. Techn.* I, *Profil*.. a Face or Head set sideways, as usually on Medals, and such a Face is said to be in Profil, or in a Side View. **1734** tr. *Rollin's Anc. Hist.* (1827) I. 139 Invented the profile to represent the side face of a prince who had lost one eye. **1833** R. Arnott *Physics* (ed. 5) II. i. 182 The shadow of a face on the wall is a correct profile.

b. A biographical sketch or character study (common in journalistic use since *c* 1920); a summary description or report.

a 1734 R. North in J. L. Clifford *Biogr. as an Art* (1962) 31 As for the many sketches or profiles of great men's lives, pretended to be synoptical or multum in parvo, we are sure there is nothing we look for in them. **1840** Dickens *Let.* 26 Nov. (1969) II. 158, I have gone through your two profiles, and marked them in pencil here and there. **1925** *New Yorker* 21 Feb. 9 (*heading*) Profiles. **1927** *Observer* 23 Oct. 6/2 No man can better give a thumbnail sketch of..a personality intimately known. In this volume we have glimpses of a few political personages... But novel 'profiles' of writers whom he has known are not to be found. **1930** H. Crane *Let.* 21 Nov. (1965) 357 One assignment is a 'profile' of Walter Teagle, president of S .ndard Oil (N.J.). **1942** *Observer* 29 Nov. 1/4 M. Maisky, the Russian Ambassador, is the subject of the 'Profile' on page 7. **1952** M. Steen *Phoenix Rising* v. 112 He's the big guy..who does the profiles in the Saturday edition. **1959** *Economist* 20 June 1096/2 He is the author of 'Profiles in Courage', a prize-winning and best-selling work of popular history. **1962** *Listener* 7 June 1004/1 A film profile of Julian Bream. **1975** *Language for Life* (Dept. Educ. & Sci.) xiv. 217 We have in mind a profile which would include diagnostic information and examples of written work. *Ibid.* xvii. 249 More reliable and productive would be a detailed profile of every child's strengths and weaknesses. **1976** *Liverpool Echo* 6 Dec. 1/5 United States President-elect Jimmy Carter was today examining profiles of 70 possible candidates for Cabinet and other senior posts.

2. ***in profile***, as seen from one side, as opposed to a front view. Also, ***in lost profile*** (see profil perdu).

a **1668** Lassels *Voy. Italy* ii. (1670) 172 The head in Profile of Alexander the great cut into marble. **1702** Addison *Dial. Medals* iii. (1726) 164 Till about the end of the third Century, when there was a general decay in all the arts of designing, I do not remember to have seen the head of a Roman Emperor drawn with a full face. They always appear in *profil*, to use a French term of art. **1746–7** Hervey *Medit.* (1818) 268 Sometimes, she appears in profile, and shews us only half her enlightened face. Anon, a radiant crescent but just adorns her brow. **1865** Lubbock *Preh. Times* xiv. (1869) 518 He excited great commotion among the Sioux by drawing one of their great chiefs in profile. 'Why was half his face left out,' they asked. **1967** W. Ames *Prince Albert & Victorian Taste* xi. 139 The Duke..is seen in lost profile, with just enough of his nose and chin showing to be unmistakable.

3. a. The actual outline or contour of anything, esp. of the human face; in quot. 1791 the horizontal contour-line of a hill. In *Physical Geogr.*, the outline of part of the earth's surface as seen in a vertical section along a straight line or a line following the course of a valley or river; ***profile of equilibrium***, the profile of a graded river or stream; a profile such that the velocity is just sufficient to transport all the load supplied to it from above; also, an analogous profile of a beach, such that the amount of sediment deposited is balanced by the amount removed.

1664 Evelyn tr. *Freart's Archit.* i. 13, I continually begin to measure the projectures of every Profile from the Central line of the Colomn. **1776** Mrs. Delany in *Life & Corr.* Ser. ii. II. 225, I..discovered him at my elbow, modelling my antiquated profil. **1791** Newte *Tour Eng. & Scot.* 434 Leading canals around the profiles of hills. [**1841** A. Surell *Étude sur les Torrents des Hautes-Alpes* i. 2 Quand on relève le profil en long du thalweg, on obtient..une courbe sensiblement continue, dont la pente s'élève, ou, si l'on aime mieux, dont la tangente s'approche de la verticale, à mesure qu'on approche du col. *Ibid.* iv. 18 Le profil longitudinal forme une courbe continue, convexe vers le centre de la terre.] **1868** *Min. Proc. Inst. Civil Engineers* XXVII. 549 The longitudinal profile of the irrigation canal, leading out of such a river should be..a regular inclined plane. *Ibid.*, The profile course of a river..described a curve, concave to the horizon throughout, but more inclined near its source than elsewhere. **1883** Stevenson *Silverado Sq.* 23 Mount Saint Helena..excelled them by the boldness of her profile. **1891** T. Hardy *Tess* i, Throw up your chin a moment, that I may catch the profile of your face better. **1894** *Jrnl. Geol.* II. 77 The profile of a consequent stream may for a time possess unequal slopes at its subsequent falls, but it soon attains a tolerably systematic curve of descent. *Ibid.*, Following certain French writers, the profile of the stream when this balanced condition has been reached has been called the profile of equilibrium. **1902** *Jrnl. Geol.* X. 1 (*heading*) Development of the profile of equilibrium of the subaqueous shore terrace. **1924** *Q. Jrnl. Geol. Soc.* LXXX. 581 There is little indication of the **U**-shaped transverse profile which is so characteristic of the Towy valley near Nant Stalwyn. **1944** A. Holmes *Princ. Physical Geol.* xiv. 292 Along a shore of submergence the slope of the initial surface may be either steeper or gentler than that of the ideal profile of equilibrium. **1950** *Geol. Mag.* LXXXVII. 430 Fig. 1 represents the profile (perpendicular to the fold-axis) of part of the quarry face. **1952** M. L. Begeman *Manuf. Process* (ed. 3) xix. 488 (*caption*) Milling profile of a locomotive side rod. **1954** W. D. Thornbury *Princ. Geomorphol.* xviii. 476 (*caption*) Comparison of topographic profiles across North America and the South Atlantic basin. **1961** L. E. Doyle *Manuf. Processes & Materials* xxxiv. 755 An optical comparator..offers one way of checking the profiles and positions of gear teeth. **1964** V. J. Chapman *Coastal Veg.* viii. 194 The beach profile is often such that it allows the waves to break close in-shore at high tide. **1968** R. W. Fairbridge *Encycl. Geomorphol.* 871/2 During the last glacial period of the Pleistocene, mean sea level was lowered by about 100 meters or more. River valleys cut down towards a new profile of equilibrium. **1969** D. J. Easterbrook *Princ. Geomorphol.* vi. 131 Below its junction with the Platte River, the profile of the Missouri River steepens because of the entry of gravel from the Platte. **1972** M. G. Cross *Oceanogr.* i. 14 A profile of the ocean bottom under the ship's track is drawn by a recorder. **1976** S. Judson et al. *Physical Geol.* xiii. 311/2 The long profile of a stream from its headwaters to its mouth is..steepest in its upper reaches.

b. *transf.* A barometric curve.

1860 Maury *Phys. Geog. Sea* (Low) xxi. §859 There is barely a resemblance between this profile of the atmosphere over the land and the profile of it over the sea.

c. The shape of a wave.

1902 *Encycl. Brit.* XXXII. 579/2 Mr Froude made the assumption that the profile of the wave was a curve of sines. **1952** R. W. Ditchburn *Light* iv. 81 A wave of irregular profile may always be regarded as the sum of a series of simple harmonic waves. **1959** E. Pulgram *Introd. Spectrogr. of Speech* ii. 33 The profiles of waves A and C are so different from one another that one cannot help wondering whether, apart from pitch, they really represent the same tone. **1975** E. Hecht *Schaum's Outl. Theory & Probl. Optics* i. 1, $g(x + vt)$ is a solution of the wave equation corresponding to an arbitrary profile $g(x)$ propagating in the negative x-direction. *Ibid.* 2 Show that $f(x - vt)$ is a progressive wave moving in the positive x-direction with an unchanging profile.

d. *transf.* A characteristic personal manner; an attitude, a policy (of a country, government, etc.). ***low profile***: see low *a.* 23.

1961 *Musical Amer.* May 14/1 In all of Prokofieff's music ..we find his profile—his 'signature'—his craftsman's attitude. **1962** *Listener* 11 Jan. 105/2 Marschner's application of a powerful declamatory style lends Heiling an extraordinary dramatic profile. **1970** *Guardian* 16 Dec. 10/2 The United States..has repeatedly committed itself to keeping its profile low. **1972** *Times* 30 Mar. 2/1 The most complicated question is the profile the Army should adopt at the start of Ulster's 'marching season'. **1972** *Guardian* 12 Apr. 14/1 The British profile during the present crisis in Vietnam has been as low as could be conceived. *Ibid.* 24 May 13/6 There is only one realistic way to deal any sort of worthwhile blow at the IRA... This is to 'raise the profile' very briefly in one.. area. **1978** S. Brill *Teamsters* ix. 323 Jackie expanded his base and his profile by joining civic groups.

4. *Arch.*, *Surveying*, and *Engineering*. A sectional drawing, generally vertical; *esp.* in *Fortif.*, a transverse vertical section of a fort.

1669 Staynred *Fortification* 7 The Profile or Section of a Fort with a Fausse-Bray and Counterscarp. **1715** Desaguliers *Fires Impr.* 141 The Profil of a Chimney, cut by a Plane perpendicular to the Hearth and to the Back. **1803** Woodington in Gurw. *Wellington's Desp.* (1837) II. 291 The profile and elevation of the western front of the fort. **1838** *Civil Eng. & Arch. Jrnl.* I. 148/2 A profile of the river was constructed, exhibiting the depth of water and mud to the rock. **1879** *Cassell's Techn. Educ.* i. 21 The profile is a vertical section at right angles to the trace, and shows the true heights and breadths of the object.

b. *transf.* The comparative thickness of an earthwork or the like (as it would appear in transverse section); hence *ellipt.* an earthwork of strong or weak thickness.

1810 Wellington in Gurw. *Desp.* (1838) VI. 39 This line ought to be taken up generally by a chain of works, closed in the rear by a weak profile connected by a line. **1865** *Reader* 4 Mar. 247/3, 172 guns of position spread over a distance of five miles, which space was fortified by field-works of the weakest profile. **1891** *Daily News* 11 Nov. 5/5 A strong profile will be required on account of the great power of penetration which is given to the present bullet by the smokeless powder employed.

c. A light wooden frame set up to serve as a guide in forming an earthwork.

1834–47 J. S. Macaulay *Field Fortif.* iii. (1851) 50 When a work is traced on the ground..two profiles should be set up on each line, to show the workmen the form of the parapet, and to guide them in the execution of their task... These profiles, when made with straight slips of deal, or other wood, shew with great accuracy the form of the parapet, &c.

d. *Soil Sci.* The set of horizons of which a soil is composed, as displayed in a vertical cross-section down to the parent material.

1906 E. W. Hilgard *Soils* x. 165 (*caption*) Soil profiles illustrating differences in soils of humid and arid regions. **1923** *Soil Sci.* XVI. 95 In this scheme of soil classification, the soil profile includes the whole thickness, upon which the soil-forming processes have operated, from the surface down to the parent rock or geologic substratum. The importance of a separation of a profile into its natural divisions is emphasized. **1927** N. C. Comber *Introd. Sci. Study of Soil* xiii. 144 Areas in which the profiles are essentially alike are grouped together and the characteristic profile is given a definite name. **1946** L. D. Stamp *Britain's Struct. & Scenery* xi. 94 Over a large part of Highland Britain..there has been insufficient time for the weathering of rocks and the formation of a complete profile. **1954** W. D. Thornbury *Princ. Geomorphol.* iv. 80 Some soils have profiles that could not have developed under a single set of soil-developing controls, but consist of a younger profile developed under existing topographic and climatic conditions superposed upon an older profile formed under different conditions. **1976** M. D. Gidigasu *Laterite Soil Engin.* xx. 512 In well-developed laterite profiles, the laterite horizon ranges in texture from gravelly soils to laterite rock.

e. *Geol.* A representation of the form of the interface between strata obtained from measurements made at points lying on a straight line; also, the line itself; ***to shoot a profile***, to make such measurements.

1929 *Colorado School of Mines Q.* Mar. 108 For a number of potential profiles covering the ground, lines of equal resistivity may be drawn in plan view, instead of equipotential lines. **1929** *Trans. Amer. Inst. Mining & Metalling Engineers* LXXXI. 597 To delimit a newly discovered dome and determine the depth to the top of the cap..profiles are shot by the refraction method. **1931** [see profiling *vbl. sb.* 3]. **1940** C. A. Heiland *Geophysical Explor.* ix. 499 In a new area a profile is first shot to determine the normal sequence of beds. *Ibid.* x. 736 The survey..is of interest because of the excellent correlation possible between resistivity profiles. *Ibid.* 739 Fig. 10-71 shows resistivity-depth curves for a dipping vein taken along three profiles, laid out 15° off strike, at increasing distances from the outcrop. **1949** *Geophysics* XIV. 57 (*heading*) Airborne magnetic profile above 40th parallel, eastern Colorado to western Indiana. **1950** *Bull. Amer. Assoc. Petroleum Geologists* XXXIV. 1384 The slope of a time-distance curve plotted from a profile across the dome usually showed salt velocity. **1960** M. B. Dobrin *Introd. Geophysical Prospecting* (ed. 2) v. 86 Figure 5-13 shows two sample refraction records shot from opposite directions, each made with a spread of 22 detectors spaced 300 ft apart along a profile in line with the shots. **1977** *Nature* 3 Nov. 23/2 (*caption*) Seismic and magnetic profiles from locations indicated in Fig. 1. Vertical scale for the seismic profiles is in seconds of two-way travel time.

f. The outline formed on a graph or chart by joining the scores that a person has obtained in tests for various personality traits, esp. in order to provide a quantified result easily comparable with the results of others or of the norm; a similar type of diagrammatic representation of measured individual attributes for purposes of comparison. Also *transf.*

1932 Darrow & Heath in K. S. Lashley *Stud. Dynamics of Behavior* 68 By repetition and comparison of tests on the same person, we find a tendency for the shape of the profile to be characteristic of a given individual. **1940** T. L. Kelley *Talents & Tasks* 28 The full line is the profile of an individual, and the dotted line that of the average participant in the type of job being considered. **1946** *Jrnl. Clin. Psychol.* II. 23/1 Several recent articles have discussed the usefulness of the Minnesota Multiphasic Personality Inventory in various clinical situations..and one has dealt with the problem of test profiles. **1948** *Eng. Stud.* XXIX. 109 Two variables are considered of prime importance in identifying specific patterns of tone in speech: the shape of the curve of speech melody, and the position of the principal stress on that curve. A given combination of shape and stress-position will be referred to as a profile. **1957** R. B. Cattell *Personality* ix. 366 The definition of a profile as a set of ordered measurements (corresponding to the mathematical definition of a vector quantity) applying to a single case. **1960** J. B. Carroll in Saporta & Bastian *Psycholinguistics* (1961) 342/1 Métraux's..'profiles' of speech development include descriptions of the tendency of the child to verbalize with regard to his own and others' behavior. **1973** *N.Y. Law Jrnl.* 24 July 4/4 To be sure, Ruiz-Estrella did fit the hijacking profile, but no one contends that this statistical survey..can come close to supplying traditional probable cause for a search. **1973** *Times* 26 July 8/2 Mr. Ehrlichman said that the need for a psychiatric profile of Dr. Ellsberg had prompted the decision to break into the office. **1974** *Physics Bull.* Nov. 505/1 Abstracts would be sent selectively to subscribers.. according to their interest 'profiles'. **1977** *Language* LIII. 186 Given that we have participants of particular socio-economic profiles—but not taking their individuality into account—and given the specific situation, these are the choices which are most expected.

g. *Astr.* (A diagram of) the way the intensity of radiation varies with wavelength from one side of a line in a stellar spectrum to the other.

1933 *Proc. Nat. Acad. Sci.* XIX. 642 (*caption*) Schematic profiles of lines in the spectrum of a nova expanding with constant high velocity. *Ibid.*, The predicted profile of a star with an effectively transparent radiation shell, ejecting matter symmetrically with respect to two hemispheres. **1953** L. H. Aller *Astrophysics* p. v, The abundance of calcium may be determined from the profile of the '*K*' line in the solar spectrum. **1957** *Encycl. Brit.* XXI. 1951/1 The profiles of faint lines are strongly affected by the resolving power of the spectrograph. **1971** *Nature* 15 Jan. 214/1 He was one of the first to measure intensity profiles of the Fraunhofer lines in the solar spectrum and to attempt to explain these by theoretical models.

h. (A diagram of) the way a quantity varies along a line, esp. a vertical line through the earth or atmosphere; more widely, any graph in the form of a line.

1953 *Jrnl. Geophysical Res.* LVIII. 519 Five temperature profiles are obtained which represent stratospheric conditions over New Mexico during October 1952. **1955** *Sci. Amer.* Sept. 168/2 If we took gravity readings all over the earth and corrected them to sea level, we would have a gravity profile of the geoid. This profile undulates. **1963** G. L. Pickard *Descriptive Physical Oceanogr.* vi. 97 Temperature/depth or salinity/depth profiles..are usually drawn as the first stage in examining oceanographic data. **1970** *Sci. Jrnl.* Apr. 50/3 The measurement of temperature profiles within the atmosphere from satellite heights. **1971** I. G. Gass et al. *Understanding Earth* v. 85/2 (*caption*) Crustal temperature—depth profiles, as a function of heat flow and surface radioactivity. **1972** *Nature* 25 Feb. 417/1 Oxygen isotope profiles through the entire depth of the ice sheets of Greenland and Antarctica..provide an excellent record of climatic changes. **1977** *Lancet* 29 Oct. 932/1 The area irradiated by the transducer was calculated from beam profiles obtained by scanning a piezo-electric probe hydrophone through the centre of the beam, parallel to the transducer face. **1978** *Nature* 20 Apr. 725/1 PAS staining of the modified bovine receptors revealed a radically different profile and showed the presence of at least four major peaks with molecular weights in the region of $3{\cdot}9 \times 10^4$, 5×10^4, $1{\cdot}25 \times 10^5$ and $1{\cdot}8 \times 10^5$.

i. *Astronautics.* A particular sequence of accelerations undergone by a space rocket in flight; the plan of a space flight as regards the nature and duration of successive trajectories.

1962 K. A. Ehricke *Princ. Guided Missile Design* I. vii. 774 (*caption*) Constant thrust acceleration profile with and without intermediate coast period. **1962** R. C. Duncan *Dynamics Atmospheric Entry* i. 16 The functional phases of the direct-entry profile are: 1. Orbital phase... 2. Departure phase... 3. Free-fall phase... 4. Approach phase... 5. Landing phase. **1966** *Electronics* 3 Oct. 131 In the Mercury and Gemini programs, and in hypothetical mission profiles, the crew's time usually limits the number of adjustments that can be made in an experiment. **1972** *Jrnl. Spacecraft &*

Rockets IX. 259 (*heading*) Thrust profile shaping for spin-stabilized vehicles.

†**5.** A ground-plan. *Obs.*

1679 MOXON *Mech. Exerc.* ix. 170 *Profile*, the same with *Ground-Plot.* **1701** J. COLLIER *Hist. Geog. Dict.* (ed. 2) s.v. *Cambalu*, It is true, that the Profil, or Draught of Cambalu, which the Portuguese have at Lisbon.. differs from that of Peking, which the Hollanders brought.

6. In *Pottery* (and *Bell-founding*). A plate in which is cut the exterior or interior outline of one side of the object to be made.

1756 *Dict. Arts* s.v. *Foundery of Bells*, The core is judged to be in perfection, when the profile carries the fresh cement entirely off, without leaving any upon the last dry lay. **1825** J. NICHOLSON *Operat. Mechanic* 462 With his fingers,.. he gives the first form to the vessel; then with different profiles, or ribs, he forms the inside of the vessel into whatever shape may be required, and smoothes it by removing the.. inequalities. **1832** G. R. PORTER *Porcelain & Gl.* 46 The instruments employed for this purpose [giving the first form to a vessel in 'throwing'] are called profiles or ribs.

7. *Theatr.* A flat piece of scenery or property on the stage of a theatre, cut out in outline.

1824 J. DECASTRO *Mem.* 43 The master carpenter had forgot to saw off one of the unpainted pieces of profile belonging to a wing. **1904** *Westm. Gaz.* 29 Jan. 10/1 A piece of 'profile' was left standing in contact with the gas-jets for twenty minutes without effect. **1906** VOLPÉ in *P.T.O.* I. 14/2 Another 'villain' and myself had to cross the stage in a boat designed on lines usually known as 'profile'.

8. *attrib.* and *Comb.*, as ***profile head, line, painter, picture, study, view, writer***; **profile board**, a flat board or plate cut to a pattern, used to test the outside measurements of an object; a gauge; **profile chart** *Ecol.* = *profile diagram*; **profile cut**, a method of cutting a diamond in which it is sliced into thin plates that are polished on one side, finely grooved on the other, and bevelled on the edge; also *attrib.* as *adj.*; **profile cutter**, a cutting tool in wood- or metal-working machines, which corresponds in shape to the profile to be produced; **profile diagram** *Ecol.*, a representation of a vertical section through a forest, showing the outlines of the individual components of the vegetation; **profile drag** *Aeronaut.*, that part of the drag on an aerofoil or aircraft which arises directly from its profile and from skin friction, i.e. those parts of the drag which are not attributable to lift; **profile grinding** *Engin.*, grinding in which the wheel extends the whole width of the work and is given a profile which when viewed at right angles to the axis of rotation is the negative of the one it is desired to produce on the work; so **profile-grind** *v. trans.*, **-ground** *ppl. a.*; also **profile grinder**, a machine for this; **profile instrument, machine**, an apparatus formerly in use for taking silhouettes; **profile machine**, a machine for shaping the profile of small parts of machinery, in which the cutting tool is guided by a pattern; **profile paper**, paper ruled with equidistant vertical and horizontal lines, for convenience in drawing to scale; **profile piece**, *Theatr.*, = sense 7; **profile shot**, a photograph or view of the human face in profile; **profile stage property** = sense 7; **profile-wing**: see quot. 1873.

1926 TANSLEY & CHIPP *Aims & Methods in Study of Vegetation* iv. 65 Profile charts record diagrammatically the vertical relations of the vegetation.. as seen in profile or 'elevation'. **1965** P. J. FISHER *Jewels* vi. 83 Normally, for the conventional brilliant cut, an octahedral diamond crystal is sawn into two halves... For the new profile cut the same crystal is sawn into four plates. **1970** R. WEBSTER *Gems* (ed. 2) xx. 378 The Profile cut allows considerably greater area of visible diamond than a brilliant cut of similar size. Viewed from above a Profile cut diamond resembles a row of baguettes joined by a common table facet. **1976** 'D. CRAIG' *Faith, Hope & Death* xxii. 156 Good stuff, like profile-cut diamonds. [**1933** DAVIS & RICHARDS in *Jrnl. Ecol.* XXI. 369 The stratification is very irregular and ill-marked, as can also be seen from the diagrammatic profile in Fig. 6.] **1952** P. W. RICHARDS *Trop. Rain Forest* ii. 24 Because the direct observation of the stratification of the Rain forest usually offers insuperable difficulties, Davis & Richards.. adopted the device of constructing profile diagrams to scale from accurate measurements of the position height and width and depth of crown of all the trees on narrow sample strips of forest. **1974** MUELLER-DOMBOIS & ELLENBERG *Aims & Methods Vegetation Ecol.* viii. 148 Profile diagrams can be used to illustrate details in vertical spacing of species. **1922** *Flight* XIV. 692/2 Prandtl calls this increment of the drag at given lift by the trailing vortex system the 'induced drag', and the drag of the wing of infinite aspect ratio and of the same section he calls the 'profile drag'. **1936** *Jrnl. Aeronaut. Sci.* IV. 13/2 The covering of cellulose acetate may be highly polished to lower the profile drag. **1979** *Nature* 20–27 Dec. 778/3 These calculations take into account the effects of lift (or, in aeronautical jargon, 'induced drag') and of the power needed to overcome direct air resistance ('profile drag'). **1941** *Automobile Engineer* XXXI. 169/3 (*caption*) Profile grinding a helical gear by the Maag gear grinding process. **1956** *Ibid.* XLVI. 348/2 The floor-to-floor time was 12 minutes, or 6 minutes per gear. To profile grind at such rates a reasonable standard of gear preparation is necessary. **1950** C. R. HINES *Machine Tools for Engineers* xi. 234 Profile or contour grinders. These grinders are similar to pantograph milling machines. **1968** S. TOLANSKY *Strategic Diamond* viii. 67 (*caption*) Shaped profile grinder roller for making ceramic spark plug. **1975** BRAM & DOWNS *Manuf. Technol.* i. 31 Microscopes are incorporated in suitable machine tools such as profile grinders. **1917** T. R. SHAW *Precision Grinding Machines* x. 155 (*heading*) Profile and form grinding. **1956** *Automobile Engineer* XLVI. 347 (*heading*) Faster profile grinding of spur gears. **1968** S. TOLANSKY *Strategic Diamond* viii. 66 Profile grinding is used extensively and ubiquitously for both large and small components which require to be of exact size or have complex shape. *Ibid.* 67 In spite of the hardness of the carbide profile grinding wheels and rollers they soon wear and lose both accurate outline and.. accuracy in dimensions. **1941** *Automobile Engineer* XXXI. 168/3 In some cases the gears are hobbed and in others pinion type profile ground cutters are employed. **1762** H. WALPOLE *Vertue's Anecd. Paint.* (1828) V. 203 John Clarke.. did two profile heads in medal of William and Mary, Prince and Princess of Orange, yet dated 1690. **1842** FRANCIS *Dict. Arts*, etc., *Silouette*, or *Profile Instrument*, a contrivance for taking the exact outline of an object, particularly the outline of a person's side face. **1897** *Outing* (U.S.) XXX. 125/2 The skull rounded with a slight peak—profile line nearly straight. **1837** DICKENS *Pickw.* xxxiii, Your likeness was took on my hart in much quicker time.. than ever a likeness was took by the profeel macheen. **1892** HASLUCK *Milling machines* 154 Fig. 134. Single-spindle profile milling machine.. used in small-arms factories for milling articles of irregular shape. **1788** BURNS *Let. to R. Ainslie* 23 June, Mr. Miers, profile painter in your town, has executed a profile of Dr. Blacklock for me. **1874** 'MARK TWAIN' *Gilded Age* xvii. 160 He plotted the line on the profile paper. **1892** *Appleton's Cycl. Techn. Drawing* 157 Profile paper can be obtained from stationers, on which are printed horizontal and vertical lines. **1793** J. WOODFORDE *Diary* 25 Nov. (1929) IV. 80 They were so kind as to bring us a profile Picture of our late worthy friend Mr. DuQuesne. **1967** P. A. WHITNEY *Silverhill* iii. 48 He could not photograph me properly. Someone less skilled had taken over, but profile shots were not the same. **1968** L. DEIGHTON *Only when I Larf* ii. 24 He swung round to give me a profile shot. **1972** I. HAMILTON *Thrill Machine* viii. 34 She always managed to turn slightly this way or that to give Joe a profile shot. **1854** A. C. MOWATT *Autobiogr.* xvii. 308, I suppose you will send some profile stage properties to my room. **1959** *N. & Q.* Feb. 84/1 An initial profile-study gives some biographical facts. **1767** MONRO in *Phil. Trans.* LVII. 503 A profile view of a small piece. **1873** *Routledge's Yng. Gentl. Mag.* Apr. 278/2 Side scenes cut out thus are termed *profile wings*. **1978** *Rugby World* Apr. 36/2 Being wholly inarticulate on any aspect of Rugby, I decided it might be wiser to confine my questioning to Gareth's second enthusiasm which, according to a generation of profile-writers, is fishing.

profile (ˈprəʊfaɪl, -fiːl, -fɪl), *v.* [ad. obs. It. *profilare* (mod. *proffilare*) to draw in outline, f. *pro*:—L. *prō*, PRO-[1] 1 a + *filare* to spin, † to draw a line:—late L. *fīlāre* to spin, f. L. *fīl-um* a thread. So mod.F. *profiler*, formerly *porfiler*, *pourfiler* (Cotgr. 1611). See also PURFLE.]

1. a. *trans.* To represent in profile; to delineate the side view or outline of; to draw in section; to outline. Also *fig.*

1715 LEONI *Palladio's Archit.* (1742) I. 21, I have profil'd the Imposts of the Arches. *Ibid.* 30 The method of profiling each Member. **1882** E. P. HOOD in *Leisure Ho.* Apr. 225 Instances in which he thus profiles his contemporaries. **1902** *Contemp. Rev.* Dec. 838 The delicate tracery of the leaves [was] profiled against the sunset sky.

b. To compose or present a profile (sense 1 b) of (a person). Also *transf.* orig. *U.S.*

1948 *Word Study* Apr. 3/1 A student publication at Wayne wrote: 'Pan Profiles Russell Beggs' *Panorama*.' **1959** J. THURBER *Years with Ross* v. 85 Ross.. took.. the flagpole sitter.. and profiled him. **1967** *Times Rev. Industry* Oct. 12/2 In February when the *Review* profiled Mr. Len Neal.. he spoke enthusiastically of his department. **1970** T. LUPTON *Managem. & Social Sci.* (ed. 2) iv. 98 Ways of measuring and 'profiling' the many structural characteristics of organizations. **1974** *Observer* 24 Mar. 29 (*caption*) Anthony Sampson profiles Mrs Katherine Graham, whose newspaper exposed the Watergate scandal. **1979** *Tucson* (Arizona) *Citizen* 20 Sept. 7B/3 Hugh Downs hosts a magazine format show. Tonight, disco star Donna Summer is profiled.

c. To summarize or register (information).

1971 *Nature* 19 Mar. 153/2 The user constructs a list of words and phrases (search terms) that summarize (profile) his information requirements. **1975** *New Yorker* 12 May 93/1 Electrical wires from the model power plants.. ran over to a control room, where electronic equipment could absorb the findings of a hundred and twenty instruments that profiled, among other things, hull pressures, mooring forces, and six degrees of freedom of motion.

2. To furnish with a profile (of a specified nature), give an outline to; also, to cause to form a profile. (In first quot. *profiled* may be an adj. = having a profile (of a certain kind), outlined.) Cf. PROFILING *vbl. sb.* 2.

1823 P. NICHOLSON *Pract. Build.* 496 The Grecian Ionic specimens of capitals,.. are, generally speaking, better profiled than those of the Romans. **1865** J. FERGUSSON *Hist. Archit.* I. II. II. i. 401 Had they [Gothic architects] carefully profiled and ornamented the exterior of the stone roofs. **1905** J. HORNER *Engineers' Turning* xv. 294 Fig. 368 is a tool in its holder used for profiling ball handles, as used on lathes, and other machine tools. **1953** G. S. SCHALLER *Engin. Manufacturing Methods* xix. 340 (*caption*) Vertical rotary-head milling machine profiling a vertical surface. **1973** J. G. TWEEDDALE *Materials Technol.* II. vi. 146 Side-cutters are often profiled axially to cut a specific shape.

3. *intr.* To present one's profile to view; *spec.* in *Bullfighting*, to stand in profile in preparation for a charge.

1932 E. HEMINGWAY *Death in Afternoon* 347 Profiling with more style, his kills would gain greatly in emotion. **1957** A. MACNAB *Bulls of Iberia* xv. 205 To get it to charge he has to profile on the contrary horn, making it feel sure it will catch him each time. **1973** *Black World* Sept. 84 Ever get tired of people posturing, Posing and profiling? **1974** F. NOLAN *Oshawa Project* ii. 14 He'll be over here.. profiling for the newsreels.

4. *trans.* To measure or investigate the profile (sub-senses of 4) of. Cf. PROFILING *vbl. sb.* 3.

1932 *Physics* II. 174 One of the earliest applications of the seismograph was its use in profiling salt domes. **1960** *Econ. Geol.* LV. 204 Sometimes the geologist wants to profile a particular stratigraphic horizon.. instead of the land surface. **1972** *Physics Bull.* Feb. 85/1 The Clarendon Laboratory at Oxford.. has improved still further its original method of profiling the atmosphere from a satellite. **1978** *Nature* 5 Jan. 49/2 Side-scan sonar has been used.. to profile icebergs, by lowering a sonar transducer vertically.. from the side of a boat.

Hence ˈ**profiled** *ppl. a.*

1715 LEONI *Palladio's Archit.* (1742) I. 15 The profil'd Architrave, mark'd F. **1902** *Encycl. Brit.* XXVII. p. xix, The profiled figures in low relief.

profiler (ˈprəʊfaɪlə(r)). [f. PROFILE *v.* + -ER[1].]

1. A profile machine.

1904 *Electr. World & Engin.* 19 Mar. 581/2 (*heading*) Motor driven profiler. **1927** *Daily Tel.* 11 May 18/3 (Advt.), Gear cutters, Profilers, Radials, &c. **1957** W. H. ARMSTRONG *Machine Tools for Metal Cutting* vii. 156 The distinguishing feature of a profiler is a profiling unit that is mounted on a spindlehead which may be fed transversely. **1963** JONES & SCHUBERT *Engin. Encycl.* (ed. 3) 1007 Most of the profilers used at the present time are hand-operated, so far as the feeding movements are concerned.

2. An instrument for measuring profiles, esp. of strata of rock or the sea bed.

1959 *World Oil* Apr. 107/2 A versatile new marine exploration device.. has been applied recently to problems in connection with petroleum exploration... Known as the ..continuous seismic profiler, the technique essentially is a continuous sound reflection device. **1969** J. W. MAVOR *Voyage to Atlantis* v. 104 We carried five basic instrument systems. First, a sonar system.. to measure depth. Three instrument systems, the seismic profiler, the magnetometer and the gravimeter. Finally, [etc.]. **1972** J. G. DENNIS *Structural Geol.* xvi. 368 Most present-day profilers work with sound sources such as high voltage sparks or air guns. **1973** *Nature* 22 June 455/2 Seismic reflexion profiler data reveal a distinct basement ridge. **1975** *McGraw-Hill Yearbk. Sci. & Technol.* 291/2 Velocity shears top to bottom are given by a free-falling electromagnetic profiler... The instrument measures minute voltages induced by the flow of sea water in the Earth's weak magnetic field. **1978** *Nature* 7 Dec. 601/2 Temperature profiles were taken from the RV Oceanographer with the microstructure profiler (MSP), a winged instrument which falls freely through the water measuring temperature, pressure, and conductivity.

profiling (ˈprəʊfaɪlɪŋ), *vbl. sb.* [f. PROFILE *v.* + -ING[1].] **1.** The drawing of profiles.

1888 W. P. P. LONGFELLOW in *Scribner's Mag.* III. 426 One of the secrets of good profiling.

2. *Engin.* The shaping of a part, orig. by means of a tool guided by a template or pattern. Freq. *attrib.*, esp. in ***profiling machine*** (= *profile machine* s.v. PROFILE *sb.* 8).

1892 HASLUCK *Milling machines* 152 Fig. 133 is a two-spindle profiling machine, and the cutter will profile or surface to the extreme limit of the table area. **1950** C. R. HINE *Machine Tools for Engineers* ix. 155 (*caption*) Four-spindle vertical Hydrotel milling machine with automatic 360-deg profiling attachment. **1957** [see PROFILER 1]. **1967** A. BATTERSBY *Network Analysis* (ed. 2) 377 This measure is likely to utilize the drilling machine inefficiently, because of the odd bits of time spent in waiting for successive small batches from the profiling machine.

3. *Geol.* and *Physical Geogr.* [f. PROFILE *sb.*] The measurement or investigation of profiles, esp. of strata; *spec.* by means of measurements made at points lying on a straight line.

1929 *Trans. Amer. Inst. Mining & Metall. Engineers* LXXXI. 598 Mapping structures.. by means of refraction profiling. **1931** F. H. LAHEE *Field Geol.* (ed. 3) xxiii. 680 Field work may be conducted according to one of three main plans: (1) fan-shooting or fanning by the refraction method; (2) profile shooting, or profiling by the refraction method; and (3) profiling by the reflection method. **1938** B. MCCOLLUM in A. E. Dunstan et al. *Sci. of Petroleum* I. VIII. 396/2 In most cases.. the profiling of this very shallow boundary cannot be successfully carried out at the present time by reflection. **1963** J. B. HERSEY in M. N. Hill *Sea* III. iv. 65 Continuous refraction profiling should prove especially valuable in the study of unconsolidated sediments in deep water. **1968** R. W. FAIRBRIDGE *Encycl. Geomorphol.* 1227/2 Sub-bottom acoustic profiling.. has demonstrated many wave-cut terraces partly hidden beneath a thin veneer of late Holocene sediments. **1977** R. J. RICE *Fund. Geol.* viii. 141 Profiling. A third approach to the analysis of hillslope forms is by measurement of representative profiles.

profilist (ˈprəʊfɪlɪst). [f. PROFILE *sb.* + -IST.] One who produces profile portraits or silhouettes.

a **1800** *Inscription Profile Portrait* in *N. & Q.* 9th Ser. VI. 357/1 Charles fecit, the first Profilist in England. **1808** LAMB *Let. to T. Manning* 26 Feb., Mrs. Beetham the Profilist or Pattern Mangle woman opposite St. Dunstan's. **1833** *New Monthly Mag.* XXXIX. 60 Likenesses.. of our host and his lady, taken in fifteen seconds by an itinerant profilist. **1905** HOLMAN-HUNT *Pre-Raphaelitism* II. 208 The profilist who did the silhouette.

profilmic: see PRO-[2] 2.

profilograph (prəʊˈfiːləʊgrɑːf, -æ-). [a. F. *profilographe* (so named by its inventor Dumoulin), f. PROFILE *sb.* + Gr. -γραφ-ος writer, delineator: see -GRAPH.] A machine which traces mechanically the contour line of the ground over which it travels; = PROFILOMETER 2.

Exhibited at Paris Universal Exhibition 1855; the subject of Eng. Patent No. 1464, but not there named. See *La Nature* (1880) II. 31.

1890 in *Century Dict.* **1941** *Jrnl. Amer. Ceramic Soc.* XXIV. 229 The closest approach to this was a profilograph which had been constructed by Abbott at the University of Michigan and a somewhat similar device which had been built in Germany by Schmaltz. These instruments used a diamond stylus mechanically mounted on a mirror in such a way that movements of the diamond point in a direction normal to the surface of the material could be magnified by an optical lever system and the results recorded on a photographic film. **1963** *Engineering* 20 Sept. 360/1 The Bump-cutter employs 110 12 in diameter saw blades impregnated with natural diamonds. The design principle is based on a profilograph with the cutting head mounted on a 16 ft long frame supported by drive wheels at the rear and steering wheels at the front. **1976** ATTEWELL & FARMER *Princ. Engin. Geol.* x. 751 Unless joint surfaces are sufficiently exposed..to lend themselves to profilograph examination, it is difficult to see how a reduction factor can be applied.

profi'lometer. [ad. F. *profilomètre* (Brocas); in Ger. *profilzeichner* (Hasting); f. PROFILE *sb.* + -OMETER.] **1.** Any instrument or device for measuring the profile of the face.

1895 in *Funk's Standard Dict.* **1939** *Jrnl. Amer. Med. Assoc.* 18 Nov. 1903/2 A description of Dr. Joseph Safian's profilometer is found in his book 'Rhinoplastic Surgery'.

2. Any instrument for measuring or recording the roughness of a surface; *spec.* (*a*) one in which a fine stylus is drawn over a metal surface; (*b*) one consisting of a wheeled frame for travelling along a road.

1937 *Metal Cleaning & Finishing* May 426 During the past two years, a new instrument called the 'Profilometer' has been developed. This instrument supplements the earlier work in this field, and enables roughness measurements to be made rapidly with a portable instrument. **1938** *Times* 26 Nov. 9/4 The profilometer—designed and constructed at the Road Research Laboratory—has been used to measure the riding qualities of a number of experimental sections. This 16-wheeled machine compares irregularities in the surface by integrating the vertical rise and fall in profile of the road above a given datum, the results being recorded as 'inches per mile'. **1949** G. SCHLESINGER *Factory* xi. 219/1 Generally the Profilometer provides only 'average' readings..determining the roughness of the surface without producing conclusions as regards the waviness. **1958** H. M. SHERRARD *Austral. Road Pract.* xvi. 302 The profilometer consists of a wheel resting freely on the road surface whose vertical movement is traced on a ribbon of paper, thus giving a profile of the road. **1966** R. ASHWORTH *Highway Engin.* xii. 254 The profilometer consists of a 16-wheeled articulated carriage arranged so as to support the recording gear at a constant height above the continuously arranged level of the road surface at these 16 wheel points. **1976** [see PROFILOMETRY below].

Hence **profi'lometry**, the use of such an instrument; **profilo'metric** *a.*

1971 T. F. J. QUINN *Applic. Mod. Physical Techniques Tribol.* i. 32 This 'microscopic' approach must involve the use of as many methods of surface examination as possible. The more conventional methods of optical microscopy..and surface profilometry..are often too coarse for this approach. **1975** D. F. MOORE *Princ. & Applic. Tribol.* ii. 15 The profilometric, cartographic, and photogrammetric measurement techniques..deal with a complete representation of surface roughness. **1976** J. HALLING *Introd. Tribol.* ii. 21 The most usual method for the study of surface geometry is profilometry. In the profilometer a very fine diamond stylus..is drawn over the surface irregularities... The vertical movement of the stylus..is measured and amplified, usually electronically, so that the recorded output provides a picture of the actual surface.

‖**profil perdu** (profil pɛrdy). Also **profile perdu**. [Fr.] (See quot. 1959.) Also *attrib.*

1959 P. & L. MURRAY *Dict. Art* 257 *Profil perdu*, (Fr. lost profile) is that view of a head in which the profile is lost because the whole head is turned so far away that only the outline of the cheek is visible. By extension, the *profil perdu* of any object is what is seen of it when it is more than half turned away from the spectator. **1961** *Times* 14 Feb. 6/6 Rubens and Velasquez repeat the idea with back views, profile or *profile-perdu* heads. **1967** E. WYMARK *As Good as Gold* xv. 214 She..stood gazing down the street, her figure a *profil perdu* against a grey sky.

‖**profi'lure.** *Obs. rare*$^{-1}$. [obs. F. *profilure*, f. *profiler* to PROFILE: see -URE.] A border.

1664 EVELYN tr. *Freart's Archit.* II. i. 89 Together with Tuscan Profilures [*les profileures Toscanes*] both at the Base and Capital.

Profintern ('prɒfintən). [Russ. *Profintérn*, f. *Krásnyĭ Internatsionál Profsoyúzov* Red International of Trade Unions, after *Komintérn* COMINTERN.] An international organization of left-wing Trade Unions, founded in 1921 and dissolved in 1937.

1928 R. W. DUNN *Soviet Trade Unions* vi. 65 Through its delegates in the Red Trade Union International (Profintern) to participate in the international labor movement. **1938** *Encycl. Brit. Bk. of Yr.* 335/1 The Red International of Labour Unions ('Profintern') was founded at Moscow in 1921 under the auspices of the Third International to work for the reorganization of the Trade Union movement throughout the world on militant and revolutionary lines. **1949** I. DEUTSCHER *Stalin* 401 Parallel with the Comintern, the *Profintern* (the International of the Red trade unions) had opposed itself to the so-called Amsterdam International. **1958** *Economist* 1 Nov. 424/2 The fact that A. Lozovsky, who had vanished previously, is also reported as dead in 1952 suggests that the former head of the International of Red Trade Unions (Profintern) may also have been a victim of the anti-Jewish drive. **1977** *N.Y. Rev. Bks.* 26 May 26/4 Nikolsky was a representative of the Profintern, the Trade Unions International.

profir, -ire, obs. forms of PROFFER.

profit ('prɒfit), *sb.* [a. OF. and mod.F. *profit* (= earlier OF. *prufit* (*a* 1140 in Godef. *Compl.*), *pur-*, *po(u)rfit*, in 15th c. *prouf(f)it*):—L. *prōfect-us* advance, progress, profit, f. L. *prōfic-ĕre* (ppl. stem *prōfect-*) to advance: see PROFICIENT.

The OF. forms in *prū-*, *prou-*, immediately represent L. *prō-*; those in *pur-*, *por-*, *pour-*, agree with the usual OF. representation of the L. prep. and prefix *prō*, in mod.F. *pour*. Of the various ME. types, *profit* coincides with later OF. and mod.F.; *prouf(f)it* reproduces the 15th c. Fr.; *profect* was a Renascence assimilation to L. *profect-us*; and *prophit*, *-phet*, an erroneous spelling after *prophet*, L. *propheta* (see PH). With *profiȝt*, *profight*, cf. the similar *perfiȝt*, *perfight*, under PERFECT *a.*]

A. Illustration of Forms.

α. 4- profit; 4-6 -ite, -yt, 4-7 -et, 5 -et(t)e, 5-6 -ett, -itte, -yte, 6 -eit; 5-6 proffet, -ette, -it, 6 -uyt, -uyte, -ute, -yte, -eit, 7 -itt.

c **1325**, *c* **1330**, etc. Profyt, Profit [see B. 1, etc.]. *a* **1340** Profet [see B. 2]. *c* **1350** *Will. Palerne* 1 For profite þat he feld. **14..** *Customs of Malton* in *Surtees Misc.* (1888) 58 All yᵉ proffettes of yᵉ sayd walles. **1460** *Lybeaus Disc.* 835 To tho Lybeaus profyte. **1464** *Rolls of Parlt.* V. 527/2 Wode, or profitte of Wode. **1466** in *Archæologia* (1887) L. I. 50 A syngler profette hyrtyth and harmyth a comyn wele. **1483** *Cath. Angl.* 292/1 A Proffet. **1500-20** DUNBAR *Poems* xiv. 53 They think no sin, quhair proffeit cumis betwene. **1521** *Knaresborough Wills* (Surtees) I. 11 Of the next profettes. *a* **1533** LD. BERNERS *Huon* lxvi. 228 Nor haue had but small profyte. **1533** GAU *Richt Vay* 20 And seikkis his awne wil and profeit. **1536** *Act 27 Hen. VIII*, c. 42 §7 The profutes yerely goyng to and for the exhibicion. **1546** in *Eng. Gilds* (1870) 196 Revenuez & proffuytes. *a* **1568** ASCHAM *Scholem.* II. (Arb.) 102 The proffet..wold conteruaile wyth the toile. **1588** Profite [B. 6]. **1604** Proffitt [B. 5].

β. 4 profiȝt, -yȝt, 5 -yht, -ith, 6 -ight, -yght, -ygth, -ygtt.

c **1315** SHOREHAM *Poems* vii. 434 ȝef hy hade be mad parfyȝt, We nedde y-haued ryȝt no profyȝt. **1387** TREVISA *Higden* (Rolls) I. 3 Medlynge to gidre profiȝtes and swetnes [orig. *utile dulci*]. **1447** BOKENHAM *Seyntys* (Roxb.) 30 To profyht of the cherche. **1538** AUDLEY in *Lett. Suppress. Monasteries* (Camden) 242 More..then eny profight in the world. **1545** BRINKLOW *Compl.* 10 b, That it make for the profyght of Antichristes Knyghtes.

γ. 4 prophit, -ite, -et, 4-5 -ete, 5 -yt.

[**1362** Prophitable [see PROFITABLE 1].] *c* **1375** *Sc. Leg. Saints* xxxiii. (*George*) 609 þat I gyf þe for þi prophit And als of wynnyng for delyt. **1387** Prophete [see B. 1]. **1473** WARKW. *Chron.* (Camden) 25 The Kynge..toke the prophete of the Archebysshopperyche.

δ. 5 prouffit, -ite, -yt, 5-6 -yte.

1456 SIR G. HAYE *Law Arms* (S.T.S.) 42 The commoun prouffit of the toune. **1488** CAXTON *Chas. Gt.* 2 For prouffyte of euery man. **1509** FISHER *Fun. Serm. C'tess Richmond* Wks. (1876) 307 We sholde more regarde our owne prouffytes.

ε. 5-6 profect, 6 proffect, profecte, -fict.

1465 MARG. PASTON in *P. Lett.* II. 188 That she may not have the profects of Clyre ys place. **1528** LYNDESAY *Dreme* 910 To thare singulare proffect. **1542** UDALL *Erasm. Apoph.* Pref., More to their profecte & benefite. **1597** J. PAYNE *Royal Exch.* 6 For commune profict.

B. Signification.

1. a. The advantage or benefit (of a person, community, or thing); use, interest; the gain, good, well-being. Formerly sometimes *pl.* when referring to several persons.

c **1315** [see A. β]. *c* **1325** *Spec. Gy Warw.* 60 þat were my ioye and my delit, And to my soule a gret profyt. *c* **1330** R. BRUNNE *Chron.* (1810) 159 It is my profit, to myn I wille þam holde. **1387** TREVISA *Higden* (Rolls) VII. 153, I have ȝitte out all my patrimony into ȝoure prophetes [L. *in commoda vestra*]. **1439** *Litt. Red Bk. Bristol* (1900) II. 156 He..schal be amercied in xijd. to the commune profite. **1481** CAXTON *Myrr.* I. iii. 10 He doth it more for his owen prouffyt than he doth it for other. **1535** COVERDALE *1 Macc.* x. 20 Yᵗ thou mayest considre what is for oure profit. **1553** T. WILSON *Rhet.* (1580) 30 Where I spake of profite..vnder the same is comprehended the getting of gaine, and the eschuyng of harme. **1648** *Eikon Bas.* xiv. 138 Profit is the Compasse, by which Factious men steere their course in all seditious Commotions. **1709** ADDISON *Tatler* No. 100 ⁋6 Posts of Honour, Dignity, and Profit. **1712** J. JAMES tr. *Le Blond's Gardening* 142 Its Wood is..fit for no Use,..so that it is a Tree of no Kind of Profit. **1810** BENTHAM *Packing* (1821) 183 The learned gentleman..of whose learning we have already made our profit. **1873** BROWNING *Red Cott. Nt.-cap* IV. 240 This power you hold for profit of myself And all the world at need.

b. *transf.* That which is to the advantage or benefit of some one or something.

1603 SHAKS. *Meas. for M.* I. iv. 61 A man..who..Doth rebate, and blunt his naturall edge With profits of the minde. **1604** —— *Oth.* III. iii. 379, I thanke you for this profit.

†**2. a.** The advantage or benefit of or resulting from something. *Obs.*

a **1340** HAMPOLE *Psalter* ix. 36 What profet has he to doe swa many illes? **1382** WYCLIF *Rom.* iii. 1 What profyt of circumcisioun? Moche by alle maner. *c* **1425** *Craft Nombrynge* (MS. Egerton 2622, lf. 140), Nexte þou most know..qwat is þe profet of þis craft. **1535** COVERDALE *Prov.* iii. 13 The gettinge of it is better then eny marchaundise of syluer, & the profit of it is better then golde. **1611** BIBLE *Transl. Pref.* 1 He had not seene any profit to come by any Synode. **1628** HOBBES *Thucyd.* (1822) 154 Both justice and profit of revenge..can never possibly be found together in the same thing.

b. With *a* and *pl.* An instance of this; a good result or effect of something. *Obs.*

1502 *Ord. Crysten Men* (W. de W. 1506) v. vii. 416 Twelue other prouffytes the whiche cometh of good werkes done in mortall synne. **1543** TRAHERON *Vigo's Chirurg.* I. i. 1 In the whych Anatomie the vtilities and profectes of the same are declared.

†**3.** Progress, advance, improvement; = PROFICIENCE, PROFICIENCY 1. *Obs. rare.*

1600 SHAKS. *A.Y.L.* I. i. 7 My brother Iaques he keepes at schoole, and report speakes goldenly of his profit.

4. That which is derived from or produced by some source of revenue, e.g. ownership of land, feudal or ecclesiastical rights or perquisites, taxes, etc.; revenue, proceeds, returns. Chiefly *pl.*

[**1292** BRITTON III. iii. §4 Tut le profit qe il prist pur le mariage soit restoré as amis et as parentz la femme.] **1387** TREVISA *Higden* (Rolls) VIII. 7 þe firste benefice þat voydede, wiþ þe fruyt and prophetes. **1447-8** SHILLINGFORD *Lett.* (Camden) 91 The amerciamentis issuys and proffits therof comyng. **1560** DAUS tr. *Sleidane's Comm.* 120 What profites arryse of the christenyng of children, of mariages, pilgrimages [etc.]. *Ibid.* 286 The Duke of Saxon..shall kepe the town and Castel of Gothe, with al the profite. **1610** HOLLAND *Camden's Brit.* (1637) 366 The fines, perquisites, amercements, and other profites growing out of the trials of such causes. **1818** CRUISE *Digest* (ed. 2) VI. 374 The limitation to F. M. to enjoy and take the profits during his life, and after his decease to the heirs male of his body.

5. The pecuniary gain in any transaction; the amount by which value acquired exceeds value expended; the excess of returns over the outlay of capital: in commercial use chiefly in pl. In *Pol. Econ.*, The surplus product of industry after deducting wages, cost of raw materials, rent, and charges. †In early use also including interest.

1604 *Aberdeen Regr.* (1848) II. 256 The soume of ane hundreth merkis..borrowit..be the toune..and to pay..the soume of four pundis, for the proffitt of the said soume for the half-yeir past. **1697** DRYDEN *Virg. Georg.* I. 137 Nor is the Profit small, the Peasant makes, Who smooths with Harrows, or who pounds with Rakes The crumbling Clods. **1764** BURN *Poor Laws* 194 The profits of any work that may be done in said hospitals to be also added to the revenue of the said hospitals. **1776** ADAM SMITH *W.N.* I. vi. (1869) I. 54 The revenue derived from labour is called wages. That derived from stock, by the person who manages or employs it, is called profit. **1825** MᶜCULLOCH *Pol. Econ.* III. v. 291 The profits of capital are only another name for the wages of accumulated labour. **1845** FORD *Handbk. Spain* I. 24 Nobody would be an innkeeper if it were not for the profit. **1893** *Law Times* XCV. 5/2 His profits diminished at the rate of 60 per cent.

6. *Phrases.* **a.** ***profit and loss*** (†***profit or loss***), an inclusive expression for the gain and loss made in a series of commercial transactions, and the gain or loss made in one transaction; esp. in ***profit and loss account***, an account in book-keeping to which all gains are credited and losses are debited, so as to strike a balance between them, and ascertain the net gain or loss at any time. In *Arithmetic*, the name of a rule by which the gains or losses on commercial transactions are calculated.

1588 J. MELLIS *Briefe Instr.* E viij, Of the famous accompt called profite or losse, or otherwise Lucrum or Damnum, and how to order it in the Leager. *Ibid.* ch. xviii, Item touching the accomptes (of profite and losse) of necessitie it must haue one accompt proper in some one place of your Leager. **1622** MALYNES *Anc. Law-Merch.* 372 Wheras you made ouer..the sum of 2300ˡˡ sterling you now receiue backe 2363ˡˡ 11ˢ, whereby your profit is 63ˡˡ 11ˢ, of this you make your Factor Debitor, and the account of Profit and Losse Creditor. **1727** A. HAMILTON *New Acc. E. Ind.* II. xlvii. 170, 500 Chests of Japan Copper..were brought into Account of Profit and Loss, for so much eaten up by the white Ants. **1882** BITHELL *Counting-ho. Dict.* (1893) 244 If the Profit and Loss Account shews a nett gain the balance is placed on the Cr. side of Capital Account; if a loss, on the Dr. side. **1891** T. HARDY *Tess* lvi, She was too deeply materialized..by her long and enforced bondage to that arithmetical demon Profit-and-Loss, to retain much curiosity for its own sake.

b. ‖***profit à prendre*** [F., = profit to take], see quot. 1876. †***to fall profit***: see FALL *v.* 46 c. ***in profit***, said of milch cattle: giving milk, in milk. †***to profit***, to a remunerative employment. †***upon profit*** (*Sc.*), at interest.

1565 *Reg. Privy Council Scot.* I. 391 The remanent of hir barnis nocht put to proffeit as yit, to the nowmer of four dochteris and ane sone. **1588** *Burgh Rec. Edinb.* (1882) IV. 520 Money [to be] gotten vpoun proffeitt for making thair charges. **1602** *Aberdeen Regr.* (1848) II. 234 The sowme of ane hundreth merkis to be..vpliftit vpon proffitt be the thesaurer. **1658** tr. *Coke's Rep.* VI. 60 b (1826), They claim not a charge, or profit apprender in the soil of another, but a discharge in their own land. **1876** DIGBY *Real Prop.* iii. 154 If the right is to take a portion of the soil or the produce of the soil of another, the right is called a *profit à prendre*. **1884** *W. Sussex Gaz.* 25 Sept., 19 excellent dairy cows and heifers ..in calf or profit.

7. *attrib.* and *Comb.*, as ***profit economy***, ***income***, ***-monger***, ***-mongering***, ***plan***, ***statement***; ***profit-bearing***, ***-conscious*** (hence ***-consciously*** adv.), ***-hungry***, ***-linked*** ***-proof*** adjs.; objective and obj. genitive, as ***profit-grinder***, ***-maximizer***, ***-producer***, ***-snatcher***;

profit-cashing, ***-generating***, ***-earning***, ***-hunting***, ***-making***, ***-maximizing***, ***-planning***, ***-pooling***, ***-seeking***, sbs. and adjs.; (instrumental, etc.) ***profit-motivated***, ***-oriented*** adjs.

1918 W. S. CHURCHILL *Let.* 10 Sept. in M. Gilbert *W. S. Churchill* (1975) IV. vii. 145 The lives they have saved and the prisoners they have taken have made these 18,000 men the most profit-bearing we have in the army. **1945** *Richmond* (Va.) *Times-Dispatch* 5 May 12/3 Profit-cashing by those who desired a clean slate over the week-end stalled numerous leaders. **1960** *Farmer & Stockbreeder* 1 Mar. 149/2 (Advt.), Every profit-conscious egg producer must have Evans Maxilay and Topscore strains. **1976** *Western Mail* (Cardiff) 22 Nov. 8/4 A number of their most profit conscious private sector industries. **1972** *Physics Bull.* June 366/3 Profit-consciously,..the company will normally supply the crawler only as part of its contract inspection service. **1943** *Sun* (Baltimore) 8 Feb. 3/2 The 'profit economy' has not always been equal to the demands of war. **1970** R. STAVENHAGEN in I. L. Horowitz *Masses in Lat. Amer.* vii. 242 Sol Tax describes the Panajackel Indians' economy as being a 'penny capitalism'..because they are oriented towards a profit economy. **1976** *National Observer* (U.S.) 14 Aug. 4/1 Profit-generating factors seem to have existed on Sundays in the Big Apple. **1893** MORRIS in Mackail *Life* (1899) II. 297 The struggle against the terrible power of the profit-grinder. **1939** *Sun* (Baltimore) 18 Aug. 6/1 The profit-hungry Celanese Corporation of America.. is creating a public resentment. **1903** *Westm. Gaz.* 13 Nov. 2/1 Germany also has a large profit-income, though on a much smaller scale than ours. **1972** *Accountant* 12 Oct. 447/3 (*heading*) Profit-linked share incentive schemes. **1973** *Times* 31 Oct. 1/1 (*heading*) Government puts limit on profit-linked rises in Phase Three changes. **1891** MISS POTTER in *Daily News* 18 July 5/1 The upper and middle-class..demand the servility of the profit-making traders. **1953** E. SMITH *Guide Eng. Traditions & Public Life* 76 'Public Schools'..are not conducted for the purpose of profit-making. If there should be any excess of income over expenditure it is used for improvements in the school. **1974** *Times* 15 Oct. 5/2 A straightforward profit-making job with very few public benefits. **1968** *Listener* 28 Mar. 403/1 A pure profit-maximiser would already be attacking these hindrances to profit if he could. **1961** *Southern Econ. Jrnl.* Oct. 163/1 Where the industry's product price has been kept below the 'profit-maximizing' and 'entry-limiting' prices due to fears of public reaction. **1968** *Listener* 4 Apr. 437/2 So much for constraints of profit-maximising. **1977** *Dædalus* Fall 92 Larger and larger fractions of the GNP are being produced in sectors..that are clearly not competitive profit-maximizing sectors. **1961** *Spectator* 2 June 808 The profitmongers have an uncanny nose for threats. **1888** *Charity Organis. Rev.* Jan. 19 The grinding exaction of the profit-monger and middleman. **1884** W. MORRIS in *Justice* 17 May 2/2 Ugliness is but a part of the bestial waste of the whole system of profit-mongering, which refuses cultivation and refinement to the workers. **1973** *Listener* 14 June 805/1 The public's distrust of..endorsements, knowing them to be profit-motivated and not spontaneous. **1978** W. GARNER *Möbius Trip* ii. 57 The tatty commercialism of profit-motivated research. **1976** *Nigerian Chron.* 18 Aug. 7/4 Government has recently decided to grant full autonomy in personnel matters to all profit-oriented parastatals. **1979** *Arizona Daily Star* 5 Aug. E3/4 'I think we need a president who is more profit-oriented,' he said. **1967** D. GOCH in Wills & Yearsley *Handbk. Managem. Technol.* 158 *Profit plan*, profit target based on a predetermined rate of return required from the invested funds represented by the fixed assets and working capital employed in carrying on a business activity. **1964** E. C. D. EVANS (*title*) Profit planning and the measurement of return on capital employed. **1599** DANIEL *Musophilus* i, Other delights than these, other desires This wiser profit-seeking Age requires. **1681** D'URFEY *Progr. Honesty* xiii, No man that's profit-proof, nor woman true. **1927** M. SADLEIR *Trollope: a Comm.* 148 The profit-seeking [of the Great Exhibition]..lay behind the pious ejaculations of an inspired Press. **1949** I. DEUTSCHER *Stalin* ii. 27 The evils of modern profit-seeking industrialism. **1965** H. I. ANSOFF *Corporate Strategy* (1968) iii. 37 It would seem..that profit-seeking, or maximization of profit, would be the natural single business objective. **1808** BENTHAM *Sc. Reform* 15 A forced increase to the multitude of profit-yielding suits. **1898** CHR. MURRAY in *Daily News* 27 Jan. 6/4 In the early days, a Colony was regarded as a profit-yielding settlement.

b. Special Combs.: **profit foul** *U.S. Basketball*, an intentional or 'professional' foul committed to prevent one's opponents from scoring (? *Obs.*); **profit margin**, the margin that remains in a business operation when the costs involved are deducted from profits, usu. considered as a percentage of the capital employed (cf. MARGIN *sb.* 2 b, quot. 1866); **profit(s motive** (usu. with *the*), the incentive that the possibility of making profits gives to individual or free enterprise; **profit-rent**, a rent of which the amount is due to a tenant's improvements; **profit-sharing**, the sharing of profits, *spec.* between employer and employed, or between capital and labour; so ***profit-sharer***; also as adj.; **profit squeeze**, the diminishment in profit margins due to costs rising relatively faster than selling prices with insufficient compensation from increased sales; **profit-taking** (*Stock-exchange*), the act of realizing the profit obtainable by the sale of stock, etc., in which a rise in price has taken place; so ***profit-taker***.

1952 *Sun* (Baltimore) 15 Jan. 17/3 Veteran Coach Murray Greason..criticized today what he termed widespread use of the '*profit foul' in basketball. **1926** *Encycl. Brit.* III. 225/2 Various measures were taken during the War to restrict profiteering, especially in belligerent countries. These included the fixing of maximum prices, and in some cases of *profit margins at each stage of production and distribution. **1974** *Guardian* 25 Mar. 22/6 The discount stores operate on narrow profit margins. **1976** B. WILLIAMS *Making of Manchester Jewry* iii. 67 The general move was in the direction of mass sales at a low profit margin. **1931** PATTERSON & SCHOLZ *Econ. Probl. Mod. Life* (ed. 2) ii. 37 The *profits motive represents the modern crystallization of the economic force of self-interest. Hence, production is guided by market value and turns toward the production of luxuries for which there is an effective demand. **1936** J. M. KEYNES *Gen. Theory Employment* xxiii. 335 In conditions in which the quantity of aggregate investment is determined by the profit motive alone, the opportunities for home investment will be governed..by the domestic rate of interest. **1947** A. E. WAUGH *Princ. Econ.* xxxvi. 863 A society that used coercion instead of the profit motive would not need to establish such institutions as those of free enterprise and free contract. **1975** *Verbatim* May 3/2 Never forget that the profit motive can sometimes be used to a customer's advantage. **1859** TROLLOPE *West Indies* xiv, The small, grasping, *profit-rent landlords. **1881** S. TAYLOR in *19th Cent.* May 802 (*title*) *Profit-sharing. **1884** —— (*title*) Profit-Sharing between Capital and Labour. **1900** *Econ. Rev.* X. 239 (*heading*) Two profit-sharing concerns. **1920** M. BEER *Hist. Brit. Socialism* II. IV. xiv. 292 Profit-sharing and Industrial Co-partnership schemes have been re-examined. **1949** *Here & Now* (N.Z.) Oct. 11/2 Far from being the predatory capitalist, he offers himself as the profit-sharing employer. **1975** *Times* 14 Jan. 14/1 Only 22 per cent of the sample belonged to profit sharing or bonus schemes related to the profits the company makes. **1979** *West Lancs. Even. Gaz.* 28 May 11 (Advt.), The company offers an attractive starting salary, operates a profit-sharing scheme and other benefits. **1891** *Chambers' Encycl.* VIII. 437/1 Those who have tested any system of profit-sharing declare that it requires much time and pains to produce substantial results; and a difficulty..is that *profit-sharers are not unfrequently unwilling to share the losses of the concern. **1958** *Wall St. Jrnl.* 8 Dec. 1/6 The outstanding feature of 1959 may be a further *profit squeeze. **1969** J. ARGENTI *Managem. Techniques* iii. 11 If margins fall, profits fall, unless the company can somehow increase sales volume—and that is not easy. This phenomenon is known as 'the Profit Squeeze' and most companies today are feeling its effects. **1552** HULOET, *Profite taker. **1968** *Economist* 5 Oct. 78/1 What does seem to have arrived is the day of the profit-taker. **1980** *Times* 5 Jan. 19 The profit takers pulled out of gold. **1896** *Daily News* 5 Nov. 7/4 A jump of 1 to 7 in prices,..brought out enormous *profit-taking sales largely by houses which bought early in London. **1897** *Ibid.* 17 July 3/1 Stocks reacted under heavy profit-taking. **1904** *Daily Chron.* 21 Sept. 1/7 At Paris the Bourse opened firm, but fell away on profit-taking. **1928** *Daily Mail* 25 July 18/3 In the Electrical group Bournemouth and Pooles eased on profit-taking. **1976** *Birmingham Post* 16 Dec. 9/10 Stocks settled for a small gain after two rally attempts were stalled by profit-taking.

c. *pl.*, as **profits tax**, a tax on business profits, *spec.* that levied on company profits, as ***excess profits tax*** (EXCESS *sb.* 6 b).

1920 [see *corporation tax* s.v. CORPORATION 7]. **1938** *Ann. Reg. 1937* 38 The Chancellor..was urged from many quarters to withdraw the profits tax and meet his requirements from a further increase in the income tax. **1947** *Western Daily Express* 14 June 1 The increased profits tax was criticized at the annual meeting of the Association of British Chambers of Commerce. **1958** *Times* 7 Jan. 15/1 The effect on capital allowances for profits tax purposes of new plants coming into operation. **1974** *Times* 17 Apr. (Ontario, Manitoba & Saskatchewan Suppl.) p. iv, Both provinces have imposed a special 'windfall profits' tax to prevent developing companies from profiting unduly from share increases in the world price of their products.

profit ('prɒfɪt), *v.* Forms: see the sb.; also 4 **profiti, profetye.** [ME. a. F. *profiter*, earlier OF. *prufiter* (*a* 1140 in Hatz.-Darm.), *po(u)rfiter*, f. *prufit, profit* PROFIT *sb.*]

I. †**1.** *intr.* To make progress; to advance, go forward; to improve, prosper, grow, increase (in some respect). *Obs.*

c **1340** HAMPOLE *Prose Tr.* 6 Ay þe mare I profette in þe luf of Jhesu þe swetter I fand it. **1382** WYCLIF *Luke* ii. 52 And Jhesu profitide in wysdom, age, and grace anemptis God and men. **1483** CAXTON *Gold. Leg.* 431/1 Prouffytyng from vertue in to vertue. **1540** R. WISDOME in Strype *Eccl. Mem.* (1721) I. App. cxv. 325 Loe!..yee se that we profect nothing at al. **1598** SHAKS. *Merry W.* IV. i. 15 My husband saies my sonne profits nothing in the world at his Booke. **1607–12** BACON *Ess., Empire* (Arb.) 296 The minde of Man is more cheared, and refreshed by profitinge in smale things, then by standing at a stay in great.

II. 2. *trans.* Of a thing: To be of advantage, use, or benefit to; to do good to; to benefit, further, advance, promote. (Orig. *intr.*, with indirect obj. (dative), which was at length treated as direct.)

1303 R. BRUNNE *Handl. Synne* 146 þey ȝeue vs grace ryȝt so to deme Vs to profyt, and god to queme. **1509** HAWES *Past. Pleas.* xi. (Percy Soc.) 45 It shall hym prouffyt yf he wyll apply To doo therafter ful conveniently. **1526** TINDALE *Matt.* xvi. 26 Whatt shall hit proffet a man [**1382** WYCLIF, what profitith it to a man], yf he shulde wyn all the whoole worlde: so he loose hys owne soule? **1605** TIMME *Quersit.* I. xiii. 62 [They] doe consist and are profited by these three beginnings. **1741–2** GRAY *Agrippina* 12 'Twill profit you, And please the stripling. **1874** SIDGWICK *Meth. Ethics* II. iii. §3. 129 The most careful estimate of a girl's pleasures.. would not much profit a young woman.

b. *intr.* To be of advantage, use, or benefit; avail. Const. *to* (= *dative*). In later use, without const., regarded as absolute use of 2.

1340–70 *Alex. & Dind.* 509 Hit profiteþ nouht to preche of oure dedus. *a* **1450** *Cursor M.* 13919 (Fairf.) Gode is to wirke euerilk day þinge þat prophetis to þe lay. **1477** EARL RIVERS (Caxton) *Dictes* 125 The sayd Galyen sayd wysdom can not proufyt to a foole. **1486** *Bk. St. Albans, Her.* f viij b, Yet shall thai [rules] profecte for thys sciens gretly. **1579** FULKE *Heskins's Parl.* 523 They profit alike to al men. **1667** MILTON *P.L.* VIII. 571 Oft times nothing profits more Then self-esteem, grounded on just and right Well manag'd. **1842** TENNYSON *Ulysses* 1 It little profits that an idle king..I mete and dole Unequal laws unto a savage race. **1904** H. BLACK *Practice Self Culture* ii. 58 Bodily exercise does profit for some things.

†**3.** Of a person: **a.** *intr.* To be profitable, bring profit or benefit, do good (*to* some one); **b.** *trans.* To be profitable to, benefit, do good to; **c.** *refl.* To benefit oneself, make one's profit; = 4.

a **1425** *Cursor M.* 5417 (Trin.) His lord he profited erly and late. **1533** ELYOT *Knowledge* Pref., I mought profyte to them whiche..wolde..reade it. **1581** PETTIE tr. *Guazzo's Civ. Conv.* II. (1586) 66 b, Hee bent himselfe rather to profite those which should reade him, than to delight them. *a* **1648** LD. HERBERT *Hen. VIII* (1683) 632 His Courtiers (especially those who had profited themselves of Abbies).

4. *intr.* (for *refl.*) To benefit oneself; to derive profit or benefit; to be benefited.

c **1400** *Apol. Loll.* 59 To w[h]as profit presthed is ȝeuen, not only þat men prest, or be boun, but þat þey prophet. **1509** FISHER *Fun. Serm. C'tess Richmond* Wks. (1876) 291 Thynges..of weyght & substaunce wherin she myghte prouffyte she wolde not let for ony payne or laboure to take vppon hande.

b. *esp.* with prepositions †*with*, *by*, *of*, *from*: To derive benefit from, be a gainer by; to avail oneself of; to make use of, take advantage of.

c **1400** *Destr. Troy* 5169 If we shall proffet with proues, or any fose wyn. **1526** *Pilgr. Perf.* (W. de W. 1531) 2, I beseche all them specyally yᵗ shall profyte by this worke to praye for me. **1578** TIMME *Caluine on Gen.* 132 He profited nothing with his outrage. **1676** DRYDEN *Aurengz.* II. 28 You might have found a mercenary Son, To profit of the Battels he had won. **1796** BURKE in *Epist. Corr. Burke & Dr. Laurance* (1827) 57 Mrs. Burke..has not profited of the bathing. **1796** BURNEY *Mem. Metastasio* I. 389 If it is not too late for him to profit from the information. **1797** *Monthly Mag.* III. 491 All of these..profited by the opportunity to effect their escape. **1871** G. MEREDITH *H. Richmond* III. 130 He was prompt in an emergency, and quick to profit of a crisis. **1873** M. ARNOLD *Lit. & Dogma* (1876) 141 To profit fully by the New Testament, the first thing to be done is [etc.].

†**5.** *trans.* To render profitable. *Obs. rare.*

1578–9 *Reg. Privy Council Scot.* III. 109 To lawbour and proffeit the ground.

III. †**6.** (?) To bring forward, present. *Obs. rare.*

1611 *N. Riding Rec.* (1884) I. 217 The executors of the late Rob. Simpson, Threasurer for the Hospitalls, shall proffitt his accompt at Pickering on April 12th.

Hence '**profited**, '**profiting** *ppl. adjs.*

1581 MULCASTER *Positions* xxxix. (1887) 203 Officious thankefullnes in the profited hearer. *c* **1605** in T. Hutton *Reasons for Refusal* (1605) 28 Sundry places of this Scripture ..left out as lesse profiting, or edifying. **1848** in W. Arnot *Life J. Hamilton* i. (1869) 33 For years I have been a profited reader of your writings. **1908** *Daily Chron.* 3 Oct. 5/4 So many profiting interests are concerned that there can be little doubt as to the ultimate formation of a syndicate.

profit(e, obs. forms of PROPHET.

profitability (ˌprɒfɪtə'bɪlɪtɪ). [f. next + -ITY.] The quality or state of being profitable; profitableness; the capacity to make a profit. Also *attrib.*

a **1340** HAMPOLE *Psalter* xxix. 11 [xxx. 9] What profetabilte is in my blode? **1893** A. A. MARTIN in *Idler* Mar. 195 If the heavenly profitability was cut off..the habit of pleasurable moving remained. **1924** J. STAMP *Current Probl. Finance & Govt.* 11, I may venture to say that we have almost reached a limit of profitability along the old lines of deductive reasoning. **1931** *Economist* 26 Sept. 548/2 In so far as an industry's profitability is improved the weight of its fixed interest charges is lessened. **1961** *Listener* 2 Nov. 691/2, I am not frightened by profits; no one should ever be frightened of profits. Profitability is the only measure of success. **1964** *Daily Tel.* 15 Feb. 9/2 (*heading*) Guthrie starts BOAC drive for profitability. **1969** *Times* 6 Jan. 7/8 But for foot-and-mouth disease, production would certainly have risen considerably and the price position would already have caused alarm among producers near the profitability margin. **1979** *Jrnl. R. Soc. Arts* CXXVII. 617/1 There is a direct connection between profitability and survival.

profitable ('prɒfɪtəb(ə)l), *a.* (*adv.*, *sb.*) Also 4–6 **prophit-, profet-, prouf(f)it-, proffet-, profect-,** etc.: see PROFIT *sb.*; also 5 **providabille.** [a. F. *profitable* (*prophitable*, 12th c., Littré): see PROFIT and -ABLE.]

1. Yielding profit or advantage; beneficial, useful, serviceable, fruitful, valuable. (Rarely of persons.) Formerly, also, useful as a remedy.

c **1325** *Spec. Gy Warw.* 4 þat i wole speke..is swiþe profitable. *a* **1340** HAMPOLE *Psalter* cvi. 38 Sympil men and profetabile. **1362** LANGL. *P. Pl.* A. VII. 262 'Bi seint Poul!' quod pers: 'þeos beoþ prophitable wordes!' **1382** WYCLIF *2 Tim.* iii. 16 Al scripture of God ynspyrid is profitable to teche, to arguwe, to reproue, for to lerne in riȝtwysnesse. **1422** tr. *Secreta Secret., Priv. Priv.* 191 More Providabille ys to a man to govern hymself than othir mene. **1450** in *Wars Eng. in France* (1861) I. 514 Marchaundisses..as shal be thoughte most behoveful and prouffuitable. **1528** in *Lett. Suppress. Monasteries* (Camden) 5 To name and appoynt.. suche one as your grace shall thinke moste mete and profightable for the place. **1562** MOUNTGOMERY in *Archæologia* XLVII. 240 Pleasaunt howses, faire gardens, and goodlie meades, whithe theire proffectable groundes. **1627** *Lisander & Cal.* I. 9 Silence or flight were much profitabler for you. **1658** *Whole Duty Man* IX. §1 Sleep was intended to make us more profitable, not more idle. **1717** BERKELEY *Tour Italy* Wks. 1871 IV. 586, B. della Regna..is profitable to the bladder, eases tenesmus and ague. **1875** JOWETT *Plato* (ed. 2) I. 290 If we are good, then we are profitable; for all good things are profitable.

2. Yielding pecuniary profit; gainful, lucrative, remunerative.

1758 R. BROWN *Compl. Farmer* (1759) 79 Geese are profitable in many ways. **1776** ADAM SMITH *W.N.* I. xi. (1869) I. 231 It becomes as profitable to employ the most fertile..lands in raising food for them [cattle] as in raising corn. **1825** McCULLOCH *Pol. Econ.* II. ii. 117 This mighty channel for the profitable employment of millions upon millions of capital. **1845** —— *Taxation* I. (1852) 111 One shipowner has a ship at sea, making a profitable voyage, while that of another is in port unemployed.

†**B.** quasi-*adv.* Profitably. *Obs. rare.*

1654 WHITLOCK *Zootomia* Pref. a iij b, That thou mayest be thine own Auditor, and write profitable for thine own perusall.

C. *absol.* as *sb.* A thing that is profitable.

1681 R. L'ESTRANGE *Tully's Offices* 6 Of Two Profitables whether is the more Profitable?

profitableness ('prɒfɪtəb(ə)lnɪs). [f. prec. + -NESS.] The quality of being profitable.

1. Advantageousness, usefulness, value, beneficial quality.

1398 TREVISA *Barth. De P.R.* v. v. (1495) giv b/1 The curtel [of the eye] that hyghte Tela arenea, and hyght soo for prouffytablynes therof to be clere & briȝte to the spirite. *c* **1450** tr. *De Imitatione* I. v. 7 We owin in scriptures raþer to seke profitabilnes þan highnes of langage. **1583** GOLDING *Calvin on Deut.* xvi. 93 To the ende that the profitableness of this doctrine may be the better knowen. **1651** CROMWELL *Lett.* 24 Mar. in *Carlyle*, To approve my heart and life to Him in more faithfulness and thankfulness, and to those I serve in more profitableness and diligence. **1824** MRS. SHERWOOD *Waste Not* II. 12 The profitableness of holiness, not only in the world to come, but also in this life.

2. Remunerativeness, lucrativeness, gainfulness.

1886 H. DUNCKLEY in *Manch. Exam.* 15 Feb. 6/1, I am speaking only of the profitableness of labour. **1892** J. J. JANNEY in A. E. Lee *Hist. Columbus* (Ohio) II. 314 Equal in ..profitableness of operation to that of any city of equal population in the Union.

profitably ('prɒfɪtəblɪ), *adv.* [f. as prec. + -LY[2].] In a profitable manner.

1. With advantage or benefit; advantageously, beneficially.

1382 WYCLIF *Tobit* vi. 5 These thingus forsothe ben profitabli necessarie to medicynes. **1495** *Trevisa's Barth. De P.R.* II. ii. bj b/2 Angels haue this vertue of werkynge myghtly swyftly and prouffitably wythout cessyng. **1538** ELYOT *Dict.*, *Vtiliter*, profytably. **1651** HOBBES *Leviath.* Rev. & Concl. 395, I think it may be profitably printed, and more profitably taught in the Universities. **1712** ADDISON *Spect.* No. 317 ⁋48 Our Hours may very often be more profitably laid out. **1899** *Allbutt's Syst. Med.* VIII. 670 The flannel garments may profitably be lined with thin washing silk.

2. With pecuniary profit; lucratively.

1839 DE LA BECHE *Rep. Geol. Cornw.*, etc. x. 287 Localities where the tin or copper can be profitably raised. **1883** GILMOUR *Mongols* xxxi. 363 A customer with whom a Chinaman can trade profitably.

profiteer (prɒfɪ'tɪə(r)), *sb.* [f. PROFIT *sb.* + -EER; cf. Fr. *profiteur* (*de guerre*).] One who profits; *spec.* one who seeks to make excessive gain, as by the extortionate sale of necessary goods. Also as second element in *war profiteer*.

1912 *Athenæum* 21 Dec. 756/3 The fundamental unfairness of the relations between the wage-earner and the 'profiteer'. **1914** *Englishwoman* Nov. 94 The tricks of the armament profiteers are fresh in the public mind. **1918** W. OWEN *Let.* 10 Aug. (1967) 568 All the stinking Leeds & Bradford War-profiteers. **1942** W. S. CHURCHILL *End of Beginning* (1943) 130 If there are any would-be profiteers of disaster who feel able to paint the picture in darker colours, they are certainly at liberty to do so. **1952** A. POWELL *Buyer's Market* ii. 137 In the twilight world of undergraduate conversation..a kind of stage 'profiteer' or 'tycoon': a man of Big Business and professionally strong will. **1975** *New Yorker* 21 Apr. 134/3 There have already been reports of some killings in several cities, where government police, tax collectors, war profiteers,..have been among the targets previously announced. **1976** *Economist* 16 Oct. 15/2 The radicals also had..strong support among ex-Red Guards and other profiteers of the 1960s cultural revolution. **1980** *Times* 9 May 15/4 Dante.. puts profiteers next door to sodomites in the Seventh Circle of Hell.

profiteer (prɒfɪ'tɪə(r)), *v.* [f. prec.] **a.** *intr.* To practise profiteering; to be a profiteer.

1916 *New Age* 17 Feb. 361/1 The companies are..not only removed from the common temptation to profiteer, but are guaranteed a practically fixed income. **1920** R. MACAULAY *Potterism* II. iii. 94 She had merely profiteered out of it all, and had a good time. **1928** R. CAMPBELL *Wayzgoose* i. 20 Journalists are..profiteering on the brains of sheep.

b. *trans.* To obtain (money) by profiteering; to exploit (a person) financially. *rare.*

1923 S. KAYE-SMITH *End of House of Alard* I. 12 He wouldn't lend us any of the money he profiteered out of those collapsible huts. **1928** *Sunday Express* 3 June 13/1 Aren't we being profiteered here?

profiteering (prɒfɪ'tɪərɪŋ), *vbl. sb.* [f. as prec. + -ING[1] (see note).] The action or fact of seeking to make an excessive profit, as by providing necessities at extortionate prices. Also *attrib.*

Quot. 1814 is apparently an independent and isolated formation. The word was revived in the early twentieth century by A. R. Orage and others.

1814 *Guernsey Star & Gaz.* in *New Age* (1919) 21 Aug. 278/2 The extortionate profiteering that is being practised by the tradesmen in the public market. **1914** *New Age* 27 Aug. 391/2 England is at war upon profiteering. *Ibid.* 15 Oct. 561/2 The profiteering braggadocio..of 'City Man' and his confederates. **1919** *Act 9 & 10 Geo. V* c. 66 (*title*) An act to check profiteering. *Ibid.* §8 This Act may be cited as the Profiteering Act, 1919. **1922** W. J. LOCKE *Tale of Triona* vi. 56 'A dog and a rose and a glass of wine,' said she, 'are a woman's due for amusing a man. But a motor-car is profiteering.' **1939** A. THIRKELL *Before Lunch* xii. 307 He said he'd take a hundred more for it than he gave. No, no, I said... No profiteering. I'll give what you gave. **1976** F. ZWEIG *New Acquisitive Society* II. v. 112 Profiteering could also cover excessive or illegitimate rents. **1978** P. BOARDMAN *Worlds of Patrick Geddes* ix. 307 The mainsprings of the Financial Age were..the perfection of profiteering-techniques.

profiter ('prɒfɪtə(r)). [f. PROFIT *v.* + -ER[1].] One who profits. †**a.** One who advances or makes progress, an improver. *Obs.*

1526 *Pilgr. Perf.* (W. de W. 1531) 73 b, The feare of profyters, that is, of them that profyteth in vertue and perfeccyon. *Ibid.* 157 The pilgrymes..as yet..but begyn the iourney of grace, or els be as yet but profyters in religyon.

b. One who makes profit or gain by anything.

1800 COLQUHOUN *Comm. Thames* iv. 178 Seven Hundred may have been Profiters by the excessive Plunder. **1835** *Tait's Mag.* II. 248 They were profiters, not inventors; eagerly adopting every improvement suggested by strangers. **1855** CHAMBIER *My Travels* III. i. 15 The affluent profiters by exchange, light or foreign coin, occupy the ground floor.

profite'role. In 6 prophitrole, 8 profitrolle, 20 also profiterolle. [a. F. *profiterole* (Littré), f. *profit* PROFIT *sb.* + *-erole*, dim. suffix. In Cotgrave *pourfiterolle* 'a cake baked vnder hot imbers', and *profiterolle*, the latter also explained (in *pl.*) as 'the small vayles, as drinking money, points, pinnes, &c., gotten by a valet or groome in his maisters seruice'. The etymological sense is thus 'small gains'.] †**a.** Some kind of cooked food: see etym. and quots. 1515, 1727. **b.** Now *spec.* a small hollow case of choux pastry usu. filled with cream and served with chocolate sauce.

1515 BARCLAY *Egloges* iv. (1570) C iv b/2 To toste white sheuers and to make prophitroles And after talking oft time to fill the bowles. **1727** BRADLEY *Fam. Dict.* s.v. *Carp*, They likewise make a pottage of profitrolles with Carp flesh minced. **1884** F. J. DELIEE *Franco-Amer. Cookery Bk.* 131 Range the profiteroles in pyramid form in the centre. **1889** A. B. MARSHALL *Cookery Bk.* xiv. 315 *Chocolate profiteroles*. .. Make a choux pastry..and force it out from the bag on to a dry baking tin in shapes about the size of a small button mushroom. **1906** *Mrs. Beeton's Bk. Househ. Managem.* lxii. 1667 *Profiteroles* (Fr.), a kind of light cake, baked in hot ashes, and filled with cream or custard. **1949** N. MITFORD *Love in Cold Climate* II. vi. 264 Chocolate profiterolles with real cream. **1960** F. RAPHAEL *Limits of Love* I. x. 129 Between dances, Andrew and Julia ate..chocolate profiteroles and hot sausages. **1972** *Daily Tel.* (Colour Suppl.) 25 Aug. 42/3, I had three puddings (40p plus each); first profiteroles which were a credit to the pâtissier, Patrice.

'profitful, *a. nonce-wd.* [See -FUL.] Profitable.

1593 BILSON *Govt. Christ's Ch.* xii. 208 Order and discipline are not onely profitefull but also needfull.

profiting ('prɒfɪtɪŋ), *vbl. sb.* [f. PROFIT *v.* + -ING[1].] The action of the verb PROFIT: †improving, advance; benefiting, etc.

1382 WYCLIF *1 Tim.* iv. 15 Thenk thou thes thingis, in these be thou, that thi profytyng be schewid [*gloss* or knowun], to alle men. *c* **1450** tr. *De Imitatione* I. xi. 12 If we put þe profitinge of religion allone in outwarde obseruaunces. **1594** CAREW *Huarte's Exam. Wits* (1616) 1 Where..he should..haue many examples and profitings of strangers. **1608** HIERON *Wks.* Ded. 689 An argument of a mans effectuall profiting by other exercises of godlinesse. **1709** STRYPE *Ann. Ref.* I. xi. 139 The Bishops once a year to oversee the profiting of the parishes.

profitless ('prɒfɪtlɪs), *a.* [f. PROFIT *sb.* + -LESS.] Void of profit; unprofitable, useless.

1599 SHAKS. *Much Ado* v. i. 4, I pray thee cease thy counsaile, Which falls into mine eares as profitlesse, As water in a siue. **1663** HAMMOND *Serm. John xviii.* 40 Wks. 1683 IV. 513 An empty, profitless, temptationless sin. **1809** MALKIN *Gil Blas* XII. vi. ⁋3 He was of an intractable and profitless age. **1885** *Manch. Exam.* 12 Mar. 5/6 After four hours of utterly profitless talk a division was taken.

Hence **'profitlessly** *adv.*, **'profitlessness.**

1822 *Blackw. Mag.* XII. 281 Our presumption..must return in profitlessness and fatigue. **1857** H. MILLER *Test. Rocks* i. 16 Human thought is not profitlessly revolving in an idle circle, but progressing Godwards. **1879** G. MEREDITH *Egoist* III. viii. 155 Dissection and inspection will be alike profitlessly practised.

†**'profitly,** *a. Obs. rare*[−1]. [f. PROFIT *sb.* + -LY[1].] Profitable.

1470–85 MALORY *Arthur* XVIII. vi. 733, I calle hym now one of the beste knyghtes..and the most profytelyest man.

†**'profity.** *Obs.* In 5 profitee, 6 profittye. [f. PROFIT *sb.* + -Y (if the examples are not erroneous ff. *profites*, pl. of PROFIT).] = PROFIT *sb.*

1432 *Rolls of Parlt.* IV. 418/2 In suynge for the gode and profitees of oure seide Soveraign Lord. **1493** *Cal. Anc. Rec. Dublin* (1889) I. 378 Fees and wages and other profitees to the said offices perteynyng. **1584** in Poulson *Beverlac* (1829) 330 All the rents, revenewes, yssues, profittyes, belonginge to the collegiate churche.

pro'flated, *ppl. a. nonce-wd.* [f. L. *prōflāt-us*, pa. pple. of *prōflāre* to blow forth, puff out (f. *prō*, PRO-[1] + *flāre* to blow) + -ED[1].] Puffed out by blowing.

1817 COLERIDGE *Biog. Lit.* xxiii. (1882) 287 Preparing the audience for the most surprising series of wry faces, proflated mouths, and lunatic gestures that were ever 'launched' on an audience to 'sear the sense'.

proflavine (prəʊ'fleɪviːn). *Pharm.* Also -in (-ɪn). [f. PRO-[2] + FLAVINE.] A yellowish-brown crystalline solid, 3,6-diaminoacridine, $C_{13}H_{11}N_3$, which is used, in the form of an orange-red hydrated sulphate, as an antiseptic.

1917 C. H. BROWNING in *Brit. Med. Jrnl.* 16 June 825/1 The Medical Research Committee's Department of Biochemistry and Pharmacology has..continued to give us valuable aid, especially by providing an experimental supply of 'proflavine'. *Ibid.* 21 July 71/1 The name 'proflavine' has been suggested to us by the Medical Research Committee. **1917** *Lancet* 3 Nov. 676/1 Proflavine..is..a preliminary product in the manufacture of acriflavine or flavine. **1945** *Times* 7 Aug. 10/2 Other interesting items included 24,000,000 hypodermic tablets, 40,000,000 acriflavine and proflavine tablets. **1958** *Nature* 11 Oct. 983/1 Proflavin, although not interfering with synthesis of deoxyribonucleic acid in phage-infected cells, inhibits the maturation of phage progeny particles. **1970** PASSMORE & ROBSON *Compan. Med. Stud.* II. xviii. 41/1 Acridine dyes, e.g. proflavine, acriflavine, are more active than aniline dyes against Gram-positive bacteria, and are also active against Gram-negative bacilli. **1971** D. J. COVE *Genetics* x. 137 The starting point of these studies was a 'phage strain which carried an *rII* mutation induced by the acridine proflavin.

profligacy ('prɒflɪgəsɪ). [f. next: see -ACY 3.] The quality, state, or condition of being profligate.

1. Self-abandonment to dissipation; reckless licentiousness or debauchery; shameless vice.

1738 BOLINGBROKE *Patriot King* (1749) 181 Hitherto it has been thought the highest pitch of profligacy to own, instead of concealing crimes, and to take pride in them, instead of being ashamed of them. **1767** COWPER *Let. to J. Hill* 16 June, [The election] occasions the most detestable scene of profligacy and riot that can be imagined. **1815** J. SCOTT *Vis. Paris* xii. (ed. 2) 203 The decorum of behaviour which profligacy preserves in the public places of Paris. **1873** SYMONDS *Grk. Poets* viii. 253 In..the Daitaleis, Aristophanes attacked the profligacy and immodesty of the rising generation.

2. Reckless prodigality or extravagance; wastefulness; hence, immoderate profusion or abundance.

1860 EMERSON *Cond. Life, Wealth* (1861) 69 Profligacy consists not in spending years of time or chests of money, but in spending them off the line of your career. **1886** P. S. ROBINSON *Valley Teetotum Trees* 121 The prodigious luxuriance and profligacy of the botany of the tropics. **1900** *Edin. Rev.* July 182 This profusion or profligacy of pictures.

profligate ('prɒflɪgət), *a.* and *sb.* [ad. L. *prōflīgāt-us* overthrown, ruined; wretched, vile, dissolute, abandoned, pa. pple. of *prōflīg-āre* to dash to the ground, cast down, overthrow, overwhelm, ruin, dispatch, f. *prō*, PRO-[1] 1 b + *-flīg-āre* for *flīgĕre* to strike down, dash.]

A. *adj.*

I. †**1.** (Const. as *pa. pple.*) Overthrown, overwhelmed, routed. (Cf. next, 1.) *Obs.*

1535 LEGH & RICE *Let. to Cromwell* in Strype *Eccl. Mem.* (1721) I. App. lvii. 145 The Canon laws..with their Author, are profligate out of this realm. *a* **1548** HALL *Chron.*, *Hen. VI.* 168 By whiche onely pollicie, the kynges armie was profligate and dispersed. **1573** *Reg. Privy Council Scot.* II. 214 The conspiratouris..wer profligat and disapointit. **1643** PRYNNE *Sov. Power Parlt.* III. 45. **1663** BUTLER *Hud.* I. iii. 728 The foe is profligate and run.

II. 2. Abandoned to vice or vicious indulgence; recklessly licentious or debauched; dissolute; extremely or shamelessly vicious.

1647 WARD *Simp. Cobler* 39 When States are so reformed that they conforme such as are profligate into good civility: civill men, into religious morality. **1750** JOHNSON *Rambler* No. 77 ⁋10 Profligate in their lives, and licentious in their compositions. **1782** PRIESTLEY *Corrupt. Chr.* I. I. 75 Paul, bishop of Samosata..said to have been of a profligate life. **1817** JAS. MILL *Brit. India* II. v. ix. 700 To corrupt the House of Commons into a profligate subservience to the views of the minister. **1849** MACAULAY *Hist. Eng.* vi. II. 68 Sir Charles Sedley, one of the most brilliant and profligate wits of the Restoration.

b. Recklessly prodigal, extravagant, or profuse.

1779 *Sylph* II. 129 Should I barter my soul to save one so profligate of his? **1875** JOWETT *Plato* (ed. 2) V. 315 The utterly bad is in general profligate, and therefore poor.

B. *sb.* A profligate or dissipated person.

1709 SWIFT *Adv. Relig.* Wks. 1755 II. I. 99 Like a sort of compounding between virtue and vice, as if a woman were allowed to be vicious, provided she be not a profligate. **1796** H. HUNTER tr. *St.-Pierre's Stud. Nat.* (1799) III. 394 Every profligate in the Country..they take care to wheedle over to strengthen their party. **1874** GREEN *Short Hist.* vii. §7. 420 The wretched profligate found himself again plunged into excesses.

profligate ('prɒflɪgeɪt), *v.* Now *rare* or *Obs.* Also 6 *pa. pple.* profligat(e. [f. L. *prōflīgāt-*, ppl. stem of *prōflīgāre*: see prec.]

1. *trans.* To overcome in battle or conflict, to overthrow, rout; to put to flight, chase away, dispel, disperse: **a.** persons (*lit.* and *fig.*).

a **1548** Hall *Chron., Hen. VI* 165 b, I..which hath subuerted so many townes, and profligate and discomfited so many of them in open battayle. *Ibid., Hen. VII* 14 b, Hys armye should..profligate and expell all the intrudors and inuadours. **1646** H. Lawrence *Comm. Angells* 117 If you..stay not till the victory be gotten, till your enemy be profligated and abased. **1692** tr. *Milton's Def. Pop.* viii. M.'s Wks. 1851 VII. 193 You have not yet profligated the Pope quite.

b. things (usually abstract, as evil, disease, error, etc.).

1542 Becon *Christmas Banquet* B vj, With how feruent herte should we profligate and chase awaye synne. **1624** Donne *Serm.* (ed. Alford) V. 274 When Christ is disseised and dispossessed, his Truth profligated and thrown out of a nation that professed it before. **1637** Brian *Pisse-Proph.* (1679) 134 To profligate your disease, and to reduce you to your former health. **1694** Salmon *Bate's Dispens.* I. (1713) 462/2 It so profligates the Humours which cause them, that it soon takes away those Diseases by the Roots. **1694** Motteux *Rabelais* v. (1737) 233 Profligating all Barbarity. **1845** *Life St. Augustine* xix. 195 A dignity..which (to use a forcible Latin word) 'profligates' calumny,—not merely wards it off, but routs, and explodes, and shames it.

c. To overthrow, ruin, destroy; in quot. *a* 1661, to waste by reckless expenditure.

1643 *Characters Richelieu* 13 Peace by Sea and Land profligated. *a* **1661** Fuller *Worthies, Warwick.* (1662) III. 122 From his Profligating of the lands of his Bishoprick.

d. To finish up, dispatch. *rare.*

1840 *Fraser's Mag.* XXI. 333 Dedicated to the glory of the *exercitus maximus* that profligated the German war in three months.

†**2.** *refl.* To abandon oneself to dissolute courses; to become profligate. *Obs. rare*—⁰.

1706 Phillips, To *Profligate one's self*, to give himself up to all manner of Vice, Lewdness and Debauchery.

†**'profligated,** *ppl. a. Obs.* [In sense 1, f. prec. + -ed¹; in sense 2, f. L. *prōflīgāt-us* pa. pple. + -ed¹: cf. profligate *a.* 2.]

1. Overthrown, vanquished; wasted, squandered; dispersed, dissipated.

1599 Nashe *Lenten Stuffe* Wks. (Grosart) V. 221 Of that profligated labour, yet my breast pants and labours. *a* **1619** Fotherby *Atheom.* I. x. §2 (1622) 67 To haue beene, in all mens eyes, so abject and profligated, as to be able to get no moe defenders. **1660** Stillingfl. *Power Excommun.* §21 (1662) 25 The other infirm and profligated argument. **1694** Salmon *Bate's Dispens.* (1713) 38/1 It draws forth the innate and profligated Heat, and restores the Warmth of the Part.

2. Abandoned, vicious; = profligate *a.* 2.

1652 Gaule *Magastrom.* 358 Dardanus, a most profligated magician, was so sordidly addicted to covetousness, that [etc.]. **1673** *Lady's Call.* I. v. §74 The most wretchless profligated state of sin. **1716** M. Davies *Athen. Brit.* II. 271 Those profligated Arians, sorry Macedonians, miserable Nestorians and wretched Eutychians.

'profligately, *adv.* [f. profligate *a.* + -ly².] In a profligate manner or degree; with reckless indulgence or open wickedness; dissolutely; with reckless prodigality, profusely, wastefully.

1694 F. Bragge *Disc. Parables* xi. 374 An utter want of that Divine grace, which they so profligately wasted while they had it. **1741** Middleton *Cicero* I. iii. 173 He was lazy, luxurious, and profligately wicked. **1791** Boswell *Johnson* 27 Mar. an. 1775 *note*, It is related, that he who devised the oath of abjuration, profligately boasted, that he had framed a test which should 'damn one half of the nation, and starve the other'. **1838** Dickens *Nich. Nick.* xvi, Mr. Gregsbury..looked like a man who had been most profligately liberal, but is determined not to repent of it. **1868** F. W. Newman in *Morn. Star* 5 June, The hard-earned wealth of our middle classes, and the honour of our nation, would be profligately squandered.

'profligateness. Now *rare.* [f. as prec. + -ness.] The quality or character of being profligate; profligacy.

1668 Wilkins *Real Char.* 195 Searedness, Profligateness. **1736** Butler *Anal.* II. Conclus. 291 Others, who are not chargeable with all this Profligateness. **1786** A. Gib *Sacr. Contempl.* I. v. iv. 65 The singular profligateness of our time. **1817** J. Gilchrist *Intell. Patrimony* 4 Extravagance of mind, and profligateness of the means of improvement.

profligation (prɒflɪ'geɪʃən). Now *rare* or *Obs.* [ad. late L. *prōflīgātiōn-em* ruin, destruction, n. of action f. *prōflīgāre*: see profligate *a.*] The action of 'profligating', overthrowing, routing; discomfiture, overthrow, rout; ruin, destruction.

1526 *St. Papers Hen. VIII*, I. 185 In the distressing of thEmperours army by see, and profligacion of the Lance-knightes. **1608** Bp. J. King *Serm. 5 Nov.* 21 To the utter..extermination of Christ and his Gospell out of the kingdome, profligation of iustice and religion. **1657** Tomlinson *Renou's Disp.* 150 Convenient for the profligation of diseases. **1815** *Q. Rev.* XIII. 351 A stern profligation of the opinions of many eminent..writers.

'profligator. Now *rare* or *Obs.* [Agent-n. in L. form from profligate *v.*: see -or.] One who or that which 'profligates'; an overthrower.

1694 Salmon *Bate's Dispens.* (1713) 305/1 That stiptick Medicaments are the chief Profligators of those Diseases.

†**pro'flige,** *v. Obs. rare*—¹. [ad. L. *prōflīg-āre* to overthrow.] *trans.* = profligate *v.* 1 a.

c **1540** tr. *Pol. Verg. Eng. Hist.* (Camden) I. 207 The brute wente in eche coste that Aluredus was profliged of the Danes.

†**profluate,** *v. Obs. rare*—¹. [irreg. f. L. *prōfluĕre* (see profluent).] *intr.* To flow forth.

1657 Tomlinson *Renou's Disp.* 215 That the blood may easily profluate.

profluence ('prəʊfluəns). Now *rare.* [ad. L. *prōfluentia* a flowing forth, f. *prōflu-ĕre* to flow forth: see profluent and -ence.]

1. †**a.** A flowing forth or onward; current, stream, flow. *Obs.*

1633 P. Fletcher *Purple Isl.* IV. xvi, A wheyish moat; In whose soft waves, and circling profluence, This Citie, like an Isle, might safely float. **1686** Plot *Staffordsh.* 49 This well will grow dry, after a constant profluence perhaps of eight or ten years. **1693** Sir T. P. Blount *Nat. Hist.* 253 As long as there is a profluence of Water through them, there is no Danger of their Entertaining such Damps.

b. *fig.* The onward flow or course (of events, etc.). *rare.*

a **1639** Wotton *Paral.* in *Reliq.* (1651) 6 In the profluence or proceedings of their fortunes. **1903** Myers *Hum. Personality* II. 289 We see it degrade the cosmic march and profluence into a manner of children's play.

2. *fig.* †**a.** Ready flow of words, fluency. **b.** Abundance, profusion. *rare.*

1568 Skeyne *The Pest* (1860) 16 Nature..disagysit be sophisticall profluence of wordis. *a* **1619** Fotherby *Atheom.* II. i. §8 (1622) 193 Africanus, had his grauitie;..Galba, his austeritie; Carbo, his profluence. **1623** Cockeram, *Profluence*, abundance. **1658** Phillips, *Profluence*, a flowing plentifully, abundance. **1950** M. Peake *Gormenghast* lxxi. 392 The windows..appeared to be sprinkled over the green facades..with an indiscriminate and wayward profluence that gave no clue as to how the inner structures held together.

†**'profluency.** *Obs. rare*—¹. [f. as prec.: see -ency.] Fluency (of speech); = prec. 2 a.

1674 Owen *Holy Spirit* (1693) 172 A Profluency of Speech, venting itself on all occasions.

profluent ('prəʊflu:ənt), *a.* [ad. L. *prōfluent-em*, pr. pple. of *prōflu-ĕre* to flow forth, f. *prō*, pro-¹ 1 a + *flu-ĕre* to flow; cf. *effluent.*] Flowing forth or onward; flowing in a full stream; in first two quots., proceeding or running out of the main body.

c **1420** *Pallad. on Husb.* XII. 56 Best is holde The croppe to kytte, and save on every side The bowes profluent for fruyte to abyde. **1578** Banister *Hist. Man* I. 32 For the subduction of..braunches of Sinewes, profluent from the spinall marey, through the holes in Os sacrum. **1667** Milton *P.L.* XII. 442 Them who shall beleeve Baptizing in the profluent streame. **1686** Plot *Staffordsh.* 42 The great and profluent river of Trent. **1717** J. Keill *Anim. Oecon.* (1738) 77 The Power of the Bladder cannot be estimated by the Motion of the Profluent Urine. **1881** J. Thomson in *Fortn. Rev.* July (1882) 37 My profluent waters perish not from life.

b. *fig.*

1848 J. Sterling in *Fraser's Mag.* XXXVIII. 308 In mild sequence forms of profluent grace Move, tuned to pipes attuning every face. **1866** Symonds in *Life* (1895) I. vii. 359 Elizabethanism..is profluent, profuse of emotion. **1905** G. Jackson in *Expositor* July 63 A babbling profluent way of talking.

†**'profluous,** *a. Obs. rare*—¹. [f. L. *prōflu-us* flowing forth + -ous.] = prec.

1585 Stubbes *Anat. Abus.* I. (1879) 105 *note*, As some be ouer largeous and profluous herein, so other some are spare enough.

†**pro'fluvious,** *a. Obs. rare.* [f. next, or L. *prōfluvi-us* adj., flowing forth + -ous.] Of the nature of, or causing, a profluvium or flux; in quot. 1616 *fig.*

1574 Newton *Health Mag.* 43 Minte..hath a speciall..efficacie against the profluvious issue of the seede, called Gonorrhea. **1616** J. Deacon *Tobacco Tortured* Title-p., The inward taking of Tobacco fumes, is..too too profluuious for many of their purses.

‖**profluvium** (prəʊ'flu:vɪəm). Pl. -ia. [L. *prōfluvium* a flowing forth, flux, f. *prōflu-ĕre*: see profluent. With variant *profluvion* cf. L. comb. form *-luvio, -ōnem* (*colluvio, diluvio*) beside *-luvium.*] A flowing forth; a copious flow or discharge, a flux. (Chiefly *Path.*)

1603 Florio *Montaigne* III. xiii. (1632) 615 An easie profluvion or aboundant running of gravell. **1670** *Phil. Trans.* V. 2075 The bloud..swels and opens the vessels, and breaks out into a Profluvium. **1835** Syd. Smith in *Mem.*, etc. (1855) II. 361, I melt away in nasal and lachrymal profluvia. **1843** R. J. Graves *Syst. Clin. Med.* xxiv. 299 The second or inflammatory stage with its well-known profluvium.

fig. **1864** E. Sargent *Peculiar* II. 108 Decorated around the bust with a profluvium of black lace.

profor, -forre, obs. forms of proffer.

proforce, profos, illiterate Sc. ff. provost.

pro-form: see pro-¹ 4 b.

‖**pro forma:** see pro A. 4.

profound (prəʊ'faʊnd), *a.* (*sb.*) Also β. 5–7 profund-e. [a. OF. *profund, profond* (*c* 1175 in Godef. *Compl.*, *parfund* 11th c. in Hatz.-Darm.), ad. L. *profund-us* deep, high, vast, obscure, profound (also *profundum* sb.), f. *prō*, pro-¹ + *fundus* bottom. The *ou* of Eng. is as in *abound, found* vb., *round*. The β-form *profund* was chiefly a conformation to L., but partly a Sc. phonetic variant.

In Latin *profundus*, the physical sense was the original, the intellectual and normal sense being transf., but in Eng. the literal sense was already expressed by *deep*, so that *profound* with its family was first used in a transferred sense, and only later in the literal sense, either in transl. French or Latin, or as a more sonorous and impressive word than *deep*. But it is convenient here to follow the original sense-development.]

1. Deep (as a physical or material quality).

a. Having great or considerable downward (or inward) measurement; of great depth.

c **1407** [implied in profoundly 1]. *c* **1530** Ld. Berners *Arth. Lyt. Bryt.* xliii. (1814) 135 An hydeous ryuer, depe & perfound. **1550** J. Coke *Eng. & Fr. Heralds* §155 (1877) 102 A kyng that wolde be lorde of the sea, must have..great and perfounde waters and havyns to kepe his shyps in. **1611** Shaks. *Wint. T.* IV. iv. 501 Not..for all the Sun sees, or The close earth wombes, or the profound sea hides In vnknowne fadomes. **1615** G. Sandys *Trav.* 23 Gainst Ioue once making head, he..flung me from the profound skie. **1629** Milton *Hymn Nativity* xxiv, Naught but profoundest Hell can be his shroud. **1715–20** Pope *Iliad* VII. 409 Ample gates ..For passing chariots; and a trench profound. **1823** Scott *Quentin D.* xxv, Surrounded by strong bulwarks and profound moats. **1860** Tyndall *Glac.* I. vii. 55 A series of profound crevasses.

β. *c* **1475** *Partenay* 1180 The diches profunde large brede gan purchas.

b. Situated or extending far beneath the surface; deep-seated, deep-reaching.

c **1430** Lydg. *Min. Poems* (Percy Soc.) 253 Of my mynde the myd poynt moost profounde. **1509** Hawes *Past. Pleas.* xix. (Percy Soc.) 88 O profounde cause of all my sekenesse. **1603** Shaks. *Meas. for M.* I. ii. 59 Which of your hips has the most profound Ciatica? **1612** Woodall *Surg. Mate* Wks. (1653) 90 Wounds made..by..a thrust profound or superficial. **1857** Dunglison *Med. Lex.* s.v. *Profundus*, Certain muscles are distinguished by the names *profound* or *deep-seated*, and *superficial*. **1884** *Pall Mall G.* 13 Sept. 5/1 The agency of heated water at profound depths. **1899** *Allbutt's Syst. Med.* VI. 591 Senile gangrene is generally more profound [than symmetrical gangrene].

β. **1707** Floyer *Physic. Pulse-Watch* 388 The profund Pulse of the Lungs indicates Hæmorrhagies, and Heat and Death.

c. Originating in, or coming from, a depth; deeply drawn, deep-fetched (as a sigh); carried far down or very low (as a bow or inclination of the body).

? *a* **1550** *Knt. of Curtesy* 184 No comforte..coude he take, Nor absteine him fro perfounde syghinge. **1602** Shaks. *Ham.* II. i. 94 He rais'd a sigh, so pittious and profound. **1603** Drayton *Odes* v. 31 Let not a Man drinke, but in Draughts profound. **1732** Lediard *Sethos* II. ix. 340 The three ambassadors..made a profound reverence. **1799** Harriet Lee *Canterbury T.* I. 199 'Why?' said Dorsain..with a profound sigh. **1877** J. D. Chambers *Div. Worship* 306 A profound inclination of the body.

2. a. Of a person: Characterized by intellectual depth; that penetrates or has penetrated deeply into a subject of knowledge, study, or thought; having great insight into or knowledge of something; very learned. In quot. 1611 (app.) Deep or subtle in contrivance, crafty, cunning (cf. deep *a.* 17).

(The earliest sense in English.)

c **1305** *Edmund Conf.* 221 in *E.E.P.* (1862) 77 Of art he radde six ȝer..& siþþe for beo more profound, to arsmetrike he drouȝ. **1481** Caxton *Reynard* (Arb.) 89 A connyng man and a profounde clerk in many sciencis. **1570** Dee *Math. Pref.* 2 The constant profound Philosopher. **1600** Shaks. *A.Y.L.* v. ii. 67 A Magitian, most profound in his Art. **1611** Bible *Hosea* v. 2 The reuolters are profound to make slaughter. *a* **1661** Fuller *Worthies* (1662) I. 121 Their Abbot..was pious, painfull, and a profound Schollar. **1734** Berkeley *Analyst* §3 Those who in this age pass for profound geometers. **1844** Disraeli *Coningsby* III. i, The greatest captain and the profoundest statesman of the age. **1869** Freeman *Norm. Conq.* III. xii. 110 The profoundest of metaphysicians and divines.

b. Of personal attributes, actions, or works: Showing depth of insight or knowledge; entering deeply into a subject; marked by great learning.

c **1412** Hoccleve *De Reg. Princ.* 363 Þe suffissant clergye, Endowyd of profound intelligence. **1497–8** *Petit. Parlt. Drogheda* (*Patent Roll 13 Hen. VII*, m. 27) They nedar canne ne dare cast dart or spear be cause they haue not the profounde wey and feate of it. **1532** Frith *Mirror* Wks. (1829) 263 If a man praise a very fool, and think his wit good and profound, then is that person, indeed, more fool than the other. **1596** Shaks. *Merch. V.* I. i. 92 To be drest in an opinion Of wisedome, grauity, profound conceit. **1664** Power *Exp. Philos.* Pref. c iij b, Their profoundest Speculations. *a* **1680** Butler *Rem.* (1759) I. 222 Learned Nonsense has a deeper Sound, Than easy Sense, and goes for more profound. **1783** Blair *Rhet.* xxxiv. (1812) II. 444 Some of the profoundest things which have been written. **1834** Mrs. Somerville *Connex. Phys. Sc.* xxi. (1849) 205 A most profound mathematical inquiry. **1855** Brewster *Newton* II. xvii. 155 His profound and beautiful letters on the existence of the Deity.

β. **1451** Capgrave *Life St. Gilbert* (E.E.T.S.) 88 He comitted al þis disposicion to þe profund councell of our Lord. **1691** Wood *Ath. Oxon.* II. 579 He was admired by great Scholars..for his profund divinity.

3. Of non-material things figured as having depth.

a. Of a subject of thought: Deep in meaning; demanding deep study or research; abstruse, recondite; sometimes connoting Difficult to 'fathom' or understand; having a meaning that does not lie on the surface.

c **1407** LYDG. *Reson & Sens.* 4856 Neuer yet was rad noo songe..so worthy of renoun, To spekyn of philosophie, Nor of profounde poetrie. **1529** MORE *Dyaloge* I. Wks. 159/1 No man is there so connyng, but he myght finde in them thinges ..farre to profounde to perce vnto. **1583** GOLDING *Calvin on Deut.* xix. 114 A higher and profounder doctrine. **1698** FRYER *Acc. E. India & P.* 365 It contains profound meanings. **1849** H. B. SMITH *Faith & Philos.* (1850) 23 Christianity..is simple as is light to the eye of the child, it is profound as is light to the eye of the sage.

β. **1596** DALRYMPLE tr. *Leslie's Hist. Scot.* I. 88 That w^t the gretter facilitie we may prepare the way sum things to reherse mair profunde.

b. Of a condition, state, or quality: Having depth or intensity; intense, thorough, extreme, very great; in which one may be intensely immersed or engaged; unbroken or undisturbed (as *profound silence, sleep, rest, peace*); deeply-rooted, deep-seated; deeply-buried, hence, concealed or involving concealment (as a *profound secret*, etc.).

1599 SHAKS. *Much Ado* v. i. 198 *Prin.* He is in earnest. *Clau.* In most profound earnest. **1610** HOLLAND *Camden's Brit.* (1637) 577 Being of a lewd disposition and profound perfidiousnesse. *a* **1659** OSBORN *Observ. Turks* Wks. (1673) 273 The fear of lapsing into grosser Idolatry, or profounder Atheism. **1711** STEELE *Spect.* No. 113 ¶2 Here followed a profound Silence. **1757** BURKE *Abridgm. Eng. Hist.* III. ix, In the profoundest peace. **1796** H. HUNTER tr. *St.-Pierre's Stud. Nat.* (1799) II. 331 The sublime impression which they produce becomes still more profound, when they recal to us some sentiment of virtue. **1805** NELSON *Let.* 11 May (in *Sotheby's Catal.* 6–9 Dec. (1905) 131), My departure for the West Indies..you will keep a profound secret. **1833** L. RITCHIE *Wand. by Loire* 35 Wearied travellers buried in profound sleep. **1837** W. IRVING *Capt. Bonneville* II. 264 The chief, and all present, listened with profound attention. **1841** MYERS *Cath. Th.* III. §7. 22 Language is most imperfect when feeling is most profound. *a* **1853** ROBERTSON *Lect. & Addr.* ii. (1858) 59 In profoundest ignorance of the opinions. **1871** L. STEPHEN *Playgr. Eur.* (1894) iv. 242 Profound melancholy seemed to haunt the hollows of the mountain ridges. **1899** *Allbutt's Syst. Med.* VII. 458 Profound unconsciousness. *Mod.* It is a subject in which I take a profound interest.

c. Said of reverence, respect, submission, or the like: often having some reference to the notion of bowing low, lowly reverence (cf. 1 c).

1526 *Pilgr. Perf.* (W. de W. 1531) 167 b, The holy fathers & sayntes..had this profounde mekenes. **1607** SHAKS. *Cor.* III. iii. 113, I do loue My Countries good, with a respect more tender, More holy, and profound, then mine owne life. **1688** *Answ. Talon's Plea* 5 Their extraordinary respect, and profoundest submission. **1721** in *Swift's Lett.* (1766) II. 305 With the profoundest regard and esteem, Sir, your most humble and most obedient servant. **1737** POPE *Hor. Epist.* II. ii. 154 They treat themselves with most profound respect. **1836** J. GILBERT *Chr. Atonem.* iv. (1852) 92 A knowledge to which the reflecting mind pays the profoundest homage. **1863** GEO. ELIOT *Romola* xxvi, The air of profound deference. **1878** STEWART & TAIT *Unseen Univ.* Introd. 12 The most profound reverence.

B. *sb.*

1. That which is profound or eminently deep, or the deepest part of something; a vast depth; an abyss. *lit.* and *fig.* chiefly *poetical*.

1640 G. SANDYS *Christ's Passion* III. 242 To raise it from that dark Profound. **1735** SOMERVILLE *Chase* III. 287 The unwieldly Beast..drops into the dark Profound. **1742** YOUNG *Nt. Th.* IV. 593 Eternity, too short to speak thy praise! Or fathom thy profound of love to man! **1813** T. BUSBY *Lucretius* II. v. Comm. p. xxiv, [Galileo] who.. taught future philosophers..to penetrate farther into the blue profound. **1839** BAILEY *Festus* iii. (1852) 30 Probe the profound of thine own nature, man!

b. *spec.* The depth of the sea or other deep water; the deep sea, 'the deep'. *poetical.*

1621 G. SANDYS *Ovid's Met.* XI. (1626) 234 On that profound Poore I was wrackt; yet thou with-out me drownd. **1725** POPE *Odyss.* VIII. 34 Expert to try The vast profound, and bid the vessel fly. **1807** J. BARLOW *Columb.* I. 202 Nor billowy surge disturbs the vast profound.

2. Intellectual depth or profundity. *rare*⁻¹.

1778 WOLCOTT (P. Pindar) *Ep. to Reviewers* ix, I never question'd your profound of head.

† **profound**, *v. Obs.* [a. obs. F. *profonder* (14th c., Oresme) 'to sound, search, pierce, or goe deepe into; to diue, or sinke vnto the bottom of; to presse downe, or put into the deepe' (Cotgr.) (in med.L. *profundāre*), f. *profond* PROFOUND *a.*]

1. *trans.* To immerse or plunge deeply; *pa. pple.* deep-seated.

? *a* **1412** LYDG. *Two Merchants* 312 Whan..Deeply profoundid is heete natural In thilke humydite i-callyd radical. **1643** SIR T. BROWNE *Relig. Med.* I. §55 Vice and the Devil put a Fallacy upon our Reasons, and, provoking us too hastily to run from it, entangle and profound us deeper in it.

2. To go deeply into; to 'sound', 'fathom'.

1643 SIR T. BROWNE *Relig. Med.* I. §13 There is no danger to profound these mysteries, no *sanctum sanctorum* in Philosophy. **1646** —— *Pseud. Ep.* I. ix. (1686) 27 To profound the Ocean of that Doctrine.

3. *intr.* To penetrate deeply, 'dive' (*into*, etc.).

1643 SIR T. BROWNE *Relig. Med.* I. §14 To profound farther, and to contemplate a reason why His Providence hath so disposed and ordered their motions. **1661** GLANVILL *Van. Dogm.* 227 Let the most confirm'd Dogmatist profound far into his indeared opinions, and..'twill be an effectual cure of confidence.

proˈfoundly, *adv.* [f. PROFOUND *a.* + -LY².] In a profound manner or degree; deeply.

1. To or at a great depth or distance from the surface. Also *fig.*

c **1407** LYDG. *Reson & Sens.* 5693 Whan I had the lettres rad, Which in the stonys..Wer profoundely and depe y-grave. *c* **1450** tr. *De Imitatione* III. xlvii. 118 þe more profoundly þat a man goþ dovn into himself and waxiþ vile to himself, þe hyer he stieþ up to god. **1840** BROWNING *Sordello* VI. 360 My soul o'ertops Each height,—than every depth profoundlier drops. **1857** DUNGLISON *Med. Lex., Profundus*,..a name given to..parts, which are seated profoundly as regards others. **1871** R. ELLIS *Catullus* xvii. 11 Where..descends most profoundly the bottom.

b. So as to come from or sink to a great depth; with a deep breath (as in sighing) or inclination (as in bowing). Sometimes with mixture of sense 3.

1480 CAXTON *Ovid's Met.* XI. xix, She wayled & sighed perfoundly. **1606** SHAKS. *Tr. & Cr.* IV. ii. 83 Why sigh you so profoundly?..tell me sweet Vnckle, what's the matter? **1700** DRYDEN *Cinyras & Myrrha* 184 The virgin started at her father's name, And sigh'd profoundly. *a* **1811** BLAKE *Poet. Wks.* (1905) 231 Then,..bowing profoundly, he said: 'A great wig'.

2. With intellectual depth; with great insight or penetration into a subject; very learnedly.

With *learned, wise*, etc., this nearly coincides with sense 3.

c **1400** MAUNDEV. (Roxb.) xvi. 73 He preched mare profoundely of Haly Writte þan oþer didd. **1561** *Godly Q. Hester* (1873) 15 In learninge and litterature, profoundely seene. **1693** *Apol. Clergy Scot.* 39 This is profoundly wise. **1711** STEELE *Spect.* No. 157 ¶7 A Person..profoundly learned in Horse-flesh. **1879** *Cassell's Techn. Educ.* IV. 63/2 Those who have not studied very profoundly.

3. Intensely, extremely, thoroughly, very greatly; to a depth of quality, state, or degree.

1502 ATKYNSON tr. *De Imitatione* III. xv. 210 Howe profoundely ought I to submytte me to thy hydde & depe iugementis. **1526** *Pilgr. Perf.* (W. de W. 1531) 167 b, Yf the herte be profoundly meke. **1654** H. L'ESTRANGE *Chas. I* (1655) 105 He..wanted money the sinews of war, his Exchequer being profoundly dry. **1719** DE FOE *Crusoe* (1840) II. ix. 209 They found all..as profoundly secure as sleep..could make them. **1849** MACAULAY *Hist. Eng.* vii. II. 175 Profoundly ignorant of the English constitution. **1871** TYNDALL *Fragm. Sci.* (1879) II. xi. 241 A poet and a profoundly religious man. **1872** YEATS *Growth Comm.* 32 The..limits were kept profoundly secret.

proˈfoundness. [f. as prec. + -NESS.] The quality of being profound; profundity.

As to chronological order of senses, see PROFOUND *a.*

1. Depth, deepness (in physical sense): = PROFUNDITY 1, 1 b. (In quot. 1642 with play on sense 2.)

1642 FULLER *Holy & Prof. St.* v. xiv. 411 The Butler makes him free..of his own fathers cellar, and guesseth the profoundnesse of his young masters capacity by the depth of the whole-ones he fetcheth off. *a* **1693** *Urquhart's Rabelais* III. xlix. 396 The Herb..never fixeth it self into the ground above the profoundness almost of a Cubit. **1851** HAWTHORNE *Ho. Sev. Gables* xi, To take a deep, deep plunge into the ocean of human life, and to sink down and be covered by its profoundness.

2. Depth of learning, thought, meaning, etc.: = PROFUNDITY 2.

1525 LD. BERNERS *Froiss.* II. ccxxviii. [ccxxiv.] 714 They that wyll seke out the profoundnesse of the mater, maye well knowe fro whence ye came. **1575** *Recorde's Gr. Artes* Pref. A iij, The ignorant sorte..do litle esteeme the profoundnesse of mannes spirit, and of reason. **1629** BURTON *Babel no Bethel* 39 Shew vs your profoundnesse.. in your reading of Bellarmine. **1709** HEARNE *Collect.* 10 Sept. (O.H.S.) II. 254 A shew of Learning passes with them for profoundness. **1874** GREEN *Short Hist.* vi. §4. 299 In originality and profoundness of thought he [Erasmus] was ..inferior to More.

b. Craft, deep or subtle contrivance.

1605 BACON *Adv. Learn.* I. viii. §3 This is what the author of the Revelation calleth the depth or profoundness of Satan [Rev. ii. 24]. **1830** HAZLITT *Party Spirit* Wks. 1904 XII. 402 Party spirit is one of the profoundnesses of Satan.

3. Intensity, extreme degree: = PROFUNDITY 3.

1612 R. SHELDON *Serm. St. Martin's* 30 What a depth of humilitie, what a profoundness of meekenesse. *Mod.* The profoundness of his ignorance was astonishing.

profre, obs. form of PROFFER.

profugate (ˈprɒfjʊgeɪt), *v. rare*⁻¹. [f. L. *prō* forth (PRO-¹) + *fugāre* to put to flight: see -ATE³.] *trans.* To drive or chase away. So **ˈprofugate** (-ət) *ppl. a. rare* [cf. L. *profugus* fugitive: see -ATE²], driven or chased away, fugitive.

1603 HARSNET *Pop. Impost.* 107 When they presented him with Frankincense, as little deeming of fuming any deuil in theyr way, or profugating a deuil from the body of our blessed Sauiour. **1866** J. B. ROSE tr. *Ovid's Met.* 28 And drive her profugate the world around. *Ibid.* 67. *Ibid.* 386 He profugate, launched forth upon the main.

profulgent (prəʊˈfʌldʒənt), *a. rare.* [f. PRO-¹ + L. *fulgent-em* FULGENT.] Shining forth, effulgent, radiant.

? *a* **1500** *Nine Ladies Worthie* in *Chaucer's Wks.* (1561) 342 b, Profulgent in preciousnes, O Sinope the queen. **1830** TENNYSON *Conf. Sensitive Mind* 145 An image with profulgent brows.

† **proˈfund**, *v. Obs. rare.* [ad. L. *pro-, prōfund-ĕre* to pour forth.] *trans.* To pour forth; *fig.* to spend profusely, to lavish.

1527 *St. Papers Hen. VIII*, I. 251 For the exchewing of grete expences, whiche shuld be profunded and consumed in the intervieu. **1657** TOMLINSON *Renou's Disp.* 264 The juice is profunded upon wallnut tree leaves.

profund, -e, obs. forms of PROFOUND.

‖ **profunda** (prəʊˈfʌndə). *Anat.* [L. fem. of *profundus* deep, PROFOUND (sc. *vēna* or *artēria*).] A distinguishing name of various deep-seated arteries and veins, in the neck, arm, leg, and other parts.

1840 E. WILSON *Anat. Vade M.* (1842) 346 The Profunda Vein is formed by the convergence of the numerous small Veins. **1846** BRITTAN tr. *Malgaigne's Man. Oper. Surg.* 260 The profunda following exactly the same course as the crural [artery]. **1879** *St. George's Hosp. Rep.* IX. 328 The profunda was blocked by a short plug.

profundal (prəʊˈfʌndəl), *a.* and *sb. Ecology.* [ad. G. *profund* PROFOUND: see -AL.]

A. *adj.* Applied to the region of the bed of a lake lying below the thermocline. **B.** *sb.* The profundal region of a lake bed.

[**1928** K. E. CARPENTER *Life in Inland Waters* viii. 180 Modern workers usually prefer to recognise a 'sub-littoral zone'.., ending at about 50 metres in lakes of the plain type .., and below this a 'profound' or 'deep-water' region.] **1931** *Ecol. Monogr.* I. 233 In fresh-water lakes few animals have proved themselves capable of living in that unusual habitat, the anaerobic profundal zone of the lake bottom. *Ibid.* 245 In Third Sister Lake the three major benthic zones have the following approximate extent: littoral, 0–3 m.; sublittoral, 3–10 m.; profundal, 10–18 m. **1957** G. E. HUTCHINSON *Treat. Limnol.* I. xv. 818 Enabling the animals of the profundal benthos to live not merely under conditions of low oxygen and high CO_2 tension. **1961** *Ekol. Polska* A. IX. 352 A total of 2300 samples was taken from the profundal of Lake Tajty. **1965** B. E. FREEMAN tr. *Vandel's Biospeleol.* i. 9 The profundal regions of lakes..constitute an environment similar to the subterranean media. **1972** *Oikos* Suppl. No. 14. 5 In the profundal of a eutrophic lake the environment is relatively homogeneous and the species diversity low compared with the littoral.

† **proˈfundeur.** *Obs. rare*⁻¹. [ad. F. *profondeur*, f. *profond* PROFOUND: cf. *grandeur*.] Depth, profundity.

1658 SIR T. BROWNE *Gard. Cyrus* iv. 162 They strictly make good their profundeur or depth. **1661** BLOUNT *Glossogr.* (ed. 2), *Profundeur*,..profundity, depth, deepness.

proˈfundify, *v. nonce-wd.* [f. L. *profund-us* PROFOUND *a.*: see -FY.] *trans.* To make profound.

1821 *Blackw. Mag.* IX. 198 They are provoked by droppings of inspiration from a stone, in which the measure and the meaning are most happily profundified.

profundipalmar (prəʊˌfʌndɪˈpælmə(r)), *a. Anat.* [f. L. *profundus* deep, PROFOUND + *palma* palm of the hand + -AR¹.] Deep-seated in the palm of the hand, as a tendon or other structure; belonging to such structure. So **proˌfundiˈplantar** *a.* [L. *planta* sole of the foot], deep-seated in the sole of the foot, or belonging to a structure so situated.

1888 *Auk* V. 105 The paper concludes with remarks..on the profundiplantar tendons.

† **proˈfunditude.** *Obs.* [f. L. *profund-us* deep + -TUDE: cf. *altitude*, etc.] = next.

1616 R. C. *Times' Whistle*, etc. (1871) 149 The body three dimensions doth include,..length, bredth, profunditude. **1645** EVELYN *Diary* 7 Feb., A lake..reported of that profunditude in the middle that it is botomelesse. **1650** ASHMOLE *Chym. Collect.* 49 A due measure of Longitude, Latitude, and Profunditude.

profundity (prəˈfʌndɪtɪ). Also 6 **profoundyte, -itie**, 7 **-ity**. [ME. *profundite*, a. OF. *profundite*, mod.F. *profondité*, ad. late L. *profunditās* depth, immensity, f. *profundus* PROFOUND: see -ITY.] The quality of being profound; that which is profound.

1. Depth, in a physical sense. † **a.** *gen.* as one of the three dimensions of bodies: Measurement or extension downwards: = DEPTH 1.

1471 RIPLEY *Comp. Alch.* II. xi. in Ashm. *Theat. Chem. Brit.* (1652) 137 Altytude, Latytude, and Profundyte. **1571** DIGGES *Pantom., Math. Disc.* ii. Y iij b, A right angled Quadrangular direct Prisma, hauing for his longitude, latitude and profunditie these three lines. **1625** N. CARPENTER *Geog. Del.* II. vii. (1635) 104 The depth or profundity is the distance betwixt the Bottome and the Superficies of the Water. **1696** J. EDWARDS *Demonstr. Exist. & Prov. God* II. 122 Its longitude was..tenfold to its profundity.

b. The quality of being (very) deep; deepness; great or vast depth; extreme lowness (of a bow).

1604 R. CAWDREY *Table Alph., Profunditie*,..deepness. **1615** G. SANDYS *Trav.* IV. 233 The ditch..of an incredible profunditie. **1794** SULLIVAN *View Nat.* I. 33 How striking the profundity of the abysses! **1832** LYELL *Princ. Geol.* II. 181 That there is life at much greater profundities in warmer regions may be confidently inferred. **1878** BESANT & RICE *Celia's Arb.* xvii, With another bow of greater profundity than would have become an Englishman.

c. *concr.* or quasi-*concr.* A very deep place; the very deep or deepest part *of* something; a (vast) depth, an abyss. Also *fig.*

1432–50 tr. *Higden* (Rolls) I. 59 The wyndes respirenge and restenge in the profundite of hit. **1552** HULOET, Profunditye, *abissus.* **1615** G. SANDYS *Trav.* 192 A great square profunditie, greene, and uneuen at the bottome, into which a barren spring doth drill. **1667** MILTON *P.L.* VII. 229 Through the vast profunditie obscure. **1851** NICHOL *Archit. Heav.* 17 A capability of sounding profundities.

2. Depth of intellect, insight, knowledge, learning, or thought; depth of meaning or content; abstruseness.

c **1450** tr. *De Imitatione* III. lxiv. 149 Thou.. art þe ende of all godes, þe hyenes of lif, þe profundite of scriptures. **1508** FISHER *7 Penit. Ps.* cii. Wks. (1876) 138 He is the profoundyte of thyn inenarrable wysdome. **1589** NASHE *Pref. Greene's Menaphon* (Arb.) 14 Which lies couched most closely vnder darke fables profounditie. **1679** C. NESSE *Antichrist* 134 It causeth me to admire the profoundity of the scripture. **1682** BUNYAN *Holy War* x. 278 To encourage you in the profundity of your craft. **1788** R. CUMBERLAND *Observer* No. 110. IV. 155 In one [Ben Jonson] we may respect the profundity of learning, in the other [Shakespeare] we must admire the sublimity of genius. **1873** SYMONDS *Grk. Poets* vii. 198 The admiration which every student of Sophocles must feel for the profundity of his design.

b. *pl.* Depths of thought or meaning; 'deep things'.

1582 N. T. (Rhem.) *1 Cor.* ii. 10 The Spirit searcheth al things, yea the profoundities of God. **1621** BURTON *Anat. Mel.* II. ii. III. (1676) 163/2, I am.. not able to dive into these profundities.: not able to understand, much less to discuss.

3. Intensity, thoroughness, extremeness of degree.

1576 NEWTON *Lemnie's Complex.* (1633) 92 In some persons it is not to be measured, so much by the number of houres, as by the soundnesse and profundity of sleeping. **1796** H. HUNTER tr. *St.-Pierre's Stud. Nat.* (1799) II. 75 The profundity of our own ignorance. **1832** L. HUNT *Sir R. Esher* (1850) 82 The profundity of his admiration.

‖**profundus** (prəʊˈfʌndəs). *Anat.* [L. (sc. *musculus* muscle): see PROFOUND *a.*] Used as distinguishing name for a deep-seated muscle, esp. the *flexor profundus perforans* of the fingers.

1704 J. HARRIS *Lex. Techn.* I, Profundus, a Muscle, which bends the Fingers. **1727–41** CHAMBERS *Cycl.* s.v. *Muscles*, Names and offices of the several muscles.. *Sublimis, Profundus*, bend the fingers. **1854–67** C. A. HARRIS *Dict. Med. Terminol.*, *Profundus*, deep-seated; also, the flexor profundus perforans muscle.

profur, obs. form of PROFFER.

profuse (prəʊˈfjuːs), *a.* [ad. L. *profūs-us* poured forth, spread out, lavish, immoderate, profuse, prop. pa. pple. of *pro-*, *prōfundĕre* to pour forth, f. *prō*, PRO-¹ + *fund-ĕre* to pour. So F. *profus* (16th c. in Littré).]

1. Of persons or agents: Expending, bestowing, or producing abundantly; lavish, liberal to excess; extravagant, wasteful, prodigal. Const. *in*, *of*.

1432–50 tr. *Higden* (Rolls) VII. 119 He was myȝhty in batelle, liberalle in ȝiffenge, and profuse in makynge festes. **1575–85** [implied in PROFUSENESS]. **1616** BULLOKAR *Eng. Expos.*, *Profuse*, wastefull, lauish in spending. **1621** BURTON *Anat. Mel.* II. i. IV. ii, Many agaiue are in that other extreame too profuse, suspitious and jelous of their health, too apt to take Physick vpon euery small occasion. **1729** FRANKLIN *Ess.* Wks. 1840 II. 259 Working-men.. are thereby induced to be more profuse and extravagant in fine apparel. **1788** GIBBON *Decl. & F.* xl. (1869) II. 477 Justinian was so profuse that he could not be liberal. **1845** BROWNING *Lett.* (1899) I. 245 Mr. Forster came yesterday and was very profuse of graciosities. **1868** E. EDWARDS *Ralegh* I. i. 11 He was.. somewhat too open-handed and profuse in his ordinary expenditure.

fig. **1667** MILTON *P.L.* VIII. 286 On a green shadie Bank profuse of Flours.

2. Of actions, conditions, or things: Very abundant; exuberant, bountiful; copious; excessive.

a **1610** HEALEY *Epictetus' Man.* (1636) 66 Let not thy laughter bee profuse, nor be led by every light occasion [cf. quot. 1608 in PROFUSED]. **1728** YOUNG *Love Fame* VI, This lady glories in profuse expence. **1802** *Med. Jrnl.* VIII. 207 Profuse sweating, great debility and loss of appetite, had begun to take place. **1876** BRISTOWE *The. & Pract. Med.* (1878) 473 When pulmonary hemorrhage.. is profuse.. the symptoms and prospects are in the highest degree grave. **1885** BIBLE (R.V.) *Prov.* xxvii. 6 The kisses of an enemy are profuse.

†**profuse** (prəʊˈfjuːz), *v.* *Obs.* [f. L. *profūs-*, ppl. stem of *profund-ĕre*: see prec. (At first perh. in pa. pple. *profused* from L. *profūsus*: see next.)] *trans.* To pour forth; to expend, bestow, or produce freely or lavishly; to lavish, squander, waste.

c **1611** CHAPMAN *Iliad* XXIV. 295 Mercury, thy help hath been profus'd Ever with most grace in consorts of travellers distress'd. **1615** —— *Odyss.* XXI. 156 Tender no excuse For least delay, nor too much time profuse In stay to draw this bow. *a* **1614** DONNE *Βιαθανατος* (1644) 58 Man snatch'd.. a new way of profusing his life to Martyrdome. **1711** STEELE *Spect.* No. 260 ⁋1 If I had laid out that which I profused in Luxury and Wantonness, in Acts of Generosity or Charity. **1771** J. FOOT *Penseroso* II. 84 With these [waters] profused is drown'd the suff'ring earth.

†**proˈfused**, *a.* *Obs.* [f. L. *profūs-us* (see PROFUSE *a.*) + -ED¹; or pa. pple. of PROFUSE *v.*] = PROFUSE *a.* Hence †**proˈfusedly** *adv.*, profusely.

1608 D. T[UVIL] *Ess. Pol. & Mor.* 96 b, Affects profused laughter [cf. L. *profusa hilaritas* (Cicero)] at a feast. **1690** NORRIS *Pract. Disc.* (1707) IV. 234 To what purpose does Dr. Wh... lay himself out so profusedly to prove that the Creatures are good?

profusely (prəʊˈfjuːslɪ), *adv.* [f. PROFUSE *a.* + -LY².] In a profuse manner; in profusion or abundance; without stint; wastefully, lavishly.

1621 BURTON *Anat. Mel.* To Rdr. (1676) 14/1 At this speech Democritus profusely laughed, (his friends.. weeping in the mean time, and lamenting his madness). **1697** DRYDEN *Virg. Past.* Pref. (1721) I. 93 A Meadow, where the Beauties of the Spring are profusely blended together. **1791** MRS. RADCLIFFE *Rom. Forest* i, After drinking profusely of some mild liquids. **1885** *Manch. Exam.* 9 July 4/7 The shipping in the harbour was profusely decked with flags.

profuseness (prəʊˈfjuːsnɪs). [f. as prec. + -NESS.] The quality or state of being profuse; lavishness; wastefulness; profusion.

1575–85 ABP. SANDYS *Serm.* (Parker Soc.) 400 There be two grand enemies of hospitality. The one is covetousness, the other profuseness. **1632** MASSINGER *City Madam* III. ii, I, That knew profuseness of expense the parent Of wretched Poverty, her fatal daughter. **1750** JOHNSON *Rambler* No. 27 ⁋7, I was convinced that their liberality was only profuseness, that.. they were equally generous to vice and virtue. **1850** *Florist* Mar. 81 Its distinctness and profuseness of bloom combine to make it a very desirable thing. **1857** BUCKLE *Civiliz.* I. xi. 631 In no age have literary men been rewarded with such profuseness as in the reign of Louis XIV.; and in no age have they been so mean spirited.

b. With *a* and *pl.* An act of profuse expenditure.

1656 EARL MONM. tr. *Boccalini's Advts. fr. Parnass.* I. xix. (1674) 20 One of those inconsiderate profusenesses used by shallow-pated Princes.

†**proˈfuser.** *Obs. rare.* [f. PROFUSE *v.* + -ER¹. So obs. F. *profuseur* (Cotgr.), late L. *profūsor.*] One who or that which lavishes; a spendthrift.

1616 *Rich Cabinet* 151 Vanitie in words.. is a lavish profuser of pretious time. **1648** HERRICK *Hesper.*, *Fortune*, Fortune's a blind profuser of her own, Too much she gives to some, enough to none.

profusion (prəʊˈfjuːʒən). [a. F. *profusion* (16th c., Montaigne), ad. L. *profūsiōn-em*, n. of action f. *profundĕre* to pour forth.]

1. The action of pouring forth; outpouring, effusion (of a liquid); spilling, shedding. Now *rare.*

1604 R. CAWDREY *Table Alph.*, *Profusion*, powring out wastfully. **1607** TOPSELL *Four-f. Beasts* (1658) 146 Some men in this extremity suffer most fearful dreams, profusion of seed, hoarseness of voyce. **1743** tr. *Heister's Surg.* 26 The effects.. are generally Profusions of Blood. **1822–34** *Good's Study Med.* (ed. 4) II. 443 [Cullen] has hence been obliged to transfer the whole of these [hæmorrhages] to another part of his system.. and to distinguish them by the feeble name of profusions instead of by their own proper denomination.

2. Lavish or wasteful expenditure or bestowal *of* money, substance, etc.; squandering, waste.

1545 JOYE *Exp. Dan.* xi. 195 b, Because of his prodigalite & profusions of giftis, he might not spare other menis goodis. *a* **1635** NAUNTON *Fragm. Reg.* (Arb.) 42 Which proved in the end a most fatall work, both in the profusion of blood and treasure. **1752** CHESTERF. *Lett.* (1774) III. 280 Be upon your guard against this idle profusion of time. **1828** D'ISRAELI *Chas. I*, II. i. 2 Charles the First has never been accused of a wanton profusion of the public wealth.

3. The fact, condition, or quality of being profuse; lavishness, wastefulness, extravagance.

1692 DRYDEN *St. Euremont's Ess.* 204 Those, that take away with violence, to disperse with profusion, are much more excusable. **1709** SWIFT *Adv. Relig.* Ded., The lustre of that most noble family.. which the unmeasurable profusion of ancestors for many generations had too much eclipsed. **1725** DE FOE *Voy. round World* (1840) 96 They were entertained with the utmost profusion and magnificence after the Spanish manner. **1838** THIRLWALL *Greece* V. xliii. 278 The profusion.. which he lavished his gold. **1876** J. PARKER *Paracl.* I. xiv. 224 You are amazed by the profusion which is characteristic of Nature; not merely a star here and there, but millions beyond all conceivable number.

4. Abundance; lavish or copious supply.

1705 ADDISON *Italy* 184 To have furnish'd out so many glorious Palaces with such a Profusion of Pictures, Statues, and the like Ornaments. **1764** GOLDSM. *Trav.* 46 Ye fields, where summer spreads profusion round. **1791** MRS. RADCLIFFE *Rom. Forest* vi, Her auburn tresses fell in profusion over her bosom. **1864** D. G. MITCHELL *Wet Days at Edgewood* 80 Wheat was growing in profusion.

proˈfusive (-sɪv), *a.* [f. L. *profūs-*, ppl. stem of *profundĕre* (see PROFUSE *a.*) + -IVE.] Characterized by or tending to profusion or lavishness.

1638 BAKER tr. *Balzac's Lett.* (vol. III) 86 Your Magnificence.. in a severer Common-wealth than ours, would be called a profusive Wast. **1685** EVELYN *Mrs. Godolphin* 222 Chearfull and even profusive Charityes. **1797** *Monthly Mag.* III. 218 Her gifts in vain profusive Plenty flings. **1861** R. QUINN *Heather Lintie* (1866) 34 Profusive smiling gleams.

Hence **proˈfusively** *adv.*; **proˈfusiveness**.

1650 EARL MONM. tr. *Senault's Man become Guilty* 230 Rivers flow profusively, their spring heads are not dried up. **1655** FULLER *Ch. Hist.* V. v. §64 His profusiveness.. not only spending the great Treasure left Him by His Father; but also vast wealth beside.

profycy(e, obs. form of PROPHECY.

profyr(e, obs. form of PROFFER.

prog (prɒg), *sb.*¹ Also 7 progg(e, 8–9 progue. [Origin obscure; perh. a variant of PRAG *sb.*¹; cf. also BROG, and PROD *sb.* and *v.*]

1. A piercing instrument or weapon; a spike; a skewer; a stiletto; a prick or prickle.

1615 G. SANDYS *Trav.* 27 Slicing it into little gobbets, prick it on a prog of iron, and hang it in a fornace. **1634** W. WOOD *New Eng. Prosp.* II. vii, The water having dank't his pistoles, and lost his Spanish progge in the bottome, the Indians swomme him out by the chinne to the shore. **1785** R. FORBES *Poems Buchan Dial.*, *Ulysses* 31 Sin the Fates hae orders gi'en To bring the progues [= arrows] to Troy. *a* **1825** FORBY *Voc. E. Anglia*, *Prog*, a curved spike or prong, to drag what is seized by it... A prog would be of no use if it could not hold and draw as well as pierce. Both these words are otherwise pronounced *progue.* **1825** BROCKETT *N.C. Gloss.*, *Prog*, a prick. —*Progly*, *a.* prickly.

2. An act of progging; a stab, thrust, sharp poke; a prod. *Sc.* and *dial.* Also *fig.*

1822 GALT *Steam-Boat* viii. 155, I.. could thole her progs and jokes with the greatest pleasance and composure. **1856** *Deil's Hallowe'en* 39 (E.D.D.) He.. gied a progue, that wasna licht. **1891** BURGESS *Rasmie's Büddie* 31 He'll mebbe need anidder proge, Frae my aald staff.

prog (prɒg), *sb.*² Also 7 progge, 7–8 progg, progue. [perh. f. PROG *v.*¹, = that which is progged or got by progging.] 'A cant word for provision, goods, or money laid up in store' (Dyche, 1740).

1. Food, victuals, provender; esp. *colloq.* provisions for a journey or excursion; *slang*, food generally, 'grub'.

1655 FULLER *Ch. Hist.* VI. ii. 290 The Abbot.. every Saturday was to visit their beds, to see if they had not shuffled in some softer matter, or purloyned some progge for them-selves. *a* **1704** T. BROWN *Sat. French King* Wks. 1730 I. 60 When first I came to town with household clog, Rings, watch, and so forth, fairly went for prog. *a* **1745** SWIFT *Direct. Servants, Cook*, You can junket together at night on your own progue, when the rest of the house are abed. **1772** MRS. DELANY in *Life & Corr.* Ser. II. (1862) I. 402, I had a letter last night from your father, who has sent me some good Xtmas prog according to custom. **1813** LADY BURGHERSH *Lett.* (1893) 13 We are obliged to carry with us all the 'prog' we want on the road. **1827** CARLYLE *Germ. Rom.* I. 80 Unless the Turk.. do freely give thee prog and lodging. **1870** SIMMONS *Oakdale Grange* 49 What a capital idea for prog (the refined expression by which scholars convey to each other the refined delicacies which tickle their palates).

b. *fig.* Food for the mind.

1783 MME. D'ARBLAY *Lett.* 12 Apr., If my letters will give you any amusement, I will write oftener.. and supply you with all the prog I get myself. **1815** IRELAND *Scribbleomania* 166 George Brewer our crew now with confidence hails, And for prog straight produces his *Siamese Tales.*

2. *dial.* A hoard (of money). Cf. PROG *v.*¹ 4.

1854 MISS BAKER *Northampt. Gloss.* s.v., He's got a fine prog of money somewhere.

3. = PROGGER¹.

1828–32 WEBSTER, *Prog*, one that seeks his victuals by wandering and begging.

4. *Comb.* **prog-basket**, a provision-basket, on a journey or 'outing'.

1855 HALIBURTON *Nat. & Hum. Nat.* I. 245 Taking out a pair of pistols and lots of ammunition from the bottom of his prog-basket. **1865** *N. Brit. Rev.* Sept. 229 During the repast a lean hungry tribe of dogs were working outside at his 'prog-basket'. They opened it; stole a goose.

prog, *sb.*³ *Undergraduates' slang.* Also proggins. [Perversion of PROCTOR, on the pattern of *Juggins* and the like.] A proctor at Oxford or Cambridge. Hence **prog** *v.*³ = PROCTORIZE *v.*

1890 BARRÈRE & LELAND *Dict. Slang* II. 152/2 *Proggins* (university), proctor. **1892** *Granta* 13 Feb. 196/1 [Proctor] What do you mean by this, Sir? You have been following me about for the last ten minutes... [Freshman] Oh—er—I only wanted to see you proggins some one! **1898** *Blackw. Mag.* Jan. 39 (Cambridge) His conversation is.. about.. the Dean or the 'Proggins'. **1900** G. SWIFT *Somerley* 137 When you lifted your arm to take your cap off to the proctor, you pulled the reins and lugged the horse's head round into the prog's mouth. **1901** *Daily Chron.* 24 Aug. 7/2 The chief offences for which the fines are imposed—or, to adopt 'Varsity parlance, for which undergraduates are 'progged' [at Cambridge]—seem to be those of smoking when wearing cap and gown, and appearing in public on Sunday evenings improperly dressed. **1935** D. SAYERS *Gaudy Night* xii. 255 The Proggins was just coming.. round the corner of Broad Street. **1935** N. MITCHISON *We have been Warned* IV. 428 'I warned him he might get progged.'.. 'We might make the progs feel a bit awkward!' **1945** G. B. GRUNDY *Fifty-Five Years at Oxford* iv. 55 He did not care a— for all the—proggins in the kingdom. **1965** *Guardian* 6 May 5/3 This evening may be the last.. on which undergraduates can be progged. *Ibid.* 5/5 The progs have chased and chased us Up and down the town.

prog (prɒg), *a.* and *sb.*⁴ *slang.* Also Prog. Abbrev. of PROGRESSIVE *a.* (*sb.*)

1958 'N. BLAKE' *Penknife in my Heart* vii. 91 The Lanes, his hosts, were a prog. couple. **1965** *N.Y. Times* 1 June 33 The 'progs' or progressives believe Tewkesbury lives too much in the past. **1968** *Listener* 29 Aug. 280/2 Chaps like us .. who don't believe in change, do far more for the Church than a thousand bloody progs like Pope John. **1971** *Progress* (Cape Town) May 1/1 (*heading*) Prog. expansion programme. *Ibid.* 1/2 (*heading*) Swing to Progs in North Rand. **1977** *Guardian Weekly* 11 Dec. 7/1 Liberal-minded South Africans cheered their favoured Progressive Federal Party... Much applause for the gains of the 'progs', as they are locally termed.

prog (prɒg), *sb.*[5] *slang.* Abbrev. of PROGRAMME *sb.* 2 e.

1975 *Listener* 11 Dec. 790/1 Nice to have you with us on the prog, we say, don't we, fans?

prog (prɒg), *v.*[1] *Obs.* exc. *dial.* Also 6 progg, 7 proague, progue. [Origin and sense-history obscure; it is not certain whether all the senses belong to one word.]

†**1.** *trans.* (?) *Obs. rare.*

1566 DRANT *Horace* I. i. Aj, Who gapes, who gawes, who pores, who pries, who proggs his mate but he?

2. *intr.* To poke about *for* anything that may be picked up or laid hold of; to search about or hunt about, *esp.* for food; to forage, (?) to purvey; also, to solicit, to beg, to go about begging.

[**1618**: cf. PROGMAN; **1622**: see PROGGING *ppl. a.*] **1624** QUARLES *Job* xiv. 60 Man digs,..He neuer rests,..He mines, and progs, though in the fangs of death. **1635** —— *Embl.* II. ii, We travel sea and soil, we pry, we prowl, We progress, and we prog from pole to pole. **1641** MILTON *Reform.* II. Wks. 1851 III. 64 Excommunication servs for nothing with them, but to prog, and pandar for fees. **1650** WELDON *Crt. Jas. I* 55 This Lake had linked himselfe in with the Scottish Nation, progging for Suits, and helping them to fill their Purses. *a* **1670** HACKET *Abp. Williams* I. (1692) 56, I never saw any of our Ministry more abstracted from their studies, continually progging at the Parliament door. **1692** R. L'ESTRANGE *Fables* 52 She went out progging for provisions again as before. **1703** A. B. *Law Succession to Benefices Just.* 37 With an impious Craft like his [Judas's] you may prog for your own Bag. *a* **1825** FORBY *Voc. E. Anglia*, *Prog*, to pry or poke into holes and corners... Those who go progging about..are likely enough to steal whatever they can lay their hands upon. **1838** MARY HOWITT *Birds & Fl.*, *House-sparrow* iii, Coarse is his nature, made to prog about. **1876** *Whitby Gloss.*, *Prooaging*,..foraging, as an animal searches for food. **1935** Z. N. HURSTON *Mules & Men* I. vi. 128 We proaged thru the woods that was full of magnolia, pine..and many kinds of trees whose name I do not know. **1949** 'J. NELSON' *Backwoods Teacher* vi. 63 He took a stick and progued around in the hole. **1949** *Sun* (Baltimore) 9 June 10/6 A progger..is a fellow that goes progging for frogs.

†**3.** *trans.* To search or hunt out; to poke out.

1654 H. L'ESTRANGE *Chas. I* (1655) 131 The subtile engineer..at length from old records progs and bolts out an ancient Precedent of raising a Tax upon the hole Kingdome, for setting forth a Navy in case of danger. **1656** HEYLIN *Extraneus Vapulans* 309 An old Skulking Statute, which..was printed and exposed to open view, and therefore needed no such progging and bolting out, as is elsewhere spoken of.

†**4.** (?) *trans.* See quot. (Cf. PROG *sb.*[2] 2.) *Obs.*

1719 SEWEL *Dutch Dict.*, *Potten, geld potten*, to Hord up money, to prog.

prog, *v.*[2] *dial.* Also 9 progue. [f. PROG *sb.*[1] Cf. PROD *v.*, and BROG *v.*, in similar sense.]

1. *trans.* To prick, stab, pierce; to prod.

1811 A. SCOTT *Poems* 114 (Jam.), I ga'e my Pegasus the spur..An' sair his flank I've proggit. **1821** CLARE *Vill. Minstr.* II. 82 While children..prog the hous'd bee from the cotter's wall. **1823** ELIZA LOGAN *St. Johnstoun* II. 168 (Jam.), I was progging up the old witch a little, to..make her confess. **1825** BROCKETT *N.C. Gloss.*, *Prog, Proggle*, to prick, to prickle. **1832-53** R. INGLIS in *Whistle-binkie* (Scotch Songs) Ser. III. 115 Again, at the battle o' red Waterloo, How they pricket and proget the French thro' and thro'. **1890** J. SERVICE *Thir Notandums* xv. 103 He progued them wi' his fork.

2. *intr.* To poke, to pierce; to prod.

1896 *Dial. Notes* (U.S.) I. 333 (E.D.D.) *Prog*, to search for anything imbedded in the mud, as clams, terrapins, or cedar logs, by means of a sounding rod. [But this may belong to PROG *v.*[1]]

prog, *v.*[3], to proctorize: see PROG *sb.*[3]

progametange to **proganosaur**: see PRO-[2] I.

progamic (prəʊ'gæmɪk), *a. Biol.* [f. Gr. πρό, PRO-[2] + γάμος marriage + -IC.] That precedes the specialization of the gametes (sexual or pairing cells). So **progamous** ('prɒgəməs) *a.*, applied to an ovum which has not been impregnated by a spermatozoon.

1891 HARTOG in *Nature* 17 Sept. 484/2 Progamic paragamy: the fusing nuclei are the normal gametonuclei of the progamous cell (ovum which has formed 1 polar body).

progenerate (prəʊ'dʒɛnərət), *ppl. a.* [In sense 1, ad. L. *prōgenerāt-us*, pa. pple. of *prōgenerāre* to beget, engender: see PRO-[1] and GENERATE *ppl. a.* In sense 2, nonce-formation after *degenerate*.]

†**1.** Propagated, begotten. (Const. as *pa. pple.* = PROGENERATED.) *Obs. rare*$^{-1}$.

1610 HEALEY *St. Aug. Citie of God* 300 Meanes for one thing to bee progenerate of another.

2. More advanced in development or type; opposed to *degenerate*.

1903 MYERS *Human Personality* I. 56 Our 'degenerates' may sometimes be in truth *progenerate*, and their perturbation may mark an evolution.

pro'generate, *v.* ? *Obs. rare.* [f. ppl. stem of L. *prōgenerāre*: see prec.] *trans.* To beget, propagate, procreate. Hence **pro'generated** *ppl. a.*

1611 COTGR., *Progenier*, to progenerate..young ones. **1770** in *Archæologia* (1773) II. 250 They were all progenerated colonies from a Scythian or Tartar race. **1824** LANDOR *Imag. Conv.*, *Pericles & Soph.* Wks. 1846 I. 145/2 He who is yet to progenerate a more numerous and far better race.

†**progene'ration.** *Obs. rare.* [ad. L. *prōgenerātiōn-em*, n. of action f. *prōgenerāre*: see above.] Procreation, propagation, begetting.

1548 UDALL *Erasm. Par. Luke* xx. 161 b, Mankynde cannot by any other possible meanes bee continued in progeneracion of issue. **1731** BAILEY vol. II, *Progeneration*, a breeding or bringing forth.

†**pro'generative,** *a. Obs. rare*$^{-1}$. [f. L. *prōgenerāt-* (see PROGENERATE) + -IVE.] Having the quality of progenerating; tending to produce.

1694 SALMON *Bate's Dispens.* (1713) 285/1 It carries off the progenerative Cause of the Scurvy, Dropsy, Stone and Gout.

†**pro'genial,** *a. Obs. rare*$^{-1}$. [f. L. *prōgeni-ēs* PROGENY + -AL[1].] Of or pertaining to progeny.

1657-83 EVELYN *Hist. Relig.* (1850) I. 159 Whether immediately produced, without any progenial traduction or radiation,..is..the dispute.

‖**progenies** (prəʊ'dʒɛniːz). *Obs. rare.* [L. *prōgeniēs* PROGENY.] = PROGENY; race, generation.

1672-3 GREW *Anat. Roots* I. i. §16 A new Progenies of Roots, from the old Head or Body, in the room of those that die yearly.

pro'genital, *a. rare.* [f. as next + -AL[1]. Cf. med.L. *prōgenitālis* (1493 in Du Cange).] = next.

1836 LYTTON *Athens* I. viii, Homer is cited in proof of the progenital humidity.

progenitive (prəʊ'dʒɛnɪtɪv), *a.* [f. L. *prōgenit-*, ppl. stem of *prōgignĕre*: see next and -IVE. So late L. *prōgenitīv-us* (Boeth.).] Having the quality of producing offspring or progeny; possessed of reproductive power or properties.

1838 *Fraser's Mag.* XVII. 679 I'm vastly popular with almost all the infant duplicates of my progenitive friends. **1845** DARWIN *Voy. Nat.* iv. (1852) 66 The Gauchos call the former [crystals of Gypsum] the 'Padre del sel', and the latter [crystals of sulphate of soda] the 'Madre'; they state that these progenitive salts always occur on the borders of the salinas when the water begins to evaporate. **1882** T. MOZLEY *Remin.* II. 433 The mighty, pregnant, progenitive atom. **1895** F. C. CONYBEARE in *Academy* 29 June 547/1 That a barren woman should bring forth a child was no ordinary progenitive act, but a result of the divine power.

Hence **pro'genitiveness,** reproductive quality.

1868 E. D. COPE *Orig. Fittest* (1887) 111 Metaphysical peculiarity or progenitiveness as isolating species.

progenitor (prəʊ'dʒɛnɪtə(r)). Also 4-6 -our. [ME. *progenitour*, a. obs. F. *progeniteur* (14th c. in Godef.), ad. L. *prōgenitōr-em* ancestor, agent-n. f. *prōgign-ĕre* to beget, f. *prō*, PRO-[1] 1 a + *gign-ĕre* to beget.]

1. A person from whom another person, a family, or a race, is descended; an ancestor, a forefather.

[**1347** *Rolls of Parlt.* II. 180/1 En salvation de lui & des almes de ses progenitours.] **1382** WYCLIF *2 Tim.* i. 3, I do thankyngis to my God, to whom I serue fro my progenitours. **1490** CAXTON *Eneydos* Prol. 4 The most renommed of alle his noble progenytours. **1542-5** BRINKLOW *Lament.* (1874) 107 Let them consider howe tyrannously the bisshoppes kyngedome hath vsed their progenitours, Kynges of Englonde. **1610** HOLLAND *Camden's Brit.* To Rdr., The English-Saxon tongue which our Progenitors the English spake. **1742-3** LD. LONSDALE in *Johnson's Debates* 23 Feb. (1787) II. 508 Another principle of government which the wisdom of our progenitors established, was to suppress vice with the utmost diligence. **1835** THIRLWALL *Greece* I. vii. 251 Their fabulous progenitor, Thessalus, was called by some a son of Hercules. **1875** JOWETT *Plato* (ed. 2) V. 70 He supposes that in the course of ages every man has had numberless progenitors.

b. *Biol.* An ancestor or ancestral species of animals or plants.

1859 DARWIN *Orig. Spec.* v. (1873) 108 We may believe that the progenitor of the ostrich genus had habits like those of the bustard. **1894** H. DRUMMOND *Ascent of Man* 240 The progenitors of Birds and the progenitors of Man at a very remote period were probably one.

2. *fig.* **a.** A spiritual, political, or intellectual 'ancestor' or predecessor.

1577 HANMER *Anc. Eccl. Hist.* (1663) 103 We take them for our progenitors, who going before, have taught us the way to follow after. **1678** R. L'ESTRANGE *Seneca's Mor.* (1776) 310 All these worthy men are our progenitors, if we will but..become their disciples.

b. The original of which anything is a copy.

1875 SCRIVENER *Lect. Text N. Test.* 5 Two several manuscripts which sprang from the same progenitor. **1883** *Glasgow Weekly Herald* 5 May 3/2 What are precedents, and how do they originate without progenitors?

progenitorial (prəʊdʒɛnɪ'tɔərɪəl), *a.* [f. L. type **prōgenitōri-us* (f. *prōgenitō r-em*: see prec.) + -AL[1].] Of or pertaining to progenitors; of the nature of a progenitor; ancestral.

1825 *Blackw. Mag.* XVIII. 289 It presents us neither with progenitorial guilt, to be visited upon the heroes, nor with predicted calamities to be inflicted. **1859** G. MEREDITH *R. Feverel* xviii, Families against whom neither..lawyer nor..physician could recollect a progenitorial blot, either on the male or female side, were not numerous. **1880** WARREN *Book-plates* xviii. 196 In the Werdenstein plate there are no less than sixteen of these 'progenitorial' shields.

pro'genitorship. [f. PROGENITOR + -SHIP.] The position or fact of being a progenitor.

1828 *Blackw. Mag.* XXIII. 171 Their dead would disown them as scornfully as Cicero would the intellectual progenitorship of a Cicerone. **1839** PYE SMITH *Script. & Geol.* 92 All land animals were created in pairs or other suitable modes of progenitorship, on one spot upon the earth's surface. **1870** TYNDALL in *Life & Lett. Huxley* (1900) I. xxiv. 330 Anything that touches progenitorship interests them.

progenitress (prəʊ'dʒɛnɪtrɪs). [f. PROGENITOR + -ESS[1].] A female progenitor, an ancestress. Also *fig.*

1611 SPEED *Hist. Gt. Brit.* IX. xvi. §34 Her selfe a Queene, and a Progenitresse of those glorious Kings and Queenes which followed. **1635** HEYWOOD *Hierarch.* VI. 343 Eue our first progenitresse. **1883** *Century Mag.* XXVI. 291 She was a worthy progenitress of a long line of most charming women novelists. **1888** *Sat. Rev.* 20 Oct. 463/1 These old cookery-books seem to bring us much nearer to our dead and gone progenitresses.

‖**progenitrix** (prəʊ'dʒɛnɪtrɪks). [a. late L. *prōgenitrix* an ancestress.] = prec. †Also with French ending, ‖**progeni'trice.** *Obs.*

1610 HEALEY *St. Aug. Citie of God* 111 [*His grandmother*] set for any progenitrix, as is often used. **1650** BP. HALL *Cases Consc.*, *Add.* i. (1654) 387 The gracious progenitrice of the Saviour of the world. **1798** *Hull Advertiser* 13 Oct. 4/4 There is now living at Allonby..a widow..who is the progenitrix of fifty eight persons. **1864** *Realm* 9 Mar. 5 In this young woman, lean, yellow, shrewd and hard, we have the type and progenitrix of the strong-minded Yankee female face, with its keen angularity.

progeniture (prəʊ'dʒɛnɪtjʊə(r)). [f. L. *prōgenit-*, ppl. stem of *prōgign-ĕre* to beget + -URE: cf. *geniture*. So F. *progéniture* (1835 in *Dict. Acad.*).]

1. Begetting of offspring; generation.

1801 HEL. M. WILLIAMS *Sk. Fr. Rep.* I. v. 38 His immense domain which descended in long succession of progeniture from his remote ancestry. **1831** T. HOPE *Ess. Origin Man* II. 21 All organic and living individuals after a time acquire the power of propagating their species by a new progeniture. **1855** W. H. MILL *Applic. Panth. Princ.* (1861) 217 All ancient testimonies respecting the Cerinthians ascribe to them also this notion of the purely celestial progeniture of the Christ.

2. Offspring, progeny.

1893 *Pall Mall Mag.* I. 38 A state of highly-strung nerves in our progeniture that may some day land them in continuous invalidism. **1894** MARQ. SALISBURY *Addr. Brit. Assoc. Oxford* 8 Aug., It is effected by their action in crossing, by their skill in bringing the right mates together to produce the progeniture they want.

pro'genity. *nonce-wd.*

†**1.** Humorous blunder for PROGENY (sense 4).

1600 HEYWOOD *1st Pt. Edw. IV*, III. Wks. I. 45 Harrys of the old house of Lancaster; and that progenity do I loue.

2. [after *humanity*: cf. CANINITY 2]. Consideration for offspring or descendants.

1902 L. STEPHEN in *19th Cent.* May 797 Progenity, or as Mr. Kidd calls it, 'projected efficiency', makes us suffer for the good of our descendants.

progeny ('prɒdʒɪnɪ). Also 4 -i, 4-5 -ye, 4-7 -ie, 6 proginie. [ME. a. obs. F. *progenie* (13th c. in Godef.), ad. L. *prōgeniē-s* descent, family, offspring, f. *prōgign-ĕre* to beget.]

1. a. The offspring (of a father or mother, or of both); issue, children collectively; more widely, descendants. (Rarely with indef. art.)

a **1300** *Cursor M.* 1361 Til him and til his progeni Wit pite sal he sceu his merci. *a* **1325** in Horstm. *Altengl. Leg.* (1878) 145 Þo Eue wist sche schuld dye, Sche cleped forþ hir progenie. *c* **1386** CHAUCER *Pars. T.* ¶250 He moste nedes dye..and al his progenye in this world. **1515** BARCLAY *Egloges* (1570) C vj b/1 In it remayneth the worthy gouernour, A stocke and fountayne of noble progeny. *c* **1586** C'TESS PEMBROKE *Ps.* CV. ii, His servantes you, O Abrahams progeny. **1604** *Bk. Com. Prayer*, *Pr. for R. Family*, All the King and Queenes Royall progenie. *a* **1618** RALEIGH *Mahomet* (1637) 26 The Mores are the progeny of such Arabians as after their Conquests seated themself in that part of Affrica. **1727** DE FOE *Syst. Magic* I. i. (1840) 13 Some think..that Noah's sons..were saved in the ark..merely for being the posterity or progeny of a righteous father. **1860** HAWTHORNE *Marb. Faun* xxvi, From this union sprang a vigorous progeny.

b. Of lower animals, and plants.

1697 DRYDEN *Virg. Georg.* III. 250 When she has calv'd, then set the Dam aside; And for the tender Progeny provide. **1843** J. A. SMITH *Product. Farming* (ed. 2) 33 A tree puts forth annually a new progeny of buds, and becomes clothed with a beautiful foliage of lungs..for the respiration of the rising brood. **1846** J. BAXTER *Libr. Pract. Agric.* (ed. 4) II. 169 In gathering seeds, choice should be made from the finest trees, as they are more likely to produce a healthy and vigorous progeny than those which are stinted in their growth.

c. *fig.* Spiritual or intellectual descendants, successors, followers, disciples.

1451 CAPGRAVE *Life St. Gilbert* (E.E.T.S.) 78 All þe priouris and souereynes of þe ordre wer sent aftir to be at þe byryng of her maystir. Whan þei wer gadered to-gidir and anoumbered þe summe of his progenie cam on-to too þousand and too hundred. *Ibid.* 88 His desire was þat his progenie schuld lyue in honest pouerte. **1616** CHAMPNEY *Voc. Bps.* 221 So are likewise the Lutherans, and all their progeny. **1768** JOHNSON *Shaks.* Pref., Wks. IX. 242 His characters..are the genuine progeny of common humanity. **1855** BREWSTER *Newton* I. xiii. 347 The intellectual progeny whom he [Newton] educated and reared.

d. More vaguely, expressing relation or character: cf. CHILD *sb.* 13.

1526 *Pilgr. Perf.* (W. de W. 1531) 90 b, Certaynly they be yᵉ housholde of Sathan & progeny of pryde. **1667** MILTON *P.L.* v. 600 Hear all ye Angels, Progenie of Light, Thrones, Dominations, Princedoms, Vertues, Powers.

2. *fig.* That which originates from or is produced by something (material or immaterial); issue, product, outcome, result.

1390 GOWER *Conf.* II. 290 Of Avarices progenie What vice suieth after this. **1751** JOHNSON *Rambler* No. 96 ¶8 False-hood was the progeny of Folly. **1837** WHEWELL *Hist. Induct. Sc.* (1857) I. 253 Art is the parent, not the progeny of Science. **1853** KANE *Grinnell Exp.* xlviii. (1856) 446 In front of it we found a progeny of bergs, crowded together so close that we could not count them. **1871** R. ELLIS *Catullus* lxiv. 90 Like earth's myriad hues, spring's progeny, rais'd to the breezes. **1871** TYNDALL *Fragm. Sc.* (1879) I. ii. 55 Are not these more rapid vibrations the progeny of the slower?

†**3.** = GENERATION 5. *Obs. rare.* (Chiefly a literalism of translation, repr. L. *prōgeniēs*.)

a **1325** *Prose Psalter* xlviii[i]. 20 Þe wicked shal entren unto þe progenie [*uel*, oþer, kynde; Vulg. *in progenies*], of his faders, and he shal se no liȝt wyþ-outen ende. **1382** WYCLIF *Exod.* xxxiv. 7 Into the thridde and the ferthe progenye. ?*a* **1500** *Chester Pl.* vi. 90 His name alwaie halowed be.. from progeny to progenye.

†**4.** A race, stock, or line descended from a common ancestor; a family, clan, tribe, or kindred.

1382 WYCLIF *Ecclus.* viii. 5 Lest he speke euele of thi progenye [Vulg. *de progenie tua*, 1388 of thi kynrede]. **1390** GOWER *Conf.* III. 22 Which al the hole progenie Of lusti folk hath undertake To feede. **1432-50** tr. *Higden* (Rolls) I. 127 The progenye of theyme descendede from Agar, seruaunte and moder of Ismael. **1565** STAPLETON tr. *Bede's Hist. Ch. Eng.* 23 The Marshes and all the progeny of the Northumbers, that is, of that people which inhabiteth the north side of the flud Humber. **1609** SKENE *Reg. Maj.* I. 70 Except remission be given with consent of the progenie and friends of him quha is vnjustlie slane. **1641** EARL MONM. tr. *Biondi's Civil Warres* II. 58 Lluelline, the last Prince of the British Progeny, being slaine. **1697** DRYDEN *Æneid* VI. 1074 Now fix your sight, and stand intent, to see Your Roman race, and Julian progeny.

†**5.** Lineage, parentage; descent, genealogy. *Obs.*

1382 WYCLIF *Gen.* xliii. 7 The man askide vs bi ordre oure progenye, if the fader lyued, if we hadden a brother. **1494** FABYAN *Chron.* v. cxii. 85 Andouera, a woman of great birth, how be it myn auctor..declarith not hir progeny. **1548** CRANMER *Catech.* 97 Let euery man be content with his proginie, office, callyng, state and degree. **1591** SHAKS. *1 Hen. VI*, III. iii. 61 All French and France exclaimes on thee, Doubting thy Birth and lawfull Progenie. **1649** ROBERTS *Clavis Bibl.* 595 This Tzephaniah, For his Progeny, is described to be the son of Chushi, the son of Gedaliah. **1775** R. CHANDLER *Trav. Asia M.* (1825) I. 299 The care of about forty families, of the same progeny as the Turks.

6. *attrib.* and *Comb.*, as **progeny test**, an assessment of the genetic value of an individual made by examining its progeny; so **progeny-test** *v. trans.*, to assess in this way; **progeny-tested** *ppl. a.*, **progeny-testing** *vbl. sb.*

1918 BABCOCK & CLAUSEN *Genetics in Relation to Agric.* xv. 293 We find that the progeny test of individual plants was first used by Le Couteur and Shirreff. But it was Louis de Vilmorin who first gave special attention to the value of the progeny test (1856). **1932** [see *performance test*]. **1953** SRB & OWEN *Gen. Genetics* xxiii. 501 The wisdom of using sires proved good by progeny tests and by careful observations on relatives has become evident to almost all breeders. **1960** *Farmer & Stockbreeder* 8 Mar. 101/2 A.I. organizations are in a favoured position, because they deal with large numbers, and can progeny-test many bulls. **1971** *Ibid.* 23 Feb. 13/3 The Milk Marketing Board's Warren Farm progeny tests.. could hardly be called a tremendous success. **1972** *Country Life* 6 Jan. 53/1 Extensive progeny testing of A1 bulls is carried out... By the use of egg transfer it should be possible to produce large numbers of calves from potential bull-breeding females and to progeny test them. **1944** *Jrnl. Agric. Res.* LXIX. 471 Use of progeny-tested dairy sires would be a little more likely to increase the rate of improvement. **1974** *Country Life* 12 Dec. 1853/1 This not only offers the advantage of the progeny-tested sire as compared with the crossing bull, which is what the farmer has to use at present, but a shorter and more concentrated calving season for the stockman. **1933** *Amer. Naturalist* LXVII. 502 Progeny testing in poultry breeding can be used in evaluating the breeding potentiality of either sire or dam. **1970** Progeny testing [see *performance testing*]. **1977** *Jrnl. Agric. Sci.* LXXXVIII. 129/1 We can calculate the expected response to selection for various types of progeny. .. We may also be able to choose between the use of different types of family or between, say, family selection and a progeny-testing programme.

progeria (prəʊˈdʒɪərɪə). *Path.* [mod.L., f. Gr. προγήρ-ως prematurely old + -IA¹.] A fatal disease of children characterized by symptoms usually associated with senility.

1904 H. GILFORD in *Practitioner* Aug. 210 The name progeria, for which I am indebted to Mr. James Rhoades and Professor Arthur Sidgwick, is not only a far better word [than micromegaly], but is a true description of the distinguishing features of the two cases. *Ibid.* 217 The name progeria..has been given in recognition of the senile characters which form such a conspicuous feature of the disease from the beginning. **1927** *Times* (Weekly ed.) 28 Apr. 475/2 Cases of premature senility in children (goblins) described as progeria, the persistence in an adult (ateleioses) of child characters (elves). **1957** L. EISELEY *Immense Journey* 108 The cause of this curious disease, known as progeria, or premature aging, is totally unknown. **1969** *Guardian* 13 Jan. 2/3 A post-mortem examination will be carried out on..a 9-year-old girl who died of a disease that gave her the physical characteristics of a 90-year-old woman. Norma.. was the second member of her family to be suffering from progeria.

Hence †**proˈgerian** *sb.*, a person with progeria; also *attrib.*; **proˈgeric** *a.*, of or being a person with progeria.

1913 *Lancet* 1 Feb. 305/1 Progerians pass from a delayed childhood into a premature old age. *Ibid.* 306/1 The total length of the progerian face from nasion to chin is only 84 mm. **1914** *Boston Med. & Surg. Jrnl.* 16 July 110/2 Progerians are usually dwarfs. **1933** R. W. B. ELLIS tr. *Apert's Infantilism* vii. 73 (*caption*) Mould of the upper and lower jaws in the same progeric patient as in figs. 11 and 12. **1945** *Amer. Jrnl. Dis. Children* LXIX. 276/2 The conditions .. are postulated for the progeric patient.. during the period from 2 to 6 years of age, when most of his subcutaneous fat vanished. **1976** *Nature* 22 Apr. 713/1 With factor VII-deficient plasma, both normal and progeric cells showed a markedly prolonged clotting time.

pro-German, -ism: see PRO-¹ 5 a, c.

progermiˈnation. *rare*⁻¹. [Noun of action f. L. *prōgermin-āre* to shoot forth + -ATION: see PRO-¹ 1 a and GERMINATION.] Springing forth; birth, propagation.

1648 HERRICK *Hesper., to Sir J. Berkley*, Sold (As other townes and cities were) for gold, By those ignoble births, which shame the stem That gave progermination unto them.

progestational (prəʊdʒɛˈsteɪʃənəl), *a.* [f. PRO-² 1 + GESTATION + -AL.] Relating to, promoting, or being part of the physiological preparations for pregnancy; applied *esp.* to substances whose physiological effects resemble those of progesterone; ***progestational proliferation***, proliferation of the endometrium in preparation for pregnancy.

1923 G. W. CORNER in *Physiol. Rev.* III. 467 It seems preferable to avoid the suggestion of falsity or imitation inherent in the prefix *pseudo* [in *pseudopregnancy*], by using the terms progravid, progestational. **1928** *Amer. Jrnl. Physiol.* LXXXVI. 78 Sections taken through the middle of the uterine horn showed that no progestational proliferation had taken place in these animals. **1929** *Ibid.* LXXXVIII. 326 It is possible that there is an antagonistic relation between oestrin and the progestational substance. **1932** *Ibid.* C. 111 The production of a progestational endometrium in the uterus of a castrate rabbit. **1944** [see PROGESTIN]. **1948**, **1949** [see GESTAGEN]. **1954** [see HYDROXYPROGESTERONE]. **1960** *Times* 19 Jan. 3/5 (Advt.), Applicants should have had considerable experience in steroid chemistry, and be well acquainted with recent work on gonadotropic, oestrogenic and progestational hormones. **1970** *Sci. Jrnl.* June 26/2 The ovaries produce ova and the oestrogenic and progestational hormones, mainly oestradiol and progesterone, which are concerned with the development and maintenance of the attributes of femaleness, including sexual receptivity and the inception of pregnancy. **1974** *Fertility & Sterility* XXV. 575/1 A special uterine reaction to the luteal hormone (progestational proliferation) was identified in the adult rabbit.

Hence **progeˈstationally** *adv.*, as regards progestational activity or state.

1948 W. H. PEARLMAN in Pincus & Thimann *Hormones* I. 441 Corticosterone..(progestationally inactive in the Clauberg test). **1958** *Jrnl. Clin. Endocrinol. & Metabolism* XVIII. 350 The highest point of formation of progestationally effective substances in the corpus luteum appears to be between the seventh and eighth day following ovulation. **1968** R. W. KISTNER in Astwood & Cassidy *Clin. Endocrinol.* II. vi. ix. 680 If an endometrial biopsy..reveals 'progestationally immature endometrium',..one tablet daily..can be prescribed.

progesterone (prəʊˈdʒɛstərəʊn). *Physiol.* [ad. G. *progesteron* (W. M. Allen et al. 1935, in *Klin. Wochenschr.* 17 Aug. 1182/1), blend of PROGESTIN and its G. synonym *luteosteron* (K. H. Slotta et al. 1934, in *Ber. d. Deut. Chem. Ges.* LXVII. 1271), f. LUTEO-, repr. *corpus luteum*: see -STERONE.] A female steroid sex hormone, $C_{21}H_{30}O_2$, which is secreted by the *corpus luteum* and also made synthetically, and is responsible for the cyclical changes in the uterus in the latter part of the menstrual cycle and also necessary for the maintenance of pregnancy. Also *attrib.* and *Comb.*

1935, etc. [see PROGESTIN]. **1949** [see GESTAGEN]. **1957** *Times* 2 Dec. p. vi/2 When P.M.S. is used in conjunction with a steroid hormone progesterone it will bring maiden sheep into season to produce an extra crop of lambs in their second summer (six months earlier than normal). **1958** [see GESTAGEN]. **1961** L. MARTIN *Clin. Endocrinol.* (ed. 3) ix. 229 Owing to its feeble progesterone-like action,..large doses must be given. **1965** LEE & KNOWLES *Animal Hormones* ii. 20 As the corpus luteum matures, increasing amounts of progesterone are produced which depress the output of LH and LTH. **1966** [see DIOSGENIN]. **1968** *Times* 11 Nov. 10/8 Udry and Morris suggest that of the two ovarian hormones, oestrogen tends to increase the likelihood of human sexual activity, and progesterone to decrease it. **1974** *Daily Colonist* (Victoria, B.C.) 25 Aug. 26/2 By 1954, Chang and Pincus had found two progesterone hormones that worked. The birth-control pill was born. **1974** *Fertility & Sterility* XXV. 575/2 The following trivial names are used in this paper:.. progesterone (pregn-4-ene-3,20-dione). **1979** *Jrnl. R. Soc. Arts* CXXVII. 417/2 It was possible to inhibit ovulation in experimental animals with progesterone.

progestin (prəʊˈdʒɛstɪn). *Physiol.* [f. PRO-¹ 5 + GEST(ATION + -IN¹.] **a.** Progesterone, esp. an unpurified preparation of it. **b.** = PROGESTOGEN, GESTAGEN.

1930 W. M. ALLEN in *Amer. Jrnl. Physiol.* XCII. 174 We have as yet proposed no name for this hormone of the corpus luteum... In so far as we are acquainted with its physiological behavior, its chief action lies in its ability, by alteration of the endometrium, to aid gestation in the castrated rabbit; and for this reason we wish to propose for it the name *progestin*, i.e., a substance which favors gestation. **1935** [see ANDROSTERONE]. **1935** W. M. ALLEN et al. in *Nature* 24 Aug. 303/2 Heretofore, two different names have been used in the literature for this hormone (progestin, luteosterone). For the sake of international uniformity, we agree to use..the name *progesterone* for the pure hormone. **1936** *Jrnl. Amer. Med. Assoc.* 23 May 1809/1 The Council adopted the following terms: (1) *progesterone* to indicate the chemically pure substance..(2) *progestin* as a general term to indicate the substance (and other chemically allied substances..in case any such compounds are subsequently discovered) without reference to the state of chemical purity. **1944** J. HOFFMAN *Female Endocrinol.* xli. 711 The term *progestin* is applied to crude extracts of corpus luteum tissue which possess progestational activity. The name progesterone describes the crystalline form of the luteal hormone. **1945** H. BURROWS *Biol. Actions of Sex Hormones* xxi. 389 More than one substance having the same kind of action as progesterone is known, and a generic name is therefore convenient. The author has used the term 'progestin' to denote chemical compounds having a biological action comparable with that of progesterone. [*Note*] 'Progestogen' has been suggested as an alternative generic name. *Ibid.* 390 The corpora lutea of the ovary are the chief natural source of progestin... The placenta is another source. **1961** J. ROCK in C. A. Villee *Control of Ovulation* xii. 228 The two artificial steroids are called 'progestins' because of the fact that their action resembles that of progesterone. **1966** *New Scientist* 15 Dec. 620/1 The synthetic progestins which are contained in all oral contraceptive tablets were in fact introduced for the wrong reason. **1976** *Sci. Amer.* Feb. 32/2 The steroid hormones.. include the male sex hormones (collectively called the androgens), the female sex hormones (the estrogens and the progestins) and the hormones secreted by the cortex.

progestogen (prəʊˈdʒɛstədʒɛn). *Physiol.* Also **progestagen.** [f. as prec. + -O + -GEN; the variant spelling may reflect the influence of GESTAGEN.] = GESTAGEN.

1941 DORLAND & MILLER *Med. Dict.* (ed. 19) 1171/2 *Progestogen*, a general term for any substance possessing progestational activity. **1945** [see PROGESTIN]. **1962** *Lancet* 12 May 1012/1 In those premature labours where relaxation of the cervix precludes uterine contractions, such measures as cervical suture and the administration of progestogens can prevent disaster. **1968** PASSMORE & ROBSON *Compan. Med. Stud.* I. xxxvii. 11/1 The principal ovarian hormones ..fall into three broad functional categories, oestrogens, progestagens and androgens. *Ibid.* 14/2 A more useful pharmacological definition of a progestagen is a substance which induces secretory changes in an oestrogen-primed endometrium. **1968** *Times* 28 Nov. 14/4 Most oral contraceptive pills contain both a progestogen and an oestrogen. **1977** *Lancet* 21 May 1101/2, 7 women..used low-dose progestagen pills.

Hence **progestoˈgenic** *a.* = PROGESTATIONAL *a.*

1949 H. E. NIEBURGS *Hormones in Clin. Pract.* viii. 176 The progestogenic preparations are mainly employed for the prevention and treatment of habitual and threatened abortion. **1969** *Sunday Times* 14 Sept. 54/3 The remedy may be a change to a more 'progestogenic brand' [of oral contraceptive]. **1973** *Nature* 9 Mar. 88/1 Administration of sex hormones or their analogues, whether androgenic, oestrogenic or progestogenic, can produce temporary remission in about one-quarter to one-third of patients with advanced breast cancer. **1977** *Lancet* 19 Nov. 1085/1 Evidence is accumulating to indicate that it is principally the œstrogenic and not the progestagenic component of combined oral-contraceptive preparations which causes the acceleration of blood-clotting.

ˈ**progger**¹. Now *dial.* [f. PROG *v.*¹ + -ER¹.] One who progs, begs, or solicits; a beggar.

1685 R. LUCAS *Happiness* (1692) I. 280 How far shou'd I prefer the..unconcernment of a poet..before the former sort of servile philosophick proggers! **1876** *Whitby Gloss.*, *Prooagers*, beggars.

ˈ**progger**². *dial.* [f. PROG *v.*² + -ER¹.] One who or that which progs or prods: **a.** One who prods for clams, etc. (*U.S.*); **b.** A butcher's stabbing instrument.

1818 MIDFORD *Coll. Songs* 46 (E.D.D.) The progger an' steel. **1887** *Fisheries of U.S.* Sect. v. II. 604 A miserable set who help the oystermen in winter and 'go clamming' in summer. They are locally known as 'proggers'.

progging (ˈprɒgɪŋ), *vbl. sb.* [f. PROG *v.*¹ + -ING¹.] Soliciting, begging; foraging.

1648 MILTON *Tenure Kings* 242 Being called to assemble about reforming the Church, they fell to progging and soliciting the parliament..for a new settling of their tithes and oblations. **1650** NEEDHAM *Case Commw.* 54 A People.. poor in Body, Pay, and other Accommodations, save what they have purchased by proguing here in England. **1715** J. CHAPPELOW *Rt. Way Rich* (1717) 87 All their plodding and

progging is for themselves. **1785** HUTTON *Bran New Wark* 412 Careful for nought but progging for belly-timber.
attrib. **1663** J. STILLINGFL. *Shecinah* Ded., The progging attempts of an ambitious phylargyrist. **1691** WOOD *Ath. Oxon.* I. 389 [He] practiced for divers years progging tricks in employing necessitous persons..to get contributions.

progging ('prɒgɪŋ), *ppl. a.* [f. as prec. + -ING².] That progs, solicits, begs, or forages.
(The sense of quot. 1642 is not clear.)
1622 FLETCHER & MASS. *Span. Curate* III. iii, That man in the Gowne in my opinion Looks like a proaguing knave. **1642** H. MORE *Song of Soul* II. i. II. xvi, But when to plantall life quick sense is ti'd, And progging phansie, then upon her guard She gins to stand. **1650** WELDON *Crt. Jas. I*, II. 185 Suppressing Promoters, and progging fellows.

proggins: see PROG *sb.*³

proglacial (prəʊ'gleɪsɪəl, -ʃəl), *a. Geomorphol.* [f. PRO-² 2 + GLACIAL *a.*] Situated or occurring just beyond the edge of an ice-sheet or glacier.
1937 WOOLDRIDGE & MORGAN *Physical Basis Geogr.* xxii. 393 The term 'extra-morainic' has been proposed to cover all such lakes, but they are evidently not literally extra-morainic in every case, and the term 'pro-glacial' is preferable. **1957** G. E. HUTCHINSON *Treat. Limnol.* I. i. 89 During the early stages of deglaciation, proglacial lakes collected between the Cary Moraine and the receding ice. **1970** R. J. SMALL *Study of Landforms* xi. 395 His reconstruction of pro-glacial drainage conditions. *Ibid.*, The waters of the lakes escaped, either into adjacent lakes or away from the pro-glacial zone altogether. **1972** R. J. PRICE *Glacial & Fluvioglacial Landforms* (1973) vii. 185 As the glacier front moves down-valley the former pro-glacial fluvioglacial deposits are overridden by the ice.

proglottic (prəʊ'glɒtɪk), *a.* [irreg. f. PROGLOTTIS + -IC.] Of or pertaining to a proglottis.
1890 in *Cent. Dict.*

proglottid (prəʊ'glɒtɪd), *Zool.* [f. Gr. *προγλωττιδ-, stem of *προγλωττίς: see next.] = PROGLOTTIS. So **proglo'ttidean** *a.* = PROGLOTTIC (*Cent. Dict.* 1890).
1878 BELL *Gegenbaur's Comp. Anat.* 129 In this way the Tænia-chain is formed, the last metameres of which (the so-called proglottids) break off at a certain stage of development, and form more or less independent individuals. **1895** *Syd. Soc. Lex.*, *Proglottid*, the same as *Proglottis*.

‖**proglottis** (prəʊ'glɒtɪs). Pl. **-ides** (-ɪdi:z). [mod.L. (Felix Dujardin, 1843 *Ann. Sci. Nat.*, ser. 2. XX. *Zoologie* 342), a. Gr. προγλωσσίς, *προγλωττίς, -ιδ- point of the tongue, f. πρό, PRO-² + γλῶσσα, γλῶττα tongue, γλωττίς glottis, mouthpiece of a pipe. So named from its shape.] A sexually mature segment or joint of a tapeworm.
Applied by Dujardin to a detached living joint; by P. J. Van Beneden, 1850, and by subsequent writers, to the joint whether attached or detached.
1855 T. R. JONES *Anim. Kingd.* (ed. 2) 136 When the gemma has grown into an adult worm (*Proglottis* of Van Beneden), the indentation, separating each from the one preceding it, increases in depth until..the segments are successively thrown off as so many distinct animals. **1870** NICHOLSON *Man. Zool.* 143 After their discharge from the body, the proglottides decompose, and the ova are liberated. **1897** *Allbutt's Syst. Med.* II. 1007 A tapeworm may therefore be regarded as a colony, and each individual proglottis as an animal complete in itself.

†'**progman.** *Obs.* [f. PROG *v.*¹ (or ? PROG *sb.*²) + MAN *sb.*¹] A man appointed to forage for victuals, etc.; a forager, purveyor.
1618 in *Wotton's Lett.* (Roxb.) 79 The same daye five prog men, common soldiers who were sent wᵗʰ money in their purses to buye victualls, were cruelly murdered.

†'**prognate,** *a.* and *sb. Obs. rare.* [ad. L. *prōgnāt-us* born or sprung from, as sb. a child, descendant, f. *prō*, PRO-¹, forth + (*g*)*nātus*, pa. pple. of (*g*)*nascī* to be born: cf. *cognate*.]
A. *adj.* Innate, congenital. (*pedantic*.)
c **1600** J. LEACH in *Lett. Lit. Men* (Camden) 75 Not myne owne nature.., but your nature, generositie prognate, and come from your atavite progenitours.
B. *sb.* Child, offspring; in quot. *fig.*
1667 WATERHOUSE *Fire Lond.* 62 If he speaks no *fiat*, folly is the best prognate of our contrivances.

prognathic (prɒg'næθɪk), *a.* [f. as PROGNATHOUS + -IC.] = PROGNATHOUS *a.*
1850 R. G. LATHAM *Var. Man* Introd. 6 When the insertion of the teeth is perpendicular, or nearly perpendicular to the base of the nose, the skull is orthognathic; when projecting forwards, prognathic. **1861** BUSK in *Trans. Ethnol. Soc.* I. 343 It is to him [Professor Retzius] that we owe the terms brachycephalic and dolichocephalic, with their respective modifications of orthognathic and prognathic. **1905** *Brit. Med. Jrnl.* 26 Aug. 455 The head small and distinctly dolichocephalic, the jaws prognathic.

prognathism ('prɒgnəθɪz(ə)m). [f. as next + -ISM (cf. *synchronous, -chronism*). So F. *prognathisme*.] The condition of being prognathous; prognathic state or condition.
1864 in WEBSTER. **1866** LAING *Preh. Rem. Caithn.* 63 The degree of prognathism, as shown by the projection of the upper jaw and teeth..is equal to that of the lowest specimens of the Negro and Australian races. **1880** MISS BIRD *Japan* II. 75 [In the Ainos] there is no tendency towards prognathism. **1896** [see ORTHOGNATHISM].

prognathous ('prɒgnəθəs), *a.* [f. PRO-² + Gr. γνάθ-ος jaw + -OUS. In mod.F. *prognathe*.] Having projecting jaws; having a low facial angle: said of a skull or person; also of the jaws: prominent, protruding. Opposed to *opisthognathous* and *orthognathous*.
1836 PRICHARD *Phys. Hist. Man.* (ed. 3) I. II. v. § 1. 282, I shall give the following terms to these two varieties in the figure of the cranium, viz. to the narrow elongated form, that of Prognathous from the prominence of the jaw. **1851** D. WILSON *Preh. Ann.* (1863) I. ix. 232 Pyramidal and prognathous skulls. **1863** [see ORTHOGNATHOUS]. **1867** BAKER *Nile Tribut.* iv. (1872) 56 They are exceedingly black, resembling..the negro, but without the flat nose or prognathous jaw.

prognathously (prɒg'næθəslɪ), *adv.* [f. PROGNATHOUS *a.* + -LY².] In a prognathous manner; with the jaw prominent or protruding.
1974 N. GORDIMER *Conservationist* 226 A jaw of fine teeth. .. Set rather prognathously, in the forward-jutting rounded arc that, in life, would make a wide white-toothed smile. **1976** T. SHARPE *Wilt* xiv. 146 He smiled prognathously.

prognathy ('prɒgnəθɪ). [f. as PROGNATH-OUS + -Y: cf. *anomal-ous, anomal-y, infam-ous, infam-y*.] = PROGNATHISM.
1890 H. M. STANLEY *Darkest Africa* I. xiv. 352 With slight prognathy of jaws. **1894** *Cosmopolitan* XVII. 43 Their features are mostly regular without that..marked prognathy of the true negro.

‖**Progne** ('prɒgni:). Also 5 **proigne**; and in Gr. form **Procne**. [L. *Prognē*, variant of *Procnē*, Gr. Πρόκνη, name of the sister of Philomela, according to Greek mythology transformed into a swallow. So F. *progné*.]
1. A poetic name for the swallow. (Cf. note on PHILOMEL.)
But the poets appear to have thought it some song-bird.
c **1374** CHAUCER *Troylus* II. 15 (64) The swalwe proigne with a sorwful lay, Whan morwe com gan make here weymentynge. [**1390** GOWER *Conf.* II. 328 And of hir Soster Progne I finde, Hou sche was torned..Into a Swalwe swift of winge.] **1577** B. GOOGE *Heresbach's Husb.* IV. (1586) 178 And Progne, on whose brest as yet is seene The blooddy marke of hands that Itys slewe. *a* **1584** MONTGOMERIE *Cherrie & Slae* 5 About ane bank..The merle and maueis micht be sene, The Progne and the Phelomene. *a* **1784** JOHNSON *Ode to Autumn* v, Soft pleasing woes my heart invade, As Progne pours the melting lay. **1803** H. K. WHITE *Clifton Grove* 230 Lorn Progne's note from distant copse behind. **1956** E. POUND tr. *Sophocles' Women of Trachis* 41 As Progne shrill upon the weeping air, 'Tis no great sound. **1980** 'A. T. ELLIS' *Birds of Air* 125 'You seem very cheerful,' she snapped... 'Oh, I am,' said Mary..Procne to mute Philomela grieving for her Itys, she thought.
2. *Ornith.* An American genus of *Hirundinidæ* or Swallows, including the common Purple Martin of the United States (*P. purpurea* or *subis*).

prognose (prɒg'nəʊz), *v.* [f. next, or its F. form *prognose*: cf. DIAGNOSE.] *trans.* To make a prognosis of.
1900 *Lancet* 27 Jan. 225/2, I venture to think that appendicitis cannot be correctly prognosed until it is possible to infer from the clinical symptoms the pathological changes proceeding within the appendix.

‖**prognosis** (prɒg'nəʊsɪs). Pl. **-oses** (-'əʊsi:z). [L. *prognōsis*, a. Gr. πρόγνωσις a recognizing beforehand, foreknowledge, in medicine a prognosis, f. προγιγνώσκειν to know beforehand: see PRO-² and GNOSIS. In F. *prognose*.]
1. *Med.* A forecast of the probable course and termination of a case of disease; also, the action or art of making such a forecast.
1655 CULPEPPER *Riverius* I. i. 3 As to the Prognosis, or Prognostical part concerning this Distemper: It is hard to cure. **1741** MONRO *Anat.* (ed. 3) 174 There will be little Difficulty in forming a just Prognosis of our Patient's Disease. **1805** *Med. Jrnl.* XIV. 397, I had arrived to that certainty of prognosis, that I could have insured the life of an individual by the treatment I recommended, and his death by any other. **1881** HUXLEY in *Nature* 11 Aug. 343/1 Pathology..was merely natural history; it registered the phenomena of disease, classified them, and ventured upon a prognosis, wherever the observation of constant co-existences and sequences, suggested a rational expectation of the like recurrence under similar circumstances.
¶**b.** A symptom: = PROGNOSTIC *sb.*¹ 3. *Obs.*
1706 PHILLIPS (Kersey), *Prognosis*..in the Art of Physick, it is the same as Prognostick Sign.
2. *gen.* Prognostication, anticipation.
1706 PHILLIPS (Kersey), *Prognosis*, a knowing before, Fore-boding, Fore-knowledge. **1872** B. HARTE *Heiress of Red Dog* (1879) 54 It is one of the evidences of original characters that it is apt to baffle all prognosis from a mere observer's standpoint. **1894** *Edin. Rev.* July 33 It is..too soon to attempt a prognosis of English culture.

†**progno'static,** *a. Obs. rare*⁻¹. In 5 **pronostatike**. Extended form of PROGNOSTIC *a.*
c **1430** LYDG. *Min. Poems* (Percy Soc.) 118 As pronostatike clerks beren witnesse.

‖**prog'nostes.** *Obs. rare*⁻¹. [a. Gr. προγνώστης one who knows beforehand.] A prognosticator; a foreteller.
1654 GATAKER *Disc. Apol.* 1, I soon perceived, that I had proved a true Prognostes, and much truer than Lilie.

prognostic (prɒg'nɒstɪk), *sb.*¹ Also 5–6 **pron-**. [ME. *pronostike, -ique*, a. OF. *pronostique* (13th c. in Hatz.-Darm.), mod.F. *pronostic*, ad. L. *prognōsticon* (*-cum*), a. Gr. προγνωστικόν a prognostic, sb. use of neut. sing. of προγνωστικός: see next.]
1. That which foreshows or gives warning of something to come, or from which the future may be foreknown; a pre-indication, token, omen.
Originally applied to things supposed to be occult or supernatural, including many now known to be natural antecedents, as the meteorological signs of the weather.
1412–20 LYDG. *Chron. Troy* IV. xxxv. (MS. Digby 232) lf. 144/2 þe Egle..þat no thyng was but tokne of Tresoun, Pronostyke and declaracioun. **1471** *Arriv. Edw. IV* (Camden) 13 A goode pronostique of good aventure. **1494** FABYAN *Chron.* VII. ccxlvi, A great comete or blasyng starre, the which..with also the foresayde eclypce, they adiudged for pronostiquykys & tokens of the kynges deth. **1598** BARCKLEY *Felic. Man* (1631) 177 Alexander received these gifts as a prognostick of his good fortune. **1657** W. MORICE *Coena quasi Κοινὴ* xix. 341 Winds..often..rise suddenly without any Prognosticks. **1716** GAY *Trivia* I. 122 From sure Prognosticks learn to know the Skies. **1761** HUME *Hist. Eng.* III. xlix. 66 A great comet appeared about the time of her death, and the vulgar esteemed it the prognostic of that event. **1830** D'ISRAELI *Chas. I*, III. xiv. 321 Laud felt it as ..the prognostic of his own doom. **1882** R. ABERCROMBY in *Nature* 12 Oct. 572/2 In common parlance any particular 'look' of the sky is called a prognostic, and it is a natural extension of the idea to call the 'look' of the sky absorption spectrum a prognostic.
2. A prediction or judgement of the future drawn from such an indication; a forecast, prophecy, anticipation.
1634 W. TIRWHYT tr. *Balzac's Lett.* (vol. I.) 225 When this young Lord came to Rome.. from the battaile of Prague, I can well witnesse..of the great Prognosticks all such gave of him. **1701** EARL OF CLARENDON in *Pepys' Diary*, etc. (1879) VI. 208, I could not but think it odd..that a man ..should give such a prognostick. **1754** RICHARDSON *Grandison* V. xliii. 274 Reflexion and Prognostic are ever inspiriting parts of the pretension of people who have lived long. **1815** *Zeluca* II. 285, I thank you for your inauspicious prognostics. **1884** H. D. TRAILL in *Macm. Mag.* Nov. 29/1 Every unpleasing phenomenon of our Parliamentary life supplies fresh material for these despairing prognostics.
3. *Med.* A symptom or indication on which prognosis is based; †formerly also = PROGNOSIS.
1544 PHAER *Regim. Lyfe* (1560) N vj, Herein haue many wise phisicions..bene deceiued, and haue euil judged of the pacientes pronostik. **1621** BURTON (*title*) The Anatomy of Melancholy, What it is, With all the kindes, cavses, symptomes, prognostickes, and severall cvres of it. **1753** N. TORRIANO *Gangr. Sore Throat* 71 Hippocrates..made a favourable Prognostic in the Squinancy, when the Humour of the Disease tended outwards. **1822–34** *Good's Study Med.* (ed. 4) III. 467 In forming our prognostic, a special regard must be had to the peculiar character of the disease. **1866** A. FLINT *Princ. Med.* (1880) 108 Prognostics are those circumstances on which a prognosis is based.

prognostic (prɒg'nɒstɪk), *a.* and *sb.*² [ad. med.L. *prognōstic-us*, a. Gr. προγνωστικός foreknowing, f. προγιγνώσκειν to know beforehand: see -IC. So mod.F. *prognostique* (Acad. 1835).]
A. *adj.* Characterized by prognosticating; foreshowing, foretelling, predictive.
1603 HOLLAND *Plutarch* Explan. Words, *Prognosticke*, foreknowing and foreshewing: as the signes in a disease which foresignifie death or recovery. **1625** HART *Anat. Ur.* I. ii. 24 There are..diuerse prognosticke signes foreshewing life or death. **1759** B. STILLINGFL. *Cal. Flora* Pref. in *Misc. Tracts* (1791) 236 A digression about birds in relation to their prognostic nature. *Ibid.* 254, I have..marked the plants which appear to be most prognostic with an asterisk. **1851** NICHOL *Archit. Heav.* 161 Movements of the leaves during a silent night, prognostic of the breeze that has yet scarce come.
b. *Med.* Of or pertaining to prognosis.
a **1648** LD. HERBERT *Life* (1886) 52 To have some knowledge in medicine, especially the diagnostic part..as also the prognostic part. **1899** *Allbutt's Syst. Med.* VII. 120 The great prognostic importance of optic atrophy.
†**B.** *sb.* One who prognosticates; a foreteller of events. *Obs. rare.*
1653 GATAKER *Vind. Annot. Jer.* 33, I might a litle question the skil of Mr. L. himself, and some of his felow Prognosticks, in that part of the Sideral Science. *Ibid.* 175 Those antiq Wizards as well..as our modern Prognostiks.

†**prog'nostic,** *v. Obs.* Also 5–6 **pron-**. [ME. *pronostike*, a. obs. F. *pronostiquer* (14th c. in Godef. *Compl.*) (ad. med.L. *prognostic-āre* (Duns Scotus, *a* 1308)), f. L. *prognostic-um*, or F. *pronostic*, PROGNOSTIC *sb.*¹]
I. *trans.* = PROGNOSTICATE *v.* 1, 1 b.
c **1400** MAUNDEV. (Roxb.) viii. 29 Many oþer thinges þai pronostic and diuines by þe colours of þa flawmes. **1477** SIR J. PASTON in *P. Lett.* III. 190 The worshypfull and vertuous dysposicion off hyr ffadr and moodr, whyche pronostikyth that..the mayde sholde be vertuous and goode. **1533** BELLENDEN *Livy* III. xx. (S.T.S.) II. 30 He wald nocht pronostok [*v. r.* pronostik] nor devyne na sic harmes to cum on þame. **1559** ABP. PARKER *Corr.* (Parker Soc.) 61 The

adversaries have good sport.. to prognostick the likelihood. **1659** H. MORE *Immort. Soul* III. v. 379 When the Sun shines waterishly and prognosticks rain.

2. *intr.* = PROGNOSTICATE *v.* 2; in quot. 1541, to make a (medical) prognosis.

1481 BOTONER *Tulle on Old Age* (Caxton) C iv b, They [old men] also remembre.. how the augurys.. sholde determyne and pronostike vpon the dyuinacions and thynges that be for to come. **1541** R. COPLAND *Guydon's Quest. Chirurg.* B ij, A Cyrurgyen.. ought to be gentyll to his pacientes.. wyly in prognostykynge. *c* **1580** JEFFERIE *Bugbears* v. viii. in *Archiv Stud. Neu. Spr.* (1897), Your daughter is well, even as I did pronostick. **1630** PRYNNE *Anti-Armin.* 280 The present tempestuous, rainie, vnseasonable weather threaten and prognosticke to vs for our apostasie.

prognosticable (prɒg'nɒstɪkəb(ə)l), *a.* [f. L. *prognostic-āre* to PROGNOSTICATE + -ABLE.]

1. Capable of being prognosticated.

1646 SIR T. BROWNE *Pseud. Ep.* VI. viii. 317 Causes.. which cannot indeed be regular, and therefore their effects not prognosticable like Ecclipses. **1652** GAULE *Magastrom.* 194 It is for any prognosticator to know any thing that is prognosticable. **1881** A. S. HERSCHEL in *Nature* 24 Feb. 384/1 One of its most marked, although not at all one of its most prognosticable, properties.

†**2.** Capable of prognosticating. *Obs. rare*⁻¹.

1562 BULLEYN *Bulwark, Dial. Soarnes & Chir.* 19 b, As in the one, be manifest tokens of death: so in the other be prognosticable signes.

prog'nostical, *a.* (*sb.*) [f. as PROGNOSTIC *a.*, or f. PROGNOSTIC *sb.* + -AL[1].]

A. *adj.* Of, pertaining to, or characterized by prognostication; prognostic. *rare.*

1588 J. HARVEY *Disc. Probl.* 79 Strange and almost incredible conclusions, as well in the Diuinatorie, as Prognostical kinde. **1652** WADSWORTH tr. *Sandoval's Civ. Wars Spain* 144 They trusted in Southsaier's Prognostical judgements. **1778** [W. MARSHALL] *Minutes Agric., Observ.* 164, I have.. given a Prognostical Arrangement of popular Maxims relative to this subject. **1894** H. LATHAM *Service of Angels* 40 Is it prognostical? Is it proleptic? **1924** KEYNES in *Econ. Jrnl.* XXXIV. 316 We come to something more prognostical of Alfred in a little device of William Marshall's latter days.

†**B.** *sb.* = PROGNOSTIC *sb.*[1] 1. *Obs. rare*⁻¹.

a **1618** SYLVESTER *Mayden's Blush* 1180 Wondring much, the King awoke withall Conceiving it some high Prognosticall.

prog'nostically, *adv.* [f. prec. + -LY[2].] In a prognostic manner; by or with prognostication.

1610 MARCELLINE *Triumphs Jas. I* 60 It produceth prognostically the most dangerous Climacteriall age of.. the Papacy. **1657** G. STARKEY *Helmont's Vind.* 51 By Rules set down to finde out the disease Diagnostically, to discover the danger of it Prognostically, and to advise the cure of it. **1716** M. DAVIES *Athen. Brit.* II. 429 To lead Prognostically and Prodromatically to the Metropolitan Crosier. **1911** *Amer. Jrnl. Med. Sci.* CXLI. 644 Studying one's cases prognostically. **1977** *Lancet* 4 June 1199/2 H.D.L. is much more important prognostically.

†**prog'nosticant**, *ppl. a. Obs. rare*⁻¹. [ad. med.L. *prognōsticānt-em*, pr. pple. of *prognōsticāre* to PROGNOSTICATE: see -ANT[1].] Prognosticating, foreshowing.

1619 BP. J. KING *Serm.* 11 Apr. 52 As significant, and prognosticant of the wrath of God as any of these wonders.

†**prog'nosticate**, *sb. Obs.* [f. med.L. *prognōsticāt-um* that which is prognosticated: see next.] A sign or token of some future event; also, a prediction, forecast: = PROGNOSTICATION 4.

1561 T. HOBY tr. *Castiglione's Courtyer* II. (1577) I j b, Yet were they.. a token of libertie, where these haue been a prognosticate of bondage. **1577–87** HOLINSHED *Chron.* I. 173/1 They neuer appeare but as prognosticats of afterclaps. **1652** GAULE *Magastrom.* 330 Behold what truth is in the vain prognosticates of fond astrologers!

†**prog'nosticate**, *a. Obs. rare.* [ad. med.L. *prognōsticāt-us*, pa. pple. of *prognōsticāre*: see next.] = PROGNOSTICANT.

1582 STANYHURST *Æneis* I. (Arb.) 32 Thee wise diuined, by this prognosticat horshead, That Moors wyde conquest should gayne with vittayl abundant.

prognosticate (prɒg'nɒstɪkeɪt), *v.* Also 6–7 pron-; 6 *pa. t.* and *pple.* -at(e. [f. ppl. stem of med.L. *pro(g)nōsticāre* to prognosticate, foreshow, foretell: see PROGNOSTIC *v.*]

1. *trans.* To know or tell of (an event, etc.) beforehand; to have previous knowledge of, to presage; to foretell, predict, prophesy, forecast.

a **1529** SKELTON *Sp. Parrot* 138 To pronostycate truly the chaunce of fortunys dyse. **1542** UDALL *Erasm. Apoph.* 61 A philosophier in Plato his tyme had prognosticate yᵉ eclipse of ye soonne. **1582** STANYHURST *Æneis* III. (Arb.) 82 By flight and chirping byrds too prognosticat aptlye. **1612** WOODALL *Surgeon's Mate* Wks. (1653) 91 To know the manner of the hurt, that he may wisely prognosticate the danger. **1709** STRYPE *Ann. Ref.* I. i. 44 Wizards and conjurers prognosticating that she should not live out a year. **1842** J. WILSON *Chr. North* (1857) II. 24 Prudent men prognosticated evil. **1884** *Pall Mall Gaz.* 19 Jan. 1/2 Other cogent reasons for prognosticating such a revolution.

b. Of things: To betoken; to give previous notice of; to indicate beforehand.

a **1533** FRITH *Another Bk. agst. Rastel* Prol., Wks. (1829) 208 Doth not this pretty pageant.. signify & prognosticate that tragedy they will play hereafter? **1549** *Compl. Scot.* vi. 39 The suannis murnit, be cause the gray goul mau pronosticat ane storme. **1600** HOLLAND *Livy* XXXVI. i. 919 Euen the very first beasts that were slain, prognosticated fortunat successe. **1684** *Contempl. St. Man* I. x. (1699) 108 The Death of a Monarch.. Prognosticated by an Eclipse or Comet. **1768** H. WALPOLE *Hist. Doubts* 106 Yet these portents were far from prognosticating a tyrant. **1825** COBBETT *Rur. Rides* 283 Everything seems to prognosticate a hard winter.

†**2.** *intr.* To make or utter a prognostication; to prophesy *of*. *Obs.*

1560 DAUS tr. *Sleidane's Comm.* 299 b, For Christ him selfe.. did prognosticate of great stormes. **1665** BRATHWAIT *Comment Two Tales* (Chaucer Soc.) 9 Albeit he could judiciously prognosticate of seasons.

b. Of a thing: To give promise or indication.

1851 NICHOL *Archit. Heav.* 296 If the aggregation of stars in the Milky Way goes on—as it prognosticates—for ages.

Hence **prog'nosticated** *ppl. a.*, **prog'nosticating** *vbl. sb.* and *ppl. a.*

1599 HAKLUYT *Voy.* II. 58 If any mans father be sick, the son straight goes vnto the.. prognosticating priest. **1613** PURCHAS *Pilgrimage* (1614) 64 Peucer.. confuteth their fiue kindes of prognosticating. **1790** BURKE *Fr. Rev.* Wks. V. 411 In order, by a proper foresight, to prevent the prognosticated evil. **1842** J. WILSON *Chr. North* (1857) II. 237 All the prognosticating sights and sounds.

prognostication (prɒgnɒstɪ'keɪʃən). Also 5–6 pron-. [ME. a. OF. *pronosticacion* (14th c. in Godef. *Compl.*), later *prognostication* (Cotgr.), n. of action from med.L. *prognōsticāre*, PROGNOSTIC *v.*]

1. The action or fact of prognosticating; foreshowing, foretelling; prediction, prophecy.

1490 CAXTON *Eneydos* vi. 29 In pronostycacyon righte happy of their fleeynge and voyage. **1548** PATTEN *Exp. Scot.* A vj b, To note the Pronosticacion and former aduertence of his future successe in this hys enterprise. **1688** BOYLE *Final Causes Nat. Things* iv. 169 The prognostication of weathers that may be made in the morning by their keeping within their hives, or flying early abroad to furnish themselves with wax or honey. **1711** ADDISON *Spect.* No. 127 ¶5 Others are of Opinion that it foretels Battle and Bloodshed, and believe it of the same Prognostication as the Tail of a Blazing Star. **1904** J. OMAN *Vision & Authority* IV. vii. 289 Prognostication beyond the limits of our duty we should discover to be only a profitless diversion.

b. with *a* and *pl.* An act or instance of prognosticating; a foreknowledge or foretelling of something; a forecast, prediction, prophecy.

1440 J. SHIRLEY *Dethe K. James* (1818) 13 The which now may well be demyd by varay demonstracions, and also pronosticacions to the Kyng, of his deth and murdur. *c* **1510** MORE *Picus* Wks. 2/2 Which pronostication one Paulinus making much of, expowned it to signifie [etc.]. **1638** JUNIUS *Paint. Ancients* 142 The Athenians for his divine prognostications erected him a statue with a golden tongue. **1750** JOHNSON *Rambler* No. 187 ¶8 This prognostication she was ordered to keep secret. **1905** *Expositor* Feb. 134 His gloomy prognostications of coming doom.

c. A conjecture of some future event formed upon some supposed sign; a presentiment, foreboding.

1760 JOHNSON *Idler* No. 92 ¶5 Will Puzzle.. foresees every thing before it will happen, though he never relates his prognostications till the event is past. **1782** MISS BURNEY *Cecilia* x. ii, At his sight, her prognostication of ill became stronger. **1812** J. J. HENRY *Camp. agst. Quebec* 49 A prognostication resulted in my mind, that we should all die of mere debility in these wilds. **1864** BOWEN *Logic* ix. 307 The prognostications of evil thus formed very often bring about their own fulfilment.

†**2.** An astrological or astrometeorological forecast for the year, published in (or as) an almanac; hence, as almanac containing this. *Obs.*

See list of such Prognostications in Forewords to *Laneham's Letter*, p. cxxxiii. et seq.

1516 (*title*) The prognosticacion of maister Iasper late.. translated into ynglissh, to the honorre of te moost noble & victorious kynge Henry the viij by.. Nicholas longwater. **1545** (*title*) A Pronostycacion or an Almanacke for the yere of our lorde MCCCCCXLV made by Andrewe Boorde of Physycke doctor. **1583** STUBBES *Anat. Abus.* II. (1882) 66 The makers of prognostications, or almanacks for the yeere. **1603** OWEN *Pembrokeshire* (1892) 142 The vsuall order annexed to the prognostications in placeing the faires of everye moneth together. **1643** *C'tess Mar's Househ. Bk.* in Ritchie *Ch. St. Baldred* (1880) 63 For ane prognostication 8d.

†**3.** *Med.* = PROGNOSIS 1. *Obs.*

1533 ELYOT *Cast. Helthe* (1541) 55 The Rules of Hipocrates in his seconde boke of pronostications. **1610** BARROUGH *Meth. Physick* VII. iv. (1639) 388 There needeth no clyster, but that prognostication is sufficient. **1767** GOOCH *Treat. Wounds* I. 96 To regulate our judgment in prognostication, we must consider, what wounds are mortal, and what not.

4. Something that foretells or foreshadows an event; an indication of something about to happen; a sign, token, portent, prognostic. Now *rare.*

1432–50 tr. *Higden* (Rolls) VII. 491 The pix.. did falle, whiche was a pronosticacion contrary to the victory of the Kynge. *a* **1548** HALL *Chron., Hen. VIII* 81 Which hideous tempest some said it was a very pronosticacion of trouble and hatred to come betwene princes. **1606** SHAKS. *Ant. & Cl.* I. ii. 54 Nay, if an oyly Palme bee not a fruitfull Prognostication, I cannot scratch mine eare. **1850** GLADSTONE *Glean.* (1879) V. cxxxviii. 254 Labouring to fix the position of the Church for our own time according to the conditions and the prognostications which the time itself not offers only but rather thrusts and forces on our view.

prognosticative (prɒg'nɒstɪkətɪv), *a.* [ad. obs. F. *prognosticatif, -ive* (1564 in Godef.): see PROGNOSTICATE *v.* and -IVE.] Characterized by prognosticating; tending to prognosticate.

1594 CAREW *Huarte's Exam. Wits* xii. (1596) 180 A phisition.. studied.. all the rules and considerations of the art prognosticatiue. **1813** HOBHOUSE *Journey* (ed. 2) 977 The comet.. was thought prognosticative of the fall of Islamism. **1824** *Blackw. Mag.* XVI. 163 The opening a new volume of poems.. accompanied by a yawn, prognosticative of the soporific nature of its contents.

prognosticator (prɒg'nɒstɪkeɪtə(r)). Also 6 pron-, -our(e. [Agent-n. in L. form from *prognōsticāre* to PROGNOSTICATE: see -OR. So OF. *pronosticateur* (15–16th c. in Godef.).] One who or that which prognosticates; one who pretends to a knowledge of the future; a soothsayer, predictor, foreteller.

1552 HULOET, Pronosticatoure, *præsagus*. **1553** BRENDE *Q. Curtius* IV. 46 He obeied the pronosticator & caused all his men to returne. **1560** BIBLE (Genev.) *Isa.* xlvii. 13 Let now the astrologers, the starre gasers, & pronosticatours stand vp, and saue thee from these things. **1604** MIDDLETON *Father Hubburd's T.* Wks. (Bullen) VIII. 60 Averring no prognosticator lies, That says, some great ones fall, their rivals rise. **1796** BURKE *Regic. Peace* iv. Wks. IX. 29 Mr. Brothers.. was a melancholy prognosticator, and has had the fate of melancholy men. **1852** S. R. MAITLAND *Ess. Var. Subj.* 207 To speak of Merlin and a train of less important prognosticators. **1891** *Pall Mall G.* 22 Sept. 3/3 A sensitive, living prognosticator, like the 'Abrus precatorius', is preferable to the inanimate barometric weather gauges, on account of the vital force which dwells in it.

†**b.** A maker or publisher of almanacs containing predictions of the weather and events of the ensuing year; also, an almanac containing these.

1601 J. CHAMBER *Agst. Judic. Astrol.* 2 Astrologers, prognosticators, almanack-makers. **1696** TRYON *Misc.* iv. 99 Our Annual Prognosticators are generally Men of little Learning. **1778** [W. MARSHALL] *Minutes Agric., Observ.* 130 Almost every supposed Prognosticator has contradicted itself.

prognosticatory (prɒg'nɒstɪkətərɪ), *a.* [f. as prec.: see -ORY[2].] Of the nature of a prognostication; serving to prognosticate.

a **1693** *Urquhart's Rabelais* III. xx. 168 The intended purpose of his Prognosticatory Response. **1832** *Fraser's Mag.* V. 584 The curl of his nose is prognosticatory of perfumes. **1893** E. A. BUTLER *Househ. Insects* 147 Its shrill chirping, prognosticatory, according to popular belief, of cheerfulness and plenty.

‖**prog'nosticon**, *sb. Obs.* Also 7 pron-. [L., a. Gr. προγνωστικόν.] = PROGNOSTIC *sb.*[1]

1588 J. HARVEY *Disc. Probl.* 97 Is not this perpetuall Prognosticon think you,.. too durable, and ouer generall to be vniuersally true? **1611** SPEED *Hist. Gt. Brit.* IX. xvi. §92 This luckie prognosticon, and ominous Meteor. **1621** BURTON *Anat. Mel.* I. iv. I. (1676) 131/1 'Tis Rabbi Moses Aphorism, the prognosticon of Avicenna, Rhasis, Aëtius.

Hence †**prog'nosticon** *v.* = PROGNOSTICATE *v.* 1.

1602 in *Archpriest Controv.* (Camden) II. 238, I do hear that ffa. Walpole doth pronosticon that the priests.. shalbe banished. I praye god it be not a pronosticon, but a practise.

†**prog'nosticous**, *a. Obs. rare.* [f. as PROGNOSTIC *a.* + -OUS.] = PROGNOSTIC *a.* 1.

1607 WALKINGTON *Opt. Glass* (1664) 142 All dreames be.. either prognosticous of some event to fall out, or false illusions. *Ibid.* 143 These.. dreames bee prognosticous of either good or badde successe.

†**prog'nostify**, *v. Obs. rare.* In 5–6 pronostify, -yfy, -efy. [ad. med.L. type **pro(g)nōstific-āre*, or OF. **pronostifier*: see PROGNOSTIC *sb.*[1] and -FY.] = PROGNOSTICATE *v.* Hence †**prog'nostifying** *vbl. sb.*

1495 *Trevisa's Barth. De P.R.* VI. xxvii. (W. de W.) o ij, Dremes.. ben somtyme open & playne, and somtyme wrappyd in fyguratyf mystyk and dymme & derke pronostifyenge & tokenynge as it faryd in Pharaoes dremes. *Ibid.* VII. lx. r vij b, They [ulcers].. ben messengers and pronostyfyen the peryll of leprehede. ? *c* **1500** *Coventry Corp. Chr. Plays* App. iv. 119 Let us haue sum commenecasion Of this seyd star be old pronostefying How hyt apperud & vnder what fassion.

progradation (prəʊgrə'deɪʃən). *Physical Geogr.* [f. next + -ATION.] The seaward advance of a beach or coastline as a result of the accumulation of river-borne sediment or beach material.

1909 W. M. DAVIS in *Geogr. Jrnl.* XXXIV. 303 There is good reason for regarding the action of the streams in terracing or degrading the former valley floors as the cause of the progradation of the strand-plain. **1937** WOOLDRIDGE & MORGAN *Physical Basis Geogr.* xxi. 332 Progradation may result from the extensive deposition of river alluvium, as in deltas. **1967** *Oceanogr. & Marine Biol.* V. 130 Brothers (1954) concluded that dune formation during subsequent periods of shoreline progradation added great quantities of sand to the foreland around Auckland. **1971** *Nature* 10 Sept. 91/2 The virtual elimination of shelf seas, during a prolonged phase of tectonic stability and peneplanation following rapid build-up of evaporites and progradation of coastal plain sediments.

prograde ('prəʊgreɪd), *a.* [f. PRO-[1] 1 + RETRO)GRADE *a.* and *sb.*] **1.** *Petrol.* Of a metamorphic change: resulting from an increase in temperature or pressure. Opp. RETROGRADE *a.* 3 e.

1967 K. G. Cox et al. *Introd. Pract. Study Crystals* x. 200 The volatile constituents, H_2O and CO_2, are expelled from the rocks with rising temperature and cease to be available for the formation of low-temperature minerals (usually rich in H_2O and CO_2) when the temperature declines at the end of prograde metamorphism. **1977** A. HALLAM *Planet Earth* 174 The metamorphism of sedimentary rocks..involves the production of water vapor, carbon dioxide and other gaseous substances... This type of metamorphism is called prograde metamorphism, and takes place principally in response to increasing temperature.

2. *Astr.* From west to east; anticlockwise as seen from north of the ecliptic; = DIRECT *a.* 3. Opp. RETROGRADE *a.* 1 a.

1969 *Nature* 19 July 243/2 Once in a prograde orbit, the tides on the Earth would begin to push the Moon outwards to its present position. **1977** *Ibid.* 3 Mar. 15/3 The overhead motion of the Sun relative to an observer fixed on the surface [of Venus] is prograde with a speed of about 4 m s^{-1}.

prograde (prəʊ'greɪd), *v.* *Physical Geogr.* [f. PRO-[1] 1 + RETRO)GRADE *v.*] **a.** *intr.* Of a shore or shoreline: to undergo progradation.

1909 W. M. DAVIS in *Geogr. Jrnl.* XXXIV. 303 After having maturely retrograded the cliffs, the waves have prograded the strand-plain. The strand-plain broadens a little opposite each valley, for now that the shore-line is prograding, the rivers have opportunity of building their deposits forward. **1929** H. MEREDITH *East Anglia* ii. 63 Its beach progrades in inverse proportion to the retrograding of the Ness itself. **1954** W. D. THORNBURY *Princ. Geomorphol.* xvii. 443 Beach features are particularly ephemeral forms along a retrograding shore line, but along a shore line that is advancing seaward or is prograding they may be semipermanent. **1967** *Oceanogr. & Marine Biol.* V. 123 Thus valley train material extending seaward off Alaska has prograded almost to the headlands. **1978** *Nature* 17 Aug. 655/1 During the Campanian, fluvial, deltaic and coastal plain systems prograded eastwards across marine strata such that by the end of the Campanian (~69 Myr BP) the area of marine deposition was greatly restricted.

b. *trans.* To cause to prograde.

1909 [see sense a]. **1919** D. W. JOHNSON *Shore Processes* v. 223 Just so long as the current aggrades (builds up) the seabottom offshore, the waves will prograde (build forward) the shore. **1939** REVELLE & SHEPARD in P. D. Trask *Rec. Marine Sediments* IV. 279 The coarse material carried to the sea by rivers may temporarily prograde the shore, forming deltas. **1968** R. W. FAIRBRIDGE *Encycl. Geomorphol.* 133/1 Marine Deposition Coasts. These are another type of Secondary coasts that have been prograded by waves and currents.

Hence **pro'graded** *ppl. a.*, **pro'grading** *vbl. sb.* and *ppl. a.*

1910 *Jrnl. Geol.* XVIII. 166 The prograding of the shore beyond the headland. **1918** *Trans. & Proc. N.Z. Inst.* L. 215 Some of the material is thrown up on the beach, so that the shore-line advances seawards, leaving a prograded strip of new land. **1919** D. W. JOHNSON *Shore Processes* v. 223 Following Davis we may call any shore which is experiencing such a long-continued advance into the sea, a prograding shore, and distinguish it from the more usual retreating or retrograding shore. The prograding of a shoreline..may continue for a few years, a few centuries, or many thousands of years. **1940** *Geogr. Jrnl.* XCVI. 261 Occasional deep lows, locally called pits and containing water, are scattered about amongst the shingle. They were usually found during rapid prograding to the lee of bends. **1968** R. W. FAIRBRIDGE *Encycl. Geomorphol.* 895/2 (*caption*) Prograded spit, Whananaki Inlet, Northland, New Zealand. **1978** *Nature* 12 July 131/1 The environment was interpreted as a prograding tidal estuary where shelf deposits pass upwards into fields of migrating dunes and megaripples.

program, programme ('prəʊgræm), *sb.* Forms: α. 7- **program**, (7 -**grame**). β. 9- **programme**. See also PROGRAMMA. [In 17–18th c. Sc. use, in spelling *program*, ad. Gr.-L. *programma*, which was itself (*c* 1656–1820) also commonly used unchanged (see PROGRAMMA); about the beginning of the 19th c., reintroduced from F. *programme*, and now more usually so spelt (though not pronounced as F.); the earlier *program* was retained by Scott, Carlyle, Hamilton, and others, and would be preferable, as conforming to the usual English repr. of Gr. -γραμμα, in *anagram*, *cryptogram*, *diagram*, *telegram*, etc. However, *program* and *programme* have become established as the standard N. Amer. and British spellings respectively, with the exception that *program* is usual everywhere in connection with *Computing*. This latter distinction is followed in this article and throughout the Dictionary in editorial matter.]

†**1.** A public notice; = PROGRAMMA 1. *Sc. Obs.*

α. **1633** W. STRUTHER *True Happines* 38 The beginning of his discourse..is like a program affixed on the entrie of a citie. **1682** *Decreit* in *Scott. Antiq.* (1901) July 4 [They] determined..without affixing any previous programe or using any examinatioune to appoint the said Mr. J. Y. **1707** (July 22) in Fountainhall *Decisions* (1759) II. 385 The Professor of Greek his place being vacant in the college of St Andrews.., there is a program emitted, inviting all qualified to dispute, and undergo a comparative trial. **1816** SCOTT *Antiq.* i, Will three shillings transport me to Queensferry, agreeably to thy treacherous program? **1824** —— *St. Ronan's* xiii, The transactions of the morning were..announced..by the following program.

2. a. A descriptive notice, issued beforehand, of any formal series of proceedings, as a festive celebration, a course of study, etc.; a prospectus, syllabus; in current use *esp.* a written or printed list of the 'pieces', items, or 'numbers' of a concert or other public entertainment, in the order of performance; hence *transf.* the pieces or items themselves collectively, the performance as a whole.

α. **1808** *Sporting Mag.* XXXII. 43 The program of the Pantomime differs materially in the exhibition. **1823** *New Monthly Mag.* VII. 2 Anticipating the amusement of the month, by a regular program (that is a nice new word I have just imported from France, to supply the hackneid common-place of a 'bill of the play')—a regular program, I say, on the second page of your coloured cover. **1831** CARLYLE *Sart. Res.* I. iii. (1858) 10 'In times like ours', as the half-official Program expressed it, 'when all things are, rapidly or slowly, resolving themselves into Chaos'. **1855** SIR E. PERRY *Bird's-Eye View India* xxviii. 169 A program of the whole was sent me the night before. **1898** G. B. SHAW *Perf. Wagnerite* 3 In classical music there are, as the analytical programs tell us, first subjects and second subjects [etc.]. **1976** *Globe & Mail* (Toronto) 16 Feb. 17/1 This was the season's final program in the Toronto Symphony's Young People's Concerts series.

β. **1805** W. TAYLOR in *Ann. Rev.* III. 68 The..catalogue sold at the door better deserved..incorporation in this work than those programmes of festivals. **1838** DICKENS *Nich. Nick.* xiv, Mrs. Kenwigs and Miss Petowker had arranged a small programme of the entertainments. **1876** GRANT *Burgh Sch. Scotl.* II. xiii. 349 According to the programme of study drawn up for the grammar school of Glasgow. **1881** in Grove *Dict. Mus.* III. 33/2 Programmes are now commonly restricted in length to 2 hours or 2½... Formerly concerts were of greater length. **1936** G. GREENE *Gun for Sale* iii. 107 They sat two programmes round at the cinema. **1975** *Cricketer* May 41/3 (Advt.), Immediate cash paid for all programmes up to 1960 £5 minimum pre-war cup finals.

b. *gen.* and *fig.* A definite plan or scheme of any intended proceedings; an outline or abstract of something to be done (whether in writing or not). Also *transf.*, a planned series of activities or events.

α. **1837** CARLYLE *Fr. Rev.* (1872) III. II. i. 60 From the best scientific program..to the actual fulfilment, what a difference! **1839** J. STERLING *Ess.*, etc. (1848) I. 332 All suggestions of the true and beautiful, which he cannot predefine and lay down in program. **1860** MOTLEY *Netherl.* (1868) I. iv. 114 In accordance with this program Philip proceeded stealthily. **1869** BROWNING *Ring & Bk.* VIII. 1765 I'm in the secret of the comedy—Part of the program leaked out long ago! **1892** SWEET *New Eng. Gram.* Pref. 9 A less ambitious program would further allow of greater thoroughness within its narrower limits. **1941** *Bull. Amer. Assoc. Petroleum Geologists* XXV. 1256 Past successes enable us now to look ahead to a difficult but orderly exploration program, rather than a frenzied, inefficient scramble for immediately needed oil. **1949** SHURR & YOCOM *Mod. Dance* 3 The fallacy of this statement became increasingly apparent as personal contact with, and participation in, teacher education programs in the colleges and universities increased. **1955** *Science* 25 Nov. 1005/2 The satellite program..is already underway. **1961** BERKNER & ODISHAW *Sci. in Space* i. 15 An orderly scientific program [of space research] cannot be conducted if the unreliability associated with new vehicles is always present.

β. **1839** *Eclectic Rev.* 1 Jan. 24 The general satisfaction which had been produced by the ministerial *programme*. **1841** MILL in *Life & Labours Fonblanque* (1874) 32 They [the Ministry] have conformed to my programme. **1860** W. COLLINS *Wom. White* II. 277 Observe the programme I now propose. **1891** J. MORLEY *Sp. Newcastle* 2 Oct., We have had a programme unfolded which is calculated to stir the deepest energy and to rouse the sincerest convictions of every man with a spark of Liberalism in him. **1976** *Liverpool Echo* 7 Dec. 17/9 On the Wirral the West Cheshire programme was reduced to three games. **1977** *Nature* 11 Aug. 487/2 A joint programme to provide a set of soil structure standards..has been under way for five years at the Universities of Warsaw and Moscow.

c. *Mus.* A sequence of objects, scenes, or events intended to be suggested by a musical composition or used to determine its structure.

1854 H. F. CHORLEY *Mod. German Mus.* II. 306 There is no parroting such a programme..to an opera as the overture to 'Leonora'. **1883** GROVE *Dict. Mus.* III. 34/2 There is a growing tendency amongst critics and educated musicians to invent imaginary 'programmes' where composers have mentioned none. **1944** W. APEL *Harvard Dict. Mus.* 605/1 In the final analysis, there are two types of program music: that which is good music regardless of the program; and that which is poor music even with a 'good' program. **1962** *Listener* 15 Mar. 489/3 While the majority of his piano pieces bear explanatory titles, in his symphonies he was far more reticent as to the underlying programme. **1974** *Encycl. Brit. Micropædia* VIII. 231/3 Only in the so-called Romantic era, from Beethoven to Richard Strauss, is the program an essential concept.

d. = *dance programme* s.v. DANCE *sb.* 7.

1899 A. E. W. MASON *Miranda of Balcony* iv. 40 He compared programmes with Miranda... Four dances must intervene before he could claim her. **1913** MRS G. DE H. VAIZEY *College Girl* xxvii. 369 The three programmes were filled to the last extra. **1949** N. MARSH *Swing, Brother, Swing* iii. 42 Her coming-out ball had been here... She felt the cord of her programme grow glossy under the nervous pressure of her gloved fingers. **1976** *Times* 11 June 14/6 Guests carry around little programmes to remind them who they are dancing with.

e. *Broadcasting.* (i) A broadcast presentation treated as a single item for scheduling purposes, being broadcast between stated times and without interruption except perhaps for news bulletins or advertisements.

1923 *Radio Times* 28 Sept. 1 From November 14th last year..we have..transmitted roughly 1,700 distinct evening programmes. **1933** *Ibid.* 14 Apr. 72/2 In the programmes for Friday next, you will find particulars of *Looking In*, first television review. **1946** *B.B.C. Year-bk.* 62 About 120 new programmes..are put on the air every week. *Ibid.*, Such famous programmes as 'Itma', 'Music Hall', and 'Workers' Playtime'. **1962** A. NISBETT *Technique Sound Studio* i. 17 Certain topical and miscellany programmes..go on the air in the form of a mixture of live and recorded segments. **1976** *Times* 21 May 2/8 Since the programme I have had about a dozen other nasty telephone calls.

(ii) A radio service providing a regular succession of programmes on a particular frequency.

1939 R. MACAULAY *Lett. to Sister* (1964) 96 I've just read the debate on B.B.C. in Hansard... The fact is we *can't* get on without 2 programmes. **1939** [see HOME *a.* 2 e]. **1945**, etc. [see LIGHT *a.*[1] 19 b]. **1946** *B.B.C. Year-bk.* 51 The Director-General promised that within ninety days of the end of hostilities in the West, the BBC would provide its listeners in the United Kingdom with two full-scale alternative programmes. *Ibid.*, It is the aim of the Home Service to provide the home programme of the people of the United Kingdom. **1968** *B.B.C. Handbk.* 48 The popular music programme on 247 metres became Radio 1. The Light Programme, on 1500 metres and VHF, became Radio 2. The Third Network, which embraces the Music Programme, the Third Programme, Study Session and the Sports Service, became Radio 3. **1980** *Times* 31 July 15/3 Radio 3 used to be the most civilized and broad-ranging programme in the world.

f. *Electronics.* Also ***programme signal***. A signal corresponding to music, speech, or other activity.

1935 NILSON & HORNUNG *Pract. Radio Communication* viii. 356 The program fed into the mixer does not always come directly from a microphone. **1948** A. L. ALBERT *Radio Fund.* xiv. 569 The frequency deviations of a program signal in frequency-modulation can be made, and is made, quite large... If the program has a wide frequency deviation, but noise does not, the signal-to-noise ratio of the output of a discriminator will be high. **1954** MOLLOY & PANNETT *Radio & Television Engineers' Ref. Bk.* IV. 12 It is necessary at times to compress the programme from a range of 50 to 22 db. **1959** K. HENNEY *Radio Engin. Handbk.* (ed. 5) xxi. 7 Program signals have very complex wave shapes. **1970** J. EARL *Tuners & Amplifiers* iv. 77 The amplifier..must process the programme signal (e.g. the signal from the pickup, radio tuner, tape recorder or whatever). **1977** *Gramophone* Nov. 937/1 The 2760 copier unit completes the system..and has automatic end-of-tape sensing and erasure of programme.

g. (i) A sequence of operations that a machine can be set to perform automatically.

1945 J. P. ECKERT et al. *Description of ENIAC* (PB 86242) (Moore School of Electr. Engin., Univ. of Pennsylvania) 1 The intended use of the ENIAC is to compute large families of solutions all based on the same program of operations. **1954** *Amer. Machinist* 25 Oct. 136/1 The operator..sets a combination of switches calling for table movements equivalent to blueprint dimensions, or a 'program', then presses a starting button. **1962** E. BRUTON *Automation* vi. 74 An automatic washing machine may be designed to wash for four minutes, empty, and spin-dry for ten. This is its programme. It can be 'programmed' in other ways. **1970** *Which?* Oct. 293/1 For most, there was a pre-rinse and a choice of two washing programmes, depending on how dirty the dishes were. **1972** *Daily Tel.* 11 Jan. 11/2 There's a Westinghouse electric clothes-dryer..which takes 12 lb of clothes and has five drying programmes: auto-dry, wash'n'wear, time dry, air fluff and low heat. **1977** *Times* 9 July 21/4 The ability of modern machines to offer merely rinse and dry programmes for clothes that have been prewashed by hand.

(ii) *Computers.* A series of coded instructions which when fed into a computer will automatically direct its operation in carrying out a specific task. Also *transf.*

1946 *Nature* 20 Apr. 527/2 Control of the programme of the operation of the machine [*sc.* ENIAC] is also through electrical circuits. **1947** *Math. Tables & Other Aids to Computation* II. 358 An important limitation upon programming is that the machine must adhere to a prescribed linear course of operation. It cannot at any point choose between two subsequent programs on the basis of results already obtained. **1950** *Phil. Mag.* XLI. 256 The problem of constructing a computing routine or 'program' for a modern general purpose computer which will enable it to play chess. **1953** *Proc. IRE* XLI. 1245/1 A large family of high-speed, large-scale, stored-program, digital computers have been built. *Ibid.* 1247/1 This conditional instruction makes it possible for the programmer to write programs which take different courses of action depending upon the results of previous computation. **1960** *Times* 4 Oct. (Computer Suppl.) p. v/3 To prepare this sequence of instructions, or program (a spelling now adopted in computer terminology), the programmer will have broken down an operation into its simplest elements. **1971** *Times Lit. Suppl.* 4 June 635/2 Were accurate estimation of the merits of such positions possible, the next world chess champion could quite conceivably be a computer programme. **1972** *Sci. Amer.* Mar. 42/3 Computer instructions are so complicated that programmers are often baffled when they look at programs they have written but have not seen for several months, and a third party usually finds them inscrutable. **1972** R. M. LEE *Short Course Basic Fortran IV Programming* i. 8 Programs are written in one of the many user-oriented languages, such as FORTRAN, and then translated into machine language... The translation is done by the computer. **1974** *Sci. Amer.* Oct. 105/1, I have described the timing and the characteristics of the coordination of the eye-head movements that are elicited by the appearance of a visual target, and have presented our evidence for the conclusion that the programs for eye-head coordination are not present in the central nervous system in their entirety. **1977** W. S. DAVIS *Operating Syst.* v. 58 Before any program can be run, it must first be set up (cards loaded in the card reader, the printer loaded with..paper.., tapes and disk packs mounted, and so on).

h. *Psychol.* and *Educ.* In human and animal learning, a series of step-by-step questions or tests (freq. designed to be used in a teaching machine operated by the learner) aimed at the establishment of learning patterns through the stimulus of rewarding correct responses or behaviour at each step.

1950 B. F. Skinner in *Psychol. Rev.* LVII. 207/2 Such a set was randomized in a program of reinforcement repeated every hour. In changing to this program from the arithmetic series..the pigeons were soon able to sustain a constant rate of responding under it. **1958** —— in *Science* 24 Oct. 971/2 The machines themselves cannot be adequately described without giving a few examples of programs. **1961**, etc. [see linear *a.* 3 b]. **1962** *Listener* 17 May 855/2 The drawback to a multiple choice programme..is that plausible wrong answers must be presented to the student, and he may remember these instead of the correct ones. **1967** Coulthard & Smith in Wills & Yearsley *Handbk. Managem. Technol.* xi. 204 Two types of programme are currently in use: 1. The linear programme—which repeats a statement just made, omitting a key word or words, and requires the trainee to remedy the omission... 2. The intrinsic programme—which provides an explanation of a key point in the subject and asks the trainee to select the correct answer to a question from several alternative answers. **1976** W. B. Kolesnik *Learning* x. 226 The program can be used in grades one through twelve in the area of language, arts, mathematics, [etc.].

3. = programma 2; *spec.* (repr. Ger. *Programm*) in German schools, an essay or disquisition on some subject, prefixed to the annual report.

1831 Carlyle *Early Germ. Lit.* in *Misc. Ess.* (1872) III. 182 A series of Selections, Editions, Translations, Critical Disquisitions, some of them in the shape of Academic Program. **1831** —— *Sart. Res.* ii. iii, Scraps of regular Memoir, College-Exercises, Programs, Professional Testimoniums. **1833** Sir W. Hamilton *Discuss.* (1852) 556 (Prussian Primary Education) The director, or one of the masters, in an official program, is to render an account of the condition and progress of the school. **1880** J. Morrison in *Expositor* XI. 461 Such is the derivation..given by Niemeyer in his Programm on the expression. **1884** *Amer. Jrnl. Philol.* V. 504 He admires greatly Hermann's program on 'Interpolations in Homer'.

4. *attrib.* and *Comb.*, as ***programme-book***, ***-card***, ***-maker***, ***-making***, ***note***, ***-seller***, ***vendor***; in sense 2 b, with reference to political 'programmes', as ***-mongering***, ***-spinner***, ***-spinning***; (sense 2 e) ***programme content***, ***director***, ***editor***, ***engineer***, ***item***, ***planner***, ***planning***, ***staff***, ***time***; (sense 2 g) ***program step***, ***tape***, ***testing***; **program counter** *Computers*, a register in the control unit of a computer which contains the address of the next instruction to be executed, this number being increased by one each time unless an instruction to do otherwise occurs; **programme boy, girl**, a boy or girl employed to sell programmes at a place of entertainment; **programme-building**, the selection of items for a concert or for a period of broadcasting; so **programme-builder**; **programme chairman** *U.S.*, one who arranges the programme of events or the agenda for a particular event for a society, etc.; **programme company**, a company authorized to make programmes and advertisements for broadcasting on British commmercial television; **programme contractor** = *programme company*, so **programme-contracting** *a.*; **program(me) control**, (*a*) = programmer 3; (*b*) control of or by a program(me); **program(me) controller** = programmer 1 c, 3; **programme girl**: see *programme boy*; **programme junction** *Broadcasting* (see quot. 1941); **program library** *Computers* = library[1] 3; **programme line** *Telecommunications* (see quot. 1940); **programme movie** = *programme picture*; **program(me)-music**, music intended to convey the impression of a definite series of objects, scenes, or events; descriptive music; **programme pencil**, a small pencil for filling in a programme-card at a dance, etc.; **programme picture**, a cinema film made relatively cheaply and intended to be shown as part of a programme that includes another film as the main feature; **program register** *Computers* = *control register* s.v. control *sb.* 5; **programme service** *Broadcasting*, a service consisting in the regular broadcasting of radio or television programmes for reception by the public; **programme symphony**, a symphony with a programme (sense 2 c).

1954 *Grove's Dict. Mus.* (ed. 5) VI. 943/2 Philip Hale's long series of notes for the Boston Symphony Orchestra made the programme-books of that orchestra valuable historic documents. **1976** *New Yorker* 9 Feb. 102/3 The wretched program book gave no texts—only excerpts from the Woolf cycle, and translations of the rest. **1921** *Dict. Occup. Terms* (1927) §889 Programme boy, girl, seller. **1928** *B.B.C. Handbk.* 73/2 The programme builders believe that ..the 60,000 hours of programmes will receive the liveliest and most general approval..by the application of a common-sense policy. **1947** *Penguin Music Mag.* Dec. 27 Every programme-builder should know the symphonic repertoire from A to Z. **1961** *Listener* 21 Dec. 1088/3, I don't know what was in the mind of the programme-builder of the concert given by the B.B.C. Symphony Orchestra. **1928** *B.B.C. Handbk.* 74/1 The best method of explaining the details of programme building is to follow a week's programmes from their first beginnings to the day on which they are broadcast. **1935** *Discovery* Sept. 277/1 It may be left safely to the B.B.C., whose experience and standards of programme building..may be relied upon to result in presentations in line with public approbation. **1948** *Penguin Music Mag.* Feb. 93 Mr. Barbirolli's extraordinary skill in programme-building. **1957** *Encycl. Brit.* IV. 208/2 It is principally under the headings (5) and (6)..that radio has created expression forms peculiar to itself, and in most other respects program-building is creative only in the sense that the program-builders can build combinations of suitable music and speech around one or another central idea. **1886** Kipling *Departm. Ditties*, etc. *My Rival*, My prettiest frocks and sashes Don't help to fill my programme-card [at a ball]. **1948** *Penguin Music Mag.* June 135 The Orchestra's first programme-card was several degrees more adventurous than any before it. **1961** *U.S. Nat. Bureau Standards Rep. Fiscal Year 1961* 57 The Bureau contributed to the planning and success of the Symposium through the efforts of..Dr. C. M. Herzfeld, Program Chairman. **1976** *Billings* (Montana) *Gaz.* 27 June 5-e/3 She is a past president, program chairman and secretary of the chapter. **1958** *New Statesman* 22 Mar. 375/3 As each programme-company in turn began broadcasting in the regions, the tale was always the same: of viewers with a choice, most chose the ITV channel most of the time. **1962** *Rep. Comm. Broadcasting 1960* i in *Parl. Papers 1961–2* (Cmnd. 1753) IX. 259 Independent television comprises not only the ITA but also the programme companies, which have at various dates since 1954 been appointed by the ITA. **1968** *Listener* 11 July 84/3 What are called the programme companies, in ITV, are set up in the first instance as contractors on the basis of the advertising franchise in their area. **1958** *New Statesman* 20 Dec. 880/1, I am not sure that I agree that the effect of the competition on the programme-content is as superficial as they seem then to have found. **1964** M. McLuhan *Understanding Media* (1967) xxviii. 293 Like the radio that it still provides with program content, the phonograph is a hot medium. **1968** *Listener* 29 Aug. 285/3 There is now hardly a significant publication, from the weekly reviews to the mass-selling dailies, which does not have equity in one or other of the programme-contracting companies. **1954** *Act 2 & 3 Eliz. II* c. 55. §2 The programmes broadcast by the Authority shall..be provided not by the Authority but by persons (hereafter in this Act referred to as 'programme contractors') who, under contracts with the Authority, have, in consideration of payments to the Authority.., the right and the duty to provide programmes or parts of programmes to be broadcast by the Authority. **1958** *New Statesman* 5 July 1/2 With commercial success and popular support behind them the existing programme contractors, and those who would like to become programme contractors, are in a much more powerful position than they were when ITV was an untried gamble. **1962** *Rep. Comm. Broadcasting 1960* 166 in *Parl. Papers 1961–2* (Cmnd. 1753) IX. 259 The [Independent Television] Authority's power to control the companies, once they are appointed programme contractors, is illusory and negligible. **1945** J. P. Eckert et al. *Description of ENIAC* (PB 86242) (Moore School of Electr. Engin., Univ. of Pennsylvania) b-5 The simplest procedure for handling the problem is to devote one multiplier program control to each of the n multiplications. **1951** M. McLuhan *Mech. Bride* (1967) 21/1 The president of the National Broadcasting Corporation ridiculed the proposal to separate business control from program control. **1953** *Proc. IRE* XLI. 1271/2 (*heading*) Program control of external units. **1957** D. M. Considine *Process Instruments & Controls Handbk.* ix. 78 The operation of a tire vulcanizer, on a completely automatic timed basis, is an example of program control. **1977** *Design Engin.* July 15/3 Eight parallel latched outputs are available as binary, BCD, or as a 7-segment-plus-decimal-point output under program control. **1957** D. M. Considine *Process Instruments & Controls Handbk.* ix. 78 By controlling sequence, intervals, and rates of change, a program controller may encompass all the operations in a complete industrial process. **1961** *Times* 4 Aug. 2/3 Independent Television in Wales..now invite application for the following key posts:. .. Programme Controller. In this position, experience of Television production, a knowledge of Welsh, and broad interests over the whole field of entertainment are essential. The Controller in Cardiff will plan and budget all programmes, and must know how and where to produce or acquire material. **1967** F. W. Clarke *Installing Small Pipe Central Heating* vi. 37 Where a boiler supplies hot water and serves the heating, the various jobs required of it can be simply co-ordinated by a programme controller. This turns the heating or the hot water on and off at selected times, as set on the clock. **1976** C. Bermant *Coming Home* ii. iv. 161, I returned to Granada and sent a memo to the programme controller. **1946** *Math. Tables & Other Aids to Computation* II. 102 Counters are used not only for arithmetic purposes, but also as a part of the programming circuits which determine when and how a given unit shall perform. Each unit whose operations consume more than one addition time has such a program counter. **1962** Huskey & Korn *Computer Handbk.* xvi. 29 In the case of a jump instruction, the address for the next instruction to be fetched comes from the address part of the present instruction... The state of the program counter must be changed to agree with this address so that it will count on from the new starting point. **1977** *Design Engin.* July 15/3 There are four parallel inputs, a testable sense input, three bi-directional control flags for use as inputs or outputs, a program counter, a two-word stack for nested subroutine calls, and an instruction-decode programmable logic array. **1961** G. Millerson *Television Production* i. 15 He may operate the buttons and faders for video switching himself, but most networks consider the programme director too preoccupied with the many other aspects of production, and delegate this job to another person. **1972** *Listener* 6 July 2/1 Michael Rice, the Programme Director, asked one of his people..to lead the production team. **1929** *Radio Times* 8 Nov. 387/3 Broadcast reading has only been tried half-heartedly. The programme editors still suffer from..fear of not pleasing everybody all day long. **1949** *Ibid.* 15 July 41/3 He returned to the BBC as a programme engineer. **1962** Programme engineer [see balance *sb.* 14 b]. **1905** *Daily Chron.* 13 Feb. 9/3 An interesting story of a medical student's love for a programme girl..was told. **1918** [see cloak-room b]. **1921** [see *programme boy*]. **1979** G. Latta tr. *Jacquemard-Sénécal's Eleventh Little Nigger* i. v. 47 The programme girls.. persuaded her to swallow a considerable amount of whisky. **1962** Programme item [see *programme planning*]. **1941** *B.B.C. Gloss. Broadcasting Terms* 25 *Programme junction*, brief interval between the end of one programme and the beginning of the next, used for switching operations whereby transmitters are linked to, or detached from, the network concerned. **1975** *Listener* 23 Oct. 532/2 There was internal machinery to see that there were common programme junctions. **1960** *Ann. Rev. Automatic Programming* I. 93 (*heading*) MERCURY autocode: principles of the program library. **1977** R. E. Harrington *Quintain* xii. 139 Sanderson gave me the constants and I just ran the program. I didn't even write it. He got it from the program library. **1940** *Chambers's Techn. Dict.* 676/2 *Programme* (or *program*) *line*, a transmission line, of superior propagation characteristics, for relaying broadcasting programmes. **1944** *Proc. IRE* XXXII. 601/1 A key located to the left of the VU meter should be used to connect this meter to the outgoing program line. **1895** *Daily News* 23 Jan. 7/3 Mr. Chamberlain is above all things a programme maker... In the year 1885 he constructed what was called an 'unauthorised programme' for the Liberal party. **1929** *Radio Times* 8 Nov. 393/1 There are people who..abuse the programme-makers! **1977** *Broadcast* 13 June 5/2 Programme makers could..put their ideas to the empirical test by means of a pilot programme. **1904** W. James *Let.* 1 Jan. in R. B. Perry *Tht. & Char. W. James* (1935) II. 201 Münsterberg has the most extraordinary power of schematization and program-making. **1949** *Penguin Music Mag.* Feb. 19 That almost perfect example of programme-making, *Music in Miniature*. **1980** *Listener* 3 Jan. 21/1 Industrial disputes [in broadcasting] took up more time than programme-making. **1935** *Movie Mirror* Dec. 106/1 Dropping into the theater, prepared for a regular program movie, my interest was caught after the first few feet and worked up to a fever pitch at the final reel. **1879** Grove *Dict. Mus.* I. 232/2 Berlioz was one of the most uncompromising champions of what, for want of a better name, has been dubbed 'programme music'. **1881** *Ibid.* III. 38/1 The Abbé Vogler..was..a great writer of programme-music. **1954** C. S. Lewis *Eng. Lit. in Sixteenth Cent.* i. ii. 139 Disorder in life rendered by disorder in art. This is in poetry what 'programme music' is in music. **1923** M. R. Werner *Barnum* 319 And then in Barnum's program notes each year appeared this notice. **1942** E. Blom *Music in England* ix. 149 Ella also wrote his own programme notes. **1958** 'E. Dundy' *Dud Avocado* i. vii. 136 I'd never seen a ballet whose story I was able to follow even when the programme-notes were in English. **1965** *Listener* 25 Nov. 874/1 The relevance of the play to the 'thirties in Britain and also to Radio in Europe Week was so admirably condensed in a programme note in *Radio Times* by the producer, Douglas Cleverdon, that it does not seem worth labouring. **1978** *Daily Tel.* 20 Jan. 13/1 To 25 years' experience before the camera can be added (I learn from the programme note) some recent experience as a director in the theatre. **1895** *Montgomery Ward & Co. Catal.* Spring & Summer 115/2 'Programme' Pencils, round, enameled in colors with gilt tip and ring. Suitable for use in lady's memorandum book. **1921** E. N. Hull *Sheik* i. 9 She hesitated, tapping her programme-pencil against her teeth. **1928** *Sunday Dispatch* 19 Aug. 14/2 A 'programme' picture is a film which costs from £6,000 to £8,000 or thereabouts, and cannot be called a 'super'. **1935** *Movie Mirror* Dec. 38/3 Your Reviewer Says: An average program picture, but Velez fans will want to see it for sure. **1956** Programme planner [see b.b.c.]. **1961** A. Wilson *Old Men at Zoo* ii. 92 The television engineers and programme planners with whom the office now seemed filled. **1974** *Guardian* 23 Jan. 1/5 If the [TV] close-down had been at 10.30 there would have been more room for manoeuvre by the programme planners. **1940** R. S. Lambert *Ariel & all his Quality* iii. 77 Charles Siepmann..was promoted to.. Director of Programme Planning. **1962** *Rep. Comm. Broadcasting 1960* 159 in *Parl. Papers 1961–2* (Cmnd. 1753) IX. 259 What particular 'time slots' each [TV company] is to occupy, and with what programme items... That is to say, the overall programme planning. **1948** *Gloss. Computer Terms* (Mass. Inst. Technol. Servomechanisms Lab. Rep. R-138) 8 *Program register*, the part of the computer used for holding orders after they are extracted from storage but before they are carried out. **1956** Program register [see *control register*]. **1962** R. V. Oakford *Introd. Electronic Data Processing Equipment* iii. 37 Information (normally instructions) can be transferred to the program register in the control unit from general memory or from the arithmetic (process) unit. **1921** Programme seller [see *programme boy*]. **1977** M. Babson *Lord Mayor of Death* v. 45 Here comes the programme seller. **1940** L. R. Lohr *Television Broadcasting* ii. 23 Televison transmitters have been in operation from time to time in Philadelphia, Schenectady,..and Bridgeport, but none of these had established a program service for the public at the time of writing. **1962** A. Nisbett *Technique Sound Studio* i. 17 The next link is a continuity suite where the entire programme service is assembled. **1940** R. S. Lambert *Ariel & all his Quality* ii. 43 Programme and administrative staff had not been divided into watertight..categories. **1977** *Listener* 28 Apr. 540/2 There has been a planned increase of programme staff, facilities and output. **1950** *High-Speed Computing Devices* ix. 157 The Type 604 can perform 60 program steps, or operations, per card; a program step includes any one of the four arithmetic operations, or a number transfer. **1956** [see command *sb.* 1 d]. **1978** *Sci. Amer.* Feb. 29/2 (Advt.), Because of this dual capability, it can..identify which program step a system was executing at the time of malfunction. **1934** C. Lambert *Music Ho!* iii. 162 Nationalism..destroys both the aristocratic quality of the eighteenth-century abstract symphony and the individualist quality of the nineteenth-century programme symphony. **1962** *Listener* 29 Nov. 941/2 The third symphony..was suggested by visits to Mycenae and Venice. Programme symphonies are even more out of fashion than the normal type, but I can only say that I tried to express the emotions aroused in me by the places rather than to paint pictures of them. **1948** *Math. Tables & Other Aids to Computation* III. 126 We can have on the first section of the program tape.. the program for arranging the data in order by age. **1964** C.

DENT *Quantity Surveying by Computer* iii. 26 In other cases the data tape is read in under control of the instructions (stored in the memory by the program tape), the data being worked on as it is read in. **1959** J. JEENEL *Programming for Digital Computers* viii. 393 In program testing one usually employs certain techniques especially developed for this purpose. **1964** F. L. WESTWATER *Electronic Computers* ix. 140 The coding is tested on the computer... (This is called 'program testing'.) **1957** *Practical Wireless* XXXIII. 529/2 Fewer programmes.. would enable the BBC to.. reject the dross which is still allowed programme time. **1977** M. BABSON *Lord Mayor of Death* xii. 82 Programme vendors.. were.. shaking their heads regretfully at would-be customers.

'program, 'programme, *v.* [f. prec. sb. The note s.v. PROGRAM, PROGRAMME *sb.* applies equally to the vb.] **1.** *trans.* To arrange by or according to a programme; to draw up a programme of; to scheme or plan definitely.

1896 *Westm. Gaz.* 12 Sept. 4/2 This match was programmed to start yesterday, but owing to the state of the weather had to be postponed. **1900** *Ibid.* 17 July 6/3 Meetings, he declares, were wrongly programmed. **1905** *Pall Mall G.* 19 Dec. 2 The devolutionist scheme was programmed and published on September 26, 1904. **1912** A. BENNETT *Jrnl.* 16 Feb. (1932) II. 44 On Wednesday morning at 7 a.m. as 'programmed' a week ago, I began 'The Regent'. **1949** *Archit. Rev.* CVI. 375/1 Let us.. consider a country like Japan where, after wholesale destruction, four million minimum dwellings are now being programmed. **1956** *Sun* (Baltimore) (B ed.) 24 Sept. 10/2 Senator Scott found.. that 75 per cent of the soil bank outlay of $261,000,000 programmed for 1956 was to be spent in twelve mid-Western farm states. **1970** *Daily Tel.* 30 Jan. 2/4 He tried to programme her day into housework and study, but with four children and a pile of nappies it did not work. **1977** *Gramophone* Feb. 1308/1 The items are programmed in a quite interesting way, the fireworks of Liszt's *Hungarian Rhapsody* No. 2 being followed by the cool renunciation of Satie's *Gymnopédie* No. 1. **1979** *Church Times* 25 May 14/5 When the ceremonies and speeches were over, the General .. was programmed to leave the gathering and walk along the red carpet to his car.

†**2.** *intr.* To write programme notes. *Obs. rare.*

1889 G. B. SHAW *London Music in 1888–89* (1937) 243 He programmed in a pat-the-young-man-on-the-back style.

3. *trans.* and *intr.* To broadcast. *U.S.*

1937 *Amer. Speech* XII. 101 *To program* means.. to broadcast. **1967** *Boston Sunday Herald* 26 Mar. II. 8/2 (Advt.), Personalities are an important ingredient in today's radio, and WCOP provides warm, personable, well established people—they program 24 hours a day with your listening pleasures in mind. **1969** *N.Y. Rev. Books* 2 Jan. 17/3 We can program twenty more hours of TV in South Africa next week to cool down the tribal temperature raised by radio last week. **1978** *Chicago* June 22/1 CSO does not program enough contemporary music.

4. a. To express (a task or operation) in terms appropriate to its performance by a computer or other automatic device; to cause (an activity or property) to be automatically regulated in a prescribed way.

1945 J. P. ECKERT et al. *Description of ENIAC* (PB 86242) (Moore School of Electr. Engin., Univ. of Pennsylvania) B-4 In this fashion, problems involving numbers of multiplications far in excess of 24 can be programmed. **1949** *Nature* 22 Oct. 684/2 The problem must be programmed, that is, it must be split up into a series of simple operations which the machine can perform. **1952** *Phil. Mag.* XLIII. 1245 When a mathematician assembles the set of orders required to work out the solution of a problem he is said to be programming this problem for the machine. **1955** *IRE Trans. Industr. Electronics* II. 3/1 Industry needs more flexible methods of programming machine cycles to achieve automatic operation of machine tools in limited-quantity production. **1958** *Times Rev. Industry* Feb. 52/2 The Burroughs Typing Sensimatic has unmatched flexibility. The control unit permits each job to be individually programmed. **1962** G. A. T. BURDETT *Automatic Control Handbk.* XIX. 2 The engineer must programme the operations which the machine is to carry out. Preferably this programming, i.e. planning in advance and in sequence all the steps of the required operations, should involve the minimum of human effort and.. a computer may be used. **1971** *Sci. Amer.* Apr. 71 Evidently an annual cycle of feeding and fasting is also programmed in the animal. **1973** A. PARRISH *Mech. Engineer's Ref. Bk.* XIX. 15 If feeds and speeds are programmed such that the spindle motor is producing its maximum horse power, any hard spots in the work piece can result in stall. **1977** *Sci. Amer.* Sept. 187 (*caption*) Typical task for a traveling-wire EDM is cutting gear teeth... When a slow and complex series of cuts is programmed, it can run unattended for 60 hours.

b. To incorporate (a property) *into* a computer or other device by programming.

1972 CARR & MIZE *MOS/LSI Design & Application* viii. 233 The uniqueness desired within the master PLA chip is often programmed into the master chip by changing only the gate mask. **1977** D. BAGLEY *Enemy* xv. 121 He's installed a scad of microprocessors in that control board... He could program his timetables into them. **1977** *Nature* 11 Aug. 571/3 This book.. deals with the problem of programming 'common sense' into a computer.

5. a. To cause (a computer or other device) automatically to do a prescribed task or perform in a prescribed way; to supply with a program. Also *absol.*

1945 J. P. ECKERT et al. *Description of ENIAC* (PB 86242) (Moore School of Electr. Engin., Univ. of Pennsylvania) B-1 The problem of programming the ENIAC. *Ibid.*, We then wish to program the first accumulator to transmit its contents twice into the second one. **1947** *Proc. IRE* XXXV. 761/1 When an accumulator is programmed to transmit subtractively, it will transmit, not the number it holds, but the complement of the number it holds. **1950** *Phil. Mag.* XLI. 256 (*heading*) Programming a computer for playing chess. **1961** K. AMIS *New Maps of Hell* i. 33 Here an airborne device, programmed to detect and forestall aggressive intentions, ends by prohibiting most kinds of human action. **1962** *Lancet* 8 Dec. 1215/2 The Pegasus computer can be programmed to punch out the desired results on standard teleprinter tape. **1973** *Daily Tel.* 8 Jan. 13 (Advt.), What you get for £505. 1. Full central heating and domestic hot water... 5. Time switch to programme the boiler. **1973** *Sci. Amer.* Sept. 87/1 Cardiographic instruments can be programmed to sound an alarm if an alarming event occurs. **1976** M. M. MANO *Computer System Archit.* ii. 74 For small quantities it is more convenient to use a programmable ROM, referred to as PROM... Each cell in a PROM incorporates a link that can be fused by application of a high current pulse. A broken link in a cell defines one binary state and an unbroken link represents the other state... This allows the user to program the unit in his own laboratory.. to achieve the desired relationship between input address and output data. **1976** *Physics Bull.* Dec. 535/3 The operation is computer controlled so that the mirrors can be programmed to follow a particular source round the sky.

absol. **1954** *Amer. Machinist* 25 Oct. 134/2 Tool Engineers .. will have to learn a new approach to tooling. Instead of designing massive fixtures or intricate mechanical controls, they will 'program'. **1958** *Oxf. Mag.* 29 May 470/1 It is not difficult to learn to program.. backed by regular university lectures in numerical analysis and computing. **1966** *Sci. Amer.* Sept. 72 The ability to write a computer program will become as widespread as the ability to drive a car. Not knowing how to program will be like living in a house full of servants and not speaking their language. **1977** *Daily Tel.* 14 Nov. 8 (Advt.), To program, just read down the column, making the appropriate keyboard entries as you go!

b. *fig.* To train to behave in a predetermined way.

1963 *Language* XXXIX. 455 He succeeded in programming the live bees that crowded around the imitation insect to head in a prescribed direction to seek and find nectar. **1966** L. JONES in A. Chapman *New Black Voices* (1972) 459 We have always been separate, except in our tranced desire to be the thing that oppressed us, after some generations of having been 'programmed'.. into believing that our greatest destiny was to become white people! **1967** *Freedomways* VII. 131 The black student is being educated in this country as if he were being programmed in white supremacy and self-hatred. **1968** *New Scientist* 19 Dec. 653/1 To what extent can astronauts, environmentally be-suited, rigidly programmed, and electrically guided to their destination, be said to resemble the courageous explorers of the past? **1975** A. PRICE *Our Man in Camelot* iv. 71 Your cover is perfect... You were trained and programmed for just such an operation as this. **1976** J. ROSS *I know what it's like to Die* ii. 12 Violent death programmed him to action in a predetermined routine; his reflexes conditioned by his training.

6. *Psychol.* and *Educ.* To form into a teaching programme (PROGRAM, PROGRAMME *sb.* 2 h).

1958 B. F. SKINNER in *Science* 24 Oct. 976/2 When material is adequately programmed, adjacent steps are often so similar that one frame reveals the response to another. **1971** PITTENGER & GOODING *Learning Theories in Educ. Practice* iii. 91 Programming complex behavior requires careful planning and sequencing of material.

7. *intr. Astronaut.* Of a spacecraft: to perform a scheduled and automatically controlled manœuvre.

1958 *Daily Progress* (Charlottesville, Va.) 11 Oct. 1/5 He said the first stage appeared to have 'programmed'—started curving on its trajectory to the northeast—higher than it should. **1962** M. CAIDIN *Man-in-Space Dict.* 156/2 *Programming*, movement of a booster vehicle through assigned trajectory maneuvers in flight, as when a booster launches from a vertical position, then programs over toward horizontal flight. **1962** J. GLENN in *Into Orbit* 189 'We're programming in roll OK,' I said.

‖**programma** (prəʊ'græmə). *Obs.* Pl. **pro'grammata.** [late L. (Cassiodorus, Justinian), a proclamation, manifesto, a. Gr. πρόγραμμα a public written notice, f. προγράφειν to write publicly, f. πρό (see PRO-[2]) + γράφειν to write.]

1. A written notice, proclamation, or edict, posted up in a public place; a public notice. (In *Gr.* and *Rom. Antiq.*, and formerly in universities.)

a **1661** HOLYDAY *Juvenal* 302 Marcilius here understands by *edictum*, not the prætor's edict, but a *programma*, or bill put up by Nero, to signifie, that after dinner he would sing Callirhoe. **1678** WOOD *Life* 6 Dec. (O.H.S.) II. 426 Programma stuck up in every College hall under the vice-chancellor's hand that no scholar abuse the soldiers.. in the night watches that they keep at the Gild hall, Peniless Bench, and at most inns doores. **1693** *Lond. Gaz.* No. 2893/1 Publick Programma's of his Expulsion [from Oxf. Univ.] are already Affixed in the three usual places. **1754** *Def. Rector Exeter Coll.* 13 We will recite the Vice-Chancellor's Programma at large. **1820** SOUTHEY *Wesley* I. 47 The vice-chancellor had, in a *programma*, exhorted the tutors to discharge their duty by double diligence.

b. Such a public notice relating to a function or celebration about to take place, with a list of the proceedings in order; hence, a play-bill, prospectus, syllabus, PROGRAM (sense 2).

1789 M. MADAN tr. *Persius* (1795) 45 *note*, A programma, a kind of play-bill, which was stuck up as ours are, in a morning. **1815** HOBHOUSE *Substance Lett.* (1816) I. 400 A programma of the fête [in France], together with the order from the minister of police was fixed to the walls. **1820** T. MITCHELL *Aristoph.* I. 227 The Prytanes.. before the meeting set up a *programma* in some place of general concourse, in which were contained the matters that were to form the subject of consideration at the ensuing Assembly.

c. An announcement of the subjects to be treated in a course of lectures or studies in a foreign university. (So F. *programme*, Ger. *programm.*)

1787 MATY tr. *Riesbeck's Trav. Germ.* lix. III. 143 When a young man comes here they commonly lay a *Programma* before him, in which all the arts are disposed according to their natural order.

2. A written preface or introduction; in *plural*, = prolegomena.

1711 tr. *Werenfels' Logomachys* 210 Prefaces, Inscriptions, and Programmata abound with Phrases.. worthy Cedar and Gold. **1715** HEARNE in *Rem.* (1857) I. 334 D[r]. Gardiner.. in a silly programma he hath published. **1761** WARTON *Bathurst* 218 [Dr. Bathurst's] programma, on preaching.. is an agreeable and lively piece of writing. **1883** J. RENDEL HARRIS *Stichometry* (1893) 36 The peculiar features of the arrangement of his [Euthalius's] text are prefaces, programmata, lists of quotations with reference to the authors.. from whom they come.

programmable ('prəʊgræməb(ə)l, -'græm-), *a.* and *sb.* Also (*rare*) **programable.** [f. PROGRAM, PROGRAMME *v.* + -ABLE.] **A.** *adj.* Of an apparatus or an operation: capable of being programmed. Also *fig.*

1959 *Times Rev. Industry* May 36/2 The investigating team.. designed a 'push-button office'... Such an arrangement would.. be a data processing system.. not based on a.. programmable computer. **1965** M. FRAYN *Tin Men* ix. 51 Filling up a football coupon is another job which a computer could easily be programmed to do... We have a range of variables which can be identified in advance and manipulated according to predetermined rules. It's programmable. **1967** COX & GROSE *Organization & Handling Bibliogr. Rec. by Computer* 11. 46 With a system such as I have described all the elaborate mechanical and studio devices used to compose pages and flats are now replaced by programmable operations generated by algorithm from simple input instructions. **1971** *Sci. Amer.* Aug. 100/1 (Advt.), Others know us as a computer company: more than 10,000 own our programmable calculators and computers. **1972** CARR & MIZE *MOS/LSI Design & Application* viii. 232 (*caption*) Programable logic array (PLA) contains multiple ROMs and flip-flop feedback elements for sequential logic elements. **1979** *Nature* 13 Sept. 131/2 The laser frequency.. and data recording were controlled by a programable calculator. **1979** B. PETERSON *Peripheral Spy* vi. 157 Predictable, hell! I'm programmable, that's what. Just like a godamned computer.

B. *sb.* A programmable calculator.

1975 *New Scientist* 27 Feb. 506 New handheld programmables will appear in 1975–76 not unlike the HP-65 at as little as £85. **1977** *Sci. Amer.* Apr. 94/2 (Advt.), All our hand-held and portable programmables incorporate HP's special RPN logic system.

Hence **,programma'bility**, the property of being programmable.

1966 *Jrnl. Assoc. Computing Machinery* XIII. 369 (*heading*) Use of multiwrite for general programmability of search memories. **1975** *Daily Tel.* 17 July 7 (Advt.), Programmability overcomes both limitations—and makes a calculator vastly more powerful. **1977** *Sci. Amer.* June 79/1 Programmability transformed the slick slide-rule calculator into an advanced scientific machine.

programmatic (prəʊgræ'mætɪk), *a.* [f. Gr. πρόγραμμα, -γραμματ-, PROGRAM + -IC.] Pertaining to or of the nature of a programme; of the nature of programme music (see PROGRAM *sb.* 4).

1896 *Godey's Mag.* Apr. 422/2 The symphony is not at all programmatic. **1898** *Century Mag.* LV. 777 A 'Bauerntanz' which is rather programmatic. **1904** G. S. GORDON *Let.* 25 Oct. (1943) 4 Pardon this very egotistical and programmatic letter dear Molly. **1935** *B.B.C. Ann.* 81/2 Announcements relating to B.B.C. policy in every respect—programmatic, engineering, or other—are issued. **1937** *Proc. Prehistoric Soc.* III. 265 There is no shortage of programmatic declarations, of resumés of problems and aims. **1941** *Mind* L. 395, I may fitly use these programmatic statements as my text on which to hang the main reflections. **1947** *Proc. IRE* XXXV. 757/1 Both digital and programmatic information must be stored: the machine must be able to remember both the numbers that are operated on and the instructions for performing the operations. **1958** *Listener* 27 Nov. 861/1 No new Pope ever makes what might be called a programmatic speech giving the policies he intends to follow. **1971** S. HERRICK *Astrodynamics* I. vii. 176 Programmatic or program-assisted singularities are destructive bits of sub-programming.. of which two are noteworthy. **1974** *Listener* 24 Jan. 121/3 A symphonic poem along Straussian programmatic lines. **1977** M. GOUDER in J. Hick *Myth of God Incarnate* iv. 65 In the programmatic opening paragraph of Acts, Luke designates the advance of the church as being in four stages. **1979** *Dædalus* Summer 105 Even the most apparently blithe comedies are far more programmatic than a haphazard jumble of anecdotal detail.

So **progra'mmatically** *adv.*, in the manner of a programme or programme music; in accordance with a programme; with regard to a programme; **pro'grammatist**, one who composes or draws up a program (in quots., in senses 2 b and 3).

1895 *Westm. Gaz.* 20 May 7/1 The organised system of gambling, which, so far as the 'programme' of the anti-gamblers is known.. it is the main purpose of the programmatists to suppress. **1899** J. P. POSTGATE in *Classical Rev.* Oct. 359/1 Each program-ist in his turn feels it his duty to set out with a prolix examination of his prolix predecessors. **1947** A. EINSTEIN *Music in Romantic Era* xi. 126 Spohr wrote a 'Characteristic Tone-Painting in the Form of a Symphony'.. which makes use of a poem as the starting-point for revivifying programmatically the traditional form of the symphony. **1952** *Word* VIII. 97 Still other American linguists are programmatically rejecting the strict asseverance of meaning from sound and the exclusion of meaning from linguistic science. **1971** S. HERRICK

Astrodynamics I. vii. 179 Programmatically or computationally, especially with automatic, automaton machinery, there is a great difference. **1974** *Times Lit. Suppl.* 29 Mar. 344/5 Beardsley's admirable drawing and programmatically tortured lettering. **1978** *Nature* 23 Feb. 785/3 The book..offers to approach flow phenomena programmatically in the framework of a general dynamic theory.

programme: see PROGRAM.

programmed (ˈprəʊɡræmd), *ppl. a.* [f. PROGRAM, PROGRAMME *v.* + -ED[1].]

1. Predetermined or controlled by a program (see PROGRAM, PROGRAMME *v.* 4a, 5a, *sb.* 2g). Also *transf.*

1947 *New Republic* 23 June 15/3 The machine, having been properly briefed.., will perform its programmed task. **1953** *Proc. IRE* XLI. 1235/1 A significant new concept in non-numerical computation is the idea of a general-purpose programmed computer—a device capable of carrying out a long sequence of elementary orders analogous to those of a numerical computer. **1958** *Engineering* 28 Feb. 263/2 After taking off vertically..the vehicle veered to the south-east along its programmed trajectory. **1959** E. M. GRABBE et al. *Handbk. Automation, Computation & Control* II. iv. 13 Programmed checks..consist of the verification of the correctness of the system operation by means of special procedures introduced by the system user. **1964** M. MCLUHAN *Understanding Media* (1967) iii. 46 In the new electric Age of Information and programmed production. **1966** P. O'DONNELL *Sabre-Tooth* xviii. 241 Willie nodded, taking the cue and moving into his role like a programmed robot. **1967** D. WILSON in Wills & Yearsley *Handbk. Managem. Technol.* 45 In addition to the validation of input data, internal programmed controls are usually included during computer processing. **1972** M. CRICHTON *Terminal Man* 106 The programmed machine could exceed the capabilities of the programmer. **1974** E. AMBLER *Dr. Frigo* III. 155, I am not referring to the immediate tactical success, but to..the programmed success of the future. **1978** G. A. SHEEHAN *Running & Being* ii. 27 It stripped off those layers of programmed activity and thinking.

2. *Psychol.* and *Educ.* Presented in the form of a teaching programme (PROGRAM, PROGRAMME *sb.* 2h), or employing such a programme.

1958 B. F. SKINNER in *Science* 24 Oct. 975/3 Immediate feedback encourages a more careful reading of programmed material. **1962** *Listener* 23 Aug. 273/2 Hundreds of thousands of Americans..are now being taught by machine, and by what are termed programmed texts. **1963** *Guardian* 15 Jan. 6/1 'Earth in Orbit'..is a geography book with a difference. It is the first programmed textbook of English origin. **1967** *Punch* 22 Mar. 407/2 The shades of Mr. Chips, let alone Dr. Arnold, have long ago fled before an influx of black-maned technicians panning stealthy TV cameras over programmed learning machines. **1967** COULTHARD & SMITH in Wills & Yearsley *Handbk. Managem. Technol.* 204 Programmed learning is already extensively used in this country in schools (teaching mathematics and the sciences), in the armed services, by the airlines, and in companies with extensive training programmes for salesmen, technicians, etc. **1968** *Brit. Universities Ann.* 10 Experiments in programmed teaching have been going on in several institutions notably at Bradford. **1970** W. S. SAHAKIAN *Psychol. of Learning* x. 187 Programmed instruction is designed so that maximal reinforcement ensues by successfully controlling environment. **1974** *Nature* 22 Mar. 300/1 (Advt.), The reader will find that his understanding of the concepts of the subject and his confidence in using them are both developed rapidly as he works through the programmed problems.

programmer (ˈprəʊɡræmə(r)). Also (*rare*) **programer**. [f. PROGRAM, PROGRAMME *sb.* or *v.* + -ER[1].] **1.** One who programmes, in various senses, as: **a.** (s.v. PROGRAM, PROGRAMME *v.*) **b.** One who devises a course of programmed instruction. **c.** One who plans or chooses programmes for broadcasting. **d.** One who arranges something according to a programme.

1890 *Cent. Dict.* s.v., The official programmer of the Jockey Club. **1958** *Science* 24 Oct. 971/1 The machine itself ..is a labor-saving device because it can bring one programmer into contact with an indefinite number of students. **1966** *Listener* 27 Jan. 147/2 It is one of the unwritten laws of programming that even if the same-only-different is to be served up it must be loudly proclaimed to be different; that at least convinces the programmers. **1966** *Punch* 27 July 146/1 It was Baden Powell who revolutionised the process of growing up... Even his most grudging admirers must admit that he was an improvement on witch doctors and tribal elders as a programmer of boys' spare time. **1975** J. DE BRES tr. *Mandel's Late Capitalism* vii. 236 The only means at the disposal of late capitalist economic programmers for the correction of actual development when they deviate from predictions, is State intervention in the economy. **1977** *Daily Tel.* 2 Dec. 16/6 Using a computer device..they can let the programmers know, while the show is in progress, that they are unhappy with what they are viewing as television entertainment. If they are in the majority, it will be taken off the air and replaced by something else. **1978** *Detroit Free Press* 2 Apr. 1C/1 One programer at ABC believes that the show will help ABC's image among those who for religious or other reasons, hold ABC and TV in general responsible for moral decay.

e. *spec.* One who writes computer programs.

1948 *Math. Tables & Other Aids to Computation* III. 45 Magnitudes of numbers at each step have to be studied by the programmer..to avoid exceeding capacity in other operations. **1951** *Electronic Engin.* XXIII. 140/1 Most machines print the results of computations at the will of the programmer by means of some electromechanical device. **1958** *Oxf. Mag.* 29 May 469/1 Numerical analysts and programmers are in great demand in the laboratories of government and industry. **1968** N. CHAPIN *360 Programing in Assembly Lang.* vi. 139 A compiler program causes the computer to accept as input the source program the programer has written... The computer translates the source program..and produces the object program. **1974** *Maclean's Mag.* (Toronto) Jan. 44/3 As any programmer will tell you, a computer is merely as good as the data fed into it. **1980** R. MCCRUM *In Secret State* iii. 12 Quitman was not a trained programmer, but he had been given the standard course in basic computer access methods.

2. = *programme picture* s.v. PROGRAM, PROGRAMME *sb.* 4.

1936 *Movie Mirror* Feb. 118/2 *Frisco Waterfront*... A better-than-average programmer that brings Rod La Rocque back to American films. **1939** *Motion Picture Herald* 11 Nov. 56/1 Very ordinary programmer. It is so simply told as to fail to arouse much for or against criticism. **1974** *Radio Times* 14 Feb. 9/3 When..Montgomery directed this Guadalcanal actionflick, everybody hoped it would certainly be a handsome cut above its other gun-toting rival *Guadalcanal Diary* made in 1943 without the benefit of real locations or scriptwriters. Instead the result was a routine action programmer with Cagney in rather restrained mood.

3. A device that automatically controls the operation of something in accordance with a prescribed programme; in quot. 1945 a part of an early electronic computer analogous to the control unit of later ones.

1945 J. P. ECKERT et al. *Description of ENIAC* (PB 86242) (Moore School of Electr. Engin., Univ. of Pennsylvania) B-2 The use of the master programmer is being stressed since it is the mechanism in the ENIAC which enables one to link the simple sequences of instructions given the other units of the computer into a complex whole. **1962** J. GLENN in *Into Orbit* 143 During the powered phase of flight..an electronic programmer inside the Atlas would guide it along the prescribed path. **1968** *McGraw-Hill Yearbk. Sci. & Technol.* 59 Until the mid-1950s this automation was in the form of special machines with mechanical programmers (cams, levers, and stops, operating in conjunction with powered lead screws) or tracer mechanisms, which cause the cutting tool to follow a path described by simultaneously moving a 'feeler' over a model of the part to be made. **1968** *Which? Guide to Central Heating* 73/1 A programmer is basically a more versatile time switch, which gives you independent control over your room heating and water heating. **1973** *Daily Tel.* 4 Dec. 11/4 If you go out for a few hours turn down the room thermostat or adjust your boiler programmer.

programming (ˈprəʊɡræmɪŋ), *vbl. sb.* Also (*rare*) **programing**. [f. PROGRAM, PROGRAMME *sb.* or *v.* + -ING[1].] †**1.** The writing of programme notes. *Obs. rare.*

1889 G. B. SHAW *London Music in 1888–89* (1937) 243 Sir George patronized everyone in his programming days.

2. *Broadcasting.* The choice, arrangement, or broadcasting of radio or television programmes.

1940 L. R. LOHR *Television Broadcasting* p. ix, The first [part] deals with television in relation to the public, that is, the programing of a television service. **1951** *Broadcasting* 15 Oct. 84/2 ZIV is delighted that NBC has taken this step.. because better programming is good for the entire industry. **1958** B. ULANOV *Hist. Jazz in Amer.* xviii. 226 WNEW, the New York radio station that has proved most adventurous in its programming of popular music. **1960** *News Chron.* 21 Sept. 6/3 Peak-time programming was reduced to the familiar diet of quizzes. **1964** M. MCLUHAN *Understanding Media* (1967) v. 63 TV caused drastic changes in radio programming. **1973** *Guardian* 16 Mar. 10/1 'Complementary programming', the principle on which BBC-2 now gives you a serious programme while BBC-1 has a light one. **1976** *Broadcast* 29 Mar. 10/2 The five station types are defined by size and programming capability.

3. Planning carried out for purposes of control, management, or administration, esp. in economics.

1943 *Sun* (Baltimore) 1 July 14/2 The President transferred from Mr. Jones' RFC to Mr. Wallace's BEW full control over the programming of imported strategic materials. **1959** *Listener* 21 May 884/2 The design of controls, the programming of production methods, and so forth. **1967** E. DUCKWORTH in Wills & Yearsley *Handbk. Managem. Technol.* 117 Operational research in general has to do with the programming function in industry and all the methods described will be found to apply to the programming problems. **1975** J. DE BRES tr. *Mandel's Late Capitalism* vii. 237 There is undoubtedly a certain reciprocal effect, of a both technical and economic character between planning of production and accumulation within individual companies and programming of the economy as a whole.

4. The operation of programming a computer; the writing or preparation of programs; ***programming language*** = LANGUAGE *sb.* 1d.

1945 J. P. ECKERT et al. *Description of ENIAC* (PB 86242) (Moore School of Electr. Engin., Univ. of Pennsylvania) B-1 An elementary programming procedure. **1947** *Electronic Engin.* XIX. 107/1 It remains to show how the automatic sequencing of operations—or programming—is achieved. **1949** *Math. Tables & Other Aids to Computation* III. 376 The most time-consuming factor occurring in the use of the ENIAC is the 'programming' (i.e. setting up the machine for a specific problem). **1954** *Sci. News* XXXIV. 60 The 'programming' of calculations to be done by computors is lengthy and tedious. **1959** *Computer Bull.* II. 81/1 This committee held three meetings starting on 24 January 1958 and discussed many technical details of programming language. **1962** *Lancet* 8 Dec. 1215/1 The final stage of programming must therefore consist in the translation of the flow diagram into actual coded orders which the machine can understand. **1967** *Economist* 8 Apr. 162/1 Programming schools are sprouting up everywhere. **1968** N. CHAPIN (*title*) 360 Programing in assembly language. **1977** *Sci. Amer.* Sept. 236/3 Most of the programming languages in service today were developed as symbolic ways to deal with the hardware-level concepts of the 1950's.

5. *Psychol.* and *Educ.* The preparation and organization of the material necessary to a course of programmed instruction.

1954 B. F. SKINNER in *Harvard Law Rev.* XXIV. 96 In addition to the advantages which can be gained from precise reinforcement and careful programming, the device will teach reading at the same time. **1969** [see LINEAR *a.* 3b]. **1976** W. B. KOLESNIK *Learning* vi. 124 The method of instruction most closely identified with the concept of learning-as-conditioning is commonly referred to as programming. *Ibid.* 125 While programming does sometimes involve the use of mechanical or electronic equipment, it need not do so.

programmist (ˈprəʊɡræmɪst). Also **programist**. [f. PROGRAM, PROGRAMME *sb.* + -IST.] One who writes programme notes.

Found only in the writings of G. B. Shaw.

1888 G. B. SHAW in *Star* 26 Nov. 2/3 The usual Dvorakian dressing of Bohemian rhythms and intervals which give the analytical programmists an opportunity of writing about 'national traits'. **1889** —— *How to become Mus. Critic* (1960) 144 Mr Joseph Bennett, the programist, says of the symphony:—'It has been described by the composer as a "little" work.' **1896** —— *Our Theatres in Nineties* (1932) II. 244 The average programmist would unblushingly write, 'Here the composer..has abruptly introduced the dominant seventh of the key of C major into the key of A flat.'

progrede (prəʊˈɡriːd), *v. nonce-wd.* [ad. L. *prōgredī*: see next.] *intr.* To go forward, advance: opp. to RETROGRADE *v.*

1866 PROCTOR *Handbk. Stars* 7 If the globe were fixed and the other circles named were made slowly to retrograde about the polar axis, the true nature of the variation due to precession would be illustrated; but as regards the variation itself, we should..obtain as effectual an illustration by making the globe progrede about the polar axis.

progredient (prəʊˈɡriːdɪənt), *a.* (*sb.*) *rare.* ? *Obs.* [ad. L. *prōgrediens, -entem*, pr. pple. of *prōgredī* to go forward, proceed, f. *prō*, PRO-[1] 1d + *gradī* to step, walk, go.] Going forward, advancing. **b.** as *sb.* One who advances. So † **proˈgrediency**, the quality or action of going forward, progress.

1650 BULWER *Anthropomet.* 131 An Index..of the Masculine generative faculty; and of that either erumpent, and progredient, or consumed. **1650** HUBBERT *Pill Formality* 54 He that is no Progredient, must needs be a Retrogredient. **1701** BEVERLEY *Apoc. Quest.* 10 The Continuation, and Progrediency of the Fourth, or Roman Monarchy.

progress (ˈprəʊɡrɪs, ˈprɒɡrɪs, -ɡrɛs), *sb.* Forms: 5–7 **progresse**, 6 **progres**, (**prograsse**, 7 **prograce**), 7– **progress**. [In 15th c. *progresse*, app. a. obs. F. *progresse* (Lett. of Louis XII, 1513 in Godef.), repr. a Romanic ***progressa**, fem. sb. from *progressus, -a, -um*, pa. pple. of *prōgredī* (see PROGREDIENT). In Fr. and Eng. the word subsequently became *progrès, progress*, by conformation to L. *progressus* a going forward, advance, progress. Cf. *egress, ingress, regress.*

a **1892** TENNYSON in Ld. Tennyson *Mem.* (1897) II. 35 Someone spoke of Diplŏmăcy and Prōgress. 'Oh!', said my father, 'why do you pronounce the word like that? pray give the ō long.']

1. a. The action of stepping or marching forward or onward; onward march; journeying, travelling, travel; a journey, an expedition. Now *rare.*

c **1475** *Partenay* 3199 Off me the werre the Giaunt doth desire, Anon shall I go hym Assail quikly. To thys forth-progresse Geffray made redy. **1590** SPENSER *F.Q.* III. xi. 20 So forth they both yfere make their progresse. **1616** R. C. *Times' Whistle* VI. 2599 It was my fortune with..others.. One summers day a progresse for to goe Into the countrie. **1621** BURTON *Anat. Mel.* II. ii. IV. (1651) 269 The most pleasant of all outward pastimes, is..to make a petty progress, a merry journey. **1678** BUNYAN (*title*) The Pilgrim's Progress from this world, to that which is to come. **1745** P. THOMAS *Jrnl. Anson's Voy.* 160 The Officers and People made a Progress round the Island. **1838** THIRLWALL *Greece* V. xl. 123 Their progress through the Persian provinces was a kind of triumph.

†**b.** *transf.* A region or distance traversed.

1601 R. JOHNSON *Kingd. & Commw.* (1603) 219 His dominion..stretcheth from the promontorie Bayador to Tanger, and from the Atlantike Ocean to the riuer Muluia. In which progresse is conteined the best portion of all Afrike.

2. *spec.* **a.** A state journey made by a royal or noble personage, or by a church dignitary; a visit of state; also, the official tour made by judges and others, a circuit; an official visitation of its estates by a college. Now somewhat *archaic.*

1461 *Rolls of Parlt.* V. 475/2 The Kyng..beyng in his progresse in the seid Counte. **1503–4** *Act 19 Hen. VII*, c. 7 §1 The justices of assises in ther cyrcuyte or progresse in that shyre. **1568** GRAFTON *Chron.* II. 597 In the time of King Henry the sixt..as he roade in Progresse. *a* **1648** LD. HERBERT *Hen. VIII* (1683) 132 Synodal Judges, going Progress yearly under pretext of Visitation. **1795** *Order of Audit Magd. Coll. Oxf.* 18 Feb., That Bills on Country Banks be accepted on the Progresses, but that the Bursars be desired to negotiate them as soon as possible. **1796** MORSE *Amer. Geog.* II. 99 Comprehended in six circuits, or annual progress of the judges. **1811** *Order Magd. Coll.* 4 June, That the Norfolk Progress do take place this year and at the expiration of three years from this time. **1849** MACAULAY *Hist. Eng.* v. I. 593 He was President of Wales and lord lieutenant of four English counties. His official tours..were scarcely inferior in pomp to royal progresses. **1901** RASHDALL & RAIT *New College* 251 New College is one of the few Colleges in which an annual 'Progress' still takes place. The Warden (or Sub-warden) accompanied by a Fellow known as 'Out-rider'..and the Steward, visit the farms on some part of the College estates.

†**b.** A state procession. *Obs.*

1533 CRANMER in Ellis *Orig. Lett.* Ser. I. II. 37 Whyche said Progresse..extendid half a myle in leyngthe by estimacion. **1613** HAYWARD *Norm. Kings* Pref., At his returne from the Progresse to his house at S. James, these pieces were delivered unto him. **1859** JEPHSON *Brittany* iii. 35 Where the Emperor was about to expose himself in a public hall and progress.

3. a. Onward movement in space; course, way.

1595 SHAKS. *John* II. i. 340 Vnlesse thou let his siluer Water keepe A peacefull progresse to the Ocean. **1601** —— *Jul. C.* II. i. 2, I cannot, by the progresse of the Starres, Giue guesse how neere to day. **1667** MILTON *P.L.* XI. 175 For see the Morn..begins Her rosie progress smiling. **1683** MOXON *Mech. Exerc.*, *Printing* xi. ¶1 If the Cheeks of the Press stand wide assunder, the sweep or progress of the..Bar will be greater than if they stand nearer together. **1712–14** POPE *Rape Lock* v. 132 The Sylphs..pursue its progress thro' the skies. **1754** GRAY *Poesy* 4 A thousand rills their mazy progress take. **1878** BROWNING *La Saisiaz* 42 Up and up we went... Call progress toilsome?

b. *fig.* Going on, progression; course or process (of action, events, narrative, time, etc.). ***in progress***: proceeding, taking place, happening.

1432–50 tr. *Higden* (Rolls) I. 395 The auctor of this presente Cronicle towchethe in his progresse other processe rather Wales then Englonde. *Ibid.* VI. 353 Of the begynnynge, progresse, and ende [of] whom [orig. *de cujus initio, progressu, et fine*] hit is to be advertisede [etc.]. **1526** *Pilgr. Perf.* (W. de W. 1531) 26 Of the iewes & theyr progresse we may lerne. **1613** SHAKS. *Hen. VIII*, v. iii. 33 In all the Progresse Both of my Life and Office, I haue labour'd ..that [etc.]. **1664** POWER *Exp. Philos.* III. 155 This virtue decayes in progress of Time (as all Odours do). **1785** REID *Intell. Powers* II. xxi, So rapid is the progress of the thought. **1849** MACAULAY *Hist. Eng.* ii. I. 179 While these changes were in progress. **1891** *Speaker* 2 May 534/1 To trace the progress of chemical knowledge and research from the earliest times.

4. a. Forward movement in space (as opposed to rest or regress); going forward, advance.

1500–20 DUNBAR *Poems* lxxxii. 52 Through streittis nane may mak progres [*rimes* incres, les], For cry of cruikit, blind, and lame. *a* **1656** USSHER *Ann.* vi. (1658) 773 Whose progresse and regresse in this journey we here set down out of Strabo. **1669** STURMY *Mariner's Mag.* IV. xvi. 200 After some progress made in your Voyage. **1784** COWPER *Task* I. 330 The folded gates would bar my progress now. **1877** BRYCE *Transcaucasia* (1896) 35 The same sense of motion without progress, which those who have crossed the ocean know so well.

b. *fig.* Going on to a further or higher stage, or to further or higher stages successively; advance, advancement; growth, development, continuous increase; usually in good sense, advance to better and better conditions, continuous improvement.

1603 KNOLLES *Hist. Turks* (1638) To Rdr., If you consider the beginning, progresse and perpetuall felicitie of this the Othoman Empire. **1686** tr. *Chardin's Trav. Persia* 24 Having made no farther progress in his Business. **1713** ADDISON *Guardian* No. 104 ¶7, I am ashamed that I am not able to make a quicker progress through the French tongue. **1742** YOUNG *Nt. Th.* IX. 1957 Nature delights in progress; in advance From worse to better: but, when minds ascend, Progress, in part, depends upon themselves. **1846** TRENCH *Mirac.* Introd. (1862) 38 The very idea of God's kingdom is that of progress, of a gradually fuller communication..of Himself to men. *a* **1862** BUCKLE *Misc. Wks.* (1872) I. 349 As civilization advances, the progress of manufactures greatly outstrips the progress of agriculture. **1874** GREEN *Short Hist.* vii. §5. 393 The moral and religious change which was passing over the country through the progress of Puritanism.

†**5.** A coming forth or proceeding *from* a source. (Cf. PROGRESSION 5.) *Obs. rare.*

c **1530** *Crt. of Love* 1067 Love is a vertue clere, And from the soule his progress holdeth he.

6. *Sc. Law.* In full, ***progress of*** (***title***) ***deeds*** or ***progress of titles***: 'such a series of the title-deeds of a landed estate, or other heritable subject, as is sufficient in law to constitute a valid and effectual feudal title thereto' (W. Bell *Dict. Law Scot.*).

1593 *Sc. Acts Jas. VI* (1816) IV. 11/2 James lindsay of barcloy pronevoy and air be progres to vmqle Johnne lindsay of wauchoip his grandschir. **1693** STAIR *Inst. Law Scot.* (ed. 2) IV. xxxviii. §19. 660 Titles by Progress, are either Retours on services of Heirs, or Confirmations of Executors, or Assignations [etc.]..from whence the conclusion of the Summons is justly and legally inferred. *a* **1722** FOUNTAINHALL *Decis.* (1759) I. 4 In buying of land, men crave a forty years clear progress, and with that think themselves secure, by the grand act of prescription 1617. **1832** SCOTT *St. Ronan's* Introd., Removed..from his legal folios and progresses of title deeds, from his counters and shelves. **1838** W. BELL *Dict. Law Scot.* s.v., Where the seller is able to show an unencumbered title..extending backwards for forty years,..the purchaser is bound to accept of this as a sufficient progress. **1868** *Act 31 & 32 Vict.* c. 101 §9 Any conveyance..forming part of the progress of title deeds of the said lands. **1874** *Act 37 & 38 Vict.* c. 94 §4 (1) When lands have been feued..It shall not ..be necessary..that he shall obtain from the superior any charter, precept, or other writ by progress.

7. *attrib.* and *Comb.*, as ***progress clerk***, ***committee***, ***department***, ***-killing***, ***man***, ***manager***, ***-paralysing***, ***payment***, adjs.; †**progress-bed**, (?) a portable bed used on a progress; †**progress block** (BLOCK *sb.* 4 b), ? the block or pattern of hat introduced for a royal progress; **progress chaser**, an employee responsible for ensuring that work is done efficiently and to schedule (cf. CHASER[1] 7); hence **progress-chasing**; †**progress house**, a temporary place of shelter erected on a journey; †**progress laundress**, a laundress employed during a progress; **progress report**, an interim report on progress made to date; †**progress-time**, the time of a royal progress.

1586 *Will of G. Scott* (Somerset Ho.), A *prograsse bedd. *c* **1614** FLETCHER, etc. *Wit at sev. Weapons* IV. i, This broad-brimm'd hat Of the last *progress block, with the young hat-band. **1939** *Daily Tel.* 18 Dec. 12/6 (Advt.), *Progress chasers wanted for aircraft work. **1943** J. B. PRIESTLEY *Daylight on Saturday* vii. 41 Even my friend Mona takes to it [*sc.* factory work] better than I do. You know she's a progress chaser now, don't you? **1977** *Lancashire Life* Mar. 49/1 The imminent threat of war found Arthur Lowe, progress chaser with Fairey Aviation, joining the Duke of Lancaster's Own Yeomanry in Manchester. **1943** J. B. PRIESTLEY *Daylight on Saturday* viii. 52 Doesn't matter what we do here—*progress chasing and..all the rest of it —we can't keep 'em to the high level. **1971** R. LEWIS *Fenokee Project* i. 10 Pete dealt with the progress chasing on outstanding contracts. **1921** *Dict. Occup. Terms* (1927) §939 **Progress clerk*,..traces and pushes forward work in its various stages from operation to operation until it is ready for delivery... Keeps a record of output, etc., in works. **1942** A. P. JEPHCOTT *Girls growing Up* iv. 77 A progress clerk ..is conscious of the superiority of her life over that of a girl who does a petty routine job all day. **1974** *Evening News* (Edinburgh) 8 Oct. 11/4 (Advt.), *Progress clerk*, £1600 plus, have you previous experience in electronics? **1914** E. T. ELBOURNE *Factory Admin. & Accounts* II. 39 (*heading*) **Progress Committee*—under Works Manager. **1925** C. L. BOLLING *Commerc. Managem.* x. 148 The managerial staff or '*progress department' will put into operation the plans of the advisory staff. **1932** S. E. THOMAS *Commerce* xxvii. 394 It is the duty of the Progress Department to follow up the various processes, to prepare job cards, material charts, etc. *a* **1631** DONNE *Serm.* (1839) IV. 177 The Tabernacle itself was but *mobilis domus*, and *ecclesia portabilis*,..a running, a *progress house. **1902** *Monthly Rev.* Oct. 46 A narrow *progress-killing formalism. **1624** MASSINGER *Parl. Love* II. i, I myself shall have..Of *progress laundresses, and market-women,..a thousand bills Preferr'd against me. **1922** *Progress man [see CHASER[1] 7]. **1957** C. SMITH *Case of Torches* ii. 26 The small offices..where the engineers and draughtsmen and progress men pored..over their columns of figures. **1925** C. L. BOLLING *Commerc. Managem.* x. 152 Each job undertaken is notified to the *progress manager. **1932** S. E. THOMAS *Commerce* xxvii. 388 The executives under the works manager may include..a *Progress Manager*, who sees that the plans of the production manager or of the planner are carried into effect and that no unnecessary delays take place as the work passes from one process to another. **1893** B. O. FLOWER in *Arena* Mar. 509 The *progress-paralyzing miasma of creeds. **1959** *Wall St. Jrnl.* 12 June 3/1 The change will affect companies that receive '*progress payments'—funds advanced by the Government, usually monthly, to help offset a company's costs as it carries out major contracts. **1977** *Herald* (Melbourne) 17 Jan. 2/6 The company had obtained nearly $120,000 in progress payments but had completed only one contract in that period it was alleged. **1929** SAUNDERS & ANDERSON *Business Reports* iv. 43 *Progress report is another report which may be limited to time, place, and handling of data similar to the informational report. **1943** J. B. PRIESTLEY *Daylight on Saturday* xxv. 189 Cheviot was now frowning hard at the progress reports on his desk. **1972** 'E. FERRARS' *Breath of Suspicion* iii. 38 So, if I see her again, you want a sort of progress report. **1607** BEAUMONT *Woman Hater* III. ii, To..make some fine jests upon country people in *progress-time.

progress (prəʊ'grɛs; see below), *v.* [f. prec. sb. So mod.F. *progresser* (neologism in Littré).

Common in England *c* 1590–1670, usually stressed like the sb., '*progress*. In 18th c. obs. in England, but app. retained (or formed anew) in America, where it became very common *c* 1790, with stress *pro'gress* (cf. *di'gress, trans'gress*). Thence readopted in England after 1800 (Southey 1809); but often characterized as an Americanism, and much more used, until later 20th c., in America than in U.K., in sense 3, in which ordinary English usage said 'go on', 'proceed'.]

1. a. *intr.* To make a 'progress' or journey; to journey, travel; *spec.* to make a state journey, travel ceremoniously, as a royal, noble, or official personage. Now *rare* or *Obs.*, or merged in 2.

c **1590** GREENE *Fr. Bacon* iv. 56 We'll progress straight to Oxford with our trains. **1607** ROWLANDS *Diog. Lanth.* 22 The Owle being weary of the night Would progresse in the Sunne. *c* **1620** Z. BOYD *Zion's Flowers* (1855) 61 He's like a mighty King, About his countreye stately progressing. **1648** EARL OF WESTMORELAND *Otia Sacra* (1879) 62 Pave me a Golden Tract to Progress in. *a* **1662** HEYLIN *Laud* 139 His Majesty progresseth towards the West.

†**b.** *trans.* To travel through; to traverse. *Obs.*

1596 DRAYTON *Leg.* i. 601 Who should have progres'd all a Kingdomes space. **1635** QUARLES *Embl.* IV. xii, When my soule had progrest ev'ry place, That love and deare affection could contrive. **1641** MILTON *Reform.* II. Wks. 1851 III. 71 Progressing the datelesse and irrevoluble Circle of Eternity.

2. *intr.* To go or move forward or onward; to proceed, make one's way, advance.

1595 SHAKS. *John* v. ii. 46 Let me wipe off this honourable dewe, That siluerly doth progresse on thy cheekes. **1624** FORD *Sun's Darling* v. i, Progress o'er the year Again, my Raybright; therein like the Sun. **1808** SCHULTZ *Trav.* (1810) II. 170 In this manner..the head [of an island] is continually progressing up the [Mississippi] river, while the lower part is proportionably wasting away. **1832** R. H. FROUDE in *Rem.* (1838) I. 359 The poor Italian, canoe, niggers, and all..were seen again about thirty yards off progressing with the crest of the wave towards the beach. **1857** THOREAU *Maine W.* (1894) 383 We had been busily progressing all day.

3. *fig.* Of action or an agent: To go on, proceed, advance; to be carried on as an action; to carry on an action.

1607 DAY *Trav. Eng. Bro.* (1881) 17 As sure as day doth progress towards night. *a* **1614** DONNE *Βιαθανατος* (1648) 213 As farre as I allowed my Discourse to progresse in this way. **1791** WASHINGTON *Lett.* Writ. 1891 XII. 52 The business of laying out the city..is progressing. **1837** LOWELL *Lett.* (1894) I. 17 'Tis a pretty good subject, but I find it enlarging as I progress. **1864** DASENT *Jest & Earnest* (1873) II. 41 If the work had progressed as it began, there ought to have been nine. **1906** J. A. HATTON *Pilgr. in Region Faith* iii. 137 The controversy is progressing.

b. *Mus.* Of melody or harmony: To proceed from one note or chord to another; cf. PROGRESSION 8 a.

1890 in *Cent. Dict.*

4. *fig.* To make progress; to proceed to a further or higher stage, or to further or higher stages continuously; to advance, get on; to develop, increase; usually, to advance to better conditions, to go on or get on well, to improve continuously.

1610 B. JONSON *Alch.* II. iii, Nor can this remote matter, sodainly Progresse so from extreme, vnto extreme, As to grow gold, and leape ore all the meanes. **1632** MARMION *Holland's Leaguer* II. iv, I began Betimes, and so progrest from less to bigger. **1791** WASHINGTON *Lett.* Writ. 1891 XII. 24 Our country..is fast progressing in its political importance and social happiness. **1796** *Ibid.* 1892 XIII. 354 The pleasure of hearing you were well..and progressing.. in your studies. **1809** SOUTHEY *Let. to G. C. Bedford* 30 Apr., Another state of being, in which there shall be no other change than that of progressing in knowledge. **1828** HAWTHORNE *Fanshawe* x, Her convalescence had so far progressed. **1832** MISS MITFORD *Village* Ser. v. 76 (*Widow Gentlewoman*) In country towns..society has been progressing (if I may borrow that expressive Americanism) at a very rapid rate. **1840** GLADSTONE *Ch. Princ.* 11 It may ..be the case that..we are actually progressing in some particulars while we retrograde in others. **1885** *Law Rep.* 10 *P.D.* 97 The melancholia had markedly progressed.

b. To proceed, as the terms or items of a series, from less to greater; to form an advancing series.

1868 HERSCHEL in *People's Mag.* Jan. 62 Squares of clear window-glass..regularly progressing in size by quarter or half inches in the side.

5. To come forth or issue *from* a source: = PROCEED *v.* 7 b. *rare.* (Cf. PROGRESS *sb.* 5.)

1850 NEALE *Med. Hymns* (1867) 179 Holy Ghost from Both progressing.

6. *trans.* To cause to move onward or advance; to push forward. *lit.* and *fig.* Also, *spec.* to cause (work, etc.) to make regular progress towards completion.

1875 *Ure's Dict. Arts* II. 131 (Dressing of Ores) The heavier portion is progressed across the table, and passed into an ore bin. **1887** *N.Y. Tribune* 7 Mar. (Cent. Dict.), Urging that the bills..be progressed as rapidly as possible. **1954** 'N. SHUTE' *Slide Rule* 184, I was chiefly occupied..in progressing the design and construction of the factory at Portsmouth. **1965** E. GOWERS *Fowler's Mod. Eng. Usage* (ed. 2) 479/2 *Progress... Prō'grĕs* is usual for the transitive verb, now much used in the manufacturing and building industries in the sense of pushing a job forward by regular stages. **1976** *Southern Even. Echo* (Southampton) 16 Nov. 13/2 (Advt.), Purchasing Administrator to work in busy spares section. Placing and progressing orders. **1978** *Observer* 12 Feb. 12/3 Welders to be trained to make more tack items to allow them to progress their own work to completion.

Hence **pro'gressed** *ppl. a.*, advanced; **pro'gressing** *vbl. sb.* and *ppl. a.*

1850 T. EDWARDS *Eng. Welsh Dict.* Addr., To meet the progressed state of the Arts and Sciences. **1850** BROWNING *Easter Day* xiv, Your progressing is slower. **1870** DICKENS *E. Drood* iii, The most agreeable evidences of progressing life in Cloisterham. **1874** THIRLWALL *Lett.* (1881) II. 304 The steadily progressing failure of my eyesight.

progression (prəʊ'grɛʃən). [a. F. *progression* (1425 in Hatz.-Darm.), ad. L. *prōgressiōn-em* a going forward, advancement, progression, n. of action f. *prōgred-ī*: see PROGREDIENT.]

1. The action of stepping or moving forward or onward. †**a.** Travel; a journey: = PROGRESS *sb.* 1. *Obs.*

c **1440** CAPGRAVE *Life St. Kath.* III. 280 Vndyr your wenge and youre proteccyon May be this viage and this progression. *a* **1548** HALL *Chron.*, *Rich. III* 53 There happened in this progression to the Earle of Richmond a straunge chaunce. *Ibid.*, *Hen. VII* 42 b, When they were with their long and tedyous iourney weried and tyred, and.. fell to repentaunce of their mad commocion and frantike progression, then he woulde..circumuent & enuyron theim.

b. Onward or forward movement (in space), locomotion; advance: = PROGRESS *sb.* 3 a, 4 a.

1588 SHAKS. *L.L.L.* IV. ii. 144 A Letter..which accidentally, or by the way of progression, hath miscarried. **1651–3** JER. TAYLOR *Serm. for Year* (1678) 54 Still the Flood [tide] crept by little steppings, and invaded more by his progressions than he lost by his retreat. **1686** GOAD *Celest. Bodies* III. i. 366, I observ'd it making a creeping Progression in the Valleys. **1849** *Sk. Nat. Hist.*, *Mammalia* III. 202 The tusks of this animal [walrus]..are instruments both of defence and of progression. **1883** *Century Mag.* XXVI. 925 This mode of progression requires some muscular exertion.

c. The moving or pushing *of* something onward.

1678 MOXON *Mech. Exerc.* v. 95 The longer to continue his several Progressions of the Saw.

2. *fig.* Continuous action figured or conceived as onward movement; going on, course (of action, time, life, etc.), proceeding, process. Now *rare* or merged in 4.

1474 CAXTON *Chesse* 133 The progressyon and draughtes of the..playe of the chesse. **1586** A. DAY *Eng. Secretary* I. (1625) 41 In all the progression of the wished life of this mighty Prince. *Ibid.* 43 Progression, continuation and determination of his most wicked and shamelesse life. **1646** SIR T. BROWNE *Pseud. Ep.* 226 All Starres that have their distance from the Ecliptick Northward not more then 23 degrees and an half..may in progression of time have declination Southward. **c 1698** LOCKE *Cond. Underst.* §20 The long Progression of the Thoughts to remote and first Principles. **1775** JOHNSON *Tax. no Tyr.* 5 Having..obtained by the slow progression of manual industry the accommodations of life. **1882** STEVENSON *Fam. Stud. Men & Bks., Thoreau* iii, There is a progression—I cannot call it a progress—in his work toward a more and more strictly prosaic level.

3. *fig.* The action of passing successively from each item or term of a series to the next; succession; a series; ***in*** (†***by***) ***progression***, in succession, one after another; gradually. (See also 6.)

1549 *Compl. Scot.* vi. 47, & sa be progressione and ordur, euyrie spere inclosis the spere that is nerest tyl it. **1660** F. BROOKE tr. *Le Blanc's Trav.* 397 The Brasilians are said originally to have come..from Peru, advancing thither by progression from time to time. **1690** LOCKE *Hum. Und.* II. xxix. §16 Of the Bulk of the Body, to be thus infinitely divided after certain Progressions,..we have no clear..Idea. **1774** BEATTIE *Minstr.* II. xlvii, The laws..Whose long progression leads to Deity. **1844** SOUTHEY *Life A. Bell* I. 175 The experiment which..had been tried..with one class, was..extended to all the others in progression.

4. *fig.* The action of going forward to more advanced or higher stages or conditions; advance; development; = PROGRESS *sb.* 4 b. Also *attrib.*

1586 A. DAY *Eng. Secretary* I. (1625) 37 His..knowledge in the Latine tongue, was so perfect, his progression in the Greeke so excellent. **1631** MASSINGER *Believe as you List* II. ii, I must..take..the boldness To reprehend your slow progression in Doing her greatness right. **a 1713** ELLWOOD *Autobiog.* (1714) 133 Having inquired divers things of me, with respect to my former Progression in Learning. **1829** I. TAYLOR *Enthus.* viii. 184 The progression of decay and perversion has been gradually and distinctly contemplated. **1871** TYLOR *Prim. Cult.* I. ii. 34 The progression-theory recognizes degradation, and the degradation-theory recognizes progression. **1877** A. B. EDWARDS *Up Nile* v. 105 To trace the progression and retrogression of the arts from the Pyramid-builders to the Cæsars.

†**5.** ? The action of proceeding forth or issuing; the fact of being produced. (Cf. PROCESSION *sb.* 4, PROGRESS *sb.* 5.) *Obs. rare.*

c 1374 CHAUCER *Boeth.* IV. pr. vi. 106 (Camb. MS.) Thilke same ordre newith ayein alle thinges growynge and fallynge a-down by semblable progression [*gloss*, issu] of sedes and of sexes. **c 1386** —— *Knt.'s T.* 2155 His ordinaunce That speces of thynges and progressions Shullen enduren by successions And nat eterne.

6. *Math.* The succession of a series of quantities, between every two successive terms of which there is some particular constant relation; such a series itself. See ARITHMETICAL *a.*, GEOMETRICAL 1 b, HARMONIC *a.* 5 a.

c 1430 *Art Nombryng* 13 Of progressioun one is naturelle or contynuelle, þat oþer broken and discontynuelle. **1542** RECORDE *Gr. Artes* (1575) 210 Arithmeticall progression is a rehearsing..of many numbers..in suche sorte, that betweene euery two next numbers..the difference be equall. *Ibid.* 229 Progression Geometricall is when the numbers increase by a like proportion. **1692** WASHINGTON tr. *Milton's Def. Pop.* vii. M.'s Wks. 1851 VII. 179 Do you not understand Progression in Arithmetick? **1763** EMERSON *Meth. Increments* 74 A series of quantities, whose construction and progression is known. **1764** BURN *Poor Laws* 153 Families..will continually increase in a kind of geometrical progression. **1884** tr. *Lotze's Metaph.* 455 Where the intensity of a sensation increases by equal differences, that is, in arithmetical progression, it implies in the strength of the stimulus an increase in geometrical progression.

7. *Astr.* **a.** Movement of a planet in the order of the zodiacal signs, i.e. from west to east; direct movement; opp. to *retrogradation.* †**b.** ***month of progression*** (*obs.*): see quot. 1615.

1551 RECORDE *Cast. Knowl.* (1556) 279 The progression, retrogradation, and station of the Planetes. **1615** CROOKE *Body of Man* 336 The moneth of Progression he calleth that space which commeth betweene one coniunction of the Moone with the Sunne and another, and it conteyneth nine and twenty dayes and a halfe. **1646** SIR T. BROWNE *Pseud. Ep.* 212. **1812** WOODHOUSE *Astron.* xix. 207 *note*, Progression is here..used technically: a motion *in consequentia*, or, according to the order of the signs.

8. *Mus.* **a.** The action of passing (in melody) from one note to another, or (in harmony) from one chord to another; a succession of notes or chords. **b.** Sometimes = SEQUENCE *sb.*

1609 DOULAND *Ornith. Microl.* 29 An authenticall progression, is the ascending beyond the Finall Key to an eight, and a tenth. **1694** W. HOLDER *Harmony* vi. (1731) 95 Degrees are uncompounded Intervals,..by which an immediate Ascent or Descent is made from the Unison to the Octave..; and by the same Progression to as many Octaves as there may be Occasion. **1877** STAINER *Harmony* v. §69 In harmonising such a progression as the following [etc.]. **1889** PROUT *Harmony* iv. §102 Such progressions are called 'hidden' octaves or fifths.

9. *Philol.* Advance in sound-development.

1877 MARCH *Comp. Gram. Ags. Lang.* 27 The first lengthening of *i* and *u* by progression is called *guna.*

10. *Spectroscopy.* A series of regularly spaced lines or bands in a spectrum which arise from transitions to or from a series of energy levels having consecutive quantum numbers.

1926 *Physical Rev.* XXVIII. 638 In other words we suppose that the absorption bands whose stimulation is associated with these series all belong to a single n' progression. **1949** P. PRINGSHEIM *Fluorescence & Phosphorescence* ii. 136 If all excited molecules of a vapor are in one definite vibrational level v' of an electronic state T', they can return from there to all existing levels v'' of the ground state and thus produce an emission spectrum in which the lines corresponding to $v'' = 0, 1, 2$..form a regular 'progression'. **1965** R. N. DIXON *Spectroscopy & Struct.* vi. 129 When an electronic spectrum is studied in absorption at moderate temperatures most of the molecules in the lower state will be in the vibrational level with $v'' = 0$, and the vibrational structure will consist of one series of bands, corresponding to consecutive values of v'. Such a series is called a progression. The bands are labelled v'-v''. Thus the absorption series 0–0, 1–0, 2–0, 3–0..is a progression in the upper state vibration frequency. **1976** *Chem. Physics Lett.* XLI. 289/2 The Raman spectrum is completely dominated by an intense band at 316 cm^{-1} and its associated overtone progression.

progressional (prəʊˈgrɛʃənəl), *a.* [f. prec. + -AL[1].] Of, pertaining to, or involving progression (in various senses: see prec.).

1570 DEE *Math. Pref.* C j b, The Venetians consideration of waight..by eight descentes progressionall, halfing, from a grayne. **1665** J. GADBURY *Lond. Deliv. Predicted* iv. 21 Venus hath a progressional motion. **1674** JEAKE *Arith.* (1696) 543 To find Numbers whose Remains shall be Arithmetically Progressional. **1800** *Hull Advertiser* 20 Sept. 2/2 Progressional Building Society. **1867** MACFARREN *Harmony* iii. (1876) 87 Its progressional treatment. **1883** F. A. WALKER *Pol. Econ.* 451 There is, M. Garnier holds, a species of increasing taxation which is rational and discreet, to which he applies the term progressional, which is held within moderate limits.

Hence **proˈgressionally** *adv.*

1658 SIR T. BROWNE *Gard. Cyrus* v. 69 So progressionally ..that from five in the foreclaw she [Nature] descendeth unto two in the hindemost.

proˈgressionary, *a. rare.* [f. as prec. + -ARY.] Of or pertaining to progression.

1859 G. MEREDITH *R. Feverel* I. iv. 62 The youth's progressionary phases were mapped out in sections, from Simple Boyhood to the Blossoming Season. *Ibid.* xv. 220 These further progressionary developments.

progressionist (prəʊˈgrɛʃənɪst). [See -IST.]

1. An advocate of or believer in progression or progress; a progressist, a progressive.

1849 *Fraser's Mag.* XL. 391 Opposed to the influence of her unconscious Toryism, a Progressionist of susceptible temperament might be in danger of abandoning his opinions. **1854** *Blackw. Mag.* LXXV. 349 None but liberals or progressionists need apply. **1883** *Standard* 28 Mar. 3/4 Old-fashioned opera is not the lifeless thing which progressionists would seek to make out. **1886** S. L. LEE *Life Ld. Herbert* Introd. 40 A sure sign that Herbert was a sincere progressionist.

2. One who holds that life on the earth has been marked by gradual progression from lower to higher forms.

1859 H. SPENCER in *Universal Review* July 81 Sir R. Murchison, who is a Progressionist, calls the lowest fossiliferous strata, 'Protozoic'. **1867** —— *Princ. Biol.* III. §140 Were the geological record complete, or did it, as both Uniformitarians and Progressionists have habitually assumed, give us traces of the earliest organic forms.

3. (See quots.) *rare*⁻⁰.

1864 WEBSTER, *Progressionist*, one who holds to the progression of society toward perfection. **1882** OGILVIE (Annandale), *Progressionist.* 1. One who maintains the doctrine that society is in a state of progress towards perfection, and that it will ultimately attain to it.

4. *attrib.* or as *adj.*

1871 TYLOR *Prim. Cult.* I. ii. 29 The unprejudiced modern student of the progressionist school. **1883** *Athenæum* 8 Sept. 305/2 The progressionist tendency of the age.

So **proˈgressionism**, the theory or principles of a progressionist, or sympathy with progress.

1861 BERESF. HOPE *Eng. Cathedr. 19th C.* 143 That wise spirit of moderate and retrospective progressionism.

progressism (ˈprəʊgrɪsɪz(ə)m). [f. PROGRESS *sb.* + -ISM.] = PROGRESSIONISM.

1921 R. BOSANQUET *Meeting of Extremes in Contemp. Phil.* 206 Men do not, under the influence of such progressism, admit that some one or more climaxes of the finite may have been attained in the past. **1922** W. R. INGE *Outspoken Ess.* 2nd Ser. 26 The 'Progressism' of much modern thought is a poor substitute for this belief in the substantial reality of the eternal values.

progressist (ˈprəʊgrɪsɪst, ˈprɒg-). [ad. F. *progressiste* = Sp. *progresista*, It. *progressista*: see PROGRESS *sb.* and -IST.] One who favours or advocates progress, esp. in political or social matters; a reformer, a progressive. (In later use chiefly in reference to foreign countries.)

For a short period *c* 1890, the term was used in London Municipal politics, but soon superseded by *progressive*: see PROGRESSIVE *a.* 4.

1848 O. A. BROWNSON *Wks.* (1884) V. 247 Socialists and progressists attempt..to defend it on humanistic principles. **1856** T. A. TROLLOPE *Girlhood Cath. de Medici* 105 The two natural and inevitable parties..conservatives and progressists. **1884** *Harper's Mag.* May 831/2 These Arabs.. were the progressists of Europe. **1890** *Illustr. Lond. News* Christmas No. 3/2 A most determined Progressist in the City Council. **1891** *Tablet* 29 Aug. 324 The citizens of Sion and those of Granada—the former city being the stronghold of the Catholics, and the latter of the Progressists. **1892** *Pall Mall G.* 20 Feb. 3/2 In your leader to-day you speak (and in my opinion correctly) of the Progressive party. On Page 6 the word 'Progressist' is used. **1894** *Current Hist.* (U.S.) IV. 432 The new [Servian] cabinet consisted of progressists and liberals.

b. *attrib.* or as *adj.* = PROGRESSIVE *a.* 4.

1889 *Pall Mall G.* 19 Jan. 2/2 (London County Council) The progressist party..is in favour of carrying out a programme so advanced [etc.]. **1907** *Hibbert Jrnl.* Apr. 496 An exponent of the progressist spirit in Catholic thought.

progressive (prəʊˈgrɛsɪv), *a.* (*sb.*) [a. F. *progressif*, *-ive* (14th c. in Hatz.-Darm.), f. L. *prōgress-*: see PROGRESS *v.* and -IVE.]

A. *adj.* **1. a.** Characterized by stepping, walking, or otherwise moving onward, as in the locomotion of men and animals generally; executed, as a movement, in this way. *Obs.* or merged in b.

1644 BULWER *Chirol.* 83 In matters of progressive motion. **1646** SIR T. BROWNE *Pseud. Ep.* 193 In progressive motion, the armes and legs doe move successively, but in natation both together. **1791** W. BARTRAM *Carolina* 173 Their ascent so easy, as to be almost imperceptible to the progressive traveller. **1816** SIR E. HOME in *Phil. Trans.* 149 Some account of the feet of those animals whose progressive motion can be carried on in opposition to gravity.

b. *generally.* Moving forward or advancing (in space); of the nature of onward motion.

1667 MILTON *P.L.* VIII. 127 Thir [the planets'] wandring course..Progressive, retrograde, or standing still. **1728** PEMBERTON *Newton's Philos.* 195 The moon..would..have partook of all the progressive motion of the earth. **1821** CRAIG *Lect. Drawing* v. 305 Water, when smooth, and having none but its progressive motion, reflects the surrounding objects.

2. a. Passing on from one member or item of a series to the next; proceeding step by step; occurring one after another, successive.

1620 T. GRANGER *Div. Logike* 178 Concerning progressiue suppartition of members [*marg.* Diuiding of parts into parts]. **1703** *Virgil's 4th Eclogue* 2 Behold the Mighty Months Progressive Shine. **1750** JOHNSON *Rambler* No. 41 ¶5 That the idea of the one was impressed at once, and continued through all the progressive descents of the species, without variation or improvement. **1811** BUSBY *Dict. Mus., Progressive Notes, those notes which succeed each other, either in ascent or descent.* **1858** HAWTHORNE *Fr. & It. Note-Bks.* II. 34 Pictures, arranged..in a progressive series, with reference to the date of the painters.

b. Applied to certain games, as euchre or whist, when played by several sets of players simultaneously at different tables, certain players passing after each round from one table to the next, according to specified rules.

1875 W. B. DICK *Amer. Hoyle* (ed. 10) 56 There is another variety to be met with occasionally, which may be styled 'Progressive Jack-Pots'. **1885** C. M. SEAVER (*title*) Standard guide to progressive euchre. **1886** I. M. RITTENHOUSE *Maud* (1939) 366 So we had a jolly little time, playing progressive euchre, and indulging in some music. **1888** A. RANDALL-DIEHL *Two Thousand Words* 169 *Progressive euchre*, a game of cards in which a player starts at one table, among the several scattered about the room. If he wins at the first table, he passes on to the next, and is credited with one game. If he wins again, he moves forward one table. **1890** *Daily News* 29 Sept. 5/4 The City Marshal of Leavenworth, Kansas, has announced that he will henceforth arrest..all persons found playing progressive euchre. **1903** R. BROOKE *Let.* 27 Dec. (1968) 5, I am going to have quite a gay time this week—progressive whist, fancy dress-balls etc. **1904** *Bridge & Progressive Bridge* 25 Progressive Bridge... The Rules of Bridge apply except that no account is taken of games or rubbers. **1906** *Daily Colonist* (Victoria, B.C.) 1 Jan. 15/1 Mrs. Piggott entertained a number of her lady friends.. progressive five hundred being the amusement. **1907** *Yesterday's Shopping* (1969) 361/1 At Home. Progressive Hearts —— o'clock. R.S.V.P. Progressive Bridge.. Progressive Whist. **1926** R. MACAULAY *Crewe Train* II. v. 118 Do you enjoy whist?.. We have very nice progressive drives on Wednesday nights. **1963** M. KENDON *Ladies' College Goudhurst* 20 In 1905 the girls were asked..for an evening of Progressive games.

c. ***progressive assimilation***, in Philol. the process whereby a sound is modified by or harmonized with one closely preceding it.

1915 G. NOËL-ARMFIELD *Gen. Phonetics* ix. 32 If the first sound carries its influence forward the assimilation is said to be progressive. **1934** M. K. POPE *From Latin to Mod. French* II. i. 64 Assimilations and dissimilations may be either *regressive* or *progressive*, i.e. a sound may be modified in anticipation of a sound following, or the articulatory position of one sound may modify the pronunciation of a later one. **1939** L. H. GRAY *Foundations of Lang.* iii. 68 Assimilation may..be either *progressive*, when the first phoneme modifies the second,..or *regressive*, when the second modifies the first. **1964** C. BARBER *Ling. Change Present-Day Eng.* iii. 63 A historical example of *progressive* assimilation is seen in words like *watch*.., where the rounded vowel..is the result of the influence of the preceding w. **1977** *Canad. Jrnl. Linguistics 1976* XXI. I. 124 Chapter 5..shows..the action of progressive and regressive assimilation in triggering errors.

d. ***progressive proofs*** (see quot. 1960).

1932 PLACE & CLUNES *Letterpress Printing* xiv. 247 *Block-Maker's Progressive Proofs.* The colour sheets of 'progressives' provided by the process block-maker must be followed with absolute exactitude. **1948** R. KARCH *Graphic Arts Procedures* vii. 221 The two preceding pages show 'progressive proofs' and the final result of four-color process printing. **1960** G. A. GLAISTER *Gloss. of Bk.* 331/1 *Progressive proofs*, the proofs made in colour-printing as a guide to shade and registration. Each colour is shown separately and imposed on the preceding ones.

e. Psychol. ***Progressive Matrices*** (see RAVEN).

1939 *Brit. Jrnl. Med. Psychol.* XVIII. 16 Progressive Matrices (Sets A, B, C, D and E 1938) obtainable from Messrs H. K. Lewis & Co. **1948** *Psychometrika* XIII. 36 In Sets E and D of the Progressive Matrices, the speed with which certain details are perceived seems to be important for the solution. *Ibid.* 41 The Progressive Matrices are loaded in several factors, plus a factor common to all of them. **1954** A. ANASTASI *Psychol. Testing* x. 261 The Progressive Matrices Test, developed in England by Raven..should also be included... This test, designed as a measure of Spearman's *g* factor, requires primarily the eduction of relationships within abstract material.

3. Characterized by progress or advance (in state or condition). **a.** Of persons or communities: Making progress, advancing (in action, thought, character, fortunes, social conditions, etc.).

1607–12 BACON *Ess., Ambition* (Arb.) 222 It is good for Princes, if they vse ambitious Men, to handle it soe, as they be still progressive, and not retrograde... For if they rise not with theire service, they will take order to make theire service fall with them. **1628** FELTHAM *Resolves* II. [I.] lxxxix. 258 He is not truely penitent, that is not progressive, in the Motion of aspiring goodnesse. **1853** J. H. NEWMAN *Hist. Sk.* (1873) II. I. iv. 187 Whatever be the natural excellences of the Turks, progressive they are not. **1857** BUCKLE *Civiliz.* I. viii. 555 For a progressive nation, there is required a progressive policy. **1859** MILL *Liberty* iii. 127 A people.. may be progressive for a certain length of time, and then stop.

b. Of things, conditions, etc.: Characterized by progress or passing on to more advanced or higher stages; growing, increasing, developing; usually in good sense: advancing towards better conditions; marked by continuous improvement.

a **1653** BINNING *Serm.* (1845) 235 The life as well as the light of the righteous is progressive. **1732** POPE *Ess. Man* I. 235 Above, how high progressive life may go! **1742** YOUNG *Nt. Th.* VII. 81 Reason progressive, Instinct is complete. **1811** BUSBY *Dict. Mus., Progressive*, an epithet..applied to lessons expressly composed for the purpose of practical improvement, and..so constructed in point of increasing execution, as to lead..by insensible degrees to those difficulties [etc.]. **1859** C. BARKER *Assoc. Princ.* ii. 45 During the fifteenth century commerce continued to be regularly and rapidly progressive. **1884** F. TEMPLE *Relat. Relig. & Sc.* vi. 182 He had to teach that the creation was not merely orderly, but progressive.

c. *Path.* Of a disease: Continuously increasing in severity or extent.

1736 BUTLER *Anal.* I. i. Wks. 1874 I. 29 Thinking that a progressive disease..will destroy those powers. **1877** tr. *von Ziemssen's Cycl. Med.* XVI. 647 In progressive pernicious anæmia unusual corpulence has been observed. **1899** *Allbutt's Syst. Med.* VII. 695 Progressive dementia with general paralysis.

d. *transf.* Characterizing or indicating progress.

1888 *Amer. Anthropologist* I. 71 Ecker..considers that unusual length [of the index-finger] is a progressive character.

e. *Educ.* Of teaching methods, types of schools, etc.: aiming to develop individual capability and character in children rather than to achieve standardized results.

1839 tr. A. Necker de Saussure (*title*) Progressive education. **1910** CHESTERTON *G. B. Shaw* 185 Shaw has always made this one immense mistake (arising out of that bad progressive education of his), the mistake of treating convention as a dead thing. **1924** *Progressive Education* Apr. 3 The Progressive Schools are increasing rapidly. **1943** [see ESSENTIALIST *adj.*]. **1946** E. HODGINS *Mr. Blandings builds his Dream House* (1947) 22 The creative, anarchistic, and sexual freedoms of a progressive school. **1959** *Listener* 5 Feb. 244/1 A man who tries to exercise authority in the manner of a sergeant-major will get short shrift in a progressive school. **1967** *Guardian* 14 Oct. 8/4 The Progressive Education Association founded..in 1915, had done its work so well that it was dissolved in 1955. **1976** *Listener* 29 Apr. 526/1 Anxious children did particularly poorly in a progressive classroom.

f. Of taxation: (see quot. 1902).

1889 G. B. SHAW *Fabian Ess. Socialism* 193 The Radical progressive income taxers singing together, and the ratepaying tenants shouting for joy. **1902** *Encycl. Brit.* XXXIII. 197/2 The question whether the burden of taxation should not be *progressive*—the proportion of the sum taken by the state from the tax-payers increasing with the wealth of the individual. *Ibid.* 199/1 A general system of progressive taxation. **1976** *National Observer* (U.S.) 21 Aug. 3/2 By using the progressive income-tax structure, state and local governments are placing the burden back on those hardest hit by raising regressive local taxes. **1978** *Times* 18 July 15/5 Progressive taxation is imposed in this country in order to moderate the unequal distribution of income.

g. ***progressive kiln***, a long kiln through which timber to be dried is slowly passed on trucks.

1920 A. L. HOWARD *Manual of Timbers of World* 397 In all progressive kilns the timber is piled on trucks, and moved at regular intervals through zones of varying temperature and humidity. **1971** *Timber Trades Jrnl.* 14 Aug. 26/1 Small mills naturally use compartment kilns for export drying, but a progressive kiln will now pay off at 60m³ per day and offers lower consumption of heating fuel and electricity.

h. *Gram.* = EXPANDED *ppl. a.* 2 b.

1924 H. E. PALMER *Gram. Spoken Eng.* II. 149 Tenses composed of the verb (bi:) and the Ing-form are called *Progressive Tenses.* **1932** *Jrnl. Eng. & Gmc. Philol.* XXXI. 252 The creation of the progressive form resulted from the desire to express the idea of progressive action, action going on: 'He *is writing* a letter to his mother.' **1946** *Trans. Philol. Soc. 1945* 130 The distinction between the 'terminate' and the 'progressive' aspects of the verb, e.g. *I go/am going, do you go/are you going?* **1957** R. W. ZANDVOORT *Handbk. Eng. Gram.* I. ii. 36 What was said..of the imperfective or durative aspect of the present participle also applies to its predicative use, as in *The ships were sailing out of the harbour.* This construction..is known as the *Progressive*, because it usually denotes an action or an activity as in progress. **1959** *Brno Studies in English* I. 13 Mod E progressive tenses must be regarded as marked counterparts of the simple tenses. **1965** N. CHOMSKY *Aspects of Theory of Syntax* ii. 64 *Frighten* is a Transitive Verb..; it takes Progressive Aspect freely.

i. Of music: modern, experimental, innovatory, avant-garde; used with reference to several distinct musical developments, as ***progressive jazz, pop, rock***, etc.

1947 *Down Beat* 13 Aug. 1/4 Stan Kenton next month returns to the band business... First recordings will be for an album to be titled Concert in Progressive Jazz. *Ibid.* 19 Nov. 1/5 Stan..abhorred references to his music as 'jazz', himself using the descriptive phrase 'progressive jazz'. **1950** S. KENTON in *Metronome* July 23/1 In modern and progressive jazz and bebop there is such an urge today for new harmonic sounds..that the music has suffered. **1952** B. ULANOV *Hist. Jazz in Amer.* xiii. 141 The movement that is variously labeled 'progressive' or 'modern' or 'new' jazz is a New York movement. **1958** in P. Gammond *Decca Bk. Jazz* xvii. 213 June Christy..might have persuaded the band to swing instead of exploiting these weary, 'progressive' jazz harmonies so thoroughly explored by Stravinsky some forty years ago. **1959** 'F. NEWTON' *Jazz Scene* vi. 117 Leading 'progressive' players like the pianist Lennie Tristano. **1963** R. I. MCDAVID *Mencken's Amer. Lang.* 744 It [*sc.* funk] also designates progressive bop containing a strong blues element which marks its Negro origin. **1970** E. LEE *Music of People* vii. 147 A new style has arisen, usually called 'progressive pop', which is of such musicality that it has been heralded by some critics as a new form of art music. **1975** *New Yorker* 21 Apr. 7/1 (Advt.), Head-hunters, a progressive disco-jazz quintet created in Herbie Hancock's image. **1977** *It* May 26/3 Patti wrote this heavy condemnation of 'progressive' rock radio as we hear it now.

4. a. Favouring, advocating, or directing one's efforts towards progress or reform, esp. in political, municipal, or social matters.

Used from *c* 1889 as a party term in municipal politics, esp. in London, to include those who were liberal or reforming in municipal and social questions, though they might not support the Liberal party in national or imperial questions. In South Africa the self-adopted appellation of those who opposed the Bond or Africander party, corresponding orig. to the British party as opposed to the Dutch.

More recently in South Africa, designating several political parties committed to a policy of multi-racialism; also, freq. a name or term adopted by radical, left-wing, or communist parties.

1884 *Pall Mall G.* 8 Jan. 8/1 The Progressive Brahmans, or, as they call their church, the 'Brahma Somaj of India'. **1889** *Ibid.* 30 Jan. 2/2 From the point of view of the Progressive majority, this is the only way to make the seat secure. **1897** *Daily News* 24 July 5/2 Progressive Conservatism is to adopt Liberal principles, and say they were always your own. **1898** LD. ROSEBERY *ibid.* 2 Mar. 4/6 One very simple demonstration of how carefully the Progressive party have cut themselves aloof from Imperial politics. **1930** W. K. HANCOCK *Australia* viii. 163 The area to be developed was also within constituencies held by the Country Progressive party, on whose support the Victorian Government was dependent. **1954** *Manch. Guardian Weekly* 16 Sept. 3/3 The ludicrous and largely Communist-dominated 'Progressive Party' campaign of 1946. **1955** *Treatm. Brit. P.O.W.'s in Korea* (H.M.S.O.) 4 The 'progressive' view—the Communist view—was the only one allowed. **1969** A. G. FRANK *Latin Amer.* xxii. 269 Concerned and progressive people everywhere scrutinize these..laws, and often criticize them. **1971** *Progress* (Cape Town) May 5/4 There had been talk of a split for a long time; the Press had even coined the term the 'Progressive Group' of the United Party. **1976** R. WILLIAMS *Keywords* 207 Nearly all political tendencies now wish to be described as progressive, but..it is more frequently now a persuasive than a descriptive term.

b. Characterized by (the desire to promote) change, innovation, or experiment; avant-garde, advanced, 'liberal'.

1908 H. G. WELLS *War in Air* ii. 35 It was always a very rhetorical and often trying affair, but in these progressive times you have to make a noise to get a living. **1949** 'J. TEY' *Brat Farrar* i. 11 The great house in the park was a boarding-school for the unmanageable children of parents with progressive ideas and large bank accounts. **1953** M. MCCARTHY *Groves of Academe* i. 4 In a progressive community where the casserole and the cocktail and the disposable diaper reigned. **1956** [see LABOUR *sb.* 2 c]. **1974** *Howard Jrnl.* XIV. 99 The Rev. W. D. Morrison, whose outspoken views in the 1890s led to the most progressive document on prison reform since the writing of John Howard himself. **1976** *Church Times* 27 Aug. 6/5 There was something either in those particular temperaments or in the 'progressive' ethos, that militated against contentment.

5. *Comb.*, as ***progressive-minded*** adj.

1955 KOESTLER *Trail of Dinosaur* 206 The worshippers of tyranny and terror usurp the rightful place of a truly progressive party and cunningly direct the energies of the progressive-minded into 'anti-Fascist' crusades. **1975** A. BERGMAN *Hollywood & Le Vine* v. 60 A bad time for progressive-minded people.

B. *sb.* **1.** One who favours, advocates, or aims at progress or reform, or claims to be in favour of it. (See note to A. 4.)

1865 BUSHNELL *Vicar. Sacr.* III. v. 277 The disappointment I may inflict on certain progressives, or disciples of the New Gospel. **1884** *Pall Mall G.* 8 Jan. 8/1 Henceforth the two parties of the Brahmans were known as the Conservatives and the Progressives. **1892** LD. ROSEBERY in *Daily News* 2 Mar. 2/6, I meant that there were Progressives who are not Liberals, but that I think there are no Liberals who are not Progressives. **1894** *Athenæum* 7 July 23/1 An attractive sketch of a Progressive of the epoch of the reforms of Alexander II. **1898** *Westm. Gaz.* 19 Nov. 2/2 The Cape will shortly be polled again, and it seems..that the result will be to give the Progressives a very small majority. **1921** J. R. HORNADY *Bk. of Birmingham* ii. 27 In the North we divide; there you will find Republicans, Democrats, Progressives, Independents, and so forth. **1954** *Britannica Bk. of Year* 638/1 Awareness of Communist thought produced the word..*Progressive*, a Communist sympathizer. **1955** *Treatm. Brit. P.O.W.'s in Korea* (H.M.S.O.) 15 'Progressives' were soon given a major rôle to play as mouthpieces of Communist propaganda. **1958** *Listener* 4 Dec. 941/1 The true Progressive was essentially urban and middle class. **1970** *Cape Times* 28 Oct. 1/1 The United Party has been a bit bitter about the Progressives, believing that they should not exist. **1971** *Rand Daily Mail* 4 Dec. 1/1 Mr. Bill Carr's decision to seek election to the Johannesburg City Council as a Progressive is more than just a coup for that particular party. **1976** *Times* 7 Aug. 12/2 When progressives seem to behave like theological scrap merchants, swopping bits and pieces in the ecumenical marketplace according to their fancy, clucking noises of disapproval are heard from the Vatican.

2. *pl.* Shortened from ***progressive proofs*** (sense A. 2 d).

1923 H. A. MADDOX *Printing* x. 125 A final set of colour proofs (progressives) is prepared for the guidance of the printer. **1932** [see sense A 2 d].

3. One who favours, advocates, or practises progressive (sense A. 3 e) educational methods.

1936 H. G. WELLS *Anat. Frustration* viii. 73 The 'natural virtue' schools of such educational 'progressives' as Neill and his associates. **1944** H. CROOME *You've gone Astray* xvi. 168 You may know the true progressive..by the fact that he calls children not boys and girls, but 'kids'. **1961** CURTIS & BOULTWOOD *Short Hist. Educ. Ideas* (ed. 3) xx. 578 Pleas by the Progressives for activity methods, informal learning, and the encouragement of self-discipline and initiative. **1969** M. ASH *Who are Progressives Now?* i. 23 Of still greater gall to the old-style progressive at the Dartington Colloquy ..was the pervasive belief of some others present, that by a well-meant concession to the independent progressive schools a niche could be found for them in the State system as recipients of..difficult children. **1976** *Times* 26 Apr. 13/3 In the past the debate between traditionalists and progressives in education has often taken place on the abstruse and abstract plane of educational philosophy.

4. *Gram.* Shortened from ***progressive form, tense***, etc. (sense A. 3 h).

1961 R. B. LONG *Sentence & its Parts* v. 127 The point of view is internal, as with all progressives. **1965** N. CHOMSKY *Aspects of Theory of Syntax* 216 Such Verbs as *own*..occur freely with or without Progressive. **1978** *Language* LIV. 418 Half of his discussion of imperfectivity (32–40) is devoted largely to an examination of the English progressive in which it is clear that he is arguing from form to meaning, rather than the reverse.

progressively (prəʊˈgrɛsɪvlɪ), *adv.* [f. prec. + -LY².] In a progressive manner; in the way of progression or progress; **a.** by continuous advance; step by step, gradually; successively; †**b.** straight forward or onward; directly (*obs.*).

1620 T. GRANGER *Div. Logike* 294 But the conforming, adapting, and disposing of them being inuented progressiuely, recedeth from vniuersals..to the most specials, or indiuiduals. **1694** HOLDER *Time* vi. 87 The reason why they fall in that order.., from the greatest Epacts progressively to the least. *a* **1716** SOUTH *Serm.* (1744) VII. i. 5 Nothing that adequately fills a place, can move in that place, unless it moves circularly; but progressively or in a direct line it is impossible. **1788** J. MAY *Jrnl. & Lett.* (1873) 96 Mountains..rising progressively to view. **1878** NEWCOMB *Pop. Astron.* I. iii. 96 The action of the sun on the moon was progressively changing.

progressiveness (prəʊˈgrɛsɪvnɪs). [-NESS.] The quality or character of being progressive.

1727 BAILEY vol. II, *Progressiveness*, the Quality of proceeding or going forward. **1795** SOUTHEY *Vis. Maid Orleans* III. 189 Those ties Which through the infinite progressiveness Complete our perfect bliss. **1845–6** TRENCH *Huls. Lect.* Ser. I. iv. 57 This progressiveness of Scripture is an important element in its fitness for the education of man. **1883** H. BONAR in *Edin. Daily Rev.* 6 June 3/8 Our progressiveness consists in the fuller discernment of all parts of revelation.

proˈgressivism. [f. PROGRESSIVE + -ISM.] The principles of a progressive or progressist; advocacy of, or devotion to, progress or reform.

1892 *St. James's Gaz.* 7 Mar., If London had been converted to Progressivism—that is Radicalism. **1896** *Westm. Gaz.* 14 May 3/1 The state of this country [Russia], in which primitivism—if I may be permitted the expression —and progressivism are sometimes so oddly mixed. **1961** CURTIS & BOULTWOOD *Short Hist. Educ. Ideas* (ed. 3) xx. 581, 1938..marked the final withdrawal of the pragmatist group from identification with progressivism. **1978** *Church Times* 17 Mar. 9/1 One might cite William Golding as representative of those intellectuals who were brought up to Wellsian rationalism and progressivism..and then rejected it. **1979** *Daily Tel.* 12 Oct. 5/1 Mr. Amin [President and Prime Minister of Afghanistan] did not refer to Communism or Socialism in his speech but stressed that the constitution would be based on 'progressivism', the word commonly used by Communists in parts of Asia where Communism is still frowned upon.

So **proˈgressivist** = PROGRESSIVE *sb.*; also *attrib.* or as *adj.*

1884 A. V. H. CARPENTER in *Chicago Advance* 1 Jan. (1885) 867 There are..no more impracticable progressivists than those who clamor for a repeal of all laws. **1904** *19th Cent.* Aug. 292 An ardent young Progressivist. **1945** K. R. POPPER *Open Society* I. iv. 39 Had he [*sc.* Plato] been a progressivist, he might have hit at the idea of a classless, equalitarian society. **1959** *Times* 23 Sept. 13/6 The younger composers..are indistinguishable in outlook from the vanguard of our English progressivists. **1969** *Daily Tel.* 13 Nov. 14/3 A favourite progressivist argument..is that people who are most vehemently against something are often the very same people who are unconsciously most inclined to it themselves. **1977** D. Watkin *Morality & Archit.* III. ii. 94 According to the progressivist view, anything which reminds one 'of the past' is regarded as a vice.

progressivity (prəʊgrɛˈsɪvɪtɪ). *rare.* [f. as PROGRESSIVISM + -ITY.] = PROGRESSIVENESS.

1882 tr. *Godet's Jesus Christ* 66 This [man's] progressivity, if I may use the word, has no limit but that of the absolute good to which he aspires. **1883** F. A. Walker *Pol. Econ.* 451 In 1848..the idea of progressivity [of taxation] was revived.

progressor (prəʊˈgrɛsə(r)). *rare.* [a. late L. *prōgressor*, agent-n. f. *prōgredī*: see PROGREDIENT.] One who progresses or makes progress; in quot. *a* 1626, one who makes a state progress or tour.

a **1626** Bacon *Digest Laws* Wks. 1879 I. 671/1 Adrian.. being a great progressor through all the Roman empire, whenever he found any decays of bridges, or highways.. gave substantial order for their repair. **1874** Neale & Littledale *Comm. Ps.* cxx. IV. 164 The beginners, the progressors, and the perfect.

proguanil (prəʊˈgwɑːnɪl). *Pharm.* [f. PRO(PYL + BI)GUAN(IDE + *-il*.] A bitter-tasting synthetic compound, 1-*p*-chlorophenyl-5-iso-propylbiguanide, $C_{11}H_{16}ClN_5$, which is used, in the form of its white crystalline hydrochloride, in the prevention and treatment of malaria. Cf. PALUDRINE.

1949 *Brit. Med. Jrnl.* 15 Jan. 88/2 (*heading*) 'Paludrine' (proguanil) in prophylaxis and treatment of malarial infections caused by a West African strain of *P. falciparum*. **1956** *Nature* 25 Feb. 368/1 Further mosquito infectivity experiments have confirmed that, in patients carrying gametocytes of a proguanil-resistant strain of *P. falciparum*, anopheline mosquitoes can be infected from a person taking 0·4 gm. proguanil daily. **1961** *New Scientist* 20 Apr. 119/1 It was found that if a strain of *P. gallinaceum* was transmitted serially from chick to chick, and the birds were treated with gradually increasing doses of proguanil, the organisms became highly resistant to its action. **1970** Passmore & Robson *Compan. Med. Stud.* II. xx. 20/1 Proguanil (paludrine) acts on the malaria parasite both in the blood and in the liver, probably by interfering with the reduction of folic acid. **1977** *Times* 5 July 7/6 Protection is easy: one of the antimalarial drugs such as proguanil should be taken.

pro-guardian: see PRO-[1].

progue, var. PROG.

‖**Progymnasium** (ˌprəʊdʒɪmˈneɪzɪəm, Ger. proːgymˈnaːzjʊm). Pl. **-ia**. [Ger. (from mod.L.): see PRO-[1] and GYMNASIUM[2].] (See quot. 1886.)

1833 Sir W. Hamilton *Discuss.* (1852) 545 Establishments..called Progymnasia and superior Burgher Schools. **1886** J. F. Muirhead in *Encycl. Brit.* XX. 17/2 The classical schools proper [in Prussia] consist of *Gymnasia* and *Progymnasia*, the latter being simply gymnasia wanting the higher classes.

‖**progymˈnasma**. *Obs. rare.* Pl. **-mata**. [ad. Gr. προγύμνασμα a preparatory exercise, f. προγυμνάζειν to train beforehand.] A preparatory or preliminary exercise or study.

1674 *Phil. Trans.* IX. 220, I consider'd that..some of those Observations..might shew me the true Quantity of the Equations of the Suns Orb... I turned over his *Progymnasmata*, and pitched on two. **1678** Cudworth *Intell. Syst.* Contents (I. v. 724) A *Progymnasma* or Prælusory attempt, towards the proving of a God from his Idea as including necessary existence.

progymnosperm: see PRO-[2] 1.

pro hac vice: see PRO 5.

proheim, -heme, -hemy, etc.: see PROEM, etc.

Prohessian (prəʊˈhɛsɪən). *Math.* [f. PRO-[1] 4 + HESSIAN *sb.*[2]] (See quots.)

1862 Salmon *Geom. Three Dimensions* xii. 338 The Hessian of any surface being of the degree $4n$–8, that of a developable consists of the surface itself, and a surface of $3n$–8 degree which we shall call the Pro-Hessian. *Ibid.* xv. 426. **1864** Cayley *Coll. Math. Papers* V. 267 The function PU, which for the developable replaces as it were the Hessian HU, is termed the *Prohessian*; and (since if r be the order of U the order of HU is $4r$–8) we have $3r$–8 for the order of the Prohessian.

proheterocyst: see PRO-[2] 1.

†**proˈhibit**, *ppl. a. Obs.* [ad. L. *prohibit-us*, pa. pple. of *prohib-ēre* to hold back, prevent, forbid, f. *prō* in front + *habēre* to hold.] Prohibited, forbidden. (Also const. as pa. pple.: see next.)

1432–50 tr. *Higden* (Rolls) II. 215 Whiche..hade not knowlege of hym selfe, whiche is comparable to brute bestes in drawenge to thynges prohibitte. **1678** Sir G. Mackenzie *Crim. Laws Scot.* I. xxxi. §2 (1699) 158 By the Civil Law likewise, the prohibit Arms were confiscat. **1683** Luttrell *Brief Rel.* (1857) I. 277 Discharging merchants..to sell or exchange any prohibite commodities with themselves or amongst others in the Kingdome of Scotland. **1714** *Fr. Bk. of Rates* 400 Arrest of the King's Council, for levying of 30 Sols per 100 upon all Cheese from Foreign Parts, except from England and Holland, which remains prohibit.

prohibit (prəʊˈhɪbɪt), *v.* Also 5 **-hibet**. [f. L. *prohibit-*, ppl. stem of *prohibēre*: see prec. For pa. pple., *prohibit* was used down to the 18th c.; but *prohibited* also appeared as early as 1532.]

1. *trans.* To forbid (an action or thing) by or as by a command or statute; to interdict.

1432–50 tr. *Higden* (Rolls) I. 237 A table of brasse prohibetenge synne [orig. *peccatum prohibens*], where the myȝhty preceptes of the lawe bene wryten. **1509** Barclay *Shyp of Folys* (1570) 148 The damnable lust of cardes and of dice, And other games prohibite by the lawe. **1532** More *Confut. Tindale* Wks. 510/2 Such folk I suppose wer better prohibited betymes. **1560** Daus tr. *Sleidane's Comm.* 91 b, Not to prohibite this newe fanglednes. **1669** W. Simpson *Hydrol. Chym.* 176 They altogether prohibite the use of wine in fevers. **1772** *Junius Lett.* lxviii. (1820) 346 They considered..what the thing was which the legislature meant to prohibit. **1812** Sir H. Davy *Chem. Philos.* 14 In England an act of parliament was passed in 5th year of reign of Henry IV prohibiting the attempts at transmutation and making them felonious. **1874** Green *Short Hist.* iv. §2. 166 The Statute of Mortmain..prohibited the alienation of lands to the Church under pain of forfeiture.

2. To prevent, preclude, hinder, or debar (an action or thing) by physical means.

a **1548** Hall *Chron., Hen. V* 59 The Frenchemen.. gathered together a greate numbre of men of warre redy to defend and prohibite the passage. **1634** R. H. *Salernes Regim.* 66 They comforte the Stomacke, and prohibite vapours and fumes. **1667** Milton *P.L.* II. 437 Gates of burning Adamant Barr'd over us prohibit all egress. **1834** Ht. Martineau *Demerara* iii, Having seen them..drop asleep, or shut their eyes so as to prohibit conversation, as much as if they were.

3. To forbid, stop, or prevent (a person):

a. *from* doing something; also, *to do* a thing (*arch.*).

1523 Ld. Berners *Froiss.* I. Pref. 1 [The reading of history] prohibyteth reprouable persons to do mischeuous dedes. *a* **1548** Hall *Chron., Hen. VII* 55 b, For the rage of the water, and contraritie of the wyndes, her ship was prohibited diuerse tymes to approche the shore and take lande. **1615** in *Buccleuch MSS.* (Hist. MSS. Comm.) I. 166 No cause why..his Majesty's subjects should be.. prohibited from any place. **1756** C. Lucas *Ess. Waters* III. 261 The patients..are peremptorily prohibited to bathe on Sundays. **1840** Macaulay *Ess., Clive* (1887) 550 There is no Act..prohibiting the Secretary of State for Foreign Affairs from being in the pay of continental powers.

†**b.** With various obsolete constructions. (Cf. FORBID.)

1432–50 tr. *Higden* (Rolls) III. 279 That he scholde prohibite hym of thynges whiche scholde not be doen. **1531** *Dial on Laws Eng.* lii. 140 Whether it stande with conscyence to prohybyt a Jury of mete & drynk tyll they be agreed. **1680** H. Dodwell *Two Lett.* (1691) 78 St. Ambrose..prohibited none for coming to him at any time.

†**c.** With direct and indirect object (dative). *Obs.* or *arch.*

1530 Palsgr. 667/2 He hath prohybyt me his house. **1619** Drayton *Past., Ecl.* vi. xv, To recall that, labour not in vain, Which is by fate prohibited returning. **1657** J. Sergeant *Schism Dispach't* 456 Those Authors, whose books are prohibited printing in England under great penalties. **1671** R. MacWard *True Nonconf.* 160 A Synod in England did prohibite the Scots any function in their Church. **1741** Middleton *Cicero* II. ix. 331 He prohibited Antony the entrance of his Province.

†**4.** Formerly with following negative expressed or implied: To command *not* to do something; to cause a thing *not* to happen or take place. *Obs.*

1555 Eden *Decades* 259 The princes of the lande are prohibite in peine of death to absteine from such stronge drinkes. **1557** North *Gueuara's Diall Pr.* (1582) 295 They did prohibit that no man shoulde..sell openly..wine of Candie or Spaine. **1561** Daus tr. *Bullinger on Apoc.* (1573) 145 b, Helyas through the power of God, did prohibit that it should not rayne. *a* **1677** Hale *Prim. Orig. Man.* I. i. 41 It cannot effectually prohibit the Heart not to move, or the Blood not to circulate. **1692** Bentley *Boyle Lect.* vii. 249 The gravity prohibiting that they cannot recede from the centers of their Motions. **1707** Earl of Bindon in *Lond. Gaz.* No. 4339/3 To Prohibit..all Coach-makers,..that they do not use Varnish'd Bullion-Nails.

Hence **proˈhibiting** *vbl. sb.*, prohibition.

1614 W. Colwall in *Buccleuch MSS.* (Hist. MSS. Comm.) I. 151 The prohibiting of white cloths to come into these countries. **1677** *Act 29 Chas. II*, c. 7 §3 Nothing in this Act contained shall extend to the prohibiting of dressing of Meate in Families or dressing or selling of Meat in Inns Cookeshops or Victualling Houses for such as otherwise cannot be provided.

proˈhibited, *ppl. a.* [f. prec. + -ED[1].] Forbidden, interdicted, debarred. ***prohibited degrees***: see DEGREE *sb.* 3. ***prohibited area***, a region which only authorized persons may enter.

1552 Huloet, Prohibited, *vetitus.* **1597** Morley *Introd. Mus* 183 Prohibited consequence of perfect cordes. **1615** G. Sandys *Trav.* 172 They say, that they marry within prohibited degrees. **1794** Mrs. Radcliffe *Myst. Udolpho* iv, Conveying prohibited goods over the Pyrenees. **1845** McCulloch *Taxation* II. ix. (1852) 338 The smuggling of prohibited and over-taxed articles. **1940** *Hansard Commons* 5 Mar. 195 *Mr. Woodburn* asked the Secretary of State for War whether, in his designation of a part of Scotland as a prohibited area, he has considered the repercussions of this decision on the Scottish tourist industry. **1948** E. Pound *Pisan Cantos* (1949) lxxxiii. 126 Bein' aliens in prohibited area. **1961** F. H. Burgess *Dict. Sailing* 164 *Prohibited area*, an area marked on a chart, where anchoring, trawling, or fishing etc., may be forbidden by authority. **1964** G. Lyall *Most Dangerous Game* vi. 48 The convictions for flying in prohibited areas.

prohibiter (prəʊˈhɪbɪtə(r)). [f. as prec. + -ER[1].] One who prohibits or forbids; = PROHIBITOR.

1608 Willet *Hexapla Exod.* 337 God..is..a prohibiter of sinnes. **1643** Milton *Divorce* II. xxii. Wks. 1851 IV. 130 The prohibiters of divorce. **1782** Miss Burney *Cecilia* IX. viii, Cecilia..cast her eyes round the church, with no other view than that of seeing from what corner the prohibiter would start. **1880** Muirhead *Gaius* III. §193 The discovery ..would subject the prohibiter to a heavier penalty.

prohibition (prəʊhɪˈbɪʃən). [a. F. *prohibition* (1237 in Godef. *Compl.*), ad. L. *prohibitiōn-em*, n. of action f. *prohib-ēre* to PROHIBIT.]

1. The action of forbidding by or as by authority; an edict, decree, or order forbidding or debarring; a negative command.

1387–8 T. Usk *Test. Love* III. iii. (Skeat) I. 54 This.. semeth to some men into coaccion, that is to saine, constrainyng, or els prohibicion that is defendyng. **1432–50** tr. *Higden* (Rolls) VII. 287 Prestes despisynge this prohibicion. **1538** Starkey *England* II. i. 160 Ther must be a prohybytyon set out by commyn authoryte. **1667** Milton *P.L.* IX. 645 So glister'd the dire Snake, and into fraud Led Eve..to the Tree Of prohibition. **1717** Lady M. W. Montagu *Let. to Abbé Conti* 1 Apr., The prohibition of wine was a very wise maxim. **1875** Jowett *Plato* (ed. 2) V. 404 The prohibition of excessive wealth is a very considerable gain in the direction of temperance.

2. *Law.* **a.** A writ issuing from a superior court, formerly from the Court of King's Bench, and sometimes from the Court of Chancery or of Common Pleas, now out of the High Court of Justice, forbidding some court, and the parties engaged in it, from proceeding in a suit, on the ground that this is beyond the cognizance of the court in question.

[**1312** *Rolls of Parlt.* I. 282/2 Ceux qi par malice purchacent prohibitions.] **1548** *Act 2 & 3 Edw. VI*, c. 13 §14 If any Party..for any Matter..sued..before the Ecclesiastical Judge, do sue for any Prohibition in any of the King's Courts. **1595** *Expos. Termes Law, Prohibition*..lieth where a man is impleded in yᵉ spiritual court of yᵉ thing yᵗ toucheth not matrimonie nor testament,..but that toucheth the kinges crowne. **1682** Burnet *Rights Princes* viii. 305 A Prohibition was served upon those Vicars. **1726** Ayliffe *Parergon* 435 Every Statute Prohibitory is a Prohibition of Law. **1863** H. Cox *Instit.* II. ii. 310 The courts of law frequently issued 'Prohibitions' against proceeding in the Ecclesiastical Courts with suits not lawfully cognizable there. **1885** *Encycl. Brit.* XIX. 793/1 A writ of prohibition is a prerogative writ—that is to say, it does not issue as of course, but is granted only on proper grounds being shown.

b. *Sc. Law.* Each of the three technical clauses in a deed of entail prohibiting the heir from selling an estate, contracting debt that would affect it, or altering the order of succession to it.

1848 *Act 11 & 12 Vict.* c. 36 §32 Disencumbering the entailed estate..and the heir of entail.. of all the prohibitions, conditions, restrictions, limitations, and clauses irritant and resolutive, of the tailzie. **1861** W. Bell *Dict. Law Scot.* 802/2 Before the passing of the act 11 and 12 Vict. c. 36, 1848, it was doubted whether an entail could be effectual which did not contain the whole of the three prohibitions;—against alienations; against the contraction of debt, so as to affect the estate; and against the succession; but it was decided, that a deed of entail containing any one of these prohibitions, properly fenced, was effectual so far as it went.

3. a. The interdiction by law of the importation of some foreign article of commerce.

1670 Temple *Let. to Ld. Arlington* Wks. 1731 II. 214 Another Point..is the Prohibition of French Commodities. **1825** McCulloch *Pol. Econ.* I. 33 Heavy duties and absolute prohibitions were interposed to prevent the importation of manufactured articles from abroad. **1872** Yeats *Growth Comm.* 302 Manufacturers in want of customers cried out for trade prohibitions.

b. A thing prohibited. *rare.*

1905 *Post Office Guide* 1 Jan. 493 Eau de cologne is a prohibition into Basutoland.

4. *spec.* The forbidding by law of the manufacture and sale of intoxicating drinks for common consumption. Now usu. with reference to the restrictions on the manufacture and sale of intoxicating drinks in the United States (1920–33) under the Volstead Act.

1851 (May) *Annual Rept. Exec. Committee Amer. Temp. Union* 27 The State of Vermont has struggled arduously to arrive at the summit level of entire prohibition. **1869** *Daily News* 6 Sept., The majority of the people of the State [Massachusetts] are..opposed to prohibition, though they would favour a good license law. **1891** (*title*) The Cyclopædia of Temperance and Prohibition (U.S.). **1899** Rowntree & Sherwell *Temperance Problems* iii. (1901) 42/1 The agitation in favour of prohibition in Maine began early in the thirties... The efforts of [Generals Appleton and Dow]..resulted in 1846 in the passage of the first Prohibitory Act. **1925** W. J. Bryan *Mem.* 186 His views on the initiative and referendum and prohibition had not altered. **1927** *New Republic* 21 Sept. 109/1 The Republicans have been laboring night and day to keep prohibition from becoming an issue in the campaign. **1931** M. F. Furness *Mem. Sixty Years* xix. 246 We of course heard much talk of Prohibition, and also saw a good deal of its absence. **1966** C. M. Bowra *Mem. 1898–1939* viii. 212 Maurice had been in the United States during the fantastic boom of the twenties. This was also the period of prohibition, which made it a matter of prestige and honour to drink too much, especially hard liquor. **1970** *Nature* 19 Sept. 1186/2 For that matter the laws [in the U.S.A.] against marihuana have become so widely abused as to appear to many as a new Prohibition.

5. *Astrology.* (See quots.)

1658 PHILLIPS, *Prohibition*,..in Astronomy it is, when two Planets are applying to Conjunction, or Aspect, and before they come to joyn themselves, another comes to Conjunction, or Aspect of the Planet applied to. **1819** J. WILSON *Dict. Astrol.*, *Prohibition*, the same as frustration.

6. *attrib.* and *Comb.* (in senses 3 and (especially) 4). Also **prohibition party**, a political party in U.S., formed in Sept. 1869 to nominate or support only persons pledged to vote for the prohibition of the liquor traffic; **prohi'bitionward** *adv.*, towards prohibition.

1869 in D. L. Colvin *Prohibition in U.S.* (1926) iv. 73 We adopt the name of the National Prohibition Party, as expressive of our primary object. **1877** *Harper's Mag.* Dec. 146/1 R. Pitman..Prohibition candidate for Governor. **1877** *Ibid.* 146/2 He argues..the prohibition system a success. **1883** *Harper's Mag.* Dec. 162/1 The prohibition amendment was defeated [in Ohio]. **1884** *N.Y. Weekly Tribune* 20 Aug. 7/1 The platform..means specifically that the prohibition law shall be enforced. **1885** G. W. BAIN in *Voice* (N.Y.) 29 Nov., It is delightful to see the tendency of public sentiment prohibitionward in the South. **1892** *Outing* Dec. 209/1 They have no beer here: North and South Dakota are prohibition states. **1897** *Westm. Gaz.* 31 Dec. 2/2 He carefully studied the Prohibition Question while there. .. In one Prohibition town he was taken to various hotels by the Dominion M.P...who..was elected on the Prohibition card—for the purpose of having a whisky-and-soda. **1901** *Daily Chron.* 10 July 7/1 Manitoba, by a law, known as the 'Liquor Law', which was passed last year, endeavoured to make itself into a 'prohibition' province. **1907** *Westm. Gaz.* 11 Dec. 8/1 The outcome of this foolish (almost wicked) retention of the Prohibition Order is that now an American Meat Trust is able to name the price that must be paid for meat by poor British consumers. **1909** G. F. PARKER *Recoll. Grover Cleveland* (1911) 71 In addition, something over 300,000 votes had been cast for the Prohibition and the Greenback candidates. **1922** S. LEWIS *Babbitt* xiii. 174 He was blind and deaf from prohibition-era alcohol. **1948** *Time* 12 Jan. 13/1 The Prohibition Party has nominated a candidate for President ever since its formation in 1869. **1949** *Daily Oklahoman* 13 Feb. D.2/2 A petition will be circulated calling for repeal of the state's liquor prohibition law. **1949** *Time* 10 Oct. 27/3 The state's church-going United Drys..were fiercely proud of living in a prohibition state. **1968** *N.Y. City* (Michelin Tire Corp.) 32 The area later became famous as the 'speakeasy belt' during the Prohibition era.

prohi'bitionary, *a.* [f. prec. + -ARY[1].] Relating to prohibition.

1894 *Pop. Sci. Monthly* June 226 The author has overlooked the fact that prohibitionary laws were enacted in Judea, Egypt, Greece and Rome.

prohibitionist (prəʊhɪ'bɪʃənɪst). [f. as PROHIBITIONARY *a.* + -IST.] One who advocates or favours prohibition, *spec.* of the manufacture and sale of intoxicating liquors. Also *attrib.*

1846 WORCESTER, *Prohibitionist*, an advocate for prohibitory measures. *For. Q. Rev.* **1854** (*title*) The *Prohibitionist* [a monthly journal in State of New York]. **1866** *Even. Standard* 13 July 6 You would probably pronounce the existing struggle as one between the Protectionists and Prohibitionists. **1883** *Manch. Guard.* 17 Oct. 5/3 If the community is really determined to have no public-houses it can carry out its wishes by filling the Town Councils with a majority of prohibitionists. **1888** BRYCE *Amer. Commw.* II. III. lvi. 372 *note*, The Prohibitionist platform of 1884.

So **prohi'bitionism**, the principles or practice of prohibition.

1889 GOLDW. SMITH (*title*) Prohibitionism in Canada and the United States. **1915** *N. Amer. Rev.* Dec. 948 All the speakers agreed that the bad saloon did more harm to the liquor trade than prohibitionism.

prohibitive (prəʊ'hɪbɪtɪv), *a.* [a. F. *prohibitif*, *-ive* (16th c. in Hatz.-Darm.): see PROHIBIT *ppl. a.* and -IVE.]

1. Having the quality of prohibiting; that forbids or restrains from some course of action; prohibitory.

1602 FULBECKE *Pandectes* 86 When it is apparant that such meetings are not made of euill intent, the prohibitiue Law ceaseth. **1765** *Act 5 Geo. III*, c. 26 *Preamble*, [They] should convey, settle, and intail the lands..with all the proper, prohibitive, irritant, and resolutive clauses. **1845** McCULLOCH *Taxation* II. v. (1852) 213 Prohibitive and protective regulations..force capital and industry into less productive channels than those into which they would otherwise flow. **1887** [see PERMISSIVE 1]. **1889** *Voice* (N.Y.) 30 May, The decrease [of saloons] being almost wholly due to the special prohibitive power of the judges of the license courts.

2. Of conditions, as taxes or prices: Such as serve to prevent the use or abuse of something.

1886 *American* XII. 100 A tax whose effect will be prohibitive. **1888** M. ARNOLD *Civiliz. U.S.* iv. 163 The cabrates are prohibitive—more than half of the people who in England would use cabs must in America use the horse-cars. **1898** *Tit-Bits* 8 Jan. 279/1 The book was published at a well-nigh prohibitive price.

3. *Gram.* That expresses prohibition; negative in an imperative use.

1875 RENOUF *Egypt. Gram.* 56 The prohibitive *em* is frequently placed before [etc.]. *Mod.* The Greek μη and Lat. *ne* with the imperative have a prohibitive force.

Hence **pro'hibitively** *adv.*, **pro'hibitiveness**.

1867 CARLYLE *Remin.* (1881) II. 296, I waved my hand prohibitively at the door. **1891** T. HARDY *Let.* 15 July (1978) I. 240 The late Lord Lytton..abolished prohibitiveness as between himself & the mass of the thinking public..by consenting to paper covers at 2s/-. **1899** *Contemp. Rev.* Dec. 829 A spirit of doctrinaire prohibitiveness.

prohibitor (prəʊ'hɪbɪtə(r)). [a. L. *prohibitor*, agent-n. from *prohibēre*: see PROHIBIT *ppl. a.*] One who prohibits.

1611 COTGR., *Prohibeur*, a prohibitor. **1655** STANLEY *Hist. Philos.* III. (1701) 85/2 Socrates..never needed any exhorter, but sometimes a prohibitor. **1857** KEBLE *Eucharist. Ador.* 27 Make it still more imperative upon the prohibitors to produce some irresistible authority.

prohibitory (prəʊ'hɪbɪtərɪ), *a.* [ad. L. *prōhibitōri-us* restraining, f. *prohibitor*: see -ORY.]

1. = PROHIBITIVE 1; esp. with reference to the common sale of intoxicating liquors, as in ***prohibitory law, movement, party***, etc.

a **1591** H. SMITH *Wks.* (1867) II. 428 Which words be most prohibitory. *a* **1602** W. PERKINS *Cases Consc.* (1619) 318 Lust may be restrained..without prohibitory lawes. **1766** BLACKSTONE *Comm.* II. xxxii. 496 This law is entirely prohibitory. **1797** BURKE *Regic. Peace* iii. Wks. VIII. 390 We have been obliged to guard it from foreign competition by very strict prohibitory laws. **1884** DOWELL *Taxation* v. ii. I. 135 An enactment prohibitory of the imposition of a subsidy on wool. **1899** [see PROHIBITION 4].

2. = PROHIBITIVE 2.

1849 MACAULAY *Hist. Eng.* iii. I. 377 The cost of conveyance amounted to a prohibitory tax on many useful articles. **1881** SIR W. THOMSON in *Nature* 8 Sept. 434/1 This..is obviously prohibitory of every scheme for economising tidal energy by means of artificial dock-basins.

3. *Gram.* = PROHIBITIVE *a.* 3.

1925 G. R. DRIVER in A. S. Peake *People & Bk.* 97 Since *lû* and *lâ* implied a precative and a prohibitory sense respectively, there was no risk of confusion between these forms.

Hence **pro'hibitorily** *adv.*, in a prohibitory way, with prohibitory effect.

1876 R. HART *Land of Sinim* (1901) 202 That foreign goods..are either differentially or prohibitorily taxed.

prohormone: see PRO-[2] 1.

proif, obs. Sc. spelling of PROOF.

proin(e, proiner, obs. forms of PRUNE, PRUNER.

pro indiviso: see PRO 6.

†**proine**, *v. Obs.* Sometimes used in sense of PRIME *v.*[1] 2.

[In the 16th c. *proine* was a very common variant of *pruine*, *prune*, both as used of a bird pruning itself and of pruning a vine, tree, etc.; for the latter PRIME *v.*[3] was also a 16–17th c. synonym. But there is no evidence of a form *prune* answering to PRIME *v.*[1] As applied in quot. 1591 *proine* is slightly earlier than PRIME in this sense.]

1591 *Garrard's Art Warre* 12 His peece readie charged, loaden with her Bullet and proind with tutch pouder. **1622** *Recov. Ship of Bristol 'Exchange'* D iv b (Arb. Garner IV. 603), And Rawlins hauing proined the Tuch-holes.

pro-infinitive, -infinitival: PRO-[1] 4 b, c.

proinsulin: PRO-[2] 1.

pro-Israeli: PRO-[1] 5 a.

project ('prɒdʒɛkt, 'prəʊdʒɛkt), *sb.* [ad. L. *prōject-um* something thrown forth or out, neut. sing. of *prōject-us* pa. pple.: see next. So F. *projet* (*pourget* 1518 in Hatz.-Darm., *project* in Cotgr.).]

†**1.** A plan, draft, scheme, or table of something; a tabulated statement; a design or pattern according to which something is made. *Obs.*

a **1400–50** *Alexander* 3331 A corone, ane þe costious þat euire kyng weryd, On þe propurest of proiecte þat euire prince bere. **1581** LAMBARDE *Eiren.* II. vii. (1588) 225, I will now adventure to run thorow all the sortes of Manslaughters and Felonies..which (for the more light) I have bestowed in this project (or Table) following. **1600** (*title*) A Projecte, conteyninge the State, Order, and Manner of Governmente of the University of Cambridge. As now it is to be seene. **1601** HOLLAND *Pliny* II. 535 Many other plots and projects there doe remaine of his [Parasius'] drawing. **1627** WREN *Serm. bef. King* 6 My sonne, love God; or, My sonne, praise God; or, My sonne, obey God;..My sonne, feare God, is a Project and Promise of them all.

†**2.** A mental conception, idea, or notion; speculation. *Obs.*

1597 SHAKS. *2 Hen. IV*, I. iii. 29 Flatt'ring himselfe with Proiect of a power, Much smaller, then the smallest of his Thoughts. **1599** —— *Much Ado* III. i. 55 She cannot loue, Nor take no shape nor proiect of affection, Shee is so selfe indeared. **1727** DE FOE *Acc. Scot.* 152 A great deal of project and fancy may be employed to find out the ancient shape of the Church.

3. Something projected or thrown out; a projection, an emanation (of some being). *rare.*

1601 B. JONSON *Ev. Man in Hum.* (Qo. 1) III. i. 22 Oh beauty is a Project of some power, Chiefely when oportunitie attends her. **1849** G. DAWSON *Shaks. & other Lect.* (1888) 416 The house should be a project of the creature who inhabits it.

†**4.** The (fact of) being thrown out or put forth.

1601 HOLLAND *Pliny* I. 535 The said branches immediatly from their project must rise somewhat vpright in maner of fingers, standing forth from the palm of ones hand.

5. a. Something projected or proposed for execution; a plan, scheme, purpose; a proposal.

1601 R. JOHNSON *Kingd. & Commw.* (1603) 81 Till they retyred, having performed the project of their journey. **1604** T. WRIGHT *Passions* v. §3. 172 Orators, whose proiect is persuasion. **1623** T. SCOT *Highw. God* 80 All our Proiects of draining surrounded grounds. **1647** CLARENDON *Hist. Reb.* I. §50 New Projects were every day set on foot for Money, which serv'd only to offend, and incense the People. **1711** ADDISON *Spect.* No. 5 ¶3 There was actually a Project of bringing the New River into the House, to be employed in Jetteaus and Water-works. **1863** GEO. ELIOT *Romola* Proem, We Florentines were too full of great building projects to carry them all out in stone and marble. **1874** GREEN *Short Hist.* vi. §6. 326 The moral support which the project was expected to receive from the Parliament.

b. *Educ.* An exercise in which pupils are set to study a topic, either independently or in co-operation, from observation and experiment as well as from books, over a period of time.

1916 D. SNEDDEN in *School & Society* 16 Sept. 420/2 Some of us began using the word 'project' to describe a unit of educative work in which the most prominent feature was some form of positive and concrete achievement. **1919** J. A. STEVENSON in *School Sci. & Math.* Jan. 57 A project is a problematic act carried to completion in its natural setting. **1924** *Progressive Education* I. 72 A distinguishing earmark of a project, then, is the whole child responding to a situation; it is child activity. **1938** *New Statesman* 8 Jan. 46/2 *New Schools for Old* shows us the changes now being introduced into American public school methods of education. Children are encouraged to cope with the practical problems of life, and emphasis laid upon the 'project' or collective enterprise. **1942** B. CLEMENTS et al. *Projects for Junior School*: *Teachers' Bk.* i. 5 When working out a project the teacher gives help only when and where necessary, since the basic principle of modern teaching is child activity and teacher guidance. **1959** *Housewife* June 16 Cristy, who in one crowded summer, enjoys a library reading project, a visit to a Kansas farm and a course in baby care. **1961** CURTIS & BOULTWOOD *Short Hist. Educ. Ideas* (ed. 3) xx. 580 Not only were large-scale projects on such topics as 'Conservation' and 'Pan-Americanism' undertaken by many schools—often all the schools of an area—as part of the curriculum, but, in addition, community service by school children became common. **1965** *Nursing Times* 5 Feb. 191/1 By etymological definition, a project is a plan, scheme or design. Educationally, it refers to any exercise in which students gather their own information on a subject, arrange it and present it in an interesting form. **1976** P. DICKINSON *King & Joker* i. 19 Can I do next term's project on it [*sc.* a toad]?

c. *N. Amer.* A government-subsidized block of houses or apartments available at low rents. ***housing project***: see HOUSING *sb.*[1] 7.

1932 *Amer. City* Aug. 82/1 (*heading*) Federal Aid Now Offered for Low-Cost Housing and Slum-Clearance Projects. *Ibid.* 82/2 All housing projects should be large-scale developments. **1958** *Hearings Housing Act 1958* (U.S. Congress, Comm. Banking & Currency) 7 July 78 There is new thinking now to break up the projects and even though they are slum sites or urban redevelopment sites, to build scattered on the site. **1966** *Listener* 29 Sept. 454/1 Jim lives in one of a group of fifteen-storey-high buildings that make up a project, a city-owned housing estate. A family can rent an apartment cheaply in a project if it has a low income. Officially intended to replace the slum neighbourhoods of ten years ago, the projects are stark, anonymous, all-brick slums now. **1968** *Globe & Mail* (Toronto) 3 Feb. 3/4 A 2,000-unit high-rise and low-rise project. **1975** *New Yorker* 29 Sept. 43/3, I lived in a project then. The floors were so new they didn't have to be covered with anything.

d. A co-operative enterprise, often with a social or scientific purpose, but also in industry, etc.

1952 D. RIESMAN in *Antioch Rev.* Dec. 426 Professor John R. Seeley is now engaged in directing a large research project. **1952** AUDEN *Nones* 61 Thou shalt not worship projects nor Shalt thou or thine bow down before Administration. **1965** H. I. ANSOFF *Corporate Strategy* ii. 17 CIT uses long-term profitability over the lifetime of the project as the yardstick for evaluation. **1966** T. PYNCHON *Crying of Lot 49* iv. 88 When they grew up they..got stuck on some 'project' or 'task force' or 'team' and started being ground into anonymity. **1969** J. ARGENTI *Managem. Techniques* v. 26 Major projects call for the co-ordination of large numbers of machines, sub-contractors, finance, local authorities, design staff and so on. **1974** *Howard Jrnl.* XIV. 37 One aspect of a larger collective project being undertaken by members of the Centre for Contemporary Cultural Studies on 'mugging'.

†**6.** A projectile, a missile. *Obs.*

1686 *Phil. Trans.* XVI. 9 (*title*) Propositions concerning..the Motion of Projects. **1706** W. JONES *Syn. Palmar. Matheseos* bj, The Doctrine of the Motion of Projects, particularly applied to Gunnery and Throwing of Bombs. **1727–41** CHAMBERS *Cycl.*, Projectile or Project.

†**7.** = PROJECTION 6. *Obs.*

1807 HUTTON *Course Math.* II. 159 [A] set of theorems, relating to projects made on any given inclined planes.

8. *attrib.* and *Comb.* (sense 5), as ***project approach, area, book, engineer, house, housing, manager, method, -monger, officer, work***.

1973 *N.Y. Law Jrnl.* 4 Sept. 5/6 We are endeavoring to try appropriation cases on a project approach. **1961** *Economist* 2 Dec. 935/3 It means accepting—as in India—the idea of a 'project area' in which all the means of modernisation will be made to converge. **1976** *Billings* (Montana) *Gaz.* 20 June 3-B/1 We joined Montana Federation of Women's Clubs because it offers prizes in all sorts of project areas. **1947** A. EINSTEIN *Mus. Romantic Era* xiii. 181 The scheme for the composition of such a work is found in Schumann's 'project-book'. **1976** *Columbus* (Montana) *News* (Fair Bk. Suppl.) 10 June 18/1 Those exhibiting must have the project books up to date and be enrolled in the project and unit in which they are exhibiting. **1931** F. L. EIDMANN *Econ.*

Control Engin. & Manuf. iv. 45 In plants where the engineering projects are large,..it has been found that a very good way of handling the work is to assign one engineer to the task of 'living' with the job from start to finish... This engineer is known as a 'project engineer' in some organizations. **1973** *Times* 12 Nov. 28/8 Let us see the professionals all take a greater share of responsibility if a project is to be a success instead of leaving it to the 'jack of all trades'—the project engineer. **1967** G. JACKSON *Let.* Nov. in *Soledad Brother* (1971) 139, I thought most blacks.. understood..that these places were built with us in mind, just as were the project houses, unemployment offices, and bible schools. **1970** D. GOLDRICH et al. in I. L. Horowitz *Masses in Lat. Amer.* v. 182 Those invaders who could qualify by 'normal' criteria for project housing would receive it. **1973** *Black Panther* 14 Apr. 7/3 Her application for project housing was refused by the Chattanooga Housing Authority. **1965** *Guardian* 31 Mar. 11/3 The truth lies..in the person of what is usually known as the project manager. **1976** *Southern Even. Echo* (Southampton) 10 Nov. 19/6 Conder, based at Winchester, are also acting as the project managers. **1916** J. C. MOORE in *School Sci. & Math.* Nov. 688 The project method in science is nothing new, though the name often calls forth an attack... The story of every great invention is the story of a project. **1925** W. H. KILPATRICK *Foundations of Method* xxi. 346 'You defend then the term 'project method'?'..'If it be thought of as a purposeful way of treating children in order to stir the best in them and then to trust them to themselves as much as possible, yes, I approve it.' **1943** H. READ *Educ. through Art* vii. 233, I am aware that serious criticisms have been made of the project method of teaching, but they seem to be based on a formless type of project. **1953** CURTIS & BOULTWOOD *Short Hist. Educ. Ideas* xvii. 476 After the Great War of 1914–18 Dewey's problem method was reinterpreted by W. H. Kilpatrick as the project method. **1630** J. TAYLOR (Water P.) *Gt. Eater Kent* 4 Some get their liuings..by their braines, as politicians, monopolists, proiect-mongers, suit-ioggers, and star-gazers. **1905** *Longm. Mag.* July 262 The old project-monger beamed with her full moon face. **1968** H. I. ANSOFF *Corporate Strategy* 1 Dr Ansoff worked for the RAND Corporation as a project officer. **1973** R. HAYES *Hungarian Game* xxxi. 183 Generally speaking, sir, agents administer *things*, while Project Officers administer *people*. **1941** *Manch. Guardian Weekly* 14 Mar. 214/4, I..discover 'underlying object of fostering project work on citizenship'. **1958** *Sunday Times* 15 June 4/8, I want more, not less, practical mathematics in junior schools..and suitably graded mathematical project work in secondary schools.

†**pro'ject**, *ppl. a. Obs.* [ad. L. *prōject-us*, pa. pple. of *prōicĕre*, *prōjic-ĕre* to throw forth, stretch out, expel, reject, give up, etc., f. *prō*, PRO-[1] + *jacĕre* to throw.] **I.** Construed as *pa. pple.*

1. Stretched out, extended.

1432–50 tr. *Higden* (Rolls) I. 295 This prouince, proiecte by the longitude of the occean, hathe on the este to hit Turonea, whom the floode callede Ligeris flowethe abowte.

2. Given up, abandoned.

1432–50 tr. *Higden* (Rolls) I. 87 Proiecte in the lustes of lechery, [þei] haue grete delectacion in women.

3. Projected, thrown.

1471 RIPLEY *Comp. Alch.* Pref. ii. in Ashm. *Theat. Chem. Brit.* (1652) 127 When thereon itt ys project,..That Mercury teynyth permanently. **1647** H. MORE *Cupid's Conflict* xxi, Whose pestilent eye into my heart project Would burn like poysonous Comet in my spright.

II. as *adj.* [= L. *prōjectus* immoderate, abject.]

4. Abandoned; abject, base.

1607 CHAPMAN *Bussy D'Ambois* II. i. Plays 1873 II. 29, I would haue put that proiect face of his To a more test, than did her Dutchesship. *c* **1611** —— *Iliad* III. Comm. (1857) 78 For which yet his Criticus hath the project impudence to tax Homer. **1616** —— *Hymn Apollo* 43 With minds project, exempt from list or lawe.

project (prəʊ'dʒɛkt), *v.* Also *South U.S. dial.* projeck, projick. [f. L. *prōject-*, ppl. stem of *prōicĕre*, *prōjicĕre*: see PROJECT *ppl. a.* (which occurs earlier than the finite vb.). OF. had in same sense *purjeter* (12th c.), *pourjeter* (14th c.), *projetter* (1452 in Godef. *Compl.*); in 16th c. Rabelais used *projecter*, Amyot *projetter*, mod.F. has *projeter*. L. had also a freq. *prōjectāre*, in the senses 'drive out' and 'reproach'.]

I. Of mental operations.

1. *trans.* To plan, contrive, devise, or design (something to be done, or some action or proceeding to be carried out); to form a project of. **a.** With simple obj. or clause. (Now a leading use.)

c **1477** CAXTON *Jason* 10 For to ymagine and proiecte the deth of his neuewe Jason. **1581** SAVILE *Tacitus' Hist.* II. lx. (1591) 88 The rest of the Legions..proiected warre in their minds [orig. *bellum meditabantur*]. **1664** EVELYN *Diary* 15 Oct., My Lord Chancellor..carried me..to see their palace, ..and to project the garden. **1671** BARROW *Serm., Ps.* cxii. 9 Wks. 1687 I. 444 Thus hath God wisely projected, that all his children should both effectually and quietly be provided for. **1679** J. GOODMAN *Penit. Pard.* III. iv. (1713) 318 Having projected the adjoining a neighbour kingdom to his own dominions. **1788** FRANKLIN *Autobiog.* Wks. 1840 I. 176, I projected and drew up a plan for the union. **1841** D'ISRAELI *Amen. Lit.* (1867) 114 He was a critical writer, projecting a system to which he strictly adhered. **1865** GROTE *Plato* I. iv. 137 Sketches projected but abandoned.

b. With *infin.* To plan, devise, or design *to do* something. Now *rare* or *Obs.*

1600 E. BLOUNT tr. *Conestaggio* 164 For that Emanuel of Portugal who had proiected to make the Prior King. *a* **1661** FULLER *Worthies, Yorks.* (1662) III. 199 King Richard.. presently projecting to repair himself by a new Marriage. **1777** ROBERTSON *Hist. Amer.* I. III. 228 He even projected to clothe the people whom he took along with him in some peculiar garments. **1810** W. TAYLOR in Robberds *Mem.* (1844) II. 293, I project already to complain of the completeness of the detail.

†**2.** *intr.* To form a plan, design, scheme, or project; to scheme. *Obs.*

1639 FULLER *Holy War* III. xxix. (1840) 170 Wise he was in projecting. **1642** —— *Holy & Prof. St.* IV. xiv. 308 About this time John Dudley Duke of Northumberland projected for the English Crown. *c* **1680** BEVERIDGE *Serm.* (1729) I. 64 The devil..projects and contrives against the church.

†**3.** *trans.* To put forth, set forth, exhibit; to present to expectation. *Obs.*

1606 SHAKS. *Ant. & Cl.* v. ii. 121, I cannot proiect mine owne cause so well To make it cleare. **1611** SPEED *Hist. Gt. Brit.* VI. xvi. §7. 96 The care that this good Emperour had for the weale of his subiects is proiected by his prouidence in making wayes passageable from place to place. **1697** DRYDEN *Virg. Georg.* I. 622 When the South projects a stormy Day, And when the clearing North will puff the Clouds away.

†**4.** To put before oneself in thought; to conceive, imagine. *Obs.*

1612 R. SHELDON *Serm. St. Martin's* 4 By their ambitious thoughts, they proiected to themselues a Messias like some Soueraigne Lord. **1657** S. PURCHAS *Pol. Flying-Ins.* 45 Which (whatsoever some have projected) is unpossible.

II. Of physical operations.

†**5.** *trans.* To throw or cast away (*lit.* and *fig.*); to reject. *Obs.*

c **1557** ABP. PARKER *Ps.* xxvii. 63 Project not me: dis-pleasantly, O Lord, my health, do not depart. **1593** NASHE *Christ's T.* 77 Abstinence and fasting, are as Corsiues to ate out the dead-flesh of gluttony, drunkennes, and concupiscence..which so proiected and eaten out, Christ.. will come and bind vp our wounds. **1603** HOLLAND *Plutarch's Mor.* 1303 There is no reason and probability, that any one should project this assertion also.

6. a. To cast, throw, hurl, shoot, impel, or cause to move forward, or onward in any direction.

1596 SPENSER *F.Q.* VI. i. 45 Before his feet her selfe she did project. **1620** VENNER *Via Recta* vii. 148 It proiecteth.. those excrements which sticke to the bowels. **1641** J. JACKSON *True Evang. T.* III. 209 In War, holy things are projected to dogges. **1704** J. HARRIS *Lex. Techn.* I. s.v. *Projectile*, The Line of Motion which a Body projected describes in the Air..is..the Curve of a Parabola. **1806** HUTTON *Course Math.* (1807) II. 151 If a body be projected upward, with the velocity it acquired in any time by descending freely, it will lose all its velocity in an equal time. **1834** MRS. SOMERVILLE *Connex. Phys. Sc.* i. (1849) 6 A body projected in space will move in a conic section. **1878** HUXLEY *Physiogr.* 53 The heat which would otherwise be projected into space.

b. To throw or cast (a substance) *in, into, on, upon* something. (Chiefly in *Alchemy* and *Chem.*)

1599 A. M. tr. *Gabelhouer's Bk. Physicke* 125/1 Take five wallenuttes with their shelles, glowe them in the fyere, then proiecte them in a gobblet with oulde wine. **1610** B. JONSON *Alch.* II. i, The great medcine! Of which one part proiected on a hundred Of Mercurie, or Venus, or the Moone, Shall turne it, to as many of the Sunne. **1800** HENRY *Epit. Chem.* (1808) 367 When projected on red-hot nitre, it [plumbago] should detonate. **1835–6** *Todd's Cycl. Anat.* I. 128/1 The pollen..is projected or falls upon the pistillum. **1849** D. CAMPBELL *Inorg. Chem.* 183 Five parts of flowers of sulphur and eight parts of iron borings are mixed together, and projected gradually into a red-hot crucible.

c. *intr.* In *Alchemy*: To make projection, i.e. to throw powder of projection (see PROJECTION 2) into a crucible of melted metal, for the purpose of transmuting the latter into gold or silver.

1610 B. JONSON *Alch.* I. i, You must be chiefe? as if you, onely, had The poulder to proiect with? *Ibid.* II. ii, My onely care is, Where to get stuffe, inough now, to proiect on, This towne will not halfe serue me. **1680** [see PROJECTION 10].

d. *South. U.S. dial.* To wander, saunter, stroll (*around*); to trifle, mess, play *with*.

1828 J. HALL *Lett. from West* 290 A man who goes into the woods..has a..great deal of *projecking* to do, as well as hard work. **1845** W. T. THOMPSON *Chron. Pineville* 107 You see what comes of your projectin' about town, when you ought to be gwine home. **1848** —— *Major Jones's Sk. Trav.* 62, I didn't know whether he was projeckin' with me or not. **1891** 'O. THANET' *Otto the Knight* 66 Quality liked projeckin' roun' de kitchin. **1893** H. A. SHANDS *Some Peculiarities of Speech in Mississippi* 51 *Projicking*, a word used by negroes and illiterate whites to mean *fooling, trifling*; as, 'If you don't stop your projickin' with me, I'll lick you.' **1906** F. LYNDE *Quickening* 135 Don't you know you oughtn't to go projecting around in the woods all alone? **1929** W. FAULKNER *Sound & Fury* 10 Don't you start no projecking with Queenie. *Ibid.* 67 Is you been projecking with his graveyard? **1957** *Daily Progress* (Charlottesville, Va.) 5 Feb. 8/1 It beats all get-out how some people are always tinkering and 'projecking' on how to do things different from the way most people do them.

7. *trans.* To place (a thing) so that it protrudes or juts out; to cause to jut out, stand out, or protrude. Now *rare.*

1624 [see PROJECTED 1]. **1679** MOXON *Mech. Exerc.* viii. 148 The better way is..to project it an Inch and a half beyond the side of the Building. **1700** DRYDEN *Fables, To Duchess of Ormund* 52 The land..had met your way, Projected out a neck, and jutted to the sea. **1765** in Picton *L'pool Munic. Rec.* (1886) II. 264 Going to project out Bow windows from their houses. **1825** *Greenhouse Comp.* I. 7 A noble conservatory or green-house may be projected from the south front. **1860** MOTLEY *Netherl.* (1868) I. v. 181 Strong structures, supported upon piers, had been projected, reaching..five hundred feet into the stream.

8. *intr.* To jut out; to stick out or protrude beyond the adjacent parts. (Now a leading use.)

1718 PRIOR *Solomon* I. 559 The craggy rock projects above the sky. **1795** BURNS *Address Miss Fontenelle* 34 As the boughs all temptingly project. **1849** MACAULAY *Hist. Eng.* iii. I. 350 The booths..projected far into the streets. **1856** STANLEY *Sinai & Pal.* vi. (1858) 267 The promontories of Tyre, Sidon, and Beirût project further..than those of Ascalon, Jaffa, Dor or Acre.

9. a. *trans.* To throw or cause to fall (light or shadow) upon a surface or into space.

1664 POWER *Exp. Philos.* I. 43 The smallest Atom..was presented as big as a Rounseval-Pea, and projecting a shade. *Ibid.* 73 If with a Prisme you strike the Rainbow-colours upon a wall, and observing where a red is projected. **1665** BOYLE *Occas. Refl.* IV. vi, The Shade my Body projected, near Noon. **1868** LOCKYER *Guillemin's Heavens* (ed. 3) 169 In all the other positions..the lunar cone of shade is projected into space away from the Earth. **1878** HUXLEY *Physiogr.* xix. 332 The shadow is said to be projected on to the flat surface.

b. To cause (a figure or image) to appear or 'stand out' *on* or *against* a background.

1831 BREWSTER *Nat. Magic* ii. (1833) 25 If a living figure had been projected against the strong light which imprinted these durable spectra of the sun. **1860** TYNDALL *Glac.* I. xi. 73 He..saw Huxley's form projected against the sky as he stood upon a pinnacle of rock. **1879** *Cassell's Techn. Educ.* II. 71/2 The mode of projecting views of objects at whatever angle they may be placed in relation to both planes.

c. To cause (an image) to be visible on a screen situated at a distance. Also *absol.*

1865 *Rep. Brit. Assoc. Adv. Sci. 1864* II. 98 The impressive character of the image projected [by a magic lantern], being often stereoscopic in aspect. **1902** *Encycl. Brit.* XXVII. 95/2 In the magic lantern an electric lamp or limelight..projects, through an objective lens, the successive images of the film upon a distant screen. **1935** *Television Today* II. 599/2 (*heading*) Projecting the cathode-ray oscillograph picture. **1946** R. LEHMANN *Gipsy's Baby* 57 Leisure employs me..as a kind of screen upon which are projected the images of persons. **1964** *Photogr. Jrnl.* CIV. 152/1 Microfilm images..can be projected directly on to printing plates. **1969** *Focal Encycl. Film & Television Techniques* 378/1 The projection cathode ray tube.. produces a very bright picture which can be projected with a suitable optical system. **1979** D. MEIRING *Foreign Body* ii. 30 Now it's film time... We'll project on the wall, just to the left of the bar.

d. To cause the image(s) on (a photograph, film, or slide) to be visible on a screen.

1896 R. W. PAUL *Brit. Pat. 4686*, My invention relates to an improved apparatus for producing representations of moving scenes, figures or objects by projecting onto a screen ..by means of.. suitable projecting apparatus, a series of photographic pictures of such scenes... In order to give a definite position to the picture on the film which is to be projected I prefer to employ the following mechanism. **1912** F. A. TALBOT *Moving Pictures* ix. 91 The film to be projected is carried upon a spool mounted on an arm or bracket above the mechanism. **1949** KIDD & LONG *Filmstrip & Slide Projection* 8 Often miniature slides can be projected in the standard projector (some of which project both miniature slides and filmstrips). **1962** L. DEIGHTON *Ipcress File* xv. 87 If they had to have a major here to project the film it might just be worth watching. **1971** L. B. HAPPÉ *Basic Motion Picture Technol.* i. 37 Corresponding prints could.. be projected by similar anamorphic lenses to show a picture filling a very wide screen. *Ibid.* 39 The proportions of the new Cinemascope format when projected were 8 units wide by 3 high.

10. *fig.* (From senses 6 and 9.)

1850 ROBERTSON *Serm.* Ser. III. x. 127 Then we project everything stamped with the impress of our own feelings. **1856** DOVE *Logic Chr. Faith* IV. ii. §1. 180 Thus we project into the realm of space a moral cause. **1869** GOULBURN *Purs. Holiness* x. 94 The very image of Christ..as it was projected upon the mind of the Jew. **1870** E. PEACOCK *Ralf Skirl.* I. 47 The realistic teaching of Holy Scripture projected itself sharply upon their uncultured minds. **1874** SYMONDS *Sk. Italy & Greece, Siena* 58 Ideas were projected from her vivid fancy upon the empty air around her. **1878** S. COX *Salv. Mundi* iv. (ed. 3) 94 Can we not project ourselves so far into the future as to anticipate the time when [etc.]? **1879** HARLAN *Eyesight* iii. 37 An excited or disordered brain may project some phantasm of its own conjuring..and see it as distinctly as if it were a tangible object. **1903** MYERS *Human Personality* I. 25 The occasional power of some agent to project himself phantasmally; to make himself manifest, as though in actual presence, to some percipient at a distance.

b. To attribute (an emotion, state of mind, etc.) to an external object or person, esp. unconsciously. Also *absol.*

1923 J. S. HUXLEY *Ess. Biologist* iv. 167 Certain neurotic types project their depression so as to colour everything that comes into their cognizance a gloomy black. **1925** A. & J. STRACHEY tr. *Freud's Coll. Papers* III. 458 It was incorrect of us to say that the perception which was suppressed internally was projected outwards; the truth is rather..that what was abolished internally returns from without. **1939** *Jrnl. Psychol.* VIII. 409 It appears that the subject projects similar patterns or configurations upon widely different materials. **1960** E. E. CUMMINGS *Let.* 30 Jan. (1969) 266 Indeed this correspondent can't help suspecting yourself of what the psychoanalysts call 'projecting'. **1966** I. G. SARASON *Personality* xii. 181 A defense mechanism through which an individual unconsciously projects his own undesirable characteristics to others than himself. **1975** K. R. SCHERER et al. *Human Aggression & Conflict* iv. 116 The subjects were projecting their needs into their imagery.

c. To convey to others, esp. by one's manner and actions (a positive image of one's personality or attributes). Usu. *absol.*

1955 *Psychiatry* XVIII. 217/2 The self-evaluation projected by his clothes and manner. **1957** *Economist* 12 Oct. 130/1 This matter of 'projection' is taken very seriously. 'He simply doesn't project' can be as final a dismissal of political aspiration as the fact that a man is known to have beaten a whole series of wives. **1959** *Encounter* Sept. 50/2 Competing with the roar of the machines..the actors struggle to project. **1960** *News Chron.* 28 July 4/5 Unable to 'project' publicly, in private he deploys considerable private charm. **1967** M. ARGYLE *Psychol. Interpersonal Behaviour* iii. 55 If a person behaves unpleasantly, or in some other way fails to live up to the image he has projected, equilibrium is disturbed.

11. *Geom.* To draw straight lines or 'rays' from a centre through every point of a given figure, so that they fall upon or intersect a surface and produce upon it a new figure of which each point corresponds to a point of the original. (With either the rays, the original figure, or the resulting figure as obj.) Hence, to represent or delineate (a figure) according to any system of correspondence between its points and the points of the surface on which it is delineated.

1679 MOXON *Mech. Exerc.* ix. 151 The manner of projecting them, is copiously taught in many Books of Architecture. *Ibid.* 152 Winding Stairs are projected on a round Profile. **1831** BREWSTER *Optics* i. 9 The truth of this rule may be found by projecting fig. 7 upon a large scale. **1854** HOOKER *Himal. Jrnls.* I. Pref. 17, I did not use instruments in projecting the outlines. **1866** PROCTOR *Handbk. Stars* 19 The whole hemisphere is projected into a circle whose radius is twice that of a great circle of the sphere. **1885** *Encycl. Brit.* XIX. 798/1 Any conic can be projected into any other conic. **1887** D. A. LOW *Machine Draw.* (1892) 116 Draw and complete the two views, as shown.., and add an end elevation, properly projected. **1895** STORY-MASKELYNE *Crystallogr.* ix. 488 It may happen that we wish to project the two crystals on a plane perpendicular to the twin-face.

b. *Chartography.* To make a geometrical or other projection or representation on a plane surface of (the earth, sky, or any portion thereof).

1855 BREWSTER *Newton* I. i. 11 We were not able to determine whether they [dials at Woolsthorpe] were executed by a tentative process..or were more accurately projected, from a knowledge of the doctrine of the sphere. **1858** HERSCHEL *Outl. Astron.* iv. §279 (ed. 5) 183 A spherical surface can by no contrivance be extended or projected into a plane without undue enlargement or contraction of some parts. **1866** PROCTOR *Handbk. Stars* 12 A simple method of projecting the meridians and parallels for any small portion of the celestial sphere. **1870** LOWELL *Among my Bks.* Ser. I. (1873) 170 As if Shakespeare's world were one which Mercator could have projected.

III. 12. a. *pass.* = next sense.

1902 J. M. BALDWIN *Dict. Philos. & Psychol.* II. 414/2 The radiations taken together are called the 'projection system', the lower centres being projected upon the cortex. **1925** *Jrnl. Neurol. & Psychopath.* VI. 5 We draw the conclusion that the upper part of the retina in apes is projected on the medial side of the corpus geniculatum externum. **1926** *Brain* XLIX. 2 The nasal part of the retina is always projected laterally to the temporal half [of the external geniculate body].

b. *intr. Physiol.* Of an area or organ of the body, or its nerves: to have or be nerve fibres extending *to* an area. Also const. *upon*.

1936 *Jrnl. Compar. Neurol.* LXIV. 37 The anterior thalamic nuclei project to a small part of the orbital surface of the frontal lobe. *Ibid.*, The nucleus ventralis posterior, projects entirely upon the cortex of the central sulcus and the postcentral convolution. **1951** T. C. RUCH in S. S. Stevens *Handbk. Exper. Psychol.* iv. 125/2 The ablation of a cortical area truncates the axons running to it, and the locus of the resulting retrograde degeneration establishes which thalamic nucleus projects to the particular area ablated. **1975** D. H. FORD *Anat. Central Nerv. Syst.* vii. 83 The white matter of the [spinal] cord..consists of association fibers.. which connect adjacent levels of the cord, longer association bundles which project up or down the various funiculi to interconnect further segments of the cord, or very long projection systems which project to supracord levels or which enter the cord from higher levels. **1978** *Sci. Amer.* July 38/1 These fibers usually branch repeatedly and may project to distant parts of the nervous system or leave the nervous system to innervate effector tissues.

projected (prəʊˈdʒɛktɪd), *ppl. a.* [-ED[1].]

1. Thrown or thrust forward; placed so as to protrude; cast upon a surface: see the verb.

1624 WOTTON *Archit.* in *Reliq.* (1651) 236 That all the projected or jutting Parts (as they are termed) be very moderate. **1692** BENTLEY *Boyle Lect.* 246 A projected transverse impulse, in tangents to their several orbs. **1695** BLACKMORE *Pr. Arth.* IV. 480 They..with projected Fires our Men assail. **1778** LOWTH *Transl. Isaiah* Notes (ed. 12) 290 Then to the rocks' projected shade retire. **1831** BREWSTER *Nat. Magic* iv. (1833) 95 The projected image of this figure..may then be accurately copied.

fig. **1904** *Daily Chron.* 16 Feb. 3/1 The command is still to 'know thyself', for only by means of an analysed and projected self can we know the minds of others.

2. Put forth as a project; planned, devised.

1706 PHILLIPS, *Projected*, designed, contrived. **1828** D'ISRAELI *Chas. I*, I. vi. 162 The difficulties of a projected invasion. **1863** H. COX *Instit.* III. v. 655 Projected treaties of commerce. **1894** S. FISKE *Holiday Stories* (1900) 73 The projected railroad..was a fact to be thought over.

Hence **proˈjectedly** *adv.*: in quots. in sense of PROJECT *ppl. a.* 4, completely, abjectly.

1660 tr. *Amyraldus' Treat. conc. Relig.* I. i. 2 There is no Nation so projectedly Savage, as to be aliens to the belief of existence of some Deity. **1665** J. SPENCER *Vulg. Proph.* 24 For they..believe no man to be so projectedly Atheistical, as to intitle God to the Visions of his own brain.

projectile (prəʊˈdʒɛktɪl, -aɪl), *a.* and *sb.* Also 7-8 -il. [ad. mod.L. *projectil-is*, f. ppl. stem of *prōjicĕre* to PROJECT. So in F. (Dict. Acad. 1762).]

A. *adj.* **1.** Of motion or velocity: Caused by impulse or projection. Now *rare* or *Obs.*

1696 WHISTON *The. Earth* I. *Lemmata* 8 From the Uniform Projectile Motion of Bodies in straight lines. **1715** CHEYNE *Philos. Princ. Relig.* I. (1716) 156 To have destroy'd the projectil Motion. **1717** J. KEILL *Anim. Oecon.* (1738) 157 The projectile Velocity of the Planets. **1828** HUTTON *Course Math.* II. 208 In case of great projectile velocities.

2. Of force, etc.: Impelling or driving forward or onward; projecting.

1715 tr. *Gregory's Astron.* (1726) I. 99 The augmentation of the projectile Force. **1801** FUSELI in *Lect. Paint.* iii. (1848) 408 The laws of attraction, the projectile and centrifuge qualities of the system. **1858** GREENER *Gunnery* 20 Its use then was more for fireworks, than as an artillerist projectile force. **1861** LYTTON *Str. Story* xxxi. In this trance there is an extraordinary cerebral activity—a projectile force given to the mind—distinct from the soul.

3. Capable of being projected by force, esp. of being thrown or used as a missile.

projectile anchor, in life-saving apparatus, an anchor adapted to be shot out of a tube towards the place where it is intended to grapple.

1865 *Morn. Star* 11 June, Everything that was projectile was brought into requisition. **1883** *Fisheries Exhib. Catal.* 42 Model Carts, Mortars, Projectile Anchors,..Signal Gun and Rocket Signals.

4. *Zool.* Capable of being thrust forward or protruded, as the jaws of a fish; protrusile.

1864 COPE in *Proc. Acad. Nat. Sci. Philad.* 226 Tongue papillose; terminal portion projectile on glosso-hyoideum.

5. *Literary Criticism.* (See quots.)

1929 I. A. RICHARDS *Pract. Criticism* 357 Aesthetic or 'projectile' adjectives..raise several extraordinarily interesting questions... In so far as they register the projection of a feeling into an object they carry a double function. **1949** BROOKS & WARREN *Fund. Good Writing* x. 351 What I. A. Richards calls 'projectile' adjectives: that is, adjectives which function, not so much to give an objective description, as to express the writer's or speaker's feelings. .. The '*miserable* wretch' may actually be smiling happily. The woman who has just been called '*a great little* wife' may be large or small.

B. *sb.* **a.** A projectile object; a body impelled through the air or through space; *spec.* a missile adapted to be discharged from a cannon by the force of some explosive.

[**1665** A. KIRCHER *Mundus Subterraneus* I. v. I. 30 De motu projectilium parabolico, et miris ejus effectibus.] **1665** *Phil. Trans.* I. 109 Of the Motion of heavy Bodies, of Pendulems, of Projectils. **1729** SHELVOCKE *Artillery* v. 312 Under the head of Missiles, by which is meant Projectiles, we will range Fire-Darts, Arrows and Javelins, Fire-Pots and Flasks. **1775** J. BANKS *Epit. Lect.* 87 Every projectile is acted upon by two forces, the impetus or projectile force, and the power of gravity. **1837** WHEWELL *Hist. Induct. Sc.* (1857) II. 44 The parabolic motion of Projectiles. **1890** *Century Dict.* s.v., Projectiles used in smooth-bore guns are ..sometimes oblong..as in the Manby, Parrott, and Lyle life-saving projectiles.

fig. **1826** *Sheridaniana* 253 The projectiles of wit.

b. *attrib.* and *Comb.*, as ***projectile-maker***, ***-trade***, etc.; ***projectile-throwing*** adj.; **projectile theory**, (*a*) that branch of mechanics which treats of the motion of projectiles, as affected by gravity and the resistance of the air; (*b*) = the emission theory of light: see EMISSION 7.

1854 *Pereira's Polar. Light* 6 The Newtonian hypothesis, or the projectile or emission theory, was started when our knowledge of the facts was but in its infancy. **1899** *Daily News* 15 May 5/4 A welcome stimulus to the projectile trade. **1907** PAYNE-GALLWEY (*title*) A Summary of the History, Construction and Effects in Warfare of the Projectile-Throwing Engines of the Ancients.

Hence **proˈjectilist**, one who studies or experiments with projectiles.

1852 COL. HAWKER *Diary* (1893) II. 338 With gunmakers, projectilists, general officers, Ordnance authorities.

projecting (prəʊˈdʒɛktɪŋ), *vbl. sb.* [f. PROJECT *v.* + -ING[1].] The action of the verb PROJECT, in various senses; = PROJECTION.

1658 *Whole Duty Man* xvi. (1684) 129 It despises all projectings for gain or advantage. **1668** MOXON *Mech. Dyalling* 4 All the Authors I have met with seem to presuppose their Reader to understand Geometry, and the projecting of the sphere already. **1688** BONNELL in W. Hamilton *Life* I. (1703) 40 Vain projectings for your escape and safety. **1726** LEONI *Alberti's Archit.* I. 48/2 The Wall may be defended by the projecting of the Cornice. **1776** G. SEMPLE *Building in Water* 25 My Plan of the Bridge, in projecting of which, I found myself..stored with Precedents. **1959** *Times Lit. Suppl.* 16 Jan. 39/1 *Introduction to Cine*..starts off the complete beginner and takes him as far as editing and projecting. **1960** E. H. GOMBRICH *Art & Illusion* xi. 385 We prefer suggestion to representation, we have adjusted our expectations to enjoy the very act of guessing, of projecting.

projecting (prəʊˈdʒɛktɪŋ), *ppl. a.* [f. as prec. + -ING[2].] That projects.

1. That puts forth projects; scheming or contriving; inventive.

1635 JACKSON *Creed* VIII. xxi. §4 Although man be a reasonable and projecting creature. **1657** THORNLEY tr. *Longus' Daphnis & Chloe* 113 Daphnis was of a more projecting wit than she. **1706** DE FOE *Jure Div.* IV. 89 Delusions and Chimeras of Projecting Statesmen. **1771** SMOLLETT *Humph. Cl.* 6 Sept., Being of a projecting spirit, some of his schemes miscarried.

2. That throws or impels forward or onward.

1727-41 CHAMBERS *Cycl.* s.v. *Projectile*, Both the projecting and the gravitating force are found in the same line of direction.

3. Jutting or sticking out beyond the general surface or adjacent parts; protruding.

1776 WITHERING *Brit. Plants* (1796) II. 225 Myosotis.. mouth closed with projecting scales. **1855** MACAULAY *Hist. Eng.* xvi. III. 622 Houses..with high gables and projecting upper stories. **1905** *Macm. Mag.* Dec. 86 A projecting twig offered a convenient prop.

Hence **proˈjectingly** *adv.*, in a projecting manner.

1774 PENNANT *Tour Scot. in 1772*, 260 A cape, placed in our maps far too projectingly. **18..** *Annals Philad. & Penn.* I. 381 (Cent.) A..hat..projectingly and out of all proportion cocked before.

projection (prəʊˈdʒɛkʃən), *sb.* [ad. L. *prōjectiōn-em* a throwing forward, extension, projection, n. of action f. *prōjicĕre*, or a. F. *projection* (13- 14th c. in Hatz.-Darm.): see PROJECT *ppl. a.*]

I. 1. The action of projecting; the fact of being projected; throwing or casting forth or forward; impulsion, ejection.

1599 A. M. tr. *Gabelhouer's Bk. Physicke* 109/1 It is commodious for the proiectione of phlegme. **1642** H. MORE *Song of Soul* (1647) 19 His [the Sun's] rays have undenied Projection. **1691** RAY *Creation* I. (1692) 23 To perswade him that this was done..by the rude scattering of Ink upon the Paper, or by the lucky Projection of so many Letters at all adventures. **1775** WESLEY *Serm.* lix. 10 Wks. 1811 IX. 128 Connect the force of projection and attraction how you can, they will never produce a circular motion. **1852** MUNDY *Our Antipodes* 117 The fall of the Viceroy's good chestnut..and the projection of his rider full ten feet over his head. **1862** G. P. SCROPE *Volcanos* 24 The immense trituration they sustain in the process of repeated projection and fall.

fig. *a* **1652** J. SMITH *Sel. Disc.* iv. 103 Shewing how all that which we call body, rather issued forth by an infinite projection from some mind.

2. a. The casting of some ingredient into a crucible; esp. in *Alchemy*, the casting of the powder of philosophers' stone (***powder of projection***) upon a metal in fusion to effect its transmutation into gold or silver; the transmutation of metals.

1594 PLAT *Jewell-ho.* III. 87 You shall make a perfect proiection your selues vpon Mercurie. **1612** WOODALL *Surg. Mate* Wks. (1653) 273 Projection is an exaltation chiefly in Metals, by a medicine cast upon them, which will suddenly penetrate and transfigurate them. **1633** T. ADAMS *Exp. 2 Peter* i. 20 Alchymists that labour to make gold by projection. *c* **1645** HOWELL *Lett.* (1650) III. 17 To do the like touching the Philosophers stone, the powder of Projection, and potable gold. **1821** SCOTT *Kenilw.* xxii, I will do projection in thy presence, my son,..and thine eyes shall witness the truth. **1836-41** BRANDE *Chem.* (ed. 5) 11 At other times the performers..purchased what was termed a powder of projection, prepared by the adepts, containing a portion of gold.

b. *fig.* Change from one thing to another; transmutation.

1630 B. JONSON *New Inn* III. ii, I feel that transmutation of my blood, As I were quite become another creature, And all he speaks it is projection. **1751** JOHNSON *Rambler* No. 111 ¶2 We laugh at the timorous delays of plodding industry, and fancy that, by increasing the fire, we can at pleasure accelerate the projection. **1820** HAZLITT *Lect. Dram. Lit.* 16 Public opinion was in a state of projection. **1828** SOUTHEY in *Q. Rev.* XXXVIII. 549 The golden opportunity is arrived, they have reached..the moment of projection. **1870** LOWELL *Among my Bks.* Ser. I. (1873) 154 The lucky moment of projection was clearly come.

II. 3. The forming of mental projects or plans; scheming, planning.

1599 SHAKS. *Hen. V*, II. iv. 46 Which of a weake and niggardly proiection, Doth like a Miser spoyle his Coat, with scanting A little Cloth. **1657** S. PURCHAS *Pol. Flying-Ins.* 142 After the projection of divers experiments. **1776** S. J. PRATT *Pupil of Pleas.* II. 230 The dead of the night..is generally my hour for projection. **1811** *Ora & Juliet* IV. 23 He was endeavouring to abet the good plans that were in projection. **1838-9** FR. A. KEMBLE *Resid. Georgia* (1863) 87 The projection of a canal. **1846** GROTE *Greece* I. xxi. II. 235 The whole plot appears of one projection, from the beginning down to the death of the suitors.

†**4.** That which is projected or planned; a project, plan, design, scheme; a proposal. *Obs.*

1633 NABBES *Tottenham Court* III. ii, The planting of hoppes was a rare projection in the Dutch. **1652** HEYLIN *Cosmogr.* II. 238 Having withall good courages and high projections. **1674** [Z. CAWDREY] *Catholicon* 9 My projection is..that this Stipulation should once be solemnly made. **1753** JOHNSON *Adventurer* No. 108 ¶13 Men are so frequently cut off in the midst of their projections. **1804** EUGENIA DE ACTON *Tale without Title* III. 218 Many other airy projections, which vanished as soon as they were formed.

III. 5. a. The action of placing a thing or part so that it sticks or stands out, or projects beyond the general line or surface; the fact or condition of being so placed as to project.

1644 BULWER *Chiron.* 30 The gentle and wel ordered Hand throwne forth by a moderate projection. **1772** HUTTON *Bridges* 97 The perpendicular projection will be equal to half the breadth..of the pier. **1806** J. DALLAWAY *Obs. Eng. Archit.* 207 The central front is rendered mean.. by the..projection of the wings. **1874** BLACKIE *Self-Cult.* 42 Let him..sit erect, with his back to the light, and a full free projection of the breast. **1875** MERIVALE *Gen. Hist. Rome* lxv. 525 The conquests..beyond the Danube constituted a deep projection of Roman civilisation into the wilds of barbarism.

b. The representation of an object in a picture in such a way as to make it appear to stand out in relief.

1603 E. Heyward in Drayton *Bar. Wars* Pref. Verses, Since affection In iudgement may, as shaddow and proiection In Lantskip, make that which is low seeme high. 1851 Carpenter *Man. Phys.* (ed. 2) 597 The idea of projection is not so strongly excited; nor are we able to distinguish with the same certainty between a well-painted picture..and the objects themselves in relief. 1883 Stevenson *Silverado Sq.* 194 The incredible projection of the stars themselves.

c. *concr.* Anything which projects or extends beyond the adjacent surface; a projecting part.

1756 Burke *Subl. & B.* III. xiv, Any ruggedness, any sudden projection, any sharp angle, is..contrary to that idea. 1815 J. Smith *Panorama Sc. & Art* I. 131 The projections at the corners..are called buttresses. 1885 *Law Rep. 15 Q.B. Div.* 316 A catch or small projection at the end of an iron pin.

IV. 6. a. *Geom.* The drawing of straight lines or 'rays' according to some particular method through every point of a given figure, usually so as to fall upon or intersect a surface and produce upon it a new figure each point of which corresponds to a point of the original figure. Hence, each of such rays, or of such points of the resulting figure, is said to be the *projection* of a point of the original one; or the whole resulting figure is said to be the *projection* of the original.

In ***central projection*** (often called simply *projection*), the rays are all drawn from one point or 'centre'; in ***axial projection***, a number of planes are similarly drawn from one line or 'axis'.

1731 W. Halfpenny *Perspective* 32 Whence, draw a Line to the Point of Distance: then is MU the Projection. 1823 P. Nicholson *Pract. Build.* 539 The most useful kinds of architectural drawing depend upon the Theory of Projection. 1831 Brewster *Optics* xxiii. 208 Supposing AOB, CPPD to be projections of great circles of the sphere. 1840 Lardner *Geom.* xv. 185 The position and form of lines in space are expressed, in the higher geometry, by determining the projection of these lines on planes placed at right angles to each other. 1885 *Encycl. Brit.* XIX. 793/2 Any figure, plane or in space of three dimensions, may be projected to any surface from any point which is called the centre of proiection.

fig. 1829 I. Taylor *Enthus.* x. 301 Metaphysical projections of the moral system, how neat soever and entire, and plausible they may seem.

b. *Math.* Any homomorphism from a vector space or the like into a part of itself such that each element of the part is mapped on to itself; also, a homomorphism from a group into a quotient group.

1942 *Amer. Jrnl. Math.* LXIV. 115 The study of groups which have projections on abelian groups. 1950 *Bull. Amer. Math. Soc.* LVI. 488 The systematic use of these injection and projection homomorphisms is at the heart of our formulation of the duality phenomena. 1976 D. E. Christie *Basic Topology* vii. 191 An indispensable tool for products is the projection, a function from the product to one of the factors.

7. a. The drawing according to scale, and on mathematical principles, of a plan, chart, or map of a surface, or a diagram on the flat of a machine or the like; *spec.* the representation of any spherical surface on the flat, e.g. of the whole or any part of the surface of the earth, more fully called ***map-projection*** (see b).

1557 Recorde *Whetst.* M ij, It serueth so many waies, in building: in proiection of plattes, for measuring of ground, timber, or stone. 1812–16 Playfair *Nat. Phil.* II. 67 In the construction of maps..by the projection of the spherical surface on a plane, such as it would be seen to the eye situated in a particular point; or by the developement, that is, the spreading out of a spherical on a plane surface. 1857 W. Binns *Elem. Treat. Orth. Project.* ii. (1862) 12 The difference betwixt perspective drawing, or scenographic projection and orthographic projection. 1869 Tyndall *Notes Lect. Light* 30 Take two drawings—projections, as they are called—of the frustum of a cone; the one as it is seen by the right eye, the other as it is seen by the left. 1887 D. A. Low *Machine Draw.* (1892) 123 Whilst the notion of projection had been imparted, projection lines being drawn, yet the student had utterly failed to realise from the sketches the form of the object he was drawing.

b. *Chartography.* A representation on a plane surface, on any system, geometrical or other, of the whole or any part of the surface of the earth, or of the celestial sphere; any one of the many modes in which this is done.

The earlier modes were actually the result of geometrical projection; but the name has been extended to representations which lie quite outside the etymological sense.

The projections (in this extended sense) that have been used to represent the whole, the half, or parts of the earth's surface, are more than thirty; they have been classified by Major C. F. Close (*Sketch of Map Projections*, 1901, *Text-bk. of Topogr. & Geogr. Surveying*, 1905, xi.) under the following heads: I. ***orthomorphic*** or *conformal* (conform, or conformable), preserving the *forms* of areas (but not their relative sizes); II. ***equal area*** (equivalent, or surface-true), in which equal areas of the surface are represented by equal areas on the map, but the forms of these, when large, are distorted; III. ***perspective***, representing the surface as seen from some point of view at the centre, on the surface, or at various distances from it; IV. ***zenithal*** (q.v.) or *azimuthal*; V. ***conical*** (q.v.); VI. ***cylindrical*** (q.v.); VII. ***conventional***, produced by arbitrary rules for convenience of drawing and the approximate representation of a number of properties; such is the *globular*, commonly used in school maps of the two hemispheres. Another conventional projection is the *two-point equidistant*, showing accurately the distances from every point to each of two chosen points. Of the varieties in actual use, many belong to two, and some to three of these classes; thus ***Mercator's projection*** is orthomorphic and cylindrical. For *gnomonic, homolographic, orthographic, polyconic, sinusoidal, stereographic*, etc. *projections*, see these adjs. Many projections are also named after their inventors, as *Mercator's*, *Bonne's* (modified conical equal-area), *Sanson-Flamsteed's* (sinusoidal equal-area), *Airy's* (balance of errors), *Cassini's* (rectangular co-ordinate) used in the 1-inch Ordnance Maps of England, and 6-inch of Great Britain, the six different projections of *Lambert*; *Albers'*, a conical equal-area projection with two standard parallels; and *Clarke's*, projected from a centre outside the globe onto a diametrically opposite plane. Projections may be *interrupted*, so that the representation is not convex but lobate or partly dissected; and *transverse*, representing a globe rotated through a right or other angle from its conventional orientation. For these see the works cited above, and other special treatises.

1570 Dee *Math. Pref.* a iv b, Of making due proiection of a Sphere in plaine. 1625 N. Carpenter *Geog. Del.* I. vii. (1635) 182 (Polar projection) This kinde of proiection, though more vnusuall,..wants not his special vse in describing the parts of the Earth neere the Pole. 1669 Sturmy *Mariner's Mag.* II. viii. 73 Charts, according to Mercator's or Wright's Projection. 1704 J. Harris *Lex. Techn.* I, *Projection of the Sphere in Plano*, is a true Geometrical Delineation of the Circles of the Sphere, or any assigned Parts of them, upon the Plane of some one Circle; as on the Horizon, Meridian, Equator, Tropick, etc. *Ibid.*, *Polar Projection*, is a Representation of the Earth, or of the Heavens, projected on the Plane of one of the Polar Circles. 1706 Phillips (ed. Kersey) s.v., Astrolabes, Quadrants, Sun-dials, Maps, &c., are Projections of the Sphere; which are of three sorts, viz. Gnomonick, Orthographick and Stereographick. 1796 Morse *Amer. Geog.* I. 56 General maps..are projected upon the plane of some great circle..and from this circle the projection is said to be meridional, equatorial, or horizontal. 1866 Proctor *Handbk. Stars* 12 *Note*, The term projection has come to be applied in mapping to any mode of construction founded on some definite geometrical principle. 1867 Denison *Astron. without Math.* 13 In Mercator's projection, which is a favourite one for maps, the globe is supposed to be stretched out on the inside of a cylinder which touches it all round the equator, and the cylinder is then cut and opened out flat or 'developed'. 1905 C. F. Close *Topogr. & Geogr. Surveying* xi. 92 The term *projection*, though sanctioned by long usage, is an unfortunate one. The great majority of useful map projections are not obtained in any geometrical way. A map projection is to be treated as the representation on a plane, by any law, of the terrestrial meridians and parallels. 1910 J. I. Craig *Theory Map-Projections* v. 45 (*heading*) Transverse conical projection... This projection is of no practical importance. *Ibid.* 53 (*heading*) Zenithal or azimuthal projections. *Ibid.* 55 Lambert's equivalent azimuthal projection. 1910 *Encycl. Brit.* XVII. 656/1 (*caption*) Clarke's perspective projection for a spherical radius of 108°. 1912 A. R. Hinks *Map Projections* i. 6 There is a class of projections sometimes named azimuthal, from the fact that the azimuths, or true bearings, from the centre of the map, of all points, are shown correctly. *Ibid.* 7 The objection to the term *azimuthal* is that it is hard to pronounce, and several writers have followed German in calling always this class of projection *zenithal*. *Ibid.* iii. 26 Albers' conical equal area projection. 1922 C. Close in *Ordnance Survey Prof. Papers* No. 5. 6 (*heading*) Two-point equidistant projection. 1927 J. A. Steers *Introd. Study Map Projections* vi. 152 (*heading*) 'Interrupted' projections. 1969 G. C. Dickinson *Maps & Air Photographs* i. 9 Distances..can be shown correctly from one, or two, but no more, chosen points on certain special projections. [*Note*] The zenithal equidistant and the two-point equidistant projections respectively. *Ibid.* 17 If a map can be broken in some areas that do not matter—the oceans if map is needed mainly for continental areas, or vice versa—and the meridians gathered together at several 'central' meridians the good qualities of the 'central' areas are more widely spread. Fig. 4F shows such an interrupted sinusoidal projection. *Ibid.* 20 Let us try projecting it [*sc.* the globe] onto a flat sheet of paper touching the globe, at the north pole to begin with, and furthermore see what happens when we move the source of light... The results form a group of projections known collectively as zenithal or azimuthal projections. *Ibid.* 24 If in relation to the parallels, the words 'their true distance apart' in the preceding specification is [*sic*] replaced by 'spaced so that the area between them is the same as that on the globe' we get Alber's projection. *Ibid.* 25 Suppose we want to make a transverse Mercator's projection based on (say) 90°W. and not the equator.

c. *Cryst.* The projection of a point in each face of a crystal upon an imaginary containing sphere, called the ***sphere of projection***.

From the centre of the sphere a line is drawn perpendicular to each face of the crystal, so that to each of these there corresponds a point on the sphere: a plane map of the sphere showing all these points is called a ***projection of the crystal***.

1878 Gurney *Crystallogr.* 32 The diameter of the sphere of projection which is at right angles to the zone plane is called the zone axis. 1895 Story-Maskelyne *Crystallogr.* ii. 27 On the sphere of projection, and the principles of its stereographic representation. *Ibid.* 28 Fig. 9 represents in orthographic projection the faces and the poles of the cubo-octahedron. *Ibid.* 29 The *plane of projection* thus bounded by a great circle of the sphere is represented by the plane of the paper on which the circle is drawn, which latter will be termed the *circle of projection* or primitive circle.

d. *Econ.* A forecast based on present trends.

1952 *Economist* 30 Aug. 526/1 The FBI's figure..amounts almost exactly in total to a direct projection of the sharp upward trend in consumption during 1950 and 1951. 1962 *Listener* 16 Aug. 235/1 When this work has reached the stage of placing the various national projections alongside one another, the foundations of planning will have been laid. 1969 *Times* 4 Sept. 7 The eminent thinker acknowledges that economic performance is not conclusive but insists that it furnishes the basic structure and framework of power. Here is his G.N.P. projection for 1980. 1976 *Time* 27 Dec. 48/2 Among those who doubt the Carter projections are the members of Time's Board of Economists.

8. a. The action of projecting, or fact of being optically projected, as a figure or image, against a background: see project *v.* 9 b. *spec.* The process of projecting (an image on) a film or transparency on to a screen for viewing.

1881 T. Webb in *Nature* 3 Nov. 10/1 Why, when a satellite passes behind the limb, is it sometimes..visible behind or through it, either from optical projection, as stars have been seen in front of the moon, or [etc.]? 1896 R. W. Paul *Brit. Pat. 4686*, I prefer to employ the following mechanism,..causing the film to be propelled instantaneously a small amount, after which it remains still for projection of the picture. 1899 *Allbutt's Syst. Med.* VI. 770 Erroneous projection and diplopia. 1912 F. A. Talbot *Moving Pictures* ix. 99 This second lens is used for the projection of lantern slides. 1953 L. J. Wheeler *Princ. Cinematogr.* vi. 193 Both lanterns must be accurately trained on the screen to give the appearance of continuous projection. 1976 *Times* 22 Apr. 11/3 Amplified sound, music, lighting, slide projection, videotape, all the tools of the professional chatterbox will be deployed to tempt conference organizers.

fig. 1901 *N. Amer. Rev.* Feb. 319 The projection of his reputation against a background of foreign appreciation, more or less luminous.

b. *Mus.* The projective quality of sound; acoustic penetration. Also *transf.* of an instrument.

1977 *Gramophone* Dec. 1045/1 So fine was the earlier recording that the later one..is not necessarily an improvement, even if the sound has slightly more clarity and projection. 1977 *Oxf. Times* 16 Dec. 16 The Allegri Quartet ..tested the viola and cello in exchanged positions. The increased projection of the viola was remarkable.

9. a. A mental figure or image visualized and regarded as an objective reality.

1836 Emerson *Nat.*, *Spirit* Wks. (Bohn) II. 167 The world proceeds from the same spirit as the body of man. It is a..projection of God in the unconscious. 1838 —— *Lit. Ethics* Nature, etc. (1883) 157 The youth, intoxicated with his admiration of a hero, fails to see that it is only a projection of his own soul which he admires. 1891 Watts in *Athenæum* 22 Aug. 259/1 If there is in any literary work a true projection of life, it must..be classed as poetry. 1903 Myers *Human Personality* I. 694, I had..been studying..various cases of astral projection in Phantasms of the Living ..making up my mind..to try..to accomplish a projection of myself by force of will-concentration.

b. *Psychoanal.* The unconscious process or fact of projecting one's fears, feelings, desires, or fantasies on to other persons, things, or situations, in order to avoid recognizing them as one's own and so as to justify one's behaviour. Also in more general use.

1909 Peterson & Brill tr. *Jung's Psychol. of Dementia Praecox* iv. 87 By the method of outward projection they frequently place the responsibility on some foreign agency. 1923 J. S. Huxley *Ess. Biologist* iv. 167 This projection, or interpretation of external reality in terms of one's self, is a curious and almost universal attribute of the human mind. 1924 J. Riviere tr. *Freud's Defence of Neuro-Psychoses* in *Coll. Papers* I. ix. 180 In paranoia the reproach is repressed in a manner which may be described as *projection*; by the defence-symptoms of distrust directed against others being erected. 1938 G. W. Allport *Personality* vi. 173 There is likewise a complementary form of projection whereby a person does not attribute his own frame of mind to others but rather one that justifies and explains his own frame of mind to himself. 1944 *Horizon* IX. 169 His [*sc.* Lenin's] fanatical hatred of the Bourgeoisie of which, in analytical terms, the Russian revolution was merely a 'projection'. 1950 T. S. Eliot *Cocktail Party* I. ii. 59 The man I saw before, he was only a projection—I see that now—of something that I wanted. 1966 R. D. Laing et al. *Interpersonal Perception* ii. 16 Projection refers to a mode of experiencing the other in which one experiences one's outer world in terms of one's inner world. 1966 *Listener* 5 May 653/2 Rogozhin..who tries to win Nastasya with money, and ends by murdering her, can be seen to be a projection of Myshkin's urge to power and destruction. 1975 K. R. Scherer et al. *Human Aggression & Conflict* iv. 117 Perhaps through the mechanism of complementary projection, they perceived the students to be particularly hostile, dangerous, and intent on overpowering the soldiers. 1976 Smythies & Corbett *Psychiatry* xv. 271 Projection means the attribution to external agencies of one's own psychological conflicts.

c. The conveying of a positive image of one's personality to others by one's manner and actions.

1955 *Times* 10 May 3/7 Attack, boldness, and what actors call 'projection' of the artist's personality, are undeniably all there. 1957 [see project *v.* 10 c].

10. *Physiol.* and *Psychol.* The process whereby a stimulus is perceived as being located at a point other than where the sensation or perception occurs (see quots.).

1887 G. T. Ladd *Elem. Physiol. Psychol.* II. vi. 387 The law of eccentric projection is generally stated thus: Objects are perceived in space as situated in a right line off the ends of the nerve-fibres which they irritate. 1890 W. James *Princ. Psychol.* II. xvii. 41 The other cases of translocation of our sensations are equally easily interpreted without supposing any 'projection' from a centre at which they are originally perceived. *Ibid.* 42, I conclude..that there is no truth in the 'eccentric projection' theory. 1892 Van Liew & Beyer tr. *Ziehen's Introd. Physiol. Psychol.* iv. 77 By 'eccentric projection' we understand the fact that a sensation produced by the stimulation of the nerve-*trunk* instead of the nerve-*ends* is regularly attributed to irritation of the peripheral ramifications of the nerve. 1902 J. M. Baldwin *Dict. Philos. & Psychol.* II. 358/2 *Projection*, the spatial objectivation of objects in sense perception... This usage is vague and descriptive, varying from the mere recognition of a spatial datum to the hypothesis of the spatial projection of states at first purely 'inner' and unspatial. It is also complicated with the hypothesis..that nervous projection.., to the periphery, sometimes extends out in lines at right angles to the sensitive surface. *Ibid.*, *Projection* (*nervous*, or '*eccentric*'), the property of the nervous system whereby stimulations are referred to the periphery of the body or to the end-organs. **1972** *Encycl. Psychol.* III. 47/1 *Projection, eccentric*, the introspective observation that sensory experiences are usually localised outside the body at the same position as the stimulus object... Thus the blue is seen as on the sky rather than in the retina.

11. *Physiol.* The spatial distribution, in the brain, or other parts of the central nervous system, of the points to which nerves or nerve impulses go from any given area or organ; const. *on*, *upon*, *to* the receiving part; also *concr.*, a tract of projection fibres.

1924 *Scand. Sci. Rev.* X. 18 [This case verified my supposition..that every limited lesion of the calcarine cortex causes a corresponding limited blind spot in the visual field, or, that there exists a mathematical projection of the peripheral retina in the calcarine cortex.] *Ibid.* 37 The projection of the retina on the calcarine cortex. **1925** *Jrnl. Neurol. & Psychopath.* VI. 3 It is very probable that the projection of the retina on the primary centres in the ape is similar to that in man. **1934** *Proc. R. Soc.* B. CXV. 504 Although the existence of the cortico-pontine fibres has long been recognized.., there has as yet been no solution of the problem of their distribution in the pons and projection on the cerebellum. **1936** *Jrnl. Compar. Neurol.* LXIV. 7 The thalamic projection to the frontal cortex has occasioned much discussion. **1938** J. F. FULTON *Physiol. Nerv. System* xv. 335 In addition to the corticospinal projections, the cerebral cortex in the higher forms gives rise to a vast extrapyramidal projection passing to many subcortical levels. **1951** T. C. RUCH in S. S. Stevens *Handbk. Exper. Psychol.* iv. 136/1 The projection of the body surface upon the posteroventral nucleus of the thalamus was worked out in greater detail. **1973** W. J. S. KRIEG *Synoptic Functional Neuroanat.* 4/2 In the pons..the cortical projections are broken into bundles, and many fibers form connections to the cerebellum here.

V. 12. *attrib.* and *Comb.*, as ***projection dynamics***, ***maker***, ***phenomenon***, ***screen***, ***surface***, ***work***; **projection booth, box** = *projection room* below; **projection-fibre**, a nerve fibre connecting one part of the central nervous system with another, esp. the cortex with the brain stem or spinal cord; **projection lens**, the objective lens in a film or slide projector, which projects an enlarged image into space; **projection measurement**: see quot. 1890; **projection printing** *Photogr.*, printing in which an optical system is placed between the negative and the printing paper, so that enlargement or reduction of image size is possible; hence **projection printer**, an apparatus for this; **projection room**, a room in a cinema or film studio designed to contain the projector and its operators, through windows in the wall of which the film is projected; **projection rule**, in *Transformational Grammar*, a rule, based on underlying phrase markers, for combining lexical senses of words so as to predict their semantic role in a given sentence; **projection system**, the nervous system by which impulses received through the senses are projected upon the consciousness; in mod. use, a system of projection fibres; **projection test** = *projective test* (see PROJECTIVE *a.* 5 b); **projection welding**, resistance welding in which welding is effected at one or more projecting points of contact previously formed in the components by pressing; so **projection weld** *sb.* and (with hyphen) *v. trans.*, **-welded** *ppl. a.*; also **projection welder**, an apparatus for projection welding.

1929 F. GREEN *Film finds its Tongue* xviii. 249 Out in the theatre, sitting in the audience, is an Observer. He has a telephone that leads to the projection booth. **1968** *Globe & Mail* (Toronto) 17 Feb. 45 (Advt.), Recreation area consisting of large family room with..projection booth and screen for home movie entertainment. **1934** S. CHESMORE *Behind Cinema Screen* ix. 85 In modern theatres the projection box is roomy..and well lit. **1966** P. O'DONNELL *Sabre-Tooth* iv. 67 The projection box was equipped with a kershaw filmstrip and slide projector. **1953** C. E. OSGOOD *Method & Theory in Exper. Psychol.* vi. 229 (*heading*) Projection dynamics in perception. **1899** *Allbutt's Syst. Med.* VII. 328 The centrum ovale..contains not only projection fibres..but also fibres which connect the cortex with the optic thalamus. **1920** S. W. RANSON *Anat. Nerv. System* xviii. 297 Many of the fibers of the medullary white center connect the cerebral cortex with the thalamus and lower lying portions of the nervous system. These are known as projection fibers, and may be divided into two groups according as they convey impulses to or from the cerebral cortex. **1970** L. J. A. DIDIO *Synopsis of Anat.* xix. 437/2 White matter of the cerebral hemispheres... It is composed of myelinated nerve fibers that may be divided into three groups: projection fibers, commissural fibers, and association fibers. *Ibid.*, Projection fibers are those that establish either ascending or descending connections between the cerebral cortex and structures outside the telencephalon. **1917** C. N. BENNETT *Guide to Kinematogr.* ix. 131 A secondary effect is often produced through the additional length of focus of the projection lens. **1962** *Which?* Mar. 68/1 The slide is put into a slide carrier in the projector and slid in front of a lamp and behind a projection lens. **1680** J. J. BECHER (*title*) Magnalia Naturæ: or, the Philosophers-stone Lately expos'd to publick Sight and Sale,..how Wenceslaus Seilerus, The late Famous Projection-maker..made away with a very great Quantity of Pouder of Projection, by projecting with it before the Emperor. **1890** BILLINGS *Med. Dict.*, *Projection measurement*, distance between lines tangent to opposite sides of the body, measured vertically to a given plane. **1962** HENDERSON & GILLESPIE *Text-bk. Psychiatry* xii. 294 When a failure of repression occurs the paranoid symptoms develop as projection phenomena. **1940** LUCAS & DUDLEY *Making your Photographs Effective* xi. 168 The apparatus required for projection printing consists of the projection printer, or enlarger,..and the easel. **1965** M. J. LANGFORD *Basic Photogr.* xviii. 324 The term 'enlarger' although common usage, is deceptive. 'Projection printer' is the more accurate description of an optical device to give prints both larger and *smaller* than the original negative. **1923** *Brit. Jrnl. Photogr.* LXX. 350 The remaining factor in contact printing is the distance between the light and the negative... The question of printing distance operates equally in projection printing. **1974** A. FEININGER *Darkroom Techniques* II. 51 Unlike contact printing,..projection printing allows a photographer a considerable amount of control as far as the final appearance of the print is concerned. **1914** R. GRAU *Theatre of Science* iii. 48 The fixture and office furniture are of massive mahogany and plate glass and the projection room is the last word in luxurious splendor. **1930** *Aberdeen Press & Jrnl.* 29 Mar. 7/4 A fire occurred in the projection room of the Swan Cinema. **1975** *Language for Life* (Dept. Educ. & Sci.) xxv. 425 Almost a quarter of the schools had a projection room. **1962** KATZ & POSTAL *Integrated Theory Ling. Descr.* iii. 64 The set of projection rules of a semantic component is..an unordered set. Each rule applies when the conditions of its application are met, and no two rules apply in the same case because no two rules have the same conditions of application. **1964** FODOR & KATZ *Struct. Lang.* xix. 493 A semantic theory must contain two components: a dictionary of the lexical items of the language and a system of rules (which we shall call *projection rules*). **1965** N. CHOMSKY *Aspects of Theory of Syntax* iv. 154 The projection rules must now be adapted to detect and interpret conflicts in feature composition. **1966** J. J. KATZ *Philos. Lang.* iv. 153 A system of *projection rules* that provide the combinatorial machinery for projecting the semantic representation for all supraword constituents in a sentence. **1977** *Language* LIII. 93, I assume..that semantic representations are complex objects, related to different aspects of syntactic structure by means of 'projection rules', or 'interpretive rules', of different types. **1946** KOESTLER *Thieves in Night* 170 You are fond of people..as projection-screens for your own feelings. **1954** —— *Invisible Writing* xxvi. 276 My emotions were self-centred, and those who inspired them served merely as projection-screens. **1890** W. JAMES *Princ. Psychol.* I. ii. 59 The entire cortex being, according to him [*sc.* Munk], nothing but a projection-surface for sensations, with no exclusively or essentially motor part. **1876** *Quain's Elem. Anat.* (ed. 8) II. 565 First projection system..between the convolutions above and the cerebral ganglia..corresponds for the most part to the corona radiata. **1890** A. HILL tr. *Obersteiner's Anat. Central Nerv. Organs* 168 Through the fibres of this system sense-pictures are projected on the perceptive cortex, and..the cortex..reflects outwards again the states of stimulation, information with regard to which is transferred to it by means of sensory nerves. The whole of these conducting paths Meynert, therefore, terms a 'projection system'. **1899** *Allbutt's Syst. Med.* VII. 98 Degeneration of the first afferent (sensory) projection systems of neurons. **1958** M. ARGYLE *Relig. Behaviour* ix. 104 The orthodox [church members] scored higher on ego-defensiveness and dependency measured by various projection tests. **1962** *Listener* 11 Jan. 62/2 Achievement motivation as measured by the projection test in which children were asked to write stories about pictures. **1967** M. ARGYLE *Psychol. Interpersonal Behaviour* i. 18 In 'projection tests' subjects are asked to tell a story about people shown in rather vaguely-drawn pictures... There is considerable doubt over the validity of such projection tests, and they cannot be said to provide very good predictions. **1950** HIPPERSON & WATSON *Resistance Welding* iii. 86 Projection welds may be made with a great variety of projection shapes and sizes. *Ibid.* 88 Unequal thicknesses of sheet may be projection welded. **1961** J. A. OATES *Welding Engineer's Handbk.* xxiii. 249 In cases where the projection welds have to be made on a narrow flange it is an advantage to use an elongated projection. **1980** L. M. GOURD *Princ. Welding Technol.* xi. 167 Reinforcing rings are frequently projection-welded around holes in sheet-metal tanks. **1950** HIPPERSON & WATSON *Resistance Welding* i. 25 A few typical projection welded applications..are shown. **1980** L. M. GOURD *Princ. Welding Technol.* xi. 166 (*caption*) Examples of projection-welded details. **1946** *Philips Resistance Welding Handbk.* i. 15 Owing to the number of spots, projection welders are of a higher kVA. than normal spot welders. **1968** ROMANS & SIMONS *Welding Processes & Technol.* v. 39 The majority of projection welders are operated by compressed air. **1918** HAMILTON & OBERG *Electric Welding* iii. 119 The welding of sheet metal is not restricted to one spot at a time, as any reasonable number of welds can be made at one operation by the method known as 'point-' or 'projection-welding'. **1975** BRAM & DOWNS *Manuf. Technol.* ii. 63 In projection welding the component is shaped to provide localised current flow, concentrating the welding heat at the areas of projection. **1905** *Brit. Med. Jrnl.* 27 May 1154 A room..fitted-up for electrometer, photo-micrographic and other 'projection' work.

† **pro'jection**, *v. Obs.* [f. prec.] *trans.* To make a projection or geometrical delineation of.

1703 MOXON *Mech. Exerc.* 346, I have taught you in the projectioning the Horizontal Dyal the original way of doing this.

pro'jectional, *a.* [f. PROJECTION *sb.* + -AL.] Of, pertaining to, or connected with projection (in various senses).

1899 *Phil. Trans.* B. CXCI. 298 The large system of fibres just described above is probably both an associational and projectional system. **1949** *Mind* LVIII. 76 If the term 'God' is really non-significant, Findlay's earlier description of the religious attitude should be translated into emotive or projectional terms.

pro'jectionist. [f. as prec. + -IST.] One who operates a film projector.

1922 A. C. LESCARBOURA *Cinema Handbk.* vii. 285 One reel must serve for a large number of projectionists. **1938** *Times* 23 May 11/1 A suggestion that the cinema projectionists' dispute in London and the home counties might be extended. **1958** X. FIELDING *Corsair Country* viii. 167 The projectionist is making the final adjustments to his Heath Robinson apparatus. **1969** B. PATTEN *Notes to Hurrying Man* 14 This is the projectionist's nightmare: A bird finds its way into the cinema..smashes into a screen. **1973** J. WAINWRIGHT *Pride of Pigs* 158 They usually employed a lad—the 'second projectionist', so-called—to carry the reels to and from the projection room. **1977** *Western Morning News* 30 Aug. 11 (Advt.), Classic Entertainment Centre. We have an immediate vacancy for a Senior projectionist. Experience on 'Kalee 21' essential.

† **projec'titious**, *a. Obs. rare*⁻⁰. [f. L. *prōjectīci-us* cast out, exposed (f. ppl. stem of *prōjicĕre* to PROJECT) + -OUS.]

1656 BLOUNT *Glossogr.*, *Projectitious*, cast out, and nourished of a stranger; flung away, as of no account.

projective (prəʊ'dʒɛktɪv), *a.* [f. L. ppl. stem *prōject-* (see PROJECT *v.*) + -IVE. So F. *projectif.*]

† **1.** Having the faculty of projecting; scheming.

1632 BROME *Court Beggar* II. Wks. 1873 I. 214 They have all projective braines I tell you. *Men.* Pray of what nature are your Projects Gentlemen?

2. *Geom.*, etc. Of, pertaining to, or produced by the projection of lines or figures on a surface.

1682 LEYBOURN (*title*) Dialling: Plain, Concave, Convex, Projective, Reflective, Refractive. **1710** J. HARRIS *Lex. Techn.* II, *Projective Dialling*, is the way of Drawing, by a method of Projection, the true Hour-lines, Furniture of Dials, &c. on any kind of Surface whatsoever. **1894** *Westm. Gaz.* 14 June 7/1 A lady exhibitor demonstrating an ingenious projective goniometer. By means of this instrument..the projection of a crystal on a sphere is accomplished, realising in practice the fundamental assumption of the theory of crystallography.

b. Capable, as two plane figures, of being derived one from the other by projection.

1885 LEUDESDORF *Cremona's Proj. Geom.* 107 If P is the point of intersection of QS and RT, then $ATPR$ is a projection of $ACA'B'$ from Q as centre, and $ATPR$ is also a projection of $ABA'C'$ from S as centre; therefore the group $ACA'B'$ is projective with $ABA'C'$, and therefore..with $A'C'AB$. *Ibid.* 163 If the point S is such that tangents can be drawn from it to the conic, each of them will be a self-corresponding line of the two projective series of tangents abc..and $a'b'c'$.

c. ***projective property***, a property (of a figure) which remains unchanged after projection. ***projective geometry***, that branch of geometry which deals with projective properties.

1885 LEUDESDORF *Cremona's Proj. Geom.* 50 Projective Geometry..dealing with projective properties (*i.e.* such as are not altered by projection), is chiefly concerned with descriptive properties of figures... Since the magnitude of a geometric figure is altered by projection, metrical properties are as a rule not projective. But there is one important class of metrical properties (anharmonic properties) which are projective, and the discussion of which therefore finds a place in the Projective Geometry. **1908** *Athenæum* 21 Mar. 359/2 'On the Projective Geometry of some Covariants of a Binary Quintic', by Prof. E. B. Elliott.

d. ***projective plane***, that two-dimensional manifold which may be regarded as a spherical shell with all pairs of antipodal points identified; it is an example of a ***projective space***, a space which may be regarded as obtained by taking a vector space of the next higher dimension, identifying all vectors which are multiples of one another, and omitting the origin.

1900 *Nature* 12 July 260/1 A purely geometric representation of all points in the projective plane. **1910** VEBLEN & YOUNG *Projective Geom.* I. iv. 97 Any such space we call a properly projective space. **1942** *Amer. Jrnl. Math.* LXIV. 137 A satisfactory analytic theory may be developed for every projective plane in which Desargues' Theorem is valid. **1960** HILTON & WYLIE *Homology Theory* iii. 133 The real projective space P^n may be defined as the image of the n-sphere S^n under identification of all pairs of antipodal points. **1962** B. H. ARNOLD *Intuitive Concepts Elem. Topology* iii. 71 A projective plane can be considered as a disk and a Möbius strip whose edges are joined. **1964** C. E. SPRINGER *Geom. & Anal. Projective Spaces* vi. 150 A projective space is orientable if the dimensionality of the space is odd and nonorientable if it is even. **1975** I. STEWART *Concepts Mod. Math.* xiii. 199 This is exactly what is happening in the projective plane: going round once things get twisted; going round twice brings them back to normal.

3. Jutting or sticking out, projecting. *rare.*

1703 T. N. *City & C. Purchaser* 20 This Jutty, or projective Building. **1844** MRS. BROWNING *Lett. R. H. Horne* (1877) II. lxi. 167 Thin colourless lips, fit for incisive meanings—a nose and chin projective without breadth.

4. Of or pertaining to projection or casting forth. *rare.*

1839–48 BAILEY *Festus* xix. (ed. 4) 217 From the projective moment of all light The moon was in the sun, and in the sun The form of earth was.

5. a. Having the quality of being mentally projected, or the power of projecting: see PROJECT *v.* 10, PROJECTION 9.

a **1834** COLERIDGE *Aids Refl.* App. C. (1858) I. 409 There is an equal intensity both of the immanent and the projective reproduction. **1908** *Edin. Rev.* Jan. 200 Kingsley's practical qualities (including a quite genuine projective imagination) were out of all proportion to the reflective.

b. *Psychol.* Of or pertaining to the projection of unconscious feelings, fears, fantasies or desires; esp. of tests designed to reveal unconscious elements of personality by responses to words, pictures, etc. Also *ellipt.* as *sb.*

1895 J. M. BALDWIN *Mental Devel. in Child* vi. 120 All of them [sc. stages of attitude] belong in the 'projective' stage of the child's sense of self, *i.e.*, they all go to furnish data which he afterwards appropriates to himself as 'subject'. **1939** *Jrnl. Psychol.* VIII. 404 No attempt has been made to provide a complete review of all the projective methods now being used. **1954** L. BELLAK *TAT & CAT in Clin. Use* p. x, The T.A.T. in common with all the other projective tests, is still far from being a properly established instrument. **1956** A. I. HALLOWELL in B. Klopfer et al. *Devel. Rorschach Technique* II. xiv. 476 Rorschach theory, as well as that underlying other projective tests, has been based on the general assumption..that 'every subject's responses..are *determined* by psychological attributes of that subject'. **1966** I. G. SARASON *Personality* xii. 180 The ideas behind projective techniques have been largely psychoanalytic. **1971** *Jrnl. Gen. Psychol.* LXXXIV. 321 The clinician using the auditory method is now able to consider stimulus properties when evaluating projective material. **1976** L. R. AIKEN *Psychol. Testing & Assessment* (rev. ed.) viii. 223 Questionnaires and projectives are useful, but the most popular psychometric device for determining attitudes is an attitude scale.

6. Having the power of projecting or throwing itself forward with energy.

1861 J. BROWN *Horæ Subs.* (1862) 155 His [Samuel Brown's] fiery, projective subtle spirit could not linger in the outer fields of mere observation.

7. ***projective verse***, a term invented by C. Olson (1910–70), American poet and poetical theorist, to describe a brand of verse propelled by its inherent energy and composed according to a system of poetic values in which structure, lay-out, and breathing have an importance not accorded them in traditional forms. Hence ***projective poet***, etc. Also *ellipt.*

1950 C. OLSON in *Poetry New York* III. 15 *Projective verse* teaches, is, this lesson, that that verse will only do in which a poet manages to register both the acquisitions of his ear *and* the pressures of his breath. *Ibid.* 20 Which gets us to.. the degree to which the projective involves a stance toward reality outside a poem [etc.] *Ibid.* 22 Eliot..has only gone from his fine ear outward rather than, as I say a projective poet will, down through the workings of his own throat to that place where breath comes from, where breath has its beginnings, where drama has to come from, where, the coincidence is, all art springs. **1962** E. MOTTRAM in *London Mag.* Dec. 71/1 Projective or open verse is a 'stance towards reality' as it brings the verse into being—'some simplicities that a man learns if he works in *open*, or what has been called *composition by field*, as opposed to inherited line, stanza, over-all form, what is the "old" base of the non-projective'. **1962** *Listener* 27 Dec. 1102/1 Of the 'projective verse' school, Ginsberg and..Edward Dorn seem to me remarkable talents. **1963** *Ibid.* 7 Mar. 435/3 A poet I liked very much is Robert Bly. In versification he is not 'projective', but in tone and attitude he is. **1967** *Book Week* (Washington Post) 19 Mar. 6/1 Here what he [*sc.* Olson] calls the Projective Open or Field verse (as opposed to the systematic Closed Forms of the past) is put to work, using *line, syllable, breath*, as principles he has preached. His one theme is energy—how a man's energy is expended in history and in space.

Hence **pro'jectively** *adv.*, in a projective manner.

1872 T. L. CUYLER *Heart Life* 27 He follows Jesus so heartily, so projectively, that he carries others along with him by his sheer momentum. **1879** G. MEREDITH *Egoist* III. x. 207 A condition in the young when their imaginative energies hold revel uncontrolled and are projectively desperate. **1885** LEUDESDORF *Cremona's Proj. Geom.* 62 The necessary and sufficient condition that two ranges, each consisting of four elements, should be projectively related.

projectivity (prɒdʒɛk'tɪvɪtɪ). *rare.* [f. prec. + -ITY.] Projective quality; power or capacity for geometrical projection.

1900 *Nature* 12 July 260/1 He then takes up the subject of chains of points, showing their application to the general theory of projectivity.

†**pro'jectment.** *Obs.* [f. PROJECT *v.* + -MENT. Cf. F. *projettement* (16th c.).] The formation of a project; a project formed, a scheme, plan, design.

a **1639** WOTTON *Disparity Buckingh. & Essex* in *Reliq.* (1651) 45 Men that were..never so dishonest in their projectments for each other's confusion. *a* **1662** HEYLIN *Laud* (1668) 405 Whether Posterity will believe..That so many great and notable Projectments could be comprehended in one Soul. **1675** PLUME *Bp. Hacket* (1865) 120 Zealous in the carrying on his great projectments for piety and charity.

projector (prəʊ'dʒɛktə(r)). [a. L. type **prōjector*, agent-n. f. *prōjicĕre* to PROJECT: see -OR. In F. *projeteur* (18th c. in Littré).]

1. a. One who forms a project, who plans or designs some enterprise or undertaking; a founder.

1596 EARL OF ESSEX in Ellis *Orig. Lett.* Ser. III. IV. 131, I think the action such as it were disadvantage to be thought the projector of it. *a* **1665** J. GOODWIN *Filled w. the Spirit* (1867) 428 How happy, then, above all worldly projectors and designers, are they whose hearts are persuaded to hearken to the counsel of God. **1738** SWIFT *Pol. Conversat.* Introd. 49 To desire a Patent granted..to all useful Projectors. **1841** MIALL in *Nonconf.* I. 1 The great design of the projectors of this paper. **1884** *Law Times* 22 Mar. 379/2 The contractors were not paid either by the projector or the company.

b. In invidious use: A schemer; one who lives by his wits; a promoter of bubble companies; a speculator, a cheat.

1616 B. JONSON *Devil an Ass* I. vii, *Tit.* What is a Proiector? I would conceiue. *Ing.* Why, one Sir, that proiects Wayes to enrich men, or to make 'hem great. **1636** FEATLY *Clavis Myst.* xxxiv. 477 Let not the Projector pretend the publike good, when he intends but to robbe the riche and to cheat the poore. *a* **1691** BOYLE *Hist. Air* (1692) 138 The women..think us still either projectors or conjurers. **1724** R. WELTON *Chr. Faith & Pract.* 470 The Judas, the worldly projector. **1787** BENTHAM *Def. Usury* iv. 37 Those, who..are distinguished by the unfavourable appellation of Projectors. **1827** WHATELY *Logic* in *Encycl. Metrop.* (1845) I. 222/1 The Sophist proceeds on the hypothesis that he who forms a project must be a projector; whereas the bad sense that commonly attaches to the latter word, is not at all implied in the former.

2. One who or that which projects or throws something forward.

1674 WALLIS in Rigaud *Corr. Sci. Men* (1841) II. 588 Which supposeth projection to be compounded of an uniform motion (impressed from the projector). **1892** *Pall Mall G.* 17 Nov. 7/2 Automatic railway fog-signal apparatus ..a box which contains the explosive cartridges or signals, and a projector which automatically places them on the rail.

3. One who forecasts.

1832 LD. COCKBURN *Jrnl.* (1874) I. 32 We confident projectors of the people's avidity to vote are a little mortified at their registering more slowly than we boasted they would.

4. a. An apparatus for projecting rays of light; a parabolic reflector or a combination of lenses.

1887 *Daily News* 15 Oct. 6/1 The electric light will be employed on both sides of the harbour, each of the four projectors displaying a light of over two thousand candle power. **1891** *Times* 28 Sept. 13/5 Projectors used as search lights are destined to play an important part in modern warfare. **1893** *Voice* (N.Y.) 14 Sept., The reflecting lens mirror used in this projector is..60 inches in diameter.

b. An apparatus containing a source of light and a system of lenses for projecting on to a screen an enlargement of an image or a slide, film, or opaque surface.

1884 in Knight *Dict. Mech.* Suppl. **1912** F. A. TALBOT *Moving Pictures* 135 In colour work the projector requires a special type of shutter. **1915** W. H. CHANTREY *Theatre Accounts* (ed. 2) 78 Cinematograph projectors should be fitted with two metal film-boxes of substantial construction. **1926** *Encycl. Brit.* II. 961/2 In June 1895 Thomas Armat of Washington..arrived at the principle of the modern projector, a device in which the film, moving intermittently, has periods of rest and illumination in large excess of the period of movement. **1962** *Movie* Oct. 12/3 The flickering blue light of the projector in the viewing theatre sequence. **1964** M. McLUHAN *Understanding Media* (1967) xxix. 311 The present dissociation of projector and screen is a vestige of our older mechanical world of..separation of functions. **1977** J. HEDGECOE *Photographer's Handbk.* 312 Projectors for 35 mm transparencies and smaller are now usually magazine loaded.

5. *Comb.*, as ***projector lamp, -man.***

1962 *Which?* Mar. 74/1 Projector lamps are expensive. **1972** *Gloss. Electrotechnical, Power Terms (B.S.I.)* IV. iii. 15 *Projector lamp*, lamp in which the luminous element is so mounted that the lamp may be used with an optical system projecting the light in chosen directions. **1927** *Observer* 17 Apr. 3 The picture is..'ridden in'—that is, the orchestra work up to an appropriate climax, and at a given bar the projector-man 'makes his throw'.

Hence **pro'jectress, pro'jectrix**, a female projector; also *Geom.*: see quot. 1890.

1709 SWIFT *Tatler* No. 32 ⁋4 A Lady who..was the Projectrix of the Foundation. **1880** 'OUIDA' *Moths* xvii. 209 'It is extremely pretty' said Vere to the projectress and protectress of it all. **1890** *Cent. Dict.*, *Projectrix*, a curve derived from another curve by composition of projections.

projecture (prəʊ'dʒɛktjʊə(r)). Now *rare.* [= F. *projecture* (1629 in Hatz.-Darm.), ad. L. *prōjectūra* a jutty, a projecture in buildings, f. *prōject-*: see PROJECT *v.* and -URE.]

1. The fact or state of projecting or jutting out beyond the general line or surface; *concr.* a projection or prominence; in *Arch.*, a projecting architectural member or moulding. Now *rare.*

1563 SHUTE *Archit.* B iv b, Then shall your vttermost compas be for the proiecture, or saylling out or hanging ouer of the foote of the pillor, which Proiecture the Grekes do name or cal it Ecphoron. *Ibid.* C j b, It hath vpon Echinus a littel edge, which seteth forth Plinthus w^t a more beautiful Proiecture. **1666** EVELYN *Mem.* 7 Sept., All the ornaments, columnes, freezes, capitals, and projectures of massie Portland stone. **1778** [W. MARSHALL] *Minutes Agric.* 28 Aug. an. 1776, The ends of the roof should have a gentle projecture. **1803** C. B. BROWN *E. Huntly* II. 49 There was no projecture which might be firmly held by the hand. **1842–76** GWILT *Archit.* Gloss., *Ecphora*,..the projecture of a member or moulding of a column.

†**2.** A projection on the flat; a plotting out, delineation. *Obs.*

1610 W. FOLKINGHAM *Art of Survey* I. xii. 44 Ground-plots are proiectures, eleuations, and all fundamentall contriuances, destinated and accomodated to some speciall and proposed ende. *Ibid.* II. i. 48.

†**3.** = PROJECTION 6. *Obs.*

1616 HALES in Rigaud *Corr. Sci. Men* (1841) I. 3 Amongst all the solutions..none there was which gave me not full and sufficient satisfaction, one only excepted,..that is concerning the projecture of an oblique circle.

†**4.** = PROJECT *sb.* 5. *Obs.*

1696 EVELYN *Let. to Ld. Godolphin* 16 June, New inventions..encouraged, or rejected without reproach as projectures, or turning the unsuccessful proposer to ridicule.

‖**projet** (prɔʒɛ). [F., ad. L. *prōject-um* PROJECT.] A proposition, proposal; the draft of a proposed treaty, etc.

1808 JEFFERSON *Writ.* (1830) IV. 108 It [the form of treaty] should be considered but as a *projet.* **1812** *Edin. Rev.* Nov. 274 After various *projets* had been offered and rejected, she made these three conditions. **1813** SCOTT *Let. to J. Ballantyne* 18 May in *Lockhart*, After many *offs* and *ons*, and as many *projets* and *contre-projets* as the treaty of Amiens, I have at length concluded a treaty with Constable.

pro'jicient (prəʊ'dʒɪʃ(ɪ)ənt), *sb.* and *a.* [ad. L. *prōjiciens, -ent-em*, pres. pple. of *prōjic-ĕre* to PROJECT.] † **A.** *sb.* One who or that which throws a thing forward or forth. *Obs.*

1677 PLOT *Oxfordsh.* 10 Though the projicient do so throw it, that it strikes at right angles with the wall.

B. *adj.* Concerned with an individual's perception of his surroundings.

1904 *Nature* 8 Sept. 465/1 [Reporting C. S. Sherrington.] In presence of the arcs of the great projicient receptors and the brain there can be few receptive points in the body the activities of which are totally indifferent to one another. **1927** J. H. PARSONS *Introd. Theory Perception* vii. 143 The projicient senses—vision.., hearing.., and smell—in the head segments provide those sensations which occupy the focus of the perceptual pattern, the field of attention. **1954** *A.M.A. Arch. Neurol. & Psychiatry* LXXII. 472 On the other hand, the admonitions from the group representative are apprehended largely by visual and auditory means; the authority figure is very much more clearly defined by 'projicient' modalities, and, we guess, is always clearer to the individual.

So **projicience** (prəʊ'dʒɪʃ(ɪ)əns), projicient activity or ability.

1906 C. S. SHERRINGTON *Integrative Action Nervous Syst.* ix. 324 It is in the leading segments that we find the 'distance-receptors'. For so may be called the receptors which, acting as sense-organs, initiate sensations having the psychical quality termed projicience. **1927** J. M. PARSONS *Introd. Theory Perception* ii. 7 At a somewhat higher level there is evidence of response to radiation of shorter wave-length—light, and perhaps ultra-violet radiation. As soon as this occurs the germ of projicience is found. **1931** *Brit. Jrnl. Psychol.* XXII. 143 Many, if not most, of the stimuli, to which man and the higher mammals respond through projicience, cannot be adequately described without using qualitative terms. **1949** A. GESELL et al. *Vision* xii. 196 This ability is a topographic discrimination, an elementary form of projicience.

prokaryon (prəʊ'kærɪən). *Biol.* Pl. **prokarya.** [f. Gr. προ- PRO-² + κάρυον nut, kernel; cf. PROKARYOTE.] The structure in a prokaryote which contains the genetic material; the prokaryotic 'nucleus'.

1957 E. C. DOUGHERTY in *Jrnl. Protozool.* IV. Suppl. 14/1 For the moneran nucleus I propose *prokaryon*.., and for that of higher organisms, *eukaryon*... From these derive.. the nouns *prokaryosis* and *eukaryosis* and their corresponding adjectives, *prokaryotic* and *eukaryotic*.., denoting, respectively, 'the condition of possessing prokarya or eukarya'. **1969** BROWN & BERTKE *Textbk. Cytol.* vi. 96/1 The more or less central region of indeterminate shape and no bounding membrane is sometimes called the nucleus but more properly the prokaryon.

prokaryote (prəʊ'kærɪəʊt). *Biol.* Also **-caryote.** [a. F. *procaryote* (É. Chatton 1925, in *Ann. des Sci. Nat.: Zool.* VIII. 76), f. as prec. + Gr. -ώτ-ης.] A prokaryotic organism. Opp. *eukaryote.*

1963 *Cold Spring Harbor Symp. Quantitative Biol.* XXVIII. 1/1 The distinction of *eukaryotes* which possess a characteristic chromosome nucleus and *prokaryotes* where the nuclear equivalent does not show any chromosome-like structures, is not bounded by a nuclear envelope, and does not divide by mitosis. **1967** KIRK & TILNEY-BASSETT *Plastids* xi. 364 This theory..makes it unnecessary to explain the separate evolution of photosynthetic ability in the prokaryotes (organisms such as bacteria and blue-green algae, with no separate membrane-bounded nucleus, or other organelles) and the eukaryotes (higher organisms, including algae and higher plants, with chromosomes inside a membrane-bounded nucleus, and other membrane-bounded organelles). **1969** LOEWY & SIEKEVITZ *Cell Struct. & Function* (ed. 2) i. 4 The genetic information in procaryotes, at least in the organisms studied so far, is located on a single chromosome that consists of a circular double strand of DNA and that lacks the basic proteins called histones. **1976** W. C. SCHEFLER *Biol.* xiii. 242/1 Procaryotes therefore have a very simple structure, which leads biologists to believe that a division of living organisms into these two basic cellular types occurred long before the evolutionary development of plants and animals as distinct groups. **1976** *Sci. Amer.* Sept. 167/2 No plant or animal is able to fix nitrogen, only prokaryotes: organisms, including bacteria and blue-green algae, that have no cell nuclei.

prokaryotic (prəʊkærɪ'ɒtɪk), *a.* *Biol.* Also **-caryotic.** [f. as prec. + -IC.] Having no nuclear membrane in its cell; belonging to the group of organisms so characterized, which comprises bacteria and blue-green algæ. Opp. *eukaryotic.*

1957 [see PROKARYON *a.*]. **1969** [see CONIDIUM]. **1974** *Taxon* XXIII. 246 Cells with a general organization between entire prokaryotic and eukaryotic cells have not been found. **1976** *Sci. Amer.* Feb. 35/2 Bacteria are prokaryotic cells, that is, their genetic material is distributed throughout the cytoplasm. **1976** W. C. SCHEFLER *Biol.* xiii.

242/1 Procaryotic cells..lack mitochondria, chloroplasts, an endoplasmic reticulum, Golgi bodies, and lysosomes.

proke (prəʊk), *v.*[1] Now only *dial.* Also 7 **proak.** [Early ME. *prokien*, app. cognate with LG. *proken*, to prod, poke, scratch, scrawl; cf. the dim. or frequent. LG., EFris. *prökeln*, Saterland *prökelje*; also, LG. *prökel* prickle, pointed instrument (Doorn.-Koolman). Not known in OE., but frequent in southern Early ME., also in late 16th c. writers, and still dial. Etymology obscure; the form and sense suggest relations with PROG *v.*[2], also PRICK *v.*, and POKE *v.*[1]]

1. *trans.* To make a thrust at; to poke; *fig.* to stir, goad, instigate, incite: = POKE *v.*[1] 1, 2.

a **1225** *Ancr. R.* 204 Hwonne þe schil and te heorte ne wiðsiggeð nout auh likeð wel, & ȝirneð al þet tet fleschs toprokeð, & helpen oðer þideward. *Ibid.* 238, & wiðsiggeð þe graunt þerof mid unwille heorte, ne prokie hit ou neuer so swuðe. *c* **1230** *Hali Meid.* 47 Al for nawt þu prokest me to forgulten. *Ibid.*, ȝif he..halt on to eili þi flesch & prokie þin herte. *c* **1325** *Poem Times Edw. II* 430 in *Pol. Songs* (Camden) 343 So the fend hem prokede uch man to mourdren other. **1556** J. HEYWOOD *Spider & F.* lxviii. 30 Nature prokth me..To take peace with the flies,..Reason prouokth me: politiklie to flee. **1609** HOLLAND *Amm. Marcell.* XIV. i. 2 The Queene ever at his elbow to pricke and proke [L. *stimulare*] him forward. **1886** *Cheshire Gloss.*, *Proke*, to poke. 'Proke th' fire a bit.'

2. *intr.* To make a thrust (*at*): = POKE *v.*[1] 4. Also *spec.* to fish for eels by thrusting bait into their lurking-places, to SNIGGLE.

1601 HOLLAND *Pliny* I. 263 The said dyuers..carry downe with them certaine sharp pricks or goads fastened to long poles: for vnlesse they [the sea dogs] be proked at and pricked with them, they will not turn their backe. *Ibid.*, Well may some from shipboord proke at the dogs aforesaid with forks; others thrust at them with Trout speares & such like weapons. **1688** [see PROKING]. **1843** N. MACLEOD *Crack aboot Kirk* (ed. 2) I. 2 If a man has a sair leg or a sick body ye needna keep prokin' at him and roarin' in his lug a' day that he's no weel. **1914** P. MACGILL *Children of Dead End* xxi. 149 I'm sick of prokin' in the gutters here. **1941** E. R. EDDISON *Fish Dinner* xiv. 261 The plague that sat dozing in her mouth's corner proked at him swiftly.

3. *intr.* To stick *out*, project: = POKE *v.*[1] 7 b.

1600 HOLLAND *Livy* XXXVIII. vii. 987 From the lid or cover ..there stood proking out long sharp pikes..for to keepe off the enemies. **1601** —— *Pliny* I. 327 There bee Insects with little hornes proaking out before their eyes.

†**proke**, *v.*[2] *Obs. rare*[−1]. [perh. ad. L. *procāre* (rare) to ask, demand, with which it is identified by Levins. Cf. PROKKE *v.*]

1570 LEVINS *Manip.* 159/45 To proke, *procare.*

prokecye, obs. form of PROXY.

ˈ**proker.** *dial.* [f. PROKE *v.*[1] + -ER[1]; or alteration of *poker* after *proke*.] = POKER *sb.*[1] 1.

1797–1802 G. COLMAN *Br. Grins, Lady of Wreck* I. ii, Before the antique Hall's turf fire Was stretch'd the Porter ..his proker in his hand. [*note*] *Hibernicè* proker, *Anglicè* poker. **1842** BARHAM *Ingol. Leg.* Ser. II. *Old Woman in Grey*, The 'prokers' are not half so hot, or so long, By an inch or two, either in handle or prong.

proker, obs. f. PROCURE.

prokeratour, proketowre, obs. ff. PROCURATOR, PROCTOR.

proket: see PRICKET.

prokinesis (prəʊkaɪˈniːsɪs, -kiːn-). *Zool.* [ad. G. *prokinetik*, f. Gr. πρό PRO-[2] + κινητικός moving: see KINETIC *a.* (*sb.*) and KINESIS.] A process, found in some birds and lizards, by which the upper bill or jaw may be raised relative to the cranium by rotation about a hinge anterior to the eyes.

1962 T. H. FRAZZETTA in *Jrnl. Morphol.* CXI. 287/2 It is here advocated that..Hofer's 'prokinesis' be modified to designate any kinetic joint anterior to the eyes. **1964** *Ibid.* CXIV. 3/1 The basic avian condition is prokinesis from which rhynchokinesis evolved. **1964**, etc. [see RHYNCHOKINESIS]. **1973** *Nature* 11 May 73/1 Prokinesis and rhynchokinesis may have evolved independently in neognathous and palaeognathous birds, or rhynchokinesis may have evolved from some form of prokinesis.

So **prokiˈnetic** *a.*

1960 *Q. Rev. Biol.* XXXV. 219/2 In view of the fact that there are so many differences in the actual operation of kinesis in the various orders [of birds], I doubt if the terms pro- and rhyncho-kinetic actually are morphologically meaningful. **1964** *Jrnl. Morphol.* CXIV. 4/2 The prokinetic condition is the most widespread and apparently the primitive condition in the class Aves. **1974** P. J. K. BURTON *Feeding & Feeding Apparatus in Waders* II. 35 An important feature of rhynchokinesis is that the pivots about which the two jaws move are relatively much further apart than in prokinetic species.

ˈ**proking,** *vbl. sb.* Now only *dial.* [f. PROKE *v.*[1] + -ING[1].] The action of the verb PROKE; poking, thrusting; sniggling for eels; *fig.* instigation. Also *attrib.* as ***proking spit*** (in quot. humorously applied to a rapier), ***proking stick.***

a **1225** *Ancr. R.* 266 Heo dude one swuche sunne iðet ilke niht, þuruh his prokiunge. *Ibid.* 294 þet beoð þe erest prokunges þet sturieð þe winȝeardes. **1597–8** BP. HALL *Sat.* IV. iv. 57 With a broad Scot, or proking spit of Spayne. **1688** R. HOLME *Armoury* III. 104/1 *Proking*, is a kind of Fishing for Eels in their holes. **1799** G. SMITH *Laboratory* II. 246 A sniggling or proking stick [for eels].

†**prokke**, *v. Obs. rare.* [Apparently a form of PROG *v.*[1], but perh. an adaptation of rare L. *procāre* to ask, demand. Cf. PROKE *v.*[2]]

c **1440** *Promp. Parv.* 414/2 Prokkyn, or styfly askyn, *procor, procito.*

pro-knock: see PRO-[1] 5 a.

prokosmial: see PRO-[2] 1.

prokyrment, obs. form of PROCUREMENT.

proˈlabial, *a.* [f. next: cf. LABIAL.] Of or pertaining to the prolabium.

1890 *Lancet* 25 Jan. 182/2 The left side of the lip was deemed the more suitable for supplying the prolabial flap.

‖**prolabium** (prəʊˈleɪbɪəm). *Anat.* Pl. **prolabia.** [med.L. *prōlabium*, f. L. *prō*, PRO-[1] + LABIUM.] The prominent or outer part of a lip.

1693 tr. *Blancard's Phys. Dict.* (ed. 2), *Prolabia*, the outmost prominent parts of the Lips. **1727–41** CHAMBERS *Cycl.* s.v. *Lips*, The lips..the fore and protuberant parts of which are red, and called *prolabia.* **1786** J. HUNTER *Venereal Dis.* IV. i. (1810) 316, I have seen a chancre on the prolabium as broad as a sixpence, caught the person did not know how. **1843** J. G. WILKINSON *Swedenborg's Anim. Kingd.* I. i. 39 Licking the fauces, gums, and prolabia.

prolactin (prəʊˈlæktɪn). *Physiol.* [f. PRO-[1] + LACT(ATION + -IN[1].] A gonadotrophic polypeptide hormone which promotes lactation.

1932 O. RIDDLE et al. in *Proc. Soc. Exper. Biol. & Med.* XXIX. 1211 We..have identified this same hormone, which we shall here call 'Prolactin' as the hitherto undefined pituitary principle which is essential for lactation in mammals. **1941** *Nature* 11 Jan. 44/2 The activity was at first ascribed to a single hormone of the pituitary which was called prolactin. Very recent work has gone to show that this activity is, in fact, due to the co-operation of two separate hormones of the anterior pituitary—prolactin and glycotropin. **1952** [see LACTOGEN]. **1974** *Sci. Amer.* Sept. 53/3 There is probably a role for a third gonadotropic hormone of the pituitary, prolactin, in maintaining the steroid-producing function of the corpus luteum for its usual 14-day life span, but there is some doubt whether this is true in humans. **1979** *Jrnl. R. Soc. Arts* CXXVII. 416/2 We know that the blood prolactin level is directly related to suckling frequency.

prolactinoma (prəʊlæktɪˈnəʊmə). *Med.* [f. prec. + -OMA.] A tumour that produces excessive quantities of prolactin.

1975 S. FRANKS et al. in *Hormone Res.* VI. 273 Pituitary tumours causing disorders of reproduction are almost without exception 'prolactinomas'. **1977** *Lancet* 9 Apr. 779/2 The incidence of prolactinoma in patients with pituitary tumours is likely to vary in different endocrine clinics.

prolamine (ˈprəʊləmiːn, -ɪn). *Biochem.* Formerly also **prolamin.** [f. PROLINE with inserted *-am* (f. AMIDE).] Any of a class of proteins which occur in the seeds of cereals and are characterized by solubility in a 70–90 per cent solution of alcohol and insolubility in water.

1908 T. B. OSBORNE in *Science* 2 Oct. 422/1 Prolamins.. form a unique and sharply differentiated group of proteins which occur in quantity in the seeds of cereals... I propose this name for the group which heretofore has been simply called alcohol-soluble proteins. The name refers to the relatively large proportion of proline and amide nitrogen which they yield on hydrolysis. **1921** *Monthly Bull. Agric. Intelligence & Plant Dis.* XII. 400 The only well-defined proteins found in oats are a venaline,..and a prolamine soluble in alcohol, and belonging to the same group as the gliadin of wheat. **1931** E. C. MILLER *Plant Physiol.* ix. 518 The prolamins..are known to occur only in the seeds of cereals. *Ibid.*, The glutelins and prolamins are collectively termed 'glutens'. **1938** *Thorpe's Dict. Appl. Chem.* (ed. 4) II. 493/1 Prolamines (gliadins) are present only in small quantities in the inner endosperm of rice. **1971** *Sci. Amer.* Aug. 36/3 The nutritional proteins in corn kernels are classified in four categories according to solubility: (1) albumins, soluble in water; (2) globulins, soluble in saline solutions; (3) prolamines, soluble in moderately strong alcohol.

prolan (ˈprəʊlæn). *Physiol.* [a. G. *prolan* (B. Zondek 1929, in *Zeitschr. f. Geburtshülfe u. Gynäkologie* XCV. 363), f. L. *prōl-ēs* progeny: see -AN.] The name given to what was formerly thought to be one female sex hormone but is now known to comprise both follicle-stimulating hormone (***prolan A***) and luteinizing hormone (***prolan B***).

1931 *Biol. Abstr.* V. 1357/2 The hormone of the anterior lobe of the pituitary body, called prolan, is an activator of the ♀ sex gland. **1936** *Brit. Med. Jrnl.* 28 Mar. 628/2 Prolan preparations are also found to be effective here [*sc.* in habitual miscarriage from no apparent cause]. **1966** ROWLANDS & PARKES in A. S. Parkes *Marshall's Physiol. of Reproduction* (ed. 3) III. xxv. 51 This gonadotrophic material, called Prolan by Aschheim and Zondek, was at first thought to be of hypophysal origin. **1971** *Path. Biol.* XIX. 1119 Estimation of..prolan B at concentrations lower than the threshold of immunological activity during various pathological conditions is rendered possible.

prolapse (prəʊˈlæps), *sb.*[1] [ad. late L. *prōlapsus*: see PROLAPSUS.]

†**1.** Gliding forward or onward; lapse, passage (of time). *Obs.*

1585 T. WASHINGTON tr. *Nicholay's Voy.* II. vii. 36 b, By long prolapse of time..the Empyre..was brought vnder the dominion of the Geneuoises.

2. *Path.* = PROLAPSUS.

1822–34 *Good's Study Med.* (ed. 4) IV. 112 A prolapse of the anus. **1869** G. LAWSON *Dis. Eye* (1874) 40 They [the ulcers] frequently perforate the cornea, and cause extensive prolapse of the iris. *Ibid.* 154 If the wound in the lens is complicated with injury to, or prolapse of the iris.

†**prolapse**, *sb.*[2] *Obs. nonce-wd.* [ad. L. *prōlapsus*, pa. pple. of *prōlābī*: see PROLAPSUS; after RELAPSE *sb.*[2]] One who has lapsed or slipped into error (in religious faith or practice).

1563 FOXE *A. & M.* [282/2 Eugenius was pronounced both an heretick & relaps. *Ibid.* 283/1 Panormitane.. disputed..he can not be perswaded that Eugenius can be called a relaps, for so muche as he neyther in the firste, neyther yet in the seconde dissolution did violate hys faythe]. *Ibid.* 283/2 This oration..this effecte it wrought, that afterwarde this worde relapse was taken out of the conclusiones and in stede therof this word *prolapse* put in.

prolapse (prəʊˈlæps), *v. Path.* [f. L. *prōlaps-*, ppl. stem of *prōlābī*: see PROLAPSUS.] *intr.* To slip forward or down out of place.

1736 AMYAND in *Phil. Trans.* XXXIX. 333 The Increase of the Tumour had been checked, and the Reduction of the Parts prolapsed thereby, rendered impracticable. **1876** *Trans. Clinical Soc.* IX. 4 In one or two..cases the iris was disposed to prolapse. **1897** *Allbutt's Syst. Med.* III. 752 Often the bowel prolapses.

Hence **proˈlapsed** *ppl. a.*, that has slipped down; also *fig.*

1738 AMYAND in *Phil. Trans.* XL. 364 It wraps up and incloses the Gut prolapsed. **1874** GARROD & BAXTER *Mat. Med.* 463 To give tone when applied to prolapsed parts. **1926** S. BALDWIN *On England* 111 We see the sentences of the ancients clean run like athletes and fit for their work as compared with the prolapsed and slovenly figures of so much of our own diction.

†**proˈlapsion.** *Obs.* [ad. L. *prōlapsiōn-em*, n. of action f. *prōlābī*: see next.]

1. A slipping or falling away into sin or error.

1601 BP. W. BARLOW *Defence* 224 Neither by his prolapsion into any sinne, his doctrine shuld be scandalized. **1627** SCLATER *Exp. 2 Thess.* (1629) 229 Particular fals we are not exempted from..yet from prolapsion, whole falling away. **1647** TRAPP *Comm. Matt.* vii. 27 From intercision, prolapsion, from utter and irrecoverable falling away, they are freed.

2. *Path.* = PROLAPSUS. *rare.*

1775 in ASH. **1797** *Encycl. Brit.* (ed. 3) XV. 583/1 *Prolapsus*, in surgery, a prolapsion or falling out of any part of the body from its natural situation. **1828** in WEBSTER; and in later Dicts.

‖**prolapsus** (prəʊˈlæpsəs). *Path.* [late L. *prōlaps-us* sb., f. ppl. stem of L. *prōlābi*, *prōlaps-*, to slip forward or down: see PRO-[1] and LAPSE *sb.*] A slipping forward or down of a part or organ, esp. of a part of the viscera, from its normal position into a cavity or through an opening; *spec.* that of the uterus or of the rectum.

prolapsus of the iris, the protrusion of the iris through an ulcer or wound of the cornea.

[**1693** tr. *Blancard's Phys. Dict.* (ed. 2), *Prolapsus Uteri.* **1753** CHAMBERS *Cycl. Supp.*, *Prolapsus oculi*..*Prolapsus uvulæ.*] **1797** M. BAILLIE *Morb. Anat.* (1807) 409 One of the most common diseases of the vagina is its inversion, or prolapsus. **1857** BULLOCK *Cazeaux' Midwif.* 317 Either a simple descent, or an incomplete or complete prolapsus may occur. **1875** H. WALTON *Dis. Eye* 574 Where the iris is on the stretch from prolapsus. **1899** *Allbutt's Syst. Med.* VIII. 513 Sometimes..associated with piles and prolapsus.

†**prolaˈtation.** *Obs.* [n. of action from L. *prōlāt-āre* to lengthen, extend, enlarge; to defer, delay; freq. of *prōferre* (see next), or ? f. *prō*, PRO-[1] + *lātus* broad: cf. *prōlongāre*, *prolongation*.]

1656 BLOUNT *Glossogr.*, *Prolatation* (*prolatatio*), a delaying, an enlarging, a deferring or prolonging. **1658–78** in PHILLIPS.

prolate (ˈprəʊleɪt), *a.* [ad. L. *prōlāt-us*, pa. pple. of *prōferre* to bring forward, produce, prolong, f. *prō*, PRO-[1] + *ferre* to carry.]

1. *Geom.* Lengthened in the direction of the polar diameter: said of a spheroid formed by the revolution of an ellipse about its longer axis. Cf. OBLATE *a.* ***prolate cycloid***: see CYCLOID 1.

1694 HALLEY in *Phil. Trans.* XXXIII. 121 His Compression of a Shell of Earth into a prolate Spheroide. **1753** SHORT *ibid.* XLVIII. 12 It will degenerate into the prolate spheroid, whose poles are *A* and *B*. **1830** KATER & LARDNER *Mech.* ix. 111 The elliptical solid, which is called a prolate spheroid. **1867** DENISON *Astron. without Math.* 7 Drawn out at the poles, like an egg with two small ends, which is called a prolate spheroid.

2. Extended or extending in width; *fig.* widely spread.

1846 DANA *Zooph.* iv. (1848) 75 By the prolate mode of growth, the polyps gradually extend outward, and new buds open, from time to time, a short distance from the edge. **1882** R. G. WILBERFORCE *Bp. Wilberforce* III. i. 3 That we had no means of repressing prolate heresy.

Hence **'prolately** *adv.*, **'prolateness**.

1767 WITCHELL in *Phil. Trans.* LVII. 38 The prolateness of his figure. **1866** B. H. KENNEDY *Public School Latin Primer* 110 The Infinitive stands... 4. Prolately, after Prolative Verbs and Adjectives. **1874** COUES *Birds N.W.* 373 Some [eggs] are ellipsoidal, or prolately spheroidal, having both ends of the same size and shape.

†**pro'late**, *v. Obs.* [ad. L. *prōlāt-āre*: see PROLATATION.] *trans.* To 'bring out', utter, pronounce; *esp.* to lengthen out in utterance.

1601 DEACON & WALKER *Answ. to Darel* 63 [A] bare commanding word, prolated and vttered abroad in the ayre with a vanishing sound. **1630** B. JONSON *New Inn* III. i, *Peck.* ...I wish he may be foundred. *Fly.* Foun-der-ed. Prolate it right. **1640** HOWELL *Dodona's Gr.* 12 The other delights in long breathed accents, which he prolates with such pauses, that before he be at a period of his sentence, one may reach a second thought. **1795** MASON *Ch. Mus.* 261 For the sake of what was deemed solemnity, every note was prolated in one uniform mode of Intonation. **1808** J. MOSER *Don Quix. in Barcelona* I. iv, Many people..prolate words which create no admiration at all.

prolating (prəʊ'leɪtɪŋ), *vbl. sb.* [f. PROLATE *v.* + -ING[1].] Increase or extension.

1919 *Empire Rev.* 256 The loss of wealth, high taxation, the dislocation of trade and industry with their attendant evils, labour unrest and the prolating of unemployment.

prolation (prəʊ'leɪʃən). [ad. L. *prōlātiōn-em*, n. of action f. *prōlāt-*, ppl. stem of *prōferre*: see PROLATE *a.*]

†**1.** The bringing forth of words; utterance. *Obs.*

1390 GOWER *Conf.* I. 256 Thurghout the Trompe into his Ere Fro hevene as thogh a vois it were, To soune of such prolacioun. **1483** CAXTON *Gold. Leg.* (1892) 65 At the prolacion and repeticion of this cantycle, that tribulacion ceassed. **1608** WILLET *Hexapla Exod.* 317 One [accent] seruing for the accenting and prolation of the word. **1636** B. JONSON *Eng. Gram.* I. iv. Wks. (1692) 676, S..softly hisseth against the teeth in the prolation. **1660** J. LLOYD *Prim. Episc.* 66 The prolation of the words of benediction. *a* **1734** NORTH *Lives* (1890) III. 74 The greatest elegance of the finest voices is the prolation of a clear plain sound.

2. In mediæval music, A term used to indicate the relative duration or time-value of the minim to the semibreve in the rhythm of a piece; see quot. 1597, and cf. MOOD *sb.*[2] 3 a, TIME.

1390 GOWER *Conf.* III. 90 Which [gamut] techeth the prolacion Of note and the condicion. *a* **1529** SKELTON *Treat. betw. Trouth & Inform.* (R.), His alterations and prolacions must be pricked treuly. **1597** MORLEY *Introd. Mus.* 12 What is Prolation?.. It is the measuring of Semi-briefes by Minoms, and is either more or lesse. The more prolation is, when the Semibrief contayneth three Minoms, his Signes be these ⊙ ⋹. The lesse prolation is when the Semibriefe contayneth but two Minoms: The Signe..is the absence of the pricke thus O C. **1782** BURNEY *Hist. Mus.* (1789) II. v. 540 The time of the musical characters from the want of bars and the use of ligatures and prolation is some-times difficult to ascertain. **1882** W. S. ROCKSTRO in Grove *Dict. Mus.* III. 459 The Thesis and Arsis of the Lesser Prolation, they say, represent the beats of the human pulse. *Ibid.*, The Greater Prolation—or, as we should now call it, Triple Time... The Lesser Prolation—the Common Time of the modern system.

†**b.** Used vaguely: Measure, strain, melody.

c **1374** CHAUCER *Boeth.* II. pr. i. 30 Musice a damoisel of oure house þat syngeþ now ly3ter moedes or prolaciouns now heuyer. **1549** *Compl. Scot.* vi. 37 Singand melodius reportis of natural music in accordis of mesure of diapason prolations, tripla ande dyatesseron.

†**3.** Bringing forth, production. *Obs. rare.*

1548–77 VICARY *Anat.* v. (1888) 43 That it might helpe the prolation of vomites. **1610** W. FOLKINGHAM *Art of Survey* I. iii. 6 Prolation and seedage of roots and herbs.

†**4.** *Theol.* The 'emission', origination, or procession of the Logos or divine 'Word'. *Obs.*

1692 tr. *Dupin's Eccl. Writers* I. 200/2 They [first ages] take the word *Generation* in another sence than we do, giving this Name to a certain Prolation, or Emission of the Word, which they imagine was done, when God resolved to create the World. **1701** tr. *Le Clerc's Prim. Fathers* (1702) 97 One might have demanded of Tertullian, whether by this Prolation he speaks of, the Reason has existed as Light from a Torch, lighted by another Torch, exists as soon as it is lighted? **1721** EARL OF NOTTINGHAM *Answ. to Whiston* 42 We have learned, that he [Christ] proceeded out of God, and by that Prolation was begotten, and therefore was said to be the Son of God.

†**5.** Advancement, progress, growth. *Obs. rare*[−1].

1610 HEALEY *St. Aug. Citie of God* XIX. v. (1620) 19 How should our Celestiall City haue euer come to originall, to prolation or to perfection, but that the Saints liue all in sociable vnion?

†**6.** A deferring, putting off, delay. (Latinism.)

1656 BLOUNT *Glossogr.*, Prolation (*prolatio*),..a delaying. **1736** AINSWORTH, Prolation, or prolonging, *Prolatio.* **1755** in JOHNSON.

prolative (prəʊ'leɪtɪv), *a.* [ad. late L. *prōlātīv-us*, f. *prōlāt-us*: see PROLATE *a.* and -IVE.]

†**1.** Characterized by being uttered or spoken. *Obs. rare*[−1].

1691 W. NICHOLLS *Answ. Naked Gospel* 93 The learned Fathers in the Church have been always careful, to distinguish between..the prolative, or enunciative word, and the essential and substantial one.

2. *Gram.* Having the function of extending or completing the predication.

1867 W. JOHNSON in Farrar *Ess. Lib. Educ.* 338 The authority which is already making 'prolative verbs' familiar in the households of many country gentlemen. **1876** KENNEDY *Publ. Sch. Lat. Gram.* (ed. 4), Index I, *Prolative Relation*,..that in which Predication is extended by an Infinitive added to Verbs, Participles, or Adjectives. **1896** *Edin. Rev.* Jan. 84 The student [of Finnish] must remember the nominative, partitive..prolative, translative, essive.. and instructive. **1902** F. RITCHIE *Pract. Engl. Gram.* 117 In analyzing such sentences as..(We must *hasten*, You can *go*) the Verb with the Infinitive may be taken together as forming a sort of Complex Verb. An Infinitive so used may be called *Prolative*.

pro'latively, *adv.* [f. PROLATIVE *a.* + -LY[2].] As a prolative infinitive.

1888 B. H. KENNEDY *Rev. Latin Primer* 163 The Infinitive of a Copulative Verb used Prolatively is followed by a Complement in the Nominative.

prole (prəʊl), *sb.* and *a.* Freq. *derogatory.*

A. *sb.* Abbrev. of PROLETARIAN *sb.*

1887 G. B. SHAW *Let.* 21 Oct. (1965) I. 176 We call the working men proles because that is exactly what they are. **1939** 'G. ORWELL' *Coming up for Air* I. ii. 18 There's a lot of rot talked about the sufferings of the working class. I'm not so sorry for the proles myself. **1939** JOYCE *Finnegans Wake* (1964) 39 The doubles of Perkin and Paullock, peer and prole. **1949** 'G. ORWELL' *Nineteen Eighty-Four* II. 209 The dumb masses whom we habitually refer to as 'the proles', numbering perhaps 85 per cent of the population. **1954** KOESTLER *Invisible Writing* III. xxi. 238, I know that these little Proles can't help being what they are—dumb, callous, primitive. **1958** *Observer* 11 May 15/2 Even the boatswain, a 'good prole' who doesn't believe in unions or democracy, is afraid to take the helm. **1967** J. POTTER *Foul Play* i. 11 Make way there, you proles. **1975** I. MURDOCH *Word Child* 10 'I'm fed up with hearing the proles binding about the price of meat,' said Freddie. **1977** J. I. M. STEWART *Madonna of Astrolabe* x. 138 In the Blunderville heyday the Mumfords were the next things to proles.

B. *adj.* Abbrev. of PROLETARIAN *a.* c.

1938 'G. ORWELL' *Let.* 20 Apr. in *Coll. Ess.* (1968) I. 314 As to the great proletarian novel, I really don't see how it's to come into existence. The stuff in *Seven Shifts* is written from a prole point of view, but of course as literature it's bourgeois literature. **1949** —— *Nineteen Eighty-Four* I. 12 A woman down in the prole part of the house suddenly started kicking up a fuss. **1959** *News Chron.* 21 Oct. 3/1 She came from prole roots in St. Pancras. **1963** *Listener* 7 Feb. 263/1 Excellent radio actresses like Gladys Young, for whom our prole dramatists write no parts nowadays. **1969** 'H. CALVIN' *Chosen Instrument* x. 132 Superior journalists..would think it Victorian and prole to know shorthand. **1977** *Times* 20 Apr. 12/2 What has happened in England is that..the proles, or to be exact the prole élite, have seized the power.

prole, obs. form of PROWL *v.*

†**prolec'tation**. *Obs. rare.* [ad. L. type **prōlectātiōn-em*, n. of action f. *prōlect-āre* to entice forth, freq. of *prolicĕre*, f. *prō*, PRO-[1] 1 a + *lacĕre* to entice.]

1. Extraction of the juices, etc., of something.

1612 WOODALL *Surg. Mate* Wks. (1653) 273 *Prolectation* is extraction by attenuation of subtil parts, so that by the inclination of their rarified nature, they may be altred from the more grosse parts. **1657** TOMLINSON *Renou's Disp.* 678 Prolectation of oleous liquors.

2. (See quot.) *rare*[−0].

1625 MINSHEU *Ductor* (ed. 2), *Prolectation*, pleasant inticement, delightsome prouocation.

pro-leg ('prəʊlɛg). *Entom.* [f. PRO-[1] 4 b + LEG.] One of the fleshy abdominal limbs or tubercles of the larvæ of some insects, e.g. of caterpillars; distinct from the true or thoracic legs.

1816 KIRBY & SP. *Entomol.* xxi. (1818) II. 237 They repose, holding strongly with their prolegs the branch on which they are standing. *Ibid.* 288 Since..they are temporary,..merely used as props to hinder its long body.. from trailing on the ground..I shall therefore call them prolegs (*propedes*). **1839** SELBY in *Proc. Berw. Nat. Club* I. No. 7. 202 It also possesses two fleshy tubercles or pro-legs. **1874** LUBBOCK *Orig. & Met. Ins.* i. 7 Larvæ..very much like caterpillars, having 3 pairs of legs, and..abdominal pro-legs as well.

pro-legate: see PRO-[1] 1.

‖**prolegomenon** (prəʊlɪ'gɒmɪnən). Pl. **-mena** (-ə). [a. Gr. προλεγόμενον, neut. of pres. pple. pass. of προλέγειν to say beforehand, f. πρό, PRO-[2] + λέγειν to say.] A preliminary discourse prefixed to a literary work; esp. a learned preface or preamble; chiefly in *pl.* introductory or preliminary observations on the subject of a book.

a **1652** J. SMITH *Sel. Disc.* I. i. (1821) 11 As a prolegomenon or preface to what we shall afterward discourse. **1659** BP. WALTON *Consid. Considered* 40 Not at all impeached by any thing maintained in the Prolegomena. **1697** EVELYN *Numism.* ii. 19 His Prolegomenon to the Polyglotte Bible. **1729** POPE (*title*) The Dunciad; with Notes Variorum and the Prolegomena of Scriblerus. **1818** SCOTT *Hrt. Midl.* To Rdr., Therefore have I chosen, in this prolegomenon, to unload my burden of thanks at thy feet. **1869** KINGSLEY *Let. to F. D. Maurice* 16 Jan., They are meant..as prolegomena to natural theology.

b. (*pl.*) Spoken preliminaries; prefatory remarks.

1892 STEVENSON & L. OSBOURNE *Wrecker* xix, He, after some ambiguous prolegomena, roundly proposed I should go shares with him.

Hence **prole'gomenal, prole'gomenary** *adjs.*, prefatory, introductory; **prole'gomenist**, one who writes prolegomena; **prole'gomenous** *a.*, (*a*) = *prolegomenary*; (*b*) given to making tedious preliminary statements; long-winded.

1897 RHYS DAVIDS in *Mind* Apr. 249 To have collected and expanded these in one *prolegomenal essay. **1846** WORCESTER, **Prolegomenary* (citing *Eclectic Rev.*). **1907** *Daily Chron.* 30 Aug. 2/6 Mr. Parsons staggers us..by a prefatory sentence of five hundred words and a mass of prolegomenary notes. **1731** *Hist. Litteraria* II. 583 There is also an Epistle from Joan. Gratian to the *Prolegomenist. **1749** FIELDING *Tom Jones* VIII. i, It may not be amiss in the *prolegomenous or introductory chapter, to say something of that species of writing which is called the marvellous. **1822** *Blackw. Mag.* XI. 162 On the title-page ominous, And in prose prolegomenous. **1881** STEVENSON *Virg. Puerisque* iv. 80 A wordy, prolegomenous babbler will often add three new offences in the process of excusing one.

prolep'sarian. *nonce-wd.* [f. next + *-arian*, as in *unitarian*, etc.] One who explains something on the theory of a prolepsis.

1694 J. SMITH *Doctr. Lord's Day* 93 The prolepsarians have a help for this: for in the room of this precept they plant Ecclesiastical Constitutions. Is not this..to pilfer from God one of his to make room for the Churches Laws?

‖**prolepsis** (prəʊ'lɛpsɪs, -'liːpsɪs). Pl. **-ses** (-siːz). Also 7 **prolepsie**, 8–9 **-sy**. [L., a. Gr. πρόληψις a preconception; in rhet. anticipation, f. προλαμβάνειν to anticipate.]

1. The representation or taking of something future as already done or existing; anticipation; also, the assignment of an event, a name, etc. to a too early date; an anachronism, prochronism.

1578 TIMME *Caluine on Gen.* 264 The answer is easy to be made, if we grant that the figure *Prolepsis* is in the speech of Moses [see *Gen.* xi. 31, xii. 1]. **1607** B. JONSON *Volpone* Ded., Such dearth of sense, so bold prolepse's, so rackt metaphor's. *a* **1633** W. AMES *Marrow of Div.* (1642) 323 This was spoken by a prolepsis or anticipation. **1699** BENTLEY *Phal.* vi. 180 A cross figure in the art of Rhetoric, called Prolepsis or Anticipation; viz. when Poets and Historians call any place by a name, which was not yet known in the times they write of. **1846** TRENCH *Mirac.* xxx. (1862) 431 St. Matthew will then relate by prolepsis..the whole of the event where he first introduces it. **1907** W. SANDY in *Expositor* May 393 That prolepsis, or prevision and apprehension of holiness which we call faith.

b. *Path.* 'Return of a paroxysm before the usual time' (*Syd. Soc. Lex.* 1895).

2. *Rhet.* and *Gram.* †**a.** A figure in which a matter is stated in a brief summary manner, before being set forth in detail. *Obs.*

1586 A. DAY *Eng. Secretary* II. (1625) 82 *Prolepsis*, where something generally first spoken, is afterwards drawne into parts, as thus, Let vs take vpon vs one selfe charge, I to direct abroad, you to order at home. **1657** J. SMITH *Myst. Rhet.* 130 Prolepsis is also a figure of Construction,..when the Congregation, or the whole doth aptly agree with the Verb, or Adjective, and then the parts of the whole are reduced to the same Verb or Adjective, wherewith notwithstanding they agree not.

b. A figure in which objections or arguments are anticipated in order to preclude their use, answer them in advance, or prepare for them an unfavourable reception; = PROCATALEPSIS.

1611 W. SCLATER *Key* (1629) 57 This Verse is added to the former by way of prolepsis, for hauing professed his desire to see them, he saw it might be demanded why he came not. **1637** SANDERSON *Serm.* II. 62 He thought it needful.., by way of *prolepsis*, to prevent whatsoever might be surmised in that kind. **1767** STERNE *Tr. Shandy* IX. xxxiii, I know it will be said, continued my father (availing himself of the *Prolepsis*), that [etc.].

c. The anticipatory use of an attribute.

1850 DONALDSON *New Cratylus* III. v. §305 (ed. 2) 484 In all three cases there is a prolepsis or tertiary predication. **1875** SCHMIDT *Shaks. Lex.* II. 1420 Prolepsis or anticipation, that is, an effect to be produced represented as already produced, by the insertion of an epithet:..'Hang his poison in the sick air'. **1882** OGILVIE (Annandale), *Prolepsis* (in rhet.), a figure by which a thing is represented as already done, though in reality it is to follow as a consequence of the action which is described.

†**3.** A pre-assumed notion, a presupposition. *Obs.*

1637 JACKSON *Serm. Matt. ii.* 17, 18, Wks. VI. 279 For the more perspicuous and facile solution of these..doubts, I must crave leave to intersert certain prolepses or prenotions. **1662** STILLINGFL. *Orig. Sacr.* III. i. §2 The existence of God, and immortality of the soul; both which seem to be supposed as general Prolepses in the writings of Moses. **1692** RAY *Disc.* II. iv. (1693) 133 That Nature should form real shells, without any design of covering an Animal, is..contrary to that innate Prolepsis we have of the Prudence of Nature.

proleptic (prəʊ'lɛptɪk, -'liːptɪk), *a.* (*sb.*) [ad. Gr. προληπτικός anticipative, f. προλαμβάνειν: see prec. and -IC. So F. *proleptique* (17–18th c.).]

1. Of, pertaining to, or characterized by prolepsis or anticipation; anticipative, anticipatory; *spec.* in *Med.* predictive, prognostic.

a **1656** USSHER *Ann.* To Rdr. (1658) 4 Having placed therefore the heads of this Period in the Kalends of January, in that proleptick year, the first of our Christian vulgar account must be reckoned the 4714 of the Julian Period. *a* **1684** LEIGHTON *Serm.* Wks. (1868) 673 Seasonable digressions, proleptic and exegetic. **1841** TRENCH *Parables, Interpr.* (1860) 39 The proleptic mind of genius may be needful to discover the law. **1882–3** *Schaff's Encycl. Relig. Knowl.* II. 878/2 The earliest proleptic signs of Gnosticism are to be looked for in Simon Magus. **1890** BILLINGS *Nat. Med. Dict.*, *Proleptic*,.. pertaining to prolepsis; anticipating; prognostic. **1905** *Westm. Gaz.* 25 Feb. 5 He suggests.. that this behaviour is, as grammarians say, rather proleptic (anglice, 'previous').

2. *Path.* Applied to a periodical disease, of which the paroxysm recurs each time at an earlier hour.

[**1693** tr. *Blancard's Phys. Dict.* (ed. 2), *Prolepticus*, a Disease always anticipating; so as if the Ague come to day at four of the Clock, then to morrow one hour sooner, and so on.] **1696** PHILLIPS (ed. 5), *Proleptick disease.* **1727–41** in CHAMBERS *Cycl.* **1867** in C. A. HARRIS *Dict. Med. Terminol.*

†**3.** Of the nature of a pre-assumption; preconceived; a priori, axiomatic. *Obs.*

1666 BP. S. PARKER *Free & Impart. Censure* (1667) 36 Propositions depending upon and orderly deduced from your first Proleptick Principles. **1679** J. GOODMAN *Penit. Pard.* I. iv. (1713) 103 That God had thus furnished the mind with such a stock of proleptick principles of knowledge.

4. *Gram.* Of, pertaining to, or exemplifying prolepsis: see prec. 2 c.

1866 JELF *Gr. Gram.* 113 *Proleptic Use of Attributive Adjectives.* An adjective is sometimes applied to a substantive, though the property expressed by it does not exist in the substantive till after the action of the accompanying verb is completed. In this construction the verb and adjective together generally form a pleonastic predicative notion. **1870** R. C. JEBB *Sophocles' Electra* (ed. 2) 15/1, ἀντίρροπον is not proleptic.

B. *sb.* (in *pl.*) *Med.* Prediction or prognosis, as a department of medical science.

1843 *Rep. Brit. Assoc.* 82 Only widely-extended and accurate observations.. can form the foundation of a science of vital proleptics. **1853** in DUNGLISON *Med. Lex.* **1895** *Syd. Soc. Lex.*, *Proleptics*, term proposed by Lacock for the science and art of prediction or prognosis.

proleptical (prəʊˈlɛptɪkəl, -ˈliːpt-), *a. rare.* [f. as prec. + -AL[1].] = prec. in various senses.

1627 W. SCLATER *Exp. 2 Thess.* (1629) 277 A prolepticall Apostrophe to the people orderly demeaning themselues after the Canon for labour. **1678** CUDWORTH *Intell. Syst.* 732 Our Knowledge here is.. in order of nature, before them, and proleptical to them. **1857** BADEN POWELL *Chr. without Judaism* 89 Some of the best commentators have regarded the passage as proleptical, or anticipatory. **1881** *Echo* 6 May 2/3 A sufficient answer must always be proleptical,.. it must anticipate every possible objection.

b. Antecedent to historical time or to record; said of a past event, etc. fixed by astronomical or other calculation, not by actual observation.

a **1646** J. GREGORY *De Æris et Epochis* Posth. (1650) 170 Historical Time is that which is deduced from the *Æra Orbis Conditi*. Proleptical is that which is fixed in the Chaos. **1659** PEARSON *Creed* i. (1839) 85 He.. who should in the Egyptian temples see the description of so many eclipses of the sun and moon, could not be assured that they were all taken from real observation, when they might be as well described out of proleptical supposition. **1839** *Fraser's Mag.* XX. 204 The old Egyptian chronicle, which disposes of the proleptical time of the great zodiacal period of 36,525 years,.. at once establishes that series.

proˈleptically, *adv.* [f. prec. + -LY[2].] In a proleptic manner; by prolepsis.

†**a.** See PROLEPSIS 2 a. *Obs.*

1611 W. SCLATER *Key* (1629) 88 They knew it, verse 19. which is proued proleptically, verse 20. by the particulars of this knowledge.

b. By way of anticipation; antecedently.

1652 URQUHART *Jewel* Wks. (1834) 292 Displaying their interrogatory part.. proleptically, with the refutative schemes of anticipation and subjection. **1678** CUDWORTH *Intell. Syst.* 733 Knowledge and Understanding, apprehend things Proleptically to their Existence. **1741** WARBURTON *Div. Legat.* II. 495 [Job] speaking proleptically, as knowing what God in a future age would do. **1867** FURNIVALL & HALES in *Percy Folio* I. 205 Sir Edward Stanley (proleptically styled Lord Mounteagle in the ballad).

proler, obs. form of PROWLER.

‖**proles** (ˈprəʊliːz). [Lat. *prōlēs* offspring.] Progeny, offspring; in phrase ***sine prole*** (abbrev. *s.p.*), without offspring or issue.

1672 *Cowell's Interpr.*, *Proles*, in English *Progeny*, is properly such as proceed from a lawful Marriage. **1706** in PHILLIPS. **1730–6** BAILEY (folio), *Proles*, the issue of a person's body; an offspring, stock, or race. **1848–83** in WHARTON *Law Lex.* **1886** in *Cassell's Encycl. Dict.*

prolet- (prəʊˈlɛt). Abbrev. [after Russ. *prolet-* in *proletkul't* for *proletárskaya kul'túra* proletarian culture] of PROLETARIAN *a.* and *sb.*, as in ***prolet-art, -cult, (-kult), -cultist, -cultural*** adj., used to designate cultural activities (esp. such as were started in Russia after 1917) which supposedly reflect or encourage a purely proletarian ethos.

1921 E. & C. PAUL *Proletcult* ii. 19 Proletarians who are alive to their class interest.. will insist upon Independent Working-Class Education, upon proletarian culture, upon Proletcult. **1921** *Glasgow Herald* 28 Dec. 11 There is little proof that there has been general misrepresentation, and it is general misrepresentation that the prolet-cultist wants. **1922** *Ibid.* 4 Jan. 5 One cannot imagine any greater stimulus to the 'Prolet-Cultural' movement. **1931** H. G. WELLS *Work, Wealth & Happiness of Mankind* (1932) xv. 732 From the Proletarian springs 'Prolet-art', for example, among the first fruits of the new spirit. It is art without individuality. **1943** E. M. ALMEDINGEN *Frossia* II. 84 Frossia told her about *Coppelia* at the neighbouring Proletcult. **1961** *New Left Rev.* May–June 27/2 The follies of *proletcult*, the stridency and crude class reductionism which passed for Marxist criticism. **1963** A. HARTLEY *State of England* ii. 26 The *Proletkult* of a philosopher such as Sartre is purely intellectual. **1967** *Oxf. Compan. Theatre* (ed. 3) 952/2 *Trades Unions Theatre*, Moscow.. was created in 1932 from the Proletcult Theatre, started after the October Revolution by Sergei Eisenstein. **1974** MOORE & PARRY *Twentieth-Cent. Russ. Lit.* (1976) ii. 24 The magazine *Proletarskaya kul'tura* incorporated the name of the movement, which itself became, in shorthand, *Proletkul't*. **1976** T. EAGLETON *Crit. & Ideology* v. 165 Such purely gestural, shamefaced materialism will provoke.. the reaction of those who press their questioning of the intrinsic élitism of literature and its aesthetics to neo-*proletkult* limits.

proletaire (prəʊlɪˈtɛə(r), prɒl-). Also as Fr. **prolétaire.** [a. F. *prolétaire* (prɔletɛr), 1748 in Hatz.-Darm. (Montesquieu, of ancient Romans, Rousseau in mod. sense), ad. L. *prōlētāri-us* a Roman citizen of the lowest class under the Servian constitution, one who served the state not with his property but only with his offspring; also adj. low, common; f. *prōl-ēs, -em* offspring. The derivatives imply an orig. stem *prōlēt-*.] = PROLETARIAN *sb.*; one of the PROLETARIAT: **a.** in sense 2 a; **b.** *Pol. Econ.*, in sense 2 b.

a. 1820 *Edin. Rev.* Aug. 28 A Despot is thus the natural representative of the *proletaires*. **1834** *Tait's Mag.* I. 222/1 The movement at Lyons was a Republican movement... It was not made by boys, or apprentices, or *proletaires*. **1859** KINGSLEY *Misc.*, *Mad World* I. 127 It [House of Commons] is not chosen by educated men, any more than it is by proletaires.

b. 1833 J. S. MILL *Let.* 2 Feb. in *Wks.* (1963) XII. 140 Those of the St. Simonians who retain their connection with the Pere Suprême and with each other, have made themselves *prolètaires*. **1853** F. BASTIAT *Ess. Pol. Econ.* 46 It creates and makes to clash two opposite interests—that of the capitalists and that of the *prolétaires*. **1890** G. B. SHAW in *Fabian Ess. in Socialism* 64 Ferdinand Lassalle said: 'Society consists of ninety-six *proletaires* and four capitalists. That is your State.' But in Lancashire there was neither capitalist nor *proletaire*.

fig. **1876** HUXLEY *Sci. Memoirs* (1902) iv. 152 The plant is the ideal *prolétaire* of the living world, the worker who produces.

proletairism (prəʊlɪˈtɛərɪz(ə)m). Also **proletarism.** [f. prec. + -ISM.] The condition of proletaires; proletaires as a body; = PROLETARIANISM.

1850 *Tait's Mag.* XVII. 658/1 The change from proletairism to proprietorship. **1870** W. R. GREG *Polit. Problems* 291 Which threatens.. to separate the *prolétairism* of the nation from the holders of property. **1880** *19th Cent.* VII. 24 The people are sinking into a very abyss of proletarism.

†**proleˈtaneous**, *a. Obs. rare*$^{-0}$. [f. late L. *prōlētāne-us* (f. *prōlēs*, **prōlēt-*, with ending *-āneus*: cf. *extrāneus*) + -OUS.] (See quot.)

1656 BLOUNT *Glossogr.*, *Proletaneous*, of a poor and base condition, that has many children, and little maintenance, or that gives nothing to the Commonwealth, but onely a supply of children. **1658** in PHILLIPS. **1775** in ASH. **1847** in WEBSTER. Hence in mod. Dicts.

proletarian (prəʊlɪˈtɛərɪən, prɒl-), *a.* and *sb.* [f. L. *prōlētāri-us* a PROLETAIRE + -AN.]

A. *adj.* Of or pertaining to the lowest class of the people. †**a.** In hostile use: Vile, low, vulgar. *Obs.*

1663 BUTLER *Hud.* I. i. 720 We that are wisely mounted higher.. Like Speculators should foresee.., Portended Mischiefs farther then Low Proletarian Tithing men. **1676** *Doctrine of Devils* 96 Much wiser (not only than the Proletarian rabble, but than they too, who profess themselves to be the great Philosophers). *a* **1734** NORTH *Exam.* I. ii. §155 (1740) 117 To have let in the rest of the Proletarian Rout of Villains, that waited without to be employed as Witnesses.

b. Of ancient Romans: cf. PROLETARIAT 1.

1839 DE QUINCEY *Casuistry Rom. Meals* Misc. I. 250 Every citizen, if he were not a mere proletarian animal kept at the public cost, with a view to his *proles* or offspring, held himself a soldier-elect.

c. Of or pertaining to the proletariat in the modern sense. ***proletarian revolution***: the stage of political development predicted by Marx when the proletarians would overthrow capitalism.

1851 SIR F. PALGRAVE *Norm. & Eng.* I. 49 The proletarian populace of the great cities. **1874** LISLE CARR *Jud. Gwynne* I. iii. 72 A she-costermonger, or other female of the proletarian classes. **1885** *Manch. Exam.* 17 Jan. 5/5 Typically the proletarian and suffering part of the metropolis. **1903** G. B. SHAW *Man & Superman* v. 196 We have been driven to Proletarian Democracy by the failure of all the alternative systems. **1925** tr. *Lenin's Proletarian Revolution* i. 11 Almost a third of this pamphlet.. is devoted by this windbag to a twaddle which must be very agreeable to the bourgeoisie, as it.. obscures the question of the proletarian revolution. **1934** C. LAMBERT *Music Ho!* IV. 248 The sleeves themselves are rolled up in the most approved proletarian fashion. **1935** W. EMPSON *Some Versions of Pastoral* 3 It is hard for an Englishman to talk definitely about proletarian art. **1966** *Guardian* 13 Dec. 8/2 [China] The example of the great proletarian cultural revolution. **1973** C. D. KERNIG *Marxism, Communism & Western Society* VII. 238/1 The proletarian revolution becomes an act of human emancipation or the self-realization of man after his self-alienation. **1975** *Chinese Econ. Stud.* VIII. IV. 3 Countless proletarian heroes have suddenly emerged. **1976** *Times* 28 Sept. (China Suppl.) 10/3 Under the banner of 'proletarian internationalism' ideological motives seem to be distinguishable features of Chinese aid. **1977** *China Now* June 4/1 Tachai is an expression of the proletarian revolution China is in the midst of today (in contrast to the democratic revolution between 1949 and 1966). **1978** *Times Lit. Suppl.* 1 Dec. 1402/5 Sociologists and realistic novelists —including proletarian novelists—find it difficult if not impossible to describe the texture of this world.

B. *sb.* A member of the poorest class of a community; *esp.* one who is without capital or regular employment; one of the proletariat.

1658 W. BURTON *Itin. Anton.* Ded. 1 The happinesse I enjoy by my Interest in our Nationall Rights (though a poor Proletarian). **1838–42** ARNOLD *Hist. Rome* II. xxxvii. 486 Even the proletarians, or the poorest class of citizens.. were now called out and embodied. **1870** *On the War* (Internat. Working-Men's Assoc.) 4 Mindful of the watchword of the International Working-men's Association: *Proletarians of all countries unite*, we shall never forget that the workmen of *all* countries are our *friends* and the despots of *all* countries our *enemies*. **1879** *Contemp. Rev.* XXXVI. 290 It is almost impossible for any but a born proletarian to understand the needs, the wants, and daily lives of the proletarian. **1898** BODLEY *France* I. II. ii. 298 Counting as proletarians politicians who utilise the blouse as a lucrative symbol. **1966** D. WILSON *Quarter of Mankind* i. 7 The peasant, not the urban proletarian, is the central character in China's drama. **1969** A. G. FRANK *Latin Amer.* (1970) xxiii. 360 The rural and slum proletarians.. tend to be quite near-sighted and to see only the land and the jobs which they want but don't have.

proleˈtarianism. [f. prec. + -ISM.] The condition of a proletarian; a state of things characterized by the existence of a proletarian class; the political principles and practice of the proletarians; also *transf.* proletarians as a class, the proletariat.

1861 J. G. SHEPPARD *Fall Rome* ii. 91 We speak of the perils of modern proletarianism, and we have cause. **1870** W. R. GREG *Polit. Problems* 326 Take the very first question .. on which property and proletarianism, statesmen and democrats, are sure to take opposite sides. **1884** *American* VIII. 411 The descent of the masses into a hopeless proletarianism. **1918** *Nation* (N.Y.) 7 Feb. 131/2 Fidelity to the cause of international proletarianism.. must stay the hands of the Bolshevik peace negotiators. **1975** D. FRANCIS *High Stakes* v. 75 If politicians.. searched diligently amongst their antecedents for proletarianism and denied aristocratic contacts.. who was I to spoil the fun?

So **proleˈtarianize** *v.*, to render proletarian; **proleˈtarianized** *ppl. a.*; **proleˈtarianizing** *vbl. sb.*

1887 *Pop. Sci. Monthly* Jan. 293 The largesses pauperized and proletarianized the populace of the great city. **1921** tr. *Rathenau's New Society* 60 To many it is not agreeable to picture to themselves the aspect of a thoroughly proletarianized country. **1937** 'C. CAUDWELL' *Illusion & Reality* vi. 115 Proletarianise the craftsman to the level of a labourer or machine-minder. **1949** 'M. INNES' *Journeying Boy* i. 6 The lower stratum of the intellectual class was being proletarianised. **1957** M. MCCARTHY *Mem. Catholic Girlhood* i. 40 The peculiarly fatigued, dusty, proletarianized character of American municipal entertainment. **1962** *Guardian* 9 Mar. 7/2 Many of the most important American cities.. have become increasingly proletarianised in the worst sense. **1965** D. E. C. EVERSLEY in Glass & Eversley *Population in Hist.* ii. 66 A fall in the death rate.. accelerated the proletarianizing process. **1966** D. WILSON *Quarter of Mankind* iii. 37 The middle class has become a captive collaborator with the Communist Party, having to work for its own downfall in the interests of a reconstructed, proletarianized nation. **1974** *Daily Tel.* 15 Jan. 14/3 Now officially referred to.. as 'Mr Tony Benn'. So the.. process by which the man who was once called Viscount Stansgate has tried so determinedly to proletarianise himself is almost complete. **1974** B. PEARCE tr. *Amin's Accumulation on World Scale* I. 27 Analogous to this process is the mobilizing of the internal colonial reserves, as with the proletarianizing of blacks in the United States. **1979** *Jrnl. R. Soc. Arts* CXXVII. 354/2 The proletarianizing of the north-east coast.

proleˌtarianiˈzation. [f. PROLETARIANIZE *v.* + -ATION.] The fact or process of rendering or becoming proletarian (sense c).

1920 *19th Cent.* Sept. 445 If State agriculture in Russia comes to be on a larger scale, will there not be a sort of proletarianisation of the peasants? **1936** 'H. MACDIARMID' *Lucky Poet* (1943) iii. 145 The line we advocate.. will.. greatly speed up the proletarianization of Scottish Arts and Letters. **1948** C. S. FOX tr. *Röpke's Civitas Humana* III. vi. 140 Proletarianisation means.. that human beings have got into a highly dangerous sociological and anthropological state which is characterised by lack of property, lack of reserves of every kind.., by economic servitude, uprooting, massed living quarters, militarisation of work..; in short, by a general devitalisation and loss of personality. **1961** L. P. HARTLEY *Two for River* 45 The appalling vulgarity of that town! Nowhere has the proletarianization of the English race gone so fast, or so far. **1966** F. SCHURMANN *Ideology & Organization in Communist China* i. 40 Given the unilinear development of history, the process of world-wide proletarianization is inevitable. **1974** *Daily Tel.* 24 May 3/2 The initiative for getting rid of the oak tables came from one or two students keen to promote the 'proletarianisation' of the college. **1977** P. JOHNSON *Enemies of Society* xiv. 190 The proletarianization of the British middle class, that leading creator and custodian of western civilization, is one of the most significant social changes of our times.

prole'tarianly, *adv.* [f. PROLETARIAN *a.* and *sb.* + -LY[2].] According to proletarian views.

1931 *Time & Tide* 3 Oct. 1130 This *rentier* has been unfeeling enough to practice what is capitalistically called virtue, but is proletarianly known as vice; *he has saved money!*

proletariat, -ate (prəʊlɪ'tɛərɪət). [ad. mod.F. *prolétariat* (prɔletarja), f. L. *prōlētāri-us* PROLETAIRE + F. *-at*, -ATE[1]. Orig. and now usually spelt *-at*, as in Fr. The spelling with the Eng. *-ate* was common *c* 1858–1920].

1. *Anc. Hist.* The lowest class of the community in ancient Rome, regarded as contributing nothing to the state but offspring. Also with reference to other ancient states.

α. **1861** J. G. SHEPPARD *Fall Rome* i. 49 In the days of Marius, its old aristocratical distinctions were abandoned in the ranks, and the proletariat admitted upon terms of equality. **1871** FARRAR *Witn. Hist.* v. 189 Athens had her slaves, Sparta her helots, Rome her proletariat.

β. **1868** 'OUIDA' *Tricotrin* I. 138 Rome—with her vast proletariate and her vast armies lulled the hungry cry. **1879** FARRAR *St. Paul* I. 558 It was from this city [Corinth] and amid its abandoned proletariate that the Apostle dictated his frightful sketch of Paganism.

2. In reference to modern society.

a. Applied to the lowest class of the community. Often with *hostile* connotation.

α. **1853** *Times* 19 Nov. 8/5 We are encouraged to fling the boroughs into the hands of a poor, ignorant, and venal proletariat. **1878** *N. American Review* CXXVII. 4 A discontented proletariat beneath. **1879** H. GEORGE *Progr. & Pov.* VII. iv. (1881) 336 To swell the ranks of the proletariat who had nothing to sell but their votes.

β. **1865** MAFFEI *Brigand Life* II. 185[It] would produce.. the wholesome effect..of destroying that savage proletariate. **1873** L. STEPHEN *Ess. Freethinking* 113 When a Church loses its hold on the intellectual classes, it can no longer maintain its sway over the 'proletariate'. **1881** MISS LAFFAN in *Macm. Mag.* XLIV. 393 He had all the cant of the advanced school; never spoke of poor people save by the term 'proletariate'.

fig. **1861** L. STEPHEN tr. *Berlepsch's Alps* vi. 47 The proletariat of vegetation, the common people of the creeping grasses, the aggregate of which forms the rich pasturage. **1881** *Nature* 24 Feb. 387/1 First..was the Sparrow, the most impudent proletariat—I had almost said Social democrat, because the whole world today has that bad word in the mouth.

b. *Pol. Econ.* That class of the community which is dependent on daily labour for subsistence, and has no reserve or capital; the indigent wage-earners; sometimes extended to include all wage-earners; working men, the labouring classes. ***dictatorship of the proletariat***: the Communist ideal of proletarian supremacy following the overthrow of capitalism and preceding the classless state.

α. **1856** GEO. ELIOT in *Westm. Rev.* X. 75 The Proletariat, or those who are dependent on daily wages. **1869** *Daily News* 31 Aug., [The system] of Partnerships of Industry..may need for its development a more cultivated proletariat and a capitalist class less anxious to be rich. **1880** WOOLSEY *Communism & Soc.* iv. §1. 127 The *proletariat*, as the agitators delighted to call the standing class of operatives: meaning by this Roman term..those who had only hands to work with and no laid-up capital. **1883** HYNDMAN *Socialism* v, The growth of the powerful capitalist class on the one hand, and of the proletariat or hand-to-mouth wage-earners on the other. **1886** tr. *Marx's Manifesto of Communists* 8 The small middle class, the artisans, merchants, mechanics, shopkeepers, and farmers, are all doomed to fall into the ranks of the Proletariat, because their small capital cannot compete with that of the millionaire, and..their skill is depreciated by new modes of production. Thus the Proletariat recruits from all classes of population. **1927** H. LASKI *Let.* 20 Nov. in *Holmes—Laski Lett.* (1953) II. 998 Did I tell you that I have traced the origins of the famous 'Dictatorship of the Proletariat' to Babeuf? **1937** E. ST. V. MILLAY *Conversation at Midnight* ii. 69 The dictatorship of the proletariat, though not yet present and in this room, is a fact! **1941** *New Statesman* 19 Apr. 407/1 Unluckily the proletariat are even more conservative in their food than the bourgeoisie. **1964** P. G. CASANOVA in I. L. Horowitz *New Sociol.* 71 Mills..could not believe that Marx's view that the proletariat was the force of history could be applied to the United States of 1960. **1972** W. LEONHARD in C. D. Kernig *Marxism, Communism & Western Society* II. 429/2 The term 'dictatorship of the proletariat' was probably coined in 1837 by Auguste Blanqui. *Ibid.* 434/1 After Stalin's death.. a change again took place in the Soviet presentation of the dictatorship of the proletariat. **1976** T. EAGLETON *Crit. & Ideology* ii. 58 In nineteenth-century England..there were sound political reasons why the proletariat should be excluded from literacy, but sound religious reasons why it should not be.

β. **1858** *Brit. Q. Rev.* LVI. 442 Who will make up his 'proletariate', or, in unambitious English, 'labouring classes'. **1884** *Illustr. Lond. News* 16 Feb. 150/2 That it is directed against the liberty of the proletariate. **1920** M. BEER *Hist. Brit. Socialism* II. III. vi. 120 O'Brien's was the policy of a relentless class war by a proletariate that was absolutely unable to convert its votes into political power.

3. *attrib.* or as *adj.*

1867 G. LUSHINGTON in *Quest. Reformed Parl.* 42 Imagine an employer of labour..placed in the dock before a Proletariat Magistrate. **1868** *Blackw. Mag.* Mar. 298 The French Revolution, by destroying the aristocratic character of the clergy, gave birth to a caste of proletariat priests. **1889** *Academy* 29 June 441/1 Efforts of philanthropy at the improvement of the proletariate classes.

Hence **prole'tariatism**, the principles and aims of a proletariat; cf. PROLETARIANISM.

1879 BARING-GOULD *Germany* II. 289 The future battle between property and proletariatism.

† **prole'tarious**, *a. Obs. rare*[−1]. [f. L. *prōlētāri-us* a PROLETAIRE + -OUS.] Pertaining to or characteristic of the proletariate; vulgar: see quot.

1656 BLOUNT *Glossogr.* s.v., A Proletarious Speech (*proletarius sermo*) the common and vulgar speech, complement or words of course; As when one says to his friend; *Pardon my boldness*, and the other answers, *You are not so bold as welcome*, or the like.

proletari'zation. [f. F. *prolétaire* PROLETAIRE + -IZE + -ATION.] = PROLETARIANIZATION. Also **'proletarize** *v. trans.*; **'proletarized** *ppl. a.*

1918 *Times* 19 Aug. 5/6 We are drifting towards the complete proletarization of the official classes. **1920** E. ANTONELLI *Bolshevist Russia* I. iii. 80 The theory of 'proletarizing' the peasants was never abandoned. **1952** GERTH & MARTINDALE tr. *Weber's Anc. Judaism* I. ii. 56 Indebted or landless, hence, proletarized Israelites. **1968** P. B. AUSTIN *On being Swedish* xiii. 86 The sinister cleavage between highbrow and lowbrow, the proletarization of the soul which lies at the root of so many of the western world's spiritual and even material ills, is here virtually unknown. **1975** *Daily Tel.* 15 Aug. 12 The real aim is the proletarisation of society.

proletary ('prəʊl-, 'prɒlɪtərɪ), *a.* and *sb.* [ad. L. *prōlētāri-us* a PROLETAIRE.]

A. *adj.* = PROLETARIAN *a.*

1609 HOLLAND *Amm. Marcell.* 138 He should gaine a number of proletairie subjects to multiplie and beget issue. **1656** J. HARRINGTON *Oceana* Wks. (1700) 184 The sixth [class] being Proletary, that is..such as thro their poverty contributed nothing to the Commonwealth but Children. **1854** J. MARTINEAU *Prospective Rev.* Ess. 1891 II. 313 The increase of a proletary class. **1884** LOWELL *Democr.* (1887) 7 The change from an agricultural to a proletary population.

B. *sb.* = PROLETARIAN *sb.*

Used in 16th and early 17th c. Reintroduced in 19th as substitute for *proletaire*.

1579 J. JONES *Preserv. Bodie & Soule* I. xix. 37 The Assyrians and Babilonians boughte their wiues.., but after vsed mariages, regarding therewith their Prolataries, as the Spartanes didde them that begatte their men children. **1610** HEALEY tr. *Vives' St. Aug. Citie of God* 125 A Proletary or Brood-man..reserued onely to beget children. **1621** BURTON *Anat. Mel.* Democr. to Rdr. (1676) 19/2 Of 15000 proletaries slain in a battel, scarce fifteen are recorded in history.

1865 SALA *Amer. in War* II. 102 The proletaries—this word, in a military sense, is not mine, but Burton's, of the 'Anatomy'—whom Columbia has summoned or forced beneath her star-spangled standard. **1879** GEO. ELIOT *Theo. Such* ix. 171 The bitterness which capitalists and employers often feel to be a reasonable mood towards obstructive proletaries. **1894** *Athenæum* 22 Sept. 381/3 [Her Socialist husband] introduces fierce proletaries into her drawing-room.

† **pro'letical**, *a. Obs. rare*[−1]. [f. L. **prōlēt-* (see PROLETAIRE) + -ICAL.] Of or pertaining to the lower orders of the community; hence, vulgar, common, popular.

1659 HOWELL *Lexicon, Proverbs* Pref. a v, Let the squeamish Reder take this Rule along with him, that Proverbs being Proleticall, and free familiar Countrey sayings do assume the Libertie to be sometimes in plain, down-right, and homely termes.

prolicide ('prəʊlɪsaɪd). [f. L. *prōl-ēs* offspring + -CIDE.] The killing of offspring; *spec.* the crime of destroying offspring either before or soon after birth. Hence **proli'cidal** *a.*, of, pertaining to, or characterized by prolicide.

1842 DUNGLISON *Med. Lex.*, *Prolicide*, a term which includes fœticide as well as infanticide. **1887** J. F. KEANE *Three Years Wand. Life* I. i. 8 The prolicidal mania which has possessed England during the last two decades.

† **pro'licient**, *a. Obs. rare*[−1]. [ad. L. *prōlicient-em*, pres. pple. of *prōlicĕre* to entice forth.] Drawing or calling forth.

a **1661** HOLYDAY *Juvenal* (1673) 196 There are also prolicient causes of tears, as violent strokes, diseases of the head, the use of mustard, onions.

† **pro'licit**, *v. Obs. rare*[−1]. [f. L. *prōlicit-*, ppl. stem of *prōlicĕre*: see prec.] *trans.* To entice, induce, provoke.

1661 RUST *Origen* in *Phenix* (1721) I. 51 That Disposition of Body which will not prolicite the Soul to join with it.

prolidase ('prəʊlɪdeɪz, -s). *Biochem.* [f. PROL(INE + IM)ID(O- + -ASE.] A proteolytic enzyme which hydrolyses peptide bonds formed with the nitrogen atom of proline or 4-hydroxy-proline.

1937 BERGMANN & FRUTON in *Jrnl. Biol. Chem.* CXVII. 191 We should like to call this enzyme *prolidase* in order to indicate that in the substrates of this enzyme the proline nitrogen is present as imido nitrogen. **1951** *Adv. Enzymol.* XII. 220 Prolidase is specifically activated by Mn^{++}. **1976** *Metabolism* XXV. 504 Prolidase is an important enzyme in completely degrading collagen to free amino acids. Prolidase is present in human intestinal mucosa.

pro-life, -lifer: see PRO-[1] 5 a.

proliferate (prəʊ'lɪfəreɪt), *v.* [Back-formation from PROLIFERATION]

1. a. *intr.* To reproduce itself by proliferation; to grow by multiplication of elementary parts.

1873 T. H. GREEN *Introd. Pathol.* (ed. 2) 277 The enlarged and granular epithelial cells may then proliferate, and thus new elements are produced. **1884** *Rep. U.S. Comm. Fish.* 988 The materials..being supplied by the mesoblast which proliferates into the median fin-fold. **1899** *Allbutt's Syst. Med.* VI. 639 The old nerve-fibres..proliferate.

b. *Zool.* To produce new individuals, esp. sexual as distinguished from nutritive zooids. Also more widely: to give rise to an increasing number of offspring, to reproduce prolifically.

1878 BELL *Gegenbaur's Comp. Anat.* §74. 95 The proliferating persons of a colony [of polyps] present various degrees of degeneration. **1926** *Socialist Rev.* Apr. 33 Those who..have neither the time to care for their children's moral well-being, nor the space which is necessary to ensure their physical welfare, proliferate, unchecked. **1955** *Sci. Amer.* May 32/3 Normal man carries throughout life a host of microbes which now and then start proliferating and cause disease.

c. *gen.* Of things, happenings, etc.: to increase greatly in numbers; to be(come) rife.

1961 *Daily Tel.* 19 Jan. 12/3 There was more than a suspicion that the system which had gradually evolved over the years was not able to produce the highest quality in British football—a quality which becomes more and more indispensable as international matches proliferate. **1972** *Sci. Amer.* Feb. 13/3 Indeed, microwave devices may proliferate as much as television sets have proliferated. **1976** *National Observer* (U.S.) 21 Aug. 6/6 In recent years, cut-rate sporting goods have proliferated to appeal to the less fussy adventurer.

2. a. *trans.* To produce or form by proliferation.

1885 A. E. SHIPLEY in *Proc. Roy. Soc.* XXXIX. 246 The mesoblastic plates..proliferate cells at their edge.

b. To produce (esp. nuclear weapons) in large quantities.

1971 *Nature* 24 Dec. 493/2 Both superpowers continue to proliferate nuclear weapons. **1974** *Daily Tel.* 24 June 1/2 The Government strongly supports international agreement not to 'proliferate' nuclear weapons.

Hence **pro'liferated, pro'liferating** *ppl. adjs.*

1873 T. H. GREEN *Introd. Pathol.* (ed. 2) 97 Some of the proliferating elements..having been left behind. **1879** *St. George's Hosp. Rep.* 691 It was..beset with numerous nuclei, as if of proliferated elements. **1904** *Brit. Med. Jrnl.* 10 Sept. 597 The great number of cells which are found wandering far and wide..are not proliferated endothelial cells. **1964** *Time* 4 Dec. 21/1 In Europe, U.S. diplomats are still trying to promote a multilateral nuclear fleed (MLF) as an alternative to proliferating national forces. **1967** *Economist* 25 Feb. 698/2 Indeed, the case for Britain (and France) going non-nuclear would become more persuasive after the signing of the treaty than it would in a treatyless, proliferating world. **1968** *Ibid.* 13 Apr. 41/1 Those who struggle on in the hospital service, taking the necessary diplomas of the proliferating specialist colleges.

proliferation (prəʊlɪfə'reɪʃən). [a. F. *prolifération*, f. *prolifère* PROLIFEROUS: see -ATION.]

1. a. *Pathol.*, etc. The formation or development of cells by budding or division.

1867 MAUDSLEY *Physiol. Mind* 402 This proliferation of connective tissue with destruction of the nerve elements has ..been already observed. **1869** E. A. PARKES *Pract. Hygiene* (ed. 3) 266 There is proliferation and rapid cell-growth. **1905** *Daily Chron.* 2 Dec. 6/3 The theory of the Imperial Cancer Research Committee that cancer is entirely due to the proliferation of cancer cells, and that to stop this proliferation would be to cure cancer.

b. *Zool.* The production of zooids, esp. of sexual zooids, by some hydrozoans.

1894 PRUDDEN in *Harper's Mag.* Mar. 633 Bacteria..are very sensitive in the matter of growth and proliferation to the conditions under which they are placed.

c. *transf.* Enlargement or extension; an increase in number (*of*); now esp. of nuclear weapons.

1920 H. G. WELLS *Outl. Hist.* II. 641/2 The British and French were at first the leading peoples in this great proliferation of knowledge. **1955** *Sci. Amer.* May 88/2 With the proliferation of cults came a tendency to worship privately without the intercession of priests. **1966** *Listener* 4 Aug. 177/3 One of the most noticeable results of setting up a Royal Commission has been the proliferation of proposals for legal solutions to industrial relations problems. **1966** SCHWARZ & HADIX *Strategic Terminol.* 89 *Proliferation*, in the context of nuclear strategy the increase of the number of states possessing independent national control over nuclear weapons, by the acquisition and development of the necessary technological capacity and industrial capabilities. **1967** *Observer* 5 Mar. 13/5 The issue is whether proliferation of bombs can be prevented without fettering peaceful nuclear developments. **1972** *Sci. Amer.* Feb. 15/3 Most of the problems are related to the fact that a large proliferation of microwave devices would make heavy demands on part of the electromagnetic spectrum. **1976** *National Observer* (U.S.) 21 Aug. 5/3 Is the United States' role..so dominant in the nuclear field that we could stop proliferation if our own policies were strict and consistent?

2. *Bot.* The condition or fact of being PROLIFEROUS (3 a); = PROLIFICATION 2 a.

1858 MAYNE *Expos. Lex.*, *Proliferatio*,..applied by Link to the appearance of a bud or flower upon a part of the plant which has not been accustomed to bear such: proliferation. **1886** in *Cassell's Encycl. Dict.*; and in later Dicts.

proliferative (prəʊˈlɪfərətɪv), *a.* [f. as PROLIFERATE + -IVE.] Characterized by or tending to proliferation. (Chiefly *Path.*)
1888 *Med. News* LIII. 507 Ulceration may be attended with proliferative vegetations which may occlude the air-passages. **1899** *Allbutt's Syst. Med.* VIII. 609 A proliferative inflammation of the vessel-sheaths. **1905** H. D. ROLLESTON *Dis. Liver* 165 A well-marked example of chronic proliferative peritonitis and perihepatitis. **1952** W. D. JACOBS *William Barnes* ii. 16 Words of the Anglo-Saxon vocabulary and their proliferative quality. **1969** E. BISHOP *Compl. Poems* 83 Our problems Becoming helplessly proliferative.

proliferator (prəʊˈlɪfəreɪtə(r)). [f. PROLIFERATE *v.* + -OR.] One that proliferates; *esp.* one that advocates or engages in the production of nuclear weapons.
1974 *Nature* 31 May 397/2 If the present nuclear countries had busied themselves more over nuclear arms control in the past 5 years, they would have a better moral platform from which they could harangue proliferators.

proliferent (prəʊˈlɪfərənt), *a. nonce-wd.* [f. as PROLIFEROUS *a.*: see -ENT.] Prolific.
1922 JOYCE *Ulysses* 377 Solicitude for that proliferent continuance.

proliferous (prəʊˈlɪfərəs), *a.* Also 8 -ferose. [f. med.L. *prōlifer* (f. L. *prōl-ēs* offspring + *-fer* bearing) + -OUS.]
†**1.** Producing offspring; procreative; prolific.
1654 GAYTON *Pleas. Notes* IV. x. 238 That her Greatnesse was augmented by the proliferous Contagion of Don Ferdinand. **1692** O. WALKER *Grk. & Rom. Hist.* 185 A Feast of such Fishes as are here expressed, Lobsters, Pulpes; such viz. as are very Proliferous and Inciters to Lust.
2. Producing many flowers; prolific. *rare.*
1682 WHELER *Journ. Greece* VI. 479 The Narcissus Flowers..so proliferous. **1796** C. MARSHALL *Garden.* xix. (1813) 373 Lily proliferous, or many flowered. **1893** E. H. BARKER *Wayfaring in Fr.* 347 Most conspicuous is the proliferous pink, with blooms unusually large and beautiful.
3. Of, pertaining to, or characterized by proliferation. **a.** *Bot.* Producing leaf- or flower-buds from a leaf or flower, or other part which is normally terminal; also, Producing new individuals from buds, as distinguished from reproduction by means of seeds.
1702 J. PETIVER in *Phil. Trans.* XXIII. 1262 The main difference..is its panicle, which is here ramose or proliferose. **1759** J. HILL (*title*) The Origin and Production of Proliferous Flowers, with the Culture at large for Raising Double from Single, and Proliferous from the Double. **1760** J. LEE *Introd. Bot.* I. xx. (1765) 60 Flowers are said to be *Proliferous*, when one Flower grows out of another. **1832** LYELL *Princ. Geol.* II. 78 These hydrophytes are in general proliferous, so that the smallest fragment of a branch can be developed into a perfect plant.
b. *Zool.* Reproducing itself or multiplying by budding; *spec.* producing sexual or generative (as opposed to nutritive) zooids.
1856 WOODWARD *Mollusca* III. 345 The embryos are attached in pairs to a double tube (or 'proliferous stolon') connected with the sinus to the right of the heart. **1878** BELL *Gegenbaur's Comp. Anat.* 392 We find, just as in the Ascidiæ, proliferous outgrowths, namely, the stolons. **1884** tr. *Claus' Zool.* vii. 237 The proliferous Polyps develop generative buds on their walls.
c. *Path.* Spreading by proliferation; = PROLIFERATIVE *a.*
1874 ROOSA *Dis. Ear* 268 The tinnitus is apt to be more troublesome in the proliferous than in the catarrhal form. **1879** *St. George's Hosp. Rep.* IX. 757 A 'proliferous' cyst by ulceration and protrusion of its contents may give rise to a wart-like excrescence that may readily be mistaken for a large wart. **1895** *Syd. Soc. Lex.*, *Proliferous cyst*, a cyst whose lining membrane proliferates, giving rise to intracystic growths. **1899** *Allbutt's Syst. Med.* VI. 317 Proliferous intima infiltrated with cells and containing tubercle-bacilli.
Hence **proˈliferously** *adv.*, by proliferation.
1846 DANA *Zooph.* (1848) 324 Folia thin,..sometimes lacerate and proliferously extended. **1864** H. SPENCER *Princ. Biol.* §192 Fronds originating proliferously from other fronds.

prolific (prəʊˈlɪfɪk), *a.* Also 7 -fique. [ad. med.L. *prōlific-us*, f. *prōl-ēs* offspring: see -FIC; or ad. F. *prolifique* (16th c. in Littré).]
1. Generating or producing offspring; generative, reproductive; fertile, not barren.
1650 BULWER *Anthropomet.* 233 The better portion of the Prolifique Seed flowes down from the Brain and spinal Marrow. **1667** MILTON *P.L.* VII. 280 Main Ocean flow'd, not idle, but with warme Prolific humour soft'ning all her Globe. **1691** RAY *Creation* I. (1692) 6 The breed of such Mixtures [of dogs] being prolifick. **1741** tr. *D'Argens' Chinese Lett.* ix. 54 By Misfortune, the prolific Virtue was quite extinct in him. **1881** MIVART *Cat* 8 The domestic cat begins..to reproduce by the end of the first year of her life, and she is prolific to her ninth.
b. *Bot.* Producing fertile seed.
1828 SIR J. E. SMITH *Eng. Flora* II. 100 Pastinaca. Parsnep... *Fl.* all regular, uniform, perfect, and generally prolific.
2. a. Producing much offspring or fruit; abundantly productive; fruitful. Also *fig.* of things.
1653 JER. TAYLOR *Serm. for Year* I. xxiii. 302 Covetousnesse being..so originall a crime, such a prolifick sin. **1775** JOHNSON *Tax. no Tyr.* 7 To attack a nation thus prolific. **1794** S. WILLIAMS *Vermont* 84 The wolf is a very prolific animal. **1832** HT. MARTINEAU *Brooke Farm* viii, We should have no idea how prolific the soil might be made. *a* **1850** CALHOUN *Wks.* (1874) III. 393 The public lands—that prolific source of corruption in the hands of the profligate. **1856** KANE *Arct. Expl.* II. xxviii. 283 One of the most prolific bird-colonies of the coast. **1875** JOWETT *Plato* (ed. 2) I. 134 Some he made to have few young ones, while those who were their prey were very prolific.
b. Abundantly productive *of*; abounding *in*.
1693 PEPYS in *Lett. Lit. Men* (Camden) 213 This age being not very prolifique of customers for such a commodity. **1795** G. WAKEFIELD *Reply 2nd Pt. Paine* 25 Whether ancient times were prolific in such stupid beings as these. **1842** J. WILSON *Chr. North* (1857) I. 141 The heather and the clover were prolific of the honey-dew. **1869** DUNKIN *Midn. Sky* 32 This constellation is very prolific in stars of the fourth and fifth magnitudes.
3. Causing abundant production; fertilizing.
1669 GALE *Crt. Gentiles* I. II. viii. 103 The Sun having such a prolific and powerful influence on al sublunaries. **1727** SWIFT *Modest Proposal* Wks. 1755 II. II. 62 Fish being a prolific dyet, there are more children born in roman catholick countries about nine months after Lent. **1738** GLOVER *Leonidas* II. 253 By Nile's prolific torrents delug'd o'er. **1858** EMERSON *Lett. & Soc. Aims, Pers. Poetry* Wks. (Bohn) III. 238 The prolific sun, and the sudden and rank plenty which his heat engenders.
b. Characterized by abundant production; fruitful.
1695 LD. PRESTON *Boeth.* Pref. 5 Born in an healthful and prolifick Climate. **1850** W. IRVING *Mahomet, Successors* xiii. (1853) 58 The country..was..adapted for the vigorous support and prolific increase of animal life. *Mod.* This has been a prolific year for apples.

prolificacy (prəʊˈlɪfɪkəsɪ). [irreg. f. med.L. *prōlific-us* (see prec.) + -ACY. The regular derivative is PROLIFICITY.] The quality or state of being prolific; fertility, productiveness, fruitfulness.
1796 MORSE *Amer. Geog.* I. 754 From the natural prolificacy of the negro race. **1802** *Eng. Encycl.* VIII. 451/2 Potatoes do not degenerate in point of prolificacy. **1834** H. O'BRIEN *Round Towers Irel.* 399 Consider..the prolificacy of its soil. **1884** *Sat. Rev.* 1 Nov. 576/1 Defoe, with all his versatility and all his prolificacy, wrote but one *Robinson Crusoe.* **1926** V. A. RICE *Breeding & Improvement of Farm Animals* v. 61 'Prolificacy' implies especially frequent or numerous production. **1962** G. MACEWAN *Blazing Old Cattle Trail* i. 3 A strong point about the longhorns was their prolificacy. **1971** *Farmer & Stockbreeder* 23 Feb. 24/2 Mr. Doane's recipe for increasing prolificacy of a flock included selection of rams with sex drive and fertility.

proˈlifical, *a.* ? *Obs.* [f. as PROLIFIC + -AL[1].]
1. = PROLIFIC *a.* 1.
1615 CROOKE *Body of Man* 200 Other parts..affoord vnto it prolificall vertue. **1647** TRAPP *Comm. John* x. 42 Place is no prejudice to the powerful operation of the word, when by the Spirit it is made prolifical and generative. **1659** *Gentl. Calling* Pref. (1660) b ij, That you would weep so long over her ashes, till that moisture had rendred them prolifical, and you see her spring out of her Urn.
b. *Astrol.* Favourable to the production of offspring; cf. PROLIFIC *a.* 3.
1647 LILLY *Chr. Astrol.* xvi. 89 If the ☽ and principall Significators be in Prolificall signes, and strong, there's no question but he shall [have children]. **1658** PHILLIPS s.v., *Prolifical* signes are *Cancer*, *Scorpio*, and *Pisces*.
2. = PROLIFIC *a.* 2.
1608 TOPSELL *Serpents* (1658) 685 They are exceeding fruitful and prolifical, and therefore also in Hieroglyphicks they are made to signifie fruitfulnesse. **1656** BLOUNT *Glossogr.*, *Prolifical*, fruitful, that breeds or brings forth issue apace. **1676** TOWERSON *Decalogue* 22 Each wound he gave it becoming strangely prolifical, and two heads starting up where there was one lopt off. **1678** E. YOUNG *Serm. at Guildhall* 17 Feb. 18 An Evil more prolifical in us then that of Adam.
Hence **proˈlifically** *adv.*, in a prolific manner; = PROLIFICLY. **proˈlificalness** = PROLIFICNESS.
1755 JOHNSON, **Prolifically*, fruitfully, pregnantly. **1895** *Westm. Gaz.* 27 Mar. 1/3 Never has the blood of the martyrs proved so prolifically the seed of the Church. **1915** C. S. JONES *Hohenzollerns* 167 He had for many years sought to win the favour of the great Frederick by writing prolifically on agriculture. **1947** O. BARFIELD in *Ess. presented to Charles Williams* 113 We owe them all to tarning, a process which we find prolifically at work wherever there is poetry. **1860** PUSEY *Min. Proph.* 490 They felt..the sterility in contrast with the exceeding *prolificalness of Babylonia. **1869** —— *Paroch. & Cathedr. Serm.* xxvi. (1883) 365 Yet sin has a terrible, infective prolificalness, a hideous progeny.

prolificate (prəʊˈlɪfɪkeɪt), *v. rare.* [f. med.L. *prōlific-āre*, or f. *prōlific-us* PROLIFIC + -ATE[3].] *trans.* To render prolific or fruitful; to fertilize.
1658 SIR T. BROWNE *Pseud. Ep.* III. xxviii. (ed. 3) 151 The sperm of the Cock prolificates and makes the oval conception fruitful. **1855** LYNCH *Lett. to Scattered* vi. 82 His gift of mercy is infinite, and through eternity renews and prolificates blessings.

prolification (prəʊlɪfɪˈkeɪʃən). [ad. med.L. *prōlificātiōn-em* (1451 in Du Cange), n. of action from *prōlific-āre* to PROLIFICATE. Cf. F. *prolification* (1550 in Godef. *Compl.*).]
1. The generation or production of offspring; also, reproductive power; fecundity, fertility.
1390 GOWER *Conf.* II. 110 Thou makst prolificacion, And dost that children ben begete. **1608** TOPSELL *Serpents* (1658) 594 The Wizards..making a sacrifice, gave answer that it betokened prolification, or birth of children. **1702** R. GIBSON in *First Dutch War* (Navy Rec. Soc.) 46 It is confessed we want people. To help this evil..prohibit all French wines (its tartar, &c., hindering prolification). **1824** J. GILCHRIST *Etym. Interpreter* 250 Specimens of the metaphoric prolification of the present literature.
†**b.** Offspring, progeny. *Obs. rare*[−1].
1646 SIR T. BROWNE *Pseud. Ep.* III. xii. 134 The offsprings of sensible creatures and prolifications descending from double originalls.
2. a. *Bot.* = PROLIFERATION 2.
1760 J. LEE *Introd. Bot.* I. xx. (1765) 61 In umbellate Flowers, the Prolification is by the Encrease of the Umbellulæ. **1887** *Nicholson's Dict. Gard.* s.v., If Prolification affects the inflorescence, it consists in the formation of leaf-buds, or of an unusual number of flower-buds.
b. *Zool.* Reproduction by budding; = PROLIFERATION 1.
1865 *Nat. Hist. Rev.* July 368 O. F. Müller, in his 'Zoologia Danica' (1788) figured a small Annelid (*Nereis prolifera*) in the act of reproducing itself by division... Quatrefages and Milne Edwards..observed prolification in Syllis and Myrianida.

prolificity (prəʊlɪˈfɪsɪtɪ). [f. med.L. *prōlific-us* PROLIFIC + -ITY: cf. *elasticity*, *rusticity*, etc.] The quality of being prolific or fruitful.
1725 BRADLEY *Fam. Dict.* s.v. *Laurus Tinus*, Excess of Vigour is a Hinderance of Prolificity. **1808** COLERIDGE in *Edin. Rev.* XII. 369 The known prolificity of the Blacks under very unfavourable circumstances. **1887** A. M. BROWN *Anim. Alkaloids* Introd. 14 The foreign cells comport themselves much in the mode that cancer cells..do, exhibiting a life, a power of prolificity so active as to rapidly invade the whole economy.

prolificly (prəʊˈlɪfɪklɪ), *adv.* [f. PROLIFIC + -LY[2].] In a prolific manner.
1895 H. CALLAN *From Clyde to Jordan* xxii. 238 The potato would grow prolificly on the sandy soil.

prolificness (prəʊˈlɪfɪknɪs). [f. as prec. + -NESS.] The quality of being prolific; prolificity, prolificacy. **a.** Capacity of bearing offspring or fruit. **b.** Great or abundant fruitfulness or productiveness.
1698 R. BURTHOGGE *Soul of World* (1699) 39 As to the Prolifickness of Matter, I should think but few will allow thereof. **1798** MALTHUS *Popul.* II. ix. (1806) II. 6 It is probable that the natural prolifickness of women is nearly the same in most parts of the world. **1853** *Jrnl. R. Agric. Soc.* XIV. II. 286 The black Tartarian [oat]..stands high for prolificness. **1884** *Manch. Exam.* 6 May 5/5 The salmon rivers of England and Wales..showed remarkable prolificness last year. **1887** A. J. BALFOUR in *Pall Mall G.* 17 June 11/1 The newspaper reporters have shown even more than their usual prolificness of resource and fertility of imagination.

prolified (ˈprəʊlɪfaɪd), *a.* [In form pa. pple. of next.] In quot. = PROLIFEROUS *a.* 3 a.
1866 *Treas. Bot.* 530/1 The Water-avens, *G[eum] rivale*,.. is frequently found in a prolified state, that is, with a branch or a second flower in the centre of the original one.

†**ˈprolify**, *v. Obs. rare.* [ad. med.L. *prōlificāre* to PROLIFICATE.] *intr.* To produce offspring.
1605 TIMME *Quersit.* II. xiv. 67 The white [of eggs].. having in [it] the prolifying power, whereof chiefly the bird is begotten. **1659** SANDERSON *Wks.* (1854) V. 338 There remained in the heart of such some piece of ill-temper unreformed, which in time prolified, and sent out great and wasting sins.

proligerous (prəʊˈlɪdʒərəs), *a.* [f. L. type (or mod.L.) **prōliger* (f. *prōl-ēs* offspring + *-ger* bearing) + -OUS; cf. F. *proligère.*]
1. Bearing offspring; generative; germinative. ***proligerous disk*** or ***layer*** (Embryol.), name given by von Baer to the aggregation of cells on the outside of an ovum, formerly supposed to be germinative. ***proligerous pellicle***, the film or membrane formed on an infusion, in which the organisms found in the infusion were supposed to originate.
1836–9 *Todd's Cycl. Anat.* II. 448/2 The centre of a granular layer..to which he [Baer] gives the name of proligerous disc or layer. *Ibid.* 449/1 A whitish opaque spot ..indicating the layer of granules or proligerous disc. **1849–52** *Ibid.* IV. 1221/2 The internal vesicle is the vesicle of Purkinje, or the proligerous vesicle. **1870** *Nature* 30 June 172/2 What Burdach named the proligerous pellicle of organic solution is made up of an aggregation of monads and bacteria in a transparent jelly-like stratum.
2. *Bot.* = PROLIFEROUS *a.* 3 a.
1890 in *Cent. Dict.*

proline (ˈprəʊliːn). *Biochem.* Formerly also prolin. [ad. G. *prolin* (Fischer & Suzuki 1904, in *Ber. d. Deut. Chem. Ges.* XXXVII. 2843), contraction of *pyrrolidin* PYRROLIDINE.] A colourless, crystalline amino-acid, pyrrolidine-2-carboxylic acid, $C_5H_9NO_2$, the lævorotatory form of which is a constituent of most proteins.
1904 *Jrnl. Chem. Soc.* LXXXVI. I. 917 (*heading*) Derivatives of prolin. *Ibid.*, The proline used was derived from gelatin. **1911** *Jrnl. Biol. Chem.* IX. 205 Prolin is ordinarily determined in the ester hydrolysis by alcoholic extraction of the amino-acids whose esters boil below 90° at less than 1 mm. pressure. **1913** *Ibid.* XIII. 513 Proline, when added to blood used for perfusing a surviving dog's liver, leads to no increase in the normal formation of acetoacetic acid, nor is the acetoacetic acid excretion of glycosuric animals markedly increased by the administration of proline. **1946** *Nature* 5 Oct. 474/2 All the proline residues appear to be situated at points roughly one third and two thirds along the length of the molecule. **1954** A. WHITE et al. *Princ. Biochem.* vii. 109 Proline is present in all proteins which have been studied. **1973** BIGGS & WOODSON *Clin. Biochem.* iii. 38 All amino acids—with the

exception of proline, which has an imino group—have an amino group on the α carbon.

prolix (ˈprəʊlɪks, prəʊˈlɪks), *a.* [a. F. *prolixe* (14th c. in Littré) or ad. L. *prōlix-us* extended, long, prolix, etc., app. etymologically, 'that has flowed forth', f. *prō-*, PRO-[1] + **lix-us*, pa. pple. of *liquēre* to flow, to be liquid.]

1. Of long duration, lengthy, protracted. **a.** In general.

1412–20 LYDG. *Chron. Troy* I. 3568 þe obseruaunce of swiche religious, Prolix in werkyng & not compendious. **1652** BENLOWES *Theoph.* XIII. xvii, He shuns prolixer lawsuits, nor does wait At thoughtful Grandies prouder gate. **1686** HORNECK *Crucif. Jesus* xv. 367 This actual preparation is either more prolix, or more compendious. The prolix, or longer actual preparation is necessary. **1726** AYLIFFE *Parergon* 81 If the Appellant appoints a Term too prolix or none at all, the Judge may then assign a competent Term. **1741** WATTS *Improv. Mind* I. xvi. §3 If the chain of consequences be a little prolix. **1744** ARMSTRONG *Preserv. Health* III. 460 While the buried bacchanal Exhales his surfeit in prolixer dreams. **1973** M. AMIS *Rachel Papers* 8 Mother's was a prolix and generally rather inelegant parturition.

b. *spec.* Of a speech or writing: Extended to great length; long; lengthy. Usually with implication of excessive length: wordy, tedious.

1432–50 tr. *Higden* (Rolls) V. 325 Iustinianus..coartede the lawes of the Romanes, occupyenge allemoste..iij. c. m[l] versus, as is prolixe [L. *prolixa*] dissonaunce, within oon volume of xij. bookes. *c* **1500** *Melusine* 214 What should I bring forth prolixe or long talkyng? **1598** DALLINGTON *Meth. Trav.* X iv, To speake thus particularly of all his seuerall humours and customes, would bee very prolixe. *a* **1651** CALDERWOOD *Hist. Kirk* (1843) II. 331 Prolixe prayers, hindering the preaching of the Word. **1717** PRIOR *Alma* III. 511 Should I, my friend, at large repeat..The bead-roll of her vicious tricks; My poem will be too prolix. **1865** GROTE *Plato* I. vi. 237 They are intolerant of all that is prolix, circuitous, not essential to the proof of the thesis in hand.

2. Of a person: Given to or characterized by tedious lengthiness in discourse or writing; long-winded.

1527 R. THORNE in Hakluyt *Voy.* (1589) 257, I should be to prolixe. **1597** MORLEY *Introd. Mus.* 184 If any man shall think me prolix and tedious in this place, I must for that point craue pardon. **1685** J. CHAMBERLAYNE *Coffee, Tea & Choc.* 108 That I may not seem too prolix, and to trespass on the Readers patience. **1758** JOHNSON *Idler* No. 1 ¶11 Conscious dulness has little right to be prolix. **1835** MARRYAT *Jac. Faithf.* vii, But not to be too prolix, it will suffice to say, that we made many trips during several months. **1871** R. ELLIS *Catullus* xcviii. 1 Asks some booby rebuke, some prolix prattler a judgment?

3. Long in measurement or extent. Now *rare.*

1650 BULWER *Anthropomet.* viii. (1653) 142 Men that were lately found.., whose Ears are so prolix, that they hang down even unto the ground. **1656** *Artif. Handsom.* 187 [A] fatherly, prolixe, and reverentiall beard. **1664** H. MORE *Myst. Iniq.* xviii. 68 Such large and prolix Shadows might Christianity cast. **1728** SWIFT *My Lady's Lament.* 77 My fingers, prolix, Are ten crooked sticks. **1784** COWPER *Tiroc.* 361 With wig prolix, down flowing to his waist. **1857** BIRCH *Anc. Pottery* (1858) I. 414 Long prolix beards appear..on some figures, to mark the virile or senile age.

†**proˈlix,** *v. Obs. rare*[−1]. [f. prec. adj.] *intr.* (with *it*). To be prolix or tedious.

1656 S. H. *Gold. Law* 88, I am afraid that I have transgrest both in quantity and quality,..so by encroaching on your Highness patience in prolixing it.

prolixed: see PROLIXT.

Prolixin (prəʊˈlɪksɪn). *Pharm.* A proprietary name in the U.S. for fluphenazine hydrochloride, $C_{22}H_{26}F_3N_3OS.HCl$, a phenothiazine derivative used as a tranquillizer.

1959 *Dis. Nervous System* XX. 170/2 The fluphenazine used in this study was supplied..under the trade name Prolixine [*sic*]. **1960** *Official Gaz.* (U.S. Patent Office) 1 Mar. TM 8/2 Olin Mathieson Chemical Corporation, New York... *Prolixin.* For central nervous system depressant preparations. First use Sept. 18, 1959. **1972** A. GOTH *Med. Pharmacol.* (ed. 6) xix. 217 The phenothiazine anti-emetics include chlorpromazine (Thorazine), fluphenazine dihydrochloride (Prolixin; Permitil), perphenazine (Trilafon), [etc.]. **1973** *Black Panther* 23 June 13/2 Do these drugs include Prolixin, a powerful mood stabilizer which includes side effects in from 50 to 100% of the cases that include pseudo-Parkinson's Disease—painful tremors and rigidity, restlessness ('the prolixin shuffle'), muscle contractions, spasms of the back, neck and throat, [etc.]?

†**proˈlixious,** *a. Obs.* Also 6 prolixous. [The regular form was *prolixous*, f. L. *prōlix-us* + -OUS: *prolixious* was due to some false analogy.]

1. = PROLIX *a.* 1 b, 2.

1527 R. THORNE in Hakluyt *Voy.* (1582) C iij, Your Lordship commaunded me to be large, and I take licence to be prolixouse. **1577** FRAMPTON *Joyfull Newes* I. (1596) 17 To repeate it, it shall be too long and to prolixious, because it is sufficiently declared before. **1630** J. TAYLOR (Water P.) *Praise cleane Linnen* Ded., To finish my prolixious..and tedious dedication. **1632** LITHGOW *Trav.* IX. 389 Many singular obseruations.., the which to recite, would proue prolixious.

2. Long in extent or duration: = PROLIX 1 a, 3.

1599 NASHE *Lenten Stuffe* Wks. (Grosart) V. 274 Well knowne vnto them by his prolixious seawandering. **1603** SHAKS. *Meas. for M.* II. iv. 162 Lay by all nicetie, and prolixious blushes. **1604** DRAYTON *Moses* I. 476 Who for the way the army was to pass,..Most part by water, more prolixious was Than present peril any whit commended.

prolixity (prəʊˈlɪksɪtɪ). Also 5–6 -ite, -yte, -itye, etc. [a. F. *prolixité* (13th c. in Littré), ad. late L. *prōlixitās*, f. *prōlix-us* PROLIX: see -ITY.] The state or quality of being prolix.

1. Lengthiness of spoken or written matter; length of discourse; copiousness and minuteness of detail; *esp.* tedious or tiresome lengthiness.

c **1374** CHAUCER *Troylus* II. 1515 (1564) But flee we now prolixite beste is. **1483** CAXTON *Cato* I. ix, For to eschewe prolyxyte and longe wordes. *c* **1555** HARPSFIELD *Divorce Hen. VIII* (Camden) 84 Which for avoiding of prolixity I do pretermit. **1678** R. R[USSELL] tr. *Geber* II. I. II. xv. 64 Without prolixity or tediousness of Words. **1755** WASHINGTON *Lett.* Writ. 1889 I. 201, I hope your Honor will..excuse the prolixity of this. **1864** BURTON *Scot Abr.* II. ii. 135 The confusion, ambiguity, and verbose prolixity of the narrative.

b. Tedious slowness of action. *rare.*

1827 LYTTON *Pelham* lviii, An appetite once thrown away can never, till the cruel prolixity of the gastric agents is over, be regained.

†**2.** Of time: Long or wearisome duration. *Obs.*

a **1548** HALL *Chron., Hen. VI* 91 Twenty other, whiche for prolixitie of tyme I thinke necessary to be omitted. **1577** HANMER *Anc. Eccl. Hist.* (1619) 187 When he hath exactly sifted every one of you by experience and prolixitie of time.

3. Material length. Now *humorous.*

1543 in Sharpe *Cal. Let. Bk. D. Lond.* (1902) p. xi, [Wearing a beard] of more notable prolyxyte or length. **1650** BULWER *Anthropomet.* 56 Haire long or short,..the prolixity or brevity whereof we cannot positively determine. **1784** COWPER *Task* I. 265 These chesnuts rang'd in corresponding lines;..The obsolete prolixity of shade. **1851** HAWTHORNE *Ho. Sev. Gables* xi, The monkey..with a thick tail curling out into preposterous prolixity from beneath his tartans, took his station at the Italian's feet.

†**proˈlixively,** *adv. Obs. rare*[−1]. [f. **prolixive* adj. (f. L. *prōlix-us* PROLIX: see -IVE) + -LY[2].] In a manner tending to prolixity; diffusely.

1633 J. DONE *Hist. Septuagint* 91 It seemes the Law intreateth more prolixively than properly.

prolixly (see PROLIX *a.*), *adv.* [f. PROLIX *a.* + -LY[2].] In a prolix manner.

1. At great length; with many words or details; copiously; verbosely, tediously.

a **1591** H. SMITH *Wks.* (1866–7) I. 3, I go upon a theme which many have traversed before me prolixly, or cursorily, or barrenly. **1687** DRYDEN *Hind & P.* III. 45 On these prolixly thankfull, she enlarg'd. **1739** POPE *Let.* in *Swift's Wks.* (1841) II. 817/1 You ask me the same question again which I have prolixly answered before. **1855** BROWNING *Epist. of Karshish* 285 Thy pardon for this long and tedious case,..Unduly dwelt on, prolixly set forth!

†**2.** For too long a time; to a tedious length. *Obs.*

1744 ARMSTRONG *Preserv. Health* III. 210 Pursued prolixly, even the gentlest toil Is waste of health.

prolixness (see PROLIX *a.*). [f. as prec. + -NESS.] = PROLIXITY.

1664 H. MORE *Apol.* Pref., The Reason of the Prolixness thereof stands upon this threefold ground. **1730** T. BOSTON *Mem.* App. (1776) 27, I hope you will pardon the prolixness of this. **1816** J. GILCHRIST *Philos. Etym.* 65 The philologer of more rapid and intuitive perceptions, will bear with my prolixness in this part of my work.

†**proˈlixt, -xed,** *a. Sc. Obs.* [Sc. var. of *prolix* (cf. Sc. *taxt* = *tax*, *vext* = *vex*, etc.), afterwards mistaken for a pa. pple.] = PROLIX *a.* 1.

c **1450** HOLLAND *Howlat* 34 All thar names to nevyn..It war prolixt and lang. **1456** SIR G. HAYE *Law Arms* (S.T.S.) 7 It war our lang and prolixit thing to count all. **1535** STEWART *Cron. Scot.* (Rolls) II. 112 His oresoun, the quhilk wes so prolixt, Wald mar my mynd and I had with it fixt. **1549** *Compl. Scot.* vi. 62 The scheiphird..endit his prolixt orison. **1585** JAS. I *Ess. Poesie* (Arb.) 20 The easiest and shortest of all his difficile and prolixed Poems.

Hence †**proˈlixitness** = PROLIXITY 1.

1508 DUNBAR *Poems* vii. 83, I lefe, for grete prolixitnes, To tell quhat feildis thou wan in Pikkardy.

proll, -e, proller, obs. ff. PROWL *v.*, PROWLER.

prolly (ˈprɒlɪ), *adv.* Representation of a corrupt pronunciation of 'probably'.

1962 J. D. MACDONALD *Key to Suite* vii. 112 The girls have dresses on today. I guess you prolly noticed. **1969** K. GILES *Death cracks Bottle* iv. 37, I don't know wot 'appen to it. The mice prolly. **1976** N. THORNBURG *Cutter & Bone* i. 29 'Some big old buck nigger prolly do it,' Ronnie said.

prolly, var. PROLY *sb.* and *a.*

proloculus (prəʊˈlɒkjʊləs). *Zool.* Also *erron.* proloculum. [f. PRO-[2] 1 + LOCULUS.] In Foraminifera, the first chamber formed by the zygote.

1928 J. A. CUSHMAN *Foraminifera* ii. 12 The initial chamber in the foraminifera is known as the proloculum. **1935** TWENHOFEL & SHROCK *Invertebr. Paleontol.* ii. 36 The zygote secretes a small shell around itself, the proloculum of the microspheric shell. **1952** R. C. MOORE et al. *Invertebr. Fossils* ii. 40/2 The size of the proloculus of megalospheric forms varies considerably in certain species. **1975** *Nature* 18 Sept. 208/2 In random thin sections these seem to arise from a cluster of small chambers or from a large initial chamber which may be the proloculus.

†**ˈprolocute,** *v. Obs. rare*[−0]. [f. ppl. stem of L. *prōloquī*: see next.] *intr.* To speak out.

1570 LEVINS *Manip.* 196/21 To Prolocute, *proloqui.*

prolocution (ˈprɒl-, prəʊləʊˈkjuːʃən). [Partly ad. late L. *prōlocūtio* a preamble (Claudianus Mamertus, fl. 470), n. of action from *prōloquī* to speak forth, declare, here identified with *prælocuī* to speak before, premise: cf. F. *prolocution* a discourse (14th c.); partly f. PRO-[1] + LOCUTION.]

1. A preliminary or introductory speech or remark. *rare.*

1597 J. KING *On Jonas* (1618) 559 The causes of this commodiousnesse and conuenience are contained in the prolocution, in those friuolous and vaine speeches that are first laide downe. **1886** STEVENSON *Kidnapped* xxvii, 'But', said he, 'these are rather alarming prolocutions'.

†**2.** The use of ambiguous language so as to mislead. *Obs.*

1679 GAVAN in *Speeches Jesuits* 6, I do not..make use of any Equivocation, or mental Reservation, or material Prolocution, or any such like way to palliate Truth. **1691** HARTCLIFFE *Virtues* 174 Their shift of Prolocution, that is, to use Words of such a sound, when they do not intend such a thing by them, as one would think, they did. **1716** M. DAVIES *Athen. Brit.* II. 142 If he is the Author himself, which he seems flatly to deny (yet not without some mental Reservation and material Prolocutions; for his Speech bewrayeth him, and agreeth to the Galilean turn of denyal, as well as to the Speech or Stile of the Book).

3. A speaking for or on behalf of others; acting as prolocutor or spokesman. *rare.*

1826 G. S. FABER *Diffic. Romanism* II. iii. 325 Had Peter been the divinely-appointed vicar of Christ upon earth; he, no doubt, acting as the Lord's special representative, would have appointed..the new suffragan apostle... But we do not find that this was the case... From these recorded circumstances I infer, that the prolocution of the zealous and warm-hearted Peter was rather incidental than official.

prolocutor (ˈprɒl-, ˈprəʊləʊkjuːtə(r), prəʊˈlɒkjʊtə(r)). Also 6–7 -our; 6 -qut-, 6–7 -quut-. [a. L. *prōlocūtor* pleader, advocate, agent-n. f. *prōloquī* to speak out; so F. *prolocuteur* (*c* 1500). In med.L. the word appears to interchange with *prælocutor* (see Du Cange), and the sense seems to hover between 'one that speaks *for*', and 'one that speaks *before* or *in precedence of* others'. Cf. the function of the 'Speaker' in the House of Commons.]

One who speaks for another or others; a spokesman. **a.** In general. Now *rare.*

[*a* **1259** MATT. PARIS *Chron.* an. 1254 (Rolls) V. 423 Congregatis universis, prolocutor domini regis et nuntius exorsus loqui, ait, etc.] *c* **1475** *Harl. Contin. Higden* (Rolls) VIII. 475 The prolocutor as for that mater was syr Thomas Percy. **1570** FOXE *A. & M.* (ed. 2) 165/1 Bishop Cedda was appointed Prolocutor for both parties in that Parliament. **1651** HOBBES *Leviath.* III. xxxvi. (1839) 412 The name of prophet signifieth in Scripture, sometimes prolocutor; that is, he that speaketh from God to man, or from man to God. **1766** GOLDSM. *Vic. W.* xi, Olivia undertook to be our prolocutor. **1807** G. CHALMERS *Caledonia* I. III. viii. 440 Margaret, who was the principal prolocutor, could only speak Saxon. **1899** *Daily News* 31 Jan. 6/3 Sir William Harcourt had called Mr. Russell the Prolocutor of the Catholic Revival.

†**b.** *Sc.* A legal spokesman in a court of law: = ADVOCATE 1. *Obs.*

1561 *Reg. Privy Council Scot.* I. 167 Maister David Makgill, prolocutour for the saidis merchandis procuratouris, protestit for coistis..expenssis, and interes. **1564** *Act Sederunt* 15 June (1790) 7 The said Lords hes declarit the sam to all the prolocutors at the bar. **1678** SIR G. MACKENZIE *Crim. Laws Scot.* II. xx. §2 (1699) 230 Advocats with us in Criminals are called Proloquutors. **1785** ARNOT *Trials* (1812) 12 The indictment being read, the prisoner.. declared that trusting to his innocence he desired no prolocutor.

c. The chairman of the Lower House of Convocation of either province of the Church of England; he is spokesman of that body in the Upper House.

[**1553** ARCHD. WIMSLEY in Strype *Eccl. Mem.* (1721) III. I. iv. 43 The Reverend Fathers..had..enjoined them to.. conclude upon the Choise of a Referendary, which they commonly called a Prolocutor.] **1560** DAUS tr. *Sleidane's Comm.* 428 b, Doctor Weston, that was proloqutour, demeaned himselfe disorderly. **1670** WALTON *Lives* I. 47 The next Parliament..he was chosen Prolocutor to the Convocation. **1761** *Chron.* in *Ann. Reg.* 175/2 The convocation of the province of Canterbury met at St. Paul's cathedral, and..afterwards chose a prolocutor. **1852** S. WILBERFORCE in R. G. Wilberforce *Life* (1881) II. iv. 140 There can..be no question as to the right of the Lower House to elect, or of the Upper to refuse to confirm the election of a Prolocutor. **1894** in *Times* 5 Feb. 14/3 That the Prolocutor be requested to convey the foregoing report and resolutions to the Upper House.

d. The presiding officer of an assembly; a chairman, 'speaker'.

1591 LAMBARDE *Archeion* (1635) 47 He [the holder of the Great Seal] is a great Personage, a Counsellor of the Estate, and Prolocutor or Mouth of the higher House of Parliament.

1663 BUTLER *Hud.* I. iii. 1099 Synods are mystical Bear-gardens, .. For Prolocutor, Scribe, and Bearward, Do differ only in a mere word. **1765** T. HUTCHINSON *Hist. Mass.* I. i. 68 Two of the elders were the moderators, or prolocutors of the assembly. **1836** H. ROGERS *J. Howe* ii. (1863) 27 Mr. Charles Herle was chosen.. Prolocutor of the Westminster Assembly. **1878** STUBBS *Const. Hist.* III. xx. 453 That an organised assembly like that of the commons could ever have dispensed with a recognised prolocutor or foreman.

Hence **prolocutorship**, the office of prolocutor.

1727 BAILEY vol. II, *Prolocutorship*, the office, etc., of a Speaker, or Chairman of a Synod or Convocation. **1861** JOWETT in *Life & Lett.* (1897) I. xi. 355, I hear that you are thinking of giving up the Prolocutorship. **1888** *Pall Mall G.* 18 Apr. 10/2 The talk as to the possibility of the Dean of York resigning the Prolocutorship [of the Convocation of the Province of York] was renewed.

† **pro'locutory.** *Obs.* *rare*$^{-1}$. [ad. med.L. *prōlocūtōri-us* adj., f. L. *prōlocūtor*: see prec. and -ORY[1].] A prologue, preface; an introduction.

1447 BOKENHAM *Seyntys* (Roxb.) 144 The prolocutorye in to Marye Mawdelen lyf.

prolocutress (see PROLOCUTOR). *rare*$^{-1}$. [f. PROLOCUTOR: see -ESS.] = next.

1737 *Gentl. Mag.* VII. 100/2 They voted..that—Miss Patty Pos shou'd take the Chair, and be the Prolocutress of this House.

† **prolocutrix** (see PROLOCUTOR). *Obs.* [a. L. *prōlocūtrix*, fem. of *prōlocūtor*.] A female prolocutor; a spokeswoman.

1613–18 DANIEL *Coll. Hist. Eng.* (1626) 141 Lady Countesse, hath the Lords made you a charter, and sent you (for that you are in eloquent speaker) to be their aduocate and prolocutrix? **1660** HOWELL *Parly Beasts* 33 A furious clash fell betwixt them who should be the Prolocutrix.

prologist ('prɒlədʒɪst, 'prəʊl-). *rare*. [f. next: see -IST.] The writer or speaker of a prologue.

1716 M. DAVIES *Athen. Brit.* III. *Diss. Drama* 5 The following Play.. The Prologist and Epilogist represent the whole Course of Literature. **1828** D'ISRAELI *Chas. I*, I. xii. 326 Such a prologist as Sir Dudley seemed scarcely to threaten.

prologize ('prɒlədʒaɪz, 'prəʊl-), *v.* See also PROLOGUIZE. [ad. Gr. προλογίζειν to speak the prologue: see PROLOGUE *sb.* and -IZE.]

intr. To compose or speak a prologue.

1608 BEAUM. & FL. *Four Plays in One* Induct., Prologues are Huishers bare before the wise; Why may not then an Huisher Prologize? *a* **1674** MILTON *Wks.* (1738) I. p. xliii, There may prologize the Spirit of Philip, Herod's Brother. **1822** *Blackw. Mag.* XII. 782 His Lordship might as dramatically..have brought forward a god or devil to prologize as of old. **1871** BROWNING *Balaust.* 166 Any who could speak A chorus to the end, or prologize, Roll out a rhesis, ..had prompt reward.

b. *trans.* To preface with a prologue; to epitomize in a prologue.

1779 *Coll. Eng. Prologues & Epil.* I. p. iii, Making every actor prologize the part he is to perform, 'I am to do, so and so'.

Hence **'prologizing** *vbl. sb.*; also **'prologizer**.

1822 *Blackw. Mag.* XII. 783 In the old dramatists of Greece, prologizing..formed..an integral portion of the structure of the piece. **1832** *Examiner* 149/1 The Westminster prologizer has been led into his error by the spirit and pure idiom of the English translation.

prologue ('prɒlɒg, 'prəʊlɒg), *sb.* Forms: 4–6 prolog, -loug, -louge, 6 -logge, 5– prologue. *β.* 4–6 prologe. [ME. *prolog*, a. F. *prologue* (*c* 1215 in Godef. *Compl.*), ad. L. *prolog-us*, a. Gr. πρόλογος the prologue of a play, also its speaker, f. πρό, PRO-[2] + λόγος speech. The *β*-form (*pro'loge* in Chaucer and Gower) represents the OF. by-form *pro'loge* (12th c. in Littré).]

1. The preface or introduction to a discourse or performance; a preliminary discourse, proem, preface, preamble; *esp.* a discourse or poem spoken as the introduction to a dramatic performance.

a **1300** *Cursor M.* 265 Now o þis prolog [*v. rr.* prolouge, prolog, prologe] wil we blin In crist nam our bok be-gin. *c* **1374** CHAUCER *Troylus* IV. 865 (893) This shorte and pleyne þeffect of my message.. For ȝe.. May to no longe prologe as now entende. **1382** WYCLIF *Matt.* Prol., Jerom in his twei prologis on Matheu seith pleynli thus. **1390** GOWER *Conf.* I. 5 Whan the prologe is so despended This bok schal after-ward ben ended. **1426** *Pol. Poems* (Rolls) II. 133 Here endith the prolog, and begynneth the translacioun. **1484** CAXTON *Fables of Æsop* i, Here begyneth the preface or prologue of the fyrste book. **1535** JOYE *Apol. Tindale* (Arb.) 47 As he bosteth himself..in his prologe. **1573** in Feuillerat *Revels Q. Eliz.* (1908) 200 Bayes for the prologges & properties. **1577–87** HOLINSHED *Chron.* III. 913/2 The hauing and reading of the new testament in English translated by Tindall, ..forbidden..that therein were prologs and prefaces sounding to heresie. **1588** SHAKS. *L.L.L.* v. ii. 305 Their shallow showes, and Prologue vildely pen'd. *a* **1679** HOBBES *Rhet.* III. xiii. (1681) 120 In other kinds it [the Proem] resembles the Prologue of a Play. **1728** POPE *Dunc.* I. 277 How Prologues into Prefaces decay, And these to Notes are fritter'd quite away. **1779** SHERIDAN *Critic* I. i, I'll undertake to read you the whole from beginning to end, with the Prologue and Epilogue. **1861** CRAIK *Hist. Eng. Lit.* I. 293 The general Prologue [of the Canterbury Tales] is a gallery of pictures almost unmatched for their air of life and truthfulness.

b. *transf.* and *fig.* An introductory or preliminary act, proceeding, or event.

1593 SHAKS. *2 Hen. VI*, III. i. 151 My death..is made the Prologue to their Play: For thousands more..Will not conclude their plotted Tragedie. **1649** JER. TAYLOR *Gt. Exemp.* III. Disc. xviii. 70 God hath provided for us certain prologues of judgement and keeps us waking with alarms. **1770** *Junius Lett.* xli. (1820) 207 Accept of this address..as a prologue to more important scenes. **1871** NAPHEYS *Prev. & Cure Dis.* I. ix. 307 The second childhood of the aged may be the prologue to a second youth.

2. One who speaks or recites the prologue to a play on the stage.

1579 J. STUBBES *Gaping Gulf* F j, She is dressing her Prologue to send him in, trust him not. **1599** [see 3]. **1606** *Choice, Chance*, etc. (1881) 45 A spruse companion..who.. as if he had bin a prologue to a play, with a wink and simper thus begins. **1761** [see PROLOGUIZE]. **1763** J. BROWN *Poetry & Mus.* xxxix. 169 The Prologue [of China] resembles that uncouth one of Greece, that is, he tells you who he is, and what is his Errand.

3. *attrib.* and *Comb.*, as ***prologue-speaker***, ***-writer***; ***prologue-like*** adv.

1560 INGELEND *Disob. Child* A ij b, Here the Prologue speaker goeth out. **1599** SHAKS. *Hen. V*, Enter Prologue... Admit me Chorus to this Historie; Who Prologue-like, your humble patience pray, Gently to beare, kindly to iudge our Play. **1713** POPE *Let. to Sir W. Trumbull* 30 Apr., This was the Case too of the Prologue-writer. **1762** GARRICK *Prol. Colman's Musical Lady*, We'll tie our prologuemonger's hands. **1898** S. EVANS *Holy Graal* 183 The Prologue-writer called himself Crestien.

'prologue, *v.* [f. prec. sb.: cf. obs. F. *prologu(i)er* (*c* 1400 in Godef.). Formerly (prə'lɒg).]

1. *trans.* To introduce or furnish with a prologue.

1701 DE FOE *True-born Eng.* II. 155 His first discourses generally appear, Prologu'd with his own wondrous Character. **1701** FARQUHAR *Sir H. Wildair* Prol., Our authors have, in most their late essays, Prologued their own, by damning other plays. **1889** *Sat. Rev.* 21 Dec. 705/1 Mr. Austin Dobson..prologues and epilogues the selection with charming verses of his own.

2. *fig.* To introduce, preface.

1601 SHAKS. *All's Well* II. i. 95 Thus he his speciall nothing euer prologues. **1680** HICKERINGILL *Meroz* 9 How were our Miseries..Prologu'd with a Noise of Arbitrary Government in the Case of Ship-Money? **1762** FOOTE *Orator* I. Wks. 1799 I. 202 A smart house, prefaced with white rails, and prologued by a red door, with a brass knocker.

† **3.** To spend (time) in introductory remarks.

1622 CALLIS *Stat. Sewers* (1647) 119, I esteem the time to be almost lost or mispent which is prologued out in preambles.

prologuer ('prɒləgə(r), 'prəʊl-). Also 6 prologer. [f. prec. sb. or vb. + -ER[1].] The speaker of a prologue at a dramatic performance.

1570 LEVINS *Manip.* 80/15 A Prologer, *prologus*. **1903** *Westm. Gaz.* 2 Dec. 5/2 In 1900 he filled the rôle of Prologuer in the Passion Play [Ober-Ammergau].

'prologuist. *rare*. [f. PROLOGUE *sb.* + -IST.] = PROLOGUIZER.

1836 *Fraser's Mag.* XIII. 455 He resolved..to eschew the manufacture of what his prologuist calls 'cast-iron lines'.

prologuize ('prɒləgaɪz, 'prəʊl-), *v.* See also PROLOGIZE. [f. PROLOGUE *sb.* + -IZE.] *intr.* To write or deliver a prologue. Hence **'prologuizing** *vbl. sb.* and *ppl. a.*; also **'prologuizer**.

1761 LLOYD *To G. Colman* Poet. Wks. 1774 I. 119 'Till, decent sables on his back (Your prologuizers all wear black) The prologue comes. **1808** JEFFREY in Lockhart *Scott* xvi. (On Marmion), The place of the prologuizing minstrel is but ill supplied..by the epistolary dissertations which are prefixed to each book of the present poem. **1812** BYRON *Let. to Ld. Holland* 10 Sept., Prologuising is not my forte. **1855** BROWNING *Old Pict. in Florence* xxxiv, How we shall prologuise, how we shall perorate. **1872** SWINBURNE *Under Microscope* 61 In vain would I try to play the part of a prologuizer before this latest rival of the Hellenic dramatists... He alone is fit, in Euripidean fashion, to prologuize for himself.

pro'long, *sb. Sc.* *rare*$^{-1}$. [= obs. F. *prolong* a delay (1542 in Godef.), f. *prolonger* to PROLONG.]

† **1.** Delay, procrastination. *Obs.*

c **1470** HENRY *Wallace* VIII. 179 Bot mar prolong throuch Lammermur thai raid.

2. A prolongation.

1905 *Electrochem. & Metall. Industry* III. 9/1 This product..is a by-product with the European smelters, who use sheet-iron 'prolongs' on the condensers to collect it.

prolong (prəʊ'lɒŋ), *v.* [Late ME. *prolonge*, a. OF. *prolonguer* (13th c. in Littré), variant of F. *prolonger* (*prolongier*, 1219 in Godef. *Compl.*), ad. late L. *prōlongāre* (in Vulgate, etc.) to lengthen, extend (f. *prō*, PRO-[1] + *long-us* long), which gradually displaced the earlier OF. forms *porloignier* and *proloignier* to put away, defer (see PROLOYNE, PURLOIN).]

1. *trans.* To lengthen out in time; to extend in duration; to cause to continue or last longer; to continue, carry on.

1432–50 tr. *Higden* (Rolls) IV. 193 Iulius Cesar.. prolongede his office [L. *protelavit dignitatem suam*] by his awne autorite by v. yere foloenge. **1525** *Aberdeen Regr.* (1844) I. 111 To set and prolong all and syndrie their fischings and takis, baith to burgh and to land, now waikand and beand in thair handis. **1533** ELYOT *Cast. Helthe* (1541) 35 b, Pollio prolonged his lyfe certayne dayes with the evaporation of honye. **1697** DRYDEN *Virg. Past.* IV. 65 To sing thy Praise, wou'd Heav'n my Breath prolong. **1738** WESLEY *Ps.* CIV. IV. ix, In praising God, while He prolongs My Breath, I will that Breath employ. **1819** BYRON *Juan* II. clxxvi, Now she prolong'd her visits and her talk. **1855** MACAULAY *Hist. Eng.* xiii. III. 253 To prolong the inter-regnum till the autumn.

† **2.** To extend (time or a period) so as to cause delay; to protract, 'waste'. *Obs.*

1426 LYDG. *De Guil. Pilgr.* 24070, I..abyde, and synge alway 'cras, cras', makyng many fals delayes, and prolonge forth my dayes, forto Resorten hom ageyn. *c* **1460** J. METHAM *Wks.* (E.E.T.S.) 64 Qwerto prolonge I the tyme? sythyn yt must nedys be That I schal dye. **1530** PALSGR. 667/2 He dothe naught els but prolonge the tyme, *il ne fait aultre chose que alonger*, or *prolonguer le temps*. **1576** FLEMING *Panopl. Epist.* 16 Set to the vttermost of your might, that we prolong no time.

† **3.** To delay, postpone, put off. *Obs.*

1412–20 LYDG. *Chron. Troy* I. 1442 Lawly besechyng þat ȝe nat prolonge My purpos now, and maketh no delay. *a* **1547** SURREY *Æneid* IV. 420 But wherto now shold I prolong my death? **1558** BP. WATSON *Sev. Sacram.* xvi. 104 Wee saye with the wicked seruaunt, my Lord prolongeth his commynge. **1681** RYCAUT tr. *Gracian's Critick* 218 Much displeased to hear of his departure, ..she..advised him to prolong it, until a time of better conveniency. **1785** J. PHILLIPS *Treat. Inland Navig.* 44 The difference of expence ..cannot now be an object considerable enough to prolong so noble and useful an undertaking.

† **b.** To put off, defer, detain, keep waiting (a person). *Obs.*

1412–20 LYDG. *Chron. Troy.* I. 3126 þe kyng requeryng no lenger hym prolonge But goodly graunt þe fyn of his emprise. **1552** T. GRESHAM in Strype *Eccl. Mem.* (1721) II. II. App. C. 146 That they [the Council] would have them [the king's creditors] prolonged for another year.

† **c.** To prorogue (parliament): see PROROGUE 2.

1485 *Plumpton Corr.* (Camden) 48 On the satterday after our Lady day, the Parlament was prolonged unto the xxvii day of January, & then it begineth agaíne. **1649** MILTON *Eikon.* 4 He never promoted the true end of Parlaments, but put them off, and prolonged them.

† **d.** To postpone payment of (a debt). *Obs.*

1552 T. GRESHAM in Strype *Eccl. Mem.* (1721) II. II. App. C. 148 He is content to prolong the 10000.*l.* due to the 20th of November for six month.

† **4.** *intr.* To delay, to put off. Also with *infin.*

c **1430** LYDG. *Min. Poems* (Percy Soc.) 167 He..that dothe prolong and tarye Withe fayre behestis, and from his promyse varie. **1555** EDEN *Decades* 2 He..appeased theyr furie, and prolonged day after day. **1598** GRENEWEY *Tacitus' Ann.* VI. x. (1622) 137 Perceiuing that they prolonged from one day to another. **1623** LISLE *Test. Antiq., Sax. Serm. Easter day* 14 Prolong not to turne unto God, lest the time passe away through thy slow tarrying.

5. *trans.* To lengthen the pronunciation of (a word or syllable); to draw out (a sound).

c **1560** in *Anglia* XIII. 464 In y[e] latter ende of y[e] syllable to prolong the sounde. **1589** PUTTENHAM *Eng. Poesie* II. xii. (Arb.) 132 Rules of shortning and prolonging a sillable. **1761** GRAY *Fatal Sisters* 60 Far and wide the notes prolong. **1810** SCOTT *Lady of L.* I. xx, 'Father!' she cried; the rocks around Loved to prolong the gentle sound.

6. To extend in spatial length; to make longer, lengthen out. *rare* before 19th c.

1573–80 BARET *Alv.* P 756 To Prolong, to drawe in length, to stretch out. **1755** JOHNSON, *Prolong*, I. To lengthen out; to continue; to draw out. **1796** [see PROLONGED]. **1828–32** WEBSTER, *Prolong*, .. 4. To extend in space or length. **1849** LYELL *2nd Visit U.S.* (1850) II. 258 We know not how much farther north or south the motion [the rise of the land] may be prolonged under water. **1860** TYNDALL *Glac.* I. xi. 77 Up to which the fault..had prolonged itself as a crevasse.

b. To extend in scope or range. *rare*.

1880 *Geol. Surv. U.S.* in *Nature* XXI. 197/2 To authorise the work of the Survey to be prolonged into States adjoining the Territories.

c. *intr.* To lengthen out; to extend.

1816 BYRON *Ch. Har.* III. cix, This page which from my reveries I feed, Until it seems prolonging without end.

† **7.** *trans.* To put away, remove. *refl.* To make off with oneself; to stay away, absent oneself; = PURLOIN *v.* I. *Obs. rare*.

c **1440** *Promp. Parv.* 417/1 Purlongyn, or prolongyn, or put fer a-wey, *prolongo, alieno*. **1591** in *10th Rep. Hist. MSS. Comm.* App. v. 452 From his servyce nether by day nor by nyght shall absent or prolong himself.

prolongability (prəʊlɒŋə'bɪlɪtɪ). [f. PROLONGABLE *a.* + -ITY.] Capacity to be prolonged or lengthened.

1950 D. JONES *Phoneme* 183 'Prolongability'..is an infallible criterion for determining which type of length a vowel or diphthong has.

prolongable (prəʊ'lɒŋəb(ə)l), *a.* [f. PROLONG *v.* + -ABLE.] Capable of being prolonged or lengthened.

a **1864** RUSH (Webster), Each syllable is a prolongable quantity. **1889** *Philos. Mag.* Ser. v. XXVII. 14 Had the rod been really indefinitely prolongable.

prolongate ('prəulɒŋgeɪt), *v. rare.* [f. ppl. stem of late L. *prōlong-āre* to PROLONG: see -ATE[3]: cf. *elongate.*] *trans.* To prolong, lengthen. Hence **'prolongated** *ppl. a.*; **'prolongating** *ppl. a.* (in quot., †extending in length).

1597 A. M. tr. *Guillemeau's Fr. Chirurg.* b iv b/1 An Ovale figure, rounde, and somwhat prolongatinge like an Egge. **1821** COMBE *Dr. Syntax, Wife* II. (1869) 282/2 His prolongated nose Should guard his grinning mouth from blows. **1828–32** WEBSTER, *Prolongate*, 1. To extend or lengthen in space; as, to prolongate a line. 2. To extend in time. (Little used.) **1852** LD. COCKBURN *Jeffrey* I. 5 Everything is hushed as death, and every dimply smile prolongated into an expression of the most serious respect. **1868** *Ch. News* 3 June 353/2 We can but be deeply sorry for the Bishop of Capetown's prolongated trials.

prolongation (prəulɒŋ'geɪʃən). [a. F. *prolongation* (14th c. in Littré), ad. late L. type **prōlongātiōn-em*, n. of action f. *prōlong-āre* to PROLONG.] The action of prolonging.

1. Lengthening or extension in time; extension of the duration of anything.

1549 *Compl. Scot.* v. 32 Oure cupidite constrenzeis vs to desire prolongatione of oure dais. **1633** EARL MANCH. *Al Mondo* (1636) 175 Prolongation [of life] is no pleasure, but so long as it goes well with us. **1748** *Anson's Voy.* II. xi. 256 This prolongation of our cruise was a very prudent measure. **1844** H. H. WILSON *Brit. India* II. 367 The escape of Apa Saheb occasioned the prolongation of military operations. **1862** SIR B. BRODIE *Psychol. Inq.* II. iv. 109 The advancement of knowledge..tends to the prolongation of the average duration of human life.

†**2.** Extension of time that defers action; delay, putting off, postponement. *Obs.*

1490 CAXTON *Eneydos* xxiii. 85 Attones wythoute prolongacion ne taryeng. **1552** T. GRESHAM in Strype *Eccl. Mem.* (1721) II. II. App. C. 146, I offered them a bargain.. for the prolongation of £25000 and to have taken £5000 in fustians. **1622** MALYNES *Anc. Law-Merch.* 470 That they shall not require (without iust cause) any time of prolongation.

3. The lengthening or prolonging of a syllable, note, or other sound.

1589 PUTTENHAM *Eng. Poesie* II. xiii. (Arb.) 127 The licence of the Greekes and Latines, who made not their sharpe accent any necessary prolongation of their times, but vsed such sillable sometimes long sometimes short at their pleasure. **1866–79** SIBSON *Wks.* (1881) IV. 259 Prolongation of the first sound is the absence of silence and the presence of the wavering,..feeble sound during the interval between the first and second sounds. **1900** H. W. SMYTH *Grk. Melic Poets* 389 A feature of great importance, [which] points..to an extensive use of the principle of prolongation (τονή).

4. Linear extension in space; increase of length; with *a* and *pl.* an instance of this; an addition by which the length of anything is increased.

1671 GREW *Anat. Plants* I. iii. §4 The Lignous Body.. being nothing else but the prolongation of the Seminal Root. **1799** KIRWAN *Geol. Ess.* 439 The old town of Damietta, anciently situated near the sea, is now by the prolongation of the land, 2 leagues from it. **1802** PALEY *Nat. Theol.* viii. (ed. 2) 123 Two remarkable processes or prolongations of the bones of the leg. **1858** MAYNE *Expos. Lex.* s.v., The medullary prolongation of the nerves.

b. *pl. humorous.* Trousers; 'continuations'.

1849 E. E. NAPIER *Excurs. S. Africa* II. 230 Blue, dungaree trowsers were substituted for white prolongations.

5. Extension of scope or range; continuation.

1848 R. I. WILBERFORCE *Doctr. Incarnation* v. (1852) 126 The ascending line of Christian truth was only the prolongation of that first principle of the Gospel, that Christ was perfect God and perfect man. **1907** *Athenæum* 19 Jan. 70/3 After the prolongation of similar stuff to the point of satiety, the book abruptly ends.

‖**prolonge** (prɔlɔ̃ʒ). *Milit.* [F. *prolonge*, f. *prolonger* to PROLONG.] A rope composed of three pieces joined by two open rings, and having a hook at one end, and a toggle at the other, forming part of the equipment of a gun-carriage, and used for various purposes, esp. for moving a gun when unlimbered.

1858 SIMMONDS *Dict. Trade, Prolonge*, a gunner's instrument. **1859** F. A. GRIFFITHS *Artill. Man* (1862) 104 One prolonge between the boxes, above the washer box. **1873** L. WALLACE *Fair God* VII. xviii. 565 All recognised a signal of attack, and halted, the slave by his prolong [sic], the knight on his horse.

prolonged (-'lɒŋd), *ppl. a.* [f. PROLONG *v.* + -ED[1].] Lengthened, extended (in space or time).

1796 *Instr. & Reg. Cavalry* (1813) 133 The adjutant.. marks the prolonged point towards the other flank. **1864** PUSEY *Lect. Daniel* (1876) 471 Each century is a prolonged victory over the destroyer of all human things. **1867** FREEMAN *Norm. Conq.* I. iv. 245 Tired of Lewis' prolonged sojourn at Rouen. **1883** H. TUTTLE in *Harper's Mag.* Nov. 814/1 The hills are neither too prolonged nor too abrupt. *Mod.* Loud and prolonged cheers followed the close of the speaker's eloquent appeal.

prolongedly (prəʊ'lɒŋɪdlɪ), *adv.* [f. PROLONGED *ppl. a.* + -LY[2].] At length, extensively, over a long period.

1934 F. ROLFE *Desire & Pursuit of Whole* xxiv. 268 Crabbe plastered a double-handful of the glutinous rice, firmly and prolongedly, over the sot's face. **1972** G. JONES *Kings, Beasts, & Heroes* p. xvii, The *Beowulf* poet's business is with a non-divine hero of wondertale descent whom he associates closely, constantly, and prolongedly with the antecedents of northern tribal history.

prolonger (prəʊ'lɒŋə(r)). [f. PROLONG *v.* + -ER[1].] One who or that which prolongs: see the verb.

1548 ELYOT *Dict., Cunctator*.., a taryar, a deferrer, a lyngerer, a prolonger of tyme. **1574** J. JONES *Nat. Beginning Grow. Things* 41 Prolongers of life. **1655** FULLER *Waltham Abb.* (1840) 265 Those common prolongers of all suits,..the heat of men's anger, and the bellows of instruments gaining by law. **1902** *Daily Chron.* 23 Apr. 7/1 He..would not be called the founder of a Mecklenburg dynasty in the Netherlands, but only the prolonger of the House of Orange-Nassau in the female line.

†**b.** A kind of save-all for a candle. Also *fig.*

1650 FULLER *Pisgah* III. ix. 428 Temperance is the best prolonger of the candle of life. **1656** in *Sussex Archæol. Coll.* I. 70, 2 prolongers and an extinguisher. *a* **1679** R. WILD *Benefice* IV. (1689) 44 If Patents and Monopolies had had Prolongers, they had not gone out yet. **1688** R. HOLME *Armoury* III. xiv. (Roxb.) 5/2 Prolongers or saue-alls..are things made after the form of a candle sockett and are set in the stick as the sockett is.

prolonging (prəʊ'lɒŋɪŋ), *vbl. sb.* [f. as prec. + -ING[1].] The action of the verb PROLONG: *spec.*

†**a.** Putting off, delay. *Obs.* **b.** Lengthening of duration.

a. **1426** LYDG. *De Guil. Pilgr.* 10534 That Rud Entendement Be somownyd to appere..ageyn a certeyn day, Wythoute prolongyng or dellay. *a* **1548** HALL *Chron., Hen. VI* 105 b, The lorde Regent..without any delaye or prolongyng, prouided vitaile, artillery and municions. *a* **1649** DRUMM. OF HAWTH. *Hist. Jas. I* Wks. (1711) 1 All unanimously..determine, without longer prolongings, to work the delivery of their native prince.

b. **1528** PAYNEL *Salerne's Regim.* D iij b, Prolongynge of tyme in eatynge moderately (as an howre space) to chawe and swolowe our meate well, is allowable. **1611** BIBLE *Dan.* vii. 12 Their lives were prolonged for a season [*marg.* a prolonging in life was given unto them]. **1722** DE FOE *Plague* 183 After several prolongings of their confinement.

prolongingly (prəʊ'lɒŋɪŋlɪ), *adv. rare*[−1]. [f. PROLONGING *vbl. sb.* + -LY[2].] At length, prolongedly.

1851 H. MELVILLE *Moby Dick* III. xlii. 243 A voice that prolongingly moulded every word.

pro'longment. *rare.* [f. PROLONG *v.* + -MENT: cf. F. *prolongement* (12th c. in Hatz.-Darm.).] The fact of prolonging or condition of being prolonged; prolongation.

1593 NASHE *Christ's T.* (1613) 178 The prolongment of a few earthly dayes. **1711** SHAFTESB. *Charac.* II. ii. §2 To decline death, and endeavour the prolongment of his own un-eligible state. *a* **1814** *Love, Honor & Interest* II. i. in *New Brit. Theatre* III. 269 The languishing prolongment of adieu. **1889** *Tablet* 7 Dec. 910 The prolongment of the actual hostilities cannot continue.

†**pro'loyne**, *v. Obs.* Also 5 -oigne. [a. OF. *proloigner*, by-form of OF. *pour-*, *por-*, *purloigner*: see PURLOIN. In form, *proloigner* is intermediate between the popular OF. *porloigner*, and the learned or latinized *prolonger*; so in Eng. *proloyne* is between *purloin* and *prolong*; it has also senses coinciding with both, and is therefore placed separately.]

1. *trans.* To entice away, kidnap (a person); to make away with, to steal; = PURLOIN *v.* 2.

1388 WYCLIF *Bible* Prol. 7 He that proloyneth his brothir which is a fre man and sillith hym, shal be slayn. **1439** *Litt. Red Bk. Bristol* (1900) II. 154 That no maister..take nor proloyne, ne schal not do take nor proloigne eny seruaunt of the seid Crafte, beyng in Couenaunt and seruice of eny other, owte of his seruice. **1581** PETTIE *Guazzo's Civ. Conv.* III. (1586) 169 b, Not content with filching from their maisters in disbursing of their moneie, and with proloyning from them otherwise, they will not be faithfull in matters touching their honour and credite.

2. To put far away; to put away, remove; = PURLOIN *v.* 1, PROLONG *v.* 7.

c **1440** *Gesta Rom.* xxxiv. 135 (Harl. MS.) Alas! for my dwellynge place is proloyned or y-made fer.

3. To put off, postpone; = PROLONG *v.* 3.

c **1450** *St. Cuthbert* (Surtees) 7941 þe bischope na langer it proloyne. *Ibid.* 8042 Forto make mens saules sure, And noght for na pecuyne Mendyng of þair lyues proloyne.

proluse (prəʊ'l(j)u:z), *v. nonce-wd.* [Back-formation from PROLUSION.] *intr.* To give an introductory discourse; to prolusionize.

1917 KIPLING *Diversity of Creatures* 330 This they permitting, he, emboldened thus, Prolused of humankind promiscuous.

prolusion (prəʊ'l(j)u:ʒən). [ad. L. *prōlūsiōn-em* a prelude, preliminary exercise, n. of action f. *prōlūd-ĕre* to play or practise beforehand.]

1. A display introductory to a game, performance, or entertainment; a prelude, preliminary essay or attempt.

1601 BP. W. BARLOW *Defence* 8 And this for our prolusion, now we meete. **1636** FEATLY *Clavis Myst.* lvii. 779 The Prophet here..useth..no prolusion after the manner of fencers. **1664** H. MORE *Myst. Iniq., Apol.* 489 That these Apparitions were ordinarily the appearing of the Son of God, and certain Prolusions to his Incarnation. **1795** MASON *Ch. Mus.* i. 47 Its extemporaneous prolusion should flow on with that equable and easy Modulation, which, while it gratifies the Ear, should not too strongly affect the intellect. **1841** WADDINGTON *Hist. Ref.* II. xxx. 338 That, which in Germany was fierce and noisy conflict, was a mere skirmish and prolusion among the Swiss.

2. A literary production intended as a preliminary dissertation on a subject which the author intends to treat more fully; a preliminary essay or article; a slight literary production.

1627 HAKEWILL *Apol.* III. vi. §1. 212 Which Famianus Strada, in the first booke of his Academicall Prolusions, relates of Francis Suarez. **1682** EVELYN in *Pepys' Diary*, etc. (1879) VI. 141 My Treatise..was intended but for a prolusion. **1713** ADDISON *Guardian* No. 115 ¶4 His prolusion on the stile of the most famous among the ancient Latin poets..is one of the most entertaining, as well as the most just pieces of criticism. *Ibid.* No. 119 ad. fin., The sequel of this prolusion shall be the work of another day. **1881** SALA in *Illustr. Lond. News* 15 Jan. 51 Penning a prolusion on Chinese metaphysics.

Hence **pro'lusionize** *v. intr. nonce-wd.*, to deliver a prolusion.

1864 *Sat. Rev.* 21 May, There were too many old stagers present, who had themselves prolusionized in rectorial addresses and lectures at country institutes.

prolusory (prəʊ'l(j)u:sərɪ), *a.* [ad. med.L. *prōlūsōri-us* (in Pandects, as var. reading of *perlusorius*) belonging to a prelude: see prec. and -ORY.] Of or belonging to prolusion; preliminary, introductory.

1868 *Contemp. Rev.* IX. 170 To prepare us, by its prolusory and mostly nugatory debates, for the time when we shall be engaged in council to decide immense realities. **1892** STEVENSON *Across the Plains* 115 The time comes when a man should cease prolusory gymnastics.

proly ('prəʊlɪ), *sb.* and *a.* Usu. *derogatory.* Also prolly. [f. PROLETARIAN *a.* and *sb.*]

A. *sb.* = PROLE *sb.*

1959 J. CARY *Captive & Free* 84 Hooper, son of a lorry driver, who worked his way through the grammar school to a varsity, had, like many of his type, a great contempt for the class from which he had sprung. He called it the prolies. He thought of a proly as a born slave and parasite. **1969** E. MCGIRR *Entry of Death* iii. 64 The politicians say that the prollies prefer to sit back and wait..rather than take direct action. **1970** K. GILES *Murder Pluperfect* viii. 166 Our Lady might have been..loving the prolies.

B. *adj.* Of working-class origin; = PROLE *a.* Also in phr. ***prolier-than-thou***, after *holier-than-thou* (see HOLY *a.* 5 c).

1971 *Listener* 2 Sept. 311/3 This 'prolier than thou' account. **1972** C. DRUMMOND *Death at Bar* iii. 69 It was one thing..for people of decent family and quite another for prolly sergeants. **1977** *Time Out* 28 Jan.–3 Feb. 3/3 The prolier-than-thou sectarianism of the new convert to Marxism is all too evident in her letter.

prom (prɒm). *colloq.* [Abbrev. of PROMENADE *sb.*]

1. *U.S.* = PROMENADE *sb.* 2 c.

1894 D. MORROW in H. Nicolson *Dwight Morrow* (1935) 41, I have..been invited over to the Smith Junior Prom. **1899** A. H. QUINN *Pennsylvania Stories* 170 All you children can get tickets of me for the Senior Prom right now. **1914** G. ATHERTON *Perch of Devil* i. 74 The Prom is anything but an exclusive affair. **1924** [see DRAG *v.* 1 e]. **1930** P. W. SLOSSON *Great Crusade* (1931) xii. 342 Dancing was a universal convention, and the formal balls, 'proms' and 'hops' became extremely expensive affairs. **1956** [see JUMP *sb.*[1] 1 d]. **1972** T. P. MCMAHON *Issue of Bishop's Blood* (1973) vii. 88 A girl.. who went into a decline because she hadn't been invited to the Junior Prom at Santa Clara University. **1977** I. SHAW *Beggarman, Thief* I. vi. 76 Girls who..went..to the proms at which he played the trumpet in the band.

2. = *promenade concert* (s.v. PROMENADE *sb.* 4 b); ***the Proms***, the Henry Wood Promenade Concerts, now given annually at the Royal Albert Hall, London (also in *sing.*).

1902 *Free Lance* 4 Jan. 358/1 There is never one of the programmes at the Proms..unworthy of the..most cultured music lover. **1913** H. WALPOLE *Fortitude* II. i. 180 A walk or two and going into the gallery at Covent Garden once or twice and the Proms sometimes. **1927** *Morning Post* 16 Aug. 6/7 (*heading*) Mozart's music at the 'Proms'. **1930** *Daily Express* 8 Sept. 6/2 Faces are certainly funny things —as you remarked when we went to the 'Prom.' at the Queen's Hall the other night. **1944** *Times* 10 June 5/4 While the L.S.O...has continued in the path it designed for itself ..the Proms have continuously evolved. **1945** *Ann. Reg.* *1944* 369 A concert in celebration of the fiftieth anniversary of the first 'Prom'. **1955** *Times* 19 Aug. 2/5 During his lifetime Henry Wood used the Proms as a stamping ground for new music. **1958** *Times* 20 June 3/6 This year is Puccini's centenary and, for the first time in a Prom, a whole act from one of his operas is included. **1973** *Listener* 14 June 810/1 Henry Wood decreed that the nine symphonies of Beethoven should be the backbone of the Proms. **1976** *Ibid.* 8 Apr. 440/1 The word 'Prom' no longer has anything to do with promenading: it means something like the Albert Hall Proms—young people of the student class enjoying high culture in a spirited, informal manner.

3. = PROMENADE *sb.* 2 a.

1909 J. A. GLOVER-KIND *I do like to be beside Seaside* (1970) (song) 4, I do like to stroll upon the Prom, Prom, Prom. **1910** *Bradshaw's Railway Guide* Apr. 1142/2 Charmingly situated on the West Prom., directly facing the Sea. **1925** *Glasgow Herald* 18 July 8/7 A scrap of conversation overheard on the 'prom' of a well-known resort. **1953** *Manch. Guardian* 21 Dec. 7/8 (Advt.), Southport.—Clifton Hotel, Prom.: A.A., R.A.C.: 86 bedrooms, lift, garage. **1973** P. LOVESEY *Mad Hatter's Holiday* i. 7 Moscrop joined the general movement in the direction of the West Pier..one of a long parade of freshly-arrived visitors taking that first bracing turn along the prom.

4. *attrib.* and *Comb.*, as (sense 1) ***prom dress, girl, night***; (sense 2) ***prom concert, -goer***.

1973 'S. HARVESTER' *Corner of Playground* II. iii. 93 She had queued to see ballet at Covent Garden, gone to Prom concerts, visited art galleries. **1976** *National Observer* (U.S.)

26 June 17/4 Prom dresses, cheers, put-downs, yearbook inscriptions...we remember them all. **1978** *Detroit Free Press* 5 Mar. (Spring fashion Suppl.) 19 (Advt.), The prom dress is back... In a big, beautiful way. **1894** *Outing* XXIV. 68/2 For two days..in January the room is crowded with 'Prom' girls and their escorts. **1947** *Penguin Mus. Mag.* II. 37 There is one body of Prom-goers who..are seen and heard too much,..a source of continual irritation to the serious Promenader. **1971** *Guardian* 26 Aug. 10/1 Tonight promises to be an adventurous evening for Prom-goers. **1974** *State* (Columbia, S. Carolina) 3 Mar. 6-F (Advt.), Sugarplum styles—beribboned with satin or velvet, strewn with flowers..to make your prom night unforgettable.

‖**promachos** ('prɒməkɒs). *Gr. Antiq.* [a. Gr. πρόμαχος, f. πρό before + μάχ-εσθαι to fight.] One who fights before or on behalf of another; a champion. Also *fig.*

1905 *Edin. Rev.* Apr. 446 It was partly chance that made Whistler such a 'promachos' in this question.

promammal, etc.: see PRO-² 1.

†**proma'nation.** *Obs. rare*⁻¹. [f. ? late L. *prōmān-āre* to flow or drop forth (Zeno Veron. in Quicherat) + -ATION.] A flowing forth; effluence, emanation.

1653 H. MORE *Conject. Cabbal.* (1713) 174 Concerning the promanation and intermixture of the Rays of Light.

promarketeer: see PRO-¹ 5 b.

promastigote (prəʊ'mæstɪgəʊt), *a.* and *sb.* *Zool.* [erron. f. Gr. πρό (? taken as opp. Gr. α-, in *amastigote*) + μαστιγ-, μάστιξ whip (used to render FLAGELLUM) + -ωτης (see -OT² and -OTE).] (Applied to) the flagellated form assumed by parasitic protozoans of the genus *Leishmania* when carried by arthropods.

1971 *Jrnl. Parasitol.* LVII. 626/2 Promastigote (leptomonad) flagellates..were from 2 strains [of *Leishmania hertigi*]... Body width frequently tapering rather abruptly.., similar to some promastigotes of *L. adleri*. **1974** *Nature* 7 June 588/1 Examination of the promastigotes of *L. hertigi* immediately revealed cytoplasmic inclusions of a type which had not been observed in any of our previous studies. **1976** *Ibid.* 19 Aug. 689/1 We present evidence that transformation from the mammalian (amastigote) stage of *L. donovani* to the insect and/or culture (promastigote) stage is inhibited by host hamster spleen homogenates.

promazine ('prəʊməziːn). *Pharm.* [f. PRO(PYL + M(ETHYL + *-azine* (f. AZ(O- + INE⁵).] The compound 10-(3-dimethylaminopropyl)phenothiazine, $C_{17}H_{20}N_2S$, which is used (in the form of its white crystalline hydrochloride) as a tranquillizer.

1956 *Jrnl. Amer. Med. Assoc.* 5 May 45/1 Treatment with promazine satisfactorily relieved the withdrawal symptoms of acute alcoholic intoxication in all patients who remained in the hospital for the complete course of therapy. **1958** *Martindale's Extra Pharmacopœia* (ed. 24) 398 Promazine has actions similar to those of chlorpromazine. It has been used for its tranquillising effect in psychotic conditions, especially those associated with hyperactivity, in acute alcoholism and delirium tremens, and in the withdrawal symptoms of drug addiction. **1965** J. POLLITT *Depression & its Treatment* iv. 46 Admission to hospital for continuous narcosis may be necessary. This may be induced by four-hourly doses of barbiturates, but these should give way as soon as possible to phenothiazine derivatives such as chlorpromazine or promazine. **1971** [see PROMETHAZINE].

†**prome.** *Obs. rare.* [a. OF. *prome*, *prosme*, *proisme* near, also as sb. a neighbour:—L. *proxim-us* nearest.] A neighbour.

[**1292** BRITTON IV. ix. §1 Et meynt homme par serment fet ..graunt ayde a soen prosme.] *c* **1400** *Rule St. Benet* 8 Luue ..ti prome als ti-self. *Ibid.* 10 þat es godis wille, þat ye foliȝ yure ordir, and luue til yure prome.

promeis, obs. form of PROMISE.

prome'nadable, *a. nonce-wd.* [f. PROMENADE *v.* + -ABLE.] Capable of being used for promenading or walking about.

1844 E. WARBURTON *Crescent & Cross* I. ii. 23 There are, probably, not less than five hundred acres of promenadable roof in, or, rather, on, the city.

promenade (prɒmɪ'nɑːd, -'eɪd, 'prɒm-), *sb.* Forms: 6 **purmenade, (purmenado),** 7 **pourmenade,** 7– **promenade.** [a. F. *promenade* (1557 in Hatz.-Darm.), f. *promener* to lead forth, take for a walk, refl., *se promener* to take a walk, altered from OF. and 16th c. F. (still in Cotgr., 1611) *pourmenade* a walk, *pourmener* 'to walke (trans.), to stirre vp and downe':—late L. *prōmināre* (Appul.) to drive onward (a beast), f. *prō* forward, forth + *mināre* to threaten, in rustic and late L. *mināre* to drive (beasts), i.e. with cries, It. *menare*, F. *mener* to conduct, lead. See also -ADE, -ADO.

1818 TODD, *Promenade*..is a common phrase of recent times.]

1. A walk taken (usually at a leisurely pace) for exercise or amusement, or (esp.) to and fro for display, or in a formal manner as part of a social ceremony. Also applied to exercise taken in this way in a carriage, on horseback, or in a boat.

1567 FENTON *Trag. Disc.* 19 The often palewalkes & purmenades he made by the gate of hys Pallais. *Ibid.* 127 He forgat not euery day..to make his purmenado on horsebacke in the street. **1675** H. WOOLLEY *Gentlewoman's Comp.* 34 Your Promenades or walks. *a* **1734** NORTH *Exam.* III. viii. §31 (1740) 606 He passed, with the Sword before him, through the Crowd... This Promenade was done more than once. **1785** G. A. BELLAMY *Apology* V. 43 She only knew how to make trimmings, to sing 'Haut de Villes', and take the promenade. **1827** SCOTT *Jrnl.* 7 Mar., To see the exhibition lit up for a promenade. **1887** RUSKIN *Præterita* II. vi. 197 He had little taste for the Sunday promenades in a town.

2. a. A place for walking or promenading; a walk; *esp.* a paved public walk for social promenades (now most freq. a paved walk raised alongside the beach at a seaside resort).

1648 W. MOUNTAGUE *Devout Ess.* I. xix. §6. 364 This little intermixture of a Garden-plat or patern..may be no unpleasant walk or promenade for the unconfined portion of some solitary Prisoner. **1656** BLOUNT *Glossogr.*, *Promenade*, see *Pourmenade*. *Ibid.*, *Pourmenade* (Fr.), a Walk. **1792** A. YOUNG *Trav. France* 20 The promenade is finely situated; built on the highest part of the rampart. **1832** G. DOWNES *Lett. Cont. Countries* I. 377 A street..running far along the shore of the Mediterranean, from which it is separated by a promenade, finely planted, and adorned with statues, fountains, &c. **1863** GEO. ELIOT *Romola* xxviii, The streets were not altogether a pleasant promenade for well-born women. **1882** ASHTON *Soc. Life Reign Q. Anne* xxxiv. II. 149 A very large barge with a saloon, and promenade on the top. **1892** B. POTTER *Jrnl.* Mar. (1966) 234, I was disappointed with the Hoe. It is exactly like the grounds of the Naval Exhibition, broad asphalt promenades, cigar kiosks, and even the lighthouse all complete. **1899** P. E. AMY *Beautiful Jersey* 69/2 *Promenades.* The chief of these is the Esplanade, a marine promenade, practically a continuation of Albert Quay. **1938** G. GREENE *Brighton Rock* I. i. 5 The ghost train diving between the grinning skeleton [sic] under the Aquarium promenade, the sticks of Brighton rock, the paper sailors' caps. **1939** *Blackpool Official Guide*, Blackpool's promenades cover the whole seaboard of seven miles in length. *Ibid.*, There is no other seafront which combines such a variety of scenery as Blackpool's famous promenade. **1958** J. BETJEMAN *Coll. Poems* 117 Prepare for an evening of dancing and cards And forget the sea-breeze on the dry promenades. **1977** *Lancashire Life* Dec. 57/1 Along the promenade at that point there were cannons at intervals.

b. *spec.* A gallery at a music-hall, frequented by demi-mondaines and their followers.

The two most notorious promenades were at the Empire and the Alhambra music-halls in Leicester Square.

1863 *Observer* 18 Jan. 6/2 The Alhambra, of all the music halls, is the one least entitled to use the name... The balcony is converted into a promenade for loose women and the simpletons who run after them. **1899** BEERBOHM *Around Theatres* (1953) 32 We bought two seats... We passed, on our way to them, into the far-famed Promenade. **1906** A. BENNETT *Whom God hath Joined* i. 20, I saw the great Charlie the other night..in the promenade at the Empire. **1914** C. MACKENZIE *Sinister St.* II. IV. ii. 870 Michael reached the Orient Palace of Varieties, and..joined the throng of the Promenade. *Ibid.* 872 On the Promenade where it was quite certain that every woman had a history to account for her presence there, how utterly living had quenched life. **1915** KIPLING in *Nash's Mag.* Oct. 133/1 He was as communicative as—as a lady in the Promenade. **1918** A. BENNETT *Pretty Lady* i. 2 Behind the audience came the restless Promenade, where was the reality which the stage reflected. **1964** C. MACKENZIE *My Life & Times* III. 236 A flash tart who frequented the promenades of the Empire or the Alhambra. **1979** R. BLYTHE *View in Winter* iv. 182 The wonderful Empire in Leicester Square..the promenade there..was frequented by the first-class ladies of the town.

c. A ball or dance at a school or college. *U.S.*

1887 *Lippincott's Mag.* Aug. 298 The most important society event of the year is the Junior Promenade. **1905** *N.Y. Herald* 22 Jan. 10 The fair guests invited to the Junior Promenade, the great event of the college year. **1933** *Fortune* Aug. 90/3 True jazz..is even losing its great popularity at college promenades. **1972** *Lebende Sprachen* XVII. 35/2 US promenade—BE school dance, college dance.

d. *Dancing.* (See quots.) Also ***promenade position.***

1953 K. AMBROSE *Beginners, Please!* vi. 43 When a pivot is made on one leg (as in Figs. 5–6–7..) the movement is termed a *promenade*. **1956** J. C. MILLIGAN *101 Scottish Country Dances* 28 *Promenade for three couples* is a formation, not a method of progression. **1957** G. B. L. WILSON *Penguin Dict. Ballet* 222 *Promenade*, (1) a slow turn on one foot while the body is held in a set position, such as an arabesque; (2) a slow turn in a pas de deux when the danseuse, on point, is turned round by her partner. **1967** CHUJOY & MANCHESTER *Dance Encycl.* 747/1 *Promenade position*, in ballroom dance, a couple in closed position moving sideways to the left, with the side of the foot leading. **1968** J. C. MILLIGAN *Introd. Scottish Country Dancing* 51 Promenade can be done by two, three or four couples. It is done in both reel and strathspey time and takes eight travelling steps.

3. *colloq.* **a.** Short for *promenade deck*: see sense 4 a.

1845 *Knickerbocker* XXV. 61 On the upper deck the engineers and sailors, ladies, emigrants and gentlemen, sat side by side upon the single seat which ran all round the promenade. **1873** W. D. HOWELLS *Chance Acquaintance* i. 1 On the forward promenade of the Saguenay boat..Miss Kitty Ellison sat. **1974** 'G. BLACK' *Golden Cockatrice* iv. 74, I..went up one deck..going out on to the open promenade which was empty.

b. Short for *promenade concert*: see sense 4 b.

1901 *Westm. Gaz.* 18 Sept. 2/1 The Promenades are with us again. **1902** *Ibid.* 11 Sept. 4/1 The Promenades go on from triumph to triumph.., if the audiences might sometimes be larger, they could not possibly be more appreciative.

4. a. *attrib.*, as ***promenade bonnet, deck, platform, terrace***; **b. promenade band,** a band that performs at a promenade concert; **promenade concert,** a concert at which the audience walk about instead of being seated or at which a proportion of the audience stands.

1823 *Repos. Arts*, etc. Ser. III. I. 184 Fashionable for promenade bonnets. **1829** *Amer. Traveller* (Boston) 14 Apr. 2 The engraving above, exhibits what may emphatically be termed a *Land Barge*..with a cabin, berths, &c. below; a promenade deck, awning, seats, &c. above. **1841** *Civil Eng. & Arch. Jrnl.* 250/1 The timber piles which carry the passengers promenade platforms. *a* **1860** ALB. SMITH *Long. Med. Stud.* (1861) 88 Mr. Jones taking refreshment with a lamplighter and two cabmen at a promenade coffee-stand near Charing Cross. **1872** HOWELLS *Wedd. Journ.* (1892) 194 The ladies drew their chairs together on the promenade deck. **1931** M. DE LA ROCHE *Finch's Fortune* vi. 114 He strode out with the best of them on the promenade deck. **1973** 'D. MARINER' *Beaufort Dossier* x. 177 The promenade deck was really a broad passage... Its roof was the..boat-deck overhead.

b. 1839 *Inventors Advocate* 5 Oct. 127/1 The Musard Promenade Band..will resume its performances at the Lyceum. **1839** DICKENS *Let.* 9 Feb. (1965) I. 640 Kate at the Promenade Concert. **1839** *Mus. World* Apr. 253 The 'gentleman pensioner' of Drury with his lions and his promenade concerts. **1865** *Pall Mall G.* 28 Aug. 11/1 When promenade concerts were first introduced into England they really deserved their name. They were then given at a place called the 'Adelaide Gallery'... The promenade concert.. was an importation from France; and Musard, Laurent, and Jullien were its importers. **1893** *World* 11 Oct. 23/2 Long before the run of a successful Savoy opera is over Sir Arthur's melodies are dinned into our ears by every promenade band and street piano. **1921** *Daily Colonist* (Victoria, B.C.) 24 Mar. 4/1 It should combine the features of a convention hall with the facilities for holding promenade concerts at which at least 3,000 persons can be accommodated. **1954** *Grove's Dict. Mus.* (ed. 5) IX. 357/1 On 30 June 1944 the Promenade Concerts were closed down ..on account of flying bombs, but they were replaced on 1 July by broadcasts from Bedford. It was there that Wood conducted his last performance on 28 July. **1962** *Listener* 2 Aug. 189/3 The programme engineer at the Promenade Concerts noticeably reduced the volume of cheers at the conclusion of Mahler's Third Symphony.

prome'nade (see prec.), *v.* Also 6 *Sc.* **prominede** (in vbl. sb. **promineding**). [f. prec. sb.]

1. a. *intr.* To make a promenade; to walk about (or take exercise on horseback, or in a carriage, etc.), esp. for amusement or display; to parade.

1588 [see PROMENADING below]. **1801** SURR *Splendid Misery* I. 128 As they were thus promenading. **1801** CHARLOTTE SMITH *Lett. Solit. Wand.* II. 280 The newspapers suffer nobody to walk—they must *promenade* (which, so used, is no word in any language). **1842** TENNYSON *Amphion* v, The poplars, in long order due, With cypress promenaded, The shock-head willows two and two By rivers gallopaded. **1871** CARLYLE in *Mrs. Carlyle's Lett.* (1883) I. 374 Promenading gently on horseback. **1877** MRS. OLIPHANT *Makers Flor.* iii. 57 Restlessly promenading up and down within sight of the windows. **1887** WASHBURNE *Recoll. Minister* I. i. 3 The *grandes dames*..promenaded in their gilded phaetons on the magnificent Avenue of the Champs Elysées.

b. With *it*, or with cognate (or advb.) acc.

1819 *Metropolis* II. 93 After promenading a few turns,.. I..sat down. *Ibid.* 94 A very high person was.. promenading it in soft whispers with his aged Venus.

2. *trans.* To make a promenade through, to walk about (a place) in a leisurely or stately way.

1818 T. BROWN *Brighton* II. i. 22 Their more fortunate comrades *promenade* Hyde Park, or the Mall. **1837** DICKENS *Pickw.* ii, The dancers promenaded the room. **1877** MAR. M. GRANT *Sun-Maid* i, I beheld two compatriots in waterproof promenading the place. **1977** *Lancashire Life* Aug. 33/2 Promenade Blackburn's bustling modern centre today, and you might find anxiety over a new town rival puzzling.

3. In causal sense (= F. *promener*): To lead (a person, etc.) about a place, esp. in the way of display. Also *fig.* (Cf. PARADE *v.* 4.)

1850 MERIVALE *Rom. Emp.* II. xxii. 512 Mystic rites, ostensibly connected with..familiar deities, were promenaded from land to land. **1873** RUSKIN *Fors Clav.* xxx. 10 The Easter ox that they had promenaded at Berne. **1886** BURTON *Arab. Nights* I. 286 The Prefect..gave him an hundred lashes with a whip and, mounting him on a camel, promenaded him round about the city. **1890** in *Pall Mall G.* 9 Aug. 1/3, I do not wish to be interviewed... I do not want to be promenaded in the papers.

Hence **prome'nading** *vbl. sb.* (also *attrib.*) and *ppl. a.*

1588 in Beveridge *Culross & Tulliallan* (1885) I. iv. 126 That all myddingis..be tane off the haill gaitts and passagis ..and all other promineding places of the samyne... That ..the places of promineding be clenyit of all muck. **1815** J. SCOTT *Vis. Paris* ix. (ed. 2) 100 Our countrymen..saw the promenading ladies. **1839** CHAMBERS *Tour Holland*, etc. 69/1 To afford space for promenading, there is a bridge of boats across the Lahn, leading to some beautiful woody banks opposite. **1865** *Reader* 26 Aug. 244/2 A promenading audience is not *blasé* to Rossini or Mozart.

prome'nader. [f. prec. + -ER¹.] **a.** One who promenades.

1830 MARRYAT *King's Own* xlvii, 'Look there!' observed one of the promenaders. **1871** R. ELLIS *Catullus* lv. 7, I hail'd each lady promenader. **1883** LD. R. GOWER *My Remin.* I. xviii. 379 The boulevards are always densely full of promenaders.

b. *spec.* One who attends a promenade concert; *esp.* one who stands.

1889 G. B. SHAW in *Star* 19 Aug. 2/4 With the floor.. hidden by a crowd of promenaders too closely packed to promenade. **1918** A. BENNETT *Roll-Call* I. ii. 36

Promenaders promenaded in and out of the corridor. **1959** *Listener* 29 Oct. 716/1 Even the Promenaders..do not respond joyfully to a reduction in the large share of familiar classics. **1966** K. S. SORABJI in 'H. MacDiarmid' *Company I've Kept* ii. 65 That archetype of the 'democratic' audiences, the Promenaders. **1977** *Times* 23 July 14/6 There was general enthusiasm among the young promenaders for the English flavour of this year's jubilee season.

Hence **prome'naderess**, a female promenader.

1837 CARLYLE *Fr. Rev.* II. VI. iv, White-muslin promenaderess, in green parasol.

promeristem: see PRO-² 1.

†**pro'merit**, *v. Obs.* [f. L. *prōmerit-*, ppl. stem of *prōmer-ēre* (also dep. *-ērī*) to deserve, merit, also, to earn, gain, win, gain over, hence in Vulgate to earn the favour of, render favourable, propitiate. See PRO-¹ and MERIT *v.*]

1. *trans.* To win the favour of; to please, gratify, propitiate.

1582 N. T. (Rhem.) *Heb.* xiii. 16 Beneficence and communication do not forget, for with such hostes God is promerited. *a* **1641** BP. MOUNTAGU *Acts & Mon.* vii. (1642) 399 As if.. God were promerited with such washing service. [**1643** OWEN *Death of Death* Wks. 1852 X. 287 The Vulgar Latin once reads *promeretur*..and the Rheimists, to preserve the sound, have rendered it *promerit*.]

2. To merit, deserve; to win or procure by merit.

1610 BP. CARLETON *Jurisd.* 201 The Princes of auncient times..when they came to make petition for the Imperiall crowne, were wont by some worthy office to promerit the fauour of the Church of Rome. **1624** BP. HALL *No Peace w. Rome* §10 That which the satisfactions of Christ haue promerited for vs. **1659** PEARSON *Creed* ii. (1839) 111 From him alone, must we expect salvation, acknowledging..there is..nothing in any other creature which can promerit or procure it to us.

3. ? To deserve well of. *rare.*

[This seems to have arisen from an erroneous analysis, connecting it with *pro merito* for or on account of merit.]

1641 BP. HALL *Serm. Jas. iv.* 8 Rem. Wks. (1660) 87 He loves not God, no not while he [God] promerits him with his favours. **1644** —— *Serm. Eph. iv.* 30 ibid. 112 A people that God had no whit promerited by his favours.

So †**pro'merit** *sb.* [ad. L. *prōmerit-um*, prop. neut. pa. pple. of *prōmerēre*: see above], merit, desert; †**pro'meritor** [agent-n. in L. form f. *prōmerēre*], one who merits or deserves.

1630 J. TAYLOR (Water P.) *Trav.* Ded., Wks. III. 76 If it fall out (not according to any Promerits of mine) but out of mine owne expectation of your..vnparallel'd disposition. **1675** J. SMITH *Chr. Relig. Appeal* I. 34 Whatsoever mischiefs befel..their posterity, though many Ages after the decease of the Promeritors.

‖**promerops** ('prɒmərɒps). *Ornith.* Pl. **pro'meropes** (-'mɛrəupiːz). [mod.L. (Réaumur) f. Gr. πρό before + μέροψ bee-eater.] A South African genus of birds, of uncertain affinity, including the Cape Promerops, *P. cafer*, a small bird with a long curved slender bill and a very long tail, and the Natal species, *P. gurneyi*. The name has been also applied to various other slender-billed birds of different families.

1827 *Perils & Captivity* (Constable's Misc.) 94 The humming birds, the red-birds, the paroquets, the promerops. **1840** tr. *Cuvier's Anim. Kingd.* 209 The Promeropses..are not crested, but possess a very long tail. **1894** NEWTON *Dict. Birds* 790 The *P[tilorrhis] magnifica* (Vieillot) of New Guinea—the '*Promerops*' of many writers. **1896** *Ibid.* 923 According to Mr. Layard, the habits of the Cape Promerops..are very unlike those of the ordinary *Nectariniidæ*.

promes, -ess(e: see PROMISE.

prometaphase (prəʊ'mɛtəfeɪz). *Cytology.* [f. PRO-² + *metaphase* s.v. META- 4.] The stage in mitotic or meiotic nuclear division, following prophase and preceding metaphase, during which the spindle is formed and the chromosomes become oriented towards it.

1931 W. J. C. LAWRENCE in *Cytologia* II. 361 The degree of repulsion gradually diminishes and diakinesis is abruptly terminated by the sudden converging of the chromosomes on the centre of the nucleus. This stage (pro-metaphase) is very brief and is characterised by the secondary association of a number of the bivalents. **1969** BROWN & BERTKE *Textbk. Cytol.* xix. 404/1 Evidence at prometaphase and anaphase seems to indicate that the centromere is 'pulled' toward the pole or poles, the arms of the chromosome apparently passively following along.

promethazine (prəʊ'mɛθəziːn). *Pharm.* [f. PRO(PYL + METH(YL + *-azine* (f. AZ(O- + -INE⁵).] A bitter-tasting antihistamine compound, 10-(2-dimethylaminopropyl)phenothiazine, $C_{17}H_{20}N_2S$, which is used chiefly as an anti-emetic and a sedative, usu. in the form of its hydrochloride, a white powder.

1951 *Lancet* 26 May 1143/2 'Avomine' (promethazine 8-chlorotheophyllinate) is a safe and effective remedy for seasickness. **1959** *Which?* July 69/2 All that is certain is that hyoscine, meclozine, cyclizine and promethazine do act to prevent travel sickness, and all have some side-effects. **1961** *Lancet* 23 Sept. 688/1 To control shivering a mixture of promethazine hydrochloride 50 mg., pethidine 50 mg., and chlorpromazine 50 mg. was made up to 20 ml. 2–4 ml. of this mixture was administered intravenously as required. **1971** B. R. JONES *Pharmacol.* iii. 15 Post-operative vomiting is reduced by including in the premedication an intramuscular injection of either an antihistamine such as Promethazine ('Phenergan') or a tranquillizer of the phenothiazine type such as Promazine.

promethea (prəʊ'miːθiːə). [L. *Promēthea*, fem. of adj. *Promētheus*: see PROMETHEUS.] In full, ***promethea moth***. The North American silk moth, *Callosamia promethea*, of the family Saturniidæ.

1889 *Cent. Dict.* s.v. Prometheus. **1901** M. C. DICKERSON *Moths & Butterflies* 119 Late in fall and winter we may find brown cocoons containing the chrysalides of the Promethea moth swinging from the branches of the wild cherry. **1905** V. L. KELLOGG *Amer. Insects* xiv. 422 The promethea-moth.., light reddish brown in female, and blackish and clay colour in male.., is perhaps the most abundant of all these giant moths. **1909** G. STRATTON-PORTER *Girl of Limberlost* xv. 300 He found a splendid Promethea on a lilac in a corner. **1949** *Nat. Hist.* Feb. 80/2 The Cecropia and Promethea have their wings wrapped around their bodies. **1954** BORROR & DELONG *Introd. Study of Insects* xxvi. 507 The promethea moth, *Callosamia promethea* (Drury), is sometimes called the spice-bush silk moth. **1972** SWAN & PAPP *Common Insects N. Amer.* 268 Promethea moth... Canada to Florida, west to the Great Plains.

Promethean (prəʊ'miːθiːən), *a.* (*sb.*) Also (erron.) 6–7 **-ian**, 7 **-æan**. [f. PROMETHEUS + -AN.]

A. *adj.* **1.** Of, pertaining to, or resembling Prometheus, in his skill, art, or punishment.

1588 SHAKS. *L.L.L.* IV. iii. 304 Womens eyes..are the Ground, the Bookes, the Achadems, From whence doth spring the true Promethean fire. **1597** DRAYTON *Mortimer.* F ij b, Like Promethian life-begetting flame. **1635** QUARLES *Embl.* IV. xiv, These vultures in my Brest Gripe my Promethian heart both night and day. **1641** MILTON *Ch. Govt.* II. iii. Wks. 1851 III. 161 With a kind of Promethean skill to shape and fashion this outward man into the similitude of a body. **1744** AKENSIDE *Pleas. Imag.* III. 410 With Promethean art, Into its proper vehicle he breathes The fair conception. **1893** *Chicago Advance* 28 Sept., Forceful utterances, promethean in snatching a flame from the very heavens.

†**2.** Applied to a kind of match: see B. 2. *Obs.*

1831 [see LUCIFER 3]. **1845** DARWIN *Voy. Nat.* iii. (1879) 41, I carried with me some promethean matches, which I ignited by biting. **1867** BLOXAM *Chem.* 160 The Promethean light was an ornamented scented paper spill, one end of which contained a small glass bulb of sulphuric acid [etc.].

3. Noting a kind of silkworm: see PROMETHEUS 2.

B. *sb.* **1.** A person likened to Prometheus.

1857 BIRCH *Anc. Pottery* (1858) II. 43 By the Athenians, potters were called prometheans [Προμηθέες], from the Titan Prometheus, who made man out of clay.

†**2.** A contrivance used, before the introduction of phosphorus or lucifer matches, for obtaining a light readily: see quots. *Obs.*

1842 BRANDE *Dict. Sci.* etc., *Prometheans*, a term applied to small glass tubes containing concentrated sulphuric acid, and surrounded with an inflammable mixture, which they ignite on being pressed, and thereby give instantaneous light. **1858** SIMMONDS *Dict. Trade*, *Promethean*, a lucifer match. **1889** TIDY *Story of Tinder Box* 28 In the year 1828 'Prometheans' were invented. They consisted of a small quantity of Chlorate of Potash, and Sugar, rolled up tightly in a piece of paper. Inside the paper-roll is placed a small sealed glass-bubble containing Sulphuric Acid. On breaking the bulb the mixture fired igniting the paper-roll.

Prometheanism (prəʊ'miːθiːənɪz(ə)m). [f. PROMETHEAN *a.* + -ISM.] Conduct or policy resembling that traditionally ascribed to Prometheus.

1957 N. FRYE *Anat. Crit.* 157 Patterns of the 'Romantic agony', chiefly sadism, Prometheanism. **1976** M. J. LASKY *Utopia & Revolution* (1977) xi. 412 He [*sc.* Locke] disdained the incendiaries of the age with their fiery images, and deplored the whole tradition of Prometheanism.

Prome'theically, *adv. nonce-wd.* [f. next + -IC + -AL¹ + -LY².] In the manner of Prometheus.

1816 T. TAYLOR in *Pamphleteer* VIII. 57 She is bound in body Prometheically and Titanically.

Prometheus (prəʊ'miːθɪuːs). [L. *Promētheus*, Gr. Προμηθεύς.]

1. *Gr. Myth.* Name of a demigod (son of the Titan Iapetus), who was fabled to have made man out of clay, and to have stolen fire from Olympus, and taught men the use of it and various arts, for which he was punished by Zeus by being chained to a rock in the Caucasus where his liver was preyed upon every day by a vulture. Hence used allusively.

1588 SHAKS. *Tit. A.* II. i. 17 Faster bound to Aarons charming eyes, Then is Prometheus ti'de to Caucasus. **1595** PEELE *Anglorum Feriæ* 180 Like Prometheus' life-infusing fire. **1711** SHAFTESB. *Charac.* (1737) II. 205 This..made me think of the manner of our modern Prometheus's, the mountebanks. **1819** SHELLEY *Prometh. Unb.* I. 445 Prometheus, the chained Titan.

2. *Entom.* **a.** = PROMETHEA. **b.** Hübner's name, 1826, for a genus of Hesperian butterflies, otherwise called *Castnia*.

1889 in *Cent. Dict.* **1972** SWAN & PAPP *Common Insects N. Amer.* 265 Efforts to reel or card the fibers of the Prometheus and Polyphemus cocoons have not been successful.

3. *Ornith.* An American species of warbler.

1884 COUES *Key N. Amer. Birds* (ed. 2) 302 *D[endrœca] blackburniæ*... Blackburn's Warbler. Prometheus... Chin, throat, and fore breast, intense orange or flame-color.

promethium (prəʊ'miːθɪəm). *Chem.* orig. **-eum**. [mod.L.: see PROMETHEUS and -IUM.] An artificially produced metallic element (traces of which have subsequently been found in nature) which is a lanthanide whose longest-lived isotope has a half-life of about 18 years. Atomic number 61; symbol Pm. Cf. ILLINIUM.

1948 MARINSKY & GLENDENIN in *Chem. & Engin. News* 9 Aug. 2348/2 We propose, therefore, the name 'prometheum' (symbol Pm) for element 61 after Prometheus,..who stole fire from heaven for the use of mankind... This name..symbolizes the dramatic way in which the element may be produced in quantity as a result of man's harnessing of the energy of nuclear fission. **1949** *Sun* (Baltimore) 22 Sept. 21/4 An element 500 times 'hotter' than radium is being studied... It is promethium, one of the rare earth metals. **1955** T. D. O'BRIEN et al. in Sneed & Brasted *Comprehensive Inorg. Chem.* IV. vi. 184 Promethium comes between neodymium and samarium in the lanthanide series. It has an oxidation number of + 3 and possibly + 4. **1959** SEABORG & VALENS *Elements of Universe* 126 Promethium was discovered as a result of its artificial production in the atomic reactor. *Ibid.*, Promethium nitrate is a rather undistinguished-looking powder. **1976** COTTON & WILKINSON *Basic Inorg. Chem.* xxvi. 450 Promethium occurs only in traces in U ores as a spontaneous fission fragment of ^{238}U. Milligram quantities of pink $^{147}Pm^{3+}$ salt can be isolated..from fission products in spent fuel of nuclear reactors.

prometryne ('prəʊmətraɪn). *Agric.* Also **-tryn** (-trɪn). [f. PRO(PYL + ME(THYL + *-tryne* (f. TRI(AZI)NE).] A herbicide, 2,4-bis(isopropylamino)-6-methylthio-1,3,5-triazine, $C_{10}H_{19}N_5S$, which is usu. employed in the form of a wettable powder against annual grasses and broad-leaved weeds.

1961 *B.S.I. News* July 28 Common names for pesticides... Prometryne. 4,6-bisisopropylamino-2-methylthio-1,3,5-triazine. **1968** *Weed Control* (Nat. Acad. Sci., Washington) x. 181 Prometryne..has..a melting point of 118°C, and a solubility of 48 ppm in water. It is highly soluble in many organic solvents. **1971** *Arable Farmer* Feb. 15/3 Resistance of..peas to prometryne..occurs as a result of such metabolic conversions within the plant. **1976** J. R. PLIMMER in Kearney & Kaufman *Herbicides* (ed. 2) II. xix. 925 Granular formations of prometryn did not cause vapor damage to cotton plants exposed to their vapor.

promette: see PROMIT *v.*

Promin ('prəʊmɪn). *Pharm.* Also **promin**. A proprietary name in the U.S. for a glucoside derivative of 4,4'-diaminodiphenyl sulphone, $C_{12}H_{12}N_2O_2S$, which has a bacteriostatic action and has been used esp. to treat leprosy.

1937 *Official Gaz.* (U.S. Patent Office) 29 June 1008/2 Parke, Davis & Company, Detroit... *Promin.* For p-amino-benzene-sulfonamide used in treatment of streptococcic infections. Claims use since April 16, 1937. **1939** *Canad. Med. Assoc. Jrnl.* XL. 319/1 The following compounds have been investigated: p-aminobenzene sulphonamide (sulphanilamide),..a glucoside derivative of 4:4' diamino diphenyl sulphone (promin). **1948** *Call-Bulletin* (San Francisco) 12 Apr. 3/6 Diasone and two companion drugs, promin and promizole, have shown promise against both tuberculosis and leprosy but they have some disadvantages. **1958** *New Scientist* 11 Sept. 798/2 Eventually it was found by Dr. John Lowe in 1948 that the simpler parent compound—diamino diphenyl sulphone ..(now called dapsone) was more active than promin. **1971** W. H. JOPLING *Handbk. Leprosy* vi. 52 Dapsone..had the advantage over Promin of being much cheaper and of being suitable for oral administration (Promin has to be given intravenously).

prominence ('prɒmɪnəns), *sb.* [a. obs. F. *prominence* (16th c. in Hatz.-Darm.), ad. L. *prōminentia* a jutting out, projection: see PROMINENT and -ENCE.]

1. The fact or condition of being prominent.

1611 COTGR., *Prominence*, a prominence; a standing, iutting, or strouting, out. **1656** in BLOUNT *Glossogr.* **1781** COWPER *Conversation* 125 His evidence,..For want of prominence and just relief, Would hang an honest man, and save a thief. **1860** TYNDALL *Glac.* I. ix. 61 Hiding by its prominence everything that might exist behind it.

2. a. That which is prominent; a projection, protuberance.

1598 FLORIO, *Prominentia*, the extending or iutting of a thing out or ouer. Also a penthouse, a prominence, by which word the Anatomists vnderstand what portion soeuer doth notably surmount the parts circumiacent in thicknes. **1681** tr. *Willis' Rem. Med. Wks.* Vocab., *Prominences*, bunchings forth, those parts that notably shew themselves above the rest, as a hill in a plain. **1865** GEIKIE *Scen. & Geol. Scot.* vii. 154 Descending into the hollows and mounting over the prominences of the rock.

b. ***solar prominence***, a projecting cloud of incandescent hydrogen, etc., above the chromosphere of the sun, best seen during an eclipse. Also *attrib.* and *Comb.*, as ***prominence-jet***, ***-spectrum***.

1871 tr. *Schellen's Spectr. Anal.* liii. 250 No bright lines were seen by Young at this prominence-spectrum. **1893** *Photogr. Ann.* 167 Reversals do not extend above the chromosphere, except in prominences; and he has not as yet obtained any prominence with the calcium lines unaccompanied by hydrogen, and corresponding to the white prominences observed at eclipses... Mr. Evershed obtained satisfactory prominence pictures, using the red hydrogen line. **1903** AGNES M. CLERKE *Astrophysics* 118 Professor Hale's daylight photographs of prominence-spectra. *Ibid.* 125 Nebular tufts, no less than prominence-jets, are resolvable into fibres.

3. a. The quality or state of being conspicuous; distinction, notoriety, conspicuousness.

1828–32 WEBSTER, *Prominence, prominency*.. conspicuousness, distinction. **1864** PUSEY *Lect. Daniel* (1876) 492 The prophet thereby gives prominence to the seeming contradiction. **1872** MORLEY *Voltaire* i. (1886) 3 Luther and Calvin.. brought into splendid prominence their new ideas of moral order. **1874** STUBBS *Const. Hist.* I. xiii. 594 Its importance comes into historical prominence.

b. *Phonetics.* The degree to which a sound or syllable stands out from its phonetic environment.

1929 I. C. WARD *Phonetics of Eng.* xiv. 135 The effect of prominence is produced by the very intimate combination of length, stress, pitch, and inherent sonority of sounds. **1949** C. E. BAZELL in *Travaux du Cercle Linguistique de Copenhague* V. 83 When two features.. are simultaneous in overt order, no distinctions of prominence (e.g. syllabic/asyllabic) can be made. **1950** D. JONES *Phoneme* 137 Prominence is an effect perceived objectively by the hearer. It is thus quite a different thing from stress which is a subjective activity on the part of the speaker. *Ibid.* 144 It is a natural tendency of English people and speakers of other stress languages to attribute all prominences to stress alone. **1962** A. C. GIMSON *Introd. Pronunc. Eng.* 219 Among the vowels prominence increases as the vowel becomes more open. *Ibid.* 221 Sound qualities also contribute to an impression of prominence but mainly through the characteristic relationship of certain qualities with unaccented syllables and others with accented syllables. **1973** *Word 1970* XXVI. 62 Not every syllable given accentual prominence in the sentence is a rhythmic accent with temporal prominence.

4. a. Any conspicuous or salient point or matter. **b.** A prominent personage (*newspaper slang*).

1827 HONE *Every-day Bk.* II. 467 These are prominences seized by his whole audiences. **1855** BREWSTER *Newton* II. xxvii. 399 He bore down with instinctive sagacity on the prominences of his subject. **1887** *Pall Mall G.* 7 Sept. 5/2 All the prominences—aristocrats, musicians, men of letters, .. &c.—sat down to a sumptuous collation.

Hence **'prominence** *v.*, to bring into prominence.

1897 T. RHONDDA WILLIAMS *Serm. on 'Just as I am'* 4 Jesus emphasized and prominenced in one life and death what God is ever doing.

prominency ('prɒmɪnənsɪ). [ad. L. *prōminēntia*: see prec. and -ENCY.]

1. = PROMINENCE 2. Now *rare.*

1645 EVELYN *Diary* 7 Feb., A perpendicular hollow cliffe .. with now and then a craggy prominency jetting out. **1703** MOXON *Mech. Exerc.* 183 Cut off the prominencies that are not concentrick to the Axis. **1813** *Examiner* 29 Mar. 205/1 All obtrusive prominencies are levelled down.

2. The quality of being prominent (*lit.* or *fig.*); conspicuousness; = PROMINENCE 1, 3.

1828–32 [see PROMINENCE 3]. **1836** *Rand. Recoll. Ho. Lords* xi. 241 Brought before the public.. with some degree of prominency. **1842** F. E. PAGET *Milf. Malv.* 203 Nobody could say that he did not give sufficient prominency to every doctrine in the circle of Christian truth. **1871** BLACKIE *Four Phases* i. 12 The prominency of.. his organs of vision.

prominent ('prɒmɪnənt), *a.* (*sb.*). [ad. L. *prōminēns, -ēnt-em*, pres. pple. of *prōmin-ēre* to jut out; f. *prō*, PRO-[1] + **minēre*, f. root of *minæ* projecting points or pinnacles, hence threats. Cf. F. *prominent* (16th c.) and EMINENT, IMMINENT.]

A. *adj.* **1.** Jutting or standing out above or beyond the adjacent surface; projecting, protuberant.

1545 JOYE *Exp. Dan.* viii. 129 b, That prominent great horne of the Gote in his most strength broken of. **1646** SIR T. BROWNE *Pseud. Ep.* 261 In the picture of Jonah.. Whales are described with two prominent spouts on their heads. **1721** BRADLEY *Philos. Acc. Wks. Nat.* 55 The Eyes of the Crab are more prominent from the Body than those of Lobsters. **1826** KIRBY & SP. *Entomol.* IV. 305 *Prominent*, when the head is in the horizontal line, and forms no angle with the trunk. **1834** MRS. SOMERVILLE *Connex. Phys. Sc.* i. (1849) 8 The prominent mass at the terrestrial equator. **1870** ROLLESTON *Anim. Life* 119 An orifice with prominent tumid lips.

2. a. Standing out so as to strike the eye; conspicuous.

1759 JOHNSON *Rasselas* x, To exhibit in his portraits of Nature such prominent and striking features, as recall the original to every mind. **1883** W. GARDNER in *Science Gossip* May 99 The most prominent object was a mountain on the other side of the valley, composed of three peaks.

b. *fig.* Standing out so as to strike the attention or notice; conspicuous; distinguished above others.

1849 MACAULAY *Hist. Eng.* ii. I. 200 Attachment to France had been prominent among the crimes imputed by the Commons to Clarendon. **1850** ROBERTSON *Serm.* Ser. III. viii. 111 God is there, accordingly self is less prominent. **1885** CLODD *Myths & Dr.* I. vi. 113 Ancestor-worship.. was the prominent feature of the old Aryan religion.

B. *sb.* †**1. a.** A protruding or projecting part; a prominence, an eminence. *Obs. rare.*

c **1611** CHAPMAN *Iliad* XI. 624 A certain city shines Upon a lofty prominent. *Ibid.* XII. 291 Till highest prominents, Hill tops, low meddows, and the fields.. are hid.

b. A prominent person. Now *N. Amer.*

1608 CHAPMAN *Byron's Trag.* v. i. Plays 1873 II. 313 *Byr.* Where shall this weight fall? on what region Must this declining prominent pour his lode? **1948** *Sun* (Baltimore) 19 June 3/2 Hillcrest Country Club, a favorite among movie prominents, was blown up today by an accumulation of gas. **1975** *Maclean's Mag.* (Toronto) 15 Dec. 62/2 Several prominents such as John Diefenbaker and Joey Smallwood pushed for a reprieve.

2. *Entom.* Collectors' name for Cuspidate moths of the genus *Notodonta*, containing many species, European and American.

1819 SAMOUELLE *Entomol. Compend.* 418 Notodonta tritopha. The great Prominent. **1832** RENNIE *Conspect. Butterfl. & M.* 35 The Pale Prominent. **1869** E. NEWMAN *Brit. Moths* 225–231 The Coxcomb Prominent,.. Maple Prominent,.. Scarce Prominent,.. White Prominent,.. Swallow Prominent [etc.]. *Mod.* The Marbled Browns belong to the same genus as the Prominents.

C. *Comb.*, as ***prominent-eyed, -nosed***, etc.

1895 S. S. BUCKMAN in *Pop. Sci. Monthly* Jan. 372 The small-jawed, long and prominent-nosed individual. **1903** *Daily Mail* 10 Sept. 2/7 The narrow-chested, the fat, the flabby, the prominent-eyed.

prominently ('prɒmɪnəntlɪ), *adv.* [f. prec. + -LY[2].]

In a prominent manner or degree. **a.** Projectingly, protrudingly. *rare.* **b.** Conspicuously, eminently.

1645 EVELYN *Diary* 23 Feb., We came to Justinian's gardens,.. so prominently built as threatning every moment to fall. **1794** SULLIVAN *View Nat.* II. 177 In Africa, how prominently they appear. **1843** BETHUNE *Sc. Fireside Stor.* 16 To bring the simple elegance of her form more prominently into view. **1883** E. B. TYLOR in *Nature* 3 May 8/2 A consideration I wish to bring prominently forward. **1885** J. K. JEROME *On the Stage* 37 All the parts were torn and greasy, except one, which was prominently clean.

So **'prominentness** (Bailey vol. II, 1727).

pro'minulous, *a.* [f. L. *prōminul-us* rather prominent + -OUS.] Slightly prominent.

1819 SAMOUELLE *Entomol. Compend.* 201 Prominulous eyes. **1858** MAYNE *Expos. Lex.*, *Prominulus*.. applied by Haüy to a crystal having ridges upon its surface, which form a very slight prominence: prominulous.

promisable ('prɒmɪsəb(ə)l), *a. rare.* [f. PROMISE *v.* + -ABLE.] That can be promised.

1796 BENTHAM *Mem. & Corr.* Wks. 1843 X. 314 Should some prosperous and scarce promisable turn in the wheel of fortune transform.. the shoulder into a leg.

pro'miscous, *a. rare*; now only *dial.* or *vulgar.* [f. L. *prōmisc-us* (collateral form of *prōmiscu-us* PROMISCUOUS) + -OUS.] = PROMISCUOUS.

1701 *Stanley's Hist. Philos.*, *Biog.* 12 The Eastern Learning was not taught in Schools to a promiscous Audience. **1903** *Eng. Dial. Dict.* s.v., He came in quite promiscous like. (E. Kent.)

Hence †**pro'miscously** *adv.* = PROMISCUOUSLY.

1635 R. CAREW in *Lismore Papers* Ser. II. (1888) III. 218 In the hall.. they sitt permiscously, not obsereuing of place or qualitie. **1678** SIR G. MACKENZIE *Crim. Laws Scot.* I. xvii. §4 (1699) 88 That absurd custom amongst Tinkers, of living promiscously.

†**pro'miscual**, *a. Obs. rare.* [f. L. *prōmiscu-us* PROMISCUOUS + -AL[1].] = PROMISCUOUS.

1604 PARSONS *3rd Pt. Three Convers. Eng.* 98 They seeme .. to haue permitted promiscuall copulation. **1610** HEALEY *St. Aug. Citie of God* III. xxv. (1620) 135 Yet worshipping those promiscuall gods they cannot.. cleare themselues of this question of Concord and Discord.

Hence †**pro'miscually** *adv.*, promiscuously. *Obs.*

1600 W. WATSON *Decacordon* (1602) 135 They proceeded .. to draw great persons, Nobles, Honours and Graces promiscually vnto them. **1610** HEALEY *St. Aug. Citie of God* 233 This he giveth promiscually to good and bad.

promiscuity (prɒmɪ'skjuːɪtɪ). [ad. F. *promiscuité* (1752 in Hatz.-Darm.), f. L. *prōmiscu-us* (see next) + *-ité*, -ITY.]

1. The condition of being promiscuous; indiscriminate mixture, confusion; promiscuousness.

a **1849** POE *Marginalia* lxxv, The God-abstractions of the modern polytheism are nearly in as sad a state of perplexity and promiscuity as were the more substantial deities of the Greeks. **1868** W. R. GREG *Lit. & Soc. Judgm.* 84 Men, women, and children huddled together in dirt, disorder, and promiscuity like that of the lower animals. **1894** *Queen* 8 Dec. 1036/2 The average Continental traveller likes a crowd, chatter, promiscuity of acquaintanceship.

2. Promiscuous sexual union.

1865 MCLENNAN *Prim. Marriage* viii. 160 Promiscuity in the connexion of the sexes. **1876** H. SPENCER *Princ. Sociol.* (1877) I. 672 Promiscuity may be called indefinite polyandry, joined with polygyny. **1900** A. LANG *Hist. Scot.* I. i. 5 The natives.. were in stages of culture which are not usually found associated with promiscuity or polyandry.

fig. **1895** SAINTSBURY *Ess. Eng. Lit.* Ser. II. 101 The adjective wedded to its proper substantive, not indulging in unseemly promiscuity.

promiscuous (prəʊ'mɪskjuːəs), *a.* [f. L. *prōmiscu-us* mixed, indiscriminate, in Gram. epicene (f. *prō*, PRO-[1] + *miscēre* to mix) + -OUS. Cf. late L. *prōmiscēre* to mix up.]

1. a. Consisting of members or elements of different kinds grouped or massed together without order; of mixed and disorderly composition or character; also, with *pl. sb.*, of various kinds mixed together.

1603 KNOLLES *Hist. Turks* 283 About them.. the promiscuous common people, doubling and redoubling the praises of the King, and Huniades. **1621** BURTON *Anat. Mel.* Democr. to Rdr. 20 Hee told him that hee saw a vast multitude and a promiscuous. **1667** MILTON *P.L.* I. 380 While the promiscuous croud stood yet aloof. **1692** BENTLEY *Boyle Lect.* ii. 41 The Apostle who was to speak to such a promiscuous Assembly. **1752** HUME *Ess. & Treat.* (1777) I. 222 The characters of nations are very promiscuous in the temperate climates. **1830** LYELL *Princ. Geol.* (1875) I. I. iii. 46 He conceived the strata to have settled down from this promiscuous mass. **1875** HELPS *Soc. Press.* xx. 291 What Milverton contemptuously would call our miscellaneous and promiscuous essays.

b. Rarely of a single thing.

1663 BUTLER *Hud.* I. i. 99 It had an odd promiscuous Tone, As if h' had talk'd three Parts in one. **1711** POPE *Temp. Fame* 22 Sudden I heard a wild promiscuous sound.

2. a. That is without discrimination or method; done or applied without respect for kind, order, number, etc.; confusedly mingled, indiscriminate.

1605 BACON *Adv. Learn.* II. vii. §3 Axioms which are promiscuous and indifferent to several sciences. **1650** HOBBES *De Corp. Pol.* 179 To forbid the promiscuous Use of Women. **1678** R. L'ESTRANGE *Seneca's Mor.* (1776) 334 The common and promiscuous lot both of good men and bad. **1751** JOHNSON *Rambler* No. 144 ¶9 Secrets are not to be made cheap by promiscuous publication. **1772**—— 31 Mar. in *Boswell*, Promiscuous hospitality is not the way to gain real influence. **1816** SCOTT *Old Mort.* ii, The profane custom of promiscuous dancing—that is, of men and women dancing together in the same party. **1853** J. H. NEWMAN *Hist. Sk.* (1873) II. I. ii. 28 At Metz he [Attila] involved in one promiscuous massacre priests and children.

b. Of an agent or agency: Making no distinctions; undiscriminating. Now esp.: indiscriminate in sexual relations (cf. PROMISCUITY 2).

1633 E. PORTER in *Donne's Poems* 405 Why should death, with a promiscuous hand, At one rude stroke impoverish a land? **1688** R. HOLME *Armoury* II. 310/1 Promiscuous Birds .. feed on Flesh, Insects, Fruit, or Grain, as the Raven. *a* **1763** SHENSTONE *Ess.* vi. (1765) 21 A well-discriminated landscape was.. to be preferred to a distant and promiscuous azure. **1900** A. LANG *Hist. Scot.* I. i. 5 People ..still polyandrous or promiscuous in the relation of the sexes. **1924** C. CONNOLLY *Let.* Dec. in *Romantic Friendship* (1975) 32, I am not promiscuous but I can't be loyal to an icicle. **1937** A. HUXLEY *Let.* 17 Dec. (1969) 430 Where it is 'done' to attach a great deal of importance to the achievement of promiscuous satisfaction.. there.. will the amount of attention given to other matters decline. **1949** *Times Lit. Suppl.* 21 Oct. 680/2 She was promiscuous in her favours, and did not at once become his alone. **1955** G. GREENE *Quiet American* II. ii. 130 One starts promiscuous and ends like one's grandfather, faithful to one woman. **1978** S. HERZEL in P. Moore *Man, Woman, & Priesthood* viii. 119 It is precisely because men *can* compartmentalize that they are more easily promiscuous than women.

3. Of common gender; epicene. *rare.*

a **1628–32** B. JONSON *Eng. Gram.* I. x, The promiscuous, or epicene, which understands both kinds. **1878** VILLARI *Life & Times Machiavelli* (1898) I. III. vii. 130 There were three sexes, male, female and promiscuous.

†**4.** That forms part of a promiscuous or mingled company; hence (*slang*), a term of depreciation or contempt. *Obs.*

1753 SMOLLETT *Cnt. Fathom* (1813) I. 162 One may see with half an eye that he is no better than a promiscuous fellow. **1785** CRABBE *Newspaper* 233 This, like the public inn, provides a treat, Where each promiscuous guest sits down to eat. **1889** GRETTON *Memory's Harkb.* 58 'Go back to bed, you promiscuous old bird!' 'Promiscuous' was just then a term in slang use.

5. Casual, carelessly irregular. *vulgar* or *colloq.*

1837 DICKENS *Pickw.* xxxiv, I walked in.. just to say good mornin', and went, in a permiscuous manner, up-stairs, and into the back room. **1883** L. OLIPHANT *Altiora Peto* I. 5 On the beach, where he will, in the most promiscuous and accidental manner, certainly go for a stroll.

6. quasi-*adv.* **a.** = PROMISCUOUSLY 1.

1671 MILTON *P.R.* III. 118 Glory he receives Promiscuous from all Nations, Jew, or Greek. **1695** ADDISON *King* 110 And Planks, and Arms, and Men promiscuous flow'd. **1747** FRANCIS tr. *Horace, Sat.* II. ii. 99 Roast, and boil'd, when you promiscuous eat, When fowl and shell-fish in confusion meet. **1813** SHELLEY *Q. Mab* II. 153 Old age and infancy Promiscuous perished.

b. = PROMISCUOUSLY 2. *vulgar.*

1826 DISRAELI *Vivian Grey* II. xii. 170, I do wish you'd come in some day quite promiscuous. **1827** *Ibid.* III. viii. 115 It's remarkable wrong to tax 'em all promiscuous. **1875** SWINBURNE *Let.* 5 Nov. (1960) III. 82 It turned up promiscuous when at last wanted after ten years. **1885** G. ALLEN *Babylon* xiv, Colin only kissed her now and again quite promiscuous like. **1901** A. FORBES *Odd Fish* 92 You get a barrel o' the reds, and send it aboard just permiscuous like.

promiscuously (prəʊ'mɪskjuːəslɪ), *adv.* [f. prec. + -LY[2].]

1. In a promiscuous manner; without distinction, discrimination, or order; indiscriminately; at random, in confusion.

1610 HOLLAND *Camden's Brit.* (1637) 100 These [coins] passed promiscuously as mony from one to another. **1641** WILKINS *Math. Magick* I. xvii. (1648) 124 Both which names are sometimes used promiscuously. **1693** *Lond. Gaz.* No. 2888/2 The body of their Fleet lay promiscuously to Leeward of one another. **1777** ROBERTSON *Hist. Amer.* (1778) II. v. 119 Horsemen and infantry plunged in promiscuously. **1840** MACAULAY *Ess., Clive* (1887) 542 The dead bodies, a hundred and twenty-three in number, were flung into it promiscuously and covered up.

†**b.** *colloq.* Without 'standing upon the order of one's going'; unceremoniously; promptly. *Obs.*

1609 Rowlands *Knaue of Clubbes* 37, I bad him vanish most Promiscuously, And not Contaminate my company.

2. *colloq.* Casually, incidentally.

1812 *Sporting Mag.* XL. 153 Witness promiscuously found the bottle..amongst some rubbishing things, quite empty. **1843** Mrs. Romer *Rhone, Darro*, etc. II. 300 'Let us go to Africa!' exclaimed a friend of mine quite promiscuously (as the Cockneys have it). **1871** L. Stephen *Playgr. Eur.* 16 The stone was dropped promiscuously by a flying dragon, and picked up by a passing peasant.

pro'miscuousness. *rare.* [f. as prec. + -ness.] The quality or state of being promiscuous; promiscuity.

1727 Bailey vol. II, *Promiscuousness*, mixedness. **1775** in Ash. **1818** in Todd; and in mod. Dicts.

promise ('prɒmɪs), *sb.* Forms: 5-6 **promis, -ys, -isse, -ysse,** 6 **-yse,** 7 **-iss,** 5- **promise.** *β.* 5 **promess,** 5-6 **-es, -esse,** 6-7 *Sc.* **-eis.** [ad. L. *prōmiss-um* a promise, sb. use of neut. pa. pple. of *prōmitt-ĕre*: see promit *v.* The *β* forms represent F. *promesse* (13th c.):—med.L. *prōmissa* a promise.]

1. A declaration or assurance made to another person with respect to the future, stating that one will do, or refrain from, some specified act, or that one will give or bestow some specified thing. (Usually in good sense, implying something to the advantage or pleasure of the person concerned.)

breach of promise: see breach *sb.* 3b.

c **1400** Maundev. (1839) v. 40 No straungere cometh before him, but that he maketh him sum promys and graunt, of that the sowdan asketh. *c* **1430** Lydg. *Min. Poems* (Percy Soc.) 39 This man for trust of femynyne promysse, Wolde telle out alle. *a* **1548** Hall *Chron., Edw. IV* 225 Geuyng them faire wordes, and makyng large promises. ?*a* **1550** *Knt. of Curtesy* 280 His promysse he wil not breke. **1605** Shaks. *Macb.* v. viii. 21 These Iugling Fiends..That keepe the word of promise to our eare, And breake it to our hope. **1613** Purchas *Pilgrimage* (1614) 631 Which Boferes after with like perfidiousnes, and breach of promise, requited on three thousand Marochians. **1768** Blackstone *Comm.* III. ix. 158 A promise is in the nature of a verbal covenant. **1785** Paley *Mor. Philos.* iii. i. v, Promises are not binding, where the performance is unlawful. **1838** W. Bell *Dict. Law Scot.*, *Promise and Offer*... An offerer is not bound until his offer is accepted. A promiser is bound as soon as the promise reaches the party to whom it is made. **1845** Stephen *Comm. Laws Eng.* (1874) II. 55 There is in strictness a distinction between a promise and a contract; for the latter involves the idea of mutuality which the former does not. **1877** Froude *Short Stud.* (1883) IV. i. v. 52 Becket had broken his promise to submit to the Constitutions.

β. *c* **1412** Hoccleve *De Reg. Princ.* 1772 Whanne I þe mette, & sy þin heuynesse, Of comfort, sone, made I þe promesse. *c* **1470** Henry *Wallace* vi. 866 A promes maid to meit Wallace but let. *Ibid.* xi. 947 The tym was past by Off the promess the quhilk at he was bund. **1489** Caxton *Faytes of A.* iv. iv. 238 Hys promesse and affyaunce made. **1530** Palsgr. 258/2 Promesse, *promesse*.

2. a. In religious use: One of the Divine assurances of future good or blessing, recorded in the Scriptures as made to particular persons on various occasions, or conceived as given to mankind through Christ; *spec.* that made to Abraham with respect to his posterity (Gen. xii. 2, etc.).

1502 Atkynson tr. *De Imitatione* iii. xviii. 211 The promes of god. **1526** Tindale *Heb.* vi. 12 Them, which thorow fayth and pacience inheret the promyses. **1567** *Gude & Godlie B.* (S.T.S.) 3 The threitning of God maid to them that brekis his commandementis, and his promeis made to them that keipis them. **1659** T. Allen (*title*) A Chain of Scripture Chronology..in VII periods, viz., From the Creation to the Flood, the Flood to the Promise, the Promise to the Law, the Law to the Temple, the Temple to the Captivity.., the Captivity to the Return, the Return to the Death of Christ. **1707** Watts *Hymn*, '*Begin, my tongue*' ii, Sing the sweet promise of his grace, And the performing God. **1819** Scott *Ivanhoe* xxxii, 'So help me the promise', ..said Isaac,..'as no such sounds ever crossed my lips!'

b. ***land of promise*** (tr. τὴν γῆν τῆς ἐπαγγελίας, Heb. xi. 9): = promised *land*. Also *fig.*

1535 Coverdale *Heb.* xi. 9 By faith was he a straunger in the londe of promes [Wycl. the loond of biheest]. **1662** Stillingfl. *Orig. Sacr.* ii. v. §8 Not..meerly a Covenant for the Land of Promise. **1851** Dixon *W. Penn* xv. (1872) 131 To all these exiled sects America was the land of promise. **1865** J. H. Ingraham *Pillar of Fire* (1872) 570 Their land of heaven is our land of promise also.

c. ***bow of promise***, the rainbow (in allusion to Gen. ix. 12-17).

1827 Sarah E. Miles *Hymn*, '*Thou who didst stoop below*' iii, To see a Father's love Beam, like a bow of promise, through the cloud. **1850** S. Dobell *Roman* viii, Thoughts that shining through To-morrow's tears shall set in our worst cloud The bow of promise.

3. *transf.* The thing promised; *contextually* (with *claim*) = the fulfilment of a promise.

1526 Tindale *1 John* ii. 25 This is the promes that he hath promysed vs, even eternall lyfe. **1594** Shaks. *Rich. III*, iii. i. 197 Ile clayme that promise at your Graces hand. **1646** H. Lawrence *Comm. Angells* 168 They hope to attaine the promise of God, that is, the thing promised. **1864** Tennyson *En. Ard.* 455 He stood once more before her face, Claiming her promise.

4. *fig.* **a.** That which affords a strong or reasonable ground of expectation of something to come, esp. of future good; a pledge, earnest, forerunner, pre-indication (*of* something); something that leads one confidently to expect (good) results.

to give (***afford***, etc.) ***promise***: to afford expectation *of* something, esp. good. ***of great*** (***high***, etc.) ***promise***: such as leads one to expect future excellence; very promising.

c **1532** Du Wes *Introd. Fr.* in *Palsgr.* 922 A gyrle..full of swete promyse. **1599** Shaks. *Much Ado* i. i. 14 A yong Florentine,..He hath borne himselfe beyond the promise of his age. **1697** Dryden *Virg. Past.* iv. 23 Fragrant Herbs (the promises of Spring). **1700** —— *Cymon & Iph.* 329 Like a fiery meteor sunk the sun, The promise of a storm. **1748** Gray *Alliance Educ. & Govt.* 21 The vernal Promise of the Year. **1828** Macaulay *Ess., Hallam* (1887) 55 A historical novel of high merit, and of still higher promise. **1832** Ht. Martineau *Hill & Vall.* i. 16 Remarking on the fine promise of fruit. **1886** E. G. White *Hist. Sk. Foreign Missions Seventh-Day Adventists* 281/2 They should be ready to counsel and instruct those who have newly come to the faith, and who give promise of possessing ability to work for the Master. *a* **1909** *Mod.* This scholarship is given for promise, rather than for attainment. **1919** T. S. Eliot *Poems*, Grishkin is nice..her friendly bust Gives promise of pneumatic bliss. **1971** *Daily Tel.* 17 June 3/3 To police he showed 'promise' of becoming a sophisticated criminal.

†**b.** A mental feeling of assurance. *Obs.*

a **1625** Fletcher *Noble Gent.* iv. iv, I have a constant promise she's my own.

5. *Comb.*, as ***promise-breach, -breaker, -maker, -monger; promise-bound(en, -crammed*** adjs.; ***promise-breaking, -fulfilling, -keeping, -making, -performing*** sbs. and adjs.

a **1548** Hall *Chron., Hen. VI* 133b, He, which is a promise breaker, escapeth not alwaie free. **1592** Nashe *P. Penilesse* Wks. (Grosart) II. 10, I am quite vndone through promise-breach. **1602** Shaks. *Ham.* iii. ii. 99, I eate the Ayre promise-cramm'd, you cannot feed Capons so. **1603** —— *Meas. for M.* i. ii. 77 He was euer precise in promise keeping. *a* **1639** W. Whateley *Prototypes* ii. xxvi. (1640) 48 A thankfull receiving of Gods promises..proveth faith to the promise-maker. **1771** Wesley *Wks.* (1872) VI. 85 It is hard to speak of..these promise-mongers, as they deserve. **1772** Fletcher *Logica Genev.* 160 A merciful, gracious promise-keeping God. **1813** Scott *Trierm.* ii. xx, As promise-bound, I bid the trump for tourney sound. **1842** Dickens *Let.* 22 Mar. (1974) III. 146 You..have set me down, I know, as a neglectful, erratic, promise-breaking and most unworthy person. **1849** Macaulay *Hist. Eng.* vi. II. 11 If..he had also turned dissembler and promise-breaker. **1864** Tennyson *En. Ard.* 835 Awed and promise-bounden she forbore. **1940** *Mind* XLIX. 231 Utilitarians have tended rather to over-estimate the disastrous consequences of promise-breaking. *a* **1974** R. Crossman *Diaries* (1975) I. 249 From the point of view of the electorate this technical promise-keeping is quite unimportant.

promise ('prɒmɪs), *v.* Forms: see prec. [Appears early in 15th c.; f. prec. sb.]

1. *trans.* To make promise of; to give verbal assurance of; to undertake or engage, by word or writing addressed to another person, to do or refrain from (some specified act), or to give or bestow (some specified thing): usually to the benefit or advantage of the person concerned. Often with dative (with or without *to*) of the person to whom the promise is made. **a.** with simple direct object, expressing the thing or act promised.

c **1420** ? Lydg. *Assembly of Gods* 227 Oon thyng suerly I will yow promyse. ?*a* **1500** *Chester Pl.* xiii. 6 Vnto whom I was promised, before the world began, to pay ther ransome and to become man. **1508** Fisher *7 Penit. Ps.* xxxii. Wks. (1876) 23 He promyseth dampnacion to them that refuseth penaunce; to them that dooth it, forgyvnes. **1548-9** (Mar.) *Bk. Com. Prayer, Catechism*, They did promise and vowe three thinges in my name. **1611** Shaks. *Wint. T.* iv. iv. 237, I was promis'd them against the Feast. **1736** Butler *Anal.* i. iii. Wks. 1874 I. 69 The wonderful power and prosperity promised to the Jewish nation in the Scripture. **1802** Mar. Edgeworth *Moral T.* (1816) I. xii. 97 She would not promise what..she could not perform. **1872** Freeman *Gen. Sketch* xvi. §5. 335 All the princes promised free constitutions to their people.

b. with obj. clause, expressing the act.

c **1420** ? Lydg. *Assembly of Gods* 482 Ye me promysyd That my myght of noon shuld haue be dyspysyd. **1470-85** Malory *Arthur* x. lix. 515, I promyse yow that I shalle be with yow by that day, yf I be vnslayne or vnmaymed. **1548-9** (Mar.) *Bk. Com. Prayer, Catechism*, Your Godfathers and Godmothers dyd promyse for you that ye should kepe Goddes commaundementes. **1690** Dryden *Don Sebastian* Pref., I dare boldly promise for this Play, that in the Roughness of the Numbers..you will see somewhat more masterly..than in..any of my former Tragedies. **1726** Swift *Gulliver* ii. viii, I made him promise he would come to see me at my house. **1864** Tennyson *Aylmer's Field* 417 Him..she promised that no force, Persuasion, no, nor death could alter her.

c. with inf., expressing the act.

1467 *Mann. & Househ. Exp.* (Roxb.) 558 [The parker] hathe promessed me to make it as wel as he kane fore me. *a* **1548** Hall *Chron., Edw. IV* 228 The Constable had promised to the kyng and the duke, to render vp to them the towne of sainct Quintynes. **1603** Shaks. *Meas. for M.* i. ii. 75 He promis'd to meete me two howres since. **1737** Pope *Hor. Epist.* ii. i. 178 When..we..promise our best Friends to rhyme no more. **1848** Thackeray *Van. Fair* xli, The Baronet promised to take charge of the lad at school.

2. *absol.* or *intr.* To make a promise; to engage to do or give something. In quot. 1869, to undertake responsibility, stand sponsor *for* another.

1447 Bokenham *Seyntys* (Roxb.) 26 Now haf I acomplysyd Brefly, lych as I you promysyd In the prologe. *a* **1533** Ld. Berners *Huon* lxxxiv. 266 Desyre hym to render to you your londes as he promysyd. **1651** Hobbes *Leviath.* ii. xx. 102 He that promiseth, hath no right in the thing promised. **1716** *Wodrow Corr.* (1843) II. 145, I cannot promise upon this so very soon, we having much public business. **1777** Burns '*I dream'd I lay*' ii, Fickle fortune..promis'd fair, and perform'd but ill. **1842** Tennyson *Dora* 44 Dora promised, being meek. **1869** —— *Pelleas & Ettarre* 15 There were those who knew him near the King And promised for him: and Arthur made him knight.

3. a. *spec.* (*trans.*) To engage to give (e.g. a daughter) in marriage to another; to betroth. ***to be promised***, to be engaged or betrothed. *arch.*

a **1548** Hall *Chron., Hen. VII* 60 The lady Mary..was promysed to kyng Charles. *a* **1553** Udall *Royster D.* iii. ii. (Arb.) 42 Haue you he will (he sayth) and haue you he must. *C. Custance.* I am promised duryng my lyfe, that is iust. **1596** Shaks. *Tam. Shr.* i. ii. 262 Her father..will not promise her to any man, Vntill the elder sister first be wed. **1738** Swift *Pol. Conversat.* i. 35 If she ben't marry'd, at least she's lustily promis'd. **1904** L. T. Meade *Love Triumphant* ii. ix. 192 If anything could induce me to promise myself to a man..it would be to Cedric Vershoyle. **1967** C. Potok *Chosen* xii. 200 My father promised my sister to the son of one of his followers when she was two years old.

†**b.** *pass.* To be engaged; to have an engagement. *Obs.*

1601 Shaks. *Jul. C.* i. ii. 293 *Cassi.* Will you suppe with me to Night, Caska? *Cask.* No, I am promis'd forth.

4. ***to promise oneself*** (something): to entertain the (pleasing) expectation of. Const. as in 1 a, b, c.

1617 Moryson *Itin.* i. 42 Nothing were more pleasant..then Sea-voyages, if a man might promise himselfe a good wind, and a reasonable gale. **1639** N. N. tr. *Du Bosq's Compl. Woman* i. 21 There are some who promise to themselves, never to discover their secrets. **1746** *Col. Rec. Pennsylv.* V. 45, I promise myself that you will proceed to some less exceptionable Method. **1832** Ht. Martineau *Each & All* iv. 53 She ran out, promising herself that she would be back in ten minutes. **1869** 'Mark Twain' *Innoc. Abr.* xii, We..promised ourselves that we would call around some time.., and finish the game.

5. *colloq.* With *obj. cl.* or *parenthetically*, and with *dat.* of person: To convey assurance of some fact, to assert confidently or emphatically, to declare; almost always in phrase ***I promise you*** = I assure you, I tell you plainly.

a. with reference to the future, as a strong assertion of one's intention. (Nearly coinciding with 1 b, but often implying a threat of something disadvantageous or unpleasant.)

c **1440** *Generydes* 1603 Thu shalt dye to morow.., And what that euer be..That wolle for the entrete.., He shall not spede I yow promysse. **1538** Starkey *England* i. i. 25, I promys you I schal neuer pretermyt occasyon..of helpyng my cuntrey. **1777** Dibdin *Quaker* i. i, You wont get a lamb out of our fold, I promise you. **1825** Thirlwall tr. *Tieck's Pictures* 80 Well, I promise you, you shall find I do not come again.

b. in assurance of a statement as to the present. (Cf. expect *v.* 6.)

1469 J. Paston in *P. Lett.* II. 349 He losythe sore hys tyme her, I promyse yow. **1535** in *Lett. Suppress. Monasteries* (Camden) 74 The comyssioners, I promyse you, have been very necligent. **1599** Shaks. *Much Ado* iv. ii. 47, I do not like thy looke I promise thee. **1655** tr. *Com. Hist. Francion* xii. 37 The Nights, I promise you, are very cold. **1705** Addison *Italy* (1733) 211 For, I promise, I long for it. **1749** Fielding *Tom Jones* xviii. i, I promise thee it is what I have desired. **1841** F. E. Paget *Tales of Village* (1852) 466, I promise you I'm preciously tired already. **1862** Thackeray *Round. Papers, Peal of Bells*, Magnificent dandies, I promise you, some of us were. **1963** J. Kennaway *Bells of Shoreditch* i. i. 12 He said, 'I promise you, you're looking very well.' **1969** [see ghastly *a.* 1 b].

6. *fig.* **a.** To afford ground of expectation of; to cause or lead one to expect (something good or bad); to give pre-indication of. Const. as in 1 a or c.

1594 ? Greene *Selimus* 1102 My life forepassed in Pleasure's court Promises weak resistance in the fight. **1617** Moryson *Itin.* i. 3 The houses promise more beauty outwardly then they haue inwardly. **1665** Sir T. Herbert *Trav.* (1677) 125 Berry is a Village which promises much at a distance, but when there, deludes the expectation. **1722** De Foe *Col. Jack* (1840) 4 He..promised to be stout when grown up. **1832** Ht. Martineau *Life in Wilds* v. 56 A plan ..which promised fair to supply the butcher with employment. **1855** Tennyson *Maud* i. i. xvii, I play'd with the girl when a child; she promised then to be fair. **1878** H. H. Gibbs *Ombre* 25 If his own hand be such as not to promise him at least two or even three tricks. **1891** *Law Times* XC. 459/2 An atmosphere of public discussion which promises future storms.

b. *absol.* or *intr.* To encourage expectation, to give tokens: usually with adv., as *fair, well.*

1601 Shaks. *All's Well* ii. i. 146 Oft expectation fails, and most oft there Where most it promises. **1686** tr. *Chardin's Coronat. Solyman* 88 The Harvest..promis'd no better then the last year. **1687** A. Lovell tr. *Thevenot's Trav.* i. 14 The weather promising fair. **1768** J. Byron *Narr. Patagonia* (1778) 153 He promised the fairest for holding out, being a very strong young man. **1847** Marryat *Childr. N. Forest* iv, Humphrey, the second, promised well. **1887** Gissing *Thyrza* I. ii. 29 It promises for another fine day to-morrow.

promised ('prɒmɪst), *ppl. a.* [f. prec. + -ed[1].] Undertaken to be done or given; of which promise is made. ***promised land***: the land of Canaan, as promised to Abraham and his posterity (Gen. xii. 7, xiii. 15, etc.); hence allusively applied to heaven, or to any place of expected felicity.

1538 ELYOT, *Sponsus*..promysed. **1545** *Ibid.*, *Desponsus*, et *desponsa*, affianced or promised in mariage. **1667** MILTON *P.L.* III. 531 Over the Promis'd Land to God so dear. **1697** DRYDEN *Virg. Georg.* III. 133 The fiery Courser..Shifts Place, and paws, and hopes the promis'd Fight. **1862** BP. C. WORDSWORTH *Hymn*, '*O day of rest and gladness*' iii, From thee, like Pisgah's mountain, We view our Promised Land. **1881** LADY HERBERT *Edith* 140 Edith was Lord St. Aubyn's promised bride. **1920** WODEHOUSE *Jill the Reckless* (1922) x. 142 The rank and file of the profession were greeted, like Moses on Pisgah, with a fleeting glimpse of the promised land, consisting of a large desk [etc.]. **1965** *Amer. N. & Q.* Apr. 128/2 Nearly 100 songs tell about travel around the Horn and across the Plains to the promised land, life in California..and the great joy of going home. **1972** D. DAKIN *Unification of Greece* 268 Just when the promised land seemed to be within their grasp, the Greeks..suffered ignominious defeat. **1975** J. CLEARY *Safe House* vi. 250 The farmers..had headed west to the Promised Land of California.

promisee (ˌprɒmɪˈsiː). Also promissee. [f. as prec. + -EE.] The person to whom a promise is made: esp. in legal use, correlative to PROMISOR.

1733 SWIFT *Advice to Freemen Dublin* Wks. 1745 VIII. 239 The persons..possessed of the sole executive power.., and hundreds of expectants, hopers, and promissees. **1785** PALEY *Mor. Philos.* III. I. v. 107 The promise is to be performed in that sense in which the promiser apprehended at the time that the promisee received it. **1846** GROTE *Greece* I. xx. II. 110 The tie which binds a man to..any special promisee towards whom he has taken the engagement of an oath. **1875** POSTE *Gaius* I. Introd. (ed. 2) 11 The intention of the promissor must accord with that of the promissee. *Ibid.* II. Comm. 203 The payee, promisee, or creditor, is..defined by the class term 'bearer' or 'holder'.

promiseful (ˈprɒmɪsfʊl), *a. rare.* [f. PROMISE *sb.* + -FUL.] **a.** Full of or accompanied by promises. **b.** Full of promise or pre-indication of good; promising.

1598 SYLVESTER *Du Bartas* II. ii. II. *Babylon* 96 Som he wins with promisefull intreats,..and som with rougher threats. **1883** *Chicago Advance* 25 Jan., From the Rocky Mountain Districts, never more promiseful, comes the unchanged cry. **1908** *Daily Chron.* 9 June 3/2 Our rivers are promiseful enough of sport.

promiseless (ˈprɒmɪslɪs), *a. rare.* [f. as prec. + -LESS.] Devoid of promise.

1882 J. A. HEWITT *Summer Songs* 3 The promiseless calm of the present Was dull with the dusk of night.

promiser (ˈprɒmɪsə(r)). [f. PROMISE *v.* + -ER[1]. (See also PROMISOR, PROMISSOR.)] One who or that which promises; the maker or giver of a promise.

1530 TINDALE *Answ. More* IV. xi. Wks. (1573) 336/2 Faith ..shall receaue according to the truth of the promiser. **1632** MASSINGER *City Madam* III. ii, I must be A doer, not a promiser. **1771** MRS. GRIFFITH *Hist. Lady Barton* II. 122 That sweet promiser Hope. **1775** JOHNSON *Tax. no Tyr.* 22 An idle promiser of kingdoms in the clouds. **1864** *Realm* 6 Apr. 2 We may always distrust the universal promiser.

promising (ˈprɒmɪsɪŋ), *vbl. sb.* [f. as prec. + -ING[1].] The action of the verb PROMISE; the making of a promise or promises.

1513 DOUGLAS *Æneis* VIII. x. 38 Lo, my reward heyr, and my promissing Fulfillit justly. **1530** PALSGR. 258/2 Promysing, trouthe plyghtynge, *fianceilles*. **1607** SHAKS. *Timon* V. i. 23 Promising, is the verie Ayre o' th' Time;.. Performance, is euer the duller for his acte.

ˈpromising, *ppl. a.* [f. as prec. + -ING[2].] That promises.

1. *lit.* That makes a promise or promises; that engages to do or give something. *rare.*

1720 SWIFT *Fates Clergymen* Wks. 1755 II. II. 30 He was hardly drawn to attend upon some promising lord. **1838** E. BROWN *Serm.* xi. 252 Will the promising God ever permit the name of Christ to be forgotten?

2. *fig.* Affording expectation of good; showing signs of future excellence or success; likely to turn out well; full of promise; hopeful. (The prevailing sense.)

1601 SHAKS. *All's Well* III. iii. 3 We..lay our best loue and credence Vpon thy promising fortune. **1654–66** EARL ORRERY *Parthen.* (1676) 544 My Prince's condition was so promising. **1709** STANHOPE *Paraphr.* IV. 512 That so promising and plentiful a crop might not be lost. **1770** HARRIS in *Priv. Lett. Ld. Malmesbury* (1870) I. 194 He is a very promising man; and will I think do honour to his name and his country. **1860** TYNDALL *Glac.* I. v. 37 The weather was not quite clear, but it was promising. **1878** BOSW. SMITH *Carthage* 90 This was not a promising beginning.

ˈpromisingly, *adv.* [f. prec. + -LY[2].] In a promising manner; so as to cause expectation of good.

a **1691** BOYLE *Hist. Air* (1692) 49, I speak the less promisingly of what I am to say in the remaining part of this paper. **1748** RICHARDSON *Clarissa* (1811) V. xxvii. 272 Clarissa must be the name, if promisingly lovely. **1861** W. BRINTON in *Peaks, Passes & Glac.* Ser. II. I. 428 The weather cleared, and left the summits of the surrounding mountains promisingly covered with snow.

So **ˈpromisingness,** promising quality.

1665 BOYLE *Occas. Refl.* IV. *Transition* (1848) 289 Notwithstanding the Serenity and Promisingness of the Morning. **1727** in BAILEY vol. II.

promisor (ˈprɒmɪsɔː(r)). *Law.* [f. PROMISE *v.* + -OR: cf. PROMISER, PROMISSOR.] The person who makes a promise: correlative to PROMISEE.

1846 in WORCESTER citing CHITTY. **1875** POSTE *Gaius* II. Comm. (ed. 2) 171 The obligation of the promisor. *Ibid.* III. §100 A stipulation to convey on the day before the death of the promisee or promisor is invalid.

†**proˈmiss,** *a. Obs. rare.* In 7 -isse. [ad. L. *prōmiss-us* hanging down, prop. pa. pple. of *prōmitt-ĕre*: see PROMIT *v.*] Hanging down; long and pendent.

1637 HEYWOOD *Dial.* iv. Wks. 1874 VI. 190, I know him by his promisse beard. **1657** TOMLINSON *Renou's Disp.* 375 Promisse and not broad leafs.

†**ˈpromissary.** *Obs. rare.* [f. L. *prōmiss-*, ppl. stem of *prōmittĕre* (see PROMIT *v.*) + -ARY[1].]

1. (?) = PROCURATOR[1].

c **1485** *Digby Myst.* (1882) III. 237, I am pylat pr[o]mmyssary and presedent.

2. = PROMISEE.

1655 T. WHITE *Grounds Obed. & Govt.* 36 He who maketh a promise to another, so it be a perfect one,..puts himselfe and his promissary into a rank of agency and patiency.

promisse, obs. form of PROMISE, PROMISS.

promissee, variant of PROMISEE.

†**proˈmission.** *Obs.* [a. F. *promission* (12th c. in Hatz.-Darm.), ad. L. *prōmissiōn-em* a promising, n. of action from *prōmitt-ĕre*: see PROMIT *v.*] = PROMISE *sb.* (esp. in sense 2): orig. and chiefly, as in PROMISE *sb.* 2 b, in phrase ***land of promission.***

c **1250** *Gen. & Ex.* 4131 [Moses] Saȝ ðe lond of promission. *a* **1300** *Cursor M.* 6924 þis Iuus, fild wit vn-resun, In-to þe land o promission Thoru moyses ne come þai noght. *c* **1400** MAUNDEV. Prol. (1839) 1 Holy Lond..men callen..the lond of Promyssioun. **1480** CAXTON *Chron. Eng.* I. (1520) 6 b/2 Eleazar and Iosue deuyded the lande of promyssyon to ye chyldren of Israell. **1588** PARKE tr. *Mendoza's Hist. China* 316 So great store of prouision y[t] it seemeth to be y[e] land of promission.

c **1440** CAPGRAVE *St. Kath.* III. 1429 At this eyte dayes ende, as was promyssion, Cometh oure lady wyth lyght doun from euene. *c* **1440** *Gesta Rom.* xxxiv. 134 (Harl. MS.) This is a grete promissioun that thowe makest to me. **1529** FRITH *Pistle to Chr. Rdr.* Wks. (1829) 469 We..are the children of promission as Isaac was. **1560** DAUS tr. *Sleidane's Comm.* 217 b, Chyldren..which are also partakers of the godly promission.

promissive (prəʊˈmɪsɪv), *a.* Now *rare.* [ad. late L. *prōmissīv-us* promising, applied to the future tense: see PROMISE and -IVE.] Conveying, implying, or having the character of a promise; promissory.

a **1635** NAUNTON *Fragm. Reg.* (Arb.) 24 She amazed them with a kind of promissive disputation. **1650** HOBBES *De Corp. Pol.* 186 All Declarations..concerning Future Actions and Omissions, are either Promissive, as 'I will do, or not do'; or Provisive, As for example, 'If this be done or not done, this will follow'; or Imperative, as 'Do this, or do it not'. **1677** GALE *Crt. Gentiles* II. IV. 356 God's Wil reveled in his Word is either promissive or preceptive. *a* **1703** BURKITT *On N.T.* Matt. xi. 12 Which words are both restrictive and promissive. **1824** L. MURRAY *Eng. Gram.* (ed. 5) I. vi. 119 Instead..of making a separate mood for every auxiliary verb, and introducing moods Interrogative, Optative, Promissive, Hortative, Precative, &c. we have exhibited such only as are obviously distinct. **1850** *Proc. Philol. Soc.* IV. 186 Shall (2, 3) and will (1) [are called] promissive.

promissor (prəʊˈmɪsə(r)). [a. L. *prōmissor* a promiser, agent-n. f. *prōmitt-ĕre*: see PROMIT *v.*]

†**1.** *Astrol.* = PROMITTOR. *Obs.*

1621 BURTON *Anat. Mel.* I. ii. I. iv, If ♄ by his revolution, or transitus, shall offend any of those radicall promissors in the geniture. *Ibid.* III. iii. I. ii. (1651) 596 By direction of the significators to their several promissors. **1696** PHILLIPS (ed. 5), *Promitters* or *Promissors*, a Term in the Genethliack part of Astrology, so called because they promise in the Radix something to be accomplished, when the Time of direction is fulfilled.

2. *Rom. Law*, etc. One who makes a promise: = PROMISOR.

1644 [H. PARKER] *Jus Pop.* 12 This wide gaping promissor. **1859** SANDARS *Instit. Justinian* III. xv. (ed. 2) 423 If the promissor attempted to defeat the condition by preventing its being fulfilled, he was treated as if he had promised *pure*, and the thing could be demanded from him at once. **1875** POSTE tr. *Gaius* I. Introd. (ed. 2) 11 The intention of the promissor must accord with that of the promissee. *Ibid.* III. Comm. 362 A unilateral convention is one where there is a single promissor and a single acceptor.

ˈpromissorily, *adv. rare.* [f. next + -LY[2].] In a promissory manner; in the way of a promise.

1646 SIR T. BROWNE *Pseud. Ep.* v. xiv. (1650) 217 Nor was he [Jephthah] obliged by oath unto a strict observation of that which promissorily was unlawfull.

promissory (ˈprɒmɪsərɪ), *a.* [ad. med.L. *prōmissōri-us* (Bonaventura *a* 1274), f. L. *prōmissor*: see above and -ORY[2].]

1. a. Conveying, containing, or implying a promise; of, pertaining to, or of the nature of a promise.

1649 JER. TAYLOR *Gt. Exemp.* II. Disc. ix. 115 [It] require[s] the sanction of promissory oaths. **1696** LORIMER *Goodwin's Disc.* vii. 71 A form of words which..was.. promissory of Eternal Life upon a possible condition. **1782** MISS BURNEY *Cecilia* VIII. viii, Her imagination,—that source of promissory enjoyment. **1851** HT. MARTINEAU *Hist. Eng.* 1800–15 II. i. (1878) 259 Popham's Circular to the British merchants, promissory of a rich trade. **1890** BRIDGETT *Blunders & Forgeries* iv. 107 The binding power of a promissory oath.

b. ***promissory note***: a signed document containing a written promise to pay a stated sum to a particular person (or to the bearer), either at a specified date, or on demand.

1710 *Lond. Gaz.* No. 4699/4 A Bill to make Promissory Notes more effectual. **1711** SWIFT *Jrnl. to Stella* 10 May, To lend Stella twenty pounds, and to take her note promissory to pay it in half a year. **1766** BLACKSTONE *Comm.* II. xxx. 446 If a man..gives a promissory note, he shall not be allowed to aver the want of a consideration in order to evade the payment. **1833** HT. MARTINEAU *Berkeley the Banker* I. iv. 81 A bank note is a promissory note for a definite sum; and it must be stamped. **1882** [see AGENT *sb.* 4]. **1911** *Oklahoma Session Laws* (3rd Legislature) 216 If any such promissory note or assessment is not paid when due, action may be brought thereon. **1960** G. DURRELL *Zoo in my Luggage* iii. 79, I paid him the two shillings, and then wrote out a promissory note for the other five shillings. **1972** *Times* 18 Feb. 20/5 In 1963 UDT..accepted a number of promissory notes.

2. *fig.* Conveying a 'promise' or indication of something to come, esp. of good; full of promise, promising; prognosticatory.

1839–48 BAILEY *Festus* xxiii. (ed. 4) 294 A promissory Being unfulfilled. **1891** *Harper's Mag.* Jan. 205/1 The tender glow of evening,..so promissory of the splendid days to come. *Ibid.* Apr. 728/1 She nodded her head with a look promissory of horrors.

†**ˈpromit,** *sb. Sc. Obs.* [f. next.] = PROMISE *sb.* 1, 2.

1501 DOUGLAS *Pal. Hon.* III. lxxvi, In thair promittis thay stude euer firme and plane. **1567** *Gude & Godlie B.* (S.T.S.) 113 My beleue is in thy word, And all thy promittis maist and leist.

†**proˈmit,** *v. Obs.* Forms: 5–6 promit, -itt(e, -yt(te (5 *pa. t.* promit, -ytt). *β.* 5 **promette.** [ad. L. *prōmitt-ĕre* to let go or send forth, to put forth; to promise, give hope of; to foretell; f. *prō*, PRO-[1] + *mitt-ĕre* to let go, send. The *β* form a. F. *promett-re* (10th c. in Godef.) to promise.]

1. = PROMISE *v.* 1, 2.

1425 *Rolls of Parlt.* IV. 297/2 Promyttyng and behotyng ..to do, kepe, observe and fulfille..al yat shall be decreed. **1432–50** tr. *Higden* (Rolls) VI. 93 Promittynge if he myȝhte escape þat pestilence, þat he wolde dye in goynge pilgremages. **1456** SIR G. HAYE *Law Arms* (S.T.S.) 141 He has payit thame all that he promyttit thame. **1527** in Fiddes *Wolsey* II. (1726) 141 Promytting..that from henceforth I shall never retorn agen to the said heresies. *a* **1584** MONTGOMERIE *Cherrie & Slae* 1131 Promitting, unwitting, Ȝour hechts ȝou neuir huiked.

β. *c* **1422** HOCCLEVE *Jereslaus's Wife* 802 If your pardon Yee me promette. **1432–50** tr. *Higden* (Rolls) V. 435 Y promette feithefully to be rulede by hym. *c* **1489** CAXTON *Blanchardyn* xxiii. 78 'Syre', sayd the pucell, 'I promette you that youre hoste shalbe al to gydre contented of you.'

b. = PROMISE *v.* 5 a.

1484 CAXTON *Fables of Æsop* v. xvi, I promytte and warne the that yf thow come nyghe me I shalle slee the with this grete clubbe.

¶ **2.** Erroneous for PERMIT: perh. scribal error.

c **1500** *Joseph Arim.* (E.E.T.S.) 32 He..commaunded hym he sholde promytte and suffre the seruauntes of almyghty god to passe out of pryson. **1523** [COVERDALE] *Old God & New* (1534) E j, They were promitted and suffred to retreate. **1565** *Reg. Privy Council Scot.* I. 330 The Quenis Majestie promittis thame to tak of her awin woddis as may serve to the bigging of neidfull houssis for the labouraris.

¶ The alleged sense 'To disclose, to publish, to confess' is a figment founded on a misquotation: see below.

a **1548** HALL *Chron., Hen. VII* 33 b, Pardone of all offences and crymes committed, and promocions and rewardes for obeynge to the kynges request. [Misquoted in *Cassell's Encycl. Dict.* 'of all offences and crimes promitted': whence in *Cent. Dict.*, and (def.) in *Funk's Stand. Dict.*].

promitochondrion: see PRO-[2] I.

promittor (prəʊˈmɪtə(r)). *Astrol.* Also 7 -er. [f. PROMIT *v.* + -OR. Cf. PROMISSOR.] A planet which 'promises' or prognosticates that some event will take place on its arriving at some particular aspect with another planet, star, or point of the heaven (the *significator*); also applied to such an aspect.

1647 LILLY *Chr. Astrol.* clxvii. 719 Consider the Profections of Significators and Promittors. **1671** SALMON *Syn. Med.* I. xxxiv. 71 The Quality of the Disease shall be discerned from the Promittor or afflicting Planet. **1696** Promitters [see PROMISSOR I]. **1819** J. WILSON *Dict. Astrol.* s.v., ♄ and ♂ are anaretic promittors, and promise to destroy the life of the native when the hyleg is directed to them. ♃ and ♀ are promittors of good when directions to them are fulfilled.

promizole (ˈprəʊmɪzəʊl). *Pharm.* Also Promizole. [f. PROMI(N + THIA)ZOLE.] A bacteriostatic agent, 2-amino-5-*p*-aminobenzenesulphonylthiazole, $C_9H_9N_3O_2S_2$, formerly used to treat leprosy and tuberculosis.

Formerly a proprietary name in the U.S.

1944 *Proc. Staff Meetings Mayo Clinic* XIX. 26 Promizole is the trade name of 4,2′-diaminophenyl-5′-thiazolesulfone [*sic*]. **1944** *Official Gaz.* (U.S. Patent Office) 11 Apr. 191/1 Parke, Davis & Company, Detroit... *Promizole.* For chemotherapeutic agent for the treatment of bacterial infections. Claims use since Dec. 23, 1943. **1948** [see PROMIN]. **1964** P. FEENY *Fight against Leprosy* xvi. 147 From every continent there was coming a steady stream of literature about the effects of promin, diasone, sulphetrone and one more weapon that had been added to the arsenal, promizole.

Prommer (ˈprɒmə(r)). *colloq.* Also **prommer.** [f. PROM 2 + -ER¹.] One who attends a promenade concert (*esp.* at the Royal Albert Hall); a promenader.

1947 *Penguin Music Mag.* May 36 Even in 1932 a Prommer could follow a score without digging his elbow into someone every time he turned a page. **1960** *Times* 30 July 9/1 (*heading*) Prommers Stay for Gerhard. **1969** *Listener* 12 June 836/3 Traditionally, of course, your average Prommer is a catholic music-lover.. who jolly well doesn't care who sees him enjoying himself on Saturdays. **1972** *Guardian* 14 Aug. 8/1 A regular Prommer who couldn't make it this particular night and is.. listening at home. **1975** *Times* 19 Sept. 9/8 The finale was a young man's reading, and seemingly much to the liking of the even younger prommers.

‖**promnesia** (prɒmˈniːsiːə). *Psychic Science.* [mod.L., f. Gr. πρό, PRO-² + -μνησία memory.] (See quot.)

1903 MYERS *Human Personality* I. p. xx, *Promnesia*, the paradoxical sensation of recollecting a scene which is only now occurring for the first time; the sense of the *déjà vu*. *Ibid.* II. 264 That sensation of already remembering what is happening or is just about to happen, to which some authors have applied the too wide term paramnesia, but for which *promnesia* seems a more exact and distinctive name.

promo (ˈprəʊməʊ), *a.* and *sb. colloq.* [Abbrev. of PROMOTIONAL *a.*, PROMOTION 2 a.]

A. *adj.* = PROMOTIONAL *a.* **B.** *sb.* Publicity, advertising; *spec.* a promotional trailer for a television programme. *Comb.*, as **promo man**, a promotion man, publicity organizer.

1963 *Amer. Speech* XXXVIII. 156 Other stump words or clipped forms such as *info*.. and *promo*. **1966** *Sat. Rev.* (U.S.) 12 Feb. 8/3 'Will Robin escape?... Will Batman arrive in time to save him? The worst is yet to come!' And sure enough, minutes later on came the second of this trilogy —*The Blue Light*. What a promo! **1971** D. E. WESTLAKE *I gave at the Office* (1972) 11, I did promo voice-overs for the new TV shows. **1972** *Village Voice* (N.Y.) 1 June 46/1 A slightly agitated promo-man-about-town stopped me one day recently as I was crossing Sheridan Square. **1973** *Publishers Weekly* 10 Sept. 54 (Advt.), With big national TV promo by the author.. Robert Rosefsky is really doing a terrific job of promoting his book on TV. **1974** *Some Technical Terms & Slang* (Granada Television), *Promo*, a short promotional trailer for a programme. **1976** *New Musical Express* 17 Apr. 22/4 Despite promo pics that make them look like 12-year-olds, their 'charisma' is more David Cassidy style. **1978** *Advertising Age* (Chicago) 16 Oct. 19 (*heading*) Oxford promo is publicity happening.

†**ˈpromont.** *Obs. rare.* [Shortened from PROMONTORY, as if f. PRO-¹ + L. *mont-em* MOUNT *sb.*¹] = PROMONTORY.

1612 DRAYTON *Poly-olb.* i. 151 A Promont jutting out into the dropping south. *a* **1627** MIDDLETON *Changeling* I. i, Our citadels Are plac'd conspicuous to outward view On promonts' tops. **1631** CHETTLE *Trag. Hoffmann* B j b, Ile to yon promonts top, and their suruey, What shipwrackt passengers the belgique sea Casts from her fomy entrailes.

†**ˈpromonˌtore.** *Obs. rare.* [f. L. *prōmontōrium* PROMONTORY: cf. F. *promontoire* (15–16 c. in Hatz.-Darm.).] = prec.

1623 LITHGOW *Trav.* I. 22 Capo Bianco in Calabria.. being the furthest promontore of Italy. *Ibid.* x. 448 Without it is quadrangled, and within round; hauing two degrees of incircling promontores, supported by Marble pillars, and Allabaster arches. **1657** THORNLEY tr. *Longus' Daphnis & Chloe* 82 Coming to a Promontore which ran into the Sea.

promontorial (prɒmənˈtɔərɪəl), *a. rare.* [f. L. *prōmontōri-um* PROMONTORY + -AL¹.] Of, pertaining to, or resembling a promontory.

1875 ALEX. SMITH *New Hist. Aberdeen.* I. i. 1 From its semicircular shape it may be called promontorial.

promontoried (ˈprɒməntərɪd), *a.* [f. PROMONTORY + -ED².] Formed into or furnished with a promontory or projection.

1649 G. DANIEL *Trinarch., Hen. V* ccxxxviii, The floating Bodies, promontoried, Reaks An Exhalation. **1844** FABER *Sir Lancelot* (1857) 51 The green hill-tops and promontoried steeps. **1891** *Cornh. Mag.* June 649 They see the promontoried backs and small heads and long necks of some of those ungainly beasts [camels].

b. as *pa. pple.* Pierced as by a promontory.

1877 BLACKMORE *Erema* II. xxxi. 141 In bays and waves of rolling grass, promontoried, here and there, by jutting copse or massive tree.

†**promonˈtorious,** *a. Obs. rare.* [f. as prec. + -OUS.] Of the nature of a promontory; lofty and prominent. (In quots. *fig.*)

1615 T. ADAMS *Eng. Sickness* Serm. ii. Wks. 1861 I. 422 The Papists brag of their numerous multitude, and promontorious celsitude. **1618** —— *Happiness Ch.* ibid. II. 497 The ambitious man's mountain is his honour, and who dares find fault with so promontorious a celsitude?

‖**promontorium** (prɒmɒnˈtɔərɪəm). [med.L.: see next.] **a.** = next, 1. **b.** = next, 2.

1652–62 HEYLIN *Cosmogr.* Introd. (1674) 19/1 Promontorium, is a high Mountain which shooteth it self into the Sea, the utmost end of which is called a Foreland, or Cape. **1831** [see next, 2]. **1871** *Daily News* 23 Jan., This long bluff.. its promontorium throws forward, as it were, two sheltering wings for batteries stationed in the narrow waist behind.

promontory (ˈprɒməntərɪ). Also 7 -ary, promentory. [ad. med.L. *prōmontōri-um*, alteration (after *mont-em* MOUNT *sb.*¹) of L. *prōmunturi-um* a mountain ridge, a headland, promontory; referred by some to *prōminēre* to jut forward.]

1. A point of high land which juts out into the sea or other expanse of water beyond the line of coast; a headland.

1548 UDALL, etc. *Erasm. Par. Acts* xiii. 46 Barnabas and Saul went to Seleucia, whiche is a great promontorye, or peake on the weste parte of Antioche. **1553** EDEN *Treat. Newe Ind.* (Arb.) 8 Euen vnto the promontorie or landes ende of the people, called *Cimbri*. **1559** W. CUNNINGHAM *Cosmogr. Glasse* 80 The parallele.., goth by the promontory of good hope. **1669** GALE *Crt. Gentiles* I. I. viii. 44 Corsica .. called by the Grecians.. the Horny Iland; because of its many Promontories, and angles. **1725** POPE *Odyss.* x. 221 From yonder Promontory's brow, I view'd the coast. **1876** GREEN *Stray Stud.* 60 Monaco stands on a promontory of rock which falls in bold cliffs into the sea.

b. *transf.* and *fig.*

1603 OWEN *Pembrokeshire* (1892) 196 The begynning of his Raigne is the Period or farthest Promontorye of the certaine antiquities of this Realme. **1832** W. IRVING *Alhambra* I. 309 They doubled the promontory of the mountains, and arrived in sight of the famous Puente del Pinos. *a* **1854** H. REED *Lect. Brit. Poets* (1857) II. xv. 205 Standing on the promontory of the present, to feel the air rising from the shadowy waters of the past. **1860** TYNDALL *Glac.* I. ix. 63 The avalanche.. was hidden from us by a rocky promontory.

2. *Anat.* Applied to certain prominences or protuberances of the body.

promontory of the sacrum, an angular prominence formed by the junction of the last lumbar vertebra with the sacrum. ***promontory of the tympanum***, a protuberance of the inner ear caused by the projection of the cochlea.

1831 R. KNOX *Cloquet's Anat.* 111 The sacrum is articulated to the fifth lumbar vertebra... Its junction with the spinal column forms a projecting angle named the Promontory (*promontorium*). *Ibid.* 567 The Promontory (*Promontorium*).. is another pretty broad tubercular eminence, of a variable form, which limits the fenestra ovalis below. **1881** MIVART *Cat* 298 Another opening, called the fenestra rotunda, lies below and behind the promontory.

3. *attrib.* (or *adj.*) Resembling a promontory, projecting, outstanding.

1579 FENTON *Guicciard.* VII. (1599) 284 On the top of the mountaine called the Promontorie hill. *c* **1590** GREENE *Fr. Bacon* iv. 6 Welcome.. To Englands shore, whose promontory cleeues, Shewes Albion is another little world. **1693** DRYDEN *Juvenal* vi. 153 A Promontory Wen, with griesly Grace, Stood high, upon the Handle of his Face. **1726** POPE *Odyss.* XIX. 281 His bending head O'er which a promontory shoulder spread. **1809** CAMPBELL *Gertr. Wyom.* III. xxv, Each bold and promontory mound.

promorph (ˈprəʊmɔːf). *Biol.* [a. Ger. *promorph* (Haeckel), f. Gr. πρό, PRO-² + μορφή form.] A primitive or fundamental form.

1889 *Nature* 28 Feb. 409/2 An addition of three pages on 'the fundamental form (promorph)'.

promorphology (ˌprəʊmɔːˈfɒlədʒɪ). *Biol.* [ad. Ger. *promorphologie* (Haeckel): see PRO-² and MORPHOLOGY.] The morphology of fundamental forms; the branch of morphology that treats of organic forms from a mathematical standpoint; stereometric morphology. So **promorphoˈlogical** *a.*, of or pertaining to promorphology; whence **promorphoˈlogically** *adv.*; **promorˈphologist**, one who is versed in promorphology.

1878 BELL *Gegenbaur's Comp. Anat.* 2 General Anatomy has to do with the fundamental forms of animal organisms (Promorphology). **1883** P. GEDDES in *Encycl. Brit.* XVI. 843/2 *note*, As promorphology develops the crystallography of organic form, so mineralogy.. becomes parallel to morphology. *Ibid.* 844/2 The classification into bilateral and radiate forms which usually does duty for more precise promorphological conceptions. *Ibid.* 845/1 These homoplastic or homomorphic forms, as Haeckel has shown, come as fairly within the province of the promorphologist. **1890** *Cent. Dict.*, Promorphologically. **1895** *Syd. Soc. Lex.*, *Promorphology*, morphology, as relating to a few fundamental types.

promotable (prəʊˈməʊtəb(ə)l), *a.* [f. next + -ABLE.] That may be or is to be promoted; deserving of promotion.

1716 M. DAVIES *Athen. Brit.* III. 31 Scarce sufferable, much less promotable or remunerable *Alibi*. **1887** MORLEY *Sp.* in *Scott. Leader* 31 Mar., Resident Magistrates are removable, and, if I may coin a word, 'promotable' by the Executive Government.

promote (prəʊˈməʊt), *v.* [f. L. *prōmōt-*, ppl. stem of *prōmov-ēre* to move forward, advance: see PRO-¹ and MOVE *v.* So obs. F. *promoter* to instigate (14th c. in Godef.).]

I. 1. a. *trans.* To advance (a person) *to* a position of honour, dignity, or emolument; *esp.* to raise to a higher grade or office; to prefer.

1387 TREVISA *Higden* (Rolls) VII. 145 þe emperour i-smyten aȝen promoted hym sone into a bisshop [L. *promovit in episcopum*]. **1401** *Pol. Poems* (Rolls) II. 94 Preestes, wich to fatte benefices wolde be promotid. **1535** COVERDALE *Ps.* xxxvi[i]. 34 He shal so promote the, that thou shalt haue the londe by enheritaunce. **1685** STILLINGFL. *Orig. Brit.* iv. 167 Leontius his way was, to promote onely those in the Church, he was beforehand sure of. **1874** GREEN *Short Hist.* iii. §5. 140 Boniface.. was promoted to.. the Archbishopric of Canterbury.

b. *Chess.* To raise (a pawn) to the rank of a piece. (Cf. to QUEEN.)

1803 [see PROMOTION 1 b]. **1900** *Westm. Gaz.* 12 May 3/3 Compelled to promote a Pawn to a piece. **1904** H. J. R. MURRAY in *Brit. Chess Mag.* Dec. 466 [In Malay chess] a pawn may be promoted to the rank of any superior piece, but promotion takes place, not when the Pawn reaches the eighth line, but only after a further diagonal move.

c. *Sport* (chiefly *Assoc. Football*). To transfer (a team) to a higher division of a league (see PROMOTION 1 d).

1924 *Times* 5 May 6/6 Bristol City,.. promoted a year ago, return to a lower division. **1949** *Times* 25 Apr. 6/2 (*heading*) Swansea Town promoted.

d. *Curling.* To move (another stone) forward by striking.

1937 T. HENDERSON *Lockerbie* 58 He left the stone alone.. deeming it safer play to promote the Minister's stone.

e. *Bridge.* To establish (a relatively low card) as a winner; to secure (a trick) by this action.

1959 *Listener* 31 Dec. 1178/3 A further spade lead will promote the nine of diamonds. *Ibid.*, The fifth heart will promote one of North's trumps. **1962** *Ibid.* 12 Apr. 662/2 The defence would take two rounds of clubs and play a third club, promoting a trick for West's nine of hearts.

2. a. To further the growth, development, progress, or establishment of (anything); to help forward (a process or result); to further, advance, encourage. (Formerly also with *on.*) *spec.* To further the sale of (an article) by advertising or other modes of publicity; to publicize (a venture, person, etc.). Also *absol.*

1515 BARCLAY *Egloges* IV. (1570) C vj/1 Such rascolde drames promoted by Thais,.. Or by suche other newe forged Muses nine. **1526** *Pilgr. Perf.* (W. de W. 1531) 12 b, This gyfte expelleth all vyce, and promoteth all vertue. **1577** HANMER *Anc. Eccl. Hist.* (1619) 236 The Emperour.. went about to promote christian religion. **1644** DIGBY *Nat. Soul* iv. §5. 390 All the causes and helpes that promote on its impotent desires. **1698–9** (Mar. 8) *Minute Bk. S.P.C.K.*, The Journal of the Honble Society for Promoting Christian Knowledge. **1703** J. TIPPER in *Lett. Lit. Men* (Camden) 305 You will promote the Sale of it as much as possibly you can. **1765** A. DICKSON *Treat. Agric.* (ed. 2) 79 Vegetation is promoted.. by communicating to the earth the food of plants, and enlarging their pasture. **1849** MACAULAY *Hist. Eng.* ii. I. 191 It could in no way promote the national interest. **1874** GREEN *Short Hist.* ii. §1. 60 Commerce and trade were promoted by the justice and policy of the Kings. **1930** *Publisher's Weekly* 31 May 2732/2 The books all to be individualized in appearance and fully promoted. **1965** *Melody Maker* 3 Apr. 7/3 With the group over here to promote their latest recording,.. they could well make the chart. **1971** D. POTTER *Brit. Eliz. Stamps* x. 117 These packs are heavily promoted, with full-page colour advertisements in the national press. **1976** *National Observer* (U.S.) 30 Oct. 9/3, I love chocolate-chip cookies, and I love to promote.

b. To support actively the passing of (a law or measure); now *spec.* to take the necessary steps for obtaining the passing of (a local or private act of parliament).

1721 *Col. Rec. Pennsylv.* III. 138 The parties concerned in promoting this Bill. **1863** H. COX *Instit.* 170 Many bills promoted as private bills, largely affect public as well as private interests.

c. *Chem.* To increase the activity or effectiveness of (a catalyst) by addition of another substance; to act as a promoter of (a catalyst) or in (a catalytic reaction). *Loosely* (passing into 2 a), to initiate, catalyse.

[**1920** *Jrnl. Physical Chem.* XXIV. 243 When more than one of the components are themselves catalysts a difficulty presents itself in choosing between 'promoter' and 'promoted'.] **1930** N. K. ADAM *Physics & Chem. of Surfaces* viii. 280 Many reactions go on at the surface of charcoal. It is a good catalyst for promoting halogenations. **1936** R. H. GRIFFITH *Mechanism of Contact Catalysis* iii. 82 The fact that a substance may act as a poison to a catalyst, and yet itself be promoted by that catalyst, is obviously quite possible. **1940** GLASSTONE *Textbk. Physical Chem.* xiii. 1128 On an ordinary iron catalyst one atom only in 2,000 appears to be able to catalyze the reaction between nitrogen and hydrogen, but when suitably promoted the proportion of active points is increased ten-fold. **1946** *Chem. Abstr.* XL. 4876 The catalytic action is promoted by a smaller quantity of BF_3. **1947** *Jrnl. Polymer Sci.* II. 41 The presence of small amounts of relatively high molecular weight mercaptans greatly promotes the copolymerization reaction. **1967** R. W. LENZ *Org. Chem. Synthetic High Polymers* x. 270 *N,N*-Dimethylaniline promotes the spontaneous decomposition of benzoyl peroxide, and this combination can be used to initiate polymerization reactions at low temperatures. **1975** P. H. EMMETT in Drauglis & Jaffee *Physical Basis for Heterogeneous Catalysis* 21 Why then is a K_2O-Al_2O_3 promoter better than Al_2O_3 alone in promoting an iron synthetic ammonia catalyst?

II. †**3.** To put forth or forward into notice or attention; to publish, promulgate; to assert, advance (a claim). *Obs.*

1480 CAXTON *Chron. Eng.* ccxxv. 230 The kynges nedes were put forth and promoted as touchyng the kyngdom of Fraunce. **1555** in Strype *Eccl. Mem.* (1721) III. App. xlvi. 139 The false surmised articles promoted by Hugh Raulins, priest. **1563** BONNER in Strype *Ann. Ref.* (1709) I. xxxiv. 342 That the oath shall be promoted in open place, where there shall be a convenient assembly of people to witness the same. **1662** STANLEY *Hist. Chaldaick Philos.* (1701) 18/1 An Intellectual incorruptible pattern, the Print of whose Form He promoted through the World. **1683** MOXON *Mech. Exerc., Printing* i, Gutenberg.. promoted His claim to the first Invention of this Art.

†**4.** To incite, prompt, move (*to* something). *Obs. rare.*

1450–1530 *Myrr. our Ladye* 27 The aungels of god.. to helpe vs in time of prayer, & to promote our prayers towarde god. **1646** H. LAWRENCE *Comm. Angells* 80 The Angell keepers.. promote to all good, oppose all evill.

5. To cause to move forward in space or extent; to extend. *Obs.* exc. *dial.*

1652 NEEDHAM tr. *Selden's Mare Cl.* 274 None of them ever attempted to promote their Empire beyond the bounds thereof. **1660** BOYLE *New Exp. Phys. Mech.* i. (1682) 16 Other eminent Astronomers would promote the Confines of the Atmosphere to exceed six or seven times that number of Miles. **1683** MOXON *Mech. Exerc., Printing* i, William Caxton (.. who first brought it to Oxford) promoted it to London also. *a***1705** RAY *Creation* I. (1714) 201 Francis Pirara promotes the life of the Brazilians beyond the term we have set it. **1872** *Spectator* 7 Sept. 1137 'Sure it's I will promote her for your honour', where the word 'promote' was used.. in its strict meaning of 'cause to move forward'.

III. †**6.** To inform against (a person); to lay an information of (a delinquency, etc.); also *intr.* or *absol.* to act as informer. Cf. PROMOTER 3. *Obs.*

14.. *Chester Pl.* (Shaks. Soc.) II. 82 Taverners, tapsters of this cittie, Shalbe promoted heare by me, For breakinge statutes of this cuntrey. **1550** LATIMER *Last Serm. bef. Edw. VI* Serm. (1562) 130 [129] There lacke men to promote the kinges officers when they do amisse, and to promote al offenders. **1566** DRANT *Horace, Sat.* iv. C j b, I am not one that doth promote, why art thou frayde of me? **1596–1623** [see PROMOTING *ppl. a.* 1].

7. *Eccl. Law.* To set in motion (the office of the ordinary or judge) in a criminal suit in an ecclesiastical court; to institute (a suit *ex officio promoto*) by permission of the ordinary.

1681 CONSET *Pract. Spir. Courts* I. ii. §1 (1700) 5 Its Official [*sc.* of the Court of Arches] is the proper and competent Judge to take cognizance of all Ecclesiastical Causes whatsoever not only at the Instance of Parties, but also of his meer Office, or when 'tis promoted. *Ibid.* I. ii. §3 (1700) 7 It is left to the election of the Plaintiff to elect in which Court he will institute or promote his Cause. **1789** SIR W. SCOTT in Haggard *Rep. Consist. Court* (1822) I. 14 This is a case of Office promoted [= *ex officio promoto*] against Thomas Calcott, for.. erecting tombs in the church-yard.. without leave of the Ordinary. **1837** LUSHINGTON in Curteis *Rep. Eccl. Cas.* (1840) 601 Mr. Williams [Vicar of Hendon], who promotes the office of the judge, has brought a charge against a parishioner of chiding and brawling. **1849** DICKENS *Dav. Copp.* xxix, The office of the judge promoted by Tipkins against Bullock for his soul's correction. **1889** (May 11) ABP. BENSON in *Read v. Bp. of Lincoln* (Roscoe) 36 The archbishop's office was promoted against him [Bp. Wood of Lichfield, 1681]. *Ibid.* 37 The suit [*Lucy v. Bp. St. Davids*] was promoted ex officio before the archbishop. **1895** SIR R. PHILLIMORE *Eccl. Law* (ed. 2) 837 In every ecclesiastical court there are two modes of procedure—the civil and the criminal. In criminal proceedings the office of the judge is promoted, [i.e.] inasmuch as all spiritual jurisdiction is in the hands of the bishop or ordinary, his office or function is set in motion. *Ibid.* 956 The Criminal Suit is open to every one whom the ordinary allows to promote his office, and the Civil Suit to every one showing an interest.

IV. 8. *slang* (orig. *U.S.*). To borrow or obtain (usu. illicitly). Also to exploit (someone) *for* material advantage.

1930 *Amer. Mercury* Dec. 457/1 *Promote*, to steal. 'We got to promote a boat to run the stuff in.' **1934** J. M. CAIN *Postman always rings Twice* 97 If I hadn't been there, and begun promoting him for something to drink that afternoon, maybe he'd be here now. **1941** *Argus* (Melbourne) *Week-End Mag.* 15 Nov. 1/4 In Army parlance to arrange something is always to 'tee up'; just as to borrow something is to 'promote' it. **1942** Z. N. HURSTON in A. Dundes *Mother Wit* (1973) 226/1 You skillets is trying to promote a meal on me.

†**pro'mote,** *ppl. a. Obs.* [ad. L. *prōmōt-us*, pa. pple. of *prōmovēre* (see prec.); or abbreviated from *promoted*.] Promoted.

*c***1530** *Crt. of Love* 1261 For where a lover thinketh him promote, Envy will grucch, repyning at his wele.

promoted (prəʊ'məʊtɪd), *ppl. a.* [f. PROMOTE *v.* + -ED[1].] That has been promoted; furthered, advanced. **1.** *Chem.* Of a catalyst: containing or influenced by a promoter (sense 1 d).

[**1920**: see PROMOTE *v.* 2 c.] **1927** *Jrnl. Amer. Chem. Soc.* XLVIII. 2821 In the case of pure iron and promoted iron catalysts for ammonia synthesis, oxygen is the type of poison which seemed best suited for such a study. **1968** E. K. RIDEAL *Concepts in Catalysis* vi. 120 Promoted iron catalysts used in the ammonia synthesis are generally prepared by reduction in hydrogen at 500°C of a mixture 95% Fe_3O_4 plus 4–5% Al_2O_3 plus 0–1% K_2O. **1975** P. H. EMMETT in Drauglis & Jaffee *Physical Basis for Heterogeneous Catalysis* 18 The carbon monoxide chemisorption indicates that about 50 percent of the singly promoted (Al_2O_3 the only promoter) catalyst is usually covered with promoter.

2. In other senses of the vb.

1962 *Listener* 6 Dec. 975/3 A splendid, and splendidly promoted, mixture of Baedeker, gazetteer, and travellers' tales. **1977** *Cleethorpes News* 6 May 31/1 Two fine individual performances destroyed promoted Cromwell-Drewery on their Premier debut.

promotee (prəʊməʊ'tiː). [f. PROMOTE *v.* + -EE[1].] One who is or has been promoted.

1958 E. H. CARR *Socialism in One Country* I. I. iii. 110 The railways, whose staff adopted.. an unwelcoming.. attitude to promotees. **1966** *Punch* 2 Feb. 174/3 Crimes of local importance have to be handled at higher and higher levels to provide something for the promotees from *Z Cars* to do. **1977** *Hongkong Standard* 12 Apr. 8/1 This promotion causes the promotee to lose money on the deal.

†**pro'motement.** *Obs. rare*[−1]. [f. PROMOTE *v.* + -MENT.] = PROMOTION 2.

1670 EVELYN *Sylva* xxii. (ed. 2) 105 Some commend the strewing a few Oats at the bottom of the fosses or pits.. for a great promotement of their taking.

promoter (prəʊ'məʊtə(r)). Forms: α. 5–6 promotour, -oure, 6 *Sc.* -ar, 6–9 -or, 5– -er. β. 6–8 promooter, 7 -mouter. [AF. and early mod.E. *promotour* = F. *promoteur* (1336 in Hatz.-Darm.) one who promotes, an official procurator in an ecclesiastical court, †a business agent, ad. med.L. *prōmōtor*, agent-n. f. *prōmovēre* to PROMOVE. But from 16th c. commonly spelt with *-er*, as if f. PROMOTE *v.* + -ER[1]. The β forms occur only in sense 3.]

I. 1. a. One who or that which promotes, advances, or furthers any movement or project; a furtherer, an encourager.

1450–1530 *Myrr. our Ladye* 237 A comforter to them that are desolate, a promoter to the rightful, an helper to the synful. **1494** FABYAN *Chron.* VII. 445 Of whiche oppynyou.. a great furtherer or promoter. **1553** BECON *Reliq. Rome* (1563) 85 The firste promoters.. to haue Images in churches. *a***1568** ASCHAM *Scholem.* (Arb.) 82 In tyme they be Promoters of both openlie. **1660** BOYLE *New Exp. Phys. Mech.* xx, That great and learned promoter of experimental philosophy, Dr. Wilkins. **1737** BRACKEN *Farriery Impr.* (1756) I. 78 A powerful Diuretic, or Promoter of Urine. **1781** D. WILLIAMS tr. *Voltaire's Dram. Wks.* II. 135 Money is the best promoter of matrimony. **1840** *Penny Cycl.* XVII. 277/1 In 1837 the bills for making four distinct lines of railway to Brighton had been referred to one committee. An unprecedented contest arose between the promoters of the competing lines. **1847** HELPS *Friends in C.* I. 106 There are two great classes of promoters of social happiness. **1878** LECKY *Eng. in 18th C.* II. v. 35 [The] leading promoter [of the University] was the Chancellor, Bishop Elphinstone.

b. *Legisl.* One who takes steps for, or actively supports, the passing of a law; now *spec.* one of those who take the necessary steps for obtaining the passing of a local or private act of parliament.

1741 MIDDLETON *Cicero* I. vi. 441 Cicero himself was the promoter of it, and procured a decree to his satisfaction. *Ibid.* 551 Cælius was the promotor of this law. [Cf. **1840** in 1.] **1863** H. COX *Instit.* I. iv. 20 With respect to these [local acts] various preliminaries.. are.. required to be observed by the promoters of the several bills. *Ibid.* I. ix. 172 The promoters of each bill are required to prove compliance with the standing orders of both Houses.

c. *Finance.* One who promotes, or takes the requisite steps for, the formation of a joint-stock company; one who is a party to the preparation or issue of the prospectus; a company-promoter. In consequence of the amount of swindling too often resorted to, the term has in popular use acquired an opprobrious sense: cf. PROMOTERISM.

1876 *World* V. No. 106. 5 A promoter, *quoad* promoter, is not necessarily a bad man. **1884** W. C. SMITH *Kildrostan* 80 He.. cursed Himself, his friend, and all the ravenous crew Of jobbers and promoters. **1889** *Times* 18 Mar. 9/3 The promoter of a company is accountable for what he omits to do, as well as for what he does. **1890** *Act 53 & 54 Vict.* c. 64 §3 A promoter in this section means a promoter who was a party to the preparation of the prospectus. **1894** *Westm. Gaz.* 15 Nov. 8/1 *Official Receiver.* Is he a company promoter? *Witness.* Oh, no; he is far too respectable for that.

d. *Chem.* A less active additive which increases the activity of a catalyst; more generally, a substance which improves a catalyst in some way. Also, a substance used as an initiator in a catalytic polymerization reaction.

1911 J. Y. JOHNSON *Brit. Pat. 19,249* 6 Very much better yields can be obtained in the synthetical production of ammonia from its elements if there be employed, as the catalytic agent, iron in admixture with certain bodies as hereinafter explained... These bodies my foreign correspondents [*sc.* Badische Anilin & Soda Fabrik, Germany], for the sake of brevity, term 'promoters'. **1927** *Jrnl. Amer. Chem. Soc.* XLVIII. 2826 The results show that the predominant effect of promoters of the type alumina and potassium aluminate is to increase the number of catalytically active atoms relative to the total number of metal atoms present. **1930** N. K. ADAM *Physics & Chem. of Surfaces* viii. 241 Many promoters are simply refractory supports for a metallic catalyst. **1961** J. N. ANDERSON *Appl. Dental Materials* (ed. 2) xxiv. 251 When these promoters meet the benzoyl peroxide in the polymer, they start a chain of events similar to that which occurs when heat is applied. **1963** P. H. PLESCH *Chem. Cationic Polymerization* iv. 149 The patent literature contains a great many combinations of a metal halide and a co-catalyst (often called promoter, especially in American patents), most of which are substances which can combine with the metal halide to form a protonic acid. **1970** G. ODIAN *Princ. Polymerization* vii. 464 The reactive cyclic ether used as a component of the catalyst system is referred to as a promoter (or a cocatalyst). **1971** *Sci. Amer.* Dec. 52/3 It has been found that iron plus a few percent of the oxides of potassium and aluminum, which are known as promoters, give a longer-lived catalyst and one with greater resistance to impurities in the feed stream.

e. One who organizes or actively supports a sporting event, entertainment, etc., esp. for profit.

1936 [see *football pool* s.v. FOOTBALL 4]. **1950** *Sport* 7–11 Apr. 22/3 This would involve the full co-operation of sports promoters and the B.B.C. **1951** *Sunday Pictorial* 21 Jan. 16/3 He's a promoter's dream and has sold £450 worth of tickets for this outing. **1956** B. HOLIDAY *Lady sings Blues* (1973) xxii. 180 If it had been left to the management and promoters, I could have shot myself long ago. **1964** *Melody Maker* 28 Nov. 3 Deejays and promoters must stop being idiots. **1971** *Daily Tel.* 27 May 2/6 The Isle of Wight County Council last night rejected all three farm sites proposed by Richard Roscoe, a promoter, for staging a pop festival.

f. *Med.* An agent that causes tumour promotion (PROMOTION 2 d) (see quot. 1978).

1947 *Brit. Jrnl. Cancer* I. 390 Dibenzanthracene is undoubtedly a potent Initiator, but a weak Promotor; benzpyrene is moderately potent both as Initiator and Promotor; croton oil, on the other hand, is exceptionally potent as a Promotor, but quite useless as an Initiator. **1969** *Progress Exper. Tumor Res.* XI. 50 When the initiating agent is given.. to mice and this is followed by repeated skin application of the promoter after a lapse of as much as 380 days, tumors arise within 32–42 days from the beginning of promoting treatment. **1970** [see PROMOTING *ppl. a.* 2 b]. **1976** *Maclean's Mag.* (Toronto) 27 Dec. 22/3 These carcinogens don't usually cause cancer unless they mix with other agents called promoters. **1978** *Nature* 20 July 271/1 Tumour promoters are compounds which are not carcinogens but which can induce tumours in mice treated with a subcarcinogenic dose of a chemical carcinogen.

g. *Genetics.* An essential part of an operon, situated between the operator and the structural gene(s), at which transcription starts. [The sense is due to F. Jacob et al., who used F. *promoteur* (*Compt. Rend.* (1964) CCLVIII. 3128).]

1967 C. R. WOESE *Genetic Code* iv. 93 The operator locus comprises both the modulation sequence and the punctuation for tape-reader attachment. Jacob and his associates.. have more recently adduced evidence for the existence of the latter, which they call *promoter*, by a study of deletions. **1971** D. J. COVE *Genetics* xi. 163 Mutations in the promoter region lead to a reduction in the rate of messenger synthesis from the whole operon. The promoter is thought to be the region for the attachment of the DNA-dependent RNA polymerase, the enzyme responsible for transcription. **1975** *Nature* 13 Mar. 118/1 The promoter has been loosely defined as the site on the DNA where the RNA polymerase recognises some signal which allows it to bind tightly and initiate transcription.

2. One who promotes or advances another in dignity or position.

14.. [see PROMOVER]. **1670** G. H. *Hist. Cardinals* III. 301 They are disinterested, and no passionate promoters of their Kindred. **1868** FREEMAN *N. Conq.* II. vii. 80 Harold.. appears as a special promoter of German churchmen.

II. 3. a. One whose business was to prosecute or denounce offenders against the law; originally an officer appointed by the crown; later, one who prosecuted in his own name and that of the sovereign, and received a part of the fines as his fee; a professional accuser, an informer. *Obs.* exc. *Hist.*

α. **1485** *Rolls of Parlt.* VI. 347/1 The Office of oure Promotoure, by us graunted unto hym by oure Lettres Patents. **1509** BARCLAY *Shyp of Folys* (1570) 140 b, Sergeaunt, Atturney, Promoter, Judge or Scribe, Will not feele thy matter without a priuie bribe. **1566** *Roy. Proclam.* 10 Nov., Such as be infourmers vpon penall lawes and Statutes, commonly called promoters. **1603** HOLLAND *Plutarch's Mor.* 421 Aristogiton the sycophant or false promotor, being condemned to death for troubling men with wrongfull imputations. **1603** [see RELATOR 2]. **1607** COWELL *Interpr.*, *Promoters*.. be those, which in popular and penall actions doe deferre the names, or complaine of offenders, hauing part of the profit for their reward... They belong especially to the Exchequer and kings bench. *a***1661** FULLER *Worthies, Northampton* (1662) 287[Henry VII] made Empson Promoter General, to press the Penal-Statutes all over the land.

β. **1573** TUSSER *Husb.* (1878) 147 His eies be promooters, some trespas to spie. **1598** GRENEWEY *Tacitus' Ann.* IV. vii. (1622) 99 The promooters [L. *delatores*], a race of men found out for a common ouerthrow and destruction. **1607** R. C[AREW] tr. *Estienne's World of Wonders* 158 Prowling promoters. **1653** MILTON *Hirelings* Wks. 1851 V. 358 Tyndarus and Rebuffus, two canonical Promooters. **1670** BLOUNT *Law Dict.*, Promooters. **1955** W. W. GREG *Shakespeare First Folio* iv. 150 The Act may well have been a dead letter except for action by professional promooters.

†**b.** An officer appointed to prosecute students before the Rector for debts or offences, in some of the Scottish universities. Now only *Hist.* repr. med.L. *promotor*.

[**1482** *Munim. Univ. Glasguensis* (Maitl. Club) II. 9 De electione Promotoris Universitatis et eius officio.] **1854** *Ibid.* II. Table p. iv, A Promotor or General Sindic to be elected annually for the recovery of University debts, and the detection of contraventions of the Statutes. The Promotor to bring offenders before the Lord Rector... The Promotor's oath.

c. *Eccl. Law.* The prosecutor of a suit in an ecclesiastical court.

1754 HUME *Hist. Eng.* I. viii. 172 Laics should not be accused in spiritual courts, except by legal and reputable promoters and witnesses. **1821** LAMB *Elia* Ser. I. *Oxford in Vacation*, Amid an incongruous assembly of attorneys, attorneys' clerks, apparitors, promoters, vermin of the law, among whom he sits 'in calm and sinless peace'. **1876** LD. PENZANCE in *Willis v. Bp. of Oxf.* in *Law Rep., Prob. Div.* II. 198 The promoter in this proceeding of 'duplex querela' complains in his libel that having been duly presented.. the bishop has refused to institute him. *Ibid.*, That the result of the examination satisfied him (the defendant) that the promoter was *non idoneus et minus sufficiens in literaturâ*. **1889** E. S. ROSCOE *Bp. of Lincoln's Case* 1 The promoters in the suit were E. Read, W. Brown, T. F. Wilson, and J. Marshall. The respondent was the Lord Bishop of Lincoln. **1895** SIR R. PHILLIMORE *Eccl. Law* (ed. 2) 992 The promoter of the office of the judge is bound not only to give in articles, but also a correct copy to the defendant.

III. 4. A descriptive appellation in the Scottish universities (or some of them) of the official who presents students for degrees.

Properly in Latin form *promotor*, but sometimes represented historically by the Eng. form.

1699 *Edin. Gaz.* 26–29 June, Monday last being the Day appointed for the publick Graduation.. Mr. William Scot.. Promoter for this year declam'd an Elegant Harangue. **1858** *Min. Univ. St. Andrews* (MS.), XVII. 415 The Senatus appoint the ex-Rector to act in the meantime as pro-Rector and Promotor. **1894** W. L. LOW *D. Thomson* iv. 93 It was his turn to act as Promotor or 'Father' of the new graduates. **1898** A. C. FRASER *T. Reid* iv. 46 In the last year of each course, as 'promoter', he presented his undergraduates to receive the Master's degree [at King's Coll., Aberdeen]. **1962** *Aberdeen Univ. Rev.* Autumn 313 The other graduands who have obtained First Class Honours are called up, one by one, by the Promotor.

Hence **pro'moterism**, the reprobated practice or conduct of promoters of joint-stock companies.

1882 (*title*) Last Words of Thomas Carlyle on Trades-Unions: Promoterism and the Signs of the Times. **1882** *Edin. Courant* 27 Oct. 6/7 Word-painting of the diabolical promoterism of the day.

promoting (prəʊ'məʊtɪŋ), *vbl. sb.* [f. PROMOTE *v.* + -ING[1].] The action of the verb PROMOTE.

1. Advancement, furtherance, helping forward; the 'getting up' of joint-stock financial companies.

1485 *Rolls of Parlt.* VI. 276/1 The.. preferring of.. Justice and promoteinge and rewardeinge Vertue. **1529** RASTELL *Pastyme, Hist. Pap.* (1811) 54 [He was accursed] for promotynge of benefices by symony. **1648** MILTON *Observ. Art. Peace* Wks. 1851 IV. 560 To give the first promoting.. to his own tyrannical designs in England. **1771** LUCKOMBE *Hist. Print.* 41 For the promoting of their pious designs. **1890** *Pall Mall G.* 3 July 2/2 Company-promoting has become a business.

†**2.** The action of a PROMOTER (sense 3); accusing, denouncing. *Obs.*

1581 SAVILE *Tacitus' Hist.* II. x. (1591) 58 Annius Faustus .. condemned of promoting.

3. *Chem.* The action of PROMOTE *v.* 2 c.

1936 R. H. GRIFFITH *Mechanism of Contact Catalysis* iii. 82 The most useful oxides, to give the promoting effect with ion-oxide catalysts, were of the unreducible type, and would give spinels of the same cubic symmetry as Fe_3O_4. **1947** *Jrnl. Polymer Sci.* II. 42 Aliphatic mercaptans in the buradiene-styrene recipe with persulfate as catalyst exert a strong promoting effect upon the copolymerization.

pro'moting, *ppl. a.* [f. as prec. + -ING[2].] That promotes, in various senses.

†**1.** That lays an information; that is a promoter or informer. *Obs.*

1596 HARINGTON *Apol. Ajax* Aa vj b, Least some hungrie promoting fellowes should beg it as a concealement. **1604** DRAYTON *Owl* 547 Steps in this false spy, this promoting wretch, Closely betrays him that he gives to each. **1623** SANDERSON *Serm.* (1657) 121 Informing, and promoting, and pettifogging make-bates.

2. a. That furthers, assists, or fosters. Chiefly in comb., as ***company-promoting***, ***health-promoting***.

1871 'M. LEGRAND' *Cambr. Freshm.* 250 Hunting the Drag.. is so innocent, so health-promoting, and in every way so praiseworthy an amusement. **1904** *Westm. Gaz.* 1 Feb. 2/2 Colossal company-promoting swindlers.

b. *Med.* That causes tumour promotion (PROMOTION 2 d).

1944 *Jrnl. Exper. Med.* LXXX. 101 (*heading*) The initiating and promoting elements in tumor production. **1966** *Lancet* 31 Dec. 1457/2 Nevertheless, should such initiated skin be subsequently treated with a promoting agent (not itself carcinogenic), the train of events leading to cancer is again accelerated so that a visible tumour appears at the initiated site. **1970** *Cancer Res.* XXX. 312/1 It is generally agreed that promoting agents cause epidermal hyperplasia.., but not all hyperplastic agents have been shown to be promoters. **1976** [see PROMOTION 2 d].

promotion (prəʊ'məʊʃən). Also 5–6 -cio(u)n, -cyon. [a. F. *promotion* (14th c. in Hatz.-Darm.), ad. L. *prōmōtiōn-em*, n. of action f. *prōmov-ēre*: see PROMOVE.]

1. a. Advancement in position; preferment.

on promotion, on the way to promotion, on trial; ***to be on one's promotion***, to conduct oneself with a view to promotion (also *colloq.* to marriage).

1429 *Rolls of Parlt.* IV. 344/2 Ne for promotion or fortheryng of any persone to Office. **1523** LD. BERNERS *Froiss.* I. cccxxvii. 511 With his promocyon of popalyte the romayns were apeased. **1540** *Test. Ebor.* (Surtees) VI. 119, I give to Dorithe and Anne my doughters xl *li*, to be equallye devyded betwixte them towarde ther mariadge or other promocion. **1613** SHAKS. *Hen. VIII*, v. ii. 23 The high promotion of his Grace of Canterbury, Who holds his State at dore 'mongst Pursueants, Pages, and Foot-boyes. **1693** LUTTRELL *Brief Rel.* (1857) III. 81 Disgusted that he was not in the late promotion made a marshall of France. **1751** EARL ORRERY *Remarks Swift* (1752) 29 In point of power and revenue, such a deanery might be esteemed no inconsiderable promotion. **1785** CRABBE *Newspaper* 312 Promotion's ladder, who goes up or down. **1857** BUCKLE *Civiliz.* I. x. 602 In that period promotion depended solely on merit.

1836 *Lett. fr. Madras* i. (1843) 4 Several Irish girls apparently on their promotion. **1848** THACKERAY *Van. Fair* xxxix, The little kitchen-maid on her promotion. *Ibid.* xliv, 'I remember when you liked 'em, though'.. 'That was when I was on my promotion, Goosey', she said. **1888** W. E. HENLEY *Bk. Verses* 4 A square, squat room (a cellar on promotion). **1902** MISS E. P. THOMPSON in *Gentl. Mag.* Dec. 583 When the canonised saints have been worked out, he has recourse to those, as it were, 'on their promotion'.

b. *Chess.* The elevation of a pawn to the rank of a higher piece.

1803 P. PRATT *Studies of Chess* (1804) I. 30 Of promoting a pawn to be a queen, rook, &c. When a pawn has penetrated to the farthest rank on the adverse side of the board, he is rewarded with promotion to the *highest vacant* dignity. **1900** *Westm. Gaz.* 12 May 3/3 If a player.. is forced.. to the promotion which involves the loss of the game. *Ibid.* 22 Dec. 3/3 A trio of promotion problems.. representing three different types of promotion side by side.

c. *Curling.* The positional advancement of a stone by striking. Cf. PROMOTE *v.* 1 d.

1897 *Encycl. Sport* I. 261/1 A canny, or quiet, draw is expected from the lead, and it is better that his stone, when spent, should be short of the tee, where it is in the way of promotion. **1937** T. HENDERSON *Lockerbie* ix. 57 Ye're a graun' curler. That yin's in the wey o' promotion.

d. *Sport* (chiefly *Assoc. Football*). Reallocation of a team to a higher division of a league on the basis of final position in a league table after a season's play.

1907 *Times* 15 Apr. 11/3 Notts Forest and Chelsea have now made themselves certain of promotion. **1949** *Times* 25 Apr. 6/2 Swansea Town assured themselves of promotion to the Second Division. **1965** [see INJECT *v.* 2]. **1967** *Listener* 17 Aug. 223/3 'Millwall must be certainties for promotion': thus Bill Nicholson, one of the two or three most analytic club managers in England.

e. *Boxing.* The organization or staging of a contest; a contest staged.

1951 *Sport* 7–13 Jan. 14/4 This show is but the first of the season at Streatham but will be the forerunner of many more value-for-money promotions at the South London hall. **1958** F. C. AVIS *Boxing Ref. Dict.* 87 *Promotion*, the organization of a boxing contest. **1962** *Listener* 27 Sept. 466/2 The odd-looking circular building would be just the place for boxing promotions.

f. *Phonetics.* The intensification of normal stress levels in verse; an instance of this.

1956 S. CHATMAN in *Kenyon Rev.* XVIII. 424 What I have called 'metrical tension' can conveniently be described as 'promotions' or 'suppressions' of the stress levels of normal non-verse speech under the pressures of the abstract metrical pattern. **1973** *Word 1970* XXVI. 55 These examples, from Prator, illustrate suppression and promotion respectively.

g. *Bridge.* The action of promoting a card or trick (see PROMOTE *v.* 1 e).

1959 *Listener* 31 Dec. 1178/2 The problem is to prevent North.. from winning a second trump trick by promotion. **1964** *Official Encycl. Bridge* 633/2 *Trump promotion*, the creation of trump tricks through forcing the premature use of the trump cards of the opposition.

h. *Transformational Gram.* The translation of material from an embedded to a main sentence.

1968 R. W. LANGACKER *Lang. & Struct.* II. v. 128 A permutation rule that we will call Not Promotion is an interesting example that accounts for a subtle type of ambiguity in negative sentences. **1973** P. SCHACHTER in *Language* XLIX. 19 The derivation of both constructions involves the *promotion* of material from an embedded into a matrix sentence.

2. a. The action of helping forward; the fact or state of being helped forward; furtherance, advancement, encouragement. *spec.* the furtherance of the sale of something by advertisement or other modes of publicity. Also *transf.*

1483 *Caxton's Chron. Eng.* v. N viij b, To the quyete state of the chyrche and to the promocion of the fayth. **1584** *Reg. Privy Council Scot.* III. 702 To the promotioun and furtherance of the gospell. **1664** POWER *Exp. Philos.* III. 188 An Authentick discouragement to the promotion of the Arts and Sciences. **1725** T. THOMAS in *Portland Papers* VI. (Hist. MSS. Comm.) 100 There is a navigable river.. which is a great promotion of the trade of the town. **1845** S. AUSTIN *Ranke's Hist. Ref.* III. 60 Institutions for the promotion of learning. **1862** SIR B. BRODIE *Psychol. Inq.* II. vii. 233 The great agent in the promotion of civilization is the advancement of knowledge. **1925** C. MORLEY *Thunder on Left* ix. 112 He spoke of the Elevated Railroad's limited appropriation for promotion, of the peculiar problems of transportation publicity. **1928** *Publishers' Weekly* 26 May 2169 Promotion cannot be done without waste... But the idea back of the new mergers is the idea of outlets, of promotion, of selling more goods. **1932** *Ibid.* 7 May 1945/2 A free gift offer in a full page Book-of-the-Month Club promotion. **1958** *Listener* 23 Jan. 148/1 Sir Miles [Thomas] .. began his business career as an adviser to Mr. W. R. Morris.. on 'sales promotion'. **1962** *Advertisers' Rev.* 26 Oct. 17/2 Price-reductions were easily preferred to all other types of promotion... Other types of promotions considered effective were sample offers, banded offers and free gifts. **1969** *Morning Star* 20 Nov. 5 Heather.. had to show a good knowledge of BEA as well as poise and charm. She will represent the airline in promotions and conferences. **1976** *National Observer* (U.S.) 13 Nov. 9/4 Some industry observers say one of those promotions could be trading stamps, although they cost four times as much as a game promotion and require a long-term commitment from a store. **1980** *Bookseller* 12 Jan. 194/1 (Advt.), Evans Brothers Limited require a Publicity Controller to deal with the promotion of their Adult and Children's Trade Books. Applicants should.. be capable of dealing with all aspects of book promotion and advertising. *Ibid.* 194/3 The successful candidate.. will have experience in organising direct mail promotions, preparing catalogues, leaflets and adverts, [etc.]

b. The getting up of a joint-stock company.

1886 *Law Times* LXXX. 310/1 The plaintiff.. was interested in the promotion of the Georgia Gold Mines Company Limited. **1898** *Westm. Gaz.* 8 June 7/1 He had not personally reaped the benefit of some of his promotions.

c. *Chem.* The action of PROMOTE *v.* 2 c.

[**1920** *Jrnl. Physical Chem.* XXIV. 263 Such an example of auto-catalysis.. is to be distinguished from simple auto-catalysis, in which a reactant or product has a direct catalytic effect on the reaction. Here the specific effect of the product is on the catalyst... From the point of view of promoter action such a term as 'auto-activation' or 'auto-promotion' would be more appropriate.] **1926** *Jrnl. Chem. Soc.* 1817 (*heading*) Promotion with iron. **1940** GLASSTONE *Text-bk. Physical Chem.* xiii. 1128, 1 per cent. of ceria gives the optimum promotion for the catalytic action of thoria on the combination of oxygen and hydrogen. **1968** E. K. RIDEAL *Concepts in Catalysis* v. 97 The V–O stretching frequency ν = 1025 cm^{-1} is shifted to longer wavelengths by promoters such as alkaline sulphates, where the order of activity in promotion is Cs > Rb > K > Na.

d. *Med.* The furtherance of neoplastic growth following its initiation by a carcinogen; the conversion of latent tumour cells into active, malignant ones; (see quot. 1964[1]).

1944 *Jrnl. Exper. Med.* LXXX. 121 Non-Specific Promotion.—It seems certain that many agents and influences which have no actual carcinogenicity will be found to stimulate the multiplication of latent neoplastic cells. **1964** *Progress Exper. Tumor Res.* IV. 209 Cocarcinogenesis is not synonymous with tumor promotion, since promotion inherently denotes a specific step in the sequence of events leading to skin tumor formation. Conversely, cocarcinogenesis describes a situation in which response to a carcinogen is increased by a second factor introduced concurrently with the carcinogen, with no implication of impact at a specific step in tumor formation. *Ibid.* 226 Apparently, there is a threshold for the amount of croton oil that must be used in each application in order to achieve promotion. **1976** *Brit. Jrnl. Cancer* XXXIV. 660/1 The events related to tumor promotion are understood better since the isolation and chemical characterization of active promoting agents by Hecker (1968) and Van Duuren (1969).

†**3.** The laying of an information against any one. *Obs.*

a **1536** TINDALE *Exp. Matt.* v–vii. 71 Couetousnes & promocion and such like,.. are that ryghte hand and right eye that must be cut of & plucked out that the whole man peryshe not. [But this quot. perh. belongs to sense 1.]

†**4.** ? Motion or stirring of the mind. *Obs.*

1526 *Pilgr. Perf.* (W. de W. 1531) 136 Passyons of ire, enuy, sclaunderous wordes or other promocyons. **1656** STANLEY *Hist. Philos.* IV. (1701) 134/1 They held.. That nothing judgeth but by interior promotion, and the judgment of true and false consists of inward touch.

†**5.** Advance, getting on, progress made. Cf. PROMOVE *v.* 5. *Obs.*

1649 JER. TAYLOR *Gt. Exemp.* I. Sect. 7. 108 Whether it were truly or in appearance, in habit or in exercise of act.., it is certain the promotions of the holy Childe [Luke ii. 52] were great, admirable, and as full of wonder as of sanctity.

6. *attrib.* (in sense 1 a) ***promotion examination***; (sense 1 d) ***promotion contender***, ***rival***; ***promotion-challenging***, ***-chasing***, ***-seeking*** sbs. and adjs.; (sense 2 a) ***promotion campaign***, ***kit***, ***man***, ***scheme***, ***stunt***; (in sense 2 b) ***promotion allowance***, ***expense***, ***money***; **promotion bar**, a notional barrier imposed to restrict a person's promotion above a certain level unless certain specified requirements are met; **promotion sheet**, a record of an employee's service showing his claim to promotion or increased pay.

1898 *Engineering Mag.* XVI. 32 *note*, The Edinburgh arbitrator took the actual cost of promotion as the test of the promotion allowance. **1973** C. MULLARD *Black Britain* II. iv. 43 Besides overt racism employers operated a promotion bar. **1962** *Listener* 19 July 116/1 The distributors were rash in putting it [*sc.* a film] on without a promotion campaign. **1972** *Oxf. Mail* 15 Feb. 12/6 Carlisle are in their customary promotion-challenging position. **1977** *Sunday Express* 30 Jan. 31/8 Big Brian Joicey grabbed two goals to earn Barnsley a well-deserved victory over promotion-chasing rivals Bournemouth. **1978** *Rugby World* Apr. 19/1 At the time of writing they still had three matches left to play, including games against fellow promotion contenders Jedforest and Selkirk. **1899** *Westm. Gaz.* 4 Dec. 10/1 To look into the promotion expenses. **1903** *Daily Chron.* 17 Oct. 3/7 The.. promotion examinations are at hand. **1964** *Bookseller* 2 May 1783/1 The Society of Young Publishers reports that the half-way mark has been reached in their appeal for £1,000 towards the production of 'promotion kits' for mailing to 2,000 booksellers and 1,000 libraries throughout the country. **1958** *Spectator* 25 July 138/1 Given a really good labour-saving idea, the British are not so reluctant to try it as many high-powered promotion men would have us believe. **1977** *Rolling Stone* 19 May 14/4 Bennett formerly worked as a Beatles promotion man. **1882** *Pall Mall G.* 13 July 6/1 The General Hydraulic Power Company... No promotion money is to be paid. **1977** *News of World* 17 Apr. 24/7 It was just as well that most of Brighton's promotion rivals faltered yesterday. **1925** C. MORLEY *Thunder on Left* xx. 250 The children had found some deceptive promotion scheme advertised in a cheap magazine. **1958** *New Statesman* 26 Apr. 548/1 Some people seem to think that there is something bogus about these promotion schemes and that their cost would be better applied in making a permanent price reduction. **1976** *Norwich Mercury* 10 Dec., The mark of a promotion-seeking team is to win when playing badly. **1909** *Daily Chron.* 23 Mar. 1/4 The manipulation of their promotion sheets, with the object of postponing the payment of justly earned increased salaries, was one of the grievances of the strikers. **1955** W. GADDIS *Recognitions* II. ii. 372 It was all fixed up about this guy who jumped out a window... It's something for a TV promotion stunt.

promotional (prəʊˈməʊʃənəl), *a.* [f. PROMOTION + -AL.] Promotive; of or pertaining to promotion (usu. sense 2) or promoters; relating to advertising.

1922 *Universalist Leader* 13 May 4 Experience has disclosed that emotional contributions are promotional of the very poverty we had felt moved to alleviate. **1926** *Publisher's Weekly* 22 May 1675/1 As a further promotional step the.. Company is displaying a letter commenting on its service. **1935** *Sun* (Baltimore) 10 Jan. 11/5 Consolidated Gas picked up more than a point on hopes of an amicable adjustment of its rate controversies with the regulatory authority through adoption of a 'promotional' schedule of charges. **1950** *Sport* 22–28 Sept. 14/1 A promotional 'war' seems certain over the privilege of staging a fight with Lee Savold. **1959** *Sociometry* Sept. 273 Some effects of promotional frustration on employees' understanding of, and attitudes toward, management. **1960** W. TAPLIN *Advertising* i. 12 Some of the ideas involved in advertising.. the complex of promotional activities of which they form part. **1963** *Guardian* 2 Feb. 12/7 What about that for promotional literature? **1978** *Incorporated Linguist* Summer 60/3 Nearly twenty years ago, a totally unknown mineral water gained national fame in France through a relatively inexpensive and brilliant promotional campaign relying solely on the slogan '*Bébé aime Charrier*' originally spelt 'B.B.' thus capitalizing instantaneously on the tempestous Bardot-Charrier romance. **1980** *Bookseller* 12 Jan. 165/2 His publishers' promotional machinery was faultlessly efficient.

promotive (prəʊˈməʊtɪv), *a.* (*sb.*) [f. as PROMOTE *v.* + -IVE, after MOTIVE *a.* Cf. Anglo-L. *prōmōtīvus* (1337 in Du Cange).] Having the quality of promoting; tending to the promotion (*of* a thing).

1644 J. GOODWIN *Innoc. Triumph.* (1645) 76 They will use [it] rather in a destructive, then promotive way thereunto. **1680** *Relig. Dutch* v. 46 Promotive to the advancement of Christian Religion. **1711** SHAFTESB. *Charac.* III. Misc. II. iii. 98 Corroborative of Religion, and promotive of true Faith. **1824** MISS MITFORD *Village* Ser. I. 277 The air is so promotive of growth. **1882** FAIRBAIRN in *Contemp. Rev.* XLII. 860 Agencies powerfully promotive of human progress.

B. *sb. nonce-use.* That which promotes or furthers something.

1793 W. TAYLOR in *Monthly Rev.* XII. 286 To evolve its real promotives.

Hence **proˈmotiveness**, the quality of being promotive; tendency to promote or further.

a **1866** J. GROTE *Exam. Utilit. Philos.* (1870) 251 He has defined utilitarianism as the philosophy which values one thing simply in regard of actions, viz. their promotiveness of happiness. **1874** P. SMYTH *Our Inher.* xi. 224 To set forth .. their promotiveness to the fulness of thought as well as the material comforts of.. man.

proˈmotor. *rare*⁻¹. [a. med.L.: see PROMOTER.] † **1.** *Obs.* A procurator, prolocutor, or proctor.

1706 tr. *Dupin's Eccl. Hist. 16th C.* II. III. i. 2 Hercules Sevecollus, Promotor of the Council.

2. *Chem.* = PROMOTER 1 d.

1931 *Chem. Abstr.* XXV. 428 The influence of various other promotors and protectors in hydrogenation is studied. **1976** J. PETRÓ in Szabó & Kalló *Contact Catalysis* II. v. 60 Additives which have a favourable effect on the operation of catalysts are termed promotors (activators).

3. Var. PROMOTER 1 f. *rare.*

† **promotorial** (prəʊməʊˈtɔərɪəl), *a. Obs.* [f. med.L. *prōmōtor* (see prec.) + -IAL; cf. obs. F. *promotoriel* (1589 in Godef.), = med.L. **prōmōtōrius*.] Of or pertaining to a procurator; ***promotorial letters***, letters of attorney.

1631–3 J. DURIE in *Presbyt. Rev.* (1887) 301 [The King] had promised to give mee Promotoriall letters to further this end. *Ibid.* 303 How.. to goe to the King of Sweden for his Promotoriall Letters towards ye Lutheran princes.

promotress (prəʊˈməʊtrɪs). [f. PROMOTER + -ESS¹.] A female promoter. So [in L. form] **proˈmotrix**, in same sense.

1622 H. SYDENHAM *Serm. Sol. Occ.* II. (1637) 107 A promotresse and bawd to error. **1678** ANTH. WALKER *Funeral C'tess Warwick* 48 The greatest Mistress, and Promotress.. of a new Science—The Art of obliging. **1892** *Cornh. Mag.* July 14 The promotress of mothers' meetings. **1660** J. LLOYD *Prim. Episc.* 17 A zealous promotrix of the Schism of the Donatists.

promovable (prəʊˈmuːvəb(ə)l), *a.* [f. PROMOVE *v.* + -ABLE.] = PROMOTABLE *a.*; esp. in phr. ***removable and promovable*** (cf. PROMOTABLE *a.*, quot. 1887), of Sc. and Ir. magistrates.

1920 W. O'BRIEN *Evening Memories* xiii. 216 Two paid magistrates removable and promovable at the caprice of Dublin Castle.

† **proˈmoval.** *Sc. Obs. rare.* [f. PROMOVE *v.* + -AL¹.] Promotion, furtherance, advancement.

1683 RENWICK *Serm.*, etc. (1776) 570 For promoval and defence of Reformation. **1687** in Shields *Faithful Contendings* (1780) 300 For the promoval and defence of these testimonies. *a* **1693** *Urquhart's Rabelais* III. xxix. 246 Steadable for the promoval of the good of that Youth.

† **proˈmove,** *v. Obs.* [ad. L. *prōmovēre* to move forward, promote: see PRO-¹ and MOVE *v.* Cf. OF. *por-, promovoir*, mod. *promouvoir*, perh. the immediate source.]

1. *trans.* = PROMOTE *v.* 1.

c **1425** *Found. St. Bartholomew's* (E.E.T.S.) 34 The sone of Stevyne.. the whiche promouyd Theobalde.. in-to the Archebisshope of Cawntirbery. **1513** DOUGLAS *Æneis* VII. Pref., Lat euery nobyll Prynce.. luf vertew and iustice, heat vyce, punys euyll men, and promowe gud men. *a* **1578** LINDESAY (Pitscottie) *Chron. Scot.* (S.T.S.) I. 62 [He] laborit daylie to promove his freindis to honour and dignatie. **1671** J. BRYDALL *Law Eng. Nobility & Gentry* (1675) 2 Nobility being then a Quality or Dignity, whereby a Man is.. promoved out of, and above the Estate of the vulgar.

2. = PROMOTE *v.* 2.

c **1400** *Apol. Loll.* 51 Prelats promouing, or secular lordis procuring þat þat clerk lord in þat maner, þei synnun deadly. **1566** *Let. Gen. Assembly Ch. Scot. to Eng. Ch.* 19 To promove the Kingdom of Jesus Christ. *a* **1641** SUCKLING *Loving & Beloved* Poems (1646) 5 It is impossible, nor can Integrity our ends promove. **1677** GALE *Crt. Gentiles* II. III. 19 Making use of the Christian Religion only as a blind or politic medium to promove their gain. **1702** C. MATHER *Magn. Chr.* IV. iv. (1852) 77 The 'sons of the prophets', whose establishment 'in the present truth', I am.. under an obligation to promove.

3. To move mentally, provoke, instigate, incite.

c **1477** CAXTON *Jason* 10 To this promouid him enuye and disloyal detraccion. **1637** GILLESPIE *Eng. Pop. Cerem.* Ep. B iij b, A Law ought to draw back men from evill,.. it ought also to promove them unto good.

4. To move outward, remove to another place. *rare.*

1535 STEWART *Cron. Scot.* (Rolls) II. 329 Tha war promouit till ane vther place At will.. of the kingis grace.

5. *intr.* To move on, advance, make progress.

1570 BUCHANAN *Chamæleon* Wks. (1892) 43 This monsture promovit to sic maturitie of aige as it could easelie flatter and imitat euery manis countenance. **1627** S. WARD *Happiness of Practice* 38 We can doe iust nothing, but lye becalmed and vnable to moue or promoue as a Ship on the Sea. **1655** GURNALL *Chr. in Arm.* I. 77 How few are there who endeavour to promove in their spiritual state.

promovent (ˈprəʊməʊvənt), *a.* (*sb.*) [ad. L. *prōmovēnt-em*, pr. pple. of *prōmovēre*: see prec.]

† **1.** That 'promoves' or promotes; causing advancement or progress. *Obs. rare.*

1625 *Debates Ho. Comm.* (Camden) 86 To shew.. the remedyes both removent and promovent. **1677** GALE *Crt. Gentiles* II. IV. 169 Religion is both the conversant and promovent cause of States. **1809** KNOX & JEBB *Corr.* I. 540 In fact, I never wish to be promovent in any thing.

† **2.** Prosecuting, suing. *Obs. rare.*

1693 WOOD *Allegation* in *Life & Times* (O.H.S.) IV. 17 *Item.* That the book entituled Athenæ Oxonienses,.. exhibited by the party promovent in this cause,.. was first enter'd in the book of the register of the company of Stationers of London.

B. *sb.* The promoter of a suit in an ecclesiastical court; = PROMOTER 3 c.

1877 *Willis v. Bp. of Oxf.* in *Law Rep., Prob. Div.* II. 192 This was a suit of duplex querela arising out of the refusal of .. the Bishop.. to institute the promovent.. to the rectory. *Ibid.* 193 Dr. Tristram on behalf of the promovent, moved the Dean of Arches.. Lord Penzance.. to give leave to the promovent to bring in his libel. *Ibid.* 203 Dr. Swabey.. moved the Court to dismiss the defendant from the suit; the promovent being dead. [So all though the case; but in the judgement Lord P. used 'promoter': see PROMOTER 3 c.]

† **proˈmover.** *Obs.* [f. PROMOVE *v.* + -ER¹.] One who or that which 'promoves' or promotes: = PROMOTER 1 (in quot. 14.. = PROMOTER 2).

14.. WYNTOUN *Cron.* VI. 1009 (Wemyss MS.) His promovare [*Cotton MS.* promotour] him oft assayit How of his part he held him payit. **1545** JOYE *Exp. Dan.* vii. 102 Bokis & heresies as they call goddis worde, to be prohibited, pressed downe, & burned with all the promouers therof. **1614** BP. FORBES *Comm. Rev.* xiii. 109 The dragon.. substituteth this viceroy.. the most effectuall promoouer of darkenesse that euer was. **1638** M. GRIFFITH in Hearne *Collect.* 7 Jan. an. 1706 (O.H.S.) I. 160 A zealous promover of good Works. **1650** *Rec. Dingwall Presbytery* (O.H.S.) 173 Plotters and prime promovers yʳoff.

† **proˈmoving,** *vbl. sb. Obs.* [f. as prec. + -ING¹.] The action of promoting, promotion; moving.

14.. tr. *Secreta Secret.* App. 249 Of promovyng of Study. **1610** DONNE *Pseudo-martyr* 204 For the promouing of Christs glorie. *a* **1631** —— *Serm.* viii. (1640) 81 Those works of ours.. that.. conduce most to the promoving of others to glorifie God. *a* **1639** SPOTTISWOOD *Hist. Ch. Scot.* II. (1677) 32 To have his advice for the promoving of some worthy person unto the place. **1721** WODROW *Hist. Suffer. Ch. Scot.* (1829) II. 170 The promoving of real religion in themselves and others.

prompt (prɒm(p)t), *sb.* [In branch I. ad. L. *promptus* readiness, f. ppl. stem of *prōm-ĕre* (see next); in II. f. PROMPT *v.*; in III. f. PROMPT *a.*]

I. † **1.** Readiness; preparedness. ***in prompt*** (= L. *in promptu*), in readiness. *Obs. rare.*

c **1425** *Found. St. Bartholomew's* (E.E.T.S.) 34 He hadde yt in prompte what sumeuer he wolde vttir to speke yt metyrly.

II. 2. a. An act of prompting; instigation; something said or suggested to incite to action, or to help the memory. Cf. PROMPT *v.* 2.

1597 J. PAYNE *Royal Exch.* 27 Common dronckards and carnall lyvers.. esteme themeselves as honest and as truly religiouse as the best, and bothe by a subtill prompt of the divill. **1721** CIBBER *Com. Lovers* v, You won't forget.. to give me a Prompt upon occasion. **1881** M. A. LEWIS *Two Pretty G.* III. 12 She.. was glad to accept a prompt from her neighbour.

b. *spec.* in *Theat.* The act of the prompter on the stage. Chiefly in *Comb.*, as **prompt-bell**, the bell used by a prompter in a theatre to summon an actor; **prompt-box**, the prompter's box on a stage; **prompt-centre**, the position on a stage half-way between the centre and the prompt-side; **prompt-copy** = PROMPT-BOOK; **prompt corner**, the prompter's corner off-stage; **prompt entrance** (see quot. 1952); **prompt script** = PROMPT-BOOK; **prompt-side**, the side of the stage where the prompter takes up his position, usu. on the actor's left (*U.S.*, on the right); **prompt table**, the table on which the prompter rests his book; **prompt-word**, a word spoken by a prompter (in quot. *transf.*).

1784 *New Spectator* No. 6. 7 Then recommences the music of the iritated Gods.. after that comes the tinkling of the *prompt bell. **1859** SALA *Tw. round Clock* (1861) 263, I happened to be almost born in a *prompt-box and weaned in a scene-painter's size-kettle. **1891** *Pall Mall G.* 30 Sept. 3/1 The prompt-box was placed in the centre of the stage; but, owing to there being no floor below the stage, our prompter.. had to raise a trap-door in the stage, and to crawl along, on hands and knees. **1884** HALLIWELL-PHILLIPPS in *Athenæum* 25 Oct. 529/2 An old *prompt copy may have wandered out of England. **1933** P. GODFREY *Back-Stage* i. 17 A good stage-manager is never far from the *prompt corner. **1967** *Listener* 21 Sept. 370/3 When the moment came, I was standing in the prompt corner with.. the stage-director. **1886** M. MACKINTOSH *Stage Reminisc.* ii. 25 It would give him a better chance with the audience to sing it from the '*prompt' entrance. **1890** B. HALL *Turnover Club* xx. 187 One evening he was standing in the 'prompt entrance' with a prominent actress who was starring at the house then. **1952** GRANVILLE *Dict. Theatr. Terms* 143 *Prompt entrance*, that way on to the stage from the prompt corner which is for the use of the stage management. **1920** WODEHOUSE *Jill the Reckless* (1922) xiv. 210 The assistant stage-director bent sedulously over the footlights.. shading his eyes with the *prompt script. **1824** R. HUMPHREYS *Mem. J. Decastro* 30 A thunder-drum, which now stands on the *prompt side of the theatre. **1838** DICKENS *Nich. Nick.* xxiii, Nicholas found himself close to the first entrance on the prompt side. **1898** *Daily Chron.* 11 Oct. 3/4 On the prompt side some picturesque little bazaars are being fitted up. **1963** C. MACKENZIE *My Life & Times* I. 90 The next thing I remember is sitting on my nurse's knee in the front of the dress circle of the Cork Opera House on the right-hand side, or as an actor would say, on the prompt side. **1844** J. COWELL *Thirty Years passed among Players* II. ii. 59/2 Every book or manuscript they have an opportunity to place upon a *prompt-table. **1967** *Listener* 21 Sept. 369/2 He caught sight of Trebel.. lurking by the prompt table. **1918** A. QUILLER-COUCH *Foe-Farrell* 176, I knew.. that I must break his fate to him. I even gave him the *prompt-word. 'Homelike', I suggested.

c. *Computing.* A request or message given by a computer in use, requiring or helping the user to respond.

1977 in A. CHANDOR et al. *Dict. Computers* (ed. 2) 330. **1984** *Personal Software* Winter 53/1 A prompt appears asking for the mode in which the picture is to be drawn. **1985** *Which Computer?* Apr. 51/2 Prompts and help messages reduce the possibility of making an error in the first place.

III. 3. *Commerce.* **a.** (ellipt. for *prompt date, day, time.*) A trade term for a limit of time given for payment of the account for produce purchased; the limit (varying with different goods) being stated on a note of reminder called a ***prompt-note***; hence = due-date.

1755 MAGENS *Insurances* I. 348 This 1 per Cent., which was left out on account of the different Prompts for Payment, must either be deducted on none or both the Accounts. **1848** MILL *Pol. Econ.* II. 64 The speculation went on at advancing prices.. till nearly the expiration of the prompt. **1858** SIMMONDS *Dict. Trade, Prompt-note*, a note of reminder of the day of payment and sum due, etc., given to a purchaser at a sale of produce. **1890** *Pall Mall G.* 24 Nov. 7/3 In goods like tea, where the prompt, or time allowed before the goods are taken up, is long, a deposit of something like one-third of the value has to be made at the time of purchase... In most.. leading goods the prompt is short. *Mod.* If you offered me corn at so much, I might reply 'At what prompt?' or 'What is the prompt?'

b. See quot.

1882 BITHELL *Counting-ho. Dict.* (1893) 245 *Prompt*... In commerce, the setting forth in a written document the record of a bargain or sale, in such a form as to render it negotiable... A prompt is an agreement between a shipper or importer on the one hand, and a merchant on the other; in which the former engages to sell certain specified goods at a given price, and the latter to take them up and pay for them at a specified date... It implies.. that the goods shall be 'promptly' paid for on delivery, if delivered before the specified date, and at the specified date, whether they are delivered or not.

c. ellipt. for *prompt goods* (see PROMPT *a.* 3): Goods sold under an agreement as to a prompt or time-limit.

prompt (prɒm(p)t), *a.* (*adv.*) [a. F. *prompt* (1219 in Godef. *Compl.*), or ad. L. *prompt-us* brought forth, brought to light, manifest; at hand, ready, quick, prepared, disposed, inclined; pa. pple. of *prōm-ĕre* to bring forth or out, produce, bring to light, f. *prō*, PRO-¹ 1 a + *em-ĕre* to take, to buy.]

A. *adj.* **1. a.** Ready in action; quick to act when occasion arises; acting with alacrity; ready and willing.

1432-50 tr. *Higden* (Rolls) V. 61 A man of lawe bloode of Briteyne, Carausius by name, but prompte in cownsel [L. *consilio et manu promptus*]. **1494** FABYAN *Chron.* v. cxvi. 91 She that was prompte & redy to all euyll, cast in her mynde that this chylde was slayne by poyson. **1549** *Compl. Scot.* Prol. 12 Thai ar mair prompt to repreif ane smal ignorant falt, nor to commende ane grit verteous act. **1555** EDEN *Decades* 58 A man of prompt wytte. **1606** SHAKS. *Ant. & Cl.* III. xiii. 75 Tell him, I am prompt To lay my Crowne at's feete, and there to kneele. **1728** POPE *Dunc.* II. 381 Three pert Templars came..Each prompt to query, answer, and debate. **1808** SCOTT *Marm.* VI. xvi, A matchless horse, though something old, Prompt to his paces, cool and bold. **1851** CARLYLE *Sterling* I. i. (1872) 5 The promptest and least hesitating of men. **1870** BURTON *Hist. Scot.* (1873) VI. lxxii. 290 The friend who had ever been prompt in the time of peril.

fig. **1525** LD. BERNERS *Froiss.* II. cxxxiii. [cxxix.] 373 Thus they went saylyng by the see freshly..the see was so prompe and so agreeable to them.

†**b.** Ready in mind; inclined, disposed. *rare.*

1606 SHAKS. *Tr. & Cr.* IV. iv. 90, I cannot sing..Nor play at subtill games; faire vertues all; To which the Grecians are most prompt and pregnant.

†**c.** Hasty, forward, abrupt, blunt. *Obs. rare.*

1768 STERNE *Sent. Journ.* (1775) I. 35 A prompt French marquis, at our ambassador's table, demanded of Mr. H——, if he was H—— the poet? No, said H—— mildly — *Tant pis*, replied the Marquis.

2. a. Of action, speech, etc.: Characterized by readiness or quickness; done, performed, etc. at once, at the moment, or on the spot.

1526 *Pilgr. Perf.* (W. de W. 1531) 234 Contemplacyon is a free & a prompte or redy syght of the eye of the mynde. **1542** (*title*) Apophthegmes, that is to saie, prompte, quicke, wittie and sentencious saiynges, of certain Emperours, Kynges,..Philosophiers and Oratours,..compiled in Latine by..Maister Erasmus..And now translated into Englyshe by Nicolas Udall. **1624** WOTTON *Archit.* in *Reliq.* (1651) 260 The reception of Light into the Body of the building, was very prompt. **1667** MILTON *P.L.* v. 149 Such prompt eloquence Flowed from their lips, in prose or numerous verse. **1706** PHILLIPS, *Prompt Payment*, a present paying of Money, a Term in Merchandize. **1766** W. GORDON *Gen. Counting-ho.* 371 His creditor..demands prompt payment in cash..in ready money. **1791** BOSWELL *Johnson* Advt., The stretch of mind and prompt assiduity. **1834** MACAULAY *Ess.*, *Pitt* (1887) 322 Those qualities which enable men to form prompt and judicious decisions. **1877** W. S. GILBERT *Sorcerer* I, We deduct 10 per cent for prompt cash.

†**b.** *transf.* Suddenly emergent; demanding instant action. *Obs. rare.*

1634 SIR T. HERBERT *Trav.* 157 Very apt in prompt occasions, to demonstrate valour and resolution.

3. *Commerce.* For immediate delivery (and payment); also, due at once, or at the date fixed. Cf. PROMPT *sb.* 3.

1879 *Expression in London Tea-trade*, When are the overland teas prompt? [The regular word for *due* in reference to the proceeds of sales of tea and other merchandise.] **1883** *Daily News* 25 Sept. 2/7 Beetroot—Old crop, 89½ per cent., sold prompt at 20*s.* 7½*d.* **1884** *St. James's Gaz.* 28 Apr. 7/2 Rates for prompt boats are not well maintained. **1888** *Daily News* 24 Dec. 2/6 The prompt figure for No. 3 [pig iron] has been 33*s.* 6*d.*; 34*s.* to 34*s.* 3*d.* is quoted January to March. **1894** *Ibid.* 31 Dec. 2/6 There have been a few odd prompt lots sold at 35*s.* No 3. **1898** *Ibid.* 16 May 8/6 Sometimes 40*s.* 7½*d.* will be taken for prompt iron by merchants.

4. *Nucl. Physics.* Of a neutron or gamma ray: emitted within a small fraction of a second as the direct result of a fission, as distinct from radiation due to the decay of fission products.

1947 M. DEUTSCH in C. Goodman *Sci. & Engin. of Nucl. Power* I. ii. 84 The average total kinetic energy of the two fission fragments from U^{236} is about 160 Mev. In addition, the prompt neutrons have kinetic energies totaling about 5 Mev. If the energy of excitation of the fission fragment immediately after its formation is insufficient to cause neutron emission, the nucleus may lose energy by the emission of prompt gamma rays. **1950** [see *delayed neutron*]. **1962** H. D. BUSH *Atomic & Nuclear Physics* vii. 140 'Prompt' γ-rays are also observed due to the excitation of the primary fission products. **1973** *Physical Rev.* VII. C. 1180/1 In Table 1 the energy emitted per fission event in the form of prompt-γ radiation and the number of γ rays per fission are given for a number of energy intervals above 0·14 MeV. **1974** S. E. HUNT *Fission, Fusion & Energy Crisis* vi. 53 Reactors are operated so that if they relied on the neutrons emitted instantaneously on fission, on so-called 'prompt' neutrons, alone, the fission chain reaction would be subcritical, i.e. the reaction would die away.

B. as *adv.* **a.** Promptly, to the minute or the fixed time; sharp.

Mod. She must be called prompt at seven o'clock.

b. Promptly; soon.

1910 W. M. RAINE *Bucky O'Connor* ii. 23 The reverend gentleman..had this diverting experience so prompt after he was wishing for it.

C. *Comb.* of adj., as ***prompt-witted***; of adv. as ***prompt-paying*** (that pays promptly); **prompt-critical** *a. Nucl. Physics*, critical even when the effect of delayed neutrons is neglected and prompt neutrons alone are considered; hence **prompt-criticality**.

1954 R. STEPHENSON *Introd. Nucl. Engin.* ii. 64 When the *k* for a U^{235} reactor is exactly equal to 1·0073, there is sufficient reactivity to maintain the chain reaction by means of the prompt neutrons alone, and the reactor is said to be prompt critical. **1956** S. GLASSTONE *Princ. Nucl. Reactor Engin.* iv. 242 The rapid increase in the flux when the reactivity exceeds the prompt-critical value would make the reactor difficult to control, and special precautions must be taken that this condition does not arise in reactor operation. **1973** D. R. INGLIS *Nucl. Energy* IV. 120 Plutonium has only about one-third as many delayed neutrons as does uranium (about 0·23 percent of neutrons are delayed), and this provides only a narrow margin for adjustments below a prompt critical condition. **1954** R. STEPHENSON *Introd. Nucl. Engin.* vii. 269 This is the condition for prompt criticality. **1974** S. E. HUNT *Fission, Fusion & Energy Crisis* vi. 53 Prompt criticality would be even more serious in a fast reactor of the Dounreay type than in the more usual thermal neutron reactors, since the neutrons do not need to be slowed down between one generation of fissions and the next. **1899** *Daily News* 6 June 8/6 Good, prompt-paying, established tenants. **1594** CAREW *Huarte's Exam. Wits* viii. (1596) 112 None, who is prompt-witted, can learne to read without stumbling.

prompt (prɒm(p)t), *v.* Also 4-5 promtt, 5-6 promp, 6 prompte, 6-7 promt. *Pa. pple.* **prompted**, rarely in 7 **prompt**. [f. prec. adj. or its F. or L. original, in sense 'to make prompt or ready to do something'.

The genesis of the verb is not clear; the first example (if certain) is earlier than any known instance of the use of the adj. in Eng., and suggests the prior use of a med.L. **promptāre* or F. **prompter* = It. *prontare*, to make ready, to prompt; of this in Fr. or med.L. no example has been found, but its agent-n. *promptātor* occurs in *Promp. Parv.*: see PROMPTER 1.]

1. *trans.* To incite to action; to move or instigate (a person, etc.) *to do*, or *to* something.

a **1340** HAMPOLE *Psalter* xxxiv. 7 þe deuel foluand & promttand. *c* **1440** *Promp. Parv.* 415/1 Promptyn, *promo, incenso, insumo.* *c* **1440** *Alphabet of Tales* 444 Anoder was with the at þou saw nott, þat stude evur and prompyd the to wurk besylie. **1592** SHAKS. *Rom. & Jul.* II. ii. 80 By whose direction found'st thou out this place?.. By Loue that first did promp me to enquire. **1607** —— *Timon* II. ii. 150 When I haue Prompted you in the ebbe of your estate, And your great flow of debts. **1657** S. PURCHAS *Pol. Flying-Ins.* 12 A hot Sun-shine or warmer aire (even in Winter) will quickly prompt them out of their Hives. **1673** O. WALKER *Educ.* (1677) 90 Defer what your passion promts you to do. **1745** *De Foe's Eng. Tradesman* vi. (1841) I. 36 Their pride prompting them to put it to the utmost trial. **1837** DISRAELI *Venetia* II. i, A mysterious instinct prompted her.

b. *absol.*

1830 S. ROGERS *Italy*, *Meillerie* 62 Records of the past That prompt to hero-worship. **1855** BAIN *Senses & Int.* II. ii. §3 (1864) 124 When two feelings prompt in opposite ways, the one that determines the conduct is said to be volitionally the stronger. **1856** KANE *Arct. Expl.* II. xiii. 133 They migrate in numbers as their necessities prompt.

2. *trans.* To assist (a speaker when at a loss) by suggesting something to be said, or (a reciter) by supplying the words that come next. Used esp. of thus helping a pupil in his recitation, or an actor in speaking his part. (Cf. PROMPT *sb.* 2 b.)

1428 *Surtees Misc.* (1888) 5 John Lyllyng come unto hym and promped hym, and bad hym say [etc.]. **1542** UDALL *Erasm. Apoph.* 241 Yᵗ euery such suter..should knowe to salute & cal euery citezen by his name without the helpe of any byddelle to prompe hym. *a* **1568** ASCHAM *Scholem.* (Arb.) 89 Let him translate it into Latin againe, abiding in soch place, where no other scholer may prompe him. **1679** *Establ. Test* 8 To stand behind the Scene, and prompt both Parties, to Act the bloody Tragedy. **1778** BP. LOWTH *Transl. Isaiah* xxx. 21 Thine ears shall hear the word prompting thee behind. **1874** BURNAND *My Time* viii. 69 It was like being prompted in an examination, and being unable to catch the word.

†**b.** To remind, put (one) in mind. *Obs.*

1599 SHAKS. *Much Ado* I. i. 306 All prompting mee how faire yong Hero is.

3. To urge, suggest, or dictate (a thing); to inspire, give rise to (thought, action).

1602 WARNER *Alb. Eng.* XIII. lxxviii. (1612) 323 That be not Two or diuers Gods is also prompt by this. **1610** SHAKS. *Temp.* I. ii. 420 It goes on I see As my soule prompts it. **1624** QUARLES *Sion's Elegies* xvii. Div. Poems (1717) 382 She prompteth how to break New languages. **1673** *Vain Insolency of Rome* 15, I shall not repent that I prompt these intimations unto you. **1717** POPE *Eloisa* 216 Whisp'ring Angels prompt her golden dreams. **1722** DE FOE *Plague* (1756) 222 To prompt due Impressions of the Awe of God on the Minds of Men. **1810** SCOTT *Lady of L.* II. i, 'Tis morning prompts the linnet's blithest lay. **1873** BLACK *Pr. Thule* xxvi, Lavender knew well what prompted these scornful comments on Borva. **1887** BOWEN *Virg. Æneid* IV. 290 The reasons that prompt this policy new.

†**b.** With direct and indirect (dative) obj. *Obs.*

1607 SHAKS. *Cor.* III. ii. 54 Not..by th' matter Which your heart prompts you. **1632** SIR T. HAWKINS tr. *Mathieu's Unhappy Prosperitie* 101 Nature so unworthily outraged, prompted him these imprecations.

Hence **'prompted**, **'prompting** *ppl. adjs.*

1588 SHAKS. *L.L.L.* IV. iii. 322 The prompting eyes, Of beauties tutors. **1671** MILTON *P.R.* I. 12 Inspire As thou art wont my prompted Song. **1826** FOSTER in *Life & Corr.* (1846) II. 80 A prompting impulse to go and look for him.

'prompt-book. [f. PROMPT *sb.* 2 b + BOOK.] A copy of a play prepared for the prompter's use, containing the text as it is to be spoken, and directions for the performance.

1809 MALKIN *Gil Blas* VII. vii. ¶23 As invariable a rule as any in the prompt book. **1820** HAZLITT *Lect. Dram. Lit.* 136 The characters of their heroes have not been cut down to fit into the prompt-book. **1867** DICKENS *Let.* 16 Sept., Going over the prompt-book carefully, I see one change in your part to which..I positively object.

prompter ('prɒm(p)tə(r)). Also 5 -ar(e, -owre, 7 -or. [f. PROMPT *v.* + -ER¹.] One who prompts.

1. One who moves or incites to action; an instigator, mover.

c **1440** *Promp. Parv.* 415/1 Promptare, or he þat promptythe (*v. r.* promptowre), *promptator.* *a* **1548** HALL *Chron., Hen. VI* 176 The Mayre aunswered that he..neded neither of prompter, nor yet of Coadiutor, either to defend or gouerne the citie. **1637** NABBES *Microcosmus* III. i, Come my best prompter, with indeavours wings Let's cut the ayre. **1722** DE FOE *Col. Jack* (1840) 244 The devil is..a..prompter to wickedness, if he is not the first mover of it. **1875** BUCKLAND *Log-bk.* 130 No greater prompter of good fellowship.

2. a. One who helps a speaker or reciter by supplying him, when at a loss, with a name, word, or something to say.

1592 GREENE *Groat's W. Wit* (1617) 13 He stoode like a trewant that lackt a Prompter. **1657** W. MORICE *Coena quasi Κοινὴ* xv. 188 The very season was a kinde of prompter to remember them of that. **1661** *Papers on Alter. Prayer Bk.* 77 We pray without a Monitor or promptor because we do it from the heart, or from our own breast. **1870** ANDERSON *Missions Amer. Bd.* II. xi. 90, After two or three years, she was able to spell out her words without a prompter.

b. *spec. Theat.* A person stationed out of sight of the audience, to prompt or assist any actor at a loss in remembering his part. Also *Comb.* in possessive, as **prompter's bell, box, copy, table** = *prompt-bell, -box, -copy, table* s.v. PROMPT *sb.* 2 b.

1604 SHAKS. *Oth.* I. ii. 84 Were it my Cue to fight, I should haue knowne it Without a Prompter. **1710** STEELE *Tatler* No. 193 ¶2 A Letter from poor old Downes the Prompter, wherein that Retainer of the Theatre desires my Advice. **1874** BURNAND *My Time* xvii. 144 Everybody being more or less inaudible, with the solitary exception of the Prompter.

1812 C. MATHEWS *Let.* 20 Jan. in A. Mathews *Mem. Charles Mathews* (1838) II. viii. 187, I..never did believe (nor will I, till I hear the prompter's bell) that Drury would be played in next winter. **1895** W. ARCHER *Theatr. World 1894* 369 Where, at the stroke of the prompter's bell, a new world is revealed to the delighted sense. **1775** F. ABINGTON *Let.* in *Private Corr. D. Garrick* (1835) II. 32 Begging leave to sit in the prompter's box. **1870** E. L. BLANCHARD *Diary* 23 Mar. in Scott & Howard *Life E. L. Blanchard* (1891) II. 381 Adelphi; Byron's new four-act drama of *The Prompter's Box: A Story of the Footlights and the Fireside*. **1770** A. MURPHY *Let.* 20 Sept. in *Private Corr. D. Garrick* (1831) I. 399 Having the prompter's copy in my drawer for above two years past. **1834** W. C. MACREADY *Diary* 10 June (1912) I. 152, I came up and was first at rehearsal; from the prompter's table I wrote a hasty note to R. Price. **1889** J. L. TOOLE *Reminisc.* I. i. 29, I was sitting at the prompter's table, when I heard a voice at my elbow.

prompting ('prɒm(p)tɪŋ), *vbl. sb.* [f. as prec. + -ING¹.] The action of the verb PROMPT; an incitement to action, an instigation.

1401 *Pol. Poems* (Rolls) II. 96 ȝit, Dawe, thou drawist in many fals promptynges. *c* **1440** *Alphabet of Tales* 294 Be prompyng of þe Holie Gaste. **1580** SIR R. MANWOOD in Boys *Sandwich* (1792) 231 In such [school] exercises, promptinge and helping one of another to be more punished then lack of well doinge. **1851** MAYNE REID *Scalp Hunt.* xxviii, In spite of the promptings of our appetites.

promptitude ('prɒm(p)tɪtjuːd). [a. F. *promptitude* (15th c. in Hatz.-Darm.), or ad. late L. *promptitūdo*: see PROMPT *a.* and -TUDE.] Quickness or readiness of action; promptness.

c **1450** tr. *De Imitatione* I. xxiii. 31 Labour of penaunce, promptitude of obedience. **1587** *Reg. Privy Council Scot.* IV. 175 His Hienes doubtis not of the lyke reddines, promptitude, and gude will. **1658** R. WHITE tr. *Digby's Powd. Symp.* (1660) 75 They unite with more promptitude. **1751** JOHNSON *Rambler* No. 113 ¶6 Assurance of address, and promptitude of reply. **1863** A. BLOMFIELD *Mem. Bp. Blomfield* II. ix. 183 His promptitude was remarkable: with him a matter would be completed, while another would be only thinking of it.

†**b.** Readiness of mind, inclination; prompting.

1660 JER. TAYLOR *Duct. Dubit.* IV. i. rule iii. §1 If our inclinations..become facilities and promptitudes to sin, they are not innocent. **1712** STEELE *Spect.* No. 497 ¶1 Those who were contented to live without Reproach, and had no Promptitude in their Minds towards Glory.

'promptive, *a. rare.* [f. PROMPT *v.* + -IVE.] Tending or calculated to prompt; apt to move or give rise to something.

1884 J. TAIT *Mind in Matter* (1892) 2 It is promptive of serious reflection that some of the greatest thinkers of past ages accounted in this way for the manifestation of Mind in providence. **1955** W. FAULKNER *Fable* 384 The third man..said,..just diffident and promptive, as you address someone ..who may have temporarily forgotten your need or forgotten you: 'Paris'.

promptly ('prɒm(p)tlɪ), *adv.* [f. PROMPT *a.* + -LY².] In a prompt manner; readily, quickly; directly, at once, without a moment's delay.

1490 CAXTON *Eneydos* xxvii. 103 Telle her that she brynge wyth her promptely the shepe & other bestes. *a* **1548** HALL *Chron., Hen. VII* 30 b, He..coulde tell all that was taught him promptly without any difficultie. **1632** LITHGOW *Trav.* VI. 244 A stranger that vnderstandeth not promptly the Italian tongue. **1817** LADY MORGAN *France* II. (1818) I. 247 To give stimulus to the promptly-exhausted attention of fasionable inanity. **1884** *Manch. Exam.* 15 May 5/4 A House was made to-day promptly at a quarter-past 12 o'clock.

promptness ('prɒm(p)tnɪs). [f. as prec. + -NESS.] The quality of being prompt or quick in action, performance, etc.; readiness, promptitude.

1526 *Pilgr. Perf.* (W. de W. 1531) 44 b, Promptness in perceyuynge, Quicknes of inuencyon. **1586** WEBBE *Eng. Poetrie* (Arb.) 64 The ready skill of framing anie thing in verse, besides the naturall promptnesse which many haue therevnto, is much helped by Arte. **1728** MORGAN *Algiers* II. iv. 278 With wonderful Promptness and Diligence, the Land-Forces, Artillery, &c., were put on Shore. **1831** J. DAVIES *Manual Mat. Med.* 304 It possesses the same virtues as morphia, but acts with more promptness and energy. **1868** FREEMAN *Norm. Conq.* II. vii. 159 The hopes of an insurrection always lie in promptness and energy.

'**promptress.** *rare.* [f. PROMPTER + -ESS.] A female prompter.

1793 COLERIDGE *To Fortune* 1 Promptress of unnumber'd sighs,.. O look, and smile!

promptuary ('prɒm(p)tjuːərɪ), *sb.* (*a.*) Now *rare.* [As sb. ad. late L. *promptuāri-um* a storeroom, repository; cf. F. *promptuaire* a manual; as adj. ad. L. *promptuāri-us* ready for distribution, f. *promptus* sb. (see PROMPT *sb.*).]

A. *sb.* **1.** A place where supplies, etc., are kept in readiness for use; a storehouse, a repository; the source whence anything is derived.

1432–50 tr. *Higden* (Rolls) I. 399 ʒiffenge that londe as a promptuary of alle hollesomme thynges. **1583** STUBBES *Anat. Abus.* II. (1882) 7, I doubt not to call hir sacred breast the promptuarie, the receptacle, or storehouse of all true virtue and godlines. **1695** WOODWARD *Nat. Hist. Earth* I. (1723) 52 The Matter is self restored to its original Fund and Promptuary, the Earth. **1774** GOLDSM. *Nat. Hist.* (1862) I. xvii. 96 The earth, the common promptuary that supplies subsistence to men, animals, and vegetables. **1977** 'E. CRISPIN' *Glimpses of Moon* xi. 222 He looked.. like a gorilla at large in an unguarded banana promptuary.

2. Applied to a handbook or note-book containing a summary or digest of information, etc.

1577 FULKE *Answ. True Christian* 108 There be also.. Promptuaries of lyes, Festiuals of lyes, and other infinite bookes of lyes. **1672** BAXTER *Life Alleine* i. (1838) 19 Such a promptuary for any one that hath not leisure to peruse.. the philosophers themselves. **1706** tr. *Dupin's Eccl. Hist. 16th C.* II. v. 157 A Moral Promptuary upon the Gospels. **1855** (*title*) Promptuary of matter for preaching.. suitable for retreats, for sermons on Sundays, and other occasions.

†**B.** *adj.* in ***promptuary art***, the art of collecting information for future use. *Obs.*

1640 G. WATTS tr. *Bacon's Adv. Learn.* v. iii. 238 To procure this ready Provision for discourse,.. Arguments may be before hand framed, and stored up, about such things as are frequently incident, and come into disceptation; and this we call promptuarie Art, or Preparation.

prompture ('prɒm(p)tjʊə(r)). *rare.* [f. L. ppl. stem *prompt-* (taken in sense of PROMPT *v.*) + -URE.] Prompting, suggestion, instigation.

1603 SHAKS. *Meas. for M.* II. iv. 178 Though he hath falne by prompture of the blood. *a* **1633** AUSTIN *Medit.* (1635) 180 His Confession meerely the prompture of the Spirit. **1798** COLERIDGE *Recoll. Love* vi, Love's prompture deep. **1877** BLACKIE *Wise Men* 191 Not from the prompture of mine own conceit, Or spur of private vantage.

†**pro'mulgate,** *ppl. a. Obs.* [ad. L. *promulgāt-us*, pa. pple. of *promulgāre*: see PROMULGE.] Promulgated, set forth. (Usu. as pa. pple.)

1526 *Pilgr. Perf.* (W. de W. 1531) 5 As soone as his holy lawe of the gospell was promulgate and publysshed. **1530** PALSGR. 668/1 Nowe that it is promulgate, we maye boldely speake of it. **1632** LITHGOW *Trav.* I. 19 Whose luxurious liues are vulgarly promulgat in this Hispanicall prouerbe. **1674** ALLEN *Danger Enthus.* 79 If they had not been commanded by a promulgate Law.

promulgate ('prɒməlgeɪt, 'prəʊ-, prəʊ'mʌlgeɪt), *v.* [f. L. *prōmulgāt-*, ppl. stem of *prōmulgāre* to expose to public view, publish: see PROMULGE. The first pronunciation is that now usual: cf. COMPENSATE, CONTEMPLATE.] *trans.* To make known by public declaration; to publish; *esp.* to disseminate (some creed or belief), or to proclaim (some law, decree, or tidings).

1530 PALSGR. 668/1, I promulgate, I publysshe, or declare openly, *je prouulgue.* **1560** DAUS tr. *Sleidane's Comm.* 353 b, Those letters.. the Byshop promulgat at Rome at the latter ende of December. **1630** PRYNNE *God no Impostor* 17 The Gospell must be thus promulgated. **1669** GALE *Crt. Gentiles* I. I. iv. 22 To.. promulgate the knowlege and worship of the great God. **1749** CHESTERF. *Lett.* (1870) 163 The arrogant pedant does not communicate, but promulgates his knowledge. **1824** L. MURRAY *Eng. Gram.* (ed. 5) I. 349 Trisyllables ending in *ce, ent,* and *ate,* accent the first syllable: as,.. 'própagate';.. unless the middle syllable has a vowel before two consonants: as, 'Promúlgate'. **1903** A. ROBERTSON *Rom. Cath. Ch. in Italy* i. (1905) 36 The Doctrine of the Immaculate Conception was promulgated in December 1854.

Hence '**promulgated** *ppl. a.*; '**promulgating** *vbl. sb.* = next.

c **1555** HARPSFIELD *Divorce Hen. VIII* (Camden) 33 Before the promulgating of the law of Moses. **1690** LOCKE *Govt.* II. xi. (Rtldg.) 136 Promulgated standing laws. **1838** CHALMERS *Wks.* XII. 176 The promulgated will of Him who is the King of Kings.

promulgation (prɒməl'geɪʃən, prəʊ-). [a. F. *promulgation* (14th c. in Hatz.-Darm.), ad. L. *prōmulgātiōn-em*, n. of action f. *prōmulgāre*: see PROMULGE.] The action of promulgating or fact of being promulgated; publication.

1604 R. CAWDREY *Table Alph.*, *Promulgation*, publishing openly, or proclaiming. **1613** JACKSON *Creed* I. To Rdr. d iij, Extant in the age immediately following the Gospels promulgation. **1794** SULLIVAN *View Nat.* V. 394 Before the promulgation of Christianity, the world was infinitely divided on this important head. **1844** H. H. WILSON *Brit. India* I. 173 The promulgation of these designs went far to effect their fulfilment. **1858** BUCKLE *Civiliz.* (1869) II. v. 233 They felt themselves bound to prevent its promulgation.

b. *spec.* The official publication of a new law, decree, ordinance, etc., putting it into effect.

1618 BOLTON *Florus* (1636) 22 The day of promulgation of the Law was come. **1699** BURNET *39 Art.* xxvii. (1700) 304 The preaching of the Apostles was of the nature of a Promulgation made by Heraulds. **1867** SMILES *Huguenots Eng.* viii. (1880) 131 One of Henry's.. greatest acts was the promulgation.. of the celebrated Edict of Nantes. **1875** STUBBS *Const. Hist.* II. xv. 205 *note*, The Writ of 1217 for the promulgation of the Charter orders the sheriff to publish it, 'in pleno comitatu [etc.]'.

attrib. **1802–12** BENTHAM *Ration. Judic. Evid.* (1827) II. 672 The use of promulgation paper, provided with a printed border, presenting, in tenor or in the way of reference, such dispositions of law as are applicable to the subject.

promulgator ('prɒməlgeɪtə(r), 'prəʊ-). [agent-n. in L. form from PROMULGATE: see -OR: cf. late L. *prōmulgātor* (Ennodius, *a* 520).] One who promulgates or publishes.

a **1665** J. GOODWIN *Filled w. the Spirit* (1867) 410 Christ .. is the dispenser, or promulgator, or minister of God unto the world of a new spiritual economy. **1766** WARBURTON *Serm. John x.* 11 Wks. 1788 V. 335 An odd Legacy to the promulgators of the Law of Liberty! **1802** *Med. Jrnl.* VIII. 146 Dr. Jenner's claim of being the promulgator or inventor of vaccine inoculation. **1885** *Manch. Exam.* 11 Feb. 5/2 Mr. C... has instructed his solicitor to deal with the promulgator of the slander.

Hence '**promul'gatress**, a female promulgator.

1660 H. MORE *Myst. Godl.* v. ix. 157 The First was the Promulgatress of the Jewish, the Second of the Christian law.

promulge (prəʊ'mʌldʒ), *v. arch.* [ad. L. *prōmulgāre* to expose to public view, publish; perh. altered from *prōvulgāre* in same sense (see PROVULGATE) by the influence of some other word. Cf. F. *promulguer* (Oresme, *a* 1400).] = PROMULGATE *v.*

1. *trans.* To publish or proclaim formally (a law or decree). Now chiefly an *official archaism.*

1488 *Rolls of Parlt.* VI. 414/1 All utlagaries into any of the said Defendauntes in the said appele named promulged. **1495** *Act 11 Hen. VII*, c. 59 *Preamble*, An utlarie upon him [is] therupon promulged. **1600** HOLLAND *Livy* LVIII. Epit. 1242 Tiberius Sempronius Gracchus.. when hee promulged an Agrarian law, that [etc.]. **1702** KENNETT *Pres. St. Convocation* 2 Their final Acts were duly promulg'd. **1766** BLACKSTONE *Comm.* II. xxvii. 410 The king.. has the right of promulging to the people all acts of state and government. **1879** *Q. Rev.* CXLVIII. 545 They would have claimed to promulge their canons and constitutions.. without license from the Crown first obtained.

2. To set forth, declare, or teach publicly (a creed, doctrine, opinion, statement); to bring before the public, to publish (a book, etc.).

1614 JACKSON *Creed* III. viii. §12 If vncleane spirits may not be permitted to promulge this, or like diuine mysteries. **1736** BUTLER *Anal.* II. vii. Wks. 1874 I. 280 A book of this nature, and thus promulged and recommended to our consideration. **1841** CATLIN *N. Amer. Ind.* I. xi. 81 From these [traditions and historic facts] when they are promulged, I think there may be a pretty fair deduction drawn. **1882–3** *Schaff's Encycl. Relig. Knowl.* II. 1515 Fanatics announced visions, and promulged prophecies.

Hence **pro'mulged** *ppl. a.*, **pro'mulging** *vbl. sb.* and *ppl. a.*

1627 MAY *Lucan* VI. 906 The popular law-promulging Draft. **1656** R. ROBINSON *Christ all* (1868) 534 His promulging of it to the world. **1659** T. PECKE *Parnassi Puerp.* 162 Tiberius by a promulg'd Edict, Prohibited Salutes. *a* **1716** SOUTH *Serm.* (1744) IX. ii. 40 At the promulging of the law from Mount Sinai. **1874** MRS. JAY *Holden with Cords* 452 The recently promulged theory of Gall.

promulger (prəʊ'mʌldʒə(r)). [f. prec. + -ER¹.] One who promulges; a promulgator.

1659 PEARSON *Creed* ii. (1839) 131 The first revealer and promulger bred in the house of a carpenter.. despised by.. all the learned in the religion of his nation. **1737** WHISTON *Josephus, Antiq.* XIV. x. §21 He had himself been the promulger of your decree. **1824** G. S. FABER *Diffic. Infidelity* (1833) 156 A tale known to be a falsehood by the very promulgers themselves.

pro'muscidate, *a.* [f. L. *promusc-is, -idem* (see next) + -ATE².] Formed as or furnished with a promuscis or proboscis: chiefly of insects.

1826 KIRBY & SP. *Entomol.* IV. xlvii. 378 Mouth promuscidate. **1840** WESTWOOD *Classification Insects* II. 414 Mouth arising from the under and hinder surface of the head, promuscidate.

‖**promuscis** (prəʊ'mʌsɪs). [L., altered form of *proboscis.* Cf. obs. F. *promuscide* (1536 in Godef.).]

†**1.** The proboscis or trunk of an elephant. *Obs.*

[**1576**: see PROBOSCIS 1.] **1600** J. PORY tr. *Leo's Africa* Introd. 40 The elephant.. will stande vp to the mid-body therein, bathing the ridge of his backe, and other parts with his long promuscis or trunke. **1607** TOPSELL *Four-f. Beasts* (1658) 153 His trunck called *Proboscis* and *Promuscis*, is a large hollow thing hanging from his nose. **1709** BLAIR in *Phil. Trans.* XXVII. 56 The *Proboscis* (or *Promuscis*, as some call it, in English the Trunk).

2. *Entom.* The proboscis in certain orders of insects: cf. PROBOSCIS 3; *spec.* that of the Hymenoptera: see quots. 1826–8.

1658 ROWLAND *Moufet's Theat. Ins.* 962 It hath very long cornicles, and the promuscis or snout doubled in or rolled up together. *Ibid.* 990 A long kinde of compact fast substance, which like a promuscis supplieth the place of a mouth and tongue. **1826** KIRBY & SP. *Entomol.* III. xxxiii. 360 *Promuscis*, the oral instrument of Hemiptera, in which the ordinary Trophi are replaced by a jointed sheath, covered above at the base by the *Labrum*,.. and containing four long capillary lancets, and a short tongue. **1828** STARK *Elem. Nat. Hist.* II. 219 [In the Hymenoptera] All these parts, as well as the labium, are often much elongated, and compose together a species of trunk or proboscis, which Illiger names *promuscis*, and which Latreille calls a spurious proboscis. **1856–8** W. CLARK *Van der Hoeven's Zool.* I. 372 *Chrysis* L.—Labium not in form of a promuscis.

†**promu'tation.** *Obs. rare.* [f. PRO-¹ 1 + MUTATION: so OF. *promutation* (1359 in Godef.).] Exchange, barter.

1560 DAUS tr. *Sleidane's Comm.* 178 In case he become.. Metropolitan of another churche, throughe promutation, or any other meane. **1660** R. COKE *Power & Subj.* 131 If in Promutation a man sets such a value upon such a thing, and does not respect the person or quality of any buyer. *Ibid.*, To observe this Arithmetical Rule which Aristotle propounds in Promutation.

‖**promycelium** (prəʊmaɪ'siːlɪəm). *Bot.* Rarely in Eng. form '**promycele.** [mod.L., f. *prō*, PRO-¹ + MYCELIUM.] The filamentous product of the germination of a spore.

1867 J. HOGG *Microsc.* II. i. 291 We see the Uromycesspores passing through the generations of promycelium, sporidia, and mycelium. **1874** COOKE *Fungi* 126 To distinguish them from such spores as are reproductive without the intervention of a promycelium. **1882** VINES *Sachs' Bot.* 335 The teleutospores.. produce promycelia on germination.

Hence **promy'celial** *a.*, of the promycelium.

1887 tr. *De Bary's Fungi* v. 177 The promycelial tube is divided by transverse walls into a series of.. short cells.

promyelocyte, -cytic: see PRO-² 1.

promys, -yse, -ysse, obs. ff. PROMISE.

proname: see PRO-¹ 4 b.

‖**pronaos** (prəʊ'neɪɒs). *Gr.* and *Lat. Antiq.* Also 7 -on, 8 -us. [L. *pronāos (-us)*, a. Gr. πρόναος (-ον) the hall of a temple, prop. adj. 'situated in front of the temple': see PRO-² and NAOS.] The space in front of the *naos*, cell, or body of a temple, enclosed by the portico and the projecting side walls; the vestibule. Also, a similar vestibule in some early Christian churches: = NARTHEX.

1613 T. GODWIN *Rom. Antiq.* xx. (1614) 17 They had their *pronāon*, or Church-porch. **1704** J. HARRIS *Lex. Techn.* I, *Pronaos* or *Pronaus*,.. a Church-Porch, or a Portico to a Palace, great Hall, or spacious Building. **1745** POCOCKE *Descr. East* II. II. III. x. 169 The architrave.. continued from the front of the portico or pronaos to the side pillars. **1833** *Penny Cycl.* I. 140/2 Inner porticoes formed by the longitudinal extension of the flank walls,.. forming what are distinguished as the pronaos and opisthodomus.

fig. **1894** HUXLEY *Evol. & Ethics* Pref. 8 If I had attempted to reply in full to the criticisms.. I know not what extent of ground would have been covered by my *pronaos.* **1897** *Bookman* Nov. 235 A roomy niche in the pronaos of Fame.

pronase ('prəʊneɪz). *Biochem.* [f. PRO(TEI)NASE.] A purified preparation of proteinase from cultures of the bacterium *Streptomyces griseus.* (A proprietary name in the U.S.)

1960 *Jrnl. Biochem.* (Japan) XLVIII. 600 The above mentioned, excellent proteolytic activity of *Streptomyces griseus* protease is expected to develop many new industrial and scientific applications, in cooperation with the success in commercial production of this enzyme. [*Note*] Partially purified *Streptomyces griseus* protease is put on the market from the Kaken Chemical Co., Ltd., in the trademark of '*Pronase*'. **1962** *Science* 2 Nov. 594/1 The zona pellucida may be removed from all stages of the mouse egg by digestion with pronase. **1963** *Official Gaz.* (U.S. Patent Office) 22 Jan. TM132/2 California Corporation for Biomedical Research, Los Angeles, Calif... *Pronase* for highly purified proteinase prepared from *Streptomyces griseus* culture broth. First use May 9, 1961. **1976** *Ann. Rev. Microbiol.* XXX. 163 Ribonuclease digestion of a phenolic extract containing the antiviral factor resulted in complete loss of activity, whereas treatments with trypsin or pronase did not lessen antiviral activity.

pronatalist (prəʊ'neɪtəlɪst), *a.* and *sb.* Also **pro-natalist.** [f. PRO-¹ 5 a + NATAL *a.*¹ and *sb.*¹ + -IST.] **A.** *adj.* Of or pertaining to the encouragement of large families, esp. by the state; in favour of or advocating large families. **B.** *sb.* A pronatalist person.

1938 *Mod. Law Rev.* II. 102 The suppression of abortion was part of the policy of the *Alliance Nationale pour l'Accroissement de la Population Française*, founded by J. Bertillon in 1896. (Three months after this had been founded, Paul Robin set up his counter organisation, '*La Ligue de la Régénération Humaine*', for advocating birth-control and attacking the pro-natalists.) *Ibid.* 105 In most countries and at most periods there have been pro-natalist policies directed at encouraging marriage and the raising of large families. **1953** *Population Stud.* VII. 39 Even the most ambitious of French pro-natalists admit to-day that policy must be directed to encouraging the birth of a third and possibly a fourth child, rather than concentrating on the large family. **1974** *Encycl. Brit. Macropædia* XIV. 818/2 Taken as a whole, Europeans in the Middle Ages were pronatalists. **1974** *Sci. Amer.* Sept. 125/3 Between the 1930's and the 1950's there was.. an increase in pronatalist intervention by the [U.S.] Government, particularly through the tax structure. **1976** *Nature* 4 Nov. 7/1 More and more governments are reversing pro-natalist policies and instituting family planning programmes. **1979** *Jrnl. R. Soc. Arts* CXXVII. 415/1 Some countries are still avowedly pro-natalist.

So **pro'natalism**, advocacy or encouragement, esp. by the state, of large families.

1938 *Mod. Law Rev.* II. 105 The semi-official (e.g. municipal) encouragement of birth-control in the first half of the nineteenth century was severely shaken by the Franco-Prussian war, which was followed by an intensive pro-natalist campaign. Similarly, a further impetus to pro-natalism was given during the last war, and the policy is now an official one. **1974** D. V. GLASS in H. B. Parry *Population* I. v. 73 Japan, too, in spite of its high Gross Reproduction Rate, included pronatalism in its imperialist policy.

'pronate, *ppl. a. rare.* [ad. late L. *prōnāt-us*, pa. pple. of *prōnāre*: see next.] Bent into a prone position; bent forward and downward.

1853 KANE *Grinnell Exp.* vi. (1856) 47 Such turf, where the tree growths of more favored regions have become pronate and vine-like. **1938** S. BECKETT *Murphy* ii. 24 He raised his left hand.. and seated it pronate on the crown of his skull.

pronate ('prəʊneɪt), *v. Physiol.* [f. late L. *prōnāt-*, ppl. stem of *prōnāre* to bend forward, f. *prōn-us* PRONE *a.*] *trans.* To render prone; to put (the hand, or the fore limb) into the prone position; to turn the palm downwards: see next. Opp. to SUPINATE.

1836–9 *Todd's Cycl. Anat.* II. 786/1 The forearm and hand were rigidly pronated. **1849–52** *Ibid.* IV. 1517/1 The patient is unwilling to attempt to pronate or supinate his hand. **1875** SIR W. TURNER in *Encycl. Brit.* I. 832/1 The range of movement at the radio-ulnar joints enables us.. to pronate the hand and fore-arm by throwing the radius across the ulna, so as to make the thumb the innermost digit.

pronation (prəʊ'neɪʃən). *Physiol.* [= F. *pronation*, ad. med.L. *prōnātiōn-em*, n. of action f. *prōnāre*: see prec.] The action of pronating; the putting of the hand or fore limb into the prone position, i.e. with the palmar surface downwards (if the limb be stretched forward horizontally) or backwards (if it be hanging vertically); the position or condition of being pronated. (Sometimes applied to a similar movement of the tibia in the hind limb.) Opp. to SUPINATION.

1666 J. SMITH *Old Age* (1676) 62 They [the muscles] can perform adduction, abduction; flexion, extension; pronation, supination. **1745** AMYAND in *Phil. Trans.* XLIII. 296 A gummatous Swelling upon the upper Head of the Radius on the right Arm, checking the Motion of this Bone in Pronation and Supination. **1872** HUMPHRY *Myology* 42 In the hind limb.. the muscular force is.. less expended on the pronation of the tibia.

†**b.** The action of placing (a body, etc.) in a prone position. *Obs.*

1698 TYSON in *Phil. Trans.* XX. 118 The First Pair of Muscles.. which.. came to be dissected, upon the Pronation of the Animal.

pronato-flexor (prəʊ,neɪtəʊ'flɛksə(r)), *a. Anat.* [f. *prōnātō-* (prop. advb. combining form of L. *prōnāt-us* pa. pple., pronated, but taken as repr. PRONATOR) + FLEXOR.] Applied to the mass of pronator and flexor muscles of the fore or hind limb.

1872 HUMPHRY *Myology* 24 Below the knee the plantar aspect.. is occupied by a broad thick pronato-flexor mass.

pronator (prəʊ'neɪtə(r)). *Anat.* [a. med.L. *prōnātor*, agent-n. f. *prōnāre*: see PRONATE *v.* Cf. F. *pronateur* (16th c. in Littré).] A muscle that effects or assists in pronation; *spec.* one of two muscles of the fore limb, *pronator* (*radii*) *teres* and *pronator* (*radii*) *quadratus*. Also *attrib.* (Opposed to SUPINATOR.)

[**1693** tr. *Blancard's Phys. Dict.* (ed. 2), *Pronatores Musculi*, one is round, the other foursquare, both move the Radius.] **1727–41** CHAMBERS *Cycl.* s.v. *Pronation*, There are peculiar muscles whereby the pronation is effected called pronators. **1770** PENNANT in *Phil. Trans.* LX. 323 The tendinous muscles.. have much the same effect on the tail as the supinator and pronators have in turning the hand. **1826** KIRBY & SP. *Entomol.* IV. xliii. 172 At first it may seem that insects.. cannot have the Supinator and Pronator muscles; but some muscle of this kind must be.. in those that have a versatile head. **1872** MIVART *Anat.* 294 The muscles of the fore-arm consist of pronators and supinators, flexors and extensors.

pro-Nazi: see PRO-[1] 5 a.

prone (prəʊn), *sb.* Also 7 prosne, 8– ‖prône. [a. F. *prône* (12th c. in Hatz.-Darm.), also *prosne*, orig. a grill, grating, railing, hence a place enclosed by such, spec. the grating or railing separating the chancel from the nave of a church, the place where notices were given and addresses delivered. Ulterior origin uncertain: see Körting s.v. *præcōno*, and articles there cited.]

†**1.** A part of a church from which notices were read out; hence the notices there given out. *Obs.*

1670 COTTON *Espernon* x. 514 Upon All-Saints day he thundred out his Excommunication against the Lieutenant of the Guards.. at the Prosnes of all the Parish Churches of the City. [*Margin.*] The *Prosnes* are the Publications of the Feasts, and Fasts of the Church, Banes of Matrimony, Excommunications, etc. **1686** —— tr. *Montaigne* II. 18 Causing it to be Proclaimed at the Prosne of her Parish-Church.

2. An exhortation or homily to be read or delivered in church. Also prayers, exhortations, etc., attached to the sermon.

a **1670** HACKET *Abp. Williams* II. (1692) 56 A saying.. out of a prosne or homily, made on purpose to be read before the clergy and laity in all Visitations. **1716** M. DAVIES *Athen. Brit.* II. 275 One Eusebius.. is said to have writ many short Prones or Exhortations upon the Gospels. [**1763** C. CORDELL *Divine Office for Use of Laity* I. p. vi, The prayers, publications, and familiar instructions used at the Parish-Mass, on Sundays.. either immediately after the Gospel, or before the Lavabo are called in France the Prône, from a Greek word signifying the Nave of the Church.] *a* **1773** A. BUTLER *Moveable Feasts Catholic Church* (1774) I. v. 78 A Person who besides Morning and Evening Prayers has devoutly attended High-mass with a Prone or Sermon. **1860** F. C. HUSENBETH *Life Monsignor Weedall* iii. 50 These sermons were called by the French name of *Prones*... In these *Prones*, however, no one surpassed Mr. Weedall. **1897** GASQUET *O. Eng. Bible* 65 Parochial sermons were, for the most part.. prones upon the Scripture lessons proper for the special Sundays. **1912** A. FORTESCUE *Mass* vii. 295 The Prayers of the Faithful.. became the *prône*, commands to pray for all classes of people, living and dead, which are still given out before the sermon. **1915** F. E. BRIGHTMAN *Eng. Rite* II. 1037 The Bidding of the Bedes has not stood alone, but has formed part of a group of vernacular devotions, instructions, and notifications, attached to the Sermon, and known as the 'Prone'. **1937** W. DOUGLAS *Church Mus. in Hist. & Pract.* v. 120 The most powerful [urge] was that toward the use of the vernacular. Both in England and in Northern Europe.. this tendency had brought about a series of vernacular public devotions called the Prone, in connection with the Sermon at High Mass. It contained a bidding prayer for intercessions, a confession and absolution, the Creed, the Lord's Prayer, and the Ten Commandments with explanation, and the Church notices. **1968** F. E. VOKES in *Studia Evangelica* V. 146 The so-called 'Prone', the vernacular instruction in the Mass. **1972** J. G. DAVIES *Dict. Liturgy & Worship* 76/2 The association between the sermon and the intercessions which is found in some of the Reformed churches is probably derived from their association in the prone. **1978** D. H. TRIPP in C. Jones et al. *Study of Liturgy* II. III. xi. 255 The normal Sunday worship was to be a preaching-service, based on the medieval prone.

prone (prəʊn), *a.* Also 4 proone, 6–7 proane. [ad. L. *prōn-us* bent or leaning forward; inclined downward, sinking; disposed, prone (to anything), favourable, easy, cf. obs. F. *prone* (1488 in Godef.).]

1. a. Having the front or ventral part downwards; bending forward and downward; situated or lying face downwards, or on the belly: said chiefly of persons or animals, or of the posture or attitude itself. Of the hand: with the palm downwards (or backwards); also, of the fore-arm, or the radius, in the corresponding position: see PRONATION. Often predicative or quasi-advb., esp. after *lie*, etc. (cf. FLAT *a.* 2). Opp. to SUPINE *a.*

1578 BANISTER *Hist. Man* IV. 62 The office of these two [muscles].. is in prone order to turne Radius. **1610** G. FLETCHER *Christ's Vict.* II. xvii, He lowted lowe With prone obeysance. **1615** CROOKE *Body of Man* 268 The position or manner of lying of the sickeman, eyther prone that is downe-ward, or supine that is vpward. **1667** MILTON *P.L.* VII. 506 A Creature who not prone And Brute as other Creatures, but endu'd With Sanctitie of Reason, might erect His Stature. **1784** COWPER *Task* V. 785 Brutes graze the mountain-top, with faces prone. **1859** TENNENT *Ceylon* II. VII. vii. 256 The dogs lie prone upon the ground, their legs extended far in front and behind. **1864** TENNYSON *En. Ard.* 775 Falling prone he dug His fingers into the wet earth.

b. Of a part of the body: So situated as to be directed downwards; under, nether, ventral.

1646 [see PRONELY 1]. **1661** LOVELL *Hist. Anim. & Min.* Introd., Their finns are foure, two in the prone part, two in the supine. **1826** KIRBY & SP. *Entomol.* IV. xlvi. 268 Prone Surface... The under surface. *Ibid.* 308 Mouth.. Prone... When the mouth is wholly under the head.

2. a. In inexact or extended sense (as if opp. to *erect*): Lying (or so as to lie) flat; in (or into) a horizontal posture; prostrate. Often predicative or quasi-advb., with *lie*, *fall*, etc. = flat down. Permissible of things that have not an upper and under side; but improper of men and animals, unless the position is as in 1. *to lie prone* is one position of *lying prostrate.*

1697 POTTER *Antiq. Greece* II. iv. (1715) 229 The Beast.. did not fall prone upon the Ground. **1784** COWPER *Task* II. 125 Ancient tow'rs.. Fall prone. **1835** WILLIS *Melanie* 280 The broken column, vast and prone. **1842** BROWNING *Count Gismond* xvi, Prone lay the false knight, Prone as his lie, upon the ground. **1890** 'R. BOLDREWOOD' *Col. Reformer* (1891) 302 One man.. lay on his side with face half upturned... The strong man had fallen prone, as if struck by lightning.

b. *transf.* Constructed for lying prone upon.

1884 *Health Exhib. Catal.* 102/1 Prone Couches. Recumbent Chairs.

3. a. Having a downward aspect or direction; having a downward or descending inclination or slope. Also *loosely*, steeply or vertically descending, headlong. Often predicative or quasi-advb.

1627 MAY *Lucan* IV. 125 Let no Streames finde prone passage to the Maine. **1654** H. L'ESTRANGE *Chas. I* (1655) 126 Edenburgh.. seated on the prone and descending part of an hill. **1695** BLACKMORE *Pr. Arth.* III. 803 The Way's so wondrous smooth, so prone and broad. **1725** POPE *Odyss.* I. 132 From high Olympus prone her flight she bends. **1820** SHELLEY *Witch Atl.* xli, Down the prone vale. **1853** C. BRONTE *Villette* xxxiv, The storm seemed to have burst at the zenith; it rushed down prone. **1864** TENNYSON *En. Ard.* 67 Just where the prone edge of the wood began To feather toward the hollow.

b. *fig.* = DECLINING *ppl. a.* 4 b.

1872 TENNYSON *Gar. & Lyn.* 94 Some comfortable bride and fair, to grace Thy climbing life, and cherish my prone year.

4. *fig.* Directed or inclined 'downwards', or towards what is base; 'grovelling', abject, base.

1645 MILTON *Colast.* Wks. 1851 IV. 354 Nothing.. but a prone and savage necessity, not worth the name of marriage, unaccompanied with love. **1742** YOUNG *Nt. Th.* II. 345 Prone to the centre; crawling in the dust. *Ibid.* VII. 1197 Erect in stature, prone in appetite! **1842** [see 2].

†**5.** *fig.* Said of action compared to following a downward sloping path: Easy to adopt or pursue; involving no difficulty or effort. (Sometimes with mixture of sense 6: = to which one is prone.) *Obs.*

1475 *Rolls of Parlt.* VI. 151/1 The moost easy, redy and prone payment. **1638** CHILLINGW. *Relig. Prot.* I. v. §87. 290 It is most prone and easy to doe so. **1654** GATAKER *Disc. Apol.* 74 Doth it not pave a plain and prone path unto Atheism? **1656** SANDERSON *Serm.* (1689) 71 There is not a proner way to Hell. **1660** H. MORE *Myst. Godl.* VII. viii. 312 There is nothing more prone then to lye and sleep on the shadie banks of a River.

6. Having a natural inclination or tendency to something; inclined, disposed, apt, liable. Const. *to* with sb., or inf. (The earliest sense in Eng., and still the prevailing one.)

a. Of persons or animals, in reference to mental disposition or the like; (*a*) to something evil.

(*a*) **1382** WYCLIF *Gen.* viii. 21 The witt.. and the thouȝt of mannus herte ben redi [*v. rr.* redi *ether* proone; prome *ether* redi] in to yuel fro his tyme of waxyng. **1483** CAXTON *Gold. Leg.* 32/2 Consyderynge.. how prone the people haue ben to worshipe fals gods. **1555** EDEN *Decades* 305 Yet are they exceadyng prone to lechery. **1611** SHAKS. *Wint. T.* II. i. 108, I am not prone to weeping (as our Sex Commonly are). **1659** PEARSON *Creed* i. (1839) 31 We shall always find all nations ..more prone to idolatry than to atheism, and readier to multiply than to deny the Deity. **1729** BUTLER *Serm.* Wks. 1874 II. 130 Men are exceedingly prone to deceive themselves. **1881** JOWETT *Thucyd.* I. 197 All are by nature prone to err.

(*b*) to something neutral or good.

1528 GARDINER in Pocock *Rec. Ref.* I. xli. 78 Much more prone to adhere to the league. *c* **1530** H. RHODES *Bk. Nurture* in *Babees Bk.* (1868) 106 Be.. Prone, inclyned to mercy. **1613** PURCHAS *Pilgrimage* (1614) 690 These seeme prone to receiue the Faith; for they beleeue in One God,.. and haue no Idols. **1665** MANLEY *Grotius' Low C. Warres* 321 More prone to concord. **1764** GOLDSM. *Trav.* 93 Every state, to one loved blessing prone, Conforms and models life to that alone. **1816** J. WILSON *City of Plague* III. ii. 25 How prone to love Is the pure sinless soul of infancy! **1844** DISRAELI *Coningsby* III. v, A mind predisposed to inquiry and prone to meditation.

b. Of things or persons, in reference to merely physical tendencies (e.g. to disease).

1607 NORDEN *Surv. Dial.* v. 222 The ground.. is good enough, and not so prone to mosse as you take it. **1804** ABERNETHY *Surg. Obs.* 35 Not being prone to inflammation. **1871** BROWNING *Balaust.* 2030 He was.. prone Already to grey hairs. **1883** *Hardwich's Photogr. Chem.* (ed. Taylor) 241 The unstable Tetrathionate of Soda, prone to liberate Sulphur. **1899** *Allbutt's Syst. Med.* VII. 579 Gouty patients or those prone to migraine or neuralgia.

c. Const. *absol.* with preceding sb. (usu. with hyphen).

1926, etc. [see ACCIDENT *sb.* 10 b]. **1973** J. M. WHITE *Garden Game* 47 They were fundamentally good boys.. but they were also violence-prone. **1974** *Times* 18 Oct. 16/4 The traditionally drought-prone areas. **1975** *Publishers Weekly* 25 Aug. 287/2 This tale of a wayward bus line founded by the author's failure-prone father.

7. Ready in mind (for some action expressed or implied); eager. *Obs.* or *arch.*

1553 T. WILSON *Rhet.* (1580) 4 Though.. our will [be] prone, yet our fleshe is so heauie. **1610** GUILLIM *Heraldry* III. xiii. (1660) 161 The Horse.. of all beests there is none.. more prone in battell or desirous of revenge. **1611** SHAKS. *Cymb.* V. iv. 208 Vnlesse a man would marry a Gallowes, and beget yong Gibbets, I neuer saw one so prone. **1728**

MORGAN *Algiers* II. v. 313 A Body of prone Warriors, never sparing of their Flesh. **1819** SHELLEY *Cenci* I. iii. 109 What deep wrongs must have blotted out First love, then reverence in a child's prone mind.

8. *Comb.*, as (sense 3) ***prone-descending, -rushing*** adjs.; (sense 7) ***prone-minded*** adj.; †**pronewise** *adv.*, with 'prone' movement, downward, easily, readily (cf. 3, 5).

1585 BANISTER *Wecker's Chyrurg.* 336 So as the matter maye freely and pronewise flowe out of the wounde. **1727-46** THOMSON *Summer* 655 Floods Prone-rushing from the clouds. *Ibid.* 1145 A deluge of sonorous hail, Or prone-descending rain. **1869** BUSHNELL *Wom. Suffrage* vii. 143 They will take in the political corruptions with a prone-minded human facility.

†**prone**, *v. Obs. rare*⁻¹. [a. F. *prôner* (*c* 1600 in Hatz.-Darm.) to address (a congregation), also to eulogize, f. *prône* PRONE *sb.*] *trans.* To read out, make proclamation of.

1683 TEMPLE *Mem.* Wks. 1731 I. 446 The Contents of this Letter were proned by the French Ambassadors at Nimeguen among the several Ministers there.

pronece: see PRONIECE.

pronely ('prəʊnlɪ), *adv.* [f. PRONE *a.* + -LY².]

1. In a prone position; face downwards; *loosely* (quot. 1578), right down, flat down (cf. PRONE *a.* 2).

1578 BANISTER *Hist. Man* I. 9 A man, in fallyng..backwardes, goeth pronely, without all hope of recouerable stay. **1616** SHELDON *Miracles Antichr.* ix. 224 The same did..pronely adore and worship at the time of eleuation. **1646** SIR T. BROWNE *Pseud. Ep.* 151 Some couple..pronely, that is by contaction of prone parts in both. *a* **1851** MOIR *Fowler* vi, We laid us down and watch'd,..Pronely, the sea-fowl and the coming dawn.

2. With a natural inclination; †readily, willingly (*obs.*); eagerly.

1556 J. CLEMENT in Strype *Eccl. Mem.* (1721) III. App. lx. 208 They knewe the trewthe, and pronely wolde confess it. *a* **1677** BARROW *Wks.* (1686) II. Serm. x. 148 Closely affixed to material things, or pronely addicted to brutish pleasures.

proneness ('prəʊnnɪs). Also 6-7 pronenes, -nesse; 7 prones, pronesse, proaness (see note s.v. -NESS). [f. prec. + -NESS.] The quality or condition of being prone.

1. Natural inclination, disposition, tendency, or propensity (*to* something, or *to do* something).

1548 ELYOT, *Pronitas*, pronenesse, inclinacion to good or euell. **1549** COVERDALE, etc. *Erasm. Par. Rom.* Prol. *v b, Pronenes and redines vnto the dede in the ground of the herte. **1613** PURCHAS *Pilgrimage* (1614) 89 The pronenesse of that sexe to teares. **1626** SIR S. D'EWES *Jrnl.* (1783) 36 My fathers prones to..change his former purposes. **1748** *Anson's Voy.* I. x. 101 A proneness to swoon on the least exertion of strength. **1859** SMILES *Self-Help* xiii. (1860) 338 What is done once and again soon gives facility and proneness.

†**b.** Readiness of mind, willingness, eagerness.

1631 MASSINGER *Believe as You List* v. ii, I..with a gentle reprehension taxde Your forwarde pronenesse. *c* **1645** T. TULLY *Siege of Carlisle* (1840) 9 Of great prudence and proneness in arms.

2. Prone position of the body. *rare.*

1646 SIR T. BROWNE *Pseud. Ep.* IV. i. 180 Though in Serpents and Lizards we may truly allow a pronenesse,..perfect Quadrupedes, as Horses, Oxen, and Camels, are but partly prone, and have some part of erectnesse. *Ibid.*, Birds or flying animals, are so farre from this kinde of pronenesse, that they are almost erect.

†**3.** Downward direction or slope; declivity. *Obs.*

1686 GOAD *Celest. Bodies* II. ii. 168 The River ebbs by the Proneness of its Streams.

pronepce: see PRONIECE.

†'**pronephew**. *Sc. Obs.* Also 5 'pronevow, -newowe, 6 -nevoy, 6-7 -nepuoy. [f. PRO-¹ 2 + NEPHEW, after F. *pronepveu* (1486 in Godef.), L. *pronepōt-em* PRONEPOT.] A great-grandson.

c **1425** WYNTOUN *Cron.* VIII. iii. 372 (Cott. MS.) Fra þe stok..Discendande persownys lynyally In þe toþir, or þe thride, degre, Newow, or pronewowe [*v.r.* pronevow], sulde be. **1535** STEWART *Cron. Scot.* (Rolls) I. 316 Ane greit nobill, that callit wes Dardane, The pronevoy of gude King Metallane. **1593** *Sc. Acts Jas. VI* (1816) IV. 11/2 James lindsay of barcloy pronevoy and air be progres to vmqle Johnne lindsay of wauchoip his grandschir. **1597** SKENE *De Verb. Sign.* s.v. *Eneya*, The son in the first degree, excludis the nepuoy in the second, and the Nepuoy excludis the pronepuoy in the thrid degree. **1623** *Kings of Scot.* 43 Lord Darnley, Sonne to Matthew, Earle of Lennox: a comelie prince, and Pronepuoy unto Henrie the seauenth, King of England. **1658** PHILLIPS, *Pronephew*, a Nephew, or Grandchilds son.

pronephron, -nephros (prəʊ'nɛfrɒn, -'nɛfrɒs). *Zool.* [mod.L., f. Gr. πρό, PRO-² + νεφρός kidney.] The anterior division of the primitive kidney or segmental organ in the embryos of lower vertebrates. Hence **pro'nephric** *a.*, of or pertaining to the pronephron; also **prone'phridian** *a.*

1877 E. R. LANKESTER in *Q. Jrnl. Microsc. Sc.* XVII. 429 The pronephron (*Kopfnieren*) aborts, the pronephric duct becomes the oviduct; it is frequently called Müller's duct. **1881** BALFOUR *Compar. Embryol.* II. II. xxiii. 601 That this body is..related functionally to the pronephros appears to be indicated..(3) by its enclosure together with the pronephridian stoma in a special compartment of the body cavity. **1887** *Amer. Naturalist* XXI. 588 Van Wijhe's view..that the primitive Craniota had no pronephric duct, the pronephros opening outwards by a pore from the gland.

†'**pronepot**. *Sc. Obs. rare.* [ad. L. *pro-, pronepos, -ōtem* great-grandson, f. *prō*, PRO-¹ 2 + *nepos* grandson: see NEPOTE.] = PRONEPHEW.

1536 BELLENDEN *Cosmogr.* ii. in *Cron. Scot.* (1821) I. p. xx, This Brutus wes nepot, or ellis pronepot, to..Eneas. [**1729** MACFARLANE *Genealog. Collect.* (S.H.S.) II. 142 Sir Thomas Maule his Pronepos..was killed at Flowdoun.]

†'**pronept(e.** *Obs.* [ad. L. *pronept-is* great-granddaughter, f. *prō*, PRO-¹ 2 + *nept-is* NIECE.] A grand-niece; = PRONIECE.

1543 *St. Papers Hen. VIII*, V. 337 Leaving behinde Him oone only doughter the Kinges Hieghnes pronepte. **1543** in *Sadler's St. Papers & Lett.* (1809) I. 152 He did well perceive..how much your highness tendred the surety and preservation of your pronepte. **1544** in Ld. Herbert *Hen. VIII*, (1649) 509 He shall fore-see that the Kings Pronept be not conveyed out of Scotland, but strive to get her person into his custody. **1545** *St. Papers Hen. VIII*, V. 420 The Quene of Scotland,..His Highnes pronept.

pronepuoy, -nepvoy, obs. ff. PRONEPHEW.

prones, pronesse, obs. ff. PRONENESS.

‖**proneur** (pronœr). [F. *prôneur*, agent-n. f. *prôner*: see PRONE *v.*] One who praises another; an extoller, eulogist, flatterer.

1812 MAR. EDGEWORTH *Vivian* vii, This depreciator..of Vivian..had been his political *proneur* and unblushing flatterer. **1822** HAZLITT *Table-t.* Ser. II. xi. (1869) 232 These *proneurs*, or satellites, repeat all their good things [etc.]. **1853** DE QUINCEY *Autobiog. Sk.* iii. Wks. 1862 XIV. 124 Her dislike..to the doctor, as their receiver, and the *proneur* of their authors.

proneural: see PRO-² 2.

pronevow, -nevoy, obs. ff. PRONEPHEW.

†**prong, prang**, *sb.*¹ *Obs.* In 5 prange, 5-6 pronge, 6 prang. [Known only from *c* 1440: app. = MLG. *prange* a pinching (Franck), Du. *prang* a pinching, confinement, †*prange* 'shackle, neck-iron, horse-muzzle' (Hexham), †*pranghe* 'coarctatio, compressio' (Kilian); f. OTeut. vbl. stem **prang-* to pinch, squeeze: cf. PRANGLE, also next and PANG *sb.*¹]

1. Urgent distress, anguish; a pang.

c **1440** *Promp. Parv.* 493/1 Throwe, womannys pronge (*K.* sekenes), *erumpna*. **1447** BOKENHAM *Seyntys* (Roxb.) 151 As thow the prongys of deth dede streyn Here hert root. *c* **1450** *Cov. Myst.* (Shaks. Soc.) 287 These prongys myn herte asondyr thei do rende. *c* **1530** *Crt. of Love* 1150 The prange of loue so straineth them to crie.

2. ? A trick, a prank. *rare*⁻¹.

Perhaps a different word.

a **1518** SKELTON *Magnyf.* 501 My frende, where haue ye bene so longe?.. I haue bene about a praty pronge.

prong (prɒŋ), *sb.*² Forms: α. 5-6 **prange**, 6 **prannge, prang.** β. 5-7 **pronge**, 6 **prongue**, 7 **prung**, 6- **prong**. See also SPRONG. [Known only from *c* 1500; origin and etymology obscure; perh. related to prec.; cf. MLG. *prange* a pinching, also a pinching instrument, a horse's barnacle (Franck). But in sense more akin to PRAG *sb.*¹, PROG *sb.*¹, as if a nasalized variant of these.]

1. a. An instrument or implement with two, three, or more piercing points or tines; a forked instrument, a fork. In many specific uses, now chiefly *dial.*; e.g. a fork to eat with, a table-fork; a long-handled fork for kitchen use; a kind of fire-iron; a rural implement, a pitchfork, hay-fork, dung-fork, digging-fork.

1492 RYMAN *Poems* lv. 4 in *Archiv. Stud. neu. Spr.* LXXXIX. 221 Dethe hathe felde me with his pronge. [Cf. lxxxv. 5 When dredefull deth to the shal come And smyte the with his spronge.] **1501** *Will of Treffry* (Somerset Ho.), A Prange of siluer for grene gynger. **1504** *Ibid.*, My best prannge for grene gynger. **1528** *Lett. & Pap. Hen. VIII*, IV. II. 2227 In casting prangs for to cast fyre and faggott. **1549** *Acts Privy Council* (1890) II. 349 Pronges of yron. **1556** WITHALS *Dict.* (1568) 19 a/2 A pronge, *bidens*. **1559-60** *Will of J. Kighley* (Somerset Ho.), A pronge of silver which they eate Sucket withall. **1567** *Wills & Inv. N.C.* (Surtees) I. 279 An Iron Chimnay, a pair of tongs, a prong vˢ. **1570** LEVINS *Manip.* 166/47 A Prongue, *hasta furcata*. **1621** G. SANDYS *Ovid's Met.* VIII. (1626) 167 Her husband..Tooke downe a flitch of bacon with a prung, That long had in the smokie chimney hung. **1637** HEYWOOD *Dial.* iv. Wks. 1874 VI. 164 Expell me With forks and prongs, as one insenc'd with ire. **1646** SIR T. BROWNE *Pseud. Ep.* 60 Culinary utensils and Irons that often feele the force of fire, as tongs, fireshovels, prongs and Andirons. **1697** DRYDEN *Virg. Georg.* II. 487 Be mindful..With Iron Teeth of Rakes and Prongs, to move The crusted Earth. **1706** PHILLIPS, *Prong*, a Pitch-fork. *a* **1742** J. HAMMOND *Love Elegies* (1745) 211 I'll press the Spade or wield the weighty Prong. **1762** FALCONER *Shipwr.* II. 74 One [fish]..glides unhappy near the triple prong. **1791** COWPER *Iliad* I. 570 Busy with spit and prong. **1813** T. DAVIS *Agric. Wilts Gloss.*, *Prong* or *Pick*, a fork for the stable, or for hay-making. **1877** *Auctioneer's Catalogue* (Shropsh.) (E.D.D.), Six superior quality electro-plated dinner prongs. **1881** JEFFERIES *Wood Magic* I. iii. 48 He wanted a prong, and a stout stick with a fork was cut and pointed for him. **1881** *Q. Rev.* Apr. 332 He shouldered a prong and assisted his haymakers. **1891** 'Q' (Quiller Couch) *Noughts & Crosses* 79 He..always dined wi' a pistol laid by his plate, alongside the knives an' prongs.

b. Any forked object, appendage, or part.

1846 GREENER *Sc. Gunnery* 145 Two iron bars, the one fixed, the other loose. In the latter there is a prong or notch to receive one end. **1905** E. CHANDLER *Unveiling of Lhasa* vi. 105 The muzzles and prongs of the Tibetan matchlocks.

2. a. Each pointed tine or division of a fork.

1697 *Lond. Gaz.* No. 3287/4, 4 Forks with 3 Prongs. **1729** SWIFT *Let. to Gay* 19 Mar., I dine with forks that have but two prongs. **1763** SMOLLETT *Trav.* (1766) I. v. 62 The poorest tradesman in Boulogne has..silver forks with four prongs. **1879** G. MEREDITH *Egoist* xxx, You were lean as a fork with the wind whistling through the prongs.

b. Any slender stabbing or piercing instrument, or projecting part of a machine or apparatus.

1649 G. DANIEL *Trinarch., Hen. V* ccii, The Stronger Squadron of the french fell in Vpon the goreing stakes; ..'mongst these officious prongs Surpriz'd; their horse entangled, plunge their way Through many wounds, to Death. **1875** [see *prong-chuck* in 4].

c. A projecting spur of any natural object (esp. of one with several such), as a tooth, a deer's horn, a rock, etc. In Southern U.S., 'a branch or arm of a creek or inlet' (Bartlett *Dict. Amer.* 1860).

1725 in *Amer. Speech* (1940) XV. 300 To a Gum on the sound side of the north prong of the Spring Swamp. **1784** G. WASHINGTON *Diary* 25 Sept. (1925) II. 311 Carpenters Creek, a branch of Jackson's..which is the principal prong of James River. **1802** *Med. Jrnl.* VIII. 120 If Mr. Reece's descriptive state of the prongs or stumps [of teeth] was correct. **1834** *Penny Cycl.* II. 71/1 The prong or antler [of the prongbuck]..is short and compressed, points forwards and a little outwards. **1834** J. M. PECK *Gazetteer Illinois* III. 217 It [*sc.* Crawford's Creek] enters the south prong of Bear creek. **1843** A. WHITE in *Zoologist* I. 29 The antennae are monstrously developed..emitting from each 'prong' a part of a distinct antennule. **1855** *Ecclesiologist* XVI. 82 The castle stands upon a narrow prong of the hill. **1858** *N. York Tribune* 9 Mar. 6/3 A..man who lives on a prong of Middle Creek [Kansas]. **1886** CHR. G. ROSSETTI *Songs for Strangers* Poems (1904) 134/2 Fair its floating moon with her prongs. **1899** BARING-GOULD *Bk. of West* I. xii. 214 Strike for some prongs of rock that appear south-east.

3. ? A prawn.

a **1820** J. R. DRAKE *Culprit Fay* (1836) 19 Some are rapidly borne along On the mailed shrimp or the prickly prong.

4. *Comb.*, as ***prong-like*** adj., ***prong-maker***; **prong-chuck** (see quot.); **prong-fork**, a large fork for agricultural purposes; **prong-hoe** *sb.*, an agricultural implement with two curving prongs, used like a hoe; = HACK *sb.*¹ 1; hence **prong-hoe** *v. trans.*, to break up or dig with a prong-hoe; **prong-pin**, a hairpin with two prongs; **prong-staff** (pl. *-staves*), the handle of a *prong-fork*.

1875 KNIGHT *Dict. Mech.*, **Prong-chuck*, a burnishing chuck with a steel prong. **1765** *Museum Rust.* IV. lviii. 245 The use of the *prong-fork that I have done my land with. **1733** TULL *Horse-Hoeing Husb.* x. 47 'Tis very profitable to Hoe that little with a Bidens, called here a *Prong-Hoe. **1753** CHAMBERS *Cycl. Supp.*, The prong-hoe consists of two hooked points of six or seven inches long, and when struck into the ground will..answer both the ends of cutting up the weeds and opening the land. **1765** *Museum Rust.* IV. lviii. 245 A prong-hoe, which is used in hop-grounds. **1892** *Board of Agric. Circular conc. Raspberry Moth*, Soot, lime ashes..might be forked or *prong-hoed into the ground. **1848** J. BISHOP tr. *Otto's Violin* App. v. (1875) 85 The three *prong-like portions of the mute. **1733** TULL *Horse-Hoeing Husb.* xxiii. 376 Made perfectly round, and of equal Diameter from one End to the other, by the *Prong-Maker. **1902** *Daily Chron.* 19 July 8/3 Tortoise-shell..is..in great request for the *prong pins that girls stick in the thick coil of hair behind their ears. *a* **1722** LISLE *Husb.* II. 256 Another part of the ash may serve for *prong-staves, rake-staves, and rath-pins for waggons.

prong, *v.* [f. prec. sb.]

1. *trans.* To pierce or stab with a prong; to turn up the soil with a 'prong' or fork; to fork.

1840 *Cottager's Man.* 45 in *Libr. Usef. Knowl., Husb.* III, Improved by deep pronging or mattocking between the rows. **1848** THACKERAY *Van. Fair* li, Silver forks with which they prong all those who have not the right of the *entrée*. **1852** R. S. SURTEES *Sponge's Sp. Tour* (1893) 174 'No, sir, no', he continued, pronging another onion.

2. To furnish with prongs, or prong-like points.

1874 T. HARDY *Far fr. Madding Crowd* xi, The indistinct summit of the facade was notched and pronged by chimneys.

prongbuck ('prɒŋbʌk). [f. PRONG *sb.*² + BUCK *sb.*¹] = PRONGHORN (strictly, the male).

1834 *Penny Cycl.* II. 71/2 The prongbuck inhabits all the western parts of North America from the 53° of north latitude to the plains of Mexico and California. **1902** T. ROOSEVELT in *Deer Family* (Sportsm. Libr.) 98 The prongbuck or pronghorn antelope, known throughout its range simply as antelope, is..the only hollow-horn ruminant which annually sheds its horns as deer do their antlers. **1903** *Q. Rev.* Jan. 44 The prong-buck..and the opossums of America being unknown in the Old World.

So '**prongdoe**, the female of the pronghorn.

1890 *Cent. Dict.* s.v. *Pronghorn*, The prongdoe regularly drops twins.

pronged (prɒŋd), *a.* [f. PRONG *sb.*² + -ED².] Furnished with or having prongs.

1767 COLLINSON in *Phil. Trans.* LVII. 466 The pronged teeth are like to agate. **1813** SCOTT *Trierm.* I. xiii, Wicket of oak..And prong'd portcullis. **1851** Mayne Reid *Scalp Hunt.* v, I observed a pronged head disappearing behind a swell in the prairie. **1863–76** Curling *Dis. Rectum* (ed. 4) 54, I..generally use the pronged forceps.

b. Often in comb. with a numeral, as ***two-, three-, four-pronged.***

1799 *Hull Advertiser* 6 July 3/3 Eating..with a three-pronged fork. **1844** Dickens *Mart. Chuz.* xxxix, Very mountebanks of two-pronged forks. **1897** *Outing* (U.S.) Feb. 440/1 A four pronged buck and a big doe running together.

pronȝe, obs. Sc. form of prune *v.*[1]

† **'pronȝeand**, *a. Sc. Obs.* [erron. or altered form of *ponȝeand*, poignant, perh. after *preen, prick*, etc.] Poignant, pricking. So † **prunȝeandlie** *adv.*, poignantly, piercingly.

1533 Bellenden *Livy* iii. xiv. (S.T.S.) I. 302 Ane other sentence, semand mare pronȝeand and scharp, was pronuncit in þe said courte, howbeit It was nocht of sa grete effect. **1596** Dalrymple tr. *Leslie's Hist. Scot.* ii. (S.T.S.) 152 Pricked sa prunȝeandlie with this law.

pronghorn ('prɒŋhɔːn). [f. prong *sb.*[2] + horn *sb.*]

1. Short for *prong-horned antelope* s.v. prong-horned *a.*

1826 J. D. Godman *Amer. Nat. Hist.* II. 324 The prong-horn..is usually called a goat by the Canadians. **1864** Webster, Prong-horn. **1877** J. A. Allen *Amer. Bison* 581 The tact and caution required in the successful pursuit of the watchful pronghorn.

2. A projecting stabbing implement (in context a gas lamp). *nonce-wd.*

1922 Joyce *Ulysses* 439 The navvy..gores him with his flaming pronghorn.

3. *attrib.*, as ***prong-horn antelope.***

1826 J. D. Godman *Amer. Nat. Hist.* II. 321 The prong-horn antelope is an animal of wonderful fleetness. **1902** [see prongbuck]. **1903** *Q. Rev.* Jan. 183 Prong-horn antelope were shot; but wapiti were scarce and shy.

prong-horned ('prɒŋ,hɔːnd), *a.* [f. prong *sb.*[2] + horned *a.*] In ***prong-horned antelope***: A North American ruminant (*Antilocapra americana*), resembling a deer, the male of which has hollow deciduous horns with a short 'prong' or snag in front; popularly reckoned as an antelope, but scientifically regarded as the sole surviving representative of a distinct family *Antilocapridæ*. Also called cabrie or *cabrit*.

1815 G. Ord *N. Amer. Zool.* (1894) 308 The Prong-Horned Antelope is found in great numbers on the plains and the high-lands of the Missouri. **1834** *Penny Cycl.* II. 71/1 The prong-horned antelope seems..to have been associated [by the ancient Mexicans] with the deer, on account of its branched horns. **1871** Darwin *Desc. Man* II. viii. 234 In the prong-horned antelope, only a few of the females..have horns.

† **'proniece.** *Obs. rare.* In 6 pronece, -nepce. [f. pro-[1] 2 + niece: see pronept.] A grand-niece.

1542 *St. Papers Hen. VIII*, V. 231 Oure Soverane and Maister, ȝour tendir nepho, is departit fra yis present life..and hes left ane Princes, ȝoure pronece, to be heretar and Quene of yis Realme. **1543** *Ibid.* 270 Oure Soverane Lady, Quene of Scotland, ȝoure best lovit pronece. *Ibid.* 281 For the performance of the mariage betwene my Lorde Princes Grace and the doughter of Scotlande, the Kinges Majesties pronepce.

† **'pronity.** *Obs.* [ad. L. *prōnitās, -ātem* inclination, propensity, f. *prōn-us* prone *a.*]

1. Steepness of descent: cf. prone *a.* 3. *rare.*

1524 Pace *Let. to Hen. VIII* in Strype *Eccl. Mem.* (1721) I. App. xi. 20, I durst not..look on my left hand, for the pronite and deepnes to the valei.

2. Propensity, proneness (chiefly to evil).

1526 *Pilgr. Perf.* (W. de W. 1531) 246 b, A pronite or redynesse to all vyce. *a* **1535** Fisher *Wks.* (E.E.T.S.) II. 440 Consideryng y[e] pronytie of mans harte to be infected with heresies. *a* **1670** Hacket *Cent. Serm.* (1675) 231 An eagerness and pronity to resist. **1672** Wallis in *Phil. Trans.* VII. 5165 Gravity or Heaviness is..reputed to be such a *Conatus* or Pronity to move downwards. **17..** Killingbeck *Serm.* xi. (1717) 227 What Restraints shall we lay upon the vicious Pronities and Inclinations of Human Nature?

pronk (prɒŋk), *v. S. Afr.* [Afrikaans, to show off, strut, prance, ad. Du. *pronken* to strut.] *intr.* Of springbok: to leap in the air, to buck, esp. as an alarm-signal. Hence **'pronking** *vbl. sb.*

1896 F. V. Kirby *In Haunts of Wild Game* ii. 49 He quickly settles down into a long 'rocking-horse' canter, or else goes 'pronking' away, as the Boers style it. **1915** *Chambers's Jrnl.* Nov. 703/1 When a whole troop of these antelopes are thus leaping..'pronking', or 'pranking', as the Boers call it. **1957** R. Campbell *Portugal* v. 90 Both the mules..began to rise off the ground as if the earth were red-hot, like springboks 'pronking', with all four feet at once, arching their backs. **1966** E. Palmer *Plains of Camdeboo* ix. 154 Every hunter in the past had his theory as to why springbuck pronk, just as every Karoo farmer has today. **1971** *Sunday Mail Family Section* (Brisbane) 10 June 6 The beautiful springbok..gives a spectacular alarm signal... It springs into the air, back arched, displaying a crest of pure white hairs. This is called 'pronking'.

pronk (prɒnk), *sb. slang.* [Origin uncertain: cf. Du. *pronker* fop.] A weak or effeminate person, a softie; a crank, fool, mug.

1959 C. MacInnes *Absolute Beginners* 25 Here the pronk half rose in his ballet tights and saluted. *Ibid.* 33 No one is going to..try to blackmail me with that crazy old mixture of threats and congratulations that a pronk like you falls for. **1972** L. Henderson *Cage until Tame* iv. 28 Whoever this pronk Durant was he had a lot to learn. **1976** —— *Major Enquiry* xv. 102 This pronk reckons he can..point out the right one [*sc.* car] with a hazel twig.

pronograde ('prəʊnəʊgreɪd), *a.* [f. L. *prōn-us* prone *a.* + *-gradus* going, walking: see grade *sb.*] Moving on all fours.

1902 [see orthograde *a.*]. **1918** F. Wood-Jones *Probl. Man's Ancestry* 22 The likeness [to man] still further diminished in the lemurs, and in the general run of pronograde quadrupedal mammals it reached a minimum. **1971** F. S. Hulse *Human Species* (ed. 2) vii. 168 For moving or standing in a pronograde position, that is, on all fours, a somewhat tube-shaped pelvis is quite adequate. **1978** *Nature* 14 Dec. 706/1 A narrow trochlea with pronounced anteromedial and posterolateral borders such as is characteristic of cercopithecoid monkeys (and many other pronograde quadrupedal mammals).

pronominal (prəʊ'nɒmɪnəl), *a.* (*sb.*) [ad. late L. *prōnōminăl-is* belonging to a pronoun (Priscian), f. L. *prōnōmen, -in-* pronoun: see -al[1]. So in F.]

A. *adj.* † **1.** Serving to indicate things, instead of naming them. *Obs. rare.*

1644 Bulwer *Chirol.* 164 The naturall validity of this indigitation of persons, and pronominall vertue of this Finger.

2. Of, pertaining to, or of the nature of a pronoun. Also, characterized by the presence of a pronoun.

1680 Dalgarno *Deaf & Dumb Tutor* 134 Our own English pronominal words are none of the most graceful pronunciation. **1751** Harris *Hermes* II. i. (1786) 233 There are the Pronominal Articles, such as, *This, That, Any, Other, Some, All, No* or *None*, &c. **1824** J. Winterbottom *Two French Words* 19 The French Pronominal Adverb *en.* **1837** G. Phillips *Syriac Gram.* 42 What are called pronominal affixes, which are added to the end of nouns. **1902** Greenough & Kittridge *Words* 170 To the second class we give the name of *pronominal roots*, because a great number of them occur in pronouns, and because they seem to express ideas of a relative nature, such as are found in pronouns and indefinite adverbs. **1924** O. Jespersen *Philos. Gram.* 303 There are two kinds of questions; 'Did he say that?' is an example of one kind, and 'What did he say?' and 'Who said that?' are examples of the other. Many names have been proposed for these two kinds: yes-or-no question or categorical question *v.* pronominal question [etc.]. **1928** H. Poutsma *Gram. Late Mod. Eng.* (ed. 2) I. vii. 381 *Sweet*..distinguishes them as general and special questions; Kruisinga..as disjunctive and pronominal questions. **1931** G. Stern *Meaning & Change of Meaning* xi. 332 German *etcetera*..may mean 'podex, crepitus ventris, devil, cacare', etc. This might be called a pronominal use. **1960** E. Delavenay *Introd. Machine Transl.* 120 Prepositions require further programming..as do pronominal verbs (s'améliorer). **1965** B. Collinder in Bessinger & Creed *Medieval & Linguistic Stud.* 28 Adolf Noreen distinguished between *expressive* and *pronominal* sememes. **1978** *Language* LIV. 369, I also argue that the pro-predicates have an especially close resemblance to 'pronominal determiners' like the italicized portions of the following.

B. *sb.* (The adj. used absol.) A pronominal word.

1871 Kennedy *Public Sch. Lat. Gram.* § 127. 279 When the Accusative of the Matter is a Neuter Pronoun or Pronominal. **1876** *Ibid.* § 31 (ed. 4) 143 The Interrogative Pronominals *qualis, quantus, quot.* **1971** *Language* XLVII. 169 The prefixes of the inflectional category include aspects such as *si-*..and *yi-*.., modals such as *ni-*..and *di-*.., and pronominals such as *yi-*..and *i-*.

Hence **pro'nominalize** *v. trans.*, to render pronominal; **pro'nominalized, pro'nominalizing** *ppl. adjs.*; **pro'nominally** *adv.*, with the force of or as a pronoun; by means of a pronoun.

1871 Earle *Philol. Eng. Tongue* § 477 We have also some substantives which have been *pronominalised to this effect, as *person, people, body, folk.* **1971** *Language* XLVII. 527 The indefinite article, when truly indefinite (when pronominalized by *one*), introduces a noun in a qualitative rather than an identifying sense. **1975** *Archivum Linguisticum* VI. 78 The subject of *ofereode* is pretty clearly the (unhappy) result of the situation outlined in the stanza; the genitive, which has been pronominalized, referring to the situation itself. **1978** *Amer. Speech* LIII. 31 In colloquial English, *they* can be said to pronominalize a [+ human, + III] antecedent of undetermined sex, regardless of number. **1961** *Amer. Speech* XXXVI. 163 These are reducible identically to the *pronominalized *each one, this one*..or finally all the way to *it.* **1977** *Language* LIII. 97 The *pronominalizing languages present in surface more of the logical structure of restrictive relative clauses than do the non-pronominalizing languages. *a* **1665** J. Goodwin *Filled w. the Spirit* (1867) 118 The..particle is to be taken adjectively..and not merely nominally or *pronominally. **1836** in Smart. **1888** Howells *Annie Kilburn* xxx, 'What was that notion of his'—they usually spoke of the minister pronominally.

pronominalization (prəʊ,nɒmɪnəlaɪ'zeɪʃən). [f. pronominalize *v.* + -ation.] The process or fact of replacing (a noun or noun phrase) by a pronoun. Also *attrib.*

1961 *Amer. Speech* XXXVI. 163 The optional deletion of the modifier..occurring in the grammar after the pronominalization. **1965** N. Chomsky *Aspects of Theory of Syntax* iii. 145 Sameness of reference requires reflexivization of the second Noun Phrase (this is also true of pronominalization). **1970** *Language* XLVI. 172 The essence of the pronominalization rule adopted..is that any noun phrase..may be expressed as a pronoun. **1971** J. P. Thorne in A. J. Aitken et al. *Edin. Stud. Eng. & Scots* 59 The rules governing pronominalisation require either that the pronoun occurs in the deep structure of the sentence or that the deep structure contains two identical noun phrases, in which case a transformational rule rewrites one of them as a pronoun in the surface structure. **1979** *Trans. Philol. Soc.* 58 Hankamer (1971)..has argued that pronominalization is a special instance of deletion.

pronomination (prəʊnɒmɪ'neɪʃən). [In sense 1 f. pro-[1] + nomination, imitating Gr. ἀντονομασία, antonomasia; in sense 2 f. L. *prōnōmen* pronoun + -ation.]

† **1.** = antonomasia. *Obs. rare.*

1611 Cotgr., *Antonomasie*, a pronomination. **1629** Mabbe tr. *Fonseca's Devout Contempl.* 134 Called..by an *Antonomasia*, or pronomination, 'The Ships of Tharshish'.

2. Indication or reference by means of a pronoun.

1899 *N. & Q.* 9th Ser. III. 448/2 Has any rule been laid down by grammarians..for the pronomination or pronounization of this word [church]?

‖ **prononcé** (prɔ̃nɔ̃se), *a.* [Fr. pa. pple. of *prononcer* to pronounce.] Pronounced, emphasized; strongly marked or defined; conspicuous, noteworthy.

1838 Mill *A. de Vigny* Diss. & Disc. (1859) I. 291 A certain monotony of goodness,..and a degree of distaste for *prononcé* characters, as being nearly allied to ill-regulated ones. **1880** Mrs. Forrester *Roy & V.* II. 151 When the flirtation between her and D'Arcy became more prononcé.

pronosophical (prəʊnəʊ'sɒfɪkəl), *a. nonce-wd.* [f. Gr. προνοεῖω to foresee + *-sophical* as in *philosophical.*] Having the wisdom of foresight; previsionary.

1922 Joyce *Ulysses* 425 Stephen: Gesture..would be a universal language, the gift of tongues rendering visible..the first entelechy, the structural rhythm. Lynch: Pronosophical theology. Metaphysics in Mecklenburg street!

pronostic, etc.: see prognostic, etc.

† **pro'notary.** *Obs.* Also 7 -notory, 8 -nothary. = protonotary. Cf. also prenotary.

1563 Abp. Parker *Corr.* (Parker Soc.) 198 The precontract..alleged for one Leonard's son, a pronotary. **1605** Daniel *Queen's Arcadia* III. i, I knew you a pronotories boy, That wrote Indentures at the towne-house-doore. **1660** R. Coke *Power & Subj.* 231 The oath..shall be taken of..Utter barristers, Benchers, Readers, Ancients, Pronotaries [citing *Act 5 Eliz.* c. 1, which has 'Prothonotaries']. **1714** *Lond. Gaz.* No. 5192/1 The Pronothary read the Oath.

‖ **pronotum** (prəʊ'nəʊtəm). *Entom.* [mod.L. *pronōtum*, f. Gr. πρό, pro-[2] + νῶτον, notum, back.] The dorsal part of the prothorax of an insect; the anterior division of the notum, as distinct from the ***mesonotum*** and ***metanotum.***

Its segments or scleres are the *pro-præscutum, proscutum, proscutellum, pro-postscutellum.*

1836 Shuckard tr. *Burmeister's Man. Entom.* 78 They [Kirby & Spence] think they have observed that some insects (*Vespa, Cimbex*) possess both a collar and a pronotum. **1877** Huxley *Anat. Inv. Anim.* vii. 399 The tergal portion of the prothorax (pronotum) is a wide shield, which overlaps the head. **1904** *Proc. U.S. Nat. Mus.* XXVII. 389 The pronotum [of *Ceratophyllus multispinosus*] has two rows of few weak bristles. **1925** A. D. Imms *Gen. Textbk. Entomol.* II. 665 In many species [of flea] the pronotum carries a row of stout spines forming the pronotal comb. **1947** C. A. Hubbard *Fleas Western N. Amer.* iv. 38 Taxonomically the only portion which has any great significance is the pronotum and the absence or presence on it of the pronotal comb or ctenidium. **1959** Southwood & Leston *Land & Water Bugs Brit. Isles* iii. 17 Head and pronotum [of the juniper shieldbug] with concolorous puncturation except sometimes near the pronotal angles. **1972** Swan & Papp *Common Insects N. Amer.* xii. 123 The head [of lace bugs] is often covered with a hood, the pronotum extended on the sides like another pair of wings.

Hence **pro'notal** *a.*, of or pertaining to the pronotum (*Cent. Dict.* 1890).

1904 *Proc. U.S. Nat. Mus.* XXVII. 395 *Ceratophyllus alaskensis*... Male: Head flattened on top as usual. Pronotal ctenidium of 22 spines. **1972** Swan & Papp *Common Insects N. Amer.* xxiii. 655 Genal and pronotal spines absent [in the human flea].

pronoun ('prəʊnaʊn). [f. pro-[1] 4 + noun, after F. *pronom*, L. *prōnōmen.*] **a.** One of the Parts of Speech: a word used instead of a noun substantive, to designate an object without naming it, when that which is referred to is known from context or usage, has been already mentioned or indicated, or, being unknown, is the subject or object of inquiry.

Personal pronouns of the first and second persons (*I, you* (*thou*), pl. *we, you*, with their cases) stand instead of the names of the speaker and the person spoken to. Those of the third person (*he, she, it, they*, with their cases, originally demonstratives) avoid the repetition of a name already mentioned or indicated. Interrogative pronouns (*who? what? which?*) ask the name, etc. of a person or thing unknown. Relative pronouns (*who, which, that*) combine the function of a personal or demonstrative pronoun with that of a conjunction, and subordinate one sentence or clause to another, as 'I met a friend *who* told me' for 'I met a friend, *and he* told me'. Possessive pronouns are adjectives arising out of the original genitive case of personal pronouns. In Eng., as in many other modern langs., they have developed two forms, one absolute or strictly pronominal (*mine, thine, ours, yours*, etc.), the other adjectival (*my, thy, our, your*, etc.).

In addition to these, several definitive adjectives are very commonly used absolutely or pronominally, and classed as *adjective pronouns* or *pronominal adjectives*. These include the DEMONSTRATIVES, *this* (pl. *these*), *that* (pl. *those*), *yon* (or *yonder*); DISTRIBUTIVES, *each, every, either, neither* (of which *every* as a pronoun is now archaic); INDEFINITE numerals, etc., *any, some, one, other* (*another*), *none*, to which some add *all, both, many, few, enough, such*, when used absolutely. *One* is often used as an indefinite personal pronoun (ONE 20); and the words *self* and *own*, used to strengthen the personal and possessive pronouns, are sometimes classed with them.

1530 PALSGR. 74 Pronownes be suche as, standynge in the stede of substantives, may governe verbes to be of lyke nombre and parson with them. **1581** W. FULKE in *Confer.* III. (1584) Tij, Whereto els hath the pronowne (*this*) relation? **1612** BRINSLEY *Lud. Lit.* vi. (1627) 55 They are either Nownes, or Pronowns. **1668** WILKINS *Real Char.* III. ii. §3 As Nouns are notes or signs of things, so Pronouns are of Nouns; and are therefore called *Pronomina, quasi vice Nominum*, as being placed commonly instead of Nouns. **1751** HARRIS *Hermes* I. v. (1786) 73 The Genuine Pronoun always stands by itself, affirming the Power of a Noun and supplying its place. **1827** HARE *Guesses* (1847) 187 They are strange and mighty words, these two little pronouns, *I* and *Thou*. **1904** ONIONS *Adv. Eng. Syntax* §62 Adjective Clauses are introduced by Relative Pronouns.., Relative Adjectives.., or Relative Adverbs.., referring to a noun or noun-equivalent called the Antecedent, expressed or implied in the Principal Clause. *Ibid.* §223 *We* is often employed colloquially, like 'you', as an Indefinite Pronoun = 'one'.

b. *Comb.*, as ***pronoun-form, -object.***

1933 L. BLOOMFIELD *Language* xvi. 269 Among the substantives there are some pronoun-forms which, by over-differentiation, do not serve as actors: *me, us, him, her, them, whom*. **1973** *Word 1970* XXVI. 81 In the first-person plural, the subject pronoun-form functions as an indirect object: *They give me the money*. **1957** R. W. ZANDVOORT *Handbk. Eng. Gram.* I. v. 78 *To do* is used as a notional verb, chiefly in its non-finite forms and with a neuter pronoun-object (*something, nothing, this, that, it, what?* etc.). **1963** F. T. VISSER *Hist. Syntax* I. iv. 425 The period of transition from Old to Middle English is characterised by a considerable number of remarkable changes in the form of most of the reflexive pronoun-objects.

pro'nounal, *a. rare.* [irreg. f. prec. + -AL[1]: cf. NOUNAL for *nominal*.] = PRONOMINAL.

1883 J. W. F. ROGERS *Gram. & Logic* I. iii. 67 Pronounal Phrase, I myself. **1884** *Brit. Q. Rev.* Apr. 499 His [Rogers'] style has serious defects. Such expressions as 'nounal' and 'pronounal' grate harshly upon the ear. **1961** R. B. LONG *Sentence & its Parts* ii. 39 Inflection for the possessive is fundamentally a nounal or pronounal variety of inflection.

†**pro'nounce**, *sb. Obs. rare.* [f. next; cf. obs. F. *prononce*, f. *prononcer* (see next): cf. It. *pronunzia*, med.L. *prōnuncia* (Du Cange).]

1. = PRONUNCIATION 2.

1600 DYMMOK *Ireland* (1843) 35 Orators, all of them having their particular excellencies in barbarisme, harshnes, and rusticall both pronounce and action.

2. = PRONOUNCEMENT 1.

1641 MILTON *Ch. Govt.* vi. Wks. 1851 III. 124 That all controversie may end in the finall pronounce or canon of one Arch-primat, or Protestant Pope.

pronounce (prəʊ'naʊns), *v.* Also 4–5 (*Sc.* 6–7) **pronunce, 4–6 -nounse, 5 -nunse, -nowns, 5–6 -nownce, 6 -nownse.** [ME. *pronunce, pronounce*, a. OF. *pronuncier* (1277 in Godef. *Compl.*), for earlier *purnuncier* (mod.F. *prononcer*):—late L. *prōnunciāre* for orig. *prōnuntiāre* to proclaim, announce, rehearse, narrate, pronounce, f. *prō*, PRO-[1] + *nunti-āre* to announce: cf. ANNOUNCE, ENOUNCE.]

I. 1. *trans.* To utter, declare, or deliver (a sentence or statement) formally or solemnly; to proclaim or announce authoritatively or officially.

c **1330** R. BRUNNE *Chron.* (1810) 315 To areson þe pape, þe right forto declare.. & þorgh his decre þe pes pronunce a day. *c* **1400** *Brut* 155 þe Pope.. grantede ful power to iiij bisshopis to pronounce þe enterdityng, if it were nede. **1485** CAXTON *Paris & V.* (1868) 7 The messagers.. had pronounced the joustes. **1548–9** (Mar.) *Bk. Com. Prayer, Matrimony*, I pronounce that they bee man and wyfe together. **1552** *Ibid., Morn. Prayer* Rubric, The absolucion to be pronounced by the Minister alone. **1586–7** *Reg. Privy Council Scot.* IV. 142 He pronunceit a Wo aganis the inhabitantis of Edinburgh. **1660** F. BROOKE tr. *Le Blanc's Trav.* 135 Then the first Prince, whose office it is, pronounces with a loud voice, that it is but necessary they should have a Prince to Govern and Rule them. **1690** LOCKE *Govt.* I. xi. §129 The pronouncing of Sentence of Death is not a certain mark of Sovereignty. **1743** J. MORRIS *Serm.* vii. 183 When he had pronounced the curse. **1850** MRS. JAMESON *Leg. Monast. Ord.* (1863) 199 The day and hour on which he pronounced his vows as an Augustine Friar. **1876** TENNYSON *Harold* II. ii, And hath King Edward not pronounced his heir? **1884** A. R. PENNINGTON *Wiclif* ix. 297 Excommunications, unjustly pronounced, must be disregarded.

2. To declare aloud, proclaim, announce, make known; to tell, narrate, report. *Obs.* or merged in 1.

c **1380** *Antecrist* in Todd *3 Treat. Wyclif* (1851) 147 To pronounce wele here nedis to begge of þe puple. *c* **1386** CHAUCER *Pard. Prol.* 7 First I pronounce whennes þat I come, And thanne my bulles shewe I alle and some. *c* **1400** *Rule St. Benet* 1003, I sal pronunce.. All my mysdedes myself ogayne. **1576** GASCOIGNE *Philomene* lxxiii, Amidde the thickest throngs.. I will pronounce this bloudie deede. *a* **1774** GOLDSM. *Hist. Greece* II. 94 A Courier.. appeared before the Prytanes, and pronounced the dreadful tidings, that the King of Macedon had taken possession of Elatea. *a* **1845** HOOD *Lamia* i. 2 Here I'll sit down and watch; till his dear foot Pronounce him to my ear. **1865** TROLLOPE *Belton Est.* ix. 98 Impassioned words, in which she pronounced her ideas of what should be the religious duties of a woman.

†**b.** *fig.* To 'declare', display. *Obs.*

1615 J. STEPHENS *Ess. & Char., Worthy Poet* (1857) 144 His workes doe.. pronounce both nourishment, delight and admiration to the readers soule. **1777** W. DALRYMPLE *Trav. Sp. & Port.* cxliii, Costly decorations to the capital, that pronounce false pride and vain glory.

3. To affirm, assert, state authoritatively or definitely; to declare as one's opinion or judgement, or as a known fact. **a.** with simple compl. or inf.

c **1380** WYCLIF *Wks.* (1880) 35 Whi schulde curatis pronounsen here breþeren a cursed. *c* **1450** tr. *De Imitatione* II. xi. 55 Lete him.. pronounce himself an vnprofitable seruant. **1613** PURCHAS *Pilgrimage* (1614) 64 The Oracle of Apollo, pronounced the Chaldæans and Hebrewes to be only wise. **1695** BLACKMORE *Pr. Arth.* II. 193 God view'd his Creatures, and pronounc'd them good. **1718** *Free-thinker* No. 57 ¶3 Pronouncing you a Genteel, Fine, Beautiful Woman. **1826** K. DIGBY *Broadst. Hon.* (1829) I. *Godefridus* 69 The twelfth century, which even Sismondi pronounces to have been a great age. **1860** TYNDALL *Glac.* II. xvi. 314 Professor Forbes.. pronounces this portion of the Mer de Glace impassable. *Mod.* The apples were pronounced excellent. The child was pronounced out of danger.

b. with simple obj. or objective clause.

1594 T. B. *La Primaud. Fr. Acad.* II. 491 Wee can not pronounce anie thing certaine of so high a nature as is that of the soule. **1629** DONNE *Serm.* xxiv. (1640) 241 Do not pronounce.. that every man is in an errour, that thinkes not just as thou thinkest. **1705** STANHOPE *Paraphr.* II. 298 Remember, how deceitful Marks all these are to pronounce one's State by. **1860** WARTER *Sea-board* II. 24 He could pronounce nothing.. as to the extent of the injury. **1875** W. S. HAYWARD *Love agst. World* 2 A stranger would at once pronounce that the three young men were brothers.

4. *intr.* To make a statement or assertion, esp., now always, an authoritative or definite one; to pass judgement, give one's opinion or decision. Now usually const. *on* or *upon*; also *for* (*in favour of*) or *against*.

c **1425** WYNTOUN *Cron.* v. 4282 Huchon of þe Aule Reale.. Has tretyt þat mater cunnandly Mar sufficiande þan to pronowns can I. *c* **1586** C'TESS PEMBROKE *Ps.* LXXIII. ii, They wanton grow, and in malicious vaine Talking of wrong, pronounce as from the skies! **1628** T. SPENCER *Logick* 98 This.. signifies properly two sentences wch pronounce against each other. *Ibid.* 158 Some propositions that pronounce of the creature be necessary, and some contingent in their truth. **1651** HOBBES *Leviath.* II. xxvi. 146 Twelve men of the common People.. pronounce simply for the Complaynant, or for the Defendant. **1725** WATTS *Logic* III. iii. §1 Some weaker People.. pronounce against the Use of the Bark or Opium upon all Occasions whatsoever. **1830** PUSEY *Hist. Enq.* II. 405 He will not presume to pronounce upon the fate of those who lived either under the darkness or the light. **1849** MACAULAY *Hist. Eng.* ix. II. 457 The majority.. pronounced in favour of William's undertaking. **1859** JEPHSON *Brittany* xviii. 295 When all France pronounced for atheism and anarchy. **1885** *Manch. Exam.* 29 May 5/3 Nor are we in a position to pronounce on the fairness of the scale fixed.

b. *refl.* To utter or avow one's opinions or intentions; to declare oneself.

1837 CARLYLE *Fr. Rev.* II. II. vi, The mutineers pronounce themselves with a decisiveness, which to Bouillé seems insolence. **1842–3** GROVE *Corr. Phys. Forces* (1846) 27 Without pronouncing myself positively upon the question.. I think it will be safer to regard the action on Photographic compounds as resulting from a function of light.

II. 5. *trans.* To give utterance to; to utter, speak, articulate (a word or words); †to make, or produce (a vocal sound) (*obs.*). Also *absol.*

1388 WYCLIF *Job* xxxiv. 1 And Helyu pronounside and spak also these thingis [*Vulg.* Pronuntians itaque Eliu, etiam hæc locutus est]. **1390** GOWER *Conf.* III. 90 Thurgh notes of acordement, The whiche men pronounce alofte. **1432–50** tr. *Higden* (Rolls) VI. 255 Instructe in the langage of Grece, in whiche.. he hade better use to understonde hit then to pronownce hit. **1553** T. WILSON *Rhet.* (1580) 222 Demosthenes beyng not able to pronounce the firste letter of that arte.. but would saie, for *Rhetorike, Letolike*, vsed to putte little stones vnder his tongue, and so pronounced, whereby he spake at length so plainly, as any manne in the worlde could doe. **1567** *Gude & Godlie B.* (S.T.S.) 110 Thay can pronunce na voce furth of thair throtis. **1667** MILTON *P.L.* IX. 553 Language of Man pronounc't By Tongue of Brute. **1711** J. GREENWOOD *Eng. Gram.* 300 They say that the Americans bordering on New England.. cannot pronounce either an *l* or *r*, but use *n* instead of it. **1841** LANE *Arab. Nts.* I. ii. 107 When she.. pronounced some words that I understood not.

b. With reference to the mode of pronunciation of a letter, syllable, word, or language. Also *absol.*

c **1620** A. HUME *Brit. Tongue* (1865) 9 *U* the south pronunces, quhen the syllab beginnes or endes at it, as eu, teu for tu, and eunum meunus for unum munus, quhilk.. I hoep I sal not need argumentes to prove it wrang. **1686** tr. *Chardin's Trav. Persia* 381 The word is sometimes pronounc'd with a *b*. **1712** STEELE *Spect.* No. 314 ¶9 My Friends flatter me, that I pronounced those Words with a tolerable good Accent. **1726** SWIFT *Gulliver* IV. iii, In speaking, they pronounce through the nose and throat. **1775** MME. D'ARBLAY *Early Diary* (1889) II. 131 He pronounces English quite different from other foreigners. **1861** CRAIK *Eng. Lit.* I. 253 Wallis.. suggested that the origin of this silent *e* probably was, that it had originally been pronounced, though somewhat obscurely, as a distinct syllable.

6. To deliver, declaim, recite: with reference to the manner. Also *absol. Obs.* (or passing into 1).

1560 DAUS tr. *Sleidane's Comm.* 342 To se the priest.. standing at the aultare, pronouncing al thinges in a strange language. **1602** SHAKS. *Ham.* III. ii. 2 Speake the Speech I pray you, as I pronounc'd it to you trippingly on the Tongue. **1612** BRINSLEY *Lud. Lit.* 211 That famous Greek Orator, when he was asked, what was the chief grace or excellency in Rhetorick, what was the second and third; he stil answered, To pronounce wel. [**1761** GRAY *Descent of Odin* 23 Thrice he.. pronounc'd, in accents dread, The thrilling verse that wakes the Dead.]

†**b.** *intr.* To deliver a sermon or address; to preach. *Obs. rare.*

1663 COWLEY *Cutter of Coleman St.* IV. v, Brother Abednego, will you not pronounce this Evening-tide before the Congregation of the Spotless in Coleman Street?

pronounceable (prəʊ'naʊnsəb(ə)l), *a.* [f. prec. + -ABLE. So F. *prononçable* (1611 Cotgr.), late L. *prōnuntiābil-is*.] That can be pronounced.

1611 COTGR., *Prononçable*, pronounceable. **1665** WITHER *Lord's Prayer* 15 There is no Name pronounceable by Men or Angels, which can define God as he is. **1875** WHITNEY *Life Lang.* iv. 68 A mere succession of consonants, though pronounceable by sufficient effort, would be an indistinct and disagreeable sputter.

pronounced (prəʊ'naʊnst), *ppl. a.* [See -ED[1].]

1. Spoken, uttered, articulated.

1577 *Fruites of Prayer* Hijb, He that by the vse of pronounced prayer is caried into the inward consolation of the minde. **1901** *Westm. Gaz.* 18 Sept. 2/1 Hymns.. chaunted by the childish choir in ill-pronounced Latin.

2. *fig.* Clearly expressed, strongly marked; such as to be clearly, easily, or readily perceived or recognized; decided.

1727–41 CHAMBERS *Cycl.* s.v. *Pronouncing*, Thus the painters, in speaking of a piece, say these or these parts are well pronounced. **1781** J. MOORE *View Soc. It.* (1790) II. xlvi. 14 The contour of the body being as distinctly pronounced through it [the light drapery] as if the figure were naked. **1818** COLEBROOKE *Import Colonial Corn* 75 Emigration from Europe has not yet taken a pronounced direction towards Southern Africa. **1860** TYNDALL *Glac.* I. vii. 54 When regarded obliquely their colour is not so pronounced. **1861** BERESF. HOPE *Eng. Cathedr. 19th C.* vi. 217 Even in the little round church of St. Sepulchre's, Cambridge, of pure Norman or Romanesque, there is a pronounced triforium. **1879** T. P. O'CONNOR *Ld. Beaconsfield* 67 Mr. Disraeli sought election at Marylebone as a Radical of the most pronounced type.

pronouncedly (prəʊ'naʊnsɪdlɪ), *adv.* [f. prec. + -LY[2].] In a pronounced manner or degree; markedly, decidedly, distinctly.

1867 F. H. LUDLOW *Fleeing to Tarshish* 143 The earl was an elegant, though most pronouncedly British man of about forty. **1881** *Times* 11 Oct., Spanish was pronouncedly dull, and all markets closed with a gloomy appearance. **1891** *Speaker* 2 May 530/2 Both.. theologies were in their doctrines of sin and grace pronouncedly Augustinian.

pronouncement (prəʊ'naʊnsmənt). [f. PRONOUNCE *v.* + -MENT: cf. OF. *prononcement* (13th c.).]

1. The action or an act of pronouncing; a formal statement, esp. one authoritatively made; an opinion or decision given; a declaration, assertion.

1593 NASHE *Christ's T.* (1613) 46 Repent yet, and I will repent me of the pronouncement against thee. **1680** J. C. *Vind. Oaths* (ed. 2) 1 The first and lowest step or degree is a bare and simple affirmation and negation, or pronouncement of the matter without more, as to say,.. 'My name is John'. **1860** W. G. WARD *Nat. & Grace* I. p. xxvii, The Catholic philosopher is bound to take care, that his conclusions are fully in accordance with the pronouncements of sound Theology. **1880** F. HALL in *19th Cent.* Sept. 424 Peremptory and unseasoned pronouncements as to what is bad English are not the least of the minor pests which vex our enlightened age.

2. The fact or condition of being pronounced or strongly marked. *rare.*

1908 *Q. Rev.* Jan. 272 It was not till the approach of the Renaissance that the feeling attained any definite pronouncement in Europe.

pronouncer (prəʊ'naʊnsə(r)). [f. PRONOUNCE *v.* + -ER[1].] One who pronounces.

c **1374** CHAUCER *Boeth.* II. pr. iii. 25 (Camb. MS.) Thow Rethoryen or pronouncere of kynges preysynges desseruedyst glorye of wit and of Eloquence. **1561–2** *Reg. Privy Council Scot.* I. 197 Quha is the gevar and pronuncear of the said decreit. **1618** *Barnevelt's Apol.* Biij b, Heere now I appeale from the Readers to the pronouncers of iudgement. **1691** WOOD *Ath. Oxon.* I. *Fasti* 696, A Pronouncer of the men of this World to be vain, in whom the knowledge of God reigneth not. **1813** LEIGH HUNT in *Examiner* 15 Feb. 98/1 The pronouncers of my sentence. **1890** *Sat. Rev.* 29 Nov. 607/2 Every intelligent pronouncer and adopter of the formularies of the Church.

pronouncing (prəʊ'naʊnsɪŋ), *vbl. sb.* [f. as prec. + -ING[1].] The action of the verb PRONOUNCE.

1. Utterance, articulation, pronunciation.

1451 CAPGRAVE *Life St. Aug.* (E.E.T.S.) 21 His forhed, chekis, his eyne and all his membres in maner laboured in pronounsyng of þese wordes. **1581** MULCASTER *Positions* v. (1887) 31 Our spelling is harder, our pronouncing harsher. **1597** HOLLYBAND (*title*) The Italian Schoole-maister; Contayning Rules for the perfect pronouncing of th' italian tongue. **1668** WILKINS *Real Char.* III. xii 366 Those Letters are stiled Consonants, in the pronouncing of which the Breath is intercepted, by some Collision or Closure.

2. Authoritative or official utterance, delivery (of a sentence, or the like).

1563-4 *Reg. Privy Council Scot.* I. 258 For the inordinat pronunceing of ane decreit aganis him. **1651** Hobbes *Leviath.* III. xlii. 275 Besides the Judgment, there is necessary also the pronouncing of Sentence. **1884** *Law Times* 1 Nov. 2/2 The decree *nisi*.. is not to be made absolute until six months from the pronouncing thereof.

b. The giving of an authoritative opinion; a decision, judgement, pronouncement.

1786 Jefferson *Writ.* (1859) I. 561 There is no pronouncing on future events. **1869** Browning *Ring & Bk.* x. 146 Here is the last pronouncing of the Church, Her sentence that subsists unto this day.

3. *attrib.*; **pronouncing dictionary**, a dictionary in which the received pronunciation of the words is indicated.

1764 W. Johnston (*title*) A Pronouncing and Spelling Dictionary. **1791** J. Walker (*title*) A Critical Pronouncing Dictionary. **1857** Pryce (*title*) English-Welsh Pronouncing Dictionary.

pro'nouncing, *ppl. a. rare.* [-ING².] That pronounces; expressing a pronouncement.

1628 T. Spencer *Logick* 153 Axiome signifieth no more, but a declaratiue or pronouncing sentence.

† **'pronounist.** *Obs. nonce-wd.* [f. PRONOUN + -IST.] One who favours the use of pronouns. So **pronouni'zation** = PRONOMINATION 2.

1625 J. Phillips *Way to Heaven* 63 These Pronounists do so glory in the phrase [*Our Lord*], that it is become a distinguishing note of a Romish Catholike. **1899** [see PRONOMINATION 2].

pronto ('pronto), *a. Mus.* [a. It. *pronto* ready, prompt, f. L. *promptus* quick: cf. next.] (See quots.)

Quot. 1740 represents quasi-*adv.* use.

1740 J. Grassineau *Mus. Dict.* 184 *Pronto*, readily, quick, nimbly, without loss of time. **1908** L. J. De Bekker *Stokes' Encycl. Mus. & Musicians* 517/2 *Pronto, It.* Quick, ready. **1938** *Oxf. Compan. Mus.* 759/1 *Pronto* (It.) 'Ready', 'prompt'. So *Prontamente*, 'promptly'.

pronto ('prɒntəʊ), *adv. colloq.* (orig. *U.S.*). [a. Sp. *pronto*, f. as prec.] Quickly; promptly, straight away.

[**1850** L. H. Garrard *Wah-to-Yah* ix. 134 Bent told him to *vamos, prento*! (go quick). *Ibid.* xi. 162 Me be off prento. *Ibid.* xvii. 225 Esta—'here'—said she... Vamos—prento, por el rancheros—'go quick for the rancheros.'] **1911** H. B. Wright *Winning of Barbara Worth* v. 96 All we have to do with it is to push for Rubio City pronto. **1926** J. Black *You can't Win* vi. 66 If we was in the city I'd take fifty cents of it purty pronto. **1934** R. Macaulay *Going Abroad* ii. 26, I bring zem wizout fail; pronto, right away. **1938** E. Bowen *Death of Heart* III. v. 405 I'm going to take you right back—now, pronto, at once. **1948** 'N. Shute' *No Highway* v. 128 Will you..get Honey back here, pronto? **1952** M. Allingham *Tiger in Smoke* x. 165 When the war ended you were slung out pronto. **1966** *Listener* 22 Dec. 927/3 He finished up by saying that there would be a punitive expedition pretty pronto if the stuff was not returned. **1976** P. Cave *High Flying Birds* iii. 33 You tell that bastard to come and see me... Pronto.

Prontosil ('prɒntəʊsɪl). *Pharm.* Also **prontosil.** [G., proprietary name.] **1.** A proprietary name for a reddish-brown crystalline bacteriostatic dye, 2′,4′-diaminoazobenzene-4-sulphonamide, $C_{12}H_{13}N_5O_2S$, which was the first of the sulphonamide drugs to be known and was given (usu. orally) in the treatment of a wide range of bacterial infections; formerly also called ***Red Prontosil.***

1936 *Proc. R. Soc. Med.* XXIX. 313 Advice will be given of a new class of substances, which have an actual chemotherapeutic action in streptococcal infections (prontosil, prontosil S). **1936** *Trade Marks Jrnl.* 15 July 874/2 Prontosil... A medicated dye preparation for human use in the prevention and treatment of Streptococcus infections. Bayer Products, Limited. **1937** *Lancet* 13 Mar. 626/1 Trefouël and others.. have shown that the soluble red azo-dye Prontosil Soluble (for injection) and the almost insoluble orange azo-dye Red Prontosil (oral) are bactericidal only after reduction to sulphanilamide. **1938** F. B. Young *Dr. Bradley Remembers* viii. 437 Some German, it seemed—it was always the Germans in those days—had compounded a new synthetic drug..marketed under the name of Prontosil. **1938** *Times* 8 Dec. 18/5 The new drug, prontosil, the value of which in treating human puerperal fever was clearly established at the Queen Charlotte's Hospital isolation blocks and research laboratories. **1942** *Endeavour* July 122/2 The origin of these and other developments of bacterial chemotherapy was the synthesis by Mietzsch and Klaren of the drug known as prontosil, and the disclosure of its therapeutic properties by Domagk. **1965** *Listener* 10 June 847/1, I can remember helping to make some quinine ampoules for the treatment of a young wife who was dying in her first pregnancy. They were useless. A few years later a proprietary drug called 'Prontosil' came to us, and by giving tablets of that by mouth we began to cure puerperal fever. **1972** 'J. Herriot' *It shouldn't happen to Vet* (1973) xxi. 143 Just a suggestion, James..I honestly think that the situation calls for a little Prontosil.

2. Special Combs. (none now current): **Prontosil Album** [L. *album*, neut. of *albus* white], a name for sulphanilamide; **Prontosil Red** or **Rubrum** [L. *rubrum*, neut. of *ruber*, *rubrus* red] = sense 1; **Prontosil soluble** (see quot. 1958).

1937 *Lancet* 27 Feb. 510/1 From the 12th to the 29th the patient also received one tablet of Prontosil Album by mouth every six hours. **1958** *Martindale's Extra Pharmacopœia* (ed. 24) 1250 Proprietary preparations of sulphanilamide were formerly marketed in Great Britain under the names Prontosil Album (Bayer Prod.) and Streptocide (Evans Medical Supplies). **1938** *Brit. Med. Jrnl.* 8 Jan. 104/2, I have obtained successful results in the treatment of erysipelas and acute dermatitis by using as a local application prontosil red, 7½ grains being dissolved in 1 oz. of distilled water. **1938** *Lancet* 10 Sept. 647/1 The new rule..will apply not only to sulphanilamide but to related substances including products sold under the following names:..Prontosil rubrum.., Prontosil Soluble, [etc.]. **1959** Evers & Caldwell *Chem. of Drugs* (ed. 3) ix. 114 Prontosil rubrum is broken down in the body to 4-aminobenzenesulphonamide. **1964** Ariëns & Simonis in E. J. Ariëns *Molecular Pharmacol.* I. 77 One of the bio-activations first recognized as such was that of Prontosil Rubrum.., the compound found by Domagk..to be effective in the protection of mice against bacterial infections. **1936** *Lancet* 11 July 107/2 There seems to be some risk of toxic reactions associated with the administration of Prontosil (soluble) intravenously. *Ibid.* 5 Dec. 1323/2 When prontosil soluble was substituted for the sulphonamide, there was no bactericidal effect. **1958** *Chambers's Techn. Dict.* 1017/2 Prontosil-soluble, which has greater antibacterial effect [than Prontosil] and is more soluble, is the disodium salt of 4′-sulphonamido phenylazo-7-acetylamino-1-hydroxy naphthalene-3·6-disulphonic acid.

‖**pronuba** ('prəʊnjuːbə). *Rom. Antiq.* [L. *prōnuba* a woman who attended a bride, f. **prōnubāre* (found in *prōnubāns*) to arrange a marriage, f. PRO-¹ + stem of *nūb-ĕre* to marry.]

1. A woman presiding over or assisting in the ceremonies and arrangements of marriage.

1513 Douglas *Æneis* IV. iv. 78 Erth, the first modir, maid a takin of wo, And eik of wedlok the pronuba Juno. **1850** Leitch tr. *C. O. Müller's Anc. Art* §429 (ed. 2) 618 The bride..is pushed forward by the pronuba to the husband who is armed with a lance. **1868** *Smith's Dict. Gr. & Rom. Antiq.* (ed. 7) 252/2 At the end of the repast the bride was conducted by matrons who had not had more than one husband (*pronubae*), to the lectus genialis in the atrium.

2. [C. V. Riley 1872, in *Nature* 26 Sept. 444/1.] In full, ***pronuba moth***. A small white North American moth of the genus formerly so called, now usually included in the genus *Tegeticula*, esp. the yucca moth, *T. yuccasella*, which pollinates yucca plants.

1872 *Nature* 26 Sept. 444/1 The larva of *Pronuba* eats through the Yucca capsule in which it fed, enters the ground and hibernates there. **1905** V. L. Kellogg *Amer. Insects* xvi. 577 (*caption*) Pronuba-moth depositing eggs in ovary of Yucca. **1929** Robbins & Rickett *Botany* xxvi. 437 Without the *Pronuba* moth the *Yucca* would not produce seeds. **1946** D. C. Peattie *Road of Naturalist* ii. 24 The smoky little Pronuba moths..come to the blossoms, mate there, hover and hide and perform small extraordinary rites without which no Joshua tree would stand and brandish arms at heaven.

Hence **'pronubal** *a. rare*: see quot.; also **pro'nubial** *a. rare* [after *connubial*], presiding over or promoting marriage.

1877 W. Jones *Finger-ring* 303 Pronubal or pledge rings passed between the contracting parties among the Romans. **1698** Congreve *Semele* I. i, Thy aid, pronubial Juno, Athamas implores.

‖**pronucleus** (prəʊ'njuːklɪəs). *Biol.* [mod.L. (E. van Beneden), f. Gr. πρό, PRO-² + NUCLEUS.] A primitive or prior nucleus; in *Zool.* the nucleus of a spermatozoön or of an ovule, before these unite to form the definitive nucleus of the fertilized ovum; in *Bot.* the nucleus of a gamete, which, by coalescing with another of the opposite sex, forms the germ nucleus.

1880 *Athenæum* 25 Dec. 868/3 In this egg,..shortly before impregnation, a clear nucleus is formed, round which the protoplasm of the egg becomes radiately striated. This is known as the female pronucleus. **1882** Vines *Sachs' Bot.* 524 One of these is the nucleus of the oosphere, and may be termed the 'female pronucleus'; the other appears to have passed into the oosphere from the pollen-tube, and is the 'male pronucleus' (*spermakern*). These two nuclei coalesce to form the definitive nucleus of the oospore. **1888** Rolleston & Jackson *Anim. Life* Introd. 25 The two pronuclei approach each other, and the granules of the surrounding protoplasm are arranged round each of them, so as to form a star or aster with a pronucleus as a centre.

pronunce, -nunse, obs. forms of PRONOUNCE.

pronunciability (prəʊnʌnsɪə'bɪlɪtɪ, -nʌnʃɪə-). [f. next + -ITY.] Capability of being pronounced.

1816 Bentham *Chrestom.* App., Wks. 1843 VIII. 191/2 The several properties..desirable in language, may be thus enumerated:—1. Clearness. 2. Correctness. 3. Copiousness. 4. Completeness. 5. Non-redundance. 6. Conciseness. 7. Pronounciability. 8. Melodiousness [*sic*]. **1881** Masson *De Quincey* xi. 156 Mere pronunciability was not enough for him, and musical beauty had to be superadded.

pronunciable (prəʊ'nʌnsɪəb(ə)l, -ʃɪəb(ə)l), *a.* [ad. late L. *prōnuntiābil-is*, f. *prōnuntiāre*: see PRONOUNCE *v.* and -ABLE.] = PRONOUNCEABLE.

1649 Jer. Taylor *Gt. Exemp.* I. Ad Sect. v. 61 Like vowels pronunciable by the intertexture of a Consonant. **1748** Hartley *Observ. Man* I. iii. 290 Words rendered pronunciable by affixing some simple or short Sound.

pronuncial (prəʊ'nʌnʃ(ɪ)əl), *a. rare*⁻⁰. [f. stem of L. *prōnunti-āre* to PRONOUNCE + -AL¹.] Of or pertaining to pronunciation.

1847 in Webster; also in later Dicts.

pronunciamento (prəʊnʌnsɪə'mɛntəʊ). [ad. Sp. *pronunciamiento* (pronunθja'mjento), lit. a pronouncement, repr. a L. type **prōnuntiāmentum*, f. *prōnuntiāre* to PRONOUNCE: see -MENT.] A pronouncement, a proclamation, a manifesto; often applied to one issued by insurrectionists, esp. in Spanish-speaking countries. Also *attrib.*

1835 *Morning Courier & N.Y. Enquirer* 23 Nov. 2/2 It is not..a question of a *pronounciamiento* in favor of federalism or centralism, or who shall govern. **1843** W. Irving in *Life & Lett.* (1866) III. 287 The besiegers calculated..upon a pronunciamento in favor of the insurrectional government. **1845** Ford *Handbk. Spain* I. 352/2 Malaga shared with Lugo ..in taking the lead in the Espartero Pronunciamento. **1886** *Cycl. Tour. Club Gaz.* June 215 The pronunciamentos of well-posted critics notwithstanding. **1889** *Spectator* 14 Dec. 835 Marshal da Fonseca..made a pronunciamiento, in Spanish fashion, against the Ministry. **1906** R. Fry *Let.* 20 Nov. (1972) I. 273 The Trustees..will pass some sort of resolution accepting my *pronunciamento.* **1929** *Times* 1 Nov. 17/4 The worst result of the Spanish doctor's pronunciamento is likely to be a regular cult of conscientious and laboured irregularity. **1939** H. G. Wells *Holy Terror* IV. iii. 439 The pronunciamento bosses of those little old republics there used to be in South America. **1951** E. Paul *Springtime in Paris* xi. 202 Then came Zhdanov's pronunciamento in Russia condemning jazz as degenerate and unfit for proletarian amusement. **1968** R. Hargreaves *Bloodybacks* x. 265 Although there was anything but unanimity of sentiment and opinion among the inhabitants of the Thirteen Colonies, the Congressional *pronunciamento* had committed them to continued resistance. **1972** *Daily Tel.* (Colour Suppl.) 10 Nov. 18/1 The political revolution consisted largely of intimidation, arbitrary rule..and windy *pronunciamientos.* **1975** *New Yorker* 20 Jan. 61/3, I wish he had prevailed on the author to drop a few samples of the writer-hero's more high-flown, phony-eloquent pronunciamentos.

† **pro'nunciate,** *ppl. a. Obs. rare.* [ad. L. *prōnuntiāt-us*, pa. pple. of *prōnuntiāre* to PRONOUNCE.] Pronounced.

In quot. 1432-50 = 'announced, predicted' (const. as *pa. pple.*); in quot. 1508 = 'publicly known, declared to be'.

1432-50 tr. *Higden* (Rolls) II. 293 And iiij. names be pronunciate [L. *quatuor nomina leguntur prænuntiata*] in the olde testamente, that is to say, Ismael, Ysaac, Sampson, and Iosias, and ij. oonly in the newe testamente, Iohn Baptiste and Criste. **1508** Kennedie *Flyting w. Dunbar* 525 Sarazene, symonyte, provit Pagane pronunciate.

† **pro'nunciate,** *v. Obs. rare*⁻¹. In 7 **-tiate.** [f. ppl. stem of L. *prōnuntiāre* to PRONOUNCE.] *trans.* To pronounce, declare.

1652 Gaule *Magastrom.* 201 To pronuntiate to the wicked and reprobates their destinated judgements and deserts.

pronunciation (prəʊnʌnsɪ'eɪʃən). Also 6-8 **-noun-**, 7 **-non-**; 6 **-cy-**, **-sy-**, 6-7 **-ti-**; 5 **-cion.** [ad. L. *prōnuntiātiōn-em*, n. of action f. *prōnuntiāre* to PRONOUNCE. Cf. F. *prononciation* (*pronunciation*, 1281 in Hatz.-Darm.).] The action of pronouncing.

1. The pronouncing or uttering of a word or words; the mode in which a word is pronounced.

1432-50 tr. *Higden* (Rolls) II. 161 Hit is to be hade in meruayle that the propur langage of Englische men scholde be made so diuerse in oon lytelle yle in pronunciacion. *Ibid.* III. 249 The seide Esdras founde newe letters, whiche were more liȝhte to the writenge and pronunciacion. **1530** Palsgr. Introd. 20 They have utterly neglected the frenche mennes maner of pronounciation, and so rede frenche as theyr fantasy or opinion dyde lede them. **1555** Eden *Decades* 124 For the ryghter pronunsyation of the names. **1613** Purchas *Pilgrimage* (1614) 4 Drusius thinkes that Galatinus was first Authour of this pronountiation *Iehoua.* **1710** *Lond. Gaz.* No. 4695/3 This William Charlton..speaks according to the Northern Pronunciation. **1889** J. D. Robertson in *Gloucester Gloss.* p. v, I have admitted a fair proportion of mere 'pronunciations' which a more competent and scientific worker would have relegated to a Glossic Appendix.

†**2.** Oratorical utterance; elocution; delivery; *spec.* elegant or eloquent delivery. *Obs.*

1430-40 Lydg. *Bochas* VI. xv. (MS. Bodl. 263) 335/1 Bi crafft he hadde a special auauntage Fauour synguleer in pronunciacioun. **1553** T. Wilson *Rhet.* 116b, Pronunciation is an apte orderinge both of the voyce, countenaunce, and all the whole bodye, accordynge to the worthines of suche woordes and mater as by speache are declared. **1612** Brinsley *Lud. Lit.* 211 Pronuntiation, beeing that which either makes or mars the most excellent speech. **1748** J. Mason *Elocut.* 8 By Pronunciation, the Antients understood both Elocution and Action; and comprehended in it the right Management of the Voice, Looks, and Gesture.

†**3. a.** The action of pronouncing authoritatively, or proclaiming; declaration, promulgation; a pronouncement. *Obs.*

c **1475** *Harl. Contin. Higden* (Rolls) VIII. 500 The chauncellor of Ynglonde made a pronunciacion in the maner of a sermon. **1538** Cromwell in Merriman *Life & Lett.* (1902) II. 112 For advoidinge..of the pronunciation of Novellties withoute wise and discrite qualification. **1564-5** *Reg. Privy Council Scot.* I. 315 Quhill the pronunciation of the decreit arbitrall. **1611** Speed *Hist. Gt. Brit.* IX. xiii. (1623) 758 The forme of pronunciation was *In the Name of God, Amen.* *a* **1674** Clarendon *Surv. Leviath.* (1676) 322 If he be not terrified with that dismal Pronunciation, *If we sin willfully* [etc.].

b. = PRONUNCIAMENTO. *rare.*

1848 *Blackw. Mag.* LXIII. 105 The declamations and 'pronunciations' of the rabble.

†**4.** The action of speaking; articulation. *Obs.*

1686 tr. *Chardin's Trav. Persia* 387 He wrought that Miracle, onely by the pronuntiation of one word. **1706** tr. *Dupin's Eccl. Hist. 16th C.* II. v. 150 That Jesus Christ continued the Pronunciation [of the Words] all the while he bless'd, and brake and distributed the Eucharist.

†**5.** *fig.* (See quot. and cf. PRONOUNCED 2.) *Obs.*

1727–41 CHAMBERS *Cycl.*, *Pronouncing, Pronunciation*, in painting, the marking and expressing the parts of all kinds of bodies with that degree of force necessary to make them more or less distinct and conspicuous.

6. *attrib.* and *Comb.*, as **pronunciation key**, a list of symbols providing a guide to pronunciation; **pronunciation-spelling**, the spelling of words in accordance with their usual pronunciation; an instance of this.

1962 C. L. BARNHART in Householder & Saporta *Probl. in Lexicogr.* 174 Two great scholars..said that the pronunciation key was of no importance whatsoever; they felt that any key that used symbols consistently was adequate. **1966** *Random House Dict. Eng. Lang.*, (*heading*) Pronunciation Key. **1944** H. J. ULDALL in E. P. Hamp et al. *Readings in Linguistics II* (1966) 149 If there have been cases of spelling-pronunciation, there have also been cases of pronunciation-spelling. **1953** K. JACKSON *Lang. & Hist. in Early Brit.* I. ii. 70 If the spelling..depended on tradition alone..there would be far more cases of pronunciation-spellings betraying lenition than the few which do exist. **1979** *Amer. Speech* LIV. 33 There are no spelling pronunciations in the corpus, although there are pronunciation spellings like the British *cuppa* and *pinta*, as in *cup of tea* and *pint of milk*.

pronunciative (prəʊˈnʌnsɪətɪv, -ˈnʌnʃ(ɪ)ətɪv), *a.* *rare.* [ad. L. *prōnuntiātīv-us*, f. ppl. stem of L. *prōnuntiāre* to PRONOUNCE + -IVE: see -ATIVE.] Characterized by pronouncement; declarative; hence, †dogmatic (*obs.*).

1619 SIR A. GORGES tr. *Bacon's Wisd. Anc.* xxvi. (1886) 104 The confident and pronunciative school of Aristotle.

pronunciator (prəʊˈnʌnsɪeɪtə(r), -ˈnʌnʃɪeɪtə(r)). *rare.* [a. L. *prōnuntiātor*, agent-n. from *prōnuntiāre* to pronounce.] One who pronounces.

1846 in WORCESTER, citing *Ch. Obs.* **1876** *Life W. S. Johnson* 166 Mr. Sheridan,..and..other..speakers at that time, began to be considered in a great degree the standard of pronunciators.

So **proˈnunciatory** *a.*, of or pertaining to pronunciation; of the nature of a pronouncement.

1806 M. SMART in *Monthly Mag.* XXI. 132 Our pronunciatory reformers in the pulpit and the theatre. **1846** in WORCESTER, citing EARNSHAW.

pronymph, -al: see PRO-² 1.

proo (pru:), *int.* *Sc.* and *north. dial.* A call to a cow or horse, inviting it to stand still or come near.

1818 SCOTT *Hrt. Midl.* xlv, [To cow] Pruh, my leddy—pruh, my woman. **1824** MACTAGGART *Gallovid. Encycl.*, *Proo*, cry, at horses when they are wanted to stand still, or, at least, not to gallop. **1853** A. SMART in *Whistle-Binkie* II. 308 Moo, moo, proochy lady! Proo, Hawkie, proo, Hawkie!

proo, obs. form of PROW *sb.*¹

pro-ode (ˈprəʊəʊd). [ad. Gr. προῳδός: see PRO-² and ODE.] An introductory ode in a Greek chorus; an overture or prelude; also, a short verse preceding a longer one: opposed to EPODE.

1850 MURE *Lit. Greece* III. 58 The epode, when prefixed to the [strophe and antistrophe], assumes the name of Proöde. **1900** H. W. SMYTH *Grk. Melic Poets* 284 A glyconic proode followed by a simmiacum.

prooemiac (prəʊˈi:mɪæk), *a.* *rare.* [ad. med.L. *prooemiac-us* (Du Cange), a. Gr. προοιμιακ-ός, f. προοίμιον PROŒMIUM, PROEM.] = PROEMIAL *a.*

1850 NEALE *East. Ch.* I. 856 The 104th [Psalm] is the Prooemiac, because it commences Vespers.

prooemial, variant of PROEMIAL.

‖**prooemium** (prəʊˈi:mɪəm). Also 5 prohemium, 8- proemium, 9 prooemion. [L. *prooemium*, a. Gr. προοίμιον; see PROEM.] = PROEM *sb.*

1456 SIR G. HAYE *Law Arms* (S.T.S.) 2 Doctour Bonnet Priour of Sallon maid his first intitulacioun and prohemium. **1650** R. GELL *Serm.* 8 Aug. 2 The *Prooemium*, wherein he calls heaven and earth to witness. **1715** M. DAVIES *Athen. Brit.* I. 311 As it appears in the very Prœmium of that Decretal it self. **1826** *Hansard Commons* 25 Apr. 590 The whole of the authorities..formed a very dry proemium to the proposal with which it [*sc.* the bill] terminated. **1857** LD. CAMPBELL *Chief Justices* III. xlvii. 125 The prooemium and the peroration of his speech. **1868** TENNYSON *Lucretius* 70 Forgetful how my rich prooemion makes Thy glory fly along the Italian field. **1933** R. TUVE *Seasons & Months* i. 11 Both analogues and influences may be found for the 'alma Venus' of Lucretius' proemium.

pro-œstrous, -œstrum: see PRO-² 1.

pro-œstrus, var. *pro-œstrum* s.v. PRO-² 1.

proof (pru:f), *sb.* Forms: α. preve, prefe, etc.; β. prove, proof, etc.: see below. [ME. *preove*, *proeve*, *preve*, etc., a. OF. *prueve* (*c* 1224 in Godef. *Compl.*), *proeve*, *preve*, *proeuve* (from 13th c. and in mod.F. *preuve*) = Pr. and Pg. *prova*, Sp. *prueba*, Cat. *proba*, It. *prova*, †*pruova*:—late L. *proba* (Ammianus *a* 400) a proof, f. *probāre* to PROVE. The α forms were the original, corresp. to OF. and to Sp. *prueba*; they continued longer in Sc. The β forms (also in late OF. *prouve*, *prove*, 14th c. in Littré) are assimilated in the vowel to F. *prouver*, Eng. PROVE *v.* The devocalization of *v* to *f* ensued upon the loss of final *e*; cf. the relation of *v* and *f* in *believe*, *belief*, *relieve*, *relief*, *behove*, *behoof*, etc.]

A. Illustration of Forms.

α. 3 **preoue, 4 proeue, prieve, 4–5 pref, preef, 4–6 prefe, preve,** *Sc.* **preiff, 5 proef, preff(e, preeff, preyf, prewe, 5–6 prief(e, preif, 6 preife, pryef, preeue, pryve,** *Sc.* **prieff; 8–9** *arch.* **prief,** *dial.* **preef, prief, preif.**

a **1225** *Ancr. R.* 154 Ich chulle, of bo two, scheawen uorbisne & preoue. *c* **1325**, **13..** Pref [see B. 2, 7]. **1340** *Ayenb.* 134 Wyþ-oute oþre proeue. *c* **1375** *Sc. Leg. Saints* i. (*Petrus*) 187 As men may preiff furth bringe. *c* **1380** Prefe [see B. 4]. *c* **1386** CHAUCER *Clerk's T.* 731 This Markys yet his wyf to tempte moore To the outtreste preeue [*v. rr.* preue, priue, proef, preef] of hir corage. **1387** TREVISA *Higden* (Rolls) I. 71 Þe fourþe witnesse and preef. **1390** GOWER *Conf.* I. 227 Sothliche I lieve And durste setten it in prieve. *c* **1400** *Ragman Roll* 122 in Hazl. *E.P.P.* I. 74 For your dedys preyf. *c* **1420** LYDG. *Thebes* 2326 That she thought forto mak a prief. **1422** tr. *Secreta Secret.*, *Priv. Priv.* 216 Wythout longe Prewe. *c* **1430** Preef; **1436** Preffe [see B. 7, 8]. *c* **1440** *Generydes* 1453 Other wise thanne he cowde make the preff. **1499** *Exch. Rolls Scotl.* XI. 436 The preve that Sir Patrik Hume offeris to produce. *c* **1570** *Pride & Lowl.* (1841) 36 Of truth and vertue for to maken pryef. **1572** Preuis; *a* **1584** Preif [see B. 1 c]. **1590** Priefe, Prief [see B. 5, 10]. **1591** SPENSER *M. Hubberd* 408 But readie are of anie to make preife. **1594** CAREW *Tasso* (1881) 18 He showes in hoarie lockes of strength the preeue. *a* **1796** BURNS *Troker* in Ainslie *Land of Burns* (1892) 188 Let's see How ye'll pit this in prief to me.

β. 4–5 **prooff, 4–5 prof, proff,** *Sc.* **pruf(f, 4–6 proue, profe,** *Sc.* **prowe, 5–6 proufe, -ffe, prove, prooue, 5–7 proofe, proffe,** *Sc.* **prufe, 6 prooffe, 7** *Sc.* **pruife, 5- proof.** (Sc. *pruife*, etc. (Y, ø).) *Pl.* **proofs; also 4–7 proues, 5 prouves, 5–7 proves, 6–7 prooves.**

c **1330** R. BRUNNE *Chron.* (1810) 341 Bi profe & gode assaies. **13..** *Cursor M.* 6865 Thoru proue [*Gött.* prof] o seluen dede. *c* **1375** *Sc. Leg. Saints* xxiii. (*VII Sleperis*) 10 Be verray prowe. *Ibid.* xxvii. (*Machor*) 941 Swa with prooff of mychtfull dede he strinthit alway godis sede. *c* **1380** WYCLIF *Wks.* (1880) 70 Þe dede doynge is proff of loue. *Ibid.* 290 Examyne here proues. **1425** Prouves; *c* **1430** Prouffe [see B. 1 c, 4 b]. *c* **1440** *Promp. Parv.* 414/2 *Proof*, idem quod *preef.* **1456** Pruf [see B. 2]. *c* **1500** *Not-br. Mayd* 470 in Hazl. *E.P.P.* II. 291, I see the proue. **1526** TINDALE *2 Cor.* viii. 24 The proffe off youre love. *a* **1562** G. CAVENDISH *Poems*, etc. (1825) II. 115 The proue in me ye may playnly se the vse. **1570** DEE *Math. Pref.* *j b, His bookes..are good profe. **1581** MULCASTER *Positions* iii. (1887) 11 No proufe at all. *a* **1595** SOUTHWELL *Wks.* (1828) II. 38 So many proofs would persuade thee. **1609** Prufe [see B. 1 b]. **1637** Proofe [see B. 2]. **1639** S. DU VERGER tr. *Camus' Admir. Events* 341 Proffes of the greatnesse of my freindship. **1683** Proves, Prooves [see B. 12, 16].

B. Signification. I. From PROVE *v.* in the sense of making good, or showing to be true.

1. a. That which makes good or proves a statement; evidence sufficient (or contributing) to establish a fact or produce belief in the certainty of something. † *to make proof*: to have weight as evidence (*obs.*).

a **1225** *Ancr. R.* 52 Þet hit beo soð, lo her þe preoue. *a* **1300** *Cursor M.* 8708 (Cott.) Proue yee see þat þar es nan. *c* **1385** CHAUCER *L.G.W.* Prol. 28 We han noon other preue. **1437** *Rolls of Parlt.* IV. 510/2 Till the said examination and previs be fully determined. **1526** *Pilgr. Perf.* (W. de W. 1531) 70 b, Very pledges and sure proues of the kynges fauoure. **1560** DAUS tr. *Sleidane's Comm.* 249 Hereof they bryng manye proues. **1659** OWEN *Div. Orig. Script.* Wks. 1853 XVI. 319 Light requires neither proof nor testimony for its evidence. **1759** ROBERTSON *Hist. Scot.* IV. Wks. 1813 I. 318 These suspicions are confirmed by the most direct proof. **1832** R. & J. LANDER *Exped. Niger* I. vi. 232 As a proof of his esteem and confidence. **1883** W. E. NORRIS *Thirlby Hall* xxxi, Which was proof positive that he had thought better of his intention. **1927** A. H. MCNEILE *Introd. to N.T.* 13 He therefore makes no use of proof-texts, and no suggestions that Christianity is the real and 'fulfilled' Judaism. His sole 'proofs' are the actual words and deeds of the Master and the effects which they produced. **1945** R. KNOX *God & Atom* iii. 42 In the long run, you felt, the first three Proofs stood or fell by the value of the causality argument.

b. *Law.* (*generally*) Evidence such as determines the judgement of a tribunal. Also *spec.* (*a*) A written document or documents so attested as to form legal evidence. (*b*) A written statement of what a witness is prepared to swear to. (*c*) The evidence which has been given in a particular case, and entered on the court records. (See also 3.)

1481 *Coventry Leet Bk.* 473 No feynied matiers but such as shall be proved be credible proves in writyng. **1483** CAXTON *Gold. Leg.* 284 b/1 Yf the preues of the lignages were fayled. **1609** SKENE *Reg. Maj.* I. 67 b, It is in the election of him quha is accused, to vnderly the prufe of the woman, or to purge him be judgement, or ane gude assise of the crime quhereof he is accused. *Ibid.* 106 b, Gif the partie defendand that day of prufe, be absent; and the party followand being present with his prufe in his hand and swa the partie defendand be not ready or present, to receiue the prufe against him. *a* **1715** BURNET *Own Time* an. 1678 (1823) II. 445 The proof did not carry it beyond manslaughter. **1768** BLACKSTONE *Comm.* III. xxiii. 368 Written proofs, or evidence, are, 1. Records, and 2. Antient deeds of thirty years standing, which prove themselves. **1818** CRUISE *Digest* (ed. 2) IV. 231 It being in proof that the draft was not completed till six months after instructions had been given for preparing it. **1863** H. COX *Instit.* I. ix. 172 A statement showing all matters required to be proved, and opposite each proof the name of the witness to prove it. **1883** *Act 46 & 47 Vict.* c. 52. Sched. ii. 7 Every creditor who has lodged a proof shall be entitled to see and examine the proofs of other creditors.

†**c.** A person who gives evidence; a witness: = EVIDENCE *sb.* 7. *Obs.* (After 1500 only *Sc.*)

1425 *Rolls of Parlt.* IV. 289/2 That the same Marchant..do brynge..two prouves of Marchantz. **1449** *Ibid.* V. 145/2 Other resonable witnesse and proves sworne. **1456** SIR G. HAYE *Law Arms* (S.T.S.) 73 Gif men suld be prufis thame selff. **1572** *Sc. Acts Jas. VI* (1814) III. 72/1 That the disobedient obstinat and relaps persounis..sall not be admittit as preuis witnessis or Assysouris aganis ony professing þe trew Religioun. *a* **1584** MONTGOMERIE *Cherrie & Slae* 761 For I myself can be ane preif And witness thairintill.

2. The action, process, or fact of proving, or establishing the truth of, a statement; the action of evidence in convincing the mind; demonstration.

c **1325** *Song of Yesterday* 171 in *E.E.P.* (1862) 137 And i say nay and make a pref. **1456** SIR G. HAYE *Law Arms* (S.T.S.) 74 Gif I faile of my pruf.., the juge may assoilȝe my party. **1480** *Coventry Leet Bk.* 461 In prove þerof the procession weye on þe South syde of the seid Churche..was where the south baye of the seid Churche ys nowe. **1637** *Star Chamb. Decree* §21 in *Milton's Areop.* (Arb.) 19 Vpon complaint and proofe made thereof. **1718** HICKES & NELSON *J. Kettlewell* II. lvi. 175 They put the King upon the Proof that they had presented such a Petition. **1848** KEBLE *Serm.* 386 The burthen of proof was of course thrown on the heresiarch. **1860** TYNDALL *Glac.* II. v. 252 This is all capable of experimental proof. *Mod.* In proof of this assertion, I may state [etc.].

3. *Sc. Law.* Evidence given before a judge, or a commissioner representing him, upon a record or an issue framed in pleading; the taking of such evidence by a judge in order to a trial; hence, trial before a judge instead of by a jury.

This distinctive development of sense has gradually taken place since the introduction of trial by jury into Scotland in 1815.

1838 W. BELL *Dict. Law Scot.* 373 The duties of commissioners in taking proofs, under authority of the Court of Session, are pointed out by the acts of Sederunt 11th March 1800, and 22d June 1809. **1845** POLSON in *Encycl. Metrop.* II. 853/1 The proof is taken in the presence of a commissioner appointed by the Lord Ordinary, who examines the witnesses, commits their depositions to writing, and reports the whole, either to the Lord Ordinary or to the court, according to his directions. **1879** MACKAY *Pract. Crt. of Session* II. 10 Under the existing practice a certain discretion is exercised by the Court in determining what causes are..fitted for proof before a judge and not by jury trial. **1890** WATSON *Bell's Dict. Law Scot.* 615/1 By §4 of the Evidence Act, 1866, proof may be taken before the Lord Ordinary, without jury, in any cause, 'if both parties consent thereto, or if special cause be shown'. **1903** J. RANKINE *Princ. Law Scot.* 551 When the Lord Ordinary takes a proof, each party adduces witnesses to prove his statements, and the proof is followed by a hearing on evidence [i.e. a hearing of counsel on the evidence]. *Ibid.*, Where the parties are agreed as to the necessity for inquiry regarding the facts, the Lord Ordinary appoints a diet of proof, or in certain cases orders issues with a view to the trial of the cause by a jury. **1908** *Scots Law Times* 14 Mar. XV. 958/1 The Lord Ordinary held that the case was one for proof not jury trial. *Ibid.* 959/1 Lord Guthrie. 'I think it ought to be sent to proof and not to jury trial.'

II. From PROVE *v.* in the sense of trying or testing.

4. a. The action or an act of testing or making trial of anything, or the condition of being tried; test, trial, experiment; examination, probation; assay. Often in phrases *to bring, put, set*, etc. (something) *in, on, to (the,* †*a) proof.*

c **1380** WYCLIF *Wks.* (1880) 384 We mot take hede to þe rewle of prefe..by her werkis ȝe schul knowe hem. *c* **1386** [see A. α]. *c* **1440** *Promp. Parv.* 412/1 Preef, or a-say(y)nge, *examinacio.* **1523** FITZHERB. *Surv.* 13 b, That there may be made due proues without fauoure, bribery, or extorcyon. **1683** MOXON *Mech. Exerc.*, *Printing* xvi, Without several Proofs and Tryings, [the mould] cannot be expected to be perfectly true. **1727** A. HAMILTON *New Acc. E. Ind.* I. p. xxix, I leave them to my Reader, with the old Proverb to accompany them, that the Proof of the Pudding is in eating it. **1805** SOUTHEY *Madoc in W.* vi. ad fin., If thy heart Be harden'd to the proof, come when thou wilt. **1842** TENNYSON *Locksley Hall* 77 Drug thy memories, lest thou learn it, lest thy heart be put to proof. **1861** FAIRBAIRN *Iron. Manuf.* 150 Some large pump-rods.. were required to stand a proof of 120,000 lbs. per square inch.

b. *Arith.* An operation serving to test or check the correctness of an arithmetical calculation.

(Sometimes understood as in sense 2.)

c **1430** *Art Nombryng* 6 The subtraccioun is none other but a prouffe of the addicioun, and the contrarye in like wise. **1594** BLUNDEVIL *Exerc.* I. iii. (1636) 9 In making which proofe or tryall you cannot likely erre. **1704** J. HARRIS *Lex. Techn.* s.v. *Multiplication*, The Proof of Multiplication can only certainly be effected by Division. **1827** HUTTON *Course Math.* I. 40 The method of Proof, and the reason of the Rule, are the same as in Simple Multiplication.

†**5.** The action or fact of passing through or having experience of something; also, knowledge derived from this; experience. *Obs.*

a 1300 *Cursor M.* 20005 (Cott.) þe apostels..þai did þam-seluen al to proue, O ded for þair lauerd be-houe. 1399 LANGL. *Rich. Redeles* Prol. 17 It passid my parceit, and my preifis also, How so wondirffull werkis wolde haue an ende. c 1400 *Destr. Troy* 5525 Epistaphus, to preue, was his pure nome. 1544 *Suppl. to Henry VIII* in *Four Supplic.* (1871) 40 Of whom they haue proue & sure knowledge. 1590 SPENSER *F.Q.* I. viii. 43 Good growes of evils priefe. *Ibid.* II. i. 48 Tell what fatall priefe Hath with so huge misfortune you opprest. 1613 PURCHAS *Pilgrimage* (1614) 392 A fountaine..of Tarre, whereof wee had good vse and proofe in our ship.

†**6.** A trial, attempt, essay, endeavour. *Obs.*

1575 CHURCHYARD *Chippes* (1817) 156 Yet diuers proues were made the breach to view, And some were slayne, that dyd assayle the same. 1628 HOBBES *Thucyd.* (1822) 119 They thought this accident (especially being their first proof by sea) very much against reason.

†**7.** That which anything proves or turns out to be; the issue, result, effect, fulfilment; esp. in phrase *to come to proof*. *Obs.*

13.. *Sir Beues* (A.) 4030 þe king Yuor hadde a þef: God him ȝeue euel pref, For þat he kouþe so wel stele! c 1430 *How Wise Man tauȝt his Son* 62 in *Babees Bk.* (1868) 50 And flee al letcherie in wil and dede Lest þou come to yuel preef. c 1489 CAXTON *Sonnes of Aymon* vii. 161 Some of you speketh now hye, that whan the dede shall come to preeff, he shall be full lowe. 1575–85 ABP. SANDYS *Serm.* xv. (Parker Soc.) 301 The timeliest fruit often cometh to least proof. 1599 HAKLUYT *Voy.* II. I. 85 The most part of the sayd mines came to no proofe though they put fire in them. 1607–12 BACON *Ess., Parents & Childr.* (Arb.) 274 The proofe is best, when Men keepe theire authoritye towardes theire Children, but not theire purse.

8. *esp.* The fact, condition, or quality of proving good, turning out well, or producing good results; thriving; good condition, good quality; goodness, substance. Now only *dial.*

[1436 *Pol. Poems* (Rolls) II. 161 The wolle of Spayne hit cometh not to preffe, But if [= unless] it be tosed and menged welle Amonges Englysshe wolle the gretter delle.] 1616 SURFL. & MARKH. *Country Farme* I. xxiv. 105 When you haue fed your Swine to his full proofe. 1725 BRADLEY *Fam. Dict.* s.v. *Sainfoin*, This sort of Grass has obtain'd the Preference above Clover-Grass in England, as continuing longer in Proof than it. 1854 *Jrnl. R. Agric. Soc.* XV. II. 404 This is not found to deteriorate their bulk, or the 'proof' or quality of keeping. 1862 *Q. Rev.* Apr. 287 Sainfoin..the aftermath is invaluable for securing the high and rapid proof of lambs. 1893 *Wilts. Gloss.*, *Proof*, of manure, hay, &c., the strength or goodness... A thriving tree is said to be in 'good proof'.

9. a. The testing of cannon or small fire-arms by firing a heavy charge, or by hydraulic pressure. ***proof of (gun) powder***, the testing of the propulsive force of gunpowder.

1669 STURMY *Mariner's Mag.* v. xii. 64 What Powder is allowed for Proof, and what for Action of each Piece. 1797 *Encycl. Brit.* (ed. 3) XV. 589/1 *Proof of Powder*, is in order to try its goodness and strength. 1859 F. A. GRIFFITHS *Artill. Man.* (1862) 57 All Ordnance..are subject to the Water proof. This is done by means of a forcing pump.

b. A place for testing fire-arms or explosives.

1760 *Chron.* in *Ann. Reg.* 146/1 At a proof at Woolwich warren, a smoke-ball burst. 1883 *Pall Mall G.* 6 Apr. 7/1 The box..proved, on investigation, to contain about 200 lb. of nitroglycerine... A sample was kept, while the bulk was taken to one of the 'proofs' on the marshes.

10. a. The condition of having successfully stood a test, or the capability of doing so; proved or tested power; *orig.* of armour and arms, whence *transf.* and *fig.*: impenetrability, invulnerability. *arch.*

Often in phrase ***armour*** (etc.) ***of proof***: cf. PROOF *a.* 1; ***at the proof***, so as to be proof; ***to the proof***, to the utmost, in the highest degree. ***proof of lead*** or ***shot*** (cf. PROOF *a.* 1), the quality of being proof against leaden bullets.

1456 SIR G. HAYE *Law Arms* (S.T.S.) 85 The traist that he has in his gude armouris makis him hardy.., for thai ar of prove. 15.. *Sir A. Barton* in *Surtees Misc.* (1888) 72 Then he put on the armere of prooffe. c 1585 *Faire Em* III. iv, Should they haue profered it, her chaste minde hath proofe enough to preuent it. 1590 SIR J. SMYTH *Disc. Weapons* 14 Manie Captaines and Officers of footmen were armed at the proofe of the Harquebuze. 1590 SPENSER *F.Q.* I. x. 24 Salves and med'cines, which had passing prief. 1621 FLETCHER *Wild Goose Chase* III. i, We must be patient; I am vex'd to th' proof too. 1678 BUNYAN *Pilgr.* I. 173, I was cloathed with Armour of proof. ? a 1700 *Judgments upon Persecutors* 50 (Jam.) Knowing he had proof of lead, [he] shot him with a silver button. 1871 PALGRAVE *Lyr. Poems* 102 Nor whether his shield be of proof.

b. Proof armour. *Hist.*

1596 DALRYMPLE tr. *Leslie's Hist. Scot.* x. 419 Corsletis of profe. a 1625 FLETCHER *Chances* I. x, Ye clap on proof upon me. 1956 W. S. CHURCHILL *Hist. Eng.-Speaking Peoples* I. II. i. 126 They..were clad in proof, but..they cast aside their ring-mail.

c. The process of stiffening hats and rendering them waterproof. Cf. PROOF *v.* 2.

1901 *Daily News* 15 Jan. 6/3 The bursting of a stove in what is called the proof shop of the works, where hats are dried after proof.

11. a. The standard of strength of distilled alcoholic liquors (or of vinegar); now, the strength of a mixture of alcohol and water having a specific gravity of 0·91984, and containing 0·495 of its weight, or 0·5727 of its volume, of absolute alcohol. Also *transf.* Spirit of this strength.

1705 tr. *Bosman's Guinea* 403 For Proof [of the brandy] there was a little Spanish Soap clapt into it, and the Scum of the Soap passed on them for the Proof. 1711 *Lond. Gaz.* No. 4790/4, 5 Pipes of French Brandy, full Proof. 1725 *Ibid.* No. 6437/1 Brandy or Spirits above Proof. 1748 H. ELLIS *Hudson's Bay* 175 All the Liquors under the Proof of common Spirits, freeze to a State perfectly solid. 1826 in Hone *Every-day Bk.* II. 862 The bar was crowded with applicants for 'full proof', and 'the best cordials'. 1856 KANE *Arct. Expl.* I. xiii. 146 A bottle of Monongahela whiskey of good stiff proof froze under Mr. Bonsall's head.

b. In sugar-boiling: The degree of concentration at which the syrup will successfully crystallize.

1753 CHAMBERS *Cycl. Supp.*, *Proof*, in the sugar trade, a term used by the refiners of sugar for the proper state of the dissolved sugar when it should be set to harden.

c. The aeration of dough by leaven before baking. Cf. PROVE *v.* 1 g.

1903 KIPLING *Five Nations* 23 There is no proof in the bread we eat or rest in the toil we ply. 1961 *Sunday Times* 5 Feb. 30/4 You knead it [*sc.* the dough] again, but this time for a few minutes only—just to 'knock out the proof', as the bakers say.

III. That which is produced as a test; a means or instrument for testing.

12. *Typog.* A trial or preliminary impression taken from composed type, in which typographical errors may be corrected, and alterations and additions made.

Applied esp. to the ***first proof***; a second or later one being called a *revise*: see REVISE *sb.* 3; see also quot. 1842.

[1563: see PROBE *sb.* 3.] 1600 W. WATSON *Decacordon* (1602) 345, I was not present..: nor had I the sight of one proofe vntill the whole booke was out in print. 1612 [see REVISE *sb.* 3]. 1613 CHAPMAN *Masque Inns of Court* Pref., Plays 1873 III. 96 The Printer..neuer sending me a proofe till he had past those speeches. 1655 tr. *Com. Hist. Francion* x. 24 We did all go to the Printers house, where we did find him correcting Proofs. 1683 MOXON *Mech. Exerc., Printing* i, The Correcter [would] not read Proves. 1771 LUCKOMBE *Hist. Print.* 440 Deliver them to the Pressmen to pull a Proof of them. 1842 BRANDE *Dict. Sc.* etc. s.v., First proof..is the impression with all the errors of workmanship. After, it is read and corrected..another impression is printed with more care, to send to the author; this is termed a clean proof. 1878 HUXLEY *Physiogr.* Pref. 9, I have carefully revised the proofs of every chapter.

13. a. *Engraving.* Originally, An impression taken by the engraver from an engraved plate, stone, or block, to examine its state during the progress of his work; now applied to each of a limited or arbitrary number of careful impressions made from the finished plate before the printing of the ordinary issue, and usually before the inscription is added (in full, ***proof before letter(s)***).

artist's or ***engraver's proof***, a proof taken for examination or alteration by the artist or engraver; ***signed proof***, an early proof signed by the artist. ***letter*** or ***lettered proof***, a proof with the signatures of the artist and engraver, and the inscription. *marked, remarque, touched, trial, wax proof*: see these words.

1797 *Encycl. Brit.* (ed. 3) XV. 590/1 Proofs of Prints were anciently a few impressions taken off in the course of an engraver's process,..and when they were complete. 1853 'C. BEDE' *Verdant Green* vii, The panels were covered with the choicest engravings (all proofs-before-letters). 1890 *Pall Mall G.* 26 Apr. 3/1 An artist's proof..originally meant that proof of an engraving which was sent to the artist for approval and remarks. But the term..is now applied to a certain number of early impressions carefully made, and signed by the artist.

b. *Photogr.* A first or trial print taken from a plate; also used as equivalent to PRINT (*sb.* 13).

1855 HARDWICH *Photogr. Chem.* v. 50 It is necessary to remove the unaltered Chloride or Iodide of Silver which surrounds the image, in order to render the proof permanent. *Ibid.* x. 180 On the use of the hyposulphite of gold in colouring photographic proofs. 1948 C. ABEL *Business of Photogr.* xxxix. 357 Ownership of the proofs submitted by a portrait photographer to a customer has long been a matter of argument in the profession. 1960 MORTENSEN & DUNHAM *How to pose Model* (ed. 3) xii. 152 As soon as you have picked out the proofs that you want to make into prints, destroy *all* the others.

14. †A coin or medal struck as a test of the die (*obs.*); also, one of a limited number of early impressions of coins struck as specimens.

These often have their edges left plain and not milled; they may also be executed in a metal different from that used for the actual coin.

1762–71 H. WALPOLE *Vertue's Anecd. Paint.* (1786) III. 176 On the proofs were the king's and queen's heads on different sides, with a rose, a ship, &c. but in 1694 it was resolved, that the heads should be coupled, and Britannia be on the reverse. 1889 J. ATKINS *Coins & Tokens of Possessions & Colonies of Brit. Empire* 5 Proofs exist of both these pieces. 1901 *Daily Chron.* 4 Nov. 5/1 A limited number were issued to certain collectors with unmilled edges—these coins being called 'proofs'—a course which was followed in the Jubilee issue. 1920 *Brit. Numismatics Jrnl. 1918* IV. 131 The same artist issued proofs either for a sixpence or a farthing. 1969 *Times* 21 July p. v/4 Proofs (special coins struck from highly polished dies mainly for collectors) have been issued for this denomination. 1977 *Times* 5 May 20/2 Jubilee crown proofs are in silver.

15. An instrument, vessel, or the like for testing. †**a.** A surgeon's probe. *Obs. rare*$^{-0}$.

(Perhaps only an etymologizing invention of Cotgrave.) 1611 COTGR., *Curette*, a Chirurgions Proofe, or Probe; an instrument wherewith he sounds the bladder [etc.]. 1656 BLOUNT *Glossogr.*, *Probe* or *Proof* (the Fr. call it *curette*) a Chyrurgeons Instrument, wherewith he tries the depth of wounds [etc.].

b. (*a*) A test-tube. (*b*) An apparatus for testing the strength of gunpowder.

1790 CRAWFORD in *Phil. Trans.* LXXX. 397 A portion of the cancerous virus, diffused through distilled water, was introduced into a small proof. *Ibid.* 406 The liquor..was put into a proof, to the bottom of which heat was applied. 1800 *Ibid.* XC. 207 A common gunpowder proof, capable of containing eleven grains of fine gunpowder, was filled with it, and fired in the usual way. 1828 BRANDE in *Lancet* 7 June 292/1 Here are some little phials, called in the glass-houses *proofs*. c 1860 FARADAY *Forces Nat.* ii. 197 *note*, Thick Glass Vessels..called Proofs or Bologna phials.

†**16.** *Typog.* A definite number of ems placed in the composing-stick as a pattern of the length of the line. *Obs.*

[The width of pages is expressed according to the number of 'ems'. *Encycl. Brit.* 1888.]

1683 MOXON *Mech. Exerc.*, *Printing* xvi, He sets up his Prooves in the Composing-stick.

17. *Bookbinding.* The rough uncut edges of the shorter or narrower leaves of a book, left in trimming it to show that it has not been cut down.

1890 ZAEHNSDORF *Bookbinding* 57 A few leaves should always be left not cut with the plough, to show that the book has not been cut down. These few leaves are called *proof*, and are always a mark of careful work. 1908 A. W. POLLARD *Let. to Editor*, Our binder's head man tells me that when I write 'not to be cropped' he translates it to the men under him as 'leave proof'.

IV. 18. *attrib.* and *Comb.* **a.** General Combs. in senses 1–4, as ***proof needle, object, paper, passage, patch, piece, test, text***; ***proof-producing, proof-proof*** adjs.; in sense 4, as ***proof-test*** vb.; in sense 9, as ***proof-butts, -charge, -ground, -house, -master, -mortar*** (MORTAR *sb.*[1]), ***-sleigh***; in senses 12–14, as ***proof coin, copy, proof-correct*** vb., to correct in proof, ***proof-correcting, -correction, -corrector, -galley, impression, -plate*** (PLATE *sb.* 6 b), ***print, -printer, -puller, -pulling, set, stage, state***.

1907 *Daily Chron.* 3 Jan. 7/1 A serious accident..at the *proof butts on Plumstead Marshes. 1727 SWIFT *Art Pol. Lying* Wks. 1755 III. I. 122 A proof-lye is like a *proof-charge for a piece of ordnance, to try a standard credulity. 1894 *Field* 9 June 815/1 The proof-charge of powder with the 4-bore is 50 per cent. greater than the proof-charge of the 8-bore. 1949 W. H. SHELDON *Early Amer. Cents 1793–1814* I. 39 *Proof coins were never struck for circulation... Proofs were first used as presentation pieces. 1969 *Coin Investor* 18 Jan. 3/1 The difference between a proof coin and a brilliant uncirculated one is that a proof coin has been specially struck on a highly polished die. 1976 *National Observer* (U.S.) 17 Jan. 17/4 (Advt.), Highly sought after by collectors, Proof coins are the ultimate expression of the minting art. Dies and solid gold blanks are polished by hand to a mirror finish. 1806 SCOTT *Let.* Oct. (1932) I. 327, I would like to see them in the *proof copy in case any minute alterations may yet occur to me. 1975 A. POWELL *Hearing Secret Harmonies* ii. 66 He held under his arm what looked like the proof copy of a book. 1803 LAMB *Let. to Coleridge* 20 Mar., I feel myself..accessory to the selection, which I am to *proof-correct. 1890 *Pall Mall G.* 29 Aug. 2/1 To have it written by other people in time for himself to proof-correct it. 1850 W. M. THACKERAY *Let.* June in H. Ritchie *Lett. A. T. Ritchie* (1924) iii. 29 Then comes printing and *proof correcting & so forth. 1855 HT. MARTINEAU *Autobiog.* II. 40, I highly enjoyed the proof-correcting. 1905 A. E. BURN *Niceta of Remesiana* Pref. 3 Little leisure for *proof-correction. 1940 *Chambers's Techn. Dict.* 677/2 *Proof corrections*, additions or emendations to a proof. They should be made in ink, and clearly indicated in the margin. 1978 *Hart's Rules for Compositors & Readers* (ed. 38) 34 (*heading*) Proof-correction marks. 1928 L. P. SMITH *Words & Idioms* 162 We are becoming more and more the slaves of schoolmasters and *proof-correctors. 1932 A. E. HOUSMAN *Let.* 19 June (1971) 322 On p. 32 the proof-corrector has again given directions for making a change which ought not to be made. 1896 T. L. DE VINNE *Moxon's Mech. Exerc., Printing* 407 The long *proof-galley of brass. 1712 *Lond. Gaz.* No. 5026/7 The Place now used for a *Proof-house. 1846 GREENER *Sc. Gunnery* 203 The Company of Gunmakers of the City of London instituted a proof-house, at which the barrels of respectable makers were all sent to be proved. 1891 *Daily News* 29 Apr. 5/6 There are in Europe five 'proving houses' or testing places for firearms. Of the Birmingham and London proof houses all people have heard. 1806–7 J. BERESFORD *Miseries Hum. Life* (1826) IX. xxii, *Proof impressions of the grain of the footman's thumb printed off..upon the rim of your plate. 1910 *Connoisseur* Oct. 93/1 How to distinguish Proof Impressions. 1707 CHAMBERLAYNE *Pres. St. Eng.* III. xi. 379 To see that all Provisions received, be good and serviceable, and duly proved, with the Assistance of..the *Proof-Masters, and marked with the Queen's Mark. 1833 J. HOLLAND *Manuf. Metal* II. 95 Government authorised the gun-makers of Birmingham to erect a proof-house of their own, with wardens and a proof-master. 1839 URE *Dict. Arts* 626 The result of more than two hundred discharges with the *proof-mortar. 1849 NOAD *Electricity* (ed. 3) 285 Suspending a small *proof needle, with a silk fibre, and causing it to oscillate horizontally opposite different points of a magnetic bar placed vertically. 1837 GORING & PRITCHARD *Microgr.* 93 Directions..for the management of *proof-objects in the Amician catadioptric engiscope. 1759 H. WALPOLE *Let. to G. Montagu* 17 Nov., You shall see the documents, as it is the fashion to call *proof papers. 1895 SALMOND *Chr. Doctr. Immort.* IV. iii. 456 Taken as one of the primary *proof-passages for the dogma of the Descent to Hell. 1816 KEATINGE *Trav.* I. 11 *note*, This place is a residue of a wreck of nature; it is a *proof-patch of former level. 1594 J. DICKENSON *Arisbas* (1878) 41 It seemed nature and vertue..had conspired to make her a peere-lesse *proofe-peece of their vnited perfections. 1783 MME. D'ARBLAY *Diary* 10 Jan., Mr. Seward has sent me a *proof plate..of an extremely fine impression of this dear Doctor [Johnson]. 1818–60 WHATELY *Commpl. Bk.* (1864) 231 [This] you can prove (to any one who is not *proof-proof). 1899 *Daily News* 20 Nov. 11/6 *Proofpuller seeks situation, Press, assist Machine, or other offer. 1900 *Ibid.* 12 Oct. 10/3 Man (young) wanted, in printing office, for *proof-pulling. 1879

H. Phillips *Notes Coins* 14 A number of fine *proof sets, and coins, of the United States mint. **1895** F. M. Ford *Let.* (1965) 8 You may tell Longmans that W.M.R. had offered to revise my chapters as they go to Press wh. is better than in the *proof stage I shd. think. **1966** N. Nicolson in H. Nicolson *Diaries & Lett., 1930–1939* 118 The name had to be altered again..at proof-stage. **1910** *Connoisseur* Oct. 93/2 To such a man even the names of the various *proof states must be a source of bewilderment. **1683** Pettus *Fleta Min.* I. (1686) 15 You must..have a Frame, in which you may heat the *Proof-Tests and Crucibles. **1951** *Sun* (Baltimore) 30 Jan. 5/3 Their major purpose..is to proof-test some slide-rule work being done by nuclear physicists and weapons experts. **1847** Webster, *Proof-text. **1874** H. R. Reynolds *John Bapt.* iv. vi. 262 Modern criticism has submitted the 'proof-texts'..to stringent examination. **1904** H. A. A. Kennedy *St. Paul's Concept. Last Things* vi. 310 Solitary proof-texts have wrought more havoc in theology than all the heresies.

b. Special Combs.: **proof-arm** *v. nonce-wd.* [? back-formation from *proof armour*], *trans.* to arm in or as in armour of proof; † **proof-favour**, favour or goodwill strong as armour of proof; **proof-gallon**, a gallon of proof-spirit; **proof-glass**, a deep cylindrical glass for holding liquids while under test; **proof-leaf**, = proof-sheet; also, the sheet of paper by means of which coloured designs are transferred from the engraved plate to the biscuit in pottery-making; **proof-letter**, a letter cast to test the accuracy of the type-mould; **proof load** *Mech.*, a load which a structure must be able to bear without exceeding specified limits of deformation; *loosely*, proof stress; **proof-man** (*Sc.*), one whose profession is to estimate the content of corn-stacks; **proof-mark**, †(*a*) in testing powder, a mark made on the ribbon by which the recoil is measured, showing the strength of powder of the standard quality (*obs.*); (*b*) a mark impressed on a fire-arm to show that it has passed the test; **proof-plane**, a small flat or disk-shaped conductor fixed on an insulating handle, used in measuring the electrification of any body; **proof-plug**: see quot.; **proof-press**, a press or machine used for taking proofs of type; **proof-read** *v. trans.*, to read (printer's proofs) and mark errors for correction; hence **proof-read** *ppl. a.*; **proof-reader**, one whose business is to read through printer's proofs and mark errors for correction; = reader 2 b; so **proof-reading** *vbl. sb.* and *ppl. a.*; **proof-slip** *Typog.* = proof-sheet; **proof-sphere**: see quot.; **proof-staff**, a metal straight-edge for testing or adjusting the ordinary wooden instrument (Knight *Dict. Mech.* 1875); **proof-stick**, a rod by means of which a sample of the contents of a vacuum sugar-boiler may be taken without admitting air; **proof strain** *Mech.*, the strain produced by the proof stress; *loosely*, proof stress; **proof strength**, = sense 11; **proof stress** *Mech.*, the stress required to produce a specified permanent deformation of a material or structure; **proof theory** (see quot. 1942); hence **proof-theoretic** *a.*, of or pertaining to proof theory; **proof-theoretically** *adv.*, in a proof-theoretic manner; **proof timber**: see quot.; **proof vinegar**, vinegar of standard strength.

a **1625** Fletcher *Hum. Lieut.* ii. iii, She..is a delicate and knows it; And out of that *proof-arms herself. **1621** —— *Pilgrim* ii. ii, All your glories in the full Meridian, The King's *proof-favour buckled on your body. **1907** *Westm. Gaz.* 18 Feb. 11/1 The total consumption of spirits in the United Kingdom during the past year amounted to 39,302,480 *proof gallons. **1765** H. Jackson *Ess. Brit. Isinglass* 73 We likewise advise them to a serious Perusal of our new-invented *Proof-glasses. **1848** *Knickerbocker* XVIII. 380 With what profound deliberation he drew his proof-glass from the bung-hole of a brandy-pipe. **1839** Ure *Dict. Arts* 1017 s.v. *Pottery*, The copper-plate is now passed through the engraver's cylinder press, the *proof leaf is lifted off and..[applied] to the surface of the biscuit. **1683** Moxon *Mech. Exerc., Printing* xvii. ¶2 Then he Casts a *Proof-Letter or two. **1858** W. J. M. Rankine *Man. Appl. Mech.* ii. iii. 287 The toughness of the bar, or the extension corresponding to the *proof load. **1930** *Engineering* 21 Feb. 241/2 This working load is equivalent to one-half the proof load, which again is almost one-half the ultimate strength of the chain. **1973** A. Parrish *Mech. Engineer's Ref. Bk.* xii. 5 A 'proof load' is a specified load which a lifting appliance shall withstand without showing permanent set exceeding a specified amount or showing other defect. **1813** W. Leslie *Agric. Surv. Nairn & Moray* 180 The quantity of grain is ascertained by the *proof-man, a professional character in the country. **1781** *Phil. Trans.* LXXI. i. 300 If the ribbon is drawn out as far or farther than the *proof mark, the powder is as good or better than the standard. **1858** Greener *Gunnery* 251 On arms of the first and third classes the definitive proof mark and view mark shall be impressed at the breech end of the barrel. **1855** Miller *Elem. Chem.* I. 284 Bring the *proof plane..into contact with any part of the outer surface of the metallic can, and an abundant charge will be obtained. **1873** Maxwell *Electr. & Magn.* (1881) I. 315 This disk, when employed in this way, is called Coulomb's Proof Plane. **1875** Knight *Dict. Mech.*, *Proof-plug, a plug screwed temporarily into the breech of a gun-barrel to be proved. **1899** Mackail *Life Morris* II. 253 A *proof-press and a printing-press were set up there. **1933** G. Stein *Autobiogr. Alice B. Toklas* v. 139 A good many years later Jane Heap said that she had never appreciated the quality of Gertrude Stein's work until she *proof-read it. **1937** W. Follett in *Atlantic Monthly* Jan. 49/1 *The New York Times*..is..the most nearly proofread of the larger metropolitan dailies. **1951** L. Hellman *Autumn Garden* i. 14 His publishers..want the manuscript... I'll have to proofread it with him tonight. **1964** F. Bowers *Bibliogr. & Textual Crit.* iv. iv. 126 The automatic assumption is surely wrong that every forme of cheap commercial printing was necessarily proof-read. **1966** 'H. B. Taylor' *Triumvirate* xx. 115 The galleys of proofread type. **1976** *Times Lit. Suppl.* 2 July 813/4 It is smoothly written, although no better illustrated than Professor Donohue's survey..and far less well proofread. **1855** I. C. Pray *Mem. J. G. Bennet* 41 From this post he was transferred to that of a *proof-reader in the printing-house of Wells & Lilly. **1883** *Harper's Mag.* Feb. 469/2 A new proof-reader seemed to be needed. **1907** *Daily Chron.* 4 Apr. 6/6 Thomas Bailey Aldrich..entered literature as a 'proof-reader'. That is the American equivalent of our 'corrector to the Press' or 'printer's reader'. **1852** Geo. Eliot *Let.* 15 June (1954) II. 36 Between theatre-going and *proof-reading, my spiritual eyes are burning as dim and bleared as gas-lights. **1937** W. Follett in *Atlantic Monthly* Jan. 49/2 Such a thing it is to be equipped, or cursed, with the proofreading eye. **1977** *Early Music* Oct. 470/2 Manuscripts..*A* and *B* show more evidence of proofreading. **1883** 'Mark Twain' *Lett. to Publishers* (1967) 162 You must glance through all the *proof-slips..for..I have added footnotes and other stuff which you have not seen. **1967** Cox & Grose *Organiz. & Handling Bibliogr. Rec. by Computer* v. 118 The material along with the worksheet and the LC proof slip or the Title II card..is then routed to the Catalogue Department... All books for which there are proof slips or Title II depository cards are processed. **1902** Sloane *Stand. Electr. Dict.*, *Proof-sphere, a small sphere, coated with gold-leaf or other conductor, and mounted on an insulated handle. It is used instead of a proof-plane, for testing bodies whose curvature is small. **1839** Ure *Dict. Arts* 1206 The *proof-stick, an ingenious brass rod for taking out a sample of syrup without admitting air. **1858** W. J. M. Rankine *Man. Appl. Mech.* ii. iii. 273 Resilience or Spring is the quantity of mechanical work required to produce the *proof strain. **1862** [see *proof stress* below]. **1888** J. G. Horner *Lockwood's Dict. Mech. Engin. Terms* 268 A proof strain would in all cases be short of that which would have a crippling effect. **1811** *Niles' Reg.* I. 311/1 The same process repeated until the ley has acquired *proof strength. **1905** *Daily Chron.* 29 July 4/5 Spirits, however, are always sold below, and generally considerably below, 'proof' strength. **1862** W. J. M. Rankine *Man. Civil Engin.* ii. i. 226 Resilience, or Spring.. is the quantity of mechanical work required to produce the *proof-stress on a given piece of material, and is equal to the product of the proof strain, or alteration of figure, into the mean load which acts during the production of that strain; that is to say, in general, very nearly one-half of the proof load. **1935** *Discovery* Apr. 112/2 By the use of aluminium alloy with a ·1 per cent. proof stress of 17 tons per square inch instead of the 15 tons per square inch alloy now used, the hull weight of such a [flying] boat could be kept as low as 12½ per cent. of the total weight. **1962** *BSI News* June 12/1 Qualities of steels determined by the ratio of the 0·2 per cent proof stress at elevated temperatures to the minimum tensile strength at room temperature. **1952** S. C. Kleene *Introd. Metamath.* xiv. 213 The *proof-theoretic equivalents provability and irrefutability refer only to the enumerable infinity of formal proofs... The set-theoretic notions are actually equivalent to the proof-theoretic ones. **1967** —— *Math. Logic* 118 The proof-theoretic approach to the predicate calculus. **1952** —— *Introd. Metamath.* xiv. 425 The axioms are 'consistent' *proof-theoretically. **1967** —— *Math. Logic* 118 We now develop some of the further results proof-theoretically. **1942** D. D. Runes *Dict. Philos.* 255/2 *Proof theory*. The formalization of mathematical proof by means of a logistic system..makes possible an objective theory of proofs and provability, in which proofs are treated as concrete manipulations of formulas (and no use is made of meanings of formulas). **1969** *Listener* 10 July 44/2 The analogy he was using was one with proof theory in logic, where from initial axioms and rules of inference you can produce true theorems—rather like doing geometry exercises in school. **1979** *Sci. Amer.* Oct. 138/3 For this purpose Hilbert introduced a new theory called proof theory, or metamathematics, in which meaningful statements about the meaningless signs and configurations of the axiomatic system could be formulated. *c* **1850** *Rudim. Navig.* (Weale) 139 *Proof timber*, an imaginary timber, expressed by vertical lines in the sheer draught, similar to the joints of the square timbers, and used nearly forward and aft, to prove the fairness of the body. **1839** Ure *Dict. Arts* 13 An excise duty of 2*d*. is levied on every gallon of..*proof vinegar.

proof (pruːf), *a.* (*adv.*) Forms: see prec. [The sb. used as adj., app. by ellipsis of *of*: cf. prec. 10.]

1. Of tried strength or quality; *esp.* of armour: of tested power of resistance; hence *transf.* and *fig.* strong, impenetrable, impervious, invulnerable. Const. *against*, *to*. † *proof o' shot*, proof against shot; in quot. *fig.*

1592 Shaks. *Rom. & Jul.* ii. ii. 73 Looke thou but sweete, And I am proofe against their enmity. **1607** —— *Cor.* i. iv. 25 Now..fight With hearts more proofe then Shields. **1631** Heywood *2nd Pt. Fair Maid of West* iii. Chorus, With two proofe targets arm'd. **1656** Earl Monm. tr. *Boccalini's Advts. fr. Parnass.* i. xxxix. (1674) 53 Venice..is fortified, and armed with the proof-Armor of Marishes and Washes. **1667** Milton *P.L.* ix. 298 Not incorruptible of Faith, not prooff Against temptation. **1697** Dryden *Æneid* iii. 317 The fated Skin is proof to Wounds. **1711** Steele *Spect.* No. 41 ¶5 Proof against the Charms of her Wit and Conversation. **1728** Ramsay *There's my Thumb* i, A heart.. proof a-shot to birth or money. **1785** Burns *To J. Smith* i, Ne'er a bosom yet was prief Against your arts. **1810** Scott *Lady of Lake* ii. xix, Proof to the tempest's shock. **1835** Lytton *Rienzi* x. iv, Dearer..than he had ever yet found the proofest steel of Milan. **1871** *Routledge's Ev. Boy's Ann.* June 344 Their thick scales..are proof against every missile.

b. Often used as the second element in compounds, as bomb-proof, bullet-*proof*, fire-proof, plot-*proof*, rain-*proof*, shot-*proof*, sound-*proof*, thief-*proof*, waterproof, weather-*proof*, etc., and many occasional or nonce formations.

1602 Manningham *Diary* (Camden) 61 Such a one is clarret proofe, *i.e.* a good wine-bibber. **1662** Hickeringill *Apol. Distressed Innoc.* Wks. 1716 I. 297 The old Powder-Plotters..are shot-free and Justice-proof by a pious charm. **1709** *Brit. Apollo* II. No. 19. 3/1 You're Impudence-Proof. **1824** Mackintosh *Sp. Ho. Com.* 15 June, Wks. 1846 III. 468 Is he bullet-proof or bayonet-proof? or does he wear a coat of mail? **1901** *Westm. Gaz.* 7 Jan. 5/1 If the heavy mackintosh overalls were expletive-proof as well as snow-proof it would not be a bad thing. **1903** *Daily Chron.* 3 Mar. 5/1 Fire-proof, and burglar-proof, and every other proof, except visitor proof!

2. Of distilled alcoholic liquors: Of standard strength; cf. proof *sb.* 11. See proof-spirit.

1709 *Brit. Apollo* II. No. 7. 2/2 Rectify'd Spirits are *Proof.*

† **B.** *adv.* To the fullest extent; to the utmost; utterly, entirely: cf. *to the proof* (proof *sb.* 10).

1613 Fletcher, etc. *Captain* i. ii, Such distemper'd spirits Once out of motion, though they be proof-valiant. **1621** —— *Isl. Princess* iii. i, Looks melancholy Wondrous proof melancholy. [**1875** Ruskin *Fors Clav.* lv. 197 She had busy blood..but, with that, well-conducted and proof-faithful [*transl. F.* fidèle à toute épreuve].]

proof (pruːf), *v.* [f. proof *sb.* or *a.*]

1. *trans.* To test, prove. **a.** *Sc.* To estimate the content of (a corn-stack); cf. *proof-man* s.v. proof *sb.* 18 b.

1834 H. Miller *Scenes & Leg.* x. (1869) 146 He was engaged in what is called proofing the stacks of a cornyard.

b. To take a proof impression of (an engraved plate, or the like): = prove *v.* 1 e.

1884 *World* 3 Dec. 15/2 The outcome is a masterpiece of etching, which is being 'proofed'.

c. To aerate (dough) by the action of yeast before baking. Cf. prove *v.* 1 g.

1875 *Encycl. Brit.* III. 253/2 After this laborious process the finished dough is covered over for some time..during which fermentation again begins, and the mass is 'proofed'. **1972** *Countryman* Autumn 45 There were three ovens, one above the other, in our bakehouse. The bottom one was small and used only for proofing buns and certain cakes.

d. = *proof-read* vb. s.v. proof *sb.* 18 b.

1960 *Times* 16 Feb. 6/1 Bristol set its own papers and printed and proofed them in the city. **1974** R. C. Dennis *Conversations with Corpse* viii. 70 Arenas was reading a pink report, making occasional corrections of grammar or punctuation... He handed me the pages he had already proofed. **1979** A. Easson *Elizabeth Gaskell* i. 44 William also proofed much of her work.

2. To render proof against or impervious to something; *esp.* to render (a fabric or article of dress) impervious to water, to waterproof.

1885 C. G. W. Lock *Workshop Receipts* Ser. iv. 3/1 Fabrics which are to be 'proofed' by spreading.

Hence **proofed** *ppl. a.*; **'proofing** *vbl. sb.*

1902 *Brit. Med. Jrnl.* 15 Feb. 378/1 *Proofing* or *stiffening* is of two kinds: (*a*) *Water Proofing* is done with shellac and resin dissolved in water with borax. *Ibid.* 378/2 The process of spirit-proofing and the subsequent drying of the 'proofed' hats. **1904** *Ibid.* 17 Sept. 635/2 The..draining of a single pool,..the 'proofing' of a single room. **1909** *Westm. Gaz.* 3 Sept. 5/2 Dr. Bartsch, of the Royal Proofing Office at Great Lichterfelde, communicates the result of experiments he has made in disinfecting large quantities of books with hot air. **1940** *Chambers's Techn. Dict.* 678/1 *Proofed tape*, cotton cloth coated with a rubber compound, wrapped round rubber-insulated cables. **1953** *News Chron.* 2 June 2/2 Squatting..in the light-weight (six pound) proofed cotton nylon tents. **1957** *Times* 20 Dec. 19/2 The moth-proofing of wool, the rot-proofing of jute, the mould-proofing of paint. **1958** *Times Lit. Suppl.* 18 Apr. 214/5 We are told nothing about the special proofings of the *Second World War* volumes. **1976** H. Wilson *Governance of Britain* viii. 157 The Conservative leader is fairly well proofed against trouble with the [party] machinery. **1977** *Broadcast* 13 June 7/2 There were..only ten days between the signature of the Report and its proofing and publication.

† **'proofful**, *a. Obs. rare.* [f. proof *sb.* + -ful.] Full of proof; convincing.

1631 Chapman *Cæsar & Pompey* ii. i. Plays 1873 III. 151 As their alacrities did long to merit With proofefull action.

proofless ('pruːflɪs), *a.* [f. proof *sb.* + -less.] Unsupported by proof or evidence; unfounded.

1610 Bp. Carleton *Jurisd.* 242, I will set downe some of his proofelesse positions. **1795** *Hist.* in *Ann. Reg.* 126/1 The injurious epithets,..being proofless, fell to the ground. **1859** Tennyson *Vivien* 552 Accusation vast and vague, Spleen-born.., and proofless.

Hence **'prooflessly** *adv.*, without proof.

1675 Boyle *Reconcileableness Reason & Relig.* v. Wks. 1772 IV. 171 The erroneous conceits..which the schoolmen and others have prooflessly fathered upon philosophy. **1685** —— *Enq. Notion Nat.* vi. 189 It has been prooflessly asserted, and..I do not think my self bound to admit it.

proofre, obs. form of proffer.

'proof-sheet. *Typog.* A sheet printed from a forme of type for the purpose of examination and correction, before it is finally printed off for use: see proof *sb.* 12.

a **1625** Fletcher *Nice Valour* iv. i. Stage direct., Enter Galoshio, with a Proof-Sheet and a Table. **1693** Clarendon in *Wood's Life* (O.H.S.) IV. 12 That the said Mr. à Wood did ..correct all or att least some of the first printed sheets or proof sheets of the said *Athenæ Oxonienses*. **1771** Luckombe *Hist. Print.* 440 A Proof-sheet ought to be pulled as clean and neat as any sheet..that is worked off. **1826** SCOTT *Woodst.* xxii, Some proof-sheets, as they are technically called, seemingly fresh from the press. **1888** BURGON *Lives 12 Gd. Men* II. x. 269 The proof-sheets, elaborately corrected throughout, I often saw in his hands.

proof-spirit. Spirit of wine, or any distilled alcoholic liquor, of proof strength: see PROOF *sb.* 11.

1790 BLAGDEN in *Phil. Trans.* LXXX. 338 It may appear odd, that no mention has been made till now of proof spirit, the standard to which most of the regulations of the excise have hitherto been referred. **1811** A. T. THOMSON *Lond. Disp.* (1818) 380 Proof Spirit..is merely rectified spirit diluted with a certain proportion of water. According to the London and Dublin Colleges, its specific gravity should be to that of distilled water as 930 to 1000; while the Edinburgh College orders it of the gravity of 935. The former.. contains 44 parts of pure alcohol and 56 of water in 100 parts; the latter..42 of pure alcohol and 58 of water in 100 parts. **1818** *Act 58 Geo. III*, c. 28 To denote as Proof Spirit that which, at the Temperature of Fifty-one Degrees by Fahrenheit's Thermometer, weighs exactly Twelve Thirteenth Parts of an equal Measure of Distilled Water. **1876** HARLEY *Mat. Med.* (ed. 6) 326 Proof Spirit is alcohol containing 49 per cent. by weight, or 42 per cent. by volume of water.

b. Formerly often in plural form, in accordance with the popular use of *spirits* for alcoholic drink.

1741 *Compl. Fam. Piece* I. iv. 244 Take Mint 2 Handfuls, Proof-spirits 2 Gallons and a half. **1800** VINCE *Hydrostat.* ii. (1806) 25 Proof spirits consists, half of pure spirits, called alcohol, and half of water.

proofy ('pruːfɪ), *a. dial.* [f. PROOF *sb.* 8 + -Y.] Having the quality of turning out well or producing good results.

1848 W. BARNES *Poems in Dorset Dial.* Gloss., *Proofy*, having much proof; likely to fatten. **1854** *Jrnl. R. Agric. Soc.* XV. II. 428 A cut of grass like a water-meadow of the most 'proofy' kind. **1886** ELWORTHY *W. Somerset Wordbk.*, *Proofy*...1. Of cattle or sheep—of a kind like to improve in size or condition...2. Of land or soil—rich in fattening qualities. Very proofy ground for young stock.

proole, proone, obs. ff. PROWL *v.*, PRONE *a.*

pro-opic (prəʊ'əʊpɪk, -'ɒpɪk), *a. Anthrop.* [f. Gr. πρό, PRO-² + ὤψ, ὠπ- face + -IC.] Having the nose and central line of the face prominent or projecting, as compared with the lateral parts: the opposite of *platyopic* or flat-faced.

1885 O. THOMAS in *Jrnl. Anthrop. Inst.* May 334 Individual skulls or races having [naso-malar] indices below 107·5, might be called *platyopic* or flat-faced; from 107·5 to 110·0, *mesopic*; and above 110·0, *pro-opic*.

Prooshian, Prooshan, Prooshun, Proosian: joc. var. PRUSSIAN *a.* and *sb.*

pro-osteon: see PRO-² 2.

‖**pro-ostracum** (prəʊ'ɒstrəkəm). *Palæont.* [mod.L., f. Gr. πρό, PRO-² + ὄστρακον potsherd, shell.] The anterior prolongation, usually lamellar, of the guard or rostrum of a fossil cephalopod, as a belemnite.

1872 NICHOLSON *Palæont.* xxvi. 297 The form of the 'pro-ostracum' varies greatly in different cases, and it affords important characters in the discrimination of specific and generic forms in the *Belemnitidæ*. **1877** HUXLEY *Anat. Inv. Anim.* viii. 542 The pro-ostracum and the rostrum together represent the pen in the Teuthidae. **1889** NICHOLSON & LYDEKKER *Palæont.* I. 876 A horny or more or less calcified plate, known as the pro-ostracum..corresponds with the 'pen' of the ordinary cuttlefishes, and from its extreme tenuity is never perfectly preserved.

Hence **pro-'ostracal** *a.*, of, pertaining to, or of the nature of a pro-ostracum.

1890 in *Cent. Dict.*

proot (pruːt), *int.* [Etym. obscure.] A command to a donkey to move faster. Hence **proot** *v. intr.* To cry proot. Cf. PROO *int.*

1879 R. L. STEVENSON *Trav. with Donkey* 18 [He] taught me the true cry or masonic word of donkey-drivers, 'Proot!' *Ibid.* 20 'Proot!' seemed to have lost its virtue. I prooted like a lion, I prooted mellifluously like a sucking-dove; but *Modestine* would be neither softened nor intimidated. **1950** L. G. GREEN *In Land of Afternoon* ix. 132 One expert driver ..encourages his mules by yelling the principal parts of Greek verbs... The word of command '*Proot!*', which appears to have come from France with the Huguenots, is more commonly heard.

pro'otic (prəʊ'əʊtɪk, -'ɒtɪk), *a.* and *sb. Comp. Anat.* [f. Gr. πρό, PRO-² + οὖς, ὠτ- ear + -IC.]

A. *adj.* That is in front of the ear; applied distinctively to one of the three bones which together form the periotic capsule.

1870 ROLLESTON *Anim. Life* 43 A glenoid cavity which is formed..by the squamosal, opisthotic, and prootic bones. **1875** HUXLEY in *Encycl. Brit.* I. 751/1 The hyoidean arch.. almost always becomes connected with the pro-otic region of the skull.

B. *sb.* The pro-otic bone.

1870 ROLLESTON *Anim. Life* 25 One for the prootic and the other for the squamosal. **1872** MIVART *Elem. Anat.* 106 The Pro-otic is the largest and most important element of the three in Vertebrates below Mammals.

prop (prɒp), *sb.*¹ Also 5–6 **proppe**. [Not known before 1440; = MDu. and early mod.Du. *proppe* a vine-prop, a support ('*pedamen, fulcimentum, fulcrum, sustentaculum*' Kilian); ulterior history uncertain. Wedgwood compares 'Piedmontese *broba, bropa*, a vine-prop, Wallachian *proptea* a prop, *propte* to prop, lean on'. Irish *propa*, Gael. *prop* are from English.

MDu. *proppe* is in form identical with, and by Kilian treated as the same word as, *proppe* 'une broche de fer' (Plantin), 'obturamentum oblongum, veruculum' (Kilian), mod.Du. *prop*, MLG. *proppe*, LG. *propp*, Da. *prop*, Sw. *propp*, Ger. *pfropf, -en* a plug, stopper, stopple, bung; but the connexion of sense is not clear. The same is true of MDu. and early mod.Du. *proppen* to prop, stay, bear up, compared with Du. *proppen* to cram, stuff full, fill up, MLG. and LG. *proppen*, Ger. *pfropfen*, Da. *proppe*, Sw. *proppa*. With this latter group cf. also OHG. *pfroffo, pfropfo* a sucker, slip, shoot, and Ger. *propfen* to graft, which are referred to L. *propāgo* a set, layer, slip, or shoot. It is thus certain that *prop* sb. and vb. have cognates in Dutch; but the connexion of the two Du. words for 'prop' and 'plug', and of the latter of these with the Ger. word for 'graft' is uncertain. See Franck and Kluge. Cf. PROP *sb.*²]

1. a. A stick, rod, pole, stake, beam, or other rigid support, used to sustain an incumbent weight; esp. when such an appliance is auxiliary, or does not form a structural part of the thing supported. Often in comb. as ***clothes-prop***.

c **1440** *Promp. Parv.* 415/1 Proppe, longe (*S.* staffe), *contus*. **1483** *Cath. Angl.* 292/2 A Prope (*A.* Proppe), *ceruus, destina...fulcimen, fulcimentum*. **1530** PALSGR. 259/1 Proppe to underset any thyng, *estaye*. **1535** COVERDALE *1 Kings* vii. 34 The foure proppes vpon the foure corners of euery seate were harde on the seate. **1555** EDEN *Decades* 226 Theyr houses are..buylded aboue the grownde vppon proppes & pyles. **1573–80** BARET *Alv.* P 784 The vine must be set vp with props. *c* **1623** in Swayne *Sarum Churchw. Acc.* (1896) 177 To make A proppe to supporte the Roofe. **1645** in *10th Rep. Hist. MSS. Comm.* App. IV. 636 The propps and standerdes upon which the Town Hall did stand. **1785** MARTYN *Rousseau's Bot.* xxxi. (1794) 484 What he [Linnæus] calls *Fulcra*, props or supports of the plant. **1870** BRYANT *Iliad* II. XIII. 8 Mighty rains Have worn away the props that held it fast.

b. *spec.* in *Coal-mining*: A piece of timber set upright to support the roof or keep up the strata. (Also *pit-prop*.)

1756–7 tr. *Keysler's Trav.* (1760) IV. 236 A fragment of a prop of fir, which had been used in a shaft in the forest of Hartz. **1851** GREENWELL *Coal-trade Terms Northumb. & Durh.* 40 *Prop*, a piece of wood, cut 2½ or 3 inches shorter than the thickness of the seam of coal, and set upright beneath the end of a crowntree, or under a headtree, for the support of the roof. **1857** J. STEWART *Sk. Sc. Charac.* 91 Cut up in lengths for coal-pit praps. **1885** *Law Times* LXXIX. 176/1 Timber props for regulating the ventilation.

c. In a vehicle: see quot. 1875.

1875 KNIGHT *Dict. Mech.*, *Prop*.., a stem fastened to the carriage bow for the attachment of the stretcher-piece, known as the *prop-joint*, and upon which the bows rest when down.

d. *pl. Entom.* See quot. 1826.

1826 KIRBY & SP. *Entomol.* IV. 353 *Prop* (*Ereisma*), a bipartite retractile glutinous organ exerted from between the legs of the genus *Sminthurus* Latr., and employed by the animal to support itself when its legs fail it.

e. *dial.* or *slang.* The leg; also, the arm extended in boxing; hence, a straight hit. (Usu. in *pl.*)

1793 *Carlop Green* II. xxvii, Wi' his stiff shank..As thick again 's his soople prop. **1828** *Craven Gloss.* (ed. 2), *Props*, legs. **1869** *Temple Bar Mag.* XXVI. 74 You take off your coat and put up your 'props' to him. **1887** *Lic. Vict. Gaz.* 2 Dec. 358/3 Ned met each rush of his enemy with straight props. **1891** *Sportsman* 20 Apr. 3/2 There are those..who assert that with such 'props' he will never successfully negociate the Epsom gradients.

f. *fig.* Any person or thing that serves as a support or stay; *esp.* one who upholds some institution.

1571 GOLDING *Calvin on Ps.* xxxvii. 17 To leane unto the prop of God's blessing. **1596** SHAKS. *Merch. V.* IV. ii. 70 The boy was the verie staffe of my age, my verie prop. **1650** HUBBERT *Pill Formality* 41 The wicked prophane Priest was a prop to the Bishops Kingdom. **1766** FORDYCE *Serm. Yng. Wom.* (1767) I. i. 15 You shall live to be the prop..of her age. **1849** ROBERTSON *Serm.* Ser. I. xii. (1866) 211 He needs no props..to support his faith.

g. *Rugby Football.* One of two outside front-row forwards who support the hooker in a scrummage.

1950 B. H. TRAVERS *Let's talk Rugger* iii. 50 In a 3-4-1 scrum the wing forwards have to push the front-row props towards the hooker all the time. **1959** *Sunday Times* 15 Mar. 40/7 Later in the half, Wood the Irish prop, was hauled back for a five-yard scrum when many people thought he had forced his way over for a try. **1960** E. S. & W. J. HIGHAM *High Speed Rugby* 154 In order to achieve a well-balanced and fairly comfortable scrum, it is desirable to pair off the two props and the two locks so that they are, as nearly as possible, of the same length of body and the same length of leg. **1971** [see LOCK *sb.*² 11 c]. **1977** *Western Morning News* 1 Sept. 10/7 Perhaps the most significant move, however, is the inclusion of Nigel Redgrave, another to rejoin Albion.. at loose head prop.

†**2. a.** A pole or stake, e.g. a boundary stake: cf. PROP *v.*¹ 3. Also **b.** A butt for shooting at.

1456 *Reg. Aberbrothoc* (Bann. Cl.) II. 89 The sowthe syde of the myre sal ly in commoun pasture..as the proppis ar sett fra the est to the west apon the northe syde throuout the myre linialy... And frae the west cors sowthe as it is proppit. **b.** **1496** *Acc. Ld. High Treas. Scot.* I. 273 Giffin to the King himself to schute at the prop with James Mersar,..x s. **1503** *Ibid.* II. 401 Item, in Strethbogy, to the King to play at the prop, ij s. iiij d. **1505–6** *Ibid.* III. 179 Item, to the King quhilk he tynt at the prop with George Campbell, vj Franch crownis.

3. [f. PROP *v.*¹ 4.] A sudden stop made by a horse when going at speed. *Australian.*

1881 A. C. GRANT *Bush Life Queensland* I. xiv. 201 A sudden fierce prop, and Roaney has shot behind Sam's horse. **1884** 'R. BOLDREWOOD' *Melbourne Mem.* xvi. 115 The 'touchy' mare gave so sudden a 'prop', accompanied by a desperate plunge, that he was thrown.

4. *attrib.* and *Comb.*, as ***prop-iron, -wood***; **prop-crib, -joint, -maul, -stay**: see quots.; **prop-foot, -leg** (of a caterpillar) = PRO-LEG; **prop forward** *Rugby Football*, = sense 1 g above; **prop-free front** *Coal-mining* (see quot. 1967); **prop-man**, a man who places and attends to the props in a coal-mine; **prop-root** [tr. G. *stützwurzel* (K. Goebel *Organographie der Pflanzen* (1901) II. 479)], a root springing from the base of a plant above ground level, providing extra support; **prop-word** (see quot. 1892).

1881 RAYMOND *Mining Gloss.*, **Prop-crib timbering*, shaft timbering with cribs kept at the proper distance apart by means of props. **1890** JULIA P. BALLARD *Among Moths & Butterfl.* 88 The hinder *prop-feet were a dark brown. **1951** *Sport* 30 Mar.–5 Apr. 6/3 The greatest surprise of the whole 26 is the omission of Bill Hopper, the young Leeds *prop forward. **1978** *Rugby World* Apr. 33/2 Mayer belonged to a by-gone age in that, despite his size, he always was scrupulously fair on the field, and the revolution in prop-forward scrummage techniques over the past few years, to some extent, passed him by. **1956** F. S. ATKINSON in D. L. Linton *Sheffield* xiv. 270 Much pioneer work has been done in the coalfield to the north-east of Sheffield and in Nottinghamshire to develop a new method of mining at the coalface, known as the '*prop-free front' system. With this method a strong, flexible scraper-chain conveyor, called an armoured conveyor, is installed in the space between the nearest roof supports and the face of coal being worked... To maintain intact the roof between the vertical supports and the wall of coal, cantilever bars are used which are supported by the props behind the conveyor. **1967** *Gloss. Mining Terms* (*B.S.I.*) XI. 11 *Prop-free front*, a system of supports in a longwall face in which props are not normally set between the conveyor and the coal. The roof above and in advance of the conveyor is supported by cantilever bars set on props on the goaf side of the conveyor. **1895** *Westm. Gaz.* 29 Mar. 2/1 Step and *prop-iron, bolt and screw. **1875** KNIGHT *Dict. Mech.*, **Prop-joint*.., the jointed bar which spreads the bows of a calash-top. **1869** PACKARD *Guide Stud. Insects* (1872) 21 These 'false' or '*prop-legs' are soft and fleshy, and without articulations. **1880** *Libr. Univ. Knowl.* (U.S.) III. 388 The [canker-worm] has six legs forward, and four stout prop-legs behind. **1888** *Times* 27 Sept. 3/3, 30 men, chiefly *propmen, continued to descend into the pit to keep the workings open and in repair. **1851** GREENWELL *Coal-trade Terms Northumb. & Durh.* 40 **Prop-maul*, an iron maul, with a handle 3 feet long, used by the deputies in drawing props. **1905** I. B. BALFOUR tr. *Goebel's Organogr. Plants* II. 277 A series of transitions..leads us from the soil-roots to those which spring from the base of the stem of many Monocotyledones, and which soon entering the soil serve as *prop-roots. **1938** FRITSCH & SALISBURY *Plant Form & Function* x. 109 These prop-roots serve the purpose of augmenting the somewhat feeble primary root-system. **1953** K. ESAU *Plant Anat.* xvii. 474 Others [*sc.* roots] serve mainly as supporting organs, such as the prop roots in the mangrove plants and, on a smaller scale, in the grasses and sedges. **1976** NORSTOG & LONG *Plant Biol.* vi. 165 A conspicuous feature of the majority of the trees [of the tropical rain forest]..is their smooth, thin, lichen-covered bark and their flaring buttresses or, in the case of some smaller trees, stilt-like prop roots. **1875** KNIGHT *Dict. Mech.*, **Prop-stay*, a transverse water-tube crossing a boiler-flue..increasing the flue-surface by the exposure of its exterior surface to the heated current. **1839** URE *Dict. Arts* 978 Columns of *prop-wood are erected betwixt the pavement and the roof. **1892** H. SWEET *New Eng. Gram.* I. 66 Another way of using the adjective without its noun in English is to substitute the unmeaning noun-pronoun *one* for the noun, the inflection of the noun being transferred to the *prop-word, as we may call it. **1914** O. JESPERSEN *Mod. Eng. Gram.* II. 248 The reason why the word *one* has been chosen to fulfil the role of a prop-word is chiefly to be sought in the frequent and quite natural use of *one* (by itself) to take the place of a substantive just mentioned. **1934** *Language* X. 370 We call *drinking* in one employment a participle, in another a gerund, *one* now a numeral, now a prop-word, now a pronoun. **1965** *Eng. Stud.* XLVI. 59 A careful survey of the propword 'one' question.

prop (prɒp), *sb.*² [= MDu. *proppe*, Du. *prop* broach, skewer, plug, stopple. As to etym., see prec.]

†**1.** A plug; a wedge. *Sc. Obs. rare.* Cf. PROP *v.*²

1513 DOUGLAS *Æneis* XI. iii. 86 The mekill syllis of the warryn tre Wyth wedgis and with proppis bene devyd.

2. a. A scarf-pin. *Thieves' Cant, Slang.*

(App. a slang application of 'broach', 'skewer'.)

1850 DICKENS *Artful Touch* in *Repr. Pieces* (1866) 210 In his shirt-front there's a beautiful diamond prop,..a very handsome pin indeed. **1891** *Sporting Times* 11 Apr. 1/2 He is proudest..of the pin,..presented to him by the Heir to the Throne... John was wearing this prop in the Paddock at Epsom.

b. A diamond; a valuable piece of jewellery. *Criminals' slang.*

1914 JACKSON & HELLYER *Vocab. Criminal Slang* 66 *Prop*. .. General circulation amongst pickpockets and looters. A diamond stud originally, now comprehending diamonds in any sense... Example: 'Any heel gun can get a breech poke, but it takes an A1 claw to grab a prop.' **1925** *Flynn's Mag.* 7 Mar. 191 *Prop*, a large diamond. **1931** [see GROIN *sb.*² 4]. **1971** S. HOUGHTON *Current Prison Slang* (MS.) 17 *Prop*, nice piece of jewellery.

3. *Comb.* (all ? *Obs.*), as **prop-getter, man, -nailer** *Criminals' slang*, one who steals props (sense 2); a pickpocket.

1901 'J. FLYNT' *World of Graft* 220/2 *Prop-getters*, thieves who make a specialty of 'lifting' scarf-pins. **1931** *Police Jrnl.* Oct. 505 *A prop getter*, a thief who steals scarf-pins. **1935** *Amer. Speech* X. 19/2 *Prop man*, a pickpocket or *snatcher* who lifts stickpins containing valuable stones. **1862** H. MAYHEW *London Labour* Extra vol. 25 'Prop-nailers', those who steal pins and brooches. **1886** H. BAUMANN *Londinismen* 146/1 Prop-nailer.

prop (prɒp), *sb.*[3] *colloq.* or *School slang.* Short for PROPOSITION *sb.*

[**1737** *Gentl. Mag.* VII. 343/2 This Author shews by way of Corollary from the preceding Prop. that [etc.].] **1871** 'M. LEGRAND' *Cambr. Freshm.* 212 To demonstrate the props of Euclid by cutting them out in note paper, and carefully piecing them together.

prop, *sb.*[4] *U.S.* [Derivation unknown.] Usually in pl. **props**: A name given to cowrie shells, used in a gambling game, and hence to the game itself, in vogue in New England chiefly from *c* 1830 to the beginning of the Civil War.

The convex backs of the shells were ground down, and the hollows thus made filled up flat with red sealing-wax. Four of the shells were shaken in the hand or in a box, and thrown after the manner of dice on a table, the stake being won or lost according to the number of white or red sides coming up. When two or four shells turned up alike, it was called a 'nick' and won; any other combination was an 'out' and lost. *dead props* were loaded shells used in cheating. Hence in Comb. *prop-box, prop-house, prop-table.*

1833 W. J. SNELLING *Expose Gaming Massach.* 11 We advanced to the prop table and held forth our hand for the props between two infamous blackguards. *Ibid.* 25 About fifty persons were shaking props... The Box eventually won the greater part of the money, by means of loaded props. **1868** *How Gamblers Win* (N.Y.) 97 It is said that there is not a prop-house in the city of New York. *Ibid.* 99 The professional provides himself with what are called dead props, with which he can throw 'nicks' or 'outs' at pleasure. *Ibid.*, A pastime so stupid and monotonous as Props. **1905** *Boston Even. Transcript* 14 Jan., When I was a boy, knowing people said prop-au. But we boys scorned this.

prop, *sb.*[5] Abbrev. of PROPRIETOR.

? **1880** in W. Whitman *Daybks. & Notebks.* (1978) I. 157 Herman Beckurts—prop: Denver *Tribune*. **1913** W. T. ROGERS *Dict. Abbrev.* 157/1 *Prop...*, proprietor. **1956** H. GOLD *Man who was not with It* III. xxviii. 264 The prop. on this busy corner was with it and for it. **1974** A. ROSS *Bradford Business* 15 A painted board.. said *Redlands Hotel —props. K. & G. Lyall.* **1980** *Guardian* 25 July 12/8 At Porters..(the Viscount Newport prop.—and head waiter on a busy Thursday evening).

prop, *sb.*[6] *colloq.* [f. PROP(ELLER.] **1.** A propeller, esp. on an aircraft.

1914 *Flight* 10 Jan. 43/2 He made a fine glide from 650ft., making a perfect landing with the 'prop' stationary. **1918** E. M. ROBERTS *Flying Fighter* 239, I crashed into a hedge, smashed my prop to bits, and then the machine landed on its nose in the next field. **1931** *Daily Express* 13 Oct. 15/3 A smiling young man jumped back from the roaring prop. **1935** C. S. FORESTER *Afr. Queen* viii. 139 Must 'a' just 'it a rock with the tip of the prop. **1969** G. MACBETH *War Quartet* 33 We ran, Clumsy in fleece and leather, to the field, Hearing the props whirl. **1974** L. DEIGHTON *Spy Story* xix. 202 The propellers came to a standstill... For a moment the sub became unstable... Then the props picked up speed.

2. *attrib.* and *Comb.* **a.** Simple *attrib.*, as ***prop swinger***; in the sense 'propeller-driven', as ***prop bomber, plane, trainer***.

1975 *New Yorker* 8 Sept. 25/2 Man's most sophisticated machines of war were sent to hover.. over the towns and villages of the Plain of Jars: light spotter planes at 2,000 feet; prop bombers, gunships, and flareships at 5,000 feet; [etc.]. **1965** J. V. PACILIO *Discovering Aerospace* 50 The aircraft engineer would say that a prop plane 'loses its efficiency' at this speed. **1973** *Black Panther* 13 Oct. 14/2 All prop planes were.. supposed to land on Runway 31-Right. **1936** F. CLUNE *Roaming round Darling* xiii. 117 The quartet of 'prop swingers' and 'contracters' departed hopefully for the aerodrome. **1974** *Daily Tel.* (Colour Suppl.) 19 Apr. 15 They make jet trainers and prop trainers.

b. Special Combs.: **prop-fan,** (an aircraft engine incorporating) an airscrew having broad blades swept back from a direction perpendicular to the rotation axis; **prop-jet** = TURBO-PROP; **prop-shaft,** a propeller shaft, esp. of a motor vehicle; **prop wash,** a surge or wash of air created by the action of a propeller; also *transf.*

1970 METZGER & GANGER *Results of Initial Prop-Fan Model Acoustic Testing I* (NASA N 71-25785) 1 In order to explore the low noise potential of a Prop-Fan as an aircraft propulsion system, a noise survey was conducted. *Ibid.* 3 The test item consisted of a 21-inch diameter, 12-bladed, manually adjustable pitch, shrouded Prop-Fan model with 22 fixed pitch recovering vanes. **1977** *Jrnl. R. Soc. Arts* CXXV. 352/1 Propeller developments in the guise of so-called prop fans are being studied in the USA. Uninstalled performances as good as those for low pressure ratio fans are estimated at high subsonic speeds. **1977** *New Scientist* 1 Dec. 567/1 The propfan.. has eight thin, swept-back blades which allow it to turn at high speeds without encountering the compressibility problems associated with conventional propellers. *Ibid.* 567/2 On a flight from New York to Miami the propfan airliner would take several minutes less than its turbofan counterpart, because of reduced climb and descent times. **1946** P. H. WILKINSON *Aircraft Engines of World* II. 264 Most of the atmospheric jet engines now in production or under development for use in piloted aircraft are turbojets or propjets. **1963** *Engineering* 1 Nov. 560/3 The Dart was the first propjet engine to go into commercial service. **1971** *Flying* Apr. 2/1 (Advt.), The MU-2F and MU-2G outperform competitive prop-jets simply because they are the only propjets in their category designed to utilize a low-drag high-speed wing. **1972** *Daily Colonist* (Victoria, B.C.) 5 Mar. 16/1 The pilot of a Mohawk Airlines propjet which crashed.. apparently knew he would not make it to the airport runway. **1964** C. BARBER *Ling. Change Present-Day Eng.* iv. 87 *Prop-shaft*..'propellor shaft'. **1965** *Listener* 17 June 914/3 Telemetering devices which can measure the vibration in a wheel or a prop-shaft. **1976** *Drive* Jan.-Feb. 78/1 Propshaft vibration is an occasional nuisance cured only by diligent garage detective work. **1941** *Amer. Speech* XVI. 168/1 *Prop wash*, an expression of disbelief. (Air Corps.) **1944** *U.S. Air Services* May 16/1 All we could feel was the breathing of tightly packed men.. and the animal shudder of the glider as it swung into the prop wash and swung out again. **1958** L. WOLFF *Low Level Mission* 19 The prop-wash blasts of the four engines would interfere with other planes to the rear. **1977** *Observer* 28 Aug. 21/4 The pilot climbed aboard... The diminutive figure.. waved bravely in the prop-wash.

prop, *sb.*[7] *Criminals' slang.* Abbrev. of PROPERTY *sb.* used in *Comb.*, as **prop game,** the practice of defrauding householders into paying exorbitant prices for unnecessary house repairs; **prop man,** one who perpetrates such a fraud. (See also PROPS *sb. pl.*)

1966 *Evening Echo* (Bournemouth) 20 Apr. 15/1 The 'prop game' appeared to be.. unique to Leeds, something that has cropped up in the last two and a half years. **1966** *Guardian* 13 Dec. 5/4 Gangs operating from Leeds are known as 'the prop men' because the racket began in Leeds when so-called property repairers made exorbitant charges after the gales of February, 1961. **1967** N. LUCAS *CID* viii. 97 The 'prop game'.. was a method by which men obtained money from old people by posing as officials.

prop (prɒp), *v.*[1] Also 6 proppe. [Known from 15th c.; app. directly f. PROP *sb.*[1]; cf. obs. Du. *proppen* 'fulcire, suffulcire' (Kilian), 'to prop, stay or bear up' (Hexham).]

1. a. *trans.* To support or keep from falling by or as by means of a prop; to hold up: said both of the prop or support itself and of the person who places it. Also with *up*.

1492-3 [see PROPPING *vbl. sb.* 1]. **1538** ELYOT, *Statumino, nare*, to proppe vp, to vnderset, to make sure... *Suffulcio*.. to proppe vp. **1582** STANYHURST *Æneis* II. (Arb.) 51 Thee wheels wee prop with a number Of beams and sliders. **1697** DRYDEN *Virg. Georg.* IV. 263 To prop the Ruins, lest the Fabrick fall. **1726** POPE *Odyss.* XVII. 228 Propt on a staff, a beggar old and bare. **1878** BROWNING *Poets Croisic* Ep. 1 Your shoulder propped my head. **1886** BESANT *Childr. Gibeon* II. i, Valentine made Lotty lie down.. and propped her up with pillows.

b. In various humorous and ironic phrases. Usu. with *up*.

1908 WODEHOUSE & WESTBROOK *Globe By The Way Bk.* 34 As regards Boarding-The-'Bus and Propping-The-Public-House-Wall, the issue is perhaps more open. But here again I look to see the representatives of the old country well to the fore. **1938** G. HEYER *Blunt Instrument* x. 196 There's a couple propping the wall up at the end of the street. You know the style: kissing and canoodling for the past hour. **1950** 'J. TEY' *To love & be Wise* xi. 133 You'll find him propping up the counter of the post-office. **1965** *Listener* 7 Oct. 539/1 He was to be seen almost every night propping up the left end of the bar in the Wheatsheaf. **1973** J. PATTINSON *Search Warrant* ii. 37 A solitary man was propping up the bar. **1978** B. PRIESTLEY *Island Emperor* iii. 25, I lay in the sun and.. I propped up Niki's bar.

2. *fig.* To support, sustain: esp. used in relation to some weak or failing cause or institution.

1549 [implied in PROPPER]. *a* **1586** SIDNEY *Ps.* XX. ii, With heavnly strength, thy early strength to prop. **1613** SHAKS. *Hen. VIII*, I. i. 59 Being not propt by Auncestry, whose grace Chalkes Successors their way. **1698** FRYER *Acc. E. India & P.* 191 Propped by these Persuasions, the Women freely Sacrifice themselves. **1763** J. BROWN *Poetry & Mus.* v. 52 An ingenious Writer toiling.. to prop a mistaken Principle. **1843** E. MIALL in *Nonconf.* III. 209 Justice should not be propped up by injustice, disinterestedness by rapacity.

†**3.** To mark out with posts, cairns, or other erections: cf. PROP *sb.*[1] 2. *Sc. Obs.*

1456 [see PROP *sb.*[1] 2]. **1540** in *5th Rep. Hist. MSS. Comm.* 609/1 Meithis and merchis.. begynnand.. in the myddis of the resk.. as is proppit be us. *Ibid.*, Ascendand up the hill carne be carne as we haif proppit to the heid of the said hill.

4. *intr.* Of a horse: To stop suddenly when going at speed. orig. *Austral.* Also *transf.*

1870 E. B. KENNEDY *Four Yrs. Queensland* xi. 194 When almost against it, the animal would stop in his stride (or prop), when the rider vaulted lightly over his head on to the verandah. **1882** *Daily News* 3 June 6/4 Another horse propped suddenly at the water-jump hurdle, and sent his rider over into the very middle of the pool. **1890** 'R. BOLDREWOOD' *Col. Reformer* i. (1891) 8, I didn't think he'd ha' propped like that. **1928** 'BRENT OF BIN BIN' *Up Country* 171 How they raced and propped and wheeled on desperate courses bristling with pitfalls. **1946** *Sun* (Baltimore) 4 Oct. 16/4 Tacato Briar was unprepared for break and propped coming out of gate. **1954** *Ibid.* 10 July 9/3 Sans Egal went to the front at once and opened a lead of some six lengths along the backstretch. However, when he entered the final straightaway, he attempted to 'prop' and lost much of his lead. **1969** T. KENEALLY *Survivor* 70 Seconds later a university sedan, driven by George the university guard, wheeled fast in through the gate and propped at the front of the house. **1970** P. WHITE *Vivisector* 602 The present mob might have trampled Rhoda underfoot if it hadn't suddenly realized she was something beyond its experience, so it propped, and divided.

5. *trans.* To hit straight; to knock down. *slang.*

1851 MAYHEW *Lond. Labour* (1861) III. 387/1 If we met an 'old bloke' (man) we 'propped him' (knocked him down) and robbed him. **1892** *Nat. Observer* 27 Feb. 378/1 Give me a snug little set-to down in Whitechapel: Nobody there that can prop you in the eye!

†**prop,** *v.*[2] *Sc. Obs. rare*[−1]. [app. a. MDu., MLG. *proppen* to cram, stuff full: cf. PROP *sb.*[2], and note in etymology of PROP *sb.*[1]] *trans.* To cram, stuff, load.

a **1568** *King Berdok* 38 in *Bannatyne Poems* (Hunter. Cl.) 406 Thay stellit gunis to the killogy laich, And proppit gunis with bulettis of raw daich [= dough].

†**prop,** *v.*[3] *Obs.* [app. a variant of dial. *brob* vb.: see *Eng. Dial. Dict.* s.v. *brob.*] *intr.* To probe (for minerals).

1747 HOOSON *Miner's Dict.* E ij, When a Miner discovers any Signs of a Vein by Proping, he falls to cutting a Square Hole, about a Yard every way. *Ibid.* H ij, The Person who owns the Land where the Miner Props and makes search for Ore. *Ibid.* P iv b, If one Miner went by himself, he took nothing but his Proping Spade, if two went together they would take a Hack and Spade to Cast with. [**1748** *Articles for High Peak Hundred* in Hardy *Miner's Guide* 22 If any Miner within the King's Field, do brob or make any Holes for the finding of any Vein or Rake.]

propædeutic (prəʊpiːˈdjuːtɪk), *a.* and *sb.* [f. Gr. type *προπαιδευτικός adj., f. προπαιδεύειν to teach beforehand, f. πρό, PRO-[2] + παιδεύειν to teach, educate: see PÆDEUTICS.]

A. *adj.* Pertaining to or of the nature of preliminary instruction; supplying the knowledge or discipline introductory or preliminary to some art or science; preliminarily educational.

1849 MORELL *Philos. Relig.* 139 Judaism was Propædeutic to Christianity. **1868** M. PATTISON *Academ. Org.* v. 262 The university course is almost wholly special; the liberal and propædeutic studies are relegated to the grammar-school. **1882-3** *Schaff's Encycl. Relig. Knowl.* II. 1704 The study of philosophy has a propaedeutic value.

B. *sb.* **1.** A subject or study which forms an introduction to an art or science, or to more advanced study generally.

1798 A. F. M. WILLICH *Elem. Crit. Philos.* 19 In the mean time Kant's system, or rather his elementary *Propedeutic* for a system, acquired still greater reputation. **1836** SIR W. HAMILTON *Discuss.* (1852) 285 If Mathematics.. do constitute the true logical catharticon, the one practical propaedeutic of all reasoning. **1855** MEIKLEJOHN tr. *Kant's Critique* Pref. 25 Logic is properly only a propædeutic—forms, as it were, the vestibule of the sciences. **1905** *Athenæum* Feb. 170 Psychology pushes its claim to be the propaedeutic of metaphysics, with dire results to intellectualism.

2. *pl.* **propædeutics.** The body of principles or rules introductory to any art, science, or subject of special study; preliminary learning.

1842 BRANDE *Dict. Sci.*, etc., *Propædeutics*.. a term used by German writers to signify the preliminary learning connected with any art or science: that in which it is necessary to be instructed, in order to study with advantage the art or science itself. **1877** A. B. ALCOTT *Table-T.* 114 Rather is it [our secular life] the propædeutics of human combination and communication, wherein spiritual life becomes a reality.

Hence **propæˈdeutical** *a.* = PROPÆDEUTIC *a.*

1867 J. H. STIRLING *Schwegler's Hist. Philos.* (1871) 205 Logic precedes both as propædeutical of the study of philosophy in general. **1893** *Nation* (N.Y.) 6 Apr. 257/3 The propaedeutical narration of various well-chosen anecdotes.

propædia (prəʊˈpiːdɪə). [ad. Gr. προπαιδεία: see PROPAIDEIA.] An introductory volume of the 15th edition of the *Encyclopædia Britannica* (published in 1974) in which information is presented in the form of short outlines. (Cf. MACROPÆDIA, MICROPÆDIA.)

1974 [see MICROPÆDIA]. **1974** *Times* 12 Jan. 12/1 The first volume, propaedia, will be introductory, setting forth a classification of all knowledge into 10 parts, each with a long essay.

propagable (ˈprɒpəgəb(ə)l), *a.* [f. L. *pro-, prōpāg-āre* to PROPAGATE + -ABLE. Cf. med.L. *propāgābil-is* (Albertus Magnus *Metaph.* v. vi. v.).] Capable of being propagated.

1651 BIGGS *New Disp.* ¶ 60 And carry about with them propagable mines. *a* **1682** SIR T. BROWNE *Tracts* 48 The Olive not being successfully propagable by seed. *a* **1707** J. FRASER *Disc. Second Sight* 36 Whether this Second Sight be Hereditary, or propagable from father to Son. **1822-34** *Good's Study Med.* (ed. 4) II. 73 A specific source of infection as in other cases of propagable contagion.

Hence ˌ**propagaˈbility,** ˈ**propagableness,** the capability of being propagated.

1685 BOYLE *Effects of Mot.* v. 46 We must grant in our Instances a wonderful propagableness of motion. **1881** W. B. CARPENTER in *19th Cent.* Oct. 554 The propagability of the micrococcus of tubercle by the milk of cows affected with tuberculosis.

propagand (prɒpəˈgænd), *sb.* Also -ande. [ad. F. *propagande*: see PROPAGANDA *sb.*] = PROPAGANDA *sb.*

1795 W. COBBETT *Bone to gnaw for Democrats* 13 Citizen David, painter to the Propagande, has represented Liberty under the form of a Dragon. **1801** HEL. M. WILLIAMS *Sk. Fr. Rep.* I. xi. 115 To.. form a propagande of the rights of man. **1806** 'C. CAUSTIC' *Democracy Unveiled* (ed. 3) I. 75 Vile propagands in every city Make smooth the path of

French banditti. **1830** *Examiner* 629/1 Europe recollected the past, and asked whether no revolutionary propagand would arise amongst them. **1879** M. Pattison *Milton* iv. 47 A grand scheme for the union of Protestant Christendom, and his propagand of Comenius's school-reform.

propagand (prɒpə'gænd), *v.* [Back-formation from PROPAGANDA.] *trans.* and *intr.* = PROPAGANDIZE *v.*

1901 *Westm. Gaz.* 11 Jan. 2/2 Being free to 'propagand' he has not hesitated to do so. **1923** *Ibid.* 16 May 8/1 Russia was spending large sums out of her Secret Service in order to propagand in the East against British interests. **1935** N. Mitchison *We have been Warned* II. 208, I expect he'll propagand me a lot. **1938** E. Hemingway *Fifth Column* (1939) 171 That typical French *ivresse* that you were propaganded to believe did not exist. **1948** W. Fortescue *Beauty for Ashes* xii. 77 Would I consent to be a voluntary speaker and 'propagand' on platforms?

Hence **propa'ganded** *ppl. a.*; **propa'ganding** *vbl. sb.* and *ppl. a.*

1920 R. Frost *Let.* 19 Sept. (1972) 94 Good luck with the propaganding. **1937** F. P. Crozier *Men I Killed* xii. 268 They discuss it in awed whispers, well away from the propaganding microphones of the B.B.C. **1958** *Times Lit. Suppl.* 24 Oct. 604/2 Faulty reasoning..and unfelicities like 'propaganding' are a few of the obstacles it [*sc.* a book] presents. **1968** *Economist* 31 Aug. 45/1 The fear-bound and self-propaganded Kremlin leaders. **1971** F. R. Leavis in *Human World* Aug. 9 To see it [*sc.* the present government] replaced by one that has an alternative party-backing, representing a proclaimed and propaganded different policy and programme.

propaganda (prɒpə'gændə), *sb.* [a. It. (Sp., Pg.) *propaganda* (F. *propagande*), from the mod.L. title *Congregatio de propaganda fide* 'congregation for propagating the faith': see sense 1.]

1. (More fully, ***Congregation*** or ***College of the Propaganda***.) A committee of Cardinals of the Roman Catholic Church having the care and over-sight of foreign missions, founded in 1622 by Pope Gregory XV.

1718 Ozell tr. *Tournefort's Voy. Levant* II. 237 The Congregation of the Propaganda gives them at present but twenty five Roman Crowns a Man. **1819** T. Hope *Anastasius* (1820) I. ix. 168 An Italian missionary of the Propaganda. **1851** Gallenga *Italy* II. iii. 70 The Propaganda was busy in Paraguay, or Otaheite.

2. Any association, systematic scheme, or concerted movement for the propagation of a particular doctrine or practice.

Sometimes erroneously treated as a plural (= efforts or schemes of propagation) with singular *propagandum*, app. after *memorandum, -da*.

1790 J. MacPherson Let. 27 Sept. in A. Aspinall *Corresp. George, Prince of Wales* (1964) II. 98 All Kings have..a new race of Pretenders to contend with, the disciples of the propaganda at Paris or, as they call themselves, Les Ambassadeurs de genre humain. **1797** *Gentl. Mag.* Aug. 687 The Propaganda, a society whose members are bound, by solemn engagements, to stir up subjects against their lawful rulers. **1842** Brande *Dict. Sci.* etc., s.v., Derived from this celebrated society, the name *propaganda* is applied in modern political language as a term of reproach to secret associations for the spread of opinions and principles which are viewed by most governments with horror and aversion. **1868** M. E. G. Duff *Pol. Surv.* 36 Their *propaganda* represents nothing more than a mere idiosyncrasy. **1879** Farrar *St. Paul* I. 208 It seems unlikely that Saul should at once have been able to substitute a propaganda for an inquisition. **1896** *Brit. Weekly* XXII. 340/2 The opportunity and occasion for a vigorous and effective propaganda.

3. The systematic propagation of information or ideas by an interested party, esp. in a tendentious way in order to encourage or instil a particular attitude or response. Also, the ideas, doctrines, etc., disseminated thus; the vehicle of such propagation.

1908 Lilley & Tyrrell tr. *Programme of Modernism* 102 The Church..soon felt a need of new methods of propaganda and government. **1911** G. B. Shaw *Blanco Posnet* 324 Though we tolerate..the propaganda of Anarchism as a political theory..we clearly cannot..tolerate assassination of rulers on the ground that it is 'propaganda by deed' or sociological experiment. **1929** G. Seldes *You can't print That!* 427 The term propaganda has not the sinister meaning in Europe which it has acquired in America... In European business offices the word means advertising or boosting generally. **1938** R. G. Collingwood *Princ. Art* ii. 32 Where a certain practical activity is stimulated as expedient, that which stimulates it is advertisement or (in the current modern sense, not the old sense) propaganda. **1957** R. N. C. Hunt *Guide to Communist Jargon* 132 The Soviet Government not only has an elaborate machinery for conducting such propaganda abroad..but also does the same at home through the press, radio, films etc. **1974** *Anderson* (S. Carolina) *Independent* 23 Apr. 4A/6 CIA went on employing propaganda fronts long after anybody except professionals on both sides was paying any attention to the propaganda. **1976** A. J. Russell *Pour Hemlock* xiv. 166 White propaganda, the truth; gray, a composition of half-truths and distortions; or black, a pack of lies.

4. *attrib.* and *Comb.*, as (sense 3) ***propaganda campaign, chief, film, fund, leaflet, meeting, play, poster, raid, technique, war, warfare, work***; **propaganda machine**, an organization responsible for the dissemination of propaganda.

1937 Koestler *Spanish Testament* vi. 133 One of the most effective propaganda campaigns launched by the rebels was that relating to the alleged shooting of hostages by the Madrid Government. **1974** *Encycl. Brit. Macropædia* XV. 39/2 Today several hundred more or less scholarly books and thousands of articles shed substantial light on the psychology, techniques, and effects of propaganda campaigns, major and minor. **1942** *Short Guide Gr. Brit.* (U.S. War Dept.) 1 The first and major duty Hitler has given his propaganda chiefs is to separate Britain and America. **1950** Koestler in *God that Failed* 27 The absurdity of a propaganda-chief who only reads his own paper. **1973** D. May *Laughter in Djakarta* x. 161 It's a propaganda film..anti-neo-colonialism. **1978** Cadogan & Craig *Women & Children First* x. 224 According to widely shown propaganda films, the most adept German spy was bound to give himself away eventually through mispronunciation. **1842** *Communist Chronicle & Communitarian Apostle* I. v. 77 The propaganda fund shall be devoted to the propagation of the doctrines of communism. **1947** F. Frenaye tr. *C. Levi's Christ stopped at Eboli* (1948) xvii. 162 When their ship came back to Trieste from Odessa, Communist propaganda leaflets were found on board. **1978** A. Waugh *Best Wine Last* xv. 178 The propaganda leaflets that our aeroplanes scattered behind the German lines. **1948** Propaganda machine [see MACHINE *sb.* 8]. **1972** H. MacInnes *Message from Malaga* ii. 35 A propaganda machine is only as effective as people are stupid. **1978** F. Maclean *Take Nine Spies* iv. 153 The Russians only responded with counter-blasts from their own propaganda machine. **1899** *Two Worlds* 6 Jan. 7/1 Propaganda meetings will be conducted in the Cowgate-street Club and the Labour Institute. **1905** *Westm. Gaz.* 24 Jan. 3/1 A propaganda play. **1945** *New Yorker* 31 Mar. 52/1 A propaganda poster pasted on the remaining walls. **1979** *Listener* 1 Nov. 604/3 English [war] propaganda posters are bland alongside those of America, Holland or Sweden. **1934** *Ann. Reg. 1933* I. 181 On July 1 occurred the first of a series of propaganda raids by German aeroplanes over the Austrian frontier, when leaflets abusing the Dollfuss Government were dropped. **1927** H. D. Lasswell (*title*) Propaganda technique in the World War. **1975** *New Yorker* 21 Apr. 133/1 The Communists are taking full advantage of their highly developed propaganda techniques. **1838** tr. *Recoll. Caulincourt, Duke of Vicenza* I. iv. 74 The English Cabinet was well aware that a propaganda war was impossible as long as Russia should continue allied to France. **1854** J. S. C. Abbott *Napoleon* (1855) II. xii. 197 Aware that a propaganda war was impossible as long as Russia should continue allied to France. **1974** D. Seaman *Bomb that could Lip-Read* vi. 49 The I.R.A...are already winning the propaganda war, the one that finally matters. **1979** *Guardian* 22 Feb. 6/1 The [Russian] propaganda war against China continues to intensify. **1942** *R.A.F. Jrnl.* 18 Apr. 31 Propaganda warfare in the field was used. **1898** *Westm. Gaz.* 25 Jan. 5/3 We would rather see our money spent in propaganda work than paying election expenses.

propaganda (prɒpə'gændə), *v.* [f. the sb.] *trans.* = PROPAGANDIZE *v.*

1921 J. F. Porter *Sir Edward Elgar* 10 Elgar..never attempted to propaganda his work. **1949** H. L. Mencken in *Philologica: Malone Anniversary Stud.* 317 There is..a desire to get rid of circumlocution and the waste of words, as in..to propaganda, to steam-roller, to belly-ache.

propa'gandic, *a. rare.* [irreg. f. PROPAGANDA *sb.* + -IC.] Pertaining to a propaganda or to propagandism.

1890 in *Cent. Dict.* **1939** W. Fortescue *There's Rosemary* xxxix. 242 Next morning I studied my newspaper to see if my propagandic statistics had been faithfully recorded and was aghast to see, in 'leaded caps', a paragraph headed *The Baby fizzled*. **1946** L. Krey in W. S. Knickerbocker *20th Cent. English* 409 Just such grossly indecent or propagandic publications as often yield fabulous returns.

propagandism (prɒpə'gændɪz(ə)m). [f. as prec. + -ISM: so F. *propagandisme*.] The practice of a propaganda; systematic work at propagating any opinion, creed, or practice.

1800 *Aurora* (Philadelphia) 8 May 3 A war undertaken by the coalesced power against the system of *Propagandism* by which they have been menaced. **1807** *Weekly Inspector* (N.Y.) 28 Mar. 75/1 We have ever been disposed to attribute the wonderful success of the French, since their revolutionary era, to *Propagandism* or, in other words, to the poison of their principles, circulated by their emissaries; and corrupting the *mind* of the nations they proposed to attack. **1818** Lady Morgan *Autobiog.* (1859) 247 If the liberty of the press is curbed, the liberty of the tongue is taken to a wonderful degree, and I am not certain that its propagandism is not the stronger of the two. **1851** Gallenga *Italy* ii. 93 The results of French propagandism in Central Italy in 1830. **1879** Farrar *St. Paul* I. 292 The best Jews despised all attempts at active propagandism.

propagandist (prɒpə'gændɪst), *sb.* (*a.*) [f. as prec. + -IST: so F. *propagandiste*.]

A. *sb.* **1.** A member or agent of a propaganda; one who devotes himself to the propagation of some creed or doctrine; a proselytizer.

1797 Burke *Two Lett. on Conduct of our Domestick Parties* 109 How can I help it if this Royal propagandist will preach the doctrine of the rights of men? **1829** Southey *Sir T. More* (1831) I. 352 The propagandist of Atheism and the Jesuit both find facile converts. **1861** Crawfurd in *Trans. Ethnol. Soc.* I. 88 The early Portuguese conquerors in India ..very active and zealous propagandists. **1876** Lowell *Among my Bks.* Ser. II. 114 Evil is a far more cunning and persevering propagandist than Good. **1885** *Sat. Rev.* 30 May 713/2 To counteract the teachings of Radical propagandists. **1929** J. Fineberg tr. *Lenin's What is to be Done?* in *Coll. Wks.* IV. II. 147 A propagandist..must present 'many ideas', so many indeed that they will be understood as a whole only by a (comparatively) few persons. **1942** *Sun* (Baltimore) 12 Jan. 8/1 The rumors have been fostered by Hitler's propagandists. **1976** *Daily Tel.* 20 July 3/1 Dr Goebbels, the Nazi propagandist, could not have invented a more vilifying tag than that of the Black Panther.

2. *spec.* A missionary or convert of the Roman Catholic Congregation of the Propaganda.

1833 A. Crichton *Hist. Arabia* I. i. 29 *note*, He exposed the errors and superstitions of the Church of Rome, so as to alarm the Propagandists, who employed a Franciscan friar to refute it. **1890** *Tablet* 6 Sept. 365 Two Catholic factions, called respectively Padroadists and Propagandists. **1893** *Dublin Rev.* Jan. 31 The Goanese, to whatever part of India they wandered, kept themselves distinct from the Catholics, whom they termed Propagandists.

B. *adj.* Given or inclined to propagandism; devoted to the propagation of doctrines or principles.

1824 D. Webster *Speech on Greek Revolution* 5 It may be easy to call this resolution *Quixotic*, the emanation of a crusading or propagandist spirit. **1833** *Blackw. Mag.* June 933 Portugal..has been abandoned..to the revolutionary spoliation and propagandist arts of France. **1856** Emerson *Eng. Traits, Race* Wks. (Bohn) II. 20 They are still aggressive and propagandist. **1885** C. Lowe *Bismarck* xii. II. 320 The authorities had been ordered to deal with the Catholic Press, and with propagandist societies under the influence of the Jesuits.

Hence **propagan'distic** *a.*, of or pertaining to propagandists or propagandism; **propagan'distically** *adv.*, in a propagandist manner.

1880 *Daily Tel.* 17 Feb., Nicholas was opposed to France, because she was propagandistically dangerous to his form of government, pure absolutism. **1890** in *Voice* (N.Y.) 30 Jan., The objects of the society are mainly propagandistic. **1941** G. G. Scholem *Major Trends in Jewish Mysticism* viii. 306 Men of tireless literary and propagandistic activity. **1957** I. Asimov *Earth is Room Enough* (1960) 19 Such propagandistic lies were not uncommon. **1976** *New Yorker* 26 Jan. 66/3 Kim Il Sung figures he has made enough headway, even propagandistically, at the United Nations for the moment. **1977** *N.Y. Rev. Bks.* 23 June 4/2 There was no such propagandistic cause as anti-communism to impel those peach-cheeked youngsters to wage a war against an enemy caught up in the thrall of a fanatical, even suicidal nationalism.

propagandize (prɒpə'gændaɪz), *v.* [f. as prec. + -IZE.] **a.** *trans.* To disseminate (principles) by organized effort; to subject to a propaganda. Also, to subject (a person) to propaganda; to encourage to a belief thus.

1844 *Fraser's Mag.* XXIX. 333 We did not fight to propagandise monarchical principles. **1878** *Ibid.* XVIII. 51 They..came..to propagandise their political and literary notions. **1892** *Echo* 4 Feb. 2/3 All the..places..where voters can be reached, will be visited and propagandized. **1928** *Observer* 11 Mar. 13/4 A crowd of the peasants..tries to 'propagandize' an American soldier. **1933** *Sun* (Baltimore) 3 Oct. 12/1 Those who have only money enough ..should not be propagandized into spending beyond their means. **1938** *Daily Tel.* 7 Jan. 12/4 They had too much common-sense to be propagandized. **1969** *Wall St. Jrnl.* 14 Feb. 1/6 South Korea..propagandizes its citizens heavily. **1974** tr. *Sniečkus's Soviet Lithuania* 31 The Party.. propagandised Marxist-Leninist theory and intensified the ideological training of its members.

b. *intr.* To carry on a propaganda. Also, to disseminate propaganda.

1889 *Voice* (N.Y.) 1 Aug., Unselfish, disinterested citizens, propagandizing for the sake of principle. **1967** *Cold Spring Harbor Symp. Quant. Biol.* XXXII. 7/2 Being honest, I always have to mention when I am propagandizing against cigarettes—that 80% of heavy cigarette smokers do *not* die of lung cancer. **1974** K. Millett *Flying* III. x. 335, I propagandize and make coffee. **1977** *New Yorker* 6 June 137/1 He propagandized for wilderness preservation as well as urban amenity.

Hence **propa'gandizing** *ppl. a.* and *vbl. sb.*

1855 J. D. Howard in *N. Amer. Rev.* LXXX. 5 The early conquests of the Saracens, then, are to be ascribed..to the propagandizing spirit of their new faith. **1860** *Even. Jrnl. Tract* No. 13. 2 What class of men north and south did Mr. Fillmore represent? The old Whig or Clay party south who had no sympathies with the slave propagandising element of the Democratic party. **1927** S. Bent *Ballyhoo* iii. 87 The propagandizing of screened officials. **1978** *N.Y. Times* 30 Mar. B2/1 Here is a perfectly legal industry..based on the commercial exploitation and propagandizing of something that is illegal. **1979** *Country Life* 8 Nov. 1687/4 'Folk song' is a silly, sentimental, misleading and propagandising concept.

'propagant, *a. rare*⁻¹. [ad. L. *propāgāns, -ānt-em*, pres. pple. of *propāgāre* to PROPAGATE.] Propagating, prolific, productive.

1895 F. Hall *2 Trifles* 30, I predict that it [the term 'scientist'] will live. Nay, who knows that..it may not get to be ambitiously propagant, engendering..*scientism, scientistic, scientistically,..scientize* [etc.]?

†**'propagate**, *ppl. a. Obs. rare.* [ad. L. *propāgāt-us*, pa. pple. of *propāgāre*: see next.] Propagated. (Const. as pa. pple.)

a **1548** Hall *Chron., Hen. VII* 30 Because he was propagate and descended of the house of Lancastre. **1671** R. MacWard *True Nonconf.* 160 A sprig of Rome's hierarchy, propagate by her ambition and deceit.

propagate ('prɒpəgeɪt), *v.* Also 6–7 *erron.* propo-. [f. ppl. stem of L. *prō-, propāgāre* to multiply (plants) by means of layers or slips, to breed, to enlarge, extend, or prolong the stock or race of, cognate with *prō-, propāgo, -āginem* a layer (esp. of a vine), a shoot or slip from which a new plant is produced, f. PRO-¹ 1 e, forth, out,

+ (perh.) *pag-*, root of *pangĕre* to fix, fasten, set, plant; hence, 'to plant or set out layers'.]

1. a. *trans.* To multiply specimens of (a plant, animal, disease, etc.) by any process of natural reproduction from the parent stock; to produce as offspring, procreate, reproduce, breed; to cause to breed; *refl.* to reproduce itself (i.e. its kind).

1570 LEVINS *Manip.* 41/6 To Propagate, *propagare.* **1606** G. W[OODCOCKE] *Hist. Ivstine* IX. 42 Hee had many other sons propagated from seuerall women. **1607** TOPSELL *Four-f. Beasts* (1658) 121 The French Dogs are derived or propagated of the Dogs of Great Britain. **1671** J. WEBSTER *Metallogr.* iii. 40 [They] have no seminary principle to propagate themselves by. *a* **1680** BUTLER *Rem.* (1759) I. 117 To plant, and propagate a Vine. **1774** GOLDSM. *Nat. Hist.* (1776) IV. 271 Men..are often content to propagate a race of slaves. **1796** C. MARSHALL *Garden.* iv. (1813) 59 Plants are propagated by seeds, suckers, slips, offsets, divisions, cuttings, layers, and graffs. **1843** R. J. GRAVES *Syst. Clin. Med.* xxvii. 349 It is then not syphilis, but the original morbid diathesis modified by syphilis which becomes propagated. **1859** DARWIN *Orig. Spec.* i. 42 Pigeons..can be propagated in great numbers and at a very quick rate. **1859** W. S. COLEMAN *Woodlands* (1866) 114 The Mistletoe may be artificially propagated by slitting the bark of a tree and inserting one of the seeds. *Mod.*, Thistles seed and propagate themselves rapidly.

b. *absol.*, or *intr.* for *refl.* To breed, to produce offspring; to reproduce itself, i.e. its kind; to multiply or spread by generation or other form of reproduction.

1601 HOLLAND *Pliny* II. Explan. Words, *Propagat*, to grow and increase, after the manner of Vine branches, which being drawne along in the ground from the mother-stock do take root. **1640** NABBES *Bride* I. i, T' increase And propagate was the best end of marriage. **1732** POPE *Ess. Man* II. 64 Fix'd like a plant on his peculiar spot, To draw nutrition, propagate, and rot. **1772** PRIESTLEY *Inst. Relig.* (1782) I. 32 Carnivorous [animals] propagate very slowly. **1858** CHR. ROSSETTI *From House to Home* ix, Fat toads were there to hop or plod And propagate in peace.

†**c.** *trans.* To produce, yield as produce. *Obs.*

1699 DAMPIER *Voy.* II. I. 116 The greatest part of the Island of Sumatra propagates this Plant [pepper].

d. *transf.* To hand down from one generation to another; to pass on to one's descendants; to reproduce in the offspring.

1601 SHAKS. *All's Well* II. i. 200 My low and humble name to propagate With any branch or image of thy state. **1754** SHERLOCK *Disc.* (1759) I. iv. 142 These Follies were propagated from Father to Son. **1866** DARWIN *Orig. Spec.* ii. (ed. 4) 47 It may be doubted whether..great deviations of structure..are ever permanently propagated in a state of nature.

†**e.** To people (*with* a race or progeny). *Obs. rare.* (Cf. PROPAGATION 1 b.)

1784 *Unfortunate Sensibility* II. 155 It has always appeared to me ridiculous for people who propagate the world with nothing but miserable dependents, to make any rejoicing at their birth.

2. *fig.* **a.** To cause to grow in numbers or amount; to cause to increase or multiply. (Often passing into 3.)

1592 SHAKS. *Rom. & Jul.* I. i. 193 Griefes of mine owne lie heauie in my breast, Which thou wilt propagate to haue it preast With more of thine. **1633** PRYNNE *1st Pt. Histrio-M.* III. iii. 103 This practise therefore of acting Vices, doth onely propagate them, not restraine them. **1729** BUTLER *Serm.* Wks. 1874 II. 105 It is the very nature of this vice to propagate itself..in a peculiar way of its own. **1875** SCRIVENER *Lect. Text N. Test.* 5 The pernicious effects of this natural fault will propagate themselves rapidly.

b. To extend (anything material or immaterial).

1647 CLARENDON *Hist. Reb.* I. §146 Not to enlarge it, by continuing and propagating the War. **1704** *Providence Rec.* (1896) X. 77 A person..Purchased severall lands, and propagated other Estate as Goods, Cattell, and Chattells. **1860** TYNDALL *Glac.* II. xvii. 317 A narrow rent opened beneath his feet, and propagated itself through the ice.

c. *intr.* for *refl.* To increase, multiply itself, grow more numerous.

1670 G. H. *Hist. Cardinals* I. II. 53 As Heresie did propagate and increase. **1868** H. LAW *Beacons Bible* (1869) 34 [Sin] quickly propagates and fearfully extends.

3. a. *trans.* To spread from person to person, or from place to place; to disseminate, diffuse (a statement, belief, doctrine, practice, etc.).

1600 [see *propagating* below]. **1605** CAMDEN *Rem.* 4 Before the yere of Christ 200, it was propagated, as Tertullian writes, to places of Britaine..whither the Romans never reached. **1657** W. RAND tr. *Gassendi's Life Peiresc* II. 261 The Family of the *Fabricii*, had its Original from Pisa, from whence..it was propagated into France. **1658** *State Papers, Domestic* 295 The Act for propagating the Gospel in the 4 northern counties. **1674** OWEN *Holy Spirit* (1693) 107 The Kingdom of Christ is preserved, carried on and propagated in the World. **1725** BERKELEY *Proposal* Wks. 1871 III. 215 To propagate the Gospel in foreign parts. *a* **1727** NEWTON *Chronol. Amended* i. (1728) 80 This year being at length propagated into Chaldæa, gave occasion to the year of Nabonassar. **1802** *Med. Jrnl.* VIII. 195, I have had the pleasure to propagate Vaccination so far as Bagdad. **1862** MERIVALE *Rom. Emp.* VII. lxiii. 241 Some critics have imagined that the Roman occupation was propagated as far as the Don. **1868** HELPS *Realmah* xii. (1876) 327 Men who made and propagated false rumours.

b. *intr.* for *refl.* To become more widely spread; to spread. *rare.*

c **1645** HOWELL *Lett.* (1650) I. 330 A religion that..did expand herself, and propagate by simplicity, humbleness, and by a meer passive way of fortitude.

4. a. *trans.* To extend the action or operation of; to transmit, spread, convey (motion, light, sound, etc.) in some direction, or through some medium. At first chiefly in *pass.*; now also *active.*

1656 tr. *Hobbes' Elem. Philos.* (1839) 216 All endeavour, whether strong or weak, is propagated to infinite distance; for it is motion. **1660** BOYLE *New Exp. Phys. Mech.* xxvii. 207 The structure of the cover..through which the sound was propagated from the Watch to the Ear. **1799** WOOD *Optics* i. (1811) 1 The vibrations of an elastic fluid are propagated in every direction. **1843** R. J. GRAVES *Syst. Clin. Med.* xxx. 406 It might be thought improbable that irritation, commencing in the kidney or in the bladder, should be propagated through sentient nerves to the spinal cord. **1853** HERSCHEL *Pop. Lect. Sc.* i. §22 (1873) 15 The manner in which an earthquake is propagated from place to place. **1854** [see PROPAGATION 5]. **1973** *Sci. Amer.* Feb. 73/2 Internal waves propagate energy through the body of a stratified fluid in much the same way that energy is propagated by waves at the surface. **1975** *Nature* 8 May 157/1 The flagellum of this organism propagates waves both distally and proximally in common with other trypanosomes.

b. *refl.* for *passive.*

1880 [see *cathode ray* s.v. CATHODE c]. **1908** tr. *Suess' Face of Earth* III. IV. i. 4 Some kind of wave propagating itself freely through the crust of the earth.

c. *intr.* for *passive.* To be propagated, to travel.

1943 F. E. TERMAN *Radio Engineers' Handbk.* III. 255 Waves of a variety of types may propagate down a wave guide. **1957** J. J. STOKER *Water Waves* x. 374 In practically all of this book we assume that the medium in which waves propagate is water. **1966** C. R. TOTTLE *Sci. Engin. Materials* vii. 168 Griffith in 1920..proposed that glass possessed many fine cracks in the surface, which could propagate through the material and cause failure. **1967** *Oceanogr. & Marine Biol.* V. 31 The elevation ζ may be specified as a function of position and time, representing an external surge propagating into the sea area. **1969** *Sci. Jrnl.* Dec. 44/3 In a waveguide the microwave energy propagates down the inside of a hollow conductor. **1971** *Nature* 3 Dec. 292/2 When a laser beam propagates through a mixture of gases. **1974** *Sci. Amer.* Jan. 38/3 In the nerves of both higher and lower animals it is the cell membrane that..enables the nerve impulse to be set up and to propagate. **1977** *Nature* 21 July 203/2 The proton is knocked out of the nucleus and could be observed propagating freely after the collision.

Hence **'propagated** *ppl. a.*, **'propagating** *vbl. sb.* and *ppl. a.*

1600 J. PORY tr. *Leo's Africa* 390 The propagating of the christian faith. **1638** QUARLES *Hieroglyph.* II. xix, Or is't a propagated Spark, rak'd out From Natures embers? *a* **1653** G. DANIEL *Idyll.* ii. 59 Such propagating Iellyes nere distill Without their Mandrakes; whose first hissings kill. **1868** *Rep. U.S. Commissioner Agric.* (1869) 320 The efforts of the pisciculturists..at their propagating establishment at Stormontfield. **1899** *Allbutt's Syst. Med.* VI. 161 The starting-point of a continued or propagated thrombus. **1971** *Sci. Amer.* June 22/1 The energy stored in the inverted population is then available to amplify a propagating light wave at a particular frequency. **1972** *Ibid.* Jan. 18/3 The muffling of seismic signals might be achieved by conducting the test in an underground material where a comparatively small fraction of the energy of the explosion would appear in a propagating seismic wave. **1973** *Physics Bull.* Nov. 657/3 It may be helpful to consider first the ways in which propagating gravitational waves are like electromagnetic waves.

propagation (prɒpə'geɪʃən). [a. F. *propagation* (13th c. in Hatz.-Darm.), or ad. L. *prō-, propāgātiōn-em*, n. of action f. *prŏpāgāre* to PROPAGATE.] The action of propagating.

1. a. The action of producing as offspring, or multiplying by such production; procreation, generation, reproduction.

a **1450** *Mankind* 181 in *Macro Plays* 7 Of þe erth & of þe cley we haue owur propagacyon. **1526** *Pilgr. Perf.* (W. de W. 1531) 170 b, He that by naturall propagacyon hath generate or begoten vs. **1601** HOLLAND *Pliny* XVII. xiii. 515 The worke of nature, in sending out these sprigs, taught us the feat to couch and lay sets in the ground by way of propagation. **1781** BURKE *Sp. Marriage Act* Wks. X. 136 Matrimony is instituted not only for the propagation of men, but for their nutrition, their education, their establishment. **1857** HENFREY *Bot.* §875 In the lower Algæ, ..the plants are continually undergoing propagation by division of the constituent cells. **1883** GOODE *Fish. Indust. U.S.A.* 74 (Fish. Exhib. Publ.) The machinery for propagation [of fish] on a gigantic scale by the aid of steam.

†**b.** The action of peopling with offspring. *Obs.*

1662 STILLINGFL. *Orig. Sacr.* III. i. §2 The propagation of the world after [the flood] by the Sons of Noah.

†**2.** That which is propagated; offspring, generation, breed, race. *Obs.*

1536 *Exhort. to the North* 86 in Furniv. *Ballads fr. MSS.* I. 307 And with that noit content, hys mallys put in vre agaynes the trew lewes of hys propagation. **1596** WARNER *Alb. Eng.* XI. lxvii. (1612) 285 With Marrage, that legitimates our propagation. **1611** RICH *Honest. Age* (Percy Soc.) 49 The Laconian women brought foorth a propagation of men of haughty courage.

†**3.** *fig.* Increase in amount or extent; enlargement; extension in space or time. *Obs.*

1603 SHAKS. *Meas. for M.* I. ii. 154 This we came not to, Onely for propogation of a Dowre Remaining in the Coffer of her friends. *a* **1716** SOUTH *Serm.* (1744) XI. ii. 39 The spoil and waste they had made..for the propagation of their empire, which they were still enlarging as their desires. **1741** MIDDLETON *Cicero* I. iii. 217 Not for the propagation of his own life.

4. Dissemination, diffusion, esp. of some principle, belief, or practice.

1588 *Reg. Privy Council Scot.* IV. 266 The propagatioun of the trew..religioun. **1615** LATHAM *Falconry* Epist., For the propagation of the noble sport. **1701** *Charter Will. III* 16 June, [To] be one Body Politick and Corporate, in Deed, and in Name, by the Name of the Society for the Propagation of the Gospel in Foreign Parts. **1751** JOHNSON *Rambler* No. 144 ¶6 Calumny is diffused by all arts and methods of propagation. **1859** MILL *Liberty* ii. 36 Forbidding the propagation of error. **1877** SPARROW *Serm.* ix. 112 The main use of agencies..in connection with religion, is the propagation of the truth.

5. Transmission of some action or form of energy, as motion, light, sound, etc.

1656 tr. *Hobbes' Elem. Philos.* (1839) 334 When..one body, having opposite endeavour to another body, moveth the same, and that moveth a third, and so on, I call that action propagation of motion. **1710** J. CLARKE *Rohault's Nat. Philos.* (1729) I. 191 The Propagation of Sound may very well be compared with Circles made in the Water, by throwing a Stone into it. **1804** SIR J. LESLIE (*title*) An Experimental Inquiry into the Nature and Propagation of Heat. **1849** NOAD *Electricity* (ed. 3) 138 We must consider the transference of the hydrogen to take place by the propagation of a decomposition through a chain of particles extending from the zinc to the platinum. **1854** *Pereira's Pol. Light* 8 The Propagation of Light.—Light emanates, radiates, or is propagated in straight lines.

†**6.** The action of branching out as a shoot (L. *propago*); *concr.* a branch, ramification. *Obs. rare.*

1650 BULWER *Anthropomet.* 10 The nerves of the Taste descend from the third and fourth Propagations, and so diffuse themselves into the tongue.

7. *Chem.* In a chain reaction, the step or series of steps in which product molecules are formed or polymer chains lengthened, but which is self-perpetuating by virtue of the regeneration or relocation of reactive centres; e.g. in polymerization, reaction of a radical with a molecule of monomer to form a longer radical. Freq. *attrib.*

1928 *Proc. R. Soc.* A. CXXII. 621 The conditions which govern the propagation of the stable reaction chains. **1940** *Ann. Rep. Progr. Chem.* XXXVI. 74 When an active molecule possesses such a long lifetime, the rate of formation and destruction of these centres plays no part in the rate of polymerisation, which is then solely determined by the velocity of the propagation reaction. **1950** *Thorpe's Dict. Appl. Chem.* (ed. 4) X. 88/1 This is followed by the propagation stage, in which successive additions of monomer molecules occur, maintaining an odd electron, characteristic of a free radical, at the end of the growing chain. **1964** J. M. CRABTREE et al. tr. *V. N. Kondrat'ev's Chem. Kinetics of Gas Reactions* ix. 613 The chain propagation processes involving HO_2 radicals are important in the so-called slow oxidation of hydrogen which occurs.. at relatively high pressures. **1973** K. J. SAUNDERS *Org. Polymer Chem.* i. 10 This new radical then adds further monomer molecules in rapid succession to form a polymer chain. In this propagation the active centre remains, being continuously relocated at the end of the chain.

8. *attrib.* and *Comb.*, as *propagation tray*; **propagation coefficient, constant,** or **factor** *Physics*, the coefficient of the distance in an equation representing the propagation of a wave (quot. 1943 represents an equivalent def.); **propagation function** *Physics*, = PROPAGATOR 3.

1943 *Gloss. Terms Telecommunications* (*B.S.I.*) 7 *Propagation coefficient, propagation constant*, the natural logarithm of the vector ratio of the steady-state amplitudes of a wave at a specified frequency, at points in the direction of propagation separated by unit length. **1911** J. A. FLEMING *Propagation Electr. Currents* ii. 68, P is a complex quantity and therefore may be written in the form $\alpha + j\beta$. It is called the Propagation constant of the line. **1963** R. W. DITCHBURN *Light* (ed. 2) ii. 28 The wave-length..is denoted by λ. An associated constant $\kappa = 2\pi/\lambda$ is called the wavelength constant (or propagation constant). **1976** G. R. OLHOEFT in R. G. J. Strens *Physics & Chem. of Minerals & Rocks* 262 All of the material properties (other than geometric boundary conditions) which are important to the description of the propagation of an electromagnetic wave (or lack of propagation) are described in the propagation constant by the quantities μ, ϵ, and σ. **1958** CONDON & ODISHAW *Handbk. Physics* IV. vii. 108/2 The solution is a plane wave..varying periodically in time with the frequency $\nu = \omega/2\pi$ and advancing in the + x direction through space with a complex propagation factor $\gamma = j\omega\sqrt{\epsilon^*\mu^*} = \alpha + j\beta$. **1949** *Physical Rev.* LXXVI. 770/1 Many of the properties of the integrals are analyzed using formal properties of invariant propagation functions. **1970** J. SCHWINGER *Particles, Sources, & Fields* iii. 145 Considering spin 0 particles and their real scalar sources,..we examine the effect of adding an additional weak source $\delta K(x)$. It is given by $\delta W(k) = \int(dx)\delta K(x)\phi(x)$, where $\phi(x) = \int(dx') \times \Delta + (x - x')K(x')$. This combination of source and propagation function, measuring the effect of pre-existing sources on a weak test source, is the *field* of the sources. **1977** *Grimsby Even. Tel.* 31 May 9/5 A hundred small cannabis plants in propagation trays, plus smoking pipes and an LSD tablet were found.

propa'gational, *a. rare.* [f. prec. + -AL[1].] Of or pertaining to propagation.

1898 LD. KELVIN in *Nature* 17 Nov. 56/2 How and about what range do we pass from the propagational velocities of 3 kilometres per second?

propagative ('prɒpəgeɪtɪv), *a.* [f. L. ppl. stem *prō-, propāgāt-* (see PROPAGATE *v.*) + -IVE.] Having the quality of propagating; belonging to, characterized by, or tending to propagation.

1660 WATERHOUSE *Arms & Arm.* 118 If the design of Loyola..were..propogative of the faith of Jesus. *a* **1677** HALE *Prim. Orig. Man.* IV. vii. 354 Every Man owes more of his Being to Almighty God than to his natural Parents, whose very Propagative Faculty was at first given..by the only virtue, efficacy, and energy of the Divine Commission and Institution. **1857** HENFREY *Bot.* §876 In the Hepaticæ and Mosses the propagative structures do not yet arrive at the condition of buds. **1883** H. DRUMMOND *Nat. Law in Spir. W.* (ed. 2) 356 A church without propagative power in the world cannot be other than a calamity.

propagator (ˈprɒpəgeɪtə(r)). [a. L. *prō-, propāgātor*, agent-n. from *prōpāgāre* to PROPAGATE: so F. *propagateur* (1516 in Hatz.-Darm.).] One who or that which propagates.

1. a. One who begets or produces offspring.

1686 GOAD *Celest. Bodies* I. ix. 32 [They] must needs depend on some prime Propagator, as all Families do. **1711** ADDISON *Spect.* No. 203 ¶7 Were I to propose a Punishment for this infamous Race of Propagators, it should be to send them..into our American Colonies..to people those Parts ..where there is a want of Inhabitants.

b. A planter; a rearer of plants.

1669 WORLIDGE *Agric.* (1681) 330 *Propagator*, a Planter.

c. A forcing-frame for plants; a propagating-house. Also, a small box with a transparent lid and a base that can be heated, for germinating seeds or raising seedlings.

1885 *Bazaar* 30 Mar. 1254/2 A well made propagator, zinc, can be heated with gas or oil lamp, very useful for raising flower seeds or striking cuttings. **1914** W. F. ROWLES *Garden under Glass* i. 16 The propagator itself may consist of a box..covered by loose sheets of glass. **1950** E. J. KING *Propagation of Plants* iii. 29 A propagator is a small frame built inside a heated greenhouse in such a way as to give even higher temperatures than those in the main part of the house. **1971** *Daily Tel.* 13 Feb. 7/3 A week or two lost in raising seeds in a heated greenhouse, or electric propagator in the home, is not a matter of extreme urgency. **1976** *Abingdon Herald* 9 Dec. 5/2 A small propagator..enables one to raise seeds at any time. **1979** *Garden* CIV (Advt.), Humex Mono-top Propagator. Pick of the bunch—the electrically heated propatray base surmounted by an.. enclosure with sliding doors for easy access.

d. The male copulative organ; the penis. Now *arch.*

1670 J. OGILBY *Africa* 451 Lastly, they have little Bellies, broad Feet, long Toes, and furnish'd, as most of the Blacks upon the Guinee Coast, with large Propagators. **1971** *Black Scholar* June 12/1 Setting foot on the shores of West Africa in 1550, the Englishman was struck by the African's religion ..and his 'Propagator', which he perceived monstrous.

2. *fig.* One who spreads abroad, disseminates, or diffuses (a statement, opinion, practice, etc.).

1613 PURCHAS *Pilgrimage* (1614) 52 The propagator of true Religion. **1664** H. MORE *Myst. Iniq.* 283 The Propagators of the worship of the Baalim. **1790** BURKE *Fr. Rev.* 167 These writers, like the propagators of all novelties, pretended to a great zeal for the poor and the lower orders. **1812** LD. ELLENBOROUGH in *Examiner* 28 Dec. 832/2 The defendant was not proved to be the institutor, but only the propagator, of the libel. **1867** FREEMAN *Norm. Conq.* I. vi. 455 A zealous propagator of Christianity.

3. *Physics.* An algebraic function that is taken as representing the propagation of a particle on the sub-atomic scale, esp. between its space-time points of creation and annihilation.

1951 *Physical Rev.* LXXXIV. 1233/1 G' (1,2), the 'quantum propagator', is a function of $(x_\mu 1 x_\mu 3)$ not containing any Dirac operators. **1958** *Ibid.* CXII. 1417/1 A coincidence arrangement appears capable of testing the electron propagator at distances approaching the nucleon Compton wavelength, which is comparable with our present limit on the photon propagator. **1973** J. A. REISSLAND *Physics of Photons* vi. 186 If the effect of a perturbation $H'(t)$ is to create a particle at position **r**′ at time t', the function (6.19) traces the propagation of that particle until it is removed at **r** at a time t. Hence the term 'propagator' for the one-particle Green's function $G(\mathbf{r},t;\ \mathbf{r}',t') \equiv i\eta(t-t') < a(\mathbf{r},t)a^{+}(\mathbf{r}',t'>$ where $a^{+}(\mathbf{r}',t')$ creates a particle at **r**′,t' and $a(\mathbf{r},t)$ destroys it at (**r**,t). **1974** *Physics Bull.* May 191/2 Propagators (or Green's functions) have been much used by physicists.

Hence ˈ**propagatress, propaˈgatrix**, a female propagator.

1653 R. BAILLIE *Dissuas. Vind.* (1655) 24 That heresie for its great and prime propogatrix had Mistresse Hutcheson. **1660** HOWELL *Parly of Beasts* 89 The prime Propagatresse of Religion and Learning. **1803** *Edin. Rev.* I. 498 This industrious propagatrix of the species.

† ˈ**propagatory**, *a. Obs. rare.* [f. as PROPAGATE *v.* + -ORY[2].] **a.** = PROPAGATIVE. **b.** Subject to propagation; = PROPAGABLE.

1647 M. HUDSON *Div. Right Govt.* II. x. 144 Which power God delegated unto man..by that propagatorie benediction, *Crescite & multiplicamini.* **1652** GAULE *Magastrom.* 196 Prophecy, as it is not hereditary by nature, so neither is it propagatory by art.

† **proˈpage**, *v. Obs. rare.* [ad. L. *propāgāre*, or F. *propage-r.*] = PROPAGATE *v.*

1695 BP. PATRICK *Comm. Gen.* 17 [The plants] at the beginning were brought out of the Earth, with their Seed in them, to propage them ever after. **1695** CONGREVE *Love for L.* II, Body o' me, what a many-headed Monster have I propaged!

propagule (prəʊˈpægjʊl). *Bot.* [ad. mod.L. *propāgul-um*, dim. of L. *propāgo* a shoot laid down in layering, a runner.]

1. See quot. *rare.*

1858 MAYNE *Expos. Lex., Propagulum*, Bot. Applied by Willdenow to the round corpuscles which are solitary or agglomerated upon the surface of the *thallus* of the *Lichenes*: a propagule.

2. A seed, spore, or other product of a plant which is disseminated to form a new individual; also, occasionally used as a name for the products of asexual reproduction in certain lower animals. Hence **proˈpagular** *a.*, of or pertaining to a propagule.

1905 F. E. CLEMENTS *Res. Methods Ecol.* iv. 241 Dormant seeds and propagules are abundant. **1959** *New Biol.* XXVIII. 80 Extrinsic barriers between breeding populations..effectively prevent or check gene flow because they are not crossed by adults, or by seeds, pollen, or other 'propagules'. **1965** BELL & COOMBE tr. *Strasburger's Textbk. Bot.* 204 Propagules may consist of single cells (spores), groups of cells (gemmae), or entire organs or complexes of organs (bulbils). **1967** *Oceanogr. & Marine Biol.* V. 494 Several hydroids are particularly adapted..to ensure asexual reproduction by means of propagular stolons whose brittle and curved extremities can catch a neighbouring leaf. **1969** *New Scientist* 20 Nov. 402/1 Any fungal propagules landing on its surface will be killed. **1974** *New Phytologist* LXXIII. 981 Wallace pointed out that the small propagules of Compositae..allowed that family to gain an early footing on islands. **1977** *Nature* 3 Nov. 48/2, I report here that the marine red alga *Centroceras* produces missile-shaped propagules which are carried away by ocean currents.

‖**propaiˈdeia.** *rare*[−1]. [a. Gr. προπαιδεία preliminary teaching, f. πρό, PRO-[2] + παιδεία teaching.] Preliminary teaching or education.

1888 GLADSTONE in *Contemp. Rev.* May 781 The marvellous propaideia of the Jewish history.

† ˈ**propalate**, *v. Obs.* [f. ppl. stem of late L. *prōpalāre*: see PROPALE and -ATE[3].] = PROPALE.

1598 in *Archpriest Controv.* (Camden) I. 209 We..almost make dowbte to propalate what answeares they have returned to some very grave, learned and worthy persons. **1633** PRYNNE *Histriomastix* 126, Christian love, which delights to cover, not propalate and divulge mens sinnes. **1716** M. DAVIES *Athen. Brit.* III. 62 Mr. Howarden..dare's propalate his Ignorance so far as to say, The Swissers have no University.

So † **propaˈlation**, publication, divulgement.

a **1677** HALE *Pomponius Atticus* 137 They would immediately before the propalation of such businesses, send for persons of greatest reputation and credit.

proˈpale, *v.* Chiefly *Sc. arch.* [ad. late L. *prōpal-āre* to make public, divulge, f. L. *prōpalam* openly, manifestly, f. *prō*, PRO-[1] 1 a + *palam* openly.] *trans.* To publish, divulge, disclose.

c **1529** in Fiddes *Wolsey* II. (1726) 170 Never to propale the same to any man lyving. **1721** WODROW *Hist. Suffer. Ch. Scot.* (1828) I. I. ii. 130 The springs of such surprising treatment..are either secret, or not very fit to be propaled. **1730** T. BOSTON *Mem.* App. 29, I do not desire it to be propaled. **1820** SCOTT *Abbot* iv, Anxious to propale their misdemeanour.

propalinal (prəʊˈpælɪnəl), *a. Physiol.* [f. Gr. πρό, PRO-[2] + πάλιν backward + -AL[1]: cf. PROAL, PALINAL.] Having a forward and backward motion: said of the lower jaw in mastication.

1888 COPE in *Amer. Nat.* Jan. 7 [*Note*] The propalinal mastication is to be distinguished into the proal, from behind forwards,..and the palinal, from before backwards. *Ibid.* 9 A fifth effect of the development of the incisors, and of the propalinal mastication, is seen in the position of the molar teeth.

propamidine (prəʊˈpæmɪdiːn). *Pharm.* [f. PROP(ANE + AMID(E + -INE[5].] A diamidine with bactericidal and fungicidal properties which is used, usu. in the form of its isethionate (a white, hygroscopic powder), in dressing minor wounds or burns; 1,3-di(4-amidinephenoxy)propane, $CH_2[CH_2 \cdot O \cdot C_6H_4.C(NH)(NH_2)]_2$.

1941, 1951 [see PENTAMIDINE]. **1964** W. G. SMITH *Allergy & Tissue Metabolism* iv. 56 Mast cell degranulation will account for the histamine liberating activity of compound 48/80. This is also true of the histamine releasing properties of..propamidine. **1976** 'J. HERRIOT' *Vets might Fly* (1977) ii. 20 Lord Hulton was a devotee of May and Baker's Propamidine Cream and used it for all minor cuts and grazes in his cattle.

propane (ˈprəʊpeɪn). *Chem.* [f. PROP(IONIC + -ANE 2 b; introduced by Hofmann, 1866.]

1. The paraffin or saturated hydrocarbon C_3H_8, the third member of the series C_nH_{2n+2}; a colourless gas occurring in petroleum, which liquefies at − 20°C. Also called *propyl hydride.*

1866 HOFMANN in *Proc. Roy. Soc.* XV. 58 *note*, The following names are formed: Methane, $(CH_4)°$, Ethane, $(C_2H_6)°$, Propane, $(C_3H_8)°$, Quartane, $(C_4H_{10})°$ [etc.]. **1868** *Fownes' Chem.* (ed. 10) 539. **1872** WATTS *Dict. Chem.* VI. 957 Propane. C_3H_8. Propyl Hydride. This hydrocarbon, the third member of the marsh-gas or paraffin series..occurs among the gases evolved from the petroleum springs of North America. **1880** CLEMINSHAW *Wurtz' Atom. The.* 215 The three carbon atoms of the new hydrocarbon, propane, will thus form a chain firmly riveted by the very affinities which would have separated them from each other. *Ibid.* 288 Propyl hydride or propane may be formed in different ways.

2. *attrib.*, as ***propane gas.***

1974 *Janet Frazer Catal.* Spring/Summer 458/4 Portable refrigerator... Suitable for use with Butane or Propane gas. **1979** 'J. ROSS' *Rattling of Old Bones* iii. 25 The propane-gas lamps..were flooding the cupboard with hissing white light.

propanediol (ˌprəʊpeɪnˈdaɪɒl). *Chem.* [f. PROPANE + DI-[2] + -OL.] = *propylene glycol* s.v. PROPYLENE 2; also, a derivative of this.

1894 G. M'GOWAN tr. *Bernthsen's Text-bk. Org. Chem.* (ed. 2) 206 Propylene glycol is known in two isomeric forms, viz.: (*a*) Tri-methylene glycol† or β-Propylene glycol,.. (*b*) α-Propylene glycol‡. [*Note*] †1-3-Propane-diol. ‡1-2-Propane-diol. **1952** *Jrnl. Pharmacol. & Exper. Therapeutics* CV. 452 The 1,3-propanediol ethers have greater protective action in electroshock seizures than the corresponding position isomers of the 1,2-propanediol series. **1966** *McGraw-Hill Encycl. Sci. & Technol.* XIV. 16/2 According to basic chemical structure, four categories of tranquilizers are delineated: phenothiazines..; rauwolfia derivatives..; propanediols, for example, meprobamate or Miltown; diphenylurethanes. **1976** *Ann. Rev. Microbiol.* XXX. 421 A clear example of evolution to reverse function in the laboratory is the evolution of propanediol catabolism through recruitment of enzymes normally involved in L-fucose and L-lactate metabolism.

propanidid (prəʊˈpænɪdɪd). *Pharm.* [Arbitrarily f. PROPAN(E.] A colourless or yellowish oily liquid which is given intravenously in solution as a short-acting anæsthetic; propyl-4-diethyl-carbamoylmethoxy-3-methoxyphenylacetate, $C_{18}H_{27}NO_5$.

1964 *Brit. Jrnl. Anaesthesia* XXXVI. 655/1 The new intravenous narcotic propanidid..displays a biphasic action on ventilation consisting of stimulation followed by depression. **1965** *Med. Jrnl. Austral.* 21 Aug. 329 Propanidid is a unique, short-acting intravenous anæsthetic agent with many interesting features—in particular, its mode of inactivation. **1971** PRYOR & MACALISTER *Gen. Anaesthetic & Sedation Techniques Dentistry* x. 63 Propanidid has made a tremendous contribution towards making the induction of anaesthesia pleasanter for the patient and working conditions easier for the dental surgeon.

propanol (ˈprəʊpənɒl). *Chem.* [f. PROPAN(E + -OL.] Either of the isomers of propyl alcohol; sometimes *spec.* normal propyl alcohol, 1-propanol (cf. *isopropanol* s.v. ISO- b).

[**1892** *Proc. Chem. Soc.* 16 June 128 Citric acid, on this system, would be named propanoltrioic acid or simply propanoltri-acid.] **1894** G. M'GOWAN tr. *Bernthsen's Text-bk. Org. Chem.* (ed. 2) 92 Normal propyl alcohol. [*Note*] 1-Propanol. *Ibid.* 93 Secondary propyl alcohol. [*Note*] 2-Propanol. **1926** H. G. RULE tr. *Schmidt's Text-bk. Org. Chem.* I. 111 Propyl alcohol, propanol, $C_3H_7.OH$. Both of the theoretically possible structural isomerides of this formula are known. **1951** I. L. FINAR *Org. Chem.* I. iv. 62 Propylene, propene, C_3H_6, may be prepared by heating propanol or *iso*-propanol with sulphuric acid. **1964** N. G. CLARK *Mod. Org. Chem.* viii. 140 Two isomeric propanols exist, of which the primary alcohol is less important. **1964** J. C. MATTHEWS *Mod. Chem. Course* xxv. 302 Add 20–25 drops of ethanol or propanol slowly with shaking.

propantheline (prəʊˈpænθəliːn). *Pharm.* [f. PROP(YL + X)ANTH(ENE + *-el* (f. E(THY)L) + -INE[5].] A white, bitter-tasting powder, $C_{23}H_{30}NO_3Br$, which is a quaternary ammonium bromide derived from xanthene, and is a parasympatholytic agent used esp. for treating the symptoms of peptic ulceration. Also ***propantheline bromide.*** Cf. PRO-BANTHINE.

1954 *Brit. Jrnl. Pharmacol.* IX. 218 (*heading*) A comparison of the peripheral parasympatholytic and autonomic ganglion blocking activities of methantheline ('Banthine') and propantheline ('Pro-Banthine') with atropine and hexamethonium. *Ibid.* Propantheline (2′-di*iso*propylaminoethyl xanthene-9-carboxylate methobromide) is the isopropyl analogue of methantheline and differs from it only in degree of activity.., its actions being qualitatively similar. **1955** *Lancet* 10 Sept. 526/2 Propantheline bromide can be used to relieve colic, whether due to spasm of the sphincter or associated with biliary reflux and pancreatitis. **1958** [see PRO-BANTHINE]. **1970** O. L. WADE *Adverse Reaction to Drugs* ii. 13 Atropine or propantheline in the doses required to reduce gastric motility and gastric secretion in the treatment of peptic ulcer may cause unpleasant dryness of the mouth or blurring of vision. **1977** *Lancet* 26 Nov. 1134/1 The effects of propantheline bromide on the eyes should be considered when the drug is used in the treatment of hyperhidrosis.

proparapteral, -on: see PRO-[2] 2.

proparasceve (prəʊˈpærəsiːv, -pærəˈsiːvɪ). *rare.* [ad. Gr. προπαρασκευή a previous preparation: see PRO-[2] and PARASCEVE.] A fore-preparation; something that precedes preparation.

1646 TRAPP *Comm. John* xi. 55 They had their parasceve, and proparasceve, their preparation and fore-preparation. **1826** H. N. COLERIDGE *West Indies* 175 Turtle..is the proparasceve of our manducatory energies.

† ˈ**pro-ˌparent.** *Obs. rare.* [f. PRO-[1] 4 + PARENT.] One who takes the place of a parent.

1653 G. FIRMIN *Sober Reply* 14 For your Pro-parent, and Adoption,..I must now answer. **1661** *Papers on Alter. Prayer Bk.* 98 Who made those Sureties Guardians of the Infants that are neither Parents, nor Pro-parents, nor Owners of them? **1661** *Grand Debate* 19 We desire that the two first Interrogatories may be put to the Parents..; and the last propounded by the Parents, or Pro-parents.

propargyl (prəʊˈpɑːdʒɪl). *Chem.* [f. *prop-* in PROPIONIC + *arg-* (in allusion to the fact that one of its proportions of hydrogen is characteristically replaceable by silver, *argentum*) + -YL.]

A hydrocarbon radical, C_3H_3, $= CH{\equiv}C{\cdot}CH_2$, also called *propinyl*, which is found isolated in the form of DIPROPARGYL, and occurs in *propargyl alcohol*, a colourless, very fragrant liquid, $CH \equiv C.CH_2.OH$, formed by the action of KOH on monobromallyl alcohol; *propargyl bromide*, $CH \equiv C{\cdot}CH_2Br$, etc. Hence **pro'pargyla,mine** $C_3H_3NH_2$; **pro'pargylate**, a compound of propargyl with another radical, as *ethyl propargylate*, $CH \equiv C{\cdot}CH_2(OC_2H_5)$; **propar'gylic** *a.*, of or containing propargyl, as *propargylic ether* = ethyl propargylate.

1866–8 WATTS *Dict. Chem.* IV. 728 Propargylic ether. **1872** *Ibid.* VI. 958 Propargylic ether.. is a liquid having an offensive odour, boiling at 72°. **1875** *Ibid.* VII. 1007 Propargyl compounds. *Ibid.*, Ethyl propargylate or propargylic ether.. was discovered in 1865 by Liebermann. *Ibid.*, Propargyl Alcohol.. is a colourless liquid of peculiar odour, boiling at 114°–115°. *Ibid.* 1008 Methyl propargylate ..Amyl propargylate. Propargyl Bromides,.. Iodide,.. Acetate,.. Sulphocyanate.

proparoxytone (prəʊpə'rɒksɪtəʊn), *a.* and *sb.* *Gram.* [ad. Gr. προπαροξύτον-ος: see PRO-² and OXYTONE; so F. *proparoxyton.*] **a.** *adj.* In *Gr. Gram.* Having an acute accent on the antepenult. Also applied to words in Latin, and sometimes in other languages, having the tonic accent or stress on that syllable. **b.** *sb.* A word so accented.

1764 W. PRIMATT *Accentus Rediv.* 106 When they [the Ionians] turned proparoxytone nouns of the.. declension in εια into ιη, at the same time they made them paroxytones. **1885** J. LECKY tr. *Paul Pierson* in *Academy* 24 Jan. 65/2 We may even predict that at some period.. there will be nothing but paroxytones and proparoxytones [in French], since these accentuations are now invading even exclamatory and interrogative phrases, while conclusive phrases are barytone already. **1887** 'Q' (QUILLER COUCH) *Dead Man's Rock* 187 It is a great thing for struggling youth to have a three-syllabled name with a proparoxyton accent.

Hence **,proparoxy'tonic**, **†,proparo'xytonous** (*rare*) *adjs.*, having or characterized by proparoxytone accent or stress; **propa'roxytone** *v. trans.*, to accent on the antepenultimate syllable.

1754 H. GALLY *Dissert. agst. pronouncing Grk. Lang. according to Accents* 143 All the Compounds of οικος are proparoxytonous. **1887** A. MOREL-FATIO in *Encycl. Brit.* XXII. 349/2 Castilian may be said to be essentially a paroxytonic language, though it does not altogether refuse proparoxytonic accentuation. **1890** *Cent. Dict.*, *Proparoxytone* vb.

proparte, -tie, obs. forms of PROPERTY.

†pro'passion. *Obs.* [ad. med.L. *prōpassiōn-em*: see PRO-¹ 1 g and PASSION *sb.* Cf. F. *propassion.*] A feeling that precedes or anticipates passion; the first stir or beginning of a passion.

1597 J. KING *On Jonas* (1618) 639 They were rather propassions and entrances into passion than passions, rather infirmities than iniquities. **1627** BP. HALL *Farew. Serm. Fam. Pr. Henry* Wks. 464 As death, so passions are the companions of infirmity: whereupon some that haue beene too nice haue called those which were incident into Christ propassions. **1649** JER. TAYLOR *Gt. Exemp.* II. Disc. ix. 122 Not the first motions are forbidden, the pro-passions, and sudden and irresistible alterations. *a* **1700** EVELYN *Hist. Relig.* (1850) I. 234 For a wise man should not be without his passions, but above them... Keep a steady hand, regulated and free from excess; for so did our Lord and Master; and therefore have divines called them propassions. **1875** H. E. MANNING *Internal Mission of Holy Ghost* xiv. 392 In our Divine Lord there were no passions... We say indeed, that there were in Him pro-passions. **1876** —— *Glories of Sacred Heart* ix. 266 All those pro-passions, as they are called—because the Church never speaks of passions when it speaks of the Sacred Heart.

‖propatagium (prəʊpə'teɪdʒɪəm). *Ornith.* [mod.L. f. PRO-² + PATAGIUM.] The so-called patagium of a bird's wing; = PATAGIUM b. Hence **propa'tagial**, **propa'tagian** *adjs.*, of or pertaining to the propatagium.

1887 *Science* Aug. 71/2 The question as to the function of the propatagial slip. *Ibid.*, A new drawing of the propatagian muscles of the swallows. **1901** *Ibis* Apr. 205 A muscular pectoral slip ends in tendons which reinforce the long and short propatagial tendons.

†'propathy. *Obs. rare.* [ad. Gr. προπάθεια: cf. προπαθεῖν to suffer beforehand. Cf. F. *propathie* a preliminary symptom.] = PROPASSION.

1657 REEVE *God's Plea* 63 Whether.. a mere nescience, pawsing delight or propathy, doe not of it selfe cause sinne. [**1858** MAYNE *Expos. Lex.*, *Propathia*, term for the presentment or first symptoms of a disease: propathy.]

proped ('prəʊpɛd). *Entom. rare.* [ad. mod.L. *prōpēs*, pl. *prōpedēs*, f. PRO-¹ 4 + *pēs*, *ped-em* foot.] = PRO-LEG. Hence **'propedal** *a.*, of or pertaining to the pro-legs.

[**1816** *Propedes*: see PRO-LEG.] **1842** BRANDE *Dict. Sci.* etc., *Propeds*, *Propedes*, the name given by Kirby to the soft, fleshy, inarticulate, pediform appendages of certain larvæ, placed behind the true feet, and disappearing in the mature insects.

propel (prəʊ'pɛl), *v.* [ad. L. *prōpell-ĕre* to drive before one, push or urge forward, f. *prō*, PRO-¹ 1 + *pell-ĕre* to drive.]

†1. *trans.* To drive forth or away; to expel. *Obs.*

c **1440** *Pallad. on Husb.* I. 1034 Fer awey propelle Horrende odour of kichen, bath, gutteris. **1658** PHILLIPS, *Propelled*,.. thrust out, or driven forward. **1666** G. HARVEY *Morb. Angl.* xxx. (1672) 89 Avicen doth witness, the blood to be frothy, thats propell'd out of a Vein of the Breast.

2. To drive forward or onward; to impart an onward motion to; to cause to move onwards.

1658 [see 1]. **1692** BENTLEY *Confut. Atheism* II. (1693) 24 Too feeble and languid to propell so vast and ponderous a Body with that prodigious velocity. **1762–9** FALCONER *Shipwr.* II. 24 Propell'd by flattering gales, the vessel glides. **1790** RUMSEY *Patent Specif.* No. 1738. 2 To cause.. the vibrating water.. to propell the vessel. **1816** R. BUCHANAN (*title*) Treatise on propelling Vessels by Steam. **1822** IMISON *Sc. & Art* I. 225 Among the.. applications of steam is that of propelling vessels by it, without the aid of sails or oars. **1855** MACAULAY *Hist. Eng.* xvi. III. 649 Each galley was propelled by fifty or sixty huge oars.

b. *fig.* To give a forward impulse to; to impel or urge onward; in quot. 1762, to accelerate.

1762 KAMES *Elem. Crit.* I. 389 The rate of succession may be retarded by insisting upon one object, and propelled by dismissing another before its time. **1830** D'ISRAELI *Chas. I* III. xiii. 279 The terror of Romanism propelled Protestantism. **1902** E. R. BEVAN *Ho. Seleucus* II. 158 He was propelled not only by the desire of glory, but by the urgent necessity of money.

propellable (prəʊ'pɛləb(ə)l), *a. rare.* [f. prec. + -ABLE.] Capable of being propelled.

1853–8 HAWTHORNE *Eng. Note-bks.* II. 133 Some [barges] are calculated to be drawn by horses; others are propellable by oars.

propellant (prəʊ'pɛlənt), *a.* and *sb.* Also 7–9 **-ent.** [ad. L. *prōpellent-em*, pr. pple. of *prōpellĕre*: see PROPEL and -ENT. The spelling with *-ant*, contrary to etymology but usual since the mid-19th c., is prob. due to the greater commonness of the suffix -ANT.]

A. *adj.* Propelling, driving forward; *spec.* (of an explosive) Adapted for propelling a bullet, etc. from a fire-arm.

1644 BULWER *Chiron.* 43 The Hand propellent to the leftward. **1858** GREENER *Gunnery* 21 Gunpowder is an explosive propellant compound... The terms, *explosive* and *propellant*,.. are not convertible; for a chemical mixture may possess the explosive power in a much higher degree than the propellant. **1919** R. H. GODDARD in *Smithsonian Misc. Coll.* LXXI. II. 6 This enables high chamber pressures to be employed.. and also permits most of the mass of the rocket to consist of propellant material. **1945** *Soap & Sanitary Chemicals* Apr. 125/3 Methyl chloride is an excellent propellant gas for aerosols to be used against insects out of doors.

B. *sb.* **a.** Something that propels; a propelling agent; *fig.* an incentive, a stimulus; *spec.* an explosive for use in fire-arms.

1814 JEBB in *Knox & J.'s Corr.* II. 189 Providence has placed me in a narrow sphere.. without any of the propellents which variety affords. **1881** GREENER *Gun* 368 In all saloon rifles and pistols the propellant is fulminating powder contained in a small copper case. **1890** *Engineer* 7 Feb. 117 Though not as a military propellant [guncotton] has been used with great success in sporting cartridges. **1917** W. S. CHURCHILL in M. Gilbert *Winston S. Churchill* (1977) IV. Compan. I. 125 What proportion of our total explosive or propellant output could be based upon 10 million gallons of whiskey? **1931** L. H. MORRISON *Amer. Diesel Engines* v. 129 The explosion of these lighter parts of the fuel provides the propellant whereby the remainder of the fuel is injected into the engine cylinder in a finely atomized condition. **1936** W. S. CHURCHILL in *Second World War* (1948) I. 538 By ammunition is meant projectiles (both bombs and shells) and cartridge-cases containing propellent. **1939** W. BEVERIDGE *Blockade & Civilian Population* 8 Fats, broadly speaking, are all directly convertible into munitions, because they can be used, and are very largely used, in making propellants. **1966** *McGraw-Hill Encycl. Sci. & Technol.* V. 153/1 Besides black powder, which is mainly used in sporting rifles, the common gun propellants are either nitrocellulose or a mixture of nitrocellulose and nitroglycerine.

b. A substance that is used (alone, or reacting with another) as a source of the hot gases that provide the thrust in a rocket engine. Cf. FUEL *sb.* 3 c, OXIDIZER 1, MONOPROPELLANT *sb.* and *a.*

1919 R. H. GODDARD in *Smithsonian Misc. Coll.* LXXI. II. 67 Let us assume, for case (a) (many small secondary rockets), as well as for case (b) (large secondary rockets), that the ratio of mass of metal to mass of propellant is the minimum reasonable amount that can be expected. **1948** M. J. ZUCROW *Princ. Jet Propulsion & Gas Turbines* xii. 467 The propellants employed in a rocket motor may be a solid, two liquids (fuel plus oxidizer), or materials containing an adequate supply of available oxygen in their chemical composition (mono-propellants). **1955** *Times* 29 June 16/3 Some five years ago we faced a difficult decision as to the most suitable propellents for the type of rockets which we were developing. **1957** *Space-flight* I. 51/1 A propellant can be either fuel or oxidizer. **1967** *New Scientist* 21 Sept. 594/2 Project officials ordered a series of critical tests to determine just how much propellant would be available for use after the main retrorocket had been fired. **1974** *Sci. Amer.* Aug. 7/1 (Advt.), Launch weight of the spacecraft was only 1,108 pounds, including 66 pounds of propellant and 122 pounds of science instruments.

c. The compressed fluid in an aerosol container or the like that causes its contents to be ejected.

1945 *Soap & Sanitary Chemicals* Apr. 127/1 Nitrous oxide also has a pressure too high for it to be practical as a propellant. **1957** H. R. SHEPHERD in E. Sagarin *Cosmetics Sci. & Technol.* xxxvi. 804 While some aerosol cosmetics are made with a single propellent, it is customary to use a mixture or a solution of propellents. **1966** *McGraw-Hill Encycl. Sci. & Technol.* V. 279/1 In the small first-aid water fire extinguisher, a propellant must be provided. Usually this is carbon dioxide. **1973** *Daily Tel.* 21 Aug. 15/7 The propellent in the anti-perspirant caused freezing in the lung tissues resulting in loss of oxygen and death. *Ibid.* 15/8 A variety of compressed or liquified bases are used in aerosols and technically known as propellents. Most are halogenated hydrocarbons, which are also refrigerants, and sniffing of such propellents is a recognised form of drug abuse in Britain and the United States. **1978** *N.Y. Times* 30 Mar. 62/3 The nitrous-oxide cartridges are made for use as the propellant in restaurant-sized equipment for whipping cream and non-dairy toppings.

propeller (prəʊ'pɛlə(r)). Also **propellor.** [f. PROPEL + -ER¹.]

1. *gen.* One who or that which propels.

c **1815** in W. H. Ireland *Scribbleomania* 6 *note*, To ye, all Authors' known propellers, I tune my lays, renown'd Booksellers! **1863** LYTTON *Misc. Prose Wks.* (1868) III. xx. 235 Every man has in his own temperament peculiar propellers to the movement of his thoughts. **1875** BUCKLAND *Log-bk.* 52 The Kangaroos did not use their tails as propellers. **1879** *Cassell's Techn. Educ.* IV. 6/2 Mr. Brunel was the first man.. in his profession who perceived the capabilities of the screw as a propeller.

2. A mechanical contrivance for propelling something, e.g. for driving machinery, or giving motion to a vehicle. In quot. 1780, a turbine water wheel.

1780 *Patent Specif.* No. 1252 A Grant unto William Bache of Birmingham, for his new invented instrument or machine which he calls by the name of a Propeller. *Ibid.*, Propeller for the use of communicating power to mills, forges, and sundry other important purposes. **1827** *Gentl. Mag.* XCVII. II. 546/1 A triple perch,.. beneath which two propellers, in going up a hill, may be set in motion, somewhat similar to the action of a horse's legs.

3. a. *spec.* An appliance or mechanism for propelling a ship or other vessel, fixed upon the vessel itself and actuated by machinery (usually by a steam-engine); most commonly applied to a revolving shaft with blades, usually three or four set at an angle and twisted like the thread of a screw (also called *screw propeller* or simply *screw*).

1809 FULTON *U.S. Patent Specif.*, The successful construction of steam boats depends on their parts being well proportioned, whether wheels or any other propellers be used. **1838** *Civil Eng. & Arch. Jrnl.* I. 385/1 The engine will be placed amidships,.. and the propeller or paddle, which is under the stern, will be worked by a communicating shaft. **1839** *Mech. Mag.* XXXI. 226 The idea of a screw propeller seems to have been formed very early in the history of steam navigation. **1843** *P. Parley's Ann.* IV. 258 A splendid boat.. of a new construction, having what is called a propeller. **1858** *Pat. Off. Abridgm.*, *Marine Propulsion* 32 In A.D. 1780 Jouffroy used an engine for his boat with the duck foot propeller. **1870** *Daily News* 22 Apr., The City of Brussels left New York on the 28th March, and lost her propeller three days afterwards. **1875** KNIGHT *Dict. Mech.* s.v., In 1729, Dr. John Allen patented the hydraulic propeller, forcing water through the stern of the ship at a convenient distance under water... In 1782, Rumsey propelled a freight-boat on the Potomac by means of the hydraulic propeller..; the water was drawn in at the bow and expelled through a trunk astern. **1885** RUNCIMAN *Skippers & Sh.* 7 The throb of the propeller ceased. **1980** *Daily Tel.* 22 Aug. 2/3 SMM Engineering.. has won an £800,000 order.. for a propellor and a bow steering unit for an 80,000-ton tanker.

b. *transf.* A steamer with a screw propeller.

1860 CAPT. MAURY in *Merc. Marine Mag.* VII. 233 Two propellers.. might be sent out. **1871** *Echo* 15 Dec., On the Welland Canal the ice is three inches thick, and eight propellers and other vessels are locked in.

c. A device on an aeroplane analogous to a ship's propeller in form and function; now always, an airscrew (formerly, a pusher as opposed to a tractor).

1842 W. S. HENSON *Brit. Patent 9478* 2 In the place of the movement or power for onward progress being obtained by movement of the extended surface or plane, as is the case with the wings of birds, I apply suitable paddle wheels or other proper mechanical propellers. **1843** G. CAYLEY in *Mechanics' Mag.* 8 Apr. 278/1 The broad horizontal rudder, or tail, H, capable of being turned on its hinge to any angle, .. gives the power of ascent and descent when the propellers are used. **1853** —— *Let.* 22 June in J. L. Pritchard *Sir George Cayley* (1961) 263 When perfected this toy [*sc.* Chinese flying top] furnishes a very beautiful specimen of the action of the screw propeller in air. **1871** *English Mechanic* 27 Jan. 448/2 Through the instrumentality of the hollow bladed screw-propeller.. shall we.. be enabled to sustain and propel the mechanism which we shall construct, in and through the atmosphere. **1888** H. MIDDLETON *Brit. Patent 9725* 5 Propellors and supporters for flying machines consisting of curved flexible wings with ribs. **1894**, etc. [see *airscrew* s.v. AIR *sb.*¹ B. III. 6]. **1908** H. G. WELLS *War in Air* viii. 271 She.. swept down to the water.. and came.. rolling and.. writhing.., halting and then coming on again, with her torn and bent propeller still beating the air. **1917** R. B. MATTHEWS *Aviation Pocket-bk. 1917* iv. 93 An airscrew is described as a tractor when placed in front of the main planes, and as a propeller when fitted behind. **1928** *Trans. Inst. Mining Engineers* LXXVI. 110 A considerable amount of research-work has been carried out on screw propellors in wind-tunnels. **1937** J. H. YOUNGER et al. *Airplane Maintenance* xv. 298 A propeller develops thrust by its reaction on a mass of air, which it pushes backward. **1968** MILLER & SAWYERS *Technical Devel. Mod. Aviation* vi. 205 The advantage of the turboprop stems essentially from the greater efficiency of the propeller than the jet as a means of propulsion at low speeds and for take-off. **1977** D. ANTHONY *Stud Game* vi. 38 A lounge decorated with.. an ancient propeller Lindbergh might have used.

4. *Angling*. An artificial bait having blades which cause it to rotate when drawn through the water.

1884 KNIGHT *Dict. Mech., Supp.* s.v., 2. (*Fishing.*) Chapman's Reversible Propeller.

5. *attrib.* and *Comb.*, as ***propeller-blade, efficiency, -screw, -shaft, -shafting, steam-ship; propeller-driven*** adj.; **propeller-engine**: see quot.; **propeller fan**, a fan that produces a flow of air parallel to the axis of rotation of its impeller; *esp.* one with the impeller unenclosed or in a very short casing that does not restrict the air flow; **propeller-mower**, a mowing-machine driven or pushed forward by the team: see quot. 1875; **propeller-pump**, a rotary pump in which the wheel resembles a screw propeller; **propeller shaft**, a shaft transmitting power from an engine to a propeller or to the driven wheels of a motor vehicle; **propeller turbine** = TURBOJET; usu. *attrib.*; **propeller-well**, a vertical cavity at the stern of a ship into which the propeller can be hoisted when not in use; **propeller-wheel** (cf. *paddle-wheel*), a screw propeller: see 3.

1898 *Daily News* 8 Aug. 9/5 Sheffield supplies cranks, crank shafts, propeller shafts, *propeller blades, and anchors. **1953** D. O. DOMMASCH *Elem. Propeller & Helicopter Aerodynamics* iii. 69 The development of the turbo-prop engine has made flight at high subsonic Mach numbers possible for *propeller-driven aircraft. **1973** *Black Panther* 13 Oct. 14/2 They had steered 553 in behind a small propeller driven plane. **1909** *Westm. Gaz.* 4 Mar. 4/2 *Propeller efficiency also constitutes one of the most serious drawbacks to the experimenter. **1875** KNIGHT *Dict. Mech.*, **Propeller-engine*, the introduction of the screw-propeller has brought into use a new class of engines of short stroke, a number being ranged in a line coincident with the line of the propeller-shaft. **1897** *Proc. Inst. Mech. Engineers* 469 The *propeller fan was for volume of air without compression, the centrifugal for volume with compression. **1937** C. KELLER et al. *Theory & Performance Axial-Flow Fans* i. 1 In axial-flow or propeller fans the air or gas flows essentially in an axial direction through the fan. **1950** T. H. F. HOLMAN et al. *Textbk. Heating & Ventilating* vi. 77 Fans are of two main types, the propellor fan.. and the centrifugal fan. **1966** W. C. OSBORNE *Fans* ii. 47 Larger propeller fans of up to 24 ft (7·5 m) or more in diameter are often really axial flow fans in very short casings, since such a design is mechanically more satisfactory. *Ibid.*, Large 'propeller' fans are commonly used on cooling towers. **1970** M. G. LUFF *Air Conditioning* viii. 261 In terms of ventilation and air conditioning there are three main types of fan, the propeller fan, the axial flow fan and the centrifugal fan. [**1875** KNIGHT *Dict. Mech.* s.v. *Mower*, One other mode of draft is to be noticed, and that is the propeller, in which the cutting apparatus is ahead of the horses, which push the implement before them.] **1875** KNIGHT *Dict. Mech.*, **Propeller-pump*, a form of rotary pump in which the wheel resembles the propeller-wheel of the marine service. *Ibid.* s.v. *Propeller*, The pitch of a *propeller-screw is the length, measured along the axis, of a complete turn. **1839** *Civil Eng. & Arch. Jrnl.* II. 442/2 The propeller consists now of two half-turns of a thread.. placed diametrically opposite to each other on the *propeller-shaft. **1841** A. S. BYRNE *Best Means Propelling Ships* 17 The propeller shafts may be detached. **1913** A. E. BERRIMAN *Aviation* iii. 24 In monoplanes the propeller-shaft is ordinarily on a level with the middle of the body. **1945** P. H. WILKINSON *Aircraft Engines of World* 345 The drive shaft.. drives the two concentric propeller shafts for the two contra-rotating propellers through planetary spur reduction gears. **1962** *Which? Car Suppl.* Oct. 143/1 New propellor shaft coupling. **1973** *Daily Tel.* 13 July 13 (Advt.), There's no ugly propeller shaft tunnel in the floor of the car to spoil the stretch of deep-pile carpets. **1898** *Daily N.* 9 Mar. 4/5 The Sturgeon.. was disabled last week by an accident to her *propeller shafting. **1851** R. B. FORBES *New Rig* 39, I believe that *propeller steam-ships.. can successfully compete with paddle-wheel steamers. **1945** *Jrnl. R. Aeronaut. Soc.* XLIX. 196/2 Perhaps the large blower of the jet or *propeller turbine unit may encourage the study of boundary layer control possibilities of higher maximum lift coefficients. **1951** *Engineering* 6 July 8/1 The propeller-turbine engine could be expected to improve appreciably in power output and specific weight as combustion temperatures were increased from current values. **1968** MILLER & SAWYERS *Technical Devel. Mod. Aviation* vi. 183 (*heading*) Propeller turbines succeed with the Viscount. *Ibid.*, The propeller-turbine engine was of more immediate interest to the airlines than the jet, and by 1950 the idea of fitting it to existing airplanes like the DC-6 and Constellation was becoming widely accepted in the United States. **1875** KNIGHT *Dict. Mech.*, **Propeller-wheel*, the blades are sections of spiral flanges winding around the shaft like screw-threads... Generally called a screw-propeller.

pro'pelling, *vbl. sb.* and *ppl. a.* [f. PROPEL *v.* + -ING[1], [2].] **a.** *vbl. sb.* The action of PROPEL *v.*; propulsion; also *attrib.* **b.** *ppl. a.* That propels. Also in *Comb.*, as ***propelling pencil***, a mechanical pencil containing a screw by which the lead may be projected and retracted.

1809 FULTON *U.S. Patent Specif.*, I give the preference to a water wheel or wheel with propelling boards. *Ibid.*, The superior advantage of a propelling wheel or wheels. **1827** STEUART *Planter's G.* (1828) 436 These propelling vessels were said to be Arteries, and the returning vessels were considered as Veins. Such is the theory of the circulation of the Sap, held forth by the earlier phytologists. **1837** *Mech. Mag.* 3 June 130 Whether it be great speed or great propelling power. **1877** W. THOMSON *Voy. Challenger* I. i. 58 The propelling engines are.. high-pressure direct-acting vertical engines of six horse-power. **1895** *Montgomery Ward Catal.* 185/1 Men's Propelling and Repelling Pencil.. takes full size and length of lead. **1933** D. L. SAYERS *Murder must Advertise* x. 169 If Bredon really wanted a propelling pencil he ought to get an Eversharp. **1955** S. BECKETT *Molloy* 136 Between my fountain-pen and my propelling-pencil. **1962** L. DEIGHTON *Ipcress File* xi. 71 Murray used a propelling pencil with changeable coloured leads. **1976** M. BUTTERWORTH *Remains to be Seen* ii. 15 Silver propelling-pencil poised over the page.

propelment (prəʊ'pɛlmənt). [f. PROPEL *v.* + -MENT.] **a.** The act of propelling; propulsion. **b.** *concr.* The propelling mechanism of a clock or other recording instrument; *spec.* an escapement in which the pallets drive the escape-wheel (instead of the reverse, as in an ordinary clock).

1890 in *Cent. Dict.*

†**pro'pend**, *v. Obs.* [ad. L. *prōpend-ēre* to hang forward or down, preponderate, be inclined or favourable, f. *prō*, PRO-[1] 1 b + *pend-ēre* to hang.]

1. *intr.* To hang or lean forward or downward; to incline or tend in a particular direction; of a scale, to weigh down, preponderate.

1545 RAYNOLD *Byrth Mankynde* 12 This seme or lyne.. propendyng, helding, hangyng or lokyng downward in to ye vault or amplytude of ye womb. **1599** SANDYS *Europæ Spec.* (1632) 48 To make that part the heavier, to which they shall propend. **1621** BURTON *Anat. Mel.* III. ii. II. i, His eyes are like a balance, apt to propend each way, and to be weighed down with every wench's looks. **1650** FULLER *Pisgah* III. i. 315 The heart.. is not so unpartially in the midst of the body, but that.. it propends to the left side. *a* **1691** BOYLE *Hist. Air* (1692) 95 [To] shew the quantity of the angle, by which when the scales propend either way, the tongue declines from the perpendicular.

2. *fig.* To have a 'leaning' or propensity; to incline, be disposed, tend (*to* or *towards* something, or *to do* something).

1606 SHAKS. *Tr. & Cr.* II. ii. 190, I propend to you In resolution to keepe Helen still. *a* **1619** FOTHERBY *Atheom.* I. ix. §1 (1622) 60 The most part of the learned did propende to that opinion. **1642** FULLER *Holy & Prof. St.* III. xiii. 185 Some sports.. more propend to be ill than well used. *a* **1711** KEN *Edmund* Poet. Wks. 1721 II. 124 Corrupted Nature might to Lust propend. **1824** LANDOR *Imag. Conv., Louis xiv & Father la Chaise* Wks. 1846 I. 150/1 If.. anyone.. is convinced of the contrary, or propends to believe so. **1844** KINGLAKE *Eöthen* xii. (1845) 174 As I went down.. from Tiberias to Jerusalem.. my thinking all propended to the ancient world of herdsmen and warriors.

Hence †**pro'pended** *ppl. a.* (*fig.*), inclined, disposed (= PROPENSE *a.* 1); †**pro'pending** *ppl. a.* (*lit.* and *fig.*: see senses above).

1681 H. MORE *Exp. Dan.* vi. Notes 216 He is more propending to the opinion that Chittim signifies the Romans. **1682** T. GIBSON *Anat.* (1697) 25 Its propending part must.. imitate the bottom of a pouch. **1693** BEVERLEY *True St. Gosp. Truth* 36 Others.. desirous, and most propended to be Teachers of the Law. *a* **1711** KEN *Edmund* Poet. Wks. 1721 II. 248 Their Souls on mutually propending Wings, Made tow'rds each other sympathetick Springs.

†**pro'pendence**. *Obs. rare*[−1]. [f. as prec. + -ENCE.] The fact of hanging forward or out.

1615 CROOKE *Body of Man* 204 Another vse of their propendence or hanging out.

†**pro'pendency**. *Obs. rare.* [f. as prec. + -ENCY.] **a.** Inclination, tendency. **b.** Weighing, deliberation.

1660 tr. *Amyraldus' Treat. conc. Relig.* III. i. 305 When a thing is equally counterpoised on both sides.. to determine the dubious propendency he observes in it. *a* **1677** HALE *Prim. Orig. Man.* I. ii. 57 An act far above the animal actings, which are sudden and transient, and admit not of that attention, *mora*, and propendency of actions.

propendent (prəʊ'pɛndənt), *a.* Also 6 erron. **-ant**. [ad. L. *prōpendēnt-em*, pres. pple. of *prōpendēre*: see PROPEND and -ENT.]

1. Hanging forward, outward, or downward.

1593 NASHE *Christ's T.* 32 So did theyr propendant breast-bones imminent-ouer-canopy theyr bellies. **1650** BULWER *Anthropomet.* 122 The Lips.. besieged with such long and propendent Mustachos. **1745** tr. *Columella's Husb.* VII. xii, [A dog] with dejected and propendent ears. **1840** PAXTON *Bot. Dict.*, *Propendent*, hanging forwards and downwards. **1846** WORCESTER cites LOUDON.

†**2.** *fig.* Inclining or inclined to something: = PROPENSE *a.* 1. *Obs. rare.*

17.. SOUTH (cited by Webster 1864).

propene ('prəʊpiːn). *Chem.* [f. as PROP-ANE + -ENE.] The olefine C_3H_6, more commonly called PROPYLENE. Also *attrib.*

1866 HOFMANN in *Proc. Royal Soc.* XV. 58 *note.* **1873** WATTS *Fownes' Chem.* (ed. 11) 596 The iodide may also be produced by the action of hydriodic acid on isopropyl alcohol, allyl iodide, propene, or propene alcohol.

†**propen'sation**. *Obs. rare*[−1]. [Bad formation.] = PROPENSION 1.

1650 R. STAPYLTON *Strada's Low C. Warres* IX. 43 He,.. in riding the great horse, and practising his weapon, more delighted to exercise his body, then his mind. (*margin*) Propensation [*mispr.* Prospensation] to Armes.

propense (prəʊ'pɛns), *a.* Now *rare.* Also 6–7 **propence**. [ad. L. *prōpens-us* hanging toward, inclining, inclined; disposed, prone, favourable, pa. pple. of *prōpend-ēre*: see PROPEND.]

1. Having an inclination, bias, or propensity to something; inclined, disposed, prone; ready, willing. Const. *to*, with *sb.* or *inf.*; rarely *towards*.

1528 FOX in Pocock *Rec. Ref.* I. liii. 143 His holiness was.. much propence to satisfy his majesty therein. *c* **1540** tr. *Pol. Verg. Eng. Hist.* (Camden) I. 86 A manne of nature somwhat to propense to the desier of glorie. *c* **1624** LUSHINGTON *Recant. Serm.* in *Phenix* (1708) II. 496 A propense and earnest Concurrence jointly to prosecute the same Good. **1671** MILTON *Samson* 455 Feeble hearts, propense anough before To waver, or fall off and joyn with Idols. **1756** JOHNSON *K. of Prussia* Wks. IV. 549 He appears always propense towards the side of mercy. **1830** FOSTER in *Life & Corr.* (1846) II. 191, I am.. little.. capable of forming.. new friendships;.. I have never been propense to contract them. **1869** GOULBURN *Purs. Holiness* xii. 111 Certain forms of sin to which all persons of strong passions.. are naturally propense.

†**b.** Inclined or biased in favour of some person, cause, etc.; propitious, favourable, partial. *Obs.*

1555 EDEN *Decades* 278 With propense and frendly persuasions. **1670** FLAMSTEED in Rigaud *Corr. Sci. Men* (1841) II. 97, I fear he was partial to Tycho, because a Calvinist, and propense to Claromontius. *a* **1797** H. WALPOLE *Mem. Geo. III* (1845) III. iv. 96 However Rigby had charged Conway with being subservient to the Favorite, no man living was less propense to him.

†**c.** Liable, subject (*to* physical influence). *Obs.*

1568 SKEYNE *The Pest* A iij, Thingis, quhilkis makis ane man propense to becum Pestilential. *a* **1713** ELLWOOD *Autobiog.*, etc. (1885) 230 Things subject to exterior sense Are to mutation most propense.

†**2.** [By association with the verbs PURPENSE, PREPENSE (q.v.), or their pa. pples.] Premeditated, deliberate, intentional: = PREPENSE *a.* *Obs.*

1650 BULWER *Anthropomet.* Ded., You will soon discern the propense malice of Satan in it. **1752** J. LOUTHIAN *Form of Process* (ed. 2) 33 Out of a murdering Design, and from a propense and premeditate Malice.

†**pro'pensed**, *ppl. a. Obs.* Also 6 **propenced**. [f. as prec. + -ED[1] 2.]

1. Favourably inclined or disposed; = prec. 1.

1530 WOLSEY in Ellis *Orig. Lett.* Ser. II. II. 33 Your most excellent nature wych hath ever be moved and propensyd to clemency and mercy.

2. [Associated with PURPENSED, PREPENSED.] Premeditated, purposed; deliberate; = prec. 2.

1512 *Helyas* in Thoms *Prose Rom.* (1828) III. 72 The treason and falsnesse that.. was propenced against me. **1567** THROCKMORTON in *Cal. Scott. Pap.* (1900) II. 369 Yff her majestie be pleasyd to dyffeste me my doyngs here, off propensyd intent (wyche God forbyd) I am les able to answer [etc.].

propensely (prəʊ'pɛnslı), *adv.* Now *rare.* [f. PROPENSE *a.* + -LY[2].]

1. With inclination or propensity; pronely.

1675 EVELYN *Terra* (1729) 35 They but too propensely sink of themselves. **1754** BLACKLOCK *Hymn Supreme Being* Poems 15 Thou behold'st the whole propensely tend To perfect happiness, its glorious end. **1829** LANDOR *Imag. Conv., Epicurus, Leontion & T.* Wks. 1846 I. 504/1 You.. will have leaned the more propensely toward this opinion.

†**2.** Premeditatedly, intentionally: = PREPENSELY. (See PROPENSE *a.* 2.) *Obs.*

1694 tr. *Milton's Lett. State* M.'s Wks. 1851 VII. 263 Nor can we apprehend.. that the Blood of the Innocent, shed by a propensely malicious Murder, is not to be aveng'd. **1775** S. J. PRATT *Liberal Opin.* cxvii. (1783) IV. 99 One fellow-creature set his heart propensely against another! **1824** LANDOR *Imag. Conv., Eliz. & Cecil* Wks. 1846 I. 28/2 Those are the worst of suicides, who voluntarily and propensely stab or suffocate their fame.

3. Favourably, readily. *nonce-use.*

1922 JOYCE *Ulysses* 409 If I had poor luck with Bass's mare, perhaps this draught of his may serve me more propensely.

propenseness (prəʊ'pɛnsnıs). Now *rare.* [f. as prec. + -NESS.] The quality of being propense.

1. Proneness, inclination, propensity; favourable disposition; liability.

1568 SKEYNE *The Pest* (1860) 13 Greit appetit, and propensnes to sleip. **1624** DONNE *Devotions*, etc. (ed. 2) 538 There is a propensnesse to diseases in the body. **1681** FLAVEL *Meth. Grace* xvii. 314 A prayer.. conceived in the heart, and not yet uttered.., is often anticipated by the propenseness of free grace. **1858** BUSHNELL *Serm. New Life* 81 Consider the vice of envy, and the general propenseness of men to be in it.

†**2.** Premeditatedness, deliberateness. (See PROPENSE *a.* 2.) *Obs.*

1708 *Brit. Apollo* No. 102. 1/1 The Sin of Cursing is.. aggravated by the Propenseness of the Malice.

propension (prəʊ'pɛnʃən). Now *rare.* [= F. *propension* (1595 in Godef. *Compl.*), ad. L. *prōpensiōn-em* inclination, propensity, n. of action f. *prōpendēre*: see PROPEND.]

1. The action, fact, or quality of 'propending' or inclining to something; inclination, 'leaning', propensity. **a.** = PROPENSITY 1 a.

c **1530** WOLSEY in Ellis *Orig. Lett.* Ser. I. II. 11 Knowyng hys Graces excellent propensyon to pyte and mercy. **1580** BABINGTON *Exp. Lord's Prayer* (1596) 144 In respect of our great propension to abuse his plenty. **1640** GLAPTHORNE *Wallenstein* IV. iii, I feele A strong propension in my braine, to court Sleepe. *a* **1677** HALE *Contempl.* II. 57 There are certain..Propensions in our Natures after certain Objects. **1705** STANHOPE *Paraphr.* (1709) IV. 268 A strong Propension to Sensuality. **1837** WHEWELL *Hist. Induct. Sc.* II. 48 The impetus, energy, momentum, or propension to motion.

b. Favourable inclination; = PROPENSITY 1 b.

1606 J. KING *Serm. Sept.* 43 Wheresoeuer they haue met with any word..that beareth any..propension and fauour towards the vpholding of the eldership. **1652–62** HEYLIN *Cosmogr.* III. (1673) 56/1 The natural propension of the People to one of their own Nation. **1759** B. STILLINGFL. *Misc. Tracts* (1775) 358 The propension of cattle to this or that plant. **1867** STUBBS *Lect. Med. & Mod. Hist.* (1886) 18 The political slang which each side uses to express their aversions and their propensions.

c. Liability, tendency; = PROPENSITY 1 c.

1626 BACON *Sylva* IX. Introd., The aptness or propension of air or water to corrupt or putrefy. **1661** FELTHAM *Resolves* II. xxviii. (ed. 8) 239 Bodies planted aboue the vapourous Orb of Air..rest there..without propension of descent, or falling. **1684** tr. *Bonet's Merc. Compit.* XIV. 506 When you see the propension of Nature, you may come safely to Diureticks.

†**2.** Tendency to move in some direction or to take some position; inclination, as of the scale of a balance. (Cf. PROPENSITY 2.) *Obs.*

1644 DIGBY *Nat. Bodies* x. (1658) 103 Bodies that of themselves have no propension unto any determinate place. **1678** HOBBES *Decam.* viii. 89 He defines Gravity to be a Natural propension towards the Centre of the Earth. **1705** C. PURSHALL *Mech. Macrocosm* 269 If the Needle were under the Equator, it would have no Propension more one way than another. **1709** *Phil. Trans.* XXVI. 324 A certain propension which some things have to one another, whereby they attract, retain, and alter each other.

Hence †**pro'pensioner** *Obs.*, one who or that which has or causes a propension to something.

1657 *Divine Lover* 21 To the greate..comfort of such an Interior Propensioner, and God-thirstinge soule.

†**pro'pensitude.** *Obs. rare.* [f. L. *prōpens-us*, PROPENSE + -TUDE.] = PROPENSENESS, PROPENSITY. **a.** Mental inclination, liking. **b.** Physical inclination, leaning.

1607 MARSTON *What you will* II. ii, An you have a propensitude to him, he shall be for you. **1683** MOXON *Mech. Exerc., Printing* xxiv. ¶2 If it have a propensitude to one side more than another, the declivety is on that side.

propensity (prəʊ'pɛnsɪtɪ). [f. as prec. + -ITY: so It. *propensità* (Florio).]

1. The quality or character of being 'propense' or inclined to something; inclination, disposition, tendency, bent. Const. *to*, *towards* (rarely *for*, *of*) with *sb.*, or *to* with *inf.* **a.** Disposition or inclination to some action, course of action, habit, etc.; bent of mind or nature.

1612 T. TAYLOR *Comm. Titus* iii. 1 A propensitie, and disposition to euery good worke. **1715** DE FOE *Fam. Instruct.* I. i. (1841) I. 21 A natural propensity in us to do evil. **1774** WARTON *Hist. Eng. Poetry* III. xxi. 42 An early propensity to polite letters and poetry. **1813** SYD. SMITH *Wks.* (1867) I. 225 That dreadful propensity which young men have for writing verses. **1844** LD. BROUGHAM *Brit. Const.* xiv. (1862) 199 He could gratify his propensity to accumulate. **1856** KANE *Arct. Expl.* I. xxix. 391 From my knowledge of the hugging propensity of the plantigrades.

b. Disposition to favour, benefit, or associate oneself with some person, party, etc.; favourable inclination, good will.

1570 FOXE *A. & M.* (ed. 2) 1219/2 Of good will and mere propensitye of hart..he is..ready to forewarne your grace. **1678** *Trans. Crt. Spain* 169 Your zeal and propensity in the service of the King and State. **1709** STRYPE *Ann. Ref.* I. x. 132 Knowing the forwardness of the Duke's nature, and his great propensity towards him. **1757** GRAY *Wks.* (1825) II. 199 If I had any little propensity it was to Julie. **1827** MOORE *Mem.* (1854) V. 236 Lord Liverpool, with all his kingly propensities, could do this [manage the King] upon occasion.

c. Tendency or liability to some physical condition or action.

1660 SHARROCK *Vegetables* 141 Why have those plants..a propensity of sending forth roots? **1731** ARBUTHNOT *Aliments* vi. (1735) 170 A great Propensity to the putrescent alkaline Condition of the Fluids.

†**2.** Tendency to move in some particular direction: cf. PROPENSION 2. *Obs. rare.*

1647 H. MORE *Poems* 163 Nature..Binding all close with down-propensities.

†**3.** An overhanging part. *Obs. rare.*

1771 LUCKOMBE *Hist. Print.* 241 The *P* is kerned, that its propensity may cover the back of the protruding angle of *A*.

†**pro'pensive,** *a. Obs.* [f. as prec. + -IVE.]

1. Having an inclination; = PROPENSE 1.

1599 NASHE *Lenten Stuffe* 12 Edward the thirde, of his propensiue minde towardes them, vnited to Yarmouth Kirtley roade. **1683** TRYON *Way to Health* 44 He that doth know..to what his Inclinations are most naturally propensive,..may thereby..shun many Inconveniences.

2. Hanging or leaning forward. *rare*$^{-1}$.

1819 H. BUSK *Banquet* III. 31 The shaft, propensive from the lightning's stroke, In vain outlives its taller rival oak.

propenyl ('prəʊpɪnɪl). *Chem.* [f. PROPENE + -YL.] The hypothetical hydrocarbon radical $C_3H_5(CH_3{\cdot}CH{=}CH)$, the trivalent hydrocarbon radical of the propyl or trityl series. Chiefly *attrib.* or in *Comb.*

1866 HOFMANN in *Proc. Royal Soc.* XV. 58 *note.* **1877** WATTS *Fownes' Chem.* (ed. 12) II. 23 Names..of the trivalent radicles [formed] by changing the final *e* in the names of the bivalent radicles, methene, etc., into *-yl*..CH''' Methenyl, C_2H_3''' Ethenyl, C_3H_5''' Propenyl [etc.]. *Ibid.* 24 Among these [nitrils] special mention must be made of a group consisting of nitrogen combined with a trivalent hydrocarbon-radicle, such as (CH)N Methenyl nitril, $(C_2H_3)N$ Ethenyl nitril, $(C_3H_5)N$ Propenyl nitril... = $CN.C_2H_5$ Ethyl cyanide. **1894** MUIR & MORLEY *Watts' Dict. Chem.* IV. 309 Propenyl Phenol = Anethol. *Ibid.*, Propenyl Bromide = Bromo-propylene C_3H_5Br. *Ibid.*, Propenyl Carbinol = Butenyl Alcohol.

Hence '**propenyla,mine,** the amine or compound ammonia of propenyl, $CH_3{\cdot}CH{=}CH{\cdot}NH_2$.

propeptone: see PRO-[2] 1.

proper ('prɒpə(r)), *a.* (*adv.*, *sb.*) Forms: 3–6 propre (4–6 propir(e, -yr(e, -ur(e, 6 propper), 4– proper. [ME. *propre*, a. F. *propre* (11–12th c. in Hatz.-Darm.):—L. *propri-us* one's own, special, particular, peculiar, whence It., Sp., Pg. *proprio*.

The sense had already undergone great development in Latin, Romanic, and French, before the word was taken into Eng., where the chronological appearance of the senses does not correspond with the logical development. As it happens, our earliest evidence for the word appears in the adv. PROPERLY sense 3, corresp. to 10 of the adj.]

A. *adj.* **I. 1.** Belonging to oneself or itself; (one's or its) own; owned as property; that is the, or a, property or quality of the thing itself, intrinsic, inherent. Usually preceded by a possessive (cf. OWN *a.* 1); sometimes also by *own. arch.* exc. in special connexions (chiefly scientific).

proper motion (Astron.), that part of the apparent motion of a heavenly body (now usually of a 'fixed' star) supposed to be due to its actual movement in space; any observed motion of a star other than those due to the rotation of the earth, to parallax, and to aberration. ***in proper person*** (L. *in propriā persōnā*), in his (or one's) own person. † ***proper thing*** = one's own thing, a property.

a **1300** *Cursor M.* 562 (Cott.) An saul has propre thinges [= properties] thre. *Ibid.* 18765 Wit his aun propur might, He stei up in þair aller sight. *c* **1330** R. BRUNNE *Chron.* (1810) 325 To haf in heritage,..als a propire þing, þat were conquest tille him. **1340** HAMPOLE *Pr. Consc.* 4958 For to sytte in dome in proper parsoun. *c* **1400** MAUNDEV. v. (1839) 37 With his own propre Swerd he was slayn. **1531** TINDALE *Expos. 1 John* ii. 21 (1538) 46 b, Some call themselues poore, wythout hauynge ony thynge proper. **1604** E. G[RIMSTONE] *D'Acosta's Hist. Indies* III. vii. 141 This proper and equal motion of the heaven. *Ibid.* IV. xxxiii. 300 Neither have they any master to whom they are proper. **1610** SHAKS. *Temp.* III. iii. 60 Euen with such like valour, men hang, and drowne Their proper selues. **1691** WOOD *Ath. Oxon.* II. 700 The said leiger-book which was then my proper book, is now in Bodlies Library. **1718** G. SEWELL *Proclam. Cupid* 9 Ill is the Bird that soils his proper Nest. **1783** HERSCHEL in *Phil. Trans.* LXXIII. 267 Astronomers have..observed what they call a proper motion in several of the fixed stars. **1850** TENNYSON *In Mem.* xxvi, To shroud me from my proper scorn. **1877** MRS. OLIPHANT *Makers Flor.* iii. 79 (transl. Dante) To judge..with my proper eyes. **1881** PIAZZI SMYTH in *Nature* XXIV. 430/1 He concludes that the cause of the 'proper' light of the comet is the illumination of its constituent molecules by electric discharge. **1893** SIR R. BALL *Story of Sun* 335 One of those stars which has a considerable proper motion.

2. a. Belonging or relating to the person or thing in question distinctively (more than to any other), or exclusively (not to any other); special, particular, distinctive, characteristic; peculiar, restricted; private, individual; of its own. Opp. to *common*. Const. *to*.

In liturgies, applied to a service, psalm, lesson, etc., specially appointed for a particular day or season. (See also C. 2, and PREFACE *sb.* 1.) In quot. 1377, = several, separate, distinct: cf. PROPERLY 1 b.

a **1300** *Cursor M.* 24921 (Cott.) Sai me..qua[t]kinwise Of hir we sal mak þis seruis, Sin þar es propre nan i knau. **1377** LANGL. *P. Pl.* B. x. 237 Three propre persones, ac nouȝt in plurel noumbre, For al is but on god, and eche is god hymselue. **1390** GOWER *Conf.* III. 100 The dreie Colre.. his propre sete Hath in the galle. *c* **1400** MAUNDEV. (Roxb.) xvii. 77 Þe folk of Caldee has a propre langage and propre lettres and figures. **1548–9** (Mar.) *Bk. Com. Prayer*, *Morn. Prayer*, Then shal folow certaine Psalmes in ordre as they been appointed..except there be propre Psalmes appointed for that day. **1607** TOPSELL *Four-f. Beasts* (1658) 3 Their feet are proper, and not like mans,..for they are like great hands. **1672** SIR T. BROWNE *Let. Friend* §14 Endemial and local Infirmities proper unto certain Regions. **1760** J. LEE *Introd. Bot.* I. viii. (1765) 16 A Proper Receptacle, is that which belongs only to the Parts of a single Fructification. **1830** LINDLEY *Nat. Syst. Bot.* 171 Flowers..having an involucrum which is either common or proper. **1870** TYNDALL *Electricity* §66. 13 The notion of two kinds of electricity, one proper to vitreous bodies,..the other proper to resinous bodies. *Mod.* Hymns, with proper Tunes. The Psalms and Canticles, with proper Chants.

b. *Gram.* Applied to a name or noun which is used to designate a particular individual object (e.g. a person, a tame animal, a star, planet, country, town, river, house, ship, etc.). Opposed to COMMON *a.* 17 a.

A proper name is written with an initial capital letter. The same proper name may be borne by many persons in different families or generations, or by several places in different countries or localities; but it does not connote any qualities common to and distinctive of the persons or things which it denotes. A proper name may however receive a connotation from the qualities of an individual so named, and be used as a common noun, as a Hercules, a Cæsar (Kaiser, Czar), a Calvary, an atlas.

c **1290** *S. Eng. Leg.* I. 462/18 Heo was icleoped in propre name 'þe Maudeleyne'. *c* **1440** *Promp. Parv.* 70/1 Charlys, propyr name, *Carolus.* **1551** T. WILSON *Logike* (1580) 4 b, In this Proposition *Cato* is the Nowne proper, whiche belongeth to one manne onely. **1690** LOCKE *Hum. Und.* III. iii. §5 If we had Reason to mention particular Horses, as often as..particular Men, we should have proper Names for the one, as familiar as for the other; and Bucephalus would be a Word as much in use, as Alexander. **1720** WATERLAND *Eight Serm.* 117 Supposing Jehovah to be meerly a proper name. **1843** MILL *Logic* I. v. §2 Proper names have strictly no meaning: they are mere marks for individual objects.

c. *Physics.* (See quot. 1924.) [tr. G. *eigen*(*zeit*) proper (time) (H. Minkowski 1908, in *Nachr. von der k. Ges. der Wissensch. zu Gottingen* (Math.-phys. Klasse) 103).]

1916 *Monthly Notices R. Astron. Soc.* LXXVI. 704 The element *ds* integrated along the geodetic line gives $s = \int ds$. This is what Minkowski calls the proper-time of the material particle. **1923** *Proc. R. Soc.* A. CII. 530 Where *m* and (− *e*) are the 'proper mass' and charge of the electron respectively. **1924** A. S. EDDINGTON *Math. Theory Relativity* i. 34 Quantities referred to the space-time system of an observer moving with the body considered are often distinguished by the prefix proper- (German, *Eigen-*), e.g. proper-length, proper-volume, proper-density, proper-mass = invariant mass. **1942** P. G. BERMAN *Introd. Theory Relativity* iv. 41 Whenever the two events can be just connected by a light ray which leaves the site of one event at the time it occurs and arrives at the site of the other event as it takes place, the proper time interval τ_{12} between them vanishes. **1952** C. MØLLER *Theory of Relativity* iv. 137 While q^0/c^2 expresses the source density of proper mass, we see that the source density for relativistic mass is $((\mathbf{f.u}) + q)/c^2$. **1964** W. G. V. ROSSER *Introd. Theory Relativity* iii. 102, l_0..is the length of the fish measured in the coordinate system in which it is at rest; l_0 is called the proper length of the fish, whilst l..is the length of the fish measured in an inertial reference frame relative to which the fish is moving with uniform velocity. **1970** *Nature* 17 Oct. 272/1 Proper mass (equivalently, rest-mass, proper energy, or rest-energy) is the most important Lorentz-invariant scalar associated with any system.

3. *Her.* Represented in the natural colouring, not in any of the conventional tinctures.

1572 BOSSEWELL *Armorie* II. 95 b, Twoo Cypres trees raguled Solis, enwrapped with Ivy proper. **1610** GUILLIM *Heraldry* III. xii. (1611) 123 By proper is euermore vnderstood his naturall colour. **1688** R. HOLME *Armoury* III. 409/1 The City of Oxford beareth Azure, a Book open, proper; with seven Seals between three Crowns Or. *c* **1710** CELIA FIENNES *Diary* (1888) 193 A turkey Cock on each Cut in stone and painted proper. **1864** BOUTELL *Her. Hist. & Pop.* xvii. §2. 272 A peacock in its pride, proper.

4. *Math.* and *Physics.* Used in collocations as a translation of G. *eigen* own, proper, characteristic.

a. Applied to a vibration or oscillation: = NORMAL *a.* 2 c.

1873 *Proc. London Math. Soc.* IV. 258 The problem of determining the proper tones of any spherical cavity bounded by rigid walls. **1909** *Westm. Gaz.* 4 Sept. 10/1 All elastic bodies, including metals, when made fast at one end, vibrate when subjected to a shock from outside. The vibrations so caused are what are known as proper vibrations. **1962** S.-I. TOMONAGA *Quantum Mech.* I. i. 16 It was possible to arrange the proper oscillations in order by giving each of them an integral number *s* which has the physical meaning that $(s - 1)$ is the number of nodes of the oscillation.

b. = EIGEN-, as ***proper function*** = EIGENFUNCTION; ***proper value*** = EIGENVALUE.

1930 RUARK & UREY *Atoms, Molecules & Quanta* xv. 526 Such an aggregate of E values is often referred to as a 'spectrum of characteristic values', or 'proper values'. **1935** PAULING & WILSON *Introd. Quantum Mech.* iii. 58 The functions $\psi_s(x)$ which satisfy Equation 9-8 and also certain auxiliary conditions..are variously called wave functions or eigenfunctions (Eigenfunktionen), or sometimes amplitude functions, characteristic functions, or proper functions. **1938** [see EIGENVALUE]. **1958** [see LATENT *a.* i]. **1975** GRAY & ISAACS *New Dict. Physics* 574/1, ψ must always be finite... The integral of $|\psi|^2$ over all space must be equal to 1... Wave functions obtained when these conditions are applied are called proper wave functions and form a set of characteristic functions of the Schrödinger wave equation. These are often called eigenfunctions and correspond to a set of fixed energy values in which the system may exist, called eigenvalues (proper values).

II. 5. a. Strictly belonging or applicable; that is in conformity with rule; strict, accurate, exact, correct; †literal, not metaphorical (*obs.*).

c **1449** PECOCK *Repr.* II. v. 166 In properist maner of speking. **1563** WINȜET *Four Scoir Thre Quest.* §4 Wks. (S.T.S.) I. 72 Qvhy diminiss ȝe or takis away..the trew and propir sentence fra ws, of this part of our Catholik beleif? **1579** FULKE *Heskins' Parl.* 236 The sense of that place is proper, and not figuratiue. **1581** [see IMPROPER *a.* 1]. **1768** PENNANT in *Phil. Trans.* LVIII. 96 The proper name of these birds is Pinguin... It has been corrupted to Penguin. **1828** MISS MITFORD *Village* Ser. III. 43 As I was walking along the common—blown along would be the properer phrase. **1875** *Encycl. Brit.* II. 272/2 Arachnids are not, in a proper sense, subject to metamorphosis.

†**b.** Very, identical. *Obs.*

1523 LD. BERNERS *Froiss.* I. cclxxxv. 426 The same proper night Sir Thomas Grantson was departed. **1582** STANYHURST *Æneis* I. (Arb.) 29 But loa, the proper image of corps vntumbed apeered In dreame to Dido. **1849** ROBERTSON *Serm.* Ser. I. x. (1866) 178 Act..like his proper self.

6. a. To which the name accurately belongs; strictly so called, in the strict use of the word; genuine, true, real; regular, normal. In mod. use often following its noun. † *proper chant* (obs.): see PROPERCHANT.

a **1400-50** *Alexander* 367 May þou hald me þis hest.. And profe þus in my presens as a propire sothe. *c* **1449** PECOCK *Repr.* 189 It is leeful in proprist maner of lefulnes that Pilgrimagis be doon. **1609** BIBLE (Douay) *Ps.* xciii. Comm., The Holie Ghost is the proper auctor, and a man is the writer. **1734** SALE *Koran* Prelim. Disc. §1 (Chandos) 1 Proper Arabia is by the oriental writers divided into five provinces. **1752** P. PETIT *Hebrew Guide* Nj, Vowels are X Proper.. and IV Improper, i.e. which are scarcely sounded. **1807** T. THOMSON *Chem.* (ed. 3) II. 89 The earths proper do not unite with oxygen... Characters of the alkaline and proper earths. **1849** RUSKIN *Sev. Lamps* i. §1. 7 Extending principles which belong..to building, into the sphere of architecture proper. **1850** ROBERTSON *Serm.* Ser. III. vii. 101 Rome asserts that in the mass a true and proper sacrifice is offered. **1899** *Allbutt's Syst. Med.* VII. 458 The concussion ..may be limited either to the cerebrum proper, or to the medulla and pons.

b. *Arith.* ***proper fraction***, a fraction whose value is less than unity, the numerator being less than the denominator.

proper prime: applied by W. H. H. Hudson to a prime number such that, when it is the denominator of a vulgar fraction, the recurring period of the equivalent decimal fraction consists of the highest possible number of figures, i.e. one less than such prime.

1674 JEAKE *Arith.* (1701) 44 Proper Fractions always have the Numerator less than the Denominator, for then the parts signified are less than an Unit or Integer. *Ibid.* 169 Nevertheless this is to be understood of Proper Fractions. **1827** HUTTON *Course Math.* I. 52. **1864** W. H. H. HUDSON in *Messenger of Math.* II. 1 If the period of d consist of $d - 1$ places, d is called *a proper prime*.

c. *Math.* (i) Applied to any subset (subgroup, etc.) that does not constitute the entire set.

1906 W. H. & G. C. YOUNG *Theory of Sets of Points* iii. 16 A set which is contained entirely in another set is called a component of the latter set, and, if there are points of the latter set not belonging to the former set, it is said to be a proper component of the other. **1937** R. D. CARMICHAEL *Introd. Theory of Groups of Finite Order* i. 28 A subgroup of G which is not identical with G is called a proper subgroup of G. **1953** A. A. FRAENKEL *Abstract Set Theory* i. 21 A subset of S which is different from S, is called a proper subset. **1965** B. MITCHELL *Theory of Categories* i. 6 If the monomorphism $\alpha: A' \to A$ is not an isomorphism, we shall call A' a proper subobject of A.

(ii) Applied to a subgroup (subring, etc.) that does not constitute the entire group, and has more than one element.

1953 W. LEDERMANN *Introd. Theory of Finite Groups* ii. 31 Every group G has two trivial or improper subgroups namely, G itself and the group which consists of the unit element by itself ($I^2 = I$); all other subgroups are called proper subgroups. **1965** PATTERSON & RUTHERFORD *Elem. Abstract Algebra* ii. 39 A subgroup of G other than G or E is called a proper subgroup. *Ibid.* iii. 100 Every non-zero ring has two ideals, namely the ring itself and the subset consisting of 0 alone. Any ideal which is not one of these two is called a proper ideal.

7. Answering fully to the description; thorough, complete, perfect, out-and-out; cf. 8. Now *slang* or *colloq.*

1375 BARBOUR *Bruce* II. 377 Quhen the king his folk has sene Begyn to faile, for propyr tene, Hys assenȝhe gan he cry. *c* **1385** CHAUCER *L.G.W.* Prol. 259 (MS. Gg. 4. 27) He nys but a verray propre fole. *c* **1470** HENRY *Wallace* III. 166 Throw matelent, and werray propyr ire. *a* **1683** OWEN *Exp. Heb.* (1790) III. 194 Not to be thankful for gifts is the most proper, that is, the most base ingratitude. *a* **1825** FORBY *Voc. E. Anglia* s.v., 'The mischievous boy got a proper licking'. 'Tom is a proper rogue'. **1853** MISS YONGE *Heir of Redclyffe* xliii, Old Markham seems in a proper taking. **1871** *Routledge's Ev. Boy's Ann.* Jan. 45 There will be a proper blow-up about this.

8. a. Such as a thing of the kind should be; excellent, admirable, commendable, capital, fine, goodly, of high quality. (Also ironically: cf. *fine.*) Now *arch.* or *vulgar.*

c **1375** *Sc. Leg. Saints* xxxvi. (*Baptista*) 243 John þe propereste profit was Of al þat aperit in manis flesch. **1377** LANGL. *P. Pl.* B. XIII. 51 'Here is propre seruice', quod pacience, 'þer fareth no prynce bettere'. *c* **1384** CHAUCER *H. Fame* II. 218, I wille Tellen the a propre skille. **1523** LD. BERNERS *Froiss.* I. cvii. 129 Ther wes many a proper feat of armes done. *a* **1548** HALL *Chron., Edw. V* 16b, She had a proper wytte & coulde both reade and wryte. **1577-87** HOLINSHED *Chron.* II. 40/2 A good humanician, and a proper philosopher. **1593** SHAKS. *2 Hen. VI*, I. i. 132 A proper iest, and neuer heard before. **1599** —— *Much Ado* IV. i. 312 Talke with a man out at a window, a proper saying. **1625** B. JONSON *Staple of N.* I. ii, Ay, she is a proper piece! that such creatures can broke for. **1788** J. MAY *Jrnl. & Lett.* (1873) 60 Major Doughty sent me a proper herring.. which I salted. **1826** DISRAELI *Viv. Grey* VI. i, Thou hast tasted thy liquor like a proper man.

Comb. **1607** MIDDLETON *Your Five Gallants* III. ii, 'Tis a pity such a proper-parted gentleman should want [see PART *sb.* 12].

b. Of good character or standing; honest, respectable, worthy. *Obs.* or merged in 11 b.

1597 SHAKS. *2 Hen. IV*, II. ii. 169 A proper Gentlewoman. **1601** —— *All's Well* IV. iii. 240 An aduertisement to a proper maide in Florence..to take heede of the allurement of one Count Rossillion. **1647** CLARENDON *Hist. Reb.* IV. §19 The other, Sr Philip Stapleton, was a proper man, of a fair extraction. **1765** GRAY *Shakespeare* 3 'Tis Willy begs, once a right proper man. **1891** T. HARDY *Tess* li, 'What about you?' 'I am not a—proper woman'.

9. Of goodly appearance or make; fine-looking, 'fine', good-looking, handsome, well-made, elegant, comely, 'fair'. Now *arch.* and *dial.*

13.. *E.E. Allit. P.* A. 685 Aproche he schal þat proper pyle. *c* **1380** *Sir Ferumb.* 5366 'Sirs', quaþ Neymes, 'comeþ ner, And seeþ a propre siȝte'. *c* **1450** HOLLAND *Howlat* 125 That was the proper Pape Iaye, provde in his apparale. **1519** *Interl. Four Elem.* in Hazl. *Dodsley* I. 26 Little Nell, A proper wench, she danceth well. **1526** TINDALE *Heb.* xi. 23 The same tyme was Moses borne, and was a propper childe [WYCLIF fair or semely; *Rheims* a proper infant]. **1648** GAGE *West Ind.* 77 These Indians..were very proper, tall and lusty men. *a* **1661** FULLER *Worthies* (1840) III. 397 One of the properest buildings north of Trent. *c* **1710** CELIA FIENNES *Diary* (1888) 129 One of white marble..the sinewes and veines..so finely done as to appear very proper. **1823** SCOTT *Quentin D.* ii, By St. Anne! but he is a proper youth. **1847-78** HALLIWELL s.v., *To make proper*, to adorn. **1865** KINGSLEY *Herew.* iv, If he had but been a head taller they had never seen a properer man.

III. 10. Adapted to some purpose or requirement expressed or implied; fit, apt, suitable; fitting, befitting; *esp.* appropriate to the circumstances or conditions; what it should be, or what is required; such as one ought to do, have, use, etc.; right.

a **1225-** [implied in PROPERLY *adv.* 3]. **1477** EARL RIVERS (Caxton) *Dictes* 70 To disordre goode thinges, and put them oute of their propre placis. **1530** PALSGR. 321/2 Proper or apte or that serveth to a purpose, *duict, duicte.* **1604** SHAKS. *Oth.* v. ii. 196 'Tis proper I obey him; but not now. **1660** F. BROOKE tr. *Le Blanc's Trav.* 132 The fruit of Cocos,..of great vertue to purge all humours, and proper for all diseases. **1694** LUTTRELL *Brief Rel.* (1857) III. 258 To enquire of the properest methods to carry on our trade. **1703** MOXON *Mech. Exerc.* 120 They sometimes use the Adz.. when the Ax, or some other properer Tool, lies not at hand. **1772** *Junius Lett.* lxviii. (1820) 337 He might introduce whatever novelties he thought proper. **1795** COWPER *Pairing Time* 64-5 Choose not alone a proper mate, But proper time to marry. **1830** LINDLEY *Nat. Syst. Bot.* 91 Boiling the chips ..until the inspissated juice has acquired a proper consistency. **1879** HARLAN *Eyesight* vi. 70 The proper time to commence using glasses.

11. a. In conformity with social ethics, or with the demands or usages of polite society; becoming, decent, decorous, respectable, genteel, 'correct'.

[**1704** SWIFT *T. Tub* Auth. Apol., How the author came to be without his papers is a story not proper to be told. **1712** ADDISON *Spect.* No. 271 ¶4 If it had been proper for them [ladies] to hear,..the Author would not have wrapp'd it up in Greek.] **1738** SWIFT *Pol. Conversat.* 79 That won't be proper; you know, To-morrow's Sunday. **1812-13** SHELLEY in Dowden *Life* (1886) I. 327 So you do not know whether it is proper to write to me? **1831** PRAED *Stanzas Boccaccio* iv, Then Guilt will read the properest books, And Folly wear the soberest looks. **1852** MRS. STOWE *Uncle Tom* xvi, When will you learn what's proper?

b. *transf.* of persons: Conforming to social ethics or polite usage; strictly decorous in manners and behaviour. (Somewhat *colloq.*)

1818 MOORE *Fudge Fam. Paris* x. 72 We dined at a tavern —La, what do I say?..a *Restaurateur's*, dear; Where your properest ladies go dine every day. **1871** BLACKIE *Four Phases* i. 30 Very proper and respectable gentlemen. **1880** SPURGEON *Serm.* XXVI. 466 You hear very proper people.. cry out against some of us.

c. ***Proper Bostonian*** = BRAHMIN b. Also *attrib.* or as *adj.*

1947 C. AMORY (*title*) The Proper Bostonians. *Ibid.* i. 12 Outside observers have claimed to be able to tell the Proper Bostonian male by waistcoat, and the Proper Bostonian female by hat. **1956** C. W. MILLS *Power Elite* iii. 58 Proper Bostonians and proper San Franciscans..would be genuinely embarrassed..[by] cheap publicity. **1969** A. LASKI *Dominant Fifth* v. 180 Daughter of a not particularly wealthy and certainly not Proper Bostonian American. **1973** R. L. SIMON *Big Fix* i. 10 Her proper Bostonian background, the old shipping family back on Lewisburg Square. **1977** J. CLEARY *High Road to China* vii. 231 She was only a mild rebel: there was still too much of the Proper Bostonian in her.

B. *adv.* = PROPERLY.

1. Excellently, finely, handsomely; genuinely, thoroughly; also, correctly, in a genteel manner (of speech). Now *dial.*, *vulgar*, or *slang.*

c **1450** HOLLAND *Howlat* 901 He lukit to his lykame..So propir plesand of prent. *c* **1470** *Gol. & Gaw.* 242 Propir schene schane the son. **1816** J. WILSON *City of Plague* II. v. 53 As proper brave a man as e'er was laid Under the turf. **1835-40** HALIBURTON *Clockm.* (1862) 201, I am proper glad you agree with me, squire, said he. **1898** DOYLE *Trag. Korosko* ix, 'Had 'em that time—had 'em proper!' said he. **1915** *Dialect Notes* IV. 188 Talk proper before your teacher. **1952** M. ALLINGHAM *Tiger in Smoke* ii. 41 Perhaps she'll 'ave another go at teachin' me to speak proper, pore soul. **1966** F. SHAW et al. (*title*) Lern yerself Scouse. How to talk proper in Liverpool. **1980** *Listener* 22 May 665/1 He has not learnt how to talk proper.

† 2. Suitably, appropriately. *Obs.*

1663 GERBIER *Counsel* a vj, Ordering each part thereof proper to its particular use. **1703** MOXON *Mech. Exerc.* 136 The Joysts lie not proper for the second Story. **1768-74** TUCKER *Lt. Nat.* (1834) II. 36 Which is properest done at those seasons when our thoughts are fresh.

C. *sb.* or quasi-*sb.*

[The adj. used *absol.*, sometimes with pl. as a sb. Cf. L. *proprium* neuter, used subst., and *own* used predicatively (*this is my own*) or *absol.* (*take of your own*).]

† 1. a. That which is one's own; private possession, private property; something belonging to oneself.

[*c* **1330** R. BRUNNE *Chron. Wace* (Rolls) 2380 Þey nolde soffre hym nought to take, Hys owen propre for to make.] *c* **1380** WYCLIF *Wks.* (1880) 40 Lyuynge in obedience, wiþouten propre. **1422** tr. *Secreta Secret., Priv. Priv.* 130 How moche thou mayste despende of thyn owyn propyr. **1456** *Regist. de Aberbrothoc* (Bann. Cl.) II. 89 The proppis that passis estwart betwix the propir and the commoun. **1524** in Strype *Eccl. Mem.* (1721) I. App. xiii. 26 Redounding to their honours & suerties, as his awne propers. **1550** BALE *Apol.* 22, I frire N. make my profession and promyse obedience to God, to S. Frances..to live without propre and in chastite accordynge to the rule of the sayd ordre.

† b. ***in proper***: in individual possession; as private property; as one's own. (Opposed to *in common.*) *Obs.*

c **1374** CHAUCER *Boeth.* II. pr. ii. 22 (Camb. MS.) Yif thow mayst shewyn me þat euere any mortal man hath reseyuyd any of tho thinges to ben hise in propre. **1401** *Pol. Poems* (Rolls) II. 101 We seyen we han riȝt nouȝt in propre ne in comoun. **1553** BECON *Reliques of Rome* (1563) 215 Christ and his Apostles had no possessions neyther in proper nor in commune. **1613** PURCHAS *Pilgrimage* VIII. vi. (1614) 768 They haue their lands and gardens in proper. **1650** JER. TAYLOR *Holy Living* iii. §3 (1727) 171 They could not have that in proper, which God made to be common.

2. *Eccl.* An office, or some part of an office, as a psalm, etc., appointed for a particular occasion or season. Opp. to COMMON *sb.* 10.

[*c* **1400** *Table of Lessons*, etc. in *Wyclif's Bible* IV. 683 First ben sett sondaies and ferials togider, and after that the sanctorum, bothe comyn and propre togider, of al the ȝeer. *Ibid.* 696 Here endith the Propre Sanctorum, and now bigynneth the Commoun Sanctorum.] **1548-9** (Mar.) *Bk. Com. Prayer, Order*, etc., The Collect, Epistle, and Gospell, appoynted for the Sundaie, shall serue all the weeke after, except there fall some feast that hath his propre. **1851** [RORISON] *Hymns & Anthems* Introd. 23 The Proper of the Season and the Proper of Saints, for which [the Prayer Book] provides Epistles and Gospels. **1874** [see COMMON *sb.* 10]. **1882-3** *Schaff's Encycl. Relig. Knowl.* 2064 The regular [R.C.] orders have also in most cases a Proper, containing offices of saints belonging to their rule.

† 3. An attribute specially or intrinsically belonging to something; an essential quality, property, characteristic. *Obs.*

1619 BP. ANDREWES *Serm., Acts* x. 34. 35 (1629) 725 The receiving of the Holy Ghost in a more ample measure [is] *opus diei*, the proper of this Day. *Ibid.* (1661) 418 That is Christ's proper. **1654** Z. COKE *Logick* 67 Every proper floweth from the Essential beginnings of his subject. **1697** tr. *Burgersdicius his Logic* 41 Propers either flow immediately from the Essence of the Subject;..Or, by the Mediation of some other Property.

† 'proper, *v.* *Obs.* [f. PROPER *a.*: cf. L. *propriāre* to make one's own, obs. F. *proprier* corresponding in form and use. In some cases perh. aphetic for *apropre*, APPROPRE *v.*]

1. *trans.* To appropriate (to oneself), to make one's own, take possession of.

c **1380** WYCLIF *Wks.* (1880) 421 Men..þat assenten to siche propring of chirchis bisyde cristis leeue. **1496** *Dives & Paup.* (W. de W.) VII. v. 281/2 They propren to themselfe by couetyse that is comon by kynde.

2. To appropriate, to make proper, to apply or ascribe specially or exclusively (*to* a person or thing).

c **1380** WYCLIF *Wks.* (1880) 353 Crist seiþ..þat by hijs manhed he had no power to ȝyue hem leue to sit on hijs riȝt side, but to þe godhed in hijs fadure is propred þis power. **1398** TREVISA *Barth. De P.R.* VI. xxvii. (Tollem. MS.), Þe liknesse þat we seeþ in sweuenis we..propreþ to him þe names of þo þinges, for liknesse of þe þingis [L. *propter similitudinem eis appropriamur*]. *Ibid.* XVII. cxl. (Bodl. MS.), Rubitum oþer Rubus is a name ipropred þer to a schrubbe þat bereþ wilde beries. *c* **1400** *Prymer* 50 God! to whom it is proprid to be merciful euere.

b. ? To make master (*of* something).

1502 *Ord. Crysten Men* (W. de W. 1506) II. xvii. 130 The person contemplatyf yt by the grace of god is truely propred of all his desyres & pleasures vayne & wordly.

¶ The alleged sense 'to make proper, to adorn', cited in *Cent. Dict.*, is due to a misreading of Halliwell: see quot. 1847-78 s.v. PROPER *a.* 9.

† 'properant, *a.* *Obs. rare.* [ad. L. *properānt-em*, pres. pple. of *proper-āre*: see next.] Hasty.

1536 BELLENDEN *Cron. Scot.* (1821) I. 138 Julius..was the mair fers and properant aganis the Scottis. **1633** T. ADAMS *Exp. 2 Peter* iii. 12 The former [action] is patient, looking for; the other is properant, hasting to.

† 'properate, *v.* *Obs.* [f. ppl. stem of L. *proper-āre* to hasten, f. *proper-us* quick.]

1. *intr.* To hasten, to go quickly.

1623 COCKERAM, *Properate*, to hasten. **1632** VICARS *Virgil* II. 43 A while to keep off death, which properates. [**1767** A. CAMPBELL *Lexiph.* (1774) 64 Misocapelus, Captator, Eubulus, and Quisquilius properated before, with a rapid oscitancy. (Here a burlesque of pedantic language.)]

2. *trans.* To hasten; to quicken the growth of.

1675 EVELYN *Terra* (1676) 109 Some [salts]..are..deadly to plants..others properate [them] too fast; and some are sluggish, and scarce advance them at all.

† prope'ration. *Obs.* [ad. L. *properātiōn-em*, n. of action f. *proper-āre*: see prec.] The action of hastening (*trans.* and *intr.*).

1628 FELTHAM *Resolves* II. [I.] xxxi. 99 Often handling of the withering Flowre..is a properation of more swift decay. **1633** T. ADAMS *Exp. 2 Peter* i. 14 Death's properation prevents their preparation.

† 'proper,chant. *Mus.* *Obs.* [f. PROPER *a.* + CHANT *sb.*] Applied to those hexachords which began on the note C (nearly corresponding to the modern 'natural scale').

1597 MORLEY *Introd. Mus.* 4 What is Properchant?.. It is a propertie of singing, wherein you may sing either *fa* or *mi* in ♭ *fa* ♮ *mi* according as it shall be marked ♭ or thus ♮ and is when the *vt* is in *C fa vt.* **1667** C. SIMPSON *Compend. Pract. Mus.* 112 From these six Notes, *Vt*, *Re*, *Mi*, *Fa*, *Sol*,

La, did arise three properties of Singing; which they [Latins] named *B Quarre*, *B Molle*, and *Properchant* or *Naturall*. *Ibid.* 113 Properchant was when their *Vt* was applyed to *C*... But in our Modern Musick, we acknowledge no such thing as Properchant.

properdin (prəʊˈpɜːdɪn). *Phys.* [f. L. *prō-* PRO-[1] + *perd-ere* to destroy (see PERDITION) + -IN[1].] A protein found in the blood and concerned with the body's response to infection.

1954 *Science* 20 Aug. 279/1 This protein, tentatively named *properdin*.., acts only in conjunction with complement and Mg^{++} and participates in such diverse activities as the destruction of bacteria, the neutralization of viruses, and the lysis of certain red cells. Properdin is a normal serum constituent and differs from antibody in many respects, particularly in its lack of specificity and in its exact requirements for its interactions. [*Note*] Hans Hirschmann.. suggested this name. **1963** C. J. C. BRITTON *Whitby & Britton's Disorders of Blood* (ed. 9) xiv. 356 Properdin levels are low in acute leukæmia. **1975** SPRAGG & GIGLI in Mathieu & Kahan *Immunol. Aspects Anesthetic & Surg. Pract.* vi. 116 Properdin has been highly purified as a distinct protein with a molecular weight of 223,000 daltons.

†**ˈproperhede.** *Obs.* [f. PROPER *a.* + -HEAD.] The quality of being 'proper', i.e. of pertaining or relating to oneself.

c **1440** *Jacob's Well* 171 þe v. spanne lengthe of þe handle of þi skeet in contricyoun muste be propyrhede; þat is to sayn, thynke of þin owen propre synnes & noȝt on oþere mennys. **1496** *Dives & Paup.* (W. de W.) VII. v. 281/1 Ther is thre maner of propertees and properhede.

properispome (prəʊˈpɛrɪspəʊm), *a.* and *sb.* *Gr. Gram.* Also, more fully, **properispomenon** (prəʊpɛrɪˈspɒmɛnɒn). [ad. Gr. προπερισπώμενον, neuter pr. pple. passive of προπερισπᾶν to circumflex on the penultimate, f. πρό, PRO-[2] + περισπᾶν: see PERISPOME.] **a.** *adj.* Having a circumflex accent on the penultimate syllable. **b.** *sb.* A word so accented.

1818 BLOMFIELD tr. *Matthiæ Gr. Gram.* 958 *Properispomena*, which have the circumflex on the penultima. **1867** tr. *Curtius' Grk. Gram.* (ed. 2) §93 Proparoxytones and properispomes.. receive also from the following enclitic another accent as acute on the last syllable. **1881** CHANDLER *Grk. Accentuation* §11 No word with a final syllable long by nature can be proparoxytone or properispomenon. *Ibid.* §971 A properispomenon followed by an enclitic receives the acute on its last syllable.., but dissyllabic enclitics after properispomena ending in ξ or ψ are oxytone. **1905** *Athenæum* 19 Aug. 250/3 He knows that an enclitic in ancient Greek throws back the accent upon a properispomenon, and consequently he writes τὸν μαῦρόν του which is not to be pronounced in modern Greek. What he actually heard was τὸ μαῦρο του.

properistoma, etc.: see PRO-[2] 1.

properly (ˈprɒpəlɪ), *adv.* [f. PROPER *a.* + -LY[2].] In a proper manner (in senses of the adj.).

1. a. In its own nature, in itself, intrinsically, essentially; in one's own person, for oneself; as one's own, as private property, privately. Now *rare* or *Obs.*

c **1380** WYCLIF *Wks.* (1880) 49 þei han grete housis proprid to hem self.. and myche hid tresour..; and þis tresour is kept proprely to idel men or fendis. **1551** T. WILSON *Logike* (1580) 5 b, To goe vpright and to speake, are properly to all menne generally. **1607** SHAKS. *Cor.* v. ii. 90 My Affaires Are Seruanted to others: Though I owe My Reuenge properly, my remission lies In Volcean brests. **1678** CUDWORTH *Intell. Syst.* 170 The whole world or heaven.. is moved properly by soul.

b. Particularly, distinctively, specially.

1340 *Ayenb.* 34 And specialliche and propreliche of the rote of auarice guoþ out manye smale roten, þet byeþ wel greate dyadliche zennes. **1486** *Bk. St. Albans* D ij, That terme draw is propurli assigned to that hawke that will slee a Roke or a Crow or a Reuyn. **1596** DALRYMPLE tr. *Leslie's Hist. Scot.* (S.T.S.) I. 19 A certane schort.. grase, quhairin scheip properlie delytes. **1651** HOBBES *Govt. & Soc.* viii. §5. 130 A subject hath nothing properly his owne against the will of the Supreme Authority. **1823** SCOTT *Peveril* xxv, One would think mischief was so properly thy element that to thee it was indifferent whether friend or foe was the sufferer.

†**c.** By itself or themselves; severally. *Obs.*

1390 GOWER *Conf.* III. 127 Thus ben the Signes propreli Divided. ? *a* **1500** *Wycket* (1828) p. xiii, A man maye take a glasse, and breake the glasse into many peces, and in euery pece properly thou mayste se thy face.

2. In the proper or strict sense; strictly speaking; †literally, not figuratively (*obs.*); in accordance with fact; strictly accurately, correctly, exactly.

a **1340** HAMPOLE *Psalter* xiv. 1 Tabernakile propirly is þe mansyon of feghtand men. *c* **1340** —— *Prose Tr.* 33 þis desire es noghte propirly lufe, bot it es a begynnynge, for lufe propirly es a full cuppillynge of þe lufande and þe lufed to-gedyre. *c* **1400** MAUNDEV. (Roxb.) xxxiii. 150 Off Paradys can I noȝt speke properly, for I hafe noȝt bene þare. **1560** DAUS tr. *Sleidane's Comm.* 24 If we wil properly and exactly speake, accordyng to the difinition of the word. **1600** SHAKS. *A.Y.L.* I. i. 8 He keepes me rustically at home, or (to speak more properly) staies me heere at home vnkept. **1674** ALLEN *Danger Enthus.* 128 Carefully avoiding to take words properly, which are spoken metaphorically. **1790** PALEY *Horæ Paul.* Rom. ii. 17 Greece properly so called, that is, as distinguished from Macedonia. **1850** MCCOSH *Div. Govt.* I. iii. (1874) 67 Virtue is not virtue, properly speaking, when it is constrained.

3. Fittingly, suitably, appropriately; as it ought to be, or as one ought to do; rightly, correctly, duly, well; in accordance with social ethics or good manners, becomingly, with propriety.

a **1225** *Ancr. R.* 98 Lokeð nu, hu propreliche þe lefdi in Canticis,.. lereð ou, bi hire sawe, hu ȝe schulen siggen, 'En dilectus meus'. **1340** *Ayenb.* 25 Huanne he.. deþ his guodes naȝt uor god properliche, ac uor þe wordle. *c* **1375** *Sc. Leg. Saints* xi. (*Symon & Judas*) 69 He send til hyme þane a paynteore.. To paynt his fygur propirly. *c* **1400** MAUNDEV. (Roxb.) xxx. 134 In þat land er many papeiais.. and þai speke of þaire awen kynde als properly as a man. *a* **1533** FRITH *Disput. Purgat.* Wks. (1829) 99 Mark.. how properly that substantial reason, wherewith they go about to establish purgatory, concludeth. **1660** F. BROOKE tr. *Le Blanc's Trav.* 372 Those famous sheep called *Pacos* which serve as properly for carriage as horses. **1776** ADAM SMITH *W.N.* I. viii. (1869) I. 82 Law can never regulate them [wages] properly. **1811** L. M. HAWKINS *C'tess & Gertr.* III. 73 He took leave affectionately and yet properly. **1852** MRS. STOWE *Uncle Tom's C.* xxi, Take the horse back, and clean him properly. **1868** LOCKYER *Elem. Astron.* VI. xxxvii. (1879) 219 If the object-glass does not perform its part properly. *Mod.* Why don't you behave properly?

4. In a goodly fashion, excellently, admirably; with goodly appearance, finely, handsomely; well. Now *arch.* or *vulgar*.

a **1375** *Lay Folks Mass Bk.* App. IV. 621 þe Orisoun.. of seynt Ambrose þat he properly in prose Made. *c* **1400** MAUNDEV. (Roxb.) xxiii. 107 Made of precious stanes so properly and so curiously þat it semez as it ware a vyne growand. *c* **1430** *Hymns Virg.* 62 'Apparaile þe propirli' quod Pride. **1519** *Interl. Four Elem.* in Hazl. *Dodsley* I. 47, I can prank it properly. **1552** HULOET, Properly or trymme, *concinne, dextre.* **1732** EARL OF OXFORD in *Portland Papers* VI. (Hist. MSS. Comm.) 159, I never saw hills so properly and so finely clothed. **1740–87** *Lett. Miss Talbot, &c.* (1808) 19 A mean dressed man got up into a tree, and from thence harangued them very properly.

5. Of degree: Thoroughly, completely, perfectly; utterly, entirely, quite; exceedingly, very. (Now *slang* or *colloq.*)

a **1400–50** *Alexander* 3283 (Dubl. MS.) þus prosperite and pride propyrly me blyndyd. *c* **1530** LD. BERNERS *Arth. Lyt. Bryt.* (1814) 57 For certayne I thoughte properly it had ben you. **1664** PEPYS *Diary* 24 June, Such variety of pictures, and other things of value and rarity, that I was properly confounded. *Ibid.* 14 July, All which, I did assure my Lord, was most properly false, and nothing like it true. **1816** SCOTT *Let. to T. Scott* 29 May in *Lockhart*, Economy is the order of the day, and I can assure you they are shaving properly close. **1895** MORRIS in Mackail *Life* (1899) II. 309 They beat us properly.. we polled about half what they did. **1896** *Daily News* 18 Mar. 3/6 The accused said he got 'properly drunk'.

6. *Math.* So as to form a proper subset or a proper subgroup (see PROPER *a.* 6 c).

1965 E. SCHENKMAN *Group Theory* iv. 125 If Π is a set of primes, a Sylow Π-subgroup of a group G is a Π-subgroup of G not properly contained in any Π-subgroup of G. **1968** E. T. COPSON *Metric Spaces* i. 6 The set A is.. properly contained in B if every member of A belongs to B and there is at least one member of B which does not belong to A. **1971** E. C. DADE in Powell & Higman *Finite Simple Groups* viii. 326 The group H.. is properly contained in G.

properness (ˈprɒpənɪs). Now *rare*. [f. as prec. + -NESS.] The quality of being proper.

1. The fact of belonging specially to something; special quality or character, peculiarity.

1630 LORD *Banians* ii. 9 The Woman to whom God had giuen that vnderstanding, to be capable of the propernesse of his speech. **1635** HEYWOOD *Hierarch.* III. Comm. 175 The Latines in regard of the propernesse of the forme, name it [Deltoton] *Triangulum*. **1727** BAILEY vol. II, *Properness*, Peculiarness.

2. Excellence, goodness; esp. of appearance: goodliness, handsomeness, elegance, comeliness.

1530 PALSGR. 258/2 Propernesse, *faictisse, factise.* **1548** UDALL, etc. *Erasm. Par. Acts* vii. 29 The propernes of the childe. *a* **1625** FLETCHER *Love's Pilgr.* IV. i, Yonder is a lady veil'd; For properness beyond comparison. **1655** FULLER *Hist. Camb.* (1840) 196 The queen, upon parity of deserts, always preferred properness of person in conferring her favours. **1706** PHILLIPS, *Properness*, Talness of Stature.

3. Fitness, suitableness; becomingness, propriety; conformity with what is 'proper'.

a **1603** T. CARTWRIGHT *Confut. Rhem. N.T.* Pref. (1618) 18 Both for propernesse of wordes, and truth of sense he hath wisely and faithfully translated. **1710** ABP. KING *Let. to Swift* 16 Sept., I am not courtier enough to know the properness of the thing. **1873** MRS. WHITNEY *Other Girls* vi, Standing off in separate properness, as people do who 'go into society'.

†**ˈpropertary**, *a.* and *sb.* *Obs. rare.* In 5 propirtarij, proprytarye. [f. PROPERTY *sb.* + -ARY[1]: cf. PROPRIETARY (to which *proprytarye* leads); also the forms of PROPERTY.] = PROPRIETARY B. 2, A. 2.

c **1400** *Rule St. Benet* 142 þe behouis liue in wilfull powerte,.. þat þu be noght propirtarij and falle in owre-hegh daunger enence þi religiun. **1497** BP. ALCOCK *Mons Perfect.* D j, Whan the relygyous men therof.. ben proprytaryes. **1526** *Pilgr. Perf.* (W. de W. 1531) 275 Some doctours thynketh that all suche propertaryes be excommunicate & accursed.

Propertian (prɒˈpɜːʃ(ɪ)ən), *a.* [f. L. *Propertius* (see below) + -AN.] Belonging to or characteristic of Sextus Aurelius Propertius, Latin elegiac poet of the first century B.C., or his poetry.

1871 J. R. LOWELL *My Study Windows* 217 Goethe, who was classic.. in his 'Hermann and Dorothea', and at least Propertian in his 'Roman Idyls', wasted his time.. on the mechanical mock-antique of an unreadable 'Achilleis'. **1918** E. POUND *Let.* 22 Nov. in *Lett. J. Joyce* (1966) II. 424, I hope my Propertian ravings will amuse you. **1930** W. S. MAUGHAM *Cakes & Ale* xiv. 161 Love lyrics and elegies in the Propertian manner. **1974** *Classical Q.* XXIV. 96 The verb of the first clause is rendered in English by the pluperfect. The Propertian passage displays a structural similarity.

propertied (ˈprɒpətɪd), *a.* [f. next + -ED[2].]

†**1.** Having a specified property, quality, nature, or disposition. *Obs.*

1606 SHAKS. *Ant. & Cl.* V. ii. 83 His voyce was propertied As all the tuned Spheres, and that to Friends. **1633** HEYWOOD *Eng. Trav.* I. Wks. 1874 IV. 9 This approues you To be most nobly propertied. [**1862** F. HALL *Hindu Philos. Syst.* 94 The expression *dharma-dharmyabhedát*, 'because of the non-difference of a property and that which is propertied.']

2. Possessed of, owning, or holding property.

1760–72 H. BROOKE *Fool of Qual.* (1809) III. 30 You are still in the flesh, in a carnal and propertied world. **1834** *Fraser's Mag.* IX. 267 They are the propertied class. **1887** M. ARNOLD *Ess. Crit.* Ser. II. viii. (1888) 296 Whatever the propertied and satisfied classes may think.

3. Furnished with theatrical properties.

1901 *Westm. Gaz.* 10 Jan. 2/1 The great picture of 'An Audience in Athens during the Representation of Agamemnon'.. is too 'staged' and 'propertied' to be very convincing. **1909** M. E. ALBRIGHT *Shakesperian Stage* 147 The Elizabethan stage.. was little more than a union of the old *sedes* and *plateæ* of the moralities, or the propertied and unpropertied stages of the interludes.

property (ˈprɒpətɪ), *sb.* Forms: α. 4–6 **proprete**, **-tee**, **-tie** (6 **-ty**); 4–6 **properte**, (4–5 **-ur-**, **-yr-**, 4–6 **-ir-**, 5–6 **-ar-**; 4–5 **-tee**, 4–6 **-te**, 5 **-ty**, 5–6 **-tie**), 5–7 **propertie** (5–6 **-tee**, 6–7 **-tye**), 6– **property**. β. 4 **proprite**, 5 **propryte**, **-tee** (6 **-tye**). [ME. *proprete*, app. ME. or AF. modification of OF. *proprieté* (12th c. in Littré), ad. L. *proprietāt-em*, n. of quality from *proprius* own, proper. The β form *proprite* corresponds to a F. dial. form *propritei* cited of 1292 in Godef. *Compl.* The F. *propreté*, which corresponds exactly to ME. *proprete*, is not cited before 17th c., and is viewed by Hatz.-Darm. as directly f. *propre* adj. + *-té*. All the forms are ultimately French or Eng. representations of the L. word (whence PROPRIETY) with or without conformation to the adj. *propre*, PROPER.]

1. The condition of being owned by or belonging to some person or persons (cf. PROPER *a.* 1); hence, the fact of owning a thing; the holding of something as one's own; the right (*esp.* the exclusive right) to the possession, use, or disposal of anything (usually of a tangible material thing); ownership, proprietorship; = PROPRIETY *sb.* 1.

c **1380** WYCLIF *Serm.* Sel. Wks. I. 317 þe cite of Beedleem was Daviþis bi sum propirte. **1390** GOWER *Conf.* I. 357 Whan that a riche worthi king,.. Wol axe and cleyme proprete In thing to which he hath no riht. **1489** *Paston Lett.* III. 349 Tyll it myth be undyrstond wedyr the propyrte ware in the Kyng or in my lord. **1582** *Reg. Privy Council Scot.* III. 501 Landis.. pertening to the said David, Erll of Craufurd,.. in propertie and tenandrie. **1641** *Termes de la Ley* 226 *Propertie* is the highest right that a man hath or can have to any thing, which no way dependeth upon another mans curtesie. **1690** LOCKE *Govt.* I. iv. §42 God.. has given no one of his Children such a Property in his peculiar Portion of the Things of this World. **1713** *Treaty of Utrecht* in Magens *Insurances* (1755) II. 501 Sea-letters or Passports, expressing the Name, Property and Bulk of the Ship. **1768** BLACKSTONE *Comm.* III. x. 190 The right of possession (though it carries with it a strong presumption) is not always conclusive evidence of the right of property, which may still subsist in another man. **1838** T. DRUMMOND *Let. to Tipperary Magistrates* 18 Apr., in B. O'Brien *Life* (1889) 284 Property has its duties as well as its rights. **1876** DIGBY *Real Prop.* x. §1. 374 Rights of property or ownership over land, meaning by property or ownership the enjoyment of those indefinite rights of user over land by virtue of which in ordinary language a person is entitled to speak of land as his property.

fig. **1601** SHAKS. *Phœnix & Turtle* 37 Either was the others mine. Propertie was thus appalled, That the selfe was not the same: Single Natures double name, Neither two nor one was called. [? = Either was claimed by the other as 'Mine'. Ownership was thus dismayed. (But Schmidt takes 'property' here as = 'particularity, individuality'.)]

2. a. That which one owns; a thing or things belonging to or owned by some person or persons; a possession (usually material), or possessions collectively; (one's) wealth or goods. (In quots. 1456, 1526, private as distinguished from common property.) Also *fig.*

(Comparatively few examples before 17th c.)

13.. *Cursor M.* 28389 (Cott.) And haue i ran bath aght and fe O þam þat had na propurte. *c* **1450** tr. *De Imitatione* III. xlii. 113 þat þou mowe be dispoiled of all maner propirte. **1526** *Pilgr. Perf.* (W. de W. 1531) 14 They.. had no property, but all was in commune. **1602** SHAKS. *Ham.* II. ii. 597 A King, Vpon whose property, and most deere life, A damn'd defeate was made. **1690** LOCKE *Govt.* II. ix. §123 He .. is willing to join in Society with others.. for the mutual Preservation of their Lives, Liberties and Estates, which I call by the general Name, *Property*. **1758** JOHNSON *Idler* No. 14 ¶3 Time therefore ought, above all other kinds of property, to be free from invasion. *c* **1796** T. TWINING *Trav. Amer.* (1894) 33 She was the property, I understood, of Mr. Francis, who had bought her some time before. **1804**

EUGENIA DE ACTON *Tale without Title* I. 13 The sole disposal of a property to the amount of a hundred thousand pounds. **1838** FONBLANQUE in *Life & Labours* (1874) 290 In 1838.. the personal property of 24 English Bishops who had died within the last 20 years amounted to £1.649.000. **1849** COBDEN in Morley *Life* xviii. (1902) 67/2 Real property always falls in value in the vicinity of barracks. **1874** GREEN *Short Hist.* vi. §4. 304 The printing press was making letters the common property of all.

b. A piece of land owned; a landed estate.

1719 DE FOE *Crusoe* (1840) I. xx. 366 They..had their properties set apart for them. **1792** A. YOUNG *Trav. France* 411 Small properties, much divided, prove the greatest source of misery that can be conceived. **1885** *Truth* 28 May 835/1 Lord Eldon..possessed one considerable property in Durham, and another in Dorset.

†**c.** ? Something belonging to a thing; an appurtenance; an adjunct. *Obs.*

a **1350** *Exalt. Cross* 58 in Horstm. *Altengl. Leg.* (1881) 128 Also ȝit gert he mak þarin Propirtese by preue gyn. **13..** *Minor Poems fr. Vernon Ms.* I. 493 þe propertes of nature Redi to þe þei be [L. *Comoda nature nullo tibi tempore deerunt*]. *a* **1661** FULLER *Worthies, Herefordsh.* (1662) II. 33 Many aged folk which in other countries are properties of the chimneyes, or confined to their beds, are here found in the feild as able..to work.

d. *ellipt.*, shares or investments in property.

1964 *Financial Times* 3 Mar. 19/5 There was a little more interest in Properties, sentiment being helped by last Friday's Gallup poll. **1977** *Evening Post* (Nottingham) 24 Jan. 16/9 Properties ran into profit-taking with Haslemere 176p, MEPC 62p, Land Securities 161p, and Stock Conversion 161p on offer.

e. A person (esp. one engaged in show business) regarded as a commercial asset, esp. in phr. ***hot property*** (cf. HOT *a.* 6 a, 9 b), a success or sensation, a 'hit'. *colloq.*

1958 J. BLISH *Case of Conscience* xiv. 153 Signor Egtverchi is now a hot property... Suddenly..he is worth a lot of money. **1969** *Rolling Stone* 28 June 22 The Hagers, potentially hot property, now have Record One. **1980** M. GILBERT *Death of Favourite Girl* xii. 114 Katie was a big property by then and..naturally I was ready to talk about her.

3. *Theatr.* Any portable article, as an article of costume or furniture, used in acting a play; a stage requisite, appurtenance, or accessory. Chiefly *pl.*

c **1425** *Cast. Persev.* 132 in *Macro Plays* 81 þese parcellis in propyrtes we purpose us to playe þis day seuenenyt. **1578** in Feuillerat *Revels Q. Eliz.* (1908) 303 Furnished in this office with sondrey garmentes & properties. **1590** SHAKS. *Mids. N.* I. ii. 108, I wil draw a bil of properties, such as our play wants. **1626** MASSINGER *Rom. Actor* IV. ii, This cloak and hat, without Wearing a beard or other property, Will fit the person. **1748** *Whitehall Even. Post* No. 371 To be Sold very cheap, Cloaths, Scenes, Properties, clean, and in very good Order. **1831** DISRAELI *Yng. Duke* III. xix, They were excessively amused with the properties; and Lord Squib proposed they should dress themselves. **1881** LD. LENNOX *Plays, Players*, etc. II. iii. 47, 'I used it as a property'. 'A what?' interrupted the..magistrate.

†**4.** *fig.* A mere means to an end; an instrument, a tool, a cat's-paw. *Obs.*

1598 SHAKS. *Merry W.* III. iv. 10 'Tis a thing impossible I should loue thee, but as a property. **1611** SPEED *Hist. Gt. Brit.* IX. xx. (1623) 965 That he was but a Puppet, or a property in the late tragical motion. **1667** *Decay Chr. Piety* xii. ¶ 1 Both religion..and those that fought for it, were only made properties to promote the lusts of those who despised both. **1764** *Low Life* (ed. 3) 54 Hackney Coachmen.. praying for rainy Weather, that they may make a Property of the People they carry in the Afternoon.

5. An attribute or quality belonging to a thing or person: in earlier use sometimes, an essential, special, or distinctive quality, a peculiarity; in later use often, a quality or characteristic in general (without reference to its essentialness or distinctiveness). **a.** Of a thing or things.

1303 R. BRUNNE *Handl. Synne* 10081 Y rede þe here how þe propertes are shewed, þoghe þe langage be but lewed. **1398** TREVISA *Barth. De P.R.* III. xxi. (1495) d vij b/1 The wytte of gropyng hath this propryte, that he is [in] al þe partyes of the body, outake heer, nayles of fete and of hondes. *c* **1470** HENRYSON *Mor. Fab.* I. (*Cock & Jasp*) ix, This joly jasp had propirteis sevin: The first, of cullour it was meruellous. **1526** *Pilgr. Perf.* (W. de W. 1531) 2 b, The philosophers had suche..desyre to knowe the natures & propertees of thynges. **1551** TURNER *Herbal* I. A iv, In pontike wormwode is there no smalle astringent propertie. **1664** POWER *Exp. Philos.* I. 35 Though heat hath that killing property, yet it seems that cold hath not. **1777** PRIESTLEY *Matt. & Spir.* (1782) I. xix. 218 Truth is only a property, and no substance whatever. **1831** BREWSTER *Nat. Magic* i. (1833) 5 The property of lenses and mirrors to form erect and inverted images of objects. **1868** LOCKYER *Elem. Astron.* VII. xli. (1879) 241 It is one of the properties of a triangle that the three interior angles taken together are equal to two right angles.

†**b.** Of a person. *Obs.*

c **1380** WYCLIF *Serm.* Sel. Wks. I. 138 Crist..telliþ þe heieste proprete þat falliþ to a good herde. **1494** FABYAN *Chron.* II. xxx. 22 Hauynge great experiences in hawkynge & huntynge and other properties apperteynynge to a Gentylman. **1556** OLDE *Antichrist* 70 b, The persone of Antichrist, his nature, disposicion,..and all his proprieties. **1642** FULLER *Holy & Prof. St.* v. xiii. 409 He hath this property of an honest man, that his word is as good as his hand. **1794** GODWIN *Cal. Williams* 313, I am sorry for your ill properties, but I entertain no enmity against you. **1821** SCOTT *Kenilw.* xxi, One of whom..he knew no virtuous property.

†**c.** A peculiar or exclusive attribute; a quality belonging only to the being in question. *Obs.*

a **1628** PRESTON *New Covt.* (1634) 38 A man that hath excellent gifts and graces himselfe, he cannot convey them to another, but that is the propertie of God, that is peculiar to him alone. **1638** CHILLINGW. *Relig. Prot.* I. v. §13. 257 This is..to..take upon you the property of God, which is to know the hearts of men.

d. *Logic.* Reckoned as one of the PREDICABLES, q.v.: see quots. 1725, 1870.

1551 T. WILSON *Logike* (1580) 5 b, Propertie is a naturall pronenesse and maner of doing, which agreeth to one kind, and to the same onely, and that euermore. **1628** T. SPENCER *Logick* 62 Properties be not adjuncts: for, adiuncts doe outwardly befall the subiect... Properties..are necessary emanations from the principles of nature. **1725** WATTS *Logic* I. ii. §3 A *secondary essential mode* is any other attribute of a thing, which is not of primary consideration; this is called a *property*: sometimes indeed it goes toward making up the essence, especially of a complex being..; sometimes it depends upon, and follows from the essence of it; so *volubility*, or aptness to roll, is the property of a bowl, and is derived from its roundness. **1870** JEVONS *Elem. Logic* xii. (1880) 102 Property..may perhaps be best described as any quality which is common to the whole of a class, but is not necessary to mark out that class from other classes.

e. *Linguistics.* An intrinsic aspect or function.

1953 C. E. BAZELL *Linguistic Form* iii. 38 The acoustic and articulatory property-complexes are 'genuine' aspects of the phonemes. **1962** E. F. HADEN et al. *Resonance-Theory for Linguistics* iv. 49 Every entity in language has a Property and a Form... The Property of each entity is internal to it, corresponding to its function in the complex of which it is a part. **1965** N. CHOMSKY *Aspects of Theory of Syntax* iv. 160 In any given linguistic system lexical entries enter into intrinsic semantic relations of a much more systematic sort than is suggested by what has been said so far. We might use the term 'field properties' to refer to these..aspects.

†**6.** Usually with *the*: The characteristic quality of a person or thing; hence, character, nature. *Obs.*

1303 R. BRUNNE *Handl. Synne* 3973 Who-so kan knowe þe properte, Enuyus man may lyknyd be To þe lawnes. *c* **1400** *Destr. Troy* 626 As the Roose in his Radness is Richest of floures,..So passis þi propurty perte wemen all. **14..** in *Babees Bk.* (1868) 332 It is þe properte of A gentilmann To say the beste þat he cann. **1559** *Bk. Com. Prayer, Prayers Sev. Occas.*, O God, whose nature and propertie is euer to haue mercy, and to forgeue. **1563** HYLL *Art Garden.* (1593) 77 The Rue of propertie doth driue away al venemous beasts and wormes. **1651** BAXTER *Inf. Bapt.* 10 It is the property of error to contradict it self. *a* **1703** BURKITT *On N.T.* Mark vi. 6 It is the property and practice of profane men, to take occasion..to dispise their persons, and to reject their doctrine.

†**7.** The quality of being proper or suitable; aptitude, fitness; the proper use or sense (of words). = PROPRIETY *sb.* 5 b. *Obs.*

c **1380** WYCLIF *Wks.* (1880) 353 þat is good love of þe fire of charite, and is clepid benignitie by propirte of word. *c* **1399** *Pol. Poems* (Rolls) II. 13 So hath the werre as ther no proprité. **1531** ELYOT *Gov.* I. xv, All kyndes of writyng must also be sought for; nat for the histories only, but also for the proprietie of wordes, whiche communely do receiue theyr autoritie of noble autours. **1627** W. SCLATER *Exp. 2 Thess.* (1629) 252 Which, though in large sense it may bee stiled Excommunication..yet, in property of speach, is not so. **1675** HAN. WOOLLEY *Gentlewom. Comp.* 54 The neatness and property of your Clothes... Property, I call a certain suitableness and convenience betwixt the Clothes and the Person. **1740** CHEYNE *Regimen* 136 With infinite Variety, Justness, and Property.

8. *attrib.* and *Comb.* **a.** In sense 1 or 2, as ***property account, -class, developer, -holder, -interest, -lawyer, -market, -owner, right, speculator, -taxation, value***; ***property-based, -holding, -loving, -owning***, etc. adjs.; **property bond**, a share or bond in property; **property mark**, a mark indicating ownership; **property qualification**, a qualification for office (e.g. of a member of parliament), or for the exercise of a right (e.g. of voting), based on the possession of property to a certain amount; **property tax**, a direct tax levied on property.

1869 *Bradshaw's Railway Man.* XXI. 417 *Expended*... *Property accounts—materials..[$]139,463. **1974** *Terminol. Managem. & Financial Accountancy* (Inst. Cost & Managem. Accountants) 58 *Real or property account*, the record of an asset, (e.g. buildings, plant and equipment, cash, etc.). **1957** K. A. WITTFOGEL *Oriental Despotism* 2 The modern *property-based system of industry. **1974** tr. *Wertheim's Evolution & Revolution* 27 Only one of the filiation lines leads to social progress, namely the one passing through the 'property-based', 'multicentered', or..'open' society. **1970** *Daily Tel.* 17 Jan. 22/3 The considerable expansion of property values since the war..is the great selling point for *property bonds, compared with other investment plans. **1972** *Accountant* 12 Oct., Property bonds ..reflect the value of the property owned by the property fund without being subject to the vagaries of the stock exchange. **1885** *Pall Mall G.* 2 Feb. 6/2 A great deal had lately been said about the *property classes, and there had been a good deal of wild talk about property. **1970** *Harper's Bazaar* Oct. 76/1 *Property developers..wreaked vandalism upon the cities and countryside of England. **1977** M. WALKER *National Front* v. 125 A property developer called Roy Bramwell. **1824** *Deb. Congress U.S.* (1856) 18th Congress 1 Sess., App. II. 3129 The memorial of the ..*property-holders of the city of Baltimore. **1856** OLMSTED *Slave States* 179 A question so important to the property-holders of the State. **1906** J. F. RHODES *Hist. U.S.* VI. Pref. 5 The educated and *property-holding people of several States. **1822** T. MITCHELL *Aristoph.* II. 227 Isæus, the great *property-lawyer of the Athenians, assures us that this was a trick in very common practice at Athens. **1899** *Amer. Anthropologist* Oct. 601 *Property marks are used very frequently by the Eskimo tribes of Alaska. They occur almost exclusively on weapons used in hunting, which, after being dispatched, remain in the bodies of large game. **1905** *Daily Chron.* 20 May 3/5 Indications that the *property market is returning to the condition of healthy activity. **1865** *Harper's Mag.* July 154/2 It is the nightmare of *property-owners. **1902** *Westm. Gaz.* 2 June 2/1 Many..district councils are under the complete domination of cottage property owners. **1941** W. TEMPLE *Citizen & Churchman* v. 75 What are the rights of property-owners in respect of the property which they own? **1979** C. E. SCHORSKE *Fin-de-Siècle Vienna* ii. 46 The property owners of the inner city.. feared the competition of vast new housing construction. **1923** *Spectator* 19 May 837/2 It remains to state as clearly as may be what means lie ready to develop a *property-owning democracy. **1978** *Countryman* LXXXIII. 37 (*title of poem*) Towards a property-owning democracy. **1807** *Deb. Congress U.S.* 16 Nov. (1852) 916 The Constitution of the United States requires no *property qualification in the elected. **1862** MERIVALE *Rom. Emp.* (1865) IV. xxxii. 10 He raised the property qualification to twelve hundred thousand sesterces. **1863** H. COX *Instit.* I. viii. 126 All property qualifications of members of Parliament are now abolished. **1870** FREEMAN *Norm. Conq.* (ed. 2) I. App. Q. 590 The strange notion..that a property qualification was needed for a seat in the Witenagemôt. **1942** W. TEMPLE *Christianity & Social Order* ii. 27 Men are sinful, so *property-rights are needed, not so much for the satisfaction of the rich as for the protection of the poor. **1968** *Listener* 27 June 847/1 A friend likened it [*sc.* a vacuum cleaner] to a *property speculator's cocktail cabinet. *a* **1974** R. CROSSMAN *Diaries* (1975) I. 46 Nobody in a Labour Cabinet is going to object to an action which is extremely popular outside London and which will only ruin property speculators. **1808** in *57th Rep. R. Comm. Hist. Manuscripts* 139 in *Parl. Papers 1902* (Cd. 931) LIII. 1 How do the farmers with you talk of the **Property Tax?* **1809** HAN. MORE *Cælebs* I. x. 118 That abominable Property-tax makes me quite a beggar. **1978** *N.Y. Times* 30 Mar. B6/3 The legislative leaders and Governor Carey agreed today to..offer low-income taxpayers, particularly the elderly, a property-tax protection program. **1844** COBDEN *Let.* 7 Dec. (in *Tregaskis' Catal.* 16 Sept. (1901) 25/2), As a leaguer we must not take up the question of direct *property-taxation, but individually I go with you entirely. **1914** *Proc. 6th Nat. Conf. City Planning* (U.S.) 102 Suddenly he finds his *property values injured..because someone has chosen to construct a small retail store. **1979** V. S. NAIPAUL *Bend in River* vi. 109 The big recent rise in property values in the town.

b. In sense 3 (*Theatr.* and *Cinemat.*): (*a*) appositive, applied to any article (often an imitation) used as a property or stage accessory, as ***property broadsword, cittern, doll, fowl***; also, to a person who appears in a scene but takes no part in the action, as ***property boy, child***; so allusively ***property clerk***; (*b*) ordinary attrib. and Comb., as ***property-maker, manager, truck, wagon, woman, workshop***; **property-man, -master**, a man who furnishes and has the charge of stage properties at a theatre; **property-plot**, a list of the properties required for a play; **property-room**, the room in which the properties are kept. See also PROPERTY BOX 2.

1685 DRYDEN *Albion & Alb.* III. ii, The Saints advance, To fill the Dance, And the *Property Boys come in. **1898** *Westm. Gaz.* 16 Feb. 2/1 It was like a man armed with a *property broadsword facing a master of fence. **1889** J. JEFFERSON *Autobiog.* i. (1891) 3, I had seen many rehearsals, ..having been taken on 'in arms' as a *property child. **1889** W. S. GILBERT *Foggerty's Fairy*, etc. (1892) 145 We also shared a '*property' clerk, who did nothing at all. **1895** *Pall Mall G.* 2 Dec. 1/2 The man who can't eat a *property fowl is no actor. **1559** in Feuillerat *Revels Q. Eliz.* (1908) 110 Wages of taylours, karvars, *propertie makers, wemen & other. **1582** *Ibid.* 352 Property makers being Paynters the firste at iiᵈ the day. **1633** SHIRLEY *Triumph of Peace* 19 There rush in A Carpenter. A Paynter... A Feather-makers Wife. A *Property-Mans Wife. **1749** W. R. CHETWOOD *Hist. Stage* 251 Property-man is the person that receives a bill from the prompter for what is necessary in every play; as purses, wine, suppers, poison [etc.]. **1856** EMERSON *Eng. Traits, Relig.* Wks. (Bohn) II. 102 The religion of the day is a theatrical Sinai, where the thunders are supplied by the property man. **1959** W. S. SHARPS *Dict. Cinematogr.* 121/2 **Property manager*, the person responsible for obtaining, storing and supplying all the inanimate items required for a set. **1888** *Scribner's Mag.* Oct. 440/2 While the *property-master and his men were fashioning the god Talepulka, the scenic artist had sketched and modelled the scenery of the opera. **1897** *Q. Rev.* Oct. 349 Rant and frippery that befit a third-rate actor or a second-hand *property-monger. **1933** P. GODFREY *Back-Stage* iv. 44 The *property-plot is a detailed list of every article of furniture and every other stage accessory used throughout the play. **1784** J. BYNG *Torrington Diaries* (1934) I. 176 In the *property room is a profusion of wigs, and truncheons. **1829** H. FOOTE *Compan. Theatres* 38 In the line with the flies, over the auditory, are carpenters' shops, property-rooms, store-rooms, &c. **1858** LYTTON *What will he do* I. vi, She had left in the property-room of the theatre her robe of spangles and tinsel. **1885** J. K. JEROME *On the Stage* 66 The dressing-rooms (two rows of wooden sheds) were situate over the property room, and were reached by means of a flight of steps. **1961** BOWMAN & BALL *Theatre Lang.* 280 **Property truck*, a wagon offstage on which properties can be placed until needed. **1963** *Movie* May 19/3 He sat in the back of the property truck writing the ending. **1895** *McClure's Mag.* V. 55/1 The baggage-wagons and the *property-wagons have stopped near the dressing-rooms. **1808** *Monthly Pantheon* I. 692/2 His wife was (in the technical language of the theatre) a dresser and *property-woman. **1829** H. FOOTE *Compan. Theatres* 38 Beneath it is the *printing-office*; and over it are *property workshops.

ˈ**property**, *v.* *Obs.* or *rare.* [f. prec. sb.]

1. *trans.* To make a 'property' or tool of, to use for one's own ends, to exploit. *Obs.*

1595 SHAKS. *John* v. ii. 79, I am too high-borne to be propertied To be a..seruing-man, and Instrument To any Soueraigne State throughout the world. **1758** *Herald* I. Ded. 5 There must..be a vast fund of stupidity amongst mankind, to make them..be continually property'd away for the interests of a few crafty leaders.

2. To make one's own property, to appropriate, to take or hold possession of.

1607 SHAKS. *Timon* I. i. 57 His large Fortune..Subdues and properties to his loue and tendance All sorts of hearts. **1833** T. HOOK *Parson's Dau.* I. x, A being like Emma—whose sentiments, whose character, are propertied by the one, one engrossing passion.

3. To imbue with a property or quality: see PROPERTIED 1.

ˈproperty box. *Theatre.* [f. PROPERTY *sb.* + BOX *sb.*²] †**1.** A seated compartment (BOX *sb.*² 8) which may be privately rented. *Obs.*

1812 *Dramatic Censor 1811* 53 And Ladies Carlisle and Jersey rent Property boxes, which reduces the number of Ladies seceders to fourteen. **1828** J. EBERS *Seven Yrs. King's Theatre* ix. 243 In this year (1825) and the preceding one, the terms existing in the property-boxes expired.

2. A box (BOX *sb.*² 1) in which stage properties are stored.

1864 P. PATERSON *Glimpses Real Life* 3 Richard's truncheon we knew was in the property-box. **1890** B. HALL *Turnover Club* ii. 28, I met on the rocks, with a 'property-box', A gloomy theatrical man.

ˈpropertyless, *a.* Also **propertiless** (cf. *merciless, pitiless*). [f. PROPERTY *sb.* + -LESS.] Devoid of property; having no property. Also *ellipt.* as *sb.*

1822 W. COBBETT *Cottage Econ.* 107 They were formerly the sons and daughters of small farmers; they are now the progeny of miserable property-less labourers. **1880** *Fortn. Rev.* Apr. 536 The population will always be the propertyless, pauperised labourers. **1886** W. GRAHAM *Soc. Probl.* 333 The fear of the uncertain morrow, with all its danger for the propertiless. **1912** BELLOC *Servile State* I. 16 Two classes of free citizens, the one capitalist or owning, the other propertyless or proletarian. **1941** R. HUMPHREYS *Latin Amer.* 20 For the Indian and the propertyless, independence meant not new freedom but new masters. **1977** *Dædalus* Summer 72 They predicted, in Hegelian fashion, an abolition of private property and class ownership of the means of production by a regenerated communism among the propertyless masses.

Hence **ˈpropertylessness,** the state of being propertyless.

1964 M. MCLUHAN *Understanding Media* xxxiii. 357 Hence the specter of joblessness and propertylessness in the electric age.

ˈpropertyship. *nonce-wd.* [f. as prec. + -SHIP.] The condition of being property; the constitution of property: the correlative of *ownership.*

1884 L. GRONLUND *Co-operat. Commw.* vi. 140 It will be decidedly inexpedient in that commonwealth to destroy any of the essential qualities of propertyship.

prophage (ˈprəʊfeɪdʒ). *Biol.* [Contraction of F. *probactériophage* (Lwoff & Gutmann 1950, in *Ann. de l'Inst. Pasteur* LXXVIII. 734): see PRO-² and PHAGE.] The form which a temperate phage has in a lysogenic bacterium: it is incorporated into and replicates with the bacterial genome, and is only potentially lytic.

1951 [see INDUCE *v.* 4 e]. **1955** *Sci. Amer.* Apr. 93/1 Some prophages control the production of substances by their hosts (e.g., diphtheria toxin) or have other important effects on them. **1969** A. M. CAMPBELL *Episomes* vi. 81 Prophage insertion is a special kind of recombination process. **1973** R. G. KRUEGER et al. *Introd. Microbiol.* xviii. 507/1 The evidence suggested that the virus resided in a novel state as a prophage and that the presence of the prophage or phage genome in the cell rendered the cell immune to vegetative replication of other similar temperate phage particles by the same mechanism that limited its own vegetative replication.

prophain(e, -phan(e, obs. forms of PROFANE.

propham (ˈprəʊfæm). [f. PRO(PYL + PH(ENYL + CARB)AM(ATE.] Isopropyl *N*-phenylcarbamate, $C_6H_5{\cdot}NH{\cdot}CO{\cdot}O{\cdot}CH(CH_3)_2$, a white crystalline substance used as a selective herbicide to control weeds among crops, esp. during germination.

1955 *Proc. Brit. Weed Control Conf. 1954* I. 183 The almost complete failure of the more insoluble propham, CIPC and CMU to give control of wild oats may also be connected with the inability of the material to reach the wild oats at the critical time at Site I, where TCA was successful. **1958** *Weed Control Handbk.* (Brit. Weed Control Council) i. 19 For the control of wild oats in sugar beet and peas, propham has given results comparable with those obtained with trichloroacetic acid when applied in the same way—before the final seed-bed cultivations. **1973** ASHTON & CRAFTS *Mode of Action of Herbicides* xiii. 202 Propham is rapidly broken down by micro-organisms in the soil; such degradation is promoted by warmth and moisture. For this reason propham has proved most useful in cool season crops.

prophase (ˈprəʊfeɪz). *Cytology.* [ad. G. *prophase* (E. Strasburger 1884, in *Arch. f. mikrosk. Anat.* XXIII. 250): see PRO-² and PHASE.] The first stage in a mitotic or meiotic nuclear division, preceding prometaphase, during which the chromosomes become visible and shorten and the nuclear envelope disappears. Also *attrib.* or as *adj.*

Prophase of the first meiotic division is divided into LEPTOTENE, ZYGOTENE, PACHYTENE, DIPLOTENE, and DIAKINESIS, in that order.

1884 *Jrnl. R. Microsc. Soc.* IV. II. 714 In both [plants and animals] we find that in the 'prophases' of nuclear division cytoplasm is collected at the future poles of the cell-nucleus. **1887** tr. *Strasburger's Bot.* xxxii. 363 With this the preparatory phases of cell-division, the *prophases*, are completed.—Now begin the phases of separation and rearrangement of the daughter-segments, the *metaphases* of division. **1898** *Ibid.* I. i. 62 The changes occurring in a mother nucleus preparatory to division are termed the prophases of the karyokinesis. **1903** *Bot. Gaz.* XXXV. 250 The first division in Salamandra is characterized by a long period of growth of the cell and nucleus during the prophase..; the first longitudinal fission taking place during the prophase and the second during the metaphase or anaphase. **1911** *Q. Jrnl. Microsc. Sci.* LVII. 27 The most important difference between the pre-meiotic and meiotic prophases is the entire absence in the former of any appearance of fusion of chromatin threads, such as takes place in zygonema. **1931** E. B. FORD *Mendelism & Evolution* I. i. 18 Blocks of genes cross over together, as would be expected if, in fact, this phenomenon is due to the twisting of the chromosome threads round each other during the prophase of the reduction division. **1948** R. A. R. GRESSON *Essent. Gen. Cytol.* v. 33 (*caption*) Prophase chromosome to show arrangement of chromonemes. **1957** C. P. SWANSON *Cytol. & Cytogenetics* iii. 49 Prophase is said to be initiated at the moment when the chromosomes become visibly distinct. **1970** AMBROSE & EASTY *Cell Biol.* ix. 296 In late prophase.. the spindle develops and the asters move apart.

Hence **proˈphasic** *a.*

1913 *La Cellule* XXIX. 311 The first indication that the prophasic changes have begun is seen in the breaking down of the anastomoses along the lines between the heavier portions of the reticulum. **1929** *Bot. Gaz.* LXXXVIII. 376 In the latter case the visible division of the chromonema would always be prophasic. **1951** H. C. BOLD in G. M. Smith *Man. Phycol.* xi. 225 The Florideae furnish a conspicuous exception in that the spermatium nucleus is usually described as in a prophasic condition at the moment of union.

‖**prophasis** (ˈprɒfəsɪs). *Med.* [mod.L., a. Gr. πρόφασις (Hippocr.), f. πρό, PRO-² + φάσις PHASE *sb.*] (See quots.)

1681 tr. *Willis' Rem. Med. Wks.* Vocab., *Prophasis*, the appearing or shewing of a thing. **1693** tr. *Blancard's Phys. Dict.* (ed. 2), *Prophasis*, a Fore-knowledge in Diseases; also an Occasion of antecedent Cause. **1858** MAYNE *Expos. Lex.*, *Prophasis*, old term for the remote, or procatarctic cause of disease; but Lindenus seems to have taken it for the antecedent, or proximate cause, and the predisposition of the body to disease. **1895** *Syd. Soc. Lex.*, *Prophasis*..the occasion which renders active or efficient a previous disposition to disease.

propheciˈographer. *nonce-wd.* [f. PROPHECY + -(O)GRAPHER.] One who writes down or records prophecies.

1817 SOUTHEY *Malory's Arthur* I. Pref. 13 One of his clerks, by name Master Anthoine, succeeded to the office of Propheciographer.

ˈprophecize, *v. nonce-wd.* [f. PROPHECY + -IZE: cf. PROPHETIZE.] *intr.* To utter prophecies.

1815 LADY GRANVILLE *Lett.* (1894) I. 87 Lord Kinnaird whispering, gesticulating, and prophecising.

prophecy (ˈprɒfɪsɪ). Forms: α. 3–4 **profecie,** 4 **-fecye,** 4–5 **-fycye, -fes(s)ye,** 5 **-fesi.** β. 3–7 **prophecie,** 3–8 **-phesie,** 4–5 **-pheci, -phessye,** 4–6 **-phecye, -phesye,** 5 **-phecij, -phesi, -phicie, -phase, -phasy,** 5–8 **-phesy,** 4– **prophecy.** γ. 5 **propheteye,** 6 **-phe(a)tie.** [a. OF. *profecie* (12th c.), mod.F. *prophétie* (pron. prɔfesi) = Pr., Pg. *prophecia*, Sp. *profecía*, It. *profezía*; ad. late L. *prophētia* (in *Itala*), *-ēcia*, a. Gr. προφητεία prophecy, f. προφήτης PROPHET. The variant spelling *prophesy* is found as late as 1709, but is now confined to the verb.]

1. The action, function, or faculty of a prophet; divinely inspired utterance or discourse; *spec.* in Christian theology, utterance flowing from the revelation and impulse of the Holy Spirit.

a **1225** *Ancr. R.* 158 He [Saint John the Baptist] ine his iborenesse upspende his feder tunge into prophecie. *c* **1290** *S. Eng. Leg.* I. 364/30 For prophesie and riȝt-wisnesse huy heolden al þat he seide. **1382** WYCLIF *1 Cor.* xiii. 2 If I schal haue prophesye, and haue knowun all mysteries,..if I schal not haue charite, I am noȝt. **1390** GOWER *Conf.* III. 67 For it was guile and Sorcerie, Al that sche tok for Prophecie. **1563** WINȜET *Four Scoir Thre Quest.* §24 Wks. (S.T.S.) I. 90 Serapion, quha..wes illuminat be the spirit of prophetie. **1619** W. SCLATER *Exp. 1 Thess.* (1638) 532 Of Prophecie we find two sorts. First, Extraordinary, that stood partly in foretelling things to come, by immediate reuelation; partly, in interpreting Scriptures with unerring faith. *a* **1704** LOCKE *Par. 1 Cor.* xii. (1709) 78 *note* 10 Prophesie comprehends these three things. Prediction, Singing by the Dictate of the Spirit, and understanding and explaining the mysterious hidden Sense of Scripture by an immediate Illumination and Motion of the Spirit. **1823** KEBLE *Serm.* iii. (1848) 44 Prophecy, or the authorized declaration of God's will. **1877** E. R. CONDER *Basis of Faith* vii. 299 Prophecy, as the term is used in the Bible, signifies not prediction, but divinely-inspired speech. Prediction was merely one function of the prophetic office, subordinate to its moral aim. **1886** C. A. BRIGGS *Messianic Proph.* i. 1 Prophecy is religious instruction. It is an essential feature of the religion of cultivated nations.

2. The spoken, or especially, the written utterance of a prophet, or of the prophets.

a **1300** *Cursor M.* 9196 Þat time was prophet Ieremi Spekand in his propheci. *c* **1315** SHOREHAM I. 1292 Ine þe alde laȝe þe redere Rede þe prophessye By wokke. **1388** WYCLIF *2 Chron.* ix. 29 Writun..in the wordis of Achie of Silo, and in the visioun [*gloss* ether prophesie] of Addo, the prophete, aȝens Jeroboam. **1560** BIBLE (Genev.) *Prov.* xxxi. 1 The wordes of king Lemuel; The prophecie which his mother taught him. **1561** DAUS tr. *Bullinger on Apoc.* (1573) 307 b, All the Scripture is called a prophesie, which is as much to say as diuine. *c* **1575** H. NICHOLAS (*title*) Revelatio Dei. The Revelation of God, and his great Propheatie, which God now, in the last Daye, hath shewed unto his Elect. **1680** BURNET *Rochester* 140 The 53rd Chapter of the Prophesie of Isaiah. **1727** DE FOE *Syst. Magic* I. i. (1840) 33 The wise men of Babylon are distinguished in the prophecy of Daniel into four classes. **1815** BYRON *Heb. Mel. Vision Belshazzar* v, The lamps around were bright, The prophecy in view. **1902** FAIRBAIRN *Philos. Chr. Relig.* II. v. 422 To be the Christ of prophecy was to be the Crucified of Judaism.

†**3.** A company or body of prophets. *Obs. rare.*

13.. *E.E. Allit. P.* B. 1308 He þe kyng hatz conquest & þe kyth wunnen..& þe pryce of þe profecie prisoners maked.

4. The foretelling of future events; orig. as an inspired action; extended to foretelling by any means; an instance of this. Now the ordinary sense.

Originally, one of the notions included in sense 1.

a **1300** *Cursor M.* 14531 He com for to dei wit wil, And sua þe prophecis to fill. *c* **1330** R. BRUNNE *Chron.* (1810) 282 A prophecie sais he salle die. **1485–6** *Plumpton Corr.* (Camden) 50 It is in actt, that all maner of profycyes is mayd felony. **1584** POWEL *Lloyd's Cambria* 3 Until the prophesies of Merlin should be fulfilled. **1605** SHAKS. *Lear* III. ii. 80 Ile speake a Prophesie ere I go. *Ibid.* 95 This prophecie Merlin shall make, for I liue before his time. **1706** PHILLIPS, *Prophecy*, a Prediction or Foretelling. **1736** BUTLER *Anal.* II. vii. Wks. 1874 I. 273 Prophecy is nothing but the history of events before they come to pass. **1810** SCOTT *Lady of L.* I. xxiii, Old Allan-bane foretold your plight,..But light I held his prophecy. **1838** DE MORGAN *Ess. Probab.* 113 There is prophecy, but not of particular events, and derived, not from inspiration, but from observation. The astronomer predicts—and all the world knows that his predictions daily come true. **1894** H. DRUMMOND *Ascent Man* 271 The amelioration of the Struggle for Life is the most certain prophecy of Science. **1897** SIR W. LAWSON in *Westm. Gaz.* 3 Dec. 2/1 One of Disraeli's delightful sayings was, 'that of all forms of error prophecy is the most gratuitous.'

b. *fig.* A foreshadowing of something to come.

1742 YOUNG *Nt. Th.* VII. 16 The world's a prophecy of worlds to come. **1822** B. CORNWALL *Ludovico Sforza* ii, Methinks she was A beautiful prophecy of thee.

5. The interpretation and expounding of Scripture or of divine mysteries: a function of the prophet in the apostolic churches; applied in the 16th and 17th centuries, and sometimes later, to exposition of the scriptures, esp. in conferences for that purpose, and to preaching. See PROPHESYING b.

1382 [see 1]. **1382** WYCLIF *1 Cor.* xiii. 8 Charite fallith not down, whether prophecyes schulen be voydid, ether langagis schulen ceesse, ether science schal be distroyed [1611 Whether there be prophecies, they shall faile]. [**1576** GRINDAL *Let.* 20 Dec. in *Mem.* (1710) 15 That Exercise in the Church St. Paul calleth *Prophesia*, and the Speaker *Prophetas*, terms very Odious in our Days to some, because they are not rightly understood; for indeed, *Propheta* in that, and the like Places of the same St. Paul..signifieth thereby the Assent and Consent of the Scriptures.] **1577** HARRISON *England* II. i. (1877) I. 17 In manie of our archdeaconries we have an exercise..called a prophesie or conference, and erected onelie for the examination or triall of the diligence of the cleargie in their studie of holie scriptures. **1577** in Stovel *Introd. Canne's Necess.* (1849) 59 Forbidding the exercises called Prophecies, as being practices and rites belonging to religion, not established by parliament and her authority. *a* **1649** WINTHROP *New Eng.* (1853) I. 60 Mr. Wilson, praying and exhorting the congregation to love, etc., commended to them the exercise of prophecy in his absence. **1709** STRYPE *Ann. Ref.* I. xxxiv. 343 One Thursday in March, at a prophesy (as it was called) in the Dutch Church in London, where Nicolas one of the ministers preached upon the doctrine of regeneration.

6. *Eccl.* **a.** An Old Testament lection, *esp.* in the eucharistic office (e.g. in the Ambrosian rite). Cf. *prophetic lesson* (PROPHETIC 1 b), PROPHET 3 b.

c **1440** *Alphabet of Tales* 324 Saynt Ambros þe bisshoppe was att mes..and as he lenyd on þe altar, betwix þe prophesie & þe epistull, he fell on slepe. **1853** DALE tr. *Baldeschi's Ceremonial* 201 When the Acolyte has finished singing the Prophecy, he genuflects to the Altar. **1872** SCUDAMORE *Notitia Euch.* 205 In the Milanese [rite] there was..a verse or two sung from the Psalms..between the Prophecy and the Epistles.

b. The canticle *Benedictus* as used in the Gallican liturgy.

[**1855** NEALE & FORBES *Anc. Lit. Gall. Ch.* 34 *marg.*, We learn from the exposition of the Gallican service ascribed to S. Germanus that the *prophetia* was the song of Zacharias.] **1872** SCUDAMORE *Notitia Euch.* 203 *note*, The reader must not be misled by the title Collectio or Oratio post Prophetiam in the Old Gothic, Frank, and Gallican Sacramentaries; for by 'the Prophecy' is there meant the *Benedictus* or Prophecy of Zacharias. **1880** —— in *Smith's Dict. Chr. Antiq.* 1738/1 The prophecy was, on some days, in most of the Gallican liturgies, followed by an 'Oratio' or 'Collectio post Prophetiam'.

ˈprophecy-ˌmonger. [f. prec. + MONGER.] One who deals in, repeats, or occupies himself with prophecies.

1655 FULLER *Ch. Hist.* IV. ii. §46 An old prophesie among the English (observed by forrainers to be the greatest

Prophecy-mongers). **1858** H. W. Beecher *Life Th.* (1859) 32 Such to me is the Bible when the pragmatic prophecy-monger and the swinish utilitarian have toothed its fruits and craunched its blossoms.

ˈ**prophesiable**, *a. rare.* In 7 -cyable. [f. as next + -able.] Capable of being prophesied.

1652 Gaule *Magastrom.* 194 It is not for every prophet to know every thing that is prophecyable.

prophesier (ˈprɒfɪsaɪə(r)). Also 5–7 -cier, 8 -syer. [f. next + -er¹.] One who or that which prophesies; *esp.* one who predicts or foreshows; a prophet; a prognostic; in 17th c. applied to Puritan preachers: cf. prophesy *v.* 1 c.

1477 Earl Rivers (Caxton) *Dictes* 11 God..hath establisshed prophetes & prophecier. *a* **1548** Hall *Chron., Hen. IV* 20 The Lorde Percy and Owen Glendor were vnwisely made beleue by a Welsh Prophecier that King Henry was the Moldwarpe. **1598** Tofte *Alba* (1880) 17 Like to the Porpose (Tempests prophesier) I play before the storme of my sad Teares. **1601** Shaks. *All's Well* iv. iii. 115 Bring forth this counterfet module, has deceiu'd mee, like a double-meaning Prophesier. **1631** Weever *Anc. Fun. Mon.* 54 Martinists, Prophesiers, Solifidians. **1754** Sherlock *Disc.* iv. (1764) 217 Temporal Prosperity was not excluded from the Prophesyer's Thoughts. **1831** *Fraser's Mag.* III. 478 What meant that old proser and prophesier?

prophesy (ˈprɒfɪsaɪ), *v.* Forms: 4–5 profecy, 5 -ecie; 4–5 prophecien, -esien, 5–6 -ecie, 5–7 -esie, -ecy, 5– prophesy. [ME. a. OF. *prophecier* (1245 in Godef.), *-phesier, -fecier, -ficier*, f. *prophecie, -fecie* prophecy. The modern differentiation of *prophesy* vb. and *prophecy* sb. was not established till after 1700, and has no etymological basis, *prophesy* being at first a mere spelling variant in both sb. and vb. For the pronunciation of the final vowel cf. verbs in *-fy*, also *multiply*.]

1. *intr.* To speak by (or as by) divine inspiration, or in the name of a deity; to speak as a prophet.

1382 Wyclif *Num.* xi. 25 And whanne the spiryte hadde restid in hem, thei profecyden, ne more ouer ceisden. **1382** —— *Jer.* xix. 14 Cam forsothe Jeremye fro Tofeth..to profecien. **1382** —— *Ezek.* xxx. 2 Sone of man, prophecy thou, and sey, Thes thingis seith the Lord God. **1382** —— *Rev.* xi. 3 And I shal ȝiue to my two witnesses, and thei shulen prophecie a thousynd dayes two hundrid and sixty. **1535** Coverdale *1 Sam.* xix. 23 And yᵉ sprete of God came vpon him [Saul] also, and he wente & prophecied likewise before Samuel... Here of came the prouerbe: Is Saul also among the prophetes? **1651** Hobbes *Leviath.* iii. xxxii. 197 The Prophet that was sent to prophecy against the Altar. **1681–6** J. Scott *Chr. Life* (1747) III. 109 He came down immediately from the Father, to prophesy to us. **1880** R. Grant White *Every-Day Eng.* 304, I would..call upon the Furies to aid me while I prophesy against this new thing.

b. *spec.* To utter predictions, to foretell future events (by inspiration, or generally).

1382 Wyclif *1 Pet.* i. 10 Prophetes..that prophecieden of the grace to comynge in ȝou. **1432–50** tr. *Higden* (Rolls) I. 419 Therefore there were ij. Merlynes; oon of them.. profeciede in Snawdonia in the tyme of Vortigernus. *a* **1450** *Knt. de la Tour* (1906) 90 Brun..was the quene of the whiche Sibille spake and profesied. **1563** Winȝet *Four Scoir Thre Quest.* §79 Wks. (S.T.S.) I. 127 Quhare he [St. Paul] propheciis of the hæretikis, that suld forbid mariage. **1601** Shaks. *Jul. C.* iii. i. 259 Ouer thy wounds, now do I Prophesie,..A Curse shall light vpon the limbes of men. **1817** Shelley *Rev. Islam* ix. vi. 9 Half-extinguished words, which prophesied of change. **1898** *Westm. Gaz.* 19 May 11/1 'Never prophesy till you know', is a safe American saying.

c. In the Apostolic churches, To interpret or expound the Scriptures, to utter divine mysteries and edifying communications (as moved by the Holy Spirit); hence, in the 16th and 17th centuries, applied by the Puritans to the interpretation and expounding of Scripture and the preaching of the Gospel. See also prophesying *vbl. sb.*

1382 Wyclif *1 Cor.* xiv. 4 He that spekith in tunge, edifieth him silf; forsoth he that prophecieth, edyfieth the chirch of God. *Ibid.* 39 So, bretheren, loue ȝe for to prophecie [**1388** profecie], and nyle ȝe forbede for to speke in tungis. **1583** Stubbes *Anat. Abus.* ii. (1882) 72 It were good..that all could prophesie, that is, that all could preach and expound the truth. **1607** Hieron *Wks.* I. 99 To *prophecy*, in Scripture, signifieth..secondly, exactly and soundly to interpret the Scripture; to which sense the word is often applyed in the New Testament. *a* **1645** Featly *Dippers Dipt* Epist. B ij, They hold their Conventicles weekly in our chiefe Cities,..and there prophesie by turnes. **1771** Wesley *Wks.* (1872) V. 28 O that, as I prophesy, there might now be 'a noise and a shaking'! **1860** Pusey *Min. Proph.* 128 Those sons and daughters of the sons of Zion, having received the Spirit, prophesied, i.e. in divers tongues they spake of the heavenly mysteries.

2. *trans.* To announce or utter by (or as by) divine inspiration; *esp.* so to announce (a future event); to predict, to foretell. **a.** with obj. clause expressing the matter announced.

1377 Langl. *P. Pl.* B. xix. 16 Patriarkes & prophetes prophecyed bifore, þat alkyn creatures shulden knelen & bowen. **1388** Wyclif *John* xi. 51 He prophesiede, that Jhesu was to die for the folc. **1470–85** Malory *Arthur* x. v. 419 Merlyon profecyed that in that same place shold fyghte two ..knyghtes. *a* **1533** Ld. Berners *Huon* lxxxiv. 265 She prophesyed that my father..sholde wynne the batayle. **1682** Dryden *Mac Fl.* 87 For ancient Decker prophesy'd long since, That in this pile should reign a mighty prince. **1802** Mar. Edgeworth *Moral T.* (1816) I. vi. 33, I prophesy you will not succeed better than I have. **1842** Tennyson *St. Sim. Styl.* 217 By the warning of the Holy Ghost, I prophesy that I shall die to-night, A quarter before twelve.

b. with simple obj.

c **1380** Wyclif *Last Age of Ch.* (1851) p. xxix, And þat þat is prophesied schal come. **1382** —— *Jer.* xx. 6 There thou shalt be biried, and alle thi frendus, to whyche thou profeciedist lesing [*quibus prophetasti mendacium*]. *c* **1400** *Three Kings Cologne* 37 Hit was þe same sterre þat was prophecied by balaam. **1481** Caxton *Myrr.* i. v. 24 Philosophres that..prophecyed the holy tyme of the comyng of ihesu cryste. **1585** T. Washington tr. *Nicholay's Voy.* iv. viii. 119 b, The first Sibille..prophesied the myracle of the fiue loaues and two fishes. **1679** Dryden *Troilus & Cr.* Ep. Ded., I am almost ready..to point out, and Prophecy the Man, who was born for no less an Undertaking. **1847** Tennyson *Princ.* i. 141 Dismal lyrics, prophesying change Beyond all reason.

c. *fig.* To indicate beforehand, foreshow.

1605 Shaks. *Lear* v. iii. 175 Me thought thy very gate did prophesie A Royall Noblenesse.

Hence **prophesied** (ˈprɒfɪsaɪd) *ppl. a.*, uttered prophetically, foretold, predicted; ˈ**prophesying** *ppl. a.*, that prophesies.

c **1440** *Promp. Parv.* 414/2 Profecyed, *prophetatus.* **1621** Brathwait *Nat. Embassie* (1877) 52 The Augur hauing left behind him his Oscines or Prophes[y]ing birds. **1708** Shaftesb. *Charact.* (1733) I. 44 The new prophesying Sect. **1742** J. Willison *Balm of Gilead* xi. (1800) 123 Unlikely this and other prophesied events may appear.

prophesying (ˈprɒfɪsaɪɪŋ), *vbl. sb.* [f. prec. + -ing¹.] The action of the verb prophesy; speaking by divine inspiration; foretelling the future; expounding divine mysteries or preaching unto edification, as practised in apostolic times.

1526 Tindale *1 Cor.* xiv. 6 Excepte I speake vnto you other by revelacion, or knowledge, or prophesying, or doctrine. **1535** Coverdale *1 Chron.* xxvi. [xxv.] 3 The children of Iedithun.., whose prophecienge was to geue thankes and to praise the Lorde. **1617** R. Fenton *Treat. Ch. Rome* 115 To reforme abuses concerning Praier, and Prophes[y]ing in the Church of Corinth. **1820** Keats *Hyperion* i. 174 So also shuddered he—Not at dog's howl,.. Or prophesyings of the midnight lamp.

b. Applied in the 16th and 17th centuries, and by some in later times, to the expounding of Scripture by those who spoke 'as the Spirit gave them utterance' in special meetings, or to preaching in public services.

1560–1 *1st Bk. Discipl. Ch. Sc.* xii, That Exercise, which Sanct Paull calleth prophecieing. **1561** Daus tr. *Bullinger on Apoc.* (1573) 42 The woman..sought to gouerne the propheciyng at her pleasure. **1569** Golding *Heminges Post.* Ded. 2 Hee opening the Gospels after the maner of our prophecyings. **1574** in Strype *Parker* iv. xxxvii. (1711) 462, I am commanded.., in the Queen her Majesty's name, that the Prophesyings throughout my Dioces should be suppressed. **1604** Bacon *Pacif. Ch.* Wks. 1879 I. 357/1 [The exercise] called prophesying; which was this: That the ministers within a precinct did meet upon a week day in some principal town... Then every minister successively, beginning with the youngest, did handle one and the same part of Scripture. **1642** T. Lechford *Plain Dealing* (1867) 41 There a Minister..preacheth and exerciseth prayer every Lords day, which is called prophesying in such a place. **1647** Jer. Taylor *Lib. Proph.* ii. 43 S. Cyprian had not learn'd to forbid to any one a liberty of prophesying or interpretation. **1655** Fuller *Ch. Hist.* ix. iv. §2 These prophesyings were founded on the Apostles precept, 'For, ye may all prophesie one by one, that all may learn, and all be comforted'. **1752** Carte *Hist. Eng.* III. 579 Setting up certain exercises, which, by the misapplication of a text of scripture, they called prophesyings. **1827** Hallam *Const. Hist.* (1857) I. iv. 197 The clergy in several dioceses set up, with encouragement from their superiors, a certain religious exercise, called prophesyings. **1849** Stovel *Introd. Canne's Necess.* 60 The prophesyings here prohibited, formed an administration of divine truth, to which the Puritans adhered as being of Divine authority.

attrib. **1679** C. Nesse *Antichrist* 184 When their prophecying-work is done.

prophet (ˈprɒfɪt), *sb.* Forms: α. 2–5 **profete**, 3 -fiete, 4 -fiȝt, -fet, 4–5 -fett, 5 -ffet, -fyt, 6 -fit(te, 7 -ffit. β. 2–6 **prophete**, 4– **prophet** (4 -phyte, -phite, 4–5 -phett, 5 -phytt, 6 *Sc.* -pheite). [ME. *prophete, -fete*, a. F. *prophète* (11th c. in Littré), ad. L. *prophēta* (*prophētēs*), ad. Gr. προφήτης an interpreter, proclaimer, spokesman, esp. of the will of the deity; an inspired person, a prophet; f. πρό forth, before, for + -φητης speaker, f. φάναι to speak.]

I. 1. a. One who speaks for God or for any deity, as the inspired revealer or interpreter of his will; one who is held or (more loosely) who claims to have this function; an inspired or quasi-inspired teacher.

In popular use, generally connoting the special function of revealing or predicting the future. (Hence sense 5.)

The Greek προφήτης was originally the spokesman or interpreter of a divinity, e.g. of Zeus, Dionysus, Apollo, or the deliverer or interpreter of an oracle, corresponding generally to the Latin *vātēs*. By the LXX it was adopted to render the Heb. *nābī*, in the O.Test. applied indiscriminately to the prophets of Jehovah, of Baal and other heathen deities, and even to 'false prophets', reputed or pretended soothsayers. In the N.T. it is used in the same senses as in the LXX, but mainly applied to the Hebrew prophets of Jehovah, also to John the Baptist, as well as to certain persons in the Early Church, who were recognized as possessing more or less of the character of the old Hebrew prophets, or as inspired to utter special revelations and predictions; also applied historically to Balaam, and by St. Paul, in the old Greek sense, to Epimenides the Cretan, while 'false prophets' are frequently mentioned. The Greek word was adopted in L. as *prophēta* chiefly in post-classical times, and largely under Christian influences; and this is the regular rendering in the *Itala*, Vulgate, and Christian Fathers. From Ecclesiastical Latin it has passed down into the Romanic and Teutonic languages. In English the earliest uses are derived from the Scriptures; but the word is currently used in all the ancient senses and in modern ones derived from them.

c **1175** *Lamb. Hom.* 5 Þa hit wes ifullet þet ysaias þe prophete iwiteȝede. *c* **1200** *Vices & Virtues* 31 For ði sade Dauið, ðe profiete. *c* **1200** Ormin 5195 Helyas wass an haliȝ mann & an wurrþfull prophete. *a* **1300** *Cursor M.* 7287 (Cott.) Prophet he was, sir samuel. *c* **1315** Shoreham iii. 60 Al he folueþ þe lawe of gode, And prophetene gestes. *c* **1380** Wyclif *Serm.* Sel. Wks. II. 74 Elisee þe profete. **1382** —— *Exod.* vii. 1, Y haue ordeyned thee the god of Pharao; and Aaron, thi brother, shal be thi prophete. **1382** —— *1 Kings* xviii. 19 The prophetis of Baal foure hundrid and fifti, and the prophetis of mawmet wodis foure hundrid, that eten of the bord of Jezebel. **1382** —— *Acts* xiii. 1 Ther weren in the chirche that was at Antioche, prophetis and doctours. **1382** —— *Tit.* i. 12 The propre prophete of hem [**1388** her propre profete], seide, Men of Crete ben euermore lyeris. *c* **1400** *Destr. Troy* 4403 Of whom the proffet of prise plainly can say, þere was no sterne in astate stode hym aboue. *a* **1450** Myrc *Festial* 110 Euer þay were lettyd by drede of þe pepull; for þe pepull heldyn hym a profyt. **1483** *Cath. Angl.* 292/1 A Profett (*A.* Profite), *propheta,..vates;..vaticinus, vatidicus; Christus.* **1526** Tindale *Acts* xiii. 6 A certayne sorserer, a falce prophet which was a iewe, named Bariesu. **1534** —— *Matt.* xiii. 57 A Prophet is not with out honoure, save in hys awne countre, and amonge his awne kynne. **1559** Bp. Scot in Strype *Ann. Ref.* (1709) I. App. vii. 13 Almyghtie God said by the profitte. **1648** *Assembly's Shorter Catech.* Q. 23 Christ as our Redeemer executeth the Offices of a Prophet, of a Priest, and of a King. **1677** Gale *Crt. Gentiles* II. iii. 61 Plato tels..The God..useth these ministers, and messengers to deliver his oracles, and divine Prophets. **1697** Dryden *Virg. Georg.* iv. 558 In the Carpathian Bottom makes abode The Shepherd of the Seas, a Prophet and a God. **1757** Gray *Bard* 21 With a Master's hand, and Prophet's fire. **1838** Thirlwall *Greece* II. 28 He [Epimenides] was a poet too as well as a prophet, and the descriptions given of his works attest the fecundity of his genius. **1841** Lane *Arab. Nts.* I. ii. 80 Suleymán is the Prophet of God. **1850** Robertson *Serm.* iv. xxv. (1882) 185 A prophet was one commissioned to declare the will of God —a revealer of truth; it might be of facts future, or the far higher truth of the meaning of facts present. **1874** H. R. Reynolds *John Bapt.* iii. iii. 194 The true *Nabi*..is the mouthpiece, the interpreter of God to man. This is unquestionably the true significance of the word 'prophet'.

†**b.** In vaguer sense: rendering L. *vātēs* or *poēta*, an 'inspired' bard. *Obs.*

1387 Trevisa *Higden* (Rolls) I. 13 So saiþ the prophete Satiricus [Higden *poeta satiricus*; *Hart. tr.* the poete Satiricus: i.e. Horace, *Ars Poet.* 304], 'I fare as the whetston þat makeþ yren sharpe and kene.' **1593** Q. Eliz. *Boeth.* iii. met. xii. 72 The Tracian profit wons His wives funeralz wailing. [**1780** Cowper *Table T.* 500 In a Roman mouth, the graceful name Of prophet and of poet was the same. **1840** Carlyle *Heroes* iii. (1858) 244 Poet and Prophet differ greatly in our loose modern notions of them. In some old languages the titles are synonymous; *Vates* means both Prophet and Poet.]

c. Sometimes applied to those who preach or 'hold forth' in a religious meeting, by those who take them to represent the 'prophets' of the Apostolic Church. Also, the official name of a grade of ministers in the 'Catholic Apostolic' or Irvingite Church.

Founded upon the references to prophets and prophesying in 1 Cor. xiv. e.g.: **1526** Tindale *1 Cor.* xiv. 29 Lett the prophetes speake two atonce, or thre atonce, and let other iudge... For ye maye all prophesy one by one, thatt all maye learne, and all maye have comforte.

1560 Daus tr. *Sleidane's Comm.* 130 At this same tyme the chiefest Prophet amonges them, for that name they doe vsurpe to themselues, Iohn Mathewe commaunded them. **1832** E. Irving in Mrs. Oliphant *Life* (1862) II. v. 278 After I have preached, I will pause a little, so that then the prophets may have an opportunity of prophesying if the Spirit should come upon them; but I never said that the prophets should not prophesy at any other time. **1845** S. Austin *Ranke's Hist. Ref.* II. 27 Of what use, said he, would learning be henceforth? They had now among them the divine prophets of Zwickau, Storch, Thomä, and Stübner, who conversed with God, and were filled with grace and knowledge without any study whatsoever. **1854** W. Wilks *E. Irving* 187 The Albury School of Prophets. **1883** R. H. Story *E. Irving* in *Scottish Divines* 269 On..Friday, April 5 [1833] the apostle, laying his hands on Irving's head, ordained him 'Angel of the Church'. At the same time elders and deacons were set apart, and the functions of prophet and evangelist were more exactly defined than hitherto.

d. *fig.* (In non-religious sense.) The 'inspired' or accredited spokesman, proclaimer, or preacher of some principle, cause, or movement.

1848 R. I. Wilberforce *Doctr. Incarnation* xiv. (1852) 407 These [Newton and Milton] and such prophets of humanity have opened to us secrets, which..ordinary faculties.. would have been unable to discover. **1874** Micklethwaite *Mod. Par. Churches* 6 Durandus himself, the prophet of symbolism. **1893** Liddon, etc. *Life Pusey* I. iii. 41 Byron was in a sense the prophet of the disappointed, and, as such, he threw a strange spell over Pusey as a young man.

2. *spec.* ***the Prophet*:** **a.** Muhammad, the founder of Islam; a rendering of the Arabic title *al-nabiy*; often used by writers on Islam. (Sometimes put for another Arabic title, *al-rasūl*, 'the apostle', or 'messenger', esp. in the formula 'There is no god but God [*Allah*];

Muhammad is the messenger of God', often rendered 'Muhammad is his prophet'.)

By Christians sometimes designated 'the False Prophet'. **1615** G. SANDYS *Trav.* I. 55 Some shaking their heads incessantly,..perhaps in imitation of the supposed trances ..of their Prophet. *a* **1618** RALEIGH *Mahomet* (1637) 16 The title of Prophet which he had obtained. **1634** SIR T. HERBERT *Trav.* 153 Their is one God, the great God and Mahomet is his Prophet. **1728** POPE *Dunc.* III. 97 His conqu'ring tribes th' Arabian prophet draws. **1731** tr. *Boulainvilliers' Life Mahomet* 256 He says that the Prophet exhorting one day his soldiers [etc.]. **1788** GIBBON *Decl. & F.* l. (1790) IX. 289 The flight of the prophet from Mecca to Medina has fixed the memorable æra of the Hegira. **1813** BYRON *Giaour* 679 He called the Prophet, but his power Was vain against the vengeful Giaour. **1824** MORIER *Adv. Hajji Baba* (1835) I. v. 33, I swear by the beard of the Prophet, that if you do not behave well, I'll burn your father. **1868** FITZGERALD *Omar Khayyam* (ed. 2) lxv, If but the Vine and Love-abjuring Band Are in the Prophet's Paradise to stand.

b. Applied by (or after) the Mormons to the founder of their system, and his successors.

1844 in *The Mormons* vii. (1851) 171 On hearing of the martyrdom of our beloved Prophet and patriarch, you will doubtless need a word of advice and comfort. **1851** *Ibid.* i. 16 The remarkable career of Joseph Smith, the Prophet of the Mormons. **1874** J. H. BLUNT *Dict. Sects* 347/1 The Prophet, his brother Hyram, and other leading Mormons, were seized. **1893** GUNTER *Miss Dividends* 121 'Don't you know ..that the prophet up there', he nods his head in the direction of Brigham Young's private residence, 'and some of the other leaders of the Church are beginning to be afraid of Tranyon?'

3. a. *pl.* The prophetical writers or writings of the Old Testament.

By the Jews the Scriptures of the O.T. are divided into the *Law* (*hat-tōrāh*), the *Prophets* (*hann'bīim*), and the *Writings* or Hagiographa (*hak-k'thūbīm*). The *Prophets* are divided into the *Former Prophets*, including the books of Joshua, Judges, 1 and 2 Samuel, 1 and 2 Kings, and the *Later Prophets*, incl. Isaiah, Jeremiah, Ezekiel, and the twelve minor prophets, Hosea to Malachi. A compendious name for the O.T. Scriptures, often used in the N.T., was *the Law and the Prophets* or *Moses and the Prophets.* In Christian usage, the Prophets or Prophetical Books are the Later Prophets of the Jews, with Daniel (which by the Jews is placed among the Hagiographa). The terms *Minor Prophets* and (to a certain extent) *Major Prophets* are also in current use.

1382 WYCLIF *Matt.* xxii. 40 In these two maundementis hangith al the lawe and prophetis. **1382** —— *Luke* xvi. 29 Thei han Moyses and the prophetis; heere thei hem. **1526** TINDALE *Acts* xiii. 15 After the lectur of the lawe and the prophetes, the ruelers of the synagoge sent vnto them. **1611** BIBLE *Transl. Pref.* 3 Saue onely out of the Prophets. *Ibid.*, *2 Macc.* xv. 9 Comforting them out of the law, and the prophets. **1652** J. MAYER (*title*) A Commentarie upon all the Prophets. **1860** PUSEY (*title*) The Minor Prophets.

b. *Liturgics.* The Old Testament or Prophetic lesson at Mass.

1832 PALMER *Orig. Liturg.* I. 127 The liturgy of Milan is found to consist of the following parts... The anthem called 'Ingressa'—'Kyrie eleison'—'Gloria in excelsis'—the Collect—the Prophet—the Psalm—Epistle—Alleluia—Gospel and Sermon [etc.]. *Ibid.* 128 The Prophet and Psalm were only more frequently used at Milan than Rome.

†**4.** *pl.* Applied to certain actors (? personifying prophets) in the church plays before the Reformation: see quots. *Obs.*

1519 *Churchw. Acc. S. Stephen, Wallbrook* (MS. Guildh. Lib.) §v. lf. 2 b, Item for hyere of a borde for a proffyt on palme sondaye ij *d.*.. [Item for] dressyng of the proffyttes. **1524–5** *Rec. St. Mary at Hill* 327 Paid..for the fframe ouer þe North dore of the chirche, þat is for þe profettes on palmesonday..iii *d.* **1536–7** *Ibid.* 373 Item, paid to Wolston ffor makyng of yᵉ stages ffor yᵉ prophettes vj *d.* **1539–40** *Ibid.* 382 Payed for bred & drynke for the prophettes on palme sondaye j *d* ob.

II. 5. a. One who predicts or foretells what is going to happen; a prognosticator, a predictor. (Without reference to divine inspiration.)

a **1225** *Ancr. R.* 212 Summe iuglurs beoð þet..makien cheres, and wrenchen mis hore muð....þeos beoð hore owune prophetes forcwiddares. **1589** PUTTENHAM *Eng. Poesie* I. xxxi. (Arb.) 76 The disorders of that age, and specially the pride of the Romane Clergy, of whose fall he [Langland] seemeth to be a very true Prophet. **1605** SHAKS. *Lear* v. iii. 71 Iesters do oft proue Prophets. **1683** *Pennsylv. Archives.* I. 72 My Friend Braithwait was a true Proffit. **1769** H. WALPOLE *Let.* 31 Jan., I protest, I know no more than a prophet what is to come. **1898** A. J. BALFOUR in *Daily News* 30 Nov. 6/3 They prophesied, and they were subject to the weakness of all prophets—the event contradicted them.

b. Of things: An omen, a portent.

1591 SHAKS. *1 Hen. VI*, III. ii. 32 Now shine it [a torch] like a Commet of Reuenge, A Prophet to the fall of all our Foes. **1847** TENNYSON *Princ.* IV. 257 The mystic fire on a mast-head, Prophet of storm.

c. *slang.* One who predicts the result of a race, etc.; a tipster.

1843 *Ainsworth's Mag.* III. 220 What's to win the Derby? .. What say the prophets? **1862** *Times* 31 Dec., Prophets, tipsters and welshers—the parasites of the ring. **1884** *Pall Mall G.* 3 May 1/2 The skilful arguments of the 'prophet' of a daily or weekly newspaper. **1894** F. LOCKWOOD *Sp. at Cambr.* (Daily News 4 June 3/4), He remembered a prophet in a north of England town. He did not mean a racing prophet. He meant a real prophet, a sort of man who foretold the end of the world once a week.

III. 6. *attrib.* and *Comb.* **a.** Appositive (= 'that is a prophet'), as *prophet-bard, -king, -painter, -poet, -preacher, -romancer, -statesman*, etc. **b.** Of or pertaining to a prophet, as *prophet-eye, -mantle, -mind, -soul, -speech, -story, -voice.* Also **c.** *prophet-bearing, -like, -tongued* adjs.

1824 PIERPONT *Hymn, O thou to whom in ancient time* v, The lyre of *prophet bards was strung. **1855** BAILEY *Mystic* (ed. 2) 6 The preview clear of prophet-bard. **1733** ARBUTHNOT *Harmony in Uproar* Misc. Wks. 1751 II. 19 Further than Mahomet ever flew on his *Prophet-bearing Ass. **1821** BYRON *Juan* IV. xxii, That large black *prophet eye seem'd to dilate. **1860** PUSEY *Min. Proph.* 556 The prophecy..was framed to prepare the Jews to expect a *prophet-king. **1857** G. H. LEWES *Biogr. Hist. Philos.* (ed. 2) II. 319 Now grave, *prophetlike, and impassioned. **1906** *Dublin Rev.* Apr. 411 Aristotle in Mohammed's *prophet-mantle. **1832** TENNYSON *'Of old sat Freedom'* 6 Self-gather'd in her *prophet-mind. **1903** *Humanitarian* Mar. 104 An honoured place among the *prophet-poets of democracy. **1875** W. CORY *Lett. & Jrnls.* (1897) 393 No eminent *prophet-preacher is so self-contradictory as Carlyle. *a* **1861** CLOUGH *Relig. Poems* iii. 71 Is there no *prophet-soul..To dare, sublimely meek..The Deity to seek? **1814** SCOTT *Ld. of Isles* III. ii, When that grey Monk His *prophet-speech had spoke. **1871** R. ELLIS *Catullus* lxiv. 325 Hark..what *prophet-story the Sesters Open surely to thee.

† **'prophet,** *v. Obs. rare. pa. t.* (in 5) prophet. [ad. late L. *prophēt-āre* to prophesy, f. *prophēt-a* a PROPHET: so OF. *propheter.*] *intr.* To prophesy.

Hence † **'propheting** *ppl. a.*

c **1450** *St. Cuthbert* (Surtees) 2966 How cuthbert prophet, þis is taught. *Ibid.* 3023 As cuthbert prophet. **1582** STANYHURST *Æneis* III. (Arb.) 93 Nor propheting Helenus.. Forspake this burial mourning.

† **prophe'tation.** *Obs. rare*⁻¹. [ad. late L. *prophētātiōn-em*, n. of action from *prophēt-āre*: see prec.] Prophesying.

1594 R. WILSON *Coblers Proph.* I. i. 178 But now must Raph trudge about his prophetation.

prophetess ('prɒfɪtɪs). Forms: 4 prophetes, 4–5 profetesse, 4–6 prophetissa, 4–7 -isse, -esse, 5 -yssa, -ice, -as, -ese, 6 -ise, 4– prophetess. [ME. a. OF. *prophetesse, -isse*, ad. late L. *prophētissa* (*a* 200 in Itala, Luke ii. 36): see PROPHET *sb.* and -ESS¹. (The L. form was sometimes retained in earlier English use.)] A woman who prophesies, a female prophet; a sibyl.

In Isa. viii. 3, the meaning may be 'a prophet's wife'.

a **1300** *Cursor M.* 11356 (Cott.) O propheci soth þis word es, For þis anna was a prophetes [*Gött.* -ess]. *c* **1375** *Sc. Leg. Saints* xxiv. (*Alexis*) 30 Fyrst, be þat noble wyf anna, þat callit was prophetissa. **1382** WYCLIF *Luke* ii. 36 And Anna was a prophetisse. **1388** —— *Isa.* viii. 3 Y neiȝede to the profetesse [1382 a prophetesse]; and sche conseyuede, and childide a sone. *a* **1400–50** *Alexander* 4412 Dame Proserpyne, a prophetese of ȝoure praysid laȝes. *c* **1420** ? LYDG. *Assembly of Gods* 1589 The nobyll prophetyssa, Sybyll men hyr call. *c* **1440** *Alphabet of Tales* 369 He callid Sybilla þe prophetice vnto hym. *c* **1540** tr. *Pol. Verg. Eng. Hist.* (Camden No. 29) 37 Ioane the maide, the prophetisse of God, as the Common sort termed her. **1542** UDALL *Erasm. Apoph.* 201 He had..made a iourney to Delphos, when the prophetisse there saied [etc.]. **1579** FULKE *Heskins's Parl.* 29 The prophetesses of the olde lawe. **1591** SHAKS. *1 Hen. VI*, I. iv. 102 The Dolphin, with one Joane de Puzel ioyn'd, A holy Prophetesse, new risen vp. **1625** K. LONG tr. *Barclay's Argenis* I. xx. 64 When she had uttered many things in this Propheticke fury, falling to a lamentable shreiking, she resembled a true possest Prophetesse. **1763** J. BROWN *Poetry & Mus.* x. 180 Miriam, a distinguished Prophetess. **1882** G. SALMON in *Dict. Chr. Biog.* III. 936/1 The frenzied utterances of the Montanistic prophetesses.

b. *spec.* A woman who foretells events.

1390 GOWER *Conf.* I. 219 For so my dowhter prophetesse Forth with hir litel houndes deth Betokneth. **1594** SHAKS. *Rich. III*, I. iii. 301 O but remember this another day:..And say (poore Margaret) was a Prophetesse. **1761** GRAY *Descent of Odin* 85 No boding Maid of skill divine Art thou, nor Prophetess of good. **1817** SHELLEY *Rev. Islam* IX. xx, Cythna shall be the prophetess of love.

prophet-flower: see PROPHET'S-FLOWER.

prophethood ('prɒfɪthʊd). [f. PROPHET *sb.* + -HOOD.] The position or office of a prophet.

1840 CARLYLE *Heroes* iii. (1858) 268 That notion of Mahomet's, of his supreme Prophethood. **1868** NETTLESHIP *Browning* i. 50 For her sake, he would give up all his power and prophethood. **1875** S. TAYLOR tr. *Oehler's O.T. Theol.* II. 314 A review of the historical development of the prophethood. **1896** C. ALLEN in *United Presb. Mag.* Oct. 435 The Universal prophethood of believers.

prophetic (prəʊ'fɛtɪk), *a.* [a. F. *prophétique* (15th c. in Hatz.-Darm.), or ad. late L. *prophēticus* (*a* 200 in Itala), a. Gr. προφητικ-ός: see PROPHET *sb.* and -IC.]

1. Of, pertaining or proper to a prophet or prophecy; having the character or function of a prophet.

1604 SHAKS. *Oth.* III. iv. 72 A Sybill..In her Prophetticke furie sow'd the Worke. **1632** MILTON *Penseroso* 174 Till old experience do attain To something like Prophetic strain. **1638** SIR T. HERBERT *Trav.* (ed. 2) 135 Shaw-meer-Ally-Hamzy a prophetique Mahomitan. **1761** GRAY *Descent Odin* 20 The dust of the prophetic Maid. **1845** S. AUSTIN *Ranke's Hist. Ref.* II. 295 That their preachers should confine themselves wholly to the Gospel and the prophetic and apostolic Scriptures. **1865** GROTE *Plato* II. xxiv. 213 A prophetic woman named Diotima. **1876** LOWELL *Among my Bks.* Ser. II. 301 Puritanism showed both the strength and weakness of its prophetic nurture.

b. *Liturgics.* *prophetic lesson* (L. *lectio prophetica*): see quot. 1878.

1872 SCUDAMORE *Notitia Euch.* 206 [tr. St. Germanus] The Prophetic Lesson keeps its due place, rebuking evil things and announcing future. [**1878** HAMMOND *Antient Liturgies* Gloss. 384 *Prophetica lectio* (or *Propheta*), (Gall.), The Lection from the Old Testament, which..in the Gallican Liturgy preceded the Epistle and Gospel.]

c. *prophetic present, perfect*: the present or perfect tense used to express a certain future.

1882 FARRAR *Early Chr.* xxii. II. 67 *note*, The perfects [in James v. 2, 3] are prophetic perfects; they express absolute certainty as to the ultimate result. **1884** G. H. WEBSTER *Gram. New Eng.* 116 Both the Historic and the Prophetic Present use a past and a future, as though they expressed the present of absolute time. *Ibid.* 117 A Prophetic preterit occurs when the simple preterit is used in the description of future contingent events.

2. Characterized by, containing, or of the nature of prophecy or prediction; predictive, presageful.

1595 SHAKS. *John* III. iv. 126 Now heare me speake with a propheticke spirit. **1605** —— *Macb.* I. iii. 78 Say..why Vpon this blasted Heath you stop our way With such Prophetique greeting? **1647** CLARENDON *Hist. Reb.* I. §49 He quickly found how Prophetick the last King's Predictions had proved. *a* **1771** GRAY *Dante* 27 Sleep Prophetic of my Woes. **1881** LADY HERBERT *Edith* 24, I feel that woman's words are prophetic.

3. Spoken of in prophecy; predicted.

1651 HOBBES *Leviath.* II. xxxi. 187 There may be attributed to God, a two-fold Kingdome, Naturall, and Prophetique. **1798** *Anti-Jacobin* No. 8 (1799) 273 Sober plodding Money-lenders..little in the habit of lending their Funds on prophetic Mortgages.

4. *Comb.* **prophetic-eyed** *a.*, having a prophetic eye or outlook.

1847 EMERSON *Poems, May-day* 61 The sparrow meek, prophetic-eyed, Her nest beside the snow-drift weaves.

pro'phetical, *a.* (*sb.*) [f. as prec. + -AL¹.]

1. Of, belonging or proper to, or of the nature of a prophet; of or pertaining to prophecy (= PROPHETIC 1).

1456 *Coventry Leet Bk.* 287 Ysay, replete with þe spirite propheticall. **1577** B. GOOGE *Heresbach's Husb.* II. (1586) 71 As the Propheticall Psalmist singeth. **1613** PURCHAS *Pilgrimage* (1614) 462 One of those youths, in that Propheticall distraction before mentioned, warned them to depart from thence. **1651** HOBBES *Govt. & Soc.* xvii. §23. 321 The Apostolicall worke indeed was universall; the Propheticall to declare their owne revelations in the Church; the Evangelicall to preach, or to be publishers of the Gospell. **1697** POTTER *Antiq. Greece* III. vii. (1715) 69 They had Recourse to the whole Train of prophetical Divinities. **1856** STANLEY *Sinai & Pal.* Pref. 18 The poetical imagery of the prophetical books.

2. Of the nature of or containing prophecy, predictive (= PROPHETIC 2).

1605 BACON *Adv. Learn.* I. iv. §5 The reprehension of Saint Paul was not only proper for those times, but prophetical for the times following. **1674** BREVINT *Saul at Endor* 269 The Man, whom the Pope in a Prophetical dream saw supporting his Lateran Church from falling. **1830** D'ISRAELI *Chas. I*, III. ix. 200 A prophetical oration announced that the future line from Charles would not be less numerous.

† **B.** *sb.* A prophetical utterance, a prophecy. *Obs.*

1615 SYLVESTER *Memory of Margarite* Wks. (Grosart) II. 294 One night, two dreams made two propheticals: Thine, of thy Coffin; mine, of thy Funerals. **1653** H. WHISTLER *Upshot Inf. Baptisme* 99 By plain coherence of these Propheticalls it appeareth.

Hence **propheti'cality** (*nonce-wd.*), **pro'pheticalness** (*rare*), prophetical quality.

1727 BAILEY vol. II, *Propheticalness*..prophetical Nature or Quality. *a* **1834** COLERIDGE in *Lit. Rem.* (1836) II. 284 (on B. Jonson's *Barth. Fair*) An odd sort of propheticality in this Numps and old Noll!

prophetically (prəʊ'fɛtɪkəlɪ), *adv.* [f. as prec. + -LY².] In a prophetical manner; in the manner of a prophet; by way of prophecy or prediction.

1577 tr. *Bullinger's Decades* (1592) 433 Saint Peter and S. Paul doe..applie this..as a thing spoken Propheticallie vnto Christ Iesus. **1644** MILTON *Judgm. Bucer* Wks. 1851 IV. 342 Which our enemies too profetically fear'd. **1752** J. GILL *Trinity* iii. 61 This is prophetically expressed in *Isa.* lxiii. 1. **1856** FROUDE *Hist. Eng.* I. v. 356 Kirwan was one of those men of whom the preacher spoke prophetically.

propheticism (-'fɛtɪsɪz(ə)m). [f. as prec. + -ISM.]

1. An expression characteristic of the Prophets.

1684 H. MORE *Answ.*, etc. 252, I suspect it to be a mere Propheticism, if I may so speak, that is, a prophetick scheme or propriety of speech, usefull for concealment.

2. Prophetic system or practice.

1701 BEVERLEY *Apoc. Quest.* 10 Which Propheticisms of the Churches, Mr. Fleming being Averse to, I will not Press them upon him.

† **pro'pheticly,** *adv. Obs. rare.* [f. PROPHETIC + -LY².] = PROPHETICALLY.

1656 J. HAMMOND *Leah & R.* (1844) 25 Although this was prophetiquely forseen by diverse merchants of London. **1704** *The Storm* vi, Often he has those Cares Prophetickly exprest.

pro'phetico-, comb. form of L. *prophetic-us* PROPHETIC, prefixed adverbially to an adj., e.g. *prophetico-Messianic*, of or pertaining to the prophetic Messiah.

1865 tr. *Strauss' New Life Jesus* II. II. lxxiii. 174 We have here a prophetico-Messianic myth of the clearest stamp.

prophetism (ˈprɒfɪtɪz(ə)m). [f. PROPHET *sb.* + -ISM.] The action or practice of a prophet or prophets; the system or principles of the Hebrew prophets. ***false prophetism***, the practice or principles of a false prophet.

1701 BEVERLEY *Apoc. Quest.* Pref. a iv b, To be waited for with Reverence; and not Reproach'd as False Prophetism. **1845** KITTO *Cycl. Bibl. Lit.* s.v. *Theology*, The freer religious enthusiasm which..had prevailed in the nation in the form of Prophetism. **1861** A. MCCAUL *Ess. Prophecy* in *Aids to Faith* 90 To have received a call and message direct from God and to deliver it constituted the essence of prophetism. **1893** HUXLEY *Evol. & Ethics* 109 Prophetism attained its apogee among the Semites of Palestine.

b. *Philos.* In the teaching of Algazzāli, an Arabian philosopher of the eleventh century, the fourth stage in intellectual development (the three preceding being Sensation, Understanding, and Reason), in which a man sees things that lie beyond the perceptions of reason.

1847 LEWES *Hist. Philos.* (1853) 310.

†**propheti'zation.** *Obs. rare*⁻¹. [f. next: see -ATION.] The action or faculty of prophesying.

1652 GAULE *Magastrom.* 221 Take the stone which is called Esmundus or Asmadus, and it will give prophetization.

†**'prophetize,** *v. Obs.* [ME. a. F. *prophétiser* (-*izer* 12th c. in Littré), ad. late L. *prophētiz-āre* (*a* 200 in Itala), a. Gr. προφητίζειν to prophesy: see PROPHET *sb.* and -IZE.]

1. *trans.* To prophesy, predict.

c **1330** R. BRUNNE *Chron. Wace* (Rolls) 16606 Til þat tyme come..þat Merlyn til Arthur prophetysed. **1483** CAXTON *Gold. Leg.* 427 b/2 He prophetysed that a recluse sholdbe seen emonge men by the vyce of couetyse. **1549** *Compl. Scot.* i. 22 In the nummyr of them that Sanct paul prophetizit in the sycond epistil to tymothie. *Ibid.* vi. 46 His father Adam hed prophetyszit that the varld sal end be vattir and be the fyir.

2. *intr.* To utter predictions; to prophesy.

1588 A. KING tr. *Canisius' Catech.* 113, I send nocht yir Prophets and thay did rime, I spak nocht to yam and thay prophetized. **1604** T. WRIGHT *Passions* v. §2. 162 Elizeus.. desiring to prophetise, called for a musitian. **1715** M. DAVIES *Athen. Brit.* I. 263 Had not he prophetiz'd against the Corruptions of the Church of Rome.

Hence †**'prophetizing** *vbl. sb.* and *ppl. a.*

1595 DANIEL *Civ. Wars* (1609) III. lxii, Nature..doth warning send By prophetizing dreames. **1598** SYLVESTER *Du Bartas* II. i. IV. *Handie-cr.* 785 The prophetizing spirit forsook him so. **1715** M. DAVIES *Athen. Brit.* I. 60 Monks and Fryars, who abetted her Prophetizing Impostures.

'prophetless, *a.* [f. PROPHET *sb.* + -LESS.] Without a prophet or inspired teacher.

1900 H. D. RAWNSLEY in *Westm. Gaz.* 16 Jan. 8/1 In prophetless despair We hear through cloud of doubt and misty air The rival Churches cry uncertain cries. **1906** *Expositor* June 517 The priest..bare rule over a kingless and prophetless people.

†**'prophetly,** *a. Obs. rare.* [f. as prec. + -LY¹.] Prophet-like, befitting a prophet.

1547–64 BAULDWIN *Mor. Philos.* (Palfr.) 11 A worthy and prophetly saying.

prophe'tocracy. *nonce-wd.* [f. as prec. + -(O)CRACY.] Government by a prophet.

1893 *Pall Mall Budget* 6 Apr. 526/1 There is little to be brought against the Mormons, except the galling prophetocracy of their government and their marriage laws.

'prophetry. *nonce-wd.* [f. as prec. + -RY.] The prophetical office, the body of prophets.

1863 MILMAN *Hist. Jews* VIII. (ed. 3) 347 Elijah..appears in the solemn scene of the Transfiguration as the representative of prophetry.

Prophet's-flower, prophet-flower. [A rendering of Persian *gul-i paighāmbar* 'rose or flower of the Apostle' (i.e. Muhammad).] A name, of Oriental origin, given to two species of *Arnebia*, N.O. *Boraginaceæ*, viz. *A. echioides*, a perennial, native of the regions west of the Upper Indus, having primrose-yellow flowers, marked with evanescent purple spots; and *A. Griffithii*, an annual, native of India.

[**1834** SIR A. BURNES *Trav. Bokhara* I. iii. 86 The violet has the name of 'gool i pyeghambur', or the rose of the Prophet, par excellence, I suppose, from its fragrance. **1861** *Bot. Mag.* tab. 5266.] **1866** *Treas. Bot.* 929/2 *Prophet's-flower*, the name given by Indian Mussulmans to *Arnebia echioides*. **1869** J. L. STEWART *Punjab Plants* 152 'Prophet's flower'..is liked by the Pathâns on account of its delightful scent, and is also held in veneration by them, as the five dark marks on the corolla are said to be those of Mahomed's fingers. **1882** *Garden* 14 Oct. 344/2 In flower just now ..*Arnebia echioides* (the Prophet's flower).

prophetship (ˈprɒfɪt-ʃɪp). [f. PROPHET *sb.* + -SHIP.] The office or function of a prophet.

1642 J. EATON *Honey-c. Free Justif.* 238 We give to Christ the glory and truth of his Prophetship. **1873** FAIRBAIRN *Stud. Philos. Relig. & Hist.* (1877) 329 It is no matter of much moment where the idea of prophetship originated. Israel alone realized it. **1899** GARVIE *Ritschlian Theol.* IX. ii. 274 Christ has founded his community through his royal prophetship and priesthood.

propho (ˈprɒfəʊ). *slang* (orig. *U.S.*). [f. PROPH(YLAXIS + -O².] Prophylaxis of venereal disease. Also *attrib.*

1919 L. L. LINCOLN *Company C, 11th Engineers* 37 In his efforts to get away with it he paid many visits to 'Doc. Propho'. **1921** J. DOS PASSOS *Three Soldiers* IV. 202 That's one thing you guys are lucky in, don't have to worry about propho. **1925** —— *Manhattan Transfer* III. i. 281 Just my propho kit. **1959** J. BRAINE *Vodi* vii. 115 Jack..had pointed out that there were no propho stations in Civvy Street.

prophoric (prəʊˈfɒrɪk), *a. rare.* [ad. Gr. προφορικός, f. προφορά utterance, f. προφέρειν to utter, to bring forth.] Characterized by utterance, enunciation, or emission.

1833 J. H. NEWMAN *Arians* II. iv. (1876) 197 A distinction had already been applied by the Stoics to the Platonic Logos, which they represented under two aspects... The terms were received among Catholics: the 'Endiathetic', standing for the Word as hid from everlasting in the bosom of the Father, while the 'Prophoric' was the Son sent forth into the world, in apparent separation from God, with His Father's name upon Him, and His Father's will to perform.

prophragm (ˈprɒfræm), ‖**prophragma** (prəʊˈfrægmə). *Entom.* [ad. Gr. πρόφραγμα a fence in front, f. πρό, PRO-² + φράσσειν, stem φρακ-, to fence in.] (See quot.)

1826 KIRBY & SP. *Entomol.* III. xxxiii. 371 *Prophragma* (the Prophragm). A partition of an elastic substance, rather horny, connected posteriorly with the Dorsolum. *Ibid.* xxxv. 550 The anterior margin of the dorsolum [is] deflexed so as to form a septum called..the prophragm. **1890** *Cent. Dict.*, Prophragma.

prophylactic (prɒfɪˈlæktɪk), *a.* and *sb.* [ad. Gr. προφυλακτικ-ός, f. προφυλάσσειν to keep guard before: see PRO-² and PHYLACTIC. So F. *prophylactique* (16th c. in Hatz.-Darm.).]

A. *adj. Med.* That defends from or tends to prevent disease; also *transf.* preservative, precautionary.

1574 J. JONES *Nat. Beginning Grow. Things* 45 Prophilacticke that preuenteth diseases. **1605** DANIEL *Queen's Arcadia* III. ii, Yoo haue not very carefull beene, T' obserue the prophilacticke regiment Of your owne body. **1661** in BLOUNT *Glossogr.* (ed. 2), *Prophylactic.* **1725** WATTS *Logic* I. vi. §10 Medicine is justly distributed into prophylactick, or the art of preserving health; and therapeutick, or the art of restoring health. **1742** W. STUKELEY in *Mem.* (Surtees) I. 326 An amuletick, averruncative or prophylactick symbol. **1798** W. BLAIR *Soldier's Friend* 2 Steady enforcement of proper prophylactic regulations. **1866** *Lond. Rev.* 17 Feb. 189/2 [Vaccination] does seem to have exercised a prophylactic or modifying influence. **1889** J. R. ILLINGWORTH in *Lux Mundi* iii. 118 With men, as with animals, suffering is largely prophylactic.

B. *sb.* **a.** A medicine or measure used to prevent, or as a precaution against, disease. Also *transf.*

1642 *Preparative for Fast* 13 Weare it as a Prophylactick about thee. **1777** G. FORSTER *Voy. round World* I. 53 It is one of the best prophylactics against the sea-scurvy. **1828** *Blackw. Mag.* XXIII. 302 A serpent's skin is still looked upon in Egypt as a prophylactic against complaints of the head. **1897** *Allbutt's Syst. Med.* II. 657 Vaccination, which has now stood the test of practice for a century, remains to-day one of the greatest medical prophylactics the world has ever known.

b. A condom.

Condoms were formerly used more for their prophylactic properties against venereal disease than for their contraceptive properties.

1943 [see PREVENTIVE *sb.* c]. **1950** 'D. DIVINE' *King of Fassarai* xviii. 143 'What were you doing before this?' 'Handin' out prophylactics in Baltimore.' **1964** G. MCDONALD *Running Scared* v. 73 Prophylactics made them [*sc.* women] more willing... People could have intercourse ..without restraint. **1972** C. POTOK *My Name is Asher Lev* III. x. 259 Along the..beach lay..beer cans, bits of paper, a prophylactic. **1975** *Listener* 27 Nov. 728/3 The GI wore his packet of prophylactics in his cap and propositioned every woman in sight.

†**prophy'lactical,** *a. Obs. rare.* [f. as prec. + -AL¹.] = prec. adj.

1628–9 BP. HALL *Serm. Acts ii.* 37–40 Wks. 1863 V. 409 Dietetical and prophylactical receipts of wholesome caution. **1657** W. COLES *Adam in Eden* cviii, It is not only Therapeuticall or restorative, but Prophylacticall or preventionall.

Hence **prophy'lactically** *adv.*, by way of prevention of disease.

1859 R. F. BURTON *Centr. Afr.* in *Jrnl. Geog. Soc.* XXIX. 135 *note*, A greybeard who had been treated at Maskat prophylactically against the pain and venom of the scorpion. **1894** *Westm. Gaz.* 26 Oct. 3/1 In the matter of vaccinating prophylactically to secure that a child shall be immune.

‖**prophy'lacticon.** *Obs. rare*⁻¹. [a. Gr. προφυλακτικόν, neut. sing. of προφυλακτικός: see PROPHYLACTIC.] = PROPHYLACTIC *sb.*

1716 M. DAVIES *Athen. Brit.* II. 354 The avow'd best Prophylacticons or Preservers of Health, be the moderate use of Medicinal Water-Drinking [etc.].

‖**prophylaxis** (prɒfɪˈlæksɪs). [mod.L., f. Gr. πρό, PRO-² + φύλαξις a watching, guarding, after PROPHYLACTIC.] *Med.* The preventive treatment of disease. Also *transf.*

1842 in DUNGLISON *Med. Lex.* **1843** R. J. GRAVES *Syst. Clin. Med.* xxvii. 342 An elaborate and critical history of the pathology, prophylaxis, and treatment of syphilis. **1866** A. FLINT *Princ. Med.* (1880) 109 The prevention of disease.. constitutes a division of medicine called prophylaxis. **1897** A. DRUCKER tr. *Ihering's Evol. Aryan* 376, I should call it the Prophylaxis of a primitive race.

prophylaxy (ˈprɒfɪlæksɪ). [= mod.F. *prophylaxie*, f. mod.L. *prophylaxis.*] = prec.

1890 *Lancet* 25 Jan. 218/1 The discussion on the prophylaxy of tuberculosis was then resumed. **1892** *Sat. Rev.* 23 Jan. 93/1 Certain vistas in the future of prophylaxy.

prophyll (ˈprəʊfɪl). *Bot.* Also 9 **prophyllon** (pl. **-phylla.** [f. PRO-² + Gr. φύλλ-ον leaf.]

1. See quots.

1898 tr. *Strasburger's Bot.* 462 The leaves borne on the stalks of the flowers are designated Bracteoles or Prophylla. **1905** I. B. BALFOUR tr. *Goebel's Organogr. Plants* II. 382 Prophylls are characterized first of all by their position. We find them..usually in pairs at the base of the lateral shoots. **1921** J. SMALL *Textbk. Bot.* vii. 75 The first few leaves on a lateral branch are described as prophylls. There are commonly two, and they may be spiny..or just small and simpler than the other leaves... The latter prophylls are usually called bracteoles. **1953** K. ESAU *Plant Anat.* xvi. 413 The first cataphylls on a lateral shoot are called prophylls. **1976** BELL & COOMBE tr. *Strasburger's Textbk. Bot.* (rev. ed.) 131 These first leaves of the side shoot, which are frequently of simple form.., are termed prophylls.

2. = PROTOPHYLL.

1971 D. W. BIERHORST *Morphol. Vascular Plants* ii. 24/2 This [*sc.* the protocorm] is a parenchymatous moss bearing ..a number of avascular, leaflike structures ('prophylls').

†**pro'pice,** *a. Obs.* Also 5–6 **-pyce,** 6 **-pise, -pysse.** [ME. a. F. *propice* (12th c. in Littré), ad. L. *propiti-us* favourable, gracious, kind.]

1. = PROPITIOUS *a.* 1.

a **1325** *Prose Psalter* 189 He shal be propice to þe londe of his folk. **1489** CAXTON *Faytes of A.* I. v. 10 To whom fortune was so propice. **1526** ABP. LEE *Let. to Wolsey* (MS. Cott. Vesp. C. iii. 213), I humblie beseched his Magestie not to geve easie and propice eares unto any such reaports. **1609** HOLLAND *Amm. Marcell.* 75 The Romanes..worship the gracious power of God, so propice and mercifull unto them. **1656** BLOUNT *Glossogr.*, *Propitious*, not displeased, merciful, favorable, propice, gentle.

2. = PROPITIOUS *a.* 2.

c **1477** CAXTON *Jason* 6 The knightes..drew hem vnto a place propice for the ioustes. **1568** GRAFTON *Chron.* II. 816 Now was the time propice and conuenient. **1618** *Barnevelt's Apol.* Pref. A iv b, A more propice and fat sacrifice at the Altar of Proserpina. **1620** THOMAS *Lat. Dict.*, *Fortunatus*.. luckie, happy, fortunate, propice.

Hence †**pro'picely** *adv. Obs.*

1541 *St. Papers Hen. VIII*, III. 298 The purchace of certeyn landes there, lyeng propicely for them. **1542** *Ibid.* V. 587 The tyme shall more propicely serve Us.

propiciable, etc., obs. ff. PROPITIABLE, etc.

†**pro'piciant,** *a. Sc. Obs. rare.* [ad. L. *propitiānt-em*, pres. pple. of *propiti-āre* to PROPITIATE.] = PROPITIOUS *a.* 1.

1533 BELLENDEN *Livy* III. vii. (S.T.S.) I. 272 We haue þe goddis mare propiciant to ws quhen we ar fechtand. **1548** *Sc. Acts Mary* (1814) II. 481/2 To aide..and defend at his powar this tender princes..as propiciant and helplyke brother.

propination (prɒpɪˈneɪʃən). [ad. L. *propīnātiōn-em* a drinking to one's health, n. of action f. *propīn-āre* to PROPINE.]

†**1.** The action of offering drink to another in pledging; the drinking to the health of any one.

1656 BLOUNT *Glossogr.*, *Propination*, a drinking to one, a bidding one drink. **1697** POTTER *Antiq. Greece* IV. xx. (1715) 393 Proteas..drank it off, and presented his Service to Alexander in another of the same Dimensions. This Propination was carry'd about towards the right Hand. *Ibid.* 398 The Propinations, and methods of Drinking, which other Nations observ'd.

†**2.** Giving, presenting, administering. *Obs. rare.*

1608 TOPSELL *Serpents* (1658) 662 Cantharides,..if you fail in their due and skilful application or propination,.. drive men into most intolerable grievous symptomes.

3. [= Ger. *propination.*] In reference to Austrian Poland: The seigniorial monopoly of brewing and distilling and selling the produce.

1886 *Daily News* 23 Dec. 5/7 This nobleman has the 'propination' or sole right of selling spirits in this part of the world. **1888** *Times* 27 Sept. 3/3 The Galician land-owners by the Spirit Tax Act passed last Session..have been deprived of the right of 'propination'—that is, of distilling and selling spirits on their estates.

propine (prəʊˈpaɪn), *sb.*¹ *Sc. Obs.* or *arch.* [a. obs. F. *propine* (16th c. in Godef.) 'drinking money, or somewhat to drinke' (Cotgr.), f. *propiner* to PROPINE; so Sp. *propina* a present, a 'tip', It. *propina* a drinking, a 'health'.]

†**1.** Drink-money. *Obs.*

[This is etymologically the earlier sense, but early evidence for it in Sc. has not been found.]

1638 RUTHERFORD *Lett.* 11 June (1664) 230 To love the bridegroom better then his gifts, his propines, or drink-money.

2. A thing presented as a gift; a present.

In the first quotation a present of wine.

1448 *Aberdeen Regr.* (1844) I. 17 To mak a propyne to our souerane lord the Kingis welcum..of twa tunnes of Gascoene wyne. **1473** *Rental Bk. Cupar-Angus* (1879) I. 169 He sal gyue to ws in name of propyne a ra or a buk. **1557–75** *Diurn. Occurr.* (Bann. Club) 67 With ane coffer quhairin wes the copburd and propyne quhilk suld be propynit to hir hienes. **1598** J. MELVILL (*title*) A Spirituall Propine of a

Pastour to his People. *a* **1619** W. Cowper *Heaven Opened* II. Ded., That I haue conioyned your Maiesties in the participation of this small propine of the first fruits of my labours. **1818** Scott *Hrt. Midl.* xxxix, We maun think of some propine for her, since her kindness hath been great. **1849** Mrs. A. S. Menteath *Lays Kirk & Covt.* (1892) 39 'Twas my first hansel and propine to heaven.

3. The power to give; gift, disposal. *rare.* (Doubtfully correct.)

a **1803** *Lady Anne* vii. in Child *Ballads* I. (1882) 227/2 If I were thine, and in thy propine, O what wad ye do to me? **1813** Picken *Poems* II. 71 The richest gift in Heaven's propine.

propine (ˈprəʊpaɪn), *sb.*² *Chem.* [f. as PROPANE + -INE⁵ 2.] Hofmann's systematic name for the gaseous hydrocarbon C_3H_4, the tri-carbon member of the acetylene series, C_nH_{2n-2}; usually called ALLYLENE, and formerly also *propinene.*

1866 Hofmann in *Proc. Royal Soc.* XV. 58 *note.* **1873** Watts *Fownes' Chem.* (ed. 11) 558 Ethine and propine are gaseous at ordinary temperatures. **1877** *Ibid.* (ed. 12) II. 63 Allylene or propine C_3H_4..is produced by the action of sodium ethylate on bromopropene.

propine (prəʊˈpaɪn), *v.* Chiefly *Sc. Obs.* or *arch.* Also 5–7 **-pyne**, 9 *dial.* **-peyne**. [ad. L. *propīn-āre* to drink to one's health, pledge; to give to drink, administer, furnish, ad. Gr. προπίν-ειν lit. to drink before or above, to drink to another, to give one to drink, also to give freely, to present, f. πρό, PRO-² + πίνειν to drink.]

1. *trans.* To offer or give to drink; to present with (drink); *fig.* to offer or give (a 'cup' of affliction, etc.). *Obs.*

c **1430** Lydg. *Commend. our Lady* viii. 52 Sum drope of graceful dewe to us propyne. **1563** Winȝet *Wks.* (S.T.S.) II. 27 Thai feir nocht to propyne the venum of hæresie til wtheris. *a* **1598** Rollock *Passion* ii. (1616) 21 The Father hath propined vnto mee a bitter cuppe of affliction. **1637** Gillespie *Eng. Pop. Cerem.* III. ii. 31 Whiles she propineth to the world the cup of her fornications. **1675** J. Smith *Chr. Relig. Appeal* II. 25 That deadly Poyson of their Religion that was propined from the Stage. *a* **1713** Pitcairn in Maidment *Scot. Pasquils* (1868) 317 A health to the King I do thee propine.

2. To offer for acceptance or as a present; to present; to put before one, propose.

Perhaps first said of a present of wine.

c **1450** Lovelich *Grail* xvii. 118 My grete veniaunce & my gret discipline, With my strengthe to ȝow it schal propine. **1500–20** Dunbar *Poems* lxxvii. 61 Ane riche present thay did till hir propyne. **1526** *Aberdeen Regr.* (1844) I. 115 That thar be propynit to the kingis grace..sax potionis of wyne. *c* **1560** Rolland *Seven Sages* 34 Of thair prettick to me ane point propyne. **1596** Dalrymple tr. *Leslie's Hist. Scot.* VIII. 92 The king propynet him the cuntries Knapden and Kintyr. *a* **1619** Fotherby *Atheom.* I. ii. §2 (1622) 11 Vnlesse we would propine, both our selues, and our cause, vnto open and iust derision. **1660** Jer. Taylor *Duct. Dubit.* I. iv. rule ii. §19 It propines to us the noblest, the highest, and the bravest pleasures of the world. **1807** J. Stagg *Poems* 67 Our past misfortunes we'd propeyne T' oblivion. **1819** Scott *Ivanhoe* xxxii, In expectation of the ample donation, or *soul-scat*, which Cedric had propined.

3. To present (a person) *with* something; to endow, reward.

c **1450** Lovelich *Merlin* 6506 For mochel worschepe by hym schalt þou se And ful gret encres to the and thyne, And thow hit worschepe & hit propyne. **1554** *Edin. Counc. Rec.* 29 Dec. II. lf. 39 (MS.) An vther goblet, with which to propine the Quenis Grace. *a* **1598** Rollock *Passion* ii. (1616) 22 If the Lord propine thee with a cup of affliction. *a* **1670** Spalding *Troub. Chas. I* (Spald. Cl.) II. 86 He, with his Quene..wes bankettit.., and thairefter propynit with 20,000 lib. sterling in ane fair coup of gold. *a* **1758** Ramsay *Three Bonnets* 62 And bought frae..Bawsy, His [bonnet]. to propine a giglet lassie. **1895** Crockett *Men of Moss-Hags* xlix, Bless God that you have had a husband..to propine Him with.

4. a. *trans.* To wish (health or the like) to some one in drinking. **b.** *intr.* To address a pledge or toast *to*; to drink a health *to.*

a **1770** C. Smart *Hop Garden* I. Poems (1810) 38/1 The lovely sorceress mix'd, and to the prince Health, peace and joy propin'd. **1887** *Blackw. Mag.* Sept. 402 And thus did he to the king propine: 'Long live the King!'

Hence †**pro'piner** *Obs. rare*⁻¹, one who 'propines', offers, or gives.

1589 Bruce *Serm.* (Wodrow Soc.) 26 There is twa propiners, twa personis that offeris and givis the Sacrament.

propinquant (prəʊˈpɪŋkwənt), *a. rare.* [ad. L. *propinquāntem*, pres. pple. of *propinqu-āre* to bring near, approach, f. *propinqu-us*: see PROPINQUE.] Near, neighbouring, adjacent.

1633 T. Adams *Exp. 2 Peter* ii. 3 That cannot be called closely propinquant..which is actually present. **1903** *T.P.s Weekly* 4 Sept. 427/3 Small vans..stationed at various squares, propinquant to busy sections of the city.

†**pro'pinquate**, *ppl. a. Obs. rare.* [ad. L. *propinquāt-us* brought near, pa. pple. of *propinqu-āre*: see prec.] Immediate, proximate.

1665 J. Gadbury *Lond. Deliv. Predicted* Concl. 40 The shutting up of People in a time of Sickness..is no small propinquate cause..of the increase of the Contagion. **1683** —— in *Wharton's Wks.* Pref., Aptly..distinguished into Causes Remote, and Propinquate.

†**pro'pinquate**, *v. Obs. rare*⁻⁰. [f. ppl. stem of L. *propinquāre* to bring near, to draw near.]

1623 Cockeram, *Propinquate*, to approach.

propinque (prəʊˈpɪŋk), *a. rare.* [ad. L. *propinqu-us* near, neighbouring, derivative of *prope* near: cf. *longinqu-us* distant, from *longe* far.]

1. Near in space, neighbouring, at hand.

1635 Swan *Spec. M.* v. §2 (1643) 81 The matter of Meteors..as it is propinque or near, it consisteth of Exhalations. **1892** J. Ashby-Sterry in *Graphic* 16 Apr. 494/1 They did not disdain..the foaming pewter from the propinque public. **1907** N. Munro in *Blackw. Mag.* Jan. 81/1 Ports more propinque to the highways of the world.

†**2.** Immediate, proximate, direct. *Obs.*

1649 Bulwer *Pathomyot.* I. iv. 18 Some more propinque and conjunct cause of motion. **1661** K. W. *Conf. Charac., Gd. old Cause* (1860) 63 The devil's the remote cause, and their hearts the approximate and neere propinque cause.

†**3.** Nearly approaching accuracy; approximate.

1680 Aubrey *Lives* (1898) II. 86 Mr. Launcelot Moorhouse..wrote against Mr. Francis Potter's booke of 666, and falls upon him, for that 25 is not the true roote, but the propinque root. **1691** Wood *Ath. Oxon.* II. 455.

Hence **pro'pinquial** *a.*, done in proximity.

1891 C. James *Rom. Rigmarole* 116 In the course of a week's propinquial (excuse my coinage) climbing.

pro'pinquitous, *a. rare.* [f. next + -OUS: cf. *calamitous.*] That is in propinquity; close at hand.

1899 *Literature* 11 Mar. 260 A propinquitous and sympathetic brother-in-arms is a welcome ally indeed. **1941** *Cold Spring Harbor Symp. Quant. Biol.* IX. 155/1 The tendency to propinquitous union. **1974** R. Adams *Shardik* xxviii. 234 Let us just step outside for a stroll in some nice, lovely place with no propinquitous walls or bushes.

propinquity (prəʊˈpɪŋkwɪtɪ). [ME. *propinquite*, a. obs. F. *propinquité* (*c* 1240 in Godef.), ad. L. *propinquitās, -tātem* nearness, f. *propinqu-us*: see PROPINQUE.] Nearness, closeness, proximity:

a. in space: Neighbourhood.

c **1460** Metham *Wks.* (E.E.T.S.) 148 He concludyth.. that the mone schuld, for her propynqwyte, sundry indysposycion..cause. **1570** Levins *Manip.* 110 24 Propinquitie, *propinquitas.* **1601** Holland *Pliny* II. 372 By reason of the propinquity and neighborhood of that region. **1725** Bradley *Fam. Dict.* s.v. *Wind*, The propinquity of the Sea, being to be consider'd. **1879** *Cassell's Techn. Educ.* IV. 307/2 It should not be in too close propinquity to the stable.

b. in blood or relationship: Near or close kinship.

c **1374** Chaucer *Boeth.* II. pr. iii. 25 (Camb. MS.) The moost presyous kynde of any propinquite or alyaunce þat may ben. **1387–8** T. Usk *Test. Love* II. ii. (Skeat) I. 101 She ..maketh nigh cosinage, ther neuer propinquite ne alyaunce in lyue was, ne shulde haue be. **1558** Knox *First Blast* (Arb.) 55 It is not birth onely nor propinquitie of blood. **1613–18** Daniel *Coll. Hist. Eng.* (1626) 105 The next day..hee put her away, pretending..propinquity of blood. **1766** Blackstone *Comm.* II. xiv. 234 Thus in the second degree, the issue of George and Cecilia Stiles and of Andrew and Esther Baker..are each in the same degree of propinquity. **1880** Muirhead *Gaius* III. §27 He does not call them in the second class immediately after the *sui heredes*,..but in the third class, on the ground of propinquity.

c. in nature, disposition, belief, association, etc.: Similarity, affinity.

1586 A. Day *Eng. Secretary* II. (1625) 117 An annexed propinquity or opposition of good and bad, vertue and vice. **1650** T. Vaughan *Anima Magica* 8 There is in Nature a Certain Chain, or subordinate propinquity of Complexions between Visibles, and invisibles. **1823** Gillies *Aristotle's Rhet.* II. x. 297 The objects of envy must always be characterised by nearness in time, place, age, reputation, in short by a sort of propinquity.

d. in time: Near approach, nearness.

1646 Sir T. Browne *Pseud. Ep.* VII i. 341 Thereby is declared the propinquity of their desolation. **1825** Lamb *Elia* Ser. II. *Superannuated Man*, Each day used to be individually felt by me..in its distance from, or propinquity to, the next Sunday.

pro'pinquous, *a. rare*⁻¹. [f. L. *propinqu-us* PROPINQUE + -OUS.] Near, close at hand, in proximity.

1832 Bentham *Deontol.* vii. (1834) I. 107 Susceptible of being brought into the mind with the vividness of that which is propinquous.

propio-, propion-, *Chem.*, a formative derived from PROPIONIC, entering into the names of compounds related to propionic acid. The chief are: **propio'lactone**, a pungent, colourless, liquid β-lactone, $\underbrace{CH_2{\cdot}CO{\cdot}O{\cdot}CH_2}$, which is used as a disinfectant; also ***β*-propiolactone**. **propi'olic** *a.* [dim. f. PROPIONIC], in ***propiolic acid***, $CH{\equiv}C.CO_2H$, obs. synonym of PROPARGYLIC *acid*; ***phenyl-propiolic acid***, $C_6H_5.C{\equiv}C.CO_2H$: see quot. **propi'ona,mide**, the amide of propionic acid, $C_3H_5O.N.H_2$: see quots. **'propionate**, a salt of propionic acid. **'propione**, di-ethyl ketone $(C_2H_5)_2.CO$, a colourless mobile liquid lighter than water, in smell resembling acetone; discovered by Frémy in 1835, and called by him *metacetone.* **propio'nitril, -ile**, the nitrile or nitrogen compound of the propyl series, C_3H_5N, derived from propionyl by substitution of N for O. **'propionyl**, the monovalent radical C_3H_5O of propionic acid; formerly called *metacetyl.*

1917 *Chem. Abstr.* XI. 2577 *Propiolactone..was prepd. by treating an aq. soln. of $CH_2ICH_2CO_2Na$ with $AgNO_3$ and stirring the resulting ppt. for 15–25 min. **1952** *Chambers's Jrnl.* Apr. 255/2 Treating natural wool with a chemical called propiolactone increases its diameter and density without appreciable effect upon its surface properties. **1966** *McGraw-Hill Encycl. Sci. & Technol.* I. 463/2 β-Propiolactone works best at high humidities and is active even below 10°C. **1872** Watts *Dict. Chem.* VI. 962 *Phenyl-*propiolic Acid.* $C_9H_6O_2$..related to phenyl-propionic acid in the same manner as stearolic to stearic acid... It crystallises from water or from carbon bisulphide in long white silky needles melting at 136°–137°. **1881** *Times* 3 June 5 Competition with the natural dye-stuff is not to be thought of until the maker can reduce the price of dry propiolic acid. **1857** Miller *Elem. Chem.* III. 239 **Propionamide* $C_6H_7NO_2$, *Butyramide* $C_8H_9NO_2$, and *Valeramide* $C_{10}H_{11}NO_2$, may all be obtained by the action of ammonia upon their respective ethers. **1875** Watts *Dict. Chem.* VII. 1009 Propionamide is colourless, readily soluble in cold alcohol and ether, from which it crystallises in radiate crystalline masses..; from chloroform it crystallises in pearly scales. **1862** Miller *Elem. Chem.* III. 350 Most of the *propionates are soluble and crystallizable. The propionates of potash and soda are deliquescent. Propionate of lime is efflorescent, but very soluble. **1851** R. I. Morley in *Q. Jrnl. Chem. Soc.* IV. 1 (*heading*) On *Propione, the Ketone of Propionic Acid. **1866** Watts *Dict. Chem.* IV. 729 Propione, $C_5H_{10}O$..is sometimes called ethyl-propionyl. **1857** Miller *Elem. Chem.* III. 166 *Cyanide of Ethyl: Hydrocyanic Ether:* **Propionitrile* ($C_4H_5Cy = C_6H_5N$)..is obtained..by the distillation of sulphethylate of potash with cyanide of potassium. **1864–72** Watts *Dict. Chem.* II. 211 Cyanide of ethyl, Propionitrile, Metacetonitrile,..discovered by Pelouze in 1834..is a colourless liquid, of specific gravity 0·78... It has a strong alliaceous odour, and is very poisonous. **1850** *Phil. Trans. R. Soc.* CXL. 129 The existence of a series of bases of the formula $C_nH_{n+1}N$, *i.e.* bases containing formyl, acetyl, *propionyl (metacetyl), butyryl, &c., appears to be still doubtful. **1857** Miller *Elem. Chem.* III. 311 Propione.., ethylide of propionyl. **1872** Watts *Dict. Chem.* VI. 962 *Propionyl bromide.* C_3H_5OBr. *Ibid.* 963 *Propionyl iodide.* C_3H_5OI.

propionic (prəʊpɪˈɒnɪk), *a. Chem.* [ad. F. *propionique* (Dumas, Malagute, & Leblanc 1847; *Comptes Rendus* XXV. 781), f. Gr. πρό, PRO-² (or πρῶτος first) + πίων, πιον- fat, in reference to its being the first in order of the actual fatty acids (formic and acetic acids, which precede it in the series, not forming unctuous derivatives).

From *propionic* are derived the names PROPANE, PROPENE, PROPYL, and the terms under PROPIO-.]

1. propionic acid, the monatomic monobasic acid of the propyl or tri-carbon series, the third acid of the fatty series, $C_3H_6O_2$, discovered by Gottlieb in 1844, and by him designated *metacetonic acid.* Its salts are PROPIONATES. Also in *comb.* as ***bromopropionic acid***, etc.

1850 [see PROPYL]. **1851** R. I. Morley in *Q. Jrnl. Chem. Soc.* IV. 1 The unfortunate term *metacetonic* or *metacetic acid*, only lately replaced by the appropriate appellation of *propionic acid*, now universally adopted. **1859** *Fownes' Chem.* 411 Under the influence of oxidizing agents, propylic alcohol..is converted into an acid analogous to acetic acid, which is called propionic acid..a colorless, transparent liquid, of a peculiar, somewhat pungent odor, similar to that of acetic acid. **1873** Ralfe *Phys. Chem.* 46 Formic, Acetic, and Propionic acids are present in sweat.

2. propionic aldehyde, $C_3H_6O = C_3H_5O.H$, (*propyl aldehyde, hydride of propionyl*), a limpid neutral liquid, having an ethereal odour. So ***propionic ethers, salts***, etc.

1866–8 Watts *Dict. Chem.* IV. 734 Propionic aldehyde.. discovered in 1847 by Guckelberger. **1880** *Libr. Univ. Knowl.* (N.Y.) VIII. 494 Acetone is isomeric with propionic aldehyde C_3H_6O.

propir(e, -te, -tie, obs. ff. PROPER, -TY.

propitiable (prəʊˈpɪʃɪəb(ə)l), *a.* [ad. L. *propitiābil-is* easy to be appeased: see PROPITIATE *v.* and -ABLE; cf. obs. F. *propiciable, -tiable* (15th c. in Godef.).]

†**1.** Able to propitiate. *Obs. rare.*

1553 T. Watson in Crowley *Soph. Dr. Watson* ii. (1569) 130 Graunt good Lord, that this sacrifice..be propitiable or a meane to obteyne mercy. **1563** Foxe *A. & M.* 979/1 In the Masse..the liuely sacrifice of the Churche, which is propitiable, as well for the synnes of the quicke, as of the dead.

2. Capable of being propitiated or made propitious.

1557 *Sarum Primer, Dirige* L vj, Almightie eternall God, ..bee propiciable to the soule of thy seruaunte. **1662** H. More *Philos. Writ.* Pref. Gen. (1712) 10 It could never enter into my mind, that he [God] was either irritable or propitiable, by the omitting or performing of any mean and insignificant services. **1890** Sarah J. Duncan *Soc. Depart.* 305 [She] is propitiable, and walks the deck daily with her former calumniators.

propitial (prəʊˈpɪʃəl), *a. rare*⁻¹. [f. L. *propiti-us* PROPITIOUS + -AL¹.] Propitiatory.

1850 Neale *Med. Hymns* (1867) 108 Luke the ox, in form propitial, As a creature sacrificial.

†**pro'pitiate**, *ppl. a. Obs. rare.* [f. L. *propitiāt-us*, pa. pple. of *propiti-āre*: see next.] Propitiated. (In quot. const. as *pa. pple.*)

1551 Bp. Gardiner *Explic.* 150 With suche sacrifices God is made fauorable, or God is propitiate, if we shall make new Englishe.

propitiate (prəʊ'pɪʃɪeɪt), *v.* [f. ppl. stem of L. *propiti-āre* to render favourable, appease (f. *propiti-us* propitious): see -ate[3].]

1. *trans.* To render propitious or favourably inclined; to appease, conciliate (one offended).

1645 Waller *To Mistris Broughton* Poems 127 You (her priest) declare What offrings may propitiate the Faire. **1759** Johnson *Rasselas* xi, That the supreme Being may be more easily propitiated in one place than in another is the dream of idle superstition. **1832** Ht. Martineau *Manch. Strike* viii, If it was indeed necessary to propitiate the masters by sacrificing him. **1875** Jowett *Plato* (ed. 2) V. 153 That they [the Gods] can be propitiated..is not to be allowed or admitted for an instant.

†**2.** *intr.* To make propitiation. *Obs. rare*[−1].

1703 Young *Serm.* II. 267 The sorrows of our Lord were propitiating for the sins of Eden.

†**3.** *trans.* To treat propitiously. *Obs. rare*[−1].

1768 [W. Donaldson] *Life Sir B. Sapskull* I. xiv. 142 The Grecians..used to enrich their victim, by tipping his horns with gold, in order to bribe the mercenary God to propitiate their appeal.

Hence **pro'pitiated, pro'pitiating** *ppl. adjs.*; **pro'pitiatingly** *adv.*

*a***1711** Ken *Hymnotheo* Poet. Wks. 1721 III. 68 And on the cross breathing his painful last, To his propitiated great Father pass'd. *a***1812** A. M'Lean *Comm. Heb.* (1847) II. xii. 196 Christ is represented as the meek and propitiating Lamb. **1873** Symonds *Grk. Poets* ix. 291 The old Oedipus, ..is made a blessed Daemon through the mercy of propitiated deities. **1890** E. L. Arnold *Phra* vii, 'Now', said the scribe propitiatingly.

propitiation (prəʊpɪʃɪ'eɪʃən). [ad. late L. *propitiātiōn-em*, n. of action f. *propiti-āre* to propitiate; cf. F. *propitiation* (14th c. in Hatz.-Darm.).]

1. The action or an act of propitiating; appeasement, conciliation; atonement, expiation.

1388 Wyclif *Lev.* xxv. 9 In the tyme of propiciacioun. **1706** Phillips, *Propitiation*, the Act of propitiating, an appeasing of the Divine Anger by Sacrifice, or Prayer; an Atonement. **1750** Johnson *Rambler* No. 10 ¶11 By what propitiation, therefore, may I atone for my former gravity? **1850** R. I. Wilberforce *Holy Bapt.* 132 The propitiation which our Lord effected on the Cross for the sins of men. **1871** Tyndall *Fragm. Sc.* (1879) II. i. 1 Propitiation of these terrible powers was the consequence.

b. A propitiatory gift, offering, or sacrifice. *arch.*

1552 *Bk. Com. Prayer, Communion* (1 John ii. 2), He is the propiciation for our synnes. **1649** Jer. Taylor *Gt. Exemp.* ii. Disc. viii. 69 Christ is our Advocate, and he is the propiciation.

†**2.** The condition or state of being propitiated or rendered favourable; favour. *Obs. rare*[−1].

1639 G. Daniel *Ecclus.* xviii. 54 That in the Day, the Day of visitation, God may looke on thee wth Propitiation.

propitiative (prəʊ'pɪʃɪətɪv), *a. rare.* [f. propitiate *v.* + -ive.] Tending to propitiate; propitiatory, conciliatory.

1928 *Observer* 19 Feb. 17/2 Where the majority of passengers have to travel in a brutalising congestion, the sight of half-empty 'firsts' next door is not propitiative.

†**propitiatoir(e**, *a. Sc. Obs. rare*[−1]. [a. F. *propitiatoire.*] = propitiatory *a.*

1580 Hay *Demandes* in *Cath. Tractates* (S.T.S.) 69 The sacrifice of the aulter..is propitiatoire and obteins remissione fra God to thame for quhilks it is offred.

propitiator (prəʊ'pɪʃɪeɪtə(r)). [a. late L. *propitiātor*, agent-n. from *propiti-āre* to propitiate; so F. *propitiateur*, in 1519 *propic-* (Hatz.-Darm.).] One who propitiates.

1571 Knox *Bk. Com. Order* (1868) 61 Look Thou to Thy dear Son..our Head..Mediator, and only Propitiator. **1624** Darcie *Birth of Heresies* vi. 23 Our Eternall Priest and Propitiator. **1742** tr. *Bossuet's Hist. Var. Prot. Ch.* (1829) I. 131 The whole Church, who acknowledged Jesus Christ for propitiator and author of justification.

propitiatorily (prəʊ'pɪʃɪətərɪlɪ), *adv.* [f. next + -ly[2].] In a propitiatory manner; by way of propitiating.

*a***1555** Bradford *Serm., Lord's Supper* (1574) I iv b, Being peruerted and vsed to a contrary ende, as of sacrificyng propitiatorely for the syns of the quicke and of the dead. **1853** W. Anderson *Exposure Popery* (1878) 184 There is not a shadow of evidence that Christ made an Offering of that bread and wine to his Father, either eucharistically or propitiatorily.

propitiatory (prəʊ'pɪʃɪətərɪ), *sb.* and *a.* [As sb. ad. late L. *propitiātōri-um* (*a* 200 in Itala) place of atonement, also propitiation, rendering Gr. ἱλαστήριον (LXX and N.T.); sb. use of neut. sing. of late L. *propitiātōri-us* adj. atoning, reconciling (whence the adj. B), f. *propitiātor* propitiator: see -ory. So OF. *propiciatorie, -s* sb. (*a* 1200 in Littré), mod.F. *propitiatoire* adj. and sb. Cf. Mercy-seat.]

A. *sb.* **1.** The mercy-seat.

[*c***1200** Ormin 1036 Tær oferr þatt arrke wass An oferrwerrc wel timmbredd þat wass Propitiatoriumm O Latin spæche nemmnedd.] *a***1300** *Cursor M.* 8281 (Cott.) And [in þat hali arke] was aarons wand,..þe gilden oyle, þe propiciatori, Tua cherubins. **1382** Wyclif *Heb.* ix. 5 Vpon whiche thingis weren cherubyns of glorie, schadewinge the propiciatorie. *c***1449** Pecock *Repr.* ii. vi. 174 The ark or chest of witnessing with propiciatorie. **1564** Harding *Answ. Jewel* xiv. 145 Two Cherubins of beaten golde,..spreading abroad their whinges,..their faces tourned toward the propitiatorie. **1643** Lightfoot *Glean. Ex.* (1648) 45 This cover..is called the Propitiatory, vulgarly in our English, the Mercy-seat. **1888** Cave *Inspir. O. Test.* v. 246 Laws.. announced from the Propitiatory of the Tabernacle.

b. *transf.* and *fig.*, esp. applied to Christ.

1549 Coverdale, etc. *Erasm. Par. Rom.* iii. 7 b, But nowe hath God declared Christ to be vnto all people the very propiciatory, mercie table, and sacrifice. **1603** Harsnet *Pop. Impost.* 118 The auncient renowmed glorious Reliques jewelled up in the Popes Propitiatorie at Rome. *a***1635** Sibbes *Confer. Christ & Mary* (1656) 2 There were two angels, one at the head, another at the feet, to shew that peace was to be expected in the true propitiatory, Jesus Christ. **1800** A. Swanston *Serm. & Lect.* I. 28 Here is the mercy-seat, the true propitiatory, the throne of grace.

2. *Theol.* A propitiation; an offering of atonement; esp. said of Christ. ? *Obs.*

1561 T. Norton *Calvin's Inst.* ii. xvii. (1634) 250 Christ, whom God hath set to be the propitiatorie by faith which is in his blood. **1650** W. Brough *Sacr. Princ.* (1659) 269 Thou hast a propitiatory for sin above all my provocations. **1726** De Foe *Hist. Devil* ii. i. (1822) 166 If Christ was put to death he would become a propitiatory.

B. *adj.* That propitiates or tends to propitiate; of or pertaining to propitiation; appeasing, atoning, conciliating, expiatory; ingratiating.

1551 T. Wilson *Logike* (1580) 29 b, No hypocriticall workes, no Propiciatorie Massyng, no meritorious praiyng, ..are yet to bee allowed before God. **1554** Coverdale *Carrying Christ's Cross* v. 64 The propiciatory sacrifyce of Chryste. **1736** Butler *Anal.* ii. v. Wks. 1874 I. 212 The general prevalence of propitiatory sacrifices over the heathen world. **1840** Dickens *Old C. Shop* ii, Mr. Swiveller ..looking about him with a propitiatory smile. **1846** Grote *Greece* i. xx. II. 130 A propitiatory payment to the relatives of the deceased.

propitious (prəʊ'pɪʃəs), *a.* Forms: 5 propycyous, 5–7 -pici(o)us, 6– propitious. [Late ME. a. OF. *propicius, -eux* (*a* 1140 in Godef.), f. L. *propiti-us* (see propice): see -ous.]

1. Disposed to be favourable; well-disposed, favourably inclined; gracious.

1447 Bokenham *Seyntys* (Roxb.) 10 To them in erthe that the serve and love Be evere propycyous. **1451** Capgrave *Life St. Gilbert* (E.E.T.S.) 75 Nature, which is propicius to helth, had withdrawe sum-what hir fauour. **1596** Spenser *Hymns* i. ii, T'asswage the force of this new flame, And make thee more propitious in my need. **1681** R. Wittie *Surv. Heavens* 56 Astrology considers some of the Planets in their Influences as propitious to Mankind. **1748** Hartley *Observ. Man* ii. ii. 112 They all endeavoured to render God propitious by Sacrifice. **1888** Anna K. Green *Behind Closed Doors* iv, If the fates are propitious we may succeed.

b. Indicative of, or characterized by, favour; of favourable import; boding well.

1586 Marlowe *1st Pt. Tamburl.* v. i, We entreat..That this device may prove propitious. **1649** Milton *Eikon.* xxviii. 238 God hath testifi'd by all propitious and evident signes..that such a solemn..act..was..a..gratefull.. Sacrifice. **1703** Maundrell *Journ. Jerus.* (1732) 26 Having first sent our Present,..to procure a propitious reception. **1734** tr. *Rollin's Anc. Hist.* (1827) VI. xv. xiii. 202 Being told that the auspices were not propitious. **1870** Bryant *Iliad* I. ii. 52 Almighty Jupiter Flung down his lightnings on the right and gave Propitious omens.

2. Presenting favourable conditions; favourable, advantageous.

1601 R. Johnson *Kingd. & Commw.* (1603) 12 The gentlenesse of the aire, with the fertilitie of the ground,..is so propitious and naturall for the increase of fruite. **1695** Addison *King* 210 May Heav'n's propitious gales attend thee home! **1781** Gibbon *Decl. & F.* xxv. (1869) I. 721 The circumstances were propitious to the designs of an usurper. **1868** Freeman *Norm. Conq.* II. viii. 206 Thurstan looked upon the moment as one propitious for revolt. **1870** L'Estrange *Miss Mitford* I. iii. 75 The weather was most propitious.

Hence **pro'pitiously** *adv.*, in a propitious manner; **pro'pitiousness**, the quality or fact of being propitious.

1593 Nashe *Christ's T.* Wks. (Grosart) IV. 61 If I had but bestowed the thousand part of the propitiousnes I haue bestowed on the progeny of Abraham. **1681** Dryden *Abs. & Achit.* 363 Yet oh that Fate, propitiously inclined, Had raised my birth, or had debased my mind. **1690** Temple *Anc. & Mod. Learn.* Wks. 1720 I. 159 The Propitiousness of Climate to that sort of Tree. **1831** Carlyle *Sart. Res.* i. ix. (1838) 58 The wreck of matter and the crash of worlds was thy element and propitiously wafting tide.

'proplasm. *rare.* [ad. L. *proplasma* (Plin.), a. Gr. πρόπλασμα a pattern, model, f. προπλάσσειν to mould or form before: see pro-[2] and plasm.] A mould, a matrix.

1695 Woodward *Nat. Hist. Earth* iv. 182 Those Shells, by that means, serving as Proplasmes, or Moulds, to the Matter which so filled them. **1704** J. Harris *Lex. Techn.* I, *Proplasm*, the same with a Mould in which any Metal or soft Matter, which afterwards will harden, is cast. **18..** *Jrnl. of Science* No. 124. 242 (Cent. Dict.) We gather that the mysterious Spirit is merely the noumenon or proplasm of physical and psychical phenomena.

†**pro'plastic**, *sb.* and *a. Obs.* [As sb. ad. mod.L. *proplasticē*, a. Gr. type *προπλαστική (sc. τέχνη) the art of moulding, f. προπλάσσειν: see prec., also plastic; as adj. ad. Gr. type *προπλαστικός, f. προπλάσσειν: see prec.]

A. *sb.* The art of forming moulds for casting.

[**1662** Evelyn *Chalcogr.* i. 2 *Sculptura*..was apply'd to several things; as,..*Proplastice* forming the future work *ex creta*, or some such matter, as the *Protypus* was of Wax for Efformation, and the *Modulus* of wood.] **1688** R. Holme *Armoury* iii. 153/2 Lysistratus..found out the Art of Proplastick, or casting of Figures in Moulds. [**1706** Phillips, *Proplastice*, the Art of making Moulds, in which any thing is cast or framed.]

B. *adj.* Of or relating to the making of moulds; forming a mould or cast.

1662 Evelyn *Chalcogr.* Table, Proplastic Art. **1821–2** Coleridge *Confess.* iii. 34 The first ferments of the great affections—the proplastic waves of the microcosmic chaos.

proplastid: see pro-[2] 1.

propless ('prɒplɪs), *a.* [f. prop *sb.*[1] + -less.] Without prop or support; unsupported.

1591 Sylvester *Du Bartas* i. vii. 94 The dull Earth's prop-less massie Ball Stands steddy still. **1652** Benlowes *Theoph.* v. xix, Tell how pond'rous Earths huge proplesse Ball Hangs poised in the fluent Hall Of fleeting Air? *a***1734** Dennis *To Thomson*, Yet shall my propless ivy, pale and bent, Bless the short sunshine which thy pity lent.

‖**propleuron** (prəʊ'plʊərən). *Entom.* Pl. **-a.** [mod.L., f. pro-[2] + pleuron.] Each of the two lateral portions of the prothorax, or first thoracic somite of an insect, lying one on each side of the pronotum. Hence **pro'pleural** *a.*, of or pertaining to the propleuron.

Each propleuron consists of three parts named *proëpimeron, proëpisternum, proparapteron.* (Cf. *mesopleuron* and *metapleuron*, with their divisions *mesepimeron, metepimeron*, etc.)

1841 E. Newman *Insects* 146 The *prothorax* has a *pronotum, prosternum*, and two *propleura.*

proplex, -exus: see pro-[2] 2.

†**pro'plexity.** *Obs.* [For *perplexity*, by confusion of prefixes.] Perplexity.

1487 *Barbour's Bruce* xii. 530 (Camb. MS.) Set in-till herd proplexite. *c***1500** Kennedy *Passion of Christ* 1332 He estounit with gret proplexite. **1547** Salesbury *Welsh Dict.*, *Kyfing gyngor*, Proplexitie. *a***1568** in *Bannatyne Poems* (Hunter. Cl.) 214 Peax is away, flemit is all proplexite.

‖**propodeon** (prəʊ'pɒdiːən). *Entom.* Improperly **propodeum.** [mod.L. (Newman) f. Gr. πρό, pro-[2] + ποδεών (-ῶνος) the neck or mouth of a wineskin, or of the bladder; hence, any narrow end.

(The Latinized form in *-podeum* was app. founded on the misconception that the Gr. word is a neuter in *-ον*.)]

That part of the thorax, principally in Hymenoptera, which precedes and partly surrounds the petiole; originally the first abdominal segment.

1833 E. Newman in *Entomol. Mag.* I. 410 The fifth segment is the Propodeon, and is, of the whole thirteen, the most difficult to determine, because in orders of the same class it appears in different modes. **1895** *Camb. Nat. Hist.* V. 491 [The term 'Propodeum'] was proposed by Newman, under the form of propodeon, and appears to be on the whole the most suitable term for this part. **1899** G. H. Carpenter *Insects* iv. 268 The partial or entire fusion of the first abdominal segment (*propodeum*) with the thorax.

propodial (prəʊ'pəʊdɪəl), *a.* and *sb. Zool.* [ad. mod.L. *propodiālis*, f. propodi-um + -al[1].]

A. *adj.* **1.** Of or pertaining to the propodium of a mollusc.

2. Of or pertaining to the proximal or upper segment of a limb, as the humerus or femur.

[**1882** Wilder & Gage *Anat. Techn.* 41 The bones of the proximal segments are the *Ossa propodialia* [= propodial bones], [etc.].]

B. *sb.* (Also in L. form *propodiāle*, plural *propodiālia.*) A propodial part or element; a propodial bone, as the humerus or femur.

1889 Cope in *Amer. Nat.* Oct. 852 (Synopsis of *Vertebrata*) Limbs consisting of one basal element, two propodials, and metapodials and digits..*Batrachia.*

propodite ('prɒpəʊdaɪt). *Zool.* [f. next + -ite[1] 3.] The penultimate joint of a developed endopodite limb, as of a crustacean.

1870 Rolleston *Anim. Life* 92 The two terminal joints.. which are known as the 'propodite' and 'dactylopodite'. **1880** Huxley *Crayfish* iv. 165 The endopodite is divided into five joints, named,—ischiopodite, meropodite, carpopodite, propodite, and dactylopodite.

Hence **propo'ditic** *a.*, of, pertaining to, or of the nature of a propodite, as *the propoditic joint.*

‖**propodium** (prəʊ'pəʊdɪəm). *Zool.* Pl. **-ia.** [mod.L., f. Gr. πρό, pro-[2] + πούς, ποδ- foot: cf. Gr. προπόδιος adj. before the feet.] The anterior lobe of the foot in some molluscs.

1853 Huxley in *Phil. Trans.* CXLIII. i. 36 The fin or propodium is flattened and fan-shaped. *Ibid.*, The posterior edge of the propodium carries a cup-shaped disk... This is commonly called the sucker... It may be called the mesopodium. **1875** Nicholson *Man. Zool.* xlvii. (ed. 4) 342

In the *Heteropoda*..and in the Wing-shells..the foot exhibits a division into three portions—an anterior, the 'propodium'; a middle, the 'mesopodium'; and a posterior lobe, or 'metapodium'. **1883** E. R. LANKESTER in *Encycl. Brit.* XVI. 653/1 The foot of the Azygobranchia..often divided into..a fore, middle, and hind lobe, pro-, meso-, and metapodium.

propodus ('prɒpədəs). *Zool.* [f. PRO-[2] + Gr. πούς, ποδ- foot.] = PROPODITE.

1945 T. H. SAVORY *Spiders Brit. Isles* (ed. 2) 196 The propodus ends in a large claw and often a pair of smaller accessory claws. **1976** *Nature* 11 Mar. 136/1 Among the factors affecting the strength of a crab's master claw is the cross-sectional area of muscle in the manus (that part of the propodus behind the apposing fingers).

‖**propolis** ('prɒpəlɪs). [L. (Plin.) a. Gr. πρόπολις a suburb, also bee-glue, f. πρό before + πόλις city. So in F. (Paré *c* 1560).] A red, resinous, aromatic substance collected by bees from the viscid buds of trees, as the horse-chestnut; used to stop up crevices, and fix the combs to the hives; bee-glue.

[**1398** TREVISA *Barth. De P.R.* XVIII. xii. (Bodl. MS.) Þe þrid tyme scheo setteþ more grete matier and þik, and þat is þe stablemente and fastenynge of þee honye combes, and many men clepeþ that mater *Propolim*. **1598** FLORIO, *Propoli*, that which Bees make at the entrance of the hiues to keepe out cold, called Beeglue.] **1601** HOLLAND *Pliny* I. 313 But Propolis consisteth of a more solid matter,..and serueth as a good defence against cold, and to stop the passage of waspes and such hurtful creatures as would do iniurie to the bees. *Ibid.* II. 338 With the like quantity of..the cereous matter in the Bee-hive called *Propolis*. **1766** *Compl. Farmer* s.v. *Bee*, She began by loosening the straw hive from the board on which it rested, and to which the bees had fastened it with propolis. **1816** KIRBY & SP. *Entomol.* xv. (1818) I. 502 M. Huber ascertained that this substance was actually propolis, collected from the buds of the poplar. **1882** *Good Words* 745 Propolis, an adhesive vegetable secretion, obtained..from various sources, the bud of the chestnut being the chief favorite.

Hence '**propolize** *v. trans.*, to cover or secure with propolis.

1884 PHIN *Dict. Apiculture* 55.

†**propomate.** *Obs.* [f. late L. *propoma*, a. Gr. πρόπομα or πρόπωμα a drink taken before eating + -ATE[1].] (See quotations.)

[**1693** tr. *Blancard's Phys. Dict.* (ed. 2), *Propoma*, a Drink made of Wine and Hony, or Sugar. **1895** *Syd. Soc. Lex.*, *Propo·ma*..a potion of wine and honey taken before meat;..also applied to other drinks and medicated wines taken before food.] **1657** *Physical Dict.*, *Propomates*, all kind of drinks made with sugar and hony.

propone (prəʊ'pəʊn), *v.* Now only *Sc.* [ad. L. *prōpōn-ĕre* to put or set forth, expose, declare, propose, intend, f. *prō*, PRO-[1] 1 a + *pōn-ĕre* to put, place. Cf. PROPOUND, PROPOSE.]

1. *trans.* To put forth, set forth, or propose for consideration, acceptance, or adoption; to propound as a question or matter for decision. Since 17th c. only *Sc.*

c **1375** *Sc. Leg. Saints* v. (*Johannes*) 297 Proponand þam þat distinctiue..þat oþire þai to dame dyane prayand, suld [etc.]. **1513** DOUGLAS *Æneis* I. i. *heading*, The poet first proponyng his entent, Declaris Junois wraith and mailtalent. **1528** GARDINER in Pocock *Rec. Ref.* I. 137 Among all which requests nothing certain is proponed. **1538** CRANMER *Let. to Cromwell* in *Misc. Writ.* (Parker Soc.) II. 359 To call my doctors unto me, and to propone the same case amongst them. **1585** T. WASHINGTON tr. *Nicholay's Voy.* I. xix. 23 b, He would gladly agree to the matter proponed. **1640** LAUD *Wks.* (1853) III. 318 These articles were sent unto me, not to be proponed to the church, but to be inserted amongst the canons thereof. **1676** W. ROW *Contn. Blair's Autobiog.* ix. (1848) 143 Mr. Livingstone proponed an overture. **1683** E. HOOKER *Pref. Pordage's Mystic Div.* 77 If hee proponed ani Quæstions to ani. **1814** SCOTT *Wav.* xvi, It did not..become them..to propone their *prosapia*. **1893** STEVENSON *Catriona* I. ii, The bits of business that I have to propone to you are rather..confidential.

2. *Civil* and *Sc. Law.* To put, bring, or state before a tribunal.

c **1425** WYNTOUN *Cron.* VIII. x. 1589 Þis Makduff til Lundyn past, And þar proponyt his qwerel. *a* **1548** HALL *Chron., Hen. VI* 163 b, Such articles, as against hym should in open parliament be bothe proponed and proved. **1609** SKENE *Reg. Maj.* II. Table 62 And quhen he compeirs, he may propon his exceptions dilatories, and others. **1786** BURNS *Addr. to Unco Guid* ii, I, for their thoughtless, careless sakes, Would here propone defences. **1838** W. BELL *Dict. Law Scot.* 795 Pleas proponed and repelled are those pleas which have been stated in a court and repelled previous to decree being given.

†**3.** *refl.* To offer oneself, to offer. *Obs.*

c **1500** *Lancelot* 2461 So that thei can them vtraly propone In his seruice thar lyves to dispone.

†**4.** *trans.* To set before any one as an example or aim; to propose or offer as a reward. *Obs.*

1555 CDL. POLE *Let.* in *Cranmer's Misc. Writ.* (Parker Soc.) II. 537 The great sophister and father of all lies..proponing ever that which is more agreeable to the sense. **1563–7** BUCHANAN *Reform. St. Andros* Wks. (1892) 10 Thair salbe twa bonnittis proponet to be given solemnly to the twa that makis best composition. **1586** A. DAY *Eng. Secretary* I. (1625) 143, I think the examples already proponed to be sufficient. *a* **1653** BINNING *Serm.* (1845) 525 It might endear this Christian virtue [love] unto us, that God propones Himself as the pattern of it.

†**5.** To put before oneself as something to be done; to purpose. Also *absol. Obs.*

1596 DALRYMPLE tr. *Leslie's Hist. Scot.* IX. 221 He propones to punise thame with al seueritie conforme to Justice. *c* **1598** D. FERGUSON *Sc. Prov.* (1785) 25 Man propones, but God dispones.

Hence **pro'poned** *ppl. a.*, put forward, proposed, 'given' as a datum; **pro'poning** *vbl. sb.*, propounding; also **pro'ponement**, proposing, nomination; **pro'poner**, one who propones, a proposer.

1533 MORE *Answ. Poysoned Bk.* Wks. 1044/1 Our sauiour ..vsed in the proponing therof vnto them diuers waies. **1535** CROMWELL in Merriman *Life & Lett.* (1902) I. 420 Prayeng you to vse your discression in the proponing of the premisses to the Frensh king and the grete Master. **1553** CDL. POLE in Strype *Cranmer* (1840) II. App. lxxv. 924 Consysteng the whole..in the proponement of the parson, that hath to put furthe the same. **1557** RECORDE *Whetst.* D iv, When any odde nomber is propounded..multiplie that proponed nomber by it selfe, and it will make a square nomber. **1576** FLEMING *Panopl. Epist.* 179 Some sentence of certaintie, touching this proponed controuersie. **1636** W. SCOT *Apol. Narr.* (Wodrow Soc.) 261 The proponers were quickly cut off.

proponent (prəʊ'pəʊnənt), *a.* and *sb.* [ad. L. *prōpōnent-em*, pres. pple. of *prōpōn-ĕre*: see prec.]

A. *adj.* That brings forward or proposes; that brings an action; that makes a proposal.

1687 DRYDEN *Hind & P.* I. 121 And for mysterious things of faith rely On the proponent Heaven's authority. **1693** WOOD *Allegation* in *Life & Times* (O.H.S.) IV. 17 This party proponent doth alledge that..there was and is att present now in force an act of parliament, entituled [etc.]. **1827** HONE *Every-day Bk.* II. 82 The landlord..swore in the 'party proponent'.

B. *sb.* **1.** One who brings forward a proposition or argument; a propounder, a proposer.

1588 FRAUNCE *Lawiers Log.* II. ix. 101 b, The Proponent who defendeth proposition or position. **1691** NORRIS *Pract. Disc.* 23 These two Ends considered Absolutely and Simply in themselves, are alike valued by their respective Proponents. **1693** WOOD *Allegation* in *Life & Times* (O.H.S.) IV. 17 This proponent doth farther allege, that the above-said book, entituled *Athenae Oxonienses*, Volume the Second, exhibited in this cause into the [Vice-Chancellor's] court..by the party promovent in this cause, was, and is printed..and published in London. **1702** KENNETT *Pres. St. Convocation* 11 The only proper Rule for interpreting the Speech of this Proponent. **1872** DE MORGAN *Budget of Paradoxes* 296 Attempt to enforce..doctrine, by arguments drawn from mathematics, the proponents being persons unskilled in that science.

2. A kind of government agent in Ceylon under the Dutch.

1860 BATEMAN *Life Bp. D. Wilson* I. xiii. 412, These men were selected by the Government, paid stipends varying from £60 to £100 per annum, and called 'Proponents'.

‖**propons** ('prəʊpɒnz). *Anat.* [mod.L., f. PRO-[1] + PONS 2.] (See quot.)

1890 in BILLINGS *Med. Dict.* **1895** *Syd. Soc. Lex.*, *Propons*, term for the arciform fibres, where they cover the anterior pyramid of the medulla immediately below the pons Varolii.

‖**Pro'pontis.** Also 7 **Propontey.** [L., a. Gr. προποντίς the Sea of Marmora, lit. the 'Fore-sea', f. πρό, PRO-[2] 2 (*a*) + πόντος a sea, spec. the Euxine.] The ancient name of the Sea of Marmora; also *transf.* a narrow channel (obs.).

1642 HOWELL *For. Trav.* xi. (Arb.) 57 Over the Propontey to divers places in Asia. **1693** J. O. tr. *Cowley's Plants* (1795) 47 Thence thro' a small propontis carried down, It makes the port, and takes the left-side town. **1865** SWINBURNE *Atalanta* (1868) 121 Where the narrowing Symplegades whitened the straits of Propontis with spray.

Hence **Pro'pontic** *a.*, of or pertaining to the Propontis; *sb.*, the Propontic Sea, Sea of Marmora.

1604 SHAKS. *Oth.* III. iii. 456 Like to the Ponticke Sea, Whose Icie Current..keepes due on To the Proponticke, and the Hellespont. **1604** DRAYTON *Owl* 792 The Fowle from the Proponticke Spring, Fild all th' Egean with their stemming Ores.

†**pro'port,** *sb.*[1] *Obs. rare*[−1]. [Short for *proportion*.] = PROPORTION *sb.* 4.

1565 *Satir. Poems Reform.* i. 383 Nature formed my feate[r] beside in such proport as advanseth my pride.

†**proport,** *sb.*[2], obs. Sc. f. PURPORT *sb.*, bearing.

1597 SKENE *De Verb. Sign.*, *Proporcitas, proportatio assisæ*, the proport, report, declaration, or deliverance of ane assise.

†**pro'port,** *v. Sc. Obs.* [a. OF. *proporte-r* (1118 in Godef.), variant of *porporter* to PURPORT.] *trans.* To convey to the mind, to express; to mean, to bear; to set forth; = PURPORT *v.* 1.

1387 *Charters &c. of Edinb.* (1871) 55 This Endenture..contenis, proportis, and beris witnes. **1434** *Reg. St. Andrews* 506 (Jam.) The endenture maid at Saint Androwis..proportis and berys witnes [etc.]. **1513** DOUGLAS *Æneis* VI. Prol. 28 Virgile..heirintill, as Seruius gan proport, His hie knawledge he schawis. **1535** STEWART *Cron. Scot.* (Rolls) I. 219 In siclike number as tha did proport. **1607** LEVER *Crucifix* lxxxv, Take for an instance him whom we proport. **1609** HUME *Admon.* in *Wodrow Soc. Misc.* (1844) 578 The historie proporteth that sum of theis byschopes seates wer aboue ane other. **1678** SIR G. MACKENZIE *Crim. Laws Scot.* I. xxi. §4 (1699) 112 As our saids Laws and Acts of Parliament in themselves proports.

proportion (prəʊ'pɔəʃən), *sb.* [ME. *proporcioun*, a. F. *proportion* (13th c. in Littré), ad. L. *prōportiōn-em* proportion, comparative relation, analogy, app. derived from the phrase *prō portiōne* for or in respect of (his or its) share: see PORTION.]

I. In general use.

1. A portion or part in its relation to the whole; a comparative part, a share; sometimes simply, a portion, division, part.

c **1386** CHAUCER *Can. Yeom. Prol. & T.* 201 What sholde I tellen eche proporcion Of thynges whiche þat we werche vpon? **1581** MARBECK *Bk. of Notes* 213 According to the working of euerie part in his proportion. **1599** SHAKS. *Hen. V*, I. ii. 304 Therefore let our proportions for these Warres Be soone collected. **1632** *High Commission Cases* (Camden) 267 What proportion of maintenance shall be allowed her for Alimony? **1654** R. CODRINGTON tr. *Iustine* v. 97 To demand their proportion in the spoils. **1700** in Picton *L'pool Munic. Rec.* (1883) I. 291 Persons may come and peticion for proportions to build on. **1711** *Fingall MSS.* in *10th Rep. Hist. MSS. Comm.* App. v. 181 The major part of them embarked..about the beginning of December... Another proportion of them departed on the 22nd of December. **1822** CHALMERS *Sp. Gen. Assembly* Wks. XVI. 158 Each parish is divided into districts called proportions, over which an elder is appointed. **1841–4** EMERSON *Ess.*, *Love* Wks. (Bohn) I. 72 The strong bent of nature is seen in the proportion which this topic..usurps in the conversation of society. **1878** HUXLEY *Physiogr.* 73 The sea which covers so large a proportion of the earth's surface.

2. The relation existing between things or magnitudes as to size, quantity, number or the like; comparative relation, ratio. Also *fig.*

1387 TREVISA *Higden* (Rolls) I. 45 Þe proporcioun of þe roundenesse aboute of a cercle is to þe brede as is þe proporcioun of two and twenty to seuene. **1557** RECORDE *Whetst.* Bj, Any .2. nombers maie haue comparison and proportion together, although thei be incommensurable. As .3. and .4. **1663** GERBIER *Counsel* e vij, The Proportion of the Sun and Moon. **1687** A. LOVELL tr. *Thevenot's Trav.* I. 33 They put in this Powder, to the proportion of a good spoonful for three Dishes or Cups full of Water. **1690** LOCKE *Hum. Und.* II. xv. §12 Finite of any Magnitude, holds not any proportion to Infinite. **1692** BENTLEY *Boyle Lect.* iii. 94 The proportion of Births to Burials is found to be yearly as Fifty to Forty. **1814** CARY *Dante, Paradise* VI. 124 It is part of our delight, to measure Our wages with the merit; and admire The close proportion. **1831** BREWSTER *Optics* v. 46 To make this image as large as we please, and in any proportion to the object. **1848** MILL *Pol. Econ.* I. x. §3 The population exhibits, in every quinquennial census, a smaller proportion of births to the population.

b. In phrase ***in*** (†***for,*** †***of,*** †***with***) ***proportion.*** Const. *to*, *unto* (†*of*), as.

1390 GOWER *Conf.* II. 212 After that sche hath richesse, Her love is of proporcion. **1637** G. SANDYS *Trav.* II. 121 His tongue, of a marvelous length for proportion [*earlier edd.* for the p.] of his body. **1660** WILLSFORD *Scales Comm.* 1 In proportion unto the rate it may be sold for. **1677** *Govt. Venice* 196 There being no Nobleman (with proportion) so well recompenced as they, no not the Doge himself. **1683** RAY *Corr.* (1848) 134 Small wings in proportion to the bulk of its body. **1723** *Present St. Russia* I. 53 Ordering how many Men each Governor is to raise in Proportion of his Jurisdiction. **1762–71** H. WALPOLE *Vertue's Anecd. Paint.* (1786) II. 28 The rooms large, but some of them not lofty in proportion. **1843** RUSKIN *Mod. Paint.* I. II. I. iii. §9 Every truth is valuable in proportion as it is characteristic of the thing of which it is affirmed. **1855** PRESCOTT *Philip II*, I. II. xii. 284 Margaret's credulity seems to have been in proportion to her hatred, and her hatred in proportion to her former friendship.

3. *transf.* A relation, other than of quantity, between things; comparison; analogy †an analogue.

1538 ELYOT *Dict.* Addit., *Analogia*, conueniency or proporcion, whose proprietie is to conferre that which is doutfull, with that whiche is like to it, whiche is more certayne, to make it more playne. **1614** SELDEN *Titles Hon.* 4 Neither is [there] in a humane Monarchie what hath not in their [i.e. the Bees'] Commonwelth some remarquable proportion. **1664** BUTLER *Hud.* II. ii. 109 Oaths are but words, and words but Wind,..And hold with deeds proportion, so As shadows to a substance do. **1690** NORRIS *Beatitudes* (1694) I. 2 He was to be a Law-giver, as well as Moses; and, to carry on the Proportion yet farther, he thought fit to imitate him in the very Manner and Circumstance of delivering his Law. **1824** MACKINTOSH *Sp. in Ho. Com.* 15 June, Wks. 1846 III. 462 What proportion does the contest bear to the country in which it prevails?

4. (= *due* or *proper proportion*.) Due relation of one part to another; such relation of size, etc., between things or parts of a thing as renders the whole harmonious; balance, symmetry, agreement, harmony.

c **1380** WYCLIF *Sel. Wks.* III. 132 Surely þo Chirche schal nevere be hool, byfore proporciouns of hir partis be broght ageyne by þis hevenly leche. **1398** TREVISA *Barth. De P.R.* IV. iii. (1495) e vij/1 Dryenesse is the worste qualyte whan it passyth the proporcyons in bodyes. **1490** CAXTON *Eneydos* xxix. 112 Well made of her membres, eche in his qualyte, and ryght egall in proporcyon, without eny dyfformyte. **1597** HOOKER *Eccl. Pol.* v. lxxiii. §2 Choise seeketh rather proportion then absolute perfection of goodnesse. **1642** FULLER *Holy & Prof. St.* III. xiii. 183 Let thy recreations..bear proportion with thine age. **1723** CHAMBERS tr. *Le Clerc's Treat. Archit.* I. 29 By Proportion I don't here mean, a Relation of Ratio's as the Geometricians do; but a Suitableness of parts, founded on the good Taste of the Architect. *a* **1832** MACKINTOSH *Revolution of 1688* Wks. 1846 II. 11 He never obtained an importance which bore any proportion to his great abilities.

b. Phrase. ***out of proportion***, having no due relation in size, amount, etc. (usu. implying excess).

1710 PALMER *Proverbs* 359 If the pomp exceed the character, and be carry'd out of proportion. **1831** KEBLE *Serm.* v. (1848) 116 Civil liberty..is usually allowed to fill a space in our thoughts, out of all proportion to that which it fills in the plan of happiness drawn out in the Bible.

5. Size or extent, relatively to some standard; relative size; also *fig.* extent, degree. ***at full proportion***, full size, life size. **b.** Now only in *pl.* Dimensions. (Cf. DIMENSION *sb.* 2.)

1390 GOWER *Conf.* III. 108 Here [the planets'] cercles more or lasse be, Mad after the proporcion Of therthe. **1551** TURNER *Herbal* I. I v, The proporcion of the lesse is much like vnto a water rose, otherwyse called nunefar. **1641** J. JACKSON *True Evang. T.* III. 230 Cornelius à Lapide,.. whose volumes are swelled to that proportion that they take up halfe a Classis in our publique Libraries. **1652** NEEDHAM tr. *Selden's Mare Cl.* 26 It may in a certain proportion bee called Servitude, inasmuch as the Republick hath been constrained to assume the total Dominion and Government thereof. *c* **1710** CELIA FIENNES *Diary* 125 Hung with pictures att full proportion of ye Royal family.

b. 1638 JUNIUS *Paint. Ancients* 10 A few very moderate and easie documents of meet proportions. **1824–9** LANDOR *Imag. Conv.* Wks. 1846 II. 155/1 Few..have beheld their contemporaries in those proportions in which they appeared a century later. **1850** ROBERTSON *Serm.* Ser. III. iv. (1872) 59 Monsters, with some part of our being bearing the development of a giant, and others showing the proportions of a dwarf. **1860** TYNDALL *Glac.* I. xvi. 96 The ice-crags.. seemed of gigantic proportions.

†**6.** The action of proportioning or making proportionate; proportionate estimate, reckoning, or adjustment. *Obs.*

c **1386** CHAUCER *Frankl. T.* 558 Whan he hadde founde his firste mansion He knew the remenant by proporcion. *a* **1483** *Liber Niger* in *Househ. Ord.* (1790) 69 To make proportion for the expenses of this houshold for an hoole yere. **1605** SHAKS. *Macb.* I. iv. 19 Would thou hadst lesse deseru'd, That the proportion both of thanks, and payment, Might haue beene mine.

7. Configuration, form, shape; a figure or image of anything. *Obs.* exc. *poet.*

a **1400–50** *Alexander* 5142 A purtrayour in preuate scho prays..to pas, And his personele proporcions in perchemen hire bring. **1530** PALSGR. 259/1 Proporcyon of a beest, *lineature.* **1535** COVERDALE *Wisd.* xiii. 13 A croked pece of wodd..he geueth it some proporcion, fashioneth it after the similitude of a man, or maketh it like some beest. **1585** T. WASHINGTON tr. *Nicholay's Voy.* III. iv. 76b, The figure following doth liuely represent vnto you the proportion of the Ianissary. **1678** WOOD *Life* II. 411 On the top of the said monument layes the short proportion of a man. **1842** TENNYSON *Two Voices* 20 She gave him mind, the lordliest Proportion, and..Dominion in the head and breast.

†**8.** A relative quantity, amount, or number *of*. (But the relativity is often not thought of.) *Obs.*

1601 R. JOHNSON *Kingd. & Commw.* (1603) 22 It bringeth not forth Mules nor Asses, but of horse infinite proportions. *c* **1618** MORYSON *Itin.* IV. (1903) 372 The Netherlanders, who make infinite proportions of hangings for houses. **1633** BP. HALL *Hard Texts, N.T.* 102 God..hath indued him with an infinite proportion thereof. **1652** HOWELL *Giraffi's Rev. Naples* II. 12 They burnt a huge proportion of bisket.

II. In technical senses.

9. *Math.* An equality of ratios, esp. of geometrical ratios; a relation among quantities such that the quotient of the first divided by the second is equal to that of the third divided by the fourth.

This was formerly distinguished as ***geometrical proportion*** (see GEOMETRICAL *a.* 16) in contrast to ***arithmetical proportion*** (now obs.). ***harmonic(al*** or †***musical proportion***: see HARMONIC *a.* 5a.

c **1391** CHAUCER *Astrol.* Prol. 1 Abilite to lerne sciencez touchinge noumbres & proporciouns. **1551** RECORDE *Pathw. Knowl.* Pref., Lycurgus..is most praised for that he didde chaunge the state of their common wealthe frome the proportion Arithmeticall to a proportion geometricall. **1571** DIGGES *Pantom., Math. Disc.* T j b, Any lyne or number is sayde to be diuided by extreame and meane proportion, when the diuision..is suche.. that the whole line or number retayne the same proportion to the greater parte that the greater doth to the lesser. **1669** STURMY *Mariner's Mag.* I. ii. 32 Two..Lines being given,..to find a third which shall be in proportion unto them. **1696** PHILLIPS (ed. 5) s.v., Arithmetical Proportion is when Three or more Numbers proceed with the same difference. Geometrical, when Three or more Numbers have the same reason, or where every Number bears the same proportion to that which preceeds. **1798** HUTTON *Course Math.* (1810) I. 110 If two or more couplets of numbers have equal ratios, or equal differences, the equality is named Proportion, and the terms of the ratios Proportionals. **1859** BARN. SMITH *Arith. & Algebra* (ed. 6) 432 Proportion is the relation of equality subsisting between two ratios.

b. *Arith.* The rule or process by which, three quantities being given, a fourth may be found which is in the same ratio to the third as the second is to the first, or (what is the same thing) in the same ratio to the second that the third is to the first; the rule of three.

1542 RECORDE *Gr. Artes* (1575) 240 The rule of Proportions..whose vse is, by three numbers knowen, to find another vnknowen. **1678** PHILLIPS (ed. 4) s.v., In Arithmetick, the Rule of proportion..is otherwise called the Golden Rule, or Rule of Three. **1691** WOOD *Ath. Oxon.* II. 129 In 1624 he transported into France the Rule of Proportion, having a little before been invented by Edm. Gunter of Gresham Coll. **1827** HUTTON *Course Math.* I. 50 *Compound Proportion*, is a rule by means of which the student may resolve such questions as require two or more statings in simple proportion.

10. *Mus.* and *Pros.* †**a.** Metrical or musical rhythm or harmony; hence, an air, tune, melody. Cf. MEASURE *sb.* 16, 17. *Obs.*

1447 BOKENHAM *Seyntys* (Roxb.) 43 Orpheus..of me wolde never take hede Nor of his armonye oo poynt me teche In musical proporcyon rymes to lede. **1513** DOUGLAS *Æneis* VI. x. 43 Orpheus of Trace..Playand proportionis and springis dyvyne Apon his harp. **1589** PUTTENHAM *Eng. Poesie* II. i. (Arb.) 79 And this our proportion Poeticall resteth in fiue points: Staffe, Measure, Concord, Scituation and figure all which shall be spoken of in their places.

b. Ratio (of duration of notes, rates of vibration, lengths of strings, etc.): = sense 2, in specific applications.

1609 DOULAND *Ornith. Microl.* 59 The Art of Musicke doth onely consider of the Proportion of inequalitie. **1658** PLAYFORD *Skill Mus.* vi. 20 Notes in Musick have two Names, one for Tune, the other for Time or Proportion of sounds... Here (according to the ordinary Proportion of Time) we account two Minums to the Semibrief. **1694** HOLDER *Treat. Harmony* v. (1731) 86 It was said..that Mercurius's Lyre was strung with four Chords, having those Proportions, 6, 8, 9, 12. **1898** STAINER & BARRETT *Dict. Mus. Terms* s.v., This system of proportion was used not only with reference to intervals but also to the comparative length of notes.

11. *Chem.* = PROPORTIONAL B. 3.

1863–72 WATTS *Dict. Chem.* I. 454 Davy..introduced the word proportion as a substitute for Dalton's word atom. *Ibid.*, Every..symbol is used to express one atomic proportion of its particular element.

proportion (prəʊˈpɔəʃən), *v.* [ME. a. OF. *proporcioner* (14th c. in Littré), mod.F. *proportionner*, ad. med.L. *prōportiōn-āre* (Bede), f. *prōportio*: see prec.]

1. *trans.* To adjust in proper proportion *to* something else, as to size, quantity, number, etc.; to make proportionate. Const. *to*, *with*.

1449 in *Calr. Proc. Chanc. Q. Eliz.* (1830) II. Pref. 55 All the remnaunt of the tymbr..shall be wele and covenably proporcioned after the scantelons of tymbr above writen. *c* **1460** FORTESCUE *Abs. & Lim. Mon.* vi. (1885) 120 Ffor aftir that [his expenses] nedith his reuenues to be proporcioned. **1530** PALSGR. 668/1, I proporcyon a thynge, I make it of juste measure and quantyte, *je proporcionne.* **1669** STURMY *Mariner's Mag.* v. xi. 46 A Gunner ought..to proportion his Charge according to the thinnest side of the Metal. **1710** PRIDEAUX *Orig. Tithes* i. 5 To proportion the means to the end. **1833** HT. MARTINEAU *Briery Creek* ii. 39 You can proportion your supply exactly to the demand. **1862** MILL *Utilit.* 85 The punishment should be proportioned to the offence.

2. To adjust or regulate the proportions of; to fashion, form, shape. *Obs.* exc. in PROPORTIONED.

a **1380** [see PROPORTIONED *ppl. a.* 2]. *c* **1400** *Destr. Troy* 3053 Coruyn by crafte, colourd with honde, Proporcionet pertly with painteres deuyse. *c* **1460** J. RUSSELL *Bk. Nurture* 210 Thow must square & proporcioun þy bred clene & evenly. **1641** J. TRAPPE *Theol. Theol.* 157 A Painter..had illfavouredly proportioned a Hen. **1687** A. LOVELL tr. *Thevenot's Trav.* I. 144 To proportion the heat to such a temperate degree, that there be neither too much nor too little. **1703** MOXON *Mech. Exerc.* 317 For thus proportioning the Divisions in the Semi-circle, you may proportion the Divisions and Sub-divisions of Hours upon the Dyal Plane.

†**3.** To bear a due proportion to, to be in proportion to; to correspond to, to equal. *Obs.*

1599 SHAKS. *Hen. V*, III. vi. 134 Bid him therefore consider of his ransome, which must proportion the losses we haue borne, the subiects we haue lost. **1652** SPARKE *Prim. Devot.* (1663) 417 Yet here her offering proportioneth her ability. **1654–66** EARL ORRERY *Parthen.* (1676) 271 Their Success had proportion'd their Virtues.

†**4.** To divide into proportionate parts; to measure or mete out: to distribute in due shares.

1535 *Act 27 Hen. VIII*, c. 27 The sayde chancellour..shal also proporcion the sayd religious houses and other the premisses in ten partes. **1647** N. BACON *Disc. Govt. Eng.* I. lxvii. (1739) 163 The Judges itinerant had their time proportioned out to every County. **1709** STEELE *Tatler* No. 87 ¶9 Proportioning the Glory of a Battle among the whole Army. **1724** DE FOE *Mem. Cavalier* (1840) 41 They agree to proportion their forces.

†**5.** To allot or assign (a thing) to a person as his portion; to apportion. Also, To assign (a person) to a lot or portion. *Obs.*

1581 PETTIE *Guazzo's Civ. Conv.* II. (1586) 96 They doe all things better then we are able to proportion them out unto them. **1612** SIR R. DUDLEY in *Fortescue Papers* (Camden) 7 *note*, Uppon the sale of those landes, I have proportioned a thankefull gratuity for you. **1642** ROGERS *Naaman* 69 Samuel proportioned Eliab to a Crowne at first sight. *a* **1711** KEN *Submission* Poems (1857) 39 They'll me proportion what for me is best. **1798** CRAIG in Owen *Wellesley's Desp.* (1877) 599 It will then remain to proportion its several parts into the different branches.

†**6.** To compare or estimate proportionately; to estimate the relative proportions of. *Obs.*

1591 *Troub. Raigne K. John* (1611) 62, I doubt not when your Highnesse sees my prize, You may proportion all their former pride. **1616** B. JONSON *Forrest, To Penshurst* 99 Now, Penshurst, they that will proportion thee With other edifices. **1635** QUARLES *Embl.* IV. ii, Fond earth! Proportion not my seeming love To my long stay. **1711** SHAFTESB. *Charac.* (1737) II. I. ii. 200 To think with more Equality of Nature, and to proportion her Defects a little better.

proportionaˈbility. *rare.* [f. next: see -ITY.] = PROPORTIONABLENESS.

1697 J. SERGEANT *Solid Philos.* 177 Take Divisibility.. Proportionability, Impenetrability, Space, Place, etc. They have, all.., some nice Formality,..which distinguishes them.

proportionable (prəʊˈpɔəʃənəb(ə)l), *a.* [a. OF. **proporcionable* (assumed from the adv. in *-ment*, 1319 in Godef.), or ad. med.L. **prōportiōnābil-is* (assumed from the adv. *-iter*, Boeth.), f. *prōportiōnāre* (see PROPORTION *v.*) + *-ābilis*, -ABLE.]

1. That is in due proportion; corresponding, agreeable, commensurate, proportional. **a.** in number, amount, or degree.

c **1374** CHAUCER *Boeth.* III. metr. ix. 87 (Add. MS.), þou byndest þe elementz by noumbres proporcionables [*Camb. MS.* porcionables]. **1538** STARKEY *England* I. iii. 83 The partys of thys body be not proporcyonabul one to a nother. **1593** SHAKS. *Rich. II*, II. ii. 125 For vs to leuy power Proportionable to th' enemy, is all impossible. **1647** N. BACON *Disc. Govt. Eng.* I. lxii. (1739) 123 No more of the Inheritance can be conveyed to any of the Children, than their proportionable parts will amount unto. **1734** tr. *Rollin's Anc. Hist.* (1827) I. I. i. 181 Twenty pillars six fathoms round of a proportionable height. **1808** J. WEBSTER *Nat. Philos.* 17 The cohesive force is proportionable to the number of parts that touch each other. *a* **1832** MACKINTOSH *Life Sir T. More* Wks. 1846 I. 424 When his son with a wife, three daughters with their husbands, and a proportionable number of grandchildren, dwelt under his patriarchal roof.

†**b.** in nature, quality, or function: Suitable, appropriate; consonant, agreeable; analogous. *Obs.*

1528 PAYNEL *Salerne's Regim.* F ij, They..engendre bludde specialye proportionable to the harte. **1577** *Test. 12 Patriarchs* (1706) 107 The Lord maketh a mans body proportionable to the spirit that he will put into it, and fitteth the spirit to the ability of the body. **1671** J. WEBSTER *Metallogr.* iv. 61 They have their species perpetuated by a spiritual substance proportionable to seed. **1754** EDWARDS *Freed. Will* II. iii. (1762) 44 That it has a Cause proportionable and agreeable to the Effect.

†**2.** *Music.* Of sounds: Having definite relations of pitch and length. *Obs.*

1597 MORLEY *Introd. Mus.* Annot., Franchinus Gausurius [defineth music] thus..A disposition of proportionable soundes deuided by apt distances. **1604** T. WRIGHT *Passions* V. iv. 197 The harmony of proportionable voices and instruments, which feed the eare. **1644** BULWER *Chiron.* 105 They had an artificiall manner of clapping their hands, to a certain measure or proportionable tune.

3. Well-proportioned; symmetrical. *Obs.* or *arch.*

1625 K. LONG tr. *Barclay's Argenis* IV. viii. 267 Nature having done her part in giving him proportionable lineaments. **1658** *Hist. Christina Alessandra Qu. Swedland* 353 She [Christina]..is in her gestures and motion most comely and gracious, of a proportionable stature, a fresh colour, and royall features. **1750** G. HUGHES *Barbadoes* 65 It is about eight inches long and every way proportionable.

†**4.** Relative, comparative. *Obs.*

1654 FULLER *Two Serm.* 34 Each of them [Jeremiah and Baruch] by proportionable Computation, above sixtie yeares of age. **1718** J. CHAMBERLAYNE *Relig. Philos.* II. xvii. §10 The Consequences that we have deduced touching the proportionable Gravity of Water and Quicksilver. **1787** R. BURROWES in *Trans. R. Irish Acad.* Pref. 12 The proportionable density of the air at its various distances from the surface of the earth.

†**5.** Capable of being proportioned. *Obs.* *rare*$^{-1}$.

1653 MILTON *Hirelings* Wks. 1851 V. 355 The Laborer; worthy somtimes of single, somtimes of double Honor, not proportionable by Tithes.

†**B.** as *adv.* = PROPORTIONABLY. *Obs.*

1600 HAKLUYT *Voy.* III. 863 That there be nothing found out of order or lacking..which euery shippe proportionable to her burthen ought to haue. **1645** EVELYN *Diary* Feb., A roome of about 10 paces long, proportionable broad and high. **1681** tr. *Belon's Myst. Physick* 16 Add..of all proportionable to the quart of Wine contained in the Vessel.

proˈportionableness. [f. prec. + -NESS.] The quality of being proportionable.

1633 T. ADAMS *Exp. 2 Peter* ii. 17 This is the proportionableness of it [i.e. punishment]. **1698** ATTERBURY *Serm.* (1723) I. 240 The fitness and proportionableness of their exceeding great recompence. **1711** SHAFTESB. *Charac.* (1737) II. II. I. iii. 96 There is found generally an exact Proportionableness,..and Regularity in all their Passions.

proportionably (prəʊˈpɔəʃənəblɪ), *adv.* [f. as prec. + -LY².] In a proportionable manner or degree; in proportion; proportionately.

1413 *Pilgr. Sowle* (Caxton) I. xxx. (1859) 34 He shal be punysshed proporcionably after the tyme of his absence. **1551** RECORDE *Cast. Knowl.* (1556) 61 Euery one of the Paralleles in the heauen hath a lyke circle in the earthe proportionably drawen. **1656** HOBBES *Six Lessons* Wks. 1845 VII. 221 Equal bodies of the same nature weigh proportionably to their magnitudes. **1781** GIBBON *Decl. & F.* xx. (1869) I. 554 As he gradually advanced in the knowledge of truth, he proportionably declined in the practice of virtue. **1857** TOULMIN SMITH *Parish* 107 Every occupier within the Parish is declared proportionably liable to contribute labour to the needful work.

proportional (prəʊˈpɔəʃənəl), *a.* and *sb.* [ad. L. *prōportiōnāl-is*: see PROPORTION *sb.* and -AL¹. So F. *proportionnel.*]

A. *adj.* **1.** Of or pertaining to proportion; relative; also, Used in obtaining proportions.

proportional compasses, compasses having two opposite pairs of legs turning on a common pivot, which is adjustable in a slide, so as to vary the distance apart of the points at each end in any desired ratio. ***proportional counter***, an ionization chamber in which the voltage between the electrodes is great enough to produce gas amplification but not so great that the output pulse ceases to be proportional to the initial ionization; so ***proportional counting***. ***proportional limit*** (Mech.), the maximum stress to which a body or material can be subjected without a departure from the proportionality of stress and strain. ***proportional scales***: see quot. 1710; also called ***logarithmical scales***.

1561 T. NORTON *Calvin's Inst.* I. 6b, To wey..the knitting together, the proportional agreement, the beautie, and vse in the frame of mannes body. *Ibid.* III. ii. (1634) 263 In these formes of speech standeth a proportionall relation. **1570** DEE *Math. Pref.* divb, The Proportionall, and Paradoxall Compasses (of me Inuented). **1690** LOCKE *Hum. Und.* II. xxviii. §1 These Relations depending on the Equality and Excess of the same simple Idea, in several Subjects, may be called..Proportional. **1690** [see LOGARITHMETICAL]. **1710** J. HARRIS *Lex. Techn.* II, *Proportional Scales*, sometimes also called *Logarithmetical*; are only the Artificial Numbers or Logarithms placed on Lines, for the ease and advantage of Multiplying, Dividing, Extracting Roots, &c. by means of Compasses or by Sliding-Rules. **1807** T. YOUNG *Lect. Nat. Philos.* I. x. 103 Proportional compasses are..of great use in reducing lines and figures to a different scale. **1906** *Proc. R. Soc.* XII. 427 Bars tested in torsion to some stress below the elastic limit (proportional limit of bar) and the direction of torsion reversed immediately. **1937** *Rev. Sci. Instruments* VIII. 254 (*heading*) Properties of the proportional (Geiger-Klemperer) counter. *Ibid.* 255/1 The proportional or Geiger-Klemperer counter which is operated in a range of potential below discharge but above the region of ionization by collision has been used in several series of experiments, notably where the detection of protons in the presence of gamma-radiation is required. **1939** *Rev. Mod. Physics* XI. 213/2 With the gases mentioned, stable proportional counting and freedom from extremely critical voltage control can only be achieved with the aid of high gain amplifiers. **1950** D. H. WILKINSON *Ionization Chambers* vi. 157 With simple precautions as to the allowed region of initial ionization the proportional counter becomes a precision instrument, and may be used as an accurate measure of particle energy. **1950** E. E. WAHLSTROM *Introd. Theoret. Igneous Petrol.* v. 115 Both the elastic limit and the proportional limit vary with the time during which the stress is applied. **1958** FAIRES & PARKS *Radioisotope Lab. Techniques* xi. 111 In order to obtain the high electric fields required to produce gas amplification, the proportional counter usually takes the form of a metal cylinder, having a fine wire, insulated at its ends, stretched along its length. **1961** G. R. CHOPPIN *Exper. Nuclear Chem.* xi. 186 This fact and the sensitivity to impurities make Geiger-Müller counting less attractive than proportional counting. **1971** *Nature* 16 Apr. 448/1 Several investigators have measured the diffuse cosmic X-ray intensity in the 1/4 keV band by means of rocket-borne gas proportional counters. **1972** MALLOWS & PICKERING *Stress Anal. Probl. S.I. Units* ii. 37 It is common..to use the proportional limit, elastic limit, and yield stress as alternatives for one another in design calculations: since they are usually close to one another, this is quite acceptable.

2. a. That is in proportion, or in due proportion; having (suitable) comparative relation; corresponding, esp. in degree or amount.

[**1396**: implied in PROPORTIONALLY 1.] **1570** DEE *Math. Pref.* biij, With some proportionall consideration for our time, and being. *a* **1631** DONNE *Serm.* xxvii. (1640) 270 We must hold them so as may be analogall, proportional, agreeable to the Articles of our Faith. **1669** STAYNRED *Fortif.* 6 To draw the Proportional Dimension of a Regular Fort of 6 Sides. **1769** ROBERTSON *Chas. V*, III. VIII. 74 Animated with a zeal in defence of their religion proportional to the fierceness with which it had been attacked. **1831** BREWSTER *Optics* vii. 70 Taking as much of each as seem to be proportional to the rays in each coloured space.

b. ***proportional representation***, a system of parliamentary representation based on numerical (rather than regional) divisions of the electorate, *spec.* one by which each party is represented in proportion to the numerical strength of the vote it receives, usually by means of a method of transferable vote (see TRANSFERABLE *a.*).

1870 *Putnam's Mag.* June 720/1 When once the theory of proportional representation is reduced to practice..it will assert its superiority. **1873** MILL *Autobiogr.* vii. 302 The two greatest improvements which remain to be made in Representative Government... One of them was Personal, or, as it is called with equal propriety, Proportional Representation. **1884** *Pall Mall G.* 19 Dec. 3/1 Proportional Representation finds little favour with the caucuses. **1909** [see TRANSFERABLE *a.*]. **1917** H. G. WELLS in *Times* 30 Mar. 7/5 The essential point to grasp is that Proportional Representation is not a novel scheme, but a carefully worked-out remedy for universally recognized ills. **1940** F. A. HERMENS *Democracy & Proportional Representation* 1 There are few devices of democratic government on which opinions differ so sharply as on proportional representation. **1952** [see GAULLIST *a.* and *sb.*]. **1963** J. GRIMOND *Liberal Challenge* xi. 314, I believe..that the best solution might be to keep the present system for the Commons but introduce proportional representation for a second chamber. **1976** *Scotsman* 24 Dec. 4/3 A series of amendments to provide for the Scottish and Welsh assemblies to be elected by proportional representation were tabled yesterday.

3. *Math.* **a.** That is in proportion (sense 9); having the same or a constant ratio.

1570 BILLINGSLEY *Euclid* v. def. 7. 131 Magnitudes which are in one and the selfe same proportion, are called Proportionall. **1594** BLUNDEVIL *Exerc.* I. xxiii. (1636) 51 Multiply the two numbers..the one by the other,..the square Root of the Product shall be the meane Proportionall number betwixt them. **1706** W. JONES *Syn. Palmar. Matheseos* 66 The Powers of Proportionals are also Proportional. **1798** HUTTON *Course Math.* (1810) I. 309 Three quantities are said to be Proportional, when the ratio of the first to the second is equal to the ratio of the second to the third. *Ibid.* 319 Triangles which have their Sides Proportional, are Equiangular. **1851** RICHARDSON *Geol.* v. (1855) 87 The planes of a crystal are said to be similar when their corresponding edges are proportional. **1871** TYNDALL *Fragm. Sci.* (1879) I. i. 15 The heat is proportional to the square of the velocity.

b. ***proportional circles, radii, spirals***: see quots.

1704 J. HARRIS *Lex. Techn.* I, *Proportional Spirals*, are such Spiral Lines as the Rhumb Lines on the Terrestrial Globe, which because they make equal Angles with every Meridian, must also..make equal Angles with the Meridians in the Stereographick Projection on the Plane of the Equator. **1825** J. NICHOLSON *Operat. Mechanic* 21 When these two circles [representing wheel and pinion] are so placed that their outer rims shall touch each other, a line drawn from the centre of the one to the centre of the other is termed the *line of centres*; and the radii of the two circles the *proportional radii*. These circles are sometimes called *proportional circles*, but by mill-wrights in general *pitch lines*.

B. *sb.* **†1.** That which is proportional; a proportionate part; a relative quantity. *Obs.*

c **1386** CHAUCER *Frankl. T.* 550 And hise proporcioneles conuenientz For hise equacions in euery thyng. **1856** *Jrnl. R. Agric. Soc.* XVII. I. 177 We get blighted leaves and straw, with too small a proportional of corn.

2. *Math.* One of the terms of a proportion.

1570 DEE *Math. Pref.* ciijb, Betwene two lines giuen, finde two middle proportionals, in Continuall proportion. **1656** tr. *Hobbes' Elem. Philos.* (1839) 168 If there be never so many continual proportionals..their differences will be proportional to them. **1743** EMERSON *Fluxions* 131 Let the Number of geometrical Proportionals be increas'd..and let the arithmetic Proportionals be in like Manner increased. **1798** HUTTON *Course Math.* (1810) I. 110 The four proportionals, 4, 2, 6, 3 are set thus, 4:2::6:3, which means, that 4 is to 2 as 6 is to 3; or thus, 4:2 = 6:3, or thus, $\frac{4}{2} = \frac{6}{3}$, both which mean, that the ratio of 4 to 2, is equal to the ratio of 6 to 3. **1827** *Ibid.* 119 The mean proportional between two numbers is the square root of their product.

†3. *Chem.* The smallest combining proportion of a chemical element or compound; a combining equivalent; the proportional weight of an atom or molecule. *Obs.*

1825 BRANDE *Man. Pharm.* 204 In its dry state it [Nitric Acid] consists of—5 proportionals of Oxygen..1 [of] Nitrogen. **1832** G. R. PORTER *Porcelain & Gl.* 164 Silica, boracic acid, and oxide of lead, brought together in single proportionals. **1836–41** BRANDE *Chem.* (ed. 5) 435 The decomposition..furnishes a good illustration of the theory of definite proportionals, both in volumes and weights. **1855** GROVE *Corr. Phys. Forces* (ed. 3) 181 No compound is known in which twenty-seven grains of iron will combine with two proportionals or sixteen grains of oxygen.

pro'portionalism. [f. prec. adj. + -ISM.]

1. *Chem.* The system, doctrine, or fact of the combination of elements in definite proportions.

1854 SCOFFERN in *Orr's Circ. Sc., Chem.* 34 The laws of definite chemical proportionalism.

2. The theory or practice of the proportional representation of electors in parliamentary and other elections.

1885 *Contemp. Rev.* Feb. 252 A sneaking kindness for proportionalism. **1954** B. & R. NORTH tr. *Duverger's Pol. Parties* II. iii. 377 In all three P.R. replaced a modified majority system (second ballot in Switzerland and Norway, some features of proportionalism in Denmark).

So **pro'portionalist**, (*a*) one who plans the proportions of anything; a designer; (*b*) an advocate of proportional representation. Also *attrib.*

1857 RUSKIN *Two Paths* iv. 147 Will your architectural proportions do as much?.. You are of use, certainly; but, pardon me, only as builders—not as proportionalists. **1884** *Q. Rev.* July 32 According to the strict proportionalist theory, seventy or eighty [members] would come to its share. **1884** *Manch. Exam.* 19 Dec. 5/4 For two or three nights this week the Proportionalists had it all to themselves. **1898** *Westm. Gaz.* 5 Mar. 7/1 The anomalies, as they seem to proportionalists, in our electoral system.

proportionality (prəʊpɔəʃə'nælɪtɪ). [ad. F. *proportionnalité* (14th c. in Littré), or ad. med.L. *prōportiōnālitās, -tātem* (Scotus Erigena, 875): see PROPORTIONAL and -ITY.]

1. a. The quality, character, or fact of being proportional.

1569 J. SANFORD tr. *Agrippa's Van. Artes* 25b, In like manner of proportion and proportionallitie, and of their species. **1701** GREW *Cosm. Sacra* II. ii. §5. 37 All Sense, so far as Grateful, dependeth upon the Equality, or the Proportionality, of the Motion or Impression which is made. **1830** HERSCHEL *Stud. Nat. Phil.* 152 Proportionality of the effect to its cause. **1854** SCOFFERN in *Orr's Circ. Sc., Chem.* 31 Definite proportionality [i.e. the fact of combining in definite proportions] may be said to be the.. characteristic of chemical combinations.

b. ***limit of proportionality*** (Mech.) = *proportional limit*.

1888 W. C. UNWIN *Testing of Materials of Construction* iii. 65 Between A and B a sensible, but slight, curvature appears in the diagram, and a sensible, though small, deviation from proportionality begins to appear in the stresses and strains. Bauschinger calls the point A the limit of proportionality. **1930** *Engineering* 3 Jan. 31/1 The figures for limit of proportionality..were obtained from stress-strain diagrams. **1971** B. SCHARF *Engin. & its Lang.* iv. 22 The following values may be obtained by means of a tensile test: limit of proportionality..; yield stress..; proof stress [etc.].

c. ***constant*** or ***factor of proportionality*** (also ***proportionality constant, factor***): the constant ratio of one variable to a second to which it is proportional.

1919 *Smithsonian Misc. Coll.* LXXI. II. 9 The cross section, S, should obviously be as small as possible; and this condition will be satisfied at all times, provided it is the following function of the mass of the rocket (M − m), S = A (M − m)$^{\frac{2}{3}}$, where A is a constant of proportionality. **1937** *Rev. Sci. Instruments* VIII. 255/1 These are all connected with..proportionality between resultant electrical impulse and initial ionization per particle. The proportionality factor should not depend much upon the kind of particle entering the counter. **1955** J. LINDHARD in W. Pauli *Niels Bohr* 188 Accordingly, ω and the average excitation potential become proportional to Z, i.e. $\hbar\omega = I = Z.I_0$. However, it was found difficult to calculate the proportionality constant I_0. **1962** F. I. ORDWAY et al. *Basic Astronautics* x. 396 The proportionality factor C_F, called thrust coefficient, is a result of the expansion of the combustion gases through the nozzle.

2. A formula affirming the proportionality of two or more quantities.

1954 A. DRESDEN tr. *van der Waerden's Science Awakening* vi. 176 The proportionality $a:b::c:a$ means that $na>mb$ implies $nc>md$, and $na = mb$ implies $nc = md$, and $na<mb$ implies $nc<md$, no matter how the integers m and n are chosen. **1976** *Nature* 27 May 301/2 The luminosity of a star of solar mass satisfies the approximate proportionality $L \propto G^7M^5 \propto t^3$.

proportionally (prəʊ'pɔəʃənəlɪ), *adv.* [f. PROPORTIONAL + -LY².]

1. In a proportional manner or degree; in proportion; in due proportion.

1396 in *Scott. Antiq.* XIV. 217, ii. c. [marks] to be payit in the yhere at four termes proportionaly. **1434** in *Exch. Rolls Scotl.* IV. 567 *note*, Ten markkis of usuale mone of oure realme at twa termes of the yheir proporcionaly. **1561** T. NORTON *Calvin's Inst.* III. iv. (1634) 297 Such a bitternesse of sorrow..as may proportionally answer the greatnesse of the fault. **1571** DIGGES *Pantom.* I. xx. F iv, Yf a parallele line be drawen to any side of a triangle it shal proportionallye cut the two other sides. **1660** R. COKE *Justice Vind., Arts & Sc.* 23 Harmonical proportion increases neither equally nor proportionally: nor do the extremes added or multiplied produce the like number with the mean. **1756–7** tr. *Keysler's Trav.* (1760) IV. 343 An elephant's tooth, three ells long and proportionally thick, was found on the banks of the Saal. **1880** L. STEPHEN *Pope* iv. 82 His friendships were keen and his hostilities more than proportionally bitter.

†b. With due or proper proportion of parts; in a well-proportioned manner. *Obs.*

1651 GATAKER in Fuller *Abel Rediv.*, *Whitaker* (1867) II. 115 A body well compact, tall of stature, upright, proportionally limbed. **1766** CLARKE in *Phil. Trans.* LVII. 78 They are..as well and proportionally made as ever I saw people in my life.

†2. Correspondingly, analogously. *Obs.*

a **1614** DONNE *Βιαθανατος* iii. (1644) 29, I presume them to speak proportionally and analogally to their other doctrine.

†pro'portionary. *Obs. rare.* [f. PROPORTION *sb.* + -ARY¹.]

1. Proportional arrangement of parts; proportion.

1494 FABYAN *Chron.* Prol. (1533) 2 So to worke yt after his proporcynary That yt may appere to all that shall yt se A thynge ryght perfyte, and well in eche degre.

2. One who is skilled in computing proportions.

1627 *Pres. St. Eng.* in *Harl. Misc.* (Malh.) III. 555 Professors of a rare and strange art or science, who are called Proportionaries... If you deliver one of these a bone of your grandfather's little finger, he will by that find the proportion of all his bones, and tell you to an inch how tall a man your grandfather was.

proportionate (prəʊ'pɔəʃənət), *a.* [ad. late L. *prōportiōnāt-us* proportioned, f. *prōportiōn-em* PROPORTION + *-ātus*: see -ATE².]

1. Proportioned, adjusted in proportion; that is in due proportion. (In early use const. as *pa. pple.*)

1398 TREVISA *Barth. De P.R.* v. ii. (Tollem. MS.), The hed schulde be mene betwene greet and lytele, and proporcionate in quantite to oþer membris [L. *ad alia membra in quantitate proportionatum*]. **1432–50** tr. *Higden* (Rolls) II. 181 A goode habitude of the mynde is signifiede when the membres be welle proporcionate as vn to figure, coloure [etc.]. **1576** FLEMING *Panopl. Epist.* 232 No more is your giuing proportionate to my liking. **1605** TIMME *Quersit.* I. iv. 18 The which..are so proportionate together ..that a manifest signe..is found in this contrarietie. **1650** BULWER *Anthropomet.* 16 If they be reciprocally equal, the Head is called Proportionate. **1758** JOHNSON *Idler* No. 1 ¶10 Ponderous bodies forced into velocity move with violence proportionate to their weight. **1875** HELPS *Soc. Press.* xxv. 403 That the justly proportionate character was the one for which we finally reserved our admiration.

†b. Adequately adapted; adequate. *Obs.*

1614 SELDEN *Titles Hon.* 115 The speaking to them, in the singular Number, is very proportionat to their proper names. **1680** ALLEN *Peace & Unity* Pref. 4 When circumstances rendred others [institutions] more accomodate and more proportionate to his end.

†2. Corresponding, analogous. *Obs. rare*⁻¹.

1612 SELDEN *Illustr. Drayton's Poly-olb.* ii. 37 It is wished ..that some iudges, proportionat to those of the Græcian Games, (who alwayes..pulled downe the statues erected, if they exceeded the true symmetry of the victors) had giuen such exorbitant fictions their desert.

†3. *Mus.* = PERFECT *a.* 10a. *Obs.*

1609 DOULAND *Ornithop. Microl.* 46 The Proportionate [tact] is that, whereby three Semibreefes are vttered against one (as in a Triple).

proportionate (prəʊ'pɔəʃəneɪt), *v.* [f. prec.: see -ATE³ 3; and cf. med.L. *prōportiōnāre*.]

1. *trans.* To make proportionate or proportional (*to* something); to adjust in proportion; = PROPORTION *v.* 1.

1570 DEE *Math. Pref.* aj, Proportionating to the Sommes bequeathed, the Contributions of eche part. **1605** TIMME

Quersit. II. iv. 116 Salt, sulphur, and mercurie,..being.. equally ballanced and proportionated,..make gold to be incorruptible. **1615** G. SANDYS *Trav.* 78 The number of the conuiuials at priuate entertainments exceeded not nine, nor were vnder three, proportionating themselues vnto the Graces and Muses. *c* **1790** IMISON *Sch. Art* I. 284 To proportionate them, so as to measure time regularly, is the design of calculation. **1840** CARLYLE *Heroes* (1858) 253 A true inward symmetry, what one calls an architectural harmony, reigns in it, proportionates it all.

†**2.** To be proportionate or in proportion to, to correspond to; = PROPORTION *v.* 3. *Obs.*

1579–80 [see *ppl. a.* below]. **1606** J. KING *Serm. Sept.* 30 Nether doth the former of these proportionate, nor the latter import any such presbytery as is now exacted. **1654–66** EARL ORRERY *Parthen.* (1676) 487 Our powers of gratitude proportionated our cause. *Ibid.* 523 Their sufferings have at least proportionated their Constancy.

†**3.** To mete out in due proportion; to allot, apportion; = PROPORTION *v.* 4, 5. *Obs.*

1650 JER. TAYLOR *Holy Living* i §2 (1727) 30 He proportionates out our trials, and supplies us with a remedy.

†**4.** To form in its full proportions; to mould, fashion; = PROPORTION *v.* 2. *Obs.*

1643 R. O. *Man's Mort.* i. 1 When God had moulded, formed, and compleatly proportionated Adam out of the Dust of the ground.

Hence **pro'portionated** *ppl. a.* = PROPORTIONED; **pro'portionating** *vbl. sb.*

1579–80 NORTH *Plutarch* (1676) 41 If they found [the child] fair, and well proportionated of all his Limbs and strong. **1610** HEALEY *St. Aug. Citie of God* v. ii. (1620) 189 This..might haue much power in the proportionating of both their natures alike. *a* **1619** FOTHERBY *Atheom.* II. ii. §1 (1622) 198 Some fitting and proportionated Obiect. **1713** DERHAM *Phys. Theol.* IV. iii. 127, I am clearly of Dr. Willis's opinion that the Use of the Ear-drum is chiefly for the proportionating Sounds.

pro'portionately, *adv.* [f. PROPORTIONATE *a.* + -LY².] In a proportionate manner or degree; in or with due proportion; correspondingly.

1659 PEARSON *Creed* xii. (1820) I. 599 To this internal perfection is added a proportionately happy condition. *a* **1677** HALE *Prim. Orig. Man.* 13 That Brightness and Splendor..is presented to us more proportionately to our Capacities and Faculties. **1847** LEWES *Hist. Philos.* (1867) I. 11 It would be impossible for all to be arranged duly and proportionately. **1877** LADY BRASSEY *Voy. Sunbeam* ix. (1878) 152 It always rains, and the vegetation is proportionately dense and luxuriant.

pro'portionateness. [f. as prec. + -NESS.] The quality of being proportionate.

1654–66 EARL ORRERY *Parthen.* (1676) 798 The length of the trouble would have been abundantly repaired by the.. proportionateness of the Present. *a* **1677** HALE *Prim. Orig. Man.* 2 The fitness and proportionateness of these objective Impressions, Qualities, or Motions, upon their respective Faculties. **1850** LYNCH *Theo. Trin.* ix. 153 The sentimentalist..his feeling is not real; or if real has no proportionateness to a right activity.

†**pro'portionative**, *a. Obs. rare*⁻⁰. [f. as PROPORTIONATE *a.* + -IVE.] Analogical. Hence †**pro'portionatively** *adv. Obs. rare*⁻¹.

1751 R. SHIRRA in *Remains* (1850) 59 [Jesus Christ] is the Word analogically, or proportionatively, in so far as he is like unto and bears the resemblance both of a mental and vocal word.

†**pro'portionator.** *Obs. rare*⁻¹. [Agent-n. in L. form from PROPORTIONATE *v.*] One who proportionates.

1610 HEALEY *St. Aug. Citie of God* 567 Why then doe those bad proportionators allow the earth to lye so high, and yet deny the water to mount higher?

proportioned (prəʊ'pəəʃənd), *ppl. a.* [f. PROPORTION *v.* and *sb.* + -ED.]

1. Adjusted in due proportion, measure, or relation to something else; proportionate.

1626 T. H[AWKINS] *Caussin's Holy Crt.* 111 The neast of the Halcyon..is so proportioned to the bird, as if it were sowed to her body. **1669** STURMY *Mariner's Mag.* I. ii. 27 In Æqui-angled Triangles all their Sides are proportioned. **1722** *Wodrow Corr.* (1843) II. 681 Even when they have little prospect of being able to make any proportioned returns. **1855** MACAULAY *Hist. Eng.* xxi. IV. 550 Great as were the offences of this bad man, his punishment was fully proportioned to them.

2. Formed with 'proportions'; composed.

a **1380** *St. Augustine* 736 in Horstm. *Altengl. Leg.* (1878) 74 Riht as i schulde [take] a medecyn Proporciont, boþe good and fyn. **1433** LYDG. *S. Edmund* I. 987 A bettir compact was ther noon a-lyue Nor proporcyownyd of fetures nor stature. **1577** B. GOOGE *Heresbach's Husb.* IV. (1586) 158 A cocke framed and proporcioned after this sort. *a* **1704** T. BROWN *Praise Drunkenness* Wks. 1730 I. 37 How strong and large are his legs, fit and proportion'd to support the noble structure above! **1791** MRS. RADCLIFFE *Rom. Forest* ii, Another apartment, proportioned like the first.

b. In combination with an adverb, as *evil-*, *ill-*, *well-proportioned*.

c **1386** CHAUCER *Sqr.'s T.* 184 The hors of bras..so heigh was, and so brood and long So wel proporcioned for to been strong. **1549** *Compl. Scot.* Prol. 12 Sche that hed ane veil proportionet body, hed euil proportionet feit. **1602** MARSTON *Ant. & Mel.* II. Wks. 1856 I. 25 My fortunes [are] as ill proportioned as your legs. **1746–7** HERVEY *Medit.* (1818) 62 It shall teach me not to think too highly of well-proportioned clay. **1877** W. THOMSON *Voy. Challenger* I. ii. 113 Supported by low, gracefully proportioned..arches.

pro'portioner. [f. PROPORTION *v.* + -ER¹.] One who or that which proportions.

1590 GREENE *Roy. Exch.* Wks. (Grosart) VII. 260 The Poet calls them inequall proportioners of duetie. **1607** J. CARPENTER *Plaine Mans Plough* 183 A Measurer, or Proportioner of monethes. **1901** *Academy* 9 Mar. 211/2 Earth is the great corrector of values, the great proportioner.

pro'portioning, *vbl. sb.* [f. as prec. + -ING¹.] The action of the verb PROPORTION; relation or adjustment of proportions.

1570 DEE *Math. Pref.* *iv b, In sundry his other accountes, ..Measurynges, and proportionynges. **1641** SIR S. D'EWES in Rushw. *Hist. Coll.* III. (1692) I. 304 The House of Commons hath done no more in rating and proportioning of these particular Summs upon your Lordships, than by the ancient Rights and Privileges of Parliament they might. **1849** RUSKIN *Sev. Lamps* v. §15 (1855) 151 The proportioning of the columns and wall of the lower story is so lovely and so varied. **1883** H. SPENCER in *Contemp. Rev.* XLIII. 15 A rational proportioning of work and relaxation.

†**pro'portionist.** *Obs. rare*⁻¹. [f. PROPORTION *sb.* + -IST.] = PROPORTIONARY 2.

1645 J. BOND *Occasus Occid.* 14 As that proportionist did draw the whole stature of Hercules by the print of his foot.

pro'portionless, *a.* [f. as prec. + -LESS.] That is without or is wanting in proportion; disproportionate, shapeless.

1665 BRATHWAIT *Comment Two Tales* (Chaucer Soc.) 86 What was she, but a sapless seer stock without verdure;..a proportionless feature without favour? **1775** R. CHANDLER *Trav. Greece* (1825) II. 190 An example of the rough outline and proportionless sketch from which it [Art] rose to correctness, precision, and sublime expression.

†**pro'portionly**, *adv. Obs. rare*⁻¹. [irreg. f. as prec. + -LY².] = PROPORTIONATELY.

1541 R. COPLAND *Guydon's Quest. Chirurg.* k ij b, It is proporcionly made to the yerde.

proportionment (prəʊ'pəəʃənmənt). [f. PROPORTION *v.* + -MENT.] The act or fact of proportioning; proportional distribution, adjustment, or arrangement; †allotment.

1697 MOLYNEUX *Let. to Locke* 20 July, Locke's Lett. (1708) 230, I doubt not but Sir R. Blackmore..had a regard to the proportionment of the projective motion to the *vis centripeta.* **1827** FONBLANQUE *Eng. under 7 Administr.* (1837) I. 77 The proportionment of the fine..for certain offences is left to the discretion of the Magistrate. **1842** *Civil Eng. & Arch. Jrnl.* V. 138/2 The machinery..in every particular of its structure, proportionment, and disposition, manifests the most eminent engineering ability.

‖**propos** (prɔpo). [F. *propos*, f. *proposer* to PROPOSE, formed to represent L. *prōpositum.*] A proposition, thesis, statement.

1890 STIRLING *Gifford Lect.* xiv. 282 It is decidedly in contradiction of his [Hume's] own propos that 'anything may be the cause or the effect of anything'.

propos, variant of PROPOSE *sb. Obs.*

proposable (prəʊ'pəʊzəb(ə)l), *a.* [f. PROPOSE *v.* + -ABLE. Cf. F. *proposable* (18th c. in Littré).] Capable of being or fit to be proposed.

1817 BENTHAM *Parl. Reform* Introd. 141 Candidates actual or proposable. **1853** RUSKIN *Stones Ven.* III. App. vii. 216 The ends which are proposable to the man, or attainable by him.

proposal (prəʊ'pəʊzəl). [f. PROPOSE *v.* + -AL¹.]

1. †**a.** The action, or an act, of putting before the mind; setting forth, propounding, statement. *Obs.*

1653 H. MORE *Antid. Ath.* I. x. (1712) 30 That which all men admit true, though upon the proposal of another, is undoubtedly to be termed true. **1667** *Decay Chr. Piety* i. ¶10 This clear proposal of the promises is most proper to encourage and inspirit our endeavours. **1678** OWEN *Mind of God* ii. 33 Revelation is the Discovery of anything, whether by the proposal of it unto us, or [etc.].

b. *Philos.* (See quots.) *rare.*

1932 W. E. JOHNSON in *Mind* XLI. 1 (*title*) Probability: the relations of proposal to supposal. *Ibid.* 5 Any statement of implication, whether formal or material, may be translated into the language of probability by taking the implicans as supposal and the implicate as proposal. **1944** *Mind* LIII. 98 Following Johnson I shall call the proposition on the left of the solidus the 'proposal' and that on the right of it the 'supposal'.

2. †**a.** A putting forward of something for acceptance; an offer. *Obs.* exc. as in b.

1673 *Lady's Call.* I. v. §4 God's Laws..are inforced upon us by the proposals both of punishments and rewards.

b. *spec.* An offer of marriage.

1749 FIELDING *Tom Jones* XVII. iii, Some Person hath made Proposals to Miss Western, which the Ladies of the Family approve. **1782** MISS BURNEY *Cecilia* II. vii, Her unaffected aversion to the proposals she had received. **1900** EL. GLYN *Visits Eliz.* (1906) 53 Dearest Mamma,—I have had a proposal! Isn't it too interesting?

3. a. The action, or usually (now always) an act, of proposing something to be done; an offer to do something; a scheme or plan of action proposed.

1657 CROMWELL *Sp.* 20 Apr. in *Carlyle*, What comes from the Parliament in the exercise of their Legislative power, as this Proposal does. **1796** MORSE *Amer. Geog.* II. 382 A proposal of annulling all the taxes. **1874** GREEN *Short Hist.* viii. §4. 493 The proposal was welcomed with..enthusiasm.

b. *Law.* (See quot.)

1848–83 *Wharton's Law Lex.*, *Proposal*, a statement in writing of some special matter submitted to the consideration of a chief clerk in the Court of Chancery, pursuant to an order made upon an application *ex parte*, or a decretal order of the court. It is either for maintenance of an infant, appointment of a guardian, placing a ward of the court at the university, or in the army, or [etc.].

c. An offer or tender. Now *U.S.*

1748 in Picton *L'pool Munic. Rec.* (1886) II. 158 A Committee..to receive proposals for doing the whole work. ..And that all proposals be given in to them..sealed up. **1914** *Chicago Tribune* 8 May 14 Sealed proposals plainly marked on the outside 'Proposals for coal'..will be received at the Indian Office. **1935** H. W. HORWILL *Dict. Mod. Amer. Usage* 244/1 *Proposal* is sometimes used in Am. in the sense of *tender*.

4. *Comb.*, as *proposal-form*; **proposal-paper**, a paper proposing a person for admission to a society, club, or the like.

1859 LANG *Wand. India* 25 A lady..actually sent round a proposal paper in her own handwriting, and by one of her own servants. She failed of course.

'**proposant.** *rare.* [a. F. *proposant*, prop. pres. pple. of *proposer* to PROPOSE: see -ANT.] One who proposes or offers himself as a candidate.

1813 A. BRUCE *Life Alex. Morus* ii. 21 All examiners of proposants for the Ministry. **1833** SOUTHEY in *Q. Rev.* XLIX. 50 [Among the Protestants in French Switzerland] the theological student, after certain examinations, is received as a *Proposant* by those who exercise the pastoral office, and employed as a lay-helper, or catechist, in their parishes.

†**pro'pose**, *sb. Obs.* Also 5 propos, 6 *Sc.* propoise. [ME. *propos*, a. F. *propos* (13th c.), f. *proposer* to PROPOSE, under the influence of L. *prŏposit-um* a thing proposed. See PURPOSE *sb.*]

1. Something proposed for discussion; a subject; a proposition.

a **1325** *Prose Psalter* lxxvii[i]. 2, Y shal speke proposes fram þe bygynnyng. *c* **1400** *Apol. Loll.* 54 Þe propos, Whas doctrine any folowiþ, his disciple he is. **1597** MORLEY *Introd. Mus.* 1 All the propose which then was discoursed vpon, was Musicke.

2. Purpose, intention.

1483 in *Lett. Rich. III & Hen. VII* (Rolls) I. 51 We remayne in the said propose. **1489** CAXTON *Faytes of A.* I. xxix. 87 Thy propos thou ought to say or shewe vnto few folke. *c* **1500** *Melusine* 228 The commynaltee of the tounne ..were in propos & wylle for to yeld the toun & themself ouer to the kyng Zodyus. **1556** *Aurelio & Isab.* (1608) K iv, The kinge of nothinge changedt his propose. **1573–4** *Reg. Privy Council Scot.* II. 329 The said Robert..is on propoise ..to purches ane licence to depart. *a* **1600** HOOKER *Eccl. Pol.* VII. xxiv. §17 If to withdraw any mite of that which is but in propose only bequeathed,..be a sin.

3. A proposal; something proposed to be done.

1600 HOLLAND *Livy* XLI. xxiv. 1112 When the same men ..gaue their accord now also to this propose. **1673** in Picton *L'pool Munic. Rec.* (1883) I. 265 After the Maior hath made his proposes every Alderman..shall have liberty to speake. *a* **1721** PRIOR *Erle Robert's Mice* 10 John the Saint, Who maketh oft propos full queint,..cried To Matthew..Come frame us now some..playsant rhime on yonder mice.

propose (prəʊ'pəʊz), *v.* [a. F. *propose-r* (12th c. in Hatz.-Darm.), f. *pro-*, PRO-¹ + *poser*, POSE *v.*¹; substituted for L. *prōpōn-ĕre* (cf. COMPOSE): see PROPONE and cf. PURPOSE *v.*]

†**1.** *trans.* To put forth, hold forth, or present to view or perception; to exhibit. *lit.* and *fig. Obs.*

1548 GEST *Pr. Masse* in H. G. Dugdale *Life* (1840) App. I. 117 Let us not grossely beholde the breade and cuppe proposed and set before our eyes, but in faythe consydere the lambe of God. **1598** CHAPMAN *Iliad* To Rdr., The worth of a skilfull and worthy translator is to obserue the sentences, figures, and formes of speech proposed in his author. *c* **1610** *Women Saints* 33 The crosse..the bishop.. at Ester doth take forth, and propose it to the people to be adored. **1644** QUARLES *Barnabas & B.* 33 Propose to mine eyes the evilness of my days. **1737** WHISTON *Josephus, Antiq.* XIV. x. §2, I will that [the decree] be openly proposed in a table of brass.

2. a. To put forward or present for consideration, discussion, solution, imitation, or other treatment; to put before the mind, bring to one's notice, call attention to; to set forth, state, propound.

The pa. pple. *proposed* following a sb. has sometimes the force of 'in question': see quot. 1715.

c **1430** [see PROPOSED]. *c* **1475** *Partenay* 6404 Sin more ther-of I can noght propose, Of-fors moste I here take rest and repose. **1568** GRAFTON *Chron.* II. 795 That they might resort to his presence to propose their entent, of which they would to none other person any part disclose. **1580** LYLY *Euphues* (Arb.) 401 Yeelding the choyce..to the discretion of the Ladie Flauia who thus proposed her minde. **1593** SHAKS. *3 Hen. VI*, v. v. 20 Where I stand, kneele thou, Whil'st I propose the selfe-same words to thee, Which (Traytor) thou would'st haue me answer to. **1646** SIR T. BROWNE *Pseud. Ep.* I. v. (1686) 13 God..hath proposed the World unto our Knowledge. **1657** SPARROW *Bk. Com. Prayer* (1661) 76 When the Priest proposes to God the people's necessities. **1715** tr. *Gregory's Astron.* (1726) I. 428 To define the Periodic time of any Planet about the Sun. Let the Planet proposed be observed in the Node. **1751** JOHNSON *Rambler* No. 90 ¶3 The poets..whom he proposed to himself for his models. **1845** M. PATTISON *Ess.* (1889) I. 9 The Church did but take into her service, and propose a fitting object to, an impulse which will vent itself in some form or other. **1892** WESTCOTT *Gospel of Life* Pref. 22 Nature herself does not give an answer to the riddles which she proposes.

†**b.** To set before one's mind as something to be expected; to look for, anticipate; in quot. 1588, 'to look forward to, to be ready to meet' (Schmidt), to face, confront. *Obs.*

1588 SHAKS. *Tit. A.* II. i. 80 A thousand deaths would I propose, To atchieue her. **1606** —— *Tr. & Cr.* II. ii. 146, I propose not meerely to my selfe, The pleasures such a beauty brings with it. **1670** COTTON *Espernon* Apology, What utility may we not propose to our selves, from the great examples both of the one, and the other? **1725** DE FOE *Voy. round World* (1840) 47 The men could propose nothing to themselves but hardships. **1749** FIELDING *Tom Jones* v. iii, The pleasure he proposed in seeing her married.

c. To set before one (usually, before onself) as an aim, end, or object; to put forward as something to be attained.

1601 SHAKS. *Jul. C.* I. ii. 110 But ere we could arriue the Point propos'd, Cæsar cride, Helpe me Cassius, or I sinke. **1602** —— *Ham.* III. ii. 204 What to our selues in passion we propose, The passion ending, doth the purpose lose. **1638** ROUSE *Heav. Univ.* vi. (1702) 79 We must propose an End worthy of God. **1715** ATTERBURY *Serm., Matt. xxvii.* 25 (1734) I. 119 The great Ends and Designs he proposed to himself in their Sufferings. **1868** J. H. BLUNT *Ref. Ch. Eng.* I. 67 As if the Cardinal had proposed it to himself simply as a costly monument of his ambition.

†**d.** To contemplate as a supposition; to imagine, fancy: = PROPOUND *v.* 5b. *Obs. rare.*

1597 SHAKS. *2 Hen. IV*, v. ii. 92 Make the case yours: Be now the Father, and propose a Sonne.

e. *Mus.* To 'give out' or sound (a subject) for imitation or contrapuntal treatment.

1879 GROVE *Dict. Mus.* I. 69/2 An answer in music is, in strict counterpoint, the repetition by one part or instrument of a theme proposed by another.

3. To put forward for acceptance. †**a.** To set before or hand to some one for him to take; to present. *Obs.*

1586 A. DAY *Eng. Secretary* II. (1625) 57 Hauing no other or better meane.., then these submissiue lines; I propose them vnto you..confessing that if any waies I haue erred vnto you..it was but as a yong man. **1609** BIBLE (Douay) *Exod.* xii. Comm., The lambe being consumed, which old tradition proposed, the Master setteth inconsumptible meate to his disciples. *c* **1611** CHAPMAN *Iliad* XI. 554 Withal so weighty was the cup, That being proposed brimful of wine, one scarce could lift it up.

b. To proffer or offer for mental acceptance or assent. In quot. 1602, To state the terms of (an oath) to be 'taken' or sworn.

1596 SHAKS. *Tam. Shr.* v. ii. 69 He whose wife is most obedient,..Shall win the wager which we will propose. **1602** —— *Ham.* I. v. 152 *Hor.* Propose the Oath my Lord. *Ham.* Neuer to speake of this that you haue seene, Sweare by my sword. **1615** G. SANDYS *Trav.* 102 The boughs thereof [the Palm] haue bin proposed as rewards for such as were either victorious in armes or exercises. **1686** tr. *Chardin's Trav. Persia* 331 A Man may have seen the Maid, propos'd him for a Wife, especially when she was little. **1780** S. J. PRATT *Emma Corbett* (ed. 4) II. 95, I will wait..to hear the event of terms that are proposing between the countries. **1883** STEVENSON *Treas. Franchard* iii. in *Merry Men*, etc. (1905) 220, I propose no wages.

c. To nominate for acceptance for some office or position, esp. as a member of a society.

1715 ATTERBURY *Serm., Matt. xxvii.* 25 (1734) I. 121 Pilate..then proposes him as the Man he was by Custom to release at the Passover. **1770** FOOTE *Lame Lover* I. 25 There is to be a ballot at one for the Ladies' Club..and lady Bab Basto has proposed me for a member. **1871** *Routledge's Ev. Boy's Ann.* Feb. 107, I propose the head boy..for chief.

d. To make a formal proposal to the company to drink (a health or toast); to offer for acceptance as a toast.

1712 W. ROGERS *Voy.* 44 They were very merry, and in their Cups propos'd the Pope's Health..; to keep up the Humour, we also propos'd William Pen's to them. **1855** MACAULAY *Hist. Eng.* xvii. IV. 7 As often as any of the great princes proposed a health, the kettle drums and trumpets sounded. **1892** *Law Times* XCII. 145/2 The second part of his duty was to propose the health of the honorary Fellows.

e. *absol.* To make an offer of marriage. Also with *for* and (more usually) *to*. (*colloq.*)

1764 GRAY *Candidate* 20 Divinity heard, between waking and dozing, Her sisters denying, and Jemmy proposing. **1800** MRS. HERVEY *Mourtray Fam.* I. 190 If a man now says three words to a girl, she immediately expects he is to propose to her. **1855** THACKERAY *Newcomes* II. xiii. 127 Perhaps neither of them will propose for her. **1856** STANLEY *Sinai & Pal.* Introd. 44 Ptolemy Physcon,..who proposed, but in vain, to Cornelia, mother of the Gracchi. **1872** A. C. STEELE *Broken Toys* II. xxv. 167, I am going to Vere Court tomorrow to propose for Nella Vere. **1911** G. B. SHAW *Getting Married* 227 *Sykes.* When her blood boils about it.. she doesnt care what she says. *Reginald.* Well: you knew that when you proposed to her. **1928** E. O'NEILL *Strange Interlude* IX. 341 Ned's just proposed to me. I refused him, Charlie. **1931** H. WALPOLE *Judith Paris* II. 311 She had been amazed when the handsome young Pomfret Herries had proposed for her in marriage. **1978** T. SHARPE *Throwback* iii. 19 Mr Flawse..took a swig of brandy to steady his nerves. The bloody woman was proposing to him.

4. *trans. spec.* with an action as obj. **a.** To put forward as a scheme or plan to be adopted; to lay before another or others as something which one offers to do, or wishes to be done. (With *simple obj.*, *obj. clause*, or *inf.*)

1647 CLARENDON *Hist. Reb.* I. §21 Not to communicate the thing proposed, before he had first taken his Own resolution. **1724** DE FOE *Mem. Cavalier* (1840) 202 The king proposed the marching to London. **1788** CLARA REEVE *Exiles* II. 237, I proposed to my wife to reside at M——. **1799** HT. LEE *Canterb. T., Old Woman's T.* (ed. 2) I. 366 Lothaire..at length proposed retiring. **1839** KEIGHTLEY *Hist. Eng.* II. 66 King James..proposed to his nobles an inroad into England. **1856** FROUDE *Hist. Eng.* I. ii. 101 It had been proposed to marry the Princess Mary to a son of the French king. **1875** JOWETT *Plato* (ed. 2) IV. 228 He proposes that they shall reassemble on the following day.

b. To put before one's own mind as something that one is going to do; to design, purpose, intend. (With *inf.* or *vbl. sb.*) Now usually with some notion of having formed a decision or intention.

1500–20 *Exhort. bef. Commun.* in Maskell *Mon. Rit.* (1847) III. 348, Y charge yow..that no man nother woman that this day proposyth here to be comenyd that he go note to Godds bord, lase than he byleue stedfastlych, that [etc.]. **1500–20** DUNBAR *Poems* lv. 6 Now propoyss thai..Off Wenus feest to fang ane fill. **1718** *Free-thinker* No. 31 ¶11 To compleat the Observations I at first proposed to make upon these Fanaticks. **1738** C'TESS OF HERTFORD *Corr.* (1805) I. 23, I..propose being there on the birth day. **1853** J. H. NEWMAN *Hist. Sk.* (1873) II. vi. 142 He had proposed to conquer Jerusalem, and to have rebuilt it, had God granted him life.

c. *absol.* To put forward a scheme, make a proposal or motion; to form a design or purpose. In quot. 1485–6 *ellipt.* = propose to go.

Prov. ***man proposes, God disposes***: see DISPOSE *v.* 7.

1340 *Ayenb.* 180 Nou [h]y leueþ, nou hi misleueþ, nou hi wylleþ, nou hi ne wylleþ, nou hi proposent, nou hit is betere. þeruore hi byeþ ase þe wedercoc þet is ope þe steple, þet him went mid eche wynde. **1485–6** *Plumpton Corr.* (Camden) 50 The Kyng proposyth northward hastyly after the Parlament. *c* **1500** [see DISPOSE *v.* 7]. *a* **1533** LD. BERNERS *Gold. Bk. M. Aurel.* (1546) G v b, I..knew the famous oratour Taurin propose diuers tymes in the senate. **1625** BACON *Apophth.* Wks. 1879 I. 327 At Athens wise men did propose, and fools dispose. **1898** *Daily News* 20 Dec. 5/3 But, 'Man proposes, God disposes'—how everlastingly true is that old saying of the good Thomas à Kempis!

†**5.** *absol.* or *intr.* To carry on a discussion; to confer, converse, discourse. *Obs. rare.* (Cf. 2.)

1599 SHAKS. *Much Ado* III. i. 3 There shalt thou finde my Cosin Beatrice, Proposing with the Prince and Claudio. **1604** —— *Oth.* I. i. 25 The Bookish Theoricke: Wherein the Tongued [*1st Quarto* toged] Consuls can propose As Masterly as he.

proposed (prəʊˈpəʊzd), *ppl. a.* [f. PROPOSE *v.* + -ED[1].] Put forward for consideration or adoption; 'given' or stated (in the premisses); intended, etc.: see the verb.

c **1430** *Art Nombryng* 8 Multiplicacioun of nombre by hym-self other by a nother, with proposide .2. nombres, [is] the fyndyng of the thirde. **1635** SWAN *Spec. M.* ii. (1643) 29 There should be a proposed point or mark. **1780** *Newgate Cal.* V. 8 Her mother..was a warm friend to the proposed marriage. **1855** MACAULAY *Hist. Eng.* xvi. III. 715 The proposed law, they said, was a retrospective penal law, and therefore objectionable.

Hence **proˈposedly** *adv. rare*, intendedly, purposely.

1777 *Sterne's Tr. Shandy* I. xix, They had proposedly [*edd.* 1–4 purposedly, *ed.* 5– purposely] been plann'd and pointed against him.

†**proˈposely**, *adv. Sc. Obs. rare*[−1]. [f. PROPOSE *sb.* + -LY[2]; cf. *purposely*.] On purpose, purposely.

1582 *Reg. Privy Council Scot.* III. 504 Procurit proposelie, as apperis, to eschew puneisment of certane odious crymes.

proposer (prəʊˈpəʊzə(r)). [f. PROPOSE *v.* + -ER[1].] One who proposes: in various senses of the vb.

†**1.** One who presents to view or exhibits something. *Obs.*

a **1690** J. COLLINGES in Spurgeon *Treas. Dav.* Ps. cvii. 43, I should view it [a picture] as curiously as I could; yet the proposer would..undertake to show me something in it which I did not observe.

2. One who propounds an argument, a question, or the like.

(In quot. 1602 erroneously explained by Schmidt 'A speaker, orator'; whence in some recent dictionaries.)

1602 SHAKS. *Ham.* II. ii. 297 Let mee coniure you by the rights of our fellowship, by the consonancy of our youth,.. and by what more deare, a better proposer could charge you withall. *a* **1714** ABP. SHARP *Answ. Quest. Rom.-Cath.* Wks. 1754 VII. App. 300 *Q.* May a man, wilfully dying a Roman-catholic, be saved? *A.* What the proposer means by wilfully dying a Roman-catholic, I know not.

3. One who makes a proposal; one who brings forward or offers a scheme or suggestion; *spec.* one who formally makes a motion, or who proposes or nominates some one for a position.

1660 MILTON *Free Commw.* Wks. 1851 V. 448 Queen Elizabeth..imprison'd and persecuted the very Proposers therof. **1762** H. WALPOLE *Vertue's Anecd. Paint.* (1765) II. i. 43 One of the first proposers of coining money by a press, instead of the former manner of hammering. **1873** TRISTRAM *Moab* vii. 117 Schwartz is the proposer of this identification. **1886** *Daily Tel.* 12 Jan. 5/5 His proposer and seconder will..conduct him to the chair. **1886** *Law Times Rep.* LIII. 761/1 In a form of proposal to an insurance office ..the residence of the proposer was stated to be [etc.].

†**b.** One who tenders for a contract.

1750 in Picton *L'pool Munic. Rec.* (1886) II. 152 Parker, paviour, the lowest proposer. [Cf. PROPOSAL 3c: quot. 1748.]

proposing (prəʊˈpəʊzɪŋ), *vbl. sb.* [f. as prec. + -ING[1].] The action of the verb PROPOSE, in various senses.

1690 LOCKE *Hum. Und.* I. ii. §21 Or doth the proposing them, print them clearer in the Mind. **1790** BEATSON *Nav. & Mil. Mem.* I. 118 To venture the proposing of Giles Earle, Esq. to be again chosen chairman of the committee. **1832** tr. *Sismondi's Ital. Rep.* vii. 153 To begin with what they called proposing; that is, taking a text from some celebrated author, either sacred or profane. **1869** FREEMAN *Norm. Conq.* III. App. E. 623 The proposing and supporting of opposing candidates.

proposita (prəʊˈpɒzɪtə). [L., fem. of *prōpositus*: see PROPOSITUS.] A female propositus.

1970 *Jrnl. Med. Genetics* VII. 180/2 The proposita.. presented as a profoundly retarded, 21-year-old girl with poor posture. **1976** *Nature* 15 Jan. 139/1 A study of 12 different blood group systems in the proposita and her parents failed to exclude paternity.

†ˈ**proposite.** *Obs.* [ad. L. *prōposit-um* a thing proposed, sb. use of neuter of *prōpositus*, pa. pple. of *prōponĕre*: see PROPONE.] Something propounded, put or set forth; a proposition.

1620 T. GRANGER *Div. Logike* I. ii. 2 Of Logicke there be two parts. The former is of the purpose, or matter propounded... The Proposite is the explication of the conceits, or meaning of the minde, instituted or framed according to sound reason. *Ibid.* iii. 7 There be two parts of euery Proposite, or matter proposed, viz. the theme, and the argument.

proposition (prɒpəʊˈzɪʃən), *sb.* [ME. *proposicioun*, a. F. *proposition* (12th c. in Littré), ad. L. *prōpositiōn-em* a setting forth, purpose, theme, statement, n. of action f. *prōpōn-ĕre*: see PROPONE.]

1. The action of setting forth or presenting to view or perception; presentation, exhibition. In quot. 1584, representation by a figure, delineation (cf. PROPOUND *v.* 5). Now *rare.*

† ***loaves of proposition***, in *Jewish Hist.*, the show-bread; so ***table of proposition***. *Obs.*

c **1380** WYCLIF *Serm.* Sel. Wks. II. 181 þe holy looves of proposicioun. **1382** —— *Exod.* xxv. 30 Thow shalt putte vpon the bord looues of propicisioun [**1388** proposicioun], euermore in my siȝt. **1549** *Compl. Scot.* ix. 76 He..reft the goldin alter..ande the tabil of propositione. **1584** LYLY *Campaspe* III. iv, *Alex.* Where doe you first begin, when you drawe any picture? *Apel.* The proposition of the face in iust compasse, as I can. *c* **1624** LUSHINGTON *Recant. Serm.* in *Phenix* (1708) II. 494 The 12 loaves of proposition. **1866** *Liturgy Ch. Sarum* 67 *note*, A proposition of Christ under the sacramental veils, to receive the adoration of the faithful.

†**2. a.** The action of putting forward or offering for acceptance; an offer. *Obs.*

1606 SHAKS. *Tr. & Cr.* I. iii. 3 The ample proposition that hope makes In all designes. **1649** JER. TAYLOR *Gt. Exemp.* I. Ad Sect. iv. 50 He..sweetly allures us by the proposition of rewards.

b. The action of proposing a person for election or admission. *rare.* (In quot. *attrib.*)

1901 *Scotsman* 21 Nov. 8/1 The proposition book did shew entries of a considerable number of names.

3. a. The action of propounding something, or that which is propounded; the setting forth of something as a subject of discourse; something proposed for discussion, or as a basis of argument; *spec.* an introductory part of a speech or literary work, in which the speaker or writer sets forth the subject to be treated. In quots. 1845, the speech with which the Emperor opened the Diet of the Holy Roman Empire. Now *rare* or *Obs.*

a **1340** HAMPOLE *Psalter* xlviii. 4, I sall oppyn in psawtry my proposicion. **1382** WYCLIF *Ps.* lxxvii[i]. 2, I shal speke proposiciouns fro the begynnyng. **1552** HULOET s.v., A proposition is an argument or matter proposed to be disputed and reasoned vpon. **1553** T. WILSON *Rhet.* 97 Proposicion is a short rehersall of that wherof we mynde to speake. **1635–56** COWLEY *Davideis* I. Note i, The custom of beginning all Poems, with a Proposition of the whole work, and an Invocation of some God for his assistance to go through with it, is..observed by all the ancient Poets. **1751** JOHNSON *Rambler* No. 158 ¶12 The proposition of the Eneid closes with dignity. **1775** BURKE *Sp. Conc. Amer.* Wks. III. 33 The plan..derives..one great advantage from the proposition and registry of that noble lord's project. **1845** S. AUSTIN *Ranke's Hist. Ref.* I. 517 The Proposition with which he opened the diet sufficiently showed that the young emperor was determined to avail himself of it. *Ibid.* III. 163 The first thing was to appoint a committee to deliberate and report upon the Proposition.

†**b.** A question proposed for solution; a problem; a riddle. *Obs.*

Also in *Logic* in a special sense: see PROBLEM 2b, quot. 1656.

1382 WYCLIF *Judg.* xiv. 18 If ȝe hadden not erid in my she calf, ȝe shulden not haue founden my proposicioun. —— *Dan.* viii. 23 There shal ryse a king..vndirstondynge proposiciouns [*gloss* or resouns]. **1600** SHAKS. *A.Y.L.* III. ii. 246 It is as easie to count Atomies as to resolue the propositions of a Louer.

c. *Music.* The proposing or 'giving out' of a subject for contrapuntal treatment; the subject so proposed.

1890 in *Cent. Dict.* **1898** STAINER & BARRETT *Dict. Mus. Terms* s.v. *Subject*, In a fugue the subject is called also the exposition, dux, proposition.

4. a. (*a*) The making of a statement about something; a sentence or form of words in which this is done; a statement, an assertion. (*b*) In *Logic*, a form of words in which something (the PREDICATE) is affirmed or denied of something (the SUBJECT), the relation between them being expressed by the COPULA; sometimes extended to the form of thought or mental process expressed by this, more strictly called a JUDGEMENT (9 b).

1387–8 T. USK *Test. Love* I. i. (Skeat) I. 71 Your mercy than passeth right. God graunt that proposicion to be verifyed in me. *c* **1530** MORE *Answ. Frith* Wks. 841/1 But lette thys fyrste proposicion passe, and come nowe to the secounde,..that is, that the body of Chryste cannot be at once in all places. **1654** BRAMHALL *Just Vind.* ii. (1661) 27 Though it be not in the power of any Councel..to make that proposition heretical,..which was not heretical ever from the dayes of the Apostles. **1802–12** BENTHAM *Ration. Judic. Evid.* Wks. 1843 VII. 81 That the proposition, two and two make four, is neither more nor less than a proposition concerning the import of words. **1879** HARLAN *Eyesight* i. 10 A proposition too plain to admit of argument.

(*b*) **1432–50** tr. *Higden* (Rolls) VII. 281 If ye redde logike, reduce to mynde a proposicion: That thynge whiche hathe effecte in the holle, hathe effecte in the parte. **1551** T. WILSON *Logike* (1580) 18 A Proposition is, a perfecte sentence spoken by the Indicatiue mode, signifying either a true thyng, or a false. **1656** STANLEY *Hist. Philos.* v. (1701) 182/1 Of that Speech which we call Proposition, there are two kinds; Affirmation and Negation. **1725** WATTS *Logic* II. ii. § 1 Propositions may be divided according to their subject into universal and particular; this is usually called a division arising from the quantity. **1827** WHATELY *Logic* ii. I. § 2 (ed. 2) 55 An act of apprehension expressed in language, is called a term; an act of judgement, a proposition; an act of reasoning, an argument. **1836–7** SIR W. HAMILTON *Metaph.* xxxvii. (1870) II. 336 The whole mental judgement, formed by the subject, predicate, and copula, is called, when enounced in words, proposition.

b. *spec.* Either of the premisses of a syllogism; *esp.* the major premiss (opposed to ASSUMPTION 12). Now *rare* or *Obs.*

1551 T. WILSON *Logike* (1580) 23 The matter [i.e. the middle term] is twise rehearsed in the firste and seconde Proposition, and entreth not into the conclusion. **1604** JAMES I *Counterbl.* (Arb.) 102 Of this Argument, both the Proposition and Assumption are false, and so the Conclusion cannot but be voyd of it selfe. **1628** T. SPENCER *Logick* 266 We learne from Aristotle, cap. 48. that, the proposition and assumption may be vniversall, yet the conclusion not vniversall. **1725** WATTS *Logic* III. ii. § 3 There is also a fourth figure, wherein the middle term is predicated in the major proposition, and subjected in the minor. **1837–8** SIR W. HAMILTON *Logic* xv. (1866) I. 281 Of the premises, the one which enounces the general rule or the relation of the greatest quantity to the lesser, is called the Major Premise, or Major Proposition or the Proposition simply.

5. *Math.* A formal statement of a truth to be demonstrated or of an operation to be performed (in the former case called distinctively a *theorem*, in the latter a *problem*); in common parlance often including the demonstration.

1570 BILLINGSLEY *Euclid.* I. 8 Propositions..are sentences set forth to be proued by reasoning and demonstrations. *Ibid.*, Propositions are of two sortes, the one is called a Probleme, the other a Theoreme. **1662** STILLINGFL. *Orig. Sacr.* II. ii. § 6 The finding out of that demonstration, which is now contained in the 47 proposition of the first of Euclide. **1718** QUINCY *Compl. Disp.* 16 These Propositions, which are demonstrated in Hydrostaticks. **1810** HUTTON *Course Math.* I. 2 A Corollary..is a consequence drawn immediately from some proposition.

6. a. The action of proposing something to be done; something put forward as a scheme or plan of action; a proposal; *spec.* in *U.S.*, (*a*) see quot. *a* 1727; (*b*) a constitutional proposal.

1382 WYCLIF *1 Kings* xviii. 24 Al the puple answerynge seith, Best the proposicioun, that Helias spac. *a* **1548** HALL *Chron.*, *Edw. V* 23 b, When the protector had harde the proposicion, he loked very strangely therat. **1579** FENTON *Guicciard.* I. (1599) 14 This proposition had no willing passage into the eares or harts of the great Lords of France. **1653** SIR E. HYDE in *Evelyn's Mem.* (1819) II. 206 Any such proposicons and expedients which you thinke fitt to offer for the promoting his seruice. *a* **1727** in Colden *Hist. Five Indian Nat.* 41 Without laying down either Bever or any Belt or Wampum, as we always do when we make Propositions. [*Note.*] The word Proposition has always been used by the Commissioners for the Indian Affairs at Albany, to signifie Proposals or Articles. *a* **1806** C. J. FOX *Reign Jas. II* (1808) 101 That a proposition to the Prince of Orange, to connect himself in politicks with Lewis, would..have been rejected. *a* **1873** WILBERFORCE *Ess.* (1874) II. 321 We hold it essential to our success..that the proposition of Sir George Clerk should be adopted. **1921** *Congress. Rec.* 21 Feb. 3537/1 If this particular proposition were a law, and the Federal Trade Commission were given the authority that is herein provided, they would protect the country and the people in it by proper license. **1979** *Tucson Mag.* Jan. 25/1 Today's mad, mad world of Proposition 13 and other horrors. **1979** *Time* 13 Aug. 24/1 County officials hope the mistake will work in their favor, on the somewhat shaky grounds that the absurdity of Proposition .004 will defeat it.

†**b.** *in proposition for*, in treaty for. *Obs.*

1677 YARRANTON *Eng. Improv.* 39 To go over into Ireland to Survey some Iron works, Woods and Lands which they were in proposition for.

7. a. An enterprise or project submitted for consideration or action; a matter, problem, or undertaking which requires attention; also with respect to ease or difficulty of performance, etc., as an ***easy***, ***serious***, ***tough proposition*** and with regard to likelihood of (commercial) success, as ***business***, ***mining proposition***. orig. *U.S.*

1877 R. J. BURDETTE *Rise & Fall of Mustache* 258 For a long time the good lady held out stoutly against the chicken proposition. **1893** *Scribner's Mag.* June 756/1 'Arn't you ashamed to tell me this?' 'Of course I am, but that isn't the proposition just now.' **1896** ADE *Artie* xviii. 168 I'm goin' against a tough proposition. **1902** O. WISTER *Virginian* ii. 19 The biggest tobacco proposition for five cents got out yet. *Ibid.* xviii. 214, I saw over in a fenced meadow..what he was pleased to call 'the proposition'. Proposition in the West does, in fact, mean whatever you at the moment please. **1906** *Daily News* 24 Jan. 12/3 Later on it was found that the Main Reef series of gold-bearing rock dipped into this property, which became an attractive mining 'proposition', as the slang phrase goes. **1909** S. E. WHITE *Rules of Game* III. ix. 181 We're the only two business propositions in this country. **1929** *Daily Express* 7 Nov. 2/5 Every industry I want to nationalize must be a business proposition. **1932** E. WILSON *Devil take Hindmost* viii. 70 Care of the worker is a money-saving proposition. **1941** *Strand Mag.* June 140/2 All I know is that I've got to find her. The question is, how? And it won't surprise you to hear that it appears to me to be a pretty stiff proposition. **1958** *Economist* 26 July 271 Once the basic capital expenditure has been made on a machine and microphone, this is definitely an economic proposition.

b. *transf.* of persons.

1901 *Tit-Bits* 27 July 416/2 He was a pretty smooth proposition himself. **1908** C. E. MULFORD *Orphan* xiv. 178 I'd rather have him with me in a mix-up than against me. He's the coolest proposition loose in this part of the country at any game. **1915** T. BURKE *Nights in Town* 19 He is educated..to regard himself as, in the Broadway phrase, a serious proposition. **1925** C. E. MULFORD *Cottonwood Gulch* vii. 92 Knife fighters are bad propositions. **1979** 'H. HOWARD' *Sealed Envelope* v. 74 Soon as I discovered she was an easy proposition I dropped out. I don't go for a twist who sleeps in anybody's bed.

8. *Comb.*, as (sense 4) ***proposition-forming*** adj.

1955 A. N. PRIOR *Formal Logic* III. iii. 261 We may define in terms of 'ε' another proposition-forming operator. **1968** HUGHES & CRESSWELL *Introd. Modal Logic* ii. 23 'It is necessary that' is thus a (monadic) proposition-forming operator on propositions.

proposition (prɒpəʊˈzɪʃən), *v.* orig. *U.S.* [f. the sb.] **1.** *trans.* To make or present a proposition to (a person). (Sometimes with unfavourable connotations.)

1924 H. C. WITWER *Love & Learn* x. 275, I finally got Ike sold on the idea that my plan was a good thought and he departed to proposition Hershel. **1927** *Collier's* 24 Dec. 36/4 He propositioned her to use his lodge at Big Bear [Lake] for her party. **1935** A. J. POLLOCK *Underworld Speaks* 91/2 *Propositioned*, asked to join in an unlawful undertaking. **1938** *Amer. Speech* XIII. 194 One need be very little of a purist to recoil from the current expression 'I *propositioned* him', meaning, of course, 'I made a proposition to him'. **1947** E. ANDREWS *Hist. Scientific Eng.* xiv. 252 It makes us more tolerant today when we hear a businessman speak of 'contacting' a customer or, worse yet, of 'propositioning' him. **1949** *Chicago Tribune* 10 Dec. 12/5 Count that day gained in which A sofomore sonny Won't proposition pop For movie money! **1949** 'J. TEY' *Brat Farrar* iii. 20 I'm propositioning you... What is wrong with the proposition? **1967** *Punch* 28 June 949/2 While being propositioned by Lord Beaverbrook about becoming the film critic of the *Evening Standard*, I nervously filled in a yawning silence by telling this anecdote. **1978** J. A. MICHENER *Chesapeake* 660 [They] sailed up river to the landing of a farm owned by an old man.., and there they propositioned him: 'You ain't gonna have much more use for your long gun... We aim to buy it.' **1979** *Dædalus* Summer 46 The deputy..proceeds to proposition her with a debased contract.

2. To request sexual favours from (a person); to solicit.

1936 J. G. COZZENS *Men & Brethren* I. 139 There's no real reason to be embarrassed because your clerical collar keeps you from feeling free to proposition every woman you meet. **1946** 'P. QUENTIN' *Puzzle for Fiends* iii. 23 You..had him proposition you in a canoe? **1949** K. MALONE in Kirby & Woolf *Philologica* 317 *To proposition*, at least in the field of amour, is not only distinct from *to propose*, but in a sense antithetical to *propose*. **1953** W. BURROUGHS *Junkie* vi. 60, I remember once he told me how he'd been propositioned by a queer who offered him twenty dollars. **1963** T. PYNCHON *V.* xi. 328 The girls were professional and tried for a while to proposition Fausto and Dnubietna. **1974** M. GILBERT *Flash Point* xii. 105 This girl stopped me, by asking me for a cigarette... There was no question of me propositioning her or annoying her. **1975** *New Yorker* 4 Aug. 25/1 In Hyde Park, that black whore had propositioned him as he walked from work toward the Tube.

propositional (prɒpəʊˈzɪʃənəl), *a.* [f. PROPOSITION *sb.* + -AL[1].] **a.** Pertaining to or of the nature of a logical proposition; consisting of or based on propositions; *spec.* applied to speech and language in which statements and assertions occur.

c **1714** POPE, etc. *Mem. M. Scriblerus* I. xii, When two of these propositional Channels empty themselves into a third, they form a Syllogism. **1725** WATTS *Logic* II. ii. § 1 If a proposition..has an indefinite subject, it is generally to be esteemed universal in its propositional sense. **1847** SIR W. HAMILTON *Let. to De Morgan* 31 The second scheme is that which logically extends the expression of quantity to both the propositional terms. **1874** J. H. JACKSON in *Med. Press & Circ.* 14 Jan. 21/1 But if *I* have to say, 'Gold is yellow', I have to revive the words, and I have to put them in propositional order. **1879** —— in *Brain* I. 312 A speechless patient may retain the word 'no', and yet have only the interjectional or emotional, not the propositional, use of it; he utters it in various tones as signs of feeling only. **1883** H. DRUMMOND *Nat. Law in Spir. W.* xi. (1884) 360 There is no worse enemy to a living Church than a propositional theology. **1892** *Mind* I. 10 There are *five* independent laws, which are necessary and sufficient for propositional synthesis. **1922** tr. *Wittgenstein's Tractatus* 45 The sign through which we express the thought I call the propositional sign. *Ibid.* 51 An expression is thus presented by a variable whose values are the propositions which contain the expression... I call such a variable a 'propositional variable'. **1926** H. HEAD *Aphasia* I. iii. 39 Occasionally he can not only use 'yes' and 'no' correctly, but can even repeat them. Here, then, we have propositional speech and voluntary utterance. **1932** LEWIS & LANGFORD *Symbolic Logic* ix. 267 In elementary functions only propositional variables occur. **1935** WEISENBURG & MCBRIDE *Aphasia* x. 277 When propositional speech is negligible, spoken expression may nevertheless be frequent. **1943** W. G. HARDY in *Cornell Univ. Abstr. of Theses* (1944) 57 Richards..now concerns himself with the educative values of propositional analysis. **1947** H. REICHENBACH *Elem. Symbolic Logic* 179 The recursive definition of the term 'propositional expression'. **1955** A. N. PRIOR *Formal Logic* I. iii. 50 We introduce the symbol 'o' as a propositional *constant*, to stand..for some arbitrarily chosen proposition. **1957** J. EISENSON in L. E. Travis *Handbk. Speech Path.* (1959) xii. 438 When linguistic symbols are used to communicate a specific idea or to elicit a specific response, we are dealing with propositional speech. **1968** N. RESCHER *Topics in Philos. Logic* v. 51 The most satisfactory course is to base the logic of belief (and of assertion) upon a propositional analysis, rather than one articulated in terms of sentences, inscriptions, utterances, or the like. **1973** J. J. ZEMAN *Modal Logic* p. v, The book..contains a detailed development of non-modal propositional logic. **1976** *Listener* 9 Dec. 743/1 The capacity for propositional speech—the synthesis of words into statements that, by their form, give extra meaning to those words. **1977** *Word 1972* XXVIII. 223 In propositional speech (both in forming constructions and in understanding them), the patient had difficulty sorting out relationships between more than two critical items.

b. In special collocations, as ***propositional attitude***, an attitude which can vary expressed towards a proposition that does not vary; ***propositional calculus***, a calculus which formalizes the basic truth-functional operations possible in logical propositions and gives notation, indicating conjunction, disjunction, negation, etc., to their sentential connectives; ***propositional connective***, a connective which is used as a logical operator in propositions; ***propositional function*** (see quot. 1910 and cf. PREDICATE *sb.* 2 a).

[**1904** B. RUSSELL in *Mind* XIII. 509 Belief is a certain attitude towards propositions, which is called knowledge when they are true, error when they are false.] **1939** *Mind* XLVIII. 479 When we disbelieve, then doubt, and finally believe a proposition, it must be the *same* proposition toward which we have these different attitudes; that is, propositions must be invariant under change of propositional attitude. **1940** B. RUSSELL *Inquiry into Meaning & Truth* xi. 204 A negative basic proposition thus requires a propositional attitude, in which the proposition concerned is the one which, on the basis of perception, is denied. **1966** W. V. QUINE *Ways of Paradox* xv. 189 Striving and wishing, like believing, are propositional attitudes and referentially opaque. **1969** J. HINTIKKA *Models for Modalities* iii. 87 (*heading*) Semantics for propositional attitudes. **1903** B. RUSSELL *Princ. Math.* ii. 12 It is not with such entities that we are concerned in the propositional calculus, but with genuine propositions. **1938** *Jrnl. Symbolic Logic* III. 83 Chapter 2 supplements the propositional calculus, in effect, with the Boolean algebra of one-place predicates. **1959** *Ibid.* XXIV. 97 Gödel proves the non-existence of a finite matrix characteristic for the intuitionist propositional calculus IC. **1966** *Mathematical Rev.* XXXI. 4/1 Since the main results are existential, a really conclusive solution requires a narrow meaning of 'propositional calculus'. **1973** J. J. ZEMAN *Modal Logic* ii. 7 Our first task will be..to set down some propositional calculi. Many systems discussed later will be presented as extensions of the propositional calculus. **1938** *Jrnl. Symbolic Logic* III. 84 A deductive system is presented which involves..the propositional connectives, and prediction and quantification with respect to individuals. **1952** S. C. KLEENE *Introd. Metamath.* iv. 73 In particular, $\supset$, &, $\vee$, $\neg$ are propositional connectives, and operators of the forms $\forall x$ and $\exists x$ are quantifiers..these six are logical operators. **1974** *Jrnl. Philos. Logic* III. 202 The propositional connectives concern statements. **1903** B. RUSSELL *Princ. Math.* ii. 13 Where there are one or more real variables, and for all values of the variables the expression involved is a proposition, I shall call the expression a *propositional function*. **1910** WHITEHEAD & RUSSELL *Principia Math.* I. i. 15 Let ϕx be a statement containing a variable x such that it becomes a proposition when x is given any fixed determined meaning. Then ϕx is called a 'propositional function'; it is not a proposition, since owing to the ambiguity of x it really makes no assertion at all. **1943, 1969** [see PREDICATE *sb.* 2 a]. **1974** *Jrnl. Philos. Logic* III. 196 A predicate, or propositional function, is a statement-valued function, i.e. a function that maps objects of some kind into statements (propositions).

Hence **propoˈsitionalist**, someone who is concerned with the logic of propositions; **propoˈsitionally** *adv.*; **propoˈsitionalness**, the quality of laying down propositions.

1864 MASSON in *Macm. Mag.* July 216 A quality..which coining a monstrous word for my purpose, I will venture to call propositionalness. It is in the main identical with that passion for intellectual generalization which we often speak of as particularly visible in the French mind. **1879** *Brain* II. 215 Then propositionally 'yes' and 'no' give assent or dissent to anything whatever. **1890** *Lancet* 12 Apr. 787/1 *note*, If he only uttered them [propositions] at random, or if they were only signs of emotion, they would not serve propositionally. **1952** *Mind* LXI. 61 The spurious character of our propositionalist's argument becomes evident. **1970** W. V. QUINE *Philos. of Logic* i. 3 The propositionalist bypasses differences between languages.

propoˈsitionize, *v.* [f. as prec. + -IZE.] *intr.* To make or utter propositions.

1868 BUSHNELL *Serm. Living Subj.* 74 By much theologizing, propositionizing, schematizing and abstractionizing, we show it builded together for the very ends and uses we have reasoned for it. **1878** *Brain* I. 312 Loss of speech is therefore the loss of power to propositionise. It is not only loss of power to propositionise aloud (to talk), but to propositionise either internally or externally. **1890** *Lancet* 12 Apr. 787/1 *note*, To speak is not merely to utter words, but to propositionize. **1920** *Brain* XLIII. 119, I believe that under the uncouth word 'propositionizing' is included what I understand by 'symbolic thinking'. **1921** *Brit. Jrnl. Psychol.* XI. 185 There are some aspects of the loss of function in aphasia which are not strictly comprised under the heading of 'propositionising'. **1955** R. JAKOBSON in H. Werner *On Expressive Lang.* 77 The patient fails to operate with contiguity, while operations based on similarity remain intact. Thus he [*sc.* an aphasic] loses the ability to propositionize. **1956** —— in Jakobson & Halle *Fund. Lang.* II. iv. 71 The impairment of the ability to propositionize, or generally speaking, to combine simpler linguistic entities into more complex units, is actually confined to one type of aphasia.

‖**propositum** (prəʊˈpɒzɪtəm). *Philos.* [L., neut. of *prōpositus*: see next.] The first premise of a syllogism; an argument, principal theme or subject propounded.

1858 A. DE MORGAN *On Syllogism* (1966) 83, I see great difference in the *propositum* between 'This house was built by Jack' and 'This is the [or even *a*] house that Jack built'. **1913** [see JUDICATUM]. **1920** S. ALEXANDER *Space, Time, & Deity* II. 249 'Proposition' contains a reference to language, and 'propositum' would be a better, though a pedantic name.

propositus (prəʊˈpɒzɪtʌs). Pl. propositi. [a. L. *prōpositus*, pa. pple. of *prōpōnere* (see PROPONE *v.*).] An individual who was the first member of a family to come to the notice of a researcher, and through whom investigation of a pedigree began. Cf. PROBAND, PROPOSITA.

1926 *Eugenics Rev.* XVIII. 248 ☛ Points to the Propositus or central figure in the pedigree. **1939** *Brit. Jrnl. Psychol.* XXX. 9 When propositi are separated into groups of comparable mental grade, defect is seen to be more common among relatives of simpletons than among relatives of idiots. **1956** *Nature* 7 Jan. 40/1 The factor was transmitted to them by the paternal grandmother (generation II) of the propositus. **1961** *Lancet* 19 Aug. 437/2 We have collected the details of 107 sibships; the propositi attended our clinics. **1977** *Ibid.* 3 Sept. 504/1 The propositus (family C) presented with pituitary insufficiency.

pro-postscutellar, -um: see PRO-[2] 2.

†**proˈposure.** *Obs. rare*[−1]. [f. PROPOSE *v.* + -URE: cf. *composure, exposure.*] The act of proposing or propounding.

1655 OWEN *Vind. Evang.* Wks. 1853 XII. 124 The proposure of a question..is the next part of our employment.

propound (prəʊˈpaʊnd), *v.* Also 6 propowne, -poune. [A later form of PROPONE, through the intermediate *propoune, propowne*: cf. COMPOUND, EXPOUND.]

1. *trans.* To put forth, set forth, propose, or offer for consideration, discussion, acceptance, or adoption; to put forward as a question for solution.

α. **1537** STARKEY *Let.* in *England* (1878) p. I, What peryl of damnatyon he declaryth in hys boke, and propownyth to honge certaynly ouer our hedys. **1542** UDALL *Erasm. Apoph.* 46 A certain person had propouned an harde reedle. **1586** B. YOUNG tr. *Guazzo's Civ. Conv.* IV. 182 Without anie question propowned to her at all. *a* **1651** CALDERWOOD *Hist. Kirk* (Wodrow Soc.) II. 38 Who..speeke nothing against the doctrine propouned.

β. **1551** T. WILSON *Logike* (1580) 26 He propounded the same vnto him, and thought thereby to haue giuen hym a foile. **1560** DAUS tr. *Sleidane's Comm.* 14 To treate, what conditions should be propounded to the Emperour. **1613** PURCHAS *Pilgrimage* I. x. 46 An Image-maker, and propounded his Images..as Gods to be worshipped. *c* **1618** MORYSON *Itin.* IV. vii. (1903) 114 No man besides himselfe [the duke] can propounde any thing in the great Counsell. **1634** SIR T. HERBERT *Trav.* 28 They propounded Articles of peace and friendship. *a* **1720** SEWEL *Hist. Quakers* (1795) II. VII. 63 To answer such questions as they shall propound to you. **1836–7** SIR W. HAMILTON *Metaph.* xliii. (1870) II. 458 In the thirteenth book..this theory is formally propounded. **1847** GROTE *Greece* II. xi. III. 171 The most extensive scheme of constitutional reform yet propounded. **1876** GLADSTONE *Homeric Synchr.* 224 No one, to my knowledge, has propounded such an idea.

b. In *Eccl. Law.* To bring forward (an allegation, etc.) in a cause: cf. PROPONE *v.* 2. (See also sense 6.)

1685 CONSETT *Pract. Spir. Crts.* I. iii. §1 (1700) 11 If the Plaintiff..does [not] propound any dilatory matter, to hinder the giving of Sentence. *Ibid.* VI. xii. §1 This Allegation is to be propounded jointly and severally, and is to be admitted as in other Causes.

c. *absol.* or *intr.* To make a proposal: in quot. 1570–6, to bring forward a charge or complaint; cf. PROPONE *v.* 2 (*obs.*).

1570–6 LAMBARDE *Peramb. Kent* (1826) 106 If any [person] of the same Townes had cause to complaine of any ..he shall be at Shipwey to propound against him. **1598** GRENEWEY *Tacitus, Ann.* xi. iv. (1622) 145 Then he [Claudius] propounded in Senate touching the colledge of southsayers, least that the most auncient discipline of Italie should come to naught by slothfulnes. **1601** SIR W. CORNWALLIS *Disc. Seneca* (1631) 63 To propound, not to conclude, is the destiny of man.

2. *trans.* To propose or nominate for an office or position, as a member of a society, etc. Now *U.S.*

1573 G. HARVEY *Letter-bk.* (Camden) 3 The Pensionars were also forthwith propoundid. **1623** BINGHAM *Xenophon* 107 They first propounded Cherisophus for an Ambassadour. *a* **1649** WINTHROP *New Eng.* (1853) I. 131 He was then (with his wife) propounded to be admitted a member [of the church]. **1673** RAY *Journey Low C., Venice* 163 His name..is by the Secretary set down..with the name of him who propounded him, and the set of Electors he was of. **1809** KENDALL *Trav.* I. vii. 63 Nor shall any person be chosen newly into the magistracy, which was not propounded in some general court before, to be nominated the next election. **1828** WEBSTER s.v., In congregational churches..persons intending to make public profession of their faith, and thus unite with the church, are propounded before the church and congregation. **1863** R. B. KIMBALL *Was He Successful?* (1864) 25 In due course he was propounded and admitted into the church.

†**3.** To hold forth or set before one as an example, reward, aim, etc. *Obs.*

1571 DIGGES *Pantom.* III. i. Qj, Of either I minde to propound an example, although one rule suffise them bothe. **1577** HANMER *Anc. Eccl. Hist.* (1619) 146 Of these, for examples sake I will propound one, with the end he made. **1609** SIR R. SHERLEY in *Harl. Misc.* (Malh.) III. 95 Kings themselues propound great gifts and rewards. **1651** HOBBES *Leviath.* I. xiv. 67 If a man propound a Prize to him that comes first to the end of a race, The gift is Free. *a* **1661** FULLER *Worthies* (1840) I. i. 1 Know then, I propound five ends to myself in this Book. *a* **1703** BURKITT *On N.T.* Matt. v. 14 The great end we propound in all the good works which we perform. **1719** D'URFEY *Pills* (1872) I. 24 For Honour and Valour Preferment's propounded.

†**4.** To propose (to do or the doing of something); to suggest (that something should be done).

1597 BACON *Coulers Gd. & Evill* iv. Ess. (Arb.) 142 The one propounded to goe downe into a deepe Well. **1658** HOWE in H. Rogers *Life* iii. (1863) 64, I propounded that this might be put into the agreement. **1668–9** PEPYS *Diary* 21 Mar., After dinner propounds to me my lending him 500*l.* **1676–7** MARVELL *Corr.* Wks. (Grosart) II. 524 It was also propounded to move the House. **1702** ECHARD *Eccl. Hist.* (1710) 200 He propounded to scourge him, and so dismiss him. **1709** STRYPE *Ann. Ref.* I. xxx. 305 In this convocation it was propounded, that an act of Parliament should be made for the relief of poor ministers.

†**b.** To set before oneself as something to be done; to purpose. *Obs.*

1596 SPENSER *F.Q.* IV. vi. 42 Fit time for him thence to depart..To follow that which he did long propound. **1598** BARCKLEY *Felic. Man* (1631) 491 He that will liue happily must propound to himselfe things possible, and be content with things present. **1604** E. G[RIMSTONE] *D'Acosta's Hist. Indies* III. xix. 178 It is the last of the three Elements, whereof wee have propounded to treate in this Booke. **1655** tr. *Com. Hist. Francion* v. 4 Propounding to themselves to become glorious by that means. **1692** R. L'ESTRANGE *Josephus, Antiq.* XI. viii. (1733) 298 To give the Macedonians Battle before they should over run the whole of Asia, which they propounded to do.

†**5.** To represent, to exhibit (by figure or description). *Obs.*

1594 BLUNDEVIL *Exerc.* II. (1636) 119 Note that whensoever any manner of angle is propounded by three letters: that the middle letter doth alwayes signifie the angle propounded. **1659** PEARSON *Creed* ii. (1662) 124 They propound the Jews senselesly offended and foolishly exasperated with those words. **1668** CULPEPPER & COLE *Barthol. Anat.* I. xvii. 46 This Table [= plate] propounds the Kidneys both whole and cut asunder.

†**b.** To set before one's mind; to conceive or imagine to oneself. *Obs.*

1634 W. TIRWHYT tr. *Balzac's Lett.* I. 64 Propound to yourself monsters in my will to be mastred. **1647** TRAPP *Comm. Rom.* xv. 33 When they pray to propound God to their minde in such notions, and under such titles, as whereby they may see in God the things they desire of God.

6. *Law.* To put forth or produce (a will, or other document making testamentary dispositions) before the proper authority, for the purpose of having its legality established.

1753 SIR G. LEE *Reports Cases* (1833) I. 420 This will..is propounded by Lady Ann. *Ibid.*, These instructions [for preparing a will] wrote by deceased..are propounded by Thomas Jekyll, one of his brothers, as a legatee. **1826** W. ROBERTS *Treat. Wills* II. VI. i. §2. 174 If the paper propounded to the ecclesiastical Court may have any effect on the estate..probate will be granted. **1829** HAGGARD *Eccles. Reports* I. 56 *margin*, A codicil..which..came out of the custody of, and was propounded by, the person solely benefitted under it. *Ibid.* 57 The paper was then propounded..as a further codicil to the will of the deceased, and asserted to be all in his own hand-writing. **1836** SIR H. JENNER in Curteis *Rep. Eccl. Cas.* (1840) I. 160 The asserted execution of the will propounded on the 19th. **1884** *Law Rep.* 9 *Probate Div.* 23 The executors named in [the will] propounded it for probate.

Hence **proˈpounded** *ppl. a.*, **proˈpounding** *vbl. sb.*

1551 T. WILSON *Logike* (1580) 61 b, The disputer must alwaies keepe hym in, and..force hym still to aunswere the propounded argument directly. **1575** GASCOIGNE *Flowers* Wks. 13 After supper they should passe the tyme in propounding of Ryddles. **1608** D. T[UVIL] *Ess. Pol. & Mor.* 64 Neither dooth she alter her propounded courses. **1656** tr. *Hobbes' Elem. Philos.* (1839) 182 Between the two propounded points, there is one strait line, by the definition of a circle, contained wholly in the propounded plane. **1807** J. BARLOW *Columb.* III. 68 Yet oh, may sovereign mercy first ordain Propounded compact to the savage train!

†**proˈpound,** *sb. Obs.* [f. prec.] A proposition.

1599 PEELE *Sir Clyom.* Wks. (Rtldg.) 511/1 The which propound within my mind doth oftentimes revolve.

propounder (prəʊˈpaʊndə(r)). [f. as prec. + -ER[1].]

1. One who propounds or sets forth, esp. for acceptance, consideration, discussion, or solution.

1561 T. NORTON *Calvin's Inst.* IV. vi. (1634) 544 There is ..no Session of Judges without a Pretor or Propounder. **1660** JER. TAYLOR *Duct. Dubit.* I. v, It..can receive no warrant in legitimation by the intention of the propounder. **1829** MARRYAT *F. Mildmay* iv, I answered every question with such fluency.., as sometimes caused the propounder to regret that he had put me to the trouble of speaking. **1837** HT. MARTINEAU *Soc. Amer.* II. 31 A country where political economy has never been taught by its only effectual propounder—social adversity. **1895** DIXON in *Fortn. Rev.* Apr. 640 Prominent among the supporters of this theory —if not its actual propounder.

†**2.** A name for the rhetorical figure PROLEPSIS. *Obs. rare*[−1].

1589 PUTTENHAM *Eng. Poesie* III. xii. (Arb.) 179 Ye haue yet another maner of speach purporting at the first blush a defect which afterward is supplied, the Greekes call him *Prolepsis*, we the Propounder, or the Explaner which ye will.

¶ The alleged sense 'A monopolist' given in modern Dicts., and suggested in Blount's *Law Dict.* (1670), is founded upon the heading of ch. 85 of 3rd pt. of Coke's *Institutes* 'Against Monopolists, Propounders, and Projectors', where the text has 'These Inventers and Propounders of evill things' [*inventores malorum*], in which the word is used as in sense 1 above.

proˈpoundment. *rare.* [f. as prec. + -MENT.] The act or fact of propounding.

1846 G. S. FABER *Lett. Tractar. Secess.* 63 The remedy.. by the very circumstance of its propoundment, affords a tacit acknowledgment, that the Theory..is defective.

proˈpoundress. *rare.* [f. PROPOUNDER + -ESS[1].] A female propounder.

1866 J. B. ROSE *Ovid's Metam.* 207 And she, propoundress of the ridding curse.

propoxur (prəʊˈpɒksʊə(r)). [f. PROP(YL + OX- I + UR(ETHANE.] An insecticide having a long-lasting ability to produce rapid incapacitation of affected insects; *o*-isopropoxyphenyl-*N*-methylcarbamate, $CH_3{\cdot}NH{\cdot}CO{\cdot}O{\cdot}C_6H_4{\cdot}O{\cdot}CH(CH_3)_2$.

1964 *Zeitschr. f. Angewandte Zool.* LI. 332 Deposits on filter paper of..carbamates (carbaryl and propoxur), prepared up to 105 days ago, were repeatedly applied to imagines of five different strains of house-flies (Musca domestica). **1977** *Time* 12 Sept. 56/3 Health authorities are now using more of other insecticides, such as Malathion and propoxur to kill DDT-resistant mosquitoes.

propoxyphene (prəʊˈpɒksɪfiːn). *Pharm.* [f. PROP(IO- + OXY- + *-phene* (f. PHEN-, PHENO-).] A mild narcotic analgesic, chemically related to methadone, which is given orally (usu. as the hydrochloride, a whitish powder) esp. in cases of chronic or recurrent pain, its effects being similar to but weaker than those of codeine; (+)-α-4-dimethylamino-3-methyl-1,2-diphenylbut-2-yl propionate, $(CH_3)_2N{\cdot}CH_2{\cdot}CH(CH_3){\cdot}C(C_6H_5)(CH_2{\cdot}C_6H_5){\cdot}O{\cdot}CO{\cdot}CH_2CH_3$.

1955 *Arch. Internat. de Pharmacodyn.* CIV. 165 The analgesic activity of Propoxyphene has been demonstrated in patients with chronic pain. **1957** *Jrnl. Amer. Med. Assoc.* 29 June 966/2 Propoxyphene is a new synthetic analgesic with the effectiveness of codeine but having less undesirable gastrointestinal side-effects. *Ibid.* 969/2 Since the preparation of this article, the Council on Drugs of the American Medical Association has changed the generic name of propoxyphene hydrochloride to dextro propoxyphene hydrochloride. **1974** M. C. GERALD *Pharmacol.* xiv. 272 In recent years propoxyphene has been among the most frequently prescribed drugs. **1976** *National Observer* (U.S.) 28 Aug. 3/1 The drug agency has suggested that the Justice Department's Drug Enforcement Administration (DEA) rule that propoxyphene-containing products be added to the list of the Controlled Substances Act's 'Schedule IV' drugs. This would mean that physicians must renew prescriptions for Darvon and similar drugs every six months.

proppage (ˈprɒpɪdʒ). *nonce-wd.* [f. PROP *v.* + -AGE.] Propping or supporting apparatus.

1827 CARLYLE *Germ. Rom.* III. 138 Hat and stick were his proppage and balance-wheel.

propped, propt (prɒpt), *ppl. a.* [f. PROP *v.* + -ED[1].] Held up or supported by or as by a prop.

1789 MRS. PIOZZI *Journ. France* II. 154 The sight of propt-up cottages which fright the fancy more than those already fallen. **1849** RUSKIN *Sev. Lamps* iii. §7. 69, I think the propped machicolations of the Palazzo Vecchio and Duomo of Florence far grander. **1894** MRS. DYAN *All in a Man's K.* (1899) 339 He sank weakly on to a chair and buried his head in his propped-up arms.

propper (ˈprɒpə(r)). [f. PROP *v.* + -ER[1].] One who props or supports.

1549 BP. POYNET *Def. Mariage Priestes* C j b, The patchers and proppers vp of this Decree.

propping (ˈprɒpɪŋ), *vbl. sb.* [f. as prec. + -ING[1].]

1. The action of the verb PROP; supporting as or with a prop.

1492–3 *Rec. St. Mary at Hill* 188 For sartayne thynges.. Repayryd in hys howse and for proppyng of the dore. **1565** COOPER *Thesaurus, Pedatio*, the propping or settinge vp of vines. **1725** RAMSAY *Gentle Sheph.* III. i, What disturbs the great, In propping of their pride and state. **1902** *Blackw. Mag.* Jan. 50/1 The miner not only gets the coal but makes all proppings and repairs.

b. *pl. concr.* Supports, stays, props.

1660 W. SECKER *Nonsuch Prof.* 181 Your weakest building needs the most under propings. **1662** GERBIER *Princ.* 28 A Moorish Ground, whereon no New Building could stand any time without Proppings.

2. Of a horse (*Australia*): Sudden stopping.

1884 'R. BOLDREWOOD' *Melb. Mem.* xxi. 152 Traveller's dam had an ineradicable taste for 'propping'.

3. The propelling of a wagon or carriage on one line of rails, by means of a pole or 'prop' extended from an engine on a parallel line, so as to push it along; a dangerous operation now illegal.

1900 *Act 63 & 64 Vict.* c. 27 Sch., 1. Brake levers on both sides of waggons. 2. Labelling waggons. 3. Movement of waggons by propping or tow roping. 4. Steam or other power brakes on engines. **1901** *Dundee Advertiser* 13 May 4 Tow-roping and 'propping'.. practices which have resulted in many accidents, are forbidden.

'propping, *ppl. a.* [f. as prec. + -ING[2].] That props; supporting.

1567 DRANT *Horace, Epist.* xvi. E vij, Propping elmes that clad with vinetrees be. **1821** CLARE *Holywell* 139 in *Vill. Minstr.* I. 77, I..loll'd me 'gainst a propping tree. **1879** BROWNING *Ivan Ivanovitch* 69 Down fell her face upon the good friend's propping knee.

'proppy, *a.*[1] *colloq. nonce-wd.* [f. PROP *sb.*[1] + -Y[1].] Resembling or suggesting a prop or pole.

1870 *Daily News* 6 June, Ashdale has the weight, but rather proppy forelegs, while Marston excels in quality and has the most hunting character about him.

proppy ('prɒpɪ), *a.*[2] *Austral. colloq.* [f. PROP *v.*[1] + -Y[1].] Of a horse: tending to prop (PROP *v.*[1] 4) or stop suddenly in mid-stride, faltering; also of other animals. Hence **'proppily** *adv.*

1945 BAKER *Austral. Lang.* 70 Another extension is the adjectival use of *proppy* for a horse that jibs and plays up when ridden or driven. **1951** H. G. LAMOND in Murdoch & Drake-Brockman *Austral. Short Stories* 213 Both [dogs] walked proppily on tiptoes. **1969** *Australian* 24 May 35/5 King's Delight had a bruised sole on the near fore, and Clare said the horse was proppy in his action.

pro-præscutal, -um: see PRO-[2] 2.

proprætor (prəʊ'priːtə(r)). [a. L. *prōprætor*, originally *prō prætōre* (one acting) for the prætor.] A magistrate of the ancient Roman republic who after holding the office of prætor was given the administration of a province not under military control, with the authority of a prætor. Also, one who acted in place of a prætor.

1579–80 NORTH *Plutarch* (1595) 1107 Junius Vindex being Proprætor of Gavle. **1600** HOLLAND *Livy* xxx. 769, P. Lentulus the Propretour. **1727–41** in CHAMBERS *Cycl.* **1832–4** DE QUINCEY *Cæsars* Wks. 1859 X. 228 *note*, In the imperatorial provinces, where the governor bore the title of Proprætor, there was provision made for a military establishment. **1840** MACAULAY *Ess., Clive* (1887) 560 The [East India] Company's servants might still be called factors... But they were in truth proconsuls, proprætors, procurators of extensive regions.

Hence **pro'prætorship**, the office of a proprætor.

1620–55 I. JONES *Stone-Heng* (1725) 9 The second Year of Julius Agricola his Proprætorship, or Lieutenancy in Britain. **1824** J. H. NEWMAN in *Encycl. Metrop.* (1845) X. 280/1 From the period of his Consulate to his Proprætorship in Cilicia.

propræ'torial, *a.* [f. prec., after PRÆTORIAL.] Of or pertaining to a proprætor; under the rule of a proprætor.

1885 J. G. FRAZER in *Encycl. Brit.* XIX. 885/1 Thus the distinction between consular (or proconsular) and prætorial (or proprætorial) provinces varied from year to year with the military exigencies of different parts of the empire.

So **propræ'torian** *a.*, in same sense.

1832–4 DE QUINCEY *Cæsars* Wks. 1859 X. 228 *note*, The whole revenues of the proprætorian (or imperatorial) provinces, from this time forward, flowed into the *fiscus*, or private treasure of the individual emperor. **1882–3** *Schaff's Encycl. Relig. Knowl.* I. 23 The proconsular as distinct from the propraetorian status of Cyprus.

propranolol (prəʊ'prænəlɒl). *Pharm.* [f. PRO(PYL + PR(OP)ANOL with reduplication of final -OL.] The compound 1-isopropylamino-3-(1-naphthyloxy)-2-propanol, $C_{16}H_{21}NO_2$, which is a β-adrenergic blocking agent used mainly (in the form of a colourless crystalline hydrochloride) in the treatment of cardiac arrhythmia.

1964 *Brit. Med. Jrnl.* 19 Sept. 720 (*heading*) Effect of propranolol (Inderal) in angina pectoris: preliminary report. **1965** J. H. BURN *Lect. Notes Pharmacol.* (ed. 8) 10 When propranolol is given, a patient performs a given amount of work at a lower heart rate and he can perform a greater amount of work without feeling pain. **1972** *Lancet* 16 Sept. 565/2 In our clinical experience, propranolol is effective in the treatment of heroin dependence. **1974** *Sci. Amer.* June 62/3 This complex series of events can be turned off by propranolol, a drug that prevents the noradrenaline from combining with the beta adrenergic receptor. **1980** *Brit. Med. Jrnl.* 29 Mar. 885/1 We have..investigated the effect of giving higher doses of a nonselective beta-blocker (propranolol)..to patients with suspected myocardial infarction.

propre, obs. form of PROPER *a.* and *v.*

proprefect, -præfect (prəʊ'priːfɛkt). [f. PRO-[1] 4 + PREFECT. So L. *prōpræfectus* (inscr.), F. *propréfet.*] A deputy prefect or commander.

1691 WOOD *Athenæ Oxon.* II. 293 He..was entertained by William Marquess of Newcastle, and by him made Proprefect or Lieutenant General of his Ordnance. **1727–41** CHAMBERS *Cycl.* s.v., The third inscription mentions proprefects of the pretorium under Gratian, in the city of Rome, and the neighbouring parts.

pro'prefecture. [f. as prec. from PREFECTURE.] The office of proprefect; deputy presidentship.

1803 *Monthly Mag.* XVI. 201 Pius the Sixth,..who was pleased..to invest me with the charge of the Pro-prefecture of the Congregation of Propaganda Fide.

† **'propremen,** *adv. Obs. rare.* [a. F. *proprement* adv., f. *propre* PROPER.] Properly, naturally.

a **1225** *Ancr. R.* 196 Þet flesch put propremen touward swetnesse & touward eise.

proprete, -tie, etc. obs. forms of PROPERTY.

† **'propriary.** *Obs. rare*[−1]. [f. L. *propri-um*, or short for *proprietary.*] A proprietor, owner.

1606 WARNER *Alb. Eng.* XIV. lxxxvii. 357 To either Propriarie so was either Realme againe Of Romaines left.

† **'propriate,** *a.* (*sb.*) *Obs.* [ad. L. *propriāt-us*, pa. pple. of *propri-āre* to make one's own, f. *propri-us* PROPER.]

1. Appropriated, assigned to a particular person; annexed as an attribute, special, peculiar: = APPROPRIATE *ppl. a.* 3, 4.

1654 *Kirk Sess. Rec.* in Campbell *Balmerino* (1899) 403 The Session, finding that rowme and place not propriat to any other. **1820** COMBE *Consol.* VII. (1869) 226/2 Without whose propriate sympathies We should be neither strong nor wise.

2. *Eccl.* Of a benefice: Appropriated to a religious house or corporation: = APPROPRIATE *ppl. a.* 1. (In quot. 1697 loosely applied to the rector of such a benefice.)

Cf. notes s. vv. IMPROPRIATE *v.* 2 and IMPROPRIATION 1.

1616 SPELMAN *De non Temer. Eccl.* (1646) b j, Thy Tithes, whether propriate or impropriate. **1697** BP. GARDINER *Adv. Clergy* 21 One cannot but wonder..that Rectors as well Impropriate as Propriate, should not take more care to fit their Chancels for this purpose.

B. *sb.* One to whom something is appropriated; a possessor, proprietor. *rare*[−1].

1660 BURNEY Κέρδ. Δῶρον (1661) 25 The Scepter..should run on in a direct line, till it came to the Essentiator of the being of Kings, the propriate of Rule, Βασιλεὺς Βασιλέων.

† **'propriate,** *v. Obs. rare*[−1]. [f. L. *propriāre* (see prec.) + -ATE[3].] *trans.* = APPROPRIATE *v.* 2.

1624 DONNE *Serm., Deut.* xxv. 5 (1649) II. 424 The covetous desires of the world, that is, the covetous propriating [*mispr.* proprieting] of all things to our selves.

propriation (prəʊprɪ'eɪʃən). *rare.* [ad. L. type **propriātiōn-em*, n. of action f. *propriāre*: see above. Cf. OF. *propriacion* (14th c. in Godef.).]

1. a. The action of making or condition of being made one's own (or some one's own): = APPROPRIATION 1. **b.** *Eccl.* = APPROPRIATION 2.

1600 W. WATSON *Decacordon* (1602) 185 By reason of more particular respects of propriation or otherwise. **1601** *Act 43 Eliz.* c. 2 Euery Occupier of Landes Houses Tithes impropriate or Propriacions of Tythes, Colemynes or saleable Underwoods. *a* **1660** *Contemp. Hist. Irel.* (Ir. Archæol. Soc.) I. 191 To be one and the same united in comon without division, or propriation. **1840** *Act 3 & 4 Vict.* c. 89 *Preamble.*

2. ? The action of taking in a 'proper', i.e. literal or strict, sense: cf. PROPER *a.* 4.

1819 COLERIDGE in *Lit. Rem.* (1838) III. 65 This propriation of a metaphor, namely, forgiveness of sin and abolition of guilt through the redemptive power of Christ's love and of his perfect obedience during his voluntary assumption of humanity,..by transferring the sameness from the consequents to the antecedents is the one point of orthodoxy (so called, I mean) in which I still remain at issue.

† **'propriatory.** [f. L. *propriāt-us* PROPRIATE *a.* + -ORY.] = PROPRIETARY *sb.* 3.

1569 BP. PARKHURST *Injunc.* in *2nd Rep. Ritual Comm.* (1868) 404/2 That no Parson Vicar, propriatorie or fermer of any benefice, doe admit any Minister or Curate to serue his said benefice, vnlesse [etc.]. **1621** BOLTON *Stat. Irel.* 317 Propriatories of large portions of land.

proprietage (prəʊ'praɪɪtɪdʒ). *rare.* [irreg. f. *propriet(or* or *propriet(y* + -AGE.] **a.** The property of individuals collectively; the whole body of personal property. **b.** The body of proprietors collectively.

1830 COLERIDGE *Ch. & St.* (ed. 2) 141 In the same sense as I at once oppose and conjoin the Nationalty to the Proprietage; in the same antithesis and conjunction I use and understand the phrase, Church and State. *Ibid.*, The Possessions of both orders, taken collectively, form the Proprietage of the Realm. **1845** J. MARTINEAU *Essays* (1891) II. 28 The interests and concerns of the whole Proprietage.

† **proprietaire.** *Obs.* Also 7 *Sc.* -ar. [a. F. *propriétaire* (1335 in Hatz.-Darm.): see also -AR[2].] = PROPRIETARY *sb.* (in various senses).

c **1491** *Chast. Goddes Chyld.* 26 This man that thus resteth vpon his owne loue to his proper persone may well be callid a propryetayre. **1619** SIR J. SEMPIL *Sacrilege Handled* App. 27 Why shall the Priestes vnder the Law be debarred from Tithes comming from Secularies? Here then, we haue the Priest, the first proprietar.

proprietarian (prəʊpraɪɪ'tɛərɪən). *nonce-wd.* [In sense 1, f. as PROPRIETARY + -AN; in sense 2, f. PROPRIET(Y + -*arian*, as in *necessitarian*, etc.]

† **1.** ? An advocate or supporter of proprietary government in the N. American colonies. *Obs.*

1776 J. ADAMS *Wks.* (1854) IX. 411 The quakers and proprietarians together have little weight.

2. A stickler for propriety.

1866 HOWELLS *Venet. Life* xx, The *Conversazioni* of the rigid proprietarians where people sit down to a kind of hopeless whist..and say nothing.

proprietariat (prəʊpraɪɪ'tɛərɪət). *nonce-wd.* [f. PROPRIETARY *a.*, after *proletariat.*] The propertied class.

1896 G. B. SHAW *Rep. Fabian Policy* 4 It [*sc.* the Fabian Society]..does not believe that the moment will ever come when the whole of Socialism will be staked on the issue of a single General Election or a single Bill in the House of Commons, as between the proletariat on one side and the proprietariat on the other. **1928** —— *Intelligent Woman's Guide Socialism* 223 The Proletariat and the Proprietariat face each other. **1950** —— *Farfetched Fables* 86 The feudal proprietariat is all for well policed private property.

† **proprie'tarious,** *a. Obs. rare*[−1]. [f. as next + -OUS.] Pertaining to a 'proprietary' (see next, A. 2); self-seeking, selfish.

1657 *Divine Lover, Summarie Perfect.* 11 Contrarie to the proprietarious or vnresigned will of our corrupt nature.

proprietary (prəʊ'praɪɪtərɪ), *sb.* and *a.* [ad. late L. *proprietāri-us* (Paulus) proprietary, in med.L. also sb. a proprietor, f. *proprietās* PROPERTY: see -ARY[1].]

A. *sb.* † **1.** One who has 'propriety' or property in something, or to whom something belongs as property; an owner: = PROPRIETOR 2. *Obs.*

1473 *Rolls of Parlt.* VI. 65/2 The first or former proprietaries and owners of the same. **1541** *Declar. War Sc.* in Hall *Chron., Hen. VIII* (1548) 252 b, Our sayd progenitour,..enioyed it, as very proprietary and owner of the realme. **1622** MALYNES *Anc. Law-Merch.* 113 If a Factor ..giueth no aduice to the owner or proprietarie of the sale of the said goods. **1707** NORRIS *Treat. Humility* vii. 299 We are not receivers, but original proprietaries of what we have. **1790** *Hist. Europe* in *Ann. Reg.* 16/2 The enraged proprietaries, with their..servants, defeated the plunderers.

† **2.** A member of a religious or monastic order who, in violation of his vow of poverty, reserved goods for himself as private property. Hence *fig.* A self-seeking or selfish person. *Obs.*

c **1450** tr. *De Imitatione* III. xxxvii. 107 All proprietaries & louers of hemself. **1502** ATKYNSON *Ibid.* 226 All proprietaries & louers of them selfe be fetered and nat fre. **1496** *Dives & Pauper* (W. de Worde) VII. xxi, One of his monkes was in harde payne of purgatorye, for he had a propryetarye vnto the tyme of his deynge. **1538** BALE *Thre Lawes* 1005 We are such mercenaryes, And subtyle proprietaryes.

† **3.** The holder of an appropriated benefice: = APPROPRIETARY. *Obs.*

c **1460** *Oseney Regr.* 161 Þe foresaide prior and Couent of Merton proprietaries and persons of þe parisch church of Dunstywe. **1540** *Act 32 Hen. VIII*, c. 7 §1 The owners proprietaries and possessours of the personnages vicarages [etc.]. **1616** SPELMAN *De non Temer. Eccl.* (1668) 96 Upon these reasons Proprietaries are still said to be Parsons of their Churches. **1661** J. STEPHENS *Procurations* 30 In such Grants..of Impropriate Rectories those payments..are.. left as a charge..upon the Proprietaries.

4. *Amer. Hist.* The grantee or owner, or one of the grantees or owners, of any one of certain North American colonies: see B. 3. Also *lord proprietary*.

1637 in *Archives of Maryland* (1883) I. 23 Insolencies, mutinies and contempts against the Lord Proprietary and the government of this place. **1683** (*title*) A Letter from William Penn, Proprietary and Governour of Pennsylvania in America. **1765** T. HUTCHINSON *Hist. Mass.* I. 329 To govern under..the lords proprietaries. **1876** BANCROFT *Hist. U.S.* I. vii. 182 To the proprietary was given the power of creating manors and courts baron.

5. A proprietary body, a body of proprietors; proprietors collectively.

1803 W. TAYLOR in *Ann. Rev.* I. 406 An incroaching but modest plan of reform which will divide the proprietary into hostile factions. **1849** BRIGHT *Sp., Burdens on Land* 15 Mar. (1876) 423 Certain burdens..borne exclusively by the landed proprietary and real property of this country. **1856** FROUDE *Hist. Eng.* I. i. 14 The advocates for a peasant proprietary. **1884** *Bazaar, Exchange & Mart* 13 June 633/2 Of the greatest importance to the proprietary of a paper.

6. The holding of something as property; proprietorship.

1624 DONNE *Devotions*, etc. (ed. 2) 559 Euen in pleasures, and in paines, there is a proprietary, a meum and tuum. **1868** *Contemp. Rev.* VIII. 610 There is a spiritual commonalty..in which he can claim no exclusive proprietary. **1886** H. GEORGE in *N. Amer. Rev.* April 395 'Peasant proprietary' or 'occupying ownership',..the names European economists give to that system of ownership.

7. Something held as property, a possession; *esp.* a landed property or estate. ? *Obs.*

1608 NORTON *Stevin's Disme* D ij, That which Land-meater shall need to doe but once, and that at the end of the casting vp of the proprietaries. **1800** *Proc. Parl.* in *Asiat. Ann. Reg.* 12/2 Nor could the estate be..divided or parcelled into shares or several proprietaries. **1846** *Blackw. Mag.* LIX. 406 To one-half of the great proprietaries of the kingdom, a diminution of rent, even by a third, would make their possessors personally bankrupt.

B. *adj.*

1. a. Belonging to a proprietor or proprietors; owned or held as property; held in private ownership.

In mod. use applied esp. to medicines or other preparations of which the manufacture or sale is, by patent or otherwise, restricted to a particular person or persons. ***proprietary name*** or ***term***, a word or phrase over which a person or company has some legal rights, esp. in connection with trade (as a trade mark).

1589 PUTTENHAM *Eng. Poesie* I. xxiv. (Arb.) 62 Worldly goods they come and go, as things not long proprietary to any body. **1701** GREW *Cosm. Sacra* III. ii. §38. 99 Though Sheep, which are Proprietary, are seldom Marked, yet they are not apt to straggle. **1818** HALLAM *Mid. Ages* (1872) I. ii. I. 147 *note*, Alodial lands are commonly opposed to beneficiary or feudal; the former being strictly proprietary. **1866** G. MACDONALD *Ann. Q. Neighb.* i, I had formerly officated as curate in a proprietary chapel. **1900** *Westm. Gaz.* 22 Mar. 9/1 [They] are now charging a shilling a pound more for certain well-known proprietary tobacco. **1911** *T. Eaton & Co. Catal.* Spring & Summer 175 (*heading*) Proprietary Medicines. **1921** W. A. CRAIGIE *Let.* 18 Feb. (Oxf. Dict. files), We have expressly recognized that it [sc. *Vaseline*] is a proprietary term. **1924** *Pocket Oxf. Dict.* 932/1 *Vaseline*... Proprietary term introduced in 1872 by R. A. Chesebrough. **1930** *Engineering* 7 Mar. 304/1 These stock, or proprietary, engines are made by..specialists. **1930** *Economist* 22 Nov. 957/1 The Economic Council was unable to agree as to whether the undertaking by retailers selling proprietary articles to charge the price fixed by the manufacturers..should be prohibited. **1933** *O.E.D.* (new impr.) s.v. *Vaseline*... A proprietary term, introduced by R. A. Chesebrough in 1872. *Ibid.* Suppl. s.v. *Ferozone*... Proprietary name. **1958** *New Statesman* 28 June 822/2 Many [doctors]..tend to prescribe a well-advertised proprietary brand because they have no time to consult their list for a cheaper standard preparation. **1972** *Physics Bull.* Aug. 489/2 'Freon' is the proprietary name for Du Pont's brand of the fluorinated derivatives of hydrocarbons used as refrigerants and aerosol propellants. **1974** *Islander* (Victoria, B.C.) 4 Aug. 10/1 By the mid-18th century, more than 200 so-called 'proprietary medicines' were being sold in Britain and in the American colonies.

b. ***proprietary company*** = *private company* s.v. PRIVATE *a.* 7 h. *Austral.*

1896 *Companies Act* (Victoria, Austral.) §2 'Proprietary Company' means a company..which..(a) has not more than twenty-five members or shareholders; (b) does not receive deposits, except from its members or shareholders..; (c) does not use its title without the addition thereto immediately before the word 'limited' of the word 'proprietary'. **1973** R. N. PURVIS *Purvis on Proprietary Companies* i. 8 A public company must have at least three directors, whereas a proprietary company need have only two.

2. Holding property; that is a proprietor, or consisting of proprietors.

a **1709** ATKYNS *Parl. & Pol. Tracts* (1734) 409 He would be the great Proprietary Owner and Disposer of all Estates. **1825** MCCULLOCH *Pol. Econ.* Introd. 45 The second, or proprietary class, consists of those who live on the rent of the land, or on the net surplus produce raised by the cultivators. **1844** LD. BROUGHAM *Brit. Const.* vi. (1862) 91 The classes who are without any property..would overpower the proprietary classes.

3. *Amer. Hist.* Pertaining or subject to the proprietor or owner of any one of certain N. American colonies, which were granted by the Crown to particular persons; being such a proprietor: see A. 4.

1704 W. PENN in *15th Rep. Hist. MSS. Comm.* App. IV. 79 How much better the Colonies thrive in proprietary hands than under the immediate Government of the Crown. **1825** JEFFERSON *Autobiog.* Wks. 1859 I. 16 The backwardness of these two colonies might be ascribed partly to the influence of proprietary power and connections. **1899** *Westm. Gaz.* 30 Aug. 3/2 The provincial governor was either royal or proprietary, and his authority was imposed on the colony by the Crown directly, or by the proprietors through rights granted by the Crown.

4. Of or relating to property or proprietorship.

a **1832** BENTHAM *Anarch. Fallacies* Wks. 1843 II. 503 Property stands second on the list,—proprietary rights are in the number of the natural and imprescriptible rights of man. **1844** H. H. WILSON *Brit. India* I. 19 The complicated questions of proprietary right to lands that had repeatedly changed masters. **1855** MACAULAY *Hist. Eng.* xviii. IV. 183 William could defend the proprietary rights of the Crown only by putting his negative on the bill.

Hence **pro'prietarily** *adv.*, in a proprietary capacity; as a proprietor.

1654 VILVAIN *Theol. Treat.* vii. 205 Their progeny.. enjoyed it [the promised land] proprietarily for many ages.

proprietor (prəʊ'praɪətə(r)). [Anomalously formed and substituted in 17th c. for the etymological word PROPRIETARY: cf. also PROPRIETORY. App. first used of the 'proprietors' of the North American colonies.

An OF. *proprieteur* (once in Godef.) and its fem. *proprieteresse* (thrice) occur each time in a legal document (1419–1533). There may have been a Law Latin **proprietor*, but it does not appear to be recorded.]

1. *Amer. Hist.* = PROPRIETARY *sb.* 4. Also ***lord proprietor***.

1639 in E. Hazard *Hist. Coll.* (1792) I. 458, I Sir Ferdinando Gorges Lord proprietor and owner of the province of Maine in New England [etc.]. **1688** *Col. Rec. Pennsylv.* I. 230 The Chieff Proprietor and Govr acquainted them that he had little more to say. **1747** FRANKLIN *Let.* Wks. 1887 II. 93 We have petitioned the Proprietor to send us some from England. **1851** DIXON *W. Penn* xxxi. (1872) 291 The future lord proprietor of Pennsylvania.

2. One who holds something as property; one who has the exclusive right or title to the use or disposal of a thing; an owner.

peasant proprietor, a person of the peasant class who is the owner of the land he cultivates.

1645 *Col. Rec. Mass.* (1854) III. 27 Mr. Glouer [and 3 others] are appointed a committee to lay out ye way and judge of ye satisfaccion yey shall give to ye proprietors. *a* **1667** COWLEY *Ess. Verse & Prose, Agric.* Wks. (1684) 99 They who are Proprietors of the Land are either too proud, or for want of that kind of Education, too ignorant to improve their Estates. **1681** LUTTRELL *Brief Rel.* (1857) I. 142 The proprietors of the 800 iron guns here..have orders ..not to dispose of them. **1736** BUTLER *Anal.* II. vii. 359 The Maker and Proprietor of the World. **1840** DICKENS *Old C. Shop* xix, One of [the travellers] was the proprietor of a giant. **1849** GROTE *Greece* II. liii. VI. 559 A large proprietor and worker of gold mines. **1861** CRAIK *Hist. Eng. Lit.* I. 98 A large proportion..of the inferior landed proprietors. *fig.* **1742** YOUNG *Nt. Th.* VI. 283 Hearts are proprietors of all applause.

b. *attrib.* (usually appositive).

1898 *Westm. Gaz.* 26 Apr. 8/3 The proprietor barber.. insisted on a gratis shave. **1901** *Daily News* 18 Feb. 6/6 Even a proprietor-manager could hardly afford such regal garments. **1903** *Westm. Gaz.* 30 Mar. 5/1 An engineer and landed proprietor-farmer.

proprietorial (prəʊpraɪə'tɔərɪəl), *a.* [f. prec. + -AL[1]: cf. *dictatorial, senatorial*, etc.] Of or pertaining to a proprietor.

1851 DIXON *W. Penn* xxii. (1872) 195 Control.., financial, civil, proprietorial, and judicial. **1866** *Pall Mall G.* 7 June 2 [To] discharge the social and proprietorial obligation devolving upon them.

b. That is a proprietor; consisting of proprietors: = PROPRIETARY *a.* 2.

1866 *Lond. Rev.* 24 Nov. 568 'Stop, stop', exclaimed the proprietorial censor, 'that won't do'. **1904** *Spectator* 3 Sept. 314/1 Directed, not towards the removal of the old proprietorial class,..but towards facilitating their remaining in the country.

Hence **proprie'torially** *adv.*, as proprietor.

1864 *Daily Tel.* 8 June, Editorially and proprietorially connected with the *World* newspaper. **1901** *Westm. Gaz.* 7 June 10/2 Alderman H. was proprietorially connected with the *Dispatch*.

proprietorship (prəʊ'praɪətəʃɪp). [f. as prec. + -SHIP.]

1. The position or condition of a proprietor; ownership. (In earlier quots. in reference to the N. American colonies: see PROPRIETOR 1.)

1669 J. LOCKE *Draft Const. Carolina* §6 in 33 *Dep. Kpr. Rep.* 258 Those who are then lords proprietors shall not have power to alienate or make over their proprietorships. **1790** *Lunenburg* (Mass.) *Proprietors' Rec.* (1897) 304 An act..for the final Settlement of the Proprietorship of the Town of Lunenburg. **1817** COBBETT *Wks.* XXXII. 17 Mr. Hammond..offered to me the proprietorship of one of those papers as a gift. **1848** DICKENS *Dombey* v, With an air of joint proprietorship with Richards in the entertainment. **1866** ROGERS *Agric. & Prices* I. iii. 62 As a rule..whenever peasant proprietorship is prevalent..hired labour..is scarce and dear. **1886** *Act 49 & 50 Vict.* c. 33 §7 To prove the existence or proprietorship of the copyright of any work first produced in a foreign country.

2. A piece of land owned by a proprietor.

1837 J. E. MURRAY *Summer in Pyrenees* II. 135 Divided as the soil is into small proprietorships, each owner of an arpen of land possesses a horse.

pro'prietory, *sb.* and *a.* [erron. or var. f. PROPRIETARY, going with the anomalous PROPRIETOR.]

A. *sb.* †**1.** = PROPRIETARY A. 1, 4. *Obs.*

1643 PRYNNE *Sov. Power Parl.* App. 168 If the king be not the proprietorie of the Realme. **1687** A. LOVELL tr. *Thevenot's Trav.* III. 102 The King of Golconda..is proprietory of all the Lands in his Kingdom. **1764** *Answ. to Queries on Proprietary Govt. Maryland* 4 The Lord-proprietory (who is hereditary governor) or his lieutenant-governor.

2. = PROPRIETARY A. 5.

1802 *Hist. Europe* in *Ann. Reg.* 267/2 This correspondence gave great uneasiness to the proprietory. **1869** *Daily News* 30 July, It is in the neighbourhood of a rich proprietory and large towns.

B. *adj.* = PROPRIETARY B.

1633 SIR J. BURROUGHS *Sov. Brit. Seas* (1651) 105 By the common Law of the land the King is proprietory Lord of our seas. **1706** LUTTRELL *Brief Rel.* (1857) VI. 16 [A bill] for better regulation of charter and proprietory government in America. **1898** *Allbutt's Syst. Med.* V. 615 An exclusive diet of one or other of the proprietory preserved foods.

proprietous (prəʊ'praɪətəs), *a.* [f. PROPRIETY + -OUS.] Characterized by (extreme) propriety or punctilious behaviour. Also *Comb.* Hence **pro'prietously** *adv.*

1844 *Ainsworth's Mag.* VI. 228 An elderly person, whose proprietous grey silk dress..conveyed the idea of a distant relative. **1845** *Ibid.* VII. 498 The rows of canvass-covered proprietous-looking [bathing] machines. **1882** 'L. MALET' *Mrs. Lorimer* I. v. 120 My dear, I feel a little stifled when I think of you guarded by these proprietous and unimaginative dragons. *Ibid.* vi. 132 Mrs. Mainwaring had lost for a moment that proprietous self-command and calm dignity of demeanour, which..were certainly liable to keep most people at a very respectful distance from her. **1913** D. H. LAWRENCE *Sons & Lovers* viii. 181 He must see a girl home from the skating rink—quite proprietously—and so can't get home. **1974** R. B. PARKER *Godwulf MS* i. 9 The elevator that took me to the fourth floor was covered with obscene graffiti that some proprietous soul had tried to doctor into acceptability. **1979** *Verbatim* Autumn 1/1 In Marvin Pope's exhaustive scholarly study of *The Song of Songs*, the Bride's vivid description of her passion for the Bridegroom as 'my bowels were moved for him'—striking in its proprietous King James context (5:4)—is rendered 'my inwards seethed for him.'

proprietress (prəʊ'praɪətrɪs). [f. PROPRIETOR + -ESS[1]: cf. obs. F. *proprieteresse*.] A female proprietor.

1692 R. L'ESTRANGE *Fables* II. cccxxiii. 282 The Proprietress..Demanded Possession again, but the Other begg'd her Excuse. **1838** DICKENS *Nich. Nick.* xvi, With his eyes fixed on a very fat old lady in a mob-cap—evidently the proprietress of the establishment. **1875** MAINE *Hist. Inst.* xi. 334 When the proprietress dies, there is a special order of succession.

pro'prietrix. [f. as prec. after L. fem.] = prec.

1837 J. D. LANG *New S. Wales* II. 425 The convict Watt ..ingratiated himself into the favour of the proprietrix of 'The Sydney Gazette'. **1884** *N. Brit. Daily Mail* 5 Aug. 4/3 Law agent for the proprietrix of the island.

propriety (prəʊ'praɪətɪ), *sb.* Forms: 5–6 propriete, (-yete(e, 6 -ietee, -ietye, -yetie), 6–7 proprietie, 6– propriety. [ME. *propriete*, a. F. *propriété* (12th c. in Littré), ad. L. *proprietāt-em*: see PROPERTY.] The quality of being proper, or that which is proper (in various senses of the adj.).

†**1. a.** The fact of being owned by some one, or of being one's own, 'ownness'; the fact of owning something, right of possession or use; ownership, proprietorship: = PROPERTY *sb.* 1. *Obs.*

In quot. 1502 *fig.* in spiritual sense: cf. PROPRIETARY *sb.* 2.

1486 *Petition to Hen. VII* in *Materials Hen. VII* (Rolls) I. 297 An othre cope, with a cover gilt,..the propriete wherof rightfully belongith to oure..moder, the countesse of Richemond & Derby. **1502** ATKYNSON tr. *De Imitatione* III. xlii. 230 Stande thou..without all propryete, & thou shalt alway wyn. **1581–90** in Willis & Clark *Cambridge* (1886) II. 412 They..can challenge no more proprietie in that grownde, then may euery seuerall Colledge of that Vniuersitie. **1652–62** HEYLIN *Cosmogr.* IV. (1682) 47 The people..live like Beasts, without propriety so much as in their Wives or Children. **1671** FLAVEL *Fount. Life* iv. 9 When men give, they transfer Propriety to another. **1707** E. CHAMBERLAYNE *Pres. St. Eng.* III. iv. (ed. 22) 297 Every Freeman hath such a full and absolute Propriety in his Goods, That no Taxes..legally can be imposed upon them, without their own Consent. **1827** HALLAM *Const. Hist.* (1876) II. xi. 309 The clergy themselves had never expected that their estates would revert to them in full propriety.

†**b.** The fact of belonging or relating specially to a particular thing or person; peculiarity, particularity, specialty. *Obs.*

1625 BACON *Ess., Unity in Relig.* (Arb.) 425 The Doctor of the Gentiles [St. Paul] (the Propriety of whose Vocation, drew him to haue a speciall care of those without) saith [etc.]. *a* **1648** LD. HERBERT *Hen. VIII* (1683) 69 The Sweating Sickness (call'd for the propriety by which it seized on the English Nation chiefly *Sudor Anglicus*).

†**c.** *Path.* (Of a pain or disease.) The fact of belonging specially to, or originating in, the part affected: see quot. 1657, and cf. IDIOPATHY 2 a. *Obs.*

1615 CROOKE *Body of Man* 190 The stone of the Kidneyes is knowne or discerned from that of the bladder by The propriety of the paine, by the scituation, and by the dulnesse. **1655** CULPEPPER *Riverius* VII. i. 146 The Breath is hindered by divers Causes, either by sympathy or propriety of parts. The hinderance of breathing by propriety, called *Idiopathica*, comes from the Lungs distempered. **1657** *Physical Dict.* s.v., A pain by propriety is when the cause of the pain is in the part pained, as when the head-ach comes from the humors in the head it's called a pain by propriety; when it proceeds of vapors sent up from the stomach or any other part it's called head-ach by consent or sympathy.

2. †**a.** Something owned, a possession: = PROPERTY *sb.* 2. *Obs.* (exc. as in b).

1571 *Satir. Poems Reform.* xxvii. 70 How þai..yitt posseidis that peoples proprietie. **1661** FELTHAM *Resolves* II. xlvi. (ed. 8) 274 How can he have a good conscience..that.. takes away what is anothers just propriety? *a* **1667** JER. TAYLOR *Serm. Eph.* v. 32–33 Wks. 1831 I. 327 So are the proprieties of a wife to be disposed of by her lord. *a* **1711** KEN *Hymnarium* Poet. Wks. 1721 II. 76 'Tis thy Propriety, and not my own.

b. A piece of land owned by some one, a private possession or estate: = PROPERTY *sb.* 2 b. *Obs.* exc. in *Amer. Hist.*: cf. PROPRIETARY *sb.* 7.

1661 FELTHAM *Resolves* II. lxxxii. (ed. 8) 365 It is the Hedge..which hinders from breaking into other mens propriety. **1690** *Andros Tracts* II. 42 The Lands of Widdows and Orphans and other peoples proprieties. **1705** BEVERLEY *Virginia* I. §92 (1722) 65 The splitting the Colony into Proprieties, contrary to the original Charters. **1889** *Athenæum* 3 Aug. 157/1 The lately established propriety of Nova Scotia was to be ceded to that power [France]. **1894** *Nation* (N.Y.) 19 July 51/1 Early in 1774 he removed to Lenox, Mass., was at once elected clerk of that 'Propriety', and was sent as its delegate to the General Court of the Colony.

3. Proper or particular character; own nature, disposition, idiosyncrasy; essence, individuality; sometimes, proper state or condition. Cf. PROPERTY *sb.* 5. Now *rare.*

1456 SIR G. HAYE *Law Arms* (S.T.S.) 29 As sais the maister of proprieteis of bestis, A scorpioun is as a worm of the erde. **1483** CAXTON *G. de la Tour* F v, I shall telle yow thensample of the lyon and of his propryete. **1549** *Compl. Scot.* v. 32 To paynt ande discriue the origyne ande propriete of the varld. **1604** SHAKS. *Oth.* II. iii. 176 Silence that dreadfull Bell, it frights the Isle, From her propriety. **1643** MILTON *Divorce* II. ix. Wks. 1851 IV. 85 It holds a strange and lawlesse propriety from all other works of God under heaven. **1659** PEARSON *Creed* v. 511 We are presented with three Particulars: First, the Action itself, ..'he rose again'. Secondly, The verity, reality, and propriety of that Resurrection, 'he rose from the dead'. **1795** [see PROPRIUM 1 b]. **1876** MOZLEY *Univ. Serm.* vii. (1877) 156 This propriety, or characteristic in the individual, which he receives from a Divine source, is a sacred deposit with him.

†**4.** A quality or attribute; esp. an essential or distinctive quality; a characteristic, a peculiarity: = PROPERTY *sb.* 5. *Obs.*

1456 SIR G. HAYE *Law Arms* (S.T.S.) 63 He was bathe honest and honourable,..and full of all gude proprieteis. **1584** R. SCOT *Discov. Witchcr.* xv. xxxiii. (1886) 383 Salomon..had full and perfect knowledge of all their proprieties. **1610** HOLLAND *Camden's Brit.* (1637) 718 A secret propriety of this ground. **1613** PURCHAS *Pilgrimage* i. (1614) 5 All the proprieties of God are infinite as they are immanent in Himself. **1678** HOBBES *Decam.* viii. 101 To tell you the several proprieties of the Magnet. **1700** ASTRY tr. *Saavedra-Faxardo* I. 55 Impatience is as it were a Propriety of Power. **1868** BUSHNELL *Serm. Living Subj.* 13 Proprieties of the incarnation.

†**5. a.** The special character, or a special characteristic, of a language; peculiarity of diction, idiom. Often, with mixture of sense 6: Correctness or purity of diction. *Obs.*

a **1568** ASCHAM *Scholem.* II. (Arb.) 87 In..Cæs. Commentaries..is seene, the vnspotted proprietie of the Latin tong. **1587** GOLDING *De Mornay* viii. (1592) 108 The Punicke tongue was but a kinde of seuerall proprietie of the Hebrew. **1621** T. WILLIAMSON tr. *Goulart's Wise Vieillard* 5 A word, which according to the Idiom and propriety of the language wherein he spake, may be translated *liues.* **1690** LOCKE *Govt.* I. iv. §31 'Tis pity the Propriety of the Hebrew Tongue had not used *Fathers of Men*, instead of *Children of Men.* **1739** *Wks. Learned* I. 140 The neglect of acquainting our youth..with the Proprieties and Beauties of their Mother Tongue. **1746–78** (*title*) An Exmoor Scolding, in the Propriety and Decency of Exmoor Language.

†**b.** The proper, strict, or literal sense of a word; strictness of meaning, literalness. *Obs.*

1641 WILKINS *Math. Magick* II. i. (1648) 145 In its stricture and propriety, it is onely appliable unto fresh inventions. **1649** JER. TAYLOR *Gt. Exemp.* II. Disc. vi. 15 The word ἀπείθεια which in propriety of language signifies mis-persuasion. **1656** [J. SERGEANT] tr. *T. White's Peripat. Inst.* 378 God, therefore, cast..a sleep upon Adam: the Propriety is, and He made a sleep fall. **1678** CUDWORTH *Intell. Syst.* 451 If we add that the propriety of this word Jupiter, does not express a Divine, but only a Humane force.

6. Fitness, appropriateness, aptitude, suitability; appropriateness to the circumstances or conditions; conformity with requirement, rule, or principle; rightness, correctness, justness, accuracy. (Cf. PROPER *a.* 4, 9.)

1615 BRATHWAIT *Strappado* (1878) 69 Displaying resolution in thy eye Courtship in cloths, in speech propriety. **1659** HAMMOND *On Ps.* vii. 40 But that was in the businesse of Absalom,..to which this Psalm hath no propriety. **1729** BUTLER *Serm.* Pref., Wks. 1874 II. 8, I shall not..justify the propriety of preaching..Discourses so abstruse as some of these are. **1824** L. MURRAY *Eng. Gram.* (ed. 5) I. 429 Propriety of language is the selection of such words as the best usage has appropriated to those ideas, which we intend to express by them. **1849** MACAULAY *Hist. Eng.* ii. I. 223 They..appointed a committee to consider the propriety of impeaching Arlington. **1870** FREEMAN *Norm. Conq.* (ed. 2) II. App. T 609 In some manuscripts..the propriety of the title is formally disputed.

7. Conformity with good manners or polite usage; correctness of behaviour or morals; becomingness, decency. ***the proprieties***: the things that are considered proper; the details of conventionally correct or proper conduct. Also, ***to play propriety***, to ensure correct moral behaviour, act as a chaperone.

[**1782** MISS BURNEY *Cecilia* v. xiii, Such propriety of mind as can only result from the union of good sense with virtue.] **178.** BURNS *Addressed to Lady whom Author feared he had offended*, Propriety's cold cautious rules Warm fervour may o'erlook. **1799** HAN. MORE *Fem. Educ.* (ed. 4) I. 76 The decorums, the proprieties, the elegancies, and even the graces, as far as they are simple, pure, and honest, would follow as an almost inevitable consequence. **1836** T. HOOK *G. Gurney* II. v. 290 She talked of some elderly body, in the shape of an aunt, who was to accompany her, and play Propriety. **1856** EMERSON *Eng. Traits, Manners* (Bohn) II. 50 The keeping of the proprieties is as indispensable as clean linen. **1865** TROLLOPE *Belton Est.* xi. 118 Her taste for decency of demeanour and propriety of life. **1877** V. LUSH *Jrnl.* 13 Feb. (1975) 187, I invited a few of the Choir here after practice, with Mrs Scott and Mrs Lloyd to play propriety and we had a very jolly evening. **1925** I. SMITH *Marriage in Ceylon* 137 Angela..had felt it would not be 'the thing' to accept hospitality of the man who in a few days' time would be her husband without someone to 'play propriety'.

proprioceptor ('prəʊprɪəʊsɛptə(r)). *Physiol.* [f. L. *propri-us* own, PROPER + -O + RE)CEPTOR.] Any sensory structure which receives stimuli arising within the tissues (other, usually, than the viscera); *esp.* one concerned with the sense of position and movement of a part of the body. Cf. EXTEROCEPTOR, INTEROCEPTOR.

1906 [see EXTEROCEPTOR]. **1927** HALDANE & HUXLEY *Animal Biol.* i. 24 The receptor organs are those parts of the living organism which are specially sensitive to the changes going on around them. Some of them are affected by the changes going on inside the body in muscles and joints and in the organ of balance (proprioceptors), others by the changes taking place in the world outside (exteroceptors). **1938** *Jrnl. Exper. Biol.* XV. 112 The campaniform sensilla will act as proprioceptors for the palps. **1940** FRAENKEL & GUNN *Orientation of Animals* iv. 37 In the knee-jerk the stimulus is translated by the proprioceptors in the leg, goes to the central nervous system and is there, so to say, reflected back to the leg, where it is translated into effect or action. **1964** J. Z. YOUNG *Model of Brain* xv. 242 Proprioceptors are probably present [in octopus arms] but it is not clear how they could appropriately signal the position of the arms. **1974** D. & M. WEBSTER *Compar. Vertebr. Morphol.* x. 200 The most studied proprioceptor is the muscle spindle.

So **proprio'ception**, the reception of information by proprioceptors and its interpretation; **proprio'ceptive** *a.*; **proprio'ceptively** *adv.* (*rare*).

1906 C. S. SHERRINGTON *Integrative Action of Nervous Syst.* iv. 130 Since in this field the stimuli to the receptors are given by the organism itself, their field may be called the proprio-ceptive field. *Ibid.* ix. 349 The supposition that the organ [*sc.* the cerebellum] is the chief co-ordinative centre or rather group of centres of the reflex system of proprioception. **1927** HALDANE & HUXLEY *Animal Biol.* v. 123 Proprioceptive organs may affect the consciousness. Thus we can tell how much our knee is bent even with our eyes shut, owing to the joint-organs, or how great a weight we are holding, owing to the muscle-organs. **1958** S. H. BARTLEY *Princ. Perception* xiv. 315 Kinesthesis and the vestibular sense have been called proprioception, since they have something to do with end results originated by the activity of the body itself. **1961** L. F. BROSNAHAN *Sounds of Language* i. 15 Articulations which are similar..must require greater precision of execution..in order to keep the resulting speech sounds distinct, both proprioceptively and auditorily. **1968** *New Scientist* 7 Nov. 315/1 Proprioceptive information..describes such things as the tension in the muscles and the location and movement of the parts of the limb. **1977** *Lancet* 5 Nov. 977/1 He had..absent vibration sense, and very reduced proprioception in the lower limbs.

proprio-spinal ('prəʊprɪəʊ,spaɪnəl), *a. Anat.* Also as one word. [f. as prec. + SPINAL *a.*] Situated wholly within the spinal cord.

1904 C. S. SHERRINGTON in *Nature* 8 Sept. 461 (*caption*) Proprio-spinal neurones. *Ibid.* 463/1 We..arrive at the following reflex chain for the scratch reflex: (i.) The receptive neurone... (ii.) The long descending proprio-spinal neurone.., from the shoulder segment to the grey matter of leg segments. **1920** H. HEAD *Studies in Neurol.* II. III. 504 If these proprio-spinal paths have been destroyed, or their functions abolished, the mass-reflex may appear in its complete form even though some sensation and voluntary movement are still present below the level of the lesion. **1959** *Brain* LXXXII. 614 We have retained the name 'fasciculi proprii' for the fibres under review, as there is no suitable English equivalent. Sherrington's name 'proprio-spinal fibres'..might be suggested. But it seems to us that a name which includes the term 'spinal' is undesirable. **1974** *Exper. Brain Res.* XXI. 188 Our results show that long propriospinal fibres stimulated a few segments caudal to the cervical enlargement.

proprite, obs. form of PROPERTY.

‖**proprium** ('prəʊprɪəm). Pl. -ia. [L., neut. sing. of *proprius* PROPER; in sense 1 a rendering Gr. ἴδιον (Aristotle).]

1. *Logic.* **a.** = PROPERTY *sb.* 5 d.

1551 T. WILSON *Logike* (1580) 4 Of the fiue predicables, otherwise called the fiue common wordes, which are spoken of other... *Genus.* The generall worde. *Species.* The kinde, or speciall. *Differentia.* The difference. *Proprium.* The propertie. *Accidens.* The thing chauncing or cleauing to the substance. **1656** STANLEY *Hist. Philos.* VI. (1701) 247/1 *Proprium* is that which declareth, not what a thing is, but is in it only, and Reciprocal with it. **1885** DAVIDSON *Logic Definit.* 46 A logical operation which..grasps the essence of a thing (to the exclusion of its accidents and propria).

b. An attribute essentially belonging to something, a distinctive characteristic; essential nature, selfhood.

1795 tr. *Swedenborg's Chr. Relig.* §189. iv. (ed. 3) 220 Who-soever worshippeth Nature instead of God, or in Preference to God, and in Consequence of such Worship maketh himself, and his own *Proprium*, the Center and Fountain of his Thoughts. [*Note*] By *Proprium*, as here applied to Man, is meant his own Propriety, or all that he has of himself, when separated from Divine Influence. **1858** BUSHNELL *Nat. & Supernat.* ii. (1864) 57 What we call their character is the majestic proprium of their personality. **1863** H. JAMES *Subst. & Shadow* xv. 256 Religion has had but one legitimate spiritual aim, namely: the softening of the self-hood or *proprium* which man derives from nature.

†**2.** Something given to a person for his own; a perquisite. *Obs.*

a **1734** NORTH *Lives* (1826) I. 208 The allowing *propriums* to the attornies, in taxing of costs, was a very great abuse.

pro-proctor (,prəʊ'prɒktə(r)). [f. PRO-[1] 4 + PROCTOR[1].] orig. One who acted for the proctor of a university (see PROCTOR[1] 3); an officer under the control of the proctors, who assisted them in executing their duties of keeping order, etc. (sometimes specially appointed for the occasion); now, an assistant or deputy proctor in the universities.

1650 in Wood *Life & Times* (O.H.S.) I. 163 At a meeting of the Delegates..Mr. Hancock proproctor the last yeare did certifie the Delegates that one Keblewhite a citizen had served him with a writ out of the Common Pleas for false imprisonment. **1663** *Ibid.* 22 Sept. 492 The 24 masters of Art,..that were to be as pro-proctors and exercise procuratorial power over schollers. *Ibid.* 23 Sept., The 24 pro-proctors placed..the Doctors and Bachelors of Divinity next to Xt. Ch. gate, and the Masters on both sides almost up to the Bull Inne. **1721** AMHERST *Terræ Fil.* Pref. 20 One of the pro-proctors for the last and the present year. *a* **1884** M. PATTISON *Mem.* (1885) 229 For the proctorial year 1847 I had acted as proproctor to Green.

pro-provincial, pro-provost: see PRO-[1] 4.

propryete, -tie, propryte, etc., obs. ff. PROPRIETY *sb.*, PROPERTY.

props (prɒps), *sb. pl. Theatrical slang.* [Short for *properties.*]

1. a. Stage requisites: see PROPERTY 3.

1841 *Spirit of Times* 16 Oct. 396/2 There we subsisted by *spouting*, not Shakespeare, but our dresses and props. **1854** E. L. BLANCHARD *Diary* 22 Nov. in Scott & Howard *Life E. L. Blanchard* (1891) I. 125 Go to Drury; see props. **1865** *Slang Dict.*, *Props*, stage properties. **1883** *Referee* 6 May 3/2 At the Theatre Royal..the scenery and props were sold by auction. **1885** J. K. JEROME *On the Stage* 32 It was..the property room, the things therein being properties, or, more commonly 'props', so called, I believe, because they help to support the drama. *Ibid.* 46 Scenery and props were not being used at this, the first, rehearsal.

b. A familiar name for a property-man or the props department.

Quot. 1831 may be an example of PROP *sb.*[5]

1831 P. EGAN *Show Folks* 23 'Good Houses' now to make him right, The *Treasury* to swell: The Actors [*sic*] need—the *Props* delight—And '*All's well, that ends well!*' **1889** *New York Trib.* 14 July (Cent.), The property-man, or, as he is always called, props for short. **1902** PATTERSON & BATEMAN *By Stage Door* 192 While he was 'Props' he was discharged ..for not yelling 'fire!' at the right time. **1921** GALSWORTHY *Six Short Plays* 128, I want 'Props'. *Ibid.* (*stage-direction*) 'Props' goes out through the French windows. **1933** P. GODFREY *Back-Stage* iv. 48 No self-respecting 'Props' will spend a penny on new materials if odd scraps will serve. **1976** M. MAGUIRE *Scratchproof* ii. 23 What do you think of our tack-room interior? Have props done a good job?

c. as *sing.* a stage property.

1911 C. POLLOCK *Footlights* 257 By-play with small articles, rehearsed twenty times, is blundered over when the player finds the 'prop' actually in his hands. **1961** M. CATTO *Mister Moses* iii. 80 The stage had been set—it awaited the last theatrical prop. **1976** *Early Music* Oct. 394/1 Each tableau, step, gesture, prop and lighting-cue must arise from necessity and have its effect at once. **1978** *Listener* 23 Mar. 366/3 Ronnie Barker's face..is,..as with all true comedians, his best prop.

2. *transf.*

1898 A. M. BINSTEAD *Pink 'Un & Pelican* vi. 146 And when at last the day came for him to go, he 'collected his props', as he called getting his belongings together, most reluctantly. **1926** *Publishers' Weekly* 10 July 120/1 Woodard-Clarke's [window-display]..took a middle course between the painted background route and the 'props' of nature. The clear blue sky was conveyed by blue cloth of chiffon-like texture. **1948** M. GILBERT *They never looked Inside* iii. 35 Have a cigarette? They are part of the office props. **1976** S. BARSTOW *Right True End* III. xiv. 224 A shot of me standing on a stone pier beside a whelk-stall, holding a huge crab by one claw. It must have been dead, lent to me as a prop by some kindly stall-holder.

3. *attrib.* and *Comb.* **a.** ***props department, girl, man***; **props room** = *property room* s.v. PROPERTY *sb.* 8 b. **b.** Formed with the *sing.*, as ***prop boy, girl, man***; **prop basket** = PROPERTY BOX 2; **prop table** (see quot. 1964); **prop wagon,** a property wagon (see quot.).

1952 GRANVILLE *Dict. Theatr. Terms* 144 It is the traditional boast of an old actor that he was born in a *prop basket* in the prompt corner. **1935** *Motion Picture* Nov. 38 Colman, who was off in a corner talking with a prop boy, heard her. **1960** K. A. OMMANNEY *Stage & School* v. xv. 413 All movable articles are stored in the props department. **1970** R. LEACH *Theatre for Youth* I. v. 43 Masks properly belong to the props department. **1964** E. CRAMPTON *Handbk. Theatre* 260 These tables are the direct responsibility of the prop-girl. **1977** S. BRETT *Star Trap* iii. 31 There's always the stage staff... Nothing like a warm little props girl to comfort a chap. **1942** BERREY & VAN DEN BARK *Amer. Thes. Slang* §605/12 *Property man*,..prop man. **1951** in H. DOWNS *Theatre & Stage* II. 818/2, I once knew a 'props' man who was..a marvel. **1971** *Esquire* July 88/3 We were watching the prop men lug the elephant tubs and the chimp- and lion-act furniture. **1978** M. PUZO *Fools Die* xxviii. 323 Script-girls, secretaries, studio accountants, cameramen, propmen, the technical crews, the actors and actresses, the directors and even the producers. **1957** Props room [see BALLOON *sb.*[1] 6 c]. **1977** C. WOOD *James Bond* xii. 103 This place..was like the props room of a folded theatrical company. **1939** BURRIS-MEYER & COLE *Scenery for Theatre* xiii. 390 Prop table, left. **1964** E. CRAMPTON *Handbk. Theatre* 260 *Prop tables*, tables set in the wings..for properties to be taken on and brought off-stage during a performance. **1927** *Hollis St. Theatre Progr.* (Boston) 19 Sept. Gloss., *Prop wagon*, wagon for transporting paraphernalia and equipment used on carnival.

props, gambling game with shells: see PROP *sb.*[4]

propternuptial (,prɒptə'nʌpʃəl), *a. Rom. Law.* [f. L. phr. *propter nupti-ās* on account of marriage + -AL[1].] That is made or given on account of marriage.

1875 POSTE *Gaius* I. (ed. 2) 116 The party who made a causeless repudium,.. was punished by pecuniary losses in respect of dos and propternuptial donations.

‖**propterygium** (prɒptəˈrɪdʒɪəm). *Ichthyol.* [mod.L., f. PRO-[2] + PTERYGIUM.] The anterior cartilaginous portion of the fin in elasmobranch fishes. Hence **propteˈrygial** *a.*, of or pertaining to the propterygium.

1878 BELL *Gegenbaur's Comp. Anat.* 478 The propterygium and the mesopterygium are evidently derived from rays which still remain attached to the shoulder-girdle. **1889** NICHOLSON & LYDEKKER *Palæont.* II. 920 In the pelvic fin of the Selachians the mesopterygium is absent, and the propterygium more or less rudimentary. **1890** *Cent. Dict.* s.v. *Pterygium*, Bearing.. the propterygial, mesopterygial, and metapterygial basalia and radialia.

‖**proptosis** (prɒpˈtəʊsɪs). *Path.* [late L. *proptōsis*, a. Gr. *πρόπτωσις* a falling forward, prolapse, f. *προπίπτειν* to fall forwards.] Prolapse or protrusion of some bodily part, esp. of the eye.

1676 J. COOKE *Marrow Chirurg.* 713 *Staphyloma*... In its progress it receives several Names, as when the Uvea sticks out above the Cornea: 'tis called *Proptosis*. **1782** E. FORD in *Med. Commun.* I. 95 [She] was brought to me.. with a *Proptosis* of the left eye. **1876** *Trans. Clinical Soc.* IX. 17 During the examination one of the eyes got dislocated forwards, and had to be replaced... The proptosis is probably accounted for by shallowness of the orbits.

So **propˈtosed** *ppl. a.*, prolapsed, protruded.

1890 *Lancet* 1 Feb. 246/2 A small portion of the bladder wall was proptosed through the deficient neck. **1900** *Ibid.* 12 May 1362/2 An elderly woman whose Right Eye on Stooping became Proptosed.

†**proˈpudious**, *a.* *Obs. rare.* [f. L. *prŏpudiōsus* shameful, infamous, f. *prŏpudi-um* a shameful action, f. *prō*, PRO-[1] + *pud-ēre* to make ashamed: see -OUS.] Shameful, infamous, disgraceful.

1629 MAXWELL tr. *Herodian* (1635) 111 Calling upon Niger.. to vindicate the Roman State, and hasten to free them from that propudious Governour. **1678** PHILLIPS, *Propudious*, (Lat.) shameful, filthy, dishonest.

†**propugn** (prəʊˈpjuːn), *v.* *Obs.* [ad. L. *prōpugn-āre* to go forth to fight; to fight for, defend, f. *prō*, PRO-[1] + *pugn-āre* to fight.] *trans.* To contend for; to defend, maintain, champion, vindicate (an opinion, doctrine, or the like). Hence †**proˈpugning** *vbl. sb.* and *ppl. a.*

c **1555** HARPSFIELD *Divorce Hen. VIII* (Camden) 48 To stand stiffly.. against our adversaries and to propugne our side. **1629** BURTON *Truth's Triumph* 218 Scriptures and Fathers were.. so strongly propugned and maintained by Luther. **1633** PRYNNE *Histriomastix* 722 To give a satisfactory answer to all their chiefe Play-propugning Objections. *a* **1660** HAMMOND (J.), For propugning of our faith. **1676** TOWERSON *Decalogue* 95 Divinations which they .. were highly concern'd to propugn as true.

†**proˈpugnacle.** *Obs.* [a. obs. F. *propugnacle* (14th c. in Godef.), ad. L. *prōpugnācul-um* a defence, bulwark, f. *prōpugn-āre*: see prec.] A bulwark, rampart; also *fig.* a defence, protection.

1550 J. COKE *Eng. & Fr. Heralds* §219 (1877) 119 A great strength, propugnacle and bulwarke for the noble realme of Englande. **1612** R. SHELDON *Serm. St. Martin's* 61 His propugnacle and defence of Christian religion which no Pontifician durst euer yet attempt to confute. **1657** HOWELL *Londinop.* 48 The Tower of London, it being the prime Fortresse and propugnacle of the City.

Hence **proˈpugnacled** *a.* *nonce-wd.*, having ramparts, battlemented.

1875 BLACKMORE *Alice L.* III. xxvii. 341 The smallest of them [opals] is larger and finer than that.. which is called 'Troy burning', from the propugnacled flash of its movement.

‖**propugˈnaculum.** [L.] = PROPUGNACLE.

1773 BOSWELL *Jrnl. Tour Hebr.* 10 Sept. (1785) 198 Before it the ocean roars, being dashed against monstrous broken rocks; grand and aweful *propugnacula*. **1864** LOWELL *Fireside Trav.* 235 No elastic propugnaculum had been interposed between the body and the axle, so that we sat, as it were, on paving-stones. **1878** *Encycl. Brit.* VI. 158/2 The Roman colonies were.. valuable as *propugnacula* of the state.

†**proˈpugnate**, *v.* *Obs. rare.* [f. L. *prōpugnāt-*, ppl. stem of *prōpugn-āre*: see PROPUGN.] *trans.* = PROPUGN. Hence †**propugnating** *vbl. sb.*

1657 TOMLINSON *Renou's Disp.* 144 If they equally conduce to the propugnating of one affection, and roborating one part.

†**propugˈnation.** *Obs.* [ad. L. *prōpugnātiōn-em*, n. of action f. *prōpugn-āre*: see PROPUGN.] Defence, protection, vindication.

1586 FERNE *Blaz. Gentrie* II. 62 Signifiyng.. that this Scottish Lyon depended wholly upon the propugnation and defence of french lilies. **1606** SHAKS. *Tr. & Cr.* II. ii. 136. **1647** HUDSON *Div. Right Govt.* II. vi. 113 Arguments alledged for the propugnation thereof.

propugnator (ˈprəʊpəgneɪtə(r)). [ad. L. *prōpugnātōr-em*, agent-n. f. *prōpugn-āre*: see PROPUGN. Cf. obs. F. *propugnateur* (1552 in Godef.).] One who champions; a defender, champion.

c **1450** *Mirour Saluacioun* 1283 Sho offrid a son to be for the Jewes propugnatoure, Marie hire son to be of alle this werld protectoure. **1549** *Compl. Scot.* Ep. Ded. 4 Of them that hes been propungnatours for the libertee of ther cuntre. **1648** CHARLES I *Gracious Mess. Peace* 73 The erectors and propugnators of the Presbyterian Discipline in Scotland. **1792** BURKE *Corr.* (1844) IV. 42 One of my father's earliest and most able propugnators. **1895** RAMSAY in Mary R. L. Bryce *Mem. Prof. Veitch* (1896) 136 The sturdy, uncompromising propugnator of any question which he took up.

So †**proˈpugnatrice** *Obs.* [prob. a. OF. fem. of *propugnateur*], a female champion or defender.

c **1450** *Mirour Saluacioun* 3254 Oure swete ladye And als our propugnatrice ouercome the feende oure enemy.

propugner (prəʊˈpjuːnə(r)). Now *rare* or *Obs.* [f. PROPUGN *v.* + -ER[1].] A defender, a champion; = PROPUGNATOR.

1597 J. KING *On Jonas* (1618) 570 the daily exclamations of the Donatists in Africke against the Orthodoxe.. was, that they were traitours against the holy books, and themselues the propugners of them. **1691** W. NICHOLLS *Answ. Naked Gospel* 96 These were the chief Propugners of this Heresie in the Primitive times. **1841** GALLENGA *Italy* II. v. i. 306 Dante found numberless propugners and disciples.

†**propulˈsation.** *Obs.* [ad. L. *prōpulsātiōn-em*, n. of action f. *prōpulsāre*: see PROPULSE. So obs. F. *propulsation* (Cotgr.).]

1. A driving forth; = PROPULSION 1. *rare*$^{-1}$.

1578 BANISTER *Hist. Man* IV. 56 As touchyng.. propulsation of the byrth in women, nature receiueth by them [transverse muscles] a large benefite.

2. A driving away; repelling.

1610 GUILLIM *Heraldry* IV. xiv. (1611) 225 The finalle end for which militarie profession is instituted viz. propulsation or reuenge of wrong. **1649** BP. HALL *Cases Consc.* III. viii. (1654) 244 The just cause of war is the propulsation of publique injuries. **1690** NORRIS *Beatitudes* (1694) I. 73 Two Enquiries offer themselves... One is, concerning the Propulsation or Repelling of Injuries; the other is, concerning the Revenging of Injuries already done.

proˈpulsatory, *a.* *rare*$^{-1}$. [f. L. *prōpulsātor*, agent-n. f. *prōpulsāre*: see next and -ORY[2].] = PROPULSIVE *a.* 2.

1842 YOUATT *Dog* ii. (1845) 34 It is by the propulsatory efforts of the muscles of the loins and thighs that the race is won.

†**proˈpulse**, *v.* *Obs.* [ad. L. *prōpuls-āre*, frequent. of *prōpellĕre* to PROPEL.] *trans.* To drive off, chase away, repel. Hence †**proˈpulsing** *vbl. sb.*

a **1548** HALL *Chron., Hen. VII* 19 By which craftie ymagened inuencion they might eyther cloke or propulse from them all suspicion. **1574** NEWTON *Health Mag.* 10 The same il humours and fumes are propulsed and dispersed and the brayne is made sincere, stronge and healthfull. **1668** H. MORE *Div. Dial.* IV. xxxvii. (1713) 396 Those Reformed Churches that can do that right to themselves by propulsing their Enemies.

propulsion (prəʊˈpʌlʃən). [a. F. *propulsion* (1642 in Hatz.-Darm.) or f. L. type **prōpulsiōn-em*, n. of action f. *prōpellĕre* to PROPEL.]

†**1.** The action of driving forth or away; expulsion, repulsion. *Obs.*

1611 FLORIO, *Propulsione*, a repelling,.. a propulsion. **1626** BACON *Sylva* §715 In joy it worketh it diversely; viz. by propulsion of the moisture, when the spirits dilate, and occupy more room. **1756** C. LUCAS *Ess. Waters* I. 210 Warm bathing.. promotes the propulsion of noxious matters.

2. a. The action of driving or pushing forward or onward; the condition of being impelled onward; also, propulsive force or effort.

1799 KIRWAN *Geol. Ess.* 434 The materials.. are.. unceasingly carried forwards by the circulation and propulsion of water into the unfathomable regions of the sea. **1807** J. E. SMITH *Phys. Bot.* 59 To conclude this subject of the propulsion of the sap. **1849** MACAULAY *Hist. Eng.* iii. I. 372 He had succeeded in constructing a rude steam engine,.. which he pronounced to be an admirable and most forcible instrument of propulsion.

b. *fig.* Impelling influence; impulse.

1800 LAMB *Lett., to Manning* 1 Mar., I set to, with an unconquerable propulsion to write, with a lamentable want of what to write. **1846** WHITTIER *Reformer* xxiv, God works in all things; all obey His first propulsion from the night. **1876** LOWELL *Among my Bks.* Ser. II. 202 The constant propulsion of an unbending will.

3. *attrib.*, as ***propulsion-jet, -system***; **propulsion gun**, a hand-held device that an astronaut can cause to eject a jet of compressed gas so as to propel him in space.

1958 C. C. ADAMS *Space Flight* viii. 196 Auxiliaries. These include taxis and propulsion 'guns' for individual men in space suits, or reaction power packages attached like outboard motors to large objects. **1965** *Life* 18 June 26/2 White himself used a camera attached to his propulsion gun, and McDivitt operated another at his window inside. **1935** BALMER & WYLIE *After Worlds Collide* i. 14 The earth around the huge metal cylinder had been melted by the blasts of its atomic propulsion-jets. **1961** *Amer. Speech* XXXVI. 170 In the years after 1919, he [*sc.* Robert Esnault-Pelterie] had taken the initiative in stimulating studies on propulsion systems for interplanetary travel. **1966** *Electronics* 14 Nov. 16/3 In addition, four panel discussions will bring together the nation's top men in the fields of space policy and launch and propulsion systems.

†**proˈpulsity.** *Obs. rare*$^{-1}$. [f. as next + -ITY.] Propulsive quality; propulsion.

1607 J. DAVIES *Summa Totalis* (Grosart) 10/1 Eternity.. was e're Time had roome To stirre it selfe, by Heau'ns propulsity.

propulsive (prəʊˈpʌlsɪv), *a.* (*sb.*) [f. L. *prōpuls-*, ppl. stem of *prōpellĕre* to PROPEL + -IVE.]

†**1.** Having the power, quality, or tendency to drive off or away; expulsive. *Obs. rare.*

1648 *Regall Apol.* 23 London-Treacle is of a temperate nature, and propulsive of Venome from the Heart. **1650** BULWER *Anthropomet.* 193 Children.. having then no further need for that propulsive cause.

2. Having the quality of propelling, or the tendency to propel; that drives or urges forward or onward.

1758 BATTIE *Madness* v. 30 The propulsive action of the heart. **1874** CARPENTER *Ment. Phys.* I. ii. §30 (1879) 30 The propulsive movement of the foot in walking. **1893** FAIRBAIRN *Christ in Mod. Theol.* I. II. I. vi. 227 An immanent, yet ever-active, impulsive and propulsive being maintaining his society.

b. *sb.* A propulsive agent or principle.

1834 *Tait's Mag.* I. 38 Misery, fun, folly, fame, honour,.. and all the host of propulsives, which to name even would be to fill divers pages.

propulsor (prəˈpʌlsə(r)). *Aeronaut.* [f. L. *prōpuls-*, ppl. stem of *prōpellĕre* to PROPEL, + -OR.] A propeller mounted in a short duct or cylinder which can usually be swivelled to vary the direction of thrust, e.g. on an airship.

1975 *SAE Preprint No. 750534* in *Engin. Index Ann.* (1976) LXXIV. 180/3 The paper reiterates the case for the Ducted Propulsor, the idea of which was introduced some time ago. **1977** *Phoenix* (Airship Assoc.) Dec. 9/2 The propulsion system is also unique, combining vectored thrust .. with ducted propulsors (giving increased thrust with reduced noise and size). **1979** *Flight Internat.* CXV. 543/2 The ducted propulsors are made by Vickers-Slingsby to Aerospace Developments' own design. **1983** *Airship* Sept. 5/2 The two engines were again started, following a forward tilt of the ducted propulsors to flood the gearboxes with oil.

proˈpulsory, *a.* *rare.* [f. as PROPULSIVE *a.* (*sb.*) + -ORY[2].] †**a.** = PROPULSIVE *a.* 1 (*obs.*). **b.** = PROPULSIVE *a.* 2; propelling.

1656 BLOUNT *Glossogr.*, *Propulsory*, that serves to put away or drive back. **1805** KNOX & JEBB *Corr.* I. 208, I had reasons propulsory for every one of them; and reasons attractive, for three out of the four.

propupa, propygidium: see PRO-[2] 1, 2.

propur(e, -te(e, -ty, obs. ff. PROPER, -TY.

propyl (ˈprəʊpaɪl, -ɪl). *Chem.* [f. PROP(IONIC + -YL: so called as being the radical of propionic acid; cf. *propane, propene*, etc.] Either of two isomeric radicals, $CH_3{\cdot}CH_2{\cdot}CH_2-$ (***1-propyl, primary*** or ***normal propyl***) and $(CH_3)_2CH-$ (***2-propyl, secondary propyl*** or ***isopropyl***); sometimes *spec.* the normal form. Chiefly *attrib.* = PROPYLIC, as ***propyl alcohol, aldehyde, bromide, hydride, nitrate, nitrite***; ***propyl series***, etc.

Of *propyl alcohol*, C_3H_7OH, there are two isomeric forms, ***normal propyl alcohol*** $CH_3.CH_2.CH_2OH$, and ***iso-*** (or ***pseudo-***) ***propyl*** or ***secondary propyl alcohol*** $CH_3.HCOH.CH_3$. So with other propyl derivatives.

1850 *Phil. Trans. R. Soc.* CXL. 127 Substances of the formula $C_{18}H_{13}N$ will also be obtained.. by fixing upon aniline the radical (propyl) belonging to the missing alcohol of propionic acid* (metacetic acid). [*Note*] *A more appropriate name for metacetic acid, proposed by Dumas, Malaguti and Leblanc.., as it is the *first* acid of the series $C_nH_nO_4$ that exhibits the character of a *fatty* acid. **1859** *Fownes' Man. Chem.* 411 Propylic alcohol, or hydrated oxide of propyl. **1866** ROSCOE *Elem. Chem.* 241 The propyl compounds.. closely resemble the foregoing ethyl series of bodies. Propyl alcohol, when oxidized, yields propionic acid. **1873** WATTS *Fownes' Chem.* (ed. 11) 594 Propyl alcohol was discovered by Chancel in 1853, in the fusel-oil of the residues left in the distillation of brandy from wine. **1873** J. COOKE *Chem.* (1875) 313 Propyl hydride [= Propane] is the third in a series of homologous compounds. **1887** MOORE & AVELING tr. *Marx's Capital* I. i. 18 Butyric acid is a different substance from propyl formate. Yet both are made up of the same chemical substances, carbon (C), hydrogen (H), and oxygen (O), and that, too, in like proportions—namely, $C_4H_8O_2$. **1950** *Thorpe's Dict. Appl. Chem.* (ed. 4) X. 223/1 *n*-Propyl radical is formed by exposing the vapour of di-*n*-propyl ketone to ultra-violet light at 2 mm. pressure. **1951** I. L. FINAR *Org. Chem.* I. viii. 122 All aldehydes can be made to undergo the Cannizaro reaction by treatment with aluminium ethoxide. Under these conditions the acid and alcohol are combined as the ester,.. *e.g.*.. propionaldehyde gives propyl propionate.

Hence ˌ**propyl-aˈcetic** *a.* = VALERIC; thence ***propyl-acetate***; ˌ**propyl-aˈcetylene** = *pentinene* (see PENTANE). ˈ**propylaˌmine**, an amine of propyl, as C_3H_9N, a bright, colourless, highly refracting, very mobile liquid, having a peculiar, strongly ammoniacal odour. ˈ**propylate**, a salt of propylic acid. ˌ**propyl-ˈbenzene** = CUMENE. ˌ**propylthioˈuracil**, any propyl derivative of a thiouracil; *spec.* 6-*n*-propyl-2-thiouracil, $C_7H_{10}N_2OS$, an antithyroid substance used to combat thyrotoxicosis.

1860 in *N. Syd. Soc. Year-Bk. Med.* 414 By adding very cautiously hydrate of lime the *propylamine is obtained.

1868 WATTS *Dict. Chem.* V. 891 Sulphate of propylamine is crystalline and deliquescent. **1880** *Athenæum* 27 Nov. 713/1 The authors..have thus prepared aluminic methylate, ethylate, *propylate. **1873** WATTS *Fownes' Chem.* (ed. 11) 767 *Propyl-benzene is a liquid which boils at 157°. **1945** *Jrnl. Clin. Endocrinol.* V. 424/1 The compounds 6-ethylthiouracil and 6-*n*-*propylthiouracil are among a group which are approximately ten times as active as thiouracil when tested in rats. *Ibid.* 424/2 It seemed fitting to test the effectiveness of ethylthiouracil and propylthiouracil in human beings suffering from hyperthyroidism. **1961** *Lancet* 23 Sept. 688/2 On 2 of these patients there was subsequent difficulty in management with a lack of the usual responsiveness to propylthiouracil. **1975** B. CATZ *Thyroid Case Stud.* 13 The dose of propylthiouracil taken daily was 600 mg.

propyla, pl. of PROPYLON.

‖**propylæum** (prɒpɪ'liːəm). Pl. **propylæa.** [L., ad. Gr. προπύλαιον, usually in pl. -αια, sb. use of neuter of προπύλαιος adj. 'before the gate', f. πρό, PRO-[2] + πύλη a gate: see PROPYLON.] The entrance to a temple or other sacred enclosure, esp. when of architectural importance; *spec.* the entrance to the Acropolis at Athens. Hence, A gateway, porch, or vestibule.

1706 PHILLIPS, *Propylæum*, (in *Architect.*) the Porch of a Temple or great Hall; a Gate-House. **1745** POCOCKE *Descr. East* II. II. III. x. 161 The propylæum was probably about the third gate, which was built at a great expence. **1849** FREEMAN *Archit.* iv. 72 These propylaea lead into a large open court. **1890** J. MARTINEAU *Seat Auth. in Relig.* I. iii. 92 This invulnerable Stoic..lingers still at the propylaeum of the temple of Duty.

b. *fig.* An introduction; *pl.* prolegomena.

1727–41 CHAMBERS *Cycl.* s.v., Hence Propylæum is also used figuratively in matters of learning, for an introduction, apparatus, or prodromus to some greater work. **1893** *Nation* 16 Feb. 128/1 The magnificent propylaea, metaphysical, psychological, historical, through which, in chapter after chapter, he advances to the sacred precincts of his particular themes.

propylene ('prəʊpɪliːn). *Chem.* [f. PROPYL + -ENE.]

1. The olefine of the tricarbon or propyl series, C_3H_6, a colourless gas; called also *propene* and *tritylene.*

1850 J. W. REYNOLDS in *Jrnl. Chem. Soc.* III. 114 It is this hydrocarbon..to which I propose to give the name of Propylene. **1850** DAUBENY *Atom. The.* (ed. 2) 489 *note*, The discovery by Captain Reynolds of another homologue of olefiant gas, namely propylene. *c* **1865** LETHEBY in *Orr's Circ. Sc.* I. 116/1 *Propylene*.., or the super-olefiant gas of Dalton and Henry.

2. Used *attrib.* or in *Comb.* in the names of derivatives: **propylene glycol**, either of two isomeric liquids, $CH_2OH{\cdot}CHOH{\cdot}CH_3$ and $CH_2OH{\cdot}CH_2{\cdot}CH_2OH$; *spec.* the 1,2-glycol (the former), which has a wide variety of uses, chiefly as a solvent or carrier, as a constituent of antifreeze, and in the food and perfume industries; **propylene imine** (also ,**propylen(e)-'imine**) [ad. G. *propylenimin* (Gabriel & Ohle 1917, in *Ber. d. Deut. Chem. Ges.* L. 815)], a synthetic, colourless, highly inflammable liquid, $CH_3{\cdot}\underline{CH{\cdot}CH_2{\cdot}NH}$, which is widely used industrially, freq. in polymerized form and esp. as a binding agent with dyes and adhesives, and in the manufacture of plastics, paper, etc.

1885 MORLEY & GREEN in *Jrnl. Chem. Soc.* XLVII. 132 From the aqueous portion of the distillate 140 grams of propylene glycol (boiling at 185–195°) can be obtained by fractional distillation. **1926** *Jrnl. Biol. Chem.* LXVIII. 416 It was..desired to convert propylene glycol into β-hydroxybutyric acid by a set of reactions which would not involve carbon atom (2). **1951** I. L. FINAR *Org. Chem.* I. xvii. 329 Lactic acid..may be prepared: (i) By oxidising propylene glycol with dilute nitric acid. **1966** *Kirk-Othmer Encycl. Chem. Technol.* (ed. 2) X. 649, 1,2-Propylene glycol, $CH_3CHOHCH_2OH$, is a colorless and odorless liquid with a slightly sweet taste. **1917** *Jrnl. Chem. Soc.* CXII. I. 564 β-Bromopropylamine and β-bromo*iso*propylamine..both yield β-bromo*iso*propylamine, this result being explicable by the intermediate compound being propylenimine. **1944** *Jrnl. Org. Chem.* IX. 133 Propylenimine was prepared from 2-amino-1-propanol. **1966** *Kirk-Othmer Encycl. Chem. Technol.* (ed. 2) XI. 527 Ethylenimine and propylenimine are colorless mobile liquids with a strong ammoniacal odor. **1971** *Nature* 16 Apr. 460/2 Propylene imine is an important chemical intermediate with a variety of applications in the production of polymers, coatings, adhesives, textiles and paper finishes.

propylic (prəʊ'pɪlɪk), *a. Chem.* [f. as prec. + -IC.] Of or belonging to propyl, containing propyl, as ***propylic*** (or propyl) ***alcohol***, $C_3H_7.OH$.

1850 J. W. REYNOLDS in *Jrnl. Chem. Soc.* III. 114 The corresponding alcohol..still unknown, for which the appellation Propylic alcohol has been suggested by Dr. Hofmann. **1857** MILLER *Elem. Chem.* III. 126 Tritylic (or propylic) Alcohol. **1897** *Allbutt's Syst. Med.* II. 843 Other members of the alcoholic series—amylic, butylic, and propylic alcohol..may exert a decidedly toxic action.

propylidene (prəʊ'pɪl-, prəʊ'paɪlɪdiːn). *Chem.* [ad. F. *propylidène* (E. Reboul 1876, in *Compt. Rend.* LXXXII. 30): see PROPYL and -IDENE.] The bivalent radical $CH_3CH_2CH{=}$; usu. *attrib.*, esp. in names of derivatives of this.

1876 *Jrnl. Chem. Soc.* XXIX. I. 894 Propionic aldehyde is treated with phosphoric chloride, and forms a propylidene dichloride homolog[o]us with ethylidene dichloride; its formula is $CH_3-CH_2-CHCl_2$, and it boils at 85°–87°. **1903** A. J. WALKER tr. *Holleman's Text-Bk. Org. Chem.* I. 146 Propylene chloride, $C_3H_6Cl_2$,..is not identical with the reaction-product obtained by treating acetone with phosphorus pentachloride..nor with that from propionaldehyde, $CH_3{\cdot}CH_2{\cdot}CHCl_2$ (propylidene chloride). **1951** I. L. FINAR *Org. Chem.* I. iv. 49 General methods of preparation of the olefins... By the action of zinc dust on methanolic solutions of *gem*-dihalogen derivatives of the paraffins.., *e.g.*, propylene from propylidene bromide. **1976** *Chem. Physics Lett.* XXXVII. 220/2 The barrier to conversion of propylidene to propylene is greater than in C_2H_4.

propylite ('prɒpɪlaɪt). *Lithol.* [f. Gr. πρόπυλ-ον (see PROPYLON) + -ITE[1]. So named by Richthofen 1867 as opening the Tertiary volcanic epoch.] A volcanic rock occurring in and considered to be characteristic of various silver-mining regions; also called *greenstone trachyte.*

Believed to be a product of the metamorphism which accompanied the formation of the metalliferous deposits.

1867 RICHTHOFEN in *Mem. Calif. Acad. Sci.* I. II. Propylite. **1877** RAYMOND *Statist. Mines* 167 Propylite. **1879** RUTLEY *Stud. Rocks* xii. 237 Propylites also occur in Transylvania and Hungary. **1889** *Q. Jrnl. Geol. Soc.* XLV. 201, I hope shortly to be able to describe some of the chief types of these rocks,..their altered forms (the 'propylites'), and their Plutonic representatives (diorites and quartz-diorites).

Hence **propy'litic** *a.*, pertaining to propylite.

1889 *Quart. Jrnl. Geol. Soc.* XLV. 179 These rocks.. exhibiting interesting examples of the so-called propylitic modification.

propylitization (,prɒpɪlɪtaɪ'zeɪʃən). *Petrol.* [f. PROPYLIT(E + -IZATION.] The hydrothermal alteration of an igneous rock to propylite.

1903 A. GEIKIE *Text-bk. Geol.* (ed. 4) II. 812 The solutions..in their progress..induce chemical and mineralogical changes in the surrounding rocks which thus undergo various transformations, being sometimes weakened by the removal of certain constituents, as in propylitisation and kaolinisation. **1965** G. V. WILLIAMS *Econ. Geol. N.Z.* viii. 87/1 The mineralization is a typical Tertiary andesitic propylitization of which there is evidence from Te Puke..in the south to Great Barrier Island in the north. *Ibid.*, They found..that zones of intense propylitization (containing known gold-bearing veins) are detectable electrically.

‖**propylon** ('prɒpɪlɒn). Pl. **-pylons**, or in Gr. form **-pyla** (**-pula**). [L., a. Gr. πρόπυλον, f. πρό, PRO-[2] + πύλη gate.] = PROPYLÆUM. Also *transf.*

1831 M. RUSSELL *Egypt* vi. (1832) 257 Between these obelisks and the propylon are two colossal statues. **1841** *Penny Cycl.* XIX. 152/2 Many of them [Pyramids of Nubia] have propyla attached to one side, as if forming the entrance to the building. **1865** FERGUSSON *Hist. Archit.* I. I. iv. 113 The cells of the temple have been excavated from the rock, but their courts and propylons are structural buildings added in front. **1875** BROWNING *Aristoph. Apol.* 4103 O hail, my palace, my hearth's propula! **1880** *Academy* 11 Dec. 418/3 Evisa..looks down between two huge propylons of red rock to the blue expanse of sea.

propyn(e, variants of PROPINE *Obs.*

propyne ('prəʊpaɪn). *Chem.* [f. PROP(ANE + -YNE.] A gaseous, unsaturated hydrocarbon, $CH_3-C{:}CH$, which resembles acetylene, from which it is formally derived by replacing a hydrogen atom by methyl; allylene.

1931 *Jrnl. Chem. Soc.* 1610 The names of hydrocarbons containing the triple linking will end in *yne*, *diyne*, etc... Examples: Propyne, heptyne. **1935** *Jrnl. Amer. Chem. Soc.* LVII. 1089/2 The gaseous product of the reaction, propyne, was not determined quantitatively, but was identified through the fact that it formed a silver salt with ammoniacal silver nitrate solution. **1969** M. JULIA in H. G. Viehe *Chem. of Acetylenes* v. 341 Acetylene itself with photolyzed diazomethane..gave propyne and allene. **1975** GUTSCHE & PASTO *Fund. Org. Chem.* viii. 208 Treatment of propyne with water (in the presence of mercuric ion..) yields 2-propenol, which immediately rearranges to..acetone.

propyr(e, -yrte(e, obs. ff. PROPER, PROPERTY.

‖**proquæstor** (prəʊ'kwiːstə(r)). *Rom. Antiq.* [Late L. *prōquæstor* (Gloss. Cyril., Gl. Philox.) for earlier *prō quæstōre* (one acting) on behalf of a quæstor.] One acting in place of or on behalf of a quæstor; an officer who was associated with a proconsul in the administration of a province after having fulfilled the quæstorship at Rome.

1706 PHILLIPS, *Pro-Quæstor*, a Deputy or Vice-Treasurer. **1727** LARDNER *Wks.* (1838) I. 88 Lucius Antonius son of Mark, proquæstor and proprætor, to the magistrates, senate, and people of Sardis, greeting. **1832** GELL *Pompeiana* II. xiii. 21 Of sufficient importance to have had a proquæstor.

‖**prora** ('prɔːrə). Pl. **-æ.** [L. *prōra* PROW.]

1. The prow of a ship; = PRORE. *rare.*

1850 LEITCH tr. *C. O. Müller's Anc. Art* (ed. 2) 432 Naked, planting the right leg on a rock, a prora or a dolphin, leaning thereon and looking abroad, a victor in combat and ruling over the vanquished.

2. *Zool.* Either of the two points of a cymba or C-shaped sponge-spicule.

1887 SOLLAS in *Encycl. Brit.* XXII. 417/2 s.v. *Sponge*, The back of the 'C' [-shaped spicule] is the *keel* or *tropis*; the points are the *prows* or *proræ*.

proral ('prɔːrəl), *a.* [f. L. *prōr-a* prow + -AL[1].]

†**a.** *Anat.* in ***proral bone***, one of the original elements of the occipital. *Obs. rare.* **b.** *Zool.* Of or pertaining to the proræ of a cymba: see prec. 2.

1831 R. KNOX *Cloquet's Anat.* 51 At birth the occipital bone..appears to be formed by four centres... These four pieces form at that period so many distinct bones, which have been described as such under the names of the proral or squamous, condyloid and basilar bones. **1887** SOLLAS in *Encycl. Brit.* XXII. 418/1 s.v. *Sponge*, By growing towards the equator the opposed proral and pleural pteres may conjoin.

‖**pro rata**: see PRO 7.

pro-rate (prəʊ'reɪt), *v.* Chiefly *U.S.* Also **prorate.** [f. *pro rata.*] **a.** *trans.* To divide or assess *pro rata*; to distribute proportionally.

1860 *Congress. Globe* 21 Dec. 180/1 The amendment.. requires this company to pro-rate passenger fare with all railroad companies or lines which terminate either at Alexandria, Washington or Baltimore. **1864** WEBSTER, *Prorate*, to divide or distribute proportionally; to assess *pro rata* (*Corrupt. U.S.*). **1881** *Chicago Times* 17 June, As to the basis for pro-rating business between the subsidized and unsubsidized portions of the railroad. **1892** in A. E. Lee *Hist. Columbus* II. 262 The Baltimore and Ohio [Railroad] to operate and maintain the road..and prorate sixty-five per cent of the gross earnings..that is to pay the Central Ohio thirty-five per cent of the gross earnings. **1921** *Oil & Gas Jrnl.* 1 July 3/1 (*heading*) Are runs to be prorated? **1926** J. ISE *U.S. Oil Policy* xii. 116 California oil was cutting deeper into the eastern markets all the time, and in July [1923] some of the pipe-line companies in the eastern fields started to prorate runs. **1963** J. MITFORD *Amer. Way of Death* v. 66 In all likelihood, idle time of employees is figured in and prorated as part of the 'man-hours'. **1978** *Time* 3 July 37/3 San Jose businessman Larry Whitaker..said he would pro-rate his own $18,921 property tax cut among his 150 California employees.

b. *intr.* or *absol.* To make arrangement or agreement on a basis of proportional distribution.

1867 *Chicago Times* 21 Mar., An act amending the charter of the Hannibal and St. Jo Road, which the latter is bound to 'pro-rate' with any and all roads coming to Hannibal. **1890** *Tribune* (New York) 6 June (Cent.), The Santa Fe [Railroad]..will hereafter refuse to prorate with them on shipments of grain and live stock.

Hence **pro-'ratable** *a.*, 'capable of being prorated or divided proportionately' (Webster *Suppl.* 1879); **pro-'rated** *ppl. a.*, **pro-'rating** *vbl. sb.*

1911 F. E. WEBNER *Factory Costs* 212 On the other hand, there is no possible way of entirely avoiding a pro-rating or averaging of expense. **1921** *Oil & Gas Jrnl.* 1 July 3/1 In order to conserve space in the containers there may be instituted in the near future a prorating program. **1967** *Boston Sunday Globe* 23 Apr. 24 (Advt.), A pro-rated portion of the purchase price.

proration (prəʊ'reɪʃən). [f. PRO-RATE *v.* + -ION.] The action or an instance of prorating; *spec.* allocation of the permitted production of oil or gas between competing operators, fields, etc.

1923 *Oil Weekly* 22 Sept. 12/1 The Eastern fields and those of the Middle West are without proration problems. **1931** *Economist* 20 June 1324/2 Oil proration, copper curtailment agreements, and railroad mergers indicate the swing of the pendulum. **1954** R. CASSADY *Price Making in Petroleum Industry* vii. 114 Under a proration scheme..a sort of floor is placed under prices by limiting the amount of oil to be withdrawn on a basis of the needs of the market. **1957** *Times* 11 Dec. 16/5 The Pembina Oilfield is subject to strict proration; but all the wells have produced the maximum allowable since they were completed. **1960** *Economist* 15 Oct. 264/1 The ideas of a petroleum exporters' cartel, miscalled 'international proration'..are not inherently unfeasible. **1971** *Nature* 28 May p. viii/1 (Advt.), Only a Wang 100 can do side calculations, analyses, prorations and serve as an adding machine.

Hence **pro'rationing** *vbl. sb.* in the same sense.

1948 E. V. ROSTOW *National Policy for Oil Industry* iii. 21 In 1932, the Supreme Court declared prorationing legal. **1959** DE CHAZEAU & KAHN *Integration & Competition in Petroleum Industry* vii. 163 Prorationing to market demand has clearly brought about orderly marketing of crude oil with much fewer and less extreme price changes. **1960** *Guardian* 15 Oct. 7/5 The Organisation of Petroleum Exporting Countries..would..try to keep prices stable by regulating production (the system known to the industry as 'pro-rationing'). **1962** W. A. LEEMAN *Price of Middle East Oil* ix. 230 In effect the Venezuelans proposed a system of world-wide 'prorationing', similar to the arrangements already established in Texas, Louisiana, Oklahoma, and a number of other states.

prore (prɔə(r)). Now *poet.* and *rare.* Also 5 **prowere**, 6 **proer.** [a. obs. F. *prore* (*a* 1527 in Godef.), ad. L. *prōra* PROW *sb.*[1]] The PROW of a ship or boat.

1489 CAXTON *Faytes of A.* II. ii. 93 The prowere whiche is the foremest partye of the shippe. **1490** —— *Eneydos* vi. 29 The prores or forship whiche lay towarde the countre of Thir, tourned anone toward the Royame of Cypre. **1553** BRENDE *Q. Curtius* E e iij, The prores did stricke against the puppes. **1582** N. LICHEFIELD tr. *Castanheda's Conq. E. Ind.* 101 They carryed certeine Ordinaunce in the proer of theyr

Boates. **1718** POPE *Iliad* II. 773 Twelve galleys with vermillion prores. **1810** SCOTT *Lady of L.* VI. xiii, The tall ship, whose lofty prore Shall never stem the billows more. **1866** CONINGTON tr. *Æneid* VI. 5 Toward the sea they turn their prores.

b. *poetically*. A ship.

c **1645** HOWELL *Lett.* (1650) II. I ij b (*The Vote*) Now I hope in a successfull prore, The Fates have fix'd me on sweet Englands shore. **1813** SCOTT *Rokeby* VI. xviii, He.. Must.. lag with overloaded prore, While barks unburthened reach the shore.

pro-rector (ˌprəʊˈrɛktə(r)). [f. PRO-¹ 4 + RECTOR; also mod.L.; Ger. *prorektor*.] The deputy or substitute of a RECTOR in a university, college, or other educational institution; a vice-rector.

Formerly in use in the Scottish universities; also in those of Germany, in some of which the king or prince of the state was formerly the nominal Rector (RECTOR 4 c), and the professor who executed the duties of the office was pro-rector. (Cf. the positions of Chancellor and Vice-chancellor at Oxford, Cambridge, and Dublin.) Also in some other German institutes of higher education.

c **1618** MORYSON *Itin.* IV. IV. i. (1903) 306 But if it happen that any Baron or Prince be Student in the University, they vse to chuse him Rector for the yeare, and he vseth to chuse for his Prorector or Substitute, him who by order and course should haue otherwise beene Rector that yeare. [**1685** (Feb. 25) *Acta Rectorum Univ. St. Andr.* III. 471 Nomina incorporatorum in Collegio D. Leonardi R.D.D. Waltero Comrio pro Rectore, Collegii Dᵃᵉ Mariae primario.] **1858** (Mar. 1) *Minutes Univ. St. Andrews* XVII. 415 (MS.) The Senatus appointed the ex-Rector to act in the meantime as pro-Rector and Promotor. **1886** *Pall Mall G.* 18 Aug. 4/2 The pro-rectors.. of the several [German] universities represented [at Heidelberg] wore their gold chains of office. **1896** *Daily News* 12 June 7/1 The Emperor.. was received .. by the Rector and Pro-Rector of the Polytechnicum, in their long brown gowns and caps. **1908** J. MAITLAND ANDERSON *Let. to Editor* 5 Mar., [At St. Andrews] Down to the date of the Ordinances following on the Universities Act of 1858 there was always a pro-Rector, or, as he was sometimes called, a vice-Rector, whose duty it was to act for the Rector in his absence.

Hence **pro'rectorate**, the office of a pro-rector.

1846 in WORCESTER (citing Wm. Howitt). **1863** DOWDING *Life Calixtus* xxii. 203 The duties of the prorectorate have occupied and distracted me.

pro-regent, prorenal: see PRO-¹ 2, PRO-² 1.

pro-re-nascent, pro re nata: see PRO 8.

†**pro'reption.** *Obs. rare.* Also 7 -sion. [n. of action f. L. *prōrēp-ĕre, prōrept-* to creep forward.] A creeping on; a slow advance.

1656 BLOUNT *Glossogr.*, *Prorepsion*, a creeping forward, a stealing forward by little and little, a growing, spreading, or coming forth. **1658** J. ROBINSON *Endoxa* x. 55 The slow proreption of every Sidus, out of his proper Sign.

‖**'pro-rex.** *Obs.* [f. L. *prō*, PRO-¹ + *rex* a king.] A deputy king, a viceroy.

1586 MARLOWE *1st Pt. Tamburl.* I. i, Create him pro-rex of all Africa. **1589** NASHE *Anat. Absurd.* Epist., As I haue no portion in any mans opinion, so am I the Prorex of my priuate thought. **1649** ROBERTS *Clavis Bibl.* 198 In the 17. year of Jehoshaphat, Jehoram his son began to reign as Pro-rex, or Vice-Roy to his father. *a* **1679** T. GOODWIN *Knowledge of God* III. xiii, Whilst the world stands he [Christ] governs it, easeth God of that burden, and is his *prorex* for him.

†**'proritate,** *v. Obs.* [f. ppl. stem of L. *prōrītāre* to provoke, incite, entice. Cf. PRORITE and IRRITATE *v.*¹] *trans.* To provoke, irritate, incite.

1620 VENNER *Via Recta* v. (1650) 109 By reason of their moyst and calorificall nature, they proritate Venus. **1669** W. SIMPSON *Hydrol. Chym.* 81 By proritating the gout. **1684** tr. *Bonet's Merc. Compit.* XIX. 705 Fontanels.. proritate and milk as it were the outer surface of the Skin.

Hence †**prori'tation** *Obs.*, provocation, irritation, incitement.

1641 *Answ. Vind. Smectymnuus* 43 Your Maimonides (after all your proritation) holds no other than faire termes with our Samaritan Chronicle. **1657** TOMLINSON *Renou's Disp.* 535 It helps such as labour under.. the Dysentery, or the frequent proritation of the Belly. **1684** tr. *Bonet's Merc. Compit.* VI. 221 The flux.. may be continued by a gentle proritation of the bloud.

†**pro'rite,** *v. Obs.* [ad. L. *prōrīt-āre*: see above. Cf. obs. F. *proriter* (Cotgr.).] *trans.* = PRORITATE.

1574 NEWTON *Health Mag.* 72 It doth prorite and tickle them to expell it.

prorogate (ˈprəʊrəʊgeɪt), *v.* Chiefly *Sc.*; now only *Sc. Law.* Pa. pple. in Sc. also **prorogate**. [f. ppl. stem of L. *prōrogāre*: see PROROGUE.]

†**1.** *trans.* = PROROGUE 1. *Obs.*

1432–50 tr. *Higden* (Rolls) IV. 193 In that he had prorogate his office by the space of v. yere. **1552** *Reg. Privy Council Scot.* I. 127 With power to thaim to prorogat thair decreit. **1607** EARL STIRLING *Julius Cæsar* Argt., He sent to the Senate to have his government of the Gaules prorogated for five years. **1685** *Sc. Acts Chas. II* (1820) VIII. 460/1 The excise of Inland and forraign Commodities Granted to King Charles the Second.. by the fourteenth act of the Parliament 1661.. and prorogat by the eight act of þe Parliament 1681 for fyve yeares therafter. *a* **1693** *Urquhart's Rabelais* III. xl. 332, I prorogate,.. wyre-draw, and shift off the Time.

2. = PROROGUE 2, 3.

1569 *Reg. Privy Council Scot.* II. 31 To prorogat the said day of thair meting. **1646** BP. MAXWELL *Burd. Issach.* in *Phenix* (1708) II. 298 He gave order to prorogate it [the Assembly] to another and longer day. **1678** SIR G. MACKENZIE *Crim. Laws Scot.* II. (1699) 290 The Council may prorogat also the Dyets appointed for Execution. **1828–40** TYTLER *Hist. Scot.* (1864) I. 66 *note*, The day of assembling was afterwards prorogated to the 2nd of August. **1868** *Act 31 & 32 Vict.* c. 100 §26 It shall not be competent of consent of parties to prorogate the time for complying with any statutory enactment.

3. *Sc.* and *Civil Law.* To extend (the jurisdiction of a judge or court) to a cause in which it would otherwise be incompetent: cf. PROROGATION 4 a.

1601 J. WHEELER *Treat. Comm.* 25 All Ciuill causes,.. arising betweene or among the brethren.. who either may or will prorogate the Iurisdiction of the said Companie, and their court. **1678** SIR G. MACKENZIE *Crim. Laws Scot.* II. (1699) 287 Custome had in this prorogat the power of inferior Judges. **1838** W. BELL *Dict. Law Scot.* s.v. *Prorogation of Jurisdiction*, Where the proper jurisdiction of the judge is confined to causes amounting to a certain value, parties may prorogate the jurisdiction to causes above that value, unless the statute conferring the jurisdiction prohibits it.

¶**4.** pa. pple. *prorogate*, app. used for 'called, summoned'. *Obs. rare.*

c **1470** HARDING *Chron.* CXVII. i (MS. Arch Seld. B. 10), Edmonde Irneside.. After Ethelrede his fadir was prorogate Vnto the Crowne of alle this roiale land.

Hence **'prorogated** *ppl. a.*

1645 RUTHERFORD *Tryal & Tri. Faith* xviii. (1845) 205 The standing and prorogated intercession and advocation of Jesus Christ.. must have a daily use. **1773** ERSKINE *Inst. Law Scot.* I. ii. §27 Prorogated jurisdiction is that which is, by the consent of parties, conferred on a judge, who, without such consent, would be incompetent. **1850** *Act 13 & 14 Vict.* c. 36 §2 The original or prorogated period, as the case may be, for lodging a revised condescendence.

prorogation (prəʊrəʊˈgeɪʃən, prɒrəʊ-). [ME. a. OF. *prorogacion* (1313 in Hatz.-Darm.), mod.F. *-tion*, or ad. L. *prōrogātiōn-em*, n. of action f. *prōrogāre* to PROROGUE.]

1. The action of lengthening in duration, or causing to last longer; extension of time; prolongation, protraction, further continuance. Now *rare* or *Obs.* exc. in *Sc. Law.*

1432–50 tr. *Higden* (Rolls) V. 185 Thro the prorogacion of his lyfe by oon day. **1542** UDALL *Erasm. Apoph.* 278 b, The senate would not geue ne graunte vnto Caesar prorogacion, that is to saie, a longer tyme in his dictature. **1647** H. MORE *Song of Soul* Notes 136/1 Distance of life makes time, and the prorogation of life continueth time. **1746–7** *Act 20 Geo. II*, c. 50 §21 By virtue of the prorogation of any lease or tack. **1838** W. BELL *Dict. Law Scot.*, *Prorogation*, in judicial proceedings,.. a prolongation of the time appointed for reporting a diligence, lodging a paper, or obtempering any other judicial order... *Prorogation of a Lease* is the extension of it. **1876** LOWELL *Among my Bks.* Ser. II. 253 He himself can count on patriarchal prorogations of existence.

2. The action of proroguing an assembly, esp. Parliament; discontinuance of meetings until the following session, without dissolution.

1472–3 *Rolls of Parlt.* VI. 31/2 Your Parlement.. by dyvers prorogations and adjornamentes, unto the xxi day of Januarii.. contynued. **1586** BURGHLEY in Ellis *Orig. Lett.* Ser. I. III. 13 We.. did procure this prorogation for the other ij. causes. [Cf. PROROGUE *v.* 2, quot. 1586.] **1638** DK. HAMILTON in *H. Papers* (Camden) 48 A great manie of them came to toune to haue protested against the prorogation [of the General Assembly]. **1765** BLACKSTONE *Comm.* I. ii. 187 A prorogation is the continuance of the parliament from one session to another, as an adjournment is a continuation of the session from day to day. **1828** SCOTT *F.M. Perth* vii, Bailie Craigdallie.. who had advised the prorogation of their civic council to the present place and hour. **1840** *Penny Cycl.* XVII. 271/1 The effect of a prorogation is at once to suspend all business until parliament may be summoned again. *Ibid.*, A bill must be renewed after a prorogation, as if it had never been introduced, though the prorogation be for no more than a day. **1878** STUBBS *Const. Hist.* §768 III. 480–1 The distinction between adjournment and prorogation.. is a modern distinction. The necessary adjournment from day to day, as well as the countermanding of a parliament called, and the longer intermission of the session, was known as prorogation. *Ibid.* note, The word 'prorogation' is constantly used for countermanding or delaying the day of meeting.

b. *transf.* The time during which Parliament stands prorogued; the interval between successive sessions.

a **1548** HALL *Chron.*, *Hen. VIII* 110 b, Duryng whiche prorogacion, the common people saied to the Burgesses, sirs, we heare saie you will graunt .iiii.*s.* of the pound, we aduise you to doo so that you maie go home. **1663** PEPYS *Diary* 18 Feb., This day the Parliament met again, after their long prorogation. **1724** SWIFT *Drapier's Lett.* ii. Wks. 1755 V. II. 42 It would seem very extraordinary, if an inferiour court in England should take a matter out of the hands of the high court of parliament during a prorogation.

†**3.** The action of deferring to a later time; postponement. *Obs. rare.*

1658 PHILLIPS, *Prorogation*, a deferring, or putting off to another time. **1703** KELSEY *Serm.* 73 He often obtained Pardon, or a Prorogation of the Punishment.

4. a. *Sc. Law.* The extension of the jurisdiction of a judge or court to causes which do not properly come within it: allowed in certain cases by consent of the parties.

1838 W. BELL *Dict. Law Scot.* s.v. *Prorogation of Jurisdiction*, In order to render prorogation effectual, the judge must have a jurisdiction susceptible of prorogation.

†**b.** *gen.* Extension. *Obs. rare.*

a **1626** BP. ANDREWES *Serm.* (1856) I. 223 Goodwill is a kind of peace, but.. with an extent or prorogation, a kind of peace peculiar to men which the other parts of the earth are not capable of.

'prorogator. *rare.* [a. L. *prōrogātor*, agent-n. f. *prōrogāre* to PROROGUE.] One who prorogates.

(In quot. app. a meaningless jingle.)

1652 GAULE *Magastrom.* 376 Against all Merlinicall arrogators, prorogators, derogators.

prorogue (prəʊˈrəʊg), *v.* Forms: 5–7 **proroge**, (5 -rouge, 6 -rog), 6– **prorogue**. [Late ME. *proroge*, a. F. *proroge-r*, obs. F. *prorogue-r* (both 14th c. in Godef. *Compl.*), ad. L. *prōrogāre* to prolong, extend, esp. a term of office; to defer; lit. to ask publicly, f. *prō*, PRO-¹ + *rogāre* to ask.

The etymological sense, according to Scheller, was perh. 'to ask the people whether the term of an office or the like may be prolonged to a person', as if to ask him *on*. But of this no example is extant in Latin.]

†**1.** *trans.* To prolong, lengthen, extend (in time or duration); to cause to last longer; to continue, protract. *Obs.* (exc. as a Latinism).

1425 *Rolls of Parlt.* IV. 289 The which Graunte was lengthed and proroged att the last Parlement.. for other two yeer. *c* **1510** MORE *Picus* Wks. 9/2 If he might haue had yᵉ space of his life proroged. **1579** FENTON *Guicciard.* (1618) 91 The truce was eftsoones proroged for a few dayes. **1579–80** NORTH *Plutarch* (1676) 599 And besides [they] did prorogue the time of his Government five years further. **1665** MANLEY *Grotius' Low C. Warres* 896 The States prorogued the space for deliberation.. from that present time, until the first of September. *a* **1716** SOUTH *Serm.* (1744) XI. 263 As long as the Spirit prorogues his workings after an obstinate resistance of them. **1878** BOSW. SMITH *Carthage* 337 The command of Scipio was prorogued, not, as on previous occasions, for a fixed period, but till such time as the war should be brought to a conclusion.

†**2.** *trans.* To put off for a time, defer, postpone.

1453 *Rolls of Parlt.* V. 233/1 To forbere and proroge, and to putte in suspence, th' execution of leviyng of the fyndyng of the seid.. men Archers. **1494** HEN. VII *Let.* in *Epist. Acad. Oxon.* (O.H.S.) II. 618 Prorouge your said election unto the tyme ye shall have furthre knowlege from us. **1592** SHAKS. *Rom. & Jul.* IV. i. 48, I heare thou must and nothing may prorogue it, On Thursday next be married to this Countie. **1632** PORY in Ellis *Orig. Lett.* Ser. II. III. 278 The Kinges journey into Scotland must be prorogued untill another yeare. *a* **1716** SOUTH *Serm.* (1744) VII. vi. 126 To stop a sinner in his return to God, by persuading his corrupt heart, that he may prorogue that return with safety.

†**b.** *absol.* or *intr.* To delay, procrastinate. *Obs.*

1593 NASHE *Christ's T.* 11 b, Why doost thou proroge till thy wretched life be at his wayes end?

3. To discontinue the meetings of (a legislative or other assembly) for a time, definite or indefinite, without dissolving it; to dismiss by authority until the next session. Originally and chiefly in reference to the British Parliament.

Originally a particular application of sense 2; the meaning being to 'put off, postpone' the assembly or sittings of a parliament which had been summoned or was in session: cf. quot. 1878 in PROROGATION 2.

1455 *Rolls of Parlt.* V. 286/1 This present Parliament to proroge, adjorne, or dissolve. **1494** FABYAN *Chron.* VII. 344 In this .xlii. yere, the kyng helde one parlyament at Westmynster, & another or ellys prorogyd yᵉ same to Wynchestre. *a* **1548** HALL *Chron.*, *Hen. V* 41 Vpon this poynct.. the parliament was proroged to Westminster. **1586** BURGHLEY in Ellis *Orig. Lett.* Ser. I. III. 13 We had gret reason to prorog our session which is rone till the 25ᵗʰ. *c* **1615** BACON *Adv. Sir G. Villiers* ii. §28 By the king's authority alone, and by his writs are they [the two houses of peers and commons] assembled, and by him alone are they prorogued and dissolved; but each house may adjourn itself. **1769** ROBERTSON *Chas. V*, VII. Wks. 1813 III. 23 The Pope ..recalled them and prorogued the Council. **1846** MᶜCULLOCH *Acc. Brit. Empire* (1854) II. 77 Parliament is called together by the King, who may prorogue or dissolve it at pleasure.

b. *intr.* in *pass.* sense: To be prorogued; to discontinue meeting until the next session.

1642 *View Print. Book int. Observat.* 8 He may command them to prorogue, or adjourn for time or place. **1680** *Roxb. Ball.* (1883) IV. 646, I mind not the Members, and makers of Laws, Let 'em Sit or Prorogue as his Majesty please. **1896** LD. LONDONDERRY in *Westm. Gaz.* 7 Sept. 2/2 No opportunity was afforded.. of discussing the question before Parliament prorogued.

Hence **pro'rogued** *ppl. a.*, **pro'roguing** *vbl. sb.*; †**pro'roguement** [cf. AF. *proroiguement* (1376 in Godef.)] = PROROGATION; **pro'roguer**, one who prorogues (in quot., one who puts off or defers).

1552 HULOET, *Proroged, *prorogatus.* **1647** CLARENDON *Hist. Reb.* III. §1 The King.. went privately.. as if it had been to a return of a prorogued or adjourn'd Parliament. **1660** R. COKE *Power & Subj.* 257 The day for the convention of the Parliament after their *Proroguement. **1597** J. PAYNE *Royal Exch.* 5 These *prorogers of wel doinge having wherwith, are here iustly reproved. **1581** in W. H. Turner *Select. Rec. Oxford* (1880) 417 A proclamacion for the *prorogyne of the Parliament. **1642** tr. *Perkins' Prof. Bk.* xi. 360 That the cause of the proroging of his induction bee in his owne default. **1680** SIR C. LYTTELTON in *Hatton Corr.* (Camden) 239 The proroguinge yᵉ parliment for 10 days. **1937** G. FRANKAU *More of Us* vi. 69 And, as he donned those shoes Shoemaker Lobb webs From toe to heel with best bespoken broguing, This house of lords seemed ripe for his proroguing.

prorsad (ˈprɔːsæd), *adv. Anat.* [f. L. *prorsum* forwards + *-ad*: see DEXTRAD.] Towards the front, forward. So **'prorsal** *a.*, forward, anterior.

1890 in *Cent. Dict.* **1895** in *Syd. Soc. Lex.*

† **pro'rump,** *v. Obs. nonce-wd.* [ad. L. *prōrumpĕre*, f. PRO-¹ + *rumpĕre* to burst.] *intr.* To burst forth.

1601 B. JONSON *Poetaster* v. iii, *Cris.* O—ô—prorumped. *Tibv.* Prorumped? what a noise it made! as if his spirit would haue prorumpt with it.

prorupt (prəʊ'rʌpt), *v. rare.* [f. L. *prōrupt-*, ppl. stem of *prōrumpĕre*: see prec.] *trans.* To cause to burst forth: hence **pro'rupted** *ppl. a.* So **proruption** (prəʊ'rʌpʃən) [ad. late L. *prōruptiōn-em*, n. of action], a bursting forth.

1646 SIR T. BROWNE *Pseud. Ep.* III. xvi. 145 The latter brood impatient, by a forcible proruption anticipate their period of exclusion. **1858** MAYNE *Expos. Lex.*, *Proruptio*, term for a bursting or breaking forth, as of the blood: proruption. **1874** *Contemp. Rev.* XXIV. 430 The Inferno is in the conical pit, the Purgatorio on the prorupted mountain.

pros (prɒs), var. PROSS.

‖ **prosa** ('prəʊzə). *Eccl.* Pl. prosae. [L.] = PROSE *sb.* 2. Cf. PROSULA.

1801 T. BUSBY *Dict. Mus.*, *Prosæ*, certain hymns used in the Romish church consisting of rhyme without measure. **1907** [see PROSULA]. **1929** *Exultet Roll* (Brit. Mus.) 5 In the South of Italy, at least from the early part of the tenth century till the thirteenth, a custom existed of writing out this prosa .. on a separate roll distinct from the other services of the day. **1957** N. FRYE *Anat. Crit.* 275 The emergence of the 'prosa' out of the sequence in medieval music. **1970** P. EVANS *Early Trope Repertory of St. Martial de Limoges* i. 9 Both the prosa and the prosula are basically literary in their conception. The prosa is created by adding a text to the pre-existent melismatic sequentia which follows the Alleluia.

prosaic (prəʊ'zeɪɪk), *a.* (*sb.*). [ad. med.L. *prōsaic-us* (6th c.), f. *prōsa* PROSE: see -IC. So F. *prosaïque* (15th c. (adv. *-ment*) in Hatz.-Darm.).]

1. Of or pertaining to prose; consisting of or written in prose; (of an author) writing in prose. Now *rare* or *Obs.*: expressed by PROSE 5 *attrib.*

1656 BLOUNT *Glossogr.*, *Prosaick*, that is in Prose and not in Meeter, pertaining to Prose. **1719** H. EELBECK (*title*) A Prosaic Translation of .. Persius Flaccus's Six Satyrs. **1780** HARRIS *Philol. Inq.* II. iii. (1781) 92 In modern Rhythm .. be it Prosaic or Poetic, he [the reader] must expect to find it governed for the greater part by Accent. **1830** W. TAYLOR *Hist. Surv. Germ. Poetry* III. 13 He [Herder] published many works, chiefly prosaic, which widely extended his literary reputation. **1878** BROWNING *La Saisiaz* lxxix, Verse which, born, demands Prosaic ministration.

2. Having the character, style, or diction of prose as opposed to poetry; lacking poetic beauty, feeling, or imagination; plain, matter-of-fact. Hence **b.** *transf.* Unpoetic, unromantic; commonplace, dull, tame. (Of persons and things.)

1746 P. FRANCIS tr. *Horace, Sat.* I. iv. 53 'Tis not enough to close the flowing Line, And in ten Syllables your Sense confine. Or write in meer prosaic Rhimes like me, That can deserve the Name of Poetry. **1795** MASON *Ch. Mus.* iii. 166 The verses were easy and .. prosaic enough to be intelligible to the meanest capacity. **1841** D'ISRAELI *Amen. Lit.* (1867) 287 (*Ship of Fools*) The verse being prosaic, preserves its colloquial ease.

b. 1813 H. & J. SMITH *Horace in Lond.* 10 When you are flat, prosaic, and insipid (which, under favor, you sometimes are). **1859** HOLLAND *Gold F.* iii. 41 Do you get impatient with the prosaic life around you—the dulness, and the earthliness and the brutishness of men? **1877** BLACK *Green Past.* vii, Marriage settlements are very prosaic things. **1892** WESTCOTT *Gospel of Life* 128 The Chinese are commonly held to be a prosaic people.

B. *sb.* † **1.** A prose author: = PROSAIST 1. *Obs.*

1589 PUTTENHAM *Eng. Poesie* I. xix. (Arb.) 56 Which occasioned the story writer to chuse an higher stile fit for his subiect, the Prosaicke in prose, the Poet in meetre.

2. *pl.* Prosaic things or subjects.

1890 CLARK RUSSELL *Ocean Trag.* I. viii. 163 She [a ship] hardened rapidly into the familiar prosaics of timber, sail-cloth and tackling.

pro'saical, *a.* [f. as prec. + -AL¹.]

† **1.** = prec. 1. *Obs.*

1652 L. S. *People's Liberty* v. 10 As we may observe both from their Poets, and Prosaicall writers. **1751** EARL ORRERY *Remarks Swift* (1752) 251 Consider the prosaical works of Milton, you will find them more nervous than elegant. **1808** DIBDIN *Sir T. More's Utopia* Introd. 73 The first prosaical work with which Rastell's ponderous folio opens is called 'The Life of John Picus'.

2. = prec. 2. Now *rare* or *Obs.*

1699 BENTLEY *Phal.* 218 As familiar and prosaical, as our Censurer would make it. **1848** MRS. CARLYLE *Lett.* (1883) II. 33, I found that now too prosaical for my romantic circumstances. **1859** KINGSLEY *Misc.* I. i. 29 It is the practical, prosaical fanatic who does the work.

pro'saically, *adv.* [f. prec. + -LY².] In a prosaic manner.

a **1834** COLERIDGE *Let. to Pickering* (*Kerslake's Catal.* June 1879), Sir Walter Scott, tho' a poet, .. manages these matters somewhat more prosaically—*i.e.* with more sense and discretion. **1839** HALLAM *Hist. Lit.* II. v. §6. 255 La Balia [of Tansillo] .. contains good advice to mothers .. very prosaically delivered. **1885** *Bookseller* 5 Mar. 241/2 The violin .. may be prosaically described as 'a hollow box 13 inches long by 8½ wide, and weighing about 8½ ounces'.

pro'saicalness. *rare.* [f. as prec. + -NESS.] = PROSAICNESS.

1844 L. HUNT *Imag. & Fancy* 47 As to prosaicalness in general, it is sometimes indulged in by young writers on the plea of its being natural. **1876** MISS YONGE *Womankind* xxi. 162 The intense prosaicalness of common life is shown in the Paston letters, where the girls pray for husbands, with apparently perfect indifference as to who they may be.

prosaicism (prəʊ'zeɪɪsɪz(ə)m). [f. PROSAIC *a.* + -ISM.] = PROSAISM.

1804 ANNA SEWARD *Mem. Darwin* 266 Those long trains of comparative prosaicism, over which we yawn. *a* **1849** POE *Marginalia* Wks. 1864 III. 500 It is the prosaicism of these two writers to which is owing their especial quotability. **1884** *Contemp. Rev.* Mar. 401 People are never weary of inveighing against the prosaicism of our time.

pro'saicness. [f. as prec. + -NESS.] Prosaic quality or character.

1887 *Jrnl. Educ.* 1 Feb. 79 That Dutch picture .. in its unadulterated materiality and prosaicness. **1890** *Athenæum* 8 Mar. 303/3 The vulgarity and prosaicness of these people and their surroundings.

pro,sai-,comi-'epic, *a. nonce-wd.* Combining the prosaic, comic, and epic.

1749 FIELDING *Tom Jones* v. i, We have laid it down as a Rule necessary to be observed in all Prosai-comi-epic Writing.

prosaism ('prəʊzeɪɪz(ə)m). [ad. F. *prosaïsme*, f. L. *prōsa* PROSE: see -ISM.]

1. Prosaic character or style. (In quot. 1855, Dull or commonplace condition or prospect.)

1787 ANNA SEWARD *Lett.* (1811) I. 352 Ever have you found me ready to acknowledge the prosaism of many lines which you have pointed out in my most favourite poets. **1855** *Fraser's Mag.* LI. 700 Not a picturesque bit of building was to be seen; .. nothing but the most arid prosaism. **1865** LEWES in *Fortn. Rev.* 1 Dec. 181 Nor could a Frenchman .. feel the whole prosaism of Wordsworth's lines—'That adequate provision should be made For all the people to be taught to read'.

2. (with *pl.*) A prosaic phrase or expression.

1817 COLERIDGE *Biog. Lit.* xviii. (1882) 185 The existence of prosaisms .. must .. be conceded. *a* **1850** WORDSW. *Prose Wks.* (1876) II. 85 Critics, who, when they stumble upon these prosaisms, as they call them, imagine that they have made a notable discovery. **1865** *Pall Mall G.* 13 Nov. 10 There are prosaisms and colloquial turns which every now and then remind us of the restraints.

prosaist ('prəʊzeɪɪst). [f. as prec. + -IST.]

1. One who writes in prose; a prose author.

1803 W. TAYLOR in *Ann. Rev.* I. 322 Known to the public as a poet, and a prosaist of eloquence and erudition. **1827** DE QUINCEY in *Blackw. Mag.* XXI. 20 The prosaist is satisfied if he impresses clear and distinct ideas. **1879** M. PATTISON *Milton* vi. 70 There is no other prosaist who possesses anything like Milton's command over the resources of our language.

2. A prosaic or unpoetic person.

1831 CARLYLE *Schiller* in *Misc. Ess.* (1872) III. 71 A man who denied that Schiller was a Poet, would himself be, from every side, declared a Prosaist. **1853** CLOUGH *Poems*, etc. (1869) I. 396 How that first of English prosaists was inspired with them [poetic lines], remains a problem.

† **'prosal,** *a. Obs.* [ad. med.L. *prōsāl-is* (6th c., Cassiod.), f. L. *prōsa* PROSE: see -AL¹. Cf. F. *prosal* (14th c.).] Pertaining to or composed in prose; in quot. 1654, written or printed in the form of prose (not in measured lines like verse).

1654 VILVAIN *Theol. Treat.* vi. 137 These Analyses in a prosal method .. are plainer .. for the vulgar sort, than such as are set in Sections. *a* **1682** SIR T. BROWNE *Tracts* xi. (1683) 177 The Priest not onely or always composed his prosal raptures into Verse.

† **'prosapy.** *Obs.* [ad. L. *prōsāpi-a* (also *-ēs*) a stock, race, family. Cf. obs. F. *prosapie* (1507 in Godef.).] Stock, race, lineage.

1432-50 tr. *Higden* (Rolls) I. 281 Soe the lineall descense of the prosapy [*L. prosapiæ*] or kynrede of Feramundus faylede by men, but hyt remaynede in Batildis sustyr to Dagoberte. **1542** UDALL *Erasm. Apoph.* 62 Beeyng a manne, and begotten to of a mannes prosapie, in manly wise. **1654** VILVAIN *Epit. Ess.* II. xxvi. 33 Two Tarquins sprung from Greekish prosapy.

‖ **prosateur** (prozatœr). [F. (Ménage 1666), ad. It. *prosatore* (in Florio): cf. med.L. *prōsātor* (Du Cange).] A prose-writer.

1880 E. W. GOSSE in *Academy* 4 Sept. 164 Shelley ceased to come before the world as a prosateur just as he began to do so seriously as a poet. **1901** *Q. Rev.* Oct. 491 There are few better examples of his charm as *prosateur*.

Also in med.L. form **pro'sator.**

1891 STEVENSON *Lett.* (1901) II. xi. 221 Not that I set much account by my verses, which are the verses of Prosator.

prosauropod (prəʊ'sɔːrəʊpɒd), *sb.* and *a. Palæont.* [ad. mod.L. name of infraorder *Prosauropoda* (F. von Huene 1920, in *Zeitschr. für Induktive Abstammungs- und Vererbungslehre* XXII. 211), f. PRO-² 1 + mod.L. *Sauropoda*: see SAUROPOD *a.* and *sb.*] **A.** *sb.* A dinosaur belonging to the infraorder Prosauropoda, which includes herbivorous, usually bipedal, saurischians. **B.** *adj.* Of or pertaining to an animal of this kind.

1951 C. C. YOUNG in *Palaeontologia Sinica* CXXXIV. 88 For the sake of convenience we may discuss the prosauropods together. **1962** E. H. COLBERT *Dinosaurs* iv. 80 The prosauropods quickly developed to become the dinosaur giants of their day. **1965** *Proc. Linn. Soc.* CLXXVI. 211 Each of the two prosauropod families transferred from the Carnosauria .. bears .. a striking resemblance to one of two existing prosauropod families. **1971** E. C. OLSON *Vertebr. Paleozool.* II. viii. 354 Some genera .. among animals often classed as prosauropods were intermediate in structures related to gait, being only partially quadrupedal. **1978** *Nature* 17 Aug. 662/1 Prosauropods probably could feed tripodally—supporting their weight on the hindlimbs and stout tail.

proscapula, -ar: see PRO-² 2.

† **pro'scarab.** *Obs. rare.* [ad. mod.L. *prōscarabæ-us*: see PRO-¹ and SCARAB; so F. *proscarabée*.] A name of the Oil-beetle, *Meloe proscarabæus*.

[**1658** ROWLAND *Moufet's Theat. Ins.* 1016 Called *Proscarabeus* in Latine .. in English it may fitly be called the Oyl-beetle, or the Oyl-clock.] **1668** WILKINS *Real Char.* II. v. §2. 123 Insects .. like a Beetle without wings, but seeming to have some little rudiments of wings, noted for being apt upon a touch to send out a yellowish oyly substance from his joynts... Proscarab.

‖ **proscenium** (prəʊ'siːnɪəm). Pl. **-a.** [a. L. *proscēnium*, ad. Gr. προσκήνιον a proscenium, also in late Gr. a stage-curtain, f. πρό, PRO-² 2 + σκηνή a booth, stage, SCENE.]

1. a. In the ancient theatre, The space between the 'scene' or background and the orchestra, on which the action took place; the stage.

1606 HOLLAND *Sueton.* 184 These Games hee beheld from the top of the *Proscenium* [*margin* The fore-stage]. **1696** PHILLIPS (ed. 5), *Proscenium*, the forepart of the Scene: an Edifice as high as the last Portico of the Theater, whose Face or Front was adorned with many ranges of Pillars. **1839** ARNOLD *Let.* in Stanley *Life & Corr.* (1844) II. ix. 160 The two marble pillars still standing in the *proscenium* of the theatre, reminded me of the Forum at Rome. **1869** TOZER *Highl. Turkey* II. 201 Of .. the proscenium there are no remains.

b. In the modern theatre, The space between the curtain or drop-scene and the orchestra; often including the curtain itself and the arch or framework which holds it.

1807 *Director* I. 244 This equivocal proscenium, as it were, dove-tails the house with the stage. **1860** *All Year Round* No. 44. 417 The appearance of the audience, as seen from the proscenium .. is highly remarkable in its union of vastness with compactness. **1908** *Q. Rev.* Apr. 453 The one determining characteristic of the Elizabethan stage .. is its lack of anything like a proscenium.

2. *transf.* and *fig.* **a.** The front, the foreground.

1648 HERRICK *Hesper.*, *Upon his Julia*, Lips she has, all rubie red, .. And a nose that is the grace And proscenium of her face. **1793** EARL MACARTNEY in J. Barrow *Life*, etc. (1807) II. 272 Several persons passed backwards and forwards, in the proscenium or fore ground of the tent. **1851** CARLYLE *Sterling* I. xiv, These thoughts .. for a good while .. kept possession of the proscenium of his mind.

b. 'The stage'; dramatic art.

1812 G. COLMAN *Poet. Vag.* (1818) 16 During his time, from the Proscenium ta'en, Thalia and Melpomene both vanished. **1907** *Edin. Rev.* Jan. 197 The Censor is still enthroned above the proscenium.

3. *attrib.*, as ***proscenium arch, box, curtain, door, drop, opening.***

1901 *Scribner's Mag.* XXIX. 466/2, I was in the box that used to be built inside the proscenium arch so that the actors themselves could watch the stage during their waits. **1875** MISS BRADDON *Strange World* I. ii. 36 That official .. unlocked a door behind the proscenium box, a door sacred to the manager, and let Penwyn through. **1828** J. R. PLANCHÉ *Paris & London* (1830) I. v. 24 (*stage direction*) A Diagonal View of the Stage of the Odeon is seen through the wings—the proscenium boxes, L. **1849** THACKERAY *Pendennis* I. xiv. 124 One of the illustrious patrons of the Museum Theatre, and occupant of the great proscenium-box, was .. the Marquis of Steyne. **1829** *Harlequin* 20 June 46 The only drop below the proscenium curtain was the very fine pierced forest limbs, which every frequenter of Drury Lane Theatre must recollect. **1975** C. HOGGET *Stage Crafts* i. 14 Pelmet for proscenium curtains should overhang reveals to allow curtains to open fully. **1827** T. DIBDIN *Reminisc.* II. 115 One artist offered to paint me a proscenium drop (as we call the painted cloth which falls between the acts). **1889** *Theatre* XIII. 292 The proscenium opening is formed by groups of columns on either side of the first proscenium box. **1974** *Encycl. Brit. Micropædia* VIII. 244/1 The proscenium opening was of particular importance to the realistic playwrights of the 19th century.

proscession, obs. form of PROCESSION.

‖ **Proscholium, -ion** (prəʊ'skəʊlɪəm, -ɪɒn). [med.L. *proscholium*, f. Gr. πρό, PRO-² 2 + L. *schola*, ad. Gr. σχολή school.] The name of a covered court forming the eastern entrance to the Divinity School at Oxford.

1676 in *Wood's Life* 1 July (O.H.S.) II. 351 Bound to be in the Proscholium of the Divinity School during the asking of his grace. **1720** HEARNE *Collect.* (O.H.S.) VII. 192 He did not stand that day in the Proscholion (commonly called Pig-market) of the Divinity School, as he ought to have done.

† **pro'scind,** *v. Obs. rare.* [ad. L. *prōscind-ĕre* to tear open in front, rend, f. *prō*, PRO-¹ 1 f + *scind-*

ĕre to cut, rend.] *trans.* To rend, to tear; also *fig.* to revile.

1659 GAUDEN *Tears of Ch.* IV. xx. 573 They did too much proscind and prostitute (as it were) the Imperial purple. **1671** R. MACWARD *True Nonconf.* 58 The.. Reproaches, where-with your Clergie during these unhappy wars did not cease continually to proscind the people of God.

†**proscission** (prəʊˈsɪʃən). *Obs. rare*⁻⁰. [ad. L. *prōscissiōn-em* breaking up (of land), first ploughing, f. *prō*, PRO-[1] + *scind-ĕre*, *sciss-um* to break or tear asunder.] (See quot.)

1656 BLOUNT *Glossogr.*, *Procission* [error for *proscission*], a cutting up, a tilling, a ploughing, a manuring of land.

prosciutto (prəʊˈʃuːtəʊ). Also (erron.) prosciuto. [It., 'ham'.] Italian spiced ham. Also (pleonastically) *prosciutto ham*.

c **1938** *Fortnum & Mason Price List* 39/2 Proscuitto [*sic*] (Hors d'Œuvre Sliced Ham)..3/9. **1945** E. WAUGH *Brideshead Revisited* I. iv. 90 Melon and prosciuto on the balcony. **1952** V. CANNING *House of Seven Flies* iii. 53 Charlie had ventured too far in search of black market *vino*, *prosciutto* and anything else he could lay his hands on. **1960** I. FLEMING *For Your Eyes Only* 153, I shall have melon with prosciutto ham. **1964** MRS. L. B. JOHNSON *White House Diary* 6 May (1970) 131 We had a gourmet lunch, beginning with prosciutto and melon. **1965** *Guardian* 4 Aug. 6/4 *Prosciutto* ham was among the delicacies on the buffet table. **1967** 'J. CROSS' *To Hell for Half-a-Crown* xv. 190 She had fixed melon with *prosciutto*. **1977** C. MCFADDEN *Serial* xx. 46/2 Kate.. sauntered up to a vantage point in front of the prosciutto.

proscolecine, -scolex: see PRO-[2] 1.

‖**proscolla** (prɒsˈkɒlə). *Bot.* Pl. -æ. [mod.L., f. Gr. πρός to + κόλλα glue.] (See quot.)

1866 *Treas. Bot.*, *Proscolla*, a viscid gland on the upper side of the stigma of orchids, to which the pollen-masses become attached.

proscribable (prəʊˈskraɪbəb(ə)l), *a.* [f. next + -ABLE.] Capable of being proscribed, or placed under legal proscription.

1881 *Echo* 16 Feb. 3/2 The offence had to be committed in a proscribable district; and it was desired that the warrant should be conclusive evidence of the proscription of the district.

proscribe (prəʊˈskraɪb), *v.* [ad. L. *prōscrīb-ĕre* to write in front of; to write before the world, publish by writing, offer in writing for sale, etc.; to 'post' a person as condemned to confiscation or outlawry, f. *prō*, PRO-[1] 1 f + *scrīb-ĕre* to write.]

†**I. 1.** *trans.* To write in front; to prefix in writing. *Obs. rare.*

Perhaps a scribal error for *prescribe*: see PRO-[1] 3.

1432-50 tr. *Higden* (Rolls) I. 21 When the compilator [Ranulphus] spekethe, the letter shall be proscribede [L. *præscribitur*] in this forme folowenge [R].

II. 2. To write up or publish the name of (a person) as condemned to death and confiscation of property; to put out of the protection of the law, to outlaw; to banish, exile. Also *fig.*

1560 DAUS tr. *Sleidane's Comm.* 33 b, He..doth condemne, & proscribe him as aucthor of Scismes. **1596** SPENSER *State Irel.* Wks. (Globe) 637/1 Ro. Vere, Earle of Oxford, was..banished the realme and proscribed. **1678** R. L'ESTRANGE *Seneca's Mor.* (1776) 200 He that proscribes me today, shall himself be cast out tomorrow. **1840** THIRLWALL *Greece* VII. lvii. 226 He was himself outlawed and proscribed in the name of his sovereign. **1842** ALISON *Hist. Europe* X. lxxvii. 840 A declaration was..signed by all the Powers, which..proscribed Napoleon as a public enemy, with whom neither peace nor truce could be concluded.

b. To ostracize, to 'send to Coventry'.

1680 EARL ROSCOM. tr. *Horace's Art Poet.* 31 Then Poetasters in their raging fits..dreaded and proscrib'd by Men of sense.

3. To reject, condemn, denounce (a thing) as useless or dangerous; to prohibit, interdict; to proclaim (a district or practice); = PROCLAIM *v.* 2 e, f.

1622 MABBE tr. *Aleman's Guzman d'Alf.* II. 319 This Custome is that vncontrouled Lord, that prescribes, and proscribes Lawes at his pleasure. **1768** HUME *Ess. & Treat.* (1777) II. Notes 507 They [plays] have been zealously proscribed by the godly in later ages. **1772** PRIESTLEY *Inst. Relig.* (1782) I. 219 The Stoics..proscribed..Compassion. **1774** GOLDSM. *Nat. Hist.* (1862) I. IV. iii. 424 Persons of taste or elegance seem to proscribe it [civet] even from the toilet. **1841** D'ISRAELI *Amen. Lit.* (1867) 342 The ecclesiastics in vain proscribed these licentious revelries. **1850** MRS. JAMESON *Leg. Monast. Ord.* (1863) 194 Before their religion was proscribed and their country confiscated.

¶ As a literalism of rendering in Rhemish N.T.

1582 N.T. (Rhem.) *Gal.* iii. 1 O sensles Galatians, who hath bewitched you, not to obey the truth, before whose eies Iesus Christ was proscribed [Gr. προεγράφη; *Vulg.* præscriptus est; 1388 WYCLIF exilid; TINDALE, COVERD. described; 1611 euidently set forth; 1881 *R.V.* openly set forth], being crucified among you?

Hence **proˈscribed** *ppl. a.*

1611 B. JONSON *Catiline* I. i, I hid for thee Thy murder of thy brother,..And writ him in the list of my proscrib'd After thy fact, to save thy little shame. **1689** SHADWELL *Bury F.* 11, As the proscribed emperor was by his perfumes betrayd. **1868** J. H. BLUNT *Ref. Ch. Eng.* I. 66 A well-known favourer of the proscribed opinions. **1869** RAWLINSON *Anc. Hist.* 447 The property of the proscribed was confiscated.

†**proscribe,** formerly for PRESCRIBE: see PRO-[1] 3.

1530 PALSGR. 668/1, *I proscrybe* (Lydgate) for *I prescrybe*.

proˈscriber. [See -ER[1].] One who proscribes.

1697 DRYDEN *Æneid* Ded., Ess. (ed. Ker) II. 219 The triumvir and proscriber had descended to us in a more hideous form than they now appear. **1869** *Daily News* 17 July, Where frequent revolutions have divided parties into proscribers and proscribed.

proscript, *a.* and *sb.*[1] [ad. L. *prōscript-us*, pa. pple. of *prōscrīb-ĕre* to PROSCRIBE. So obs. F. *proscript*, F. *proscrit*.]

†**A.** *adj.* (prəʊˈskrɪpt). Proscribed: see PROSCRIBE *v.* 2. *Obs.*

1582-8 *Hist. James VI* (1825) 29 The disobeyers war maid proscript and forefaltit, to the end he mycht be also anoyntit with the fatnes of thair lands and rents. **1600** HOLLAND *Livy* LXXXIX. Epit. 1252 Cn. Domitius, one of the proscript outlawes. **1628** tr. *Mathieu's Powerfull Favorite* 29 A Proscript man who to enioy the goods of his wife, told her that he would kill himselfe, she added that she would accompanie him.

B. *sb.* (ˈprəʊskrɪpt). One who is proscribed.

1576 FLEMING *Panopl. Epist.* 148 L. Cæsar, her brother, when hee was a proscript or outlawe. **1652-62** HEYLIN *Cosmogr.* I. (1682) 240 So high an estimat did they set upon the casual death of this Proscript. **1835** SHOBERL tr. *Chateaubriand's Trav.* Introd. (ed. 3) I. 37 Proscripts never open a public school of philosophy. **1899** *Blackw. Mag.* June 1003/2 No proscript could find a refuge beyond the reach of the Cæsars.

†**proscript,** *sb.*[2] *Obs. rare.* [ad. L. *prōscript-um*, pa. pple. neut. of *prōscrīb-ĕre* to PROSCRIBE.]

A prohibition, an interdict.

1570 FOXE *A. & M.* (ed. 2) 374/1 He should be within the daunger of this proscript. *Ibid.*, Princes to auoyd the paine of thys proscript, were ready to do whatsoeuer the pope would haue them..do.

proscription (prəʊˈskrɪpʃən). [ad. L. *prōscriptiōn-em*, n. of action f. *prōscrīb-ĕre* to PROSCRIBE. Cf. F. *proscription* (1486 in Godef.).]

1. The action of proscribing; the condition or fact of being proscribed; decree of condemnation to death or banishment; outlawry. Also *fig.*

1387 TREVISA *Higden* (Rolls) VII. 443 In þat tyme [in] Engelond was robberie under kyng William þe Rede, and proscripciouns and excilinges and takynge into [the] kynges hond. **1412-20** LYDG. *Chron. Troy* IV. xxxiv. (MS. Digby 230) lf. 159/1 Exile, werre, cheynes, and presoun, Proscripcioun and captiuite. *a* **1533** LD. BERNERS *Gold. Bk. M. Aurel.* (1546) B viij, The tyme of Sylla, whan he made the vniuersall proscription agaynste the Marians. **1600** DYMMOK *Ireland* (1843) 14 This cuntry..was very well quieted by a proscription of the O'Connors made by the erle of Kildare. **1738** BOLINGBROKE *On Parties* Ded. 16 To hang up the Tables of Proscription, without the Power of sending Centurions to cut off every Head that wears a Face disliked at Court, would be Madness in a Prince. **1874** GREEN *Short Hist.* ix. §8. 675 William..was resolved that no bloodshed or proscription should follow the revolution.

2. Denunciation, interdiction, prohibition by authority; exclusion or rejection by public order.

1659 in *Burton's Diary* (1828) IV. 284 The saving of their rights is the clear proscription of their rights. **1775** JOHNSON *Tax. no Tyr.* 62 A proscription published by a Colony against the Mother-country. **1854** MILMAN *Lat. Chr.* IV. vii. (1864) II. 342 Iconoclasm..was a mere negative doctrine, a proscription of those sentiments which had full possession of the popular mind. **1877** C. GEIKIE *Christ* liii. (1879) 627 A land afflicted by social proscription.

proscriptive (prəʊˈskrɪptɪv), *a.* [f. L. *prōscript-*, ppl. stem of *prōscrīb-ĕre* to PROSCRIBE + -IVE.] Characterized by proscribing; tending to proscribe; of the nature or character of proscription.

1757 FOOTE *Author* I. Wks. 1799 I. 134 A most noble triumvirate; and..as proscriptive and arbitrary, as the famous Roman one. **1781** GIBBON *Decl. & F.* xxxv. (1788) VI. 143 The Imperial ministers pursued with proscriptive laws, and ineffectual arms, the rebels whom they had made. **1853** HOLLAND *Mem. J. Badger* i. (1854) 23 The powerful and established party..becomes proscriptive towards the new and weaker organizations.

Hence **proˈscriptively** *adv.*, by way of proscription; **proˈscriptiveness**, the quality of being proscriptive.

1882 OGILVIE (Annandale), Proscriptively. **1886** RAVLIN *Progr. Th. Grt. Subj.* v. 70 The proscriptiveness of ecclesiastical intolerance is a characteristic of a dead church.

proscutal, proscutellar, etc.: see PRO-[2] 2.

prose (prəʊz), *sb.* Also 6 proese, proase, *Sc.* pross, prois. [a. F. *prose* (13th c. in Littré), ad. L. *prōsa* (*ōrātio*), lit. straightforward discourse, sb. use of fem. of *prōs-us*, for earlier *prors-us* adj. straightforward, straight, direct, contr. from *prōvers-us*, pa. pple. of *prōvert-ĕre* to turn forwards. Hence med.L. *prōsa* an accentual hymn, in which the prose pronunciation and order is used.]

1. a. The ordinary form of written or spoken language, without metrical structure; esp. as a species or division of literature. Opposed to *poetry*, *verse*, *rime*, or *metre*.

c **1330** R. BRUNNE *Chron. Wace* (Rolls) 10975 But ffrensche men wryten hit in prose, Right as he dide, hym for to alose. *c* **1386** CHAUCER *Melib.* Prol. 19 Gladly quod I by goddes sweete pyne I wol yow telle a litel thyng in prose. **1483** CAXTON *Cato* 3 Two partyes—the fyrst is in prose and the second in verse. **1575** LANEHAM *Let.* (1817) 15 The thing which heer I report in vnpolisht proez, waz thear pronounced in good meeter and matter. **1596** DALYRYMPLE tr. *Leslie's Hist. Scot.* x. 468 Monie vther thingis baith in prois and verse he wrote. **1667** MILTON *P.L.* I. 16 Things unattempted yet in Prose or Rhime. **1718** LADY M. W. MONTAGU *Let. to Abbé Conti* 31 July, I..will..continue the rest of my account in plain prose. **1800** WORDSW. *Lyr. Ball.* (ed. 2) Pref. *note*, Much confusion has been introduced into criticism by this contradistinction of Poetry and Prose... The only strict antithesis to Prose is Metre. **1833** COLERIDGE *Table-t.* 3 July, The definition of good prose is—proper words in their proper places. **1880** M. ARNOLD *Ess. Crit.*, *Stud. Poet.* (1888) 39 The needful qualities for a fit prose are regularity, uniformity, precision, balance.

b. with *a* and *pl.* A piece of prose, as opp. to a poem; a composition in prose; a prose exercise. Now *rare* or *Obs.* exc. in school or college use.

1589 PUTTENHAM *Eng. Poesie* III. xvi. (Arb.) 184 The Greekes vsed a manner of speech or writing in their proses, that went by clauses, finishing the words of like tune. **1646** J. HALL *Poems* I. 5 Gently to amble in a York-shire prose. **1865** CARLYLE *Fredk. Gt.* XIX. viii. V. 607 New Verses or light Proses. **1901** *Punch* 9 Jan. 20/1 When my tutor fond supposes I am writing Latin proses.

¶ **c.** In ME., A (prose) story or narrative.

(The pl. was app. sometimes confounded with *proses*, *proces*, PROCESS *sb.* 4; this being, as in F., sing. and pl.)

c **1400** *Laud Troy Bk.* 6357 He fond her bokes bothe two ..In siker proses and no romaunce. *c* **1400** *Destr. Troy* 11523 All the pepull in þat presse, þat the prose herd, Afermyt hit as fyn þat þe freike said. *a* **1400-50** *Alexander* 2062 And slike a pas, sais þe prose, to Persy he ridis. *Ibid.* 2397 A croune all of clere gold, clustrid with gemmes, Of fyfty ponde with þe payse, as þe prose tellis.

2. *Eccl.* A piece of rhythmical prose or rimed accentual verse, sung or said between the epistle and gospel at certain masses: also called a *sequence*.

Called *prōsa* in Latin in distinction from *versus* applied to the ancient quantitative metres: see P. Wagner *Introd. Gregorian Melodies* (Eng. transl. 234, etc.).

c **1449** PECOCK *Repr.* (Rolls) 201 Also in the prose clepid a sequence which is sungun in the Feeste of the Cross is Hiȝing, aftir that manye spechis there ben mad to the cros. **1486** *Rec. St. Mary at Hill* 16 Euery persone..syngyng a Respond of Seynte Stephen with the prose therto. **1561** T. NORTON tr. *Calvin's Inst.* III. xx. (1634) 427 In all their Letanies, Hymnes, and Proses, where no honour is left ungiven to dead Saints, there is no mention of Christ. **1822** K. DIGBY *Broadst. Hon.* III. (1848) 90 The stanzas of the new worship proposed as more worthy of God than the ancient proses of the Church. **1882** ROCKSTRO in Grove *Dict. Mus.* III. 465 In the Middle Ages it [Sequence] was called a Prose; because, though written for the most part in rhymed Latin..the cadence of its syllables was governed, not as in classical Poetry, by quantity, but by accent—a peculiarity which deprived it of all claim to consideration as Verse of any kind. **1885** *Cath. Dict.*, *Sequence*, In the revision of the Roman Missal in the sixteenth century, only four sequences were retained: 'Victimæ Paschali'.., 'Veni, Sancte Spiritus'.., 'Lauda, Sion'.., the 'Dies Iræ'... A fifth prose, 'Stabat Mater'..must have been added very recently, since neither Le Brun nor Benedict XIV. recognise it.

†**b.** Hence, *in prose* is used in the following instances app., as = in rimed, as opposed to quantitative verse. *Obs.*

1486 *Surtees Misc.* (1888) 54 Which shall salute the king w[t] wordes folowing in prose... Most reverend, rightwose regent of this rigalitie, Whos primative patrone I peyre to your presence [*rimes* citie..prehemynence.]. *Ibid.* 55 Saying the wordes folowing unto the king in prose..Most prudent prince of pruved prevision [etc.].

3. *fig.* (from 1). Plain, simple, matter-of-fact, (and hence) dull or commonplace expression, quality, spirit, etc. (The opposite of POETRY 5.)

1561 T. NORTON tr. *Calvin's Inst.* I. 18 For the plaine prose hereof is to cleare to be subject to any cauillations at all. **1641** MILTON *Ch. Govt.* II. Pref., Wks. 1851 III. 143 Sitting here below in the cool element of prose. **1742** YOUNG *Nt. Th.* IV. 645 That Prose of Piety, a lukewarm Praise. **1876** LOWELL *Ode 4th July* III. iii, To see things as they are, or shall be soon, In the frank prose of undissembling noon. **1900** 'SARAH GRAND' *Babs* xv, Mrs. Normanton was a broad embodiment of the prose and commonplace of her class.

4. a. A dull, commonplace, or wearisome discourse or piece of writing; a prosy discourse. Also, a dull, prosy person. *colloq.*

1688 R. HOLME *Armoury* III. 175/2 Mr. Guillims had not needed to have used such a long prose. **1813** BYRON in *Daily News* (1899) 29 June 6/1, I have sent you a long prose. I hope your answer will be equal in length. **1840** J. H. NEWMAN *Lett.* (1891) II. 300 All this is a miserable prose. **1844** DICKENS *Mart. Chuz.* xxxvii. 439, I verily believe you have said that fifty thousand times, in my hearing. What a Prose you are! **1897** *Life & Lett. B. Jowett* I. v. 129 He received many a 'prose' from Jowett on the philosophy of law and on the various questions of the hour.

b. *Old colloq.* Familiar talk, chat, gossip; a talk.

1805 MRS. CREEVEY in *C. Papers*, etc. (1904) I. 68, I had a great deal of comfortable prose with her. **1807** EARL MALMESBURY *Diaries & Corr.* III. 385 Long prose with the Duke of Portland till one in the morning. **1825** BROCKETT *N.C. Gloss.*, *Pross*, talk, conversation—rather of the gossiping kind. 'Let us have a bit of *pross*.' **1848** R. D. HAMPDEN in *Some Mem.* (1871) 162 She does not forget the long friendly proses that you have had together, and she longs to have another talk-out with you.

5. *attrib.* (often hyphened to the following word). **a.** Consisting of, composed or written in prose.

(In this and the following, substituted for PROSAIC 1.)

1711 SHAFTESB. *Charac.* (1737) III. 254 Which after the manner of my familiar prose-satir I presume to criticize. **1718** POPE *Let. to Dk. Buckhm.* 1 Sept., There had been a very elegant Prose-translation before. **1817** COLERIDGE *Biog. Lit.* 23 In verse or prose, or in verse-text aided by prose-comment. **1862** STANLEY *Jew. Ch.* (1877) I. xi. 206 Here we have..the prose account. **1875** LOWELL *Spenser* Wks. 1890 IV. 322 Bunyan..is the Ulysses of his own prose-epic.

b. Composing or writing in prose.

1668 DRYDEN *Evening's Love* III. i, The prose-wits playing, and the verse-wits rooking. **1711** SHAFTESB. *Charac.* (1737) I. 235 Poets and prose-authors in every kind. **1866** J. MARTINEAU *Ess.* I. 172 In..First Principles we have a kind of prose Lucretius.

c. *fig.* Having the character of prose; plain, matter-of-fact, commonplace: = PROSAIC 2.

1818 HAZLITT *Eng. Poets* viii. (1870) 194 Poets are not ideal beings; but have their prose-sides. **1864** WEBSTER s.v., The prose duties of life. **1905** *Q. Rev.* Oct. 485 For the poet the aesthetic value of the Gospels is independent of their prose-truth.

6. *Comb.*, as ***prose book, work; prose-inditing*** sb. and adj., ***prose-like*** adj.; **prose fiction**, the genre of fictional narratives written in prose; †**prose-master**, a master of prose, one who excels in prose composition; **prose-poem**, a prose work having the style or character of a poem; so **prose-poet, prose-poetry**; †**prose-printer**, a printer of prose (in quot. = prose author); **prose sense**, the meaning of a poem as it can be paraphrased in prose; **prose style**, characteristic manner of writing in prose; **prose-writer**, one who writes or composes prose, an author who writes in prose; so ***prose-writing***.

1940 DYLAN THOMAS *Let.* 13 May (1966) 248, I do not want to write another straight *prosebook yet. **1382** WYCLIF *Job* Prol., The litle distinccioun that leueth with *prose enditing is wouen. **1841** *Prose-fiction [see PERFECT *a.* 4 a]. **1848** MILL *Pol. Econ.* I. II. xiv. 467 The most successful writer of prose fiction (Scott). **1919** V. WOOLF in *Times Lit. Suppl.* 10 Apr. 189/2 It is for..[the historian of literature] to ascertain whether we are now at the beginning, or middle, or end, of a great period of prose fiction. **1957** *Encycl. Brit.* XVI. 573/2 Dickens, perhaps the most remarkable genius in the history of English prose fiction. **1742** P. FRANCIS tr. *Horace's Art P.* 138 For Telephus or Peleus..must complain In *prose-like Style. **1656** EARL MONM. tr. *Boccalini's Pol. Touchstone* (1674) 270 *Prose-Master Major to his Majestie. **1842** POE in *Graham's Mag.* Jan. 69/1 Criticism is *not*..an essay, nor a sermon, nor an oration,..nor a *prose-poem. **1850** C. KINGSLEY *Alton Locke* I. ix. 139 That great prose poem, the single epic of modern days, Thomas Carlyle's 'French Revolution'. **1906** *Daily Chron.* 15 Jan. 3/4 The so-called prose-poem is very rarely attempted. **1711** SHAFTESB. *Charac.* (1737) I. 162 They have vulgarly pass'd for a sort of *prose-poets. **1860** GEN. P. THOMPSON *Audi Alt.* III. cxiii. 42/2 The prose-poet Bunyan's 'Holy War'. **1887** SAINTSBURY *Hist. Elizab. Lit.* ii. 41 Sidney commits himself..to the pestilent heresy of *prose-poetry, saying that verse is 'only an ornament of poetry'. **1581** SIDNEY *Apol. Poetrie* (Arb.) 68 Peculier to Versifiers, and..not..among *Prose-printers. **1947** C. BROOKS *Well Wrought Urn* xi. 182 The '*prose-sense' of the poem is not a rack on which the stuff of the poem is hung. **1852** THACKERAY *Esmond* III. iii. 88 His [*sc.* Addison's] *prose style I think is altogether inimitable. **1906** R. BROOKE *Let.* 10 May (1968) 51 This effort has..worked..havoc in my carefully elaborated prose-style. **1959** G. D. PAINTER *Proust* I. viii. 115 His [*sc.* Proust's] prose style was..faded and artificial. **1976** N. FREELING *Lake Isle* xiii. 120 Someone, presumably..has been phoning somebody. A prefect to judge from the prose style. *c* **1827** MILL *Speech* in *Adelphi* (1924) I. 692 The very small number of good *prose works which have been published for many years past, except indeed novels. **1934** J. JOYCE *Let.* 1 June (1966) III. 306, I work every day alone at my big long wide high deep dense prosework. **1978** W. WHITE *Whitman's Daybks. & Notebks.* I. p. xxiii, Every name of a person, place, book, poem, prose work, or a 'situation' in Whitman's life and times that seemed to me to call for annotation, I have annotated. **1611** WHITAKER in *Coryat's Crudities* Panegyr. Verses d v, The most peerelesse Poeticall *Prose-writer. **1697** DRYDEN *Virg., Ess. Georg.* (1721) I. 202 Where the Prose-writer tells us plainly what ought to be done, the Poet often conceals the Precept in a Description. **1847** GROTE *Greece* II. xxix. IV. 130 The philosopher Pherekydês of Syros, about 550 B.C., is called by some the earliest prose-writer. **1769** R. WOOD *Ess. Homer* 60 It is allowed on all hands, that *Prose writing was unknown in Greece, till long after the Poet's time. **1787** SIR J. HAWKINS *Johnson* 255 A taste in morals, in poetry, and prose-writing.

prose (prəʊz), *v.* [f. prec. sb.; cf. F. *proser* (*a* 1613 in Littré) to turn into or write in prose.]

1. *trans.* To express, compose, or write in prose; to translate or turn into prose.

c **1393** CHAUCER *Scogan* 41 Al schal passyn þat men prose or ryme. *c* **1450** J. SHIRLEY in *B.M. Addit. MS.* 16,165 lf. 4 Boicius de consolacione prosed in Englische by Chaucier. **1785** BURNS *2nd Ep. to J. Lapraik* vi, An' if ye winna mak it clink, By Jove I'll prose it! **1893** JACOBS *More Eng. Fairy T.* (1894) p. viii, I have had no scruple in prosing a ballad or softening down over-abundant dialect.

b. *intr.* To compose or write prose. Also *to prose it.*

1805 SOUTHEY in Robberds *Mem. W. Taylor* II. 77, I am prosing, not altogether against my will. **1812** COMBE *Picturesque* I. (Chandos) 7 I'll prose it here, I'll verse it there, And picturesque it every where. **1834** *Tait's Mag.* I. 378 I've rhymed, I've prosed..In short done everything.

2. *intr.* To discourse in a prosy manner; to talk or write prosily; *old colloq.* and *dial.* to converse familiarly, chat, gossip.

1797 TWEDDELL *Rem.* xxxii. (1815) 171 The time that you and I, my good Mother, used to prose over the parlour-fire, till you drove me away to bed. **1813** MOORE *Post-bag*, etc. (ed. 2) 48 To wait till the Irish affairs were decided—That is, till both houses had prosed and divided. **1819** KEATS *Otho* I. ii. 189 Pray, do not prose, good Ethelbert, but speak What is your purpose. **1879** A. LANG in *Academy* 11 Jan. 25/1 That mythical stage of man's existence when he was eternally prosing about the weather. **1885** FRANCES E. TROLLOPE in *Graphic* 21 Feb. 190/1, I won't keep you here prosing with me.

b. *trans.* with *adv.* or *phr.* To bring into some specified condition by prosing; to talk or lecture *into* or *to* (some state).

1825 R. H. FROUDE in *Rem.* (1838) I. 178, I think I must come to you to be prosed and put into a better way. **1883** F. M. PEARD *Contrad.* II. 192 In spite of my having prosed you to death. **1897** KER *Epic & Rom.* 275 The important things of the story may be made to come with the stroke and flash of present reality, instead of being prosed away by the historian.

prosecretin: see PRO-² 1.

prosect (prəʊ'sɛkt), *v. rare.* [Formed (after next) on L. *prōsect-*, ppl. stem of *prōsecāre* to cut away or off, cut up, f. PRO-¹ 1 + *secāre* to cut.] *trans.* To dissect (a dead body, or part of one) in preparation for anatomical demonstration; *absol.* to perform the office of a prosector. So **prosection** (prəʊ'sɛkʃən), dissection for purposes of anatomical demonstration; the function of a prosector.

1890 *Cent. Dict.*, Prosect..Prosection.

prosector (prəʊ'sɛktə(r)). [a. late L. *prōsector* (Tertull.) a cutter up, an anatomist, agent-n. f. L. *prōsec-āre* to cut up. So F. *prosecteur* (1835 in *Dict. Acad.*), after which the English designation was prob. introduced.] One whose business is to dissect dead bodies in preparation for anatomical research or demonstration, as assistant to a lecturer on anatomy, a surgeon, or a zoological society.

1857 DUNGLISON *Med. Dict.*, *Prosector*, dissector. **1858** MAYNE *Expos. Lex.*, *Prosector*, term for an anatomist; applied to one who prepares the subject for the lecturer on anatomy; the same as *Dissector*. **1861** HULME tr. *Moquin-Tandon* II. v. ii. 267 M. Robelin, Prosector to the Faculty of Sciences at Montpellier. **1883** *Manch. Exam.* 24 Nov. 5/3 The Council of the Zoological Society have decided to employ a prosector, whose chief duty will be that of dissecting animals that may die in the gardens.

Hence **prosec'torial** *a.*, of or pertaining to a prosector; ‖**prosec'torium** [mod.L.: see -ORIUM], a room or building for prosection; the place of operation of a prosector; **pro'sectorship**, the position or office of prosector.

1881 *Nature* 20 Oct. 579/2 If the Zoological Society had not in 1865 established its prosectorship, we should have seen little of the really solid advances in our knowledge of the anatomy of the two higher classes of vertebrated animals. **1883** *Athenæum* 28 Apr. 544/1 Prof. Garrod, Mr. Forbes's predecessor in the prosectorial office. **1901** *Ibis* Apr. 344 The rich collections of the British Museum, the Zoological Society's Prosectorium, and other leading institutions.

prosecutable ('prɒsɪkjuːtəb(ə)l), *a.* [f. PROSECUTE *v.* + -ABLE.] That may be prosecuted; liable to prosecution.

1802–12 BENTHAM *Ration. Judic. Evid.* (1827) V. 436 Cases prosecutable in the way of indictment. **1836** CHALMERS *Wks.* V. 377 Its violation shall be made a prosecutable offence. **1892** STEVENSON *Across the Plains* 230 A claim not prosecutable in any court of law.

prosecute ('prɒsɪkjuːt), *v.* Also 6 **proseqwuit**, **-quut**, 6–7 **-qute**; 7 *pa. pple.* (*Sc.*) **prosecute**. [f. L. *prōsecūt-*, ppl. stem of *prōsequī* to follow, pursue, attend, accompany; to honour or present (a person) with; f. *prō*, PRO-¹ 1 + *sequī* to follow. So obs. F. *prosecuter* (1519 in Godef.).]

1. a. *trans.* To follow up, pursue; to persevere or persist in, follow out, go on with (some action, undertaking, or purpose) with a view to completing or attaining it.

1432–50 tr. *Higden* (Rolls) V. 51 Origenes sende an epistole..preyenge and comfortenge his fader to prosecute [*L. prosequi*] that he hade begunne. **1509** FISHER *Fun. Serm. Hen. VII* A ij, As this honorable audyence now is here assembled to prosecute the funeral obseruaunces [etc.]. **1568** *Reg. Privy Council Scot.* I. 624 Quhill thai renew thair forceis and prosequute thair formair detestabill interpryise. **1614** RALEIGH *Hist. World* III. (1634) 102 How the Army came into the Territorie of Synope, and there prosequuted the same purpose. **1643** DRUMM. OF HAWTH. *Skiamachia* Wks. (1711) 192 That the late articles of the treaty of peace ..may be carefully and truly prosecute. **1676** RAY *Corr.* (1848) 126 If still you prosecute the same studies and inquiries. **1754** RICHARDSON *Grandison* xxvii. (1781) II. 251 Determined to prosecute their intended tour. **1836** H. COLERIDGE *North. Worthies* I. 40 The Dutch war, commenced without necessity, and prosecuted..with ill-judged parsimony. **1874** CARPENTER *Ment. Phys.* I This inquiry..has not until recently been systematically prosecuted.

b. *intr.* or *absol.* To continue, go on.

a **1529** SKELTON *Replyc.* 158 What shullde I prosecute, Or more of this to clatter? **1585** T. WASHINGTON tr. *Nicholay's Voy.* I. xix. 22[He] sued..for licence too prosecute on his iourney. **1588** PARKE tr. *Mendoza's Hist. China* 357 Here hee doth prosecute in things which the saide fathers did see.

2. *trans.* To carry out, perform; to engage in, carry on, practise, exercise, follow.

1576 FLEMING *Panopl. Epist.* 342 Those exercises, that are vsually prosequuted in the common schooles. **1610** WILLET *Hexapla Dan.* 141 True repentance..may not be deferred or put off but speedily prosequuted. **1707** MORTIMER *Husb.* (1721) II. 177 It is a piece of great neglect amongst us, that the sowing of them is not more prosecuted. **1824** J. MARSHALL *Const. Opin.* (1839) 307 These privileges.. cannot be enjoyed unless the trade may be prosecuted. **1883** GOODE *Fish. Indust. U.S.* 23 (Fish. Exhib. Publ.) The salmon and other fisheries of Puget Sound are prosecuted chiefly by the aid of Indian fishermen.

3. To follow out in detail; 'to proceed in consideration or disquisition of' (J.); to go into the particulars of, investigate; to treat of or deal with in greater detail.

1538 STARKEY *England* II. i. 162 Yf I schold partycularly prosecute euery thyng..perteynyng to thes materys, we schold not fynysch our communycatyon thys xv. days and more. **1577** HANMER *Anc. Eccl. Hist.* (1619) 10 The which Josephus hath prosecuted at large in his histories. **1612** BRINSLEY *Lud. Lit.* xiii. (1627) 178 Speciall rules and directions giuen, for writing their Theames,..prosecuting the seuerall parts of the Theame. **1672** CAVE *Prim. Chr.* III. iii. (1673) 304 This Argument Eusebius particularly prosecutes. **1743** EMERSON *Fluxions* Pref. 14 As to the Resolution of Problems by infinite Series, I have been more sparing of that, because it has been well prosecuted by others. **1873** H. ROGERS *Orig. Bible* ii. (ed. 3) 63, I do not further prosecute this subject.

†**4.** To follow up (an advantage); to improve, take advantage of (an opportunity). *Obs.*

1594 PLAT *Jewell-ho.* I. 27 They prosecuted this good happe of theirs further the next yeare. **1654** tr. *Martini's Conq. China* 24 The Tartars..prosecute the victory with all quickness and diligence. **1754** HUME *Hist. Eng.* (1761) I. ix. 191 The French Army..left Henry free to prosecute his Advantages against his other Enemies.

†**5. a.** To follow quickly with hostile intent (a fleeing man or beast); to chase; = PURSUE. *Obs.*

1568 GRAFTON *Chron.* II. 166 The king..prosecuted Dauid the brother of Lewlyn from towne to towne. **1607** TOPSELL *Four-f. Beasts* (1658) 24 These wild asses..cast backward with their heels stones with such violence, as they pierce the brests of them that prosecute them. **1648** CROMWELL *Let.* 20 Aug. in *Carlyle*, We..prosecuted them home to Warrington Town. **1697** DRYDEN *Virg. Georg.* III. 619 The Mastiffs gen'rous Breed,..who, for the Folds Relief, Will prosecute with Cries the nightly Thief.

absol. **1549** LATIMER *1st Serm. bef. Edw. VI* (Arb.) 24 Pharao..what tyme he hard of the passage of Goddes people,..he did prosecute after, entendyng to destroye them. **1607** TOPSELL *Four-f. Beasts* (1658) 4 The Munkeys ..fling stones at them that prosecute to take them.

†**b.** To follow with vengeance; to revenge (injuries, etc.). *Obs.*

1551 ROBINSON tr. *More's Utop.* II. (1895) 245 But whether it were righte or wrong, it was with so cruell and mortal warre reuenged... So egerly the Vtopians prosequute the iniuries done to ther frindes, yea, in money matters; and not their owne likewise.

6. *Law.* **a.** To institute legal proceedings against (a person) for some offence; to arraign before a court of justice for some crime or wrong.

1579 *Reg. Privy Council Scot.* III. 159 To be apprehendit and prosequutit be justice. **1647** CLARENDON *Hist. Reb.* I. §11 Any Person..who was not either immediately Prosecuted by the Court, or in evident Disfavour there. **1769** BLACKSTONE *Comm.* IV. xxiii. 315 If he made his peace with the king, still he might be prosecuted at the suit of the party. **1780** BENTHAM *Princ. Legisl.* xi. §24 You prosecute him for the cheat. **1818** SCOTT *Hrt. Midl.* xxxi, Are you aware of the law of this country—that if you lodge this charge you will be bound over to prosecute this gang? *Mod.* Notice. Trespassers will be prosecuted as the law directs.

b. with the crime or offence as object.

1680 OTWAY *Orphan* II. iv, If the offence be found Within my reach..I'd prosecute it with severest Vengeance. **1769** ROBERTSON *Chas. V*, *View St. Europe* I. 42 Resentment was almost the sole motive for prosecuting crimes. **1863** H. COX *Instit.* I. x. 235 The House of Commons had given up the practice of prosecuting state crimes.

c. In phrase ***to prosecute an action, a claim.*** †Formerly also ***to prosecute an accusation, the law.***

1596 BACON *Max. & Use Com. Law* II. (1636) 12 Hee also then bindeth to appeare those that give testimony and prosecute the accusation. *Ibid.* 64 If hee prosecuted the law against the thiefe and convict him of the same felony, he shall have his goods again. **1654** SIR E. NICHOLAS in *N. Papers* (Camden) II. 51 The strange accusation violently prosecuted against Sʳ Edw. Hyde at the Council Board at Paris. **1709** STRYPE *Ann. Ref.* I. xxiv. 246 They did not put or continue them in prison, nor prosecute the law upon them. **1817** LD. CASTLEREAGH in *Parl. Deb.* 1853 Nothing but a deep sense of the duty which I owed to the public could..have induced me to prosecute that action. **1818** CRUISE *Digest* (ed. 2) V. 242 That the parties included in the exception should have five years clear from every disability there mentioned, to prosecute their claim.

d. *intr.* or *absol.* To institute or carry on a prosecution, to be prosecutor.

1611 B. JONSON *Catiline* v. vi, When they are done, the laws may prosequute. **1657** W. RAND tr. *Gassendi's Life Peiresc* II. 2 He durst not prosecute against the party he supposed had stollen them. **1765** BLACKSTONE *Comm.* I. vii.

268 He [the king] is therefore the proper person to prosecute for all public offences and breaches of the peace, being the person injured in the eye of the law. **1817** *Parl. Deb.* 418 He had at that time prosecuted for high treason, because he disdained to bring the persons.. before a jury for any other crime than that of which he was conscientiously satisfied they were guilty. **1865** *Chambers's Encycl.* VII. 799/1 If a person is murdered, some one of the relatives naturally prosecutes. **1901** G. B. SHAW *Capt. Brassbound's Conversion* III. 286 The counsel for the prosecution can proceed to prosecute. The floor is yours, Lady Waynflete. **1966** *Listener* 9 June 828/1 Even when the police prosecute, committal for trial cannot be left entirely to their discretion. **1971** *Reader's Digest Family Guide to Law* 743/1 A private individual has the right in most cases to follow the same procedure, even if the police have decided not to prosecute.

†**7.** To seek to gain or bring about; to follow after, strive for. *Obs.*

1595 *Blanchardyn* vii. B iij b, Her beautie hath carryed such prayse and commendation throughout the world, that all the neighbouring Princes haue prosecuted her loue. **1604** T. WRIGHT *Passions* I. iii. 14 Selfe-love.. inticeth.. to prosecute pleasures. **1641** J. JACKSON *True Evang. T.* III. 224 Let peace be prosecuted, and followed, by the safest and surest rule of this pursuit. **1722** WOLLASTON *Relig. Nat.* ix. (1738) 218 [We] at the same time [shall] prosecute our own proper happiness.

†**8.** To follow (*fig.*) *with* honour, regard, execration, or other feeling or its expression. (A figure from literally following a person with shouts of acclamation, execration, etc.) *Obs.*

1538 BALE *Thre Lawes* 1981 To worshyp one God aboue And hys poore neyber to prosecute with loue. *c* **1540** tr. *Pol. Verg. Eng. Hist.* (Camden) I. 206 The Danes didd.. with honorable sepulture, prosecute the corps of Hubo. **1632** MASSINGER *City Madam* v. iii, Prosecuted with the fatal curses Of widows, undone orphans, and what else. **1664** JER. TAYLOR *Dissuas. Popery* II. II. ii. (1667) 21 Prosecuting the Lord Jesus Christ with a singular honour. **1741** WARBURTON *Div. Legat.* II. 168 The same Animal was prosecuted, in one place, with divine Honours.

†**9.** To pursue (a person) vindictively or with malice; to persecute. *Obs.*

1588 *Let.* in *Harl. Misc.* (Malh.) II. 67 Not maliciously bent to have men prosecuted to death, only for their religion. **1665** SIR T. HERBERT *Trav.* (1677) 61 The eldest sonne of Aben Babur.. who was sadly prosecuted through the power and malice of Mirza Kameron his younger Brother. **1678** CUDWORTH *Intell. Syst.* I. i. §24. 24 He acknowledged Dæmons or Angels; declaring that some of these fell from Heaven, and were since prosecuted by a Divine Nemesis. **1704** *Clarendon's Hist. Reb.* III. Ded. 8 Prosecuting this Author with unjust and false accusations.

Hence **ˈprosecuting** *vbl. sb.* and *ppl. a.*

1603 KNOLLES *Hist. Turks* (1638) 194 Godly wars.. from prosecuting whereof he was.. by his violence withdrawn. **1643** DRUMM. OF HAWTH. *Skiamachia* Wks. (1711) 208 The prosecuting and effectuating of such a blessed and necessary work. **1832** *Jrnl. Indiana Ho. Representatives* 6 Dec. 33 Duly elected Prosecuting Attorney of the 2d Judicial Circuit. **1848** DICKENS *Dombey* iv, The prosecuting of a ship's discoveries. **1870** *Standard* 7 Dec., The borough prosecuting solicitor. **1912** M. NICHOLSON *Hoosier Chron.* 180 The Republican prosecuting attorney of Ranger County joined with the local bank in certifying Miles's probity. **1959** *Granta* 6 June 33/2 'Where were you?' shouted the bluff prosecuting counsel. **1976** *Daily Mirror* 16 July 9/2 Prosecuting authorities are now more sensitive to the need to investigate suspicions of corruption.

prosecution (prɒsɪˈkjuːʃən). Also 6 prosequutioun, -quitioun, 6–7 -quution. [a. OF. *prosecution* (1294 in Godef.), or ad. late L. *prōsecūtiōn-em*, n. of action f. *prōsequī* to PROSECUTE.] The action of prosecuting.

1. The following up, continuing, or carrying out *of* any action, scheme, or purpose, with a view to its accomplishment or attainment.

1567 *Reg. Privy Council Scot.* I. 529 Proceding still in the prosequutioun of that rychtuous querrell. **1589** *Ibid.* IV. 440 The prosequutioun of hir jornay. **1607** TOPSELL *Four-f. Beasts* (1658) 543 The same devises, diligence, labour, prosecution, and observations, are to be used in the hunting of the Boar. **1682** *Enq. Elect. Sheriffs* 13 The Design, in prosecution whereof, they are so zealous. **1747** *Col. Rec. Pennsylv.* V. 142 For the present to lay aside the prosecution of the intended Expedition. **1852** H. ROGERS *Ecl. Faith* (1853) 198 In the prosecution of their object. **1884** *Manch. Exam.* 22 May 5/2 Nothing was to be gained by the further prosecution of the war.

†**b.** *concr.* A continuation. *in prosecution*, in the sequel, subsequently, in due course. *Obs.*

a **1641** BP. MOUNTAGU *Acts & Mon.* iv. (1642) 255 Antipater his eldest son, of whom we shall heare much in prosecution. **1688** R. HOLME *Armoury* III. 454/1 This Chapter is a prosecution of the latter end of the foregoing.

2. The carrying on, exercise, performance, or plying *of* a pursuit, occupation, etc.

1631 WEEVER *Anc. Fun. Mon.* To Rdr. 7 In the prosequution of this businesse. **1707** ADDISON *Pres. St. War* (1708) 1 Their Prosecutions of Commerce, and Pursuits of Universal Monarchy. **1823** SCORESBY *Jrnl. Whale Fish.* p. xv, The original design of the voyage.. was the prosecution of the Whale-Fishery. **1879** *Cassell's Techn. Educ.* IV. 76/2 Well calculated for the successful prosecution of ostreoculture.

†**3.** The following out *of* anything minutely or in detail; investigation. *Obs.*

1615 CROOKE *Body of Man* 300 My purpose was onely to touch the heads of things, reseruing my selfe to heereafter for the particular prosecution. **1659** T. BUSHELL (*title*) Abridgement of the Lord Chancellor Bacon's Philosophical Theory in Mineral Prosecutions. *a* **1677** HALE *Prim. Orig. Man.* I It is not here seasonable to make a large prosecution of the particular instances. **17..** in *Westm. Gaz.* 16 Oct. (1906) 2/3 Promises.. which he design'd certainly to have comply'd with, had not a Tide of new Things flow'd in, and prevented the Method of his Prosecutions.

†**4.** The action of pursuing; a literal pursuit, chase, or hunting. *Obs.*

1567 *Reg. Privy Council Scot.* I. 530 The prosequutioun of the committaris of the said cruell murthour. **1582** *Ibid.* III. 53 In the prosequutioun of the saidis thevis and brokin men. **1610** GUILLIM *Heraldry* III. xvi. (1611) 147 Dogges of prosequution, as Beagles Terriers and such like. **1649** JER. TAYLOR *Gt. Exemp.* Exhort. §16 Let us therefore press after Jesus, as Elisha did after his Master, with an inseparable prosecution, even whithersoever he goes.

fig. **1606** SHAKS. *Ant. & Cl.* IV. xiv. 65 When I should see behinde me Th' ineuitable prosecution of disgrace and horror.

†**b.** Action or effort to obtain or get possession *of* property or a benefice. *Obs.*

1564 *Reg. Privy Council Scot.* I. 309 Quhilkis gudis the saidis Bonauenture Bodeker and Conradt Van Boekert causit to be persewit. And in the prosequitioun thairof, the materis cumin to that end, that the saidis gudis ar put, be inventure, in the handis of certane cautionaris. **1628** PRYNNE *Cens. Cozens* 41 These are so taken vp with.. the eager prosecution of some fat Benefice.

5. *Law.* **a.** In strict technical language: A proceeding either by way of indictment or information in the criminal courts, in order to put an offender upon his trial; the exhibition of a criminal charge against a person before a court of justice. **b.** In general language: The institution and carrying on of legal proceedings against a person. **c.** Loosely: The party by whom criminal proceedings are instituted and carried on. Also *attrib.*

1631 MASSINGER *Beleeve as You List* III. i, [To] commit Unto your abler trust the prosecution Of this impostor. **1765** BLACKSTONE *Comm.* I. vii. 268 In criminal proceedings, or prosecutions for offences, it would still be a higher absurdity, if the king personally sate in judgement; because in regard to these he appears in another capacity, that of prosecutor. **1769** *Ibid.* IV. xxi. 289 The regular and ordinary method of proceeding in the courts of criminal jurisdiction.. may be distributed under twelve general heads... 1. Arrest; 2. Commitment and bail; 3. Prosecution; 4. Process; 5. Arraignment, and it's incidents; 6. Plea and issue; 7. Trial, and conviction; [etc.]. **1817** W. SELWYN *Law Nisi Prius* (ed. 4) II. 993 Of the Action on the Case for a Malicious Prosecution, and in what Cases such Action may be maintained. **1832** tr. *Sismondi's Ital. Rep.* xi. 243 His third criminal prosecution began, like the two others, with torture. **1891** *Daily News* 30 Sept. 2/5 [He] contended that.. two of the prosecution witnesses had really favoured the case of the defendant. **1901** *Ibid.* 2 Mar. 7/3 The prosecution's theory was that prisoner wanted to get rid of his wife.

d. *director of public prosecutions*: an English law officer, appointed in 1879 by Act 42 & 43 Vict. c. 22, to institute and conduct criminal proceedings in the public interest. Cf. *public prosecutor* below.

1879 *Act 42 & 43 Vict.* c. 22 §2 A Secretary of State may from time to time appoint an officer to be called the Director of Public Prosecutions... It shall be the duty of the Director of Public Prosecutions, under the Superintendence of the Attorney General, to institute, undertake, or carry on such criminal proceedings.. as may be.. prescribed by regulations under this Act. **1884** *Act 47 & 48 Vict.* c. 58 §2 On and after the passing of this Act.. the person for the time holding the office of Solicitor for the affairs of Her Majesty's Treasury shall be Director of Public Prosecutions. **1902** L. L. SHADWELL in *Encycl. Brit.* XXVIII. 1/2, The director of public prosecutions attends the trial [of election petitions] personally or by representative.

†**6.** = PERSECUTION 1. *Obs.*

1647 CLARENDON *Hist. Reb.* III. §122 An Instance of as great Animosity, and Indirect Prosecution,.. as can be given. **1759** HUME *Hist. Eng.* II. ii. 491 Requiring him.. to desist from the farther prosecution of his Queen's party.

†**prosecutive,** *a. Obs. rare.* Also 7 -quutive. [f. as PROSECUTE *v.* + -IVE: cf. obs. F. *prosecutif, -ive* (1569 in Godef.) and *executive.*] Having the quality or function of prosecuting.

1617 COLLINS *Def. Bp. Ely* I. i. 48 The virtues of the prosequutiue part rule not the intellectual, but are ruled rather. **1759** R. SHIRRA in *Rem.* (1850) 111 Give place to Him in the elective faculty, the will; in the prosecutive faculty, the affections.

prosecutor (ˈprɒsɪkjuːtə(r)). [a. med.L. *prōsecūtor*, agent-n. f. *prōsequ-ī* to PROSECUTE.]

1. One who follows up or carries out any action, project, or business.

1599 SANDYS *Europæ Spec.* (1632) 83 These Iesuites.. endeavour.. to imbreed that fiercenesse and obstinacie in their schollers, as to make them hote prosecutors of their owne opinions. **1632** SPELMAN *Hist. Sacrilege* (1698) 193 The Lord Cromwel was conceived to be the principal mover, and prosecutor thereof.

†**2.** A pursuer. *Obs.*

1607 TOPSELL *Four-f. Beasts* (1658) 75 Shooting forth their darts, one against the front of the enemy, and the other against the prosecutors and followers. **1741** *Compl. Fam.-Piece* II. i. 299 He is observed to take her Measures from her Prosecutors, well knowing that she can out-run the Dogs at Pleasure.

3. One who institutes and carries on proceedings in a court of law, esp. in a criminal court. (In quot. 1670 = PROMOTER 3.) *public prosecutor*, a law officer appointed to conduct criminal prosecutions on behalf of the crown or state or in the public interest: *spec.* in Scotland, the Procurator fiscal in each county, etc.; the single officer recently appointed with this function in England is officially styled Director of public prosecutions: see PROSECUTION 5 d.

1670 BLOUNT *Law Dict.*, *Prosecutor*, is he that followeth a Cause in an others name. See *Promooters.* **1765** BLACKSTONE *Comm.* I. vii. 268 [see PROSECUTION 5]. **1769** —— *Ibid.* IV. xxvii. 362 On a conviction of larceny in particular, the prosecutor shall have restitution of his goods. **1783** W. GORDON tr. *Livy's Rom. Hist.* (1823) III. lvi. 282 Virginius was pitched on as the first prosecutor. **1839** *Encycl. Brit.* (ed. 7) XIX. 759/2 (Scotland) There seems little doubt but that in early times the king was public prosecutor... In process of time.. this office of public prosecutor naturally devolved upon the crown counsel. The principal of these is the lord advocate. *Ibid.* 760/1 The procurators fiscal of the county and burgh courts, who are the public prosecutors in their respective districts, may also be regarded as deputies of the lord advocate. **1848** WHARTON *Law Lex.*, *Public prosecutor*, the Queen, in whose name criminals are prosecuted, because all offences are said to be against the Queen's peace, her Crown, and dignity. **1877** E. ROBERTSON in *Encycl. Brit.* VI. 590/2 The distinguishing feature of Scotch criminal law is the existence of a public prosecutor. **1907** *Expositor* Feb. 187 Among them appears the Satan, a sort of Prosecutor General.

†**4.** One who prosecutes with malice; a PERSECUTOR. *Obs.*

1704 *Clarendon's Hist. Reb.* III. Ded. 10 His malicious Prosecutors afterwards scandalized him, as being the Author of such Counsels.

Hence **ˈprosecutorship,** the office of a (public) prosecutor.

1870 *Echo* 8 Dec., Mr. E. W. C—— has been appointed to the Senior Crown Prosecutorship of County Mayo.

prosecutorial (prɒsɪkjuːˈtɔərɪəl), *a.* [f. PROSECUTOR + -IAL.] Of or pertaining to a prosecuting official or his duties. Also *transf.*

1973 *N.Y. Law Jrnl.* 19 July 1/8 To our minds the participants' attempt to set up a federal crime for which these defendants stand convicted went beyond any proper prosecutorial role. **1975** *Columbia Law Rev.* LXXV. 130 Prosecutorial discretion is the power held by an agency or official charged with enforcement of the law to exercise selectivity in the choice of occasions for the law's enforcement. **1978** *N.Y. Times* 30 Mar. B3/5 The Midtown Enforcement Project has received a Federal grant.. to bring innovative enforcement and prosecutorial methods to the area from 30th Street to 60th Street from river to river. **1978** *Listener* 29 June 848/1 His closely-argued, mercilessly prosecutorial book.

prosecutrix (prɒsɪˈkjuːtrɪks). Pl. -trices (-trɪsiːz). [a. mod.L. *prōsecūtrix*, fem. agent-n. f. as PROSECUTOR + -TRIX.] A female prosecutor.

1748 SMOLLETT *Rod. Rand.* xxiii, Not one of them had compassion enough to mollify my prosecutrix. **1812** COLLINSON *Idiots & Lunaticks* I. 530 (Jod.) The prosecutrix stated that she was married. **1907** *Westm. Gaz.* 26 July 5/1 One of the prosecutrices.. described in detail how she gave the prisoner at different times various sums.

prosefy: see PROSIFY.

proseity (prəʊˈsiːɪtɪ). *Metaph.* [f. L. *prō sē* for oneself + -ITY.] The quality or condition of existing for itself, or of having itself for its own end.

1899 A. E. GARVIE *Ritschlian Theol.* ii. 48 The isolated thing will be thought of as its own cause (aseity) and its own purpose (proseity). *Ibid.* iii. 98 He [Frank] put instead of it [the absolute] the expression being through, in, and for self (aseity, inseity, proseity). **1899** P. T. FORSYTH in *Speaker* 23 Dec. 319/1 He.. calls attention to.. the proseity of Christ's work, to its nature as an ethical calling in which everything that he did was done for himself as a personality and not in an official capacity.

proselachian (prəʊsɪˈleɪkɪən). *Zool.* [PRO-[2] 1.] A hypothetical primitive selachian.

proselenic (prəʊsɪˈliːnɪk), *a. rare.* [f. PRO-[2] 1 + Gr. σελήνη moon + -IC.] Existing before the moon.

1641 H. L'ESTRANGE *God's Sabbath* 97 Though Papists inform their disciples of I know not what pro-selenique antiquitie it hath, yet sure we are that.. it was not in being above a thousand years after our Saviour.

prosely'tation. *rare.* [f. PROSELYTE *v.* + -ATION.] Proselytizing; conversion.

1826 G. S. FABER *Diffic. Romanism* (1853) 383 For the instruction and proselytation of the English Laity.

proselyte (ˈprɒsɪlaɪt), *sb.* Forms: 4 proselyt, -ilite, 4–8 -elit(e, 7 -ylite, 6– -proselyte. [ad. late L. *prosēlyt-us* (fem. *-a*), *a* 200 in Itala, Tertullian, a. Gr. προσήλυτ-ος one who has come to a place, also a convert to Judaism, prop. adj. f. προσηλυθ-, 2nd aorist stem of προσέρχ-εσθαι to come to, approach. Cf. F. *prosélyte*, OF. *proselite* (13th c. in Littré).]

1. One who has come over from one opinion, belief, creed, or party to another; a convert.

1382 WYCLIF *Matt.* xxiii. 15 Woo to ȝou, scribis and Pharisees, ypocritis, that cumpassen the se and the lond, that ȝee maken o proselite [*gloss* that is, a conuertid to ȝoure ordre; **1388** prosilite; **1535** COVERDALE proselyte]. **1611** SHAKS. *Wint. T.* v. i. 108 Would she begin a Sect, might.. make Proselytes Of who she but bid follow. **1638** SIR T. HERBERT *Trav.* (ed. 2) 27 The Portugall has preacht Christ, but have few Proselites. *a* **1639** T. CAREW *Poems* Wks. (1824) 121 Both rendred Hymen's pros'lits by thy muse. **1799** *Med. Jrnl.* I. 492 These difficulties procured the theory of Boerhaave a great number of proselytes. **1871** FREEMAN

Norm. Conq. IV. xvii. 16 The Danes were the pupils and proselytes of the English.

2. *spec.* A Gentile convert to the Jewish faith. *proselyte of righteousness* or *of the covenant*: see quot. 1831–3. *proselyte of the gate*, a proselyte who did not submit to all the ordinances of the law, esp. to circumcision, nor participate in all the privileges of an Israelite.

c **1375** *Sc. Leg. Saints* xxxvi. (*Baptista*) 1060 He [Herod] is proselit; þat is til vndirstand, þu treu, Of a payane cumyne a Iow. **1382** WYCLIF *Acts* ii. 10 Jewis, and proselitis, men of Crete and Arabye. **1581** MARBECK *Bk. of Notes* 879 They were Proselites which were Gentiles borne, and embraced the Jewish Profession. **1611** BIBLE *Transl. Pref.* 8 The Translation of Aquila a Proselite, that is, one that had turned Iew. **1831–3** E. BURTON *Eccl. Hist.* iv. (1845) 84 The Proselytes of righteousness, i.e. Gentiles who adopted circumcision and every other ordinance of the Mosaic Law. **1879** FARRAR *St. Paul* I. 139 One who was only a proselyte of the gate, one who held back from the seal of the covenant made to Abraham, would not be regarded as a full Christian any more than he would be regarded as a full Jew.

3. *attrib.* or *adj.*

1646 R. BAILLIE *Anabaptism* (1647) 135 The right of proselyte infants under the Law to the Covenant and the Sacrament which then did seal it. **1826** J. GILCHRIST *Lect.* 33 It is certain that Proselyte Baptism existed among the Jews at and previously to the time of John the Baptist. **1858** J. MARTINEAU *Stud. Chr.* 113 How would the effect of this great revolution be described to the proselyte Gentiles?

proselyte (ˈprɒsɪlaɪt), *v.* [f. prec. sb.] *trans.* To make a proselyte of; to cause to come over or turn from one opinion, belief, creed, or party to another; *esp.* to convert from one religious faith or sect to another; to proselytize.

1624 BP. MOUNTAGU *Gagg* To Rdr., I then delivered unto my neighbour the partie that should have been proselyted. **1657–83** EVELYN *Hist. Relig.* (1850) II. 133 In whose name they were to baptize and proselyte all nations. **1680** *Visor pluckt off R. Thompson* 2 In less than two years he proselyted many Anabaptists and Quakers. **1702** ECHARD *Eccl. Hist.* (1710) 85 Thus Sichem..was the first place proselyted to the Gospel. **1831** SOUTHEY in *Q. Rev.* XLV. 409 [He] endeavoured to proselyte them to his own miserable state of unbelief.

†**b.** *refl.* and *intr.* To become a proselyte. *Obs.*

1657–83 EVELYN *Hist. Relig.* (1850) II. 244 Though many proselyted, yet remains there a part, who would never be recovered to that Church. **1672** P. HENRY *Diaries & Lett.* (1882) 254 Wee reason'd long; but neither hee proselyted to mee nor I to him. **1716** M. DAVIES *Athen. Brit.* II. 254 The Arian Court-Mongring Bishops persuaded the Emperor Constantius to Proselyte him into their Arian Heterodoxy.

c. *absol.* To make proselytes, to proselytize.

1799 R. HALL *Wks.* (1833) I. 73 They would never disturb the quiet of the world by their attempts to proselyte. **1827** J. J. GURNEY in *Memoir* (1854) I. 334 His liberality enables him to proselyte more successfully. **1888** LEA *Hist. Inquisition* I. 242 To carry it out fully, they should have proselyted with the sword.

Hence **ˈproselyted** *ppl. a.*, made or become a proselyte, converted; **ˈproselyting** *vbl. sb.* and *ppl. a.*; also **ˈproselyter**, one who proselytizes or makes proselytes.

1652 EVELYN *Diary* 13 Apr., Deane Cosin's proselyted son. **1660** STILLINGFL. *Iren.* I. ii. (1662) 67 The use of Baptism in proselyting. **1785** PALEY *Mor. Philos.* (1818) II. 319 A polemical and proselyting spirit. *a* **1834** COLERIDGE in *Lit. Rem.* (1836) II. 366 An eager proselyter and intolerant. **1931** H. F. PRINGLE *Theodore Roosevelt* II. xiii. 456 Mrs. Storer went on with her proselyting. **1948** *Richmond* (Va.) *Times-Dispatch* 13 Feb. 30/1 San Francisco..was guilty of one of the worst cases of out-and-out..proselyting and subsidizing yet seen.

proselytess (ˈprɒsɪlaɪtɪs). [f. PROSELYTE *sb.* + -ESS[1].] A female proselyte; *spec.* a female convert to Judaism.

1621 AINSWORTH *Annot. Pentat.* Deut. xxii. 19 A virgin an Israelitesse..an heathen that was become a proselytesse..was free from the mulct. **1711** J. GALE *Refl. Wall's Hist. Inf. Bapt.* 356 A woman baptiz'd or wash'd, tho for uncleanness only, does nevertheless thereby become a proselytess or Jewess. **1879** FARRAR *St. Paul* (1883) 351 Among the women sat a Lydian proselytess.

†**proseˈlytical**, *a. Obs. rare.* [f. as prec. + -ICAL. Cf. F. *prosélytique* (Littré).] Of or pertaining to proselytes or to proselytism.

1581 HANMER *Jesuites Banner* B j b, Who blazed abroad at the beginning of this parliament, to vphold the proselytical Papists, that they stoode in good hope the Romishe religion would bee restored presently in England. **1658–9** EVELYN *Let. to G. Tuke* Jan., We must commit to Providence the successe of tymes & mitigation of Proselytical fervours.

proselytism (ˈprɒsɪlaɪt-, -lɪtɪz(ə)m). [In sense 1 f. PROSELYTE *sb.* + -ISM: so F. *prosélytisme* (1721 in Hatz.-Darm.); in sense 2 from PROSELYTIZE.]

1. The fact of becoming or being a proselyte; the state or condition of a proselyte.

a **1660** HAMMOND *Serm. Gen. xxxi.* 13 Wks. 1684 IV. 500 Spiritual Proselytism, to which the Jew was wont to be wash'd, as the Christian is baptized. **1683** HICKES *Case Inf. Baptism* 59 Capable of Proselytism, or entring into the Covenant after the Jewish manner. **1823** LINGARD *Hist. Eng.* V. 364 The converts laboured to diffuse the new light with all the fervour of proselytism. **1844** —— *Anglo-Sax. Ch.* (1858) I. i. 23.

2. The practice of proselytizing.

1763 HUME *Hist. Eng.* (1825) VIII. lxxi. 290 Such was his zeal for proselytism, that..he plainly stopped not at toleration and equality. **1790** BURKE *Fr. Rev.* 226 The spirit of proselytism attends this spirit of fanaticism. **1829** *Blackw. Mag.* XXV. 59 The very word proselytism was scarcely known to the English language, until it was added to it a few years ago by the barbarous jargon of Catholicism. **1870** *Daily News* 16 Apr., If any religionists..persist in making day schools engines of proselytism.

proselytist (ˈprɒsɪlaɪt-, -lɪtɪst). [f. PROSELYTIZE + -IST.] One who proselytizes; a proselytizer.

1859 *Athenæum* 5 Mar. 315 Other proselytists of milder character were for gentler measures. **1876** *New York Evangelist* 22 June (Cent.), The Mormon proselytists report unusual success in their missionary work.

Hence **proselyˈtistic** *a.*, of or pertaining to proselytists or proselytism.

1900 B. CHAMPNEYS *Mem. C. Patmore* II. iii. 39 He had resented the proselytistic raids which had been made on him and his first wife.

ˌproselytiˈzation (see next). [f. next + -ATION.] The action or work of proselytizing.

1871 H. MARSHALL *For Very Life* I. v, The parents, regarding the act in the light of proselytization to some damnable heresy, took the silver coin from the child. **1890** *Spectator* 25 Jan., A worthy old lady..whose heart is..devoted to the work of Christian proselytisation there [India].

proselytize (ˈprɒsɪlaɪtaɪz, -lɪtaɪz), *v.* [f. PROSELYTE *sb.* + -IZE.]

1. *intr.* To make proselytes; = PROSELYTE *v.* c.

1679 L. ADDISON *Mahumedism* xiv. 71 As he was zealously proselytizing at Medina, news came that Abusophian Ben-Hareth was going into Syria. **1831** CARLYLE *Sart. Res.* III. xii. (1858) 180 Not without some touch of the universal feeling, a wish to proselytise. **1840** DE QUINCEY *Essenes* Wks. 1859 X. 286 A sect that proselytized was at any rate a hazardous sect in Judæa.

2. *trans.* To make a proselyte of; = PROSELYTE *v.* a.

1796 BURKE *Let. Noble Ld.* Wks. VIII. 51 One of these whom they endeavour to proselytize. **1847** DISRAELI *Tancred* II. v, His lordship..was all for proselytising Ireland again. **1865** MORLEY *Mod. Characteristics* 85 We do not expect a bigot to live in much harmony with people whom he cannot proselytize.

Hence **ˈproselytizing** *vbl. sb.* and *ppl. a.*

1828 CARLYLE in *For. Rev. & Cont. Misc.* II. 439 The influence of this proselytizing bigotry. **1842** PUSEY *Crisis Eng. Ch.* 98 In our own day, any exhibition of ourselves as a proselytizing Church would unsettle many of our own children. **1881** MONIER WILLIAMS in *19th Cent.* Mar. 504 Proselytising has never been attempted by the Zoroastrians since their arrival on Indian soil. **1883** FROUDE *Short Stud.* IV. iii. 269 A proselytising religion was a new phenomenon.

proselytizer (ˈprɒsɪlaɪt-, -lɪtaɪzə(r)). [f. prec. vb. + -ER[1].] One who proselytizes; one who makes or endeavours to make proselytes.

1848 GILFILLAN in *Tait's Mag.* XV. 280 He is the least in the world of a proselytizer. **1904** SIR R. RODD *Sir W. Raleigh* i. 7 [He] with the zeal of a proselytiser, began to take her to task for carrying beads.

proseman (ˈprəʊzmən). [f. PROSE *sb.* + MAN *sb.*[1]] A man who writes prose, a prose author.

1589 PUTTENHAM *Eng. Poesie* III. xviii. (Arb.) 202 The figure which the Greeks call Hiperbole..must be vsed very discreetly,..for although a prayse or other report may be allowed beyond credit, it may not be beyond all measure, specially in the proseman. **1733** POPE *Hor. Sat.* II. i. 64 Verse-man or Prose-man, term me which you will. **1887** SAINTSBURY *Hist. Elizab. Lit.* ix. (1890) 343 For the meditative reading of instructed persons he [Browne] is perhaps the most delightful of English prosemen.

proseminary (prəʊˈsɛmɪnərɪ). [f. PRO-[2] 1 + SEMINARY *sb.* So G. *proseminar.*] A preparatory seminary or school.

1774 WARTON *Hist. Eng. Poetry* lv. (1840) III. 282 *note*, Merchant-Taylors' school in London..was then just founded as a proseminary for saint John's college, Oxford. **1893** *Home Miss.* (N.Y.) July 192 The German pro-seminary at Crete..prepares students for the Chicago Theological Seminary.

†**proˈseminate**, *v. Obs.* [f. ppl. stem of L. *prōsēmināre* to sow, propagate: see PRO-[1] 1 and SEMINATE.] *trans.* To sow, to propagate; to disseminate.

1657 R. CARPENTER *Astrol.* 36 These errours..procreated and proseminated by Astrologers. **1657–83** EVELYN *Hist. Relig.* (1850) II. 222 To proseminate his curious cockles, dissensions, and factions..in this goodly plantation.

So †**prosemiˈnation** *Obs.*, propagation by seed; spreading abroad as if sown, dissemination.

1611 SPEED *Hist. Gt. Brit.* v. vii. §4. 38 That first beginning of the vniuersall pro-semination of Mankind. *a* **1677** HALE *Prim. Orig. Man.* I. iii. 79 The eternal succession of the Species, whether of Men, Animals, or Vegetables by natural propagation or prosemination.

‖**prosencephalon** (prɒsɛnˈsɛfəlɒn). *Anat.* Pl. **-a.** [mod.L., f. Gr. πρός toward (but here used as if = πρό, PRO-[2] 2) + ἐγκέφαλον, -ος brain, ENCEPHALON.] The anterior part of the brain, consisting of the cerebral hemispheres and other structures; sometimes including the olfactory lobes (*rhinencephalon*) and the optic thalami and adjacent parts (*thalamencephalon*); the fore-brain.

1846 OWEN *Anat. Vert.* I. 181 *note*, Influenced by the inapplicability of the term 'hemispheres'..I shall apply the term 'prosencephalon' to the constant division of the brain in question, and prosencephalic lobes or prosencephala to its commonly distinct moieties. **1856** TODD & BOWMAN *Phys. Anat.* II. 600 The prosencephalon soon increases in size, and becomes much larger than all the others. **1880** GÜNTHER *Fishes* 99 The prosencephalon, mesencephalon, and metencephalon are contiguous.

Hence **prosencephalic** (prɒsɛnsɪˈfælɪk) *a.*, pertaining to or connected with the prosencephalon: applied esp. to parts of the skull in animals.

1846 [see above]. **1854** OWEN *Skel. & Teeth* in *Orr's Circ. Sc.* I. *Org. Nat.* 251 The rhinencephalic fossa..in the lion..is defined by a well-marked angle..from the prosencephalic compartment. **1880** GÜNTHER *Fishes* 86 Prosencephalic arch, composed of pre-sphenoid, orbito-sphenoid, frontal and postfrontal.

prosenchyma (prɒsˈɛŋkɪmə). *Bot.* Also in form **prosenchym**. [mod. f. Gr. πρός to, toward + ἔγχυμα infusion, after PARENCHYMA. So F. *prosenchyme*, Ger. *prosenchym.*] Tissue consisting of elongated cells closely placed with their ends interpenetrating, and often with the terminal partitions obliterated so as to form ducts or vessels; found in different systems of tissues, but most typically in the fibro-vascular tissue (wood, bast, etc.); hence sometimes used as synonymous with 'fibro-vascular tissue'. Also *attrib.*, as *prosenchyma cell.* (Distinguished from PARENCHYMA 2.)

1832 LINDLEY *Introd. Bot.* 9 Professor Link distinguishes Parenchyma and Prosenchyma [*so ed.* **1835**; *ed.* **1848** Prosenchym]. **1849** LANKESTER tr. *Schleiden's Sci. Bot.* 56 Thus originates in the place of parenchyma a peculiar tissue which is called prosenchyma. **1875** BENNETT & DYER *Sachs' Bot.* 78 If the cells are pointed at the ends, [etc.], then the tissue is termed *Prosenchyma*. *Ibid.* 79 The cells of such a tissue are usually elongated in the direction of its length,..and we then have Prosenchyma bundles. The most important of these are the Fibro-vascular Bundles.

prosenchymatous (prɒsɛŋˈkɪmətəs), *a.* [f. prec.: cf. PARENCHYMATOUS.] Belonging to, consisting of, or having the nature of prosenchyma.

1848 LINDLEY *Introd. Bot.* (ed. 4) I. 57 The tubes which stand in contact with prosenchymatous cells. **1861** [see PARENCHYMATOUS 2]. **1875** BENNETT & DYER *Sachs' Bot.* 281 The ascending and descending lobes dove-tailing in a prosenchymatous manner.

proseneschal: see PRO-[1] 4.

prosˌenneaˈhedral, *a. Cryst. rare.* [f. F. *prosenneaèdre* (Haüy) (f. Gr. πρός approaching to + *enneaèdre*) + -AL[1], after ENNEAHEDRAL.] (See quot.) Also **prosenneˈëdrous** *a. rare*[−0].

1805–17 R. JAMESON *Char. Min.* (ed. 3) 208 *Prosenneahedral*,..having nine faces on two adjacent parts, as in the prosenneahedral tourmaline..; in which the prism has nine sides, and one of the extremities nine planes, and the other only three. **1858** MAYNE *Expos. Lex.*, *Prosenneædrus, Min.*, having nine faces upon two adjacent parts. Applied by Haüy to a variety of tourmaline..: prosenneëdrous.

pro-sentence: see PRO-[1] 4 b.

proseology (prəʊˈzɒlədʒɪ). *colloq. rare.* [f. PROSE *sb.* + -OLOGY.] Prolix, turgid, or confusing prose.

1909 *Daily Chron.* 19 July 3/4 To plough through all the extracts from journals, letters, &c., which form the book needs not a little patience and sticking power. Doubtless, those who can get beneath all this proseology will find much to excite them. **1968** *Economist* 29 June p. xi/2 The usual, easy proseology reviling the accursed folk or crying the beloved country.

†**proseˈpilogism.** *Logic. Obs. rare.* [f. Gr. πρός in addition + EPILOGISM. Cf. PROSSYLLOGISM.] (See quot.)

1620 T. GRANGER *Div. Logike* 281 The proofe of the premises of the Prossyllogisme, is called an Epilogisme; and the proofe of any part hereof also is called a Prosepilogisme.

prosequut(e, etc., obs. forms of PROSECUTE, etc.

proser (ˈprəʊzə(r)). [f. PROSE *v.* + -ER[1].]

1. A writer of prose; = PROSAIST 1.

1627 DRAYTON *Elegy H. Reynolds* in *Agincourt*, etc. 206 And surely Nashe, though he a Proser were A branch of Lawrell yet deserues to beare. **1815** L. HUNT *Feast Poets*, etc. 14 Such prosers as Johnson, and rhymers as Dryden. **1854** LOWELL *Jrnl. in Italy* Prose Wks. 1890 I. 125 Poets and prosers have alike compared her [Italy] to a beautiful woman.

2. One who proses; one who talks or writes in a prosy, dull, commonplace, or tiresome way.

1769 *St. James's Chron.* 29–31 Aug. 4/2 Bore... My Father's Word for this intolerable Animal was a Proser. **1810** CRABBE *Borough* v. 39 The proser who..has tales of three hours' length. **1886** DOWDEN *Shelley* II. v. 210 He would find Gisborne a proser, and a sieve through which much learning had passed.

proses, prosesioun, -session, etc., obs. forms of PROCESS, PROCESSION.

†**ˈproset.** *Obs. nonce-wd.* [f. PROSE *sb.* + -ET[1].] A little or insignificant piece of prose.

1625 LISLE *Du Bartas' Noe* Pref. 1 Among the sundrie versets or prosets which I have, or shall set out if you find some that savour of my younger time.

‖**proseucha** (prɒˈsjuːkə). Pl. **-æ**; in 7 **-a's**. [late L. (Juv.), ad. Gr. προσευχή prayer, a place of prayer, f. προσεύχ-εσθαι to offer prayers, f. πρός toward + εὔχ-εσθαι to pray.] A place of prayer in ancient times, an oratory; among the Jews, usually an unroofed place set apart for prayer, as distinct from a synagogue.

a **1638** MEDE *Wks.* (1672) 66 Proseucha was a plot of ground encompassed with a wall or..other..inclosure, and open above... A Synagogue was..a covered edifice... Synagogues were within the Cities, as Proseucha's were without. **1879** J. MARTINEAU *Hours Th.* (1880) II. 345 The unadorned proseucha that sufficed for apostolic disciples. **1891** tr. *Father Didon's Jesus Christ* I. 25 [The Jews] built synagogues and proseuchae at the entrances of towns.

proseys, obs. form of PROCESS.

pro shop: see PRO *abbrev.* 2 c.

prosify (ˈprəʊzɪfaɪ), *v.* Chiefly *humorous.* Also **prosefy**. [f. late L. *prōsa* or PROSE *sb.* + -FY: in sense 2, after *versify*. The spelling *prosefy* is app. after *stupefy*, etc.]

1. *trans.* To turn into prose; to make prosaic.

1774 MISS CARTER *Let. to Mrs. Montagu* 28 June, Either the poetry confounds..the lesson, or the lesson prosifies the poetry. **1830** *Blackw. Mag.* XXVIII. 882 In such a frozen atmosphere would not eloquence be congealed on the lips of an Ulysses, and poetry prosified on those of an Apollo! **1850** *Tait's Mag.* XVII. 547/1 [He] maltreats the glorious lines of Burns,..prosefying his poetry and twaddleising his vigour.

2. *intr.* To make or write prose.

1816 SOUTHEY *Let. to G. C. Bedford* 4 Feb., I cannot write verses in the presence of any person,..but I can prosify, let who will be present. **1828** *Blackw. Mag.* XXIII. 36 Prosifying where there was prose enough before, and poetising what was poetical enough already.

So **prosification** (ˌprəʊzɪfɪˈkeɪʃən), the action of 'prosifying', conversion into prose, making prosaic; **prosifier** (ˈprəʊzɪfaɪə(r)), one who or that which 'prosifies'.

1788 ANNA SEWARD *Lett.* (1811) II. 12 The *that's*, the *which's*, the *who's*, and the *whom's*, are prosefiers,..injurious to the melody of verse. **1847** L. HUNT *Jar Honey* iv. (1848) 43 This prosification of a fine bit of poetry.

prosilient (prəʊˈsɪlɪənt), *a. rare.* [ad. L. *prōsilient-em*, pres. pple. of *prōsilīre* to leap forth.] *lit.* Leaping forth; *fig.* outstanding, prominent. So †**proˈsiliate** *v.* [erron. form] *intr.*, to be prominent, project, 'stand out'; **proˈsiliency** [see -ENCY], †the fact of leaping forth (*obs.*); *fig.* prosilient quality, great prominence; †**prosiˈlition** [n. of action f. L. *prōsilīre*: see -TION], the action of leaping or starting out.

1653 R. SANDERS *Physiogn.* 173 The minde is..apertly conversant in the eyes..: the minde resolute, the eyes *prosiliate, being humble, they subsidate. **1665** GLANVILL *Def. Vanity Dogm.* 61 A Repentine *Prosiliency jumping into Being. **1827** COLERIDGE in *Lit. Rem.* (1839) IV. 402 He has given it such prominence, such prosiliency of relief. **1902** GERTR. ATHERTON *Conqueror* v. i, Hamilton,..not excepting Washington,..was to Europeans the most *prosilient of Americans. **1657** TOMLINSON *Renou's Disp.* 485 That the Powder..may pass..without any loss by *prosilition.

prosily (ˈprəʊzɪlɪ), *adv.* [f. PROSY + -LY².] In a prosy manner; with dull and tedious utterance; in a matter-of-fact way, prosaically.

1849 MISS MULOCK *Ogilvies* xxiii, This speech, delivered rather prosily and oracularly. **1874** T. HARDY *Far fr. Madding Crowd* I. ii. 23 Oak knew her..as the heroine of the yellow waggon..: prosily, as the woman who owed him twopence.

†**prosiˈmetrical**, *a. Obs. rare*⁻⁰. [f. med. or mod.L. *prōsimetric-us*, f. *prōsa* prose + *metricus* METRICAL.] (See quot.)

1656 BLOUNT *Glossogr.*, *Prosimetrical*, consisting partly of Prose, partly of Meeter or Verse.

prosimian (prəʊˈsɪmɪən), *a.* and *sb. Zool.* [f. mod.L. *Prōsimia*, generic name (Brisson 1756), *Prosimiæ* pl. (Storr 1780), *Prosimii* pl. (Illiger and Goldfuss 1811) (f. *pro-* (? PRO-¹ 4, or PRO-² 1) + *simia* ape) + -AN.]

A. *adj.* Of, belonging to, or designating prosimians. So **proˈsimious** *a.* **B.** *sb.* A mammal belonging to the suborder Prosimii, a group of primitive, mostly arboreal primates, which includes lemurs, lorises, galagos, and tarsiers.

1858 MAYNE *Expos. Lex.*, *Prosimius*... Applied by Illiger and Goldfuss to a Family (*Prosimi*..) of the *Mammifera*, comprehending those which, under different relations, approach the *Simiæ*: prosimious. **1890** *Cent. Dict.*, *Prosimian* [adj. and sb.]. **1925** *Bull. Geol. Soc. China* IV. 142 In some area intermediate between the Oriental and Ethiopian regions the centre of prosimian dispersal was located. **1945** *Bull. Amer. Mus. Nat. Hist.* LXXXV. 181/2 It seems quite possible that New World and Old World monkeys arose independently from Eocene prosimians... Their prosimian ancestors, if distinct, must have been closely allied. **1959** *New Scientist* 10 Dec. 1175/1 Professor Schultz considers that the very important exploratory function of the hands of simians superseded the tactile sense of the prosimians (such as the lemurs). **1966** [see HIGH *a.* 6 d]. **1972** T. A. VAUGHAN *Mammalogy* vii. 117 (*caption*) Hands and feet of some prosimian primates. **1974** *Sci. Amer.* Apr. 127/1 The prosimians and the tenrecs, unlike any other mammals, respond sharply to external temperature. **1977** P. NAPIER *Lemurs, Lorises & Bushbabies* i. 9 The lemurs, lorises and bushbabies are called prosimians.

prosiness (ˈprəʊzɪnɪs). [f. PROSY + -NESS.] Prosy or prosaic quality; commonplaceness; dullness and tediousness of writing or speech.

1814 SIR G. JACKSON *Diaries & Lett.* (1873) II. 448 Settling down again to the prosiness of their every-day life. **1870** LOWELL *Among my Bks.* Ser. I. (1873) 291 Those well-regulated minds which, during a good part of the last century found out a way, through rhyme, to snatch a prosiness beyond the reach of prose.

prosing (ˈprəʊzɪŋ), *vbl. sb.* [f. PROSE *v.* + -ING¹.] The action of the verb PROSE.

1. Prose-writing, prose composition.

1641 MILTON *Ch. Govt.* II. Pref., Wks. 1851 III. 144 Prosing or versing, but chiefly this latter. **1801** MOORE *Morality* 2 Dozing O'er books of rhyme and books of prosing. **1840** HOOD *Up the Rhine* 6 Should I ever get beyond prosing, my verses belong to her.

2. Dull or tedious talking; prosy discourse.

1775 MASON *Mem. Gray* G.'s Poems (1775) 139 *note*, But what shall we say..when a writer whom Mr. Gray so justly esteemed as M. Marivaux is now held in such contempt, that *Marivauder* is a fashionable phrase amongst them [the French], and signifies neither more nor less, than our own fashionable phrase of *prosing*? **1816** SCOTT *Antiq.* xix, The unceasing prosing of his worthy companion. **1874** L. STEPHEN *Hours in Library* (1892) I. ii. 61 His moral prosings savour of the endless gossip over a dish of chocolate.

ˈprosing, *ppl. a.* [f. as prec. + -ING².] That proses; talking or writing prosily; also said of a writing or discourse (= PROSY).

1775 MME. D'ARBLAY *Early Diary*, *Let.* 24 Apr., Remember how prosing, affected, and very fine he is. **1809** G. ELLIS in Smiles *Mem. J. Murray* (1891) I. vii. 159 A dull prosing piece of orthodoxy may have its admirers. **1865** GROTE *Plato* I. 125 Prosing beggars, in mean attire and dirt.

Hence **ˈprosingly** *adv.*, in a prosing manner.

1822 *Blackw. Mag.* XI. 735 You will not need to hear us prosingly speak of it.

prosiopesis (prɒsɪəʊˈpiːsɪs). *Gram.* [f. Gr. προ- before + σιώπησις taciturnity, f. σιωπᾶν to be silent.] Jespersen's term for ellipsis of the beginning of a grammatical structure in speech.

1924 O. JESPERSEN *Philos. Gram.* x. 142 The subject must generally be expressed, and those few cases in which it is omitted, may be explained through prosiopesis, which sometimes becomes habitual in certain stock exclamations like *Thank you*. **1927** —— *Mod. Eng. Gram.* III. 226 *It* is occasionally left out through prosiopesis. **1935** H. STRAUMANN *Newspaper Headlines* 41 Whether such sentences should be considered as incomplete or elliptic or as aposiopesis and prosiopesis is a question of terminology. **1966** G. N. LEECH *Eng. in Advertising* viii. 78 One marginally casual feature of advertising language is the occurrence of what..has been termed prosiopesis.

prosiphon (prəʊˈsaɪfən). *Zool.* [f. PRO-² 1 + SIPHON.] The primitive siphon in an embryonic ammonite, a kind of ligament attached to the protoconch. Hence **proˈsiphonal** *a.*, pertaining to the prosiphon.

1890 *Cent. Dict.*, Prosiphon, Prosiphonal. **1895** *Cambr. Nat. Hist.* III. 387 The protoconch is present, and contains a prosiphon.

prosiphonate (prəʊˈsaɪfənət), *a. Zool.* [f. *prō*, PRO-¹ 1 a + SIPHON + -ATE² 2.] Of a chambered shell: Having the siphonal funnel directed forward, as in the *Prosiphonata*, a primary group of chambered cephalopods now extinct.

1935 TWENHOFEL & SHROCK *Invertebr. Paleont.* ix. 378 Prosiphonate ones [*sc.* septa] are found in Mesozoic forms [of cephalopod]. **1952** R. C. MOORE et al. *Invertebr. Fossils* ix. 371/1 In late Paleozoic and Mesozoic ammonoids, this structure [*sc.* the siphuncle] is mostly confined to immature stages, and forward-pointing septal necks appear in submature whorls. This condition is described as prosiphonate. **1970** R. M. BLACK *Elements Palaeont.* viii. 86 Short septal necks encircle the siphuncle where it passes through the septa; the septal necks project forwards (prosiphonate) in the later formed septa of Mesozoic ammonites.

prosis(se, obs. forms of PROCESS.

prosish (ˈprəʊzɪʃ), *a. nonce-wd.* [f. PROSE *sb.* + -ISH¹.] Partaking of the nature of prose; somewhat prosaic.

1797 COLERIDGE *Lett., to Southey* (1895) 223 The five lines are flat and prosish.

prosist (ˈprəʊzɪst). *rare.* [f. PROSE *sb.* + -IST.] A prose-writer: = PROSAIST 1.

1809 COLERIDGE *Lett., to Southey* 555 Lessing, the best German prosist. **1850** LYNCH *Theo. Trin.* ix. 154 Imaginative thinkers, whether they be poets or prosists.

‖**prosit** (ˈproːzɪt), *int.* [L., usu. through Ger., 'may it benefit'.] Used to wish good health, success, etc., esp. as a toast in German-speaking countries.

1846 R. FORD *Gatherings from Spain* xv. 182 '*Muchas gracias, buen provecho le haga á usted*', 'Many thanks—much good may it do your grace', an answer which is analogous to the *prosit* of Italian peasants after eating or sneezing. **1916** J. BUCHAN *Greenmantle* iii. 40 He filled us two long tankards of very good Munich beer. '*Prosit*,' he said, raising his glass. **1930** AUDEN *Poems* 12 Thanks. Prosit! **1937** E. AMBLER *Uncommon Danger* x. 131 Vodka..should be poured straight down the throat. I will show you. *Prosit!* **1944** W. LOWRIE tr. *Kierkegaard's Attack upon 'Christendom'* 170 For one who belongs essentially to the criminal world..the taking of an oath is no more than saying 'Prosit' to one who sneezes, or adding Esq. to a letter. **1951** F. BROWN *Murder can be Fun* ii. 24 'Prosit!' said Tracy. They drank. **1973** WILSON & MICHAELS tr. *M. Bar-Zohar's Third Truth* v. 73 Schneider said '*Prosit*,' and lifted his glass.

‖**proslambaˈnomenos.** [L. (Vitruv.) a. Gr. προσλαμβανόμενος (sc. τόνος) the note taken in addition, i.e. added below the ὑπάτη, HYPATE.] The name of the lowest note, added below the lowest tetrachord, in the later scales or systems of ancient Greek music.

1694 HOLDER *Harmony* (1731) 104 In this Scale of Disdiapason..the Mese is an Octave below the Nete Hyperbolæon, and an Octave above the Proslambanomenos. *Ibid.* 105 The Hypodorian Mood, the Proslambanomenos whereof was fix'd upon the lowest clear and firm Note of the Voice or Instrument..of the deepest settled Pitch. *Ibid.* 106 The Proslambanomenos of the Hypermixolydian Mood was just an Eighth higher than that of the Hypodorian. **1782** BURNEY *Hist. Mus.* (1789) II. ii. 86 The proslambanomenos or most grave sound in all their systems. **1894** R. C. HOPE *Med. Music* iii. 25 The lesser or conjunct system comprised the scale of Sappho, the proslambanomenos or added note below, with the upper tetrachord of Terpander's.

pro-slavery, etc.: see PRO-¹ 5.

prosne, obs. form of PRONE *sb.*, a homily.

‖**prosneusis** (prɒsˈnjuːsɪs). *Astron.* [a. Gr. πρόσνευσις a nodding to, inclination towards; in Ptolemy as in sense a below; f. προσνεύειν to nod to, incline towards.] In the Ptolemaic astronomy: **a.** ***prosneusis of the epicycle.*** A supposed deviation in the axis of the moon's epicycle, assumed as a correction to the lunar anomaly. **b.** The angle between the ecliptic and the great circle joining the centres of the moon and of the earth's shadow in a lunar eclipse.

1906 DREYER *Hist. Planetary Syst.* ix. 196 The principle of rigorously uniform motion had been violated both by introducing a point outside the centre of the deferent, with regard to which the angular motion was uniform, and by the prosneusis. *Ibid.* xi. 252 He [Bertrand]..showed that Abu'l Wefa did not add his 'mohazat' to the prosneusis, the latter not being included in his 'second anomaly'. **1908** —— *Let. to Editor* 20 Aug., [In reference to sense b] This is the prosneusis of the eclipsed part [of the moon].

prosobranch (ˈprɒsəʊbræŋk), *sb.* (*a.*) *Zool.* [f. mod.L. *Prosōbranchia*, neut. pl., f. Gr. πρόσω forwards + βράγχια gills.] A prosobranchiate gastropod: see next. **b.** *adj.* = next.

1851 WOODWARD *Mollusca* I. 50 The sexes are distinct in the most highly organized (or diœcious) mollusca:..the prosobranchs pair. **1861** CARPENTER in *Smithsonian Rep.* 171 In the Prosobranchs, the breathing cavity is at the back of the head. **1877** HUXLEY *Anat. Inv. Anim.* viii. 511 No Prosobranch is..symmetrical. **1887** *Amer. Naturalist* XXI. 557 A Contribution to the Embryology of the Prosobranch Gasteropods.

Hence **ˈprosoˌbranchism**, the condition of being prosobranchiate.

prosobranchiate (-ˈbræŋkɪət), *a.* (*sb.*) *Zool.* [f. mod.L. *Prosōbranchiāta* = *Prosōbranchia*: see prec. and -ATE² 2.] Having the gills in front of the heart, as the aquatic gastropod molluscs of the group or order *Prosōbranchia*. **b.** *sb.* = prec.

1877 HUXLEY *Anat. Inv. Anim.* viii. 508 Nearly related forms are sometimes opisthobranchiate, sometimes prosobranchiate. **1880** G. W. TRYON *Man. Conchol.* II. 6 An external shell..is common to all the prosobranchiates.

prosocial (prəʊˈsəʊʃəl), *a. Social Psychol.* Also **pro-social**. [f. PRO-¹ 5 + SOCIAL *a.*] Of or pertaining to the type of behaviour that is automatically loyal, sometimes in a rigid and conventional manner, to the moral standards accepted by the established group; freq. contrasted with antisocial or asocial types of response.

1961 R. R. SEARS in *Jrnl. Abnormal Psychol.* LXIII. 471/2 Prosocial aggression is aggression used in a socially approved way for purposes that are acceptable to the moral standards of the group. **1972** *Jrnl. Social Psychol.* LXXXVI. 223 The subjects who made more flexible, social moral judgements felt less concern about doing well ..than those who were more conventional and prosocial. **1973** PATTERSON & COBB in J. F. Knutson *Control of Aggression* 176 The analysis of stimulus control for prosocial responses required that the interaction involve two persons who had not interacted with each other during the preceding eighteen months. **1977** *New Society* 5 May 244/2 Little work has been done on measuring the positive effects of 'prosocial' programmes which may help correct the imbalance in British television of, on average, four violent 'incidents' an hour.

prosodal (ˈprɒsəʊdəl), *a. Zool.* [f. PROSODUS + -AL¹.] Pertaining to or of the nature of a prosodus; incurrent.

1887 SOLLAS in *Encycl. Brit.* XXII. 415/1 (*Sponges*) The extension of the prosodal or adital canals into long tubes.

prosode (ˈprɒsəʊd). *Gr. Antiq.* [ad. Gr. προσόδιον.] = PROSODION.

1777 R. POTTER *Æschylus* (1779) II. 33 Prosode. Supreme of Kings, Jove; and thou friendly night [etc.]. This ode.. begins with a sublime and manly address to Jupiter.

prosodeme (ˈprɒsəʊdiːm). *Linguistics.* [f. PROSOD(IC *a.* 2 + -EME: cf. F. *prosodème.*]

A prosodic feature with phonemic status; a suprasegmental phoneme. Hence **prosoˈdemic** *a.*

1940 *Language* XVI. 249 The discussion of the vowel systems is thoroughly confused by the lack of separation between segmental and prosodic phonemes, so that one never knows whether, say, a long and a short vowel pair consists of two vowel phonemes or of a single vowel with two different prosodemes of quantity. **1945** *Ibid.* XXI. 283 He says that there are two prosodemes of vowel quality. **1949** *Ibid.* XXV. 282 Any significant sound feature whose overlap of other features is temporally correlated to syllabic contour should be called a prosodeme, and should be treated by itself in a manner appropriate to its special nature. **1955** *Archivum Linguisticum* VII. II. 134 The Polish accent.. being separated from the end of the word which it indicates by its position, by the intervention of another prosodeme. **1964** L. S. HULTZÉN in D. Abercrombie et al. *Daniel Jones* 85 The treatment is primarily at prosodemic level. **1971** D. CRYSTAL *Linguistics* iv. 184 Contrastive units in suprasegmental phonology were sometimes called prosodemes, or prosodic phonemes.

prosodia, L. = PROSODY; pl. of PROSODION.

prosodiac (prɒˈsɒdiæk), *a.*[1] and *sb.* [ad. late L. *prosodiac-us*, ad. Gr. προσοδιακός, f. προσόδιον PROSODION.]

A. *adj.* **a.** Pertaining to or used as a prosodion; processional. **b.** Of or pertaining to the verse described in B.

1850 [see PROSODION].

B. *sb. Anc. Pros.* A verse consisting of three anapæsts, for the first of which a spondee or iambus may be substituted.

prosodiac (prɒˈsəʊdiæk), *a.*[2] [ad. late L. *prosōdiacus* = Gr. προσῳδιακός (Victorinus and Martianus Capella, 4th and 5th c.) (*p. metrus, numeri*), with sense 'of or pertaining to prosody'.

But Gr. προσῳδιακός is, according to Liddell and Scott, an erroneous form of προσοδιακός (f. προσόδιον (μέλος) a processional song), an adj. denoting the metrical foot (— —∪) in processional songs, and unconnected with προσῳδία, though app. confused with it in Latin (which had only o for Gr. ο and ω; hence in the mod. langs. referred to PROSODY.]

= PROSODIC.

1890 in *Cent. Dict.*

prosodiacal (prɒsəʊˈdaɪəkəl), *a.* [f. as prec. + -AL[1].] Of or pertaining to prosody; = PROSODIC.

1774 MITFORD *Ess. Harmony Lang.* 132 A living writer, whose.. criticisms I.. admire, tho obliged to combat his prosodiacal tenets. **1831** *Fraser's Mag.* III. 429 The measure and rhyme force you to prosodiacal propriety. **1873** WAGNER tr. *Teuffel's Hist. Rom. Lit.* I. 110 The prosodiacal licences of the dramatic poets.

Hence **prosoˈdiacally** *adv.* = PROSODICALLY.

1836 in SMART.

prosodial (prɒˈsəʊdiəl), *a.*[1] [f. L. *prosōdi-a* PROSODY + -AL[1].] Of or pertaining to prosody; = PROSODIC.

1775 T. SHERIDAN *Art Reading* 214 The measure.. to speak in the prosodial language, becomes purely amphibrachic. **1789** —— *(title)* A complete Dictionary of the English Language,.. to which is prefixed a Prosodial Grammar [*ed.* 1 Rhetorical Grammar]... The Second Edition, Revised, Corrected and Enlarged. **1885** *Athenæum* 1 Aug. 138/2 A poet.. not occupied with.. prosodial or metrical systems, or traditional models of.. style.

proˈsodial, *a.*[2] [f. PROSODI-ON + -AL[1].] = PROSODIAC *a.*[1]

1874 SYMONDS *Italy & Greece* 215 Chapleted youths singing the praise of Pallas in prosodial hymns.

prosodian (prɒˈsəʊdiən), *sb.* and *a.* [f. L. *prosōdia*, Gr. προσῳδία prosody + -AN.]

A. *sb.* = PROSODIST.

1623 COCKERAM II, The Art of accenting, or the rule of pronouncing wordes truely long or short, *prosodie.* One skild in that Art, *prosodian.* **1646** SIR T. BROWNE *Pseud. Ep.* VII. i. 339 That the Forbidden fruit.. was an Apple, is commonly beleeved,.. and some have been so bad Prosodians, as from thence to derive the Latine word *Malum*; because that fruit was the first occasion of evill. **1852** BLACKIE *Stud. Lang.* 13 The word *female* is, according to the technical style of Prosodians, a Spondee.

B. *adj.* = next.

1817 COLEBROOKE *Algebra* IV. vi. 49 *note*, Commentators appear to interpret this as a name of the rule here taught; *sád' hárana*, or *sád'hárana-ch'handó-gańita*, general rule of prosodian permutation: subject to modification in particular instances; as in music.

prosodic (prɒˈsɒdɪk), *a.* [f. L. *prosōdia* PROSODY + -IC. Cf. F. *prosodique.* (The reputed Gr. προσῳδικός, is, according to Liddell and Scott, an erroneous spelling of προσοδιακός.)]

1. Of, pertaining or relating to prosody.

1774 WARTON *Hist. Eng. Poetry* (1840) I. Diss. ii. p. cvi, The strict.. attention of these Latin poets to prosodic rules. **1886** J. EGGELING in *Encycl. Brit.* XXI. 270/2 The normal instrumental ending *â*, preserved for prosodic reasons. **1906** SAINTSBURY *Eng. Prosody* I. Pref. 6 To make the book a history of prosodic study as well as of prosodic expression.

2. *Linguistics.* Of or pertaining to suprasegmental features of pitch, juncture, stress, etc. Also, of or pertaining to prosodies (PROSODY 3); esp. ***prosodic analysis***, the type of linguistic analysis associated with J. R. Firth and his followers, which employs as fundamental concepts the phonematic unit (see PHONEMATIC *a.* b) and the prosody.

1940 *Language* XVI. 31 There are a number of vowel phonemes, each of which may be accompanied by either short quantity or long quantity, these being prosodic phonemes. **1942** BLOCH & TRAGER *Outl. Linguistic Anal.* 41 We now turn our attention to those modifications of the segmental bounds to which we have given the names of *quantity*, *accent* and *juncture*... The methods of analysis are in principle the same for these prosodic features as for segmental phonemes... The product of the analysis will be an inventory of what may be called the *prosodic* or *suprasegmental phonemes.* **1949** J. R. FIRTH in *Trans. Philol. Soc. 1948* 136 The prosodic diacritica included tone, voice quality, and other properties of the sonants. **1952** A. COHEN *Phonemes of Eng.* 19 Other elements of speech, such as length, stress, or pitch, which according to the terminology of Prague are called prosodic features or 'suprasegmental phonemes' in American usage. **1955** *Bull. School of Oriental & Afr. Stud.* XVII. 134 The difference in theoretical basis between the prosodic approach and the phoneme theory is reflected firstly in the setting up of a total *system* to account for the phonetic material presented here, and secondly in the stating of that system not in relation to the *syllable* but to the *word.* **1957** *Proc. Univ. of Durham Philos. Soc.* I. Ser. B (Arts) I. 3 The aim of prosodic analysis in phonology is.. a phonological analysis in terms which account take [*sic*] not only of paradigmatic relations and contrasts, but also of the equally important syntagmatic relations and functions which are operative in speech. **1968** J. LYONS *Introd. Theoret. Linguistics* iii. 131 By virtue of their occurrence in words of one prosodic class rather than another, they are realized phonetically in different ways. **1971** *Archivum Linguisticum* II. 68 The mainspring of prosodic analysis in phonology was the recognition of phonetic features whose domains extended beyond those of the (more practical) phoneme. **1974** R. QUIRK *Linguist & Eng. Lang.* i. 20 His [*sc.* Dickens's] characters' speeches are.. repeatedly accompanied by instructions as to tempo, stress, pitch, rhythm, and other prosodic features.

prosodical (prɒˈsɒdɪkəl), *a.* [f. as prec. + -AL[1]: see -ICAL.] = prec.

1774 WARTON *Hist. Eng. Poetry* (1840) II. xxxiii. 505 A burlesque Latin poem,.. yet not destitute of prosodical harmony. **1878** *N. Amer. Rev.* CXXVI. 554 He has attempted.. the 'absolute prosodical reproduction' of the originals.

proˈsodically, *adv.* **a.** In relation to prosody.

1882 in OGILVIE.

b. With regard to prosodic features (PROSODIC *a.* 2).

1949 *Trans. Philol. Soc. 1948* 144 The Danish glottal stop is.. best considered prosodically as a feature of syllabic structure and word formation. **1964** M. A. K. HALLIDAY et al. *Linguistic Sciences* iii. 69 The vowel phoneme /iː/, is prosodically marked: it is characterized by the movement of the tongue towards a certain position, rather than by its attainment of a fixed position for a fixed segment of time. **1973** *Nature* 13 Apr. 481/1 The early utterances of the child which consist of only single morphemes are nevertheless 'sentences' since they are prosodically marked and because they are productively used.

‖**prosodiencephalon** (ˌprɒsəʊdaɪenˈsɛfəlɒn). *Anat.* Pl. **-ˈcephala**. Also in anglicized form **-ˈcephal.** [mod.L., f. Gr. πρόσω forward + DIENCEPHALON.] In Wilder's nomenclature, the prosencephalon and diencephalon taken together. Hence **prosodiencephalic** (-sɪˈfælɪk) *a.*, pertaining to the prosodiencephalon.

1889 *Buck's Handbk. Med. Sc.* VIII. 130/2 The compacted motor and sensory conductors between the prosodiencephal and the metepencephal. **1890** *Cent. Dict.*, *Prosodiencephalic.*

‖**prosodion** (prɒˈsɒdiən). *Gr. Antiq.* Also in L. form **-ium.** Pl. **prosodia.** [a. Gr. προσόδιον (μέλος) a processional song, neut. sing. of προσόδιος adj. processional, f. πρόσοδος an approach, procession: see PROSODUS.] A hymn sung in procession at a religious festival in ancient Greece.

1850 MURE *Lit. Greece* III. 73 The prosodion was the hymn sung by the choristers in their procession to the altar or sanctuary... The prosodion, accordingly, is occasionally classed under the general head of Pæan, by the special title of Prosodiac, or Processional, pæan. *Ibid.*, Such, apparently, was the style of the celebrated Delian prosodium of Eumelus. **1873** SYMONDS *Grk. Poets* v. 116 Processional hymns, or *Prosodia*, were sung at solemn festivals by troops of men and maidens walking, crowned with olive, myrtle, bay, or oleander, to the shrines.

prosodist (ˈprɒsədɪst). [f. L. *prosōdia* PROSODY + -IST.] One skilled or learned in prosody.

1779–81 JOHNSON *L.P.*, *Pope* Wks. IV. 121 Here are the swiftness of the rapid race, and the march of slow-paced majesty, exhibited by the same poet in the same sequence of syllables, except that the exact prosodist will find the line of *swiftness* by one time longer than that of *tardiness.* *c* **1800** J. WALKER *Key to Classical Pronunc.* (ed. 2) Advt., If it convinces future prosodists that it is not worthy of their attention. **1885** LECKY in *Philol. Soc. Proc.* p. iii, Prosodists assumed that the quantity of an English syllable depended on the number of sounds it contained; that, for example, *ask* was longer than *ass* (*vide* Guest).

‖**prosodus** (ˈprɒsədəs). *Zool.* [mod.L., ad. Gr. πρόσοδος an approach, f. πρός to + ὁδός a way.] An incurrent opening or channel in a sponge.

1887 SOLLAS in *Encycl. Brit.* XXII. 415/1 (*Sponges*) The prosopyles.. may remain unchanged.. or at the most be prolonged into very short tubes, each a *prosodus* or *aditus.*

prosody (ˈprɒsədɪ). Also *β.* 6–8 in L. form **proˈsodia.** [ad. L. *prosōdia* the accent of a syllable, a. Gr. προσῳδία a song sung to music, an accompaniment; the tone or accent of a syllable, a mark to show it; later also, a mark of quantity; f. πρός to + ᾠδή song, ODE. Cf. F. *prosodie* (1562 in Hatz.-Darm.).]

1. The science of versification; that part of the study of language which deals with the forms of metrical composition; formerly reckoned as a part of grammar (see note s.v. GRAMMAR 1), and including also the study of the pronunciation of words (now called *phonology* or *phonetics*), esp. in relation to versification. Also, a treatise on this.

c **1450** *Cov. Myst.* xx. (Shaks. Soc.) 189 Amonges alle clerkys we bere the prysse, Of gramer, cadens, and of prosodye. **1580** G. HARVEY *Let. to Spenser* Wks. (Grosart) I. 76, I would gladly be acquainted with M. Drants Prosodye. *a* **1637** B. JONSON *Eng. Gram.* i. (tr. Scaliger), Prosody, and orthography, are not parts of grammar, but diffused like the blood and spirits through the whole. **1749** *Numbers in Poet. Comp.* 10 There is a very wide Difference between the Latin and English Prosody. And it's in vain to think of introducing the Rules of the former into the latter; since the English Language is not so framed as to admit of it. **1824** L. MURRAY *Eng. Gram.* (ed. 5) I. 345 Prosody consists of two parts: the former teaches the true pronunciation of words, comprising accent, quantity, emphasis, pause, and tone; and the latter, the laws of versification. **1871** R. ELLIS *Catullus* Pref. 17, I have bound myself to avoid certain positions forbidden by the laws of ancient prosody.

β. **1586** W. WEBBE *Eng. Poetrie* Pref. (Arb.) 19 If English Poetrie were truely reformed, and some perfect platforme or *Prosodia* of versifying were.. sette downe. *Ibid.* 62 Though our wordes can not well bee forced to abyde the touch of Position and other rules of *Prosodia.* **1693** DRYDEN *Examen Poeticum* Ded., Ess. (ed. Ker) II. 11 For the benefit of those who understand not the Latin *prosodia.* **1702** ADDISON *Dial. Medals* i. (1726) 28, I should as soon expect to find the *Prosodia* in a Comb as Poetry in a Medal.

2. Correct pronunciation of words; the utterance of the sounds of a language according to rule; observance of the laws of prosody. *rare.*

1616 BULLOKAR *Eng. Expos.*, *Prosodie*, true pronouncing of wordes. *a* **1637** B. JONSON *Eng. Gram.* i, A letter is an indivisible part of a syllabe, whose prosody, or right sounding, is perceived by the power. **1837** CARLYLE *Fr. Rev.* (1872) III. v. ii. 178 She expressed herself with a purity, with a harmony and prosody that made her language like music. **1842** MRS. GORE *Fascin.* 128 He heard a pure and eloquent voice recite with the most elegant and perfect prosody, these verses from the first satire of Persius.

3. *Linguistics.* In the theories of J. R. Firth and his followers: a phonological feature having as its domain more than one segment.

Prosodies include the class of 'suprasegmental' features such as intonation, stress, and juncture, but also some features which are regarded as 'segmental' in phonemic theory, e.g. palatalization, lip-rounding, nasalization.

1949 J. R. FIRTH in *Trans. Philol. Soc. 1948* 129 We may abstract those features which mark word or syllable initials and word or syllable finals or word junctions from the word, piece, or sentence, and regard them syntagmatically as prosodies, distinct from the phonematic constituents which are referred to as units of the consonant and vowel systems. **1951** *Bull. School of Oriental & Afr. Stud.* XIII. 945 The prosodies abstracted by these treatments have included not only aspiration but also, e.g. yotization, labiovelarization, rhotacization, affrication, friction, and voice. **1957** *Proc. Univ. of Durham Philos. Soc.* I. Ser. B (Arts) I. 3 *Prosodic analysis*.. makes use of two types of element, Prosodies and Phonematic Units... Phonematic units refer to those features or aspects of the phonic material which are best regarded as referable to minimal segments, having serial order in relation to each other in structures... Structures are not, however, completely stated in these terms; a great part.. of the phonic material is referable to prosodies, which are, by definition, of more than one segment in scope or domain of relevance, and may in fact belong to structures of any length. **1964** R. H. ROBINS *Gen. Linguistics* iv. 161 The relevant phonetic data may be assigned to such different categories of prosody as sentence prosodies, sentence part prosodies, word prosodies, syllable prosodies, and syllable part prosodies. **1966** J. T. BENDOR-SAMUEL in C. E. Bazell *In Memory of J. R. Firth* 31 There are three word prosodies: nasalization, yodization, and the absence of nasalization and yodization. **1968** [see PHONEMATIC *a.* b]. **1971** *Archivum Linguisticum* II. 68 In phonology, too,.. the Firthian view was to reject the phoneme in favour of a syntagmatic concept, which was termed—perhaps not too happily—the 'prosody'.

4. *attrib.*

1877 HALES *Spenser* (Globe) p. xxviii, Allying himself with these Latin prosody bigots, Spenser sinned grievously against his better taste.

prosogaster (prɒsəʊˈgæstə(r)). *Anat.* [mod.L., f. Gr. πρόσω forward + γαστήρ belly.] The anterior or upper section of the alimentary canal, extending from the pharynx to the pylorus, and including the œsophagus or gullet and the stomach; the foregut.

1890 in *Cent. Dict.* **1895** *Syd. Soc. Lex.*, *Prosogaster*, syn. for Foregut.

prosognathous (prɒˈsɒgnəθəs), *a.* [f. as prec. + Gr. γνάθος jaw + -OUS.] = PROGNATHOUS.
1890 in *Cent. Dict.* **1895** in *Syd. Soc. Lex.*

‖**prosoma** (prəʊˈsəʊmə). *Zool.* Also in anglicized form **prosome** (ˈprəʊsəʊm). [mod.L., f. Gr. πρό, PRO-[2] + σῶμα body.] The anterior or cephalic segment of the body in certain animals, as cephalopods, lamellibranchs, and cirripeds.
1872 NICHOLSON *Palæont.* 272 The body in the Cephalopoda is symmetrical.. there is a tolerably distinct separation.. into an anterior cephalic portion (prosoma) and a posterior portion, enveloped in the mantle.. (metasoma). **1877** HUXLEY *Anat. Inv. Anim.* vi. 293 The thoracic segments, which succeed the prosoma, gradually taper posteriorly.

Hence **proˈsomal**, **prosoˈmatic** *adjs.*, belonging to the prosoma or anterior part of the body.
1890 *Cent. Dict.*, Prosomal, Prosomatic. **1895** in *Syd. Soc. Lex.* **1900** W. H. GASKELL in *Jrnl. Anat. & Physiol.* July 465 The Prosomatic Appendages of the Merostomata. *Ibid.* 471 The metastoma represented the fused last pair of prosomatic appendages, and so formed a ventral lip to a prosomatic or oral chamber.

‖**prosonoˈmasia.** *Obs.* [mod.L., a. Gr. προσονομασία a naming, appellation, f. προσονομάζειν to call by a name, f. πρός to + ὀνομάζειν to name.] Properly, a calling by a name, a nicknaming. (By Day confused with PARONOMASIA.)
1586 A. DAY *Eng. Secretary* I. (1625) 110 Hee is somewhat a foolosopher, for he carries all his possessions about him [*margin* Prosonomasia]. **1589** PUTTENHAM *Eng. Poesie* III. xviii. (Arb.) 212 If any other man can geue him a fitter English name, I will not be angrie, but I am sure mine is very neere the originall sence of the Prosonomasia, and is rather a by-name geuen in sport, than a surname geuen of any earnest purpose. As, Tiberius the Emperor, because he was a great drinker of wine, they called him.. Caldius Biberius Mero, in steade of Claudius Tiberius Nero: and so a iesting frier that wrate against Erasmus, called him.. Errans mus, and are mainteined by this figure Prosonomasia, or the Nicknamer.

prosopagnosia (ˌprɒsəʊpægˈnəʊsɪə). *Med.* [mod.L., ad. G. *prosopagnosie* (J. Bodamer 1948, in *Arch. f. Psychiatrie* CLXXIX. 6), f. Gr. πρόσωπ-ον face, person + ἀγνωσία ignorance.] An inability to recognize a face as that of any particular person.
1950 *Q. Cumulative Index Medicus* XLIV. 125/2 Agnosia in recognition of physiognomy (prosopagnosia). **1953** *Brain* LXXVI. 542 There is still to be considered the seeming contradiction between the patient's severe prosop-agnosia and his better achievements in the perception of Snellen's types, in time reading and counting of fingers. **1976** *Lancet* 30 Oct. 967/1 She can read N6 slowly and complains of inability to recognise faces (prosopagnosia): people are recognised by their voices. **1979** *Sci. Amer.* Sept. 162/3 The lesions that cause prosopagnosia are as stereotyped as the disorder itself.

‖**prosopalgia** (prɒsəʊˈpældʒɪə). *Path.* [mod.L., f. Gr. πρόσωπ-ον a face (f. πρός to + ὤψ, ὠπ- eye, face) + ἄλγος pain. Cf. F. *prosopalgie.*] Facial neuralgia; face-ache.
1831 SOUTH *Otto's Pathol. Anat.* 454 It is not surprising that.. prosopalgia, ischias nervosa, &c. should be considered as arising from inflammation of the medullary part and sheaths of the nerves. **1862** *New Syd. Soc. Year-bk. Med. & Surg.* 150 Case of Prosopalgia from a cranial tumour. **1876** tr. *von Ziemssen's Cycl. Med.* XI. 100 Prosopalgia is one of the forms of neuralgia.. most frequently met with.

Hence **prosopalgic** (-ˈældʒɪk) *a.*, pertaining to or affected with prosopalgia.
1890 in *Cent. Dict.* **1895** in *Syd. Soc. Lex.*

prosopial (prɒˈsəʊpɪəl), *a. Ornith.* [f. PROSOPIUM + -AL[1].] Belonging to the prosopium.
1895 MIVART in *Proc. Zool. Soc.* 369 On either side a large aperture, the two forming the posterior prosopial nares.

‖**prosopis** (prɒˈsəʊpɪs). [In sense 1, late L. *prosōpis*, a. Gr. προσωπίς (an unidentified plant), applied as generic name (Linnæus 1767); in sense 2, mod.L. generic name (Fabricius 1804).]
1. *Bot.* A tropical and subtropical genus of leguminous trees and shrubs, of the suborder *Mimoseæ*, often prickly or thorny, bearing spicate green or yellow flowers, and usually fleshy pods. *Prosopis juliflora* is the mesquit or honey-locust.
1851 MAYNE REID *Scalp Hunt.* xxxii, Peering cautiously through the leaves of the prosopis.
2. *Zool.* A genus of solitary bees of the family *Andrenidæ.*
1887 JEFFERIES *Field & Hedgerow* (1889) 205, I think there were four species of wild bee at these early flowers, including the great bombus and the small prosopis with orange-yellow band. **1901** LD. AVEBURY in *Daily Chron.* 25 May 3/1 On the evolution of the hive bee from the less highly organised Prosopis—which has a short, simple tongue, no brushes or baskets on the legs, and leads a solitary life.

prosopite (prɒˈsəʊpaɪt). *Min.* [ad. G. *prosopit* (Th. Scheerer 1853), f. Gr. πρόσωπον face, mask: see -ITE[1].] A hydrous fluoride of aluminium and calcium, occurring in colourless, white, or greyish crystals.
1854 DANA *Min.* 502 Prosopite.. occurs at the tin mines of Altenberg. **1899** *Amer. Jrnl. Sc.* Ser. IV. VII. 53 If the assumptions made in the foregoing are justified, the Utah mineral is prosopite.

‖**prosopium** (prɒˈsəʊpɪəm). *Ornith.* Pl. **-ia.** [mod.L. (Mivart 1895), ad. Gr. προσωπεῖον a mask, f. πρόσωπον face.] Term for the whole of the bones and ossifications in front of the cranio-facial articulation in parrots.
1895 MIVART in *Proc. Zool. Soc.* 365 The Bony Beak or Prosopium. [*Note*] By this term I intend to denote the whole ossified mass in front of the cranio-facial articulation and the articulations of the zygomata and palatines. It includes the premaxilla, the maxillæ, maxillo-palatine processes, the nasals, and the ethmoidal and turbinal ossifications of the beak. *Ibid.* 369 The greater extension ventrad of the apex of the prosopium.

proso-poetical (ˌprəʊzəʊpəʊˈɛtɪkəl), *a. rare.* [f. *proso-*, assumed comb. form of L. *prōsa* PROSE (see -O[1]) + POETICAL.] Properly 'of the nature of prose poetry'; but in quots. app. taken in the sense 'of the nature of metrical prose or prosaic verse'.
1858 C. A. COLE *Mem. Hen. V*, p. xliii, The present Metrical, or rather Proso-poetical, History. **1895** *Month* June 230 Thomas of Elmham—in his.. proso-poetical History of Henry V.

prosoˈpography. [f. Gr. πρόσωπον face, person: see -GRAPHY. Cf. F. *prosopographie.*]
†**1.** A description of the person or personal appearance. *Obs.*
1577 tr. *Bullinger's Decades* (1592) 613 Prosopographie is a picturing or representing of bodily lineaments. **1577–87** HOLINSHED *Chron.* (1807) II. 110 Thus farre of the acts and deeds of Stephan: now.. touching the prosopographie or description of his person. **1654** Z. COKE *Logick* 212. **1813** *Monthly Mag.* XXXVI. 330 An historic character, says a German professor, should consist of two parts, the *proso[po]graphy*, or description of the person, and the *ethopea*, or description of the mind and manners.
2. [tr. mod.L. *prosopographia.*] A study or description of an individual's life and career; hence, historical inquiry, esp. in Roman hist., concerned with the study of (political) careers and family connections; a presentation of evidence relating to this study.
The German word *prosopographie* is attested at an earlier date than the English form, but with less specific methodological implications.
1929 R. M. DAWKINS *Sanctuary of Artemis Orthia at Sparta* x. 292 Account has been taken of the lettering, the formulae, and the prosopography. **1934** R. SYME in *Jrnl. Roman Stud.* XXIV. 80 Of recent years prosopography, as it may conveniently be called, has been the object of a heightened interest coincident with the detailed study of the development and working of the imperial administration. **1954** A. MOMIGLIANO in *Cambr. Jrnl.* Mar. 345 He [*sc.* M. I. Rostovtzeff] was lucky in being born early enough to escape the present ridiculous adoration of so-called prosopography (which, as we all know, claims to have irrefutably established the previously unknown phenomenon of family ties). **1959** A. G. WOODHEAD *Study Gk. Inscriptions* iv. 47 A prosopography for the Argolid.. and another for Macedonia.. mark the beginnings of similar coverage for other parts of Greece. **1961** *Encounter* Jan. 40/1 The technique which.. has come to be known as *prosopography*: 'the study of personalities'. **1968** L. DURRELL *Tunc* ii. 62 A queer sort of prosopography reigns over this section of time. **1969** H. B. A. PETERSSON *Anglo-Saxon Currency* iv. 71 *Prosopography*, the comparative study of the personnel charged with the minting of a coinage. **1970** *Times Lit. Suppl.* 13 Nov. 1326/4 Arthur Schlesinger, Jr., takes Mr. Powell as an exponent of 'prosopography', a term borrowed from the ancient historians. A prosopographer investigates 'the common background characteristics of a group of actors in history by means of a collective study of their lives'. **1971** A. H. M. JONES et al. (*title*) The prosopography of the later Roman Empire. **1973** *Proc. Brit. Acad.* LVII. 429 The third and very important and permanent by-product of [A. H. M.] Jones's needs is the *Prosopography of the Later Roman Empire*... The other scholars who have brought the *Prosopography* into being will in the end have done the major part of the huge task, but Volume I at least will stand as a particular and lasting monument to Jones. **1973** *Jrnl. Interdisciplinary Hist.* III. 543 (*heading*) The Prosopography of the Tudor University. *Ibid.* 544 On the theme of prosopography (or collective biography), the argument has tended to revolve around two distinct but related issues: the social status and numbers of those attending the universities. **1975** *Anglo-Saxon Eng.* IV. 168 Dolley.. infers from prosopography that the missing first element of the moneyer's name on this cut-halfpenny is not *Ægel-* but some form of *Leof-*. **1976** *Times Lit. Suppl.* 18 June 734/4 He [*sc.* C. E. Stevens] had a preoccupation.. with 'gutting the source'.. and so likewise, whether their field be history (social, political, military or economic), historiography or prosopography, do the contributors whose work is assembled here to do him honour.

Hence **prosoˈpographer**, one who undertakes or is concerned with prosopography; **prosopoˈgraphic(al)** *a.*, denoting the method of historical inquiry which makes use of prosopography; **prosopoˈgraphically** *adv.*, in a prosopographical manner; as regards prosopography.
1930 *Antiquity* IV. 526 During the period from the 4th. century to the Roman rehandling of the site a series of dedicatory inscriptions, mostly of the latter 1st. and 2nd. century A.D., accumulated. These Mr. Woodward describes with much prosopographic detail. **1933** R. SYME in *Classical Q.* XXVII. 144 A mistake or a change of name must be assumed—or else we must believe that the grandfather received a second consulate from Augustus... The whole question has a more than prosopographical value. **1939** —— *Roman Revolution* p. viii, The index is mainly prosopographical in character. *Ibid.* p. ix, Many of them are bare names.. and most of them will be unfamiliar to any but a hardened prosopographer. **1940** A. MOMIGLIANO in *Jrnl. Roman Stud.* XXX. 77 Prosopographical research has the great virtue of reaching individuals or small groups, but does not explain their material or spiritual needs: it simply presupposes them. **1954** *Antiquity* XXVIII. 127 The essay on prosopographical method is a useful introduction. **1959** A. G. WOODHEAD *Study Gk. Inscriptions* iv. 46 This prosopographical study is particularly valuable for the social historian, but it may have its bearing on a variety of problems. *Ibid.* 47 Ptolemaic Egypt is prosopographically served by the *Prosopographia Ptolemaica.* **1961** *Encounter* Jan. 40/2 Namier found his métier as the pioneer applier of the prosopographical technique. **1961** DOLLEY & SKAARE in R. H. M. Dolley *Anglo-Saxon Coins* 70 We believe that there is both epigraphical and prosopographical evidence to warrant a division of the coinage of Æthelwulf into four distinct phases. **1967** A. N. SHERWIN-WHITE *Racial Prejudice in Imperial Rome* II. 53 Finally the sons of successful procurators become senators. This is a familiar tale in this prosopographical age. **1970** Prosopographer [see above]. **1971** *Dædalus* C. 55 The attitude toward the workings of politics taken by the early prosopographers appears to owe little to the writings of political theorists. *Ibid.* 66 The monks have also been studied prosopographically. **1971** A. H. M. JONES et al. *Prosopography of Later Roman Empire* I. p. v, The project of a prosopographical dictionary of the Later Roman Empire was originated by Theodor Mommsen. **1973** *Times Lit. Suppl.* 23 Feb. 209/4 A prosopographical register of some 779 wealthy individuals who lived in Athens during the sixth, fifth, or fourth centuries. **1975** D. W. S. HUNT *On Spot* ix. 176 While I am in the prosopographical vein I shall imitate Plutarch by completing the other leaf of the diptych with a portrait of Lieutenant-Colonel Emeka Odumekwu Ojukwu, the Military Governor of the Eastern Region.

prosopolespsy (prɒˈsəʊpəʊˌlɛpsɪ, -ˌliːpsɪ). ? *Obs.* [ad. Gr. προσωποληψία (a Hebraism of the N.T.) acceptance of the face or person, f. προσωπολήπτης an acceptor of the face or person, f. πρόσωπον face + λαμβάνειν to take, accept.] Acceptance or 'acception' of the face or person of any one (see ACCEPTION 2, PERSON 13); respect of persons, undue favour shown to a particular person; partiality.
1646 BUCK *Rich. III* Ded., The Historiographer, veritable; free from all Prosopolepsyes, or partiall respects. **1678** CUDWORTH *Intell. Syst.* I. iv. §36. 567 The Assumption of it was neither Fortuitous nor Partial, or with Prosopolepsie (the Acception of Persons) but bestowed upon it justly for the Merit of its Vertues. **1849** E. B. EASTWICK *Dry Leaves* 116 The English rule is a model of justice. There is no prosopolepsy in it; no respect of persons. All men are equal, and have equal rights.

Hence †**prosopoˈlepsian** *Obs.*, one given to 'prosopolepsy'; a 'respecter of persons'.
1647 J. HEYDON *Discov. Fairfax* 11 God's no Prosopolepsian, he respects the poore as well as the rich.

prosopologist (prɒsəʊˈpɒlədʒɪst). *nonce-wd.* [f. Gr. πρόσωπον face + -LOGIST.] One who studies or treats of the face. So **prosoˈpology** (*rare*⁻⁰) the scientific study of the face, physiognomy.
1820 *Blackw. Mag.* VI. 651 As this author limits his observations to the face, we propose to term him, and all such, prosopologists, discoursers on the face. **1858** MAYNE *Expos. Lex.*, *Prosopologia*, term for a dissertation on the countenance: prosopology.

prosopon (ˈprɒsəʊpɒn). [a. Gr. πρόσωπον face.]
1. *Theol.* A conception or external presentation of one of the three Persons of the Trinity; = HYPOSTASIS 5.
1900 J. S. BANKS *Devel. Doctrine in Early Church* I. vii. 101 John of Damascus.. says, Father, Son, and Spirit are one God or one substance (*ousia*, nature, essence), but not one person (*hypostasis, prosopon*). **1932** A. C. MCGIFFERT *Hist. Christian Thought* I. xii. 238 As creator and governor God is called Father, as redeemer he is called Son, as regenerator and sanctifier he is called Holy Spirit. But it is one and the same God, one and the same divine person, who acts in all these ways. The difference is not in being or person, but in function or activity. Each of these functions or activities —Father, Son and Spirit—was called by Sabellius prosopon (*πρόσωπον*), the Greek word of which the Latin translation is persona. The word means not person but face, and was used for the mask worn by actors in the theatre or for the part they played. **1936** G. L. PRESTIGE *God in Patristic Thought* iii. 55 Christ, who was called the prosopon of God with no less assurance (if with less frequency) than He was called God's Word or Wisdom. **1950** [see ALLOGENOUS *a.*] **1969** *Dict. Christian Theol.* 279/1 *Prosopon* is a term used as an alternative to *Hypostasis*.. to express the plurality of the Godhead. **1973** J. A. T. ROBINSON *Human Face of God* vii. 215 The prosopon, the face or person, of the Son is henceforth the faces of men and women.
2. Outward appearance or aspect.
1947 AUDEN in *Amer. Scholar* XVI. 406 Even the dinner waltz.. is a voice that assaults International wrong,.. Completely delivering to the sick, Sad, soiled prosopon of our ageing Present the perdition of all her rage.

†**proˈsopopey.** *Obs.* Also **-eie, -eye.** [ad. L. *prosōpopœia*: see next, and cf. F. *prosopopée* (16th c. in Littré).] = next.
1577 tr. *Bullinger's Decades* (1592) 613 Prosopopeie is wher those are brought in to speake that do not speake. **1605** *Answ. Supposed Discov. Rom. Doctr.*, etc. 2 He warreth.. against poetically or childishlie feigned Prosopopeis, and

Chimeres of his owne creation. *a* **1641** BP. MOUNTAGU *Acts & Mon.* (1642) 89 The Prophet himselfe..speaks by Prosopopey concerning them. *a* **1693** *Urquhart's Rabelais* III. Prol., Who with their very countenance..express their consent to the Prosopopeie.

‖**prosopopœia** (prɒsəʊpəʊˈpiː(ɪ)ə). Also 6 **-oiia**, 6–9 **-eia**, (*erron.* 6–8 **-œa**, 7 **-oia**). [L. (Quintil.), a. Gr. προσωποποιία personification, representation in human form or with human attributes, f. πρόσωπον face, person + ποιεῖν to make.]

1. A rhetorical figure by which an imaginary or absent person is represented as speaking or acting; the introduction of a pretended speaker.

1561 DAUS tr. *Bullinger on Apoc.* (1573) 91 We vnderstand these things to be spoken by a figure called Prosopopeia: that is, by the fayning of a person. **1581** SIDNEY *Apol. Poetrie* (Arb.) 24 His notable Prosopopeias, when he maketh you as it were, see God comming in his Maiestie. **1609** R. BARNARD *Faithf. Sheph.* 67 Prosopopeia; the feigning of a person: when wee bring in dead men speaking, or our selues doe take their person vpon vs, or giue voice vnto senselesse things. **1787** GREGORY tr. *Lowth's Lect.* (1816) I. xiii. 280 Prosopopœia, or Personification. Of this figure there are two kinds: one, when action and character are attributed to fictitious, irrational, or even inanimate objects; the other, when a probable but fictitious speech is assigned to a real character. **1877** MORLEY *Crit. Misc.* Ser. II. 153 This is his one public literary Equivocation..it was resorted to..to give additional weight by means of a harmless prosopopoeia to an argument for the noblest of principles.

2. A rhetorical figure by which an inanimate or abstract thing is represented as a person, or with personal characteristics: = PERSONIFICATION I. (Formerly included in prec. sense: see quots. 1609, 1787 there.)

1578 TIMME *Caluine on Gen.* 142 Clemency and gentleness..is attributed thereto, by a figure called Prosopopoiia. **1649** ROBERTS *Clavis Bibl.* 276 The universall triumph and gladnesse as it were of all creatures (in an elegant Prosopopeia) is intimated. **1732** BERKELEY *Alciphr.* v. §22 Sentiments, and vices, which by a marvellous prosopopœia he converts into so many ladies. **1884** A. LAMBERT in *19th Cent.* June 947 Prosopopœia has no place even in popular science.

b. *transf.* Applied to a person or thing in which some quality or abstraction is as it were embodied; an impersonation, embodiment (*of* something).

1826 DISRAELI *Viv. Grey* I. x, Don't start..and look the very Prosopopeia of Political Economy! **1867** MACFARREN *Harmony* iv. (1876) 152 Everywhere at once..the prosopopœia of ubiquity.

Hence **prosopoˈpœial**, **prosopoˈpœic**, **-ical** *adjs.*, pertaining to, of the nature of, or involving prosopopœia.

1577 tr. *Bullinger's Decades* (1592) 622 To this place now doo belong the *Prosopopeiall speeches of God. **1652** URQUHART *Jewel* Wks. (1834) 292, I could have used..apostrophal and prosopopœial diversions. **1883** COTTERILL *Does Science Aid Faith?* (1886) 57 A poetic and *prosopopœic representation of the attribute of Divine wisdom. **1576** FLEMING *Panopl. Epist.* 192 He hath a *Prosopopoical speach to his countrie.

prosopulmonate (prɒsəʊˈpʌlmənət), *a. Zool.* [f. Gr. πρόσω forward + PULMONATE.] Pulmonate in front: applied to those pulmonate or air-breathing gastropod molluscs which have the pulmonary sac in front (opp. to *opisthopulmonate* (see OPISTHO-); cf. PROSOBRANCHIATE).

1877 HUXLEY *Anat. Inv. Anim.* viii. 514 The animal is thus more or less prosopulmonate.

prosopyle (ˈprɒsəʊpaɪl). *Zool.* [f. Gr. πρόσω forward + πύλη a gate.] A small aperture by which an endodermal chamber in a sponge communicates with the exterior. Hence **prosopylar** (prɒˈsɒpɪlə(r)) *a.*, pertaining to, having, or constituting a prosopyle.

1887 SOLLAS in *Encycl. Brit.* XXII. 413/2 (*Sponges*) To avoid ambiguity we shall for the future distinguish [this] kind of opening as a prosopyle. **1888** —— in *Challenger Rep.* XXV. p. xiv, The recesses, known as flagellated chambers, communicate with the cavity of the sac (*paragaster*) each by a single wide mouth (*apopyle*), and with the exterior by a small pore (*prosopyle*). **1890** *Cent. Dict.*, *Prosopylar.*

pro-Soviet, -ism: see PRO-[1] 5 a, c.

prospect (ˈprɒspɛkt), *sb.* [ad. L. *prōspect-us* a look out, view, f. *prōspic-ĕre* to look forward, f. *prō*, PRO-[1] + *specĕre* to look. Cf. F. *prospect* (16th c. in Littré).]

I. 1. a. The action or fact of looking forth or out, or of seeing to a distance; the condition (of a building, or station of any kind) of facing or being so situated as to have its front in a specified direction; outlook, aspect, exposure. *Obs.* passing into 2.

1430–50 tr. *Higden* (Rolls) I. 147 The water of Cilicia, which hathe prospecte ageyne the yle of Cipresse [L. *sinum qui prospicit contra insulam Cyprum*]. *Ibid.* II. 11 Briteyne is ..sette as vn to the prospecte of Speyne [*ad prospectum Hispaniæ sita est*]. **1560** BIBLE (Genev.) *Ezek.* xl. 44 Without the inner gate were the chambers of the singers in the inwarde courte..and their prospect was towarde the South. **1601** HOLLAND *Pliny* I. 119 [Armenia] confineth vpon the Medians, and hath a prospect to the Caspian sea. **1691** RAY *Creation* II. (1692) 4 This [erect] Figure is most convenient for Prospect, and looking about one. **1845** STOCQUELER *Handbk. Brit. India* (1854) 265 The atmosphere tolerably clear,..and the prospect, for the most part, clear and open: this is the autumn, if autumn there be at Dorjeling.

†**b.** A place which affords an open and extensive view; a look-out. *Obs.*

c **1586** C'TESS PEMBROKE *Ps.* CII. xi, From the prospect of thy heav'nly hall Thy eye of earth survey did take. **1611** CORYAT *Crudities* 164 People may from that place as from a most delectable prospect contemplate and view the parts of the City round about them. **1667** MILTON *P.L.* III. 77 Him God beholding from his prospect high,..Thus..spake. **1885** BIBLE (R.V.) *1 Kings* vii. 4 And there were prospects [1611 windowes] in three rows, and light was over against light in three ranks.

2. a. An extensive or commanding sight or view; the view of the landscape afforded by any position.

1538 ELYOT, *Prospectus*..a syght farre of, a prospecte. **1594** NORDEN *Spec. Brit. Pars* (Camden) 23 A..howse of pleasure vpon the topp of a mount..: it is seene farr of, and hath most large and pleasant perspecte [*sic*]. **1613** PURCHAS *Pilgrimage* (1614) 436 The streets are strait, yeelding prospect from one gate to another. **1634** SIR T. HERBERT *Trav.* 216 [St. Helena] giues a large prospect into the Ocean. **1657–83** EVELYN *Hist. Relig.* (1850) I. 28 Take we next a prospect of the earth's surface, and behold from the lofty mountains how the humble valleys are clothed with verdure. **1778** M. CUTLER in *Life*, etc. (1888) I. 68, I had a fine prospect of the whole army as it moved off. **1818** MISS MITFORD in L'Estrange *Life* (1870) II. ii. 23 There is but one place in all Berkshire which has a really fine commanding prospect. **1853** PHILLIPS *Rivers Yorksh.* iv. 128 A most striking prospect over sea and land. **1860** TYNDALL *Glac.* I. vii. 49 The prospect was exceedingly fine.

b. *in* (*within*) or *into prospect*: in or into a position making it possible to see or to be seen; within the range or scope of vision; in or into sight or view; within view. Also *fig. arch.*

1555 EDEN *Decades* 13 Within the prospecte of the begynnynge of Cuba, he founde a commodious hauen. **1599** SHAKS. *Much Ado* IV. i. 231 Euery louely Organ of her life, Shall come..Into the eye and prospect of his soule. **1605** [see 8]. **1664** BUTLER *Hud.* II. iii. 486 The Knight..Was now in prospect of the Mansion. **1685** BAXTER *Paraphr. N.T.* Matt. iv. 8 By all Kingdoms is meant, many that were within prospect. **1738** GRAY *Tasso* 5 Nor yet in prospect rose the distant shore. **1800–24** CAMPBELL *Dream* iv, Yon phantom's aspect..would appal thee worse, Held in clearly measured prospect.

3. a. That which is looked at or seen from any place or point of view; a spectacle, a scene; the visible scene or landscape.

a **1633** AUSTIN *Medit.* (1635) 278 What a prospect is a well-furnish'd Table? **1662** J. DAVIES tr. *Mandelslo's Trav.* 58 The windows of all the houses..were beset with Lamps, before which were placed Vessels of Glass fill'd with waters of several colours, which made a very delightful prospect. **1693** *Humours Town* 3, I had rather look up to see the welcome prospect of your House. **1711** SWIFT *Jrnl. to Stella* 25 Aug., He is ravished with Kent, which was his first prospect when he landed. **1727–46** THOMSON *Summer* 1438 Heavens! what a goodly prospect spreads around, Of hills, and dales, and woods, and lawns, and spires. **1763** JOHNSON in *Boswell* 6 July, But, Sir, let me tell you, the noblest prospect which a Scotchman ever sees, is the high road that leads him to England. **1798** WORDSW. *Peter Bell* I. xvi, On a fair prospect some have looked. **1859** DICKENS *Lett., to Mrs. Watson* 31 May, A snug room looking over a Kentish prospect.

‖**b.** A vista; a long, wide, straight street; an avenue of houses. Cf. PROSPEKT.

†**4.** The appearance presented by anything; aspect. *Obs. rare.*

1604 SHAKS. *Oth.* III. iii. 398 It were a tedious difficulty, I thinke, To bring them to that Prospect. **1709** MRS. E. SINGER *Love & Friendship* 36 in *Prior's Poems*, On the Plain when she no more appears, The Plain a dark and gloomy Prospect wears. **1715** LEONI *Palladio's Archit.* (1742) II. 8 By Prospect is understood the first show or appearance that a Temple makes to such as approach it... Those which have their Porticos only in front, may be said to have the Prospect *Prostylos*.

†**5.** A pictorial representation of a scene or the like; a view, a picture, a sketch. *Obs.*

1649 EVELYN *Diary* 20 June, I went to Putney and other places on the Thames to take prospects in crayon to carry with me into France, where I thought to have them engrav'd. **1695** E. BERNARD *Voy. fr. Aleppo to Tadmor* in *Misc. Cur.* (1708) III. 119 We have since procured a Curious Prospect of these Noble Ruins, taken on the Place. **1708** J. CHAMBERLAYNE *St. Gt. Brit.* II. III. x. (1737) 435 The Prospects of it [the Bass], as represented in Slezer's Theatrum Scotiæ, will sufficiently shew the Difficulty of Access to it. **1762–71** H. WALPOLE *Vertue's Anecd. Paint.* (1786) II. 180 His works are mentioned in the royal catalogue, particularly prospects of his majesty's houses in Scotland.

II. †**6.** A mental view or survey; a look, inspection, examination; also, an account or description. *Obs.*

1625 BACON *Ess.*, *Truth* (Arb.) 501 'To see the Errours.. in the vale below': So alwaies, that this prospect, be with Pitty. *a* **1648** LD. HERBERT *Hen. VIII* (1683) 10 Our King being thus setled in his Throne, took several prospects upon all his neighbouring Princes. **1677** *Govt. Venice* 266 Let us now take a Prospect of their Governours, I mean, consider the Manners and Maxims of their Nobility. *a* **1718** PENN *Tracts* Wks. 1726 I. 248, I take a Serious Prospect of the Spiritual Nature and Tendency of the Second Covenant. **1764** GOLDSM. (*title*) The Traveller; or, a Prospect of Society.

7. A scene presented to the mental vision, esp. of something future or expected; a mental vista.

1641 DENHAM *Sophy* v. i, Man to himselfe Is a large prospect. **1672** GREW *Anat. Plants, Idea Philos. Hist.* §63 How far soever we go, yet the surmounting of one difficulty is wont still to give us the prospect of another. **1736** BUTLER *Anal.* I. Concl., Wks. 1874 I. 144 All expectation of immortality..opens unbounded prospect to our hopes and our fears. **1785** T. BALGUY *Disc.* 26 True knowledge will perpetually mortify us with the prospect of our own weakness and ignorance. **1879** *Cassell's Techn. Educ.* IV. 95/1 The torch which illuminated the path of the youth, and opened new prospects to his eager views.

8. a. A mental looking forward; consideration or knowledge of, or regard to something future.

1605 SHAKS. *Macb.* I. iii. 74 To be King Stands not within the prospect of beleefe. **1662** EVELYN *Chalcogr.* 102 Not.. without Prospect had to the benefit of such as will be glad of instruction. *a* **1703** BURKITT *On N.T.* John xix. 22 The providence of God hath a prospect beyond the understanding of all creatures. **1779–81** JOHNSON *L.P.*, *Dryden* Wks. II. 400 His prospect of the advancement which it [navigation] shall receive from the Royal Society. **1862** STANLEY *Jew. Ch.* (1877) I. viii. 157 It was a Pisgah, not of prospect, but of retrospect.

b. *esp.* Expectation, or reason to look for something to come; that which one has to look forward to. Often *pl.*

1665 MANLEY *Grotius' Low C. Warres* 281 For the future, nothing remained, but a prospect of Tyranny and slavery. **1667** MARVELL *Corr.* Wks. (Grosart) II. 223 If anything be particularly in your prospects,..you will do well to give us timely advice. *c* **1775** JOHNSON *Lett., to Mrs. Thrale* (1788) I. 259 Our gay prospects have..ended in melancholy retrospects. **1849** MACAULAY *Hist. Eng.* v. I. 535 The prospect which lay before Monmouth was not a bright one. **1860** TYNDALL *Glac.* I. xxiii. 165 Seeing no prospect of fine weather, I descended to Saas. **1881** FROUDE *Short Stud.* (1883) IV. II. iii. 196 He was careless about his personal prospects.

c. *in prospect*: within the range of expectation; expected, or to be expected: now chiefly of something personally advantageous.

1779 BURKE *Corr.* (1844) II. 286 Every thing in prospect appears to me so very gloomy. **1833** HT. MARTINEAU *Manch. Strike* iv. 55 Allen longed to..forget all that had been done, and all that was in prospect. *Mod.* He has nothing in prospect at present.

d. A person or thing considered to be suitable for a particular purpose, *spec.* a potential or likely purchaser, customer, client, etc.

1922 S. LEWIS *Babbitt* vi. 68 He drove a 'prospect' out to view a four-flat tenement in the Linton district. **1922** *Glasgow Herald* 19 Dec. 8/8, I consider my bull calves excellent prospects for next season's fairs. **1926** *Publishers' Weekly* 16 Jan. 161/2 What the newspaper advertisement is for is to carry your helpful suggestions to the people who would be logical prospects for you. **1927** *Observer* 27 Nov. 11/1 There are thousands of 'prospects' who simply will not decide about a car until they have seen the new Ford. **1932** *New Yorker* 9 Apr. 32 She naturally considered her friends her best prospects. **1958** LICKORISH & KERSHAW *Travel Trade* v. 149 To define your market, use this check-list: Is the price of your service..right for the likely prospects?.. How often are the prospects likely to buy your service? *Ibid.* vii. 236 The ultimate purpose of both paid advertising and 'editorial' publicity is to increase the number of prospects who will buy the tickets and tours offered by the travel trade. **1967** N. FREELING *Strike Out* 49 A bank manager..would certainly regard her as a good prospect for a mortgage. **1973** R. C. DENNIS *Sweat of Fear* ix. 60 He told them he had a prospect looking at the house now. **1976** *Daily Mirror* 16 July 5/5 Carter men even checked the health and mental stability of the final six vice-presidential prospects.

e. A selected victim of a thief or pickpocket; a dupe.

1931 'D. STIFF' *Milk & Honey Route* viii. 91 Always approach a male prospect from the rear. *Ibid.* ix. 103 It is seldom that as he approaches one prospect after another he is not moved as much by speculative curiosity as by the need of sustenance. **1937** [see *lemon-game* s.v. LEMON *sb.*[1] 7].

III. †**9.** Short for *prospect-glass*: see 11. *Obs.*

1639 R. BAILLIE *Lett., to W. Spang* 28 Sept., The King himself beholding us through a prospect, conjectured us to be about 16 or 18,000 men. **1685** BURNET *Lett.* iii. (1686) 169, I looked at this Statue..through a little prospect that I carried with me. **1743** HUME *Ess.*, *Rise Arts & Sc.* (1817) I. 106 A man may as reasonably pretend to cure himself of love, by viewing his mistress through the artificial medium of a microscope or prospect.

IV. 10. *Mining.* **a.** A spot giving prospects of the presence of a mineral deposit.

1839 MARRYAT *Diary Amer.* Ser. I. II. 129 Finders, who would search all over the country for what they called a good prospect, that is, every appearance on the surface of a good vein of metal. **1882** *Rep. to Ho. Repr. Prec. Met. U.S.* 180 There are also a number of prospects being opened up in the vicinity. **1895** in *Daily News* 11 July 5/4 This demand [in California] is more for developed properties than for mere 'prospects' which may or may not become mines. **1975** *Offshore* Sept. 73/1 Finding oil and natural gas at prospect Cognac off the Louisiana coast, whether the field turns out to be large or not, is an important reminder of what this offshore exploration business is all about.

b. An examination or test of the mineral richness of a locality or of the material from which the ore, etc. is extracted.

1855 *Melbourne Argus* 10 Jan. 4/6 The result of a few prospects that have been made at a spot..has been very satisfactory.

c. A sample of ore or 'dirt' for testing; also, the resulting yield of ore.

1879 ATCHERLEY *Boërland* 115 The thrill of pleasure.. with which the digger contemplates his first good 'prospect' in the pan. There they are—some bright and yellow, others inky black, little rounded nuggets of every shape. **1890** 'R. BOLDREWOOD' *Miner's Right* (1899) 33/1 When the first 'prospect', the first pan of alluvial gold-drift, was sent up to be tested, we stopped work and joined the anxious crowd, who pressed around. **1891** *Melbourne Age* 2 Sept. 5/3 The average prospect will not exceed from 2 to 6 oz. per dish.

V. 11. *attrib.* and *Comb.*, as (from 1 b) ***prospect ground, tower***; (from sense 2) ***prospect-hunter***; (from 10) ***prospect hole, operation, pan, shaft, work***; **prospect-glass**, a 'prospective glass', telescope, field-glass.

1617 *Fight at Sea* A iij, Who in a *prospect glasse perceiued them to bee the Turkes Men of Warre. **1871** CARLYLE in *Mrs. Carlyle's Lett.* (1883) I. 257 Susan..had from her windows, with a prospect-glass, singled me out on the..deck of the steamer. **1848** BUCKLEY *Iliad* 406 They rushed by the *prospect-ground and the wind-waving fig-tree. **1877** RAYMOND *Statist. Mines & Mining* 303 Most of these are as yet mere *prospect-holes, and can boast of but little rich ore. **1803** D. WORDSWORTH *Jrnl.* 27 Aug. (1941) I. 271 The ferryman...would often say, after he had compassed the turning of a point, 'This is a bonny part,' and he always chose the bonniest, with greater skill than our *prospect-hunters and 'picturesque travellers'. **1880** SUTHERLAND *Tales of Goldfields* 12 He stood up with the dripping *prospect-pan in his hand. **1877** RAYMOND *Statist. Mines & Mining* 56 As determined by the *prospect-shafts, the channel falls toward his end on a steep grade. **1900** *Daily News* 25 Sept. 5/1 The Lord of the Manor determined to restore it to its original purpose of a *prospect-tower. **1882** *Rep. to Ho. Repr. Prec. Met. U.S.* 290 *Prospect work is all that has thus far been done.

† **ˈprospect**, *ppl. a.* *Obs. rare*⁻¹. [ad. L. *prōspect-us*, pa. pple. of *prōspic-ĕre*: see prec.] Open to view, clearly visible.

a **1619** FLETCHER, etc. *Q. Corinth* III. i, I wear a Christall casement 'fore my heart... Let it be prospect unto all the world.

prospect (see below), *v.* [In branch I, ad. L. *prōspect-āre*, frequent. of *prōspic-ĕre*: see above; in branch II, a new formation from PROSPECT *sb.* IV.]

I. (prəʊˈspɛkt).

† **1.** *intr.* To look forth or out; to front or face; to afford a prospect in some direction. *Obs.*

1555 EDEN *Decades* 79 It prospecteth towarde that parte of Aphrike. **1598** SYLVESTER *Du Bartas* II. i. IV. *Handie-Crafts* 206 Sixteen fair Trees..Whose equall front in quadran form prospected As if of purpose Nature them erected. **1613** PURCHAS *Pilgrimage* (1614) 437 Their houses are low..and prospect into the streets.

† **2.** *trans.* Of a person: To look out upon or towards; to look at, view, see at a distance. Of a building or the like: To front, face; to lie or be situated towards; to command a view of. *Obs.*

1555 EDEN *Decades* 140 The highest towre of his palaice, from whense they myght prospecte the mayne sea. **1578** BANISTER *Hist. Man* I. 20 Openyng the window of light, on the clearer side, prospecting the Sunne. **1579** FENTON *Guicciard.* (1618) 223 He cast a mine on that side which prospects Pizifalcona. **1677** [see PROSPECTING *vbl. sb.* 1]. **1698** FRYER *Acc. E. India & P.* 150 The College of the Carmelites is on an high Mount, prospecting the whole City.

† **3.** *trans.* To foresee, look for, expect; to anticipate. *Obs. rare.*

1652 GAULE *Magastrom.* 152 How many accidents fall out fatally, that can have no second cause ordinatly assigned to them, much less prospected in them. **1671** FLAVEL *Fount. Life* xviii. Wks. 1731 II. 52/1 The infinite Wisdom, prospecting all this, ordered that Christ should first be deeply humbled.

II. *Mining*, etc. (ˈprɒspɛkt, -ˈspɛkt). Orig. *U.S.*

4. *intr.* To explore a region *for* gold or other minerals.

1848 [see PROSPECTING *ppl. a.* 2]. **1850** B. TAYLOR *Eldorado* ix. (1862) 88 Dr. Gillette came down..with a companion, to 'prospect' for gold among the ravines in the neighborhood. **1872** BESANT & RICE *Ready Money Mortiboy* iii, 'Went prospecting to Mexico'—'What's prospecting, Dick?' 'Looking for silver'. **1885** MRS. C. PRAED *Head Station* (new ed.) 64 I've sent my mate to prospect for a new claim. **1898** MORRIS *Austral Eng.*, *Prospect v.*, to search for gold. In the word, and in all its derivatives, the accent is thrown back on to the first syllable.

b. *fig.* To search about, look out *for* something.

1867 E. NASON in *N. Eng. Hist. & Gen. Reg.* XXI. 5 Mr. Webster..finding himself almost penniless,..came to Boston, 'prospecting' for employment. **1870** LOWELL *Study Wind.* I. 7, I hope she was prospecting with a view to settlement in our garden. **1872** R. B. MARCY *Border Rem.* 145 A professional mesmerist..'prospecting' for subjects to exercise his powers upon after a lecture. **1884** *N. Eng. Hist. & Gen. Reg.* XXXVIII. 340, I have prospected in the records, from the middle of the sixteenth to the middle of the seventeenth centuries.

5. *trans.* **a.** To explore or examine (a region) for gold or other minerals. **b.** To work (a mine or lode) experimentally so as to test its richness.

1858 *N. York Tribune* 20 Sept. 7/2 [He] left Cherry Creek, near Pike's Peak, on the 27th of July, having satisfactorily 'prospected' a rich gold region. **1865** VISCT. MILTON & CHEADLE *N.W. Passage* xii. (1901) 222 The three miners.. discovering that they were close to the Athabasca, had turned back to prospect the sources of the McLeod. **1877** RAYMOND *Statist. Mines & Mining* 162 A shaft is being sunk to prospect the ground.

c. *fig.* To survey as to prospects.

1864 D. A. WELLS *Our Burden & Strength* 10 Let us now cautiously prospect the resources of the future. **1867** F. FRANCIS *Angling* vii. (1880) 264 Prospect the place, look for an open space. **1892** *Daily News* 12 Apr. 5/5 In prospecting the new year, he saw grounds for caution, but none for alarm.

6. *intr.* Of a mine, reef, or ore: To give (good or bad) indications of future returns; to 'promise' (well or ill). Also, to turn out, prove (rich or poor) on actual trial.

1868 F. WHYMPER *Trav. Alaska* xxv. 282 If a speculation promises well, they may answer, 'It prospects well'. **1877** RAYMOND *Statist. Mines & Mining* 60 The dirt on the bedrock is very rich, having prospected from $5 to $10 to the pan. **1897** *Daily News* 3 Nov. 9/5 This stone is very rich in places, and some of it prospects fully 20 ounces to the ton.

prospecting, *vbl. sb.* [f. prec. + -ING¹.] The action of the verb PROSPECT.

† **I. 1.** (prəʊˈspɛktɪŋ) Viewing, seeing. *Obs.*

1677 GILPIN *Demonol.* (1867) 416 The expression.. intimates that the way which Satan took was different from common prospecting or beholding.

II. *Mining* (ˈprɒspɛktɪŋ, now usu. prəˈspɛktɪŋ).

2. a. Surveying as to prospects; exploring or examining for minerals; the experimental working of a mine or reef.

1848 W. COLTON *Jrnl.* 18 Oct. in *3 Yrs. in Calif.* (1850) xxi. 292 Half their time is consumed in what they call prospecting; that is, looking up new deposits [of gold]. **1849** C. T. JACKSON in *Ex. Doc. 31st U.S. Congress 1 Sess. House* No. 5. 457 It is obvious that the shallow pits now sunk on the vein [of copper] show only its surface, and that they can only be regarded..as mere superficial explorations, or '*prospecting diggings*', as they are called in the west. **1857** J. D. BORTHWICK *3 Years California* vi. 124 We abandoned it [our claim], and went 'prospecting'. **1872** RAYMOND *Statist. Mines & Mining* 283 Little real mining has been carried on, while much prospecting has taken place. **1887** R. MURRAY *Geol. & Phys. Geog. Victoria* 157 Tracts..which,..in spite of careful prospecting, failed to yield gold.

b. *attrib.* Used, made, or done in prospecting, as ***prospecting camp, dish, drill, mill, pan, shaft, trip, work***; **prospecting claim**, the first claim, marked out by the discoverer of the deposit.

1851 in *Occasional Papers Univ. Sydney Austral. Lang. Res. Centre* (1966) No. 9. 19 The sediment which is composed of dirt, small stones and the particles of Gold which appear at and in the different compartments at the bottom are now emptied thro' two plugholes into a..tin dish, called a prospecting pan. **1869** *Overland Monthly* Mar. 279/1 Over one of the hoisting shafts there is a large wooden bucket with a rope and rude windlass such as you might see on the prospecting shaft of the poorest miner. **1877** RAYMOND *Statist. Mines & Mining* 37 Prospecting-drills will be used..to make a thorough examination of the best-appearing veins on the whole estate. **1880** *Cimarron News & Press* 22 July 2/2 New Mexico ought to become one vast prospecting camp for the next five years. **1880** *Daily Tel.* 3 Dec., Hundreds of men..began to sink what are called 'prospecting shafts', and a vast amount of low grade mineral was brought to bank. **1890** 'R. BOLDREWOOD' *Miner's Right* v, This..would be but half the size of the premier or prospecting claim. **1931** V. PALMER *Separate Lives* 183 Men ..had been trickling in from the prospecting-camps and copper-shows of the dry country. **1944** F. CLUNE *Red Heart* 62 He now knew how to twirl a prospecting dish. **1948** P. JOHNSTON *Lost & Living Cities Calif. Gold Rush* 52/2 A number of miners disappeared while on prospecting trips, leaving no trace of their fate.

fig. **1891** *Athenæum* 23 May 662/2 Nothing could well look less promising..than the first appearances which..greeted Dr. Atkinson on his prospecting visit to Danby.

prospecting, *ppl. a.* [f. as prec. + -ING².]

† **1.** That looks forward or foresees; provident.

1681 FLAVEL *Meth. Grace* Ep. to Rdr. 14 Man being a prudent and prospecting creature, hath the advantage of all other creatures in his foreseeing faculty.

2. *Mining* (ˈprɒspɛktɪŋ). That prospects or searches for indications of gold, etc.

1848 *N. York Lit. World* 3 June (Bartlett), Two or three men with a bucket, a rope, a pick-axe, and a portable windlass... This..is a prospecting party. **1882** H. LANSDELL *Through Siberia* I. 213 There must be a prospecting party made up.

prospection (prəʊˈspɛkʃən). Now *rare.* [n. of action f. L. *prōspic-ĕre*: see PROSPECT *sb.*]

1. The action of looking forward; anticipation; consideration of or regard to the future; foresight.

1668 H. MORE *Div. Dial.* I. ix. (1713) 18 A Principle that has a Prospection for the best, that rules all. **1668** HOWE *Bless. Righteous* (1825) 185 This is great wisdom in prospection; in taking care of the future. **1802** PALEY *Nat. Theol.* xviii. (1819) 282 That the prospection, which must be somewhere, is not in the animal, but in the Creator. **1831** CARLYLE in *Misc. Ess.* (1872) III. 238 Such retrospections and prospections bring to mind an absurd rumour.

b. A seeing or beholding, a view.

1897 in *Chicago Advance* 29 July 135/2 The higher sense gives prospection of a spiritual King and a spiritual Canaan.

2. The action of prospecting for gold or the like: see PROSPECT *v.* II.

1908 *Westm. Gaz.* 31 Mar. 11/3 The directors authorised ..the prospection of the swampy land..with a view to ascertaining the possibility of working this.

prospective (prəʊˈspɛktɪv), *a.* and *sb.* [As adj. ad. obs. F. *prospectif, -ive*, or med.L. *prōspectīv-us* belonging to or affording a prospect, f. L. *prōspect-*, ppl. stem of *prōspic-ĕre*: see PROSPECT *sb.* and -IVE. As sb. a. obs. F. *prospective* (1553 in Godef.) a view, prospect; but in senses 1 and 2 short for *prospective glass.* Sometimes corresponding to the earlier PERSPECTIVE, q.v.]

A. *adj.* **1.** Characterized by looking forward into the future; also, †having foresight or care for the future; provident (*obs.*).

c **1590** GREENE *Fr. Bacon* xiii. 12 By prospective skill I find this day shall fall out ominous. **1658** A. FOX tr. *Würtz' Surg.* II. xiv. 100 Be moderate, prospective, and cautious in stitching, and not too hasty. **1690** CHILD *Disc. Trade* Pref. (1694) C vj b, The French King and King of Sweden are.. circumspect, industrious and prospective too in this Affair. **1850** L. HUNT *Autobiog.* II. ix. 7 He was a retrospective rather than a prospective man.

† **2.** Used or suitable for looking forward or viewing at a distance (*lit.* and *fig.*). ***prospective stone***: cf. PROSPECTIVE GLASS 1. *Obs.*

1603 H. CROSSE *Vertues Commw.* (1878) 128 That olde Witch Lamea, who as the Poets frame, had broade prospectiue eyes to pull out and in at pleasure. *a* **1635** NAUNTON *Fragm. Reg.* (Arb.) 60 It seemes nature..to pleasure him the more, borrowed of Argus, so to give unto him a prospective sight. **1652** ASHMOLE *Theat. Chem. Brit.* Prol. 8 By the Magicall or Prospective Stone it is possible to discover any Person in what part of the World soever.

† **3.** Fitted to afford a fine prospect or extensive view. Hence *fig.* Elevated, high, lofty. *Obs.*

1588 GREENE *Metamorphosis* Wks. (Grosart) IX. 88 Desirous to heare what the meaning of this monument seated so prospectiue to Neptune, should be. **1632** LITHGOW *Trav.* IV. 139 Being situate on moderate prospectiue heights. *Ibid.* IX. 416 A pleasant and prospectiue Countrey. *a* **1814** *Apostate* III. iii. in *New Brit. Theatre* III. 328 It..cannot be, that one so great, So lofty and prospective in his virtue, Should fall to such perdition. *a* **1817** T. DWIGHT *Trav. New Eng.*, etc. (1821) II. 106 Above this plain, after ascending a moderate acclivity, lies another: both of them handsome grounds, and the latter finely prospective.

4. a. That looks or has regard to the future; operative with regard to the future.

1800 *Proc. E. Ind. Ho.* in *Asiat. Ann. Reg.* 112/1 The usages and customs of this country have authorised a certain species of oaths, which he would denominate prospective oaths, as they generally are so. **1802** PALEY *Nat. Theol.* xiv. §2 (ed. 2) 275 It is not very easy to conceive a more evidently prospective contrivance, than that which, in all viviparous animals, is found in the milk of the female parent. **1828** MACAULAY *Ess.*, *Hallam* (1887) 58 A prospective law, however severe,..would have been mercy itself compared with this odious act. **1868** M. PATTISON *Academ. Org.* v. 188 The fellowship should convey a prospective obligation to the prosecution of the studies intended to be promoted by the endowment. **1884** SIR J. PEARSON in *Law Rep. 27 Chanc. Div.* 354 The language of the 26th section is entirely prospective and not retrospective.

b. *Gram.* Denoting a tense of a verb which is present in form but implies a future action or state.

1931 O. JESPERSEN *S.P.E. Tract* XXXVI. 528 This leads to the use of *is going to* with an infinitive as what may be called a prospective present, and *was going to* as a prospective past. **1963** L. R. PALMER *Interpretation of Mycenaean Gk. Texts* 51 On the 'prospective' form *e-ke-qe*, which I formerly interpreted phonetically as a future, see p. 190. *Ibid.* 190 The facts thus suggest that the addition of the particle *-qe* to the verb gives it 'prospective' force.

5. That looks forward or is looked forward to; that is in prospect; expected, hoped for; future.

1829 SOUTHEY *Sir T. More* (1831) I. 372 No measure which indicates prospective policy was taken. **1853** C. BRONTE *Villette* xii, All the pupils above fourteen knew of some prospective bridegroom. **1863** FAWCETT *Pol. Econ.* II. iii. 150 Not only a large prospective but even a large immediate profit would be returned. **1884** *Truth* 13 Mar. 376/2 A silly lordling and prospective peer.

B. *sb.* Formerly (ˈprɒspɛktɪv).

† **1.** A magic mirror: = PROSPECTIVE GLASS 1. Also *fig. Obs.*

[*a* **1430** *Chaucer's Sqr.'s T.* 226: see PERSPECTIVE *sb.* 2.] **1595** DANIEL *Delia* xxii, This heart made now the prospectiue of care. **1596** FITZ-GEFFRAY *Sir F. Drake* (1881) 76 Highe throne, wherein all vertues made their seate, True prospective of immortalitie. **1604** DANIEL *Vis. 12 Goddesses* Ded., And withal delivers her a Prospective, wherein she might behold the Figures of their Deities, and thereby describe them. **1625** BACON *Ess.*, *Seeming Wise* (Arb.) 215 It is a Ridiculous Thing..to see what shifts these Formalists haue, and what Prospectiues, to make Superficies to seeme Body, that hath Depth and Bulke. **1626** —— *Sylva* §98 Such Superficiall Speculations they have; Like Prospectives, that shew things inward, when they are but Paintings.

† **2.** A field-glass, spy-glass, or telescope; *pl.* spectacles; = PROSPECTIVE GLASS 2. Also *fig. Obs.*

1630 J. TAYLOR (Water P.) *Fennor's Defence* Wks. II. 149/2, I haue look't ouer with my best Prospectiues, And view'd the tenor of thy base Inuectiues. *a* **1635** CORBET *Poems* 91 Lastly of fingers, glasses we contrive, And every fist is made a prospective. **1657** W. MORICE *Coena quasi Κοινή* ii. 35 Turning the wrong end of the Prospective, to make things at hand seem to be far off. **1674** *Depos. Cast. York* (Surtees) 233 To follow his calling..of pollishing glasses for prospectives and specktacles and mycroscopes. **1727** A. HAMILTON *New Acc. E. Ind.* I. i. 14 Those on board the Ship, saw, by their Prospectives, what was acted Ashore.

3. The action of looking out (*lit.* or *fig.*); cf. PROSPECT *sb.* 1. † ***at prospective***: on the look-out (*obs.*). ***in prospective***: in view (*lit.* or *fig.*); in prospect or anticipation. Now *rare.*

1599 B. JONSON *Cynthia's Rev.* II. Wks. (Rtldg.) 79/1 A quarter past eleven, and ne'er a nymph in prospective. **1616** J. LANE *Cont. Sqr.'s T.* XI. 19 But lo, as Canac stoode at prospective, Her glasse discried from farr a troopes arive. **1746–7** HERVEY *Medit.* (1818) 217 Now the day is gone, how short it appears! When my fond eye beheld it in prospective, it seemed a very considerable space. **1866** MRS. H. WOOD *St. Martin's Eve* ix, Four thousand a year now, and six in prospective! **1978** *Times Lit. Suppl.* 20 Jan. 69/5 Its rather curious title 'Mankind in Prospective' perhaps accords with the book's New World spelling—has 'prospective' already evolved into a noun there?

†**4.** A scene, a view: = PROSPECT *sb.* 3. *Obs.*
1599 PORTER *Angry Wom. Abingd.* in Hazl. *Dodsley* VII. 269 As prospectives, the nearer that they be, Yield better judgment to the judging eye. *a* **1639** WOTTON *Life Dk. Buckhm.* in *Reliq.* (1651) 93 The whole Scene of affairs was changed from Spain to France; there now lay the prospective. **1745** P. THOMAS *Jrnl. Anson's Voy.* 188 When the Canal runs in a strait Line, as they usually do, it makes a Prospective at once stately and agreeable.

†**5.** A pictorial view; *fig.* a description: cf. PROSPECT *sb.* 5, 6. *Obs. rare.*
1658 T. HIGGONS tr. *Busenello* (title), A Prospective of the Naval Triumph of the Venetians over the Turk. **1660** *(title)* A Landskip: or a Brief Prospective of English Episcopacy, Drawn by three skilfull hands in Parliament: Anno 1641.

†**6. a.** A place for viewing, a look-out: = PROSPECT *sb.* 1 b. *Obs. rare*$^{-1}$.
1616 R. C. *Times' Whistle*, etc. 145 Be ther placd A prospective vpon the top o' th' mast, Wherin 'tis fitt that carefull diligence Keep evermore his watchfull residence.

†**b.** A point of view. *Obs.*
1603 DANIEL *Def. Rhyme* H iv, Men, standing according to the prospectiue of their owne humour, seeme to see the selfe same things to appeare otherwise to them, than either they doe to other, or are indeede in themselues.

†**7. a.** The art of drawing in perspective: = PERSPECTIVE *sb.* 3; also, a perspective view. *Obs.*
1601 B. JONSON *Poetaster* III. i, I studie architecture too.. I'd haue a house iust of that prospectiue. **1620–55** I. JONES *Stone-Heng* (1725) 42 The whole Work in Prospective, as when entire. *Ibid.*, The Ruin yet remaining drawn in Prospective. **1662** GERBIER *Princ.* (1665) 5 An Exact Architect must have the Art of Drawing, and Prospective. **1684** *Contempl. St. Man* I. ii. (1699) 22 Those who work in Prospective, will so paint a Room, that the Light entring only through some little Hole, you shall perceive beautiful and perfect Figures and Shapes.

b. *Her.* (See quot.) Also *Comb.* **prospective-wise**, in perspective.
c **1828** BERRY *Encycl. Herald.* I. Gloss., *Perspective*, or *Prospective*, is used, in blazon, to express divisional lines forming a kind of pavement with diminishing squares in perspective, as *paly barry*, or *barry bendy, in perspective*, or *prospective wise*.

† **pro'spective glass.** *Obs.*
1. A magic glass or crystal, in which it was supposed that distant or future events could be seen. Also called ***glass prospective***. Also *fig.*
a **1584** *Tom Thumbe* 298 in Hazl. *E.P.P.* II. 190 This cunning doctor tooke A fine prospective glasse, with which he did in secret looke Into his sickened body downe. *c* **1590** GREENE *Fr. Bacon* v. 110 In a glasse prospectiue I will shew Whats done this day in merry Fresingfield. **1609** ROWLEY *Search for Money* (Percy Soc.) 26 If every conjurer had such a prospective glasse of his owne, they would never deale so much with the Divell as they doe. **1628** MILTON *Vacation Exerc.* 71 A Sybil old.. That.. in Times long and dark Prospective Glass Fore-saw what future dayes should bring to pass.

2. A spy-glass, field-glass, telescope. Also *pl.* spectacles, binocular glasses. Cf. PERSPECTIVE *a.* 2.
1626 CAPT. SMITH *Accid. Yng. Seamen* 33 The Gunners scale is made in brasse at Tower Hill, with prospectiue glasses. **1672** *Phil. Trans.* VII. 5065 He likewise shew'd his Highness a little Prospective Glass, made according to Mr. Newtons new Invention. **1696** tr. *Du Mont's Voy. Levant* xiii. 168 He frequently observ'd what was done in the City from his Seraglio, by the help of some excellent Prospective-Glasses. **1738** NEAL *Hist. Purit.* IV. 22 Discovering by prospective glasses that they were coming down to attack him.
fig. **1634** WITHER *Emblemes, Medit. on Pict.*, A glimpes farre off, through Faith's prospective glasse. **1641** MILTON *Animadv.* Wks. 1851 III. 191 These free-spoken, and plaine harted men that are the eyes of their Country, and the prospective glasses of their Prince. **1678** *Donna Olimpia* 150 And with the Prospective Glasses of their Ambition daily surveyed all Italy.

pro'spectively, *adv.* [f. PROSPECTIVE + -LY².] In a prospective manner.
1. With outlook upon or consideration of the future, with foresight; also, in anticipation or expectation of something to come.
1826 J. S. MILL in *Wks.* (1967) IV. 75 The few who watch prospectively the signs of future supply and demand. **1828** *Blackw. Mag.* XXIII. 418 Prospectively maintaining the same harmony between the existing powers of the tree, and the exigencies of its new situation. **1868** M. PATTISON *Academ. Org.* iv. 103 An annual outlay.. is applied—prospectively as scholarship, or retrospectively as fellowship.

2. With bearing upon or application to the future.
1863 H. COX *Instit.* I Rules which.. prospectively declare the rights and obligations which the State will enforce. **1885** *Law Times Rep.* LII. 168/2 The Judicature Act 1875.. cannot.. apply prospectively to the Bankruptcy Act of 1883.

†**3.** = PERSPECTIVELY *adv.* 3 (for which in quot. it may be an error; but cf. PROSPECTIVE *sb.* 7).
1557 RECORDE *Whetst.* Hj, These numbers can not be expressed aptly in flatte, but prospectiuely, as Dice maie be made in protracture.

pro'spectiveness. [f. as prec. + -NESS.] The quality or character of being prospective.
1817 COLERIDGE *Biog. Lit.* xviii. (1882) 172 There is a want of that prospectiveness of mind, that surview, which enables a man to foresee the whole of what he is to convey. **1824** T. E. HOOK *Sayings & Doings* III. 343 The symptomatic prospectiveness of the disease.

prospectless ('prɒspɛktlɪs), *a.* [See -LESS.]
1. Having no prospect or outlook.
1656 S. H. *Gold. Law* 103 Wert thou hous'd in some dark or Prospectless ground room. **1770** H. WALPOLE *Let. to G. Montagu* 11 June, A palace as dismal and prospectless as if it stood 'on Stanmore's wintry wild!'

2. Without prospects for the future.
1878 FLOR. MONTGOMERY *Seaforth* III. i, Your boys.. were born as penniless and as prospectless as mine. **1889** MRS. OLIPHANT *Poor Gentleman* II. ii. 27 A penniless, prospectless young man.

prospector (prəʊ'spɛktə(r), 'prɒspɛktə(r)). Also -er. [a. late L. *prōspector* one who looks out, foresees, or provides, agent-n. f. *prōspic-ĕre*: see PROSPECT *sb.*] One who prospects; in quots., one who explores a region for gold or the like: see PROSPECT *v.* 4, 5.
1857 J. D. BORTHWICK *3 Years California* vi. 124 A 'prospecter' goes out with pick and shovel, and a wash-pan; and.. digs down till he reaches the dirt in which it may be expected that the gold will be found. **1862** *Times* 8 Apr., Mr. Disraeli may be a good prospecter, and he may make the best of his 'claim', but the result is nil. **1884** *Ibid.* 18 Apr. 8 All the trains.. bring in new settlers and prospectors.

prospectus (prəʊ'spɛktəs). Pl. **prospectuses** (rarely in L. form **prospectūs**). [a. L. *prōspectus* (-*ūs*) a view, PROSPECT *sb.* So F. *prospectus* (1723 in Hatz.-Darm.).] A description or account of the chief features of a forthcoming work or proposed enterprise, circulated for the purpose of obtaining support or subscriptions. Also, a description or account of the activities of a school or other educational institution.
1765 D. GARRICK *Let.* 27 Jan. in R. B. Peake *Mem. Colman Family* (1841) I. v. 136, I could be glad that something was put into the St James's Chronicle.. for my friend Monnet. You have seen his prospectus by this time. **1777** *Life Goldsmith* G.'s Wks. 1786 I. Pref. 31 A design for executing an universal dictionary of arts and sciences, the *prospectus* of which he actually printed and distributed among his acquaintance. **1791** BOSWELL *Johnson* an. 1747, His 'Dictionary of the English Language', was announced to the world by the publication of its Plan or Prospectus. **1823** COGSWELL & BANCROFT *(title)* Prospectus of a school to be established at Round Hill, Northampton, Massachusetts. **1832** F. TROLLOPE *Domestic Manners* II. xxx. 163 Whilst at New York, the prospectus of a fashionable boarding-school was presented to me. **1845** R. W. HAMILTON *Pop. Educ.* iv (ed. 2) 62 The extent of injurious influence upon the public mind of certain *prospectūs* of education. **1855** MACAULAY *Hist. Eng.* xix. IV. 322 To put forth a lying prospectus announcing a new stock. **1890** SIR R. ROMER in *Law Times Rep.* LXIII. 685/2 The plaintiff applied for shares in this company on the faith of the prospectus. *a* **1908** *Mod.* He has obtained the prospectuses of several schools. **1937** *Discovery* Jan. p. ii/1 (Advt.), Boys' Preparatory School... Boarders only; six graduate staff, entire charge if required. Prospectus on request. **1980** *Times* 15 July 5/2 (Advt.), Tuition by post. Free prospectus... Wolsey Hall, Oxford.
attrib. **1895** *Pall Mall Gaz.* 3 July 3/1 A rich specimen,.. though not for prospectus purposes. **1900** *Westm. Gaz.* 19 Apr. 9/1 The results.. are distinctly disappointing when compared with the prospectus estimates.

pro'spectusless, *a.* [f. PROSPECTUS + -LESS.] Of a company or its shares: for which no prospectus has been issued.
1898 *Westm. Gaz.* 26 Oct. 8/1 It is a lesson to those who deal in prospectusless shares... We said we should not buy the shares until some official prospectus has been issued. *Ibid.* 11 Nov. 8/1 It is not a sound business principle to buy the shares of a prospectusless company. **1907** *Sat. Rev.* 20 Apr. 486/1 We are by no means opposed to prospectusless companies, thinking that when the public are not asked to subscribe, there is no reason why the public should be informed of the details of other people's business. **1928** *Daily Mail* 9 Aug. 18/1 A good deal of interest has been aroused.. by our references yesterday to statements published by prospectusless companies.

‖**Prospekt** ('prɒspɛkt). Also with small initial. [a. Russ. *prospékt.*] In the Soviet Union: a long, wide street; an avenue, a boulevard. Esp. used of the great avenues of Leningrad, e.g. *Nevsky Prospekt*. Cf. PROSPECT *sb.* 3 b.
1866 *Chamber's Encycl.* VIII. 427/2 About ten of the other streets of the city [*sc.* St. Petersburg] are distinguished for their grandeur, though none of them equals the Nevski Prospekt. **1966** L. DEIGHTON *Billion-Dollar Brain* xxvi. 274 There were signs of a thaw. All along the Prospekt the huge drainpipes were groaning. **1979** O. SELA *Petrograd Consignment* 105 Petrograd.. was a tedious panorama of featureless white. Sleds slipped noiselessly along the *prospekts*.

†**prosper,** *a. Obs. rare.* [ME. *prospere*, a. F. *prospère* (14th c. in Littré) or ad. L. *prosper*, *prosper-us* favourable, fortunate, prosperous: of uncertain origin. The form *prospre* is a. OF. *prospre* (12th c. in Littré).] Prosperous, successful.
c **1374** CHAUCER *Boeth.* I. pr. iv. 8 (Camb. MS.) Thilke man.. þat maade alwey assawtes ayeins the prospere [*v.r.* prospre] fortunes of poore feeble fookkes. **1513** DOUGLAS *Æneis* VIII. v. 59 We pray the vissie, that thou may cum heyr Wyth prosper presens and full happy fute. *Ibid.* XI. xiv. 88 The pepill Tuscane.. Seand the exempill and prosper chans that tyd Of thar stowt duke.

prosper ('prɒspə(r)), *v.* [a. F. *prospére-r* (14th c. in Littré), ad. L. *prospe'rā-re* to cause (a thing) to succeed, to render fortunate, also absol., in late L. also to propitiate (God), in pass. to prosper, f. *prosper* adj.: see prec.]
1. a. *intr.* Of a person, community, etc.: To be prosperous, fortunate, or successful; to flourish, thrive, succeed, do well.
c **1460** FORTESCUE *Abs. & Lim. Mon.* xvi. (*heading*), How the Romaynes prospered whiles thai hade a grete counsell. **1526** *Pilgr. Perf.* (W. de W. 1531) 16 b, They wente hole togyder, and prospered ryght well in theyr iourney. **1651** HOBBES *Leviath.* III. xxxiii. 202 Why wicked men have often prospered in this world. **1786** *Scotch Paraphr.* VII. iii Who, that tries th' unequal strife Shall prosper in the end? **1864** TENNYSON *En. Ard.* 48 Enoch.. so prosper'd that at last A luckier or a bolder fisherman.. did not breathe. **1884** RUSKIN *Pleas. Eng.* 75 No false knight or lying priest ever prospered, I believe, in any age.

b. *intr.* Of things: To flourish; to turn out well.
c **1529** in *Archæologia* (1882) XLVII. 51 We will the said religion to prospere according unto the foundacion of the house. **1535** COVERDALE *Ps.* i. 3 What soeuer he doth, it shal prospere. *a* **1720** SEWEL *Hist. Quakers* (1795) II. VII. 11 If such doings as this ever prosper. **1870** MORRIS *Earthly Par.* (1890) 358 Well did all things prosper in his hand.

c. *intr.* Of plants: To thrive, to flourish.
1553 EDEN *Treat. Newe Ind.* (Arb.) 41 There were also vynes.. planted in this Ilande, where they prosper so wel, that [etc.]. **1682** SIR T. BROWNE *Chr. Mor.* III. §4 Where such Plants grow and prosper. **1731** P. MILLER *Gardeners' Dict.* s.v. Phaseolus. In the West-Indies it [*sc.* the pigeon-pea].. will thrive on barren land which has been worn out, where scarcely any thing else will prosper. **1946** D. C. PEATTIE *Road of Naturalist* iii. 34 Nature out of her vast variety has provided forms that prosper even there [*sc.* in Death Valley].

2. *trans.* To cause to flourish; to promote the prosperity or success of; to be propitious to.
1530 PALSGR. 668/1, I beseche Jhesu prospere you in all your busynesses. **1593** NASHE *Christ's T.* 61 b, God.. cherrisht and prosperd them with all the blessings hee could. **1642** *Declar. Lords & Com., Ordinance* 13 Apr. 3 For prospering the common cause. **1784** COWPER *Task* VI. 1024 Whose frown can disappoint the proudest strain, Whose approbation prosper—even mine. **1855** KINGSLEY *Westw. Ho!* xxiii, If Heaven prospered them, they might seize a Spanish ship.
Hence **'prospering** *vbl. sb.* and *ppl. a.*
c **1557** ABP. PARKER *Ps.* xx, This prayth for kinges Good prosperinges, Theyr realmes to have defence. **1604** EARL STIRLING *Parænesis to Pr. Henry* lxxvii, Every State by long experience findes, That greatest blessings prosp'ring Peace imparts. **1854** E. G. HOLLAND *Mem. J. Badger* xviii. 349 The pastor of a prospering church.

†**'prosperable,** *a. Obs. rare.* [f. prec. + -ABLE.] **a.** Prosperous, likely to prosper. **b.** Able or inclined to give prosperity; propitious.
c **1422** HOCCLEVE *Learn to Die* 112 Horrible is thy presence and ful greeuable To him þat yong is strong and prosperable. **1611** SPEED *Hist. Gt. Brit.* IX. xxiii. §46 Vnlesse God be prosperable to his purpose.

†**'prosperance.** *Obs. rare*$^{-1}$. [f. L. *prosperāre* to PROSPER: see -ANCE.] = PROSPERITY.
1502 ARNOLDE *Chron.* (1811) 162 God the yeuar of all goodnes graunte the prosperaunce and happy encreses.

†**'prosperately,** *adv. Obs. rare*$^{-0}$. [f. **prosperate*, ad. late L. *prosperāt-us* prospered + -LY².]
1573–80 BARET *Alv.* P 786 Prosperately, fortunately, with good lucke, *secundis auibus*.

prosperation (prɒspə'reɪʃən). *rare.* Now only *dial.* [ad. late or med.L. *prosperātiōn-em*, n. of action f. *prosper-āre* to PROSPER. Cf. obs. F. *prosperation* (1512 in Godef.).] Prosperity.
c **1470** HARDING *Chron.* LXXXVII. xii. (MS. Arch. Seld. B. 10) þe Churche [might haue be] preserued in greate prosperacioun. **1828** *Craven Gloss.* (ed. 2), *Prosperation*, success, good luck. **1856** HINCHLIFFE *Hist. Barthomley* 145 One old song.. was always sung at these meetings [Annual Churchwardens' Dinner],.. which I insert below... 'Come, brave boys, prosperation Be to the Church and Nation!' **1883** BURNE *Shropsh. Folk-Lore* 471 [At Much Wenlock] each of the new burgesses was required to stand up in turn and empty the cup to the toast of 'Prosperation To the Corporation'.

'prospered (-əd), *ppl. a.* [f. PROSPER *v.* + -ED¹.] Caused to prosper, blest with prosperity.
1651 CROMWELL *Let. to Speaker* 4 Sept. in *Carlyle*, That the fear of the Lord, even for His mercies, may keep an Authority and a People so prospered, and blessed,.. humble and faithful. **1661** BOYLE *Style of Script.* (1675) 230 Wherein her Prospered Sedulousness gave her an Understanding much above her Age and Sex.

prosperer ('prɒspərə(r)). *rare.* [f. as prec. + -ER¹.] **a.** One who is prosperous or flourishing. **b.** One who causes prosperity.
1633 D. R[OGERS] *Treat. Sacram.* I. 161 A man that is no prosperer in grace. **1643** TRAPP *Comm. Gen.* xlix. 10 Others render *Shiloh*.. The Peace-maker, The Prosperer.

prosperity (prɒ'spɛrɪtɪ). [ME. a. F. *prospérité* (*prosperitet a* 1140 in Littré), ad. L. *prosperitās*, *-tātem* good fortune, success, prosperity, f. *prosper*, *prosper-us*: see PROSPER *a.* and -ITY.] The condition of being prosperous, successful, or thriving; good fortune, success, well-being.
a **1225** *Ancr. R.* 194 Uor þe uttre uondunge is mislicunge in aduersite, & ine prosperite þet limpeð to sunne. **1382** WYCLIF *1 Macc.* ii. 47 The werk hadde prosperite in her hondis. **1406** HOCCLEVE *La male regle* 34 Prosperitee is blynd, & see ne may. **1500–20** DUNBAR *Poems* lxxx. 11 God

giue the guid prosperitie, Fair fortoun and felicitie. **1607** SHAKS. *Cor.* II. i. 188 You haue, I know, petition'd all the Gods for my prosperitie. **1638** BAKER tr. *Balzac's Lett.* (vol. II.) 68 A Moderatour in prosperitie; and a guide in adversitie. **1795** BURKE *Corr.* (1844) IV. 284 Prosperity is not apt to receive good lessons, nor always to give them. **1862** RUSKIN *Unto this Last* iv. 143 The prosperity of any nation is in exact proportion to the quantity of labour which it spends in obtaining and employing means of life. **1874** GREEN *Short Hist.* vii. §2. 357 The cause which prosperity had ruined revived in the dark hour of persecution.

b. *pl.* Instances of prosperity, prosperous circumstances.

1340 *Ayenb.* 24 Þe guodes of hap byeþ heȝnesses, richesses, delices, and prosperites. **1598** GRENEWEY *Tacitus, Ann.* VI. v. (1622) 128 The vitious and bad triumph with so great prosperities. **1632** SIR T. HAWKINS tr. *Mathieu's Unhappy Prosperitie* 231 Shewing all prosperities of the world were but trifles, and counterfet gems, compared with eternall felicitie. **1856** MRS. BROWNING *Aur. Leigh* II. 467 What then, indeed, If mortals are not greater by the head Than any of their prosperities?

c. *attrib.* and *Comb.*

1647 TRAPP *Comm. Mark* iv. 17 These are prosperity-proselytes, holy-day servants,..neuter passive Christians. **1889** *Standard* 16 Apr., The Budget which Mr. Goschen introduced..might have been a 'Prosperity' Budget, had the requirements of the country been normal. **1901** *Lady's Realm* X. 655/2 Households, who shall watch the prosperity-bringing fire with mingled joy and awe.

prosperous ('prɒspərəs), *a.* [a. obs. F. *prospereus* (15th c. in Godef.) = It. *prosperoso*: see PROSPER *a.* and -OUS.]

1. Having continued success or good fortune; consistently successful; flourishing, thriving.

1472-3 *Rolls of Parlt.* VI. 30/2 The first yere of your moost prospereux reigne. **1531** TINDALE *Exp. 1 John* (1537) 58 Oure brethren were in prosperouser state then we. **1591** SHAKS. *1 Hen. VI*, I. i. 32 The Battailes of the Lord of Hosts he fought: The Churches Prayers made him so prosperous. **1638** JUNIUS *Paint. Ancients* 88 In this same plaine and prosperous way of emulation. **1771** *Junius Lett.* l. (1820) 260 In the most prosperous state of his fortune he was always the very man he is at present. **1878** JEVONS *Prim. Pol. Econ.* 7 Political Economy inquires into the causes which make one nation more rich and prosperous than another.

2. Promoting or conducing to success; bringing prosperity; favourable, auspicious, propitious.

1445 in *Anglia* XXVIII. 273 While goodis be had in habundaunce & prosperous chauncis be falle. *c* **1460** J. METHAM *Wks.* (E.E.T.S.) 153 Yt ys prosp[er]us that day to pase the see with marchaundyse, and to wedde a wyfe. **1555** EDEN *Decades* 247 We sayled euer with prosperous wynde. **1599** NASHE *Lenten Stuffe* (1871) 58 To try what kind of flesh-meat was most nutritive and prosperous with a man's body. **1772-84** *Cook's Voy.* (1790) V. 1697 We..had a prosperous gale, and plenty of provisions. **1871** R. ELLIS *Catullus* lxiv. 237 A prosperous hour shall bring to thee happy returning.

3. *Comb.*, as ***prosperous-looking*** adj.

1899 CROCKETT *Kit Kennedy* 31 'But, Lilias, you are well dressed, and prosperous-looking', said the man.

prosperously ('prɒspərəslı), *adv.* [f. prec. + -LY².] In a prosperous manner.

1. Successfully, with continued good fortune.

1503-4 *Act 19 Hen. VII*, c. 38 §2 Your moste noble & royall Estate longe prosperously to endure. **1617** MORYSON *Itin.* I. 251 Vpon Friday the eleuenth of October, we sayled prosperously. *a* **1714** SHARP *Wks.* V. iv. 297 We are willing to trust God with any other concern, so long as that concern goes on prosperously. **1849** MACAULAY *Hist. Eng.* vi. II. 71 For a time the intrigue went on prosperously and secretly.

2. Favourably, propitiously. *rare.*

1596 DRAYTON *Leg.* iv. 39 Be now abundant prosp'rously to aide The Pen prepar'd.

prosperousness ('prɒspərəsnıs). [f. as prec. + -NESS.] The quality or condition of being prosperous; prosperity, success.

1648 BOYLE *Seraph. Love* i. (1700) 3, I seldom use endeavours, whose prosperousness is more welcome to me, than those that aspire to serve Lindamor. **1812** G. CHALMERS *Dom. Econ. Gt. Brit.* 459 Yet, was that prosperousness accompanied, by unfavourable exchanges, and several bankruptcies.

‖**prosphora** ('prɒsfɒrə). [a. Gr. προσφορά.] A religious offering, esp. the bread offered for use in the Eucharist (see quots.).

1874 GLADSTONE in *Contemp. Rev.* Oct. 676 Uniting the humble and unworthy *prosphora* with the one full perfect and sufficient Sacrifice, to offer it upon the altar of the heart. **1945** G. DIX *Shape of Liturgy* v. 111 The Greek terminology is throughout the pre-Nicene period quite clear... The communicant 'brings' (*prosenegkein*) the *prosphora*; the deacon 'presents' it or 'brings it up' (*anapherein*); the bishop 'offers' (*prospherein*) it. **1957** *Oxf. Dict. Christian Church* 1115/1 *Prosphora*.., in the E. Church, the altar bread. **1961** D. ATTWATER *Christian Churches of East* I. 224 *Prosphora*.., the Byzantine altar-bread, like a small loaf or cake.

prosphygmic (prəʊ'sfıgmık), *a. Phys.* [f. PRO-² + Gr. σφυγμ-ός the pulse + -IC: cf. SPHYGMIC.] Preceding the beat of the pulse.

1898 *Allbutt's Syst. Med.* V. 469 This is the period of 'getting up pressure', the 'prosphygmic interval' as Allbutt terms it. *Ibid.* 930 This apparent origin of the murmur is suggested by the great protraction of the 'prosphygmic' interval.

‖**prosphysis** ('prɒsfısıs). *Path.* Pl. -es (-iːz). [mod.L., a. Gr. πρόσφυσις a growing on or to something, an attachment, adhesion, f. πρός to + φύσις growth, cf. προσφύεσθαι to grow to or upon.] An adhesion; morbid adhesion of parts.

1693 tr. *Blancard's Phys. Dict.* (ed. 2), *Prosphysis*, a Coalition, or growing together, as when two Fingers are connected to each other. **1704** J. HARRIS *Lex. Techn.* I. **1727-41** CHAMBERS *Cycl.* s.v. *Adhesion*, Anatomists sometimes observe prosphyses, or Adhesions of the lungs to the sides of the thorax, the pleura, and diaphragm. **1842** DUNGLISON *Med. Lex.*, *Prosphysis*, adhesion... In a more limited sense, this word means morbid adhesion of the eyelids, either between themselves, or with the globe of the eye.

† **pro'spicient**, *a. Obs. rare.* [ad. L. *prōspiciens, -entem*, pr. pple. of *prōspic-ĕre* to look forward.] Having foresight; provident. So † **pro'spicience** *Obs.*, † **pro'spiciency** *Obs.*, the action or quality of looking forward; foresight.

1654 R. CODRINGTON tr. *Iustine* xliii. 503 But fortune prospicient to the Original of Rome, did provide a Woolf to give suck to the children. **1656** BLOUNT *Glossogr.*, *Prospicience*, providence, fore-sight. [So **1775** in ASH; **1828** in WEBSTER; and in recent Dicts.] **1817** T. L. PEACOCK *Melincourt* vii, Well-grounded prospiciencies of hopelessness and helplessness. *Ibid.* xvi, The second [reason] is most refined, abstract, prospicient, and canonical.

† **pro'spicuous**, *a. Obs. rare.* [f. L. *prōspicu-us* that may be seen afar, conspicuous (f. *prōspic-ĕre*: see prec.) + -OUS.] Conspicuous; also, app., distinguished, 'fair to behold'.

1605 A. WARREN *Poore Mans Passions* E iij, Dutifull Loyalty would humbly greete My Person, passing the prospicuous streete. **1632** LITHGOW *Trav.* x. 499 The incircling Coast a nest of Corporations; and Meandring Forth from tip-toed Snadoun, the prospicuous mirrour for matchlesse Maiesty. **1656** BLOUNT *Glossogr.*, *Prospicuous*, goodly or fair to see or behold, or which may be seen afar off. **1688** R. HOLME *Armoury* III. 393/1 An Eagles head..is an adornment only added to the handle to make it more prospicuous.

prosporangium: see PRO² 1.

pross, pros (prɒs). A slang abbrev. of PROSTITUTE *sb.* 1 a.

1905 *Sessions Paper* 8 Feb. 556 She is only a *pros.*; you know her. **1937** in PARTRIDGE *Dict. Slang.* **1942** BERREY & VAN DEN BARK *Amer. Thes. Slang* §507/2 *Prostitute*,..pross. **1969** C. BURKE *God is Beautiful, Man* 55 You heard that you should go out on a date with a pross, but I tell you, you better not even think about it. **1972** J. MILLS *Report to Commissioner* 104 I'm a pros, man, I shoot up in my thighs. **1973** J. SEABROOK *Loneliness* 75 She's been hanging round the Cherry Tree—that's the pub where all the old prosses go—and she's been going down there since she was thirteen. **1975** J. F. BURKE *Death Trick* iii. 48 'Why is the man naked?' 'He was tricking with a pross.'

pross, obs. Sc. and mod. dial. f. PROSE.

prosse, obs. erron. f. PROWESS; var. of PRUCE *Obs.*

prosses(se, obs. ff. PROCESS.

prossession, obs. f. PROCESSION.

prossie ('prɒsı, -zı). *slang* (orig. *Austral.*). Also prossy, prozzy. [f. PROSS + -Y⁶, -IE.] = PROSS.

1941 BAKER *Dict. Austral. Slang* 57 *Pros, prossie*, a prostitute. **1942** BERREY & VAN DEN BARK *Amer. Thes. Slang* §507/2 *Prostitute*,..pross, prossy. **1945** B. NAUGHTON in C. Madge *Pilot Papers* I. 102 The average prossy is very soft-hearted at the bottom of her. **1961** H. S. TURNER *Something Extraordinary* vii. 144 She reserves her whole-hearted contempt for the 'prossies'. Prostitution is wrong. **1971** F. RAPHAEL *Who were You with Last Night?* 74 A shipmate of mine had this gag... 'What's in a prossy's telegram?' Answer, 'Come at once.' **1971** J. WAINWRIGHT *Dig Grave* 107 Gawd! A prozzy with pretentious tastes in T.V. drama.

† **prossyllogism.** *Logic. Obs. rare.* [f. Gr. πρός in addition (added) to + SYLLOGISM. Cf. PROSYLLOGISM.] A syllogism added after either premiss of the principal syllogism, and furnishing the proof of that premiss.

1620 T. GRANGER *Div. Logike* 281 A Prossyllogisme is a reason, or proofe set after the principall Syllogisme, or some part thereof... Here both the proposition, and assumption are prooued by their Prossyllogismes.

prostacyclin (prɒstə'saıklın). *Biochem.* [f. as next + CYCL(IC *a.* + -IN¹.] A derivative of prostaglandin $F_{1\alpha}$ which is generated by the arterial walls from prostaglandins and is an anti-coagulant and vasodilator.

1976 R. A. JOHNSON et al. *Prostaglandins* XII. 915 The chemical structure of prostaglandin X..from prostaglandin endoperoxides, is 9-deoxy-6,9α–epoxy–Δ^5-$PGF_{1\alpha}$... The trivial name prostacyclin is proposed for [this]. **1977** *Lancet* 1 Jan. 18/1 Fresh rings of arteries and veins obtained from surgical specimens generated an unstable substance, prostacyclin (prostaglandin X..) which is a potent inhibitor of platelet aggregation. **1979** *Nature* 6 Sept. 14/3 Many papers dealt with the newly discovered prostacyclin. Because of its vasodilator and platelet antiaggregating properties it has already been tested for treatment of peripheral artery diseases. **1980** *Brit. Med. Jrnl.* 29 Mar. 939/3 The enhanced platelet release reaction in patients with poor prognosis may be related to decreased prostacyclin activity.

prostaglandin (prɒstə'glændın). *Biochem.* [a. G. *prostaglandin* (U. S. von Euler 1935, in *Klin. Wochenschr.* 17 Aug. 1183/1), f. G. *prosta(ta* or Eng. PROSTA(TE *sb.* (*a.*) + GLAND² + -IN¹.] Any of a group of closely related unsaturated, oxygenated, cyclic fatty acids which occur in seminal fluid and many tissues in male and female mammals and have numerous marked physiological effects (notably the contraction of smooth muscle, esp. that of the uterus). Cf. next.

1936 U. S. VON EULER in *Jrnl. Physiol.* LXXXVIII. 233 In secretion and extracts from the prostate and seminal vesicles of man and the vesicular gland of the sheep a pharmacodynamically highly active substance, prostaglandin, has been demonstrated. **1957** *Acta Chem. Scand.* XI. 1086/1 We have succeeded in obtaining one 'prostaglandin' factor (PGF) in crystalline form. **1960** *Ibid.* XIV. 1693 (*heading*) The isolation of prostaglandin F from sheep prostate glands. **1965** *Sun* 2 Nov. 11/1 It is thought that prostaglandins may work by acting on the woman's reproductive muscles, so helping the process of conception. **1970** *New Scientist* 3 Sept. 468/1 All 14 of the closely related prostaglandins discovered so far occur naturally in minute amounts in the human body. **1971** *Daily Tel.* 15 Oct. 2/2 An extra dose of prostaglandins is being tried as a 'once-a-month' pill for women, but a deficiency of prostaglandins in semen has been associated with infertility. **1973** J. R. WEEKS in Kahn & Lands *Prostaglandins & Cyclic AMP* 2 The prostaglandins are among the most potent substances known, acting in some systems at concentrations of 0·01 ng/ml *in vitro*. **1977** *Martindale's Extra Pharmacopoeia* (ed. 27) 1328/2 An important source of prostaglandins is the cortex of a Gorgonia coral, *Plexaura homomalla* or sea whip, from the Caribbean. **1979** F. H. STEWART et al. *My Body, my Health* i. 17 Researchers suspect that prostaglandin released by the uterus may play a role in menstrual cramps.

prostanoic (prɒstə'nəʊık), *a. Biochem.* [f. prec. after **heptanoic acid* (cf. -OIC).] ***prostanoic acid***: the 20-carbon carboxylic acid from which the prostaglandins are formally derived, the molecule of which consists of a saturated five-membered ring to which a saturated chain of eight carbon atoms and one of seven are attached at adjacent positions, the shorter chain ending with a carboxyl group; 7-(2-octylcyclopentyl)heptanoic acid.

1963 *Jrnl. Biol. Chem.* CCXXXVIII. 3563/2 Recent isolation of additional prostaglandins..have necessitated introduction of a new nomenclature for this class of compounds. This is being based on the trivial name prostanoic acid for the parent C_{20} acid. **1970** *New Scientist* 3 Sept. 468/2 Prostanoic acid..itself has no hormone-like action. **1972** *Lancet* 4 Nov. 5 (Advt.), All natural prostaglandins contain 20 carbon atoms and have the same basic carbon skeleton—prostanoic acid.

prostaphæresis, etc., obs. erron. ff. PROSTH-.

† **prostasy.** *Obs. rare*⁻¹. In 7 proes-. [ad. L. *prostasia* office of a president, a. Gr. προστασία a standing before or in front, f. προστάτης one who stands in front.] Precedence, pre-eminence.

1661 H. D. *Disc. Liturgies* 41 [We] shall willingly allow him proestasie in that Art and Practise.

prostate ('prɒsteıt), *sb.* (*a.*) *Anat.* [ad. med.L. *prostat-a* the prostate, ad. Gr. προστάτ-ης one who stands before, agent-n. from προϊστάναι to set before: cf. στατός placed, standing. (So F. *prostate.*)] A large gland, or each of a number of small glands, accessory to the male generative organs, surrounding the neck of the bladder and the commencement of the urethra, in man and other Mammalia.

(In first quot. app. confounded with the seminal vesicles.)

1646 SIR T. BROWNE *Pseud. Ep.* 189 An Horse or Bull may generate after castration, that is, from the stock..of seminall matter, already prepared and stored up in the Prostates or glandules of generation. *c* **1720** W. GIBSON *Farrier's Guide* I. ii. (1738) 17 There are several glandular bodies situated.. immediately before the seed bladders [in the horse], and are therefore called Prostates. **1804** ABERNETHY *Surg. Obs.* 234 The chief cases..are those of enlarged prostates. **1847-9** *Todd's Cycl. Anat.* IV. 146/1 In shape the prostate resembles a Spanish chesnut. **1888** ROLLESTON & JACKSON *Anim. Life* 31 It is in accordance with general usage to speak of both of [the two other] sets of glands [in the male rabbit] as 'prostates', the smaller as the 'anterior' and the larger as the 'posterio prostates'.

b. *attrib.* or *adj.*, esp. in ***prostate gland***.

(In first quot. applied to the gland of Bartholin in the female, the homologue of the Cowperian gland.)

1754-64 SMELLIE *Midwif.* I. 94 On each side of the *Meatus urinarius* are two small..openings the tubes of which.. come from the prostate gland. **1840** G. V. ELLIS *Anat.* 582 The prostate gland..is situated at the front of the pelvis, and near the symphysis pubis.

Hence **prosta'talgia**, pain in the prostate (Dunglison, 1842); **prostatectomy** (prɒstə'tɛktəmı) [Gr. ἐκτομή cutting out], excision of the prostate, or of part of it; ‖**prostatitis** (-'aıtıs) [-ITIS], inflammation of the prostate; hence **prostatitic** (-'ıtık) *a.*; **pro'statolith** [-LITH], a calculus formed in the prostate; **prosta'tometer** [-METER], 'an instrument for measuring the prostate' (*Syd. Soc. Lex.*); ‖**ˌprostato'rrhœa** (-'riːə) [Gr. ῥοία flux], a discharge, esp. of mucus, from the prostate; **prostatotomy** (-'ɒtəmı) [Gr. τομή cutting], incision of the prostate; **ˌprostato-**

'vesical *a.* [L. *vesica* bladder], belonging to the prostate and bladder.

1890 BILLINGS *Nat. Med. Dict.*, *Prostatectomy. **1904** *Brit. Med. Jrnl.* 17 Dec. 1641 Prostates removed by perineal prostatectomy. **1890** *Cent. Dict.*, *Prostatitic. **1895** *Syd. Soc. Lex.*, *Prostatitic*, belonging to, or affected with, prostatitis. **1844** DUNGLISON *Med. Lex.*, **Prostatitis*. **1860** SIR H. THOMPSON *Dis. of Prostate* (1868) 53 The morbid anatomy of acute prostatitis. **1895** *Syd. Soc. Lex.*, **Prostatolith*... **Prostatometer*. **1858** MAYNE *Expos. Lex.*, **Prostatorrhœa*. **1899** CAGNEY *Jaksch's Clin. Diagn.* ix. (ed. 4) 425 Their presence in large numbers..indicates prostatorrhœa. **1890** BILLINGS *Nat. Med. Dict.*, **Prostatotomy*. **1878** T. BRYANT *Pract. Surg.* (1879) II. 85 The dumb-bell calculus is usually *prostato-vesical or encysted.

prostatic (prəʊ'stætɪk), *a.* [f. as PROSTATE + -IC: cf. F. *prostatique* and Gr. προστατικός.] Pertaining to, produced by, or connected with the prostate. ***prostatic body, gland***, the prostate.

1836–9 *Todd's Cycl. Anat.* II. 459/1 Very little is known as to the uses of the prostatic body. **1846** G. E. DAY tr. *Simon's Anim. Chem.* II. 359 The prostatic fluid..mixes with the semen..at the moment of emission. **1870** ROLLESTON *Anim. Life* Introd. 54 [Birds have no] accessory glands..appended to the generative canals.., as..the Cowperian, the prostatic glands, and the vesiculae seminales.

prostatism ('prɒsteɪtɪz(ə)m). *Med.* [ad. F. *prostatisme*, f. *prostat-e* PROSTATE + *-isme* -ISM.] Any condition due to disease of the prostate gland, esp. difficulty in urination.

1900 DORLAND *Med. Dict.* 540/1 *Prostatism*, a morbid state of mind and body due to prostatic disease. **1904** *Boston Med. & Surg. Jrnl.* CL. 451/2 The frequent, painful, feeble and usually incomplete emptying of the bladder seen in elderly men, which we term prostatic obstruction or prostatism, is not dependent on any single lesion of the prostate. **1920** *Ibid.* CLXXXII. 79/1 Prostatism is the best word I know to express that condition which results from obstruction to urination at the bladder neck due to adenomatous or sclerotic changes in the glands of the prostate itself, or of the posterior urethra. **1956** V. F. MARSHALL *Textbk. Urol.* iv. 61 An abnormally small prostate can cause prostatism, usually by fibrosis. **1977** *Jrnl. Urol.* CXVII. 70/1 Most patients have symptoms commonly referred to as prostatism, which include hesitancy, deterioration in the urinary stream, postmicturition dribble, urgency, frequency and nocturia.

prostemmate (prəʊ'stɛmət). *Zool.* [f. PRO-[2] 2 + Gr. στέμμα, -ματ- a wreath: see STEMMA.] An organ of unknown function situated in front of the eyes in some apterous insects of the lowest type of the order *Collembola*. Hence **proste'mmatic** *a.*, pertaining to or of the nature of a prostemmate.

1895 *Cambr. Nat. Hist.* V. 193 Some of the Collembola possess a very curious structure called the prostemmatic or ante-ocular organ... The prostemmate is placed slightly in front of the group of ocelli.

†**pro'stern**, *v. Obs.* [a. F. *prosterner* (15th c. in Littré), ad. L. *prōsternĕre* to strew in front, throw down, prostrate, f. *prō*, PRO-[1] 1 b + *sternĕre* to lay flat.] *trans.* To cast down, lay flat, prostrate. (Chiefly *refl.* or *pass.*) Hence †**pro'sterning** *vbl. sb.* = PROSTERNATION.

c **1489** CAXTON *Blanchardyn* xxv. 93 His doughter Beatryse..prosterned or casted her self doune byfore her faders feet, on her knees humbly. **1588** A. KING tr. *Canisius' Catech.* 79 We maist humblie and laulie prosterne our selfs. **1612** J. GORDON Ειρηνοκοινωνία E iij, In..prayers there is a threefold kinde of gesture..: the first is a falling downe or prosterning of the body: the second is..a bowing downe of the head to the ground. The third is kneeling.

prosternal (prəʊ'stɜːnəl), *a. Entom.* [f. PROSTERNUM + -AL[1].] Of or pertaining to the prosternum of an insect.

1868 *Rep. U.S. Commissioner Agric.* (1869) 93 They [*Elateridæ*] extend the prothorax so as to bring the prosternal spine..to the anterior part of the mesosternal cavity.

†'**prosternate**, *v. Obs.* [f. ppl. stem of med.L. *prōstern-āre*, collateral form of L. *prōsternĕre*: see PROSTERN.] *trans.* = PROSTERN *v.*

1593 NASHE *Christ's T.* (1613) 78 Wholy haue I bequeathed my penne and my spirit, to the prosternating and ensorrowing the frontiers of sinne. **1651** BIGGS *New Disp.* §85 Trip up and prosternat our strength. **1653** E. CHISENHALE *Cath. Hist.* 394 Prosternating her lofty Spires, ..to the ground.

†**proster'nation**. *Obs.* [a. F. *prosternation* (1599 in Hatz.-Darm.), n. of action from F. *prosterner* or L. *prōstern-āre*: see prec.] The action of prostrating or condition of being prostrated; prostration. Also *fig.*

1622 DONNE *Serm.* (ed. Alford) V. 93, I shall rise..from the prostration, from the prosternation of Death. **1650** CHARLETON *Paradoxes* 17 Before the Patient hath suffered too great a prosternation of spirits. *a* **1652** J. SMITH *Sel. Disc.* II. i. (1821) 33 Prosternations, uncouth gestures, and strange rites of worship. **1768** [W. DONALDSON] *Life Sir B. Sapskull* I. xii. 127 To the humiliating attitude of prosternation. **1819** H. BUSK *Banquet* II. 30 You call the oaks to witness the deceit, In prosternation at their aged feet.

‖**prosternum** (prəʊ'stɜːnəm). *Entom.* [mod.L., f. PRO-[2] 2 + STERNUM.] The sternal, ventral, or under segment of the prothorax of an insect.

1826 KIRBY & SP. *Entomol.* III. xxxv. 544 The *sternum* or breast-bone of insects consists mostly of three distinct pieces..the first of these pieces, the *sternum* of the *antepectus* or *prosternum*. **1833** E. DOUBLEDAY in *Entomol. Mag.* I. 474 The prosternum..occupies the lower part of the prothorax. **1895** *Cambr. Nat. Hist.* V. 102.

‖**prosthaphæresis** (prɒsθə'fɪərɪsɪs). *Astr.* Pl. **-eses** (-ɪsiːz). Also 7–8 *erron.* **prosta-**; 8–9 **-eresis**. [mod.L., a. Gr. προσθαφαίρεσις previous subtraction, f. πρόσθε(ν before + ἀφαίρεσις: see APHÆRESIS.] The correction necessary to find the 'true', i.e. actual apparent, place of a planet, etc. from the mean place; the equation of the centre. (In quot. 1677 in more general sense.)

1633 H. GELLIBRAND in T. James *Voy.* R ij, The Prosthaphæresis of the ☉ orbe. **1669** STURMY *Mariner's Mag.* II. 102 To Rectifie the Tables of the Sun's Declination ..by Prostaphæreses. **1677** R. CARY *Chronol.* I. I. I. vii. 19 The Months alternatively of 29, and 30 Days, except where necessity did require a Prosthaphæresis, either a Subduction, or else an Adjection of one or more Days. **1810** VINCE *Astron.* x. 96 The difference of these two angles is called the equation of the planet's center, or prosthapheresis. **1882** MORTON *Astronomers* 51 Tables of the prosthapheresis and nychthemeron are given.

Hence **prosthaphæ'retical** *a.*, of, pertaining to, or involving prosthaphæresis. *rare* or *Obs.*

1635 GELLIBRAND *Var. Magn. Needle* 5 Its..necessary for the Seaman who sailes by his Compasse, continually to search the variation, that so by the Prosthaphæreticall application thereof, the true point of the compasse..may be rectified. **1690** LEYBOURN *Curs. Math.* 813 Called the Prosthaphaeretical Time, because it is wont sometimes to be added to, sometimes..taken from the Time of the middle Syzygy.

‖**prostheca** (prɒs'θiːkə). *Entom.* [mod.L., ad. Gr. προσθήκη an addition, appendage, f. προστιθέναι to put to, add. Cf. F. *prosthèque.*] A process on the mandibles in certain coleopterous insects. Hence **pros'thecal** *a.*, pertaining to the prostheca.

1826 KIRBY & SP. *Entomol.* III. xxxiii. 356 *Prostheca*.., a subcartilaginous process attached to the inner side, near the base, of the *Mandibulæ* of some *Staphylinidæ*. **1879** J. WOOD-MASON in *Trans. Entomol. Soc. Lond.* 152, I refer to the prostheca of Kirby and Spence, and to the structures homologous with it in beetles other than Staphylinidæ.

prosthenic (prəʊs'θɛnɪk), *a.* (*sb.*) [f. Gr. πρό (PRO-[2] 2) + σθένος strength + -IC.] Having preponderance of strength in the anterior limbs or part of the body. *sb. pl. Ent.* Insects so characterized.

1863 DANA [see *Metasthenic* in META- 3].

‖**prosthesis** ('prɒsθɪsɪs, -'θiːsɪs). [L., a. Gr. πρόσθεσις addition, f. προστιθέναι to put to, add. Cf. F. *prosthèse*.]

1. *Gram.* The addition of a letter or syllable at the beginning of a word.

(The qualification 'at the beginning' may have arisen from associating προς- with προ-.)

1553 T. WILSON *Rhet.* (1580) 180 *Prosthesis*. Of Addition. As thus: He did all to berattle hym. Wherin appeareth that a sillable is added to this woorde (rattle). **1657** J. SMITH *Myst. Rhet.* 170 *Prosthesis*... A figure (contrary to *Aphæresis*) whereby a letter or syllable is added to the beginning of a word. **1876** DOUSE *Grimm's Law* 208 'Prosthesis' belongs to a..class of terms..denoting arbitrary processes, whose intrusion into the realm of language should be viewed with..suspicion.

2. *Surg.* (usu. pronounced prɒs'θiːsɪs).

a. That part of surgery which consists in supplying deficiencies, as by artificial limbs or teeth, or by other means.

1706 PHILLIPS (ed. Kersey) s.v., In Surgery *Prosthesis* is taken for that which fills up what is wanting, as is to be seen in fistulous and hollow Ulcers, filled up with Flesh by that Art: Also the making of artificial Legs and Arms, when the natural ones are lost. **1902** *Encycl. Brit.* XXVII. 417/2 Dental Prosthesis.

b. (Pl. **prostheses**.) An artificial replacement for a part of the body.

1900 in DORLAND *Med. Dict.* **1926** T. G. ORR *Mod. Methods Amputation* vi. 90 These prostheses, while excellent, are not so practical for use in civil life because they are usually not available. **1945** THOMAS & HADDAN *Amputation Prosthesis* vii. 262 If the leg amputee is to be a successful member of society he must first learn to walk and travel on his prosthesis. **1959** *New Scientist* 10 Dec. 1181/2 (*caption*) A plastic prosthesis has been inserted and blood flow restored. **1959** L. SMITH *One Hour* (1960) v. 66 Her hand touched the empty trouser leg... It was before I had learned to use the prosthesis. **1976** *Evening Post* (Nottingham) 15 Dec. 22/3 (Advt.), Had a mastectomy? We offer a discreet and efficient fitting service. Stockists of the Camp Tru-life Prosthesis. **1977** D. FRY *Homo Loquens* x. 140 Everyone understands the need for supplying prostheses to, say, a thalidomide baby at the earliest possible opportunity.

prosthetic (prɒs'θɛtɪk), *a.* and *sb. pl.* [ad. mod.L. **prosthetic-us*, ad. Gr. προσθετικός of the nature of addition, giving additional power, f. πρόσθετος added, vbl. adj. of προστιθέναι: see prec. and -IC. Cf. F. *prosthétique*.]

A. *adj.* **1.** *Gram.* Pertaining to, or of the nature of prosthesis; prefixed, as a letter or syllable.

1837 G. PHILLIPS *Syriac Gram.* 60 Some verbs are found to have Olaph prosthetic. **1852** *Proc. Philol. Soc.* V. 145 A prosthetic *s* in the Norwegian *skrucke*, to shrink. **1859** MAX MÜLLER *Sc. Lang.* (1873) II. 291 Prosthetic vowels are very common in Greek before certain double consonants. **1875** RENOUF *Egypt. Gram.* 63 The prosthetic use of *a* is not confined to words beginning with two consonants.

2. *Surg.* Pertaining to or of the nature of prosthesis: see prec. 2.

1902 *Brit. Med. Jrnl.* 19 July 180/1 The history of operative and prosthetic dentistry. **1966** *Lancet* 31 Dec. 1447/1 Prosthetic valve replacement avoids this complication, but a mechanical valve cannot grow with the patient. **1977** C. SAGAN *Dragons of Eden* viii. 205 Perhaps some day it will be possible to add a variety of cognitive and intellectual *prosthetic* devices to the brain—a kind of eyeglasses for the mind.

3. *Biochem.* Applied to a non-protein group forming part of or combined with a protein, e.g. in an enzyme. [This sense is due to A. Kossel (1892), who used G. *prosthetisch* (*Arch. f. Anat. u. Physiol.* (*Physiol. Abt.*) (1893) 157).]

1898 J. A. MANDEL tr. *Hammarsten's Text-bk. Physiol. Chem.* (ed. 2) ii. 48 The nucleoproteids..may be considered as combinations of a proteid nucleus with a side chain, which Kossel calls the prostetic [*changed to* prosthetic *in ed.* 4 (1904)] group. **1932** *Science* 10 June 615/2 It is of fundamental importance to decide whether the activity of insulin is a function of the whole molecule or of a prosthetic group, non-proteid in composition, which is attached to the protein complex. **1939** *Nature* 25 Nov. 886/2 It is now known also that vitamin B_1, including its pyrophosphate derivative, is identical with the prosthetic group of the enzyme carboxylase. **1954** K. J. LAIDLER *Introd. Chem. Enzymes* v. 94 The cytochromes are there-fore complete enzymes in themselves, their prosthetic groups being successively reduced and oxidized during the course of a biological oxidation. **1964** G. H. HAGGIS et al. *Introd. Molecular Biol.* iii. 42 The total structure of a protein molecule often includes, in addition to its peptide chains a component of different chemical constitution, known as a prosthetic group. The haem component of haemoglobin is an example of a group of this kind. **1973** R. G. KRUEGER et al. *Introd. Microbiol.* vii. 238/1 Prosthetic groups are usually permanently attached to the enzyme, having been built into the enzyme when it was synthesized.

Hence **prost'hetically** *adv.*, in the way of prosthesis; as a prefix.

1875 RENOUF *Egypt. Gram.* 63, *n* is also sometimes used prosthetically.

B. *sb. pl.* The branch of surgery concerned with the replacement of defective or absent parts of the body by artificial substitutes.

1894 in G. M. GOULD *Illustr. Dict. Med. & Biol.* **1911** G. H. WILSON *Man. Dental Prosthetics* Pref., This book has been written in response to the oft-repeated request by teachers and members of the dental profession for a concise modern text-book on Dental Prosthetics. **1963** *New Scientist* 28 Nov. 525 Here is only one more instance of a remarkable flowering of techniques..ranging from prosthetics to chromosomal manipulations, which have tremendous potential for good, but also allow a mockery of nature.

prosthetist ('prɒsθɪtɪst). *Surg.* [f. PROSTHET(IC *a.* + -IST.] One who designs and fits prostheses.

1902 *Buck's Ref. Handbk. Med. Sci.* (ed. 2) V. 513/2 Napoleon..certainly made many cripples and should be hailed as the patron saint of prosthetists. **1924** D. D. CAMPBELL *Full Denture Prosthesis* x. 235 It scarcely need be observed that no prosthetist, sure of his method of securing central occlusion, will avail himself of such a mechanical aid. **1953** H. R. B. FENN et al. *Clin. Dental Prosthetics* xix. 453 (*caption*) If this type of denture is to be successful it requires absolute accuracy on the part of both the prosthetist and the technician. **1970** M. VITALI in G. Murdoch *Prosthetic & Orthotic Pract.* xiii. 531 The prosthetist..could not say when the pylon is going to be ready for delivery but it has helped a lot to understand some of the problems of the amputee.

prosthion ('prɒsθiːɒn). *Anat.* [Neut. of Gr. πρόσθιος foremost (f. πρόσθεν before, in front): cf. -ION[2].] The lowest or the most forward point of the maxilla between the two central incisors.

1925 *Biometrika* XVII. 55 If there be two points used, the prosthion and the alveolar point..then the computation of the angles and sides of the fundamental triangle of the skull becomes impossible. **1933** *Jrnl. R. Anthrop. Inst.* LXIII. 42 Some modern craniometricians speak of the prosthion and the alveolar point as if they were coincident. **1937** *Amer. Jrnl. Physical Anthrop.* XXII. 486 Prosthion has..been generally used to designate both the most forward and the lowest points, in accordance with the measurement being taken. The distinction is made, however, by Buxton and Morant, who call the most forward point prosthion and the lowest the alveolar point. **1937** [see NASION]. **1974** MOORE & LAVELLE *Growth of Facial Skeleton in Hominoidea* iv. 196 Up to the stage of eruption of the first permanent molar, the face of the orang utan is growing strongly downwards and forwards. Subsequently, the face begins to tilt so that the prosthion, instead of moving downwards and forwards, moves forwards and somewhat upwards.

prosthodontia (prɒsθəʊ'dɒntɪə). *Dentistry.* [f. as next + -IA[1].] Prosthodontics.

1917 F. A. PEESO *Crown & Bridge-Work* viii. 151 (*heading*) Relations of prosthodontia and orthodontia. **1934** F. W. FRAHM *Princ. & Technics Full Denture Construction*, p. xiv, The term 'prosthetic dentistry', or 'prosthodontia', may..be defined as an account of methods for the replacement of any lost or missing parts of the dental organism by artificial substitutes. **1947** H. H. HORNER *Dental Educ. Today* ix. 266 The School of Dentistry.. offers graduate courses in orthodontia, prosthodontia, and oral surgery.

prosthodontics (prɒsθəʊˈdɒntɪks), *sb. pl. Dentistry.* [f. as next + -IC; cf. ORTHODONTICS *sb. pl.*] The branch of dentistry concerned with the design, manufacture, and fitting of artificial replacements for teeth and other parts of the mouth; prosthetic dentistry.
1947 H. H. HORNER *Dental Educ. Today* ix. 266 Post-graduate and refresher courses are offered in orthodontics.., prosthodontics.., [etc.]. **1977** M. M. HUDIS *Dental Lab. Prosthodontics* p. xv, The basic concepts will be developed so that they may be integrated into the total concept of prosthodontics. **1978** *Who's Who* 1495/2 Formerly Professor and Chairman of the Prosthodontics Department, University of Southern California.

prosthodontist (prɒsθəʊˈdɒntɪst). *Dentistry.* [f. PROSTH(ESIS + Gr. ὀδοντ-, ὀδούς tooth + -IST.] One who practises prosthodontics.
1917 F. A. PEESO *Crown & Bridge-Work* viii. 151 Quite frequently when the services of an orthodontist has been employed the coöperation of the prosthodontist is necessary to complete and render his work permanent. **1934** F. W. FRAHM *Princ. & Technics of Full Denture Construction* vi. 74 The prosthodontist should avail himself of the use of the very best appliances and technics that will help him to develop and adapt the very finest that is possible in the construction of dentures. **1977** *Daily Colonist* (Victoria, B.C.) 21 May 34/3 'I don't like to go to the dentist myself,' says Dr.. Tregaskis.. dental professor and prosthodontist.

†ˈ**prostibule.** *Obs. rare*$^{-0}$. [ad. L. *prōstibulum* a prostitute, also a brothel, f. *prōstāre* to stand forth publicly as for sale, f. *prō*, PRO-[1] 1 + *stāre* to stand.] (See quot.)
1623 COCKERAM, *Prostibule*, an Harlot, or the Stewes.

†**proˈstibulous,** *a. Obs. rare.* [f. as prec. + -OUS.] Pertaining to a prostitute, meretricious; addicted to the company of prostitutes.
1550 BALE *Image Both Ch.* II. G vb, The great gouernours, and learned lawers of the world, hath she made in maner of beastlye dronkerdes, witlesse, faythlesse, and gracelesse, by their prostibulous doctrine. *Ibid.* III. A a iv, The aduouterouse cardenals,.. the prostibulouse prelates and priestes.

prostie, var. PROSTY.

Prostigmin (prəʊˈstɪgmɪn). *Pharm.* Also **-ine** (-iːn), and with small initial. A proprietary name for neostigmine (s.v. NEO- 1 b).
1931 *Trade Marks Jrnl.* 11 Nov. 1500/2 Prostigmin... Chemical substances prepared for use in medicine and pharmacy. The Hoffmann-La Roche Chemical Works Limited... London. **1935** *Times* 9 Mar. 9/4 Later, using a drug known as prostigmin, she obtained much better results in the treatment of a severe case of myasthenia. **1946** *Official Gaz.* (U.S. Patent Office) 19 Mar. 327/1 *Prostigmin.* For medicinal preparation... Claims use since Apr. 29, 1931, in the form 'Prostigmine'; and since Nov. 8, 1931, on the mark as shown. **1956** LD. AMULREE in A. Pryce-Jones *New Outl. Mod. Knowl.* II. 217 The use of prostigmine in the treatment of myasthenia gravis and of the extract of thyroid and of its synthetic substitute thyroxin in the treatment of diseases of the thyroid, are further examples of the way in which modern therapy can overcome hitherto irremediable diseases. **1961** *Lancet* 2 Sept. 512/1 Various unsuccessful regimens were tried, including a diabetic diet, acetylcholine derivatives, and prostigmine. **1967** H. BECKMAN *Dilemmas in Drug Therapy* 47/1 In sinus and nodal tachycardia, neostigmine (Prostigmin) may occasionally effect a conversion to normal rhythm. **1974** M. C. GERALD *Pharmacol.* vii. 132 Such reversible inhibitors,.. neostigmine (Prostigmine), for example, act for several hours after a single dose.

prostisciutto (ˌprɒstɪˈʃuːtəʊ). *nonce-wd.* [Blend of PROSTITUTE *sb.* and PROSCIUTTO.] A female prostitute regarded metaphorically as an item on a menu.
1930 S. BECKETT *Whoroscope* 1 What's that? A little green fry or a mushrooming one? Two lashed ovaries with prostisciutto?

†ˈ**prostite.** *Obs. rare*$^{-1}$. App. a shortening, for the sake of rhythm, of PROSTITUTE B. 2 c.
1721 D'URFEY *Athen. Jilt* Operas 184 Fortune.. thinking now her Prostite had For Youth's Excursions dearly paid.

†ˈ**prostitue,** *v. Obs. rare.* [a. F. *prostituer*, ad. L. *prōstituĕre*: see next.] = PROSTITUTE *v.*
1530 PALSGR. 324 b/2 Better.. to lyue in wedlocke.. than thus to prostytue thy selfe and be at commaundement of all comers. **1631** A. WILSON *Swisser* III. iii, I must sue for what You prostitude to him. Am I less worthy?

prostitute (ˈprɒstɪtjuːt), *ppl. a.* and *sb.* [ad. L. *prōstitūt-us* (fem. *prōstitūta* a prostitute), pa. pple. of *prōstitu-ĕre* to place before, expose publicly, offer for sale, prostitute, f. *prō*, PRO-[1] 1 + *statu-ĕre* to cause to stand, set up, place.]
A. *adj.* **1.** Offered or exposed to lust (as a woman), prostituted; also more generally, abandoned to sensual indulgence, licentious. (Sometimes const. as *pa. pple.*) Now *rare* or *Obs.* (exc. as *attrib.* use of B. 1).
1572 tr. *Buchanan's Detection Mary Q. Scots* G iij, One of hir awne traine, one past all shame and of prostitute vnchastitie. **1584** R. SCOT *Discov. Witchcr.* IV. ii. (1886) 59 The divell lieth prostitute as *Succubus* to the man. *a* **1613** OVERBURY *A Wife*, etc. (1638) 118 Shee baits her desires with a million of prostitute countenances and enticements. **1621** BURTON *Anat. Mel.* I. ii. IV. vii. (1651) 165 Noblemens daughters.. were prostitute to every common souldier. **1706** *Reflex. upon Ridicule* 155 Women of a prostitute character. *a* **1721** PRIOR *Henry & Emma* 454 Made bold by want, and prostitute for bread. **1756** C. SMART *Horace's Sat.* I. iv. (1826) II. 39 His dissolute son, mad after a prostitute mistress, refuses a wife with a large portion.
2. *fig.* Debased or debasing; abandoned; basely venal, devoted to infamous gain; corrupt. Now *rare*.
1563 MAN *Musculus' Commonpl.* 43 These prostitute images openly sette up in Churches doe this harme, that they doe withdrawe mennes mindes.. from the consideration of God's maiestie shewed in his liuely Creatures. **1626** MEADE in Ellis *Orig. Lett.* Ser. I. III. 229 We might.. draw a general contempt and hatred upon the University as men of most prostitute flattery. **1704** SWIFT *T. Tub* Auth. Apol., Illiterate scribblers prostitute in their reputations, vicious in their lives and ruined in their fortunes. **1754–62** HUME *Hist. Eng.* (1818) VIII. 236 No courtier, even the most prostitute, could go farther than the parliament itself towards a resignation of their liberties. **1788** A. HAMILTON *Federalist* No. 67 II. 226 So shameless and so prostitute an attempt to impose on the citizens of America.
†**3. a.** Given over, devoted; exposed, subjected (*to* something usually evil). Const. as *pa. pple. Obs.*
1603 DRAYTON *Bar. Wars* I. xxvi, Honour deiected from that soueraigne state,.. Now prostitute to infamy and hate. **1610** HEALEY *St. Aug. Citie of God* (1620) 120 The Moone can be eclipsed but at her full, and in her farther positure from the Sunne: then is she prostitute to obnubilation. **1651** HOBBES *Govt. & Soc.* Pref., As a matter of ease, exposed and prostitute to every Mother-wit, and to be attained without any great care or study. **1708** *Erasmus' Life Colet* in *Phenix* II. No. 17. 16 The Dean's table, which.. had been too much prostitute to excess, he reduc'd to frugality.
†**b.** Debased by being made common or cheap; hackneyed. *Obs.*
1630 B. JONSON *New Inn, Ode to Himself* v, Leave things so prostitute, And take the Alcaic lute. **1652** H. L'ESTRANGE *Amer. no Jewes* 19 This is so cheap and prostitute a custome all the World over. **1761** HUME *Hist. Eng.* II. xxxviii. 318 Yet was not the gracious reception which she gave prostitute and undistinguishing.
¶**4.** Laid low before some one: perh. confused with PROSTRATE *a.* (Cf. B. 2 c, and next, 4.)
1621 QUARLES *Esther* K iv b, Once more the Queen prefers an earnest suit, Her humble Body lowly prostitute Before his Royal feet. *a* **1648** LD. HERBERT *Hen. VIII* (1683) 627, I your most humble Subject prostitute at your foot, do most humbly beseech your Highness to be my good and gracious Lord.
B. *sb.*
1. a. A woman who is devoted, or (usually) who offers her body to indiscriminate sexual intercourse, esp. for hire; a common harlot.
1613 PURCHAS *Pilgrimage* VIII. iv. 627, I haue seene houses as full of such prostitutes, as the schooles in France are full of children. **1645** EVELYN *Diary* 28 Feb., [During the Carnival at Rome] The streetes swarm with prostitutes, buffoones, and all man'er of rabble. **1768** GOLDSM. *Good-n. Man* v. i, Your friendship as common as a prostitute's favours. **1840** MACAULAY *Ess., Ranke* (1887) 591 A prostitute, seated on a chair of state in the chancel of Nôtre Dame.
†**b.** A catamite. *Obs. rare.*
1654 R. CODRINGTON tr. *Iustine* xxx. 380 Her Brother Agathocles, a prostitute of an aspiring comeliness. *Ibid.*, Agathocles the Prostitute being joined to the side of the King, did govern the city.
c. A man who undertakes male homosexual acts for payment; usu. ***male prostitute***.
1948 [see *male prostitute* s.v. MALE *a.* 1 e]. **1958** L. DURRELL *Balthazar* vii. 157 A magnificent-looking male prostitute whose oiled curls hung down his back and whose eyes and lips were heavily painted. **1967** *Listener* 1 June 718/2 Few of them ever told me what they were in for, though in the case of Ralph, a male prostitute known to the wing as Suzanne, it was only too obvious. **1975** *Daily Tel.* 24 July 3/6 Many of the boys became male prostitutes.
2. a. A person given over to infamous practices of any kind; an abandoned person. **b.** *esp.* One who debases himself for the sake of gain, a base hireling, a corrupt and venal politician.
1647 N. BACON *Disc. Govt. Eng.* I. lxiv. (1739) 134 To serve one man, a stranger, and a prostitute to all manner of licentiousness. **1693** DRYDEN *Persius* i. (1697) 407 Base Prostitute, thus dost thou gain thy Bread? Thus dost thou feed their Ears, and thus art fed? **1760–72** H. BROOKE *Fool of Qual.* I. 50 The faithful and the perfidious, the prostitute and the patriot are confounded together. **1804** CURRIE in *Creevey Papers* (1904) I. i. 30 He [Lord Brougham] is a notorious prostitute, and is setting himself up to sale. **1889** G. B. SHAW *Let.* 31 Aug. (1965) 223 The radical who writes conservative articles is considered a prostitute. **1980** C. FITZGIBBON *Rat Report* vi. 122 You damned us.. for turning scientists into military prostitutes.
†**c.** A person entirely or abjectly devoted to another; a 'slave'. *Obs.* Cf. PROSTITUTE *v.* 3 a.
1624 DARCIE *Birth of Heresies* Ep. Ded., Your Highnes most Humble and deuoted prostitute Ab. Darcie. **1634** J. CLAVELL *Recant.* Ded., Your most humbly devoted prostitute, J. C. **1721** AMHERST *Terræ Fil.* No. 45 (1754) 241 All this did not satisfy the revengeful president, and the abandon'd prostitutes, his creatures.

prostitute (ˈprɒstɪtjuːt), *v.* [f. L. *prōstitūt-*, ppl. stem of *prōstitu-ĕre*: see prec.]
1. *trans.* To offer (oneself, or another) to unlawful, esp. indiscriminate, sexual intercourse, usually for hire; to devote or expose to lewdness. (Chiefly *refl.* of a woman.)
1530 PALSGR. 668/1, I prostytute, as a comen woman dothe her self in a bordell house, *je prostitue.* **1603** B. JONSON *Sejanus* I. i, He prostituted his abused body To that great gourmond, fat Apicius; And was the noted pathic of the time. **1611** BIBLE *Lev.* xix. 29. **1653** R. SANDERS *Physiogn.* 59 She is an Adulteress, impudent, prostitutes her self publiquely. **1788** GIBBON *Decl. & F.* xlii. (1869) II. 563 He recovered his liberty by prostituting the honour of his wife. *fig.* **1860** PUSEY *Min. Proph.* 30 Israel, being wedded to God, estranged herself from Him.. and prostituted herself to her idols.
†**b.** *intr.* for *refl.* To play the prostitute; to commit whoredom. Also *fig. Obs. rare.*
1631 T. POWELL *Tom All Trades* (1876) 143 Before it have defiled the bed of its reputation by prostituting to the adulterous imbracings of a Citie Scrivener. **1747** *Gentl. Mag.* 193 Ambitious Chloe prostitutes for fame.
c. *trans.* To seduce, debauch (a woman). *rare.*
1658 GURNALL *Chr. in Arm.* verse 14. II. ii. 30 It were a hard work for the adulterer to convince her he would prostitute, that the fact is lawful. **1890** M. DAVITT in *Echo* 11 Dec. 3/2 [He] will not succeed in prostituting the Irish cause as easily as he prostituted the wife of his friend.
2. *fig.* To surrender or put to an unworthy, vile, or infamous use or purpose; to sell for base gain or hire; to defile, dishonour, profane, corrupt.
1593 NASHE *Christ's T.* 38 Thou hadst a Prophecie that thy Sanctuary should not be prostituted. **1610** G. FLETCHER *Christ's Tri.* I. xiii, When Eve to Sinne her soul did prostitute. *a* **1674** CLARENDON *Hist. Reb.* x. §149 This Argumentation.. made a great impression upon all Men who had not prostituted themselves to Cromwell and his Party. **1681** NEVILE *Plato Rediv.* 64 Certain Wits, who prostituted the noble flame of Poetry.. to flatter the Lust and Ambition of the Roman Tyrants. **1781** GIBBON *Decl. & F.* xix. II. 127 *note*, Posides,.. in whose favour the emperor prostituted some of the most honourable rewards of military valour. **1874** GREEN *Short Hist.* vii. §1. 340 Justice was prostituted in the ordinary courts to the royal will.
†**3. a.** To offer with complete devotion or self-negation; to devote. *Obs.*
c **1540** tr. *Pol. Verg. Eng. Hist.* (Camden) I. 255 And here mie selfe am preste and readie ethir to prostitute mie bodie as a sacrifice for mie realme, or to throwe mie selfe into the mideeste of mine enemies. **1611** RICH *Honest. Age* (Percy Soc.) 12, I doe honour them, and I doe prostitute my selfe for euer to doe them humble seruice. *a* **1677** BARROW *Serm.* (1687) I. ix. 120 If God should in requital exact, that we.. adventure our health and prostitute all our earthly contents to his service.
†**b.** To expose, exhibit, subject, submit (to any destructive agency). *Obs.*
1607 MARKHAM *Caval.* II. (1617) Ded., To publish my rude collections, and prostitute to your censuring the depth of my knowledge. **1683** *Brit. Spec.* Pref. 7 [That] would prostitute the Lives of all his fellow Subjects to the Arbitrary Power of any prevailing Faction.
†**c.** To expose to shame; to expose, in a degrading manner to public view, or for public sale.
1613 PURCHAS *Pilgrimage* III. i. (1614) 233 The women couer their faces, contented to see with one eie, rather then to prostitute the whole face. **1657** G. STARKEY *Helmont's Vind.* 68 Are not now all vulgar preparations of Minerals, prostituted in every Apothecaries shop? *a* **1680** BUTLER *Rem.* (1759) I. 322 To vail their Faces from public View, only to avoid prostituting the Majesty of their Persons to common Eyes.
¶**4.** Misused for PROSTRATE *v.* (Cf. prec., A. 4.)
1620 SHELTON *Quix.* (1746) IV. ix. 69 He flung himself from his Horse, and with great Humility, went to prostitute himself before the Lady Teresa. **1624** DARCIE *Birth of Heresies* xv. 61 Prostituting themselues before the Images. **1662** J. CHANDLER *Van Helmont's Oriat.* 94 Places wherein the Quellem is immediately prostituted beneath the Clay.
Hence ˈ**prostituting** *vbl. sb.* and *ppl. a.*
1611 COTGR., *Abandonnement*, an abandonning.. giuing ouer,.. prostituting vnto others. **1646** SIR T. BROWNE *Pseud. Ep.* 247 She is plainly termed πορνη, which signifies not an Hostesse, but a pecuniary and prostituting Harlot. **1667** MILTON *P.L.* XI. 716 All now was turn'd to jollitie and game,.. Marrying or prostituting, as befell.

prostituted (ˈprɒstɪtjuːtɪd), *ppl. a.* [f. prec. vb. + -ED[1].]
1. Devoted to lewdness, esp. for hire, as a woman.
1565 T. STAPLETON *Fortr. Faith* 123 Make.. of professed nonnes prostituted harlots. **1678** R. L'ESTRANGE *Seneca's Mor.* II. xviii. (1696) 279 Forced to Banish his Daughter Julia, for her Common, and Prostituted Impudence. **1781** BURKE *Sp. Marr. Act Repeal Bill* Wks. X. 140, I should feel for a son who married a prostituted woman, or a daughter who married a dishonourable and prostituted man.
2. *fig.* Devoted to base or shameful purposes, esp. to infamous gain; degraded, debased, corrupted. Of persons (now *rare*) or things.
1579 G. HARVEY *Letter-bk.* (Camden) 63, I woulde.. that all the ilfavorid copyes of my nowe prostituted devises were buried. *a* **1659** OSBORN *Wks.* (1673) 284 A too prostituted Familiarity breeds contempt. **1798** PENNANT *Hindoostan* II. 104 The encouragement which his prostituted Ministry had given to vices. **1829** LYTTON *Devereux* I. i, That galaxy of prostituted genius of which Charles II was the centre.

†ˈ**prostitutely,** *adv. Obs. rare*$^{-1}$. [f. PROSTITUTE *a.* + -LY[2].] In a 'prostitute' or abandoned manner; lewdly.
1594 CHAPMAN *Shadow Night* Ded., To think that she should prostitutely show them her secrets, when she will scarcely be looked upon by others.

prostitution (prɒstɪˈtjuːʃən). [ad. late L. *prōstitūtiōn-em*, n. of action f. *prōstitu-ĕre* to PROSTITUTE. Cf. F. *prostitution* (13th c. in Hatz.-Darm.).] The action of prostituting or condition of being prostituted.

1. a. Of women: The offering of the body to indiscriminate lewdness for hire (esp. as a practice or institution); whoredom, harlotry.

1553 EDEN *Treat. Newe Ind.* (Arb.) 17 By whiche common prostitucion of the quene [in Calicut], he may well iudge that the chyldren borne of her are not to be estemed as his owne. **1613** PURCHAS *Pilgrimage* (1614) 339 The most noble of that Nation there (dedicating shall I say? or) prostituting their daughters; where after long prostitution with their Goddesse, they are giuen in marriage, none refusing such matches. **1711** STEELE *Spect.* No. 155 ¶4 As if they stood there to sell their Persons to Prostitution. **1878** C. L. WAKE *Evol. Morality* II. 89 Prostitution seems never to have been recognised at Rome as a legal institution.

b. *personified.*

1784 COWPER *Task* III. 60 Till prostitution elbows us aside In all our crowded streets.

†**c.** *transf.* A prostitute, a harlot. *Obs. rare*⁻¹.

1607 MIDDLETON *Michaelm. Term* III. i, I may grace her with the name of a Curtizan, a Backslider, a Prostitution, or such a Toy, but when all comes to al tis but a plaine Pung.

d. Of men: the undertaking of homosexual acts for payment.

1886 R. F. BURTON *Terminal Ess.* in *Arabian Nights' Entertainments* X. 242 According to Gomara there were at Tamalipas houses of male prostitution. **1975** P. MCCUTCHAN *Very Big Bang* xiii. 122 Porn, poncing, male prostitution—you name it, the court'll send you down for it. **1975** *Times* 21 June 2/3 Runaway boys..were procured for a male prostitution ring by offers of food and shelter.

2. *fig.* Devotion to an unworthy or base use; degradation, debasement, corruption.

1647 WARD *Simp. Cobler* 47 Peoples prostrations of ..[Civill Liberties and Proprieties] when they may lawfully helpe it, are prophane prostitutions. **1704** *Clarendon's Hist. Reb.* III. Ded. 14 A prostitution of all Manners in contempt of all Government. **1711** STEELE *Spect.* No. 103 ¶1 Many Professions of Kindness and Service..are a Prostitution of Speech, seldom intended to mean Any Part of what they express. **1740** JOHNSON *Sir F. Drake* Wks. IV. 457 The honour of knighthood..; an honour in that illustrious reign not made cheap by prostitution. **1874** L. STEPHEN *Hours in Library* (1892) I. vi. 229 They live..on the prostitution of their talents to gratify..personal animosities.

¶**3.** app. misused for PROSTRATION, overthrow.

1593 NASHE *Christ's T.* (1613) 39 Heauen..shall be made an Artillery-house of Haile-stones, and no Planner shall reuolue any thing but prostitution and vastity.

prostitutor (ˈprɒstɪtjuːtə(r)). Also 7 -er. [a. late L. *prōstitūtor*, agent-n. f. *prōstitu-ĕre* to PROSTITUTE: see -OR. Cf. F. *prostituteur*.] One who prostitutes (usually in *fig.* sense: see the vb.).

1611 COTGR., *Abandonneur*, an abandonner..giuer ouer, prostitutor of. **1665** BOYLE *Occas. Refl.* v. viii. (1848) 325 Difference betwixt the Contentment of this calm admirer of Beauty, and that of a greedy and unconfin'd Prostituter of his Heart to it. **1761** HURD *Let. to Warburton* 18 Mar., Lett. (1809) 321 A reproof..of the Prostitutors of the Lord's Supper. **1896** *Voice* (N.Y.) 11 June 3/3 They believe they have facts sufficient..to put some of the prostitutors of the ballot behind the bars.

‖**prostomium** (prəʊˈstəʊmɪəm). *Zool.* [mod.L., ad. Gr. προστόμιον, lit. a fore-mouth, or something before the mouth: see PRO-² and STOMA.] The part of the body situated in front of the mouth in certain invertebrates, as molluscs and worms, and in embryos; the pre-oral region. Hence **proˈstomial** *a.*, pertaining to, constituting, or situated on the prostomium; **proˈstomiate** *a.*, furnished with or characterized by having a prostomium.

1870 NICHOLSON *Man. Zool.* 149 There is always a considerable portion of the body situated in front of the mouth, constituting the so-called 'præ-oral region', or prostomium. **1883** E. R. LANKESTER in *Encycl. Brit.* XVI. 639/2 The Mollusca are sharply divided into two great lines of descent or branches, according as the prostomial region is atrophied on the one hand or largely developed on the other. **1886** A. G. BOURNE *ibid.* XXI. 6/1 The development of a prostomiate condition. **1888** ROLLESTON & JACKSON *Anim. Life* 484 [Mollusca] Eyes absent on the prostomial region of the adult. *Ibid.* 315 Plate XII. Earthworm (*Lumbricus terrestris*). The fifteen anterior somites,..the 'prostomial segment' counting as the first.

prostrate (ˈprɒstrət), *a.* (*sb.*) [ad. L. *prōstrāt-us*, pa. pple. of *prōstern-ĕre*: see PROSTERN.]

1. In strict use, Lying with the face to the ground, in token of submission or humility, as in adoration, worship, or supplication; more loosely, Lying at full length or with the body extended flat (on the ground or other surface), in a horizontal position. Often predicative or quasi-adv. with *lie*, *fall*, etc.

a **1380** *Savinian* 259 in Hortsm. *Altengl. Leg.* (1878) 97 Prostrat heo fel þen to grounde And preyed to God þus in þat stounde. *c* **1450** tr. *De Imitatione* I. xxv. 36 He fel doun prostrate in his praiers before an auter in þe chirche. **1485** CAXTON *St. Wenefr.* 15 Here we lye prostrate for to offre our prayers to god. **1533** ELYOT *Cast. Helthe* II. xxx. (1541) 48 To them, which haue feeble digestion, it is good to slepe prostrate on their bealies. **1642** H. MORE *Song Soul* I. III. i, Whiles we on grassie bed did lie prostrate. **1726** SWIFT *Gulliver* III. i, Finding us all prostrate upon our faces (for so I gave order) they pinioned us. **1814** SCOTT *Ld. of Isles* II. xv, O'er my prostrate kinsman stood The ruthless murderer. **1877** A. B. EDWARDS *Up Nile* ii. 27 Some lay prostrate, their foreheads touching the ground.

b. Of things usually erect, as trees, walls, pillars, etc.: Levelled with the ground, overthrown.

a **1677** HALE *Prim. Orig. Man.* II. vii. 191 Great quantities of subterraneous Woods, lying 10 and 20 Ells below the Superficies of the Ground, prostrate towards the East. **1807** WORDSW. *Wh. Doe Ryl.* VII. 340 The mournful waste Of prostrate altars.

†**c.** Sometimes const. as pple. = PROSTRATED.

1591 SPENSER *Virg. Gnat* 558 For loftie type of honour.. is downe in dust prostrate.

2. *fig.* Laid low in mind or spirit; submissive; overcome, overthrown, powerless.

1591 SHAKS. *1 Hen. VI*, I. ii. 117 Looke gracious on thy prostrate Thrall. **1749** SMOLLETT *Regicide* v. i, Let us avoid the opposite extremes Of negligence supine, and prostrate fear. **1802** WORDSW. *Sonn., Calais*, Ye men of prostrate mind, A seemly reverence may be paid to power. **1849** MACAULAY *Hist. Eng.* ii. I. 278 The violent reaction which had laid the Whig party prostrate. **1867** SMILES *Huguenots Eng.* xvii. (1880) 294 William III took active steps to restore the prostrate industry of the country.

b. In a state of physical exhaustion or complete weakness; unable to rise or exert oneself.

1871 MACDUFF *Mem. Patmos* vii. 90 Puts nerve and sinew into the most prostrate arm. **1880** J. W. SHERER *Conjuror's Daughter*, etc. 284 'How was she?' 'Very prostrate and at this hour feverish'. **1887** *Sportsman* 25 July 2/1 At the present moment we are so 'prostrate', that we have not strength enough to go to the treasure chamber.

3. *Bot.* In its habit of growth, lying flat upon the ground; procumbent.

1776 WITHERING *Brit. Plants* (1796) II. 430 Stem prostrate, striking root. *Ibid.* III. 62 Stem and root-leaves prostrate, longer than the branches. **1836** *Penny Cycl.* VI. 432/1 *C[erasus] prostrata*, the spreading cherry. A small prostrate bush, found on the sea-coast of Candia. **1861** MISS PRATT *Flower. Pl.* I. 3 A prostrate stem runs along the ground, and never becomes erect.

b. Closely appressed to the surface; lying flat: as, prostrate hairs or setæ.

B. *sb.* One who is prostrate, or lying flat, as a suppliant, a vanquished foe.

1654 TRAPP *Comm. Job* i. 20 The ancient Prophets and holy men were called *Nephalim procidentes*, or *Prostrantes*, that is prostrates or Fallers downe. **1676** OTWAY *Don Carlos* I. i, To lie a Prostrate at her feet. **1691** HEYRICK *Misc. Poems* 40 'Twill sully all your former glorious Fame To say, You such a Prostrate overcame.

b. = PROSTRATOR 2.

a **1600** HOOKER *Eccl. Pol.* VI. v. §8 Being taken and admitted to the next degree of prostrates, at the feet yet behind the back of that angel representing God, whom the rest saw face to face. *a* **1711** KEN *Hymnotheo* Poet. Wks. 1721 III. 77 The Prostrates near the Sacred Desk are plac'd, By Self-humiliations more debas'd.

prostrate (ˈprɒstreɪt), *v.* Pa. t. and pple. **prostrated**; also 6 **prostrate**. [f. L. ppl. stem *prōstrāt-*: see prec. Sense 1 may have arisen out of the reflexive sense 3; but the latter has not been found so early. (Formerly stressed *proˈstrate*.)]

†**1.** *intr.* To become prostrate; to fall down flat before some person or thing, in token of reverence or submission: = sense 3. *Obs.*

c **1400** *Rule St. Benet*, etc. 143 Þan þe nouice sall prostrate downe be-fore þe gree, when 'Kirieleison'. **1604** R. CAWDREY *Table Alph.*, *Prostrate*, to fall downe flat on the ground. **1712** ARBUTHNOT *John Bull* III. x, When I am Lord of the Universe, the sun shall prostrate and adore me! **1755** AMORY *Mem.* (1769) I. 268 We must even prostrate before the block they call her image.

2. *trans.* To lay flat on the ground, etc.; to throw down, level with the ground, overthrow (something erect, as a house, a tree, a person).

1483 *Caxton's Chron. Eng.* e viij b, He prostratit mony a M. **1531–2** *Act 23 Hen. VIII*, c. 5 To..prostrate and ouerthrowe all suche mylles..lockes..hebbinge weares, and other impedimentes. **1594** SPENSER *Amoretti* lvi, A storme, that all things doth prostrate [*rime* ruinate]. **1692** RAY *Disc.* II. v. (1732) 232 These Trees..were broken down and prostrated by the force of..tempestuous Winds. **1726** POPE *Odyss.* XIX. 581 Heav'n..Shall prostrate to thy sword the Suitor-crowd. **1856** KANE *Arct. Expl.* II. xxi. 213 They tied the dogs down..and prostrated themselves to escape being blown off by the violence of the wind. **1878** BROWNING *Poets Croisic* xxxiv, Pebble from sling Prostrates a giant.

†**b.** *fig.* To overthrow (a measure, etc.). *Obs. rare.*

1642 SLINGSBY *Diary* (1836) 82 My Lord of Newcastle.. would not give any new commission unless some just cause was shown to prostrate yᵗ yᵉ King had given.

3. *refl.* To cast oneself down prostrate; to bow to the ground in reverence or submission.

1530 PALSGR. 668/2 So soone as ever he came byfore the sacrament, he prostrate hym selfe with moost hyghe reverence. *a* **1548** HALL *Chron.*, *Hen. VII* 24 The Moores.. prostrated and humbled them selues before the sayde great Master. **1687** A. LOVELL tr. *Thevenot's Trav.* I. 49 When they prostrate themselves, that signifies that they adore God. **1732** LEDIARD *Sethos* II. x. 455 Sethos, upon entring, prostrated himself at his feet. **1883** GILMOUR *Mongols* xviii. 211 Going the rounds of the sacred place, prostrating himself at every shrine.

4. *trans. fig.* To lay low, overcome; to make submissive or humble; to reduce to helplessness.

1562 EDEN *Let.* 1 Aug. (in *Decades*, etc. (Arb.) p. xliii/1), The greefes of aduerse fortune..dyd so muche prostrate my mynde. **1655** FULLER *Ch. Hist.* IX. vi. §46 Her Adversaries conceive; had she not been laid there, the happiness of England had been prostrated in the same place. *a* **1711** KEN *Man. Prayers* Wks. (1838) 370 When you read any great mystery recorded in holy writ, you are to prostrate your reason to divine revelation. **1838** THIRLWALL *Greece* XXX. IV. 159 It was adverse to any treaty which would not completely prostrate Athens under its rule.

b. To reduce to extreme physical weakness or exhaustion: said of disease, fatigue, and the like.

1829 H. MURRAY *N. Amer.* II. III. iii. 368 On calling for a lady, he was told that she was 'quite prostrated', which on explanation proved to be ill in bed. **1843** R. J. GRAVES *Syst. Clin. Med.* xiii. 145 He appeared exceedingly low and prostrated. **1865** LIVINGSTONE *Zambesi* xx. 412 Fever rapidly prostrates the energies.

†**5.** To lay down at the feet of a person; to submit, present, or offer submissively or reverently. *Obs.*

1583 H. D. *Godlie Treat.* 4 Being bold in all humilitie to prostrate this little booke before your honour. **1588** CAVENDISH in Beveridge *Hist. India* (1862) I. I. ix. 210 All which services, with myself, I humbly prostrate at her majestie's feet. **1669** FLAMSTEED in Rigaud *Corr. Sci. Men* (1841) II. 87 This I desire I may have the liberty..to prostrate to the most illustrious Royal Society. **1681** R. KNOX *Hist. Ceylon* 76 Before them they prostrate Victuals.

†**b.** To let down, lower *to* the level or cognizance of. *Obs. rare.*

a **1718** PENN *Tracts* Wks. 1726 I. 605 God never prostrates his Secrets to Minds disobedient to what they do already know.

Hence **ˈprostrated** *ppl. a.*, **ˈprostrating** *vbl. sb.* and *ppl. a.*

1545 JOYE *Exp. Dan.* vii. 96 b, A lyon is a cruell beast yf he be exasepered, and gentle yf the man fal downe naked before him; and except it be in great honger he hurteth not siche humble prostrated proyes. **1580** HOLLYBAND *Treas. Fr. Tong*, *Prostration*, a prostrating, or falling at ones feete. **1656** EARL MONM. tr. *Boccalini's Advts. fr. Parnass.* I. viii. (1674) 10 By humble prostrating of their service. **1859** CORNWALLIS *New World* I. 354 That gentleman reported the prostrated hopes of the over-sanguine goldhunters. **1890** *Athenæum* 4 Jan. 17/2 To fight so long and bravely against the prostrating effects of a wasting illness.

ˈprostrately, *adv. rare.* [f. PROSTRATE *a.* + -LY².] In a prostrate manner or position.

1556 J. HEYWOOD *Spider & F.* lxxxviii. 189 The hour is cum: wherin the flie must die, For which he weilth, at spiders foote prostratlie. **1632** SIR T. HAWKINS tr. *Mathieu's Unhappy Prosperitie* 183 Those..who prostrately bowed their knees to adore him, now jested at him.

prostration (prɒˈstreɪʃən). [a. F. *prostration* (14th c. in Hatz.-Darm.) or ad. late L. *prōstrātiōn-em*, n. of action f. *prōstern-ĕre*: see PROSTERN.]

1. The action of prostrating oneself or one's body, esp. as a sign of humility, adoration, or servility; the condition of being prostrated, or lying prostrate.

1526 *Pilgr. Perf.* (W. de W. 1531) 237 b, And there with genufleccyons or knelynges, inclynacyons, prostracyons, or other reuerence, to aske yᵉ mercy of god. **1622** [see PROSTERNATION]. *c* **1645** HOWELL *Lett.* IV. xxxvi. (1655) 86 The comely prostrations of the body..in time of Divine Service, is very exemplary. **1672** CAVE *Prim. Chr.* III. v. (1673) 369 After his usual Prostrations in the Church as if unworthy either to stand or kneel. **1758** J. S. *Le Dran's Observ. Surg.* (1771) 183 No Prostrations could reduce the Herniæ. **1823** GILLIES tr. *Aristotle's Rhet.* I. 178 Among barbarians honour is denoted by humble prostrations of the body. **1879** H. SPENCER *Princ. Sociol.* §384 Though the loss of power to resist which prostration on the face implies, does not reach the utter defencelessness implied by prostration on the back, yet it is great enough to make it a sign of profound homage. **1883** 'OUIDA' *Wanda* I. 5 The villagers ..came timidly around and made their humble prostrations.

2. *fig.* The mental attitude which is implied in prostrating the body; veneration; abject submission, adulation; humiliation, abasement.

1646 SIR T. BROWNE *Pseud. Ep.* I. vii. 25 Nor is only a resolved prostration unto Antiquity a powerfull enemy unto knowledge, but also a confident adherence unto any Authority. **1755** YOUNG *Centaur* iv. Wks. 1757 IV. 199 For that bountiful grant, what adoration is due? With prostration profound I cannot but adore. **1823** ROSCOE *Sismondi's Lit. Eur* (1846) II. xxxii. 341 The prostration of the intellect. **1849** TWEEDIE *Life J. Macdonald* iii. 255 To read the record of his profound prostration and abasement is at once humbling and joyous.

3. *fig.* Debasement of any exalted principle or faculty.

1647 [see PROSTITUTION 2].

4. Extreme physical weakness or exhaustion; also extreme mental depression or dejection.

1651 BAXTER *Inf. Bapt.*, *Apol.* 14, I can hardly..speak above an hour without the prostration of my strength. **1732** ARBUTHNOT *Rules of Diet* (1736) 358 There is a sudden Prostration of the Strength or Weakness attending this Colick. **1803** *Med. Jrnl.* X. 109 Distinguished..by the unusual prostration of strength. **1828** WEBSTER, *Prostration* ..3. Great depression; dejection: as, a prostration of spirits. **1865** DICKENS *Mut. Fr.* III. x, Exhibiting great wretchedness in the shivering stage of prostration from drink. **1887** *Spectator* 15 Oct. 1377 An appreciable number of the guilty died of nervous prostration.

5. The reduction of a country, party, or organization to a prostrate or powerless condition.

1844 THIRLWALL *Greece* VIII. lxvi. 472 The prostration of Greece under the Turkish yoke. **1844** H. H. WILSON *Brit.*

India III. 224 The result of the war was the complete prostration of Persia before the power of Russia. **1851** GALLENGA *Italy* 295 The exaggerated notions of the utter prostration and dissolution of the empire then prevalent.

prostrative ('prɒstrətɪv), *a. rare.* [f. L. ppl. stem *prōstrāt-* (see PROSTRATE *v.*) + -IVE.]

a. Having the quality or faculty of prostrating. **b.** Characterized by prostration or abjectness.

1817 BENTHAM *Parl. Reform* Introd. 131 The more palpable the deficiency..the more prostrative, the more irresistible the force. **1890** CLARK RUSSELL *Ocean Trag.* I. xiii. 278 Not much relishing the prostrative nature of the fellow's respectfulness I walked aft.

prostrator ('prɒstreɪtə(r), prɒ'streɪtə(r)). *rare.* [a. late L. *prōstrātor*, agent-n. f. *prōstern-ĕre*: see PROSTERN.]

1. One who overthrows or throws down prostrate.

1659 GAUDEN *Tears Ch.* II. xii. 189 Common people..are the great and infallible prostrators of all Religion, vertue, honour, order, peace, civility and humanity, if left to themselves. **1818** BENTHAM *Ch. Eng.* 165 [The] Bishop of London..Prostrator-General of understandings and wills.

2. *Eccl. Hist.* Used (chiefly *pl.*) as a rendering of Gr. γονυκλίνοντες, ὑποπίπτοντες, or L. *genuflectentes*, *prostrati*, the third order of penitents in the early Church (see quots.). Cf. KNEELER 2.

1709 J. JOHNSON *Clergym. Vade M.* II. 51 Next above the Hearers were the ὑποπιπτοντες, *Prostrators*, so call'd because tho' they were dismissed with the Catechumens, yet not before they had prostrated themselves before Bishop, Clergy, and Communicants. **1711** HICKES *Two Treat. Chr. Priesth.* (1847) II. 303 They put down those..into the station of penitents and prostrators. **1843** HAMMOND *Def. Faith Œcum. Councils* 31 The third order of penitents, called ..kneelers or prostrators, because they were allowed to remain and join in certain prayers particularly made for them, whilst they were kneeling, or prostrate on the ground.

prosty ('prɒstɪ). *U.S. slang.* Also **prostie**. Abbrev. of PROSTITUTE *sb.* 1 a. Cf. PROSSIE.

1930 *Bookman* Dec. 397/2 These song writers exploit motherhood into a mania, and go Rotary about any old half-baked, klux-ridden Dixie backwash. They make love in kindergarten terms, turn Sunday-school superintendent about prosties whom they term 'faded roses' or 'butterflies', and otherwise trade on primitive mass ideas. **1941** [see HOPPY *sb.*[2]]. **1951** GREEN & LAURIE *Show Biz* 571/1 *Prostie*, prostitute. Variety's sensitized way of describing female characters comparable to those in early Mae West plays. **1972** G. BAXT *Burning Sappho* vii. 128 The prostie in the orange wig. **1976** J. HAYES *Missing* i. 29 If she was a prostie, he couldn't afford her fee.

prostyle ('prəʊstaɪl), *sb.* and *a. Anc. Arch.* [ad. L. *prostȳlos* adj. having pillars in front, also sb. (Vitruv.) a. Gr. *πρόστυλος: see PRO-[2] and STYLE *sb.* Cf. F. *prostyle* (1691 in Hatz.-Darm.).]

A. *sb.* A portico in front of a Greek temple, of which the columns, never more than four in number, stood in front of the building.

1697 EVELYN *Architects & Archit.* (1723) 30 The Prostyle, whose Station being at the Front consisted of only four Columns. **1710** J. HARRIS *Lex. Techn.* II, *Prostyle*,..whose Station was in the front of a Temple, or other great Building.

B. *adj.* Having a prostyle.

1696 PHILLIPS (ed. 5), *Prostyle*, that which has Pillars before only; which was one sort of the Temples of the Ancients. **1810** *Rudim. Anc. Archit.* (1821) 125 *Prostyle*,.. according to Vitruvius, the second order of temples. **1850** LEITCH tr. *C. O. Müller's Anc. Art* §288 (ed. 2) 317 Temples are divided into..prostyle, with porticoes on the front, and amphiprostyle, at the two ends. **1883** J. T. CLARKE *Reber's Anc. Art* 200 The next step was the removal of these side walls [*antæ*]..and the prostyle temple was thus obtained.

pro-substantive, -ly: see PRO-[1] 4.

‖**prosula** ('prəʊsʊlə). *Eccl.* Pl. -æ. [mod.L., dim. of L. *prosa* PROSA; see -ULE.] (See quots.)

1907 ORME & WYATT tr. *Wagner's Introd. Gregorian Melodies* xiv. 245 A second kind of trope, which also goes back to Tutilo, resembles the Sequences, and is often like them called *Prosa*, or, when of lesser extent, *Prosula*. **1958** W. APEL *Gregorian Chant* iii. 433 Twenty-five of the Offertoires..are further amplified by the addition of a *prosula*..that is, a new text appended to the end of a verse, usually the last. *Ibid.*, The music for the *prosula* or, as we would say, for the trope, is identical with the closing passage of the verse. **1970** [see PROSA]. **1975** *Anglo-Saxon England* IV. 134 A Kyriale, beginning imperfectly with part of the prosula to the *Kyrie eleison* entitled *Clemens rector*. *Ibid.* 135 A number of Kyries do not have prosulae.

†**prosult.** *Obs. rare*$^{-1}$. [ad. L. **prōsult-um*, neut. pa. pple. of *prōsilīre* to leap forth; or f. PRO-[1] after RESULT *sb.*] That which issues forth: the resulting issue.

1647 WARD *Simp. Cobler* (1843) 35 What is amisse in the mould, will misfashion the prosult.

prosy ('prəʊzɪ), *a.* [f. PROSE *sb.* + -Y.]

1. Resembling, or having the character of, prose. Sometimes = PROSAIC 2, commonplace, matter-of-fact; but usually with emphasis rather on the tiresome effect than on the intrinsic quality: commonplace and tedious; dull and wearisome.

1814 JANE AUSTEN *Let.* 9 Sept. (1952) 402 The scene with Mrs. Mellish, I should condemn; it is prosy & nothing to the purpose. **1823** SCOTT in *Ballantyne's Novelist's Library* V. p. lxxxvi, Perhaps, to be circumstantial and abundant in minute detail, and in one word, though an unauthorized one, to be somewhat *prosy*, is one mode of securing a certain necessary degree of credulity in hearing a ghost-story. **1837** DICKENS *Pickw.* xxi, During this prosy statement of the ghost's. *Ibid.* xxxi, This address..was of a very prosy character. **1838** MILL *Diss. & Disc., A. de Vigny* (1859) I. 327 If prolix writing is vulgarly called *prosy* writing, a very true feeling of the distinction between verse and prose shows itself in the vulgarism. **1849** MISS MULOCK *Ogilvies* xxvii, Mrs. Pennythorne..went on talking to his friend in her own quiet, prosy way. **1885** *Law Times* LXXIX. 351/2 To be preferred to the prosy monotony of judicial life.

2. Of persons: Given to talking or writing in a commonplace, dull, or tedious way; prosing.

1838 LYTTON *Alice* II. ii, A sensible..though uncommonly prosy speaker. **1859** GREEN *Oxf. Stud.* II. xvi. (O.H.S.) 181 The parents are all benevolent, affable and prosy.

prosylite, obs. form of PROSELYTE.

pro-syllable, -syllabic: see PRO-[1] 4 b, c.

prosyllogism (prəʊ'sɪlədʒɪz(ə)m). *Logic.* [ad. med.L. *prosyllogism-us* (Boeth.), ad. Gr. προσυλλογισμός: see PRO-[2] and SYLLOGISM.] A syllogism of which the conclusion forms the major or minor premiss of another syllogism.

1584 FENNER *Def. Ministers* (1587) 43 Which reason with the prosilogismes of the antecedent being..reduced vnto a sillogisme,..he answered. **1697** tr. *Burgersdicius Logic* II. xiii. 58 A Prosyllogism is then when two Syllogisms are so contained in five Propositions, as, that the Conclusion of the First becomes the Major or Minor of the Following, as, For Example, this; Every living thing is nourished; But every Plant is a living thing; And therefore every Plant is nourished. But no Stones are nourished: And therefore no Stones are Plants. **1725** WATTS *Logic* III. ii. §6. **1884** tr. *Lotze's Logic* §96 Every conclusion of a syllogism may.. become the major premiss of another syllogism: the first is then called the *prosyllogism* of the second, and each one that follows the *episyllogism* of the one which preceded it.

So **prosyllo'gistic, prosyllo'gistical** *adjs.*, of the nature of or pertaining to a prosyllogism.

1588 FRAUNCE *Lawiers Log.* I. iii. 19 This nowe is a new and prosyllogisticall argument, fet from the very naturall definition of the argument it selfe. **1652** URQUHART *Jewel* Wks. (1834) 292 Mounting the scale of their probation upon the prosyllogistick steps of variously-amplified confirmations.

Prot (prɒt), *sb.* and *a.* Also **prot.** A colloq. abbrev. of PROTESTANT *sb.* 2 a and *a.* 1; *spec.* opp. to *Catholic* (freq. in derog. or contemptuous use). Cf. PROD *sb.*[3] and *a.*

1725 J. THORNTON *Let.* in *Dublin Rev.* (1916) Apr. 318 Sir George Brown, I hear, is got to Gant, there be-moaning his folly in having tied himself up to an old Prot, who cunningly settled all she had out of his reach. **1737** R. CHALLONER *Let.* 15 Sept. in *Recusant Hist.* (1970) X. 351 Our Prelate here, has..absolutely refused to consent to the Parties being married first by a Priest and then by a Prot. minister. **1843** M. EDGEWORTH *Let.* 3 Dec. (1971) 599 The average salary of the Irish priest is £290 per Annum and average of Prot— £120 or £130. **1900** C. M. YONGE *Mod. Broods* v. 50 Oh, she is a regular old Prot..almost a Dissenter. **1900** M. CREIGHTON *Let.* 16 Nov. (1904) II. 454 The position was 'I would meet you if I could: but I am not going to be bullied by a handful of Prots.' **1937** AUDEN & MACNEICE *Lett. from Iceland* xiii. 204, I know a Prot Will never really kneel, but only squat. **1955** E. POUND *Section: Rock-Drill* (1957) lxxxvi. 24 Yes yr/ Holiness, they are all of them prots. **1971** B. SLEIGH *Smell of Privet* x. 87 'You must never say cup, always chalice. Don't be such a Prot, my dear!' I had no idea what a 'Prot' was, but vowed to myself I would never be one again. **1977** P. WAY *Super-Celeste* 100 Back in Belfast.. there were Prot bombs and Catholic bombs and SAS bombs.

prot-, the form of PROTO- used before a vowel.

pro'tactic, *a. rare.* [ad. Gr. προτακτικ-ός placed in front, f. προτάσσειν to place before or in front.] Placed in front; giving a previous explanation, introductory.

1847 in WEBSTER.

protactinium (prəʊtæk'tɪnɪəm). *Chem.* Also **protoactinium** (ˌprəʊtəʊæk'tɪnɪəm). [mod.L., coined (as *protactinium*) in Ger. (Hahn & Meitner 1918, in *Physik. Zeitschr.* XIX. 211/1) see PROTO- and ACTINIUM 2. So named because the principal isotope produces actinium by radioactive decay.] A radioactive metallic element of the actinide series, which occurs in small quantities as a decay product in uranium ores, and whose longest-lived isotope has a half-life of about 33,000 years. Atomic number 91; symbol Pa.

The spelling *protactinium* is that adopted by the International Union of Pure and Applied Chemistry.

1918 *Jrnl. Chem. Soc.* CXIV. II. 346 Assuming that 8% of the uranium atoms disintegrating produce 'protoactinium', the quantity in the 73 mg. is that in equilibrium with 86 grams of uranium. **1919** *Chem. Abstr.* XIII. 1181 Protactinium is one of the 5 new radioactive elements occupying a place in the periodic table hitherto vacant. **1934** *Nature* 8 Sept. 386/1 The protoactinium was precipitated with zirconium as phosphate in the earlier stages, partly freed from zirconium by fractional crystallization and precipitated together with tantalum. **1934** *Times* 13 Sept. 9/4 The successful isolation of protactinium, the parent element in the actinium series of radioactive changes, was announced yesterday. **1959** *New Scientist* 17 Dec. 1264/3 From 60 tons of waste material from the production of uranium from its ores, chemists at Windscale have with some difficulty extracted 100 grammes of protactinium. **1962** COTTON & WILKINSON *Adv. Inorg. Chem.* xxxii. 906 Protactinium as ^{231}Pa..occurs in pitchblende, but even the richest ores contain only about 1 part Pa in 10^7. The isolation of protactinium..is difficult, as indeed is the study of protactinium chemistry generally, owing to the extreme tendency of the compounds to hydrolyze. **1970** J. W. GARDNER *Atoms Today & Tomorrow* vi. 99 The decay chain proceeds from thorium (atomic number 90) via protactinium (atomic number 91) to uranium. **1973** PHILLIPS & MILNER in J. C. Bailar et al. *Comprehensive Inorg. Chem.* V. 79 Protactinium is the third member of the actinide series, but it possesses many of the properties of the Group V elements in its chemical reactions... The stable valency state in solution is Pa(V), and the existence of Pa(IV) is also possible.

protagon ('prəʊtəgɒn). *Physiol. Chem.* [a. G. *protagon* (Liebreich), f. Gr. πρῶτ-ος first + ἄγον, neut. pres. pple. of ἄγειν to lead.] A highly complex crystalline substance, containing nitrogen and phosphorus, found in brain and nerve tissue.

1869 ROSCOE *Elem. Chem.* xli. 407 The Brain and other nerve-centres contain a substance termed Protagon. **1871** H. SPENCER *Princ. Psychol.* (ed. 2) I. I. v. 83 Fibrous nerve-tissue is chemically distinguished from..vesicular nerve-tissue by the presence..of a substance called *protagon.* **1904** TITCHENER tr. *Wundt's Physiol. Psychol.* I. 54 Protagon, a highly complex body, to which Liebreich [*Ann. Chem. & Phar.* CXXXIV. (1865) 29] has assigned the empirical formula $C_{116}H_{241}N_4PO_{22}$.

protagonist (prəʊ'tægənɪst). [ad. Gr. πρωταγωνιστ-ής an actor who plays the first part, f. πρῶτος first + ἀγωνιστής one who contends for a prize, a combatant, an actor, f. ἀγωνίζεσθαι: see AGONIZE. So F. *protagoniste* (1835 in *Dict. Acad.*).]

1. The chief personage in a drama; hence, the principal character in the plot of a story, etc. Also *pl.*, the leading characters in a play, story, contest, etc.

Fowler's classification of the plural as an absurd use (*Dict. Modern English Usage* p. 471; maintained in Sir E. Gowers' second edition, p. 489) may be challenged on the grounds that derivation from Greek πρῶτος *first*, does not preclude a plural form, and limitation to the singular is strictly relevant only in the context of ancient Greek drama.

1671 DRYDEN *Even. Love* Pref., Ess. (ed. Ker) I. 141 'Tis charg'd upon me that I make debauch'd Persons..my protagonists, or the chief persons of the drama. **1770** BARETTI *Journ. fr. Lond. to Genoa* III. 27 The Devil in.. Spanish plays..is generally the protagonist of those in which he is introduced. **1857** BIRCH *Anc. Pottery* (1858) I. 321 The earth-shaker Poseidon, the sea god, appears as a subordinate in many scenes, and as a protagonist in others. **1950** G. B. SHAW *Shakes versus Shav* 135 Living actors have to learn that they too must be invisible while the protagonists are conversing, and therefore must not move a muscle nor change their expression. **1952** *Sunday Times* 6 July 4/8 The soliloquy is a special problem on the screen but in 'Julius Caesar' there are only two of them, both short. Mr. Mankiewicz has told me that he hopes to use an intimate technique, giving importance above all to the characters of the protagonists. **1962** L. AUCHINLOSS in I. Howe *Edith Wharton* 35 The change..comes with the infiltration of the other protagonists of the drama, the Spraggs, the Wellington Boys, the Gormers, [etc.].

2. A leading personage in any contest; a prominent supporter or champion of any cause. Also *pl.*, the most prominent or most important individuals in a situation or course of events.

1839–52 BAILEY *Festus* xxxv. (ed. 5) 554 Thou the Divine Protagonist of time, The everlasting sacrifice. *a* **1859** DE QUINCEY *Conversat.* Wks. 1860 XIV. 169 The great talker —the protagonist—of the evening. **1877** MORLEY *Crit. Misc.* Ser. II. 53 If social equity is not a chimera, Marie Antoinette was the protagonist of the most..execrable of causes. **1930** D. L. SAYERS *Strong Poison* viii. 109 I'm getting a certain amount of light on the central figures in the problem—what journalists like to call the protagonists. **1976** *Times* 29 Oct. 1/1 Strong opposition to more cuts in public expenditure were voiced at a meeting of the Cabinet on Tuesday. The protagonists were Mr Crosland..Mr Shore..and Mr Benn.

¶ **3.** [Through confusion of sense 2 with PRO-[1] 5 a.] A proponent, advocate, or supporter (of a cause, idea, etc.).

In this use the notion of 'a leading personage' is not implied. In some contexts there is ambiguity between this sense and sense 2.

1935 *Hansard Commons* 4 June 1718/2 My right hon. Friend the Member for Epping and others on the right have come out in this House as the protagonists of self-determination. **1935** A. P. HERBERT *What a Word!* iv. 99, I heard with horror..that the word 'protagonist' is being used as if it were pro-tagonist—one who is *for* something, and opposed to ant-agonist, one who is against it. **1952** *Times* 2 Apr. 5/4 As a protagonist, in and out of Parliament and especially in the county of Sussex of the fullest use of land for food production, I feel impelled to reply to my friend Miss Nancy Price's letter..and to defend the town council of Worthing. **1961** L. R. KLEIN et al. *Econometric Model of U.K.* iv. 122 Professor Robbins, a firm protagonist of the importance of the influence of demand over the period. **1972** *Observer* 15 Oct. 39/6 In practical terms, I wish I thought that, in 1975, we shall read..alongside *protagonist*, not just '*also*: proponent' but '*also, improperly*: proponent'. **1974** *BSI News* Sept. 12/3 Over the last few years the relative merits of the pascal and the bar have been discussed interminably... Protagonists of the pascal do not think its magnitude of any relevance to its choice. **1975** *Times Lit. Suppl.* 22 Aug. 939/2 Kōkan was..an unabashed protagonist of the technical superiority of Western civilization. **1979** *Jrnl. R. Soc. Arts* CXXVII. 334/2 A protagonist of and expert on the Added Value concept.

Hence ¶**proˈtagonism** *rare*, the defence or advocacy of a cause, idea, etc.

1909 *N.Y. Even. Post* 27 Nov. 6 The principal character ..is gradually drawn into a protagonism of common sense, candour, and progress. **1937** *Mind* XLVI. 511 This method, the validity of which depends upon the progressive series of experiments developed in the *Phenomenology*, is dramatic; it requires the experimenter to be protean in his factitious protagonism.

Protagorean (prəʊtægəˈriːən), *a.* and *sb.* [f. *Protagoras* (Gr. Πρωταγόρας) the name of a Greek philosopher of the 5th century B.C. + -AN.] **A.** *adj.* Of or pertaining to Protagoras or his philosophy. **B.** *sb.* An adherent or admirer of the philosophy of Protagoras. Hence **Protagoˈreanism**, the Protagorean philosophy.

1678 R. CUDWORTH *True Intell. Syst.* i. 10 The Protagorean Philosophy made all things to consist of a Commixture of Parts (or Atoms) and Local Motion. **1845** *Encycl. Metrop.* II. 614/1 The need of such a measure, he asserts, in opposition to the Protagorean notion of man being the measure of all things, which he treats as a silly truism. **1887** *Encycl. Brit.* XXII. 236/1 Socrates rested his scepticism upon the Protagorean doctrine that man is the measure of his own sensations and feelings. *Ibid.*, In the review of theories of knowledge which has come down to us in Plato's *Theætetus* mention is made..of certain 'incomplete Protagoreans'. **1907** *Hibbert Jrnl.* Jan. 439 A Protagorean treatise of the fifth century B.C. **1921** T. R. GLOVER *Pilgrim* 176 The idea of Christian charity has been perverted,..to mean a Protagorean acceptance of the equal value of all opinions. **1932** *Times Lit. Suppl.* 21 Apr. 282/2 It supplies the key to the interpretation of the refined Protagoreanism which the author avows. **1954** *Essays in Crit.* IV. 55 There Arnold figures as a Protagorean sceptic. **1958** *Times Lit. Suppl.* 17 Jan. 26/2 For Professor Guthrie this is a genuine outline of Protagorean thought.

protalus (prəʊˈteɪləs). *Physical Geogr.* Also **pro-talus.** [f. PRO-² + TALUS¹.] A rocky ridge or lobe on the lower edge of an existing or former snow-bank, composed of frost-fractured boulders and other debris that have slid or rolled over the snow from a talus or scree higher up the slope, or been transported by solifluction from the talus. Usu. *attrib.*, as ***protalus lobe, rampart.***

1934 K. BRYAN in *Geogr. Rev.* XXIV. 656 The word 'nivation' is the name of a process of excavation around snowbanks described by Matthes. The use of the same word for these ramparts of blocks is likely to prove misleading, and the reviewer suggests that 'protalus rampart' would be appropriate for the features. **1962** *Prof. Papers U.S. Geol. Survey* No. 324. 61/2 Many deposits thin downslope to a featheredge, but in the mountains some terminate in a lobate mass bearing one or more arcuate ridges in which the fragments tend to be oriented imbricate to the slope... Such protalus lobes appear to have flowed slowly forward as a unit, presumably by solifluction. **1970** R. J. SMALL *Study of Landforms* xi. 378 The disintegrated material may slide across the bank of firn below, and accumulate to give moraine-like piles of debris ('pro-talus') running approximately parallel to the headwall. **1976** *Scottish Geogr. Mag.* XCII. 182 An excellent example of a protalus rampart occurs in Wester Ross 10 km south-east of Gairloch. *Ibid.* 184 The protalus complex lies at the foot of a scree slope that rises through a vertical height interval of 100–200 m.

protamine (ˈprəʊtəmiːn). *Biochem.* and *Med.* Also †-in (-ɪn). [ad. G. *protamin* (F. Miescher 1874, in *Verhandl. d. Naturforsch. Ges. in Basel* VI. 153): see PROTO- and AMINE.] **1.** Any of a class of basic proteins of relatively low molecular weight which occur combined with nucleic acids in the sperm of many species of fish, and which have the property of countering the anti-coagulant action of heparin; orig. *spec.* that obtained from the salmon.

1874 *Jrnl. Chem. Soc.* XXVII. 794 Nuclein occurs in the salmon roe in the form of an insoluble compound with the new base protamine, the latter constituting no less than one-fourth of the weight of the roe. **1896** *Ibid.* LXX. i. 582 The names *salmine* and *sturine* are suggested by [*sic*] the two protamines. **1902** *Encycl. Brit.* XXXI. 724/1 These Protamins..take up water and yield the bases above referred to. **1928** W. V. THORPE tr. *Kossel's Protamines & Histones* II. i. 2 Increasing knowledge of the hydrolysis products of the protamines confirmed Kossel's view..that the protamines belonged to the protein group and were the most elementary type of this..class of compounds. **1954** A. WHITE et al. *Princ. Biochem.* ix. 195 The protamines are relatively small and simple proteins, deficient in many amino-acids and extremely rich in arginine. **1970** R. W. MCGILVERY *Biochem.* xxvi. 653 The effects of heparin can be reversed by giving protamine, the highly basic small protein associated with nucleic acids in fish sperm. **1971** D. R. WILLIAMS *Metals of Life* iii. 27 The threshold between polypeptides and proteins is arbitrarily set at MW 5000 since the smallest physiologically active polymers, the protamines (found in spermatozoa), have molecular weights commencing at this value. **1973** B. A. BROWN *Hematol.* iv. 132/1 At the completion of surgery, protamine is administered in order to neutralize the effects of the heparin.

2. *attrib.* and *Comb.* **a.** In various combs., as ***protamine-insulin, protamine-zinc(-insulin)***, denoting suspensions of insulin with a protamine, and usu. also zinc chloride, which have greater stability and a more prolonged hypoglycæmic action than insulin alone.

1935 C. L. HEEL tr. N. B. Krarup (*title*) Clinical investigations into the action of protamine insulinate. **1936** *Canad. Public Health Jrnl.* XXVII. 157/2 In the preparation of protamine insulin for injection, a suitable quantity of protamine, buffered with sodium phosphate, is added to regular insulin. **1936** *Canad. Med. Assoc. Jrnl.* XXXV. 240/1 The other solution contained a buffer phosphate, 1 c.c. of which, when added to the protamine-zinc-insulin complex, adjusted the reaction so that the hydrogen-ion concentration..was identical with that of blood. **1956** *Nature* 4 Feb. 223/2 Robinson and Fehr were able to estimate the percentage of insulin in protamine insulin by using the upper phase from a butanol/acetic/water.. mixture as a chromatographic solvent. **1960** M. SPARK *Bachelors* vii. 100 Protamine zinc for more prolonged coverage throughout the evening and the following night. She needs 80 units. **1962** H. BURN *Drugs, Med. & Man* xiv. 148 While the maximum time of action of insulin alone was six hours, that of protamine-insulin was 12–18 hours, and finally that of zinc-protamine-insulin was 24–30 hours.

b. protamine sulphate, a salt of a protamine and sulphuric acid, given as an aqueous solution to neutralize the anti-coagulant effect of heparin; **protamine titration**, a test of the clotting ability of blood in which blood is first made incoagulable with heparin and then titrated against protamine sulphate until clotting occurs; a value so obtained.

1936 *Jrnl. Pharmacol. & Exper. Therapeutics* LVIII. 80 After standing 4 or 5 days the precipitated protamine sulfate has settled and is removed by centrifugation. **1962** *Listener* 3 May 769/2 Certain mixtures of large molecules—for example, mixtures of starch, gelatin, and protamine sulphate—will form drops which have great stability. **1971** S. I. RAPAPORT *Introd. Hematol.* xxiv. 311 One-tenth volume of 1 per cent protamine sulfate is added to plasma, and the plasma is examined for a precipitate after 15 minutes at 37°C. **1949** J. G. ALLEN et al. *Jrnl. Lab. & Clin. Med.* XXXIV. 473 (*heading*) A protamine titration as an indication of clotting defect in certain hemorrhagic states. **1949** *Jrnl. Amer. Med. Assoc.* 30 Apr. 1251/1 The blood.. showed an increased protamine titration when the prothrombin level was normal or near normal, when fibrinogen levels were not abnormal and when fibrinolysin was not grossly disturbed. **1973** B. A. BROWN *Hematol.* iv. 132/1 The protamine titration..is used to estimate the minimum required dose of protamine.

protamnion, etc.: see PROTO- 2 b.

protan (ˈprəʊtæn), *sb.* (*a.*). *Ophthalm.* [f. *protan-* in PROTANOMALY, PROTANOPIA, etc.] A protanomalous or protanopic person. Also as *adj.*

1944 D. FARNSWORTH in *Inter-Society Color Council News Let.* LVI. 8 There are 3 or more types of Anomaly (chromatic imbalance). 1. n. Protan; adj. Protanous: reduction of red-bluegreen discrimination relative to interesting axis. **1962** *Lancet* 15 Dec. 1269/1 The former includes protan and deutan defects with 3 or more alleles at each locus, and the latter includes true hæmophilia and Christmas disease. **1968** [see ISHIHARA]. **1974** *Nature* 23 Aug. 653/1 It is highly probable that there are at least two gene loci involved in each of four X-linked diseases: colour blindness (protan and deutan), haemophilia (A and B), muscular dystrophy (Duchenne and Becker), and retinal degeneration (retinoschisis and Norrie's disease).

protandrous (prəʊˈtændrəs), *a.* [ad. G. *protandrisch* (F. H. G. Hildebrand *Die Geschlechter-Vertheilung bei den Pflanzen* (1867) 17), f. PROT(O)- + -ANDROUS.]

1. *Bot.* = PROTERANDROUS; opposed to *protogynous.*

1870 A. W. BENNETT in *Jrnl. Bot.* VIII. 317 (*heading*) Protandrous. **1875** BENNETT & DYER *Sachs' Bot.* 812 Dichogamous Flowers are either protandrous or protogynous. **1880** GRAY *Struct. Bot.* vi. §4 (ed. 6) 219 Dichogamous flowers are Proterandrous (or Protandrous), when the anthers mature and discharge their pollen before the stigma of that blossom is receptive of pollen. **1965** BELL & COOMBE tr. *Strasburger's Textbk. Bot.* 602 Many apparently protandrous flowers..were borne in the axils of the dead leaves.

2. *Zool.* = PROTERANDROUS *a.* 2.

1897 PARKER & HASWELL *Textbk. Zool.* I. vi. 285 A few forms [of Nematoidea] are hermaphrodite, but, instead of having a double set of reproductive organs, as in Platodes, organs of the ordinary female nematode type are present, and the gonads produce first sperms and afterwards ova. Such animals are said to be protandrous (male products ripe first). **1929** *Amer. Naturalist* LXIII. 571 The lengths of males [of *Pandalus danae* Stimpson] indicated that they were in two year-groups... On the other hand the females seemed to belong to a third year-group... This appeared to suggest that the form under consideration was protandrous. **1973** *Nature* 5 Oct. 262/2 Both protandrous and protogynous hermaphroditism have been reported in fishes, and there is some evidence that smaller and younger specimens of *U*[*mbra*] *limi* are predominantly males, while larger and older individuals are mostly females.

So **proˈtandric** *a.* = PROTANDROUS (*Cent. Dict.* 1890); **proˈtandrism** (Webster 1890), **proˈtandry** = PROTERANDRY: opposed to *protogyny.*

1870 [see PROTOGYNY]. **1887** *Bergens Museums Aarsberetning* VII. 29 It may not be amiss to draw a comparison between the protandric hermaphroditism of Myxine and the hermaphroditism of the few other hermaphroditic vertebrates known. **1892** J. A. THOMSON *Outl. Zool.* 632/2 (Index), Protandry of Myxine. **1897** WILLIS *Flower. Pl. & Ferns* I. 87 When the pollen is ripe before the stigma..termed protandry. **1932** *Proc. 6th Internat. Congr. Genetics* II. 26 Several of the oviparous species show a large percentage of intersexuality when young, with a strong tendency toward protandry. *Ibid.* 27 This species is regularly protandric, each young animal producing many thousands of sperm balls. **1951** [see *gonochoric* adj. s.v. GONO-]. **1970** *Nature* 11 July 189/2 Gross examination of gonads in larger males and smaller females showed no evidence of protandry. **1975** *Ibid.* 15 May 221/2 He considered it likely that *A. equina* is a protandric hermaphrodite which mainly self-fertilises and retains larvae within the parent.

protanomal (prəʊtəˈnɒməl). *Ophthalm.* [ad. G. *protanomale* (W. A. Nagel 1907, in *Zeitschr. f. Psychol. und Physiol. d. Sinnesorgane*: *Abt. II* XLII. 67), f. Gr. πρωτ- PROT- + G. *anomal* anomalous.] A person with protanomaly.

1915 J. H. PARSONS *Introd. Study Colour Vision* II. iii. 183 Of the partial protanopes (protanomal, Nagel) Donders and König do not record any case, v. Kries one only, whereas Nagel, Guttman, and Abney and Watson record a considerable number. **1973** *Jrnl. Optical Soc. Amer.* LXIII. 236/1 In Fig. 2, the red primary is assigned a value of 637 nm for normals and deuteranomals, and 629 nm for protanomals.

Hence **protaˈnomalous** *a.*, having protanomaly; also *absol.*

1911 *Amer. Jrnl. Psychol.* XXII. 370 It is now customary ..to distinguish two groups of anomalous trichromates, upon the analogy of the two groups of dichromates,—the red-anomalous or protanomalous trichromates, whose sensitiveness to red is below normal, and the green-anomalous or deuteranomalous trichromates, whose sensitiveness to green is below normal. **1938** [see PROTANOMALY]. **1965** *Science* 9 July 186/1 The protanomalous subject can match all colors of the spectrum with mixtures of three hues but requires more red in each mixture than the normal subject. **1975** *Sci. Amer.* Mar. 172/3 Some have considered that the protanomalous need more red in their mixture because, although they have normal cone pigments, the red signals are too weak.

protanomaly (prəʊtəˈnɒməlɪ). *Ophthalm.* [f. prec. + -Y³.] A form of anomalous trichromatism marked by a reduced sensitivity to red and subnormal discrimination between red, yellow, and green hues.

1938 *Proc. Physical Soc.* L. 674 As the results for only one protanomalous observer are given, it is impossible to talk of any stages of protanomaly except by comparison with the results for the deuteranomalous observers. **1946** W. D. WRIGHT *Res. Normal & Defective Colour Vision* xxiv. 297 Anomalous trichromatism is subdivided into three corresponding groups—protanomaly, deuteranomaly and tritanomaly—from the fact that each group has characteristics intermediate between those of the trichromat and the corresponding dichromat. **1973** *Vision Res.* XIII. 2033 The condition of anomalous trichromacy thus includes the categories of simple and extreme protanomaly and simple and extreme deuteranomaly.

protanope (ˈprəʊtənəʊp). *Ophthalm.* [ad. G. *protanop* (J. von Kries 1897, in *Zeitschr. f. Psychol. und Physiol. d. Sinnesorgane* XIII. 248), f. PROT- + Gr. priv. ἀν- + ὤψ, ὠπ- eye, face.] A person with protanopia.

1908 *Psychol. Bull.* V. 298 When red and blue are mixed to match blue-green the protanope requires a relative excess of red in his purple mixture; and in similar determinations with red and yellow the protanope may demand five times as much red as the deuteranope. **1924** tr. J. von Kries in *Helmholtz's Treat. Physiol. Optics* II. 402 In order to have brief descriptive terms for the relation that has been found to exist here, without expressing any theoretical bias, the writer suggests the names *protanopes* and *deuteranopes* to describe the two kinds of dichromats, that is, persons who lack the first component or the second component, respectively, of the normal visual organ. **1953** *Jrnl. Physiol.* CXXI. 565 The protanopes confuse red with green and are characterized by a very low sensitivity to light of long wavelengths. **1959** [see DICHROMAT, DICHROMATE *sb.*²]. **1971** *Vision Res.* XI. 1034 Protanopes are deficient in some red-sensitive cone pigment that is present in normal eyes.

protanopia (prəʊtəˈnəʊpɪə). *Ophthalm.* [mod.L., f. prec. + -IA¹.] A form of dichromatic colour-blindness marked by an insensitivity to red and an inability to distinguish between red, yellow, and green hues.

1902 J. M. BALDWIN *Dict. Philos. & Psychol.* II. 371/1 In ..the so-called red-blindness, the red end of the spectrum is shortened, and the maximum brightness is further towards the green (protanopia). **1923** L. C. MARTIN *Colour* x. 146 In complete protanopia or deuteranopia we have the spectrum consisting (broadly speaking) of two parts of differing hue separated by a grey or white. **1950** *Jrnl. Optical Soc. Amer.* XL. 46/2 If the scores at either + 5 or − 5 are incorrect the subject has complete red-green color deficiency, i.e. either protanopia or deuteranopia. **1974** *Ophthalmic Res.* VI. 281 Colour discrimination as tested with the Ishihara plates and Nagel anomaloscope..was typical for protanopia.

Hence **protaˈnopic** *a.*

1908 *Psychol. Bull.* V. 298 Certain individuals..make their mixtures much redder, and other individuals much greener than the average. Here again we must distinguish between a protanopic and a deuteranopic sub-type. Investigations since Rayleigh's pioneer publication have shown that the former sub-type is much more numerous than the latter. **1973** *Vision Res.* XIII. 1762 The reduction in gradient of the deuteranopic isochromatic line through the blue-green and purple region suggests an explanation of why some deuteranopes cannot distinguish either the protanopic or the deuteranopic diagnostic figures in the Ishihara test.

pro tanto: see PRO 9.

protarch (ˈprəʊtɑːk). *rare.* [ad. Gr. πρωτάρχ-ης, f. πρῶτος first + ἀρχός ruler.] A chief ruler.

1656 BRAMHALL *Replic.* v. 190 In the age of the Apostles ..the highest Order in the Church, under the Apostles, were nationall Protarchs or Patriarchs.

protargol (prəʊˈtɑːgɒl). *Med.* [a. G. *protargol* (A. Neisser 1897, in *Dermatologisches Centralblatt* I. 5), f. *prot-eïn* PROTEIN + L. *argentum* silver; cf. -OL.] A substance made from protein and various compounds of silver, used as a mild antiseptic and a stain.

1898 *Boston Med. & Surg. Jrnl.* 25 Aug. 194/2 In the few cases of purulent ophthalmia that have been treated with protargol the length of the course of the disease has apparently only been slightly shortened, but the severity of the attack has been decidedly lessened. **1907** J. H. PARSONS *Dis. Eye* xxix. 580 In more severe cases..protargol, 15 to 20 per cent., should be rubbed into the margins of the lids with a stumpy camel's hair brush. **1938** *Stain Technol.* XIII. 154 Protargol exhibits an isoelectric point roughly about pH 4, at which acidity it is precipitated, hence it might be expected to behave somewhat like a dye by having its selectivity altered by variation of pH of the staining mixture. **1976** *Acta Zool.* LVII. 117 The figures demonstrate the close connection between the surface cilia as shown by SEM [*sc.* scanning electron microscopy] and the subsurface kinetosomes revealed by the protargol impregnations.

protarsal (prəʊˈtɑːsəl), *a. Ent.* [f. PROTARS(US + -AL.] Of or pertaining to the protarsus.

1902 R. I. POCOCK in *Proc. Zool. Soc.* II. 391, 2nd leg with superior basal and anterior apical femoral spine, three inferior apical protarsal spines..and one inferior medium tarsal spine.

‖**protarsus** (prəʊˈtɑːsəs). *Entom.* Pl. -si (-saɪ). [f. PRO-² 2 + TARSUS.] The tarsus of the first or fore leg of an insect.

1890 in *Cent. Dict.*

‖**protasis** (ˈprɒtəsɪs). [Late L., a. Gr. πρότασις a stretching forward, a proposition, (major) premiss, a hypothetical clause, a problem, the first part of a play, f. πρό, PRO-² + τάσις, n. of action f. τείνειν to stretch.]

1. That which is put forward; a proposition, a maxim. *rare.*

1656 BLOUNT *Glossogr.*, *Protasis*, a Proposition or Declaration. **1755** in JOHNSON. **1806** *Monthly Mag.* XXII. 210 It is a universally received protasis among grammarians that the first terms of every language were nouns, which were turned into verbs by putting them in action.

2. In the ancient drama, The first part of a play, in which the characters are introduced and the subject entered on, as opposed to the *epitasis* and *catastrophe*. Also *fig.*

a **1568** ASCHAM *Scholemaster* (1570) 57 He began the Protasis with *Trochaijs Octonarijs*. **1616** R. C. *Times' Whistle*, etc. (1871) 111 Thou shalt be both the protasis & catastrophe of my epistle. **1632** B. JONSON *Magn. Lady* I. i, Do you look, master Damplay, for conclusions in a protasis? I thought the law of comedy had reserved [them] to the catastrophe. **1713** SWIFT *Frenzy J. Dennis* Wks. 1755 III. I. 143, I am sick..of the diction, of the protasis, of the epitasis, and the catastrophe.—Alas, what is become of the drama? **1815** *Mr. Decastro* I. 259 Thus far by way of protasis to the matter..the epitasis whereof..comes next. **1961** *Listener* 5 Oct. 527/2 For a good deal of his new novel one might as well be reading the protasis of a fair-to-middling detective story.

3. *Gram.* and *Rhet.* The first or introductory clause in a sentence, *esp.* the clause which expresses the condition in a conditional sentence; opposed to the *apodosis*. Also *fig.*

1588 W. KEMPE *Educ. Children* sig. G.4 ᵛ, Only the protasis or first part of our similitude is attributed but to Cato, for want of a like similitude garnished with like authoritie. *a* **1638** MEDE *Wks.* (1672) 77 Let us examine and consider a little of the Protasis, whereof the words I have now read are the Apodosis. **1879** ROBY *Lat. Gram.* IV. §1025 A subordinate (relative, temporal, causal, concessive, or conditional) sentence is often called the protasis, the principal (i.e. demonstrative, conditioned, &c.) sentence is often called the apodosis. **1904** [see *if-clause* s.v. IF *conj.* (*sb.*) 10]. **1922** JOYCE *Ulysses* 704 Positing what protasis would the contraction for such several schemes become a natural and necessary apodosis? **1971** *Language* XLVII. 81, I use the term 'conditional sentence' to cover the entire complex sentence consisting of a protasis and an apodosis.

4. *Ancient Prosody.* The first colon of a dicolic line or period.

1890 in *Cent. Dict.*

protastacine, -astacus: see PROTO- 2 b.

protatic (prəʊˈtætɪk), *a.* [ad. late L. *protatic-us*, a. Gr. προτατικ-ός, f. πρότασις: see PROTASIS. Cf. F. *protatique.*] Of or pertaining to the or a protasis; in *protatic character, person*, appearing only in the protasis (sense 2).

1668 DRYDEN *Dram. Poesy* Ess. (ed. Ker) I. 61 There are indeed some protatick persons in the Ancients, whom they make use of in their plays, either to hear or give the relation. **1881** *Birm'ham Daily Post* 20 July 7/4 The protatic character of Davies found a competent representative.

Hence **proˈtatically** *adv.*, in the protasis.

1865 F. HALL in *Reader* 1 Apr. 371/3 He will have made out his case completely on showing..that *quha* or *who* was employed, so early as 1556, as equivalent, save protatically, to *he who*, or rather to *whoso, whosoever*.

protaxonial: see PROTO- 2 b.

‖**protea** (ˈprəʊtɪə). *Bot.* [mod.L. *Prōtea*, generic name (Linnæus *Hortus Cliffortianus* (1737) 29), f. *Prōteus* (see PROTEUS), in allusion to the great variety of form of the different species.] An evergreen shrub or small tree of the genus so called, belonging to the family Proteaceæ, usually native to southern Africa or Australia, and bearing cone-like heads of small flowers with prominent bracts. Also *attrib.*

1753 CHAMBERS *Cycl. Supp.*, *Protea*, in the Linnæan system of botany, a genus..which takes in the lepidocarpodendron, and the hypophyllocarpodendron of Boerhaave. **1770** R. WESTON *Universal Botanist* I. 221 Cape Protea or Silver-tree. **1804** H. ANDREWS *Botanists Repository* V. tab. cccxlix, From the great number of the divided leaved Proteas, we are led to conjecture, that they are as numerous as those with entire leaves. **1825** *Greenhouse Comp.* I. 131 Banksias, proteas, acacias, melaleucas, and a few other Cape and Botany Bay plants. **1850** R. G. CUMMING *Hunter's Life S. Afr.* (ed. 2) I. 19 The splendid protea, whose sweets never fail to attract swarms of the insect tribes. **1901** L. H. BAILEY *Cycl. Amer. Hort.* III. 1438/2 Proteas are tender shrubs which are among the most attractive and characteristic plants of the Cape of Good Hope. **1951** [see DISA]. **1972** J. BURMEISTER *Running Scared* 13 Their daughter had been chosen to present a protea, South Africa's unlovely national flower, to the President. **1972** PALMER & PITMAN *Trees S. Afr.* I. xxiv. 503 The close-set protea leaves may yield as important a source of food to sugarbirds and sunbirds as do the flowers.

proteaceous (prəʊtɪˈeɪʃəs), *a.* [f. mod.L. *Prōteāce-æ*, f. prec.: see -ACEOUS.] Of or pertaining to the *Proteaceæ*, a natural order of trees, shrubs, or (rarely) perennial herbs, mainly S. African and Australian, typified by the genus *Protea.*

1835 *Penny Cycl.* III. 123/2 Multitudes of proteaceous plants, with their hard and woody leaves [near Port Jackson, S. Australia]. **1880** DAWKINS *Early Man* ii. 26 There were cypresses..and proteaceous plants allied to the banksia.

protead (ˈprəʊtiːæd). *Bot. rare.* [f. PROTEA: see -AD I d.] Lindley's name for a plant of the order *Proteaceæ.*

1846 LINDLEY *Veg. Kingd.* 532 A happier name than that of Proteads could not have been devised, for the diversity of appearance presented by the various genera is such as it would be hard to parallel in the same Natural Order. **1882** *Garden* 10 June 398/1 Hakea cucullata and various other Proteads..cultivated in the temperate house.

Protean (ˈprəʊtiːən, prəʊˈtiːən), *a.* (*sb.*) Also protean. [f. PROTEUS + -AN: cf. F. *Protéen.*]

A. *adj.* **a.** Of or pertaining to Proteus; like that of Proteus; hence, taking or existing in various shapes, variable in form; characterized by variability or variation; variously manifested or expressed; changing, varying.

1598 MARSTON *Pygmal.* ii, I shall stand in doubt What sex thou art, since such Hermaphrodites Such Protean shadowes so delude our sights. **1613** PURCHAS *Pilgrimage* (1614) 793 Hee escaped by his Protean Arts; now appearing like an Eagle, the second time like a Tygre, the third like a Serpent. **1679** *Establ. Test* 3 Their Protean Faculties of Dissimulation, Perjury, and Putting on so many Shapes. **1834–5** J. PHILLIPS *Geol.* in *Encycl. Metrop.* VI. 559/2 Its geological relations should always be consulted before deciding on the name of this Protean rock. **1859** DARWIN *Orig. Spec.* ii. (1878) 35 Genera which have been called 'protean' or 'polymorphic', in which the species present an inordinate amount of variation. **1860** TYNDALL *Glac.* I. xiv. 97 The scene had time to go through several of its Protean mutations. **1899** *Allbutt's Syst. Med.* VIII. 346 General paralysis is of necessity a protean malady.

b. *spec.* *Zool.* Varying in shape; of or pertaining to the proteus-animalcule; amœboid, amœbiform, proteiform.

1802 BINGLEY *Anim. Biog.* (1813) III. 492 The Protean Vibrio... A species which has derived its name from its very singular power of assuming different shapes. **1835–6** *Todd's Cycl. Anat.* I. 645/1 The Protean animals..do not undergo ..any further metamorphosis.

c. Of a theatrical performer: characterized by the ability to take several parts in the same piece; quick-change; also *transf.* of such a performance. orig. *U.S.* Cf. sense B 1 b.

1897 *Daily Tel.* 10 Mar. 4/5 Few will deny that Leopoldi Fregoli..is..alert, versatile, neat in his business, quick as lightning in his changes, and..the best 'protean' entertainer that the oldest playgoer has ever seen. **1909** WEBSTER, *Pro'te-an*... 3..*Theat.* Noting an actor who plays different parts in a play; hence, noting a performance of this kind. *Slang.* **1952** GRANVILLE *Dict. Theatr. Terms* 145 *Protean act*, an act performed by a: *Protean entertainer*, a lightning-change artiste. An impersonator. **1961** BOWMAN & BALL *Theatre Lang.* 282 Protean actor, protean artist. Hence protean act, protean drama, etc.

d. Of animal behaviour: unpredictable, following no obvious pattern.

1959 CHANCE & RUSSELL in *Proc. Zool. Soc.* CXXXII. 67 We therefore propose the term 'Protean Displays'. The mythical Proteus frustrated would-be captors by constantly changing his shape, so that they had nothing systematic to which to react. *Ibid.* 68 Protean displays involve rapid, sudden transitions, as one obvious component of their confusing effect. **1967** *New Scientist* 13 July 96/2 The term protean behaviour was coined to cover behaviour that is sufficiently unsystematic to prevent the predator from predicting in detail the positions, actions or both, of the prey. **1970** *Nature* 6 June 968/1 We have surveyed the occurrence of such protean behaviours and defined them as behaviours which are sufficiently unsystematic in appearance to prevent a reactor predicting in detail the position and/or actions of the actor. *Ibid.*, The erratic nature of a protean display defeats anticipation by the predator.

B. *sb.* †**1. a.** One who constantly changes; and inconstant or equivocal person. *Obs. rare*⁻¹

1598 MARSTON *Pygmal.* ii, These same Proteans, whose hipocrisie, Doth still abuse our fond credulity.

b. An actor who takes several parts in the same piece. orig. *U.S.*

1890 in *Cent. Dict.*

2. *Zool.* = PROTEID² (*Cent. Dict.* 1890).

Hence ˈ**Proteanly** *adv. rare*⁻¹, in a protean manner, with variation of form.

1678 CUDWORTH *Intell. Syst.* I. i. §29. 36 Matter..only Proteanly transformed into different shapes.

protease (ˈprəʊtiːeɪs). *Physiol. Chem.* [f. PROTEO(LYSIS + -*ase* in DIASTASE; first formed as F. *proteinase* (G. Malfitano 1900, in *Ann. de l'Inst. Pasteur* XIV. 420).] A proteolytic enzyme or ferment; a proteinase or peptidase.

1903 *Ann. Bot.* XVII. 237 There is at present evidence that enzymes which digest proteids (proteases) occur..in certain lowly Algae, in some fungi, and in various Phanerogams. **1904** VINES in *Annals of Bot.* XVIII. 289 (Article) The Proteases of Plants... Hitherto the proteases of both plants and animals have been classified as 'peptic' or as 'tryptic', in accordance with their general resemblance to either the pepsin or the trypsin of the animal body... But with the discovery of erepsin by Cohnheim, this simple classification of the proteases has become inadequate, for erepsin is neither 'peptic' nor 'tryptic'. *Ibid.* 316 It appears ..that erepsin is present in the onion without any other protease. **1923** [see PEPTIDASE]. **1931** [see PROTEINASE]. **1949** ABRAHAM & HEATLEY in H. W. Florey et al. *Antibiotics* I. ii. 85 This can happen..by the secretion of destructive exocellular enzymes such as penicillinase, protease, or peptidase. **1962** A. SPECTOR in A. Pirie *Lens Metabolism Rel. Cataract* 330 An endopeptidase called β-protease..will attack lens protein in acid pH and a second enzyme, the α-protease,..attacks the breakdown products produced by the endopeptidase. **1973** ZEFFREN & HALL *Study of Enzyme Mechanisms* ix. 168 Chymotrypsin is one of several proteolytic enzymes or proteases which function collectively in the mammalian small intestine. **1976** *Path. Ann.* XI. 380 This may be related in part to the presence of protease inhibitors in connective tissues.

†**protect**, *ppl. a. Obs.* [ad. L. *prōtect-us*, pa. pple. of *prōteg-ĕre* to cover in front, protect, defend, f. *prō*, PRO-¹ + *teg-ĕre* to cover.] Protected. (Const. as *pa. pple.*)

1432–50 tr. *Higden* (Rolls) I. 111 Like as a doȝhter is protecte [*orig.* protegitur] of the moder, and subiecte to her. **1544** tr. *Littleton's Tenures* (1574) 41 b, The things by which a man is protect & holpen.

protect (prəʊˈtɛkt), *v.* [f. ppl. stem of L. *prōteg-ĕre*: see prec. Cf. rare obs. F. *protecter* (15th c. in Godef.).]

1. a. *trans.* To defend or guard from injury or danger; to shield from attack or assault; to support, assist, or afford immunity to, esp. against any inimical agency; to preserve intact, or from encroachment, invasion, annoyance, or insult; to keep safe, take care of; to extend patronage to. Also *absol.*

1526 *Pilgr. Perf.* (W. de W. 1531) 12 b, Whome god almyghty..protected, defended, saued, and gouerned. **1593** SHAKS. *2 Hen. VI*, I. iii. 5 The Lord protect him..Iesu blesse him. **1651** HOBBES *Leviath.* II. xviii. 91 To every man remaineth..the right of protecting himselfe. **1750** GRAY *Elegy* xx, These bones from insult to protect. **1793** BURKE *Corr.* (1844) IV. 183, I trust that Providence protects you and your illustrious brother for some great purpose. **1857** BUCKLE *Civiliz.* I. xi. 646 Whenever a government undertakes to protect intellectual pursuits, it will almost always protect them in the wrong place and reward the wrong men. **1879** HARLAN *Eyesight* vii. 96 The simplest forms of spectacles are those used merely to protect the eyes from mechanical injury or excessive light. **1894** E. FAWCETT *New Nero* ii. 26 Music..was always an expression of..that soulless and mysterious will-to-live, which for ever creates, protects, and perpetuates. **1934** W. B. YEATS tr. *Sophocles' Oedipus at Colonus* in *Coll. Plays* 543 *Theseus*... If God sent you hither, you need no protection of mine, but God or no God my mere name will protect.

b. To act as official or legal protector (PROTECTOR 1) or guardian of.

1593 SHAKS. *2 Hen. VI*, II. iii. 29, I see no reason, why a King of yeeres should be to be protected like a Child. **1594** —— *Rich. III*, II. iii. 21 Then the King, Had vertuous Vnkles to protect his Grace.

c. To attempt to preserve (a threatened plant or animal species) by preventing collecting, hunting, etc.; to restrict access to (land valued for its wild life or its undisturbed state).

1893 *Zoologist* XVII. 390 If a particular species were declining, and were known to frequent a particular place, the County Council should..be called upon to protect that restricted area. **1935** *Discovery* Oct. 304/1 To protect a bird proved..to be noxious simply brings bird-protection into contempt. **1969** F. N. HEPPER in J. Fisher et al. *Red Bk.* 360/1 The need to protect plants for their own sake is becoming increasingly accepted by those in authority.

2. *Pol. Econ.* To assist or guard (a domestic industry) against the competition of foreign productions by means of imposts on the latter.

1789 *Deb. Congress U.S.* 9 Apr. (1834) 106 [Measures] calculated to encourage the productions of our country, and protect our infant manufactures. **1825** J. S. MILL in *Westm. Rev.* III. 415 The various classes of manufactures are protected from foreign competition. **1827–39** GEN. P. THOMPSON *Catechism Corn Laws* (1839) § 160 If no trade can be 'protected' but at the expense of some other trade first, and of the consumers a second time besides, it will be very difficult to make out a case for 'protection'. **1868** ROGERS *Pol. Econ.* xvii. (1876) 233 If every producer of every kind were protected, foreign trade might cease... It would be certainly futile, to protect everybody. **1885** LD. DUNRAVEN in *Daily Tel.* 29 Sept. 2/6 Their industries were protected and ours were not.

3. *Comm.* To provide funds to meet (a commercial draft or bill of exchange); cf. COVER *v.*[1] 18.

1884 *Law Times Rep.* LI. 16/1 Please protect the draft as advised above and oblige drawer.

4. a. To furnish with a protective covering; *spec.* in reference to war-ships.

1839 URE *Dict. Arts* 615 When the gilder has protected the burnished points, he dries the piece. **1884** [see PROTECTED].

b. To provide (machinery, etc.) with devices or appliances to prevent injury from it.

1900 *Daily News* 14 Apr. 2/5 The different systems of 'safety' or 'protected' rifle ranges in use.

c. To provide (an electrical device or machine) with safeguards against too high a current or voltage.

1875 *Telegr. Jrnl.* III. 60/2 Lightning protectors invented to protect telegraph lines. **1888** D. SALOMONS *Managem. of Accumulators & Private Electric Light Installations* (ed. 3) II. ii. 97 Put a safety fuse in every switch and wall plug... Every lamp is protected in this way..against accidental short-circuits. **1935** MONSETH & ROBINSON *Relay Syst.* xiii. 458 The first zone..is protected by an instantaneous balanced-beam impedance element. **1975** D. G. FINK *Electronics Engineers' Handbk.* VII. 27 Two types of fast-blow fuses are used to protect power-tubes.

5. *Chem.* **a.** To prevent the alteration or removal of (a particular group or part of a molecule) in a reaction, by first causing it to form an unreactive derivative from which the original structure can later be regenerated.

1889 G. M'GOWAN tr. *Bernthsen's Text-bk. Org. Chem.* 352 When it is wished to prepare the mono-nitro-compounds, the aniline must again be 'protected', either by using its acetyl compound or by nitrating in presence of excess of concentrated sulphuric acid. **1929** MITCHELL & HAMILTON *Biochem. Amino Acids* i. 90 In other words, the chloracetyl group, introduced to protect the amino group of the amino acid is, after it has performed its protective function, itself transformed into an amino acid group. **1951** I. L. FINAR *Org. Chem.* I. xi. 203 If the synthesis requires reaction with one halogen atom only, the most satisfactory procedure is to 'protect' the other halogen atom by ether formation and subsequently decompose the ether with concentrated hydrobromic acid. **1964** N. G. CLARK *Mod. Org. Chem.* vi. 90 By forming the dibromide..the double bond is 'protected' from the ensuing reaction, and may be restored later to the compound by zinc treatment. **1971** D. R. WILLIAMS *Metals of Life* ix. 134 Freeman *et al.* have found that the amide bonds in simple peptides which are usually easily hydrolysed to give amino acids again are protected by transition metal ions, the best protectors being copper (II) and nickel (II).

b. To render (a hydrophobic sol) inert to the flocculating action of small concentrations of an electrolyte.

[**1903** *Jrnl. Chem. Soc.* LXXXIV. I. 135 The capacity of colloidal solutions to protect a colloidal solution of gold against the precipitating action of an estimated quantity of sodium chloride is expressed as the gold number.] **1909** J. ALEXANDER tr. *Zsigmondy's Colloids & Ultramicroscope* iii. 77 Another colloid which protects the nascent colloidal gold was discovered by Faraday, and called by him 'jelly'. **1939** *Thorpe's Dict. Appl. Chem.* (ed. 4) III. 287/2 A quartz suspension protected by gelatine will possess the cataphoretic velocity and isoelectric point of gelatine. **1966** GUCKER & SEIFERT *Physical Chem.* xxii. 665 A lyophobic sol is often stabilized by addition of a lyophilic sol, which is then termed a protective colloid. An example is gelatin, which protects the silver bromide sol used in photographic emulsions.

Hence **pro'tecting** *vbl. sb.*, the action of the verb; protection.

*c*1630 SANDERSON *Serm.* II. 275 The curbing of the one sort, and the protecting of the other.

pro'tectant, *a.* and *sb.* [irreg. f. prec. + -ANT.]

A. *adj.* **a.** = PROTECTIVE *a.* 1. **b.** Protecting (esp. plants) against disease.

1670 *Conclave wherein Clement VIII was elected Pope* 29 He would be his friend, and would always be graciously protectant of his Majesty. **1943** *Phytopathology* XXXIII. 627 (*heading*) The slide-germination method of evaluating protectant fungicides. **1954** *Jrnl. Econ. Entomol.* XLVII. 462 (*heading*) Protection of stored shelled corn with a protectant dust in Indiana. **1977** *Protecting World's Crops* (Shell Internat. Petroleum Co.) 2 Protectant fungicides, if applied before the disease occurs, kill or inhibit the development of fungal spores or mycelia (strands of fungus) before they can damage plant tissues.

B. *sb.* An agent that protects, esp. a plant against disease.

1935 *Jrnl. Pomol. & Hort. Sci.* XIII. 262 The effects of the wetting agents..upon the biological activities of the protectant..have to be determined. **1940** *Phytopathology* XXX. 2 Synthetic organic chemicals developed by the Crop Protection Institute were efficient, non-injurious seed protectants for combating damping-off in Lima beans. **1960** *New Scientist* 4 Aug. 344/1 Removal of the dark green colouring matter present in crude preparations of pyrethrum markedly increased its stability in sunlight, and further improvement was achieved by the addition of..a number of antioxidants... The data suggest that these compounds act primarily as protectants for pyrethrin II and cinerin II, whereas the absence of 'chlorophyll' pigments enhances the stability of pyrethrin I and cinerin I. **1975** *Nature* 22 May 329/1 It is clear that as a protectant, sclareol is highly specific for rust fungi.

protected, *ppl. a.* [f. PROTECT *v.* + -ED.]

a. That enjoys protection; receiving legal immunity or exemption.

1836 WHEATON *Elem. Internat. Law* I. ii. 63 The sovereignty of the inferior ally or protected state remains, though limited and qualified by the stipulations of the treaties of alliance and protection. **1872** BAGEHOT *Physics & Pol.* (1876) 82 This principle explains..why the 'protected' regions of the world..are of necessity backward. **1878** H. H. GIBBS *Ombre* 22 He keeps only the trumps and perhaps the Kings or at most a protected Queen. **1884** SIR T. SYMONDS in *Pall Mall G.* 25 Sept. 1/2 Twenty-three battle ships..(of which four are protected cruisers). **1885** *Athenæum* 3 Oct. 433/3 Toul [was]..a protected state dependent upon France. **1888** *Nation* (N.Y.) 6 Dec. 454/1 Whatever increased profits our manufacturers of 'protected' articles get..must come from other classes..the consumers of their products. **1900** [see PROTECT *v.* 4 b]. **1926** *Brit. Gaz.* 12 May 2/6 The London Central Meat Market, at Smithfield, is now a protected area, and barriers have been drawn across all the approaches. **1942** *Ann. Reg. 1941* 27 Now they [*sc.* men above the reservation age] were to be reserved only if engaged on what was called 'protected work', i.e. work which the Government recognised as of national importance. **1944** *Manpower* (Ministry of Information) 112 Firms were divided into 'protected' and 'unprotected' establishments, according to the urgency of the work they were doing. **1956** J. C. SWAYNE *Conc. Gloss. Geogr. Terms* 114 *Protected state*, a territory, e.g. Brunei, Kuwait, under a ruler who receives the protection of another state. The protecting state controls foreign affairs, but has no jurisdiction over internal matters. **1968** 'C. AIRD' *Henrietta Who?* vii. 64 You're a protected tenant... No one can make you leave. **1975** 'J. BELL' *Victim* i. 12, I took in my second lot of tenants. Protected tenure. **1978** *Country Life* 20 July 148/3 Jersey has no statutory list of protected buildings as has existed in Britain for the last three decades.

b. Of a species whose survival is threatened: affected by laws preventing collecting, hunting, etc.

1930 J. S. HUXLEY *Bird-Watching & Bird Behaviour* vi. 115 The National Trust and the Royal Society for the Protection of Birds..are..paying watchers to see that protected birds are not shot or robbed of their eggs. **1936** *Discovery* Feb. 34/2 Any local authority may now, on application to the Ministry [of Agriculture] take the bird [*sc.* the little owl] off the protected list. **1959** E. F. LINSSEN *Beetles Brit. Isles* I. 156 In an effort not to bring about its [*sc.* the Great Silver Beetle's] total destruction, naturalists refrain from publishing records regarding its distribution... It should be treated as a 'protected' species and left alone. **1976** *Hortus Third* (L. H. Bailey Hortorium) 798/1 In most cases it is better to leave these plants to live where they are native and protected than to move them to gardens. **1978** *Vole* Dec. 18/1 It seemed like every damn animal on this planet should be a protected species.

protectee (prəʊtɛk'tiː). [f. PROTECT *v.* + -EE.] One who is under protection. *spec.* **a.** A protégé. **†b.** In 16–17th c., An Irishman who had accepted the protection of the English government (*obs.*). **c.** *Pol. Econ.* A manufacturer or merchant whose trade is protected.

1602 in Moryson *Itin.* (1617) II. 238 By prey-beeues gotten from the Rebels, and good numbers had of the protectees,..we haue vsed a great kind of sparing of the victuals in the store. **1633** T. STAFFORD *Pac. Hib.* I. xiii. (1810) 147 If the Protectees had meant in their hearts as they professed with their tongues. **1807** W. TAYLOR in Robberds *Mem.* II. 198 Your protectee, White, was clerk to my cousin. **1894** J. S. MORTON in *Forum* (U.S.) June, Protection.. compels him [the farmer] to be always the chained customer of the protectee.

protecter: see PROTECTOR.

pro'tectful, *a. nonce-wd.* [f. PROTECT *v.* + -FUL.] Careful to protect.

1883 G. H. BOUGHTON in *Harper's Mag.* Apr. 696/1 They are more proud and protectful of them than in most..Dutch towns.

pro'tectible, *a. rare*$^{-1}$. [f. PROTECT *v.* + -IBLE.] Capable of being protected.

1858 CARLYLE *Fredk. Gt.* IX. iii. (1872) III. 89 Not mere fanatic mystics..protectible by no Treaty.

protecting (prəʊ'tɛktɪŋ), *ppl. a.* [f. PROTECT *v.* + -ING[2].] **a.** That protects; preserving or shielding from harm or danger; extending patronage.

*c*1586 C'TESS PEMBROKE *Ps.* LXI. iii, To thy wings protecting shade My self I carry will. **1617** MORYSON *Itin.* I. 194 Saint Denis (the Protecting Saint of the French). **1785** *Daily Universal Reg.* 1 Jan. 2/3 The Protecting Duties, so generally called for in Ireland. **1818** COBBETT *Pol. Reg.* XXXIII. 521 Say, whether there be any protecting law for the people. **1820** *Ann. Reg.* 73/2 The American timber being of an inferior quality to that from the Baltic, required a protecting duty. **1821** in Bischoff *Woollen Manuf.* (1842) II. 18 Lord Milton and Mr. Wortley both conceive, that a protecting duty of sixpence per lb. on the wool exported will be conceded to the manufacturers if required. **1879** HARLAN *Eyesight* vii. 96 Protecting glasses are not worn nearly so much as they should be.

b. *spec.* in *Chem.*, applied to a group introduced into a molecule in order to protect a feature of that molecule in a reaction. (Cf. PROTECT *v.* 5 a.)

1947 *Nature* 12 Apr. 500/1 The use of another protecting unit easily removed by hydrolysis in combination with the carbobenzoxy method would considerably extend the use of the latter. **1952** L. J. DESHA *Org. Chem.* (ed. 2) xiii. 246 Finally, the protecting acetyl group is removed by hydrolysis. **1968** I. L. FINAR *Org. Chem.* (ed. 4) II. xiii. 584 This enamine can react with another amino-acid, and the protecting group is removed by mild bromination.

Hence **pro'tectingly** *adv.*; **pro'tectingness**.

1828 *Blackw. Mag.* XXIV. 49 One of Blackie's hands is protectingly placed across her neck. **1869** MISS MULOCK *Woman's Kingd.* II. 238 This little..child hovered about her handsome mother with a tender protectingness rather amusing. **1881** MISS BRADDON *Asph.* III. 165 Edgar, drawing protectingly near her, as they turned a sharp corner.

protection (prəʊ'tɛkʃən). Also 4 prott-, 4–5 proteccioun(e, -ione, 5–6 -ion, -yon, (4 -texcion, 6 -texion), 6 protectione, -ioun. [ME. a. F. *protection* (12–13th c.), ad. late L. *prōtectiōn-em*, n. of action f. *prōteg-ĕre* to PROTECT.]

1. a. The action of protecting; the fact or condition of being protected; shelter, defence, or preservation from harm, danger, or evil; patronage, tutelage.

*c*1375 *Sc. Leg. Saints* iii. (*Andreas*) 943, I can fynd place na-quhare, þat to me sa gaynand ware, as vndir ȝour proteccione. **1387–8** T. USK *Test. Love* III. i. (Skeat) I. 122 And ye innocence..safely might inhabyte by protexcion of safe conducte. **1453** *Rolls of Parlt.* V. 267/1 That everyche other persone..stand and be putte oute of youre protection. *c*1489 CAXTON *Sonnes of Aymon* xvi. 388, I leve this castel in your proteccyon & sauff garde. **1596** SHAKS. *Merch. V.* v. i. 235 Be well aduis'd How you doe leaue me to mine owne protection. **1651** HOBBES *Leviath.* II. xxvii. 152 When there is no such Power, there is no protection to be had from the Law. **1795** BURKE *Corr.* (1844) IV. 313 Ireland, constitutionally, is independent; politically, she can never be so. It is a struggle against nature. She must be protected, and there is no protection to be found for her, but either from France or England. **1809** *Proclam.* 2 Oct. in Hertslet *St. Pa.* III. 251 *note*, We present ourselves to you, Inhabitants of Cephalonia, not as Invaders, with views of conquest, but as Allies who hold forth to you the advantages of British protection. **1809** ROLAND *Fencing* p. vii, Offering the present Work to your kind protection. **1879** LUBBOCK *Sci. Lect.* ii. 45 The prevailing color of caterpillars is green, like that of leaves. The value of this to the young insect, the protection it affords, are obvious.

b. *euphem.* The keeping of a concubine or mistress in a separate establishment.

1677 H. SAVILE in *12th Rep. Hist. MSS. Comm.* App. v. 43 One Mrs. Johnson a lady of pleasure under his Lordship's protection. **1809** WILBERFORCE *Sp. Ho. Com.* 15 Mar. in Cobbett *Parl. Deb.* XIII. 590 That which used to be called 'adultery', was now only 'living under protection'. **1874** J. HATTON *Clytie* (ed. 10) 171 While she was living under his lordship's protection at Gloucester Gate.

c. Freedom from molestation obtained by paying money to a person who threatens violence or retribution if payment is not made; hence protection money itself. Also in other extended uses.

1860 [implied at *protection-rent* below]. **1903** *Independent* 15 Jan. 148/2 I'm sure that no one man knows all ends of this business of 'protection'. **1930** *Economist* 25 Oct. 754/1 A gangster would take it upon himself, say, to organise the selling of fish in one district in Chicago... The fishmonger who did not care for protection would find his shop bombed. **1938** G. GREENE *Brighton Rock* II. i. 78 I've got protection. You be careful. **1938** F. D. SHARPE *Sharpe of Flying Squad* xix. 202 A man offered to sell 'protection' to the bookmakers —at a price. **1962** D. FRANCIS *Dead Cert* ix. 106, I..asked the owners straight out if they were paying protection. **1977** 'W. HAGGARD' *Poison People* III. iv. 123 A man whose prosperous business had kicked at increasing demands for protection and had therefore finally gone to the wall.

d. An attempt to preserve certain animals, plants, or undisturbed areas of land by enforcing rules governing access, collecting, hunting, etc.

1880 *Act 43 & 44 Vict.* c. 35 It is expedient to provide for the protection of wild birds of the United Kingdom during the breeding season. **1894** W. H. HUDSON *Lost Brit. Birds* 1 It was thought best to leave out any species represented by at least three or four pairs that have some measure of protection afforded to them when breeding. **1895** G. S. ANDERSON in Roosevelt & Grinsell *Hunting in Many Lands* 377 (*heading*) Protection of the Yellowstone National Park. **1930** J. S. HUXLEY *Bird-Watching & Bird Behaviour* vi. 115 Protection has brought the bittern back to breed and boom in Norfolk. **1936** *Discovery* Sept. 293/1 From time to time the moose is over-hunted in some districts, but after a few years' protection they come back again. **1952** H. L. EDLIN *Changing Wild Life of Brit.* v. 71 The Harriers, typical hawks of the marshes, became very rare, but under protection a few continue to nest. **1969** F. N. HEPPER in J. Fisher et al. *Red. Bk.* 360/2 The I.U.C.N. itself has taken the principal lead in this field by initiating a scheme for the protection of plant species.

e. *Electr. Engin.* The action or result of PROTECT *v.* 4 c.

1890 SLINGO & BROOKER *Electr. Engin.* xvii. 725 The way in which it [*sc.* the cut-out] affords this protection is by automatically disconnecting the circuit when the current.. exceeds a certain predetermined limit. **1920** *Whittaker's Electr. Engineer's Pocket-Bk* (ed. 4) 428 Merz-Price protection may operate by a balance of voltages or a balance of currents. The former is used for the protection of cables, and the latter for the protection of transformers and alternators. **1962** *Newnes Conc. Encycl. Electr. Engin.* 612/1 The fuse forms the basis of most small, simple distribution-system protection, combining overcurrent protection and fault isolation. **1977** R. W. SMEATON *Switchgear & Control Handbk.* xxvi. 27 The proper choice of protection is based on equipment size, application reliability, shutdowns, probability of faults, and economics.

f. *Chem.* The action of PROTECT *v.* 5 a and b.

1909 J. ALEXANDER tr. *Zsigmondy's Colloids & Ultramicroscope* xviii. 185 The origin of the protection of the gold can be most simply explained by the assumption that specific attractive forces bring about a union of the ultramicrons of metal and protective colloid. **1939** *Thorpe's Dict. Appl. Chem.* (ed. 4) III. 287/1 The protection of sols is of great importance and has been practised empirically since ancient times. **1947** *Nature* 12 Apr. 500/1 The use of the carbobenzoxy reagent for protection of amino-groups in the course of peptide synthesis has..some limitations. **1951** I. L. FINAR *Org. Chem.* I. xii. 215 'Protection' of the double bond is conveniently carried out by the addition of bromine which is subsequently removed by zinc dust in methanolic solution. **1958** J. W. MULLIN in Cremer & Davies *Chem. Engin. Pract.* VI. xi. 459 Protection is effected by a number of lyophilic molecules which envelop a lyophobic particle and cover it with a monomolecular layer.

g. *Bridge.* (See quot. 1967.)

1952 I. MACLEOD *Bridge* vii. 88 Naturally, if there is an element of protection about your bid,..partner will realize that you may be quite a bit weaker. **1958** *Listener* 30 Oct. 709/3 This is a situation in which I cannot look for protection. **1967** *Bridge Players' Encycl.* 393/2 *Protection*, reopening with a bid or double when the opposing bidding has stopped at a low level.

h. *Mountaineering.* (See quot. 1971.)

1966 C. BONNINGTON *I chose to Climb* iii. 46 There was no protection and it was now necessary to pivot round on one's toes to grasp the smooth, square-cut edge of the bulge. **1971** —— *Annapurna South Face* Gloss. 323 *Protection*, quantity and quality of running belays used to make a pitch safe to lead.

2. A thing or person that protects.

1388 WYCLIF *Prol.* 33 It is a comyn proteccioun ȝens persecuscioun of prelatis and of summe lordis. *c* **1410** HOCCLEVE *Mother of God* 120 Be yee oure help and our proteccioun. **1552** ABP. HAMILTON *Catech.* (1884) 38 Our singular defence and protectioun. **1750** GRAY *Long Story* 96 His quiver and his laurel 'Gainst four such eyes were no protection. **1823** F. CLISSOLD *Ascent Mt. Blanc* 17 We all put on our veils, as a protection from the heat and light.

3. A writing or document that guarantees protection, exemption, or immunity to the person specified in it; a safe-conduct, passport, pass; †*esp.* (also, ***letter of protection***) a writing issued by the king granting immunity from arrest or lawsuit to one engaged in his service, or going abroad with his cognizance (*obs.*). In U.S. a certificate of American citizenship issued by the customs authorities to seamen.

[**1312** *Rolls of Parlt.* I. 286/1 Par Protections graunteez as gentz qe se feignent d'aler en service le Roi.] *c* **1450** *Godstow Reg.* 665 A proteccion of kyng Richard, worde by worde, after the proteccion of kyng henry afore I-writte. *a* **1500** in Arnolde *Chron.* (1811) 40 That our protecions..to ani persones to be made and graunted wᵗ vs to gon and dwellen in our viage..from hensforth shul not be allowed in plees of dett for vytayles..bought vpon yᵉ viage, wherof in such proteccions mencion befallith to be made. **1502–3** *Plumpton Corr.* (Camden) 174 It hath pleased the Kings highnes to grant unto your father his letter of protexion. **1595** *Expos. Terms Law* 150b, *Protection* is a writ, and it lyeth where that a man will passe ouer the Sea in the kings seruice, then..by this writ hee shall be quit of all manner of plees between him & any other person, except plees of dower [etc.]. **1607** COWELL *Interpr.* s.v., *Protection*..in the speciall signification is vsed for an exemption, or an immunitie giuen by the King to a person against suites in lawe, or other vexations, vpon reasonable causes him there-unto moouing. **1658–9** *Burton's Diary* (1828) IV. 1 Moved that the speaker sign protections for such persons as are called before the Committee for inspecting Treasury and Revenue. **1775** DE LOLME *Eng. Const.* II. xvi. (1784) 244 Having been detected in selling protections. **1897** KIPLING *Day's Work* (1898) 119 Jan Chinn never broke a protection spoken or written on paper.

4. *Pol. Econ.* The theory or system of fostering or developing home industries by protecting them from the competition of foreign productions, the importation of these being checked or discouraged by the imposition of duties or otherwise.

1789 *Deb. Congress U.S.* 15 Apr. (1834) 150 He conceived it the duty of the committee to pay as much respect to the encouragement and protection of husbandry..as they did to manufactures. **1820** *Hansard Lords* 26 May 579 Let your lordships consider..what would be the effect..if the existing system of protection were abolished, and a fixed duty..were substituted. **1828** MᶜCULLOCH *Adam Smith's W.N.* Notes 364 Without entitling them to a protection from foreign competition. **1830** GEN. P. THOMPSON *Exerc.* (1842) I. 194 Suppose then that every individual in the community was a producer of some kind, and that every one had a 'protection' upon his particular trade. **1838** C. P. VILLIERS 15 Mar. in *Free Trade Speeches* (1883) I. i. 7 What is the principle of the Corn Laws? I believe that I adopt the phrase which is current in reply when I say that it is Protection—Protection of the landed interest. **1841** MIALL in *Nonconf.* I. 228 Protection means shutting out the best chapman and the best food. **1875** T. HILL *True Ord. Stud.* 127 Earnest debates..concerning protection and free trade. **1881** *Oracle* 12 Nov. 311 Protection means the taxing of commodities imported from foreign countries, so that home manufacturers or producers may be protected from being undersold..by foreign manufacturers or producers. **1904** A. J. BALFOUR *Sp. at Edin.* in *Times* 4 Oct. 4/3 The object of protection is to encourage home industries. The means by which it attains that object is by the manipulation of a fiscal system to raise home prices.

5. *attrib.* and *Comb.* Of, pertaining to, or for protection, as ***protection fee, grant, plate, wall, work***; ***protection-burdened*** adj.; **protection act**, an act of parliament for the protection of classes of persons, of wild birds, etc.; **protection forest**, a forest whose purpose is to provide a dense cover of vegetation which helps to inhibit erosion and conserve water; **protection money**, money paid to secure protection (sense 1 c); **protection racket**, an illegal scheme for the levying of protection money; † **protection rent** = *protection money*.

1881 W. E. FORSTER *Let. to Gladstone* 1 Nov., in Reid *Life* (1888) II. viii. 361 We made up our minds to arrest the leaders under the *Protection Act. **1888** REID *Ibid.* II. vii. 306 The passing of the Protection Act [1881] had been succeeded by a lull in the progress of the outrages in Ireland. **1899** *Westm. Gaz.* 18 Dec. 2/3 We are afraid that no number of orders under the Wild Birds Protection Act would render them safe. **1908** *Daily Chron.* 11 May 1/7 Contrast between social reform possibilities in Free Trade Britain and *Protection-burdened Germany. **1820** W. TOOKE tr. *Lucian* I. 514 They never once think of paying their *protection-fees. **1902** *Westm. Gaz.* 10 July 9/1 A large number of the claims so abandoned..were not worth protection fees. **1889** W. SCHLICH *Man. Forestry* I. i. 47 Already in the middle ages so-called '*Protection Forests' existed. **1928** R. S. TROUP *Silvicultural Syst.* ix. 116 To afford protection against erosion, landslips, and avalanches in mountainous regions, to conserve the water-supply in catchment areas and to prevent floods; forests maintained for such purposes are termed 'protection forests'. **1974** LONGMAN & JANÍK *Trop. Forest* vi. 123 Forest reserves are also particularly appropriate in steep terrain to prevent erosion and rapid run-off of water in catchment areas, and these have been recognised for many years as 'protection forests'. **1923** *Nation* (N.Y.) 24 Oct. 449 The men that help unload get $1 a case, and the revenue officers $2 *protection money. **1934** R. GRAVES *I, Claudius* xx. 289 Shopkeepers in the town and farmers in the country had to pay secret 'protection money' to the local captains; if they refused to pay there would be a raid at night by masked men, their house would be burned down and their families murdered. **1972** T. LILLEY *'K' Section* vi. 29 The opium dens and brothels closed. The coffee-shops that now refused to pay protection money. **1937** E. AMBLER *Uncommon Danger* x. 149 His business then was intimidating shopkeepers—the '*protection racket', as it is called now in America. **1954** T. S. ELIOT *Confidential Clerk* II. 62 Colby doesn't need your protection racket So far as I'm concerned. **1976** D. DAICHES in D. Villiers *Next Year in Jerusalem* 275 The characteristics of a Chicago gangster tale: a leader organizing a protection racket, violent measures taken against those who refuse protection money. **1860** *Leisure Hour* 19 July 460/2 In return for black-mail or *protection-rent, they shared the property of those who paid it, and engaged to defend it from aggressions. **1901** *Westm. Gaz.* 21 Mar. 5/2 The cliff *protection works..have been seriously damaged by the gale.

Hence **pro'tectional** *a.*, of or pertaining to protection; **pro'tectionary**, that which provides protection; **pro'tectionate** *a.*, of or pertaining to the economic theory of protection: = PROTECTIONIST *a.*; *sb.* = PROTECTORATE *sb.*

1888 J. T. GULICK in *Linn. Soc. Jrnl., Zool.* XX. 226 *Protectional Segregation is Segregation from the use of different methods of protection against adverse influences in the environment. **1900** MORLEY *Cromwell* IV. i. 277 The protectional establishment of national commerce. **1653** URQUHART *Rabelais* II. xi, The bankrupt *Protectionaries of five yeares respit. **1853** *Blackw. Mag.* LXXIII. 764 What has become of all the *Protectionate croaking about low prices? **1882** *Contemp. Rev.* Jan. 32 A military occupation of, or British Protectionate over, Egypt.

protectionism (prəʊ'tɛkʃənɪz(ə)m). [f. prec. + -ISM. Cf. F. *protectionnisme* (? from Eng.).] The economic doctrine of protection; the policy or system of protection.

1852 *Punch* 31 July 53/1 If a steam-boat does accidentally 'put in' with a few voyagers, it is met, in the first place, by a spirit of Protectionism and high prices in the shape of pier dues. **1858** *Sat. Rev.* 20 Nov. 496/1 Up to the moment when Free-trade triumphed there remained a stolid mass of Protectionism against which argument was hopeless. **1878** *N. Amer. Rev.* CXXVII. 179 The leanings of America towards protectionism. **1889** *Times* 27 Nov. 5/4 Italy is the first Continental country which has had the courage to break with protectionism. **1895** *Ibid.* 10 Jan. 9/4 In the struggle against old-world protectionism..Mr. Villiers did admirable work in the House of Commons. **1945** K. R. POPPER *Open Society* I. vi. 97 What I demand from the state is protection..for my own freedom and for other people's. ..[This] view..may be called 'protectionism'. **1955** *Times* 4 June 5/1 The Canadian Government's decision to amend the Customs tariff—the changes are due to come into effect today—has a suggestion of protectionism. **1969** *Listener* 14 Aug. 201/1 This protectionism..was originally intended to stave off the intrusions of the American cinema. **1977** *Time* 30 May 51/1 In times of recession, nations inevitably turn toward protectionism as a means of shielding jobs from the threat of foreign goods.

protectionist (prəʊ'tɛkʃənɪst), *sb.* (*a.*) [f. as prec. + -IST. Cf. mod.F. *protectionniste.*] One who supports the economic theory or system of protection; one who advocates the protection of domestic industries from foreign competition by the imposition of duties on imports, or by other means.

1844 LD. FITZWILLIAM in G. Pryme *Autobiog.* (1870) 306 *Protectionists*, as they are now called, though I do not think it a good name to have given them, as I fear it will be rather a popular title. **1845** *Ann. Rept. U.S. Treasury* 483 The protectionist says, Tax us on, tax us on, until we have a home market for all our agricultural produce. **1849** COBDEN *Speeches* 34 If there be protectionists who think that the old protection principle can be restored, I am willing that they should vote against me on this occasion. **1876** FAWCETT *Pol. Econ.* (ed. 5) III. vii. 393 In America and Australia the great body of the working men are ardent protectionists. **1904** A. J. BALFOUR *Sp. at Edin.* in *Times* 4 Oct. 4/3, I now proceed to say that I individually am not a protectionist... The Conservative party, indeed, after the Peelite split, was a protectionist party. It was based upon protection.

B. as *adj.* Favouring or supporting protection.

1846 SIR R. PEEL *Speech* 27 Jan. (Flügel) My plan will meet the approval of neither the freetrade nor the protectionist party. **1861** MAY *Const. Hist.* (1863) II. viii. 72 Sir Robert Peel..ventured in the face of a protectionist Parliament, wholly to abandon the policy of protection. **1865** *Daily Tel.* 28 Nov. 6/4 The repeal of protectionist duties is among the wisest measures embraced in our statute book. **1880** DISRAELI *Endym.* III. xv. 153 The protectionist ministry were to remain in office, and to repeal the corn laws.

protectionize (prəʊ'tɛkʃənaɪz), *v.* [f. as prec. + -IZE.] *trans.* To render protectionist; to convert to protectionism.

1905 *Westm. Gaz.* 7 Sept. 1/3 Mr. Chamberlain..is confident of his ability to complete in Opposition the task of Protectionising the Unionist Party.

protective (prəʊ'tɛktɪv), *a.* (*sb.*) [f. PROTECT *v.* + -IVE. Cf. med.L. *prōtectīvus*:

a **1259** MATTH. PARIS *Cron. Maiora* anno 1250, Manus regis..que utique manus defensiva esse tenetur et protectiva.]

A. *adj.* **1. a.** Having the quality or character of protecting; tending to protect; defensive; preservative.

1661 FELTHAM *Resolves* II. lix. (ed. 8) 310 [The] accidents of Life deny us any safety, but what we have from the favour of protective Providence. **1728–46** THOMSON *Spring* 781 The stately-sailing swan..Bears forward fierce, and guards his osier-isle, Protective of his young. **1793** SMEATON *Edystone L.* §328 To apply the protective coat, before any rust could be formed. **1833** LAMB *Let. to Serjeant Talfourd* Feb., Those canvas-sleeves protective from ink. **1871** DARWIN *Desc. Man* II. xvi. 224 There are twenty-six species ..which manifestly have had their plumage coloured in a protective manner. *a* **1909** *Mod.* Examples of protective colouring are numerous among insects. **1938** *Encycl. Brit. Bk. of Year* 467/1 The term 'protective foods' was originally applied to milk and green leaf vegetables, because they made good the deficiencies commonly found in human diets... It has come to include..foodstuffs..which protect the body against disturbance in structure or function of its organs and parts..which protect, in short, against 'disease'. **1940** *Topeka* (Kansas) *State Jrnl.* 19 Apr. 1/8 De Geer in his broadcast declared The Netherlands would resist with arms any attempt by a foreign power to extend protective help to her. **1944** J. S. HUXLEY *On living in Revol.* xiii. 139 Agriculture..can be devoted mainly to providing protective foodstuffs. **1955** *Gloss. Terms Radiol.* (*B.S.I.*) 67 *Protective material*, material which is used to provide protection against ionizing radiation. **1974** *Times* 2 Feb. 18/7 The Inland Revenue accepts that in certain trades the employee has to supply his own tools, protective clothing, etc. *a* **1977** *Harrison Mayer Ltd. Catal.* 4/1 Always wear suitable protective clothing.

b. ***protective coloration, colouring***, an animal's colouring that blends with its habitat, enabling it to conceal itself. Also *fig.*

1892 F. E. BEDDARD *Animal Coloration* iii. 86 A South American bittern..affords an excellent instance of the advantages which result from a protective coloration. **1918** G. H. THAYER *Concealing-Coloration in Animal Kingdom* ii. 25 We have..Obliterative Coloration, and Mimicry, as the two main principles of Protective Coloration. **1934** *Proc. Nat. Acad. Sci. Washington* XX. 559 (*heading*) Does protective coloration protect? **1937** KOESTLER *Spanish Testament* II. 372, I was able to observe..what direct biological forces this process of protective coloration exerts. Guilty or innocent, the prisoner changes form and colour, and assumes the mould that most easily enables him to secure a maximum of those minimal advantages possible within the framework of the prison system. **1941** A. CHRISTIE *Evil under Sun* x. 183 Protective colouring is your line. Remain rigidly nonactive and fade into the background! **1949** N. MITFORD *Love in Cold Climate* iii. 30 As far as my fellow guests were concerned, I was clearly endowed with protective colouring;..I might just as well not have been there at all. **1957** T. W. KIRKPATRICK *Insect Life in Tropics* viii. 214 This instance of protective coloration is unlike most others. **1977** B. COLLOMS *Victorian Country Parsons* xi. 211 To avoid trouble he became over-anxious to please and grew adept at assuming protective colouration [*sic*]. **1979** *Books & Bookmen* Jan. 16/1 One strand of English (and American) poetry, the strand that reflects nineteenth-century bourgeois values at their most unequivocal, can only survive by adopting the protective colouring of a game.

c. *Electr. Engin.* Providing protection against too high a current or voltage.

1896 R. ROBB *Electric Wiring* v. 171 All conductors.. must be provided near the point of entrance to the building with some protective device which will operate to shunt the instruments in case of a dangerous rise in potential, and will open the circuit and arrest an abnormal current flow. **1922** [see BIAS *v.* 5]. **1962** *Newnes Conc. Encycl. Electr. Engin.* 612/1 A great variety of protective equipment is marketed for distribution systems because of its influence on capital expenditure on such items as switchgear. **1976** *Billings* (Montana) *Gaz.* 6 July 3-D/1 A protective relay adjacent to a Kemmerer, Wyo., power plant was blamed Monday for the Fourth of July electrical black-out that darkened most of Utah. **1978** *Gramophone* Apr. 1796/3 There is also a mains voltage adjuster and twin 2.5A protective mains fuses.

2. *Pol. Econ.* **a.** Of or relating to the economic doctrine or system of protection.

1820 *Ann. Reg.* 771/1 The protective or restrictive system. **1829** *Edin. Rev.* L. 73 Such was the state of the silk trade under the protective system. **1876** FAWCETT *Pol. Econ.* (ed. 5) III. vii. 394 Few can now be found in England, who would favour the re-imposition of protective duties. **1904** A. J. BALFOUR *Sp. at Edin.* in *Times* 4 Oct. 4/3 A Protective policy, as I understand it, is a policy which aims at supporting or creating home industries by raising home prices. The raising of prices is a necessary step towards the encouragement of an industry under a Protective system.

b. in comb., as ***protective-prohibitive.***

1906 *Month* Jan. 38 By mitigating the protective-prohibitive system he [Canning] promoted commerce.

c. ***protective arrest, custody***, the detention (of a person) either allegedly or truly for his own protection.

[**1933** R. BERNAYS *Special Correspondent* xliii. 222 Jews, Socialists, pacifists, Liberals—anyone who has engaged in political agitation or is believed to be hostile to the New Germany—are incarcerated without trial and for an indefinite period. The German name is *Schutzhaft* (protective detention), the idea being that they are asylums ..for men who otherwise might suffer grievous bodily harm for their political opinions at the hands of their infuriated countrymen.] **1935** S. LEWIS *It can't happen Here* xv. 154 It was blandly explained..that they were merely being safeguarded. Sarason did not use the phrase 'protective arrest'. **1936** *Sun* (Baltimore) 17 Feb. 8/3 He is declared to have been placed under protective custody. Now this phrase is a deliberate steal from the vocabulary of Nazi Germany, its purpose being to cast a pall of dignity around the proceeding when Brown Shirts take an opponent into a Brown House for the purpose of beating him with a rubber hose. *Ibid.*, 'Protective arrest' sounds better than 'ganging up' and gives the impression that the State in its beneficent wisdom is protecting somebody when the only need for protection is protection against the protectors. **1940** *Topeka* (Kansas) *State Jrnl.* 8 May 3/1 When I was asked to take some letters..I agreed readily thinking they might be an open sesame for sleeping quarters. They were—under British 'protective arrest' in Spillum. **1940** C. V. WEDGWOOD *William the Silent* vii. 192 He was even forced to take monks and priests into protective custody—and it really was protective custody, though the catholics represented it as plain imprisonment. **1947** P. WOODRUFF *Wild Sweet Witch* 7 The Deputy Commissioner of the day did take a man into protective custody to prove he was not the panther. **1964** N. MARSH *Dead Water* iii. 79, I wish I could put you under protective custody. **1973** 'D. SHANNON' *No Holiday for Crime* viii. 128 Pat's reformed pusher ready to tell all sitting safe in protective custody.

3. *Chem.* **a.** Having the quality or property of protecting a sol (cf. PROTECT *v.* 5 b); *spec.* in ***protective colloid***, a lyophilic colloid whose presence in small quantities protects a lyophobic sol.

1906 *Jrnl. Soc. Chem. Industry* 31 May 484/1 To insure the satisfactory production of bright deposits it is in all cases essential to employ clear, well filtered solutions. The authors explain the observed phenomena by supposing that the bright deposit is formed by causing the metal to retain its amorphous condition and preventing it from becoming crystalline. The mutual protective effect of colloids upon one another..is probably the chief factor. **1909** J. ALEXANDER tr. *Zsigmondy's Colloids & Ultramicroscope* iii. 77 Lobry de Bruyn (1898), characterized gelatin jelly as a protective colloid (Schutzkolloid). **1939** *Thorpe's Dict. Appl. Chem.* (ed. 4) III. 287/1 Zsigmondy showed that the sharp colour change from red to blue displayed by gold sols under the influence of electrolytes could be used as a means of obtaining a quantitative comparison of the protective action of different colloids. **1950** E. K. FISCHER *Colloidal Dispersions* vi. 247 In the manufacture of colored pigments, protective colloids aid in keeping the particle size small. **1960** [see PEPTIZATION]. **1967** G. P. A. TURNER *Introd. Paint Chem.* xi. 160 If the protective colloids are not truly compatible with the film-former, gloss will be reduced and the film weakened.

b. = PROTECTING *ppl. a.* b.

1932 *Chem. Abstr.* XXVI. 5072 The method of synthesizing peptides which consists in stabilizing the amino group of 1 acid with a protective group R, then so altering the CO_2H group as to enable it to couple with a 2nd amino acid and removing the group R after the coupling has been effected. **1968** I. L. FINAR *Org. Chem.* (ed. 4) II. xiii. 582 Bergmann (1932) introduced carbobenzoxy chloride as an amino protective group, and this appears to be the most widely used method of protection.

B. *sb.* Anything employed to protect; e.g. in *Surgery*, carbolized oiled silk used for the protection of wounds. Also, a contraceptive sheath.

1875 H. C. WOOD *Therap.* (1879) 589 *Protectives*... Those materials used by the physician as external applications to exclude the air and to protect inflamed dermal or other tissues. **1885** CLODD *Myths & Dr.* I. ii. 18 The passage..to the use of charms as protectives against the evil-disposed. **1898** P. MANSON *Trop. Diseases* xxxi. 487 In dressing it is of importance that the raw surfaces be covered by some aseptic non-fibrous protective. **1971** *It* 2–16 June 23/3 (Advt.), Protectives by post:..Durex Gossamer Doz. 50p. **1977** *Lancet* 15 Oct. 811/1 Although the condom, or male protective, is marketed primarily as a method of contraception, some stress is laid both by the manufacturers and by the medical profession on its value as a prophylactic against sexually transmitted diseases.

pro'tectively, *adv.* [f. prec. + -LY².]

1. In a protective or protecting manner; by way of protection; so as to afford protection.

1839 *Blackw. Mag.* XLV. 682 Coachee bows protectively to the man of tickets. **1881** G. ALLEN *Vignettes fr. Nat.* iv. 37 Butterflies close their wings and display only the outer surface, which is imitatively and protectively coloured. **1898** *Westm. Gaz.* 5 Nov. 5/3 A race of protectively coloured mice that are found on a sandy island in the Bay of Dublin. **1899** *Harper's Mag.* Feb. 363 She held up a yellow telegram protectively in front of her.

2. *Pol. Econ.* So as to protect from competition; by protective imposts, etc.

1872–3 W. M. WILLIAMS *Sc. in Short Chapters* (1882) 231 Protectively nursed and sickly imitations of English manufactures. **1881** *Times* 3 June 9/5 To maintain..that the passenger duty operates protectively for the competing omnibus and especially for the tramcar traffic.

protectiveness (prəʊ'tɛktɪvnɪs). [f. as prec. + -NESS.] Protective quality, power, or function.

1847 MISS AGUILAR *Home Influence* III. i. 5 The caressing protectiveness of an elder for a younger. **1857** *Parl. Rep. Hist. Vaccination*, Evidence on the protectiveness of vaccination must now be statistical. **1891** T. HARDY *Tess* xxxvii, If he had entered with a pistol in his hand he would scarcely have disturbed her trust in his protectiveness.

protector (prəʊ'tɛktə(r)), *sb.* [ME. a. OF. *protectour* (14th c. in Hatz.-Darm.), mod.F. *protecteur*, ad. post-cl. L. *prōtector*, *-ōrem*, a protector, a body-guard, agent-n. f. *prōteg-ĕre* to PROTECT.]

1. a. One who protects, defends, or shields from injury or harm; a defender; a guardian, a patron.

cardinal protector, a cardinal who has charge of the interests of a country, or a religious order or college, at Rome. ***Protector of the Poor***, a term of respect formerly used in British India, as by Indian servants to their masters.

c **1375** *Sc. Leg. Saints* vi. (*Thomas*) 21 To þa fel yndis hald þi way; for þi protectour sal I be. **1484** CAXTON *Fables of Æsop* III. xiii, The wulues kyld the dogges whiche were capytayns and protectours of the sheep. *a* **1586** SIDNEY *Ps.* XLIII. i, Judg me, And protector bee Of my cause. **1670** G. H. *Hist. Cardinals* I. II. 62 The Cardinals Protectors of the several orders about Rome. **1738** WESLEY *Ps.* III. iii, By my kind Protector kept, Safe I laid me down and slept. **1839** THIRLWALL *Greece* xlvi. VI. 61 He had indeed been a useful ally: but he was something more; he was a powerful protector. **1890** KIPLING in *Macmillan's Mag.* June 149/2 The news does not come from my mouth, Protector of the Poor. **1894** —— *Jungle Bk.* 165 'Was it to help thee steal green corn?..'Not green corn, Protector of the Poor—melons', said Little Toomai. **1901** in *Daily Chron.* 23 Nov. 6/5 It will give him [the King] great satisfaction to assume and bear the honorary title of Protector of the University of Wales. **1910** *Blackw. Mag.* Feb. 167 They sent him to Lord Caerlaverock, for the ex-viceroy loved to be treated as a kind of consul-general for India. But this Protector of the Poor proved a broken reed. **1911** F. H. BURNETT *Secret Garden* iv. 25 The native servants..in India..called them [*sc.* their masters] 'protector of the poor' and names of that sort. **1952** J. MASTERS *Deceivers* ix. 99 Protector of the Poor, at first cockcrow the villain called for a lotah for purposes of nature.

b. A thing that protects; a guard; *esp.* a device or contrivance serving to prevent injury to or from something, the object being often indicated by a prefixed word; e.g. *chest-protector*, *cuff-protector*, *ear-protector*, *point-protector* (for a pencil), etc.

1849 NOAD *Electricity* (ed. 3) 140 When the metallic protector was from $\frac{1}{90}$ to $\frac{1}{150}$, there was no corrosion or decay of the copper. **1860** TYNDALL *Glac.* II. viii. 265 Such a mass is..a protector of the ice beneath it. **1867** G. H. SELKIRK *Guide to Cricket Ground* ii. 33 *Pads*, leg guards and protectors for the abdomen. **1898** *Sci. Abstr.* I. 240 (*heading*) Telephone line protectors. **1902** *Westm. Gaz.* 1 Dec. 8/3 The second item was a head protector. **1904** *Daily Chron.* 8 Dec. 5/4 Footprints showing the marks of boot-protectors were found in the garden. **1906** *Westm. Gaz.* 4 Jan. 5/2 The boots had been mended with English protectors. **1922** *Lillywhites' Sports Requisites* 7 Wicket-keeping Sundries. Palmer's Abdominal Protectors. **1934** *Jrnl. Inst. Electr. Engineers* LXXIV. 236/2 Protectors are connected to every open-wire Post Office line.

attrib. **1901** *Daily News* 3 Jan. 6/4 Venturing outside upon the framework between the protector arms.

c. *Rom. Antiq.* A member of the life-guard or body-guard. *rare*⁻¹.

1781 GIBBON *Decl. & F.* xvii. II. 57 From the seven schools two companies of horse and foot were selected, of the protectors, whose advantageous station was the hope and reward of the most deserving soldiers.

d. (*a*) A man who keeps a mistress; (*b*) a man who looks after a prostitute in return for her earnings, a pimp. Cf. PROTECTION 1 b.

1905 [see *man's woman* s.v. MAN *sb.* 21]. **1938** F. D. SHARPE *Sharpe of Flying Squad* x. 116 Prostitutes and their protectors were roped into the stations by the dozen. **1954** *Britannica Bk. of Year* 637/2 A group of criminals making a living from organized prostitution was referred to as a Vice-Ring, the leader of such a group being a Vice-Chief..or—with reference to the prostitutes controlled by him—a Protector.

e. One by whom protection from harassment is assured or who collects protection money. Cf. PROTECTION 1 c.

1933 H. G. WELLS *Shape of Things to Come* II. 153 The man who wanted to be left alone in peace..was pressed to pay his tribute to the gang. Or he would not be left in peace. And even if his particular 'protectors' left him in peace, there might still be other gangs about for whom they disavowed responsibility and with whom he had to make a separate deal. **1977** J. WAINWRIGHT *Nest of Rats* iii. 15, I was wise enough to choose my own 'protector'.

2. *Eng. Hist.* **a.** One in charge of the kingdom during the minority, absence, or incapacity of the sovereign; a regent.

1427 *Rolls of Parlt.* IV. 326/1 Yat ye be protectour and defendour of yis Lond, and so named and called. *c* **1450** *Brut* (E.E.T.S.) 431 The Duke of Gloucestre, to ben Protectour and deffendour of the Rewme. **1560** DAUS tr. *Sleidane's Comm.* 278 An honorable style [was] geuen him, that he should be called the Protectour of the kyng and his Realme. **1593** SHAKS. *2 Hen. VI*, I. ii. 56 My Lord Protector, 'tis his Highnes pleasure, You do prepare to ride vnto S. Albons. *a* **1658** CLEVELAND *Definition of Protector* Wks. (1687) 343 What's a Protector? He's a stately Thing, That Apes it in the Non-age of a King. **1670** PETTUS *Fodinæ Reg.* 15 John Duke of Bedford, Regent of France, and Protector of England. *a* **1771** GRAY *Corr.* (1843) 293 His great patron the protector, Humphry, Duke of Gloucester. **1863** H. COX *Instit.* III. iii. 623 The appointment of a protector, guardian, or regent, when the heir-apparent of the Crown has been very young.

b. The official title of the head of the executive during part of the period of the Commonwealth; in full ***Lord Protector of the Commonwealth***: borne by Oliver Cromwell 1653–8, and by his son Richard 1658–9.

1653 in *Acts & Ordin. Parl.* (1658) 275 From and after the six and twentieth day of December 1653 the Name, Style, Title and Teste of the Lord Protector..of the Commonwealth, of England, Scotland, and Ireland..shall be used. **1653–4** *Weekly Intelligencer* 14–21 Mar., The Privy Lodgings for his Highness the Lord Protector in Whitehall are now in readiness, as also the Lodgings for his Lady Protectoress. **1658** EVELYN *Diary* 22 Oct., Saw the superb funerall of the Protector. *a* **1674** CLARENDON *Hist. Reb.* XIV. §23 The Declaration of the Council of Officers was read, whereby Cromwell was made Protector. **1827** HALLAM *Const. Hist.* (1876) II. x. II. 244 Cromwell's assumption, therefore, of the title of Protector was a necessary and wholesome usurpation. **1849** MACAULAY *Hist. Eng.* I. I. 135 The kingly prerogatives were intrusted to a lord high protector..called not His Majesty but His Highness.

3. *Law.* ***protector of the settlement***: see quot. 1876.

1833 *Act 3 & 4 Will. IV*, c. 74 §22 The Person who shall be the Owner of the prior Estate, or the first of such prior Estates if more than One,..shall be the Protector of the Settlement so far as regards the Lands in which such prior Estate shall be subsisting. **1865** *Pall Mall G.* 20 Oct. 1 The renewed collision which is certain to take place between the Liberal and Conservative parties, now that 'the protector of the settlement', as the lawyers say, is gone, will pretty certainly produce the desire for Reform, if it does not now exist. **1876** DIGBY *Real Prop.* v. §2. 219 The Protector of the settlement is usually the tenant for life in possession; but the settlor of the lands may appoint in his place any number of persons not exceeding three to be together Protector during the continuance of the estates preceding the estate tail.

4. A rendering of L. *tutor* in college use.

1886 WILLIS & CLARK *Cambridge* I. Introd. 90 The earliest statutable recognition of stranger-students at Oxford is at Magdalen College (1479)... Waynflete's statute is copied at Corpus Christi College (1517) where the number of such students is limited to four, or six at the outside, and a person is named who is to be responsible for them, termed protector (*tutor*) [cf. Statutes of C.C.C. 1517, c. 34, quamdiu sint sub tutoribus et honeste se gerant].

Hence †**pro'tectordom** *Obs.*, a state under the rule of a Protector.

1660 FULLER *Mixt Contempl.* (1841) 227 We have been in twelve years a kingdom, commonwealth, protectordom, afterwards under an army, parliament, &c.

pro'tector, *v. nonce-wd.* [f. prec.] *trans.* **a.** To treat or deal with as Protector. **b.** To make or proclaim Protector.

1658–9 *Burton's Diary* (1828) III. 180 When the army see they are yours, they will be protectored by you. **1670** PENN *Truth Rescued fr. Impost.* 25 The then English Army was the remainder of those Souldiers, that not only subverted the Kings Forces, but Protector'd Oliver Crumwell.

protectoral (prəʊ'tɛktərəl), *a.* (*sb.*) [f. as prec. + -AL¹: cf. *doctoral*, *electoral*, *pastoral*. So F. *protectoral* (16th c. in Littré).] Of or pertaining to a protector, *esp.* in *Hist.* to the Protector of a kingdom or commonwealth.

1657 *Narr. Late Parlt.* 27 Less burthensome and chargable to the people then the instrument of Protectorall Government, or the present Government. **1798** W. TAYLOR in *Monthly Rev.* XXV. 503 This body, during the civil wars, and during the protectoral republic, fostered an excessive zeal for regal power. **1848** *Fraser's Mag.* XXXVIII. 244 This was the signal for the advance of troops by the Emperor of Russia in his protectoral character. **1885** *Athenæum* 22 Aug. 232 The notices of the Commonwealth and Protectoral taxation are good and trustworthy.

†**B.** *sb.* = PROTECTORATE *sb.* 1. *Obs. rare*⁻¹.

1661 J. DAVIES *Civil Warres* 366 With the dissolving of this Parliament was an Exit likewise given to the Protectorall.

protectorate (prəʊ'tɛktərət), *sb.* [f. PROTECTOR *sb.* + -ATE¹; cf. *doctorate*; so F. *protectorat* (18th c. in Hatz.-Darm.), = L. type **prōtectōrāt-us*.]

1. The office, position, or government of the Protector of a kingdom or state; the period of administration of a Protector; *spec.* in *Eng. Hist.* the period (1653–9) during which Oliver and Richard Cromwell held the title of Lord Protector of the Commonwealth.

1692 WOOD *Ath. Oxon.* II. *Fasti* 797 He [Richard Cromwell] being designed to be his Fathers successor in the Protectorate, was..sworn a Privy Counsellour. **1770** GUTHRIE *Geog. Hist. & Comm. Gram.* (1771) 314 During the continuance of his protectorate, he was perpetually distrest for money, to keep the wheels of his government going. **1836** H. COLERIDGE *North. Worthies* (1852) I. 18 The Short Parliament of 1658–9, summoned after the death of Oliver, during the brief Protectorate of Richard Cromwell. **1846** MᶜCULLOCH *Acc. Brit. Empire* (1854) II. 379 During the Protectorate the university [of Dublin] was nearly extinct, but was revived again,..according to its previous forms, at the Restoration.

2. The office, position, or function of a protector or guardian; protectorship, guardianship. In *Internat. Law*: **a.** originally, The relation of a strong to a weaker state to which it gives its protection. **b.** The relation of a suzerain to a vassal state; suzerainty. **c.** now *spec.* The relation of a European power to a territory inhabited by tribal groups lacking political organization, and not ranking among the nations as a state.

With a. cf. PROTECTION 1, quot. 1809; PROTECTED, quot. 1836. In sense c. the term acquired international recognition in the proceedings of the Berlin Conference of 1885. See also Ilbert *Govt. India* (1898) vii. 427, *Encycl. Laws Eng.* (1908) XII. 42.

1836 WHEATON *Elem. Internat. Law* 64 The city of Cracow in Poland, with its territory, was declared by the congress of Vienna to be a free, independent, and neutral state, under the protection of Russia, Austria, and Prussia. . . Its sovereignty still remains, except so far as it is affected by the protectorate which may be lawfully asserted over it in pursuance of the treaties of Vienna. **1844** *Times* 30 July 4/5 Queen Pomane [of Tahiti] had been forced to accept the 'Protectorate' of the French flag. **1845** S. AUSTIN *Ranke's Hist. Ref.* II. 387 The King of England, it was hoped, would accept the protectorate of the alliance. **1851** GALLENGA *Italy* i. 51 Not a word more was said about the high protectorate hitherto exercised by Austria on the minor Italian States. **1860** MOTLEY *Netherl.* (1868) I. ii. 64 To request England and France to assume a joint protectorate over the Netherlands. **1864** WOOLSEY *Introd. Internat. Law* App. II. (1879) 485 The seven Ionian islands—..Great Britain's abandonment of her protectorate having been accepted—are to form a part of the Greek monarchy. **1884** *Daily News* 18 Oct. 3/1 The setting up of a British protectorate over south-eastern New Guinea, as announced..a few days ago. **1885** tr. *Acte Générale Confer. Berlin* 26 Feb. in *Parl. Papers Eng.* (1886) XLVII. 110 In all parts of the territory..where no Power shall exercise rights of sovereignty or Protectorate, the International Navigation Commission of the Congo.. shall be charged with supervising the application of the principles proclaimed..by this Declaration.

3. A state or territory placed or taken under the protection of a superior power; *esp.* a protected territory inhabited by tribal peoples.

1860 E. B. ANDREWS in G. E. Metcalfe *Gt. Brit. & Ghana* (1964) 285/1 The Protectorate on this side of the Volta. **1871** *Act 34 Vict.* c. 8 Whereas the inhabitants of certain territories in Africa adjoining Her Majesty's settlements of Sierra Leone, Gambia, Gold Coast, and Lagos, and the adjacent protectorates. **1884** *Daily News* 18 Oct. 3/1 The coasts even of our new protectorate [in New Guinea] are incompletely known. **1889** *Pall Mall G.* 18 Nov. 5/2 H.M.S. Egeria has..just completed a remarkable cruise of annexation, formally declaring as protectorates of Great Britain no fewer than thirteen islands in the South Pacific. **1891** *Times* 9 Jan. 3/2 The missionaries appealed to the Governor of the Protectorate. **1899** C. W. C. OMAN *Eng. 19th Cent.* x. 256 The programme sketched out by Mr. Rhodes, of drawing a continuous chain of British protectorates from Cape Colony to the Nile valley. **1908** *Whitaker's Almanack* 557 The islands of Zanzibar and Pemba form a British Protectorate, and the East Africa Protectorate extends from the Umba to the river Juba. **1921** *Brit. Year Bk. Internat. Law 1921–2* 114 Virtually colonies; constitutionally foreign soil—that is the definition of 'protectorates': juridical monsters. **1923** *Publ. Permanent Court Internat. Justice* B. IV. 27 The extent of the powers of a protecting State in the territory of a protected State depends, first, upon the Treaties between the protecting State and the protected State establishing the Protectorate, and, secondly, upon the conditions under which the Protectorate has been recognised by third Powers as against whom there is an intention to rely on the provisions of these Treaties. **1955** *Sci. Amer.* Mar. 60/2 The protectorate borders on the vast jungle belt of central Africa in which yellow fever is endemic. **1961** L. VAN DER POST *Heart of Hunter* I. vii. 110 Although Lobatsi was in a British Protectorate the railway itself belonged to Southern Rhodesia.

4. *attrib.* (all in senses 2, 3), as ***protectorate force, form, idea, land, law, official, ordinance, regiment, system, troops***, etc.

1897 *Daily News* 16 Feb. 6/2 It was arranged that the Protectorate force..should occupy the next place in the marching order. *Ibid.* 19 Oct. 7/5 An extraordinary change ..in the Benin country owing to the energy of Sir Ralph Moor and the Protectorate officials. **1899** *Westm. Gaz.* 12 Apr. 5/2 A strong body of Protectorate troops has set out for the interior of Benin to capture Ologbosheri. **1901** *Daily Chron.* 13 Dec. 4/6 Political questions..arising out of the Protectorate Ordinance of 1896. **1936** *Discovery* June 189/1 Nigeria is in the peculiar state of having both mandated and protectorate lands within its boundaries. **1961** L. VAN DER POST *Heart of Hunter* I. vii. 112 The provincial commissioner..would have up the station-master and draft instructions to ensure that the station was run in the spirit as well as the letter of Protectorate Law.

Hence **pro'tectorate** *v. trans.*, *nonce-wd.* to assume or annex as a protectorate.

1881 GORDON *Let.* 21 May (in *Pearson's 76th Catal.* (1894) 25), England to protectorate Egypt, France to do Ditto to Tunis. **1884** W. G. LAWES in *Nonconf. & Indep.* 24 Apr., If we are to be annexed, attached, appropriated, or protectorated, it should be by the Imperial rather than by any Colonial Government.

protectoress, obs. var. PROTECTRESS.

protec'torial, *a.* [f. late L. *prōtectōri-us* PROTECTORY + -AL[1].] Of or pertaining to a protector, or a protecting state.

1806 NOBLE *Biog. Hist. Eng.* III. 70 He was in some degree, allied to the Protectorial family, by his uncle's.. marriage with Ann, a daughter of Richard Cromwell. **1885** *Manch. Exam.* 3 Jan. 5/3 The fact that we either had or had not protectorial rights over New Guinea.

†**Protec'torian**, *a.* and *sb.* [f. as prec. + -AN.]

A. *adj.* Of or pertaining to the Protector (Cromwell), or to the Protectorate; Cromwellian.

1659 J. HARRINGTON *Ways & Means*, etc. Wks. (1700) 540 Now says the Protectorian Family, O that we had set up the equal Commonwealth! *a* **1661** FULLER *Worthies, Hereford* (1662) II. 47 During the Tyranny of the Protectorian times. **1682** *New News fr. Bedlam* 13 Witness of late their Protectorian Praise, For which some say, Our Laureat won the Baies.

B. *sb.* A supporter of Cromwell's protectorate; a Cromwellian.

1659 in *Trans. Roy. Hist. Soc.* XVII. 114 Leiut. Coll. Kingwell a greate courtier, and a Protectorian. **1661** J. DAVIES *Civ. Warres* 344 This the Protectorians endeavoured to have made no question.

protectorist (prəʊ'tɛktərɪst). *Hist.* [f. PROTECTOR *sb.* + -IST.] = PROTECTORIAN *sb.*

1913 J. WILLCOCK *Life Sir H. Vane* xvi. 275 About half the members of the Commons were Protectorists or supporters of the constitution prescribed in *The Petition and Advice.*

pro'tectorless, *a.* [f. PROTECTOR + -LESS.] Having no protector.

1847 in WEBSTER.

Protectorly (prəʊ'tɛktəlɪ), *a. rare.* [f. as prec. + -LY[1].] Befitting or appropriate to a protector, esp. to the Lord Protector.

1654 in *Rump Songs* I. (1662) 365 Enthron'd in his Chair ..He took such Protectorly courses. **1672** T. JORDAN *London Triumphant* 14 The Captain of a Troop of Horse,.. The Crown, King and Kingdom did divorce; And put the Land into a Protectorly course, By Excision.

protectorship (prəʊ'tɛktəʃɪp). [See -SHIP.]

1. The office of Protector of the realm: = PROTECTORATE *sb.* 1; also, with possessive pronoun, as title of a protector.

c **1460** *Brut* 523 þe Duke of Yorke was sent fore to Grenewiche, & þer was dischargied of þe protectorshipp. **1593** SHAKS. *2 Hen. VI*, II. i. 30 *Glost.* As who, my Lord? *Suff.* Why, as you, my Lord, An't like your Lordly Lords Protectorship. **1659** *England's Conf.* 3 The most probable competitor for succession in the Protectorship. **1738** NEAL *Hist. Purit.* IV. 150 Cromwell's Protectorship was built only upon the authority of the Council of Officers. **1847** *Nat. Encycl.* I. 971 Under the 'protectorship' of the Khedive.

2. The position, character, or function of a protector; guardianship, patronage.

1576 FLEMING *Panopl. Epist.* 12 The loue of good men, obteined through his behauiour in the protectourship of the people. **1670** G. H. *Hist. Cardinals* II. I. 105 Those Kings bestow not those Protectorships upon the Cardinals to receive, but to confer honour upon them. **1792** MARY WOLLSTONECR. *Rights Wom.* vii. 282 Not the libidinous mockery of gallantry, nor the insolent condescension of protectorship. **1807** ROBINSON *Archæol. Græca* I. xii. 51 Minerva, contending with Neptune for the protectorship of Athens. **1864** BRYCE *Holy Rom. Emp.* xx. (1889) 346 Napoleon found that the protectorship of the Church strengthened his position in France.

protectory (prəʊ'tɛktərɪ), *a.* and *sb.* [As adj. ad. late L. *prōtectōri-us* of or belonging to the body-guard, f. *prōtector* (see PROTECTOR and -ORY[2]). As sb. f. as PROTECT *v.* + -ORY[1]: cf. *refectory*, *reformatory*, etc., and med.L. *prōtectōri-um* protectorship, sb. use of neut. of *prōtectōrius*.]

A. *adj.* Having the quality of protecting; protective.

1658 CLEVELAND *Rustic Rampant* Wks. (1687) 471 The King..sends his Letters Protectory to the Abbot in these Words.

B. *sb. R.C. Ch.* An institution for the care and education of destitute or delinquent children.

1868 [see quot. 1893]. **1885** *Pall Mall G.* 10 Oct. 8/2 The cardinal was very active in..philanthropic work, having established protectories for destitute children [etc.]. **1888** HURLBERT *Ireland under Coercion* (ed. 2) I. i. 42 The Catholic demand for the endowment of Catholic schools and protectories. **1893** *Tablet* 16 Sept. 450/2 The New York Catholic Protectory, founded in 1868.

protectress (prəʊ'tɛktrɪs). Also *β.* 7–8 **protectoress.** [f. PROTECTOR + -ESS.]

1. A female protector; a patroness.

1570 FOXE *A. & M.* (ed. 2) 660/1 Straightly enioyning you ..to worship our Lady Mary the mother of God, and our patronesse and protectresse, euermore in all aduersity. **1621** BP. MOUNTAGU *Diatribæ* 505 Pallas, Patronesse of Athens, and Protectresse. **1774** PENNANT *Tour in Scot. in 1772*, 297 The fair protectress of a fugitive adventurer. **1878** GLADSTONE *Prim. Homer* ii. 19 Athenè, the personal protectress of Achilles, of Odusseus, and of Diomed.

β. **1680** HICKERINGILL *Meroz* Ded. 3 In making Choice of such a Protectoresse. **1682** WHELER *Journ. Greece* III. 285 Juno of Samos, the Protectoress of that Island. **1704** *Addr. Devon* 3 Oct. in *Lond. Gaz.* No. 4066/8 A Protectoress of Your own Dominions.

b. Applied to a thing.

1615 G. SANDYS *Trav.* I. 76 Christians: whose pouerty is their onely safety and protectresse. **1835** I. TAYLOR *Spir. Despot.* v. 225 If the Papacy were inherently the protectress of humanity.

2. A female Protector or regent of a kingdom or commonwealth; also, the wife of a Protector.

1577–87 HOLINSHED *Chron.* III. 1081/1 Katharine Par.. was by patent made protectresse of the realme of England, when king Henrie the eight went in person to the wars of Bullongne. **1643** PRYNNE *Sov. Power Parl.* App. 70 Ferdinand the fourth,..being but a childe when his father Sancho died, was in ward to his mother Queen Mary, his Protectresse. **1845** CARLYLE *Cromwell* (1871) III. 125 At Norborough..the Lady Protectress, Widow Elizabeth Cromwell, after the Restoration, found a retreat.

β. **1653–4** [see PROTECTOR 2 b]. **1660** TATHAM *Rump* II. i, She will be a Protectoress whether he be a Protector or not.

protec'trice. now *rare.* Also 5 -yse, 5–6 -yce. [ME. a. F. *protectrice*, ad. med.L. *prōtectrix*, *-trīcem*: see PROTECTRIX] = prec.

c **1375** *Sc. Leg. Saints* xliv. (*Lucy*) 310 As agatha, my cystire fre, is protectryse of þis cyte. *c* **1450** *Mirour Saluacioun* 255 How gods modire is oure protectrice. **1513** BRADSHAW *St. Werburge* II. 1741 'Patrones of Chestre', protectrice of the countre. **1654** in Morley *Cromwell* v. vii. (1900) 451 At the table of my Lady Protectrice dined my Lady N. **1740** tr. *De Mouhy's Fort. Country-Maid* (1741) II. 137 She found a Protectrice, the Character she gives of her exactly suited Madame. **1974** J. FLINT *Cecil Rhodes* v. 105 Lobengula...had imagined that Queen Victoria was now his ally and protectrice.

‖**protectrix** (prəʊ'tɛktrɪks). [med.L., fem. of L. *prōtector.*] = PROTECTRESS.

c **1500** KENNEDY *Poems* (Schipper) iv. 9 Sancta Maria, Virgo virginum! Protectrix till all pepill penitent. **1562** A. SCOTT *Poems* (S.T.S.) i. 39 Preiss ay to be protectrix of þe pure. **1647** A. ROSS *Myst. Poet.* viii. (1675) 152 Hecate was said to be the goddess or protectrix of witches. **1832** *Blackw. Mag.* XXXI. 23 England, the mother and the protectrix of heresies. **1883** *N. Eng. Hist. & Gen. Reg.* XXXVII. 244 The duchess was an eminent protectrix of literary men and scholars.

†**pro'tecture.** *Obs. rare*[−1]. [f. as PROTECT *v.* + -URE.] The action or office of a protector.

a **1485** FORTESCUE *Wks.* (1869) 501 The Churche hath approved him and his reigning by accepting of his Protecture.

protégé *masc.*, **protégée** *fem.* ('prɒtɛʒeɪ). [F., '(one) protected', pa. pple. of *protéger*, ad. L. *prōtegĕre* to PROTECT.] One who is under the protection or care of another, esp. of a person of superior position or influence.

1778 SHERIDAN *Camp* II. iii, And very *à propos*, here comes your ladyship's *protégée*. **1786** *Lounger* (1787) II. 243 She looked upon me as her particular *protegée*. **1787** BECKFORD *Italy* (1834) II. 206 An immense tray of dried fruits..which one of his hundred and fifty *protégés* had sent him. **1801** MAR. EDGEWORTH *Belinda* (1831) II. xxv. 178 He may be a protegé of Lady Anne Percival. **1818** SCOTT *Hrt. Midl.* xxiv, Mrs. Saddletree..distressed about the situation of her unfortunate *protegée*. **1825–9** MRS. SHERWOOD *Lady of Manor* IV. xxiv. 172 The little orphan girl, who had been the protegée of my dear husband. **1908** *Athenæum* 1 Feb. 126/1 As a distinguished physician and as the protégé of prominent personages in Church and State.

protegulum (prəʊ'tɛgjuːləm). *Zool.* [mod.L., f. PRO-[2] I + L. *tegulum* covering.] In brachiopods, the embryonic form of the shell.

1891 C. E. BEECHER in *Amer. Jrnl. Sci.* XLI. 344 All brachiopods, so far as studied by the writer, have a common form of embryonic shell, which may be termed the protegulum. **1904** *Amer. Jrnl. Sci.* CLXVII. 283 The protegulum of this species [sc. *Stropheodonta perplana*] is nearly circular. **1935** TWENHOFEL & SHROCK *Invertebr. Paleont.* viii. 269 Growth proceeds around the protegulum, mainly along the anterior and lateral margins of the two valves. **1959** L. H. HYMAN *Invertebrates* V. xxi. 531 Each valve begins as a minute plate, the protegulum, presumably composed of periostracum. **1973** P. TASCH *Paleobiol. Invertebrates* vii. 263/2 The outer surface of the mantle flaps (lobes) became white and smooth, indicating initial shell formation (protegulum).

†**pro'teic**, *a. Chem. Obs.* [f. PROTE(IN + -IC.] Of, of the nature of, or consisting of protein.

1857 W. A. MILLER *Elem. Chem.* III. 647 The proteic principles have been termed the plastic materials of nutrition. **1867** *N. Syd. Soc. Biennial Retrosp. Med. & Surg.* 30 A newly-formed proteic compound.

proteid[1] ('prəʊtiːɪd). *Chem.* Also **proteide.** [f. PROTE(IN: see -ID[4].] A term applied in England from 1871 to the class of organic compounds previously known as 'protein bodies' or 'substances' (Ger. *proteïn-stoffe*), and now by preference called 'proteins': see PROTEIN, and Note there.

1871 WATTS tr. *Gmelin's Handbk. Chem.* XVIII. 252 The term *proteides* is here used in the comprehensive sense, which permits the grouping together of the non-crystallisable nitrogenous animal and vegetable substances possessing reactions in common. **1872** —— *Genl. Index of Jrnl. Chem. Soc.* 1841–72, Proteids. **1872** NICHOLSON *Biol.* 68 It is a common and often a very convenient practice to speak of the various albuminoid substances of animals or vegetables as 'proteids'. **1873** WATTS *Fownes' Chem.* (ed. 11) 955 Albuminous Principles—Albuminoids or Proteids [*ed. 10 Index*, Protein]. **1876** FOSTER *Phys.* I. i. (1879) 14 Proteids ..form a large portion of all living bodies and an essential part of all protoplasm. **1891** *Pall Mall G.* 5 Feb. 6/3 Some months ago Mr. Hankin discovered a class of organisms to which he gave the name of 'Protective Proteids'. These substances..appear to be a sort of natural antiseptic, possessing..the power of destroying the bacilli of anthrax and other maladies. **1897** *Allbutt's Syst. Med.* II. 810 The work of this accomplished author [Weir Mitchell] on the venom of the rattlesnake, formed the first step in our knowledge of toxic proteids. **1897** WILLIS *Flower. Plants* I. 207 The first downward step in the decomposition of protoplasm into proteids. **1907** *Recommendations of Committee* in *Proc. Physiol. Soc.* 26 Jan. p. xviii. 1 The word Proteid—which is used in different senses in this country and in Germany—should be abolished.

b. *attrib.* and *Comb.* = PROTEIN *attrib.*

1872 HUXLEY *Phys.* i. 3 That compound known to chemists as proteid matter. **1878** KINGZETT *Anim. Chem.* 159 A man confined to a purely proteid diet must eat a prodigious quantity of it. **1883** *American* VI. 173 The crotaline venom contains three distinct proteid bodies. **1897** *Trans. Amer. Pediatric Soc.* IX. 130 The more proteid material the body is called upon to metabolize the more likely we are to have an excess of [uric acid, etc.].

proteid[2] ('prəʊtiːɪd). *Zool. rare.* [f. mod.L. generic name *Prōteus* + -ID[3].] An amphibian of the family *Proteidæ*, typified by the genus *Proteus* (PROTEUS 3 b). So **proteidean**

(prəʊtiːˈɪdiːən) *a.*, belonging to this group of amphibians.

proteiform (ˈprəʊtiːɪfɔːm), *a.* [f. PROTE-US + -(I)FORM.] Changeable in form, or assuming many various forms, like the fabled Proteus or the 'proteus-animalcule'; protean, multiform, extremely variable or various.

1793 *Critical Rev.* IX. 183 Pathologists have, within these last years, differed greatly respecting the cause of this Proteiform disease [*sc.* gout]. **1833** B. G. BABINGTON tr. *Hecker's Black Death* ii. (1888) 20 This violent disease..is proteiform in its varieties. **1849–52** *Todd's Cycl. Anat.* IV. 1224/2 Proteiform expansions of the Amœba and other inferior animals. **1853** H. LUSHINGTON *Ital. War* (1859) 237 [They] must imagine to themselves such a string as never was put together before of..all the possible proteiform transformations of an absolute and impartial egotism. **1862** H. SPENCER *First Princ.* II. xix. §152 (1875) 414 When we turn from these proteiform specks of living jelly..we find differences of tissue. **1944** S. PUTNAM tr. *E. da Cunha's Rebellion in Backlands* ii. 84 The proteiform mestizo of the seaboard.

protein (ˈprəʊtiːɪn, now ˈprəʊtiːn). *Chem.* Also 9 -ine. [a. F. *protéine* (Mulder 1838), Ger. *proteïn*, f. Gr. πρωτεῖ-ος primary, prime (so named as a primary substance or fundamental material of the bodies of animals and plants): see -IN[1].

It seems likely that in proposing the word *protéine* Mulder was adopting a suggestion made to him by Berzelius: see *Nature* (1951) 11 Aug. 244.]

†**a.** Name given by Mulder to a complex residual nitrogenous substance, of tolerably constant composition, obtained from casein, fibrin, and egg albumin, to which he assigned the formula $C_{40}H_{62}N_{10}O_{12}$, and which he regarded as the essential constituent of organized bodies, animal or vegetable (*obs.*). **b.** In current use, any one of a class of organic compounds, the *proteins*, consisting of carbon, hydrogen, oxygen, and nitrogen, with a little sulphur, in complex and more or less unstable combination; forming an important part of all living organisms, and the essential nitrogenous constituents of the food of animals; obtained as amorphous solids, differing in solubility and other properties, and usually coagulable by heat. Also called *albuminoids*, and very generally *proteids* (see PROTEID[1]).

When the advance of chemical knowledge showed that there was no such definite compound as Mulder's 'protein', the albuminoid substances of which he had considered it to be the basis continued to be known as the *protein bodies* or *substances*, Ger. *proteïn-stoffe* (see c). To render the latter, the term *proteids* (at first *proteides*) was used by H. Watts in 1871 in his translation of Gmelin's *Handbook of Chemistry*, also in the Journal of the Chemical Society, and the 11th ed. of Fownes' Chemistry, 1873, and became common (though not universal) in English use. *Proteïd* had however in German been applied to designate compounds still more complex, e.g. hæmoglobin (see Hoppe-Seyler, *Handbch.*, ed. 5, 1883, 290). Thence arose confusion in nomenclature, to remedy which a Committee on Proteid Nomenclature was appointed, and in 1907 recommended the disuse of the term *proteid* in either sense, and the use of *proteins* as the collective name for the *proteïn-stoffe* or protein bodies. This recommendation was adopted by the International Congress of Physiologists at Heidelberg in the same year.

The simple proteins are the *protamines*, *histones*, *albumins*, and *globulins* (derivatives of which are fibrin and myosin). The combination compounds are the *sclero-proteins* (e.g. gelatin and keratin), *phospho-proteins* (e.g. vitellin, caseinogen, and casein), *conjugated proteins* (incl. *nucleo-proteins*), *gluco-proteins* (e.g. mucin), *chromo-proteins* (e.g. hæmoglobin). Derivatives of protein are *meta-proteins* (acid-albumin, alkali-albumin), improperly called 'albuminates'; *proteoses* (e.g. albumose, globulose, gelatose); *peptones*, *polypeptides*. See *Journal of Physiology* XXXV. *Proc.* 26 Jan. 1907, pp. xvii–xx, and *Proc. Chem. Soc.* XXIII. 56.

[**1838** MULDER in *Bulletin des Sciences Phys. en Néerlande* 111 La matière organique, étant un principe général de toutes les parties constituantes du corps animal..pourrait se nommer *Protéine* de πρωτεῖος primarius.] **1844** DUNGLISON *Med. Lex.*, *Protein*, a product of the decomposition of albumen, &c., by potassa. **1851** CARPENTER *Man. Phys.* (ed. 2) 9 Proteine and Gelatine are remarkable, not only for containing four elements, but for the very large number of atoms of these components which enter into the single compound atom of each. **1854** BUSHNAN in *Orr's Circ. Sc.* I. *Org. Nat.* 45 According to a view which has excited much attention, these three proximate elements [albumen, fibrine, and caseine] are merely slightly modified forms of the one proximate element, proteine. Mülder [is] the author of this view. **1868** HUXLEY *Phys. Basis of Life* in *Fortn. Rev.* Feb. (1869) 135 All forms of protoplasm..yet examined, contain the four elements carbon, hydrogen, oxygen, and nitrogen, in very complex union... To this complex combination, the nature of which has never been determined with exactness, the name of *Protein* has been applied. **1896** *Allbutt's Syst. Med.* I. 415 In many [foods] the amount of protein is too small. *Ibid.* 520 Of the true chemical character of the enzymes we are ignorant. They are probably proteins. **1907** *Jrnl. Physiol.* XXXV. *Proc.* 26 Jan. *Rept. on Proteid Nomencl.* p. xviii, The word Protein is recommended as the general name of the whole group... It is at present so used both in America and Germany.

c. *attrib.* and *Comb.*

1846 G. E. DAY tr. *Simon's Anim. Chem.* II. 417 Acetic acid..renders them gelatinous and tough, but takes up no protein-compound. **1847–9** *Todd's Cycl. Anat.* IV. 104/1 The main element of this material is of protein-basis. **1857** *G. Bird's Urin. Deposits* (ed. 5) 45 Sort of transition stage between the protein elements and urea. **1860** *N. Syd. Soc. Year-Bk. Med. & Surg.* 70 The pancreas as well as the stomach secretes a substance capable of transforming protein matters into peptone. **1875** H. WALTON *Dis. Eye* 734 The protein element, crystallin, is at its least quantity. **1881** MIVART *Cat* 250 The ovum is a minute spheroidal mass of protein substance. **1883** *Chambers' Encycl.* s.v. *Protein*, The term *protein bodies*, or *protein compounds*, is..commonly retained both by physiologists and chemists, as being the most convenient one for representing a class of compounds, which..deserve their name from their constituting the group which form the most essential articles of food. **1898** *Allbutt's Syst. Med.* V. 890 The fibres become finely granular from the deposition in them of fine protein granules. **1917** *Nature* 15 Feb. 471/2 Just as the protein supply in meat may be compensated for by the greater utilisation of the protein-rich pulses. **1925** C. H. BROWNING *Bacteriol.* iii. 46 Instead of adding peptone a useful procedure is to digest the minced meat at the commencement by pancreatic extracts containing the protein-splitting ferment trypsin, which produces peptone bodies in the mixture and yields a very suitable basis for nutritive medium. **1928** *Physiol. Rev.* VIII. 418 If, as is stated by Mathews.., Fischer was induced to turn his attention to protein chemistry by Kossel, the debt science owes this great biochemist is beyond estimation. **1946** *Nature* 19 Oct. 556/2 Estimations are made on protein-free filtrates, prepared by adding to 0·2 c.c. serum, 11 c.c. water and 0·5 c.c. of each of the Folin-Wu reagents. **1953** *Amer. Naturalist* LXXXVII. 255 The heterogeneity which is the dismay of the protein chemist attempting to solve purification problems may be the very basis for his existence as a human being. **1956** *Nature* 28 Jan. 190/1 Although reticulocytes have practically their full complement of hæmoglobin, evidence from amino-acid incorporation studies suggests that these cells..still have protein-synthesizing capacity. **1960** *Farmer & Stockbreeder* 9 Feb. 110/2 (Advt.), Lobolettes are protein-packed, rich in energy and fully fortified with vitamins, minerals and trace elements. **1961** *Lancet* 29 July 258/1 These figures may be explained by the presence of one or more insulin antagonists ..or by protein-binding of the insulin in the blood. *Ibid.* 5 Aug. 284/1 Rona and Takahaski first demonstrated..that.. the plasma-calcium consisted of a diffusible fraction and a non-diffusible protein-bound fraction. **1972** J. MADDOX *Doomsday Syndrome* iii. 75 Protein deficiency is still a serious cause of stunted development..among poor people even in advanced societies. **1979** *Arizona Daily Star* 5 Aug. (Parade Suppl.) 14/3 Protein-rich foods such as meat, dairy products and nuts should be eaten.

d. Special Combs.: **protein plastic**, a plastic in which protein is the chief component; *esp.* a casein plastic; **protein shock** *Med.*, a disturbed state produced by the parenteral introduction into the body of a foreign protein; also, protein therapy; **protein therapy**, *Med.*, the production of protein shock for therapeutic purposes.

1936 STURKEN & WOODRUFF *U.S. Patent 2,040,033* 1/1 Our invention relates to the production of protein plastics which may be cured in the mold without the necessity of a prolonged cure in formaldehyde solution or formaldehyde vapor. In the past, protein plastics such as casein have found many uses in the light plastics field. **1943** H. R. FLECK *Plastics* iv. 82 The two most widely known and industrially important protein plastics are those formed from casein.. and those formed from the proteins present in soya beans. **1969** *Encycl. Polymer Sci. & Technol.* XI. 696 The term 'protein plastic' is specifically interpreted commercially to mean casein plastic. **1917** *Jrnl. Exper. Med.* XXVI. 699 The mechanism of recovery following the so called 'protein shock therapy'. *Ibid.* 705 By means of the protein shock, antibody-rich fluids (serum) are forced into the lymph channels. **1935** F. P. GAY *Agents of Dis. & Host Resistance* lxiii. 1506 Symptomatic disturbances during protein shock are an increased pulse rate, sweating, decreased blood pressure, increased peristalsis, increased lymph flow and lymph volume, and a mobilization of the serum enzymes. **1964** S. DUKE-ELDER *Parsons' Dis. of Eye* (ed. 14) xiv. 149 In certain aspects the response to cortisone resembles that to fever therapy by 'protein shock'. **1917** *Jrnl. Amer. Med. Assoc.* 8 Sept. 766/2 The application of foreign protein therapy to the acute, sub-acute and chronic arthritides. **1940** B. I. COMROE *Arthritis* xv. 195 Substances..now employed for non-specific protein therapy include bacterial vaccines. **1967** *Biol. Abstr.* XLVIII. 7122/1 (*heading*) The use of protein therapy for gastric and duodenal ulcers.

Hence **proteinaceous** (-ˈneɪʃəs), **proteinic** (-tiːˈɪnɪk, -ˈtiːnɪk), **proteinous** (prəʊˈtiː(ɪ)nəs) *adjs.*, of the nature of, or consisting of, protein.

1844 DUNGLISON *Med. Lex.*, **Proteinaceous*, proteinous. **1868** HUXLEY in *Fortn. Rev.* Feb. (1869) 135 If we use this term with..caution..it may truly be said that all protoplasm is proteinaceous. **1870** NICHOLSON *Man. Zool.* 8 The proteinaceous matter or protoplasm which constitutes the physical basis of life. **1876** tr. *Schützenberger's Ferment.* 81 Yeast cannot elaborate *proteinic matter under these conditions. **1844** DUNGLISON *Med. Lex.* s.v., A *proteinous alimentary principle. **1859** *Todd's Cycl. Anat.* V. 391/1 Nucleated cells; the membranous walls of which consist of a proteinous substance.

proteinase (ˈprəʊtiːneɪz, -s). *Biochem.* [a. G. *proteinase* (Grassmann & Dyckerhoff 1928, in *Zeitschr. f. physiol. Chem.* CLXXIX. 41): see PROTEIN and -ASE.] Any enzyme that hydrolyses proteins to smaller polypeptides.

1929 *Chem. Abstr.* XXIII. 615 Plant proteases... The proteinase and the polypeptidase of yeast. **1931** *Biochem. Jrnl.* XXV. 256 In their main conclusions these authors agreed that green malt contains (1) a protease or proteinase (to adopt the nomenclature of Grassmann) which appears to attack..crystalline egg-albumin..and (2) at least one peptidase which attacks the dipeptide leucylglycine. **1941** *Adv. Enzymol.* I. 76 Pepsin, trypsin, and chymotrypsin represent the three best recognized proteinases. **1963** *Biochem. Jrnl.* LXXXVI. 100/1 The purified proteinase probably liberated peptides from a boiled sample of α_2-crystallin, and it seems probable that the lens proteinase is an endopeptidase. **1970** PASSMORE & ROBSON *Compan. Med. Stud.* II. xviii. 33/1 Potent bacterial proteinases and collagenases decompose muscle tissue and collagen.

proteinoid (ˈprəʊtiːnɔɪd), *sb.* (*a.*) *Biochem.* [f. PROTEIN + -OID.] A protein-like polypeptide or mixture of polypeptides obtained by heating a mixture of amino-acids. Also *attrib.* or as *adj.*

1956 S. W. FOX in *Amer. Scientist* XLIV. 353 Evidence that proteinoids can be formed by heating one or two amino acids has now accumulated. *Ibid.* 354 The appearance of aspartic acid after hydrolysis is part of the evidence for a proteinoid product. **1968** *New Scientist* 4 Apr. 41/1 When Sidney Fox first discovered this form of amino acid condensation ten years ago, he was immediately attracted by the idea that these quasi-proteins—or proteinoids,..might represent the first evolutionary step..that led to the true proteins. *Ibid.* 41/2 Perhaps the most striking similarity that proteinoids bear to true proteins..is that..they act like enzymes. **1971** *Nature* 7 May 42/1 In contrast to the plausible explanations for proteinoid formation, there seems to be no satisfactory concept for the genesis of polynucleotide templates in the presumed conditions of the primitive Earth. **1977** A. HALLAM *Planet Earth* 236 (*caption*) Cell-like structures called 'proteinoid microspheres' have been produced by evaporating organic chemicals on hot lava beds.

proteinosis (prəʊtiːˈnəʊsɪs). *Path.* [mod.L., ad. G. *lipoid*)*proteinose* (E. Uhrbach in J. Jadassohn *Handb. der Haut- und Geschlechtskrankheiten* (1932) XII. 336): see PROTEIN and -OSIS.] The abnormal accumulation or deposition of protein in tissue.

1937 *Arch. Dermatol. & Syphilol.* XXXV. 357 A subsequent microscopic examination revealed the tinctorial and cellular features of lipoid proteinosis. **1954** *Ann. Internal Med.* XLI. 163 Lipoid proteinosis is a peculiar abnormality of fat deposition characterized by the appearance of white or yellow plaques and nodules in the skin and mucous membranes, producing hoarseness due to vocal chord involvement. **1958** *New England Jrnl. Med.* 5 June 1123 (*heading*) Pulmonary alveolar proteinosis. **1961** *Lancet* 30 Sept. 733/2 A man aged 36 gave a 2-year history of increasing breathlessness with diffuse shadowing on the chest radiograph. 15 months after the onset of symptoms a lung biopsy..showed that he had pulmonary alveolar proteinosis. **1974** *Arch. Dermatol.* CX. 594/2 This finding suggests that lipid accumulation in lipoid proteinosis lesions is not due to a primary defect in lipid metabolism, but could be due to secondary adherence to glyco-proteins.

proteinuria (prəʊtiːˈn(j)ʊərɪə). *Med.* [mod.L., ad. F. *protéinurie* (L. Hugounenq 1901, in *Lyon Médical* CXVI. 87): see PROTEIN and -URIA.] The presence of abnormal quantities of protein in the urine.

1911 *Jrnl. Physiol.* XLII. 238 It seemed important to determine how far an individual suffering from so grave a disturbance of protein metabolism as this condition of proteinuria betokens, could be in nitrogenous equilibrium. *Ibid.* 241 Of some significance is the fact that the excretion of creatin appears to be characteristic of Bence-Jones proteinuria. **1976** *Acta Med. Biol.* XXIV. 9 These patients with symptomless persistent proteinuria appear to constitute a distinct clinical group which is characterized by normal renal function..and a more favorable prognosis.

Hence **proteiˈnuric** *a.*, of, pertaining to, or suffering from proteinuria.

1932 *Dorland's Med. Dict.* (ed. 16) 1042/2 Proteinuric. **1969** *Metabolism* XVIII. 556/1 A polypeptide exhibiting diabetogenic and anti-insulin properties has been isolated from the urine of 33 of the 35 proteinuric diabetic patients. **1977** *Lancet* 21 May 1108/2 Groups divided up according to whether they remained normotensive or developed mild pre-eclampsia or proteinuric pre-eclampsia as defined by Nelson.

pro tem., pro tempore: see PRO 10.

protembryo, protembryonic, protencephalon: see PROTO- 2 b.

‖**protenchyma** (prəʊˈteŋkɪmə). *Bot.* [mod.L., f. Gr. πρῶτ-ος first + ἔγχυμα infusion, after PARENCHYMA.] A term used by Nägeli for the primary meristem and those tissues (the epidermal and fundamental) which arise immediately from it: contrasted with *epenchyma*.

1875 BENNETT & DYER tr. *Sachs' Bot.* 103 Nägeli says.. that he would call the primary meristem and all parts of the tissue which arise immediately from it..Protenchyma (or Proten); the cambium, on the other hand, and everything which..originates from it Epenchyma (or Epen)... But.. there is no reason for bringing into prominence only the contrast between fibro-vascular and non-fibro-vascular masses (Epenchyma and Protenchyma)..; the protenchyma of Nägeli therefore splits up, according to me, into three kinds [primary meristem, epidermal tissue, fundamental tissue] of equal value with his epenchyma. **1884** BOWER & SCOTT *De Bary's Phaner.* 6.

protend (prəʊˈtɛnd), *v.* Now *rare.* [ME. ad. L. *prōtend-ĕre* to stretch forth, extend: f. PRO-[1] 1 a + *tendĕre* to stretch; cf. obs. F. *protend-re* (1404 in Godef.) to extend, a variant of *portendre*: see PORTEND.]

I. 1. *trans.* To stretch forth; to hold out in front of one. Also *fig.*

1432–50 tr. *Higden* (Rolls) VI. 217 In whiche yere ij. horrible blasynge sterres apperede..protendenge [orig. *protendentes*] grete flammes from theym into the northe. **1656** BLOUNT *Glossogr.*, *Protend*, to set, put, cast, or stretch forth. *a* **1688** CUDWORTH *Immut. Mor.* IV. i. (1731) 127 Not stamps or impressions passively printed upon the soul from without, but ideas vitally protended or actively exerted from within it self. **1715-20** POPE *Iliad* XV. 888 [Ajax] Now shakes his spear, now lifts, and now protends. **1852** GROTE *Greece* II. lxix. IX. 25 The spears were protended, the trumpets sounded.

b. *intr.* for *refl.* To stretch forward; to stick out, protrude.
1726 LEONI *Alberti's Archit.* II. 66/1 Its two horns or wings protending forwards. **1848** CLOUGH *Bothie* III, Prone, with hands and feet protending.

2. *trans.* To extend in length, or in one dimension of space; to produce (a line); usually *pass.* to extend, stretch, reach (from one point to another). Also *fig.*
1432-50 tr. *Higden* (Rolls) I. 49 The thridde parte, which is Affrica, is protendede from the weste in to the meridien in to the coste of Egipte. *Ibid.* II. 35 Kynge Offa causede a longe diche to be made.. whiche.. protendethe hit vn to the durre of the floode of Dee behynde Chestre. **1654** H. L'ESTRANGE *Chas. I* (1655) 126 One entire street.. protended in a right line from the Castle to Holy-rood-house. **1778** *Phil. Surv. S. Irel.* 3 London is more protended in length. **1876** ALEXANDER *Bampton Lect.* (1877) 9 Whether, and how far, the thought and personality of the Psalmists were protended to, and absorbed by, the Divine object of their contemplation.

b. To extend in magnitude or amount.
1659 H. L'ESTRANGE *Alliance Div. Off.* 319 Protending and contracting it.. according to the rate and assise of the Office. **1675** R. BURTHOGGE *Causa Dei* 244 He begetteth or Principleth the Number next in Nature, and that is Two... The Monad is Protended, which begetteth Two.

3. To extend in duration; to protract, prolong.
1432-50 tr. *Higden* (Rolls) VI. 189 Hit awe to be protended unto þe eve of the xxj[ti] day. **1659** H. L'ESTRANGE *Alliance Div. Off.* 150 All.. high Fasts were protended and reached to the evening thereof. **1836** SIR W. HAMILTON *Discuss.* (1852) 301 The starry Heaven.. protends it also to the illimitable times of their periodic movement.

II. †**4.** To portend, foretoken. (In quot. 1589 *absol.*) *Obs.*
1589 GREENE *Menaphon* (Arb.) 22 That Comets did protend at the first blaze. **1610** HEALEY *St. Aug. Citie of God* 205 This protendeth the birth of a beast and not of a man.

Hence **pro'tended** *ppl. a.*, **pro'tending** *vbl. sb.* and *ppl. a.*
1659 H. L'ESTRANGE *Alliance Div. Off.* 267 The protending of the Hand towards the West. **1697** DRYDEN *Æneid* II. 299 They lie protected there, By her large buckler, and protended spear. **1756** P. BROWNE *Jamaica* 26 A huge protending rock. **1816** KIRBY & SP. *Entomol.* xxi. (1818) II. 224 The terrific and protended jaws of the stag-beetle.

†**pro'tense,** *sb. Obs. rare*$^{-1}$. [f. L. *protens-*, ppl. stem of *prōtendĕre* to PROTEND.] = PROTENSION 3.
1590 SPENSER *F.Q.* III. iii. 4 By dew degrees, and long protense [*2nd and later edd.* pretense].

†**pro'tensed,** *ppl. a. Obs. rare*$^{-1}$. [f. L. *prōtens-us*, pa. pple. of *prōtendĕre* to PROTEND + -ED[1].] Stretched forward, extended in length.
1578 BANISTER *Hist. Man* I. 30 The head of the ioynt, after a certaine manner long, and forward protensed.

protension (prəʊ'tɛnʃən). Also (sense 3 b) **protention.** [ad. late L. *prōtensiōn-em*, n. of action f. *prōtendĕre* to PROTEND.] The action or fact of protending.
1. A stretching or reaching forward. Also *fig.*
1681 tr. *Willis' Rem. Med. Wks.* Vocab., *Protension*, a stretching forth at length. **1836-7** SIR W. HAMILTON *Metaph.* xli. (1870) II. 426 There could be no tendency, no protension of the mind to attain this object as an end. **1858** J. MARTINEAU *Stud. Chr.* (1873) 9 There are minds whose power is shed, if we may say so, in protension, precipitated forwards in narrow channels with impetuous torrent.
2. Extension in length; linear extent; length.
1704 NORRIS *Ideal World* II. vii. 359 The rays.. will be of an unequal protension. **1890** W. JAMES *Princ. Psychol.* II. xx. 222 In the case of protension or mere farness it [*sc.* the neural process] is more complicated.
3. a. Extension in time; duration.
1852 SIR W. HAMILTON *Discuss.* App. i. (A.) (1853) 605 Time, Protension or protensive quantity, called likewise Duration, is a necessary condition of thought. **1935** *Philos. of Sci.* II. 236 In a similar reaction against Wundtian atomism Külpe also added duration (protension) to the list.
b. (With spelling **protention**, after G. *protention* (E. Husserl 1922 in *Jahrb. f. Philos. u. phänomenol. Forsch.* I. III. ii. §77.145), perh. infl. by RETENTION 2 c.) In Phenomenology, extension of the consciousness of some present act or event into the future. Hence **pro'tentional** *a.* Cf. RETENTION 2 c.
1931 W. B GIBSON tr. *Husserl's Ideas* III. ii. 216 The same holds good, according to the naïvely natural view, in respect of *anticipation*.., or previsional expectation. At first there comes in the immediate '*protention*' (as we might put it). *Ibid.* 237 Continuous changes in an opposite direction: 'after' corresponding to 'before', a protentional continuum corresponding to the retentional. **1941** *Philos. & Phenomenol. Res.* II. 341 These expectations—Husserl calls them.. 'protentions'—belong, of course, to our present acting. **1966** A. GURWITSCH *Phenomenol. & Psychol.* ix. 149 The notions of protention and particularly of retention are at the center of the Husserlian theory concerning the experience of time. **1974** D. CARR *Phenomenol. & Probl. of Hist.* iv. 103 It is the act conceived as the living present, with its horizons of retention and protention, which is 'responsible' for the original or primary givenness of anything.

pro'tensity. [f. *protense, ad. L. *prōtens-us* (see next) + -ITY.] 'The character of being protensive or of taking up time' (*Cent. Dict.*).
1915 G. F. STOUT *Man. Psychol.* (ed. 3) II. i. 212 In all sense presentations we can discern Quality, Intensity, and Protensity or Duration. **1920** S. ALEXANDER *Space, Time, & Deity* II. 130 The 'protensity' of sensation is nothing but its continuance, that is, again, a continuous repetition of the sensation in time. **1935** *Philos. of Sci.* II. 236 The four classical attributes of sensation are quality, intensity, extensity and protensity. **1964** JAKOBSON & HALLE in D. Abercrombie et al. *Daniel Jones* 99 The tense/lax opposition should.. be.. viewed as a separate, 'protensity' feature which.. corresponds to the quantity features in the prosodic field. **1972** *Language* XLVIII. 31 This difference between laxness diphthongization and all other types is a simple consequence of the fact that laxness is a protensity feature.

protensive (prəʊ'tɛnsɪv), *a. rare.* [f. L. *prōtens-*, ppl. stem of *prōtend-ĕre* to PROTEND + -IVE.] Having the quality of protending.
1. Extending in time; continuing, lasting, enduring.
1643 [implied in PROTENSIVELY]. **1671** FLAVEL *Fount. Life* xxix. Wks. 1731 II. 88 Our Patience is.. according to the Will of God, when it is as extensive as intensive, and as protensive as God requires it to be. **1836-7** SIR W. HAMILTON *Metaph.* xxxviii. (1870) II. 372 Time is a protensive quantity, and, consequently, any part of it, however small, cannot, without a contradiction, be imagined as not divisible into parts. **1870** *Outline Hamilton's Philos.* 217 Examples of the sublime.. are manifested in the extensive sublime of Space and in the protensive sublime of Eternity.
2. Extending lengthwise; relating to or expressing linear extension, or magnitude of one dimension.
1836 SIR W. HAMILTON *Discuss.* (1852) 310 In the study of Mathematics we are accustomed.. to a protensive, rather than to either an extensive, a comprehensive, or an intensive, application of thought. **1843** *Blackw. Mag.* LIII. 763 Distance in a direction from the percipient or what we should call protensive distance.

Hence **pro'tensively** *adv.*, (in quots.) in respect of duration or extension in time.
1643 TRAPP *Comm. Gen.* vi. 5 All the thoughts extensively are intensively onely evil, and protensively continually. **1882-3** *Schaff's Encycl. Relig. Knowl.* III. 2322 Space cannot be thought of except as extensively, nor time except as protensively, infinite.

protention. See PROTENSION 3 b.

proteo- (prəʊtiːəʊ-), comb. form of PROTEIN; **proteo'clastic** *a.* [see CLASTIC *a.*] = PROTEOLYTIC *a.*; **proteoglycan** (-'glaɪkæn) (see quot. 1969); **proteo'lipid, -ide,** a complex that contains protein and lipid moieties and is insoluble in aqueous media but soluble in organic solvents; cf. *lipoprotein* s.v. LIPO-. Also PROTEOLYSIS, etc.
1929 I. F. & W. D. HENDERSON *Dict. Sci. Terms* (ed. 2) 260/2 Proteoclastic. **1959** W. ANDREW *Textbk. Compar. Histol.* v. 195 The granular amoebocytes or granulocytes of the oyster carry out intracellular digestion by means of sucroclastic, lipoclastic, and proteoclastic enzymes. **1969** HASCALL & SAJDERA in *Jrnl. Biol. Chem.* CXLIV. 2384/2 We refer to this fraction, which is a basic building block for the cartilage matrix, as proteoglycan subunit. Because of the selectivity of the techniques used in its purification we presume that it contains only covalently bound protein. The second component is a glyco-protein fraction. [*Note*] The term 'proteoglycan' is used to describe macromolecules which consist primarily of polysaccharide which is presumed to be bound covalently to the small amount of protein present. 'Glycoprotein' is used to indicate a macromolecule which is primarily protein, but which contains covalently bound saccharide. **1974** *Sci. Amer.* May 67/1 It does appear, however, that the wet surfactants on the ocean, which are known to be glycoproteins and proteoglycans, are reasonably good carriers of phosphate, of various organic molecules, of the scarcer ions of seawater and of heavy metals. **1977** *Lancet* 4 June 1190/2 The major proteins of cartilage are proteoglycan.. and type-II collagen. **1950** FOLCH & LEES in *Federation Proc.* IX. 171/2 (*heading*) Brain proteolipides, a new group of protein-lipide substances soluble in organic solvents and insoluble in water. **1971** [see *lipoprotein* s.v. LIPO-]. **1976** *Nature* 25 Mar. 348/1 The L-glutamate binding proteins of insect and crustacean muscle are hydrophobic proteins (that is, proteolipids) extractable with organic solvents.

proteolite ('prəʊtiːəʊlaɪt). *Min.* [f. PROTE-US + -LITE.] A synonym of CORNUBIANITE, q.v.

‖**proteolysis** (prəʊtiː'ɒlɪsɪs). *Phys. Chem.* [mod.L., f. *prōteo-, assumed combining form of PROTEIN + Gr. λύσις a loosening, solution.] A term for **a.** The separation of the proteins from a protein-containing mixture; **b.** The splitting up of proteins by ferments. (*Syd. Soc. Lex.*)
Although parallel in form to *electrolysis* and *hydrolysis* (decomposition by the agency of electricity and of water), *proteolysis* is not parallel in sense: see quot. 1907.
1880 *Nature* XXIII. 169/1 The second lecture chiefly relates to pepsin and the digestion of proteids; digestive proteolysis; the milk-curdling ferment. **1888** *Lancet* 4 Feb. 234/2 An examination of the contents of the stomach proved that the gastric juice was diminished in quantity, and proteolysis impaired. **1890** BILLINGS *Nat. Med. Dict.*, *Proteolysis*, the separation of proteids from a mixture. **1896** *Allbutt's Syst. Med.* I. 97 Of these [substances] the more important are ferments, the results of proteolysis. **1907** *Recommendations of Committee* 8 in *Jrnl. Physiol.* XXXV. *Proc.* 26 Jan., Derivatives of Proteins. Of these, the products of protein-hydrolysis (a term preferable to proteolysis) are those which require special attention. (*Note.* Terms such as proteolysis fail to convey a meaning in harmony with that which is conveyed by the terms electrolysis and hydrolysis (on which they are moulded) of decomposition *by.*)

Hence **proteolyse** ('prəʊtiːəʊlaɪz), *v. trans.*, to decompose or split up (proteins).
1902 in *Daily Chron.* 22 Nov. 6/6 These experiments [of Professor Vines] definitely establish the fact.. that an enzyme which actively proteolyses the simpler forms of proteid is present in all parts of the plant body. **1904** VINES *Proteases of Plants* in *Ann. Bot.* Apr. 291 The results show that these Fungi can peptolyse Witte-peptone, with formation of leucin and tyrosin, and can proteolyse fibrin.

proteolytic (prəʊtiːəʊ'lɪtɪk), *a.* [f. as prec. + Gr. λυτικ-ός able to loose, dissolving.] Having the quality of decomposing proteins. Hence **proteo'lytically** *adv.*, as regards or by means of proteolysis or proteolytic enzymes.
1877 FOSTER *Phys.* II. iv. (1878) 319 An aqueous solution of the precipitate is both amylolytic and proteolytic, i.e. appears to contain some of both the salivary (pancreatic) ferment and pepsin. **1890** BILLINGS *Nat. Med. Dict.*, *Proteolytic*, having the power to decompose or digest proteids. **1896** *Allbutt's Syst. Med.* I. 724 The organism at the primary seat of lesion secretes a potent proteolytic enzyme. **1903** *Ann. Bot.* XVII. 613, I have further succeeded in preparing a proteolytically active glycerin-extract from the roots. **1970** *Nature* 12 Dec. 1097/1 Plasmin.. proteolytically degrades fibrin and fibrinogen preferentially to other substrates. **1978** *Ibid.* 21 Sept. 182/2 One current speculation is that the two forms of fibronectin may be the same gene product, but the surface form is proteolytically processed to the slightly smaller plasma form.

proteose ('prəʊtiːəʊs). *Phys. Chem.* [f. PROTE(IN + -OSE[2].] One of a class of products of protein-hydrolysis: see quots. and PROTEIN.
1890 BILLINGS *Nat. Med. Dict.*, *Proteoses*, primary cleavage-products formed in the digestion of proteids with gastric or pancreatic juices or their equivalents, or by the hydrolytic action of boiling dilute acids. They are intermediate between the original proteid and peptone. **1897** *Allbutt's Syst. Med.* II. 811 Venoms contain proteids which possess.. characteristics of the albumins or globulins and.. those of proteoses. **1907** *Recommendations of Committee on Proteid Nomencl.* 8 Derivatives of Proteins.. b. Proteoses. This term includes albumose, globulose, gelatose, etc.

proter ('prəʊtə(r)). *Biol.* [a. F. *proter* (Chatton & Lwoff 1936, in *Arch. Zool. expér. et gen.* LXXVIII. 85), f. Gr. πρότερος in front.] In ciliate protozoa, the anterior of the two organisms formed by transverse fission. Cf. OPISTHE.
1950 A. LWOFF *Probl. Morphogenesis in Ciliates* xi. 73 In ciliates of the *Leucophrys* type, the proter and the opisthe are modelled in the anterior and posterior parts of the parent. **1961** MACKINNON & HAWES *Protozool.* iv. 222 At binary fission.. the oral structures then go to the anterior daughter, or proter.

proter-, shorter form of PROTERO-, used before a vowel, as in the words here following.

proterandrous (prɒtə'rændrəs), *a.* [f. PROTERO- + -ANDROUS: cf. PROTANDROUS. In both senses opp. to PROTEROGYNOUS.]
1. *Bot.* Having the stamens or male organs mature before the pistil or female organ.
1875 LUBBOCK *Wild Flowers* v. 130 Cross-fertilisation is.. favoured by the flower being proterandrous. **1879** A. W. BENNETT in *Academy* 33 Pentstemon is proterandrous (therefore cross-fertilized).
2. *Zool.* Of a hermaphrodite animal, or a colony of zooids: Having the male organs, or individuals, sexually mature before the female. (Cf. quot. 1887 s.v. PROTERANDRY below.)
Hence **prote'randrousness**, the quality or fact of being proterandrous; so **prote'randry.**
1875 LUBBOCK *Wild Flowers* v. 132 Cross-fertilisation is secured.. in Echium and Borago by proterandrousness (if I may be permitted to coin the word). **1887** *Nature* 29 Dec. 213/1 If the polypides are unisexual, then the proterandry refers only to the colony as a whole. **1895** *Syd. Soc. Lex.*, *Proterandry*, the condition, in a Phanerogam, in which the stamens of the flower mature before the pistil.

proteranthous (prɒtə'rænθəs), *a. Bot.* [f. as prec. + Gr. ἄνθ-ος flower + -OUS.] Having flowers appearing before the leaves.
1832 LINDLEY *Introd. Bot.* 401.

†**pro'terical,** *a. Obs. rare*$^{-1}$. [f. Gr. πρωτερικός early-bearing, precocious (πρωτερική συκῆ a kind of early fig) + -AL[1].] Early-bearing.
a **1682** SIR T. BROWNE *Tracts* (1684) 73 This great variety of Figg Trees, as precocious, proterical, biferous, triferous, and always-bearing Trees.

protero- (prɒtərəʊ), before a vowel proter- (prɒtər), combining form from Gr. πρότερος fore, former, anterior, in place, time, order, rank; used in a few scientific terms.
'proterobase (-beɪs) *Min.* [after DIABASE], an eruptive rock resembling diabase, but in a more advanced stage of alteration. **,protero'glossate**

a. Zool. [Gr. γλῶσσα tongue], belonging to Günther's division *Proteroglossa* of batrachians, having the tongue free in front. **ˈproterosaur** (-sɔː(r)) [Gr. σαῦρος lizard], a saurian of the extinct genus *Proterosaurus* or group *Proterosauria*, comprising some of the oldest known reptiles; so **ˌproteroˈsaurian** *a.*, belonging to the *Proterosauria*; *sb.* a proterosaur. **ˈproterotome** (-təʊm) *a. Zool.* [Gr. -τομος cutting], applied to mastication in which the molars of the lower jaw move forwards against those of the upper, as in the Carnivora. **ˌproteroˈzoic** *a. Geol.* [cf. PROTOZOIC]: see quots. See also PROTERANDROUS, PROTEROGYNOUS, etc.

[**1872** NICHOLSON *Palæont.* 356 In the Permian Rocks the first undoubted Reptilian remains occur, the *Proterosaurus of this period being probably a Lacertilian.] **1896** COPE *Primary Factors Evol.* vi. 318 The inferior molar shears forwards on the superior molar. *Proterotome mastication. **1905** CHAMBERLIN & SALISBURY *Geol.* I. i. 17 In these four great series of sedimentary rocks there are, here and there, intrusions of igneous rocks, and in some places the sedimentary beds have been metamorphosed into crystalline rocks by heat and pressure. This is particularly true in the lowest of these series, the *Proterozoic, where a large part of the sediment is metamorphosed, and where there is much igneous rock. *Ibid.* II. iv. 162 To the *Proterozoic era is assigned the time that elapsed between the close of the formation of the igneous complex and the beginning of the lowest system which is now known to contain abundant well-preserved fossils. [*Note*] Proterozoic, as here used, is a synonym of *Algonkian* as used by the U.S. Geol. Surv. **1906** *Athenæum* 18 Aug. 191/2 Between the close of this long archæan period and the beginning of the palæozoic ages.. there was another vast stretch of geological time, distinguished as the Proterozoic era. **1971** *Nature* 25 June 498/1 The establishment of global subdivisions for the Upper (Late) Pre-Cambrian, or the Proterozoic, is particularly important. **1977** A. HALLAM *Planet Earth* 189 The Proterozoic was, compared with the Archaean, dominantly a period of crustal reworking.

proterogenesis (prɒtərəʊˈdʒɛnɪsɪs). *Biol.* [mod.L. (coined in Ger. by O. H. Schindewolf 1925, in *Neues Jahrb. f. Min., Geol. und Paläont.* LII. B. 337): see PROTERO- and -GENESIS.] The anticipation of future evolutionary development in the early stages of an organism's life. Hence **ˌproterogeˈnetic** *a.*, **-geˈnetically** *adv.*

1938 *Rep. Brit. Assoc. Adv. Sci.* 79 Among the examples quoted by Schindewolf in support of the principle of proterogenesis is one drawn from the cephalopod family the *Clymendiæ* which lived during the Devonian period. It consists of a number of genera and species in which, at one end of the series, the shell has the normal type of spiral coil .. with an almost circular outline throughout development. In the next member of the series the innermost portion of the spiral has a triangular outline. In other members of the series the latter form of outline finds every degree of expression up to one in which it prevails at all stages of growth, including the adult. The series as it stands may be quoted in support of either the proterogenetic or the tachygenetic view, according to which end of the series is taken as the starting point. Schindewolf adopts the former. *Ibid.* 82 Trend characters, on the other hand, arise either cœnogenetically or deuterogenetically and proceed proterogenetically or tachygenetically towards later or earlier stages in life-history respectively in successive generations. **1947** A. M. DAVIES *Introd. Palæont.* (ed. 2) iv. 139 In some cases this change is contrary to the rule of palingenesis, since the youthful whorl-shape foreshadows the adult whorl-shape of forms that come later in time... This reverse sequence to that of palingenesis is termed proterogenesis or cænogenesis, and has been observed in other animal phyla, particularly in the Graptolites. **1947** H. H. SWINNERTON *Outl. Palæont.* (ed. 3) x. 195 The significance of the inner capricorn whorls in alimorphs may accordingly become anticipatory or recapitulatory, proterogenetic or palingenetic according to which view is adopted. **1966** DAVIS & LANGERL tr. *Hennig's Phylogenetic Systematics* iii. 228 The theory of the 'early ontogenetic origin of types' assumes a special place in discussions of the origin of higher categories or new types. Equivalent or nearly equivalent are the concepts of 'proterogenesis' (Schindewolf), paedomorphism (Garstang), and—as Wettstein 1942 emphasizes—the designations diametagenesis.., fetalization.., and neomorphosis.

proteroglyph (ˈprɒtərəʊglɪf). *Zool.* [ad. F. *protéroglyphe*, mod.L. *Proteroglypha* (A. H. A. Duméril 1853, in *Mem. Acad. Sci.* XXIII. 415), f. PROTERO- + Gr. γλυφή carving.] A venomous snake belonging to a group characterized by grooved fangs in the front of the mouth. So **proteroˈglyphous** *a.*

1895 G. S. WEST in *Proc. Zool. Soc.* 813 It is undoubtedly the homologue of that structure present in the Viperine and Proteroglyphous forms. **1896** *Proc. Zool. Soc.* 616 In the Proteroglyphs adapted to life in the sea, a similar series of modifications takes place. **1956** L. M. KLAUBER *Rattlesnakes* II. xi. 715 The front-fanged snakes whose fangs are permanently erect are referred to as proteroglyphs. **1965** R. & D. MORRIS *Men & Snakes* viii. 177 With the sea-snakes and the cobras, we come to a condition known as Proteroglyphous. Here there has been a reduction in the structure of the upper jaw, the front region having disappeared, bringing the poison fangs to the fore... These are the so-called 'fixed-front-fang' snakes. **1969** A. BELLAIRS *Life of Reptiles* I. v. 193 According to this hypothesis the viperids would have had a separate ancestry from the proteroglyphs (elapids and sea snakes).

proterogynous (prɒtəˈrɒdʒɪnəs), *a.* [f. PROTERO- + -GYNOUS. Cf. PROTOGYNOUS. In both senses opposed to PROTERANDROUS.]

1. *Bot.* Having the pistil or female organ mature before the stamens or male organs.

1875 LUBBOCK *Wild Flowers* iii. 51 *Caltha palustris*... The species.. are said by Hildebrand to be proterogynous. **1877** DARWIN *Forms of Fl.* Introd. 10 Other individuals, called proterogynous, have their stigma mature before their pollen is ready. **1883** THOMPSON tr. *Müller's Fert. Flowers* 12 *note*, Sprengel calls this species of dichogamy, *female-male*..; Hildebrand, *protogynous*; Delpino, *proterogynous*.

2. *Zool.* Of a hermaphrodite animal, or a colony of zooids: Having the female organs, or individuals, sexually mature before the male.

So **proteˈrogyny**, the quality or state of being proterogynous.

1890 in *Cent. Dict.* **1895** *Syd. Soc. Lex.*, *Proterogyny*, the maturation of the pistil of a flower before the stamens.

†**proˈterve**, *a. Obs. rare.* [ad. L. *proterv-us* forward, bold, pert, wanton, impudent; cf. obs. F. *proterve* (*c* 1277 in Godef.).

Etymol. of L. *protervus* doubtful. Walde suggests after Fröhde **pro-pterguos*, f. PRO-[1] 1 + cogn. of Gr. πτέρυξ wing.]

Forward, wayward, untoward, stubborn; peevish, petulant. Hence †**proˈtervely** *adv.*

1382 WYCLIF *2 Tim.* iii. 4 Men schulen be.. traitours, proterue [*gloss* or ouerthwert, *Vulg.* protervi]. **1526** *Pilgr. Perf.* (W. de W. 1531) 117 Who so euer by his owne reason or sentence wyll defende proteruely or styfly that thynge yᵗ he loueth. **1567** *Satir. Poems Reform.* vi. 31 Man of his awin nature is so proterue.

protervious, erron. form of PROTERVOUS.

protervity (prəʊˈtɜːvɪtɪ). Now *rare.* [ad. obs. F. *protervité*, ad. L. *protervitātem* forwardness, pertness, etc.: see prec.] Waywardness, frowardness, stubbornness; pertness, sauciness, insolence; peevishness, petulance; an instance of this.

?*c* **1500** *Proverbis* in *Antiq. Rep.* (1809) IV. 409 They that of protervite will not tewne well, *Ve, ve, ve*, theyre songe shal be in hell. **1613** DAY *Festivals* viii. (1615) 233 If.. we adde Protervitie, Stubbornesse, and rude Behaviour. **1654** H. L'ESTRANGE *Chas. I* (1655) 59 The queen, who formerly showed so much waspish protervity and waywardnesse. **1726** C. D'ANVERS *Craftsman* i. (1727) 10 The peevishness and protervity of age. **1838** G. S. FABER *Inquiry* 516 The protervity of heretics in the very efforts of their falsehood. **1882** STEVENSON *Fam. Studies* 36 In his [Hugo's] poems and plays there are the same unaccountable protervities.

†**b.** *fig.* Applied obscurely (or erroneously) to a bodily deformity or disfigurement. *Obs.*

1661 FELTHAM *Resolves* II. iv. (ed. 8) 183 Some deformity in the mind.. (as in certain naturall protervities in the body) they are seldome taking, but often begett a dislike.

†**proˈtervous**, *a. Obs.* Also *erron.* **protervious**. [f. L. *proterv-us* (see PROTERVE) + -OUS.] = PROTERVE.

1547 BALE *Exam. Anne Askewe* 65 b, Slacke eare gaue Pylate to the prestes:.. he detected their proteruouse madnesse. **1624** F. WHITE *Repl. Fisher* 8 No such apparant Victorie was gotten of proteruious Heretiques. *Ibid.* 9 The Scriptures are a meanes to conuict proteruious error.

protest (ˈprəʊtɛst, formerly prəʊˈtɛst), *sb.* [ME. = OF. *protest* (1479 in Hatz.-Darm.), mod.F. *protêt* (= med.L. *prōtest-um*, It., Sp., Pg. *protesto*), f. F. *protester* to PROTEST. Cf. obs. F. *proteste*, It., Sp. *protesta* fem.] An act of protesting.

1. A solemn declaration; an affirmation; an asseveration; an avowal; = PROTESTATION 1.

c **1400** *Beryn* 3905 And in protest opynly, here a-mong ȝewe all, Halff my good.. I graunt it here to Geffrey. **1596** SHAKS. *1 Hen. IV*, III. i. 260 Sweare me.. a good mouth-filling Oath: and leaue in sooth, And such protest of Pepper Ginger-bread, To Veluet-Guards, and Sunday-Citizens. **1654** WHITLOCK *Zootomia* 17 They would cousen.. their Neighbours with Protests of good Usage. **1876** MOZLEY *Univ. Serm.* i. 19 A statement or protest is, compared with the reality, a poor thing.

2. The action taken to fix the liability for the payment of a dishonoured bill; *spec.* a formal declaration in writing, usually by a notary-public, that a bill has been duly presented and payment or acceptance refused.

1622 MALYNES *Anc. Law-Merch.* 399 The Notarie may.. leaue afterwardes the copie of the Protest with some of the house, or throw the same within doores, and keepe a note of it against the next time. **1682** SCARLETT *Exchanges* 71 If a Bill be presented for Acceptance, and the Acceptant refuse absolutely to accept it, then the Possessor of the Bill is obliged instantly without delay to make Protest for Non-Acceptance. **1698** *Act 9 & 10 Will. III*, c. 17 Which Protest .. shall within Fourteen Days after making thereof, be sent, or otherwise due Notice shall be given thereof, to the Party from whom the said Bill or Bills were received. **1726** SHELVOCKE *Voy. round World* 23, I gave the Protest to Capt. Clipperton in the South-Seas. **1882** *Act 45 & 46 Vict.* c. 61 §51 (4) When a bill has been duly noted, the protest may be subsequently extended as of the date of the noting. *Ibid.* (7) A protest must contain a copy of the bill, and be signed by the notary making it.

3. A written declaration made by the master of a ship, attested by a justice of the peace or a consul, stating the circumstances under which injury has happened to the ship or cargo, or under which officers or crew have incurred any liability.

1755 MAGENS *Insurances* I. 87 The Insurers ask for the Protest; which is a Declaration upon Oath, usually made by the Master, and some of his People, before a Justice, Notary or Consul, at any Place where they first arrive. **1848** WHARTON *Law Lex.*, *Protest*,.. a writing attested by a justice of the peace or consul, drawn by a master of a vessel, stating the severity of the voyage by which the ship has suffered, and showing that the damage was not occasioned by his misconduct or neglect.

4. a. A formal statement or declaration of disapproval of or dissent from, or of consent under certain conditions only to, some action or proceeding; a remonstrance.

1751 *Parl. Hist.* I. 38 This Answer of the Barons to the King [in 1242].. being in the Nature of a Protest, is the First of that Kind we meet with in History; we shall, therefore, give it at length as follows. **1769** ROBERTSON *Chas. V*, III. x. 221 Protests and counter-protests were taken. **1822** J. HAGGARD *Rep. Consist. Crt.* I. 5 The husband appeared under protest, and prayed to be dismissed on the ground [etc.]. **1846** MCCULLOCH *Acc. Brit. Empire* (1854) II. 291 On the first day (18th May) of the meeting of the general assembly of 1843, the ministers and elders, members of that body, opposed to the right of patronage and in favour of the veto, gave in a Protest, stating.. that 'The courts of the church as now established, and members thereof, are liable to be coerced by the civil courts in the exercise of their spiritual functions'. **1885** SIR W. B. BRETT in *Law Rep. 14 Q. Bench Div.* 876 The meaning of paying under protest necessarily is that the party paying the money does not pay it by way of rightful payment, but claims it still as his money in the hands of the person to whom it is paid. **1893** *Times* 30 Dec. 9/4 Meetings of protest began to be held all over Ireland.

b. A written statement of dissent from any motion carried in the House of Lords, recorded and signed by any Peer of the minority. (The earlier term was PROTESTATION 3 b.)

1712 (*title*) The Protest of the L[ord]s, upon A[ddressing] Her M[ajesty] for Her Sp[eech]: With the Names of the L[or]ds. **1721** *Jrnls. Ho. Lords* XXI. 695/2 Ordered, That on Thursday next, this House will take into Consideration the Nature of Protests, and the Manner of entering them. **1721** (*title*) Another Protest of their Lordships, on Sir George Byng's Attacking the Spanish Fleet. **1765** BLACKSTONE *Comm.* I. ii. 168 Each peer has also a right, by leave of the house, when a vote passes contrary to his sentiments, to enter his dissent on the journals of the house, with the reasons of such dissent; which is usually stiled his protest. **1854** MACAULAY *Biog.* (1867) 16 Some of the most remarkable protests which appear in the journals of the peers were drawn up by him [Atterbury]. **1875** ROGERS (*title*) A Complete Collection of the Protests of the Lords.. 1624–1874. *Ibid.* Pref. 13 It was not assumed or acted on before the Long Parliament, though the six Peers who make the first protest, with or without reasons, state that they 'demanded their right of protestation'. *Ibid.* Pref. 15 The first protest with reasons entered in the Journals of the Irish House of Lords was in 1695,.. the practice was plainly borrowed from English procedure.

c. In Adlerian psychology, a personal, perhaps unconscious, dissent or attempted dissociation from one's self or circumstances; esp. ***masculine protest*** (see quots. 1917 and 1972).

1917 GLUECK & LIND tr. *Adler's Neurotic Constitution* (1921) iii. 49 The dynamics of the neurosis can therefore be regarded (and is often so understood by the neurotic because of its irradiation upon his psyche) as if the patient wished to change from a woman to a man. This effect yields in its most highly colored form the picture of that which I have called the 'masculine protest'. **1939** H. ORGLER *A. Adler* v. 128 The second little theft was carried out as a protest against his being released on parole. **1972** H. PAPANEK in Freedman & Kaplan *Interpreting Personality* iii. 127 The term 'masculine protest' refers to the attitude of a boy or girl who is raised in a patriarchal culture, in which the real man is respected and admired and the feminine role connotes submissiveness and immaturity.

d. The expressing of dissent from, or rejection of, the prevailing social, political, or cultural mores.

1953 S. A. BROWN in A. Dundes *Mother Wit* (1973) 40/2 We go then to what is called the New Negro Movement, then to.. Social Protest. **1967** *Listener* 8 June 752/3 Mr Woodcock.. traces the development of protest from the first tramps of *Down and Out in Paris and London* to the final achievement of Big Brother. **1968** *Ibid.* 4 July 22/3 Unlike many American authors of his generation, he has [not].. the rather breathy enthusiasm of those who have jumped alongside the youthful millions on the band-wagon.. of Protest. **1975** A. POWELL *Hearing Secret Harmonies* ii. 72, I was watching a programme.. dealing with protest, counterculture, alternative societies.

5. *attrib.* and *Comb.* **a.** Demonstrating or representing a protest against a specific action or proceeding, as ***protest banner, button, camp, group, meeting, movement, rally, resolution, strike***; designating a literary or artistic medium which seeks to register or portray dissatisfaction with a given event, style, etc., as ***protest art, literature, music, poetry, song***; also ***protest-singer, -singing***; (sense 4 c) ***protest mechanism***; also ***protest-oriented*** adj. **b.** Special combs.: **protest march** = MARCH *sb.*[4] 1 a; hence as *v. intr.*; also **protest marcher**; **protest vote**, a vote placed with a minor faction and considered to represent a protest against the policies of a greater; so **protest voting**.

1973 S. HENDERSON *Understanding New Black Poetry* 16 Not 'protest' art but essentially an art of liberating vision. **1976** *Milton Keynes Express* 18 June 3/3 Their threat to swamp the area with protest banners had been lifted at the last minute. **1972** *Sat. Rev.* (U.S.) 27 May 6/2 A large protest button, reading: 'Memorial Day, 1969, 35,000 GI's dead in Vain. No More.' **1968** 'O. Mills' *Sundry Fell Designs* i. 9 This..must be her eleventh protest camp, not counting non-overnight demonstrations in Trafalgar Square but counting the Aldermaston marches. **1895** *Daily News* 9 Sept. 5/5 Lord Dunraven did not, as many expected.., hoist the protest flag after the finish. **1961** B. R. Wilson *Sects & Society* 1 The sect, as a protest group, has always developed its own distinctive ethic. **1973** *Freedom* 1 Sept. 4/1 The various 'protest' groups had lost interest in The Bomb. **1960** *Times Lit. Suppl.* 5 Feb. 77/1 Mr. Klaus Roehler's stories..invite automatic comparison with other outcrops of post-war protest literature. **1975** *Listener* 16 Jan. 69/1 A..flood of protest literature which circulated through the underground channels of *samizdat*, or clandestine publishing. **1959** 'M. Derby' *Tigress* iv. 151 What was he..doing in Ceylon? Leading a hydrogen bomb protest march? **1963** *Economist* 9 Nov. 550/2 The people were protest-marching. **1966** C. Achebe *Man of People* i. 4 Protest marches and demonstrations were staged up and down the land. **1967** *Punch* 8 Nov. 699/1, I see an army with banners, protest-marching up and down Charing Cross Road. **1976** *Eastern Even. News* (Norwich) 9 Dec. 3/1 The meeting held at the Hippodrome theatre after a protest march with banners through the town centre. **1960** *Guardian* 12 Oct. 8/5 Sir Edgar Whitehead..failed to..speak to the patient thousands of protest marchers. **1976** J. Wainwright *Bastard* v. 74 The leather-stampers [*sc.* policemen] who stroll alongside the protest marchers. **1920** *Challenge* 21 May 45/1 Adler..has shown how this protest mechanism is responsible for neurotic manifestations of another kind. **1852** Mundy *Our Antipodes* (1857) 209 The protest meetings occurred on the 11th and 18th. **1902** *Daily Chron.* 27 June 8/1 A protest meeting was held at ten o'clock. **1939** L. MacNeice *Autumn Jrnl.* vii. 30 In the sodden park on Sunday protest Meetings assemble. **1965** S. T. Ollivier *Petticoat Farm* x. 137 The Richards brothers..called a protest meeting of all suppliers. **1909** *Westm. Gaz.* 5 Nov. 5/2 A protest movement is being organised in Belgium against the interference of England in the internal policy of Belgium, especially in regard to the Congo question. **1974** tr. *Wertheim's Evolution & Revolution* iv. 114 In such a case, it should not be called a counterpoint any more, but a social protest movement. **1969** *Listener* 5 June 806/1 Can he [*sc.* Bob Dylan] have forgotten entirely the horrors that gave such a fine edge to his protest music? *Ibid.* 6 Feb. 163/3 Mr Desmond Bird spoke of our 'protest-oriented' society. **1973** S. Henderson *Understanding New Black Poetry* 25 There has been, despite denials, some protest poetry in the sixties. **1960** *Guardian* 11 July 5/3 A protest rally was held in Trafalgar Square. **1977** W. H. Manville *Good-bye* ii. 16 A lot of show-biz people were going to sing and tap-dance at a last-ditch protest rally. **1968** *Guardian* 19 Sept. 9/4 Brave new causes for brave new protest singers. **1969** *Listener* 5 June 805/3 Bob Dylan's *Nashville Skyline* LP completes his recent renunciation of the rebellious, CND-oriented protest-singer image in favour of that of a fun-loving country boy. **1966** *Punch* 19 Jan. 70/2 Anyone tired of protest singing must have been cheered to learn that a group in California..is rapidly climbing the charts with seventeenth-century songs. **1953** J. Greenway *Amer. Folksong of Protest* 3 Protest songs are unpleasant and disturbing. **1966** *Punch* 9 Feb. 208/2 The rise of the protest songs seems to be doing something for the audibility of lyrics. **1979** *Oxford Times* 21 Dec. 15 What happened to protest songs? Well, here's one, asking: 'Do you find it attractive to be radioactive?' **1974** T. Allbeury *Snowball* xxii. 138 A million workers were due to vote on protest strikes. **1973** *Irish Times* 2 Mar. 9/3 In the event, West Mayo threatened a protest vote. **1976** *Times* 3 Feb. 7/5 A substantial part of the [French] communist vote is a protest one. **1948** in M. McLuhan *Mech. Bride* (1967) 6/6 A blank ballot is the only means of protest voting.

protest (prəʊ'tɛst), *v.* [a. F. *proteste-r* (14th c. in Littré), ad. L. *prōtest-ārī* (also in late L. *-āre*) to declare formally in public, testify, protest, f. pro-[1] 1 a + *testārī* to be or speak as a witness, to declare, aver, assert.]

1. a. *trans.* To declare or state formally or solemnly (something about which a doubt is stated or implied); to affirm, asseverate, or assert in formal or solemn terms. Const. with *subord. cl.*, *compl.*, or *simple obj.*

1440 Humphrey Dk. Glouc. *Advice* in Rymer *Fœdera* (1710) X. 767/1, I Protest, for myn Excuse and my Discharge, that I never was, am, nor never shal be Consentyng..to his Deliverance. **1530** Palsgr. 668/2, I protest that I wyll nothyng obstynatly affyrme that [etc.]. **1561** T. Norton *Calvin's Inst.* i. 33 Likewise Thomas in protesting him to be his lord and his God, doth professe that he is that only one God whome he hath alway worshipped. **1561** in Calderwood *Hist. Kirk* (Wodrow Soc.) II. 119 Forasmuche as no man speeketh against this thing, you, N., sall protest heere, before God, and his holie congregatioun, that you have taken, and are now contented to have, M., heere present, for your lawfull wife. **1621** Jas. I in Ellis *Orig. Lett.* Ser. i. III. 169 Till then I proteste I can have no joye in the going well of my owin bussienesse. **1709** Steele *Tatler* No. 3 ¶7, I protest to you, the Gentleman has not spoken to me. **1759** Robertson *Hist. Scot.* vii. Wks. 1813 I. 512 She protested in the most solemn manner, that she was innocent of the crime laid to her charge. **1839** Keightley *Hist. Eng.* II. 38 She then..with dignity and calmness solemnly protested her innocence.

b. *intr.* To make protestation or solemn affirmation.

1560 Bible (Genev.) *1 Kings* ii. 42 Did I not make thee sweare..& protested vnto thee, saying [etc.]? —— *Jer.* xi. 7, I haue protested vnto your fathers.., rising earely & protesting, saying, Obey my voyce. **1602** Shaks. *Ham.* iii. ii. 240 *Ham.* Madam, how like you this Play? *Qu.* The Lady protests to much, me thinks. **1611** Bible *Gen.* xliii. 3 The man did solemnly protest vnto vs, saying, Ye shall not see my face, except your brother be with you. —— *1 Sam.* viii. 9 Protest solemnly vnto them, and shew them the maner of the King that shall reigne over them. **1850** Robertson *Serm.* Ser. iii. v. 75 Every mother..who ever, by her hope against hope for some profligate, protested for a love deeper and wider than that of society.

c. As a mere asseveration; cf. declare *v.* 6 b.

1587 Turberv. *Trag. T.* (1837) 136, I lovde, I doe protest, And did of worldlie men account that worthie knight the best. **1612** Dekker *If it be not good* Wks. 1873 III. 313, I will doe it I protest. **1771** *Junius Lett.* xlix. (1820) 253, I cannot ..call you the..basest fellow in the Kingdom. I protest, my lord, I do not think you so.

d. *trans.* With direct speech as obj.

1903 E. Childers *Riddle of Sands* v. 48 'I'm not boring you, am I?' he said suddenly. 'I should think not,' I protested. **1919** V. Woolf *Night & Day* xii. 154 'But I do read De Quincey,' Ralph protested 'more than Belloc and Chesterton.' **1952** M. Laski *Village* xvi. 218 'But it's quite a good idea,' protested Martha. **1976** B. Freemantle *November Man* iii. 36 'And why the hell not?' he protested.

2. a. *trans.* To make a formal written declaration of the non-acceptance or non-payment of (a bill of exchange) when duly presented. Also *fig.*

1655 *Nicholas Papers* (Camden) II. 194 Permitting a Bill to be protested by Mr Webster. **1667** Pepys *Diary* 13 Dec., If the bill of 200*l.*..be not paid..and..if I do not help him about it, they have no way but to let it be protested. **1765** *Act 5 Geo. III*, c. 49 §5 The person..who shall have protested such note. **1866** Crump *Banking* v. 112 The acceptor may procure the funds necessary to meet the bill, and prevent its being protested.

†**b.** To protest the bill of (a person). *Obs. rare.*

1622 Fletcher *Beggar's Bush* iv. i, I'm sure 'twould vex your hearts, to be protested; Ye're all fair merchants. **1632** Massinger *City Madam* i. iii, I must and will have my money, Or I'll protest you first, and, that done, have The statute made for bankrupts served upon you.

c. *U.S. Football.* To lodge a protest against (a player); to object to as disqualified.

1905 *McClure's Mag.* June 118/2 Princeton protested Thomas J. Thorp, one of Columbia's best men. Columbia returned the compliment by protesting Davis, Princeton's captain and end-rush.

†**3.** To assert publicly; to proclaim, publish; to declare, show forth. *Obs.*

a **1548** Hall *Chron., Edw. IV* 227 In case y[e] he did refuse so to do, then he [the herald] dyd protest the harme that should ensue, in the forme and maner, that in suche a case is..accustumed to be done. **1599** Shaks. *Much Ado* v. i. 149 Do me right, or I will protest your cowardise. *c* **1620** [see protested 1]. **1641** (Sept. 9) in Rogers *Protests of Lords* (1875) I. 6 Therefore to acquit ourselves of the dangers and inconveniences that might arise..we do protest our dissasents to this vote, and do thus enter it as aforesaid. [Cf. sense 7.] *a* **1644** Quarles *Sol. Recant.* Sol. xii. 46 Remember thy Creator; O protest His praises to the world.

†**4.** To vow; to promise or undertake solemnly.

1560 Daus tr. *Sleidane's Comm.* 432 That suche [married priests] as by the consent of their wiues, wil proteste to make a diuorsement they do handle more gently. **1590** Shaks. *Mids. N.* i. i. 89 On Dianaes Altar to protest For aie, austerity, and single life. **1624** *Brief Inform. Affairs Palatinate* 36 As for the Dignitie Imperiall, the Elector Palatine hath alwayes protested to recognize him for Emperor. *c* **1660** in Gutch *Coll. Cur.* II. 455 The Scots seriously protested the performance of all these.

†**5.** To make a request in legal form; to demand as a right; to stipulate. Const. with *subord. cl.*, also *intr.* with *for*. *Sc. Obs.*

1508 Kennedie *Flyting w. Dunbar* 331 Syne ger Stobo for thy lyf protest. **1574** *Reg. Privy Council Scot.* II. 410 The said Maister Johnne protestit that the said Lord Robert sould not be haldin to answer to the saidis letters. **1678** Sir G. Mackenzie *Crim. Laws Scot.* ii. xx. §3 (1699) 230 When Advocats assist Pannels, especially in Treason, they use to protest that no escape of theirs in pleading, may be misconstructed. **1752** J. Louthian *Form of Process* (ed. 2) 113 Of old, before inclosing the Jury, the Lord Advocate or Prosecutor used to protest for an Assize of Error against the Inquest, if they assoilzied.

†**6.** To call to witness; to appeal to. *Obs.*

1555 W. Watreman *Fardle Facions* App. 339 Protesting God, that he entended not to tourne aside, or hide..any thing that is another mannes. **1667** Milton *P.L.* x. 480 Unoriginal Night and Chaos wilde..with clamorous uproare Protesting Fate supreame. **1675** Hobbes *Odyssey* (1677) 9 Protest the gods against their injuries; And let the whole assembly know your case.

7. a. *intr.* To give formal expression to objection, dissent, or disapproval; to make a formal (often written) declaration *against* some proposal, decision, procedure, or action; to remonstrate. Also const. *at*.

1608 Armin *Nest Ninn.* (1842) 48 This lusty jester..in fury draws his dagger, and begins to protest. **1634** Sir T. Herbert *Trav.* Ded. A ij b, Such imprest money I doe not like, but protest against it. **1641** (Dec. 24) in Rogers *Protests of Lords* (1875) I. 7, I do protest against the deferring the debate thereof until Monday, to the end to discharge myself of any ill consequence that may happen thereby. **1718** (Feb. 20) *Ibid.* I. 240 We, whose names are subscribed, do protest against the resolution for refusing the other instruction, moved to be given to the same Committee on the Mutiny Bill, for the reasons following: 1st, Because [etc.]. **1762** Goldsm. *Cit. W.* xxxiii, This I protested against, as being no way Chinese. **1873** J. H. Newman *Hist. Sk.* II. Pref. 12 A minister of religion may fairly protest against being made a politician. **1947** Partridge *Usage & Abusage* 46/1 The following from a newspaper placard, *The Daily Worker*, Feb. 6, 1938, —40,000 protest at food prices. **1969** *Daily Tel.* 22 Apr. 29 Conservatives protested angrily..at the Government's failure to announce new contribution rates.

b. *trans.* To protest against (an action or event); to make the subject of a protest. Chiefly *U.S.* Cf. 2 c.

1904 *Brooklyn Eagle* 5 June **5/6 Many of the students are much incensed at the judges and will probably protest the decision. **1927** E. G. Mears *Resident Orientals on Pacific Coast* i. 6 The Peking Foreign Office has regularly protested acts of injustice and violence. **1930** C. Johnson *Negro in Amer. Civilisation* xx. 297 They are protesting the disposition of public school officials to ignore vocational training for Negro youth. **1944** *Sun* (Baltimore) 22 July 2/1 For Hitler it was sufficient that this former chief of staff resigned in 1938 to protest Hitler's march into Austria. **1951** *Newsweek* 27 Sept. 74/3 The residents of Follanshee..have protested the sale, claiming it would throw 2,441 persons out of work. **1956** [see heel *sb.*[1] 11]. **1966** H. Kemelman *Saturday Rabbi went Hungry* ii. 15 For one thing, I protest their having been singled out. They were pushed and one of them fell. **1977** H. Fast *Immigrants* ii. 82 Dan protested naming the child after Jean's mother. **1978** *Dædalus* Summer 188 They protest the brutal simplicities, the unilinearity and determinism of the great cruel myths of modernization.

†'**Protestancy.** *Obs.* [f. next + -cy.] The condition of being a Protestant; the Protestant religion, system, or principles; = Protestantism 1. In 17th c., *spec.* the system of the reformed Church of England, as distinguished on the one hand from Popery, on the other from Presbyterianism and Puritanism.

1604 *Supplic. Masse Priests* §41 Puritanisme differing from Protestancie in 32 articles of doctrine (as their owne bookes and writings doe witnesse). **1612** J. Chamberlain in *Crt. & Times Jas. I* (1848) I. 162 He renounced all religions, Papistry, Protestancy, Puritanism, and all other, and took himself only to God. **1655** G. Hall (*title*) The Triumphs of Rome over Despised Protestancie. **1687** *Refl. upon Pax Vobis* 32 Presbytery..would crush Protestancy if it could. **1688** Penn *Let.* Wks. 1726 I. *Life* 137 The Common Protestancy of the Kingdom. **1822** J. Milner *Vind. Ends Relig. Controv.* 59 Recanting the whole system of Protestancy.

b. The Protestant community: = Protestantism 2.

1711 in *10th Rep. Hist. MSS. Comm.* App. v. 196 This death miserably contristated the whole Protestancy of the three nations.

Protestant ('prɒtɪstənt), *sb.* and *a.* [a. Ger. or F. *protestant*, in pl. the designation of those who joined in the protest at Spires in 1529, ad. L. *prōtestāns*, pl. *prōtestānt-ēs*, pres. pple. of *prōtest-ārī* to protest. In French also †one who protests in any sense, e.g. who protests devotion, sb. use of pres. pple. of *protester* (cf. sense 3 a).]

A. *sb.* **I.** *Eccles.*

1. *Hist.* usually *pl.* The name given to those German princes and free cities who made a declaration of dissent from the decision of the Diet of Spires (1529), which re-affirmed the edict of the Diet of Worms against the Reformation; hence, a general designation of the adherents of the Reformed doctrines and worship in Germany.

In the 16th c., the name *Protestant* was generally taken in Germany by the Lutherans; while the Swiss and French called themselves *Reformed*.

1539 Wyatt *Let. to Cromwell* in *MS. Cotton Vesp. C. vii.* lf. 26 b, The Launsegrave the Duke of Saxone and the other of the Liegue whiche they cal the Protestantes. *Ibid.* lf. 28 b, This must be other against the Turk or the Protestantes, or for Geldres. **1540** Wotton *Let. to Cromwell* in *St. Papers Hen. VIII*, VIII. 287 They reken heere that the Protestantes will make no leage nor truecis with thEmperour, but under suche wordes, as shalbe able to ynclude the Duke of Cleves to. **1542** Coverdale *Actes Disput.* Contents, The namys of all them which are called protestantys. **1551** J. Hales *Let. fr. Augsburg to Cecil* 27 Apr. (S.P. For., Edw. VI, VI. No. 328, P.R.O.), In most places the Papistes and Protestauntes haue ther servyce in one churche, one after thother. **1559** Bp. Scot in Strype *Ann. Ref.* (1709) I. App. vii. 17 It is declared..that earnest sute was made by the protestantes to have three things graunted and suffered to be practyssed within that realme [of Polonia]. **1560** Daus tr. *Sleidane's Comm.* 82 b, Vnto this protestation of Prynces, certen of the chief cities..did subscribe..this is in dede y[e] first original of the name of Protestauntes, which not only in Germany, but also emonges foreyn nations, is nowe common and famous. **1624** Bedell *Lett.* ii. 4 *Protestants.* A name first given to the Princes and free Cities of Germany, that sought reformation in the Diet at Spire, Anno 1529. **1659** Milton *Civ. Power* Wks. 1738 I. 547 Which Protestation made by the first publick Reformers of our Religion against the Imperial Edicts of Charles the fifth, imposing Church-Traditions without Scripture, gave first beginning to the name of Protestant. **1761** Hume *Hist. Eng.* II. xxx. 174 The Lutheran princes..had combined in a league for their own defence at Smalcalde; and because they protested against the votes passed in the imperial diet, they thenceforth received the appellation of Protestants. **1899** B. J. Kidd *39 Art.* I. i. §2. 7 In church ornaments,..while the Lutherans or Protestants were willing to retain everything that was not expressly forbidden in Scripture, the Swiss or Reformed excluded everything but what was positively enjoined.

2. a. A member or adherent of any of the Christian churches or bodies which repudiated the papal authority, and separated or were severed from the Roman communion in the Reformation of the sixteenth century, and generally of any of the bodies of Christians descended from them; hence in general language applied to any Western Christian or member of a Christian church outside the

Roman communion. Opposed to *Papist*, *Roman Catholic*, or *Catholic* in the restricted sense.

1553 E. Underhill in *Narr. Reform.* (Camden) 140 Your honors do knowe thatt in this controversy thatt hathe byn, sume be called papistes and sume protestaynes. **1554** Coverdale *Lett. Mass* (1564) 345 The more parte doe parte stakes wythe the papistes and protestantes, so that they are become maungye Mongrelles. **1556** M. Huggard (*title*) The displaying of the Protestantes, & sondry their practises, with a description of diuers their abuses.. frequented within their malignaunte church. **1561** (*title*) The Confession of the Faythe and Doctrine beleued and professed by the Protestantes of the Realme of Scotlande. **1562** A. Scott *Poems* (S.T.S.) i. 145 Protestandis takis þe freiris auld antetewne, Reddie ressauaris, bot to rander nocht. **1594** Nashe *Unfort. Trav.* 60, I must saie to the shame of vs protestants, if good workes may merit heauen they [Romans] doe them, we talke of them. **1610** Holland *Camden's Brit.* (1637) 327 William Lambard.. was the first Protestant that built an Hospitall. **1659** Baxter *Key Cath.* Pref. 3 A Protestant is a Christian that holdeth to the holy Scriptures as a sufficient Rule of faith and holy living and protesteth against Popery. **1659** Evelyn *Diary* 21 Oct., A private Fast was kept by the Church of England Protestants in towne. **1678** *Act 30 Chas. II*, Stat. ii. §2, *Declar.* 3, I do make this Declaration.. in the plain and ordinary Sense of the Words read unto me, as they are commonly understood by English Protestants, without any Evasion, Equivocation or mental Reservation whatsoever. **1685** Evelyn *Diary* 3 Nov., The French persecution of the Protestants raging with the utmost barbarity. **1686** *Ibid.* 5 May, The Duke of Savoy, instigated by the French King to extirpate the Protestants of Piedmont. **1689** Sancroft in Gutch *Coll. Cur.* I. 447 We are true Englishmen and true Protestants, and heartily love our Religion and our Laws. **1798** Sophia Lee *Canterb. T., Young Lady's T.* II. 255 He could not, as a protestant, claim sanctuary with the monks. **1864** J. H. Newman *Apologia pro Vita Sua* vii. 425 If Protestants wish to know what our real teaching is,.. let them look, not at our books of casuistry, but at our catechisms. **1895** Ld. Acton *Stud. Hist.* (1896) 24 The centre of gravity, moving.. from the Latin to the Teuton, has also passed from the Catholic to the Protestant. **1900** C. M. Yonge *Mod. Broods* v. 50 You seem to me like the Roman Catholic child, who said there were five sacraments, there ought to be seven, but the Protestants had got two of them. **1903** F. W. Maitland in *Camb. Mod. Hist.* II. xvi. 571 The word 'Protestant', which is rapidly spreading [*c* 1559] from Germany, comes as a welcome name. In the view of an officially inspired apologist of the Elizabethan settlement, those who are not Papists are Protestants. **1938** O. C. Quick *Doctrines of Creed* II. xiii. 134 Neither Thomistic orthodoxy nor the modernism of the Liberal Protestants can take such an interpretation seriously. **1955** R. Macaulay *Let.* 5 Feb. in *Last Lett. to Friend* (1962) 190 It is this tendency to rule out Protestants (including Anglicans) from the Church of Christ that is so tiresome and silly. **1962** C. Quin tr. *E. Amand de Mendieta's Rome & Canterbury* viii. 183 After the Reformation movement had led to a vigorous reaction among Protestants against excessive devotion to the Virgin Mary, Roman Catholic theologians have always regarded the defence of the legitimacy of such devotion as one of their chief tasks. **1966** D. E. Jenkins *Guide to Debate about God* iii. 65 Protestants have tended not to be very concerned about the collapse of reason in relation to awareness of God. **1973** *Ann. Reg. 1972* 376 In Northern Ireland the most sinister development was sectarian assassination; 81 Catholics and 40 Protestants.

b. *spec.* In reference to the Church of England the use has varied with time and circumstances. In the 17th c., *Protestant* was generally accepted and used by members of the Established Church, and was even so applied to the exclusion of Presbyterians, Quakers, and Separatists, as was usual at least until the early 20th c. in parts of England and Ireland. In more recent times the name has been disfavoured or disowned by many Anglicans. Also, a Low Church member of the Church of England.

In the 17th c., 'protestant' was primarily opposed to 'papist', and thus accepted by English Churchmen generally; in more recent times, being generally opposed to 'Roman Catholic', or (after common Continental and R.C. use) to 'Catholic' (see catholic A. 7, B. 2, 3), it is viewed with disfavour by those who lay stress on the claim of the Anglican Church to be equally Catholic with the Roman. (see also sense c below).

1608 Chapman, etc. *Eastward Hoe* v. i, I have had of all sorts of men.. under my Keyes; and almost of all religions i' the land, as Papist, Protestant, Puritane, Brownist, Anabaptist,.. etc. **1608** D. T[uvil] *Ess. Pol. & Mor.* 64 Betweene the Catholick and the Protestant, the Protestant and the Puritan, the Puritan and others. **1642** Mrs. Eure in *Verney Mem.* (1892) II. v. 96 Neither papist, nor puritan, aye nor protestant, but will be the loosers by it. **1661** Jer. Taylor *Serm. at Opening Parl. Irel.* 8 May ¶ 11, I hope the presbyterian will join with the protestant, and say, that the papist, and the Socinian, and the independent, and the anabaptist, and the quaker, are guilty of rebellion and disobedience. **1820** tr. *Cosmo's Trav.* 425 The Puritans.. sworn enemies of the Catholics, as also of the Protestants. [Cf. p. 412 Protestants or those of the Established Religion.] **1830-3** W. Carleton *Traits & Stories Irish Peasantry* (1860) I. 185 The population of the Catholics on the one side, and of Protestants and Dissenters on the other. **1834** J. H. Newman *Let.* 30 July (1891) II. 59 The word Protestant does not, as far as I know, occur in our formularies. It is an uncomfortable, perplexing word, intended to connect us.. with the Protestants abroad. We are a 'Reformed' Church, not a 'Protestant'. **1874** J. H. Blunt *Dict. Sects* 447/2 High Churchmen of modern times.. have.. objected to the designation of Protestant as being (1) one of too negative a character to express at all justly the principle of Catholic resistance to the uncatholic pretensions and practices of Rome: and (2) as being a name which is used by so many sects as to be inclusive even of heresy. **1890** Healy *Insula Sanctorum*, etc. 291 His memory is cherished not only by Catholics but by Protestants and even by Presbyterians also. **1900** Rev. C. B. Mount *Let. to Editor*, Forty years back in Dorset, I frequently heard the word 'Protestant' used as distinctive name for members of the Established Church of England, in distinction from 'Dissenters', 'Chapel-goers', and the like. **1913** C. Mackenzie *Sinister St.* I. ii. vi. 239 'Finding out for yourself,' echoed Chator with a look of alarm. 'I say, you're an absolute Protestant.' 'Oh, no I'm not,' contradicted Michael. 'I'm a Catholic.' **1933** G. Faber *Oxf. Apostles* iii. 73 They [*sc.* the Tractarians] were hostile to Roman pretensions.. but they claimed the same title of Catholic.. and they loathed the title of Protestant only less than that of Dissenter. **1960** *Daily Tel.* 15 Nov. 12/8 Surely Canon Lionel Lydekker is mistaken when he writes that the original meaning of Protestant was 'protesting against any tampering with the Holy Catholic Faith'. *Ibid.*, Canon Lydekker's definition of 'Protestant' is in line with 18th-century usage when, in this country, it meant Anglican, as distinct from Nonconformist, just as on the Continent it still means Lutheran as distinct from Calvinist (or 'reformed'). **1813** A. Knox in *K. & Jebb's Corr.* (1834) II. 122 What perverse influence the nick-name of protestant has had on our church. **1905** A. Cooper-Marsdin *Church or Sect* i. 7, I refuse to call myself a Protestant except.. when I wish to declare.. that I am not a Papist.

c. A member of a nonconformist or non-episcopal Church.

1958 M. Argyle *Relig. Behaviour* xii. 157 By Protestants we mean to refer to the main 'nonconformist' denominations such as Methodists, Presbyterians and Baptists. **1963** Auden *Dyer's Hand* 350 In New England Protestants of Anglo-Scotch stock consider themselves a cut above Roman Catholics and those of a Latin race. **1977** R. L. Wolff *Gains & Losses* 8 Dissenters or Non-conformists, Protestants of many varying sects, who dissent from the Church of England.

II. *General.* Often stressed (prəʊˈtɛstənt).

3. One who protests. **a.** One who makes protestation or declaration; *esp.* one who protests devotion [Fr. *protestant*]; a suitor. *rare.*

1648 Herrick *Hesper., To Anthea, who may command*, etc. i, Bid me to live, and I will live Thy Protestant to be. **1904** *Daily Chron.* 5 May 3/3 That is how we find among her 'protestants' Mr. Denis O'Hara, whose love-chase is the theme of this, as of the earlier story.

b. One who protests against error (partly etymological, partly *fig.* from 1 or 2).

1836-7 Sir W. Hamilton *Metaph.* (1877) I. v. 91 We must be protestants, not infidels in philosophy. **1903** G. F. Browne *St. Aldhelm* 297 Abbat Failbe was the first Protestant in these islands, for Adamnan says that he 'protested'... A Protestant is one who asserts his own belief in a definite and positive form.

c. One who makes protest *against* any decision, proceeding, practice, custom, or the like; a protester. (Often with allusion to senses 1 and 2.)

1853 Maurice *Proph. & Kings* xix. 328 The protestant against sensual and divided worship. **1862** —— *Mor. & Met. Philos.* IV. ix. §108. 629 To hope that he would be the effectual protestant against all North West passages. **1885** *Century Mag.* June 328/1 No great moral value can be attached to a protest against evil doing at which the protestant has connived. **1896** Bp. Gore *Rom. Cath. Claims* (1904) App. i. 206 When John the Baptist appeared, he appeared as a protestant against the actual development which the inspired religion had received. **1906** *Daily Chron.* 4 May 3/4 Lawrence Rivers, protestant against compulsory games, champion of the right to do with schoolboy leisure as schoolboy pleases.

B. *adj.* **1. a.** Of, pertaining to, or of the nature of Protestants or Protestantism; usu. in a broad sense, designating Christian bodies, beliefs, etc., outside the Communion of Rome and the Eastern Communions; occas. (*b*) more narrowly, in sense A. 2 c above. (In the earliest quots., = *protesting*, and, in reference to the Continent, = *Lutheran*.)

1539 Cromwell in *St. Papers Hen. VIII*, I. 605 The States Protestantes have geven their petition more then 4 dayes passed, but as yet thEmperours Commissioners have geven no answer therto. **1542** Coverdale *Actes Disput.* 195 These be the Prynces and estates protestantys & all which do stond to the confessyon geuen at Augspurg called the germanys confession. **1584** *Leycesters Commw.* (1641) 97 Complaining on all hands of our protestants Bishops and Clergy. **1607** Topsell *Four-f. Beasts* Ep. Ded., D. Gesner.. was a Protestant Physician. **1644** Evelyn *Diary* 6 Mar., To heare & see the manner of the French Protestant Churches service. **1648** *Eikon Bas.* xxvii. 277 That scarce any one [of them].. either was, or is a true Lover,.. or Practiser of the Protestant Religion, established in England. **1654** (Dec. 7) *Resolution in Jrnls. Ho. Comm.* VII. 397/2 The True Reformed Protestant, Christian Religion, as it is contained in the Holy Scriptures,.. shall be asserted and maintained, as the publick Profession of these Nations. **1679** Evelyn *Diary* 28 Nov., This Duke [Monmouth], whom for distinction they call'd the Protestant Duke.., the people made their idol. *c* **1687** Burnet *Orig. Mem.* i. (1902) 153 She does the protestant interest more service than all her ill-affects can do it a prejudice. **1688** Kennett in *Magd. Coll. & Jas. II* (O.H.S.) 258 There was a Protestant, or rather Providential, wind. **1688** *Act 1 Will. & Mary* c. 6 (Coronation oath), Will you to the utmost of your Power maintain the Laws of God, the true Profession of the Gospel and the Protestant Reformed Religion established by Law? **1689** Sancroft in Gutch *Coll. Cur.* I. 447 The Bishops and Clergy of England are unmoveably fixt to the Protestant religion; and absolutely irreconcileable both to Popery and arbitrary power. **1700** Pepys *Let.* 12 Apr., All the King of France does against his Protestant subjects. **1828** *Act 9 Geo. IV*, c. 17. §2 (*Declaration*) The Protestant Church as it is by Law established in England. **1854** [see catholic B. 3]. **1899** Bp. Stubbs *Visitation Charges* (1904) 343 *The Protestant Religion* is, I think, the historical and reasonable expression for collective application. **1861** C. M. Yonge *Young Stepmother* xxix. 448, I wonder if the omnibus is too protestant to leave a parcel at the convent. **1903** F. W. Maitland in *Camb. Mod. Hist.* II. xvi. 594 That Protestant principle which refers us to the primitive Church. **1930** T. Parsons tr. *Weber's Protestant Ethic* i. 35 Business leaders and owners of capital, as well as the higher grades of skilled labour, and even more the higher technically and commercially trained personnel of modern enterprises, are overwhelmingly Protestant. *Ibid.* iii. 80 The conception of the calling thus brings out that central dogma of all Protestant denominations which the Catholic division of ethical precepts into *præceptia* and *consilia* discards. **1935** E. Gill *Lett.* (1947) 342 Prudishness is more typically the vice of the protestant puritan. **1940** R. Niebuhr *Christianity & Power Politics* i. 18 This is the issue upon which the Protestant Reformation separated itself from classical Catholicism. **1954** B. Griffiths *Golden String* vii. 114 When his mother heard that it would be necessary for him to attend a Protestant service, she had replied that she would rather go to the workhouse with her eleven children than submit to that. **1958** B. Pym *Glass of Blessings* xiv. 164 It was absurd to have this suspicious Protestant attitude towards convents. **1960** *Daily Tel.* 10 Nov. 14/7 The Rev. John Castle asks: 'Where in her formularies is the Church of England described as "Protestant"?' The answer is (albeit singly and solely) in the Coronation Service. Whether or no the contention that the oath then taken by the Sovereign regarding the 'Protestant Religion' is merely one imposed by the State without the fiat of the Church, is beside the point. **1965** C. E. Pocknee *Parson's Handbk.* (ed. 13) i. 7 These quotations from well-known Roman Catholic writers are sufficient to disprove the idea that there is something 'protestant' or anti-Roman in the custom of bowing as the normal act of reverence. **1976** *Listener* 29 Apr. 526/2 'The Good Lord' may have Protestant connotations, which would be inappropriate in translating ['le Bon Dieu' in] a Catholic poem. **1976** *Times* 28 Sept. 2/1 Mr. Mason, Secretary of State for Northern Ireland, yesterday made a determined attempt to win the hearts and minds of Ulster's disgruntled population, Roman Catholic and Protestant, by pledging himself to tackle their serious economic ills.

(*b*) **1864** J. H. Newman *Apologia pro Vita Sua* v. 248 They [*sc.* Anglican Bishops] were.. fraternizing.. with Protestant bodies, and allowing them to put themselves under an Anglican Bishop, without any renunciation of their errors. **1942** J. Bailie *Invitation to Pilgrimage* x. 71 Some of the lesser Protestant sects, Quaker, Methodist, and others,.. tended to be 'perfectionist'—sometimes even to a greater degree than Mediaeval Catholicism has ever been. **1954** R. Macaulay *Let.* 19 Aug. in *Last Lett. to Friend* (1962) 166 Conversions.. from the unlovely Protestant churches. **1963** Auden *Dyer's Hand* 350 In New England.. the most respectable Protestant denominations are the Congregationalists and the Unitarians. **1973** *Times* 16 Apr. 1/7 He will meet Roman Catholic, Anglican and Protestant church leaders, and Mr Whitelaw, Secretary of State for Northern Ireland. **1977** R. L. Wolff *Gains & Losses* 13 Those who were more Protestant than the legally established Church of England had their own troubled history.

b. Protestant ascendancy, the Anglo-Irish ruling class in pre-Republican Ireland, which became Protestant at the Reformation, as opp. the native Irish who remained Roman Catholic; also *transf.*; **Protestant Dissenter**: see dissenter 2 c; **Protestant Episcopal**, official style of the church in U.S. descended from and in communion with the Church of England; hence **Protestant Episcopalianism**, **Episcopalism**; **Protestant ethic**, the ethical outlook towards business enterprise which, according to Max Weber's analysis, first evolved in protestant Europe through the teachings of Calvin that to be successful through hard work was a person's duty and responsibility; also **Protestant work ethic**.

1827 Barrington *Personal Sk.* 243 The term 'Protestant ascendancy' was coined by Mr. John Gifford.. and became an epithet very fatal to the peace of Ireland. **1875** F. Arnold *Our Bishops & Deans* I. iii. 148 What idea of Protestant truth was conveyed to the Roman Catholics by the favourite phrase 'Protestant ascendancy'? **1922** R. Dunlop *Ireland from Earliest Times* v. 129 The Treaty of Limerick marks the beginning of a new period known as that of the Protestant Ascendancy. **1936** R. M. Douglas *Irish Bk.* 138 He [*sc.* the Catholic Irishman] was 'loyal', and.. became an informer, a policeman, or a soldier serving the Protestant ascendancy. **1966** C. M. Bowra *Memories 1898–1939* xii. 272 His mother, an O'Reilly, was a true daughter of the Protestant Ascendancy. **1977** *Herald* (Melbourne) 17 Jan. 7/3 The neglect of the Castle Hill uprising reflects the prejudices of the Protestant ascendancy in Australia. **1672** Dk. Buckhm. *Sp.* in *Proc. Ho. Lords* (1742) I. 165 That you would give me leave to bring in a Bill of Indulgence to all Protestant Dissenters. **1688, 1689, 1826, 1839** [see dissenter 2 c]. **1780** in W. S. Perry *Hist. Amer. Episcopal Ch.* (1885) II. 21 On motion of the Secretary it was proposed that the Church known in the province as Protestant be called 'the Protestant-Episcopal Church', and it was so adopted. **1857** *Church Rev.* Jan. 562 The Protestant Episcopal is representative—republican; but not democratic. **1920** *Catholic World* Sept. 777 The best they can offer now as a way out of the hated 'Protestant Episcopal' is 'Protestant Catholic' church! **1961** *N. & Q.* June 236/2 His thesis is that the name 'Protestant Episcopal', though historically justifiable, is a liability to the missionary efforts of American Anglicans and should be replaced by 'The American Episcopal Church'. **1977** *Time* 10 Oct. 37/1 Social relations executive of the Protestant Episcopal Diocese of Massachusetts. **1956** R. Macaulay *Towers of Trebizond* i. 14 My aunt had inherited.. strong prejudices against.. all American religious bodies except Protestant Episcopalianism. **1836** *Southern Lit. Messenger* II. 282 In regard to Protestant Episcopalism in America, it may be safely said that, prior to this publication of Dr. Hawks, there were no written memorials extant. [**1904** M. Weber in *Archiv. f. Sozialwissenschaft und Sozialpolitik* XX. 1 (*title*) Die protestantische Ethik und der 'Geist' des Kapitalismus.] **1926** R. H. Tawney *Relig. & Rise of Capitalism* 320 Both 'the capitalist spirit' and 'Protestant ethics'..were a good deal more complex than Weber seems to imply. **1930** T. PARSONS tr. *Weber's Protestant Ethic* iii. 89 We thus take as our starting-point in the investigation of the relationship between the old Protestant ethic and the spirit of capitalism the works of Calvin, of Calvinism, and the other Puritan sects. **1944** *Social Res.* Feb. 61 Weber's original intention in *The Protestant Ethic* must be seen against the background of his time. **1956** W. H. WHYTE *Organization Man* I. i. 6 The organization man..needs..something that will do for him what the Protestant ethic did once. **1968** C. ARMSTRONG *Balloon Man* xii. 146 She was tough. In her own way, Protestant ethic or whatever, she was. **1977** *Listener* 7 Apr. 455/1 Infant prodigies..are the ultimate denial of the Protestant Ethic—hard work can produce lesser rewards than sheer talent. **1980** *Country Life* 24 Apr. 1283/3 Mrs Smith had the Protestant work-ethic in the very marrow of her bones.

2. Also (prəʊˈtɛstənt). Protesting; making a protest.

1844 LD. HOUGHTON *Mem. Many Scenes, Tintern Abbey* 182 We of this latter, still protestant age, With priestly ministrations of the sun,.. Maintain this consecration. **1890** G. S. HALL in *Amer. Jrnl. Psychol.* Jan. 61 A private protestant tribunal, where personal moral convictions preside. **1899** *Echo* 1 Nov. 1/4 Artlessly protestant against the vicious vanities of smart society.

Hence **ˈProtestantdom**, the Protestant communities collectively; **ˈProtestant,like** *a.*, like or after the manner of a Protestant; **ˈProtestantly** *adv.*, in a Protestant manner; consistently with Protestantism.

1579 FULKE *Refut. Rastel* 739 An argument of authority negatiue, is naught and protestantlike. **1659** MILTON *Civ. Power* Wks. 1851 V. 312 To protestants..nothing more protestantly can be permitted then a free and lawful debate. **1676** *Doctrine of Devils* 21 If there have not been..even in Protestantdom some too, that..give heed to such doctrines. **1896** D. L. LEONARD in *Papers Ohio Ch. Hist. Soc.* VII. 98 Probably by most of Christendom, if not also by most of 'Protestantdom', we are as yet unheard of.

†**Proteˈstantical**, *a. Obs.* [f. prec. + -ICAL.] Of, pertaining to, or of the nature of a Protestant; inclined to or of the nature of Protestantism; = PROTESTANT *a.* 1. (Sometimes with hostile or opprobrious implication.)

1592 BACON *Observ. Libel* Wks. 1879 I. 382/2 A third kind of gospellers called Brownists..affirm that the protestantical church of England is not gathered in the name of Christ, but of Antichrist. **1612** T. JAMES *Corrupt. Scripture* IV. 97 They had euery where almost omitted Photius words, being very Protestanticall in this Translation.

ˈProte,stantish, *a. rare.* [f. as prec. + -ISH[1].] = prec. Hence **ˈProte,stantishly** *adv.*

1680 R. L'ESTRANGE *Answ. Litter of Libels* 8 Something..which might give the Protestantish Authour occasion of that flourish. **1685** H. MORE *Refl. Baxter* 24 As if he insinuated himself Popishly and Protestantishly affected in one Breath. **18..** in Flügel *Eng.-Germ. Dict.* (1891), Louis Philip has been very Protestantish in his predilections.

Protestantism (ˈprɒtɪstən,tɪz(ə)m). [f. as prec. + -ISM. Cf. F. *protestantisme.*]

1. The religion of Protestants, as opposed to Roman Catholicism; the condition of being Protestant; adherence to Protestant principles.

1649 MILTON *Eikon.* xv. 142 In the setling of Protestantism, thir [Papists'] aid was both unseemly and suspicious. **1726** JOS. TRAPP *Popery* III. 205 There were Schisms..long before Popery, and consequently much longer before Protestantism..was in Being. **1775** BURKE *Sp. Conc. Amer.* Wks. III. 53 But the religion most prevalent in our northern colonies is a refinement on the principle of resistance: it is the dissidence of dissent, and the protestantism of the protestant religion. **1790** —— *Fr. Rev.* 30 It was still a line of hereditary descent..though an hereditary descent qualified with protestantism. **1849** MACAULAY *Hist. Eng.* vi. II. 54 When the Jesuits came to the rescue of the papacy..Protestantism..was stopped in its progress, and rapidly beaten back from the foot of the Alps to the shores of the Baltic. **1862** J. H. NEWMAN *Let.* 28 June (1970) XX. 216, I do hereby profess *ex animo*..that Protestantism is the dreariest of possible religions; that the thought of the Anglican service makes me shiver. **1864** —— *Apologia pro Vita Sua* v. 181, I held a large bold system of religion, very unlike the Protestantism of the day, but it was the concentration and adjustment of the statements of great Anglican authorities. **1895** BP. GORE *Creed of Christian* x. (ed. 7) 60 She [Ch. of Eng.], more than any other branch of the Church Catholic, holds together Church authority, Bible authority, and individual conscience. The Church of Rome makes much of one; Protestantism makes much of the other two. **1930** T. PARSONS tr. *Weber's Protestant Ethic* 27 We are dealing with the connection of the spirit of modern economic life with the rational ethics of ascetic Protestantism. **1938** O. C. QUICK *Doctrines of Creed* ii. 12 While the error of scholasticism was to tie down Christianity to a particular philosophy, the error of much modern Protestantism has been to disparage philosophy altogether. **1952** P. TILLICH *Courage to Be* v. 114 Protestantism..was established as a strictly authoritarian and conformist system, similar to that of its adversary, the Roman Church of the Counter-reformation. **1964** A. WATTS *Beyond Theol.* vi. 155, I am not speaking of modern 'liberal Protestantism', but of that 'old-time Bible religion'. **1974** *Encycl. Brit. Macropædia* XV. 136/2 Providence..may also be experienced as personal guidance. This latter phenomenon is common..in some forms of Protestantism in which generally each person is expected to have a private experience of divine guidance. **1976** B. GRIFFITHS *Return to Centre* xv. 106 Protestantism opened the Bible to the private interpretation of every man. **1976** *Times* 13 Aug. 13/6 What gives them their weight and validity is their promulgation by the *magisterium* and surely it is this authority that the traditionalists are ready to defy. Is not this nearer to the heart of Protestantism? **1977** B. COLLOMS *Victorian Country Parsons* xii. 228 William Kingsley was a broadminded parson whose sermons and services were suitable for most brands of Protestantism.

2. Protestants, or the Protestant churches, collectively.

1662-3 SOUTH *Serm.* (1727) V. 60 The only thing that makes Protestantism considerable in Christendom, is the Church of England. *a* **1677** J. HARRINGTON *Grounds Monarchy* II. §108 The slow assistances sent to his Daughter, in whose safety and protection Protestantism was at that time so much concern'd. **1902** *Daily Chron.* 28 July 7/3 Protestantism, meaning by that all the non-Roman Catholic persuasions, has held its own, but the Roman Catholics are still steadily dwindling. **1948** F. W. DILLISTONE in M. Warren *Triumph of God* iii. 80 The energy of young Protestantism was bound to be poured out in the effort to consolidate its own position within the hostile environment by which it was surrounded.

3. The condition of protesting; an attitude of protest or objection. *rare.*

1854 H. SPENCER in *Westm. Rev.* Apr. 388 There, needs, then, a protestantism in social usages. **1855** THACKERAY *Newcomes* I. 366 How his protestantism against her doctrines should exhibit itself on the turf.

Protestantization (,prɒtɪstəntaɪˈzeɪʃən). [f. PROTESTANTIZE *v.* + -ATION.] The action or fact of rendering Protestant; conversion to Protestantism.

1880 W. JAMES in *Atlantic Monthly* Oct. 447/2 After Charles IX. and Louis XIV., no general protestantization of France. **1977** S. SCHOENBAUM *Shakespeare* v. 54 Further forays into Protestantization followed.

Protestantize (ˈprɒtɪstən,taɪz), *v.* [f. as PROTESTANTISM + -IZE.] **a.** *trans.* To render Protestant; to convert to or permeate with the principles of Protestantism. **b.** *intr.* To follow Protestant practices. Hence **ˈProtestan,tized** *ppl. a.*, **ˈProtestan,tizing** *vbl. sb.* and *ppl. a.*; also **ˈProtestan,tizer**, one who protestantizes.

1834 *Fraser's Mag.* X. 720 The grants which they still retain for the express purpose of Protestantising Ireland. **1851** J. H. NEWMAN *Cath. in Eng.* 339 Are Protestantizing priests and monks the only evidence of the kind which they could get? **1891** BP. R. T. DAVIDSON, etc. *Abp. Tait* II. xxiv. 199 He would further 'Protestantise' the Church of England. **1895** *Daily News* 24 May 5/6 He belonged to a Protestantised Jewish family, eminent in the financial world. **1906** W. WALKER *Calvin* vii. 203 Another considerable element valued the Protestantising of Geneva more for its political than for its religious results. **1908** *Dublin Rev.* Apr. 308 He was a Protestantizer who formed a party of Calvinists in his Church.

protestation (prɒtɪˈsteɪʃən). [a. F. *protestation* (13th c. in Littré), ad. late L. *prōtestātio* (in Itala, 2 Macc. vii. 6), n. of action f. *prōtest-ārī* to PROTEST.] The action of protesting; that which is protested.

1. A solemn affirmation of a fact, opinion, or resolution; a formal public assertion or asseveration. ***to make protestation***, to protest in a solemn or formal manner.

1340 HAMPOLE *Pr. Consc.* 9593, I make here a protestacion, þat I wil stand til þe correccion Of ilka rightwyse lered man. *c* **1386** CHAUCER *Miller's Prol.* 29 First I make a protestacioun, That I am dronke I knowe it by my soun. **1526** *Pilgr. Perf.* (W. de W. 1531) 98 With a meke protestacyon deny it, & clere your selfe. **1559** *Declar. Doctrine* in Strype *Ann. Ref.* (1709) I. viii. 116 Although in our last protestation made before the honourable auditory at Westminster, we sufficiently set forth in few words the sum of our faith. **1591** SHAKS. *Two Gent.* IV. iv. 133, I know they are stuft with protestations, And full of new-found oathes, which he will breake As easily as I doe teare his paper. **1663** COWLEY *Verses & Ess., Cromwell* (1669) 64 If there had been any faith in mens vows and protestations. **1733** NEAL *Hist. Purit.* II. 437 They entered into a solemn Protestation to stand by each other with their lives and fortunes. **1838** DICKENS *Nich. Nick.* xxviii, Many protestations of friendship, and expressions anticipative of the pleasure which must inevitably flow from so happy an acquaintance. **1899** *Westm. Gaz.* 4 Oct. 10/1 The great 'Church of the Protestation', which is being erected at Spires as a memorial of the origin of the name 'Protestant' at the famous Reichstag in that city in 1529.

†**b.** *by, with, under* (*a*) ***protestation***, with the assertion of the reservation or stipulation, under the condition (*that*). Cf. PROTEST *v.* 5. *Obs.*

1425 *Rolls of Parlt.* IV. 267/2 Yat he myghte speke under protestation, to yat ende. **1480** *Coventry Leet Bk.* 444 With a protestacion that the seid Priour & Couent may be at their liberte at all tymes to refourme & adde more. *Ibid.* 454 The answeres..made..to þe bill of Compleynt made be þe priour of Couentre, be protestacion þat þis answer at all tymes hereafter may be altered, added þerto, amended or otherwyse reformed at eny tyme requisite. **1576** *Reg. Privy Council Scot.* II. 577 Under protestatioun that thay na wayis grant the narrative..to be of veritie.

2. *Law.* †**a.** In pleading, an affirmation or denial, introduced in form of a protest, of some allegation the truth of which the pleader cannot directly affirm or deny without duplicating his plea, and which he cannot pass over lest he should be held to have tacitly waived or admitted it (see quot. 1628). *Obs.*

by protestation, by way of or in the form of a protestation.

1471-3 in *Calr. Proc. Chanc. Q. Eliz.* (1830) II. Pref. 55 Thomas seith, by protestacion, that the mater contened in the seid bill is insufficient to put hym to answer therto. **1551** in Leadam *Sel. Cas. Crt. Requests* (Selden) 57 And he beyng thereof so seysed dyed of such estate thereof by protestacion seysed. **1579** *Expos. Terms Law* 162 b/2 *Protestation* is a sauinge to the partie (that so pleadeth by protestation) to bee concluded by any matter alledged or obiected against him, vpon which he cannot ioin issu. **1628** COKE *On Litt.* 124 b, Protestation..is an exclusion of a conclusion that a party to an action may by pleading incurre, or it is a safegard to the party which keepeth him from being concluded by the plea he is to make, if the issue be found for him. **1797** TOMLINS *Law Dict.* s.v., The use of a Protestation in pleading seems to be this, *viz.* When one party alleges or pleads several matters, and the other party can only offer, or take issue on one of them, he protests against the others.

b. *Sc. Law.* (See quot. 1838.)

1571 *Reg. Privy Council Scot.* II. 92 Thay will proceid and minster justice alsweill be geving of protestationis and decretis. **1633** *Acts of Sederunt* 12 Dec. (1790) 46 Act anent Expences in Protestations. **1739** *Ibid.* 7 July 325. **1838** W. BELL *Dict. Law Scot.* s.v., Where a pursuer, advocator or suspender, after having raised an action, fails to insist in it, his opponent, by means of protestation, may compel him either to proceed or to suffer the action to fall... [This] is done by delivering to one of the Outer-house clerks, a note for insertion in the minute-book of the Court of Session... This note..is called a protestation.

3. A solemn or formal declaration of dissent or objection; = PROTEST *sb.* 4.

1641 J. JACKSON *True Evang. T.* III. 194 After a thousand Complaints, Dissertations, Protestations against their Errors. **1661** WOOD *Life* 1 Apr. (O.H.S.) I. 391 Mr. Brent desir'd them..to read a paper..containing a protestation in the name of all the fellowes, under a public notarie's hand, against the admission of Sir Thomas Clayton to the wardenship of Merton coll. **1793** *Acc. Proc. Camb. agst. W. Frend* 194, I Robert Tyrwhitt, a non-regent master of arts, do, within ten days, make this open and legal protestation against the said grace. **1803** JEFFERSON *Writ.* (1830) IV. 7 Spain had entered into a protestation against our ratification of the treaty. **1849** STOVEL *Introd. Canne's Necess.* p. xxxiii, Its burning fetters have provoked..protestation, resistance, dissent, in various forms, civil and sacred.

b. = PROTEST *sb.* 4 b.

1624 (May 26) in Rogers *Protests of Lords* (1875) I. 2 Therefore the Lords, spiritual and temporal, in the higher House of Parliament, now assembled, do hereby declare and pronounce, and cause this protestation to be entered on record, in the rolls of this Parliament. **1641** (Sept. 9) *Ibid.* 6 [The first formal protest with Reasons in the Journals of the House] We whose names are underwritten did disassent, and having, before the putting of the question, demanded our right of protestation, did accordingly make our protestation: That [etc.]. **1700** (April 4) *Ibid.* 139 We cannot but enter this our protestation against a second reading of this Bill. **1722** *Jrnls. Ho. Lords* XXII. 73/1 The restraining the Assertions, used in Protestations, to the Apprehension or Opinion of the Lords protesting.

4. *attrib.*, as ***protestation meeting***, ***money*** (2 b).

1589 *Pappe w. Hatchet* (1844) 36, I drew neere the sillie soule whom I found quiuering in two sheetes of protestation paper [alluding to the Marprelate tract 'The Protestation']. **1661** *Acts of Sederunt* 4 July (1790) 78 The supplication of Richard Wairde, lately clerk of the bills, under the usurpers, mentioning him to have in his hands severall sums of money, consigned as protestation-money. **1908** *Nation* (N.Y.) 6 June 342/2 Protestation meetings have been held.

protestator (ˈprɒtɪsteɪtə(r)). *rare*$^{-0}$. [a. mod.L. *prōtestātor*, agent-n. from *prōtestārī* to PROTEST.] One who protests; a protester.

1847 in WEBSTER.

protestatory (prəʊˈtɛstətərɪ), *a. rare.* [f. L. *prōtestāt-*, ppl. stem of *prōtestārī* to PROTEST + -ORY[2]. So F. *protestatoire.*] Pertaining to or of the nature of a protest.

a **1624** BP. M. SMITH *Serm.* (1632) 27 The answere is partly indignatory..partly protestatory. **1887** *Standard* 23 Dec. 3/2 These concessions were not favourably received by the National Party, who went so far as to threaten further protestatory elections.

proˈtested, *ppl. a.* [f. PROTEST *v.* + -ED[1].]

1. Solemnly or †publicly asserted.

1605 MARSTON *Dutch Courtezan* IV. i, And don all the offices of protested gallantrie for your sake. *c* **1620** FLETCHER & MASS. *Lit. Fr. Lawyer* I. i, Thou wouldst not willingly Live a protested coward, or be call'd one?

†**2.** That has made or joined in a protest or protestation. *Obs. rare*$^{-1}$.

1641 MILTON *Animadv.* iv. Wks. 1851 III. 219 In this age ..God hath renewed our protestation against all those yet remaining dregs of superstition. Let us all goe, every true protested Brittaine throughout the 3 Kingdoms, and render thanks to God the Father of light.

3. That is protested against, objected to, or done or given under protest. ***protested bill***: see PROTEST *v.* 2.

1849 THACKERAY *Friendship* Wks. 1900 VI. 626, I will disown you, and cut you off with a protested shilling. **1864** O. W. HOLMES *Banker's Secret* Poet. Wks. (1895) 310 The moral market had the usual chills Of Virtue suffering from protested bills.

protester (prəʊˈtɛstə(r)). [f. as prec. + -ER[1].]

1. One who makes a protestation or solemn affirmation.

1601 SHAKS. *Jul. C.* I. ii. 74 Were I a common Laugher, or did vse To stale with ordinary Oathes my loue To euery new Protester.

2. a. One who make a protest or remonstrance.

1651 C. CARTWRIGHT *Cert. Relig.* I. 103 To annex their Religion as a codicill to an appeal of a company of Protesters against a decree at Spira. **1794** BURKE *Rep. Lords' Jrnls.* Wks. 1842 II. 601 The reasons against the article, alleged in the protest, were by no means solely bottomed in the practice of the courts below, as if the main reliance of the protesters was upon that usage. **1812** L. HUNT in *Examiner* 25 May 322/2 The Grenvilles and other protesters against improper expenses. **1885** *Manch. Exam.* 14 May 6/1 The motion was carried by 54 to 4, the protesters being [etc.].

b. *Sc. Hist. pl.* (usu. with cap. initial.) Those Presbyterians who in 1650 protested against the union with the Royalists; also applied to those who on various later occasions formally protested against acts or decisions of the church courts.

1660 DOUGLAS in Wodrow *Hist. Suff. Ch. Scot.* (1721) I. Introd. 12 That it may be they were mistaken for some of their Brethren the Protesters, to whom..the King's Return is Matter of Terror. **1722** *Wodrow Corr.* (1843) II. 630 His pieces he wrote in the debate with the Protesters contain.. many things as to the History of this Church. **1816** SCOTT *Old Mort.* v, They had parted..at the time when the kingdom of Scotland was divided into Resolutioners and Protesters. **1855** *Summary Principles U.P. Ch.* 2 In May 1733 the Assembly refused to hear fully the reasons which the protesters had to urge. **1882–3** *Schaff's Encycl. Relig. Knowl.* I. 409/2 His father..belonged to the extreme Covenanting party of Protesters.

c. An opponent of the established order, esp. one who actively remonstrates over an issue of public importance; a demonstrator.

1960 *Times Lit. Suppl.* 1 Jan. 3/2 Those cold-water apartments where hipsters and protesters..try to go their own way. **1968** *Listener* 4 July 22/3 Absolutely and actively in sympathy with the protesters over most issues, he can.. trace out the roots of their discontents. **1971** 'E. LATHEN' *Longer the Thread* vii. 65 Thatcher..would not believe.. that homicide investigations came to a halt whenever youthful protesters threatened to act up. **1976** 'R. B. DOMINIC' *Murder out of Commission* v. 41 Protesters picked up some pretty strange habits during the Vietnam War.

3. One who protests a bill or other commerical document.

1849 DE QUINCEY *Eng. Mail Coach* Wks. 1862 IV. 295 If it is by bills at ninety days after date that you are made unhappy—if noters and protesters are the sort of wretches whose..shadows darken the house of life.

pro'testing, *vbl. sb.* [f. PROTEST *v.* + -ING[1].] The action of the verb PROTEST. **a.** Protestation, solemn declaration; remonstrance. **b.** The formal declaration of the non-payment of a bill when duly presented.

1599 ? SHAKS. *Pass. Pilgr.* vii, Yet in the mids of all her pure protestings, Her faith, her othes, her teares, and all were ieastings. **1702** ROWE *Tamerl.* I. i. 344 'Twas well my Heart was cautious of believing Thy Vows, and thy Protesting. **1722** *Jrnls. Ho. Lords* XXII. 74/1 The Liberty of Protesting, with Reasons, being an unquestionable Right and essential Privilege of the whole Peerage. **1809** R. LANGFORD *Introd. Trade* 20 The..act..authorises the protesting of inland bills for non-acceptance.

pro'testing, *ppl. a.* [f. as prec. + -ING[2].] That protests: in various senses of the verb.

1681 WOOD *Life* 6 June (O.H.S.) II. 542 The outrage committed on the old lady Lovelace..they pluck'd her out of her coach, and called her 'old protesting bitch'. **1703** ROWE *Ulyss.* v. i. 1967 A protesting, faithless, villain Friend.

pro'testingly, *adv.* [f. prec. + -LY[2].] In a protesting manner; by way of protest.

1888 R. DOWLING *Miracle Gold* I. vii. 125 She looked at him protestingly. **1894** *Temple Bar Mag.* CII. 328 The maid ..stood protestingly in the background.

protestor (prəʊ'tɛstə(r)). [Early mod.E. *protestour*, ad. obs. F. *protesteur*, f. *protester*: see PROTEST *v.* and -OR.]

†**1.** = PROTESTER 1. *Obs.*

1550 BALE *Image Both Ch.* I. v. 64 The present protestours of the veritie, here liuing in the world. **1691** WOOD *Ath. Oxon.* II. 493 He was..a protestor for a Community of wealth, as well as of women.

2. = PROTESTER 2 a.

1706 HEARNE *Collect.* 5 Feb. (O.H.S.) I. 178 Dr. Cawley was the more taken notice of upon Acc[t] of his Being one of the Protestors. **1780** *Hist. Eur.* in *Ann. Reg.* 121/2 He contended, that the protestors..possessed property equal, if not superior, to the petitioners. **1885** *Manch. Exam.* 13 Feb. 5/1 It is asserted by the protestors that three names should have been so forwarded.

b. = PROTESTER 2 b. Also *attrib.*

1693 *Apol. Clergy Scot.* 78 They pretend..that the generality of the Godly did adhere to the Protestors, that the Publick Resolutioners had made defection. *a* **1715** BURNET *Own Time* I. (1724) I. 55 A great division followed in the Kirk: Those who adhered to these resolutions were called the Publick Resolutioners: But against these some of those bodies protested, and they, together with those who adhered to them, were called the Protestors. **1834** H. MILLER *Scenes & Leg.* viii. (1857) 110 Urquhart of Cromarty..had lately 'counterfeited the Protestor'. **1900** *U.P. Mag.* May 209/2 When the foundations of the Protestor Synod were laid [1737–8], he was one of seven.

protetrarch: see PRO-[1] 1.

‖**Proteus** ('prəʊtju:s, 'prəʊti:əs). [L. *Prōteus*, a. Gr. Πρωτεύς proper name.]

1. *Gr.* and *Rom. Mythol.* A sea-god, the son of Oceanus and Tethys, fabled to assume various shapes.

c **1400** *Rom. Rose* 6319 Protheus, that coude him chaunge In every shap, hoomly and straunge. **1620** T. GRANGER *Div. Logike* 137 More mutable then Proteus. **1639** S. DU VERGER tr. *Camus' Admir. Events* a j b, Falsehood is..capable of more different formes, than the..Proteus of Poets. **1806** WORDSW. *Sonn., The world is too much with us* 13 So might I..Have sight of Proteus rising from the sea; Or hear old Triton blow his wreathèd horn.

2. Hence allusively, One who, or that which, assumes various forms, aspects, or characters; a changing, varying, or inconstant person or thing.

1585 J. HART *Æsop's Fables* 111 A Protheus..vnstedfast in word and ded. **1589** COOPER *Admon.* 28 Such a subtile Protheus hee is, that he can turn himself into all maner of shapes. **1685** *Gracian's Courtier's Orac.* 76 He is a wise Proteus that is holy with the holy,..serious with the serious, and jovial with the merry. **1703** MAUNDRELL *Journ. Jerus.* 4 Mar. (1810) 17 Being such Proteus's in religion, that no body was ever able to discover what shape or standard their consciences are really of. **1823** R. HALL *Wks.* (1841) V. 62 Mental phenomena form a Proteus which is constantly changing its aspect.

3. *Zool.* and *Biol.* **a.** A name for the protozoon now called AMŒBA. (Now disused as a generic name.) Also ***proteus animalcule***, † ***p. insect***.

1802 BINGLEY *Anim. Biog.* (1813) III. 492 Some..if viewed in a microscope, will be found to contain, among several other animalcules, the Proteus. **1806** PRISCILLA WAKEFIELD *Dom. Recreat.* vi. 85, I shall find plenty of the Proteus insect in it. **1888** ROLLESTON & JACKSON *Anim. Life* 256 *Amœba Proteus* or *A. princeps*, the Proteus animalcule.. is to be found in the upper layers of soft ooze at the bottom of still clear lakes, ponds, and ditches.

b. A genus of tailed amphibians with persistent gills, having four short slender legs and a long eel-like body, found in subterranean caves in Austria. [Adopted as the name of a genus by J. N. Laurenti in his *Synopsis Reptilium* (1768) 35.] = OLM.

a **1829** H. DAVY *Consolations in Travel* (1830) iv. 190 The same infinite power..has given the Proteus to the deep and dark subterraneous lakes of Illyria,—an animal to whom the presence of light is not essential. **1835** KIRBY *Hab. & Inst. Anim.* II. xxii. 419 The Proteus is about a foot in length.. the body is cylindrical. **1854** OWEN *Skel. & Teeth* in *Orr's Circ. Sc.* I. *Org. Nat.* 188 In the proteus the last segment of the fore-limb divides into three rays. **1860** GOSSE *Rom. Nat. Hist.* 76 The proteus, a strange sort of salamander found in the lakes of immense caverns in Illyria. **1902** BASKETT & DITMARS *Story of Amphibians & Reptiles* vii. 48 *Proteus*.. lives in a cave in Austria. **1965** B. E. FREEMAN tr. *Vandel's Biospeleol.* iii. 23 *Proteus* represents a veritable giant amongst the European cave fauna, because it reaches a length of 30 cm.

c. The name given to a group of bacteria, some of which are saprophytes and some pathogenic.

1896 *Allbutt's Syst. Med.* I. 529 The list of putrefactive organisms includes various forms of proteus (vulgaris, mirabilis, Zenkeri), for which formerly the name bacterium termo had to do duty. **1897** *Ibid.* III. 748 Dr. Booker states that a group which he calls the 'proteus' group of bacteria was represented in fifteen out of nineteen cases.

4. a. *attrib.* Changeable like Proteus, protean. ***proteus animalcule, insect*** = sense 3 a. **b.** *Comb.* as ***Proteus-like*** adj. and adv.

1687 DRYDEN *Hind & P.* III. 818 O Proteus Conscience, never to be tied! **1718** *Entertainer* No. 34. 233 Who it is, that Proteus like has so often shifted his Meaning. **1733** CHEYNE *Eng. Malady* II. viii. §4 (1734) 196 In such a Proteus-like Distemper. **1834** *Tait's Mag.* I. 599/1 The fantastic tricks of this Proteus principle, become most amusing. **1839** CARLYLE *Chartism* iv. (1858) 22 English commerce with its ..immeasurable Proteus Steam-demon, makes..all life a bewilderment.

Hence [irreg.] †**Pro'teusian** *a. Obs.* = PROTEAN.

1689 T. PLUNKET *Char. Gd. Commander* 51 Proteusian pranks, unthought of mysteries.

protevangel (prəʊtɪ'vændʒəl). Also irreg. ˌ**proto-e'vangel** (see PROTO-). [ad. next: cf. EVANGEL[1]. So F. *protévangile*.] = next, 2.

1875 *Expositor* 413 It is entirely absent even from his interpretation of the Protevangel of Gen. iii. **1878** F. FERGUSON *Pop. Life Christ* x. 105 The meaning of Eden's protevangel. **1882–3** *Schaff's Encycl. Relig. Knowl.* I. 503 The grace under which the patriarchal protevangel manifested itself.

‖**Protevangelium** (prəʊtˌɛvæn'dʒɛlɪəm). Also (after Gr.) -ion. [mod.L., f. Gr. πρῶτ-ος first, primitive (see PROTO- 1) + L. *evangelium*: see EVANGELY.] A primitive or original gospel.

1. Name of an apocryphal gospel, attributed to St. James the Less.

1715 Proto-Evangēlion [see PSEUDEPIGRAPHAL]. **1851** LONGF. *Gold. Leg.* III. *Nativity* Introitus 11 The Nativity of our Lord, As written in the old record Of the Protevangelion.

2. Applied to the promise concerning the seed of the woman implied in the curse upon the serpent (Gen. iii. 15), regarded as the earliest utterance of the gospel. (In quot. 1892 in extended sense.)

1874 H. R. REYNOLDS *John Bapt.* ii. 113 Going right back to the protevangelium uttered in paradise. **1892** WESTCOTT *Gospel of Life* 186 The whole narrative of the Creation and the Fall, and not one isolated verse, contains, when rightly apprehended, the real Protevangelium, the primitive Gospel of the world.

So **prote'vangelist**, a first or original evangelist or bringer of good tidings.

1864 CARLYLE *Fredk. Gt.* XVI. viii. IV. 371 *note*, The true protevangelist of the thing.

protext ('prəʊtɛkst). *rare.* [f. PRO-[1] 3 or PRO-[2] + TEXT *sb.*; cf. *context*.] The preceding context of a passage.

1641 J. JACKSON *True Evang. T.* II. 141 The..alliance that the text hath with the protext, or verse immediately foregoing. **1886** *N. & Q.* 7th Ser. II. 279/1 See Baring-Gould's 'Curious Myths of the Middle Ages', p. 600 (ed. London, 1881), and the protext.

‖**prothalamion** (prəʊθə'leɪmɪən). Also (in mod. Dicts.) -ium. [Invented by Spenser, after *epithalamion*, EPITHALAMIUM: see PRO-[2].] 'A preliminary nuptial song' (Stanf.).

1597 SPENSER *(title)* Prothalamion, or a Spousall Verse. **1612** DRAYTON *Poly-olb.* xv. Argt. 8 At Oxford all the Muses meet her And with a Prothalamion greet her. **1627** —— *Miseries Q. Margaret* Poems (1748) 141 Poets write prothalamions in their praise Until men's ears were cloy'd with the report. [**1896** *Spectator* 31 Oct. 594/1 'Prothalamion'. Spenser must have invented this word, as it does not exist in either Greek or Latin, to express the idea of a song of greeting to happy lovers before the actual wedding-day had arrived.]

prothallial (prəʊ'θælɪəl), *a. Bot.* [f. next + -AL[1].] Pertaining to or of the nature of a prothallium; *spec.* applied to a small cell formed at an early stage in the development of the male gametophyte of certain gymnosperms, or a similar structure in certain pteridophytes. So **pro'thallic, pro'thalline** *adjs.*

1876 J. H. BALFOUR in *Encycl. Brit.* IV. 160/1 In Ferns the alternation consists of two dissimilar generations,—a sexual or prothallial generation, and an asexual generation. **1882** J. M. CROMBIE *ibid.* XIV. 555/2 Their fecundating influence is rather exercised on the prothalline elements of the growing thallus. **1890** *Cent. Dict.*, *Prothallic.* **1892** *Ann. Bot.* VI. 214 Judging from the obvious continuity of the dividing wall with the lateral walls of the prothallial chambers..there can hardly exist a doubt that the two cavities result from a primary transverse division of the cell. **1910** COULTER & CHAMBERLAIN *Morphol. Gymnosperms* vi. 277 The appearance of two evanescent vegetative (prothallial) cells is a feature only of the Abietineae. **1929** ROBBINS & RICKETT *Botany* xxii. 326 Two are very small cells (prothallial cells) which die and disintegrate almost as soon as formed. **1965** BELL & COOMBE tr. *Strasburger's Textbk. Bot.* 593 In the originally unicellular microspore (pollen grain) [of *Pinus*] one or two (or sometimes more) small cells are formed at a particular spot just inside the wall; these prothallial cells often degenerate after a time. **1969** F. E. ROUND *Introd. Lower Plants* xi. 132 The microspore divides within the spore wall to form a single 'prothallial' cell and an antheridial initial cell. **1973** A. CRONQUIST *Basic Bot.* xvi. 262 The prothallial cell [of *Selaginella*] is considered to be an evolutionary vestige of the body of the gametophyte.

‖**prothallium** (prəʊ'θælɪəm). *Bot.* Pl. **prothallia.** [mod.L., f. PRO-[2] 1 + Gr. θαλλίον, dim. of θαλλός: see PROTHALLUS, THALLUS.] In vascular cryptogams (ferns, horsetails, club-mosses, etc.), A minute cellular structure or thallus, produced by the germination of the spore, and bearing the sexual organs (antheridia and archegonia); forming the first of the two alternate generations, much simpler than, and as it were introductory to, the fully-developed (asexual) plant. (Sometimes including also the similar PROTONEMA of mosses.) Also, a homologous structure in the development of certain gymnosperms.

1858 CARPENTER *Veg. Phys.* §402 This Marchantia-like expansion has received the name of *prothallium*, and it is on this little membranous body, that the archegonia and pistillidia make their appearance. **1872** OLIVER *Elem. Bot.* II. 286 From the germinating spore [of Ferns] arises a small, green, leafy expansion, called a prothallium, which gives off delicate root-fibres from its under surface. **1875** BENNETT & DYER *Sachs' Bot.* 335 In the Ferns and Equisetaceæ the prothallium resembles the thallus of the lowest Hepaticæ. **1892** J. B. FARMER in *Ann. Bot.* VI. 213 *(title)* On the occurrence of two prothallia in the embryo sac of *Pinus.* **1935** C. J. CHAMBERLAIN *Gymnosperms* xiii. 309 In some heterosporous pteridophyte ancestor [of the conifers], the prothallium (gametophyte) became included within the spore..and finally disappeared entirely.

prothalloid (prəʊ'θælɔɪd), *a.* [f. next + -OID.] Resembling, or having the form of, a prothallus.

1890 in *Cent. Dict.* **1897** *Naturalist* 178 The brown radicles are a prothalloid growth.

‖**prothallus** (prəʊ'θæləs). *Bot.* Pl. **prothalli** (-aɪ). [mod.L., f. PRO-[2] + Gr. θαλλός shoot: see THALLUS.] = PROTHALLIUM.

1854 J. H. BALFOUR in *Encycl. Brit.* V. 144/1 *Equisetaceæ.* .. The spore when sprouting, produces a pro-embryo or pro-thallus, which at first appears as a green-lobed leaf supported on a stalk. **1857** BERKELEY *Cryptog. Bot.* §32. 45 The spores germinate and produce a more or less foliaceous mass, which after impregnation bears fruit containing bodies like the original spores, or a plant capable of bearing such spores, in which case it is called a prothallus. **1908** *Athenæum* 16 May 608/1 The fern plant..is typically a land-plant... But one phase of its life-cycle, the small green prothallus or fore-plant, is essentially an aquatic phase. **1940** *Chambers's Techn. Dict.* 680/1 The term prothallus is extended to cover homologous stages in the life-cycle of Gymnosperms. **1965** K. R. SPORNE *Morphol. Gymnosperms* i. 19 Cell-walls are being laid down between the nuclei of the female prothallus, a process which, in most gymnosperms, continues until the whole of the prothallus becomes circular.

protheca: see PRO-[2] 1.

prothelminth, -ic, -thelmis: see PROTO- 2 b.

‖**prothesis** (ˈprɒθɪsɪs). [a. Gr. πρόθεσις a placing before or in public, as in the phrase οἱ ἄρτοι τῆς προθέσεως the showbread (LXX and N.T.), f. PRO-[2] 2 + θέσις placing: cf. προτιθέναι to place before, set out (food, etc.).]

1. *Eccl.* The placing of the elements, etc., in readiness for use in the eucharistic office; hence, the table upon which these are placed, a credence-table, or the part of a church where this stands.

In the Greek Church, the preparation and preliminary oblation of the elements, performed by the priest and deacon (more fully *office of prothesis*); hence, the table upon which this is done (*table* or *altar of prothesis*), or the place where this table stands (*chapel of prothesis*).

1672 CAVE *Prim. Chr.* I. vi. (1673) 140 The Prothesis, or place where things were prepared in order to the Sacrament. **1711** HICKES *Two Treat. Chr. Priesth.* (1847) I. 322 The use of a Prothesis, or another table from whence he may fetch them [bread and wine]. **1883** BERESF. HOPE *Worship & Ord.* 92 We have the Altar with its attendant table of Prothesis.

2. (See quots.)

1812–29 COLERIDGE in *Lit. Rem.* (1838) III. 93, I would thus class the pentad of operative Christianity:—

Thesis, the Scriptures. *Prothesis*, Christ, the Word. *Mesothesis*, the Holy Spirit. *Synthesis*, the Preacher. *Antithesis*, the Church.

1830 *Ibid.* IV. 429 *note*, As a synthesis is a unity that results from the union of two things, so a prothesis is a primary unity that gives itself forth into two things.

3. *Gram.* The addition of a letter or syllable at the beginning of a word: commonly, but less etymologically, called PROSTHESIS.

1870 MARCH *Ags. Gram.* §48. 31 Real prothesis is pretty common in Greek. **1968** P. M. POSTAL *Aspects Phonol. Theory* vii. 144 The Prothesis rule is that which inserts an [i] in the front of verbs containing less than one vowel. **1976** *Language* LII. 307 Evidence for prothesis in Spain dates from the Vulgar Latin of the 2nd century.

¶**4.** *Surg.* Erron. used for PROSTHESIS 2.

1842 DUNGLISON *Med. Lex.*, *Prothesis* [ed. 1857 adds *Prosthesis*], that part of surgery, whose object is to add to the human body some artificial part, in place of one that may be wanting.

prothetely (prəʊˈθɛtəlɪ). *Ent.* [ad. G. *prothetelie* (H. J. Kolbe 1903), in *Allgemeine Zeitschr. f. Entom.* VIII. 1), f. Gr. προθεῖν to run before + τέλος end: see -Y[3].] In certain insect larvæ, the development of one part of the body, esp. the wings, at a faster rate than that of the rest. Hence **protheˈtelic** *a.*, of or pertaining to this type of development.

1934 FOLSOM & WARDLE *Entomol.* (ed. 4) iii. 169 As a rare abnormality a holometabolous larva may possess two pairs of true external wing-pads... The phenomenon is termed prothetely. **1940** R. GOLDSCHMIDT *Material Basis of Evolution* iv. 283 The actual working of this timing mechanism can be inferred from cases of so-called prothetely, where a single larval organ, e.g. wings or antennae, metamorphoses alone. *Ibid.* 284 (*caption*) Head of prothetelic caterpillar of *Lymantria dispar* with pupal antennae. **1960** H. OLDROYD tr. *Jeannel's Introd. Entomol.* iv. 83 (*caption*) Prothetelic larva of *Tenebrio molitor*.. showing rudiments of wings. *Ibid.*, Prothetely. Quite often when bred artificially, but more rarely in nature, insect larvae may have rudiments of wings, which have matured at a greater rate than the rest of the body. **1978** *Nature* 23 Mar. 350/2 They..obtained morphogenetic effects (precocious-prothetelic adults after administration to young instars) only in Heteroptera.

prothetic (prəʊˈθɛtɪk), *a.* [ad. Gr. προθετικ-ός having a purpose in view, also of or for prefixing, prepositional, f. προτιθέναι to place before.]

1. *Gram.* Prefixed at the beginning of a word; also, less etymologically called PROSTHETIC.

1833 S. KENRICK in *Philol. Museum* II. 348 That the ω in the longer form is merely prothetic and no part of the root. **1888** *Athenæum* 24 Nov. 704/2 In II. 156 Prof. Sterrett has again misunderstood this prothetic iota; read ἰσφαγεντι. **1900** H. HARRISON in *N. & Q.* 9th Ser. VI. 514/2 Wrayton... Its prothetic *w* is due to false analogy.

2. That is posited before; antecedent. *rare*[−1].

1839–52 BAILEY *Festus* xix. (ed. 5) 301 In hope to know the great unknowable, The all prothetic universal I.

¶**3.** *Surg.* Erron. used for PROSTHETIC 2.

1899 *Nature* 23 Nov. 77/1 The introduction of a section upon prothetic appliances.

proˈthetical, *a.* [f. as prec. + -AL[1].] ? Having the quality of putting forth into view, or exhibiting.

1837 *Fraser's Mag.* XVI. 91 A poet is necessarily a synthetical, if, indeed, he be not rather a higher, a prothetical agent. *Ibid.* 258 The language of Scripture..the style not being so much symbolical or typical as *prothetical*, if we may coin the word; the natural things which we too generally understand as figures of speech..being used not only as direct exponents of the spiritual,..but as one and the same with them.

proˈthetically, *adv.* [f. prec. + -LY[2].]

1. (Cf. prec.)

1838 *Fraser's Mag.* XVII. 167 The genuine poet works synthetically, or even in higher guise, prothetically, and never analytically.

2. *Gram.* By prothesis or prefixion.

1885 *Trans. Amer. Philol. Assoc.* XVI. App. 33 Letters added prothetically.

prothistorian: see PROTO- 1.

prothocall, -coll, -gall, -goll, obs. ff. PROTOCOL.

†**prothodaw.** *Obs. humorous nonce-wd.* [f. *protho-*, PROTO- + DAW *sb.* 2 a.] A prime simpleton, a noodle of the first rank.

a **1548** HALL *Chron.*, *Hen. V* 73 That an Arche foole cannot forge a lye for his pleasure, but a prothodawe wyll faine a glose to mainteine his folish fantasie.

prothonotary, etc., var. PROTONOTARY, etc.

prothoplasmator, -pla(u)st(e: see PROTO-.

prothoracic (prəʊθɒˈræsɪk), *a.* *Entom.* [f. mod.L. *prothōrax*, *-thōrācem* (see next) + -IC: cf. PRO-[2] 2, and *thoracic*.] Of or pertaining to the front of the thorax; pertaining to or situated on the prothorax.

1826 KIRBY & SP. *Entomol.* III. xxxiv. 412 The lower margin of the prothoracic cavity has a notch. **1836–9** *Todd's Cycl. Anat.* II. 883 In the Coleoptera..the pro-thoracic.. segments are largely developed. **1887** *Athenæum* 16 Apr. 518/1 The existence of prothoracic glands in certain species.

‖**prothorax** (prəʊˈθɔəræks). *Entom.* [mod.L.: see PRO-[2] 2 and THORAX.] The first of the three thoracic somites, or divisions of the thorax of an insect, which bears the first pair of legs. Its upper surface consists of the *pronotum* or central ridge, and the two *propleura*, one on each side.

[**1824** AUDOUIN in *Ann. des Sc. Nat.* I. 119 Nous nommerons *Prothorax* le premier segment... Le prothorax, le mésothorax, et le métathorax réunis, constituent le Thorax.] **1826** KIRBY & SP. *Entomol.* III. xxxv. 531, I adopt likewise the terms..*prothorax*, *mesothorax*, *metathorax*, to signify the three segments into which the thorax of Linné, or the upper side of the trunk, is resolvable. **1877** HUXLEY *Anat. Inv. Anim.* vii. 437 The longicorn Beetles produce a sound by the friction of the tergum of the prothorax upon a process of that of the mesothorax.

prothrombin (prəʊˈθrɒmbɪn). *Phys.* [a. G. *prothrombin* (A. Schmidt *Zur Blutlehre* (1892) xii. 202), f. Gr. πρό PRO-[2] + θρόμβ-ος clot, THROMBUS: see -IN[1].] A protein formed in the liver and normally present in blood, whose conversion into thrombin is an essential part of the clotting process.

1898 E. A. SCHÄFER *Text-bk. Physiol.* I. 160 A fibrin ferment (thrombin), or its precursor (prothrombin), producing the formation of fibrin from fibrinogen. *Ibid.*, The fibrin ferment is sometimes spoken of as 'thrombin', and the nucleo-proteid material in the plasma from which it is produced is then termed 'prothrombin'. **1912** J. G. MCKENDRICK *Princ. Physiol.* viii. 117 The theory at present in vogue is that when blood is shed there is at once the death of many colourless cells. These contain a protein called prothrombin, which, in turn, produces an enzyme known as thrombin. **1936** [see *hypoprothrombinæmia* s.v. HYPO- II]. **1946** [see *oxalated* ppl. a. s.v. OXALATE *v.*]. **1957** *Sci. News* XLIV. 31 In the presence of ionized calcium, of a further globulin component of the plasma, and probably of other factors, thromboplastin converts prothrombin, by what must be a relatively minor change in its molecule, to thrombin. This last substance now reacts directly with fibrinogen, changing it to fibrin. **1974** R. M. KIRK et al. *Surgery* ii. 10 Vitamin K analogue, 10 mg intramuscularly each day, replaces the deficiency but if there is concomitant liver damage, prothrombin is not synthesised. **1976** [see *proconvertin* s.v. PRO-[2] 1].

b. *attrib.*, as **prothrombin time**, the time taken for blood or plasma to clot when an excess of a calcium salt and possibly other natural components of the clotting mechanism (besides prothrombin) are added.

1935 *Amer. Jrnl. Med. Sci.* CXC. 505 By omitting the addition of excess thromboplastin, but otherwise following the directions of the method outlined for the determination of prothrombin, one determines the clotting time of recalcified plasma, which for normal plasma is from 90 to 130 seconds. This method is still commonly called Howell's Prothrombin Time. **1957** A. J. QUICK *Hemorrhagic Dis.* ii. 44 The prothrombin time of normal human plasma is consistently 12 seconds, whereas when measured by the two-stage test, it varies from 244 to 452 units. **1972** *Daily Colonist* (Victoria, B.C.) 1 Feb. 2/1, I am on anticoagulants and have a prothrombin time test taken weekly to determine dosage.

prothyalosomal: see PROTO- 2 b.

prothyl, -yle, variants of PROTYLE.

‖**prothyrum** (ˈprɒθɪrəm). [L. (generally in pl. *prothyra*), ad. Gr. πρόθυρον a front-door, a porch, f. πρό, PRO-[2] + θύρα a door.] The porch or vestibule of an ancient Greek or Roman house.

1706 PHILLIPS, *Prothyrum*, a Porch at the outer Door of an House, a Fence of Pales or Rails, to keep off Horses or Carts from the Door. **1834** *Gentl. Mag.* CIV. I. 53 The Roman Villa after Vitruvius... The principal features noticed are the Prothyrum, vestibule, or lobby.

prothysteron, protichnite: see PROTO- 2 b.

protic (ˈprəʊtɪk), *a.* *Chem.* [f. PROT(ON + -IC.] Of a liquid, esp. a solvent: possessing protons whose binding is sufficiently loose for them to participate in protonation; hydrogen-bonded.

1944 *Jrnl. Physical Chem.* XLVIII. 53 In all protic solvents, protons enter strongly into any consideration of acid-base properties. **1965** PHILLIPS & WILLIAMS *Inorg. Chem.* I. xv. 556 Similarly, in other 'protic' solvents a special role is played by substances producing H^+ ions, or the characteristic anion of the solvent (e.g. NH_2^- in NH_3, F^- in HF, and HSO_4^- in H_2SO_4). **1973** E. J. KING in Covington & Dickinson *Phys. Chem. Org. Solvent Syst.* iii. 333 We first distinguish two broad classes [of solvent] based on dielectric constant. In solvents of high dielectric constant, often referred to loosely as polar solvents, ion-pairing is minimal, even negligible in dilute solutions... By contrast, in solvents of low dielectric constant, loosely called non-polar solvents, ion-pairing is important and acid strength depends on the choice of standard base... Each broad class in turn is sub-divided into hydrogen-bonded and non-hydrogen-bonded solvents. The term *protic* is frequently used for the first sub-division, *aprotic* for the second. **1975** *Nature* 3 Jan. 40/1 These reactions show that molecular nitrogen can be reduced at a single metal site in a protic medium with negligible discharge of dihydrogen or displacement of dinitrogen by hydride ligands.

protide (ˈprəʊtaɪd). *Biochem.* Also -id (-ɪd). [a. F. *protide* (G. Bertrand 1923, in *Bull. de la Soc. de Chim. biol.* V. 102), f. *protéine* PROTEIN: see -IDE.] A generic term for a protein, peptide, or amino-acid. Hence **proˈtidic** *a.*

The scheme of nomenclature proposed by Bertrand met with little favour among English-speaking scientists (see *Chem. & Engin. News* (1952) 5 May 1910). *Protide* is now to be found almost exclusively in translations or abstracts from French.

1936 A. P. MATHEWS *Princ. Biochem.* xxii. 215 The International Union of Pure and Applied Chemistry suggested that the proteins be called 'protides' in consonance with the 'glucides' and 'lipides'. **1958** (*title*) Protides of the biological fluids. *Ibid.* p. v, Some biochemical constituents of protidic nature or origin in the living animal are considered in a further nine original papers. **1962** *Biol. Abstr.* XXXIX. 948/1 (*heading*) Study of the protidic fraction of Digitaria exilis. **1973** *Compar. Biochem. & Physiol.* B. XLV. 225 (*heading*) Protides of the Mustelidae: comparative study of plasma lactate dehydrogenases. **1975** *Biol. Abstr.* LX. 4700/2 Some data.. suggest that the initiation of growth is strictly dependent in [*sic*] nutritional factors (mainly protids). **1977** *Lancet* 10 Dec. 1242/2 The 26th colloquium on protides of the biological fluids will be held in Bruges on May 1–5.

‖**protiˈmesis.** *Obs.* [mod.L., a. Gr. προτίμησις, n. of action f. προτιμᾶν to honour before or above.] Estimation of one thing above another; preference.

a **1638** MEDE *Wks.* (1672) 285, 'I will have mercy and not sacrifice'; it is no Antithesis, but a Protimesis, that 'I had rather have mercy than sacrifice'.

protiodide (prəʊˈtaɪədaɪd). *Chem.* Also **protoiodide.** [*prot-*, PROTO- 3.] A combination of iodine with another element or radical, containing the smallest proportion of iodine: opposed to PER-IODIDE. Formerly also called †**protiˈoduret.** Now usually otherwise expressed, as *protiodide of iron* = ferrous iodide, FeI_2; *protiodide* or *protioauret of mercury* = mercuric iodide, HgI_2.

1836 J. M. GULLY *Magendie's Formul.* (ed. 2) 120 Preparation of the Proto-Ioduret of Mercury. **1836–41** BRANDE *Chem.* (ed. 5) 677 Iodide of Calcium..may also be obtained by digesting hydrate of lime with protiodide of iron. **1854** SCOFFERN in *Orr's Circ. Sc.*, *Chem.* 499 The protoiodide [of mercury]..is a beautiful red compound.

‖**Protista** (prəʊˈtɪstə), *sb. pl.* *Biol.* [mod.L. (= Ger. *Protisten*, Haeckel 1868), a. Gr. πρώτιστα, neut. pl. of πρώτιστ-ος the very first, superl. of πρῶτος first.] A third kingdom of organized beings, proposed by Haeckel to include those of the simplest structure, not definitely distinguished as either animals or plants (thus comprising the Protozoa and Protophyta, with those forms indeterminately assigned to either group); corresponding to the *Primalia* of Wilson and Cassin (see PRIMAL 5).

1878 BELL *Gegenbaur's Comp. Anat.* 75 The plan of uniting all the lower organisms which cannot be regarded as Animals or Plants into the Kingdom of the Protista. **1908** M. HARTOG in *Contemp. Rev.* Apr. 486 The physiology of the Protista (organisms which have the character of isolated cells).

Also **protist** (ˈprəʊtɪst), an organism of the group *Protista*, a protozoon or protophyte [f. mod.L. *Protista*, f. G. *protisten* (E. Haeckel *Generelle Morphologie der Organismen* (1866) I. 203): see PROTISTA *sb. pl.* above]; also *attrib.* = *protistan*; **proˈtistan** *a.*, of or belonging to the *Protista*; *sb.* = *protist*; **proˈtistic** *a.*, of the *Protista*.

1869 HUXLEY *Crit. & Addr.* xii. (1873) 314 Some of the *Monera* acquired tendencies towards the Protistic, others towards the Vegetal, and others towards the Animal modes of life. **1877** F. BATEMAN *Darwinism* 33 The second group of the Protistic Kingdom—the Amœboida or Protoplasta. **1889** GEDDES & THOMSON *Evol. Sex* x. 129 In [Volvox], which is best regarded as a multicellular protist. *Ibid.* xi. 152 Loose protist colonies like Volvox or Ampullina. **1897** *Nat. Science* Oct. 234 The modes of reproduction among Protists are many and various. **1905** J. MCCABE tr. *Haeckel's Evol. Man* I. vi. 98 In the case of the protists, the entire organism usually consists of a single autonomous cell throughout life. **1908** M. HARTOG in *Contemp. Rev.* Apr. 489 The Protistic parent that loses its individuality in its offspring when it divides. **1926** C. M. WENYON *Protozool.* I. i. 4 A typical Protist consists of a small portion of cytoplasm and a nucleus. **1940** [see METACHRONAL *a.*]. **1965** B. E. FREEMAN tr. *Vandel's Biospeleol.* vi. 62 Not a single free-living aquatic protist can be considered as a true cavernicole. **1975** *Nature* 7 Aug. 467/2 These [phytoflagellates] were the ancestors of all plants, and . . of non-photosynthetic protists and animals.

protistology (prəʊtɪ'stɒlədʒɪ). [f. PROTIST, PROTISTA *sb. pl.* + -OLOGY.] The study of organisms included in the Protista. Hence **proti'stologist**, one who studies protists.

1911 J. A. THOMSON *Introd. Sci.* iv. 110 It might also be convenient to have a special science of Protistology for the minute and simple organisms which seem to hesitate between plant and animal life. **1911** *Q. Jrnl. Microsc. Sci.* LVI. 396 Cytologists and protistologists alike have been content . . with assuming that the Bacteria are a group of simple organisms. **1926** C. M. WENYON *Protozool.* I. I. 4 It is safer to regard them all as one large group, the Protista, the study of which is known as Protistology. **1951** *John o' London's Weekly* 17 Aug. 501/2 A scholar . . may spend his days at the microscope and read only treatises on protistology. **1965** B. E. FREEMAN tr. *Vandel's Biospeleol.* vi. 61 The disappearance of pigments in *Euglena* placed in darkness is a common occurrence, well known to protistologists. **1973** *Microscopy* XXXII. 325 He [*sc.* Georges Deflandre] . . was soon deep in studies of protistology (the biology of unicellular organisms).

protium ('prəʊtɪəm). *Chem.* [mod.L., f. Gr. πρῶτ-ος first + -IUM.] The 'normal', most abundant isotope of hydrogen, having only a proton in the nucleus and forming at least 99·98 per cent (by volume) of naturally occurring hydrogen; symbol ^1H (also H^1). Cf. DEUTERIUM, TRITIUM.

1933 [see DEUTERIUM]. **1936** *Nature* 12 Dec. 1021/1 Several attempts have been made to determine the ratio protium-deuterium (^1H: ^2H) in ordinary water, and the results mostly fall into two groups, either near 5500 or near 9000. **1957** G. E. HUTCHINSON *Treat. Limnol.* I. iii. 211 Hydrogen has two stable isotopes, H^1, sometimes called protium, and H^2 or D, usually called deuterium. **1972** *Nature* 31 Mar. 202/1 Of late, both Cornforth and Arigoni have developed techniques for the solution of this problem based in the chemical synthesis of CH_3 – groups containing one atom each of the three hydrogen isotopes, protium, deuterium and tritium. **1975** *Physics Bull.* May 211/1 In the case of the neutron diffraction experiments D_2O was used instead of H_2O as deuterium is a better coherent scatterer than protium.

proto- (prəʊtəʊ), before a vowel or *h* properly prot- (prəʊt), or with *h* (prəʊθ), repr. Gr. πρωτο-, combining form of πρῶτος first, which became πρωτ- before a simple, and πρωθ- before an aspirated vowel.

In compounds already used in Greek, and many of later formation, the Greek practice (represented by the forms *proto-*, *prot-*, *proth-*) is retained, but in modern formations, esp. in group 2 below, the tendency is to leave *proto-* unchanged: e.g. *proto-apostate*, *proto-hippus*.

Words in *proto-* requiring for any reason individual treatment will be found as main words; those not so treated follow here, in three groups, showing the use of *proto-*, (1) in general language; (2) in terms of zoology and biology; (3) in chemical terminology.

1. In various words of rare occurrence or noncewords, often self-explaining: *proto-* (which, when prefixed to a word already in English, is usually hyphened) denoting (*a*) 'First in time, earliest, original, primitive', as in ***proto-apostate***, ***-bishop***, ***-chemistry***, ***-chronicler***, ***-culture***, ***-god***, ***-heresiarch***, ***-history***, ***-ideal***, ***-metaphrast***, ***-music***, ***-novelist***, ***-parent***, ***-pattern***, ***-phoneme***, ***-poet***, ***-protestant***, ***-scientist***, ***-sinner***, ***-tyrant***; (*b*) 'First in rank or importance, chief, principal', as in †***proto-abbaty*** (= abbacy), ***-architect***, ***-chemist***, ***-devil***, ***-groomship***, ***-justiciaryship***, ***-magnate***, ***-rebel***, ***-traitor***; also the following: **proto'cultural** *a.*, belonging to such origins as can be surmised of human cultural development. **proto-'deacon** (**-diacon**) [Gr. πρωτοδιάκονος], a chief deacon (in the Greek Church). †**proto-'forester** (**protho-**) [med.L. *protoforestarius*], chief forester. **proto-'gospel** = PROTEVANGELIUM. †**'protogram** *Obs.*, an acronym. **'protograph** [see -GRAPH], a first or original writing. †**proto'graphic** *a. Obs.*, acronymic. **proto-hi'storian**, (*a*) (also †**prot-**) the earliest or original historian; (*b*) one who studies proto-history. **proto-hi'storic** *a.*, belonging to or relating to primitive history, or the beginnings of historical records. **proto-hi'storical** *a.* = *proto-historic* adj. **'proto-literate** *a.*, characterized by the most primitive kind of writing. **proto-'Mark**, an assumed original writing which formed the basis of the existing Gospel of Mark; so **proto-'Matthew**. †**proto-'natural** *a. Obs.*, primarily natural, belonging to the original nature of a thing. †**proto-no'tator**, a first or principal recorder of a court. **proto-patri'archal** *a.*, belonging to a chief patriarch. †**'proto-plot** *Obs.*, an original plot or scheme. **proto-'presbyter** = PROTOPOPE. †**proto-'primitive** *a.*, earliest among the primitive, most primitive. **proto-scien'tific** *a.*, belonging or relating to primitive science, or to an early stage in scientific development. †**proto-'scriniary** (*erron.* **scrinerary**), a chief keeper of records, etc. **'protosyntax** (see quot. 1940); hence **protosyn'tactical** *a.* **protosyn'tactically** *adv.* **'prototheme** (see quot. 1897). **proto-ty'pographer**, the earliest or chief printer. **proto'vestiary** [med.L. *prōtovestiārius*], the chief keeper of a (royal) wardrobe. **proto'zeugma** (see quot.). Also PROTOCANONICAL, PROTOMARTYR, PROTOPOPE, PROTOTYPE, etc.

a **1661** FULLER *Worthies, Somerset.* (1662) III. 21 Glassenbury being the *Proto-Abbaty then and many years after. **1827** HALLAM *Const. Hist.* xv. II. 475 *note*, Sir James Montgomery, the false and fickle *proto-apostate of whiggism. **1859** HOBHOUSE *Italy* I. 93 Sansovino was *proto-architect to the empire of St. Mark. **1641** HEYLIN *Hist. Episc.* II. (1657) 18 James the *Proto-Bishop, the first that ever had a fixt Episcopall Sea, was ordained Bishop of Hierusalem, by Peter, James and John the sonnes of Zebedee. **1907** *Edin. Rev.* Jan. 34 Anastasius . . sent the *proto-chemist, Johannes Isthmius, to end his fraudulent career in the Fortress of Petra. **1650** T. VAUGHAN (*title*) Anthroposophia Theomagica: Or a Discourse of the Nature of Man and his state after death; Grounded on his Creator's *Proto-Chimistry. *Ibid.* 9 He that knows how to imitate the Proto-Chymistrie of the Spirit by Separation of the Principles wherein the Life is Imprisoned. **1976** *Times Lit. Suppl.* 12 Nov. 1418/2 The development of alchemy and proto-chemistry [in China]. **1604** PARSONS *3rd Pt. Three Convers. Eng., Relat. Trial* 61 Though he be the Protestants *Protochronicler. **1961** A. I. HALLOWELL in S. L. Washburn *Social Life Early Man* 237, I suggested that the level of development represented by cultural adaptation can be focused more sharply in evolutionary perspective if we hypothecate a *protocultural phase in hominid evolution. **1976** *Sci. Amer.* Oct. 104/2 The difference is not necessarily related to the confinement of our troop but may simply reflect protocultural differences. **1971** R. M. & F. M. KEESING *New Perspectives Cultural Anthropol.* 48 There must have been 'protomen' with '*protoculture'. **1698** J. CRULL *Muscovy* 314 He hath also a *Proto-Deacon. **1896** *Westm. Gaz.* 27 May 6/2 Two archpriests, accompanied by proto-diacons, come forward. **1694** MOTTEUX *Rabelais* v. xiii, Oh you Devils, . . *Proto-Devils, Panto-Devils, you would wed a Monk, would you? [**1617** MINSHEU *Ductor*, **Protoforestarius*, was he whom the auncient Kings of this Realme made cheefe of Winsour Forest.] **1631** WEEVER *Anc. Fun. Mon.* 644 This Hugh was high Iustice, Gardian, or Prothoforester of England. **1900** *Nature* 8 Mar. 437/2 So stangely complex a pantheon was set up that the *protogod was almost whelmed by the sanctifications of himself. **1924** *Glasgow Herald* 27 Sept. 4 'Anzac' is one of the first *protograms to which the war gave birth. It is used . . to describe anything pertaining to the 'Australian and New Zealand Army Corps'. **1933** H. WENTWORTH *Blend-Words in Eng.* 3 Words formed from the initials of other words—called *letter words* . . and *protograms* (F. H. Vizetelly)—are fewer. **1841** MYERS *Cath. Th.* III. §46. 176 If it be admitted that an authentic *protograph of the Bible, with incontestably Divine signature . . does not exist. **1974** *Bible Translator* July 317 According to Russian biblical scholarship these basic sections are . . (1) the protographs of the Septuagint and the New Testament [etc.]. **1924** *Glasgow Herald* 27 Sept. 4 The great majority of words of the *protographic type have been coined within the last decade. **1822** *New Monthly Mag.* V. 342 The *protogroomship of the horse. **1844** W. KAY in *Fleury's Eccl. Hist.* III. 188 *note*, The words . . may simply refer to the fact of Simon's being the *proto-heresiarch. **1647** M. HUDSON *Div. Right Govt.* I. viii. 63 All Histories and Chronicles . . since Moses the *Prothistorian of the world. **1949** *Proc. Prehist. Soc.* XV. 196 That difficult problem so often shirked by prehistorian and proto-historian—the mechanics of cultural diffusion. **1880** *Trans. Royal Hist. Soc.* VIII. 191 The great school of *protohistoric mythology. **1901** *Pilot* 26 Jan. 102/2 Our knowledge of prehistoric and protohistoric times . . increases daily. **1928** V. G. CHILDE *Most Anc. East* viii. 176 The implements of the *protohistorical period were almost entirely of metal. **1950** A. HUXLEY *Themes & Variations* 54 That Golden Age of Peace, which not long since was regarded as a mere myth, but is now revealed by the light of archaeology as a proto- and pre-historical reality. **1920** R. R. MARETT *Psychol. & Folk-lore* xi. 249 The value of *proto-history, as it is sometimes termed. **1947** H. C. E. ZACHARIAS (*title*) Proto-history. An explicative account of the development of human thought from Palaeolithic times to the Persian monarchy. **1980** *Encounter* May 66/1 We—the workers in British protohistory during the last 30 years—have suffered corporately from inadequate preliminary education, leading to the mental counterparts of asthma, myopia and strabismus. **1716** M. DAVIES *Athen. Brit.* III. *Diss. Physick* 40 The same *Proto-Ideal Purpose of drawing out the Primogenial Physick of the Grecians to its first aboriginal Offspring. **1611** SPEED *Hist. Gt. Brit.* IX. ix. §31. 588 The Earle of Kent, whom . . the King remooued from the *Proto-Iustitiariship (or high office of his Chiefe Iustice). **1942** DELOUGAZ & LLOYD *Pre-Sargonid Temples* i. 123 The architectural history of the Sin Temple bears out . . the subdivision of the Early Dynastic period into three and the *Proto-literate into at least two distinct phases. **1971** Proto-literate [see *pictographic* adj. s.v. PICTOGRAPH]. **1822** *New Monthly Mag.* V. 342 Creating him a *protomagnate of Persia. **1883** SCHAFF *Hist. Ch.* II. XII. lxxix. 600 He used the Hebrew Matthew . . or a lost *proto-Mark. **1865** DE MORGAN in *Athenæum* 13 May 653/3 Billingsley, the English *protometaphrast of Euclid. **1963** AUDEN *Dyer's Hand* 474 A music which sounds remarkably like primitive *proto-music. **1977** *Rolling Stone* 21 Apr. 41/3 Ultimately, *14 Canons* is a unique type of protomusic—a series of potentially extendible alchemical exercises. *a* **1653** BINNING *Serm.* (1845) 68 This is the *protonatural obligation. **1720** STRYPE *Stow's Surv.* II. v. xxviii. 387/1 The Maior's Clerk, together with the Common Clerk of the City, and the Sheriff's Clerks sat before them, to note . . all the Matters objected. . . And one was *Protonotator, from whose Note all the rest took each his Copy of Writing. **1976** *Times Lit. Suppl.* 19 Nov. 1459/4 Bunyan's humanity and his raciness and his humour and everything that makes him a *proto-novelist. **1603** J. DAVIES *Microcosm.* (Grosart) 23/1 Since our *Proto-parents' lowest fall, Our wisdome's highest pitch (God wot) is low. *c* **1810** COLERIDGE in *Lit. Rem.* (1838) III. 218 Aye! here is the *ovum*, . . the proto-parent of the whole race of controversies. **1658** BRAMHALL *Schism Guarded* IV. I. x, His *Protopatriarchal power was acknowledged. **1657** J. WATTS *Vind. Ch. Eng.* 86 We are to . . eye Christ beyond them, especially, as the *Proto-Patterne. **1960** H. M. HOENIGSWALD *Lang. Change & Ling. Reconstruction* xii. 132 If a split affects the same *proto-phoneme in each daughter language, the partial likeness between the sets of correspondences is impaired. **1974** R. W. WESCOTT in *Language Origins* 116 Only eight proto-phonemes (which are more nearly equivalent to contemporary morphophonemes than to contemporary Phonemes) appear in all five of their formulations. The eight are p, t, k; m, n; y, w; e. **1584** *Leycesters Commonw.* (1641) 91 Their Architipe or *Proto-plot which they follow (I meane the conspiracy of Northumberland and Suffolke in King Edwards dayes). **1963** AUDEN *Dyer's Hand* 34 Whatsoever Adam called every living creature, that was . . its Proper Name. Here Adam plays the role of the *Proto-poet. **1882–3** *Schaff's Encycl. Relig. Knowl.* III. 1942 There is a *proto-presbyter or proto-pope at each cathedral . . in the Græco-Russian Church. **1694** J. SMITH *Doctr. Lord's Day* 70 Sunday was accounted by the *Protoprimitive Fathers the Seventh day in the order of Creation. **1604** PARSONS *3rd Pt. Three Convers. Eng.* 355 One of the first *Protoprotestants of England. **1714** LOCKHART *Mem. Affairs Scot.* 9 His son . . thence acquired the title of *proto-rebell. **1907** A. LANG *Hist. Scot.* IV. iv. 80 Queensberry, now regarded by Cavaliers as 'the proto-rebel', was Privy Seal. **1934** WEBSTER, **Protoscientific*, adj. **1968** M. BUNGE in R. Klibansky *Contemp. Philos.* II. 4 In the underdeveloped (protoscientific) disciplines, fact-collecting passes for the sole respectable occupation. **1978** *Sci. Amer.* Jan. 69/1 Overshadowed by scholasticism, the work of the *protoscientists was ignored or treated as heresy, and its proponents endured ridicule and some persecution. **1670** G. H. *Hist. Cardinals* I. III. 85 He had under him twelve Scrineraries, and one *Proto-Scrinerary. **1702** *Burlesque L'Estrange's Quevedo* 279 Lucifer, the *Proto-Sinner of Heaven. **1940** W. V. QUINE *Math. Logic* vii. 292 The part of syntax which omits membership will be called *protosyntax. . . *Protosyntactical definability is intended not as an approximation to constructivity, but as something more inclusive. The notion of a non-theorem, e.g., is *protosyntactically definable, yet presumably not constructive. **1943** *Mind* LII. 272 A restricted portion of the syntax (that which omits membership) is distinguished by the label 'protosyntax'. **1964** *Amer. Philos. Q.* I. 265/1 The entire construction is done . . within Quine's protosyntax. **1897** *Prototheme [see *deuterotheme* s.v. DEUTERO-]. **1905** *N. & Q.* III. 176/1 These protothemes in familiar intercourse, or even on more serious occasions, often received the termination *-a*, *Seax*, for instance, becoming *Seaxa*. **1570–6** LAMBARDE *Peramb. Kent* (1826) 284 Thomas that *Prototraitour and rebell to his Prince. **1656** BLOUNT *Glossogr.*, **Prototypographer* . . , the cheif Printer. **1880** BLADES in *Athenæum* 18 Dec. 814/3 He left Bruges to return to his native country and become its proto-typographer. **1931** *Library* XII. 109 This volume is printed with the type of Johannes de Salsburga and Paulus de Constantia, the prototypographers of Barcelona. **1976** *Times Lit. Suppl.* 22 Oct. 1328/2 Thanks to Caxton, England had a native prototypographer who worked with patriotic gusto in the national language. **1657** W. RAND tr. *Gassendi's Life Peiresc* Ep. Ded. 4 Nimrod the mighty Hunter, and *Proto-Tyrant of the world. **1774** WARTON *Hist. Eng. Poetry* (1840) I. iii. 132 *Protovestiary or wardrobe keeper of the palace of Antiochus at Constantinople (*c* 1070). **1657** J. SMITH *Myst. Rhet.* 180 **Protozeugma*, . . when the Verb or Adjective is expressed in the beginning of the clause or sentence; and omitted after.

2. In numerous modern scientific and technical terms (sbs. and adjs.). The second element is properly of Greek origin, less frequently of Latin.

a. Prefixed to adjs. from names of countries or races, forming adjs. denominating primitive or original peoples, writings, works of art or manufacture, styles of architecture, etc.; in *Philol.*, forming sbs. and adjs. designating the earliest attested or hypothetically-reconstructed form of a language or family of languages (cf. PRIMITIVE *a.* 4b): as ***proto-Algonquian***, ***-Arabic***, ***-Aryan***, ***-Athapaskan***, ***-Australian***, ***-Australoid***, ***-Austronesian***, ***-Babylonian***, ***-Caucasic***, ***-Celtic***, ***-Corinthian***, ***-Doric***, ***-Egyptian***, ***-Elamite***, ***-Gallo-Romance*** (also ***-Romanic***), ***-Germanic***, ***-Greek***, ***-Hattic***, ***-Indo-European***, ***-Ionic***, ***-Italic***, ***-Malay***, ***-Medic***, ***-Phœnician***, ***-Polynesian***, ***-Romance***, ***-Semitic***, ***-Slavonic***. Also with nouns denoting natives or inhabitants, as ***proto-Mede***; with geographical names and sbs., as ***proto-Atlantic***, ***-Nile***, ***-ocean***, ***-Thames***; and with astronomical names, as ***proto-earth***, ***-Jupiter***, ***-sun*** (hence ***protosolar*** adj.). Also *protocloud*, *-cluster* in 2b, PROTOCONTINENT, PROTOGALAXY, PROTOPLANET, PROTOSTAR. **proto-'Hittite**, the language of the Hattian people, philologically unrelated to Hittite.

1939 L. BLOOMFIELD in C. Hockett *Bloomfield Anthol.* (1970) 352 Our basic forms are not ancient forms, say of the *Proto-Algonquian parent language. **1974** *Canad. Jrnl. Linguistics* XIX. 145 As was mentioned above, Proto-Algonquian palatalization came down into Fox pretty much unscathed. **1889** SAYCE in *Contemp. Rev.* Dec. 905 An alphabet and language which have been termed *Protoarabic. **1904** G. S. Hall *Adolescence* II. xviii. 657 The Todas of India, whom some call *proto-Aryans. **1938** Partridge *World of Words* iv. 126 The Latin may be traced to an Aryan original; but the proto-Aryan form.. was caused by some accidental circumstance. **1964** M. E. Krauss in *Internat. Jrnl. Amer. Linguistics* XXX. 118 (*title*) *Proto-Athapaskan-Eyak and the problem of NaDene: the phonology. **1966** J. T. Wilson in *Nature* 13 Aug. 676/1 It is proposed that, in Lower Palaeozoic time, a *proto-Atlantic Ocean existed so as to form the boundary between the two realms, and that during Middle and Upper Palaeozoic time the ocean closed by stages. **1972** *Sci. Amer.* Nov. 62/3 In Devonian times an order of jawless freshwater fishes, cousins to the orders that once flourished on opposite sides of the proto-Atlantic, inhabited the streams of the region that is now the European and Asiatic flanks of the Urals. **1918** *Phil. Trans. R. Soc.* B. CVIII. 382 This fossil human skull of a not yet adult *Proto-Australian presents.. the general picture of a cranium similar in all respects to the cranium of the Australian of to-day. *Ibid.*, The Proto-Australian is, in some very important features, to be sharply differentiated from Neanderthal man. This is nowhere more clearly seen than in the palate and teeth. **1923** R. B. Dixon *Racial Hist. Man* IV. ii. 374 The Australian population thus appears to be made up almost entirely of two types, the *Proto-Negroid and *Proto-Australoid, of which the former is concentrated in the north and northwest, the latter in the south and southeast. **1959** Proto-Australoid [see gerontomorphic *a.*]. **1963** G. B. Milner in C. Mohrmann et al. *Trends in Mod. Linguistics* 68 Dempwolff had found a sufficient body of evidence to justify his setting up a Proto-Melanesian language.. as he had reconstructed a Proto-Polynesian language, both of which he regarded as ultimately descended from *Proto-Austronesian. **1976** *Language* LII. 221 The systematic reconstruction of Proto-Austronesian.. phonology and lexicon was first attempted by Otto Dempwolff. **1889** I. Taylor *Orig. Aryans* iii. 182 The higher culture of the Semites, which again was derived from the *proto-Babylonian people. **1899** R. Munro *Prehist. Scot.* III. 246 The horned weapons are products of the *proto-Celtic stratum which lies chronologically between the earlier megalithic chambers and the later Gaulish tumuli. **1894** E. Robinson in *Nation* (N.Y.) 31 May 405/2 Of the early styles,.. and, most of all, the so-called '*proto-Corinthian'. **1907** *Athenæum* 6 July 20/2 In one of the primitive graves laid bare.. in the Forum was found a small vase of the proto-Corinthian class. **1932** *Times Lit. Suppl.* 8 Sept. 622/4 Corinth, where the Protocorinthian style forms a natural transition between the Geometric and the Orientalizing. **1973** *Univ. Oxf. Ann. Rep. 1970–71* 8 Publications: 'A Protocorinthian Dinos and Stand'. **1876** Birch *Rede Lect. Egypt* 21 The architect invents the *protodoric column. **1969** *Times* 18 July 6/4 The *proto-earth may have swept up from the dust cloud much more silicate material than it now possesses. **1977** A. Hallam *Planet Earth* 18/2 Most probably, the Moon formed from a dense atmosphere, generated by the high temperatures of solid-particle accretion at the surface of the proto-Earth. **1901** A. J. Evans in *Oxf. Univ. Gaz.* 12 Feb. 339/1 A survival of this *Proto-Egyptian class in the Libyan regions. **1950** *Language* XXVI. 9 A concrete example of how this type of intermediate reconstruction can be done and what it gives us can be seen in the phonological system of *Proto-Gallo-Romance. **1964** *Ibid.* XL. 32 If Provençal should turn out to belong to it, 'Proto-Gallo-Romance' is the obvious choice. **1946** *Stud. in Philol.* XLIII. 463 Then with a similarly acquired statement of Proto-Provençal, we can formulate *Proto-Gallo-Romanic. **1934** Priebsch & Collinson *German Lang.* iv. 236 The Proto-Italic and *Proto-Germanic peoples. **1960** *Amer. Speech* XXXV. 227 From pre-Scandinavian or Proto-Germanic to Old and Modern Icelandic. **1964** *Language* XL. 294 Next he reviews the history of the problem of the Proto-Germanic long stops. **1972** *Ibid.* XLVIII. 407 Proto-Germanic, which should be based on the internal reconstructions of the individual dialects. **1901** *Pilot* 26 Jan. 103/1 Hitherto.. called 'Mycenæan' or *proto-Greek art. **1959** T. Burton-Brown *Early Medit. Migrations* iii. 66 There were established, from at least as early as the end of the Third Millennium, some kind of 'proto-Greek' people. **1964** E. Palmer tr. *Martinet's Elem. Gen. Linguistics* v. 149 Tsakonian is a proto-Greek dialect. **1968** W. S. Allen *Vox Graeca* i. 30 It may be mentioned that in Proto-Greek, and still preserved in Mycenaean, there was a series of 'labio-velars'. **1933** E. H. Sturtevant *Compar. Gram. Hittite Lang.* i. 29 There seems to be no need for the cumbrous terms '*Proto-Hattic' or 'Proto-Hittite'. **1948** D. Diringer *Alphabet* v. 89 Some scholars call them 'Proto-Hattic' or 'Proto-Hittite'. **1924** A. H. Sayce in *Jrnl. R. Asiatic Soc.* 245 *Proto-Hittite is the name given by Dr. Forrer to the prefixal language, examples of which are found in the cuneiform texts of Boghaz Keui. **1952** O. R. Gurney *Hittites* vi. 122 The name Proto-Hittite has been widely adopted in order to avoid confusion with the official Hittite, but is somewhat misleading, since it suggests an earlier stage of Hittite, whereas it is a language totally unrelated to the latter. The name Hattian is preferable. **1947** R. S. Wells in *Word* III. 15 Linguists have reconstructed large parts of the vocabulary of *Proto-Indo-European. **1955** W. P. Lehmann in *Language* XXXI. 355 (*title*) Proto-Indo-European Resonants in Germanic. **1960** *Amer. Speech* XXXV. 227 Specific laryngeal problems in Proto-Indo-European phonology. **1979** *Amer. Speech 1978* LIII. 266 We have virtually no evidence for the earlier history of Proto-Indo-European forms. **1890** *Cent. Dict.* s.v., [Figure] *Proto-Ionic Capital, discovered in the Troad. **1968** *Language* XLIV. 269 On the evidence of Latin, Oscan, and Umbrian, *Proto-Italic still had the phrasally prior final consonants that have disappeared in Proto-Romance. **1976** *Archivum Linguisticum* VII. 62 Oscan *-tt-* represents a proto-Italic cluster *-ky-. **1976** *Sci. Amer.* May 113/1 James B. Pollack and his co-workers.. suggest that exactly the same process would have taken place within the miniature solar system of the Jovian satellites, with the *proto-Jupiter the source of the heat. **1909** A. C. Haddon *Races of Man* 18 *Indo-Chinese, Parcæans* or *Southern Mongols*:.. Those members who spread into the East Indian Archipelago are often called Oceanic Mongols, but a better term is *Proto-Malays; and it is from these the true Malay is derived. *Ibid.* 14 The broadening of the head is probably due to an early mixture with a Proto-Malay stock. **1947, 1958** Proto-Malay [see Jakun]. **1964** W. A. Hamid in W. Gungwu *Malaysia* III. xii. 179 The Proto-Malays are the tribes to be found in the interior forests among the foothills of the Malay archipelago. **1889** I. Taylor *Orig. Aryans* iii. 184 Non-Aryan tribes, such as the *proto-Medes,.. the Etruscans, and the Picts. **1877** A. H. Sayce in *Trans. Philol. Soc. 1875–6* 136 In *Protomedic and Susianian.. the initial is similarly always dropped in the plural of the verb. **1880** —— *Introd. Sci. Lang.* II. x. 321 The Protomedic group of languages to which Accadian belongs, in the Ural-Altaic family. **1894** Protomedic [see Medic *sb.*²]. **1972** *Sci. Amer.* Apr. 116/1 Primate forms found in fossil forest beds deposited 35 million years ago beside the *proto-Nile. **1975** *Nature* 29 May 376/1 Young rift oceans (*proto-oceans) are commonly the site of large scale evaporite deposition. **1893** F. Adams *New Egypt* 38 An expedition of acquisition, a truly *Proto-Phœnician trait! **1930** R. Paget *Human Speech* vii. 145 Several other gesture-words from *Proto-Polynesian. **1973** *Amer. Speech 1970* XLV. 118 The reconstruction of some proto-Polynesian forms. **1949** *Archivum Linguisticum* I. 151 The *Proto-Romance consonant clusters... We use this term, instead of the vague..'Vulgar Latin'. **1978** *Language* LIV. 182 There is no discussion of proto-morphophonemics, which might conceivably have raised the issue of umlaut in Proto-Romance. **1948** D. Diringer *Alphabet* 214 The *proto-Semitic alphabet. **1969** *Word* XXV. 115 The Proto-Semitic consonant system is generally assumed to have had a voiced velar stop phoneme */g/ as established by a set of correspondences throughout the Semitic family. **1920** *Trans. Philol. Soc. 1916–20* 128 In *Proto-Slavonic all final consonants fell out. *Ibid.* 130 Beside the palatalization there is another sweeping tendency in Proto-Slavonic phonology. **1951** *Archivum Linguisticum* III. 205 The work is a succinct presentation of Protoslavonic morphology. **1975** *Nature* 11 Sept. 91/1 S. Ramadurai.. argued that carbonaceous chondrites contain interstellar graphite grains from the *protosolar nebula. **1978** *Ibid.* 16 Mar. 239/2 Further conditions which must be satisfied are.. penetration of this element into the protosolar cloud. **1974** *Sci. Amer.* Mar. 51/3 At a distance of perhaps 20 million miles from the *protosun, a fifth of the way to the present orbit of the earth, a very few nonvolatile materials could have condensed into solid particles. **1969** Bennison & Wright *Geol. Hist. Brit. Isles* xv. 346 The consequent drainage pattern developed on the eastwards-tilted Mesozoic rocks included the *proto-Thames.

b. In terms, chiefly of Zoology or Biology: usually designating an (actual or hypothetical) original or primitive form, type, organism, structure, etc. ‖**pro'tamnion**, a hypothetical primitive amniotic animal, the supposed common ancestor of mammals, birds, and reptiles. ‖**prota'mœba**, a genus of Protozoa having lobate pseudopodia like the amœba (cf. protogenes); hence **prota'mœban**, *a.* belonging to or having the characters of this genus; *sb.* a member of this genus; **prota'mœboid** *a.*, resembling a protamœba. **pro'tamphirhine**, the ancestral type of the amphirhine or double-nostrilled vertebrates. ‖**pro'tastacus** [Gr. ἀστακός lobster, crayfish], the ancestral type of the *Astacidæ* or crayfishes; hence **pro'tastacine** (-saɪn) *a.* **prota'xonial** *a.*, in *Morphology*, having the parts arranged about a single primary or main axis; of or pertaining to *Protaxonia*. **pro'tembryo**: see quot.; hence **protembry'onic** *a.* ‖**proten'cephalon**, the first of the three primary cerebral vesicles of the embryo. **prot'helminth** [Gr. ἕλμινς, ἑλμινθ- worm], a protozoön of the order *Prothelmintha*, comprising most of the *Infusoria*, regarded as representing an ancestral type of worms; hence **prothel'minthic** *a.*; so ‖**prot'helmis**, a hypothetical ancestral type of worms. **prothyalosomal** (prəʊθaɪələʊ'səʊməl) *a.*, pertaining to the *prothyalosoma* [Gr. ὕαλος glass + σῶμα body], 'Van Beneden's name (1883) for the envelope of the nucleolus of an ovum' (*Syd. Soc. Lex.*). ‖**prothysteron** (prəʊ'θɪstərɒn) *Rhet.* [Gr. πρωθύστερον] = hysteron proteron. **protichnite** (-'ɪknaɪt), *Palæont.* [see ichnite], one of the fossil tracks found in the Potsdam sandstone of Canada, supposed to be those of a trilobite or allied animal. **proto-'biface** *Archæol.*, an early form of biface. **'protoblast** [see -blast], (*a*) a cell of a primitive or simple form, consisting of a mass of protoplasm with no investing membrane or cell-wall; (*b*) 'the nucleus of the ovum' (*Syd. Soc. Lex.*). **proto'blastic** *a.* = holoblastic. **proto'blastoderm**, the primitive blastoderm or investing layer of the fertilized ovum. **proto-'carinate**, *a.* belonging to those primitive birds having a carinate or keeled breast-bone; *sb.* one of such birds. **'protocell**, a body postulated as ancestral to the cell. **proto'cercal** *a.*, *Ichth.*, having a tail-fin of the primitive form, continuous with the dorsal and ventral fins. **'protocere** (-sɪə(r)) [Gr. κέρας horn], the rudiment of the antler of a deer, the process developed in the first year. ‖**proto'cerebrum**, (*a*) the anterior cerebral vesicle of the embryo, which develops into the cerebrum; (*b*) the anterior segment of the brain of an arthropod; hence **proto'cerebral** *a.* **protocœ'lomate**, an animal belonging to the *Protocœ'lomata*, a proposed division of *Metazoa* characterized by a primitive enteric cavity with simple cœlomic sacs, as most sponges; hence **protocœlo'matic** *a.* **'protocloud** *Astr.*, a protogalactic cloud. **'protocluster** *Astr.* = prec.. **protocneme** ('prəʊtəʊkniːm) *Zool.* [Gr. κνήμα tibia; cf. cnemial *a.*], one of six pairs of primary mesenteries which are found in corals of the order Scleractinia. **'protoconch** (-kɒŋk) [see conch], the embryonic shell in certain cephalopods; hence **proto'conchal** *a.* **proto'dipnoan**, a hypothetical primitive dipnoan. **proto'dolomite** *Min.*, a mineral with a composition near that of dolomite, $CaMg(CO_3)_2$, but an imperfect crystal structure. **'protodome** *Cryst.*, a primary dome. **protody'nastic** *a.*, *Anc. Hist.*, belonging to the first or earliest (Egyptian) dynasties. **proto'enstatite** *Min.*, an artificial, high-temperature form of the magnesium silicate $MgSiO_3$. **proto'fibril** *Biol.*, a filament of protein that is a component structural element of a fibril or *spec.* of a microfibril. **proto'filament** *Biol.*, a filament of protein, about 5 nanometres in diameter, a group of which constitute a microtubule. **protoˌfora'minifer** (pl. **-forami'nifera**), a primitive foraminifer. ‖**proto'gaster** [Gr. γαστήρ stomach]: see quot. **proto'gastric** *a.* [as prec.], (*a*) a term designating two lobes, one on each side, towards the front of the gastro-hepatic area of the carapace in brachyurous Crustaceans; (*b*) pertaining to the protogaster. **proto'human** *sb.* and *a.* *Anthrop.*, (pertaining to or being) one of the man-like prehistoric creatures from which man is held to have evolved. **proto'lemur**, a term including various extinct insectivorous mammals as the supposed ancestral types of the lemurs. **'protolife**, inanimate existence representing a late stage in the evolution of life. **'protolith** *Petrol.* [Gr. λίθ-ος stone] (see quot. 1972). **proto'lithionite** *Min.* [ad. G. *protolithionit* (F. Sandberger *Untersuchungen über Erzgänge* (1885) ii. 169): cf. lithionite], a variety of zinnwaldite containing a higher proportion of lithium and a lower proportion of iron. ‖**proto'mala** [L. *māla* jaw], each member of the first pair of jaws or mandibles in the Myriapoda; hence **proto'malal**, **proto'malar** *adjs.* **proto'meristem** *Bot.*, the meristem or generating tissue of the youngest parts of plants; primary meristem (Russow (in Ger.) 1872). **pro'tomerite** [Gr. μέρος part], the first or anterior segment of a polycystid gregarine, as distinguished from the larger posterior segment (*deuteromerite* or *deutomerite*); hence **proto-me'ritic** *a.* **pro'tomesal** *a.*, *Entom.* [Gr. μέσος middle], applied to a series of cells in the wings of hymenopterous insects; now called the second, third, and fourth submarginal or cubital cells. **'protomorph** [Gr. μορφή form], a primitive or original form; so **proto'morphic** *a.*, having the primitive or simplest form or structure. **proto'myxoid** *a.*, resembling *Protomyxa* [Gr. μύξα slime], a genus of myxopodous Protozoa. **proto-Neo'lithic** *a.* *Archæol.*, belonging to or characteristic of the earliest Neolithic period; also *absol.* as *sb.* **protone'phridium** *Zool.* [mod.L., coined in Ger. by B. Hatschek *Lehrb. der Zool.* (1889) II. 160: see nephridium], in certain invertebrates, esp. flatworms, an excretory system made up of solenocytes opening into ducts leading to pores in the exterior surface; also, a larval nephridium of this type; so **protone'phridial** *a.* ‖**proto'nephron** [Gr. νεφρός kidney], the primitive kidney in the embryo of vertebrates, consisting of the *pronephron*, *mesonephron*, and *metanephron*; hence **proto'nephric** *a.* **proto'nucleate** *a.*, having a primitive nucleus; belonging to the *Protonucleata*, a hypothetical group of Protozoa regarded as the ancestors of all other animals. **proto-'organism**, a primitive or unicellular organism, animal or vegetable; a protozoön or protophyte. **proto-'ornithoid** *a.* [Gr. ὄρνις, ὀρνιθ- bird], of the most ancient or primitive birdlike type. **ˌprotoperi'thecium**, in some fungi, an ascogonium from which have grown out one or more trichogynes, some of which develop into part of a perithecium if spermatization occurs; hence **ˌprotoperi'thecial** *a.* **protope'troleum** [mod.L., coined in Ger. by C. Engler 1897, in *Ber. d. Deut. Chem. Ges.* XXX. 2360], an intermediate product in the formation of petroleum from organic debris. **'protophenomenon** *Philos.*, a primary phenomenon. **proto'phloem** *Bot.*, the tissue from which the phloem is developed; the primitive phloem of a fibro-vascular bundle (Russow (in Ger.) 1872). [a. G. *protophloëm* (E. Russow 1873, in *Mém. Acad. Impér. Sci. St.-Pétersbourg* 7 sér. XIX. 4]. **'protopod** *a. Ent.* [ad. It. *protopodo* (A. Berlese 1913, in *Redia* IX. 127)], of an insect larva, lacking abdominal segmentation and limbs. **proto'podial** *a.*, pertaining to a *protopodium*. **pro'topodite** [see PODITE], in Crustacea, the first or basal joint of a limb, which articulates with its somite; hence **protopo'ditic** *a.* ‖**proto'podium** [see PODIUM 2b], a primitive or typical foot in Molluscs. **'protoprism** *Cryst.*, a primary prism. **proto'proteose** *Biochem.*, any of a class of proteoses that are soluble in water and dilute salt solutions and are formed during gastric secretion. **proto'pyramid** *Cryst.*, a primary pyramid. **proto'scolex** *Zool.*, a vesicle formed from the germinal layer of a hydatid cyst and capable of development into a scolex or a secondary cyst. **proto'seismograph** [see SEISMOGRAPH], an instrument for recording the beginning or first trace of an earthquake shock. **proto'siphon**, the primitive or rudimentary siphon or siphuncle in the protoconch of certain cephalopods; also ‖**protosi'phonula**. **proto'somite**, each of the rudimentary somites or segments of the embryo in arthropods and annelids. hence **protoso'mitic** *a.* **'protospasm** *Path.*, a local spasm preceding a general convulsion. **proto'spermatoblast** [see SPERM and -BLAST], term for certain cells from which spermatozoa are formed: see quot. **proto'spongian** *a.*, designating a primitive stage in the development of a sponge. **'protospore** *Bot.*, a primary spore or spore-like body in certain fungi, corresponding to the prothallium in higher cryptogams. **'protostele** *Bot.* [STELE 2], a simple type of stele in which a central core of xylem is surrounded by a cylinder of phloem: hence **protostelic** (-'sti:lɪk) *a.* **pro'tostoma** [Gr. στόμα mouth]: see quot. for *protogaster*. **protosyste'matic** *a.*, *Cryst.*, belonging to a primary system. **proto'tergite** *Entom.* [L. *tergum* back], the first dorsal segment of the abdomen of an insect. **'prototheca** *Zool.* [THECA], a cup-shaped basal plate which is formed at the start of the development of a colony of stony corals. **proto'toxin**: see quot.; so **proto'toxoid** = *protoxoid*: see TOXIN and TOXOID. **'prototroch** *Zool.* [Gr. τροχός wheel], a pre-oral ciliated ridge encircling the body of the trochosphere larva of certain invertebrates, including polychæte worms and some annelids and molluscs. **protover'miculite** *Min.*, a mineral similar in composition to vermiculite but containing more water, and found as large yellow or brown scales. **proto'vertebra**, (*a*) *Comp. Anat.* in Carus's nomenclature (1828) applied to the ribs reckoned as the first set of vertebræ; (*b*) *Embryol.* each of the segments, formerly considered as primitive (temporary) vertebræ, in the early embryo of a vertebrate; hence **proto'vertebral** *a.*, pertaining to or of the nature of a protovertebra. **proto'vertebrate** *a.*, (*a*) furnished with protovertebræ; (*b*) belonging to the *Protovertebrata*, the hypothetical ancestral forms of vertebrate animals. ‖**pro'tovum**, an ovum in its first or primitive stage, e.g. before impregnation, or (in the case of a meroblastic ovum) before the formation of the food-yolk (cf. METOVUM). **protoxylem** (-'zaɪləm) *Bot.*, the tissue from which the xylem is developed; the primitive xylem of a fibro-vascular bundle. [a. G. *protoxylem* (E. Russow 1873, in *Mém. Acad. Impér. Sci. St.-Pétersbourg* 7th Ser. XIX. 3)]. **proto'zonite** *Entom.* [Gr. ζώνη girdle], each of the primitive or rudimentary segments of the body of an insect in the embryonic stage. **pro'tureter**, the primitive ureter, the excretory duct of the *protonephron*. See also PROTOHIPPUS, PROTOPHYTE, PROTOZOA, etc.

1879 tr. *Haeckel's Evol. Man* xviii. II. 134 This unknown common parent-form is the Primitive Amnion Animal (**Protamnion*). In external appearance the Protamnion was most probably an intermediate form between the Salamanders and the Lizards. **1877** HUXLEY *Anat. Inv. Anim.* ii. 79 It is open to doubt..whether either **Protamœba, Protogenes*, or *Myxodictyum* is anything but one stage of a cycle of forms. **1883** J. E. ADY in *Knowledge* 15 June 355/2 The thousands of other *protamœboid creatures. **1869** HUXLEY *Crit. & Addr.* xii. (1873) 317 From this '*Protamphirhine' were developed, in divergent lines, the true Sharks, Rays, and Chimæræ; the Ganoids, and the Dipneusta. **1880** —— *Crayfish* vi. 344 The common *protastacine form is to be sought in the Trias. **1878** —— in *Proc. Zool. Soc.* 787 A Crustacean..which we may call provisionally **Protastacus*. **1887** *Proc. Boston Soc. Nat. Hist.* 397 The stages of holoblastic ova may be..classified as follows..(1) The ovum or Monoplast..; (2) the first stage of segmentation..; (3) the second stage of segmentation... We have proposed to classify these stages under the name of *Protembryo. **1887** T. J. PARKER in *Proc. Zool. Soc.* 37 The ..unpaired portion of the *protencephalon (embryonic fore-brain). **1879** tr. *Haeckel's Evol. Man* xvii. II. 76 The common parent-form of the whole Worm tribe (the **Prothelmis*). **1873** DAWSON *Earth & Man* iii. 45 Some of the most ancient sandstones have their surfaces covered with rows of punctured impressions (**Protichnites*, first foot-prints). **1880** *Libr. Univ. Knowl.* (U.S.) VII. 772 The sandstone beds which contain the protichnites. **1975** *Nature* 7 Aug. 470/2 Some protohandaxes may have one face made entirely of cortex, so not all of these artefacts can be called *protobifaces and the term protohandaxes is preferable. **1976** *Ibid.* 8 July 104/2 Other tool forms, such as.. protobifaces..occur with less frequency. **1872** PACKARD *Embryol. Stud. Hexapodous Insects* (Peabody Acad. Sci. I. Mem. III.) 6 The primitive blastodermic skin..or as it might be termed, *protoblastoderm. **1901** *Ibis* Apr. 343 That in Rhea we have represented the *proto-carinate wing-type of to-day. **1965** S. W. FOX *Orig. Prebiol. Syst.* 372 The explanation has been extended to permit us to visualize a spontaneous synthesis of protein-like material sufficiently similar to yield a *protocell which could spontaneously include ATP-splitting ability. **1974** PONNAMPERUMA & GABEL in Carlile & Skehel *Evolution in Microbial World* 407 Oparin does not in any way imply that the coacervates he and his associates have studied were the actual precursors of the protocell. **1977** A. HALLAM *Planet Earth* 236 Carbonaceous meteorites also contain organic spheres, and mineral grains coated with organic sheaths, that have been likened to 'protocells'. **1892** J. A. THOMSON *Outl. Zool.* xx. 403 The end of the notochord in the tail is quite straight (*protocercal and diphycercal). **1885** WILDER in *N. York Med. Jrnl.* 28 Mar. 354 *Proto-cerebrum, a monomial.. significant equivalent for..cerebral rudiment. **1897** *Q. Jrnl. Microsc. Sci.* XL. 261 Viallanes has shown, by his very careful researches on the structure of the adult brain.., that it consists in insects of three segments... The first or protocerebrum, including the optic centres, corresponds to the first segment in Peripatus. **1969** *New Scientist* 10 July 56/2 It is generally known that the regulating clock mechanism of insects lies in the protocerebrum. **1970** *Nature* 31 Oct. 412/1 A *protocloud formed at that time would initially expand with the Universe, but at a reduced rate. **1971** *Proc. Internat. School of Physics 'Enrico Fermi'* XLVII. 336 The density fluctuations associated with *protoclusters—and *a fortiori* protogalaxies—would be too small to be detected. **1976** *Nature* 11 Nov. 114/2 Four stages might usefully be distinguished: (1) the creation of a massive protocluster cloud; (2) the separation of individual protostars from such a protocluster cloud; [etc.]. **1900** *Protocneme [see *metacneme* s.v. META- 4]. **1916** H. S. PRATT *Man. Common Invertebr. Animals* 138 The gullet is joined with the body wall by all of the protocnemes. **1940** L. H. HYMAN *Invertebrates* I. vii. 589 These original twelve septa, which arise as couples, are called protocnemes. **1956** J. W. WELLS in R. C. Moore *Treat. Invertebr. Paleont.* F 333/2 When the first 6 mesenteric pairs (comprising 12 protocnemes) have developed the embryonic period [of scleractinians] is terminated. **1884** HYATT in *Proc. Boston Soc. Nat. Hist.* 113 Anatomically, the Sponges may be called Metazoa protocœlomata... We can readily transform a *protocœlomate into a trochocœlomate by destroying the horizontal parts of the partitions. **1888** *Ibid.* XXIII. 542 The *protoconch of Owen, in Cephalopods, is the early shell which precedes the conch, or true shell. Professors Hyatt and Brooks consider the protoconch in cephalous molluscs as..probably derived from the periconch of Scaphopods. **1955** GRAF & GOLDSMITH in *Bull. Geol. Soc. Amer.* LXVI. 1566 These poorly ordered near dolomites, or *protodolomites, also have been observed to form during the rapid cooling of dry periclase-calcite assemblages through the dolomite stability field. *Ibid.* 1567 In view of their relatively narrow compositional range, it appears probable that protodolomites have a relatively high degree of short-range Ca-Mg order, rather than being merely metastable, disordered, high-magnesium calcites. **1967** *Oceanogr. & Marine Biol.* V. 151 The deficiency of magnesium in the Red Sea brine might be caused by dolomitization of the carbonate rocks (some evidence of which is found in the presence of crystals of protodolomite in the core from the Discovery Deep). **1878** GURNEY *Crystallogr.* 52 The former [dome] is distinguished as the *protodome. **1902** *Daily Chron.* 6 Oct. 3/1 The period of the first three dynasties..requires a designation of its own,.. the word '*proto-dynastic' appears to be suitable. **1902** *Nature* 6 Nov. 14/2 [Professor E. Smith] intends to give a full account of the structure of the brain in the predynastic and protodynastic Egyptians. **1962** S. E. FINER *Man on Horseback* vii. 89 These are the traditional monarchies where the ideals of nationality, liberty, equality and popular sovereignty have not yet penetrated. Another and better description is perhaps the proto-dynastic societies, societies where allegiance is owed to the dynasty. **1977** G. CLARK *World Prehist.* (ed. 3) v. 236 There can be no doubt of the existence precisely at the period of transition from the Predynastic to the Protodynastic or Archaic period of Egyptian history of innovations that stemmed from Mesopotamian sources. **1939** *Jrnl. Amer. Ceramic Soc.* XVIII. 110/1 Constitution of steatite... On heating to 800°, talc lost its H_2O and was transformed into *protoenstatite. **1962** *Ibid.* XLV. 156/2 The rate of the metastable inversion of protoenstatite to clinoenstatite during cooling is very sensitive to particle size. **1965** L. BRAGG et al. *Crystal Struct. Minerals* xii. 236 The detailed shape and relative positions of the silicate chains depend on the relative positions of the Mg atoms and their surrounding, octahedrally coordinated, oxygens. In protoenstatite the chains are fully extended, whereas in enstatite and clinoenstatite they are slightly different in shape and not fully extended. **1961** FILSHIE & ROGERS in *Jrnl. Molecular Biol.* III. 785 It can be observed ..that a high concentration of lead has entered each microfibril and become bound to preferred sites, revealing a composite structure consisting of filamentous subunits relatively unstained by lead (henceforth to be referred to as *protofibrils) each of the order of 20 Å in diameter. **1966** *New Scientist* 24 Feb. 480/2 Protofibrils, some 20 angstroms wide, may be observed to occur in a regular array, and it is widely accepted that they aggregate around an annulus, with perhaps nine outer protofibrils and two further protofibrils inside. **1971** *Nature* 22 Jan. 253/1 Wood fibres are hollow tubes composed of layers of cellulosic protofibrils embedded in a matrix of hemicellulose and lignin. **1971** *Proc. Nat. Acad. Sci.* LXVIII. 1766 If we assume a *protofilament arrangement of monomeric subunits..in a microtubule, it becomes apparent that a homofilament microtubule can be constructed only if the number of protofilaments is even (i.e. 12 or 14 in the usual model) while a heterofilament microtubule always results if an odd number (11 or 13) of protofilaments are assembled. **1977** *Jrnl. Protozool.* XXIV. 4/1 Microtubules..can be thought of as protofilaments that are end-to-end polymers of dimers which are then bound together to form a tube with an open lumen. **1875** DAWSON *Dawn of Life* viii. 215 Eozoon [etc.], our *protoforaminifera. **1879** tr. *Haeckel's Evol. Man* viii. I. 194, I shall call the central cavity of the Gastrula-body the primitive intestine (**protogaster*), and its opening the primitive mouth (*protostoma*). **1877** HUXLEY *Anat. Inv. Anim.* vi. 343 The latter is..sub-divided into two epigastric lobes, two *protogastric lobes, a median mesogastric lobe, two metagastric lobes and two urogastric lobes. **1910** *Daily Chron.* 9 Apr. 6/2 The Oceanic negro is far removed from primitive man, but..he inherits, as we all do, but happily in a lesser degree, the savage instincts of the *proto-human. **1954** L. C. EISELEY in W. L. Thomas *Current Anthropol.* 69/1 We have..stumbled into the world of essentially cultureless or almost cultureless proto-human types which are diverse in form because they represent evolution still at work upon the parts of the body. **1954** W. LA BARRE *Human Animal* iv. 83 The linearity of man, his relative hairlessness, his clothing, and his culture-based carnivorousness suggest that the proto-humans, like the anthropoids, were warm-climate-adapted animals. **1971** R. M. & F. M. KEESING *New Perspectives in Cultural Anthropol.* 45 Sharing must be viewed as a crucial protohuman innovation. **1978** *Sci. Amer.* Apr. 94/1 Excavation of these protohuman sites has revealed evidence suggesting that two million years ago some elements that now distinguish man from apes were already party of a novel adaptative strategy. **1887** HEILPRIN *Distrib. Anim.* III. ii. 348 By Trouessart they [certain mammals of tertiary age] are all ranged with the Insectivora as the group of the *proto-lemurs. **1966** *Palaeogeogr., Palaeoclimatol., Palaeoecol.* II. 54 The formation of cobionts and *protolife through inorganic photosynthesis stopped at the beginning of this period of transition. **1977** A. HALLAM *Planet Earth* 236/1 The stromatolites are universally regarded as the remains of true life: the earlier microscopic fossils may well also represent the remains of blue-green algae, but it is perfectly probable that they represent some form of primitive protolife. **1972** *Gloss. Geol.* (Amer. Geol. Inst.) 571/2 **Protolith*, the unmetamorphosed rock from which a given metamorphic rock was formed by metamorphism. Syn: *parent rock.* **1974** *Nature* 15 Mar. 199/1 This investigation attempts to decipher the premetamorphic age of the protolith of a recrystallised breccia from Apollo 16. **1892** *Dana's Syst. Min.* (ed. 6) VI. 627 **Protolithionite*, a lithium-iron mica from the granite of the Erzgebirge, Fichtelgebirge, etc. Color dark. Optically nearly uniaxial... Sandberger regards it as the source of the zinnwaldite, hence the name. **1959** *Amer. Mineralogist* XLIV. 1297 It is a lithium-iron mica, closely related to zinnwaldite and containing a large amount of the protolithionite component of the lepidolite series. **1883** PACKARD in *Proc. Amer. Philos. Soc.* June 198 [In *Myriapoda*] the *protomala consists of two portions, the *cardo* and *stipes*, while the hexapodous mandible is invariably composed of but one piece,..which corresponds to the stipes of the myriapodous protomala. *Ibid.* 203 The *protomalal and deutomalal arthromeres. **1881** *Nature* XXIII. 288/1 Dr. Jakob Eriksson describes in a lengthened paper the *protomeristem of the roots of Dicotyledons. **1882** VINES *Sachs' Bot.* 550 The young anther consists at first of a small-celled proto-meristem in which a fibro-vascular bundle becomes differentiated lying in the axis of the connective. **1885, 1921** *Protomerite [see EPIMERITE]. **1888** ROLLESTON & JACKSON *Anim. Life* 858 [In] the *Polycystidea* [the body] is divided by two septa into three segments... The first segment is the epimerite; it is the part from which the other two segments bud out... The second segment is the protomerite, the third and by far the largest, the deuteromerite. **1962** J. D. SMYTH *Introd. Animal Parasitol.* vi. 73 In some forms [of gregarines], the protomerite is drawn out into a specialised region for attachment. **1826** KIRBY & SP. *Entomol.* III. xxxv. 632 The medial areolets of the Intermediate Area..form three distinct series; these may be called the *protomesal, deuteromesal, and tritomesal, reckoning from the postcostal areolets. **1876** J. J. G. WILKINSON *Hum. Sc. & Div. Rev.* 58 The growth of evils from their first wicked thoughts or germs, from their true *protomorphs, tiny and unperceived, to monstrous destructions. **1859** *Todd's Cycl. Anat.* V. 476/1 The integumentary *protomorphic line. **1867** H. SPENCER *Princ. Biol.* §290 II. 289 A protomorphic layer, which differentiates in opposite directions. **1883** P. GEDDES in *Encycl. Brit.* XVI. 846/2 The writer has attempted to explain the forms of free and united cells as specializations of a (*protomyxoid) cycle in which variations of functional activity are accompanied by the assumption of corresponding forms. **1921** R. A. S. MACALISTER *Text-bk. European Archaeol.* I. x. 549 A culture independent of any of those which we have now considered, namely the '*Protoneolithic' Campignian. **1924** [see ASTURIAN *a.* and *sb.*]. **1931** *Antiquity* V. 520 Menghin distinguishes a Protoneolithic, and a Mixoneolithic, in the latter of which the Neolithic arts found their full expression. **1960** C. WINICK *Dict. Anthropol.* 440/2 *Protoneolithic*, in some classifications, the lower, or early, Neolithic era, consisting of the Campignian and Ertebole cultures. **1879** tr. *Haeckel's Evol. Man* xxv. II. 412 In all low Skulled Animals (*Craniota*), without amnion..the primitive kidneys (**protonephra*), though much modified,..act permanently as urine-secreting glands. **1895** *Protonephridial [see *protonephridium* below]. **1963** R. P. DALES *Annelids* v. 98 The metanephridial funnels or protonephridial solenocytes lie in the coelomic fluid. **1895** E. S. GOODRICH in *Q. Jrnl. Microsc. Sci.* XXXVII. 479 The nephridia of the Planarians ..are formed of a main duct, which branches out into fine tubules ending blindly internally in flame-cells; they do not develop beyond this 'protonephridial' condition—

*protonephridium of Hatschek. **1900** *Ibid.* XLIII. 742 For its [*sc.* the nephridium's] closed representation..and for closed 'head-kidneys', the term Protonephridium might, perhaps, be used with advantage. It is the name proposed by Hatschek for the closed nephridia of the Platyhelminths. **1930, 1967** [see *metanephridium* s.v. META- 4]. **1949** A. S. ROMER *Vertebrate Body* ii. 19 The excretory organs [of Amphioxus]..are tiny tubes (protonephridia) of a type found in certain invertebrates. **1978** L. C. OGLESBY in P. J. Mill *Physiol. Annelids* xiv. 619 In only one group, the Rotifera, is there direct evidence that the protonephridia serve an osmoregulatory role. **1861** *N. Syd. Soc. Year-bk. Med.* 113 Genesis of the *Proto-organisms found in Calcined Air, and in Putrescible Substances that have been heated to 150°. **1895** *Syd. Soc. Lex.*, *Protoörganism*, one of the simplest of organised beings, capable of being referred either to the animal or vegetable kingdom. **1883** W. SIKES in *Harper's Mag.* Feb. 332/2 Slab..extending the..area of *proto-ornithoid forms of life from longitude 72° to 4°. **1955** G. M. SMITH *Cryptogamic Bot.* (ed. 2) I. xii. 450 If appropriate spermatidia or conidia are not available for the trichogynes, there is no further development beyond the *protoperithecial stage. **1976** *Ann. Rev. Microbiol.* XXX. 98 Nutritional control is important for the initiation of protoperithecial development and conidiogenesis. **1941** *Bot. Rev.* VII. 396 A haploid mycelium or a multicellular trichogyne of *Neurospora sitophila*.., through which nuclei of opposite sex are passing *en route* to the ascogonium in a *proto-perithecium, where they are destined to take part in the formation of the first pair or pairs of conjugate nuclei. **1974** *Nature* 24 May 383/1 In *N*[*eurospora*] *crassa*, protoperithecia have been induced to develop into fruiting bodies, albeit sterile. **1909** *Econ. Geol.* IV. 625 Engler thus enumerates the various stages which in his opinion occur in the formation of petroleum from organic matter:..4. Formation of liquid hydrocarbons and violent reaction with 'cracking' into light or gaseous products = formation of *protopetroleum. **1938** B. T. BROOKS in A. E. Dunstan et al. *Sci. of Petroleum* I. 52/1 Accordingly it might be expected that protopetroleums in transition stages will be found in geologically recent strata in the form of solid or semi-solid material. **1973** R. E. CHAPMAN *Petroleum Geol.* ii. 32 There is general agreement that the main source of petroleum is the organic matter buried with a fine-grained sediment (usually a clay); and that diagenesis of this organic matter leads to a 'protopetroleum' which, before or during migration, becomes modified by the physical and chemical environment—particularly by increasing temperature during burial—until it eventually becomes petroleum. **1953** G. E. M. ANSCOMBE tr. *Wittgenstein's Philos. Investigations* I. 167 Our mistake is to look for an explanation where we ought to look at what happens as a '*proto-phenomenon'. That is, where we ought to have said: *this language-game is played*. **1966** *Amer. Philos. Q.* III. 7/1 We should look simply at what is said as a proto-phenomenon. **1884** BOWER & SCOTT *De Bary's Phaner.* 390 The first primitive elements of the phloem, Russow's *protophloem. **1898** tr. *Strasburger's Bot.* I. i. 105 In fully-developed vascular bundles the protoxylem and protophloem cease to perform their functions. **1902** Protophloem [see *metaphloem* s.v. META- 4]. **1953** K. ESAU *Plant Anat.* xii. 286 The primary phloem may be divided into protophloem and metaphloem. **1965** Protophloem [see *metaphloem* s.v. META- 4]. **1925** A. D. IMMS *Gen. Textbk. Entomol.* 179 In the *protopod phase metamerism is incomplete, the abdomen being imperfectly differentiated. **1934** FOLSOM & WARDLE *Entomol.* (ed. 4) iii. 172 The protopod larva is characterized by a lack of differentiation of the internal and external organs. **1969** R. F. CHAPMAN *Insects* xx. 400 Among the parasitic Hymenoptera the first instar larva hatches as a type known as a protopod larva. **1870** ROLLESTON *Anim. Life* 94 (Common Crayfish) The appendages of the..post-abdominal segments consist of a biarticulate '*protopodite' [etc.]. **1877** HUXLEY *Anat. Inv. Anim.* vi. 273 Two pairs of appendages, composed each of a protopodite, terminated by an endopodite and exopodite. **1880** GILL in *Smithsonian Rep.* 361 The valve of the siphon [in Cephalopods] is a true foot or *protopodium, and the two lateral folds are pteropodia. **1895** STORY-MASKELYNE *Crystallogr.* 283 The hexagonal deutero-prism..is identical in features with the *proto-prism... The horizontal sections of the proto- and deutero-prisms are regular hexagons. **1891, 1916** *Protoproteose [see *heteroproteose* s.v. HETERO-]. **1936** A. P. MATHEWS *Princ. Biochem.* xxii. 221 'Proto-proteoses', precipitated by half saturation of their solutions by ammonium sulphate. **1895** STORY-MASKELYNE *Crystallogr.* 291 The trigonal *proto-pyramid may be regarded..as being a limiting case of the ditrigonal proto-pyramid. **1971** *Exper. Parasitol.* XXX. 233/1 Protein synthesis in larval *Echinococcus granulosus* *protoscolices occurs by the pathway involving amino acyladenylates and amino acyl-tRNA as intermediates. **1976** *Lancet* 9 Oct. 811/2 Since the Lebanese also eat raw liver a hydatid of the tonsil might arise from implantation of a protoscolex in a tonsillar crypt. **1881** *Friends' Intelligencer* XXXVIII. 556 The *protoseismograph and the microseismograph,..with which Professor Palmieri..may detect the first faintest quiver which hints the coming earthquake. **1893** HYATT in *Proc. Boston Soc. Nat. Hist.* 103 An aperture through which the *protosiphonula communicated with the protoconch. **1877** HUXLEY *Anat. Inv. Anim.* v. 243 Generally, the development of the *proto-somites, as these segments might be called, does not occur until some time after the embryo has been hatched. *Ibid.* vi. 250 As with Annelids, the segmentation of the body results from the subdivision of the mesoblast by transverse constrictions into protosomites. **1890** *Cent. Dict.*, *Jacksonian epilepsy*.., epilepsy in which the spasms are local... Such spasms are also called *monospasms*, or, when they are followed by general convulsions, **protospasms*. **1899** *Allbutt's Syst. Med.* VII. 289 With this monospasm or protospasm there is often a tendency to generalisation. **1889** *Q. Jrnl. Microsc. Sc.* Dec. 251 *note*, The spermatozoa of the Decapods studied by him [Sabatier] arise in large cells, the '*protospermatoblasts'. **1884** HYATT in *Proc. Boston Soc. Nat. Hist.* 86 We have not been able to separate the *Protospongian stage of Haeckel from the ascula. **1901** L. A. BOODLE in *Ann. Bot.* XV. 705 A centrally placed solid stele (*protostele), consisting of a central mass of xylem..surrounded by a continuous ring of phloem. **1919** F. O. BOWER *Bot. Living Plant* xxi. 330 Generally in young sporelings there is a simple stele of a type called a 'protostele', having a solid xylem-core, and phloem surrounding it. **1957** H. C. BOLD *Morphol. Plants* xxiii. 446 The most primitive genera and the juvenile stages of most others have stems that contain protosteles. **1975** J. D. HAYNES *Botany* xxii. 331 The stele of most members of this group [*sc.* lycopods] is a protostele. **1902** *Encycl. Brit.* XXV. 413/2 There is good reason to suppose that the *protostelic condition is primitive in evolution. **1957** H. C. BOLD *Morphol. Plants* xxiii. 447 Internally the roots are exarch and protostelic. **1878** GURNEY *Crystallogr.* 72 These are sometimes called the *protosystematic planes. **1895** STORY-MASKELYNE *Crystallogr.* 110. **1904** H. M. BERNARD in *Ann. Mag. Nat. Hist.* XIII. 4 The parent colony of a calicle rises out of a basal cup—the *Prototheca... The term 'prototheca' was suggested to me in conversation by my friend Prof. Jeffrey Bell. **1906** S. J. HICKSON in Harmer & Shipley *Cambr. Nat. Hist.* I. xiv. 386 The calicoblasts form ..a skeletal plate at the aboral end of the coral embryo, which becomes turned up at the edges to form a shallow saucer or cup. This cup is called the 'prototheca'. **1935** TWENHOFEL & SHROCK *Invertebr. Paleont.* iv. 78 The embryonic skeleton of a typical coelenterate has the shape and appearance of a little, hollow, conical cup and is known as the prototheca. **1904** *Brit. Med. Jrnl.* 10 Sept. 567 We have three different toxins with different toxicity and different avidities to the antitoxin, viz. the *prototoxin, the deuterotoxin, and the tritotoxin. *Ibid.* 568 The prototoxin with the greatest avidity for the antitoxin and with the greatest toxicity..but..being comparatively labile it changes after some time into *prototoxoid. **1897** A. T. MASTERMAN in *Q. Jrnl. Microsc. Sci.* XL. 291 There are three prominent ciliated bands, the preoral (or *prototroch), the collar-band..and the trunk band. **1904** *Amer. Naturalist* XXXVIII. 500 Cells arising from the first quartette..make up a cell row which very probably forms at least a part of the second ciliated band on the head of the adult, in a position corresponding with that of the prototroch of the annelid larva. **1932** BORRADAILE & POTTS *Invertebrata* vii. 207 A band of cilia round the base [of the Pilidium larva] constitutes the prototroch. **1959** *Q. Jrnl. Microsc. Sci.* C. 89 The ectoderm of the mouth region [of the pre-adult *Scoloplos armiger*]..includes transitorily the prototroch cells. **1978** K. S. RICHARDS in P. J. Mill *Physiol. Annelids* ii. 48 In the prototroch, the compounding of cilia helps to eliminate such lateral stresses. **1877** *Proc. Acad. Nat. Sci. Philadelphia* 269 Professor Geo. A. König described a micaceous mineral from Magnet Cove, Ark., to which he gave the name *Protovermiculite... The mineral occurs in large foliated plates, loose in the soil. **1948** *Amer. Mineralogist* XXXIII. 656 Protovermiculite from Magnet Cove, Arkansas. Large golden yellow scales. **1877** HUXLEY *Anat. Inv. Anim.* v. 225 The mesoblast becomes divided into a series of quadrate masses, like the *protovertebrae of a vertebrate embryo. **1881** MIVART *Cat* 325 On each side of the medullary groove and notochord a series of quadrate thickenings appear, termed protovertebræ. **1890** BILLINGS *Nat. Med. Dict.*, *Protovertebra*, primitive segment of the mesoderm; myotome. When the name was given the myotomes were supposed to be the rudiments of the vertebræ. **Protovertebral column* or *plate*, a thick column of cells lying along the medullary groove, from which by segmentation the protovertebræ are formed. **1879** tr. *Haeckel's Evol. Man* I. 223 The **protovum* is thus transformed into the *metovum* (after-egg) which is many times larger..but..is only a single..cell. **1887** tr. *Strasburger's Bot.* viii. 86 We have found..in the wood portion (the xylem) of the fibro-vasal bundle, the primary wood, the *Protoxylem, composed of primary wood-parenchyma and of vessels. **1898** *Ibid.* I. i. 105 The protoxylem occupies the innermost, the proto-phloem the outermost side of a procambium strand. **1902** *Phil. Trans. R. Soc.* B. CXCV. 135 The protoxylem is separated from it [*sc.* the pith] by a large mass of primary metaxylem. **1974** *New Phytologist* LXXIII. 979 The helically thickened protoxylem..is stretched during the elongation of the axis. **1871** PACKARD *Embryol. Stud. Diplax* etc. (Peabody Acad. Sci. I. Mem. II.) 16 The primitive arthromeres, or segments of the body (*protozonites [mispr. *protozoonites*] of Claparède). **1872** —— *Hexapodous Insects* (Mem. III.) 6 The cephalic lobes and succeeding protozonites are formed. **1879** tr. *Haeckel's Evol. Man* xxv. II. 406 We find a long tube, the primitive kidney duct (**protureter*..), on each side.

c. More widely, prefixed to adjs. and sbs. designating an original, early, or undeveloped form of an artistic or political movement, as ***proto-Baroque***, ***-Cubist*** adjs., ***-Fascism*** (hence ***-Fascist*** sb. and adj.), ***-Marxian*** adj., ***-Renaissance*** (also *attrib.*), ***-romantic*** adj.

1935 *Burlington Mag.* Apr. 159/1 Why are the artists working about the year 1800 gothic-manneristic, classicistic, proto-Baroque, high Baroque? **1977** *Dædalus* Summer 2 Titian's removal of the Virgin..to the right side of the worshipers in his Pesaro Madonna—once considered a protobaroque stylistic invention. **1979** *Jrnl. R. Soc. Arts* Nov. 767/2 If I can use the historical analogy again, with sixteenth-century Italy, the proto-Baroque or Mannerist period, which seems to have had the same kind of doubts and plu[r]alism characteristic of our age. **1959** H. READ *Conc. Hist. Mod. Painting* v. 156 The metamorphic *Three Dancers* is in fact a turning point in Picasso's art almost as radical as was the proto-cubist *Demoiselles d'Avignon*. **1938** *New Statesman* 19 Feb. 302/1 It [*sc.* racism] is proto-Fascism, based on mysticism on the one hand, and pseudobiology on the other. **1945** H. READ *Coat of Many Colours* i. 3 Lucian, one of those romantic exiles who brought some light and liberty into a proto-fascist world. **1959** —— *Conc. Hist. Mod. Painting* iv. 119 Anarchists.., proto-fascists in some cases, the Dadaists, adopted Bakunin's slogan: destruction is also creation! **1973** *Black Panther* 28 Apr. 8/3 The danger in a 'professional' national police force is the same as that of a volunteer army. In both we find an elitist, racist, proto-fascist orientation and esprit. **1977** M. WALKER *National Front* i. 15 Proto-fascist, crypto-fascist,..quasi-fascist; the sub-groups..multiply and do little to impose meaning on the confusion. **1969** P. A. ROBINSON *Freudian Left* 168 Portrait of Hegel as loyal son of the Enlightenment and proto-Marxian critic of the European social order. **1909** *Cent. Dict.* Suppl., *Proto-Renaissance*.., a revival movement in art and literature preceding the Renaissance proper, especially that which began in the reign of the Emperor Frederick II. (1194–1250). **1911** *Encycl. Brit.* XX. 468/1 A 'Proto-Renaissance', the characteristic of which was a fresh interest in surviving remains of classical antiquity. **1942** N. PEVSNER *Outl. Europ. Archit.* iv. 61 The Tuscan Proto-Renaissance of S. Miniato..i.e., the architecture of Florence in the 11th century, and nothing else. **1945** *Burlington Mag.* Jan. 23/2 Such, however, was the popular 'proto-Renaissance' in our country. **1948** N. PEVSNER *Outl. Europ. Archit.* (rev. ed.) v. 82 Of Romanesque or Proto-Renaissance connections there are here none left. **1963** *Times Lit. Suppl.* 26 Apr. 312/4 'Proto-Renaissance' Romanesque 'antique' models. **1947** A. EINSTEIN *Mus. Romantic Era* viii. 81 Many of the traits in Mozart's works can be considered 'Romantic' or proto-romantic. **1971** *Country Life* 12 Aug. 392/1 The drawings are large in scale..and far removed from the experimental, proto-romantic work that we associate with Brown.

3. In Chemistry. **a.** With names of binary compounds in -IDE (formerly *-uret*), designating that in which the element or radical combines in the first or smallest proportion with another element; e.g. PROTOXIDE, PROTOCHLORIDE (†*protochloruret*), PROTIODIDE, PROTOSULPHIDE (†*protosulphuret*), q.v. So **proto'bromide** (*protobromuret*), **protocarbide** (*-carburet*), **protocyanide** (*-cyanuret*), **protophosphide** (*-phosphuret*), etc., a compound of bromine, carbon, cyanogen, phosphorus, etc., with another element or radical, in which the bromine, etc., is present in the smallest proportion, or in a smaller proportion than in another (designated by *per-*). Also in the generalized term **proto-compound**. Hence, in derived verbs, ppl. adjs., etc., as PROTOXIDATE, PROTOXIDIZE, ***proto-cabureted***, ***-phosphureted***, ***-sulphureted***, now rarely used.

This use of *proto-* was introduced in 1804 by Dr. T. Thomson, in his *System of Chemistry* ed. 2, for combinations of oxygen with a metal; *protoxide* being used to denote the first degree or 'minimum of oxidizement': see quot. s.v. PEROXIDE. It was extended by later chemists to similar combinations of other elements, as in 1815 to PROTOCHLORIDE, and so on. In later chemical nomenclature, names in *proto-* have been to a great extent superseded by others with more definite numerical prefixes, or in which the constitution of the substance is differently expressed (e.g. *protoxide of manganese* by *manganese monoxide*, or *manganous oxide*; *protochloride* and *protoxide of iron*, by *ferrous chloride*, *ferrous oxide*; *protocarburet of hydrogen* by *light carburetted hydrogen*, *methyl hydride*, *or methane*. But the *proto-* forms are retained in some cases, especially when they correspond with *mono-* compounds, and in pharmacy and popular use.

b. In ternary compounds *proto-* was formerly used to designate salts produced from protoxides (cf. PROTOSALT), which thus contain the smallest (or smaller) proportion of the acid radical. Thus, ***proto-carbonate*** or ***proto-chlorate of iron***, = the earlier expressions, 'carbonate' or 'chlorate of the protoxide of iron', i.e. the salts formed by the action of carbonic and chloric acid on the protoxide of iron. The latter is now *ferrous oxide*, and the salts are called *ferrous carbonate* and *ferrous chlorate* respectively. So with organic salts, as ***protacetate***, ***protoxalate***; as ***protoxalate of tin***, the salt produced by the action of oxalic acid upon the protoxide of tin (*stannous oxide*); now called *stannous oxalate*. So †***proto-hydrochlorate*** (***proto-muriate***), †***proto-haloid salt***, a salt formed by the action, on a metallic protoxide, of hydrochloric (muriatic) acid or other haloid acid (see HALOID). †***proto-hydrate***, the hydrate of a protoxide, as proto-hydrate of lime $CO.H_2O$. Hence †***proto-combination***, combination of the protoxide.

These terms are common in chemical writings of the first half of the nineteenth century, but now belong mostly to the history of chemistry.

c. In Organic and Physiological Chemistry and Pharmacy, *proto-* occurs in senses having little or no connexion with a or b, but rather akin to its use in 1 or 2.

Thus in ***proto-catechuic acid*** ($C_7H_6O_4$) the name was given because the substance has some resemblance to *catechuic* acid or *catechu* (? $C_{19}H_{18}O_8$), but has a simpler composition. ***proto-albumoses*** were the albumoses first produced in the process of digestion from the 'acid-albumins', and are now called *primary proteoses*. ***protalbinic acid*** is the first product of the action of alkalis upon albumin or protein.

1836–41 BRANDE *Chem.* (ed. 5) 1315 Acetic acid..forms a well-defined class of salts, *acetates*... Some of the peroxides convert part of this acid into carbonic acid and water, by which they are reduced to a soluble state, and form *protacetates. **1876** HARLEY *Mat. Med.* (ed. 6) 85 The bromine and the iron, in equivalent proportions unite to form a *protobromide of iron. **1858** MAYNE *Expos. Lex.*, *Protobromuret; protocarburet; protochloruret; protocyanuret; protofluoruret; protohydrioduret; protophosphuret; protoseleniuret; protosulphuret. **1876** DUHRING *Dis. Skin* 84 Iron may be prescribed in the form of the *protocarbonate, citrate, pyrophosphate [etc.]. **1858** MAYNE *Expos. Lex.*, *Protocarbonated. **1826** HENRY *Elem. Chem.* I. 422 Carbureted Hydrogen Gas. This gas has been distinguished also by the name of..gas of marshes, hydro-carburet, *proto-carburet of hydrogen. **1849** R. V. DIXON *Heat* I. 136 *Protocarburetted hydrogen and bicarburetted hydrogen..are yet sensibly more compressible than air. **1876** HARLEY *Mat. Med.* (ed. 6) 385 Vanillin is the methylic aldehyd of *proto-catechuic acid. **1885** REMSEN *Org. Chem.* (1888) 303 Proto-catechuic acid, $C_6H_3.CO_2H.(OH)_2$, is a frequent product of the fusion of organic substances with caustic potash. **1854** SCOFFERN in *Orr's Circ. Sc.*, *Chem.* 436

In almost every case..this metal [manganese] will be found in the state of *proto-combination,—either as an oxygen salt of the protoxide, or as a *protohaloid salt. *Ibid.* 443 With *proto-compounds of iron it [red prussiate of potash] yields a white, with per-compounds a blue precipitate. *Ibid.* 499 It ..is..the *protocyanide, or *protocyanuret of mercury. **1826** HENRY *Elem. Chem.* I. 577 In this compound, the lime is to the water, according..To Berzelius, as 100 to 32·1... It is, therefore, strictly a *proto-hydrate. **1836** J. M. GULLY *Magendie's Formul.* (ed. 2) 17 A solution of *proto-hydrochlorate of tin. **1826** HENRY *Elem. Chem.* II. 100 Corresponding with the two chlorides of copper, we have also a *protomuriate and permuriate. **1838** T. THOMSON *Chem. Org. Bodies* 63 When this salt is dropt into a solution of *protonitrate of mercury, a copious white precipitate falls. **1858** MAYNE *Expos. Lex.*, *Protophosphoratus*.., applied to hydrogen gas containing the first of the different proportions of phosphorus with which it combines: *protophosphorated. **1854** SCOFFERN in *Orr's Circ. Sc., Chem.* 457 Add carbonate of potash or soda to a *protosolution of zinc. **1836–41** BRANDE *Chem.* (ed. 5) 1185 The *protoxalate [of iron] crystallizes in green prisms.

proto-abbaty: see PROTO-.

protoactinium, var. PROTACTINIUM.

proto-Algonquian: see PROTO- 2 a.

protoanemonin (prəʊtəʊəˈnɛmənɪn). *Chem.* [Coined in Japanese as *purotoanemonin* (Asahina & Fujita 1920, in *Jrnl. Pharmaceut. Soc. Japan* XL. 3): see PROTO- and ANEMONIN (cf. quot. 1920).] A poisonous, vesicant, pale yellow oil, which is isolated from many plants of the family Ranunculaceæ, and is an unsaturated lactone, $CH_2{=}C{\cdot}CH{=}CH{\cdot}CO{\cdot}O$, having bacteriostatic and fungistatic properties.

1920 *Chem. Abstr.* XIV. 1384 The sharp, oily substance volatile with steam obtained from *Ranunculus scleratus* L., consists in the main of the mother substance of anemonin, and has been given the name *protoanemonin*, which under spontaneous union of 2 mols. passes into anemonin. **1949** H. W. FLOREY et al. *Antibiotics* I. xiv. 605 Protoanemonin ($C_5H_4O_2$) was obtained as a pale yellow irritating oil. It solidified to give anemonin within a few hours at room temperature but was stable at 5°C. in 1 per cent. aqueous solution. **1958** *New Biol.* XXVI. 44 All three species [of buttercup] contain a glycoside 'ranunculin' which is readily broken down in damaged tissues to give glucose and an unsaturated lactone—protoanemonin. This lactone is poisonous and blistering, and makes *R. bulbosus* and *R. acris* very unpalatable to stock. **1972** *Science* 5 May 512/2 Lesser in toxicity are the vitamin antagonists such as protoanemonin..and amino acid antagonists such as mimosine.

proto-Aryan to **-Austronesian**: see PROTO- 2 a.

proto-Baroque, -biface: PROTO- 2 c, b.

protobiont (-ˈbaɪɒnt). *Biol.* [f. Gr. πρωτο- PROTO- + βιοντ-, pres. pple. stem of βιοῦν to live, f. βίος life.] A small drop of fluid surrounded by a membrane, hypothesized as ancestral to living cells.

1964 A. SYNGE tr. *Oparin's Chem. Origin of Life* iii. 61 The droplets would come to contain a constantly increasing concentration of the corresponding catalysts when the mass of the droplet increased as it grew by polymerising the monomers of the surrounding medium. Such coacervate droplets with an improved organisation are still only hypothetical but, for convenience of discussion, we shall refer to them in what follows by the provisional name of 'protobionts'. **1970** A. L. LEHNINGER *Biochem.* xxxiv. 782 Oparin..has suggested that the first cells, which he called protobionts, arose when a boundary or membrane formed around one or more macromolecules possessing catalytic activity, presumably proteins. **1971** *Sci. Amer.* May 30/1 Judging from the various forms of life we know today, the first protobionts were probably microscopic in size and single-celled in structure. **1978** *Ibid.* Sept. 65/1 To Oparin the reproductive machinery and DNA are only the ultimate biochemical subtleties that turned metabolically competing protobionts into living cells.

protoblast: see PROTO- 2 b.

protocanonical (ˌprəʊtəʊkəˈnɒnɪkəl), *a.* [f. mod.L. *prōtōcanonic-us* (see PROTO- 1 + CANON) + -AL[1].]

See quots.: opp. to DEUTEROCANONICAL.

[**1566** A. F. SIXTUS SENENSIS *Bibl. Sancta* I. (1575) 13 Canonici primi ordinis, quos Protocanonicos appellare libet, ..de quorum autoritate nulla vnquam in Ecclesia catholica fuit dubitatio, aut controuersia.] **1629** T. ADAMS *Medit. Creed* Wks. 1862 III. 86 [The Creed] is the word of God,..not protocanonical scripture, yet the key of the holy Scripture. **1684** N. S. *Crit. Enq. Edit. Bible* App. 263 In the first [Classis] he reckons those [Books] which he calls Protocanonical, or Canonical of the first Order. **1727–51** [see DEUTEROCANONICAL]. **1849** W. FITZGERALD tr. *Whitaker's Disput.* 49 The proto-canonical [books] are those which are counted in the legitimate and genuine canon.

protocarbide, etc.: see PROTO- 3 a.

protocell, -cerebrum: see PROTO- 2 b.

protochemistry: PROTO- 1

ˌprotoˈchloride. *Chem.* [PROTO- 3 a.] A compound of chlorine with another element or radical, containing the minimum proportion of chlorine; hence, antithetical to *perchloride*. Formerly also called **protoˈchloruret**. (Now usually otherwise expressed, as ***protochloride of iron*** = ferrous chloride, $FeCl_2$).

1815 HENRY *Elem. Chem.* (ed. 7) I. xiv. 418 The different compounds of chlorine with one base, might have been designated in the way proposed by Dr. Thomson for the oxides, the first being called proto-chloride, the second deuto-chloride, and so of the rest. **1836** J. M. GULLY *Magendie's Formul.* (ed. 2) 169 Exposed to a moderate heat, it passes to the state of proto-chloruret. **1842** PARNELL *Chem. Anal.* (1845) 89 A solution of protochloride of tin containing a little perchloride of tin.

protoˈchlorophyll. *Biochem.* [a. G. *protochlorophyll* (N. A. Monteverde 1893, in *Acta Horti Petropolitana* XIII. 210): see PROTO- and CHLOROPHYLL.] A naturally occurring photoactive precursor of chlorophyll.

1894 *Jrnl. R. Microsc. Soc.* 702 The same author [*sc.* Monteverde] finds, in etiolated leaves, besides xanthophyll and carotin, a pigment to which he gives the name *protochlorophyll*. It displays a distinct red fluorescence. **1928** *Science* 7 Dec. 570/2 Protochlorophyll is not a decomposition product of some other organic substance, as leucophyll, but is a pigment which develops without the influence of light and changes photochemically into chlorophyll upon exposure to light. **1951** *Ann. Rev. Plant Physiol.* II. 131 Protochlorophyll is a pale greenish pigment containing two hydrogen atoms less than chlorophyll. **1956** E. I. RABINOWITCH *Photosynthesis* II. xxxvii. 1759 Up to 90% of the protochlorophyll, accumulated in the dark, are quantitatively converted, within a minute or less of moderately strong illumination, into chlorophyll *a*. **1976** *Photochem. & Photobiol.* XXIV. 555 We now extract cells with acetone... Protochlorophyll is obtained by extracting this solution with petroleum ether..and extracting this petroleum ether fraction with 80% acetone to remove substances which interfere with subsequent chromatography.

protoˈchordate, *sb.* and *a.* *Zool.* [ad. mod.L. *Protochordata* (F. M. Balfour *Treat. Compar. Embryol.* (1881) II. xii. 27), f. PROTO- + CHORDATE *a.* and *sb.*] **A.** *sb.* A small marine animal belonging to one of the subphyla Hemichordata or Cephalochordata, which form a group considered to be related to ancestors of the vertebrates, and are characterized by a dorsal nerve cord, a notochord, and gill slits. **B.** *adj.* Of, pertaining to, or resembling an animal of this kind.

1894 A. WILLEY *Amphioxus & Ancestry of Vertebrates* v. 242 Of the free-living protochordates, the lowest type of organisation is undoubtedly presented by the *Enteropneusta* (Hemichorda). *Ibid.* 282 There is no *a priori* reason for doubting that the Vertebrate mouth is completely homologous with the Protochordate mouth. **1918** H. F. OSBORN *Orig. & Evol. Life* viii. 246 The principal.. secretory glands..doubtless had their beginnings among the ancestors (protochordates) of the vertebrated animals. **1933** L. A. ADAMS *Introd. Vertebrates* i. 17 All these modern protochordates are small and live in the sea. **1951** C. K. WEICHERT *Anat. Chordates* ii. 12 The animals included in this category [*sc.* Acrania] are believed to show similarities to the ancestors of the chordates and for this reason are sometimes called the protochordates. **1978** *Nature* 5 Jan. 61/2 Attention has focused on the protochordate endostyle since the demonstration that certain of its cells could bind iodine.

protocloud to **-cneme**: see PROTO- 2 b.

‖**Protococcus** (prəʊtəʊˈkɒkəs). *Bot.* Pl. protococci (-ˈkɒksaɪ). [f. Gr. πρῶτο-ς first, primary (see PROTO-) + κόκκος grain, seed.] A genus of microscopic unicellular algæ, of spheroidal form.

The common species *P. viridis* is abundant everywhere on trunks of trees, old palings, walls, etc., forming green patches or layers; *P. nivalis* is an alpine species constituting the so-called 'red snow'.

1842 *Penny Cycl.* XXII. 168/1 A field of green snow.. accompanied..with the Protococcus, giving a red colour. **1860** H. SPENCER in *Westm. Rev.* Jan. 97. **1875** HUXLEY & MARTIN *Elem. Biol.* (1883) 16 Get some water that is quite green from containing a large quantity of Protococcus.

Hence **protoˈcoccal** *a.*, of or pertaining to *Protococcus*; **protoˈcoccoid, protocoˈccoidal** *adjs.*, having the form of or resembling *Protococcus*.

1879 *Jrnl. Quekett Microsc. Club* 46 My impression,.. from an examination of many *Amœbæ*, is that they are the results of changes from the Protococcal state. **1965** F. E. ROUND *Biol. Algae* i. 3 The unicells may be sub-divided into non-motile (Protococcoidal), 'amoeba'-like (Rhizopodial) and motile cells (Flagellate). **1967** M. E. HALE *Biol. Lichens* iii. 45 The common protococcoid algae are soon killed off by the fungus.

protocœlomate, -atic: see PROTO- 2 b.

protocol (ˈprəʊtəʊkɒl), *sb.* Forms: 6 prothocoll, protocole, (prothogoll, 6–8 -gall, -call, 7 protocal), 8 protocoll, 7– protocol. [Early mod.E. *prothocoll*, a. OF. *prothocole* (*a* 1200 in Godef. *Compl.*), *prothecolle*, mod.F. *protocole* (= Prov. *prothcolle*, It. *protocollo*, Sp. *protocolo*), ad. med.L. *prōtocoll-um*, ad. Gr. πρωτόκολλ-ον the first leaf of a volume, a fly-leaf glued to the case and containing an account of the MS., f. πρωτο-, PROTO- first + κόλλα glue.

The history of the sense-development of this word belongs to mediæval Latin and the Romanic languages, esp. French; in the latter it has received very considerable extensions of meaning: see Du Cange, Cotgr., Littré, Hatz.-Darm., etc. The word does not appear to have at any time formed part of the English legal vocabulary; in Sc. from 16th c. probably under French influence; otherwise used only in reference to foreign countries and their institutions, and as a recognized term of international diplomacy in sense 2, until its comparatively recent entry into the general vocabulary of English in senses 5 b, c.]

1. a. The original note or minute of a transaction, negotiation, agreement or the like, drawn up by a recognized public official, notary, etc. and duly attested, which forms the legal authority for any subsequent deed, agreement, or the like based on it; †sometimes applied to a book or register in which these were written by the official concerned, as they were drawn up by him; = *protocol book*: see 7 (*obs.*).

In the parts of the United States acquired from Mexico, the name is used for the original record of a grant, transfer, etc. of land; under the Spanish law this was an entry made in his book by the official recorder of such transactions.

1541 [see 7]. **1552** HULOET, *Prothocoll*, loke in wrytynge fyrste drawen. **1560** ROLLAND *Crt. Venus* IV. 309 The prothogoll heirof I wald haif drawin In writ, for cost to be my Vidimus. **1578** in *Maitland Cl. Misc.* (1840) I. 6 The prothogall of the chancellarie of France. **1682** SCARLETT *Exchanges* 223 In all Fairs there are but few,..and in some but one Notary Publick allowed of, who is to protest, and must keep a Protocal of every Protest, to which every one must have free access to see and know what Bills for Non acceptance, and what Bills for Non-payment are protested. **1726** AYLIFFE *Parergon* 304 An Original is in other Terms stiled the Protocol, or *Scriptura Matrix*; and if the Protocol, which is the Root and Foundation of the Instrument, does not appear, the Instrument is not valid. **1745** in Scott *Wav.* l, A corresponding entry was made in the protocol of the Lord High Chamberlain. **1752** J. LOUTHIAN *Form of Process* (ed. 2) 283 The current Price of the Vellum or Parchment for the Time. For the first Sheet that it fills up of the Clerk's Prothocall as Notary 4 0 0.

b. *fig.* An original authority.

1580 J. HAYE in *Cath. Tract.* (S.T.S.) 37 Hawing for all learning ane onlie protocole of thair preachings, some Inglishe buikes, quhilks skairslie thay wnderstude thame selwes.

2. a. *spec.* The original draught, minute, or record of a dispatch, declaration, negotiation, treaty, stipulation or other diplomatic document or instrument; *esp.* a record of the propositions agreed to in a conference, signed by the parties, to be embodied in a formal treaty. Also *fig.*

1697 LUTTRELL *Brief Rel.* (1857) IV. 222 The plenipotentiaries have agreed that point shal be entred in the protocol or register of the mediator. **1700** RYCAUT *Hist. Turks* III. 563 The Minutes or Protocolls of what was propounded. **1711** *Lond. Gaz.* No. 4802/2 The Ministers.. have given in their Reasons to be entred in the Protocoll. **1815** EARL CATHCART in Gurw. *Wellington's Desp.* (1839) X. 119 A copy of the Protocol of the military conference on the 19th Instant which has been signed by all the Field Marshals and general officers who were present. **1829** MACKINTOSH *Sp. Ho. Com.* 1 June, Wks. 1846 III. 515, I consider the protocol as the minutes of conferences, in which the parties verbally agreed on certain important measures, which, being afterwards acted upon by others, became conclusively binding. **1868** *Daily News* 18 Nov., The representatives of all the Powers signed the protocol, whereby the question.. is satisfactorily settled. This protocol is to serve as the basis of an international convention.

fig. a **1861** MRS. BROWNING *Garibaldi* vii, Men feared this man At Como, where this sword could seal Death's protocol with every stroke. **1923** A. HUXLEY *Antic Hay* xii. 184 The parting kiss..was already in the protocol, as signed and sealed before her departure by giggling Molly.

b. *transf.* (*familiar*) A preamble, a preliminary.

1897 MRS. RAYNER *Type-writer Girl* xi. 126 When all protocols were settled he went on, 'Can you come in at once?'

c. [In Gr. sense.] The first sheet of a roll of papyrus, bearing the manufacturer's official mark; this mark itself.

1885 *Encycl. Brit.* XVIII. 233/1 The first sheet of a roll was named πρωτόκολλον... On the Arab conquest of Egypt in the 7th century, the manufacture was continued, with the substitution of Arabic in marking the protocol. **1905** W. E. CRUM *Catal. Coptic MSS. Brit. Mus.* 181 Upon the 1st *selis*, above the Coptic text, is part of the protocol in large Kufic characters. **1912** E. M. THOMPSON *Introd. Gk. & Lat. Palaeogr.* 25 After their conquest of Egypt in the seventh century, the Arabs continued the manufacture of papyrus and also affixed protocols to their rolls.

d. ***Protocols of the (Learned) Elders of Zion***: a spurious publication of Russian origin purporting to describe Jewish plans for the domination of the world. Also, ***Protocols of Zion***.

1920 (*title*) The Jewish peril: protocols of the Learned Elders of Zion. **1921** *Times* 16 Aug. 9/6 The so-called 'Protocols of the Elders of Sion' were published in London last year under the title of 'The Jewish Peril'. **1937** H. G. WELLS *Star-Begotten* vii. 128 These Reds—Moscow—Bernard Shaw—New Dealers—Atheists—Protocols of Zion, all of that—mere agents. **1941** —— *You can't be too Careful* v. i. 238 You can study how the new pogromism was revived in that curious and impudent forgery, *The Protocols of the Elders of Zion*. **1974** *Jewish Chron.* 20 Dec. 15/4 The antisemitic Protocols of the Elders of Zion have gone through more editions in Arabic than any other language.

1979 O. SELA *Petrograd Consignment* 142 Wasn't he desperate to read the Protocols of the Elders of Zion again; wasn't another pogrom all he lived for.

e. *Philos.* A statement which forms an essential part of a person's description of something experienced or perceived; a basic statement that can be verified or assessed.

1936 *Mind* XLV. 275 N[eurath] expresses Protocol-propositions in the form 'Charles's protocol (there is a table in the room perceived by Charles)'. **1956** J. O. URMSON *Philos. Analysis* viii. 121 Protocols are direct reports of the given and are justified with reference to the given... I choose between the possible protocols 'This is red' and 'This is green' by seeing which correctly reports experience. **1965** P. CAWS *Philos. Sci.* xi. 74 A set of protocol sentences .. constitutes a *protocol*.

3. A formal or official statement of a transaction or proceeding; *spec.* the detailed record of the procedure and results in a scientific experiment; hence, experimental procedure.

1880 *Times* 9 Feb. 11/6 [In] St. Petersburg .. all .. vehicles which carry lamps .. are compelled to light their lamps simultaneously with the lighting of the street lamps. Should the coachman fail to comply with this regulation, the police draw up a 'protocol' of the case, which is handed to a justice of the peace. **1884** [cf. quot. in 7]. **1887** *Amer. Jrnl. Psychol.* I. 136 The protocol here is admirable, taken on the spot by Mr. Birchall and printed in full, and Mr. Guthrie is very positive in stating that there were a large number of 'complete successes'. **1897** *Trans. Amer. Pediatric Soc.* IX. 104 Autopsy... Made and protocol dictated by Dr. Flexner. **1910** *Amer. Jrnl. Physiol.* XXVII. 36 The protocols of the experiments above discussed follow. **1923** [see *intratracheally* adv. s.v. INTRA-]. **1929** I. A. RICHARDS *Pract. Crit.* 4, I lectured the following week partly upon the poems, but rather more upon the comments, or protocols, as I call them... I asked each writer to record on his protocol the number of 'readings' made of each poem. **1947** *Ann. Rev. Microbiol.* I. 357 The data are not given, but from the protocols it appears probable that the hemagglutinin persists while toxicity and infectiousness are lost. **1961** *Lancet* 22 July 213/2 Not only the urinary but also the fæcal porphyrin excretion must be considered. Protocols of published cases [of porphyria] frequently lack this vital information. **1973** *Jrnl. Genetic Psychol.* CXXII. 192 Each *S*'s protocol was scored in terms of the number of responses to critical items which indicated a preference for balance. **1976** *Amer. Speech 1974* XLIX. 12 The phonetic transcriptions and marginal notes made from that record and entered in the workbooks are a protocol, and they are regarded as working notations. **1977** *Lancet* 9 Apr. 805/1 The most common treatment protocol appears to have been a series of 6 treatments (range 1–30) at a dose of 250 (range 100–400) roentgens per treatment.

4. An official of police in some foreign countries.

1865 BARING-GOULD *Werewolves* xiv, When taken before the Protokol at Dabkow.

5. a. In France, The formulary of the etiquette to be observed by the Head of the State in official ceremonies, relations with ambassadors, foreign sovereigns, etc.; the etiquette department of the Ministry of Foreign Affairs; the office of the Master of the Ceremonies. Also used of analogous departments in other countries.

1896 *Daily News* 4 Mar. 7/7 M. Crozier, who fills the, to the public, mysterious office of Director of the Protocol, came up to the President and informed him that Mr. Gladstone, on a visit to Cannes, desired to pay him his respects. **1899** *Westm. Gaz.* 21 Feb. 2/1 This will be a change indeed, for in M. Faure's time the contrary was the rule, thanks largely to the Protocol, to whose flummery the deceased President so weakly surrendered himself. *Ibid.* 9 Mar. 10/1 People interested in French matters have read something about the Protocol, which is virtually the etiquette department of the Ministry of Foreign Affairs. **1975** M. SINCLAIR *Long Time Sleeping* xii. 150 'I wonder when was the last time we refused to accept an Ambassador?' 'I'll ask Protocol in the morning.' **1980** J. HONE *Flowers of Forest* I. 13 His job .. had been in Protocol. .. It was his function to control liaison .. between our own and other allied intelligence services.

b. An official form of procedure and etiquette in affairs of state and diplomatic relations; the observance of this.

1945 in WEBSTER Add. **1949** *Washington Post* 22 Mar. 1/3 He [*sc.* President Truman] felt that it would not be good protocol for him to be away hobnobbing with an Englishman out of office at the very time that the man now in charge of Britain's foreign affairs is in Washington. **1953** *Economist* 12 Dec. 799/1 Alleged breaches of diplomatic protocol at the Bermuda conference. **1957** *Listener* 5 Sept. 337/2 Dr Adenauer .. chatted gaily and frankly... Protocol and affairs of state were set aside. **1980** J. CARTWRIGHT *Horse of Darius* iii. 46 Our sovereign is coming here... The protocol is very important. Who comes to visit. How we keep in touch with Tehran.

c. In extended and general uses, any code of conventional or proper conduct; formally correct behaviour.

1952 *Daily Express* 27 Mar. 4/3 He punctuates his work with a gay laugh .. and a first-name informality with colleagues... Not that protocol is in danger. For behind his exuberance is a tough grasp of ceremonial and what is due. **1954** W. FAULKNER *Fable* 18 The old generalissimo turned, his two confreres .. flanking him in rigid protocol. **1954** *Times* 27 Nov. 6 The ceremony was taking its course in accordance with academic protocol. **1959** *Woman's Own* 20 June 37/2 Prince Edward and Princess Alexandra had a childhood as free from protocol as their mother's had been. **1971** B. W. ALDISS *Soldier Erect* 20 That sort of American approach was even harder to master than the Ancient British protocol but, once mastered, it gave positive results.

6. *Diplomatics.* The official formulas used at the beginning and end of a charter, papal bull, or other similar instrument, as distinct from the *text*, which contains its subject-matter.

The ***initial protocol*** consists, according to Giry, of the *Invocation* (e.g. In the name of God, Amen); the *Subscription* or *Superscription* (e.g. We, Edward, by the grace of God .. King); the *Address* (e.g. To all our faithful subjects), and the *Salutation* (e.g. Greeting). The ***final protocol***, sometimes called *eschatocol*, consists of the *Date*, the *Apprecation* (anciently 'feliciter', 'Deo gratias', or 'Amen'), and the *Validation* (signatures and seals of witnesses).

[**1867** DE SICKEL *Acta Karolinorum* I. 208 Das Protokoll oder Formular. **1894** A. GIRY *Manuel de Diplomatique* 528 Le texte et le protocole réunis forment la teneur de l'acte.] **1908** HUBERT HALL *Eng. Official Hist. Doc.* 189 The distinction between the Protocols, or official formulas which occur at the beginning and end of the charter, and the Text, or body of the instrument, is not indicated at all. *Ibid.* 192 The description of the boundaries .. is .. usually inserted between the Text and the Final Protocol.

7. *attrib.* as ***protocol book, register*** (one in which protocols were written, a notary's register); (sense 2 c) ***protocol sheet***; (sense 5 a) ***protocol department, section***.

1541 *Records of Elgin* (New Spald. Cl. 1903) I. 64 Ane .. instrument transsumit out of Master Androu Cheves prothogall buik. **1857** J. PATERSON *Hist. Regality Musselburgh* 31 The burgh had a protocol record. **1865** *Daily Tel.* 18 Oct. 6/5 The 'Protocol' King, as German newspapers delighted to call Christian IX, was really and truly the lawful heir and successor of Frederick VII. **1884** *Mind* Jan. 103 A second person sitting at the other side of the table reads off and records in the protocol-book the distance of each excursion. **1899** *Daily News* 6 Oct. 5/3 M. Loubet .. has no taste for those pomps and protocol ceremonies which his predecessor so intensely enjoyed. **1912** E. M. THOMPSON *Introd. Gk. & Lat. Palaeogr.* 24 Among the Romans the protocol-sheet was inscribed with the name of the Comes largitionum .. and with the date and the name of the place where it was made. **1958** L. DURRELL *Mountolive* vi. 133 Then, turning, he completed his devoirs to the Protocol section. **1977** 'S. LEYS' *Chinese Shadows* (1978) viii. 182 Masses can always be arranged by appointment: one should apply at the Protocol Department in the Ministry of Foreign Affairs.

b. *spec.* in *Philos.* (sense 2 e), as ***protocol language, proposition, sentence, speech, statement***.

1933 *Philosophy* VIII. 98 Carnap then considers the 'protocol language'. Scientific evidence is derived from protocol propositions that describe our perceptions, feelings, thoughts, etc. *Ibid.*, Finally, Carnap develops the thesis that protocol speech is part of physical speech. **1935** *Analysis* II. 59 The form of protocol statements cannot be found, but must be fixed by a convention. **1937** A. SMEATON tr. *Carnap's Logical Syntax of Lang.* v. 317 The statement of the protocol-sentences is the affair of the physicist who is observing and making protocols. **1965** P. CAWS *Philos. of Sci.* xi. 73 A protocol sentence must be such that a decision as to its empirical truth or falsity can be reached after a finite number of observations.

ˈprotocol, *v.* [f. prec. sb. Cf. med.L. *prōtocollāre*, Ger. *protokollieren*.]

1. *intr.* To draw up protocols.

1832 [see PROTOCOLLING *vbl. sb.*]. **1835** MARRYAT *Olla Podr.* vii, Lord Palmerston protocol-ed while Marshal Gerard bombard-ed. **1837** CARLYLE *Fr. Rev.* II. vi. iii, Serence Highnesses, who sit there protocolling, and manifestoing. **1871** *Daily News* 17 Jan., The diplomatists .. will have an opportunity to prose and protocol over Turkey.

2. *trans.* To bring (into something) as by a protocol, or by diplomatic means. *nonce-use.*

1832 *Examiner* 663/1 [Her] half-coaxing, half-bullying manner of protocolling him into submission was inimitable.

3. To record in a protocol.

1886 W. J. TUCKER *E. Europe* 286 They succeeded in protocolling their direct descent from the Romans, and even boldly laid claims to hereditary distinctions by the aid of various armorial and heraldic forgeries which they most cunningly devised. **1895** *Daily Chron.* 8 Nov. 4/5 We do not say the whole should be protocolled.

Hence **ˈprotocolling** *vbl. sb.*

1832 *Lincoln Herald* 13 Jan. p. iv, That our wise whig ministers were completely over-reached in the art of protocoling in the affair of Belgium. **1864** DK. MANCHESTER *Court & Soc.* I. xxiii. 391 In spite of all this protocolling .. the young people .. patiently bided their time.

‖**protocolaire** (prɔtɔkɔlɛr), *a.* [Fr.] Characterized by a strict regard for protocol; formal, ceremonial.

1934 'A. BRIDGE' *Ginger Griffin* xviii. 232 But of course James wouldn't—he's too *protocolaire*. **1958** *Spectator* 24 Jan. 101/1 Less *protocolaire* than Trooping the Colour. **1962** T. ZINKIN *Caste Today* 29 Occasionally there are festivals or private ceremonies... On those occasions, as in the most protocolaire of royal banquets, the place and part to be taken by each are known to all. **1975** N. FREELING *What are Bugles blowing For?* xxiii. 137 A list .. of engagements .. ranging from the unavoidable to the purely *protocolaire*. **1979** H. WILSON *Final Term* viii. 161 Duncan Sandys .. said that even in pre-Amin days he had always insisted on the title 'Britain' despite protocolaire objections.

protocolar (ˈprəʊtəʊkɒlə(r)), *a. rare.* [f. PROTOCOL *sb.* + -AR[1]: cf. prec.] Of, pertaining to, or characterized by (a) protocol; formal, *protocolaire*.

1905 *Truth* 22 June 1589/1 To some extent it [sc. *The Mikado*] is protocolar, but one must not for that think it an empty form. **1960** *News Chron.* 12 Apr. 6/7 The Canadian Prime Minister, found himself in the peculiar protocolar position of sending a message of sympathy .. at the same time as he was sending a vigorous protest.

protocolic (prəʊtəʊˈkɒlɪk), *a. rare* [f. as PROTOCOL *v.* + -IC.] Of or pertaining to protocols. So **protocolist** (ˈprəʊtəʊkɒlɪst), one who draws up a protocol; **protocolize** (ˈprəʊtəʊkɒˌlaɪz) *v.* **a.** *intr.* to draw up protocols; to diplomatize; = PROTOCOL *v.* 1; **b.** *trans.* (*a*) = PROTOCOL *v.* 2; (*b*) = PROTOCOL *v.* 3; hence **ˈprotocoˌlizer**.

1836 DISRAELI *Runnymede Lett.* (1885) 152 To learn that his favourite portfolio was now in your Lordship's *protocolic custody. **1969** *Punch* 8 Jan. 60/3 It .. cuts out all your time-consuming Ambassadorial summonses, stern notes .. and general argy-bargy in protocolic triplicate. **1828–32** WEBSTER **Protocolist*, in Russia, a register or clerk. TOOKE. **1872** *Daily News* 5 Aug., The second meeting of the Sugar Conference was held at the Foreign-office on Saturday... Mr. F. G. Walpole attended as Secretary, and Mr. H. Austin Lee as Protocolist. **1833** *Westm. Rev.* Jan. (unpaged leaf), Will not the Whigs now *protocolize a little in Portugal? **1836** F. MAHONY *Rel. Father Prout, Plea Pilgr.* (1859) 35 *note*, The Irish Pozzo di Borgo .. kept protocolising with soft promises and delusive delays. **1854** SARAH AUSTIN *Germany* 141 To protocolize the business of the Counts. **1836** *Fraser's Mag.* XIV. 507 The hopes and expectations of our great *protocoliser. **1855** *Westm. Rev.* Apr. 404 Lord Aberdeen .., the most pacific and *protocolizing of British statesmen.

proto-combination, proto-compound, *Chem.*: see PROTO- 3.

protoconch: see PROTO- 2 b.

ˈprotocone. *Zool.* [f. PROTO- + CONE *sb.*[1]] An inner cusp on the front corner of a mammalian upper molar tooth.

1888 H. F. OSBORN in *Amer. Naturalist* XXII. 1072 (*table*) Proposed terms... Protocone... Protoconule... Protoconid. **1896** *Proc. Zool. Soc.* 573 In the deciduous 4th premolar [of *Centetes*] likewise the protocone develops first. **1922** [see *deuterocone* s.v. DEUTERO-]. **1933** A. S. ROMER *Vertebr. Paleont.* xii. 248 A single cusp is found at the inner apex; this was originally believed to represent the original reptilian cone and hence is called the protocone. **1968**, **1971** [see METACONULE]. **1976** *Nature* 5 Aug. 464/2 The upper first deciduous molar displays spatial dominance of the protocone.

protoconid (-ˈkəʊnɪd). *Zool.* [f. prec. + -ID[5].] A cusp on a mammalian lower molar tooth corresponding to the protocone on an upper molar.

1888 [see prec.]. **1896** *Proc. Zool. Soc.* 568 In the lower molar [of *Gymnura*] the protoconid evidently develops fast. **1907** [see *deuteroconid* s.v. DEUTERO-]. **1933** [see METACONID]. **1971** W. D. TURNBULL in A. A. Dahlberg *Dental Morphol. & Evolution* ix. 168 (*caption*) The eocristid and its associated primary cusp, the protoconid or eoconid .. are shown. **1976** *Nature* 5 Aug. 464/2 There is a spatially dominant protoconid with a large flat buccal face, a lingually facing anterior fovea, and an inferiorly projecting mesiobuccal enamel line.

ˈprotocontinent. *Geol.* [f. PROTO- + CONTINENT *sb.*] = SUPERCONTINENT. Hence **ˌprotocontiˈnental** *a.*

1958 L. KING in *Continental Drift* (Univ. of Tasmania) 13 Recent studies .. suggest once more the validity of continental drift, with two proto-continents Laurasia and Gondwana. **1968** *Sat. Rev.* (U.S.) 2 Mar. 48 (*caption*) The hegira of the Indian subcontinent about 60,000,000 years ago is suggested on the above map of earth's proto-continent. **1977** *Sci. Amer.* Mar. 104/2 As long as the fairly coherent supercontinent could move in relation to its adjacent ocean floor, the ocean floor could have been subducted, partially melted and chemically differentiated to manufacture typical continental crust at the leading edge of the protocontinent. **1978** *Nature* 10 Aug. 547/1 The protocontinental tectosphere produced in island-arc environments or along the active margins is probably thin, chemically heterogeneous and poorly consolidated.

protoconule (-ˈkəʊnjʊl). *Zool.* [f. PROTOCON(E + -ULE.] An intermediate cusp between the protocone and the paracone of a mammalian upper molar tooth.

1888 [see PROTOCONE]. **1905** [see METACONULE]. **1933** A. S. ROMER *Vertebr. Paleont.* xii. 248 Between protocone and paracone there is often a smaller cusp, the protoconule. **1968** R. ZANGERL tr. *Peyer's Compar. Odontogr.* 187 Intermediate cusps occurred along the trigon, a protoconule between protocone and paracone and a metaconule between protocone and metacone.

ˈprotocorm. *Bot.* [ad. F. *protocorme* (M. Treub 1890, in *Ann. Jard. Bot. Buitenzorg* VIII. 30), f. PROTO- + CORM[2].] A tuber-like body produced in the seedling stage of certain pteridophytes and orchids which grow in association with mycorrhiza. Also *attrib.*

1891 F. O. BOWER in *Proc. R. Soc.* L. 267 The sporophyte [of *Phylloglossum*] consists of two parts:—(i) the protocorm, with its protophylls and roots, and (ii) the strobilus. **1905** I. B. BALFOUR tr. *Goebel's Organogr. Plants* II. 232 The chief mass of the seedling [of orchids] is formed of the 'protocorm'. **1938** G. M. SMITH *Cryptogamic Bot.* II. vii. 180 A massive globose structure (the protocorm) .. grows through the gametophyte. **1959** S. SHUSHAN in C. L. Withner *Orchids* iii. 53 Continued enlargement of the embryo, which can henceforth be called the protocorm, results in either a smooth or irregular globular mass of cells. **1962** K. R. SPORNE *Morphol. Pteridophytes* iv. 64 The protocorm might well be regarded as a derivative and retrograde development. **1967** *New Scientist* 14 Sept. 551/1 By subculturing every few weeks, protocorm formation may be kept going indefinitely. **1977** J. Arditti *Orchid Biol.* 211 Within 4–6 months, a mass of protocorms is formed.

proto-Cubist: see proto- 2 c.

proto-cultural, -culture: proto- 1.

proto-cyanide, -uret, *Chem.*: see proto- 3.

ˌproto-ˈdiasystem. *Linguistics.* [f. proto- + *diasystem* (1954), f. Gr. διά through + system.] A hypothetical reconstruction of the system of linguistic relationships in a proto-language (see also quot. 1969).

1964 *Word* XX. 376 If I use the term proto-language for a reconstruction and proto-dialect for the real speech, my implication is that the reconstruction is in fact a proto-diasystem. **1968** *Language* XLIV. 485 Proto-languages are to be understood as proto-dia-systems, with over-all sets of correspondences between related linguistic structures. **1969** S. P. Durham *Computer in Reconstruction of Proto-Diasystem: Franco-Provençal* I. i. 14 Since a diasystem is a combination into one single descriptive statement of the features of several dialects viewed horizontally, a proto-diasystem can be considered a combination into one single statement of the features of several dialects viewed vertically, that is, historically. **1972** *Computers & Humanities* VII. 6 A corpus of about 1000 words, chosen from eleven villages, provided a concordance to suggest a reconstruction of the Franco-Provençal proto-diasystem and a tentative phonology.

protodolomite to **-filament**: see proto- 2.

ˈproto-form, *sb.* (and *a.*) *Linguistics.* [f. proto- + form *sb.* 5 c.] A hypothetical form of a word or part of a word from which actual words have been derived. Also *attrib.* or as *adj.*

1964 *Language* XL. 145 We must use different symbols to represent the proto-forms. **1965** *Canad. Jrnl. Linguistics* X. 94 Reconstruction of proto-form phonological shapes. **1965** *Language* XLI. 305 There is no reason to assume stress on a first syllable of the proto-form. **1976** *Archivum Linguisticum* VII. 63 Both of these assumed proto-forms might appear surprising in view of the dearth of direct evidence in Latin texts and inscriptions.

ˈprotogalaxy. *Astr.* Also with hyphen. [f. proto- + galaxy *sb.*] A vast mass of gas, not yet formed into stars, postulated as a preliminary stage in the evolution of a galaxy.

1959 *Astrophysical Jrnl.* CXXX. 43 These nuclei had already originated before the protogalaxy condensed into stars. **1969** *Monthly Notices R. Astron. Soc.* CXLV. 417 The central part of the cloud begins to collapse, and the collapsing region gradually grows until it eventually includes almost the entire mass of the proto-galaxy. **1977** *Sci. Amer.* Oct. 43/3 Shapley's work laid the foundation for the present view that the globular clusters were formed 10 to 13 billion years ago during the gravitational collapse of the protogalaxy, a vast cloud of gas consisting of hydrogen and helium.

Hence **protogaˈlactic** *a.*, of, pertaining to, or being a protogalaxy.

1969 *Monthly Notices R. Astron. Soc.* CXLV. 407 We assume for simplicity that the proto-galactic material consists of pure hydrogen. **1977** *Sci. Amer.* Oct. 44/2 As the protogalactic cloud contracted local regions of higher density became self-gravitating and condensed within a relatively short time into globular star clusters.

proto-Gallo-Romance, -Romanic: see proto- 2 a.

protogenal (prəʊˈtɒdʒɪnəl), *a.* [irreg. f. Gr. πρωτογενής: see protogenes + -al[1]. (A more etymological form would be **protogeneal*: cf. next.)] First generated; primitive or primordial as an organism.

1868 Owen *Vertebr. Anim.* III. 817 Sarcode or the 'Protogenal' jelly-speck.

†**protoˈgeneous,** *a. Obs. nonce-wd.* [f. Gr. πρωτογενής (see next) + -ous. (Cf. *homogeneous.*)] Of the first or highest kind or nature.

1660 Burney Κέρδ. Δῶρον (1661) 68 So Kings and Princes have the same sense correspondent to their several Titles, .. and are Homogeneous and Protogeneous in the decreeing of Justice.

‖**protogenes** (prəʊˈtɒdʒɪniːz). *Biol.* [mod.L. (Haeckel), a. Gr. πρωτογεν-ής first-born, primeval, f. πρωτο-, proto- + γένος, γενε-, origin, race, nature, kind, f. stem γεν- to give birth to.] (See quots.)

1868 H. Spencer *Princ. Psychol.* §55 In the *Protogenes* of Professor Haeckel, there has been reached a type distinguishable from a fragment of albumen only by its finely-granular character. **1872** Mivart *Elem. Anat.* i. (1873) 8 In the lowest grade of the animal kingdom is a creature *Protogenes*, at once structureless and devoid of any form, as its shape varies like that of Proteus himself. **1884** Tait *Mind in Matter* (1892) 118 All along the line of evolution, from the 'protogenes' to the mammoth, there have been marked deviations to the right and the left.

protogenetic (ˌprəʊtəʊdʒɪˈnɛtɪk), *a. Bot.* [f. Gr. πρωτο-, proto- + genetic.] = next, c.

1884 Bower & Scott *De Bary's Phaner.* 200 The stomata of the epidermis .. are a special case of schizogenetic and protogenetic spaces, which usually contain air. *Ibid.* 525 The occurrence of protogenetic secretory passages in the soft-bast has already been .. noticed.

protogenic (prəʊtəʊˈdʒɛnɪk), *a.*[1] [irreg. f. Gr. πρωτογεν-ής first-born, primeval (see protogenes) + -ic.] Primitive, or primitively formed.

a. Of or belonging to an original race or lineage.

1851 D. Wilson *Preh. Ann.* (1863) I. ix. 254 The former adheres to the protogenic character of the Celtae.

b. *Geol.* Applied to the primary or originally-formed igneous rocks: opposed to *deuterogenic*. *fig.* c **1850** H. Reeve in *Academy* 8 Oct. (1898) 22/1 [Weighing Macaulay against Newton and Bacon, as a mind] essentially of the tertiary formation; [theirs] protogenic.

c. *Bot.* Applied to intercellular spaces, etc. formed in early stages of growth: opp. to hysterogenic.

1885 Goodale *Physiol. Bot.* (1892) 99 *note*, A distinction .. between those intercellular spaces which are formed when the tissues begin to differentiate,—*protogenic*,—and those formed in older tissues,—*hysterogenic*.

protogenic (-ˈdʒɛnɪk), *a.*[2] *Chem.* [f. proto(n + -genic.] Of a solvent (or solute): having a tendency to protonate most solutes (or solvents). Opp. protophilic *a.*

1931 N. F. Hall in *Chem. Rev.* VIII. 194 The protogenic and protophilic character of very weak acids and bases is largely masked by the overwhelming prominence of the similar properties of water. **1940** Glasstone *Textbk. Physical Chem.* xii. 958 For convenience solvents are divided roughly into three categories according as the molecules are (*a*) proton acceptors, i.e., basic, or protophilic, (*b*) proton donors, i.e., acidic, or protogenic, or (*c*) neither donors nor acceptors, i.e., aprotic. **1969** R. G. Bates in Coetzee & Ritchie *Solute-Solvent Interactions* ii. 51 The four classes of solvents, 'amphiprotic', 'protogenic', 'protophilic', and 'aprotic', are not clearly restrictive and the proper classification of many solvents is in doubt. **1973** E. J. King in Covington & Dickinson *Physical Chem. Org. Solvent Syst.* iii. 333 Formic acid is an obvious example of an acidic or protogenic solvent, but it has weak basic properties too.

ˌproto-geoˈmetric, *a.* Also proto-Geometric and as one word. [f. proto- + geometric *a.* d.] Designating the period preceding the Geometric Age in Greece, or the pottery attributed to this period, contemporaneous with the collapse of Mycenæan civilization on the mainland and the period of cultural decline that followed it (*c* 1100–*c* 900 B.C.).

1926 *Cambr. Anc. Hist.* IV. xvi. 580 Between the flourishing of the Creto-Mycenaean civilization, and the geometric period proper, there lies a long period which has been named, not very happily, the proto-geometric: a period of cultural decay. **1933** *Jrnl. Hellenic Stud.* LIII. 162 Cremation first appears in connexion with the proto-Geometric style in pottery. **1939** J. D. S. Pendlebury *Archaeol. Crete* iv. 243 This type of tomb, square with a circular vault above, continues in Lasithi and the neighbourhood into Proto-geometric times. **1950** H. L. Lorimer *Homer & Monuments* i. 42 Simple as the proto-Geometric culture is, it marks a period, not of decline, but of renascence. **1953** *Antiquity* XXVII. 75 The Protogeometric iron sword of about 30 inches long, when new, was quite as effective for cutting as for thrusting. **1961** *Oxf. Mag.* 16 Feb. 232/1 The earliest Proto-geometric wares found at Smyrna can be dated about 1000 B.C. **1973** J. Boardman *Greeks Overseas* (ed. 2) i. 3 The finds in Athens cemeteries show that after a very short while, probably by about 1050 B.C., the new 'Protogeometric' style of vase-painting had been evolved from the debased Mycenæan forms.

proto-Germanic: see proto- 2 a.

protogine (ˈprəʊtədʒɪn). *Geol.* [a. F. *protogine* (1806, Jurine, *Journ. des Mines*, Paris, XIX. 372), irreg. f. Gr. πρῶτο-ς first + γίν-εσθαι to be born or produced (intended to express 'first-produced', the rock being assumed to be the most ancient of all).] A variety of granite occurring in the Alps, in which chlorite often takes the place of biotite (secondary white micas being sometimes developed), and in which a foliated structure has frequently been produced by dynamic action.

It was for a long time erroneously supposed to contain talc, and called *talcose granite*; its foliated structure also led to its being classed as a variety of gneiss. It abounds esp. in the chain of Mont Blanc, of which mountain it forms the summit.

1832 De la Beche *Geol. Man.* (ed. 2) 37 Crystalline compounds, arranged in strata, such as saccharine marble, .. gneiss, protogine, &c. **1849** Dana *Geol.* xiii. (1850) 564 Some of the veins in this Mellaca Hill consist of protogine, or a grayish-white granular compound of feldspar and compact talc. **1869** Bristow tr. *Figuier's World Bef. Deluge* ii. 35 Protogine is a talcose granite, composed of felspar, quartz, and talc or chlorite, or decomposed mica. **1879** Rutley *Stud. Rocks* xii. 212 Protogine is a gneiss in which, in addition to the ordinary constituents of granite, a greenish, pearly, or silvery, talcose mineral is present.

proto-god: see proto- 1.

protogonous (prəʊˈtɒgənəs), *a. rare.* [f. Gr. πρωτόγον-ος first-born, first-created + -ous.] First-created, primitive.

1847 J. W. Donaldson *Vind. Protest. Princ.* 140 An obvious attempt to biographize the protogonous and archetypal man.

proto-gospel to **-groomship**: see proto-.

protogynous (prəʊˈtɒdʒɪnəs), *a.* [ad. G. *protogynisch* (F. H. G. Hildebrand *Die Geschlechter-Vertheilung bei den Pflanzen* (1867) 17), f. proto- + -gynous.]

1. *Bot.* = proterogynous *a.* 1: opp. to protandrous. Hence **protogyny** (prəʊˈtɒdʒɪnɪ) = proterogyny: opp. to protandry.

1870 A. W. Bennett in *Jrnl. Bot.* VIII. 315 The terms Protandry and Protogyny used by Hildebrand to express, in the one case the development of the stamens before the pistils, in the other case the development of the pistil before the stamens, are so convenient and expressive that I have adopted them in this paper. *Ibid.* 320 *Chlora perfoliata* .. is protogynous. **1875** Bennett & Dyer *Sachs' Bot.* 812 Dichogamous Flowers are either protandrous or protogynous. *Ibid.* 813 In protogynous flowers the stigma is receptive before the anthers in the same flower are mature. **1896** *Henslow's Wild Flowers* 56 Sometimes .. the stigmas mature first. This is called protogyny. **1909** J. R. A. Davis tr. *Knuth's Handbk. Flower Pollination* III. 221 The flowers [of *Bartsia alpina*] in Greenland were found by Warming to be feebly protogynous, the anthers dehiscing soon after the maturation of the stigma. **1940** *Nature* 30 Mar. 485/2 Protandry, protogyny, special floral arrangements and other devices could also be listed. **1972** *Science* 12 May 601/2 In these plants, dioecism, protandry, protogyny .. are common. **1973** *Nature* 23 Mar. 275/2 Some cross-pollination may occur because the flowers are protogynous and have some insect visitors.

2. *Zool.* = proterogynous *a.* 2.

1931 F. A. E. Crew in W. Rose *Outl. Mod. Knowl.* 285 In quite a number of forms protandrous .. or protogynous .. hermaphroditism is the rule, it being usual for an individual first to function as a female or male, and then, later, as a male or female. **1973** *Nature* 12 Oct. 333/1 This system is an illustration of the phenomenon of social determination of phenotype, which includes social control of sex reversal in protogynous fishes.

protohæm, -heme (ˈprəʊtəʊhiːm). *Biochem.* [a. G. *protohäm* (H. Fischer et al. 1931, in *Zeitschr. f. physiol. Chem.* CXCV. 21): see proto- and hæm, heme.] A ferrous chelate derivative of a protoporphyrin; *spec.* = hæm, heme a.

1931 *Chem. Abstr.* XXV. 2157 By using a technic which excludes the possibility of oxidation, etioheme, protoheme, mesoheme and meso-ester heme were obtained cryst. from the corresponding porphyrins. **1963** R. P. Dales *Annelids* iv. 88 In haemoglobin the haem is the red protohaem, in chlorocruorin it is the green chlorocruorohaem. **1963** C. H. Doering tr. *Karlson's Introd. Mod. Biochem.* ix. 183 Peroxidases oxidize substrates by employing H_2O_2 as an oxidizing agent. Depending on their origin, they may contain either a red heme (protoheme or closely related ones) or a green heme. **1970** R. W. McGilvery *Biochem.* xxi. 499 The normal product of porphyrin synthesis is protoheme IX, which is quickly bound by globin peptides and protected from oxidation.

proto-haloid to **-Hattic**: see proto-.

‖**protohippus** (prəʊtəʊˈhɪpəs). *Palæont.* [mod.L., f. Gr. πρωτο-, proto- + ἵππος horse. The Gr. word would have been *πρωθίππος, **prothippus*.] An extinct genus of quadrupeds, ancestrally related to the horse, whose fossil remains are found in the Pliocene of North America.

1876 *Times* 7 Dec. (Stanf.), In the recent strata was found the common horse: in the Pleiocene, the Pleiohippus and the Protohippus or Hipparion. **1877** Le Conte *Elem. Geol.* III. (1879) 509 Next came .. the *Protohippus* of the United States and allied *Hipparion* of Europe.

proto-historic: see proto- 1.

ˈproto-language. *Linguistics.* [f. proto- + language *sb.*] A hypothetical parent language from which actual languages or dialects have been derived.

1948 W. F. Twaddell in *Language* XXIV. 139 Our reconstruction of a proto-language is theoretical and partial. **1950** H. M. Hoenigswald in *Ibid.* XXVI. 357 We may refer to Meillet's rule that in reconstructing the vocabulary of a proto-language we need the testimony of three, rather than two, independent witnesses. **1955** *Orbis* IV. 428 Many distinguished linguists have expressly declared that the assumption of a uniform proto-language conflicts with all we know about languages actually observed. **1964** *Word* XX. 376 The reconstructed proto-language is a formula, a statement on relationships, albeit in a diachronic rather than synchronic direction, and does not therefore represent, at least not necessarily, a genuine speech form that ever existed. **1977** R. Williams *Marxism & Lit.* I. ii. 25 In one area this movement was 'evolutionary' in a particular sense: in its postulate of a proto-language (proto-Indo-European) from which the major 'family' had developed.

protolemur to **protolife**: see proto- 2 b.

protolinˈguistic, *a.* [f. proto- + linguistic *a.*] Descriptive of communication or signs which are understood without the use of verbal language (see quot. 1964); of communication, etc., from which language is presumed to have developed. Also, relating to the study of proto-language. Hence **protolin'guistics** *sb. pl.*

1964 *Discovery* Oct. 32/3 Those [*sc.* symbols]..which are commonly translated into or from ordinary language; and those which are not so translated—like clothes, architectural design and furniture... We are concerned here with symbols of this latter kind and with behaviour to which a meaning is attached when it occurs in a specific setting. In both these kinds of strictly non-verbal communication we are dealing with messages which are not para-linguistic, but proto-linguistic. **1975** M. Critchley in E. H. & E. Lenneberg *Foundations Lang. Devel.* I. i. 6 One point must ..be kept well to the fore when ruminating upon this topic of protolinguistics. From an anatomic, physiological angle, speech is a parasitic function. **1976** R. W. Wescott in *Ann. N.Y. Acad. Sci.* CCLXXX. 104 As used here, the term 'protolinguistics' will mean the analytic and comparative study of protolanguages. *Ibid.* 115 Some protolinguistic problems, finally, are due almost exclusively to lack of information. **1978** *Sci. Amer.* Apr. 104/3 If, as I suppose, the hominids under observation communicated only as chimpanzees do or perhaps by means of very rudimentary protolinguistic signals, then the observer might feel he was witnessing the activities of some kind of fascinating bi-pedal ape.

proto-literate, -lith: see proto- 1, 2 b.

proto'lithic, *a. Archæol.* [f. proto- + Gr. λίθος stone, after *neolithic*, etc.] **1.** A term introduced by the American ethnologist W. J. McGee to designate a type of primitive stone implements formerly in use amongst the Seri Indians of eastern Mexico (see quots.).

1897 *Amer. Anthropologist* X. 326 In this stage of development (called *protolithic* after McGee) stone implements come into more or less extended use in connection with implements of shell, tooth, etc. **1898** W. J. McGee in *17th Ann. Rep. Bur. Amer. Ethnol. 1895–6* i. 295 None other so well represents protolithic culture.

2. Belonging to the earliest stone age: eolithic.

1931 *Antiquity* V. 518 In the new terminology three major divisions are recognised, the old Lower and Middle Palaeolithic being grouped together as 'Protolithic', the Upper Palaeolithic and Mesolithic as 'Miolithic', the 'Neolithic' continuing as usual though now including the old Aeneolithic. **1962** A. D. Krieger in Jennings & Norbeck *Prehist. Man in New World* 29 Menghin..employs six culture stages applied to both Old and New World, namely, (1) Protolithic (2) Epiprotolithic, (3) Miolithic, (4) Epimiolithic, (5) Neolithic, and (6) Chalcolithic. The first two are more or less equivalent to Lower Paleolithic as used by Old World archeologists... Menghin is careful to avoid any suggestion that such stages in the New World are of an age equal to those of the Old World; even his Protolithic in America may be no more than twenty thousand years old.

protolithionite: see proto- 2 b.

protologue ('prəʊtɒlɒg). *Taxonomy.* Also **protolog.** [f. proto- + -logue.] The description and other details accompanying the first publication of the taxonomic name of a plant or animal.

1905 Schuchert & Buckman in *Science* 9 June 900/1 For the sake of accuracy we suggest that the original description by words (type-description) be called the protolog. **1939** *Jrnl. Bot.* LXXVII. 206 A 'protologue' is the printed matter (description etc.) accompanying the original publication of a name or epithet. **1957** W. T. Stearn *Linnaeus's Species Plantarum* xiii. 126 For each Linnaean species all the constituent elements in Linnaeus's protologue must be taken into consideration. **1970** *Watsonia* VIII. 43 The entire protologue reads as follows.

pro'tology (prəʊ'tɒlədʒɪ). [ad. Gr. πρωτολογία the right of speaking first; see proto- and -logy.]

†**1.** *Obs. rare*$^{-0}$. (See quots.)

1623 Cockeram, *Protologie*, a preface. **1658** Phillips, *Protologie*, a fore-speech, or Preface.

2. The study of or enquiry into origins. Hence **proto'logical** *a.*, that pertains to what is original or primitive.

1903 *21st Ann. Rep. Bur. Amer. Ethnol. 1899–1900* 138 In the quaint protology, or science of first things, of the Iroquois things are derived from things through transformation and evolution. **1937** *Proc. Prehist. Soc.* III. 188 When man began to control his environment to a greater extent, 'things' became for him imbued with 'force', and in this way arose the magical and protological conception of the world. **1974** *Archiv für Rechts- und Sozialphilosophie* LX. 385 We have found that the learning of basic logical principles and methods via protological calculus has also a didactic advantage. **1977** M. Goulder in J. Hick *Myth of God Incarnate* iv. 75 In place of the primitive eschatology, the stress would now fall on protology.

protolytic (-'lɪtɪk), *a. Chem.* [f. proto(n + -lytic.] Applied to a reaction or process in solution which consists in the transfer of a proton from one molecule to another, one of the molecules usu. being of the solvent; also applied to the solvent itself. Also **pro'tolysis,** a protolytic reaction; proton transfer in solution.

1931 N. F. Hall in *Chem. Rev.* VIII. 191 Acid-base or protolytic reaction may be defined by the general equation ..A ⇌ B + ⊕ (acid ⇌ base + proton). **1934** *Chem. Abstr.* XXVIII. 5740 Acids and bases are designated [by J. N. Brønsted] 'protolyte' and their reaction 'protolysis'. **1959** I. M. Kolthoff in Kolthoff & Elving *Treat. Analytical Chem.* I. i. xi. 411 It is clear that a base can be of any charge type, its charge being one less positive than that of its conjugate acid, for example, $Al(OH)_2{}^+$, NH_3, $HCO_3{}^-$, $CO_3{}^{-2}$. Its reaction with an acid solvent is called a protolysis reaction and no distinction is made between a dissociation (NH_3 in water) and hydrolysis (cyanide in water). **1968** V. Gutmann *Coordination Chem. in Non-Aqueous Solutions* i. 6 Acids and bases are defined as proton donors and proton acceptors respectively and acidbase reactions are regarded as being due to proton transfer reactions (protolysis). **1969** T. R. Blackburn *Equilibrium* ii. 66 If a solvent is both appreciably acid and appreciably basic (as water is), it will have a measurable autoprotolysis constant. Such solvents are called protolytic.

‖**protoma** ('prɒtəmə). Pl. **-æ, -as.** [mod.L., ad. Gr. προτομή protome.] = protome.

1931 *Antiquity* V. 330 Fragments of horns and ears of the stone protomas of the bulls forming the capitals. **1953** *Proc. Prehist. Soc.* XIX. 45 From Ghar Dalam there are two protomae of animals, in the same ware, and having a similar decoration to the pottery described above.

protomagnate to **-Marxian:** see proto-.

protomartyr (prəʊtəʊ'mɑːtə(r)). Forms: 5 prothomartir, -er, 5–6 prothomartyr, 6– protomartyr. [Late ME. *prothomartir*, a. OF. *prothomartir* (1326 in Godef.), mod.F. *protomartyr*, or a. med.L. *prōtomartyr* (in Beda), a. eccl. Gr. πρωτόμαρτυρ: see proto- and martyr *sb.*] The first martyr; the earliest of any series of martyrs (for Christianity, or for any cause); *spec.* applied to St. Stephen, the first Christian martyr.

1433 Lydg. *St. Edmund* iii. 43 The prothomartir seyn Steuene with his stonys. *Ibid.* 58 Seynt Albon Prothomartyr off this regioun. *a* **1555** Ridley in Coverdale *Lett. Martyrs* (1564) 73 Agayne I blesse God in our deare brother and of thys tyme protomartyr Rogers, that he was also..a prebendarye preacher of London. **1594** Carew *Huarte's Exam. Wits* (1616) 187 That [declaration] which S. Stephen the Prothomartyr made in his discourse to the Iewes. *c* **1661** *Mrq. Argyle's Last Will* in *Harl. Misc.* (Malh.) II. 508 Archibald, Marquis of Argyle, the Devil's viceroy in the Highlands, and the most sacred covenant's protomartyr in the Low. *a* **1749** Boyse *Triumphs Nat.* Poems (1810) 537/1 With Hampden firm assertor of her laws, And protomartyr in the glorious cause. **1877** Shields *Final Philos.* 205 As early as the twelfth century Arnold of Brescia,..protomartyr of civil liberty, had perished.

‖**protome** ('prɒtəmiː). [mod.L., a. Gr. προτομή the foremost or upper part of anything, a bust or half-figure, f. προτέμνειν to cut off in front; cf. τομή cutting.] A bust. Now *spec.* the forepart of an animal represented decoratively, as in (ancient) sculpture.

1737 W. Stukeley in *Mem.* (Surtees) III. 57 A very ancient protome of our Saviour's effigies over the south porch. **1868** *Ecclesiologist* XXIX. 72 A finely benignant head, or rather protome of the Saviour. **1886** A. J. Evans in *Jrnl. Hellenic Stud.* VII. 14 The horse's head, or protomê, as is well known, is introduced generally in a sunken square. **1933** C. Seltman *Greek Coins* v. 60 The device of the foreparts of two lions facing one another. The son.. replaced one of the half-lions by the forepart of a bull, and at first the two *protomes* were back to back. **1942** *Antiquity* XVI. 356 But there is one motive, the bull's protome, that does seem really distinctive of the Halaf style. **1972** *Scripta Hierosolymitana* XXIV. 41 A Greek artist conceived the strange idea of..combining two traditional elements..by uniting a lion *protome* with a swinging handle. **1978** W. A. P. Childs *City-Reliefs of Lycia* 13 The lintel was decorated with four winged bull-protomes.

proto-Medic: see proto- 2 a.

protomer ('prəʊtəmə(r)). [ult. f. Gr. πρῶτος first + -mer.] **1.** *Chem.* [f. proto(n or proto(tropy.] Any prototropic tautomer.

1923 [see prototropy]. **1968** *Jrnl. Amer. Chem. Soc.* XC. 1575/2 Analysis of the protomer stabilities in terms of relative chemical binding energies is risky. **1979** C. Roussel et al. in J. V. Metzger *Thiazole & its Derivatives* ii. vii. 379 Protic solvents stabilize more the form giving the stronger hydrogen bond: so the mercapto protomer..should become apparent in the ultraviolet spectra recorded in ethanol.

2. *Biochem.* [f. prot(ein.] Any of the protein subunits of which an oligomeric protein is built up.

1965 J. Monod et al. in *Jrnl. Molecular Biol.* XII. 89 The identical subunits associated within an oligomeric protein are designated as protomers. *Ibid.* 106 Within oligomeric proteins the protomers are in general linked by a multiplicity of non-covalent bonds, conferring both specificity and stability on the association. **1970** *Nature* 28 Nov. 828/1 By definition a protomer constitutes one primitive cell. **1980** *Biophysical Chem.* XI. 49/1 The treatment has been extended to include aggregated structures containing from two to five protomers, thus encompassing almost the whole spectrum of oligomeric proteins likely to be encountered.

Hence **proto'meric** *a.*

1923 *Jrnl. Chem. Soc.* CXXIII. 828 The two forms of the ion are tautomeric..; but they yield protomeric hydrides, and isomeric derivatives with radicles such as methyl and ethyl. **1968** *Jrnl. Amer. Chem. Soc.* XC. 1575/1 In the cases of the heteroaromatic isomers, the protomeric equilibrium has been..found to favor the amide in solution. **1974** *Nature* 24 May 316/1 The accumulation of data on the protomeric units of several synthetases. **1979** R. Barone et al. in J. V. Metzger *Thiazole & its Derivatives* ii. vi. 20 When the electro-negativity of the substituent borne by the amino group increases, the protomeric equilibrium is expected to be shifted towards the imino structure.

protomeristem to **-metaphrast:** see proto-.

†**'protomist.** *Obs. rare.* [For **protomyst*, ad. med.L. *prōtomyst-ēs* or *-a* (Sidonius), a. eccl. Gr. πρωτομύστ-ης a chief priest, a bishop, f. πρωτο-, proto- + μύστης one initiated.] A chief priest.

1635 Pagitt *Christianogr.* App. 17 They have a Protomist or Bishop whom they highly reverence. **1638** Sir T. Herbert *Trav.* (ed. 2) 152 They [Armenians] have two Patriarchs or Protomists. *Ibid.* 261 The Meccan Protomist sends a sanctified Camell by an adopted sonne, who is welcom'd to Spahawn by many thousand Mussulmen.

protomorph to **protomusic:** proto-.

proton ('prəʊtɒn). [a. Gr. πρῶτον, neut. sing. of πρῶτος first; but see sense 2 below.]

‖**1.** *Biol.* (See quot. 1895.)

1893 *Nation* 11 May 350/2 Mark translates it [Ger. *anlage*] *fundament*. Minot adopts it as an English word... Neither seems to have thought of reverting to Aristotle, whose phrases..ἡ πρώτη οὐσία, τό πρῶτον, suggest the short word *proton*. **1895** *Buck's Handbk. Med. Sc.* IX. 104 (*note*), This neuter noun [proton] is employed to designate the primitive, undifferentiated mass or rudiment of a part, thus in the sense of *Anlage* of the German embryologists. **1898** *Nature* 15 Dec. 156/2 Dr. Arthur Willey recently suggested in these columns..the word *primordium* as an accurate..rendering of *Anlage*. Prof. B. G. Wilder.. thinks the shorter word *proton*, already familiar in numerous compounds, and used by many biologists, is a better equivalent.

2. *Physics.* A stable sub-atomic particle which has a positive charge numerically equal to that of the electron, forms a part (or in the commonest isotope of hydrogen the whole) of all atomic nuclei, and is a baryon with a mass of 938·3 MeV (1836 times that of the electron), spin of $\frac{1}{2}$, and isospin of $\frac{1}{2}$; it is now usu. regarded as a particular state of a nucleon. [Perh. suggested by, if not derived from, the name of William *Prout* (1785–1850), English chemist and physician, who suggested that hydrogen was a constituent of all the elements.]

1920 *Engineering* 17 Sept. 382/3 Sir Ernest [Rutherford], replying, said that..a clear nomenclature was certainly wanted; the term 'prouton' for [*read* or] 'proton' might be suitable for the H nucleus. **1922** J. Mills *Within Atom* ii. 13 The hydrogen atom is composed of only one proton and one electron. **1926** *Nature* 9 Oct. 526/2 Recourse was had to passing fairly large amounts of hydrogen—up to one litre —through heated palladium, in the hope that at the moment of exit a fraction of the protons and electrons would combine to form the helium nucleus. **1942** J. D. Stranathan *'Particles' Mod. Physics* xi. 416 By firing alpha particles through a cloud chamber filled with nitrogen, it has been possible to photograph the track of the proton leaving the nitrogen nucleus. **1955** *Sci. News Let.* 10 Sept. 170/1 The number of protons in the nucleus determines the kind of matter the atom forms, whether hydrogen, uranium, iron, carbon or any other. **1962** H. D. Bush *Atomic & Nucl. Physics* iii. 62 Isotopes will occur where atomic nuclei have the same number of protons but differing numbers of neutrons. **1968, 1972** [see neutron]. **1979** *Nature* 7 June 483/2 A novel prediction of many such grand unified models is that baryon number is not absolutely conserved; so the proton may actually decay!

3. Special Comb. (all for sense 2): **proton accelerator**, a particle accelerator designed to accelerate protons; **proton acceptor, donor**, a substance or species which is able to accept protons from, or give them up to, a substrate; also ***proton donator***; so ***proton-accepting, donating*** ppl. adjs.; **proton gradiometer**, a rod with a proton magnetometer at each end, which may be stood on the ground in a vertical position to measure local variations in field strength at ground level due to features just below the surface; **proton magnetometer**, a magnetometer in which the magnetic field strength is determined from the frequency of the voltage induced by the precession of protons in hydrogen atoms (e.g. in water) following the removal of a stronger magnetic field applied to orient the protons; **proton-precession magnetometer** = prec.; **proton synchrotron**, a synchrotron designed to accelerate protons.

1947 Proton accelerator [see bevatron]. **1961** Livingston & Blewett *Particle Accelerators* xiii. 438 The synchrocyclotron, which has been so successful as a proton accelerator in the 100- to 700-Mev range, requires a solid-core magnet. **1969** *Times* 5 Feb. 13/6 Four new particles of matter have been discovered in two independent experiments using the proton accelerators at Brookhaven.. and at the European Nuclear Research Centre. **1925** *Jrnl. Chem. Soc.* CXXVII. i. 1383 All prototropic changes appear to involve..(i) the removal of a proton from one part of a molecule to some outside basic or proton-accepting component of the system, and (ii) the addition to another part of the molecule of a proton..from some acidic or proton-donating component of the system. **1966** Gucker & Seifert *Physical Chem.* xix. 537 Many a neutral molecule is amphiprotic because it has an ionizable proton and a proton-accepting oxygen or nitrogen atom. **1925** *Jrnl. Chem. Soc.* CXXVII. i. 1378 We..regard the acid as a proton donator and the base as a proton acceptor. **1940** Glasstone *Text-bk. Physical Chem.* xii. 958 It is unlikely that free protons exist to any extent in solution, and so the acidic or basic functions of any species cannot become manifest unless the solvent molecules are themselves able to act as proton acceptors or donors, respectively: that is to say, the medium itself must have basic or acidic properties. **1953** L. C. Jackson tr. *Ketelaar's Chem. Constitution* 85 A base, according to Brönsted, is a proton-acceptor just as an acid is a proton-donor. **1973** A. W. Adamson *Textbk. Physical Chem.* xii. 544 NH_3 is a much better proton acceptor than is H_2O. **1925**

Proton-donating, donator [see *proton-accepting, acceptor* above]. **1940, 1953** Proton donor [see *proton acceptor* above]. **1977** HELMPRECHT & FRIEDMAN *Basic Chem.* vii. 149 H_2SO_4 is a more effective proton donor and a stronger acid than HSO_4-. **1960** M. J. AITKEN in *Archaeometry* III. 38 Previous articles.. have described the use of the proton *magnetometer* for archaeological prospecting. The proton *gradiometer* is a development which not only has advantages in operation, but is also less complex and therefore cheaper to construct. *Ibid.* 39 With the two-bottle system of the proton gradiometer all these large-scale effects are avoided for they affect both bottles equally. **1970** *Oxf. Univ. Gaz.* C. Suppl. VI. 25 Comparative surveys using proton gradiometer, pulsed magnetic induction, and soil conductivity meter. **1959** Proton magnetometer [see EYE *sb.*[1] 3 g]. **1961** *Antiquaries' Jrnl.* XLI. 44 In an attempt to locate these burials.. a survey with proton magnetometer followed by selective excavation was organized. **1975** *New Yorker* 12 May 58/3 With a proton magnetometer, the geologists began aeromagnetic surveys to develop a general view of the region's geological structure. **1976** W. M. TELFORD et al. *Appl. Geophysics* iii. 136 The important advantages of the proton magnetometer are that it measures absolute field strength and that its sensitivity (~ 1γ) is higher than any of the instruments considered so far. The fact that it requires no orientation or levelling makes it very attractive for marine and even more for airborne operations. **1958** *Jrnl. Geophysical Res.* LX. 880 The proton-precession magnetometer has been successfully adapted.. for measuring the horizontal and vertical components of the earth's magnetic field. **1971** I. G. GASS et al. *Understanding Earth* xvi. 236/1 Fluxgate and proton-precession magnetometers were developed to measure magnetic fields to one part in 10^5. **1947** *Proc. Physical Soc.* LIX. 677 (*heading*) Theory of the proton synchrotron. **1966** *Daily Tel.* 25 Nov. 26/3 Nimrod, a proton-synchrotron, is essentially a circular racetrack, round which bursts of sub-atomic particles are repeatedly accelerated until they approach the speed of light. **1975** *McGraw-Hill Yearbk. Sci. & Technol.* 208/2 The collision of protons of energy 28 GeV from the CERN proton synchrotron with a metal target yielded.. charged pions and kaons.

protonate ('prəʊtəneɪt), *v. Chem.* [f. PROTON + -ATE[3].] **a.** *trans.* To transfer a proton to (a molecule, group, atom, etc.), a co-ordinate bond being formed to the proton. **b.** *intr.* To receive a proton in this way. So **'protonated** *ppl. a.*, having received a proton; bonded to an additional proton; **'protonating** *vbl. sb.*

As used by Pitzer (quot. 1945), *protonated* had a slightly different, more restricted sense, being applied to the two bonds (each with a bridging hydrogen atom) which link the boron atoms in the electron-deficient compound diborane, B_2H_6.

1945 K. S. PITZER in *Jrnl. Amer. Chem. Soc.* LXVII. 1127/1 Let us call it a proton containing double bond or, shorter, a protonated double bond. **1951** *Jrnl. Amer. Chem. Soc.* LXXIII. 3647/2 With the carbinols.. the fact that one *p*-amino grouping was never protonated is consistent with the view that only one of the rings is involved in resonance interactions. **1958** *Ibid.* LXXX. 3715/1 Compounds such as tri-*p*-aminophenylmethanol.. when dissolved in sulfuric acid form stable carbonium ions in spite of the strong electron-withdrawing groups present in the form of protonated amino substituents. **1966** SMITH & CRISTOL *Org. Chem.* xlii. 795 Pyrrole.. does protonate in the presence of very strong acids with the destruction of the aromatic sextet. **1969** T. R. BLACKBURN *Equilibrium* ii. 66 Any acid stronger than the hydronium ion will simply protonate water molecules to produce an equal quantity of H_3O^+. **1972** COTTON & WILKINSON *Adv. Inorg. Chem.* (ed. 3) v. 176 Even protonated carbonic acid, or more properly, the trihydroxycarbonium ion, $C(OH)_3{}^+$.. has been observed in solutions of carbonates or bicarbonates in FSO_3H-SbF_5-SO_2 solutions at − 78°. *Ibid.* 182 Fluorosulfuric is one of the strongest of pure liquid acids. It is commonly used in presence of SbF_5 as a protonating system. **1975** *Nature* 30 Oct. 823/2 Calculations.. show that this spectral shift can be associated with the formation of the protonated $C = N^+$ bond.

protonation (prəʊtə'neɪʃən). *Chem.* [f. prec. + -ION.] The action or result of protonating.

1948 *Jrnl. Biol. Chem.* CLXXV. 249 The effectiveness of the positively charged ammonium group in preventing appreciable protonation of the carboxyl group of the L-leucine cation in 100 per cent sulfuric acid can be appreciated when it is remembered that both acetic acid and monochloracetic acid are completely ionized in this solvent. **1958** *Jrnl. Amer. Chem. Soc.* LXXX. 3715/1 If one of the benzene rings in diphenyl- or triphenylmethanol is replaced by a pyridine ring, protonation of the nitrogen atom would be expected to decrease the stability of the carbonium ion produced in sulfuric acid. **1970** *Nature* 25 July 370/1 The double helix denatures abruptly at both low and high *p*H because of protonation of amine groups near *p*H 3 and ionization of hydroxyl groups near *p*H 11·5. **1976** *Sci. Amer.* June 43/3 The release and uptake of protons by intact cells was clearly different from the change in protonation observed during the photo-reaction of isolated purple membrane.

†**protone** ('prəʊtəʊn). *Biochem. Obs.* [ad. G. *proton* (A. Kossel 1898, in *Zeitschr. f. physiol. Chem.* XXV. 174), f. *pro(tamin* PROTAMINE + *pep)ton* PEPTONE.] Any of various peptone-like substances produced as the primary products of hydrolysis of protamines.

1898 [see HEXONE 1]. **1916** A. P. MATHEWS *Physiol. Chem.* iv. 136 It has been suggested by Taylor that the protamine, salmin, may be made up of these tri-peptides, or protones, united as follows. **1928** A. T. CAMERON *Textbk. Biochem.* viii. 115 According to Kossel protamines are hydrolysed first into protones which are compounds containing two radicals of arginine.. united with one of alanine, or serine, or proline, or valine.

‖**protonema** (prəʊtəʊ'niːmə). *Bot.* Pl. -'**nemata**. Also (in mod. Dicts.) in anglicized form **protoneme** ('prəʊtəʊniːm). [mod.L., f. Gr. πρωτο-, PROTO- + νῆμα thread.] In mosses (and some liverworts), The confervoid or filamentous thallus which arises from the germination of the spore, and produces the full-grown plant by lateral branching. (Also called *pro-embryo.*)

1857 BERKELEY *Cryptog. Bot.* §509. 462 This mass.. is called the Protonema, and is always distinguished by the cells containing chlorophyl. **1858** CARPENTER *Veg. Phys.* §738 When the spores of mosses are sown they do not.. directly produce a young moss, but they put forth conferva-like filaments, which are called the *protonema*. **1875** BENNETT & DYER *Sachs' Bot.* 150 A new Moss-plant is.. constituted by the formation of a leaf-bearing shoot out of a branch of the alga-like Protonema, which branches, strikes root (by root-hairs), and is independently nourished.

Hence **proto'nemal, proto'nematal** *adjs.*, pertaining to or of the nature of a protonema; **proto'nematoid** *a.*, resembling a protonema.

1875 BENNETT & DYER tr. *Sachs's Text-bk. Bot.* II. 318 These latter [leaves] then put forth protonemal filaments, which produce first of all a flat pro-embryo; and upon this finally new leaf-buds arise. **1900** *Nature* 9 Aug. 340/1 Leaves which,.. with greater or less intervention of protonematal filaments give birth to new individuals. **1938** G. M. SMITH *Cryptogamic Bot.* I. ii. 135 The protonematal initial develops into a green filament (the primary protonema), also differentiated into nodes and internodes. **1958** *Nature* 19 Apr. 1139/2 In the course of studies on protonematal regeneration and growth in the moss *Splachnum ampullaceum* (L.) Hedw., the effect of gibberellic acid on the growth of the protonemata was also tested. **1969** F. E. ROUND *Introd. Lower Plants* viii. 101 The protonemal stage is.. generally ignored in the description of liverworts.

proto-Neolithic to **-nephron**, etc.: see PROTO- 2 b.

protonic (prəʊ'tɒnɪk), *a.*[1] *rare*[−0]. [f. PRO-[2] + TONIC.] A more etymological form for PRETONIC.

1890 in *Cent. Dict.*

protonic (prəʊ'tɒnɪk), *a.*[2] [f. PROTON + -IC.]
a. Of, pertaining to, or characteristic of, a proton or protons.

1929 A. N. WHITEHEAD *Process & Reality* 127 Each proton is a society of protonic occasions. **1932** E. MOLLOY *Compl. Wireless* 113/1 If.. an atom happens to lose one or more of its planetary electrons.. some of the protons become unbalanced, and there is a surplus of protonic force. **1953** R. B. BRAITHWAITE *Scientific Explanation* 93 Hydrogen atoms behave.. as if they were solar systems each with an electronic planet revolving round a protonic sun. **1961** G. R. CHOPPIN *Exper. Nuclear Chem.* i. 1 The existence of nuclei means, therefore, that there must also be another force present which is strong enough to counterbalance the protonic repulsion and hold the nucleons together. **1976** *Nature* 23 Sept. 298/2 It is important at each step to vary the *p*H of the aqueous buffered component to keep the protonic activity of the solvent constant.

b. *Chem.* Of an acid, solvent, etc.: possessing a proton which can be used in protonation. Of a hydrogen atom in a molecule: available for use in protonation; possessing some positive charge.

1951 *Jrnl. Polymer Sci.* VI. 518 If we use this value for both the methyl and butyl salts in the protonic solvents, we obtain the *B* values given in.. Table VIII. **1953** AUDRIETH & KLEINBERG *Non-Aqueous Solvents* ii. 28 Why should not any protonic solvent, capable of undergoing limited self-ionization into hydrogen ion and some base-analog ion, serve as a parent substance of a system of acids, bases, and salts? **1966** PHILLIPS & WILLIAMS *Inorg. Chem.* II. xxxiii. 563 Organometallic compounds undergo typical reactions with compounds which contain protonic hydrogen, i.e. which act as acids towards them... Of these reactions, hydrolysis is one of the most important. **1968** [see HYDRIDIC *a.*]. **1969** T. C. WADDINGTON *Non-Aqueous Solvents* i. 8 In terms of Brønsted-Lowry or protonic acids, the strongest acid in a solvent is the protonated form of that solvent and the strongest base the deprotonated form.

Hence **pro'tonically** *adv.*

1979 *Science* 7 Dec. 1157/2 The semifluid bimolecular lipid membrane and the plug-through complexes form a condensed, continuous nonaqueous (protonically insulating) sheet that acts as the osmotic barrier and separates the aqueous proton conductors on either side.

proto-Nile: see PROTO- 2 a.

protonmotive (ˌprəʊtɒn'məʊtɪv), *a. Physics* and *Biochem.* Also **proton motive**. [f. PROTON + MOTIVE *a.*] Of, pertaining to, or characterized by the movement of protons in response to an electric potential gradient; *protonmotive force*: a force analogous to the electromotive force, which acts on the proton gradient across cell membranes and comprises the sum of the electric potential difference and the pH gradient across the membrane.

1966 P. MITCHELL in *Biol. Rev.* XLI. 494 The operation of the proton-translocating ATPase and o/r chain systems in an ion-tight membrane would create both a pH differential and a membrane potential, conveniently described together as a protonmotive force.. by analogy with electromotive force. **1977** HALL & BAKER *Cell Membranes & Ion Transport* iv. 79 The energy derived from the proton gradient (the proton motive force) may be used to drive oxidative phosphorylation. **1978** *Nature* 7 Sept. 14/3 Bonner suggested that a modified protonmotive ubiquinone cycle satisfies the kinetics of cytochrome interactions. **1979** *Science* 7 Dec. 1153/3 The first protonmotive device conceived by man was the electromotive hydrogen-burning fuel cell, invented by William Grove in 1839. **1980** *Federation Proc.* XXXIX. 1706/1 According to Mitchell's chemiosmotic hypothesis, a protonmotive force.. energizes the synthesis of ATP by a proton-translocating ATPase.

protonosphere (prəʊ'tɒnəsfɪə(r)). [f. as prec. + -O + SPHERE *sb.*] (See quot. 1960.)

1960 F. S. JOHNSON in *Jrnl. Geophysical Res.* LXV. 578/1 The name protonosphere is adopted here to describe the ionized medium above about 1800 km where protons are the principal ionized constituent, the name ionosphere being reserved for the lower region consisting of heavier atmospheric ions, such as atomic oxygen. **1973** *Q. Jrnl. R. Astr. Soc.* XIV. 197 Estimates of the flux of ionization into and out of the protonosphere. **1975** *Physics Bull.* July 338/3 (Advt.), There are vacancies for three Research Students, to commence in October 1975 and work for the degree of PhD. .. 2. Ionosphere and protonosphere by satellite radio transmissions.

Hence ˌ**protono'spheric** *a.*

1971 *Radio Science* VI. 849/1 The observed fluxes must be lower limits to the total protonospheric fluxes, since H^+ ions may also be differing from the protonosphere and contributing to the *F*-region via charge exchange below 800 km. **1978** *Nature* 2 Feb. 428/1 Temporal changes of protonospheric content are indicative of the filling and draining of this region.

protonotary, prothonotary (ˌprəʊtəʊ-, ˌprəʊθəʊ'nəʊtərɪ; prəʊ'tɒn-, prəʊ'θɒnətərɪ). Forms: α. 5- **prothonotary**; β. 6- **protonotary**; also 5 **-notur, -nothayr**, (6-7 **-natory, -natary**). [ad. late L. *prōtonotāri-us* (*c* 400 Ammianus in Du Cange), in med.L. also *protho-* (Hoveden); a. Gr. πρωτονοτάρι-ος (in Sophronius *c* 634), f. πρωτο-, PROTO- + νοτάριος, ad. L. *notārius* NOTARY *sb.* In 15th c. also after obs. F. *prothonotaire*, mod. *protonotaire*.

The pronunciation *pro'tonŏtary* is old in Eng., the absence of stress on *-notary* being shown by the 16th c. spelling *-natary, -natory*; cf. the corresponding spellings of PRENOTARY. It may have originated in the med.L. *pro,tono'tārius* and F. *pro,tono'taire*, with the English gradual change of the (accidental) secondary into primary stress. The analytical spelling *proto-notary*, and pronunciation *ˌprōto-'nōtary* are also evidenced from 16th c. Both pronunciations, with the variants *proto-* and *protho-* are now in official use in different quarters.]

1. A principal notary, chief clerk, or recorder of a court: originally, the holder of that office in the Byzantine court; also, applied by early English writers to similar officers in other ancient countries.

(But this latter application may have been suggested by the English use, sense 2.)

α. **1447** BOKENHAM *Seyntys* (Roxb.) 141 Oon Theophyl.. Wych prothonotarye was of þat kyngdam [Cappadocia]. **1727-41** CHAMBERS *Cycl.*, *Prothonotary, Protonotarius, Protonotary*,.. was anciently the title of the principal notaries of the emperors of Constantinople.

β. **1600** HOLLAND *Livy* XLIII. xvi. 1166 Shut up and locked all the offices of the Chauncerie, and discharged for the time the publicke clarkes and protonotaries attending upon that court. **1885** *Cath. Dict.* (ed. 3), *Protonotary*, in early times this title, which seems to have been first used at Constantinople, meant 'the chief of the notaries', and corresponded to *primicerius notariorum*, the term then in use at Rome. After 800, the title of protonotary was introduced in the West.

2. In England, formerly, The chief clerk or registrar in the Courts of Chancery, of Common Pleas, and of the King's Bench; also, in other courts of law, in some of which the term is still in use: see quots.

α. *c* **1460** J. RUSSELL *Bk. Nurture* 1063 A provincialle, a doctoure devine, or boþe lawes, þus yow lere, A prothonotur apertli, or þe popis collectoure, if he be there. **1467-8** *Rolls of Parlt.* V. 578/1 Oure Prothonotary in oure Chauncery. **1658** *Practick Part of Law* (ed. 5) 2 The Subordinate Officers [of the Court of Common-Pleas] are.. Three Prothonotaries (who by themselves and their Clarks, draw all pleadings and enter them, and exemplifie and record all common Recoveries). **1766** ENTICK *London* IV. 385 There are the same judges as in the Marshalsea-court, and a prothonotary, a secondary, and deputy prothonotary. **1825** *Act 6 Geo. IV*, c. 59 §4 The.. deposit of the price.. in the hands of the prothonotary or clerk of such court. **1854** *Act 17 & 18 Vict.* c. 125 §101 All the Provisions.. applicable to Masters of the said Courts at Westminster shall apply to the respective Prothonotaries of the Court of Common Pleas at Lancaster and Court of Pleas at Durham. **1868** *Lond. Gaz.* 14 July 3937/2 The Queen has been pleased to appoint Edward Thomas Wylde, Esq., to be Registrar or Prothonotary and Keeper of Records of the Supreme Court of the Colony of the Cape of Good Hope.

β. **1599** *Life Sir T. More* in Wordsw. *Eccl. Biog.* (1818) II. 147 His Father.. had procured for him the Protonotaries office of the King's Bench. **1658** BRAMHALL *Consecr. Bps.* iv. 108 Two of them were the Principall Publick Notaries in England, that is, Anthony Huse protonotary of the See of Canterbury, and Thomas Argall Registerer of the Prerogative Court. **1674** G. HUXLEY (*title*) A second Book of Judgements.. with Addition of some Notes, by George Townesend Esq; Second Prothonotary of the Common Pleas. Very Useful and Necessary for all Prothonotaries, Secondaries, Students [etc.]. **1707** E. CHAMBERLAYNE *Pres. St. Eng.* II. xv. (ed. 22) 197 There are three Protonotaries [of the Court of Common Pleas].. ; they are chief Clerks of this Court, and by their Office are to enter and enroll all Declarations, Pleadings.. Assizes, Judgments and Actions; to make out Judicial Writs, etc. for all English Counties except Monmouth.

3. a. *R.C. Ch.* A member of the college of twelve (formerly seven) prelates, called ***Protonotaries Apostolic(al***, whose function is to register the papal acts, to make and keep records of beatifications, to direct the canonization of saints, etc. Formerly also a title of certain papal envoys.

a. **1494** FABYAN *Chron.* VII. 435 Master Godfrey de Plessys, prothonothayr of yᵉ courte of Rome. **1550** BALE *Apol.* 92 Of lykelyhode ye are some prothonotary of Rome. **1725** tr. *Dupin's Eccl. Hist. 17th C.* I. II. viii. 73 Anthony Goosode, Doctor in Divinity, and Apostolick Prothonotary. **1845** S. AUSTIN *Ranke's Hist. Ref.* II. iii. I. 477 How proud and elated was Eck on reappearing in Germany with the new title of papal prothonotary and nuncio.

β. **1555** EDEN *Decades* 1 Counsiler to the kyng of Spayne and Protonotarie Apostolicall. **1682** *News fr. France* 36 The most renowned John Baptist Lauri, Protonotary Apostolick, and Auditor of the Apostolick Nunciature in France. **1758** JORTIN *Erasm.* I. 11 The Popes Protonotary of Ireland. **1898** *Westm. Gaz.* 28 Sept. 1/2 Monsignor Weld..was the oldest Protonotary Apostolic attached to the Papal household.

b. *Gr. Ch.* The principal secretary of the Patriarch of Constantinople.

1835 F. SHOBERL tr. *Chateaubriand's Trav. Jerus.*, etc. I. Introd. (ed. 3) 19 The first [letter] is addressed in 1575, by Theodore Zygomalas, who styles himself Prothonotary of the great church of Constantinople, 'to the learned Martin Crusius [etc.]'.

4. A chief secretary in some foreign courts; also *transf.* and *fig.*

a. **1502** *Privy Purse Exp. Eliz. of York* (1830) 4 A servaunt of the prothonotarye of Spayn. *c* **1570** *Pride & Lowl.* (1841) 70, I wrote never day with prothonotory. **1756** NUGENT *Gr. Tour, Germany* II. 93 This senate [of Hamburg] consists of four burgomasters,..twenty-four senators,..four syndics, ..and four secretaries, the chief of whom is called Prothonotary.

β. **1633** T. ADAMS *Exp. 2 Peter* iii. 2 They [i.e. the prophets] were the protonotaries of heaven, the registers of the truth, the secretaries of the Holy Ghost. **1852** MISS YONGE *Cameos* (1877) III. xxx. 304 Bayard had come out of his ambush too soon, and only dispersed the suite of secretaries, protonotaries, and all the rest.

5. *Comb.* **prothonotary warbler**, an American warbler, *Protonotarius citrea*, of the family Parulidæ, distinguished by a deep yellow head and breast, green back, and blue-grey wings.

1783 J. LATHAM *Gen. Synopsis Birds* II. II. 494 Prothonotary W[arbler]... This inhabits Louisiana, where it has obtained the name of *Protonotaire.* **1811** A. WILSON *Amer. Ornithol.* III. 72 Prothonotary Warbler... They are abundant in the Mississippi and New Orleans territories, near the river. **1874** E. COUES *Birds of Northwest* 47 Prothonotary Warbler... This species..only reaches the lowermost Missouri. **1977** *Daily Tel.* 24 Jan. 10/4 Bird-watchers..already know what a prothonotary warbler is.

Hence **proto-, prothonotarial** (-ˈɛərɪəl) *a.*, of or pertaining to a protonotary; **proto-, prothonotariat** (-ˈɛərɪæt), the college of protonotaries; **proto-, protho'notaryship**, the office of a protonotary.

1547 *Acts Privy Council* (1890) II. 517 Sir John Godsalve ..was required to repaire hether to attend his office of the Signete and Protonotorieship. **1691** WOOD *Ath. Oxon.* I. 452/3 Her Majesty who also gave him [George Carew] a Prothonotaryship in the Chancery. **1893** *Westm. Gaz.* 12 Apr. 2/1 The ancestor..drew a profit from the Prothonotaryship, and shared in the subsequent pension.

proto-notator to **protonovelist**: see PROTO-.

protonym (ˈprəʊtənɪm). *rare.* [f. PROT(O- + Gr. ὄνομα, ὄνυμα name, after *synonym.*] The first person or thing of the name; that from which another is named.

1880 *Scribner's Mag.* Mar. 667/2 The wrecked canal-boat, the *Evening Star*,..quenched in the twilight, with its heavenly protonym palpitating in the vapor above it. **1882** *Daily News* 26 Juen 5/2 Faugh-a-Ballagh..a colt of no mean ability..was, like his famous protonym, bred in Ireland.

proto-organism to **-ornithoid**: see PROTO-.

‖**protopapas** (prəʊtəʊˈpæpəs). Also 7 **-pappa.** [a. eccl. Gr. πρωτοπαπᾶς chief priest, f. πρωτο-, PROTO- + παπᾶς priest (see POPE *sb.*²); cf. med.L. *prōtopāpa*, and see PROTOPOPE.] = PROTOPOPE.

1682 WHELER *Journ. Greece* I. 32 The Protopappa, or Chief Priest. **1718** OZELL *Tournefort's Voy.* I. 274 The Greeks have full 200 Papas subject to a Protopapas. **1820** T. S. HUGHES *Trav. Sicily* I. iv. 141 They inhabit a certain quarter where they have a church called the Catholicon, and a protopapas or high-priest.

protoparent: see PROTO- I.

protopathic (prəʊtəʊˈpæθɪk), *a.* [f. PROTO- + Gr. πάθ-ος suffering, disease + -IC: cf. for form, Gr. παθικ-ός PATHIC.]

1. *Path.* Of the nature of a primary disease or affection: opp. to *deuteropathic.*

1858 MAYNE *Expos. Lex.*, *Protopathicus*, term applied the same as *Primary*, to the symptoms of disease;..protopathic. **1896** *Allbutt's Syst. Med.* I. 738 This primary debility of the heart..constitutes the primary or protopathic malignity of the older writers. **1899** *Ibid.* VII. 176 The atrophy was regarded as secondary to the lateral sclerosis, and hence these cases are called deuteropathic, in opposition to the protopathic cases of progressive muscular atrophy.

2. *Neurology.* In the theory that there are two (or three) sets of nerves and sensory receptors supplying the skin, the epithet of the coarser and more primitive sensibility (involving pain and temperature) and of the parts of the nervous system on which it is based.

1905 H. HEAD et al. in *Brain* XXVIII. 106 The position of the point stimulated cannot be recognised and each stimulus causes a widespread radiating sensation... To this form of sensibility we propose to give the name 'protopathic'. **1912** J. G. MCKENDRICK *Princ. Physiol.* xiii. 224 If a sensory nerve to an area of skin is divided, sensibility may return if the ends unite. The sensations that return first have been termed protopathic, and depend on heat, cold, and pain spots. **1920** [see EPICRITIC *a.*]. **1942** *Brain* LXV. 110 Head's protopathic and epicritic fibres..come to grief when they make contact with the hard facts of anatomy. **1951** W. L. JENKINS in S. S. Stevens *Handbk. Exper. Psychol.* xxx. 1172/1 Also abandoned for the lack of experimental confirmation are Head's proposal of a dual system of four epicritic and four protopathic skin senses [etc.]. **1958** *Ann. N.Y. Acad. Sci.* LXXIV. 30 Return of protopathic sensibility commences about six weeks following section of the sensory nerves and is completed within six months. **1974** M. & D. WEBSTER *Compar. Vertebr. Morphol.* xii. 278 The often unmyelinated protopathic fibres..arise from small cell bodies in the dorsal root ganglia. **1977** *Lancet* 11 June 1271/2 Head, in his model of the protopathic and epicritic nervous system,..introduced the notion of processing of sensory input at the level of entry into the central nervous system.

protopathy (prəʊˈtɒpəθɪ). *rare.* [ad. mod.L. *prōtopathīa*, a. Gr. πρωτοπάθεια (Galen), a first feeling, f. πρωτοπαθεῖν to suffer or feel first: see PROTO- and -PATHY. So F. *protopathie.*] Primary suffering; pain or other sensation immediately produced; in *Path.* a primary disease or affection, i.e. one not produced by or consequent on another. (Opp. to DEUTEROPATHY and SYMPATHY.)

1636 JACKSON *Creed* VIII. xii. §6 The grief and sorrow which in the Garden he [Christ] suffered could not be known by sympathy. The protopathy was in Himself, and no man..could so truly sympathize with Him in this grief, as he had done with them. **1647** H. MORE *Song of Soul* Notes 163/2 If any man strike me, I feel immediately; because my soul is united with this body that is struck: and this is protopathy. **1858** MAYNE *Expos. Lex.*, *Protopathia*, term for a first or original suffering, opposed to sympathy: protopathy.

proto-patriarchal: see PROTO- I.

proto'pectin. *Biochem.* [ad. G. *protopektin* (A. Tschirch-Bern 1907, in *Ber. d. Deut. Pharm. Ges.* XVII. 242): see PROTO- and PECTIN.] = PECTOSE.

1908 *Chem. Abstr.* II. 431 (*heading*) On pectin and protopectin. **1922** *Biochemical Jrnl.* XVI. 704 The soluble pectin probably develops from an insoluble pectic substance contained in the cell wall... This insoluble pectin corresponds to the protopectin of Fellenberg, and to the pectose of earlier investigators. **1951** Z. I. KERTESZ *Pectic Substances* iii. 55 Protopectin is now believed by some to represent very large (and therefore water-insoluble) pectinic acid molecules. **1962** S. M. SIEGEL *Plant Cell Wall* i. 16 The constitutional differences between protopectin and the other pectic substances remain unclear. Empirically, the protopectins are distinguished by their insolubility, and, in general, by a higher molecular weight. **1973** J. J. DOESBURG in L. P. Miller *Phytochemistry* I. x. 272 In most plant tissues, the pectic substances are present in the form of water-insoluble protopectin. Ripe fruits are the main exceptions having a part present in soluble form, which is formed from protopectin during the ripening process. **1976** BELL & COOMBE tr. *Strasburger's Textbk. Bot.* (rev. ed.) 64 Protopectin can..be regarded as a cementing substance holding the cells of a tissue together.

Hence **proto'pectinase** [-ASE] (see quots.).

1927 *Bot. Gaz.* LXXXIII. 331 Protopectinase.—The term applied to the enzyme which hydrolyzes or dissolves protopectin, with the resultant separation of the plant cells from each other, usually spoken of as maceration. *Ibid.* 338 Various strains of potatoes, of a wide range of mealiness, were used as test tissue for protopectinase activity, with the idea that the most mealy might have middle lamellae most easily hydrolyzed by the enzyme. **1951** Z. I. KERTESZ *Pectic Substances* xiv. 335 Until a few years ago it was believed that protopectinase is distinct from the enzyme which hydrolyzes the 1,4 glycosidic linkages in pectinic acids... However, there is now a growing tendency toward the view that the two enzymes (protopectinase and pectin-polygalacturonase) are identical. **1973** J. J. DOESBURG in L. P. Miller *Phytochemistry* I. x. 281 In the past a specific enzyme, protopectinase, was thought to produce soluble pectic material from protopectin... Since there is no adequate proof of the existence of such a specific enzyme.. it is believed that the action of 'macerating' enzymes is exerted by one or more of the pectic enzymes mentioned hereafter.

protoperithecium to **-phenomenon**: see PROTO- 2 b.

proto'philic, *a. Chem.* [f. PROTO(N + -PHILIC.] Of a solvent (or solute): having a tendency to remove a proton from most solutes (or solvents). Opp. PROTOGENIC *a.*² Also **'protophile** (*rare*), such a substance.

1930 N. F. HALL in *Jrnl. Chem. Educ.* VII. 787 The terms *protophilia* and *hydrophilia* have been proposed to describe the tendency of a molecule to unite with proton, and it would seem that some such word as *protophile*, forbidding as it is, would arouse less prejudice than the term *base* used in such a broad and subversive manner. *Ibid.* 792 Next there is the basic strength, or protophilic tendency of the solvent. **1931, 1940** [see PROTOGENIC *a.*²]. **1953** AUDRIETH & KLEINBERG *Non-Aqueous Solvents* ii. 33 Amphiprotic solvents occupy a position intermediate between those of marked protophylic [*sic*] character, such as ammonia and the amines, and those of distinct protophobic character, such as acetic and hydrogen fluoride. **1969** [see PROTOGENIC *a.*²]. **1973** E. J. KING in Covington & Dickinson *Phys. Chem. Org. Solvent Syst.* iii. 334 Ethanolamine and dimethyl sulphoxide are basic or protophilic solvents.

protophloem, -phoneme: see PROTO- 2 b, I.

protophosphide, -uret: see PROTO- 3.

'protophyll. *Bot.* [f. PROTO- + Gr. φύλλ-ον leaf.] In club-mosses, a structure resembling a leaf produced on the upper surface of the protocorm or tuber.

1891 F. O. BOWER in *Proc. R. Soc.* L. 267 The sporophyte [of *Phylloglossum*] consists of two parts:—(i) the protocorm, with its protophylls and roots, and (ii) the strobilus. **1902** *Encycl. Brit.* XXXII. 74/1 The plant [sc. *Phylloglossum*] is produced by tubers, which resemble the protocorm in bearing first a number of protophylls. **1938** G. M. SMITH *Cryptogamic Bot.* II. vii. 180 From the upper surface of the protocorm arise a few to many erect, conical outgrowths (protophylls) which are leaf-like in function. **1962** K. R. SPORNE *Morphol. Pteridophytes* iv. 64 Further protophylls appear in an irregular manner.

‖**Protophyta** (prəʊˈtɒfɪtə), *sb. pl. Bot.* [mod.L., pl. of *prōtophytum*, f. Gr. πρῶτος first, PROTO- + φυτόν plant.] A primary division of the vegetable kingdom (corresponding to PROTOZOA in the animal kingdom), comprising the most simply organized plants (usually of microscopic size), each individual consisting of a single cell. (Formerly more vaguely used: see quot. 1858.)

1855 [see PROTOZOA]. **1858** MAYNE *Expos. Lex.*, *Protophytum*, applied (*Protophyta*, nom. pl. n.) by Fries to the *Algæ*, which he regarded as the first productions of the vegetable kingdom... Mackay established under this name a division containing the *Mucores* and *Lichenes*: a protophyte. **1860** H. SPENCER in *Westm. Rev.* Jan. 99 The lowest forms of animal and vegetal life—*Protozoa* and *Protophyta*—are chiefly inhabitants of the water. **1895** *Westm. Gaz.* 14 Sept. 8/2 The oysters thrive best upon the living protophyta and protozoa.

protophyte (ˈprəʊtəʊfaɪt). [ad. mod.L. *prōtophytum*: see prec. So F. *protophyte.*] A plant belonging to the division *Protophyta*; a unicellular plant. (Used as the Eng. singular of *Protophyta.*)

1853 in DUNGLISON *Med. Lex.* **1862** DANA *Man. Geol.* II. i. 270 The plants thus far observed are sea-weeds and Protophytes. **1884** *Trans. Victoria Inst.* 78 The protophyte obtains the materials of its nutrition from the air and moisture that surround it.

protophytic (prəʊtəʊˈfɪtɪk), *a.* [f. PROTOPHYT-A + -IC.] Of, pertaining to, derived from, or having the characters of the *Protophyta.*

1882 *American* V. 122 The protophytic origin of the mineral.

'protopine. *Chem.* [f. PROTO- 3 c + OPIUM + -INE⁵.] A white crystalline alkaloid, $C_{20}H_{19}NO_5$, occurring in very small quantities in opium.

1894 MUIR & MORLEY *Watts' Chem. Dict.* IV. 345.

'protoplanet. *Astr.* [f. PROTO- + PLANET *sb.*¹] A large diffuse body of matter in a solar or stellar orbit, postulated as a preliminary stage in the evolution of a planet.

1949 *Astrophysical Jrnl.* CIX. 309 A simple model is therefore considered first, consisting of two spherical masses ('protoplanets') in near contact, located inside the gaseous disk surrounding the sun. **1952** H. C. UREY *Planets* i. 13 First, a spherical or irregular cloud must rapidly collapse to a flat disk... Second, the disk of gas would break up into a Kolmogoroff spectrum of turbulent eddies... Finally a system of protoplanets, one for each of the planets, would be left at the appropriate distance from the sun. **1971** I. G. GASS et al. *Understanding Earth* ix. 135/2 This conclusion suggests..that a considerable degree of fractionation had already taken place in the protoplanet before it condensed into a solid body. **1974** *Sci. Amer.* Mar. 57/3 The second compositional class would have consisted of protoplanets formed just after the metallic iron-nickel alloy condensed out of the solar nebula.

Hence **proto'planetary** *a.*, of, pertaining to, or being a protoplanet.

1962 *Lancet* 13 Jan. 89/1 Meteorites are generally assumed to have originated by the disruption of protoplanetary bodies in the region now occupied by the asteroids. **1977** *Nature* 13 Oct. 584/1 When the cloud collapses and a new hot star is created in its centre, the flattened protoplanetary disk formed from the remnants of the cloud continues to be cold.

protoplasm (ˈprəʊtəʊplæz(ə)m). *Biol.* [ad. Ger. *prōtoplasma* (H. von Mohl, 1846), f. Gr. πρωτο-, PROTO- + πλάσμα moulded thing, figure, form. (*Prōtoplasma* was used in late L. by Venantius Fortunatus *a* 600, in sense of 'first created thing, protoplast', and was prob. used in Chr. Greek.) Before von Mohl coined the word in this sense it had been used (also in Ger.) with a slightly different meaning by J. E. Purkinje (*Uebersicht der Arbeiten und Veränderungen der schlesischen Ges. für vaterländische Kultur 1839* 82).]

a. A viscid, semifluid, semitransparent, colourless or whitish substance, consisting of oxygen, hydrogen, carbon, and nitrogen (often with a small amount of some other elements) in extremely complex and unstable combination, and manifesting what are known as vital properties, i.e. irritability, contractility, spontaneous movement, assimilation, and reproduction; constituting 'the physical basis of life' (Huxley) in all plants and animals, and forming the essential substance of the cells (see CELL *sb.*[1] 12) out of which their bodies are built up. Also called BIOPLASM, CYTOPLASM, and (in animals) formerly SARCODE.

[**1846** VON MOHL *Saftbewegungen im Inneren der Zellen* in *Botan. Zeitung* 73 tr. Henfrey (1852) 37 The remainder of the cell is more or less densely filled with an opake, viscid fluid, of a white colour, having granules intermingled in it, which fluid I call protoplasm.] **1848** LINDLEY *Intod. Bot.* (ed. 4) I. 10 The first layer of matter is invariably soft and azotised, and now bears the well-contrived name of *protoplasm*, proposed by Professor Mohl. **1854** EMERSON *Lett. & Soc. Aims, Poet. & Imag.* Wks. (Bohn) III. 141 Indicating the way upward from the invisible protoplasm to the highest organisms. **1866** [see CELL *sb.*[1] 12]. **1868** HUXLEY in *Fortn. Rev.* 1 Feb. (1869) 129, I have translated the term Protoplasm which is the scientific name of the substance.. by the words 'physical basis of life'. **1875** BENNETT & DYER *Sachs' Bot.* 3 Since.. no further process of development can take place in the cells which no longer contain protoplasm, it may be concluded that the latter is the proximate cause of growth. **1903** MYERS *Human Personality* I. 117 In the protoplasm or primary basis of all organic life there must have been an inherent adaptability to the manifestation of all faculties which organic life has in fact manifested.

fig. **1894** H. DRUMMOND *Ascent Man* 189 These [primeval times] were the days of the protoplasm of speech. **1906** D. S. CAIRNS *Chr. Mod. World* iii. 150 Here is the true protoplasm of Christianity out of which.. all the theologies and all the ritual.. have sprung.

b. *Comb.* as *protoplasm-mass*, *-sac*, etc.

1875 BENNETT & DYER *Sachs' Bot.* 2 The cavity enclosed by the protoplasm-sac is filled with a watery fluid, the Cell-sap. **1882** VINES *Sachs' Bot.* 7 The formation of a new cell always commences with the re-arrangement of a protoplasm-mass round a new centre. **1895** in *Daily News* 3 Oct. 2/2 The protoplasm-containing cells of his brain.

proto'plasmal, *a. rare.* [f. prec. + -AL[1].] = PROTOPLASMIC. (*Cent. Dict.*)

1885 W. S. GILBERT *Mikado* I. 7, I can trace my ancestry back to a protoplasmal primordial atomic globule.

protoplasmatic (ˌprəʊtəʊplæz'mætɪk), *a.* [f. Gr. type *πρωτοπλάσματ- + -IC: the etymological derivative after Greek analogies.] = PROTOPLASMIC.

1866 A. FLINT *Princ. Med.* (1880) 40 By protoplasmatic off-shoots from pre-existing capillaries. **1893** NEWTON *Dict. Birds* 196 The germinal vesicle,.. like the white yolk, consists of numerous protoplasmatic spherules.

†**protoplasmator.** *Obs. rare.* In 6 protho-. [? med.L.: see PROTO- and PLASMATOR, and cf. PROTOPLASM.] First framer or moulder, creator: = PROTOPLAST[2].

c **1550** R. BIESTON *Bayte Fortune* A iij, Thou knowest howe god the hygh prothoplasmator Of erth hath formed man after hys owne ymage.

protoplasmic (prəʊtəʊ'plæzmɪk), *a.* [f. PROTOPLASM + -IC. So F. *protoplasmique*.] Of, pertaining to, or having the nature of protoplasm.

1854 J. H. BALFOUR in *Encycl. Brit.* (ed. 8) V. 67/1 The formation of nuclei or cells in a protoplasmic matrix. **1859** *Todd's Cycl. Anat.* V. 217/1 The protoplasmic membrane divides.. into particles. **1861** BENTLEY *Man. Bot.* 56 All cells originate.. either free in the cavities of older cells, or at least in the protoplasmic fluid elaborated by their agency; or by the division of such cells.

fig. **1888** *Athenæum* 7 Jan. 13 The metrical systems of the banished *régime*.. have, no doubt, a primitve and even a protoplasmic simplicity. **1891** *Daily News* 20 Oct. 2/6 The barber-surgeon and medicine man of ancient times, who furnished the protoplasmic material out of which the art of medicine and surgery had been evolved.

b. Relating to protoplasm; acting upon or affecting protoplasm.

1876 BARTHOLOW *Mat. Med.* (1879) 148 Quinia.. is a protoplasmic poison, and arrests the amoebiform movements of the white corpuscles. **1903** MYERS *Human Personality* I. 117 Which.. to avoid the ambiguities of the word Darwinian, I will call the protoplasmic solution.

'protoˌplasmist. *rare.* [f. as prec. + -IST.] One who treats of protoplasm.

1884 C. A. BARTOL in *Homilet. Monthly* (N.Y.) July 550 Amid the slime protoplasmists tell of at the bottom of the sea.

protoplast[1] ('prəʊtəʊplæst). Also 6 **prothoplauste.** [a. F. *protoplaste* (16th c. *prothoplauste*), or ad. late L. *prōtoplast-us* (14th c. *-plaustus*), ad. Gr. πρωτόπλαστ-ος (LXX. *Wisd.* vii. 1), f. πρωτο-, PROTO- + πλαστ-ός moulded, formed, vbl. adj. f. πλάσσ-ειν to form, mould.]

1. That which is first formed, fashioned, or created; the first-made thing or being of its kind; the original, archetype. **a.** The first man; the first created of the human race.

c **1532** DU WES *Introd. Fr.* in *Palsgr.* 1049 Comyng from God to the firste father or prothoplauste [Fr. *premiér pére ou prothoplauste*] it goeth and retourne to God from father to the sonne. **1600** W. WATSON *Decacordon* (1602) 202 In Salem citie was Adam our protoplast created. **1794** COLERIDGE *Dest. Nations* 282 Night A heavy unimaginable moan Sent forth, when she the Protoplast beheld. **1888** *Q. Rev.* Apr. 300 The Book [Wisdom of Solomon] has given to modern science the term 'protoplast', which it twice uses of Adam.

†**b.** The first man of some line or series. *Obs.*

1644–7 CLEVELAND *Char. Lond. Diurn.* 1 The originall sinner in this kind was Dutch; Galliobelgicus the Protoplast; and the moderne Mercuries but Hans-en Kelders. **1737** BRACKEN *Farriery Impr.* (1757) II. 55 The Pedigree we often lay Claim to would produce a Drummer, as frequently as a Colonel, for his Protoplast.

c. The first example; the original, model.

1612 STURTEVANT *Metallica* viii. 67 The first windmilne that the inuentioner euer set vp to grinde corne was the Protoplast and example from whence all other wind-milnes sprange and were deriued. **1651** BIGGS *New Disp.* ¶ 238 The protoplast or primitive ordainment of a Cautery, had excretion for its object. **1819** H. BUSK *Vestriad* IV. 172 No more the protoplast of active beauty. **1863** *Macm. Mag.* May 63 If Hebrew was the protoplast of speech.

d. *attrib.* in apposition; or *adj.*

1617 COLLINS *Def. Bp. Ely* II. ix. 406 Ignatius, the Protoplast Iesuite. **1695** J. SAGE *Article*, etc. Wks. 1844 I. 204 Andrew Melville, the Protoplast Presbyterian in Scotland.

2. *Biol.* **a.** A unit or mass of protoplasm, such as constitutes a single cell; a bioplast. Sometimes applied to a unicellular organism; *spec.* one of the suborder *Protoplasta* of rhizopods.

[**1858** MAYNE *Expos. Lex.*, *Protoplast, Physiol.*, a primary formation.] **1884** *Standard Nat. Hist.* (1888) I. 14 The filose protoplasts seem to be in nowise different from the Foraminifera, except that the shells of the latter are usually calcareous. **1898** tr. *Strasburger's Bot.* I. i. 52 Within the walled protoplasts, the granular protoplasm often exhibits internal flowing movements.

b. The living contents of a cell; *esp.* in recent usage, a living cell whose cell wall has been removed or destroyed.

1884 *Rep. Brit. Assoc. 1883* 536 When the protoplast is in its normal position lining the cell wall, this core of protoplasm filling the pore would offer great resistance to a bodily passage of the cell sap. **1895** *Jrnl. Microsc. Soc.* 563 For the protoplast of the Cyanophyceæ and Schizomycetes the author proposes the term *archiplast*. **1925** E. B. WILSON *Cell* (ed. 3) i. 22 Cytosome and nucleus taken together form a living unit or protoplasmic system that is often spoken of as the protoplast (Hanstein) or sometimes as the energid (Sachs). **1953** C. WEIBULL in *Jrnl. Bacteriol.* LXVI. 690/2 The spherical bodies obtained by lysis in sucrose will be designated as 'protoplasts'. **1970** AMBROSE & EASTY *Cell Biol.* viii. 271 The outer wall and capsule in many bacteria can be digested away by enzyme treatment leaving the protoplast, which is surrounded by a membrane still retaining the main permeability characteristics of the original bacterium.

'protoplast[2]. Also 6 prothoplast. [ad. med.L. *prōtoplast-ēs*, a. Gr. *πρωτοπλάστ-ης, f. πρωτο-, PROTO- + πλάστης, agent-n. f. πλάσσειν: see prec.] The first former, fashioner, or creator.

1600 W. WATSON *Decacordon* (1602) 100 The followers of a prothoplast or first Author of a profession. [**1650** BULWER *Anthropomet.* Ep. Ded., The honour and reputation of the great Architect, man's Protoplastes.] **1676** NEWTON in Rigaud *Corr. Sci. Men* (1841) II. 389 Nature,.. became a complete imitator of the copies set her by the protoplast. **1872** BROWNING *Fifine* cxxiv, Those mammoth-stones, piled by the Protoplast Temple-wise in my dream!

protoplastic (prəʊtəʊ'plæstɪk), *a.* [f. PROTOPLAST[1] + -IC: cf. PLASTIC.]

1. Of the nature of a protoplast (see PROTOPLAST[1] 1); first formed; original, archetypal.

a **1652** J. SMITH *Sel. Disc.* v. viii. (1821) 170 Which issuing forth from God.. is the protoplastic virtue of our being. **1660** HOWELL *Lexicon* Poems 1 When our Protoplastick sire Lost Paradis. **1716** M. DAVIES *Athen. Brit.* II. To Rdr. 7 A more correct Edition of the Protoplastick Copy. **1840** F. BARHAM *Alist* 5 This divine or protoplastic Adam.. is the divine idea or exemplar of humanity.

2. *Biol.* = PROTOPLASMIC.

1855 BADEN POWELL *Ess.* 436 *note*, What the author terms the 'primary mucus', 'schleim-substanz', or protoplastic matter. **1898** tr. *Strasburger's Bot.* I. i. 52 Rotation is the more frequent form of protoplastic movement in the cells of water-plants, while in land plants circulation is.. the rule.

proto-plot to **-Polynesian**: see PROTO-.

protopope ('prəʊtəʊpəʊp). [ad. Russ. *protopop*ᵘ: see PROTO- and POPE *sb.*[2]; after eccl. Gr. πρωτοπαπᾶς PROTOPAPAS. So F. *protopope*.] A chief priest, or priest of higher rank, in the Greek Church.

1662 J. DAVIES tr. *Olearius' Voy. Ambass.* 136 A Protopope of Casanskey, whose name was Juan Neronou, began to inveigh against the honour done to Images. **1784** COXE *Trav. Poland*, etc. II. 103 The highest dignity to which they can ever attain, as long as they continue married, is that of protopope of a cathedral. **1900** *Pilot* 7 July 6/2 One formerly a playmate, but now the fiercest opponent of Nikon, the protopop Avvakum.

proto'porphyrin. *Chem.* [a. G. *protoporphyrin* (Fischer & Lindner 1925, in *Zeitschr. f. physiol. Chem.* CXLII. 147): see PROTO- and PORPHYRIN.] Any of a group of fifteen isomeric porphyrins, $C_{34}H_{34}N_4O_4$, in which the porphin nucleus has four methyl, two vinyl, and two propionic acid substituents; one isomer (*protoporphyrin IX*) occurs widely in living organisms, notably as hæm (its ferrous chelate derivative).

1925 *Chem. Abstr.* XIX. 1714 The esters of ooporphyrin, Kämmerer's porphyrin, Papendieck's porphyrin and CO_2- and HCl-porphyrins are identical... The name 'protoporphyrin' is proposed for all of these. **1937** *Jrnl. Biol. Chem.* CXVIII. 521 Probably the most important porphyrin in nature is protoporphyrin IX... There are fifteen possible isomers of this compound, but this one.. is the only one so far demonstrated in nature. **1961** *Lancet* 26 Aug. 450/2 This man.. produced no abnormal quantity of uroporphyrin but excessive amounts of protoporphyrin which were localised mainly within his circulating red cells. **1964** A. WHITE et al. *Princ. Biochem.* (ed. 3) xlii. 792 A common pathway exists for the synthesis of heme and of chlorophyll leading to formation of protoporphyrin IX... Insertion of iron into the latter results in heme formation. In plants, in addition to synthesis of heme, magnesium is inserted into protoporphyrin IX to form magnesium protoporphyrin, which is converted in plastids to chlorophyll. **1975** *Nature* 26 June 706/1 The prosthetic group of haemoglobin has a protoporphyrin structure (ferrohaem) in which the ion atom is ionically bound.

Hence ˌ**protopor'phyria** *Med.*, the presence of protoporphyrin in the red blood cells.

1956 in *New Gould Med. Dict.* (ed. 2) 975/1. **1961** I. A. MAGNUS et al. in *Lancet* 26 Aug. 451/2 The absence of uroporphyrin clearly distinguishes this syndrome from congenital porphyria. It seems to be a hitherto undescribed erythropoietic condition for which we suggest the name 'erythropoietic protoporphyria'. **1975** *Sci. Amer.* July 73/1 Investigators can easily induce these typical symptoms without serious consequences in patients suffering from mild forms of erythropoietic protoporphyria, so that the disease is one of the few of its kind where the action spectrum for a direct effect of light has been studied in detail. **1977** *Proc. R. Soc. Med.* LXX. 572/2 Erythropoietic protoporphyria (EPP) is a disorder, usually of autosomal dominant inheritance, in which large amounts of protoporphyrin are found in erythrocytes.

proto-presbyter to **-proteose**: see PROTO-.

‖**protopterus** (prəʊ'tɒptərəs). *Ichth.* [mod.L. generic name (Owen, 1837), f. Gr. πρωτο-, PROTO- + πτερ-όν wing (taken in sense 'fin').] A genus of dipnoan fishes, formerly included in *Lepidosiren*, containing only the African mud-fish (*P. annectens*); characterized by having the pectoral and ventral fins reduced to long fringed filaments; also, a fish of this genus.

1837 (June) OWEN in *MS. Catal. Museum of Coll. Surg.* Protopterus. **1841** *Penny Cycl.* XIX. 59/2. **1854** OWEN *Skel. & Teeth* in *Orr's Circ. Sc.* I. *Org. Nat.* 186 The protopterus and lepidosiren, which are the most reptile-like of fishes. **1894** *Daily News* 10 Apr. 5/4 The biggest protopterus at the Zoo is not more than two feet long.

Hence **pro'topteran**, *adj.* of the nature of a *Protopterus*; having a primitive or simple type of fin; *sb.* a fish of the order *Protopteri* (a synonym of *Dipnoi*); ‖**protopter** (prəʊ'tɒptər) [= Fr. *protoptère*] = prec. sb.; **pro'topterous** = prec. adj.

protopterygian (ˌprəʊtəʊptə'rɪdʒɪən), *a. Ichth.* [f. Gr. πρωτο-, PROTO- + πτερύγιον fin + -AN.] Introduced by Ryder to designate the first-fin stage when the embryonic fin rays first appear.

1884 *Rep. U.S. Comm. Fish.* (1886) 987 The protopterygian stage of development of the permanent fin-rays.

protopyramid: see PROTO- 2 b.

†**proto'quamquam.** *Obs. nonce-wd.* [f. PROTO- + L. *quamquam* although, albeit, notwithstanding that.] Humorous imitation of PROTONOTARY, referring to the exceptive and concessive conjunctions used in legal documents.

1670 G. H. *Hist. Cardinals* II. III. 180 Who in case of his Unkles exaltation, would be the *Protoquamquam* in Rome.

protosalt ('prəʊtəʊsɔːlt). *Chem.* [f. PROTO- 3 + SALT[1].] A salt formed by combination of an acid with the protoxide of a metal, e.g. a salt of ferrous oxide, FeO, as ferrous sulphate, $FeSO_4$.

1820 FARADAY [see PERSALT]. **1836–41** BRANDE *Chem.* (ed. 5) 592 The protosalts of iron are in these cases preferable to those of tin, inasmuch as the resulting peroxide of iron is retained in solution, and the precepitated metal is pure. **1866** R. M. FERGUSON *Electr.* (1870) 42 Among paramagnetic substances are proto salts of iron. **1869** ROSCOE *Elem. Chem.* (1871) 239 The ferrous- or proto-salts are distinguished by their light green colour.

So **proto-so'lution**, a solution which contains a protosalt.

1854 SCOFFERN in *Orr's Circ. Sc., Chem.* 457 Add carbonate of potash or soda to a protosolution of zinc.

proto-scrinerary to **-spasm**: see PROTO-.

'protosome. *Genetics.* [f. PROTO- + -SOME[4].] The larger of two particles which together were postulated to constitute a gene; cf. EPISOME. (No longer current.)

1931, **1966** [see EPISOME a].

‖**protospatharius** (ˌprəʊtəʊspəˈθɛərɪəs). Also in Fr. form **protospat(h)aire**. [med.L. *prōtospathārius*, ad. Byzant. Gr. πρωτοσπαθάριος, f. πρωτο-, PROTO- + σπαθάριος swordsman.] Title of the captain of the guards in the Byzantine empire.

1788 GIBBON *Decl. & F.* liii. (1846) V. 267 Whilst he exercised the office of *protospathaire*, or captain of the guards, Photius was sent ambassador to the caliph of Bagdad. **1831** SCOTT *Ct. Robt.* ii, Every one..hath understood this much, that the great Protospathaire..hath me at hatred. **1853** J. STEVENSON *Ch. Historians Eng.* I. 648 The protospataire was sent to summon Sergius. **1854** MILMAN *Lat. Chr.* II. 140 The protospatharius, the officer of the Emperor, was driven with insult from the city.

protospermato- to **protostele**: see PROTO-.

ˈ**protostar.** *Astr.* [f. PROTO- + STAR *sb.*[1]] A contracting mass of gas in which nucleosynthesis has not yet begun, representing an early stage in the formation of a star.

1954 H. ALFVÉN *Orig. Solar Syst.* xii. 188 This condensation may have taken place from a 'protostar' of the type considered by Spitzer and others. **1972** *Sci. Amer.* Aug. 49/3 It has been suggested that protostars are formed when some of the gas and dust associated with the spiral arms of the galaxy piles up into clouds. **1976** [see OBSERVATIONALLY *adv.*]. **1977** J. NARLIKAR *Struct. Universe* ii. 27 Such a cloud contracts as a whole, but subsequently breaks up into smaller subunits or 'protostars' when instability develops in the system.

Also **protoˈstellar** *a.*, of, pertaining to, or being a protostar or protostars.

1973 *Nature* 17 Aug. 425/1 Conditions are therefore appropriate for the formation of solid planets if the nature of the protostellar body is such that dispersal of the particulate matter does not take place soon after its formation. **1975** *Ibid.* 6 Feb. 393/2 The initially low metal abundance could radically alter both the cooling of the gas required for protostellar collapse and the mechanisms which limit the greatest mass which can condense into a star. **1976** *Astron. Jrnl.* LXXXI. 1092/2 There is..a cluster of protostellar objects..southwest of M17 at the apparent edge of fragment B.

ˌ**protoˈsulphide.** *Chem.* [PROTO- 3.] A compound of sulphur with another element or radical containing the minimum proportion of sulphur. Formerly also called **protoˈsulphuret**. (Now usually otherwise expressed: as ***protosulphide*** or ***-sulphuret of iron*** = ferrous sulphide, FeS.) So †**protoˈsulphate**, a salt formed by sulphuric acid with the protoxide of a metal, as ***protosulphate of iron***, = ferrous sulphate, copperas, or green vitriol.

1856 MILLER *Elem. Chem.* II. 726 Potassium..combines with this element [sulphur] in..five different proportions, KS, KS_2, KS_3, KS_4, and KS_6... The *protosulphide, KS [New Notation K_2S], etc. *c* **1865** J. WYLDE in *Circ. Sc.* I. 376/2 The proto-sulphide is..produced by passing sulphuretted hydrogen through a solution of a copper salt. **1826** HENRY *Elem. Chem.* II. 35 Two compounds of iron and sulphur have been proved to exist, the one with a smaller..proportion of sulphur..which is distinguished by the property of being magnetic, is the *proto-sulphuret. **1819** J. G. CHILDREN *Chem. Anal.* 430 Sulphuretted hydrogen destroys the colour of the red compound of strychnine, as does..*protosulphate of iron. *c* **1865** J. WYLDE in *Circ. Sc.* I. 146/1 Protosulphate of iron is well known under the name of green copperas.

proto-syntax to **-tergite**: see PROTO-.

protoˈtaxic, *a. Psychol.* [f. PROTO- + TAX(IS + -IC.] Applied to a hypothetical first or basic stage of experiencing or receiving impressions; also, related to a primal type of experience. See also PARATAXIC, SYNTAXIC *adjs.*

1945 P. MULLAHY in *Psychiatry* VIII. 183/2 Prototaxic symbolization seems without reference to an ego, to 'I' or 'me' because the infant has no, or only a rudimentary, self. **1953** H. S. SULLIVAN *Interpersonal Theory of Psychiatry* (1955) ii. 28 These modes are: the prototaxic, the parataxic, and the syntaxic. I shall offer the thesis that these modes are primarily matters of 'inner' elaboration of events. *Ibid.* 29 The prototaxic mode, which seems to be the rough basis of memory, is the crudest..the earliest, and possibly the most abundant mode of experience. **1969** A. NEEL *Theories of Psychol.* xx. 247 The first state he [*sc.* Sullivan] called the prototaxic. **1972** L. SALTZMAN in Freedman & Kaplan *Interpreting Personality* vi. 176 (*heading*) Prototaxic mode of experience. **1975** J. C. GOWAN *Trance, Art & Creativity* ii. 24 The prototaxic mode is notable for the scary, hair-raising aspect of the numinous.

proto-Thames to **-theme**: see PROTO- 1, 2 a, b.

‖**prototheria** (prəʊtəʊˈθɪərɪə), *sb. pl. Zool.* [mod.L. (Gill, 1872), f. Gr. πρωτο-, PROTO- + θηρία beasts.] The lowest subclass of Mammals (correlative with *Eutheria* and *Metatheria*), comprising the single order *Monotremata*, with their hypothetical ancestors. Sometimes confined to the latter, as the primitive mammalian type. Hence **prototheré** (ˈprəʊtəʊθɪə(r)), a member of the *Prototheria*; **prototherian** (prəʊtəʊˈθɪərɪən), *a.* belonging to the *Prototheria*; *sb.* = *protothere*.

1880 HUXLEY in *Proc. Zool. Soc.* 653 It will be convenient to have a distinct name, *Prototheria*, for the group which includes these, at present, hypothetical embodiments of that lowest stage of the mammalian type, of which the existing Monotremes are the only known representatives. **1881** —— in *Nature* XXIII. 229/1 There is no known Monotreme which is not vastly more different from the Prototherian type. **1885** W. K. PARKER *Mammalian Desc.* ii. 48 *note*, A thoroughly clear idea of what a primary mammal, an original, ancient 'Protothere' must have been like. **1903** *Q. Rev.* Jan. 65 The astrapothere and prototheres died out without descendants.

protothetic (-ˈθɛtɪk). *Logic.* [ad. G. *protothetik* (S. Leśniewski 1929, in *Fundamenta Math.* XIV. 4), f. Gr. πρωτο- PROTO- + θετικός fit for placing, positive, f. θετός, ppl. adj. of τιθέναι to set, place.] A type of propositional calculus on the basis of which Leśniewski developed his system of logic (see quots. 1945, 1955). Also **protoˈthetics** *sb. pl.* in the same sense.

1940 *Jrnl. Symbolic Logic* V. 83 Protothetic involves not only propositional variables..but also truth-function variables. **1945** Z. JORDAN in *Polish Sci. & Learning* VI. 24/2 Lesniewski's system consists of three parts. The first of them, called Protothetic, corresponds to what is known as the 'calculus of equivalent statements'..or the 'theory of deduction', together with that of the apparent variable. It makes use of one axiom and of one logical constant only. **1946** [see MEREOLOGY]. **1955** A. N. PRIOR *Formal Logic* III. iii. 293 The basis of Leśniewski's logic is the 'protothetic', i.e. propositional calculus enriched with functional variables and quantifiers,..and on this he builds two further disciplines called 'ontology' and 'mereology'. **1963** O. WOJTASIEWICZ tr. *Łukasiewicz's Elem. Math. Logic* iv. 92 The sentential calculus can be extended by the introduction of variable functors and what are called *quantifiers*. One such system, containing the sentential calculus, is S. Leśniewski's *protothetics*. **1974** *Jrnl. Philos. Logic* III. 231 The extended propositional calculus which serves as a basis for this theory is not full protothetic.

prototoxin to **prototroch**: see PROTO-.

prototroph (ˈprəʊtəʊtrəʊf, -trɒf). *Genetics.* [f. as next.] A strain (usu. of bacteria or fungi) which can grow on the simplest medium necessary for the growth of its species, without supplementary nutrients.

1946 RYAN & LEDERBERG in *Proc. Nat. Acad. Sci.* XXXII. 172 We propose to designate as a prototroph any strain which has the nutritional requirements of the 'wild type' from which it was derived irrespective of how it became prototrophic. **1952** *Genetics* XXXVII. 720 The occurrence of prototrophs, thus selected, from platings of thoroughly investigated auxotroph parents has been taken as *prima facie* evidence of crossing. **1958** *Heredity* XII. 269 Bursts of white, prototrophic cells frequently arise from colonies of certain strains of red, adenine-requiring yeasts. The occurrence of prototrophs appears to result from back-mutation at the locus for adenine requirement. **1975** J. B. JENKINS *Genetics* viii. 311 Prototrophs are cells that can grow on minimal medium.

Hence ˈ**prototrophy**, the state of being a prototroph.

1952 *Genetics* XXXVII. 720 The methionineless stock is, fortunately, so stable that back mutations to prototrophy are undetectable under the conditions of crossing experiments. **1974** *Nature* 8 Feb. 387/1 *E. coli* strain H/r 30 R requiring arginine was used for measurement of mutation to prototrophy. **1975** *Ibid.* 26 June 736/2 It was impossible to grow the population for long periods without reversion to prototrophy.

prototrophic (-ˈtrəʊfɪk, -ˈtrɒfɪk), *a.* [f. Gr. πρωτο- (see PROTO-) + τροφ-ή nourishment + -IC.] **1.** *Bot.* [ad. G. *prototroph* (A. Fischer *Vorlesungen über Bakterien* (1897) v. 47).] = *autotrophic* adj. s.v. AUTO-[1].

1900 A. C. JONES tr. *Fischer's Struct. Bacteria* v. 48 A better classification would be to divide the bacteria, according to their mode of life, into three biological groups, prototrophic, metatrophic, and paratrophic. *Ibid.*, Prototrophic species are those which either require no organic compounds at all for their nutrition (nitrifying bacterium), or which, given the smallest quantity of organic carbon, can derive all their nitrogen from the atmosphere (bacteria of root-nodules). With them may be classed..sulphur and iron bacteria. **1923** F. O. BOWER *Bot. Living Plant* (ed. 2) xxviii. 430 On the basis of nutrition Bacteria have been classified into three groups: (i) Prototrophic, those which require no organic compounds at all for their nutrition. These are represented by the nitrifying Bacteria which live in open nature, in the soil, and are never parasitic. (ii) Metatrophic... (iii) Paratrophic. **1940** *Nature* 26 Oct. 541/2 If virus was the first form of life, it ought to be possible to find prototrophic viruses which feed on inorganic materials.

2. *Genetics.* Being a prototroph.

1946 [see PROTOTROPH]. **1952** *Genetics* XXXVII. 721 Prototrophic stereomycin-sensitive (S^s) stocks were crossed to S^r (streptomycin-resistant) auxotrophs by plating the parents on minimal-streptomycin agar. **1958** [see PROTOTROPH]. **1978** *Nature* 29 June 753/2 When complementary auxotrophs of opposite mating type are conjugated and plated on minimal medium (MM), several types of prototrophic colonies grow up.

Hence **protoˈtrophically** *adv.*

1978 *Nature* 20 Apr. 731/1 These cells..now grow prototrophically at a reduced rate identical to that of the spermidine-deficient cells.

prototropy (prəʊˈtɒtrəpɪ, ˈprəʊtəʊtrɒpɪ). *Chem.* [f. PROTO(N + Gr. τροπή turn, turning.] Tautomerism in which the forms differ only in the position of a proton; migration of a proton from one part of a molecule to another.

1923 T. M. LOWRY in *Jrnl. Chem. Soc.* CXXIII. 828 Prototropy, or the reversible change of protomers, which differ from one another in the position of a proton or hydrogen nucleus. **1953** C. K. INGOLD *Structure & Mechanism in Org. Chem.* v. 219 Proton migration is considered always to depend on proton-transfer processes..and is of such outstanding importance, that it is usually designated by the special name prototropy. **1964** N. G. CLARK *Mod. Org. Chem.* xv. 296 The behaviour of ethyl acetoacetate is another example of the phenomenon of tautomerism, in particular of prototropy.

Hence **protoˈtropic** *a.*, of, pertaining to, or exhibiting prototropy.

1925 *Jrnl. Chem. Soc.* CXXVII. 1382 Prototropic changes, which involve only the migration of a proton, are catalysed both by acids and by alkalis, like the hydrolysis of an ester. **1947** *Nature* 11 Jan. 68/1 Dislocation of α-hydrogen in glutamic acid can be interpreted as due to reversible condensation of the amino-group with the carbonyl in the prosthetic component of aminopherase to form a prototropic system. **1953** C. K. INGOLD *Structure & Mechanism in Org. Chem.* x. 579 When 2-hydroxypyridine, or α-pyridone, as it is usually named after its prototropic tautomer, is alkylated..the formed quaternary ammonium ion passes into its anhydro-base, the N- alkyl-α-pyridone. **1976** *Nature* 6 May 15/1 Ganellin showed that dynamic structure-activity relationships are capable of analysing quite complex situations, such as relative ionic populations in a prototropic equilibrium mixture.

prototypal (ˈprəʊtəʊtaɪpəl), *a.* [f. next + -AL[1].] Of the nature of, or constituting, a prototype; of or pertaining to a prototype; archetypal.

a **1693** *Urquhart's Rabelais* III. xxxviii. 319 Prototypal and precedenting fool. **1716** M. DAVIES *Athen. Brit.* III. *Arianism* 4 The prototypal Schemes and original Ideas of that Præ-Arian primitive Anti-Christianity. **1888** DAWSON *Geol. Hist. Plants* ii. 24 Survivors of that prototypal flora. **1893** *Cornh. Mag.* Sept. 262 The mole..is the prototypal navvy.

prototype (ˈprəʊtətaɪp). Also 7 **-tipe.** [a. F. *prototype* (Rabelais, 16th c.) f. mod.L. PROTOTYPON, q.v.]

1. a. The first or primary type of anything; the original (thing or person) of which another is a copy, imitation, representation, or derivative, or to which it conforms or is required to conform; a pattern, model, standard, exemplar, archetype.

1603 DANIEL *Panegyric to King* xxiii, There great Exemplare Prototipe of Kings, We finde the good shal dwel within thy Court. **1649** BP. GUTHRIE *Mem.* (1702) 10 The framing of the Petition having been committed to him, he had yet the Prototype by him. **1762–71** H. WALPOLE *Vertue's Anecd. Paint.* (1786) I. 90 He and..Charles Brandon were the prototypes of those illustrious heroes, with which Mademoiselle Scuderi has enriched the world of chivalry. **1845** DARWIN *Voy. Nat.* iv. (1879) 200 The Apteryx..as well as its gigantic extinct prototype the Deinornis, possess only rudimentary representatives of wings. **1869** TOZER *Highl. Turkey* II. 284 For the prototype of this tale we must look to the story of 'Brynhildr and Sigurd'.

b. *spec.* That of which a model is a copy on a reduced scale.

1920 *Flight* 8 Jan. 57/2 Anyone can make a model resembling a full-size prototype that won't fly; this is not a scientific model. **1924** H. GREENLY *Model Railways* i. 6 *Tonnage coefficient* is the scale equivalent of the weight of a train or loco. in tons actual of the particular prototype. **1942** *Model Railway News* Jan. 24/2 Were the Americans to enter the British market (i.e. the market based on British prototypes) the story would..be different. **1955** E. A. STEEL *Model Mech. Engin.* i. 1 The working model must be an engineering job. A model locomotive is built to the scale of 1½ in. to the foot or one-eighth the size of a prototype of similar design. **1967** C. J. FREEZER *Model Railway Terminol.* No. 18. 2/2 On the prototype the gauge is always expressed in feet and inches, or metric measurements. In the model it can be similarly expressed, but..it is customary to use numbers or letters to describe the gauges. **1975** *Railway Modeller* Jan. 18/1 An hour or two beside a main line..can provide one with quite a collection of short trains suitable for modelling. A study of prototype railway magazines is another prolific source.

2. *Electr.* A basic filter network (usu. having series and shunt reactances in inverse proportion) with specified cut-off frequencies, from which other networks may be derived to obtain sharper cut-offs, constancy of characteristic impedance with frequency, etc. Freq. *attrib.*

1923 *Bell Syst. Technical Jrnl.* II. 28 Mid-series and mid-shunt sections derived from prototypes other than the 'constant-*k*' wave-filter..are other possible units. **1932** W. L. EVERITT *Communication Engin.* vii. 170 The fundamental data required for a filter are the pass band or, in the case of a low-pass filter, the cut-off frequency, and the impedance into which it is to work. From these data the prototype is computed. **1962** *Newnes Conc. Encycl. Electr. Engin.* 298/2, *m*-Derived Sections. These are 'derived' from the prototype sections above... The result is to introduce resonance into the shunt arm and/or antiresonance into the series arm,..so that the attenuation rises much more steeply. **1977** M. H. KLAYTON *Fund. Electr. Technol.* xviii. 578 This band-pass filter is another form of the constant-*k* prototype circuit. The same elements can be rearranged to form a constant-*k* prototype band-suppression filter, sometimes called a wave trap.

3. The first full-size working version of a new vehicle, machine, etc., or a preliminary one made in small numbers so that its performance and methods of mass-production can be evaluated. Freq. *attrib.*

1932 *Flight* 26 Feb. 170/1 The A.B. 20 was actually begun as a three-engined machine, like its prototype the D.B. 70. **1935** C. G. BURGE *Compl. Bk. Aviation* 261/1 The first experimental machine of a new type is usually made by a special department in the factory... This first or 'prototype' machine is, to a large extent, hand-made. **1939** *Flight* 28 Dec. 530*a*/1 Of these one or two, such as the Ha 138 flying boat, may have been put into production, but in the main the machines are 'prototype only'. **1948** J. S. MURPHY *Production Engin.* ii. 20 The previous model forms an ideal basis for the prototype, and experimental work can be carried out under practical conditions. **1948** 'N. SHUTE' *No Highway* i. 16 That was the prototype Reindeer, the one we had here for the trials. **1955** *Times* 10 Aug. 8/4 The American figures assumed the large-scale development 15 to 20 years hence of types of reactor now at the prototype stage. **1964** *Jrnl. Geophysical Res.* LXIX. 2399/1 The development of a prototype lunar transponder.. demonstrates the feasibility of designing future transponders for hard landings on the moon. **1970** P. H. HILL *Sci. Engin. Design* iii. 47 When entering the experimental stage of the design process.. one should first deal with the mock-up, then the model, and finally the prototype after the mock-up and model have proven the real worth of the design. **1978** *Daily Tel.* 7 Apr. 2/5 Three camels from Longleat Wildlife Park.. were driven 80 miles to Reading.. where the prototype of the camel-milking machine.. had been set up.

ˌprototyˈpembryo. *Biol. rare.* [f. as prec. + EMBRYO. (Hyatt.).] Term for a later stage of the embryo, at which it exhibits the essential characters of the group to which it belongs. Hence **ˌprototypembryˈonic** *a.*

1890 in *Cent. Dict.*

prototypic (prəʊtəʊˈtɪpɪk), *a.* [f. PROTOTYPE + -IC, after Gr. τυπικ-ός; = mod.F. *prototypique.*] = next.

a **1878** SIR G. G. SCOTT *Lect. Archit.* (1879) II. 66 Deviation from the design of St. Stephen's which was at once rectified by adding them to the prototypic building. **1926** *Physiol. Rev.* VI. 322 The author.. advanced the view that the blood plasma of Vertebrates and Invertebrates with a closed circulatory system is.. but a reproduction of the sea water of the remote geological period in which the prototypic representatives of such animal forms first made their appearance. **1963** A. FARRER in Mascall & Box *Blessed Virgin Mary* 28 A change which is prototypic of our own adoption, and the breaking of our bondage. **1965** LD. NORTHBOURNE tr. *Schuon's Light on Anc. Worlds* iv. 76 Semi-divine beings, the prototypic and normative personages whom earthly man has to imitate in all things. **1974** H. ASHLEY *Engin. Anal. of Flight Vehicles* i. 7 During the first decade of powered flight, 1903–1913, configuration was going through rapid, somewhat haphazard evolution. There were therefore many deviations from the prototypic arrangement outlined in Section 1.2, e.g., the Wright Flyers.. employed anti-symmetric warping of the wing structure for roll control.

prototypical (prəʊtəʊˈtɪpɪkəl), *a.* [f. as prec.: see -ICAL.] Of the nature of or serving as a prototype; prototypal.

1650 T. VAUGHAN *Anthroposophia* 45 The Symbollicall exteriour Descent from the Prototypicall planets to the created spheres. **1871** H. MACMILLAN *True Vine* iii. 99 The leaf is the basis of the whole—the essential, and prototypical plant. **1890** E. JOHNSON *Rise of Christendom* 58 The prototypical myth of Romulus slaying Remus. **1964** GOULD & KOLB *Dict. Social Sci.* 257/1 Fads, unlike fashions, may occur even in simple societies which have merely prototypical class systems. **1967** D. COOPER *Psychiatry & Anti-Psychiatry* i. 19 In the popular mind the schizophrenic is the prototypical madman. **1978** J. SACKS in P. Moore *Man, Woman, & Priesthood* iii. 30 The claim of Korah was the prototypical denunciation of chosenness in the name of equality. **1979** *Amer. Speech 1978* LIII. 281 The prototypical instances of interruption are perhaps those in which the interrupting material is semantically connected to what is interrupted.

Hence **ˌprotoˈtypically** *adv.*

1890 E. JOHNSON *Rise of Christendom* 379 A dramatic scene in which Christ prototypically performs the act [washing of feet]. **1957** H. READ *Tenth Muse* xxx. 281 An attempt to find in architecture a new universal art.. represented proto-typically by Greek architecture and later by Byzantine architecture.

prototyping (ˈprəʊtəʊtaɪpɪŋ), *vbl. sb.* [f. PROTOTYPE + -ING[1].] The design, construction, or use of a prototype. Freq. *attrib.*

1951 *Chem. Age* LXV. 833/1 Prototyping of machines, instruments, and of chemicals is an essential step in this development. *Ibid.* 833/2 Prototyping may also prove of value in the estimation of costs. **1965** *Economist* 13 Nov. 738/1 Means for using the accumulated facts are to be developed through such techniques as experimentation, prototyping, intervention and micromodelling. **1976** HILBURN & JULICH *Microcomputers/Microprocessors* i. 4 Most microprocessor manufacturers have development systems, sometimes called prototyping systems, available for the designer. **1977** *Sci. Amer.* Sept. 99/2 (Advt.), There's room for eight plug-in options such as a prototyping board for experimenting with interfaces to other equipment.

proto-typographer to **-xylem**: see PROTO- 1, 2 b.

‖**proˈtotypon.** *Obs.* Pl. proˈtotypa, -ons. [mod.L., a. Gr. πρωτότυπον prototype, prop. neut. sing. of πρωτότυπ-ος adj. (in med.L. *prōtotypus*) in the first form, original, primitive: see PROTO- and TYPE *sb.*] = PROTOTYPE 1.

1596 *Foxe's A. & M.* (ed. 5) 299/2 The copie of the said letter followeth agreeing with the prototypon or originall. **1611** W. SCLATER *Key* (1629) 110 Whether their worship had the terme in the images without reference to the prototypa, the things which their images represented. **1625** JACKSON *Creed* v. xxxii. §1 These for the most part delight in pictures for their prototypons sake. **1715** M. DAVIES *Athen. Brit.* I. 290 Saxon Prototypons of the Lord's Prayer, according to the different gradual Changes of that Idiom.

prototyrant to **protovum**: see PROTO-.

protoxide (prəʊˈtɒksaɪd). *Chem.* [PROT-, PROTO- 3 a.] That compound of oxygen with another element or radical which contains the smallest proportion of oxygen, as ***protoxide of hydrogen***, H_2O = water.

Now commonly otherwise named, as ***potassium protoxide***, K_2O = potassium oxide (or monoxide); ***protoxide of iron***, FeO = ferrous oxide.

1804 T. THOMSON [see PEROXIDE]. **1804** HATCHETT in *Phil. Trans.* XCIV. 323. **1812** SIR H. DAVY [see PEROXIDE]. **1836–41** BRANDE *Chem.* (ed. 5) 609 Potassium.. forms two definite compounds with oxygen, which we may call the *protoxide* and *peroxide*. **1847** *Turner's Elem. Chem.* (ed. 8) 190 Water (protoxide of hydrogen). **1865–8** WATTS *Dict. Chem.* III. 808 Manganese forms four oxides of definite composition, viz. (1) Protoxide or Manganous oxide MnO. .. (4) Dioxide or Peroxide MnO_2. The protoxide is a strong base, forming with acids a class of very stable salts. **1880** CLEMINSHAW *Wurtz' Atom. Th.* 61 The composition of protoxides.

Hence †**proˈtoxidate**, †**proˈtoxidize** *vbs. trans.*, to convert into a protoxide. *rare*$^{-0}$.

1828–32 WEBSTER, *Protoxydize*, to oxydize in the first degree. **1858** MAYNE *Expos. Lex.*, *Protoxydatus*, that which is converted into the state of a protoxide, as *Ferrum protoxydatum*: protoxidated.

protoxoid [PRO-[2]]: see TOXOID.

protoxylem, -zeugma: see PROTO- 2 b, 1.

‖**Protozoa** (prəʊtəʊˈzəʊə), *sb. pl. Zool.* [mod.L. (Goldfuss, 1818 in *Isis*, June), f. Gr. πρωτο-, PROTO- + ζῷα animals.] One of the two (or three) great divisions of the animal kingdom, comprising animals of the simplest or most primitive type, each consisting of a single cell, usually of microscopic size: correlated with METAZOA (and MESOZOA). Also in sing. **protozoon** (-ˈzəʊɒn), a member of the division *Protozoa*, a unicellular animal.

Under his *Protozoa* (= *Urthiere*) Goldfuss included also such higher forms of life as sponges, hydroids, corals, crinoids, *Rotifera*. Von Siebold, *Anatomie d. wirbillosen Thiere*, 1845, restricted it to the *Infusoria* and *Rhizopoda*, excluding the sponges, etc., which are now recognized as *Metazoa*.

a **1834** COLERIDGE *Aids Refl.* xv. (1839) 64 The lowest class of animals or *protozoa*.. have neither brain nor nerves. **1853** DUNGLISON *Med. Lex.*, *Protozoon*. **1855** H. SPENCER *Princ. Psychol.* III. v. 377 Those lowest organisms classed as protophyta and protozoa. **1859** J. R. GREENE *Man. Anim. Kingd.* I. *Protozoa* i. 1 The sub-kingdom *Protozoa* includes a number of animal beings of simple organisation, many of which have, until recently, been associated with the lower members of the vegetable kingdom. **1869** *Spectator* 24 July 877 The analogy between the development of the species from the original protozoon and of the individual from the germ is quite Spencer's own. **1901** G. N. CALKINS *Protozoa* 28 *note*, The name 'Protozoa' given by Goldfuss, meant the same as Oken's 'Urthiere'. It did not acquire its present significance until 1845, when von Siebold gave it a new meaning.

protozoal (prəʊtəʊˈzəʊəl), *a.* [f. prec. + -AL[1].] Of, pertaining to, or connected with protozoa; in *Path.* caused, as a disease, by a parasitic protozoon.

1890 *Lancet* 8 Feb. 308/2 Bütschli's classification of these protozoal forms. **1898** P. MANSON *Trop. Diseases* Introd. 13 In 'fly disease', the protozoal organism which is the direct cause of the disease is carried from one animal to another on the mandibles of the tsetse fly. **1904** *Brit. Med. Jrnl.* 17 Sept. 643 Malaria and other protozoal diseases.

protozoan (prəʊtəʊˈzəʊən), *a.* and *sb.* [f. as prec. + -AN.] **A.** *adj.* Of or belonging to the *Protozoa* or a protozoon; also = prec. **B.** *sb.* An animal of the division *Protozoa*; a protozoon.

1864 DANA in WEBSTER s.v., The protozoans.. include the rhizopods, sponges, and many of the so-called animalcules. **1888** ROLLESTON & JACKSON *Anim. Life* 822 Conjugation.. is generally if not universally connected with reproductive activity in some Protozoan classes. **1901** *Westm. Gaz.* 30 Mar. 6/2 His contention is that the organism of cancer is undoubtedly a protozoan. **1904** *Brit. Med. Jrnl.* 17 Sept. 656 As to the nature of this new protozoan disease.

protoˈzoary. *rare*$^{-0}$. [ad. mod.F. *protozoaire*, f. PROTO- + Gr. ζωάριον, dim. of ζῷον animal.] A Protozoon.

1890 in *Cent. Dict.*

protozoic (prəʊtəʊˈzəʊɪk), *a.* [In sense 1, f. Gr. πρωτο-, PROTO- + ζωή life + -IC; in sense 2, f. PROTOZO-A + -IC.]

1. *Geol.* and *Palæont.* Applied to those strata which contain the earliest remains or traces of living beings; also to fossils found in such strata.

1838 SEDGWICK in *Proc. Geol. Soc.* II. 684 Class 1. Primary stratified Groups... Should organic remains appear unequivocally in any parts of this class, they may be described as the *Protozoic System*. **1841** J. PHILLIPS *Palæoz. Foss. Dev. & Cornw.* 160 Mr. Murchison [after Sedgwick] called the part of the series to which his attention was most directed 'Protozoic', for which Professor Sedgwick [subsequently] proposed to substitute Palæozoic. **1854** MURCHISON *Siluria* i. (1867) 2 To develope the succession of deposits that belong to such protozoic zones. **1859** PAGE *Handbk. Geol. Terms*, *Protozoic*... Applied to the earlier fossiliferous epoch and strata; equivalent to Primordial.

2. *Zool.* and *Path.* = PROTOZOAN *a.*

1864 WEBSTER, *Protozoic*, of, or pertaining to, the protozoa. **1877** HUXLEY *Anat. Inv. Anim.* i. 47 A similar process takes place in sundry Protozoa and gives rise to a protozoic aggregate, which is strictly comparable to the Morula. **1896** *Allbutt's Syst. Med.* I. 211 Appearances characteristic of a protozoic life history. **1906** *Q. Rev.* Apr. 522 The protozoic origin of malaria.

protozonite: see PROTO- 2 b.

protozoology (ˌprəʊtəʊzəʊˈɒlədʒɪ). [f. PROTOZO-A + -(O)LOGY.] That department of zoology, or of pathology, which deals with protozoa, esp. with parasitic disease-producing protozoa.

1904 *19th Cent.* Dec. 901 To establish.. two new chairs, one for medical protozoology and one for medical helminthology. **1906** *Q. Rev.* Apr. 522 The establishment, by the aid of the Quick bequest, of a chair of protozoology. **1974** *Nature* 3 May 89/3 In former times protozoology was considered to be a suitable subject by which students could be introduced to biology.

Hence **ˌprotozooˈlogical** *a.*, of or pertaining to protozoology; **protozoˈologist**, an expert or specialist in protozoology.

1906 *Nature* 29 Nov. 117/2 When the protozoologist has worked out his life-histories and obtained his results, then the medical man steps in and carries off the honey to the medical hive. **1922** *Daily Mail* 17 Nov. 1 (Advt.), Botanical, zoological and protozoological work. **1944** L. E. H. WHITBY *Med. Bacteriol.* (ed. 4) vii. 90 The most commonly used preparations in protozoological work are Leishman's stain and Siemsa's stain. **1956** *New Biol.* XXI. 88 Probably more is known of *E. histolytica* than of any other amoeba, and what is revealed is not only of practical importance to medical science but is of the greatest interest to protozoologists. **1971** *Daily Tel.* 18 June 25 (Advt.), A Protozoologist.. is required to join a team responsible for the maintenance and supply of free living protozoa and to assist in the research programme of the Centre. **1972** *Nature* 3 Mar. 44/2 Most of his 500 publications deal with protozoological problems.

protoˈzoon, sing. of PROTOZOA.

protoˈzoum (*rare*$^{-0}$), latinized f. PROTOZOON.

1858 in MAYNE *Expos. Lex.*; and in later Dicts.

‖**protracheata** (prəʊtrækɪˈeɪtə), *sb. pl. Zool.* [mod.L., f. PRO-[2] + *Trachēāta*: so called as representing the supposed ancestral form of all the tracheate *Arthropoda* (i.e. insects, myriapods, and most arachnids).] A class of arthropodous animals, represented by the single genus *Peripatus* (PERIPATUS[2]). Hence **proˈtracheate**, *a.* belonging to the *Protracheata*; *sb.* an animal of this class.

1878 BELL *Gegenbaur's Comp. Anat.* 255 In the Protracheata the nervous system remains in a lower condition. **1879** *Athenæum* 19 July 83/1 One of his hypothetical animals, a protracheate, may be said to have been actually discovered.. in the primitive air-breathing Arthropod Peripatus.

protract (prəʊˈtrækt), *sb.* [ad. L. *prōtractus* a prolonging, protraction, f. *prōtract-*, ppl. stem of *prōtrah-ĕre*: see next.]

†**1.** Prolongation or extension (of time); hence, delay, procrastination. *Obs.*

1536 *St. Papers Hen. VIII*, II. 298 The doing therof will aske a protracte of tyme. *a* **1640** SIR J. OGLE in *Sir F. Vere's Comm.* (1657) 143 By protract of time, and casualties of war, he found his numbers wasted. **1646** *Unhappy Game at Scotch & Eng.* 4 The difference would only be in the protract of time, not in the nature of the thing.

†**2.** A delineation, drawing. Cf. PORTRAIT. *Obs. rare.*

1585 T. WASHINGTON tr. *Nicholay's Voy.* II. xix. 53 b, I made the draughtes and protractes heere represented vnto you [orig. *ie fey les pourtraicts icy representez*].

3. [f. the vb.] A 'protracted meeting': see PROTRACTED 1, quot. 1860. *U.S. colloq.*

1908 *Mission Field* Jan. 343 There is always a great religious awakening at the annual revival or 'protract'... When the 'protract' is over their emotions are calmed and every man returns to his own 'vine and fig tree'.

protract (prəʊˈtrækt), *v.* Also 7 -traicte. [f. L. *prōtract-*, ppl. stem of *prōtrah-ĕre* to draw forth, to prolong, extend, defer, f. *prō*, PRO-[1] 1 + *trah-ĕre* to draw. With sense 6 cf. PORTRAY, the direct repr. of *prōtrahĕre* through OF. *portraire.*]

I. †**1.** *trans.* To extend or prolong (time) so as to cause delay; to waste (time). *Obs.*

a **1548** HALL *Chron., Edw. IV* 240 b, All these faire wordes wer onely delaies to protracte tyme. *a* **1660** *Contemp. Hist. Irel.* (Ir. Archæol. Soc.) II. 84 His father would protraicte time the best he could. **1769** ROBERTSON *Chas. V*, II. Wks. 1813 V. 296 This they did merely to protract time.

2. To lengthen out (an action); to cause to continue or last longer; to extend in duration; to prolong. (The chief current sense.)

1563 [see PROTRACTING *vbl. sb.* 1]. **1591** SHAKS. *1 Hen. VI*, I. ii. 120 Else ne're could he so long protract his speech. **1614** SYLVESTER *Bethulia's Rescue* II. 439 But, with thy Dayes thy Dolours to protrack, Thou shalt from hence unto Bethulia pack. **1700** DRYDEN *Sigism. & Guiscardo* 334 But I.. Protracting life have liv'd a day too long. **1838** THIRLWALL *Greece* V. xxxix. 101 Their stay was protracted for some weeks. **1855** MOTLEY *Dutch Rep.* v. iii. (1866) 699 The dance upon the sward was protracted to a late hour.

†**3.** To put off, defer, postpone (an action). *Obs.*

(The date of the first quotation is very doubtful.)

[**1477** NORTON *Ord. Alch.* Introd. in Ashm. (1652) 3 Sin protracts the gifts of Heaven.] **1553** *Act 7 Edw. VI*, c. 1 §16 If any Auditor.. willingly protract or delay the taking of the same Accompt. *a* **1648** LD. HERBERT *Hen. VIII* (1683) 369 If the Interview.. must needs follow (which yet he wished were protracted). **1776** GIBBON *Decl. & F.* v. (1869) I. 97 He attempted, however, to prevent, or at least to protract, his ruin. **1808** ELEANOR SLEATH *Bristol Heiress* IV. 219 Lord L——s' marriage, which had been protracted.. was celebrated in Grosvenor-square.

†**b.** To put off, defer (a person). *Obs. rare.*

1737 WHISTON *Josephus, Antiq.* XI. iv. §4 Desire.. to delay and protract the Jews in their zeal.

†**4.** *intr.* To make delay, to delay. *Obs.*

1611 BIBLE *Neh.* ix. 30 Yet many yeres diddest thou forbeare [*marg.* protract ouer] them. **1677** *Govt. Venice* 293 They had not lost the Battle of Vaila, had they.. protracted but ten days.

II. 5. *trans.* To extend in space or position.

a **1658** J. DURHAM *Exp. Rev.* vi. (1680) 31 Concerning Christs Body on earth, or ubiquitie of his humanitie, or bodily presence with his churches, or for protracting of his Body. **1749** SMOLLETT *Regicide* v. vii, To save his country, and protract his blaze Of glory, farther still! *a* **1850** WORDSW. (Ogilvie), Many a ramble, far And wide protracted, through the tamer ground Of these our unimaginative days.

†**b.** To extend or amplify the signification of anything; to 'stretch'. *Obs. rare.*

1698 FRYER *Acc. E. India & P.* 363 If any thing happen to oppose common Sense, they protract the meaning [of the prophecy] Mysteriously or Anagogically.

III. 6. To draw, represent by a drawing [so med.L. *prōtrahĕre*]; *spec.* to draw to scale; to delineate by means of a scale and protractor (lines, angles, a figure); to plot out.

1563 SHUTE *Archit.* B ij b, An Architecte must.. haue experte knowladg in drawing and protracting the thinge, which he hath conceyued. **1607** [see PROTRACTION 5]. **1669** STURMY *Mariner's Mag.* v. 6 After you have taken the Angles.. You must Protract or lay down the Figure. **1766** *Compl. Farmer* s.v. *Surveying*, How to measure a close, or parcel of land, and to protract it, and give up the content. **1881** E. HULL in *Nature* 22 Dec. 177/2 If we protract to a true scale the outlines of certain tracts of the British Isles.

protracted (prəʊˈtræktɪd), *ppl. a.* [f. prec. + -ED¹.]

1. Lengthened, extended, prolonged; **a.** in time; *spec.* in ***protracted meeting***.

1746–7 HERVEY *Medit.* (1767) I. 62 (*Tombs*) The divine Redeemer expired in tedious and protracted Torments. **1832** *Patriot & Farmer's Monitor* (Kingston, Ontario) 10 Apr. 2/6 It is now required of the Episcopal Methodist preachers, to make the public acquainted with their motives for establishing Protracted Meetings. **1855** HALIBURTON *Nat. & Hum. Nat.* i. I. 2 It's a gentleman that calculates to hold a protracted meeten here to night. **1860** BARTLETT *Dict. Amer.*, *Protracted Meeting*, a name given in New England to a religious meeting, protracted or continued for several days. **1864** BRYCE *Holy Rom. Emp.* xix. (1875) 354 The miseries of a protracted war. **1925** W. J. BRYAN *Mem.* 17 A protracted meeting held in a Christian Church. **1948** *Chicago Tribune* 21 Nov. VII. 1/7 Loafers' Glory.. acquired that name years ago when a protracted meeting was held in the little log schoolhouse.

b. in space.

1784 COWPER *Task* I. 257 Their shaded walks And long protracted bowers.

2. Drawn out; = PROLATE *a.* 1.

1816 tr. *Lacroix's Diff. & Int. Calculus* 662 The protracted or contracted cycloid.

†**3.** Delayed, tardy. *Obs.*

1838 tr. *Strauss' Early Life Lutheran Clergym.* ii. 12 A cart laden with the protracted produce of the fields.

4. Drawn to scale; plotted out; see prec. 6.

1696 *Col. Rec. Pennsylv.* I. 498 The Courses and protracted figure thereof. **1808** PIKE *Sources Mississ.* II. App. 51 Lieutenant Wilkinson has copied and carries with him a very elegant protracted sketch of the route.

Hence **proˈtractedly** *adv.*, in a protracted or long-continued way; **proˈtractedness**, long continuance or extent.

1847 WEBSTER, *Protractedly.* **1862** F. HALL *Hindu Philos. Syst.* 29 Pursuing it with due heed, continuously, and protractedly. **1893** F. ADAMS *New Egypt* 122 When.. he told me that he himself.. had received an order.. I whistled protractedly, and decided offhand on going up to Cairo. **1888** TALMAGE *Serm.* in *N. Y. Witness* 29 Feb., In regard to what is the protractedness and immensity of influence of one good woman in the church and world.

protracter, obs. variant of PROTRACTOR.

(The only form in BAILEY (originally), and in JOHNSON; also a variant in later Dicts.)

proˈtractible, *a.* [f. as PROTRACT *v.* + -IBLE.] Capable of being protracted or lengthened out.

1830 *Westm. Rev.* Oct. 434 In the infinitely protractible part with which, under his plan,.. jury trial is preceded.

protractile (prəʊˈtræktɪl, -aɪl), *a. Zool.* [f. as prec. + -ILE: cf. *contractile.*] Capable of being lengthened out or extended.

1828 STARK *Elem. Nat. Hist.* I. 135 Echidna... Toothless, but the palate aculeated;.. tongue protractile. **1861** HULME tr. *Moquin-Tandon* II. v. 268 A special organ.. sometimes internal and protractile. **1878** BELL *Gegenbaur's Comp. Anat.* 298 A narrow coiled continuation of this leads to the protractile ovipositor.

Hence **protracˈtility**, the quality or fact of being protractile.

1849–52 *Todd's Cycl. Anat.* IV. 1146/2 The Chameleon presents us with the most complete protractility of the organ [the tongue].

protracting (prəʊˈtræktɪŋ), *vbl. sb.* [f. PROTRACT *v.* + -ING¹.] The action of PROTRACT *v.*

1. Lengthening out, prolonging, extending (of time, or of action in time); †dilatory action (*obs.*).

a **1548** HALL *Chron.*, *Hen. VI* 89 b, The duke of Bedford ..not content with their whisperynges and protractyng of tyme. **1563** GOLDING *Cæsar* I. (1565) 31 b, The Galles were now weary with long protracting of the war. **1601** FULBECKE *1st Pt. Parall.* (1602) 75 The tedious and odious protracting of suits. **1622** CALLIS *Stat. Sewers* (1647) 114 If any danger be likely to ensue by the protracting of time.

†**b.** The putting off or postponement of an action; deferring. *Obs.*

1581 SAVILE *Tacitus, Hist.* III. xx. (1591) 125 More oftentimes profiteth and helpeth hee by protracting, then venturing rashly. **1608** *Mem.* in *Buccleuch MSS.* (Hist. MSS. Comm.) 76 The protracting of a plantation until the Ward come to years.

2. Extending in space. *rare.*

a **1658** [see PROTRACT *v.* 5].

3. Drawing or plotting out to scale; delineation.

1669 STAYNRED *Fortification* Title-p., The Scale, for speedy Protracting of any Fort. **1766** *Compl. Farmer* s.v. *Surveying*, These squares and long squares need no protracting; for you need only to multiply the chains and links of the length, by the chains and links of the breadth.

4. *attrib.* and *Comb.*, denoting instruments used in protracting (sense 3), as ***protracting-bevel, -needle, -pin***; **protracting quadrant**, a protractor.

1669 STURMY *Mariner's Mag.* IV. xi. 178 To know the Rhomb between any two Places.. by a Protracting Quadrant. **1701** MOXON *Math. Instr.* 16 *Protracting Pin*, a taper piece of brass with a Point of Silver, to draw black Lines on Mathematical Paper, and a small Head.. which holds a fine Needle to prick off any Degree and part from the Protractor. **1766** *Compl. Farmer* s.v. *Surveying*, Having drawn lines with the point of the compasses, or a protracting-needle, the intersections represent the angles. **1875** KNIGHT *Dict. Mech.*, *Protracting-bevel*, a plotting-instrument having a protracting sector and a prolongation of one radius, which forms a rule.

protracting (prəʊˈtræktɪŋ), *ppl. a.* [f. as prec. + -ING².] That protracts, delays, or defers; delaying, time-consuming.

1600 R. CHURCH *Fumée's Hist. Hungary* 29 He might rather molest them by a protracting fight. **1822** 'B. CORNWALL' *Dram. Scenes, Jul. the Apostate* i, Never! A dull, protracting, melancholy word That in an alien language, talks despair.

protraction (prəʊˈtrækʃən). [a. F. *protraction* (1499 in Godef.), or ad. late L. *prōtractiōn-em*, n. of action from *prōtrah-ĕre*: see PROTRACT *v.*] The action of protracting.

I. 1. The lengthening out or extension of time or of the duration of anything; drawing out, prolongation; †delay, postponement (*obs.*).

1535 *Act 27 Hen. VIII*, c. 4 §1 Without longe tarienge and protraction of time. **1608** D. T[UVIL] *Ess. Pol. & Mor.* 112 By reason of his protractions and delayes. **1610** HEALEY *Vives' Comm. St. Aug. Citie of God* (1620) 10 That Fabius that.. by his cunning protraction blunted the fury of Hannibal. *a* **1677** HALE *Prim. Orig. Man.* 92 As to the fabulous protractions of the age of the World by the Egyptians or others, they are uncertain idle Traditions. **1734** tr. *Rollin's Anc. Hist.* IV. VIII. xiii. 83 Such are his usual protraction, delays, distrusts and fearful precaution. **1868** E. EDWARDS *Ralegh* I. xxi. 473 The long protraction of the suit must have been occasioned by difficulties.

2. Drawing forth or out.

1681 tr. *Willis' Rem. Med. Wks.* Vocab., *Protraction*, a drawing forth at length. **1895** *Syd. Soc. Lex.*, *Protraction*, extraction; as of a foreign body from a wound.

3. A stretching out or extension; the action of a protractor (muscle).

1890 in *Cent. Dict.* **1899** *Allbutt's Syst. Med.* VII. 285 In this area one may distinguish, more or less completely, protraction and retraction of the upper arm.

4. The lengthening of a vowel, syllable, or word; = PROLONGATION 3.

a **1849** POE *Fancy & Imag.* Wks. 1865 III. 381 He also too frequently draws out the word Heaven into two syllables —a protraction which it never will support.

II. 5. The drawing to scale or laying down of the figure of any surface, esp. of a piece of land.

1607 NORDEN *Surv. Dial.* III. 128 The difference is onely in the protraction: for where the one protracteth the worke, by the degrees, found by the fall of the wandring Index: so the other protracteth from the degree, whereupon the needle falleth. **1669** J. FLAMSTEAD in *Phil. Trans.* IV. 1109 The protraction of the Star's way in this appearance will be facile. **1774** M. MACKENZIE *Maritime Surv.* 66 Protract carefully, with a large Protractor, the several Angles written in the Field-book; and also calculate trigonometrically the most material Distances: judge of the Accuracy of the Protraction by its Agreement with the Calculation. **1823** SCORESBY *Jrnl. Whale Fish.* 268 The distances by protraction, and the estimated distances of five or six headlands,.. generally coincided to within 1½ miles. **1866** LIVINGSTONE *Last Jrnls.* (1873) I. x. 270 By protraction Rua Point was distant 33 miles.

b. That which is protracted; a chart or plan drawn or laid down to scale; a survey.

1669 STURMY *Mariner's Mag.* II. viii. 73 Any Chart or Protraction whatsoever. **1810** G. CHALMERS *Caledonia* II. 62 Employing five years in drawing their protractions of the country.. on a vast scale of 3000 feet to an inch.

†**proˈtractive**, *a. Obs.* [f. L. *prōtract-* (see PROTRACT *v.*) + -IVE.] Characterized by or tending to protraction; lengthening out, delaying.

1606 SHAKS. *Tr. & Cr.* I. iii. 20 Our workes,.. nought else But the protractiue trials of great Ioue. **1687** DRYDEN *Hind & P.* III. 1103 He saw, but suffer'd their Protractive Arts. **1796** *Mod. Gulliver's Trav.* 149 By this protractive work, fresh mischief grows. **1819** H. BUSK *Vestriad* IV. 675 Protractive alleys the trim grove deform.

protractor (prəʊˈtræktə(r)). Also 7–8 -er. [a. med.L. *prōtractor*, agent-n. f. *prōtrah-ĕre* to PROTRACT.] One who or that which protracts.

1. One who lengthens out or prolongs time or any action; †one who puts off, delays, or postpones action (*obs.*).

1611 COTGR., *Delayeur*, a delayer, deferrer, protractor, prolonger, lingerer, wiredrawer... *Prolongeur*, a prolonger, protracter, wyre-drawer, delayer. **1661** BLOUNT *Glossogr.* (ed. 2), *Protractor* (Lat.), a prolonger or drawer out. **1697** BURGHOPE *Disc. Relig. Assemb.* 144 The protractors and delayers of due preparation. **1727** BAILEY (vol. II.), *Protracter*, one who protracts. **1737** BOLINGBROKE *Stud. & Use Hist.* viii. (1777) 277, I know not what part the protractors of the war.. intended to take. **1755** JOHNSON, *Protracter*, one who draws out any thing to tedious length.

2. An instrument, generally having the form of a graduated semicircle, used in setting off and measuring angles.

1658 PHILLIPS, *Protractor*, a certain Mathematical instrument made of brasse, consisting of the Scale and Semicircle, used in the surveying of Land. **1669** PEPYS *Diary* 4 Feb., This parallelogram is not, as Mr. Sheres would, the other day, have persuaded me, the same as a Protractor. **1712** J. JAMES tr. *Le Blond's Gardening* 92 Measure the Angle marked upon the Plan with the Protractor. **1727** BAILEY and **1755** JOHNSON, *Protracter.* **1889** *Anthony's Photogr. Bull.* II. 421 The application of an ordinary horn protractor will at once show the angle included in every instance.

3. A surgical instrument: see quots.

1727–41 CHAMBERS *Cycl.*, *Protractor*, an instrument used in surgery, to draw out any foreign or disagreeable bodies from a wound or ulcer; in like manner as the forceps. **1731** BAILEY, *Protracter.* **1736** *Ibid.* (folio), *Protracter, Protractor.* **1895** *Syd. Soc. Lex.*, *Protractor*, an instrument for extracting foreign bodies from wounds.

4. *Anat.* A muscle which serves to protract or extend a limb or member. Also ***protractor muscle***.

1861 HULME tr. *Moquin-Tandon* II. v. ii. 276 Four muscles, two of which are protractors, and two retractors. **1870** ROLLESTON *Anim. Life* Introd. 96 One pair of protractor muscles may be present. **1871** HUXLEY *Anat. Vertebr. Anim.* 49 The *psoas minor*.. is a protractor of the pelvis.

5. (See quot.)

1875 KNIGHT *Dict. Mech.*, *Protractor*,.. an adjustable tailor's pattern, expansible to agree in its proportions with the particular measurements and capable of being secured in the obtained adjustment.

†**proˈtracture.** *Obs.* Also *erron.* 6–7 -our, -or. [f. as PROTRACT *v.* + -URE: cf. *portraiture.*]

1. Representation by a figure; drawing.

1551 RECORDE *Pathw. Knowl.* I. Defin., Without perspectiue knowledge, it is not easy to iudge truly the formes of them in flatte protracture. **1557** —— *Whetst.* G iv, I will.. set forth a brief explication of their names, with the protracture of the figures. **1613** M. RIDLEY *Magn. Bodies* 51 Having the formes and protractors of creeping things.. drawne in past-boord. **1634** W. WOOD *New Eng. Prosp.* II. xx. (1865) 107 They make curious baskets with intermixed colours and protractures of antique Imagerie.

2. Figure, shape, form, outline.

1551 RECORDE *Pathw. Knowl.* II. lv, Circles are regulare formes, that is to say, such formes as haue in their protracture a iuste and certaine proportion. **1581** DERRICKE *View Irel.* II. E iij b, His skirtes be verie shorte.. And Irishe trouzes more to put their straunge protractours out. **1607** TOPSELL *Four-f. Beasts* (1658) 411 It is her fashion and protracture to lie thus when she [the hamster] is angry.

protraicte, obs. form of PROTRACT *v.*

protreptic (prəʊˈtrɛptɪk), *a.* and *sb.* [as adj. ad. Gr. προτρεπτικ-ός fitted to urge on, hortative, instructive, f. πρό, PRO-² + τρέπ-ειν to turn, direct the course of; as sb. ad. late L. *protrepticon* (*-um*) = Gr. προτρεπτικόν, neuter of the adj.]

A. *adj.* Directive, instructive, didactic.

1658 PHILLIPS, *Protreptick*, doctrinal, or giving instructions. **1850** MAURICE *Mor. & Met. Philos.* (1854) I. 47 The discipline of the habit or character he [Clement] would call protreptic.

B. *sb.* A book, writing, or speech intended to exhort or instruct; an exhortation, instruction.

1656 BLOUNT *Glossogr.*, *Protreptick*, a book of instruction, a doctrinal. **1678** CUDWORTH *Intell. Syst.* 125 To rank Anaximander amongst the Divine Philosophers, as he [Clement] doth in his Protreptick to the Greeks. *Ibid.* 371 That this Pythagorick Prayer was directed to the Supreme Numen and King of Gods, Jamblichus thus declares in his Protrepticks. **1899** A. B. COOK in *Classical Rev.* Nov. 418/1 In the mind of Ischomachus' wife the bear-dance.. bulked larger than the protreptics of her husband.

So **pro'treptical** *a.*, of protreptic nature.
1667–8 BP. WARD *Serm. Infidelity* (1670) 3 The means used..are partly Didactical, and partly Protreptical. **1895** R. G. MOULTON *Proverbs* p. x, Early proverbs are philosophical, not protreptical.

protriæne ('prəʊtraɪˌiːn). *Zool.* [f. PRO-[2] + TRIÆNE.] In sponges, a triæne whose three prongs or cladi project forwards from the shaft.
1887 SOLLAS in *Encycl. Brit.* XXII. 417/1 (*Sponges*) The arms make different angles with the shaft: when recurved a grapnel or *anatriæne* is produced, when projecting forwards a *protriæne*, and when extended at right angles an *orthotriæne*.

protribune: see PRO-[1] 4.

protrichocyst: see PRO-[2] 1.

protriptyline (prəʊ'trɪptɪliːn). *Pharm.* Also (*erron.*) protryptiline, protryptyline. [f. PRO(PYL + TRI- + *he*)*ptyl* (s.v. HEPTANE) + -INE[5].] A tricyclic antidepressant, 5-(3-methylamino-propyl)dibenzo[*a*, *e*] cycloheptatriene, $C_{19}H_{21}N$, given as the hydrochloride, a white bitter-tasting powder.
1963 *Amer. Jrnl. Psychiatry* CXX. 594/1 In an attempt to evaluate a derivative of amitriptyline, MK-240 (protriptyline), where the 'sleepiness' was removed by a change in the chemical formula, the drug was studied in 61 patients with various types of depression. **1965** *Psychosomatics* VI. 346/1 Protriptyline is at least five times as active as amitriptyline against depressive reactions. **1966** *Canad. Med. Assoc. Jrnl.* XCIV. 1220/1 Protryptiline gave chemical results that compared favourably with those of antidepressants of established value. **1978** *Nature* 23 Mar. 330/1 The tricyclic anti-depressant drugs which are tertiary amines..were more potent inhibitors than those which are secondary amines (desmethylimipramine, nortriptyline, protriptyline).

†**pro'trite,** *a. Obs.* [ad. L. *prōtrīt-us* worn away, in late L. trite, vulgar, pa. pple. of *prōter-ĕre* to tread under foot: see PRO-[1] and TRITE *a.*] Worn out, trite, threadbare, hackneyed.
1604 T. WRIGHT *Passions* I. iii. 12 The fourth [Passion] most protrite and manifeste unto the world, is their Inconstancie. *Ibid.* v. 214 What else meane those protrite words of the Psalme. **1659** GAUDEN *Tears Ch.* II. xv. 195 They are but old and rotten errours, protrite and putid opinions of the ancient Gnosticks.

protrudable (prəʊ'truːdəb(ə)l), *a.* [f. next + -ABLE.] Capable of being protruded, protrusible.
1881 DARWIN *Veg. Mould* (1882) 17 This part corresponds..with the protrudable trunk or proboscis of other annelids.

protrude (prəʊ'truːd), *v.* [ad. L. *prōtrūd-ĕre* to thrust or push forward or forth, f. *prō*, PRO-[1] 1 a + *trūd-ĕre* to thrust.]
†**1.** *trans.* To thrust forward (some detached body); to push or drive onward. *Obs.*
1620 VENNER *Via Recta* vii. 112 They protrude and driue downe the meates from the stomacke, before they be digested. *a* **1704** LOCKE (J.), When the stomach has performed its office upon the food, it protrudes it into the guts. **1769** E. BANCROFT *Guiana* 284 The arrow is by a single blast of air from the lungs, protruded through the cavity of the reed. **1822–34** *Good's Study Med.* (ed. 4) IV. 121 A series of spasmodic contractions..gradually increase in strength ..and protrude the child into the world.
fig. **1654** H. L'ESTRANGE *Chas. I* (1655) 169 Nothing is more familiar than for several Factions..to protrude and drive on one and the same design.
†**b.** *intr.* To shoot out. *Obs.*
1626 BACON *Sylva* §328 If the spirits be not merely detained, but protrude a little, and that motion be confused and inordinate, there followeth putrefaction.
2. *trans.* To push or thrust into any position; to thrust forth or stick out (an organ or part) into a projecting position; to cause to project; to extend.
1646 SIR T. BROWNE *Pseud. Ep.* III. xx. 156 If beholding a candle we protrude either upward or downeward the pupill of one eye, the object will appeare double. **1664** POWER *Exp. Philos.* I. 36 Those black filaments or optick nerves, which are sheathed in her [the snail's] horns which she can retract or protrude. **1730–46** THOMSON *Autumn* 1311 When young Spring protrudes the bursting gems. **1828** G. W. BRIDGES *Ann. Jamaica* II. xv. 236 The linen jacket which he wore was protruded by a broken rib. **1841–71** T. R. JONES *Anim. Kingd.* (ed. 4) 131 From each tube a polyp is protruded, of a brilliant grass-green colour.
†**b.** *transf.* To bring to the surface, as a rash.
a **1776** R. JAMES *Diss. Fevers* (1778) 17 Let the physician but remove the fever, and..no miliary eruptions will be protruded.
c. *fig.* To obtrude, put forth obtrusively.
1840 THACKERAY *Pict. Rhapsody* Wks. 1900 XIII. 321 Critics, who..protrude their nonsense upon the town. **1841** CATLIN *N. Amer. Ind.* II. lviii. 255, I would protrude my opinion to the world.
3. *intr.* To stick out; to project or jut out beyond the surrounding parts.
a **1626** BACON (Webster 1828–32), The parts protrude beyond the skin. **1771** [see PROTRUDING below]. **1802** *Med. Jrnl.* VIII. 219 If the other hand should protrude, it may be encountered by a similar expedient. **1860** TYNDALL *Glac.* I. xxii. 155 The rocks which protrude from the snow at the base of the last spur of the mountain. **1868** FARRAR *Seekers* I. vi. (1875) 75 A common soldier had spied a pair of feet protruding from under the curtains.
Hence **pro'truded, pro'truding** *ppl. adjs.*
1771 LUCKOMBE *Hist. Print.* 241 The *P* is kerned, that its propensity may cover the back of the protruding angle of *A.* **1810** SOUTHEY *Kehama* II. xi, The protruded brow. **1841–71** T. R. JONES *Anim. Kingd.* (ed. 4) 7 The protruded filaments are able to coalesce. **1904** W. M. RAMSAY *Lett. to Seven Ch.* xxvii. 394 A coiled serpent with raised head and protruding tongue.

protrudent (prəʊ'truːdɪnt), *a.* [ad. L. *prōtrūdent-em*, pres. pple. of *prōtrūd-ĕre* to PROTRUDE.] Protruding, projecting, protuberant, prominent.
1891 LD. HOUGHTON *Bookworm* in *Stray Verses* 9 Earnest underlip protrudent. **1893** *Scribner's Mag.* Aug. 180/2 The lofty, protrudent corner made by the dropping of the high-road into the curious transverse valley.

protrusible (prəʊ'truːsɪb(ə)l), *a.* [f. L. *prōtrūs-*, ppl. stem of *prōtrūd-ĕre*: see prec. and -IBLE.] Capable of being protruded or thrust out.
1836–9 *Todd's Cycl. Anat.* II. 400/1 A sharp horny dart.. readily protrusible through the aperture. **1870** ROLLESTON *Anim. Life* Introd. 58 The tongue may be..protrusible, as in other Reptiles.

protrusile (prəʊ'truːsɪl, -aɪl), *a.* [f. as prec. + -ILE, after L. type **prōtrūsilis.*] Adapted to be extended or thrust out, as a limb, tentacle, etc.
1847 in WEBSTER citing GARDNER. **1849** JOHNSTON in *Proc. Berw. Nat. Club* II. No. 7. 366 Mandibles large and protrusile. **1867** J. HOGG *Microsc.* II. iii. 574 The mouth is furnished with a protrusile proboscis.

protrusion (prəʊ'truːʒən). [a. F. *protrusion*, ad. L. type **prōtrūsiōn-em*, n. of action f. *prōtrūd-ĕre* to PROTRUDE.]
1. The action of protruding (in various senses of the vb.); the fact or condition of being protruded. †**a.** Thrusting forward or onward. *Obs.*
1646 SIR T. BROWNE *Pseud. Ep.* VII. xviii. 381 He was.. not to bee removed by the force or protrusion of three men. **1660** BOYLE *New Exp. Phys. Mech.* I. 21 You will finde the Sucker forcibly carryed up to the top of the Cylinder, by the protrusion of the external Air. **1727** BRADLEY *Fam. Dict.* s.v. *Cantharides*, Such Motions as are necessary for the Protrusion forwards or Ejectment of the Water.
b. The action of thrusting or pushing out an attached part; the condition of being protruded.
1646 SIR T. BROWNE *Pseud. Ep.* III. xvii. 148 That the distinctive parts of sexes are onely different in position, that is inversion or protrusion. **1783** POTT *Chirurg. Wks.* II. 13 The falling down or protrusion of some part. **1833** LYELL *Princ. Geol.* III. 340 The notion of deluges accompanying the protrusion of mountain-chains. **1880** C. & F. DARWIN *Movem. Pl.* 62 Shortly before the protrusion of the leaves.
c. The fact of projecting or jutting out.
1853 KANE *Grinnell Exp.* viii. (1856) 56 The protrusion of these abutting faces into the waters of the sound.
2. *concr.* That which protrudes or juts out; a protruded part, a protuberance, a prominence.
1704 SWIFT *T. Tub* xi. Wks. 1760 I. 123 [They] looked upon all extraordinary dilatations of that member as protrusions of zeal, or spiritual excrescencies. **1805** *Med. Jrnl.* XIV. 19 Between this ridge and the protrusion above-mentioned. **1862** S. LUCAS *Secularia* 96 The fantastic gables, pinnacles, and protrusions, which intercepted the light. **1884** BOWER & SCOTT *De Bary's Phaner.* 66 They.. are covered by a protrusion of the epidermis.

protrusive (prəʊ'truːsɪv), *a.* [f. L. *prōtrūs-*, ppl. stem of *prōtrūd-ĕre* to PROTRUDE + -IVE.]
1. Having the power or tendency to thrust forward or onward; propulsive.
1676 H. MORE *Remarks* 172 Though it add nothing to the elasticity of the Air, seeing it has a pressure and protrusive force in it. **1718** J. CHAMBERLAYNE *Relig. Philos.* (1730) I. iv. §13 The Protrusive Motion of the Bowels. **1822–34** *Good's Study Med.* (ed. 4) IV. 144 The protrusive force of the surrounding muscles.
2. Characterized by thrusting oneself forward; obtrusive.
1840 CARLYLE *Heroes* iii. (1858) 267 A true English heart breathes, calm and strong, through the whole business; not boisterous, protrusive. **1893** *Chicago Advance* 16 Nov., His protrusive, unrestrained, ill-regulated idiosyncracies.
3. Protruding, projecting, protuberant.
1858 CARLYLE *Fredk. Gt.* III. iv. (1872) I. 156 The 'Austrian lip'—protrusive underjaw, with heavy lip disinclined to shut. **1876** GEO. ELIOT *Dan. Der.* vii, The chin protrusive, and the cervical vertebræ a trifle more curved.
Hence **pro'trusively** *adv.*, **pro'trusiveness.**
1831 CARLYLE *Sart. Res.* I. x, To him thou, with sniffing charity, wilt protrusively proffer thy hand-lamp. **1890** *Cent. Dict.*, Protrusiveness. **1975** H. THOMSON *Occlusion* ix. 156 The whole procedure is repeated for the outgoing movements beginning at intercuspal position and moving laterally on each side and then protrusively.

protrypsin: see PRO-[2] 1.

prottore, -our, obs. ff. *prouder*, comp. of PROUD.

protuberance (prəʊ'tjuːbərəns). [f. PROTUBERANT: see -ANCE. So F. *protubérance* (1738 in Hatz.-Darm.).]
1. The fact or condition of being protuberant; bulging out or projecting in a rounded form.
1681 tr. *Willis' Rem. Med. Wks.* Vocab., *Protuberance*, a bunching forth above the rest. **1756–82** J. WARTON *Ess. Pope* (ed. 4) I. vii. 361 The firmness and protuberance of the Muscles in each limb. **1836** *Random Recoll. Ho. Lords* xiv. 342 His eyes have a sunken appearance, owing to the protuberance of his eye-brows. **1874** *Imperial Gazetteer* s.v. *Australia*, The whole figure..very well proportioned, but frequently marred by the protuberance of the abdomen.
2. a. That which is protuberant; a rounded prominence, projection, or swelling; a knob, a bump.
1646 SIR T. BROWNE *Pseud. Ep.* III. xix. 154 A cartilagineous substance without any spondyles, processes, or protuberance whatsoever. **1658** —— *Gard. Cyrus* iii. 47 The Rhomboidal protuberances in Pineapples maintaining this Quincuncial order unto each other. **1794** S. WILLIAMS *Vermont* 82 Under the throat there is a fleshy protuberance. **1859** W. S. COLEMAN *Woodlands* (1866) 106 On the leaf of the Poplar..large reddish-coloured protuberances.
b. *solar protuberance* = solar PROMINENCE (2 b).
1869 *Jrnl. Franklin Inst.* LVII. 317 The first protuberance which I observed, is represented by Fig. 1. Above an intensely luminous peak-shaped mass, rising from the border of the sun, is spread a cloud-like formation. **1874** tr. *Lommel's Light* 167 The so-called protuberances afforded an instant and crucial test of the truth of Kirchhoff's hypothesis. **1907** *Daily News* 25 Dec. 4 Janssen was in the Malay Peninsula making his observations of the solar 'protuberances', otherwise masses of blazing hydrogen.

pro'tuberanceless, *a.* [f. PROTUBERANCE + -LESS.] Without a protuberance; flat, regular.
1954 W. FAULKNER *Fable* 353 The entire earth one unbroken machined de-mountained dis-rivered expanse of concrete paving protuberanceless by tree or bush or house.

pro'tuberancy. [f. as PROTUBERANCE + -ANCY.]
1. Protuberant condition; bulging out; = PROTUBERANCE 1.
1654 GAYTON *Pleas. Notes* IV. xxii. 276 When..a protuberancy of the lip should be the certeine signe of the true heir to the Crowne. **1692** RAY *Disc.* I. iii. (1693) 34 The protuberancy of the dry Land above the common Superficies of the Ocean. **1718** J. CHAMBERLAYNE *Relig. Philos.* (1730) II. xx. §23 The Earth..is not perfectly globular, but has a greater Protuberancy under the Equator. **1822–34** *Good's Study Med.* (ed. 4) III. 185 The other [cause of squinting arises] from an oblique position and greater protuberancy of the cornea.
†**2.** A rounded projection; = PROTUBERANCE 2 a. *Obs.*
1653 H. MORE *Antid. Ath.* II. x. (1712) 72 Why has he four Knees,..as also a Protuberancy under his Breast to lean on? **1760** MILLES in *Phil. Trans.* LI. 537 Small protuberancies sometimes appear, like the knots of trees.

protuberant (prəʊ'tjuːbərənt), *a.* [ad. late L. *prōtūberānt-em*, pres. pple. of *prōtūber-āre* to swell or bulge out, f. L. *prō*, PRO-[1] + *tūber* a hump, swelling. So F. *protubérant* (16th c. in Littré).]
1. Bulging or swelling out beyond the surrounding surface; prominent.
1646 SIR T. BROWNE *Pseud. Ep.* III. iv. 113 These.. follicles are found in both sexes, though somewhat more protuberant in the male. **1661** GLANVILL *Scepsis Sci.* xxvi. (1665) 162 One mans eyes are more protuberant, and swelling out. **1747** HERVEY *Medit.* II. 122 Mountains vastly uneven and protuberant. **1807** G. CHALMERS *Caledonia* I. II. vi. 292 Eocha III..is remembered for his protuberant nose. **1869** PHILLIPS *Vesuv.* iv. 130 The protuberant northern base of the dome of Vesuvius.
b. *fig.* That forces itself upon notice, prominent.
1822 GALT *Provost* xxxiii, The effect of this, however, was less protuberant in our town than in many others. **1895** R. BURTON in *Forum* (N.Y.) Apr. 251 A foil to the protuberant ugliness of the theory.
†**2.** Moulded or done in the round; figured in relief, or rising above the surface. *Obs.*
1676 TOWERSON *Decalogue* 109 God..forbade all images whatsoever, particularly all protuberant ones. **1696** BP. PATRICK *Comm. Exod.* xx. 4 The former was a protuberant Image, or a Statue made of Wood, Stone, &c. *Ibid.* xxviii. (1697) 538 Abarbinel saith the Letters were protuberant as they are upon Coins, or upon Wax.
Hence **pro'tuberantly** *adv.*, in a protuberant, bulging, or prominent manner.
1836 LANDOR *Peric. & Asp.* cliii. Wks. 1846 II. 417/1 They serve as graven images, protuberantly eminent and gorgeously uncouth.

protuberantial (prəʊtjuːbə'rænʃəl), *a.* [f. L. type **prōtūberānti-a* PROTUBERANCE + -AL[1]. So F. *protubérantiel.*] Of the nature of, or belonging to (the solar) protuberances.
1880 *Nature* XXI. 436/2 The mixture of protuberantial vapours in the sun. **1882** *Ibid.* XXVII. 111/1 The spectrum is that of protuberantial gases and of matter still unknown.

protuberate (prəʊ'tjuːbəreɪt), *v. rare.* [f. late L. *prōtūberāt-*, ppl. stem of *prōtūberāre*: see PROTUBERANT.] *intr.* To bulge out; to form a rounded prominence.
1578 BANISTER *Hist. Man* I. 26 The inner region..hath cauities..which on the outer side agayne do protuberate and giue forth. **1650** BULWER *Anthropomet.* 11 Hippocrates.. writes, That the head sometimes doth more remarkably protuberate at the eares, then either forward or backward. **1721** BRADLEY *Philos. Acc. Wks. Nat.* 126 We see the.. Fore-legs half out, and the other just beginning to protuberate through the skin. **1822–34** *Good's Study Med.*

(ed. 4) II. 483 Mesenteric enlargement..felt in the form of knots protuberating in the abdomen.

b. *trans.* To cause to bulge out or project. *rare.*

1884 A. A. WATTS *Life A. Watts* I. 302 The manly breast protuberated by waistcoats fashioned like a doublet.

Hence **pro'tuberated** *ppl. a.*, swollen or bulged out; **pro'tuberating** *vbl. sb.*, a swelling; **pro'tuberating** *ppl. a.*, bulging out.

1683 A. SNAPE *Anat. Horse* v. xii. (1686) 221 The fourth Bone..is smooth, not being hollow nor *protuberated as the rest are. **1755** NEDHAM in *Phil. Trans.* XLIX. 239 The circumference of which was full, and protuberated. **1667** *Phil. Trans.* II. 564 Suffering grievous *Protuberatings of the bones in his Arms. **1615** CROOKE *Body of Man* 977 These Rack-bones haue in the middle *protuberating, round and embowed bodies. **1776** WITHERING *Brit. Plants* (1796) I. 285 In others, the nectary is blunt, scarcely protuberating.

†**protube'ration.** *Obs.* [n. of action f. late L. *prōtūberāre* to PROTUBERATE.] A swollen or bulged part, a protuberance.

1615 CROOKE *Body of Man* 903 The sixt Nerue..neare the inner protuberation of the arme distributeth many surcles.. into the skinne of the cubit. **1670** H. STUBBE *Plus Ultra* 125 A..Souldier..having grievous protuberations of the bones in his armes. *c* **1720** W. GIBSON *Farrier's Guide* I. vi. (1738) 97 The foremost of which receives the Protuberation of the Stifle bone.

†**pro'tubered,** *ppl. a. Obs. rare*$^{-1}$. [f. late L. *prōtūber-āre* (see PROTUBERANT) + -ED[1].] Swollen or bulged out.

1578 BANISTER *Hist. Man* I. 21 The cauities wherin the protubered heads of the ribbes are setled.

†**pro'tuberous,** *a. Obs. rare*$^{-1}$. [f. stem *protuber-* of PROTUBERANT, etc. + -OUS, after *tuberous*.] = PROTUBERANT. So **protube'rosity,** = PROTUBERANCE; a rounded bulge or boss. *rare.*

1666 J. SMITH *Old Age* (1676) 183 The one being protuberous, rough, crusty, and hard; the other, round, smooth, spongy, and soft. **1859** R. F. BURTON *Centr. Afr.* in *Jrnl. Geog. Soc.* XXIX. 314 The forehead converges to a central protuberosity, where phrenologists locate eventuality.

pro'turb, *v. humorous nonce-wd.* [ad. L. *prōturb-āre* to drive forth in confusion, f. *prō*, PRO-[1] 1 a + *turbāre* to confuse: cf. *perturb, disturb*.] *trans.* To drive forth or chase out.

1845 STANLEY in *Life* I. x. 342 Some undergraduates.. saw Ward rush out from the Theatre—'proturbed', as they imagined by the Bedell.

protureter: see PROTO- 2 b.

pro-tutor (prəʊ'tjuːtə(r)). *Sc. Law.* [f. PRO-[1] + TUTOR *sb.* Cf. med.L. *prōtūtor*, F. *protuteur* (1762 in *Dict. Acad.*).] One who acts as 'tutor' or guardian to one in the state of pupillarity, though not legally appointed as such. So **pro-'tutory,** the charge of a pro-tutor.

1665 *Acts of Sederunt* 10 June (1790) 93 Whatsoever person or persons shall..intromett with the means and estate of any minor, and shall act in his affairs as pro-tutors, haveing no right of tutory or curatory established in their persons, they shall be lyable. **1681** [see PRO-CURATOR[2]]. *a* **1722** FOUNTAINHALL *Decis.* (1759) I. 10 Kilrie had medled with the charter-chest..which the Lords did not find sufficient to make him protutor. **1773** ERSKINE *Inst. Law Scot.* I. vii. §28 Pro-tutors..may be sued by the minor in an action for accounting, even during the pro-tutory, though proper tutors or curators are not bound to account till their office determine. **1838** in W. BELL *Dict. Law Scot.*

‖**protyle** ('prəʊtaɪl). Also **prothyle, -yl.** [irreg. f. Gr. πρωτ(ο-, PROT(O- first, primary, primitive + ὕλη 'timber, material', in philosophical lang. 'matter'; see HYLE, and cf. πρώτη ὕλη first matter or substance (Aristotle *Metaph.*).

If a combination of the two words had been made in Greek, it would have been *πρωθύλη, in Latin form *prōthylē*. Moreover, in Eng., ὕλη as second element usually becomes *-yl*, as in *methyl, ethyl, carbonyl*, etc.; thus the regular form would be *prothyl*.]

A name proposed for the hypothetical original undifferentiated matter, of which the chemical substances provisionally regarded as elements may be composed.

1886 W. CROOKES *Address* in *Rep. Brit. Assoc.* 568 Let us picture the very beginnings of time... Before even the sun himself had consolidated from the original protyle. [*Note*] We require a word analogous to protoplasm to express the idea of the original primal matter existing before the evolution of the chemical elements. The word I have ventured to use for the purpose is compounded of πρό (earlier than) and ὕλη (the stuff of which things are made). **1891** [F. C. S. SCHILLER] *Riddles of Sphinx* 189 Prothyle, the undifferentiated basis of chemical evolution. **1903** *Daily Chron.* 24 Apr. 5/1 That hypothetical substance—the 'prothyl'—of which the entire material universe, suns, planets, comets, and nebulæ, is made. **1905** *Academy* 4 Feb. 108/1 At present theory seems to suggest that this ether, originally 'invented' to account for the phenomena of light, and called the 'luminiferous ether', is really the *prima materia* of the ancients, the *Urstoff* of the Germans, the *protyle* of Sir William Crookes.

‖**protypon** ('prɒtɪpɒn). *Anc. Arch.* Pl. **-a.** [a. Gr. πρότυπον, f. as next.] (See quots.)

1601 HOLLAND *Pliny* II. 552 To set up Gargils or Antiques at the top of a Gavill end, as a finiall to the crest tiles, which in the beginning he called *Protypa.* [*margin*] Moulds or patternes. **1857** BIRCH *Anc. Pottery* (1858) I. 167 These early reliefs, called *protypa*, or bas reliefs, and *ectypa*, or high-reliefs, were also used for decorating houses and halls.

‖**protypus** ('prɒtɪpəs). *Obs.* Also in anglicized form '**protype.** [f. Gr. πρό, PRO-[2] + τύπος TYPE.] (See quot. 1656.)

1656 BLOUNT *Glossogr.*, *Protype*.., that is made for an example or copy; an image or form whereof moulds are made, in which things of mettal or earth are cast. **1662** EVELYN *Chalcogr.* (1769) 16 The *protypus* was of wax for efformation.

prou, obs. f. PROW *sb.*[1] and [2]; var. PROW *v. Obs.*

proud (praʊd), *a.* (*sb.*, *adv.*) Forms: see below. [Late OE. *prūt, prūd* = ON. *prúð-r* brave, gallant, magnificent, stately (whence Icel. *pruður*, MSw. *prudh*, MDa. *prud*); both prob. a. OF. *prūd, prōd*, nom. *prūz, prōz* (= **prūt-s*, **prōt-s*) valiant, doughty, gallant (11th c. in Godef.), in mod.F. *preux* = Prov. *proz, pro*, Cat. *prou*, It. *prode* valiant, Rhæto-Rom. *prus* pious:—late L. **prōd-is* profitable, advantageous, useful (*prōde* neut. in Itala *a* 200); app. either the source of, or taken from, the first element of L. *prōd-esse* to be of value, be good. See also PREUX, PROW *a.*, and cf. PRIDE.]

A. Illustration of Forms.

α. 1–5 **prút,** 5 **prute,** 3–5 **prout, -e,** 5–6 **prowte.** *Compar.* 4 **prottore, -our,** 5 **prutter, -yr.**

a **1050** *Liber Scintill.* xlvi. (1889) 152 Pryte heaȝe utawyrpð & wiþerwyrdnyss prute [*sublimes*] ȝenyþerude. *a* **1225** *Ancr. R.* 276 Eaðe meiht tu beon prut! *c* **1290** *S. Eng. Leg.* I. 225/197 Oure maister was so prout, Lucefer, for his fairhede, þat he ful sone out. **1297** R. GLOUC. (Rolls) 9539 King stefne was þe boldore & þe prottore [*v.r.* prottour] uor þis cas. *c* **1440** *Eng. Conq. Irel.* 57 Ne for no good chaunce, he was not the Pruttyr [*v.r.* prutter]. *Ibid.* 145 Spare the meke, and wreke Ham on the Prowte. *c* **1440** *Gesta Rom.* lxv. 280 (Harl. MS.) And when he was this i-hyed, he wex prout. **1553** *Respublica* (Brandl) v. vii. 17 Zo thieke prowte howrecop.

β. 1–4 **prúd,** 4–6 **prude,** (4–5 **prode**), 4–6 **proude,** 4–7 **prowd(e,** 4– **proud.** *Compar.* 3 **pruder, prudder,** 5 **prodder.** *Superl.* 3 **prudest,** 4 **pruddest, proddest,** 5 **pruddist.**

c **1000** in Napier *O.E. Gloss.* 226/233 *Arrogantes*, modiȝ: *vel* prud. *c* **1175** *Lamb. Hom.* 57 Prud ne wreiere ne beo þu noht. *a* **1225** *Ancr. R.* 296 He is þinge prudest, and him is scheome loðest. *c* **1330** R. BRUNNE *Chron.* (1810) 289 þe proude kyng Pharaon, þat chaced Israel. *c* **1350** *Will. Palerne* 2942 þe proddest of hem alle. **13..** *E.E. Allit. P.* B. 1300 þe pruddest of þe province. *Ibid.* 1772 þe prowde prynce of Perce. **13..** *Cursor M.* 2415 (Cott.) Fra þaa prude folk had hir sen. *Ibid.* 27571 Oft bitides þat man es Bicummen prode for halines. *a* **1400–50** *Alexander* 4375 þe playne purperyn see full of prode fischis. *c* **1400** *Destr. Troy* 2743 The pruddist of payone, prise men of honde. *a* **1450** MYRC 1129 Hast þou.. þe prodder þe mad, For any ofyce þat þow hast had? **1535** COVERDALE *Job* xxxv. 12 Because of the wickednesse off proude tyrauntes.

B. Signification.

Senses 6 and 7 come nearest to the OF. and ON. The unfavourable sense, so early in Eng., may be due to the aspect in which a Norman *prud barun* or *prode chevalier* presented himself to the English peasant or townsman. (Cf. the two senses of L. *superbus*.)

I. 1. a. Having or cherishing a high or lofty opinion of oneself; valuing oneself highly on account of one's position, rank, attainments, possessions, etc.; Usually in a bad sense: Disposed to take an attitude of superiority to and contempt for others; arrogant, haughty, overweening, supercilious.

a **1050** *Liber Scintill.* xvii. (1889) 85 Sawl prutes byð forlaeten. *c* **1175** *Lamb. Hom.* 5 Ne beo þu þereuore prud ne wilde. *Ibid.* 43 Prud heo wes swiðe and modi. *c* **1290** *Beket* 980 in *S. Eng. Leg.* I. 134 [He] is prouȝt and conteckor. **1362** LANGL. *P. Pl.* A. III. 172 Ne to depraue þi persone with a proud herte. **1484** CAXTON *Fables of Æsop* IV. xx, None ought to be prowd ageynst his lord, but ought to humble hym self toward hym. **1526** *Pilgr. Perf.* (W. de W. 1531) 18 Some be as proude as Nabugodonosor. **1560** DAUS tr. *Sleidane's Comm.* 119 They are as bragge and as proude as pecockes. **1613** SIR E. HOBY *Countersnarle* 54 Hee was a proud insolent Delegate. **1711** SWIFT *Jrnl. to Stella* 20 Nov., Lord Strafford is as proud as Hell. **1782** MISS BURNEY *Cecilia* IX. vi, They say he's as proud as Lucifer. **1784** COWPER *Task* VI. 96 Knowledge is proud that he has learned so much; Wisdom is humble that he knows no more. **1820** BYRON *Mar. Fal.* II. i. 210 The vile are only vain; the great are proud. **1841** W. SPALDING *Italy & It. Isl.* II. 16 Claims not less arrogant than those of the proudest popes in the middle ages. **1859** TENNYSON *Geraint & Enid* 347 Turn, Fortune, turn thy wheel and lower the proud.

b. Const. *of* (the thing, quality, action, etc. which constitutes the ground of pride). See also 2.

1422 tr. *Secreta Secret., Priv. Priv.* 154 Haue knowynge of thy-Selfe, and be not Prute of so hey vyrchipp. *c* **1510** MORE *Picus* Wks. 17/2 If thou haste receiued it: why arte thou prowde therof, as thoughe thou haddst not receiued it. **1593** SHAKS. *2 Hen. VI*, IV. x. 77 Iden farewell, and be proud of thy victory. **1616** R. C. *Times' Whistle* III. 959 Most of our women are extreamly proud Of their faire lookes. **1707** NORRIS *Treat. Humility* vii. 317 If a man were to be proud of anything, it should be what the angels were proud of,.. their intellectual endowments. **1809–10** COLERIDGE *Friend* (1865) 140, I should be more inclined to be ashamed than proud of myself if they had. **1859** GEO. ELIOT *A. Bede* ii, An ornament of which she was much prouder than of her red cheeks.

c. Preceded by a sb. in comb. = proud of...

1682, etc. [see PURSE-PROUD]. **1863** W. C. BALDWIN *Afr. Hunting* viii. 354, I could make four or five spans of..good and well-matched oxen..and I am now becoming a little ox-proud. **1904** *Globe* 27 Oct. 4/4 No one can prevent the woman who is jewel-proud..from bedecking herself with gems on every possible and a few impossible occasions.

2. Highly sensible of, or elated by, some honour done to one; feeling oneself greatly honoured by some act, fact, or relation; taking pride or having high satisfaction in something; in early use (as still in *dial.*) sometimes merely = gratified, pleased, glad. Often const. *of*, or with *inf.*

c **1250** *Gen. & Ex.* 1414 Wið gold, and siluer, and wið srud, Ðis sonde made ðe mayden prud. **1377** LANGL. *P. Pl.* B. XIII. 59 Pacience was proude of þat propre seruice, And made hym muirth with his mete. *c* **1400** *Destr. Troy* 262 Pelleus of the proffer was proude at his hert. **1593** SHAKS. *Rich. II*, III. iii. 191 Faire Cousin, you debase your Princely Knee, To make the base Earth prowd with kissing it. **1677** DRYDEN *Apol. Heroic Poetry* Ess. (Ker) I. 182 The author of the *Plain Dealer*, whom I am proud to call my friend. **1781** COWPER *Charity* 308 A divine ambition, and a zeal, The boldest patriot might be proud to feel. **1784** BURNS '*There was a lad*' iv, He'll be a credit to us a', We'll a' be proud o' Robin. **1902** LD. KITCHENER in *Westm. Gaz.* 30 July 5/1 This..will, I am sure, be well understood by the Army I have been so proud to command. **1938** M. K. RAWLINGS *Yearling* viii. 69 Be proud things come so bountiful. *Ibid.* xv. 163 I'd be proud to eat breakfast before I go. **1949** H. HORNSBY *Lonesome Valley* xxiii. 302 I'm just as proud to see you..as if you was one of my own young 'uns! **1951** H. GILES *Harbin's Ridge* x. 99, I was sure proud Granny was there that day.

3. Having a becoming sense of what is due to or worthy of oneself or one's position; unwilling to stoop to what is beneath one; characterized by lofty self-respect; feeling or showing a proper pride.

1738 POPE *Epil. Sat.* II. 205 *F.* You're strangely proud. *P.* So proud, I am no Slave: So impudent, I own myself no Knave. **1761** GRAY *Sketch* 1 Too poor for a bribe and too proud to importune. **1828** CARLYLE *Misc.*, *Burns* (1857) I. 233 Many a poet has been poorer than Burns; but no one was ever prouder. **1833** TENNYSON *Lady Clara Vere de Vere* ii, Your pride is yet no mate for mine, Too proud to care from whence I came.

4. *transf.* Of actions, etc.: Proceeding from or indicating pride; arrogant, haughty, presumptuous; arising from lofty self-respect.

1390 GOWER *Conf.* II. 379 Ther was..many a proud word spoke also. **1535** COVERDALE *Prov.* vi. 17 There be sixe thinges, which the Lorde hateth... A proude loke, a dyssemblynge tonge [etc.]. **1701** *Stanley's Hist. Philos.*, *Biog.* 9 This Philosophy [the Stoick] has..charmed a World of People by its Proud and Ostentatious Principles. **1790** COWPER *Mother's Picture* 110 Higher far my proud pretensions rise—The son of parents pass'd into the skies. **1853** tr. *F. Bremer's Homes New World* II. xxvii. 311 The Indians, like the Greenlanders, look down upon the white race with proud contempt.

5. That is ground or cause of pride; of which one is or may be proud (now usually in good sense); affording high satisfaction or gratification.

a **1340** HAMPOLE *Psalter* xix. 8 þai ere on heghe, and has þaire delite in proude honurs and vayn. *a* **1577** GASCOIGNE *Herbs, Weeds*, etc. Wks. (1587) 304 Not one of these rebuketh avarice And yet procureth prowd pluralities. *c* **1600** SHAKS. *Sonn.* xxv, Let those..Of publike honour and proud titles bost. **1746–7** HERVEY *Medit.* (1767) I. 57 (*Tombs*) Where is Honour, with her proud Trophies of Renown? **1831** LAMB *Elia* Ser. II. *Ellistoniana*, One proud day to me he took his roast mutton with us in the Temple. **1840** DICKENS *Barn. Rudge* xlviii, 'It is a proud sight', said the secretary. **1868** FREEMAN *Norm. Conq.* II. vii. 44 The proud inheritance of their stainless loyalty.

II. 6. As a poetic or rhetorical epithet. **a.** Of persons, their name, etc.: Of exalted station, of high degree, of lofty dignity; lordly.

a **1250** *Prov. Ælfred* 5 in *O.E. Misc.* 102 Eorles prute, knyhtes egleche. *c* **1374** CHAUCER *Anel. & Arc.* 147 A noþere ladye proude and nuwe. *c* **1425** WYNTOUN *Cron.* IV. viii. 1148 Donald-Erchsone-Heggeboud King wes xiiii. winter provd. **1599** SHAKS. *Much Ado* III. i. 50 Nature neuer fram'd a womans heart, Of prowder stuffe then that of Beatrice. **1742** GRAY *Spring* ii, How low, how little are the Proud. **1805** SCOTT *Last Minstr.* VI. i, High though his titles, proud his name, Boundless his wealth as wish can claim. **1854** CHR. G. ROSSETTI *Poems* (1904) 180/1 In the grave will be no space For the purple of the proud.

b. Of things: Stately, majestic, magnificent, grand, 'gallant', splendid. (Referring to aspect.)

c **1290** *S. Eng. Leg.* I. 301/41 A noble churche huy founden þare, with walles faire and proute. *a* **1300** *Cursor M.* 3249 Ring and broche war selli prude. *c* **1400** *Destr. Troy* 435 With pelur and pall & mony proude rynges. **1530** PALSGR. 321/2 Prowde or stately, *fier*. **1602** MARSTON *Antonio's Rev.* III. ii, Tis not yet prowde day: The neat gay mist[r]es of the light's not vp. **1678** WOOD *Life* 28 June (O.H.S.) II. 410 The ruins..do shew that it hath been a verie statelie and proud fabrick. **1794** MRS. RADCLIFFE *Myst. Udolpho* xv, And through the waters view on high The proud ships sail, and gay clouds move. **1840** THIRLWALL *Greece* VII. lv. 91 Ecbatana..one of the proudest cities of the ancient world.

†**c.** *transf.* Highly pleasing (to other senses), 'grand'. *Obs. rare.*

c **1375** *Sc. Leg. Saints* vii. (*Jacobus minor*) 705 Persawand prowd sawoure þare Of sottyne [sodden] flesche.

7. Characterized by great vigour, force, or vitality, such as indicates or suggests pride: in various applications. †**a.** Of warriors (or their acts): Valiant, brave; mighty; esp. in phr. ***proud in pres*** (***prece***), valiant in conflict (see PRESS *sb.*[1] 1 b).

c **1320** *Sir Tristr.* 57 To Marke þe king þai went Wiþ kniȝtes proude in pres. *c* **1400** *Destr. Troy* 2132 To purvey a pepull pruddest of werre. *Ibid.* 6719 Preset hym with payne, & with proude strokes. *c* **1420** *Avow. Arth.* xlvii, Thenne he wente to the dece, Be-fore the pruddust in prece. **1523** LD. BERNERS *Froiss.* I. ccl. 371 The ii squiers within were right hardy and prowde. **1591** CONINGSBY *Jrnl. Siege Rouen* in *Camden Misc.* I. 58 Thus have you the most prowd sally that any capten here can tell of to their memorie. **1697** DRYDEN *Virg. Georg.* IV. 27 The youthful Prince, with proud allarm, Calls out the vent'rous Colony to swarm.

b. Of animals: Spirited, high-mettled; marked by vigorous and fearless activity; moving with force and dignity. (Chiefly *poet.*)

c **1407** LYDG. *Reson & Sens.* 3714 Bestys that be proude: As boors, lippardys, and lyouns. **1588** SHAKS. *Tit. A.* II. ii. 21, I haue dogges my Lord, Will rouze the proudest Panther in the Chase. **1667** MILTON *P.L.* IV. 858 The Fiend repli'd not,.. But like a proud Steed reind, went hautie on, Chaumping his iron curb. **1780** COWPER *Table-Talk* 523 Give me the line that ploughs its stately course Like a proud swan, conquering the stream by force.

c. Of the sea or a stream: Swelling, swollen, high, strong, in flood.

1535 COVERDALE *Job* xxxviii. 11 Here shalt thou laye downe thy proude and hye wawes. **1590** SHAKS. *Mids. N.* II. i. 91 Which falling in the Land, Hath euerie petty Riuer made so proud, That they haue ouer-borne their Continents. **1611** BIBLE *Ps.* cxxiv. 5 Then the proud waters had gone ouer our soule. **1828** BUCHAN *Ballads N. Scot.* I. 247 The wind was loud, the stream was proud, And wi' the stream gaed Willie. **1894** *Field* 1 Dec. 838/1 In the big rivers of upper Sweden and Norway, the grayling lives in the turmoil and 'proud' water.

d. Of organic structures: Overgrown, exuberant, too luxuriant; swelling or swollen, tumid. (*a*) Said of the sap: Swelling; rising or circulating vigorously; also, said locally of plants, or parts of them, as buds, shoots, grain. (See also WINTER-*proud*.) (*b*) Applied to overgrown flesh in a healing wound: see also PROUD FLESH.

[**1586** A. DAY *Eng. Secretary* II. (1625) 78 *Metaphora*.. as if we should say.. corne by the stately length and weighty eare it carrieth, to be proud.] **1593** SHAKS. *Rich. II*, III. iv. 59 As we.. wound the Barke, the skin of our Fruit-trees, Least being ouer-proud with Sap and Blood, With too much riches it confound it selfe. **1607** TOPSELL *Four-f. Beasts* (1658) 219 Used by Physitians for taking down of proud swelling wounds. **1648** MARKHAM *Housew. Gard.* III. x. (1668) 79 Now sap in flowers is strong and proud. **1664** EVELYN *Sylva* 32 About the beginning of March (when the buds begin to be proud and turgid). **1764** *Museum Rust.* III. xxxiv. 152 Ten acres of wheat, which, after Christmas, seemed proud. **1825** BROCKETT *N.C. Gloss.*, *Proud*, luxuriant. 'Corn's varra proud.' **1844** STEPHENS *Bk. Farm* II. 515 If the winter has been open and mild, the autumn-wheat plant will have grown luxuriantly,.. so.. that it may have become *proud*, that is, in a precocious state of forwardness for the season. **1970** *Country Life* 1 Oct. 856/1 Your case is the same as that of the farmer who sows his winter wheat too early; by the time the cold weather arrives the crop is 'proud'—too lush and forward.

8. a. Sensually excited; 'swelling', lascivious. ? *Obs.*

1590 SPENSER *F.Q.* I. x. 26 In ashes and sackcloth he did array His daintie corse, proud humors to abate. **1593** SHAKS. *Lucr.* 712 The flesh being proud, Desire doth fight with grace. **1641** HINDE *J. Bruen* vii. 27 Who having made their flesh proud by pampering, do now.. cast off all feare of God.

b. *spec.* Of certain female animals, as bitches, mares, elephants: In a state of sexual excitement; 'in heat'. ? *Obs.*

1575 TURBERV. *Venerie* vii. 17 A fayre Bitch.. the whiche you may make to goe proude in this wyse. **1590** COKAINE *Treat. Hunting* B iij b, A Brach is.. nine daies full proude. **1615** tr. *De Monfart's Surv. E. Indies* 17 To take them [wild elephants].. they make vse of a female, when shee goeth proud, in her heate [etc.]. **1727** BRADLEY *Fam. Dict.* I. Ee j b/2 Make Broth thereof and of this give her some twice or thrice, and she will infallibly grow proud. **1781** P. BECKFORD *Hunting* (1802) 62 Watch over the bitches with a cautious eye, and separate such as are going to be proud, before it be too late.

9. orig. *dial.* or *local.* 'Large; projecting in any direction; of a roof: high-pitched'; also 'said of a fulcrum when it is placed too near the lever end' (*E.D.D.*); also *techn.*: slightly raised or projecting; and see quots.

1825 JAMIESON, *Proud*, applied to a projection in a hay-stack, during the act of rearing it, whence it needs dressing in a particular quarter. **1857** P. COLQUHOUN *Comp. 'Oarsman's Guide'* 13 It has been the custom to fill oars very square, to make them row proud; but there are few men capable of enduring proud oars for any length of time.. not rowing the stroke out is attributable to these proud fillings. **1886** *S.W. Linc. Gloss.* s.v., 'The nails [in a horseshoe] stand out too proud'; 'The board's a bit too proud, it wants spoke-shaving off.' *a* **1909** *Mod.*, 'You are too proud': said of or to a person who, trying to raise something with a crowbar or other lever, places the point too far under the object to be lifted (= too far beyond the fulcrum). **1960** R. C. BELL *Board & Table Games* vii. 172 The inlay pieces.. were fitted into them [*sc.* recesses], leaving an excess standing proud. **1971** P. AUDEMARS *Stolen like Magic Away* vi. 92 The exposed rails of the track.. stand proud and quite high above the flints. **1974** *Good Motoring* July/Aug. 18/2 The horn push, sited right across the central spoke of the steering wheel, is well proud of the spoke and this gives rise to occasional, accidental blasts.

10. *Phrases.* **a.** ***proud tailor***: a local name for the goldfinch, from its showy plumage.

1770 D. BARRINGTON in *Archæologia* (1775) III. 33 A gold-finch still continues to be called a proud tailor in some parts of England. **1829** *Glover's Hist. Derby* I. 151 *Fringilla Carduelis*, Goldfinch, Thistle-Finch, Proud Tailor. **1876–82** *Yarrell's Brit. Birds* (ed. 4) II. 118 *note*, In some of the Midland counties it is termed 'Proud Tailor'.

b. ***to do*** (a person) ***proud*** (colloq.): to make proud, confer an honour upon, gratify highly.

1819 *Metropolis* I. 220 'You do me proud', said the general. **1837** THACKERAY *Ravenswing* i, Madam, you do me proud. **1884** *Milnor* (Dakota) *Teller* 22 Aug., The people of Milnor have done themselves proud in building a school house. **1899** *Daily News* 1 June 6/4 The sun did himself proud... For once the tents were not actually crammed throughout the afternoon.

†**c.** ***to make it proud***: to behave proudly or haughtily. *Obs.* (See MAKE *v.*[1] 68 b.)

c **1460** *Towneley Myst.* xxx. 263 She can make it full prowde with iapes and with gynnes. **14..** *Tundale's Vis.* 486 Þis hogy best.. His sette to swolo covetous men þat in erþe makyȝt hit prowd and towȝe.

†**C.** as *sb.* *Obs.*

1. A proud person; one of high degree.

c **1400** *Destr. Troy* 13696 Pirrus with that proude presit to þe temple, Weddit þat worthi, & as wif held. **1535** STEWART *Cron. Scot.* (Rolls) II. 24 Wes neuir proud of sic auctoritie Moir wirschip wan. *a* **1586** in Pinkerton *Anc. Scot. Poems* (1786) 190 He luifit that prowde in paramouris.

2. Pride. *rare.* (*Prude* (*ü*) was also early southern ME. spelling of *pryde*, PRIDE.)

c **1440** *Gesta Rom.* i. 4 (Harl. MS.) Alle þat is in þe wordle oþer it is fals couetise of flesch, or fals couetise of yen, or prowde of lif.

D. as *adv.* Proudly, in a proud manner (in various senses).

13.. *Cursor M.* 28515 Lucheri has don me scrud Me-self and bere my bodi prud. *c* **1425** *Cast. Persev.* 1793 in *Macro Plays* 130 Heyl, prinse, proude prekyd in palle! **1534** MORE *Treat. Passion* Wks. 1272/2 Men maye call hym a foole that beareth hymselfe prowde, because he ietteth about in a borowed gown. **1857** [see 9 above].

E. *Comb.* **a.** parasynthetic, as ***proud-arsed***, ***-blooded***, ***-crested***, ***-lidded***, ***-minded***, ***-necked***, ***-paced***, ***-pillared***, ***-plumed***, ***-quivered***, ***-spirited***, ***-stomached***, ***-visaged***: see also PROUD-HEARTED. **b.** adverbial, as ***proud-arching***, ***-blind*** (blinded by pride), ***-exulting***, ***-fed***, ***-glancing***, †***-pied*** (proudly or splendidly variegated), †***-pight***, ***-prancing***.

1919 A. HUXLEY in *Coterie* Sept. 61 The swan's *proud-arching opulent loveliness. **1952** AUDEN *Nones* 56 When the *proud-arsed broad-shouldered break and run. **1599** *Broughton's Let.* ix. 32 Put on your spectacles you purblind and *proud-blind Pharisee. **1759** MASON *Caractacus* Poems (1774) 261 *Proud-crested soldier! **1944** BLUNDEN *Shells by Stream* 57 And look, those birds with perfect ease, Proud-crested. **1796** *Poetry* in *New Ann. Reg.* 168 To leave him, *proud-exulting in his pains. **1929** BLUNDEN *Near & Far* 37 A *proud-fed but a puny rill. **1948** C. DAY LEWIS *Poems 1943–47* 88 Palpable calm, visible reticence, *Proud-lidded water. **1596** SHAKS. *Tam. Shr.* II. i. 132, I am as peremptorie as she *proud minded. **1934** T. S. ELIOT *Rock* ii. 75 Yet they walk in the street *proudnecked, like thoroughbreds ready for races. **1616** *Marlowe's Faust.* Wks. (Rtldg.) 120/2 On a *proud-pac'd steed, as swift as thought. *c* **1600** SHAKS. *Sonn.* xcviii, When *proud pide Aprill (drest in all his trim) Hath put a spirit of youth in euery thing. **1912** C. MACKENZIE *Carnival* xlii. 373 When April pauses to survey her handiwork, assuming in the contemplation of the proud pied earth the warmth and maturity of midsummer. *c* **1400** *Laud Troy Bk.* 11191 Many a *proude pight pynacle Stode a-boute that tabernacle. **1949** BLUNDEN *After Bombing* 9 With a sounding *proud-plumed company By a glittering sea. **1901** L. F. BEGBIE in *Academy* 28 Sept. 258/1 *Proud-prancing Æschylean words. **1838** DICKENS *Nich. Nick.* xiii, *Proud-stomached teachers. **1844** J. R. LOWELL in *Graham's Mag.* July 15 Though these *proud-visaged hopes, once turned to fly, Hurl backward many a deadly Parthian dart.

†**proud**, *v.* *Obs.* [OE. *prútian*, ME. *prouden*, f. *prút* PROUD *a.*]

1. *intr.* To be proud; to behave proudly.

a **1000** *Aldhelm Gloss.* 1161 in Napier *O.E. Gloss.* 32/1 *Fastu*, .i. *elatione*, prutunge. *c* **1000** *Corp. Chr. Coll. Cambr. MS.* 191, 29 þæt hi wyllon modiȝȝan oððe prutian. *Ibid.* 168 Hwanon hi modiȝian maȝon oððe prutian. *c* **1325** *Deo Gratias* 18 in *E.E.P.* (1862) 129 A noþur Mon proudeþ as doþ a poo. **1382** WYCLIF *Job* xv. 20 Alle his daȝis the vnpitous man proudeth. *a* **1618** SYLVESTER *Henry Gt.* 117 There prowdeth Pow'r, here Prowesse brighter shines.

b. To be lively or wanton. (Cf. PROUD *a.* 8.)

c **1330** *Arth. & Merl.* 264 Mirie time is Auerille.. ȝong man wexeþ jolif, & þan proudeþ man & wiif.

2. *trans.* To make proud; to puff up with pride.

c **1425** *St. Mary of Oignies* II. ii. in *Anglia* VIII. 153/12 Nor she was depressed wiþ reproues ne prouded wiþ hir preisynges. **1606** WARNER *Alb. Eng.* XVI. cii. 403 Yee whom Nature hath or Fortune prowded. **1606** SYLVESTER *Du Bartas* II. iv. II. *Trophies* 1333 As Sin breeds Sin, and Husband marr's the Wife, Sister prouds Sister, Brother hardens Brother, And one Companion doth corrupt another.

Hence †'**prouded** *ppl. a.*, made proud, over-swollen; †'**prouder**, ? one who behaves proudly.

1602 WARNER *Alb. Eng.* IX. lii. 236 The prouded Flesh from sins excesse to waine. **1565** W. ALLEN *Def. Cath. Doctr. Purgatory* II. viii. 191 Goddes Churche.. hathe by the spirite of God beaten downe your proudders, the Arrians: the Macedonians: the Anabaptistes. **1577** FULKE *Confut. Purg.* 298 [quoting prec.] Our prowders the Arians.

proudens, obs. form of PRUDENCE.

†'**proudfall.** *Obs.* *rare*$^{-1}$. [f. PROUD *a.* + (?) FALL *sb.*[1]] ? The front hair, the forelock.

c **1400** *Destr. Troy.* 3025 The shede þurghe the shyre here shone as þe lilly, Streght as a strike, straght þurgh the myddes, Depertid the proudfall pertly in two, Atiret in tressis trusset full faire.

proud flesh. [See PROUD *a.* 7 d (*b*).] Overgrown flesh arising from excessive granulation upon, or around the edges of, a healing wound.

c **1400** *Lanfranc's Cirurg.* 78 An hori elde wounde þat haþ summe greete crustis, or ellis.. sum gret proud fleisch to hiȝe [Lat. *carnem superfluam grossam*]. **1597** A. M. tr. *Guillemeau's Fr. Chirurg.* 50 b/2 Aboue the ordinary fluxions, therin engendreth proude fleshe. **1685** BOYLE *Enq. Notion Nat.* vii. 323 In wounds, proud-flesh, and perhaps funguses, are as well produced and entertained by the aliment brought to the wounded part, as the true and genuine flesh. **1779** *Gentl. Mag.* XLIX. 80 If fungus, commonly called proud-flesh, should appear, a dressing of dry lint will mostly soon repress it. **1880** M. MACKENZIE *Dis. Throat & Nose* I. 526 The formation of 'proud flesh' on the edges of the wound.

Hence '**proud-flesh** *v. trans.*, to cause a growth of proud flesh upon (in quot. *fig.*).

1876 S. LANIER in *Life & Lett. B. Taylor* (1884) II. xxviii. 693 The additional forcing of such a tendency.. becomes postively hurtful through proudfleshing the artistic conscience.

proudful ('praʊdfəl), *a.* Now *dial.* [f. PROUD *a.* + -FUL: cf. PRIDEFUL.] Full of pride; abounding in pride; proud. (In quot. 1900 as *adv.*)

1340 *Ayenb.* 217 Prouduol cloþinge ne wynþ naȝt of god. *a* **1578** LINDESAY (Pitscottie) *Chron. Scot.* (S.T.S.) I. 81 [They] began to delet [= delate] his proudfull ambitioun and disdainning of the pepill. **1881** W. C. SMITH in *Mod. Sc. Poets* III. 243 She leaves his proudfu' mither Draggin through the dowie heather. **1900** 'ZACK' (GWEN. KEATS) *Tales Dunstable Weir* (1901) 135 (Devon dial.) He moved that free and yet that proudful I couldn't but call to mother to mark him.

'**proud-'hearted**, *a.* Having a proud heart or spirit; proud, haughty.

? *a* **1366** CHAUCER *Rom. Rose* 1491 Proude-herted Narcisus. **14..** in *Harrow. Hell* Introd. 25 The horss hath xxv propertes,.. iiii off a lyon.. prowd-herted, brod-brestid, iiii good legis, and a stowte stern. **1456** SIR G. HAYE *Law Arms* (S.T.S.) 116 Oft dois hautane proud-hartit men to wyn los in armes, mare for pride na prow. **1593** SHAKS. *3 Hen. VI*, v. i. 98 And so, prowd-hearted Warwicke, I defie thee. *a* **1803** *Young Benjie* iv. in Child *Ballads* IV. (1886) 282/1 And he was stout, and proud-hearted, And thought o't bitterlie. **1861** TROLLOPE *Framley P.* I. xi. 236 It is hardly possible that the proud-hearted should love those who despise them; and Lucy Robarts was very proud-hearted.

So '**proud-heart** *sb.*, a name for a proud-hearted person; *a.*, proud-hearted.

1362 LANGL. *P. Pl.* A. v. 45 Pernel proud-herte [C. VII. 3 proute-herte] platte hire to grounde,.. And beo-hiȝte to him þat vs alle maade, Heo wolde [etc.]. **1819** KEATS *Lamia* II. 285 Leaving thee forlorn.. For all thine impious proud-heart sophistries. **1887** MORRIS *Odyss.* II. 324 Those young and proud-heart lords.

proudish ('praʊdɪʃ), *a.* [f. PROUD *a.* + -ISH[1].] Somewhat proud, rather proud.

1658 COKAINE *Trappolin* IV. i, I do remember my self well enough, yet Eo, Meo, and Areo, have made me something proudish. **1688** PENTON *Guard. Instruct.* (1897) 44 Especially when they are a little proudish. **1827** DISRAELI *Viv. Grey* VI. i, He said this with a proudish air.

†'**proudling.** *Obs. rare.* [f. as prec. + -LING[1].] A proud person; a 'son' or 'daughter of pride'.

a **1618** SYLVESTER *Henry Gt.* 152 Milde to the Meek, to Proudlings sterne and strict. **1628** SIR W. MURE *Doomesday* 196 There, the Ambitious.. Of base contempt is made the pryse; The Proudling pestred downe.

†'**proudly**, *a.* *Obs.* *rare*$^{-1}$. [f. as prec. + -LY[1].] Of proud manner; proud-looking.

c **1400** *Laud Troy Bk.* 2136 Duk Nestor was ful of wratthe and ire Toward Antenor, that proudely sire.

proudly ('praʊdlɪ), *adv.* Forms: see PROUD *a.* and -LY[2]. [Late OE. *prútlíce*: see -LY[2]; ME. *prudeliche*.] In a proud manner; with pride.

1. With excessive self-esteem; with an attitude or air of superiority; haughtily, arrogantly.

a **1050** *Liber Scintill.* lviii. (1889) 178 Prutlice [*superbe*] witan. *a* **1225** *Leg. Kath.* 577 Þa onswerede þe an swiðe prudeliche, þus, to þe prude prince. *c* **1380** *Sir Ferumb.* 534 Fyrumbras ansuerde him agayn prouteliche & sayde;.. 'Ich hem wolde wel conquere wiþ my swerd trenchaunt'. **14..** *Tourn. Tottenham* 30 in Hazl. *E.P.P.* III. 84 How prudly among vs thy doȝter he craues. **1560** DAUS tr. *Sleidane's Comm.* 192 b, He aunswered contemptuously & proudlye. **1621** MOLLE *Camerar. Liv. Libr.* III. x. 178 [She] thinketh the proudlier of herselfe. **1671** MILTON *Samson* 55 Proudly secure, yet liable to fall By weakest suttleties. **1788** COWPER *Negro's Compl.* 56 Prove that you have human feelings, Ere you proudly question ours! **1831** FOSTER in *Life & Corr.* (1846) II. 197 A long and proudly imperious reign of corruption.

b. With lofty satisfaction or self-respect; with a high sense of honour done to one, or of what is worthy of one; with elation or exultation.

1753 A. MURPHY *Gray's Inn Jrnl.* No. 23 Rather than drag a feverish Life under an huge Load of Misery, he proudly resolves to put an End to his Sufferings. **1855** MACAULAY *Hist. Eng.* xiii. III. 290 A rule which, as far back as the days of the Plantagenets, had been proudly declared by the most illustrious sages of Westminster Hall to be a distinguishing feature of the English jurisprudence. **1871** FREEMAN *Norm. Conq.* IV. xvii. 79 A conquest which is proudly contrasted with the petty exploits of the first Cæsar in the same island.

2. With an aspect or manner suggesting pride; grandly, magnificently, splendidly; †gallantly, valiantly (quot. *c* 1420); with spirited and dignified movement; with vigour or force, exuberantly.

c **1050** *Byrhtferth's Handboc* in *Anglia* (1885) VIII. 313 Eac hiȝ prutlice ȝymað þæs miotacismus ȝefleard. *c* **1200** *Vices & Virt.* 107 Ne he ne scal to prudeliche bien isc(r)edd. **13..** *K. Alis.* 3413 (Bodl. MS.) Many stede there proudely lep. *c* **1400** *Destr. Troy* 371 A chamber full choise.., þat proudly was painted with pure gold ouer. *c* **1420** *Brut* 370 Proutly & manly he quitte hym on his aduersarye. *a* **1547** SURREY *Æneid* II. (1557) C ij, The pillers eke proudly beset with gold, And with the spoiles of other nations. **1597** SHAKS. *2 Hen. IV*, v. ii. 130 The Tide of Blood in me, Hath prowdly flow'd in Vanity, till now. **1670** CAPT. J. SMITH *Eng. Improv. Reviv'd* 73 The best season is when the Sap is ready to stir, not when it is proudly stirring. **1671** MILTON *P.R.* IV. 34 An Imperial City.. With Towers and Temples proudly elevate On seven small hills. **1899** F. T. BULLEN *Way Navy* 40 We swept proudly up to the anchorage off Buncrana.

proudness ('praʊdnɪs). Now *rare*. [f. PROUD *a.* + -NESS.] The quality of being proud; pride.

1. Lofty self-esteem, arrogance, haughtiness.

1500–20 DUNBAR *Poems* ix. 116, I synnit.. In he exaltit arrogance and folye, Prowdnes, derisioun, scorne and vilipentioun. **1552** LATIMER *Serm. Gospels* iv. 173 He fell.. in suche a hatred and proudenes agaynst God. **1588** A. KING tr. *Canisius' Catech.* K j, Thair proudnes is intolerable. **1860** PUSEY *Min. Proph.* 465 Isaiah accumulates words, to express the haughtiness of Moab.. as if we were to say 'pride, prideful, proudness, pridefulness'. **1902** E. H. COOPER *20th Century Child* xii. (1905) 231 They [crabs] should be kept in a bucket for a week, said a small child firmly, 'to calm down their proudness'.

2. Proud show, splendour, magnificence.

1606 WARNER *Alb. Eng.* XVI. ci. 401 Nature wrongd by Arte, of Prowdnes more than need.

proues, -ese, -esse, obs. ff. PROWESS.

prouey(e, obs. f. PURVEY.

prouffer, -ffre, obs. ff. PROFFER.

prounȝe, obs. Sc. form of PRUNE *v.*[1]

Proustian ('pruːstɪən), *sb.* and *a.* [f. the name of Marcel *Proust*, French writer (1871–1922), + -IAN.]

A. *sb.* An admirer or imitator of Proust.

1919 R. FRY *Let.* 28 Oct. (1972) II. 464 I've.. got Proust's second volume... I forget whether you are a Proustian or not. **1928** *Sunday Express* 26 Feb. 5/2 If you desire to be a Jurgenist you must toil at Jurgenism as the Proustian toils at Proustery. **1936** A. HUXLEY *Eyeless in Gaza* xiv. 183 You're a Proustian, I take it? **1958** *Times* 6 Mar. 13/5 Proustians will be glad to have these 'moves on the chess-board of Time' in a volume that stimulates endless new ideas. **1973** *Listener* 2 Aug. 155/3 An ardent Proustian who was trying to persuade me to.. plunge into the full 12-volume *fleuve*.

B. *adj.* Of, pertaining to, or characteristic of Proust, his writings, or his style.

1926 A. HUXLEY *Jesting Pilate* I. 139 The decaying relics of feudalism.. form the stormy background to the Proustian comedy. **1929** [see IMITATION 5]. **1931** *Times Lit. Suppl.* 2 Apr. 274/2 The Proustian distinction between 'involuntary memory'.. and 'voluntary memory'. **1936** L. P. SMITH *Reperusals & Re-Collections* ii. 23 An immense leisurely, true novel, written with a Tolstoyan or Proustian amplitude, which allows space for an immense copiousness of detail and for infinite digressions. **1943** J. LEES-MILNE *Ancestral Voices* (1975) 186 Lady Crewe believes no relationship, no emotion, no motive to be straightforward, and suspects everything and everyone. This is truly Proustian. **1958** *Spectator* 10 Jan. 51/1 Too often the adjective 'Proustian' evokes a kind of decadent Barsetshire. **1976** A. POWELL *Infants of Spring* viii. 123 A lack of interest for individuals in what might be called the Proustian sense was perhaps characteristic, too, of the whole of the Arts Society.

Hence **'Proustery** *nonce-wd.*, a Proustian manner; **Prousti'ana**, memorabilia of Proust.

1928 Proustery [see PROUSTIAN *sb.* above]. **1965** *Guardian* 20 Dec. 6/5 She invited me to her home to see her Proustiana. **1973** *Times* 4 Oct. 17/2 Considering the volume of Proustiana.. it requires an artist's skill to pick out the white stones of this life and work.

proustite ('pruːstaɪt). *Min.* [a. F. *proustite* (1832), after J. L. Proust, a French chemist, the discoverer: see -ITE[1].] Native sulpharsenide of silver, occurring in crystals or granular masses of a cochineal-red colour; also called *ruby silver* or *light-red silver ore*.

1835 C. U. SHEPARD *Min.* II. II. 120 Proustite. Aphotistic Melacone-Blende. **1872** *Catal. Min. W. Nevill* 20 Proustite in large crystals. **1893** CHAPMAN *Blowpipe Pract.* 156 Proustite.. is recognized by its deep or bright red colour.

prout(e, prouwis, obs. ff. PROUD, PROWESS.

provable, proveable ('pruːvəb(ə)l), *a.* Also 4–5 prevable, (5 -bulle), 6 proov(e)able. [a. OF. *pro(u)vable* (*c* 1225 in Godef.) that can be proved, worthy of approbation, ad. L. *probābilis* PROBABLE. The form *prevable* is f. *preve* (see PROVE); *proveable* (usual from 17th to early 19th c.) affects direct formation from PROVE *v.*]

1. Capable of being proved; of which the truth or validity can be established; demonstrable.

c **1400** *Rom. Rose* 5414 And if thee thinke it is doutable, It is thurgh argument provable [*orig.* c'est bien par argument prouvable]. *c* **1400** *Apol. Loll.* 7 It is not aȝen þe feiþ, or prouable aȝen þe trowþ. **1561** T. NORTON *Calvin's Inst.* I. xv. (1634) 79 They seem to say somewhat by reason proveable, yet.. there is no stedfast certainty in their reasons. **1651** BAXTER *Inf. Bapt.* 272 He makes it fully proveable from Scripture. **1729** BUTLER *Serm., Hum. Nat.* i. *note*, [This] is a mere question of fact.. not proveable immediately by reason. **1873** M. ARNOLD *Lit. & Dogma* (1876) 280 This being proveable from Scripture. **1889** *Spectator* 23 Nov., The steady prosecution of every provable case of sanitary neglect.

†**2.** Such as approves itself to the mind; worthy of acceptance or belief; plausible; = PROBABLE 2.

c **1400** tr. *Secreta Secret., Gov. Lordsh.* 118 Whenne þou shal fynde dyuers tokenynges & contrary, holde þe all-dayes to þe bettyr & more preuable party. *c* **1450** *Mirour Saluacioun* 2359 Ȝit is prouable y[t] crist lufed the Sinagoge wele more. **1570–6** LAMBARDE *Peramb. Kent* (1826) 327 It is more prooveable to affirme, that he was buried at Horsted here. **1588** PARKE tr. *Mendoza's Hist. China* 230 The Spaniards did giue their discharge in such prouable maner, that the captaines.. were satisfied of the false opinion.

†**3.** Worthy to be approved; commendable, praiseworthy, meritorious. *Obs.*

1382 WYCLIF *Ecclus.* xlii. 8 Thou shalt ben lerned in alle thingus, and prouable [1388 comendable] in the siȝte of all men. **1387** TREVISA *Higden* (Rolls) VII. 135 Of whom are tolde prevable and famous þinges [L. *feruntur fuisse insignia*]. *c* **1420** *Avow. Arth.* xxxvi, As prest knyȝte, and preuabulle, With schild and with spere. **1483** CAXTON *Gold. Leg.* 427 b/1 He proufferyd hym to god in al thynges pryuables and wythoute confusyon in his werkys.

†**4.** That proves or turns out well; that yields a profit. Cf. PROVE *v.* 10. *Obs. rural.*

a **1722** LISLE *Husb.* (1757) 474 The most proveable pig is the cheapest, though dearest at first cost. **1884** *Cheshire Gloss.*, *Provable*, said of corn that yields well.

Hence **prova'bility, 'provableness**, the quality of being provable; demonstrability.

1864 WEBSTER, *Provableness.* **1902** *Month* May 453 The Church.. affirms the provability of the Divine existence. **1908** SIR E. RUSSELL in *Hibbert Jrnl.* July 773 There is at present no such evident provableness in them as can make them effective in motive.

provably, proveably ('pruːvəblɪ), *adv.* [f. prec. + -LY[2]. Cf. AF. *provablement* (Act 25 Edw. III. Stat. v. c. 2, 1351–2).] In a provable manner: †**a.** so as to approve itself to the mind, with likelihood (*obs.*); **b.** as may be proved; demonstrably.

1395 PURVEY *Remonstr.* (1851) 77 It semeth preuabli to feithful men that newe determinacioun of fleshli prelatis is suspect of eresie eithir of errour. *c* **1400** *Apol. Loll.* 8 Þus prouabli a feiþful man miȝt in ȝering mani messis geit on a day seuenti [*MS.* þewenti] þowzand ȝer of pardoun. **1460** *Rolls of Parlt.* V. 379/1 If eny persone.. therof provably be atteinte. **1549** COVERDALE, etc. *Erasm. Par. Titus* 26 If thou knowe any man of that maners and vpright lyuinge, that no faulte can proueably be layed to him. **1857** *Chamb. Jrnl.* VIII. 119/1 Supposing her to be, provably, Lucy Hamblin. **1890** *Sat. Rev.* 4 Oct. 392/2 The most provably conservative of all religious rites.

†**proval**. *Obs. rare*⁻¹. [f. PROVE *v.* + -AL[1]: cf. OF. *prouvaille* proof (in Godef.); also *trial.*] The act of proving or testing; = PROOF *sb.* 4; something that proves or tests.

1622 MABBE tr. *Aleman's Guzman d'Alf.* II. 325 [A Prison] is.. a forced tryall of a mans patience,.. a prouall of a mans friends, and a revengement of his enemies.

provand ('prɒvənd). Also 4–5 provande. [= MLG. and early mod.Du. *provande* (Plantin, Kilian, Hexham 1678); app. ad. F. *provende*: see PROVEND *sb.* In quot. 1481 immediately from Flemish; but in earlier examples perh. from OF.]

Food, provisions, provender; *esp.* the food and fodder provided for an army.

c **1341** [see b]. ? *a* **1400** *Cursor M.* 3317 (Fairf.) Prouande [*other MSS.* fodder] and hay þou sal finde boun. *c* **1450** *Bk. Curtasye* 608 in *Babees Bk.* (1868) 319 A pek of prouande on a day; Euery horse schalle so muche haue. **1481** CAXTON *Reynard* xxvii. (Arb.) 60, I wolde ofte sende them for prouande [*orig.* wt seynden om prouande]. **1590** SIR J. SMYTH *Disc. Weapons* Ded. ***iij b, That their Soldiers, in steade of pay with money, should be payed in Prouand, which was bread and cheese. **1607** SHAKS. *Cor.* II. i. 267 Cammels.. haue their Prouand Onely for bearing Burthens. **1828** *Craven Gloss.* (ed. 2), *Provand*, provender. **1890** G. HOOPER *Wellington* 141 The Marshal.. got some provand from that unwasted country.

b. *attrib.* Cf. PROVANT 3.

c **1341** *Durham Acc. Rolls* (Surtees) 541 In Canabo empt' pro j Provandpok. **1590** SIR J. SMYTH *Disc. Weapons* Ded. (10 b), Turning their Prouand money.. into their owne purses.

provang, obs. form of PROBANG.

provant ('prɒvənt), *sb.* Also 5–7 provent(e. [app. a. MLG. *provant*, later form of *provande* PROVAND; perh. sometimes confounded with PROVENT *sb.* Formerly *pro'vant*.]

1. Provand, provender; an allowance of food.

c **1450** *Mankind* 61 in *Macro Plays*, The chaff, to horse xall be goode provente; When a man ys for-colde, þe straw may be brent. **1592** NASHE *P. Penilesse* (ed. 2) 22 From the flesh pots of Egipt, to the Prouant of the Lowe Countreyes. *a* **1623** FLETCHER *Love's Cure* II. i, One peaze was a souldier's provant a whole day, at the destruction of Jerusalem. **1698** FRYER *Acc. E. India & P.* 34 On the Shoulders of the Coolies they load their Provant, and what Moveables necessary. **1809** W. IRVING *Knickerb.* VI. viii. (1861) 224 It severed off a deep coat pocket, stored with bread and cheese, which provant rolling among the armies, occasioned a fearful scrambling between the Swedes and Dutchmen. **1885** BURTON *Arab. Nts.* (1887) III. 96 Then she applied herself to making ready the wants of the way, to wit provaunt and provender.

†**2.** One who deals in provant; a sutler. *Obs.*

1608 BEAUM. & FL. *Four Plays in One* I. i, Oh, gods of Rome, was Nicodemus To bear these braveries from a poor provant!

3. *attrib.* or as *adj.* **a.** Of or belonging to the provant or soldier's allowance; hence, of common or inferior quality. (Cf. AMMUNITION *sb.* 3.) *arch.*

1598 B. JONSON *Ev. Man in Hum.* III. i, *Step*... He swore it was a Toledo. *Bob.* A poor provant rapier, no better. **1627** HAKEWILL *Apol.* (1630) 118 The provant wine ordained for the army being frozen, was divided with hatchets. **1628** R. S. *Counter-Scuffle* C j, Commanders, That hither come, compell'd by want, With rustie Swords, and Suits Prouant. *a* **1639** WEBSTER *Appius & Virg.* I. iv, All our provant apparel's torn to rags. [**1819** SCOTT *Leg. Montrose* ii, The good wheaten loaves of the Flemings were better than the provant rye-bread of the Swede. **1863** SALA *Capt. Dangerous* I. i. 16 Those that handle the backsword and are quick at finish with the provant rapier.]

†**b.** That serves or engages for provant; mercenary; also in *Comb.* as **provant-man**, a mercenary. *Obs.*

c **1624** LUSHINGTON *Resurr. Serm.* (1659) 43 Why yet do they say they were asleep? The reason is, they are.. mercenary Souldiers, hired to it by the Priests with a large piece of money. The Provantman will undertake to say any thing, yea, to do any thing for money. **1663** KILLIGREW *Parson's Wed.* I. i, Hang him, lean, mercenary, provant Rogue.

Hence † **provant** *v. trans.*, to provision. *Obs.*

1599 NASHE *Lenten Stuff* 6 Yarmouth.. should not onely supply her inhabitants with plentifull purueyance of sustenance, but prouant and victuall moreouer this monstrous army of strangers.

† **'provant-,master**. *Obs.* [f. PROVANT *sb.* + MASTER *sb.*[1]: cf. Du. *provand-meester* (Kilian; mod. *proviand-*), G. *proviant-meister*.] The officer in charge of the commissariat; the commissary; also ? a supplier of or dealer in provisions.

1607 TOPSELL *Four-f. Beasts* (1658) 399 When the Scythians understood that Darius with his great Army stood in need of victuals, they sent unto him a Provant-master with these presents or gifts, a Bird, a Mouse, a Frog, and five darts. *a* **1618** MORYSON *Itin.* IV. II. v. (1903) 244 Agayne our Prouant masters for apparrelling the soldier, dealt as corruptly as the rest, not sending halfe the proportion of Apparrell due to the soldier. **1620** MARKHAM *Farew. Husb.* II. xviii. (1668) 97 According to the opinions of antient Husbandmen and other provant Masters.

prove (pruːv), *v.* Forms: *α.* prove, etc.; *β.* preove, preve, etc.: see below. Inflected **proved, proving;** Pa. pple. also (orig. in Sc. legal use) **proven**. [a. OF. *prove-r* (11th c. in Littré), in mod.F. *prouver* = Pr. *proar*, Sp. *probar*, Pg. *provar*, It. *probare*:—L. *probāre* to test (a thing) as to its goodness, to try; to approve; to make good, prove, demonstrate; f. *prob-us* good. In OF. the Lat. *o* when unstressed became *o*, later *ou* (*probāre*, *prover*; so *provant*, *provė*, *provons*), but in the stressed syllable, *ue* (*oe*, *eo*, *ē*), later *eu* (*probat*, *prueve*, later *preuve*), as in the sb. *preuve* PROOF. In modern F. all forms of the verb are levelled under *ou* (*prouver*, *prouve*). In ME. the two OF. inflexional types gave origin to two concurrent forms of the vb., *prove* and *preove*, *preve*. In Standard Eng. *prove* alone survives; *preve* is seldom found after 1500, but was usual in literary Scotch, and still exists (written *preeve*, *prieve*, *preave*, *preeave*) in Sc. and north. Eng. dialects. Cf. the parallel phonetic history of MOVE *v.* The pa. pple. *proven*, orig. Sc., from *preve*, follows the strong vbs., e.g. *cleave*, *cloven*, *weave*, *woven*.]

A. Illustration of Forms.

1. Present stem.

α. 2–3 prouwe, 2–7 proue, (3 proui, -y, y-proue), 4–5 prof, profe, 4–6 *north. dial.* and *Sc.* pruve, prufe, pruf, preve, 5 *Sc.* pruff, 5–6 proove, proufe, 6 (prooeyve), *Sc.* pruiff, proife (*pa. pple.* prute), 6–7 prooue, proove, (7 proov), 5– prove.

c **1175** *Lamb. Hom.* 17 He.. prouwede deð for al moncun. *c* **1200** *Trin. Coll. Hom.* 93 Proue ech man him seluen. *c* **1330** R. BRUNNE *Chron. Wace* (Rolls) 12632 Com to morn, & prof [*v.r.* proue] þy day. **1387** TREVISA *Higden* (Rolls) VII. 99 He perceyved and i-proved þe deceyvynge of Edrik. *c* **1400** *Destr. Troy* 11665 As prouit is of old. **1472** *Presentm. Juries* in *Surtees Misc.* (1888) 23 It may be prowyd. **1535** STEWART *Cron. Scot.* (Rolls) III. 363 As it mycht weill be prute [*rime* mute]. **1542** UDALL *Erasm. Apoph.* 181 b, Alexander in prouvyng maisteries would not bee matched but with kynges. **1560** DAUS tr. *Sleidane's Comm.* 222 b,

Prophecyes, wherof the ende prooued some trewe. **1576** *Lichfield Gild Ord.* (E.E.T.S.) 27 Prooeyvinge the saide supplycacion. **1599** CHAPMAN *Hum. Dayes Myrth* Wks. 1873 I. 71 You are come to tempt and proove at full the spirit of my wife. *c* **1600** MONTGOMERIE *Cherrie & Slae* 1235 Experience can proife. **1652** GATAKER *Antinom.* 13 Such.. arguments proov nothing.

β. 3–5 **preoue**, 4–5 **proeue, -ve, prefe**, 4–6 **preue, preve**, 4–8 **prieve**, 5–6 **pref, preiue, preif, prewe**, 6 **preaue, pryve**, *Sc.* **preiff, prief**, 7 (8 *Sc.*) **prive**. See also the contracted form PREE.

a **1225** *Ancr. R.* 182 Hwon heo is ipreoued hit seið:.. Vor al so preoueð God his icorene. *c* **1374** CHAUCER *Boeth.* v. pr. iii. 120 (Camb. MS.) Ne I ne proeue nat thilke same reson. *c* **1386** —— *Merch. T.* 994 Thexperience so preueth euery daie. **1390** GOWER *Conf.* III. 88 Which in som cas upon believe Stant more than thei conne prieve. **1393** LANGL. *P. Pl.* C. XII. 39 And putteþ forþ presompcions to preouen þe sothe. *c* **1440** *Promp. Parv.* 412/2 Prevyn, or provyn. *a* **1450** *Cursor M.* 5374 (Fairf.) Wele ys him has hap to prefe. *c* **1450** tr. *De Imitatione* I. xiii. 14 Ffire preueþ golde. *c* **1470** HENRYSON *Mor. Fab.* IV. (*Fox's Confess.*) xvii, Or heid, or feit, or paynchis let me preif. **1535** STEWART *Cron. Scot.* (Rolls) I. 12 Nane be so pert to prewe.. Of thair awin blude to mak ane king agane. **1596** SPENSER *F.Q.* VI. xii. 18 Her countenaunce and her likely hew.. do surely prieve That yond same is your daughter. *c* **1600** *Scot. Poems 16th C.* (1801) II. 186 Priests, prief you men. **1634** S. R. *Noble Soldier* I. ii. in Bullen *O. Pl.* I. 272 To prive thy sonne,.. Spaines heire Apparant. *a* **1758** RAMSAY *Masque* 184 Skink 't up, and let us prive.

2. *Pa. pple.* Illustration of the form **proven** (also 6 **-in**). (Properly in passive.) Now common in the U.S.

c **1536** NISBET *New Test. in Scots* (S.T.S.) III. 335 It is evidently knawin ande cleirly provin. **1633** W. STRUTHER *True Happines* 8 When a number serveth not necessitie, all are proven to be weak. **17..** *Erskine's Princ. Sc. Law* (1890) 598 A verdict of 'not proven' is allowable—and common—in Scotland, and involves acquittal and dismissal from the bar. **1818** R. P. KNIGHT *Symbolic Lang.* (1876) 175 Some who had proven themselves prolific. **1828** LANDOR *Imag. Conv., Wolfgang & Henry of Melctal* Wks. 1846 I. 317/1 Did not this same.. man.. call thee a felon? not having proven thee such. **1846** MCCULLOCH *Acc. Brit. Empire* (1854) II. 225 A verdict of Not Proven indicates suspicion, but a want of proof of guilt. **1850** GLADSTONE *Glean.* (1879) V. 224 Whatever can be proved from his mouth.. may be regarded as proven *a fortiori*. **1872** TENNYSON *Gareth & Lyn.* 1390 Being after all their foolish fears.. only proven a blooming boy. **1899** *Allbutt's Syst. Med.* VI. 247 It is generally assumed..; but this is by no means proven. **1916** *Nat. Real Estate Jrnl.* (U.S.) 15 Mar. 110/2 Time has proven the jurisdiction of our creation for we have advanced with a knowledge and better understanding of ourselves and our profession. **1927** E. O'NEILL *Marco Millions* II. i. 106, I believe that what can be proven cannot be true. **1931** C. KELLY *U.S. Postal Policy* iv. 81 How little he understood the will of the American people is proven by their unyielding demand for this service. **1934** *Dict. Amer. Biogr.* XIV. 531/1 He had already proven himself a bold operator in various speculative fields. **1943** W. ROUGHEAD *Art of Murder* 131 Our national nostrum, 'Not Proven'.. a verdict which has been construed by the profane to mean 'Not Guilty, but don't do it again'. **1944** *Scots Mag.* Aug. 387 That his volume had a very large circulation for some generations is proven from a statement quoted by Stevenson. **1957** B. & C. EVANS *Dict. Contemp. Amer. Usage* 399/1 The participle *proven* is respectable literary English. In the United States it is used more often than the form *proved*. In Great Britain *proved* is used more often and *proven* sounds affected to many people. **1959** I. EPSTEIN *Judaism* xviii. 201 This doctrine of resurrection.. cannot be proven philosophically. **1963** L. HUGHES in *Liberator* July 4/1 Savages have proven a point. **1971** *Sci. Amer.* July 5 (Advt.), The MGB's 1798 c.c. twin-carb engine is proven time and again in competition. **1976** *Brit. Jrnl. Sociol.* XXVII. 315 Many of its specific predictions have been proven wrong by the course of events over the last century. **1979** *Economist* 11 Aug. 74/1 If it means a form (or rather, forms) of involvement that seem profitable to employees and employers alike, both can be proven right. **1980** *Daily Tel.* 18 Mar. 15/3 As yet.. chloracne is the only disorder proven to result from human contact with olioxin.

B. Signification.

I. To make trial of, try, test.

1. a. *trans.* To make trial of, put to the test; to try the genuineness or qualities of; to try, test. *arch.* exc. in technical uses (see b, etc.).

c **1200** [see A. 1 *a*]. *a* **1225** [see A. 1 *β*]. **1297** R. GLOUC. (Rolls) 9373 Þis noblemen.. Þat in armes iproued beþ binorþe & bisouþe. *a* **1300** *Cursor M.* 8115 (Cott.) Þe might o þam þou latt vs proue. **1382** WYCLIF *Jas.* i. 3 The prouyng of ȝoure feith werchith pacience. *c* **1440** *Alphabet of Tales* 43 How þe fadir taght his son for to prufe his frende. **1526** TINDALE *John* vi. 6 This he sayde to prove hym, For he hym sylfe knewe what he wolde do. **1585** JAS. I *Ess. Poesie* (Arb.) 27 No flesh nor bone Can preif the honnie we from Pinde distill. **1611** BIBLE *1 Thess.* v. 21 Proue [WYCLIF **1382** prove, **1388** preue ȝe, *Rhem.* prooue, TINDALE to *Geneva* examen] all things: hold fast that which is good. **1704** OLDMIXON *Blenheim* xxii, In vain they prove again the bloody Field. **1807** WORDSW. *White Doe* III. 340 Nor did he turn aside to prove His Brothers' wisdom or their love. **1867** FROUDE *Short Stud., Crit. & Gosp. Hist.* (ed. 2) 160 To prove all things—to try the Spirits whether they be of God. [The prevailing use in Bible of 1611 (34 instances) and retained in Revised Version 1881–85.] **1881** 'MARK TWAIN' *Prince & Pauper* xxv. 198 He seized Miles by the arm, dragged him to the window, and began to devour him from head to foot with his eyes.. stepping briskly around him and about him to prove him from all points of view.

b. To subject to a testing process (any natural, prepared, or manufactured substance or object).

a **1340** HAMPOLE *Psalter* xi. 7 Syluyre examynd in fire, proued of þe erth, purged seuenfald. **1428** *Surtees Misc.* (1888) 1 Þat metaill.. whilk was proved and founden fals. **14..** *Ibid.* 61 All maner of mesurys.. schall be schewed and prevyd. **1502** ATKYNSON tr. *De Imitatione* I. xvii. 165 As golde is proued in the fournes. **1720** MRS. MANLEY *Power of Love* (1741) 328 He saw a Gentleman cheapning and proving Swords. **1788** J. MAY *Jrnl. & Lett.* (1873) 50 This afternoon I proved my rifle-gun. **1872** *Routledge's Ev. Boy's Ann.* 135 The monster cannon now only requires to be vented and proved.

c. *Arith.* To test the correctness of (a calculation). Also *intr.* in *pass.* sense.

Sometimes understood in sense 5.

1806 HUTTON *Course Math.* I. 15 There are three different ways of proving Multiplication. *Ibid.* 16 Multiplication is also very naturally proved by Division. **1862** *Temple Bar Mag.* VI. 542 My friend's moral arithmetic was wrongly squared, and wouldn't prove.

d. *Mining.* (See quot. 1883.)

1839 MURCHISON *Silur. Syst.* I. viii. 124 The coal has been proved, if not worked out, under every part of it. **1869** *Trans. N.Z. Inst.* II. 368 At Coromandel.. the [gold-bearing] lodes have been 'proved' to a depth of over 300 feet from the surface. **1883** GRESLEY *Gloss. Coal Mining, Prove*, ..to ascertain by boring, driving, etc., the position and character of a coal seam, a fault, &c... To examine a mine in search of fire-damp, &c., known as proving the pit. **1883** J. BRADSHAW *N.Z. as it was & Is* xii. 178 In the Coromandel and Thames gold-fields, reefs have been 'proved' to a depth of over 600 feet below the sea level. **1978** *Nature* 6 Apr. p. xix/1 The Steeple Aston Borehole (1970–1971) proved Jurassic, Upper Coal Measures, Upper Devonian and igneous intrusive rocks. **1979** *Jrnl. R. Soc. Arts* Jan. 84/2 Figure 1 shows the extent of the coalfield under the land and also shows that about 10 kilometres of coal measures under the sea have been proven.

e. To take a proof impression of (composed type or an electro- or stereotype plate).

1797 *Encycl. Brit.* (ed. 3) XV. 590/1 [The engraver] proved a plate in different states, that he might ascertain how far his labours had been successful. **1847** *Nat. Encycl.* I. 958 The plate is.. sent to the printer to prove.

f. *Homœopathy.* [tr. G. *prüfen* (Hahnemann).] To give (a drug) to healthy persons to ascertain the symptoms it produces.

[**1833** C. H. DEVRIENT tr. *Hahnemann's Organon of Healing Art* 216 Employ those medicines whose pure effects have been proved upon a healthy person in the manner best suited to the cure of diseases homœopathically.] **1843** *Brit. Jrnl. Homœopathy* I. 160 It is essential that a preparation precisely similar to that proved should be always employed. **1910** *Encycl. Brit.* XIII. 645/2 To ascertain the curative virtues of any drug it must be 'proved' upon healthy persons—that is, taken by healthy individuals of both sexes in a state of health in gradually increasing doses. **1974** *Homoeopathy* June/July 93, I got Nelsons to potentise fulmar oil, and I wanted it proved, but no one would cooperate.

g. *intr.* Of dough: to become aerated by the fermentation of yeast prior to baking; to rise. Also of yeast: to cause such aeration.

1854 C. TOMLINSON *Cycl. Useful Arts* I. 181/1 The whole of the flour is.. left about an hour.. to *prove*. **1854** A. E. BAKER *Gloss. Northamptonshire Words & Phrases* II. 139 In making a cake, if it rises well, 'it *proves* well'. A baker will often say 'It is good yeast, it *proves* so well'. **1909** MRS. BEETON *Cookery Bk.* (new ed.) 265/2 Knead well, and leave dry, cover over with a clean cloth, and let it prove for 1½ hours. **1911** JACK & STRAUSS *Woman's Bk.* 214/2 After shaping the loaves, place them on a baking-sheet.. and set them to prove for fifteen or twenty minutes. **1923** W. G. R. FRANCILLON *Good Cookery* (ed. 2) xxi. 386 *Currant loaf*... Set to prove. Then bake in a quick oven for about fifteen minutes. **1959** *Woman* 14 Mar. 21/1 Put the dough to rise and prove in a warm but not too hot place. **1972** *Guardian* 30 June 11/3 Form the dough into a ball... Cover with a clean cloth and stand in a warm place to prove.

†**2.** *intr.* To make a trial (*of* something), esp. by tasting; to taste (*of*). Cf. PREE *v.* *Obs.*

a **1300** *Cursor M.* 3656 Þou bidd him rise þar-of to proue. **1552** LYNDESAY *Monarche* 1113 Geue thay of that tre had preuit, Perpetuallye thay mycht haue leuit. **1622** R. HAWKINS *Voy. S. Sea* (1847) 36 Some of my company proved of them, and they caused vomits and purging.

3. *trans.* To find out, learn, or know by experience; to have experience of, to experience, 'go through', suffer; also with compl., to find by experience (a person or thing) to be (something). Cf. APPROVE *v.*[1] 9. *arch.*

c **1175** [see A. 1 *a*]. *a* **1300** *Cursor M.* 4383 If i liue þou sal me proue An iuel freind to þi be-houe. **1509** BARCLAY *Shyp of Folys* (1874) I. 228 That thoughe a man had hym delyvered than The same peryll wolde he haue proved agayne. **1588** ALLEN *Admon.* 10 Other inconueniences which they had proued, and mighte easely fall againe. **1662** COKAINE *Tragedy of Ovid* v. ii, I may prove The like sad destiny Clorina did, Should I become your Wife. **1738** WESLEY *Ps.* II. xiii, They only shall his Mercy prove. **18..** M. ARNOLD *Farewell* x, In the world I learnt, what there Thou too wilt surely one day prove, That will, that energy, though rare, Are yet far, far less rare than love.

†**4. a.** To try, endeavour, attempt, strive. Usually const. with *inf.*, also with *if, whether, how, and.* Cf. APPROVE *v.*[1] 8. *Obs.*

c **1330** *Amis & Amil.* 347 Euer he proued with nithe and ond, To bring him into care. **1382** WYCLIF *Rom.* xv. 26 Forsoth Macedonye and Achaye proueden for to make sum collacioun. *c* **1400** *Sowdone Bab.* 183, I shall prove with al my myghte To breke there bothe spere and shelde. *c* **1475** *Rauf Coilȝear* 304, I sall preif the morne.. To bring Coillis to the Court. **1560** DAUS tr. *Sleidane's Comm.* 6 He wyl proue and do the best he can to make the same decree and his questions to accorde. **1600** HOLLAND *Livy* XXIII. xix. 487 They within the towne were driven.. to plucke off the lether from their shields & bucklers, and make them soft in skalding water, and prove [*conari*] how they could eat them. *a* **1610** PARSONS *Leicester's Ghost* (1641) 13, I did also prove To winne their handmaids.

†**b.** *intr.* or *absol.* To set oneself to do something; to try, strive, essay. *Obs. rare.*

1612 DRAYTON *Poly-olb.* A j, From any example, either of ancient or modern, that have proved in this kind. *a* **1659** OSBORN *Observ. Turks* Wks. (1673) 272 Yet he proved against this inconvenience, with as much caution as a by-past error is capable to admit.

II. To make good, establish.

5. *trans.* To establish (a thing) as true; to make certain; to demonstrate the truth of by evidence or argument. (The subject may be a person, a fact, evidence, etc.)

In this sense the Sc. pa. pple. *proven* is often used, esp. in the verdict 'Not proven', which is admitted, besides 'Guilty' and 'Not guilty', in criminal trials in Sc. Law. See examples in A. 2.

a. With subord. cl., or obj. and compl.

a **1225** *Ancr. R.* 68 So þet þe witnesse ne preoue heom ualse. *c* **1230** *Hali Meid.* 23 Ha is an hundred degrez ihehet toward heuene hwil ha meidenhad halt, as þat frut preoueð. *c* **1290** *S. Eng. Leg.* I. 95/98 I-chulle proui þat he ne miȝte a-liue beo. **1387** TREVISA *Higden* (Rolls) VII. 259 Þat ooth was i-preved untrewe. **1422** tr. *Secreta Secret., Priv. Priv.* 218 Here is I-prowid that the sowle sueth the condycionys of the bodyes. **1560** DAUS tr. *Sleidane's Comm.* 101 b, He went about also to proue hym selfe a Germayne. **1594** R. ASHLEY tr. *Loys le Roy* 63 b, Thother goeth about to proue that the world is eternall. **1715** DE FOE *Fam. Instruct.* Introd., I shall take up no time in proving this matter to be a duty. **1874** GREEN *Short Hist.* iii. §5. 137 Able as he proved himself, his task was one of no common difficulty. **1885** *Law Times Rep.* LIII. 60/2 The plaintiff and the surveyor proved that the *I.C.U.* carried proper lights.

b. with simple obj.

c **1320** R. BRUNNE *Medit.* 18 Y wyl no þyng seye But þat ys preued by crystes feye. *c* **1384** CHAUCER *H. Fame* II. 300 Who so seyth of trouthe I varye Bid hym proven the contrarye. **1387** TREVISA *Higden* (Rolls) VII. 345 As it fil afterward þe soþe was i-preoved. **1428** in *Surtees Misc.* (1888) 4 Any thyng agayne ye kynges pease yat myght be proved apon hym lawfully. **1551** T. WILSON *Logike* (1580) 33 An example is a maner of argumentation, where one thyng is proued by an other. **1605** CAMDEN *Rem.* 33 If they should be forced to prooue descent. **1681** FLAVEL *Meth. Grace* ix. 186 A thousand witnesses cannot prove any point more clearly than one testimony of conscience doth. **1782** G. SELWYN in *15th Rep. Hist. MSS. Comm.* App. VI. 563 The endeavour to prove too much has made more Atheists than any book wrote on purpose to establish Infidelity. **1837–8** SIR W. HAMILTON *Logic* xxvi. (1866) II. 39 To prove, is to evince the truth of a proposition not admitted to be true, from other propositions the truth of which is already established. **1844** MRS. BROWNING *Lady G.'s Courtship* lxx, When my footstep proved my coming.

c. *to fend and prove*: see FEND *v.* 2.

d. *to prove too much*, to pursue an argument too far; to establish by argument a proposition so inclusive as to yield unhelpful results.

1791 J. MACKINTOSH *Vindiciæ Gallicæ* iv. 215 To this I answer, *first*, that such reasoning will prove too much, and that, taken in its proper extent, it impeaches the great system of morals, of which political principles form only a part. **1801** T. JEFFERSON *Let.* 9 Sept. in Koch & Peden *Life T. Jefferson* (1944) 565 It may be objected that this proves too much, as it proves you cannot enter the ship of a friend to search for contraband of war. **1870** J. H. NEWMAN *Gram. of Assent* vi. 153 The theory to which I have referred cannot be carried out in practice. It may be rightly said to prove too much. **1893** 'L. CARROLL' *Sylvie & Bruno Concluded* iii. 41 But surely that involves the logical fallacy of *proving too much*?

6. To show the existence or reality of; to give demonstration or proof of by action; to evince.

a **1300** *Cursor M.* 1077 Proued was son his sari pride. *c* **1375** *Sc. Leg. Saints* xxx. (*Theodera*) 186 Scho went on to pref hir arte. *c* **1500** *Lancelot* 3476 No man shall eschef Frome yhow this day, his manhed for to pref. **1697** DRYDEN *Virg. Georg.* IV. 105 Ev'ry Knight is proud to prove his Worth. **1872** MORLEY *Voltaire* i. (1886) 2 They should prove their love of him whom they had not seen, by love of their brothers whom they had seen.

7. a. To establish the genuineness or validity of (a thing or person); to show to be such as is asserted or claimed.

1517 TORKINGTON *Pilgr.* (1884) 41 The holy crosse was provyd by resyng of a Dede man. **1531** in *Sel. Cas. Crt. Requests* (1898) 33 Your seid Orator hath noo especyaltie ne wrytyng prouyng the seid contracte. **1642** FULLER *Holy & Prof. St.* v. iii. 365 It is very hard to prove a Witch. **1866** NEALE *Seq. & Hymns* 89 If the purple proves the King.

b. *spec.* To establish the genuineness and validity of (a will); to obtain probate of.

1439 *Rolls of Parlt.* V. 22/1 By the seid Testament yet nought proeved. **1521** in *Bury Wills* (Camden) 120 Item in expenses.. or the will cowd be proved. **1609** B. JONSON *Sil. Wom.* v. iii, You can proue a Will, master Doctor, you can proue nothing else. **1726** S. SEWALL *Diary* 28 Mar., I prov'd Elder Preston's Will. **1818** CRUISE *Digest* (ed. 2) II. 435 The heir's joining would supply the want of proving the will. **1885** *Whitaker's Alm.* 421 One [executor] alone is competent to prove a will and carry out its provisions.

c. *refl.* To evince proof of one's abilities or prowess.

1961 *She* Mar. 38 But no one could help him, in his agonising struggle to save them—and prove himself. **1964** *Harper's Mag.* Dec. 95/1 A third such student, Caesar, came from a Latin-American country where a man is expected to prove himself by having many affairs, and a mistress after marriage. **1973** *Times* 1 Dec. 13/6 You have to prove yourself to your father, don't you?

8. *intr.* for *refl.* To show itself to be (something); to be shown or found by experience or trial to be (so and so); to turn out (to be). **a.** with complement (sb., adj., or infin. phr.).

13.. *E.E. Allit. P.* B. 704 Wel nyȝe pure paradys moȝt preue no better. **1447** *Shillingford Lett.* (Camden) 101

Which offence preveth to be done by the consent [etc.]. **1551** T. WILSON *Logike* (1580) 73 A ragged Colte maie proue a good horse. **1584** R. SCOT *Discov. Witchcr.* x. vi. (1886) 147 Dreames proove contrarie. **1596** SPENSER *F.Q.* IV. xi. 35 If old sawes prove true. **1617** MORYSON *Itin.* II. 83 One accident, that might have proved of great consequence. *a***1680** BUTLER *Rem.* (1759) I. 65 For Things said false, and never meant, Do oft prove true by accident. **1789** W. BUCHAN *Dom. Med.* (1790) 285 When the disease proves violent. **1823** SCORESBY *Jrnl. Whale Fish.* 107 The land.. nearest to us was Wollaston Foreland, which, by my late surveys, proves to lie in latitude 74° 25'. **1870** TYNDALL *Lect. Electr.* I This gas when collected proves to have the specific gravity of hydrogen.

b. With adv. or advb. phrase, as *to prove well* (obs. or dial.), to turn out well; now only with such advbs. as *how, so, otherwise*.

1447 *Shillingford Lett.* (Camden) 119 So hit proveth by the seide boke of Domesdey. *c***1460** METHAM *Wks.* (E.E.T.S.) 146 Howe the yere schuld preue, afftyr that Crystmes day fallyth vpon ony day off the weke... Qwydyry[t] schuld preue fayr or foule. **1575–85** ABP. SANDYS *Serm.* (Parker Soc.) 327 Such marriages seldom or never prove well. **1648** GAGE *West Ind.* 79 Ships which have proved as well at sea, as those that are made in Spain. **1695** LUTTRELL *Brief Rel.* (1857) III. 482 Engineer Richards has proved the..new invented mortars, which proved to admiration. **1794** SMEATON *Edystone L.* §98 In case the weather should be then in our favour; but it proving otherwise, we returned to Plymouth. *a***1825** FORBY *Voc. E. Anglia* s.v., 'How did that beast prove?' is a question often asked of the butcher by the farmer. **1886** C. SCOTT *Sheep-Farming* 157 Breeders are beginning to understand that it is to their interest to have their sheep prove well.

†**c.** *to prove well*: to be well seen, to be evident. *Obs. rare.*

*c***1386** CHAUCER *Prol.* 547 (Harl. MS.) Ful big he was of braun and eek of boones, That preuede wel, for ouer al þer he cam At wrastlynge he wolde bere away þe Ram. **1470–85** MALORY *Arthur* x. viii. 425 He is a grete enemy to alle good knyghtes, and that preueth wel, for he hath chaced oute of that Countrey syr Tristram.

9. To come to be, become, grow. *arch.*

1560 DAUS tr. *Sleidane's Comm.* 3 This Thomas.. went.. after to Paris, and proued best learned of al men in his time. **1615** G. SANDYS *Trav.* 136 Neither.. will other races in that soile proue blacke. **1697** DRYDEN *Virg. Georg.* III. 814 To Birds their Native Heav'ns contagious prove, From Clouds they fall, and leave their Souls above. **1842** TENNYSON *Lord of Burleigh* 66 Then her countenance all over Pale again as death did prove.

†**10.** *intr.* To turn out well; to prosper; to thrive; to succeed. *Obs.*

*c***1386** CHAUCER *Can. Yeom. Prol. & T.* 659 Ye shul se wel thanne How þat oure bisynesse shal thryue & preeue. *c***1440** *Promp. Parv.* 415/2 Provyn, or chevyn, *prosperor*. **1543** *Act 35 Hen. VIII*, c. 17 §1 Standils or Storers, likely to prove and to be Timber-trees. ?*a***1550** *Hye Way to Spyttel Ho.* 690 in Hazl. *E.P.P.* IV. 55 Inholders that lodge hoores and theues, Seldon theyr getyng ony way preues. **1578** LYTE *Dodoens* I. xxvi. 39 Orpyne proueth wel in moyst shadowy places. **1604** E. HAKE *No Gold, No Goodnesse* in Farr *S.P. Jas. I* (1848) 255 Nothing proves where gold is skant. **1698** FRYER *Acc. E. India & P.* 376 All the Eggs laid under one Hen do not always prove.

†**11.** *trans.* = APPROVE *v.*[1] 6. *Obs.*

1387 TREVISA *Higden* (Rolls) VII. 337 Kyng William his dedes,..[beeþ] worþy to be i-preved. *c***1400** *Destr. Troy* 4942 Part of þat pepull prouyt hit for wit. **1545** T. FORSTER *Disc.* in Tytler *Hist. Scot.* (1864) III. 33 He thinketh that that adventure would be proved; for he saith.. the cardinal is.. smally beloved in Scotland.

12. prove up. a. To adduce or complete the proof of right to (something); *spec.* to show that one has fulfilled the legal conditions for taking up (a grant of government land), so that a patent may be issued. Also *absol. N. Amer.*

1867 A. D. RICHARDSON *Beyond Mississippi* xi. 138 He does not see the land again until ready to 'prove up' which he may do after thirty days. Then he revisits his claim. **1878** J. H. BEADLE *Western Wilds* ii. 43 My wife proved up on her Cherokee blood. **1890** L. C. D'OYLE *Notches* 49 As I had advertised to prove up, I persuaded him to stay a week longer.. and be one of my witnesses. **1892** *Harper's Mag.* June 95/2 As they 'prove up' those claims in the fulness of time, each will get her one hundred dollars. **1893** *Kansas Hist. Coll.* (1896) V. 91 'Money to loan to prove up' was the device on many a little board building. **1921** *Daily Colonist* (Victoria, B.C.) 11 Mar. 12/5 Proved up, with hard work, a wild and forest covered homestead. **1958** J. G. MACGREGOR *North-West of 16* v. 67 They also had to bring fifteen acres under cultivation and to erect some sort of abode. (Carrying out these obligations and getting title to the land was termed 'proving up'.) **1963** G. H. THOMSON *Crocus Country* xix. 124 The homesteaders, however, were obliged to fence so many acres before they could 'prove up' or be given the patent to their land. **1969** *Islander* (Victoria, B.C.) 16 Nov. 12/2 Mr. James Foulds, widower, proved up on his homestead.. in 1910 or thereabouts. **1977** *New Yorker* 11 July 37/2 He tried to educate people in the responsibilities of living on public estate, so they could stay within the rules, legalize their occupancy, prove up.

b. = sense 1 d. Also *absol.* orig. *N. Amer.*

1921 *Daily Colonist* (Victoria, B.C.) 13 Oct. 2/4 Several claims staked up and down the channel from the discovery have proved up in a similar manner. **1926** *Ibid.* 17 Jan. 35/5 The richest mineralization that has been proved up in the whole district. **1975** *Offshore* Aug. 87/2 The company is aiming to prove up about 20 trillion cubic feet of the fuel to justify an initial transmission line to southern markets. **1977** *Bulletin* (Sydney) 22 Jan. 42/1 It frequently takes as much as 10 to 12 years from an initial discovery to prove up a viable mine, arrange finance and forward sales-contracts.

13. prove out. To establish (something) as correct or workable; to test (a system or process) exhaustively. Also *intr.* for *refl.* orig. *U.S.*

1959 *Wall St. Jrnl.* 13 May 14/2 Fishermen are pondering the commercial possibilities of pollock... If pollock proves out, the trawlers could stay closer to U.S. shores. **1964** D. F. GALOUYE *Counterfeit World* xii. 98 Of all the metaphysical concepts.. mine was the only one open to final verification. It could be proved out conclusively. **1967** *Electronics* 6 Mar. 28 (Advt.), We'll run a sufficient number of samples to prove out the process. **1969** *Daily Mail* 15 Jan. 5/7 The Moon is a convenient body on which to prove out our systems and programmes. **1972** *Daily Tel.* (Colour Suppl.) 10 Nov. 10/1 A duration of 50 to 60 hours was required really to prove out the plane. **1976** N. THORNBURG *Cutter & Bone* iv. 102 If your hundred-to-one chance proves out, and Wolfe actually is the one.

†**prove,** *sb. Obs. rare.* [f. PROVE *v.*: cf. obs. F. *prouve* a probe (1549 in Godef.), also PROOF *sb.* 15 a.] A surgeon's probe.

1541 R. COPLAND *Guydon's Quest. Chirurg.* L iv, The maner to take theym [seames] of is to put the tayle of the proue vnder the fyst, & to cut the threde of the sayd tayle of the proue, and in puttynge the flat of the proue aboue the lyppe wherby ye threde is drawen out, for drede of dyuydynge the wounde.

proveable, -ably: see PROVABLE, -ABLY.

†**pro'vect,** *a.* (*sb.*) *Obs.* [ad. L. *prōvect-us* advanced, pa. pple. of *prōvehĕre*: see next. Cf. obs. F. *provect* (1545 in Godef.).] Advanced (in years); mature, adult. **b.** *sb.* Something grown or become old.

1531 ELYOT *Gov.* I. iv, Litle infantes assayeth to folowe.. the faictes and gesture of them that be prouecte in yeres. **1630** DAVENANT *Cruel Brother* II, Dull Caytife, leaue these abortiue Prouects, And talke in the newest fashion. **1636** BRATHWAIT *Rom. Emp.* Ep. Ded. A iij, It is the nature of some trees not to bring forth fruite until they come to be provect.

provect (prəʊˈvɛkt), *v.* [f. L. *prōvect-*, ppl. stem of *prōvehĕre* to carry or conduct forward, to advance, f. *prō*, PRO-[1] 1 + *vehĕre* to carry.]

†**1.** *trans.* To carry forward or onward. *Obs.*

1652 GAULE *Magastrom.* 17 They were miraculously provected, and, as it were, carried along in the ayr. *a***1776** R. JAMES *Diss. Fevers* (1778) 103 A continual fever, which.. is too often provected to malignity.

2. *Philology.* To change or 'mutate' a consonant in the direction of the sound-shift (*lautverschiebung*) formulated for Teutonic in Grimm's Law (LAW 17); *esp.* in Celtic, to change a voice consonant into a breath consonant of the same series (e.g. *d* to *t*, *v* to *f*).

1861 WHITLEY STOKES *Middle-Cornish Poem* in *Trans. Philol. Soc.* App. 83 *G* is provected into *h* after *y* in *y hyller* (*gyller*). **1877** RHŶS *Lect. Welsh Philol.* ii. 85 As an initial, it [*gw* reduced to *w*] was some time or other modified from *w* to *v*, which was subsequently provected into *f*. **1879** RHŶS in *Academy* 23 Aug. 144 Even supposing.. that the Teutons were by nature endowed with a sort of a *lautverschiebung* sense, whereby they provected the consonants of other nations.

pro'vectant. *Math.* [f. L. *prōvect-* (see prec.) + -ANT: cf. *evectant*.] In *Invariant Algebra* (*Quantics*): A covariant considered as the resultant of the operation of a provector on a contravariant.

1858 [see PROVECTOR].

provection (prəʊˈvɛkʃən). [ad. late L. *prōvectiōn-em*, n. of action f. *prōveh-ĕre*: see above.]

†**1.** Advance, proficiency; advancement. *Obs.*

1652 URQUHART *Jewel* Wks. (1834) 264 Master Duncan Liddel was then of that maturity of age and provection of skil in most of the disciplines mathematical. **1660** J. LLOYD *Prim. Episc.* 8 He [Clemens Alexandrinus] saith, that here in the Church the provections or proficiencies of Bishops, Presbyters, Deacons, be imitations of the angelical glory.

2. *Philology.* **a.** The sound-shift (*lautverschiebung*) of consonants formulated for Teutonic langs. in Grimm's Law; *esp.* in Celtic, the mutation of voice consonants to breath consonants (e.g. of *g, d, b, v* to *k, t, p, f*), which occurs in certain circumstances in the Celtic languages.

1861 WHITLEY STOKES *Middle-Cornish Poem* in *Trans. Philol. Soc.* App. 83 Observe the provection [of *d* to *t*] after *y*; the reason being that *y* stands for *yt* = *ate*; thus: *ma-y trehevys* [from *drehevys*]. **1873–5** RHŶS in *Revue Celtique* II. 331 Other instances of this kind of provection of mute consonants following *l* or *r*. **1877** —— *Lect. Welsh Philol.* ii. 67 When *gg* becomes *cc* and the like: this kind of mutation may, in default of a more appropriate term, be called *provection*. *Ibid.* vii. 348 When it is said.. that the *f* of [*feather*] is the *p* of [πτερον] subjected to provection.

b. The carrying on of the final letter of a word to the succeeding one.

1868 KEY *Philol. Ess.* 177 The *t* [in *tother*] is due to.. Provection, having been transferred from the end of the preceding word, just as in 'for the nonce', in place of 'for then once'. **1872** F. HALL *Rec. Exemp. False Philol.* 6 A like instance of the provection of *n* is seen in the 'no nother cause of varyaunce' of Sir Thomas More.

3. The carrying forward of something into the place of something else; substitution.

1891 RHŶS *Stud. Arthur. Leg.* vii. 165 To be explained as a result of another mythological provection, which in some instances thrust the Culture Hero into the place of the more ancient head of the Celtic pantheon.

pro'vector. *Math.* [See VECTOR *sb.* and PROVECT.] **a.** *Quaternions*: see quot. 1853. **b.** Name for a particular kind of operator in the theory of Invariant Algebra.

1853 SIR W. R. HAMILTON *Quaternions* (1866) I Successive vectors, such as AB and BC, or B − A and C − B, are occasionally said to be vector and provector. *Ibid.* 4 If a provector BC be added to a vector AB, the sum is the transvector AC; or in symbols, I..(B − A) + A = B; and II..(C − B) + (B − A) = C − A. **1858** CAYLEY *Coll. Math. Papers* II. 514 The Provector operating upon any contravariant gives rise to a contravariant, which may of course be an invariant. Any such contravariant, or rather such contravariant considered as so generated, may be termed a Provectant.

proved (pruːvd), *ppl. a.* Forms: see PROVE *v.* [f. PROVE *v.* + -ED[1].]

1. Tried, tested; hence, That has stood a trial or test; approved, trustworthy, trusty.

*a***1340** HAMPOLE *Psalter* xvii. 25 þe temptaciouns of proued men. **1451** CAPGRAVE *St. Aug.* (E.E.T.S.) 14 He, with ful good a-vise, sent hem Austyn, a preued maystir. **1568** GRAFTON *Chron.* II. 36 The best proued men that they coulde finde. **1587** MASCALL *Govt. Cattle* Title-p., Search herein, and thou shalt find, of prooued remedies quickly. **1850** LYNCH *Theo. Trin.* ix. 176 The saved companies of heaven will be.. happy societies of proved men.

2. Shown to be true, or to be as stated; demonstrated. Hence, †Known as such, notorious (*obs.*).

14.. *Stockh. Med. MS.* I. 77 in *Anglia* XVIII. 297 þis is prowyd thinge for þe suth [*MS.* syth]. **1562** *Child-Marriages* 207 [She] said he was 'a provid thief, & all his kinne'; and apon that, he callid her 'provid hoore'. **1875** MAINE *Hist. Inst.* xi. 326 A custom of proved antiquity. **1941** A. TARSKI *Introd. Logic* I. vi. 118 Statements established in this way are called *proved statements* or *theorems*. **1965** B. MATES *Elem. Logic* vi. 97 We may wish to use previously proved theorems.

3. Of which probate has been granted.

1890 *Whitaker's Alm.* 640 (*heading*) Where to find a proved will.

Hence ˈ**provedly** *adv.*

1628 FELTHAM *Resolves* II. [I.] lxxvii. 221 One would thinke it strange,.. yet it is provedly true. **1892** R. KIPLING in *Pall Mall G.* 24 Mar. 3/2 Having.. reverence only for that which was indubitably and provedly stronger than themselves. **1901** *N. & Q.* 9th Ser. VIII. 455/1 Of the plays contained in the present volume two only are provedly his.

proveditor (prəʊˈvɛdɪtə(r)), also in It. form ‖**proveditore** (provediˈtore). Also α. 7 proveditour, -videto(u)r, -vidator, 7 -viditor; β. (as It.) 6–7 providitore, 7 -videtore, 9 provv-; *pl.* -veditori (7 -vidatory). [ad. obs. It. *proved-*, mod. *provveditore*, provider, purveyor, agent-n. from *provedere* to PROVIDE: so in F. *provéditeur*.]

1. The title of certain officers of the Venetian republic: e.g. a commissioner or delegate who acted as adviser to the commander of a military force; the governor of a dependency; a governor, overseer, inspector.

α. **1585** T. WASHINGTON tr. *Nicholay's Voy.* II. i. 32 We came too an anker vppon good wyll and request of the Proveditor. **1601** R. JOHNSON *Kingd. & Commw.* 97 With the armie they sende diuers of their gentlemen as legats or prouiditors. **1668** *Lond. Gaz.* No. 222/2 The Proveditor of Candia Seignior Lorenzo Pisani. **1693** J. EDWARDS *Author. O. & N. Test.* 216 Joseph.. was Grand Proveditor of that country. **1756** NUGENT *Gr. Tour, Italy* III. 82 Besides these the Venetians have.. a common proveditor who takes care of the bridges and keeps the city neat. **1832** tr. *Sismondi's Ital. Rep.* xvi. 361 The patriots, warned in time, arrested the proveditor himself.

β. **1549** THOMAS *Hist. Italie* 82 They create a *Proueditore*, who (out of Venice) is of no lesse authoritee, than the Dictatour was wont to be in Rome. **1696** tr. *Du Mont's Voy. Levant* xxvi. 242 Both the City and the Harbour are commanded by a very fine Castle, where the Proveditore.. resides. **1825** SCOTT *Talism.* xxiv, 'I protest against such a combat', said the Venetian *proveditore*.

2. A purveyor, caterer, steward. Also *fig.*

α. **1697** T. SMITH *Voy. Constantinople* in *Misc. Cur.* (1708) III. 30 Nor did I ever see any in their Fish-Markets, or one of them brought to the Ambassador's Table by the Providetor for curiosity. *a***1716** SOUTH *Serm.* (1744) XI. vii. 164 He.. made the liberality of heaven the instrument of his vanity and the very proveditor for his lust. **1720** DE FOE *Capt. Singleton* ix. (1840) 163 Our new providitor ordered some of our negroes to plant it. **1765** BLACKSTONE *Comm.* I. viii. 288 Ready money in open market.. being found upon experience to be the best proveditor of any. **1861** THACKERAY *Four Georges* iii. (1862) 130 He.. is proud, he says, to be that gentleman's proveditor. **1872** *City Press* 20 Jan., A committee dinner of the Ironmongers' Company took place at the hall, Mr. Webster being the proveditor.

β. **1599** NASHE *Lenten Stuffe* 38 This well meaning *Pater patriæ*, and prouiditore and supporter of Yarmouth [the herring]. **1649** JER. TAYLOR *Gt. Exemp.* I. Sect. viii. 113 The entertainment, that S. John's Proveditore the Angel gave him. *a***1716** SOUTH *Serm.* (1823) I. 420 Can any one dare to make him [Christ].. his providetore for such things as can only feed his pride, and flush his ambition?

3. Comb. *proveditor-general* [cf. GENERAL *a.* 10].

1701 *Lond. Gaz.* No. 3706/1 Proveditore-General Molino, who has the Chief Command of the Venetian Forces in Italy. **1724** *Briton* No. 23. 100 Vinegar, who is Proveditor-General of Cudgels for the inferior Class of Combatants at the Bear-Garden. **1725** DE FOE *Voy. round*

World (1840) 275 By the help of our proveditor-general we fared very well. **1730** A. GORDON *Maffei's Amphith.* 80 Physician to the Proveditor-General [of Candia].

provedore (prɒvɪˈdɔə(r)). Also 6 proveador, -vedor, 7 -vido(u)r, 7–9 -vidore, 8 -viedore. [ad. various Romanic forms, as Pg. *provedor*, Sp. *proveedor*, ? Venetian dial. *providore*, all the agent-n. from the vb. repr. L. *prōvidēre* to PROVIDE; cf. prec. and F. *pourvoyeur* PURVEYOR.]

1. A chief officer; a commander, governor, overseer; = PROVEDITOR 1.

1578 in HAKLUYT *Voy.* (1600) III. 701, I talked with the *Prouedor* and the Captaine. **1598** W. PHILLIP *Linschoten* 4/2 By fauour and good will of the *Proueador*, which is the chiefe officer of the Admiraltie. **1615** G. SANDYS *Trav.* 6 The Gouernor of the Iland [Zante]..whom they call the Prouidore, with two Consiglieri, all gentlemen of Venice. **1658** PHILLIPS, *Proveditor*, (..as it were a providour) a great Military Officer among the Venetians. **1805** T. LINDLEY *Voy. Brazil* 130 Till they should obtain the permission also of the provedore of the custom-house.

2. A purveyor, caterer, steward; = PROVEDITOR 2.

1686 GOAD *Celest. Bodies* II. xiv. 355 A Providore, who looks abroad into the Country for the supply of his Charge. **1719** DE FOE *Crusoe* 249 The Proviedore, or Steward of the Monastery, had taken great Care all along. **1814** SCOTT *Swift's Wks.* II. 182 *note*, Mr Richard Estcourt, a player.. was *Providore* of the Beef-steak Club. **1878** LADY BRASSEY *Voy. Sunbeam* I. xiv. 231 Watching our *proveedor*, as he went about collecting things by ones and twos.

fig. **1693** *The Rake, or Libertine's Relig.* Pref. A ij b, [He] considers the whole Creation as only his Garden and Confectionary, and the God of it as no more than his Providore. **1826** T. I. WHARTON in *Pa. Hist. Soc. Mem.* I. 151 Jewels and diamonds to be sold by Robert Bell, humble provedore to the sentimentalists.

†**3.** A storehouse, a larder. *Obs. rare*⁻¹.

1658 R. FRANCK *North. Mem.* (1821) 68 To observe.. what stock of provisions is stored in their providors.

proveist, obs. Sc. form of PROVOST.

proven (ˈpruːv(ə)n, ˈprəʊv(ə)n), *ppl. a.* [pa. pple. (orig. Sc.) of *preve*, PROVE *v.*, after strong vbs. as †*chese* (*choose*), *chosen*, *cleave*, *cloven*, *weave*, *woven*.]

1. = PROVED 2. (Orig. in *Sc. Law*: see note s.v. PROVE *v.* 5.) In some uses passing into sense 2 ('tested, approved, shown to be successful').

1653 R. BAILLIE *Dissuas. Vind.* (1655) 63 This is no answer to a proven challenge. **1829** LANDOR *Imag. Conv.*, *Penn & Ld. Peterb.* Wks. 1846 I. 534/1 They never abandon a proven falsehood or an iniquitous demand. **1897** *Allbutt's Syst. Med.* II. 264 We must accept it as a proven fact. **1963** *Automobile Engineer* LIII. 231/1 One..well known manufacturer is experimenting with an automatic stepped ratio transmission based upon proven principles. **1964** *Archivum Linguisticum* XVI. 125 A few relatively recent histories of the language..continue to repeat seemingly contradictory, debatable and even erroneous statements on this subject as if they were proven facts. **1968** *Globe & Mail* (Toronto) 17 Feb. B6 (Advt.), We seek an ambitious, mature university graduate possessing a proven sales background preferably in pharmaceutical sales. **1975** *Daily Tel.* 27 Nov. 29/1 (Advt.), Applicants should possess..a proven success record within a national consumer goods environment. **1976** *Sunday Times* 8 Feb. 66/3 (Advt.), The ideal candidate will above all have a proven profitable track record as a manager. **1977** T. M. BERNSTEIN *Dos, Don'ts & Maybes of Eng. Usage* 181 The form *proven* is used as an attributive adjective..and particularly in certain technical locutions, such as 'a *proven* oil field'.

2. = PROVED 1. pseudo-*arch.* Also (of a person, etc.) in wider use.

1870 MORRIS *Earthly Par.* IV. 150 He..Had got his proven sword into his hand. **1872** TENNYSON *Gareth & L.* 27 Gawain..Ask'd me to tilt with him, the proven knight. **1942** W. FAULKNER *Go down, Moses* 144 Boon and the negroes..ran the coons and cats, because the proven hunters..scorned such other than shooting..to test their marksmanship. **1961** *Sunday Express* 8 Oct. 30 Game little *Angazi* is a proven mudlark. **1968** *Globe & Mail* (Toronto) 17 Feb. B6 (Advt.), An outstanding opportunity exists for a proven manager to join a new management team.

provenance (ˈprɒvənəns). [a. F. *provenance* (prɔvnɑ̃s) *Dict. Acad.* 1835, f. *provenant*, pres. pple. of *provenir* to come forth, arise, ad. L. *prōvenīre*: see PROVENE.] **a.** The fact of coming from some particular source or quarter; origin, derivation.

1785 E. SHERIDAN *Jrnl.* (1960) 61 Miss Anstruther as I before mention'd Elegant, fashionable in her appearance, but nothing of that *provenance* in her manner that caught me so much in Miss Brook. **1861** C. W. KING *Ant. Gems* (1866) 80 Supposing this statement as to the provenance of the hoard to be essentially true. **1884** A. LANG *Custom & Myth* 13 He would have some difficulty in guessing its provenance, and naming the race from which it was brought. **1893** J. T. BENT *Ruined Cities Mashonaland* vi. 204 Beads of doubtful provenance, though some of them may be considered as Egyptian of the Ptolemaic period. **1906** H. B. SWETE *Apocalypse* Introd. ii. §5. 25 How hard it is to determine the date and provenance of Jewish apocalypses.

b. The history or pedigree of a work of art, manuscript, rare book, etc.; *concr.*, a record of the ultimate derivation and passage of an item through its various owners.

A distinction is often drawn between the 'origin' and the 'provenance' of an article, as in quot. 1960.

1926 J. BUCHAN *Dancing Floor* I. vi. 111 If I knew the provenance of the manuscript, I might be able to understand it better. **1946** 'M. INNES' *From London Far* II. x. 146 That aspect of the history of art which collectors call provenance? Who owned the picture last..and who before that. The ideal is to trace it right back to the studio. **1947** A. CHRISTIE *Labours of Hercules* xi. 220 Sir Reuben would have purchased a Renaissance goblet, *provenance* unspecified. **1960** E. A. LOWE *Eng. Uncial* 21 A Canterbury origin is probable, Canterbury provenance is certain. **1966** *Listener* 10 Feb. 207/1 At gallery number three on Madison Avenue I was introduced to a man who asked if I had a *provenance* or any sort of papers for the picture. **1967** J. N. BARRON *Lang. Painting* 156 *Provenance*, a history or pedigree of a painting: the establishment of the identity of successive owners since its execution. Also included would be all published documents, catalogues, and journals that contain references to the painting, along with reproductions, exhibitions, and sales records, as well as correspondence, especially of the artist, in which mention of it may be made. **1974** A. PRICE *Other Paths to Glory* II. ix. 223 'He was only interested in where it came from, eh?' *Provenance.*

c. *Forestry.* The location in which tree seed is collected. Also, seed from a specific location.

1933 *Empire Forestry Jrnl.* XII. 198 The problem of seed origin embraces both the geographical location where the seed was collected..and the genetic character of the mother trees... In European literature the term 'provenance'..has come to be used for the first phase of the problem. **1942** H. I. BALDWIN *Forest Tree Seed* iii. 29 Provenance is of tremendous significance to the outcome of plantations. **1956** M. L. ANDERSON tr. *Köstler's Silviculture* iii. 89 The first experimental planting, with thirty different provenances of pine, had been carried out as early as 1821. **1970** H. L. EDLIN *Collins Guide to Tree Planting & Cultivation* vi. 100 The true origin of each stock is called its provenance. *Ibid.* 101 A second generation of the same stock would still have that provenance.

Hence **ˈprovenanced** *a.*, provided with a record of provenance; established as to origin.

1939 *Nature* 20 May 848/2 Only adequately provenanced objects should be collected; only so can we hope to map, ultimately, the cultural regions of pre-industrial Britain. **1971** J. MANN *Charitable End* iii. 27 Most of it's [*sc.* an art collection is] not provenanced, you know. **1975** *Numismatic Chron.* 198 (*heading*) Some provenanced finds of Crusader bezants.

Provençal (prɒvɑ̃ːˈsɑːl), *a.* and *sb.* Also 6–7 provenzal(l, 7–8 provencial, 8– Provençale. [a. F. *provençal* of Provence:—L. *prōvinciāl-is* PROVINCIAL: see PROVENCE.]

A. *adj.* **1.** Of or pertaining to Provence and its inhabitants. (See next.)

1589 NASHE *Pref. Greene's Menaphon* (Arb.) 10 Those that are neither prouenzall men, nor are able to distinguish of Articles. **1650** [see PICARD *adj.*]. **1723** POPE *Let. to Lady* 26 Sept., Pieces of the old provençal poets. **1771** [see LANGUEDOCIAN *a.* and *sb.*]. **1819** KEATS *Ode to Nightingale* 14 Dance, and Provençal song, and sunburnt mirth! **1855** MILMAN *Lat. Chr.* IX. viii. IV. 220 The high Provençal patriotism of the Troubadour. **1902** *Speaker* 5 Apr. 9/2 The Provençal shepherd does not drive his flock but leads it. **1936** A. W. CLAPHAM *Romanesque Archit.* iv. 78 A not uncommon feature of the Provençal apse is its polygonal external form. **1971** *Guardian* 16 Feb. 9/3 A quilted skirt in fine wool Provençal print.

2. Designating a style of cookery characteristic of Provence, typically containing rich savoury ingredients.

1841 THACKERAY in *Fraser's Mag.* June 720/1 You know what a *Provençale* sauce is?.. A rich, savoury mixture, of garlic and oil. **1966** *Harrod's Food News* Sept. 2/2 Individual Scampi Provençal—per carton 9/6. **1974** *Times* 23 May 7/6 Try my favourite Provençal mixture with tomatoes, herbs and anchovies.

B. *sb.* **1.** An inhabitant of Provence.

1600 SURFLET *Country Farm* 31 The Gascoin is hot... The Prouenciall is haughtie and cannot indure to be reproued. **1804** C. B. BROWN tr. *Volney's View Soil U.S.* 136 A collateral wind, called, by the Provençals, the mistral. **1865** KINGSLEY *Herew.* viii, Her mother was a Provençale. **1902** *Speaker* 5 Apr. 9/1 With all his imagination, the Provençal betrays a curious realism of his own.

2. The Romanic language spoken in Provence.

1642 J. HOWELL *Forraine Travell* x. 124 The French have three dialects, the Wallon..the Provensall..and the speech of Languedoc. **1671** J. GAILHARD *Pres. St. Italy* (ed. 2) 173 About Piemont..they speak a corrupt Italian, which hath most of the Provenzal in it. **1743** COLLINS *Ep. to Hanmer on Edit. Shaks.* 40 The soft Provencial pass'd to Arno's stream. **1792** [see CATALAN]. **1901** *Q. Rev.* Oct. 484 One wished that the periodical should be bi-lingual and the other that it should be solely in Provençal. **1964** *Archivum Linguisticum* XVI. 34 Occitan—or Provençal, as it is more usually known—was one of the major European literary languages... *Provençal* is ambiguous, referring as it does both to the language as a whole and to one particular dialect, that of Provence. **1977** *Listener* 28 July 118/1 The verbal texts..are sung in the original Provençal.

3. *Cookery.* (See quots.)

1960 *Times* 5 Sept. 13/5 *Provençale*, a dish which contains tomatoes, garlic and peppers. **1977** *Times* 28 Nov. 31/3 Particularly recommended are..*provençales* (with garlic, tomatoes and herbs, served somewhat like a pizza).

Hence **Provenˈçalism**, an idiom or mode of expression typical of the Provençal language; **Provençalist**, a student of Provençal language and literature; **Proˈvençalize** *v.*, *trans.* to influence by or assimilate to Provençal modes.

1903 H. LYNCH *G. Paris' Med. Fr. Lit.* 95 It is probable that we have lost the earliest lyric poetry of the Provençalised school. **1934** *Times Lit. Suppl.* 30 Aug. 587/1 Mr. W. P. Shepard, himself no mean Provençalist. **1958** Provençalism [see CATALANIST]. **1975** *Times Lit. Suppl.* 12 Sept. 1023/4 A brilliant essay..that Provençalists ignore at their peril. **1978** *Language* LIV. 428 The Berlin school was spearheaded by K. A. F. Mahn, who, as a Provençalist, became something of a rival of Raynouard and Diez.

Provence (‖prɔvɑ̃s, ˈprɒvəns). [a. F. *Provence*:—L. *prōvincia* PROVINCE.

The southern part of ancient Gallia (*Narbonensis*), which came under Roman rule long before the other parts, was familiarly styled (*nostra*) *Provincia*, 'the (or our) province'.]

The name of a former province in the south-east of France east of the Rhone; used *attrib.*, as in ***Provence oil***, olive oil from Provence; ***Provence rose***, the cabbage rose, *Rosa centifolia*, or a variety of it, esp. one bearing fragrant red flowers, or a hybrid produced by crossing *R. centifolia* and *R. gallica*; also, a flower of one of these plants.

There is a long-established confusion between Provence and Provins roses, reflected in quots. 1597 and 1905. Quot. 1578 probably refers to the Provins rose: cf. *province rose* s.v. PROVINCE 10.

1578 LYTE *Dodoens* VI. i. 653 The third kind are they which some call Roses of Prouince. **1597** GERARD *Herball* III. i. 1801 The Damaske Rose is called..of some *Rosa provincialis*, or Rose of Provence. **1707** J. MORTIMER *Whole Art Husbandry* I. xviii. 477 The Red Provence Rose, whose Branches and Leaves are bigger and greener than those of the common Red Rose. **1765** H. ST. JOHN *Let. to G. Selwyn* 11 Jan. in Jesse *S. & Contemp.* (1843) I. 347 My brother desires you would be so good as to send him some very good Provence oil. **1817** *Repository of Arts* (Ackermann) Jan. 53/1 A..bonnet..ornamented with Provence roses and fancy flowers. *a* **1821** KEATS *Cap & Bells* in R. Monckton-Milnes *Life Keats* (1848) II. 219 She..wetted three or four White Provençe rose-leaves with her faery tears. **1837** T. RIVERS *Rose Amateur's Guide* 2 It is therefore very probable that it [*sc. Rosa centifolia*] was called the Provence Rose from growing more abundantly in that province. *Ibid.*, Hybrid roses, between this [*sc. R. centifolia*] and *Rosa gallica*, are called Provence Roses by the French amateurs of the present day. **1847** C. M. YONGE *Scenes & Characters* xxv. 301 Those are some Provence roses for Miss Weston. **1850** LOUDON *Encycl. Gard.* 1053/2, 55 *R*[*osa*] *centifolia*.. Provence or Cabbage rose. **1848**, **1869** [see GALLICA]. **1905** *Westm. Gaz.* 31 July 10/1 The misnamed Provence rose was first introduced into France by the Crusaders at Provins (Seine and Marne). **1909** R. G. KINGSLEY *Roses* iii. 39 The Moss Rose,..originally a sport from the common Provence or Cabbage Rose, was also introduced into England from Holland in 1596. **1955** G. S. THOMAS *Old Shrub Roses* xii. 139 *Rosa gallica* (the 'French Rose' or 'Rose of Provins'). The title Provins is also found in the old name, *Rosa provincialis*, but must not be confused with the Provence Rose, *Rosa centifolia*. **1978** J. HARKNESS *Roses* xiii. 180 These old roses [*sc.* centifolias] have mostly been known by three common names: Cabbage roses, Provence roses and Cent-feuilles.

†**provencion**, obs. erron. form of PREVENTION 2a: cf. PRO-¹ 3.

a **1548** HALL *Chron., Hen. VIII* 109 Also by his power Legantine he gaue by prouencions, all benefices belongyng to spirituall persones.

provend (ˈprɒvənd), *sb. Obs.* or *arch.* Also 4–6 provende. [a. F. *provende* (12th c. in Littré) †a prebend, a supply of food, provender = It. *profenda*, †*provenda*, provender, med.L. *provenda* (13th c. in Du Cange):—Romanic type **prōvenda* (whence also OSax. *prôvenda*, OHG. *pfrovinta* (G. *pfründe*), MLG., MDu. *proven(d)e*, ON. *próvenda*, *prófenda*, etc.); altered form of L. *præbenda*, *prēbenda*, PREBEND (with *pro-* for *præ-*, *pre-* (see PRO-¹ 3), and Romanic *v* from *b*): cf. PROVOST, and OF. *provoire* for *prevoire*:—*presˈbytˈrum* priest. See also PROVENDER, and PROVAND, PROVANT, PROVIANT, representing the same word.

(Cf. Tobler in Cohn's *Suffixw.* 81, Körting *Rom. WB.* no. 7360.) Diez (s.v. *prebenda*) suggests that the word has been influenced by L. *prōvid-ēre* to PROVIDE.]

1. = PREBEND 1; also, the portion or allowance of food supplied to each inmate of a monastery; stipend.

[**1292** BRITTON II. xvii. §6 Touz prelatz et religious demaundauntz tenementz estre apurtenauntz a lour eglises ou a lour provendes.] *c* **1330** R. BRUNNE *Chron.* (1810) 210 þei rene þam prouendes, þorgh power þat þei haue. *c* **1400** *Rom. Rose* 6931 If we seen hym wynne honour Richesse or preis thurgh his valour Prouende rent or dignyte. **1483** CAXTON *Gold. Leg.* 415/2 The other dayes he gaue his prouende to poure peple. **1727–41** CHAMBERS *Cycl.* s.v., In monasteries, when the religious go to meals, they are said to go to provend. **1873** LONGF. *Wayside Inn* III. *Monk of Casal-Maggiore* vii, Brother Anthony..Drove him [the ass] before him..Safe with his provend to the convent gate.

2. Food, provisions; *esp.* (in early use always) dry food for horses, as corn and hay; = PROVENDER 2.

c **1330** R. BRUNNE *Chron. Wace* (Rolls) 10730 Mete & drynke, & hors prouende. **1570** LEVINS *Manip.* 65/1 Prouende, *pabulum, i.* *a* **1687** COTTON *Winter* xxx, With Hail instead of Provend fed. **1853** *Fraser's Mag.* XLVIII. 423 He gives us an elaborate account of the provend and *cuisine*. **1855** ROBINSON *Whitby Gloss.* s.v., 'Tis a proud horse that won't carry its own proven. **1900** CROCKETT *Fitting of Peats* iii. in *Love Idylls* (1901) 24 It shall never be said that Adam Home took another man's horse and provend without asking his leave.

†ˈ**provend**, *v. Obs.* [f. prec. sb.] *trans.* To supply with provender; to feed, to fodder.

1581 A. HALL *Iliad* II. 30 Do throughly prouend wel your Horsse. *c* **1746** J. COLLIER (Tim Bobbin) *View Lanc. Dial.* Wks. (1862) 67 I'll fodder an Provon the Tits for the.

provender ('prɒvɪndə(r)), *sb.*[1] Also 4-5 provendre, 5 -dour, -dere, -dyr, 6 provander, prawnder. [a. OF. *provendre* (13th c. in Godef.), a phonetic variant of *provende* PROVEND.]

†**1.** A prebend. *Obs.*

[**1306** *Rolls of Parlt.* I. 219/1 Le Roi & les ditz Countes & Barons..deivent presenter a les Provendres, & les Eglises Parochieles.] *c* **1380** WYCLIF *Wks.* (1880) 419 Cathedral chirchis þat han prouendris approprid to hem. **1387** TREVISA *Higden* (Rolls) VIII. 95 Þe monkes were disparpled, and what þey hadde was i-ordeyned to provendres to clerkes [L. *in præbendas clericorum redactis*]. **1393** LANGL. *P. Pl.* C. IV. 32 And porchace ȝow prouendres while ȝoure pans lasteþ. *c* **1425** *St. Mary of Oignies* II. vi. in *Anglia* VIII. 167/27 Anoþere..whan hee hadde a prouendour menely sufficient to hym..receyued anoþer prouendere þat was gretter of dignite and rentys. *c* **1440** *Promp. Parv.* 415/2 Prouender..(*K.* provendyr, benyfice, *S.* prebend, benfyce, *P.* probender, benfice), *prebenda*.

2. Food, provisions; *esp.* dry food, as corn or hay, for horses, etc.; fodder, forage. In reference to human beings, now *humorous*.

1340 *Ayenb.* 35 Seruices ulessliche of hors, of carten, oþer prouendres to ham, oþer to hare children. **1377** LANGL. *P. Pl.* B. XIII. 243, I fynde payne for þe pope and prouendre for his palfrey. *a* **1400** *Siege of Troy* 409 in *Archiv neu. Spr.* LXXII, Provandre, corn and hay. **1547** BOORDE *Introd. Knowl.* xxxvii. (1870) 216 The Camel..kneeled downe to haue eaten hys prouender. **1567** TURBERV. *Ovid's Epist.* 91 b, And in unwilling mouth my meate and yrksome prawnder greene. **1591** SHAKS. *1 Hen. VI*, I. ii. 11 They must be dyeted like Mules, And haue their Prouender ty'd to their mouthes. **1703** MAUNDRELL *Journ. Jerus.* (1732) 2 Meat, Drink, Bed, Fire, Provender; with these it must be every ones care to furnish himself. **1836** MARRYAT *Midsh. Easy* xiii, The coxswain had examined the provender in the ship. **1863** HOLLAND *Lett. Joneses* iii. 53 He..salutes any flag under which he can win plaudits and provender. **1907** *Westm. Gaz.* 3 Jan. 12/1 The vacant canonry of St. Albans—at present a stall without provender.

3. *Thieves' slang.* (See quot.)

a **1700** B. E. *Dict. Cant.*, *Provender*, he from whom any Money is taken on the Highway. **1725** *New Cant. Dict.*, *Provender*, Money taken from any one on the Highway.

†**provender**, *sb.*[2] *Obs.* Also 4 prouendere, -dre. [In sense 1, ME. *provendere*, a. OF. *provendier*, *-der* (11th c. in Godef.):—L. *præ-*, *prēbendārius* PREBENDARY, f. *præbenda* prebend: see PROVEND *sb.* In sense 2, perh. for *provander*, f. PROVAND + -ER[1].]

1. A prebendary.

c **1330** R. BRUNNE *Chron.* (1810) 81 Of þe þan is þis house þat are was prouendere, now is religiouse. *Ibid.* 261 Neuer bisshop, ne person, ne riche prouendere [*printed* perronendere], Ne erle, ne baron, ne knyght, ne squiere. **1387-8** T. USK *Test. Love* II. ii. (Skeat) l. 50 Nowe is losell for his songes, personer and prouendre alone, with whiche many thriftye shulde encrease.

2. A purveyor, one who provides supplies. *rare.*

1515 BARCLAY *Egloges* iii. (1570) B vj b/2 For if thou liue in court, thou must rewarde this rable... Butlers and Butchers, prouenders and Bakers.

†**provender**, *a. Obs. rare*[—1]. (?) (Perhaps an error of some kind.)

1643 MILTON *Divorce* iv. 9 Even then most unquencht, when the importunity of a provender burning is well anough appeas'd.

provender ('prɒvɪndə(r)), *v.* [f. PROVENDER *sb.*[1] Cf. OF. *provender* to furnish with or to take provender, to provide with a prebend, f. *provende* PROVEND.]

†**1.** *trans.* To provide with a prebend or benefice. *Obs.*

1377 LANGL. *P. Pl.* B. III. 149 She blesseth þise bisshopes.., Prouendreth persones and prestes meynteneth.

2. To provide (horses, etc.) with provender; to fodder. Also *fig.*

1584 *Leycesters Commw.* (1641) 151 The white Paulfrey when hee..is well provendred, is proud and fierce. **1641** MILTON *Prel. Episc.* Wks. 1851 III. 90 Their resolved decree of reducing into Order their usurping and over provender'd Episcopants. **1707** MORTIMER *Husb.* (1721) I. 207 That the Horse be well provender'd, and drink but little over Night. **1905** HOLMAN-HUNT *Pre-Raphaelitism* I. 438 He had our horses stabled and provendered.

3. *intr.* To partake of provender; to feed *on*. *rare.*

1819 KEATS *Let.* 9 June (1931) II. 376 Infidel Rooks do not provender with Elisha's Ravens. **1891** C. GRAVES *Field of Tares* IV. vi. 241 Leaving the iron horse provendering on coal and water..we follow the footsteps of the man with the black valise.

Hence '**provendering** *vbl. sb.*, the providing of provender.

1620 SHELTON *Quix.* (1746) III. xxv. 172 Let me make an End of provendering my Beast. *a* **1628** PRESTON *New Covt.* (1630) 183 The provendering of his horse is a dispatching of his Iourney.

†'**provendrer.** *Obs.* [f. PROVENDER *sb.*[1] + -ER[1]; cf. PROVENDER *sb.*[2] 1, also *fruiterer*, *upholsterer*.] The holder of a prebend; a prebendary.

[**1347-8** *Rolls of Parlt.* II. 219/1 Thomas de Trillek Provendrer de la Provendre de Matton en Eglise de Welles.] **1362** LANGL. *P. Pl.* A. III. 145 Prouendreres, persuns, Preostes heo meynteneþ. *c* **1380** WYCLIF *Sel. Wks.* III. 211 Alle siche ben symonieris þat occupien bi symonye þe patrimonye of Crist, be þei popis..or provendereris.

†'**provendry.** *Obs. rare.* [f. PROVEND *sb.* + -RY.] = PREBEND 1, 2: cf. PREBENDRY.

[**1327-8** *Year Bk.* 41 *Edw. III* (1600) 5 b, Le roy port Quare impedit vers W. leuesque de Sarum del prouendry appelle Minor pars altaris in ecclesia beate Marie Sarum.] **1483** *Cath. Angl.* 292/2 A Prouandry [*pr.* Promandry], *prebenda, prebendarius qui habet prebenda*[*m*]. **1708** *Termes de la Ley* 469 Provendry in the Church of Sarum, is called the lesser part of the Altar in the Church of St. Mary 41 E. 3. 5. b.

†**pro'vene**, *v. Obs. rare.* [a. F. *provenir*, or ad. L. *prōvenīre* to come forth, arise, originate, f. *prō*, PRO-[1] 1 a + *ven-īre* to come.] *intr.* To come as proceeds or produce; to proceed, arise (*from* any source of revenue or profit).

1505 *Will of W. Clarke* (Somerset Ho.), The cropp therof provenyng. **1584** *Sc. Acts Jas. VI* (1814) III. 370/2 To transport þe samin and all vtheris mynerallis and metalles and vtheris thingis provening thairof..beȝond sea. **1733** tr. *Renaudot's Acc. India & China* 63 The Sums provening from this great Quantity of Gold are distributed to those of the Royal Household.

provenience (prəʊ'viːnɪəns). [f. L. *prōvenient-em*, pr. pple. of *prōvenīre* to PROVENE: see -ENCE. Preferred to PROVENANCE by those who object to the French form of the latter: cf. CONVENANCE, CONVENIENCE.] = PROVENANCE. Now chiefly *U.S.* (and to some extent *Canad.*).

Elsewhere *provenance* is the more usual form.

1882 *Century Mag.* Aug. 632/2 Wherever..its *provenience* is stated, I received the information from General Cesnola in person. **1895** A. J. EVANS in *Jrnl. Hellenic Stud.* XIV. 276 Engraved stones of other types..of uncertain provenience were obtained in Candia. **1899** R. ELLIS in *Class. Rev.* 131/2 The readings reported as coming from the Gyraldinus were not always to be treated as if we had any certainty of their provenience. **1955** J. R. HULBERT *Dicts. Brit. & Amer.* 54 It would be redundant and space consuming to give two pronunciations and indicate their provenience every time a word containing an *r* in this position turned up. **1968** P. M. POSTAL *Aspects Phonol. Theory* iv. 71 Thus in English the gross divisions seem to correspond to the Germanic, Romance, and Greek provenience of forms. **1978** *Maledicta 1977* Winter 133, I am concerned here particularly with some lexical reflections of the dislike of foreigners, as those reflections appear in English, although they are certainly not all of English provenience. **1978** *New York* 3 Apr. 81/2 Why should the hero's hypertrophic sense of smell—heightened to the point where, blindfolded, he can ferret out olfactorily the exact provenience and writing thickness of a ballpoint pen—be the means for his blowing up the world?

†**pro'venient**, *a. Sc. Obs. rare.* [ad. L. *prōvenient-em*: see prec.] Forthcoming.

1554 *Sc. Acts Mary* (1814) II. App. 601/1 W[t] all þe.. Contributionis and taxationis of oure said realme and dominionis to be falling or provenientis sen þe deceiss of oure said derrest fathir.

'**provenly**, *adv.* [f. PROVEN *ppl. a.* + -LY[2].] In a proven manner.

1887 G. B. SHAW *Let.* 27 May (1965) 170 The provenly heroic Annie Besant. **1967** *Times Rev. Industry* July 33/2 The uncommitted clearing banks are staying firmly on the sidelines until the industry has provenly made its way. **1972** *Daily Tel.* 30 Dec. 18 The otter is provenly beneficial to fishing. **1975** *Ibid.* 30 Aug. 11/2 The doctor concerned was fully trained and provenly competent.

†**pro'vension**, obs. erron. form of PREVENTION 2 a: cf. PRO-[1] 3.

1655 FULLER *Ch. Hist.* IV. ii. §8. 158 The King..promised to take order with the Popes Provisions and Provensions, that so learned men might be advanced.

†'**provent.** *Obs.* [ad. L. *prōvent-us* a coming forth, produce, supply, increase, f. *prōvent-*, ppl. stem of *prōven-īre* to come forth, PROVENE. So OF. *provent* (1382 in Godef.).] = PROVENUE.

1432-50 tr. *Higden* (Rolls) VI. 361 This kynge divided alle his proventes [L. *proventus suos*] into ij. partes. *Ibid.* VIII. 335 He..occupied the wolles of alle men, and the ix[the] parte of alle cornes, of which proventus he commaunded lordes of townes that were nye to þeym to ȝiffe an answere. *c* **1460** *Oseney Reg.* 57 Offrynges, and oþer parishall prouentes or profittes. **1544** *Supplic. to Hen. VIII* (E.E.T.S.) 47 There greate lordships and domynions, with the yerely prouentes of the same. **1593** *Sc. Acts Jas. VI* (1816) IV. 26/2 þat hir maiestie is lykwyis infeft in lyverent in..all proventis rentis and emolumentis of the same propirtie. **1664** EVELYN *Pomona, Aphorisms Cider* 45 A Neighbour having a good provent of Purelings (an Apple of choice account with us).

provent(e, obs. variant of PROVANT.

proventricular (prəʊvɛn'trɪkjʊlə(r)), *a.* [f. next + -AR[1].] Pertaining to the proventriculus.

1835-6 OWEN in *Todd's Cycl. Anat.* I. 319/1 The secretion of the proventricular or gastric glands is analogous to the gastric juice in man. **1874** COUES *Birds N.W.* 683. **1895** *Athenæum* 30 Mar. 412/3 A description of the proventricular crypts he had found in..the African tantalus.

‖**proventriculus** (prəʊvɛn'trɪkjʊləs). *Zool.* [mod.L., f. *prō*, PRO-[1] + *ventriculus* VENTRICLE, dim. of *venter* belly.]

a. *Ornith.* The glandular or true stomach of birds, which lies between the crop and the gizzard.

1835-6 OWEN in *Todd's Cycl. Anat.* I. 319/1 The proventriculus varies..in form and magnitude in different birds. **1870** ROLLESTON *Anim. Life* Introd. 51 In adult Birds, the digestive tract is characterized by the absence of teeth.., and by the presence of a horny beak, and of a muscular gizzard placed posteriorly to a glandular proventriculus. **1886** *Athenæum* 30 Jan. 171/3 The ostrich's proventriculus.

b. A glandular expansion of the lower part of the œsophagus in some Mammalia.

1875 C. C. BLAKE *Zool.* 52 The proventriculus of the Dormouse and Beaver.

c. In Invertebrata: in some insects, the crop or ingluvies, an expansion of the œsophagus having thick muscular walls armed with horny prominences; in worms, a muscular crop.

1877 HUXLEY *Anat. Inv. Anim.* vii. 411 The proventriculus leads posteriorly into a narrow, thick-coated canal. **1904** *Brit. Med. Jrnl.* 17 Sept. 665/2 The intestinal canal [of the larva] commences as a short oesophagus, which ends in a proventriculus.

†'**provenue.** *Obs.* [a. obs. F. *provenu* (1670 in Godef.) produce, revenue, prop. pa. pple. of F. *provenir* to come forth, arise: cf. PROVENT.] The sum arising from something; the proceeds, returns, produce, profit, revenue.

1640 BP. HALL *Chr. Moder.* (ed. Ward) 9/2 The rich and dainty provenues of our gardens and orchards. **1671** HOWE *Van. Man* (ed. Rogers) I. 424 Born to consume such an estate, and devour the provenue of so many farms and manors. **1755** MAGENS *Insurances* I. 25 By the Provenue (or Produce) of the Kersies and Tin, bought with the £1000 lent.

prover ('pruːvə(r)). Also 4 -ere, 5 -ar, -owr, (prower), 5-6 provour; β. 4 preuere, 5 prever. [In sense 1, f. PROVE + -ER[1]: = OF. *proveor*, *prouvour*. In 2 = Anglo-L. *probātor* (Bracton, Fleta II. lii. §§42, 44), AF. *provour*, *pruvour* (Britton).]

I. 1. a. One who tries, tests, or puts to the proof. In quot. 1686, an assayer of metals. *Obs.* or *arch.*

1382 WYCLIF *Jer.* vi. 27 A stalwrthe prouere [**1388** preuere, Vulg. *probatorem*] Y ȝaf thee in my puple, and thou shalt wite, and preue the weie of them. *c* **1450** tr. *De Imitatione* III. iii. 67, I am rewarder of all gode men, & a miȝty prever of all deuoute men. **1535** COVERDALE *Jer.* vi. 27 The haue I set for a prouer of my harde people, to seke out and to trye their wayes. **1686** *Lond. Gaz.* No. 2194/4 Chief Prover (or Assay-Master General of the Empire of Germany).

b. An instrument or apparatus for testing.

1751 D. JEFFERIES *Treat. Diamonds* (ed. 2) 18 An instrument useful for examining the size and depth of any diamond, called a prover. **1862** *Catal. Internat. Exhib.* II. XIII. 10 Woollen and linen provers.

c. *Engraving.* A skilled workman employed to print proof impressions: cf. PROVE *v.* 1 e.

1875 *Ure's Dict. Arts* II. 289 In the principal houses there are generally employed from two to six men..whose duty it is to print proof impressions only [of an engraved plate]; they are called *provers*. **1900** *Daily News* 18 Sept. 8/4 Process block prover on Albion Press wanted.

d. *Homœopathy.* A healthy person on whom the effect of a drug is tested. Cf. PROVE *v.* 1 f.

1843 *Brit. Jrnl. Homœopathy* I. 162 The prover should choose a period when he is in the best of health. **1848** C. J. HEMPEL tr. C. Hering in *Jahr's New Manual* I. p. viii, Every lover of homœopathy must bestow the most unbounded praise and admiration on the Austrian provers. **1902** *Encycl. Brit.* XXIX. 312/2 The manifestations of drug action thus produced are carefully recorded, and this record..after being verified by repetition on many 'provers', constitutes the distinguishing feature of the homœopathic materia medica. **1931** J. E. BARKER *Miracles of Healing* vii. 102 It may seem easy to match the symptoms of a patient with a drug producing the same symptoms in healthy provers who have experimentally taken it. In reality this is exceedingly difficult. **1974** *Homoeopathy* June/July 89 After taking the thirty powders the provers have a rest for a month, and then have a further thirty powders.

II. †**2.** One who confesses a felony and gives evidence against his accomplices in order to secure their conviction; one who turns king's or state's evidence; one who undertakes to prove a criminal accusation against another: = APPROVER[1] 1. *Obs.*

[**1235-6** *Bracton's Note-bk.* (1887) III. 174 Appellum unde duellum..inter quemdam probatorem et alium quemdam quem idem probator de societate appelauit contra coronam..Regis. **1275** *Act 3 Edw. I* (1st Stat. Westm.) c. 15 Ceus queux sont appellez de provurs taunt come le provur vist. **1292** BRITTON I. ii. §16 Qe les Corouners receyvent les reconisaunces de felonies fetes par provours en presence del viscounte.] *c* **1400** *Apol. Loll.* 69 Oiþer he schal dampne þe prouar, or..schal iuge þe vngilty. **1444** *Rolls of Parlt.* V. 111/2 He knowleched diverse Felonies and Tresons, and becam a provowr. **1456** SIR G. HAYE *Law Arms* (S.T.S.) 264 Jugement is done before a juge be a provour and a defendour and witnes. **1588** LAMBARDE *Eiren.* III. ii. 344 A Prouour.. must beginne with confession of his owne fault, before he may be permitted to burthen an other man. **1611** SPEED *Hist. Gt. Brit.* IX. xxiv. 851/2 Suffer neither the said prouer, nor defender to take any of their weapons. **1769** BLACKSTONE *Comm.* IV. xxv. 330 He is called an approver or prover, *probator*, and the party appealed or accused is called the *appellee*.

3. One who shows something to be true; a demonstrator. *rare.*

1738 WARBURTON *Div. Legat.* III. II. App. 34 He will bring several Testimonies to prove it... And on such Occasions..he is a most unmerciful Prover. **1850** BROWNING *Christmas-Eve* iv, Truth remains true, the fault's in the prover.

proverb (ˈprɒvɜːb), *sb.* Also 4-7 **proverbe**. [ME. a. F. *proverbe* (12th c. in Hatz.-Darm.), ad. L. *prōverbium* an old saying, adage, proverb, in late L. also a byword, f. *prō*, PRO-¹ 1 + *verb-um* word + *-ium*, collective suffix, hence app. 'a (recognized) set of words put forth'; cf. *adāgium* adage.]

1. a. A short pithy saying in common and recognized use; a concise sentence, often metaphorical or alliterative in form, which is held to express some truth ascertained by experience or observation and familiar to all; an adage, a wise saw.

c **1374** CHAUCER *Troylus* III. 250 (299) Prouerbes kanst þi self I-now and woost Aȝens þat vice. **1382** WYCLIF *Ezek.* xvi. 44 Loo! eche man that seith euery where..a prouerbe in thee shal take it to..As the modir, so and hir douȝter. **1481** CAXTON *Reynard* iv. (Arb.) 7 It is a comyn prouerbe, An Enemyes mouth saith seeld wel. **1553** T. WILSON *Rhet.* (1580) 122 What neede I heape all these together, seeyng Heiwoddes Prouerbes are in Printe? **1577** B. GOOGE *Heresbach's Husb.* (1586) 47 As the Prouerbe in Englande is, Set a Knaue on horsebacke, and you shall see him shoulder a Knight. **1601** J. WHEELER *Treat. Comm.* 58 For it is merry in Hall, where beards wagge all, according to that olde right English Prouerbe of our Ancestours. **1659** HOWELL *Lexicon, Proverbs* a iv, Proverbs may not improperly be called the Philosophy of the Common Peeple, or, according to Aristotle, the truest Reliques of old Philosophy. *a* **1716** SOUTH *Serm.* (1823) I. 437 What is a proverb, but the experience and observation of several ages, gathered and summed up into one expression? **1840-1** WRIGHT & HALLIWELL (*title*) The Proverbs of King Alfred. **1850** HT. MARTINEAU *Hist. Peace* II. IV. xii. 159 Hence it was that those words..passed..into a proverb. **1870** LOWELL *Study Wind.* 162 Sambo, with his stock of proverbs, the ready money of human experience.

b. *spec.* ***the Book of Proverbs***, a didactic poetical book of the Old Testament, consisting of maxims ascribed to Solomon and other authors.

1303 R. BRUNNE *Handl. Synne* 11904 Salamon seyþ, þat ys wys, Yn a boke of Prouerbyys. **1390** GOWER *Conf.* III. 48 Of Salomon and the proverbes, Of Macer al the strengthe of herbes. **1526** *Pilgr. Perf.* (W. de W. 1531) 212 b, Than shall it be veryfyed that Salomon sayth in his prouerbes. **1635** R. BOLTON *Comf. Affl. Consc.* i. 14 This Book of Proverbs is compared to a great heape of gold rings rich and orient severally; and every one shining with a distinct sense by itselfe. **1880** W. W. NEWTON *Serm. Boys & Girls* (1881) 203 He turned to the third chapter of Proverbs and read it over.

c. Phr. ***to a proverb***, to an extent that has become proverbial; proverbially.

1743 in A. D. Candler et al. *Georgia Rec.* (*c* 1913-16) XXIII. 513 He had then recourse to his Usual Salve, (well known, to all persons at Savannah with whom he converses, even to a proverb) That He was Seventy Years of Age, His Memory decayed, etc. **1766** FORDYCE *Serm. Yng. Wom.* (1767) II. xiii. 231 That revengeful disposition, of which your sex have been accused even to a proverb. **1796** MORSE *Amer. Geog.* I. Pref. 7 To depend on foreigners, partial, to a proverb, to their own country. **1817** J. EVANS *Excurs. Windsor*, etc. 482 A country, swampy even to a proverb. **1849** MACAULAY *Hist. Eng.* viii. II. 275 The new chief justice, Sir Robert Wright, was ignorant to a proverb.

2. a. A common word or phrase of contempt or reproach, a byword; †hence *transf.* a person or thing to which such a phrase is applied: = BYWORD 2 (*obs.*).

1382 WYCLIF *1 Kings* ix. 7 And Irael shal be into prouerbe and into fable, to alle puplis [1535 COVERD. shall be come a byworde and fabell amonge all nacions]. **1535** COVERDALE *Hab.* ii. 6 Shall not all these take vp a prouerbe agaynst him, and mocke him with a byworde..? **1560** BIBLE (Genev.) *Deut.* xxviii. 37 And thou shalt be a wonder, a prouerbe & a commune talke among all people. **1680** BURNET *Rochester* 173 One of the Glories of his Age was become a Proverb. **1791** BOSWELL *Johnson* (1851) III. 34 He should take care not to be made a proverb.

b. *transf.* A thing that is proverbial or a matter of common talk.

1655 STANLEY *Hist. Philos.* II. III. 13 Abdera a Town of Thrace, noted for the simplicity of the Inhabitants which grew even to a proverb. **1707** E. CHAMBERLAYNE *Pres. St. Eng.* I. iii. (ed. 22) 10 Buckinghamshire Bread and Beef is a Proverb for their Goodness. **1712** STEELE *Spect.* No. 509 ¶8 Mr. Hobson,..when a Man came for a Horse,..obliged him to take the Horse which stood next to the Stable-Door... From whence it became a Proverb..to say 'Hobson's Choice'. **1853** J. H. NEWMAN *Hist. Sk.* (1873) II. I. ii. 61 Siberia goes for a proverb for cold: India is a proverb for heat. **1855** BAIN *Senses & Int.* III. iv. §21 (1864) 212 The mental absorption of Archimedes is a proverb.

†**3.** An oracular or enigmatical saying that requires interpretation; an allegory, a parable. *Obs.*

1382 WYCLIF *John* xvi. 25, I haue spokun to ȝou thes thingis in prouerbis [*gloss* or derke saumplis]; the our cometh, whanne now I schal not speke to ȝou in prouerbis, but opynly. **1526** TINDALE *ibid.* 29 His disciples sayd vnto hym: loo nowe speakest thou playnly, and thou vsest no proverbe. **1611** BIBLE *Prov.* i. 6 To vnderstand a prouerbe, and the interpretation; the wordes of the wise, and their darke sayings. **1841** TRENCH *Parables* i. (1877) 7 Those are called 'proverbs' in St. John, which, if not strictly parables, yet claim much closer affinity to the parable than to the proverb, being in fact allegories.

4. A play of which a proverb is taken as the foundation of the plot. Called in French *proverbe*; in Eng. chiefly used of French plays so called.

1842 BRANDE *Dict. Sci.*, etc. 994/1 *Proverb*..In dramatic literature..the term has been applied to short pieces, in which some proverb or popular saying is taken as the foundation of the plot... Carmantelli was the most successful writer of proverbs at the time of their highest popularity. **1879** JOS. KNIGHT in *Athenæum* 28 June, [in reference to the *Comédie Française* then in England] The comedies or the proverbs of Musset meanwhile defy the translator, and their representation calls for a class of acting of which our stage knows nothing. **1893** *Nation* (N.Y.) 20 July 50/3 She [Comtesse de Chambrun]..was fond of acting in her own private theatre... Sometimes she wrote a 'proverb' herself, and created the principal part.

5. *pl.* A name for various round games played with proverbs or popular sayings.

A common form is the guessing of such a saying by asking questions of the circle of players, whose answers must introduce in order each word of the proverb.

1855 *Home Games for People* 104 *Proverbs.* One of the party is sent out of the room: the rest busying themselves with thinking of a proverb..to be discovered by him on his return. **1867** 'AUNT CARRIE' *Popular Pastimes for Field & Fireside* 188 *Proverbs.* The company select some one to leave the room; those remaining agree upon a proverb [etc.]. **1879** 'L. HOFFMANN' *Drawing-Room Amusements & Evening Party Entertainments* ii. 50 Proverbs. This is another 'guessing' game. **1895** *Montgomery Ward & Co. Catal.* Spring & Summer 236/3 Proverbs. The old standard game revised, consisting of 100 cards containing the best proverbs. **1910** W. OWEN *Let.* 27 Dec. (1967) 66 We have been playing games (e.g. Proverbs, Memory Tray, etc.) this evening. **1975** *Way to Play* 257/2 *Proverbs...* It is sometimes called hidden proverbs, or guessing proverbs.

6. *attrib.* and *Comb.*, as ***proverb-card***, ***-hunting***, ***-monger***, ***-wisdom***; ***proverb-like*** adj. and adv.

c **1586** C'TESS PEMBROKE *Ps.* XLIV. vii, Proverb-like our name is worn. **1709** O. DYKES *Eng. Prov. & Refl.* (ed. 2) 274 A Pack of Proverb-Cards, lately printed, and curiously engrav'd with Figures. **1857** MRS. GATTY *Leg. Tales* (1858) 4 A genuine proverb-monger—he who chills off your enthusiasm by a tame truism. **1902** F. E. HULME *Proverb-Lore* 89 Proverb-hunting is a very pleasant recreation. **1966** S. MANN *Collecting Playing Cards* vii. 141 *Proverb Cards*, containing pleasant Devices, suited to the most witty English Proverbs. Made c. 1700... The value is indicated by a single suit-mark at top right. **1977** *Jrnl. Playing-Card Soc.* Nov. 44 There seem to be two packs of Proverb cards that could conceivably be the one referred to by Lenthall.

proverb (ˈprɒvɜːb), *v.* [f. prec. sb.; cf. med.L. *prōverbi-āri*, It. *proverbiare* to speak in proverbs.]

1. *trans.* To utter in the form of a proverb; to speak of proverbially; to make a byword of.

c **1374** CHAUCER *Troylus* III. 244 (293) Þis wise clerkes that ben dede han euere this prouerbed to vs ȝong. **1599** PORTER *Angry Wom. Abingd.* (Percy Soc.) 41 You haue most learnedly prouerbed it, commending the vertue of patience or forbearance. **1671** MILTON *Samson* 203 Am I not sung and proverbd for a Fool In every street? **1791-1823** D'ISRAELI *Cur. Lit., Philos. Proverbs*, Nations proverb each other; counties flout counties. **1841** LD. J. MANNERS *Eng. Trust* ii. 64 One short month should hear his dastard name Proverbed as emblem of disgrace and shame.

2. To furnish or provide with a proverb. *rare.*

1592 SHAKS. *Rom. & Jul.* I. iv. 37, I am prouerb'd with a Grandsier Phrase, Ile be a Candle-holder and looke on.

3. *intr.* To utter or compose proverbs. *rare.*

1648 MILTON *Observ. Art. Peace* Wks. 1851 IV. 580 All thir pains tak'n to seem so wise in proverbing, serves but to conclude them downright Slaves.

Hence ˈ**proverbed** *ppl. a.*

1788 BURNS *Let. to Mrs. Dunlop* 2 Aug., Unlike sage proverb'd wisdom's hard-wrung boon. **1845** S. TURNER *Rich. III*, Pref. 8 A regular story, corresponding with this proverbed King's real story, or rather biography.

proverbial (prəʊˈvɜːbɪəl), *a.* (*sb.*) [ad. late L. *prōverbiāl-is*, f. *prōverbi-um*: see PROVERB *sb.* and -AL¹. So F. *proverbial* (1556 in Hatz.-Darm.).]

A. *adj.* **1.** Resembling, characteristic of, or of the nature of a proverb; expressed in a proverb or proverbs. Also *absol.*

1432-50 [implied in PROVERBIALLY 1]. **1548** UDALL, etc. *Erasm. Par. John* xviii. 507 b, Jesus did vouchsafe to aunswere hym by a riddle and a prouerbiall saying. **1646** SIR T. BROWNE *Pseud. Ep.* 98 Although proverbs bee popular principles, yet is not all true that is proverbiall. **1712** STEELE *Spect.* No. 509 ¶1 Delivered in his own homely Maxims, and a Kind of Proverbial Simplicity. **1908** *Q. Rev.* Apr. 338 Popular expressions of proverbial wisdom. **1961** *N. & Q.* Feb. 76/2 The description given certainly enlightens the reader as to a number of characteristics of the proverb, but equally certainly leaves him doubtful about where the proverbial leaves off.

2. That has passed into a proverb, or into common talk; used or current as a proverb; notorious. Also used with allusive force to introduce a word or expression that is familiar as (part of) a proverb or catch-phrase.

1571 GOLDING *Calvin on Ps.* xliv. 14 The name of them flew comonly abrode among prouerbyall figures in way of reproche. **1589** GREENE *Menaphon* (Arb.) 71 That grounded tranquilitie, which made it prouerbiall to the world, *No heauen but Arcadie.* **1711** STEELE *Spect.* No. 145 ¶2 What Hudibras says of such Disputants, which is so true, that it is almost Proverbial. **1878** HUXLEY *Physiogr.* 45 The proverbial London fog owes its density and darkness to the smoke. **1924** *Argosy* 27 Sept. 463/1 In the more than proverbial nick..of time. **1928** W. A. WOLFF *Trial of Mary Dugan* xxiv. 282 Like the proverbial man from Missouri, I have to be shown. **1931** H. ASHBROOK *Murder of Steven Kester* xv. 225 The whole thing is rather ideal—the proverbial house party, a murder, everyone under suspicion. **1937** M. ALLINGHAM *Dancers in Mourning* viii. 108 White Walls normally contained an excitable household... This morning..the proverbial monkey-wrench had landed squarely in the middle of the brittle machinery. **1976** J. SNOW *Cricket Rebel* 19 Having bowled a short ball at a batsman during one match he sarcastically patted the pitch almost in front of my feet. This is the proverbial red flag to a fast bowler. **1976** 'D. FLETCHER' *Don't whistle 'Macbeth'* 212 The proverbial penny had dropped... It certainly made me very uncomfortable.

†**3.** Addicted to the use of proverbs. *Obs.*

1665 BRATHWAIT *Comment Two Tales* 138 He was a most Proverbial Jenkin, and could twit his testy Wife with store of such Proverbs as these.

†**B.** *sb.* **a.** One addicted to the use of proverbs. **b.** A proverbial saying, a proverb. *Obs.*

1599 PORTER *Angry Wom. Abingd.* (Percy Soc.) 39 Why, what doth this prouerbial with vs? *a* **1673** J. CARYL in Spurgeon *Treas. Dav.* Ps. ii. 12 In our proverbials, to take a thing in snuff, is to take it in anger. **1778** *Learning at a Loss* II. 157 A few more pretty Proverbials.

Hence **proˈverbialism**, a proverbial saying; also = PROVERBIALITY a.

1832 W. MOTHERWELL in A. Henderson *Scottish Proverbs* p. xiv, Zachary Boyd, Rector of Glasgow University, has..given quite a cento of common proverbialisms. **1846** in WORCESTER, citing *N. Amer. Rev.* **1935** *Times Lit. Suppl.* 14 Dec. 854/4 We pick them [*sc.* proverbs] up every now and then from great men's epigrammatic sayings and above all from books... This aspect of modern proverbialism should not be ignored. **1976** *Hiroshima Stud. Eng. Lang. and Lit.* XXI. 72 His resort to such proverbialisms indicates his dependence on the world of experience.

proˈverbialist. [f. as prec. + -IST.] One who originates, uses, or records proverbial sayings.

1709 *Brit. Apollo* II. Supernum. No. 5. 2/2 He [Solomon] was so celebrated a Proverbialist. **1815** W. H. IRELAND *Scribbleomania* 317 *note*, Luckily for the proverbialist, the good Pope knew nothing of the Greek language. **1898** *N. & Q.* 9th Ser. II. 430/2 If Ray is the only proverbialist who notes it.

proverbiˈality. [f. PROVERBIAL *a.* + -ITY.]

a. The quality of being proverbial. **b.** Addiction to the use of proverbs.

1852 E. FITZGERALD *Lett.* 27 Feb. (1889) I. 216 To show why Books of that kind are dull: what sort of writers ought to be quoted &c.; proverbial writers: and what constitutes proverbiality. **1892** *Athenæum* 11 June 758/2 Coarseness and 'proverbiality' are the only leading features we can detect in the scanty fragments of Sophron.

proˈverbialize, *v.* [f. as prec. + -IZE.]

1. *intr.* To make or utter proverbs. Hence **proˈverbializing** *vbl. sb.*

1683 KENNETT tr. *Erasm. on Folly* 125, I forbear from any farther Proverbializing. **1818** COLERIDGE in *Lit. Rem.* (1836) I. 129 Perhaps the best specimen of Sancho's proverbializing.

2. *trans.* To make or convert into a proverb; to use proverbially; to speak of in a proverb. *rare.*

a **1827** GOOD cited in WEBSTER (1828-32).

proverbially (prəʊˈvɜːbɪəlɪ), *adv.* [See -LY².]

1. In a proverbial manner; by way of, by means of, or as a proverb; according to the proverb.

1432-50 tr. *Higden* (Rolls) V. 55 Of whom hit was seide proverbially that his lyfe was lyke to his doctryne, slepenge not in bedde, and tastenge neither wyne ne flesche. **1571** GOLDING *Calvin on Ps.* lxxiii. 9 As we say proverbyally in English, to looke uppon one as the divile looketh over Lincoln. **1613** PURCHAS *Pilgrimage* (1614) 621 A coward braggart is prouerbially called a Lion of Agla. *a* **1754** FIELDING *1st Olynthiac Demosth.* Wks. 1766 IX. 240 It is proverbially said, that if a man preserves the wealth he attains, he is greatly thankful to fortune. **1855** MACAULAY *Hist. Eng.* xii. III. 204 His ancestors.., though originally English, were among those early colonists who were proverbially said to have become more Irish than Irishmen.

2. To a degree that has become proverbial, or matter of common talk; notoriously.

1665 GLANVILL *Def. Vanity Dogm.* 15 So uncertain and proverbially inconstant a cause as the Winds are. **1796** MORSE *Amer. Geog.* I. 313 The name of Benedict Arnold has become proverbially contemptible. **1892** MONTEFIORE *Hibbert Lect.* ii. 96 The argument from silence is proverbially dangerous.

proˈverbic, *a. rare.* [f. L. *prōverbi-um* or Eng. *proverb* + -IC.] Of, pertaining to, or of the nature of proverbs.

1902 F. E. HULME *Proverb-Lore* 123 The Talmud as a mine of proverbic wealth.

proverbiˈology. [f. L. *prōverbi-um* PROVERB + -O)LOGY.] The scientific study of proverbs; *transf.* proverbs collectively. Hence **proverbiˈologist**, a student or investigator of proverbs.

1868 *Q. Rev.* July 243 The richness of Spanish proverbiology is like 'good wine that needs no bush!' **1893** *Athenæum* 18 Feb. 216/1 His excellent book is..sure to meet with a hearty welcome on the part of all proverbiologists.

†ˈ**proverbize**, *v. Obs. rare*⁻¹. [f. PROVERB *sb.* + -IZE.] *trans.* To style or call proverbially.

1591 SYLVESTER *Du Bartas* I. vii. 653 For house-hold Rules, read not the learned Writs Of the Stagyrian (glory of good Wits): Nor his, whom [*i.e.* Xenophon], for his hony-steeped stile, They proverbiz'd the Attick Muse yer-while.

provett (pruːˈvɛt). *rare.* [Aphetic form of EPROUVETTE.] An eprouvette, an instrument for testing the strength of gunpowder.

1817 *Sporting Mag.* I. 107 Employed by the Board of Ordnance, to make their provetts for ascertaining the strength of gunpowder.

†**proˈvexity.** *Obs. rare*⁻⁰. [Ultimately from L. *prōvect-us* advanced, pa. pple. of *prōvehĕre*: see PROVECTION. For the form, cf. *convex*, *convexity*.] An advanced condition or state.

1674 BLOUNT *Glossogr.* (ed. 4), *Provexity*.., greatness of age, the being well grown in years, or well studied in any Art.

†**proˈvey,** obs. variant of PURVEY *v.*

†**proviable,** *a. Obs. rare*⁻¹. [a. OF. *proveable* (13th c. in Godef.), var. of *por-*, *pourveable*, 'qui pourvoit à tous les besoins': see PURVEYABLE.] ? Suitable, convenient; or ? get-at-able.

1450 *Paston Lett.* I. 176, I desyre that and [= if] John Berney..can mete wyth Dallyng, that fals undre eschetor, in onye place proviable, that he may [be] by force brought to Castre..to be kept yn hold.

†**proviˈance.** *Sc. Obs. rare.* Also 4 pruwiance. [a. OF. *proveance* (13th c. in Godef.), variant of *por-*, *pourveance*, *-voyance*, semi-popular representatives of L. *prōvidēntia*: see PURVEYANCE.] Provision; providence.

c **1375** *Sc. Leg. Saints* xxxiii. (*George*) 213 In þe tyme come a knycht..I treu, of goddis pruwiance—Quhare þe maydine abad hir chance. **1552** LYNDESAY *Monarche* 6197 Thocht presentlye, be Goddis prouiance, Beistis, fowlis, and fyschis in the seis, Ar necessar, now, for mannis sustenance.

proviant (ˈprɒvɪənt). Also 7 proveant, 9 proviand. [a. G. *proviant*, Du. *proviand*, in It. *provianda*, apparently an altered form of *provenda* PROVEND, influenced by OF. *proveant* providing, *proveance* provision. Brought into Eng. by soldiers who served in the Thirty Years' War, 1618–48.

The German word is treated by Kluge as from the It.; but *provianda* is not in Florio 1598–1611, who has only *provenda* 'provander for horses or fodder for cattle'. Diez referred the word to L. *providenda* things to be provided.]

Provision; food supply, esp. for an army; commissariat; = PROVAND, PROVANT 1.

1637 R. MONRO *Exped.* I. 7 Receiving all necessaries fitting for our march, as ammunition, proviant, and waggons, for our baggage. **1647** *Sc. Acts Chas. I* (1814) VI. 270/1 That all Regiments..be put and kept in equality, either in Money, Proveant, or Provision, according to their strength. **1832** CARLYLE in Froude *Life* (1882) II. xii. 313 We want for nothing in the way of earthly proviant, and have many reasons to be content and diligent. **1885** A. FORBES *Souvenirs* (1894) 135 On one occasion, before Plevna, his imperturbable coolness stood him in good stead in the matter of 'proviand'.

b. *attrib.* = PROVANT 3 a.

1637 R. MONRO *Exped.* I. 5 We were entertained on proviant bread, beere and bacon. **1870** *Daily News* 5 Dec., It was the wheel of his [own] gig that he had seen stuck on to the proviant waggon. **1880** A. FORBES in *19th Cent.* VII. 233 Marshall was hustling proviant columns up along the line of communications.

pro-vicar, -vicariate: see PRO-¹ 4.

ˌpro-vice-ˈchancellor. [f. PRO-¹ 4 + VICE-CHANCELLOR.] One of the deputies appointed by the vice-chancellor of a university on his election; an assistant or deputy vice-chancellor.

1660 WOOD *Life* 30 June (O.H.S.) I. 320 The same day the doctors and provicechancellor at home put off the Act. **1663** *Ibid.* 23 Sept. 492 When they were there the provicecancellor and the 24 proproctors placed them. **1721** AMHERST *Terræ Fil.* No. 35 (1754) 185 The gentlemen..went to Dr. Dobson, president of Trinity college, who was at that time pro-vice-chancellor. **1898** *Daily News* 10 Oct. 9/1 The new Vice-Chancellor..appointed as his Pro-Vice-Chancellors the Principal of Hertford, the Provost of Queen's, the Master of University, and the President of Corpus.

providable (prəʊˈvaɪdəb(ə)l), *a. rare.* [f. PROVIDE *v.* + -ABLE.] Capable of being provided.

1891 *Dict. Nat. Biog.* XXVIII. 224/2 He would have provided for Rousseau had Rousseau been providable for.

providator, providatory: see PROVEDITOR.

provide (prəʊˈvaɪd), *v.* Also 5–6 provyde, *Sc.* -wyde, -wide, 6 -vyd. [ad. L. *prōvid-ēre* to see before, foresee, look after, attend to, be cautious, f. *prō*, PRO-¹ + *vidēre* to see. Cf. PURVEY, a doublet of this through OF., in earlier Eng. use. *Provide* was app. introduced in 15th c. as a direct repr. of the L. verb in certain senses, and its use may have been promoted by the fact that *providence* was already in use for *purveyance*.]

I. †**1.** *trans.* To foresee. *Obs.*

1423 JAS. I *Kingis Q.* ix, So vncouthly hir werdes sche deuidith, Namly In ȝouth, that seildin ought prouidith. **1545** RAYNOLD *Byrth Mankynde* 91 Euident and sufficient signes, whereby maye be prouided & foresene the aborcement before it come. **1607** B. JONSON *Volpone* Ded., Seuere and wiser patriots..prouiding the hurts these licentious spirits may doe in a state. **1640** YORKE *Union Hon.* 137 Of especiall counsell and advice, in providing and foreseeing the event of any deepe designes.

2. *intr.* To exercise foresight in taking due measures in view of a possible event; to make provision or adequate preparation. Const. *for*, *against*.

c **1407** LYDG. *Reson & Sens.* 3556 Huge boolys of metal..Brent[en] al that kam be-syde: Ther koude no man hym provyde To save him that he was brent. **1432–50** tr. *Higden* (Rolls) III. 47 Men of Lacedemonia provide for a batelle ageyne men of Micena. **1529** MORE *Dyaloge* I. Wks. 132/2 Go to Christes gospell & loke on his first miracle, whither he might not haue prouided for wine without miracle. **1568** GRAFTON *Chron.* II. 689 The olde adage, saiyng in tyme of peace, prouide for war, and in tyme of war, prouide for peace. **1665** BOYLE *Occas. Refl.* II. xi. (1848) 131 We may be often sollicitous to provide against many Evils and Dangers that possibly may never reach us. **1796** BURKE *Corr.* (1844) IV. 393 The first duty of a state is to provide for its own conservation. **1878** JEVONS *Prim. Pol. Econ.* i. §2. 10 Suffering from misfortunes which could not have been provided against. **1883** E. T. PAYNE in *Law Times* 27 Oct. 432/2 An inn or hotel is an establishment, the proprietor of which undertakes to provide for the entertainment of all comers, especially travellers.

†**b.** To see to it or take care beforehand; to make provision (*that* something shall not happen). *Obs.*

c **1430** LYDG. *Min. Poems* (Percy Soc.) 186, I wil be ware and afore provide, That of no fowler I wil no more be japed. **1509** FISHER *Fun. Serm. C'tess Richmond* Wks. (1876) 296 To..prouyde by her owne commaundement that nothynge sholde lacke. **1538** STARKEY *England* II. ii. 181 We must prouyd..that by no prerogatyfe he vsurpe apon the pepul any such authorysyd tyranny. **1573–80** BARET *Alv.* P 801 To prouide that a thing happen not, *precaueo*. *Ibid.* 803 To prouide that one take no harme, *cauere alicui*.

c. To make it, or lay it down as, a provision or arrangement; to stipulate *that*. Cf. PROVIDED 5, PROVIDING *pr. pple.*, PROVISION 5.

1423 [see PROVIDING *pr. pple.*]. **1560** DAUS tr. *Sleidane's Comm.* 114 b, The Mayers wyfe of the citie prouided in her wyll, that she would be buried without any pompe or noyse. **1596** DALRYMPLE tr. *Leslie's Hist. Scot.* I. (S.T.S.) 116 Qⁿ sa our lawis provydes, that the eldest succeides. **1849** MACAULAY *Hist. Eng.* i. I. 13 Another regulation, providing that every person who was found slain should be supposed to be a Frenchman, unless he were proved to be a Saxon. **1891** *Law. Rep.*, *Weekly Notes* 72/2 The clause did not provide that the costs of references..should be in the discretion of the arbitrators.

II. 3. *trans.* To prepare, get ready, or arrange (something) beforehand. Now *rare*.

c **1420** ? LYDG. *Assembly of Gods* 216 What pyne or greef ye for me prouyde, Without any grogyng I shall hit abyde. *c* **1470** HENRY *Wallace* x. 620 Wallace in haist prouidyt son his ost. **1526** *Pilgr. Perf.* (W. de W. 1531) 8 b, Of certayne benefytes that god hath prouyded for vs. **1535** COVERDALE *Prov.* vi. 7 In the sommer she prouideth hir meate, & gathereth hir foode together in yᵉ haruest. **1697** DRYDEN *Virg. Georg.* I. 271 The wise Ant her wintry Store provides. **1809** MALKIN *Gil Blas* v. i. ¶ 103 He had provided a gown of coarse dark cloth, and a little red horse-hair beard.

†**4.** *intr.* To prepare, make preparation, get ready. Const. with *inf.*, or *absol. Obs.*

1493 *Petronilla* (Pynson) 105 Felliculla gan afore prouyde, Maugre flaccus, to lyue in maydynhede. **1568** GRAFTON *Chron.* II. 165 He prouyded to sende men and victualles to strengthen the castels of Flynt and Rutlande. **1601** R. JOHNSON *Kingd. & Commw.* (1603) 195 Let them not thinke to begin anie long warre, much lesse to continue it, unlesse they throughly provide aforehand. **1616** HIERON *Wks.* I. 589 Your respectiue saluting vs, your prouiding to entertaine vs. **1626** B. JONSON *Staple of N.* IV. i, But stay, my Princesse comes, prouide the while, I'lle call for't anone. **1692** tr. *Sallust* 116 He toyls, provides, and..sets all his Trains and Engines at work by Treachery to ruine Hiempsal. **1727** POPE *Th. Var. Subj.* Swift's Wks. 1755 II. I. 231 Very few men..live at present, but are providing to live another time.

†**b.** *trans.* with *vbl. sb.* (*provide your going* = prepare or make ready to go). *Obs.*

1606 SHAKS. *Ant. & Cl.* III. iv. 36 Prouide your going, Choose your owne company, and command what cost Your heart ha's mind to.

5. *trans.* To supply or furnish for use; to yield, afford. Const. †*to* (obs.), *for*, or with dative.

1447 BOKENHAM *Seyntys* (Roxb.) 37 Al that longyth to thy necessyte Shal be provydyd be god and me. **1538** STARKEY *England* I. i. 10 Al thyng that God and nature hath prouydyd to hym. **1552** *Bk. Com. Prayer, Communion*, The bread and wyne for the Communion shall be prouyded by the Curate, and the churchwardens, at the charges of the Parishe. **1581** in *Confer.* III. (1584) R iv, Prouide me ynke and paper, and I will write. **1634** MILTON *Comus* 186 Such cooling fruit As the kind hospitable Woods provide. **1772** *Junius Lett.* lxviii. (1820) 344 This very act provides a remedy for such persons. **1898** BESANT *Orange Girl* II. xxvi, The contractors..do honestly provide the convicts the rations prescribed by the Government.

6. To furnish or appoint (an incumbent) *to* a vacant benefice (rarely, a person *to* a pension); *esp.* of the pope: To appoint (a person as successor) *to* a benefice not yet vacant, thus setting aside the right of the patron. Cf. PROVISION *sb.* 4, PROVISOR 1. Now only *Hist.*

[**1388** *Act 12 Rich. II*, c. 15 Item qe null liege du Roy..passe le meer..pur soy providre ou purchacer ascun benefice de seinte Esglise ove cure ou sanz cure en le dit roialme.] **1426** *Paston Lett.* I. 25 Ther arn ij. other persones provided to the same bysshopriche yet lyvyng, beforn my seyd adversarie. **1580** *Reg. Privy Council Scot.* III. 324 His brother german, being lauchfullie providit to ane yeirlie pensioun.., wes slane,.. in quhais place the said Alexander, being providit to the said pensioun, bruikit the samin peciabillie. **1593–4** *Exch. Rolls Scotl.* XXII. 393 Johnne Balfour, providit of auld to the chapellanie of Sanct Thomas. *a* **1639** SPOTTISWOOD *Hist. Ch. Scot.* II. (1677) 59 Shevez posted to Rome..and was himself provided to the Archbishoprick. **1887** LUPTON *Life Colet* 121 He was provided, in 1504, to the vacant see of St. David's. **1899** TREVELYAN *Eng. Age Wycliffe* 120 The Papal power of 'providing' to benefices.

III. 7. To equip or fit out (a person, etc.) with what is necessary for a certain purpose; to furnish or supply with something implied. In quot. 1628, to provide or furnish with a lodging.

1465 in *Exch. Rolls Scotl.* VII. 321 *note*, Gevin..in parte of sustentacione of him unto the tyme that he be bettir providit, ten poundis. **1536** *MS. Acc. St. John's Hosp., Canterb.*, Payd to Colney for to provide hym selfe away xijd. **1588** PARKE tr. *Mendoza's Hist. China* 121 They do take so much fish, that they do prouide the whole kingdome for all the yeare. **1628** EARL MANCH. in *Buccleuch MSS.* (Hist. MSS. Comm.) I. 268 Werden tells me he hath provided you not far from the Parliament. **1656** H. PHILLIPS *Purch. Patt.* (1676) B ix b, The first Builder is sufficiently provided by his workman to testifie his cost. **1838** DICKENS *Nich. Nick.* xliii, I..mean to look out for another situation; so provide yourselves, gentlemen, if you please.

†**b.** *refl.* To equip or prepare oneself, to make oneself ready, prepare (*to do* something, *for* or *against* something). Cf. 3 and 4. *Obs.*

c **1489** CAXTON *Blanchardyn* xlvii. 182 [They] ordeyned & prouyded theym self soo, that they fered but lytyl Subyon or nouȝte. *c* **1594** CAPT. WYATT *R. Dudley's Voy. W. Ind.* (Hakl. Soc.) 2 A speciall commaundement..that they should generallie provide themselves to goe with him the Sonday followinge..to the church. **1600** SHAKS. *A.Y.L.* I. iii. 89 You Neice prouide your selfe. **1602** —— *Ham.* III. iii. 7 *King*... Therefore prepare you... *Guild.* We will our selues prouide. **1650** FULLER *Pisgah* II. x. 212 Hence the Sea running Southward, provides itself to entertain a nameless Brook. *a* **1652** J. SMITH *Sel. Disc.* x. ii. (1856) 469 If we will provide ourselves against the devil who never misseth any opportunity..to tempt us.

8. To furnish or supply (a person, etc.) with something. Often in indirect passive. **a.** Const. *with*.

14.. in *Tundale's Vis.* (1843) 98 With help of her..So prudently with vertu hus to provyde. **1500–20** DUNBAR *Poems* xiv. 3 How that this realme, with nobillis owt of nummer, Gydit, provydit sa mony ȝeiris hes bene. **1605** CAMDEN *Rem.* 1 Prouided with all complete prouisions of Warre. **1798** SOPHIA LEE *Canterb. T.*, *Yng. Lady's T.* II. 167 His valet [was] provided with phosphoric matches, by which he had now lit a taper. **1841** LANE *Arab. Nts.* I. 71 They..provide themselves with sweet cakes, bread, dates. **1860** TYNDALL *Glac.* I. xxii. 151 The waiter then provided me with a ham sandwich.

†**b.** Const. *of*. *Obs.*

1547 BOORDE *Introd. Knowl.* xiv. (1870) 160 Howbeit the good townes be prouyded of vitels. **1556** *Aurelio & Isab.* (1608) P iij, Provyde you of trew contricion and patience. **1657** W. RAND tr. *Gassendi's Life Peiresc* I. 172 Viassius..providing him of a ship, sent him away. **1723** CHAMBERS tr. *Le Clerc's Treat. Archit.* I. 142 When an Architect is not provided of an able Painter fit to manage a Work of this kind.

†**c.** Const. *in*. *Sc. Obs.*

1586–7 *Rot. Scacc. Reg. Scot.* XXI. 61 [He] sall..provyid and furneis his majesteis hous and haill tabillis..in naiprie, fyireweschell, and tyneveschell.

9. *intr.* with *for*: to make provision *for* a person, his needs, etc. Often in indirect passive.

1535 COVERDALE *1 Chron.* xxiii. 5 Therfore wyl I prouyde for him. **1597** SHAKS. *2 Hen. IV*, v. v. 105 His wonted Followers Shall all be very well prouided for. **1632** J. HAYWARD tr. *Biondi's Eromena* 194 The old King seeing his sonnes thus well match'd, and Polimero so well provided for and setled. **1764** BURN *Poor Laws* 202 Thus hath the wisdom of the nation..been employed for ages, in providing properly for the poor, and yet they are not properly provided for. **1856** FROUDE *Hist. Eng.* I. i. 44 The essential duty of every man being to provide honestly for himself and his family.

†**ˈprovide,** *a. Obs. rare*⁻¹. [ad. L. *prōvidus* foreseeing, f. *prōvidēre*: see prec.] Prudent, foreseeing, provident.

c **1475** *Harl. Contin. Higden* (Rolls) VIII. 445 He was moderate in cures temporalle, provide in cownsaille [WALSINGHAM *Chron.* 'In curis temporalibus providus'].

provided (prəʊˈvaɪdɪd), *ppl. a.* and quasi-*conj.* [Pa. pple. of PROVIDE *v.*]

I. *ppl. a.* †**1.** Prearranged, preconcerted. *Obs.*

1562 *Burgh Rec. Peebles* 4 Oct. (Rec. Soc.) 280 The greit providit slauchteris oppresiones and skaithis done to ws.

2. Prepared, ready; in a state of readiness.

1579 LYLY *Euphues* (Arb.) 136 Demosthenes being sent for to declaime amiddest the multitude, stayd and saide, I am not yet prouided. **1594** SHAKS. *Rich. III*, III. i. 132 With what a sharpe prouided wit he reasons. *a* **1604** HANMER *Chron. Irel.* (1633) 89 Hawlaffe came in the night..hee hasted to Adelstanes Tent, but he was provided, and in armes. **1719** DE FOE *Crusoe* (1840) II. xiv. 284 The company was..well armed, and provided for all events.

3. Furnished or equipped (with what is needed).

1873 TRISTRAM *Moab* xii. 217 *note*, Offering an easy opportunity for a rightly provided collector. **1880** J. E. WATT *Poet. Sk.* 45 (E.D.D.), I was ance weel providit, an' deemed mysel' thrang, A-boukin' an' bleachin' haill wabs o' new sheetin'.

4. That is supplied, furnished, or afforded.

1878 BROWNING *La Saisiaz* 446 Man..makes for the provided room Where the old friends want their fellow. **1891** *Pall Mall G.* 21 Sept. 3/2 Heligoland..was not..an average tourist's haunt. It was less..in the matter of 'provided' amusements.

b. *provided school*, a public elementary school provided by the local education authority, under the Education Act of 1902.

[**1902** *Act 2 Edw. VII*, c. 42 §7 A school maintained but not provided by the local education authority. *Ibid.* §8 Where the local education authority or any other persons propose to provide a new public elementary school. *Ibid.*, That a school provided by the local education authority, or not so provided, as the case may be, is better suited to meet the wants of a district than the school proposed to be provided.] **1902** *Westm. Gaz.* 29 July 2/2 The House stopped at..the management of provided schools; the whole question of the Voluntary (or unprovided) schools has still to come. **1902** *Daily Chron.* 17 Oct. 5/7 What guarantee is there that they would not turn the school into a 'provided' or Board School?

II. *pa. pple.* and quasi-*conj.*

5. With the provision or condition (that); it being provided, stipulated, or arranged (that): used chiefly in legal and formal statements; also, in general use, more loosely: On the condition, supposition, or understanding (that). **a.** with *that.*

c **1460** FORTESCUE *Abs. & Lim. Mon.* xiv. (1885) 143 Provided alway, that no man be harmyd..in the arrerages off such livelod. **1488** *Act 4 Hen. VII*, c. 3 Provided alwey that this present Acte begyn to take effecte at the fest of Annunciacion of oure Lady next coming, and not afore. **1591** SHAKS. *Two Gent.* IV. i. 71, I take your offer, and will liue with you, Prouided that you do no outrages On silly women, or poore passengers. **1637** *Decree Star Chamb.* §15 in *Milton's Areop.* (Arb.) 16 Prouided that they exceed not the number of Twentie. **1818** CRUISE *Digest* (ed. 2) VI. 575 Provided that, if such child should die before 21..the reversion should go to other persons named. **1879** BAIN *Higher Eng. Gram.* 113 Provided that all is safe, you may go.

b. without *that*: = if only.

[**1600** E. BLOUNT tr. *Conestaggio* 17 Always prouided, if the Turk sent not an armie into Italy.] **1604** SHAKS. *Ham.* v. ii. 210 (2nd Qo.) Now or whensoeuer, prouided I be so able as now. **1611** —— *Cymb.* I. iv. 166. **1687** A. LOVELL tr. *Thevenot's Trav.* I. 60 For the common sort of People, provided you'll give them Drink enough, they are wholly at your service. **1716** ADDISON *Freeholder* No. 30 ¶4 Provided there be a Pudding upon the Table, no matter what are the other Dishes. **1857** BUCKLE *Civiliz.* I. xiv. 761 The circumstances..may always be known, provided the evidence is ample and authentic. **1871** B. STEWART *Heat* §60 Provided the temperature remain the same the volume which a gas occupies is inversely proportional [etc.].

providence ('prɒvɪdəns), *sb.* [a. F. *providence* (12th c. in Hatz.-Darm.), ad. L. *prōvidentia* foresight, precaution, providence, f. *prōvidēre* to PROVIDE: see -ENCE.]

†**1.** The action of providing; provision, preparation, arrangement; chiefly in phrase *to make providence*, to make provision. *Obs.* exc. *dial.* In this sense, and in b, *dial.* also (prəʊ'vaɪdəns).

1426 LYDG. *De Guil. Pilgr.* 8785 Yiff thow lyst maken prouydence Off any konnyng or scyence. **1432–50** tr. *Higden* (Rolls) VII. 115 God schalle make providence [of a king] after hym [TREVISA God schal purveie, L. *providebit Deus*]. *a* **1533** LD. BERNERS *Gold. Bk. M. Aurel.* (1546) R iij b, Sodeyn death came to the fathers, and no prouidence made for the doughters. **1547** *Bk. Marchauntes* e v b, That they maye make suche prouidens and remedy that the vengeaunce of God do not fall on the poore peopel. **1878** *Cumberland Gloss.*, *Providance*, a providing of victuals, etc.

†**b.** That which is provided; a supply, a provision. Cf. PROVIDING *vbl. sb.* b. *Obs.* exc. *dial.*

[**1390** *Earl Derby's Exp.* (Camden) 5 Expense pro providenciis contra viagium Prucie.] **1475** *Bk. Noblesse* (Roxb.) 68 Yn every castelle..or towne he wolde hafe grete providence of vitaille, of cornys, of larde, and beoffes. [**1706** PHILLIPS, *Providentia*, Providence.... In some old Records, Provision of Meat or Drink.] **1868** ATKINSON *Cleveland Gloss.*, *Providance* (with the *i* long), the matters or supply provided; to wit, the meat and other eatables for a burial entertainment; the cakes,..&c. for a tea-party.

2. Foresight, prevision; *esp.* anticipation of and preparation for the future; 'timely care' (J.); hence, prudent or wise arrangement, management, government, or guidance. Also, an instance of this.

1382 WYCLIF *Wisd.* vi. 17 In his weis it shal shewe itself to them, and gladsumli in alle prouydence [*gloss* or bifore ordeynyng, 1611 in every thought, *R.V.* purpose], it shal aȝen come to them. **1390** GOWER *Conf.* I. 203 He made Edwyn his lieutenant,..and thus be providence Of alle thinges wel begon He tok his leve. **1470–85** MALORY *Arthur* I. vi. 43 The Archebisshop..by Merlyns prouydence lete purueye thenne of the best knyghtes that they myghte gete. *a* **1548** HALL *Chron.*, *Edw. IV* 189 b, In compassyng and bryngyng greate thynges to passe, there lacked no industrie, nor prouidence. **1622** BACON *Hist. Gt. Brit.* Wks. 1879 I. 796/1 In this matter the providence of king Henry the seventh was in all men's mouths. **1702** *Eng. Theophrast.* 379 This is not to exclude that providence of tracing premisses into consequences and causes into their effects. **1867** MAURICE *Patriarchs & Lawg.* vi. (1877) 134 The creature who bears His image is intended to exercise providence.

b. Regard to future needs in the management of resources; foreseeing economy, thrift, frugality.

1608 HEYWOOD *Rape Lucrece* III. v. Wks. 1874 V. 209 We must be carefull, and with providence Guide his domestick businesse. **1620** E. BLOUNT *Horæ Subs.* 105 They that spend more then they haue, want gouernment: they that spend all, Prouidence. **1848** MILL *Pol. Econ.* I. xiii. §1 (1876) 117/2 [It] renders the increase of production no longer exclusively dependent on the thrift or providence of the inhabitants themselves. **1857** RUSKIN *Pol. Econ. Art* 8 When there should have been providence there has been waste. **1885** LD. PEMBROKE in *Pall Mall G.* 23 May 2/1 The providence which is all that is necessary in a rich country like ours to bring material prosperity to the labouring class.

3. In full, *providence of God* (etc.), *divine providence*: The foreknowing and beneficent care and government of God (or of nature, etc.); divine direction, control, or guidance.

13.. *St. Erkenwolde* 161 in Horstm. *Altengl. Leg.* (1881) 269 Þe prouidens of þe prince þat paradis weldes. **1382** WYCLIF *Wisd.* xiv. 3 Thou, fader, governest bi prouydence [Gr. πρόνοια, 1388 puruyaunce]. *c* **1400** *Three Kings Cologne* 35 Almyȝty god, whos prouidence in hys ordinaunce faileþ noȝt. **1483** CAXTON *Gold. Leg.* 121/2 He was in hys chyldhode sette to studye whereby dyuyne prouydence he floured in double science. **1553** T. WILSON *Rhet.* (1580) 57 Nature by her prouidence, mindeth vnto vs a certaine immortalitie. **1587** GOLDING *De Mornay* ix. (1592) 132 What else is Prouidence, than the will of God vttered foorth with Reason, and orderly disposed by vnderstanding? **1632** LITHGOW *Trav.* x. 471 Thy Bookes..are miraculously Translated by her [i.e. the Virgin Mary's] speciall prouidence. **1676** W. HUBBARD *Happiness of People* 36 Creation and providence are the issues of the same Being and Power. **1727** DE FOE *Hist. Appar.* iv. (1840) 38 Providence which is..the administration of heaven's government in the world. **1854** MILMAN *Lat. Chr.* III. vii. (1864) II. 150 That the ordinary providence of God gave place to a perpetual interposition of miraculous power.

†**b.** The lot assigned to one by Providence. *Obs. nonce-use.*

a **1661** FULLER *Worthies, Camb.* (1662) I. 152 Stephen de Fulborn..Going over into Ireland to seek his Providence (commonly nicknamed his fortune)..became..Bishop of Waterford.

4. Hence applied to the Deity as exercising prescient and beneficent power and direction.

1602 WARNER *Alb. Eng.* XIII. lxxviii. 321 Whom if yee Nature call (saith One) yee call him not amis... Or Prouidence, whose acting power doth all begin and end. **1691** NORRIS *Pract. Disc.* 219 No Man is too little and despicable for the notice of Providence, however he may be overlook'd by his Fellow-Creatures. **1704** DE FOE in *15th Rep. Hist. MSS. Comm.* App. IV. 88 What Providence has reserved for me he only knows. **1842** ALISON *Hist. Europe* lxxviii. X. 1013 Moreau expressed a fact of general application, explained according to the irreligious ideas of the French Revolution, when he said, that 'Providence was always on the side of dense battalions'. **1894** BARING-GOULD *Queen of L.* II. 59, I am not one to fly in the face of Providence.

b. *transf.* A person who acts or appears in the character of Providence. *colloq.*

1856 EMERSON *Eng. Traits, Aristocr.* Wks. (Bohn) II. 86 'They might be little Providences on earth', said my friend, 'and they are, for the most part, jockeys and fops'. **1886** P. S. ROBINSON *Valley Teet. Trees* 28 Man is the Providence of the goose and..it is well that we should..generously condescend to sympathy with it. **1895** *Daily News* 30 May 6/5 The Providence of the officers who were sent to stay at St. Petersburg was Mlle. Georges.

5. An instance or act of divine intervention; an event or circumstance which indicates divine dispensation. *special providence*, a particular act of direct divine intervention.

1643 [ANGIER] *Lancash. Valley of Achor* 1 Gods eternall Counsells..are in time turned into..Prayers, Prayers into Providences, and Providences into Praises. **1651** MRQ. ORMONDE in *Nicholas Papers* (Camden) I. 279 The King being by an eminent and high providence escaped the bloody hands of the Rebells is arived at Paris. **1719** DE FOE *Crusoe* I. x. 175 How can he sweeten the bitterest providences! **1861** PEARSON *Early & Mid. Ages Eng.* 233 Here the event would no doubt be classed by some modern religionists under the head of special providences. **1871** TYNDALL *Fragm. Sc.* (1879) II. ii. 11 The miracle of the Thundering Legion was a special providence.

b. Applied esp. to a disastrous accident, or fatality, regarded as an act of God. *Obs.* or *dial.*

1740 WESLEY *Wks.* (1872) I. 290, I was informed of an awful providence. **1809** KENDALL *Trav.* lxxxv. III. 292 The phrase a providence..in New England..appears to be more frequently used for that which is disastrous but which is at the same time to be regarded and submitted to as the act of God. **1814** *Connecticut Courant* 1 Mar. 3/2 Distressing Providence.—On Wednesday last as John N. Olcott..was scating on Connecticut river..he..broke in and drowned.

Hence **'providence** *v. nonce-wd.*, *trans.* to act the part of Providence towards; to be a providence to.

1901 *Pall Mall G.* 28 May 4/1 She grew up in an obscure country parsonage..providenced by a high-minded..father.

†**'providency.** *Obs. rare.* [ad. L. *prōvidenti-a*: see prec.] The quality of being provident; foresight and preparation; = prec. 2.

1600 W. WATSON *Decacordon* (1602) 258, I haue..often doubted whether Saint Ambrose deserued more commendation for his prouidencie in attempting such a matter: or the emperor for his patience and obedience in taking the same in so good part. **1617** MORYSON *Itin.* II. 204 Yet we haue not been wanting in our prouidency. **1644** DIGBY *Nat. Bodies* xxxviii. §1. 327 Of prescience of future euentes, prouidencies, the knowing of thinges neuer seene before; and such other actions.

provident ('prɒvɪdənt), *a.* [ad. L. *prōvidēns, -ēntem*, pres. pple. of *prōvidēre* to PROVIDE. Cf. F. *provident* (16th c. in Godef.).]

1. Foreseeing; that has foresight of and makes provision for the future, or for some future event; exercising or characterized by foresight. *provident society* = *friendly society* (FRIENDLY *a.* 8). Also *provident club.*

1429 *Pol. Poems* (Rolls) II. 143 Provident, with Brutus Cassius; Hardy as Hector, whan tyme doth require. **1487** [implied in PROVIDENTLY 1]. **1548** UDALL *Erasm. Par. Luke* vi. 67 b, He is like to a prouident and circumspect builder, that buildeth his house, nor for a vain braggue or shewe onely. **1663** BOYLE *Usef. Exp. Nat. Philos.* I. ii. 50 By Solomon God sends the Sluggard to school to the Ant, to learn a provident Industry. **1694** ADDISON *Virg. Georg.* IV. 189 Each provident of cold, in summer flies Thro' fields and woods to seek for new supplies. **1783** BURKE *Affairs India* Wks. XI. 315 The order..was (for its matter) provident and well considered. **1846** *Lit. Gaz.* 7 Nov. 957/2 National Provident and Benevolent Institution. **1847** MARRYAT *Childr. N. Forest* xxi, It was fortunate that Humphrey had been so provident in making so large a quantity of hay. **1858** M. TUCKETT *Diary* 12 Nov. (*c* 1975) 18 We betook ourselves to the Polytechnic where a stall awaited us, in the sale for the Provident Society. **1869** *Bradshaw's Railway Manual* XXI. App. 98 The United Kingdom Railway Officers' and Servants' Association, and Railway Provident Society. **1968** A. BRYANT *Hist. Brit. United Provident Assoc.* 2 During the 'twenties and 'thirties many Provident Clubs became linked with particular hospitals. **1973** P. GOSDEN *Self-Help* vi. 49 During the first half of May, 1836, petitions were received by the Commons from a number of societies in South Lancashire... These included..the Provident Society of Salford. **1978** P. SUTCLIFFE *Oxf. Univ. Press* II. xii. 63 He started a provident club for medical aid and a clothing club.

2. Economical; frugal, thrifty, saving.

1596 BP. W. BARLOW *Three Serm.* iii. 133 Let the poore be prouident in a plentifull haruest. **1655** JER. TAYLOR *Guide Devot.* (1719) 54 Thou wilt be more provident of thy Time and of thy Talent. **1700** DRYDEN *Pal. & Arcite* III. 527 A Prince so gracious and so good, So just, and yet so provident of blood! **1743** BULKELEY & CUMMINS *Voy. S. Seas* 124 If we are not exceedingly provident in Regard to serving out Provisions, we must all inevitably starve. **1888** F. HUME *Mme. Midas* I. iii, He will always be poor, because he never was a provident man.

providential (prɒvɪ'dɛnʃəl), *a.* (*sb.*) [f. L. *prōvidēntia* PROVIDENCE + -AL[1]. So F. *providentiel* (18–19th c. in Hatz.-Darm.).]

†**1.** Of the nature of or characterized by providence or foresight; provident, prudent. *Obs.*

1663 BUTLER *Hud.* I. i. 758 Sure some mischief will come of it Unless by providential wit Or force we averruncate it. **1673** H. STUBBE *Further Vindic. Dutch War* 17 Neither is it providential for a weak Prince..to run Precipitously into a War. **1794** T. TAYLOR *Pausanias* I. 33, I especially admire ..his providential care with respect to future contests. *a* **1845** HOOD *Open Question* xiii, The tender Love Bird—or the filial Stork? The punctual Crane—the providential Raven?

2. Of, pertaining to, or ordained by divine providence. †*providential right*, the 'divine right' of kings (*obs.*).

1648 *Eikon Bas.* x. 83, I do not think that I can want any thing which providentiall necessity is pleased to take from me. *a* **1677** HALE *Prim. Orig. Man.* I. i. 34 The necessity of a Providential Regiment of the parts of the Universe. **1695** J. SAGE *The Article* Wks. 1844 I. 345 Sure I am, here [i.e. in Knox's Letter] is the providential right, so plainly taught that no glosses can obscure it. **1736** BUTLER *Anal.* I. v. Wks. 1874 I. 94 A providential disposition of things. **1768** in Picton *L'pool Munic. Rec.* (1886) II. 277 Unless sickness or other providential accident hinders him. **1869** M. PATTISON *Serm.* (1885) 187 The existence of a first cause and providential governor.

b. That is, or is thought to be, by special interposition of providence; opportune; lucky, fortunate. (Now the most common use.)

1719 DE FOE *Crusoe* (1858) 264, I knew nothing that night of the supply I was to receive by the providential driving of the ship nearer the land. **1790** BURKE *Fr. Rev.* 25 [It] was by them considered as a providential escape. **1856** KANE *Arct. Expl.* II. i. 27 Petersen caught another providential fox.

B. *sb.* A providential occurrence; an interposition of Providence. *rare.*

1658–9 in *Burton's Diary* (1828) III. 267 If you consider affairs in the providentials; all providences have rather bent that way. **1893** *Boston Congregationalist* 14 Sept., Providentials... To consider whether certain particular occurrences were specially prepared to fit certain exigencies.

Hence **provi'dentialist**, *nonce-wd.*, a maintainer of the 'providential' or divine right of sovereigns.

1695 J. SAGE *The Article* Wks. 1844 I. 343 [Knox] may chance to be honoured as a Father by the Providentialists.

provi'dentialism. [f. PROVIDENTIAL *a.* + -ISM.] The belief that events are predestined, whether by God or by fate.

1927 J. S. HUXLEY *Relig. without Revelation* 18 The release of God from the anthropomorphic disguise of personality also provides release from that vice which may be termed Providentialism. **1934** H. G. WELLS *Exper. Autobiog.* I. v. 264 The ultimate adoption of the Five Year Plan and its successor has been the completest change over from the providentialism of Marx to the once hated and despised method of the Utopists. **1954** C. S. LEWIS *Eng. Lit. in 16th Cent.* I. ii. 148 His [*sc.* Fabyan's] philosophy of history is a simple Providentialism which leaves him completely agnostic about second causes.

provi'dentially, *adv.* [f. PROVIDENTIAL *a.* (*sb.*) + -LY[2].] In a providential manner.

†**1.** With foresight; providently, prudently. *Obs.*

1614 RALEIGH *Hist. World* V. i. §10. 366 The victuallers, which the Consull Iunius, more hastily than prouidentially, had sent before him towards Lilybæum. **1619** J. CHAMBERLAIN in *Crt. & Times Jas. I* (1848) II. 184 Enabling himself to live more providentially hereafter.

2. By the ordination of divine providence.

1651 G. W. tr. *Cowel's Inst.* 64 But there is another Species of accession which is providentially naturall and is made by the cooperation of divine and humane nature from whence a property is acquired. **1654** CROMWELL *Speech* 12 Sept. in *Carlyle*, A desire..to be quit of the power God had most providentially put into my hands, before he called me to lay it down. **1712** STEELE *Spect.* No. 432 ¶2 The Geese were providentially ordained to save the Capitol. **1857** RUSKIN *Pol. Econ. Art* 111 Pines and lettuces.. don't grow Providentially sweet and large unless we look after them.

b. By special intervention of Providence; by special chance; opportunely, fortunately. (Now the most common use.)

1719 DE FOE *Crusoe* (1840) II. viii. 179 Providentially it was so. **1771** *Hist.* in *Ann. Reg.* 68/2 Providentially a happier temper prevailed in general. **1838** DICKENS *Nich. Nick.* xv, Several frowns and winks from Mrs. K., which providentially stopped him. **1888** BURGON *Twelve Good Men* I. i. 34 A great separation was thus providentially averted.

So **provi'dentialness.**

1727 BAILEY vol. II, *Providentialness*, the Happening of a Thing by divine Providence, Providential effect. **1903** E. WHARTON *Sanctuary* I. i. 10 The sense of general providentialness on which Mrs. Peyton reposed.

'providently, *adv.* [f. PROVIDENT + -LY².] In a provident manner.

1. With foresight and providing care; prudently.

1487 *Rolls of Parlt.* VI. 403/2 The Kyng.. hath been besied.. so that [neither] his Grace nor yet his moost Honorable Councill myght.. provydently make Leesez [etc.]. **1553** T. WILSON *Rhet.* (1580) 74 Did he enuie them, or els did he prouidently forsee vnto them bothe, when he tooke theim bothe from vs. **1603** KNOLLES *Hist. Turks* (1638) 137 He prouidently foresaw in what danger the Oguzian state stood. **1765** BLACKSTONE *Comm.* I. Introd. ii. 51 Our laws might be providently made, and well executed, but they might not always have the good of the people in view. **1889** GRETTON *Memory's Harkb.* 61 He brought first a clean handkerchief, which his bed-maker had providently supplied.

b. With economy that looks ahead; thriftily.

1576 FLEMING *Panopl. Epist.* 228 The ant.. more prouidently employing her paines then the grasshopper. **1607** *Stat.* in *Hist. Wakefield Gram. Sch.* (1892) 57 Providentlie to lay out for the schole wants. **1641** *Epitaph* in Hissey *Holiday on Road* (1887) 404 Prudently simple, providently wary, To the world a Martha, and to heaven a Mary. **1694** MOTTEUX *Rabelais* v. Prol., Providently to save Charges.

†**2.** = PROVIDENTIALLY *adv.* 2, 2 b. *Obs.*

1600 HAKLUYT *Voy.* III. 708 And also prouidently defeated their dangerous and almost ineuitable fire-works. **1681** E. MURPHY *State Ireland* §18 Providently one John Mackeevir going by.

So **'providentness** *rare*, the quality of being provident or foreseeing.

1727 BAILEY vol. II, *Providentness*, Thriftiness, Savingness. **1761** *Ascham's Wks., Toxoph.* 83 Companions of shotinge, be providentness [*earlier edd.* prouidens], goode heede geving, true meetinge, honest comparison.

provider (prəʊ'vaɪdə(r)). Also 6 -or. [f. PROVIDE *v.* + -ER¹.] One who provides or supplies; a purveyor. *lion's ~~provider~~*: see LION 2 f.

1523 in W. H. Turner *Select. Rec. Oxford* (1880) 34 No purveyor, providor, or taker of victualls for the King's howshould. **1550** BALE *Eng. Votaries* II. Pref., This chaplayne of the deuyll was a generall prouyder for the oyled fathers there. **1698** G. THOMAS *Pensilvania* 41 Gratitude to our Plentiful Provider, the great Creator of Heaven and Earth. **1774–1831** Lion's provider [see LION 2 f]. **1827** D. JOHNSON *Ind. Field Sports* 91 We heard at a distance the Pheäll (commonly called the Lion or Tigers provider) which is a jackal. **1852** JERDAN *Autobiog.* II. viii. 88 Our skilful provider for popular curiosity brought over Buonaparte's coachman. **1879** *Daily News* 25 Mar. 4/7 Mr. Whiteley,.. equally well known as the Universal Provider.

Hence **pro'videress,** a female provider. *rare*⁻⁰.

1611 COTGR., *Pourvoyeuse*, a Prouideresse, or Purueyeresse.

providetor, -our, obs. forms of PROVEDITOR.

pro'viding, *vbl. sb.* [f. PROVIDE *v.* + -ING¹.] The action of the verb PROVIDE; furnishing, supplying; provision; †preparation (*obs.*).

1603 KNOLLES *Hist. Turks* (1638) 282 Mony enough for the prouiding of all things needfull. **1616** [see PROVIDE 4]. **1760–72** H. BROOKE *Fool of Qual.* (1809) III. 122 The auctioneer and bidders proved of Mr. Snack's providing. **1885** *Athenæum* 26 Dec. 843/2 Little or none of the money has been of English providing.

b. That which is provided; outfit; *spec.* a bride's stock of linen and household requisites (*Sc.*); also, a stock of food or equipments.

1820 *Glenfergus* III. xxxii. 255 Rachel's apparel and 'providing'.. were packed up in trunks, chests, and boxes. **1864** *Cornh. Mag.* Nov. 614 His sweetheart.. has managed .. to save money enough to buy what is called her 'providing', which comprises the napery and other household linen. **1895** *Outing* (U.S.) XXVI. 3/1 All our providings and personnel were such as in India nobody supposes he can do without. **1900** CROCKETT *Fitting of Peats* iii. in *Love Idylls* (1901) 23, I will put plenty of providing for man and beast behind the park dyke.

pro'viding, *pr. pple.* and quasi-*conj.* [The pr. pple. of PROVIDE *v.* used absolutely.]

a. *pr. pple.* with *that.* Making the proviso or stipulation *that*, it being provided or stipulated *that*; = PROVIDED 5 a.

1423 *Rolls of Parlt.* IV. 256/2 Prouydyng euir more that thei.. may have [etc.]. **1463** *Bury Wills* (Camden) 33 Provydyng alwey that she be made sewr of hire levving. **1579** *Reg. Privy Council Scot.* III. 177 Providing alwyis that the said Andro beir not forther eventure of the said money nor he dois of his awin propir geir and himself. **1632** LITHGOW *Trav.* VI. 246 Hee cared little for our Faith, and Patience, prouiding, that our purses could answere his expectation. **1901** *Times* 2 Oct. 3/6 The owners have unanimously expressed their willingness to proceed to arbitration.. providing that all sections.. were agreeable to this course.

b. quasi-*conj.* (without *that*). On condition that; in case that, if only; = PROVIDED 5 b.

1632 LITHGOW *Trav.* x. 495 The Wooll.. is nothing inferiour to that.. of Spaine: providing they had skill to fine, Spin, Weaue, and labour it as they should. **1795** EARL MALMESBURY *Diaries & Corr.* III. 198 Freytag proposes a concert, providing somebody will pay for it. **1839** GEO. ELIOT in *Life* (1885) I. 50 Always providing our leisure is not circumscribed by duty. **1874** RUSKIN *Fors Clav.* xlv. 203 Providing they pay you the fixed rent.

providitor, providore: see PROVED-.

province ('prɒvɪns). Also 4 (*Sc.*) prowince, 5 prouynse. [a. F. *province* (13th c. in Godef. *Compl.*), ad. L. *prōvincia* an official duty, a charge, a province. Of uncertain derivation: that which offers itself at first sight, from *prō*, PRO-¹ 1 + *vincĕre* to conquer (although it may in later times have affected the application of the word) does not explain the earliest known use in Latin. See Walde *Lat. Etym. Wbch.* s.v.

1904 W. M. RAMSAY in *Expositor* Oct. 243 A 'Province' to the Roman mind meant literally a 'sphere of duty', and was an administrative, not a geographical fact; the Province of a magistrate might be the stating of law in Rome, or the superintendence of a great road, or the administration of a region or district of the world; but it was not and could not be, except in a loose and derivative way, a tract of country.]

I. 1. a. *Rom. Hist.* A country or territory outside Italy, under Roman dominion, and administered by a governor sent from Rome. (In L. also the official charge or administration of such a territory.)

a **1380** *St. Augustin* 64 in Horstm. *Altengl. Leg.* (1878) 62 Austin þe doctour.. Boren was in þe prouince of Affrican. **1382** WYCLIF *Acts* xxiii. 34 Whanne he hadde rad, and axid, of what prouynce he was,.. knowinge for he was of Cilice. *c* **1400** *Destr. Troy* 100 Tessaile.., A prouynce appropret aperte to Rome. **1615** G. SANDYS *Trav.* 144 His Ethnarchy reduced into a Romane Prouince, and the gouernment thereof committed vnto Pontius Pilate by Tyberius Cæsar. **1755** W. DUNCAN tr. *Sel. Orat. Cicero* xi. (1816) 389 You obtained a consular province. **1904** W. M. RAMSAY in *Expositor* Oct. 244 The Province was the aspect in which Rome presented itself to the people of Asia; and conversely the Province was the form under which the people of Asia constituted a part of the Empire.

†**b.** The country of Provence in South Eastern France, which was one of the earliest Roman provinces. *Obs.*

1560 DAUS tr. *Sleidane's Comm.* 140 b, He marched through the myddest of Italye.. tyll he came in to prouynce of Fraunce. *Ibid.* 219 Ther be in the French prouince a people called Valdois. **1563** *Homilies* II. *Idolatry* II. (1640) 28 Massile, the head Towne of Gallia Narbonensis (now called the Province).

2. a. An administrative division of a country or state; any principal division of a kingdom or empire, esp. one that has been historically, linguistically, or dialectally distinct, as the provinces of Ireland, Spain, Italy, Prussia, Russia, India, and the old provinces of France; *spec.* in recent use, Northern Ireland. Formerly sometimes applied to the shires of England.

1382 WYCLIF *Esther* iii. 13 And the lettris.. ben sent bi the corouris of the king to alle his prouyncis. **1387** TREVISA *Higden* (Rolls) I. 259 Franconia is, as it were, þe myddel prouynce of Germania, and haþ in þe est side Thuryngia, in þe west Sueuia. *Ibid.* II. 87 The prouince of Yorke extendethe hit oonly now from the arche of the floode of Humbre on to the floode of Teyse. *c* **1400** MAUNDEV. (Roxb.) xxv. 119 Þe land.. es diuided in XII. prouincez. **1494** FABYAN *Chron.* vi. xc. 67 Thenne Hengiste beganne his Lordshyp ouer the Prouynce of Kent. **1593** SHAKS. *2 Hen. VI*, I. i. 120 Aniou and Maine? My selfe did win them both: Those Prouinces, these Armes of mine did conquer. **1610** HOLLAND *Camden's Brit.* (1637) 182 My perambulation through the Provinces or Shires of Britaine. **1617** MORYSON *Itin.* II. 274 The Lord President.. left the Prouince of Mounster to meet the Lord Deputy at Galloway in Connaght. **1625** N. CARPENTER *Geog. Del.* II. xv. (1635) 260 Our mountainous Prouinces of Deuon and Cornwall haue not deserued so ill. **1706** PHILLIPS s.v., The United Provinces of the Netherlands, the Seven Northern Provinces of the Low-Countries, that made a firm Alliance at Utrecht, A.D. 1579, by which they united themselves, so as never to be divided. **1794** MRS. RADCLIFFE *Myst. Udolpho* i, On the pleasant banks of the Garonne, in the province of Gascony. **1804** *Europ. Mag.* XLV. 35/2 They divided the country into four provinces, viz. Ulster, Leinster, Munster and Connaught, each of which had its King. **1841** W. SPALDING *Italy & It. Isl.* III. 383 Corsica.. is still a province of that kingdom [France]. **1908** *Whitaker's Alm.* 491/1 The Central Provinces [of India] were formed in 1861 out of territory taken from the North-West Provinces and Madras. **1972** *Ann. Reg.* *1971* 26 A horrifying escalation of violence in the Province. **1977** [see sense 10 below].

†**b.** Applied to the North American Colonies of Great Britain, now provinces of Canada; also formerly to several of those which after the War of Independence united to form the United States of America.

Of the latter, chiefly applied to those colonies which were denominated provinces in their charters, some being so termed from the first, others only at a later date. Generally, but not universally, colonies having a royal governor, and some having proprietary governors, were 'provinces'.

1622 (Aug. 10) *Grant* in *Capt. John Mason* (Prince Soc.) 180 All that part of yᵉ maine land in New England.. wᶜʰ the said Sʳ Ferdinando Gorges and Capt. John Mason.. intend to name yᵉ Province of Maine. **1682** (Mar. 4) *Charter Chas. II to W. Penn* in Poore *Fed. & St. Constit.* II. 1510 We do hereby erect the aforesaid Country and Islands into a Province and Seigniore, and doe call itt Pensilvania. **1691** I. MATHER in *Andros Tracts* II. 289 Now that the Massachusets Colony is made a Province. **1717** *Commission to J. Wentworth* (*N.H. Provl. Pa.* II. 712), We have constituted and appointed Samuel Shute Esq. our Captain General and Governor in chief in and over our Province of New Hampshire, in New England, in America. **1758** *Commission to F. Bernard* (*N.J. Docts.* IX. 23), The Division of East and West New Jersey in America, which we have thought fit to reunite into one Province and settle under one entire Government. **1832** *Encycl. Brit.* (ed. 7) VI. 55 In the year 1791 it [Canada] was divided, by an act of the British parliament, into the two provinces of Upper and Lower Canada. **1878** *Whitaker's Alm.* 246 By an act passed in 1867, the provinces of Canada (Ontario and Quebec), Nova Scotia, and New Brunswick, were united under the title of 'Dominion of Canada', and provision was made.. for the admission at any subsequent period of the other provinces and territories of British North America. **1898** E. B. GREENE *Provincial Govnr. in Eng. Colonies of N.A.* 15 When James Duke of York became king, New York ceased to be a proprietary colony and became a royal province.

c. *fig.* A main division of any 'realm'.

1869 J. MARTINEAU *Ess.* II. 172 Our earth is but a province of a wider realm. **1880** SWINBURNE *Stud. Shaks.* 73 Their spotted souls.. hovering for an hour.. on the confines of either province of hell.

3. *Eccl.* **a.** The district within the jurisdiction of an archbishop or a metropolitan (in quot. 1377 applied to a diocese); formerly, also, that within the jurisdiction of a synod of a Presbyterian church.

1377 LANGL. *P. Pl.* B. xv. 562 Euery bisshop.. is holden, Thorw his prouynce to passe and to his peple to shewe hym. **1425** *Rolls of Parlt.* IV. 291/1 Write to the Chirche of York for that Provynce. **1454** *Ibid.* V. 249/1 The Clergie of the Province of Caunterbury. **1580** *Register of Privy Council Scot.* III. 277 The diocie or province of Louthiane. **1610** HOLLAND *Camden's Brit.* (1637) 181 The Provinciall Synods in both Provinces. **1649** (*title*) An Apologetic Declaration of the conscientious Presbyterians of the Province of London. **1852** HOOK *Ch. Dict.* 617. **1861** J. G. SHEPPARD *Fall Rome* xii. 644 To the parochial cities were attached bishops, to the provinces metropolitans, to the dioceses patriarchs.

b. One of the territorial divisions of an ecclesiastical or ecclesiastico-military order, as the Knights Templars, the Franciscans, the Jesuits, or of the Propaganda.

1727–41 CHAMBERS *Cycl.* s.v., The general of the order has several provinces under him. **1839** *Penny Cycl.* XIII. 110/2 Although they [the Jesuits] had also their respective generals residing at Rome, yet their authority over the distant convents of the various provinces was very limited. **1848** *Secr. Societies, Templars* 244 Besides these offices of the Order [the Templars] there were the Great-priors, Great-preceptors, or Provincial Masters.. of the three Provinces of Jerusalem, Tripoli, and Antioch.

4. More vaguely, A country, territory, district, or region; a part of the world or of one of its continents.

c **1330** R. BRUNNE *Chron.* (1810) 332 His sonne Edward þe prince, & fiftene for his sake, þre hundred of þe prouince, knyghtes wild he make. **1484** CAXTON *Fables of Æsop* IV. viii, They came in to the prouynce of the apes. **1555** EDEN *Decades* 52 Owre men fownde certen trees in this prouince [Cartagena], which bore greate plentie of sweete apples. **1604** E. G[RIMSTONE] *D'Acosta's Hist. Indies* III. x. 151 Distinct seas, taking their names from the Provinces they bathe. **1751** JOHNSON *Rambler* No. 142 ¶7 The whole province flocks together as to a general festivity. *Ibid.* No. 165 ¶14 Some had long moved to distant provinces.

5. *pl.* A comprehensive designation for all parts of a country outside the capital or chief seat of government; e.g. of France apart from Paris, or England apart from London. Cf. PROVINCIAL A. 4.

[Of French origin, and referring to the old Provinces of France as distinct from L'Île de France and its capital Paris. Cf. Littré, *la province* 'all that is in France outside the capital (often with the notion of that which is behind in fashion, manners, or taste)'. Sometimes also in the plural *les provinces* (1671 in Mme. de Sévigné). In reference to England chiefly an expression of the London newspapers, or of London actors who 'star the provinces'.]

[**1638** BAKER tr. *Balzac's Lett.* (vol. III.) 31 This sweete ayre of the wide world, and these dainties of the spirit, which are not common in our Provinces.] **1789** *Ann. Agric.* XI. 293 All the animation, vigour, life, and energy of luxury, consumption, and industry, which flow with a full tide through this kingdom, wherever there is a free communication between the capital and the provinces. **1804–6** SYD. SMITH *Mor. Philos.* (1850) 168 Those opnions go down by the mail-coach, to regulate all matters of taste for the provinces. **1849** THACKERAY *Pendennis* xix, She had .. starred the provinces with great eclat and had come back to London. **1874** L. STEPHEN *Hours in Library* Ser. I. vi. 341 The provinces differ from Paris in the nature of the social warfare. **1882** PEBODY *Eng. Journalism* xii. 88 In the provinces, as in London, Liberal journalists outnumber the Conservatives. **1882** FREEMAN in *Longm. Mag.* I. 89, I have even known a New York paper speak of the rest of the United States as 'the provinces'. **1882** [see PROVINCIAL *a.* 4]. **1896** *Cosmopolitan* XX. 442 Mr. Pastor's company all came back from giving pleasure to what English writers would call 'the provinces'. **1896** *Law Times* CI. 573/2 The full force of the Bench is required to deal effectually with the work in London and the provinces.

6. a. *Nat. Hist.* A faunal or floral area less extensive than a 'region', or containing a distinctive group of animal or plant communities; a sub-region.

1847 H. C. Watson *Cybele Britannica* I. 14 Eighteen 'Provinces', or groups of counties, have been marked out on the map; and..they will be found more natural sections of the island than are the counties themselves. **1860** *Q. Jrnl. Geol. Soc.* XVI. p. xxxv, Thus natural provinces are constituted, each including a considerable number of forms peculiar to itself. **1877** Huxley *Anat. Inv. Anim.* 19 Certain areas of the earth's surface are inhabited by groups of animals and plants..not found elsewhere... Such areas are termed Provinces of Distribution. **1885** Lyell *Elem. Geol.* (ed. 4) 96 The sea and land may be divided into..distinct areas or provinces, each peopled by a peculiar assemblage of animals and plants. **1932** Fuller & Conard tr. *Braun-Blanquet's Plant Sociol.* xiv. 355 The province is.. characterized by at least one climax community. **1947** R. Good *Geogr. Flowering Plants* ii. 38 This classification divides the floras and floristic units of the world first into kingdoms, then into regions.., and finally into provinces. **1957** P. Dansereau *Biogeography* i. 54 Each area (the provinces here) holds a more or less heterogeneous residue of the units that have fared variously in the course of its total history. **1973** J. W. Valentine *Evolutionary Paleoecol. Marine Biosphere* iii. 74 The regions that constitute distributional units of organisms are called bio-geographical regions or provinces (biotic provinces, faunal provinces, floral provinces, and so on). **1974** *Sci. Amer.* Apr. 83/3 The marine faunas today are partitioned into more than 30 provinces, among which there is in general only a low percentage of common species.

b. In full ***petrographic*** or ***petrographical province***. An area of igneous rocks that appear to have been formed during the same period of igneous activity, presumably from the same magma. [cf. G. *geognostisch bezirk* (H. Vogelsang 1872, in *Zeitschr. d. deutsch. geol. Ges.* XXIV. 525).]

1886 J. W. Judd in *Q. Jrnl. Geol. Soc.* XLII. 54 There are distinct petrographical provinces, within which the rocks erupted during any particular geological period present certain well-marked peculiarities in mineralogical composition and microscopical structure, serving at once to distinguish them from the rocks belonging to the same general group, which were simultaneously erupted in other petrographical provinces. **1886** F. Rutley in *Ibid.* XLII. 96 Lavas of totally distinct characters are poured out from the same vent, so that the use of the term 'petrographic province' seemed to be of rather doubtful propriety. **1910** Lake & Rastall *Text-bk. Geol.* xiii. 230 The occurrence of chemical peculiarities running through all or nearly all the igneous rocks of a province shows that they are not all brought together by chance, but that there must be some real relationship between the different types. **1941** *Amer. Jrnl. Sci.* CCXXXIX. 542 (*heading*) Compositions (less anorthite) of the salic portions of residual magmas in New Zealand petrographical provinces. **1954** H. Williams et al. *Petrography* i. 10 The markedly potassic, leucitic lavas of the region around Rome and Naples..form a petrographic province. **1962** P. T. Broneer tr. *Beloussov's Basic Probl. in Geotectonics* xxxii. 657 At first it was thought..that different geographic areas were characterized by the predominance of different magmas. This was the origin of the study of petrographic provinces.

c. In full now ***physiographic province***. An extensive region all parts of which have a broadly similar geology and topography and which differs significantly from adjacent regions.

1893 J. W. Powell in *14th Ann. Rep. U.S. Geol. Survey, 1892–3* I. 71 One of the results of this interpretation is the recognition of geologic provinces... The geologic province is the unit of past geography; throughout each the successive deposits represent a definite chronologic sequence, and throughout each there may generally be found definite, consistent, and mutually corroborative series of records of geologic events. **1895** B. Willis *Northern Appalachians* (Nat. Geogr. Monogr. I. No. 6) 197 The plains were the homes of the most populous Indian tribes... The ranges of the mountains..were a barrier to intercourse long after the several topographic provinces had come under one national government. **1914** *Ann. Assoc. Amer. Geographers* IV. 85 The confusion will be worse when the plotting of census and other statistics by physiographic provinces has become common. **1936** *Bull. Amer. Assoc. Petroleum Geologists* XX. 1278 (*caption*) Outline map of Mexico showing principal physiographic provinces. *Ibid.* 1297 Although geologists and travellers subdivide the mountainous area of Chiapas into several sections, differing in their topographic and geologic aspects, nevertheless, their related and combined features can be taken as a whole to form one large province. **1974** *Physics Bull.* Oct. 430/2 Another striking feature of the Mercurian surface is the asymmetry in distribution of the major physiographic provinces (also a characteristic of the moon and Mars).

†**d.** *Soil Science.* In full ***soil province***. (See quots.) *Obs.*

1909 *Bull. Bureau of Soils* (U.S. Dept. Agric.) No. 55. 26 The complete scheme of classification, so far as perfected by the Bureau of Soils, also provides for the grouping of these series..into thirteen great soil provinces, as shown in the map. **1913** *Ibid.* No. 96. 7 A soil province is an area having the same general physiographic expression, in which the soils have been produced by the same forces or groups of forces and throughout which each rock or soil material yields to equal forces equal results. **1924** F. E. Bear *Soil Managem.* iv. 30 Province refers to a large land area in which either the mode or the source of origin, or both, of the soil have been quite similar throughout. Thus the Glacial and Loessial Province of the Bureau of Soils includes the entire land area in the United States over which the glacial processes were most important in the formation of the original soil.

e. = ***oil province*** s.v. oil *sb.*[1] 6 e.

1926 [see *oil province* s.v. oil *sb.*[1] 6 e]. **1933** *Bull. Amer. Assoc. Petroleum Geologists* XVII. 1107 The earliest..trap to form in many American petroleum provinces was a reservoir rock which was wedged out and overlapped by an impervious cap rock. **1966** *McGraw-Hill Encycl. Sci. & Technol.* X. 61/2 Underground occurrences of petroleum may be classified as pools, fields, and provinces. **1971** *Daily Tel.* 29 Dec. 5/3 This huge oil yield from the northern 'province' of the North Sea will have important consequences for this country.

II. 7. The sphere of action of a person or body of persons; duty, office, business, function, department.

a **1626** Bacon *Q. Eliz.* Mor. & Hist. Wks. (Bohn) 480 This is not a subject for the pen of a monk, or any such cloistered writer... Certainly this is a province for men of the first rank. **1651** Hobbes *Leviath.* xxii, This word province signifies a charge, or care of business, which he whose business it is, committeth to another man. **1702** *Clarendon's Hist. Reb.* I. Pref. 2 It is a difficult Province to write the History of the Civil Wars of a great and powerful Nation. **1773** *Life N. Frowde* 32, I rose softly, and dressed myself, a Province I was grown very alert at. **1775** *Sterne's Sent. Journ.* III. 192 (*The Story*) My province was..to carry home the goods. **1776** G. Semple *Building in Water* 149, I presume it is quite out of our Province. **1787** Jefferson *Writ.* (1859) II. 103 It is neither in my province, nor in my power, to remedy them. **1806** A. Hunter *Culina* (ed. 3) 262 The province of the cook, is to dress the meat according to the modern costume, and..to dish it up in an elegant manner. **1849** Macaulay *Hist. Eng.* x. II. 657 James had invaded the province of the legislature. **1888** M. Robertson *Lombard St. Myst.* xii, How he had secured an entrance..it is not our province to inquire.

III. *fig.* from I.

8. A department, division, or branch of learning, science, art, government, or any subject.

1690 Locke *Essay Hum. Und.* iv. xx. 362 They seemed to me to be the three great Provinces of the intellectual World, wholly separate and distinct one from another. **1709** Berkeley *The. Vision* §115 The two distinct provinces of sight and touch. **1710** —— *Princ. Hum. Knowl.* §101 The two great provinces of speculative science,..Natural Philosophy and Mathematics. **1756–82** J. Warton *Ess. Pope* (ed. 4) II. xi. 262 He early left the more poetical provinces of his art, to become a moral, didactic and satiric poet. **1838–9** Hallam *Hist. Lit.* IV. iv. vii. §8. 296 In the provinces of erudition and polite letters..some tendency towards a coalition began to appear. **1874** Carpenter *Ment. Phys.* ii. xii. (1879) 505 In the provinces of Æsthetics and Morals.

†**9.** *Zool.* and *Bot.* A sub-kingdom. *Obs. rare.*

1866 Owen *Anat. Vertebr. Anim.* I. Pref. 9 Illustrations.. will be found in the chapters on the Articulate Province and other parts of the 'Lectures on Invertebrates'.

IV. 10. *attrib.* and *Comb.* Of, belonging or pertaining to a (or the) province, as ***province cost, man, seal, store***; **province-line**, see quot. 1809; **province rose** = *Provins rose* s.v. Provins or *Provence rose* s.v. Provence; also *absol.*; **province-wide** *a.*, extending throughout or pertaining to a whole province.

1597 Gerard *Herball* iii. i. 1802 The greate Rose..is generally called the greate Province Rose. **1629** J. Parkinson *Paradisi in Sole* cix. 413 Some Gentlewomen have caused all their damaske stockes to be grafted with province Roses, hoping to have as good water, and more store of them. *Ibid.*, The flowers are..of a sent not so sweete as the damaske Province. **1648** B. Plantagenet *Descr. New Albion* 6 Having obtained under the Province Seal my grant of my Manor of Belvill. **1731** P. Miller *Gard. Dict.* s.v. Rosa. The Damask, Province, and Frankfort Roses grow to the Height of seven or eight Feet. **1758** L. Lyon in *Milit. Jrnls.* (1855) 14 There was a regiment of province men come up to Schenacata. **1758** S. Thompson *Diary* (1896) 20 We eat supper and breakfast on Province cost. **1763** J. Woolman *Jrnl.* (1840) 114 Going down the river to the province-store at Shaniokin. **1809** Kendall *Trav.* III. 277 The bay itself..is intersected by what is called the province-line; that is, by the forty-fifth degree of north latitude, which is the southern boundary of Lower Canada. **1964** P. Worsley in I. L. Horowitz *New Sociol.* 380 Government intervention in province-wide infrastructural fields, such as air-ways, bus-lines, insurance etc. **1977** *Belfast Tel.* 22 Feb. 8/8 The old Loyalist merry-go-round of..province-wide protests and rallies for the converted are discarded.

provincial (prəʊˈvɪnʃəl), *a.* and *sb.* [a. F. *provincial* (13th c. in Hatz.-Darm.), or ad. L. *prōvinciāl-is*, f. *prōvincia*: see prec. and -al[1].]

A. *adj.* Of or belonging to a province or provinces.

1. Of or pertaining to an ecclesiastical province.

1377 Langl. *P. Pl.* B. xi. 56 For whiles fortune is þi frende, Freres wil þe louye..and for þe biseke, To her priour prouyncial a pardoun forto haue. *c* **1380** Wyclif *Wks.* (1880) 40 þe mynystris prouyncials, to whom only..be grauntid leue to resceyue freris. **1483** *Caxton's Chron. Eng.* iv. (1520) 33/1 Yf the cause were shewed in the provyncyall counsel of bysshops. **1529** More *Dyaloge* i. Wks. 109/1 That the clargye of this realme hath..by a constytucion prouincial prohybited any boke of scripture to bee translated into the englyshe tonge. **1560** Daus tr. *Sleidane's Comm.* 70 b, It was necessarye to haue a lawfull counsell, eyther prouinciall, or general. **1578** *2nd Bk. Discipl. Ch. Scot.* vii. §18 Provinciall assemblies we call lawful conventions of the pastors doctors and uther eldaris of a province. **1649** Milton *Eikon.* xiii. Wks. 1851 III. 444 Not Presbytery but Arch-Presbytery, Classical, Provincial, and Diocesan Presbytery. **1726** Ayliffe *Parergon* p. xxxvii, A Law made in a Provincial Synod is properly term'd a Provincial Constitution. **1851** Hussey *Papal Power* i. 4 He had good reason to appeal from a provincial judgment of his case.

2. a. Of or belonging to a civil province, *e.g.* an ancient Roman province, or a province of a modern country or state; rarely, of an English county; now specifically of Canada.

1594 O. B. *Quest. Profit. Concern.* 15, I am a poore wretched vnderling, and no prouinciall man, neither warden of my company. **1633** T. Stafford *Pac. Hib.* i. ii. (1821) 36 By the perswasion of the Provinciall rebells. **1647** N. Bacon *Disc. Govt. Eng.* i. iii. (1739) 4 In this provincial way of Government of Britain, under the Roman Lieutenants. **1690** Temple *Misc.* ii. iv. *Poetry* 36 The common People used that [Latin language] still, but vitiated with the base allay of their Provincial Speech. **1795** *Quebec Gaz.* 8 Jan. 3/1 Clerk of the Provincial Court for the District of Three Rivers. **1796** Burke *Corr.* (1844) IV. 363, I believe that place has more of the stuff of a good provincial capital, than any town in England. **1804** *Europ. Mag.* XLV. 35/2 At the head of these four provincial Kings [of Ulster, Leinster, Munster, and Connaught] was placed a supreme Monarch. **1835** Thirlwall *Greece* I. viii. 307 The provincial land was tributary to the state. **1849** J. E. Alexander *L'Acadie* I. 35 It was found necessary to intermingle the newly arrived regulars with the Glengarry light infantry, a provincial corps. **1874** Parker *Goth. Archit.* ii. 283 These round towers, or campaniles of Ravenna seem to constitute a provincial type. **1878** *Herald* (Ottawa) 24 Jan. 1/4 Two whiskey informers..were under the protection of the Provincial Police. **1965** *Globe & Mail* (Toronto) 10 Mar. 1/6 Provincial police said the single-engined plane..struck the lines with its undercarriage. **1968** *Ibid.* 3 Feb. 11/1 He said his department is seeking to have provincial services extended to Indians. **1976** *Telegraph-Jrnl.* (St. John, New Brunswick) 12 Aug. 1/1 He will recommend a *provincial* tax hike.

b. Of the American provinces or colonies of European states, *esp.* of the British colonies; colonial. Cf. B. 4 b. *Obs.* exc. *Hist.*

1688 *Col. Rec. Pennsylv.* I. 228 At a Meeting of the Deputy Governor and Provinciall Councill. **1760** *Hist.* in *Ann. Reg.* 59/2 The whole regular, and no small part of the provincial force, which remained in Canada. **1764** *Answ. to Queries on Govt. Maryland* 16 Like the provincial rattle-snake coiled up, whose poison is best prevented by a switch. **1776** *N. Jersey Archives* Ser. ii. I. 55 Elected..to represent the County of Bergen in Provincial Congress, to be held at Trenton. **1882** Freeman *Lect. to Amer. Audiences* ii. iv. 320 The word *provincial* was, with a near approach to accuracy, often applied to your Thirteen Colonies, while they were still dependencies of Great Britain. **1898** E. B. Greene *The Provincial Govnr. in Eng. Colonies of N.A.* Pref. 5 The term 'Provincial Governor' has been chosen to designate the chief executive of the Royal and proprietary colonies.

†**3.** Having the relation of a province to a sovereign state. Also *fig.* *Obs.*

1576 Fleming *Panopl. Epist.* 243 He being a Prince of a Prouinciall iurisdiction. **1602** Warner *Alb. Eng.* Epit. (1612) 363 As of the aforesaid Countrie called Angel or Angulus, now prouincial to Denmarke. **1649** Bulwer *Pathomyot.* Ep. Ded. 1 The Argument of it [this Book] is Provinciall to Physick. **1685** Dryden *Pref. Albion & Albanius* Ess. (ed. Ker) I. 272 The other parts of it..are still as much provincial to Italy, as..in the time of the Roman Empire. **1708** J. Chamberlayne *St. Gt. Brit.* i. i. i. (1737) 2 The whole Provincial Britain..was..divided into Britannia Prima, Britannia Secunda, and Maxima Cæsariensis.

4. a. Of or belonging to a province or provinces as distinguished from the nation or state of which it or they form a part; local; hence (inaccurately), of the 'provinces' (see province 5) as distinguished from the capital (the usage of which is taken as national); situated in 'the provinces'.

(A French idiom, referring orig. to the provinces of France.)

1638 Baker tr. *Balzac's Lett.* (vol. II.) 190 You know provinciall spirits [orig. (1624) *esprits provinciaux*] are extremely greedy. **1674** Dryden *Prol. at Opening New House* 22 That, like the ambitious monarchs of the age, They give the law to our provincial stage. **1772** Gouv. Morris in Sparks *Life & Writ.* (1832) I. 17 Those many barbarisms which characterize a provincial education. **1787** Grose *Provinc. Gloss.* Pref. 3 Provincial or local words are of three kinds, the first, either Saxon or Danish, in general grown obsolete from disuse. **1809–10** Coleridge *Friend* (1865) 154 An article in a provincial paper of recent date. **1844** Ld. Brougham *Brit. Const.* ix. §2 (1862) 120 In Paris and the great provincial towns. **1855** Macaulay *Hist. Eng.* xviii. IV. 142 Merchants resident at Bristol and other provincial seaports. **1867** *Harper's Mag.* Dec. 96/1 The provincial theatres compare favorably with those of London. **1880** Swinburne *Stud. Shaks.* 113 His [Shakspere's] patriotism was too national to be provincial. **1882** Freeman *Lect. to Amer. Audiences* ii. iv. 320 In Great Britain there are no provinces, for every spot of the land has equal rights with every other. Little Pedlington is no more provincial than London. **1952** Granville *Dict. Theatr. Terms* 145 *Provincial theatre*, the stage outside London.

b. *transf.* Said of foxhunting outside the 'shires'.

1861 Whyte Melville *Mkt. Harb.* i. v. 35, I could have made you, now, a particular neat *provincial* boot; but with this pattern it's exceedingly difficult to attain the correct appearance for the flying countries. **1899** *Westm. Gaz.* 1 Dec. 4/2 Good sport has not been confined to the shires... Provincial packs have enjoyed their full share.

c. *spec.* Of a university other than the older universities of Oxford and Cambridge (or other than that of Oxford only).

1914 C. Mackenzie *Sinister St.* II. iii. ix. 688 It was still natural to regard Cambridge as a provincial university, and to take pleasure in shocking the earnest young Cambridge man with the metropolitan humours and airy self-assurance of Oxford. **1955** *Ann. Reg. 1954* 351 *Lucky Jim*..was an example of the work of the new 'provincial school' about which there was much talk in the year. **1958** *Times Lit. Suppl.* 17 Jan. 30/4 Talk of..'the red-brick intellectuals', though no Movement founder-member had done more than *teach* at one of the provincial universities. **1966** C. M.

BOWRA *Memories 1898–1939* xiii. 320 In the United States the academic profession had ties all over the country and was not divided as in England into Oxford and Cambridge on the one side and 'provincial' universities on the other. **1978** *Encounter* July 8/1, I studied at an English provincial university.

5. Having the manners or speech of a province or 'the provinces'; exhibiting the character, especially the narrowness of view or interest, associated with or attributed to inhabitants of 'the provinces'; wanting the culture or polish of the capital.

[*a* **1745** SWIFT (J.), A country 'squire having only the provincial accent upon his tongue, which is neither a fault, nor in his power to remedy.] **1755** JOHNSON, *Provincial*,.. rude; unpolished. *a* **1774** HARTE *Eulogius* Poems (1810) 385/2 His mien was awkward; graces he had none; Provincial were his notions and his tone. **1813** M. EDGEWORTH *Let.* 6 Apr. (1971) 10 He..speaks excellent language but with a strong provincial accent which at once destroys all idea of elegance. **1817** CHALMERS *Astron. Disc.* vi. (1852) 136 Christianity is not so paltry and provincial a system as Infidelity presumes it to be. **1863** TROLLOPE *Rachel Ray* I. vi. 118 Mrs. Rowan perceived at once that Mrs. Tappitt was provincial,.. but she was a good motherly woman. **1864** BAGEHOT *Lit. Stud.* (1878) II. 126 'Tristram Shandy'..Its mirth is boisterous. It is provincial. **1864** M. ARNOLD *Ess. Crit.* ii. (1875) 77 The provincial spirit, again, exaggerates the value of its ideas for want of a high standard at hand by which to try them. **1899** J. MCCARTHY *Reminisc.* II. xxxv. 252 Rather tall, very angular, surprisingly awkward..with a rough provincial accent and an uncouth way of speaking. **1909** A. W. EVANS tr. *A. France's Penguin Island* VII. ix. 312 Provincial women, since they wear low heels, are not very attractive, and preserve their virtue with ease. **1954** C. S. LEWIS *Eng. Lit. in 16th Cent.* I. i. 68 Scotch poetry had already a considerable achievement behind it and was by no means a local or provincial department of English poetry.

6. ***Provincial Letters***, the collection of letters of Blaise Pascal 1656–7, called (in ed. 1657) *Les Provinciales, ou les Lettres écrites par Louis de Montalte, à un Provincial de ses Amis*, letters written by L. de M. to a provincial of (= among) his friends.

1659 (*title*) An answer to the Provinciall Letters [of B. Pascal] Published by the Jansenists, Under the Name of Lewis Montalt. **1845** MAURICE *Mor. & Met. Philos.* in *Encycl. Metrop.* II. 658/1 Whether there may not be something in the *Provincial Letters* of that very spirit which they are attacking.

†**7. a.** = PROVENÇAL. *Obs.*

c **1440** *Pallad. on Husb.* III. 309 A dight vine in prouyntial manere That lyke a busshe vpstont.

b. Consisting of or designating a Provins (or 'province') rose (= '*Rose de Provence*, the Province Rose, the double Damaske Rose', Cotgrave; *Rosa provincialis*, Gerarde's Herbal, 1597). *Obs.*

1602 SHAKS. *Ham.* III. ii. 288 Would not this Sir, and a Forrest of Feathers,..with two Prouinciall Roses on my rac'd Shooes, get me a Fellowship in a crie of Players? **1633** FORD *Broken H.* I. ii, That I myself..have wrought To crown thy temples, this Provincial garland.

B. *sb.* [Absolute or elliptical uses of the adj.]

†**1.** A variety of the game of backgammon. *Obs.*

13.. *MS. Kings* 13 *A. XVIII* (Brit. Mus.) lf. 159/1 Prouincial. Est etiam alius ludus qui vocatur prouincial.

2. a. *Eccl.* The ecclesiastical head of a province; the chief of a religious order in a district or province.

1362 LANGL. *P. Pl.* A. VIII. 178 A powhe ful [*v.r.* pokeful] of pardoun þer with Prouincials lettres. *c* **1380** *Antecrist* in Todd *3 Treat. Wyclif* 125 To abbotes & priours, mynistris & wardeyns, & to þise provynciales & to þe popes chapileyns. **1412** in *Laing Charters* (1899) 24 Frere Willyam Cokar, than beande prouincial of the Quite Freris of Scotlande. **1534** LEE in *Lett. Suppress. Monasteries* (Camden) 41 We receyved your lettres by the provynciall of the Augustyn ffriers. **1599** SANDYS *Europæ Spec.* (1632) 69 These Generalls have under them their Provincialls as Lievtenants in every Province or State of Christendome. **1718** *Entertainer* No. 32. 215 A Hooker in his Country Cottage may be as upright and conscientious as his Provincial invested with his Pastoral Staff. **1839** *Penny Cycl.* XIII. 111/2 The general [of the Jesuits] receives monthly reports from the provincials, and quarterly ones from the superiors of professed houses. **1916** JOYCE *Portrait of Artist* (1969) 48 If the minister did it he would go to the rector: and the rector to the provincial: and the provincial to the general of the jesuits. **1960** [see DEFINITORY *sb.*]. **1973** *Franciscan* XV. 168 The Community Retreat conducted by Brother Luke, the American Provincial.

†**b.** Applied to a procuress (cf. F. *abbesse*). *Obs. slang.*

c **1640** [SHIRLEY] *Capt. Underwit* III. i, New yeares guifts From soder'd virgins and their shee provintialls Whose warren must be licenc'd from our office.

†**3.** The governor of a province. *Obs.*

1590 R. HICHCOCK *Quintess. Wit* 59 Those Cities which are vsed to liue free, or accustomed to gouerne themselues by their Prouincialls. **1593** NASHE *Christ's T.* (1613) 77 Thou suffredst him..to resist the Romane Prouinciall Florus.

4. a. A native or inhabitant of a province (Roman or modern); in *pl.* auxiliary troops raised in a province; formerly applied to the native Irish.

1605 CAMDEN *Rem.* (1657) 54 They took Roman names when they were provincials. **1617** MORYSON *Itin.* II. 118 (Rebell. Earl of Tyrone) So as if the Spaniards should land the Lord President might be enabled to keepe the Prouincials from reuolt. *Ibid.* 274 Lord Barry with 1600 Prouincials vnder him. *a* **1638** MEDE *Wks.* (1672) 674 The Inhabitants of Arabia Petræa, which were never yet Provincials of the Turkish Empire. **1781** GIBBON *Decl. & F.* xxii. (1869) I. 615 The grateful provincials enjoyed the blessings of his reign. **1808** PIKE *Sources Mississ.* III. (1810) 268 To be sent to America..to discipline and organize the Spanish provincials. **1907** GRIFFITH JOHN *Voice fr. China* xi. 245 Mr. Peng was..like most of his fellow provincials bitterly anti-foreign.

b. An inhabitant of the North American Colonies before the revolution; applied esp. to those engaged in military service. Cf. A. 2 b.

1758 *Hist.* in *Ann. Reg.* 72/2 He embarked upon Lake George with near 16000 troops, regulars and provincials. **1759** *Ibid.* 33/2 The French..collected all the regular troops and provincials, which they could draw from all their posts about the lakes. **1775** M. CUTLER in *Life*, etc. (1888) I. 49 We obtained an exact account of the number of Provincials that were killed and wounded in the battle [of Lexington] of the 19th ultimo. **1876** BANCROFT *Hist. U.S.* III. xiii. 196 Nine thousand and twenty-four provincials, from New England, New York, and New Jersey, assembled on the shore of Lake George.

c. In Canada: a member of a provincial police force.

1936 W. B. MOWERY *Paradise Trail* 4 On his flight across the provinces he had..slipped out of several tight squeezes with the Provincials. **1952** H. GARNER *Yellow Sweater* 143 One of the Provincials took me upstairs. **1963** J. N. HARRIS *Weird World Wes Beattie* xi. 137 The provincials were extremely dubious about trying to find a weapon in the depths of Lake Muskoka in March.

5. One who dwells in or comes from the 'provinces' as distinguished from an inhabitant or native of the capital; hence, a 'countrified' person.

1711 SHAFTESBURY *Charac.* (1737) II. II. II. i. 133 This we may observe in the hardy remote Provincials. **1775** T. SHERIDAN *Art Reading* p. x, By the aid of which all foreigners and provincials may..acquire a just pronunciation. **1843** tr. *Custine's Empire of Czar* II. 153 On the same principle that, in France, the Provincial distrusts the Parisian. **1865** LOWELL *New Eng. Two Cent. Ago* Prose Wks. 1890 II. 73 After that time they sank rapidly into provincials, narrow in thought, in culture, in creed. **1913** C. MACKENZIE *Sinister St.* I. II. v. 210 She used to laugh and tell him he was a regular old 'provincial'. **1954** C. S. LEWIS *Eng. Lit. in 16th Cent.* I. i. 83 Until we have trained ourselves to feel that 'gudeman' is no more rustic or homely than 'husband' we are no judges of Douglas as a translator of Virgil. If we fail in the training, then it is we and not the poet who are provincials.

†**6.** An ordinance of a provincial synod; also, a rescript addressed to an ecclesiastical province. *Obs.*

a **1529** SKELTON *Ware the Hawke* 133 Decrees or decretals ..Or els provincials. **1605** CAMDEN *Rem.* i. 5 And the Kings of Scotland, as appeereth in an antient Roman Provinciall, had next place before Castile. **1659** H. L'ESTRANGE *Alliance Div. Off.* 317 Considering that Provincial in Lindwood, where the Arch-Deacons are enjoyned in their visitations, diligently to take into their care..the fabrique of the Church.

†**7.** A provincial synod: cf. PROVINCE 3. *Obs.*

1637–50 ROW *Hist. Kirk* (Wodrow Soc.) 25 A partie conceaveing himself wronged by a session, may appeall to the Provinciall and Superintendent, (Presbyteries were not as yit erected). **1643** R. BAILLIE *Lett. & Jrnls.* (1841) II. 70 At our last Provinciall in Glasgow we resolved to be no longer silent. **1654** LAMONT *Diary* (Maitl. Cl.) 81 The fast (appointed by the provinciall of Fyfe, at Kirkekaldie, 1654).

†**8.** A kind of lizard. *Obs. rare.*

1575 TURBERV. *Falconrie* 301 Take the dung of a Lyzart, (which is called a Provinciall) and beate it into powder.

9. In other elliptical uses: e.g. a provincial newspaper.

1892 *Pall Mall G.* 7 Apr. 2/1 All four men included here are commonly given a full report in the *Times*, and on first-class occasions a full report in the greater provincials. **1961** *Listener* 31 Aug. 325/1 His thoughts about Beckford and Beckett, Jouhandeau and Camus, the *anti-roman* and the English provincials. **1973** *Times* 2 July 15/6 The London papers stood out for a long time after the provincials had joined with him.

pro'vincialate. [f. PROVINCIAL *sb.* 2 + -ATE[1].] The office or period of office of a provincial; ecclesiastical headship.

1906 *Tablet* 29 Sept. 482 It was during his Provincialate that the fourth Congregation of Westminster took place. **1911** A. BRENNAN *Life St. Lawrence of Brindisi* xviii. 179 During his Provincialate the Friars of Piedmont..renewed their petitions. **1930** T. S. WESTBROOK *Glimpses Catholic Eng.* 70 During the Provincialates of Agnellus..and of his successor Albert of Pisa..the brethren at Oxford lived in the strictest poverty. **1960** J. B. DOCKERY *Christopher Davenport* viii. 121 During the Provincialate of Sancta Clara the community were well clothed. **1976** *Oxford Times* 3 Dec. 13/3 For the Jesuit student, as later for all his religious brethren during his Provincialate, he came as a breath of fresh air.

provincialism (prəʊ'vɪnʃəlɪz(ə)m). [f. PROVINCIAL *a.* + -ISM. So mod.F. *provincialisme*.]

1. *Politics.* Attachment to one's own province, its institutions, interests, etc., before those of the nation or state of which it is a part; provincial patriotism; desire for the autonomy of the province or provinces rather than national unity.

1820 *Hist.* in *Ann. Reg.* I. 245/2 The prevalence of a spirit of provincialism—and the factions into which the capital was split. **1860** MOTLEY *Netherl.* (1867) III. 27 The inherent view of the Netherland polity was already a tendency to decentralisation and provincialism. **1873** *Spectator* 23 Aug. 1061/1 The Welsh themselves admit that the meeting tends to maintain their provincialism, their separateness, and their pride of pedigree. **1902** *Daily Chron.* 26 June 4/3 The key-note of Spanish life, both in town and country, is provincialism. His *pueblo* and his province are infinitely more to a Spaniard than his mother country.

2. a. Provincial character or peculiarity; the manner, fashion, mode of thought, etc., which characterize a particular province, or 'the provinces' generally, as distinct from that which is (or is held to be) national, or which is the fashion of the capital; hence, narrowness of view, thought, or interests, roughness of speech or manners as distinct from the polish of the court or capital.

1836 HOR. SMITH *Tin Trump.* (1876) 296 There is a provincialism of mind as well as of accent—a nationality of counties. **1861** SMILES *Engineers* II. 491 It might be said that there was narrowness and provincialism in this. **1870** LOWELL *Study Wind.* 204 Perhaps the narrowest provincialism is that of Self. **1872** —— *Dante* Prose Wks. 1890 IV. 182 Dante was..incapable of intellectual provincialism. **1902** *Westm. Gaz.* 16 Oct. 2/2 This idea was fostered by the London Unionist Press, but that Press was afflicted with a sort of metropolitan provincialism.

b. with *a* and *pl.* A peculiarity confined to a certain area; a local peculiarity or variety.

1845 FORD *Handbk. Spain* 127 Ecclesiastical architecture has its provincialisms like dialects. **1848** *Rickman's Goth. Archit.* (ed. 5) p. xxxvii, Windows of this character are common in the northern part of Oxfordshire, and may be considered as a provincialism.

3. *esp.* The manner of speech characteristic of a particular province; with *pl.*, A local word, phrase, or peculiarity of pronunciation which is not part of the standard language of a country.

1770 *Monthly Rev.* XLII. 180 His language..is, moreover, frequently debased with certain provincial*isms*. **1793** MARSH *Michaelis' New Test.* I. iv. §13. 176 Inscriptions ..of singular service..in explaining the provincialisms and idiotisms. **1798** SOUTHEY in Robberds *Mem. W. Taylor* (1843) I. 221 Perhaps you will find many of the expressions provincialisms, which are familiar to my ears. **1851** GALLENGA *Italy* I. III. ii. 305 The style was thought to be harsh and uncouth; the language full of Lombard provincialism. **1864** BURTON *Scot Abr.* II. i. 28 Buchanan, Bellenden, and Johnston had their provincialisms and peculiarities, as Livy the Paduan, and Sallust the Sabine had.

4. *Ecol.* The development of biogeographical provinces. Cf. PROVINCE 6 a.

1969 *Spec. Papers Geol. Soc. Amer.* No. 119. 1 Provincialism increased by the addition of the Malvinokaffric Province. **1975** *Nature* 22 May 353/2 Why should the early Devonian faunas exhibit more provincialism, for instance, than those of the late Silurian.

provincialist (prəʊ'vɪnʃəlɪst). [f. as prec. + -IST.]

1. A native or inhabitant of a province, or of the 'provinces', as distinct from the capital; = PROVINCIAL *sb.* 4, 5.

Originally in reference to the French provinces.

1656 EARL MONM. tr. *Boccalini's Advts. fr. Parnass.* I. xli. (1674) 57 Provincialists are more troubled at the immodesty of an Officers favorite, than at a foul insolency committed by a Townsman. **1796** W. MARSHALL *W. England* I. 26 A fact of which the mere Provincialists..do not appear to be yet sufficiently apprized. **1817** W. TAYLOR in *Monthly Rev.* LXXXII. 204 Such practical skill comes of itself in condensed masses of population, and it is this which gives the Londoner his advantage over the provincialist. **1834** *Blackw. Mag.* XXXV. 969 He thus spared the [ancient Roman] provincialists those burthens which must else have alighted upon them. **1871** H. R. HAWEIS *Thoughts for Times* (1872) 44 His ways are inscrutable to small-minded provincialists.

b. (See quot.) *rare*[−0].

1882 OGILVIE, *Provincialist*, one who uses provincialisms.

c. An actor in 'provincial' theatres.

1902 *Westm. Gaz.* 21 Apr. 4/3 The grievance at the Théâtre Français might well be aired by our 'provincialists', both male and female.

2. A supporter or advocate of provincialism, or of the rights or claims of a province. Cf. PROVINCIAL *sb.* 4 a, b.

1708 OCKLEY *Saracens* (Bohn) 446 There was only a small party, supported by a few provincialists, in the interest of Abdallah. **1766** *Gazetteer* 11 Feb. 1/2 The latest accounts from New-York..seem to indicate, that a repeal of the Stamp Act will only encrease those provincialists to further demands.

provinciality (prəʊvɪnʃɪ'ælɪtɪ). [f. PROVINCIAL *a.* + -ITY.] **1. a.** The quality or condition of being provincial; the pettiness or narrowness of interests, feeling, or view that is apt to be associated with this; an example of this, a provincial trait.

1805 W. TAYLOR in *Ann. Rev.* III. 243 This Scotch spirit, this provinciality of public zeal, pervades the pamphlet before us. **1864** M. ARNOLD *Ess. in Crit.* ii. (1875) 70 In the bulk of the intellectual work of a nation which has no centre, no intellectual metropolis..there is observable a note of provinciality. Now to get rid of provinciality is a certain stage of culture. **1869** —— *Cult. & An.* Pref., In what we call *provinciality* they [the Nonconformists] abound, but in what we may call *totality* they fall short. **1886** *Pall Mall G.* 28 Aug. 1/1 The petty personalities, the mean ambitions, and narrow provincialities of too many of his opponents.

b. *spec.* in reference to speech or writing.

1782 T. WARTON *Enq. Poems Rowley* 46 That circumstance must have added greatly to the provinciality, and consequently to the unintelligibility, of the poem. **1798** ANNA SEWARD *Lett.* (1811) V. 150 A hardness in sounding the consonants, which mark the provinciality of Derbyshire and Lancashire. **1805** *Monthly Mag.* XX. 30 The provinciality of their accent..greatly offends the English ear.

2. *Ecol.* The restriction of the distribution of a plant or animal community to a particular province or group of provinces. Cf. PROVINCE 6 a.

1969 *Spec. Papers Geol. Soc. Amer.* No. 119. 3 The waxing and waning of provinciality displayed by Lower Devonian invertebrate faunas can be viewed in another way. **1971** J. G. JOHNSON in *Amer. Jrnl. Sci.* CCLXX. 257 Degrees of faunal resemblance..can be measured by a Provinciality Index (PI) consisting of a weighted ratio of common and endemic genera. **1976** *Nature* 24 June 695/1 It is noteworthy that an abrupt increase in phyletic rate commonly coincides initially with the brief upsurge in cladogenetic rate accompanying major provinciality increase.

provinciali'zation. [f. PROVINCIALIZE *v.* + -ATION.] A making or becoming provincial; conversion into a province.

1924 *Glasgow Herald* 16 Sept. 7 In a vigorous speech [he] emphasised the provincialisation and Indianisation aspect of the Report. **1967** A. N. SHERWIN-WHITE *Racial Prejudice in Imperial Rome* I. 24 Critognatus contrasts Roman imperialism, as revealed by the permanent exploitation and provincialization of southern Gaul (Gallia Narbonensis) unfavourably with the former temporary devastation of the country by the Cimbri. **1976** *Northern Miner* (Toronto) 19 Aug. 6/1 The government of Saskatchewan took the first step in the provincialization of the potash industry.

provincialize (prəʊ'vɪnʃəlaɪz), *v.* [f. PROVINCIAL *a.* + -IZE.]

1. *intr.* To write or speak in a provincial dialect.

1803 W. TAYLOR in *Monthly Mag.* XVI. 306 As it appears that Peter provincialized and was unlearned, he probably wrote in the vernacular tongue.

2. *trans.* To make provincial; to give a provincial character or name to.

1829 *Blackw. Mag.* XXVI. 171 That nothing be done which would have the effect of provincialising the literature. **1849** *Zoologist* VII. 2392 None of your correspondents have provincialized the names of our water-birds. **1885** *Pall Mall G.* 31 Dec. 2/1 Every branch of [Indian] expenditure, in fact, that was not of necessity Imperial..was provincialized.

3. *intr.* To become provincial.

1892 *Black & White* 6 Aug. 150/1 Men's minds do not always widen, they sometimes 'provincialise' with the process of the suns.

pro'vincialized, *ppl. a.* [f. PROVINCIALIZE *v.* + -ED[1].] Made, or having become, provincial; having become a province.

1955 *Times* 23 June 11/6 A country which had felt itself neglected and provincialized under the Danish and, especially, the Swedish connexion. **1974** *Sci. Amer.* Apr. 85/3 A widespread, soft-bodied fauna of low diversity gave way to a slightly provincialized, skeletonized fauna of somewhat higher diversity.

pro'vincially, *adv.* [f. PROVINCIAL *a.* + -LY[2].] In a provincial manner or capacity.

1628 J. DOUGHTY *Serm. Church-schismes* 25 About Lent and autumne they ordained councels provincially to be held. **1681** NEVILE *Plato Rediv.* 79 We have the same Foundations that all other Aristocracies have, who Govern but one City, and have no Territory but what they Govern Provincially. **1704** *Addr. Durham* in *Lond. Gaz.* No. 4049/1 We.., the Clergy of this Diocese, having been already Provincially Represented to Your Majesty.

pro'vincialship. [f. PROVINCIAL *sb.* + -SHIP.] The office or dignity of a provincial in an ecclesiastical or religious order.

1629 WADSWORTH *Pilgr.* iii. 29 His place..was Prefect of the English Mission, which is now by dispensation from the Pope conuerted into a Prouinciall-ship. **1679** OATES *Narr. Popish Plot* 7 The Father General of the Society of Jesus.. had conferred the Provincialship upon Thomas White. **1867** R. PALMER *Life P. Howard* 79 The provincialship was made an honorary title.

provinciate (prəʊ'vɪnʃɪət), *sb.* [f. L. *prōvincia* PROVINCE + -ATE[1].] = prec.

1857 G. OLIVER *Cath. Relig. Cornw.* 465 Filling the office of the provinciate from 1806 to 1810.

†**pro'vinciate,** *ppl. a. Obs. rare.* [f. as prec. + -ATE[2].] Reduced to the state of a province.

1671 R. MACWARD *True Nonconf.* 19 Restoring the jews to their own Land, Religion and Laws, but only with a provinciat liberty.

pro'vinciate, *v.* [f. as prec. + -ATE[3].] *trans.* To reduce to the condition of a province or of provincials. Hence **pro'vinciated** *ppl. a.*

1629 MAXWELL tr. *Herodian* (1635) 209 *note*, He means the Provinciated part of Britaine. **1640** HOWELL *Dodona's Gr.* 56 When there was a Designe to Provinciate the whole Kingdome. **1783** W. F. MARTYN *Geog. Mag.* II. 391 The greatest part of Britain becoming provinciated. **1881** W. MARSHALL *Hist. Scenes Perth.* 374 The provinciated Britons were employed to cut down the woods.

provine (prəʊ'vaɪn), *v.* [ad. F. *provignier* (3rd s. *provigne*), *-vaignier*, *-veignier* (13th c. in Godef. *Compl.*), f. OF. *provain*, mod.F. *provin*:—L. *prōpāgin-em* young shoot, slip, or layer. See PROPAGATE *v.*] *trans.* To propagate (a vine or the like) by layering. Also *absol.*, and *intr.* in *pass.* sense. Hence **pro'vining** *vbl. sb.*

c **1440** *Pallad. on Husb.* XII. 31 Now also to prouyne is not the werst [L. *Nunc et propago iure ducetur*]. *a* **1577** SIR T. SMITH *Commw. Eng.* I. xii. (1589) 14 The father and mother sendeth them out in couples as it were by prouining or propagation. [*Margin*] Prouining, or propagation, is when a man layeth a branch of a..tree into the ground, so that it taketh roote of it self. **1707** *Curios. in Husb. & Gard.* 198 This was not the right Cinnamon-tree, but..'twas impossible to make it provine. **1866** FLEMING & TIBBINS *Fr. Dict.* II. 844/1 *Provignement*,..provining. *Provigner*, to provine, to lay a branch of a vine in the ground to take root, to layer.

proving ('pruːvɪŋ), *vbl. sb.* Forms: see PROVE *v.*; also 3 **preofunge**, 6 **preeving**. [f. PROVE *v.* + -ING[1].] The action of PROVE *vb.*

1. a. Testing, trial, probation; †experience. Now *arch.* or *techn.* (See also 6.)

c **1325** *Spec. Gy Warw.* 335 Man, woltou make a god prouing, Wher þu loue þe heuene king? *a* **1340** HAMPOLE *Psalter* ix. 10 þai at haf felid the suetnes in þaire saule.., and knawis it be prouynge. **1382** WYCLIF *Jas.* i. 3 The prouyng [**1388** preuyng] of ȝoure feith werchith pacience. *a* **1450** MYRC *Festial* 18 Hegh preuyng of our fay. **1591** SPENSER *M. Hubberd* 1366 [He] Bad him stay at ease till further preeving. **1837** WHITTOCK, etc. *Bk. Trades* (1842) 287 (*Gun-maker*) Proving..consists in loading each barrel with a ball of its own size upon as much powder as the ball weighs. **1846** TRENCH *Mirac.* i. (1862) 112 A proving of men's temperance ..in the midst of abundance.

b. *Homœopathy.* The testing of a drug (see PROVE *v.* 1 f).

1843 *Brit. Jrnl. Homœopathy* I. 291 In the provings of the insoluble substances, such as calcarea, silica, &c., the symptoms produced by the first doses are rarely experienced ..in the subsequent ones. **1881** *Encycl. Brit.* XII. 126/2 The record of such provings constitutes a large part of the literature of homœopathy. **1905** J. H. CLARKE *Homœopathy Explained* xvi. 122 There is always this check in homœopathy—the provings can be tested in practice. **1936** H. A. ROBERTS *Princ. & Art of Cure by Homœopathy* i. 16 The results of such investigation would enrich the homœopathic materia medica by completing provings of some of the older remedies, and by bringing out provings of new remedies. **1975** C. H. SHARMA *Man, Homoeopathy & Natural Med.* i. 16 Before a homoeopathic remedy can be used by a physician, it has to go through a series of 'provings'.

†**2.** A proof, a demonstration. *Obs.*

a **1225** *Ancr. R.* 160 Sutel preofunge is þet heo was muchel one, þe heold so silence.

3. The obtaining probate (of a will).

c **1440** *Jacob's Well* 25 For provyng of testamentys. **1633** SPELMAN *Prob. Wills* Wks. 1723 II. 129 The ancient manner of opening, publishing, or as we call it, proving of Wills.

4. a. The action of showing to be true, genuine, or valid; demonstration.

a **1533** FRITH *Another Bk. agst. Rastell* 336 The proving of good works doth neither make for purgatory nor against it. **1827** WHATELY *Logic* II. iii. (ed. 2) 246 One might..define Proving, 'the assigning of a reason or argument for the support of a given proposition'. **1898** SIR W. CROOKES in *Daily News* 8 Sept. 6/3 It has been said that 'Nothing worth the proving can be proved nor yet disproved'.

b. *N. Amer.* The action of establishing a claim. Also with *up*. Cf. PROVE *v.* 12.

1958 J. G. MACGREGOR *Northwest of 16* v. 67 They also had to bring fifteen acres under cultivation and to erect some sort of abode. (Carrying out these obligations and getting title to the land was termed 'proving up'.)

†**5.** Turning out; issue; thriving. (PROVE *v.* 10.)

a **1529** SKELTON *El. Rummyng* 185 God gyve it yll preuynge.

6. *attrib.* chiefly in sense 1, orig. in names of things used in some testing process.

1858 SIMMONDS *Dict. Trade*, *Proving-press*, an apparatus for testing the strength of iron girders, and other castings, by pressure. **1875** KNIGHT *Dict. Mech.*, *Proving-machine*, one for testing the resistance of springs or the strength of materials... *Proving-pump*, a forcing-pump for testing boilers, tubes, etc. **1881** RAYMOND *Mining Gloss.*, *Proving-hole*, a small heading driven to find and follow a coal-seam, lost by a dislocation. **1899** *Westm. Gaz.* 27 July 5/2 Experiments are being made at the Sandy Hook proving grounds. **1944** *Air News Yearbk.* II. 188 Poland and Norway represented the 'proving ground'. **1948** 'N. SHUTE' *No Highway* i. 28 They did a whole lot of proving flights over the route before they put it into regular operation. **1959** *Listener* 15 Jan. 147/2 And, finally, proving time: once you have reconstituted the yeast and made a dough, carry on with your normal timing. **1971** M. LEE *Dying for Fun* ix. 55 All over his desk were scattered invitations—art galleries, press conferences..air trips and proving flights. **1975** *Harpers & Queen* May 27/1 The other day, I and my dough came to be separated at a crucial point in the 'proving' process. **1979** *Nature* 8 Feb. 430/1 Scientists have used astronomy as a proving ground for theories of gravity ever since Newton explained the sizes and shapes of the planetary orbits.

proving ('pruːvɪŋ), *ppl. a.* [f. as prec. + -ING[2].] That proves, in various senses: Trying, testing; affording proof; thriving: see the verb.

1620 *Form of Service* in Sprot *Scott. Liturgies Jas. VI* (1901) 5 After experience both of thy manifold goodness and proving corrections. **1670** EACHARD *Cont. Clergy* 26 To think, that one such proving lad should make recompense.. for those many weak ones. **1824** H. CAMPBELL *Love Lett. Mary Q. Scots* Pref. 9 The proving argument was in them.

provinour. In 5 provy'nour. [a. OF. *provigneur*, agent-n. from *provignier*: see PROVINE *v.*] A propagator. (In quot. app. a multiplier or disseminator of a narrative.)

1426 LYDG. *De Guil. Pilgr.* 277 Go fforth thow dreme! I sende the By all the placys wher thow hast be; I send the to thy provynours, By all the pathys & the tovrs.

Provins (prɔvɛ̃s). The name of a French town, thirty miles east of Melun, used attrib. to designate a variety of *Rosa gallica*, formerly known as *Rosa provincialis*, the apothecary's red rose, which has long been cultivated there. Cf. *province rose* s.v. PROVINCE 10.

1837 T. RIVERS *Rose Amateur's Guide* 11 In France, this [sc. *Rosa gallica*] is called the 'Provins Rose'. **1902** JEKYLL & MAWLEY *Roses for Eng. Gardens* ii. 13 These two names, Provence and Provins, for two classes of garden rose..are so much alike... Provence is the Cabbage Rose (*R. centifolia*); Provins is *Rosa gallica*, the garden kinds being mostly striped. **1955** C. C. HURST in G. S. Thomas *Old Shrub Roses* ix. 61 The Provins Roses were also much appreciated in India and in England. **1978** J. HARKNESS *Roses* xiii. 173 It [sc. *Rosa gallica officinalis*] is also known as the Apothecary's Rose, a reference to its uses in medicine, and as the Provins rose, because that French town specialized in making conserves and medicine from it.

provirus (prəʊ'vaɪərəs). *Biol.* [f. PRO-[2] + VIRUS, after PROPHAGE.] The form which a DNA or RNA virus has when incorporated into, and able to replicate with, the DNA of a host cell.

1952 *Physiol. Rev.* XXXII. 419 Most of the cells perpetuate the potentiality of producing virus, although the virus itself is rarely detectable in them. For this reason, such cells are considered as infected with a provirus, a perpetuating, but immature and nonlytic agent. **1953** S. E. LURIA *Gen. Virol.* xiv. 277 We may suppose that in the recovered plant the virus is mainly in a condition (provirus) similar to the prophage. **1964** *Proc. Nat. Acad. Sci.* LII. 323 It has been suggested that the provirus of Rous sarcoma virus-infected cells is composed of DNA. **1970** *Nature* 5 Sept. 1023/1 It is widely believed that cells transformed with Rous sarcoma virus (RSV) contain a DNA transcript of the viral RNA, the so-called 'provirus'.

Hence **pro'viral** *a.*

1969 C. D. DARLINGTON in C. W. M. Whitty et al. *Virus Dis. & Nervous Syst.* 137 Diseases such as Kuru and Scrapie having combined genetic, cytoplasmic and pro-viral components. **1976** *Nature* 15 July 190 (*heading*) Proviral sequences of baboon endogenous type C RNA virus in DNA of human leukaemic tissues.

†**pro'visal.** *Obs. rare*[−1]. [f. as PROVISE *v.* + -AL[1].] An arrangement, provision.

1641 EARL MONM. tr. *Biondi's Civil Warres* IV. 28 So were the difficulties of making new provisals wonderfully great.

†**pro'vise,** *sb. Obs. rare.* [ad. L. *prōvīs-um*, neut. pa. pple. of *prōvidēre* to PROVIDE; cf. PROVISO.] That which is provided or arranged beforehand; a provision, arrangement; a stipulation, proviso.

1466 in *Archæologia* (1887) L. I. 50 Here is the Copye of the provyse for the lyuelote of the churche. **1523** FITZHERB. *Surv.* xi. 22 The grauntour maye make a prouycion in his graunt... And this prouyse had, the landes be charged and the person discharged. **1570** LEVINS *Manip.* 148/7 A Próuise, *prouisum, i.*

†**pro'vise,** *v. Obs. rare.* [f. L. *prōvīs-*, ppl. stem of *prōvidēre* to foresee, PROVIDE.]

1. *trans.* To foresee; = PROVIDE *v.* 1.

14.. in *Hist. Coll. Citizen London* (Camden) 178 Men provysyde be-fore þat the vyntage..shulde come owre Scheters Hylle. **1625** WALTER *Diary* (Camden) 84 A fleet of seven or nine Hollanders not far from, provising some disturbance in their ships, drew near.

2. To provide, furnish, or supply beforehand.

1484 CAXTON *Fables of Æsop* I. iv, The dogge provysed and broughte with hym fals wytnes.

provision (prəʊ'vɪʒən), *sb.* Also 4–6 with *y* for *i*, *c* for *s*, *ou* for *o* (5 *Sc.* **-wisioune**, 6 **-vysshion**, **-vytyon**, *Sc.* **-visiun**, 7 **-vission**). [a. F. *provision* (1320 in Hatz.-Darm.), ad. L. *prōvīsiōn-em* a foreseeing, forethought, precaution, providing, prevention, n. of action f. *prōvidēre* to PROVIDE.]

†**1.** Foresight, PREVISION; *esp.* (with trace of sense 2) foresight carefully exercised; looking ahead. *Obs.*

c **1430** LYDG. *Min. Poems* (Percy Soc.) 22 For all cometh of Jhesu—Conseul, confort, discrecion, and prudence, Provysion for sight and provydence. **1515** BARCLAY *Egloges* iv. (1570) C vj b/2, But goodly vertue a lady moste ornate Within gouerneth with great prouision. *c* **1530** H. RHODES *Bk. Nurture* 276 in *Babees Bk.* (1868) 89 Giue with good will, and auoyde thy ennemye with prouisyon.

2. a. The action of providing; seeing to things beforehand; preparing, or arranging in advance; the fact or condition of being prepared or made ready beforehand.

1456 *Coventry Leet Bk.* 292 Payd to Joh. Wedurby..for þe provicion and makyng of these premisses of the welcomyng of oure Souerayn lady the quene. **1549** *Compl. Scot* Prol. 13 [Phormion] persauand thir tua princis entir in his scule,..but prouisione, he began to teche the ordour of the veyris. **1602** *2nd Pt. Return fr. Parnass.* v. ii. (Arb.) 67 Letts both go spend our litle store, In the prouision of due furniture. **1610** SHAKS. *Temp.* I. ii. 28. **1655** MRQ. WORCESTER *Cent. Inv.* §6 According to occasion given and means afforded, *Ex re natâ*, and no need of Provision beforehand. **1879** HUXLEY *Hume* i. (1881) 15 Due provision for education..is a right and, indeed, a duty of the state.

b. *esp.* The providing or supplying of necessaries for a household, an expedition, etc.
1484 CAXTON *Fables of Alfonce* v, This thre felawes made so grete prouysyon of flour for to make theyr pylgremage. **1557** *Order of Hospitalls* D viij b, Such necessaries and prouisions as are to be made, as of Butter, Cheese, Hering, Wood, Cole, and other whatsoeuer. **1630** *R. Johnson's Kingd. & Commw.* 52, I would not have him live at his owne provision, (especially in France) it will hinder his profiting, and onely further him with some few kitchen and market phrases. **1818** COLEBROOKE *Import Colonial Corn* 23 It is the same surplus of population above the provision of necessaries, that is availing for the promotion..of the arts of peace.

c. Phr. ***to make*** (†***have, take***) ***provision***, to make previous arrangement or preparation *for*, or for the supply or benefit of; to provide *for*. †***to put provision to***, to provide against (*obs.*). †***to take provision of***, to have recourse to (*obs.*).
1432-50 tr. *Higden* (Rolls) III. 321 The man imprisonede askede respite that he myȝhte make ordinaunce and prouision for his wife and childer. *c* **1470** HENRY *Wallace* III. 272 Quhill eft for him prowisioune we may mak. **1480** *Coventry Leet Bk.* 435 Þe wardeyns shuld..pay for their costes vnto such tyme that provision myght be taken howe such charge & coste shuld be boron. *c* **1489** CAXTON *Blanchardyn* xxvii. 101 But yf thou putte a prouysyon therto shortly, thou shalt, are thre dayes be passed, see thy self beseged wythin the cyte. **1523** LD. BERNERS *Froiss.* I. 241 All this season the kynge of Englande made great provisyon to come into France. **1538** STARKEY *England* I. iv. 111 Some prouysyon for the second bretherne, by the ordur of law, also wold be had. **1622** *Buccleuch MSS.* (Hist. MSS. Comm.) I. 209 If there were not a present surrendry made, England must take provision of arms. **1766** FRANKLIN *Ess.* Wks. 1840 II. 358 The more public provisions were made for the poor, the less they provided for themselves. **1833** HT. MARTINEAU *Vanderput & S.* viii. 125 No provision made for his daughter's residence. **1879** *Cassell's Techn. Educ.* IV. 64/2 Provision should be made for the illustrations of the lectures by monster diagrams.

3. The action of God in providing for his creatures; the divine ordination and over-ruling of events; the providential dealing of the Divine Being; providence; the action of Providence.
c **1450** *Mankind* 188 in *Macro Plays* 8 To..yelde ws wndur Godis provycyon. **1483** *Caxton's Chron. Eng.* III. (1520) 27/1 In his dayes peas was over all the worlde thrugh the provysyon of the very god. **1538** STARKEY *England* I. iii. 90 When the prouysyon of God sendyth vs sesonabul weddur. **1552** ABP. HAMILTON *Catech.* (1884) 13 The conservatioun, provisioun, protectioun and governans quhilk God hes of all his creaturis. **1559** BP. SCOT in Strype *Ann. Ref.* (1709) I. App. x. 32 If we woulde consider all things well, we shall see the provision of God marvellous in it.

4. *Eccl.* Appointment to a see or benefice not yet vacant; *esp.* such appointment made by the pope in derogation of the right of the regular patron: cf. PROVIDE *v.* 6. Also, the document conferring such an appointment. *Obs.* exc. *Hist.*
[**1350-1** *Act 25 Edw. III*, Stat. IV. (Stat. of Provisors), Et en cas qe dascune Erceveschee, Eveschee, dignite ou autre quecunqe benefice, soit reservacion, collacion, ou provision faite per la courte de Rome, en desturbance des eleccions, collacions ou presentacions [etc.].]
c **1380** WYCLIF *Sel. Wks.* II. 416 Bigynne we at eleccioums or provysyouns of þe pope. **1387** TREVISA *Higden* (Rolls) VIII. 339 Þe kyng fordede provisiouns þat þe pope hadde i-graunted, and hoted þat no man schulde..brynge suche provisiouns upon peyne of prisonement. **1538** FITZHERB. *Just. Peas* 142 The statute of Kynge Rycharde the seconde ..of prouisyon and premunire. **1612** DAVIES *Why Ireland*, etc. (1787) 62 The Bishops of Rome..drew away all the wealth of the realm by their provisions and infinite exactions. **1769** BLACKSTONE *Comm.* IV. viii. 107 Papal provisions were the previous nomination to such benefices, by a kind of anticipation, before they became actually void; though afterwards indiscriminately applied to any right of patronage exerted or usurped by the pope. **1852** HOOK *Ch. Dict.* 617. **1899** *Reg. John de Grandisson* III. Pref. 5 He held this Office till his Provision to the Bishoprick of Exeter.

5. Something provided, prepared, or arranged in advance; measures taken beforehand; a preparation, a previous arrangement; a measure provided to meet a need; a precaution.
1494 FABYAN *Chron.* I. xcix. 73 Augmentynge his Kyngdome by knyghtly batayles, and other worldly prouycyons. **1538** STARKEY *England* I. i. 15 Excepte ther be joynyd some gud prouysyon for theyr [the seeds'] spryngyng vp and gud culture. **1561** T. NORTON *Calvin's Inst.* I. xvii. (1634) 91 Hee hath given us provisions and remedies. **1697** DRYDEN *Virg. Georg.* III. 497 By how much less the tender helpless Kind, For their own Ills, can fit Provision find. **1764** BURN *Poor Laws* 129 It will follow.. that a provision which was proper for the time, may not be now effectual. **1832** HT. MARTINEAU *Ella of Gar.* ii. 33 There was no step for a mast, nor provision for a rudder. **1907** *Q. Rev.* Apr. 538 Trinity College is not, however, a sufficient provision for the educational needs of Ireland.

6. a. A supply of necessaries or materials provided; a stock or store of something.
1451 CAPGRAVE *Life St. Gilbert* (E.E.T.S.) 68 Þat þei [monks and nuns] schuld not fayle of here dayly prouysion. *a* **1533** LD. BERNERS *Huon* lvii. 193 He..hath slayn my men & led away all my bestes & prouysyon. **1535** COVERDALE *Ps.* civ. 16 He called for a derth vpon the londe and destroyed all the prouysion of bred. **1578** BOURNE *Inventions* 3 He [ship's surgeon]..to have all such prouisions as is meete for his purpose in readinesse, to the end to dresse the hurt men. **1628** DIGBY *Voy. Medit.* (Camden) 59, I stayed here to gett some prouisions, as hoopes, tallow, tarre, pitch, wine, bread. **1690** LOCKE *Hum. Und.* III. xi. §27 The Provision of Words is so scanty in respect of that infinite Variety of Thoughts, that Men..will..be forc'd often to use the same Word, in somewhat different Senses. **1715** LEONI *Palladio's Archit.* (1742) I. 57 The Wood, and other numberless Country Provisions. **1796** MORSE *Amer. Geog.* I. 202 Here they deposit their provision of nuts and acorns.

†**b.** *transf.* A warrant for such a supply. *rare.*
a **1533** LD. BERNERS *Gold. Bk. M. Aurel.* (1546) Ff iv b, I sende the a prouision, to the entente that a shyp maie be gyuen the.

7. *spec.* A supply of food; food supplied or provided; now chiefly *pl.*, supplies of food, victuals, eatables, and drinkables; in *W. Indies* = *ground-provisions* s.v. GROUND *sb.* 18 a.
[See 1451, *a* 1533 in 6.]
1610 HOLLAND *Camden's Brit.* (1637) 394 The English for want of provisions were forced to breake up Siege. **1671** MILTON *P.R.* II. 402 With that Both Table and Provision vanish'd quite. **1758** JOHNSON *Idler* No. 35 ¶8 She condemns me to live upon salt provision. **1773** *Observ. State Poor* 65 A period, wherein the price of provisions is exorbitant. **1808** J. STEWART *Acct. Jamaica* 100 Ground provisions (as they are called), or roots... These roots, or ground provisions, are so productive (particularly the yam), [etc.]. **1827** [see *ground-provisions* s.v. GROUND *sb.* 18 a]. **1839** *Penny Cycl.* XIII. 75/1 A variety of wholesome and nutritious roots cultivated in [Jamaica] are called by the name of *ground provisions*; such as the yam [etc.]. **1860** NARES *Naval Cadets' Guide* 68 *Wet provisions.* Beef, pork, suet, vinegar, rum and lime juice... *Dry provisions*, Peas, oat-meal, chocolate, tea, flour, raisins, sugar. **1866** *Morn. Star* 8 Mar., Mr. Poland said..he should contend that tea was not 'provisions' within the meaning of the Act. Mr. Baylis said he should contend that it was. If a provision merchant were victualling a ship, and did not put tea amongst his provisions, he would not be considered to have provisioned her. **1955** *Caribbean Q.* IV. I. 51 A large number of the contractors used these payments to acquire small plots of land in which they planted cocoa, provisions, and later, nutmeg trees. **1965** 'LAUCHMONEN' *Old Thom's Harvest* i. 11 Bet we can grow some whopping good crop of provision on that piece of land, Pa.

8. Each of the clauses or divisions of a legal or formal statement, or such a statement itself, providing for some particular matter; also, a clause in such a statement which makes an express stipulation or condition; a proviso.
Applied in English History to certain early statutes or ordinances. *Provisions of Oxford*, ordinances for checking the king's misrule, and for the reformation of the government, drawn up at a meeting of the barons (nicknamed the Mad Parliament) held at Oxford, under the leadership of Sir Simon de Montfort, in 1258 (38 Henry III). Among the chief of these provisions were that parliaments should be held thrice in the year, and that four knights should be chosen by the freeholders of each county to ascertain and lay before parliament all wrongs committed by the royal officers. The refusal of the King to abide by these Provisions led to the Barons' War in 1264.
1473 *Rolls of Parlt.* VI. 74/2 So alwey, that this Provision be not available or beneficiall to the persones afore-named. **1523** [see PROVISE *sb.*]. [**1701** *Cowell's Interpr.* s.v., The Acts to restrain the exorbitant abuse of Arbitrary Power made in the Parliament at Oxford 1258, were called *Provisiones*, being to provide against the King's Absolute Will and Pleasure.] **1781** T. GILBERT *Relief Poor* 14, I think some Provisions may be introduced into this Bill..for encouraging the Marriage of Persons who have been placed out by the Parishes as Servants or Apprentices. **1818** COBBETT *Pol. Reg.* XXXIII. 106 The principles and the provisions of the Bill would have shown..precisely what we wanted. **1827** HALLAM *Const. Hist.* (1876) II. xi. 330 These provisions struck at the heart of the presbyterian party. **1878** STUBBS *Lect. Med. & Mod. Hist.* viii. (1900) 204 The half-brothers of..Henry III..had been banished in consequence of their opposition to the Provisions of Oxford.

†**9.** A commission or percentage charged on mercantile transactions by an agent or factor. *rare.*
(So F. *provision*, Ger. *provision*, in same sense.)
1589 WOTTON *Lett.* (see ed. 1907 I. 228), I have..two billes of exchaunge to his factor in Stode, there to receave the like summ in the currant money of that Cuntrie, without any manner of provision as the merchantes call it, a pacefied word for it. **1682** SCARLETT *Exchanges* 135 For Courtagie of Exchanges, whether in drawing or remitting, usually one *per mille* is allowed for Provisions for drawing and remitting, each half *per cent. Ibid.* 170 Provision is the Reward the Factor receives from his Principal..for his trouble.

10. *attrib.* and *Comb.*, mainly in sense 7, as ***provision-bag, -basket, -boat, book, contractor, -craft, -dealer, -depot, farm, farmer, house, importer, man, -merchant, -money, pit, -sack, shop, store, -trade, train, wagon***; **provision-ant**, the provident ant; **provision-ground**, in the W. Indies, etc., ground allotted for the growing of food-stuffs; **provision-making**, the making of provision; **provision pay**, pay in kind.
1838 J. HODGSON in J. Raine *Mem.* (1858) II. 379 They were careful like the *provision-ant. **1856** KANE *Arct. Expl.* II. xvi. 168 Our *provision-bags were of assorted sizes. **1876** 'MARK TWAIN' *Tom Sawyer* xxviii. 268 The gay throng filed up the main street laden with *provision baskets. **1748** *Anson's Voy.* III. ix. 394 One of the principal thieves was.. in a *provision-boat along-side. **1922** *Beaver* Apr. 9/2 A record of the provisions stocked, with their weight or quantities, was entered as they were received in the '*Provision Book', in which was also entered the allowances as they were given out. **1800** *Hull Advertiser* 27 May 3/2 A *provision contractor of the first eminence. **1849** GROTE *Greece* II. xxxviii. V. 45 Crews of the *provision-craft and ships of burthen. **1834** *Picture of Liverpool* 73 Mr. Edward Thomas, *provision dealer. **1877** *Harper's Mag.* Jan. 284/2 They sold some grapes and apples and pears to the provision dealer in exchange for beef and chicken. **1958** J. CAREW *Black Midas* i. 9 At the back of the village were rice-fields, small *provision farms..and wild-cane reeds. **1953** E. MITTELHOLZER in *Caribbean Anthol. Short Stories* 41 Hoolcharran had begun as a *provision farmer, and lived in a mudhouse. **1766** *Chron.* in *Ann. Reg.* 155/2 Great damage was done to the *provision-grounds. **1871** KINGSLEY *At Last* xvi, The 'provision grounds' of the Negros are very interesting. **1798** W. TOMISON *Jrnl.* 2 Feb. in A. M. Johnson *Saskatchewan Jrnls. & Corr.* (1967) 108 The rest employed bringing ice for the *provision house. **1804** J. ORDWAY in *Jrnls. Lewis & Ordway* (1916) vi. 166 We continued building, raised a provision & Smoak house 24 feet by 14 f. **1903** *N.Y. Times* 15 Oct. 1 Deacon Cotten..was dickering with representatives of meat and provision houses for supplies. **1885** *List of Subscribers, Classified* (United Telephone Co.) (ed. 6) 174 *Provision importers. **1564** BECON *Wks.* Gen. Pref. A v, With hospitalitie, or *prouision making for the poore. **1872** *Boston* (Mass.) *Ordin.* (1873) 193 The vehicles of market or *provision men. **1858** SIMMONDS *Dict. Trade*, **Provision-merchant*, a general dealer in articles of food. **1683** *Rec. East Hampton, N.Y.* (1887) II. 131 For his Wages hee is to be payd the some of thirty five pound in *probision pay. **1692** S. SEWALL *Lett.-Bk.* (1886) I. 7 Some of the Provision-Pay was Wheat, which I sold, for Indian Corn. **1887** *Courier-Jrnl.* (Louisville, Kentucky) 3 Feb. 7/4 Within a very few minutes after the opening the crowd in the *provision pit increased. **1854** M. S. CUMMINS *Lamplighter* XV. 115 Willie accompanied them as far as the *provision-shop. **1796** *Boston* (Mass.) *Directory* s.v. *Fletcher*, *Provision store. **1830** *Reg. Deb. Congress U.S.* 11 May 429/2 The *provision trade of the West. **1895** CROCKETT *Bog-Myrtle & Peat* IV. ii, The latest canons of..retail provision-trade taste. **1896** *Harper's Mag.* Apr. 764/1 Blücher..found that he had captured..all the enemy's hospital outfit, his field-smithies, and his *provision-train. **1765** R. ROGERS *Jrnls.* p. viii, I tarried till August 26th, and was then ordered with 100 men to escort the *provision-waggons. **1925** G. STUART *40 Yrs. on Frontier* I. 97 Three days were consumed in getting together the equipment of men and horses with provision wagons and everything necessary.

provision (prəʊˈvɪʒən), *v.* [f. prec. Cf. F. *provisionner* (1556 in Godef.).] **a.** *trans.* To supply with provisions or stores; *esp.* to supply with a stock of food. Also *refl.* **b.** *intr.* (for *refl.*) To supply oneself with provisions; to lay in provisions. Also with *up*.
[**1805**: see PROVISIONED *ppl. a.*]. **1809** A. HENRY *Trav.* 47 Maize..is depended upon, for provisioning the canoes. **1818** TODD, *Provision*, to supply with provision. **1836** *Tait's Mag.* III. 428 Tempted to laugh at the style in which the Wyatts have provisioned. **1851** DIXON *W. Penn* xxiii. (1872) 203 Every man had to be provisioned for the longer term. **1859** LANG *Wand. India* 101 He raised a regiment of horse and provisioned it. **1903** R. BEDFORD *True Eyes* viii. 48 Why didn't you provision from home? **1928** *Daily Express* 11 Aug. 4/6 The main thing to remember in going to the islands is to provision-up for your stay well ahead. **1941** *Pitman's Business Educ.* Oct. 152 Without access to overseas supplies of oil, Germany has attempted to provision herself by the seizure of Rumania and by the invasion of Russia. **1973** *Animal Behaviour* XXI. 306/2 We suspect that the females were provisioning separate cells.
Hence **proˈvisioning** *vbl. sb.*
1868 HELPS *Realmah* xii. (1876) 335 The provisioning of the town for a protracted siege. **1869** FREEMAN *Norm. Conq.* III. xiv. 339 An excellent point for the gathering and provisioning of armies.

provisional (prəʊˈvɪʒənəl), *a.* (*sb.*) [f. PROVISION *sb.* + -AL[1]. So obs. F. *provisionnal* (*c* 1485 in Hatz.-Darm.), mod.F. *provisionnel.*]
A. *adj.* **1. a.** Of, belonging to, or of the nature of a temporary provision or arrangement; provided or adopted for present needs or for the time being; supplying the place of something regular, permanent, or final; also, accepted or used in default of something better. ***provisional callus***: see quot. 1856. ***Provisional Government***: now *spec.* a government set up to rule until constitutional self-government can be established; ***Provisional I.R.A.***: the unofficial wing of the Irish Republican Army instituted in 1970; ***provisional (driving-)licence***: a licence issued to a learner-driver; ***provisional order***: (see quot. 1963).
1601 J. WHEELER *Treat. Comm.* 41 Hee and they were glad and fayne to come to a prouisionall agreement. **1617** MORYSON *Itin.* II. 68 Sir Arthur Sauage..was appointed prouisionall Gouernour of the Prouince of Connaght. **1726** AYLIFFE *Parergon* 192 The Church should not be without a provisional Pastor. **1803** M. CUTLER in *Life*, etc. (1888) II. 148 Look at the power given to the President by the provisional government of Louisiana. **1848** *Act 11 & 12 Vict.* c. 63 s. x, They shall make a Provisional Order under their Hands and Seal of Office. **1856** DRUITT *Surg. Vade Mecum* 217 The formation of what is called a provisional callus, that is to say, a ferrule of new bone encircling both fragments. **1870** *Act 33 & 34 Vict.* c. 1 §2 Any Select Committee of the House of Commons to which any Bill for confirming Provisional Orders has been referred in relation to any Provisional Order therein contained may examine witnesses upon oath. **1873** HAMERTON *Intell. Life* XI. i. (1875) 399 The intellectual spirit does not regard its conclusions as being at any time final, but always provisional. **1893** TUCKEY tr. *Hatschek's Amphioxus* 158 This primary caudal fin..is only a provisional formation. **1916** WELLS & MARLOWE *Hist. Irish Rebellion of 1916* ix. 47 At the Post Office was established the Headquarters of the 'Provisional Government of the Irish Republic'. **1931** *R.A.C. Guide 1931-32* 34 To enable an applicant suffering from a disability to learn to drive a motor vehicle of any special construction..the Licensing Authority may..grant him a provisional licence for a period of three months. **1963** J. F. GARNER *Administrative Law* iii. 42 Provisional orders are made by a Minister of the Crown under the authority of a statute, and they are therefore sometimes described as a form of delegated or subordinate legislation, but they have no legal force until they have been included (usually by way

of reference in a schedule) in a Provisional Orders Confirmation Act. **1965** J. CH'ÊN *Mao & Chinese Revolution* (1967) I. viii. 172 Under the Constitution, the Provisional Soviet Government was elected with Mao as its chairman. **1970** TIERNEY & MACCURTAIN *Birth Mod. Ireland* 131 Pearse then stepped out on to the portico and read the Proclamation of the Provisional Government of the Irish Republic. **1970** *Times* 9 Apr. 12/2 The recent formation of a 'provisional' I.R.A. Council. **1971** S. A. DE SMITH *Constitutional & Administrative Law* xv. 342 Provisional orders, which do not have legal effect till confirmed by Act of Parliament and are therefore not a form of delegated legislation at all. **1973** *Times* 11 Oct. 2/5 Mr McMorrow had been active in the Provisional IRA in Londonderry. **1974** *Guardian* 22 Mar. 8/7 The Environment Department has turned down a plea for stricter eyesight tests for people applying for their first provisional driving licence. **1976** *Burnham-on-Sea Gaz.* 20 Apr. 24/4 Mrs —— told the court that she only held a provisional licence and this had now expired. **1978** *Times* 6 Mar. 2/6 Under the Provisional IRA's new structure, each active service unit is largely self-contained, and in contact only with the central command.

†**b.** Preparatory, preliminary. *Obs.*

1619 HALES *Gold. Rem.* II. (1673) 83 That Sessions consultatory and Provisional shall be private, but Sessions wherein they discuss and conclude shall be publick.

†**2.** Characterized by or exhibiting careful foresight; provident. *Obs. rare.*

1620 E. BLOUNT *Horæ Subs.* 523 Either from a pressing necessity, or a foreseeing and prouisionall carefulnes. *a* **1677** HALE *Prim. Orig. Man.* 370 The Wise God that foresaw this Sin..was not wanting in providing a fit provisional Remedy against it. **1763** GOLDSM. *Misc. Wks.* (1837) II. 505 This provisional care in every species of quadrupeds, of bringing forth at the fittest seasons.

†**3.** Of, belonging to, or done with a proviso; conditional. *Obs.*

1656 BLOUNT *Glossogr.*, *Provisional*,..done by way of *Proviso*. **1706** PHILLIPS, *Provisional*..belonging to a Proviso. **1808** BENTHAM *Sc. Reform* 3 There is enough in it to afford an ample justification to the provisional acceptance your Lordship has been pleased to give to it.

4. Of or relating to provisions or supplies. *rare.*

1812 W. TAYLOR in *Monthly Mag.* XXXIII. 228 Both words [plenty and abundance]..are metaphorically applied to the provisional state of the country, to its eatable stock. **1823** *Blackw. Mag.* XIV. 509 From Covent garden..we must take a peep at the other points of provisional concentration about town.

B. *sb.* **1.** Something that is provisional.

1895 *Westm. Gaz.* 23 Aug. 3/1 'Provisional' labels had to be issued while the real stamps were being engraved. The collector treasures a 'provisional' above most things.

†**2.** One for whom provision is made; one provided for. *Obs.*

1716 M. DAVIES *Athen. Brit.* II. 316 A Popish Pervert and a Protestant Convert are indeed two different Provisionals.

3. a. One whose tenure of office is of a temporary nature; a provisional governor.

1848 A. H. CLOUGH *Let.* 26 Feb. in J. Bertram *N.Z. Lett. of T. Arnold* (1966) 78 Will the army and Nationals rally around this government, or allow the people to set up their Provisionals. Inasmuch as the Provisionals are all in the Ministry, I suppose they may please themselves.

b. A member of the Provisional I.R.A.

1971 *Guardian* 11 Aug. 1/5 Some senior members of the IRA Provisionals, known to have been in Belfast recently, have..arrived. **1974** *Listener* 14 Mar. 323/1 The Provisionals' traditional method of discipline: putting a gun barrel behind a man's knee and blowing off his knee cap.

Hence **provisio'nality**, provisionalness.

1821 *Examiner* 821/2 Open your eyes..and you will see that provisionality itself is infused into all the branches of your system. **1891** *Harper's Mag.* Oct. 765/1 There was a terrible provisionality about the whole business.

pro'visionally, *adv.* [f. prec. + -LY².] In a provisional manner; as a temporary measure.

1602 in Moryson *Itin.* II. (1617) 247 We are content prouisionally to warrant your proceedings in any thing you doe or publish in Our name. **1692** *Lond. Gaz.* No. 2729/3 The Place..is given provisionally to the Count de Clermont, till the arrival of the Elector of Bavaria. **1793** BURKE *Corr.* (1844) IV. 149 His personal virtues..make him the fittest to authorize this arrangement provisionally. **1878** NEWCOMB *Pop. Astron.* III. ii. 266 This hydrogen is always mixed with another substance, provisionally called helium.

pro'visionalness. [f. as prec. + -NESS.] The quality of being provisional.

1874 MORLEY *Compromise* 168 It is no reason why [they] should think solely of the utility and forget the equally important element of its provisionalness. **1891** CHEYNE *Bampton Lect.* p. xxviii, Our arguments must for the most part bear the stamp of provisionalness.

provisionary (prəʊ'vɪʒənərɪ), *a.* Now *rare.* [f. PROVISION *sb.* + -ARY¹.]

1. = PROVISIONAL *a.* 1.

1617 MORYSON *Itin.* II. 88 His Lordship..appointed Sir Iohn Barkeley to supplie his place of Prouisionarie Gouernour of the Prouince of Connaght. **1776** GIBBON *Decl. & F.* xv. I. 456 A provisionary scheme intended to last only till the coming of the Messiah. **1794** HERON *Inform. Powers at War* 30 A provisionary government was appointed. **1876** MOZLEY *Univ. Serm.* iii. 58 In practical life probable evidence only raises a provisionary belief.

†**2.** That forsees and provides for the future; provident; = PROVISIONAL *a.* 2. *Obs.*

1647 N. BACON *Disc. Govt. Eng.* I. lii. (1739) 93 To cast the government of the persons of their Wards out of the view of the Lords provisionary care. **1699** SHAFTESB. *Charac.* (1711) II. II. i. iii. 89 [Nature's] provisionary Care and Concern for the whole Animal. **1784** SIR J. REYNOLDS *Disc.* xii. (1876) 47 The provisionary methods Demosthenes and Cicero employed to assist their invention.

3. Of or pertaining to papal provisions: see PROVISION *sb.* 4.

1736 DRAKE *Eboracum* II. i. 436 The Archbishop of York ..was by the pope's provisionary bulls translated to Canterbury. **1856** MRS. H. O. CONANT *Eng. Transl. Bible* iii. (1881) 19 *note*, The sale of these provisionary grants was a source of large income to the Papal courts.

†**4.** Of or pertaining to provisions or food-supply; = PROVISIONAL *a.* 4. *Obs. rare*⁻¹.

1613–18 DANIEL *Coll. Hist. Eng.* (1626) 41 For his prouisionary reuenues..the Kings Tenants..payd no money at all; but onely Victualls, Wheate, Beifes, Muttons [etc.].

5. Of, pertaining to, or of the nature of a proviso, a provision, or provisions (in a law, etc.).

1774 BURKE *Amer. Tax.* 8 The preamble of this law..has the lie direct given to it by the provisionary part of the act.

pro'visioned (-ənd), *ppl. a.* [f. PROVISION *sb.* or *v.* + -ED.] Supplied with provisions; *esp.* furnished with a stock of food.

1805 PIKE *Sources Mississ.* (1810) 40 We were now provisioned, but were still in want of water. **1855** MACAULAY *Hist. Eng.* xx. IV. 414 The ships of war were not half manned or half provisioned. **1896** *Westm. Gaz.* 13 Nov. 2/1 We clattered down to the second 'Hospice'—a sort of provisioned hut—and took what luncheon we could get.

pro'visioner. [f. PROVISION *v.* + -ER¹.] One who provisions; one who supplies or deals in provisions. Hence **pro'visioneress**, a female provisioner.

1866 HOWELLS *Venet. Life* vii. 102 Provisioners..who bring fresh milk in bottles. **1894** —— in *Cosmopolitan* XVII. 58 The display was on either side of the provisioner's door. **1886** BURTON *Arab. Nts.* (abr. ed.) I. 79 Then arose the provisioneress and..set the table by the fountain.

pro'visionless, *a.* [f. PROVISION *sb.* + -LESS.] Having no provision; without provisions.

1796 COLERIDGE *Destiny of Nations* 236 The air clipt keen, the night was fanged with frost, And they provisionless! **1894** *Columbus* (Ohio) *Dispatch* 9 June, There is the suffering of those whose interests are directly affected by the strike, the penniless purses and the provisionless pantries.

pro'visionment. [f. PROVISION *v.* + -MENT.] The supplying or supply of provisions.

1827 SOUTHEY *Hist. Penins. War* II. xxiii. 363 His last remaining anxiety was for the provisionment of Barcelona. **1834** *New Monthly Mag.* XLII. 42 Profiting by the facilities afforded..towards the provisionment of his capital.

†**pro'visive**, *a. Obs. rare.* [f. L. *prōvīs-*, ppl. stem of *prōvid-ēre* to PROVIDE + -IVE.]

a. Conditional, contingent; = PROVISIONAL *a.* 3. **b.** Prudent, foreseeing; = PROVIDENT *a.* 1.

1650 HOBBES *De Corp. Pol.* 186 Declarations..concerning Future Actions..Promissive..or Provisive, as for example, 'If this be done or not done this will follow'. **1677** GALE *Crt. Gentiles* II. IV. 443 God therefore is the Maker and Provisor, and his good wil is the effective, contentive and provisive Virtue.

proviso (prəʊ'vaɪzəʊ). Pl. **-oes** (6–7 **-os**). [a. L. *prōvīsō*, abl. neut. sing. pa. pple. of *prōvid-ēre* to PROVIDE, as used in med.L. legal phrase *prōvīsō quod* 'it being provided that' (1350 in Du Cange).]

‖**1.** The L. ablative absolute = 'it being provided', used conjunctively. *Obs. rare.*

1596 BACON *Max. & Use Com. Law* (1635) 47 Not extendable for the debts of the party after his death: *proviso*, not to put away the land from his next heire. **1686** GOAD *Celest. Bodies* II. xiv. 350 If this be an excursion, let it be pardoned, *Proviso*, that we remember that the Planets have the great hand in this remarkable Tempest.

2. A clause inserted in a legal or formal document, making some condition, stipulation, exception, or limitation, or upon the observance of which the operation or validity of the instrument depends; a condition; hence, generally, a stipulation, provision.

1467 *Mann. & Househ. Exp.* (Roxb.) 421 Item, [the price] for do makenge of provyso is xx.*d.* **1473** *Rolls of Parlt.* VI. 84/2 Grauntes made by us..excepte and forprised oute of this proviso. **1485** *Act 1 Hen. VII*, c. 9 Notwithstondyng eny acte ordenance graunt or proviso in this present parliament made. **1489** in *Trevelyan Papers* (Camden) 93 With the same condicions and provisoes. *Ibid.* 94. **1509–10** *Act 1 Hen. VIII*, c. 15 The seid acte of restitucion wyth the Provysowes conteyned in the same. **1610** *Histrio-m.* VI. 236 Sirs, those provisos will not serve the turn. **1672** PETTY *Pol. Anat.* (1691) Advt., The papists *per proviso* were such as had provisoes in that act [the Act of Settlement]. **1765** *Museum Rust.* IV. 260 Lucerne will grow very well in clay land, with proviso the ground works well. **1864** BOWEN *Logic* ix. 298 The Major Premise of the sophism is not true except with a proviso or limitation. **1878** F. HARRISON in *Fortn. Rev.* Nov. 692 There are some other provisoes with which I think it is necessary to guard Austin's analyses of primary legal notions.

†**b.** ***trial by proviso***: a trial at the instance of the defendant in a case in which the plaintiff, after issue joined, did not proceed to trial. *Obs.*

[**1607** COWELL *Interpr.*, *Proviso*,..if the plaintife or demandaunt desist in prosecuting an action, by bringing it to a triall, the defendant or tenent may take out the *venire facias* to the Shyreeue: which hath in it these words, *Prouiso quod*, &c. to this ende, that if the plaintife take out any writ to that purpose, the shyreeue shall summon but one Iurie vpon them both.] **1768** BLACKSTONE *Comm.* III. xxiii. 357 The defendant..willing to discharge himself from the action, will himself undertake to bring on the trial... Which proceeding is called the trial by *proviso*; by reason of the clause then inserted in the sheriff's *venire*, viz. '*proviso*, that if two writs come to your hands..you shall execute only one of them'.

3. *Naut.* See quot. 1867.

1627 CAPT. SMITH *Seaman's Gram.* ix. 45 To more a Prouiso, is to haue one anchor in the riuer, and a hawser a shore, which is mored with her head a shore. **1710** in J. HARRIS *Lex. Techn.* II. **1867** SMYTH *Sailor's Word-bk.*, *Proviso*, a stern-fast or hawser carried to the shore to steady by. A ship with one anchor down and a shore-fast is moored *a proviso*.

provisor (prəʊ'vaɪzə(r), -ɔ(r)). [ME. *provisour*, a. AF. *provisour* (quot. 1339 in 1) = F. *proviseur* (14th c. in Hatz.-Darm.), ad. L. *prōvīsōr-em* a provider, agent-n. f. *prōvid-ēre* to PROVIDE.]

I. 1. The holder of a provision or grant (esp. from the pope) giving him the right to be presented to a benefice on the occurrence of the next vacancy. (See PROVISION *sb.* 4.) *Obs.* exc. *Hist.*

Statute of Provisors, the act 25 Edw. III, 1350–1, enacted to prevent the granting of these provisions by the pope; subsequent laws to the same effect were also so called.

[**1339** *Year Bk. Mich. 13 Edw. III*, pl. 3 (Rolls) 5 Et il, nient aresteant la prohibicion, a la request dun provisour,.. fist clore le huys del Eglise..en contempt du Roy, et encontre la prohibicion. **1350–1** *Act 25 Edw. III*, Stat. IV, Et en cas qe les presentes le Roi, ou les presentes dautres patrons..soient desturbez per tieles provisours..adonqes soient les ditz provisours attaches per lour corps.]

1362 LANGL. *P. Pl.* A. III. 142 Heo is priue with þe Pope, Prouisours hit knowen. **1455** *Rolls of Parlt.* V. 303/1 The penaltee of the Statutes of provisours. *a* **1648** LD. HERBERT *Hen. VIII* (1683) 349 The King..granted them a Pardon for all offences against the Statutes of Provisors. **1769** BLACKSTONE *Comm.* IV. viii. 111 Sharp and penal laws were enacted against provisors. **1856** FROUDE *Hist. Eng.* (1858) I. ii. 104 Morton had gone beyond the limits of the statute of provisors in receiving powers from Pope Innocent. **1886** L. O. PIKE *Year Bks. 13 & 14 Edw. III*, Introd. 61 The Provisor became practically the King's presentee at a time when the Abbey was not vacant.

II. One who provides, purveys, or takes charge.

[In many specific uses in med.L.: cf. Du Cange: *Provisores Ecclesiarum* nuncupati Laici, qui earum bona & possessiones administrabant... *Provisores Exteriorum*, apud Præmonstratenses..'ad quos pertinet exteriora providere'. ..*Provisor Monasterii*, cui thesaurus Monasterii commissus erat.]

†**2.** One who is in charge; a manager, a supervisor; an agent, a deputy. *Obs.*

1390 GOWER *Conf.* II. 224 There be nou many suche, I gesse, That lich unto the provisours Thei make here prive procurours, To telle hou ther is such a man, Which is worthi to love. *c* **1450** tr. *De Imitatione* II. i. 40 Whan þou hast crist ..he shal be þi prouisour, þy true procutour in all þinges. **1474** CAXTON *Chesse* IV. ii. Kiv, That kynge is not wel fortunat that lesith hym to whom his auctorite delegate aperteyneth who..was prouysour of al the royame. *a* **1533** LD. BERNERS *Gold. Bk. M. Aurel.* (1535) 154b, And reson whiche is prouisour declareth.

†**3.** One who provides or cares for another; a provider; a guardian, protector. *Obs.*

1503 HAWES *Examp. Virt.* VII. xliv, A kynge to be..Vnto his subiectes..a good prouysour. **1610** HEALEY *St. Aug. Citie of God* XIX. xiv. (1620) 724 The prouisors are the commanders, as the husband ouer his wife; parents ouer their children and masters ouer their seruants: and they that are prouided for obey. **1653** H. COGAN tr. *Pinto's Trav.* lxxvii. 312 The poor Licentiat Gaspar Jorge, who termed himself Auditor Generall of the Indiaes, great Provisor of the deceased and Orphelins, and Superintendent of the Treasure of Malaca. **1677** [see PROVISIVE]. **1730** T. BOSTON *View Covt. Grace* (1771) 162 Their Shepherd, Provisor, Protector, King, Husband, Head.

†**4.** One who has charge of getting provisions; a purveyor; the steward or treasurer of a house, a monastery, etc. *Obs.* exc. *Hist.*

1498 *Acc. Ld. High Treas. Scot.* I. 390 Item,..giffin to the Gray Freris prouisour in Striuelin, to the bigging, lxvj lib. xiij s. iiij d. **1574** *Reg. Privy Council Scot.* II. 364 The saidis ministeris, redaris, and provisor of oure Soverane Lordis hous. **1578–9** *Ibid.* III. 93 The said Alexander being provisour of the saidis houssis..payment sould have bene maid to him. **1584** *Ibid.* 655 Cuikis, and utheris provisouris of victuellis. **1631** HEYLIN *St. George* 106 The Caterer forsooth, or Provisor generall of Hogs-flesh for the armie. **1683** CAVE *Ecclesiastici*, *Athanasius* 142 Provisor General of Pork for the Army. **1848** MOZLEY *Ess.* (1878) I. *Luther* 360 John Kestner of Wittenberg, provisor of the Cordeliers.

†**5.** = PROVEDITOR 1. *Obs. rare.*

1579 FENTON *Guicciard.* II. (1599) 84 The army..but little disposed (specially the prouisors of the Venetians) to put them selues any more in the arbitrement of fortune. **1596** DANETT tr. *Comines* (1614) 280 As touching these prouisors whom they send in person with their armies vppon the land.

6. *R.C. Ch.* An ecclesiastic assisting an archbishop or bishop, and acting in his stead; a vicar-general; a deputy-inquisitor.

[Cf. Du Cange: *Provisor Episcopi*, Qui ejus vices gerit, nostris *Grand-Vicaire*.]

c **1560** FRAMPTON *Narration* in Strype *Ann. Ref.* (1709) I. xx. 231, I was sent for, and brought before the Bishop, the two Inquisitors, and the Provizor. **1600** HAKLUYT *Voy.* III. 453 The Bishop of Mexico, and his Prouisor. **1617** MORYSON *Itin.* I. 252 The Lord Nicholas Donati Generall Prouisor and Inquisitor in the Kingdome of Candia. **1625** *Gonsalvio's Sp. Inquis.* 44 Where all the Inquisitors..sit in their seates of Maiestie, and besides them the Prouisor, as they tearme him, or deputy Ordinary of the Diocesse. **1823**

SOUTHEY *Hist. Penins. War* I. 623 D. Francisco Castanedo, Canon of the holy Church of Jaen, Provisor and Vicar-general of that diocese. **1841** J. L. STEPHENS *Centr. Amer.* (1854) 10 A Roman Catholic priest..on his way to Guatimala by invitation of the Provisor, by the exile of the Archbishop the head of the church.

provisorily (prəʊˈvaɪzərɪlɪ), *adv.* [f. PROVISORY + -LY².] In a provisory way; provisionally.

1801 *St. Papers* in *Ann. Reg.* 278/1 The elections must provisorily be suspended. **1836–7** SIR W. HAMILTON *Metaph.* xxxix. (1870) II. 396 It can only..be admitted provisorily. **1892** *Monist* II. 199, I thus formed provisorily the view that Nature has two sides—a physical and a psychological side.

‖**provisorium** (prəʊvɪˈzɔərɪəm). [Ger.] A provisional or interim measure or condition.

1957 *Listener* 28 Nov. 867/1 Since it has not been possible to reach such understandings subsequently..the provisorium flowing from these circumstances has endured. **1963** *Economist* 3 Aug. 428/1 Bonn was not a 'provisorium' but a 'transitorium'.

provisorship (prəʊˈvaɪzəʃɪp). *rare.* [See -SHIP.] The office or position of a provisor.

1623 WEBSTER *Duchess of Malfi* I. i, What's my place? The provisorship o' the horse? **1651** N. BACON *Disc. Govt. Eng.* II. xxvii. (1739) 122 The King hath no power thereby to confer Church-livings by Provisorship.

provisory (prəʊˈvaɪzərɪ), *a.* [ad. F. *provisoire* or ad. med.L. **prōvīsōri-us*: see PROVISOR, -ORY².]

1. Subject to a provision or proviso; conditional.

1611 COTGR., *Provisoire*, prouisorie, conditionall, implying a limitation, including a prouiso. *a* **1665** J. GOODWIN *Filled w. the Spirit* (1867) 442 'Abide in me, and I in you'; if we take it provisory, Abide in me, and know that I shall then abide in you; or let me abide in you, or that I may abide in you. **1857** MAYNE REID *War-Trail* lxv, 'If yet in time'—ay, such provisory parenthesis was in my mind.

†**2.** Granting an ecclesiastical provision. *Obs.*

1631 WEEVER *Anc. Fun. Mon.* 744 He was likewise by the Popes prouisorie Bulles, translated to Canterbury.

3. = PROVISIONAL *a.* 1.

1788 JEFFERSON *Writ.* (1859) II. 540 There remains an expression in the *Arret*, that it is provisory only. **1830** R. KNOX *Béclard's Anat.* 275 Bichat, M. Dupuytren,..and others, have admitted that these external and internal ossifications are provisory. **1895** *Daily News* 20 June 5/7 It has been resolved..that the nomination of a Provisory Government will be the best way out of the difficulty.

4. That makes provision for eventualities.

1843 *Blackw. Mag.* LIII. 222 To communicate secrets, delivered to her in strictest confidence, and imparted by her again with equal caution and provisory care, was the choicest occupation of her..life.

provitamin (ˈprəʊvɪtəmɪn). *Biol.* Also pro-vitamin. [a. G. *provitamin* (Windhaus & Hess 1926, in *Nachr. von der K. Ges. d. Wissensch. zu Göttingen* (1927) 175): see PRO-² and VITAMIN.] A substance which is converted into a vitamin within an organism. (Freq. with following capital letter indicating relationship to a specific vitamin.)

1927 ROSENHEIM & WEBSTER in *Lancet* 5 Feb. 306/2 These observations suggest that the provitamin (we propose to use this convenient term, suggested by Prof. Windhaus, for the parent substance of vitamin D) is destroyed by bromine. **1943** *Endeavour* Apr. 73/2 It became evident that, though the diets of the tropical natives were often deficient in the calcifying vitamin,..they really had ample supplies because of the action of sunlight on the provitamin. **1952** *New Biol.* XIII. 40 Doubling the number of chromosomes in pure yellow corn caused a 40% increase in the carotenoid pigment content, including the active provitamin A fraction of the carotenoids. **1971** *Nature* 22 Jan. 255/2 Vitamin D.. is produced in the skin when ultraviolet radiation is absorbed by the pro-vitamin 7-dehydrocholesterol. **1976** H. CAMPION et al. in B. E. C. Nordin *Calcium, Phosphate & Mineral Metabolism* xii. 445 The two principal pro-vitamins D, ergosterol..and..7-dehydrocholesterol..are formed in vivo by two very similar routes.

provo¹, **provoe** (prəʊˈvəʊ). Also with capital initial.

1. A spelling of PROVOST, representing a pronunciation after F. *prévôt* (prevo, *formerly* prəˈvoː): cf. PROVOST *sb.* 7. Also *transf.*, a provost-cell.

c **1675** VILLIERS (Dk. Buckhm.) *Satire Follies Age* Wks. (1752) 112 But if I laugh when the court-coxcombs show, To see the booby Sotus dance provoe;..To me the name of railer strait you give. **1692** *Siege Lymerick* 6 The Prisoners were immediately put into the Provo's Custody. **1705** *Lond. Gaz.* No. 4183/4 Duncan Robinson..was..sent to the Provo's. **1746** M. HUGHES *Jrnl. Late Rebell.* 7 The Duke.. ordered that seven Rebels should go down into the Well, take their dead Bodies out and bury them; which the Captain of the Provo saw done. **1779** *New-Jersey Jrnl.* (Chatham, N.J.) 13 Apr. 3/1 The other two are safely lodged in the provo of the continental troops. **1832** W. DUNLAP *Hist. Amer. Theatre* iv. 43 The Jail, then called the provo, where American prisoners suffered for asserting the rights of their country, scowled on the east. **1865** W. REID in *Cincinnati Daily Gaz.* 13 Dec. 1/3 He was boasting of his success with the 'cussed free niggers'. We've got a Provo' in our town that settles their hash mighty quick. He's a downright high-toned man, that Provo', if he is a Yankee.

2. *Comb.*, as **provo-marshal**: cf. PROVOST-MARSHAL.

1919 G. B. SHAW *Peace Conference Hints* vii. 102 The estimate of military crime which any statistician can give.. without consulting a provo-marshal. **1934** —— *Too True to be Good* II. 50 Offences which cannot be stated on a charge sheet and dealt with by the provo-marshal.

provo, Provo² (ˈprəʊvəʊ). [a. Du. *provo*, abbrev. of F. *provocateur*.] A member of a group of young Dutch agitators of anarchist persuasion, whose policy was to provoke the authorities; the Dutch anarchist group or movement. Also *attrib.*

1966 *Times* 15 June 1/5 For several weeks there has been unrest in Amsterdam. Young men and women calling themselves 'provos', from the French *provocateur*, who reject any authority or discipline, have gathered in certain parts of the city to provoke police intervention. **1967** *Listener* 19 Jan. 83/2 A somewhat riotous group of youngsters, who called themselves Provos, organized themselves and started to prove the validity of their organization's name by provoking the authorities. **1967** J. EASTWOOD *Little Dragon from Peking* x. 97 Hitch-hikers, *autostops, Blousons noirs*, provos from Amsterdam. **1968** *Listener* 22 Feb. 233/1 Police action against a Provo demonstrator when Princess Beatrice of the Netherlands was married in 1966. **1970** *New Yorker* 8 Aug. 50/3 One of the most interesting aspects of Provo, the Dutch movement that was among the first and brightest of the radical movements of the last decade, was that it blossomed forth with a number of responsible civic ideas. **1976** J. VAN DE WETERING *Corpse on Dike* v. 58 You look funny..but you don't look like a hippie or a provo or a bird-of-protest.

provo, Provo³ (ˈprəʊvəʊ, ˈprɒvəʊ). *colloq.* [abbrev. of PROVISIONAL *a.* (*sb.*).] A member of the Provisional I.R.A. Also *attrib.* or as *adj.*

1971 *Guardian* 14 Aug. 9/7 In their bombing campaign the Provos seem to have hit on a policy..described as being the best way to bring down Stormont. **1972** *New Yorker* 19 Feb. 52/2 There are still no more than a few thousand I.R.A. men, Provo or Official, in the Six Counties. The Officials have less than half as many members as the Provos. **1973** *Daily Tel.* 27 Jan. 1/2 IRA men who recognise courts are automatically disowned by the Provos. **1976** *Church Times* 26 Nov. 5/2 The march squelched on to a new rallying point as a mob of Provo IRA thugs had barred the way into Falls Park. **1977** *Cork Examiner* 8 June 16/2 The Provos also claim that two soldiers were killed in a bomb explosion in West Belfast.

provocable (ˈprɒvəkəb(ə)l), *a. rare.* [ad. late L. *prōvocābil-is*, f. L. *prōvocāre* to PROVOKE: see -ABLE.] = PROVOKABLE.

1613 JACKSON *Creed* I. xxiii. §5 Vespasian..scarce prouocable to reuenge practice of treason. **1673** O. WALKER *Educ.* (1677) 55 Pardoning injuries..and not provocable to injure another. **1770** RAWLINS *Serm. Worcester* 8 An unsteady Man, unmerciful, of a Spirit easily provocable, and revengeful. **1850** A. H. CLOUGH *Let.* 3 Jan. in J. Bertram *N.Z. Lett. of T. Arnold* (1966) 188 There is a great blessing ..in being set down among uncongenial people—for me at least who am over provocable.

Hence **provocaˈbility**.

1834 *Autobiog. Dissenting Minister* 174 Cultivate a habit of placidity, in preference to..provocability.

provocant (ˈprɒvəkənt). *rare.* [a. F. *provocant* (18th c. in Hatz.-Darm.) or ad. L. *prōvocānt-em*, pr. pple. of *prōvocāre* to PROVOKE.] One who provokes.

1894 WEYMAN *My Lady Rotha* xviii, It was very evident she was the provocant.

†**ˈprovocate**, *ppl. a. Obs. rare.* [ad. L. *prōvocāt-us*, pa. pple. of *prōvocāre* to PROVOKE.] Provoked, stimulated, incited. Const. as *pa. pple.*

1432–50 tr. *Higden* (Rolls) I. 7 Y, wyllenge to folowe the descriptores of the storye.., and as provocate thro thexemple of theim. *Ibid.* 15 Thro whiche labour..grete men schalle be prouocate to exercise.

†**ˈprovocate**, *v. Obs. rare.* [f. L. *prōvocāt-*, ppl. stem of *prōvocāre* to PROVOKE.] *trans.* To provoke, call forth, incite.

1432–50 tr. *Higden* (Rolls) IV. 363 Guiderius..did prouocate gretely the hate of the Romanes ageyne him. **1570** LEVINS *Manip.* 41/5 To Prouocate, *prouocare*.

Hence †**ˈprovocating** *ppl. a.*, provoking. *rare.*

1774 DIBDIN *Waterman* I. i, What a provocating creature!

‖**provocateur** (prɔvɔkatœr). [Fr., = 'instigator, provoker'.] One who provokes a disturbance; an agitator; an *agent provocateur*. Also *attrib.*

1922 U. SINCLAIR *They call me Carpenter* xxvii. 94 The poor devils who went on strike were locked out of the factories..and their policies bedevilled by provocateurs. **1925** L. TROTSKY *Whither England?* v. 99 It must also thoroughly understand that the strike will fail to be immediately defeated only if it is able to offer the necessary resistance to the strike-breakers, provocateurs, Fascisti, etc. **1934** C. STEAD *Seven Poor Men of Sydney* iv. 112 What y' raisin' 'ell for; where y' come from? You're a *provocateur*. **1940** 'G. ORWELL' *Inside Whale* 142 To say 'I accept' in an age like our own is to say that you accept..submarines, spies, provocateurs, press censorship, [etc.]. **1956** A. L. GOODHARD in A. Pryce-Jones *New Outl. Mod. Knowl.* 581 The most important task..is the final extirpation..of all the remnants of these *provocateur* fabrications. **1961** C. COCKBURN *View from West* vi. 67 It looked much as though there might have been some *provocateurs* at work. **1974** T. P. WHITNEY tr. *Solzhenitsyn's Gulag Archipelago* I. I. viii. 319 The trial of the provocateur R. Malinovsky. **1976** 'J. DAVEY' *Treasury Alarm* i. 13 So you want me to..tell you if he's a genuine bloated capitalist or some sort of provocateur.

provocation (prɒvəʊˈkeɪʃən). [a. F. *provocation* (12–13th c.), ad. L. *prōvocātiōn-em*, n. of action f. *prōvocāre* to PROVOKE.] The action of provoking.

I. †**1.** The action of invoking the office of a court or judge; *esp.* the action of appealing to a higher ecclesiastical court against a judgement; an appeal. *Obs.*

1426 *Paston Lett.* I. 25, I made an appell and a procuracie, and also a provocacion, at London. **1532–3** *Act 24 Hen. VIII*, c. 12 §6 There to be diffinitiuely..adiudged..without any appelacion or prouocacion to any other..courte. **1604** PARSONS *3rd Pt. Three Convers. Eng.* 434 This insolent bragg and prouocation to scripture by these artificers. **1726** AYLIFFE *Parergon* 72, I shall define such an Appeal to be a Provocation from an Inferiour to a Superiour Judge. *Ibid.*, A Provocation is every Act whereby the Office of the Judge or his Assistance is ask'd and implor'd. [**1894** MRS. HOPE *First Divorce Hen. VIII* 337 Bonner repeated his protest, and presented Henry's 'provocation'.]

†**2.** The action of calling out to fight; a challenge, a defiance. *Obs.*

1484 CAXTON *Fables of Poge* ix, The frensshman prouoked the Janueye to bataylle... The Januey accepted the prouocacion & came in the day assigned in to the felde. **1494** FABYAN *Chron.* IV. lxiv. 44 By meanes of prouocacion on eyther party vsed, lastly the Romaynes Issued oute of the Cytie and gaue Batayl to the Brytons.

3. The action of calling, inviting, or summoning; invitation, summons. *Obs.* exc. as coloured by 4.

1548 LD. SOMERSET *Epist. Scots* Cj, God..Whose callyng & prouocacion, we haue & will followe, to the beste of oure powers. *a* **1569** KINGESMYLL *Man's Est.* xiii. (1580) 97 Following the prouocation of the Prophete, whiche calleth men to the consideration of God's mercie by this call. **1827** SCOTT *Surg. Dan.* Pref., I daily expected..a card to drink tea with Misses Fairscribe, or a provocation to breakfast, at least, with my hospitable friend. **1878** BROWNING *La Saisiaz* 116 The sudden light that leapt At the first word's provocation, from the heart-deeps where it slept.

II. 4. The action of inciting; incitement, impulse; instigation; an incentive, a stimulus.

c **1425** WYNTOUN *Cron.* VIII. 2976 Qwhat he did agayn þat nacion, þai made hym prowocacion. **1451** CAPGRAVE *St. Gilbert* (E.E.T.S.) 71 Whan he was compelled be þe prouocacion of natur to go to bed and to rest. **1511–12** *Act 3 Hen. VIII*, c. 22 *Preamble*, The Kyng of Scottis..cruell and haynous provocacions of Werre hath moeved..ayenst your Highnesse. **1602** J. CLAPHAM *Hist. Eng.* I. 56 Those common prouocations of vices, namely sumptuous Galleries, hote baths, and exquisite banquetings. **1678** R. BARCLAY *Apol. Quakers* V. xi. 134 It is a constant Incitement and Provocation, and lively Incouragement to every Man, to forsake Evil. **1848** W. H. BARTLETT *Egypt to Pal.* xii. (1879) 265 If his statements were true, he had some provocation to call them by some of the hard names which he bestowed upon them. **1858** DORAN *Crt. Fools* 112 It does not appear that wit was always the provocation to royal laughter.

5. a. The action or an act of provoking or exciting anger, resentment, or irritation.

1539 BIBLE (Great) *Ps.* xcv. 8 Harden not youre hertes, as in yᵉ prouokacion. **1540** *Act 32 Hen. VIII*, c. 38 §2 To the vtter destruction of their own soules, and the prouocacion of the terrible wrath of god. **1618** ROWLANDS *Sacred Mem.* 34 Then answered he, O faithlesse generation, How long shall I endure your Prouocation? **1736** BUTLER *Anal.* I. ii. (1874) 46 Suppositions..that he must be incapable of offence and provocation. **1876** BLACK *Madcap V.* xvii, You ought not to give way to your temper, under whatever provocation.

b. A cause of irritation, anger, or resentment.

1716 ADDISON *Freeholder* No. 40 ¶1 Writing is indeed a Provocation to the Envious and an Affront to the Ignorant. **1819** WORDSW. *Waggoner* IV. 178 This complicated provocation A hoard of grievances unsealed. **1878** T. L. CUYLER *Pointed Papers* 170 A most irritating provocation is thrown like a torpedo at our feet.

III. 6. *attrib.* **provocation test** *Med.*, a test to ascertain whether or not a person is alive.

1966 *Lancet* 31 Dec. 1466/2 On Oct. 12, 1965, patient was anæsthetized with halothane for a few minutes as a provocation test. **1971** *Essentials from Rep. Organtranspl.* (Netherlands Red Cross) 12 Provocation-tests and the best possible recording techniques should be used.

provocative (prəʊˈvɒkətɪv), *a.* and *sb.* [As adj. a. obs. F. *provocatif* (1486 in Godef.), or ad. late L. *prōvocātīv-us*: see PROVOCATE *ppl. a.* and -IVE; as sb. ad. L. *prōvocātīv-um* neut. sing.]

A. *adj.* **1.** Having the quality of provoking, calling forth, or giving rise to (const. *of*); *spec.* apt or tending to excite or enrage; stimulating, irritating.

1649 JER. TAYLOR *Gt. Exemplar* II. Ad Sect. xii. 99 Not to be hasty, rash, provocative, or upbraiding in our language. **1791** PAINE *Rights of Man* (ed. 4) 44 The people..accosted him with reviling and provocative language. **1812** L. HUNT in *Examiner* 7 Dec. 769/1 Hard of digestion or provocative of fever. **1832** tr. *Sismondi's Ital. Rep.* xv. 331 Pescara.. determined on adopting the part of provocative agent instead of rebel. **1868** M. PATTISON *Academ. Org.* v. 208 Rich endowments have not been found in practice invariably provocative of mental activity.

2. *spec.* Serving to excite appetite or lust. Now limited to sexual contexts.

1621 T. WILLIAMSON tr. *Goulart's Wise Vieillard* 65 To seeke after meats and provocatiue drugs, to enflame and stirre vp their beastly lustes. **1769** E. BANCROFT *Guiana* 381 Diseases..have been augmented by cookery, with its stimulating provocative arts. **1933** [see EXOTIC A. 2b]. **1960** [see BEEHIVE 1d]. **1980** I. ST. JAMES *Money Stones* I. vii. 24 Her provocative teasing looks.

B. *sb.* **1.** That which provokes, excites, or draws forth; an incentive.

1638 SIR T. HERBERT *Trav.* (ed. 2) 118 The Pagans.. made the fury and anger of the English meere provocatives of scorne and laughter. **1711** ADDISON *Spect.* No. 47 ¶5 To examine into the several Provocatives of Laughter in Men of superior Sense and Knowledge. **1874** BLACKIE *Self-Cult.* 66 Vanity is another provocative of lies.

2. *spec.* Anything that excites appetite or lust; *esp.* an aphrodisiac. (The earliest sense.)

c **1412** HOCCLEVE *De Reg. Princ.* 1608 þei receyuen eeke prouocatyues Tengendre hem luste. *a* **1631** DRAYTON *David & Goliah* 734 His locks of hayre,.. Tost to and fro, did with such pleasure moue, As they had beene prouocatiues for loue. **1790** BURKE *Fr. Rev.* Wks. V. 127 Swallowing down repeated provocatives of cantharides. **1817** COLERIDGE *Biog. Lit.* 236 Men of palsied imaginations.. greedy after vicious provocatives.

Hence **pro'vocatively** *adv.*, in a provocative manner, provokingly; **pro'vocativeness**, provokingness.

1661 H. D. *Disc. Liturgies* 59 To convince us, over whom he so provocatively insults. **1882** STEVENSON *New Arab. Nts.* II. 192 A red flower set provocatively in her corset. **1682** R. BURTHOGGE *Argt. Infants Bapt.* (1684) 83 Sensible of the great Provokativeness, and of the as great Unfitness and Undecency of it. **1881** RUSKIN in *19th Cent.* Oct. 526 It is.. only when he has lost his temper that the inherent provocativeness comes out.

provocator ('prɒvəkeɪtə(r)). [ad. Fr. *provocateur.*] A provoker or challenger; = PROVOCATEUR.

1896 W. LE QUEUX *Secret Service* iv. 79 From Paris 'flying brigades' of spies and provocators are sent out. **1913** *Amer. Yearbk. 1912* 392/2 This.. has caused a reawakening of the revolutionary movement.. the old Terrorist wing having practically disappeared.. on account of the exposure of the activity of Eugene Azeff and his staff of police spies and provocators within its ranks. **1918** A. GRAY tr. *Grelling's Crime* II. ii. 132 If even the creator of the defensive Entente of 1904 was regarded as a dangerous provocator, [etc.].

provocatory (prəʊ'vɒkətərɪ), *a.* (*sb.*) *rare.* [ad. late L. *prōvocātōri-us*, f. L. *prōvocātor*, agent-n. f. *prōvocāre* to PROVOKE: see -ORY². So obs. F. *provocatoire* (Cotgr. 1611).] Calculated or tending to provoke; = PROVOCATIVE *a.*

1630 J. TAYLOR (Water P.) *Bawd* Wks. II. 97/2 Amorous actions, prouocatory gestures, effeminate glances. **1870** *Pall Mall G.* 28 Nov. 2 It is impossible that provocatory action should be undertaken. **1892** *Times* 2 Feb. 8/6 It is scarcely to be feared that any combative or provocatory course.. will be adopted.

†**b.** As *sb.* (See quot.) *Obs.*

1611 COTGR., *Provocatoire*, a Prouocatorie; a writing, etc., whereby one is prouoked; a challenge.

provocatrix (prɒvəʊ'keɪtrɪks). [a. late L. *prōvocātrix*, fem. of L. *prōvocātor*, agent-n. from *prōvocāre* to PROVOKE. So F. *provocatrice* (Littré).] A female provoker or challenger.

1904 *Daily Chron.* 23 Feb. 4/6 Cries this scribe.. it is for England, the provocatrix, that M. Jaurès reserves his favours.

‖**provodnik** (prəvad'nik). [Russ.] In the U.S.S.R.: **a.** A guide. **b.** An attendant or guard on a train.

1888 J. C. MURRAY tr. *S. Maimon's Autobiogr.* xviii. 148, I was once seized as a prowodnik myself. **1927** *Contemp. Rev.* June 729 Two *provodniks*, or train attendants, looked after our coach. **1936** P. FLEMING *News from Tartary* ii. 23, I went back to my compartment and found the provodnik. **1976** *National Observer* (U.S.) 21 Feb. 7/2 A provodnik is shaving in one of the two lavatories at the height of the morning rush.

provokable (prəʊ'vəʊkəb(ə)l), *a.* [f. PROVOKE *v.* + -ABLE: cf. the earlier PROVOCABLE.] Capable of being provoked or excited to anger or impatience.

1678 CUDWORTH *Intell. Syst.* I. iv. 188 The inferior gods, ..being also irascible, and therefore provokable by our neglect of them. **1711** SHAFTESB. *Charac.* (1737) I. 41 An unsteddy, changeable, easily provokable, and revengeful man.

provoke (prəʊ'vəʊk), *v.* [a. OF. *provoke-r* (14th c. in Godef. *Compl.*), mod.F. *provoquer* (learned word taking the place of the earlier *purvuchier*), ad. L. *prōvocāre* to call forth, challenge, appeal, excite, f. *prō*, PRO-¹ + *vocāre* to call.]

I. †**1.** *trans.* To call forth, call upon, call for, invoke; to summon, invite. Also *absol. Obs.*

c **1477** CAXTON *Jason* 29 The peple.. knelid down tofore him and prouoked the goddes vnto his ayde and helpe. **1483** *Caxton's Chron. Eng.* III. (1520) 25 b, Hircanum her sone she prouoked to the bysshopryche. **1589** PUTTENHAM *Eng. Poesie* I. viii. (Arb.) 33 Horace.. was.. prouoked to be Secretarie of estate to Augustus th' Emperour. **1667** WATERHOUSE *Fire Lond.* 123, I humbly provoke the Nation to humiliation before God. **1697** DRYDEN *Virg. Georg.* II. 771 The Herdsmen.. provoke his Health in Goblets crown'd. **1708** POPE *Ode St. Cecilia* 36 But when our Country's cause provokes to Arms, How martial music ev'ry bosom warms!

†**2.** *intr.* To call to a judge or court to take up one's cause; to appeal (*from* a lower *to* a higher ecclesiastical tribunal). *Obs.*

1533 CRANMER *Let. to Boner* in Burnet *Hist. Ref.* (1715) III. App. 46, I have provoked from his Holyness to the General Counsell. **1666** J. SERGEANT *Let. of Thanks* 113 Tertullian is the unlikeliest man in the world to provoke to the Scriptures. **1682** DRYDEN *Relig. Laici* 346 Even Arius and Pelagius durst provoke To what the centuries preceding spoke.

†**b.** *trans.* To bring or carry (an appeal). *rare.*

1532-3 *Act 24 Hen. VIII*, c. 12 §3 Where.. any of the Kinges Subjectes.. haue vsed to pursue provoke or procure any appele to the See of Rome.

†**3.** *trans.* To call out or summon to a fight; to challenge, to defy. *Obs.*

1484 [see PROVOCATION 2]. **1560** DAUS tr. *Sleidane's Comm.* 258 Them wold he haue prouoked to exarmouche. *a* **1578** LINDESAY (Pitscottie) *Chron. Scot.* (S.T.S.) I. 347 Thair was ane combatt of singular battell betuix the laird of Drumlanrick and the laird of Hempsfeild quho provockit wther in barras to fight to deid. **1657-83** EVELYN *Hist. Relig.* (1850) I. 383 Tertullian.. provokes all the world to contradict it, if they could. **1697** DRYDEN *Æneid* VI. 252 Swoln with applause, and aiming still at more, He now provokes the sea-gods from the shore.

II. 4. To incite or urge (a person or animal) *to* some act or *to do* something; to stimulate to action; to excite, rouse, stir up, spur on. Also with *simple obj.* or *absol.* Now *arch.* except as involving mixture of 5.

1432-50 tr. *Higden* (Rolls) III. 45 Bothe Numetor and the ij. breþer were provokede in to the dethe off Amulius. *c* **1440** *Promp. Parv.* 415/2 Provokyn, or steryn to good, or badde. **1462** *Litt. Red Bk. Bristol* (1900) II. 128 Diuers.. Weuers.. for ther singuler profit, provokyn and stere diuers marchauntz and othour to bryng in.. people.. not born vndir the Kynges obeisaunce. **1526** TINDALE *Heb.* x. 24 Let vs consyder one another to provoke vnto love, and to good workes. **1535** COVERDALE *1 Kings* xviii. 28 They cried loude, and prouoked themselues with knyues & botkens. **1600** SHAKS. *A.Y.L.* I. iii. 112 Beautie prouoketh theeues sooner then gold. *c* **1600** — *Sonn.* l, The bloody spurre cannot prouoke him on. **1671** R. MACWARD *True Nonconf.* 10 To alleage, that the Prophets did not provock to such courses. **1743** J. MORRIS *Serm.* ii. 46 He.. provokes them who are rich to liberality. **1868** M. PATTISON *Academ. Org.* 1 In the hope that these pages may provoke others to come forward.

b. *trans.* To stir up, agitate.

1675 HOBBES *Odyssey* XII. 167 And with our Oars in hand provok'd the Deep.

5. To incite to anger (a person or animal); to enrage, vex, irritate, exasperate. Also *absol.*

1432-50 tr. *Higden* (Rolls) IV. 51 Anthiocus Magnus, provokede thro that, had occupiede alle Egipte [TREVISA, Antiochus was wrooþ]. **1535** COVERDALE *Ps.* lxxvii[i]. 17 For all this they synned agaynst him, and prouoked the most hyest in the wildernesse. *Ibid.* xciv. [xcv.] 8 Harden not youre hertes, as when ye prouoked in tyme of temptacion in the wildernes. **1678** R. L'ESTRANGE *Seneca's Mor.* (1776) 231 A shadow provokes the asp. **1715** DE FOE *Fam. Instruct.* I. iv. (1841) I. 74 You had better let her alone, you will but provoke her. **1800** MRS. HERVEY *Mourtray Fam.* I. 90 Mrs. Mourtray, quite out of patience,.. exclaimed, 'you are really enough to provoke a saint'. **1880** MRS. FORRESTER *Roy & V.* I. 47 'Don't provoke me,' exclaims Netta.

6. To excite, stir up, arouse (feeling, action, etc.); to give rise to, call forth.

1533 GAU *Richt Vay* 16 Thay that prouokis ony ewil desir ..in thair selff or in oders with sangis or wordis. **1610** SHAKS. *Temp.* I. ii. 140 My Tale prouokes that question. **1653** WILKINS *Gift Prayer* vi. 51 The meditation of his bounty and goodness will provoke Love and Gratitude. **1774** GOLDSM. *Nat. Hist.* (1776) III. 301 Their natures are too opposite ever to provoke mutual desire. **1804** *Med. Jrnl.* XII. 263 The discussions it has provoked, and the train of experiments it has induced. **1881** FROUDE *Short Stud.* (1883) IV. II. v. 233 The Oxford revivalists had provoked the storm, but had no spell which would allay it.

b. *transf.* To excite, give rise to, induce, bring about (a physical action, condition, etc.).

1551 TURNER *Herbal* I. M iv, Saffron.. hath the propertye ..to prouoke vryne. **1563** T. GALE *Antidot.* II. 15 It prouoketh slepe, the temples beynge annoynted with it. **1642** ROGERS *Naaman* 207 Lukewarm water will not sooner provoke vomiting, then thou dost the Lord to vomit thee out of his mouth. **1732** ARBUTHNOT *Rules of Diet* in *Aliments*, etc. 262 All things which provoke great Secretions, especially Sweat. **1871** TYNDALL *Fragm. Sc.* (1879) II. xii. 262 Does the yeast-plant stand alone in its power of provoking alcoholic fermentation?

Hence **provoked** (prəʊ'vəʊkt), *ppl. a.*, having received provocation; irritated, angry, annoyed.

1552 HULOET, Prouoked, *concitatus*, *impulsus*. **1698** VANBRUGH (*title*) The Provok'd Wife: a Comedy. **1719** DE FOE *Crusoe* (1840) II. vi. 151 There may be a time when provoked mercy will no longer strive.

pro'voke, *sb. rare.* [f. prec.]

1. An act of provoking; a provocation; a challenge; a cause of offence.

1773 J. ROSS *Fratricide* II. 589 (MS.) By just provoke made ireful. **1824** SCOTT *Let. to Ld. Montagu* 14 Apr., Were you to consider this letter as a provoke requiring an answer.

2. An invitation.

1842 *Blackw. Mag.* LI. 375 He regretted to hear that Sunday was our only open day, but finally, summing up courage, he hazarded a provoke for Sunday.

provokee (prɒvəʊ'kiː). *nonce-wd.* [f. as prec. + -EE¹.] One who is provoked.

1827 CARLYLE *Germ. Rom.* III. 130 The provokee, therefore, determined that the plebeian provoker.. should never more speak to him.

†**pro'vokement.** *Obs.* [f. PROVOKE *v.* + -MENT. Cf. obs. F. *provoquement* (15–17th c. in Godef.).] The action of provoking; that which provokes, instigates, or excites; a provocation.

1553 BRENDE *Q. Curtius* IV. 55 b, Thou hast done it without enye peruokement [*ed.* **1570** prouokement] of my parte. **1581** J. BELL *Haddon's Answ. Osor.* 391 Speciall prickes and prouokementes to sturre vpp such as were fallen. **1597** BEARD *Theatre God's Judgem.* (1612) 462 Giges.. vsurped the crowne at the prouokement of the Queene his mistresse. **1644** FARY *God's Severity* (1645) 20 Notwithstanding the daily provokements and grievances that are done against him by the children of men.

provoker (prəʊ'vəʊkə(r)). [f. as prec. + -ER¹.] One who or that which provokes (in various senses); a challenger, instigator, inciter, irritator, etc.

1432-50 tr. *Higden* (Rolls) VI. 435 A noble yonge man, Hew by name,.. toke the batelle for the kynge, and did sle his provoker. *a* **1541** WYATT *Penit. Ps.* xxxviii. 62 My provokers.. That without cause to hurt me do not cease. **1605** SHAKS. *Macb.* II. iii. 27 Drinke, Sir, is a great prouoker of three things. *a* **1656** BP. HALL *Rem. Wks.* (1660) 162 Fear ..is a just provoker of our tears. **1711** ADDISON *Spect.* No. 47 ¶11 Men who are such Provokers of Mirth in Conversation, that it is impossible for a Club or Merry-meeting to subsist without them. *a* **1860** J. A. ALEXANDER *Gosp. Christ* xxx. (1861) 401 The foolhardiest provoker of temptation.

Hence **pro'vokeress**, a female provoker.

1611 COTGR., *Concitatrice*, a concitatrix; incitresse, prouokeresse.

provoking (prəʊ'vəʊkɪŋ), *vbl. sb.* [f. as prec. + -ING¹.] The action of the verb PROVOKE; stirring up, incitement, provocation.

1530 PALSGR. 259/1 Provokyng to angre, *irritation.* **1535** COVERDALE *1 Kings* xv. 30 With yᵉ prouokynge wherwith he displeased the Lorde God of Israel. **1591** PERCIVALL *Sp. Dict.*, *Açomamiento*, prouoking, stirring vp.

provoking (prəʊ'vəʊkɪŋ), *ppl. a.* [f. as prec. + -ING².] That provokes.

1. That incites or instigates; provocative.

1530 PALSGR. 321/2 Provokyng or movyng to a thynge, *incitatif.* **1630** MASSINGER *Renegado* II. iv, Provoking dishes passing by, to heighten Declined appetite. **1644** MILTON *Areop.* (Arb.) 52 God therefore left him [Adam] free, set before him a provoking object, ever almost in his eyes.

2. Causing anger or irritation; exasperating, irritating.

1642 J. SHUTE *Sarah & Hagar* (1649) 163 As he shall be powerfull, so he will be provoking and cruell. **1658** *Whole Duty Man* Pref. (1684) 6 The abuse of mercy, which is of all sins the most provoking. ? **1710** LADY M. W. MONTAGU *Lett., to Mrs. Hewet* (1887) I. 29 It is a provoking thing to think.. we should always be asunder so many dirty miles. **1849** MACAULAY *Hist. Eng.* viii. II. 327 This answer, far more provoking than a direct refusal. **1884** *Fortn. Rev.* June 812 Joseph, unquestionably, must have been a very provoking younger brother.

Hence **pro'vokingness**.

1840 L. HUNT *Leg. Florence* II. ii, You take Ways of refined provokingness to wreak it.

pro'vokingly, *adv.* [f. prec. + -LY².]

1. In a way that incites, instigates, or tempts.

1615 G. SANDYS *Trav.* 78 The women did sit, when admitted..: for them to lie along, [was] esteemed too prouokingly lasciuious. **1731** A. HILL *Adv. Poets* Epist. 12 What they daily heard, and saw, so provokingly praised. **1887** J. ASHBY STERRY *Lazy Minstrel* (1892) 221 When rosy lips, like Cupid's bow, Assault provokingly invite.

2. In an irritating manner; so as to cause irritation; exasperatingly; to a provoking degree.

1786 MME. D'ARBLAY *Diary* 28 Nov., He smiled a little provokingly, and said, 'We agree'. **1881** GEIKIE in *Macm. Mag.* XLIV. 238 Your progress becomes provokingly slow and laborious.

provolone (prɒvəʊ'ləʊnɪ). [It., f. *provola* cheese made from buffalo's milk.] An Italian smoked cheese, often made in a variety of shapes, as spherical, pear-shaped, etc. Also *attrib.*

1946 A. SIMON *Conc. Encycl. Gastron.* IX. 22/1 *Provelone*, an all-the-year-round Italian cheese. **1952** S. KAUFFMANN *Philanderer* (1953) xii. 198 Madeline had gone shopping.. to get him the anise and java ring and provolone that he loved. **1967** *Boston Sunday Globe* 23 Apr. (Advt. Section) 7/2 For color and flavor contrast add some sliced Swiss cheese, Italian Provolone. This last is light in color, sharp, tangy, cuts without crumbling, and has an agreeable flavor. **1968** V. & M. PETTITT *Len Deighton's Continental Dossier* 25 *The Basilicata*—a rather remote wild area where Romans caught bears for the Colosseum... Specialities: Provolone cheese, Aglianico di Vúlture—a full red wine. **1975** *New Yorker* 4 Aug. 20/3 Authentic Philadelphia hoagies, which are sort of submarines made of Genoa salami, cooked salami, provolone, capicola, lettuce, tomato, olive oil, and assorted spices. **1978** *Detroit Free Press* 16 Apr. (Detroit Suppl.) 7/1 The house specialty ($1.25–$6.50) is made from eight kinds of Italian luncheon meat, salamis, provolone cheese, Italian bread and sweet peppers.

†**provo'lution.** *Obs. rare*⁻¹. [ad. L. type *prōvolūtiōn-em, n. of action f. *prōvolvĕre* to roll or tumble forwards, prostrate oneself (before another).] A tumbling down; prostration.

1664 H. MORE *Myst. Iniq.* I. xxi. §5 This Anniversary Provolution therefore of a Penitent upon the floor at the feet of a formal Confessor.. is no part of true Christian Discipline.

provost ('prɒvəst), *sb.* Forms: α. 1 pra(?prá)fost, -uost, -fast, -uast, -fest. β. 1 pro(?pró)fost, 2–6 prouost, 4 prouast, prouos, 4–6 provest, *Sc.* -west, 4, 8 proves, 5 -veste, 5–6 prowost, -voste, 6–7 -vist, 7 *Sc.* -veist, 4– provost. See also PREVOST, PROVO¹. [Corresponds to OE. *profost* (? *pró-*), beside *prafost* (? *prá-*), and also to early OF. and Anglo-Fr. *provost* (12th c.), found beside *prevost* (mod.F. *prévôt*); representing early med.L. *propositus*, occurring beside and in the sense of *præpositus*, 'a prefect, president, head, chief, overseer, director, commander', sb. use of *præpositus*, placed, or set before or over, placed at the head, appointed as chief, pa. pple. of *præpōnĕre*, f. *præ* before + *pōnĕre* to place, put.

As to the etymological and phonetic relations of the OE. and Teutonic forms, see Note below.]

One set or placed over others; a superintendent, president, head, chief; used generally as an equivalent of the uses of PRÆPOSITUS in ancient and med.Latin, and of the descended terms in French and other languages, and *spec.* as the proper title of certain ecclesiastical and secular officers in England and Scotland, or as a rendering of French *prevost, prévôt*, formerly used to designate various officials: see Cotgr. s.v. *Prevost*, and cf. PREVOST.

I. In ecclesiastical and scholastic use.

1. The head or president of a chapter, or of a community of religious persons; in conventual bodies properly the official next in rank to the abbot, = PRIOR 1 (in quot. *c* 1375 the prioress of a body of nuns); also the chief dignitary of a cathedral or collegiate church, corresponding to the existing dean (but see DEAN[1] 4). Now chiefly *Hist.*

α. *c***961** ÆTHELWOLD *Rule St. Benet* (MS. *c* 1000) lxv. (1885) 124 Be mynstres prafaste [*MS. F. c* 1100 profaste]... þurh þæs ʒeendebyrdan profostes [*MS. T. c* 1075 prauostes] misfadunge. *a* **1066** *Charter of Eadweard* in Kemble *Cod. Dipl.* IV. 233 [Witnesses] Gisa bisceop, and Ælfsie abbod, and Wulʒeat abbod, and Ælfnoð mynster prauost.

β. *a* **900** *Martyrol.* 20 Mar. 42 þa ondranc se þæs wætres ond sealde hit þæm breðer þe him ætstod, þæs mynstres profoste [*v.r.* prauast]. **970** (Aug. 10) in *MS. 'Ritual of Durham'* lf. 84/2 (ed. 1840 p. 185), Be suðan wudiʒan gæteæt aclee on west sæxum on laurentius mæssan dæʒi on wodnes dæʒi ælfsiʒe ðæm biscope in his ʒetelde aldred se profast ðas feower collectæ on fif næht aldne mona ær underne awrat. *c* **1000–1100** [see *α c*961]. *a* **1122** *O.E. Chron.* an. 1066 Ða cusen þa munecas to abbot, Brand prouost. forðan þæt he wæs swiðe god man. *c* **1375** *Sc. Leg. Saints* x. (*Mathou*) 307 þar dowchtyre..of his hand þe vail scho [Ephigenea] tuk ..& wes mad proves but wene Of twa hu[n]dricht virginis clene. *c* **1450** HOLLAND *Howlat* 688 Abbotis of ordouris, Prowestis and priouris. *a* **1552** LELAND *Itin.* VI. 1 Wyngham ..Ther is a Provoste, VI. Prebendaries, besydes othar Ministers of the Churche. **1561** *Reg. Privy Council Scot.* I. 194 All Denis, Archdenis, Subdenis, Chantouris, Subchantouris, Provestis, Personis, Vicaris. **1641** *Sc. Acts Chas. I* (1817) V. 520/1 Ane dissolutione made be the proveist and first prebendar of the Colledge kirk of Corstorphine with advyse and consent of George Lord Forrester of Corstorphine vndoubted Patrone of the said Provesterie. **1688** R. HOLME *Armoury* III. 177/1 (Benedictine Rules) That the Provost or Prepositus be chosen by the Abbot to whom he must be subject. **1824** G. CHALMERS *Caledonia* III. III. viii. 307 In place of the nunnery [of Linncluden], he established a collegiate church, consisting of a provost, and twelve canons. **1878** *Clergy List* 458 The Episcopal Church in Scotland.. United Diocese of Moray, Ross, and Caithness..Provost of the Cathedral [Inverness] the Bishop. *Ibid.* 459 St Ninian's Cathedral [Perth] John Burton, Provost. **1898** *Beverley Chapter Act Bk.* (Surtees) I. Introd. 40 At York, Hugh the Chanter says, on Thomas rebuilding the Canons' Hall he..'established a Provost [*Præpositum constituit*] to preside over them and provide for them'.

b. In modern use, a rendering of Ger. *propst*, Da. *provst*, etc., as the title of the Protestant clergyman in charge of the principal church (*hauptkirche*) of a town or district.

1560 DAUS tr. *Sleidane's Comm.* 414 b, The fellowes or prebends of that Colledge [at Eluange = Elbing] haue authority to chuse the Prouost, as they commonly call him. **1780** tr. *Von Troil's Iceland* 173 The provost and minister of Hiardarholt..is justly celebrated. **1796** MORSE *Amer. Geog.* II. 23 The Danish clergy consists of bishops, provosts, and ministers. **1845** S. AUSTIN *Ranke's Hist. Ref.* II. 507 Support..from their two provosts—patricians of Nürnberg —in the appointment of evangelical preachers.

†**c.** Applied by Caxton to a Muslim muezzin [mistransl. obs. F. *provoire* a priest].

1481 CAXTON *Godeffroy* clxx. 252 On the cornes ben hye towres, vpon whiche the prouostes were woonte to goo vp at certayn howres for to warne and somone the peple to praye.

2. The specific title of the heads of certain educational colleges.

In earlier instances, a survival from the ecclesiastical establishments in which these originated; in later instances an extension of the name to subsequent foundations. The title is borne by the heads of Oriel, Queen's, and Worcester Colleges at Oxford, King's College, Cambridge, and Trinity College, Dublin; also of Eton College, and now or formerly of certain other colleges in England, Scotland, the United States, etc.

1442 *Rolls of Parlt.* V. 45/2 The Provost and the College of the same place [Eton]. **1531–2** *Act 23 Hen. VIII*, c. 19 Archedeacons maisters prouostes presidentes wardens felowes bretherne scholers. **1581** MULCASTER *Positions* xli. (1887) 241 Being himselfe prouost of the kings college in Cambridge. **1638** CHILLINGW. *Relig. Prot.* I. v. §47. 270 That D. Potter cannot leave being Provost of Q. Colledge. **1672** PETTY *Pol. Anat.* (1691) 40 There is an University at Dublin..wherein are a Provost and seven Senior and Ruling Fellows. **1691** WOOD *Ath. Oxon.* I. 45 He.. professed Theology in the Coll. of S. Salvator at S. Andrews, whereof he was made Provost. **1812** *Orig. Charter Columbia Coll.* (1836) 35 The trustees of Columbia college have, by their petition, prayed that the provost of the said college may be eligible as a trustee of said college. **1838–9** HALLAM *Hist. Lit.* II. III. i. §8. 374 From a press established at Eton by himself, provost of that College. **1846** N. F. MOORE *Hist. Sk. Columbia Coll.* 78 The trustees determined to divide the powers and duties of the presidential office between a president and an officer to be styled Provost.

transf. **1669** GALE *Crt. Gentiles* I. III. ix. 93 He concludes with a Curator or Provist of the whole Discipline [Plato's Sacred College].

II. A secular officer, etc.

†**3.** One appointed to preside over or superintend something; usually the representative of the supreme power in a district or sphere of action; formerly used as a translation of various Latin titles, as *præpositus, prætor, proconsul, procurator*, etc.; also in the sense of viceroy, prime minister, and the like. Sometimes without explicit reference to his delegated or appointed position, = Ruler, chief, head, captain, etc.: see 4. *Obs.*

α. *a* **900** *O.E. Martyrol.* 13 Aug. 144 Valerianus, Decies prafest þæs caseres. *c* **1000** ÆLFRIC *Exod.* v. 16 þa comun Israela folces prafostas [Vulg. *præpositi filiorum Israel*] & clypodon to Pharaone & þus cwædon. *a* **1100** *Voc.* in Wr.-Wülcker 309/33 *Prepositus*, ʒerefa, oððe prafost.

β. *c* **1375** *Sc. Leg. Saints* VI. (*Thomas*) 9 Gundoforus..þare kynnge..has send his proveste here Abney [*orig.* præpositum Abbanem], bis[i]ly fore to spere A man, þat sic palace can make. ? *c* **1400** *Warres of Jewes* (Laud MS. 22) in Warton *Hist. Eng. Poetry* (1840) II. 105 Pylot was provost under that prynce ryche. *c* **1440** CAPGRAVE *Life St. Kath.* IV. 1028 The prouost of perse was there also. **1456** SIR G. HAYE *Law Arms* (S.T.S.) 110 A kingis provost may have na mare power na has his maister. **1491** CAXTON *Vitas Patr.* (1495) 111 A Provoste or Capytayne of men of warre. *a* **1518** SKELTON *Magnyf.* 1480 The prowde prouoste of Turky lande. **1549** *Compl. Scot.* xi. 87 He [Darius] send his prouest tasifernes victht gold and siluer to lacedemonia. **1581** SAVILE *Tacitus, Hist.* I. (1591) 25 Flauius Sabinus they ordeyned Prouost of the citty [L. *urbi præfecere*]. **1600** HOLLAND *Livy* VIII. xi. 289 Their Pretor or Provost [L. *prætor*] named Millionius, spake these words. **1631** T. POWELL *Tom All Trades* (1876) 145 Free-Schooles... Some of them..are commonly in the gift of the King, or his Provost or Substitute, in that behalfe.

†**b.** *transf.* Applied to the archangel Michael as leader of the heavenly host. *Obs.*

1413 *Pilgr. Sowle* (Caxton) I. ii. (1859) 3, I wil bringe hym bifore Mychael the prouost of heuene. **14..** HOCCLEVE *Compl. Soule* 267 Wks. 1897 III. p. lix, Sere prouost Michael graciows. **1521** in *Market Harb. Records* (1890) 216 The holy Archangell Mychell, the provest off paradyse.

4. An officer or official in charge of some establishment, undertaking, or body of men; an officer who had the management of a royal or feudal establishment and the collection of dues; a ruler, manager, steward, overseer, keeper. Now *Hist.*

The title *prevost, prévôt* was formerly extensively given in France to officials having administrative and judicial functions: see Cotgrave s.v. *prevost*, and cf. PREVOST 2.

1340 *Ayenb.* 37 þe greate [thieves] byeþ..þe ontrewe reuen, prouos, and bedeles, and seruons þet steleþ þe amendes, and wyþdraʒeþ þe rentes of hire lhordes. *c* **1374** CHAUCER *Boeth.* I. pr. iv. 8 (Camb. MS.) Trygwille prouost of the Kynges hows [*regiæ præpositum domus*]. **1382** WYCLIF *Judg.* xx. 28 And Phynees, the sone of Eliazar, sone of Aaron, was prouost of the hows. **1382** —— *Isa.* xxii. 15 Weend in to hym, that dwelleth in the tabernacle, to Sobnam, prouost of the temple. *c* **1400** *Rom. Rose* 6812 Taylagiers, and these monyours, Bailifs, bedels, provost, countours. **1570** DEE *Math. Pref.* d iv b, The Architect..is ..the Hed, the Prouost, the Directer..of all Artificiall workes, and all Artificers. **1598** BARRET *Theor. Warres* v. iv. 136 A Prouost ouer the horses which draw the Artillery. **1611** COTGR., *Prevost des Monnoyes*, the Prouost of the Mint; the Iudge of controuersies arising by reason of the Mint, or among Mintmen. **1615** BEDWELL *Arab. Trudg.*, *Amir, Præses fidelium*, The prouost of the faithfull. **1696** *Lond. Gaz.* No. 3219/4 Mr. John Braint, Provost of His Majesty's Mint at the Tower of London. **1766** ENTICK *London* IV. 342 (At the Mint) A provost,..blanchers, moniers, &c. **1863** H. Cox *Instit.* III. ix. 727 Relieving them [burgesses] from the interference of Royal provosts in the collection of the King's revenue.

†**5.** The chief magistrate of a town. **a.** In obsolete or historical uses, esp. (*b*) in reference to French, Flemish, or other foreign cities, in which also it sometimes passes into sense 6.

[? *a* **1135** *Leges Willelm. Conq.* (MS. *c* 1230) I. ii. §1 E si aucuns vescunte u provost mesfait as humes [de sa baillie]. [And if any sheriff or provost does wrong to the men of his jurisdiction.] *Ibid.* v. Cil kis claimed, durrad [al gr(efe) s(ive) al provost aveir] pur la rescussiun viii den. [He who claims them shall give to the provost for the recovery 8 pence.] **1200** *Charter Ipswich* in Grose *Gild Merch.* II. 115 Reddendo per annum rectam et solitam firmam ad terminum Sancti Michaelis per manum Gippeswici prepositi ad scaccarium nostrum. [*transl.* I. 7, Paying annually at our Exchequer the right and customary ferm at Michaelmas term, by the hand of the provost of Ipswich.] **1292** BRITTON I. iii. §1 Le provost de chescune vile. **1306** *Rolls of Parlt.* I. 270/1 Le Provost des Villes.] **1485** *Rolls of Parlt.* VI. 378/1 The Office of Provost of your Towne of Middelton, in the forsaid Countie [Kent].

(*b*) *c* **1330** R. BRUNNE *Chron.* (1810) 294 þe prouest of þe toun [Bruges] a wik traytour & cherle, He þouht to do tresoun vnto his lorde þe erle. *c* **1386** CHAUCER *Prioress' T.* 164 The cristene folk that thurgh the strete wente..hastily ..for the Prouost sente. **1494** FABYAN *Chron.* VII. ccxxxi. 263 This foresayde Charlis was sore hated of the prouoste of Brudgys. *a* **1533** LD. BERNERS *Huon* vii. 15 Than they sent for ye provost of Gerone. **1547** *Bk. Marchauntes* ciij, The hygh prouost of these marchants..kepeth his bank vnder exchang to all people—conuertynge leade into golde. [**1611** COTGR. s.v. *Prevost, Prevost des Marchands à Paris*, the Lord Mayor of Paris; different from the Prouost of Iustice, who is called, *Le Prevost de Paris*.] **1706** PHILLIPS, *Provost of Merchants*, the chief Magistrate or Mayor of the City of Paris in France.

b. *spec.* The title of the head of a Scottish municipal corporation or burgh; equivalent to *mayor* in England: cf. MAYOR 1.

The provosts of some of the more important corporations, viz. Edinburgh (since *c* 1486), Glasgow (since 1690), Aberdeen, Perth, Dundee, are styled *Lord Provost.*

[**13..** in *Sc. Stat.* (1844) I. 683 [319] Et facto hujusmodi sacramento osculari debet prepositum et vicinos si frater Gilde fuerit.] **1387** *Charters &c. of Edinb.* (1871) 35 Androw Yutsoun prowest of the Burgh of Edynburgh. ? **1495** *Acc. Ld. High Treas. Scot.* I. 219 The provest of the toune beand present. *a* **1515** *Interl. Droichis* 21 in *Dunbar's Poems* (S.T.S.) 315 Prowest, baillies, officeris, And honerable induellaris,..Of all this fair towne. **1563** WINJET *Four Scoir Thre Quest.* §29 Wks. (S.T.S.) I. 94 The prouestis and ballies of euiry burgh. **1639** DK. HAMILTON in *H. Papers* (Camden) 70 A letter of yours derected to the prouist and balleifes of Edinburg. **1727–41** CHAMBERS *Cycl.* s.v., The provost of Edinburgh has the title *lord.* **1806** *Gazetteer Scotl.* (ed. 2) 7 Aberdeen... Its civil government is vested in a provost, denominated lord provost, 4 bailies, a dean of guild, treasurer, and town-clerk, a town-council, and 7 deacons of the incorporated trades. **1882** GRANT *Old & New Edinb.* II. 278/1 In 1377 John of Quhitness first appears as Provost or Prepositus, on the 18th of May. *Ibid.* 278/2 Patrick Hepburn, Lord Hailey [*c* 1486] was the first designated 'my Lord Provost', probably because he was a peer of the realm.

†**6.** An officer charged with the apprehension, custody, and punishment of offenders. *Obs.*

In France many of the officials called *prevost* (*prévôt*) were specially charged with the keeping of public order and the apprehension, custody, trial, and punishment of offenders, for which they had considerable powers of summary jurisdiction: hence the military use in 7.

? *a* **1400** *Morte Arth.* 1611 Be-teche þam þe proveste [of Paris] in presens of lordez, O payne and o perelle þat pendes there too. **1525** LD. BERNERS *Froiss.* II. clxxxv. 564 The kyng commaunded hym and sayd: Prouost, get you men togyther well horsed, and pursewe that traytour syr Peter of Craon. **1603** SHAKS. *Meas. for M.* I. ii. 118 Here comes Signior Claudio, led by the Prouost to prison. *Ibid.* III. ii. 219 Prouost,..Claudio must die to morrow: Let him be furnish'd with Diuines, and haue all charitable preparation. **1604** E. G[RIMSTONE] *D'Acosta's Hist. Indies* VII. xix. 552 A few dayes after hee sent a provost..to take this Sorcerer. **1611** [see 5 a (*b*)]. **1617** MORYSON *Itin.* III. 289 (Netherlanders Commonwealth) Among the apprehenders, the chiefe are called Prouosts, and they of old had power to hang vagabonds. **1841** JAMES *Brigand* xxvii,'Fetch the provost', exclaimed another. **1873** J. LEWES *Census* 1871. 204 (Guernsey) The provost or Queen's sheriff [cf. PREVOST 2 b].

7. *spec. Milit.* An officer of the military police in a garrison, camp, or the field: see PROVOST-MARSHAL, and *provost-sergeant* in 9.

In this sense usually pronounced (prəʊ'vəʊ) (after F. *prévôt*) and sometimes written PROVO[1].

1692–1746 [see PROVO[1]]. **1799** WELLINGTON in Gurw. *Desp.* (1837) I. 37, I wish you would send the Provost here. .. Until some of the plunderers are hanged it is vain to expect to stop the plunder. **1894** 'J. S. WINTER' *Red-Coats* 44 Perhaps she had less cause for bitterness..owing to her superior position as the wife of the Provost.

b. Short for *provost-cell*: see 9.

1890 in *Cent. Dict.*

†**8.** An assistant fencing-master. (So F. *prévôt.*)

1545 ASCHAM *Toxoph.* I. (Arb.) 97 Of fence..there is not onely Masters to teache it, wyth his Prouostes [*Wks.* (*ed.* 1761) provosters] Vshers Scholers and other names of arte and Schole. **1599** B. JONSON *Cynthia's Rev.* v. ii, We..do give leave and licence to our provost, Acolastus-Polypragmon-Asotus, to play his master's prize, against all masters whatsoever. **1615** in Strutt *Sports & Past.* III. vi. §22 They which desire to be taught at their admission are called scholars, and, as theyr profit they take degrees, and proceed to be provosts of defence.

9. *attrib.* and *Comb.*: **provost-cell**, a cell for confining military prisoners; †**provost-place**, in phr. *to sit provost-place*, to preside; †**provost-seal**, the official seal of a provost of a borough; **provost-sergeant**, a sergeant of the military police: cf. sense 7.

1902 WEBSTER Suppl., **Provost cell*, in the British service, a military prison for soldiers confined, by order of the commanding officer or by sentence of court martial, for periods not exceeding forty-two days. **1748** J. WALLIS in *Gentl. Mag.* (1779) XLIX. 495 If the proud gentleman that thinks himself slighted should happen to sit *provost-place as they call it, he sits at the head of his table in all the agonies of concealed ill-nature. **1466** *Cal. Anc. Rec. Dublin* (1889) I. 322 Undre the *Prowost seall of the saide citte. **1868** *Regul. & Ord. Army* ¶824 The *Provost Serjeant is to cause the prisoners to wash themselves once a day.

Hence, chiefly *nonce-wds.*, †'**provostage**, some impost duty in some countries; '**provostess**, a female provost; in quot. (after Ger. *pröpstin*) applied to the prioress of a (Protestant) conventual foundation; **provo'storial** *a.*, of or pertaining to a provost, provostal.

1766 W. GORDON *Gen. Counting-ho.* 281 The ship *Jenny* arrives at Bilboa, and there Bradson sells 1640½ quintals of fish..and delivers for *provostage 2½ per cent. in specie of fish. **1905** *Westm. Gaz.* 20 Mar. 2/1 The dismantled apartments are hung with the portraits of the Abbesses since the Reformation... One looks, instinctively, for Aurora von Königsmark; and she, having been only *provostess, is missing... Certainly she is the lady of Quedlinburg. **1855** J. STRANG *Glasgow & Clubs* (1856) 212 During his *provostorial sovereignty the provost haugh was purchased.

[*Note.* The forms of this word in the cognate continental langs. are ON. *prófastr* (*c* 1160 in Norway), Icel. *prófastur*,

Norw. *provast, -est*, MSw. *provast, -est, proast, -est, proost*, Sw. *prost*, MDa. *provæst, -est*, Da. *provst* (*propst*); MLG. *provest, prōfst, prōst*, MFris., MDu. *prōvest*, MDu. also *proo(f)st*, Du. *proost* (*provoost*); OHG. *probost, -ist*, MHG. *probest*, Ger. *probst, propst*: all in eccl. sense. It is not clear whether the OE. *profost* was historically connected with any of these, except as representing the same Latin word; *prafost* stands quite alone. The length of the stress-vowel in OE. can only be determined by inference; most lexicographers have marked it as long, as in ON.; but Pogatscher (*Lautl. der Gr. Lat. Lehnworte im Altengl.*) gives reasons for short *a* and *o* (so Sievers and Napier); the *o* in Ger. and Du. appears also to have been short. Pogatscher takes *prafost* as repr. late L. or Romanic *prepost-* from *præpositus*, and *profost*, late L. or Romanic *propost-* from *propositus*; which latter gave OHG. *probost* and all the continental cognate forms. The early 12th c. *prouost* = *provost* might mean either the OE. *pro-vost* or the Anglo-Fr. *pro'vost*. While the Teutonic langs. have favoured the *propost-* form, the Romanic have preferred the *prepost-* from *præposit-*, though in earlier times they had also forms in *pro-*. Cf. OF. *prevost*, also *provos(t, pourvost, prouvos(t, preuvost, proost, prost, pros* (Godef. *Compl.*), Anglo-Fr. *provost*, mod.F. *prévôt*; Pr. *prebost*, Sp., Pg. *preboste*, It. *prevosti*, formerly also *provosto* (Florio).]

'provost, *v. rare.* Also provo' (cf. PROVO[1]). [f. prec. sb. sense 7.] *trans.* To hand over to the provost-marshal to be dealt with summarily and (formerly) to receive corporal punishment. Hence **'provosting** *vbl. sb.*

Apparently a short-lived word used *c* 1837.

1837 MAJOR RICHARDSON *Brit. Legion* ix. (ed. 2) 241 Men found to be incorrigible, have first been provosted, then marched forth disgracefully by beat of drum from their regiments. **1837** C. SHAW *Mem.* II. xxxv. 541 There is a good deal of provosting, of which I rather approve, as it prevents serious punishments. **1839** A. SOMERVILLE *Hist. Brit. Legion* iii. 69 He [an officer] was a decided enemy to provo'ing. *Ibid.* xi. 242 In four months he had been eleven times provosted, and once flogged by sentence of a court-martial.

provostal (prəʊ'vɒstəl), *a. rare.* [f. PROVOST *sb.* + -AL[1], after obs. F. *prevostal* (Cotgr. 1611), mod.F. *prévôtal*.] Of or pertaining to a provost.

1611 COTGR., *Prevostaire*, prouostall, of a Prouost. **1656** BLOUNT *Glossogr.*, *Provostal*, of or pertaining to a Provost. **1706** in PHILLIPS. **1905** *Daily News* 10 Aug. 6 It is earnestly to be hoped..that no 'confession' will be created in any mayoral or provostal bosom by the selection of such a date as the 13th, and such a day as Friday.

[provoster, error for PROVOST.

The quot. cited in Richardson from Ascham *Toxoph.* is given s.v. PROVOST 8, q.v.

a **1661** FULLER *Worthies, Buckingh.* (1662) I. 131 Fellow and Provoster of Eaton.]

provost guard. *U.S.* A body of soldiers acting as military police under a provost-marshal; also, the quarters used by these.

1778 *Jrnls. U.S. Continental Congress* (1908) X. 74 About thirty [officers] who have been confined in the provost guard and in the most loathsome gaols. **1864** O. W. NORTON *Army Lett.* (1903) 212 Company K is provost guard and river patrol. **1883** SWEET & KNOX *On Mexican Mustang through Texas* xlii. 595 We may be caught by the provost-guard, and put in the bull-pen. **1887** G. B. MCCLELLAN *McClellan's Own Story* iv. 69 These..I at once brought to the city and employed as a provost-guard.

provost-marshal. Also 6 propheest-, 6, 9 -martial. [f. PROVOST *sb.* 6, 7 + MARSHAL *sb.*, commonly held to be an irregular representation of OF. *prevost des mareschaus (de France)*, 'provost of the marshals (of France)', 15th c. in Littré: see Note below.]

An officer (= PROVOST 6, PREVOST 2) attached to a military or naval force, whose duties and powers have varied at different times and in different countries. Now, in the army: An officer appointed to a force in camp or on active service, as the head of the police, having duties which include the preservation of order, the prevention of pillage, the custody of prisoners charged with offences till trial, the carrying into effect of the punishments awarded, etc. In the navy, the 'Master-at-Arms' of the ship in which a court-martial is to be held (being the Chief Petty Officer in charge of the ship's police) is appointed by warrant Provost-marshal for the occasion.

1535 *St. Papers Hen. VIII*, II. 237 They wer..arrayned before the propheest marshall and capitannes, and ther, upon ther awne confessions, adjudged to die. *a* **1548** HALL *Chron., Hen. VIII* 12 b, The lorde Darcie..sent forth his Prouost Marshal, which scarcelie with peyne refrayned the yomen archers. **1571** *Reg. Privy Council Scot.* II. 102 Tak the personis, and use thame as presoners, and deliver thame to the Provest Marcheall. **1591** *Garrard's Art Warre* 157 They shall by the Provost Martiall be punished. **1600** HOLLAND *Livy* XXIX. xxix. 731 Amongst whom was Hanno also the Provost Marshall [*præfectus*], a noble young gentleman. *a* **1642** SIR W. MONSON *Naval Tracts* III. (1704) 342/1 The Boatswain serves for a Provost-Marshal. **1706** PHILLIPS, *Provost-Marshal*,..also an Officer in the Royal Navy, who has charge of the Prisoners taken at Sea. **1809** WELLINGTON in Gurw. *Desp.* (1835) IV. 455 The appointment of Assistant Provost Marshals, I am sorry to say, is but too necessary. **1833** MARRYAT *P. Simple* lxi, I was put under the custody of the provost-martial. **1844** *Regul. & Ord. Army* 275 The Officer appointed to the situation of Provost-Marshal has the rank of Captain in the Army: the appointment is one of great responsibility, and requires the utmost vigilance and activity. **1897** GEN. H. PORTER in *Cent. Mag.* June 211 Provost-marshal's guards seized all available citizens..and impressed them into the service. **1908** *Admiralty Memo. on Court-Martial Procedure* 35 The Convening Authority..shall, by warrant..appoint a provost-marshal to take the accused into his custody and safely keep him until he shall have been delivered in due course of law.

b. Used as equivalent of obs. F. *prevost des mareschaux* and of other names of semi-military officers of public order.

1580 HOLLYBAND *Treas. Fr. Tong*, *Vn prevost de mareschaulx*, a prouoste Marshall, that hath in charge to hang vp theues. *c* **1620** FLETCHER & MASS. *Lit. Fr. Lawyer* v. iii, *Provost.* I have been provost-marshal twenty years, And have truss'd up a thousand of these rascals. **1823** SCOTT *Quentin D.* vi, They bore the palm [as the object of fear and execration] over every hangman in France, unless it were their master, Tristan l'Hermite, the renowned Provost-Marshal, or his master, Louis XI. *Ibid. passim.* **1845** S. AUSTIN *Ranke's Hist. Ref.* II. 261 A provost-martial of the name of Aichili traversed Swabia and Franconia..; it is calculated that within a small district, he hung forty evangelical preachers on trees by the roadside.

c. The chief police official of some of the states or colonies in the West Indies, etc.

1737 J. CHAMBERLAYNE *St. Gt. Brit.* II. III. 204 Governors and Officers in the West Indies..Peter Forbes Esq.; Provost Marshall. *Ibid.* 205 Bermuda..George Tucker, Esq.; Secretary and Provost-Marshal. [Given also as the title of an official in Barbadoes, Leeward Islands, South Carolina.] **1908** *Whitaker's Alm.* 539 The Bahamas..Provost-Marshal and Commandant of Constabulary. *Ibid.* 542 Barbados..Provost-Marshal.

[*Note.* The functions of the *prevost des mareschaus de France* in the 15th c. appear to have been those of a military provost-marshal, although they were subsequently extended and changed; thus Cotgrave 1611 explains *Prevost des Mareschaux* as 'A Prouost Marshall (who is often both Informer, Judge, and Executioner) punishes disorderlie Souldiors, Coyners, Free-booters, high-way robbers, lazie rogues, or vagabonds, and such as weare forbidden weapons'; Littré has '*prévôt des maréchaux*, an officer appointed to watch over the safety of the highways within the limits of a *généralité*, called also *prévôt de la maréchaussée* [i.e. provost of the marshalcy]'; in which the military functions have disappeared. For these Littré has *prévôt de l'armée, prévôt du régiment*, and in the navy, *prévôt général de la marine*, and *prévôt marinier*. The 15th c. F. *prevost des mareschaus* might have been rendered 'marshals' provost', but it is not easy to see how it became *provost-marshal*, unless perhaps under the influence of *court-martial, law martial*, and the 16th c. confusion of *marshal* and *martial*, whereby we find also *law marshal* and *provost martial*, showing that the latter was sometimes at least taken to be 'war provost'.]

provostry ('prɒvəstrɪ). Now *Hist.* [f. PROVOST + -RY: cf. F. *Provoterie*, local name (in Godef.), variant of OF. *prevosterie* the tribunal of a *prévôt*.]

†**1.** The office or jurisdiction of a provost. Formerly applied to a Roman prætorship or prefecture; also to the provostship of a Scottish burgh. *Obs.*

c **1374** CHAUCER *Boeth.* III. pr. iv. 58 (Camb. MS.) Certes the dignite of the prouostrye [*praetura*] of Rome was whylom a gret power, now is it nothyng but An Idel name. *Ibid.*, What thyng is now more owt cast than thylke prouostrye. **1413** *Pilgr. Sowle* (Caxton) I. xxxix. (1859) 43 He shalle spoylen the thy worshyp and of thy prouostry with grete shame and shendeshyp. **1545** *Aberdeen Regr.* (1844) I. 214 His office of prouestry quhilk he had of the said tovnn. *a* **1639** SPOTTISWOOD *Hist. Ch. Scot.* VI. (1677) 383 There had been a long and old emulation betwixt the two Families ..for the Wardenry of the middle Marches, and the Provostry of Jedburgh.

2. The benefice of a collegiate provost: see PROVOST 1; the revenue derived from such a benefice; rarely, the office of provost of an educational college; = PROVOSTSHIP 1 b. Now *Hist.*

c **1450** T. BECKINGTON *Corr.* (Rolls) II. 164 Amovyd and pryved perpetually frome provestre of the same collage Royall. **1548–9** in E. Green *Somerset Chantries* (1885) 5 The parsonage ther is appropriat to the Provostrie of Wells. **1581** in Grant *Burgh Sch. Scotl.* II. xv. (1876) 446 An Act of Parliament ordaining all provostries and prebends to be given to scholars. **1641** [see PROVOST *sb.* 1 β]. **1702** *Anguis in Herba* 48 She had conceded to her Luxemburg with its Provostry. **1889** HUNTER-BLAIR tr. *Bellesheim's Hist. Cath. Ch. Scot.* III. 222 To retain..the provostry of St. Mary's and the rectorship of the University. **1898** *Beverley Chapter Act Bk.* (Surtees) I. Introd. 38 In the latter part of its existence, the Provostry of Beverley was a peculiar institution.

†**b.** The residence of a provost. *nonce-use.*

1825 LOCKHART *Let.* 18 July in *Life Scott*, A superb *dejeuner* in the Provostry [at Trinity College, Dublin].

'provostship. [f. PROVOST + -SHIP.]

1. The office or position of a provost: e.g. **a.** of a Roman prefect; **b.** of the provost of an ecclesiastical or educational college; **c.** of the provost of a municipal corporation, esp. in Scotland; **d.** of an officer of public order (in quot. as a title).

a. **1546** LANGLEY *Pol. Verg. De Invent.* II. iii. 38 b, During that office [viz. of Dictator], all other magistrates were abrogated except the Tribunate or Prouostship of the Commons. **1598** GRENEWEY *Tacitus, Ann.* XIV. xii. (1622) 213 But whom shall any mans dignitie warrant, seeing the Prouostship [*præfectura*] of the citie auailed not? **1678** WANLEY *Wond. Lit. World* VI. x. §12. 579/2 Piso..was advanced to the Provostship of the City of Rome.

b. **1514** in Burton & Raine *Hemingbrough* 381 The preferment of the Priour of Drax..to the provestship of Hemmyngburgh. **1549** LATIMER *2nd Serm. bef. Edw. VI* (Arb.) 67 Hauynge the profyt of a Prouestshyp and a Deanry, and a Personage. **1623** in *Crt. & Times Jas. I* (1849) II. 390 The provostship of Eton seems not to be so assured to Sir William Beecher. **1631** WEEVER *Anc. Fun. Mon.* 199 He was preferred..vnto..the Prouostship of Beuerley. **1714** *Lond. Gaz.* No. 5231/1 The Provostship of Oriel-College in Oxford. **1871** FRASER *Life Berkeley* ii. 18 He entered Trinity College in June 1682... He was raised to the Provostship in August 1699.

c. *a* **1578** LINDESAY (Pitscottie) *Chron. Scot.* (S.T.S.) II. 150 [She] dischargit the lord Ruthven of his provistschipe and maid the laird of Kinphans prowest and captane of the toun. **1820** RANKEN *Hist. France* VII. v. i. 393 The townhall was rebuilt..under the provostship of the celebrated Miron. **1890** GROSS *Gild Merch.* I. 23 On Thursday, June 29, the whole community of the borough [Ipswich, an. 1200] elect two bailiffs to take charge of the provostship of the borough.

d. **1823** SCOTT *Quentin D.* vi, 'And it please your noble provostship' answered one of the clowns; 'he was the very first..to cut down the rascal whom his Majesty's justice most deservedly hung up.'

†**2.** A collegiate society, house, or church under a provost. *Obs.*

1762 tr. *Busching's Syst. Geog.* IV. 201 A little royal town ..containing a collegiate-church or provostship. *Ibid.* 202 Oberndorf, a provostship of regular canons of the order of St. Augustine. *Ibid.* 324 Coppenberg, a noble provostship of Præmonstratenses..seated on an agreeable eminence.

'provosty. *rare.* Now only *Hist.* [a. OF. *provosté* (13th c. in Godef. *Compl.*), var. of *prevosté*, mod.F. *prévôté*: = med.L. *præpositātus*; also repr. OF. *provostie* (15th c. in Godef.), MLG. *prōvestīe*, MG. *probistîe*, G. *prostei, propstei*, Du. *proosdij*: see -Y.]

= PROVOSTSHIP, in various senses; *esp.* (= F. *prévôté*) the jurisdiction of the *prévôt de Paris*, the supreme officer of the Châtelet, and that of the *prévôt de l'Île de France*, the chief officer who had charge of the safety of the highways of Paris and its environs.

c **1483** CAXTON *Dialogues* 30 Benet the chorle Is lieutenant Of the baylly of amyas And of the prouostye [*de la prevostie*]. **1483** —— *Gold. Leg.* 289 b/2 Phelyp hadde taken of the Senate the prouostye of Allexandrye. **1494** FABYAN *Chron.* VII. 375 The prouosty, or chief rule or offyce, was in yᵉ handes of the cytezeyns of Parys. **1670** COTTON *Espernon* I. II. 68 One Nicholas Poulin, a Lieutenant in the Provosty of the Isle of France. **1849** SCHOBERL tr. *Hugo's Hunchback* 154 Robert d'Estouteville, knight..keeper of the provosty of Paris [*garde de la prévôté de Paris*].

†**provulgate**, *v. Obs. rare.* [f. late L. *provulgāt-*, ppl. stem of *provulg-āre*: see PROVULGE.] *trans.* To make public, publish, promulgate; to disseminate, propagate.

a **1540** BARNES *Wks.* (1573) 331/2 These decrees were prouulgated ouer all Italy. **1586** FERNE *Blaz. Gentrie* II. 40 Lyons, Leopards, Beares, Wolfes, Hyens, and such lyke.. afterward being prouulgated into these parts of Europe.

†**provul'gation.** *Obs. rare*[−1]. [n. of action f. L. *provulgāre*: see next and -ATION.] Publication, promulgation.

1566 PAINTER *Pal. Pleas.* I. Ded. A ij b, Some which I deemed most worthy the prouulgation in our natiue tongue.

†**pro'vulge**, *v. Obs. rare.* [ad. late L. *provulgāre* to make known publicly, f. *prō*, PRO-[1] 1 a + *vulgāre* to publish, f. *vulg-us* the people. Cf. obs. F. *provulguer* (16th c. in Godef.).] *trans.* To make publicly known, proclaim; = PROMULGE.

1512 *Act 4 Hen. VIII*, c. 4 §1 Any outlawrie..had or provulged ageynst any person. **1532–3** *Act 24 Hen. VIII*, c. 12 §12 Any excommengement..or any other censures..to be fulminate, prouulged, declared, or put in execucion.

provysowe, obs. f. PROVISO.

prow (praʊ), *sb.*[1] Now chiefly *literary*. Forms: 6 proo, 7 proe, pro; 6–8 prowe, 7 prou, -e, 7– prow. [a. F. *proue* (in 14th c. *proe, proue*), or ad. the cognate *proa* (Pg., Sp., Cat., Pr., Genoese), in It. *prua*; all prob. ultimately from L. *prōra*, a. Gr. πρῷρα, earlier πρώϊρα prow. For details, and the pronunciation, see Note below.]

1. The fore-part of a boat or ship; the part immediately about the stem.

1555 EDEN *Decades* 231 They had a west and north weste wynd in the proos of theyr shyppe. **1601** HOLLAND *Pliny* I. 129 To auoid the necessitie of turning about in these seas, the ships haue prows at both ends, and are pointed each way. *Ibid.* 252 A shel-fish..fashioned with a keele like to a barge or barke, with a poupe embowed and turned vp: yea and armed as it were in the proe with a three-forked pike. **1610** —— *Camden's Brit.* I. 244 He used the Helme of a Ship for a Seale..like as Pompeie [had] the Stemme or Pro thereof in his coines. **1697** DRYDEN *Æneid* v. 188 The brushing oars and brazen prow [*rimes* row, below]. **1757** GRAY *Bard* 74 Youth on the prow, and Pleasure at the helm. **1830** TENNYSON *Arab. Nts.* v, The sparkling flints beneath the prow [*rimes* low, flow]. **1833** L. RITCHIE *Wand. by Loire* 27 The pointed prow and flat bottom of the boats. **1853** SIR H. DOUGLAS *Milit. Bridges* (ed. 3) 172 From this part it tapers in plan, and rises in section, to the prow and stern. **1887** BOWEN *Æneid* III. 277 Anchors are cast forthwith from the prows, sterns laid on the sand.

†**b.** Formerly sometimes applied specially to the fore gun-deck holding the bow-guns, and

hence to a discharge of shot from these. Cf. CHASE *sb.*[1] 6. *Obs.*

1600 HAKLUYT *Voy.* III. 566 They..came vpon our quarter star-boord: and giuing vs fiue cast pieces out of her prowe, they sought to lay vs aboord. **1627** CAPT. SMITH *Seaman's Gram.* ii. 10 The Prow is the Decke abaft the Fore-castle, whereon lyeth the Prow peeces. *Ibid.* xiii. 60 Giue him..your prow and broad side as before. **1704** J. HARRIS *Lex. Techn.* I, *Prow* of a Ship, is that part of her Fore-castle which is aloft, and not in the Hold; and is properly that which is between the Chase and the Loofe.

†**c.** Phr. ***prow and poop***, the whole ship; *fig.* the whole. *Obs.*

1561 T. NORTON *Calvin's Inst.* IV. xvii. (1634) 691 As if the enclosing of Christ under bread were (as the proverbe is) the prowe and poupe of godlinesse. *a* **1632** in Lithgow *Trav.* VII. 328 Both Proue and puppe, do answere to the Helme.

2. A point or pointed part projecting in front, like the prow of a ship; *spec.* in *Zool.* = PRORA 2.

1656 BLOUNT *Glossogr.*, *Prow*,..Also a point advancing it self out of a building, as the Prow out of a Ship. **1812–16** PLAYFAIR *Nat. Phil.* (1819) I. 209 If a prow, in the form of a wedge, be drawn through a fluid [etc.]. **1819** SHELLEY *Prometh. Unb.* IV. i. 232 A guiding power directs the chariot's prow Over its wheelèd clouds. **1887** SOLLAS in *Encycl. Brit.* XXII. 417/2 (*Sponges*) The back of the 'C' [-shaped spicule] is the *keel* or *tropis*; the points are the *prows* or *proræ*.

3. *transf.* A ship. *poet.* (Cf. KEEL *sb.*[1] 2.)

1738 GRAY *Propertius* iii. 51 Prows, that late in fierce Encounter mett. **1819** BYRON *Juan* II. clxxiv, At last her father's prows put out to sea.

4. *attrib.* and *Comb.*, as ***prow gun, ornament, side***; **prow-decked** *a.*, having an ornamental prow; **prow-shaped** *a.*, of the shape of a ship's prow, i.e. projecting in a point in front.

1615 CHAPMAN *Odyss.* IX. 131 Nor place the neighbour Cyclops their delights, In braue Vermilion *prow-deckt ships. **1790** BEATSON *Nav. & Mil. Mem.* II. 41 The grabs attacked at a distance with their *prow-guns. **1838** *Civil Eng. & Arch. Jrnl.* I. 394/2 High pressure steam, length of stroke, and *prow-shaped bows..are not all necessary for speed. **1899** *Allbutt's Syst. Med.* VIII. 200 The small head, with narrow forehead presenting marked interfrontal ridge—the prow-shaped cranium—indicates the worst pathological type. **1653** H. COGAN tr. *Pinto's Trav.* lxvi. 267 Rocks and shelves of sand, which were on the *Prow side.

Hence **prowed** (praʊd) *a.*, having a prow.

1884 A. J. EVANS in *Archæologia* XLIX. 46 A wooden bridge..supported on pillars..prowed so as to look like a row of vessels breasting the current. **1895** K. MEYER *Voy. Bran* I. 18 The prowed skiff in which Bran is.

[*Note.* The loss of the *r* of L. *prōra* in the Romanic *proa* is unusual, but is said to be exemplified in Genoese, which may be the source of the other Mediterranean forms, and of It. *prua* and F. *proue*. But F. *proue* might also represent a Romanic **prōda* (or **prōta*) preserved in It. *proda* prow, brink, which may have arisen from L. *prōra* by dissimilation, *r* becoming *d* after *r* preceding, as in It. *rado* = L. *rārus* rare. But some would refer It. *proda* to OHG. *prort, prot* (= OLG. *brood*) prow, brink. See Diez s.v. *prua*, Körting s.v. *prora*, and articles there referred to.

The earlier Eng. spellings *proo, pro, proe* point to the pronunciation (pro:); but *proo* may also have meant (pru:) = F. *proue*. *Prow, prowe*, are ambiguous: Dryden and Scott rime *prow* with *below, glow*; Shelley with *flow*, but also with *now*; Tennyson in 1830 with *low, flow*, but later with *brow* and *now*. Walker 1791 cites 5 orthoepists for each pronunciation. Smart 1836 gives only (pro:). It is possible that there were in 16th c. two forms (pro:) and (pru:), corresp. to Romanic *proa*, F. *proe*, and to F. *proue* respectively, the form (pru:) being in 18th c. diphthongized to (praʊ); but this pronunciation may also have arisen in the 18th c., as in *prowl*, merely from the ambiguity of the spelling *ow*.]

†**prow** (pru:), *sb.*[2] *Obs.* Forms: 3–4 pru, pruu, prw, 3–5 prou, 4–6 prowe, 4–7 prow, (5 prowȝ). See also PREW. [ME. *pru, prou*, a. OF. *pru, prou* (earlier *prod, prot, prut, prout*) profit, advantage (= It. *prode*, Sp., Pg. *pro*), subst. use of OF. *pru, prou* (*prod, prud*), It. *prode*, adj.: see next. Cf. IMPROVE *v.*[2]] Advantage, profit, benefit, weal, good.

c **1290** *Beket* 356 in *S. Eng. Leg.* I. 116 Þe bischopriches fullen boþe, In-to þe kingus hond, For-to onder-fonge al þe prov þare-of. *Ibid.* (Percy Soc.) 302 That he myȝte the more prou afonge. **1303** R. BRUNNE *Handl. Synne* 10717 As weyl haue þe quyke, þe pru, As þe dede. *c* **1330** —— *Chron.* (1810) 278 His barons did also for þe comon prow. **13..** *Cursor M.* 29470 (Cott.) Þe neuent es for þin aun pruu [*C. Galba* prow]. *c* **1386** CHAUCER *Nun's Pr. T.* 130, I shal my self to herbes techen yow That shul been for youre hele and for youre prow. *c* **1470** HARDING *Chron.* XCVIII. ix, It maye bee for his prowe, To thynke on it. **1535** STEWART *Cron. Scot.* (Rolls) II. 144 Dissaitfullie..he gart him trow, That he wrocht ay for his plesour and prow. *c* **1570** *Pride & Lowl.* (1841) 34 Syr ..gladlye would I doon ye prowe, If in this matter I had halfe the skyll.

prow (praʊ, *bef.* 1600 pru:), *a. arch.* [ME. a. OF. *prou* adj. (earlier *prod, pro, prud, pru*, nom. *proz, prus*), in later OF. *preu*, mod.F. *preux* = It. *prode*, Pr. *proz, pro*:—late L. **prōdis*, neut. *prōde* (in Itala), = the first element in L. *prōd-esse* to be useful or profitable, to do good: see PROUD, also the ME. forms PREU, *pru, prew, preus*, corresp. to later OF.] Good, worthy, valiant, brave, gallant.

(A doublet of the earlier *prút, prúd*, PROUD, introduced anew in the French sense, after *proud* was specialized in its English sense = *superbus*. App. obsolete from 16th c. (cf. PREU), but the superlative *prowest* was much affected by Spenser, whence it has come down in later poets. Some modern writers have also revived the positive *prow*.)

c **1400** tr. *Secreta Secret., Gov. Lordsh.* 115 He þat hauys a long nose rechinge to þe mouth, ys prow and hardy. *a* **1555** PHILPOT *Exam. & Writ.* (Parker Soc.) 360 Christ, our most prowest Master, keepeth silence of them. **1590** SPENSER *F.Q.* I. iv. 41 The prowest knight that ever field did fight. *Ibid.* III. iii. 28 Proofe of thy prow valiaunce Thou then shalt make. **1591** HARINGTON *Orl. Fur.* XLVI. vii, The noblest, stoutest, and the prowest knight. **1671** MILTON *P.R.* III. 342 Angelica His Daughter, sought by many Prowest Knights Both Paynim, and the Peers of Charlemane. **1818** HALLAM *Mid. Ages* (1872) I. i. II. 52 They might claim to be the prowest knights in Europe. **1851** C. L. SMITH tr. *Tasso* III. lix, A man more wise of head or prow of hand. **1869** TENNYSON *Pelleas & Ettarre* 342 From prime to vespers will I chant thy praise As prowest knight and truest lover. **1898** T. HARDY *Wessex Poems* 69 Carl Schwartzenberg was in the plot, And Blücher, prompt and prow.

†**prow**, *v. Obs. rare.* In 4 prowe, prou. [f. PROW *sb.*[2] or *a.*; possibly, 'to prow', in *him to prow, the folk to prow* = 'for advantage to him, to the people', was mistaken for a verb infinitive. Cf.

c **1330** R. BRUNNE *Chron. Wace* (Rolls) 8820 When þe kyng herde of þer vertu, þat þey myght falle þe folk to prw, He had longyng for hem to go..þe stones to Bretaigne for to brynge.]

intr. To be of advantage; to be profitable or beneficial. Const. *to* or *dative*.

c **1330** R. BRUNNE *Chron.* (1810) 298 Þat no þing suld be left, þat myght to Inglond prowe. **13..** *Cursor M.* 27127 (Cott.) And es he for a fule to trou, þat will noght do þat mai him prou.

prow, Malay boat: see PROA.

prowd(e, obs. f. PROUD.

prowdence, obs. f. PRUDENCE.

†**prower**. *Obs. rare.* Also 4 -or, -our. [ad. OF. *provere-s* nom. (13th c. in Godef.), obl. *proveur*, var. of *porveor* PURVEYOR, f. *por-, purveeir* to PURVEY.] 'Purveyor, provider of necessaries' (Skeat, *Notes to P. Pl.*).

1377 LANGL. *P. Pl.* B. XIX. 255 My prowor and my plowman, Piers shal ben on erthe [*v. rr.* prowyour, purveour; C. XXII. 260 prower, *v. rr.* prowour, prouour, puruyour]. *c* **1449** PECOCK *Repr.* IV. viii. 467 Crist which was ..oure beest prower, ordeyned al that was best for us to haue.

prowere, obs. f. PRORE, prow of a ship.

prowess (ˈpraʊɪs). Now chiefly *literary*. Forms: 3–5 prouesse, 3–7 prowesse, prowes, 4–5 pruesse, 5 prowez, -is, -ys, prouwis, prouese, -es, proes, -esce, 5–6 prosse, 5–7 proesse, 6 pruice, prowse, 6– prowess. [ME. *prowesse*, a. OF. *proec(c)e, -eisse, -oise*, in mod.F. *prouesse* = Prov., Sp. *proeza*, Cat. *proesa*, It. *prodezza*: f. *pro, prou*, PROW *a.* and -ESS[2]. (In 15–17th c. often a monosyllable.)]

1. Valour, bravery, gallantry, martial daring; manly courage, active fortitude.

c **1290** *S. Eng. Leg.* I. 397/163 More prouesse ne miȝte be þan was of þis kniȝte. **1297** R. GLOUC. (Rolls) 279 Vor þe noble kinne þat þou art of & vor þi prowesse iwis. *c* **1330** R. BRUNNE *Chron.* (1810) 118 Of pruesse had he fame. **1375** BARBOUR *Bruce* IX. 503 Schir yngerame vmphrevell, that ves Renownit of so hye prowes. **1422** tr. *Secreta Secret., Priv. Priv.* 154 That euery man..sholde haue hope to come to glorie of a Prynce or of an empyre, by prosse and vasselage. **1436** *Pol. Poems* (Rolls) II. 200 Science, proesce, devocion, equyté, Of moste estate his magnanimité. *c* **1470** *Gol. & Gaw.* 1207, I aught as prynce him to prise for his prouese. *c* **1489** CAXTON *Blanchardyn* xxix. 109 Thourgh þ[e]..hyghe proesse of Blanchardyn. *a* **1533** LD. BERNERS *Huon* lv. 188 His hye prowes was suche that no paynym durst abyde him. *Ibid.* lix. 207 By the prowess of .xiiii. persons. **1567** DRANT *Horace, Epist.* II. ii. H ij, Prease on with luckie foote to where thy pruice calleth the. **1586** WARNER *Alb. Eng.* I. v. (1612) 16 Philoctes trustlesse of his prowse. **1603** OWEN *Pembrokeshire* (1892) 209 A mightye, and valiant gentleman of no small power or prowes. **1610** HOLLAND *Camden's Brit.* (1637) 7 Whom they matched every way in manhood and proesse. **1667** MILTON *P.L.* XI. 789 First seen in acts of prowess eminent And great exploits. **1788** GIBBON *Decl. & F.* xli. (1869) II. 548 Their prowess was always conspicuous in single combats. **1809** WELLINGTON in Gurw. *Desp.* (1837) IV. 538 So glorious a display of the valor and prowess of his troops. **1877** RUSKIN *Arrows of Chace* (1880) II. 216 Military distinction is no more possible by prowess.

b. An act of bravery; a valiant deed; a daring feat or exploit. (Chiefly in *pl.* = deeds of valour.)

1340 *Ayenb.* 59 Þe zenne of þan þet zuo bleþeliche recordeþ hare dedes and hare prowesses. **1422** tr. *Secreta Secret., Priv. Priv.* 205 Vayne glory of this forsayde proesses. **1553** T. WILSON *Rhet.* (1580) 13 By these men, worthie prowesses haue been dooen. **1604** E. G[RIMSTONE] *D'Acosta's Hist. Indies* V. ix. 352 To do those actes and prowesses which shall be spoken of. **1843** CARLYLE *Past & Pr.* III. i, If he speaks of his excellencies and prowesses.

†**2.** Moral goodness or excellence; virtue. *Obs.*

c **1374** CHAUCER *Boeth.* IV. pr. vi. (E.E.T.S.) 138 What oþer þing semeþ hele of corages but bounte and prowesse. *c* **1386** —— *Wife's T.* 273 (Ellesm.) For god of his goodnesse [6 *texts* prowesse, prouesse] Wole that of hym we clayme oure gentillesse.

†**prowessed** (ˈpraʊɪst), *a. Obs. rare.* [f. prec. + *-d* = -ED[2], app. through a misunderstanding of the superl. *prowest* (see PROW *a.*) in Spenser and Milton.] Endowed with prowess; valiant.

1717 E. FENTON *Odyss.* XI. Poems 111 Feminine Deceit, To them more fatal than the prowess'd Foe. **1726** POPE *Odyss.* XVIII. 139 Our freedom to thy prowess'd arm we owe.

ˈ**prowessful**, *a. rare.* [f. PROWESS (in 16–17th c. *prow's, prowse*) + -FUL.] Full of prowess; valorous, valiant.

1598 SYLVESTER *Du Bartas* II. ii. II. *Babylon* Argt. 3 Nimrod vsurps: his prow's-full Policy, To gain himselfe the Goal of Soveraignty. **1608** *Ibid.* II. iv. IV. *Decay* 839 But, the brave Prince cleaves quicker then the rest His slender Firr-poles, as more prow's-full prest. **1610** GUILLIM *Heraldry* I. i. (1660) 3 Worthy prowesfull exploits performed in Martiall services. **1899** J. H. METCALFE *Earldom Wiltes* 9 The Scropes have been no less distinguished and prowessfull in the battle-field.

pro-West, -Western: see PRO-[1] 5 a.

prowl (praʊl), *v.* Forms: α. 4–6 prolle, (5 pralle), 6–8 proll, prole, 7 prool(e. β. 6–7 proule, prowle, 7–8 proul, 7– prowl. [ME. *proll-en*, origin unknown: there is app. no related word outside English. The change to *proul, prowl*, was at first merely one of spelling (cf. BOWL *sb.*[1]), but has since *c* 1750 perverted the pronunciation from (pro:l, proʊl) to (praʊl).]

1. a. *intr.* Originally, To go or move about, esp. in search of or looking for something; hence, to go, rove, roam, or wander about, in search of what can be found, esp. of plunder or prey, or with predatory intent. Orig. chiefly of persons; in mod. use (cf. PROWLING *ppl. a.*, quot. 1667), characteristically of wild beasts, or persons acting like them.

α. *c* **1386** CHAUCER *Can. Yeom. Prol. & T.* 859 Though ye prolle ay ye shul it neuere fynde Ye been as boold as is Bayard the blynde That blondreth forth. *c* **1440** *Promp. Parv.* 415/1 Prollyn, as ratchys, *scrutor*. **1530** PALSGR. 667/2, I prolle, I go here and there to seke a thyng, *je tracasse*... The felowe prolleth aboute, but it cometh nat to effecte. **1579** SPENSER *Sheph. Cal.* Sept. 160 [Wolves] Priuely prolling two and froe. **1608** TOPSELL *Serpents* (1658) 655 Some do prole after Wasps, and kill them. **1687** DRYDEN *Hind & P.* III. 413 You..range around the realm without controll Among my sons, for Proselytes to prole. **1735** SOMERVILLE *Chase* I. 309 [Robbers] Then proling far and near, whate'er they seize Becomes their Prey.

β. **1538** [see PROWLING *vbl. sb.* β]. **1563** B. GOOGE *Eglogs* viii. (Arb.) 68 Whose gredy Pawes, do neuer ceas, in synfull fluds to prowle [*rime* soule]. **1697** DRYDEN *Virg. Georg.* III. 802 The nightly Wolf, that round th' Enclosure proul'd To leap the Fence; now plots not on the Fold. **1778** MME. D'ARBLAY *Diary* Aug., I then prowled about to choose some book. **1791** *Ibid.* 1 Aug., We determined..to prowl to the churchyard, and read the tombstone inscriptions. *c* **1850** NEALE *Hymn, 'Christian, dost thou see them'* i, How the troops of Midian Prowl and prowl around. **1866** ALGER *Solit. Nat. & Man* I. 20 The leopard prowls through the jungle alone. **1888** BESANT *Inner House* v, We have prowled about the old building.

†**b.** To search, seek *for* something (without moving about). *Obs. rare.*

c **1460** J. RUSSELL *Bk. Nurture* 280 Youre hed ne bak ye claw, a fleigh as þaughe ye sought, ne youre heere ye stryke, ne pyke, to pralle for a flesche mought. **1687** *New Atlantis* III. 520 Thoughtful and dull..Stood Bavius, proling for his barren Muse.

†**c.** *fig.* To seek for gain or advantage in a mean, grasping, or underhand way; to 'cadge'. *Obs.*

α. **1530** [see PROWLING *vbl. sb.* α]. **1550** CROWLEY *Waie to Wealth* Wks. (1872) 145 Purchaisinge and prollynge for benefices. **1563–87** FOXE *A. & M.* (1596) 261/1 An other pretie practise of the pope to proll for monie, was this. **1669** MARVELL *Corr.* Wks. (Grosart) II. 272 A Corporation of your dignity dos not proll for advantage upon gentlemen your neighbours.

β. **1550** BALE *Eng. Votaries* II. Nij, This legate..went banketynge and prowlynge from bishope to bishope. **1603** H. CROSSE *Vertues Commw.* (1878) 129 It is not equall..for a man to liue prowling and shifting by the labours of other men.

†**2. a.** *trans.* To obtain (something) by stealth, cheating, or petty theft; to get in a clandestine way; to pilfer, to filch. *Obs.*

1530 *Proper Dialogue* in *Rede me*, etc. (Arb.) 137 What soeuer we get with sweate and labour That prolle they awaye with their prayour. **1592** WARNER *Alb. Eng.* IX. xlvii. (1612) 220 For from my fault could not, as chanst, the Somner prole a fee. **1622** MABBE tr. *Aleman's Guzman d'Alf.* II. 132 If we found any breach in any wall of a house, we would prie what we could proule from thence. *a* **1677** BARROW *Pope's Suprem.* Wks. 1687 I. 183 By how many tricks did he proll money from all parts of Christendom?

b. *intr.* To plunder, steal, pilfer. *Obs.*

1571 CAMPION *Hist. Irel.* II. v. (1633) 84 Surfeited with flesh and acquauitae all the Lent long, prolled and pilled insatiably without neede. **1573** TUSSER *Husb.* (1878) 143 The champion robbeth by night, And prowleth and filcheth by day. **1658** GURNALL *Chr. in Arm.* II. 4 That he, who hath no hope of another world, be made to shark and prole to get some of this.

c. *trans.* To plunder, rob (a person). *Obs.*

1603 FLORIO *Montaigne* 503, I overwhelme and contemne it then in great, by retayle it spoyles and proules me. **1672** MARVELL *Reh. Transp.* I. 111 Were it not for prolling or molesting the People, his Majesty would give Mr. Bayes the Patent for it.

3. To traverse (a place or region) esp. on the look out for prey; to traverse stealthily. †In quot. 1649, to steal in through (*obs.*).

a **1586** SIDNEY *Arcadia* II. Poems (Grosart) II. 64 He proules each place, still in new colours deckt, Sucking one's ill, another to infect. **1649** G. DANIEL *Trinarch., Hen. V* cclxxv, The invading Brine Prolls everie Seame. **1750** GRAY *Long Story* 45 Who prowl'd the country far and near. **1879** MISS YONGE *Cameos* Ser. IV. xx. 213 He prowled the streets in disguise.

b. *Criminals' slang* (in U.S.). To examine, search, or inspect (a place or person), esp. before committing a robbery; to 'case'; to rob.

1914 JACKSON & HELLYER *Vocab. Criminal Slang* 67 *Prowl*, noun... An expeditionary investigation; a survey in transit; a search of the person or of a place in the sense of '*frisk*'; a burglary; a sneak; a saunter. Also used as a verb in the same senses. **1926** J. BLACK *You can't Win* xi. 136 I'd rather 'prowl' one of them than any business man. *Ibid.* xx. 318 He magnanimously suggested that I 'prowl the joint' he lived in. **1938** in *Amer. Speech* XIII. 158/1 Store is prowled. **1943** R. CHANDLER *Lady in Lake* xii. 71, I went back to the kitchen and prowled the open shelves above and behind the sink. **1977** 'M. INNES' *Honeybath's Haven* xv. 137 Some sort of sneak-thief had conceivably been prowling the dead man's property.

prowl (praʊl), *sb.* [f. prec. vb.] **a.** An act or the action of prowling; roaming or roving about, esp. in search of plunder or prey. ***on*** or ***upon the prowl***, prowling about; now freq. in search of an amorous partner.

1803 *Sporting Mag.* XXII. 54 A poor miserable thief had been all night upon the prowl. **1836** W. IRVING *Astoria* II. xxviii. 118 The Crow Indians.. are apt to be continually on the prowl about the skirts of the mountains. **1876** 'ANNIE THOMAS' *Blotted out* iii. 31 Let us clear off this business as soon as we can, and then go out for a prowl. **1895** *19th Cent.* Sept. 482 Through all the intricacies of their hunting prowl we followed them. **1922** JOYCE *Ulysses* 600 A figure of middle height on the prowl, evidently, under the arches saluted again, calling: *Night!* **1946** *Sun* (Baltimore) 3 July 4/5 That big cat.. is reputedly on the prowl again. **1959** W. BROWN *Cry Kill* iii. 31 Not a beauty like Lola Stuart, but good enough to catch the eye of any guy on the prowl. **1966** *N.Y. Times Bk. Rev.* 27 Mar. 35/1 Including his memorable encounters with an emancipated American college girl on the prowl. **1972** F. WARNER *Lying Figures* II. 9 Out on the prowl tonight, lover-boy? **1973** 'E. PETERS' *City of Gold & Shadows* iii. 45 A normal minor wolf on the prowl, with.. an eye cocked for congenial company.

b. *Comb.*, as **prowl car** orig. *U.S.*, a police patrol car having a radio link with headquarters; **prowl dog** = *guard dog* s.v. GUARD *sb.* 18.

1937 *Sun* (Baltimore) 6 Sept. 2/7 The man.. climbed into the rear seat of our prowl car. **1953** H. CLEVELY *Public Enemy* xxix. 229 There's a prowl car outside... You were followed here. **1963** J. JOESTEN *They call it Intelligence* IV. xix. 188 A prowl car, manned by Western police, providentially arrived on the scene. **1967** N. LUCAS *C.I.D.* xi. 169 The presence of one of the Austin vans in the area had not passed unnoticed by the alert crew of a Berkshire County Police wireless prowl car. **1971** *Islander* (Victoria, B.C.) 16 May 11/1 Meantime another prowl car pulled into the yards. **1971** *Southerly* XXXI. 71 A prowl car told us to switch our parkers on. **1974** W. GARNER *Big enough Wreath* xii. 163 We got patrols. We got prowl dogs.

prowler ('praʊlə(r)). Forms: α. 6–7 **proller**, 7–8 **proler**. β. 6– **prowler**, (6 **prouler**). [f. as prec. + -ER[1].] One who prowls; one who goes about on the look-out for what he can find or seize; one who sneaks about in search of prey or plunder; also, †one who seeks gain or advantage by any underhand or dishonourable means; a parasite, a 'sponge'; a pilferer, impostor, cheat, plunderer (*obs.*); a burglar, a sneak thief.

α. **1519** HORMAN *Vulg.* 28 b, He is a good proller for the bely. *a* **1520** *Vox Populi Vox Dei* 712 in Hazl. *E.P.P.* III. 292 Customers and comptrollers, Purvyours and prollers. **1550** LEVER *Serm.* (Arb.) 63 Couetous greedyguttes and ambicious prollers. **1632** BURTON *Anat. Mel.* II. iii. VIII. (ed. 4) 366 No sharkers, no Cunnicatchers, no prolers. **1735** SOMERVILLE *Chase* IV. 398 O'er the dank rushy Marsh The sly Goose-footed Proler [the otter] bends his Course.

β. **1557** NORTH *Gueuara's Diall Pr.* IV. vii. (1568) 125 b, Greedy gluttons, and shameles prowlers. **1670** MILTON *Hist. Eng.* III. Wks. 1851 V. 130 Suttle Prowlers, Pastors in Name, but indeed Wolves. **1791** COWPER *Iliad* xv. 712 Some prowler of the wilds. **1861** DICKENS *Tom Tiddler* i, You attract all the disreputable vagabonds and prowlers. **1912** D. LOWRIE *My Life in Prison* i. 5 Inadvertently we had left the back door open one night and a nocturnal prowler had taken advantage of it. **1926** J. BLACK *You can't Win* xix. 295 What a fox he is, to roll his money up in the curtain... What chance would a prowler have of finding his money? **1955** H. KURNITZ *Invasion of Privacy* (1956) xv. 99 It was Zorn's first ride in a police car. The radio chattered endlessly.. of prowlers, burglars, rapists. **1976** *Flintshire Leader* 10 Dec. 1/7 Many of them are elderly or handicapped and live in fear of prowlers, car accidents and falls on uneven pathways.

†'**prowlery.** *Obs. rare*[−1]. [f. as prec. + -ERY.] The action or practice of a prowler; a mode of plunder or dishonest gain; a swindle.

a **1670** HACKET *Abp. Williams* I. (1692) 51 Before the month of March expir'd, thirty-seven monopolies, with other sharking prouleries, were decried in one proclamation.

'**prowling,** *vbl. sb.* Forms: see PROWL *v.* [f. as prec. + -ING[1].] The action of the verb PROWL in various senses.

α. *c* **1440** *Promp. Parv.* 415/1 Prollynge, or sekynge, *perscrutacio*. **1530** PALSGR. 259/1 Prolyng for a promocyon, *ambition*. **1606** WARNER *Alb. Eng.* XIV. lxxx. 339 Seauenth Henry.. Of his Retriuers Proolings much (as well he might) repented. **1687** *New Atlantis* II. 194 Such proling is unworthy our great Name.

β. **1538** BALE *Thre Lawes* 1584 By prowlynge and lyenge ye fryers wolde all haue. **1632** SANDERSON *Serm.* 173 There would not be that insolency of Popish Recusants, that licence of Rogues and wanderers, that prouling of Officers. **1908** *Daily News* 6 July 6 All the odds and ends that he picks up on his prowlings along the coast.

'**prowling,** *ppl. a.* Forms: see PROWL *v.* [f. as prec. + -ING[2].] That prowls, in various senses.

α. **1565** DRANT *Reply to Epit. on C. Scotte by R. Shacklock*, No golden Andwerpe, no of truth they seke no gold of thyne, A cheat of thanks for popysh priests to cram their prolling pine. **1607** R. C[AREW] tr. *Estienne's World of Wonders* 137 Prolling pettifoggers. **1710** *Life of Stillingfleet* 116 The Patent 13th Jacobi to explain it, was called a Proling Patent and of no Effect in Law.

β. **1560** PILKINGTON *Expos. Aggeus* (1562) 66 The gredy carle and prowling poller, that is neuer filled. **1667** MILTON *P.L.* IV. 183 A prowling Wolfe, Whom hunger drives to seek new haunt for prey. **1860** EMERSON *Cond. Life, Behaviour* Wks. (Bohn) II. 385 There are asking eyes, asserting eyes, prowling eyes; and eyes full of fate. **1882** *Pall Mall G.* 10 July 4/1 The system of prowling hansoms may be gainful to cabdrivers, and perhaps.. convenient to the public.

Hence '**prowlingly** *adv.* (in mod. dicts.).

prown(e, obs. forms of PRUNE *sb.* and *v.*

prowor, -our, variants of PROWER *Obs.*

proword: see PRO-[1] 4 b.

†'**prowous,** *a. Obs. rare.* [f. PROW *sb.*[2] or *a.* + -OUS.] Brave, valiant: = PROW *a.*

c **1400** tr. *Secreta Secret., Gov. Lordsh.* 91 He þat berys it with hym shal be prowous and hardy. **1422** *Ibid., Priv. Priv.* 176 By Speche of the Pepille, a coward may be as Prowos as Ector of troi.

prowse, prowte, obs. f. PROWESS, PROUD.

†**prox**[1] (prɒks). *U.S. local* (*Rhode Island*). *Obs.* [abbrev. of PROXY: see quot. 1843.] (See quots., and cf. PROXY *sb.* 4.)

1698 *Rhode Island Col. Rec.* (1861) III. 333 Voted, That Capt'n Nathaniel Coddington, Capt'n Robert Carr, are appointed to open the prox votes on the day of Election. **1768** *Ibid.* VI. 551 Upon this plan.. only one prox will be printed. **1816** PICKERING *Vocab. U.S.* s.v. *Proxies*, The abbreviation *Prox* is also used in Rhode Island, for the Ticket; that is, the List of Candidates at Elections. **1843** STAPLES *Ann. Providence* 64 Such of the colony as could not attend the General Assembly had the right to send their votes for these officers by some other persons; hence the origin of the terms prox, and proxy votes, as applied to the present mode of voting for state officers in Rhode-Island.

prox.[2], abbrev. of PROXIMO.

1881 G. B. SHAW *Let.* 14 July (1965) 39 After the 1st prox. my address will be 37 Fitzroy Street W. **1935** A. P. HERBERT *What a Word!* iii. 64 There must be millions of our citizens who have not the least notion what is meant by your *inst.*, *prox.*, and *ult.* **1962** *Daily Tel.* 10 Dec. 12/7 'Inst', 'prox' and 'ult', which even today are scattered broadcast.

proxemics (prɒk'siːmɪks). *Sociol.* [f. PROX(IMITY + *-emics*; cf. EMIC *a.*] The study of the spaces that people feel it necessary to set between themselves and others as they vary in different social settings, or between different social groups or cultures; also the study of the feeling for space between people as it is manifested in aspects of culture such as the planning of houses or towns, in language, etc.

1963 E. T. HALL in *Amer. Anthropologist* LXV. 1003 Proxemics, the study of how man unconsciously structures microspace—the distance between men in the conduct of daily transactions, the organization of space in his houses and buildings, and ultimately the layout of his towns. **1969** *Guardian* 29 Sept. 7/2 Though territoriality and its effects has been studied for many years now in connection with animal life, Dr Hall is.. the first person to link the concept direct with human beings and.. has coined a purely human word for it: proxemics. **1974** *Language Sciences* Aug. 32/3 Ever since Edward Hall.. made public the results of his research on man's use of space, the interrelated observations and theories of which he calls proxemics, [etc.]. **1976** U. ECO *Theory of Semiotics* 10 *Kinesics and proxemics*: the idea that gesturing depends on cultural codes is now an acquired notion of cultural anthropology.

Hence **pro'xemic** *a.*, of, relating or pertaining to proxemics.

1963 E. T. HALL in *Amer. Anthropologist* LXV. 1003 (*title*) A system for the notation of proxemic behavior. **1965** [see KINESIC *a.*]. **1971** *Times Lit. Suppl.* 4 June 653/4 In man 'proxemic' behaviour ranges from the distance two people maintain while engaged in conversation or the way a group of people arrange themselves, to architecture and city planning. **1976** J. F. KESS *Psycholinguistics* vi. 145 A detailed notational system for proxemic behaviors along a number of dimensions.

†'**proxenete.** *Obs.* Also 7 -et. [a. F. *proxénète* (16th c. in Littré), or ad. L. *proxenēta*, ad. Gr. προξενητής a negotiator, agent, agent-n. f. προξενεῖν to be one's πρόξενος (see next), to manage for another.] One who negotiates something, esp. a marriage; an agent, go-between, match-maker.

1659 H. MORE *Immort. Soul* III. III. xiii. (1662) 203 He being the common proxenet or contractor of all natural matches and marriages betwixt forms and matter. *a* **1693** *Urquhart's Rabelais* III. xli. 341 To supply the place of a.. Proxenete or Mediator. **1813** F. DOUGLAS *Anc. & Mod. Greeks* 108 He then applies to some respectable matron.. who assumes the name and character of the ancient Proxenete.

‖**proxenus** ('prɒksɪnəs). Also in Gr. form **proxenos.** Pl. **proxeni** (-aɪ). [mod.L., a. Gr. πρόξενος, f. πρό, PRO-[2] + ξένος a guest, stranger.] In *Gr. Antiq.*, A resident citizen of a state appointed by another state to represent and protect its interests there: see quot. 1842. Hence *transf.*

1838 THIRLWALL *Greece* III. xxi. 193 Laco son of Aimnestus, was *proxenus* of Sparta. **1842** SMITH *Dict. Gr. & Rom. Antiq.* 491/1 The office of proxenus.. bears great resemblance to that of a modern consul or minister-resident. .. When a state appointed a proxenus, it either sent out one of its own citizens to reside in the other state, or it selected one of the citizens of this state, and conferred upon him the honour of proxenus. **1850** GROTE *Greece* II. lxv. VIII. 375 Nikias.., the friend and proxenus of Sparta at Athens. **1887** *Pall Mall G.* 18 Oct. 5/1 Mr. Childs.. has been to them a sort of British proxenos in Philadelphia.

proxeny ('prɒksɪnɪ). [ad. Gr. προξενία, f. πρόξενος PROXENUS: so F. *proxénie*.] The office or function of a *proxenus*; the system of *proxeni*.

1842 SMITH *Dict. Gr. & Rom. Antiq.* 491/2 Privileges.. not necessarily included in the proxeny. **1846** GROTE *Greece* II. vi. II. 518 No multiplication of proxenies (or standing tickets of hospitality) between the important cities. **1890** *Smith's Dict. Antiq.* I. 979/1 The Delphian decree.. conferring the proxeny on the Athenian priestess Chrysis.

'**proxically,** *adv. humorous nonce-wd.* [f. PROXY + -ICAL + -LY[2].] In the way of a proxy or substitute; as representing another.

1828 SOUTHEY *Lett.* (1856) IV. 113, I must thank you on my own part, as well as proxically for Mrs. S.

proximad ('prɒksɪmæd), *adv. Anat.* [f. as next + *-ad*: see DEXTRAD.] In the direction of its point of attachment: opp. to DISTAD.

1803 BARCLAY *New Anat. Nomencl.* 167 In both kinds of extremities, Proximad will signify towards the proximate aspect. **1808** —— *Muscular Motions* 395 Where the olecranon is drawn proximad upon the anconal aspect of the humerus. **1889** *Buck's Handbk. Med. Sc.* VIII. 536/2 The shoulder is proximad of the elbow, the elbow is proximad of the wrist.

proximal ('prɒksɪməl), *a.* (*sb.*) [f. L. *proxim-us* nearest + -AL[1].]

A. *adj.* **1.** †**a.** Lying very near or close *to* something: in quot. *fig. Obs.* **b.** Proximate, immediate. *rare.*

1727 *Philip Quarll* 71 Qualifications so proximal and suitable to my Inclinations. **1828** in WEBSTER. **1884** *American* VII. 233 The proximal cause of the glory.

2. a. *Anat.* Situated towards the centre of the body, or the point of origin or attachment of a limb, bone, or other structure: opp. to DISTAL.

1803 BARCLAY *New Anat. Nomencl.* 7 The first, second, and third, or what I would call the *proximal*, *medial*, and *distal* phalanxes. *Ibid.* 124 We may.. denominate the end [of a limb] which is nearest to the trunk the *Proximal* end, and that which is farthest from it the *Distal*. **1877** HUXLEY & MARTIN *Elem. Biol.* 213 A third bone.. articulates only with the carpal bones on the proximal and distal sides of it.

b. *transf.*

1882 D. HOOPER in *Standard* 10 Oct. 2/2 The drainage-pipes are.. very imperfectly.. connected at their proximal or house termination. **1886** *Pop. Sci. Monthly* XXVIII. 650 A brace or bracket made out of an unhewed piece of timber, generally the proximal portion of some big branch.

c. *Dentistry.* Of, pertaining to, or being opposing surfaces of adjacent teeth in the same arch.

1908 G. V. BLACK *Work on Operative Dentistry* II. 3 Cavities occurring in the proximal surfaces of the teeth are called proximal cavities. **1944** S. HEMLEY *Fund. Occlusion* vi. 150 The teeth in the same arch in the adult dentition are normally in proximal contact with each other on both the mesial and the distal surfaces. **1963** C. R. COWELL et al. *Inlays, Crowns, & Bridges* iv. 35 The restoration covers the incisal edge of the tooth as well as the affected proximal surface. **1975** G. T. CHARBENEAU *Princ. & Pract. Operative Dentistry* xi. 262/1 The annoyance of food impaction between such teeth with an open proximal contact will be the initial concern of the patient.

3. *Psychol.* Applied to the stimuli immediately responsible for a perception or sensation.

1935 K. KOFFKA *Princ. Gestalt Psychol.* iii. 80 The table.. can be called a stimulus for our perception of a table;.. the excitations to which the light rays coming from the table give rise are called the stimuli for our perception. Let us call the first the distant stimulus, the second the proximal stimuli. **1955** F. H. ALLPORT *Theories of Perception* v. 147 The gestaltists point out the necessary differences between the proximal stimulus-pattern and the percept,.. and attribute the 'way things look' to the organizing forces of the brain-field. **1971** *Jrnl. Gen. Psychol.* LXXXV. 3 A relation between the various aspects of perception and the proximal and distal stimuli is clearly revealed in almost all experiments.

B. as *sb.*, *ellipt.* for *proximal end* or *part.*

1886 in *Cassell's Encycl. Dict.*

Hence '**proximally** *adv.*, in a proximal position; towards or near the proximal part or end.

1880 DUNCAN in *Jrnl. Linn. Soc.* XV. 140 The second is partly hidden proximally, by the meeting of the side arm-plates. **1899** *Allbutt's Syst. Med.* VI. 581 The colour change beginning at the tips and advancing proximally.

proximate ('prɒksɪmət), *a.* [ad. late L. *proximāt-us*, pa. pple. of *proxim-āre* to draw near, approach, f. *proxim-us* nearest.]

1. a. Closely neighbouring, immediately adjacent, next, nearest (in space, serial order, quality, etc.); close, intimate (quot. 1864).

1597 [implied in PROXIMATELY 1]. **1755** JOHNSON *Pref. to Dict.* ¶48 Words are seldom exactly synonymous... It was then necessary to use the proximate word; for the deficiency of single terms can very seldom be supplied by circumlocution. **1836** *Blackw. Mag.* XXXIX. 138 Parts of the..valley are distinguished by [the name] of some proximate village. **1864** PUSEY *Lect. Daniel* i. (1876) 27 Crete, with which both Assyria and Tyre were in proximate intercourse.

b. Coming next or very near in time, closely approaching.

1845 STODDART *Gram.* in *Encycl. Metrop.* (1847) I. 61/1 A distinct form of imperative for the proximate and distant future. **1862** MERIVALE *Rom. Emp.* VII. lxiii. 197 In choosing him for their prince, the nobles..may have looked to another proximate vacancy. **1889** *Science* 4 Oct. 228 The enormous consumption of petroleum and natural gas.. raises the question as to the..proximate exhaustion of the supply.

2. Coming next (before or after) in a chain of causation, agency, reasoning, or other relation; immediate: opposed to *remote* or *ultimate*.

proximate principle, constituent, or ***element*** (*Chem.*), one of those compounds of which a more complex body is directly made up, and which are therefore first arrived at in the process of analysis: so ***proximate analysis***.

1661 GLANVILL *Van. Dogm.* xii. 114 We hastily conclude that impossible, which we see not in the proximate capacity of its Efficient. **1771** SMOLLETT *Humph. Cl.* 6 May, The proximate cause of her breach with Sir Ulic Mackilligut. **1819** CHILDREN *Chem. Anal.* 271 The proximate principles of vegetable and animal bodies. **1831** [see ANALYSIS 3]. **1857** W. A. MILLER *Elem. Chem.* III. i. 6 The separation of wheat flour into starch, sugar, gluten, ligneous fibre, and oily matter, affords an instance of proximate analysis. **1881** WESTCOTT & HORT *Grk. N.T.* Introd. §295 Readings that are explicable by the supposition of a common proximate original. **1951** CAMPBELL & GIBB *Methods of Analysis of Fuels & Oils* i. 1 The proximate analysis of coal, which is carried out on coal ground to pass a 72 B.S. sieve and air-dried, involves the direct determination of (*a*) moisture, (*b*) volatile matter, and (*c*) ash, the remainder, the so-called 'fixed carbon', being obtained by difference. **1971** M. F. MALLETTE et al. *Introd. Biochem.* ix. 314 The crude lipid of the proximate analysis found on..certain food labels refers to the nonvolatile material derived by weighing the residue after evaporation of the extraction solvent.

3. Nearly accurate or correct; approximate.

1796 in Morse *Amer. Geog.* I. 667 The proximate breadth behind the toes. **1863** KINGLAKE *Crimea* I. xiv. 281 In searching for a proximate notion of the extent of the carnage. **1863, 1902** [implied in PROXIMATELY 3].

†**proximate**, *v. Obs. rare*⁻⁰. [f. L. *proximāre*: see prec. and -ATE³.] (See quot.)

1623 COCKERAM, *Proximate*, to aproach or draw neere.

'**proximately**, *adv.* [f. PROXIMATE *a.* + -LY².]

1. In an immediately adjacent situation (in space, serial order, etc.); next; closely.

1597 A. M. tr. *Guillemeau's Fr. Chirurg.* 32b/2 On that parte which nexte and proximately thervnto is situated. **1822** T. TAYLOR *Apuleius* 283, I manifestly drew near..and proximately adored them.

2. In the way of immediate agency, etc.; by direct relation; as the next (preceding or following) term in a series of causes or the like; immediately: opposed to *remotely* or *ultimately*.

1675 BAXTER *Cath. Theol.* II. v. 105 Was it not proximately in my nearer Parents? **1691** —— *Nat. Ch.* i. 2 Tho' it meant Christ remotely and eminently, it meant his Successors proximately. **1745** WESLEY *Answ. Ch.* 18 Faith..is Proximately necessary thereto; Repentance, Remotely. **1878** GLADSTONE in *19th Cent.* Mar. 594 Where our partners ..are both more proximately and more deeply concerned than ourselves.

3. With approach to accuracy; approximately.

1863 FAWCETT *Pol. Econ.* III. 361 This..may proximately be regarded as the amount of gold which England annually requires to maintain her metallic currency. **1902** J. H. ROSE *Napoleon I*, I. xii. 297 The same remark is proximately true of the literary life of the First Empire.

'**proximateness.** [f. as prec. + -NESS.] The fact of being proximate; nearness in position.

1881 WESTCOTT & HORT *Grk. N.T.* II. 217 The question of its remoteness or proximateness to the two extant MSS. remains undecided.

†'**proxime, proxim,** *a. Obs.* [ad. L. *proxim-us* nearest, superl. adj. f. *prope* near.]

1. Next in position, adjacent: = PROXIMATE *a.* 1.

1651 [impl. in PROXIMELY]. **1661** GLANVILL *Van. Dogm.* xx. 200 The agitated parts of the Brain begetting a motion in the proxime Æther. **1832** W. STEPHENSON *Gateshead Poems* 65 They..Would sit proxime and snatch a stolen kiss.

2. Next in causation, reasoning, etc.: = PROXIMATE *a.* 2.

1662 HIBBERT *Body Div.* I. 264 The punishment it self which is the remote term and the obligation to it, which is the proxime term of pardon. **1693** J. BEAUMONT *On Burnet's Th. Earth* I. 46 We must not look after proxim Causes in Nature for it. **1725** WATTS *Logic* III. i. § 1 The three terms are called the remote matter of a syllogism; and the three propositions the proxime or immediate matter of it.

Hence †'**proximely** *adv. Obs.* = PROXIMATELY.

1651 BIGGS *New Disp.* ¶295 Although simility doth proximely include familiarity.

‖**proxime accessit** ('prɒksɪmiː æk'sɛsɪt). [Lat. phr. = 'he (or she) has come very near (or next).'] A phrase indicating that the person in question has obtained the next place in merit to the actual winner of a prize, scholarship, etc.; hence as *sb.* applied to the person himself, or his position. Also *colloq.* abbreviated *proxime*.

1878 LOCKHART *Mine is Thine* I. xi. 224, I..was *proxime accessit* for the Chancellor's medal at Cambridge. **1882** SIR F. LEIGHTON in *Standard* 11 Dec. 3/2 They had..reserved an honourable mention, as *proxime accessit*. **1896** J. S. COTTON in *Academy* 13 June 488/3 He won the Ireland in his second year, though for the Hertford and the Craven he came out only as proxime.

†**proximi'ority.** *Obs. nonce-wd.* [irreg. f. L. *proxim-us* (see PROXIME *a.*) + L. *-ior*, suffix of compar. degree + -ITY. (The correct formation f. L. compar. *propior* nearer, would be **propiority*.)] The fact of being nearer; greater proximity.

1720 STRYPE *Stow's Surv.* I. I. vi. 32/1 If to the Proximiority which the Moon has to the Earth, by moving in her Eclipsis, there be added that Proximiority which she hath in her Eccentrick (or opposite Angles).

proximity (prɒk'sɪmɪtɪ). [a. F. *proximité* (14th c. in Hatz.-Darm.), ad. L. *proximitāt-em* nearness (etymologically, state of being nearest, 'nextness'), f. *proxim-us* nearest: see PROXIME.]

1. The fact, condition, or position of being near or close by; nearness, neighbourhood: **a.** in space.

1579 FENTON *Guicciard.* I. (1599) 16 The proximitie and neighbourhood of Myllan with France. **1682** SIR T. BROWNE *Chr. Mor.* III. §9 Tempt not Contagion by proximity, and hazard not thy self in the shadow of Corruption. **1794** G. ADAMS *Nat. & Exp. Philos.* III. xxv. 67 The effect of the proximity was a strong adhesion of the bodies. **1845** MCCULLOCH *Taxation* I. iii. (1852) 101 Our proximity to Ireland. **1872** JENKINSON *Guide Eng. Lakes* (1879) 286 Owing to the close proximity to the sea.

b. in abstract relations, as kinship (the earliest use: usually in phr. ***proximity of blood***); affinity of nature, nearness in time, etc.

1480 CAXTON *Ovid's Met.* XIII. ii, By reson of proxymyte I oughte haue them, syth thᵗ cometh none nerrer heyre than I am. **1521** LD. DACRE in Ellis *Orig. Lett.* Ser. II. I. 283 Bi reason of the nerenes and proximitie of blood. **1603** FLORIO *Montaigne* II. xii. (1632) 327 Marriages in proximity of blood are amongst us forbidden. **1762** WARBURTON *Doctr. Grace* Pref., A dark conceit and a dull one have a great proximity in modern wit. **1765** BLACKSTONE *Comm.* I. iii. 201 Nor is it to this day decided..whether the order of the stocks, or the proximity of degree, shall take place. **1876** GLADSTONE *Homeric Synchr.* 69 The inferences..are in favour of the Poet's proximity in time to the War of Troy.

2. *attrib.* **proximity fuse**, a detonator in a missile that employs radar to operate it automatically when within a predetermined distance of a target; so **proximity-fused** *a.*; **proximity talks**, diplomatic discussions or negotiations in which opposing parties do not meet but are in close proximity to each other and talk through intermediaries.

1945 *Sci. News Let.* 6 Oct. 214/1 The *proximity fuze, a tiny radio set device in the nose of the projectile, is rated as the U.S.A. No. 2 secret weapon. **1956** A. H. COMPTON *Atomic Quest* 53 Applications of radar in the form of the 'proximity fuse' were critically important in bringing victory [in World War II]. **1972** *Guardian* 11 Jan. 11/2 In the Chinese campaign in Hongkong..the guerrillas eventually produced bombs equipped with photo cells, magnetic and proximity fuses, and vibration detectors that would set off the charge if you so much as looked at it. **1978** R. V. JONES *Most Secret War* xliv. 427 The new proximity-fused shells.., although originally a British invention, had been developed and engineered in America. **1975** *Economist* 26 Apr. 15/1 '*Proximity' talks, which means that the intermediary would have to shuttle a shorter distance, between Israeli and Egyptian teams sitting in next-door rooms. **1986** *Christian Science Monitor* 23 June 15/1 Pakistan,..a key party in the continuing United Nations-sponsored 'proximity' talks in Geneva,..wants Soviet troops out of Afghanistan as soon as possible.

Hence **pro'ximitive** *a.* [irreg., on false analogy], of, belonging to, or arising from proximity.

1888 'H. S. MERRIMAN' *Phantom Future* II. vi. 85 To get farther from a proximitive influence which was becoming too strong for her.

‖**proximo** ('prɒksɪməʊ). [L. *proximō* (sc. *mense*) 'in the next month'.] In or of next month. (Following the ordinal numeral denoting the day.) Abbreviated *prox*.

1855 *N. & Q.* ser. I. I. 10 Of the common phrases *ultimo*, *instant*, and *proximo*. **1864** WEBSTER s.v., On the 3d proximo. **1885** *Times* (weekly ed.) 18 Dec. 4/4 About the 1st proximo.

proximocephalic (ˌprɒksɪməʊsɪ'fælɪk), *a. Anat.* [f. *proximo-*, taken as combining form of L. *proximus* nearest + Gr. κεφαλή head + -IC: cf. *cephalic*.] *prop.* Nearest or next to the head.

1889 *Buck's Handbk. Med. Sc.* VIII. 536/2 In numbering the individual elements [the carpal bones] the first is the most proximo-cephalic, that is the scaphoid.

†'**proximous,** *a. Obs. rare*⁻¹. [f. L. *proximus* (see PROXIME *a.*) + -OUS.] = PROXIMATE *a.* 2.

1768–74 TUCKER *Lt. Nat.* (1834) II. 390 This righteousness then is the proximous cause operating to salvation.

proxy ('prɒksɪ), *sb.* Forms: 5 **procusie, prokecye,** 6 **prockesy;** 5 **proccy, proxci,** 6–7 **proxi, -ie, -ye,** (6 **proxe,** 7 **procsey**), 6– **proxy.** [= *proc'cy*, contracted from PROCURACY, as *Proctor* from *Procurator*.]

I. 1. The agency of one who acts by appointment instead of another; the action of a substitute or deputy: = PROCURACY 1, PROCURATION 2.

Chiefly in phr. ***by proxy***, by the agency of another; by or through a substitute; not in person.

c **1440** *Promp. Parv.* 414/2 Prokecye, *procuracia*. **1530** PALSGR. 258/2 Prockesy, *procuration*. *a* **1548** HALL *Chron., Hen. VI* 146b, [They] by proxie affied the young Lady. **1628** WITHER *Brit. Rememb.* 234 The voice by Proxi hold I not the least. **1647** N. BACON *Disc. Govt. Eng.* I. lxvi. (1739) 155 They..appeared either personally or by proxy. **1762–71** H. WALPOLE *Vertue's Anecd. Paint.* (1786) III. 193 Not content to acquire glory by proxy. **1850** HT. MARTINEAU *Hist. Peace* II. IV. xiii. 174 The marriage had taken place by proxy. **1857** TOULMIN SMITH *Parish* 170 Which latter may even vote by proxy.

2. †**a.** A document empowering a person to represent and act for another; a letter of attorney: = PROCURACY 2, PROCURATION 2b. *Obs.* exc. as in b.

c **1460** *Oseney Reg.* 149 By A procuratour..in whos procusies whas i-conteyned that [etc.]. *c* **1475** *Harl. Contin. Higden* (Rolls) VIII. 501 This proccy redde and expressede, syr Iohn Busche, speker..rehersede þese wordes. **1484** *Indenture* in G. T. Clark *Cartæ Glamorgan* (1893) IV. 396 A proxci ofe theire fulle auctorite commyttede to the same Richarde. **1561** *Nottingham Rec.* IV. 126 A sufficient proxye or letter of atturney. **1726** AYLIFFE *Parergon* 421 The Warrant and Authority..which we in English call a Proxy.

b. *spec.* A writing authorizing a person to vote instead of another, at an election, a meeting of shareholders, etc., or as formerly in the House of Lords; hence, a vote so given. (Cf. also 4.)

1587 HARRISON *England* II. viii. (1877) I. 175 The consent of this [upper] house is giuen by each man seuerallie, first for himselfe..then..for so manie as he hath letters and proxies directed vnto him. **1642** CHAS. I *Answ. to 19 Propos. both Ho. Parl.* 25 They shall not be admitted to sit in the House of Peers, but onely to give their Proxies to such Protestant Lords as they shall chuse. **1648** *Art. Peace* xi. in *Milton's Wks.* (1851) IV. 517 That no Nobleman or Peer of this Realm..shall be hereafter capable of more Proxies then two, and that blank Proxies shall be hereafter totally disallowed. **1808** *Hansard's Parl. Debates* X. 1053 The house then divided on lord Arden's motion: Contents 52, Proxies 32 —84; Non-contents 45, Proxies 39—84. The numbers.. being equal, the non-contents, according to the usage of the house, carried it. **1856** EMERSON *Eng. Traits, Aristocr.* Wks. (Bohn) II. 82 Has not the Duke of Wellington at this moment..the proxies of fifty peers in his pocket? **1868** *Jrnls. Ho. Lords* 31 Mar. 99/2 Standing Order xxxii *a*. Ordered, That the Practice of calling for Proxies on a Division shall be discontinued.

1832 LEWIS *Use & Ab. Pol. Terms* xii. 97 Representation, in its primary political sense, means..holding another's proxy. **1840** ARNOLD in *Life & Corr.* (1844) II. ix. 201, I cannot hesitate for an instant which side to take, and I will send you my proxy without a moment's hesitation. **1880** *Beeton's Everybody's Lawyer* 1287 Whoever votes upon the authority of an unstamped proxy is liable to the same penalty as the person who executed it. **1900** *Whitaker's Alm.* 433 *Stamps and Taxes* Proxy to vote at a meeting o. o. 1d.

3. a. A person appointed or authorized to act instead of another; an attorney, substitute, representative, agent. (Cf. PROCTOR¹ 2, PROCURATOR¹ 2.)

1614 JACKSON *Creed* III. xxxii. §4 They..thus absolutely betrouth them to his Proxy or principall Agent here on earth. *a* **1618** SYLVESTER *Elegie to M. D. Hill* 178 Make mee thy Proxie. **1765** BLACKSTONE *Comm.* I. ii. 168 Another privilege is, that every peer..may make another lord of parliament his proxy, to vote for him in his absence. **1812** WELLINGTON in Gurw. *Desp.* (1838) IX. 237, I am very much..flattered by your having been my proxy at the Installation of the Knights of the Bath. **1878** VILLARI *Life & Times Machiavelli* (1898) I. iv. 181 Don Federigo her uncle as her proxy received the nuptial ring.

b. *fig.* of things.

1639 FULLER *Holy War* II. xiii. (1840) 67 Where the deed could not be present, the desire was a sufficient proxy. *a* **1683** OLDHAM *Passion Byblis* Poet. Wks. (1686) 135, I should myself have gone Nor made my pen a Proxy to my Tongue. **1853** PATMORE *Poems, Girl of All Periods* (1906) 422 'Twixt her shapely lips, a violet Perch'd as a proxy for a cigarette.

†**4.** *U.S. local* (*Rhode Isl. and Conn.*). orig. A written vote for the legislative assembly sent by a deputy: hence, loosely applied to the voting-papers or votes generally (cf. quot. 1843 s.v. PROX); and hence to the election or day of election. *Obs.*

1660 (Apr. 11) in *Conn. Col. Rec.* I. 346 The remote Plantations that use to send Proxies at the Election by their Deputies. **1679** *Rhode Isl. Col. Rec.* (1861) III. 30 Voted,.. that Capt'n Samuell Gorton and Mr. Caleb Carr shall open the proxies. **1755** DOUGLASS *Summary* (1760) II. 89 (Rhode I.) Formerly..the proxies or voters never exceeded 1300:.. and anno 1749, the proxies were only 888. **1809** KENDALL *Trav.* I. v. 32 The written votes or ballots which through a mistake or else abuse of terms, the statutes occasionally call proxies. *a* **1816** *Connecticut Newspr.* (Pickering), Republicans of Connecticut, previous to every proxies you have been assaulted on every side... On the approaching proxies we ask you to attend universally. **1816** PICKERING *Vocab. U.S.* 156 This use of the term *proxies* is not known ..in any of the States, except Rhode Island and Connecticut. It is also used sometimes as equivalent to *election*, or *election-day*. **1828** in WEBSTER. **1846** in WORCESTER.

II. †**5.** *Eccl.* Provision or entertainment for a visiting bishop or his representative; an annual payment by incumbents to the ordinary, in commutation of this; = PROCURACY 3, PROCURATION 3. *Obs.*

1534 HEN. VIII in J. Bacon *Liber Regis* (1786) p. xiv, Except only suche annuell and perpetuall rentts, pensions, ..proxis, and fees for officers, as before specyally ys mencyoned. **1661** J. STEPHENS *Procurations* 37 The Bishop of Meth..had a Proxie of 15*s.* 4*d* payable yearly out of the Commandery of Kells. *Ibid.* 46 'Twas noted that the same which we call Proxie or Procuracy, is termed by the Canonists *Procuratio*, because that in every Visitation the persons visited procured necessary provision for the Visitors... But afterwards..Proxies [were] reduced to a certain sum of money payable yearly in the nature of a Pension to the Ordinary, who had power of visitation. **1725** SWIFT *Let. to Sheridan* 28 June, The other fifty must go in a curate and visitation charges,—proxies I mean. **1848** in WHARTON *Law Lex.* [but see PROCURATION 3, quot. 1895.]

III. 6. a. *attrib.* and *Comb.*; done by proxy, as *proxy help*, *marriage*, *prayer*, *vote*; **proxy form**, a form on which a proxy vote is registered; **proxy-man**, = sense 3; **proxy sitting** *Spiritualism*, a sitting arranged with a medium and attended by one person at the request of another, usu. unknown, person who hopes for news of someone recently dead; **proxy war** *U.S.*, a war limited in scale or area, instigated by a major power which does not itself become involved; **proxy-wedded** *a.*, wedded by proxy.

1930 *Economist* 6 Sept. 453/2 Accordingly they may, and should, use the company's money for the printing and postage of proxy forms. **1696** *Growth Deism* 16 Whether an Oath of Abjuration laid upon the Jacobites Proxy-men, will put an end to this Corruption. **1900** *Everybody's Mag.* III. 574/1 It all comes of those proxy marriages. *a* **1845** HOOD *Stag Eyed Lady* vi, And drummed with proxy-prayers Mohammed's ear. **1927** N. WALKER *Bridge* III. iv. 139, I had known about practically nothing that was mentioned in the two previous proxy Leonard sittings. **1933** *Proc. Soc. Psychical Res.* XLI. cxxx. 139 (*title*) A consideration of a series of proxy sittings. **1948** *Mind* LVII. 393 Telepathy is again invoked as the source of supernormal material: a well-worn hypothesis, which fails to cover the data obtained by proxy-sittings, cross-correspondences and so forth. **1962** C. D. BROAD *Lect. Psychical Res.* xv. 352 The essentials of a proxy-sitting are the following. The experimenter.. receives in writing from some person, often a complete stranger to him, a few distinctive facts about a certain recently deceased individual... The specified facts are such as would suffice to enable the experimenter to recognize with some probability that the medium was referring to the individual in question. **1716** *Rhode Isl. Col. Rec.* (1861) IV. 208 This act has no reference to proxy votes, which are to be signed according to former custom. **1843** W. R. STAPLES *Ann. Providence* 65. **1955** *N.Y. Times* 9 Jan. 8E/5 A threat that the United States would instantly retaliate with atomic weapons against the heart of the Communist world if the Commies started another proxy or brush-fire war. **1978** *Amer. Polit. Sci. Rev.* Sept. 971/2 Proxy wars, as the Athenians discovered in trying to rule their empire indirectly, are extremely costly. **1847** TENNYSON *Princ.* I. 33 She to me Was proxy-wedded with a bootless calf At eight years old.

b. *Petrol.* and *Min.* Applied to a mineral that proxies another.

1931 [see PROXY *v.* 2]. **1949** F. H. HATCH et al. *Petrol. Igneous Rocks* (ed. 10) I. ii. 69 These Al''' atoms which function as silicons are 'proxy Al's', and each unit contains two of these. **1965** A. W. G. WHITTLE in G. J. Williams *Econ. Geol. N.Z.* x. 150/2 It is probable that an appreciable amount of 'proxy-nickel' was leached during the hydrothermal alteration of the pendotites to serpentinites.

Hence **ˈproxyhood**, **ˈproxyship**, the office or function of a proxy or substitute.

1776 in Doran *Mann & Manners* (1876) II. xiii. 301 My *proxy-hood made a pompous article in the Italian Gazettes. **1674** BREVINT *Saul at Endor* xvi. 394 The same Correspondency, and *Proxiship between these Spirits, and their Images.

ˈproxy, *v.* [f. the sb.]

1. *intr.* To act or vote by proxy.

a **1832** MACKINTOSH cited in Worcester (1846) for Proxy *v.*

2. *Petrol.* and *Min. rare. trans.* To occur in place of, esp. in a crystal lattice. Also *intr.*, const. *for*.

1922 A. JOHANNSEN in *Jrnl. Geol.* XXX. 640 The [German] author says a 'gabbro tendency' is shown, and that diallage is proxied by an amphibole of similar chemical composition. **1925** *Amer. Jrnl. Sci.* CCIX. 313 It is not possible for Br atoms to proxy for Na atoms in halite; they can occupy only places of Cl atoms. **1931** A. JOHANNSEN *Descr. Petrogr. Igneous Rocks* I. 189 'Proxy-minerals' is a translation of the German words *stellvertretende Gemengteile*, used by von Leonhard [in 1823] for minerals which take the place of other minerals in a rock; i.e., proxy them but do not replace them in the sense of molecular replacement... Thus if a certain type rock contains biotite, and another is like it in every way except that the dark mineral is hornblende, then in the latter the hornblende proxies biotite, and hornblende is the proxy-mineral. **1946** *Amer. Mineralogist* XXXI. 423 In tetrahedral positions Al proxies part of the Si. **1963** W. A. DEER et al. *Rock-Forming Minerals* II. 353 The richterite..has an unusually high content of titanium some of which may proxy for silicon in tetrahedral positions.

Hence **ˈproxying** *vbl. sb.*

1946 *Amer. Mineralogist* XXXI. 424 Other variables in the chemical composition [of the montmorillonite group of minerals] are..the proxying of OH by F as in the micas.

proye, obs. form of PREY.

proyn(e, obs. form of PREEN *v.*², and PRUNE.

pro-Zionist: see PRO-¹ 5 a.

prozoic (prəʊˈzəʊɪk), *a. Geol.* [mod. f. Gr. πρό, PRO-² 1 + ζωή life + -IC; cf. F. *prozoïque* (Huet).] Belonging to the period before the appearance of life on the earth.

1858 in MAYNE *Expos. Lex.* **1877** F. M. ENDLICH in *11th Rep. U.S. Geol. & Geog. Surv. Territories* (1879) 66 This occurrence of prozoic rocks is one of great interest... We found that the prozoic granite..disappeared altogether in the main chain, except northward.

prozone (ˈprəʊzəʊn). *Immunol.* [Contraction of *pro*-agglutinoid *zone*, f. PRO-¹ + AGGLUTINOID + ZONE *sb.*] The range of relative quantities of precipitin (or agglutinin) and antigen within which the expected precipitation (or agglutination) fails to occur when they are mixed; the mixture so produced, usu. containing antibody in excess. Freq. *attrib.*

[**1914** H. ZINSSER *Infection & Resistance* vi. 162 In the study of agglutinin and precipitin reactions, phenomena exactly analagous to the Neisser-Wechsberg effect have been noticed, in the case of the agglutinins, the so-called 'pro-agglutinoid' zone being a case in point.] **1916** *Jrnl. Immunol.* I. 6 The fourth line in this table represents the so-called prozone in which excess of precipitinogen inhibits precipitation. **1934** ZINSSER & BAYNE-JONES *Textbk. Bacteriol.* (ed. 7) xvi. 222 The specificity of the prozones is demonstrable in two ways. In the first place, bacteria that have been subjected to the action of serum showing such a prozone, without being agglutinated, will no longer agglutinate when subsequently emulsified in a potent agglutinating serum. Again, absorption of a prozone serum with the homologous bacteria will remove the prozone. **1964** D. F. GRAY *Immunol.* xi. 114 The 'constant antibody' precipitin reaction illustrates a phenomenon of diagnostic importance that may occur in agglutination tests, viz. the prozone, in which antigen: antibody aggregation is interfered with in the presence of an excess of antigen or of antibody. **1970** PASSMORE & ROBSON *Compan. Med. Stud.* II. xxii. 15/2 The prozone phenomenon..is probably due to the stabilizing effects of high protein concentration on the particles; the protein coating increases the net charge of the particles and brings about increased electrostatic repulsion between individual particles, thus opposing the efforts of the antibody molecules to link them together.

prozoosporange, -zygapophysis: see PRO-².

Prozymite (ˈprɒzɪmaɪt). *Eccl. Hist.* [ad. late Gr. προζυμίτης, f. προζύμιον leaven, f. πρό before, etc. + ζύμη leaven.] One who uses leavened bread in the Eucharist: a hostile appellation for members of the Greek Church. (Cf. AZYMITE.)

1850 TORREY *Neander's Ch. Hist.* VI. 418 [At Byzantium in 1054] The two parties called each other by the heretical names, Azymites and Prozymites. **1880** *Libr. Univ. Knowl.* (U.S.) II. 76 The Latins retorted [to the stigma 'azymites'] with 'prozymites'.

prozymogen (prəʊˈzaɪməʊdʒɛn). *Phys. Chem.* [f. Gr. πρό, PRO-² 1 + ZYMOGEN.] A substance produced by certain cells in the stomach of a newt, afterwards converted into a zymogen.

1900 *Lancet* 11 Aug. 447/2 As the cell parted with its zymogen a new substance—prozymogen—was produced by the nucleus at the expense of the chromatin.

prozzy, var. PROSSIE.

Pru (pruː). Colloq. abbrev. of *Prudential Assurance Company*; *esp.* in phr. ***(the) man from the Pru***, a representative of the Company who calls regularly at private houses to collect life insurance premiums (see quot. 1963).

1927 W. E. COLLINSON *Contemp. Eng.* 111 The best known English company, the Prudential, is often called the Pru. **1961** C. COCKBURN *View from West* ii. 19 To what extent..is our entire view of life..determined by what is told us by the Men from the Pru? **1963** *Times* 24 Apr. 12/3 The Prudential Assurance Company has discontinued the issue of life insurance policies paid by weekly premiums. This does not mean that 'the man from the Pru' will no longer be calling from door to door: all new 'industrial' life policy premiums will ordinarily be collected every four weeks instead of weekly. **1973** A. BEHREND *Samarai Affair* xiii. 141 She..said with no more emotion than if addressing a man from the Pru, 'My husband's told me what you've come for.' **1978** *Guardian Weekly* 15 Jan. 21/3 Next year I hope the Cottesloe [Theatre] will offer us, like the man from the Pru, a definite policy.

pru, var. of PROW *sb.*² and *v.*, PREU, PROO.

pruan, -ant, obs. forms of PRUNE *sb.*

†**pruance.** *Obs. rare*⁻¹. [f. *pru*, PREU, PROW *a.* + -ANCE.] Prowess.

c **1330** *Arth. & Merl.* 8150, Y no miȝt it nouȝt ful rede, þe pruaunce of Wawaines dede.

†**Pruce.** *Obs.* Forms: 4 pruys, 4–5 prus, 4–8 pruce, 5–7 pruse, (5 prewce, prews(e, 8 pruss, pruche). [ME. *a. Prus*, a. AF. *Pruz*, *Prus*, *Pruys*; *β. Pruce*, a. AF. *Pruce*, mod.F. *Prusse*, Prussia: see PRUSSIAN, and SPRUCE *sb.*]

1. *Geog.* Prussia.

[? *a* **1300** in *Liber Albus* (Rolls) I. 238 De c de stokfisshe venaunt del Pruz, quart.] *c* **1386** CHAUCER *Prol.* 53 Abouen alle nacions in Pruce. [**1390** *Earl Derby's Exped.* 1 En les parties de Barbarye et de Pruz. *a* **1440** WALSINGHAM *Hist. Angl.* (Rolls) II. 197 Dominus Henricus..profectus est in le Pruys.] **1436** *Libel Eng. Policy* in *Pol. Poems* (Rolls) II. 169 Of the commoditees of Pruse. **1460** CAPGRAVE *Chron.* 254 In this yere Ser Herry, erl of Derby, sailed into Prus. **1627** DRAYTON *Agincourt* 11 Six Hulks from Hull..Which had them oft accompanied to Pruce.

b. ***of Pruce***: Of or from Prussia; hence, Made (*a*) of Prussian or spruce fir wood, (*b*) of Prussian leather. Cf. SPRUCE *sb.*

[**1390** *Earl Derby's Exped.* 109 Presentanti dominum cum j tabula commensali de Prucia.] **1462** *Maldon, Essex, Court-Rolls* Bundle 37, No. 4b, 1 mensa de prewse. **1495** *Nottingham Rec.* III. 38 Unam cistam de pruce. **1700** DRYDEN *Pal. & Arc.* 1307 Some for defence would leathern bucklers use..others shields of Pruce.

2. *attrib.* **a.** Of Prussia, Prussian; comb. ***Pruceland***, ***Pruceman***. **b.** Of spruce fir, as ***pruce beer***; ***pruce chest***, ***coffer***, ***hutch***, ***table*** (but in these prob. orig. = Prussian, without specification of the wood).

a. 1377 LANGL. *P. Pl.* B. XIII. 392 If I sent ouer see my seruauntz to Bruges, Or in-to Pruslonde my prentys [*v. rr.* pruys londe, Pruce lond, spruce land; C. VII. 279 prus, spruce, pruys lond]. **1390** *Earl Derby's Exped.* 51 Per manus Nichel Pruceman [Here app. a surname]. **1402** *Nottingham Rec.* II. 16 Pro cariagio iiij^or carect[atarum] cum prusware. *c* **1500** *Blowbol's Test.* in Halliw. *Nugæ Poet.* 7 An hundreth marke of pruce money fyne.

b. 1448 in *Bury Wills* (Camden) 12, j. pruce hutche. **1463** *Ibid.* 23 As for the prews coffre alwey I wille remayne to my hefd place. **1478** *Maldon, Essex, Court-Rolls* Bundle 50, No. 6 Attachiatus est per 1 pruce tabyll. **1480** *Ibid.* Bundle 51, No. 4 Attachiatus est per 1 pruce chest. **1576** NEWTON *Lemnie's Complex.* (1633) 204 Of colour darke yellowish, like unto pruse Byer. **1760–72** tr. *Juan & Ulloa's Voy.* (ed. 3) II. 379 Turned into pruche or spruss beer.

prud, prudder, -est, obs. ff. PROUD, *-er*, *-est*.

prude (pruːd), *a.* and *sb.* [a. mod.F. *prude* adj. and sb., said of a woman in same sense as the Eng. (Molière in Littré), in OF. *prude*, *prode*, *preude*, in a laudatory sense, good, virtuous, modest, respectable; either a back-formation from *prudefemme* (cf. PRUDHOMME) or a later fem. form of *prod*, *pro*, *pru*: see PREUX, PROW *a.*]

A. *adj.* That maintains or affects extreme propriety of speech and behaviour, especially in regard to the relations of the sexes; excessively modest, demure, or prim; prudish: usually applied adversely. Now *rare*.

1709 MRS. MANLEY *Secret Mem.* (1720) IV. 318, I can't understand what you and my prude Cousin Aurelia mean by being belov'd. **1752** H. WALPOLE *Lett.* (1846) II. 449 He is jealous, prude, and scrupulous. **1900** H. G. GRAHAM *Soc. Life Scot. 18th C.* (1901) III. ii. 95 The prudest might go and enjoy Vanbrugh's *Provoked Husband*..under guise of innocently listening to Corelli's Sonatas.

B. *sb.* A woman who maintains or affects excessive modesty or propriety in conduct or speech; one who is of extreme propriety: usually applied adversely with implication of affectation.

1704 CIBBER *Careless Husb.* V. i, For you I have..stood the little Insults of Disdainful Prudes, that envy'd me perhaps your Friendship. **1709** STEELE *Tatler* No. 102 ¶5 *Prudes*, a Courtly Word for Female Hypocrites. **1781** MME. D'ARBLAY *Diary* Aug., He is an actual male prude! **1847** TENNYSON *Princ.* Prol. 141 If our old halls could change their sex, and flaunt With prudes for proctors, dowagers for deans. **1882** MISS BRADDON *Mt. Royal* III. x. 195 Prudes and puritans may disapprove our present form.

Hence **ˈprudelike** *a.*, of the nature of, or characteristic of, a prude; **ˈprudely** *adv.*, in the manner of a prude.

1718 *Freethinker* No. 145 ¶7 The same idle Charms, by which the gay Pamphilus ensnared the prudelike Honoria. **1789** WOLCOTT (P. Pindar) *Expost. Odes* iii. 22 Scorning Moderation's Prude-like stare. **1883** *Mem. Alex. Maclean* 125 Mock her not, ye prudely pure.

prude (pruːd), *v.* [f. the sb.] *intr.* To conduct oneself in the manner of a prude; to act prudishly. Hence **ˈpruding** *vbl. sb.*

1737 H. CAREY *Musical Century* 13 Crowds of coxcombs thus deluding, Cringing, chatt'ring, oggling, flatt'ring By coquetting and by pruding, All are victims to my art. **1850** C. M. YONGE *Henrietta's Wish* x. 151 'Pruding,' said Beatrice, 'showing openly that you like it to be observed how prudent and proper you are.' **1923** V. L. SILBERRAD *Lett. Jean Armiter* ix. 194 Girls aren't brought up in cotton wool nowadays as you were. We do as we jolly well like! It's no good preaching and pruding.

prude, obs. form of PROUD.

prudence (ˈpruːdəns). Also 6 *Sc.* prowdence, proudens. [a. F. *prudence* (13th c. in Littré), ad. L. *prūdēntia* foresight, sagacity, skill, prudence, contr. from *prōvidēntia* PROVIDENCE.] The quality of being prudent.

1. Ability to discern the most suitable, politic, or profitable course of action, esp. as regards conduct; practical wisdom, discretion.

1340 *Ayenb.* 125 Prudence lokeþ þane scele þet hi ne bi becaȝt. *c* **1430** LYDG. *Min. Poems* (Percy Soc.) 9 With a mantelle of prudens clad thou be. **1500–20** DUNBAR *Poems* ix. 77 Enarming me, With fortitude, prowdence, and temperance. *c* **1560** A. SCOTT *Poems* (S.T.S.) vi. 39, I will.. pleiss hir proudens to imprent it. *a* **1639** W. WHATELEY *Prototypes* I. xi. (1640) 102 Prudence is a vertue by which a man doth worke rightly to happinesse. **1752** HUME *Ess. & Treat.* (1777) I. 3 Beyond all bounds of prudence and discretion. **1820** BYRON *Mar. Fal.* I. ii, You so forget All prudence in your fury. **1850** S. DOBELL *Roman* vii, Prudence, the soul's stern sacristan.

b. An instance of this; a prudent act.

1667 WATERHOUSE *Fire Lond.* 36 In despight of those wonted prudences, and usual resistances. **1890** 'R. BOLDREWOOD' *Col. Reformer* (1891) 291 A night when the ordinary prudences and severities of conscience might be.. placed behind the perceptions.

†**2.** Wisdom; knowledge of or skill in a matter. Cf. JURISPRUDENCE. *Obs.*

c **1375** *Sc. Leg. Saints* iii. (*Andreas*) 1019 For, gyf hym wantis sic prudence [to answer questions], he suld nocht cum in ȝour presence. **1382** WYCLIF *Eph.* iii. 4 As ȝe redinge mown vndirstonde my prudence in the mysterie of Crist. **1388** —— *Jas.* Prol., In othere epistolis.. hou myche fro oure otheris making discordith, I leue to the prudence of the redere. **1609** BIBLE (Douay) *Baruch* iii. 9 Harken with your eares, that you may know prudence. **1660** STANLEY *Hist. Philos.* IX. (1701) 350/2 He.. resigned him-self to the most exact prudence of the Magi to be formed. *a* **1859** R. CHOATE *Addresses* (1878) 235 In his [Webster's] profession of politics, nothing.. worthy of attention had escaped him; nothing of the ancient or modern prudence.

†**3.** Foresight, providence. *Obs.*

a **1619** FOTHERBY *Atheom.* II. xi. §6 (1622) 320 Then must it be, either by Chance, or by Prudence. **1685** BOYLE *Enq. Notion Nat.* vi. 239 'Tis my settled opinion that Divine prudence is often at least conversant in a peculiar manner, about the actions of men.

†**4.** Alleged term for a 'company' of vicars. *Obs.*

1486 *Bk. St. Albans* F vj, A Prudens of vikeris.

†'**prudency.** *Obs.* [ad. L. *prūdēnti-a*: see prec. and -ENCY.] = prec.

1539 TAVERNER *Gard. Wysed.* II. 8 b, To fense our selfes agaynst the wyly and craftye foxes with columbyne prudencie. **1620** J. PYPER tr. *Hist. Astrea* I. x. 361 Change to the better, I call prudency, But to the worse shewes small discretion. **1656** S. HOLLAND *Zara* (1719) 77 How many Inchantments expect a period from the prudency of my Courage.

prudent ('pruːdənt), *a.* [a. F. *prudent* (*c* 1300 in Godef. *Compl.*), or ad. L. *prūdēns, -ēntem* foreseeing (very rare), knowing, skilled, experienced, versed in a thing, sagacious, circumspect, contr. from *prōvidēns* PROVIDENT, with weakening or entire loss of the notion of 'foreseeing'.]

1. Of persons (rarely of inferior animals): Sagacious in adapting means to ends; careful to follow the most politic and profitable course; having or exercising sound judgement in practical affairs; circumspect, discreet, worldly-wise.

1382 WYCLIF *Luke* xvi. 8 The sones of this world ben more prudent [*Vulgate* prudentiores] in her generacioun than the sones of liȝt. *c* **1386** CHAUCER *Doctor's T.* 110 She was so prudent and so bounteous. *c* **1450** *Cov. Myst.* xxv. 246 As a primat most preudent I present here sensyble Buschopys of the lawe with al the cyrcumstawns. **1508** DUNBAR *Tua Mariit Wemen* 508 Thai suld.. wirk efter hir wordis, that woman wes so prudent. **1610** GUILLIM *Heraldry* I. v. (1660) 29 That most prudent Prince King Henry the Seventh. **1667** MILTON *P.L.* VII. 430 So stears the prudent Crane Her annual Voiage, born on Windes. **1745** *De Foe's Eng. Tradesman* vi. (1841) I. 36 All rash adventurers are condemned by the prudent part of mankind. **1842** TENNYSON *Two Voices* 415 The prudent partner of his blood.. Wearing the rose of womanhood. **1875** JOWETT *Plato* (ed. 2) V. 74 A prudent man will avoid sinning against the stranger.

†**2.** Wise, discerning, sapient. *Obs.* (exc. as included in 1).

a **1425** *Wyclif's Bible* Matt. xi. 25 Thou hast hid these thingis fro wijse men and ware [*MS. New Coll.* 67 prudent]. *c* **1430** LYDG. *Min. Poems* (Percy Soc.) 13 Be the sentence of prudent Salaman. **1526** TINDALE *Matt.* xi. 25 Thou hast hyd these thynges from the wyse and prudent, and hast opened them vnto babes. **1549** *Compl. Scot.* xv. 129 The philosophour socrates, quhilk va iugit to be the maist prudent man in the vniuersal varld. **1579** W. WILKINSON *Confut. Familye of Loue* Ep. Ded., Salomon the sonne of holy Dauid a prudent Kyng.

3. Of conduct, action, etc.: Characterized by, exhibiting, or proceeding from prudence; politic, judicious. ***the prudent***: that which is prudent.

1412–20 LYDG. *Chron. Troy* III. 3707 þoruȝ her prudent medyacioun.. With kyng Thoas she myȝt eschaunged be. **1509** HAWES *Past. Pleas.* v. (Percy Soc.) 22 They folowed not theyr fleshe so vycious, But ruled it by prudent governaunce. **1673** *Lady's Call.* II. i. §17 'Tis prejudice enough against the prudentest advice, that it comes from their parents. **1707** HEARNE *Collect.* 30 Sept. (O.H.S.) II. 57 'Tis the prudenter Way not to know it. **1790** *Bystander* 247 Then touching upon the prudent, he entreated it might remain some little time a secret. **1845** S. AUSTIN *Ranke's Hist. Ref.* II. III. i. 29 His.. prudent and enlightened policy had ever been crowned with ultimate success. **1871** FREEMAN *Norm. Conq.* IV. xviii. 127 There were those to whom William found it prudent to be gentle.

prudential (pruː'dɛnʃəl), *a.* (*adv.*), *sb.* [f. L. *prūdēntia* PRUDENCE + -AL[1]. Cf. med.L. *prūdēntiālis* (9th c. in *Acta Sanct. Boll.* (1887) 64).]

A. *adj.* **1.** Of, belonging to, or of the nature of prudence; involving prudence; characterized or prescribed by forethought and careful deliberation.

1641 LD. DIGBY *Sp.* 21 Apr. in Rushw. *Hist. Coll.* III. (1692) I. 227 We must not piece up.. the Defailance of Prudential Fitness, with a Pretence of Legal Justice. **1652** E. WALSINGHAM (*title*) Arcana Aulica: or.. Manual of Prudential Maxims for the States-man And the Courtier. **1711** ADDISON *Spect.* No. 181 ¶7 To this I might add many other religious, as well as many prudential Considerations. **1770** *Junius Lett.* xli. (1820) 217 Here, too, we trace the little prudential policy of a Scotchman. **1863** FAWCETT *Pol. Econ.* II. vi. (1876) 195 The life of a hired labourer can exert no influence.. towards cultivating prudential habits.

b. in New England: cf. next sense and B. 1 a.

1644 *First Cent. Hist. Springfield, Mass.* (1898) I. 175 Power to order in all the prudential affaires of the Towne.

2. Of persons: Exercising prudence; (in New England) Appointed to conduct the affairs of a town, society, etc.: cf. B. 1 a.

1642 H. MORE *Song of Soul* I. II. lxxix, Prudentiall men and of a mighty reach. **1648** *N. Eng. Hist. & Gen. Reg.* (1850) IV. 30 It is this day ordered by.. the prudentiall men for the affaires of the Towne that [etc.]. **1795** J. SULLIVAN *Hist. Maine* 221 In the year 1661, seven men were chosen to take care of the town affairs, under the denomination of prudential men. **1823** SCOTT *Peveril* iv, The side of the Puritans was also deserted at this period by a numerous class of more thinking and prudential persons, who never forsook them till they became unfortunate.

†**3.** as *adv.* = PRUDENTIALLY. *Obs. rare.*

c **1400** *Beryn* 381 The hoost of Southwork.. al thing wrouȝt prudenciall, as sobir man & wise.

B. *sb.* **1.** *pl.* **a.** Matters that fall within the scope or province of prudence; *esp.* (in *U.S.*) matters of local government and administration for which there is no need to go to the law courts: cf. quots. 1644 in A. 1 b. and 1648, 1795 in A. 2.

1646 *Col. Rec. Massachusetts* 4 Nov. II. 180 Every township, or such as are deputed to order the prudentialls thereof, shall have power to present to the Quarter Court all idle and unprofitable persons. **1648** T. HILL *Serm. Truth & Love* 32 Divers things may be.. better, and more safely settled as Prudentials, as Humane Constitutions, then as Divine Constitutions. **1697** *Boston Rec.* (1881) VII. 228 Voted that the prudentials of the town is left to the judgment and discretion of the Selectmen. **1774** E. WHEELOCK in F. Chase *Hist. Dartmouth Coll.* (1891) I. 263 Agreed with Frederick Earnest.. to take the care of the kitchen, and inspect and conduct the prudentials of it. **1891** F. CHASE *ibid.* I. 565 The condition of the College in its prudentials was such as might well have led any one to hesitate to take the helm.

b. Prudential considerations.

1658–9 in *Burton's Diary* (1828) IV. 23, I hear prudentials much pressed upon us, why we should not call the old Peers. **1726** DE FOE *Hist. Devil* II. x. (1840) 322 Prudentials restrain him in all his other actings with mankind. **1838** SOUTHEY *Lett.* (1856) IV. 565 As regards the prudentials of such an engagement, there will be additional means more than equal to any additional expenditure.

†**c.** Prudential faculties. *Obs.*

1679 R. MAYHEW in Spurgeon *Treas. Dav.* Ps. cxxxv. 4 Will not a man that is not defective in his prudentials secure his jewels? **1690** C. NESSE *O. & N. Test.* I. 282 He puts forth his prudentials in providing for his safety.

†**2.** A prudential maxim or precept. *Obs.*

1719 DE FOE *Crusoe* 184 Religion joined in with this Prudential, and I was convinced [etc.]. **1734** WATTS *Reliq. Juv.* xlii. (1789) 119 The maxims of that philosopher are everlasting truths; and his prudentials will stand the test in all ages.

3. A person who urges prudence. *rare.*

1864 DE MORGAN in Graves *Life Sir W. Hamilton* (1889) III. 604, I shall shock all the mathematical prudentials by standing up for the bare uncloaked infinitesimals.

pru'dentialism. [f. prec. + -ISM.] A system or theory of life based upon, or having chief regard to, prudential considerations; also *pl.* prudential principles.

1835 DE QUINCEY in *Tait's Mag.* II. 549 With respect to Paley, and the naked prudentialism of his system, it is true that.. Paley disclaims that consequence. *a* **1866** J. GROTE *Exam. Utilit. Philos.* ii. (1870) 28, I have called utilitarianism.. superficial, because.. it rests so much on mere prudentialisms. **1898** A. B. BRUCE in *Expositor* July 10 It is better far to have the hero with all his drawbacks than to have nothing in human life that rises above prudentialism, commonplace, and humdrum.

So **pru'dentialist**, one who is professedly guided by, or acts from, prudential motives.

1833 COLERIDGE in *Lit. Rem.* (1838) III. 403 Mr. Legality, a prudentialist offering his calculation of consequences as the moral antidote to guilt and crime. *a* **1860** J. YOUNGER *Autobiog.* xxv. (1881) 318 The dogmas of starch prudentialists.

prudentiality (pruːdɛnʃɪ'ælɪtɪ). *rare.* [f. as prec. + -ITY.] The quality of being prudential; prudential nature or character.

1646 SIR T. BROWNE *Pseud. Ep.* I. iii. 9 Being uncapable of operable circumstances, or rightly to judge the prudenciality of affairs. *a* **1849** H. COLERIDGE *Ess.* (1851) II. 103 Being more personal and subjective than episcopal prudentiality would allow, at least in public worship.

prudentially (pruː'dɛnʃəlɪ), *adv.* [f. as prec. + -LY[2].] In a prudential manner; in accordance with prudence; on prudential grounds.

1641 LD. DIGBY *Sp.* 21 Apr. in Rushw. *Hist. Coll.* III. (1692) I. 227 What is Prudentially and Politickly fit for the good and preservation of the whole. **1710** STRYPE *Life Grindal* I. vii. 71 This he ordered prudentially as well as piously. **1828** SOUTHEY in *Q. Rev.* XXXVII. 572 Marriages.. when prudentially deferred. **1893** GLADSTONE in *Westm. Gaz.* 28 Sept. 5/2 The manifestation of the opinion may have been prudentially restrained.

pru'dentialness. [f. as prec. + -NESS.] = PRUDENTIALITY.

1666 J. SERGEANT *Let. Thanks* 63 The prudentialness of their obligation.. was enough to make them miscarry. **1681** *Impartial Acc. Nat. & Tendency late Addresses* 17 They would have esteem'd themselves very.. unsufficient Judges of the prudentialness of that exercise of Royal Power.

prudently ('pruːdəntlɪ), *adv.* [f. PRUDENT *a.* + -LY[2].] In a prudent manner; with prudence, circumspection, discretion, or practical wisdom; discreetly, wisely, judiciously.

1382 WYCLIF *Luke* xvi. 8 The lord preiside the fermour of wickidnesse, for he hadde don prudently. **1484** CAXTON *Fables of Æsop* II. ii, He dothe prudently and wysely whiche taketh good hede to the ende. **1538** STARKEY *England* II. i. 143 Remedys prudentely to be applyd to such sorys and dyseasys. **1694** KETTLEWELL *Comp. Persecuted* 151 That I may answer.. so prudently, as not to prejudice myself. **1776** GIBBON *Decl. & F.* xiii. I. 365 Constantius had very prudently divided his forces. **1828** DISRAELI *Chas. I*, II. ii. 68 It sometimes happens.. that old officers act more prudently than happily. *Mod.* Others prudently waited for further news.

So '**prudentness**, prudence (Bailey, II. 1727).

prudery ('pruːdərɪ, 'pruːdrɪ). [ad. F. *pruderie* (Molière 1666), f. *prude* PRUDE: see -ERY.] The characteristic quality of a prude; the character of being prudish; excessive regard for the proprieties in speech or behaviour; extreme or affected modesty or demureness.

1709 STEELE *Tatler* No. 126 ¶2 If she has any Aversion to the Power of inspiring so great a Virtue.. she.. is still in the State of Prudery. **1716** LADY M. W. MONTAGU *Let. to Lady Rich* 20 Sept., Good.. ladies long since retired to prudery and ratifia. **1745** H. WALPOLE *Lett.* (1846) II. 49, I intend to have infinite fun with his prudery about this anecdote. **1813** *Salem Gaz.* 2 July 4/1 A lady in the west end of the town has carried her prudery so far, as to separate the writings of male and female authors in her library. **1880** VERN. LEE *Stud. Italy* IV. iv. 174 Ecclesiastical prudery would suffer no woman on the stage.

b. *pl.* Prudish acts or words.

1828 SCOTT *F.M. Perth* iv, She has stopped my mouth over-long with her pruderies and her scruples.

†**prud'homme.** Also as Fr. ‖prud'homme (prydɒm). [a. F. *prud'homme*:—OF. *prod(h)ome*, oblique case, f. *pros*, obl. *prod, pro*, PROW *a.* + *om*, obl. *ome, homme* man.

(The nom. appears to have been orig., as in Prov., *prozom, prosom*, i.e. *pros* + (*h*)*om*; but *prosdom, prodom*, occur, app. with intrusive *d* from obl. *prodome.* Tobler suggests as the orig., nom. *pros d'ome*, obl. *pro d'ome*, with prep. *de.*)]

1. *Hist.* A man of valour and discretion, a 'good man and true'; a knight or freeholder who was summoned to sit on the jury or to serve in the king's council.

[**1292** BRITTON I. xxxi. §6 Tauntost face jurer xii. des plus leaus prudeshommes qe eux verité presenterount des articles. *Ibid.* II. xxvii. §5 Adounc face le viscounte trier xii. prodeshommes [twelve good men. *Note.* The word *prodehomme*, as well as the similar.. *good and lawful man*, implied the possession of a freehold].] **1701** *Cowell's Interpr.*, *Prodes Homes*, this is a Title often given in our old Books to the Barons, or other Military Tenents, who were call'd to the King's Council, and was no more than *Discreti & Fideles Homines.* **1865** KINGSLEY *Herew.* vii, The chatelain sent word to Baldwin that the newcomer was a prudhomme of no common merit. **1883** W. J. LOFTIE *Hist. London* I. v. 128 The 'prudhommes' were arrayed at every election, at every hustings, against the lesser folk.

‖**2.** A member of a French tribunal appointed to decide labour disputes.

1887 *Pall Mall G.* 14 Feb. 14/1 The English law.. confounds prud'hommes with arbiters, which is a capital fault. The prud'hommes called on to decide certain particular cases deliver what in reality are judgments.

†**prudhommie.** *Obs. rare.* In 5 preudhommye, prudommye. [a. OF. *prudhommie* (15th c. in Littré), in mod.F. *prud'homie*, f. *prud'homme* (see prec.) + *-ie*, -Y.] The character of a 'prudhomme'; approved loyalty and discretion.

c **1477** CAXTON *Jason* 28 b, I put myn armee and my men vnder the conduyte of youre preudhommye and your wysedom. **1490** —— *Eneydos* i. 11 Renommed of beaulte, wysedome, and prudommye, scyence, prowesse, valyaunce.

prudish ('pruːdɪʃ), *a.* [f. PRUDE + -ISH[1].]

1. Having the character of a prude; maintaining or affecting extreme propriety of behaviour.

1717 POPE *Challenge* vii, Should you catch the prudish itch. **1766** [ANSTEY] *Bath Guide* xv. 32 A prudish old Maid By Gaiety brought to Despair. **1801** MAR. EDGEWORTH *Pop. Tales, Contrast* (1832) 109 Fanny was neither prudish nor censorious. **1880** L. STEPHEN *Pope* ii. 38 We need not be prudish in our judgment of impassioned poetry.

2. *fig.* Of things: Extremely prim, formal, or rigid.

1771 SMOLLETT *Humph. Cl.* 8 Aug. Let. ii, The trees are planted in prudish rows. **1886** *Edin. Rev.* CLXIII. 133 A verse, not fettered in its movements, or prudish in its expressions. **1888** LOWELL *Fitz Adam's Story* Poems (1891) 505/2 There was a parlour in the house, a room To make you shudder with its prudish gloom.

Comb. **1825** J. NEAL *Bro. Jonathan* II. 176 The window was..set full of nice, prudish-looking..quaker flowers.

prudishly (ˈpruːdɪʃlɪ), *adv.* [f. prec. + -LY[2].] In a prudish manner; with prudery.

1742 POPE *Dunc.* IV. 194 Nor wert thou, Isis! wanting to the day, (Though Christ-church long kept prudishly away). **1742** H. WALPOLE *Lett. to Mann* (1834) I. 199 No yeoman's daughter could have acted more prudishly. **1859** KINGSLEY *Misc.* (1860) I. vi. 259 They prudishly despised the anatomic study of the human figure.

prudishness (ˈpruːdɪʃnɪs). [f. as prec. + -NESS.] The quality of being prudish; prudery.

1840 HOOD *Up Rhine* 68 A shrinking delicate female, with sensitive feelings, nearly akin to prudishness. **1887** MISS BRADDON *Like & Unlike* vi, She withdrew herself suddenly from her lover's arm, with a touch of prudishness.

prudist (ˈpruːdɪst). [f. PRUDE + -IST.] One who makes a principle or practice of strict propriety.

1894 C. H. COOK *Thames Rights* 111 The prudists are simply blasphemous. **1908** *Westm. Gaz.* 12 May 5/1 Prudists to-day ask severely, 'What are we coming to? Are we again to see the licence of the directoire period?'

prudity (ˈpruːdɪtɪ). *nonce-wd.* [f. PRUDE *a.* + -ITY.] = PRUDERY.

1891 M. MAARTENS *Old Maid's Love* I. ix. 86 He recoiled equally from the one old woman's purity—prudity—and from the other old woman's vulgar innuendos.

prue, var. PREU *Obs.*

pruen, pruin(e, obs. ff. PRUNE *sb.*

pruesse, pruice, obs. ff. PROWESS.

pruf, -e, -ff, obs. Sc. ff. PROOF, PROVE.

pruinate (ˈpruːɪnət), *a. Nat. Hist.* [f. L. *pruīna* hoar-frost + -ATE[2].] = PRUINOSE.

1858 MAYNE *Expos. Lex.*, *Pruinatus*, *Pruinosus*,.. pruinate: pruinous.

pruinescence (pruːɪˈnɛsəns). *Nat. Hist. rare*⁻⁰. [f. as prec., after *efflorescence*, etc.] The condition of being pruinose.

1890 in *Cent. Dict.*

pruinose (ˈpruːɪnəʊs), *a. Nat. Hist.* [ad. L. *pruīnōs-us* frosty, f. *pruīn-a* hoar-frost: see -OSE.] Covered with a fine whitish powdery substance giving the appearance of hoar-frost; frosted.

1826 KIRBY & SP. *Entomol.* IV. xlvi. 284 *Pruinose*,..when the splendour of the surface is somewhat obscured by the appearance of a bloom upon it like that of a plum, but which cannot be detached. **1847** W. E. STEELE *Field Bot.* 54 Barren stem pruinose. **1861** HAGEN *Synops. Neuropt. N. Amer.* 70 Sides yellow pruinose, with a broad superior brassy-brown stripe. **1887** W. PHILLIPS *Brit. Discomycetes* 165 Cup sessile, ..chalky white, pruinose.

pruinous (ˈpruːɪnəs), *a.* [ad. L. *pruīnōs-us*: see prec. and -OUS.]

†**1.** Of or pertaining to frost; frosty. *Obs.*

1588 J. HARVEY *Disc. Probl.* 97 Much icie and pruinous cold to be expected. **1686** GOAD *Celest. Bodies* II. ix. 284 In a Frosty morning the pruinous Atoms lye floating in the Air.

2. = PRUINOSE. *rare*⁻⁰. See PRUINATE.

prun- (pruːn). *Chem.* [f. PRUN(US.] A formative element used in the names of several substances which occur in trees of the genus *Prunus*, as **ˈprunase** [-ASE], an enzyme which hydrolyses β-glucosides (notably prunasin), liberating glucose, and occurs chiefly in bitter almonds and yeast, as well as in the fruit of several *Prunus* species; **ˈprunasin** [f. prec. + -IN[1]], a crystalline substance found in a number of trees, notably the bird cherry, *P. padus*; the racemic form of a glucoside of the nitrile of mandelic acid, $C_6H_5{\cdot}CH(CN){\cdot}OC_6H_{11}O_5$; **ˈprunetin** [-ETIN], a colourless crystalline isoflavone derivative, $C_{16}H_{12}O_5$, which is the monomethyl ether of prunetol and occurs combined as glycosides in the wood and bark of several trees; **ˈprunetol** [f. prec. + -OL] = GENISTEIN; **ˈprunitrin** [*-trin* prob. after DEXTRIN], a colourless crystalline glucoside of prunetin.

The quotations follow in chronological order.

1910 H. FINNEMORE in *Pharmaceutical Jrnl.* XXXI. 604/1 This aqueous solution was shaken with ether, which at once precipitated a nearly colourless, semi-crystalline product, consisting mainly of a new dihydric phenol, $C_{16}H_{12}O_5$, to which the name prunetin is assigned. *Ibid.*, Prunetin contains a single methoxy group, and when demethylated by boiling with hydriodic acid yields the corresponding trihydric phenol, prunetol, $C_{15}H_{10}O_5$. *Ibid.*, Further treatment of the aqueous solution yielded a colourless glucoside which when hydrolysed gave prunetin, and was obviously the mother substance of that phenol, and to which the name prunitrin is accordingly given. **1912** H. E. ARMSTRONG et al. in *Proc. R. Soc.* B. LXXXV. 360 It appears to be desirable to assign a distinct name in future to the enzyme in 'emulsin' by which the resolution of the simple cyanophoric glucoside is effected; as it occurs very generally in the various species of Prunus, we propose to term it Prunase; also it will be convenient to use the name Prunasin in speaking of the glucoside (d-mandelonitrile glucoside) which, hitherto, we have termed Fischer's glucoside. **1918** PERKIN & EVEREST *Natural Org. Colouring Matters* vii. 205 Prunetin,..colourless needles, melting-point 242°, dissolves in alkalis with a slight yellow colour. **1936** W. STILES *Introd. Princ. Plant Physiol.* v. 106 The prunasin is now hydrolysed by means of prunase into glucose and mandelonitrile. **1940** *Thorpe's Dict. Appl. Chem.* (ed. 4) IV. 283/1 This β-glucosidase is also called prunase and latterly, β-phenylglucosidase. **1956** I. L. FINAR *Org. Chem.* II. vii. 244 The enzyme zymase hydrolyses amygdalin into one molecule of glucose and a glucoside of (+)-mandelonitrile (this compound is identical with prunasin, a naturally occurring glucoside). **1959** N. CAMPBELL in E. H. Rodd *Chem. Carbon Compounds* IVB. viii. 925 Genistein (prunetol), 5:7:4′-trihydroxyisoflavone, $C_{15}H_{10}O_5$, colourless needles,..occurs along with luteolin in dyers broom. *Ibid.*, Prunetin,..genistein 7-methyl ether, ..is isolated from the bark of a wild cherry related to *Prunus emarginata*..and the commercial timber muninga (*Pterocarpus angolensis*). *Ibid.* 926 Prunitrin, prunetin 4′-glucoside..occurs in *Prunus Serotina* L. and is synthesised by methylating sophoricoside. **1976** *Nature* 15 Apr. 604/1 The ecological success of bracken is partly.. because of its ability to synthesise various secondary compounds which deter predators and phytopathogens. These compounds include the cyanogenic glycoside, prunasin, toxic because on enzymatic hydrolysis HCN is released.

prunable (ˈpruːnəb(ə)l), *a. rare.* [f. PRUNE *v.*[2] + -ABLE.] Capable of being pruned.

a **1750** A. HILL *Wks.* (1753) I. 248 Of a less grateful and prunable kind. **1801** BENTHAM *Mem. & Corr.* Wks. 1843 X. 372 The prunable matter would be completed.

†**prunall.** *Obs.* [ad. F. *prunelle* a sloe, also the pupil of the eye: see PRUNELLA[1].] The pupil of the eye.

1597 LOWE *Chirurg.* I. xi. (1634) 31 Eyes overwhelmed with some cataract or faye which covereth the prunall, called the windowe of the eye. **1600** VAUGHAN *Direct. Health* (1626) 89 Some other times the Prunall of the eye is grieued.

prune (pruːn), *sb.* Forms: see below. [a. F. *prune* (13th c. in Littré):—med.L. *prūna*, fem. sing. from *prūna*, neut. pl. of L. *prūn-um*, a. Gr. *προῦν-ον*, later form of *προῦμν-ον* a plum.]

A. Illustration of Forms.

4 prunne, 4– prune; 5–6 proyne, 6 prown, preune, 6–7 proine, 7 prewyn, pruine, 7–8 (9 *dial.*) pruin, pruen, pruan, 8 pruant.

1345–6 Prunnes [see B. 2]. *c* **1400** *Lanfranc's Cirurg.* 74 Drie prunis [*v. r.* prunes] of damascenes. *c* **1430** Prune [see B. 2]. **1481–90** *Howard Househ. Bks.* (Roxb.) 338 On Crystemas even my Lord resseyved be the caryer..iiij. lb proynes. **1519** in W. M. Williams *Ann. Founders' Co.* (1867) 52 Item, iij lb of Prownys. **1530** Prune [see B. 1]. *c* **1532** DU WES *Introd. Fr.* in *Palsgr.* 1073 Preunes. **1598** Proines [see B. 2]. **1602** *How to Choose Gd. Wife* III. iii. (1614) G j b, Pies, with Raisins, and with proines. **1603** SHAKS. *Meas. for M.* II. i. 93 Longing..for stewd prewyns. *Ibid.* 103. *Ibid.* 110. **1624** CAPT. SMITH *Virginia* II. 26 The fruit..they..preserue..as Pruines. **1658** PHILLIPS, *Jubeb*,..a kind of Pruan [**1696** Pruen, **1706** Prune]. **1659** WOOD *Life* 9 Apr. (O.H.S.) I. 277 Lemmons, oranges, pruins. **1711** *Lond. Gaz.* No. 4790/4, 24 small Barrels of new..Pruants. **1714** *Fr. Bk. of Rates* 20 Old Rags, Paper, Cards, Pruens, &c. **1719** *Accomplisht Lady's Delight* (ed. 10) 21 To make Conserve of Pruants. **1719** W. WOOD *Surv. Trade* 94 Wines, Brandies,..Pruans, Linins and wrought Silk. **1773** Pruin sauce [see B. 5].

B. Signification.

1. † **a.** The fruit of the plum-tree; a plum; also, the tree, *Prunus domestica. Obs.* (exc. as in c. and 2).

1530 PALSGR. 259/1 Prune a kynde of frute, *prune*. **1585** T. WASHINGTON tr. *Nicholay's Voy.* II. vii. 37 Gardens.. filled with..prunes, abricots, dates & olues. **1626** BACON *Sylva* §319 In Drying of Peares, and Prunes, in the Ouen, and Remouing of them often as they begin to Sweat. **1698** FRYER *Acc. E. India & P.* 247 Peach, Apricot, Prunello's, Figs, Prunes,..and all those we call Wall-Fruit.

† **b.** ***damask prune*** = DAMSON: see DAMASK 2.

[*c* **1400**: see A.] **1533** ELYOT *Cast. Helthe* (1539) 22 The damaske prune rather bindeth than lowseth. **1579** J. JONES *Preserv. Bodie & Soule* I. xvi. 29 Also Medlars, Peaches, Cheries, Grapes,..damaske proynes so they be sweete.

c. *U.S.* A variety of plum suitable for drying.

1902 *Westm. Gaz.* 14 Feb. 12/2 Prunes grow in many countries, and it is said California is 'full of them'.. The crop in 1900 was about 140,000,000 pounds. **1902** *Daily Chron.* 18 Sept. 5/1 After three years the prunes grow, the deep-blue ripe fruit being most plentiful at the end of August and beginning of September.

d. *slang* (orig. *U.S.*). A disagreeable or disliked person; a simpleton; spec., *Royal Air Force*, the personification of stupidity and incompetence (also, as a fictitious title, ***P.O. Prune***). Hence **ˈprunery**; **ˈprunish** *a.*

1895 W. C. GORE in *Inlander* Dec. 112 *Prune*, one who is disagreeable, and irritable. **1941** BAKER *Dict. Austral. Slang* 57 *Prune*, a simpleton, fool. **1942** *Tee Emm* (Air Ministry) II. 67 All because the Prunes of the Air Force *will* ignore the existence of A.A. Danger Areas. **1942** *Observer* 4 Oct. 7/2 The Royal Air Force has adopted him [*sc.* P.O. Prune] now, and an official magazine is devoted to the purpose of trying to cure him of his prunery! *Ibid.*, One day, I think, in some solemn dictionary Prune will become immortal. **1942** T. RATTIGAN *Flare Path* I. 30 They call me P.O. Prune—he's a character in The Training Manual—sort of crazy, good-tempered, half-witted sort of bloke..and I—well, I kind of act P.O. Prune for them. *Ibid.* II. i. 53 He's not quite so prunish as he lets on. **1943** C. H. WARD-JACKSON *Piece of Cake* 49 *Prune, Pilot Officer*, a fictitious character who behaves as every officer should not, created by Squadron Leader Anthony Armstrong and the artist RAFF (L. A. C. W. Hooper)... Prune was created to teach pupils and other flying personnel how things should not be done. **1944** 'N. SHUTE' *Pastoral* ii. 35 He wished..that he knew what it was that worried her, whether it was some prune that she had left at her last station. **1961** G. SMITH *Business of Loving* viii. 201 Snap out of it, you moonstruck old prune. **1963** *Listener* 28 Feb. 392/3 No horse-play, no gremlins: in Mr Barr's script the Prunes have all been turned into serious-minded Prisms. **1970** *Women Speaking* Apr. 5/1 If a man doesn't like a girl's looks or personality, she's a..prune, lemon. **1978** J. KRANTZ *Scruples* xiii. 368, I think she's a bit of a prune.

2. The dried fruit of several varieties of the common plum-tree, produced in France, Germany, Southern Europe, California, etc., and largely used for eating, raw or stewed; a dried plum. Formerly distinguished as ***dry prune***.

(The finest kind imported from France are also called *French plums*.)

1345–6 *Ely Sacr. Rolls* (1907) II. 130 In ij lb. de Prunnes empt. 1*s.* 4*d.* *c* **1400** Drie prunis [see A.]. *c* **1420** *Liber Cocorum* (1862) 40 Do dates þerto..and raysyns and prunus also. *c* **1430** *Two Cookery-bks.* 52 Plante þe cofynne a-boue with Prunez, & with Datys. **1584** COGAN *Haven Health* cv. (1636) 104 The Damasin Plummes are woont to be dried and preserved as figges, and are called in English, Prunes. **1598** *Epulario* B ij, Stuffe them with sweet hearbes, dry proines, soure grapes. **1633** HART *Diet Diseased* I. xvi. 63 In France and Spaine..they drie their plummes..these kinds wee commonly call..prunes. **1752** BERKELEY *Th. Tar-water* Wks. 1871 III. 503 Stewed prunes, and other diet of an opening kind. **1893** E. H. BARKER *Wand. Southern Waters* 295 Upon the sill were plums laid out on wooden trays to dry in the sun and become what English people call prunes.

3. *transf.* The dark reddish purple colour of the juice of prunes; also called ***prune-purple***. Also *attrib.*

1884 *Chr. World* 17 Jan. 52/1 All wool Rich Ottoman Dress material..in..Prune. **1884** *Pall Mall G.* 2 Sept. 4/1 Prune and a large variety of greys are likewise on the list of fashionable colours. **1899** *Westm. Gaz.* 20 May 1/3 Miss Debby arrayed in a prune silk gown. **1922** JOYCE *Ulysses* 690 A sofa upholstered in a prune plush. **1976** *Vogue* Jan. 74/1 Prune silk crepe de chine with tiny white print.

4. Phrase. ***prunes and prism***: see quot. 1855. Thence, applied to a prim and mincing manner of speaking, and to superficial 'accomplishments'. Also adj. phrs. ***prunes and prismy***, ***pruny and prismy***.

1855 DICKENS *Dorrit* II. v, 'Father is rather vulgar, my dear... Papa..gives a pretty form to the lips. Papa, potatoes, poultry, prunes and prism, are all very good for the lips: especially prunes and prism. You will find it serviceable in the formation of a demeanour, if you sometimes say to yourself in company or on entering a room, "Papa, potatoes, poultry, prunes, and prism, prunes and prism."' *Ibid.* vii. *heading*, Mostly, Prunes and Prism. **1888** *Brit. Weekly* 28 Sept. 353/1 He has none of the 'prunes and prism' style, and is, perhaps, addicted to strong language. **1892** W. G. JENKINS in *Amer. Ann. Deaf* Apr. 91 Surface accomplishments, the prunes and prisms of education. *c* **1909** D. H. LAWRENCE *Collier's Friday Night* (1934) i. 8 She says this in a very quaint 'prunes-and-prisms' manner, with her chin in the air and her hand extended. **1922** JOYCE *Ulysses* 365 Say prunes and prisms forty times every morning, cure for fat lips. **1931** *Time & Tide* 4 July 802/2 A tougher-minded generation than ours may find it altogether too prunes-and-prismy. **1940** G. D. H. & M. COLE *Counterpoint Murder* v. 50 She's forty if she's a day, and all pruny and prismy. **1979** *Daily Tel.* 22 Nov. 14/7 She regales us with an amusing chronicle of Lady Lytton's attempts to find a congenial companion among the straightlaced Indian Civil Service wives, whose 'prunes and prisms' expressions she found most off-putting.

5. *attrib.* and *Comb.* (see also sense 3), as ***prune-orchard***, ***-packer***, ***plum***, ***-rancher***, ***sauce***, ***-stone***, ***-whip***; ***prune-coloured***, ***-dark*** adjs.; **prune-brandy**, an alcoholic beverage prepared from prunes; **prune-juice**, the juice of prunes; also *attrib.* in reference to its colour (see 3); also (*U.S. slang*), nonsense; **prune picker** *U.S. colloq.*, a Californian; **prune-tree**, (*a*) a plum-tree (now in sense 1 c); (*b*) *Prunus occidentalis*, a West Indian timber-tree (*Treas. Bot.* 1866).

1895 M. PEMBERTON *Impregnable City* vi. 41 Drink that, and when you've drained the bumper, we'll have some *prune brandy. **1872** *Young Englishwoman* Nov. 595/1 A hat of duck-green turquoise is trimmed with *prune-coloured velvet. **1923** *Blackw. Mag.* Oct. 499/2 The foothills..were covered with a shadow over which prune-coloured clouds hung. **1941** L. MACNEICE *Plant & Phantom* 64 With *prune-dark eyes, thick lips, jostling each other. **1863** AITKEN *Sc. & Pract. Med.* (1866) II. 729 The so-called '*prune juice' expectoration characteristic of the third stage of pneumonia. **1873** T. H. GREEN *Introd. Pathol.* (ed. 2) 91 A rusty or prune-juice colour. **1957** J. KEROUAC *On Road* (1958) III. iv. 199 Here we were dealing with the pit and prunejuice of poor beat life. **1965** WODEHOUSE *Galahad at Blandings* x. 170 We decided that a big Society wedding was a lot of prune juice and we wanted no piece of it. **1921** *Chambers's Jrnl.* Mar. 173/1 *Prune-orchards do not need irrigating. **1905** *Daily News* 8 Dec. 6 The French *prune-packers, it is said, often import Californian prunes,..repack them,..and sell them to the Americans. **1918** L. E. RUGGLES *Navy Explained* 112 *Prune picker*, a native of California. So called because of the abundant prune crops. **1929** *Papers Mich. Acad. Sci., Arts & Lett.* X. 316 *Prune picker*, a Californian. **1891** *Ibid.* 24 Oct. 5/4 *Prune plums, damsons, and bullaces are the principal other fruit. **1921** *Chambers's Jrnl.* Mar. 174/2 With proper pruning and cultivation the *prune-rancher has an assured..living. **1773** GOLDSM. *Stoops to Conq.* I I, To men that are hungry, pig, with *pruin sauce is very good eating. **1599** PEELE *Sir Clyom.* Wks. (Rtldg.) 500/1 This fear hath made me beray myself with a *proin-stone that was not digested. **1617** *Janua Ling.* 98 The *prune tree and cherry tree do wither with frost. **1902** *Daily Chron.* 18 Sept. 5/1 A peach or apricot seed is planted, and when the little tree is a year old it is cut to the ground, and a piece of live prune-tree fastened to it. **1942** 'R. WEST' *Black Lamb & Grey Falcon* II. 26 Their coffee-brown beauty which fastidious nostrils, secretive lips and eyes like *prune-whip made refined and romantic.

prune (pru:n), *v.*[1] *Obsolescent.* [ME. *prune, pruyne, proyne*, of uncertain origin, but in its phonetics apparently French; agreeing in form with PRUNE *v.*[2], of which it has been supposed to be a specialized fig. application. This is not impossible; but PRUNE *v.*[2] is not found till later, nor was it common till about 1550, and its original, OF. *proignier*, is not used in this sense.

To identify them, it would be necessary to assume that in Anglo-Fr. (? in Falconry) the verb had acquired this changed use, and been taken into Eng., long before its original French sense was adopted. Evidence of the vb. in Anglo-Fr. has not been found. There appears to be some relationship between this and the synonymous *prene*, PREEN *v.*[2] Cf. the Chaucer quot. *c* 1386 in A. *β*]

A. Illustration of Forms.

α. 4- **prune**, (5 **prowne**, 6-7 **prewne**).

1390- Prune [see B.]. *c* **1450** *Bk. Hawkyng* in *Rel. Ant.* I. 298 Put her oute a-gayn to prowne and spalch herself, and a-non after that proynyng draw her in agayn. **1592**, *a* **1625** Prewn(e [see B. 4; PRUNING *vbl. sb.*[1] c].

β. 4 **pruyne**, 5-7 **proyne**, 6 **proine**, **proign**, 6-7 **proin**, **proyn**.

a **1380** Pruynen [see B. 1 b]. *c* **1386** CHAUCER *Merch. T.* 768 (*Corp. MS.*) He kembiþ him and proyneþ him and pikeþ [*so Cambr., Petw., Lansd.; Ellesm.* preyneth, *Heng.* prayneth, *Harl.* 7334 pruneth]. **1508** Proyne [see B. 1]. **1575** TURBERV. *Falconrie* 133 That they may..proine and picke their feathers. **1588** Proign [see PRUNING *vbl. sb.*[1] b]. **1623** B. JONSON *Underwoods, Celebr. Charis* v, Where I sit and proin my wings After flight.

γ. Sc. 5-6 **prunȝe**, 6 **prunȝa**, **pronȝe**, **prounȝe**, **prwnȝe**, **prunȝie**.

c **1450** HOLLAND *Howlat* 21 Birdis..Pransand and prunȝeand, be pair and be pair. **1508** DUNBAR *Tua Mariit Wemen* 374, I wald me prunȝa plesandly in precius wedis. **1513** DOUGLAS *Æneis* v. iii. 50 A standand place quhar skarthis with their beikis, Forgane the son, glaidlie thaim pronȝe and bekis. *c* **1560** Prounȝe [see B. 2 b]. **1571** *Satir. Poems Reform.* xxxvii. 56 Persaue..þe papingo þat prwnȝeis. *a* **1585** MONTGOMERIE *Flyting* 86 As proud as ȝee prunȝie, ȝour pennes sall be plucked.

B. Signification.

1. Of a bird (or any being so figured): To trim or dress the feathers with the beak: = PREEN *v.*[2] **1. a.** *trans.* (*refl.*, or with the feathers, etc. as *obj.*)

1390 GOWER *Conf.* III. 75 For there he [i.e. the eagle] pruneth him and piketh, As doth an hauk. **1490** CAXTON *Eneydos* xvi. 63 As a byrde that pruneth or pycketh her. **1508** FISHER *Penit. Ps.* cii. Wks. (1876) 154 There she proyneth & setteth her feders in ordre. **1590** SPENSER *F.Q.* II. iii. 36 She gins her feathers fowle disfigured Prowdly to prune, and sett on every side. **1704** SWIFT *Batt. Bks.* Misc. (1711) 235 Friend, said the Bee (having now prun'd himself). **1735** POPE *Donne Sat.* iv. 186 Where Contemplation prunes her ruffled wings. **1820** SCOTT *Abbot* vii, The falcon instantly settled on his wrist, and began to prune itself. **1874** HOLLAND *Mistr. Manse* v, The pigeon pruned his opal breast.

b. *absol.* or *intr.* for *refl.*

a **1380** *Pistill of Susan* 81 þe popeiayes perken and pruynen for proude. **1423** JAS. I *Kingis Q.* lxiv, The birdis ..said, 'wele is vs begone,..We proyne and play without dout and dangere'. **1649** G. DANIEL *Trinarch., Hen. IV* lxxiv, Harry prunes safe, and brings fresh feathers on T' enlarge his wing.

2. Of a person: To trim, dress up with minute nicety; to prink, deck out, adorn. **a.** *trans.* (or *refl.*): cf. PREEN *v.*[2] 2. (In quot. *c* 1450, ironical.)

c **1386** [see A. *β*]. *c* **1450** *Cov. Myst.* xvii. (Shaks. Soc.) 164, I xal prune that paddok and prevyn hym as a pad. **1513** DOUGLAS *Æneis* IV. v. 80 His hair enoynt weill prunȝeit ondir that. **1599** B. JONSON *Cynthia's Rev.* Induct., Another.. with more beard than brain prunes his mustaccio. **1629** MASSINGER *Picture* IV. ii, The younger Prunes up himself, as if..he were To act a bridegroom's part. **1737** *Songs Costume* (Percy Soc.) 220 Adorn thy mind the more within, And prune thy person less. **1789** E. DARWIN *Bot. Gard.* II. 13 So Ninon pruned her wither'd charms.

b. *absol.* or *intr.* for *refl.*

c **1560** A. SCOTT *Poems* (S.T.S.) xxxiv. 95 Swa ladeis will no[t] sounȝe With waistit wowbattis rottin, Bot prowdly thay will prounȝe, Quhair geir is to be gottin. **1678** DRYDEN *All for Love* Epil. 13 He grows a fop..Prunes up, and asks his oracle, the glass, If pink or purple best become his face. **1684** OTWAY *Atheist* III. i, A vain, pert, empty Rogue, That can prune, dance, lisp, or lie very much.

†**3.** *refl. fig.* To plume oneself, pride oneself. *Obs.*

1643 TRAPP *Comm. Gen.* xi. 7 He turned Nebuchadnezzar a grazing among beasts, for pruning and priding himself upon this Babel. **1657** W. BLOIS *Mod. Policies*, etc. (ed. 7) E iij b, The Great Turk may justly exsult and prune him-self in discourses of this nature. **1672** MARVELL *Reh. Transp.* I. 43 Divines..who pruned themselves in the peculiar Virulency of their Pens.

†**4.** *trans.* To set in order. *Obs. rare.*

1592 WARNER *Alb. Eng.*, *Æneidos* 195 A hunting was generally appoynted,..the Standes were prewned; the Toyles pitched.

prune (pru:n), *v.*[2] Forms: *α.* 5 **prouyne**, 6-7 **proin(e**, **proyne**; *β.* 7 **pruin(e**, **pruyn(e**, 6- **prune**. [In 15th c. *prouyne*, in 16th c. *proine*, a. OF. *proöing(n)ier, proögnier*, later *proignier*, in 16th c. *progner, prougner*, to prune or cut back (the vine): cf. *L'aultre sa vigne y prougne ou taille* (E. Damernal ed. 1597).

The ulterior history of the OF. is uncertain; it is quite distinct in sense and form from *provaigner, provigner* to layer a vine-shoot; PROVINE *v.*; although in mod.F. dialects the latter is reduced to *preugner, progner*.]

1. a. *trans.* To cut or lop superfluous branches or twigs from (a vine, tree, or shrub), in order to promote fruitfulness, induce regular growth, etc.; to trim.

α. **1547** *Homilies* I. *Falling fr. God* II. (1859) 87 As long as a man doth proine his vines, doth dig at the roots, and doth lay fresh earth to them, he hath a mind to them, he perceiveth some token of fruitfulness. **1553** T. WILSON *Rhet.* (1580) 49 He is coumpted no good Gardener, that.. doeth diligently proine his old Trees, and hath no regard either to ympe or graffe young settes. **1670** W. HUGHES *Compl. Vineyard* 15 In Germany..they Proin not their Vines the first year.

β. **1575** FENTON *Gold. Epist.* (1577) 93 The tree..by the high way giues more shadowe to the passenger, than fruite to the owner that prunes it. **1611** BIBLE *Lev.* xxv. 3 Sixe yeeres thou shalt prune thy Vineyard. **1624** CAPT. SMITH *Virginia* II. 26 Vines..covered with fruit, though never pruined nor manured. **1711** ADDISON *Spect.* No. 98 ¶1 Like Trees new lopped and pruned. **1870** YEATS *Nat. Hist. Comm.* 76 In France, the vine is pruned down to the size of a gooseberry bush.

b. *absol.*

1584 R. SCOT *Discov. Witchcr.* IX. ii. (1886) 136 Times and seasons to sowe, to plant, to proine. **1612** DRAYTON *Polyolb.* iii. 357 Heere set, and there they sowe; here proine, and there they plant. **1648** SANDERSON *Serm.* (1681) II. 243 What Husbandman would plow and sow and plant and prune..if he did not hope..to Inn the fruits? **1847** EMERSON *Repr. Men, Montaigne* Wks. (Bohn) I. 347 On the whole, selfishness plants best, prunes best, makes the best commerce, and the best citizen.

2. To cut or lop off (branches, boughs, shoots).

α. **1572** MASCALL *Plant. & Graff.* (1575) 12 Ye must proyne or cut the braunch of commonlye in winter. **1612** *Two Noble K.* III. vi. 242 Doe men proyne The straight yong bowes that blush with thousand blossoms? **1626** BACON *Sylva* §432 A Tree..[with] the lower boughes onely maintained, and the higher continually proined off.

β. **1612** WOODALL *Surg. Mate* Wks. (1653) 390 After the dead boughs are pruned off. **1846** J. BAXTER *Libr. Pract. Agric.* (ed. 4) I. 99 [They] should have their bottom side-shoots carefully pruned, cutting them close to their stem.

3. *fig.* **a.** To 'cut down', mutilate (quot. 1565); to rob, spoil (quot. 1640); *esp.* to cut down or reduce by rejecting superfluities; also to rid or clear *of* what is superfluous or undesirable.

α. **1426** LYDG. *De Guil. Pilgr.* 244 Many a thyng, yt ys no nay, Mot be prouyned, & kut a-way, And yshape of newe entaylle. **1565** JEWEL *Repl. Harding* (1611) 274 It is neither indifferent, nor true dealing, thus to nip, and to proine the Doctours sayings. **1608** MACHIN *Dumb Knight* III. i. F j b, Hee proind him well and brought him vp to learning. **1640** HOWELL *Dodona's Gr.* 50 They might oppresse, spoyle, rob, peele, proyne, and grubbe them up at pleasure.

β. **1605** BACON *Adv. Learn.* II. xxiii. §49 Howe they [laws] are to bee pruned and reformed from time to time. **1659** STANLEY *Hist. Philos.* XII. (1701) 475/1 When I considered, how difficult it were so to prune it [a treatise], as to please all Persons. **1711** ADDISON *Spect.* No. 135 ¶10 Some..Authors ..began to prune their Words of all superfluous Letters. **1796** SOUTHEY *Lett. fr. Spain* (1799) 201 [The lamp] has three branches;..a small pincers to prune it, and a bucket to deposit the snuff in. **1836** J. H. NEWMAN in *Brit. Mag.* X. 137 Prune thou thy words. **1838** PRESCOTT *Ferd. & Is.* (1846) II. xx. 194 Pruning it of all superfluous phrases. **1925** B. BEETHAM in E. F. Norton *Fight for Everest, 1924* 368 Bow to the inevitable, countenance what you deem to be reasonable, but prune early with a firm pencil anything excessive. **1970** *Railway Mag.* Oct. 546/1 The locomotive-hauled stock of British Railways has been drastically pruned in recent years.

b. To take away or remove (superfluities, deformities). Also with *out*.

c **1680** WALLER *On Earl of Roscommon* 9 Horace will our superfluous Branches prune. **1766** BLACKSTONE *Comm.* II. v. 77 Even *magna carta* itself..only pruned the luxuriances that had grown out of the military tenures. **1869** TOZER *Highl. Turkey* II. 117 Establishing a standard and pruning away deformities [in language]. **1955** *Bull. Atomic Sci.* Mar. 94/2 Undoubtedly, these will be pruned out in the next edition. **1973** *Sci. Amer.* June 93/3 Shannon therefore proposed that the computer should not consider all possible moves from each position but should prune out the most obvious of bad moves.

pruned (pru:nd, *poet.* 'pru:nɪd), *ppl. a.*[1] *arch.* [f. PRUNE *v.*[1] + -ED[1].] Trimmed, as a bird's feathers with the beak; also *fig.*: see PRUNE *v.*[1]

1595 BARNFIELD *Sonn.* vii, My siluer Swan is swimming: Against the sunne his pruned feathers trimming. **1641** G. SANDYS *Paraphr. Song Sol.* v. iv, Black as the newly pruned Crow.

pruned, *ppl. a.*[2] [f. PRUNE *v.*[2] + -ED[1].] Trimmed, as a tree or shrub, by cutting off superfluous branches, etc.; cut off, as a superfluous branch; also *fig.*: see PRUNE *v.*[2]

1552 HULOET, Pruned and cutte, *resex, sectiuus.* **1649** JER. TAYLOR *Gt. Exemp.* III. Disc. xiv. 11 Peace sheds no blood but of the pruned vine. **1895** *Westm. Gaz.* 11 Sept. 8/2 A persecuted cause, they no doubt reflect, flourishes like a pruned fruit tree.

†**pru'nel.** *Obs.* Also 6 **-elle**, 6-8 **-ell.** [a. F. *prunelle*, a variant of *brunelle* BRUNEL; so G. *prunelle* (obs. *braunelle*), med.L. *brunella, prunella*: see PRUNELLA[2].] The herb Self-heal (*Prunella vulgaris*); formerly often including the Bugle (*Ajuga reptans*).

1578 LYTE *Dodoens* I. xc. 132 There be two kindes of Prunell. The first is called Bugle. And the second reteyneth still the name of Prunell. *Ibid.* 133 Prunell..is also a soueraigne remedie against that disease which the Brabanders do name *den Bruynen*, that is, when the tongue is inflamed and waxeth blacke and is much swollen, so that the generall remedies haue gone before. **1597**, **1611** [see BRUNEL]. **1610** W. FOLKINGHAM *Art of Survey* I. x. 25 The sowing of the seede of Trefoyle, or Clauers, Melilot, Prunel, Milfoyle, &c...doth much inrich Meddowes. **1727** BRADLEY *Fam. Dict.* s.v. *Cut*, Take some prunel or else some nettles, and [apply to a cut].

Comb. **1599** A. M. tr. *Gabelhouer's Bk. Physicke* 78/2 Prunelle-water.

prunelet ('pru:nlɪt). [f. PRUNE *sb.* + -LET (app. arbitrarily).] 'A liquor made from sloes or wild plums' (Simmonds *Dict. Trade* 1858).

prunella[1] (pru:'nɛlə). Also 7-9 **prunello**; *β.* 8 **prenel**, 9 **prunelle**. [Of uncertain history: identical with mod.F. *prunelle*, but this is cited by Littré only from 1780, though it may occur earlier. Littré derives the name from *prunelle*, sloe, in reference to its dark colour. The forms *prunella, -ello* have the appearance of It. or Sp., but do not occur in dicts. of these langs. in the 17th c.; they may have been merely Eng. grandiose alterations, as in some words in *-ada, -ado*, etc. The *β* form *prunelle* follows the French.]

1. A strong stuff, orig. silk, afterwards worsted, formerly used for graduates', clergymen's, and barristers' gowns; later, for the uppers of women's shoes.

leather and prunella: a misquotation and misapplication of Pope's 'leather or prunella': see LEATHER *sb.* 1 d.

1656 *Bk. Values* in Scobell *Acts & Ordin. Parl.* (1658) 474 Wrought Silks called..Prunellos, broad, the Ell 00. 15. 00. **1670** LADY M. BERTIE in *12th Rep. Hist. MSS. Comm.* App. v. 21 Upon the Queene's Birthday most wore..plaine black skirts of Morella, Mohair, Prunella, and such stuffs. **1688** R. HOLME *Armoury* III. 199/1 Bachelors of Art..have a full Gown..of Stuff, Silk, Prunella, or the like. **1734** POPE *Ess. Man* IV. 204 Worth makes the man, and want of it, the fellow; The rest is all but leather or prunella. *a* **1761** CAWTHORN *Poems, Wit & Learning* (1771) 191 He..Gave him a robe of sleek prunella. **1811-1879** [see LEATHER *sb.* 1 d]. **1864** SALA *Quite Alone* I. i. 2 Everybody..trips in soft sandalled prunella, or white satin with high heels. **1882** BECK *Draper's Dict.*, *Prunella, Prunello*, a stuff only rescued from complete oblivion by Pope's famous couplet.

β. **1710** *Lond. Gaz.* No. 4706/4 For Sale.., black Prenels and Russerines. **1840** J. P. KENNEDY *Quodlibet* ix, Agamemnon Flag..in boots of drab prunelle. **1857** JAMES *Hist. Worsted Manuf.* x. 362 There were different sorts of lastings, as prunelles wrought with three healds.

2. (See quot. A modern trade use.)

1904 *Woollen Draper's Terms* in *Tailor & Cutter* 4 Aug. 479/3 *Prunella*, a superior make of doeskin having a fine diagonal twill on it.

3. *attrib.* Made or consisting of prunella.

1706 E. WARD *Wooden World Diss.* (1708) 41 He wears his Prunella Gown, as chearily as he does his Honesty. **1862** RUSSELL *Diary North & South* (1863) II. 20 White jean trousers, strapped under a pair of prunella slippers. **1872-6** VOYLE & STEVENSON *Milit. Dict.*, *Lasting Cloth*, a material similar to prunella cloth. **1907** in *Daily News* 2 Oct. 4, I brushed her [Marie Antoinette's] pretty black prunella shoes.

Hence **pru'nella'd** *a.*, wearing prunella gowns.

1812 H. & J. SMITH *Rej. Addr.* xv, Nods the prunella'd bar, attorneys smile.

‖**pru'nella**[2]. *Bot.* [Bot. L., alteration of *Brunella*, generic name in Tournefort and Linnæus, recently restored in English Floras. *P. vulgaris* is said to have been so named from being a specific against the disease *brunella* or *prunella*: see BRUNEL, PRUNEL, and Note to next.] A genus of herbaceous labiates, of general distribution in both temperate zones. *P. vulgaris*, Self-heal, is a common weed in Britain. (Formerly also taken to include the Bugle, *Ajuga reptans*.)

[**1578** LYTE *Dodoens* I. xc. 133 The second kinde is also called *Consolida media*, but most commonly *Prunella* or *Brunella*: in English Prunell.] **1599** A. M. tr. *Gabelhouer's Bk. Physicke* 74/2 This vngvent is also excellent..for sore throtes, when as we intermixe the same with water of Prunella. **1664** EVELYN *Kal. Hort.* (1729) 205 May... Flowers in Prime,..Pansis, Prunella, purple Thalictrum. **1706** PHILLIPS (ed. Kersey), *Prunella*..also the Herb Self-heal, good against a Quinsy, and other Diseases of the Mouth and Jaws. **1844** EMERSON *Ess.* Ser. II. vi. 158 All over the wide fields of earth grows the prunella or self-heal.

‖**pru'nella**[3]. *Obs.* Also 9 **prunelle**. [mod.L., earlier *brunella*, according to 16th c. writers, orig. the L. name of an infectious epidemic called in Ger. *die bräune* or *breune* (Grimm), in Du. *de bruyne*, lit. 'the browns' or 'brownness', in which the tongue was covered with a brown crust. *Brunella* was thus a dim. of med.L. *brūnus* brown: cf. *jaundice*, F. *jaunisse*, and such names of diseases as *whites*, *yellows*, *blues*, etc. The corruption *prunella* may have been due to High German pronunciation, or to a later fancied etymology, taking it as dim. of L. *prūna* 'burning coal'. See also BRUNEL, PRUNEL, PRUNELLA[2], name of the herb reputed as a specific for the disease; and Note below.]

1. *Path.* A name given to the Hungarian or camp-fever which prevailed among the imperial troops in Germany in 1547 and 1566, considered by Hecker to have been petechial. In later times, applied to other disorders of the throat or fauces, esp. to quinsy: see quots. In quot. 1658 app. used for Inflammation.

1658 A. Fox *Würtz' Surg.* I. v. 20 Many use Phlebotomy ..supposing to prevent hereby the prunella in wounds. **1669** W. Simpson *Hydrol. Chym.* 83 The spaw water avails nothing in..plurisies, prunella's, poysons. **1693** tr. *Blancard's Phys. Dict.* (ed. 2), *Prunella*, is sometimes taken for *Apthæ*, White, Black or Red, sometimes for a Quinsie or the Hungarick Fever. **1895** *Syd. Soc. Lex.*, *Prunella*... term for *Angina pectoris*; also, for *Cynanche*; also, for thrush, *Aphthous stomatitis*.

2. *Pharmacy.* Chiefly in comb. **prunella salt, prunelle salt**, in mod.L. *sal prunellæ*, *prunellæ sal*, also *lapis prunellæ* 'prunella stone', SAL-PRUNELLA, name for a preparation of fused nitre.

So called as used for the disorder of the throat.

1627 *Pharmacop. Lond.* (ed. 3) 189 Lapis Prunellæ. **1669** tr. *Schroder's Dispensatory* 254 Lapis Prunellæ, Nitre tabulated or prepared. **1681** [see SAL-PRUNELLA]. **1706** Phillips (ed. Kersey), *Sal Prunellæ*..is sometimes called *Lapis Prunellæ*, and *Crystal Mineral*; being usually given to cool and provoke Urine in Feavers and Quinsies. **1741** *Compl. Fam.-Piece* I. ii. 103 Put to it 4 Pounds of Bay Salt, ..2 Ounces of Prunella Salt. **1830** Maunder *Dict.*, *Prunella*, purified saltpetre. **1864** Webster s.v., *Prunella salt*, or *prunella*, fused niter, molded into cakes or balls, and used for chemical purposes. **1866–8** Watts *Dict. Chem.* IV. 740 *Prunelle Salt* or *Nitrum tabulatum*, fused saltpetre.

[*Note.* For the etymology of *brunella*, and the derivation thence of the name of the herb, cf. quots. under BRUNEL, PRUNEL, and PRUNELLA[2], also Gerarde *Herbal* (1636) 508. As to the camp-fever of 1547, 1566, see Hecker *Epidemics of the Middle Ages*, Eng. tr. by Babington, ed. 3, 1859, 277–8. Grimm cites Kirchhof (1602) *Milit. Discipl.* 202 'viel seucht und krankheiten (im lager), sonderlich die breune'. Kilian (1599) has '*Bruyne*..oris vitium cum linguæ tumore, exasperatione, siccitate, & nigredine: vnde et nomen teutonicè habet, vulgo *brunella*: quo nomine et herba vocatur quæ huic morbo medetur'. As to *sal prunellæ*, Boerhaave, *Elem. Chemiæ* (1732) 389, says (tr. P. Shaw 1741 II. 245), This has obtained the name of *sal prunellæ* from the Germans, who observing that a certain kind of epidemical camp-fever, attended with a dangerous black quinsey, which they call *die braune*, was happily cured by the use of this powder; they thence called it by that name: and for the same reason they give the same appellation to the plant self-heal or *prunella*, because this cures the same distemper.]

prunella, variant of PRUNELLO.

prunelle: see PRUNEL, PRUNELLA[1], [3], PRUNELLO.

prunello (pruːˈnɛləʊ). Also 7, 9 **prunella**, 8 **-elle**, 9 **-elloe**. [Altered from obs. It. *prunella* 'any kind of little plumbe or Prune' (Florio), dim. of *pruna* (mod. *prugna*) plum, prune. Cf. F. *prunelle* (*-ele* c 1270 in Godef. *Compl.*) a sloe.]

†**a.** Name for a variety of plum or prune, fresh or dried. *Obs.* **b.** The finest kind of prunes or dried plums, made from the greengage and other varieties.

1616 Bullokar *Eng. Expos.*, *Prunellas*, a fruite like small Figges, good for restoratiue, and to comfort the heart. **1622** Fletcher *Sea Voy.* III. i, Nor julips, Nor guaiacums, prunellos, camphire pills,..come not near your old woman. **1662** J. Davies tr. *Mandelslo's Trav.* II. (1669) 120 The fruit at first is green..a little bitter, like our Prunelloes. **1712** tr. *Pomet's Hist. Drugs* I. 168 We sell abundance of Prunes and Prunelles, as the Large and the Small. **1741** *Compl. Fam.-Piece* I. iii. 239 Lay them drying till they be as dry as Prunello's. **1786** Sir J. E. Smith in *Mem.* (1832) I. 195 Dined at Brignolle, famous for the *Prunes de Brignolle*, which we have corrupted into Prunellas. **1812** J. Smyth *Pract. of Customs* (1821) 185 Prunelloes are a sort of French Prunes, of which large quantities are annually gathered in Provence. **1895** *Syd. Soc. Lex.*, *Prunelloe*, a popular name for the *Prunum brignolense*.

prunello, variant of PRUNELLA[1].

pruner (ˈpruːnə(r)). Forms: see PRUNE *v.*[2] [f. PRUNE *v.*[2] + -ER[1].]

1. One who prunes trees or shrubs.

1586 W. Webbe *Eng. Poetrie* (Arb.) 75 (Virgil *Ecl.* I. 57) Vnder a Rock side here will proyner chaunt [*canet frondator*] merrie ditties. **1587** Golding *De Mornay* xxi. (1592) 322 The inuention..of the proiner of Vines. **1611** Speed *Theat. Gt. Brit.* xiii. (1614) 25/2 These grafts..were cut downe by the Pruiner. **1761** Beattie *Hares* 86 An ancient Wood..By pruner's axe yet unprofaned. **1887** Bowen *Virg. Eclogue* IV. 40 Glebe shall be free from the harrow, the vine no pruner fear.

fig. a **1763** Shenstone *Economy* I. 256 Youth is fair virtue's season, virtue then Requires the pruner's hand. **1876** Spurgeon *Commenting* 4 Calvin..was no trimmer and pruner of texts.

2. A tool used for pruning trees or shrubs.

1895 *Montgomery Ward Catal.* Spring & Summer 391/3 This pruner, being made with the shear cut, will work with double the ease of any other pruner. *Ibid.*, Waters' Improved Tree Pruner. **1916** L. H. Bailey *Pruning Man.* vi. 192 (*caption*) Double-lever and single-lever pole pruner. **1949** E. Hyams *Not in Our Stars* xiii. 160 The long-arm pruner had tired his arms and shoulders. **1971** *Country Life* 14 Oct. 955/3 My arm aches from using the sickle, and the heavy pruner. **1975** E. Wigginton *Foxfire 3* 26 Got to where I couldn't press the pruners enough to cut a big limb.

prung, obs. form of PRONG *sb.*[2]

prunȝe, obs. Sc. form of PRUNE *v.*[1]

prunȝeandlie: see PRONȜEAND.

pruˈniferous, *a. rare.* [f. L. *prūn-um* PRUNE *sb.* + -(I)FEROUS.] Bearing plums or stone-fruits; drupiferous.

1668 Wilkins *Real Char.* II. iv. §7. 112 Trees may be distinguished according to their Fruit or Seed.. Pruniferous. **1688** R. Holme *Armoury* II. 119/1 Pruniferous Trees..bear Fruit with Stones in them. **1750** G. Hughes *Barbadoes* 174 Shrubs and plants of the Pruniferous kind.

pruniform (ˈpruːnɪfɔːm), *a.* [f. mod.L. *prūniform-is*: see -(I)FORM.] Having the form or appearance of a plum.

1858 Mayne *Expos. Lex.*, *Pruniformis*,..pruniform.

pruning (ˈpruːnɪŋ), *vbl. sb.*[1] *arch.* Forms: see PRUNE *v.*[1] [See -ING[1].] The action of PRUNE *v.*[1]; preening. **a.** Of birds.

c **1450** [see PRUNE *v.*[1] A. a]. **1486** *Bk. St. Albans* A vj, An hawke wolde not be letted of hir proynyng. **1555** Digges *Prognost.* B ij b, If they busy them selues in proyning or washing..looke for rayne. **1611** Cotgr., *Onction feable*, the pruining, or annointing which a Hawke giues her feathers, by the moisture she sucks from her Crupper.

b. Of a person: see PRUNE *v.*[1] 2.

1588 Kyd *Househ. Phil.* Wks. (1901) 256 Those [women] that are faire with that filthy spunging, proigning, painting, and pollishing themselues. a **1652** A. Wilson *Inconstant Ladie* II. ii, Your prunings, paintings, and bare necks.

c. *concr. fig.* from use in Falconry.

a **1625** Fletcher *Love's Pilgr.* III. ii, Dare she think..My love so fond..That I must take her prewnings: stoop at that sh'has tyr'd upon?

ˈpruning, *vbl. sb.*[2] Forms: see PRUNE *v.*[2] [f. PRUNE *v.*[2] + -ING[1].] The action of PRUNE *v.*[2]

1. a. Of plants: see PRUNE *v.*[2] 1.

1548 Elyot *Dict.*, *Castratio arborum*, the ofte cuttyng or prunyng of trees. **1615** W. Lawson *Country Housew. Gard.* (1626) 6 Trees..loaden with wood, for want of proyning. **1706** London & Wise *Retir'd Gard.* I. 108 Pruning makes a tree look handsome. **1858** Glenny *Gard. Everyday Bk.* 50/2 Pruning is better done in the latter months of the year, when the leaves have fallen. **1941** P. P. Pirone *Maintenance of Shade & Ornamental Trees* v. 58 Proper and systematic pruning helps trees better to withstand adverse environmental conditions. **1972** G. E. Brown (*title*) The pruning of trees, shrubs and conifers.

b. *concr.* (*pl.*) Portions cut off in pruning.

1832 *Planting* 4 in *Libr. Usef. Knowl.*, *Husb.* III, Affording a quicker return of profit in prunings and thinnings. **1884** Roe *Nat. Ser. Story* vii, The prunings of the shrubbery.

2. *fig.*: see PRUNE *v.*[2] 3.

a **1603** Q. Eliz. in Nichols *Progr. Q. Eliz.* (1823) I. 10, I plucke up the goodlisome herbs of sentences by pruning. **1625** Bacon *Ess.*, *Studies* (Arb.) 9 Naturall Abilities are like Naturall Plants, that need Proyning by Study. **1907** *Nation* (N.Y.) 23 Nov. 271/1 The prunings and chastenings of his fancy. a **1930** D. H. Lawrence *Last Poems* (1932) 289 Humanity needs pruning. **1969** *Listener* 6 Mar. 322/1 It is a surprise to find the *Lyric Symphony*..a highly charged, expansive outpouring in seven longish movements of which the first three could themselves do with some pruning. **1970** T. Lupton *Managem. & Social Sci.* (ed. 2) ii. 47 A drastic alteration of working practices and some pruning of manpower. **1971** *Nature* 16 July 206/2 If a second edition is prepared, the editors would do well to perform some judicious pruning.

3. *attrib.* and *Comb.*, esp. in the name of tools or implements used in pruning, as ***pruning-bill***, ***-chisel***, ***-saw***, ***-scissors***, ***-shears***, PRUNING-HOOK, -KNIFE.

c **1586** C'tess Pembroke *Ps.* LXXX. iii, Thou..Nor planting care didst slack, nor pruning paines. **1822** Loudon *Encycl. Gard.* 319 The Pruning-Bill is generally a hooked blade..attached to a handle of from one to four feet in length. *Ibid.*, The Pruning-Saw is a blade of steel, serrated in what is called the double manner on one side. *Ibid.* 320 The Pruning-Shears differ from the common sort, in having a moveable centre for the motion of one of the blades, by which means, instead of a crushing-cut, they make a draw-cut.

ˈpruning, *ppl. a.* [f. PRUNE *v.*[2] + -ING[2].] That prunes (*lit.* or *fig.*): see PRUNE *v.*[2]

1649 G. Daniel *Trinarch.*, *Hen. IV* cccxxv, Soe stands the vineyard of Humanitye..Where pruneing Lawes lye by. a **1845** Barham *Cousin Nicholas* iv, Under the pruning and training hand of a skilful master.

ˈpruning-hook. *arch.* [f. PRUNING *vbl. sb.*[2] + HOOK *sb.*[1] 3.] A curved cutting implement used for pruning. Also *fig.* (cf. PRUNE *v.*[2] 3).

1611 Bible *Isa.* ii. 4 They shall beate their swords into plow-shares, and their speares into pruning hookes [*marg.* or, sythes]. **1688** South *Serm.* (1727) V. ix. 354 The great Husbandman of Souls takes this Course with his spiritual Vines, to add the Pruning-hook of his Judgments to the more gentle Manurings of his Mercy. **1697** Dryden *Virg. Georg.* II. 577 When peaceful Vines from Pruning-hooks are free. **1706** London & Wise *Retir'd Gard.* I. 261 The Gard'ner..will have Occasion for a Pruning-Hook to trim them.

ˈpruning-knife. A knife used for pruning. Also *fig.* (cf. PRUNE *v.*[2] 3).

1589 Warner *Alb. Eng.* VI. xxx. (1612) 147 Bacchus [needeth thee] for prewning Kniues. c **1610** in *Alleyn Papers* (1843) 39 And, if it thee please, use eke thy proinynge knife. **1717** Berkeley *Tour in Italy* Wks. 1871 IV. 575 They wear each by his side a broad pruning-knife. **1851** Dickens *Let. to Miss M. Boyle* 21 Feb., You will not be alarmed by my use of the pruning-knife.

prunoid (ˈpruːnɔɪd), *a.* [f. L. *prūn-um* PRUNE *sb.* + -OID.] Having the shape of a plum; ellipsoidal. So **pruˈnoidean** *a. Zool.*, belonging to the suborder *Prunoidea* of radiolarians, characterized by an ellipsoidal lattice-shell.

1888 Rolleston & Jackson *Anim. Life* 875 A lattice-shell,..in shape spherical, ellipsoidal (prunoid), discoidal [etc.]. **1895** *Funk's Stand. Dict.*, *Prunoidean.*

prunt (prʌnt). [perh. a provincial form of *print.*] A piece of ornamental glass, frequently of the blackberry form, attached or laid on to a body of glass, as a vase: also the tool with which this ornament is moulded or impressed with its pattern. Hence **ˈprunted** *a.*, ornamented with prunts.

1891 *Sale Catal. Glass Wks. Stourbridge*, No. 204 Pair of large fluted tools. 205 Three prunts. **1902** *Jrnl. Archæol. Inst.* Mar. 3 The 'prunts' on early glass. **1907** *Academy* 11 Oct. 6/1 The remarkable series of vessels from Anglo-Saxon graves, of which..the prunted vases appear to be the earliest, and to have been imported into England in the latter half of the sixth century.

‖**prunus** (ˈpruːnəs). [L. *prūnus* plum-tree, ad. Gr. προῦνος = προύμνη; also (*prūnus silvestris*) a sloe-bush. Adopted by Linnæus (*Hortus Cliffortianus* (1737) 186) as the name of a genus.]

1. *Bot.* (Also with capital initial.) A genus of trees and shrubs, N.O. *Rosaceæ*, containing the common sloe, bullace, plum, apricot, myrobalan, and many other species or sub-species, bearing drupaceous fruits. Also, a tree or shrub belonging to this genus, esp. one of many varieties of cherry cultivated for the sake of their ornamental, pink or white flowers.

1706 in Phillips. **1901** L. H. Bailey *Cycl. Amer. Hort.* III. 1445/2 It is an important point in the growing of these grafted Prunuses to remove all sprouts from the stock as soon as they appear. **1945** J. Betjeman *New Bats in Old Belfries* 22 Pinkly bursts the spray Of prunus and forsythia across the public way. **1966** *New Statesman* 7 Jan. 25/2 The evergreen prunus we call cherry-laurel. **1972** *Countryman* Summer 48 The old prunus on the lawn..immediately caught my eye.

2. In *Oriental Pottery.* A representation of a Chinese and Japanese species, *P. mume*, on porcelain, etc. Hence ***prunus decoration***.

1878 A. W. Franks *Catal. Coll. Oriental Pottery* (ed. 2) 245 The plum-tree or prunus (Chinese *mei*, Japanese *mume*..) forms the decoration of the pottery, erroneously termed 'may-flower' or 'hawthorn' pattern. **1898** *Daily News* 11 July 10/5 A bowl of fine pale green jade, carved on the exterior with birds and prunus in low relief. **1905** Bushell *Chinese Art* I. 111 The *prunus* because it throws out flowering twigs from its leafless stalks up to extreme old age. **1908** C. F. Bell *Let. to Editor*, *Prunus decoration* is now more generally understood as decoration with the sprigs of the flowers and thorny stems of the Chinese wild plum.

prurience (ˈprʊərɪəns). [f. as PRURIENT: see -ENCE.]

1. The physical fact or sensation of itching.

a **1688** Cudworth *Immut. Mor.* (1731) 83 Pruriences and Titillations of the Body.

2. *fig.* Mental itching or craving.

1829 I. Taylor *Enthus.* ix. 231 An irresistible prurience asking for the marvellous. **1837** [see PRURIENTLY]. **1879** F. Harrison *Choice Bks.* (1886) 29 This literary prurience after new print unmans us.

3. = PRURIENCY 3.

1781 Cowper *Conversat.* 31 There is a prurience in the speech of some, Wrath stays him, or else God would strike them dumb. **1926** H. W. Fowler *Mod. Eng. Usage* 473/1 *Prurience*, *-cy*. There is no differentiation; *-ence* is recommended. **1974** C. Ricks *Keats & Embarrassment* i. 15 Prurience, pruriency, and prurient came fully into their modern meaning (from 'itching') in the eighteenth century.

pruriency (ˈprʊərɪənsɪ). [f. as prec.: see -ENCY.]

1. The quality of itching, itchingness. *rare.*

1669 W. Simpson *Hydrol. Chym.* 164 An incipient putrefaction which begets a pruriency or itching in the blood. **1814** Cary *Dante* (Chandos) 90 Each one Plied quickly his keen nails, through furiousness Of ne'er abated pruriency.

2. *fig.* The quality or condition of mental itching.

1711 Steele *Spect.* No. 151 ¶2 A general Impatience of Thought, and a constant Pruriency of inordinate Desire. **1824–9** Landor *Imag. Conv.* Wks. 1846 I. 142/1 We have scourges in store for the pruriency of dissatisfaction.

3. Liking for or tendency towards impure or lascivious thought; an instance of this.

1795 Roscoe *Lorenzo de Medici* I. i. 51 A pruriency of imagination, not excuseable at any time of life. **1867** Burton *Hist. Scot.* (1873) I. vi. 225 The pruriency that stains the classical mythology. **1880** 'Ouida' *Moths* 40 She will have learned what..the wrapt-up pruriencies intend.

prurient ('prʊərɪənt), *a.* (and *sb.*) [ad. L. *prūriens, -entem*, pres. pple. of *prūrīre* to itch, long, be wanton. Cf. obs. F. *pruriant* (1598 in Godef.).]

1. That itches physically, itching. *rare.*

1639 ['I find the word in use in 1639, but in a passage not worth citing' (Todd 1818)]. **1648** HERRICK *Hesper.*, *To Detractor*, Some numbers prurient are, and some of these Are wanton with their itch; scratch, and 'twil please. **1832** TENNYSON *Pal. Art* 201 In filthy sloughs they [swine] roll a prurient skin, They graze and wallow.

2. *fig.* Having an itching desire or curiosity, or an uneasy or morbid craving. *rare.*

1653 GAUDEN *Hierasp.* Pref. 14 Politick affectations of piety, which grow as scurfe or scabs, over those prurient novelties of opinion. **1664** H. MORE *Myst. Iniq.* II. I. ii. §1. 212 Upon which fiery and prurient itch after the knowledge of Futurities Providence has cast this bridle. **1850** KINGSLEY *Alt. Locke* xiv, The reading public..in its usual prurient longing after anything like personal gossip. **1859** TENNYSON *Vivien* 485.

3. Given to the indulgence of lewd ideas; impure-minded; characterized by lasciviousness of thought or mind. Also *absol.* or as *sb.*

1746 SMOLLETT *Reproof* 176 Debauch'd from sense, let doubtful meanings run, The vague conundrum, and the prurient pun. **1774** WARTON *Hist. Eng. Poetry* lxv. (1840) III. 451 Marston..gratifies the depravations of a prurient curiosity. **1836** *Johnsoniana* I. 37 Solitude is the surest nurse of all prurient passions. **1874** L. STEPHEN *Hours in Library* (1892) II. vi. 202 His morality is..far superior to the prurient sentimentalism of Sterne. **1911** G. B. SHAW *Blanco Posnet* 334 The farcical comedy which has scandalized the critics in London..is played to the respectable dress circle of Northampton with these same jests slurred over so as to be imperceptible by even the most prurient spectator. **1969** *Punch* 29 Jan. 159/1 We've had the prudes and the prurients, the 'Love-Outs' and the love-ins, sex without marriage and marriage without sex. **1974** C. RICKS *Keats & Embarrassment* i. 15 The prurient is characterized by a particular attitude..of cherishing, fondling or slyly watching.

4. Unduly forward or excessive in growth.

1822–34 *Good's Study Med.* (ed. 4) I. 60 The teeth [are sometimes]..buried..by a prurient growth of the substance of their own gums. **1844** N. PATERSON *Manse Gard.* II. 192 By pinching off the prurient bud, good keeping bulbs may be secured. **1850** R. SIMPSON *Mem. Worth* v. 71 To prune the prurient branches of some promising fir.

5. *Bot.* Applied to plants which cause an itching or slightly stinging sensation. *rare.*

1858 in MAYNE *Expos. Lex.* **1887** *Nicholson's Dict. Gard.*, *Prurient*, stinging; causing an itching sensation. **1895** *Syd. Soc. Lex.*, *Prurient*, see *Pruriens*. *Pruriens*,..applied to certain plants or parts of plants furnished with hairs, because these are readily driven into the skin and then detached, causing considerable itching.

6. *Comb.*, as ***prurient-minded*** adj.

1899 KIPLING *Stalky* iii. 91 But about those three [boys]. Are they so prurient-minded?

'pruriently, *adv.* [f. prec. + -LY[2].] In a prurient manner. **a.** With itching or uneasy desire. **b.** With lascivious inclination or suggestion.

1837 CARLYLE *Fr. Rev.* II. III. i, All things..are got into hot and hotter prurience; and must go on pruriently fermenting, in continual change. **1840** —— *Heroes* vi. (1858) 352 Examine the man who lives in misery because he does not shine above other men;..pruriently anxious about his gifts and claims. **1907** *Academy* 9 Mar. 234/1 Pruriently presenting to the mind pictures which have no merit but their salaciousness.

pruriginous (prʊ'rɪdʒɪnəs), *a.* (Also 8 **-genous**, 9 **-ginious.**) [ad. F. *prurigineux* (1495 in Godef. *Compl.*), ad. late L. *prūrīginōs-us* adj., f. *prūrīgo*, *-inem*: see next and -OUS.]

1. Affected by or liable to prurigo or itching; pertaining to or of the nature of prurigo.

1656 BLOUNT *Glossogr.*, *Pruriginous*, full of the itch. **1705** GREENHILL *Embalming* 164 Their Blood becoming Pruriginous..wou'd..produce Mange, Scabs and Leprosies. **1742** C. OWEN *Serpents* II. 151 Its Bite..produces..pruriginous Pain in the Flesh. **1899** *Allbutt's Syst. Med.* VIII. 814 A general eruption which was in parts very pruriginous.

†**2.** Characterized by mental itching, curiosity, or uneasiness; irritable, excitable, fretful. *Obs.*

1609 BP. W. BARLOW *Answ. Nameless Cath.* 99 [He] hath not yet purged the pruriginous humor of his scoffing braine. **1678** R. L'ESTRANGE *Seneca's Mor.* II. ix. (1696) 198 In these [brooding or morose] Dispositions there is a kind of pruriginous Phancy that makes some People take delight in Labour, and Uneasiness.

†**3.** As a term of abuse; cf. MANGY *a.* 3. *Obs.*

1712 [OLDISWORTH] *Odes Horace* III. 17/2 Heinsius unfortunately fell into that Prurigenous blunder, by having too much regard for Julius Scaliger. **1825** HOGG in *Blackw. Mag.* XVII. 113 If thou'rt a Cotquean by my soul, I'll split thy pruriginous nowl.

‖**prurigo** (prʊə'raɪgəʊ). [L., an itching, lasciviousness, f. *prūrīre* to itch.] An itching; *spec.* in *Path.*, a diseased condition of the skin attended by a violent and chronic itching, and characterized by the presence of flat slightly red papules, and a thickening of the part affected. Formerly including other irritant skin diseases. Also *attrib.*

a **1646** J. GREGORY *Posthuma* (1650) 102 A Fever hee had, but not of anie acute kinde: an unsufferable Prurigo over all his bodie. **1706** PHILLIPS, *Prurigo*, an itching or tickling, an Itch. **1831** J. DAVIES *Manual Mat. Med.* 144 The skin..becomes the seat of a very lively pricking, of prurigo, and of an abundant perspiration. **1876** BRISTOWE *The. & Pract. Med.* (1878) 357 According to the latter authority, prurigo is a disease of remarkable intractableness, if not incurable.

'pruriousness. *rare.* [f. **prurious*, repr. late L. *prūriōs-us* adj., f. *prūrīre* to itch (see -OUS) + -NESS.] = PRURIENCY 3.

1823 *New Monthly Mag.* VII. 432 Outraged nature inciting them to avenge the mortification of the body by the pruriousness of the mind.

'prurit. *rare.* [a. F. *prurit* (16th c. in Littré), or ad. L. *prūrīt-us.*] = PRURITUS.

1597 LOWE *Chirurg.* v. xi. (1634) 146 Vngula..happeneth after Ophthalmies evill cured: it is accompanied with prurit, teares, and rednesse. **1953** S. BECKETT *Watt* 182 A diffuse ano-scrotal prurit.

†**'pruritan**, *a.* and *sb.* *Obs. nonce-wd.* Satirical perversion of *puritan*, in allusion to L. *prūrītus* itching.

1589 NASHE *Pasquil's Returne* Wks. (Grosart) I. 95 *Pasq.* ..I frequented the Churches of the Pruritane Preachers... *Marf.* I pray you, Syr, why doe you call them Pruritanes? *Pasq.* A *pruritu*. They haue an itch in their eares.

†**pruri'tation.** *Obs. rare*[−1]. [n. of action from assumed L. **prūrītāre*, freq. of *prūrīre* to itch.] A continual or recurring itching; *fig.* a restless desire, a craving.

1654 Z. COKE *Logick* 9 A pruritation and itch after knowledge (innate to every man).

pruritic (prʊə'rɪtɪk), *a.* [f. PRURITUS + -IC.] Pertaining to or of the nature of pruritus.

1899 *Allbutt's Syst. Med.* VIII. 490 It [urticaria] is a frequent complication of many pruritic dermatoses.

prurition (prʊə'rɪʃən). *rare*[−1]. [f. PRURIT(US + -ION.] = PRURITUS.

1922 JOYCE *Ulysses* 695 He scratched imprecisely with his left hand, though insensible of prurition, various points and surfaces of his partly exposed..skin.

‖**pruritus** (prʊə'raɪtəs). [L. *prūrītu-s* (*u*-stem), f. *prūrīre* to itch. In mod.L. sometimes erron. *pruritis* after words in -ITIS.] Itching; *esp.* itching of the skin without visible eruption. (Sometimes used as synonymous with *prurigo*.) Also *fig.*

[*c* **1400** *Lanfranc's Cirurg.* 248 Rubedo *id est* reednes, pruritus *id est* icchinge.] **1653** JER. TAYLOR *Serm. for Year* I. xxiii. 299 If there be a *pruritus* or itch of talking, let it be in matters of Religion. **1693** tr. *Blancard's Phys. Dict.* (ed. 2), *Pruritus*, the Itch, a dry Unevenness of the Skin, caused by Saline fixed Particles, pricking the Skin. **1799** HOOPER *Med. Dict.*, *Pruritis*, a violent itching of the skin. **1899** *Allbutt's Syst. Med.* VIII. 606 Hebra protested against the indiscriminate use of the names 'prurigo' and 'pruritus'.

†**'prurity.** *Obs. rare*[−1]. [f. stem of L. *prūrīre* (see above) + -ITY.] = PRURIENCY 3.

1600 THYNNE *Epigrams* xiii. 1 Pruritie of wemenn, by lecherous direction, Seekes pluritie of men.

Prus, Pruse, Pruss, obs. variants of PRUCE.

prushun ('prʌʃən). *U.S. slang.* [Origin obscure.] A boy who travels with a tramp and begs for him.

1893 *Century Mag.* Nov. 106/1, I once knew a kid, or prushun, who averaged in Denver nearly three dollars a day. **1899** 'J. FLYNT' *Tramping with Tramps* 396 *Prushun*, a tramp boy. An 'ex-prushun' is one who has served his apprenticeship as a 'kid' and is 'looking for revenge', *i.e.*, for a lad that he can 'snare' and 'jocker', as he himself was 'snared' and 'jockered'. **1907** J. LONDON *Road* (1914) 235 If he travels with a 'profesh', he [*sc.* 'a road-kid'] is known possessively as a 'prushun'. **1927** *Dialect Notes* V. 459 The tramp lives in idleness while the boy goes about begging food for both. Many continue as *prushuns* until middle life, and when their master dies are left helpless.

‖**prusiano** (pru'sjano). [Sp., = PRUSSIAN.] A finch or bunting (*Passerina versicolor*) of Mexico and Texas, so called from its Prussian blue colour.

1890 in *Cent. Dict.*

prusik ('prʌsɪk), *a.* *Mountaineering.* Also (*erron.*) **prussik**, and with initial capital. [f. the name of Karl *Prusik*, Austrian mountaineer.] Used to designate a method invented by Dr. Prusik of ascending a climbing rope by means of two separate continuous loops, each attached to it by a special knot (***prusik knot***) which tightens when weight is applied and slackens when it is removed, thus enabling the loop to be moved up the rope. Also *ellipt.* as *sb.* Hence as *vb.*, to climb with the aid of prusik loops or similar devices; **'prusiking** *vbl. sb.*

1937 E. A. M. WEDDERBURN *Alpine Climbing* vi. 101 By employing the Prusik method he [*sc.* a man who has fallen] may be able to get himself out of a crevasse unaided... He first attaches the middle-sized loop of cord to the climbing rope as high as he can reach with a Prusik knot.., passes it through his waist loop, [etc.]. **1946** J. E. Q. BARFORD *Climbing in Brit.* v. 68 The Prusik Knot or Friction Hitch. This is a new and very useful hitch which is used for attaching a subsidiary rope or sling to the main rope. **1955** M. BANKS *Commando Climber* v. 83 We..moved on carefully, realising that, despite Prussik slings, rescue operations are extremely difficult. **1956** C. EVANS *On Climbing* vii. 105 Each person in the party should have two Prusik loops (nine-foot lengths of Italian hemp cord spliced to make a rope ring). **1959** H. MERRICK tr. *Harrer's White Spider* 199 It is..obvious that Longhi was unfamiliar with the 'Prusik-knot' technique. *Ibid.* 200 It would not have taken Longhi half an hour to 'Prusik' himself by his own efforts up to the overhang. **1968** [see JUMAR]. **1972** D. HASTON *In High Places* i. 8 He can use a special wrap-around knot to attach himself to the rope. This is called a prussik knot, after its German inventor. *Ibid.* ix. 103 Mike and I prussiked up in two hours to the high point. *Ibid.* xi. 120 A carry from Camp IV, up the overhanging prussiks, along the horizontal horrors of the ice ridge and up the never-ending icefields above. **1977** *Guardian Weekly* 20 Mar. 19/2 Two of the instructors..help to provide a wide variety of experience in the arts of prusiking, abseiling, and all the necessary techniques, to both the advanced specialist and to schoolchildren.

†**pruss.** *Obs. rare.* [var. of PRUCE.] Pruce or spruce beer.

1783 JUSTAMOND tr. *Raynal's Hist. Indies* V. 337 A liquor called *Pruss*, which is only an infusion of the bark of a tree.

Prussian ('prʌʃən), *a.* and *sb.* Also *joc.* **Prooshian** ('pruːʃən), **Prooshan, Prooshun, Proosian.** [ad. mod.L. *Prussiān-us* adj., f. *Prussi-a*: see Note below. So F. *prussien*.]

A. *adj.* **1.** Of or pertaining to Prussia or its inhabitants; also, designating things actually or reputedly coming from Prussia.

Prussian binding (see quot. 1882); ***Prussian carp***, a smaller form of the common carp, now naturalized in England and other countries; ***Prussian collar*** (see quot. 1955).

1565 R. SHACKLOCK tr. *Hosius's Hatchet of Heresies* (*title-page verso*), Fixing his eye on Prussian grounde, He sawe holy Hosius makyng this boke. **1702** TOLAND *Acc. Court of Prussia* (1705) 36 'Tis at Berlin that his Prussian Majesty dos commonly keep his Court. **1754** [W. FAUCITT] (*title*) Regulations for the Prussian Infantry. **1796** H. HUNTER tr. *St.-Pierre's Stud. Nat.* (1799) II. 422 A Prussian Author..has lately favoured the World with various productions. **1837** *Penny Cycl.* VIII. 260/2 The Crucian Carp, or Prussian Carp..is another species of this genus now naturalized. **1844** W. SIBORNE *Hist. War in 1815* ii. (1894) 67 The Commander of the Prussian Army in this memorable campaign, the veteran Marshal Prince Blücher von Wahlstadt. **1852** G. W. JOHNSON *Cott. Gard. Dict.* 531/2 *Lactuca*, Lettuce... Imperial Grand Admirable, Prussian, Large Roman. **1880** *Queen* 19 June (Advt.), Sun umbrella cover..bound Self, Scarlet, Green, or Blue Prussian Binding. **1882** CAULFIELD & SAWARD *Dict. Needlework* 412/2 *Prussian bindings*. These are designed for the binding of mantles, dressing-gowns, and waterproofs... They consist of a silk face and cotton back, having a diagonal twill. **1883** *Chambers' Encycl.* VII. 815 This tendency to over-legislation has long been the predominating evil feature of Prussian administration. **1932** D. C. MINTER *Mod. Needlecraft* 113/1 Neaten the bottom of a fitting sleeve with lute ribbon or Prussian binding. **1955** J. E. LIBERTY *Pract. Tailoring* (ed. 2) xi. 211 The Prussian or Double collar, is made to button up to the neck and has a small stand. There are variations of this type, from the style very like the double linen collar worn with a tie, to that where the fall lies flatter on the fronts and does not fit so closely to the stand, 2 to 3¼ in. fall, as on uniforms. **1968** J. IRONSIDE *Fashion Alphabet* 52 *Prussian collar*, a fairly high-standing turned-down collar, as on military great-coats.

2. a. Prussian blue: a deep blue pigment of great body and covering power, consisting essentially of hydrated ferric ferrocyanide, $Fe'''_4(Fe''Cy_6)_3.18(H_2O)$, generally mixed with varying quantities of potassioferrous ferricyanide, $(KFe'').Fe'''Cy_6$. Also *ellipt.*

Called *Prussian* from being accidentally discovered by Diesbach, a colour-maker in Berlin, in 1704, and announced as a pigment in the Berlin Miscellanies for 1710. (See T. Thomson *Chemistry* ed. 3, 1807, Watts *Dict. Chem.* IV. 741.)

Hence the uses of *Prussian* in Chemistry and Colouring, also PRUSSIATE, PRUSSIC, PRUSSOUS, etc.

1724 *Phil. Trans.* XXXIII. 17 A Process for making the Prussian blue. **1732** J. PEELE *Water-Colours* 45 Prussian Blue is next to the Ultramarine for Beauty. **1807** T. THOMSON *Chem.* (ed. 3) II. 329 This powder was called Prussian blue; and the method of procuring it remained concealed, because it had become a lucrative article of commerce, till Dr. Woodward published a process in the Philosophical Transactions for 1724. **1835** [see ANTWERP]. **1838** MRS. MARCET *Conversations Land & Water* xi. (1848) 104 Prussian blue and carmine are derived from the animal kingdom. **1868** E. L. ORMEROD *Brit. Soc. Wasps* 14 Prussian-blue, known to washerwomen as stone-blue. **1911** O. ONIONS *Widdershins* iv. 154 The daylight had gone, but I knew that 'Prussian' would be about the colour for the eyes. **1940** [see ANTWERP].

attrib. **1848** THACKERAY *Bk. Snobs* xxi, Her relations with the Prussian-blue trade.

b. *adj.* and *sb.*, as name of the colour of this substance, sometimes called *royal blue*; also *sb.*, applied to a person dressed in a blue uniform or coat. In Dickens, prob. a variant or intensive of 'true blue'.

1837 DICKENS *Pickw.* xxxiii, 'Vell, Sammy', said the father. 'Vell, my Prooshun Blue', responded the son. **1899** *Westm. Gaz.* 30 Aug. 3/2 We have no doubt that the true solution [of 'my Prooshan blue'] is simple enough. The expression is a reference to a public-house sign common enough in the Pickwickian age, and often pictorially presented, namely, the portrait of the 'King of Prussia' in a blue uniform. *Mod.* The colour varies from azure to Prussian blue.

c. Prussian brown, Prussian green, pigments derived from or allied to Prussian blue.

1842 FRANCIS *Dict. Arts, Prussian Green*, a celebrated pigment, consisting of an imperfect Prussian blue, containing excess of the oxyde of iron, to which the yellow tincture of French berries is added. **1873** E. SPON *Workshop Receipts* Ser. I. (1888) 95 *Prussian Green.*—The sediment of the process of making Prussian Blue from bullock's blood or horns, before it has had the hydrochloric acid added to it. **1875** *Ure's Dict. Arts, Prussian brown*, a fine deep brown colour obtained by adding the yellow prussiate of potash (ferrocyanide of potassium) to a solution of sulphate of copper.

d. A variety of pea with large, bluish seeds. Also *ellipt.*

1804 J. GARDINER *Amer. Gardener* 43 Spanish morottos, rouncivals, prussians, green and white, marrowfats, and other large late peas are the kinds to sow this month. **1824** J. C. LOUDON *Encycl. Gardening* (ed. 2) III. viii. 618 The egg, the Moratto, the Prussian blue, and the Rouncivals,..are all very fine eating peas. **1832** J. TOD *Annals Rajast'han* II. 765, I never saw finer crops of Prussian-blues,..cauliflowers, celery, and all that belongs to the kitchen-garden. **1915** *N. & Q.* 6 Nov. 370/1 Prussian blues are a particular description of peas. Those and Marrowfats were in my early days considered the best varieties of that vegetable.

†**3.** Hence, *Chem.* **Prussian acid** = PRUSSIC *acid*; **Prussian alkali,** potassium ferrocyanide.

1788 *Trans. Soc. Arts* VI. 134 Yielded a blue precipitate on adding the Prussian Alkali. **1796** KIRWAN *Elem. Min.* (ed. 2) I. 487 *Prussian*, or *Prussiated alkali*, formerly called the phlogisticated alkali, is an alkali united to a particular tinging substance by the intermediation of iron, calcined. *Ibid.* 488 Iron..forms, with the Prussian acid, compounds of two different kinds; the one fully saturated, the other unsaturated. **1825** J. NICHOLSON *Operat. Mechanic* 757 A determinate quantity of the Prussian alkali must be tried previously.

B. *sb.* **1.** A native or inhabitant of Prussia (the ethnic territory, or the former duchy or kingdom).

1554 W. PRAT tr. *Discr. Aphrique* sig. B6[v], The Germaynes, Italyons, Spanyardes, Frenchemen, Scottes, Iryshmen, the Danes, Liuones Prussiens. **1565** R. SHACKLOCK tr. *Hosius's Hatchet of Heresies* f.2[v] This agrement of fayth..floryshed among..the Germanes.. Catholyke Russians, Prussians, or Masouians. **1677** E. BROWNE *Trav. Germany* 82 To the Classis, or Natio Saxonum, were reduced Saxons.., Prussians, Livonians. **1746** H. WALPOLE *Lett.* (1846) II. 112 The King of Sardinia ..has made himself as considerable in the scale as the Prussian. **1844** W. SIBORNE *Hist. War in 1815* ii. (1894) 67 He was eminently fitted to be both the representative and the leader of the Prussians. **1879** *Smith's Smaller Hist. Eng.* xxxv. 310 The Prussians strained every nerve to reach the field [of Waterloo].

joc. **1843** DICKENS *Mart. Chuz.* (1844) xix. 239 Some people..may be Rooshans, and some may be Prooshans; they are born so, and will please themselves. **1871** F. C. BURNAND *More Happy Thoughts* (ed. 2) xxix. 214 The Gay Prooshians have no end of ships. **1878** W. S. GILBERT *H.M.S. Pinafore* II. 28 For he might have been a Roosian, A French, or Turk, or Proosian, Or perhaps Itali-an! **1899** KIPLING *Stalky & Co.* 128 'My word!' said M'Turk,..'The Prooshian Bates has an infernal straight eye.' **1914** R. BROOKE *Let.* 24 Aug. (1968) 611 To Hell with the Prooshians. **1922** JOYCE *Ulysses* 324 The Prooshians and the Hanoverians.

2. = OLD PRUSSIAN *sb.* b.

1888 J. WRIGHT tr. *Brugmann's Elem. Compar. Gram. Indo-Gmc. Lang.* I. 11 The Baltic division consists of Prussian, Lithuanian, and Lettic. **1972** W. B. LOCKWOOD *Panorama Indo-European Lang.* 139 A catechism, in Prussian and German, was twice printed in 1545.

[*Note.* The name *Prussia* (in early writers *Pruscia, Pruschia, Prucia, Prusya, Prusia*) was a deriv. of *Pruzzi, Prutzci, Pruci, Prussi, Prusi*, latinized forms, in the mediæval writers, of the name of a Balto-slavonic people, who inhabited a territory now included in the Baltic Republics of the Soviet Union and in Poland, which was conquered in the 12th c. by the Knights of the Teutonic Order, and afterwards became a dukedom or duchy, at length under the rule of the elector of Brandenburg, who in 1700 thence assumed the title of *König von Preuzen*, King of Prussia. In 1947 the territory of Prussia was divided among East and West Germany, Poland, and the Soviet Union.

The German forms are *ein Preusze* a Prussian, *Preuszen* Prussians and Prussia. For the French and ME. forms see PRUCE. Other med.L. names were *Borussi*, and *Prut(h)eni*, whence the adj. *Prut(h)enicus* PRUTENIC.]

†**'prussianated,** *a. Chem. Obs.* [f. PRUSSIAN *a.* 3 + -ATE[3] + -ED[1].] = PRUSSIATED.

1791 PEARSON in *Phil. Trans.* LXXXI. 321 Prussianated alkali of tartar occasioned no alteration.

'Prussianism. [f. PRUSSIAN *a.* + -ISM.] The national spirit or political system of Prussia. Also, the militaristic concepts and disciplinary methods regarded as typical of the Prussian system. Hence **'Prussianist** *a.*

1856 *Mem. F. Perthes* II. xxiv. 362 Germanism is a noble thing unless it be a synonym for Prussianism. **1896** *Daily News* 11 June, Arrogant, overbearing Prussianism. **1915** *Chambers's Jrnl.* Oct. 664/2 Then we are getting ..'Prussianism', 'Prussianisation',.., with all their meanings. **1916** A. HUXLEY *Let.* 31 Mar. (1969) 95 One discusses too the collapse of English civilisation, whose rapid decay under the sinister influence of Prussianism is everywhere apparent. **1922** Prussianist [see GOOSE-STEP]. **1942** *R.A.F. Jrnl.* 2 May 6 Yet there *is* discipline... It is all done without Prussianism. **1944** F. A. HAYEK *Road to Serfdom* 7 It was the prevalence of socialist views and not Prussianism that Germany had in common with Italy and Russia. **1945** K. R. POPPER *Open Society* II. xii. 27 Hegel.. became the first official philosopher of Prussianism. **1978** *Christian* V. 18 Pope Leo XIII decided..to come to terms with both French Republicanism and Prussianism.

Prussianize ('prʌʃənaɪz), *v.* [f. PRUSSIAN *a.* + -IZE.] *trans.* To render Prussian or like Prussian in organization or character. Also *intr.*, to act in a manner regarded as typical of Prussians. Hence **'Prussianized** *ppl. a.*, **'Prussianizing** *vbl. sb.*; also **Prussiani'zation,** the action or process of Prussianizing; **'Prussianizer,** one who Prussianizes.

1861 M. ARNOLD *Pop. Educ. France* 167 To Prussianise his people or to Americanise it. **1872** *Spectator* 7 Sept. 1132 The attempted Prussianisation of the separated provinces of France. **1885** *Pall Mall G.* 7 Nov. 10/1 The very embodiment of didactic bureaucracy and Prussianized pedagogy. **1891** *Athenæum* 22 Aug. 250/2 The recent efforts of Japan to prussianize her institutions. **1893** *Cycl. Rev. Current Hist.* (U.S.) III. 365 The 'Prussianizing' of Germany. **1905** *Westm. Gaz.* 28 Oct. 2/1 The Prussianisers have received a set-back by the decision of the Supreme Court in the Lippe-Detmold Regency case in favour of Count Ernest of Lippe Bielefeld. **1909** *Q. Rev.* CCX. 664 A similar policy pursued in a neighbouring territory—the attempted prussianisation of the inhabitants of Prussian Poland. *Ibid.*, Since his [*sc.* Bismarck's] time there has been a steady attempt to prussianise them. *Ibid.*, So far, the prussianising policy had wholly failed. **1915** [see PRUSSIANISM]. **1927** 'IXION' *Further Motor Cycle Reminisc.* 82 The victim [of the practical joke] occupied a minor official position, by dint of which he Prussianized rather too freely. **1963** *Times Lit. Suppl.* 18 Jan. 45/2 The Poles in Prussia's eastern provinces were not only devout Catholics but also Polish patriots who..offered stubborn resistance to Bismarck's Prussianization policy. **1976** *Listener* 19 Feb. 202/1 After 60 years, some Hanoverians, especially the military, had become Prussianised.

'Prussianly, *adv.* [f. PRUSSIAN *a.* + -LY[2].] In a manner regarded as typical of Prussians.

1917 *Daily Chron.* 26 July 2/5 People don't shove quite so selfishly, don't scowl at each other so Prussianly. **1932** BLUNDEN *Face of England* 72 He stumped, yet more Prussianly, into the pavilion. **1979** F. MORTON *Nervous Splendour* i. 7 Helmet Prussianly spiked.

prussiate ('prʌs-, 'prʌʃɪət), *sb. Chem.* [a. F. *prussiate* (Morveau, etc. *Nomencl. Chim.* 1787), f. *pruss-ique* PRUSSIC + -ATE[1].] A salt of prussic acid; a cyanide. Also, a ferro- or ferri-cyanide, as ***yellow prussiate*** (of potash) = potassium ferro-cyanide, K_4FeCy_6; ***red prussiate*** (of potash) = potassium ferricyanide, $K_6Fe_2Cy_{12}$.

c **1790** tr. *Lavoisier's etc. Tabl. Chem. Nom.* (*Encycl. Brit.* (ed. 3) IV. 598), Names newly invented or adopted.. Prussiate of potash..Prussiate of iron. **1791** HAMILTON *Berthollet's Dyeing* I. I. I. i. 11 The prussiat of alkali. **1800** tr. *Lagrange's Chem.* II. 360 The prussiates of ammonia, lime, barytes, &c. **1842** PARNELL *Chem. Anal.* (1845) 68 The red prussiate of potash is as delicate and characteristic a test for protoxide of iron, as the yellow prussiate of potash is for the peroxide. **1875** *Ure's Dict. Arts* III. 598 Ferro-cyanide of potassium or Yellow prussiate of potash.

'prussiate, *v. Chem.* [f. prec.] *trans.* To convert into a prussiate.

1796 KIRWAN *Elem. Min.* (ed. 2) I. 504 They make use of the same sort of Berlin blue in Prussiating their alkali.

Hence **'prussiated** *ppl. a.*, converted into a prussiate; combined with prussic acid.

1796 KIRWAN *Elem. Min.* (ed. 2) II. 356 The prussiated Metals heated to redness. **1800** HENRY *Epit. Chem.* (1808) 334 The prussiated alkalies also precipitate muriate of alumine. **1826** —— *Elem. Chem.* II. 537 The prussiated alkalis decompose..all metallic solutions.

prussic ('prʌsɪk), *a. Chem.* [ad. F. *prussique* ('acide prussique, matière colorante du bleu de Prusse', Morveau, etc. *Nomencl. Chim.* 1787), f. *Prusse* Prussia + *-ique*, -IC. See PRUSSIAN *a.* 2.] Of, pertaining to, or derived from Prussian blue. Chiefly in ***prussic acid*** = HYDROCYANIC *acid*, CNH; also *attrib.* and *fig.*

1790 KERR tr. *Lavoisier's Elem. Chem.* 121 We are only acquainted with six animal acids..They are, Lactic,.. Saccho-lactic,..Bombic,..Formic,..Sebacic,..Prussic acid. **1800** tr. *Lagrange's Chem.* II. 355 Scheele has shewn that the red oxide of mercury takes the colouring matter from Prussian blue; and this property is employed for obtaining Prussic acid. **1813** SIR H. DAVY *Agric. Chem.* (1814) 108 The vegetable prussic acid is procured by distilling laurel leaves, or the kernels of the peach, and cherry, or bitter almonds. **1838** *Penny Cycl.* XII. 388/2 *Hydrocyanic acid*..obtained by Scheele in 1782..as it was procured, though intermediately, from Prussian blue, it was originally called prussic acid. **1860** MRS. GASKELL *Let.* ?28 June (1966) 912 The thunder yesterday gave me a dreadful headache so I had to..have my prussic acid medicine made up. **1881** *Med. Temp. Jrnl.* XLIX. 23 No more poisonous agent can be found than prussic acid. **1927** D. H. LAWRENCE *Mornings in Mexico* 12 Such a suave, prussic-acid sarcasm.

Prussification (prʌsɪfɪ'keɪʃən). [f. PRUSSI(AN *a.* + -FICATION.] = PRUSSIANIZATION. So **'Prussify** *v. trans.*, to Prussianize.

1898 *Daily News* 21 Jan. 4/5 The Bill to increase the fund for the Prussification of the Polish provinces of the kingdom. **1904** *Daily Chron.* 23 Nov. 4/6 His proposal was successfully opposed by the other kingdoms as tending to the Prussification of the new empire. **1924** *Contemp. Rev.* Mar. 301 The Russians were trying their hardest to russify, and the Prussians were trying their hardest to prussify their Polish provinces.

†**'prussin.** *Chem. Obs.* Also -ine. [f. PRUSS-IAN *a.* 2 + -INE[5] (as in *chlorine*, etc.).] An early name for CYANOGEN, CN (or a polymer of it), as a derivative of Prussian blue.

1837 *Penny Cycl.* VIII. 247/1 Cyanogen..is a gaseous compound sometimes termed *Prussine* or *Prussine gas.* **1866–8** WATTS *Dict. Chem.* IV. 742 *Prussin*, or *Prussian*, a name applied by Graham to a hypothetical radicle, C_3N_3 = Cy_3 or Pr, polymeric with cyanogen, which may be supposed to exist in the ferro- and ferricyanides.

†**'prussite.** *Chem. Obs.* [a. F. *prussite*, f. *Prusse* PRUSSIA: see -ITE[1] 4 b and PRUSSIAN *a.* 2.]

a. (*a* 1800) = *Prussian alkali*, potassium ferro-cyanide. **b.** A sulpho-cyanate, as ***prussite of potash***, KCyS. So †**'prussous** *a.*, in ***prussous acid***, early name for sulphocyanic acid (CN.HS).

1791 MACIE in *Phil. Trans.* LXXXI. 388 From this solution Prussite of Tartar..instantly threw down a very copious Prussian blue. **1796** KIRWAN *Elem. Min.* (ed. 2) II. 428 Precipitation by Soda would answer better than by Prussite. **1809** R. PORRETT in *Trans. Soc. Arts* XXVII. 99 This liquor I have named..*prussous acid*, and its salts *prussites*, of which the liquid B contained one in solution, namely the prussite of potash. **1819** CHILDREN *Chem. Anal.* 325 Sulphocyanic acid was discovered by Mr. Porrett in 1808..he first called it prussous acid.

prut (prʌt), *int.* and *sb.* Also 4 **tprut**, 8 **prute.** [Echoic, repr. a slight explosive sound, as of breaking wind.]

1. An exclamation of contempt.

c **1300** in Langtoft *Chron.* (MS. Fairfax 22, lf. 4), Tprut! Skot riveling, In unsel timing crope thu out of cage. **1303** R. BRUNNE *Handl. Synne* 3014 And seyþ 'prut for þy cursyng, prest!' *a* **1779** D. GRAHAM *Janet Clinker's Orat.* Writ. 1883 II. 150 If they had tell'd me tuts, or prute no, I laid them o'er my knee, and a com'd crack for crack o'er their hurdies. **1870** LUBBOCK *Orig. Civiliz.* viii. 282 From pr, or prut, indicating contempt.

2. The sound of a rifle shot.

1898 *Blackw. Mag.* Dec. 837/2 To the prut of the magazine rifles was added the under chorus of the clicking mechanism. **1899** *Westm. Gaz.* 2 Jan. 2/1 Time passed; the fight, short anyhow, dwindled to prut..prut..prut-prut.. prut.

prut, prute, obs. forms of PROUD.

†**Prutenic** (pruː'tɛnɪk), *a.* (*sb.*) *Obs.* [ad. med.L. *Prutenic-us*, f. *Prut(h)en-i* Prussians: see -IC. Cf. F. *pruténique.*] Prussian; in ***Prutenic tables***, the Copernican planetary tables published in 1551 by Erasmus Reinhold (*Cælestium Motuum Prutenicæ Tabulæ*); so named in compliment to Albert, Duke of Prussia. Also as *sb.* in *pl.* **Pru'tenics,** the Prutenic tables.

1615–16 H. BRIGGS *Let.* 10 Mar. in *Ussher's Lett.* (1686) 36 Concerning Eclipses..Mullerus in his *Phris. Tabulis* hath mightily discouraged me, for he hath weakned the Prutenicks, my Foundation, in three places of his Book at least. **1643** MILTON *Divorce* i. Wks. 1851 IV. 22, I trust anon ..to perfect such Prutenick tables as shall mend the Astronomy of our wide expositors. **1678** PHILLIPS (ed. 4), *Prutenick Tables*, certain Tables for the finding out of the Celestial motions... First publish in the year 1551.

So †**Pru'tenical** *a.*, in same sense.

1594 BLUNDEVIL *Exerc.* I. xxix. (1636) 79 Taught by Reinoldus in the beginning of his Prutenicall Tables. **1640** WILKINS *New Planet* I. (1707) 152 The Man that calculated the Prutenical Tables from Copernicus his Observations.

pruu, prw, var. PROW *sb.*[2] and *v. Obs.*, profit.

pruwiance, pruys, var. PROVIANCE, PRUCE.

†**pry,** *sb.*[1] *Obs.* Also 6 **prie.** [Derivation unknown.] A local name of the small-leaved lime or linden (*Tilia parvifolia*). Also ***pry-tree.***

1573 TUSSER *Husb.* (1878) 79 Lop popler and sallow, elme, maple, and prie. **1707** MORTIMER *Husb.* 355 The wild kind [of Lime-tree] bearing a smaller leaf than the other, by which I suppose, he [Evelyn] means the Tree which they call the Pry-tree, which grows the most plentiful in Essex.

pry (praɪ), *sb.*[2] Now only *dial.* Also 7–8 **prie,** 9 **prye.** [Derivation unknown.] A name given locally to various rigid glaucous grasses and species of *Carex*, esp. *C. panicea*. Also ***pry-grass.***

1610 W. FOLKINGHAM *Art of Survey* I. iii. 7 Harsh, reddish, blewish spirie and prie-grass bewray a cold, vnkind ..soile. *Ibid.* ix. 22 Rushes, ranke sower grasse, Prie and Quitch-grasse. **1798** R. DOUGLAS *Agric. Surv. Roxb.* 108 Different species of *Carex*, here called pry, and by Ainsworth interpreted sheer-grass. **1877** SIR W. ELLIOT in *Hist. Berw. Nat. Club* (1879) VIII. 454 *note, Prye, Pry*, is called 'the bottom of *spret*', which alone is eaten by sheep when the spret gets old and hard. Several plants are included under this term, as:—*Poa trivialis*,..*Holcus lanatus*... *Carex panicea* also is considered a prye grass, as are other species of *Carex*.

pry (praɪ), *sb.*[3] [f. PRY *v.*[1]]

1. An act or the action of prying; a peeping or inquisitive glance.

1750 C. SMART *Noon-piece* 50 Secluded from the teizing pry Of Argus Curiosity. **1817** KEATS *To* —— 30 They seldom meet the eye Of the little loves that fly Round about with eager pry.

2. An inquisitive person. Cf. *Paul Pry*, PAUL 3.

a **1845** HOOD *Ode to Rae Wilson* vi, The spy On fellow souls, a Spiritual Pry. **1874** R. BLACK tr. *Guizot's Hist. France* III. xxix. 152 Froissart is an insatiable pry who revels in all the sights of his day.

pry (praɪ), *sb.*[4] *dial.* and *U.S.* Also pray. [f. PRIZE, PRISE *sb.*[4], with final *s* (*z*) lost as in *pea*, *cherry*, etc.: cf. PRY *v.*[2]] An instrument for prying or prizing; a lever or crow-bar; = PRIZE *sb.*[4] 1.

1823, 1828 [see PRY *v.*[2]]. *a* **1825** [see PRIZE *sb.*[4]]. **1872** TALMAGE *Serm.* 45 The enemies of this book have tried to marshal on their side the astronomer's telescope and geologist's pry. **1884** *Science* 22 Feb. 226/2 A dozen strong wooden poles served us as pries over many a lake and river bar of sand, gravel, and mud.

pry (praɪ), *v.*[1] Also 4–6 prien, 4–7 prie, prye, 5 pri. [ME. *prien*, of unknown origin.

The verbs PIRE and PEER, which come near in form and sense, are of later appearance.]

1. *intr.* To look, *esp.* to look closely or curiously; to peep or peer, to look narrowly; to peer inquisitively or impertinently; to spy.

c **1306** in *Pol. Songs* (Camden) 222 After socour of Scotland longe he mowe prye, Ant after help of Fraunce wet halt hit to lye? *c* **1350** *Will. Palerne* 96 At þe last lelly a litel hole he findes. þere pried he in priuely. *Ibid.* 5019 Burgeys with here burdes.. weyteden out at windowes.. to prie on þe puple þat priked in þe stretes. *c* **1412** HOCCLEVE *De Reg. Princ.* 114 Whanne.. day gan at my wyndowe in to prye. **1423** JAS. I *Kingis Q.* lxxii, The long[ë] day thus gan I prye and poure Till phebus endit had his bemes bryght. **1571** *Latimer's Serm. at Stamford* 92 b, Spying, tooting, and looking, watching & prying [*ed.* 1550 catching], what they might heare or see against the sea of Rome. **1579** W. WILKINSON *Confut. Familye of Loue* 38 b, [They] bryng their wares to the light, and prie, and pore on them. **1667** MILTON *P.L.* IX. 159 Thus.. glide obscure, and prie In every Bush and Brake. **1750** GRAY *Long Story* 65 They.. Into the Drawers and China pry. **1858** DORAN *Crt. Fools* 71 He went prying about into the corners of the hall.

2. *pry into*: to search inquisitively into (something secret or private); to investigate curiously or impertinently; to make private investigations into.

1629 H. BURTON *Truth's Triumph* 323 To prye into this Arcanum. **1638** JUNIUS *Paint. Ancients* 4 To prie into the most profound mysteries of Nature. **1754** SHERLOCK *Disc.* (1759) I. iii. 114 Endeavour to pry into the nature.. of the Almighty. *a* **1859** MACAULAY *Hist. Eng.* xxiv. (1861) V. 196 A longing to pry into those mysteries of the grave from which human beings avert their thoughts.

b. *gen.* To inquire into or investigate closely.

1610 GUILLIM *Heraldry* II. viii. (1660) 92 To occasion them to prie more narrowly into these curious and nice manners or bearing, which numbers of them so sleightly passe over. **1638** WILKINS *New World* I. (1707) 9 Not.. to be rejected, but rather to be pry'd into with a diligent Enquiry. **1713** DERHAM *Phys.-Theol.* I. iii. 23 If strictly pried into, will be found owing to natural Causes. **1860** MOTLEY *Netherl.* (1868) I. ii. 54 He pries into all the stratagems of Camillus.

†**3.** *trans.* To look for, look through, or look at closely; to observe narrowly. *Obs.*

1553 *Respublica* III. iv. 760 What nowe, brother Honestie? what prye ye this waie? Is there eni thing here that ys yours, can ye saie? **1582** STANYHURST *Æneis* III. (Arb.) 91, I pryed al quarters. **1632** J. PORY in Ellis *Orig. Lett.* Ser. II. III. 276 An horseman of the enemy prying the King steadfastly in the face, said [etc.].

b. *pry out*: to search or find out by prying.

a **1548** HALL *Chron., Hen. VII* 32 b, He secretly sent wise espialles.. to searche & prye oute of what progeny thys misnamed Rycharde was dissended. **1760** DODD *Hymn to Gd.-Nature* Poems (1767) 4 Never.. to pry out littleness and faults, Where merit claims my praise.

pry (praɪ), *v.*[2] *dial.* and *U.S.* [Shortened from PRIZE, PRISE *v.*[3], app. through confusing the final consonant with the *-s* of the 3rd pers. sing. pres.: cf. PRY *sb.*[4]] *trans.* To raise or move by force of leverage; to force up; = PRIZE *v.*[3] Also *fig.* Hence **'prying** *vbl. sb.*

1823 E. MOOR *Suffolk Words & Phrases* 292 *Pray*, or *Praise*, or *Prize*, or *Pry*, to lift any thing with a lever—the lever is called a *pray* or *lewer*... To pray a door or lid open, is to open it with a handspike, or lever of any sort. **1828** WEBSTER, *Pry*, to raise or attempt to raise with a lever. This is the common popular pronunciation of *prize* in America. The lever used is also called a *pry*. **1850** LOWELL *Lett.* (1894) I. iii. 209 This seems to be the only lever to pry them over with. **1858** [see HUB[1] 3]. **1878** *Scribner's Mag.* XVI. 56/2 You must pry it up with a stick or trowel. **1896** C. M. SHELDON *His Brother's Keeper* iii. 66 We managed to pry out of him that he had seen you and Eric go down the ladders. **1897** GEN. H. PORTER *Campaigning w. Grant* ix. 146 In prying off the cross ties. **1903** [In *Eng. Dial. Dict.* from Suffolk and Essex. Common with workmen in many parts.] **1921** E. O'NEILL *Diff'rent* II. 245 It was always like pryin' open a safe for me to separate him from a cent. **1926** *Harper's Mag.* Feb. 363/1, I stood rooted to the spot and you could not have pried me away. **1927** S. ERTZ *Now East, Now West* ii. 21 He walked about the decks.. hand in hand with Cleve, whenever that friendly child could be pried loose from some new and fascinating acquaintance. **1933** D. GARNETT *Pocahontas* v. 46 Holding out his clenched fist for her to pry his fingers open. **1947** S. BELLOW *Victim* (1948) i. 14 Philip pried off the caps on the handle of a metal cabinet in the kitchen. **1954** T. S. ELIOT *Confidential Clerk* I. 18 She's come to pry some cash from the money-box. **1968** J. AIKEN *Whispering Mountain* iii. 64 Owen's teeth were pried open and the neck of the bottle forced between them. **1976** *Time* 20 Dec. 1/2 When Watergate raised questions about the integrity of the Executive Branch, Congress appointed an independent prosecutor to pry out all the facts. **1978** C. TOMLINSON *Shaft* 14 As if this place could be pried out of now.

pryan, prian ('praɪən). *dial.* [a. Corn. *pryan*, *prian* clayey ground (Jago).] A Cornish miner's term for soft white clay. Also *attrib.*

1710 J. HARRIS *Lex. Techn.* II, *Pryan Tin*, is a sort of Tin that is found mix'd with a Gravelly Earth, sometimes White, but usually Red. **1881** RAYMOND *Mining Gloss.*, *Pryan*, ore in small pebbles mixed with clay. **1882** JAGO *Cornw. Gloss.*, *Pryan lode*, a flookan lode, as a soft clayey vein of tin.

prycate, prycket(te, obs. ff. PRICKET.

pryce, obs. f. PRICE, PRISE, PRYSE.

pryck, pryde, pryef, obs. f. PRICK, PRIDE, PROOF.

†**pryelle.** *Obs. rare*[−1]. [ad. OF. *prayel*, *pra(i)el*, *preël* (mod.F. *préau*):—med.L. *prātell-um*, dim. of *prāt-um* a meadow. Cf. MDu. *pryel*, *prieel* (mod. *prieel*).] An open space in the middle of a cloister, an open court.

c **1483** CAXTON *Dialogues* 45 Rolande the handwerker Shall make my pryelle [F. *mon prayel*] An hegge aboute.

pryer, var. PRIER.

pryght, obs. pa. t. of PRICK *v.*

prygnatory, obs. f. PRENOTARY.

'prying, *vbl. sb.*[1] [f. PRY *v.*[1] + -ING[1].] The action of PRY *v.*[1]; narrow peering or examination; inquisitive search.

1611 SPEED *Hist. Gt. Brit.* VIII. i. §9. 377 There with a narrow prying was sought out the fibra, or veine of the heart on the left side. **1894** *Athenæum* 24 Feb. 238/3 Their prying into every detail of private life.

prying, *vbl. sb.*[2]: see PRY *v.*[2]

'prying, *ppl. a.* [f. PRY *v.*[1] + -ING[2].] That pries; unduly or impertinently curious; inquisitive; diligently inquiring.

1552 HULOET, Priynge knaues, *limaces uiri*. **1608** D. T[UVIL] *Ess. Pol. & Mor.* 90 b, A prying eye, a listning eare, and a prating tongue, are all birds of one wing. **1693** J. EDWARDS *Author. O. & N. Test.* 20 Such things as.. no prying historian is able to discover. **1778** FOOTE *Trip Calais* III. Wks. 1799 II. 365 She is as suspicious and prying as a customhouse officer. **1822–34** *Good's Study Med.* (ed. 4) III. 57 Analyzed in turn, by the most dextrous and prying anatomists of England, France, Germany, and Italy, but with no satisfactory result. **1845** JAMES *A. Neil* II. iv, They are a sad prying, gossiping race.

'pryingly, *adv.* [f. prec. + -LY[2].] In a prying manner; narrowly, closely, inquisitively.

1628 GAULE *Pract. The.* (1629) 50 That they will dare pryingly to sift out. **1720** S. PARKER *Biblioth. Bibl.* I. 427 Without examining too pryingly and sollicitously into the reasons of so unparallel'd a Transformation. **1853** *Chamb. Jrnl.* XX. 424/2 The writer appears to have wandered pryingly into the alleys and by-places.

pryis(s, obs. f. PRICE *sb.*[1], PRIZE *v.*[1]

pryk(e, prykk, obs. ff. PRICK.

prykel(le, prykyl, obs. ff. PRICKLE.

pryket, -ett(e, obs. ff. PRICKET.

prylle, obs. f. BRILL *sb.*[1], PRILL[1].

pryme, prymer, obs. ff. PRIME, PRIMER.

'pry-pole. [f. PRY *v.*[2] or *sb.*[4] + POLE *sb.*[1]] A pole used as a 'pry' or lever.

1828 J. M. SPEARMAN *Brit. Gunner* (ed. 2) 188, 7. Assists number 3 at the lever, slings and unslings the gun, and lashes it to the pry-pole. **1859** F. A. GRIFFITHS *Artil. Man.* (1862) 123 One prypole, fitted with a prypole rope.

prys, obs. f. PRICE, PRIZE *sb.*[1], *v.*[1], PRYSE.

prysage, prysar, obs. ff. PRISAGE[1], PRIZER[1].

†**prysauntere.** *Obs. rare*[−1]. [ad. OF. *prisautier*, *prinsautier* (12th c. in Godef.), mod.F. *primesautier* precipitate in action, presumptuous, f. OF. *prin saut* 'first leap'.] (See quot.)

c **1440** *Partonope* 6842 Comenly suche menne mow not last Prysaunteres suche folke callyth he.. Suche last not but lytylle while. [*Fr.* Qui ne sont pas si prinsautier Qui s'espargnent dusqu'al tierc jor.]

pryse, pryce. *Hunting. arch.* Also 4 priis, 5 prise, 6 prys. [ME. a. OF. or AF. *pris* 'taken', pa. pple. of *prendre* to take, or OF. *prise* 'taking, capture', thence formed: cf. PRISE *sb.*[1], PRIZE *sb.*[3]] In phrase *to blow the pryse*, i.e. to blow 'Taken!' or 'Capture!', to sound a blast on the hunting-horn as a signal that the stag is taken. Also *transf.*

c **1320** *Sir Tristr.* 2749 Tristrem on huntinge rade,.. He blewe priis as he can þre mot oþer mare. *c* **1410** *Master of Game* xxxiv. (1904) 99 þan shuld.. who so is grettest of þe hunters blowe þe pryce at couplyng vp. **1470–85** MALORY *Arthur* IV. vi. 125 Thenne kynge Arthur blewe the pryse and dyghte the herte. **1513** DOUGLAS *Æneis* X. xii. 123 And blew the prys triumphall for his [Orodes'] deth. *a* **1533** LD. BERNERS *Huon* lii. 177, I can mew a sparhawke, and I can chase the herte and the wyld bore, and blowe the pryce. **1802** SCOTT *Cadyow Castle* xvii, Sound, merry huntsmen! sound the pryse!

pryse, pryss, obs. ff. PRICE, PRISE, PRIZE.

‖**prytaneum** (prɪtə'niːəm). *Gr. Antiq.* Also 9 -eium, -eion. [L. *prytanēum*, a. Gr. πρυτανεῖον, f. πρύτανις: see next.] The public hall of a Greek state or city, in which the sacred fire was kept burning; *esp.* in ancient Athens, the hall in which those who had done distinguished service to the state (and also foreign ambassadors) were entertained at the public charge, together with the successive presidents of the senate.

1600 HOLLAND *Livy* XLI. 1108 At Cizicum, he gave freely to the Prytaneum. **1718** OZELL tr. *Tournefort's Voy. Levant* II. IX. 335 A Publick House, or *Prytaneum*, wherein they ate on the great Feasts of the publick Games. **1846** GROTE *Greece* I. xiv. I. 380 He assigned to the new hero a consecrated spot in the strongest and most commanding portion of the Sicyonian prytaneium. **1865** —— *Plato* I. i. 13 Like the public hearth or perpetual fire maintained in the prytaneum of a Grecian city.

b. *transf.* A public hall or house.

1673 RAY *Journ. Low C.* 86 Last of all feasts the Professors in the room called the *Prytaneum*, which is now used as the Divinity-Schools. **1869** FREEMAN *Norm. Conq.* III. xi. 27 The hearth and Prytaneion of the English nation. **1888** *Athenæum* 7 July 31/1 The poet and the novelist, the historian and the sage, will then live blithe and blameless in the Prytaneum.

‖**prytanis** ('prɪtənɪs). *Gr. Antiq.* Pl. -nes (-niːz). Also 7 in Anglicized form prytan, -ane. [L. *prytanis*, a. Gr. πρύτανις a prince, ruler, chief, at Athens a president.]

1. In ancient Athens, A member of that division of the Council of Five Hundred which was presiding at the time.

1656 J. HARRINGTON *Oceana* (1700) 79 The Prytans were a Committee or Council sitting in the Great Hall of Pantheon. **1727–41** CHAMBERS *Cycl.* s.v., All the fifty *prytanes* of the tribe did not govern together during those five weeks; but in companies, ten at a time, chosen by lot; seven days each company. **1874** MAHAFFY *Soc. Life Greece* xii. 372 The prytanes referred their case to the council.

2. The chief magistrate of a Greek state, as of Rhodes, Lycia, or Miletus.

1682 WHELER *Journ. Greece* III. 267 He was Prytane, or Chief Magistrate among them. **1737** WHISTON *Josephus*, *Antiq.* XIV. x. §22 The decree of those of Pergamus:—'When Cratippus was prytanis, on the first day of the month Desius'. **1868** *Smith's Dict. Gr. & Rom. Antiq.* (ed. 7) s.v. *Prytaneium*, Officers called *prytanes* (πρυτάνεις) were entrusted with the chief magistracy in several states of Greece, as Corcyra, Corinth, Miletus.

3. *transf.* A president, chief.

1847 GROTE *Greece* II. x. III. 101 It is probable also that the functions of that senate [the Areopagus], and those of the prytanes of the naukrars, were of the same double and confused nature. **1898** A. LANG *Making Relig.* xvii. 317 In polytheism that conception is necessarily obscured, showing itself dimly either in the *Prytanis*, or President of the Immortals, such as Zeus; or in Fate.

Hence **'prytan** *a. rare*, pertaining to or consisting of prytanes; presiding in the Council of Five Hundred at Athens; **'prytanize** *v. intr.*, of a division or individual: to exercise the prytany; whence **'prytanizing** *vbl. sb.* and *ppl. a.*

1866 FELTON *Anc. & Mod. Gr.* II. I. vi. 95 Every prytan body of fifty was divided into five committees of ten each; and its period of office into five of seven days each. **1847** GROTE *Greece* II. xxxvi. IV. 484 *note*, Conformable to their order in prytanising, as drawn by lot for the year. *Ibid.* 485 *note*, First in the order of prytanising tribes for the year.

prytany ('prɪtənɪ). *Gr. Antiq.* Also prut-. [ad. Gr. πρυτανεία, f. πρύτανις PRYTANIS.]

1. The presidency of the Athenian senate; the office or dignity of a prytanis. Also *transf.*

1885 *Trans. Amer. Philol. Assoc.* XVI. 169 If Schömann's older view is correct, the presiding officer.. must always belong to the tribe which holds the prytany at the time. **1898** A. LANG *Making Relig.* xv. 286 Modified by a weak reminiscence of the old kingship in the not very effective sovereignty (or *prytany*) of Zeus.

2. Each of the ten divisions of the Athenian Council of Five Hundred during its presidency; also the period of five weeks during which each division presided.

1807 ROBINSON *Archæol. Græca* I. xxxi. 115 If these officers did not carry their rents before the ninth prytany, they were to pay double. **1847** GROTE *Greece* II. xi. III. 163 *note*, The division of the year into ten portions of time, each called by the name of a *prytany*.. [does] not belong to the Solonian Athens. **1886** *Athenæum* 14 Aug. 216/1 A building called a Tholos, in which statues were dedicated and sacrifices were performed by the prutanies.

pr'ythee, obs. form of PRITHEE.

pryys, obs. form of PRICE *sb.*[1]

Przewalski (preɪjə'vælskɪ). Also Prejevalsky, Przevalsky. The name of N. M. *Przewalski* (1839–1888), Russian explorer, used *attrib.*, *ellipt.*, and in the possessive to designate a wild horse, *Equus przevalskii*, collected by him in 1876 in Central Asia, its native land, and named after him by I. S. Poliakov in 1881 (*Izvestiya Imper. Russ. Geogr. Obshchestva* XVII. 1).

1881 *Ann. Mag. Nat. Hist.* VIII. 16 (*heading*) Prejevalsky's Horse. **1884** *Nature* 21 Aug. 391/2 Przevalsky's wild horse has warts on its hind-legs as well as on its fore-legs. *Ibid.*, Nor has Przevalsky's horse any dorsal stripe. **1928** *Daily Tel.* 3 Jan. 5/1 Of the numerous arrivals at the zoo during the past year, the following are amongst the rarest or most valuable:..a Prejevalski's wild horse,..and two Komodo monitor lizards. **1951** G. G. SIMPSON *Horses* iii. 17 It is usually said that the only living true wild horse.. is the central Asiatic race or subspecies called Przewalski's horse. **1969** J. FISHER et al. *Red Bk.* 101/1 Przewalski's horse..is the sole surviving species of wild horse. *Ibid.*, 101/2 The Przewalski horse can be mistaken for the kulan, or Mongolian wild ass. **1972** *Guardian* 22 May 7/3 (*caption*) A young Przewalski filly. Only about 30 of these Mongolian wild horses are..left in the mountains of China. **1973** *Daily Tel.* 23 Aug. 14 The Przewalski, whose primitive characteristics include a hog mane and mealy muzzle, is the only true horse now living in a wild state in the Gobi Desert, where it is almost extinct.

P.S., a common abbreviation of L. *post scriptum*, POSTSCRIPT, often pronounced as written (ˈpiːˈɛs).

1616 T. ROE *Let.* 30 Nov. in *Embassy to Court of Gt. Mogul* (1899) II. 359 P.S.—I humbly desire your Honor to doe me the fauour to thanck Sir Thomas Smyth in my behalfe. **1757** J. LIND *Lett. Navy* ii. 62 This defect is remedied by a law mentioned in the P.S. **1771** J. WEDGWOOD *Let.* 11 May (1965) 108 PS The letter to which this is a ps I did not like to send by the post. **1842** ORDERSON *Creol.* xviii. 221 As a little P.S...we will here note. **1842** DICKENS *Let.* 1 May (1974) III. 228 Look over leaf for the PS. **1853** MRS. GASKELL *Cranford* ix. 163 So she ended her letter; but in a P.S. she added, she thought she might as well tell me what was the peculiar attraction to Cranford just now. *a* **1909** *Mod.* (At end of a letter.) P.S. Since writing the above I have received your telegram, and am relieved to know that the missing luggage has turned up. Good-bye! **1969** *Listener* 15 May 682/3 PS. These are only hints. Please do not repeat verbatim.

Similarly **P.P.S., P.P.P.S.,** (*post*) *post post scriptum*.

1841 DICKENS *Let.* 9 July (1969) II. 325 P.S. Half asleep. .. P.P.S. They speak Gaelic here. **1900** G. B. SHAW *Let.* 30 Dec. (1972) II. 216 PPS I have been reading 'Herod' (I never go to the theatre now). *c* **1921** E. E. CUMMINGS *Sel. Lett.* (1969) 81 P.S. am waiting for you... P.P.S. Elaine writes your painting is awfully good... P.P.P.S. Enjoyed the Krazy [Kat] you sent B. **1967** *Listener* 21 Dec. 814/2 PS: There'll be a special Christmas edition of *Round the Horne*. PPS: The new series of *Round the Horne* starts in February. PPPS: No advertising.

ps-. Words beginning with this consonant combination (with the exception of a few interjectional monosyllables, *psa, pshaw, pst*) are all taken or formed from Greek, in which language the combination is frequent, and has been represented from about 550 B.C. by the single letter Ψ, ψ. In words beginning thus the only pronunc. current is that with initial (s); the indication of an alternative (ps) in the following main entries would be misleading and is accordingly not shown.

The only words in *ps-* which go back to Old English times are the ecclesiastical terms *psalm* sb. and vb., and *psalter*. *Psalterion* and *psaltery* appear in the 13th c.; *pseudo*, and some five of its compounds, occur in Wyclif. All the other *ps-* words are of Modern English formation, few before 1600, the great majority of the 19th c. In *psalm* the initial *p* was dropped already in OE., as in OF. and the cognate languages, and in English has never been restored in pronunciation (as it has been in French and German). This appears to have served as a precedent for dropping the *p* in the pronunciation of other words, an unscholarly practice often leading to ambiguity or to a disguising of the composition of the word. As the *p* is now pronounced in French, German, and other languages, as well as by Englishmen in reading Greek, and by many scholars in English also (there being no organic defect in the English mouth to prevent it), it is here marked, except in the *psalm, psalter* group, as an optional pronunciation which is recommended especially in all words that retain their Greek form (e.g. *psora, psyche*), and in scientific terms generally, which have not been irretrievably mutilated by popular use.

psa: see PSHAW.

psalidodect (ps-, ˈsælɪdəʊˌdɛkt), *a. Comp. Anat.* [f. Gr. ψαλίς, ψαλιδ- a pair of shears + δήκτης biter, f. δάκνειν to bite.] (See quot.)

1896 COPE *Primary Factors Org. Evol.* vi. 318 Inferior molars work within superior molars, but not between them. Psalidodect mastication.

psalloid (ps-, ˈsælɔɪd), *a. Anat.* [ad. mod.L. *psalloïdes*, irreg. f. Gr. ψάλλειν (see PSALM) + εἶδος form: see -OID.] Resembling a stringed instrument: applied to a part of the *fornix* of the brain (*corpus psalloïdes*), from the lines on it suggesting the strings of a musical instrument, whence also called *lyra* (see LYRA 4).

[**1756** DOUGLAS tr. *Winslow's Struct. Hum. Body* (ed. 4) II. 245 For which reason the Ancients called it Psalloides and Lyra. **1811** HOOPER *Med. Dict., Psalloides*.. Applied..to the inner surface of the fornix of the brain.] **1858** MAYNE *Expos. Lex.* 1029/1 Resembling a psalter, harp, or *cithara*: psalloid. **1895** *Syd. Soc. Lex., Psalloid*... Resembling a harp in shape.

psalm (sɑːm), *sb.* Forms: see below. [ad. L. *psalm-us*, a. Gr. ψαλμ-ός a twitching (of the strings of the harp), the sound of the cithara or harp, a song sung to the harp, f. ψάλλ-ειν to twitch, twang, play (with the fingers), sing to a harp (in LXX and N.T.). The OE. (*p*)*sealm* was cogn. with OHG. *salm, salmo*, also *psalmo, -ma* (MHG. *salm, salme, psalme*, Ger. *psalm*, pl. *-en*, Du. *psalm*), ON. (*p*)*salmr* (mod.Icel. *sálmur*, Norw. *salm*(*e* m. (*salma* f.), MSw. (*p*)*salm*, Sw. *psalm* (*p* mute), Da. *salme* (*psalme*), all from L.; whence also OF. *salme, saume, psalme*, (*p*)*seaume*, F. from 15th c. *psaume* (= psoːm), Pr. *salme, psalm*(*e*, Cat. *salm*, Sp., It. *salmo*, Pg. *psalmo*. From the early forms in the cognate langs. as well as Eng., it is seen that the initial *p* was often dropped at an early period; in many of the langs. it has been restored after the L. and Gr. original, and in that case is also pronounced. Eng. is almost alone in spelling *ps*, and sounding only *s*. The ME. spelling (*p*)*saume*, and modern pronunciation (sɑːm), are due to F. (*p*)*saume*: cf. *balm, calm*, etc.]

A. Illustration of Forms.

α. 1- **psalm**, 1 **psealm**; 4-7 **psalme**, 7 *Sc.* **pschalme**, (6 **spalme**, 7 **sphalme**).

c **961** Hu fela psealma [see B. 2]. *c* **1000** ÆLFRIC *Gloss.* in Wr.-Wülcker 129/41 *Canticum*, psalm æfter hærpansang. *a* **1225** *Ancr. R.* 30 Hwose wule mei siggen þesne psalm. **13..** *Cursor M.* 18889 (Cott.) þe psalm [*Gött.* salme] sais, thoru þe haligast. *a* **1340** HAMPOLE *Psalter* xxii. 9 þis psalme is songen in þe office of ded men. **1398** TREVISA *Barth. De P.R.* IX. xxix. (Bodl. MS.), þe one and fifti psalme..is a psalme of penaunce. **1599** *Acc.-Bk. W. Wray* in *Antiquary* XXXII. 242 A service booke with spalmes. **1605** *Montgomerie's Poems* (S.T.S.) Notes 388 The xxiij Sphalme translait be Montgumry. **1626** BERNARD *Isle of Man* (1627) 260 A Psalme of mercy. **1644** *Direct. Publ. Worship* 40 Singing of Psalms. **1649** ROBERTS *Clavis Bibl.* 380 Psalmes with instruments musicall.

β. 1-3 **sealm**, 1-5 **salm**, 2 **selm** (3 Orm. **sallm**).

c **825** *Vesp. Psalter* xvii[i]. 50 Salm ic cweoðu. *c* **961** ÆTHELWOLD *Rule St. Benet* Contents 6 [ch.] xix, þa sealmas. *c* **1175** Of þe salm [see B. 1]. *c* **1200** *Vices & Virtues* 61 Ðe spekð..ðurh ðene selm. *c* **1200** ORMIN 15579 Upponn hiss hallȝhe sallme. **1388** WYCLIF *Jas.* v. 13 Seie he a salm [1382 psalme]. *c* **1400** Saulm [see B. 2]. *c* **1420-30** *Primer* (E.E.T.S.) 31 Y schal seie salm.

γ. 3 **saume**, 3-6 **salme**, (4 **same**), 5 **saulme**.

c **1290** *S. Eng. Leg.* I. 66/447 He bi-gan one saume of euesongue. *c* **1300** Same [see B. 2]. *a* **1325** *Prose Psalter* xxvi[i]. 11, I shal synge and saie salme to our Lord. *c* **1440** *Promp. Parv.* 441/1 Salme, *psalmus*. **1530** PALSGR. 265/1 Salme of saulter, *pseaulme*. *c* **1597** HARINGTON *Nugæ Ant.* (1779) II. 158 Singing salmes, and himms, and spirituall songs.

B. Signification.

1. In a general sense: Any sacred song that is or may be sung in religious worship; a hymn: esp. in biblical use. (In quot. *c* 1175 applied to the Creed.) Also more generally, any song or ode of a sacred or serious character.

c **825** *Vesp. Psalter* xciv. [xcv.] 2 In salmum wynsumie we him. *c* **825** *Vesp. Hymns* iii. in *O.E. Texts* 403, & salmas ure we singað [*Isa.* xxxviii. 20]. *c* **1000** [see A. α]. *c* **1175** *Lamb. Hom.* 75 þe salm þet heo alle þus writen wes ihaten. Credo . efter þan formeste word of þe salm. *a* **1300** *E.E. Psalter* lxv[i]. 3 [4] Alle land loute þe, and sing to þe sal, And salme sai to þi name with-al. **1382** WYCLIF *Col.* iii. 16 In salmes, and ymnes, and spiritual songis, in grace syngynge in ȝoure hertis to the Lord. *c* **1511** *1st Eng. Bk. Amer.* (Arb.) Introd. 31/2 Hymnes & psalmes & other orasouns haue they. **1645** MILTON *At Solemn Music* 15 Hymns devout and holy Psalms Singing everlastingly. **1838** LONGF. (*title*) A Psalm of Life. What the heart of the young man said to the Psalmist.

2. a. *spec.* Any one of the sacred songs or hymns of the ancient Hebrews which together form the 'Book of Psalms' (see b); a version or paraphrase of any of these, esp. as sung (or read) in public or private worship. (The prevailing use throughout.)

psalms for the day: the particular psalms appointed for each day so that the whole Psalter is said or sung in the course of a definite period, e.g. a week or (as in the Church of England), a month. ***proper psalms***: see PROPER *a.* 2. † ***seven psalms***: (spec.) the seven PENITENTIAL psalms.

c **961** ÆTHELWOLD *Rule St. Benet* Contents 6 [ch.] x, Hu fela psealma on nihtlicum tidum to singenne synt... xviii, Hu fela sealma þurh þa sylfan tida sceolan beon ȝecwedene. *c* **1000** *Ags. Ps.* (Th.) lvi. 9 þæt ic Gode swylce sealmas singe. *c* **1175** *Lamb. Hom.* 7 þis witeȝede dauid þe þe salm scop in þe saltere. *a* **1300** *Cursor M.* 7969-70 (Cott.) Of al þe psalmes o þe sauter, þis psalme [*Gött., etc.*, salme] o penance has na per. *c* **1300** *Beket* 1084 He..seide furst þe set sames [*S. Eng. Leg.* I. 137/1086 þe seuen salmes] and siþþe þe letanye. *a* **1340**, **1398** [see A. α]. *c* **1400** *Rule St. Benet* 1768 When gloria efter þe first saulm es said. **1548-9** (Mar.) *Bk. Com. Prayer*, The Table and Kalendar, expressing the Ordre of the Psalmes and Lessons, to bee sayd at Matyns and Euensong. **1660** WOOD *Life* Dec. (O.H.S.) I. 359 The singing of psalmes after supper..on the Lord's day. **1712** STEELE *Spect.* No. 284 ⁋6, I had one Day set the Hundredth Psalm. **1856** *Amy Carlton* 35 They now read the psalms for the day, taking each a verse in turn. **1903** *Daily Chron.* 21 May 7/2 The Psalm [cvii] is usually read as part of the simple services which take place on Sunday on ships at sea. For that reason it is known as the Sailors' Psalm.

b. ***the Psalms, the Book of Psalms***. Name of one of the books of the Old Testament, forming the hymn-book of the Jewish church, and used also in Christian worship from the earliest times; the Psalter. Often called ***the Psalms of David***, in accordance with the belief that they, or part of them, were composed by David king of Israel.

In Luke xxiv. 44 used for that division of the Old Testament containing the Psalms: = HAGIOGRAPHA.

c **950** *Lindisf. Gosp.* Luke xxiv. 44 Alle ða awritteno sindon in æ moses & witȝo & salmas of mec. **1382** WYCLIF *ibid.*, Alle thingis..whiche ben writun in the lawe of Moyses, and in prophetis, and in salmes, of me. **1581** *Acc.-Bk. W. Wray* in *Antiquary* XXXII. 117 Another boke of St. Chrysostomes upo' the salmes. **1817** D'OYLY & MANT *Bible II. Psalms* Introd., The Book of Psalms..contains the productions of different writers. These..are called however the Psalms of David, because a great part of them were composed by him. **1896** ADENEY *How to read the Bible* II. I. iv. 88 Even in the reading of the Psalms we cannot afford to neglect..the historical method.

3. *attrib.* and *Comb.*, as ***psalm-droner, -expounder, -maker, -poet, -translator***; ***psalm-quoting, -saying, -singing*** sbs. and adjs.; **psalm-meˈlodicon** (see quot.); **ˈpsalm-singer**, one who sings psalms; *spec.* one who maintains the singing of (biblical) psalms (as opposed to hymns) in public worship; (both this and *psalm-singing* frequently have somewhat derogatory connotations); † **ˈpsalm-song** *Obs.*, (*a*) in OE. (*sealmsang*), the singing of psalms; (*b*) in Ormin (*sallmsang*), the Book of Psalms (or the Hagiographa: see 2 b); **ˈpsalm-tone**, any one of the Gregorian tones or chants to which the Psalms were (or are) sung; **psalm-tune**, a tune set to a metrical version of a psalm. See also PSALM-BOOK, -WRIGHT.

1866 J. H. NEWMAN *Gerontius* iv. 27 Who..gave... Each forfeit crown To *psalm-droners And canting groaners. **1382** WYCLIF *2 Sam.* xxiii. 1 A solempne *salm maker of Yrael. **1876** STAINER & BARRETT *Dict. Mus. Terms*, *Psalm Melodicon, an instrument invented in 1828 by Schuhmacher Weinrich. It was a wind instrument with keys and ventages, imitating the tone of several orchestral instruments. **1705** HICKERINGILL *Priest-cr.* IV. (1721) 208 Hopkins and Sternhold, or the more modern *Psalm-Poets. **1563** FOXE *A. & M.* 1499/1 The *psalmsaying friars brought him to his standing, & there left him. **1806** *Med. Jrnl.* XV. 211 He was the best *psalm-singer in the whole congregation. **1818** 'A. BURTON' *Adventures J. Newcome* 254 *Psalm-singer*, an epithet of the greatest possible contempt. **1908** J. M. SULLIVAN *Criminal Slang* 17 *Psalm singer*, a prison trusty; an informer. **1909** *Daily Chron.* 15 Dec. 5/5 Cromwell, the greatest ruler England ever had, was, with his glorious Ironsides, a Psalm-singer. **1650** R. STAPYLTON *Strada's Low C. Warres* III. 61 At this *psalm-singing and these night-sermons, tumults were raised in both Cities, between such as favoured and such as hated them. **1818** 'A. BURTON' *Adventures J. Newcome* 59 Ye skulking, d—d psalmsinging crew! **1847** L. HUNT *Men, Women & B.* II. xi. 280 The psalm-singing old seamen of the Commonwealth. **1909** *Daily Chron.* 15 Dec. 5/5 In our war with the Boers we found Psalm-singing Dutchmen more than a match for our troops. **1964** Psalm-singing [see *Bible-banging* ppl. adj. s.v. BIBLE III]. *c* **1050** *Byrhtferth's Handboc* in *Anglia* (1885) VIII. 319 Mid *sealmsange godes lof up ahebban. *c* **1200** ORMIN 14291 þa bokess..wærenn Moysæsess boc, & Sallmsang, & Profetess. **1889** W. S. ROCKSTRO in Grove *Dict. Mus.* IV. 655/2 The Gregorian *Psalm-Tones are..the oldest Melodies now known to be in existence. *Ibid.* 656/2 The Psalm-Tones..are eight in number—one in each of the first eight Modes. **1709** WATTS *Lyric Poems* Pref., Wks. 1813 IX. 224, I have too often fettered my thoughts in the narrow metre of our old *psalm-translators. **1632** (*title*) All the French *Psalm tunes with English words. Being a collection of Psalms accorded to the verses and tunes generally vsed in the Reformed Churches of France and Germany. **1856** EMERSON *Eng. Traits, Aristocr.* Wks. (Bohn) II. 80 To an American, whose country is whitewashed all over by unmeaning names..or named at a pinch from a psalm-tune. **1871** R. B. VAUGHAN *St. Thomas of Aquin* I. 549 In the above *psalm-words, three things are touched upon.

psalm, *v.* Also 1 **salmian**; 4 **salme**. [f. prec. sb.: cf. *to hymn*.]

1. † **a.** *intr.* To sing psalms. *Obs.* **b.** *trans.* To sing or celebrate in psalms.

c **1000** *Ags. Ps.* (Spelm., MS. M.) cvii. 1 Ic singe and sealmiȝe [L. *cantabo et psalmum dicam*]. *a* **1300** *E.E. Psalter* vii. 18, I sal..salme [L. *psallam*] to name of lauerd heghist es. *a* **1400** HYLTON *Scala Perf.* (W. de W. 1494) II. xlii, To psalme & synge the louynges of god wyth goostly myrthe. **1598** SYLVESTER *Du Bartas* II. i. IV. *Handie-crafts* 72 That we her subjects..Psalming his praise, may sound the same the higher. **1622** H. SYDENHAM *Serm. Sol. Occ.* (1637) 30 He that only sings unto God..he doth but talk of his wondrous workes; but he that Psalmes it..he glories in his holy Name. **1849** tr. *St. Augustine's Expos. Ps.* lxviii. III. 315 He psalmeth to His name, that worketh unto His glory.

2. *trans.* To say or sing a psalm to or over. *rare.*

1800 KEATINGE in Southey *Comm.-pl. Bk.* Ser. II. (1849) 51 We cured our wounds with oil, and by a soldier called Juan Catalan, who blessed us and psalmed us,..we found our Saviour Jesus Christ was pleased to give us strength. **1807** SOUTHEY *Espriella's Lett.* II. 342 He who psalms a sick man, or fancies that the oil from his saint's lamp will heal him of all his complaints.

Hence **psalmed** *ppl. a.* (in quot. ? composed as psalms, or in the form of sacred poetry); **ˈpsalming** *vbl. sb.* and *ppl. a.*

13.. *St. Erkenwolde* 277 in Horstm. *Altengl. Leg.* (1881) 272 He says in his sothe psalmyde writtes: þe skilfulle & þe vnskathely skeltone ay to me. **1652** BENLOWES *Theoph.* III. lix, The Psalming Harp was 'bove thy swaying Scepter priz'd. *Ibid.* v. lii, My psalming Tongue Made th' Orbs suspend their vsual Song, To hear Cœlestial Hymns the glist'ring Quires did throng. **1850** *Elder's House* 141 Sweet the psalming, borne on high.

'psalm-book. In 1 ***sealm-bóc**, 2–3 **salm boc**. [Cf. ON. *psalma-bók*, mod.Icel. *sálma-bók*, Norw. *salmebok*, Sw. *psalmbok*, Da. *salmebog*; Ger. *psalmbuch*, Du. *psalmboek*.] †**a.** The Book of Psalms: see PSALM *sb.* 2 b. *Obs.* **b.** A book or volume containing the Psalms, esp. a metrical version of them for use in public worship.

c **1200** *Trin. Coll. Hom.* 69 Bete we gerne, and ben afterward þe edinesse þe þe salm boc of specð. **1579–80** *Reg. Privy Council Scot.* III. 266 That houshaldaris have Bybillis and Psalme buikis. **1644** *Direct. Publ. Worship* 40 Every one that can reade is to have a Psalm-book. **1816** SCOTT *Antiq.* iii, See this bundle of ballads.. I wheedled an old woman out of these, who loved them better than her psalm-book. **1842** I. WILLIAMS *Baptistery* I. iv. (1874) 42 'Tis Israel's Psalm-book sweet by inspiration wrought.

psalmic ('sælmɪk, 'sɑːmɪk), *a. rare.* [f. PSALM *sb.* + -IC, or ad. Chr. Gr. ψαλμικ-ός, f. ψαλμός PSALM: cf. F. *psalmique*.] Of, pertaining to, or having the character of a psalm or psalms.

1835 *Tait's Mag.* II. 581 The sudden ebullition of a psalmic chorus. **1875** J. MORISON in *Expositor* I. 194 Who has a right to say that the wings of the Psalmic bards were so feeble that [etc.]? **1898** J. ROBERTSON *Poetry & Relig. Ps.* xiii. 323 The greater part of the seventh chapter of Micah is quite psalmic in thought and expression.

psalmist ('sɑːmɪst, 'sælmɪst). [ad. late L. *psalmista* (5th c. Jerome), f. *psalm-us*: see -IST. In OF. *psalmistre* (12th c.), *psalmiste*, *salmiste*, *saumiste*, *samistre*; mod.F. *psalmiste*. Cf. Ger., Du., Da. *psalmist*.]

1. The author of a psalm or psalms; almost always with def. art. as a title for David considered as the author of the Psalms, or as a designation of the author of any one of them.

1483 CAXTON *Cato* G viij b, As the psalmyste sayth. **1539** BIBLE (Great) *2 Sam.* xxiii. 2 The noble Psalmist of Israel. **1623** GOUGE *Serm. Extent God's Provid.* §4 The Psalmist noteth it as a branch of Gods incomparable glory. *a* **1720** J. HUGHES *Div. Poetry* 23 She tun'd to pious notes the psalmist's lyre. **1838** [see PSALM B. 1]. **1875** MANNING *Mission H. Ghost* iv. 103 To say out of the depth of your own experience what the Psalmist said. **1890** KIRKPATRICK *Bk. Psalms* I. Introd. i. 10 The Psalmists celebrate *the moral law* as the guide of human conduct. **1895** *Ibid.* II. xliv. 235 A Maccabaean Psalmist.

2. *Eccl.* A member of one of the minor clerical orders (formerly recognized in some sections of the Church) discharging the functions of a chorister or cantor. *Hist.*

1565 JEWEL *Def. Apol.* II. iii. (1567) 98 The Psalmistes or Singers office was, to singe the Psalmes. **1624** BEDELL *Lett.* xi. 140 As if all that are made Priests among you were Psalmists, Sextens, Readers, Exorcists, Torch-bearers, Subdeacons, and Deacons before. **1726** AYLIFFE *Parergon* 184 Some in the [*i.e.* the Roman] Church exclude a Bishop; and others therein make nine Orders, by including the Bishop and Psalmist. **1829** SOUTHEY *All for Love* IX. ii, Choristers and Monks and Priests And Psalmists there, and Exorcists. **1901** BP. J. WORDSWORTH *Ministry of Grace* 197 Psalmists or choirmen are not mentioned in the Church till the latter half of the fourth century.

3. As the title of a book of psalmody, or of a tune-book for use in public worship.

1842 (*title*) The Psalmist. **1858** (*title*) The Congregational Psalmist: a Companion to all the New Hymn-books, providing Tunes, Chorales, and Chants [etc.].

4. *fig.* One who extols or 'sings the praises' of some one or something. *rare.*

1884 *West. Morn. News* 11 Sept. 4/3 The psalmists of the rising diplomatist tell how.. he succeeded in Syria.

5. *attrib.* and *Comb.* (in sense 1).

1843 CARLYLE *Past & Pr.* II. xvi, A kind of Psalmist solemnity. **1858** —— *Fredk. Gt.* IX. iii. (1872) III. 86 Going out to witness it, with something of a poetic, almost of a psalmist feeling. **1892** ESPINASSE *Voltaire* xi. 177 He breaks forth into almost Psalmist-like praises of the wisdom and beneficence of the Creator.

†**psalmister.** *Obs.* Also **salm-**. [a. OF. (*p*)*salmistre*: see prec.] **a.** A person appointed to sing psalms: = prec. 2. **b.** = prec. 1.

1387 TREVISA *Higden* (Rolls) VII. 195 Þat..ȝe have psalmystres [HIGDEN *psalmicines*] or saienge of psalmes of þe psawtre fourty nyȝtes. **1395** PURVEY *Remonstr.* (1851) 58 The salmistere seith to God, 'I am parteneer of alle that dreden thee'. *c* **1440** *Jacob's Well* 6 He may seye with þe psalmystre: 'Torrentes iniquitatis conturbauerent me'. **1483** *Cath. Angl.* 317/1 A Salmister, *psalmista*.

†**'psalmistry.** *Obs.* [f. PSALMIST + -RY.] The office or work of a psalmist in either sense.

1535 STEWART *Cron. Scot.* (Rolls) I. 101 In sanctuar for to make ceremonie, Witht..psalmistrie for to be said and sung. **1649** MILTON *Eikon.* i. 10 From such a kind of Psalmistry, or any other verbal Devotion, without the pledge and earnest of sutable deeds. **1650** J. COTTON *Sing. Ps.* 37 He would inspire some or other Member of the Church with such a.. Spirit of Psalmistry.

'psalmless, *a. rare.* [f. PSALM *sb.* + -LESS.] Without a psalm; unaccompanied by a psalm.

1623 HOLYDAY *Serm.* (1626) 16 You shall never find him in a Psalmelesse action.

psalmodic (sæl'mɒdɪk), *a.* [f. Gr. type *ψαλμῳδικ-ός (cf. late Gr. ψαλμῳδικῶς, Eustathius *c* 1160): see PSALMODY and -IC, and cf. F. *psalmodique*.] Of or pertaining to psalmody; having the style or character of psalmody. *loosely* = PSALMIC.

1749 *Numbers in Poet. Comp.* 31 Psalmodic Musick thus improved comes nearer to Recitative. **1774** WARTON *Hist. Eng. Poetry* xlv. (1840) III. 148 The..design was..to accommodate every part of the service to the psalmodic tone. **1823** BYRON *Juan* XI. lvii, Pegasus has a psalmodic amble. **1898** J. ROBERTSON *Poetry & Relig. Ps.* xiii. 323 The books of Nahum and Habakkuk have each a chapter entirely psalmodic in construction.

So **psalmodial** (-'məʊdɪəl), **psalmodical** (-'mɒ-) *adjs.*

1848 K. H. DIGBY *Compitum* I. 315 Their language became psalmodial. **1795** MASON *Ch. Mus.* 170 If Queen Elizabeth patronized Cathedral Music exclusively, she did not interdict Psalmodical. [Cf. quot. 1774 above.]

psalmodist ('sɑːmədɪst, 'sælm-). [f. PSALMODY + -IST, or f. PSALMODIZE: see -IST.]

1. One who practises or is skilled in psalmody; a singer of psalms.

1659 HAMMOND *On Ps.* Pref. ¶2 The Spirits and inflamed Affections, and Voices of Psalmodists. **1740** *Univ. Spectator* 19 July 1/3 A young Man, who was a Member of a Society of Psalmodists. **1796** BURNEY *Mem. Metastasio* III. 370 Like a company of psalmodists in a country church.

b. = PSALMIST 2. ? *Obs.*

1726 J. HEALEY *Prim. Liturgy* 11 Let the Psalmodist say, To the praise of God, let us sing a Part of the —— Psalm, verse the —— &c. **1726** AYLIFFE *Parergon* 400 The Canonists make nine Orders in the Church, reckoning the Psalmodist and the Tonsura into the Number.

†**2.** A writer of psalms: = PSALMIST 1. *Obs.*

a **1652** J. SMITH *Sel. Disc.* vi. 252 The writers of these Hagiographa might be termed psalmodists. **1669** GALE *Crt. Gentiles* I. III. i. 15 Plato's Rapsodist.. seems exactly parallel to.. the Jewish Psalmodist. **1886** W. R. SMITH in *Encycl. Brit.* XX. 29/1 He [Solomon] is not recognized as a psalmodist by the most ancient tradition.

b. The author of a metrical version or paraphrase of the Psalms for singing: cf. PSALMODY 1 b.

1885 DIXON *Hist. Ch. Eng.* III. 495 *note*, The English Psalmodists, Cox, Whittingham, Heath, and others, were at work in this reign.

psalmodize ('sɑːmədaɪz, 'sælm-), *v.* [ad. med.L. *psalmōdizāre* (Du Cange), f. *psalmōdi-a*: see -IZE.] *intr.* To practise psalmody; to sing psalms. Hence **'psalmodizing** *vbl. sb.* and *ppl. a.*

1513 BRADSHAW *St. Werburge* II. 620 Secular chanons, of great humilitie, To synge and psalmodise oure sauiour vnto. **1759** J. G. COOPER tr. *Gresset's Ver-vert* II. 45 In short, the bird perform'd his part In all the psalmodising art. **1817** LADY MORGAN *France* (1818) II. VII. 173 A kind of nasal psalmodizing.

psalmody ('sɑːmədɪ, 'sælmədɪ), *sb.* Also 5 **salmody**, (6 **salmede**). [ad. late L. *psalmōdia* (4th c. in Jerome), a. Gr. ψαλμῳδία singing to the harp, f. ψαλμῳδός psalmist, f. ψαλμός psalm + ᾠδή song; in Chr. Gr., psalm-singing, composing of psalms.]

1. The action, practice, or art of singing psalms (or sacred vocal music in general, including hymns and anthems), esp. in public worship.

Now almost exclusively used of the art or practice.

a **1340** HAMPOLE *Psalter* v. 1 Lord persayue my wordis þ[t] is þe psalmodye of my mouth. *c* **1450** *St. Cuthbert* (Surtees) 4051 All þe matyns tyme he stode, And psalmody sange and sayde. **1483** *Cath. Angl.* 317/1 A Salmody, *psalmodia*. **1513** BRADSHAW *St. Werburge* I. 2272 In prayer and psalmody for his helthe and solace. **1685** BAXTER *Paraphr. N.T.* 1 Cor. xiv. 26 Let all your Gifts, whether of Psalmody, or Doctrine, or Languages, or Revelation, or Interpretation, be used to Edification. *a* **1711** KEN *Sion* Poet. Wks. 1721 IV. 363 When God the grace of Psalmody infus'd. **1841** D'ISRAELI *Amen. Lit.* (1867) 327 The passion for psalmody itself is a portion of the history of the Reformation.

attrib. **1868** STEVENSON *Let.* July in *Scribner's Mag.* (1899) XXV. 31/1 As we went home we heard singing... It was a psalmody class.

b. The arrangement of psalms for singing; hence, psalms and hymns so arranged, collectively.

1554–5 *Rec. St. Mary at Hill* 399 Paid for a boke of salmede, ij s. **1718** WATTS (*title*) A Short Essay toward the Improvement of Psalmody. *Ibid.* Wks. 1813 IX. 7 We are to suit part of our psalmody to the gospel-state, as well as borrow part from the Old Testament. **1879** M. PATTISON *Milton* vii. 89 Milton's paraphrase of the Psalms belongs to history, but to the history of psalmody, not that of poetry.

†**2.** The Book of Psalms. *Obs. rare*$^{-1}$.

1471 RIPLEY *Comp. Alch.* III. iii. in Ashm. *Theatr. Chem. Brit.* (1652) 139 Thus spoken by the Prophet yn the Psalmody.

†**3.** The place where psalms are sung; the choir of a church. *Obs. rare*$^{-1}$.

1674 PLAYFORD *Skill Mus.* Pref. A vij, It is reported, that he went often into the Psalmody and sung himself.

'psalmody, *v. rare.* [In 15th c., ad. F. *psalmodier* (12th c. in Littré); in mod. use f. prec. sb.] **a.** *intr.* = PSALMODIZE. **b.** *trans.* To celebrate as in psalmody; to 'hymn'. Hence **'psalmodying** *vbl. sb.*

c **1450** *Cov. Myst.* xli. (Shaks. Soc.) 388 Of qwyche hefne and erthe eche tyme pshalmodyeth. **1491** CAXTON *Vitas Patr.* (W. de W. 1495) 260 They herde the sayd Joseph and his bretheren whiche songen and psalmodyed. **1837** CARLYLE *Misc. Ess.* (1857) IV. 119 The French Revolution ..is an event..still to be celebrated and psalmodied. **1850** —— *Latter-d. Pamph.* i. 10 My dear household, cease singing and psalmodying; lay aside your fiddles, take out your work-implements, if you have any.

†**'psalmograph.** *Obs.* [ad. late L. *psalmograph-us*, a. Gr. ψαλμογράφ-ος, f. ψαλμ-ός psalm, + -γραφος writing, a writer. So mod.F. *psalmographe*.] The author of a psalm or psalms: = PSALMIST 1.

1542 BECON *David's Harp* viii. Wks. 1564 I. 159 As the Psalmograph saith: The vngodly hath the ouerhand, and the pore is brent. **1570** FOXE *A. & M.* (ed. 2) 216/1 The sayeng of king Dauid the Psalmograph. **1657** J. SMITH *Myst. Rhet.* 145 The Psalmograph having in the former part of the 2. Psalm spoken of the terrors of Gods indignation.

So †**psal'mographer**, †**psal'mographist** *rare*$^{-0}$, in same sense; †**psal'mography** *rare*$^{-0}$, the writing of psalms.

1611 LOE *Blisse Bright. Beauty* (1614) 52 (T.) The psalmographer setteth him out, in the person of Solomon, to be of surpassing beauty. **1648** *Hunting of Fox* 10 The Psalmographers Prophecy, if applyed to these times will prove..an exact History. **1656** BLOUNT *Glossogr.*, *Psalmography*, the writing of Psalms. **1727** BAILEY vol. II, *Psalmographist*, a Writer of Psalms.

†**'psalmonize,** *v. Obs. rare*$^{-1}$. [irreg. ? after *harmonize*, or error for *psalmodize*.] *intr.* To sing psalms: = PSALMODIZE.

1483 CAXTON *Gold. Leg.* 416b/1 In syngnyng, psalmonysyng, & glorefyeng god.

†**'psalmwright.** *Obs.* Forms: 1 **psalm-, sealmwyrhta**, 2 **salmwurhta**, 3 **psalm-, salmwurhte, salmwrihte, -wruhte.** [f. PSALM *sb.* + OE. *wyrhta* worker, WRIGHT.] = PSALMIST 1.

c **1000** ÆLFRIC *Hom.* II. 82 Efne se psalmwyrhta understod on hwilcum ȝedeorfum þis mennisce lif is ȝelogod. *c* **1000** —— *On O. & N. Test.* (Grein) 1 Swa swa se sealmwyrhta þus sang. *c* **1175** *Lamb. Hom.* 117 For þon cweð þe salmwurhta. *a* **1225** *Ancr. R.* 256, & sigge mid te salmwurhte, 'Corripiet me justus [etc.]'. *c* **1230** *Hali Meid.* 3 Dauid þe salmwrihte spekeð iþe sauter. *a* **1240** *Lofsong* in *Cott. Hom.* 215 þus seið þe salmwruhte dauið iþe sawter.

psalmy ('sɑːmɪ), *a. nonce-wd.* [f. PSALM *sb.* + -Y.] Apt or disposed for a psalm.

1858 BAILEY *Age* 113 When once a man feels sermonish or psalmy.

'psaloid, *a.*, an alteration of PSALLOID, due to an assumed derivation from Gr. ψαλίς, ψαλιδ- pair of shears, also a vault (= L. *fornix*): see quots.

Psaloid from ψαλίς is as incorrectly formed as *psalloid* from ψάλλειν; its correct form would be **psalidoid*.

1858 MAYNE *Expos. Lex.*, *Psaloides*, *adj.* (As if *Psalidoeides*, which, correctly, it ought to be, from ψαλίς, an arched work: terminal -*īdēs*.) *Anat.* Resembling an arch; arch-like; arched: psa'loid... The *Corpus psaloides* is another term for the *Fornix*, simply meaning the arched body. **1895** *Syd. Soc. Lex.*, *Psa'loid*, like an arch, arched.

psalter ('sɔːltə(r)). Forms: see below. [In OE. (*p*)*saltere* (= OHG. *psalteri*, *-tare*, mostly *saltari*, *-târe*, *-teri*, MHG. *salter*, Ger. *psalter*; ON. (*p*)*saltari*, Icel. *saltari*, Sw. *psaltere*, Da. *salter* (*psalter*)), ad. L. *psaltērium*. In ME. *sauter*, a. AF. *sauter* = OF. *sautier* (*ps-*), *saltier*, *saultier* (*ps-*), in F. *psautier* (16th c.) = Pr. (*p*)*salteri*, *sauteri*, Sp., It. *salterio*, Pg. *psalterio*; all:—L. *psaltērium*, a. Gr. ψαλτήριον a stringed instrument played by twanging, f. ψάλλειν to twang; also in Christian Greek and Latin writers (e.g. Jerome *a* 420) a name for the 'Psalms of David'. The initial *ps-*, rare in OE. and ME. as in OF., frequent from 14th c., has been the established spelling from 16th c., but the *p*, pronounced in Fr., Ger., Du., etc., remains mute in Eng. The *l* was preserved in OE., was inserted occasionally in ME. as in OF., and usually from 15th c.; it is now always pronounced.]

A. Illustration of Forms.

1. α. 1–3 **saltere.** β. 2–6 **sauter, sawter**, 3–5 **sautere**, 4 **sautre, -tir**, 4–5 **sawtere**, 5 **sauteer, sawtyr, -tre**, 6 **sater.** γ. 4–6 **salter, -tere**, 5 **saulter, sawlter.**

α. *a* **900** tr. *Bæda's Hist.* III. xix. [xxvii.] (1890) 242 þæt æȝhwelce dæge alne saltere..asunge. *c* **1000**, *c* **1175** Saltere [see B. 1]. *c* **1200** *Vices & Virtues* 113 Bi ðessere holi mihte is iwriten on ðe saltere.

β. *c* **1175** *Lamb. Hom.* 155 On ane stude in þe sauter. *a* **1240** *Lofsong in Cott. Hom.* 215 þus seið..dauið iþe sawter. *a* **1300** *Cursor M.* 11616 (Cott.) Þan com þe propheci al cler, To dede, þat said es in sauter [*other MSS.* clere, sautere]. **1362** LANGL. *P. Pl.* A. VIII. 47 So seiþ the sauter and sapience boþe. ? *a* **1400** *Morte Arth.* 3317 The sexte hade a sawtere semliche bowndene. **1430–40** LYDG. *Bochas* IX. xiv. (MS. Bodl. 263) 420/1 Vpon a vers write in the Sauteer. *c* **1440** *Nom.* in Wr.-Wülcker 720/1 *Hoc psalterium*, a sawtyr. **1530** PALSGR. 265/1 Sauter a boke, *psaltier*. **1547–8** *Rec. St. Mary at Hill* 317 Item, for vj new sawters in englisshe for the quyer.

γ. *c* **1375** *Sc. Leg. Saints* x. (*Mathou*) 566 A prophet til hym dere, And makare of þe saltere. **1474** CAXTON *Chesse* 67 Dauyd preyseth moche in the sawlter the trewe labourers. *c* **1540** *Invent.* in *Trans. Lond. & Middx. Archæol. Soc.* IV. 371 Itm on bothe sydes the quyer iij salters.

2. *α.* 1 **psaltere.** *β.* 4 **psauter, psawtre,** 4–5 **psautere,** 4–6 **psawter.** *γ.* 5– **psalter** (5 **psaltyr,** 6 **spalter).**

α. c **1000** *Sax. Leechd.* III. 202 Cimbalan oððe psalteras. *β. a* **1340** HAMPOLE *Psalter* Prol. 3 Þis boke is cald þe psautere. **1387** TREVISA *Higden* (Rolls) VII. 195 þat ȝe have psalmystres or saienge of psalmes of þe psawtre fourty nyȝtes. *c* **1400** MAUNDEV. (1839) xxv. 261 David seythe in the Psautere. **1511** FABYAN *Will* in *Chron.* (1811) Pref. 5 To say oon tyme our Lady psawter.

γ. c **1470** Psaltyr [see B. 6]. **1509** FISHER *Fun. Serm. C'tess Richmond* Wks. (1876) 295 Many other prayers & psalters of Dauyd. **1513** BRADSHAW *St. Werburge* I. 2546 And deuoutely say..Dauyd spalter holly knelynge with great reuerence. **1530** (*title*) The Psalter of David, in Englishe.

B. Signification.

I. 1. The Book of Psalms, as one of the books of the Old Testament.

a **900** [see A. 1]. *c* **1000** ÆLFRIC *On O. & N. Test.* (Grein) 7 Se saltere ys an boc, þe he [David] ȝesette þurh god betwux oðrum bocum on þære bibliothecan. *c* **1175** *Lamb. Hom.* 7 Dauid þe þe salm scop in þe saltere. *a* **1225** *Ancr. R.* 288 Dauid, iðe sauter, cleopeð hine dogge. *a* **1300, 1362, 1474** [see A. 1 *β*, *γ*]. **1548–9** (Mar.) *Bk. Com. Prayer* Introd., The Psalter shalbe red through once euery Moneth. **1651** HOBBES *Leviath.* III. xxxiii. 202 The Psalter was compiled, and put into the form it now hath, after the return of the Jews. **1782** PRIESTLEY *Corrupt. Chr.* II. IX. 152 [Pay] by twenty repetitions of the psalter. **1864** *Reader* 11 June 740 We put ourselves in a right position towards the Psalter by regarding it as the national Hymn-book of the Jewish people.

b. A translation or particular version (prose or metrical) of the Book of Psalms: e.g. a Latin, English, Chinese Psalter; the Prayer-book Psalter, the Scotch Metrical Psalter, etc.

Roman, Gallican, and ***Hebraic Psalters***: the three successive forms of the Latin version of the Psalms, prepared by St. Jerome; the first a slight recension of the Old Latin text, after the LXX; the second a more thorough recension, based on Origen's Hexaplar text of the LXX; the third a new translation by Jerome from the Hebrew. The first was adopted in the Roman liturgy; the second was extensively used in Gaul, and north of the Alps, and was subsequently adopted in the Vulgate, in which Jerome's Hebraic Psalter (which properly belonged to the Vulgate) failed to supersede it. ***Prayer-book Psalter,*** the English version of the Psalms used in the Book of Common Prayer, and not displaced by the later version in the Bible of 1611.

c **1050** *Charter of Leofric* in Kemble *Cod. Dipl.* IV. 275 Nu ðaer synd..tropere and II. salteras and se þriddan saltere swa man singð on Rome. **1387** TREVISA *Higden* (Rolls) V. 183 Ierom..amended also þe sauter of þe seventy þat was þoo i-used wel nyh in alle chirches, and þat psauter was eft appeyred, and he translated it newe aȝen;..þat sauter [is] i-cleped þe Frensche sawter, psalterium Gallicanum; ȝit he made þe þridde translacioun of þe psawter from word to word. **1549** (*title*) The Psalter or Psalmes of Dauid after the Translacion of the great Bible, poynted as it shall be songe in Churches. **1723** GIBSON *Life Spelman* in *S.'s Wks.* Pref. Cj b, In the Year 1640 he [John Spelman] publish'd the Saxon Psalter from an ancient MS. of Sir Henry's. **1756–7** tr. *Keysler's Trav.* (1760) I. 250 Dr. R...fetched out of his closet a Chinese psalter, sent him as a curiosity by the cardinal de Tournon. **1889** H. E. WOOLDRIDGE in Grove *Dict. Mus.* IV. 752 Sternhold's translations [1549], [are] the nucleus of the metrical Psalter which has come down to us. **1905** W. ALDIS WRIGHT in *Westm. Gaz.* 29 July 2/1 Coverdale's first translation of the Bible was published in 1535, and he was employed in producing the Great Bible of 1539, known as Cromwell's, and the edition of April 1540, which first had Cranmer's preface. From the versions of the Psalms which appeared in these three Bibles the Prayer-book Psalter has been formed.

c. A copy of, or a volume containing, the Psalms, esp. as arranged for liturgical or devotional use.

c **1000** *Canons of Ælfric* §21 in Thorpe *Laws* II. 350 Þa halȝan bec, saltere & pistol-boc & godspell-boc & mæsse-boc. *a* **1225** *Ancr. R.* 44 Verslunge of hire sautere, redinge of Englichs, oðer of Freinchs, holi meditaciuns. ?*a* **1366** CHAUCER *Rom. Rose* 431 A sauter held she faste in honde. *c* **1380** WYCLIF *Wks.* (1880) 41 Deuyn officis..out taken þe sautir, of wheche þei may haue breuyaries, þat is smale sauteris or abreggid. **1431** *Rec. St. Mary at Hill* 27 Also iiij grayels & iij sawters. **1603** KNOLLES *Hist. Turks* (1638) 164 Hauing a Psalter in his hand. **1833** J. HOLLAND *Manuf. Metal* II. 74 In an old psalter, written and illuminated by Eadwine, a monk, about the time of king Stephen.

†**2.** A selection from, or portion of, the Psalms, said or sung at a particular service or for a particular purpose. *Obs.*

In the quots. applied to the psalms recited in the Office of the Dead.

c **1000** in Thorpe *Dipl. Angl. Aevi Sax.* (1865) 614 Ælc ȝemænes hades broður [singe] tweȝen salteras sealma..vi. mæssan oððe .vi. salteras sealma. *c* **1300** *Havelok* 244 Sauteres deden he manie reden, þat god self shulde his soule leden Into heuene. **1389** in *Eng. Gilds* (1870) 26 Euery brother and sister shal payen..a peny to a sauter for ye dedes soule. *c* **1420** *Chron. Vilod.* 3101 Tylle he hadde sayde hurre sawter alle. **1508** KENNEDIE *Flyting w. Dunbar* 318 Thow says for thame few psaltris, psalmis, or creidis.

3. *transf.* ***Our Lady's psalter***: a name given to the rosary on account of its containing the same number (150) of Aves as there are psalms in the Psalter; also, a book containing this. ***Jesus psalter***: a form of devotion consisting of 15 petitions, each beginning with a tenfold repetition of the name Jesus (which is thus said 150 times).

1380 *Lay Folks Catech.* (Lamb. MS.) 220 So myȝt pardoun be gotun to sey yche day a lady sawter. **1425** *Ord. Whittington's Alms-ho.* in Entick *London* (1766) IV. 354 Say three or two sauters of our lady at the least: that is to say, threies seaven Ave Marias, with xv Pater Nosters, and three credes. **1500** *Will of Odingsellis* (Somerset Ho.), A paire of small corall bedys with the hoole psalter of our lady. **1605–6** *Act 3 Jas. I*, c. 5 §25 No person..shall bring from beyond the Seas, nor shall print, sell, or buy any Popish Prymers, Ladies Psalters, Manuells, Rosaries, Popishe Catechismes. **1632** *High Commission Cases* (Camden) 305 That we are as carefull in printeing the Bible as they are of their Jesus' psalter. **1888** *Guardian* 21 Nov. 1766/1 The version in the Anglican manual already mentioned..retains the title of *Jesus Psalter*, while by its direction that each principal petition should be said once, instead of ten times, it abolishes the reason for which the name of Psalter was applied.

4. Applied to certain old Irish chronicles in verse (***Psalter of Cashel, Psalter of Tara*** or ***Temor***).

1685 STILLINGFL. *Orig. Brit.* v. 270 This Psalter of Cashel is one of the most Authentick Histories among them, and so called because done in Verse. **1793** HELY tr. *O'Flaherty's Ogygia* II. 240 A book..which we call the Psalter of Temor, in which are compiled the archives of the Kingdom. **1830–3** W. CARLETON *Traits & Stories Irish Peas.* (1860) I. 117 *note*, There were properly only two Psalters, those of Tara and Cashel. The Psalters were collections of genealogical history, partly in verse. **1893** JOYCE *Short Hist. Irel.* 31 A book of annals called the Psalter of Cashel was compiled by Cormac Mac Cullenan.

II. 5. A stringed musical instrument: = PSALTERY 1. *Obs.* or *arch.*

c **1000** *Sax. Leechd.* III. 202 Cimbalan oððe psalteras oððe strengas ætrinan saca hit ȝetacnað. *a* **1100** *Voc.* in Wr.-Wülcker 278/11 *Sambucus*, saltere. *a* **1325** *Prose Psalter* xlviii[i]. 4, Y..shal open in þe sauter myn purpose. **14..** *Eger & Grine* 265 in Furniv. *Percy Folio* I. 362 Shee laid a souter upon her knee Thereon shee plaid full lovesomlye. **1483** *Cath. Angl.* 320/1 A Sawtre (*A.* Sawter), *nablum, organum, psalterium.* **1552** HULOET, *Psalter*:..also an instrument of musicke lyke a harpe. **1632** QUARLES *Div. Fancies* II. lxxvii, T' one makes the Sermon, t' other tunes the Psalter. **1878** B. TAYLOR *Deukalion* I. i. 19 The strings of the psalter, The shapes in the marble, Our passing deplore.

†**b.** *Her.* Applied to a kind of wind instrument. *Obs. rare.*

1688 R. HOLME *Armoury* III. xvi. (Roxb.) 56/2 He beareth Azure, a psalter... This may also be termed, a Recorder, or a Shawm, or a Wyate... Note that all these kind of wind Instruments, or any other, which receiueth the sound from the wind of the mouth of a man are euer placed in Armes with their mouth vpwards.

III. 6. *Comb.* **psalter-book** = senses 1 and 2.

c **1200** *Trin. Coll. Hom.* 17 Dauið in þe salter boc. **13..** *S. Eng. Leg.* (MS. Bodl. 779) in Herrig's *Archiv* LXXXII. 308/72 In þe sauter-book it is I-write also. *c* **1470** HENRY *Wallace* XI. 1393 A Psaltyr buk Wallace had on him euir. **1545** JOYE *Exp. Dan.* v. 61 What els is the psalter boke then the glasse of the most holy trinite? **1551–2** in Swayne *Sarum Churchw. Acc.* (1896) 96 For a sawter booke, xvj d. **1559** *Rec. St. Mary at Hill* 411 Payd for iiij sater bookes..xij *s.* **1571** in Nicolson and Burn *Hist. & Antiq. Westmorld. & Cumbld.* (1777) II. 90 Also four psalter books in metre.

†'**psalterer.** *Obs.* In 4 sautreour, sauterer, sawtrer. [ME. *sautreour*, app. an Anglo-Fr. formation from *sautre*; subseq. conformed to Eng. agent-sbs. in -ER.] A player on the psaltery.

In first quot. used as = psaltery, app. for the sake of rime.

c **1330** R. BRUNNE *Chron. Wace* (Rolls) 11386 Many mynestrales þorow out þe toun, Som blewe trompe and clarioun, Harpes, pypes, and tabours, Ffyþeles, sitoles, sautreours. Belles, chymbes, and symfan. **1382** WYCLIF *2 Kings* iii. 15 Now forsothe the bryngith to me an sawtrer. And whanne the sawtrer songe [etc.].

psalterial (psæl-, sɒl'tɪərɪəl), *a.* *Anat.* and *Zool.* [f. PSALTERI-UM + -AL[1].] Pertaining to the psalterium (in either sense: see PSALTERIUM 3).

1865 *Reader* No. 120. 429/2 Only the psalterial fibres. **1880** BASTIAN *Brain* 274 The mode in which the Corpus Callosum and the Fornix are united posteriorly by the psalterial fibres. **1890** *Cent. Dict.*, *Psalterial*, as, the psalterial aperture of the reticulum; the psalterial laminæ.

psalterian (psæl-, sɒl'tɪərɪən), *a.* [f. L. *psaltērium* PSALTERY, PSALTER + -AN.] **a.** Of, like, or having a sound like that of, a psaltery. **b.** Pertaining to, or having the style of, the Psalter.

1819 KEATS *Lamia* 114 Then once again the charmed God began An oath, and through the serpent's ears it ran Warm, tremulous, devout, psalterian. **1893** A. H. KEENE in *Academy* 11 Feb. 121/1 Mrs. Barbauld's *Hymns in Prose for Children* with their psalterian stateliness.

‖**psalterion** (psæl-, sɒl'tɪərɪɒn). Also 3 salteriun. [In ME. a. OF. *sal-*, *sar-*, *saterion* (Wace 11th c.), mod.F. *psaltérion*, ad. L. *psaltērium*; in mod. use a transliteration of Gr. ψαλτήριον PSALTERY, PSALTER.]

1. = PSALTERY 1. Now *poet.*

c **1205** LAY. 7000 Of harpe & of salteriun, of fiðele & of coriun. **1530** PALSGR. 165 *Psalterión*, a psaltrion. **1579** NORTH *Plutarch, Themistocles* (1895) I. 283 He could no skill to tune a harpe, nor a violl, nor to playe of a psalterion. **1696** tr. *Du Mont's Voy. Levant* 275 The only tolerable Instrument they have is the Psalterion. **1875** BROWNING *Aristoph. Apol.* 5677, I sent the tablets, the psalterion, so Rewarded Sicily. **1897** F. THOMPSON *New Poems* 31 My fingers thou hast taught to con Thy flame-chorded psalterion.

2. *R.C. Ch.* = PSALTER 1 or 2.

1893 *Month* Feb. 221 With regard to Vespers, the Psalterion lays down the law in this way.

'**psalterist.** [f. PSALTER + -IST.] = PSALTERER.

1891 F. THOMPSON *Sister-Songs* (1895) 56 Yon Apollonian harp-player, Yon wandering psalterist of the sky.

‖**psalterium** (psæl-, sɒl'tɪərɪəm). [L. *psaltērium*, ad. Gr. ψαλτήριον PSALTERY, PSALTER.]

I. 1. = PSALTERY 1. (Not in Eng. use.)

1872 *Sacristy* Aug. I. 201 The *psalterium*, which must not be confounded with the *psalterion* of the 13th century, was a little portable harp. **18..** *S. Kensington Art Handbk.* No. 5. 35 The psalterium was a kind of lyre of an oblong square shape... It was played with a rather large plectrum.

2. = PSALTER 1 or 2. (Not in Eng. use.)

1882 in OGILVIE: hence in later Dicts.

II. 3. *Anat.* and *Zool.* **a.** = LYRA 4. Cf. PSALLOID. **b.** The third stomach of a ruminant; the omasum or manyplies.

1857 DUNGLISON *Med. Dict.*, *Psalterium*, Lyra. **1858** MAYNE *Expos. Lex.*, *Psalterium*, another name for the Lyra. **1868** OWEN *Vertebr. Anim.* III. 473 The muscular walls.. close the entry to the first and second cavities, and, drawing that of the psalterium, nearer to the gullet, conduct the remasticated bolus into the third cavity. **1871** HUXLEY *Anat. Vertebr. Anim.* viii. 379 When this portion of the stomach is slit open, longitudinally, the lamellæ fall apart like the leaves of a book, whence it has received the fanciful name of the *Psalterium* from anatomists, while butchers give it that of *Manyplies*. **1879** WRIGHT *Anim. Life* 11 After the mass has been thoroughly ground down by the teeth, it is again swallowed, when it passes along the oesophagus into the third stomach, called the manyplies, or psalterium.

psaltery ('sɔːltərɪ), *sb.* Forms: *α.* 3–5 **sautre,** 4 **sawtree, sauteray,** 4–5 **sawtrie, -ye,** 4–6 **sautrie,** 5 **sawtre, sautry, -triȝe,** 5–6 **sawtrey,** 5 (–9) **-try,** 6 **sawtery, saltry;** *β.* 4 **psautery,** 6 **psautry,** 6–7 **psalterie;** 5– **psaltery.** [a. OF. *saltere, sautere*, and *sauterie, psalterie* (12th c. in Godef.), ad. L. *psaltērium*, ad. Gr. ψαλτήριον; a learned form from L. for the name of the instrument, after *sautier* had become confined to the Psalter; subseq. superseded by *sauterion, psalterion*. Retained in Eng. as the name of the instrument (rarely in error put for *psalter*).]

1. An ancient and mediæval stringed instrument, more or less resembling the dulcimer, but played by plucking the strings with the fingers or a plectrum; differing from the harp in having the soundboard behind and parallel with the strings. Also, a modern imitation of this.

Chiefly in biblical translation or reference (after L. *psaltērium* of the Vulgate, usually rendering Heb. *nēbel*), or in vague poetic or rhetorical use; mostly coupled with other instruments.

a **1300** *E.E. Psalter* xxxii[i]. 2 Schriues to lauerd, in harpe and sautre Of ten stringes to him singe yhe. *a* **1340** HAMPOLE *Psalter* xxxii. 2 In psautery of ten cordis syngis til hym. *c* **1386** CHAUCER *Miller's T.* 27 And all aboue ther lay a gay Sautrie [*v.rr.* Sautrye, sawtrie] On which he made a nyghtes melodie. ?*c* **1400** *R. Gloucester's Chron.* (Rolls) App. H. 245 Nas þer noman in londe þat so muche of song couþe..Ne of sautriȝe ne of coriun. *a* **1440** *Sir Degrev.* 35 [He] gretlech yaff hym to gle, To harp and to sautre. *c* **1450** HOLLAND *Howlat* 757 The psaltery, the sytholis, the soft sytharist. *a* **1529** SKELTON *Replyc.* 340 Dauid..harped so melodiously ..in his decacorde psautry. **1530** PALSGR. 265/1, 2 *Saltry*,.. *Sautrie* an instrument. *a* **1557** in *Tottell's Misc.* (Arb.) 197 Bothe his harpe and sawtrey he [Apollo] defide. **1607** SHAKS. *Cor.* v. iv. 52 The Trumpets, Sackbuts, Psalteries, and Fifes, Tabors, and Symboles, and the showting Romans. **1700** DRYDEN *Flower & Leaf* 358 The sawtry, pipe, and hautboi's noisy band. **1808** SCOTT *Marm.* IV. xxxi, Sackbut deep, and psaltery, And war-pipe with discordant cry. **1864** PUSEY *Lect. Daniel* i. (1876) 33 The Psaltery, as described by S. Augustine, corresponds with the 'Santour', as recognised ..on the bas-relief of Babylon. **1901** W. B. YEATS *Let.* 20 July (1954) III. 354 Dolmetsch has interested himself in the chanting..and has made a psaltery for Miss Farr. It has 12 strings. **1975** *Gramophone* Oct. 709/1 The psaltery heard here is a bigger instrument than those we see in old paintings... It has seventy-three strings..and is played with both hands, the instrument lying flat on a table.

†**2. a.** = PSALTER 1, 2. *rare.*

1628 J. HUME *Jewes Deliv.* v. 82 The princely Prophet throughout all his Psalterie makes out onely a generall confession of Gods blessings. **1822** LAMB *Elia* Ser. I. *Dreamchildren*, She knew all the Psaltery by heart, ay, and a great part of the Testament besides. **1890** HEALY *Insula Sanctorum* 156 The entire psaltery seems to have been recited during the daily office at least at certain times of the year.

b. = PSALTER 4. *rare*[−1]. (*erron.*)

1809 CAMPBELL *O'Connor's Child* vi, Their tribe, they said, their high degree, Was sung in Tara's psaltery.

'**psaltery,** *v.* *rare.* In 4 sautrien. [ME., prob. repr. an AF. or OF. *sautrier*, f. *sautier*, PSALTER.] *intr.* To play on the psaltery.

1393 LANGL. *P. Pl.* C. XVI. 208 Ich can..Noþer sailen ne sautrien ne singe with þe giterne. **1903** G. B. SHAW *Let.* 11 June in *Florence Farr, Shaw, Yeats* (1946) 17 Are you too busy psalterying to copyright my new play at the Bayswater theatre?

psaltress ('sɔːltrɪs). *rare*; now only *poetic.* [app. short for *psalteress*, fem. of *psalter*, PSALTERER.] A female player on the psaltery.

c **1559** R. HALL *Life Fisher* (1655) 3 [John's] Head was beg'd of King Herod, at a banquet of Wine by a Psaltresse, or woman dancer. **1652** BENLOWES *Theoph.* IX. liv, Rare Psaltresse, with Heav'n-drops inebriate. **1835** BROWNING

Paracelsus v. 666 Earth is a wintry clod: But springtide, like a dancing psaltress, passes Over its breast to waken it. **1875** —— *Aristoph. Apol.* 98 Chantress and psaltress, flute-girl, dancing-girl.

psammic ('sæmɪk), *a. Ecol.* [f. Gr. ψάμμ-ος sand + -IC 1.] Inhabiting areas of sand or gravel.

1938 J. R. CARPENTER *Ecol. Gloss.* 222 *Psammic*, concerning communities on sand or gravel. **1965** B. E. FREEMAN tr. *Vandel's Biospeleol.* vii. 69 The banks of rivers and lakes contain numerous psammic Rotifera.

psammite ('psæmaɪt, 'sæmaɪt). *Min.* [a. F. *psammite*, f. Gr. ψάμμος sand + -ITE: cf. Gr. ψαμμίτης sandy.] Orig., a fine or smooth-grained sandstone: see quot. 1859. In later use, a sediment or sedimentary rock composed of medium-sized particles (now commonly defined to be between 1/16 mm and either 2 or 4 mm diameter); also, a metamorphic derivative of a sandstone.

1837 J. T. SMITH tr. *Vicat's Mortars* Pref. 9 Other words, used for the purpose of defining substances hitherto classed by us under a more general category..such as 'arenes', 'psammites', &c., I have thought it advisable to convert at once into English terms. *Ibid.* App. 178 The species of sandstone called grey-wackes by the Germans, and psammites by M. Brogniard. **1859** PAGE *Handbk. Geol. Terms, Psammite*,..a term in common use among Continental geologists for fine-grained, fissile, clayey sandstones, in contradistinction to those which are more siliceous and gritty. **1879** RUTLEY *Study Rocks* xiv. 299. **1882** A. GEIKIE *Text-bk. Geol.* 154 (*heading*) Gravel and sand rocks (psammites). **1933** *Geogr. Jrnl.* LXXXI. 158 If the water table approaches the surface evaporation takes place, causing a concentration of the salts carried down. These salt-sand crusts are psammites. **1962** READ & WATSON *Introd. Geol.* I. v. 260 (*heading*) The psammites: sand, sandstone, greywacke, arkose. **1977** A. HALLAM *Planet Earth* 174 Meta-sandstones are sometimes called psammites.

Hence **psammitic** (-'mɪtɪk) *a.*, pertaining to, containing, or of the nature of psammite; consisting, as a sandstone, of fine rounded grains; also, derived by metamorphism from a sandstone.

1847 in WEBSTER. **1879** [see PSEPHITIC]. **1882** A. GEIKIE *Text-bk. Geol.* 87 *Psammitic*, or sandstone-like, composed of rounded grains, as in ordinary sandstone: when the grains are larger (often sharp and somewhat angular) the rock is *gritty*, or a grit. **1910** *Q. Jrnl. Geol. Soc.* LXVI. 377 They may be conveniently divided into (1) a Psammitic Group, consisting chiefly of flaggy quartz-felspar granulites..; and (2) a Pelitic Group, consisting chiefly of garnetiferous mica-schists (or gneisses) which are often coarse and quartzose. **1921** G. W. TYRRELL in *Geol. Mag.* LVIII. 501 It is suggested that the terms *psammitic* and *pelitic* might usefully be restricted to the hard metamorphic rocks which have been changed beyond the limits implied by the corresponding Latin terms [sc. *arenaceous* and *argillaceous*]. **1956** E. W. HEINRICH *Microsc. Petrogr.* iv. 99 Psammitic and pelitic rocks may be further subdivided on the basis of mineralogical composition. **1959** *Trans. R. Soc. Edin.* LXIII. 554 In a series of psammitic and slightly calcareous pelitic schists, such as those of Morar, there is great difficulty in discovering the metamorphic grade in relation to that of other areas. **1962** READ & WATSON *Introd. Geol.* I. ix. 539 Psammitic gneisses commonly form massive pinkish rocks composed principally of quartz and feldspar.

psammo- (psæməʊ, sæməʊ), before a vowel **psamm-**, repr. Gr. ψαμμο-, combining form of ψάμμος sand, entering into some scientific terms. **psammobiid** (-'məʊbɪɪd), *Zool.*, a bivalve mollusc of the family *Psammobiidæ*, typified by the genus *Psammobia* [Gr. βίος life]; so **psa'mmobioid** *a.* ‖**,psammocarci'noma**, *Path.* (pl. **-ata**), a carcinoma containing concretions resembling sand (Billings *Nat. Med. Dict.* 1890). **psammodontid** (-məʊ'dɒntɪd), *Ichth.*, a fish belonging to the extinct *Psammodontidæ*, a family of rays with flat quadrate teeth, typified by the genus *Psammodus* [Gr. ὀδούς, ὀδοντ- tooth]. **psammolithic** (-'lɪθɪk) *a.*, *Geol.* [Gr. λίθος stone], consisting of sandstone: used of groups of strata. **'psammophile** *sb.* and *a. Bot.* [a. F. *psammophile* (J. Thurmann *Essai de Phytostatique* (1849) I. xiii. 268): see -PHIL, -PHILE], (a plant) thriving best in sandy soil. **psammo'philic** *a.* = *psammophilous* adj.; **psammophilous** (-'ɒfɪləs) *a. Bot.* [Gr. φίλος loving], sand-loving, frequenting or growing in sandy soil, as an insect or a plant. ‖**'psammophis** [Gr. ὄφις snake, serpent], name of a genus of snakes, a sand-snake or desert-snake; hence **'psammophid, 'psammophine** *adjs.*, of or belonging to the family *Psammophidæ*, and subfamily *Psammophinæ*, typified by *Psammophis*. **'psammophyte**, a plant characteristic of sandy habitats. ‖**,psammosar'coma** *Path.* (pl. **-ata**), a sarcoma or fleshy tumour with sand-like calcareous particles. **'psammosere** *Ecol.* [SERE *sb.*[2]], a plant succession having its origin on sand.

1888 F. A. LEES *Flora W. Yorkshire* 69 Others [*sc.* plants] ..are quite as much *psammophiles, if their stations be any guide. **1901** C. MOHR *Plant Life Alabama* 131 The slender, wiry culms of this grass..render the species one of the most striking types of psammophile plants. **1973** M. A. SLEIGH *Biol. Protozoa* xi. 264 These *psammophilic forms [of Protozoa] have been studied by J. Dragesco. **1869** TRIMEN & DYER *Flora Middlesex* 361 In the list of *psammophilous species..the majority do not show a decided bias for any soil. **1888** F. A. LEES *Flora W. Yorkshire* 78 (*heading*) Arenaceous soils and psammophilous species. **1909** E. WARMING *Oecol. Plants* lxviii. 263 The fourth formation, composed of large dune-grasses, is much more psammophilous than halophilous. **1961** R. D. MANWELL *Introd. Protozool.* xv. 305 Some species [of Sarcodina] appear to be restricted to beach sands... Such species are said to be 'psammophilous'. **1903** W. R. FISHER tr. *Schimper's Plant-Geogr.* II. i. 80 The formations of the sandy sea-shore and of dunes serve as excellent examples of the vegetation of *psammophytes. **1909** E. WARMING *Oecol. Plants* lxix. 264 *Triticum junceum*..is one of the halophilous psammophytes that begin the production of dune. **1973** F. DI CASTRI in di Castri & Mooney *Mediterranean Type Ecosystems* ii. 22 The psammophyte *Ambrosia chamissonis* was remarkably similar in the coastal fringe of Chile and western North America. **1901** *Lancet* 26 Jan. 251/1 A *psammosarcoma as large as an orange had grown from the falx cerebri, compressing both prefrontal lobes. **1916** *Psammosere [see *lithosere* s.v. LITHO-]. **1929** WEAVER & CLEMENTS *Plant Ecol.* iv. 74 The differences of hardness and stability result in very dissimilar seres. These are distinguished as (rock) lithoseres and (sand) psammoseres, respectively. **1964** V. J. CHAPMAN *Coastal Vegetation* vi. 150 The dune succession..is quite clearly a prisere, and since it develops on sand it is often known as a Psammosere.

‖**psammoma** (psæ'məʊmə). *Path.* Pl. **-'omata**. [mod.L., f. Gr. ψάμμος sand + *-ōma* as in *carcinoma*, etc.] A tumour containing calcareous particles like grains of sand; usually occurring in the membranes or other parts of the brain. Hence **psa'mmomatous** *a.*, of or pertaining to a psammoma.

1876 tr. *Wagner's Gen. Pathol.* (ed. 6) 433 Psammoma is a for the most part very vascular tumor..most often of cellulo-sarcomatous nature..distinguished by the constant occurrence of variously abundant, round or rounded concentrically laminated chalky masses. **1899** *Allbutt's Syst. Med.* VIII. 241 Occasionally psammomata are found attached to the choroid plexuses. **1919** J. EWING *Neoplastic Dis.* xx. 309 In other tumors of nerve-trunks the structure is that of typical perivascular endothelioma as occurring in the dura mater, and psammomatous changes may appear in them. **1974** *Radiology* CXIII. 34/2 The second characteristic of psammomatous calcification is its diffuse extent throughout the abdomen due to serosal and omental implants.

†**psa'mmurgical**, *a. Obs. rare*$^{-1}$. [f. Gr. ψάμμο-ς sand + -εργός, -ουργος, working, worker + -ICAL: cf. METALLURGICAL.] A word meaning literally 'pertaining to the working of (or in) sand'; an esoteric term in Alchemy: see quot.

1559 MORWYNG *Evonymus* Pref. A ij b, A heauenlye water or rather diuine of the Chymistes..wherof potable gold, and that philosophers stone much spoken of, but not yet fond, consisteth. Hereupon also is the name geuen vnto the art calling it Psammurgicall and misticall, and Annophysiall and holy, and greatest; as thoughe it had certaine secreate letters, and such as it should be conueniente to kepe and restrain the profane commun people from.

psarolite ('psærəʊlaɪt). *Palæont.* [f. Gr. ψάρ starling (or ψᾱρός speckled) + λίθος stone (see -LITE); app. rendering G. *starstein*, f. *star* starling + *stein* stone.] Name for the silicified stems of tree-ferns found in the Permian or Lower New Red Sandstone, from the speckled markings which they exhibit in section. Also **'psaronite** [f. mod.L. *Psaronius*, the generic name (L. *psārōnius*, name of some precious stone, Pliny) + -ITE].

1859 PAGE *Handbk. Geol. Terms, Psarolites* or *Psaronites*. .. From this speckled appearance, which is visible to the naked eye, these fossils have also obtained the popular name of *Staaren-stein*. **1865** *Ibid.*, *Psaronites* also occur in the Upper Coal-measures of France, United States, &c. [**1873** DAWSON *Earth & Man* vi. 129 The stems of the tree-ferns of the Carboniferous [age] strengthened themselves by immense bundles of cord-like aerial roots, which look like enormous fossil brooms, and are known under the name Psaronius.] **1882** OGILVIE, *Psarolite, Psaronite*.

psauter, psawter, -tery, -try, obs. ff. PSALTER, PSALTERY.

psaw: see PSHAW.

‖**pschent, p-skhent** (psxɛnt). *Egyptol.* Also **pshent**. [a. Gk. ψχέντ, = Egyptian Demotic *p-skhent*, i.e. *p* def. article 'the' + *skhent*:—Hierogl. *sekhen, sekhent, sekhet, sekhte*, the double crown of Egypt.] The double crown of ancient Egypt, combining the white crown of Upper Egypt with the red crown of Lower Egypt, used after the union of the two kingdoms under Menes. (See Budge, *Decrees of Memphis* (1904) II. 32.)

The word came into use through the discovery of the Rosetta Stone in 1798; in this, line 9 of the Egyptian text has a hieroglyph read *sekhet*, line 26 of the Demotic text has *p-skhent*, and line 44 of the Greek text has ψχέντ.

[**1802** PLUMTRE in *Gentl. Mag.* LXXII. 1108 In the midst of which shall be the crown called ψοχεντ (an Egyptian word probably). **1809** PORSON in Clarke *Greek Marbles* 64 The *basileia* called ΨΟΧΕΝΤ.] **1814** T. YOUNG in *Archæologia* XVIII. 69 There shall be placed in the midst of them..the crown Pschent, which ornament he then wore. **1857** BIRCH *Anc. Pottery* (1858) I. 87 *Mut*, the mother goddess, the companion of Amen-Ra, wearing on her head the *pschent* or Egyptian crown. **1877** A. B. EDWARDS *Up Nile* xvi. 431 The King is crowned with the pschent. **1888** *Chambers' Encycl.* I. 22/2 These are the largest figures of Egyptian sculpture, being 66 feet high from the feet to the *pschent* with which the king's head is covered. **1922** JOYCE *Ulysses* 500 On his head is perched an Egyptian pshent.

pselaphognath (ps-, 'siːləfəʊ,gnæθ). *Zool.* [f. mod.L. *Psēlaphognatha* neut. pl., f. Gr. ψηλαφᾶν to grope about + γνάθος jaw.] A member of the *Pselaphognatha*, a division of diplopod *Myriapoda*, having the second pair of jaws pediform. So **pselaphognathous** (-'fɒgnəθəs) *a.*, belonging to this division.

psellism (ps-, 'sɛlɪz(ə)m). *Path.* [ad. Gr. ψελλισμός stammering, f. ψελλίζειν to stammer, f. ψελλός stammering. Cf. mod.F. *psellisme* (Littré).] Any defect of enunciation, as stammering, lisping, etc., due either to nervous affection or to malformation of the vocal organs. So **psellis'mologist, psellis'mology**, *nonce-wds.*

[**1799** HOOPER *Med. Dict.*, *Psellismus*, defect of speech. **1842** in DUNGLISON *Med. Lex.*] **1856** *Househ. Words* Nov. 464 Professors of Psellismology have existed for some time past. **1890** *Cent. Dict.*, *Psellism*. **1895** in *Syd. Soc. Lex.*

psephism (ps-, 'siːfɪz(ə)m). *Gr. Antiq.* Also in Gr.-Lat. form **pse'phisma**, pl. **-ata**. [ad. Gr. ψήφισμα, f. ψηφίζειν to vote, prop. with pebbles, f. ψῆφος pebble.] A decree enacted by a vote of a public assembly, esp. of the Athenians.

1656 BLOUNT *Glossogr.*, *Psephism* (*psephisma*), a decree, Statute, Law or Ordinance. **1697** POTTER *Antiq. Greece* I. xxvi. (1715) 149 No Psephism shall pass to the Commons, before [etc.]. **1860** MILL *Repr. Govt.* (1865) 41/1 In the Athenian Democracy,..in the time of its most complete ascendancy, the popular Ecclesia could pass Psephisms (mostly decrees on single matters of policy), but laws, so called, could only be made or altered by..the Nomothetæ.

psephite (ps-, 'siːfaɪt). *Min.* [mod. f. Ger. *psephit*, F. *pséphite*, f. Gr. ψῆφος pebble, round stone + -ITE[1] 2 b.] A breccia or conglomerate composed of pebbles or small rounded stones. Hence **psephitic** (-'ɪtɪk) *a.*, of, of the nature of, small pebbles; composed as a conglomerate of small rounded pebbles or stones.

1879 RUTLEY *Study Rocks* xiv. 299 The clastic rocks, which he divides into the psephitic (from ψῆφος, a small stone); the psammitic, and the pelitic.

psepho-, comb. form of Gr. ψῆφος pebble, used esp. in terms relating to voting (cf. PSEPHISM).

psephocracy (sɪ'fɒkrəsɪ). *rare.* [f. prec. + -CRACY.] The form of government which results from election by ballot; representative government. So **'psephocrat**, an elected ruler, or an adherent or supporter of government by election.

1966 *New Statesman* 15 Apr. 531/1 How then did Britain ..become a democracy?.. It never did... What we do have is representative government, or the rule of the ballot-box, or (in one word) psephocracy. *Ibid.*, 531/2 Psephocracy on the British model has been extended, thanks to the advice of British psephocrats, to a couple of dozen nations. **1970** *Sci. Jrnl.* Feb. 27/1 The present system [of government] is more of a leadership than a referred system—the so called 'psephocracy'.

†**psephograph** ('siːfəʊgrɑːf, -æf). *Obs.* [f. PSEPHO- + -GRAPH.] A machine for the automatic recording of votes.

1906 *Westm. Gaz.* 18 Dec. 7/2 The machine, of which a young Italian, Signor Boggiano, is the inventor, and which is known as the 'Psephograph', or vote-recorder, has the appearance of an upright box. **1907** *Daily Chron.* 11 Mar. 6/2 The plebiscite taken by means of the vote recording psephograph..has resulted as follows:—For the Tunnel, 3,212; against, 812.

psephology (sɪ'fɒlədʒɪ, sɛf-). [f. PSEPHO- + -OLOGY.] The study of public elections, and statistical analysis of trends in voting; *loosely*, the prediction of electoral results.

1952 D. E. BUTLER *Brit. Gen. Election of 1951* 1 It..seems appropriate to preface this book with a discussion of why elections merit study and an examination of how much has been..learnt from psephology... I am indebted to Mr. R. B. McCallum for the invention of this word to describe the field of research in which he is so eminent a pioneer. It is derived from ψῆφος—the pebble which the Athenians dropped into an urn to vote. **1952** *Economist* 4 Oct. 18 (*heading*) British psephology. **1957** *Ibid.* 21 Sept. 917/2 Even with the present degree of Liberal revival in the country, prudent (as distinct from roseate) psephology suggests that the only new seats the Liberals might pick up [etc.]. **1958** *Times* 6 Nov. 6/5 (*heading*) Material for psephology—Chichester figures anxiously awaited. **1973** *Guardian* 25 May 12/2 Even with the aid of psephology, it remains difficult to detect what precisely turns votes.

So **psepho'logical** *a.*, **psepho'logically** *adv.*; **pse'phologist**, a political scientist who specializes in the study of elections; an electoral analyst or commentator.

1952 *N.Y. Herald Tribune* 8 Aug. (Late City Ed.) 12/3 He [*sc.* R. B. McCallum] suggested I [*sc.* D. E. Butler] call myself a psephologist. **1952** *Daily Express* 30 Sept. 4/3 (*heading*) Psephologically speaking: you may vote for a good-looking party. **1955** D. E. BUTLER *Brit. Gen. Election* *of 1955* p. v, Acknowledgements.. Mr. R. B. McCallum and Mr. H. G. Nicholas, my psephological mentors, gave me much valuable help. **1958** *New Scientist* 27 Mar. 32/1 The next General Election should provide the first opportunity modern Britain will have seen of testing a little-known and much neglected psephological law. **1958** *Times* 6 Nov. 6/5 The psephologists at Central Office and Transport House will be.. ready to read into the results of Chichester, and all the other by-elections pending, sinister or cheering evidence. **1962** *Times* 16 Mar. 13/2 Psephologically, and even more psychologically, it [*sc.* the Orpington by-election] is in a class by itself. **1964** *Time* 4 Nov. 3 By 9 p.m., when Vermont had plopped into the Democratic column and television's psephologists flatly declared Johnson the winner, the answer became obvious: very, very, big. **1969** *Daily Tel.* 9 Sept. 17/6 If psephological calculations mean anything, enough votes will be mustered by Spain to secure an adverse vote against Britain. **1977** *Oxford Times* 29 Apr. 10/2 Whatever happens next Thursday will be psephologically interesting. **1977** *Times* 25 July 8/4 The repercussion of this estrangement (the psephological importance of which has yet to be fathomed) was felt in the economy. **1977** *Time* 21 Nov. 28/2 Psephologists will be sorting out the particulars for months to come, but one trend was clear in last week's off-year election returns: a solid vote for sanity.

psephomancy (ps-, 'siːfəʊmænsɪ). [f. Gr. ψῆφος pebble + -MANCY.] See quot.

1727 BAILEY vol. II, *Psephomancy*,.. a Divination by Pebble-Stones, distinguished by certain Characters, and put as Lots into a Vessel; which, having made certain Supplications to the Gods to direct them, they drew out, and according to the Characters, conjectured what should happen to them. **1852** ROGET *Thesaurus* §511.

†**pse'ttaceous**, *a. Obs. rare*⁻¹. [f. L. *psētta* (Pliny), a. Gr. ψῆττα a turbot or other flat fish + -ACEOUS.] Belonging to the group of flat fishes.

1661 LOVELL *Hist. Anim. & Min.* Introd., The Psettaceous, or plain and spinose, have a spine that seemeth to be divided in the midd'st.

psettine (ps-, 'setaɪn), *a.* (*sb.*) *Ichth.* [f. mod.L. *Psettīnæ* pl., f. *Psetta*, name of the typical genus: see prec. and -INE¹.] Belonging to the subfamily *Psettinæ* of flat fishes, including the turbot, brill, etc. **b.** *sb.* A fish of this subfamily.

pseuchomachy, variant of PSYCHOMACHIA *Obs.*

pseuchrolutist, obs. variant of PSYCHROLUTIST.

pseud (sjuːd), *a.* (*sb.*) *colloq.* [f. the Gr. stem ψευδ- false, or as a shortening of PSEUDO quasi-*adj.* or PSEUDO-.] = PSEUDO *adj.* B. Also *absol.* as *sb.* ***Pseuds'*** or ***Pseud's Corner***, used of the pretentious or insincere generally (with allusion to the use in quot. 1968²).

1962 *Spectator* 26 Oct. 656 Present-day trend-setters, pseud as they come. **1964** *Ibid.* 20 Mar. 379/1 The pseuds and intellectual craze-mongers seem to have dropped *cinéma-vérité* almost as quickly as they took it up. **1968** *Jazz Monthly* Apr. 28/2 As well as being the creator of an avant-garde film on human buttocks, Miss Ono has a long list of other achievements which must put her in the running for the title of Pseud of the Century. **1968** *Private Eye* 22 Nov. 3/3 (*heading*) Pseuds' Corner. **1971** *Guardian* 21 Oct. 14/2 Woodstock, the drug scene, the race war, Vietnam... The genre is familiar, and the path through it can verge dangerously close to Pseud's Corner. **1973** P. DICKINSON *Green Gene* I. i. 20 A few big firms.. which.. don't mind spending a bit on a pseud paper which makes people.. think it's all not so bad as all that... It's a real pseud. **1976** *Listener* 25 Mar. 362/2 His ability to ad lib flowery prose with panoramic views overlooking Pseud's Corner. **1977** *Ibid.* 7 Apr. 447/1 A dreamy piano solo, recalling both Beiderbecke's 'In a Mist' and (I know this sounds pseud) early Schoenberg. **1980** *Oxford Times* 11 Jan. 13/1 Both strike me as the slightly pseud face of rock 'n' roll.

pseud-aconitine to **pseudandry**: see PSEUDO-.

†**,pseuda'postle.** *Obs.* Also pseudo-apostle. [ad. Gr. ψευδαπόστολος (2 Cor. xi. 13), f. ψευδ- (see PSEUDO-) + ἀπόστολος APOSTLE.] A false or pretended apostle.

[*c* **1449**: see PSEUDO.] **1555** LATIMER *Let. Sir E. Baynton* in Foxe *A. & M.* (1563) 1322/1 And what the pseudoapostles [*ed.* **1583** pseudapostles], aduersaries to saynt Paule, wolde so haue taken them. **1624** BP. HALL *Serm. Phil. iii.* 18 Rem. Wks. (1660) 14 For these Philippian Pseudapostles; Two wayes were they enemies to the Cross of Christ. **1709** *Let. to Ld. M[ayor]* 4 This sanguinary Pseudapostle. **1721–1800** BAILEY, *Pseudapostle.* [**1846** WORCESTER, *Pseudo-apostle.*]

So †**,pseudapo'stolical** *a. Obs.*

1605 M. SUTCLIFFE *Brief Exam.* 61 An idle declamation in prayse of this pseudapost[ol]icall petition.

‖**pseudechis** (ps-, 'sjuːdekɪs). *Zool.* [mod.L. generic name, f. Gr. ψευδ-, PSEUD(O- + ἔχις viper.] A genus of very venomous snakes of the family *Colubridæ*, series *Proteroglyphæ*, subfamily *Elapinæ*, including the Black Snake or Purple Death-adder, *P. porphyriacus* of Australia. Hence attrib. ***pseudechis poison, poisoning.*** Also **pseu'dechic** *a.*, of or pertaining to the Pseudechis.

1897 *Allbutt's Syst. Med.* II. 811 The toxic proteids of the poison of pseudechis. *Ibid.* 812 Cobra poison contains proto-albumose, and so does pseudechis poison. *Ibid.* 824 In the case of pseudechis poisoning. *Ibid.* 822 Effects of the injection of pseudechic venom.

pseudelephant, -elminth: see PSEUDO- 2.

pseudentity: see *pseudo-entity* s.v. PSEUDO- 2 a.

pseudepigram (sjuː'depɪgræm). *nonce-wd.* [f. *pseud-* (see PSEUDO-) + EPIGRAM, punning on *pseudepigraph.*] A pretended epigram.

c **1905** F. ROLFE *Nicholas Crabbe* (1958) viii. 60 The frolicsome Thorah screamed pseudepigrams everywhere.

‖**pseudepigrapha** (ps-, sjuːdɪ'pɪgrəfə), *sb.* [a. Gr. neut. pl. of ψευδεπίγραφ-ος 'with false title', f. ψευδ-, PSEUD(O- + ἐπιγράφειν to inscribe (see EPIGRAPH). Cf. APOCRYPHA.] *pl.* A collective term for books or writings bearing a false title, or ascribed to another than the true author; spurious writings; *spec.* applied to certain Jewish writings composed about the beginning of the Christian era, but ascribed to various patriarchs and prophets of the Old Testament. Also *sing.* in anglicized form **pseudepigraph** (-'epɪgrɑːf, -græf).

1692 RAY *Disc.* 37 The Verses now extant under the Name of Sibylline Oracles are all suspected to be false and pseudepigrapha. **1884** C. A. BRIGGS *Bibl. Study* 155 The book of Jubilees of the first century and other pseudepigraphs of the time. **1886** —— *Messianic Proph.* xiii. 412 We have an example of such a pseudepigraph in Ecclesiastes. **1906** H. B. SWETE *Apocalypse* Introd. xv. §1. 170 The Jewish pseudepigrapha bear the names of Old Testament patriarchs, kings, or prophets.

Hence **pseude'pigraphal, pseudepi'graphic, -ical** [see EPIGRAPHIC], **pseude'pigraphous** *adjs.*, pertaining to or having the character of pseudepigrapha; falsely or erroneously ascribed to some author; spurious; **pseude'pigraphy** [see EPIGRAPHY], false ascription of authorship.

a **1638** MEDE *Wks.* (1672) 388, I will not set my rest upon a *Pseudepigraphal Testimony. **1715** M. DAVIES *Athen. Brit.* I. Pref. 6 Amongst these Pseudo-Epigraphal Pamphlets of such early Pretensions, must be plac'd St. James's Proto-Evangelion. **1904** H. A. A. KENNEDY *St. Paul's Concept. last Things* ii. 65 The pseudepigraphal literature of Judaism anterior to and contemporary with St. Paul. **1879** J. JACOBS in *19th Cent.* Sept. 498 Its history is obscured by a mass of *pseudepigraphic writings. **1867** *Sat. Rev.* 30 Mar. 408/2 Into the wild chaos of so-called *pseudepigraphical writings.. they threw their own gospel. **1678** CUDWORTH *Intell. Syst.* I. iv. §17. 296 To conclude the Orphick Poems to have been *Pseudepigraphous. **1894** G. C. M. DOUGLAS in *Lex Mosaica* 75 [That] the whole of the prophets and historical books are pseudepigraphous or pseudonymous. **1842** BRANDE *Dict. Sc.* etc., **Pseudepigraphy*, the ascription of false names of authors to works.

†**pseude'piscopy.** *Obs. rare.* Also 8 pseudepiscopacy. [f. Gr. ψευδεπίσκοπος a spurious bishop: see EPISCOPY.] The rule or existence of a spurious or pretended bishop or bishops.

1641 MILTON *Animadv.* Pref. 2 A long usurpation and convicted Pseudepiscopy of Prelates [*altered in 18th c. edd. to* pseudepiscopacy].

pseudeponymous (ps-, sjuːdɪ'pɒnɪməs), *a. Gr. Hist.* [f. Gr. ψευδεπώνυμος falsely named after some one (f. ψευδ- PSEUDO- + ἐπώνυμος given as a name) + -OUS: see EPONYM, EPONYMOUS.] That gives an erroneous name to the year, that is wrongly named (as archon of the year).

1853 GROTE *Greece* II. xc. XI. 673 *note*, This decree.. bears date on the 16th of the month Skirrophorion (June), under the archonship of Nausikles. This archon is a wrong or pseud-eponymous archon.

pseudergate: see PSEUDO- 2 a.

pseudery ('sjuːdərɪ). *colloq.* [f. PSEUD *a.* (*sb.*) + -ERY.] An affected or pompous manner of expression, usu. with intellectual pretensions; an example of this.

1972 *Guardian* 24 Feb. 10/3 There's nothing like an overt piece of pseudery to make one feel all lilywhite. **1975** *Daily Tel.* 30 Aug. 6/2 In another paper, a psychiatrist solemnly reported his finding that 'in general fat people do not go to university'... These farragoes of improbable pseudery.. tend to be prefaced by an enormously portentous address. **1976** *Broadcast* 12 Jan. 9/3 Capital's Sunday pseudery gets the boot. **1978** *Daily Tel.* 19 Jan. 12/6 Best of all is Mr Ward's pithy dismissal of the sort of supernatural pseudery that has enthralled the credulous since the beginning of time.

pseudhæmal to **-imago**: see PSEUDO- 2.

pseudish ('sjuːdɪʃ), *a. colloq.* [f. *pseud-* (see PSEUDO-) or PSEUD *a.* (*sb.*) + -ISH¹.] Of architecture: imitative and exaggerated. Of other arts: affected, spurious. Also *ellipt.* as *sb.* Hence **'pseudishness** = PSEUDERY.

1938 O. LANCASTER *Pillar to Post* 66 Pseudish. This style which attained great popularity both in this country and in America (where it was generally known as Spanish-colonial), is actually our old friend Pont Street Dutch with a few Stockholm trimmings and a more daring use of colour. **1945** *Archit. Rev.* XCVII. 165/1 The Georgian Movement slid into Pseudish, but the ideal—of chaste simplicity—remained. **1972** *Jazz & Blues* Nov. 30/3 Other contributions are getting dangerously pseudish. **1975** *Times Lit. Suppl.* 28 Nov. 1429/2 This style, which surely earns Betjeman's label 'pseudish'. **1976** *Listener* 23 Dec. 814/1 Better, perhaps, than the pseudish silences that have been creeping over telly art in the past year. **1978** *Punch* 6 Sept. 374/1 We're accustomed to pseudishness in Arts Council catalogues.

'pseudism. *nonce-wd.* [f. Gr. ψευδ-ής false + -ISM.] A false statement.

1899 *Q. Rev.* Apr. 424 Conventional pseudisms have been incessantly meted out to him.

‖**pseudisodomon** (psjuːdaɪ'sɒdəmɒn). *Anc. Arch.* [neut. of Gr. ψευδισόδομος adj. (Vitruvius), f. ψευδ- (see PSEUDO-) + ἰσόδομος (see ISODOMON).] A method of building in which the courses were of unequal height, length, or thickness, but the blocks alike in each course. Hence **pseudi'sodomous** *a.*, of the nature of or pertaining to this.

1601 HOLLAND *Pliny* II. 593 In case they be not euen laid nor ranged streight, but that some part of the wall is thicker than others, they terme it Pseudisodomon. **1706** PHILLIPS, *Pseudisodomon*,.. a kind of Building, the Walls of which are made of Stone of an unequal Thickness. **1850** LEITCH tr. *C. O. Müller's Anc. Art* §222 (ed. 2) 219 The walls are isodomous or pseudisodomous, often with oblique joints.

pseudo ('sjuːdəʊ, *formerly also* 'psjuːdəʊ), quasi-*adj.* (*sb.*, *adv.*) and *adj.* [The combining element PSEUDO- as a separate word.]

A. quasi-*adj.* (*sb.*, *adv.*) **a.** False, counterfeit, pretended, spurious. (Now usually hyphened to the following noun: see PSEUDO- 1.) †Also *absol.* †**b.** *sb.* (with *pl.*) A false person, a pretender. †**c.** *adv.* Falsely. *rare.*

c **1380** WYCLIF *Wks.* (1880) 308 Hou men shal knowe siche pseudoes. *Ibid.* 479 Many pseudois may speke myche wiþ-oute ground. **1390** GOWER *Conf.* II. 190 It were thanne litel nede Among the men to taken hiede Of that thei hieren Pseudo telle, Which nou is come forto duelle. **1402** *Pol. Poems* (Rolls) II. 55 Ffor thou and other pseudo han marrid hem in the way. *c* **1449** PECOCK *Repr.* III. xi. 342 So manye pseudo or false Apostlis. *Ibid.* 343 What so greet myscheef schulde bi likelihode haue come bi habundaunce of ricches in tho pseudo, as came bi her pouerte in hem, whanne thei diffameden the trewe Apostlis. **1581** MARBECK *Bk. of Notes* 42 Such *Pseudo* apostles was among vs sometimes. **1679** in *Reg. Synod of Dunblane* (1877) 150 By the said Bishop and a committee of his *pseudo* Synod deposed from the exercise of my ministrie. **1810** SCOTT *Let. to Morritt* 2 Mar. in *Lockhart*, Luxuries which, when long gratified, become a sort of pseudo necessaries. **1854** MRS. OLIPHANT *M. Hepburn* II. 221 'Your reverent worship has acquaintance with my kinswoman', said the pseudo youth.

B. *adj.* Pretentious, insincere, sham, affected, meaningless; having aspirations beyond true worth. Also *absol.* as *sb.*, a pretentious or insincere person. Pl. **pseudoes, pseudos.**

Now used independently of its relation to the combining form PSEUDO- which characterizes the senses in A.

1945 *Archit. Rev.* XCVII. 110/1 The flamboyant, the vulgar, the monumental and the 'pseudo' have had their day. **1958** *Times* 11 Dec. 6/2 The whole conception was 'pseudo'. **1959** K. TYNAN in J. Feiffer *Sick Sick Sick* (ed. 2) Introd., The real Bohemians of Greenwich Village as well as the pseudoes. **1959** K. R. POPPER *Logic Sci. Discovery* ii. 51 Nothing is easier than to unmask a problem as 'meaningless' or 'pseudo'. **1962** *John o' London's* 19 Apr. 371/1 So all the pseudos flocked in. **1964** J. SYMONS *End of Solomon Grundy* III. ii. 150 That's the trouble with the country to-day, too many pseudo people in it... This garage trouble, now, it comes from the pseudos like that man Grundy. **1967** *Observer* (Colour Suppl.) 28 May 14/2 The undiscriminating, arty chat of a campus pseudo. **1977** *Time* 18 Apr. 1/1 Intellectuals all over the world, real or pseudo, proudly proclaim that 'democracy' won.

pseudo- (sjuːdəʊ, *formerly also* ps-), before a vowel usually **pseud-**, repr. the Gr. combining element ψευδο-, ψευδ-, 'false, falsely', from stem of ψευδ-ής adj. false, ψεῦδ-ος falsity, falsehood, ψεύδ-ειν to deceive, cheat, ψεύδ-εσθαι to be false, speak falsely. Forming in Greek many compounds; with sbs., as ψευδομάρτυς, -τυρ false witness, ψευδαπόστολος a false apostle or messenger, ψευδάριθμος a false number, ψευδάργυρος mock-silver; with adjs. or adj. formatives = falsely, as ψευδολόγος speaking falsely, ψευδόπλουτος feigned to be rich; and sometimes with verbs, as ψευδοποιεῖν to falsify.

Some of these Gr. substantives and adjectives were adopted in later Latin, esp. terms of natural history, as *pseudanchūsa* bastard alkanet, *pseudosphēx* false wasp, *pseudosmaragdus* false emerald, and words of Christianity, as *pseudapostolus, pseudochrīstus, pseudoprophēta*, etc. In later times, *pseudo-* was prefixed also to L. words, as *pseudoflāvus* bastard yellow, *pseudoliquidus, pseudopastor* (Jerome). Thence it bacame common in med.L., as in *pseudodoctor, pseudonuncius*, etc.: see Du Cange.

In English, *pseudo-* appears first in Wyclif, viz. in adaptations of L. words of the Vulgate, as PSEUDO-CHRIST, PSEUDOPROPHET, and in words formed after these, as *pseudo-clerk, pseudo-frere* (= friar), *pseudo-priest.* Few examples occur in the 15th and 16th c., and in these *pseudo* was usually written separately, as an adj.: see prec. word. But after 1600 the combination of *pseudo-* with a sb. became common: at least 20 examples appear before 1700, and 20 more before 1800. By 1800 *pseudo-* had become a living element prefixable at will, instead of the adjective *false* or *spurious*, to any sb., and the examples during the 19th c. are very numerous. To adjectives *pseudo-* began to be prefixed in the 17th c.; but examples are not numerous till the 19th c., when the use with an adj. became nearly as free as with a sb.

In this dictionary, words in *pseudo-* are dealt with in three groups: 1. Those in which the two elements have their obvious and ordinary sense, *pseudo-* being thus equivalent to an adj. or adv.

2. Scientific and technical terms, not in general use, in which either the element with which *pseudo-* is combined, is not a separate word in English, or if it is, the combination is a permanent term, with a special meaning.

3. Important combinations and compounds, in general use, or of long history, or having derivatives: these are treated as Main words.

1. Prefixed to any noun or adjective, forming combinations, often nonce-wds., with the sense 'false, pretended, counterfeit, spurious, sham, falsely so called or represented; falsely, spuriously, apparently but not really'. Here *pseudo-* is properly hyphened.

a. Prefixed to sbs. ***pseudo-antithesis***, ***-argument***, ***-art***, ***-artist***, ***-ascetic***, ***-bible***, ***-book***, ***-chemist***, ***-Clementine***, ***-clerk***, ***-communism***, ***-communist***, ***-conversation***, ***-criticism***, ***-definition***, ***-democracy***, ***-difficulty***, ***-education***, ***-emotion***, ***-enthusiast***, ***-fact***, ***-folk*** (in examples *attrib.*), ***-Freud***, ***-friar***, ***-gentility***, ***-gentleman***, ***-grammar***, ***-historicity***, ***-history***, ***-intellectual***, ***-isle***, ***-knowledge***, ***-language***, ***-legislator***, ***-life***, ***-linguistics***, ***-literature***, ***-logic***, ***-medic***, ***-minister***, ***-moralist***, ***-morality***, ***-Moses***, ***-mystic***, ***-mysticism***, ***-need***, ***-Nicodimite***, ***-objectivity***, ***-parson***, ***-passive***, ***-passivization***, ***-patriot***, ***-patron***, ***-perspective***, ***-philanthropist***, ***-philosopher***, ***-philosophy***, ***-politician***, ***-presager***, ***-priest***, ***-principle***, ***-procedure***, ***-proverb***, ***-question***, ***-religion***, ***-simplicity***, ***-theologician*** (*obs.*), ***-theology***, ***-thesis***, ***-word***, ***-zealot***, etc.

1949 KOESTLER *Insight & Outlook* xi. 169 The biological approach..makes these appear..as a typical pseudoantithesis. **1943** *Mind* LII. 139 The methodological unification here attempted..helps to eliminate pseudo-arguments. **1977** *Theology* May 173 That 'many people would prefer' to do something is an alarmingly Benthamite pseudo-argument. **1960** *Encounter* Mar. 83/1 The dull air of *acedia* that hangs over the mass pseudo-arts. **1934** DYLAN THOMAS *Let.* Dec. (1966) 147 This is the quarter of the pseudo-artists. **1711** SHAFTESB. *Charac.* (1737) I. 165 These may be term'd a sort of pseudo-asceticks. **1809** BYRON *Bards & Rev.* viii, O'er taste awhile these pseudo-bards prevail. **1835** SOUTHEY *Doctor* Interch. ix. III. 27 As justly entitled to the name of the Koran as the so called pseudo-bible itself. **1928** D. H. LAWRENCE *Let.* 1 Apr. (1932) 718 That was very nice of you, to send me that little pseudo-book full of red gold. **1674** G. THOMSON (*title*) 'Ορθομέθοδος 'Ιατρο-χυμικὴ.. The Character of an Ortho-Chymist and Pseudo-Chymist. **1879** FARRAR *St. Paul* II. 54 Those who..vented their hatred of Paul in the Pseudo-Clementines. [Cf. *Ibid.* I. 677 The forgeries known as the Clementine Homilies, the Clementine Recognitions.] *c* **1380** WYCLIF *Sel. Wks.* I. 200 And so pseudo-clerkes..spuylen symple men as wolves doone sheepe. **1945** KOESTLER *Yogi & Commissar* III. iii. 225 The spreading of Russian pseudo-communism over Europe can be stopped only by a true socialist movement. **1948** *Civil & Mil. Gaz.* (Lahore) 11 Apr. 1/1 Nineteen workers of the Lahore Mint, suspected to be Communists or pseudo-Communists, were arrested. **1926** D. H. LAWRENCE *Glad Ghosts* 30 The pseudo-conversation was interrupted. **1951** N. FRYE in D. Lodge *20th Cent. Lit. Crit.* (1972) 423 The literary chit-chat which makes the reputations of poets boom and crash in an imaginary stock exchange is pseudo-criticism. **1956** J. H. WOODGER tr. *Tarski's Logic, Semantics, Metamath.* 285 The sentences under (2), clearly related to the axiom of reducibility of *Principia Mathematica*, can be called pseudodefinitions in accordance with the proposal of S. Leśniewski. **1965** *Language* XLI. 37 Looked on as a theory, traditional grammar consists of primitive notions only. Its definitions are pseudodefinitions, mere embellishments. **1960** KOESTLER *Lotus & Robot* I. v. 161 The result is a pseudo-democracy in a political vacuum. **1977** M. EDELMAN *Polit. Lang.* vii. 130 One of the few psychiatrists to examine such meetings as political phenomena concludes that the self-government is in fact 'pseudodemocracy'. **1905** W. JAMES *Ess. Radical Empiricism* (1912) xi. 254 Closely connected with this pseudo-difficulty is another one of wider scope and greater complication. **1963** J. LYONS *Structural Semantics* ii. 18 A pseudo-difficulty created by posing a pseudo-question. **1901** *Daily Chron.* 9 Sept. 3/7 Pseudo-education is spoiling born workers and stifling thinkers in the birth. **1949** KOESTLER *Insight & Outlook* xv. 206 The scientist..dismissed them with a shrug as pseudoemotions and purely conventional attitudes. **1751** SMOLLETT *Per. Pic.* (1779) II. lxiii. 192 This pseudo-enthusiast proposed to visit the great church. **1787** JEFFERSON *Writ.* (1859) II. 240 These Pseudo-evangelists pretended to inspiration. **1938** R. G. COLLINGWOOD *Princ. Art* iv. 61 He would not have based his theory on a pseudo-fact. **1972** S. FISHER *Female Orgasm* (1973) xv. 390 A tremendous volume of pseudofact is being transmitted to people of all age levels about the nature of sexual response. **1962** *Times* 25 July 13/1 The reach-me-down pseudo-folk poetry. **1976** A. MURRAY *Stomping Blues* xi. 212 No less pretentious..are those pseudo-folk blues musicians. **1951** M. LOWRY *Let.* 25 Aug. (1967) 252 You might call it pseudo-Freud and the philosophy of 'nothing but'. **1963** *Times Lit. Suppl.* 31 May 391/2 The mystique is Victorian home-life made..intellectually respectable by pseudo-Freud. *c* **1380** WYCLIF *Sel. Wks.* I. 176 Siche novelries of pseudo-freris shulden prelatis and alle men aȝen stonden. **1853** HAWTHORNE *Eng. Note-Bks.* (1883) I. 418 They..have no pseudo-gentility to support. **1821** *New Monthly Mag.* 304, I..propose..that we use the term *Pseudo-Gentleman*, to signify gentleman in its..abused sense. **1927** L. BLOOMFIELD in C. F. Hockett *Leonard Bloomfield Anthol.* (1970) 190 Prescientific notions about language, with the dismal study of pseudo-grammar, still prevail in our schools. **1935** *Mind* XLIV. 407 For the general public of Goethe's day (including Goethe himself and other imaginative writers) the concept 'Hellenic' was as little historical as is that of 'Aryan' for the modern Nazis;..like it, it entailed a terrific parade of pseudo-historicity. **1958** T. F. T. PLUCKNETT *Early Eng. Legal Lit.* i. 11 Then there is the pseudo-historicity of our law. **1880** A. H. SAYCE *Introd. Sci. of Lang.* II. ix. 239 An attempt was made to extract a pseudo-history from the Greek myths. **1946** R. G. COLLINGWOOD *Idea of Hist.* 180 Meyer's great merit lies in his effective criticism of the openly positivistic sociological pseudo-history fashionable in his time. **1973** B. J. WILLIAMS *Evolution & Human Origins* iv. 48/2 These taxonomies were used, in turn, to construct pseudo-histories. **1938** *Sun* (Baltimore) 16 Apr. 8 Attacks on the profit motive by many of the pseudo-intellectuals who have supported and colored so much of the Administration's policy in the past. **1977** P. JOHNSON *Enemies of Society* xvi. 218 The fatuous Mary Wimbush, the pseudo-intellectual. **1844** in *Archæol. Jrnl.* (1845) I. 347 The pseudo-isle of Purbeck. **1842** W. NEWNHAM *Reciprocal Influence of Body & Mind* ii. 24 That pseudo-knowledge..would leave its possessor without a single ray of duty. **1957** C. DAY LEWIS *Poet's Way of Knowledge* 16 If you like to think of science as 'knowledge', and poetry as at best some kind of 'pseudo-knowledge', no one can stop you, but you will be thinking in terms unacceptable to many scientists today. **1979** *Dædalus* Spring 15 The critics accuse the positivists of surreptitiously.. transforming a pseudo-knowledge into a power which..can only be exerted 'in the interests of the dominant class'. **1960** Pseudolanguage [see INTERLANGUAGE *sb.*]. **1978** *Amer. Speech* LIII. 61 Samarin suggests that glossolalia is on the same continuum as actual language and is closely related to other kinds of 'pseudolanguage' which can be produced by any sufficiently uninhibited person who is merely playing with language-like sounds. **1802–12** BENTHAM *Ration. Judic. Evid.* (1827) V. 617 Whether in the character of legislator or pseudo-legislator. **1942** F. BROWN in *Unknown Worlds* Mar. 6/2 A formula for giving pseudolife to inanimate objects. **1978** G. A. SHEEHAN *Running & Being* ii. 32 His solution..is not to impersonate the achiever... This would be a pseudolife. **1962** H. A. GLEASON in Householder & Saporta *Probl. in Lexicogr.* 86 The reaction to popular pseudo-linguistics. **1964** M. A. K. HALLIDAY et al. *Linguistic Sci.* i. 6 Workers in other fields have gone on working with their own do-it-yourself pseudo-linguistics, being content..with inexact observations and *ad hoc* categories. **1972** *Language* XLVIII. 438 It is indicative of Arens' conservatism and his appreciation of neo-Humboldtian pseudo-linguistics in Germany that he should expand this last chapter. **1944** *Mind* LIII. 185 He therefore can only distinguish 'true literature' (the expression and communication of an experience) from 'pseudo-literature' (*e.g.* advertisement, propaganda, pot-boiling, Collingwood's 'magic' and 'entertainment'). **1964** *Listener* 9 Jan. 61/1 How can John Raymond in *The Sunday Times* deal with seven volumes of verse in just over 1,000 words?.. He can afford to generalize and chat, and in this way he provides a kind of pseudo-literature. **1960** K. AMIS *New Maps of Hell* i. 21 Time travel..is inconceivable, but..an apparatus of pseudo-logic..is set up to support it. **1657** TOMLINSON *Renou's Disp.* 130 He derides the Vanity..of the Pseudomedick. **1680** G. HICKES *Spirit of Popery* 2 This Rebellious Pseudo-Minister. **1964** A. WYKES *Gambling* ii. 50 The Victorian pseudo-moralists who screamed..of the dangers of drink and gambling were for the most part unthinking pleasure-stiflers. **1943** *Mind* LII. 19 This is the morality of obedience at its best and surest. Doubtless it is easily confused with the pseudo-morality of sanctions. **1613** PURCHAS *Pilgrimage* (1614) 158 Nicephorus mentioneth a Pseudo-Moses of the Iewes..destroied..with his Complices in a like rebellion. **1961** *Encounter* Feb. 78 Hugh Kingsmill described Lawrence as 'a pseudo-mystic'. **1964** P. F. ANSON *Bishops at Large* ix. 344 The pseudo-mysticism propagated by Mrs Besant and leading members of the Theosophical Society. **1960** *Commentary* June 472/2 The continual creation of pseudo-needs as a basis for production. **1979** *Time* 8 Jan. 72/3 Lasch detects narcissism nearly everywhere, in the buzz words of the 'human potential' movements, in the 'pseudo needs' created by advertisers for restless consumers. *a* **1658** J. DURHAM *Exp. Rev.* xiv. i. 500 This doctrine was urged against the Pseudo-nicodimites. **1946** KOESTLER in *New Writing & Daylight* VII. 82 Novels date more than drama and poetry. The reason for this is the novel's pseudo-objectivity. **1973** MATIAS & WILLEMEN tr. M. Cegarra in *Screen* Spring/Summer 185 The pseudo-objectivity of the film. **1753** SMOLLETT *Cnt. Fathom* (1784) 208/2 The pseudo-parson was very much affected by this generous proffer. **1964** *Language* XL. 77 Smx_2 marks indefinite voice, or pseudopassive. **1965** N. CHOMSKY *Aspects of Theory of Syntax* ii. 104 It is now possible to account for 'pseudo-passives', such as 'the proposal was vehemently argued against',..by a slight generalization of the ordinary passive transformation. *Ibid.* 106 Where 'on the boat' is a V[erb]-Complement in 'John decided on the boat' (meaning 'John chose the boat'), it is subject to pseudopassivization by the passive transformation. **1755** *Monitor* No. 1. I. 8 Pseudo-patriots, who under the mask of liberty and public virtue, concealed their self-interested.. designs. **1768** BLACKSTONE *Comm.* III. xvi. 248 The writ of *quare impedit* commands the disturbers, the bishop, the pseudo-patron, and his clerk, to permit the plaintiff to present a proper person..to such a vacant church. **1851** RUSKIN *Stones Ven.* (1874) I. xx. 213 Inlaid with mock arcades in pseudo-perspective. **1887** *Daily News* 19 Oct. 2/7 The artisans' dwellings..the sites of which were sold to pseudo-philanthropists so cheaply. **1828** DISRAELI *Voy. Capt. Popanilla* iv. 35 A state of existence which has puzzled many pseudo philosophers. **1842** W. NEWNHAM *Reciprocal Influence of Body & Mind* 159 It is also employed by many pseudo-philosophers as a convenient term. **1966** *Eng. Stud.* XLVII. 154 In the mid-twentieth century the typical Bohemian has become the beatnik poet or pseudo-philosopher. **1817** JANE AUSTEN *Sanditon* (1925) vii. 92 It were Hyper-criticism, it were Pseudo-philosophy to expect from the soul of high toned Genius, the grovellings of a common mind. **1838–9** HALLAM *Hist. Lit.* III. III. iii. §18. 13 A dogmatic pseudo-philosophy, like that of Paracelsus. **1897** Pseudo-philosophy [see IRRATIONALIST]. **1743** POPE *Dunc.* Mock-Advt., A certain Pretender, Pseudo-Poet, or Phantom, of the name of Tibbald. **1628** BURTON *Anat. Mel.* I. iii. II. iv. (ed. 3) 195 So must I needs..bitterly taxe those tyrannising Pseudopolititians. **1649** HEYLIN *Relat. & Observ.* II. To Rdr., A Combination or Faction of Pseudo-Polititians, and Pseudo-Theologitians, Heretics and Schismaticks. **1652** GAULE *Magastrom.* 365 Praestigious sacrificers, and pseudo-presagers. *c* **1380** WYCLIF *Sel. Wks.* II. 173 3if pseudo-preestis prechen amys. **1879** W. JAMES in *Mind* IV. 337 Illusory simplification..is made by invoking some sham term, some pseudo-principle, and conglomerating it and the data into one. **1964** M. A. K. HALLIDAY et al. *Linguistic Sci.* vii. 218 Where he has learned ..such a sheer quantity of linguistic material..testing all of it becomes a 'pseudo-procedure'; it just cannot be done. **1965** *Language* XLI. 206 Scholastic pseudo-procedures of discovery. **1949** KOESTLER *Insight & Outlook* vii. 101 A similar pseudo-proverb is, 'He never works between meals'. **1934** R. CARNAP *Unity of Sci.* 40 The danger may arise of being diverted by the material mode of speech into considering pseudo-questions. **1947** D. RYNIN *Johnson's Treat Lang.* 353 On this assumption, 'Is everything known to God?' is for us not a genuine question, but a pseudo-question. **1963** Pseudo-question [see *pseudo-difficulty* above]. **1927** A. HUXLEY *Proper Stud.* 220 There is a powerful religion, or rather pseudo-religion, of sexual purity. **1956** R. C. ZAEHNER in A. Pryce-Jones *New Outl. Mod. Knowl.* 66 The modern pseudo-religions the most obvious of which was Hitlerism. **1969** *Daily Tel.* 24 Apr. 20/3 The pseudo-religion of Social Justice. **1931** E. SAPIR in *Amer. Mercury* XXII. 205/2 The simplicity of English in its formal aspect is..really a pseudo-simplicity or a masked complexity. **1951** M. MCLUHAN *Mech. Bride* (1967) 141/2 It is the weak and confused who worship the pseudosimplicities of brutal directness. **1649** Pseudo-theologitian [see *pseudo-politician* above]. **1940** C. S. LEWIS *Let.* 17 Jan. (1966) 176 You will presently see both a Leftist and a Rightist pseudo-theology developing. **1961** 'F. O'BRIEN' *Hard Life* x. 75 His talk is always full of 'ifs' and 'buts', rawmaish and pseudo-theology. **1977** *Rolling Stone* 30 June 62/2 There has also been the startling growth of psychological technology: all the encounter groups and how-to manuals, all the new therapies and analyses, all the pseudotheologies and gurus and disciplines. **1935** R. CARNAP *Philos. & Log. Syntax* 21 All these philosophical theses are deprived of empirical content, of theoretical sense; they are pseudo-theses. **1963** —— in P. A. Schilpp *Philos. of R. Carnap* 51, I argued in detail that the thesis of materialism was just as much a pseudo-thesis as that of idealism. **1951** S. ULLMANN *Princ. Semantics* II. 59 In view of the hybrid nature of particles, it might be convenient to label them *pseudo-words*. **1954** *Archivum Linguisticum* VI. 18 Ullmann..speaks of 'pseudo-words' which would have no full semantic status. **1680** G. HICKES *Spirit of Popery* 70 Twenty six..of these Heroical Pseudo-Zealots.

b. Prefixed to adjs. ***pseudo-American***, ***-antique***, ***-Aristotelian***, ***-divine***, ***-dramatic***, ***-Elizabethan***, ***-existing***, ***-Georgian***, ***-historic(al)***, ***-infantile***, ***-intellectual***, ***-literary***, ***-localizing***, ***-logical***, ***-Marxist***, ***-medical***, ***-medieval***, ***-military***, ***-mystical***, ***-patriotic***, ***-perpetual***, ***-philosophic(al)***, ***-poetic***, ***-psychological***, ***-reformed***, ***-religious***, ***-revolutionary***, ***-romantic***, ***-sophisticated***, ***-Spanish***, ***-technical*** adjs.

1938 Pseudo-American [see KIDDO]. **1964** C. BARBER *Present-Day Eng.* ii. 20 English pop-singers have developed a special pseudo-American accent of their own. **1936** *Burlington Mag.* May 219/2 The Byzantine pseudo-antique character. **1959** Pseudo-antique [see KATHAREVOUSA]. **1850** GROTE *Greece* II. lxvii. VIII. 503 In one of the Aristotelian or Pseudo-Aristotelian treatises. **1950** D. GASCOYNE *Vagrant* 33 To be with God, and not pseudo-divine Scorn-inspired self-deceivers. **1872** LOWELL *Milton* Prose Wks. 1890 IV. 65 Impertinent details of what we must call the pseudo-dramatic kind. **1946** BLUNDEN *Shelley* 205 One of the endless pseudo-Elizabethan or at least post-Elizabethan compositions. **1956** Pseudo-Elizabethan [see MIMSEY *a.*]. **1904** B. RUSSELL in *Mind* XIII. 353 False propositions, according to Meinong, are the non-subsisting, merely pseudo-existing objectives of erroneous judgments. **1905** E. WHARTON *House of Mirth* I. i. 7 Its marble porch and pseudo-Georgian façade. **1936** J. BUCHAN *Island of Sheep* vii. 125 The house was..a pseudo-Georgian edifice of red brick with stone facings. **1919** M. BEER *Hist. Brit. Socialism* I. I. v. 51 The soul of moral philosophy was *ius naturale*, which is..pure ethics in a pseudo-historic guise. **1905** O. JESPERSEN *Growth & Struct. Eng. Lang.* x. 246 That pseudo-historical and anti-educational abomination, the English spelling. **1927** W. E. COLLINSON *Contemp. Eng.* 7 Pseudo-infantile forms like pinny (pinafore). **1977** D. MORRIS *Manwatching* 185 The pseudo-infantile woman displays pouted lips, wide-open eyes, and child-like body postures. **1944** KOESTLER in *Horizon* Mar. 173 The pseudo-intellectual hangers-on whose primary motive is..neurosis pure and simple. **1956** A. S. C. ROSS in M. Black *Importance of Lang.* (1962) 99 To say *Miss Austen* instead of *Jane Austen* is either precious or pseudo-intellectual. **1824** DIBDIN *Libr. Comp.* 585 The literary, or rather the pseudo-literary history of the first half of the sixteenth century. **1899** *Allbutt's Syst. Med.* VII. 658 The pseudo-localising symptoms..are apt to lead to an erroneous opinion as to the exact position of the new growth. **1886** *Macm. Mag.* Mar. 427 Scholastic fancies ..clothed with pseudo-logical forms. **1938** *Ann. Reg. 1937* 197 M. N. Pokrovsky... His 'school' is now persecuted as holding pseudo-Marxist, anti-Leninist and therefore unscientific conceptions. **1945** H. READ *Coat of Many Colours* xliv. 219 If Balzac had followed the advice of our pseudo-Marxist critics, he would have made his works subservient to his political theories. **1908** *Jrnl. Amer. Med. Assoc.* 28 Nov. 1860/2 Among the pseudo-medical institutions that have been investigated and closed through fraud orders by the Post-office Department was a Cincinnati concern known as the Epileptic Institute. **1977** *Gay News* 24

Mar. 18/3 Old pseudo-medical myths die hard. **1978** J. UPDIKE *Coup* (1979) iii. 108 Some..calibrated diet whose pseudo-medical niceties were catered to even in the depths of our famine. **1883** Pseudo-medieval [see HIGH *a.* 6 a]. **1967** E. SHORT *Embroidery & Fabric Collage* iv. 117 Too often a designer who happily experiments with plant forms and animals will, when confronted with the human figure, resort to the hackneyed, pseudo-medieval figure in the nebulous draped garment which is so often seen in church work. **1841** THACKERAY *Men & Coats* Wks. 1900 XIII. 604 In a sort of pseudo-military trim. **1933** *Mind* XLII. 184 It is indeed to the Greeks, or at any rate to Plato, that this argument, not inconsistently with its quasi-Kantian, Christian or Hebraic (and some will say, pseudo-mystical) flavour, harks back. **1960** KOESTLER *Lotus & Robot* II. xi. 245 The rest is pseudo-mystical verbiage. **1961** *Encounter* Feb. 78 This credo is expressed in pseudo-mystical terms. **1880** SWINBURNE *Stud. Shaks.* 113 Too deeply ingrained..to be perverted by any provincial or pseudo-patriotic prepossessions. **1677** PLOT *Oxfordsh.* 235 A Pseudo-perpetual motion made by the descent of several guilt bullets upon an indented declivity. **1914** J. LONDON *Let.* 26 Mar. (1966) 418, I have played with philosophy, expositing the power of mind over matter... While this is..pseudo-philosophic, nevertheless it will make it most palatable to..the folk who will read it. **1922** C. BELL *Since Cézanne* 82 We shall then be armed..against the portentous 'Ist', whose parthenogenetic masterpiece we are not in a state to relish till we have sucked down the pseudo-philosophic bolus that embodies his eponymous 'Ism'. **1933** M. OAKESHOTT *Experience* IV. 243 A psychology which is not scientific certainly exists, and certainly would not be superseded by a science of psychology... Nevertheless, such a psychology..would be a pseudo-philosophical form of experience. **1940** *Mind* XLIX. 99 The encumbrance of these largely parasitic philosophical and pseudo-philosophical ideas. **1817** COLERIDGE *Biog. Lit.* 19 Pope's..translation of Homer, which, I do not stand alone in regarding as the main source of our pseudo-poetic diction. **1684** EVELYN *Diary* 23 Feb., A pseudo-politic adherence to the French interest. **1946** *Mind* LV. 360 When we ask what in fact constitutes the order or form of the vegetative realm or any below the highest one, the answer is given in terms derived from human experience and purpose. Or else it is a worse answer in pseudo-mechanical, pseudo-psychological terms, like 'vital force'. **1964** *Eng. Stud.* XLV. 419 Professor Bodelsen's work..eschews..the flights of pseudo-psychological fancy of the gaudier school of criticism. **1865** PUSEY *Eiren.* 365 The pseudo-reformed and unbelieving philosophers of those times. **1673** H. MORE *Brief Reply* App. 3, I add superstitious..; and by superstitious, I understand pseudoreligious, if I may so speak, that is, false or depraved religious worship. **1938** *Burlington Mag.* Jan. 44/1 Even in old Siena..there were, not only pagan painters, but also pseudo-religious artists..who substituted prettiness for piety. **1943** K. MANNHEIM *Diagnosis of our Time* vii. 102 It is not a matter of chance that both Communism and Fascism try to..superimpose a pseudo-religious integration. **1957** J. S. HUXLEY *Relig. without Revelation* iii. 59 Only in high civilisations does art become emancipated from religious or pseudo-religious domination. **1978** *China Reconstructs* Nov. 5/1 Their pseudo-revolutionary line and its counter-revolutionary aims are being thoroughly criticized. **1979** *Dædalus* Winter 132 This leads them sometimes..to become unexpected allies..of pseudorevolutionary, violent minorities. **1854** DE QUINCEY *Autobiog. Sk.* Wks. II. 271 As yet..false taste, the pseudo-romantic rage, had not violated the most awful solitudes. **1927** R. H. WILENSKI *Mod. Movement in Art* 29 The degenerate romantic and pseudo-romantic art of the nineteenth century. **1961** D. G. JAMES *Matthew Arnold* i. 26 We may call it 'Romantic' if we like; it is better to call it pseudo-romantic or even sentimental. **1977** *Time* 19 Sept. 11/1 Against such alienation, the pseudo-romantic exploits of Andreas Baader and Ulrike Meinhof hardly needed ideological underpinnings to strike a responsive chord. **1935** W. G. HARDY *Father Abraham* 134 Abraham saw a quiet, controlled, secretive man with that indefinable air of assurance which travel imparts—considerably different, indeed, from the pseudo-sophisticated Lugal of argumentative days but yet recognizable. **1960** A. L. HENCH in *Amer. Speech* XXXV. 73 One of my brighter students recently asked me..why I had used the word *sophisticated* to praise a literary critic... The student said he understood the word meant 'artificial', 'adulterated', 'tarnished', even 'slightly corrupt'... I told him that of course the word sometimes was used to mean 'artificial' or 'false' but that I thought persons who used it this way actually meant *pseudosophisticated*. **1928** H. CRANE *Let.* 31 Jan. (1965) 315 The perfect labyrinth of 'villas'—some pseudo-Spanish, some a la Maya. **1964** H. KÖKERITZ in D. Abercrombie et al. *Daniel Jones* 143 In America, *Don Quixote* and *Don Juan* have assumed a pseudo-Spanish pronunciation. **1945** *Mind* LIV. 185 The philosopher..must be particularly conscious of the pitfalls of language, and especially of all pseudo-technical and emotive language. **1964** P. STREVENS in D. Abercrombie et al. *Daniel Jones* 120 They all commonly bear the same pseudo-technical label.

2. Special combinations: nearly all terms of modern science, (*a*) indicating close or deceptive resemblance to the thing denoted by the second element, without real identity or affinity with it; or sometimes simply denoting an abnormal or erratic form or kind of the thing; (*b*) denoting something which does not correspond with the reality, or to which no reality corresponds, as false perceptions, errors of judgement or statement.

The second element is properly Greek, but very frequently Latin, and occasionally English; in the last case almost always hyphened, but not so usually in the other two except when the full form *pseudo-* is used before a vowel.

These words, like those in 1, are practically unlimited in number; the more important are entered in their alphabetical places as main words; others of less importance follow here.

pseud-a'conitine (formerly **-'nitia**) *Chem.*, a highly poisonous alkaloid occurring in *Aconitum ferox* (also **pseudo-aconitine**) (improper use of prefix.); ‖**pseudæs'thesia** *Path.* [mod.L.: cf. ANÆSTHESIA], false or depraved sensation, as that occurring apparently in an amputated limb; **pseudambu'lacrum** *Zool.* (pl. **-a**), name for each of five spaces or areas resembling ambulacra in certain Crinoids; so **pseudambu'lacral** *a.*, simulating an ambulacrum, or of the nature of a pseudambulacrum (*Cent. Dict.*); **pseuda'mœboid** *a. Zool.*, deceptively resembling an amœba; **pseu'dandry** [Gr. ἀνήρ, ἀνδρ- man], the use by a woman of a male pseudonym; ‖**pseudaphia** (-'dæfɪə) *Path.* [mod.L., f. Gr. ἁφή touch], false or perverted sense of touch (Mayne 1858, Billings *Nat. Med. Dict.* 1890); **pseuˌdapose'matic** *a. Zool.* [Gr. ἀπό away, σῆμα sign, mark], applied to deceptive markings or colouring of an animal, having a tendency to repel the attacks of another species, e.g. by suggesting something dangerous or unpleasant; †**pseudarachnidan** (-ə'ræknɪdən) *a.*, of or pertaining to a division of the Tracheate Arachnida, also termed Adelarthrosomata, containing the Pseudo-scorpions, *Solpugidæ*, and Harvestmen; as *sb.*, an arachnidan of this order; ‖**pseudar'throsis** *Surg.* (pl. **-oses**) [Gr. ἄρθρωσις articulation], the formation of a false joint, as when the two parts of a fractured bone fail to unite; **pseuda'taxic** *a. Path.*, resembling but not really of the nature of ataxy; **pseu'daxine** *a. Zool.*, applied to a group of *Cervidæ* or deer closely resembling the Axis (AXIS[2]); **pseu'daxis** *Bot.* (also **pseudo-'axis**: pl. **-es**), an apparent axis or main shoot formed by the series of stronger branches of the successive bifurcations in dichotomous branching; **pseu'delephant** *Zool.*, an animal resembling an elephant, as a mastodon; **'pseudelminth, pseudhelminth,** *Path.* [Gr. ἕλμινς, ἑλμινθ- worm], something deceptively resembling an entoparasitic worm; ‖**pseu'delytron** (pl. **-a**) *Entom.*, a spurious or degenerate elytron or wing-sheath in certain insects; **pseu'dembryo** *Zool.*, a spurious embryo; a term applied to various larval forms in sea-urchins, starfishes, and sponges; hence **pseudembry'onic** *a.*; ‖**pseuden'cephalus** *Path.* [Gr. ἐγκέφαλος brain], a monster having a vascular tumour in place of the brain (Dunglison 1844); ‖**pseudepiploon** (-ɪ'pɪpləʊɒn) *Ornith.*, a membrane in the abdomen of certain birds, resembling the epiploon in mammals, but not investing the intestines; hence **pseudepi'ploic** *a.*; **pseuˌdepise'matic** *a. Zool.* [Gr. ἐπί upon, σῆμα sign, mark], applied to markings or colouring deceptively resembling those called *episematic*, which serve to allure or attract other individuals of the species; **pseu'dergate** *Zool.* [a. F. *pseudergate* (Grassé & Noirot 1947, in *Compt. Rend.* CCXXIV. 219): see ERGATE], in certain genera of termites, a blind, wingless member of the colony, carrying out some of the functions of the workers; **pseud'hæmal, pseudo-hæmal** *a. Zool.* [Gr. αἷμα blood], of or pertaining to the circulating fluid in some invertebrates, analogous to but not really blood, and to the vessels which contain it; ‖**pseudhalteres** (-hæl'tɪəriːz) *sb. pl. Entom.* [see HALTERES], a name for the *pseudelytra* (see above); **pseud-idea**: see *pseudo-idea* below; ‖**pseudi'mago** *Entom.*, an imperfect imago or winged stage in certain insects, as the *Ephemeridæ*, succeeding the pupal stage: also called *subimago*; hence **pseudi'maginal** *a.*; **pseudo-a'cacia**, the tree *Robinia Pseudacacia* (= ACACIA[1] 2, LOCUST-TREE 2); **'pseudo-ˌacid** *Chem.* [tr. G. *pseudosäure* (A. Hantzsch 1899, in *Ber. d. Deut. Chem. Ges.* XXXII. 577)], a compound which is not itself an acid but which exists in equilibrium with, or is easily converted into, an acidic form and thus undergoes some typical reactions of acids; hence **pseudo-a'cidic** *a.*; **pseudo-a'cidity**; **pseudo-a'conitine** = *pseudaconitine*; **pseudo-'alkaloid** *Chem.*, a substance allied to the alkaloids, but not strictly one of them; **'pseudo-ˌangle** *Geom.*, an angle in non-Euclidean geometry; **pseudo-apo'plectic** *a. Path.*, simulating apoplexy; **pseudo-articu'lation** *Zool.*, a structure having the appearance of an articulation but not really forming one; **ˌpseudo-a'symmetry** *Chem.*, the property of an atom of being bonded to two enantiomorphic groups; hence **ˌpseudo-asy'mmetric** *a.*; **pseudo-'axis** = *pseudaxis* (see above); ‖**pseudo-ba'cillus** (pl. **-i**), false bacillus, one of the minute fat crystals sometimes found in sputum; ‖**pseudo-bac'terium** (pl. **-ia**), a formation simulating a bacterium; **'pseudo-base** *Chem.* [a. G. *pseudobase* (A. Hantzsch 1899, in *Ber. d. Deut. Chem. Ges.* XXXII. 595)], a compound which is not itself a base but which exists in equilibrium with, or is easily converted into, a basic form and thus undergoes some typical reactions of bases; hence **pseudo-'basic** *a.*; **ˌpseudo-ba'sicity**; ‖**pseudoba'sidium** *Bot.* (pl. **-ia**), name for formations resembling and accompanying the basidia in certain fungi; **pseudo'bedding** *Geol.*, a structure in which an appearance of stratification has been produced by a cause other than deposition in the apparent planes of stratification; ‖**pseudo'blepsia** (erron. **-blepsis**) *Path.* [mod.L., f. Gr. βλέψις looking, sight], false or perverted vision (= *pseudopsia*); **pseudoboléite, -boleite** (-'bəʊlɪaɪt) *Min.* [a. F. *pseudoboléite* (A. Lacroix 1895, in *Bull. du Muséum d'Hist. naturelle* I. 40), f. *boléite*, similar mineral named after *Boleo*, near Santa Rosalia, Lower California, Mexico, where both were first found], a hydroxide-chloride of lead and copper occurring as translucent blue crystals; ‖**pseudobrachium** (-'breɪkɪəm) *Ichth.* (pl. **-ia**) [mod.L., f. L. *brachium* arm], the elongated base of the pectoral fins, resembling an arm, in pediculate fishes; hence **pseudo'brachial** *a.* (Gill cited in *Cent. Dict.*); **'pseudobranch** (-bræŋk), ‖**pseudo'branchia** (pl. **-iæ**), ‖**pseudo'branchium** (pl. **-ia**), *Ichth.* [Gr. βράγχια gills], names for an organ or structure in certain fishes, resembling, but not having the function of a gill; hence **pseudo'branchial** *a.*, pertaining to or of the nature of a pseudobranch, etc.; **pseudo'branchiate** *a.*, furnished with or having a pseudobranch, etc.; **pseudo'brookite** *Min.*, oxide of titanium and iron, occurring in small tabular crystals resembling brookite; **pseudo-'bulb** *Bot.*, the enlarged base of the stem (resembling a bulb but solid) in many epiphytic orchids; **pseudo-'bulbar** *a. Path.*, applied to a form of paralysis, in symptoms but not in origin, resembling bulbar paralysis (Billings 1890); **pseudo-'bulbil** *Bot.*, an outgrowth producing antheridia and archegonia, which sometimes takes the place of the sporangia in ferns; **pseudo-'bulbous** *a. Bot.*, apparently but not really bulbous; of the nature of or having a pseudo-bulb; **pseudo-'carcinoid** *a.* and *sb. Zool.* [Gr. καρκίνος crab], applied to certain macrurous crustaceans which simulate brachyurous ones or crabs (Huxley); **ˌpseudo-ceratophorus** (-sɛrə'tɒfərəs) *a. Zool.* [Gr. κέρας, κερατ- horn, -φορος bearing], apparently horn-bearing; resembling the buds of horns; ‖**pseudocer'caria** *Zool.*, a stage in certain *Gregarinida* resembling a *Cercaria*; **ˌpseudocholi'nesterase** *Biochem.*, an enzyme present in the blood and in the liver, brain, and certain other organs which acts on the same esters as cholinesterase and some others besides; ‖**pseudochromia** (-'krəʊmɪə) *Path.* [Gr. χρῶμα colour], false or perverted perception of colour (Dunglison 1857, Billings 1890); **pseudochronism** (-'dɒkrənɪz(ə)m) [after ANACHRONISM], a false dating, an error in date; **ˌpseudochro'nologist**, a false chronologist, one who attributes a false date to some occurrence; **pseudo-'chrysalis** *Entom.* = *pseudo-pupa* (see below); **pseudo'chrysolite** *Min.* [cf. Gr. ψευδοχρυσόλιθος (Diodorus Siculus)], a mineral resembling chrysolite; †**pseudocirrhosis** *Path.* [after G. *pseudolebercirrhose* (F. Pick 1896, in *Zeitschr. f. klin. Med.* XXIX. 395)] = PICK'S DISEASE 1; **'pseudocode** *Computers*, a programming language that is not a machine language and has to be translated by a computer before it can be executed; **'pseudocœle** (-siːl) *Anat.* [Gr. κοῖλος hollow], (*a*) applied to the body-cavity of certain invertebrates, derived from spaces developed secondarily in the mesoblast, not directly from the blastocœle or original cavity of the embryo; (*b*) applied to the fifth ventricle of the brain; hence **pseudo'cœlian** *a.* in sense (*b*), **pseudo'cœlic** *a.* in sense (*a*); **pseudo'cœlome** [cf. CŒLOME] = *pseudocœle* (*a*); ‖**ˌpseudocolu'mella** *Zool.*, a structure in corals simulating a columella (see quot.); hence **pseudocolu'mellar** *a.*; **pseudo-'commissure** *Zool.* [mod.L. *pseudocommissūra*], a kind of commissure, consisting of connective tissue, not of nerve-substance [see COMMISSURE 4], joining the olfactory lobes in certain batrachians; hence **pseudo-co'mmissural** *a.*; **ˌpseudo-compati'bility** *Bot.*, the fertilization of flowers by pollen which would normally be incompatible (INCOMPATIBLE *a.* 6b); ‖**pseudo-concha** (-ˈkɒŋkə) *Ornith.* [see CONCHA 4c], a turbinated structure in the nose of birds, in front of and below the turbinal proper; ˈ**pseudocone** *Entom.*, a fluid or gelatinous cone in the eyes of certain *Diptera*, as distinct from the solid crystalline cone in the eyes of other insects; also *attrib.* or *adj.*; **pseudoconˈglomerate** *Geol.* (see quot. 1972); **pseudo-ˈcorneous** *a. Zool.*, composed of a substance simulating true horn, as the base of the horn in the pronghorn antelope, which consists of agglutinated hairs; ‖**pseudoˈcortex** *Bot.*, a false cortex, as that formed by the secondary branches closely adpressed to the main branch in certain seaweeds (*Cent. Dict.* 1890, *Syd. Soc. Lex.* 1895); ‖**pseudoˈcosta** *Zool.* (pl. **-æ**) [L. *costa* rib], each of the slightly projecting parts between the septa of certain corals; **pseudoˈcostate** *a.*, (*a*) *Bot.* applied to a leaf in which the veins are confluent so as to form an apparent marginal or intramarginal vein (*Treas. Bot.* 1866); (*b*) *Zool.* having pseudocostæ; **pseudocoˈtunnite** *Min.* [ad. G. *pseudocotunnit* (G. vom Rath 1877), alteration of It. *pseudocotunnia* (A. Scacchi 1873, in *Atti della R. Accad. delle Sci., Fis. e Matem. di Napoli* VI. IX. 38), f. *cottunia*, similar mineral named after D. *Cotungo* (1736–1822), It. anatomist], a potassium lead chloride, K_2PbCl_4, found as dull yellowish or whitish crystals on Vesuvius; †ˌ**pseudocotyˈledon** *Bot. Obs.*, a name for the germinating threads of the spores of cryptogams, formerly considered analogous to the cotyledons of phanerogams (*Cent. Dict.* 1890); so ‖**pseudocotyˈledonæ** (mod.L.) *pl.*, cryptogamous plants; **pseudo-ˈcrisis** *Path.* (see quot.); ˈ**pseudo-ˌcroup** *Path.*, a disorder simulating croup, as *laryngismus stridulus* (Dunglison 1853); **pseudo-ˈcubic, -ˈcubical** *adjs. Cryst.*, said of a composite crystal of lower symmetry simulating a simple one of the cubic system; **pseudoˈcumene** *Chem.*, a hydrocarbon isomeric with cumene, being a modification of trimethylbenzene, $C_6H_3(CH_3)_3$, occurring in coal-tar oil; ‖**pseudocyˈclosis** *Biol.* [mod.L.: see CYCLOSIS], 'the apparent circulation of food-particles within the body of an amœba' (*Syd. Soc. Lex.*); ‖**pseudocyesis** (-saɪˈiːsɪs) *Phys.* [mod.L., f. Gr. κύησις conception], spurious conception or pregnancy (Dunglison 1842); cf. PSEUDOPREGNANCY 1; **pseudocyˈphella** *Bot.* [CYPHELLA], a small pore in the lower surface of certain lichens; ˈ**pseudocyst** (-sɪst) [see CYST], (*a*) *Zool.* a protoplasmic body occurring in certain *Gregarinida*; (*b*) *Bot.* each of several protoplasmic bodies formed by the breaking up of the filaments of certain *Protophyta*; (*c*) *Path.* a false cyst, as a part of the peritoneal cavity closed by adhesion of the viscera in peritonitis; ‖**pseudo-delˈtidium** *Zool.*, a simple shelly plate which takes the place of the deltidium in certain brachiopod shells; ˈ**pseudo-ˌdike** *Geol.*, a fissure filled up with sedimentary or other matter, having the appearance of a dike (DIKE *sb.*[1] 9, 9b); ‖**pseudo-diphˈtheria** *Path.*, a disease simulating diphtheria; also *attrib.* as *pseudodiphtheria bacillus*; so ˌ**pseudo-diphtheˈritic** *a.* [cf. DIPHTHERITIC]; **pseudo-ˈdistance** *Geom.*, distance in non-Euclidean geometry (*Cent. Dict.*); **pseudoˈdominance** *Genetics*, the expression of a recessive allele as a result of the deletion of the part of the chromosome bearing the corresponding dominant allele; so **pseudo-ˈdominant** *a.*; ˈ**pseudodont** *a. Zool.* [Gr. ὀδούς tooth], having horny epidermic teeth, as the *Ornithorhynchus*; ˈ**pseudo-entity, pseuˈdentity** *Philos.*, something falsely called or regarded as an entity; **pseudo-eryˈsipelas** *Path.*, any inflammatory disease resembling erysipelas; so ˌ**pseudo-erysiˈpelatous** *a.*; †**pseudo-erythrin** *Chem.*, 'an old name of ethylic orsellinate' (Watts *Dict. Chem.*); ˈ**pseudo-existence** *Philos.* (see quots.); **pseudoˈfæces** *Zool.*, a mixture of mucus and particulate matter from the water that collects in the mantle cavity of a mollusc and is expelled without passing through the digestive system; hence **pseudoˈfæcal** *a.*; ‖**pseudo-fiˈlaria** *Zool.*, a stage in the development of certain *Gregarinida*, resembling a thread-worm of the genus *Filaria*; hence **pseudo-fiˈlarian** *a.*; ˌ**pseudo-foliˈaceous** *a.Bot.*, simulating a leaf, leaf-like; **pseudoˈfovea** *Ophthalm.*, a point of maximum sensitivity on the retina other than the fovea, such as may develop in a squinting eye; hence **pseudoˈfoveal** *a.*; ˈ**pseudofracture** *Med.*, a defect in bone that appears on a radiograph as one of a series of narrow, well-defined lines of translucence; ˈ**pseudo-ˌfruit** *Bot.*, a fruit formed by growth and modification of other parts besides the ovary (e.g. a fig, a strawberry, etc.): = PSEUDOCARP; **pseudogaˈlena** *Min.*, native zinc sulphide, resembling lead sulphide or galena: = BLACK JACK 2, BLENDE; ‖**pseudoˈgaster** *Zool.*, a spurious gastric cavity produced by fusion in sponges; ‖**pseudoˈgastrula** *Embryol.*, an invaginated blastosphere simulating a gastrula; ˈ**pseudogene** *Genetics*, a section of a chromosome that is an imperfect copy of a functional gene; **pseudo-ˈgeneral** *a.*, in *Path.* applied to a kind of paralysis simulating general paralysis; **pseudo-geˈneric** *a. Nat. Hist.*, apparently but not really generic; having the character of a pseudo-genus; **pseudo-ˈgenus** *Nat. Hist.*, a spurious genus of animals or plants, e.g. one based upon forms which are really stages in the development of some species; ‖**Pseudogeusia** (-ˈgjuːsɪə), **-ˈgeustia** *Path.* [mod.L., f. Gr. γεῦσις taste, γευστός to be tasted], false or perverted sense of taste; ˈ**pseudogley** *Soil Science* [a. G. *pseudogley* (W. L. Kubiëna *Bestimmungsbuch und Systematik der Böden Europas* (1953) 295)], a gley resulting from temporary or seasonal waterlogging due to poor drainage of surface water, rather than from the permanent existence of a high groundwater table; **pseudogliˈoma** *Ophthalm.*, any condition that gives rise to signs similar to those of retinoblastoma; **pseudoˈglobulin** *Biochem.* [a. G. *pseudoglobulin* (F. Hofmeister 1899: see *Zeitschr. f. physiol. Chem.* (1900) XXXI. 140, *Beiträge z. chem. Physiol.* (1901) 361)], the fraction of serum globulin that is soluble in pure water and saline solutions but precipitated by half-saturation with ammonium sulphate; ˈ**pseudogout** *Path.*, a joint disorder resembling gout but produced by deposits of crystals of calcium pyrophosphate rather than sodium urate and occurring most often in the knee; ˈ**pseudogyne** (-dʒɪn) *Entom.* [Gr. γυνή female], one of the agamic females of aphides and other insects, which reproduce parthenogenetically; so **pseudogynous** (-ˈdɒdʒɪnəs) *a.*; **pseuˈdogyny** *Ent.*, pseudogynous condition; **pseudogyrate** (-ˈdʒaɪərət) *a. Bot.* [Gr. γῦρος ring], said of a fern having the annulus confined to the vertex of each sporangium (*Treas. Bot.* 1866); **pseudoˈhæmal** *a.*: see *pseudhæmal* above; ˌ**pseudo-halluciˈnation**, an isolated, brief, and vivid sensory experience, commonly auditory or visual, occurring in clear consciousness and in the absence of any external stimulus; so ˌ**pseudo-halluciˈnatory** *a.*; ˈ**pseudo-ˌheart** *Zool.*, each of several tubular organs, formerly described as hearts, forming a communication between the body-cavity and the pallial chamber in brachiopods; **pseudo-herˈmaphrodite** *a. Biol.*, apparently hermaphrodite but actually unisexual; hence **pseudo-herˈmaphroditism**, apparent hermaphroditism, as that due to an abnormal structure of the external sexual organs (*Cent. Dict.* 1890; *Syd. Soc. Lex.* 1895); **pseudo-hexˈagonal** *a. Cryst.*, said of a composite crystal of lower symmetry simulating a simple one of the hexagonal system; ˌ**pseudohomoˈsexual** *a.*, pertaining to or designating homosexual behaviour which acts as an outlet for the expression of fear, aggression, dependency, dominance, etc., rather than being genuinely sexual; hence ˌ**pseudohomosexuˈality**; **pseudo-hyˈpertrophy** *Path.* [see HYPERTROPHY], enlargement of an organ by growth of fat or connective tissue, with atrophy of its proper substance; so **pseudo-hyperˈtrophic** *a.*, applied to a form of paralysis caused by pseudo-hypertrophy of the muscles; ˌ**pseudoˌhypoparaˈthyroidism** *Med.*, a familial disorder in which the features of hypoparathyroidism are accompanied by skeletal and developmental abnormalities and which is caused by a failure of tissues to respond to parathyroid hormone; so ˌ**pseudo-ˌhypoparaˈthyroid** *a.*; ˈ**pseudo-idea, ˈpseud-idea**, a meaningless or false idea; ˈ**pseudo-instruction** (also ***pseudo instruction***) *Computers*, an instruction similar to a computer instruction in form that is not executed as an instruction by hardware but used to control a compiler or assembler; ˌ**pseudo-isochroˈmatic** *a. Ophthalm.*, composed of different colours that appear the same to a colour-blind person; **pseudoˈixiolite** *Min.*, an oxide of iron, manganese, tantalum, and niobium that has a highly disordered orthorhombic structure and is similar to ixiolite, differing in changing to tantalite or columbite on heating and in lacking tin; ˈ**pseudokarst** *Geomorphol.* [cf. It. *pseudocarsico* adj., *-carsismo* sb. (G. B. Floridia 1941, in *Boll. della Soc. di Sci. nat. ed econ. di Palermo* XXIII. 12), and see quot. 1960[1]], karst-like topography in ground other than limestone produced by subterranean erosion rather than solution; hence **pseudoˈkarstic** *a.*; ‖**pseudoˈlabium** *Zool.*, a part in chilopodous Myriapoda (see quot.); hence **pseudoˈlabial** *a.*; **pseudo-ˈlateral** *a. Bot.*, 'having a tendency to become lateral when it is normally terminal, as the fruit of certain *Hepaticæ*' (*Cent. Dict.*); ‖**pseudoleuchæmia** (-ljuːˈkiːmɪə) (erron. **-leucæmia, -leukæmia**), ‖ˌ**pseudo-leucocyˈthæmia**, *Path.* [see LEUKÆMIA, LEUCOCYTHÆMIA], names for HODGKIN'S DISEASE, as resembling leukæmia, but not involving increase in the number of leucocytes; **pseudo-leucocyte** (-ˈljuːkəsaɪt) *Path.*, a morbid formation resembling a leucocyte; **pseudo-lichen** (-ˈlaɪkɪn) *Bot.*, a parasitic fungus resembling a lichen, but without the presence of an alga in the thallus; **pseudo-ˈlobar** *a. Path.* (see quot. 1895); **pseudomalachite** (-ˈmæləkaɪt) *Min.*, hydrous phosphate of copper, occurring in dark-green masses resembling malachite; **pseudo-lymˈphoma** *Path.*, any of various conditions involving enlargement of lymph nodes which bear some resemblance to lymphoma but are not malignant; hence **pseudolymˈphomatous** *a.*; **pseudo-ˈmembrane** *Path.*, a false membrane (see MEMBRANE 1d); **pseudo-memˈbranous** *a. Path.*, applied to conditions in which mucous membranes are covered with a sheet formed of exudate; ˈ**pseudo-memory**: see quot.; **pseudo-meˈtallic** *a.*, resembling, but not of the nature of, a metal; of lustre: see quot.; **pseudo-ˈmica**, a mineral simulating mica; ˌ**pseudo-ˌmonocotyˈledonous** *a. Bot.*, falsely or apparently monocotyledonous, either by union of the cotyledons into one mass, or by abortion of one of them; so ˌ**pseudo-ˌmonocotyˈledon**, a pseudo-monocotyledonous plant; **pseudoˈmorphia, -ˈmorphine** *Chem.* [see MORPHIA, MORPHINE], one of the alkaloids contained in opium; also called *oxymorphine*; ‖**pseudomorula** (-ˈmɒrələ) *Embryol.*, an aggregate of unicellular organisms or spores resembling a morula; hence **pseudoˈmorular** *a.*; **pseudoˈmucin** *Med.* [a. G. *pseudomucin* (O. Hammarsten 1882, in *Zeitschr. f. physiol. Chem.* VI. 209)], the thick, tenacious, semi-opaque liquid present in pseudomucinous cysts; hence **pseudoˈmucinous** *a.*, epithet of the commonest kind of ovarian cyst, containing mucin; ˌ**pseudo-multiˈlocular** *a. Bot.*, apparently but not really multilocular; so ˌ**pseudo-multiˈseptate** *a.*; ˌ**pseudomycoˈrrhiza** *Biol.* [a. Sw. *pseudomykorrhiza* (E. Melin *Studier över de Norrländska Myrmarkernas Vegetation* (1917) II. v. 358)], an association of tree roots and fungi, often mildly pathogenic ones, in the absence of true mycorrhiza; so ˌ**pseudo-mycoˈrrhizal** *a.*; ‖ˌ**pseudo-naviˈcella, -naˈvicula** (pl. **-æ**) *Zool.* [see quot. 1867], an elliptical spore with pointed ends, forming a stage in the development of certain *Gregarinida*; hence ˌ**pseudo-naviˈcellar, -naˈvicular** *adjs.*; ‖ˌ**Pseudoneuˈroptera** *sb. pl. Entom.*, an order of insects in some classifications, resembling the *Neuroptera* but with incomplete metamorphosis; hence ˌ**pseudoneuˈropter** *sb.*, ˌ**pseudoneuˈropterous** *a.*; **pseudoneuˈrotic** *a. Psychol.*, of or pertaining to types of mental illness in which superficial symptoms of neurosis are found in conjunction with underlying symptoms of psychosis, esp. of schizophrenia; ˈ**pseudo-object** *Gram.*, a noun or pronoun that appears to be, but actually is not, an object; ˈ**pseudo-operation** (also ***pseudo operation***) *Computers* = *pseudo-instruction* above; ˈ**pseudo-order** *Computers* = *pseudo-instruction* above (see also quot. 1955); **pseudopaˈralysis** *Path.*, a disease simulating paralysis; so ‖**pseudo-paraˈplegia**; **pseudo-ˈparasite** *Biol.*, an organism apparently but not really or strictly parasitic; e.g. an external parasite, a commensal, or a saprophyte; so ˌ**pseudo-para'sitic** *a.*; ‖ **pseudoparenchyma** (-pə'rɛŋkɪmə) *Bot.*, a tissue in fungi resembling parenchyma, but composed of interlaced and united hyphæ; hence ˌ**pseudoparen'chymatous** *a.*; ‖ **pseudo'paresis** *Path.*, a disease simulating paresis; an apparent or spurious paresis (*Syd. Soc. Lex.* 1895); ˌ**pseudo-**ˌ**partheno'genesis**, a form of reproduction: see quot. 1870; **pseudo-pediform** (-'pɛdɪfɔːm) *a. Zool.* [L. *pes, ped-* foot: see -FORM], having the form of a pseudopodium, pseudopodial; **pseudo-pe'lade** *Path.* [a. F. *pseudo-pelade* (L. Brocq. et al. 1905, in *Annales Dermatol. et Syph.* VI. 1): cf. PELADA], the appearance of multiple bald patches on the scalp; ‖ **pseudo'perculum** *Zool.*, a secondary lid or operculum closing the aperture of the shell in certain gastropods; hence **pseudo'percular** *a.*, belonging to or of the nature of a pseudoperculum; **pseudo'perculate** *a.*, furnished with a pseudoperculum; ‖ **pseudope-'ridium** *Bot.*, that form of peridium or investment occurring in an æcidium (1832 Lindley, *Introd. Bot.* 207); **pseudo-peri'odic** *a.*, 'quasi-periodic' (*Cent. Dict.*); 'approximately periodic' (*Funk's Stand. Dict.*); ˌ**pseudo-peri'thecium** *Biol.*, in fungi belonging to the order Laboulbeniales, a structure resembling a perithecium in which the vestigial walls have degenerated; **'pseudophone** (-fəʊn) *Acoustics* [Gr. φωνή sound], an apparatus invented by Dr. S. P. Thompson for investigating the phenomena of hearing, and producing acoustical illusions, esp. as to the direction of sound; ˌ**pseudo-pigmen'tation** (see quot.); **pseudo-'plankton** *Biol.*, organisms attached to drifting debris or vegetation; so **pseudoplank'tonic** *a.*; **'pseudoplasm** *Path.* [Gr. πλάσμα: see PLASMA], a tumour or morbid formation of heterologous tissue; **pseudo-plas'modium** *Biol.*, a structureless aggregate of distinct unicellular organisms; **pseudo'plastic** *a.* and *sb.*, (a liquid) that is non-Newtonian, esp. in having a viscosity that decreases with increasing shearing stress; hence ˌ**pseudopla'sticity**; **'pseudopore** *Zool.*, a 'false pore' in sponges, connected with a *pseudogaster* (see above); **pseudo-po'ssession** *Psychics*, a mental state simulating 'possession' (see POSSESSION 5); **pseudo-'pregnancy** *Path.*, a condition or affection simulating pregnancy (1860 Tanner *Pregn.* i. 7); **pseudo-pre'sentiment** *Psychics* (see quot.); **pseudo-'primitive** *a.*, apparently but not really primitive; **pseudopro'boscis** *Entom.*, a structure simulating a proboscis; **'pseudoproct** *Zool.* [Gr. πρωκτός anus], (*a*) the anal opening in the pseudembryo of an echinoderm; (*b*) a term suggested instead of PSEUDOSTOME in relation to sponges; hence **pseudo'proctous** *a.*; ˌ**pseudo-**ˌ**pseudohypopara'thyroidism** *Med.*, a familial disorder in which the skeletal and developmental abnormalities of pseudohypoparathyroidism are present without the biochemical abnormalities common to hypoparathyroidism and pseudohypoparathyroidism; ‖ **pseu'dopsia** *Path.* [mod.L., f. Gr. ὄψις seeing, vision], false or perverted vision; a hallucination or illusion of sight (Billings 1890); ‖ **pseudo-'pupa** *Entom.* (pl. **-æ**), a name for the 'coarctate pupa' constituting one stage of certain insects, as those which undergo hypermetamorphosis; hence **pseudo'pupal** *a.*; **'pseudopupil** *Ent.* [ad. G. *pseudopupille* (S. Exner *Physiol. d. Facettirten Augen v. Krebsen u. Insecten* (1891) ii. 18)] (see quot. 1977); **pseudoquadraphony** (-'rɒfənɪ), sound reproduction in which signals from two sources are fed to four speakers in such a way as to give a partial effect of quadraphony; **pseudo'rabies,** (*a*) (see quots. 1897, 1912) (? *obs.*); (*b*) *Vet. Sci.*, an infectious viral disease of the central nervous system that causes intense pruritus and usu. death in cattle and affects other domestic animals in varying ways; **pseudora'cemic** *a. Chem.*, applied to a racemic substance consisting of mixed or intergrown crystals of the optically active isomers; so **pseudo'racemate**; **pseudo-ra'mose** *a. Bot.* [L. *rāmus* branch], forming false branches, as the filaments of certain algæ, in which the terminal part detaches itself, and then attaches itself laterally to a special cell (heterocyst) of the filament; **'pseudo-ray** *Geom.*, a ray or straight line in non-Euclidean geometry (*Cent. Dict.*); **'pseudoreaction** *Physiol.*, a spurious positive response to a test; † **pseudore'duction** *Cytology*, the apparent halving of the number of chromosomes through synapsis; **pseudor'ganic** *a.*, † (*a*) applied to the elements sulphur and phosphorus, as occurring generally but not universally in organized bodies (*obs.*); (*b*) applied to inorganic formations closely resembling organic structures; **pseudorheu-'matic** *a. Path.*, simulating rheumatism; ˌ**pseudo-rhombo'hedral** *a. Cryst.*, applied to a composite crystal of lower symmetry simulating a simple one of the rhombohedral system; **pseudoro'tation** *Chem.*, a change in molecular configuration involving concerted displacements of the constituent atoms, which is equivalent to a rotation of the molecule coupled with a permutation of some of the constituents, but does not involve any actual rotation of the molecule; hence **pseudoro'tational** *a.*; also **pseudoro'tate** *v. intr.*, to undergo such a change; **pseudoro'tated** *ppl. a.*; **pseudo'rutile** *Min.*, an oxide of iron and titanium, $Fe_2Ti_3O_9$, that is formed as an intermediate stage in the change of ilmenite to rutile; **'pseudo-salt** *Chem.*, a compound which is normally covalent but which under certain conditions exists as or in equilibrium with an ionized, salt-like form; **pseudoscinine** (-'dɒsɪnaɪn) *a. Ornith.*, belonging to the *Pseudoscines*, an anomalous group of OSCINES, containing the lyre-bird and some other Australian birds; ‖ **pseudoscle'rosis** *Path.*, an affection simulating sclerosis (see quot.); **pseudo-'scorpion** *Zool.*, an arachnid or pseudarachnidan of the group *Cheliferidæ* or *Pseudoscorpionidæ*, resembling little scorpions, without tail or poison-glands; ‖ **pseu'dosculum** *Zool.* [see OSCULUM 3a], a 'false osculum' in sponges, connected with a *pseudogaster* (see above); = PSEUDOSTOME 2; **pseudose'matic** *a. Zool.* [Gr. σῆμα sign, mark], belonging to or characterized by deceptive markings or colouring imitating some other species or object; pertaining to or exhibiting mimicry; **psuedo'septate** *a., Nat. Hist.*, (*a*) apparently but not really septate; (*b*) having pseudosepta (*Cent. Dict.*); ‖ **pseudo'septum** *Zool.* (pl. **-a**), a septum in corals not corresponding with or representing a mesentery; **pseudo'siphon** *Zool.*, name for the vertical trace (continuous with the siphon) in the plug of the shell in certain fossil cephalopods; hence **pseudo'siphonal** *a.*; also **pseudosi'phuncle** = *pseudosiphon*; † **'pseudoskink**, † **-scink** *Obs.*, a kind of lizard resembling a skink; ‖ **pseu'dosmia** *Path.* [mod.L., f. Gr. ὀσμή smell], false or perverted sense of smell (Dunglison 1853); **'pseudosocial** *a.*, exhibiting or designating seemingly social behaviour that arises from individual reactions to a need or external stimulus rather than from genuinely social reasons; **'pseudospecies**, a term used for the different national or racial groups to denote the illusory nature of the belief that they have evolved genetically into different and separate species (inferior to one's own); so ˌ**pseudospeci'ation**, a false division into species following these lines; ‖ **pseudo'spermium** *Bot.* [mod.L., f. Gr. σπέρμα seed: cf. *achænium*], a small indehiscent fruit in which the pericarp invests the seed so closely that the whole fruit resembles a simple seed; so **pseudo'spermic**, **pseudo'spermous** *a.*, of the nature of such a fruit; **pseudo'spherical** *a. Geom.*, being or pertaining to a surface or space whose curvature is everywhere equal and negative; hence **'pseudo'sphere**, the pseudospherical surface that is generated by rotating a tractrix about its asymptote; **pseudo-'spiracle** *Zool.*, a structure or marking in certain insects and arachnidans, resembling a spiracle but not perforated; ‖ **pseudospo'rangium** (also anglicized **-spo'range**) *Bot.*, an organ resembling a sporangium, but producing gemmæ instead of spores; **'pseudospore** *Bot.*, (*a*) a peculiar spore in certain parasitic fungi, also called a TELEUTOSPORE; (*b*) a reproductive bud: = GEMMA 2b; **pseudo'squamate** *a. Zool.*, apparently but not really squamate or scaly; **'pseudo-squeeze** *Bridge*, play whereby an opponent is, or may be, misled into discarding or unguarding a potentially winning card, although he has alternative discards; cf. SQUEEZE *sb.*; ˌ**pseudo-stalac'titical** *a.*, simulating a stalactite; **'pseudo-statement**, an expression that formally resembles a statement but does not refer or correspond to an objective fact, being rather used for its subjective effect on the hearer or reader; **'pseudostem**, the apparent trunk of a banana plant or a closely related species, which is made up of closely packed leaf sheaths enclosing a stem; **pseudo'stereoscope**, a binocular microscope in which inversion of the image is not corrected; hence ˌ**pseudo-stereo'scopic** *a.*, ˌ**pseudostere'oscopism**; ‖ **pseudo'stigma** *Zool.* (pl. **-ata**), each of two respiratory organs resembling stigmata in certain acarids; hence **pseudostig'matic** *a.*; ˌ**pseudostratifi'cation** *Geol.* = *pseudobedding* above; ‖ **pseudo'stratum** *Geol.* (pl. **-a**), a mass of rock resembling a stratum but not produced by deposition; **pseudo'symmetry** *Cryst.*, simulation of higher symmetry, as in certain composite crystals; **pseudo-syphilis** (-'sɪfɪlɪs) *Path.*, a disease simulating syphilis; hence ˌ**pseudo-syphi'litic** *a.*; **pseudo'tachylyte, -ite** *Petrogr.*, a dark glassy rock resembling tachylyte that results from vitrification by frictional heat generated during dynamic metamorphism; **pseudo-te'tragonal** *a. Cryst.*, said of a composite crystal of lower symmetry simulating a simple one of the tetragonal system; ˌ**pseudote'tramerous** *a. Entom.* [see TETRAMEROUS], belonging to the division *Pseudotetramera* of beetles, having tarsi apparently four-jointed, a fifth joint being very small and hidden; **'pseudotill** *Geol.*, a deposit similar to a till but non-glacial in origin; **pseudo'tillite** *Geol.* [ad. G. *pseudotillit* (M. Schwarzbach *Das Klima der Vorzeit* (ed. 2, 1961) v. 34], a deposit similar to tillite but non-glacial in origin; **pseudo-'trachea** *Ent.*, a fine food-channel in the mouthparts of many flies; also, an organ found in certain woodlice which resembles an insect trachea; **pseudotra'cheal** *a. Entom.*, simulating a trachea; having a series of rings like those of the trachea; **pseudo'trimerous** *a. Entom.* [see TRIMEROUS], belonging to the division *Pseudotrimera* of beetles, having the tarsi apparently three-jointed, one of the four joints being very small and hidden; ˌ**pseudotubercu'losis** *Vet. Sci.* [mod.L., coined in Ger. as the specific epithet of the *Pasteurella* species causing the disease (A. Pfeiffer *Ueber die bacilläre Pseudotuberculose bei Nagethieren* (1889) 5)], any of several diseases clinically and anatomically similar to tuberculosis that occur chiefly in rodents, birds, and warm-blooded animals, esp. sheep, and are caused by species of *Pasteurella* or *Corynebacterium*; **pseudotu'berculous** *a.*, resembling (that of) tuberculosis; **'pseudo-'tumour** *Path.*, a swelling or other condition that gives rise to the clinical signs of a neoplasm but is not neoplastic, i.e. is not characterized by the persistent proliferation of cells having no physiological function; **pseudo-uni'septate** *a. Nat. Hist.*, apparently but not really uniseptate; **pseudo'uracil** *Biochem.*, the uracil residue in pseudouridine; **pseudo-'uric** *a. Chem.*, an organic acid, $C_5H_6N_4O_4$, in composition allied to uric acid; hence **pseudo-'urate**, a salt of pseudo-uric acid; **pseudo'uridine** *Biochem.*, a nucleoside, 5-ribosyluracil, found in transfer RNA and differing from uridine in that the sugar residue is attached to the base at a carbon rather than a nitrogen atom; **pseudo-'velum** *Zool.*, a kind of velum in some *Scyphomedusæ*, distinct from the true velum of the *Hydromedusæ*; hence **pseudo-'velar** *a.*; **pseudo'viperine** *a. Zool.*, resembling a viper but not venomous; belonging to the group *Pseudoviperæ* or *Acrochordidæ* of serpents, called in English 'wart-snakes'; **pseudo-vis'cosity**, a property of some solids resembling viscosity; plasticity; **'pseudovitamin** *Biochem.*, a compound that is not a vitamin but closely resembles some particular vitamin in molecular structure; **pseudovi'tellus** *Ent.* = MYCETOME; **pseudo-vol'canic** *a.*, apparently but not properly volcanic; belonging to or produced by a pseudo-volcano; **pseudo-vol'cano**, a burning mountain that emits smoke, flame, or gases, but no lava; **pseudo'wavellite** *Min.* [ad. G. *pseudo-wavellit* (F. Henrich, after Laubmann, 1922, in *Ber. d. Deut. Chem. Ges.* LVB. 3016)], a hydrated basic phosphate of calcium and aluminium, $CaAl_3(PO_4)_2(OH)_5.H_2O$, found as white, grey, or yellow crystals (see quot. 1951); **'pseudo-**ˌ**whorl** *Bot.*, an apparent whorl produced by displacement of leaves or other members, originally arranged spirally, to the same level around the axis; **pseudo'wollastonite** *Min.* [a. F. *pseudowollastonite* (A. Lacroix *Minéral. de la France* (1893–5) I. 624)], the high-temperature form of the calcium silicate $CaSiO_3$, which normally changes to wollastonite at ordinary temperatures; **pseudoxanthine** (-'zænθi:n) *Chem.*, a leucomaine resembling xanthine, occurring in muscular tissue; **pseudoxan'thoma (e'lasticum)** *Path.* [mod.L., coined in Ger. (J. F. Darier 1896, in *Monatschr. für prakt. Dermatol.* XXIII. 616): cf. XANTHOMA], a congenital disease in which there is widespread disturbance of connective tissue formation, leading to soft, yellowish papules and plaques in the skin, cardiovascular disorder, and ultimately death.

[**1875** H. C. WOOD *Therap.* (1879) 171 Böhm and Ewens have physiologically studied the alkaloid of Aconitum ferox under the name of *pseudaconitia*.] **1876** HARLEY *Mat. Med.* (ed. 6) 777 The variety of aconitia obtained from this plant has been very improperly termed *pseud-aconitine or pseud-aconitia. **1842** DUNGLISON *Med. Lex.*, **Pseudæsthesia*. **1855** J. R. REYNOLDS *Dis. Brain* viii, Pseudaesthesiae are common. **1872** NICHOLSON *Palæont.* 133 Each *pseud-ambulacrum is furrowed by a longitudinal groove. **1880** W. S. KENT *Infusoria* I. iii. 57 [These] can revert at will to a *pseud-amœboid and repent state. **1928** H. M. PAULL *Literary Ethics* xvii. 189 All sorts of devices are adopted by the author, who does not wish his name to be known. He may.. disguise it in various ways, using initials, asterisks, a reversed name, or one of the opposite sex,.. respectively initialism, asterism, boustrophedon and *pseudandry. **1961** T. LANDAU *Encycl. Librarianship* (ed. 2) 294/1 *Pseudandry*, a woman author writing under a masculine pseudonym. **1890** POULTON *Colours Anim.* xvii. 337 *Pseudaposematic colours.. are special.. instances of Procryptic colours.. and deceptively resemble Aposematic colours. **1835** KIRBY *Hab. & Inst. Anim.* II. xix. 302 *Pseudarachnidan Condylopes. This Class, which is formed from the Tracheary Arachnidans of Latreille, differs from the preceding principally in the organs of Respiration and Circulation. *Ibid.* 303 The most remarkable genus of the second Order of Pseudarachnidans is one described in the Linnean Transactions in which the posterior legs exhibit a raptorious character. **1842** DUNGLISON *Med. Lex.*, **Pseudarthrosis*. **1876** tr. *Wagner's Gen. Pathol.* (ed. 6) 290 Extremities of bones in stumps after amputation diminish in pseudarthrosis. **1899** *Allbutt's Syst. Med.* VII. 388 There were motor disorders.. at first *pseudataxic. **1877** A. H. GARROD in *Proc. Zool. Soc.* 18 *Dama vulgaris* [etc.].. are intimately allied to the *Pseud-axine group. **1875** BENNETT & DYER *Sachs' Bot.* 157 The apparent primary shoot, which in fact consists of the bases of consecutive bifurcations, may .. be termed a *Pseud-axis or Sympodium. *Ibid.* 158 Two principal forms of Cyme may be distinguished, according as a Pseud-axis.. is formed or not. **1767** HUNTER in *Phil. Trans.* LVIII. 38 A *pseud-elephant, or *animal incognitum*. **1890** *Cent. Dict.* cites COUES. **1866** COBBOLD *Tapeworms* Introd. 9 Sometimes these *pseudelminths are really so worm-like that a mere naked eye examination is insufficient to determine their nature. **1826** KIRBY & SP. *Entomol.* IV. xlvii. 370 *Pseud-elytra twisted, attached to the anterior leg. **1840** WESTWOOD *Classif. Insects* II. 294 *note*, The pseudelytra [Mr. Newman] considers as analogous to the tippets of the Lepidoptera. **1877** *Pseud-embryo [see *pseudoproct* below]. **1880** W. S. KENT *Infusoria* I. 191 The coalescing amœbiform zooids.. form by repeated segmentation a pseud-embryo, or so-called ciliated larva. **1883** W. F. R. WELDON in *Proc. Zool. Soc.* 640 In all the Anatidæ.. the representative of the horizontal septum is attached to the ventral abdominal wall,.. so that it does not cover any of the intestine coils. *Note.* This septum has been mentioned by various authors... From its resemblance to a modified Mammalian mesentery, I would propose to call it '**pseudepiploön*'. **1890** POULTON *Colours Anim.* xvii. 337 *Pseudepisematic colours.. are special instances of Anticryptic colours.., and may depend for success upon the deceptive resemblance to Episematic colours. **1957** RICHARDS & DAVIES *Imms's Gen. Textbk. Entomol.* (ed. 9) III. 380 *Pseudergates occur in *Zootermopsis* and.. the so-called workers of *Mastotermes* are probably also of this form. **1969** R. F. CHAPMAN *Insects* xxxiv. 706 The pseudergate is a central form from which various others can be derived. **1979** R. M. ALEXANDER *Invertebrates* xix. 436 Pseudergates also remove the eggs as the queen lays them. **1867** J. HOGG *Microsc.* II. iii. 562 In the Hirudinidae.. a system of vessels homologous with the *pseud-haemal system exists. **1877** HUXLEY *Anat. Inv. Anim.* i. 57 In the Arthropoda no segmental organs or pseud-haemal vessels are known. **1840** WESTWOOD *Classif. Insects* II. 292 These organs have been termed prébalanciers, præhalteres, *pseudhalteres, pseudelytra, or anterior wings. **1836–9** *Todd's Cycl. Anat.* II. 880/2 The condition of the insect previously to this change [i.e. after throwing off the pupa-covering, but before ridding themselves of the delicate enveloping membrane] has been called by Mr. Curtis the *pseudimago state. **1867** F. FRANCIS *Angling* vi. (1880) 195 It is only a half complete insect, and is termed the *pseud-imago*, or false image. **1775** A. BURNABY *Trav. N. Amer.* 69 It produces.. the *pseudo-acacia, or locust-tree. **1903** *Daily Chron.* 19 May 7/1 The acacia to be tried is.. the pseudo-acacia introduced from North America, where it is called the locust tree. **1899** *Jrnl. Chem. Soc.* LXXVI. I. 399 The author [*sc.* Hantzsch] describes as *pseudo-acids those substances which do not contain a hydrogen atom directly displaceable by metals, but which are capable of changing into a salt-forming isomeride. **1910** [see *pseudo-acidity* below]. **1929** P. WALDEN *Salts, Acids, & Bases* v. 127 In the homogeneous condition pseudo-acids are associated, usually in the dimolecular form. The carboxylic acids are typical pseudo-acids. **1952** TURNER & HARRIS *Org. Chem.* ix. 135 Primary and secondary nitroparaffins are pseudo-acids, dissolving in aqueous alkali.. to give the ions of the *aci*-nitroparaffin or true (nitronic) acid. **1953** C. K. INGOLD *Struct. & Mechanism in Org. Chem.* x. 576 The pseudo-basic carbinol corresponds to the *pseudo-acidic phenylnitromethane. **1910** N. V. SIDGWICK *Org. Chem. Nitrogen* vii. 144 The nitroparaffins are typical instances of pseudo-acids. In fact it was in this connexion that Hantzsch developed the theory of *pseudo-acidity. **1927** Pseudo-acidity [see *pseudo-basicity* below]. **1887** A. M. BROWN *Anim. Alkaloids* 5 They might be some *pseudo-alkaloid.., such as kreatine or kreatinine, amides rather than alkalies. **1899** *Allbutt's Syst. Med.* VII. 666 In *pseudo-apoplectic attacks the application of cold to the head, blistering [etc.].. are the best remedial measures. **1852** DANA *Crust.* II. 1204 Possibly the last transverse *pseudo-articulation is incorrectly so considered. **1907** J. B. COHEN *Org. Chem.* ii. 93 *Pseudo-asymmetry of the character of the trihydroxyglutaric acids.. is afforded by cyclo-propane derivatives. *Ibid.* 94 The cyclic carbon atoms 2 and 4 are asymmetrical *per se*; 3 is symmetrical though structurally identical with 2 and 4. It follows.. that 1 and 3 are *pseudo-asymmetric. **1962** E. L. ELIEL *Stereochem. Carbon Compounds* iii. 28 Such a pseudoasymmetric atom does not give rise to dissymmetry in the molecule as a whole. **1975** *Nature* 13 Nov. 96/3 Some of these ideas have now appeared in a very general paper.. which was followed by two detailed papers on compounds showing axes and planes of pseudo-asymmetry. **1899** CAGNEY *Jaksch's Clin. Diagn.* ii. (ed. 4) 105 In diphtheria the *pseudo-bacillus appears less frequently. **1884** *Science* 13 June 739 *Pseudobacteria were produced by the heating of blood. **1899** *Jrnl. Chem. Soc.* LXXVI. I. 400 *Pseudo-bases are substances which, by isomeric change, are capable of giving a true base of the ammonium hydroxide type from which the salts are derived. **1951** C. R. NOLLER *Chem. Org. Compounds* xxx. 591 The *N*-alkyl-α-pyridones are obtained by the oxidation of the quaternary hydroxides. These strong bases appear to be in equilibrium with the α-hydroxydihydropyridines, which are called pseudo bases. **1960** K. W. BENTLEY *Natural Pigments* i. 14 The α- and γ-pyranols are, in fact, pseudo bases, forming a salt and water on treatment with acid. **1921** *Jrnl. Chem. Soc.* CXIX. 1470 One of the more characteristic reactions of *pseudo-basic carbinols is the formation of ethers by simple treatment with alcohols. **1927** *Ann. Rep. Progr. Chem.* XXIV. 115 In the same way that in mobile cation tautomerism the hydrogen ion forms a more or less stable covalent link with (negative) carbon, whereas the sodium ion tends to remain in the electro-valent state (thus giving rise to the phenomena of pseudo-acidity), so.. the hydroxide ion tends to co-ordinate with positive carbon, whereas very stable anions like chloride.. tend to retain their ionic condition..: thus arises the phenomenon of *pseudo-basicity. **1850** D. T. ANSTED *Elem. Course Geol., Mineral., & Physical Geogr.* 579/1 (Index), *Pseudo-bedding. **1893** *Q. Jrnl. Geol. Soc.* XLIX. 395 Cracks, small at first, have little by little grown into deep joints, and so the pseudo-bedding has been gradually produced. **1939** *Jrnl. Geol.* XLVII. 72 The result of this nonuniformity in distribution of sand is that a type of pseudobedding is developed by concentration or combining of laminae representing the approach slopes of the ripple deposits. **1970** R. J. SMALL *Study of Landforms* xi. 365 Many of the polished surfaces observable in glaciated valleys represent pseudo-bedding planes which have been revealed by removal of overlying sheets of rock by a quite different mechanism. **1799** HOOPER *Med. Dict.*, **Pseudoblepsis*. **1842** DUNGLISON *Med. Lex.*, *Pseudoblepsia*, a generic name, used by Cullen, for perversion of vision. **1890** BILLINGS *Nat. Med. Dict.*, *Pseudoblepsia*, false vision; hallucination of sight. **1897** *Mineral. Mag.* XI. 333 *Pseudo-boleite... Between boleite and cumengeite. Boleo, Lower California. **1951** C. PALACHE et al. *Dana's Syst. Mineral.* (ed. 7) II. x. 81 Pseudoboleite and boleite have been considered to be identical but the evidence favors the individual character and tetragonal symmetry of the former species. **1964** *Mineral. Abstr.* XVI. 457/2 The mineralogy of the metalliferous areas of Iran is systematically described. Rarer species include.. pseudoboléite. **1884** *Stand. Nat. Hist.* (1888) III. 43 This gill is not functional—it receives only already aërated blood, and is therefore known as a false gill or *pseudobranch. **1871** HUXLEY *Anat. Vertebr. Anim.* iii. 161 A *rete mirabile*, which lies in the inner side of the hyomandibular bone, and sometimes has the form of a gill. This is the **pseudobranchia*. **1875** C. C. BLAKE *Zool.* 205 An accessory organ in the form of an opercular gill,.. different from a *pseudobranchium. **1878** *Amer. Jrnl. Sc.* Ser. III. XVI. 398 *Pseudobrookite. Occurs in minute tabular crystals. **1832** LINDLEY *Introd. Bot.* 58 The *Pseudobulb is an enlarged aerial stem, resembling a tuber, from which it scarcely differs. **1840** *Penny Cycl.* XVI. 477/2 By degrees large masses of pseudo-bulbs are formed by a single individual. **1890** W. WATSON *Orchids* ii. 18 Usually only one pseudo-bulb is developed at the apex or growing point of each rhizome yearly. **1934** R. STOUT *Fer-de-Lance* xvii. 292 Check.. the shipment of pseudo-bulbs. **1959** T. B. MORRIS *Death among Orchids* x. 77 Fat pseudo-bulbs and leaves had been torn and bruised by the fall. **1979** B. & W. RITTERSHAUSEN *Orchids in Colour* 14 The plants [*sc.* cymbidiums] produce a number of well rounded pseudo bulbs. **1840** *Penny Cycl.* XVI. 477/2 (Orchidaceæ) Some of the species of Dendrobium are remarkable for having the *pseudo-bulbous form at one end of their stem, and the common state at the other. **1845** *Florist's Jrnl.* 19 *Oncidium pubes*. A pretty little pseudo-bulbous plant; bulbs 2 inches long. **1901** L. H. BAILEY *Cycl. Amer. Hort.* III. 1166/2 The pseudo-bulbous species.. should be hosed over thoroughly. **1976** *Hortus Third* (L. H. Bailey Hortorium) 798/2 The rhizomes of such pseudobulbous genera, when well grown, regularly develop one or more new pseudobulbs each season. **1860** COBBOLD in *Proc. Zool. Soc.* 105 The existence [in the giraffe] of *pseudoceratophorous epiphyses permanently invested by a hairy integument. **1888** ROLLESTON & JACKSON *Anim. Life* 861 (Gregarinida) A 'pseudo-filaria' stage, followed by a '*pseudocercaria' stage, i.e. one with a slender tail and large body like a *Cercaria*. **1943** MENDEL & RUDNEY in *Biochem. Jrnl.* XXXVII. 59/1 It is the purpose of this paper to show that there exist in the animal body two esterases capable of hydrolysing acetylcholine: a true cholinesterase acting exclusively on choline esters, and a non-specific enzyme, which hydrolyses not only esters of choline but a variety of non-choline esters as well. Moreover, experiments with both enzymes at high and low concentrations of acetyl-choline, have revealed a decisive difference between the two esterases, calling for a sharp distinction of the true cholinesterase from the non-specific enzyme, for which we venture to suggest the name *pseudo-cholinesterase. **1974** M. C. GERALD *Pharmacol.* iii. 52 Alcohol.. and the skeletal muscle relaxant succinylcholine are broken down by the enzymes alcohol dehydrogenase and pseudo-cholinesterase, respectively. **1683** T. SMITH *Acc. Prusa* in *Misc. Cur.* (1708) III. 61 Mahomet.. in his Alcoran.. is guilty of vile and absurd *Pseudo-chronismes. **1728** MORGAN *Algiers* I. iii. 63 Some will needs be such *Pseudo-Chronologists, that they make those three Pastors to have flourished.. more than 400 years later. **1879** RUTLEY *Study Rocks* xi. 187 *Pseudo-chrysolite ..occurs as rounded pebbles in sand. **1900**, **1940** *Pseudocirrhosis [see PICK'S DISEASE 1]. **1953** *Proc. IRE* XLI. 1252/1 Problems are submitted to the computer expressed in *pseudo code. An 'interpretive' routine then decodes the input information and calls the subroutines into play as required. **1954**, **1958** [see INTERPRETER 5 b]. **1959** M. H. WRUBEL *Primer of Programming for Digital Computers* ii. 24 Pseudo-codes are often easier to learn than the machine language; only a single pseudo-code instruction is needed to generate frequently used functions such as square root.. and log *x*. **1969** J. E. SAMMET *Programming Languages* iv. 129 The early compiling work done in the United States by Dr. Grace Hopper initially involved very artificial pseudo-codes rather than mathematical notation. **1979** *Personal Computer World* Nov. 61/2 Some [programmers] use pseudocode, a written problem definition language that looks like PL/1 or Pascal. **1887** A. SEDGWICK in *Jrnl. Microsc. Sc.* Mar. 491 The adult body cavity [in the Cape species of Peripatus] comes entirely from *pseudocœle; the enterocœle has no part in its formation. This statement applies also to the heart and pericardium. These are both *pseudocœlic, and have nothing to do with enterocœle. **1889** *Buck's Handbk. Med. Sc.* VIII. 136/1 Three kinds of surfaces.. viz.: entocœlian, lined by endyma; ectocœlian, covered by pia; and *pseudocœlian, with no distinct membrane. **1890** *Cent. Dict.*, *Pseudocœlom*. **1895** *Syd. Soc. Lex.*, *Pseudocœlom*,.. false cœlom. One of the interstitial spaces found in certain of the *Invertebrata*, not lined with epithelium. **1888** *Q. Jrnl. Geol. Soc.* XLIV. 210 The more prominent septa extend to the centre of the corallite, and then either unite.. or curve round each other.. forming a structure to which the name of *pseudocolumella has been given. **1890** *Cent. Dict.*, **Pseudocolumellar*. **1895** in *Syd. Soc. Lex.* [**1882** WILDER & GAGE *Anat. Techn.* 420 In the frog.. [the lobes] are united by connective tissue constituting a **pseudo-commissura*.] **1943** *Nature* 16 Jan. 70/1 *N*[*icotiana*] *Forgetiana* and *N. alama* show pseudo-compatibility only in exceptional circumstances, that is, the actions of the various allelomorphs of the switch gene are always distinctive... *Pseudo-compatibility marks the breakdown of the distinction between the types produced by the *S* [*sc.* sterility] allelomorphs. **1977** *Jrnl. Hort. Sci.* LII. 475 Pseudocompatibility was maximized by pollinating old flowers with large quantities of pollen. **1878** BELL *Gegenbaur's Comp. Anat.* 547 This *pseudo-concha separates the vestibule of the nose from the internal nasal cavity. **1888** ROLLESTON & JACKSON *Anim. Life* 502 The *pseudocone eyes of *Diptera Brachyura*. **1896** C. R. VAN HISE in *16th Ann. Rep. U.S. Geol. Survey* I. 679 The autoclastic rocks which readily show their origin may be called dynamic breccias, and those which resemble ordinary conglomerates may be called *pseudo-conglomerates. **1957** F. J. PETTIJOHN *Sedimentary Rocks* (ed. 2) viii. 367 (*caption*) Brecciated siltstone... Brecciation was contemporaneous with sedimentation; a pseudoconglomerate. **1972** *Gloss. Geol.* (Amer. Geol. Inst.) 574/1 *Pseudoconglomerate*, a rock that resembles, or may easily be mistaken for, a true or normal (sedimentary) conglomerate; e.g... a sandstone packed with many rounded concretionary bodies, or an aggregate of rounded boulders produced in place by spheroidal weathering and surrounded by clayey material. **1888** *Q. Jrnl. Geol. Soc.* XLIV. 213 *note*, The flattened or rounded interspaces between the septa of these corals, which stand out slightly in relief, are generally termed **pseudo-costæ*. **1889** J. L. LOBLEY *Mount Vesuvius* x. 313 *Pseudocotunnite... Chloride of Lead with Chloride of Potassium... This mineral, which has the composition of a combination of Cotunnite and Sylvine, was obtained from the sublimations of the crater of Vesuvius following the great eruption of 1872. **1933** *Mineral. Abstr.* V. 269 New records of minerals from Vesuvius are thenardite, pseudocotunnite,.. and hieratite. **1830** LINDLEY *Nat. Syst. Bot.* 308 What green have we in Mosses or Ferns, or other *Pseudocotyledonæ, more intense than in Ulva? **1890** *Cent. Dict.*, **Pseudocrisis*. **1895** *Syd. Soc. Lex.*, *Pseudo-crisis*, an apparent crisis occurring in the course of acute lobar pneumonia, consisting in a temporary fall of 2° F to 7° F., with a subsequent rebound. **1895** STORY-MASKELYNE *Crystallogr.* vi. § 166 Complicated structures in which twelve orthorhombic crystals are united into a single *pseudo-cubic combination. **1881** *Nature* 24 Feb. 398/2 The isometry of radiate *pseudocubical groups. **1881** WATTS *Dict. Chem.* VIII. 1282 **Pseudocumene*. **1885** REMSEN *Org. Chem.* (1888) 249 Pseudocumene has been made synthetically from brom-para-xylene and methyl iodide. **1817** J. M. GOOD *Physiol. System Nosology* v. iii. 415 *Pseudocyesis. Symptoms of pregnancy without impregnation... Spurious Pregnancy. **1859** *Med. Times & Gaz.* 3 Sept. 225/1 There are two varieties of pseudo-cyesis or spurious pregnancy, a *local* and a *constitutional*. **1950** H. B. FRIEDGOOD in R. H. Williams *Textbk. Endocrinol.* x. 657 The sensation of fetal movements is reported usually during the fourth or fifth months of pseudocyesis and seems to be caused by intermittent contractions of the abdominal musculature. **1975** S. L. ROMNEY et al. *Gynecol. & Obstetr.* x. 152/2 Special forms of psychogenic amenorrhea include pseudocyesis or false pregnancy.. and anorexia nervosa. **1980** *Daily Tel.* 15 Mar. 3/3 Pseudocyesis, or spurious or phantom pregnancy as it is variously known is a psychological disorder in which a woman has the false but fixed belief that she is pregnant. It is a not uncommon condition, often around the menopause. **1882** *Encycl. Brit.* XIV. 554/1 They [*sc.* cyphellæ] are generally naked, but are often also pulverulent or sorediiferous, in which latter case they are called *pseudo-cyphellæ. **1964** *Oxf. Bk. Flowerless Plants* 64/1 The inner layers of the plant [sc. *Pseudocyphellaria crocata*].. show as conspicuous spots through small holes (pseudocyphellae) scattered over the lower surface. **1976** M. E. HALE in D. H. Brown et al. *Lichenology* i. 6 They [*sc.* foliose and fruticose lichens] have pores, pseudocyphellae or cyphellae, for gas exchange. **1888** ROLLESTON & JACKSON *Anim. Life* 860 (*Gregarinida*) The protoplasm not used up [for sporoblasts].. in *Stylorhynchus* ..collects into a central spherical mass, the *pseudocyst. **1897** *Allbutt's Syst. Med.* III. 648 The density of the walls of these pseudo-cysts and their very restricted vascularity doubtless explains this retention. **1862** Dana *Man. Geol.* 180 A triangular prominence called a *pseudo-deltidium. **1895** *Cambr. Nat. Hist.* III. 498 This pseudo-deltidium is a primitive character, and arises in an early stage of the development. **1849** Dana *Geol.* xvii. (1850) 655 Another small *pseudo-dike, six inches wide. **1895** *Syd. Soc. Lex.*, **Pseudo-diphtheria*, term for membranous pharyngitis or tonsillitis closely resembling diphtheria in its symptoms. **1899** Cagney *Jaksch's Clin. Diagn.* ii. (ed. 4) 105 A micro-organism..named the pseudo-diphtheria-bacillus. **1895** S. T. Armstrong in *Pop. Sci. Monthly* Feb. 515 The difficulty of distinguishing..the diphtheritic from the *pseudo-diphtheritic inflammation. **1930** *Amer. Naturalist* LXIV. 561 An actual loss or inactivation of chromatin material, leading to exaggeration and *pseudo-dominance. **1938** *Yearbk. Carnegie Inst.* XXXVII. 306 The 'Minute' effect is lethal when homozygous..and gives pseudo-dominance to straw in hybrids. **1969** W. D. Stansfield *Schaum's Outl. Theory & Probl. Genetics* viii. 157 When an organism heterozygous for a pair of alleles, *A* and *a*, loses a small portion of the chromosome bearing the dominant allele, the recessive allele on the other chromosome will become expressed phenotypically. This is called pseudodominance, but it is a misnomer because the condition is hemizygous rather than dizygous at this locus. **1965** *Science* 26 Nov. 1123/3 This *pseudodominant expression of *fa* can be understood by considering *N* as a deficiency for salivary band 3C7, wherein lies the wild-type allele of *fa*; the facet phenotype is expressed because the wild-type allele is missing. **1975** J. B. Jenkins *Genetics* iv. 165 The white-eye mutant allele was pseudodominant in deletions numbered 258-11..and 264-31. **1896** W. Caldwell *Schopenhauer's System* iii. 149 A *pseudo-entity..like 'mere matter' or a mere Epicurean god in the interstellar spaces. **1912** *Mind* XXI. 214 'Matter' is..a pseudentity. **1937** B. Russell *Princ. Math.* (ed. 2) p. xi, I do not mean that statements apparently about points or instants or numbers, or any of the other entities which Occam's razor abolishes, are false, but only that they need interpretation which shows that their linguistic form is misleading, and that, when they are rightly analysed, the pseudo-entities in question are found to be not mentioned in them. **1944** M. Black in P. A. Schilpp *Philos. B. Russell* 231 Vocabulary, by promoting the hypostatization of pseudo-entities, encourages false beliefs concerning the *contents* of the world. **1956** J. Holloway in A. Pryce-Jones *New Outl. Mod. Knowl.* 31 Metaphysical jargon could be abandoned once for all, and so could all pretended references to pseudo-entities which could never conceivably be observed. **1895** *Syd. Soc. Lex.*, **Pseudo-erysipelas*... An inexact term for conditions resembling erysipelas. **1876** tr. *Wagner's Gen. Pathol.* (ed. 6) 340 In so-called phlegmonous, or *pseudo-erysipelatous inflammations. **1838** T. Thomson *Chem. Org. Bodies* 403 This substance is the result of the action of boiling alcohol on erythrin... Heeren has distinguished it by the name of **pseudo-erythrin*. **1904** B. Russell in *Mind* XIII. 207 What is called the existence of an object in presentation is not really existence at all: it may be called *pseudo-existence. **1934** *Mind* XLIII. 375 Confronted with Meinong's obscure and tentative utterances about immanence and pseudo-existence, Mr. Russell reasonably protested. **1953** *Phil. Trans. R. Soc.* B. CCXXXVII. 360 The *pseudofaecal strings are conveyed to the end of the waste canals and so into the angle between the inner lobe of the mantle edge and the ctenidial membrane.., above which they are caught in the exhalant current and carried away. **1967** J. H. Day in G. H. Lauff *Estuaries* 401/2 It feeds at low tide levels, spooning up the surface silt with its chelae, sucking out the detritus, and discarding the silt as pseudo-fecal pellets. **1975** *Jrnl. Marine Biol. & Ecol.* XVII. 4 Since filtration rate and pseudofaecal production determine the amounts of material ingested they are important in studying the efficiency with which bivalves control their rates of ingestion. **1936** *Q. Jrnl. Microsc. Sci.* LXXIX. 207 It was mostly through this aperture ventral to the siphons that collections from the mantle (*pseudo-faeces) were expelled on sudden closure of the valves. **1976** B. L. Bayne et al. in *Marine Mussels* v. 145 All material to be removed is transferred to the rejection tracts of the mantle edge. These tracts convey the material to the posterior margin of the inhalant siphon, adjacent to the exhalant opening, where it is deposited as pseudofaeces and is carried away by the exhalant current. **1877** Huxley *Anat. Inv. Anim.* ii. 94 The *pseudo-filaria passes into the condition of the adult Gregarina. **18..** Underwood in *Bulletin Illinois State Lab.* II. 6 *Pseudo-foliaceous forms, in which the thallus is lobed, the lobes assuming leaf-like forms. **1937** *Mind* XLVI. 252 A patient suffering from hemianopia developed a '*pseudo-fovea' in the sound halves of his eyes. **1967** Lyle & Wybar *Lyle & Jackson's Pract. Orthoptics in Treatm. of Squint* (ed. 5) ix. 208 The definition of the image (visual acuity) at the 'pseudo-fovea' will be less clear than at the 'suppressed' fovea. **1946** N. A. Stutterheim *Squint & Convergence* xii. 37 The technique is ..to have the non-squinting eye occluded in order to encourage the true fovea and to discourage *pseudo-foveal inclinations. **1930** *Amer. Jrnl. Roentgenol.* XXIV. 31/1 Fromme considers the point of involvement of those spontaneous *pseudofractures to be about 1 inch below the epiphyseal line. **1950** Shank & Kerley *Textbk. X-Ray Diagnosis* (ed. 2) xi. 136 Pseudo-fractures or *umbauzonen* are always associated with systemic disease or malacic processes, such as Paget's diseases, adolescent rickets.., fibrous dysplasia and osteomalacia. **1976** Gordan & Vaughan *Clin. Managem. Osteoporoses* vii. 80 The pathognomonic x-ray finding of osteomalacia is the presence of bilateral symmetrical pseudofractures, described by Looser in 1920 and therefore often called Looser zones. **1887** H. M. Ward tr. *Sachs' Physiol. Plants* xxviii. 464 The Fig..is a so-called *pseudo-fruit. **1796** Kirwan *Elem. Min.* (ed. 2) II. 242 As it has much the aspect of Galena, and yet contains little or no lead, it has been called *Pseudo Galena. **1888** Rolleston & Jackson *Anim. Life* 791 (Porifera) Such fusion frequently leads to the enclosure of spaces really external to the sponge-body, which form a false gastric cavity (*pseudogaster) opening by a false osculum (pseudosculum s. pseudostome) and false pores (pseudopores). **1888** Sclater in *Q. Jrnl. Microsc. Sc.* Feb. 349 The outer layer of the *pseudogastrula forms in later stages the wall of the embryonic vesicle. **1977** C. Jacq et al. in *Cell* XII. 109/1 The 5S DNA of Xenopus laevis, coding for oocyte-type 5S RNA, consists of many copies of a tandemly repeated unit of about 700 base pairs. Each unit contains a '*pseudogene' in addition to the gene. The pseudogene has been partly sequenced and appears to be an almost perfect repeat of 101 residues of the gene. *Ibid.* 109/2 This homologous structure was nearly as long as, and almost an exact repeat of, the gene itself; hence the name—pseudogene. **1978** *Nature* 19 Jan. 205/2 The GC-rich region of 5S DNA also contains a pseudogene which is identical to the first 101 base pairs of the gene at all but 10 sites. **1882** J. M. Crombie in *Encycl. Brit.* XIV. 557/2 They occur only in a gonidial or rudimentary state, constituting the *pseudo-genus *Lepraria* of the older botanists. **1855** Dunglison *Med. Lex.*, **Pseudogeusia*, false taste. **1857** *Ibid.*, **Pseudogeustia*, pseudogeusia. **1953** W. L. Kubiëna *Soils of Europe* 242 The modification of 'gley-like soil' to **pseudogley* has been made here to make it conform to the rules of nomenclature, whereby the type designation should be expressed by a noun. *Ibid.* 244 In typical pseudogley the concretions are extremely numerous and are readily visible to the naked eye. **1965** B. T. Bunting *Geogr. of Soil* xiv. 163 Soils on elevated sites on clayey parent materials develop the mottling typical of gleization at some depth beneath a dark brown, granular or blocky structured surface horizon. Such soils have been termed pseudogleys. **1973** J. Mulqueen in Schlichting & Schwertmann *Pseudogley & Gley* 713 The pseudogley soils at Ballinamore are stratified into essentially two layers. **1884** H. R. Swanzy *Handbk. Dis. Eye* xvii. 307 Purulent inflammation of the vitreous humour (to which unfortunately the name *pseudo-glioma is sometimes applied). **1946** Berens & Zuckerman *Diagnostic Exam. Eye* ix. 258 In children retinoblastoma (glioma) should be differentiated from an abscess of the vitreous (pseudoglioma). **1962** *New Scientist* 5 Apr. 801/1 Ophthalmologists had been used to examining babies with an abnormal mass of organized tissue behind the lens of the eye, and the non-committal and portmanteau term of 'pseudoglioma' had served as a diagnosis in many of their cases. **1905** *Jrnl. Physiol.* XXXII. 329 A portion of the globulin solution was dialysed... The euglobulin which fell out was removed... The fluid remaining after dialysis contained the *pseudo-globulin. **1964** W. G. Smith *Allergy & Tissue Metabolism* vi. 69 Bradykinin is present in normal blood as an inactive precursor, bradykininogen, which is a component of the pseudoglobulin fraction of plasma. **1962** D. J. McCarty et al. in *Ann. Internal Med.* LVI. 711 (*heading*) The significance of calcium phosphate crystals in the synovial fluid of arthritic patients: the '*pseudogout syndrome'. *Ibid.* 712/1 It is suggested that these patients represent a discrete type of arthritis, labeled 'pseudo-gout' because in some respects it resembles classical gouty arthritis. **1972** *Daily Colonist* (Victoria, B.C.) 2 Mar. 2/2 Pseudo-gout is an attack that resembles an attack of gout, in that it strikes at a joint (usually the knee) with dramatic suddenness and with just as severe pain. **1975** *Amer. Jrnl. Roentgenol.* CXXIII. 532/1 Acute attacks of pseudogout have occurred following surgery, trauma, and injection of mercurial diuretics. **1884** *Nature* 15 May 69/1 The solitary egg of the female [aphis]..develops into a gall-making aphis, the foundress *pseudogyne. This produces..winged young (emigrant pseudogynes). **1851** *Zoologist* IX. p. cxlii, This class of phenomena might be called *Pseudogynous, that is, falsely or imperfectly female. **1903** *Jrnl. R. Microsc. Soc.* 172 E. Wasmann returns with fresh light to a discussion of '*pseudogyny' in *Formica sanguinea*. **1890** W. James *Princ. Psychol.* II. xix. 116 From ordinary images of memory and fancy, *pseudo-hallucinations differ in being much more vivid, minute, detailed..abrupt and spontaneous, in the sense that all feeling of our own activity in producing them is lacking. **1902** A. R. Defendorf *Kraepelin's Clin. Psychiatry* 7 This group of hallucinations, which has been variously designated as psychic hallucinations.., pseudohallucinations (Hagen), and apprehension hallucinations,..involves several or all of the sensory fields, and..stands in close relation to the other contents of consciousness. **1903** Myers *Human Personality* I. p. xvii, A pseudo-hallucination is a quasi-percept not sufficiently externalised to rank as a 'full blown' hallucination. **1968** P. McKellar *Experience & Behav.* iv. 120 What is sometimes called 'pseudo-hallucination'.. involves a projected perceptual-like image, but one in which the person concerned recognizes the subjective nature of the occurrence. **1902** W. James *Var. Relig. Exper.* x. 251, I refer to hallucinatory or *pseudo-hallucinatory luminous phenomena, *photisms*, to use the term of the psychologists. **1877** Huxley *Anat. Inv. Anim.* viii. 465 It is probable that these '*pseudo-hearts' subserve the function both of renal organs and of genital ducts. **1890** *Cent. Dict.*, **Pseudohexagonal*. **1895** Story-Maskelyne *Crystallogr.* vii. §308 Fig. 261 represents a crystal of witherite, and illustrates the pseudo-hexagonal aspect of many crystals in this [the orthorhombic] system. **1955** L. Ovesey in *Psychiatry* XVIII. 17 The dependency and power components..seek completely different, non-sexual goals, but make use of the genital organs to achieve them... For this reason, I have designated these two components as *pseudo-homosexual. *Ibid.*, This paper consists of a case study that provides clinical documentation for the concept of *pseudohomosexuality. **1962** I. Bieber et al. *Homosexuality* i. 10 A neurosis divisible into true and pseudohomosexual types. **1966** I. B. Weiner *Psychodiagnosis in Schizophrenia* xiv. 309 Pseudohomosexual concerns often emerge in the course of these reflections because the thought, 'I am a failure', readily translates into ideas of being something less than an adequate man and hence a homosexual. **1878** D. F. Lincoln tr. Eulenburg in *Ziemssen's Cycl. Pract. Med.* XIV. 155 More and more stress is laid on the connection between *pseudo-hypertrophy and progressive muscular atrophy. **1890** Billings *Nat. Med. Dict.*, **Pseudo-hypertrophic paralysis*, a rare disease of infancy and childhood... *Pseudohypertrophy*. **1896** *Allbutt's Syst. Med.* I. 184 Duchenue's paralysis, in which pseudo-hypertrophy occurs. **1954** *Arch. Dis. in Childhood* XXIX. 404/1 Any effect of chronic hypocalcaemia on physique is likely to be more evident if the disease is present early, and the preponderance of dwarfism among *pseudo-hypoparathyroid cases may be in part a reflection of the fact that in them the disorder is probably present from birth. **1942** F. Albright et al. in *Endocrinology* XXX. 922 (*heading*) Pseudo-hypoparathyroidism—an example of 'Seabright-Bartan Syndrome'. **1966** Wright & Symmers *Systemic Path.* II. xxxii. 1126/2 In pseudohypoparathyroidism, because hypocalcaemia is present from birth, the epiphyses and sutures close early, with the result that the patient is short and thickset in stature and has a characteristic round face. **1976** *Lancet* 20 Nov. 1106/2 Among suggested causes [of neonatal hypocalcæmia] are..decreased responsiveness of end-organs to parathyroid hormone (a form of pseudohypoparathyroidism), and vitamin-D deficiency. **1863** H. Spencer *First Princ.* ii. 36 We can entertain them [*sc.* hypotheses] only as we entertain such *pseud-ideas as a square fluid and a moral substance. **1879** W. James *Coll. Ess. & Rev.* (1920) 130 Professor Bain would no doubt say that nonentity was a pseud-idea not derived from experience and therefore meaningless. **1911** —— *Some Probl. of Philos.* xii. 197 The pseudo-idea of a connection which we have, Hume then goes on to show, is nothing but the misinterpretation of a mental custom. **1957** D. D. McCracken *Digital Computer Programming* xv. 182 The very first order of business on jumping into the interpretive routine is to increase index 1 by 1 so that it contains the location of the first *pseudo instruction. **1967** P. A. Stark *Digital Computer Programming* xii. 198 In addition to all the arithmetic and input-output instructions ..the symbolic language has a number of pseudo-instructions to the symbolic assembler. **1975** R. M. Graham *Princ. Systems Programming* 388 Pseudo instructions are used to define symbols, define constants, reserve space in the object segment, and provide the assembler with other information. **1879** T. J. Dills tr. J. Stilling in *Arch. Ophthalm.* VIII. 182 If we intermix the different shades of both inter-changeable colors in smaller or larger squares, in such manner that the squares of the one color form letters and figures, and those of the other the groundwork, so that the different intensities alternate in ground and letter..the question as to judgment of colors is rendered unnecessary, the inquiry being merely about letters, numbers, figures. This is the principle of the *pseudo-isochromatic plates. **1949** H. C. Weston *Sight, Light & Efficiency* vii. 241 For distinguishing between the varieties of colour-sense deficiency,..what are called pseudo-isochromatic plates are available. **1970** R. A. Moses *Adler's Physiol. of Eye* (ed. 5) xxi. 638/1 Pseudoisochromatic color plates are patterns of colored and gray dots that reveal one pattern to the normal, another to the color deficient. **1963** E. H. Nickel et al. in *Amer. Mineralogist* XLVIII. 976 The ixiolite-like minerals that convert to columbite-tantalite on heating cannot be considered as true ixiolites. For want of a better name, it is suggested that they be referred to as disordered columbite-tantalite, or as '*pseudo-ixiolite'. **1971** *Canad. Mineralogist* X. 758 In all other pegmatites, pseudo-ixiolite forms either tabular grains in a medium-grained albite + quartz + muscovite + garnet assemblage in the internal parts of the pegmatite bodies. **1954** W. R. Halliday *Pseudokarst* (Technical Note No. 25, Nat. Speleological Soc., U.S.) 1 Because the non-solugenic processes are analogous rather than homologous, it seems preferable that they should be considered as independent phenomena, i.e. *pseudokarst. *Ibid.*, Pseudokarst may be recognized in three major non-calcareous realms: basalt flows, glaciers, and certain soils. **1960** *Bull. Nat. Speleol. Soc.* XXII. II. 109/1 About 25 years ago, European geologists began to discuss features of non-solutional origin which are analogous to those of areas of karstic geomorphology. These they termed pseudokarst... Hans Peter Kosack, noted German geomorphologist, believes that the term *pseudokarst* was first employed in print in an Italian publication in 1941... However, as Dr. Kosack has pointed out (pers. comm.),..H. Cramer employed the term in an unpublished study of the karst of the British Isles which was prepared in 1936, and believes that the term was in use in Europe as early as 1930. *Ibid.*, Areas showing pseudokarstic features are distributed quite widely throughout the Western United States. **1968** R. W. Fairbridge *Encycl. Geomorphol.* 849/2 Pseudokarsts produced by piping display disappearing streams, sinkholes, ..residual hills and caves. **1971** J. N. Jennings *Karst* i. 5 More obviously pseudokarstic are larger caves..and collapse depressions. **1883** Packard in *Proc. Amer. Philos. Soc.* XXI. 201 (Chilognaths) The sternite of the sub-basilar plate is usually a very large plate..with teeth on each side, and forms the 'labium' of Newport. It may..be termed the '*pseudolabium'. **1890** Billings *Nat. Med. Dict.*, **Pseudoleukæmia*, enlargement of the spleen and lymphatic glands with anæmia, or Hodgkin's disease. **1890** *Cent. Dict.*, *Pseudoleucæmia*. **1904** *Brit. Med. Jrnl.* 17 Sept. 654 The *pseudo-leucocytes that are present in the blood in trypanosomiasis. **1890** Billings *Nat. Med. Dict.*, **Pseudoleucocythæmia*. **1895** *Syd. Soc. Lex.*, **Pseudo-lobar pneumonia*, a syn. for *Lobular pneumonia*. **1897** *Trans. Amer. Pediatric Soc.* IX. 146 The case may have been one of pseudo-lobar or mixed pneumonia. **1963** *Cancer* XVI. 928/2 A primary lymphocytic tumour of the lung will be defined as either a malignant lymphoma of the lymphocytic type or an inflammatory *pseudolymphoma that originally involves only the lung, or the lung and its regional lymph nodes, and in which there is no evidence of dissemination of the tumor for at least 3 months after the diagnosis is established. **1976** *National Observer* (U.S.) 25 Sept. 14/3 'What did you find?' I asked. 'A lesion, very rare,' he exulted. 'It is called pseudolymphoma.'..'Is it cancer?' 'No.' **1972** *Clin. & Exper. Immunol.* X. 202 The diagnosis was localized *pseudolymphomatous changes in the parotid glands and regional lymph nodes. **1976** *Chest* LXX. 358/1 Apparently these 'pseudolymphomatous' lesions have the potential to regress with appropriate therapy..or may progress to frank neoplasia. **1835** Shepard *Min.* II. II. 122 *Pseudo-Malachite. Hemi-prismatic, copper-barite. **1835–6** *Todd's Cycl. Anat.* I. 399/2 A consistence little..superior to that of mucous *pseudo-membranes. **1878** Habershon *Dis. Abdomen* (ed. 3) 21 The disease termed *pseudomembranous stomatitis. **1924** *Arch. Pediatrics* XLI. 565 (*heading*) Report of a case of pseudomembranous ileocolitis. **1952** *Gastroenterol.* XXI. 212 Acute pseudo-membranous inflammation involving portions of the intestinal tract after abdominal operations has been a subject of major importance within the past decade. **1977** *Lancet* 16 Apr. 839/1 Pseudomembranous enterocolitis may arise..as a complication of colonic obstruction. **1882** tr. *Ribot's Dis. Mem.* 186 *Pseudo-memory..consists in a belief that a new state has been previously experienced, so that when produced for the first time it seems to be a repetition. **1728** Nicholls in *Phil. Trans.* XXXV. 407 A *pseudo-metallick Substance, by the Miners term'd *Glist*. **1828–32** Webster s.v., Pseudo-metallic luster is that which is perceptible only when held towards the light; as, in minerals. *Phillips*. **1849** Dana *Geol.* ix. (1850) 515 The *pseudo-mica was nothing but altered chrysolite. [**1819** Lindley tr. *Richard's Obs. Fruits & Seeds* 74 *Pseudomonocotyledones.] **1832** Lindley *Introd. Bot.* 188 A cohesion of the cotyledons takes place in those embryos, which Gærtner called *pseudomonocotyledonous, and Richard macrocephalous. **1866** *Treas. Bot.* **1880** GRAY *Struct. Bot.* ii. (ed. 6) 26 A Pseudo-monocotyledonous embryo occasionally occurs, .. of which one cotyledon is wanting through abortion. **1890** *Cent. Dict.*, **Pseudomorphia*. **1836** *Amer. Jrnl. Sc.* XXX. 179 M. Pelletier announces the discovery of two new substances in opium, which he terms Paramorphine and *Pseudomorphine. **1874** GARROD & BAXTER *Mat. Med.* (1880) 194 Pseudomorphine ($C_{17}H_{19}NO_4$). **1883** *Jrnl. Chem. Soc.* XLIV. 875 Paralbumin is only a mixture of a mucoid substance, *pseudomucin, with varying proportions of albumin. **1901** J. L. ROTHROCK in C. A. L. Reed *Text-bk. Gynecol.* xl. 603 Pseudomucinous (Proliferating) Cysts.—To this group belong the greater proportion of ovarian cysts. **1968** J. W. HUFFMAN *Gynecol. Childhood & Adolescence* xiv. 279/2 Pseudomucinous Cystadenomas. These tumors owe their name to their contents, a gel-like fluid, pseudomucin, secreted by the cells of the epithelium lining the locules within the cysts. **1819** LINDLEY tr. *Richard's Obs. Fruits & Seeds* 5 To recognize the true loculation of fruit .. above all of those that are *Pseudomultilocular or cellular. **1887** W. PHILLIPS *Brit. Discomycetes* 393 Sporidia 8, fusoideo-filiform, straight or curved, *pseudo-multiseptate. **1927** M. C. RAYNER *Mycorrhiza* viii. 142 These *pseudomycorrhizas are usually simple and unbranched. **1934** *Forestry* VIII. 102 These pseudomycorrhizas show aberrant structure in many respects. **1952** S. A. WAKSMAN *Soil Microbiol.* iii. 88 Pseudo-mycorrhiza .. are endotrophic in nature. **1959** J. L. HARLEY *Biol. Mycorrhiza* iv. 69 The name pseudomycorrhiza must be used with some care... Those who held a pseudoreligious belief that mycorrhizas 'benefited' their hosts .. would refute, by the suggestion that the state being observed was pseudomycorrhizal rather than mycorrhizal, any observation which looked contrary to their own belief. **1867** J. HOGG *Microsc.* II. ii. 367 The Gregarinidae .. multiply by .. dividing into a multitude of minute objects called *pseudo-navicellae from their resemblance in shape to the ship-like diatoms (naviculae). **1877** HUXLEY *Anat. Inv. Anim.* ii. 94. **1890** *Cent. Dict.*, **Pseudo-navicula*. **1878** BELL *Gegenbaur's Comp. Anat.* 245 This condition is permanent in the *Pseudoneuroptera, Neuroptera, and Orthoptera. **1949** *Psychiatric Q.* XXIII. 249 In establishing the diagnosis of the *pseudoneurotic form of schizophrenia, it will be necessary to demonstrate the presence of the basic mechanisms of schizophrenia. **1966** I. B. WEINER *Psychodiagnosis in Schizophrenia* xvi. 398 Borderline and pseudoneurotic are two of many nosological terms that have been proposed to identify fairly stable personality states in which schizophrenic features are implied but not overtly manifest. **1971** *Brit. Med. Bull.* XXVII. 77/1 There are schools which diagnose simple or pseudo-neurotic forms of schizophrenia. **1965** *Language* XLI. 399 Both reject the same *pseudo-objects: From .. *The candidate spoke two hours*: .. (*They reported*) *the speaking of two hours by the candidate... Two hours were spoken by the candidate.* **1966** *Eng. Stud.* XLVII. 54 *It* (as a kind of pseudo-object) appears with transitive and intransitive verbs, and finally with original nouns and adjectives (to lord it, to queen it, to rough it) indicating the verbal function of these nominal parts of speech. **1956** *Jrnl. Assoc. Computing Machinery* III. 299 One of the principal objectives of the PACT I compiler has been to eliminate as much as was immediately feasible of the book-keeping and rudimentary thinking which is involved in the preparation of a computational problem for a large-scale, high-speed digital computer. To this end, a set of PACT *pseudo-operations was developed. These operations are more closely related to the computational problem than the machine operands. **1976** W. G. RUDD *Assembly Lang. Programming* v. 62 The START pseudo-operation orders the assembler to begin the assembly process. **1951** M. V. WILKES et al. *Preparation of Programs for Electronic Digital Computer* 17 A converse of the fact that orders are represented in the machine by numbers is that numbers may be represented outside the machine by '*pseudo-orders', that is, tape entries which are punched in the same form as orders but which are merely intended to be used as constants and are never to be obeyed as orders. **1955** *Jrnl. Assoc. Computing Machinery* II. 1 It is well known that programming may be simplified by the use of pseudoorders. We define these as additional orders (like square root..) which the machine cannot perform. [*Note*] In Wilkes, Wheeler and Gill [1951: see prec. quot.] .. what we call pseudoorder is denoted there by 'order', whilst the word pseudoorder is used in a different context. **1964** F. I. WESTWATER *Electronic Computers* ix. 143 Each sub-routine was allocated a code number, and 'pseudo-orders' were written using these numbers as functions. **1890** *Cent. Dict.*, **Pseudoparalysis*. **1895** *Syd. Soc. Lex.*, *Pseudoparalysis*, spurious paralysis. A syn. for *Dystaxia*. **1879** *St. George's Hosp. Rep.* IX. 37 *Pseudo-paraplegia. **1857** DUNGLISON *Med. Lex.*, **Pseudo-parasites*, ectozoa. **1849** BALFOUR *Man. Bot.* §1139 *Pseudo-parasitic plants, or Epiphytes. **1866** *Treas. Bot.*, *Pseudo-parasites*, including those plants which only attack dead tissues... Such plants are pseudo-parasitic. **1882** VINES *Sachs' Bot.* 245 Those Protophytes which contain chlorophyll live chiefly in water, or at least in damp localities, sometimes as pseudo-parasites. **1875** BENNETT & DYER *Sachs' Bot.* 258 The space between the enveloping layer and the coils of the ascogonium is filled by a *pseudo-parenchyma. **1890** *Cent. Dict.*, **Pseudoparenchymatous*. **1895** in *Syd. Soc. Lex.* **1864** H. SPENCER *Princ. Biol.* §75 I. 214 *Pseudo-parthenogenesis. It is the process familiarly exemplified in the *Aphides*. Here, from the fertilized eggs laid by perfect females, there grow up imperfect females, in the pseud-ovaria of which there are developed pseud-ova. **1870** ROLLESTON *Anim. Life* Introd. 112 In a second class of cases, females with a more or less imperfect reproductive apparatus produce either ova, as .. the 'workers' amongst the social Hymenoptera ..; or embryos, as in the case with *Aphis*... This form of asexual genesis is called 'pseudoparthenogenesis'. **1847–9** *Todd's Cycl. Anat.* IV. I. 5/2 Body provided with variable *pseudopediform prolongations. **1909** *Brit. Jrnl. Dermatol.* XXI. 27 Dr. J. M. H. Macleod showed a case of *pseudo-pelade (Brocq) or cicatricial alopecia in a man, aged 34 years, affecting chiefly the vertex of the scalp. **1975** S. L. MOSCHELLA et al. *Dermatol.* II. xxv. 1206 The etiology of pseudopelade is a mystery. **1887** H. E. F. GARNSEY tr. *A. de Bary's Compar. Morphol. & Biol. Fungi* v. 275 The hymenium [of Uredineae] and the rows of spores which proceed from it are enclosed in a membranous envelope composed of a single layer of cells (the peridium, *pseudo-peridium or paraphyses-envelope). **1965** BELL & COOMBE tr. *Strasburger's Textbk. Bot.* 512 In some genera .. all the spores of the peripheral chains and the terminal spores of the other chains lose their spore-like character before breaking through the epidermis and cohere as a firm investment (pseudoperidium). **1832** J. LINDLEY *Introd. Bot.* I. iii. 207 *Pseudoperithecium; Pseudohymenium; Pseudoperidium; terms used by Fries to express such coverings of Sporidia as resemble in figure the parts named perithecium, hymenium, and peridium in other plants. **1895** [see IMPERFECT *a.* 8 b]. **1903** *Bot. Gaz.* XXXV. 154 The head, which strongly suggests the pseudoperithecium, if it may so be termed, of the more highly differentiated species of Gymnoascus, is thus a remarkable combination of two elements of independent origin. **1928** C. W. DODGE tr. *Gäumann's Compar. Morphol. Fungi* xxiv. 365 At maturity, the vestigial walls of the perithecium [of *Coreomyces*] degenerate, leaving the developing ascogonium surrounded only by the walls of the original cells of the distal region, a pseudoperithecium. **1879** *Engineering* 5 Sept. 194/1 A new instrument .. to which he [Dr. S. P. Thompson] has given the name '*pseudophone'. **1876** tr. *Wagner's Gen. Pathol.* (ed. 6) 316 *Pseudo-pigmentation or pseudo-melanosis is a gray or blackish coloration, caused by the presence of sulphide of iron. **1916** B. D. JACKSON *Gloss. Bot. Terms* (ed. 3) 312/1 *Pseudoplankton .. organisms accidentally found floating. **1935** P. S. WELCH *Limnology* ix. 208 Pseudoplankton—debris mingled in plankton. **1947** R. RUEDEMANN *Graptolites N. Amer.* I. 19 The majority of the typical graptolites lived as pseudoplankton. **1898** *Amer. Naturalist* XXXII. 14 It is highly probable that many graptolites were indeed *pseudo-planktonic. **1969** BENNISON & WRIGHT *Geol. Hist. Brit. Isles* v. 105 The graptolites were planktonic or pseudoplanktonic. **1847** tr. *Feuchtersleben's Med. Psychol.* (Syd. Soc.) 265 Traumatic influences, .. (among which we must reckon the *pseudo-plasms). **1885–8** FAGGE & PYE-SMITH *Princ. Med.* (ed. 2) I. 97 [Certain tumours] were accordingly termed pseudo-plasms or neo-plasms or new growths. **1892** R. THAXTER in *Bot. Gaz.* XVII. 392 The essential characters of a *pseudo-plasmodium are common to both groups. **1966** *McGraw-Hill Encycl. Sci. & Technol.* XI. 44/1 Labyrinthulidae .. are uninucleate marine organisms... An aggregate of many individuals may form a motile pseudoplasmodium. **1929** R. V. WILLIAMSON in *Industr. & Engin. Chem.* Nov. 1108/1 Certain types of dispersions do not flow in accordance with the laws of either ideal fluids or ideal plastics. The flowing properties of such dispersions are similar in many respects to the flowing properties of ideal plastics; therefore we shall refer to them as pseudoplastics. The primary difference between pseudoplastic flow and ideal plastic flow is the absence of a real yield value in *pseudoplastic flow. **1958** *Ibid.* Jan. 10/2 Aqueous solutions of the poly(ethylene oxide) with intrinsic viscosity of 9 exhibit a mucous-like stringiness, and when observed in a variable shear-rate viscometer can be classed rheologically as pseudoplastic. **1962** *Lancet* 15 Dec. 1263/1 They suggest that the plastic or pseudoplastic flow of abnormally viscous bile caused by metallic ions is converted into a newtonian flow by the action of chelating agents. **1979** A. L. LYDERSEN *Fluid Flow & Heat Transfer* i. 2 (*caption*) Velocity gradient du/dy as a function of the shear stress $\tau = F/A$. a, dilatant fluid; b, Newtonian fluid; c, pseudo-plastic fluid; d, Bingham plastic fluid. **1938** WEISS & LOUIS in A. E. Dunstan et al. *Sci. of Petroleum* II. xx. 1128/2 The phenomenon of *pseudo-plasticity is of importance in the physico-chemical examination of the large molecules present in petroleum. **1958** *Industr. & Engin. Chem.* Jan. 11/2 The initially high viscosity and the low shear rate pseudo-plasticity are reduced. **1967** *New Scientist* 9 Feb. 334/3 Pseudoplasticity describes the fall of viscosity with increasing shear rate. **1903** MYERS *Human Personality* I. 65 A duplication of personality .. a *pseudo-possession, if you will—determined in a hysterical child by the suggestion of friends. *Ibid.* 644 What I shall .. call *pseudo-presentiments, i.e. .. hallucinations of memory which make it seem to one that something which now .. astonishes him has been prefigured in a recent dream. **1896** *Ibis* Jan. 11 The Ratite shoulder-girdle seems more primitive, and it is difficult to suppose that its condition is secondary and due to retrogression, or, in other words, that it is '*pseudo-primitive'. **1834** MᶜMURTRIE *Cuvier's Anim. Kingd.* 430 The *pseudo-proboscis is much shorter than the body. **1877** F. H. BUTLER in *Encycl. Brit.* VII. 631/2 The pseud-embryo or echinopædium .. becomes .. wedge-shaped; at its broad end appears the mouth or pseudostome, and at the other the anus or *pseudoproct. **1887** SOLLAS *ibid.* XXII. 416/1 (Sponges) In one sense the oscule is always a pseudostome; it would be better if the term *pseudoproct* could be substituted. **1952** F. ALBRIGHT et al. in *Trans. Assoc. Amer. Physicians* LXV. 339 We wish to present today a case with all of the characteristics of pseudohypoparathyroidism except that she has no manifestations suggesting hypoparathyroidism—no hyperphosphatemia, no hypocalcemia. Thus she might be said to have .. a '*pseudo-pseudo-hypoparathyroidism'. **1962** *Lancet* 19 May 1075/1 (*heading*) Chromosomal analysis in gonadal dysgenesis with pseudopseudohypoparathyroidism. **1975** *Arch. Dermatol.* CXI. 90/1 A 31-year-old woman with the characteristic features of pseudopseudohypoparathyroidism, such as shortened metacarpals and metatarsals, round facies, and normal serum calcium values, was studied. **1899** D. SHARP in *Cambr. Nat. Hist.* VI. 273 The vesicular larva [of the Bee] .. changes to a *pseudo-pupa... The majority .. wintering as pseudo-pupae. **1887** *Entomologist's Mag.* Dec. 149 The female larva [of the Phengodini] goes through a *pseudo-pupal state prior to the final moult. **1971** *Kybernetik* IX. 159/1 The *deep *pseudopupil* of Dipterans is not to be confused with the *corneal pseudo-pupil* .. and especially not with the *reduced corneal pseudopupil* .., in spite of the remarkable similarity of these phenomena. **1977** *Sci. Amer.* July 108/2 Looking at the eye of an insect, we frequently see a black spot in the center of the eye. As the insect rotates its head the black spot always points in the direction of the observer. The spot is known as the pseudopupil: the facets in it look black because they reflect less light in the direction of the observer than the facets in the rest of the eye. **1975** G. J. KING *Audio Handbk.* 2 *Pseudo-quadraphony .. is designated 2–2–4, which implies that the four loudspeakers obtain their signals from the two-channel source. **1976** *Which?* May 99/3 Apart from these, there is a sort of 'fake' quad called, variously, Hafler (after its inventor), ambiophony, or pseudoquadrophony. With this system, you can derive some quadrophonic effect from ordinary stereo recordings and broadcasts. **1897** *Lippincott's Med. Dict.* 840/2 **Pseudorabies*, hysteria resembling rabies, or a condition in animals resembling rabies. **1906** *Jrnl. Nerv. & Mental Dis.* XXXIII. 741 Pseudo-Rabies.—Five cases are cited of pathological alcoholic intoxication in which the patients were wild, making murderous attacks, attempting to bite persons or even trees, bed clothes, etc. **1912** J. J. WALSH *Psychotherapy* xx. ii. 753 There seems no doubt that .. pseudo-rabies occurs; that is, persons are bitten by a dog, become seriously disturbed over the possibility of rabies developing, and .. there is either a neurosis simulating many symptoms of true rabies, or .. even death may take place. **1931** *Jrnl. Exper. Med.* LIV. 246 Among the laboratory animals, rabbits are stated to be more susceptible to pseudorabies than guinea pigs. **1957** SMITH & JONES *Veterinary Path.* ix. 258 Pseudorabies may be suspected in disease outbreaks in which animals die shortly after showing very severe pruritus limited to a segment of the skin. **1926** *Jrnl. Chem. Soc.* II. 2779 Whether he is dealing with a racemate or a *pseudo-racemate. **1973** S. F. MASON in Ciardelli & Salvadori *Fund. Aspects & Rec. Devel. Optical Rotatory Dispersion & Circular Dichroism* iii. 212 A pseudoracemate of *lel* and *ob* diastereoisomers is not optically inactive. **1897** KIPPING & POPE in *Jrnl. Chem. Soc.* LXXI. 991 Whilst retaining the name racemic compound for a substance belonging to class (*a*), we propose .. to call those belonging to class (*b*) *pseudoracemic, in order to distinguish them from mere mixtures of the two antipodes on the one hand, and from racemic compounds on the other. **1951** S. COFFEY tr. *Wibaut's Org. Chem.* viii. 218 Cases are also known in which mixed crystals of the optical antipodes separate (pseudo-racemic mixed crystals). **1972** R. A. JACKSON *Mechanism* v. 84 If the two compounds have opposite configurations no such solid solution will in general be possible, and either a simple eutectic mixture or a 'pseudo-racemic' compound will be formed. **1900** DORLAND *Med. Dict.* 544/2 **Pseudoreaction*, a clumping or other bacterial reaction not due to the presence of the typhoid bacillus. **1928** L. E. H. WHITBY *Med. Bacteriol.* xxiii. 238 A reaction occurs in both arms, that on the control being a pseudo-reaction whereas that on the test arm is a combination of a pseudo and a positive reaction. **1977** *Compar. Biochem. & Physiol.* B. LVI. 272/2 The nature and origin of the pseudo-reaction of the marine molluscan tissues remains obscure. **1899** *Jrnl. Morphol.* XV. Suppl. 71 It may be stated .. in regard to the number of chromosomes, that it is plainly greater than in the first spermatocyte division, which is known to be post-synaptic, *i.e.*, after the *pseudo-reduction. **1931** W. SHUMWAY *Textbk. Gen. Biol.* vi. 149 The split .. develops so that when the metaphase occurs only half the diploid number of chromosomes may be counted *but* each of these has four parts. There has been no reduction in the sense that any chromosomes have been lost; they have merely united in pairs so that the change in the number of visible chromosomes is called pseudo-reduction. **1858** CARPENTER *Veg. Phys.* §25 In plants and animals, four of the [elements] are universally present, and are called organic; two are found very generally present, and are called *pseud-organic. **1898** *Nature* 2 June 118/1 Some of the 'pseudorganic' structures described in rocks might really be the casts or replacements of dried streaks. **1897** *Allbutt's Syst. Med.* III. 70 To explain the relationship of the *pseudo-rheumatic troubles to the urethral discharge. **1895** STORY-MASKELYNE *Crystallogr.* Index, *Pseudo-rhombohedral crystals. **1972** COTTON & WILKINSON *Adv. Inorg. Chem.* (ed. 3) xiii. 400 A cyclic 5-coordinate intermediate is formed which then *pseudorotates. **1960** *Rev. Mod. Physics* XXXII. 451/1 (*caption*) The *pseudorotated figure (b) corresponds to sending (a) through a clockwise rotation of $\frac{2}{3}\pi$ and permuting nuclei 1 → 3, 3 → 2, and 2 → 1. **1947** *Jrnl. Amer. Chem. Soc.* LXIX. 2484/2 (*heading*) *Pseudo-rotation of ring puckering. **1960** *Jrnl. Chem. Physics* XXXII. 937/1 One .. attractive mechanism for the exchange process in PF_5 and PCl_5 is a purely internal pseudorotation. **1974** *Nature* 31 May 474/2 By dynamic reversal of the H_2O binding step before pseudorotation, the two oxygens in the pair of oxoniums could equilibrate with the H_2O oxygens of the medium. **1976** EMSLEY & HALL *Chem. of Phosphorus* ii. 60 A shorthand notation is required for the *tbp* structures and their *pseudorotational transformations. **1966** TEUFER & TEMPLE in *Nature* 9 July 180/1 As a result of an investigation of several altered ilmenite concentrates by X-ray techniques hitherto not applied to this problem, a new crystalline phase has been identified as a major constituent of altered ilmenite. The new phase crystallizes in a disordered structure of hexagonal symmetry and has the theoretical composition $Fe_2O_3 \cdot 3TiO_2$. We propose the name '*pseudorutile' for this new mineral. **1975** *Amer. Mineralogist* LX. 905/2 The electrochemical corrosion model is consistent with the pseudorutile composition being a stable alteration product of ilmenite in which all the iron is in the ferric state. **1910** N. V. SIDGWICK *Org. Chem. Nitrogen* vii. 152 The mercury must migrate from one position to the other, according to the solvent, just as the hydrogen atom does with a pseudo-acid, and hence mercuric nitroform should be called a *pseudo-salt. **1930** *Chem. Abstr.* XXIV. 4021 In alc. soln. there can exist an equil. between the pseudo-salts and the true salts. **1953** C. K. INGOLD *Struct. & Mechanism in Org. Chem.* x. 577 Pseudo-salt formation can be seen in the reactions of methylquinolinium salts with various sources of carbanions, for instance Grignard reagents, or pseudo-acidic carbonyl or nitro-compounds. [**1880** P. L. SCLATER in *Ibis* Ser. IV. IV. 345 To place the Acromyodi abnormales of Garrod .. at the end of the Passerine series under the name *Pseudoscines. **1890** BILLINGS *Nat. Med. Dict.*, **Pseudosclerosis*, name given by Westphal to cases presenting many of the symptoms of disseminated sclerosis, but in which no anatomical lesions were discovered. **1835** KIRBY *Hab. & Inst. Anim.* II. xix. 303 Two Orders .. which may be denominated, *Pseudo-scorpions and Phalangidans. **1877** HUXLEY *Anat. Inv. Anim.* vii. 378 The Pseudo-scorpions resemble the Scorpions. **1890** POULTON *Colours Anim.* xvii. 336 Mimetic Resemblance and Alluring Colouration are called *Pseudosematic Colours, because they usually resemble Sematic or Warning and Signalling Colours. **1895** *Syd. Soc. Lex.*, *Pseudosematic*, belonging to protective disguises, as, *e.g.*, the leaf-like appearance of the leaf-insect. **1889** NICHOLSON & LYDEKKER *Palæont.* I. xx. 331 Tabulate tubes of two sizes, the larger of these being furnished with radiating *pseudosepta. **1883** HYATT in *Proc. Boston Soc. Nat. Hist.* XXII. 258 The central trace compares with the *pseudosiphon of the plug. **1890** *Cent.*

Dict., **Pseudosiphonal*, **Pseudosiphuncle*. **1895** in *Syd. Soc. Lex.* **1608** Topsell *Serpents* (1658) 693 There are..certain *Pseudoscinks..sold by Apothecaries, that are nothing else but a kinde of water Lizard. **1964** M. Argyle *Psychol. & Social Probl.* v. 60 One very common type of juvenile delinquent is the '*pseudo-social' delinquent, so called because he is perfectly well behaved towards other members of his gang, but not to people outside of it. **1968** Hebb & Thompson in Lindzey & Aronson *Handbk. Social Psychol.* II. 734 It is important also to exclude pseudosocial behavior, in which grouping occurs only because of some stimulus external to the group: examples are animals running from a forest fire. **1974** *Black Panther* 16 Mar. 11/3 Without new insights, we must really fear new outbreaks of that reactionary *pseudospeciation which found (we hope) its climax in Hitler. **1975** *N.Y. Times* 26 Jan. x. 1/1 Erikson calls this 'pseudospeciation'..meaning that man has falsely created divisions where there are none. **1965** E. Erikson in *Amer. Jrnl. Psychiatry* CXXII. 246/1 Sociogenetic evolution has split mankind into *pseudo-species, into tribes, nations and religions..which bind their members into a pattern of individual and collective identity, but alas, reinforce that pattern by a mortal fear of and a murderous hatred for other pseudo-species. **1968** —— *Identity* i. 41 Man as a species has survived by being divided into what I have called *pseudospecies*. **1974** *Black Panther* 23 Feb. 10/2 That means we have a common faith..that each pseudospecies and each empire in some dialectical way added new elements to a more universal sense of humanity. **1835** Henslow *Princ. Bot.* II. vi. 277 In *pseudospermic Fruits..we may include all fruits whose pericarp is so closely attached to the seed, that it cannot readily be distinguished from one of its integuments. **1890** *Cent. Dict.*, **Pseudospermium*. **1895** in *Syd. Soc. Lex.* **1849** Balfour *Man. Bot.* §531 Such fruits are called **pseudo-spermous*.., and are well seen in the grain of wheat. **1889** *Cent. Dict.*, *Pseudosphere. **1909** L. P. Eisenhart *Treat. Differential Geom. Curves & Surfaces* viii. 274 The surface of revolution of a tractrix about its asymptote is called the pseudosphere, or the pseudospherical surface of the parabolic type. **1926** J. E. Campbell *Differential Geom.* ii. 28 The formulae of spherical trigonometry or of pseudospherical trigonometry will apply to any surfaces which have the same ground form as the sphere or the pseudosphere. **1947** L. P. Eisenhart *Introd. Differential Geom.* iv. 284 The length of the segment of a tangent to a meridian from the point of contact to the axis of rotation is *a*, and consequently the meridian curve is a tractrix... These pseudospherical surfaces are said to be of the parabolic type. They are called pseudospheres. **1965** J. D. North *Measure of Universe* iv. 60 In 1868 E. Beltrami.. showed that Lobachevsky's plane geometry holds in Euclidean space on certain surfaces of constant negative curvature (the pseudospheres) and that these could be conformally represented on a plane. **1883** Ball in *Encycl. Brit.* XV. 664/2 Were space really *pseudospherical, then stars would exhibit a real parallax even if they were infinitely distant. **1884** tr. *Lotze's Metaph.* II. ii. 233 It is clear to us what we are to think of as a spherical or pseudo-spherical surface, but not clear what can be meant by a spherical or pseudo-spherical space, designations which we meet with.. without any help being given to us in comprehending their meaning. **1909**, **1926** Pseudospherical [see *pseudosphere* above]. **1956** J. R. Newman *World of Math.* I. IV. 645 All we know about space, he [*sc.* von Helmholtz] said, is what we have learned from experience. If we lived in a spherical or pseudo-spherical space our sensible impressions of the world would dictate the adoption of the non-Euclidian geometries of Riemann or Lobachevsky; nothing in our intuition would require us to adopt a 'flat-space' Euclidean system. **1826** Kirby & Sp. *Entomol.* III. 714 In spiders..the open ventral spiracles of the scorpion are replaced by *pseudo-spiracles; these..in *Epeira cancriformis*,..are dark red spots with an elevated rim and centre exactly resembling spiracles, except that they are not perforated. **1900** B. D. Jackson *Gloss. Bot. Terms*, *Pseudo-sporange, pseudosporangium, a simulated sporangium. **1874** Cooke *Fungi* 71 These *pseudospores are at first produced in chains, but ultimately separate. **1900** *Gloss. Bot. Terms*, *Pseudospore*,..a gemma or asexual vegetative bud. **1852** Dana *Crust.* I. 425 Either part is rugate or *pseudo-squamate. **1939** N. de V. Hart *Bridge Players' Bedside Bk.* xi. 54 The term *pseudo-squeeze should be reserved for those occasions when a player by ruse or subterfuge deliberately creates in the mind of an opponent the illusion that it is safe to discard from a certain suit and fatal to discard from another, when in fact the reverse is the case. **1975** *Times* 22 July 5/1 Careful defence was needed by the British pair..to avoid being caught in a pseudo-squeeze. **1845** Darwin *Voy. Nat.* xix. (1873) 450 A hard *pseudo-stalactitical stone. **1926** I. A. Richards *Sci. & Poetry* vi. 56 We must confine ourselves to the other function of words, or rather..to one form of that function, let me call it *pseudo-statement. *Ibid.* 59 A pseudo-statement is a form of words which is justified entirely by its effect in releasing or organizing our impulses and attitudes..; a statement, on the other hand, is justified by..its correspondence..with the fact to which it points. **1933–5** Wittgenstein *Blue & Brown Bks.* (1958) 71 One of the reasons why we are tempted to make our pseudo-statement is its similarity with the statement 'I only see this.' **1940** *Kenyon Rev.* 271 Poetry consists essentially of pseudo-statements. **1947** D. Rynin *Johnson's Treat. Lang.* 333 Only if the expression has statement meaning shall we consider it a genuine statement; otherwise we shall call it a pseudo-statement, provided it satisfies the purely grammatical requirements. **1894** *Kew Bull.* 231 The stem (*pseudo-stem) in Musas usually arises from a perennial rootstock. **1927** *Bot. Gaz.* LXXXIV. 337 If..the trunk is cut across..it is found to be a pseudostem composed of the overlapping close-fitting leaf sheaths alone. **1957** *New Biol.* XI. 71 The sappy, leafy banana trunks..are really pseudostems consisting of the overlapping leaf-bases. **1972** J. W. Purseglove *Trop. Crops: Monocotyledons* II. 357 The last leaves are produced at nodes on the flowering stem in the centre of the pseudostem. **1892** *Jrnl. Quekett Microsc. Club* July 45 Orthostereoscopism and *pseudostereoscopism. *Ibid.* 51 *note*, The first arrangement ..when applied to the compound microscope gave *pseudostereoscopic pictures... There was transposition without a cross-over; it was, therefore, a *pseudostereoscope. **1884** Michael *Brit. Oribatidæ* I. ix. 130 The *Pseudo-stigmata... The conspicuous organs ordinarily called stigmata, one on each side. *Ibid.* 131 Each pseudo-stigma has an organ proceeding from it..which I call a *pseudo-stigmatic organ. **1874** *Q. Jrnl. Geol. Soc.* XXX. 253 The great masses of gabbro in Rum often exhibit that *pseudo-stratification so often observed in igneous rocks. **1941** *Amer. Jrnl. Sci.* CCXXXIX. 1 (*heading*) The development of pseudo-stratification by metamorphic differentiation in the schists of Otago, New Zealand. **1959** *Econ. Geol.* LIV. 1161 Even, regular layering is the commonest type of pseudostratification in the section. **1833–4** J. Phillips *Geol.* in *Encycl. Metrop.* (1845) VI. 766/1 The great mass of basalt..lies in a *pseudostratum of most irregular thickness. **1890** *Cent. Dict.*, **Pseudosymmetry*. **1895** Story-Maskelyne *Crystallogr.* Index, Pseudo-symmetry. **1819** Byron *Juan* I. cxxxi, Their real lues, or our *pseudo-syphilis. **1843** R. J. Graves *Syst. Clin. Med.* xxvii. 343 Mercury, with its *pseudo-syphilitic cutaneous affections. **1917** S. J. Shand in *Q. Jrnl. Geol. Soc.* LXXII. 199 The name *pseudotachylyte has been adopted in recognition of the fact that these rocks have a great similarity to tachylyte. **1954** H. Williams et al. *Petrography* xi. 202 X-ray investigation and measurement of the refractive index have shown some pseudotachylytes to be cryptocrystalline products of extreme crushing of rocks such as granite, without actual melting. **1971** *Nature* 17 Sept. 189/1 More than half of the rocks consist of a very irregular pattern of small black veins embracing gneiss fragments—'pseudotachylytes'. **1977** A. Hallam *Planet Earth* 177 Very rarely temperature may rise enough for melting, and such frictionally-produced melts are called pseudotachylites. **1895** Story-Maskelyne *Crystallogr.* Index, *Pseudo-tetragonal crystals. **1836–9** *Todd's Cycl. Anat.* II. 862/2 The third tribe, *Phytophaga*..is..composed of *pseudo-tetramerous insects. **1957** J. K. Charlesworth *Quaternary Era* I. xxvii. 569 Solifluxion..produces stony clays or *pseudo-tills. **1966** *Earth-Sci. Rev.* II. 249 None of these thickness criteria, alone, can distinguish tills..from pseudo-tills. **1963** R. O. Muir tr. *Schwarbach's Climates of Past* v. 39, I would recommend that the term tillite be applied not only to undoubted moraines but to all moraine-like sediments of probable or possible glacial or glacio-marine origin. Those later shown to be..of non-glacial origin, may then, more properly, be called *pseudo-tillites. **1963** D. W. & E. E. Humphries tr. *Termier's Erosion & Sedimentation* x. 205 These graywackes, which must be deposited in deep water.., consist of grains of angular sand set in an argillaceous groundmass, sometimes with boulders or fragments (pseudo-tillites) not unlike the material of glacial moraines. **1968** R. W. Fairbridge *Encycl. Geomorphol.* 473/2 Any sort of 'accidental' mixture such as is caused by a gravitational flow..can easily be taken for a glacial till, i.e., it is a pseudotillite. **1890** B. T. Lowne *Anat., Physiol., Morphol., & Devel. of Blow-Fly* I. iv. 146 The *Pseudotracheæ are cylindrical channels on the oral surface of the disc. **1925** A. D. Imms *Gen. Textbk. Entomol.* III. 595 Fine trachea-like food channels or pseudotracheæ become evident [in Diptera]. **1954** *New Biol.* XVII. 44 Those species [of woodlice] which can withstand drier conditions are also those which possess these 'pseudotracheae'. **1975** *Nature* 27 Mar. 325/1 On each half labellum of *Drosophila* there are..some 25 taste pegs between the pseudotracheae. **1900** Miall & Hammond *Harlequin Fly* ii. 70 The salivary ducts..have a ring ('*pseudotracheal') structure. **1896** G. M. Sternberg *Text-bk. Bacteriol.* II. xvi. 608 Preisz (1894) has compared the bacillus of *pseudo-tuberculosis described by Nocard with that of Pfeiffer, of Parietti, and of Zagari, and finds them identical. **1899** E. O. Jordan tr. *Hueppe's Princ. Bacteriol.* iv. 201 If tubercles occur in which, instead of the tubercle bacillus, other bacteria are found the affection is called pseudo-tuberculosis. **1959** R. Lovell in Stableforth & Galloway *Infectious Dis. Animals* I. vi. 250 Caseous lymphadenitis of sheep. This is a chronic disease frequently referred to as pseudo-tuberculosis and widely distributed in South America, Australia and New Zealand. **1977** Andrewes & Walton *Viral & Bacterial Zoonoses* xxviii. 145 The numerous cases of pseudotuberculosis in zoos and research establishments are most probably due to the contamination of feeding-stuffs and water by wild birds and rodents. **1907** *Jrnl. Compar. Path. & Therapeutics* XX. 53 Mainly on account of the acid-fast character of the bacilli, the disease has been referred to as a pseudo-tuberculosis, and Bang has suggested that it should be called 'chronic bovine *pseudo-tuberculous enteritis'. **1957** S. L. Robbins *Textbk. Path.* xxix. 1101/1 Pseudotuberculous (giant cell) thyroiditis. This form of inflammation of unknown etiology is so named because of its histologic appearance. **1962** *Lancet* 19 May 1042/1 We describe here a further case of pseudotuberculous mesenteric adenitis,..together with evidence that 3 other children in the same family and a pet dog had also been infected with *Past. pseudotuberculosis*. **1901** A. P. Ohlmacher in Hektoen & Riesman *Text-bk. Path.* I. 288 Of the various pathogenic blastomycetic species obtained from morbid processes in man or under saprophytic conditions, all failed to produce anything else than '*pseudo-tumors'. **1938** Smith & Gault *Essent. of Path.* xxiii. 232 This resemblance [to true tumors] ceases on microscopic study when the histologic evidence of neoplastic change of the cells is found to be lacking. The cells in such pseudo-tumors will show evidence of inflammatory hyperplasia. **1944** J. F. Brailsford *Radiol. Bones & Joints* (ed. 3) xvii. 241 A pseudo-tumour of the spinal cord was recorded by W. E. Dandy—this was found to be a shell of bone surrounding the posterior half of the spinal cord. **1974** Passmore & Robson *Compan. Med. Stud.* III. xxxiv. 12/1 A pseudotumour is one of the names given to a syndrome of raised intracranial pressure unassociated with a space-occupying lesion. **1887** W. Phillips *Brit. Discomycetes* 407 Sporidia..becoming *pseudo-uniseptate. **1964** G. H. Haggis et al. *Introd. Molecular Biol.* ix. 218 In 5-ribosyl-uracil ('*pseudo-uracil') the uracil ring is attached to the backbone ribose through the carbon at position 5 in the uracil ring, rather than through the nitrogen at position 3. **1970** Ambrose & Easty *Cell Biol.* iv. 133 It contained, like most tRNA molecules, a number of unusual bases, such as inosine..and pseudouracil.., and certain methylated forms of normal bases. **1978** *Sci. Amer.* Jan. 62/3 In some systems the control function is associated with a particular modified nucleotide in the tRNA molecule, for example a uracil that has been converted into a pseudouracil. **1866–8** Watts *Dict. Chem.* IV. 745 The *pseudo-urates are easily obtained by the action of the acid on the corresponding hydrates, carbonates, or acetates. **1866** Odling *Anim. Chem.* 140 *Pseudo-uric acid is a recent discovery. **1959** *Biochimica et Biophysica Acta* XXXII. 571 It is proposed (by Dr. A. Michelson) that this substance be called *pseudouridine, with the symbol ψ for the prefix 'pseudo' in abbreviations. **1964** A. White et al. *Princ. Biochem.* (ed. 3) xxx. 607 Formation of pseudouridine may also occur at the polynucleotide level, but the mode of synthesis is unknown. **1978** *Sci. Amer.* Jan. 55/1 (*caption*) Other structural modifications also occur. For example, the nucleoside pseudo-uridine (ψ) has its base attached to the ribose through a carbon atom instead of a nitrogen atom. **1881** Lankester in *Encycl. Brit.* XII. 555/2 The edge of its [the medusa's] disc..is not provided with a velum (hence 'Acraspeda' of Gegenbaur), excepting the rudimentary velum of Aurelia and the well-developed vascular velum (*pseudo-velum) of Charybdæa. **1894** *Daily News* 22 Aug. 5/3 It is this *pseudo-viscosity of ice that enables a glacier to accommodate itself to the bed over which it flows. **1951** *Abstr. of Papers 120th Meeting Amer. Chem. Soc.* 22c (*heading*) Crystalline *pseudovitamin B_{12}. **1956** *Nature* 28 Jan. 188/1 Several substances, such as factor *A* and pseudo-vitamin B_{12}, are closely related to cobalamin. **1967** *Oceanogr. & Marine Biol.* V. 383 As in many other crustaceans, vitamin B_{12} is found in *Nephrops*... It occurs as the analogs Factor B and pseudovitamin B_{12}. **1858** T. H. Huxley in *Trans. Linn. Soc.* XXII. 208 The central mass.. completely simulates the vitellus of an impregnated ovum; and I will therefore term it a '*pseudovitellus'. **1899** D. Sharp in Harmer & Shipley *Cambr. Nat. Hist.* VI. viii. 588 There exists [in aphids]..a peculiar structure, the pseudo-vitellus, a sort of cellular, double string. **1924** *Philippine Jrnl. Sci.* XXIV. 150 Henneguy..also described the origin of the 'pseudovitellus' from the follicular epithelium. **1946** Pseudovitellus [see MYCETOME]. **1796** Kirwan *Elem. Min.* (ed. 2) I. 394 The fires from which many minerals derive their form and aggregation are either volcanic or *pseudo-volcanic. **1828** Stark *Elem. Nat. Hist.* II. 499 Volcanic Rocks..are divided into true volcanic and pseudo-volcanic; ..the second comprehending clays and ironstones, indurated and partially melted by the heat from beds of burning coal. **1796** Kirwan *Elem. Min.* (ed. 2) I. 419 *Pseudo-volcanos are so called, because, like volcanos, they emit smoke, and sometimes flame, but never lava... Most of these are coal mines which have accidentally taken fire. **1925** *Mineral. Mag.* XX. 463 *Pseudowavellite... Hydrated phosphate of aluminium with lime, ferric iron, and rare-earths; occurring as white encrustations (trigonal needles) on limonite and wavellite at Amberg, Bavaria. So named because of its resemblance to wavellite, of which it is perhaps an alteration product. **1942** [see LEWISTONITE]. **1951** C. Palache et al. *Dana's Syst. Min.* (ed. 7) II. 837 Available evidence indicates that crandallite and pseudowavellite are best considered as a single species with some variation of composition, the name crandallite having priority. **1875** Bennett & Dyer *Sachs' Bot.* 368 Each cycle of segments or turn of the spiral produces a whorl, which therefore, strictly speaking, is a *pseudo-whorl, because resulting from subsequent displacement. **1906** *Amer. Jrnl. Sci.* CLXXI. 105 *Pseudo-wollastonite appears either in the form of small irregular grains often tabular in shape or in short prisms or fibers arranged in parallel or divergent groups. **1942** *Ibid.* CCXL. 729 It is a most remarkable fact that, if powdered glass of the composition $CaSiO_3$ is crystallized at any temperature, the product always consists almost exclusively of pseudo-wollastonite, but lumps of the same glass will crystallize readily to wollastonite with only a trace of pseudo-wollastonite present at temperatures between 800° and 1100°. **1970** R. W. Andrews *Wollastonite* 2 There are two polymorphs of calcium monosilicate: wollastonite the low temperature form, and pseudowollastonite..the high temperature form. *Ibid.* 5 Natural pseudowollastonite has been reported from only one locality, in Iran, near the head of the Persian Gulf. **1887** A. M. Brown *Anim. Alkaloids* 87 *Pseudoxanthine,..whose resemblance to xanthine has led to some confusion. **1890** Billings *Nat. Dict.*, *Pseudoxanthin*... Leucomaine found by Gautier in muscular tissue..resembling xanthin. **1900** Dorland *Med. Dict.* 545/1 **Pseudoxanthoma*, a disease resembling xanthoma. **1901** *Brit. Jrnl. Dermatol.* XIII. 232 The author ranges himself with Darier, and considers the condition to be due to a degeneration of elastic tissue... The qualification 'pseudo'-xanthoma should be insisted upon. **1933** *Arch. Dermatol. & Syphilol.* XXVIII. 553 The histologic evidences of pseudoxanthoma elasticum are fragmentation and degeneration of the elastic tissue. **1961** *Lancet* 12 Aug. 356/2 Although the lesions attributable to pseudo-xanthoma elasticum may be widely distributed through the tissues and organs of the body, it is more commonly recognised by dermatologists and ophthalmologists than by general physicians. **1977** *Proc. R. Soc. Med.* LXX. 569/1 Instead of the well ordered wavy collagen bundles of normal skin, the middle and lower dermis in pseudo-xanthoma elasticum shows an irregular network of tangled, curled and branching fibres.

b. *Cytology*. **pseudo'diploid** (**-'tetraploid**, etc.) *adjs.*, having a chromosome complement which differs from the normad diploid (tetraploid, etc.) complement in constitution but not in number. So **pseudo'diploidy**, etc.

1923 *Bot. Gaz.* LXXVI. 330 Of two plants from our cultures, each of which had a total of 48 chromosomes in their somatic cells.., one appears to have been a chromosomal mutant of the type ($4n + 1 - 1$) and the other a mutant of the type ($4n + 1 + 1 - 1 - 1$). Such forms obviously cannot properly be called $4n$ or tetraploid. They ..may be classified as modified tetraploids, or at most as 'pseudotetraploids'. **1977** *Lancet* 30 Apr. 961/1 Pseudo-diploidy, 46,XX,D_9+,17q−, was observed in 14 marrow and in 10 blood-cells by the Giemsa staining method. **1978** *Nature* 16 Mar. 262/1 Stable diploid, or occasionally pseudodiploid transformed cell lines have been obtained after transformation by various tumour viruses.

pseudoallele (sjuːdəʊ'æliːl). *Genetics*. [f. PSEUDO- + ALLELE, or a back-formation from PSEUDOALLELISM.] Each of two or more mutations that resemble alleles of a single gene functionally, in affecting the same process or property, but differ structurally, in that crossing-over is possible between them.

1948 *Genetics* XXXIII. 113 The bithorax mutants, *bx* and bx^3 (locus, 3-58·8), are pseudo-alleles of bithoraxoiddominant, *bxd*[D]. **1956** *Nature* 17 Mar. 504/2 Phenomena such as position effect and pseudoalleles make the classical corpuscular picture of the gene obsolete in modern genetics. **1962** W. R. SINGLETON *Elem. Genetics* xiv. 235 In any organism susceptible of precise analysis, pseudo-alleles have turned out to be the rule rather than the exception. **1975** V. GRANT *Genetics of Flowering Plants* iv. 75 The pseudoalleles are so close on the genetic map that crossovers between them occur only very rarely.

So **pseudoa'llelic** *a.*, behaving as or consisting of pseudoalleles; **pseudoa'llelism**, pseudoallelic state or property.

1938 *Yearbk. Carnegie Inst.* XXXVII. 305 Any dominant mutant which is lethal when homozygous and which shows pseudo-allelism to a dissimilar, non-allelomorphic but neighboring mutant is probably a deficiency. **1948** *Genetics* XXXIII. 113 Pseudo-allelism is characterized by the presence of closely linked genes, which seem to act developmentally like one. **1953** *Adv. Genetics* V. 208 The most completely investigated pseudo-allelic series is the case of 'lozenge'. **1975** J. B. JENKINS *Genetics* ix. 388 Primarily as a result of the analysis of pseudoallelic series, the gene emerged conceptually as a unit of function, or cistron. **1975** V. GRANT *Genetics in Flowering Plants* iv. 74 The phenomenon of crossing-over within the limits of what had been considered a gene became known as pseudoallelism.

pseudo-American to **-apoplectic:** see PSEUDO-.

pseudo-apostle: see PSEUDAPOSTLE.

pseudo-archaic (ps-, ˌsjuːdəʊɑːˈkeɪɪk), *a.* Having the appearance or profession of being ancient, but not really so; artificially archaic in style, language, etc. So **pseudo-'archaism**, false or artificial archaism; **pseudo-'archaist**, one who invents or uses sham archaisms, esp. in language.

1882 SYMONDS in *Macm. Mag.* XLV. 320 These fragments of a genuinely antique composition make the pseudo-archaism of the ballad..more glaring. **1883** C. C. PERKINS *Ital. Sculpture* III. iv. 344 *note*, It is possibly a pseudo-archaic work of the fifteenth century. **1895** J. A. H. MURRAY in *Nation* (N.Y.) 3 Oct. 239/1 The 'word' *derring-do* (if it be a word) belongs only to nineteenth-century pseudo-archaists. **1904** H. BRADLEY *Making of English* 228 Spenser's language, 'pseudo-archaic' as it may be called.

pseudo-articulation, etc.: see PSEUDO- 2.

pseudo'breccia. *Geol.* Also with hyphen. [f. PSEUDO- + BRECCIA.] A limestone in which partial and irregular dolomitization has produced a texture similar to that of a breccia. So **pseudo'brecciated** *a.*; **ˌpseudobrecci'ation**, the structure or state of a pseudobreccia.

1907 A. STRAHAN et al. *Geol. S. Wales Coal-Field* VIII. (Mem. Geol. Survey No. 247) 10 Mr. [R. H.] Tiddeman notes that some of the limestones of Mumbles Head..and Oxwich exhibit pitted bedding-surfaces and a pseudo-brecciated structure. *Ibid.*, The structure referred to as pseudo-brecciation gives the rock the appearance of having been crushed into small angular fragments and re-cemented. *Ibid.* 12 In Callencroft Quarry a pseudo-breccia ..is exposed, but dolomitisation appears to have taken place along a fault also. **1913** *Jrnl. Geol.* XXI. 407 That this is actually a case of pseudobrecciation, and not a brecciated structure due to the cementation of a dolomite breccia in a calcareous matrix, is evident from a microscopical examination. **1963** D. W. & E. E. HUMPHRIES tr. *Termier's Erosion & Sedimentation* XIV. 301 This bed is a pseudo-brecciated layer of Early Malm (Late Jurassic) age. *Ibid.*, The compaction of the sediment was due to migration of 'imbibed' water... This compaction is probably associated with the pseudo-brecciation. **1969** BENNISON & WRIGHT *Geol. Hist. Brit. Isles* ix. 189 The limestones of the D Zone are oolitic or rubbly with pseudobreccias and are highly fossiliferous.

pseudo-bulb to **-carcinoid:** see PSEUDO-.

pseudocarp (ps-, ˈsjuːdəʊkɑːp). *Bot.* [mod. f. PSEUDO- + Gr. καρπός fruit. In F. *pseudocarpe*, mod.L. *pseudocarpus*, *-carpium*.] Term for a fruit formed by the modification and enlargement of other parts of the flower besides the ovary, or of parts of the plant not belonging to the flower.

a **1835** in *Encycl. Metrop.* (1845) VII. 50/1 Of spurious fruits, or pseudocarps.—In *Pollichia* the bracteas are fleshy, and therefore resemble fruit. **1875** BENNETT & DYER *Sachs' Bot.* 518 Sometimes the..series of..changes induced by fertilisation extends also to parts which do not belong to the ovary, and even to some which have never belonged to the flower... A structure of this kind (such as the fig, strawberry, and mulberry) may be termed a *Pseudocarp.* **1877** BENNETT tr. *Thomé's Bot.* (ed. 6) 405 The fleshy calyx-tube..of the rose forms an edible pseudocarp known as the hip.

So **pseudo'carpous** *a.* (also **-'carpious**), of the nature of or pertaining to a pseudocarp.

1858 MAYNE *Expos. Lex.* 1031/2 Pseudocarpious. **1890** *Cent. Dict.*, Pseudocarpous.

pseudo-'catholic, *a.* and *sb.* [PSEUDO- 1.]

A. *adj.* Falsely or erroneously called or claiming to be catholic.

1605 WILLET *Hexapla Gen.* 413 The pseudocatholike papists. **1613** PURCHAS *Pilgrimage* IX. xv. (1614) 918 Not written in hatred of their Nation, because they are Spaniards, but of their Pseudo-catholike Religion. **1908** *Westm. Gaz.* 19 May 2/3 The..minority who wish to turn the Church of England into a pseudo-Catholic sect.

B. *sb.* A Catholic falsely so called.

In 17th c. a hostile term for Roman Catholic.

1601 BP. W. BARLOW *Defence* 106 The whole rout of Pseudo-catholikes. **1647** TRAPP *Comm. Matt.* x. 17. **1849** W. FITZGERALD tr. *Whitaker's Disput.* 480 Such are the popish pseudo-catholics, who have derived their catholic errors not from the scriptures, but from the inventions of men.

So. † **pseudo-ca'tholical** *a.*, **-ca'tholicism.** *Obs.*

1601 BP. W. BARLOW *Defence* 17 The whole cluster of Pseudocatholicall scriblers against vs. **1679** *Hist. Jetzer* Pref. A j b, That Principle which obliges them..to Advance their Pseudo-catholicism, and to extirpate Heresie.

pseudo-ceratophorus, etc.: see PSEUDO- 2.

pseudo-Christ (ps-, ˈsjuːdəʊkraɪst). [ad. late L. *pseudochrīstus* (Itala *a* 200), Gr. ψευδόχριστος (Mark xiii. 22): see PSEUDO- and CHRIST.] A false Christ; one pretending to be the Christ or Messiah.

c **1380** WYCLIF *Sel. Wks.* II. 402 þer shulen rise, seiþ Crist, pseudo-Cristis and pseudo-prophetis. **1600** W. WATSON *Decacordon* (1602) 123 That absurd pseudochrist Hacket had so many followers. **1677** GALE *Crt. Gentiles* II. III. 127 Some Pseudochrist or Antichrist..in the apostles times. **1865** tr. *Lange's Comm. Mark* xiii. 11 (ed. 6) 131/2 Be on your guard against the seductions of the pseudo-Christs.

ˌpseudo-'Christian, *a.* (*sb.*) [= late L. *pseudochristianus c* 360.] **A.** *adj.* Falsely called or professing to be Christian. **B.** *sb.* A Christian falsely so called, a pretended Christian. So **ˌpseudo-Christi'anity**, false or spurious Christianity; **ˌpseudo-Chri'stology**, a false or erroneous Christology.

1579 FULKE *Heskins' Parl.* 158 They questioned how it might be, euen as the Pseudochristians do. **1664** H. MORE *Myst. Iniq.* 101 The fraudulent End that this pseudo-Christian Church might drive at. **1685** —— *Paralip. Prophet.* xlvi. 408 The Earthly Church drunk up the floud by proselyting those Barbarians to its Pseudo-Christianity. **1865** tr. *Lange's Comm. Mark* xiii. 5 (ed. 6) 131/1 Pseudo-Christs, pseudo-Christianities, false prophets. **1877** SCHAFF *Christ & Christianity* (1885) 172 The..humanitarian pseudo-Christologies of the nineteenth century.

pseudocide (ˈsjuːdəʊsaɪd). Also with hyphen. [f. PSEUDO- + SUI)CIDE *sb.*[1] and *sb.*[2]]

a. A pretended attempt at suicide, undertaken with the intention of failure. **b.** One who makes such an attempt. Hence **'pseudocidal** *a.*

1959 LENNARD-JONES & ASHER in *Lancet* 30 May 1138 (*heading*) Why do they do it? A study of pseudocide. *Ibid.* 1140/1 People are described who deliberately harm themselves or take an overdose of tablets without wishing to die. We have termed these actions 'pseudocide'. **1970** *Hospital Tribune* 23 Mar. 22/1 Another characteristic of the pseudocidal persons was found to be 'their understandable propensity to leave suicide notes'. *Ibid.* 22/2 The typical pseudocide is remarkably different from the usual picture associated with actual suicidal persons. **1976** *New Society* 22 Jan. 147/1 The reason this attempt is called 'pseudo-cide' is that it is invariably a gesture and is not meant to succeed —witness the fall in the number of attempts during the junior doctors' strike, when relief was not necessarily at hand.

pseudocirrhosis to **-compatibility:** see PSEUDO-.

pseudo-'classic, *a.* That pretends or is mistakenly held to be classic. So **pseudo-'classical** *a.*; also **ˌpseudo-classi'cality**, **pseudo-'classicism**, false or spurious classical style, sham classicism.

1866 LOWELL *Biglow P.* Introd., Poems 1890 II. 202 The impertinence of our pseudo-classicality. **1871** —— *Pope* Prose Wks. 1890 IV. 8 A pseudo-classicism, a classicism of red heels and periwigs. **1887** *Athenæum* 8 Oct. 461/3 Given over to rococo triviality or elephantine pseudo-classicism. **1899** *Westm. Gaz.* 15 Sept. 3/2 A solid-looking stone mansion,..built in the pseudo-classic style.

'pseudo-concept. *Philos.* Also without hyphen. [f. PSEUDO- + CONCEPT *sb.*] A notion which is sometimes treated as a concept though it cannot be properly conceptualized or grasped by the mind.

1866 H. L. MANSEL *Philos. of Conditioned* 93 It is not to be wondered at..that our positive conception of God as a Person cannot be included under this pseudo-concept of the Infinite. **1901** A. E. TAYLOR *Probl. Conduct* viii. 439 The religious experience..may for all we know prove to be itself a mere illusion, and the Absolute a mere pseudo-concept. **1917** D. AINSLIE tr. *Croce's Logic* ii. 37 'Conceptual fictions' is a manner of speech... For brevity's sake we shall call them pseudoconcepts. **1937** *Mind* XLVI. 228 The consequence is rigidly deduced that the 'transcendent' One cannot even without contradiction be said to be *One*; this it is apparently a 'pseudo-concept'. **1956** J. O. URMSON *Philos. Analysis* 91 There are two objects with a certain relation between them, in spite of the fact that the concept 'object', thus used, is a metaphysical pseudo-concept. **1967** *Encycl. Philos.* II. 266/2 The work of economists, like that of all other scientists, belongs to the category of utility itself, not to that of truth. 'Economic man' is a paradigm case of a pseudo concept.

pseudoconglomerate to **diphtheritic:** see PSEUDO-.

pseudodipteral (ps-, sjuːdəʊˈdɪptərəl), *a. Anc. Arch.* [f. late Gr. ψευδοδίπτερ-ος (Vitruv.) + -AL[1]; see PSEUDO- and DIPTEROS: in F. *pseudo-diptère*.] Having, as a temple or other building, a single peristyle or surrounding row of columns, placed at the same distance from the walls as the outer of the two rows in the DIPTEROS. So † **pseudo'dipter**, ‖ **pseudo'dipteron**, a building of this type; also, **pseudo'dipterally** *adv.*

1696 PHILLIPS (ed. 5), *Pseudodipter.* **1706** *Ibid.*, *Pseudodipteron*,..a kind of Temple among the Ancients, which was surrounded with but one Row of Pillars; yet the Row from the Wall was set at the Distance of two Rows. **1821** *New Monthly Mag.* II. 304 We have pseudodipteral, pseudology,..and many similar words. **1841** *Penny Cycl.* XX. 74/1 The temple of Venus and Roma... This main edifice was..remarkable as being not only decastyle, but pseudo-dipteral also. **1842–76** GWILT *Archit.* Gloss. s.v. *Temple*, The pseudo-dipteral temple was constructed with eight columns in front and rear and with fifteen on the sides, including those at the angles. **1875** *Encycl. Brit.* II. 471/1 The portico of University College, London, is pseudo-dipterally arranged, the returning columns on the ends or sides not being carried through behind those in front.

pseudodox (ps-, ˈsjuːdədɒks), *sb.* [ad. Gr. ψευδόδοξ-ος holding a false opinion, ψευδοδοξία a false opinion or notion; f. ψευδο-, PSEUDO- + δόξα opinion.] A false or erroneous opinion. So **'pseudodox**, † **pseudo'doxal** *adjs.*, of the nature of, or holding, a false opinion; **'pseudodoxy** [after *orthodoxy*, etc.], the holding of false opinions.

1615 T. ADAMS *Engl. Sicknesse* ii. Wks. (1629) 337 To maintaine the atheisticall..*pseudodox, which iudgeth evill good and darknesse light. **1631** R. H. *Arraignm. Whole Creature* ii. 13 One Proposition, truely Orthodox (though.. it seeme a Paradox, or Pseudodox). **1858** MAYHEW *Upper Rhine* Introd. (1860) 8 In this the modern Arcadia, the pseudodox still lingers. **1720** T. GORDON *Creed Indep. Whig* p. i, There is not a Tenet which can justly be called *Pseudodox. **1638–48** G. DANIEL *Eclog.* ii. 127 Strange *Pseudo-doxal fancies. **1651** HOWELL *Venice* 157 That the new name of blind obedience..is a Pseudo-doxall tenet. **1662** PETTY *Taxes* x. §28 There is no *pseudodoxy so great, but may be muzled from doing much harm..without either death, imprisonment, or mutilation. **1879** MCCLINTOCK & STRONG *Cycl. Bibl. Lit.* VIII. 760 Pseudodoxy..designates a false or deceptive opinion, and hence is employed for *superstition* and *error*.

pseudo-dramatic to **-erysipelas** etc.: see PSEUDO-.

'pseudo-event. orig. *U.S.* [PSEUDO- 1.] An event arranged or brought about merely for the sake of the publicity which it generates. Hence **pseudo-e'ventful** *a.*

1962 D. J. BOORSTIN *Image* i. 9 A pseudo-event..is not spontaneous, but comes about because someone has planned, planted, or incited it. Typically, it is not a train wreck or an earthquake, but an interview. *Ibid.* iv. 161 A pseudo-eventful by-product of the [celebrity] star system is what *Time* magazine has accurately described as 'non-books.' These are printed matter between covers, usually put together by someone other than the ostensible autobiographer. **1962** *Spectator* 22 June 823/2 Another pseudo-event three thousand miles away. On March 17, I had stood on Fifth Avenue, barred from crossing Manhattan by a quarter of a million people..parading..in ..rosettes and badges saying 'Kiss Me, I'm Irish.' **1963** *Guardian* 21 Jan. 8/2 By enthroning the pseudo-event at the heart of an £800 million industry [*sc.* football pools], the promotors have made clear..that nothing..is what it seems. **1966** D. JENKINS *Educated Society* i. 36 The centre of the public stage will be occupied by performers, whether politicians or 'celebrities', who live out a life of highly publicised pseudo-events for the delectation of multitudes. **1969** *Daily Tel.* (Colour Suppl.) 1 Aug. 10/4 Beauty Festivals are pseudo-events of almost clinical purity. **1976** *Listener* 28 Oct. 524/3 The [US] election campaign became a perfect pseudo-event..a game played on..trains, in.. planes, and in shopping precincts.

pseudo-existence to **-Freud:** see PSEUDO- 1 a, b, 2 a.

pseudogamy (sjuːˈdɒgəmɪ). *Biol.* [ad. G. *pseudogamie* (W. O. Focke *Pflanzen-Mischlinge* (1881) vii. 510): see PSEUDO- and -GAMY.]

a. In an apomictic plant, development of an embryo following pollination without fertilization.

1900 B. D. JACKSON *Gloss. Bot. Terms* 213/2 *Pseudogamy*, parthenogenetic fruiting, as pollination without impregnation of ovules. **1908** *Ann. Bot.* XXII. 42 *Humaria rutilans* is..an example of the so-called apogamous development of the ascocarp, or pseudogamy. **1956** *Nature* 21 Jan. 141/2 A third group of populations [of *Culex pipiens*] is interfertile with the others in one direction only. Parthenogenesis, with pseudogamy, predetermination and multiple compatibility genes can be excluded as causative mechanisms. **1974** *New Phytol.* LXXIII. 1243 Pseudogamy is a type of agamospermic reproduction in which seed development is stimulated by pollination although the male nucleus does not fuse with the egg. **1976** BELL & COOMBE tr. *Strasburger's Textbk. Bot.* (rev. ed.) 403 In many angiosperms embryos develop from diploid unfertilized egg-cells (parthenogenesis and angiospermy..), but sometimes this development requires the stimulus of pollination (pseudogamy).

b. The fusion of two vegetative nuclei.

1907 *Annales Mycologica* V. 422 Fusion of two vegetative nuclei: pseudogamy. **1928** C. W. DODGE tr. *Gäumann's Compar. Morphol. of Fungi* iv. 13 The sexual processes occurring outside in the thallus between two sexually differentiated vegetative cells..called pseudo-mixis (pseudogamy of Hartmann). *Ibid.*, Since the copulating cells are not morphologically distinguished from other vegetative cells and since only the release of specific developmental stimuli..marks this anastomosis of two vegetative cells as a sexual process, pseudogamy is often distinguished with difficulty from the usual pseudo-sexual anastomoses which are brought about by food relations.

Hence **pseu'dogamous** *a.*

1932 C. D. DARLINGTON *Rec. Adv. Cytol.* xv. 434 Moderate or even high pollen fertility is sometimes found in the pseudogamous *Potentilla* species. **1964** W. WILLIAMS *Genetic Princ. & Plant Breeding* viii. 290 Hybrid endosperms in pseudogamous apomicts derived from crosses between unrelated parents promote stronger growth in apomictic seedlings. **1974** *New Phytol.* LXXIII. 1246 The three pseudogamous species..would set seed when pollinated by each other or intraspecifically, but not when pollinated by any of quite a large selection of different *Potentilla* species.

pseudogene to **-globulin**: see PSEUDO-.

pseudo-'Gothic, *a.* That pretends or is erroneously held to be Gothic (in style), and is not; sham-Gothic; also as *sb.*

1876 FREEMAN *Hist. Sk.* 201 The Renaissance inherited from the pseudo-Gothic of Italy. **1902** *Monthly Rev.* Aug. 136 It is difficult to understand how they could be deceived for a moment by the pseudo-Gothic style of the 'Castle of Otranto'.

pseudograph (ps-, 'sjuːdəʊgrɑːf, -æ-). [ad. late L. *pseudograph-us* (Cassiod.), a. Gr. ψευδογράφ-ος drawing or writing falsely, a writer of falsehoods: see PSEUDO- and -GRAPH.]

†**1.** 'A counterfeit writer' (Cockeram, 1623). *Obs. rare*$^{-0}$.

2. A spurious writing; a literary work purporting to be by another than the real author. (Cf. PSEUDEPIGRAPHA.)

1828-32 WEBSTER, *Pseudograph*, *Pseudography*, false writing. **1864** *Athenæum* 27 Aug. 274/3 The..cleverest..people are..deceived by pseudographs. **1866** *Reader* 31 Mar. 317/2 A pseudograph of the thirteenth century. **1905** J. ORR *Probl. O.T.* viii. 249 Views differ as to how the book is to be regarded—whether as a pseudograph (forgery) or as a free composition in the name and spirit of Moses.

pseu'dographer. *rare*$^{-1}$. [f. as prec. + -ER: see -GRAPHER.] A false writer; in quot. one who counterfeits another's handwriting, a forger.

1818 *Edin. Rev.* Sept. 438 M. Villette, a pseudo-grapher of the greatest eminence, counterfeited the handwriting and signature of Marie Antionette.

pseu'dographize, *v.* *rare*$^{-1}$. [f. as PSEUDOGRAPH + -IZE.] *intr.* To write (in quot. to spell) falsely.

1873 F. HALL *Mod. Eng.* 159 If we account this error [*president* for *precedent*] typographical, there must have been a wide-spread conspiracy among old printers to pseudographize.

pseudography (ps-, sjuː'dɒgrəfɪ). [ad. Gr. ψευδογραφία false drawing, writing, or description, f. ψευδογράφ-ος: cf. late L. *pseudographia* (*a* 525): see PSEUDOGRAPH and -GRAPHY.] False writing.

1. The writing of words falsely, i.e. not according to the sound, or not according to usage; false, incorrect, or bad spelling; an instance of this.

1580 G. HARVEY *Lett.* Wks. (Grosart) I. 104 See what absurdities thys yl fauoured orthographye, or rather Pseudography, hath ingendred. **16..** B. JONSON *Eng. Gram.* I. iv, To add a superfluous letter, as there are too many in our pseudography. **1734** HEARNE *Collect.* 17 May, Shakespeare wanted learning. He was guilty of pseudography, sometimes perhaps designedly. **1804** MITFORD *Inquiry* 408 Those who would make our speech bend to what he justly calls our pseudography.

2. False argument. *rare.*

1603 SIR C. HEYDON *Jud. Astrol.* xxii. 467 Most absurd Pseudographie is this in Astrologie.

pseudogyne, etc.: see PSEUDO- 2.

pseudo'halogen. *Chem.* Also with hyphen. [a. G. *pseudohalogen* (Birckenbach & Kellermann 1925, in *Ber. d. Deut. Chem. Ges.* LVIII. 786): see PSEUDO- and HALOGEN.] Any of a class of compounds (in some cases hypothetical) which have small molecules built up from atoms of electronegative elements and which closely resemble the halogens in many respects.

1925 *Chem. Abstr.* XIX. 1996 (*heading*) Pseudo halogens. **1954** R. C. BRASTED in M. C. Sneed et al. *Comprehensive Inorg. Chem.* III. ix. 223 The similarities between the pseudohalogens and the halogens are as follows: 1. They are in general fairly volatile. 2. They show affinity for metals, with which they combine directly to form salts. 3. The silver, lead, and mercury (I) salts are insoluble in water. [Etc.] **1962** COTTON & WILKINSON *Adv. Inorg. Chem.* xxii. 465 The most important pseudohalogens are $(CN)_2$, cyanogen; $(OCN)_2$, oxycyanogen (existence in free state uncertain); $(SCN)_2$, thiocyanogen; $Se(CN)_2$, selenocyanogen; and $(SCSN_3)_2$, azido-carbon disulfide. **1965** PHILLIPS & WILLIAMS *Inorg. Chem.* I. xii. 467 All the pseudo-halogen anions enter into simple acid-base reactions with the proton in aqueous solution.

Hence **pseudo'halide** [HALIDE], a compound, ion, or radical formed by a pseudohalogen.

1925 *Chem. Abstr.* XIX. 1996 An attempt was made to prep. $(SeCN)_2$, $(CNO)_2$ and $(TeCN)_2$ by electrolysis of K pseudo halides in alc. solns. **1965** PHILLIPS & WILLIAMS *Inorg. Chem.* I. xii. 467 The difference between the two series of anions, halides and pseudo-halides, lies in the unsaturation of a pseudo-halide which is most marked in CN^-. The unsaturation places the pseudo-halides high relative to the halides in the spectrochemical series. **1967** *New Scientist* 28 Dec. 766/1 A novel method of making carbonyl pseudohalides by simple substitution. In this way they could obtain from potassium cyanide the pseudohalide carbonyl cyanide.

,pseudoher'maphroditism. *Med.* Also with hyphen. [f. PSEUDO- + HERMAPHRODITISM.] The condition of having the gonads and chromosomes of one sex and some anatomical and secondary characteristics of the other sex.

Contrasted with true hermaphroditism, in which there are gonads or gonadal tissue of both sexes.

1881 *Amer. Jrnl. Obstetr.* XIV. 105 The case is..an interesting and rare one, whether it be a case of double congenital ovarian hernia..or whether it proves to be that equally rare malformation, masculine pseudo-hermaphroditism with feminine external genitals. **1924** R. MUIR *Text-bk. Path.* xix. 705 General hypoplasia of the uterus is observed in ovarian defect and may be attended by other abnormalities, e.g. pseudo-hermaphroditism. **1950** H. B. FRIEDGOOD in R. H. Williams *Textbk. Endocrinol.* x. 633 Another example of the importance of considering functional as well as structural changes in making a diagnosis is seen in the differentiation of intersexuality of genetic origin from female pseudo-hermaphroditism due to congenital adrenal hyperplasia. **1974** PASSMORE & ROBSON *Compan. Med. Stud.* III. xxiii. 70/2 In males the resulting lack of testicular androgen during intrauterine development leads to..pseudohermaphroditism, the baby being born with apparently female genitalia despite a normal male chromosome complement.

So **,pseudoher'maphrodite**, a person with this condition.

1895 *Amer. Jrnl. Obstetr.* XXXII. 528 The sexual instincts of this anomalous male being were directed toward men, not women—a fact which leads the author to remark that hermaphrodites and pseudo-hermaphrodites are *degenerates*. **1928** L. LOEB in E. V. Cowdry *Special Cytol.* II. xxxiv. 1184 In male pseudo-hermaphrodites..a development of the mammary gland may occur in certain cases. **1975** FRASER & NORA *Genetics of Man* iv. 53/1 A 46,XY male with a chromatin-negative buccal smear who is female in external appearance is a male pseudohermaphrodite.

pseudo-historic to **-literature**: see PSEUDO- 1 a, b, 2 a.

pseudoism (ps-, 'sjuːdəʊɪz(ə)m). *nonce-wd.* [irreg. f. PSEUDO- + -ISM: cf. PSEUDISM.] (See quot.)

1879 MCCLINTOCK & STRONG *Cycl. Bibl. Lit.* VIII. 760 The word *pseudoism* is of recent formation, and means a general inclination to the false, which shows itself in thoughts, words, and doctrines, as well as in acts and in the social intercourse of life.

pseudolatry (ps-, sjuː'dɒlətrɪ). *rare.* [ad. Chr. Gr. ψευδολατρεία (Cyril): see PSEUDO- and -LATRY.] False worship; the worship of false gods.

1879 MCCLINTOCK & STRONG *Cycl. Bibl. Lit.* VIII. 760 Pseudolatry has also penetrated into the Christian Church.

pseu'dologer. [f. Gr. ψευδολόγ-ος speaking falsely, a liar + -ER¹.] A maker of false statements, a (systematic) liar. So **pseudo'logical** *a.* [cf. Gr. ψευδολογικ-ός false], pertaining or relating to pseudology (hence **pseudo'logically** *adv.*); **pseu'dologist** [in Gr. ψευδολογιστ-ής], (*a*) = *pseudologer*; (*b*) one versed in pseudology (sense 2).

1656 BLOUNT *Glossogr.*, **Pseudologer*, a false teacher, a liar. **1884** *Sat. Rev.* 19 July 77/1 He was hampered by the inferiority of the *pseudological tools of his day. **1867** VISCT. STRANGFORD *Selection* (1869) II. 43 *Pseudologically speaking, the first intimation..rested on a miscalculation rather than a direct falsehood. **1805** *Miniature* No. 26 (1806) II. 65, I hear..that a work is in the press, and will speedily be published, entitled The *Pseudologist or Complete Liar, in twenty-one volumes folio, with complete indices. **1867** *Pall Mall G.* 4 Jan. 10 Everybody..becomes, by the very nature of things, a comparative pseudologist.

‖**pseudologia fantastica** (sjuːdəʊ'ləʊdʒɪə fæn'tæstɪkə). *Psychol.* Also **pseudologia phantastica.** [mod.L., ad. Gr. ψευδολογία falsehood + Gr. fem. φανταστική or med.Lat. fem. *phantastica* imaginary.] A condition, often associated with other abnormal traits, in which a person fabricates stories about himself in order to inflate his importance but readily changes or abandons them when challenged. Also *ellipt.* as *pseudologia.*

1909 *Westm. Hospital Rep.* XVI. 68 There are some cases of moral imbecility in which this [lying] is the chief..feature, yet so pronounced that it has been looked upon by some as a distinct disease, and has been given a name all to itself: 'Pseudologia Fantastica'. **1917** C. E. LONG tr. *Jung's Coll. Papers Analytical Psychol.* i. 71 Our case has another analogy with *pseudologia phantastica*: The development of the phantasies during the attacks. **1934** OWEN & ZILBOORG tr. *Fenichel's Outl. Clin. Psychoanal.* xi. 443 The most remarkable feature in pseudologia is that the patient really is speaking the truth..and that unwittingly the phantastic lies are distorted expressions of his repressed infantile sexual history. **1949** *Horizon* Mar. 216 A hysteric, suffering from *pseudologia phantastica*. **1960** I. BENNETT *Delinquent & Neurotic Children* iii. 87 Imaginative or pathological lying (pseudologia fantastica).

pseudologic: see PSEUDO- 1 a.

pseudologue ('sjuːdəʊlɒg). [f. as PSEUDOLOGER: see -LOGUE.] A compulsive liar; someone suffering from *pseudologia fantastica*; a pseudologer.

1949 *Psychiatric Q.* XXIII. 19 Pseudologues have little or no insight into real behavior or into the harm they may cause others.

pseudology (ps-, sjuː'dɒlədʒɪ). [ad. Gr. ψευδολογία false speaking, f. ψευδολόγ-ος: see PSEUDOLOGER and -LOGY.]

1. False speaking; the making of false statements, esp. when humorously represented as an art or system; the 'art of lying'.

[**1577** FULKE *Confut. Purg.* 327 That part of cunning where in you are better learned, called *Pseudologia*.] **1658** PHILLIPS, *Pseudologie* (Gr.), a false speaking, or lying. **1727** SWIFT *Art Polit. Lying* Wks. 1755 III. I. 119 Not..according to the sound rules of pseudology. **1805** *Miniature* No. 26 (1806) II. 65 It is not my intention..to enter into a disquisition upon the noble art of Pseudology.

2. The science or subject of false statements; a false or pretended science.

1867 *Pall Mall G.* 4 Jan. 10 Laying the foundation of the new science of comparative pseudology. **1907** *Westm. Gaz.* 26 Nov. 3/2 To prevent his further researches in this insanitary section of the field of Pseudology ['occultism'].

pseudolymphoma: see PSEUDO- 1 b.

pseudomancy (ps-, 'sjuːdəʊmænsɪ). [ad. med.L. *pseudomantia*, a. Chr. Gr. ψευδομαντεία (Cyril), f. ψευδο-, PSEUDO- + μαντεία divination: see -MANCY.] False or pretended divination. So **pseudo'mantic** *a.*, of or pertaining to pseudomancy; ‖**pseudo'mantis** [a. Gr. ψευδόμαντις], **pseudo'mantist**, a false prophet or diviner.

1652 GAULE *Magastrom.* 371 Alexander, a pseudomantist, ..rotted loathsomely, and so died, miserably eaten up of worms. **1656** BLOUNT *Glossogr.*, *Pseudomancy*, a false or counterfeit Divination. **1894** *N. & Q.* 8th Ser. VI. 358/2 The same..wonderfully pseudomantic remark. **1901** D. SMITH in *Expositor* Aug. 145 A vulgar charlatan, strikingly like the pseudomantis, Alexander of Abonoteichos. **1902** *Q. Rev.* Oct. 596 Every kind of pseudo-mantic literature was to be rooted out.

pseudomania (ps-, sjuːdəʊ'meɪnɪə). *rare.* [f. PSEUDO- + -MANIA after *kleptomania.*] A mania for lying; an insane tendency to make false statements. Hence **pseudo'maniac**, a person affected with pseudomania.

1895 W. S. LILLY in *19th Cent.* Oct. 629 Most of us have personally known sufferers from pseudomania. I once heard of a pseudomaniac who excused himself on the ground that he did not care to plagiarise from fact. **1903** —— in *Fortn. Rev.* June 1009 There is a class of pseudomaniacs just as there is a class of kleptomaniacs.

pseudo'martyr. [mod. a. Gr. ψευδομάρτυς, -τυρ false witness, f. ψευδο-, PSEUDO- + μάρτυς, -τυρ, witness, MARTYR. So in med.L. and F.] A false or pretended martyr; a martyr falsely so called.

1587 FLEMING *Contn. Holinshed* III. 1362/2 What trust is to be given to the words of such pseudomartyrs [as Campion]. **1610** DONNE (*title*) Pseudo-Martyr. **1656** BLOUNT *Glossogr.*, *Pseudomartyr*, a false witness or martyr.

So **,pseudo-'martyrdom.**

1641 J. JACKSON *True Evang. T.* II. 155 Beware of that dangerous Rock of pseudo-Martyrdome.

pseudo-membrane, etc.: see PSEUDO- 2.

pseudomonas (sjuːdəʊ'məʊnəs). *Biol.* [mod.L. (W. Migula 1897, in *Arbeiten aus dem Bakteriol. Inst. der Technischen Hochschule zu Karlsruhe* I. 237), f. PSEUDO- + Gr. μονάς unit.] A bacterium of the genus *Pseudomonas*, which comprises aerobic Gram-negative species that occur chiefly in soil and water, are generally rod-shaped, frequently produce soluble pigments, and include many plant pathogens but few animal pathogens. Freq. *attrib.*

1917 *Jrnl. Bacteriol.* II. 174 The vibrios are..closely akin to the fluorescent (or pseudomonas) bacteria. **1950** C. J. WITTON *Microbiol.* xxvi. 366 Pseudomonas intestinal infections of infants and pseudomonas bronchopneumonias have also been reported. **1961** *Lancet* 22 July 179 Recurrence of Pseudomonas infection while on I.M. polymixin after sterile culture for 16 days. **1966** *New Scientist* 21 July 150/1 Currently, research is centred on fish bacteria which cause disease, such as vibrio and pseudomonas. **1977** *Time* 24 Jan. 55/3 These have sharply reduced infection from pseudomonas bacteria, which once killed nearly a third of all burn victims.

So **pseudo'monad**, a bacterium of the genus *Pseudomonas*, or one of the family Pseudomonadaceæ that includes it, or one of the order Pseudomonadales that includes the family.

1921 R. E. BUCHANAN *Agric. & Industr. Bacteriol.* xxxiv. 407 The organism is a typical yellow pseudomonad in morphology, culture and physiology. **1958** Pelczar & Reid *Microbiol.* xii. 125/1 Many *Pseudomonas* species, or 'pseudomonads', produce water-soluble pigments. **1966** *McGraw-Hill Encycl. Sci. & Technol.* XI. 63/1 Pseudomonads, as members of the genus are familiarly known. *Ibid.* 64/1 *Aeromonas* is composed of pseudomonads which physiologically resemble bacteria of the genus *Aerobacter*. **1973** J. Levy et al. *Introd. Microbiol.* xiii. 334 Order Pseudomonadales... The pseudomonads are ubiquitous in nature, are largely free-living.., and have achieved economic importance in that they are the most common cause of food spoilage. **1975** *Nature* 24 Apr. 671/1 The most striking metabolic capability of pseudomonad organisms is their versatile utilisation of organic compounds as sole sources of carbon, nitrogen and energy.

pseudomoralist, -morality: see PSEUDO- 1 a.

pseudomorph (ps-, 'sju:dəʊmɔ:f). [mod. f. Gr. ψευδο-, PSEUDO- + μορφή form: cf. Gr. ψευδόμορφ-ος disguising one's form. So in Ger.; F. *pseudomorphe*.] A false or deceptive form; *spec.* in *Min.* a crystal or other body consisting of one mineral but having the form proper to another, in consequence of having been formed by substitution, or by chemical or physical alteration.

1849 Dana *Geol.* App. II. (1850) 731 This author.. described certain dolomitic pseudomorphs. **1876** A. H. Green *Phys. Geol.* (1877) 27 We find crystals of Quartz having the exact shape and angles of a rhombohedron of Carbonate of Lime. Such a crystal is called a *Pseudomorph* ..of Quartz after Carbonate of Lime. *Ibid.* 185 These crystals [of salt] being afterwards dissolved leave a cast which is filled up by sediment, and so models in sand or mud are formed, known as Pseudomorphs.

attrib. **1871** *Proc. Amer. Phil. Soc.* XII. 111 Recent analysis of Pseudomorph Corundums.

So **pseudo'morphic** *a.*, pertaining to, or of the nature of, a pseudomorph; hence **pseudo'morphically** *adv.*; **pseudo'morphism**, the formation or occurrence of pseudomorphs, or the condition of a pseudomorph (in quot. 1871 with reference to plants); **pseudo'morphose** (-əʊs) *a.* = *pseudomorphic*; **pseudo'morphous** *a.* = *pseudomorphic*; hence **pseudo'morphously** *adv.* [Cf. mod.F. *pseudomorphique*, *-morphisme*, *-morphose*, *-morphoser*]. Also **pseudo'morphose** (-əʊz) *v. trans.*, to convert into a pseudomorph; **pseudomor'phosis** (pl. -'oses), conversion into a pseudomorph; **pseudo'morphosing** *vbl. sb.* Also **'pseudomorph** *v. trans.* = PSEUDOMORPHOSE *v.*; **'pseudomorphed** *ppl. a.*, **'pseudomorphing**,

1923 *Trans. R. Soc. Edin.* LIII. 371 Olivine, *pseudomorphed by brownish-green serpentine, is quite common. **1960** *Jrnl. Petrology* I. 211 In the aureole of the Glen Doll diorite the rocks of high oxidation ratio..have been reduced, hematite being pseudomorphed by magnetite. **1975** *Nature* 17 Jan. 183/2 The large amount of pseudomorphed olivine..suggests that the older dykes were very basic olivine basalts. **1804** *Edin. Rev.* III. 299 The *pseudomorphique crystals of quartz. **1894** *Thinker Mag.* V. 342 Phenomena like the devitrification of natural glasses oscillate from paramorphic to pseudomorphic. **1931** *Econ. Geol.* XXVI. 595 Features..preserved *pseudomorphically. **1971** *Canad. Jrnl. Earth Sci.* VIII. 634/1 Some of the large embayed chromites are pseudomorphically replaced and rimmed by a.. garnetiferous aggregate. **1959** *Trans. R. Soc. Edin.* LXIII. 554 The schists exhibit distinct retrogressive characteristics, notably in the common *pseudomorphing of once-idiomorphic garnet by chlorite-free assemblages. **1849** Dana *Geol.* App. II. (1850) 731 An article on *pseudomorphism. **1871** *Jrnl. Bot.* IX. 253 The term 'Pseudomorphism' suggested as a convenient substitute for those cases where a plant abandoned the facies of the Natural family to which it belonged, and assumed that of another. *a* **1822** E. D. Clarke *Cadmium* 7 Stalactites..had coated over the crystals of other bodies, and destroyed them; appearing in hollow *pseudomorphose forms. **1888** *Q. Jrnl. Geol. Soc.* Aug. 452 A crystal of augite..moulded by hornblende and partially *pseudomorphosed. **1875** Dawson *Dawn of Life* iii. 45 Most strange and incredible *pseudomorphoses of mineral substances. **1876** F. Zirkel *Microsc. Petrogr.* vi. 114 The alteration did not happen in a proper *pseudomorphosing manner, since the contours of the hornblende are..no longer recognizable. **1816** W. Phillips *Introd. Min.* (1819) p. xcii, Minerals exhibiting impressions of the forms peculiar to the crystals of other substances are said to be *pseudomorphous. **1851** Woodward *Mollusca* 40 Fossil shells are often pseudomorphous,—or mere casts..of cavities once occupied by shells. **1943** *Amer. Jrnl. Sci.* CCXLIII. A. 539 The early soft mineral, franckeite, was found strongly replaced, *pseudomorphously, by minerals of higher-temperature significance, such as pyrrhotite. **1962** W. A. Deer et al. *Rock-forming Minerals* V. 50 A mineral occurring pseudomorphously after loparite..has been named metaloparite.

pseudo-morphia to **-neurotic:** see PSEUDO-.

pseudonym (ps-, 'sju:dənɪm). Also **-yme**. [f. med. or mod.L. type **pseudōnymum*, a. Gr. ψευδώνυμον, neuter of ψευδώνυμ-ος under a false name, falsely named, f. ψευδο-, PSEUDO- + ὄνομα name. Cf. HOMONYM, SYNONYM.] **a.** A false or fictitious name, *esp.* one assumed by an author.

1833 J. S. Mill in *Tait's Edin. Mag.* III. 347 *Junius Redivivus* is the (somewhat inappropriate) pseudonyme of a writer who is one and indivisible. **1847** De Quincey *Sp. Mil. Nun* §8 As a Frenchman says,..'Chance is but the *pseudonyme* of God for those particular cases which he does not choose to subscribe openly with his own sign manual'. **1860** Holland *Miss Gilbert* xiv. 254 We would not invade the secret of the musical masculine pseudonym she has assumed. **1880** *Lit. World* 1 Oct. 209/1 Owen Meredith,.. under which pseudonym the present Lord Lytton first appeared as an author.

b. *Nat. Hist.* A name erroneously applied to some other species than that to which it properly belongs; e.g. *Nasturtium* is a pseudonym of *Tropæolum majus*, or Indian Cress.

1884 Coues in *Auk* Oct. 321 *Pseudonym*... (In a special zoological sense) A nickname; a vernacular name, inadmissible in onymy.

So †**pseu'donymal, pseudo'nymic** *adjs.* [f. as next + -AL, -IC] = PSEUDONYMOUS.

1656 Blount *Glossogr.*, *Pseudonymal*, that hath a false or counterfeit name. **1837** Beddoes *Let.* Mar., Poems (1851) p. xcviii, I only print it..for such readers as the pseudonymic lawyer mentioned. **1874** *Supernatural Relig.* II. II. vii. 141 The..pseudonymic literature of the first centuries.

pseudonymity (ps-, sju:dəʊ'nɪmɪtɪ). [f. med. or mod.L. *pseudōnym-us* (see next) + -ITY: cf. *anonymity*.] The character or condition of being pseudonymous; the use of a pseudonym or assumed name.

1877 *World* VII. No. 169. 14 Shielded by the mask and cloak of pseudonimity. **1892** *Sat. Rev.* 9 Apr. 423/1 The momentary fad for anonymity and pseudonymity.

pseudonymous (ps-, sju:'dɒnɪməs), *a.* [f. med. or mod.L. *pseudōnym-us* (a. Gr. ψευδώνυμ-ος: see PSEUDONYM) + -OUS. Cf. F. *pseudonyme* adj.]

1. Bearing or assuming, esp. writing under, a false or fictitious name; belonging to or characterizing one who does this.

1706 Phillips, *Pseudonymous*, that has a counterfeit Name. **1715** M. Davies *Athen. Brit.* I. Pref. 8 The Pseudonymous Inconsiderableness of those Libelling Insults. **1796** Pegge *Anonym.* (1809) Advt., Whether the person be of known and established character, anonymous, or pseudonymous. **1812** W. Taylor in *Monthly Rev.* LXVII. 532 The pseudonymous refugees of political persecution. **1869** *Pall Mall G.* 14 July 10 A Parisian has just taken the trouble to write a book..to unmask all his pseudonymous contemporaries.

2. Written under an assumed or fictitious name; bearing the name of another than the real author.

1727-41 Chambers *Cycl.* s.v., The greater epistles of St. Ignatius, &c., are usually supposed to be pseudonymous. **1882** Halkett & Laing (*title*) A Dictionary of the Anonymous and Pseudonymous Literature of Great Britain. **1906** H. B. Swete *Apocalypse* Introd. xv. §1. 170 A Christian apocalypse, if pseudonymous, would naturally have been attributed to an Apostle.

Hence **pseu'donymously** *adv.*, in a pseudonymous manner, under a false or fictitious name.

1836 in *Byron's Wks.* (1846) 428/2 Pieces published anonymously or pseudonymously. *a* **1845** Barham *Ingol. Leg.*, *Jerry Jarvis's Wig*, A stuff by drapers most pseudonymously termed 'everlasting'. **1882-3** *Schaff's Encycl. Relig. Knowl.* II. 1276 [Languet's] *Vindiciae contra tyrannos*, published pseudonymously in 1579.

pseudony'muncle, -'uncule. [f. L. type **pseudōnymuncul-us*, dim. of *pseudōnymus*: see prec. and -UNCLE.] A petty or insignificant person who writes under a pseudonym.

1875 Reade *Wand. Heir* Pref. 22 She makes the public believe 'C. F.' is a clue to her whole name; so she is not a Pseudonymuncule. **1875** Swinburne *Chapman* 71 The dirty tactics of a verminous pseudonymuncle.

pseudo-object to **-passivization:** see PSEUDO- 1 a, 2.

'pseudopatient. [f. PSEUDO- + PATIENT *a.* and *sb.*] Someone who pretends to have the signs, symptoms, and history of a medical case in order to gain admission to a hospital as a patient. Cf. MUNCHAUSEN b.

1973 *Science* 19 Jan. 251/1 If the sanity of..pseudo-patients were always detected, there would be prima facie evidence that a sane individual can be distinguished from the insane context in which he is found. **1974** *Med. Jrnl. Austral.* II. 385/2 The fact that studies using pseudo-patients as a means of evaluating health services have until the present been poorly conceived should not blind us to the possible values of the technique. **1977** *Times Lit. Suppl.* 4 Feb. 125/1 Research workers and journalists are increasingly lying their way into hospitals with the intention of writing up their experiences. It is high time that the World Health Organisation added the diagnostic category of 'pseudo-patient' to its International Classification of Diseases.

pseudo-pelade to **-plasticity:** see PSEUDO- 1 a, b, 2 a.

‖**pseudoperipteros, -on** (psju:dəʊpə'rɪptərɒs, -ɒn). *Anc. Arch.* Also 7 (after F.) **pseudoperipter.** [a. late Gr. ψευδοπερίπτερος (Vitruv.), f. ψευδο-, PSEUDO- + περίπτερος PERIPTER, -EROS. In F. *pseudo-périptère* (Littré).] A form of temple or other building with free columns forming a portico in front (and sometimes in rear) as in a peripteral building, but the rest of the columns engaged in the walls instead of standing free. Hence **pseudope'ripteral** *a.*, having the structure of a pseudoperipteros.

1696 Phillips (ed. 5), *Pseudoperipter* [**1706** *Pseudoperipteron*], a sort of Temple, where the side Pillars were put in the Wall of the inner Side of the Temple. **1850** Leitch tr. *C. O. Müller's Anc. Art* §288 (ed. 2) 317 Temples ..pseudo-peripteral with engaged columns around. **1875** *Encycl. Brit.* II. 410/1 There are but two known examples of Greek antiquity of a pseudo-peripteral structure—the gigantic fane of Jupiter Olympius at Agrigentum, and the nine-columned edifice at Pæstum. **1883** Clarke tr. *Reber's Anc. Art* 219 It would be difficult to decide whether this peculiar pseudo-peripteros [at Agrigentum] owed its conformation to the building-stone at disposal.

pseudopod (ps-, 'sju:dəʊpɒd). Also **-pode**. [In sense 1, ad. mod.L. PSEUDOPODIUM; in senses 2 and 4, f. Gr. ψευδο-, PSEUDO- + πούς, ποδ- foot; in sense 3, f. mod.L. *Pseudopoda* neut. pl.]

1. *Zool.* and *Bot.* = PSEUDOPODIUM. Also *fig.*

1874 Lubbock *Orig. & Met. Ins.* v. 101 The processes or pseudopods [in *Magosphæra planula*] grow gradually longer, thinner, and more pointed. **1904** *Brit. Med. Jrnl.* 10 Sept. 596 Cells with elongated blunt pseudopods. **1951** V. Nabokov *Speak, Memory* xi. 162 The undulating plump shadows of older foliage on the water..were rhythmically palpitating, extending and drawing in dark pseudopods. **1975** *N.Y. Times Bk. Rev.* 8 June 21/2 Gifts of memory and mimicry, and pseudopods of learning, extend what is only an essay into a thick 'Anatomy' of cosmic..speculation.

2. *Zool.* A process or projection serving as a foot in the larvæ of certain insects. (Cf. PRO-LEG.)

1900 Miall & Hammond *Harlequin Fly* ii. 33 Pseudopods, or provisional larval feet, occur in most of the families.

3. *Zool.* A member of the former division *Pseudopoda* of Infusorians, comprising those having pseudopodia (now usually classed as Rhizopoda).

1890 in *Cent. Dict.*

4. *Spiritualism.* (See quot. 1920.)

1920 E. E. Fournier d'Albe tr. *Schrenk Notzing's Phenom. Materialisation* 25 The recent investigations by W. J. Crawford have shown that white light acts destructively on the pseudopods or psychic projections from the medium's body. **1945** N. Collins *London belongs to Me* I. viii. 88 The medium was invited to materialise the ectoplasmic hand inside the wax. Then when the séance was over a cast of the pseudopod could be cast in plaster.

pseudopodal (ps-, sju:'dɒpədəl), *a.* *Biol.* [f. mod.L. *Pseudopod-a* (see prec.) + -AL[1].]

a. Belonging to the *Pseudopoda* (see prec. 3); having pseudopodia. **b.** = next.

1880 W. S. Kent *Man. Infusoria* I. 236 *Monas obesa*... Body elongate..the periphery usually produced at variable points into one or more..pseudopodal prolongations.

pseudopodial (ps-, sju:dəʊ'pəʊdɪəl), *a.* *Biol.* [f. PSEUDOPODI-UM + -AL[1].] Of the nature of, pertaining to, or connected with a pseudopodium.

1865 Carpenter in *Intell. Observer* No. 40. 290 The most delicate pseudopodial threads. **1875** Huxley & Martin *Elem. Biol.* (1883) 135 Nucleated corpuscles..which throw out very long pseudopodial prolongations.

So **pseudo'podian** *a.*, in same sense; **pseudopodic** (-'pɒdɪk) *a.* = PSEUDOPODAL.

1865 *Nat. Hist. Rev.* Apr. 298 Representing the sarcode that filled the chambers, pseudopodian tubules and stolon passages. **1890** *Cent. Dict.*, Pseudopodic.

‖**pseudopodium** (ps-, sju:dəʊ'pəʊdɪəm). *Biol.* Pl. **-ia**. [mod.L., f. Gr. ψευδο-, PSEUDO- + *-podium*, ad. Gr. πόδιον, dim. of πούς, ποδ- foot.]

1. *Zool.* **a.** In certain Protozoa (esp. Rhizopoda), Each of a number of processes temporarily formed by protrusion of any part of the protoplasm of the body, and serving for locomotion, prehension, or ingestion of food. Also, a similar formation in an amœboid cell, as a leucocyte. Also *fig.*

1854 J. Hogg *Microsc.* II. ii. (1861) 265 Finger-like processes, called pseudopodia, which it appears to have the power of shooting out from any part of its substance. **1875** Huxley & Martin *Elem. Biol.* (1877) 18 Each pseudopodium is evidently, at first, an extension of the denser clear substance (*ectosarc*) only. **1901** G. N. Calkins *Protozoa* 17 *note*, The term 'pseudopodia' was given by von Siebold to replace Dujardin's more descriptive phrase 'changeable processes' (*expansions variables*). *a* **1902** S. Butler *Note-bks.* (1912) xii. 196 My reviewers felt no sense of need to understand me... When the time comes that they want to do so they will throw out a little mental pseudopodium without much difficulty.

b. The tapering caudal extremity or 'foot' of a Rotifer, serving for swimming, attachment, etc.

1898 Sedgwick *Textbk. Zool.* I. viii. 299 The posterior end of the body tapers, and is called the foot or pseudopodium;..the joints are often telescopically retractile.

2. *Bot.* A false pedicel or foot-stalk; applied to certain elongations of the stem in mosses, as those supporting the gemmæ in *Aulacomnion*, or the sporogonium in *Sphagnum*.

1861 H. Macmillan *Footnotes fr. Page Nat.* 32 Several species of mosses are furnished with gemmæ or pseudopodia, which consist of powdery or granulated heads terminating an elongated and almost leafless portion of the stem. **1876** J. H. Balfour in *Encycl. Brit.* IV. 161/2 In Sphagnum, the sporogonium is fully developed within the epigonal leaves, and when complete the axis beneath it elongates, forming the pseudopodium.

pseudo-pore, etc.: see PSEUDO- 2.

'pseudopotential. *Physics.* [f. PSEUDO- + POTENTIAL *a.* and *sb.*] A potential distribution assumed for the purposes of calculation as an approximation to the actual potential.

1956 C. Herring in R. Breckenridge et al. *Proc. Conf. Photoconductivity, Atlantic City, 1954* 86 The idea of using such a repulsive pseudopotential is due to Hellman.. and has been applied with some success to molecules.. and metals. **1965** *Rev. Mod. Physics* XXXVII. 388/2 Since we are making the Born approximation, the best choice for $v(r)$ is a pseudopotential that fits free (p, p) scattering. **1968** *Times* 2 Dec. 17/1 The theory, known as the 'pseudopotential method', does not allow the properties of the metal to be calculated without guessing either the shape of the wave or the force exerted by the atoms on the electrons. **1976** Coles & Caplin *Electronic Struct. Solids* iv. 93 Pseudopotential methods are now sufficiently finely developed that not only can accurate band structures be calculated for metals (and alloys) but also meaningful estimates can be made of the difference in energy of different crystallographic structures for an element.

pseudo'pregnancy. [f. PSEUDO- + PREGNANCY[1].] **1.** *Med.* An abnormal condition in which many of the signs and symptoms of pregnancy are present in a woman who is not pregnant; = *pseudocyesis* s.v. PSEUDO- 2 a.

1860 T. H. Tanner *Signs & Dis. Pregnancy* i. 7 The term *pseudo-pregnancy* is also sometimes applied to diseases which simulate pregnancy. **1893** T. M. Madden *Clin. Gynæcol.* xl. 463 Symptoms of Pseudocyesis.—In cases of pseudopregnancy we frequently find all the general symptoms of pregnancy counterfeited with an exactitude that might well seem marvellous if we did not take into consideration the circumstances. **1972** M. M. Garrey et al. *Gynæcol. Illustr.* v. 92 Amenorrhœa... Causes. 1. Pregnancy and missed abortion. 2. Psychological. (a) Stress and emotional disturbance. (b) Pseudopregnancy. (c) Anorexia nervosa.

2. *Zool.* A state marked by changes in the reproductive organs and mammary glands similar to those of early pregnancy, occurring naturally in many female mammals after ovulation when fertilization has not occurred and also capable of being induced experimentally.

1913 Hill & O'Donoghue in *Q. Jrnl. Microsc. Sci.* LIX. 135 As the œstral cycle in Dasyurus differs considerably from that of the Eutherian mammal, it has been found necessary to introduce two new terms, viz. Post-œstrus, to designate the period which intervenes between œstrus and ovulation; and Pseudopregnancy, to designate the period which, in the non-pregnant animal, follows ovulation, and in which the changes in the ovary, mammary glands and uteri are essentially similar to those in the pregnant female. **1940** *Endocrinology* XXVII. 125 We produced pseudopregnancy [in mice] by three methods. (*a*) Females obtained from a low fertility group were allowed to copulate frequently but did not become pregnant. (*b*) Females were mated with vasectomised males. (*c*) Females were stimulated daily on the cervix uteri with a glass rod. **1970** W. B. Yapp *Introd. Animal Physiol.* (ed. 3) viii. 293 In those animals, such as mice, in which there is scarcely any pseudopregnancy, the corpora lutea develop very little and soon degenerate unless copulation occurs.

So **pseudo'pregnant** *a.*, of, in, or characteristic of the state of pseudopregnancy.

1913 *Q. Jrnl. Microsc. Sci.* LIX. 159 Comparison of our preparations of pseudo-pregnant uteri with those of normal post-partum uteri demonstrates.. that the regressive changes in the glands are identical in the two. **1932** S. Zuckerman *Social Life Monkeys & Apes* v. 73 The pseudo-pregnant state is generally shorter than the pregnant, and varies in degree from animal to animal. **1972** *Theol. Stud.* XXXIII. 432 The resulting embryos could be transplanted to a dozen or a hundred pseudo-pregnant healthy but genetically nondescript surrogate mother cows.

pseudo-principle: see PSEUDO- 1 a.

'pseudo-problem. [f. PSEUDO- + PROBLEM.] A problem which is unreal either because it has no possible solution or because there exists a confusion in the elements of which it is composed.

1911 W. James *Some Probl. Philos.* x. 156 There is a pseudo-problem, 'How can the finite know the infinite?' which has troubled some English heads. **1923** Ogden & Richards *Meaning of Meaning* vii. 268 When the pseudo-problems due to cross vocabularies are removed. **1933** *Mind* XLII. 339 The difficulty which, I think, led Russell to his theory of descriptions had its source in a mistake which logicians are prone to make, and which has given rise to many pseudo-problems. **1938** C. W. Morris in *Internat. Encycl. Unified Sci.* I. II. 57 Current scientific formulations embody many pseudo problems which arise from the confusion of statements in the language of semiotic and the thing-language. **1956** E. Copleston *Contemp. Philos.* xii. 209 Some would wish to define a pseudo-problem as a question which we are unable to answer, not simply because we here and now lack the means of answering it,.. but because no way of answering it is conceivable. **1979** *Trans. Philol. Soc.* 209 The pseudo-problems introduced by prematurely formed classificatory schemes or prejudiced reactions to them.

pseudo-procedure: see PSEUDO- 1 a.

pseudoprophet (ps-, sjuːdəʊ'prɒfɪt). [ad. late. L. *pseudoprophēta* (Itala *a* 200), Gr. ψευδοπροφήτης (Matt. xxiv. 11): see PSEUDO- and PROPHET. So F. *pseudo-prophète* (13th c. in Littré).] A false prophet; one who falsely pretends to be a prophet, or who prophesies falsely.

c **1380** Wyclif *Sel. Wks.* II. 394 And þes newe ordris.. ben clepid of Crist pseudo-profetis. *c* **1420** ? Lydg. *Assembly of Gods* 708 Pseudo prophetes, false sodomytes. **1587** Holinshed *Chron.* III. 180/1 An heremit, whose name was Peter, dwelling about Yorke.. This pseudoprophet or false foreteller of afterclaps. **1634** Sir T. Herbert *Trav.* 199 At Medina is the Pseudo-prophets Sepulchre. **1837** W. Irving *Capt. Bonneville* III. 203 As soon as a preacher, or pseudo prophet.. gets followers enough, he.. sets up for an independent chief and 'medicine man'.

So **pseudo'prophetess**, a false prophetess; **pseudopro'phetic, -ical** *adjs.*

1680 H. More *Apocal. Apoc.* ii. 21 'Which calleth herself a Prophetess', but is indeed a *Pseudoprophetess.. and seducer of my servants. **1668** —— *Div. Dial.* v. iv. (1713) 406 That Chair of Infallibility that he and his *Pseudoprophetick Body boast they sit in. **1588** J. Harvey *Disc. Probl.* 45 The fantasticall books of Brigit full fraught with such *pseudopropheticall wonderments. **1664** H. More *Exp. 7 Epist.* (1669) 130 The Bestian and Pseudoprophetical power.. is burnt and destroyed.

'pseudo-proposition. *Philos.* [f. PSEUDO- + PROPOSITION.] An apparent proposition which is unreal because it does not have intelligible meaning.

1883 *Mind* VIII. 24 It is unnecessary here to occupy space with examples of these three familar kinds of pseudo-proposition. **1934** *Mind* XLIII. 335 A pseudo-proposition being a series of words that may seem to have the structure of a sentence but is in fact meaningless. **1966** *Philos. Rev.* LXXV. 315 In the pseudo-propositions of the *Tractatus* we see how things really are.

pseudoprostyle (ps-, sjuːdəʊ'prəʊstaɪl), *a.* and *sb. Arch.* [f. PSEUDO- + PROSTYLE.] (See quot.)

1881 *Archit. Publ. Soc. Dict., Pseudoprostyle*, a portico projecting less than an intercolumniation; a term used by Hosking. **1886** in *Encycl. Dict.* **1890** in *Cent. Dict.*

pseudo-proverb to **-racemic**: see PSEUDO-.

pseudo'random, *a. Math.* Also with hyphen. [f. PSEUDO- + RANDOM *a.*] Satisfying one or more statistical tests for randomness but produced by a definite mathematical procedure.

1949 *Seminar on Sci. Computation, Nov.* (Internat. Business Machines) 104/2 A random number c lying between 0 and 1 is selected from a store, or a pseudo-random number c lying between 0 and 1 is computed arithmetically. **1954** *Jrnl. Assoc. Computing Machinery* I. 88 Modern-day usage of high-speed electronic digital computing machines frequently involves the consumption of a very large quantity of random numbers. It is desirable that the machine.. be able to manufacture its own random or pseudo-random numbers. **1966** A. Battersby *Math. in Managem.* vii. 170 For convenience, genuinely random numbers are replaced by 'pseudo-random' numbers; these are generated by fairly simple calculations which are known to produce strings of numbers indistinguishable in the short run from truly random ones. **1973** *Sci. Amer.* May 19/1 The recipient of a coded message can then be provided with a generator that operates exactly like the one used to add pseudorandom digits to the original message.

Hence **pseudo'randomly** *adv.*

1963 *IBM Jrnl. Res. & Devel.* VII. 233/2 A periodic pseudorandomly generated 256-bit pattern. **1976** *New Scientist* 3 June 529 Each alarm is interrogated pseudo-randomly every 2-3 seconds and a small PDP8 computer identifies the change of state on a visual display unit.

pseudo-'rational, *a.* [f. PSEUDO- + RATIONAL *a.*] Assumed to be, or treated as, rational although beyond experience or proof. So **pseudo-'rationalism**, a theory or system based on pseudo-rational arguments or assumptions; **pseudo-'rationalist**, an adherent or advocate of such a theory; **,pseudo-ratio'nality**, pseudo-rational quality or nature; **,pseudo-rationali'zation**, unjustified or spurious rationalization.

1909 W. James *Pluralistic Universe* v. 211 Hegel was the first non-mystical writer to face the dilemma squarely and throw away the ordinary logic, saving a pseudo-rationality for the universe by inventing the higher logic of the 'dialectic process'. **1927** A. Huxley *Proper Stud.* 207 And though the earliest philosophies and religions may seem intellectually very remote from ourselves, we feel, none the less, that the emotions and intuitions to which they give rational, or pseudo-rational, expression are recognizably akin to our own. **1929** N. K. Smith tr. *Kant's Critique Pure Reason* 394 If in employing the principles of understanding we do not merely apply our reason to objects of experience, but venture to extend these principles beyond the limits of experience, there arise pseudo-rational doctrines which can neither hope for confirmation in experience nor fear refutation by it. **1936** *Mind* XLV. 268 It is the mark of a pseudo-rationalist to refer to *the* real world, or to speak of the *certainty* of any propositions, or to assume that sense-data support only one system. **1952** K. R. Popper *Open Society* (ed. 2) xxiv. 227 What I shall call 'pseudo-rationalism' is the intellectual intuitionism of Plato. **1960** Koestler *Lotus & Robot* I. i. 51 This combination of mystic assertion and pseudo-rational proof is as old as the world. *Ibid.* ii. 100 There is a tendency in the human mind never to leave a symbol alone, an itch to debase it by pseudo-rationalizations. **1976** *Contemp. Psychoanal.* XII. 93 Any dialogue of ideological infrastructures through overt discussions.. should.. reflect the irretrievable ambivalence of ideas.. which.. are pseudo-rational in that they unify human experience according to semiotic rules but conflict with strictly scientific statements, because they cannot be experimentally demonstrated.

pseudoreaction to **-salt**: see PSEUDO- 1 a, b, 2 a.

'pseudoscalar, *sb.* and *a. Math.* and *Physics.* [f. PSEUDO- + SCALAR *a.* and *sb.*] **A.** *sb.* **a.** A quantity that transforms as a scalar under rotation but changes sign under reflection. **b.** A sub-atomic particle whose wave function is such a quantity, the particle having zero spin and odd parity.

1938 N. Kemmer in *Proc. R. Soc.* CLXVI. 137 The quantities occurring in our possible fundamental equations are one scalar (ϕ), two 4-vectors (χ_α and ϕ_α), two antisymmetrical tensors of the second order ($\chi_{\alpha\beta}$ and $\phi_{\alpha\beta}$), two 'pseudovectors', that is, totally antisymmetrical tensors of the third order ($\chi_{\alpha\beta\gamma}$ and $\phi_{\alpha\beta\gamma}$), and finally one 'pseudoscalar' (χ_{0123}). **1950** *Physical Rev.* LXXVIII. 805/2 It then follows.. that the π-meson is a pseudo-scalar. **1966** *McGraw-Hill Encycl. Sci. & Technol.* IX. 566/2 Thus **S·p** is a pseudoscalar, and so such a term cannot occur in the angular distribution of a parity conserving process.

B. *adj.* Involving or being a pseudoscalar.

1941 *Physical Rev.* LX. 151/2 Pseudo-scalar theories can give a scattering small enough to agree with that observed. **1947** *Rev. Mod. Physics* XIX. 5/1 The initial vector meson is decomposed into a pseudoscalar meson and a photon. **1949** [see *coupling constant* s.v. COUPLING *vbl. sb.* 8]. **1974** *Physics Bull.* Dec. 579/2 Pions are pseudoscalar objects and cannot condense out in states of zero momentum (in infinite nuclear matter) because they do not have the quantum numbers of the vacuum.

'pseudo-science. Also **pseudoscience.** [f. PSEUDO- + SCIENCE.] A pretended or spurious science; a collection of related beliefs about the world mistakenly regarded as being based on scientific method or as having the status that scientific truths now have.

1844 *Northern Jrnl. Med.* I. 387 That opposite kind of innovation which pronounces what had been before recognised as a branch of science, to have been a pseudo-science, composed merely of so-called facts, connected together by misapprehensions under the disguise of principles. **1859** Saxe *Poems, Progress* 190 The march of Progress let the Muse explore In pseudo-science and empiric lore. **1911** G. B. Shaw *Doctor's Dilemma* p. xcii, The pseudo science of the commercial general practitioner, who foolishly clamors for the prosecution.. of the Christian Scientists when their patients die. **1911** J. G. Frazer *Golden Bough: Magic Art* (ed. 3) I. iii. 113 Magic as a pseudo-science. **1912** J. J. Walsh *Psychotherapy* I. v. 38 Astrology, is the typical example of pseudo-science in medicine. **1928** C. Dawson *Age of Gods* vi. 134 These pseudo-sciences were held in higher honour by the Babylonians themselves than the more utilitarian branches of knowledge. **1937** *Brit. Jrnl. Psychol.* XXVII. 246 We may.. consider.. psychoanalytical theory as illustrative of the manner in which various influences combine to produce what we may call pseudo-science. **1957** J. S. Huxley *Relig. without Revelation* iii. 47 Theology has been, as my grandfather T. H. Huxley said, only a pseudo-science. **1960** *Guardian* 9 Dec. 5/3 The pseudo-science of the academic pollster. **1977** A. Giddens *Stud. in Social & Polit. Theory* i. 58 His [*sc.* K. Popper's] endeavour to establish clear criteria of demarcation between science and pseudo-science shares much of the same impetus as the concern of the logical positivists to free science from mystifying, empty word-play.

Hence **pseudo-scien'tific** *a.*, **'pseudo-scientist.**

1873 *Q. Rev.* CXXXV. 192 The pseudo-scientific teachers of what has.. been termed.. the Agnostic Philosophy. **1898** [see COLLECTIVE *a.* (*sb.*) A. 2 d]. **1902** A. Machen *Hieroglyphics* v. 126 The only people who have always a plain answer to a plain question are the pseudo-scientists.. who think that one can solve the enigma of the universe with a box of chemicals. **1902** *Encycl. Brit.* XXV. 472/1 This was the pseudo-scientific note of the new anti-Semitism, the theory which differentiated it from the old religious Jew-hatred. **1914** R. A. S. Macalister *Philistines* ii. 44 The pseudo-scientific hypothesis that Samson (like Achilles, Heracles, Max Müller, Gladstone, and other demonstrated characters of mythology) was a solar myth. **1926** Fowler *Mod. Eng. Usage* 348/1 *Mentality*.... Some like it because it is longer than *mind*;.. and some because it has a pseudo-scientific sound about it that may impress the reader. **1928** R. Macaulay *Keeping up Appearances* xix. 213 The pseudo-scientists.. like Freud, poor old man, who's hypnotised himself with observing diseased eroto-maniacs and thinking them normal. **1960** Hanrahan & Bushnell *Space Biol.* vii. 109 Not only fiction-writers but also some pseudo-scientists have dabbled in anti-gravity. **1964** M. A. K. Halliday et al. in J. A. Fishman *Readings Sociol. of Lang.* (1968) 164 The spurious rigour of some pseudo-scientific 'measurements' of the 'efficiency' of language. **1973** C. Sagan *Cosmic Connection* (1975) viii. 59 An enormous interest is apparent in a range of pseudo-scientific or borderline-scientific topics—astrology, scientology, the study of unidentified flying objects, [etc.]. **1975** *Times* 26 Sept. 19 (*heading*) Lord Zuckerman deplores pseudo-scientists.

pseudoscope (ps-, 'sjuːdəskəʊp). [f. PSEUDO- + -SCOPE.] An optical instrument invented by Wheatstone, containing two reflecting prisms which can be so adjusted as to produce an apparent reversal of the convexity or concavity of an object.

1852 Wheatstone *Physiol. Vision* §23 in *Phil. Trans.* 11 As this instrument conveys to the mind false perceptions of all external objects, I have called it the Pseudoscope. **1855** H. Spencer *Princ. Psychol.* (1872) I. III. x. 380 When looked at through the Pseudoscope, convex objects seem concave.

1879 H. GRUBB in *Proc. Royal Dubl. Soc.* 180 If we place it in a pseudoscope—*i.e.* an instrument which enables us to view the right picture with the left eye, and the left with the right—it stands up like a solid body, just the reverse of the effect in the stereoscope.

So **pseudoscopic** (-'skɒpɪk) *a.*, pertaining to the pseudoscope; involving apparent reversal of convexity and concavity, or other optical illusion (hence **pseudo'scopically** *adv.*); **pseudoscopy** (-'ɒskəpɪ), the use of the pseudoscope; the production of optical illusions such as are caused by it.

1857 GROVE *Contrib. Sc.* in *Corr. Phys. Forces* (1874) 444 With terrestrial objects the effect of the binocular..is in many instances pseudoscopic. **1872** *Contemp. Rev.* XIX. 411 When we look pseudoscopically at the face of a plaster bust, or at the outside of a mask, it is only after a lengthened gaze that such 'conversion of relief' occurs. **1951** L. P. DUDLEY *Stereoptics* i. 21 If the two components of a stereogram be transposed so that the 'left-eye' view is seen by the right eye, and the 'right-eye' view by the left eye, the result is no longer a true stereoscopic effect, but is what is termed pseudoscopy. **1960** *New Scientist* 14 July 142/3 In 1953, when interest in 3-D had a temporary revival, I took up experiments..on a new line. These were based on the observation that 'pseudoscopy'—that is to say, the effects of the left eye seeing what the right eye ought to have seen, and *vice versa*—were not at all as bad as one would expect.

pseudoscorpion, etc.: see PSEUDO- 2.

'pseudosex. [f. PSEUDO- + SEX *sb.*] Pseudo-sexual activity; also, perverted sexual activity.

1951 E. BERGLER *Neurotic Counterfeit-Sex* iii. 104 In analyzing this type of pseudo-sex, one is surprised at the seeming contradiction in the mechanical performance. **1964** *Listener* 12 Nov. 754/2 Pseudosex..takes up much of the zoo monkey's time; like violence itself, it is a symptom and a reliable index of stress in society. **1972** *Ibid.* 9 Mar. 320/2 He related the present craze for pseudo-sex to an equally current repressed hostility in society—pointing out that the kinky aim is to put us off the pleasures of real sex. **1978** M. PUZO *Fools Die* xii. 129 This was a group of publications that drowned the American public with information, pseudoinformation, sex and pseudosex: culture and hard-hat philosophy.

pseudo'sexual, *a.* Also pseudo-sexual. [f. PSEUDO- + SEXUAL *a.*] **1.** *Zool.* In certain crustaceans (see quots.).

1925 A. M. BANTA in *Zeitschr. für Indukt. Abstammungsund Vererbungslehre* XL. 28 *(heading)* A thelytokous race of Cladocera in which pseudo-sexual reproducton occurs. *Ibid.* 37 Since these eggs are apparently in every way like sexual eggs in other Cladocera, except that they develop without fertilization, they will be referred to as pseudo-sexual eggs and this type of reproduction will be referred to as pseudo-sexual reproduction as contrasted with the usual type of parthenogenesis and the normal sexual reproduction in Cladocera. **1957** *New Biol.* XXIII. 56 The story of reproduction in *Daphnia* is made more complex by certain races, particularly in arctic regions, which have a process of pseudo-sexual reproduction. **1967** G. E. HUTCHINSON *Treat. Limnol.* II. xxiv. 510 Ruttner-Kolisko (1946)..found that in *Keratella hiemalis* pseudo-sexual resting eggs are produced parthenogenetically at the height of the development of the population..in July.

2. Applied to sexual behaviour motivated by the fear of aggression, desire for dominance, etc., that frequently results from overcrowded social conditions, rather than by genuinely sexual aims.

1951 E. BERGLER *Neurotic Counterfeit-Sex* iii. 141 All their sexual (one should say, rather, *pseudo-sexual*) activity is but a blind for totally unrelated baby-conflicts. **1960** *Jrnl. Nerv. & Mental Dis.* CXXXI. 203/1 The difference in status shows itself very soon by a pseudo-sexual act. **1961** C. & W. RUSSELL *Human Behav.* iii. 175 A real sexual relationship between two people lies in the fact that each is proportionately freed from pseudosexual involvement. **1969** *Sci. Jrnl.* Apr. 86/2 To the extent that such behaviour looks sexual, but in fact relates almost entirely to agonism, it can be described as pseudosexual.

Hence **pseudo'sexually** *adv.*

1964 *Listener* 12 Nov. 755/1 Neglectful mothering.. produces juvenile delinquent monkeys, precociously aggressive and pseudosexually active.

pseudo-simplicity, -social: see PSEUDO- 1 a, 2 a.

,pseudo-solari'zation. *Photogr.* [f. PSEUDO- + SOLARIZATION.] = *Sabatier effect* s.v. SABATIER, SOLARIZATION 1 b.

1889 R. MELDOLA *Chem. of Photogr.* vi. 219 The observation of Sabatier, that a collodion wet plate becomes reversed if, towards the end of development, day-light is suddenly admitted to the room, relates to cases of what may be called pseudo-solarisation. **1969** M. J. LANGFORD *Adv. Photogr.* xi. 228 The effect discussed here, although described by photographers as solarisation, is the Sabattier effect or 'pseudo-solarisation'. The effect is easily distinguished—the reversal of weakest densities, and the formation of a thin contour line around strong tone boundaries. **1972** *Exper. Mechanics* XII. 423 A method is described for obtaining well-defined fringes..in photoelastic stress analysis. It is based on an edge effect which occurs during the pseudo-solarization of films during development.

'pseudosoph (-sɒf). [ad. Gr. ψευδόσοφ-ος falsely wise, f. ψευδο-, PSEUDO- + σοφός wise: cf. *philosoph.*] One who falsely affects, or supposes himself, to be wise; a pretender to wisdom. So **pseu'dosopher, pseudo'sophical** *a.*, **pseu'dosophy** [Gr. ψευδοσοφία]. (All *nonce-wds.*)

1863 DE MORGAN *From Matter to Spirit* Pref. 25 This will only be done by the pseudosophs. **1884** SWINBURNE *Misc., Wordsw. & Byron* (1886) 112 The excuse which may be pleaded alike for the transatlantic and the cisatlantic pseudosopher. **1885** *Ibid., Lamb & Wither* 197 Disbelievers in his pseudosophy. **1902** —— in *Q. Rev.* July 31 So consummate and pseudosophical a quack.

pseudo-sophisticated to **-stigmatic:** see PSEUDO-.

‖**pseudostoma** (psju:'dɒstəmə). Pl. **pseudostomata** (-əʊ'stɒmətə). [mod.L. Cf. Gr. ψευδόστομα the false or blind mouth (of a river), f. ψευδο-, PSEUDO- + στόμα mouth.]

1. *Anat.* A point on the surface of a serous membrane, regarded by some as the mouth of one of the absorbents or lymphatic vessels which begin in such membranes.

1886 *Cassell's Encycl. Dict., Pseudostomata,..Anat.* Flattened connective-tissue corpuscles passing up from the interior to the surface of the serous membranes. **1895** *Syd. Soc. Lex., Pseudostoma,* one of the deeply-stained areas seen under the microscope in a silver-stained section of endothelium. Klein believes many of them to be the stained processes of connective-tissue cells.

2. *Zool.* = PSEUDOSTOME 1.

1895 *Syd. Soc. Lex., Pseudostoma*... Also, the oral opening of an Echinoderm larva (echinopædium).

3. *Zool.* A synonym of *Geomys*, a genus of American rodents with external cheek-pouches (called in Eng. *pocket gophers* or *pouched rats*).

1823 *Long's Exped. to Rocky Mts.* III. 231.

Hence **pseudo'stomatous** *a.*, pertaining to a pseudostoma, or having pseudostomata (sense 1).

pseudostome (ps-, 'sju:dəʊstəʊm). *Zool.* [ad. mod.L. *pseudostoma*: see prec.]

1. The mouth or oral opening of the pseudembryo of an echinoderm.

1877 [see *pseudoproct* s.v. PSEUDO- 2].

2. In a sponge, a false osculum or excurrent opening, the mouth of a secondary canal arising from fusion; also called *pseudosculum* (see PSEUDO- 2).

1887 SOLLAS in *Encycl. Brit.* XXII. 416/1 *(Sponges)* The opening..to the exterior being termed a false oscule or pseudostome. The faulty use of the term oscule..is here obvious; for in one sense the oscule is always a pseudostome.

3. A rodent of the genus *Pseudostoma* (see prec., sense 3).

So **pseu'dostomine** *a.*, belonging or allied to the genus *Pseudostoma*; having external cheek-pouches, as a pocket-rat; **pseudosto'mosis**, the formation of a pseudostome (sense 2); **pseudosto'motic** *a.*, pertaining to or exhibiting pseudostomosis; **pseu'dostomous** *a.* [Gr. ψευδόστομ-ος having false mouths], belonging to a pseudostome, or having pseudostomes (sense 2).

1887 SOLLAS in *Encycl. Brit.* XXII. 416/1 In some sponges..secondary independent openings, deceptively like oscules, are added. This pseudostomosis is due to a folding of the entire sponge, so as to produce secondary canals or cavities. **1890** *Cent. Dict., Pseudostomine..Pseudostomotic.. Pseudostomous.* **1895** *Syd. Soc. Lex., Pseudostomotic.. Pseudostomous.*

pseudo'stratified, *a.* [PSEUDO-.] **1.** *Geol.* Exhibiting, or of, pseudostratification (see PSEUDO- 2.)

1874 *Q. Jrnl. Geol. Soc.* XXX. 245 When the northern face of this mountain is viewed from a little distance, the whole mass presents the appearance of being made up of a number of concentrically curved beds. This pseudo-stratified appearance is..very frequently presented by masses of undoubted igneous origin. **1940** *Trans. Geol. Soc. S. Afr.* XLII. 59 The rocks in this area are very clearly pseudostratified and form hilly country.

2. *Histology.* Applied to epithelium composed of a single layer of columnar cells each in contact with the basal lamina but whose nuclei are at varying distances from it, so that they give the appearance of several layers of cells.

1905 J. S. FERGUSON *Normal Histol. & Microsc. Anat.* ii. 30 Diagram showing the manner in which all the epithelial cells of pseudo-stratified ciliated epithelium reach the basement membrane. **1974** J. G. A. RHODIN *Histology* iii. 72/1 Non-ciliated pseudo-stratified columnar epithelium occurs in parts of the male urethra, excretory ducts of many glands, the ductus epididymis.., and the ductus deferens.

pseudostratum, etc.: see PSEUDO- 2.

pseudosuchian (sju:dəʊ'su:kɪən), *sb.* and *a.* *Palæont.* [f. mod.L. *Pseudosuchia* (K. A. von Zittel *Handbuch der Palæont.* (1890) Abth. I. III. 637), f. PSEUDO- + Gr. σοῦχ-ος crocodile: see -IAN.] **A.** *sb.* A small fossil reptile belonging to the suborder Pseudosuchia of the order Thecodontia, which includes primitive, often bipedal, carnivores, whose remains have been found in Triassic formations. **B.** *adj.* Of or pertaining to an animal of this kind.

1913 R. BROOM in *Proc. Zool. Soc.* II. 624 The type of this Pseudosuchian is a fairly complete skeleton from Elgin. *Ibid.* 631 The Pterodactyl and Pseudosuchian skulls are almost exactly similar in essentials. **1926** *Glasgow Herald* 14 Aug. 4/2 The Pseudosuchians have long since passed, but they fulfilled their promise and gave us birds. **1971** *Nature* 12 Nov. 75/2 The pseudosuchians and the ornithischians would seem, in fact, to be quite irreconcilable in terms of pelvis and ankle structure. *Ibid.* 76/1 It may be deduced that the ornithischians arose from pseudosuchian reptiles which are at present unknown.

pseudotachylite to **-uridine:** see PSEUDO- 1 a, b, 2 a, b.

pseudovary (ps-, sju:d'əʊvərɪ). *Zool.* Also in Lat. form **pseudovarium** (-əʊ'vɛərɪəm), pl. **-ia.** [ad. mod.L. *pseudovārium*, f. Gr. ψευδ- (PSEUDO-) + *ovārium* OVARY.] **a.** The ovary or generative gland of certain imperfect female insects which reproduce parthenogenetically, and usually viviparously, as in aphides. **b.** = *proligerous pellicle*: see PROLIGEROUS *a.* 1. So **pseu'doval** *a.*, pertaining to or containing pseudova (see below); **pseudo'varian** *a.*, pertaining to a pseudovary; **pseu'doviduct**, the duct of a pseudovary; **pseu'dovum** (pl. **-ova**), an ovum or egg produced by a pseudovary, and developing without fertilization; a parthenogenetic ovum.

1858 T. H. HUXLEY in *Trans. Linn. Soc.* XXII. 208 The number of chambers..is necessarily regulated by the..rate at which new pseudova are detached from the pseudovarium. *Ibid.*, The germ increases in size, and gradually becomes separated from the terminal chamber by the successive development..of new pseudova. **1864** H. SPENCER *Princ. Biol.* §75 I. 214 In the *Aphides*..from the fertilized eggs laid by perfect females, there grow up imperfect females, in the pseud-ovaria of which there are developed pseud-ova. **1870** ROLLESTON *Anim. Life* Introd. 112 This form of asexual genesis is called 'pseudoparthenogenesis', and the reproductive gland a 'pseudovarium'. *Ibid.*, The 'pseudovaria' [in certain dipterous larvæ] being destitute of any 'pseudoviduct'. **1877** HUXLEY *Anat. Inv. Anim.* vii. 383 It tears the pseudoval sac. *Ibid.* 447 The young are developed within organs which resemble the ovarioles of the true females..and may be termed pseudovaries. The terminal or anterior chamber of each pseudovarian tube is lined by an epithelium. **1878** BELL *Gegenbaur's Comp. Anat.* 302 The so-called pseudova have been distinguished from the eggs.

'pseudovector, *sb.* and *a.* *Math.* and *Physics.* [f. PSEUDO- + VECTOR.] **A.** *sb.* A vector whose sign is unchanged when the signs of all its components are changed.

1923 A. S. EDDINGTON *Math. Theory of Relativity* vi. 179 R^{μ} is the pseudo-vector representing the displacement from the charge (ξ, η, ζ, τ) to the point (x, y, z, t) where x^{μ} is reckoned... We call it a pseudo-vector because it behaves as a vector for Galilean coordinates and Lorentz transformations. **1938** [see PSEUDOSCALAR *sb.*]. **1966** *McGraw-Hill Encycl. Sci. & Technol.* II. 413/1 In general, vectors associated with rotations belong to the category of pseudovectors. In particular, the angular velocity vector associated with the motion of a rigid body is a pseudovector. **1972** *Jrnl. Physics* B. V. 992 It is convenient to express in the standard way the (real) antisymmetric tensor $A''(t)$ in terms of the pseudovector $V(t)$ which it uniquely defines.

B. *adj.* Involving or being a pseudovector.

1947 *Rev. Mod. Physics* XIX. 2/2 We are left with mesons of spin 0..or possibly spin 1 (vector or pseudovector fields). *Ibid.* 3/1 Little attention has been shown to the pseudovector theory. **1964** *Cambr. Rev.* 24 Oct. 51/1 The assumed conservation of the pseudovector current.

pseudo-velum to **-xanthoma:** see PSEUDO-.

pshalmody, obs. form of PSALMODY.

pshaw (pʃɔː, ʃɔː), *int.* and *sb.* Also 8 **pshah, sha, 'pshaw,** 8–9 **psha,** 9 **p'shaw,** (**psa, psaw**). [A natural expression of rejection.]

A. *int.* An exclamation expressing contempt, impatience, or disgust.

1673 WYCHERLEY *Gentl. Dancing Master* III, *Mons.* Pshaw! wat do you tell me of the matche! **1710** SWIFT *Jrnl. to Stella* 12 Dec., Why, it seems your pacquet-boat is not lost: pshah, how silly that is. **1710** MRS. CENTLIVRE *Bickerstaff's Burying* 15 Sha, sha; I tell thee thou art mistaken. **1798** FRERE, etc. in *Anti-Jacobin* No. 31 (1852) 174 'Pshaw! what, ever blundering!—you drive me from my patience. **1814** *Sporting Mag.* XLIV. 162 P'shaw, exclaims some old sportsman. **1862** MRS. H. WOOD *Mrs. Hallib.* III. xiv, 'Pshaw!' was the peevish ejaculation of Mr. Dare. **1887** J. W. GRAHAM *Neæra* I. x. 110 Psa! it is excusable in a woman. *Ibid.* II. v. 168 Psaw!

B. as *sb.*

1712 STEELE *Spect.* No. 438 ¶3 Pishes and Pshaws, or other well-bred Interjections. **1768** BARETTI *Mann. & Cust. Italy* I. 277 To answer me with an angry pshaw. **1840** HOOD *Kilmansegg, Her precious Leg* x, She writh'd with impatience more than pain, And uttered 'pshaws!' and 'pishes!' **1845** STODDART *Gram.* in *Encycl. Metrop.* I. 179/1 *Pish* and *pshaw* ..express different shades of contempt, the latter showing more of ill humour and vexation than the former.

pshaw (pʃɔː, ʃɔː), *v.* [f. prec.]

1. *intr.* To say 'pshaw!' Often with *at.*

1759 STERNE *Tr. Shandy* I. xvii, My father travelled homewards..in none of the best of moods—pshawing and pishing all the way down. **1822** SCOTT *Nigel* viii, And why pshaw at my Lord Mayor, sweetheart? *a* **1864** [see PISH *v.* 1]. **1891** *Longm. Mag.* Sept. 455 Don't 'Pshaw!' at me.

2. *trans.* To depreciate or show contempt for by saying 'pshaw!'

1848 THACKERAY *Bk. Snobs* xxix. [xxii.], They psha'd the French fleet. **1901** *Blackw. Mag.* Feb. 247/1 He pshawed his melancholy vapours.

pshent, var. PSCHENT, P-SKHENT.

psht, pshut (pʃt, pʃʌt), *int.* [A natural utterance of whispered sound: cf. *pst, whisht.*] An utterance enjoining caution or expressing impatience.

1770 FOOTE *Lame Lover* III. Wks. 1799 II. 84 Pshut!—Somebody's coming. **1868** YATES *Rock Ahead* I. viii, 'Psht!' said the old gentleman to himself.

psi[1] (psaɪ, saɪ). [Gr. ψεῖ.] **1. a.** The name of Ψ, ψ, the 23rd letter of the Greek alphabet.

c **1400** MANDEVILLE *Trav.* (1725) iii. 25 What Lettres thei ben,..with the Names..α Alpha, β Betha,..χ Chi, ψ Psi, [etc.] **1848** [see CHI]. **1955** W. PAULI *Niels Bohr* 30 A general agreement was reached following the substitution of abstract mathematical symbols, as for instance psi, for concrete pictures.

b. *Nuclear Physics.* A neutral, strongly interacting particle that is distinguished by an exceptionally long lifetime in relation to its mass of 3·1 MeV, has a spin of + 1, zero hypercharge, zero isospin, and negative parity, and is produced by the collision either of protons or of electrons and positrons at high energies; freq. written ψ. Also (*psi prime* or ψ′), a similar particle of mass 3·7 MeV that decays into a psi and two pions.

Also designated J.

1974 *Times* 18 Nov. 1/8 American physicists yesterday announced the discovery of a new kind of elementary particle which has been given the name Psi. **1974** J.-E. AUGUSTIN et al. in *Physical Rev. Lett.* 2 Dec. 1406/2 We have observed a very sharp peak in the cross section for $e^+e^- \to$hadrons, e^+e^-, and possibly $\mu^+\mu^-$... The resonance has the parameters $E = 3{\cdot}105 \pm 0{\cdot}003$ GeV, $\Gamma \leq 1{\cdot}3$ MeV. .. We suggest naming this structure ψ(3105). **1974** G. S. ABRAMS et al. in *Ibid.* 9 Dec. 1453/2 The recent discovery of a very narrow resonant state coupled to leptons and hadrons has raised the obvious question of the existence of other narrow resonances also coupled to leptons and hadrons. We therefore began a systematic search..and quickly found a second narrow resonance decaying to hadrons. The parameters of this new state (which we suggest calling ψ(3695)) are $M = 3{\cdot}695 \pm 0{\cdot}004$ GeV, $\Gamma < 2{\cdot}7$ MeV. **1975** *Physics Bull.* Jan. 12/3 Discussion between the two groups soon established the authenticity of the 'J' particle, as Brookhaven called it (Stanford suggests calling it ψ). **1975** *Physical Rev. Lett.* 7 July 1/1 Although the newly discovered narrow boson resonances at $M = 3{\cdot}095$ GeV (ψ or *J*) and at $M' = 3{\cdot}684$ GeV (ψ′) have yet to be fully explored, the data so far indicate that these particles are of a hadronic nature with quantum numbers $J^P = I^-$ and $I^{GC} = O^{--}$. **1978** *Sci. Amer.* Mar. 50/2 The main significance of the discovery of the psi particle was that it provided compelling evidence for the existence of a fourth kind of quark, which had earlier been named the 'charmed' quark.

2. Paranormal phenomena or faculties collectively; the psychic force supposed to be manifested by these. Freq. *attrib.* and *Comb.*

1942 R. H. THOULESS in *Proc. Soc. Psychical Res.* XLVII. 5, I suggest that we should use a term proposed by Dr Wiesner, and call this group of effects [*sc.* extra-sensory perception] the 'psi phenomena', a term which has the important negative merit that it implies no theory as to their nature. *Ibid.* 8 Accepting the reality of *psi*, we may seek to fit it into the existing framework of scientific explanation. **1946** *Jrnl. Parapsychol.* X. 146 *Psi*, a general term to identify personal factors or processes in nature which transcend accepted laws. It approximates the popular use of the word 'psychic' and the technical one, 'parapsychical'. **1948** J. B. RHINE *Reach of Mind* ix. 112 How general psi capacities are we do not yet know. **1950** *Times Lit. Suppl.* 9 June 361/2 The whole field of 'the Unseen', survival after death, ghosts, mediums, precognition, gypsies, astrology, spiritual healing, in short, what it is now fashionable to call 'psi'. **1955** A. HUXLEY *Let.* 27 Aug. (1969) 761 The effects [of amanita] ..are quite alarmingly powerful, and it will obviously take a lot of very cautious experimentation to determine the right psi-enhancing dose of the mushroom. **1968** *New Scientist* 10 Oct. 77/1 He was even starting to produce scores that were significantly *below* chance (a well-known effect which parapsychologists call 'psi-missing'). **1969** J. I. M. STEWART *Cucumber Sandwiches* 31 'Are individuals any longer described as psychic, Arthur?'.. 'The jargon changes. The 'psi-factor' is all the go now.' **1976** *Jrnl. Soc. Psychical Res.* XLVIII. 267 Empirical evidence exists to the contrary; i.e. that psi can act independently of the brain without following the limiting characteristics of space, time and physical causality. **1977** *N.Y. Rev. Bks.* 13 Oct. 45/3 The very essence of sound experimental design in parapsychology is to close all cheating loopholes. Until they are closed, no experiment indicating sensational psi powers is worth publishing.

psi[2], var. *p.s.i.* s.v. P II.

psicho-, psicro-, erron. ff. PSYCHO-, PSYCHRO-.

psilanthropic (psaɪlænˈθrɒpɪk), *a.* [f. as next + -IC: cf. *philanthropic.*] Of, pertaining to, or in accordance with psilanthropism.

a **1834** COLERIDGE in *Lit. Rem.* (1839) IV. 13 The purport was to give a psilanthropic explanation and solution of the phrases, Son of God and Son of Man.

psilanthropism (psaɪˈlænθrəpɪz(ə)m). [f. eccl. Gr. ψιλάνθρωπ-ος merely human (f. ψιλός bare, mere + ἄνθρωπος man) + -ISM.] The doctrine that Jesus Christ was a mere man.

c **1810** COLERIDGE in *Lit. Rem.* (1838) III. 260 The conclusion is, that between the Homoousian scheme and mere Psilanthropism there is no intelligible medium. **1825** —— *Aids Refl.* (1848) I. 163 The true designation of their characteristic tenet..is Psilanthropism, or the assertion of the mere humanity of Christ. **1866** J. MARTINEAU *Ess.* I. 368 He embraced..the 'Psilanthropism' of the sect.

So **psiˈlanthropist**, one who holds this doctrine; = HUMANITARIAN 1; **psiˈlanthropy** = PSILANTHROPISM.

c **1810** COLERIDGE in *Lit. Rem.* (1838) III. 241 Against those *Psilanthropists who as falsely, as arrogantly, call themselves Unitarians. **1883** *Ch. Q. Rev.* XV. 280 Socrates ..says he cannot treat Nestorius as a Psilanthropist. **1864** WEBSTER, **Psilanthropy.* **1876** E. MELLOR *Priesth.* vii. 339 To allege that [they] see in the phrase, 'son of man', nothing more than a barren psilanthropy.

psilo- (psaɪləʊ-, saɪləʊ-), before a vowel **psil-**, combining form of Gr. ψιλός bare, smooth, mere, used in a few scientific terms:

psiloceratite (-ˈsɛrətaɪt) *Palæont.* [Gr. κέρας, κερατ- horn + -ITE[1]], a fossil cephalopod of the Jurassic genus *Psiloceras.* **psilodermatous** (-ˈdɜːmətəs) *a. Zool.* [Gr. δέρμα, δερματ- skin, DERMA + -OUS], having the skin naked or without scales, as an amphibian of the *Psilodermata.* **psilology** (-ˈɒlədʒɪ) *nonce-wd.* [see -LOGY], mere or empty talk. **psilopædic** (-ˈpiːdɪk) *a. Ornith.* [Gr. παῖς, παιδ- a child + -IC], of a bird: hatched naked or without down; opposed to *ptilopædic.* **psiˈlosophy** *nonce-wd.* [see -SOPHY], shallow philosophy; so **psiˈlosopher**.

1888 *Proc. Boston Soc. Nat. Hist.* 22 In studying the *Psiloceratites of Central Europe. **1820-30** COLERIDGE in *Lit. Rem.* (1838) III. 33 Schools of *psilology (the love of empty noise) and misosophy. **1884** COUES *Key N. Amer. Birds* (ed. 2) 88 A more exact distinction may be drawn by using the terms *ptilopædic* and **psilopædic*..respectively for those birds which are hatched feathered or naked. **1882** OGILVIE (Annandale) Suppl., **Psilosopher*, a would-be or pretended philosopher. **1817** COLERIDGE *Biog. Lit.* iii. (1882) 34 *note*, I was decried as a bigot by the proselytes of French Phi- (or to speak more truly, *Psi-)losophy. *Ibid.* x. 85 Their adoption of French morals with French psilosophy.

psilocin (ˈsaɪləʊsɪn). *Chem.* [a. G. *psilocin* (A. Hofmann et al. 1958, in *Experientia* XIV. 108): f. as next.] The alkaloid 3-(2-dimethyl-aminoethyl)-4-hydroxyindole, $C_{12}H_{16}N_2O$, which is the active hallucinogenic metabolite of psilocybin and is found in traces in psilocybin-containing mushrooms.

1958 A. HOFMANN et al. in *Experientia* XIV. 109/1 A second substance, closely related to *Psilocybin* but found only in traces, has been called *Psilocin.* **1963** *Listener* 7 Feb. 238/2 Psilocin, which occurs as a compound in a hallucination-causing Mexican mushroom, has also been recently synthesized by military scientists. **1974** M. C. GERALD *Pharmacol.* xvii. 324 Cross-tolerance has been demonstrated between LSD and mescaline, psilocybin, and psilocin. **1975** BRIMBLECOMBE & PINDER *Hallucinogenic Agents* iv. 108 The active principles of teonanacatl, the sacred mushroom of Central America, are the alkaloids psilocin..and psilocybin... Most species of *Psilocybe* and a number of *Stropharia* and *Conocybe* species contain these compounds.

psilocybin (saɪləʊˈsaɪbɪn). *Chem.* [a. G. *psilocybin* (A. Hofmann et al. 1958, in *Experientia* XIV. 108), f. mod.L. *psilocybe* (see below), f. Gr. ψιλός bare, smooth + κύβη head: see -IN[1].] An alkaloid, $C_{12}H_{15}N_2O{\cdot}H_2PO_3$, which is the phosphate ester of psilocin and is the hallucinogen present in several Central American species of mushroom (notably *Psilocybe mexicana*), producing effects similar to those of LSD but less strongly and for a shorter time.

1958 A. HOFMANN et al. in *Experientia* XIV. 109/1 The compound has been given the name *Psilocybin*; it possesses indole characteristics and contains phosphorus. **1962** A. HUXLEY *Let.* 18 Sept. (1969) 939 Mescalin, LSD and psilocybin all produce a state of affairs in which verbalizing and conceptualizing are in some sort bypassed. One can talk about the experience—but always with the knowledge that 'the rest is silence'. **1966** T. PYNCHON *Crying of Lot 49* i. 17 Effects of LSD-25, mescaline, psilocybin, and related drugs on a large sample of suburban housewives. **1970** K. PLATT *Pushbutton Butterfly* (1971) iv. 43 He would be selling grass, meth, acid..psilocybin-coated grass, peyote buttons. **1975** [see PSILOCIN].

psilomelane (psaɪˈlɒməleɪn). *Min.* Also **-melan**. [f. PSILO- + Gr. μέλαν, neuter of μέλας black.] A common ore of manganese, a hydrated oxide, occurring in smooth black amorphous masses, or in botryoidal or stalactitic shapes.

Chemically it is a mechanical combination of the hydrated dioxide and protoxide, the latter often partly replaced by other protoxides, chiefly baryta and potash.

1831 *Trans. Royal Soc. Edin.* II. 130 The name psilomelane..is formed in allusion to the black colour and smooth hematitic shapes of the mineral. **1870** YEATS *Nat. Hist. Comm.* III. (1872) 367 The principal ores of manganese are *Pyrolusite* and *Psilomelane*, both binoxides, the former anhydrous, the latter containing 1 per cent. of water.

Hence **psilomeˈlanic** *a.*, of or of the nature of psilomelane; **psiloˈmelanite** = PSILOMELANE.

1883 *Encycl. Brit.* XV. 479/2 The writer found [in a manganese nodule dredged up by the 'Challenger' expedition]..a total of 21·04 per cent. of the psilomelanic part. **1839** DE LA BECHE *Rep. Geol. Cornw.*, etc. 610 Psilomelanite [is found] at Upton Pyne, and near Launceston. **1879** *Cassell's Techn. Educ.* IV. 255/1 Psilomelanite and braunite..are hydrated peroxide and sesquioxide of manganese.

‖**psilosis** (psaɪˈləʊsɪs). [mod.L., a. Gr. ψίλωσις, n. of action from ψιλοῦν to strip bare, make bald: see -OSIS.]

1. *Path.* A stripping bare, as of hair or flesh.

1842 in DUNGLISON *Med. Lex.* **1858** in MAYNE *Expos. Lex.* **1897** *Allbutt's Syst. Med.* III. 368 In psilosis or sprue, the œsophagus is denuded of epithelium. *Ibid.* 776 'Psilosis' (ψιλός, bare) is suggested by Phin in one of his valuable papers as a substitute for 'sprue'.

2. *Greek Gram.* The substitution of a *tenuis* for an aspirate, as in ῥάπυς for ῥάφυς, or of the *spiritus lenis* instead of the *spiritus asper.*

1904 J. H. MOULTON in *Expositor* May 361 Occasional deaspiration is part of the general tendency towards psilosis which started from Ionic influences and became universal, as modern Greek shows.

Hence **psilotic** (psaɪˈlɒtɪk) *a.*, of or pertaining to psilosis.

†**ˈpsilother, -othre.** Also 5 -otre, 7 psyl-. [ad. L. *psīlōthrum*, or a. F. *psilothre*: see next.]

1. A substance that removes hair; a depilatory.

1585 T. WASHINGTON tr. *Nicholay's Voy.* II. xxi. 59 A Psilothre..is a paste whiche..doeth foorthwith cause the haires to fall out. **1657** TOMLINSON *Renou's Disp.* 204 Every Psylother..doth not only attenuate, but evell hairs.

2. *Herb.* Bryony (*Bryonia dioica*), supposed to have a depilatory property.

c **1440** *Pallad. on Husb.* I. 917 Wattrid cucumber seed, or comyn grounde, Lupyne, or psilotre, kest on the grounde.

‖**psiˈlothron.** *Obs.* Also 7 psylo-, psilothrum. [L. *psīlōthrum*, a. Gr. ψίλωθρον a depilatory, f. ψιλοῦν to bare, with instrumental suffix.]

1. = prec. 1.

[*c* **1400** *Lanfranc's Cirurg.* 294 þou schalt anointe al þe place with psilatro [i.e. *cum psilatro*]. *a* **1387** *Sinon. Barthol.* 35 *Psilotrum*, depilatorium idem.] **1661** LOVELL *Hist. Anim. & Min.* 59 The milk..With the gall of an hedghog, and braine of a Bat, it is a psilothron. *Ibid.* 131 [etc.].

2. = prec. 2.

1601 HOLLAND *Pliny* XXIII. i. II. 149 There is a certain wild white vine, which..others [call] Melothron or Psilothrum... This know the curriours well who dresse skins, for they use it much. **1706** PHILLIPS, *Psilothron*, the Herb Briony or white Vine.

psionic (saɪˈɒnɪk), *a.* [f. PSI[1] + *-onic*, as in *electronic.*] Pertaining to or involving 'psi'. So **psiˈonics** *sb. pl.* [-IC 2], (the study of) the paranormal; **psiˈonically** *adv.*

1952 *Astounding Sci. Fiction* XLIX. 119/2 The psionic translator in his belt would have brought him the sense of every syllable, and enabled even these psionic illiterates to understand him. **1953** T. STURGEON *More than Human* III. 207 A gravity generator, to increase and decrease..weight. .. Gravitics is the key to everything. It would lead to the addition of one more item to the Unified Field—what we now call psychic energy, or 'psionics'. **1960** P. ANDERSON in 'E. Crispin' *Best SF Five* (1963) 228 Research has taught us just enough about psionics to show we can't imagine its potentialities. **1966** *Analog Science Fact/Fiction* Nov. 29/1 I'm going to have to do the real end of the work—the psionics end. **1975** *Homes & Gardens* Nov. 63/3 In the years since Lakhowski first talked of fundamental, or psionic, energy in cells, radiesthesia has not come very far. **1976** *Psionic Med.* XI. 6 Dr. Wright wondered whether the case histories of patients treated psionically would throw any light on these questions. **1978** C. HUMPHREYS *Both Sides Circle* xix. 202 Dr Lawrence, at the age of ninety, founded The Psionic Medical Society... This drew together homoeopathy and radiaesthesia.

psithurism (ˈpsɪθjʊərɪz(ə)m). *rare.* [irreg. for *psithyrism*, ad. Gr. ψιθύρισμα or ψιθυρισμός, f. ψιθυρίζ-ειν to whisper.] Whispering; a whispering noise, as of leaves moved by the wind.

1872 M. COLLINS *Pr. Clarice* II. xix. 218 Psithurism of multitudinous leaves made ghostly music. **1875** —— *Blacksmith & Scholar* (1876) II. 12 The wind wooed them with a whispering psithurism.

psittac (ˈpsɪtæk). *rare.* Also 5 **psitake.** [ad. L. *psittac-us*, a. Gr. ψιττακός parrot.] A bird of the genus *Psittacus*; a parrot.

[*c* **1400** MAUNDEV. (1839) xxvii. 274 And there ben manye Popegayes that thei clepen Psitakes in hire langage.] **1881** *Academy* 1 Oct. 252/1 To him parrots are psittacs.

psittaceous (psɪˈteɪʃəs), *a. Ornith.* [f. L. *psittac-us* parrot (see prec.) + -EOUS.] Of or belonging to the parrot family of birds, *Psittacidæ.* So **psiˈttacean, ˈpsittacid** *adjs.* (in mod. dicts.).

1835 KIRBY *Hab. & Inst. Anim.* I. ii. 71 The Psittaceous or Parrot tribes.

psittacine (ˈsɪtəkaɪn, ˈpsɪtəsaɪn), *a.* (*sb.*) [a. mod.L. subfamily name *Psittacinæ*, f. generic name *Psittacus* (Linnæus *Systema Naturæ* (1735)), a. L. *psittacus* parrot: see -INE[1].]

A. *adj.* Of or belonging to a parrot or to the parrot family; *fig.* parrot-like. B. *sb.* A bird of this family.

1874 *Proc. Zool. Soc.* 592 Many deductions can be made as to the mutual relations of the several genera of the Psittacine suborder. **1888** *Sat. Rev.* 22 Sept. 343/2 The glibness of these psittacine politicians. **1890** A. B. MEYER in *Ibis* Jan. 26 On the Coloration of the Young in the Psittacine Genus *Eclectus.* **1895** *Athenæum* 16 Mar. 348/3 Showing that it was completely psittacine. **1901** *Trans. Linn. Soc: Zool.* VIII. 257 It is possible to derive the Psittacine type as a very apocentric modification of this metacentre. **1973** *Observer* 4 Nov. 5/3 Medical evidence and a growing suspicion..are adding urgency to demands..that import restrictions should be placed on the 'psittacines'. **1976** *Amer. Speech 1973* XLVIII. 265 The psittacine linguistic and cultural relativity with which the argument begins is a very dead duck at the argument's conclusion.

psittacinite (psɪ'tæsɪnaɪt). *Min.* [Named 1876; f. as prec. + -ITE[1] 2.] A hydrous vanadate of lead and copper, of a parrot-green colour, occurring as a pulverulent coating on quartz.

1876 *Amer. Jrnl. Sci.* Ser. III. XII. 36 Psittacinite occurs sometimes associated with gold. **1893** CHAPMAN *Blowpipe Practice* 197 Psittacinite from Montana.

psittacism ('sɪtəsɪz(ə)m). [ad. F. *psittacisme* (Leibnitz *Nouveaux Essais sur l'entendement humain* (1765) II. 145) or G. *psittazismus*, f. Gr. ψιττακός parrot: see -ISM.] The mechanical repetition of previously received ideas or images that reflects neither true reasoning nor feeling; repetition of words or phrases parrot-fashion, without reflection, automatically. Hence **'psittacist; psitta'cistically** *adv.*

1896 A. G. LANGLEY tr. *Leibnitz' New Ess. conc. Hum. Und.* II. xxi. 196 All that they do think about it [*sc.* the future life] is but a *psittacism*, or gross and vain images after the Mahometan fashion, in which they themselves see little likelihood. **1901** J. WILSON in *N. & Q.* 9th Ser. VIII. 183/1 The words *in nomine Domini nostri J.C.* being, I fear, too often repeated psittacistically. **1902** *Amer. Jrnl. Sociol.* VII. 751 Leibnitz characterized human progress as a psittacism. **1904** *Amer. Jrnl. Religious Psychol. & Educ.* May 107 Then followed monographs on psittacism and symbolic thought, heredity, and laughter. **1923** OGDEN & RICHARDS *Meaning of Meaning* vi. 230 There will be some to whom a word is merely a stimulus to the utterance of other words without the occurrence of any reference—the psittacists, that is to say, who respond to words much as they might respond to the first notes of a tune which they proceed almost automatically to complete. *Ibid.* x. 349 Psittacism is the use of words without reference. **1936** *Amer. Speech* XI. 173/2 This procedure would reduce a science to the level of a fastidious psittacism—a blind alley leading to the dead end of a circumscribed habit. **1938** S. CHASE *Tyranny of Words* iv. 35 Speaking without knowing is called 'psittacism', but is a practice not confined to parrots. **1975** *Jrnl. Roman Stud.* LXV. 187 Military matters are also the subjects of contributions from two younger British scholars, which are remarkable not least for being unencumbered by the needlessly repetitive anthologies of modern literature, a healthy immunity from that pernicious psittacism too widespread in this volume.

'psittacoid, *a.* [f. Gr. ψιττακ-ός, parrot + -OID.] Like or akin to the *Psittacidæ* or parrots.

1895 in *Funk's Standard Dict.*

psittacosis (sɪtə'kəʊsɪs, formerly also ps-). [mod. L., f. L. *psittacus* (see PSITTACINE *a.*) + -OSIS.] A contagious disease of birds transmissible (esp. from parrots) to human beings as a form of pneumonia. Cf. ORNITHOSIS.

1897 *Westm. Gaz.* 3 May 10/1 The *British Medical Journal* sounds a note of warning to those who make pets of parrots. These birds are the source of a disease, psittacosis, which has lately occurred at Genoa. The disease takes the form of malignant pneumonia. **1930** *Aberdeen Press & Jrnl.* 10 Jan. 5 Recently three persons were reported to have died from 'parrot plague' at Berlin and two at Prague. The disease is rare and is known to medical science as psittacosis. **1955** *Times* 16 Aug. 4/2 Psittacosis, or 'parrot disease', may attack or be carried by birds other than parrots. It is not yet known how the zoo budgerigars caught the disease. **1966** *Listener* 3 Nov. 652/3, I remember as a child that my father bought a pair of brightly coloured and rather handsome parakeets, almost at the same time as the great psittacosis scare started, so we got rid of our nice new parakeets. **1970** I. MURDOCH *Fairly Honourable Defeat* I. v. 52 It was called psittacosis because people thought you could only get it from parrots, but in fact you can get it from any bird. Pigeons are notorious carriers of psittacosis. **1973** *Times* 29 Oct. 15/8, I have at the moment under my care five patients with psittacosis all infected by a recently imported parrot which was ill when purchased and died a week later.

Hence **psitta'cotic** *a.*

1947 W. P. BLOUNT *Dis. Poultry* xliii. 389 Mice inoculated with psittacotic material often die about the seventh day.

psoadic (psəʊ'ædɪk), *a.* [irreg. f. next + -IC.] Of or pertaining to the psoas muscle.

185. OWEN (Annandale 1882), The psoadic plexus. **1858** MAYNE *Expos. Lex.*, *Psoadicus*,..of or belonging to the loin, or to the *psoæ* muscles: psoadic.

psoas ('psəʊæs). *Anat.* [Properly pl. of *psoa*, a. Gr. ψόα, usually in pl. ψόαι, acc. ψόας, the muscles of the loins. From the rare occurrence of the sing., the pl. *psoas* has been erroneously taken as sing.] The name of two muscles of the hip: (*a*) ***psoas magnus***, a large flexor muscle of the hip-joint which arises from the lumbar vertebræ and sacrum and is inserted along with the iliac into the lesser trochanter of the femur; cf. ILIOPSOAS. (*b*) ***psoas parvus*** or ***minor***, a muscle (inconstant in man) which in many mammals forms a powerful flexor of the pelvis upon the spine.

α. sing. *psoa*, pl. *psoas*.

1681 tr. *Willis' Rem. Med. Wks.* Vocab., *Psoa*, a great muscle beginning at the 11th rib, and going through the bowels to the privie-members. **1684** tr. *Blancard's Phys. Dict.* (1693), *Psoas*, Muscles of the Loins, which proceed from about the two lowermost Vertebres of the Thorax. **1777** HUNTER in *Phil. Trans.* LXVII. 610 Where the colon passes over the psoas and iliac vessels.

β. *psoas* taken as sing.

1704 J. HARRIS *Lex. Techn.* I, *Psoas Magnus*, or *Lumbalis* ..*Psoas Parvus.* **1871** HUXLEY *Anat. Vertebr. Anim.* ii. 49 The *psoas minor*..is a protractor of the pelvis.

b. *attrib.*, as ***psoas abscess, muscle***, etc.

1813 J. THOMSON *Lect. Inflam.* 153 The disease called psoas abscess. **1804** ABERNETHY *Surg. Obs.* 214, I..carried it upwards by the side of the psoas muscle. **1870** ROLLESTON *Anim. Life* 3 The two psoas muscles.

Hence **pso'atic** *a. rare* [irregular] = PSOADIC; **pso'itis** (see quot. 1842).

1842 DUNGLISON *Med. Lex.*, *Psoitis*, inflammation of the psoas muscles. **1877** tr. *von Ziemssen's Cycl. Med.* XVI. 96 Psoitis also occurs..as an independent disease.

psocid ('səʊkɪd, -sɪd). *Ent.* [f. mod.L. family name *Psocidæ*, f. generic name *Psocus* (J. C. Fabricius *Supplementum Entomologiæ Systematicæ* (1798) 198), f. Gr. ψώχ-ειν to grind: see -ID[3].] A small winged or wingless insect with long, segmented antennæ, belonging to the family Psocidæ or the order Psocoptera, which includes book-lice and other pests feeding on fungi, algæ, cereal products, or decaying vegetable or animal matter.

1891 *Insect Life* IV. 188 The correspondence is less striking than that of a Mallophagan with a Psocid. **1922** *Entomol. Monthly Mag.* LVIII. 104 The occurrence of various species of Psocids..inside houses, has been frequently observed. **1959** [see *bark-louse*]. **1967** M. E. HALE *Biol. Lichens* xi. 159 Psocids, lice-like insects that infest larch trees, also eat lichens. **1975** R. D. HUGHES *Living Insects* ix. 226 Psocids are omnivorous, feeding on fragments of plant or animal materials.

psophometer (sɒ'fɒmɪtə(r)). *Electr.* [f. Gr. ψόφος noise + -METER.] An instrument for giving a reading approximately proportional to the subjective aural effect of the noise in a communication circuit.

1938 *Jrnl. Inst. Electr. Engineers* LXXXIII. 261/1 The circuit noise meter (or psophometer) is an instrument which has been designed for measuring the disturbing effect of power induction on telephone communication. **1953** *P.O. Electr. Engineers' Jrnl.* XLVI. 112/1 The use of the psophometer has extended in recent years from the function of power circuit noise interference measurement to the measurement of overall noise on [telephone] transmission lines and equipment. **1975** J. E. FLOOD *Telecommunication Networks* ii. 48 Noise is usually measured by a meter having a frequency-weighting network which has been standardised by the CCITT. Such instruments are called psophometers.

Hence **psopho'metric** *a.* (see quot. 1943); **psopho'metrically** *adv.*

1943 *Gloss. Terms Telecommunications (B.S.I.)* 15 *Psophometric voltage*, the voltage at 800 c/s between two points in a telephone system which, if it replaced the disturbing voltage, would produce the same degree of interference with a telephone conversation as the disturbing voltage. **1951** *Electronic Engin.* XXIII. 35 Typical figures permitted are 2 mV of weighted (psophometric) ripple. **1975** J. E. FLOOD *Telecommunication Networks* ii. 48 For white noise in the band 0-4 kHz, the effect of psophometric weighting is to reduce the noise level by 3·6 dB. *Ibid.*, Noise power is..measured in units of pWp (picowatts psophometrically weighted) or dBmp (decibels relative to 1 mW psophometrically weighted).

‖**psora** ('psɔərə). [L. *psōra*, a. Gr. ψώρα itch, mange, = L. *scabies.*] A contagious skin disease; scabies, the itch.

1681 tr. *Willis' Rem. Med. Wks.* Vocab., *Psora*, the scabbado, or scabbiness with pustles. **1803** tr. *Heberden's Comment.* xxiii. (1806) 115 There is an appearance exactly like it..yet differs from the true psora by being very little, if at all infectious. **1895** *Syd. Soc. Lex.*, *Psora*, the Itch... Also, mange, applied to men and beasts. **1899** *Allbutt's Syst. Med.* VIII. 551 From his [Celsus'] time down to that of Willan we find the names Psora and Lepra applied loosely to all kinds of squamous diseases.

psoralen ('sɔərəlɛn). *Chem.* and *Pharm.* Also -ene (-iːn). [f. mod.L. *Psoral-ea* (f. Gr. ψωραλέος itchy, mangy), generic name of an Indian leguminous herb, *P. corylifolia*, from seeds of which it was first isolated + *-en* (cf. -ENE).] A crystalline tricyclic lactone, $C_{11}H_6O_3$, containing fused coumarin and furan ring systems, which occurs in certain plants and is taken orally or applied in ointments to treat certain skin disorders; any derivative of this compound.

1933 H. S. JOIS et al. in *Jrnl. Indian Chem. Soc.* X. 46 A petroleum ether extract of the seeds of *Psoralea corylifolia* gave a dark reddish-brown oil and a crystalline solid $C_{11}H_6O_3$ now named Psoralen, melting at 162°. **1959** N. CAMPBELL in E. H. Rodd *Chem. Carbon Compounds* IVB. viii. 883 Examples of the furocoumarins are found in psoralene and angelicin, which differ from each other in the points of attachment of the furan ring to the aromatic nucleus of coumarin. **1969** *Observer* 26 Jan. 5/5 Patients who are prescribed psoralens—drugs sensitive to ultra-violet light and taken to bring a healthy glow back to unnaturally white patches of skin—should resist the temptation to use them as 'suntan pills'. **1978** *Lancet* 11 Mar. 538/1 Psoralens form photoadducts and interstrand cross-links with D.N.A. in the presence of U.V.-A. and mounting evidence indicates that these events are mutagenic.

psoriasiform (sɒraɪ'æsɪfɔːm, sɒ'raɪəsɪfɔːm), *a. Med.* [f. PSORIASI(S + -FORM.] Having the form or appearance of psoriasis.

1897 *Brit. Jrnl. Dermatol.* IX. 477 Dr. Fox brought the case again to demonstrate a curious psoriasiform eruption disseminated about the wrists. **1977** *Lancet* 3 Sept. 475/2 Exfoliative dermatitis and psoriasiform, eczematous, lichenoid, erythematous, and mixed rashes were observed.

‖**psoriasis** (ps-, sɒ'raɪəsɪs). [mod.L., a. Gr. ψωρίασις, f. ψωριᾶν to have the itch, f. ψώρα itch. The etymological pronunciation is (ˌpsɔərɪ'eɪsɪs), but that given is in ordinary use.] A disease of the skin characterized by the appearance of dry reddish patches covered with glistening imbricated scales.

1684 tr. *Blancard's Phys. Dict.* (1693), *Psoriasis*, a dry itching Scab. **1818–20** E. THOMPSON *Cullen's Nosol. Method.* (ed. 3) 324 Psoriasis is not contagious. **1878** T. BRYANT *Pract. Surg.* I. 81 The psoriasis commonly appears on the palms of the hands and the soles of the feet.

attrib. & *Comb.* **1879** *St. George's Hosp. Rep.* IX. 748 A profuse eruption, of a psoriasis character. **1898** J. HUTCHINSON *Archives of Surgery* IX. No. 36. 365 Covered with psoriasis-lupoid eruption of a very severe character. **1899** *Allbutt's Syst. Med.* VIII. 559 A psoriasis patient.

Hence **psoriatic** (psɔərɪ'ætɪk) *a.*, of the nature of or affected with psoriasis; *sb.* one who suffers from psoriasis; **psori'atiform** *a.*, = PSORIASIFORM.

1883–4 *Med. Ann.* 50/2 Applied to the psoriatic patches. **1899** *Allbutt's Syst. Med.* VIII. 534 Ichthyosis..is sometimes found in psoriatic families. *Ibid.* 558 There are psoriatiform, gyrate, and popular forms of seborrhœa. *Ibid.* 571 The view which would convert our psoriatics..into a class of neurotics and cripples.

psoric ('psɔərɪk), *a.* and *sb.* [ad. Gr. ψωρικ-ός, f. ψώρα PSORA. In F. *psorique.*]

A. *adj.* Of or pertaining to psora or itch.

1822–34 *Good's Study Med.* (ed. 4) IV. 203 He had psoric excoriations on the legs.

B. *sb.* A remedy for the itch [cf. Gr. ψωρικά].

[**1684** tr. *Blancard's Phys. Dict.* (1693), *Psorica*, Medicines against the Scab.] **1895** *Syd. Soc. Lex.*, *Psoric*..a medicine for curing the itch.

So **'psoroid, 'psorous** *adjs.*

1858 MAYNE *Expos. Lex.*, *Psorodes*,..having or full of itch: psorous..*Psoroides*,..resembling *psora* or itch: psoroid.

‖**psorophthalmia** (psɔərɒf'θælmɪə). Also **'psorophthalmy.** [mod.L. f. Gr. ψώρα itch, or ψωρός itching + OPHTHALMIA: cf. F. *psorophthalmie.*] Scurfy inflammation of the eyes.

1656 BLOUNT *Glossogr.*, *Psorophthalmy*, scurviness of the brows, with an itch. **1684** tr. *Blancard's Phys. Dict.* (1693), *Psorophthalmia.* **1704** J. HARRIS *Lex. Techn.* I, *Psorophthalmy*, an Ophthalmy, or Inflammation of the Eyes with itching. **1780** WARE (*title*) Remarks on the Ophthalmy, Psorophthalmy, and purulent Eye. **1803** WITTMAN *Trav. Turkey* 539 Psorophthalmy is common among the Syrians and Egyptians. **1858** in MAYNE.

Hence **psoroph'thalmic** *a.*

1858 MAYNE *Expos. Lex.*, *Psorophthalmic*,..of or belonging to psorophthalmy.

pso'roptic, *a. Path.* [Arbitrarily f. Gr. ψώρα itch, after *sarcoptic.*] Of the nature of psora.

1900 *Field* 7 July 46/3 Sarcoptic mange when the burrowing mites are the invaders, and psoroptic mange when the common surface mite is the cause of the itching and other effects.

psorosperm ('psɔərəʊspɜːm). [f. as prec. + Gr. σπέρμα seed.] An individual of a group of Sporozoa (*Psorospermiæ*), parasitic protozoa found in the mucous membranes, muscles, and liver of domestic animals, and sometimes in man.

1866 COBBOLD *Tapeworms* 8 The human psorosperm. [**1876** *Beneden's Anim. Parasites* 253 The disease of silk worms, known by the name of 'pébrine', has been attributed to the development of psorospermiæ.] **1880** tr. *von Ziemssen's Cycl. Med.* IX. 494 Psorosperms have thus far only been found twice in the liver of man. **1897** *Allbutt's Syst. Med.* II. 1003 The prevalence of a disease caused by psorosperms..in the lower animals.

So **psoro'spermial, psoro'spermian, psoro'spermic** [= F. *psorospermique*], *adjs.*, of, belonging to, or of the nature of *Psorospermiæ*; **psorosper'mosis**, the occurrence or development of psorosperms in animals.

1867 J. HOGG *Microsc.* II. ii. 368 Observations..on the psorospermial sacs obtained from the hair of a peasant. **1875** tr. *von Ziemssen's Cycl. Med.* III. 655 The Miescherian (or Raineyan or psorospermian) sacs. **1896** *Allbutt's Syst. Med.* I. 209 Psorospermosis could not be induced..by rubbing in psorospermial material obtained direct from the livers of other rabbits. **1898** *Ibid.* V. 174 The pébrine disease, which is caused by a psorospermial organism. **1899** *Ibid.* VIII. 879 The disease was a cutaneous psoropermosis.

psst, *int.* An onomatopoeic sound expressing a hiss, often to attract attention.
1922 JOYCE *Ulysses* 285 What is she? Hope she. Psst! **1938** M. K. RAWLINGS *Yearling* xvi. 188 Buck hissed at him. 'Psst. You got him. Leave him lay.' **1963** V. NABOKOV *Gift* v. 302 One could already hear the energetic '*psst, psst*' of Shahmatov, who had been served the wrong order. **1972** W. M. ESTES *Streetful of People* i. 63 '*Psst!* You're going the wrong way,' hissed Calvin Turnbough. **1975** *New Yorker* 13 Jan. 28/3 So now everybody is responding. Bresson is like that. *Psst, psst, psst*—the steam gathers, then the lid blows off. **1976** *Times* 21 May 16/4 Psst! Have you heard the latest?

pst, *int.* [So in Ger.] A whispered signal for silence.
1872 *Routledge's Ev. Boy's Ann.* Aug. 576/1, I said, 'Pst, pst'. 'Qui vive?' he whispered.

psucology, obs. form of PSYCHOLOGY.

psy- (saɪ). orig. *U.S.* Abbrev. of PSYCHOLOGICAL *a.*, used esp. in *psy-war*: see *psychological warfare* s.v. PSYCHOLOGICAL *a.* 3.
1954 *Britannica Bk. of Year* 638/1 Mental tensions were reflected in *psy-war* (psychological warfare). **1965** *Wall St. Jrnl.* 27 July 1/1 In the local bureaucratic jargon, this can come under the heading of 'civic action' or 'rural reconstruction' or 'psy war'. **1966** *New Statesman* 14 Oct. 549/1 As psy-op cadres take the field And start to reconsolidate. **1971** *Times Lit. Suppl.* 7 May 519/1 In one sense, 'psywar' is not the same as propaganda—is its opposite even: while propaganda aims to influence belief, psywar influences action, and above all persuades those it is directed at into inaction. **1974** *Jrnl. R. United Services Inst.* June 38/1 Good Psy-Ops must be addressed to the need level in force and this need level is determined by multiple factors, not simply by the efficiency of an army's logistical services or the level of combat losses. **1974** *Black Panther* 16 Mar. 13/3 Such tactics amount to nothing less than psychological warfare, or as they say in Vietnam—'psy-war'.

psych (saɪk), *sb. colloq.* Also **psyche**. [f. PSYCH(OLOGY, PSYCH(IATRY, etc.] **1.** Psychology or psychiatry. Freq. *attrib.*
1895 W. C. GORE in *Inlander* Nov. 64 *Psych.* n., psychology. **1910** in *Dialect Notes* (1914) IV. 129 He was feeling sadly as he thought of Psych and Chem. **1946** P. CARTER in Aldiss & Harrison *Decade 1940s* (1975) 111 Shut up or I'll have the psych corpsman go over you. **1951** *Galaxy Sci. Fiction* May 138/1 He had put the entire student body through interrogation and a psych check. **1953** 'T. STURGEON' *More than Human* III. 204 He went through medical school too, and psych. **1960** *Analog Science Fact/Fiction* Nov. 12/1, I checked with one of our own psych men... Lefferts has definite paranoid tendencies, he says. **1975** R. RIMMER *Premar Experiments* (1976) I. 78 Since I didn't feel like watching TV in the sitting room, I concentrated on my psych book. **1976** *Amer. Speech 1973* XLVIII. 297 In most large, metropolitan hospitals, there are customarily two or more units devoted to psych.
2. a. *pl.* Psychical research.
1927 *Observer* 2 Oct. 7 The story of his magic and his mysticism is good, but it is not half such satisfying spookery as is going out..from the offices of the S.P.R. Beginners in 'Psychs' may get a thrill or two from the book.
b. A psychic person.
1975 *Publishers Weekly* 7 Apr. 81/3 He has great ESP powers, so he volunteers to help his friend Ahmed of the Rescue Squad trace psyches in distress.
3. A psychologist, psychiatrist, or psycho-analyst.
1946 P. CARTER in Aldiss & Harrison *Decade 1940s* (1975) 113 The psychs probably have a spy or two planted in this room. **1947** L. MACNEICE *Dark Tower* 181 You don't mean a psycho-analyst?.. We do not believe in the psych. **1962** P. MORTIMER *Pumpkin Eater* xvi. 146 It's only that the doctor, that psyche, did say that I shouldn't have another child. I'm in the middle of treatment, Jake says, for depression. **1964** R. PETRIE *Murder by Precedent* x. 156 He'd better see a psych—no, his family doctor. **1968** *Listener* 19 Dec. 810/1 'That would be very foolish, but also of some inconvenience to me,' the psych said.
4. *Bridge.* (Usu. as **psyche**.) A psychic bid.
1965 [see PSYCH *v.* 2]. **1969** A. TRUSCOTT *Gt. Bridge Scandal* 272 His rather puerile psyche clearly indicates that he knew nothing about the hearts opposite. **1973** L. MEYNELL *Fatal Flaw* iv. 33 Vyvyan already knew Nancy's play..very dependable; no 'psyches' or fancy tricks. **1980** *Oxford Times* (City ed.) 25 Jan. 11/6 Barry Rigal reports on the two methods of dealing with psyches—the successful and the unsuccessful—against Surrey.

psych (saɪk), *v. colloq.* Also **psyche**. [f. PSYCH(OANALYSE *v.*, etc.: cf. prec.] **I. 1.** *trans.* To subject to psychoanalysis.
1917 *Metropolitan Mag.* Jan. 20/1 Well, she went to this psychoanalyzer; she was 'psyched'. **1928** *Daily Express* 31 Dec. 2/5 While for some patients being 'psyched' may be a step towards being cured, to others it may amount to being infected. **1943** F. BROWN *Angels & Spaceships* (1955) 178 It isn't *fair* to psych a guy when he doesn't know what he's talking about. **1965** P. WYLIE *They both were Naked* I. i. 20 I've been psyched so much I can hardly daydream as I used to. **1973** K. GILES *File on Death* i. 10 He's been psyched to the best of our skill.
II. 2. *intr.* In *Bridge*, to make a bid that misrepresents one's hand in order to deceive one's opponents.
1952 [implied in PSYCHING *vbl. sb.*]. **1965** *Sunday Times* (Colour Suppl.) 31 Jan. 38/2 'Obviously Jones has psyched... Don't tell me you wouldn't try five-spades.'.. You catch them out in a full-blooded psyche. **1969** A. TRUSCOTT *Gr. Bridge Scandal* 271 He had no technical reason to suppose that his partner had psyched. **1977** *Detroit Free Press* 11 Dec. 22-C/1 The psychic bid was invented by Dorothy Rice Sims in the early 1930s. It soon became the vogue to 'psyche', usually with hit and miss results.
III. 3. *trans.* To influence (someone) psychologically; to excite, stimulate; (usu. with *up*) to prepare (oneself or another) mentally for a special effort or the like; (usu. with *out*) to gain a psychological advantage over, to intimidate, to demoralize. Freq. as pa. pple. or ppl. adj. orig. and chiefly *U.S.*
1957 *Venture Sci. Fiction* Jan. 18/2 A growing moodiness had driven her..to get out alone... She couldn't understand the pull she felt... Ever since those moments in the Monster's cage... *Damn* the Monster! Had the thing psyched her? **1961** *Milwaukee Jrnl.* 8 Nov. 11. 16/3 'We didn't think we could beat Maine with an orthodox offense,' Hatch said. 'And also we hoped this way to provoke some defensive miscues and also to " psych" our own kids into believing they had something extra going for them.' **1963** *Amer. Speech* XXXVIII. 205 *Get psyched out*, v. phr., slang term applied to losing one's nerve while skiing downhill. **1966** *Time* 29 Apr. 35 Having discovered psychology, the cops induce 'truth' by psyching the subject. **1967** J. SEVERSON *Great Surfing* Gloss., *Psyched out*, mentally incapacitated; generally referring to a surfer's reaction to the big surf. To become frightened, shook up. **1968–70** *Current Slang* (Univ. S. Dakota) III–IV. 96 *Psyched up*, adj., excited. **1968** *New Yorker* 10 Aug. 78 He's never tried to psych us, or insult us with a pep talk. **1969** *Ibid.* 14 June 72/3 It's not that I'm psyched out by him, but I'm playing great and he hits three all-time winners. **1970** N. ARMSTRONG et al. *First on Moon* xiii. 318 He always likes to get you psyched up for tragedy. **1971** E. BULLINS in W. King *Black Short Story Anthol.* (1972) 63 Dandy thought that the way she managed things and worked the love and affection from people was like a pimp who psychs out his whores. **1972** *N.Y. Times* 4 June 4/8 At tiring moments she tried to psyche herself up by muttering, 'McGovern, McGovern, I've got to win for McGovern.' **1973** P. A. WHITNEY *Snowfire* vii. 131 He was absolutely without fear. Nothing ever psyched him out before a race. **1973** *Massachusetts Daily Collegian* 26 Apr. 8/1 The states get psyched... New England..has begun to get just a little excited about the upcoming bicentennial of the American Revolution. **1974** H. L. FOSTER *Ribbin'* vi. 252 The teacher psychs himself—that is, puts himself in a certain frame of mind so that he can deal with the realities of his teaching assignment. **1974** *Canad. Mag.* 21 Sept. 27/1 It's harder for me to get myself up for practices but I still get myself up for a game. Only you have to psych yourself harder as time goes by. *a* **1976** J. QUARRY in *6,000 Words* 165 Pressure doesn't psych me. **1977** I. SHAW *Beggarman, Thief* III. viii. 313, I had no business being at the net. I was trying to psyche you into missing the shot. *Ibid.* ix. 318, I could see something was psyching him out and it worried me. **1978** *Telegraph* (Brisbane) 28 Sept. 23/4 For months we had been psyching ourselves up for this very rare entertainment delight. **1979** *Chatelaine* (Canada) Jan. 22/3 Psych yourself into ignoring your pet's emotional pleas for more food. **1979** *Tucson* (Arizona) *Citizen* 20 Sept. 6D/1 It's hard for our kids to get psyched up for a dual meet, especially this early in the season.
4. *trans.* With *out*. To analyse in psychological terms; to work out.
a **1961** D. HULBURD in *Webster* s.v., I psyched it all out by myself. **1973** *Daily Tel.* (Colour Suppl.) 30 Nov. 38/1, I would have come away from his [*sc.* Geller's] various feats as from any others I could not psych out—certain there was a simple, logical, rather ordinary explanation that escaped me. **1974** K. MILLETT *Flying* (1975) IV. 435 Mother's X-ray eyes met Celia once, had it all psyched out in three minutes. **1978** S. BRILL *Teamsters* iii. 88 Most others could never approach Hoffa's ability..to psyche out the opposition's thinking so consistently.
5. *intr.* With *out*. To break down mentally; to become confused or deranged.
1970 *Atlantic Monthly* Feb. 84, I psyched out. I'll be damned if I know how. **1971** J. MANDELKAU *Buttons* xiv. 155, I psyched out! **1972** R. BLOCH *Night-World* (1974) xiv. 90 It had been a real rip-off, and at first Tony had psyched out on the whole scene. **1973** *To our Returned Prisoners of War* (U.S. Secretary of Defense, Public Affairs) 8 *Psych out*, ..to become confused or disturbed.
Hence **'psyching** *vbl. sb.*
1952 I. MACLEOD *Bridge* vii. 95 The other main rule for intelligent psyching is to read your partner's bid as phoney before the opponents find out, and to thicken the smoke screen. **1974** *Times Lit. Suppl.* 22 Feb. 182/5 The reading and psyching of an opponent is quite as fascinating as chess. **1974** H. L. FOSTER *Ribbin'* vi. 250 The psyching function helps them overcome their middle class, nonphysical, open personality. **1975** *Time Out* 16 May 13/2 None of the heavy 'psyching' or banal superstitions that I'd expected. **1977** *Washington Post* 7 Sept. E9 In time the players realized that 'psyching' was not a dividend payer.

psychagogic (ps-, saɪkəˈgɒdʒɪk), *a.* [ad. Gr. ψῡχαγωγικός attractive to the mind, persuasive, f. ψῡχαγωγία winning of the mind, persuasion, f. ψῡχαγωγός: see next. In mod.F. *psychagogique.*]
1. Influencing or leading the mind or soul; persuasive, attractive.
1846 GROTE *Greece* I. xvi. I. 573 When we examine the psychagogic influences predominant in the society among whom this belief originally grew up. **1871** MORLEY *Vauvenargues* in *Crit. Misc.* Ser. I. 15, Essential conditions of psychagogic quality.
†**2.** (= Gr. ψῡχαγωγός.) Conjuring up or evoking the spirits of the dead. *rare*$^{-1}$.
1892 *Edin. Rev.* CLXXV. 423 In the play of the 'Choëphoræ' [Agamemnon's] royal shade, powerful in the realm of death, is wrought upon by the long psychagogic odes to succour his avengers.
3. *Med.* (See quots.)
1890 BILLINGS *Med. Dict.*, *Psychagogic*,..having power to arouse or restore consciousness or mental activity. **1895** *Syd. Soc. Lex.*, *Psychagogic*,..epithet applied to restorative medicines.
So **psycha'gogical** *a.*, that leads the mind; hence **psycha'gogically** *adv.*, persuasively.
1822 GROTE *Anal. Infl. Nat. Relig.* II. ii. §6. 139 The mental (or psychagogical [*ed.* 1875 psychological]) machinery of the priest-hood is excellent; but they are unhappily deficient in physical force. **1849** J. WILSON in *Blackw. Mag.* Nov. 645 Has any more versed and profound master in criticism, before or since, authentically and authoritatively,..psychagogically, propounded..the Dogma?

'psychagogue (-əgɒg). Also **psychogogue**. [f. Gr. ψῡχή PSYCHE + ἀγωγός leading, leader; in form = Gr. ψῡχαγωγός leader of departed souls, said of Hermes. So mod.F. *psychagogue.*]
1. One who directs or leads the mind. *rare.*
1847 tr. *von Feuchtersleben's Med. Psychol.* (Syd. Soc.) 343 All this must be effected and enforced by the physician, as a psychagogue or instructor of the mind.
2. One who calls up departed spirits; a necromancer.
1843 LIDDELL & SCOTT *Grk. Lex.*, Ψυχαγωγός,..as *subst.* a necromancer, psychagogue. **1882** *Daily News* 12 Dec. 5/4 Our modern psychagogues, the members of the Psychical Society, have not been much more fortunate in calling up spirits than their ancient models. **1928** AUDEN *Poems* 20 Eyes Look in the glass, confess The tightening of the mouth; Know the receding face A blemished psychogogue; But symmetry will please.
3. *Med.* (See quot.)
1867 C. A. HARRIS *Dict. Med. Terminol.* (ed. 3), *Psychagogues*.., medicines which resuscitate, as in cases of syncope.

'psychal, *a. rare.* [f. Gr. ψῡχή PSYCHE + -AL[1].] Of or pertaining to the soul; spiritual; psychical.
1844 POE *Mesmeric Revelation* Wks. 1864 I. 111 Certain psychal impressions which of late have caused me much anxiety and surprise. *a* **1849** —— *Marginalia* xxxvi. ibid. III. 505 To reconcile the psychal impossibility of refraining from admiration, with the too-hastily attained mental conviction that, critically, there is nothing to admire. **1864** WEBSTER cites BAYNE. **1900** *Westm. Gaz.* 10 Sept. 2/3 Ah God, that loves should roses be! Their thorns our psychal pains.

psychalgia to **psychasthenia**: see PSYCHO-.

psyche (ˈpsaɪkiː, ˈsaɪkiː). [a. Gr. ψῡχή (in L. *psȳchē*) breath, f. ψύχειν to breathe, to blow, (later) to cool; hence, life (identified with or indicated by the breath); the animating principle in man and other living beings, the source of all vital activities, rational or irrational, the soul or spirit, in distinction from its material vehicle, the σῶμα or body; sometimes considered as capable of persisting in a disembodied state after separation from the body at death.
In Mythology, personified as in 1 c. By Plato and other philosophers extended to the *anima mundi*, conceived to animate the general system of the universe, as the soul animates the individual organism. By St. Paul (developing a current Jewish distinction between *ruaχ*, πνεῦμα, spirit or breath, and *nephesh*, ψυχή, soul) used for the lower or merely natural life of man, shared with other animals, in contrast with the πνεῦμα or spirit, conceived as a higher element due to divine influence supervening upon the original constitution of unregenerate human nature: see PSYCHIC *a.* 2, PSYCHICAL 2. (For this and other developments in pre-Christian Judaism, and the N.T. writings, see R. H. Charles, *Hist. of the Doctrine of a Future Life*, 1899.)]
1. The soul, or spirit, as distinguished from the body; the mind.
1658 SIR T. BROWNE *Hydriot.* iv. 61 Why the *Psyche* or soul of Tiresias is of the masculine gender. **1794** SULLIVAN *View Nat.* II. 279 The two essentials in the composition of all sublunary things were, by the ancient Greeks, termed *psyche* and *hyle*, that is, spiritus et materia, soul and body. **1877** tr. *Virchow* in Tyndall *Fragm. Sc.* (1879) II. xv. 407 If I explain attraction and repulsion as exhibitions of mind, as psychical phenomena, I simply throw the Psyche out of the window, and the Psyche ceases to be a Psyche. **1879** LEWES *Study Psychol.* 73 The most accredited [ancient] thinkers not only detached Man from Nature, but the Mind from the Organism; they invented a Psyche as the source of all mental phenomena. **1888** *New Princeton Rev.* Mar. 272 Psychology is the science of the *psyche* or soul. **1896** P. GARDNER *Sculptured Tombs Hellas* 24 The psyche, to Homer, is not in the least like the Christian Soul, but is a shadowy double of the man, wanting alike in force and wisdom. **1905** E. J. DILLON in *Contemp. Rev.* Aug. 287 It is difficult to realise the position and to picture the psyche of Rozhdestvensky [the Russian admiral who fired on the North Sea fishing fleet].
†**b.** The animating principle of the universe as a whole, the soul of the world or *anima mundi.*
1647 H. MORE *Song of Soul* Notes 138/2 Such is the entrance of Psyche into the body of the Vniverse, kindling and exciting the dead mist. **1678** CUDWORTH *Intell. Syst.* I. iv. §21. 388 This is taken by Plotinus to be the Eternal Psyche, that actively produceth All Things, in this Lower World, according to those Divine Ideas. *Ibid.* §23. 406 But in other places..he frequently asserts, above the Self-moving Psyche an Immovable and Standing Nous or Intellect, which was properly the Demiurgus.
c. In later *Greek Mythology*, personified as the beloved of Eros (Cupid or Love), and represented in works of art as having butterfly wings, or as a butterfly; known in literature as the heroine of the story related in the *Golden Ass* of Apuleius. Hence *attrib.* in sense 'like that of

Psyche', as in ***Psyche-knot*** (of hair), ***Psyche-mould***, ***Psyche task***.

1876 GEO. ELIOT *Dan. Der.* lxi, In the Psyche-mould of Mirah's frame there rested a fervid quality of emotion sometimes rashly supposed to require the bulk of a Cleopatra. **1888** A. R. DIEHL *Two Thousand Words* 170 *Psyche knot*, the style of wearing the hair in a projecting coil in the middle of the back of the head. **1895** S. B. KENNEDY in *Outing* (U.S.) Oct. 8/2 Do you think this Psyche knot suits the special cut of my features? **1901** *Westm. Gaz.* 28 May 2/4 After many Psyche tasks Fate-encumbered now unravelled, Hoping there's no more to do. **1904** *Ibid.* 30 Nov. 4/2, I am not quite sure I know what is 'a Psyche knot', which was what the lady's jet-black hair was transformed to. **1968** J. UPDIKE *Couples* v. 404 Her hair was pinned up in a psyche knot.

d. *Psychol.* The conscious and unconscious mind and emotions, esp. as influencing and affecting the whole person. Also *Comb.*

1910 C. G. JUNG in *Amer. Jrnl. Psychol.* XXI. 226 Disease is an imperfect adaptation; hence in this case we are dealing with something morbid in the psyche. *Ibid.* 254 This explains a part of the conflict in the child's psyche. **1940** H. G. BAYNES *Mythol. of Soul* v. 154 Split off from the psychic hierarchy as an infantile *idée fixe*, it resisted the decisive transition from the infantile to the cultural psyche. **1949** J. STRACHEY tr. *Freud's Outl. Psycho-Anal.* i. 1 We know two things concerning what we call our psyche or mental life: firstly, its bodily organ and scene of action, the brain (or nervous system), and secondly, our acts of consciousness. **1958** *Times Lit. Suppl.* 23 May p. xii/2 The transformation and re-birth of the psyche in the individual's development towards maturity and integration. **1959** *Ibid.* 23 Jan. 44/5 If the stability of the self is threatened by too much division the psyche asserts itself by projecting an image of wholeness upon the sphere of consciousness. **1961** *Times* 4 Sept. 5/7 This democratic and psyche-conscious age. **1976** *Jrnl. Analytical Psychol.* XXI. 193 A heart ailment..need not arise from the heart only; it can also arise from the psyche of the sufferer.

2. a. (After Gr.) A butterfly.

1820 M. EDGEWORTH *Let.* 19 Aug. (1979) 224 You know the prints of the Berne Costume. Pray look at the *butterfly wing* caps—Brobdignag butterflies... This picturesque Psyche costume. **1878** EMERSON *Sov. Ethics* Wks. (Bohn) I. 373 The poor grub..expands into a beautiful form with rainbow wings... The Greeks called it Psyche, a manifest emblem of the soul. **1896** *Cosmopolitan* XX. 396/1 Lovelier than any psyche of the sun floating with moons of velvet jet on wings of heaven's blue.

b. *Entom.* A genus of day-flying bombycid moths, typical of the family *Psychidæ*.

1832 RENNIE *Conspect. Butterfl. & Moths* 44 Psyche (Schrank [1801]). The Brown Muslin (*Psyche fusca*)..; pale greyish-brown, without spots;..the female without wings. **1857** STAINTON *Man. Brit. Butterfl. & Moths* 165 Family xi. Psychidæ... The female of *Psyche*, not only without wings, but deprived of legs or antennæ... The males fly by day in search of the females.

3. *Astron.* Name of one of the asteroids.

1883 *Chambers' Encycl.* s.v. *Planetoids*, No. 16. Psyche, [discovered] 1852, Mar. 17 [by] De Gasparis.

4. A cheval-glass; also ***psyche-glass***.

[Mod.F. In *Dict. Acad.* 1835. Said to be so called from Raphael's full-length painting of the fabled Psyche.]

1838 LYTTON *Alice* I. v, 'How low the room is..!' said Caroline;..'And I see no Psyche'. **1887** *Athenæum* 18 June 803/3 A girl combing her fair hair before a psyche.

Hence **Psyˈchean** *a. rare*, of or pertaining to Psyche; **ˈpsycheism** (see quot. 1895).

1828 *Lights & Shades* II. 186 You might have sprained it [your ankle] with more grace in a Psychean quadrille. **1849** J. W. HADDOCK (*title*) Somnolism and Psycheism, otherwise Vital Magnetism, or Mesmerism: considered Physiologically and Philosophically. **1895** *Syd. Soc. Lex.*, *Psycheism*, the somnolent condition induced by mesmerism; now most commonly termed the hypnotic state.

psyche, var. PSYCH.

psychedelia (saɪkɪˈdiːlɪə). [Back-formation from next: see -IA².] Psychedelic articles or phenomena collectively; the subculture associated with psychedelic drugs.

1967 *Melody Maker* 27 May 9 Apparently today's hippie must be expanded and experienced in the whys and wherefores of psychedelia but it cannot be said that the products of this society are all 'junkie'. **1967** *Listener* 10 Aug. 169/2, I am unfriendly to the whole idea of psychedelia and the very notion of a chemical paradise with all those tangerine trees and marmalade skies seems absurd and slightly tatty. **1968** *Rat* 13–16 May 17/2 Buttons, posters, trip glasses, zodiac pendants, psychedelia. **1972** D. SALE *Love Bite* xiv. 172 The crazy jumble of sights and sounds and smells... Here was psychedelia that could never be achieved artificially in a discothèque; a relaxed and happy sense of awareness without the use of pills or pot. **1976** *Maclean's Mag.* 15 Nov. 4/1 In the Sixties his [*sc.* Dr. Timothy Leary's] name was synonymous with psychedelia.

psychedelic (saɪkɪˈdɛlɪk, -ˈdiːlɪk), *a.* and *sb.* Also occas. **psychodelic**. [Irreg. f. Gr. ψυχή (see PSYCHE) + δηλ-οῦν to make manifest, reveal (f. δῆλος manifest, visible) + -IC.

Proposed by H. Osmond in a letter to Aldous Huxley early in 1956: see G. Smith *Lett. of Aldous Huxley* (1969) 795.]

A. *adj.* **1. a.** Of a drug: producing an expansion of consciousness through greater awareness of the senses and emotional feelings and the revealing of unconscious motivations (freq. symbolically); usu., = PSYCHOTOMIMETIC *a.*

1957 H. OSMOND in *Ann. N.Y. Acad. Sci.* LXVI. 429, I have tried to find an appropriate name for the agents under discussion: a name that will include the concepts of enriching the mind and enlarging the vision... My choice, because it is clear, euphonious, and uncontaminated by other associations, is psychedelic, mind-manifesting. **1959** *Times Lit. Suppl.* 13 Nov. 665/3 He is so far from condemning the use of psychedelic drugs as to believe that, if wisely directed, they may help to open closed minds to dimensions of experience which would otherwise remain closed to them. **1965** *Jrnl. Amer. Med. Assoc.* 11 Jan. 104/1 The use of hallucinogenic (psychotomimetic, dysleptic, psychedelic) substances to produce altered states of consciousness is not new. **1965** *Brit. Jrnl. Philos. Sci.* XVI. 150 The popular issue of consciousness-expanding, or psychodelic drugs. **1967** *New Statesman* 3 Feb. 154/3 Mr. Andrews stands for many poets..who are trying to reach beyond ordinary experience, in his case through the 'mental voyages' of psychedelic drugs. 'This LSD is pure hero food.' **1970** R. C. ZAEHNER *Concordant Discord* iii. 42 If psychedelic drugs attest the existence of a timeless heaven, they none the less point to the existence of a timeless hell. **1970** H. PERRY *Human Be-In* 111 The core society's preoccupation with psychedelic drugs has been a way of avoiding their real hang-up: the attack of the young on middle-class values, particularly status and property. **1974** *Howard Jrnl.* XIV. 99 He compares religious experience to the chemical experience induced by psychedelic drugs. **1975** BRIMBLECOMBE & PINDER *Hallucinogenic Agents* i. 4 The psychedelic drug is said to enrich the mind, to enlarge the vision, and to create a mystic insight, but the term has achieved its maximum use and notoriety in the lay rather than the scientific literature.

b. Of, pertaining to, or produced by such a drug.

1963 (*title of periodical*) The psychedelic review. **1965** G. CUMMINS *Swan on Black Sea* 116 He said that yours was possibly a psychedelic condition. **1966** *New Statesman* 16 Sept. 387/1 LSD-takers, or acidheads, look upon Aldous Huxley as a sort of John the Baptist... Huxley baptised with mescalin, but now there is this larger psychedelic vision. **1967** *Punch* 22 Feb. 280/1 How..would one set about 'integrating LSD into the fabric of American society', as one sober supporter of the psychedelic experience suggested? **1970** G. GREER *Female Eunuch* 172 The state induced by the kiss is actually self-induced, of course, for few lips are so gifted with electric and psychedelic possibilities.

c. Concerned with or characterized by the use of such drugs.

1966 *New Statesman* 4 Mar. 305/2 The work done by the 'psychedelic' specialists Timothy Leary, R. Alpert and R. Metzner in the United States has explored the possibilities of expanding awareness by the use of hallucinogenic drugs, in particular LSD-25. **1967** *Times* 3 July 7/4 Since the drug aspect of the psychedelic cult attracted a great deal of unfavourable publicity and a number of unsavoury hangers-on, Dr. Timothy Leary..was asked to resign his appointment as Professor of Clinical Psychology at Harvard Medical School. **1967** *Los Angeles Free Press* 10 Nov. 8/3 If you want a big picture of Brando on his bike, why travel to a psychedelic shop when you can get it at the drug store. **1967** *Amer. Jrnl. Psychiatry* CXXIII. 1202/1 The rationale of psychedelic therapy with alcoholic patients is focused on the alienation-breaking potential of 'peak' or psychedelic experiences induced with the aid of LSD. **1972** M. D. DE RIOS *Visionary Vine* ii. 26 While some societies such as those in Peru have thousands of years of psychedelic tradition behind them, advanced industrial societies often find themselves in deep trouble as segments of their society are suddenly discovering the use of powerful mind-altering substances. **1976** *New Musical Express* 31 July 8/2 This obsession with the bizarrity came out of the psychedelic '60s.

2. Producing an effect or sensation held to resemble that produced by a psychedelic drug; *spec.* having vivid colours, often in bold abstract designs or in motion.

1965 *Los Angeles Free Press* 5 Nov. 4/1 (Advt.), The record stores won't sell and the radio banned..The Psychedelic Sound of 'The Trip' (original version). **1966** *Life* Sept. 61/1 The world of art is 'turning on'. It is getting hooked on psychedelic art. **1966** *Melody Maker* 12 Nov. 9/1 Bobby Darin..has come back after years of absence..right in the middle of psychedelic pop, freak-outs and happenings. **1967** *Wall St. Jrnl.* 9 Feb. 1/4 Psychedelic fabrics are becoming the rage. **1967** *Daily Tel.* 24 Oct. 19 Dupont showed its spring news in the new Royal Lancaster, where a batch of whirling lights and psychedelic patterns enlivened the theatre. **1968** *Globe & Mail* (Toronto) 3 Feb. 23/4 'Topless' dancers gyrating in the glow of psychedelic slides and lights. **1968** *Southerly* XXVIII. 279 He is wearing his psychedelic union jack trousers and tee-shirt. **1969** *Observer* 12 Jan. 8/3 The very latest psychedelic colours, electric purples and greens. **1971** *Hi-Fi Sound* Feb. 71/1 A discotheque with a psychedelic lighting display making you virtually blind. **1973** C. & R. MILNER *Black Players* v. 139 He drives a secondhand Volkswagen van, which had been gaily painted in psychedelic designs by its previous owners. **1977** B. PYM *Quartet in Autumn* ii. 22 He..proceeded to check the items in his shopping-bag—a 'psychedelic' plastic carrier, patterned in vivid colours, hinting at some unexpected aspect of his character.

B. *sb.* **1.** A psychedelic drug.

1956 H. OSMOND *Let.* in G. Smith *Lett. Aldous Huxley* (1969) 795 To fathom Hell or soar angelic, Just take a pinch of psychedelic (Delos to manifest). **1957** —— in *Ann. N.Y. Acad. Sci.* LXVI. 429 The psychedelics help us to explore and fathom our own nature. **1959** R. C. JOHNSON *Watcher on Hills* x. 162 Experience under the psychedelics may have an important contribution to make to Art. **1965** A. HUXLEY *Let.* 22 July (1969) 803 As you say in your letter, we still know very little about the psychodelics. **1974** M. C. GERALD *Pharmacol.* xvii. 318 Drugs in this same category are also termed hallucinogens, psychedelics, psychotogens, psychodysleptics, and so forth. **1977** *Martindale's Extra Pharmacopoeia* (ed. 27) 880/2 The group of drugs termed variously psychodysleptics, psychotomimetics, in some cases psychodelics, or, more usually but often inappropriately, hallucinogens are substances which as their principal action provoke abnormal mental changes, particularly in cognitive and perceptual spheres. **1977** *Rolling Stone* 16 June 24/3 Ergot also contains a powerful psychedelic: lysergic acid amide, a close relative of LSD, with about ten percent of that drug's mind-altering potency.

2. A person who takes a psychedelic drug or has a psychedelic life-style.

1966 *Time* 11 Mar. 43 Such dangers do not deter the acid heads or 'psychedelics'—even though some users are willing to admit that they found no great 'show', or had a 'freak trip' (a bad one) or 'tripped out' (the worst kind). **1967** *Economist* 17 June 1240/1 The East Village has supplanted Greenwich Village as a new meeting ground for poets, beats, psychedelics and plain old-fashioned bohemians.

Hence **psycheˈdelically** *adv.*, in psychedelic colours; also various *nonce-words*, as **ˈpsychedel**, **psychedeliac** (-ˈdiːlɪæk) = PSYCHEDELIC *sb.* 2; **ˌpsychedelicaˈtessen**, a shop selling psychedelic articles.

1966 *Life* 9 Sept. 68/3 True 'acid rock' goes deeper psychedelically than just lyrics. **1967** *Times* 24 Feb. 55 In Los Angeles, the leading psychedelicatessen is the Headquarters. **1967** *Listener* 24 Aug. 252/1 Those bells which announce the approach of psychedels like medieval lepers. **1970** V. CANNING *Great Affair* xvi. 300 Troops.. wearing combat helmets—some psychedelically painted. **1975** *Time Out* 9 May 55 Zig Zag badges are optional but retired psychedeliacs requesting 'Andmoreagain' are asking for disappointment and maybe even a bunch of fives. **1976** *Homes & Gardens* July 39/1 The front door of their old rectory is painted psychedelically and Shirley opens it wearing a comfortable kaftan.

psychedelicize (saɪkɪˈdɛlɪsaɪz), *v. colloq.* [f. prec. + -IZE.] *trans.* To make psychedelic; to render more colourful and lively.

1966 *Life* 9 Sept. 68/4 Buttons with the slogan 'Psychedelicize Suburbia'. **1975** *Time Out* 15 Aug. 12/4 Reviewing style became a bizarre psychedelicised variant of the traditional 'Good beat. Chart chance' mode.

psychiater (ps-, saɪˈkaɪətə(r)). [mod. f. Gr. ψυχή PSYCHE + ἰατήρ, ἰατρός healer, physician. So mod.F. *psychiatre* (Littré).] One who treats mental disease; an alienist.

1857 DUNGLISON *Med. Lex.*, *Psychiater*, one who treats diseases of the mind—a Mad-doctor. **1884** *Scotsman* 30 Aug., The psychiater, to whose sympathetic care the unfortunate victim of morbid incitements..is to be committed. **1902** *Daily Chron.* 23 Dec. 4/7 Professor Kraft Ebing, the renowned psychiater of the Vienna University.

psychiatric (-ɪˈætrɪk), *a.* (*sb.*) [f. as prec. + -IC: cf. Gr. ἰατρικ-ός of or pertaining to a healer or to medicine.] **A.** *adj.* Of or pertaining to psychiatry. Also, connected with or affected by mental illness that can be treated medically; ***psychiatric social work***, social work designed to support and supplement psychiatric treatment; so ***psychiatric social worker***.

1847 tr. *von Feuchtersleben's Med. Psychol.* (Syd. Soc.) Ed. Pref., He turned his attention to the revival of the study of psychiatric medicine. **1890** H. ELLIS *Criminal* ii. 37 [Lombroso] initiated..a psychiatric museum. **1896** *Daily News* 22 Sept. 5/2 The introduction of psychiatric institutions under State control. **1919** M. C. JARRETT in *Mental Hygiene* Apr. 215 There is a misconception..that the psychiatric social worker has a different function from other social workers. *Ibid.* 219 The future social worker.. will have included in her professional education some knowledge of all the different branches of social work—psychiatric social work, medical social work, family rehabilitation, child welfare, community service. **1940** HINSIE & SHATZKY *Psychiatric Dict.* 13/1 Affectation... It is perhaps more commonly observed among those who are not, strictly speaking, psychiatric, though it may..appear prominently in hysteria. **1957** *Times* 15 Oct. 14/5 Britain's first psychiatric prison, which is to be built at Grendon Underwood in Buckinghamshire, is expected to be ready for occupation in 1962. **1962** N. E. WHITTEN in A. Dundes *Mother Wit* (1973) 408/1 Cases such as the following have been given..by a white psychiatric social worker. **1965** J. POLLITT *Depression & its Treatment* i. 6 It is rarely necessary for the patient to realise that evidence for a psychiatric reaction is being sought. **1971** E. D. SMIGEL *Handbk. Study of Social Probl.* 12 Beginning in the 1920s psychiatric sociology has been a developing subdiscipline. **1976** S. B. GUZE (*title*) Criminality and psychiatric disorders. **1977** E. AMBLER *Send no more Roses* xi. 253 The book..may..be of some sociological interest to specialists, particularly in the field of psychiatric social work.

B. *sb.* **psychiˈatrics** (rarely **-atric**, **-atrik**). The theory or practice of psychiatry.

1847 tr. *von Feuchtersleben's Med. Psychol.* (Syd. Soc.) 1 When we come to the study of psychiatrics proper—the doctrine of the diseases of the mind. **1861** *N. Syd. Soc. Year-bk. Med. & Surg.* 179 On Psychiatrik in its Legal Relations. **1904** *Daily Chron.* 9 Aug. 3/2 Psychology,.. sociology, criminology, psychiatrics, have pronounced it guilty.

So **psychiˈatrical** *a.*; **psychiˈatrically** *adv.*

1847 tr. *von Feuchtersleben's Med. Psychol.* (Syd. Soc.) 287 There is in these words ethically and psychiatrically an important intimation of the dangerous weakness of man. **1884** *Scotsman* 30 Aug., Both parties—the psychiatrical and the philanthropic. **1896** *Allbutt's Syst. Med.* I. 37 [They] work at the subject from the psychiatrical point of view. **1921** 'M. B., OXON' *Cosmic Anat.* ix. 122 It is quite possible that *psychiatrically* Jung's deduction was right. **1965** J. POLLITT *Depression & its Treatment* vi. 85 Out-patient treatment and short-stay admission is now widely practised for all psychiatrically ill patients. **1975** *Times* 5 Aug. 2/8 The drugs would be administered only to people who had recovered from a period of depression and were psychiatrically well.

psychiatrist (ps-, saɪˈkaɪətrɪst). [f. PSYCHIATRY + -IST.] A practitioner of psychiatry; also, a student or professor of psychiatry.

1890 in *Cent. Dict.* **1897** URQUHART in *Dict. Nat. Biog.* LII. 320/2 It recalled..the attention of psychiatrists to the physical basis of mental aberration. **1922** R. S. Woodworth *Psychology* i. 16 According to the psychiatrists, mental disturbance is primarily an affair of emotion and desire rather than of intellect. **1931** F. L. Allen *Only Yesterday* viii. 198 Psychiatrists were installed in business houses to hire and fire employées. **1959** *Daily Tel.* 9 Apr. 1/3 There would be psychiatrists, social psychologists, and penologists on the staff so that they could approach the problem of crime from all points of view. **1971** *Lancet* 29 May 1124/1 A radiologist to the N.H.S. is medical and a radiographer non-medical, and similarly with..psychiatrist and psychologist, ophthalmologist and optician.

psychiatrize (saɪˈkaɪətraɪz), *v.* [f. PSYCHIATR(Y, + -IZE.] *trans.* To treat psychiatrically; ***psychiatrize away*** (nonce-use), to do away with by means of psychiatry or its concepts. Hence **psyˈchiatrized** *ppl. a.*; **psyˌchiatriˈzation**.

1929 *Sunday Dispatch* 6 Jan. 3/5 Parents may also be psychiatrised to study their traits and home-life. **1954** E. Jenkins *Tortoise & Hare* vi. 59 He couldn't be psychiatrized against his will. **1964** P. Meadows in I. L. Horowitz *New Sociol.* 451 Psychiatrized conformity masked as true individuality. **1977** *Times Lit. Suppl.* 6 May 565/3 The psychiatrization of 'perverse' pleasures. **1978** *Church Times* 10 Feb. 11/1 We have psychiatrised away the Seven Deadly Sins. Pride, anger, avarice, envy, sloth, gluttony and lust have been made respectable. They have become self-fulfilment, stress, incentive, insecurity, inertia, defective metabolism and emotional tension.

psychiatry (-ˈaɪətrɪ). [f. Gr. ψῡχή PSYCHE + ἰατρεία healing, medical treatment (f. ἰᾱτρός healer). Cf. mod.F. *psychiatrie* (1867 in Littré).] The medical treatment of diseases of the mind.

1846 in Worcester, citing *Monthly Rev.* **1862** *N. Syd. Soc. Year-bk. Med. & Surg.* 167 Reports in Psychiatry. **1886** A. B. Bruce *Mirac. Element Gosp.* v. 183 A problem in psychology and psychiatry. **1902** *Brit. Med. Jrnl.* 3 May 1092 The intervention of psychiatry in the reform of criminals.

psychic (ˈpsaɪkɪk, ˈsaɪkɪk), *a.* (*sb.*) [ad. Gr. ψῡχικ-ός of the soul or life: in mod.F. *psychique*, as in English.]

A. *adj.* **1. a.** Of or pertaining to the human soul or mind; mental: = PSYCHICAL *a.* 1. Also, having a psychical rather than a physical or physiological origin (cf. PSYCHICAL *a.* 1 a).

psychic blindness = *psychical blindness* s.v. PSYCHICAL *a.* 1 a; ***psychic determinism*** = *psychical determinism* s.v. PSYCHICAL *a.* 1 a; ***psychic energizer***, an antidepressant drug, esp. one effective against psychotic states; ***psychic unity***, a supposed similarity of the mental make-up of all mankind.

1873 Wagner tr. *Teuffel's Hist. Rom. Lit.* I. 422 In its refined descriptions of psychic events the poem recalls Virgil's manner. **1883** *Brit. Q. Rev.* July 14 The varied stimuli, psychic and physical. **1890** W. James *Princ. Psychol.* I. ii. 41 Munk..was the first to distinguish in these vivisections between sensorial and *psychic* blindness... Psychic blindness is inability to recognize the *meaning* of the optical impressions, as when we see a page of Chinese print but it suggests nothing to us. **1896** *Alienist & Neurologist* XVII. 520 Hysteria, is a constitutional psycho-neuropathy with morbid impulsions, caprices, delusions, hallucinations, and illusions, psychic and sensory. We see it displayed..in men with psychical impotency and in women after the menopause. **1902** Buchan *Watcher by Threshold* 131 Among women his psychic balance was so oddly upset that he grew nervous and returned unhappy. **1910** *Jrnl. Abnormal Psychol.* V. 68, I have successfully treated by Freud's psychoanalytic method cases of homosexuality, psychic impotence..and many other so-called perversions. **1924** E. & C. Paul tr. *Wittels's S. Freud* 267 By psychoanalysts the term 'sexual' is used with wide connotations, so that 'libido' becomes almost synonymous with 'psychic energy', with conation and also with what Bergson terms the 'vital impetus'. **1925** J. Laird *Our Minds & their Bodies* ii. 32 'Psychic' tumours or false pregnancies have deceived skilled observers. **1931** W. B. Gibson tr. *Husserl's Ideas* I. ii. 89 Blindness to ideas is a kind of psychic blindness. **1943** *Jrnl. Nerv. & Mental Dis.* XCVIII. 184 Freud's theory of psychic determinism does not ignore human values. **1953** G. Devereux *Psychoanal. & Occult* ii. 38 Due partly to the psychic unity of mankind..and partly to the limitation imposed upon the general direction of thought processes by the ethos of the culture area [etc.]. **1955** *Internat. Jrnl. Psycho-Anal.* XXXVI. 355 Although the concept of psychic determinism is generally accepted without qualification as an aspect of scientific causality, it sometimes appears difficult to reconcile it with the feeling of free will. **1957** N. S. Kline in *Congr. Rep. 2nd World Congr. Psychiatry* I. 212 Psychic Energisers. We have found that iproniazid (Marsilid) may represent a new principle of drug action since it is capable of increasing psychic energy. **1961** Psychic energizer [see *psychostimulant* sb. and adj. s.v. PSYCHO-]. **1963** *Listener* 7 Feb. 238/2 Such 'psychic poisons' as lysergic and diethylamide, LSD-25, which produces extreme mental confusion. **1967** J. J. Honigman *Personality in Culture* iv. 97/2 The assumption of psychic unity permits an investigator to apply the same principles of psychology to many people and to use his experience in his own culture (or with other cultures he has studied) as controls. **1968** *New Scientist* 2 May 226/1 The so-called 'psychic poisons', capable of inducing temporary or even permanent insanity. **1970** Aguilera & Messick *Crisis Intervention* i. 2 Psychic determinism is the theoretical foundation of psychotherapy and psychoanalysis. **1974** S. Arieti *Amer. Handbk. Psychiatry* I. iii. 67/1 Regardless of national boundaries, great rapidity has characterized the use of these new drugs, be these 'tranquilizers'..or 'psychic energizers'. **1974** M. Mendelson *Psychoanalytic Concepts of Depression* (ed. 2) vii. 254 Unlike the energy of science..psychic energy is directional.

b. Characterized by being susceptible to psychic or spiritual influence.

1905 *Daily News* 16 Feb. 12 The Welsh are what is termed a 'psychic' race—that is, their senses are very highly strung, which gives them a tendency to second sight, or clairvoyance, also clairaudience and telepathy.

c. Physically delicate or frail; 'spirituelle'.

1891 H. Herman *His Angel* 14 The girl was a frail and delicate creature..with tiny, pointed, psychic, rosy-tipped hands.

d. ***psychic income*** (Econ.): the non-monetary or non-material satisfactions that accompany an occupation or economic activity.

1904 F. A. Feller *Princ. Econ.* xlii. 402 It is well to recall also the distinction between wealth income, money income, and psychic income... The money expression of psychic income can be only approximately attained. **1937** Gemmill & Blodgett *Economics* I. iii. 56 Psychic income means the actual enjoyment or gratification which comes to a person through the consumption of commodities and services. **1948** M. H. Umbreit et al. *Fund. Econ.* xxii. 346 The fact that individuals desire to work in..pleasant occupations has led to the concept of psychic income. **1975** *New Society* 3 July 3/2 Views of metal rooftops have been replaced by grass and flowers or attractive paving, giving office workers an inflation-proof bonus in what economists call psychic income.

2. Pertaining to, or characterized by, the 'lower soul' or animal principle, as distinguished from the spirit or 'higher soul'; natural, animal; = PSYCHICAL 2.

After St. Paul's use of ψυχικός, 1 Cor. ii. 14, etc.

1858 J. Martineau *Stud. Chr.* 259 It was necessary that the Logos..should..by preoccupation have neutralized the action of the natural (or psychic) element throughout all the years of his continuance among men. **1868** Gladstone *Juv. Mundi* ix. 376 What St. Paul calls the flesh and the mind, the psychic and the bodily life. **1889** *Bibliotheca Sacra* July 399 The psychic, or animal, man, is the natural man of this present age.

3. a. = PSYCHICAL *a.* 3.

psychic research = *psychical research* s.v. PSYCHICAL *a.* 3; so ***psychic researcher***, ***psychic surgery***, surgery that is ostensibly performed by psychic or paranormal means; so ***psychic surgeon***.

1836 *Discovery* June 185/1 A curious outbreak of what the African calls *kupagawa na pepo*, i.e., to be 'ridden by demons' has occurred recently in Mombasa..and other East African towns, almost in the form of a psychic epidemic. **1880** *Spiritualist* XVI. 18/2 (*heading*) Psychic action from a distance. [**1881** *Dr. Gheist, an Autobiogr.* 39 When the 'psychic figure' disappears, or is sucked back into the body of the medium.] **1887** F. Johnson *New Psychic Stud.* i. 7 These studies are termed psychic in a modified sense; they pertain not to the ordinary operations of the mind, but to the unusual, such as thought-transference, somnambulism, mesmerism, clairvoyance, spiritualism, apparitions of the living, haunted houses, ghosts [etc.]. **1895** Mrs. Besant in *Daily Chron.* 15 Jan. 5/5 A man..possessing some psychic gifts. **1939** 'N. Blake' *Smiler with Knife* iii. 54 He'll write up the Yarnold Cross ghost, and that'll bring a horde of sightseers and psychic researchers up to the farm. **1968** S. Hynes *Edwardian Turn of Mind* v. 145 His spectrum of interests—biology, psychic research, and socialism—make him an Edwardian radical in spirit. *Ibid.*, The psychic researchers' arguments against scientific scepticism. **1975** Milner & Smart *Loom of Creation* iv. 250 The greatest problem I have experienced in describing and substantiating psychic surgery is that previously most authors have reported something akin to conventional surgery in hospitals. **1975** W. & M. Uphoff *New Psychic Frontiers* iii. 165 (*caption*) [He] witnessed eleven and filmed ten 'psychic surgeons' in the Philippines. **1977** *Time* 12 Dec. 46/2 One part reported on 'psychic surgery', in which Filipino healers supposedly diagnose tumors and other problems, and then use psychic forces—not scalpels—to make incisions and treat them.

b. ***psychic force***, a supposed force, power, or influence, not physical or mechanical, exhibiting intelligence or volition, and assumed as the cause of certain so-called spiritualistic phenomena.

1871 W. Crookes in *Q. Jrnl. Sci.* July 17 Respecting the cause of these phenomena, the nature of the force to which ..I have ventured to give the name of *Psychic* [etc.]. **1874** Carpenter *Ment. Phys.* II. xvi. (1879) 632 The table was actually raised, either by his own 'psychic force', or by the agency of disembodied spirits. **1900** tr. *Flammarion's Unknown* vi. 228 We are compelled to admit the existence of an unknown *psychic force*, emanating from the human being, and capable of making itself felt at great distances. **1908** Sir W. Crookes *Let. to Editor*, It is not improbable that Sergeant Cox might have suggested the term *psychic force* to me in conversation before June 1871.

4. *Bridge.* Of a bid, bidder, or bidding: deliberately misrepresenting the player's hand so as to deceive the opponents.

1932 D. R. Sims *Psychic Bidding* ii. 18, I shall attempt to outline a few types of psychic bids. *Ibid.* 22 A clever psychic bidder will now employ the barricade bid of two or even three No Trumps. **1936** E. Culbertson *Contract Bridge Complete* I. iii. 55 How do the experts distinguish a bona fide bid from a psychic one? **1952** I. Macleod *Bridge* i. 13 In the years 1932–5 two notable teams were pre-eminent in duplicate Bridge in this country. One captained by Harry Ingram..devastated their opponents with their psychic bidding. **1975** *Times* 20 Dec. 10/8 A player has made a psychic opening bid and does not hold a possible trick. **1977** *Washington Post* 7 Sept. E. 9 In the early 1930s, just after the birth of psychic bidding, many players indulged in this mania of fabricating bids.

B. *sb.* **1. a.** One who is particularly susceptible to 'psychic' influence (see PSYCHICAL 3); a 'medium'.

1871 E. W. Cox *Let. to W. Crookes* in *Q. Jrnl. Sci.* July 19, I venture to suggest that the force be termed the *Psychic Force*; the persons in whom it is manifested in extraordinary power *Psychics*; and the science relating to it *Psychism*, as being a branch of *Psychology*. **1874** —— *What am I?* II. II. xxiii. 289 He had previously exhibited considerable power as a Psychic. **1890** *Sat. Rev.* 1 Nov. 507/2 Hypnotisms, mesmerisms, spiritualisms, and spiritisms, the two latter kept rigidly separate by the orthodox psychic.

b. The realm of perceptual, mental, or physical phenomena that seem to transcend known physical laws (see PSYCHICAL *a.* 3).

1909 [see OIL *v.* 1 b]. **1960** R. F. C. Hull tr. *Jung's Nature of Psyche* in *Coll. Wks.* (1969) VIII. 181 It appears the psychic is an emancipation of function from its instinctual form and so from the compulsiveness which..causes it to harden into a mechanism.

2. *Ch. Hist.* See quot., and cf. 2 above.

1874 J. H. Blunt *Dict. Sects* (1886), *Psychics*, a party name given to the orthodox by the Tertullianists, who called themselves 'Spirituals'... The distinction was drawn from St. Paul's First Epistle to the Corinthians, where he writes of the ψυχικός..and the πνευματικός.

3. *Bridge.* A psychic bid (see sense A. 4 above); ***controlled psychic***: (see quots. 1959, 1962).

1932 D. R. Sims *Psychic Bidding* i. 15 The strategical bids which, under the name of 'psychics', are being extensively misused. **1936** *Punch* 2 Dec. 639/3 Unless North's last bid was a pure psychic, he should certainly hold the King of Spades himself. **1959** T. Reese *Bridge Player's Dict.* 40 A controlled psychic, as opposed to an ordinary psychic, is one made in accordance with a prearranged system. **1962** *Listener* 8 Nov. 786/1 The British pair in the open room were playing what are known as 'controlled psychics'. That is to say, a player would sometimes open the bidding on very slight values without taking a great risk, for there would be a built-in mechanism to prevent the partnership going too high.

psychical (ps-, ˈsaɪkɪkəl), *a.* [f. as prec. + -AL[1]: see -ICAL.]

1. a. Of or pertaining to the soul or the mind; mental, as distinguished from *physical*; *spec.* in *Path.*, due to mental affection or influence.

(By Henry More distinguished from intellectual; ? = spiritual.) ***psychical blindness***, ***deafness***, inability of the brain to interpret impressions received by the visual or auditory organs; ***psychical determinism***, the theory that an individual's mental responses and actions are determined by his previous mental actions or his unconscious mind; ***psychical distance***, the mental distance from subjective emotions or involvement supposed necessary for the appreciation of the aesthetic qualities inherent in some kinds of experience (see quot. 1976); ***psychical paralysis***, see quot. 1893; ***psychical unity*** = *psychic unity* s.v. PSYCHIC *a.* 1 a.

1642 H. More *Song of Soul* II. i. III. xxiii, The first we name Nature Monadicall, The second hight Life Intellectuall, Third Psychicall. *Ibid.* Interpr. Gen. Q iv, I understand by life Psychicall, such centrall life as is capable of Æon and Ahad. **1831** Carlyle *Sart. Res.* I. ix. (1858) 36 This physical or psychical infirmity..I have..thought right to publish. **1847** tr. *von Feuchtersleben's Med. Psychol.* (Syd. Soc.) 18 The proper subject of our inquiries—spirit in its relation to corporeal life, organism in its relation to psychical life. **1863** J. F. Collingwood tr. *Waitz's Introd. Anthropol.* I. II. i. 273 If theology feared that an original difference of language..would involve the original unity of the human species..the science of language restores to theology the psychical unity of mankind. **1874** Bucknill & Tuke *Psych. Med.* (ed. 3) 28 The psychical symptoms must then inevitably arrest our attention first in the study of Insanity. **1876** W. James *Coll. Ess. & Rev.* (1920) 29 We have no space to discuss the sources of the English prejudice in favor of psychical determinism. **1877** Foster *Phys.* III. ii. (1878) 397 The difficulty of distinguishing between the unconscious or physical and the conscious or psychical factors. **1890** Billings *Med. Dict.* s.v., *Psychical blindness*, soul-blindness. *Psychical deafness*, word-deafness. **1893** *Syd. Soc. Lex.*, *Psychical paralysis*, a paralysis dependent upon psychical defect... Hysterical paralysis may be considered a psychical paralysis. **1897** C. H. Judd tr. *Wundt's Outl. Psychol.* v. 323 The ability to produce purely qualitative effects..which we designate as psychical energy. **1899** *Allbutt's Syst. Med.* VIII. 566 Such symptoms as hysteria, neurasthenia and psychical over-strain. **1902** D. G. Brinton *Basis of Social Relations* i. 19 When we have such evidence as this for the psychical unity of the human species [etc.]. **1912** E. Bullough in *Brit. Jrnl. Psychol.* V. 87 (*heading*) 'Psychical distance' as a factor in art and aesthetic principle. **1913** E. Jones *Papers on Psycho-Anal.* ii. 21 When the sublimation process is not sufficiently potent to provide an outlet for the accompanying psychical energy, other paths of discharge have to be forged. **1938** R. M. Ogden *Psychol. of Art* vii. 142 The illusion of 'psychical distance' is destroyed when the actors appear in the audience. **1960** J. Strachey *Freud's Compl. Wks.* VI. p. xiv, This is the truth which he [*sc.* Freud] insists upon..: it should be possible in theory to discover the psychical determinants of every smallest detail of the processes of the mind. **1976** Rader & Jessup *Art & Human Values* iii. 54 The phrase 'psychical distance' was employed..to denote 'the marvelling unconcern of the mere spectator' in the moment of aesthetic contemplation. Because the word 'psychical' has a misleading connotation..some recent aestheticians have preferred the term 'aesthetic distance'.

b. Dealing with mental phenomena.

1854 Bucknill *Crim. Lunacy* 14 The purely psychical school of insanity has scarcely gained a footing in this country.

2. Representing Gr. ψυχικός: Of or pertaining to the animal or natural life of man, as opposed to the spiritual (πνευματικός). (See PSYCHE, note.)

The Gr. ψυχικός in *1 Cor.* ii. 14, xv. 44, 46, is opposed to πνευματικός spiritual, and is rendered in the Vulgate by *animālis* (whence in Wyclif *beestli*), in Tindale, Cranmer, Coverd., Geneva, and 1611 by *natural(l*, in Rheims by *sensual* and *natural*.

1708 H. Dodwell *Nat. Mort. Hum. Souls* 46 The Psychical Body must be cloathed upon with a Pneumatical Body, must be transformed and transfigured, like the glorious Body of Christ. **1872** Liddon *Elem. Relig.* iii. 92 The word of God is described..as having..an analytical efficacy which separates as clearly between the spiritual and psychical elements of man's immaterial nature, as between the life of sensation and the life of motion in his corporeal nature. **1875** E. WHITE *Life in Christ* III. xx. (1878) 263 A life which, notwithstanding the possession of a spiritual faculty, persists in being animal, or psychical only, is by divine decree transitory and perishable. **1882** *Ch. Q. Rev.* Apr. 128 To try the effect of psychical and carnal methods, because apparent failure attends the use of spiritual methods.

3. Of or pertaining to phenomena and conditions which appear to lie outside the domain of physical law, and are therefore attributed by some to spiritual or hyperphysical agency. ***psychical research***, investigation of such phenomena. ***psychical researcher***, one who studies or investigates psychical phenomena.

It has been objected that, as these phenomena, etc. are not explained by ordinary known psychical facts and relations, it is an assumption to class them as 'psychical'.

1882 (Feb. 20) *Proc. Soc. Psych. Res.* I. (1883) p. v, The name of the Society is.. The Society for Psychical Research. **1886** GURNEY, etc. *Phantasms of Living* I. 5 'Psychical' phenomena. [*Note.*] The specific sense which we have given to this word needs apology. But we could find no other convenient term, under which to embrace a group of subjects that lie on or outside the boundaries of recognised science. **1888** BARING-GOULD in *Chambers' Encycl.* s.v. *Apparitions*, In 1882 a Society for Psychical Research was founded for the scientific and systematic investigation of reported apparitions, clairvoyance, haunted houses, hypnotism, thought-reading, and the phenomena called spiritualistic. **1892** W. JAMES *Coll. Ess. & Rev.* (1920) 320 The 'psychical researchers', though kept at present somewhat out in the cold, will inevitably conquer the recognition which their labors also deserve. **1901** *Daily Chron.* 14 May 3/2 Why, he asks, call the subject matter of their investigation 'psychical research', when it is really, so far as it is a legitimate matter for scientific inquiry, only a branch of morbid psychology? **1912** J. BUCHAN *Moon Endureth* iv. 135 The Presences might be..spirits.. behaving as psychical researchers think they do. **1931** A. HUXLEY *Music at Night* 102 There is the scientific Psychical Researcher, whose views on the future life..seem to be almost indistinguishable from those held by Homer and the author of Ecclesiastes. **1965** *Jrnl. Soc. Psychical Res.* XLIII. 32 Mr Priestley..has..a number of interesting and original suggestions to offer that are well worth the serious consideration of psychical researchers.

4. ***psychical moment***: see PSYCHOLOGICAL *a.* 2 b.

1904 *Sat. Rev.* 19 Nov. 633 The position of vantage indicated as the psychical moment to strike in.

ˈpsychically, *adv.* [f. prec. + -LY[2].] In a psychic or psychical manner; with reference to the soul or mind; mentally.

1849 H. MAYO *Pop. Superstit.* (1851) 76 What is sleep psychically considered? **1856** *Lamps of Temple* (ed. 3) 105 A little Leo IX—more like him personally and psychically than any other pope. **1886** GURNEY, etc. *Phantasms of Living* I. 97 A state psychically or physically abnormal.

psychicism (ps-, ˈsaɪkɪsɪz(ə)m). [f. PSYCHIC *a.* + -ISM.] The theory or study of psychical or so-called spiritualistic phenomena. So **ˈpsychicist**, one who studies psychicism or pursues psychical research.

1885 *Athenæum* 21 Feb. 247/2 We felt it our duty to submit this extraordinary case to an eminent psychicist. **1887** GURNEY *Tertium Quid* I. 254 We psychicists render unto Caesar the things that are Caesar's. **1892** *Daily News* 4 Mar. 5/1 More alluring than the theories of Psychicism.

psychics (ps-, ˈsaɪkɪks). [f. PSYCHIC *a.*, after earlier sbs. in *-ics* = Gr. *-ικά*: see -IC 2.]

1. The science of psychical or mental phenomena; psychology.

1811–31 BENTHAM *Logic* App., Wks. 1843 VIII. 284/1 Somatology,.. or somatics; psychology, psychognosy, or psychics—to one or other of these denominations will every branch of science, which has for its subject the field of, to us, perceptible existence.., be found referable. **1864** WEBSTER, *Psychics*, psychology. **1908** MISS B. HARRADEN *Interplay* 334 The joint researches in psychics and physics.

2. = *psychical research*: see PSYCHICAL *a.* 3.

1895 in *Funk's Stand. Dict.* **1942** 'M. INNES' *Daffodil Affair* III. i. 80 She represents a rare but fairly well-understood morbid condition—that of one individual split up into several personalities... I should have imagined it to be pretty well off the slate of serious psychical inquiry. Lucy is psychopathology, not psychics. **1977** *Gramophone* June 31/2 In a quite separate field, that of psychics, Percy Wilson's passing will have saddened many friends and associates.

psychism (ps-, ˈsaɪkɪz(ə)m). [f. Gr. ψῡχή PSYCHE + -ISM; in sense 1, ad. F. *psychisme.*]

1. See quot.

1857 W. FLEMING *Vocab. Philos.* 407 *Psychism*..is the word chosen by Mons. Quesne (*Lettres sur le Psychisme*, Paris, 1852) to denote the doctrine that there is a fluid, diffused throughout all nature, animating equally all living and organized beings, and that the difference which appears in their actions comes of their particular organization.

2. The attribution of a living soul to the universe, or to inanimate objects and natural phenomena; = ANIMISM.

1890 HATCH *Influence Grk. Ideas* ix. 246 A survival of the primitive psychism which peopled the whole universe with life and animation.

3. The doctrine or theory of the existence of forces unexplainable by physical science in connexion with so-called spiritualistic phenomena.

1871 [see PSYCHIC B. 1]. **1872** GEO. ELIOT *Let.* 4 Mar. (1956) V. 253 Ideas of spirit-intercourse, 'psychism' and so on, have come before me in the painful form of the lowest charlatanerie. **1895** *Folk-Lore* VI. 79 Analysed under the dry light of anthropology, its psychism [*sc.* that of psychical research] is seen to be only the 'other self' of barbaric spiritual philosophy 'writ large'. **1899** GIBIER (*title*) Psychism: Analysis of Things Existing. **1974** *Christian* I. 322 They want to know more about apparently unusual goings-on, and this interest is not far removed from the curiosity about psychism and the occult.

4. The character of being psychic or mental.

1890 in *Cent. Dict.* **1895** in *Syd. Soc. Lex.* **1962** *Times* 4 May 9/6 Psychism is, of course, a function of the brain and ..when psychism is disturbed the brain function is affected. **1970** G. ORDISH tr. *Chauvin's World of Ants* vii. 171 *Myrmica*..is an ant relatively low on the ladder of ant psychism.

So **ˈpsychist**, (*a*) a psychologist; (*b*) one who believes in psychic force, or who engages in psychical research (*Cassell's Encycl. Dict.* 1886); (*c*) a bridge-player who practises psychic bidding.

1895 *Syd. Soc. Lex.*, *Psychist*, one who makes a special study of Psychics [= psychology]. **1900** W. W. PEYTON in *Contemp. Rev.* Apr. 493 The healing of a leper may be done by suggestion, as the psychists tell us. **1952** I. MACLEOD *Bridge* vii. 95 The stupid psychist..would perhaps bid Three No Trumps.

psycho (ˈsaɪkəʊ), *sb.* and *a. colloq.* [Abbrev. of various words beginning with this element.]

A. *sb.* **1.** Psychoanalysis or psychology. Also *attrib.* or as *adj.*

1921 R. MACAULAY *Dangerous Ages* v. 102 'Psycho-analysis, I mean.' 'Oh, psycho... Not that insomnia is always a case for psycho, you know.' **1938** N. MARSH *Artists in Crime* x. 148 The psycho people say one shouldn't repress things. **1939** 'J. BELL' *Death at Half-Term* vii. 133 Now don't you let loose any of your high-faluting psycho-stuff on me. **1946** J. CARY *Moonlight* xix. 138 She gave you a guilty complex... My psycho man says that's the worst kind, it's so unreasonable. **1960** *Times* 25 June 12/3 The mind was so important in this work [*sc.* radionics] that it excluded all physical considerations. They were coming down solidly on the psycho side, but not the psychic side.

2. A psychologist.

1925 A. HUXLEY *Let.* 5 Mar. (1969) 243 The psychos imagine that they have shed some light on art by affirming that the origin of art is an infantile coprophily.

3. A psychopath.

1942 [see MENTAL *sb.*]. **1947** *Sat. Rev. Lit.* (U.S.) 18 Jan. 19/3 A large percentage of 'psychos' were exposed to unwholesome mother-influence. **1959** C. MACINNES *Absolute Beginners* 11 Wiz has for all oldies..the same kind of hatred psychos have for Jews or foreigners or coloureds. **1973** R. C. DENNIS *Sweat of Fear* vii. 45 He's some kind of psycho. He gets freak vibes—you know, like pictures in the head. **1980** *Daily Tel.* 7 Nov. 15/4 He finally runs down the psycho in a morgue, of all appropriate places, where he is pursuing a girl called Amy.

B. *adj.* **1.** Psychological.

1927 *Variety* 1 June 314 Psycho drama flops... The Compagnie des Jonchets, a private club, was over its head with the psychological drama 'Le Souffle sur la Flamme'. **1976** *Denbighshire Free Press* 8 Dec. 6/2 The programme is completed by the psycho thriller 'Night Caller', AA certificate film.

2. Psychopathic.

1936 R. CHANDLER *Man who liked Dogs* in *Black Mask* Mar. 19/1 Since when can a cop sign as complaining witness on a psycho case? **1957** J. D. MACDONALD *Executioners* ii. 22 Maybe I didn't act worried enough... I think he's psycho. **1958** A. WILSON *Middle Age of Mrs. Eliot* II. 149 Honestly I think she's a bit psycho at times. **1976** R. BARNARD *Little Local Murder* ix. 109 That sort of bloke ought to be locked away. They're psycho, that's what they are.

psycho (ˈsaɪkəʊ), *v. colloq.* [f. PSYCHOANALYSE *v.* or prec. sb.] *trans.* = PSYCH *v.* 1.

1925 [see INTENSE *a.* 4 b.]. **1925** *Christian World* 4 June 7/2 How many of us spend twenty minutes a day in consciously 'psychoing' ourselves..? **1928** C. MACKENZIE *Extraordinary Women* xviii. 343 A friend of mine took me to be psychoed last spring... It's the latest thing since the war. **1937** A. THIRKELL *Before Lunch* xi. 293 He has had every inhibition psychoed and is perfectly free. **1946** J. CARY *Moonlight* xix. 138 'It's a complex,' said Kathy. 'We ought to get her psychoed.' **1960** N. MARSH *Fake Scent* ii. 66 You'd better get yourself psychoed, my poor Charles.

psycho- (ˈpsaɪkəʊ-, ˈsaɪkəʊ-), before a vowel regularly **psych-**, repr. Gr. ψῡχο-, ψῡχ-, combining form of ψῡχή breath, life, soul. In modern use, since the 17th c., taken as a formative in the sense of 'mind', 'psychic organism', 'mental', 'psychical', mainly in scientific compounds, for the more important of which see their alphabetical places. The following are chiefly 19th or 20th century formations. (The second element is properly from Greek, but in some cases from Latin.)

psychæsthetic, var. *psycho-æsthetic* below; **psyˈchalgia** [Gr. ἄλγος pain], (see quot.); † **psyˈchandric** *a.* [irreg. f. Gr. ἀνηρ, ἀνδρ- man], ? pertaining to the mind of man; **psychasˈthenia** [ad. F. *psychasthénie* (P. M. F. Janet 1893, in *Rev. gén. des Sci. pures et appliquées* IV. 176); cf. ASTHENIA], (see quot. 1908); hence **psychasˈthenic** *a.*, pertaining to or affected with psychasthenia; also as *sb.*, a person with psychasthenia; **psychoˈactive** *a.* = PSYCHOTROPIC *a.*; hence **psychoacˈtivity**; **psycho-æsˈthetics**, the study of the psychological aspects of æsthetic perception; hence **psycho-æsˈthetic** (also **psychæsthetic**) *a.*; **psycho-ˈauditory** *a.*, connected with the mental perception of sound (*Syd. Soc. Lex.* 1895); **ˈpsychobabble** *colloq.* (orig. *U.S.*), jargon that is much influenced by the concepts and terminology of psychology and is used esp. by laymen in referring to their own personality or relationships; hence **ˈpsychobabbler**, one who uses such jargon; **ˈpsychoblast** [-BLAST], the germ from which the psychic organism is (hypothetically) developed; **psychoˈcentral** *a.*, having its centre in the mind; **psychoˈcentric** *a. Psychol.*, treating the psyche or mind, rather than the body, as the important factor in human behaviour; **psychoˈchemical** *a.*, pertaining to the relationship between chemicals and the mind, esp. the way the former can be used to modify the latter; also (of a chemical), psychotropic; also as *sb.*, a psychotropic chemical; **psychoˈchemistry**, the chemistry of the mind; **psychoˈcoma** [COMA[1]], mental stupor; **psychoˈcultural** *a.*, relating to the interaction of the culture in which individuals live and their psychological characteristics; **psychoˈcurative** *a.*, of or pertaining to the healing of mental or psychological disorders; **ˌpsychodiagˈnosis**, **-diagˈnostics** *Psychol.* [after Ger. (H. Rorschach *Psychodiagnostik* (1921))], the investigation of a subject's personality, esp. by means of Rorschach and other projective tests; hence **ˌpsychodiagˈnostic** *a.*; **psychoˈdometer** [cf. ODOMETER], an instrument proposed for measuring the duration of mental processes; **psychodysˈleptic** [Gr. δύσληπτος hard to take hold of] = PSYCHOTOMIMETIC *sb.*; **psychoˈendocrine** *a.*, relating to or involving both the endocrine glands and mood and behaviour; **ˌpsychoendocriˈnology**, the branch of science concerned with the relationship between the secretions of the endocrine glands and a person's mood and behaviour; hence **ˌpsychoendocrinoˈlogic** *a.*, **-endocrinoˈlogically** *adv.*, **-endocriˈnologist**; **psycho-ˈethical** *a.*, of or pertaining to inborn moral ideas; **psychoˈfugal** *a.* [after CENTRIFUGAL], tending away from the mind; **psychogeˈography**, that branch of psychological speculation or investigation which is concerned with the effects on the psyche of the geographical environment; so **psychogeoˈgraphic**, **-ical** *adjs.*; **psychogeusic** (-ˈgjuːsɪk) *a.* [Gr. γεῦσις taste], relating to mental perception of taste; **psychognosy** (-ˈɒgnəsɪ), also in mod.L. form **psychognosis** (-əʊgˈnəʊsɪs), (*a*) the investigation or knowledge of mental phenomena; (*b*) thought-reading; **psycho-ˈhylism** [HYLISM], the belief that the soul is material; so **psycho-ˈhylist**, one who holds this belief; **psyˈcholatry**, excessive reverence for the soul; worship of departed spirits; **ˈpsycholepsy** [Gr. λῆψις seizing], 'possession', ecstasy; so **psychoˈleptic** *a.*, (*a*) characterized by psycholepsy; (*b*) characterized by a sudden fall in psychic tension; (*c*) (of a drug) sedative; **psycholytic** (-ˈlɪtɪk) *a.* [-LYTIC], applied to a drug such as LSD which can disturb or disrupt certain emotional reactions that have become fixed in the unconscious or can block normal channels of response; chiefly in ***psycholytic therapy***, therapy that combines controlled use of low dosages of such drugs with psychotherapeutic instruction for the patient and subsequent discussion; **psychomiˈmetic** *a.* and *sb.* = PSYCHOTOMIMETIC *a.* and *sb.*; **psychoˈmonism** [MONISM]: see quot.; **psychomoˈtility** *Psychol.*, physical movement which reflects or is evidence of mental activity; **psycho-ˈneural**, of or pertaining to the relationship or interaction between the mind and the nervous system; **ˌpsychoneuroˈendocrine**, **-ˌneuroˌendocrinoˈlogic**, **-ˈlogical** *adjs.*, of or pertaining to the joint or mutual action of the nervous system, the endocrine system, and behaviour; so **ˌpsychoˌneuroendocriˈnology**, the branch of science concerned with this; **psychoneuˈrology**, the division of neurology which deals with psychology (cf. NEURO-PSYCHOLOGY); hence **ˌpsychoneuroˈlogical** *a.*; **psyˈchonomy** [see -NOMY], the branch of psychology dealing with the laws of mental action; **psychono'sology** [NOSOLOGY], the branch of medical science which treats of mental disease (Dunglison *Med. Lex.* 1853); **psycho-'optic** *a.*, relating to the mental perception of sight (*Syd. Soc. Lex.*); so **psycho-'optical** *a.*; **psycho-'osmic** [Gr. ὀσμή smell], pertaining to mental perception of smell (Billings *Med. D.* 1890); **psycho'paresis** [PARESIS], mental debility; **psy'chopetal** *a.* [after CENTRIPETAL], tending towards the mind; **ˌpsycho-pharma'ceutical** *a.* and *sb.*, (a drug) that is psychotropic; **'psycho-philosophy**, philosophical reasoning based on subjective criteria, or on subjective psychic criteria; hence **'psycho-philosopher**; **psy'chophony** [Gr. φωνή voice]: see quot.; **ˌpsychoˌphysicothera'peutics** *nonce-wd.*, remedial treatment of mind and body; **psycho-po'litical** *a.*, characterized by the interaction of politics or political events and behaviour; so **psycho-'politics**; **psycho-'prismatism** [cf. PRISMATIC *a.* 2] (see quot.); **psy'choptic** *a.*, producing vision of the mind or soul; **psycho'pyrism** [Gr. πῦρ fire], the belief that fire is the substance of the soul; so **psycho'pyrist**, one holding this belief; **psycho-'reflex** *a.*, of or pertaining to 'reflex' action of the mind; **psy'chorrhagy**, ‖**psycho'rrhagia** [Gr. ῥαγή breaking, rupture], detachment of the soul or psychic element; hence **psycho'rrhagic** *a.*; **'psychorrhythm**, an alternating or rhythmic psychic condition (*Syd. Soc. Lex.*); **psycho'sarcous** *a.* [Gr. σάρξ, σαρκ- flesh], having a spiritual body; **'psychoscope**, a means or instrument for inspecting the mind or soul; **psycho-sen'sorial** *a.*, of or pertaining to percepts not produced by any real action on the senses; so **psycho-'sensory** *a.* (Billings 1890), pertaining to the conscious perception of sensory impulses; **psycho-socio'logical** *a.*, pertaining to sociology as connected with psychology; so **psycho-soci'ologist**, **-soci'ology**; **psy'chosophy**, the philosophy or metaphysics of mind (*Cent. Dict.*); so **psy'chosophist**; **'psychosphere**, the sphere or realm of consciousness; cf. NOOSPHERE; **psycho'stimulant** *sb.* and *a.*, (a drug that is) antidepressant; **'psychosyndrome**, a syndrome in which the symptoms are psychological; **psycho-'synthesis**, the integration of disjoint elements of the psyche or personality by means of psychoanalysis; hence (*nonce-wds.*) **psycho-'synthesist**, one who practises or advocates this; **psycho-syn'thetic** *a.*; **psycho'theism** [Gr. θεός God], the doctrine of the absolute spirituality of God; **psycho-'visual** *a.*, pertaining to psychological factors associated with vision, such as the emotive connotations of particular colours, and to the centre in the brain associated with such processes; see also *visuo-psychic* s.v. VISUO-; **psycho-'vital** *a.*, pertaining to the mind as connected with life; **psycho'zoic** *a.*, of or belonging to the geological period of living creatures having souls or minds, i.e. the human period.

1890 BILLINGS *Med. Dict.*, *Psychalgia, painful melancholy state of mind. **1716** M. DAVIES *Athen. Brit.* III. *Diss. Physick* 21 The great *Psycandrick as well as Somandrick Secret of the Chymical Grand Elixir. **1900** S. B. COLLINS tr. *M. de Fleury's Medicine & Mind* v. 206 *Psychasthenia..seemed to be modified..parallel with the oscillations of the blood pressure. **1906** *Contemp. Rev.* Feb. 229 All the neuroses should be classified with neurasthenia under one generic title Psychasthenia. **1908** E. WORCESTER *Relig. & Med.* (N.Y.) 115 Psychasthenia..a form of nervous weakness in which the psychical element is dominant. **1926** [see EXTROVERT *sb.* (*a*.)]. **1968** *New Scientist* 5 Sept. 500/1 Rupp suffered from a psychasthenia which led him to ascribe fictional properties to positrons. **1901** C. R. CORSON tr. *Janet's Mental State of Hystericals* vi. 520 It is very rare to meet a *psychasthenic patient who is, if we may so speak, a pure type of this affection. *Ibid.* 521 Abulia is a common characteristic with hystericals and psychasthenics. **1906** W. JAMES *Let.* 6 May (1920) II. 254 Pierre Janet discussed lately some cases of pathological impulsion or obsession in what he has called the 'psychasthenic' type of individual. **1908** E. WORCESTER *Relig. & Med.* (N.Y.) 115 Psychasthenic patients find it difficult to come to a decision..and this inability troubles them. **1977** A. SHERIDAN tr. *J. Lacan's Écrits* ii. 16 States as diverse as phantasmatic fear, anger, active sorrow, or psychasthenic fatigue. **1961** *Perspectives in Biol. & Med.* IV. 428 Asynchrony [prevails] after application of analeptic and *psychoactive drugs. **1967** *New Scientist* 19 Jan. 128/1 Glossy magazines and sombre journals of opinion alike have discovered an intense interest in psychoactive drugs, drugs which affect the way people behave and feel. **1974** M. C. GERALD *Pharmacol.* xviii. 350 These medicines are most often tranquilizers, sedatives, and other psychoactive agents. **1975** *Daily Colonist* (Victoria, B.C.) 19 Oct. 17/2 Advisers..avoided taking any position on the two most commonly used 'psychoactive or mood-altering' drugs—alcohol and tobacco. **1977** *Rolling Stone* 30 June 123/2 (Advt.), Psychoactive mushrooms... Chart, illustrations—tests for chemicals—105 alkaloid mushrooms, 42 psilocybin. **1971** *McGraw-Hill Yearbk. Sci. & Technol.* 357/2 These tribesmen, having discovered that the narcotic constituent of the mushroom is excreted with almost undiminished *psychoactivity, incorporated a ritual urine-drinking ceremony. **1973** *Nature* 6 Apr. 367/3 These two amphetamine derivatives, which show profound psychoactivity in man. **1925** W. H. J. SPROTT tr. *Kretschmer's Physique & Character* II. xiv. 258 An indefinite number of individual temperamental shades emerge from the *psychæsthetic and diathetic proportions. **1943** [see *psychomotility* below]. **1951** *Jrnl. Aesthetics* X. 2 Our discussion will have to go in two directions: (1) What are the specific attributes of the art of the blind? (2) What psycho-aesthetic implications result from it for the world of the normal-sighted? **1973** *Screen* Spring/Summer 65 While there is perhaps no 'eternal and immutable essence' of the cinema as opposed to the theatre.., there is at least a psycho-aesthetic conditioning of each art by the technical constraints which define and constitute them. **1909** *Encycl. Relig. & Ethics* II. 448/2 **Psycho-æsthetics*,..the application of psycho-physiology to the study of æsthetic states... Helmholtz in Germany, and Grant Allen in England, tried to determine the physiological concomitants of certain phenomena of the Beautiful. **1939** *Time & Tide* 8 Apr. 454/1 Your temperament told from your taste in Old Masters. A stimulating essay in psycho-æsthetics. **1976** *National Observer* (U.S.) 8 May 15/1 For the consumer who doesn't understand *psycho-babble, trying to sort out the various specialties can be downright mind-boggling: Gestalt, TA (Transactional Analysis), bio-energetics, sex therapy, behavior modification, [etc.]. **1977** R. D. ROSEN (*title*) Psychobabble. **1977** *Proc. R. Soc. Med.* LXX. 806/1 This was yet another American death book, full of psychobabble and journalistic cuttings from every other American death book. **1980** *Times Lit. Suppl.* 16 May 544/3 The book is written in colloquial American spliced with psychobabble, a language in which the highest commendation is to say of someone 'She was a person.' **1977** *N.Y. Times Mag.* 20 Nov. 124/4 The *psychobabblers not only outnumber the rest of us, but..they have The Force on their side. **1978** *Guardian Weekly* 22 Jan. 19/1 She mocked the manners and morals and especially the 'mindless prattle' of the psychobabblers among whom she lives [in California]. **1889** *Athenæum* 5 Jan. 12/1 Instead of the association of mental atoms, we are coming to the idea of segmentation of a *psychoblast, if we may invent such a term. **1892** *Monist* II. 293 In experimental psychology, psychopetal, psychofugal, and *psychocentral processes are distinguished. **1936** J. O. WISDOM in *Proc. Aristotelian Soc.* XXXVI. 62, I shall try to establish my *psychocentric analysis of *right*. **1949** *Mind* LVIII. 390 There is the traditional 'psychocentric' conception..: the dualistic conception, which regards the human being as a compound of two distinct but interacting entities, mind and body. **1956** J. B. RHINE in A. Pryce-Jones *New Outl. Mod. Knowl.* 205 There have been psychocentric schools of psychology..but none of these psychocentric views has ever prevailed widely in academic psychology. **1958** *Psychochemical [see PSYCHOTOMIMETIC *a.*]. **1959** *New Scientist* 20 Aug. 222 The Committee appears to have been particularly impressed by what the US Army's chemists told it about the so-called psychochemical weapons. *Ibid.*, Whatever the intrinsic power of 'psychochemicals' may prove to be, the picture of a bloodless war painted by the Congressional committee is hard to believe. **1965** B. INGLIS *Drugs, Doctors & Disease* iii. 110 Nowhere has the evidence of the power of placebo effect been more striking than in the new market for psycho-chemicals: pep pills and tranquillisers. **1972** G. WATSON (*title*) Nutrition and your mind: the psychochemical response. **1973** 'A. HALL' *Tango Briefing* xiv. 176 Obviously psychochemicals but not related to mescaline or lysergic acid. **1977** *Rolling Stone* 21 Apr. 46/4 The Soviet Union was hard at work in psychochemical research. **1900** *Amer. Jrnl. Psychol.* XI. 600 The writer takes up..passive and then active sadness, morbid joy, their original mechanism, their psycho-physiology, *psycho-chemistry, [etc.]. **1931** *Chem. News* 23 Jan. 51/1 Colloidal and physiological chemistry have advanced to the extent that we should now be able to envisage a Psychochemistry, or Chemical Psychology. **1883** CLOUSTON *Clin. Lect. Mental Dis.* i. 18, I can devise no better name than the usual one of Stupor... '*Psychocoma' would express this condition. **1951** M. A. STRAUS in *Amer. Sociol. Rev.* June 374 One is led to what Frank has called a '*psychocultural' rather than a purely psychological explanation of the phenomena of bilingual inferiority. **1977** *Canada Jrnl. Linguistics* 1976 XXI. 226 The wider implications of language as a psychocultural, evolutionary phenomenon. **1901** A. C. HALPHIDE *Psychic & Psychism* i. 21 There are many schools of *Psycho-curative systems, all of which might be classified under the title Mental Medicine. **1953** *Cape Times* 14 Feb. 5/2 The doctors believe that the installation of a pigeon loft at the hospital may have a psycho-curative effect. **1940** *Proc. R. Soc. Med.* XXXIII. 173 (*heading*) Myokinetic *psychodiagnosis: a new technique of exploring the conative trends of personality. **1969** J. E. EXNER *Rorschach Systems* i. 5 Rorschach might well be appalled were he to perceive how the technique is utilized in contemporary psychodiagnosis. [**1930** *Amer. Jrnl. Psychiatry* X. 50 The Rorschach 'Psychodiagnostik' test, consisting of ten symmetrical ink-blots.] **1937** *Amer. Jrnl. Orthopsychiatry* VII. 320 With this paper we want to introduce a new concept in the theory and a new tool in the practice of Rorschach's *psychodiagnostic ink blot test. **1949** S. ROSENZWEIG *Psychodiagnosis* i. 1 As a psychodiagnostic art clinical psychology derives historically from two chief sources—the psychometric and the psychodynamic. **1932** *Character & Personality* I. 2 The proper aim of a quarterly for *psychodiagnostics and allied studies seems to us to be to establish an organic connection among the numerous specialized branches of psychology. **1960** H. J. EYSENCK *Exper. Personality* I. p. ix, Experiments in psychogenetics, psychopharmacology, psychodiagnostics [etc.],..all..form part of the programme of research. **1970** *Jrnl. Aesthetics* XXIX. 105 (*heading*) The ink blot test, 'psychodiagnostics' and Hermann Rorschach's aesthetic views. **1890** *Cent. Dict.*, *Psychodometer. **1892** D. HACK TUKE *Dict. Psychol. Med.* II., **Psychodometer*, an instrument for measuring the rapidity of psychic events. **1961** KALINOWSKY & HOCH *Somatic Treatments in Psychiatry* ii. 8 *Psychodysleptics or psychotomimetics. This refers to a group of drugs which can produce the so-called 'model psychoses' and which have characteristically hallucinogenic and mildly stimulant properties. **1967** *WHO Chron.* XXI. 465/2 Three classes of psychotropic drugs are particularly dependence-producing: the anxiolytic sedatives, the psychodysleptics (hallucinogens), and the psychostimulants. **1974** *Nature* 27 Sept. 314/1 Some psychodysleptics (mescaline sulphate and LSD), when injected during the photosensitive larval period, suppress diapause induction as if the larvae were subjected to a long 16-h photophase. **1946** *Psychosomatic Med.* VIII. 176 (*heading*) *Psychoendocrine relationships in pseudocyesis. **1958** M. REISS *Psychoendocrinol.* i. 13 The psychoendocrine concept is based on the discovery that the activity of the pituitary is related to the function of the hypothalamus. **1977** *Proc. R. Soc. Med.* LXX. 513/2 Psychoendocrine relationships in affective disorders. **1961** *Psychosomatic Med.* XXIII. 449/1 (*heading*) *Psycho-endocrinologic studies in a male with cyclic changes in sexuality. **1958** M. REISS *Psychoendocrinol.* 27 No doubt people like Tamerlane ..who had undescended testicles..have seemed brilliant just because they were *psychoendocrinologically not completely mature, and therefore more accessible to new impressions and situations. *Ibid.* i. 20 The responsibility of the *psychoendocrinologist in such a case has become very grave indeed. **1975** S. ARIETI *Amer. Handbk. Psychiatry* IV. 554/2 Psychoendocrinologists have been mainly preoccupied with the basic psycho-physiological exploration of the significance of hormonal responses as reflections of intrapsychic processes. **1953** M. REISS in *Internat. Rec. Med.* CLXVI. 196 *Psychoendocrinology will become in psychiatric research a much more recognized branch than it is at present. **1975** S. ARIETI *Amer. Handbk. Psychiatry* IV. 555/1 By the late 1950s, then, it was generally recognized not only that psychoendocrinology rested on a solid experimental foundation, but that psychological stimuli were, in fact, among the most potent of all natural stimuli to the pituitary-adrenal cortical system. **1892** *Psychofugal [see *psycho-central* above]. **1953** J. L. MORENO *Who shall Survive?* III. 440 The *psychogeographic mapping of the community shows..the relationship of local geography to psychological processes. **1963** *Listener* 14 Feb. 299/1 The kind of psychogeographic studies made by the Situationists are all very well in communicating a feeling about man/environment relationships. **1958** *Archit. Rev.* CXXIV. 1/1 It shows 'quartiers d'états d'âme' and 'gradients of *psychogeographical drift'—factors not generally taken into account by the average planning authority. **1953** J. L. MORENO *Who shall Survive?* III. 436 There is also in *psychogeography in respect to a certain criterion either a yes or a no, whatever the motivation of this yes or no may be. **1958** *Archit. Rev.* CXXIV. 1/1 This microclimatology of the psyche is something to which every town-dweller can testify, and in a city like Paris..it is a more than personal affair—that document of psychogeography, André Breton's *Nuit du Tournesol*, which ought on the face of it to be an entirely private exercise in erotic topography, can be read with understanding, even by those who have never visited Paris. **1974** *Times Lit. Suppl.* 14 June 630/2 The book promises to become a midwife's guide to the birth of a new discipline, which one expects will be inelegantly dubbed 'psychogeography', rather than 'geopsychology'. **1890** BILLINGS *Med. Dict.*, **Psychogeusic centre*, supposed centre for perception of taste, in the gyrus uncinatus. **1891** *Daily News* 16 Feb. 3/6 '*Psychognosis' at the Royal Aquarium.—This is the title which M. Guibal has adopted for a new and certainly very remarkable development of.. the thought-reading process. **1811–31** *Psychognosy [see PSYCHICS 1]. **1682** H. MORE *Annot. Glanvill's Lux. O.* 194 There being nothing absurd in Psychopyrism but so far forth as it includes *Psycho-Hylism, and makes the soul material. *Ibid.* 193 There is no more harshness in calling him Psychopyrist, than if he had called him *Psycho-Hylist. **1868** W. CORY *Lett. & Jrnls.* (1897) 229 There is that *psycholatry in it which is characteristic of the writer. **1878** MAX MÜLLER *Lect. Orig. & Growth Relig.* ii. 116 Psycholatry. Lastly, great reverence is paid to the spirits of the departed. **1886** MAUDSLEY *Nat. Causes & Supernat. Seemings* 351 Theologian and philosopher alike exhibit the strained functions of a sort of *psycholepsy. *Ibid.* 352 His success in such *psycholeptic sleights of thought. **1925** E. & C. PAUL tr. *Janet's Psychol. Healing* I. x. 558 Individuals in whom psychological tension is unstable, suffer from sudden relaxations of this tension, succumb to psycholeptic crises. **1940** H. G. BAYNES *Mythol. of Soul* xi. 882 We could then regard the whole drama as a psycholeptic crisis with its characteristic feeling-symptom of the end of the world. **1961** KALINOWSKY & HOCH *Somatic Treatments in Psychiatry* ii. 8 Delay has proposed the following classification of the new drugs based upon their predominant action. (A) Psycholeptics or Sedatives... (C) Psychodysleptics or psychotomimetics. **1971** ZIRKLE & KAISER in A. Burger *Med. Chem.* (ed. 3) II. lv. 1412/1 The antipsychotic agents were originally given such names as tranquilizers.., ataraxics.., psycholeptics, and psychosedatives. **1962** D. D. JACKSON in *Jrnl. Nerv. & Mental Dis.* CXXXV. 436/1 More accurately, perhaps, we should speak of *psycholytic drugs given by psychosogenic therapists. **1963** R. A. SANDISON in R. Crocket et al. *Hallucinogenic Drugs* 34 This total experience of the unconscious, brought about by the power of LSD to loosen the psyche, has led to a feeling that the hallucinogenic drugs should be renamed the psycholytic drugs. This name, which is free from the many objections attached to the word 'hallucinogenic' was first suggested and adopted at Göttingen last year. **1964** D. F. DOWNING in M. Gordon *Psychopharm. Agents* I. xiii. 606 In this context they [*sc.* psychotomimetic agents] are frequently known as psycholytic drugs because of their power to loosen the psyche. **1974** ARIETI & BRODY *Amer. Handbk. Psychiatry* (ed. 2) III. 425/1 *Psycholytic therapy*, this technique consists of a series of drug sessions in which small doses of LSD.. are given to a number of patients in an outpatient setting. These sessions are associated with individual or group therapy. **1964** M. MCLUHAN *Understanding Media* xxxi. 308 Our children are striving to carry over to the printed page the all-involving sensory mandate of the TV image. With perfect *psycho-mimetic skill, they carry out the commands of the TV image. **1967** *WHO Chron.* XXI. 464/2 Psychodysleptics, also called 'hallucinogens', 'psychomimetics', or 'psychodelics', are compounds that produce abnormal mental phenomena, particularly in the cognitive and perceptual spheres. **1969** *Listener* 28 Aug. 295/2 *Grand Hotel, The Age of Innocence, Dr. Finlay's Casebook*..all inextricably jumbled together into a deliriously psychomimetic paradise. **1974** S. ARIETI *Amer. Handbk. Psychiatry* (ed. 2) I. 67/2 Exaggerated expectations about the uncritical use of 'psychomimetics' (mainly LSD

25) in the treatment of mental disorders and especially about the power of some drugs to enlarge the field of consciousness and provide new philosophical and religious insights are unrealistic. **1904** *Contemp. Rev.* Apr. 497 Their *psychomonism asserts..one thing only exists and that is my own mind. **1925** W. J. H. Sprott tr. *Kretschmer's Physique & Character* ix. 134 The *psychomotility of the cycloid is even and adequate to the stimulus, and motor expressions and movements are well rounded, fluid, and natural. **1934** E. B. Strauss tr. *Kretschmer's Text-bk. Med. Psychol.* iv. 43 In a mild degree traces of these Parkinsonian features often typify the psychomotility of advanced old age. **1943** H. Read *Educ. through Art* iv. 79 Within the main cycloid and schizoid groups, there are a considerable number of psychaesthetic variants and a considerable degree of psychomotility. **1969** H. E. King in Zubin & Shagass *Neurobiol. Aspects of Psychopathol.* vi. 99 (*heading*) Psychomotility: a dimension of behavior disorder. **1890** W. James *Princ. Psychol.* II. xx. 164 Thus we should escape the responsibility of explaining, by falling back on the everlasting inscrutability of the *psycho-neural nexus. **1923** J. S. Huxley *Ess. Biologist* iv. 134 The mind, or shall we say the psycho-neural organization. **1949** [see hypnoanalysis]. **1969** *Word 1967* XXIII. 469 Nor can we yet identify all of the psychoneural factors which enter into the final stage of speech perception, 'understanding'. **1954** M. Reiss in *Jrnl. Mental Sci.* 701 The influence of the various treatments on a *psycho-neuro-endocrine cycle. **1972** *Science* 9 June 1115/3 The relationships of such psychoneuroendocrine studies to the clinical observations on man are dealt with in papers by Abrams. **1954** M. Reiss in *Jrnl. Mental Sci.* C. 687 Such efforts are unavoidable if progress is to be made in *psycho-neuro-endocrinologic problems. **1971** —— in D. H. Ford *Influence of Hormones on Nervous System* p. xix, Our association was named *Psychoneuro-endocrinological because it emphasizes not only the beginning but also the end of the most important patho-physiological vicious circle in the body. **1972** *Science* 9 June 1115/2 A group of scientists ..have organized an International Society of *Psychoneuroendocrinology. **1978** *Nature* 14 Dec. p. xii. (Advt.), Psychoneuroendocrinology is an attempt to provide the essential interdisciplinary approach to research in human reproduction. **1921** *Edin. Rev.* Jan. 61 In London the *Psycho-Neurological Society has been formed..for the study and discussion of problems in psychotherapy. **1928** H. P. Weld *Psychol. as Science* viii. 156 (*heading*) Psychoneurological theories. **1865** R. T. Stothard (*title*) *Psychoneurology: A Treatise on the Mental Faculties, as governed and developed by the Animal Nature. **1895** in *Syd. Soc. Lex.* **1943** *Amer. Jrnl. Psychiatry* C. 181/2 Apart from the therapeutic implications of the transsection of the anterior thalamic radiations, the method has important implications for experimentation in clinical neurology and in psychoneurology. **1803** J. Stewart *Opus Maximum* Title-p., *Psyconomy: or, the science of the moral powers. **1841** *Proc. Amer. Phil. Soc.* II. 76 *Psychonomy*, or the laws of mind, comprising the study of Languages, Metaphysics, Jurisprudence and Religion. **1865** R. Beamish (*title*) The Psychonomy of the Hand; or, the Hand an Index of Mental Development. **1885** Landois & Stirling *Text-bk. Human Physiol.* II. xiii. 921 The *psycho-optic centre,..according to Munk, embraces the outer convex part of the occipital lobe of the dog's brain. **1937** *Arch. Neurol. & Psychiatry* XXXVII. 1173 Both kinds of movement belong to the so-called psycho-optic reflexes because, being produced by visual stimuli, they are performed more or less instinctively. **1954** S. Duke-Elder *Parsons' Dis. Eye* (ed. 12). xxvii. 462 The involuntary reflexes which depend on vision (fixation, fusional movements, convergence, etc.)—the psycho-optical reflexes—are centred in the visual cortex of the occipital lobe. **1883** Clouston *Clin. Lect. Mental Dis.* i. 18 When the morbid condition is one of mental enfeeblement it is called Dementia or Amentia... It might be called *Psychoparesis. **1892** *Psychopetal [see *psychocentral* above]. **1964** *Dis. Nerv. System* XXV. 233/2 The effects of discontinuing *psychopharmaceuticals in a large group of long-term schizophrenic patients. **1965** *New Scientist* 18 Mar. 719/1 So far medical researchers have largely had to rely on a patient's behaviour pattern to assess the effects of the so-called psychopharmaceutical drugs—those which can be used nowadays with considerable effect against certain types of nervous disorders. **1969** *Sci. News* 20 Dec. 581 One advantage of doxepin is its apparently low toxicity compared to other psycho-pharmaceuticals. **1966** *New Statesman* 18 Feb. 243/2 (Advt.), ESP *Psycho-philosopher, having evolved new theory concerning influence on environment at a distance and through thought, seeks volunteers to co-operate in test. **1960** *IRE Trans. Electronic Computers* IX. 524/1 The pragmatic philosophy of C. S. Peirce helped save much of philosophy from the sterilizing effect of *psycho-philosophy. **1876** A. Blackwell *Kardec's Medium's Bk.* 447 **Psychophony*, the communication of spirits by the voice of a speaking medium. **1922** Joyce *Ulysses* 659 Heliotherapy, *psychophysicotherapeutics, osteopathic surgery. **1921** *Q. Rev.* Oct. 397 The exaggeration..would..have made its dogmatic definition sooner or later inevitable, but Manning's championship of it assisted its appearance at the *psycho-political moment. **1934** H. G. Wells *Exper. Autobiogr.* II. ix. 798 This psycho-political autobiography. **1948** J. Towster *Polit. Power in U.S.S.R.* iv. 57 While the unification of nations is the goal *ne plus ultra*, there are enormous psycho-political obstacles in the way. **1971** K. Millett *Sexual Politics* II. iii. 73 The psycho-political tactic here is a pretence that the indolence and luxury of the upper-class woman's role..was the happy lot of all women. **1961** *Guardian* 2 Nov. 8/2 Robert Jungk..wanted to do his thesis on what he called '*psychopolitics', the interaction between mass psychology and mass psychology movements and politics. **1980** *Boston Globe* 3 Feb. B1 Kantor claims that people's current patterns of interaction, or 'psychopolitics', are based on 'critical identity images'. **1934** H. Hiler *Notes Technique Painting* 332 **Psycho-prismatism*, the affective psychology of colour. The study of the reactions of human beings or animals to the various colours. **1744** 'J. Philander' (*title*) The Golden Calf, the Idol Worship,.. with Account of the *Psychoptic Looking Glass, lately invented by the author. **1682** *Psychopyrism [see *psycho-hylism*]. **1681** H. More *Answ. Lett. Psychopyrist* To Rdr., in *Glanvill's Sadducismus* (ed. 2), The *Psychopyrists..make the Essence or Substance of all created Spirits to be Fire. **1899** *Allbutt's Syst. Med.* VII. 338 The doubtful relation of the optic thalamus to *psycho-reflex mimetic movements. **1903** Myers *Hum. Personality* I. 263, I propose to use the Greek word *ψυχορραγῶ*..'to let the soul break loose', and from which I form the words **psychorrhagy* and **psychorrhagic*. *Ibid.* 270 A clairvoyant excursion (of a more serious type than the mere psychorrhagies already described). *Ibid.* II. 75 Those phantasms of the living which I have already classed as psychorrhagic. **1902** W. M. Alexander *Demonic Possession in N.T.* i. 33 They [demons] are 'half spirits' and are therefore possessed of a semi-sensuous or *psycho-sarcous constitution. **1885** Myers in *Proc. Soc. Psych. Research* May 61 Somnambulism, double-consciousness, epilepsy, insanity itself, are all of them natural *psychoscopes. **1886** Gurney, etc. *Phantasms of Living* I. Introd. 71 The first attempts of his rude psychoscopes to give precision and actuality to thought will grope among 'beggarly elements'. *Ibid.* I. 463 If Baillarger did not carry his view of hallucinations to this length, the whole development exists by implication in the term by which he described them—*psycho-sensorial. **1899** *Allbutt's Syst. Med.* VII. 775 In those patients who experience such *psycho-sensory auræ there is a strong tendency to mental derangement. **1910** W. A. Turner *Three Lect. Epilepsy* 25 He has described the psycho-motor, psycho-sensory, psycho-visual, and psycho-auditory centre in close relation to the motor, sensory, visual, and auditory centres. **1947** H. C. Elliott *Textbk. Nervous Syst.* xix. 238/1 Caudal to its upper part [*sc.* that of the sensory cortex] lies..the psychosensory region. **1959** S. Duke-Elder *Parsons' Dis. Eye* (ed. 13) iv. 38 The pupils participate in several reflexes, three of which are of clinical importance:.. 3. The psycho-sensory reflex, whereby a dilatation occurs on psychic and sensory stimuli. **1903** Greenstreet tr. *Duprat* (title) Morals: A Treatise on the *Psycho-Sociological Bases of Ethics. **1928** *Amer. Jrnl. Sociol.* Nov. 447 Knowing these [laws of suggestion], we could follow their lead into greater knowledge of phenomena of a psycho-sociological nature. **1970** Touraine & Pécaut in I. L. Horowitz *Masses in Lat. Amer.* iii. 67 The resulting normative and psychosociological changes [in the social system] are analyzed..as a function of the change in values judged necessary to attain the industrialized state. **1966** *Punch* 9 Mar. 332/3 Those big black career advertisements and their rich esoterica about openings for crystallographers, systems analysts and industrial *psycho-sociologists. **1908** *Science* 10 July 54 *Psycho-sociology. **1957** R. K. Merton *Student-Physician* 53 A middle ground which has been described as social psychology (or, by some, psycho-sociology). **1973** *Screen* Spring/Summer 151 Various revelatory and therapeutic methods belonging to modern psycho-sociology. **1820** L. Hunt *Indicator* No. 22 (1822) I. 176 A part of wisdom which our modern *psycho-sophists are so apt to forget. **1913** J. Murray *Ocean* x. 228 We may say that within the biosphere a sphere of reason and intelligence has been evolved in man, who attempts to interpret and explain the cosmos; this may be called the *psycho-sphere. **1957** P. B. Sears *Ecology of Man* 10 To these might be added *Mind*—the Psychosphere, studied by psychologists, anthropologists and other social scientists. **1975** O. L. Reiser *Cosmic Humanism & World Unity* iii. 97 The Psychosphere may be regarded as a psychic-magnetic environment, an 'auric field', beyond the Van Allen Radiation Belt. **1961** Musser & O'Neill *Mod. Pharmacol. & Therapeutics* (ed. 2) xix. 361 Prior to the development of these newer drugs, called *psycho-stimulants or psychic energizers, apathetic and depressed patients were treated with caffeine and the amphetamines. **1963** *Wall St. Jrnl.* 21 Jan. 12/4 The three areas in which the largest number of new agents are being investigated were psycho-stimulants, broad spectrum antibiotics and cholesterol-reducing agents. **1966** J. D. P. Graham *Pharmacol.* iv. 26/2 This drug [*sc.* dexamphetamine sulphate] is given to mentally depressed patients. It may therefore be termed a psychostimulant drug. **1967** [see *psychodysleptic* above]. **1971** T. A. Ban in O. Vinăr et al. *Advances in Neuropsychopharmacol.* 212 Conflict tolerance in humans may also increase under the influence of psychostimulants in general. **1973** *Proc. R. Soc. Med.* LXVI. 359/2 Would-be psychiatrists are taught to describe, define and treat disembodied *psychosyndromes instead of learning to apply modern investigative science to finding causes. **1976** Smythies & Corbett *Psychiatry* vii. 113 Non-specific endocrine psychosyndromes occur with apathy, depression and lability of mood. **1919** C. E. Long in M. K. Bradby *Psycho-Anal.* p. vi, We aim at a reconstruction of life which can only be conceived as a *psycho-synthesis. **1924** J. Riviere tr. *Freud's Coll. Papers* II. xxxiv. 395 The neurotic human being brings us his mind racked and rent by resistances; whilst we are working at analysis of it and removing the resistances, this mind of his begins to grow together; that great unity which we call his ego fuses into one all the instinctual trends which before had been split off and barred away from it. The psycho-synthesis is thus achieved during analytic treatment without our intervention. **1940** H. G. Wells *Babes in Darkling Wood* 9 The mental break-down of Gemini..bring [*sic*] the methods of a leading psycho-analyst and modern psychosynthesis into the story. **1975** M. & N. Samuels *Seeing with Mind's Eye* iii. 37 Currently, visualization is being used in a number of different psychotherapeutic techniques—including.. directed day-dreams, Psychosynthesis, and behaviorist desensitization. **1944** H. G. Wells *'42 to '44* 172 What a psycho-analyst calls the Unconscious, but which, according to the *psycho-synthesist, is merely a multitude of reaction systems out of contact with the main directive system. **1940** —— *All Aboard for Ararat* ii. 80 The core of the new world must be (listen to these words!) Atheist, Creative, *Psycho-synthetic. **1842** Marg. Fuller in *Mem.* (1862) I. 246 It would seem to approach the faith of some of my friends here, which has been styled *Psychotheism. **1910** *Psycho-visual [see *psycho-sensory* adj. above]. **1969** G. C. Dickinson *Maps & Air Photographs* iv. 63 The conventional colour sequence, which follows spectrum order from violet through shades of blue, green, yellow and orange to red (or more commonly brown), accords well with the psycho-visual properties of colours—blues for submarine areas are 'recessive', reds for hills 'stand out'—but there can be unfortunate suggestive overtones. **1971** *Nature* 19 Mar. 180/1 It is hoped that a laboratory equipped for psychovisual studies will..report on the degree to which descriptions of 'artificial' ball lightning resemble those of the natural phenomenon that are recorded in the scientific literature. **1877** Le Conte *Elem. Geol.* (1879) 269 The *Psychozoic era, or era of Mind. *Ibid.* 561 The Neolithic commences the Psychozoic era, or reign of man.

psycho-a'coustic, *a.* [f. psycho- + acoustic *a.*] Pertaining to the perception of sound and the production of speech or to the study of these. Also **psycho-a'coustical** *a.*, **-a'coustically** *adv.*

1885 W. Stirling tr. *Landois's Text-bk. Human Physiol.* II. xiii. 922 The psycho-acoustic centre..lies, in the dog,.. in the region of the second primary convolution. **1946** *Jrnl. Aeronaut. Sci.* XIII. 255 The Psycho-Acoustic Laboratory, Harvard University. **1953** *Electronic Engin.* XXV. 24/2 Acoustic and psycho-acoustic distortion. These forms of distortion occur through imperfections in the acoustics of studios and listening rooms, the use of mon-aural (single channel) reproducing chains, [etc.]. **1953** *Language* XXIX. 85 Measurement of fidelity has to be made psycho-acoustically in terms of the whole speech signal, not just in terms of its linguistic content. **1958** *New Scientist* 30 Oct. 1165/1 A great deal of psycho-acoustical work has concerned simple sounds, like pure tones, or sharp clicks. **1971** *Computers & Humanities* V. 312 Use of the computer in investigating psycho-acoustical phenomena. **1975** G. J. King *Audio Handbk.* vii. 163 Several psycho-acoustical principles govern the subjective assimilation of quadraphony. **1976** *Gramophone* Jan. 1269/2 Now the physical and psycho-acoustic conditions for correct perception of direction of sound can be expressed by equations. **1977** *New Scientist* 1 Dec. 574/2 Ways and means of psychoacoustically handling the retrieved signals so that they produce a realistic surround of sound.

So **psycho-a'coustics**, the science of the perception of sound and the production of speech; **,psycho-acou'stician**, an expert or specialist in psycho-acoustics.

1948 *Mind* LVII. 388 Harvard divided psychology into two Departments—the Department of Social Relations.. and the Department of General Psychology, with three.. laboratories of General Psychology, Physiological Psychology and Psycho-Acoustics. **1958** *New Scientist* 30 Oct. 1165/3 The science of acoustics..has branched out into two fields which are essentially modern in idea and purpose. .. The first field is ultrasonics... The second field is psycho-acoustics, which is, essentially, the study of hearing, but more especially the whole speech-hearing process. **1963** Ervin & Miller in *Child Psychol.* (*62nd Yearbk. Nat. Soc. Study of Educ.* 1) iii. 111 Information on the actual phonetic cues used by the child could be obtained by using artificially constructed vocalic stimuli. Such studies have been conducted by psychoacousticians on adults, but not on children **1976** *Canad. Jrnl. Linguistics* XXI. 1. 2 It would be pointless, e.g., to try to incorporate all of the practically infinite variations of the acoustic wave form into a descriptive system for psycho-acoustics when what is required is an adequate description of those specific properties of the sound pattern which significantly affect the perception of speech. **1977** *Rolling Stone* 30 June 41/2 Next I met David Wessel, a psychoacoustician (one who studies human perception of sound) from Michigan State University.

psychoactive, -activity, -æsthetic(s: see psycho-.

psycho'analyse, *v.* Also with hyphen. [Back-formation from next, after *analysis*, *analyse*.] *trans.* To subject to or treat by psychoanalysis; = analyse *v.* 3 b. Also *absol.*

1911 *Amer. Jrnl. Psychol.* July 423 It is..hoped that Freud will..psychoanalyze Goethe. **1922** J. Macy in D. H. Lawrence *Sons & Lovers* p. ix, Let whoever cares to try analyze or psychoanalyze. **1924** C. Mackenzie *Heavenly Ladder* xxiii. 288, I could psycho-analyse all Bloomsbury now. They all suffer from an inferiority complex. **1969** *Listener* 14 Aug. 219/2 Professor Baker scrupulously does not diagram, hypothesise or psycho-analyse. **1973** *Amer. N. & Q.* XI. 78/1 To psychoanalyze a dramatic hero is to treat him as a human being.

Hence **psycho'analysed** *ppl. a.*

1928 'R. West' *Strange Necessity* 240 A psycho-analysed person who has made the realization that all persons he dreams of are disguised versions of himself.

psychoa'nalysis. Also with hyphen and (*rare*) as **psychanalysis.** [ad. F. *psychoanalyse* (S. Freud 1896, in *Rev. Neurologique* IV. 166): see psycho- and analysis.

Freud earlier used *psychische analyse* and *klinischpsychologische analyse* (*Neurol. Centralbl.* (1894) XIII. 364).]

a. A therapeutic method originated by Freud for treating disorders of the personality or behaviour by bringing into a patient's consciousness his unconscious conflicts and fantasies (which are attributed chiefly to the development of the sexual instinct) through the free association of ideas, analysis and interpretation of dreams and parapraxes, etc., and allowing him to relive them by transference. **b.** A theory of personality and psychical life derived from this, based on concepts of the ego, id, and super-ego, the conscious, pre-conscious, and unconscious levels of the mind, and the repression of the sexual instinct; more widely, a branch of psychology dealing with the unconscious.

[**1898** H. Ellis in *Alienist & Neurologist* XIX. 610 The influence of fear is not denied by Breuer and Freud, but they have found that careful psychic analysis frequently reveals that the shock of a commonplace 'fear' is really rooted in a lesion of the sexual emotions.] **1906** *Jrnl. Abnormal Psychol.* I. 28 Their importance with relation to treatment (by the method of 'psycho-analysis') is made clear. **1913** *Q. Rev.* Jan. 143 'Psycho-analysis' has been strongly advocated by some men in the medical profession... It consists in carefully and systematically resuscitating the patient's past memories, thus making him aware of his buried and unconscious mental processes, when those are brought before his present consciousness. **1924** W. B. SELBIE *Psychol. of Relig.* 286 Psycho-analysis is the name given to the process by which the hidden depths of the individual consciousness can be revealed. **1932** *Sun* (Baltimore) 12 Sept. 6/3 Psychanalysis for the majority of informed Marylanders is not..a new kind of gypsy dreambook. **1938** *Internat. Jrnl. Psycho-Anal.* XIX. 1 Everything of importance that we know concerning the play of instinctual forces and the course they follow in the homosexual we have derived from psycho-analysis. **1958** THORPE & SCHMULLER *Personality* ix. 215 According to psychoanalysis, all of us are characterized by primitive impulses, but our parents and the culture have required us to develop standards of behavior which lead to the repression of these impulses, forcing them into the unconscious. **1964** A. ANASTASI *Fields of Applied Psychol.* xiv. 383 It is apparent that active interpretation by the therapist is a major feature of psychoanalysis. **1964** M. ARGYLE *Psychol. & Social Probl.* ii. 26 Neither of the two major theoretical approaches in psychology—psychoanalysis or learning theory—can explain the phenomena of childhood socialization satisfactorily. **1966** *Times* 13 Jan. 11/4 Freudian and Jungian psychanalysis.. has had its day. **1974** J. MITCHELL *Psychoanal. & Feminism* II. ii. 153 His theories of the nature of sexuality and the evidence of its repression..were developed in a double intellectual context, that of Marxism and of psychoanalysis. **1975** A. RYLE *Frames & Cages* iii. 19 In psychoanalysis, the therapist will..embark on a relationship with the patient, the understanding and evolution of which is the central process of therapy... It is through this process that unconscious primitive fantasies are replaced by freer and less idiosyncratic apprehension of the self and the world.

psychoˈanalyst. Also with hyphen. [f. prec., after *analysis*, *analyst*.] One who practises or has training in psychoanalysis.

1911 *Amer. Jrnl. Psychol.* July 434 The business of the psychoanalyst is to provide a means by which the emotion attached to a repressed complex may find expression, by being transformed. **1918** *Jrnl. Educ.* Mar. 153/1 Dr. Pfister devotes a couple of pages to an exposition of the need for the psychoanalyst to be himself 'free from complexes'. **1921** R. MACAULAY *Dangerous Ages* v. 88 The psycho-analyst doctor would really want to hear details. **1947** A. HUXLEY *Let.* 9 Mar. (1969) 567 Marlow is one of those classical cases, so dear to psychoanalysts, with a fixation on his mother. **1977** A. SHERIDAN tr. *J. Lacan's Écrits* iii. 105 Of all the undertakings that have been proposed in this century, that of the psychoanalyst is perhaps the loftiest.

ˌpsychoanaˈlytic, *a.* Also with hyphen and (*rare*) as **psychanalytic.** [f. as prec., after *analysis*, *analytic*, or ad. G. *psychoanalytisch*.] Of, pertaining to, or employing psychoanalysis.

1906 *Jrnl. Abnormal Psychol.* I. 31 The strict 'cathartic', psycho-analytic method advocated by Freud. **1932** *Sun* (Baltimore) 12 Sept. 6/3 In the twenties the works of Freud, Jung, Jones and others of the psychanalytic schools sold like novels. **1979** *N.Y. Rev. Bks.* 25 Oct. 23/2 *Patricide*..draws on some of the best recent psychoanalytic literature.

So **ˌpsychoanaˈlytical** *a.*, in the same sense; **ˌpsychoanaˈlytically** *adv.*, by means of, in respect of, or towards psychoanalysis.

[**1857** *Russell's Mag.* Nov. 163/2 [Poe] chose..the psycho-analytical. His heroes are monstrous reflections of his own heart in its despair, not in its peace.] **1908** *Jrnl. Abnormal Psychol.* III. 209 It would have added greatly to the interest of this question if a psycho-analytical investigation had been resorted to. **1919** *N.Y. Tribune* 22 Dec. 10/6 'Psychoanalytically speaking,' he writes, 'I think you were wrong about H. third and the carving knife.' **1927** *Observer* 12 June 12/4 The interesting question of whether medical men may treat a patient psycho-analytically was dealt with in Court the other day. **1931** R. CAMPBELL *Georgiad* i. 13 Nor would he dogmatise his pet perversions With psycho-analytical assertions. **1959** B. WOOTTON *Social Sci. & Social Path.* iv. 145 Even the psychoanalytically inclined are beginning to allow a rather less rigid, and therefore less dismal attitude. **1962** *Lancet* 22 Dec. 1311/1 He begins his book with an account of Freud's philosophical theories as a background to the later development of psychoanalytical concepts by the neo-Freudians. **1971** *Times* 1 Feb. 20/4 (Advt.), Psycho-analytically Orientated Group counters inhibition, anxiety, depression. **1977** C. STORR *Tales from Psychiatrist's Couch* x. 104 The strict, psycho-analytical view that it is utterly improper for the analyst to have anything to do with the husbands, wives, parents, children ..of his patients.

psychobabble, -er: see PSYCHO-.

psychobiˈography. [f. PSYCHO- + BIOGRAPHY.] **a.** A biography dealing esp. with the psychology of the subject.

1931 *Brit. Jrnl. Psychol.* XXII. 96 The majority of 'psychobiographies' and pseudo-scientific works on the psychology of character. **1969** *Daily Tel.* 20 Mar. 22/2 Frank E. Manuel, the American historian,..in this 'psycho-biography' attempts to analyse aspects of Newton's conduct. **1974** *Publishers Weekly* 13 May 56/2 To understand Mishima's death, Scott-Stokes thinks, one must understand his life. With this useful psycho-biography he would seem to have made his case. **1977** *N.Y. Rev. Bks.* 23 June 23 (Advt.), An iconoclastic psychobiography of Freud's disciple.

b. The art of writing psychobiographies; the interpretation of life histories in psychological terms, or the psychological analysis of a historical person.

1965 *Hist. & Theory* IV. 357 This is still psychobiography, but the psychopathological model has given way to a model of man in history. **1975** *Times Lit. Suppl.* 24 Jan. 90/2 The problem..is how to read the personality into the action, and it is the claim of psychobiography that this can not only be done but that it can be done systematically. The classic exercise in psychobiography is Erik Erikson's *Young Man Luther*.

Hence **psychobiˈographer**, a writer of psychobiography; **ˌpsychobioˈgraphic, -ical** *adjs.*; **ˌpsychobioˈgraphically** *adv.*

1972 *N.Y. Times Bk. Rev.* 10 Dec. 36 It [*sc.* a book] makes no large historiographical, mythological or psycho-biographical assumptions. **1975** *Times Lit. Suppl.* 24 Jan. 90/2 A psychobiographer would naturally reply that this is to take too literal and simplistic a view of the information that is contained in the sources. **1977** *Oxf. Lit. Rev.* II. III. 8/1 This touches on processes which are not consonant either with the communal norms of cultural expectations or with the detective work of psycho-biographers. **1977** *N.Y. Rev. Bks.* 15 Sept. 40/4 He is a psychobiographical critic.., interested in the poem not as artifact but as evidence. **1978** *Dædalus* Spring 229 It is..contrary to the psychobiographic drive of most of the younger scientists. **1979** *N.Y. Times* 15 July 11. 19 Leopold cuts a rather poor figure, psychobiographically, emerging as the standard narcissistic parent who sees his child only as an extension of his own ego.

psychobiˈology. Also with hyphen. [f. PSYCHO- + BIOLOGY.] The study of the biological basis of behaviour or mental phenomena; the interaction of mental and biological factors in an organism.

1902 *Encycl. Brit.* XXXII. 65/2 This connection of vegetal and animal functions remains one of the obscurest in all psycho-biology. **1923** A. MEYER in E. Winters *Coll. Papers* (1952) IV. 244 In connection with psychiatric work, but from an angle quite different from Freudism, there had developed during the last twenty-five years a less spectacular objective psychobiology. **1966** [see SOCIOBIOLOGY]. **1966** *New Scientist* 24 Feb. 464/3 Dr Allan Jacobson..reported that, by taking extracts from the brains of rats that had been taught to perform certain tasks, and injecting them into untrained rats, the latter seemed to acquire a degree of memory for these tasks... New experiments, however, undertaken by five workers from the departments of psychobiology, and of molecular and cell biology, University of California, Irvine, appear to cast considerable doubts on the validity of Dr Jacobson's conclusions. **1975** *Sci. Amer.* Dec. 7/2 (Advt.), *A Primer of Psychobiology* is a brief, informative introduction to what is known about the structure and function of the nervous system and how these relate to behavior.

So **ˌpsychobioˈlogic, -ˈlogical** *adjs.*, of or pertaining to psychobiology; both psychological and biological; **ˌpsychobioˈlogically** *adv.*, in a psychobiological manner; in relation to psychobiology; **psychobiˈologist**, an expert or specialist in psychobiology.

1901 *Amer. Jrnl. Psychol.* XII. 206 The experiments must conform to the psycho-biological character of an animal if sane results are to be obtained. **1934, 1935** [see FIELD *sb.* 17 d]. **1935** ADAMS & ZENER tr. *Lewin's Dynamic Theory of Personality* iii. 79 The environment is..to be defined not physically but *psychobiologically*, that is, according to its quasi-physical, quasi-social, and quasi-mental structure. **1941** *Amer. Speech* XVI. 216 All human behavior is a social psychobiological continuum in which there is no real dichotomy. **1946** *Nature* 24 Aug. 252/2 This is unfortunate at a time when a lot of young men are coming out of the medical services with the idea that there is something in psychosomatic medicine... It is high time we began to try to find out what this is instead of mouthing big phrases such as 'psychobiologic unit'. **1961** WEBSTER, Psychobiologist. **1971** *Amer. Jrnl. Psychiatry* CXXVIII. 706/1 The psychobiologic changes occurring during the [menstrual] cycle do not appear to produce a specific behavioral effect since the form and severity of the symptomatology differ among the various studies. **1973** *Sci. Amer.* Sept. 25/1 We strike a balance..in graduate medical education between the preparation of technologically based specialists and psychobiologically trained generalists. **1977** *Proc. R. Soc. Med.* LXX. 690/1 The underlying pathology of anorexia nervosa may comprise one extreme of the psychobiological nutritional disturbances possibly common to many cases of 'periodic oedema'. **1977** D. M. RUMBAUGH et al. in *Language Learning by Chimpanzee* iv. 89 Yerkes was a very insightful, pioneering psychobiologist. **1979** *Time* 2 Apr. 47/2 People with titles like biochemist, psychobiologist, neurophysiologist and psychopharmacologist are.. replacing traditional psychiatrists as chairmen of hospital psychiatry departments.

psychocentric, -chemical, -chemistry, -cultural, -curative: see PSYCHO-.

psychodelic, var. PSYCHEDELIC *a.* and *sb.*

psychodiagnosis, -diagnostic(s: see PSYCHO-.

ˈpsychodrama. Also with hyphen. [f. PSYCHO- + DRAMA.] **1.** A form of psychotherapy in which a patient acts or performs extempore with or in front of fellow patients and therapists in a way that dramatizes the patient's problems or difficulties; an extempore psychotherapeutic play of this kind. Also *fig.*

1937 J. L. MORENO in *Sociometry* I. 9 The psychodrama is human society in miniature, the simplest possible setup for a methodical study of its psychological structure. **1952** W. J. H. SPROTT *Social Psychol.* xi. 241 The meetings of the various committees..became in effect..psycho-dramas in which the emotional undercurrents came to the surface and were duly interpreted. **1965** *New Statesman* 9 July 38/1 Conflicts came to a head last February at the Mapai convention, a psychodrama in which BG's [*sc.* Ben Gurion's] ex-colleagues acted out years of resentment against the power and personality of the old leader. **1968** *Daily Tel.* (Colour Suppl.) 20 Dec. 15 Its methods centre around group therapy, psychodrama (Stanislavsky for tired businessmen), massage and Oriental philosophy. **1977** *Time Out* 28 Jan.–3 Feb. 59/1 (Advt.), Community. A University for the Person... Using encounter, gestalt, bioenergetics, reichian massage, re-enactment psycho-drama, transactional analysis, [etc.]. **1978** *Listener* 19 Oct. 500/1 Another therapy which believes the answer may lie in obtaining access to buried pains, repressed feelings and hidden desires is the treatment known as 'psychodrama'.

2. A play or film in which psychological elements are the main interest.

[**1927**: see PSYCHO *a.* 1.] **1963** *Movie* Apr. 22/2 A kind of psycho-drama about racial relationships. **1975** C. JAMES *Fate of Felicity Fark* IX. 87 *Flick's Wedding*..was a waking dream, a psychodrama. **1977** *Time* 5 Sept. 26/2 Now comes *Equus*, Sidney Lumet's film of the long-running Broadway psychodrama.

psychodraˈmatic, *a.* [f. prec., after *drama*, *dramatic*.] **1.** Of or by means of therapeutic psychodrama.

1937 J. L. MORENO in *Sociometry* I. 25 When we apply psychodramatic principles to art, especially in the theatre, one notes that the presentation of the role is often interrupted by foreign elements, foreign to the role, betraying the private personality of the actor. **1977** A. SHERIDAN tr. *J. Lacan's Écrits* ii. 9 Psychodramatic treatment..seeks its efficacity in the abreaction that it tries to exhaust on the level of play.

2. Pertaining to or of the nature of a psychodrama (sense 2).

1943 *Sewanee Rev.* LI. 309 It could just as easily be accidental in the psychodramatic reverie of an insane and uneducated son grieving for his dead mother. **1946** *N.Y. Times* 15 Oct. 29/1 'Frontiers of the Mind', a collection of six dramatized case histories, will be presented..under the auspices of the Denes Psychodramatic Theatre.

So **psychodraˈmatics,** (*a*) the use of psychodrama as therapy; (*b*) psychological dramatics; **psychoˈdramatist,** (*a*) one who directs or takes part in therapeutic psychodrama; (*b*) one who writes psychodramas (sense 2).

1937 J. L. MORENO in *Sociometry* I. 10 But in interpersonal therapy, especially in one of its forms which can be called psychodramatics, the task is enormously more complicated. **1953** J. L. MORENO *Who shall Survive?* p. xvi, Therefore I became a psychodramatist and roleplayer. **1957** V. NABOKOV *Pnin* ii. 45 He went on with his Slavic studies, she with her psychodramatics. **1973** *Nation Rev.* (Melbourne) 31 Aug. 1455/2 These uncertainties..are the ruination of most politico-philosophical series produced by the modern school of psychodramatists. **1979** C. E. SCHORSKE *Fin-de-Siècle Vienna* vii. 345 The harsh psycho-dramatics of [the play] *Murderer, Hope of Women* helped the painter [*sc.* Kokoschka] to liberate himself.

psychodynamic (ps-, ˌsaɪkəʊdɪˈnæmɪk), *a.* [f. PSYCHO- + DYNAMIC *a.*] Of or pertaining to mental powers or activities. Hence **psychodyˈnamics**, the science of the laws of mental action; (the study of) the activity of and interrelation between the various parts of an individual's personality or psyche.

1874 LEWES *Probl. Life & Mind* I. 134 *Psychodynamics.* From the biological stand-point our first division of the Organism is into Affective and Active, which division represents the reception of stimulus, and the discharge of force: sensation, and movement. *Ibid.* 142 Here we may note two Psychodynamic laws, 1°, of Irradiation, and, 2°, of Restriction. **1899** *Westm. Gaz.* 13 July 1/3 He was appointed assistant to the Professor of Psycho-Dynamics. **1950** *Psychosomatic Med.* XII. 113/1 Prior to the emergence of psychodynamics, interest was focused in the main on constitutional and hereditary factors in their relationship to organic disease. **1957** 'T. STURGEON' *Thunder & Roses* 175 Psychodynamics has come a long way, but it hasn't begun to alter the fact that human beings are the most feral, vicious.. and self-destructive creatures God ever made. **1960** H. J. EYSENCK *Exper. in Personality* II. 105 (*heading*) Experiments in psychodynamics. The excitation-inhibition balance in neurotics and in normals. **1963** J. A. JOHNSON *Group Therapy* v. 164 The therapist will have formed an opinion of the psychodynamics of each member from previous meetings and should now use this information as a helpful guide in anticipating as well as evaluating behavior associated with separation. **1975** ROSENBAUM & BEEBE *Psychiatric Treatm.* xii. 228/1 Psychodynamics broadly refers to an understanding of the interactions of conscious, unconscious, and reality.

Hence also **psychodyˈnamically** *adv.*

1961 in WEBSTER. **1972** L. J. SAUL (*title*) Psychodynamically based psychotherapy. **1973** *Pediatric Clinics N. Amer.* XX. 743 As a reflection of our Freudian legacy in medicine, the traditional approach to parents in the pediatric setting has been psychodynamically oriented.

psychodysleptic, -endocrine, -endocrinology, etc.: see PSYCHO-.

psychogalˈvanic, *a.* [ad. G. *psychogalvanisch(er reflex)* (O. Veraguth 1907, in *Monatsschr. f. Psychiatrie und Neurol.* XXI. 387): see PSYCHO- and GALVANIC *a.*] Involving changes in the electrical conductivity of the skin associated with emotional changes; chiefly in *psychogalvanic reflex* or *response* (abbrev. *PGR* s.v. P II) = *galvanic skin response.*

1907 *Brain* XXX. 191 It is of interest to ascertain whether the psycho-galvanic reflex runs a parallel course with the complex indices. **1917** C. R. PAYNE tr. *Pfister's Psycho-Anal. Method* 336 Secretion of tears, sighing, psychogalvanic phenomena, changes in the pulse, etc. **1936** *Discovery* July 201 Some remarkable results have been obtained from 'psycho-galvanic' experiments. **1949** WIMSATT & BEARDSLEY in D. Lodge *20th Cent. Lit. Crit.* (1972) 352 The affective critic is today actually able..to measure the 'psychogalvanic reflex' of persons subjected to a given moving picture. **1960** KOESTLER *Lotus & Robot* I. iii. 119

The psycho-galvanic reflex (used in lie detectors) reflects changes in the electrical properties of the body surface in response to emotional stimuli. **1973** *Times* 17 Feb. 14/5 Orme-Johnstone, in a study of the psycho-galvanic response .. showed that meditators had fewer responses than control subjects.

Hence **ˌpsychogalvaˈnometer**, a galvanometer used to measure the psychogalvanic response; **ˌpsychogalvanoˈmetric** *a.*

1935 H. F. DUNBAR *Emotions & Bodily Changes* iii. 87 The usefulness of the psychogalvanometer for the measurement of emotions or for research in the field of psychosomatic relationships. *Ibid.* 592 (Index), Psychogalvanometric apparatus. **1936** K. DUNLAP *Elements of Psychol.* iv. 183 For the simplest psychogalvanometric use, a d'Arsonval galvanometer is connected directly to two electrodes. **1956** *Electronic Engin.* XXVIII. 36 The earliest psycho-galvanometer consisted of a Wheatstone bridge connected to the palms of the subject's hands by means of metal electrodes. **1959** *Listener* 17 Sept. 443/1 A horrid array of forceps, scalpels, stethoscopes, electrocardiographs, and psychogalvanometers.

psychogenesis (ps-, saɪkəʊˈdʒɛnɪsɪs). [f. PSYCHO- + GENESIS 4.]

1. The genesis or origin of the soul or mind.

1838 *Fraser's Mag.* XVII. 27 Was there any tradition on the earth, below the earth, or above the earth, of the Psychogenesis? **1874** LEWIS *Probl. Life & Mind* I. 226 Psychogenesis.. teaches that Instinct is organized Experience, i.e. undiscursive Intelligence. **1889** MIVART *Orig. Hum. Reason* 262 Whether we look to the psychogenesis of the individual or that of the race.

2. a. Origin or evolution due to the activity of the soul or mind itself.

1881 MIVART *Cat* 526 This mode of origin may—as opposed to the hypothesis of natural selection—be fitly termed Psychogenesis. **188.** —— in *Forum* VII. 102 (Cent. Dict.) Specific change must be, above all, due to the action of an organism's innermost life:.. it must be a result of a process of psychogenesis.

b. The psychical origin or cause to which mental illness or behavioural disturbance may be attributed.

1920 S. FREUD in *Internat. Jrnl. Psycho-Anal.* I. 125 (*heading*) The psychogenesis of a case of female homosexuality. **1939** C. G. JUNG in *Jrnl. Mental Sci.* LXXXV. 1002 Psychogenesis of schizophrenia.. in the first place means the question: Can the primary symptom.. be considered as an effect of the psychological conflicts and other disorders of an emotional nature or not? **1972** O. L. ZANGWILL in Cox & Dyson *20th-Cent. Mind* II. vii. 188 There was also greater tolerance for the deviants and eclectics, provided that they subscribed to the general idea of psychogenesis—i.e. the belief that neurosis has a psychological rather than a physical cause. **1979** *N.Y. Rev. Bks.* 25 Oct. 25/1 Schorske's seeming demolition of Freud's Oedipal concept may in fact provide clues.. for liberating Freud's heroic Complex from its imprisonment in the depths of individual psychogenesis.

So **psychogeˈnetic** *a.* = PSYCHOGENIC *a.*; **psychogeˈnetical** *a.*, of or pertaining to psychogenesis; **psychogeˈnetically** *adv.*, in relation to, or in respect of, psychogenesis; **psychogeny** (-ˈɒdʒɪnɪ) = PSYCHOGENESIS 1.

1874 LEWES *Probl. Life & Mind* I. 140 All such distinctions are psychological, not psychogenetical. **1874** J. FISKE *Cosmic Philos.* I. I. viii. 221 Psychogeny.. endeavours to interpret the genesis of intellectual faculties and emotional feelings in the race, and their slow modifications throughout countless generations. **1879** LEWES *Study Psychol.* 157 The Psychologist must include Psychogeny in his investigations, as the Physiologist includes Embryogeny. **1881** *Jrnl. Specul. Philos.* XV. 161 Hardly a day passes in which there is not an observation to enter in the diary, which is of value psychogenetically. **1889** *Athenæum* 5 Jan. 12/1 Psychogenetically Mr. Romanes's position is opposed to all we know or can conjecture as to the beginnings of mind in the animal world or in the human individual. **1896** *Amer. Naturalist* XXX. 443 There is a great series of adaptations secured by conscious agency, which we may throw together as 'psycho-genetic'. **1904** *Jrnl. Philos., Psychol. & Sci. Methods* I. 328 Hume.. had quite unwittingly furnished what.. should have been regarded as a logical deduction and justification—rather than the mere psychogenetic description, which it purported to be—of the realistic belief. **1915** M. PRINCE *Psychol. of Kaiser* viii. 67 So long as these so-called psycho-genetic thoughts are there unmodified.. he [*sc.* the Kaiser] could not get rid of his fixed fear of the democracy if he would. **1975** *Times Lit. Suppl.* 24 Oct. 1253/4 If he really did regard [Queen] Anne's physical disorders as psycho-genetic, eighteenth-century medicine was of precious little use to her case anyway.

psychogeˈnetics. [f. PSYCHO- + GENETICS.]

1. The branch of psychology which is concerned with the effects of breeding or inheritance on behaviour.

1951 C. S. HALL in S. S. Stevens *Handbk. Exper. Psychol.* ix. 304/1 This encouraging trend will ultimately give status and stature to an interdisciplinary science of psychogenetics. The psychogeneticist of the future will presumably be trained in the methods and techniques of both genetics and psychology. **1954** *Brit. Jrnl. Psychol.* XLV. 309 This book should be studied.. by the psychogeneticists. **1960** P. L. BROADHURST in H. J. Eysenck *Exper. in Personality* I. i. 5 The use of different strains, particularly of rats and mice, has long been a favourite method of psychogenetics. Bagg was a pioneer in the application of 'the methods of genetics to the study of conduct'. **1975** *Nature* 30 Oct. 832/2 The perspectives of ethology, physiological psychology, psychogenetics, social psychology.. are all represented to some degree.

2. = PSYCHOGENESIS 1.

1964 *Eng. Stud.* XLV. Suppl. 104 Locke's empiricism takes its place in the field of psychogenetics; he asks the question: where does human understanding come from?

psychogenic (-ˈdʒɛnɪk), *a.* [f. PSYCHO- + -GENIC.] Having a mental or psychological origin or cause.

1902 BALDWIN *Dict. Philos. & Psychol.* II. 382/2 The paralyses and anaesthesias of hysteria,.. the pains and fears of neurasthenia, the ameliorations following appeals to faith or prayer are instances of psychogenic action. **1926** J. I. SUTTIE tr. *Ferenczi's Further Contrib. Theory & Technique Psycho-Anal.* viii. 107 A psychogenic disturbance of the voice. **1964** M. CRITCHLEY *Developmental Dyslexia* xii. 71 Only too often the backwardness in reading is deemed either an environmental, or a psychogenic problem, or both. **1973** *Sci. Amer.* Sept. 124/1 Whatever the cause of a psychotic disorder, be it biological or psychogenic, the mental content of the psychosis must reflect the input to the mind and how that input is refracted by the mind's history and functional state.

Hence **psychoˈgenically** *adv.*

1933 *Jrnl. Nerv. & Mental Dis.* LXXVII. 587 (*heading*) 'Colitis'—psychogenically motivated. **1973** *Lancet* 9 June 1296/1 The psychogenically impotent subject can in fact learn to induce erection at will.

psychogeography, -geographic(al: see PSYCHO-.

ˌpsychogeriˈatric, *a.* and *sb.* Also with hyphen. [f. PSYCHO- + GERIATRIC *a.*] **A.** *adj.* Of or pertaining to mental illness or disturbance in the old. Of a person: old and mentally ill or disturbed.

1961 *Guardian* 19 June 8/4 The number of psychogeriatric patients is certainly rising with increased longevity. **1965** *Lancet* 18 Sept. 583/2 A psycho-geriatric unit was established at Severalls Hospital in 1961. **1971** *Brit. Med. Jrnl.* 23 Oct. 235/1 Among psychogeriatric patients those most likely to respond appear to be those whose initial degree of memory and intellectual impairment was not of an extreme degree. **1973** *Radio Times* 1 Feb. 41/1 A 69-year-old widow, who lives with her unmarried son and regularly attends a local authority psychogeriatric Day Centre. **1975** *Daily Tel.* 1 Dec. 13/1 There was an acute shortage of psychogeriatric beds in hospitals. **1977** *Lancet* 1 Jan. 27/1 Many doctors and social workers cannot formulate a 'psychogeriatric' problem in any other terms but as the need to get it instantly off their hands.

B. *sb.* An old person who is mentally ill or disturbed.

1971 *Observer* 12 Dec. 8/4 The psycho-geriatrics form only one category of the.. mentally ill. **1973** *Listener* 19 Apr. 507/1 They're all referred by the GP... They're all psychogeriatrics.

Hence **ˌpsychogeriˈatrics,** the branch of medicine concerned with mental illness and disturbance in old people.

1967 *Brit. Jrnl. Psychiatry* CXIII. 175/1 The sub-speciality of geriatric psychiatry is coming to be known as 'psycho-geriatrics', an abbreviation which is not a very happy one, but which seems to be becoming generally accepted. **1972** *Lancet* 8 July 73/2 The working party are not convinced.. that there is any need for the recognition of a specialty of psychogeriatrics.

psychogeusic, etc.: see PSYCHO-.

psychogogue, var. PSYCHAGOGUE.

psychogony (-ˈɒgənɪ). [ad. Gr. ψῡχογονία generation of the soul, f. ψῡχο-, PSYCHO- + -γονία begetting, generating.] = PSYCHOGENESIS 1. So **psychoˈgonic** [ad. Gr. ψῡχογονικ-ός], **psychoˈgonical** *adjs.*, of or pertaining to psychogony.

[**1678** CUDWORTH *Intell. Syst.* I. iv. 214 Plutarch.., in his Timæan psychogonia,.. does at large industriously maintain the same.] **1874** SIDGWICK *Meth. Ethics* (1877) 185 The psychogonical question of their origin, and the ethical question of their validity. **1886** *Athenæum* 21 Aug. 235/3 It deals rather with psychogony, or how mind came to be what it is, than with psychology, or the description of mind as it is.

ˈpsychogram (ps-, ˈsaɪkəgræm). **1.** [f. PSYCHO- + -GRAM.] A 'spirit-writing'; a writing or message supposed to come from a spirit, or to be produced by psychical agency.

1885 in Pember *Earth's Earliest Ages* (1893) Pref. 13 Pains in the lower part of the back, which cease as soon as the psychogram is completed. **1896** *Dublin Rev.* Apr. 426 This psychogram, as Mr. Rogers calls it, certainly competes in interest with the now famous skeleton hand of Professor Röntgen.

2. *Psychol.* [ad. G. *psychogramm* (W. Stern *Differentielle Psychol.* (1911) III. xxii. 327).] A summary or diagram of someone's personality, esp. one based on his psychological history, responses to tests, etc.

1918 J. WARD *Psychol. Princ.* xviii. 433 It will be possible to construct what has been called a psychogram of the concrete individual. **1924** *Jrnl. Nerv. & Mental Dis.* LX. 227 Neither was it possible to mention so much of the history of the disease as would have been necessary to prove .. the correctness of the psychogram. **1935** H. READ in *Social Credit Pamphleteer* XII. 13 The æsthetic criterion is overcome by the force of the creative invention; the picture becomes a 'psychogram'. **1948** L. SPITZER *Linguistics & Lit. Hist.* 15 Linguistic deviations, of which the philologist may take stock in order to build up his 'psychogram' of the individual artist.

ˈpsychograph. [f. as prec. + -GRAPH.]

1. A photographic image attributed to a supernatural or spiritualistic cause.

1882 'M. A. OXON.' *Psychography* (ed. 2) 11 The book is illustrated by thirty fac-similes of Psychographs thus obtained. *Ibid.* 12 He.. obtained his.. Psychographs by the simple process of putting blank paper on the table of his room. **1920** *London Mag.* July 443/1 Most puzzling of all forms of super-normal pictures is the psychograph—so-called because it is assumed to be psychic in its origin and production. **1939** H. PRICE *Fifty Yrs. Psychical Res.* i. 35 If a message in writing or a drawing spontaneously appears on a photographic plate, with or without it being exposed in the camera it is known as a scotograph or a psychograph. **1973** D. A. SPENCER *Focal Dict. Photogr. Technologies* 496 All available evidence suggests that these psychographs were fakes or the result of a combination of chemical fog and wishful thinking.

2. = PSYCHOGRAM 2.

1909 *Q. Rev.* Oct. 500 This is no caricature, but almost a psychograph of the spirit which permeates many if not most of the descriptive reports of cricket matches in popular sporting papers. **1921** *Education* XLI. 513 A character psychograph of the individual is obtained. **1932** C. LANDIS in K. S. Lashley *Stud. in Dynamics of Behav.* 299 In order to visualize more clearly the results of the tests, three psychographs were drawn to represent the performance of each subject.

3. = PSYCHOBIOGRAPHY a.

1932 *Sunday Times* 6 Mar. 8/2 It was with some anxiety I saw Dame Una Pope-Hennessy was committed to writing a psychograph of Walter Scott. **1961** *Times Lit. Suppl.* 29 Sept. 637/2 Professor Edward Wagenknecht has been driven to compose a 'psychograph', in which he competently balances opinion against opinion in the hope of discovering what Hawthorne was really like. **1967** *Amer. N. & Q.* Sept. 14/2 Forrest, first of the American tragic actors in this assemblage of 'psychographs'. **1974** *Times Lit. Suppl.* 11 Oct. 1130/3 Dickens was the principal exemplar, and Wilson's penetrating psychograph, 'The Two Scrooges', coincided with George Orwell's revaluation in focusing upon a great novelist whose very popularity had caused him to be critically neglected.

psyˈchographer. [f. PSYCHOGRAPH + -ER[1]; see -GRAPHER.] **1.** An instrument or medium by which psychographs (sense 1) or spirit-writings are written; (see also quot. 1876).

1854 DICKENS *Lett., to Rev. J. White* 7 Mar., A thing called a Psychographer, which writes at the dictation of spirits. **1876** A. BLACKWELL *Kardec's Medium's Bk.* 447 *Psychographer*... A person who writes by psychography; a writing medium.

2. = PSYCHOBIOGRAPHER.

1912 G. BRADFORD *Lee the American* 269 The prince of all psychographers is incontestably Sainte-Beuve. **1930** *London Mercury* Feb. 378 He does not attempt a new 'life', but only a new character-study from the point of view of the 'psychographer'.

psychographic (ps-, saɪkəʊˈgræfɪk), *a.* [f. next + -IC.] Of or pertaining to psychography; in quot., in sense 2.

1884 *Manch. Exam.* 1 Nov. 5/1 Mr. Gladstone has paid a visit to.. the spirit-writing medium.. witnessing psychographic phenomena of a very high order.

psychography (ps-, saɪˈkɒgrəfɪ). [f. Gr. ψῡχο-, PSYCHO- + -γραφία, -GRAPHY.]

1. The history, description, or delineation of the mind or soul, or of mind in the abstract; the descriptive branch of PSYCHOLOGY. Also, = PSYCHOBIOGRAPHY.

[*a* **1850**: cf. *autopsychography* s.v. AUTO-[1].] **1883** SAINTSBURY in *Academy* 20 Jan. 36/3 This faculty of what may be called psychography, of drawing the landscape of moods with atmosphere and environment suitable and complete. **1895** W. ARCHER in *Daily Chron.* 6 Nov. 3/1 You aim, then, at a sort of spiritual biography of your subject —what has recently been called a psychography. **1929** G. BRADFORD in E. C. Wagenknecht *Man C. Dickens* p. xi, Psychography discards chronology, does not concern itself in any way with the sequence of external fact, except in so far as such is absolutely necessary to make clear the background. *Ibid.* i. 13 Before proceeding definitely to the psychography of Dickens, it is interesting and amusing to speculate on just what his own attitude toward this sort of inquiry would be.

2. Supposed 'spirit-writing' by the hand or intervention of a medium; cf. PNEUMATOGRAPHY 1.

1876 A. BLACKWELL *Kardec's Medium's Bk.* 447 *Psychography*, the writing of spirits by a medium's hand. **1887** *Pall Mall G.* 6 Sept. 3/1 He laughed at the Psychical Society... But he would slate-write before anybody. Psychography, he called it.

3. *Psychol.* The making of a psychogram (sense 2); the systematic experimental examination of an individual's personality. [ad. G. *psychographie* (W. Stern *Differentielle Psychol.* (1911) III. xxii. 327).]

1921 *Education* XLI. 510 Psychography may be defined as the science of making graphic records of mental traits. **1927** A. A. ROBACK *Psychol. of Character* xxiii. 426 Psychography .. records a person's *total* reactions (moral, temperamental, physical and intellectual) under all sorts of conditions. **1938** G. W. ALLPORT *Personality* xv. 404 Psychography has a striking advantage to offset its limitations. It is a method particularly well suited to the *comparative* study of personality, which.. demands the use of common traits.

psycho-hiˈstorical, *a.* Also without hyphen. [f. PSYCHO- + HISTORICAL *a.* (*sb.*)]

1. Pertaining to the history of the mind or soul.

1840 LOWELL *Lett.* (1894) I. 60, I am going to write a tragedy... It will be psycho-historical.

2. Of or pertaining to the psychological analysis or interpretation of historical events and characters. Also **psycho-hi'storic** *a.*, in the same sense.

1945 I. Asimov in *Astounding Sci. Fiction* Apr. 10/1 It would be a psycho-historic experiment of my own. *Ibid.* 30/2, I know quite a detailed version of Hari Seldon's psycho-historical claptrap. **1964** E. Erikson *Insight & Responsibility* v. 206 What we may call psycho-historical actuality, that is, the sum of historical facts and forces which are of immediate relevance to the..anticipations and..apprehensions in the individuals involved. **1970** R. J. Lifton *Hist. & Human Survival* 3 This psycho-historical approach..stems from a general uneasiness among practitioners of both psychology and history about the capacity of their traditional methods to describe and explain man during the latter part of the twentieth century.

Hence **psycho-hi'storically** *adv.*

1957 W. Abell *Collective Dream in Art* 5 Psycho-historically considered, art is one of the cultural symbols into which society projects existent states of underlying tension. **1968** *Partisan Rev.* 27 The principle of 'death and rebirth' is as valid psychohistorically as it is mythologically.

psycho-'history. Also without hyphen. [f. psycho- + history *sb.*] **a.** The analysis and interpretation of historical events with the aid of psychological theory; also = psychobiography b.

1934 *Reunion* I. 34 Judged by this profound philosophical test, so many of the glibly clear solutions of psycho-history are unsatisfactory. **1942** I. Asimov in *Astounding Sci. Fiction* June 30/2 The terms I use are at best mere approximations, but none of you are qualified to understand the true symbology of Psycho-History. **1957** W. Abell *Collective Dream in Art* 7 The energies involved in such conflicts are neither exclusively material nor exclusively psychological. .. The further we penetrate into the insights of psycho-history, the more likely we are to discover the means of mastering its disruptive forces. **1972** *Sat. Rev.* (U.S.) 25 Mar. 98/2 The roots of psycho-history may go back to Sigmund Freud's *Leonardo da Vinci: A Study in Psychosexuality*, published in Vienna in 1916. **1976** *Times Lit. Suppl.* 30 Jan. 117/1 Attempts have been made to explain Hitler's personality and ideology, in part at any rate, in terms of his childhood experiences. These works of psychohistory vary in their perceptiveness.

b. A treatise on or study in psycho-history; a psychobiography.

1972 *Sat. Rev.* (U.S.) 25 Mar. 98/3 Another psycho-history to be published..next fall is a study of Hitler by Dr. Walter Langer. **1976** *New Yorker* 17 May 60/1 Erik Erikson, in 'Gandhi's Truth', a biographical exploration that he calls a 'psycho-history', attaches considerable importance to their relationship.

So **psycho-hi'storian**, an expert in or writer of psycho-history.

1934 *Reunion* I. July 34 The psycho-historians have created a new and uneasy fashion; and while we can welcome an *exposé* of some of the lies of history such as Mr. Belloc is making, there are other much-quoted verdicts of ecclesiastical historians which are more epigrammatic than true. **1949** *Astounding Sci. Fiction* Nov. 21/1 It is enough for a Psychohistorian..to know his Biostatistics and his Neurochemical Electromathematics. **1970** *Daily Tel.* 23 Feb. 9/6 A trained psycho-historian..who had witnessed the Franco-Prussian War of 1870, would have realised that the probability of a World War had been raised to higher than 70 per cent. **1975** L. de Mause *Bibliogr. of Psychohist.* p. viii, What the new psycho-historians are creating is a radical empiricism.

psychohylism, etc.: see psycho-.

psychoid ('saɪkɔɪd), *sb.* and *a.* [f. psych(e or Gr. ψυχή + -oid.] **A.** *sb.* A name variously given to vital forces that appear to direct the functions and reflex actions of the living body.

1908 H. Driesch *Sci. & Philos. of Organism* III. iii. iii. 82, I therefore propose the very neutral name of 'Psychoid' for the elemental agent discovered in action. 'Psychoid'—that is, a something which though not a 'psyche' can only be described in terms analogous to those of psychology. **1930** E. Bleuler in *Psychiatric Q.* IV. 43 Bodily functions, too, are integrated to a high degree... Hence we have good grounds for bringing the bodily functions, too, under *one* conception. This summary, the body soul, I have called the psychoid... We cannot do otherwise than regard the psyche as a specialization of the psychoid of the organism. **1931** A. Wolf in W. Rose *Outl. Mod. Knowl.* 575 Just as the development of an animal is directed by an entelechy, so its behaviour is directed by an analogous psychoid, or an inborn intelligent urge to action. **1935** H. F. Dunbar *Emotions & Bodily Change* i. 47 Let us therefore call the body-soul the psychoid. Now the relationship of psyche to soma becomes clear.

B. *adj.* Pertaining to these forces (see also quot. 1960).

1930 *Psychiatric Q.* IV. 43 With human beings we have a number of reactions which are half psychoid and half psychic... When we scratch ourselves..how much of this is reflex action, and how much conscious action? **1934** E. B. Strauss tr. *Kretschmer's Text-bk. Med. Psychol.* iv. 39 The discrete components of an intended act are associated with a minimal degree of conscious participation or are even unconscious; i.e. they are predominantly psychoid. **1944** J. S. Huxley *On Living in Revolution* iv. 50 All the activities of the world-stuff are accompanied by mental as well as material happenings; in most cases, however, the mental happenings are at such a low level of intensity that we cannot detect them; we may perhaps call them 'psychoid' happenings, to emphasize their difference in intensity and quality from our own psychical or mental activities. **1960** R. F. C. Hull tr. *Jung's Structure & Dynamics of Psyche* in *Coll. Wks.* VIII. iii. 177 If I make use of the term 'psychoid' I do so with three reservations: firstly, I use it as an adjective ..; secondly no psychic quality in the proper sense of the word is implied, but only a 'quasi-psychic' one such as the reflex-processes possess; and thirdly, it is meant to distinguish a category of events from merely vitalistic phenomena..and from specifically psychic processes.

psychoki'nesis. Also with hyphen. [f. psycho- + kinesis.] **1.** A psychic power by which some people are held to be able to move objects by other than physical means. Cf. *telekinesis* s.v. tele-. Abbrev. *PK.*, *Pk.* s.v. P II.

1914 H. Holt *On Cosmic Relations* (1915) I. xiv. 216 Now assuming Telekinesis to be established, perhaps we are as nearly ready to consider what I shall call Psychokinesis as people were a generation ago to consider Telekinesis. **1943** *Jrnl. Parapsychol.* VII. 22 Psychokinesis seems better for a general term to cover both effects than telekinesis, which leaves out the psychical and emphasizes distance. **1952** *Sci. News* XXIII. 53 In particular the proponents of telepathy, clairvoyance, psychokinesis and the like have reached the conclusion that these phenomena are not affected by distance or orientation. **1957** *Times Lit. Suppl.* 13 Dec. 760/3 Mr. Rose seeks to establish the power of alleged rain-makers by testing their ability to will (by 'psychokinesis') the fall of a die. **1973** *Times* 1 Dec. 16/4 The other group of tests dealt with..psychokinesis, and included Mr Geller's apparent ability to bend spoons, nails and other metal objects.

2. Activity or development within the psyche or spirit. *rare.*

1920 H. L. Eno *Activism* iv. 46 The collective activity of psychons, also, which we shall call 'psychokinesis' differs, with its various combinations upon its own plane, in intensity.

psychoki'netic, *a.* Also with hyphen. [f. psycho- + kinetic *a.* (*sb.*).] **1.** Of or pertaining to psychokinesis (sense 2).

1904 G. S. Hall *Adolescence* II. xviii. 724 We are now coming to study and utilize every psycho-kinetic equivalent or analogue between the higher and the lower faith. **1948** J. G. Bennett *Crisis in Human Affairs* vii. 133 This we shall call the 'psycho-static' view, according to which the *psyche*, or essential nature of man, is unchangeable... The alternative we shall call the 'psycho-kinetic' view, which asserts the possibility of movement or transformation within man's psyche.

2. Of or pertaining to psychokinesis (sense 1).

1943 [see *PK.*, *Pk.* s.v. P II]. **1950** *Mind* LIX. 453 The random number generator will be subject to the psycho-kinetic powers of the interrogator. **1962** V. Nabokov *Pale Fire* 165 Hazel was involved in some appalling 'psychokinetic' manifestations.

psycholeptic: see psycho-.

psycholin'guistic, *a.* and *sb.* [f. psycho- + linguistic *a.* and *sb.*] **A.** *adj.* Of or pertaining to psycholinguistics (see sense B below).

1936 J. Kantor *Objective Psychol. of Grammar* iv. 55 (*heading*) The psycholinguistic situation analyzed. **1948** *Mind* LVII. 531 The psycholinguistic point of view does not allow one to answer a question such as 'What is a number?' without having ascertained first the purpose of the question. **1953** J. B. Carroll *Study of Lang.* iv. 120 Psycholinguistic analysis might suggest the units of selection in messages and better ways of gauging their semantic content. **1959** Schuell & Jenkins in L. F. Sies *Aphasia Theory & Therapy* (1974) xi. 212 Osgood (1953) has presented a psycholinguistic model for aphasia..; the model was constructed and deficits which should result from interruptions of psycholinguistic rather than neurological processes were deduced. **1967** D. G. Hays *Introd. Computational Linguistics* xi. 187 Psycholinguistic evidence is now regarded as relevant to decisions about syntax. **1970** *Language* XLVI. 87 It was evident that the phonemes as analysed did indeed match the psycholinguistic units that the subject was manipulating in the use of his own language. **1977** P. Strevens *New Orientations Teaching of Eng.* ii. 32 Modern psycho-linguistic studies of the way a small child learns his mother tongue.

B. *sb. pl.* (const. as *sing.*). The branch of linguistics which deals with the inter-relation between the acquisition, use, and comprehension of language, and the processes of the mind. Cf. *linguistic psychology* s.v. linguistic *a.* b.

1936 Allport & Odbert *Psychol. Monogr.* XLVII. i. 25 From the standpoints of the psychology of personality and psycho-linguistics the complete record is of more value. **1948** *Mind* LVII. 530 *Psycho-linguistics*.., a term which is intended to cover the spoken and written word, as well as gestures and such physical actions as are used by human being[s] to influence each other's activities. It also studies the associations which relate such acts with the mental processes which occur in the minds of the parties concerned. **1952** *Language* XXVIII. i. 115 Psycholinguistics is not linguistics plus psychology; it is a resultant of the two. **1959** *Word* XV. 192 Psycholinguistics is a relatively new discipline developing along the border between linguistics and psychology. **1967** S. Saporta *Psycholinguistic Theories & Generative Grammars* 7 Let us understand the central question in psycholinguistics to be the study of whatever psychological processes contribute to the acquisition, production, and comprehension of language. **1974** P. Dickinson *Poison Oracle* ii. 36 My field is psycholinguistics. .. The study of the effect of language on the mind. **1978** *English Jrnl.* Dec. 63/2 The findings of social linguistics and psycholinguistics are presented in terms meaningful to the younger reader.

Hence **psycho'linguist**, a student of or specialist in psycholinguistics; **psycholin'guistically** *adv.*; **,psycholingui'stician** *rare* = psycholinguist.

1953 J. B. Carroll *Study of Lang.* iv. 121 It is also possible that the mass statistics..will provide the psycholinguist with a rewarding set of material for study. **1964** *Language* XL. 226 The problem of isolating the psycho-linguistically distinctive units of sequential encoding..has elicited some interesting experiments with pausal phenomena. **1970** *New Scientist* 24 Sept. 615/1 It is a widely held view among psycholinguists..that phonology and syntax are unique to man. **1975** M. Bradbury *History Man* vi. 106 Do you mean am I a structuralist or a Leavisite or a psycho-linguistician or a formalist or a Christian existentialist or a phenomenologist? **1976** *Amer. Speech 1974* XLIX. 80 We can answer it psycho-linguistically by claiming that two items are collocates of each other if they belong to a single remembered set. **1977** *Verbatim* Dec. 1/1 The psycholinguists working with infants by and large ignored the obvious; eye contact and touch between mother and child.

psychologer (ps-, saɪ'kɒlədʒə(r)). [f. psycholog(y + -er[1]: cf. *astrologer*.] = psychologist.

1848 Hare *Guesses* Ser. ii. (ed. 2) 44 He..may be a skilful logician or psychologer, but has no claim to the high title of a philosopher. **1851** Mansel *Proleg. Logica* ii. 52 In the present state of Psychology..no one division having been so universally adopted by philosophers,..as to render imperative its adoption as the division κατ' ἐξοχὴν of psychologers.

psychologese (saɪkɒlə'dʒiːz). *colloq.* [f. psycholog(y + -ese.] Language in which technical terms in psychology are used for effect.

1961 R. Hoggart *Auden* iv. 118 On occasions..he wrote 'psychologese' in poor verse. **1974** *Publishers Weekly* 4 Nov. 70/1 The mixture of psychologese and unctuous 'poetry' goes far toward placing this among the sillier books of its sort. **1979** *N.Y. Rev. Bks.* 25 Oct. 11/3 To paraphrase Chris Edwards's psychologese, 'His new ego identity is being built up as the old one is being destroyed.'

psychologian (-əʊ'ləʊdʒɪən). [f. mod.L. *psychologia* psychology + -an.] = psychologist.

1860 W. G. Ward *Nat. & Grace* i. 288 It is commonly held..by psychologians. **1873** —— *Ess. Philos. Theism* (1884) I. 123 We consider that no really profound psychologian can be..a phenomenist.

psychologic (-əʊ'lɒdʒɪk), *a.* [f. as psycholog(y + -ic.] Of or belonging to psychology. Now freq. *poet.*

a **1787** Maty *Germ. Writers to 1780* (T.), His psychologic knowledge and experience. **1809** W. Taylor in *Crit. Rev.* Ser. iii. XVI. 453 The psychologic part of the commentary. **1875** Whitney *Life Lang.* xiv. 304 Force it into a psychologic mould and conduct it by psychologic methods. **1903** Myers *Human Personality* I. 319 Interesting from a psychologic, as well as clinical point of view. **1943** I. A. Richards *Basic Eng. & its Uses* i. 17 No one yet knows what the fundamental factors [in changes of population] are. They may be economic, but they may equally well be psychologic. **1948** M. W. Thorner *Psychiatry in Gen. Pract.* vi. 162 For a disease so pronounced in its clinical symptoms and so apparently free of a demonstrated psychologic cause, manic-depressive disease is singularly barren of any distinguishing physical findings. **1951** R. Graves *Poems & Satires* 26 Their hairy bellies warming With buzz of psychologic wit And homosexual swarming. **1954** [see gerontology]. **1967** *Listener* 19 Jan. 91/3 You've said too much, The lot of you, of psychologic such and such, A more grotesque miscellany I've never read.

Hence **psycho'logics**, *rare*, psychological matters or doctrines; psychology.

1819 Shelley *P. Bell Third* vi. xiv, Five thousand crammed octavo pages Of German psychologics. **1893** M. Beerbohm *Let.* 15 Aug. (1964) 50 *Me voici* talking self and psychologics. **1943** *Amer. Speech* XVIII. 220 General semantics, as a psychology (or 'psychologics', as Korzybski prefers to call it),..claims to put the Prince of Denmark back into *Hamlet*.

psychologic ('saɪkəʊlɒdʒɪk, saɪkə'lɒdʒɪk), *sb.* Also with hyphen. [f. psycho(logy + logic *sb.*] The practice of logical reasoning based on psychological observations and judgements rather than on abstract propositions.

1912 F. C. S. Schiller *Formal Logic* xxiv. 393 Provided he [*sc.* the formal logician] will let us frame a science which will concern itself with the aspects of intellectual functioning which are excluded from the Ideal of Pure Thought, let him restrict 'logic' to what *he* means thereby. We shall merely..adopt another term. Let us call this other study Psychologic... Formal Logic may be left to its own devices henceforth, and Psychologic will study real knowing without impediment. **1931** N. Isaacs in *Proc. Aristotelian Soc.* XXXI. 225 The term 'psycho-logic' has been used by Dr. Schiller in connection with his position. Before I met it in his writings, I happened to be led to the same coinage, some years ago, under the pressure, as I believe it to be, of the same facts... In my view (as in Dr. Schiller's) logic needs to be based on psychology through and through... That is the purport of 'psycho-logic': an expressly intermediate study that starts from clearly psychological facts, but examines these with logical intent, and attempts to show that a logic emerges from them, and of what kind. **1935** *Mind* XLIV. 471 The purely empirical *psychologic* which substitutes judgments for propositions as the subjects of logical discourse, frankly seeks the co-operation of psychology and is willing to be a handmaid of the sciences. **1953** Mays & Whitehead tr. *Piaget's Logic & Psychol.* iii. 25 These three difficulties force us to interpolate between psychology and axiomatic logic a *tertium quid*, a 'psycho-logic',..related to these in the same way as mathematical physics is related to pure mathematics and experimental physics. **1967** *Listener* 19 Oct. 492/2 The most likely resolution is a form of psychologic: the person gradually and unconsciously changes his values and beliefs so as to make them consistent with what he says and does. **1973** I. L. Child *Humanistic Psychol.* vii. 95 An account of 'psycho-logic' that he..worked out several years ago.

psychological (ps-, saɪkəʊˈlɒdʒɪkəl), *a.* (*sb.*) [f. as PSYCHOLOG(Y + -ICAL.]

A. *adj.* **1.** Of, pertaining to, or of the nature of psychology; dealing with or relating to psychology. Also *fig.* and *absol.*

a **1688** R. CUDWORTH in J. H. Muirhead *Platonic Tradition in Anglo-Saxon Philos.* (1931) 64 Wherefore we have proposed another psychological hypothesis: that.. there must of necessity be in the soul one common focus or centre in which all these kinds may meet. **1802** *Monthly Mag.* XIV. 35/1 The grand drama of the Leipzig Easter-fair is certainly.. very attractive and entertaining, whether one belong to the crowd of busy actors, or be only an idle looker-on—whether one have on his nose a pair of statistical, or psychological spectacles. **1812** D'ISRAELI *Calam. Auth.* Pref. 5, I would paint what has not been unhappily called the psychological character. [*Note*] From the Grecian *Psyche*, or the soul, the Germans have borrowed this expressive term. **1818** COLERIDGE *Diss. Sc. Method* ii. 40 Shakespeare was pursuing two Methods at once; and besides the Psychological Method, he had also to attend to the Poetical. [*Note*] We beg pardon for the use of this insolens verbum: but it is one of which our Language stands in great need. We have no single term to express the Philosophy of the Human Mind. **1873** H. SPENCER *Stud. Sociol.* xv. 382 Whether the minds of men and women are or are not alike; are obviously psychological questions. **1879** G. ALLEN *Colour Sense* iii. 27 To trace out a few of the main steps in the evolution of such organs, from the strictly psychological point of view. **1951** M. MCLUHAN *Mech. Bride* (1967) 143/2 They have a more organic approach than the Germans, whose attitude is closer to the psychological. **1974** R. ASSAGIOLI *Act of Will* (1975) v. 48 This knowledge.. enables us to make countless.. applications of those psychological laws.

2. a. Loosely used for PSYCHICAL: Of or pertaining to the objects of psychological study, of or pertaining to the mind, mental: opposed to *physical*. More recently, affecting or pertaining to the mental and emotional state of a person.

1794 G. ADAMS *Nat. & Exp. Philos.* II. xvii. 272 Powers peculiar to that psychological unity which we call the mind. **1823** BENTHAM *Not Paul* 258 Some physical process, to which in so many minds, the psychological effect in question has, by the influence of artifice on weakness, been attached. **1842** PRICHARD *Nat. Hist. Man* 63 The greatest variations, both in structure and in psychological characters. **1870** DISRAELI *Lothair* lxxxii, Discourse about the Suez Canal.. can be carried on without any psychological effort. **1907** ILLINGWORTH *Doctr. Trin.* xi. 223 Different generations have lived on very different psychological levels, and with very different degrees of psychological intensity. **1929** *Language* V. 212 Linguistics may thus hope to become something of a guide to the understanding of the 'psychological geography' of culture in the large. **1942** E. FROMM *Fear of Freedom* iii. 49 Significant changes in the psychological atmosphere accompanied the economic development of capitalism. **1958** R. I. PERUSSE in Daugherty & Janowitz *Psychol. Warfare Casebk.* ii. 34 The expressions ..'psychological operations', and 'target' should..be avoided. US observers can vouch for the discomfiture of foreign peoples at being considered by us as a fitting subject for manipulation. **1958** *Times* 15 July 11/5 Mr. Sylvester.. said that to have coal stocks lying at the pithead or anywhere else had a psychological effect on the men in the industry. **1962** E. CLEAVER in A. Dundes *Mother Wit* (1973) 11/1 The destructive psychological impact of this standard of beauty. **1974** M. TAYLOR tr. *Metz's Film Lang.* viii. 190 Since the advent of the talking film, we have had the 'psychological comedy' and the 'dramatic comedy'.

b. ***psychological moment***, = F. *moment psychologique*, applied to 'the moment in which the mind is in actual expectation of something that is to happen' (Hatzfeld *Dict. Général*); the psychologically (or rather, *psychically*) appropriate moment; often misused for 'the critical moment', 'the very nick of time', without any reference to psychology or to the mind.

The French expression arose in Paris in December 1870, during the Siege, when it was asserted to have been used by the German *Kreuz Zeitung* in reference to the bombardment of the city, and explained to mean that, as the bombardment had as its aim to act upon the imagination of the Parisians, it was necessary to choose the very moment when this imagination, already shaken by famine and perhaps by civil dissension, was in the fittest state to be effectively acted upon. (Sarcey, *Le Siège de Paris*, 1871, p. 263; Eng. tr. p. 242.) But the phrase with its explanation was due to an error of translation, in which the expression actually used by the German journal, *das psychologische Moment*, the psychological 'momentum', potent element, or factor, in the case (see MOMENTUM 5, MOMENT 9), was mistaken for *der psychologische Moment*, the psychological moment of time. The article in the *Neue Preussische* (Kreuz) *Zeitung* of 16 Dec. 1870, p. 1, col. 3, says that very cogent psychological considerations spoke against opening the bombardment before the hopes built by the Parisians upon the raising of the siege by armies of relief should be overthrown; and continued 'in all considerations the psychological momentum or factor must be allowed to play a prominent part, for without its co-operation there is little to be hoped from the work of the artillery'. Thus attributed to German pedantry, the nonsensical *moment psychologique* was ridiculed by the Parisians, and became a jocular phrase or 'tag' for 'the fitting or proper moment'; and with this connotation it passed equally nonsensically into English journalese.

1871 tr. *Sarcey's Siege of Paris* x. 243 The phrase became current and even fashionable. One used to say 'I feel hungry; it is the psychological moment for sitting down to table'. **1891** *Daily News* 29 Apr. 3/4 Unless we cable to New York, there is nothing to do but to forego turns and commissions at the very psychological moment. **1897** *Westm. Gaz.* 30 Oct. 2/1 The Prince is always in the background, and turns up at the psychological moment—to use a very hard-worked and sometimes misused phrase. **1901** *Scotsman* 17 Mar. 7/5 This was the psychological moment of the whole operations and..De Wet took advantage of it. **1907** *Expositor* Sept. 270 'Hour' in this Gospel means.. a psychological moment in the evolution of the Messianic consciousness full of significance for the Saviour's purpose.

c. = MENTAL *a.*[1] 1 c. *colloq.*

1952 M. ALLINGHAM *Tiger in Smoke* i. 18 If it's Elginbrodde himself, he's 'psychological'.

3. Special collocations: ***psychological hedonism*** (*Philos.*), the theory that the constitution of the human mind is such that one will always choose what is pleasurable; hence ***psychological hedonist***; ***psychological novel***, a type of novel in which the main interest lies in the mental and emotional aspects of the characters; hence ***psychological novelist***; ***psychological warfare***, the use of propaganda or other means designed to undermine the morale or allegiance of one's opponents; so ***psychological war*** (cf. *psy-war* s.v. PSY-); ***psychological weapon***, some particular action or reasoning designed to undermine resolution or morale in an opponent.

1884 H. SIDGWICK *Methods of Ethics* (ed. 3) I. iv. 40 There is, however, one view of the feelings which prompt to voluntary action... I mean the view that volition is always determined by pleasures or pains actual or prospective. This doctrine—which I may distinguish as Psychological Hedonism—is often connected and not seldom confounded with the method of Ethics which I have called Egoistic Hedonism. **1943** *Mind* LII. 45 Butler is, in fact, right in rejecting Psychological Hedonism. **1961** J. HOSPERS *Human Conduct* iv. 147 We must distinguish two varieties of psychological hedonism: the variety which says all that people ever desire is pleasure or satisfaction..and the variety which says that people desire many things but these things are all desired solely for the sake of the pleasure or satisfaction they will bring to the agent. **1903** G. E. MOORE *Principia Ethica* iii. 70 It is these two different theories which I suppose the Psychological Hedonists to confuse. **1969** F. VIVIAN *Thinking Philosophically* v. 114 The psychological hedonist pushes these discoveries about our motives to what seems a logical conclusion. **1855** GEO. ELIOT in *Westm. Rev.* July 288 After courses of 'psychological' novels..where life seems made up of talking and journalizing. **1959** *Oxf. Compan. French Lit.* 676/1 He has produced..purely psychological novels, depending for plot and interest on the workings of the characters' minds and their reaction to the outside world. **1960** BECKSON & GANZ *Reader's Guide Lit. Terms* (1961) 176 This term *psychological novel* is descriptive of content rather than form or technique and is applied to work as formally conventional as the novels of C. P. Snow and as unconventional as those of James Joyce. **1915** A. D. GILLESPIE *Let.* 14 Mar. in *Lett. from Flanders* (1916) 49 He can tell a rattling good story, which many of those modern psychological novelists, with their elaborate analysis of character and of sensation, quite fail to do. **1970** G. JACKSON *Let.* 22 Mar. in *Soledad Brother* (1971) 187 The truth would aid the convict in the psychological war—con against cop. **1940** *Current Hist.* Jan. 52 (*heading*) Psychological warfare and how to wage it... Psychological warfare is the fight conducted by the state with psychological weapons to strengthen its own prestige.. and to weaken that of the enemy. **1946** L. J. MARGOLIN (*title*) Paper bullets: a brief story of psychological warfare in World War II. **1949** *Sun* (Baltimore) 5 Feb. 17 Miss Gillars ..is accused..of betraying her country by aiding Hitler's psychological warfare program over a period of more than four years. **1957** G. E. WRIGHT *Bibl. Archaeol.* ix. 161/1 Tiglathpileser..says that he 'overwhelmed' Menahem (evidently not by actual fighting but by psychological warfare!). **1974** M. BABSON *Stalking Lamb* xxi. 157 We have no objection at all to helping in what she calls her 'psychological warfare'. **1940** Psychological weapon [see *psychological warfare* above]. **1944** J. S. HUXLEY *On Living in Revolution* iv. 44 Incomplete or unsatisfactory peace aims, which will have a..lower efficiency as psychological weapons.

B. *sb.* (elliptical use of adj.: cf. MEDICAL B. 1). A student or professor of psychology.

1863 READE *Hard Cash* II. 355, I have accumulated..a large collection of letters from persons deranged in various degrees, and studied them minutely, more minutely than most Psychologicals study anything but Pounds, Shillings, and Verbiage. *Ibid.* III. 366 Oh, logic of psychologicals!

Hence **psychoˈlogicalism** *nonce-wd.*, a psychological system or practice.

1893 J. REINACH in *Athenæum* 1 July 14/3 Midway between the naturalism of M. Zola and the 'psychologicalism' (the barbarous word must be forgiven) of M. Bourget.

psychoˈlogically, *adv.* [-LY[2].] In a psychological manner; in relation to psychology.

1830 MACKINTOSH *Eth. Philos.* Wks. 1846 I. 63 That the whole of Hobbes's system..depended on his political scheme; not indeed logically, as conclusions depend upon premises, but (if the word may be excused) psychologically, as the formation of one opinion may be influenced by a disposition to adapt it to others previously cherished. **1839** *Fraser's Mag.* XX. 712 Which, contemplated historically, psychologically, morally,..holds out..abundant matter. **1879** GLADSTONE *Glean.* I. i. 57 A certain reception of Christ, not easy to describe psychologically.

psychoˈlogico-. *rare.* [f. by analogy with LOGICO-.] Taken as comb. form of PSYCHOLOGICAL *a.*, PSYCHOLOGY in the sense 'psychological and...'.

1869 W. JAMES *Let.* 22 May in R. B. Perry *Tht. & Char. W. James* (1935) I. 296 Charles S. Peirce has been writing some very acute and original psychologico-metaphysical articles in the St. Louis philosophic *Journal*. **1942** *Mind* LI. 178 At this stage of our ignorance we should concentrate on psychologico-mathematical patterns.

psychologism (-ˈɒlədʒɪz(ə)m). [f. PSYCHOLOG(Y + -ISM.] **a.** *Philos.* Idealism as opposed to sensationalism: see IDEALISM 1.

1858 O. A. BROWNSON *Wks.* V. 230 The philosophy of old school Presbyterianism in so far as it recognizes the activity of the subject at all..is mere psychologism. **1874** MORRIS tr. *Ueberweg's Hist. Philos.* II. App. II. 479 The philosophic revolution which began with Descartes..manifested itself in the two forms of Psychologism (or Idealism), and Sensualism,—represented by Descartes and Malebranche on the one side, and by Locke and Condillac on the other. **1907** in *Expositor* July 27 The transcendental logical tendency which, excluding all empiricism and psychologism, aims to deduce the fundamental characteristics and categories of knowing from pure concepts.

b. The tendency to explain in psychological terms matters which are considered to be more properly explained in other ways.

1905 *Mind* XIV. 530 Psychologism..has been universal in English philosophy from the beginning. **1937** D. KATZ in R. B. Cattell et al. *Human Affairs* iii. 36 According to this tendency logic is nothing but the psychology of thinking, mathematics nothing but the psychology of mathematical thinking... This tendency is usually called psychologism. **1945** K. R. POPPER *Open Society* II. xiv. 87 The structure.. of the social environment, as opposed to the natural environment, is man-made; and therefore it must be explicable in terms of human nature, in accordance with the doctrine of psychologism. **1950** R. CARNAP *Logical Found. Probability* ii. 40 One of the important achievements in the development of modern logic has been the gradual elimination of psychologism. **1975** *Times Lit. Suppl.* 9 May 502/2 From Descartes onwards, with some notable exceptions, philosophical semantics was crippled by psychologism.

psychologist (ps-, saɪˈkɒlədʒɪst). [f. PSYCHOLOG(Y + -IST: cf. *physiologist*.] **1. a.** One who makes a study of, or is skilled in psychology; a student or teacher of the science of mental phenomena.

1727 BAILEY vol. II, *Psychologist*, one who treats concerning the soul. **1817** COLERIDGE *Biog. Lit.* I. vi. 113 Many eminent physiologists and psychologists visited the town. **1834** SOUTHEY *Doctor* xi. (1862) 30 A metaphysician, or as some of my contemporaries would affect to say, a psychologist. **1859** *Edin. Rev.* Oct. 290 The real point of separation between the à priori and the à posteriori psychologists.

b. A person who is not an expert in psychology, yet has, or claims to have, insight into the motivation of human behaviour. *colloq.*

1896 W. CUCHER *Theatrical World of 1896* 56 In a word (though he would probably not know the meaning of the word), he must be a profound psychologist. **1951** A. P. HERBERT *Number Nine* xv. 203 Why on earth had he answered all those perilous questions?.. The 'mad Admiral' ..must be a pretty subtle psychologist. **1957** P. LAFITTE *Person in Psychol.* 1 Psychology has several meanings... It may mean the person's ordinary conduct of his affairs and it does mean this when he has done something ingenious or subtle and so thinks of himself as a bit of a psychologist.

2. Phr. ***psychologist's fallacy*** (see quots.).

1890 W. JAMES *Princ. Psychol.* I. vii. 196 The great snare of the psychologist is the confusion of his own standpoint with that of the mental fact about which he is making his report. I shall hereafter call this the 'psychologist's fallacy' *par excellence*. **1902** BALDWIN *Dict. Philos. & Psychol.* II. 382/2 *Psychologist's fallacy*, the fallacy, to which the psychologist is peculiarly liable, of reading into the mind he is examining what is true of his own; especially of reading into lower minds what is true of higher. **1931** *Brit. Jrnl. Psychol.* XXI. 243 A danger to be avoided known as the 'psychologist's fallacy'. This arises from the fact that the experimenter is apt to suppose that the subject will respond to a stimulus or an order in the same way as he himself would respond in the circumstances.

psychologistic (ˌsaɪkɒləˈdʒɪstɪk), *a.* [f. PSYCHOLOG(ISM + -ISTIC.] Of, pertaining to, or characterized by psychologism.

1929 *Mind* XXXVIII. 360 His sustained and masterly demonstration of the self-ruinous character of all such 'psychologistic' theories. **1931** W. B. GIBSON tr. *Husserl's Ideas* 18 Within this view of things there grows up..a transcendental-phenomenological Idealism in opposition to every form of psychologistic Idealism. **1935** *Amer. Speech* X. 247/1 That the distinction between *langue* and *parole* does not imply any psychologistic assumptions, is shown.. by the fact that it has served as a starting point to the phoneme conception of Professor Twaddell, who resolutely protests against all psychologistic definitions of the phoneme. **1957** G. RYLE in M. Black *Importance of Lang.* (1962) 165 Where Frege attacked psychologistic accounts of thinking from the outside, they attacked them from the inside. **1976** *Brit. Jrnl. Sociol.* XXVII. 304 A sociological approach is apt to imply that such groups collude in their subordinate position and then to provide psychologistic interpretations of their behaviour.

Hence **ˌpsycholoˈgistically** *adv.*

1964 I. C. JARVIE *Revolution in Anthropol.* iii. 97 The psychological problems of religion..are the only problems of religion that can be tackled psychologistically.

psychologize (ps-, saɪˈkɒlədʒaɪz), *v.* [f. PSYCHOLOG(Y + -IZE.]

1. *intr.* To study or treat of psychology; to theorize, speculate, or reason psychologically.

1830 W. JACOBSON *Let.* in J. F. Maurice *Life F. D. Maurice* (1884) I. ix. 111 Neither stay away rusticating and psychologizing, but come here and mind your books. **1836** *Blackw. Mag.* XL. 255 *note*, When a man comes to bound the subjects of human enquiry, by showing how in nature the human mind does, and can become possessed of the matter of its knowledge, he is then . . psychologizing. **1884** W. JAMES in *Mind* IX. 5 Why, since the feeling has no proper subjective name of its own, we should hesitate to psychologise about it as 'the feeling of that relation'. **1967** *Listener* 19 Jan. 91/2 'Let us please psychologize In this wise,' Suggested Freud. **1974** *Sci. Amer.* Aug. 115/1 The texts still like to simplify; generally we psychologize about the local event and regard the suffused experience as secondary.

2. *trans.* To analyse or describe psychologically.

1856 MASSON *Ess., Milton's Youth* 46 When, by psychologizing a man, it is supposed we can tell what course of life he is fit for. **1891** F. M. WILSON *Primer Browning* 16 He is as interested in psychologising a Paris jeweller as a queen.

3. To render psychological.

[**1811-31**: implied in PSYCHOLOGIZATION: see below.] **1940** V. J. MCGILL in M. Farber *Philos. Ess.* 231 This work was a reaction against his earlier volume in which he [*sc.* Husserl] had attempted to psychologize arithmetic. **1957** *Listener* 9 May 743/2 We have been led to psychologize (to use John Dewey's rather horrid word) and to humanize learning.

4. To subject to 'psychical' influence.

1877 D. D. HOME *Lights & Shadows of Spiritualism* v. 264 Dear old gullible souls who could be readily psychologized into believing that they were eating a piece of the moon in shape of 'green cheese'. **1885** A. P. SINNETT *Karma* II. 11 Quite unaware of the fact that he had been psychologized so as to wish this. **1886** *Atlantic Monthly* Nov. 592/1 Is the non-concurrence of the obstinate juryman in a righteous verdict owing to an honest conviction, or has he been unconsciously psychologized by the lawyer who has the biggest fee in his pocket?

Hence **psy'chologizing** *vbl. sb.*; also *attrib.*; also **psy'chologized** *ppl. a.*; **psychologi'zation**, the action of making psychological.

1811-31 BENTHAM *Lang.* Wks. 1843 VIII. 318/2 Spiritualization or psychologization, in so far as any name of any physical substance, operation, or quality [is applied] to any correspondent . . psychological substance, operation, or quality. **1860** *Chr. Remembr.* XL. 477 No doubt that psychologizing is dangerous. **1895** W. JAMES *Coll. Ess. & Rev.* (1920) 393, I never find myself actively taking up the soul, so to speak, and making it to do work in my psychologizing. **1922** C. E. M. JOAD *Common-Sense Theol.* v. 233 The so-called 'psychologising' tendency in modern thought. **1956** E. H. HUTTEN *Lang. Mod. Physics* vi. 224 We are once more in danger of falling victims to the psychologizing attitude of epistemology. **1961** E. NAGEL *Structure of Science* iii. 45 Various psychologized versions of the Aristotelian requirement have enjoyed wide currency. **1966** J. J. KATZ *Philos. Lang.* v. 261 This argument is a psychologization of an argument of Goodman's in some recent work of his on the concept of confirmation in science. **1970** A. TOFFLER *Future Shock* (1974) x. 221 The key to the post-service economy lies in the psychologization of all production. **1976** *Spare Rib* Oct. 38/4 A continuous stream of psychologising and explaining . . leaves a reader little room to breathe or get curious about the characters.

psychologizer (saɪ'kɒlədʒaɪzə(r)). [f. prec. + -ER[1].] One who psychologizes, in any sense.

1895 'MARK TWAIN' in *N. Amer. Rev.* CLX. 49 The Observer of Peoples has to be a Classifier, a Grouper, a Deducer, a Generalizer, a Psychologizer. **1931** W. B. GIBSON tr. *Husserl's Ideas* III. iii. 273 The psychologizers everywhere will take offence at this; they are already disinclined to distinguish between judging as an empirical experience and judgment as 'Idea', as essence. **1966** *Listener* 4 Aug. 174/1 The 'spiritualizers' are giving way to the 'psychologizers'. Enter 'psychological man'.

'psychologue (-əlɒg). *rare.* [a. F. *psychologue* (Ch. Bonnet 1760 in Hatz.-Darm.), f. L. type **psȳchologus*: see next.] = PSYCHOLOGIST.

1872 MORLEY *Voltaire* 178 Psychologues like Sulzer might declare that the scourge of right thinking was to be found in 'those philosophers who . . assume that they have overthrown by a single smart trope truths only to be known by combining a multitude of observations'. **1890** W. JAMES *Let.* 8 July (1920) II. 1 A great chance for some future psychologue to make a greater name than Newton's. **1971** K. MILLETT *Sexual Politics* (1972) III. vi. 330 It is vaguely depressing to see a literary man vending the same trash as those hundreds of psychologues and quacks.

psychology (ps-, saɪ'kɒlədʒɪ). Also (erron.) 7 psuco-, 7-8 psyco-, 8 psicho-. [ad. mod.L. *psȳchologia* (16th c.), f. Gr. ψῡχο-, PSYCHO- + -LOGY; in F. and Ger. *psychologie*. See note below.]

1. a. The science of the nature, functions, and phenomena of the human mind (formerly also of the soul).

comparative psychology, the study of mind or intelligence as developed in man and animals.

1653 tr. *J. de Back's Discourse* in W. Harvey *Anat. Exercises* sig. H7v, I call the generall doctrine of man *Anthropologie*, the parts of which, I do ordain to be, according to this division, *Psychologie*, *Somatologie*, and *Hæmatologie*, into the doctrine of the soul, bodie, and blood. . . *Psychologie* is a doctrine which searches out mans Soul, and the effects of it. *Ibid.* sig. H8v, I do bind up the order of *Psychology* in few words. *a* **1680** R. CUDWORTH *Treat. Freewill* (1838) 19 The vulgar psychology, or the now generally received way of philosophizing concerning the soul, doth either quite baffle and betray this liberty of will, or else render it absurd, ridiculous, or monstrous. **1693** tr. *Blancard's Phys. Dict.* (ed. 2) 13/2 *Anthropologia*, the Description of a Man, or the Doctrin concerning him. Bartholine divides it into Two Parts; viz. *Anatomy*, which treats of the Body, and *Psycology*, which treats of the Soul. *Ibid.* 22/1 *Psucologie*, which Treats of the Soul. **1748** HARTLEY *Observ. Man* I. iii. 354 Psychology, or the Theory of the human Mind, with that of the intellectual Principles of Brute Animals. **1800** *Med. Jrnl.* IV. 187 A circumstance very interesting with respect to Psichology. **1836-7** SIR W. HAMILTON *Metaph.* (1877) I. viii. 129 Psychology . . strictly so denominated, is the Science conversant about the phaenomena or modifications, or States of the Mind, or Conscious Subject, or Soul or Spirit, or Self or Ego. **1837** WHEWELL *Hist. Induct. Sc.* IV. iv. (1857) I. 241 Hugo de St. Victor . . the first of the scholastic writers who made psychology his special study. **1842** PRICHARD *Nat. Hist. Man* 486 Psychology is, with respect to mankind, the history of the mental faculties. **1879** HUXLEY *Hume* II. i, Psychology is a part of the science of life or biology. . . As the physiologist inquires into the way in which the so-called 'functions' of the body are performed, so the psychologist studies the so-called 'faculties' of the mind. **1892** W. JAMES *Coll. Ess. & Rev.* (1920) xx. 317, I wished, by treating Psychology *like* a natural science, to help her to become one. **1897** C. H. JUDD tr. *Wundt's Outl. Psychol.* i. 3 The assignment of this problem to psychology, making it an empirical science coordinate with natural science and supplementary to it, is justified by the method of all the *mental sciences*, for which psychology furnishes the basis. **1910** *Amer. Jrnl. Psychol.* XXI. 72 Although great writers and poets have frequently made the most penetrating generalisations in practical psychology, the world has always been slow to profit by their discoveries. **1930** W. KÖHLER *Gestalt Psychol.* vi. 167 In psychology too, the influence of *gestalt* has been demonstrated . . in very primitive behaviour. **1973** C. D. KERNIG *Marxism, Communism & Western Society* VII. 98 Starting from the assumption that Soviet psychology is grounded on dialectical materialism, psychological historiography attempts to show how far materialist, and later dialectical and finally Marxist-Leninist thinking moulded the character of psychology.

b. A treatise on, or system of, psychology.

1791 *Gentl. Mag.* LXI. II. 779 He [Mr. John Seymour] had likewise just completed the printing of a volume from the French intituled 'Psychology'. **1866** FERRIER *Grk. Philos.* I. x. 231 The doctrine taught in all our logics and psychologies. **1884** J. TAIT *Mind in Matter* (1892) 110 The Philosophy of Spinoza results in the Psychology of Hume.

c. In mod. usage, the signification of the word has broadened to include (*a*) the scientific study of the mind as an entity and in its relationship to the physical body, based on observation of the behaviour and activity aroused by specific stimuli; and (*b*) the study of the behaviour of an individual or of a selected group of individuals when interacting with the environment or in a given social context. So ***experimental psychology***, the experimental study of the responses of an individual to stimuli; ***social psychology***, the study of the interaction between an individual and the social group to which he belongs.

(*a*) **1895** *Amer. Jrnl. Psychol.* VII. 78 Experimental Psychology was in its origin, and has remained for a considerable extent in its development, a German science. **1927** *Psychol. Rev.* XXXIV. 126 They adopt in regard to them [*sc.* instincts] the attitude common to the stimulus-response school of psychology, which purports to base the development of human behavior, of character and personality, upon the innately determined reactions of the organism to objective stimuli. **1940** HILGARD & MARQUIS *Conditioning & Learning* i. 2 The conditioned response was called the unit of habit by psychologists to whom habit was the most important concept in psychology. **1953** C. E. OSGOOD *Method & Theory in Exper. Psychol.* p. v, I have covered the major portion of what is called experimental psychology including sections on sensory processes, perception, learning, and symbolic processes. **1968** *Internat. Encycl. Social Sci.* XIII. 78/2 Existential psychology is a comprehensive psychology whose aim is an integration of the observations of different psychologies into an explanatory theory about human behavior in its lived international entirety. **1976** H. BROWN *Brain & Behaviour* i. 5 The study of the relation between brain structure and behavior gives physiological psychology the unique mission of trying to resolve an old and basic puzzle of philosophy and science, often referred to as the 'mind-body problem'.

(*b*) **1896** G. LE BON *Crowd* ii. 32 What we know of the psychology of crowds shows that treatises of logic need on this point to be rewritten. **1908** W. MCDOUGALL *Social Psychol.* 18 Social psychology has to show how, given the native propensities and capacities of the human mind, all the complex mental life of societies is shaped by them and in turn reacts upon the course of their development and operation in the individual. **1922** E. GLOVER *Roots of Crime* (1960) 4 For the first time in the history of British criminology a meeting of Justices of the Peace has invited a psycho-analyst to lecture on the psychology of crime. **1948** A. L. KROEBER *Anthropol.* (rev. ed.) viii. 323 Clinical psychology was the first recognized branch of psychology that attempted to deal with whole human beings, as distinct from . . special aspects of the mind. **1963** GOUGH & JENKINS in M. H. Marx *Theories Contemp. Psychol.* xxix. 456 The study of verbal learning has not led to the study of verbal behavior in general, to the psychology of language. **1975** W. S. SAHAKIAN *Hist. & Syst. Psychol.* xix. 425 The World War II years found him interested in the psychology of morale and human engineering psychology.

2. a. The attitude or outlook of an individual or a group on a particular matter or on life in general.

1899 G. LE BON *Psychol. of Socialism* iv. 39 We find in the working classes two well-defined subdivisions, each with a different psychology. **1908** F. M. FORD *Let.* Dec. (1965) 29 Thanks for yr. letter: of course I understand yr. psychology &, God forbid that you shd. restrain yr. irritation before men of good will. **1928** *Daily Tel.* 11 Sept. 10/5 The psychology of the workaday world has infected him with its disquiet. **1931** F. L. ALLEN *Only Yesterday* ii. 20 War-time psychology was dominant; no halfway measure would serve. **1954** KOESTLER *Invisible Writing* xxiv. 264 Was not the psychology of the masses an infinitely more complex phenomenon?

b. The nature *of* an event or phenomenon considered from the point of view of psychology.

1892 C. G. CHADDOCK tr. *Krafft-Ebing's Psychopathia Sexualis* p. iv, It is not the intention of the author to lay the foundation of a psychology of the sexual life, though without doubt psychopathology would furnish many important sources of knowledge to psychology. **1929** B. RUSSELL *Marriage & Morals* xvi. 182 The psychology of adultery has been falsified by conventional morals. **1932** F. C. BARTLETT *Remembering* ii. 16 There is . . adequate reason for beginning our detailed study of the psychology of remembering with an investigation into the character and conditions of perceiving and imagining. **1964** B. B. GILLIGAN tr. I. Lepp (*title*) The psychology of loving.

3. *attrib.*, as ***psychology journal, student***.

1971 D. CRYSTAL in E. Ardener *Social Anthropol. & Lang.* 194 This research, largely reported in psychology journals . ., is methodologically unsatisfactory in many respects. **1890** W. JAMES *Princ. Psychol.* II. xviii. 56, I have myself for many years collected from each and all of my psychology-students descriptions of their own visual imagination. **1972** G. W. KISKER *Disorganized Personality* (rev. ed.) xv. 494 Psychology students were employed by one investigator as 'companion counselors'.

[*Note.* Neither this word nor any of the group existed in Greek. *Psychology* began, in the modern Latin form *psychologia*, in Germany in the 16th c. It is said by Volkmann von Volkmar, *Lehrbuch der Psychologie*, 1875, I. 38, to have been used by Melanchthon as title of a prelection, and it was employed by J. T. Freigius in 1575; but was introduced into literature, 1590-97, by Goclenius of Marburg and his pupil Casmann (*Psychologia anthropologica. sive animæ humanæ doctrina*). It was thenceforth usual to consider *Psychologia* and *Somatotomia* or *Somatologia* as the two parts of *Anthropologia*, and in this sense the word is found frequently in the medical writers of the 17th c., as in Blancard's *Lexicon Medicum*, 1679, and in French in Dionis, *Anatomie de l'Homme*, 1690. Our first Eng. quot. of 1693 is from a transl. of Blancard. In French, according to Hatzfeld-Darmesteter, it had been used in the 16th c. by Taillepied in the sense of 'the science of the apparition of spirits'. In a philosophical sense, it was used by some (Latin) writers, as by Thomas Govan (*Ars Sciendi sive Logica*, 1682), by whom *Physica* or Natural Science was divided into the domains of *Pneumatologia* the science of spirits or spiritual beings, and *Somatologia* or *Physiologia* the science of material bodies; *Pneumatologia* contained the three subdivisions, *Theologia* the doctrine of God, *Angelographia* (incl. *Demonologia*) the doctrine of angels (and devils), and *Psychologia* the doctrine of human souls. The modern sense begins with Chr. von Wolff (*Psychologia Empirica* 1732, *Psychologia Rationalis* 1734); followed by Hartley in England 1748, and Bonnet in France 1755. The term was also employed by Kant, but was not much used in the modern languages before the 19th c.]

psychomachia (saɪkəʊ'mɑːkɪə). Also (now less frequently) **psychomachy** (ps-, saɪ'kɒməkɪ). [ad. late L. *psȳchomachia* 'conflict of the soul' (title of a poem of Prudentius *c* 400); cf. Gr. ψυχομαχία 'fight for life' (Polybius); f. Gr. ψυχή life, soul + μάχη fight.] Conflict of the soul.

1629 GAULE *Holy Madnesse* 112, I haue prophesied the number, order, and event of a Mysticall Pseuchomachie. **1656** BLOUNT *Glossogr.*, *Psychomachy*, a war betwixt the soul and body. **1658** PHILLIPS, *Psychomachy*, a conflict, or war of the Soul.

[**1927** H. WADDELL *Wandering Scholars* i. 20 In his most famous and most considerable work, the *Psychomachia*, the Battle of the Soul, he [*sc.* Prudentius] has done more than set the stage for the struggle between the spirit and the flesh.] **1936** C. S. LEWIS *Allegory of Love* ii. 55 The favourite theme of the Middle Ages—the battle of the virtues and the vices, the Psychomachia, the *bellum intestinum*, the Holy War. *Ibid.* 73 A good man, even in a panegyric, can now be good only as a result of a successful psychomachy. **1954** —— *Eng. Lit. in Sixteenth Cent.* I. i. 92 'Bewtie and the Prisoneir' is a neat but slightly frigid psychomachy. **1955** D. DAVIE *Brides of Reason* 22 There were minds Aware of themselves, and figuring this In psychomachia. **1972** *Times Lit. Suppl.* 10 Nov. 1353/1 Ruskin's criticism . . becomes a psychomachia dramatizing his own mental state.

psychomancy (ps-, 'saɪkəʊmænsɪ). [ad. Gr. type *ψῡχομαντεία, f. ψῡχόμαντις a necromancer: see PSYCHO- and -MANCY.]

†**1.** (See quot.) *Obs. rare*$^{-1}$.

1652 GAULE *Magastrom.* 165 Psychomancy, divining by mens souls, affections, wills, religious or morall dispositions.

†**2.** Divination through communication with the spirits of the dead; necromancy. *Obs.*

1684 I. MATHER *Remark. Provid.* (1856) 150, I dare not believe that the Holy God or the true Samuel would seem so far to countenance necromancie or psycomancy as this would be, should the soul of Samuel really return into the world when the witch called for him. **1702** C. MATHER *Magn. Chr.* III. II. xxviii. (1852) 503.

b. Occult intercommunication between souls or with spirits.

1865 *Sat. Rev.* 2 Dec. 710 American novels . . are constantly running off into a strange religious transcendentalism, and psychomancy, and all sorts of mystic extravagances. **1883** *Pall Mall G.* 17 May 11/1 He found so many facts beyond his power of explanation, that . . he concluded to start a rational search into psychomancy.

So **psycho'mantic** *a.*, of or pertaining to psychomancy.

1890 in *Cent. Dict.*

psychometer (-'ɒmɪtə(r)). [f. PSYCHO- + -METER (cf. PSYCHOMETRY: in sense 1 as in *geometer*).]

1. One who has the psychometric faculty, or practises psychometry (sense 1).

1863 DENTON *Nature's Secrets* 97, I have repeatedly tried to influence the minds of Psychometers, when making examinations, and at all times without success. **1878** J. R. BUCHANAN *Psychophysiol. Sc.* 72 The psychometer is not allowed even to see the manuscript, which is used by placing it on the centre of his forehead. **1903** *Daily Rec. & Mail* 10 Sept. 5 If you be a good psychometer you will by and bye be able to see as in a mental photograph the person who formerly possessed the object.

2. A means of, or (supposed) instrument for, appreciating the quality and powers of a mind.

1867 O. W. HOLMES *Guard. Angel* xiii. (1891) 157 To know whether a minister, young or still in flower, is in safe or dangerous paths, there are two psychometers. **1889** G. HUNTINGTON in *Chicago Advance* 31 Jan., I seriously believe that I have grown an intellectual inch... Is there such an instrument as a psychometer, do you know?

psychometric (-ˈmɛtrɪk), *a.* and *sb. pl.* [f. PSYCHOMETRY + -IC.] **A.** *adj.* Of, pertaining to, or of the nature of psychometry (in either sense).

1854 J. R. BUCHANAN *Lect. Neurolog. Syst. Anthropol.* 124 Old manuscripts requiring an antiquary to decipher their strange old penmanship, were easily interpreted by the psychometric power. **1878** —— *Psychophysiol. Sc.* 73 Physicians who..use their psychometric power for the diagnosis of the condition of patients at a distance. **1879** *Brain* II. 149 (*heading*) Psychometric experiments. **1906** *Daily Chron.* 22 Mar. 7/7 According to Mr. Brailey, the psychometric influence of relics and charms has been proved. **1943** *Amer. Jrnl. Psychiatry* C. 181/2 The various psychometric tests can only touch the surface of this situation. **1970** *Jrnl. Gen. Psychol.* LXXXII. 101 Intelligence measures included two psychometric indices of 'general intelligence'. **1973** R. C. DENNIS *Sweat of Fear* vi. 37, I had to find a way of telling her I had psychometric knowledge of her predicament.

B. *sb. pl.* (const. as *sing.*). The science of measuring mental capacities and processes; the application of methods of measurement to the various branches of psychology.

1930 *Proc. & Addr. Amer. Assoc. Stud. Feeble-Minded* XXXV. 94 To most persons who know the term at all, psychometrics is fairly synonymous with the use of intelligence tests. **1934** J. O'CONNOR (*title*) Psychometrics: a study of psychological measurement. *Ibid.* p. xiv, Every measuring instrument has two major aspects. In the field of psychometrics these are called reliability and validity. **1958** *Times* 27 May 2/2 (Advt.), Applications are invited for the post of Lecturer in Education with special interests in psychometrics, statistics and educational psychology. **1972** *Guardian* 24 Feb. 13/8 Psychometrics is unable to investigate the nature of intelligence. **1973** *Nature* 23 Mar. 279/2 Professor Meredith delivers a blistering attack on traditional psychometrics (i.e., the alleged 'measurement' of IQs, reading ages, and so on).

So **psychoˈmetrical** *a.* = sense A above; **psychoˈmetrically** *adv.*, according to psychometry, in the manner of a psychometer; **psyˈchometrize** *v. trans.*, to practise psychometry upon; to deal with psychometrically.

1868 DIXON *Spir. Wives* II. 253 She was a medium possessed of *psychometrical powers. **1922** E. WALLACE *Crimson Circle* ii. 14 The police might sneer at Yale's psychometrical powers. **1863** DENTON *Nature's Secrets* 130 A lady who, on examining a specimen *psychometrically, not only goes to the spot from which the specimen was obtained, but has the sensation of travelling while doing so. **1903** *Nature* 3 Sept. 409/1 It appears doubtful if any other community, European or Polynesian, has been psychometrically investigated under more favourable conditions as regards both absence of disturbing factors and simplification of method. **1977** *Lancet* 1 Jan. 7/2 These children have been re-examined medically and psychometrically. **1863** DENTON *Nature's Secrets* 99 The complete identification at times of the Psychometer with the thing *psychometrized..is one of the remarkable facts developed by our experiments. **1894** P. TYNER in *Boston Arena* June 44 Through the sense of physical touch..one is first brought, on 'psychometrizing' an object, into a vivid perception of an aura or atmosphere surrounding it. **1950** P. TABORI *Harry Price* ix. 183 He proposed..to have the box psychometrized first by the best mental mediums he could obtain. **1975** *Weekend Mag.* (Montreal) 18 Oct. 20/1 Learning of McMullen's psychic abilities, he asked him to psychometrize some artifacts.

psychometrician (ˌsaɪkəʊmɪˈtrɪʃən). [f. prec. + -IAN.] An expert in or practitioner of psychometrics.

1950 in WEBSTER Add. **1953** J. B. CARROLL *Study of Lang.* i. 4. The psychometrician..tries to make tests of 'verbal intelligence' or tests of achievement in various language arts. **1965** *Language* XLI. 353 Factor analysis has been intensively cultivated by psychologists, particularly psychometricians. **1975** *Sci. Amer.* July 128/1 In seeking to devise 'culture-free' tests of intelligence psychometricians are pursuing a chimera.

psychometrist (saɪˈkɒmɪtrɪst). [f. PSYCHOMETER + -IST.] **1.** = PSYCHOMETER 1.

1864 T. L. NICHOLS *40 Yrs. Amer. Life* II. ii. 20 Then came psychometrists, who could tell the lives, characters, fortunes, and diseases of people they had never seen. **1879** *Spiritual Notes* May 148/1 The psychometrist enters a room and is impressed with a vision of events that in some mysterious way have left their traces on its material fabric. **1900** *Referee* 4 Mar. 2, I enter into rivalry with the palmists and psychometrists and prophetesses and prophets. **1903** W. T. STEAD in *Review of Rev.* July 32/1 A psychometrist.. was to give a demonstration of her capacity. **1966** E. PALMER *Plains of Camdeboo* xvii. 289 Hearing of a psychometrist in Johannesburg, I took my piece of wood to her and asked her what she could tell me of its history. **1976** *Oxford Times* 6 Feb. 15/1 Guest speakers and demonstrators include..a psychometrist—for whom vibrations received from personal belongings create a mental picture of the owner.

2. = PSYCHOMETRICIAN.

1932 *Psychol. Exchange* I. 11 The deserving psychometrists are often not discriminated from those who have just taken up mental testing. **1964** M. CRITCHLEY *Developmental Dyslexia* xiv. 82 The formal intelligence quotient was given as 65, but this was certainly a serious underestimate due to lack of cultural rapport with the psychometrist. **1974** *Maclean's Mag.* (Toronto) May 12/2 He worked as a psychometrist measuring the abilities of children.

psychometry (ps-, saɪˈkɒmɪtrɪ). [f. Gr. ψῡχο-, PSYCHO- + -μετρια measuring; lit. 'soul-' or 'mind-measuring', but the application in sense 1 does violence to the etymology.]

1. The (alleged) faculty of divining, from physical contact or proximity only, the qualities or properties of an object, or of persons or things that have been in contact with it.

1854 J. R. BUCHANAN *Lect. Neurolog. Syst. Anthropol.* 125 The influence of Psychometry will be highly valuable..in the selection from candidates for appointments to important offices. **1863** DENTON *Nature's Secrets* Introd. 9 Mrs. Denton, by means of this science of Psychometry, professes to be able, by putting a piece of matter..to her forehead, to see, either with her eyes closed or open, all that that piece of matter, figuratively speaking, ever saw, heard, or experienced. **1903** W. T. STEAD in *Review of Rev.* July 33/2 An experiment in psychometry. **1922** E. WALLACE *Crimson Circle* vi. 38 'Nothing is absurd,' said the Commissioner quietly. 'The science of psychometry has been practised for years.' **1959** *Times Lit. Suppl.* 1 May 254/4 Such objects.. enjoy a semi-consciousness drawn from the human beings who have known them. In this there is an undeniable truth, as the modern practice of 'psychometry' proves. **1966** E. PALMER *Plains of Camdeboo* xvii. 290 Most of us can on occasions sense atmosphere, and psychometry seems to be this power greatly developed. **1975** G. W. KNIGHT *Jackson Knight* i. 44, I know now, from the witness of psychometry, that inanimate objects can indeed become impregnated by qualities gathered during their past.

2. The measurement of the duration and intensity of mental states or processes. Also, psychometrics (see PSYCHOMETRIC *a.* and *sb.* B).

1879 F. GALTON in *Brain* II. 149 Psychometry..means the art of imposing measurement and number upon operations of the mind, as in the practice of determining the reaction-time of different persons. **1883** *Athenæum* 7 July 20/2 He [Mr. F. Galton] has established by his example and initiation the science of psychometry, and pointed to the line of inquiry on which the scientific portions of psychology can alone become scientific. **1897** *Westm. Gaz.* 29 Sept. 2/1 Dr. Scripture's experiments in the psychometry of time, energy, and space. **1971** *Brit. Med. Bull.* XXVII. 35/1 Hughes and his colleagues are conducting further studies, including the use of electro-encephalography and psychometry. **1976** H. M. VAN PRAAG in *Advances in Drug Therapy of Mental Illness* (World Health Organization) 127 The third field in which psychotropic drugs have served as a pacemaker, that of psychometry... One wants to know (that is, to measure) what it [*sc.* the drug] does, and what it does not do.

psychomimetic, -motility: see PSYCHO-.

ˈpsycho-ˈmotor, *a.* Also without hyphen. [f. PSYCHO- + MOTOR.] **a.** Inducing movement by psychic or mental action; involving such movement.

1878 tr. *von Ziemssen's Cycl. Med.* XIV. 699 Neither do I see any advantage to be gained from the use of the term 'psycho-motor' to denote voluntary movements. **1879** *Jrnl. Mental Sci.* XXIV. 677 The 'Psychiatrischer Centralblatt' for August.., 1877, gives a *résumé* of the inaugural dissertation..of Dr. Pasternaki, who has studied the question of what he calls the Psychomotor Centres of the Brain. **1890** BILLINGS *Med. Dict.*, *Psycho-motor centres*, brain-centres producing voluntary movements. *P.-m nerve-fibres*, cortico-muscular nerve-fibres. **1899** *Allbutt's Syst. Med.* VIII. 392 This phenomenon has been described under the name of psycho-motor verbal hallucination. **1961** *Aeroplane & Astronautics* CI. 679/1 It was agreed that the animals selected for this programme should be capable of learning simple psycho-motor tasks which could be performed during flight. **1976** SMYTHIES & CORBETT *Psychiatry* v. 62 In depressed patients speech tends to be slow, monotonous, and sad-sounding, in keeping with the general psychomotor slowing.

b. *Med.* Applied to a partial seizure or epileptic attack (distinct from grand mal and petit mal) characterized by a state of altered consciousness in which simple or complex automatisms may be performed for which there is subsequently at least partial amnesia.

1938 *Amer. Jrnl. Psychiatry* XXV. 268 The three main manifestations of epilepsy (grand mal, petit mal and psychomotor epilepsy) are each accompanied by a distinct pattern of disrhythmia. **1961** *Listener* 7 Dec. 967/2 An attack of psychomotor epilepsy. **1974** M. C. GERALD *Pharmacol.* xi. 212 Diphenylhydantoin..is also useful against psychomotor seizures.

Hence **psychomoˈtoric, -moˈtorical** *adjs.*, of or pertaining to psychomotor activity; **psychomoˈtorically** *adv.*

1964 L. KAISER in D. Abercrombie et al. *Daniel Jones* 102 Both ways of coding and decoding show a high degree of similarity, psychomotoric patterns based on language leading to neuromuscular activity, which in its turn leads to spatial coding in both cases. **1969** *Indian Mus. Jrnl.* V. 83 Music is a much directer form of expression (psychomotorically), than painting, sculpture..and ornaments. *Ibid.* 84 These psychomotorical expressions are not in the least outbursts of uncontrolled emotions. The hands of the singers accompany in refined movements the path of the voice.

psychon (ˈsaɪkɒn). [f. PSYCHO- + -ON[1].] A hypothetical unit of nerve impulse or energy. Hence **psyˈchonic** *a.*

[**1906** H. W. ARMIT tr. *A. Forel's Hypnotism* i. 6 It is here that one must seek the transition from the conceived to the unconceived, and not in the strong and repeatedly conceived 'psychomes'. [*Note*] The author apologizes for this term. He has introduced it for brevity['s] sake to express each and every psychical unit.] **1920** H. L. ENO *Activism* iv. 45 Since we are already familiar with one form at any rate of this higher activity in the psychic processes, let us call these units 'psychons'. *Ibid.*, The term 'psychone' was proposed by Forel for the psychic aspect of a hypothetical unit of the nerve process. **1927** P. & W. R. BOUSFIELD *Mind* i. 22 As the basis of the 'immaterial substance' we may postulate a second order of 'ons' which are, like protons and electrons, fashioned out of the ether. Let us call these 'ons' by the name of 'psychons'. **1931** W. M. MARSTON et al. *Integrative Psychol.* xiii. 314 There is no doubt whatsoever that the psychons in the sensory system differ from those in the motor system. *Ibid.*, We suggest, therefore, that from the point of view of an objective psychology, exterior to its subjects, this psychonic energy is consciousness. **1968** C. L. BURT *Psychol. & Psychical Res.* 45 As unit I would rather start with the 'pure ego', which I envisage as a sort of Leibnizian monad. This, I think, on the plane of natural science we might justifiably treat as an 'elementary particle'—a 'psychon', as I styled it.

psychoneural, -neuroendocrine, -neuroendocrinology, -neurology, etc.: see PSYCHO-.

psychoneuˈrosis. *Psychol.* Also with hyphen. [f. PSYCHO- + NEUROSIS.] Any of various functional nervous disorders attributed to emotional or psychological causes, often accompanied by manifestations of anxiety, and distinguished from a psychosis by the maintenance of contact with the external world; also, in psychoanalytic theory, a mental disorder attributed to repressed unconscious conflict or fantasy (as distinguished from an 'actual' neurosis, attributed to anxiety caused by present frustration of sexual drive).

1883 CLOUSTON *Clin. Lect. Mental Dis.* i. 18 The insane temperament or *neurosis insana*, or, to keep up uniformity of the classification, Psychoneurosis. **1903** W. JAMES in *Proc. Soc. Psychical Res.* XVIII. 32 The parasitic ideas of psychoneurosis, and the fictitious personations of planchette-writing and mediumship. **1913** E. JONES *Papers on Psycho-Anal.* v. 125 Freud has pointed out that it is necessary to separate the 'actual neuroses' from the 'psychoneuroses'. *Ibid.* 129 We next come to the psychoneuroses proper... The symptoms result from the activity of certain unconscious mental processes..which the patient is unable spontaneously to recall to his memory. **1924** J. RIVIERE et al. tr. *Freud's Coll. Papers* II. xxi. 253 There always remains as a common feature in the ætiology both of the psychoneuroses and the psychoses the factor of frustration. **1938** *Jrnl. Aviation Med.* IX. 177/2 McFarland and Barach found that patients, on whom a diagnosis of psychoneurosis had been made, appeared to be more severely affected at an atmosphere of 10 per cent oxygen than were the normal controls. **1948** *Sci. News* VIII. 109 The conditions which benefit most from group psychotherapy are the psychoneuroses—particularly anxiety states and reactive depressions. **1959** J. STRACHEY *Freud's Compl. Wks.* XX. 79 In these cases—in the psychoneuroses—the reason for the accumulation of undischarged excitation was a psychological one: repression. But what followed was the same as in the 'actual' neuroses. **1972** ZAX & COWEN *Abnormal Psychol.* viii. 231 The one feature common to all forms of psychoneurosis is the presence of anxiety. *Ibid.* 232 In DSM-I (1952) six types of psychoneuroses were delineated: anxiety reaction; conversion reaction; dissociative reaction; phobic reaction; obsessive-compulsive; and depressive reaction. **1977** MILLER & SWIFT *Words & Women* iv. 67 Hysteria now refers in technical use to a specific psychoneurosis that may affect anyone, male or female.

psychoneuˈrotic, *sb.* and *a.* *Psychol.* Also with hyphen. [f. PSYCHO- + NEUROTIC *sb.* and *a.*] **A.** *sb.* A person suffering from a psychoneurosis.

1902 *Buck's Handbk. Med. Sci.* (rev. ed.) V. 28/1 In the psychoneurotic..the tendency toward imperfect mental development becomes more and more accentuated. **1924** *Proc. 7th Internat. Congr. Psychol.* 148 Though a genius is frequently a psycho-neurotic, it would be quite untrue to say that the majority of psycho-neurotics tend towards genius. **1936** *Psychoanal. Rev.* XXIII. 1 Thoughts of death and dying occur as every-day symptoms among psychoneurotics of the anxiety, hysterical and obsessive types. **1972** ZAX & COWEN *Abnormal Psychol.* viii. 231 The psychoneurotic maintains good contact with reality.

B. *adj.* Of, pertaining to, or characterized by psychoneurosis.

1909 *Jrnl. Abnormal Psychol.* June–July 144 Every psycho-neurotic symptom is to be regarded as the symbolic expression of a submerged mental complex of the nature of a wish. **1938** *Jrnl. Aviation Med.* IX. 177/2 When 50 per cent oxygen was given, the physiologic symptoms of the psychoneurotic patients were less marked. **1967** *Spectator* 1 Dec. 679/1 When one looks at the incidence of psychoneurotic disorders..it is found that these also were commoner in..flat-dwellers.

psycho-optic(al to **-osmic:** see PSYCHO-.

psychopannychy (psaɪkəʊˈpænɪkɪ). *Obs.* exc. *Hist.* [ad. med.L. *psȳchopannychia*, f. Gr. ψῡχο-, comb. f. ψῡχή soul + παννύχιος lasting all night.] All-night sleep of the soul; a state in which (according to some) the soul sleeps between death and the day of judgement. So **psychopannychian** (ˌpsaɪkəʊpəˈnɪkɪən), **-ˈpannychist, -ˈpannychite**, one holding this doctrine; **psychoˈpannychism**, the doctrine of the psychopannychists; **ˌpsychopannyˈchistic** *a.*, pertaining to the psychopannychists or their belief.

[**1545** CALVIN (*title*) Psychopannychia, qua refellitur [eorum] error, qui animas post mortem usque ad ultimum iudicium dormire putant.] **1872** tr. *Lange's Comm. 1 Thess.* iv. 13. 73/1 Calvin and others oppose with reason the *Psychopannichians. **1877** SHIELDS *Final Philos.* 195 The first of these views was known as *psychopannychism, or the total sleep of the soul. **1659** GAUDEN *Tears Ch.* 283 No more ..than the Saducees might deny and overthrow the resurrection against Christ; or the *Psychopannuchists, the souls immortality. **1891** *New Rev.* July 19 Another state, either *psychopannychistic, that is, of sleep till the resurrection; or of reward, punishment, or suspense. **1642** H. MORE *Song of Soul* III. I. xii, Go now you *Psychopannychites! **1682** —— *Annot. Glanvill's Lux O.* 110 Unless we will be so dull as to fall into the drouzie dream of the Psychopannychites. **1642** —— *Song of Soul* III. I. iii, Plain death's as good as such a *Psychopannychie. **1847** BUCH tr. *Hagenbach's Hist. Doctr.* II. 139 A revival of the earlier notion of the death of the soul..under the milder form of the sleep of the soul (*Psychopannychy*).

psychopath (ps-, ˈsaɪkəʊpæθ). [f. PSYCHO- + Gr. -παθής, f. πάθος suffering. Cf. *neuropath*, etc.] One affected with psychopathy; a mentally deranged person. Cf. PSYCHOPATHY.

1885 *Pall Mall G.* 21 Jan. 3/2 Psychopathy... We give M. Balinsky's explanation of the new malady. 'The psychopath ..is a type which has only recently come under the notice of medical science... Beside his own person and his own interests, nothing is sacred to the psychopath'. **1890** *Univ. Rev.* 15 Mar. 310 He was what Russians call a 'psychopath', a being whom Russian laws refuse to punish even for murder. **1902** W. JAMES *Varieties Relig. Exper.* 7 From the point of view of his nervous constitution, Fox was a psychopath or détraqué of the deepest dye. **1927** *New Republic* 21 Sept. 128/2 Terms not so long ago confined to specialists are handled familiarly by the laity: moron, inferiority complex, mental age,..paranoid delusions, psychopaths. **1955** D. J. WEST *Homosexuality* ix. 106 Psychopaths are the last people to try to battle against their instincts; they just obey first impulses regardless of social codes. Being incapable of prolonged or deep personal attachments, they seek only an immediate outlet for their lust. **1967** *Listener* 20 Apr. 529/3 The term psychopath is bandied about in such a way as to make it cover almost any mental disorder... However the psychopath has now achieved legal status in the Mental Health Act of 1959 as having 'a persistent disorder or disability of mind..which results in abnormally aggressive or seriously irresponsible behaviour'. **1967** M. ARGYLE *Psychol. of Interpersonal Behaviour* i. 21 It is one of the marks of the psychopath that he will engage in social behaviour in so far as it is..profitable to do so, but he has no intrinsic attraction to other people at all. For the psychopath there is no particular difference between people and things. **1972** *Observer* 31 Dec. 23/4 If she's a psychopath I'm a fruit cake. She's just a girl who needs love.

psychopathic (ps-, saɪkəʊˈpæθɪk), *a.* (*sb.*) [f. PSYCHOPATHY + -IC.]

A. *adj.* **1. a.** Of, pertaining to, or of the nature of mental disorder, now *spec.* psychopathy. **b.** Subject to or affected with mental disorder, now *spec.* psychopathy; mentally deranged. **c.** Engaged in the treatment of mental disorder.

1847 tr. *Feuchtersleben's Med. Psychol.* (Syd. Soc.) 65 A public address to the psychopathic physicians of Germany. **1899** [see HEREDITARY *a.* 2a]. **1901** *Lancet* 20 Apr. 1126/2 This condition..proves its psychopathic basis. **1902** W. JAMES *Varieties Relig. Exper.* 157 He [Bunyan] was a typical case of the psychopathic temperament, sensitive of conscience to a diseased degree. **1932** *Sun* (Baltimore) 19 Sept. 2/2 The court.. found that Duker is afflicted with a definite mental ailment or disorder known as psychopathic personality, which had reduced his mental and moral responsibility and control but that he is sane according to the legal standard. **1949** *Brit. Jrnl. Psychol.* XL. 12 The Psychopathic Personality (P.P.P.) is one of the major problems of the Prison Commission. **1957** R. F. C. HULL tr. *Jung's Compl. Wks.* I. 111 In many psychopathic illnesses there are persons who think unclearly and are prone to flights of ideas, who are ruthlessly egocentric..but who can hardly be said to be suffering from chronic mania. **1959** *Mental Health Act 7 & 8 Eliz. II* c. 72. I. §4 In this Act 'psychopathic disorder' means a persistent disorder or disability of mind (whether or not including subnormality of intelligence) which results in abnormally aggressive or seriously irresponsible conduct on the part of the patient, and requires or is susceptible to medical treatment. **1968** [see MORAL *a.* 7a]. **1976** *Times* 4 Aug. 5/7 All we can do is protect society from them. Grossly psychopathic people cannot be befriended. **1977** P. WAY *Super-Celeste* I. 53 Such men..work to please whatever passions and psychopathic urges drive them personally.

2. Of or pertaining to the treatment of disease by 'psychic' means, as by hypnotism.

1890 in *Cent. Dict.*

B. *absol.* as *sb.* = PSYCHOPATH.

1890 in *Cent. Dict.* **1896** MISS F. P. COBBE in *Daily News* 13 Apr. 7/7 They are 'psychopathics'—a term which Prof. James, of Harvard University, employs to denote an inborn aptitude to immoral actions in any direction.

Hence **psychoˈpathically** *adv.*

1961 in WEBSTER. **1972** *Lancet* 18 Nov. 1069/2 The psychopathically aggressive, the rigidly authoritarian.

psyˈchopathist. [f. PSYCHOPATHY + -IST.] One who studies or treats psychopathy or mental disease; an alienist.

1854 BUCKNILL *Crim. Lunacy* 7 Whether the doctrines of spiritualism or of materialism find favor with psychopathists is of the utmost importance. **1894** tr. *Swedenborg's Spir. Columbus* ix. 147 The Psychopathist and physician are furnished with materials for the treatment of social corruption in all its phases.

ˌpsychopaˈthology. Also with hyphen. [f. PSYCHO- + PATHOLOGY.] **a.** The pathology of the mind; the science of mental disorder or the mental or psychological causation of disorders and abnormalities.

1847 tr. *Feuchtersleben's Med. Psychol.* (Syd. Soc.) 70 Psychopathology has not yet acquired sufficient light respecting these critical processes. **1895** *Syd. Soc. Lex.*, *Psychopathology*, the science treating of the legal aspect of insanity. Also, the pathology of insanity. **1951** D. B. KLEIN *Abnormal Psychol.* 5 The study of mental disorder bulks large in the field of abnormal psychology, so that a good portion of this field might be regarded as coterminous with that of psychopathology. **1964** GOULD & KOLB *Dict. Social Sci.* 555/1 This psycho-analytic psychopathology has.. been employed to explain..not only mental symptoms but also the physical lesions of so-called psychosomatic diseases; not only disease but also the traits and quirks of normal or deviant personalities. **1968** J. ZUBIN in Zubin & Shagass *Neurobiol. Aspects of Psychopathology* 289 If we define personality as the systematic aspect of a person's behavior, and psychopathology as those aspects of this systematic behavior attributable to illness, an important question arises regarding the possible connections between premorbid personality and psychopathology. **1969** T. FREEMAN *Psychopathology of Psychoses* i. 2 Psychopathology has a wider subject-matter than the study of 'conscious psychic events'... To be comprehensive it must take account of psychoanalysis... It must also be based on certain aspects of neurology and internal medicine.

b. A mentally or behaviourally disordered state.

1947 D. JONES in R. Hague *Dai Greatcoat* (1980) II. 139 *Everything* one does is conditioned by one's psychopathology. **1952** METTLER & CURRY in F. A. Mettler *Psychosurgical Problems* i. 16 It does not follow because a patient is discharged that his psychopathology is fundamentally altered. **1970** *Jrnl. Gen. Psychol.* LXXXIII. 61 Classifying states of psychopathology into discrete, mutually exclusive categories..does not seem to be possible. **1973** SANDLER & DAVIDSON *Psychopathology* i. 8 Tests designed to reveal the developmental history of the patient's psychopathology.

Hence **ˌpsychopathoˈlogical** *a.*; **ˌpsychopaˈthologist**, a student of or expert in psychopathology; also **ˌpsychopathoˈlogic** *a.*, **ˌpsychopathoˈlogically** *adv.*

1863 *D. D. Home's Incidents Life* Introd. 15 To the psychopathologist.. this detail may serve to advance an important scientific purpose. **1891** *Ann. Rep. Board of Regents Smithsonian Inst. 1889–90* 636 One can thus see the links which form the psycho-pathologic chain of human life, at one end of which we may find insanity and at the other criminality. **1892** *Nation* (N.Y.) 15 Sept. 203/3 A volume on saints, in which the whole subject of hagiology will be investigated from a psychopathological point of view. **1919** W. S. MAUGHAM *Moon & Sixpence* i. 7 The mystic sees the ineffable and the psycho-pathologist the unspeakable. **1928** *Guy's Hosp. Rep.* LXXVIII. 458 Psychopathologically, from the content of the hypochondriacal complaints..an anal-erotic basis for some hypochondrias is strongly suggested. **1936** *Jrnl. Nerv. & Mental Dis.* LXXXIV. 450 Psychopathologically, we undertake an analysis of the situation. **1971** J. J. SHAPIRO tr. *Habermas's Toward Rational Society* iii. 42 The use of psychopathological concepts has become necessary for the identification and explanation of a political state of affairs. **1976** *Observer* 11 Jan. 21/4 Interesting little psychopathological tour de force —or, as they say in Soho, kinks and kicks.

psychopathy (ps-, saɪˈkɒpəθɪ). *Path.* [f. Gr. ψῡχο-, PSYCHO- + -πάθεια from πάθος suffering: hence sense 1 is etymologically correct; sense 2 follows *homœopathy*, *hydropathy*, etc.: see -PATHY.]

1. Mental disease or disorder; 'mental disorder considered apart from cerebral disease' (Billings). In mod. use, personality disorder that lacks a physiological basis, characterized by markedly impulsive, egocentric, irresponsible, and antisocial behaviour, and an inability to form normal relationships with others, sometimes accompanied by aggressiveness or charm and manifested at all levels of intelligence; the state of such a disorder.

sexual psychopathy, mental disease connected with sexual disorders.

1847 tr. *Feuchtersleben's Med. Psychol.* (Syd. Soc.) 343 The cure of the psychopathies..is different according to their several forms. **1885** [see PSYCHOPATH]. **1899** *Allbutt's Syst. Med.* VIII. 312 Influenza may set up psychopathy. **1902** *Daily Chron.* 23 Dec. 4/7 Professor Kraft Ebing's fame dates from the publication of his work on sexual psychopathy. **1923** C. MACKENZIE *Parson's Progress* xix. 263 Personally I have found my knowledge of psychopathy of the greatest value in the confessional. **1948** *Amer. Jrnl. Sociol.* LIII. 361/1 Caldwell indicates nomadism, inability to withstand tedium, and irresponsibility as characteristics of psychopathy. **1953** I. SKOTTOWE *Clin. Psychiatry* ii. 32 Three qualities may be discerned biographically which are a common expression of psychopathy. The first is the lack of persistence..; the second is a curious coldness of heart..; the third is an inability to defer the immediate satisfaction of appetites and desires. **1972** G. SERENY *Case of Mary Bell* II. i. 148 The condition of psychopathy is not generally identified with mental retardation. **1972** ZAX & COWEN *Abnormal Psychol.* x. 312 In trying to understand the causes of psychopathy a variety of emphases can be identified, including hereditary, neurological, environmental, and sociocultural. **1976** *Church Times* 12 Mar. 5/2 He turned loving eyes on the tormenting thugs... They, in their psychopathy, could not see him as a man like themselves.

2. The treatment of disease by 'psychical' influence, e.g. by hypnotism.

1891 *Blackw. Mag.* 406 Mesmerism is to psychopathy what alchemy was to chemistry. **1893** *Century Mag.* July 435 The importance of adopting psychopathy as a means for the relief of disease.

3. (See quot.)

1863 DENTON *Nature's Secrets* 95 All fossil remains of animals are imbued with the feelings of the animals of which they formed a part, and, under their influence, the Psychometer..feels all that was felt by them... This branch of Psychometry may be termed Psychopathy.

psychopetal, etc.: see PSYCHO-.

psychopharmaceutical: see PSYCHO-.

ˌpsychopharmaˈcology. Also with hyphen. [f. PSYCHO- + PHARMACOLOGY.] The branch of science concerned with the way drugs affect the mind and behaviour.

1920 D. MACHT in *Johns Hopkins Hosp. Bull.* XXXI. 167/1 The number of contributions to the domain of what we may be permitted to call 'psychopharmacology' is certainly very meagre. **1935** *Jrnl. Nerv. & Mental Dis.* LXXXI. 161 The psycho-pharmacology of sodium amytal. **1958** A. HUXLEY *Let.* 2 Feb. (1969) 845, I have been asked ..to do a piece on the ethical, religious and social implications of psychopharmacology. **1969** *New Scientist* 10 Apr. 80/1 LSD..may be remembered as a herald of psychopharmacology. **1970** A. TOFFLER *Future Shock* (1971) viii. 160 New knowledge..in psychopharmacology, made many Freudian therapeutic measures seem quaintly archaic.

Hence **ˌpsychopharmacoˈlogic** (chiefly *U.S.*), **-ˈlogical** *adjs.*, of or pertaining to psychopharmacology; (of a drug) psychoactive; **ˌpsychopharmacoˈlogically** *adv.*; **ˌpsychopharmaˈcologist**, an expert or specialist in this subject.

1939 *Jrnl. Mental Sci.* LXXXV. 406 (*heading*) A psychopharmacological study of schizophrenia with particular reference to the mode of action of cardiazol, sodium amytal and alcohol in schizophrenic stupor. **1958** *Science* 10 Jan. 61/2 Depressions not accompanied by anxiety and tension are less apt to be ameliorated by a psycho-pharmacologic agent. **1960** *Clin. Pharmacol. & Therapeutics* I. 257/2 Studies by psychopharmacologists and comparative psychologists concerning the effects of the new psychotropic drugs on experimentally conditioned emotional responses of animals. **1964** M. GORDON *Psychopharmacol. Agents* I. i. 3 One of the new psycho-pharmacological agents, reserpine, had a difficult time gaining acceptance in the Western hemisphere. **1967** *Guardian* 1 July 12/3 A psychopharmacologist said: 'I wouldn't be dismayed if the use of marijuana were made legal.' **1970** *Nature* 5 Sept. 1008/1 Psychopharmacological experiments are beginning to yield data relevant to urban crowding as a health hazard. **1971** *Amer. Jrnl. Psychiatry* CXXVIII. 695/1 Peyote contains more than ten alkaloids, the most psychopharmacologically significant of which is mescaline. **1977** M. E. JARVIK *Psychopharmacol. in Pract. of Med.* 21 In complicated cases the individual should be referred to a psychopharmacologically oriented psychotherapist. **1979** [see PSYCHOBIOLOGIST].

psycho-philosopher, -philosophy: see PSYCHO-.

psychophoˈnetics, *sb. pl.* (const. as *sing.*). *Linguistics.* Also with hyphen. [f. PSYCHO- + PHONETICS *sb. pl.* Cf. Pol. *psychofonetych* (J. B. de Courtenay 1894, in *Rozprawy Akad. Umiejebności*: *Wydział Filol.* 2nd Ser. V. 129).] That branch of phonetics which deals with the mental correlates of speech-sound production. So **psychophoˈnetic** *a.*, **psychophoˈnetically** *adv.*

1934 *Maître Phonétique* Jan.–Mar. 3, ɔːl ðiːz difrənsiz in prənʌnsieiʃn..duː nɔt igzist saikoufənetikəli. **1934** *Ibid.* Apr.–June 44 Doctor Arend..naturally quotes from the later one [*sc.* work by J. B. de Courtenay] published in 1901, though there was a much later work on phonetics and psycho-phonetics published in 1927. **1936**, **1950** [see PHYSIOPHONETICS *sb. pl.*]. **1956** JAKOBSON & HALLE *Fundamentals of Lang.* ii. 11 *The mentalist view*... In the oldest of these approaches,..the phoneme is a sound imagined or intended, opposed to the emitted sound as a 'psychophonetic' phenomenon to the 'physiophonetic' fact. **1966** M. PEI *Gloss. Linguistic Terminol.* 225 *Psychophonetics*, the treatment of a phoneme as the image aimed at in the speaker's mind (Courtenay, Entwistle). **1968** J. W. F. MULDER *Sets & Relations in Phonol.* 20 Articulatory phonetics has achieved results that are more widely accepted and provide a safer guide than the younger acoustic phonetics (let alone the still younger 'perceptive' phonetics, which could well be called 'psycho-phonetics'). **1968** BLACK & SINGH in B. Malmberg *Man. Phonetics* v. 106 For the sake of convenience, psycho-phonetics will be treated here as (a) speech production, (b) speech acoustics, and (c) speech perception.

psychophysic (ps-, saɪkəʊˈfɪzɪk), *a.* and *sb.* Also with hyphen. [f. Gr. ψῡχο-, PSYCHO- + φυσικ-ός physical.]

A. *adj.* = PSYCHOPHYSICAL, esp. in ***psychophysic law***, 'the law expressing the relation between a change of intensity in the stimulus and the resulting change in the sensation' (Billings).

1887 *Amer. Jrnl. Psychol.* I. 140 The conditions are as infinitely complicated as the psycho-physic constitution of man. **1890** BILLINGS *Nat. Med. Dict.* 404 The psychophysic law requires that the just observable difference shall be a constant fraction of the mean of the two stimuli.

B. *sb.* Commonly in pl. **psycho'physics.** [= Ger. *Psychophysik* (Fechner 1859): see PHYSIC *sb.* 1, PHYSICS.] The science of the general relations between mind and body; *spec.* the investigation of the relations between physical stimuli and psychic action in the production of sensations; 'experimental psychology' (*Syd. Soc. Lex.*).

1878 *Rep. Brit. Assoc. Adv. Sci. 1877* II. 95 Most of you are aware of the recent progress of what has been termed Psycho-physics, or the science of subjecting mental processes to physical measurements and to physical laws. **1879** LEWES *Stud. Psychol.* 184 It has been found possible to introduce quantitative relations between stimuli and sensations, and a new branch of science, called Psychophysics, has arisen. **1893** *Pall Mall G.* 30 Jan. 2/3 Mr. F. Galton was to lecture at the Royal Institution on 'The Just-Perceptible Difference'... It turned out to be a discourse on the somewhat vague science known to experts as psycho-physics. **1937** *Amer. Speech* XII. 228/1 On the psycho-physics of speech. **1944** *Jrnl. Optical Soc. Amer.* XXXIV. 66/1 Physicists..have surrendered almost the entire field of psychophysics to the psychologist. **1973** C. D. KERNIG *Marxism, Communism & Western Society* VII. 91/2 A distinction is made between (a) classical psychophysics in which the physiology of the senses is studied with the help of refined..techniques..; (b) activation (arousal) research, which is concerned with..conditions for the release and course of affective and motivational states. **1976** S. GEORGE *Fatal Shadows* 37 The new scientists, men whose discoveries of gifted psychics had shot them to the top of psychophysics.

psycho'physical, *a.* Also with hyphen. [f. as prec. + -AL[1]: cf. *physical.*] Of or pertaining to psychophysics; having to do with psychology and physics, or the connexion of the psychical and the physical.

psychophysical isomorphism (see quot. 1932). ***psychophysical law*** = PSYCHOPHYSIC *law.* ***psychophysical methods***, 'methods of experimenting in determining the sensibility for small differences of sensation' (Billings). ***psychophysical movement***, 'a hypothetical activity assumed by Fechner to explain the discrepancy between the increase of the stimulus and that of the sensation' (Billings).

1847 H. E. LLOYD tr. *Feuchtersleben's Med. Psychol.* iii. 151 Habit, likewise, greatly modifies the psycho-physical character. **1872** *Westm. Rev.* XLII. 177 As a result of experiments according to all these three methods, Fechner arrives at what he calls a general 'psycho-physical law', and also 'Weber's law'. *Ibid.* 188 Fechner's law..embodies and illustrates the law of relativity; but it has a psycho-physical value over and above this. **1884** tr. *Lotze's Metaph.* 442 In my eyes, nothing is gained in the way of clearness by the invention of the name 'psycho-physical occurrence', or 'psycho-physical process'. I admit that the expression may have a meaning when applied to a single element, in which, as I said before, we conceive physical and psychical stimulations to exist together. **1886** GURNEY, etc. *Phantasms of Living* I. Introd. 43 Artificial displacements of the psycho-physical threshold. **1892** C. G. CHADDOCK tr. *Krafft-Ebing's Psychopathia Sexualis* v. 403 Large lips, idiotic expression,..and an awkward attitude complete the picture of psychophysical degeneration. **1894** CREIGHTON & TITCHENER tr. *Wundt's Human & Animal Psychol.* 448 The principle of psychophysical parallelism..refers always to a parallelism of elementary physical and psychical processes. **1903** MYERS *Hum. Personality* II. 142 The psycho-physical parallelism—which insists that every mental phenomenon must have a physical correlative. **1932** B. PETERMANN *Gestalt Theory* II. iii. 110 He commences with a general leading principle, that of psychophysical isomorphism. This is the assumption that a co-ordination exists between the domain of the experiences and that of the physiological processes..and that it is a co-ordination in the sense of congruence or isomorphism in regard to their systematic properties. **1941**, etc. [see INTERACTIONISM]. **1942** W. KOEHLER *Dynamics in Psychol.* ii. 43 If an experience *A* may vary in a specific way, its correlate *a* must be capable of corresponding variations. When consistently applied, this point of view leads to the principle of psychophysical isomorphism. **1972** *Sci. Amer.* May 30/1 Young's celebrated three-color theory of color vision, published in 1802, was formulated entirely on psychophysical evidence. **1972** O. L. ZANGWILL in Cox & Dyson *20th-Cent. Mind* II. vii. 174 While still at Chicago, Watson had been much troubled by the psychophysical mould in which instruction in experimental psychology was still cast.

Hence **psycho'physically** *adv.*, by psychophysical means; as regards psychophysics.

1847 H. E. LLOYD tr. *Feuchtersleben's Med. Psychol.* v. 307 The so-called proximate cause of idiocy can..be no other than a psycho-physically impeded or depressed vital process. **1894** W. JAMES *Coll. Ess. & Rev.* (1920) 360 Do they mean that introspection acquaints them with a part of the emotional excitement which it is psycho-physically impossible that incoming currents should cause? **1948** L. SPITZER *Linguistics & Lit. Hist.* iv. 139 Man, this psychophysically conditioned being. **1973** *Nature* 21 Sept. 159/2 Gibson and others have shown psychophysically that the gradient of density of visual texture is an important clue to the orientation in depth of textured surfaces.

psycho'physicist. Also with hyphen. [f. PSYCHOPHYSIC + -IST.] One versed in psychophysics.

1886 GURNEY, etc. *Phantasms of Living* I. Introd. 44 We look..for aid to the most recent group of physiological inquirers, to the psycho-physicists. **1901** *Oxford Mag.* 4 Dec. 141/1 The experimental school of the modern psychophysicists is ignored. **1951** S. S. STEVENS *Handbk. Exper. Psychol.* i. 43/2 The psychophysicists have elaborated subtle measures that try to transcend the inconstancy of the mercurial response. **1975** *Nature* 20 Nov. 201/1 Even though psychophysicists do not necessarily share this confidence, it is worth trying to relate the neurophysiology to measurable psychophysical function.

psychophysicotherapeutics: see PSYCHO-.

,psychophysi'ology. Also with hyphen. [f. PSYCHO- + PHYSIOLOGY.] The department of physiology which deals with mental phenomena; physiological or experimental psychology. Hence **,psychophysio'logic** *a.* (chiefly *U.S.*), **,psychophysio'logical** *a.*, of or pertaining to psychophysiology; **,psychophysio'logically** *adv.*; **,psychophysi'ologist**, a student or teacher of psychophysiology.

1839 S. ADAMS (*title*) Psycho-Physiology, viewed in its connection with Mysteries of Animal Magnetism and other Kindred Phenomena. **1839** *Amer. Bibl. Repos.* Ser. II. I. 367 The great centre of psycho-physiological sympathy. **1865** *Pall Mall G.* 15 Aug. 1 How far do numbers alter the case?—we mean from the psycho-physiological point of view. **1892** VAN LIEW & BEYER tr. *Ziehen's Introd. Study of Physiol. Psychol.* vii. 144 The projection and arrangement of our sensations with reference to time, the same as with reference to space, cannot be explained psychophysiologically. **1903** *Daily Chron.* 10 Feb. 3/1 The modern experimental psycho-physiologist shows that the unity of consciousness on which the supposed unity of the ego is based is a mere illusion. **1909** WEBSTER, Psychophysiologic. **1912** L. BLOOMFIELD in C. F. Hockett *Leonard Bloomfield Anthol.* (1970) 37 Sound-change and analogy..are, respectively, psycho-physiologic and psychologic processes. **1927** J. RIVIERE tr. *Freud's Ego & Id* ii. 31 Psycho-physiology has fully discussed the manner in which the body attains its special position among other objects in the world of perception. **1936** *Psychol. Rev.* XLIII. 411 The loudness scale will probably be utilized extensively by psychophysiologists and acoustical engineers. **1958** A. R. RADCLIFFE-BROWN in M. N. Srinivas *Method Social Anthropol.* I. iii. 45 The determination of what mental differences are correlated with these differences of cerebral structure is a task for the psychologist or psychophysiologist. **1960** *Times Lit. Suppl.* 3 June 335/1 The new sciences of sociology and psychophysiology have both increasingly proposed that whether dealing with the crowd or the creative mind there are new skilled and precise ways of obtaining obedience, consent and, indeed, cooperation. **1972** *Sci. Amer.* June 91/1 The psycho-physiological basis of how contrast enables the visual system to distinguish contours. **1976** *Jrnl. Psychiatric Res.* XIII. 7 Three members of each group received a secondary or tertiary diagnosis of 'psychophysiologic gastrointestinal disorder'. **1977** *Nature* 28 Apr. 831/1 The intragroup social pressure determines the gonadal development of the subdominants. Their testes are smaller and show little or no mature testicular tissue. Low ranking males are psychophysiologically castrated.

'psychoplasm (-plæz(ə)m). [f. Gr. ψῡχή soul, mind + πλάσμα anything formed, PLASM.] A name for the basis of consciousness conceived as a substance corresponding and correlative to PROTOPLASM. Hence **psycho'plasmic** *a.*, pertaining to or of the nature of psychoplasm.

1874 LEWES *Probl. Life & Mind* I. 118 The vital organism we have seen to be evolved from the Bioplasm, and we may now see how the psychical organism is evolved from what may be analogically called the Psychoplasm... The movements of the Bioplasm constitute Vitality; the movements of the Psychoplasm constitute Sensibility. *a* **1881** A. BARRATT *Phys. Metempiric* (1883) 219 This leads to the question of the evolution of foci or monads from impersonal consciousness or psychoplasm. **1890** *Cent. Dict.*, Psychoplasmic.

psycho-political, -politics: see PSYCHO-.

psychopomp (ps-, 'saɪkəʊpɒmp). Also **'psychopompos.** [ad. Gr. ψῡχοπομπός, f. ψῡχή soul + πομπός conductor, guide.] A conductor of souls to the place of the dead. Also, the spiritual guide of a (living) person's soul; a person who acts as a guide of the soul.

In Greek, a name applied to Charon; more commonly to Hermes, the Anubis of Egypt, and to Apollo (Plut. 2. 758 B).

1863 W. K. KELLY *Curios. Indo-Europ. Trad. & Folk Lore* 111 The other Aryan psychopomp, the cow. **1879** M. D. CONWAY *Demonol.* I. II. v. 129 The appearance of mice prognosticated of old the appearance of the præter-natural rat-catcher and psychopomp. **1920** WEBSTER, Psycho-pomp .., psycho-pompos. **1941** AUDEN *New Year Let.* I. 27 For though the Janus of a joke The candid psychopompos spoke. **1946** *Antiquity* XX. 168 Hermes psychopompos, the mediator between the upper and the nether world. **1951** K. W. BASH tr. *Jacobi's Psychol. C. G. Jung* (ed. 5) III. 135 It is therefore 'an important function of the higher..superpersonal animus that it guides and accompanies as a true Psycho-pompos the wanderings and transformations of the soul'. **1958** L. DURRELL *Balthazar* vi. 144 If I had been in your shoes and the whole damn thing wasn't just a lie to make yourself more interesting to the psychopomps—I'd..well, I'd bloody well try and sleep with him again. **1965** M. BRADBURY *Stepping Westward* vii. 336 He's a psychopomp, that's what he calls himself. You know that word? I think he gets it from Jung. A soul-saver, or something. A man who leads the spirit onward. **1971** *Southerly* XXXI. 12 The concept of the nymphet as psychopomp seems..a grotesque travesty of the Beatrice myth.

Hence (*rare*) **psycho'pompal, psycho'pompous** *adjs.*, of or pertaining to a psychopomp; **psycho'pompically** *adv.*

1855 BAILEY *Mystic*, etc. 8 The god of psychopompous function, round Circling the sun with fourfold force. **1885** STEWART *'Twixt Ben Nevis & Glencoe* xxxix. 291 The psychopompal vehicle, the 'fiery chariot' in which the spirit was conveyed. **1908** R. BROOKE *Lett.* (1968) 121, I, Hermes-like, am coming to fetch you psychopompically to Hell.

psycho-prismatism: see PSYCHO-.

,psychoprophy'laxis. *Med.* Also with hyphen and (*rare*) anglicized as **-prophylaxy.** [f. PSYCHO- + PROPHYLAXIS.] A method intended to reduce or eliminate labour pains in which prenatal women are given an understanding of natural childbirth in order to obtain their physical co-operation with the process.

1958 I. BONSTEIN *Psychoprophylactic Preparation for Painless Childbirth* 5 It will be necessary to use them [*sc.* drugs] each time various difficulties prevent a confinement, prepared by psychoprophylaxy, from being continued until the end. **1960** D. A. MYSHNE tr. *Velvovsky's Painless Childbirth through Psychoprophylaxis* viii. 167 By psychoprophylaxis of labour pain we imply a system of measures aimed at preventing the appearance and development of labour pain and effected through influences exerted on the higher divisions of the central nervous system. **1965** *Observer* 1 Aug. 5/6 Dr. Pierre Vellay..has made Paris a world centre of psycho-prophylaxis. **1972** J.-P. CLERC in N. Morris *Psychosomatic Med. in Obstetr. & Gynæcol.* 76 The first object of psychoprophylaxis is to eliminate the pain which is due to socio-cultural factors and may thus be regarded as psychosomatic. **1978** *Jrnl. R. Soc. Med.* LXXI. 663 Attempts have been made to measure psychological factors.., the benefits of psychoprophylaxis ..and attitudinal aspects to antenatal education, but none have the precision of outcome which the obstetrician expects from tests of somatic function.

So **,psychoprophy'lactic** *a.*, **,psychoprophy'lactically** *adv.*

1958 I. BONSTEIN *Psychoprophylactic Preparation for Painless Childbirth* 5 The theory of the superior nervous activity, established by I. P. Pavlov.., is the basis of the psychoprophylactic preparation for painless childbirth. **1960** D. A. MYSHNE tr. *Velvovsky's Painless Childbirth through Psychoprophylaxis* viii. 199 Most of the time we consider the use of drugs for the purpose of 'enhancing' the pain prevention in psychoprophylactically well prepared women unnecessary. **1964** *New Statesman* 4 Dec. 874/3 Women in this country are most carefully taught how to cooperate with the ordinary maternity unit without abandoning their psychoprophylactic training. **1965** *Observer* 1 Aug. 5/6 The French Government is showing great interest in psycho-prophylactic obstetrics. **1972** E. D. BING in N. Morris *Psychosomatic Med. in Obstetr. & Gynæcol.* 71 Soon our first psychoprophylactically trained women gave birth, and our teachers had become the *monitrices* in order to assist the young mother in labor and delivery.

psychopyrism to **-sensory:** see PSYCHO-.

psycho'sexual, *a.* Also with hyphen. [f. PSYCHO- + SEXUAL *a.*] Involving the mental and emotional aspects of the sexual impulse.

1897 H. ELLIS *Stud. Psychol. Sex* I. iii. 73 (*heading*) Psychosexual inversion. *Ibid.* iv. 99 In other cases there is some degree of psycho-sexual hermaphroditism. **1913** A. A. BRILL tr. *Freud's Interpretation of Dreams* v. 200 Anxiety in dreams may be of a psychoneurotic nature, or it may originate in psychosexual excitements, in which case the anxiety corresponds to a repressed *libido.* **1946** *Mind* LV. 347 There are chapters sketching types of psycho-neurosis, psychosis, psycho-sexual disorder and other social disorders. **1963** *New Yorker* 29 June 84 The great unresolved psychosexual dilemma of modern man and woman. **1970** G. GREER *Female Eunuch* 43 Not all the massage in the world will ensure satisfaction, for it is a matter of psycho-sexual release. **1970** *Nature* 17 Oct. 203/2 Experimental studies to determine the psycho-sexual effects of pornography. **1976** S. HYNES *Auden Generation* v. 147 The [poem's] problem is set entirely in psycho-sexual terms.

Hence **,psychosexu'ality; psycho'sexually** *adv.*

1910 *Jrnl. Abnormal Psychol.* Apr.–May 67 Not only must the physician himself be able to approach the subject without prudishness and lewdness, but he must perforce know something about psychosexuality. **1912** A. A. BRILL tr. *Freud's Sel. Papers on Hysteria* (ed. 2) xi. 202 We..prefer to speak of psychosexuality, thus laying stress on the fact that the psychic factor of the sexual life should neither be overlooked nor underestimated. **1925** Psychosexuality [see FIXATION 3 b]. **1934** WEBSTER, Psychosexually. **1956** *Nature* 14 Jan. 54/2 Through anthropological investigations, we have some idea how they develop psychosexually in other cultures. **1971** CAUTHERY & COLE *Fundamentals of Sex* v. 170 They are pathologically promiscuous but rarely obtain much pleasure from sex and are usually underdeveloped psychosexually.

‖**psychosis** (ps-, saɪ'kəʊsɪs). Pl. **-oses** (-'əʊsi:z). [a. late Gr. ψυχωσις animation, principle of life, f. ψῡχόω I give soul or life to: but in mod. use taken as = condition of the psyche or mind.]

1. *Path.* Any kind of mental affection or derangement; esp. one which cannot be ascribed to organic lesion or neurosis (cf. NEUROSIS 1). In mod. use, any mental illness or disorder that is accompanied by hallucinations, delusions, or mental confusion and a loss of contact with external reality, whether attributable to an organic lesion or not.

1847 tr. *Feuchtersleben's Med. Psychol.* (Syd. Soc.) 11 The nosography which aims at exhibiting the phenomena, the natural history, and the so called system of psychoses. **1874**

MAUDSLEY *Respons. in Ment. Dis.* i. 33 No wonder that the criminal psychosis, which is the mental side of the neurosis, is for the most part an intractable malady, punishment being of no avail to produce a permanent reformation. **1879** LEWES *Stud. Psychol.* 26 Pathologists call it a psychosis, as if it were a lesion of the unknown psyche. **1924** J. RIVIERE tr. *Freud's Coll. Papers* I. iv. 72 The ego rejects the unbearable idea.. and behaves as if the idea had never occurred to the person at all. But, as soon as this process has been successfully carried through, the person..will have developed a psychosis, and his state can only be described as one of 'hallucinatory confusion'. **1939** E. GLOVER *Psycho-Analysis* iv. 34 When deep guilt erupts, as in the depressive psychoses, we find that the self-accusations are not justified in reality. They are delusional. **1946** R. B. CATTELL *Description & Measurement of Personality* ii. 30 Psychoses are both endogenous and exogenous, organic and psychogenic... Some exogenous psychoses are..organic, in ..that the provoking environmental influence—e.g., alcohol or syphilis—is organic. **1957** C. PFEIFFER in H. Abramson *Neuropharmacol.* (1959) 231 We have tried the Akerfeldt test in the model LSD psychosis in human volunteers. **1973** *Sci. Amer.* Sept. 117/3 The severe mental disorders we have learned to deal with more effectively are the psychoses, the most prominent of which are schizophrenia and manic-depressive psychosis. Psychoses are severe disorders characterized by profound and pervasive alterations of mood, disorganization of thought and withdrawal from social interactions into fantasy.

2. *Psychol.* A change in the psychic state; an activity or movement of the psychic organism, as distinguished from neurosis (NEUROSIS 2).

1871, **1882** [see NEUROSIS 2]. **1907** RAMSAY in *Expositor* Sept. 213 Feelings, moods, emotional consciousnesses or psychoses.

psycho-'social, *a.* Also without hyphen. [f. PSYCHO- + SOCIAL *a.*] Pertaining to the influence of social factors on an individual's mind or behaviour, and to the interrelation of behavioural and social factors; also, more widely, pertaining to the interrelation of mind and society in human development.

1899 F. W. MOORE tr. *Gumplowicz's Outl. Sociol.* II. 83 There are also psycho-social phenomena, such as language, customs, rights, religion etc., arising from the action of social elements with or upon the individual mind. **1903** *Amer. Jrnl. Sociol.* VIII. 762 In another quarter it is held that sociology is concerned only with the action of human groups on one another—social phenomena—and the influence of the group on its individual members—psycho-social phenomena. **1927** OGBURN & GOLDENWEISER *Social Sci.* xxiv. 303 Economics should also profit from such studies as the social psychologists, in the light of their knowledge of psycho-social mechanisms, see fit to make of specific institutional influences and controls. **1953** J. S. HUXLEY *Evolution in Action* i. 12 We may call these three phases [of evolution] the inorganic or, if you like, cosmological; the organic or biological; and the human or psycho-social. *Ibid.* vi. 134 Psycho-social evolution.. operates by cultural transmission. **1954** [see IDENTITY 10 c]. **1958** *Listener* 3 July 12/1 The possibility of conscious purpose arose and for the first time became a factor in man's subsequent evolution, which may be defined by Sir Julian Huxley's term as psycho-social. **1970** *Nature* 31 Oct. 422/1 The original aim of this investigation was to compare the psychosocial characteristics of a group of heroin pushers with those of a group of heroin users who did not sell drugs. **1971** I. G. GASS et al. *Understanding Earth* ix. 125/1 The noösphere..produces idea-systems by processes of psycho-social evolution. **1977** P. B. & J. S. MEDAWAR *Life Science* vi. 53 It is because of the primacy of language as the agency which provides the link between one generation and the next that exosomatic evolution is often referred to as 'cultural' or 'psychosocial' evolution.

Hence **psycho-'socially** *adv.*

1946 [see PSYCHOSOMATICALLY *adv.*]. **1972** *Sci. Amer.* July 81/3 Is it in fact possible to attribute the retarded growth of psychosocially deprived children to sleep patterns that inhibit the secretion of growth hormone?

psycho-socio- to **-sophy**: see PSYCHO-.

psychoso'matic, *a.* and *sb.* [f. PSYCHO- + SOMATIC *a.* and *sb.*] **A.** *adj.* **a.** Involving or depending on both the mind and the body as mutually dependent entities.

1863 C. READE *Hard Cash* II. xi. 119 The nocturnal and diurnal attendance of a Psycho-physical physician, who knows the Psychosomatic relation of body and mind. **1930** M. W. CALKINS in C. Murchison *Hist. Psychol. in Autobiogr.* I. 44 This biological form of personalistic psychology studies the psychophysical, or better the psychosomatic organism. **1933** H. DEVINE *Rec. Adv. Psychiatry* (ed. 2) i. 1 The purpose of this chapter is to discuss the modern concept of 'psychosomatic unity', or, as it is sometimes termed, the concept of 'the organism-as-a-whole'. **1956** E. L. MASCALL *Christian Theol. & Nat. Sci.* vii. 270 A human being is not just a spirit that is temporarily condemned to inhabit a material garment, but is a highly complicated psycho-somatic unity, in which the body is an essential constituent. **1976** *Verbatim* Sept. 11/2 The biblical view of personality was psychosomatic (and distinct from Platonic dualism—'the body is the prison-house of the soul'). So in both the Hebrew and Christian Scriptures, what we would call psychic or spiritual states are freely ascribed to physical organs and other parts of the human anatomy.

b. Applied to physical disorders caused or aggravated by mental, emotional, or psychological factors, and (less commonly) to mental or emotional disorders caused or aggravated by physical factors.

1938 S. BECKETT *Murphy* x. 219 Murphy..did not suffer from this—er—psychosomatic fistula. **1947** J. STEINBECK *Wayward Bus* 170 She called her mother's [headaches] psychosomatic and psychotic. **1950** A. HUXLEY *Themes & Variations* i. 67 Hypertension, neurosis, psychosis and all the varieties of psycho-somatic disorders. **1957** *New Biol.* XXII. 83 These are the so-called psychosomatic disorders. The distinctive feature of these illnesses is that, although they are of nervous origin, they come to the attention of patient and physician through some malfunctioning of an organ. **1958** H. L. & R. R. ANSBACHER *Indiv. Psychol. of Adler* II. xi. 286 The role of organ inferiority in psychosomatic disturbances proper will be discussed in the next chapter. **1964** *Ann. Reg.* *1963* 414 Mental strain..had often led to psychosomatic illness. **1975** B. WOOD *Killing Gift* v. iii. 150 We've built up a really solid case, at least statistically, for psychosomatic influence on breast-cancer incidence.

c. Applied to the branch of medicine concerned with the relations between the mind and the body.

1939 (*title of periodical*) Psychosomatic medicine. **1939** *Psychiatry* II. 465/1 Psychosomatic Medicine covers a different and broader field. Its object is to study in their interrelation the psychological and physiological aspects of all normal and abnormal bodily functions and thus to integrate somatic therapy and psychotherapy. **1946** *Jrnl. R. Aeronaut. Soc.* L. 263/2 The American Army had a separate section of the Medical Service dealing with what was called psychosomatic medicine. **1960** *20th Cent.* Mar. 267 Psychosomatic research has revealed that almost every common disease can have an emotional component. **1971** *Country Life* 9 Sept. 646/4 Psychosomatic medicine today appears to be making a full-circle exploration.

B. *sb. pl.* (const. as *sing.*). The field of study concerned with the relationship between mind and body.

1941 *Amer. Jrnl. Psychiatry* XCVII. 781 We will take up the present day research trends in the following order:.. psychosomatics (psychophysiology). **1941** *Psychosomatic Med.* III. 332, I surveyed ten years' literature in the field of psychosomatics. **1946** B. MITTLELMAN in P. L. Harriman *Encycl. Psychol.* 678 It is obvious..from its problems and methods that psychosomatics represents a synthesis of several streams of psychological and medical investigation. **1966** *N.Y. State Jrnl. Med.* LXVI. 3157/1 The view of the skin as a major organ of communication is not a new one; it is a basic concept of psychosomatic medicine. But if the ECM proposed here are more fully identified, some of the 'metaphors' of psychosomatics will turn out to be descriptions of real events. **1975** B. WOOD *Killing Gift* IV. i. 131 His very next paper..was on psychosomatics... He chaired a ..conference on the psychosomatics of cancer.

Hence **psychoso'matically** *adv.*, in a psychosomatic manner; *esp.* through the (unconscious) effect of the mind on the body; **psychoso'maticist**, an expert or specialist in psychosomatic medicine; **psycho'somatism** (*rare*), psychosomatics; **psycho'somatist** = PSYCHOSOMATICIST.

1854 J. C. BUCKNILL *Unsoundness of Mind* 15 The psycho-somatists find in the liability of the cerebral instrument to disease, a reasonable basis for the irresponsibility of the insane. **1946** *Lancet* 10 Aug. 190/2 Epidemiology..was founded and formulated mainly upon experience gained by the study of infectious diseases, but its use as a framework of interpretation is equally applicable to many modes of morbid behaviour that are manifestations of disturbances of emotional development—i.e., of 'life' viewed psychologically, psychosomatically, and psychosocially. **1957** *Time* 4 Nov. 56/2 It was the story of a girl who went psychosomatically deaf in emotional flight from her role as the ears of a deaf father, mother and brother. **1960** *20th Cent.* Mar. 268 Psychosomatists believe..that each of us possesses a built-in homeostatic mechanism designed to keep us healthy. *Ibid.* 269 This does not mean that psychosomatists attribute all illnesses, invariably, to states of mind. *Ibid.*, Psychosomatism is not, therefore, a 'craze'. Until less than a century ago every great medical school—Hippocratean and Christian alike—subscribed to what Mr. Jelly sneers at as the 'argot' of treating 'the whole man'. **1960** *Spectator* 14 Oct. 555 The first practising psychosomatist—if the term is allowable—that I had met. **1962** N. E. WHITTEN in A. Dundes *Mother Wit* (1973) 418/1 The only reason that the effects of a spell can be removed is that they are psychosomatically caused in the first place. **1962** C. L. BUXTON *Study of Psychophysical Methods for Relief of Childbirth Pain* i. 2 The very environment thought by psychosomaticists to contribute to difficult, prolonged and painful labor is everywhere present in this episode. **1971** *Time* 7 June 96/2 The family physician bucks the case to a psychosomaticist, who flounders in jargon. **1976** *Times Lit. Suppl.* 10 Sept. 1105/2 She was psychosomatically deaf for a week.

psychosomimetic: see PSYCHOTOMIMETIC *a.* and *sb.*

psychosphere: see PSYCHO-.

psychostasy (-ˈɒstəsɪ). Also in Gr. form **psychostasia** (-ˈsteɪzɪə). [ad. Gr. ψῡχοστασία, f. ψῡχή life, soul + στάσις putting, setting, weighing.] A weighing of souls; in *Anc. Mythol.* supposed to take place during a combat, the combatant having the lighter soul being slain.

1850 LEITCH tr. *C. O. Müller's Anc. Art* §397 (ed. 2) 527 The *Psyche* or *Eidolon* appears floating away from dying persons on the vase..at the psychostasy. **1871** P. SMITH *Anc. Hist. East* ix. §21 (1881) 177 The judgement of the dead is often represented on coffins and in the Ritual, under the figure of weighing the souls (*psychostasy*). **1892** W. E. BARNES *Test. Abraham* 71, I have failed to detect any clear description of the Psychostasy in the Apocalyptic literature.

psychostatics (-ˈstætɪks). [f. Gr. ψῡχή soul + στατικ-ός pertaining to weighing: see prec. and STATICS.] †**a.** = PSYCHOSTASY. *Obs.* **b.** *Psychol.* The study of the conditions of mental phenomena.

1719 *Freethinker* No. 149 ¶1 Sufficient to warrant my calling this Paper by the mechanical Term of Psycho-staticks; or, in plain English, the Weighing of Souls. **1874** LEWES *Probl. Life & Mind* I. 115 The conditions of these [organic] phenomena..may be classed (by a serviceable extension of the term statics) under the heads of Biostatics and Psychostatics. **1879** W. L. COURTNEY in *Fortn. Rev.* Sept. 326 The Criticism of Mr. Lewes on Kant is that he confused a question of Psychogenesis, or the growth of intelligence, with a question of Psycho-statics (if the expression may be allowed), that is, an analysis of the developed human mind.

So **psycho'static, psycho'statical** *adjs.*, of or pertaining to psychostatics; hence **psycho'statically** *adv.*, in reference to psychostatics.

1719 *Freethinker* No. 149 ¶5 Beneath this Psychostatical Experiment, One may see a mixt multitude, made up of several of the Religious Orders in the Romish Church. **1874** LEWES *Probl. Life & Mind* I. 121 Corresponding with the Biostatical laws..there are three Psychostatical laws. *Ibid.* 216 The Mind, considered psychostatically. **1890** *Cent. Dict.*, Psychostatic.

psychostimulant: see PSYCHO-.

psycho'surgery. [f. PSYCHO- + SURGERY.] Brain surgery intended to alter the behaviour of patients with certain kinds of severe mental stress or disorder.

1936 *Q. Cumul. Index Medicus* XIX. 249/1 First attempts at psychosurgery using leukotome; technic and results. **1938** *Jrnl. Nerv. & Mental Dis.* LXXXVIII. 589 (*heading*) Psychosurgery. Effect on certain mental symptoms of surgical interruption of pathways in the frontal lobe. **1952** METTLER & CANDIS in F. A. Mettler *Psychosurgical Probl.* xvi. 319 As a result of such adverse criticism practitioners of psychosurgery were forced to restrict the operative procedure to more rostral areas. **1973** *Nature* 23 Mar. 222/3 Unlike the classical lobotomy operation,..psychosurgery now rarely involves actually cutting into the brain... Psychosurgery, which is designed to alter behaviour, is usually distinguished from the treatment of epilepsy and the removal of brain tumours. **1977** M. EDELMAN *Political Lang.* iv. 58 Some psychiatrists..see political demonstrators or ghetto rioters as sick, calling for drugs or psychosurgery.

Hence **psycho'surgical** *a.*; also **'psycho-surgeon**, a surgeon specializing in psycho-surgery.

1945 WEBSTER Add., Psychosurgeon. **1946** *Canad. Med. Assoc. Jrnl.* LV. 435/1 In 1941 the research unit of the Toronto Psychiatric Hospital embarked upon the psychosurgical treatment of hopelessly mentally ill patients. **1949** M. CLARK *Medicine on March* v. 99 Summing up their ten years' work, the two psychosurgeons declared: 'The results are sufficiently good to warrant the use of prefrontal lobotomy..for the relief of the very serious and chronic forms of mental disease.' **1950** [see LEUCOTOMY]. **1952** B. WOLFE *Limbo '90* (1953) xxii. 368 The phony rapist's phony premises become the premises of the psycho-surgeon's science. **1972** *Lancet* 8 July 70/1 The modern psychosurgeon must be versatile enough to employ different operations for different symptom complexes. **1972** M. CRICHTON *Terminal Man.* vi. 46 Computer scientists and neurobiologists had worked together for several years. From that association had come Form Q, and programs like George and Martha, and new psychosurgical techniques.

psychosyndrome, -synthesis, etc.: see PSYCHO-.

psycho-technic (-ˈtɛknɪk), *sb.* and *a.* Also without hyphen. [ad. G. *psychotechnik* sb. (H. Münsterberg *Grundzüge der Psychotechnik* (1914) i. 1): see PSYCHO- and TECHNIC *a.* and *sb.*]

A. *sb.* = PSYCHOTECHNOLOGY. Also *pl.*

1926 *Psychol. Rev.* XXXIII. 402 In the applied division [of psychology], sometimes called psychotechnics, the aim is to make psychological facts useful in many different directions. **1927** *Daily Express* 17 June 12/3 The value of psycho-technic..is that it enables the railway company to eliminate at once the employee who will not be reliable. **1928** H. P. WELD *Psychol. as Sci.* xv. 266 Applied psychology is evidently to be classed with the technical sciences. It may be considered as psycho-technics. **1952** *Brit. Jrnl. Psychol.* XLIII. 83 He is continental in tending to leave to 'psychotechnics' areas which in England would fall within respectable occupational psychology.

B. *adj.* = PSYCHO-TECHNICAL *a.*

1932 *Brit. Jrnl. Psychol.* XXV. 77 These results are of value in..forcing us to realize the importance of attitudes in all judgements..in the ordering of psychotechnic test results. **1957** W. ABELL *Collective Dream in Art* 4 The result has been the gradual emergence of a synthesis which we may call the..'psycho-technic' theory of culture. **1973** *Daily Tel.* 27 Nov. 12/6 Peter Riding's programme vividly simulated part of the 'psycho-technic test' to be undertaken as well as a medical check, written questions on motoring and..an examination in actual driving.

psycho-'technical, *a.* Also without hyphen. [f. PSYCHO- + TECHNICAL *a.*] Pertaining to or concerned with the application of psychological facts or knowledge to practical problems in industry, employment, education, etc.

1903 H. MÜNSTERBERG in *Harvard Psychol. Stud.* I. 654 The science of pedagogy is a psycho-technical discipline which makes education mechanical. **1927** *Daily Express* 17 June 12 Electrical machinery, levers, mechanical puzzles, and complete paraphernalia for psycho-technical tests. **1962** *Guardian* 20 July 5/7 To the applicants for jobs, the 'psychotechnical' examinations were at once ludicrous and frightening.

,psychotech'nology. [f. PSYCHO- + TECHNOLOGY.] The area of study concerned with the practical application of tested knowledge about the human mind or brain.

Hence ˌ**psychotech'nologist**, an expert or specialist in this.

1923 F. A. Kingsbury in *Ann. Amer. Acad. Pol. & Social Sci.* CX. 5/1 Psychotechnology, or applied psychology, is interested in acquiring facts and principles only in so far as they can be turned directly to account in the solution of practical problems, in industry, selling, teaching or other fields of human endeavour. *Ibid.* 8/2 The careful psychotechnologist submits his hypothetical solution of concrete problems to prolonged and severe experimental tests. **1928** H. P. Weld *Psychol. as Sci.* xv. 280 Psychotechnology is a product of this century, and there can be little doubt that it will, in years to come, extend its activities. **1947** *Harvard Univ. Comm. Place of Psychol. in Ideal Univ.* 11 Values of the science and of psychotechnology may be exemplified more readily than enumerated. *Ibid.* 23 Already the demand greatly exceeds the supply of trained psychologists, psychotechnologists, .. etc. **1953** J. B. Carroll *Study of Lang.* vii. 196 In Europe applied psychology is widely identified as psychotechnology. **1973** *Sci. Amer.* Sept. 117/1 The potential power of this developing 'psychotechnology' is .. creating concern about unwarranted intrusions into personal privacy and individual rights. **1973** R. L. & R. K. Schwitzgebel (*title*) Psychotechnology: electronic control of mind and behavior.

psychotheism: see psycho-.

psychotherapeutic (ps-, ˌsaɪkəʊθɛrə'pjuːtɪk), *a.* and *sb.* Also with hyphen. [f. psycho- + therapeutic.]

A. *adj.* Of or pertaining to the treatment of disease by 'psychic', i.e. hypnotic, influence. Also, of, pertaining to, or characterized by psychotherapy.

1890 in *Cent. Dict.* **1901** *Westm. Gaz.* 2 Apr. 5/2 For the study of mesmerism, hypnotism, and other psychic phenomena and their adaptation to the cure and prevention of disease, the London Psycho-Therapeutic Society was inaugurated yesterday. **1914** A. A. Brill tr. *Freud's Psychopathol. Everyday Life* v. 93 The psychotherapeutic procedure which I employ in the solution and removal of neurotic symptoms. **1957** *Times Lit. Suppl.* 1 Nov. 659/4 That organized religion has been the greatest psychotherapeutic system ever invented is one of Jung's most famous dicta. **1963** A. Heron *Towards Quaker View of Sex* 51 All the large teaching hospitals have psychiatric out-patient departments of varying size and with more or less psychotherapeutic help to hand. **1970** *Jrnl. Gen. Psychol.* LXXXIII. 194 Laffal has applied this approach in studies of .. psychotherapeutic interviews. **1976** *Times Lit. Suppl.* 16 July 872/2 The spiritual healers either operate on the margin or they must be certified members or associates of a recognized psychotherapeutic fraternity.

B. *sb.* in pl. form ˌ**psychothera'peutics**. The subject of the treatment of disease by 'psychic', i.e. hypnotic, influence. Also = psychotherapy. Rarely in sing. form **psychotherapeutic**.

1872 D. H. Tuke *Illustrations of Influence of Mind on Body* p. ix, The medical reader .., I hope, may be induced to employ Psycho-therapeutics in a more methodical way than heretofore. **1887** Miss F. P. Cobbe in *Contemp. Rev.* June 797 Who will step forward and help to clear the way for this science of Psycho-Therapeutics? **1889** C. L. Tuckey (*title*) Psycho-Therapeutics; or, Treatment by Sleep and Suggestion. **1900** Hopkirk tr. *Moll* (*title*) Hypnotism: Including a Study of the Chief Points of Psycho-therapeutics and Occultism. **1903** F. W. H. Myers *Hum. Personality* II. 515 Suggestions involving .. bodily odour and chemical conditions have thus far been confined to psycho-therapeutics. *Ibid.* 527 That form of psycho-therapeutic which consists in a clairvoyant diagnosis .. followed perhaps by advice avowedly based upon a recollection of earthly learning. **1906** *Boston Med. & Surg. Jrnl.* 8 Nov. 542/1 A fundamental difficulty in psychotherapeutics up to this time has been a lack of method. **1933** *Mind* XLII. 114 Abnormal psychology .. has generalised with a freedom astonishing to those who are familiar with the logical austerities of science. This may be allowed to psychotherapeutics, but not to anything that calls itself psychology.

So ˌ**psychothera'peutical** *a.* = psychotherapeutic; **psychothera'peutically** *adv.*, by means of psychotherapy, in a psychotherapeutic manner; ˌ**psychothera'peutist**, one skilled in or practising psychotherapeutics.

1902 *Academy* 12 Apr. 388/1 For two and a half centuries a psycho-therapeutical institution has flourished in hundreds of English towns and villages, but it is usually called a Friends' Meeting. **1905** *Daily Chron.* 5 May 4/4, 'I would suggest', said Mr. Arthur Hallam, of the Psychotherapeutists or Mind-Healers, 'that you come and see us at work'. **1906** *Amer. Jrnl. Med. Sci.* Oct. 499 The neurasthenic women .. rested in bed, were isolated, and treated 'psychotherapeutically' much as were the hysterical. *Ibid.* 520 The psychotherapeutist should be an honest man and an expert clinician. **1909** H. Münsterberg *Psychotherapy* p. ix, Since that time I have never ceased to work psycho-therapeutically in the psychological laboratory. **1957** *Listener* 12 Sept. 401/1 The psycho-therapeutist .. no longer confines his attention to the classical mental disorders, but, .. has set up advisory centres to deal with problems of life or .. mental hygiene, arising at almost any phase from infancy to senescence. **1962** J. Money *Reading Disability* i. 17 Reading tuition is individualized, scholastically and psychotherapeutically, as much as economics permit.

psycho'therapy. [f. psycho- + therapy.] The treatment of disease by 'psychic' methods. In mod. use, the treatment of disorders of the mind or personality by psychological or psychophysiological methods. [Cf. van Renterghem & van Eeden *Clinique de Psychothérapie Suggestive* (Brussels, 1889).]

Quot. 1853, an isolated use, represents a different sense.
1853 *Jrnl. Psychol. Med. & Mental Path.* VI. 268 (*heading*) Psychotherapeia, or the remedial influence of mind. **1892** F. W. van Eeden in *Med. Mag.* I. 233 As a general term for our treatment we selected in 1889, 'Suggestive Psycho-therapy'. We called psychotherapy every description of therapeutics that cures by means of the intervention of the psychical functions of the sufferer. This title is borrowed from Hack Tuke... Psycho-therapy .. has .. had the misfortune to be taken in tow by hypnotism. **1897** T. H. Kellogg *Text-bk. Mental Dis.* xi. 497 By the term psychotherapy is signified .. every means and every possible agency which primarily affects the psychical rather than the physical organization of the patient in a curative direction. **1904** *Westm. Gaz.* 1 June 4/2 Though the word 'Psychotherapy' be new, and popular in America—the land of Faith-Healers—mental therapeutics acting through the 'unconscious mind' is no new thing. **1906** *Amer. Jrnl. Med. Sci.* CXXXII. 499 Prof. Dejerine was treating the psychoneuroses, especially hysteria and neurasthenia, by isolation and psychotherapy. **1947** *Nature* 4 Jan. 38/2 Psychotherapy may be useful for the criminal, but it is prolonged, and an impractical treatment with present resources. **1958** *Sunday Times* 15 June 13/3 By psychotherapy is meant the systematic application of psychological principles to the treatment of psychogenic ill-health and maladjustment. **1963** A. Heron *Towards Quaker View of Sex* 50 A number of psychotherapy clinics which give treatment for sexual difficulties. **1976** Smythies & Corbett *Psychiatry* ii. 19 Psychotherapy consists very largely in helping people to grow up, to exchange the egocentric child's role for the mature role of the adult.

Hence **psycho'therapist**, a specialist in or practitioner of psychotherapy.

1909 A. A. Brill tr. *Freud's Sel. Papers Hysteria* iii. 55, I was not always a psychotherapist but like other neuropathologists I was educated to the use of focal diagnosis and electrical prognosis. **1923** *Daily Mail* 19 Jan. 7 An earnest warning to nervous persons to avoid spiritualism is given by Dr. W. Stekel, the Viennese neurologist and psycho-therapist. **1930** R. S. Woodworth *Psychology* (ed. 8) xiii. 568 Many psychotherapists avoid the use of hypnosis because, as they say, it does not get to the root of the trouble. **1976** Smythies & Corbett *Psychiatry* xvii. 291 Most psychotherapists refuse to give specific advice as to what their patient's conduct should be in cases where ethical problems are concerned.

psychotic (-'ɒtɪk), *a.* and *sb.* [f. Gr. type *ψῡχωτικ-ός, f. ψύχωσις: see psychosis and -otic.]

A. *adj.* **a.** Of or pertaining to psychosis. **b.** = psychagogic *a.* 3.

1890 Billings *Nat. Med. Dict.*, *Psychotic*, psychagogic. **1895** *Syd. Soc. Lex.*, *Psychotic*, belonging to Psychosis. Also, used as synonymous with *Psychagogic* or *Analeptic*. **1920** C. S. Read *Milit. Psychiatry in Peace & War* ii. 21 These figures .. include pure epilepsy without any psychotic complications. **1949** *Endeavour* VIII. 37/1 The use of electric shock therapy for the treatment of certain types of psychotic patients is sometimes complicated by injuries suffered during the electrically produced convulsions. **1957** *Jrnl. Brit. Interplanetary Soc.* XVI. 8 Among psychologists, 'psychotic break' refers to the breaking loose of feeling from its previously adequate controls. **1965** J. Pollitt *Depression & its Treatment* i. 4 In advanced states the patient lacks insight and becomes psychotic. **1971** *Brit. Med. Bull.* XXVII. 77/1 An equally strong case can be made for the opposite view, that psychotic and neurotic forms of depression lie on the same continuum.

B. *absol.* as *sb.* A person with a psychosis.

1910 *Jrnl. Nervous & Mental Disease* XXXVII. 633 Thus arise the well-known 'explanation-delusions' of the psychotic. **1921** E. J. Kempf *Psychopathology* xiv. 718 Many ask the question .., 'Why do all neurotics and psychotics have sexual difficulties?' **1939** J. Dollard in A. Dundes *Mother Wit* (1973) 278/2 Psychotics in American hospitals display disorders of perception. **1958** M. Argyle *Relig. Behaviour* ix. 109 Many psychotics believe themselves to be religious leaders, prophets or mystics. **1962** *Lancet* 8 Dec. 1212/1 It might be that because some beds had been freed from psychotics, patients with neuroses or personality disorders .. could be admitted to hospital. **1975** B. Meggs *Matter of Paradise* vii. 189 You're asking .. whether .. we might hope to identify a deteriorated psychotic *before* he enters government.

Hence **psy'chotically** *adv.*

1961 in Webster. **1977** *Irish Press* 29 Sept. 6/5 The ingredients include a weak and unsuccessful father who died young and an over protective mother whose motives were selfish rather than loving, and who was almost psychotically indifferent to George's progress except to record the inconvenience it caused her.

psychoticism (saɪ'kɒtɪsɪz(ə)m). [f. psychotic *a.* + -ism.] The condition or state of being psychotic or of displaying psychotic tendencies; esp. as a factor showing liability to psychosis included in certain types of personality assessment.

1950 H. J. Eysenck in *Jrnl. Personality* XIX. 129 His [*sc.* Kretschmer's] theory can best be represented in terms of two orthogonal axes, one measuring schizothymia-cyclothymia, the other normality-psychotic abnormality or 'psychoticism'. **1955** *Jrnl. Mental Sci.* CI. 876 The effect of insulin therapy is not dependent upon the initial degree of psychoticism as used in the present sense. **1957** R. B. Cattell *Personality & Motivation* xvi. 719 At present a psychoticism measure would be considerably contaminated and distorted. **1957**, etc. [see neuroticism]. **1960** Payne & Hewlett in H. Eysenck *Exper. in Personality* II. 11 It was demonstrated that only one factor was necessary to account for the differences observed between the three groups. This factor was labelled 'psychoticism'. **1964** [see introversion 1 b]. **1977** *New Society* 7 Apr. 33/3 This book aims to establish psychoticism .. alongside neuroticism, extraversion and intelligence... The attribute it measures is a halfway stage to psychosis, as neuroticism is to neurosis.

psychotogenic (saɪˌkɒtəʊ'dʒɛnɪk), *a.* [f. as next + -genic.] = psychotomimetic *a.*

1956 *Arch. Neurol. & Psychiatry* LXXV. 122/1 To the neurologist the psychotogenic agents offer a special challenge. **1962** *Lancet* 27 Jan. 200/2 There is impressive evidence of the psychotogenic effects of some adrenaline derivatives. **1971** *Nature* 19 Nov. 152/2 The differential behavioural response of subjects to *d* and *l*-amphetamine might provide clues to psychotogenic mechanisms.

Hence (as back-formations) **psy'chotogen**, a psychotomimetic substance; **psyˌchoto'genesis**, the production of a psychosis or psychosis-like state.

1959 *Neuropharmacology: Trans. 4th Conf., 1957* 223 Relationship between endogenous substances that are found in the brain—epinephrine, norepinephrine, and .. serotonin —and the possible relationship to the exogenous psychotogens. **1960** *Clin. Pharmacol. & Therapeutics* I. 251/2 The recovery of a chronically psychotic patient coincidentally with the administration of some drug is as dramatic as .. the drug-induced psychosis. Recovery, however, is an even less satisfactory foundation for a psychopharmacologic theory than is psychotogenesis. **1971** *Nature* 19 Nov. 152/2 If noradrenergic mechanisms and behaviourally correlated motor stimulation were critical in psychotogenesis then one might expect *d*-amphetamine to have ten times the potency of the *l* form in inducing psychosis as a behavioural effect. **1974** M. C. Gerald *Pharmacol.* xvii. 318 Drugs in this same category are also termed hallucinogens, psychedelics, psychotogens, psychodysleptics, and so forth. **1976** *Nature* 8 Apr. 490/1 For many years the presence of an endogenous psychotogen in schizophrenia has been sought. **1977** *Lancet* 27 Aug. 449/2 Further study of psychotogenesis and of the relation between morphinoids and endogenous neurotransmitters and neuromodulators will probably .. clarify the biochemistry both of addiction and of schizophrenia.

psychotomimetic (saɪˌkɒtəʊmɪ'mɛtɪk, -maɪ'mɛtɪk), *a.* and *sb.* Also †**psychoso-**. [Orig. formed as *psychosomimetic*, f. psychos(is + -o + mimetic *a.*, and later altered to match psychotic *a.*] **A.** *adj.* Having an effect on the mind orig. likened to that of a psychotic state, with abnormal changes in thought, perception, and mood and a subjective feeling of an expansion of consciousness; of or pertaining to a drug with this effect.

1956 R. W. Gerard in *Neuropharmacology: Trans. 2nd Conf., 1955* 132 Let us at least agree to speak of 'so-called' psychoses when we are dealing with them in animals... Along that same line, I have liked a term which I have been using lately—'psychosomimetic'—for these agents instead of 'schizophrenogenic'. **1957** *Neuropharmacology: Trans. 3rd Conf., 1956* 205 (*heading*) Effects of psychosomimetic drugs in animals and man. **1957** H. Osmond in *Ann. N.Y. Acad. Sci.* LXVI. 417 The designation 'psychotomimetic agents' for those drugs that mimic some of the mental aberrations that occur in the psychoses had been suggested by Ralph Gerard and seemed especially appropriate. **1958** M. Jarvik in H. H. Pennes *Psychopharmacology* ix. 204 They have been called psychoso- or psychotomimetic, psychotherapeutic, tranquilizing, ataraxic, .. or, as a general class, psychochemical, neurotropic, .. and a number of other names. **1962** Henderson & Gillespie *Text-bk. Psychiatry* xi. 258 The hallucinogenic (or psychotomimetic) drugs most often employed have been mescaline and lysergic acid (LSD 25). **1964** D. F. Downing in M. Gordon *Psychopharmacological Agents* I. xiii. 562 Psilocybin and psilocin produce a psychotomimetic effect in man .. which is similar to that produced by mescaline or LSD-25. **1967** *Sunday Mail* (Brisbane) 27 Aug. 5/1 In the field of drugs, a medical friend says that if you want another term for psychedelics you could call them .. psychotomimetic. **1970** E. Goode *Marijuana Smokers* vii. 172 The general psychotomimetic questions include: 'Is your skin sensitive?' 'Are you happy?' 'Are colors brighter?' **1970** D. H. Efron *Psychotomimetic Drugs* 5 The use of these psychotomimetic substances in ancient times was either for religious, ceremonial or recreational purposes. **1975** Brimblecombe & Pinder *Hallucinogenic Agents* i. 3 It has been pointed out several times .. that there are well-defined differences between mental states induced by the majority of pyschotomimetic drugs and those encountered in mental illness.

B. *sb.* A psychotomimetic drug.

1957 *Ann. N.Y. Acad. Sci.* LXVI. 418 We are using Gerard's term 'psychotomimetics' generally for compounds that have been called schizogens, psychotica, psychotogens, phantastica, hallucinogens and elixirs. If one believes that the importance of these compounds lies in their capacity to mimic the mental illnesses called psychoses, psychotomimetics would be the choice. **1970** A. T. Shulgin in D. H. Efron *Psychotomimetic Drugs* 25 Ibogaine .. is another example in the family of psychotomimetics, with complex structures and no resemblance to known metabolic materials. **1974** M. C. Gerald *Pharmacol.* xvi. 299 The psychotomimetics (hallucinogens) such as LSD or mescaline produce profound alterations in behavior.

Hence **psyˌchotomi'metically** *adv.*

1963 *Tetrahedron* XIX. 2073 Hashish (marihuana), the psychotomimetically active resin of the female flowering tops of *Cannabis sativa L.* **1970** L. Harmon in D. H. Efron *Psychotomimetic Drugs* 349 So for Dan's N.I.M.H. hospitality (T'was psychotomimetically hip) Great thanks for new lights on mentality And a most unforgettable TRIP. **1973** R. Mechoulam *Marijuana* p. xiii, The structure of only one [cannabinoid], the psychotomimetically inactive cannabinol, had been fully elucidated.

psychotropic (saɪkəʊ'trəʊpɪk, -'trɒpɪk), *a.* and *sb.* Also **-trophic** (-'trəʊfɪk). [f. psycho- + -tropic, -trophic.] **A.** *adj.* Affecting a person's mental state; psychoactive; *spec.* =

PSYCHOTOMIMETIC *a.*; of or pertaining to a drug of this kind.

1956 M. RINKEL in *Neuropharmacology: Trans. 2nd Conf., 1955* 240, I had considerable conversation on this subject with Dr. Goodman..and Dr. Loewi of Utah University. They made the very good proposal of calling all these drugs which affect the mind 'phrenotropic or psychotropic'. This general term would allow for a number of subdivisions: drugs that are beneficial; those which may cause psychosis; [etc.]. **1962** *Listener* 13 Dec. 1003/1 In recent years extravagant hopes have been centred on the psychotropic drugs, drugs which will relieve agitation and depression. **1968** *Sunday Mail* (Brisbane) 10 Nov. 1/2 Traffic in psychotropic drugs—ranging from LSD to sedatives—had reached 'epidemic proportions', the International Narcotics Control Board warned yesterday. **1968** A. GOLDSTEIN et al. *Princ. Drug Action* vi. 474 Despite the nearly universal exposure of the population to the 'legal' psychotropic drugs (alcohol, caffeine, and nicotine), some become habituated and some do not. **1970** *Nature* 7 Feb. 485/1 The essence of the commission's code is a catalogue of drugs of dependence —'psychotrophic drugs' as they are now called. **1972** J. I. M. Stewart *Palace of Art* vii. 66 Art, like a tomtom or a psychotropic drug, can loosen up the mind of an individual exposed to it. **1977** *It* June 2/4 If you enter a state of non-ordinary reality, as you do when you use psychotropic plants, it is only to draw from it what you need in order to see the miraculous character of ordinary reality. **1977** *Lancet* 24–31 Dec. 1326/1 None of the subjects were taking psychotrophic medication at the time of admission. **1978** *Guardian Weekly* 1 Jan. 10/1 Large numbers of prisoners are being given psychotropic drugs as a form of social control rather than medical treatment.

B. *sb.* A psychotropic drug.

1976 *Nature* 29 Apr. p. ix (Advt.), Astra Chemicals is the UK subsidiary of Scandinavia's largest pharmaceutical group which specialises in the research, manufacture and marketing of ethical drugs in the fields of local anaesthetics, bronchodilators, cardiovasculars and psychotropics. **1977** *Proc. R. Soc. Med.* LXX. 766/2 The majority are adults who have deliberately swallowed an overdose of drugs, chiefly in the category of 'psychotropics'.

Hence **psycho'tropically** *adv.*

1962 *Jrnl. Sci. & Industr. Res.* XXIA. 421/2 The psychotropically active hydrazines having a monoamine oxidase inhibiting effect are pronounced antidepressants.

psycho-visual, -vital, -zoic: see PSYCHO-.

psychro- (saɪkrəʊ), comb. form of Gr. ψυχρός cold (cf. PSYCHROMETER, etc.).

psychro'philic *a. Biol.* [-PHILIC], (of an organism, esp. a bacterium) capable of growing at temperatures close to freezing, or having an optimum temperature that is low; so **'psychrophil, -phile** *sb.*, a psychrophilic organism; also as *adj.*, = prec.; **'psychrosphere**, the colder, deeper part of the oceans; hence **psychro'spheric** *a.*; **psychro'tolerance** *Biol.* [ad. G. *psychrotoleranz* (Horowitz-Wlassowa & Grinberg 1933, in *Zentralbl. f. Bakteriol., Parasitenkunde und Infektionskrankheiten* (Abt. 2) LXXXIX. 58)], the property of being able to grow at temperatures close to freezing; (introduced, like *psychrotropic*, because of the ambiguity of *psychrophilic*); so **psychro'tolerant** *a.*; **psychro'trophic** *a. Biol.* [-TROPHIC] = *psychrotolerant* adj. above; so **'psychrotroph**, a psychrotrophic organism.

1928 P. H. FOSTER in C. M. Hilliard *Textbk. Bacteriol.* viii. 95 Psychrophiles are organisms which develop at or very near the freezing point. **1956** *Nature* 16 June 1106 Such barophilic bacteria..are also psychrophil and very stenothermal. **1959** *New Scientist* 3 Dec. 1111/1 Psychrophils also ferment carbohydrates, decompose proteins,..and generally go about their business like other bacteria, except that their metabolism seems to be somewhat slowed up. **1959** *Bacteriol. Rev.* XXIII. 99/1 The unique property of psychrophilic bacteria is the ability to grow well at 0 C. This was recognized from the very beginning of the study of psychrophiles... The essentially erroneous concept that psychrophiles are distinguished by their ability to grow most rapidly below 20 C did not arise until later. **1969** *Nature* 15 Mar. 1031/1 Obligate psychrophiles—organisms able to grow well at 0°C but incapable of growth at moderate temperatures—provide suitable test organisms in this respect. When the obligate psychrophile *Micrococcus cryophilus* is grown in optimal conditions at 20°C, and then transferred to 30°C–5°C above the maximum for this organism—growth halts very quickly. **1897** LEHMANN & NEUMANN *Atlas & Essentials of Bacteriol.* 98 Psychrophilic bacteria: minimum at 0°, best at 15°–20°, maximum at about 30°. These varieties usually live in water. **1958** W. C. FRAZIER *Food Microbiol.* xxiv. 304 At refrigerator temperatures, proteolysis by psychrophilic bacteria like *Pseudomonas* is most likely, and molds may follow. **1963** J. L. STOKES in N. E. Gibbons *Rec. Progress Microbiol.* 190 The maximum growth temperatures of many psychrophilic micro-organisms can be quite high. **1964** [see *mesophilic* adj. s.v. MESO-]. **1975** R. R. GILLIES *Lect. Notes Med. Bacteriol.* iii. 15 Psychrophilic bacteria, i.e. those which grow best at temperatures below 20°C, are non-pathogenic for man but exist in soil and water. **1956** A. T. BRUUN in *Nature* 16 June 1106 (*in figure*) Psychrosphere. **1957** —— in *Mem. Geol. Soc. Amer.* LXVII. 641 The division of the hydrosphere into a warm troposphere and a cold stratosphere, or the Warmwassersphäre and Kaltwassersphäre in the terms of Wüst (1950) is the most pronounced division in the oceanic water masses. In the following the terms thermosphere and psychrosphere are used for these divisions to stress this salient ecological factor. *Ibid.*, The limit of the psychrosphere may be at about 100 meters in the eastern parts of the oceans where there is upwelling, whereas in western regions it may be as deep as 700 meters. **1976** *Nature* 8 Apr. 513/2 Three major elements were involved in the evolution of oceanic circulation during the Cainozoic... The third involves the development of the present-day system of bottom waters of the world ocean, the 'psychrosphere'. **1977** *Ibid.* 2 June 399/2 Aside from benthic foraminifera, psychrospheric ostracods also occur in some Early and Middle Miocene cores, indicating water-depths in excess of 1000 m. **1977** *Sci. Amer.* June 50/3 The bacteria's only way to adapt to the environmental conditions of the deep sea appears to be the acquisition of barotolerance and psychrotolerance. **1959** *Bacteriol. Rev.* XXIII. 98/2 The recognition that low temperatures are not optimum for organisms that grow at 0 C led to the introduction of several other names as replacement for psychrophile. These included..psychro-tolerant. **1970** *Sci. Jrnl.* May 19 Slime is caused by cold resistant, or psychrotolerant, bacteria which are not a health hazard but which produce an objectionable smell. **1979** *Nature* 21 June p. x (Advt.), An excellent survey is thus provided of the importance of psychrotrophic bacteria and of techniques involving psychrotolerant and psychrotrophic micro-organisms. **1963** M. INGRAM in N. E. Gibbons *Rec. Progress Microbiol.* 185 To avoid such misconceptions, the term psychrotroph..has recently been proposed for all organisms able to grow at temperatures near 0 C. **1968** *New Scientist* 18 Apr. 117/2 Farm contamination from..unclean dairy equipment, will allow psychrotrophs to proliferate if milk is stored at 5°–10°C. **1960** B. P. EDDY in *Jrnl. Appl. Bacteriol.* XXIII. 189 The writer considers that the word psychrotrophic..suggested by Dr. D. A. A. Mossel, should be used for bacteria able to grow at + 5° and below, whatever their optimum temperatures. **1975** CAMPBELL & MARSHALL *Sci. of providing Milk for Man* xxiii. 499 Bulk cooling and storage..have made psychrophilic and psychrotrophic bacteria the primary organisms in raw milk.

psychrolute (ps-, 'saɪkrəljuːt). [ad. Gr. ψυχρολούτ-ης a bather in cold water, f. ψυχρολουσία bathing in cold water, f. ψυχρός cold + λούειν to bathe.] One who bathes in the open air daily throughout the winter; *spec.* a member of a society formed *c* 1840 to promote this practice.

1872 BP. SELWYN in Morgan *Univ. Oars* (1873) 302 Many were also psychrolutes, bathing in winter in all states of the river. **1897** *Dict. Nat. Biog.* LI. 339/2 [Sir L. Shadwell] was president of the Society of Psychrolutes, the qualification for the membership..being the daily practice of bathing out of doors from November to March.

So † **psychro'lutist** *Obs.* (*erron.* **pseuchro-**), an advocate of bathing in cold water.

1702 FLOYER *Hot & Cold Bath.* I. iv. (1709) 181 Every Physician will in the next Age be a Pseuchrolutist.

psychrometer (-'ɒmɪtə(r)). *Meteorol.* [f. Gr. ψυχρό-ς cold + -METER; lit. a measurer of cold, a low-temperature thermometer. Badly employed in current use.] *orig.* A thermometer; now, An instrument for measuring the relative humidity of the air; a wet-and-dry-bulb thermometer; a kind of hygrometer.

1727–41 CHAMBERS *Cycl.*, *Psychrometer*, an instrument for measuring the degree of coldness of the air; more usually called thermometer. **1838** *Encycl. Brit.* (ed. 7) XVII. 533/2 Two thermometers are now mounted on the same scale, and the indications of the wet and dry bulbs seen at the same time. This instrument has been termed a psychrometer. **1876** DAVIS *Polaris Exp.* ix. 219 In it were placed the standard thermometer, the wet and dry bulb psychrometers.

Hence **psychro'metric, psychro'metrical** *adjs.*, of or pertaining to the psychrometer or to psychrometry; hygrometrical; **psy'chrometry**, the ascertainment of the degree of humidity of the atmosphere by means of a psychrometer.

1864 WEBSTER, Psychrometrical instruments... Psychrometrical observations. Psychrometry. **1880** *Nature* 4 Mar. 426/2 The values deduced..agree with the observed only with a psychrometric difference of 4°.

‖**psychrophobia** (ps-, ˌsaɪkrəʊ'fəʊbɪə). Also in anglicized form, †'**psychrophoby**. [mod.L. f. Gr. ψυχρό-ς cold + -PHOBIA.] Dread of or sensitiveness to cold; *esp.* dread of cold water.

1727 BAILEY vol. II, *Psychrophobia* [*ed.* **1731** Psychrophoby], a Fear of, or an Aversion to cold Things. **1830** MAUNDER *Dict.*, *Psycrophobia*, a dread of anything cold. **1853–** in DUNGLISON.

psychrophore (ps-, 'saɪkrəfɔə(r)). *Surg.* [f. Gr. ψυχροφόρ-ος carrying cold, f. ψυχρός cold + -φόρος bearing: see -PHORE.] (See quot.)

1890 BILLINGS *Nat. Med. Dict.*, *Psychrophore*, a double-current catheter without an eye; for the application of cold to the urethra, also called refrigerating sound.

†'**psychroˌtechny.** *Obs.* Also ‖**-techne**. [f. as prec. + Gr. τέχνη art.] (See quot. 1730–6.)

1669 *Phil. Trans.* IV. 1141 Specious hopes to attempt something in Psychrotechne. **1730–6** BAILEY (folio) Pref., *Psychrotechny*, the Art of Distillation by Means of Cold.

psychurgy (ps-, 'saɪkɜːdʒɪ). [f. Gr. ψυχο-, PSYCHO- + -εργία working: cf. AUTURGY.] Mental operation or activity.

1896 *N. Brit. Daily Mail* 10 Oct. 4 The Director of the Laboratory of Psychology and Psychurgy at Washington.

psycology, obs. form of PSYCHOLOGY.

'psyctic. *rare.* Also *erron.* **psychtic.** [ad. Gr. ψυκτικ-ός cooling, sb. pl. τὰ ψυκτικά refrigerants.] A cooling medicine; a refrigerant.

[**1693** tr. *Blancard's Phys. Dict.* (ed. 2), *Psyctica*, cooling Medicines.] **1846** SMART Suppl., *Psychtics*, refrigerating medicines. **1864** WEBSTER, *Psychtic*, a refrigerating medicine.

‖**psydracium** (psɪ'dreɪsɪəm). *Path.* Pl. **-ia.** [med.L., ad. Gr. ψυδράκιον a white blister on the tongue-tip, said to be caused by lying, a lie-blister, dim. of ψύδραξ, L. *psydrax*, pl. *psydraces*, f. ψυδρός lying, false.] (See quots.)

1693 tr. *Blancard's Phys. Dict.* (ed. 2), *Psydracia*,..are little Ulcers of the Skin of the Head, like those which are wont to burn the Skin. [*Ibid.*, *Psydraces*,..are little Pustles or Pimples, which break out upon the Skin, like Bubbles, by reason of the Winter Cold.] **1726** QUINCY *Lex. Phys.-Med.*, *Psydracium*, is a pointed white Pustule or Tumor upon the Skin, containing a serous Humour. **1842** in DUNGLISON *Med. Lex.* **1890** in BILLINGS *Nat. Med. Dict.*

Hence **psy'dracious** *a.* (*erron.* **-eous**), pertaining to or of the nature of psydracia.

1822–34 *Good's Study Med.* (ed. 4) IV. 473 *note*, Psydracious pustules may accidentally present themselves. **1842** BURGESS tr. *Cazenave's Man. Dis. Skin* 138 The successive development of psydraceous pustules. **1858** in MAYNE *Expos. Lex.* **1890** BILLINGS *Nat. Med. Dict.*, *Psydracious.*

‖**psykter** ('psɪktə(r)). *Gr.* and *Rom. Antiq.* Also **psycter.** [a. Gr. ψυκτήρ a wine-cooler, agent-n. f. ψύχειν to breathe, blow, cool.] A jar for cooling wine.

1849 SMITH *Dict. Grk. & Rom. Antiq.* (ed. 2), *Psycter*, a wine-cooler,..sometimes made of bronze..or silver. **1857** BIRCH *Anc. Pottery* (1858) II. 67 The psycter, or cooler to prepare it [wine] for drinking. **1931** *Times Lit. Suppl.* 16 July 563/1 There is a psykter signed by Duris. **1948** A. LANE *Gk. Pottery* iv. 48 Cooler (psykter) to be filled with ice or water and lowered into a wine-krater. **1973** 'D. HALLIDAY' *Dolly & Starry Bird* vi. 75 The tables were crowded with skyphoi and kylikes and psykters.

psylla ('sɪlə). *Ent.* Also **Psylla.** [mod.L. (E. F. Germar *Systematis Glossatorum Prodromus* (1811) 14), f. Gr. ψύλλα flea.] Any of the jumping plant-lice belonging to the genus so called or closely related genera, which include several pests.

1852 T. W. HARRIS *Treat. Insects Injurious to Vegetation* (ed. 2) 203 The pear-tree, in Europe, is subject to the attacks of..the pear-tree Psylla. **1891** *Insect Life* IV. 127 We had occasion some time since to abstract Dr. F. Loew's remarks on the Psyllas which inhabit the pear. **1918** W. A. DAVIS *Study Indigo Soils Bihar* 8 In 1907, two diseases appeared simultaneously—the so-called 'wilt' disease and the less serious insect pest 'psylla'. **1933** *Jrnl. R. Hort. Soc.* LVIII. 283 'Eucalyptus Psylla'... Deals with a Psylla attacking Eucalypti in English greenhouses. **1972** SWAN & PAPP *Common Insects N. Amer.* xiii. 141 Pear Psylla... A major pest of pears, first introduced into the East in 1832.

psyllic ('psɪlɪk, 'sɪl-), *a. rare.* [f. L. *Psylli*, Gr. Ψύλλοι, an African people, famed as snake-charmers.] Of or pertaining to snake-charming.

1861 GOSSE *Rom. Nat. Hist.* Ser. II. 288 Fatal terminations to these exhibitions of the psyllic art now and then occur.

psyllid ('sɪlɪd). *Ent.* Also **Psyllid.** [ad. mod.L. *Psyllid-æ*, family name, f. PSYLLA: see -ID³.] A jumping plant-louse belonging to the family Psyllidæ, which includes several species that damage plants by causing galls or spreading virus diseases. Also *attrib.*

1899 D. SHARP in *Cambr. Nat. Hist.* VI. viii. 580 Sometimes these Psyllid galls are mere changes in form of a limited part, or parts, of a leaf. **1909** H. MAXWELL-LEFROY *Indian Insect Life* 743 Kieffer describes Indian gall-making Psyllids. **1922** *Nature* 3 June 714/1, I also find a winged termite, a psyllid,..some small spiders. **1954** S. H. SKAIFE *Afr. Insect Life* xi. 111 The jumping plant lice, or psyllids.., are small insects about the size of aphids and they look something like tiny cicadas. **1962** [see LERP]. **1969** *New Scientist* 2 Oct. 19/1 The Australian plantsucking psyllid bug *Cardiaspina albitextura*..lives on eucalyptus leaves. **1972** SWANN & PAPP *Common Insects N. Amer.* xiii. 141 The psyllids, or jumping plantlice, are tiny insects.

‖**psyllium** ('psɪlɪəm). Also 6 **psylly.** [L. *psyllium*, a. Gr. ψύλλιον, f. ψύλλα flea.] The herb *Plantago psyllium*; = FLEAWORT; also, (a preparation of) the seeds of this plant or of *Psillium ovata* or *P. indica*, used as a laxative. Also *attrib.*

1598 SYLVESTER *Du Bartas* II. i. III. *Furies* 176 The dropsie-breeding, sorrow-bringing psylly, Here called fleawort. **1601** HOLLAND *Pliny* II. 239 Psyllium, Fleawort, is good for the vlcers thereof. **1706** PHILLIPS, *Psyllium*, the Herb Flea-bane or Flea-wort. **1897** W. T. FERNIE *Herbal Simples* (ed. 2) 436 In France these Psyllium seeds..are widely prescribed as a laxative. **1932** R. C. WREN *Potter's Cycl. Bot. Drugs* (ed. 4) 281 Psyllium is used successfully in dysentery in the tropics. **1959** *Times* 30 Dec. 8/6 The mailman dragged in a sack of black Psyllium seeds from France. **1977** *Martindale's Extra Pharmacopoeia* (ed. 27) 929/1 Psyllium, on account of its content of mucilage, is used as a demulcent.

psy-op, -war: see PSY-.

pt-. Words beginning with this combination of consonants are all (with the exception of the fancifully mis-spelt *ptarmigan*) from Greek, in which the combination is frequent. The *p* is pronounced in French, German, and other languages, as well as by Englishmen in reading

Greek, and by some scholars in English but in English words beginning with *pt-* the initial *p* is no longer pronounced.

ptarmacan, -gan, obs. forms of PTARMIGAN.

ptarmic (ˈptɑːmɪk, ˈtɑːmɪk), *a.* and *sb.* [ad. L. *ptarmic-us*, a. Gr. πταρμικ-ός causing to sneeze, f. πταρμός a sneeze: see -IC.]

A. *adj.* Exciting or causing sneezing; errhine.

1858 MAYNE *Expos. Lex.*, *Ptarmicus*, causing to sneeze; sternutatory: ptarmic.

B. *sb.* A substance that excites sneezing.

1684 tr. *Bonet's Merc. Compit.* III. 66 The use of Ptarmicks does rather encrease..a defluxion of humours from the head. **1822–34** *Good's Study Med.* (ed. 4) III. 203 Those, who have habituated themselves to snuff for years, can hardly be excited to sneeze by the most violent ptarmics.

So ‖ˈ**ptarmica** [L., a. Gr. πταρμική] name of a plant, sneezewort, now botanically called *Achillæa Ptarmica*; ˈ**ptarmical** *a.*, ptarmic.

1657 TOMLINSON *Renou's Disp.* 179 Ptarmicall or neezing powder, when its used for Errhins. **1706** LONDON & WISE *Retir'd Gard.* 97 Ptarmica, or Eternal Flower. **1707** *Curios. in Husb. & Gard.* 69 This Sap..becomes..ptarmical, carminative, sudorifick, diuretick. **1741** *Compl. Fam.-Piece* II. iii. 397 You have now in Flower..double Ptarmica or Sneezing-wort.

ptarmigan (ˈtɑːmɪgən). Forms: α. 6 **termigan, termigen**, 7 **termigant, termagant, tormichan**, 8 **tormican, tarmichen, tarmachan**. β. 7– **ptarmigan**, (9 **ptarmacan, -gan**). [In Lowland Sc. use before 1600; = Gaelic *tàrmachan*; ulterior history and origin unknown; see Note below. Originally with initial *t*; the spelling with *pt* appears first in Sibbald 1684, and was app. pseudo-etymological, after words from Greek, presumably *ptarmic*, *ptarmical*, then known in medicine. Being unfortunately taken from Sibbald by Pennant in 1768, it has passed into ornithological and general English use.]

A bird of the grouse family (*Lagopus alpinus* or *mutus*) which inhabits high altitudes in Scotland and Northern Europe, the Alps and Pyrenees. The plumage changes from ash-grey and black in summer to white in winter. Also called the White or Rock Grouse. **b.** The name is extended generically to other species of *Lagopus*, as *L. albus* of Europe and Asia, *L. rupestris* of N. America, etc.

α. **1599** *Sc. Acts Jas. VI* (1816) IV. 180/2 They discharge ony persone quhasumeuir..To sell or by ony..partridgis muir foullis blak cokis aithehenis Termiganis. **1600** *Ibid.* 236/2 Termigenis. **1621** *Ibid.* 628/2 Termigantis. **1617** JAS. I *Let. to Ld. Tullibardine* in Gray *Birds W. Scotl.* (1871) 230 The known commoditie yee have to provide capercaillies and termigantis. **1618** J. TAYLOR (Water P.) *Pennyles Pilgr.* Fj. Capons, Chickins, Partridge, Moorecoots, Heathcocks, Caperkellies and Termagants. **1685** *Sc. Acts Jas. VII* (1820) VIII. 475/2 That all persons forbear to Slay any Muirfoul, Heathfoul, Partridge, Quail, Duck or Mallard, Taile or Ataile or Tormichan from and after the first day of Lent to the first of July. **1726** *Macfarlane's Geog. Collect.* (S.H.S.) I. 222 Black cock, muire fowles, tarmichen. *c* **1730** BURT *Lett. N. Scotl.* xxi. (1754) II. 169 The Tormican is near about the Size of the Moor-Fowl (or Groust). **1799** J. ROBERTSON *Agric. Perth* 461 Grouse, heath-fowl and Tarmachans in abundance inhabit every hill.

β. **1684** SIBBALD *Scotia Illustr.* II. III. iii. 16 Lagopus Avis *Aldrov.* Perdix alba *Sabaudis*..Nostratibus the *Ptarmigan*. **1768** PENNANT *Zool.* I. 206 The tail of the Ptarmigan consists of sixteen feathers. **1808** *Sporting Mag.* XXXII. 214 A number of muir fowl..ptarmacans, rats, mice &c. **1810** SCOTT *Lady of L.* II. xxv, His eagle eye The ptarmigan in snow could spy. **1868** Q. VICTORIA *Life Highl.* 68 Albert left me to go after Ptarmigan.

b. **1893** NEWTON *Dict. Birds* 389 It is to [the Willow-Grouse, *Lagopus albus*] that belong, almost without exception, the thousands of birds sold in our markets as 'Ptarmigan'.

Comb. **1904** *Westm. Gaz.* 7 Sept. 3/1 Ptarmigan-shooting would be tame sport were it not for the savagery of the sublime and sterile surroundings.

[*Note.* The existing Gaelic *tàrmachan* evidently goes back, through the cited *tarmichen* and *tormican*, to *tormichan* in 1685, and prob. much earlier. It has the form of a diminutive of *tàrmach* (cf. *balachan*, dim. of *balach* boy, *tulachan*, dim. of *tulach* hillock, etc.); and *tàrmach* is given as a synonym in living use in Armstrong's and the Highland Society's Dictionaries. The word has thus all the appearance of being native; *à priori*, also, it is natural that the name of a bird found only on the Highland mountains should have been Gaelic. But *tàrmach* has no obvious derivation in Gaelic; and some Celtic scholars think that it may be a foreign word which has put on a Celtic guise. On the other hand, the word, if not from Gaelic, is without any etymology in Lowland Sc., for *termagant* can only be considered a popular perversion of the 'sparrow-grass' order.]

ptenoglossate (pt-, ˌtiːnəʊˈglɒsət), *a. Zool.* [f. Gr. πτηνό-ς feathered + γλῶσσα tongue + -ATE[2].] Of certain molluscs: Having no median teeth on the odontophore, but a large number of lateral teeth resembling the barbs of a feather.

ptenopleural (ˌtiːnəʊˈplʊərəl), *a. Zool.* [f. mod.L. *Ptēnopleura* (f. Gr. πτηνό-ς feathered + πλευρά the side) + -AL[1].] Of or pertaining to the *Ptenopleura*, a division of the *Insectivora*, represented by the flying lemurs; having the sides winged or alate; having a flying membrane.

pteranodont (pt-, təˈrænəʊdɒnt), *sb.* (*a.*) *Palæont.* [ad. mod.L. *Pteranodon*, f. Gr. πτερ-όν wing + ἀνόδους, -οδοντ- toothless.] A pterosaur of the genus *Pteranodon*, characterized by the absence of teeth. **b.** *adj.* Belonging to this genus.

1882 GEIKIE *Text-bk. Geol.* VI. III. iii. §1. 811 Pterosaurs have likewise been obtained characterized by an absence of teeth (*Pteranodonts*). **1885** C. F. HOLDER *Marvels Anim. Life* 202 The great bat-like creature..was at one time very common on this continent [America], and was a flying reptile known as the Pteranodon. It differed from the European Pterodactyles in being toothless.

‖**pteraspis** (pt-, təˈræspɪs). *Palæont.* [mod.L., f. Gr. πτερόν wing + ἀσπίς, ἀσπιδ- shield.] A fossil genus of ganoid fishes of the Devonian age.

1857 in H. Miller *O.R. Sandst.* viii. (ed. 23) 149 *note*, *Cephalaspis rostratus* is a *Pteraspis*; and Prof. Huxley and Mr. Salter describe *Cephalaspis Lewisii* and *Lloydii* as *Pteraspides*. **1880** GÜNTHER *Fishes* 354 Pteraspis, with the cephalic shield finely striated or grooved, composed of seven pieces.

Hence **pteraˈspidian** *a.*, belonging to this genus.

1872 W. S. SYMONDS *Rec. Rocks* vii. 257 Remains of Pteraspidean fishes. **1887** *Athenæum* 4 June 741/2 A canal system..in the shields of pteraspidian fishes.

ptere (ptɪə(r), tɪə(r)). *Zool.* [a. F. *ptère*, ad. Gr. πτερόν feather, wing.] A wing-like organ or part; *spec.* in sponges, A lobe of the prora, pleura, or tropis of a cymba.

1887 SOLLAS in *Encycl. Brit.* XXII. 418/1 (Sponges) By growing towards the equator the opposed proral and pleural pteres may conjoin.

‖**Pterichthys** (pt-, təˈrɪkθɪs). *Palæont.* [mod.L., f. Gr. πτερόν wing + ἰχθύς fish.] A fossil genus of fishes of the Devonian period, having a pair of wing-shaped lateral appendages.

1842 H. MILLER *O.R. Sandst.* iii. (ed. 2) 70 There are none of the fossils of the Old Red Sandstone which less resemble anything that now exists than its Pterichthys. *Ibid.* vi. 140 The oar-like arms of the Pterichthys and its tortoise-like plates. **1873** DAWSON *Earth & Man* v. 98.

So **pteˈrichthyid**, a member of the family of fishes typified by the *Pterichthys*.

1862 DANA *Man. Geol.* 279 The Pterichthyids, or 'winged fishes'..have no caudal fin for swimming, but, instead, a pair of powerful paddles.

pterideous (pt-, təˈrɪdiːəs), *a. Bot.* [f. mod.L. *Pterideæ* (f. PTERIS) + -OUS.] Belonging to the tribe *Pterideæ* of ferns, typified by the genus *Pteris*.

1858 in MAYNE *Expos. Lex.*

pteridine (ˈtɛrɪdiːn). *Chem.* Also †-in. [ad. G. *pteridin* (C. Schöpf et al. 1941, in *Ann. d. Chem.* DXLVIII. 83): see PTERIN and -IDINE.] A synthetic yellow crystalline solid, $C_6H_4N_4$, which has a bicyclic structure formed from fused pyrazine and pyrimidine rings; any derivative of this, many examples of which occur naturally, esp. as insect pigments and vitamins of the B group.

1943 *Brit. Chem. & Physiol. Abstr.* A. II. 281 The structure of leucopterin..as 2-imino-6:8:9-trihydroxy-pteridine is confirmed. This and similar CO compounds are named as (enolic) OH-derivatives of pteridine. **1948** *Nature* 2 Oct. 524/2 Reaction of the diaminopyrimidine in aqueous solution with glyoxal bisulphite gives pteridine which crystallizes from alcohol in pale yellow plates, m.p. 140°. **1951** *Jrnl. Chem. Soc.* 474 All natural pteridines have at least one amino- and one hydroxy-substituent. **1962** [see DROSOPHILA]. **1968** L. A. PAQUETTE *Princ. Mod. Heterocyclic Chem.* xi. 384 Another vitamin of the B group, B_2 or riboflavin.., also contains the basic pteridine ring system.

pterido- (pt-, tɛrɪdəʊ), before a vowel **pterid-**, combining form of Gr. πτερίς, πτεριδ- fern. **pteriˈdography** [-GRAPHY], a description of ferns. **pteriˈdology** [-(O)LOGY], that branch of botany which treats of ferns; hence ˌ**pteridoˈlogical** *a.*, pertaining to pteridology; **pteriˈdologist**, one versed in the study of ferns. ˌ**pteridoˈmania** *nonce-wd.*, a mania or enthusiasm for ferns. **pteriˈdophilist** [Gr. φίλ-ος loving], a lover of ferns; so **pteriˈdophilism**, love of ferns. ˈ**pteridophyte** [ad. mod.L. *Pteridophyta* pl. (E. Haeckel *Generelle Morphologie der Organismen* (1866) II. p. xxxix), f. Gr. φυτόν plant], a member of the *Pteridophyta*, a division of plants including the ferns and their allies; a vascular cryptogam; also *attrib.*; so **pteridoˈphytic** *a.* ˈ**pteridosperm** [ad. mod.L. *Pteridospermeæ* (Oliver & Scott (1904) in *Phil. Trans. R. Soc.* B. CXCVII. 239)], a fossil plant belonging to the class Pteridospermeæ or the order Pteridospermales, which include seed-bearing plants resembling ferns.

1884 BOWER & SCOTT *De Bary's Phaner.* 299 The..literature..of *Pteridography and Palæontology. **1854** *Phytologist* V. 151 The author intends the 'glossary' as a general, not as a *pteridological one. **1892** *Gard. Chron.* 27 Aug. 245/1 The British Pteridological Society. **1845** E. NEWMAN in *Phytologist* I. 273, I am disposed to believe that our *Pteridologists have rarely taken that comprehensive view of the characters of ferns which is requisite for their classification in accordance with nature. **1856** W. L. LINDSAY *Pop. Hist. Brit. Lichens* 13 Many ladies have..taken a high stand as Algologists and Pteridologists. **1866** MOORE in *Treas. Bot.* 917 One of the principal genera into which the old genus *Aspidium* is broken up by modern pteridologists. **1979** *N.Z. Jrnl. Bot.* XVII. 98/1 These two eminent pteridologists do not yet entirely agree on a classification for the Cyathaceae. **1855** G. B. WOLLASTON in *Phytologist* New Ser. I. 171, I venture with the greatest diffidence,.. single-handed, into the battle-field of *Pteridology. **1866** *Pall Mall G.* 12 Sept. 10 He has studied pteridology for forty years. **1882** MOORE in *Gard. Chron.* XVII. 672 Mr. James Backhouse, who, in the annals of pteridology is not unknown to fame. **1980** *Nature* 7 Feb. 608/1 An overview of the..biochemical, physiological and genetical research which has taken place during the past 40 years in experimental pteridology. **1855** KINGSLEY *Glaucus* (ed. 2) 4 Your daughters..have been seized with the prevailing '*Pteridomania', and are collecting and buying ferns. **1969** D. E. ALLEN *Victorian Fern Craze* p. xi, No one ..would have thought of filling empty carboys with greenery and building up their present vogue had not Ward himself first prepared the ground... A twentieth-century 'Pteridomania'? **1970** *New Scientist* 7 May 296/1 Pteridomania had many social aspects yet it seems to have been almost forgotten outside botanical circles. **1866** *Pall Mall G.* 12 Sept. 10 Our own *pteridophilism being of a less pronounced and practical kind. *Ibid.*, *Pteridophilists being, after all, in plain English, nothing but lovers of ferns. **1880** C. E. BESSEY *Botany* xx. 437 The epidermis of Angiosperms does not differ in any marked way from that of the Gymnosperms and the *Pteridophytes. **1897** *Nature* 11 Nov. 45/2 The bryophyte-like ancestors of the pteridophytes. **1910** COULTER & CHAMBERLAIN *Morphol. Gymnosperms* i. 4 (*heading*) Vascular anatomy of pteridophytes. **1938** J. C. SCHOUTE in F. Verdoorn *Man. Pteridol.* i. 3 By these discoveries the range of the Pteridophyte canon of morphology was much enlarged. **1956** B. COBB *Field Guide to Ferns* 36 Each of the four classes of the Pteridophytes has its own characteristic behavior in producing, bearing, and propagating its spores. **1978** *Fern Gaz.* XI. 349 The pteridophyte flora of Réunion Island is characterized by a high number of species. **1898** *Bot. Gaz.* XXV. 305 In *pteridophytic types of embryogeny..it is always possible to distinguish the segment which is the homologue of the originally distal segment. **1977** A. HALLAM *Planet Earth* 252 This has been effected by the elimination of the free-living sexual stage (prothallus) of the pteridophytic plants. **1904** OLIVER & SCOTT in *Phil. Trans. R. Soc.* B. CXCVII. 240 The further development of our knowledge of the *Pteridosperms will form one of the chief objects of palæo-botanic investigation in the near future. **1931** A. C. SEWARD *Plant Life through Ages* ix. 147 Evidence ..eventually proved that the great majority of the Carboniferous 'ferns' were seed-bearing plants—pteridosperms. **1940** J. WALTON *Introd. Study of Fossil Plants* xi. 138 The seed cupules of the Pteridosperms..were borne on fronds or leaves. **1974** G. W. BURNS *Plant Kingdom* xix. 449/1 Ovules of the Paleozic pteridosperm *Medullosa* were probably terminally attached on the pinnae.

pteridoid (pt-, ˈtɛrɪdɔɪd), *a.* and *sb.* [f. Gr. πτερίς, πτεριδ- fern + -OID.] **a.** *adj.* Of the nature of or allied to the ferns, filicoid. **b.** *sb.* A fernlike plant; a pteridophyte.

1866 *Pall Mall G.* 12 Sept. 10 His treatise on the culture of pteridoids... Cultivation of the pteridoid forms of life.

pterin (ˈtɛrɪn). *Chem.* Also -ine. [a. G. *pterin* (Wieland & Schöpf 1925, in *Ber. d. Deut. Chem. Ges.* LVIII. 2178), f. Gr. πτερ-όν wing, feather: see -IN[1].] Any of a class of naturally occurring pteridine derivatives found esp. as insect pigments; more generally, any pteridine.

1934 *Chem. Abstr.* XXVIII. 1353 (*heading*) Occurrence of pterins in wasps and butterflies. **1943** A. H. COOK tr. *Mayer's Chem. Natural Coloring Matters* v. 264 The pterins occur as small colored or colorless granules in association with chitin. **1950** *Thorpe's Dict. Appl. Chem.* (ed. 4) X. 264/1 The name 'pterin' denotes a group of heterocyclic compounds, of both natural and synthetic origin, the molecules of which contain..a pyrazine ring fused to a pyrimidine ring. **1954** *Sci. News* XXXIV. 91 The purines and pterines constitute a major source of colour to the wings of butterflies;..the latter as white, red, yellow, and orange pigments, which are also found in the integument of wasps. **1970** A. L. LEHNINGER *Biochem.* xxiv. 543 Folic acid..contains three characteristic building blocks (1) a substituted pterin, (2) *p*-aminobenzoic acid, and (3) glutamic acid.

‖**pterion** (ˈptɛrɪən). *Anat.* [mod.L., f. Gr. πτερόν wing (referring to the wing of the sphenoid): one of a series of terms in *-ion* (after κρανίον, ἰνίον) used in craniology and craniometry.] The H-shaped suture of the wing of the sphenoid with the parietal, frontal, and temporal bones.

1878 BARTLEY tr. *Topinard's Anthrop.* II. ii. 234 *Pterion*.., the region where the frontal, parietal, temporal, and sphenoid bones meet, in the form of an H. **1888** FLOWER in *Anthropological Jrnl.* Aug. 7 In the region of the pterion in the male, the squamosal articulates with the frontal on the right side for a space of 4 mm. **1899** *Allbutt's Syst. Med.* VIII. 168 The seat [of temporal headache] is about opposite the pterion on each side.

‖**Pteris** (ˈptɛrɪs, ˈtɪərɪs). *Bot.* [L. (Pliny), a. Gr. πτέρις a fern with feathery leaves.] Name of a widely diffused genus of ferns, of which the best known is *P. aquilina*, the common Bracken.

1706 PHILLIPS, *Pteris*, Fern or Brake; the Herb Osmund. **1875** HUXLEY & MARTIN *Elem. Biol.* (1877) 61 *Pteris* presents a remarkable case of the alternation of generations.

‖**pterna** (ˈptɜːrnə). [mod.L., a. Gr. πτέρνα heel.] †**a.** *Anat.* The heel-bone, *os calcis. Obs.* **b.** *Ornith.* The heel-pad or sole of the foot in birds.

1684 tr. *Blancard's Phys. Dict., Pterna,* see *Calx.* **1706** PHILLIPS, *Pterna,* the second Bone of the Foot. **1895** in *Syd. Soc. Lex.*

ptero- (pt-, tɛrəʊ), before a vowel **pter-**, combining form of Gr. πτερόν feather, wing; an element of many scientific words. ˈ**pterobranch** [ad. mod.L. *Pterobranchia*, f. F. *ptérodibranche* (H. de Blainville 1816, in *Bull. Sci. Soc. Philomatique* XXVIII. 122)], a small marine, usually colonial, animal belonging to the class Pterobranchia of the phylum Hemichordata; also *attrib.*; **pterobranchiate** (-ˈbræŋkɪət) *a. Zool.* [Gr. βράγχια gills], of or pertaining to the *Pterobranchia*, an order of pteropods in the classification of J. E. Gray, or a subsection in Lankester's classification of molluscoids; so **pteroˈbranchious** *a.*: see quot. **pteroˈcardiac** *Zool.* [Gr. καρδία heart], (*a*) *adj.* denoting an ossicle in the stomach of the crayfish, which is wing-like in shape; (*b*) *sb.* the pterocardiac ossicle. **pteroˈcarpous** *a. Bot.* [Gr. καρπός fruit], having winged seeds or fruit (Mayne). ‖**pteroˈcarpus**, a genus of tropical timber trees, N.O. *Leguminosæ.* **pteroˈcymba**, a cymbate flesh-spicule of a sponge having winged or expanded proræ, giving an anchor-like figure; hence **pteroˈcymbate** *a.* (*Cent. Dict.* 1890). **pteroˈglossal** *a.* [Gr. γλῶσσα tongue], having a tongue finely notched or divided like a feather, as a toucan of the genus *Pteroglossus*; so **pteroˈglossine** *a.* **pteˈrographer** [Gr. -γράφος writer], a writer on feathers or plumage. **pteˈrography** [-GRAPHY], the description of feathers or plumage; hence **pteroˈgraphic**, **pteroˈgraphical** *adjs.*, of or pertaining to pterography. ˈ**pterolite** *Min.* [Gr. λίθος stone]: see quot. **pteˈrology** [Gr. λογία, -LOGY], the department of entomology which deals with the wings of insects; hence **pteroˈlogical** *a.*, pertaining to pterology. ˈ**pteromorph(a)** [-MORPH], in certain mites, a wing-like appendage attached to the cephalothorax. ‖**pteroˈpædes** *sb. pl. Ornith.* [mod.L., f. Gr. παῖς, παιδ- child], birds which are fully fledged when hatched; hence **pteroˈpædic**, of or of the nature of the Pteropædes. ‖**pteroˈpegum**, pl. **-a** [mod.L., f. Gr. πηγός fastened], the socket of the wing of an insect; hence **pteroˈpegal**, **pteroˈpegous** *adjs.* **pteroˈpleuron** *Ent.*, in Diptera, the section of the thorax from which the wings arise. ˈ**pterorhine** *a. Ornith.* [Gr. ῥίς, ῥῑν- nose], of or pertaining to the *Pterorhīna*, a division of *Alcidæ* or auks having the nostrils feathered (*Cent. Dict.* 1890). **pteroˈstigma** *Entom.* [Gr. στίγμα spot, mark], a peculiar mark or spot on the wings of some insects, esp. Hymenoptera; the stigma; hence **pteroˈstigmal**, ˌ**pterostigˈmatic**, ˌ**pterostigˈmatical** *adjs.*, of, pertaining to, or characterized by a pterostigma. ‖**pteroˈtheca** *Entom.* [mod.L., f. Gr. θηκή sheath], the wing-case of an insect in the pupa.

1949 *New Biol.* VI. 118 The construction of the tubes in which both Graptolites and *Pterobranchs live gives good reason for accepting Kozlowski's thesis. **1962** D. NICHOLS *Echinoderms* xiv. 175 Grobben has shown the principal transformations necessary to convert a pterobranch hemichordate into an echinoderm. **1968** A. S. ROMER *Procession of Life* vii. 141 The pterobranchs are tiny animals, only a fraction of an inch in size, living in colonial fashion within branching tubes, with, superficially, the appearance of tiny stemmed flowers. **1978** *Nature* 23 Nov. 318/3 Examples of arborescent growth occur among sponges, hydroids, graptolites, pterobranchs. **1885** E. R. LANKESTER in *Encycl. Brit.* XIX. 436/1 A serious error has been made in comparing the contractile stalk of the *Pterobranchiate polypide to the 'funiculus' or cord-like mesentery of Eupolyzoa. **1858** MAYNE *Expos. Lex., Pterobranchius,* applied by Blainville to an Order..of the..*Pteropoda,* having the *branchiæ* in form of wings or fins: *pterobranchious. **1870** ROLLESTON *Anim. Life* 103 A small ossicle, the '*pterocardiac', articulates with either outer angle of the cardiac. **1877** HUXLEY *Anat. Inv. Anim.* vi. 319 A small curved triangular antero-lateral or pterocardiac ossicle. **1866** LIVINGSTONE *Last Jrnls.* (1873) I. ii. 48 One tree of which bark cloth is made, **pterocarpus*, is abundant. **1887** SOLLAS in *Encycl. Brit.* XXII. 417/2 A common form of anchorate, the **pterocymba*, results. **1887** *Amer. Naturalist* XXI. 585 Particular styles of imbrication of the cubital coverts with certain structural peculiarities—osteological, myological, visceral, and *pterographical. **1896** CHESTER *Dict. Min.,* **Pterolite*..an altered lepidomelane, found in fan-shaped or feather-shaped aggregations. **1907** *Nature* 12 Dec. 142/2 The species [of mites] are to be called *Oribata bostocki*, distinguished by the *pteromorphæ being attached to the anterior margin of the abdomen instead of its lateral margin. **1952** BAKER & WHARTON *Introd. Acarology* viii. 387 Within the Aptyctima we find several natural groups based on..the possession or lack of pteromorphs or wings. **1959** T. E. HUGHES *Mites* viii. 113 When big pteromorphae are present, they can usually be depressed by special muscles. **1962** *New Scientist* 20 Sept. 628/2 One group of mites is unique in possessing hinged outgrowths similar to wings, called pteromorphs. **1972** L. GOZMÁNY tr. *Balogh's Oribatid Genera of World* 22 The pteromorpha is a horizontal or inferiorly deflected chitinous lamella. **1885** *Standard Nat. Hist.* IV. 3 A few birds remain so long within the egg that the feathers are developed when the shell bursts, ..these might be called *Pteropædes. **1826** KIRBY & SP. *Entomol.* III. xxxiii. 372 **Pteropega* (the Wing-socket), the space in which the organs for flight are planted. **1858** MAYNE *Expos. Lex., Pteropega, Entomol.*, applied by Kirby to the portion of the mesothorax and metathorax to which the superior and inferior wings are attached: *pteropegous. **1884** C. R. OSTEN-SACKEN in *Trans. Entomol. Soc.* 503 *Pteropleura, situated under the insertion of the wing, and behind the mesopleural structure. **1951** COLYER & HAMMOND *Flies Brit. Isles* 24 The wings arise from the pteropleuron. **1977** RICHARDS & DAVIES *Imms's Gen. Textbk. Entomol.* (ed. 10) II. III. 961 The pteropleuron (= dorsal part of mesepimeron) lies below the root of the wing. **1861** HAGEN *Synops. Neuropt. N. Amer.* 9 *Pterostigma triangular. *Ibid.*, Wings with obscure black veins, *pterostigmal spot absent. *Ibid.* 149 Two angulose bands, the one nodal, the other *pterostigmatical. **1886** *Proc. Boston Soc. Nat. Hist.* 265 The wider venation and..the brown pterostigma without darker nebula separate this species from all related ones. *Ibid.* 288 Wings pale, yellow in the pterostigmatical part. **1826** KIRBY & SP. *Entomol.* III. xxxi. 250 The breast (*pectus*)..from which proceed the wing-cases (**Ptero-theca*) and leg-cases (*Podo-theca*).

pteroclomorphic (pt-, tɛrɒkləʊˈmɔːfɪk), *a. Ornith.* [irreg. f. mod.L. *Pterocles* (f. Gr. πτερόν, PTERO- + κλείς key) + Gr. μορφή form + -IC.] Having the structure and affinities of the *Pteroclidæ*, a family of sand-grouse typified by the genus *Pterocles.*

1868 HUXLEY in *Proc. Zool. Soc.* 304 The tarso-metatarsus is quite Pteroclomorphic.

pterodactyl (tɛrəʊˈdæktɪl). Also †**-yle.** [ad. mod.L. *Pterodactylus*, f. Gr. πτερόν wing + δάκτυλος finger.] **1.** *Palæont.* A winged reptile or pterosaur of the extinct genus *Pterodactylus.*

1830 LYELL *Princ. Geol.* I. 123 The pterodactyle might flit again through umbrageous groves of tree-ferns. **1873** DAWSON *Earth & Man* viii. 205 The Pterodactyles, the reptile bats of the Mesozoic. **1882** GEIKIE *Text-bk. Geol.* VI. III. iii. §2. 813 The earliest known birds present characters of strong affinity with the Deinosaurs and Pterodactyles.

attrib. **1883** *Century Mag.* Dec. 201/1 Colossal monsters of the Pterodactyl period.

2. *Aeronaut.* Also **Pterodactyl.** An obsolete kind of tailless pusher aeroplane with swept-back wings and a very short fuselage.

1926 G. T. R. HILL in *Jrnl. R. Aeronaut. Soc.* XXX. 528 During the summer of 1925, all outstanding design questions were finally settled, and I therefore propose..to give a more detailed description of the main features of the aeroplane, which I have called the Pterodactyl, on account of its supposed resemblance to the prehistoric lizards of that breed. **1935** *Jrnl. R. Aeronaut. Soc.* XXXIX. 823 A recent proposal for a large tailless flying boat having a pterodactyl wing plus stubs. **1960** C. H. GIBBS-SMITH *Aeroplane* xiii. 103 The *Pterodactyls* contributed to a development culminating in the swept-back and delta-wing forms of today.

Hence **pterodactylian** (tɛrəʊdækˈtɪlɪən) *a.*, of or belonging to the pterodactyl, or the genus *Pterodactylus*; *sb.*, an animal of this genus; **pterodacˈtylic**, **pteroˈdactylous** *adjs.*, of the nature of a pterodactyl; **pteroˈdactylid**, an animal of the pterodactyl family; **pteroˈdactyloid** *a.*, having the form or characters of a pterodactyl.

1858 MAYNE *Expos. Lex.*, Pterodactylous. **1884** *Daily News* 2 Sept. 2/2 The very pterodactylic-looking blue-clad fishers. **1890** *Cent. Dict.*, Pterodactylian. **1895** *Funk's Stand. Dict.*, Pterodactylid, -oid.

pteroic (ˈtɛrəʊɪk), *a. Biochem.* [f. PTER(IDINE + -OIC.] *pteroic acid*: a synthetic crystalline solid from which the pteroylglutamic acids are formally derived by peptidic linkage of glutamic acid residues to the carboxyl group; *p*-(2-amino-4-hydroxypteridin-6-ylmethyl) aminobenzoic acid, $C_{14}H_{12}N_6O_3$.

1946 [see PTEROYLGLUTAMIC *a.* a]. **1954** A. WHITE et al. *Princ. Biochem.* xii. 263 The linkage coupling the *p*-aminobenzoic acid..and glutamic acid is a peptide bond. Hydrolysis of this bond gives pteroic acid and glutamic acid. **1963** W. SHIVE in Florkin & Stotz *Comprehensive Biochem.* XI. vii. 90 Among the synthetic derivatives, pteroic acid, because it is effective in replacing folic acid for *S[treptococcus] faecalis* R but not for *L[actobacillus] casei*, and the pteroyldiglutamate..are of biological interest. **1970** T. SHIOTA in *Ibid.* XXI. 126 The mechanism involving successive additions of L-glutamic acid residues to pteroic acid and folic acid is supported by the work of Griffin and Brown.

pteroid (pt-, ˈtɛrɔɪd), *a.* and *sb.* [f. Gr. πτερόν feather, wing, or (irreg.) πτερίς fern + -OID.]

A. *adj.* **1.** Resembling a wing.

1858 in MAYNE *Expos. Lex.*

2. *Bot.* Resembling a fern; fern-like, PTERIDOID.

1890 in *Cent. Dict.*

B. *sb.* A slender bone or ossified ligament in the pterodactyl extending from the carpal region towards the humerus.

1890 in *Cent. Dict.*

‖**pteroma** (ptəˈrəʊmə). Pl. **-ata.** [L. *pterōma*, a. Gr. πτέρωμα the colonnade of a temple.]

1. *Arch.* The walk between the cella and the columns of the peristyle of a Greek temple; the *ambulatio.*

1846 ELLIS *Elgin Marb.* I. 72 The walks round the exterior of the body of the temple were called *pteromata.*

2. *Ornith.* Also **pterome.** (See quot.)

1858 MAYNE *Expos. Lex., Pteroma,* applied by Illiger to the internal *tectrices* of the wings, which are generally longer than the others: a pterome.

pterope, -opid, -opine: see PTEROPUS.

pteropod (ˈtɛrəpɒd). [ad. mod.L. *Pteropoda*, a. F. *ptéropode* (G. Cuvier 1804, in *Ann. Mus. Hist. Nat.* IV. 232): see PTEROPODA.] **a.** *Zool.* A pelagic marine gastropod belonging to the class Pteropoda, which includes molluscs having a modified foot bearing lobes which act as fins; a sea butterfly.

1835 KIRBY *Hab. & Inst. Anim.* I. ix. 269 The Pteropods ..having no means of fixing themselves like most of the bivalves, float continually in the ocean. **1877** T. H. HUXLEY *Man. Anat. Invertebr. Animals* viii. 505 In all Pteropods and Branchiogasteropods, the mantle secretes a cuticular shell. **1883** C. F. HOLDER in *Harper's Mag.* Jan. 187/1 With what grace the little pteropod Cleodora moves along! **1890** [see *butterfly snail*]. **1934** W. BEEBE *Half Mile Down* ix. 167 At 1825 feet coiled pteropods..appeared by the dozen. **1956** A. HARDY *Open Sea* I. xii. 228 The deep-water pteropods are dark in colour. **1976** *Sci. Amer.* July 95/1 The pteropods, wing-footed marine snails, collect phytoplankton on floating webs of sticky mucus.

b. **pteropod ooze**, a calcareous marine sediment rich in the remains of the tests of pteropods.

1891 MURRAY & RENARD in *Rep. Sci. Results Voy. H.M.S. Challenger: Deep-Sea Deposits* iii. 223 Pteropod Ooze. This name was employed by Mr. Murray during the cruise of the Challenger to designate those deep-sea deposits in which a very large part of the calcareous organisms consists of the dead shells of Pteropods and Heteropods. **1894** S. J. HICKSON in *Pop. Sci. Monthly* XLIV. 470 The pteropod ooze has only twenty-five per cent. of carbonate of lime. **1929** A. CONAN DOYLE *Maracot Deep* 17 We would bring up ..a scoop of pteropod ooze. **1967** *Oceanogr. & Marine Biol.* V. 51 To the South of New Caledonia..there is a small zone of pteropod ooze.

‖**Pteropoda** (pt-, təˈrɒpədə), *sb. pl. Zool.* [mod.L., = Gr. πτερόποδα, neuter pl. of πτερόπους wing-footed.] A class or division of *Mollusca*, having the mesopodium or middle part of the foot expanded into a pair of lobes, like wings or flippers (the *pteropodium*), with which the animal swims.

1835 *Todd's Cycl. Anat.* I. 113 Pteropoda... Able to swim by means of two lateral musculo-cutaneous finlike expansions. **1851** WOODWARD *Mollusca* 7 The pteropoda only inhabit the sea, and swim with a pair of fins, extending outwards from the sides of the head. **1874** WOOD *Nat. Hist.* 651 The Pteropoda or Wing-footed Molluscs.

Hence **pteˈropodan** *a.*, pertaining to the Pteropoda; *sb.* a pteropod.

‖**pteropodium** (pt-, tɛrəʊˈpəʊdɪəm). *Zool.* [mod.L., f. as prec.: see PODIUM 2 b.] The foot, or mesopodium, of a pteropod: see PTEROPODA. Hence **pteroˈpodial** *a.*, of or belonging to the pteropodium.

1883 E. R. LANKESTER in *Encycl. Brit.* XVI. 673/2 The pteropodial lobes of the foot. **1890** *Cent. Dict.*, Pteropodium.

pteropodous (pt-, təˈrɒpədəs), *a.* [f. PTEROPOD(A + -OUS.] Of or belonging to the Pteropoda; pertaining to or characteristic of a pteropod.

a **1843** *Encycl. Metrop.* VII. 287/2 *Paracephals.* By this term Blainville designates Cuvier's Gasteropodous and Pteropodous Classes of Molluscs. **1851** WOODWARD *Mollusca* 121 Mr. Adams observed the pteropodous fry of Cypræa annulus..adhering in masses to the mantle of the parent.

‖**pteropus** (pt-, ˈtɛrəpəs). *Zool.* Pl. **-i.** Also in anglicized form ˈ**pterope** (-əʊp). [mod.L., ad. Gr. πτερόπους wing-footed.] A genus of tropical and sub-tropical bats having membranous wings, known as flying foxes or fruit-bats; an animal of this genus. Hence ˈ**pteropid**, ˈ**pteropine** *adjs.*, belonging to or having the characteristics of the *Pteropidæ* or flying-fox family.

1835 *Proc. Zool. Soc.* III. 149 Mr. Bennett called the attention of the Meeting to a Pteropine Bat..recently.. obtained from the neighbourhood of the river Gambia... In one of the two other species of *Pteropi* previously obtained, ..the same backward position of the wings exists. **1887** *Athenæum* 26 Mar. 421/1 A new genus of pteropine bats. **1890** *Ibid.* 5 Apr. 438/3 Not unlike a Pteropus or flying fox. **1890** *Cent. Dict.*, Pterope.

pterosaur (ˈtɛrəʊsɔː(r)). *Palæont.* [ad. mod.L. name of order *Pterosauria*, f. generic name *Pterosaurus* (L.F.J.F. Fitzinger *Systema Reptilium* (1843) 15), f. PTERO- + Gr. σαῦρ-ος (= σαύρα) lizard.] A member of the *Pterosauria*, an extinct order of Mesozoic saurian reptiles, having the fifth digit of each fore-foot prolonged to a great length for the purpose of supporting a membrane for flight.

1862 DANA *Man. Geol.* 346 Pterosaurs..or Flying Saurians. **1882** GEIKIE *Text-bk. Geol.* VI. III. iii. §1. 810 According to a recent enumeration made by Mr. Cope.. there were known 18 species of deinosaurs, 4 pterosaurs, 14 crocodilians. **1907** *Proc. Zool. Soc.* I. 226 It has been frequently assumed that the Pterosaurs enjoyed a bipedal locomotion. **1926** G. HEILMANN *Orig. Birds* IV. 140 The Pterosaurs are of interest chiefly because they are flying reptiles. **1933** A. S. ROMER *Vertebr. Paleont.* viii. 176 The brain of the pterosaurs..was exceedingly large for a reptile. **1973** J. UPDIKE *Museums & Women* 196 The iguanodon despised these pterosaurs' pretensions. **1975** *Times* 12 Apr. 12/1 The surprise created in the popular mind by Douglas Lawson's discovery of an immense pterosaur—a beast whose wings spanned about 51 feet according to the most reliable computer estimate—is only paralleled by the bewilderment experienced in scientific circles.

Hence **ptero'saurian**, *adj.* of the nature of a pterosaur; of or belonging to the order *Pterosauria*; *sb.* a pterosaur.

1882 GEIKIE *Text-bk. Geol.* VI. III. ii. §1. 778 The pterosaurians or flying reptiles..were likewise peculiar to Mesozoic time. **1888** *Nature* 19 Apr. 599/1 The Pterosaurian skull..resembles more the Lacertilian than any other type of Reptile skull. **1981** *Sci. Amer.* Feb. 95/1 The triangle wing was supported at the wrist by a uniquely pterosaurian innovation, the pteroid bone.

pterotic (pt-, tə'rəʊtɪk), *a.*[1] (*sb.*) *Anat.* [f. Gr. πτερόν wing, + *-otic* in *periotic*, *pro-otic*, etc.] Applied to a wing-like expansion of the petrosal bone or periotic capsule, occurring in some vertebrates. **b.** as *sb.* The pterotic bone or expansion.

1870 FLOWER *Osteol. Mammalia* x. 150 A lamelliform expansion of the upper edge of the periotic (*pterotic*, Parker) forms part of the lateral wall of the cranium. **1872** MIVART *Elem. Anat.* 106 In Fishes, it appears as a bone projecting at the postero-external angle of the roof of the skull. It is called the pterotic. **1890** in *Cent. Dict.*

pte'rotic, *a.*[2] *nonce-wd.* [f. Gr. πτερωτός winged + -IC.] Winged.

1884 BLACKMORE *Tommy Upm.* II. vi. 89 A frame of unusual elasticity, partaking rather of the pterotic character.

pteroylglutamic (ˌtɛrəʊaɪlgl(j)uː'tæmɪk), *a.* *Biochem.* GLUTAMIC *a.*]

a. *pteroylglutamic acid*: any of a series of derivatives of pteroic acid which have a side chain consisting of one or more glutamic acid residues, and include certain members of the vitamin B complex and other animal growth factors; folic acid.

1946 R. B. ANGIER et al. in *Science* 31 May 669/1 For the compounds formed from *p*-aminobenzoic acid and *p*-aminobenzoyl-*l*(+)-glutamic acid, the names pteroic acid and pteroylglutamic acid are suggested. **1949**, **1955** [see FOLACIN]. **1967** PIKE & BROWN *Nutrition* iii. 65 At one time both p-aminobenzoic acid and pteroylglutamic acid were considered to be vitamins, but it is now apparent that the species requirement is for one or the other of the two.

b. With inserted prefix indicating the number of glutamic acid residues present, as *pteroylmonoglutamic acid* (cf. FOLIC ACID), etc. Also *pteroylpolyglutamic acid*.

1946 *Ann. N.Y. Acad. Sci.* XLVIII. 287 Whereas vitamin B_c..contains one glutamic acid residue, vitamin B_c conjugate contains seven. In the system of nomenclature suggested by the authors [*sc.* C. W. Waller et al.], vitamin B_c conjugate is therefore pteroylheptaglutamic acid. **1954** A. WHITE et al. *Princ. Biochem.* xlix. 1035 Animal tissues contain an enzyme, 'vitamin B_c conjugase', which hydrolyzes the naturally occurring pteroylpolyglutamic acid compounds to pteroylmonoglutamic acid and free glutamic acid. **1955** *Chem. & Engin. News* 6 June 2433/1 The pure substance hitherto known as folic acid, folacine, or vitamin B_c shall be named pteroylmonoglutamic acid. Compounds analogous to it but containing several glutamic acid residues united by amide linkages may be named pteroyltriglutamic acid, pteroylheptaglutamic acid, etc. **1970** PASSMORE & ROBSON *Compan. Med. Stud.* II. vii. 7/1 Folic acid in therapeutics means synthetic pteroylmonoglutamic acid but the term is sometimes used to embrace all naturally occurring substances with folic acid activity.

Hence **ˌpteroyl'glutamate**, (a compound or anion of) any of these acids. (Also with inserted prefix.)

1950 R. J. WILLIAMS et al. *Biochem. of B Vitamins* C. ii. 290 Both pteroic acid and formylpteroic acid are inactive for *L*[*actobacillus*] *casei* or humans, while pteroylheptaglutamate is inactive for bacteria. **1958** FRUTON & SIMMONDS *Gen. Biochem.* (ed. 2) xxxix. 999 The pteroyltriglutamate and heptaglutamate both occur in nature and are as active as folic acid in the nutrition of higher animals. **1963** [see PTEROIC *a.*]. **1970** R. W. MCGILVERY *Biochem.* xviii. 411 (*caption*) The structure of the vitamin, pteroylglutamate, more commonly known as folate. **1970** PASSMORE & ROBSON *Compan. Med. Stud.* II. vii. 7/1 In foods, folates are found free and in conjugated forms, the latter being polyglutamates such as pteroyltriglutamate and pteroylheptaglutamate.

‖**pterygium** (ptə'rɪdʒɪəm). [L., a. Gr. πτερύγιον little wing, fin, dim. of πτέρυξ wing.]

1. *Anat.* (See quot.) ? *Obs.*

1684 tr. *Blancard's Phys. Dict.*, *Pterygium*, is the Wing or round Rising of the Nose or Eye, or the Process of the Bone *Sphenoides* which is like a Wing... Also the Nymphæ of a Womans secret Parts.

2. *Path.* **a.** A diseased condition of the conjunctiva of the eye: see quots.

1657 *Physical Dict.*, *Pterygium*, or haw in the eyes called unguis. **1875** H. WALTON *Dis. Eye* 144 Pterygium generally grows as a flat triangularly-shaped tumour on the ocular conjunctiva, at the inner corner of the eye. **1884** G. TURNER *Samoa* xi. 137 Connected with diseases of the eye, pterygium is common.

b. A growth of the epidermis over the nails.

1899 J. HUTCHINSON in *Archives of Surg.* X. No. 38. 147 The nail-fold over the lunula is prolonged forwards, over the bed, as a fan-shaped, fleshy pterygium.

3. *Entom.* (See quot.)

1826 KIRBY & SP. *Entomol.* III. 381 *Pterygium*.., in under-wings this is a small wing-like appendage, fixed at the base of the wing in some Lepidoptera.

4. *Bot.* Term applied to petals and other appendages when shaped like wings.

1895 in *Syd. Soc. Lex.*

pterygo- (pt-, 'tɛrɪgəʊ), before a vowel **pteryg-**, combining form of Gr. πτέρυξ, πτερυγ- wing, fin.

1. In general sense of 'wing', 'fin', or 'winglike appendage'.

'pterygoˌblast *Ichth.* [Gr. βλαστός germ], a germinal fin-ray. **ˌpterygo'branchiate** (-'bræŋkɪət) *a.*, *Zool.* [see BRANCHIATE], of a group of isopodous crustaceans: having feathery gills. ‖**ˌpterygo'podium** *Ichth.* [Gr. πούς, ποδ- foot], one of the claspers of a shark, etc. **ˌpterygo'spermous** *a.*, *Bot.*, having winged seeds (Mayne *Expos. Lex.* 1858). ‖**ptery'gosteum** *Entom.* [Gr. ὀστέον bone], one of the nervures or veins of an insect's wing. **'pterygoˌstome** [Gr. στόμα mouth], the space between the anterior edges of the carapace in crabs and other crustacea; hence **pterygo'stomial, pterygo'stomian** *adjs.*

1884 J. A. RYDER in *Rep. U.S. Commission Fish* (1886) 985 The term..*pterygoblasts refers to the protoplasmic bodies from which the embryonic fin-rays are developed. **1897** PARKER & HASWELL *Text-bk. Zool.* II. 157 In all recent Elasmobranchs the male has, connected with the pelvic fins, a pair of grooved appendages—the claspers or *pterygopodia—which subserve copulation. **1852** DANA *Crust.* I. 367 The *pterygostome has a smooth channel parallel with the sides of the buccal area. **1877** HUXLEY *Anat. Inv. Anim.* vi. 341 The edges of the carapace pass completely in front of the bases of the limbs, and then turn suddenly forwards, parallel with one another and with the axis of the body, as the *pterygostomial plates of Milne-Edwards. **1835–6** *Todd's Cycl. Anat.* I. 780/1 *Pterygostomian portions of the carapace. **1893** STEBBING *Crustacea* v. 52 On the under side [are] the pterygostomian regions, 'the wings of the mouth'.

2. Used as combining form of PTERYGOID, denoting attachment or relation to the pterygoid processes of the sphenoid bone.

pterygo-malar (-'meɪlə(r)) *a.*, belonging to or connected with the pterygoid process of the sphenoid and the malar bone. **pterygo-'maxillary** *a.* [L. *maxilla* jaw], belonging to or connected with the pterygoid processes and the superior maxillary bone. **pterygo-'palatal, -'palatine** *adjs.*, of or belonging to the pterygoid and the palatine bones. **pterygo-pharyngeal** (-fə'rɪndʒiːəl), **-pha'ryngean** *adjs.*, connected with the pterygoid process and the pharynx. **pterygo-quadrate** (-'kwɒdrət) *a.*, pertaining to or combining the pterygoid and quadrate bones. **pterygo-'sphenoid** *a.*, belonging to the pterygoid and the sphenoid bones; spheno-pterygoid. **pterygo-'spinous** *a.*, pertaining to the pterygoid process and the spine of the sphenoid. **pterygo-'staphyline** *a.* [Gr. σταφυλή uvula]: see quot. 1858. **pterygo-tra'becular** *a.*, of or pertaining to the pterygoid and the trabeculæ of the skull.

1859 OWEN in *Encycl. Brit.* (ed. 8) XVII. 150/1 On the inferior surface the palato-nasal, the pterygo-sphenoid and the *pterygo-malar vacuities. **1840** G. V. ELLIS *Anat.* 68 The constrictor is attached behind the *pterygo-maxillary ligament. **1872** MIVART *Elem. Anat.* 89 The pterygo-maxillary [fissure] runs up between the posterior border of the maxilla and the adjacent pterygoid process. **1831** R. KNOX *Cloquet's Anat.* 37 The *Pterygo-palatine canal,.. gives passage to vessels, and is completed by a process of the palate bones. **1858** MAYNE *Expos. Lex.*, *Pterygo-pharyngean. **1886** *Proc. Zool. Soc.* 220 The *pterygo-quadrate cartilage..varies considerably in depth at different points. [**1704** J. HARRIS *Lex. Techn.* I, **Pterigostaphilinus Externus*, is a Muscle which moves the Uvula.] **1858** MAYNE *Expos. Lex.*, *Pterygostaphylinus*, of or belonging to the pterygoid process of the sphenoid bone and *uvula*: *pterygostaphyline. **1886** *Proc. Zool. Soc.* 222 A well-marked *pterygo-trabecular eminence.

pterygode (pt-, 'tɛrɪgəʊd). *Entom.* [f. mod.L. *pterygōda* pl., f. Gr. πτερυγώδης: see next.] Each of two movable appendages on the pronotum and thorax of certain Lepidoptera; the patagium.

[**1834** tr. *Latreille* in *Cuvier's Anim. Kingd.* III. 336 Before the superior wings of these Insects are two species of epaulettes—*pterygoda*—which extend posteriorly along a portion of the back on which they are laid.] **1895** *Proc. Zool. Soc.* 264 The pterygodes are purplish black at base, with a large patch of white before the terminal fringe.

pterygoid (pt-, 'tɛrɪgɔɪd), *a.* (*sb.*) *Anat.* [ad. Gr. πτερυγοειδής, contr. πτερυγώδης like a wing, f. πτέρυξ, -υγ- wing: see -OID.] **A.** *adj.* Having the form or appearance of a wing, wing-like, wing-shaped.

1. *pterygoid process* (πτερυγοειδὴς ἀπόφυσις, Galen): Each of two processes of bone descending (on each side) from the junction of the body and great wing of the sphenoid bone.

The *external pterygoid process* is a process or extension of the alisphenoid, or great wing of the sphenoid, having no independent centre of ossification, and is in no vertebrate a distinct part. The *internal pterygoid process* is in origin a distinct bone, the *pterygoid bone* proper, which in lower vertebrates remains distinct and freely articulated, but in mammalia is ankylosed with the sphenoid, and sutured with the palatal bone. (In fishes there are several distinct pterygoid bones.) The external and internal pterygoid processes (or bones) are also called the *pterygoid plates*.

1722 QUINCY *Lex. Physico-Med.* (ed. 2) 12 *Aliformes Musculi*, are Muscles arising from the Pterygoide Bone, and ending in the Neck of the lower Jaw. **1741** MONRO *Anat.* (ed. 3) 119 It runs above the inner Wing of the pterygoid Process. **1808** BARCLAY *Muscular Motions* 504 The pterygoid processes of the sphenoides. **1837** *Penny Cycl.* VIII. 162/1 The auditory bone..and the pterygoid apophyses are fixed to the skull as in the tortoises. **1881** MIVART *Cat* iii. 70 Two complex bony plates:..each of these is called a pterygoid plate.

b. Connected with the pterygoid processes.

pterygoid fossa, the deep concavity between the external and internal pterygoid plates. *pterygoid muscles* (external and internal), the muscles of mastication which arise from the respective pterygoid processes, and are inserted into the lower jaw-bone, to effect its forward-and-backward and lateral movements. *pterygoid ridge*, the ridge traversing the outer surface of the alisphenoid which gives attachment to the external pterygoid muscle. *pterygoid tubercle*, the rough prominence on the lower jaw for attachment of the internal pterygoid muscle.

1746 R. JAMES *Introd. Moufet's Health's Improv.* 4 The external Pterygoide Muscles, and some Fibres of the Masseter, draw the intire inferior Jaw forwards. **1869** *Proc. Amer. Phil. Soc.* XI. 583 A single pterygoid tooth was found in the matrix. **1872** HUMPHRY *Myology* 44 Bounding the orbit behind, and filling up the wide pterygoid fossa on the side of the skull. **1881** MIVART *Cat* 70 The very small space included between this last and the hamular process, is called the pterygoid fossa.

2. *pterygoid chest*, a form of the thorax in which the shoulder-blades stick out on each side.

1870 S. GEE *Auscult. & Percussion* I. ii. 27 It is instructive to compare the raising of the shoulders and the non-prominence of the shoulder-blades with the opposite conditions in the opposite form of chest, the pterygoid. **1898** *Allbutt's Syst. Med.* V. 202 The first [abnormal form of chest] named alar or pterygoid by Galen and Arctæus and in our own day by Dr. Gee.

B. *sb.* **a.** The pterygoid bone. **b.** Each of the pterygoid muscles.

[**1693** tr. *Blancard's Phys. Dict.* (ed. 2), *Pterygoides*, the Processes and Muscles of the Wedge-like Bone.] **1831** R. KNOX *Cloquet's Anat.* 239 In the substance of a muscle, as in the masseter and pterygoid. **1854** OWEN *Skel. & Teeth* in *Orr's Circ. Sc.* I. *Org. Nat.* 179 The palatine and pterygoids forming the roof of the mouth. **1875** HUXLEY in *Encycl. Brit.* I. 754/2 Each pterygoid is a triradiate bone.

So **ptery'goidal** *a.*; **ptery'goidean** *a.* (*sb.*).

1704 J. HARRIS *Lex. Techn.* I. s.v. *Pterigopalatinus*, The Tendon of this passes over the Pterigoidal Process. **1843** *Penny Cycl.* XXV. 58/2 The descending part of the parietal and pterygoïdean bones. *Ibid.* 59/1 The jugal proceeds from the posterior angle of the orbit..touching a little behind and below the pterygoïdean. **1851** MANTELL *Petrifactions* iii. §3. 199 Saurians without pterygoidal teeth.

‖**Pterygota** (ptɛrɪ'gəʊtə), *sb. pl.* *Entom.* [mod.L., f. Gr. πτερυγωτός winged.] A primary division of Insects, containing all the winged kinds. Hence **'pterygote** *a.*, furnished with wings, winged; belonging to the *Pterygota*.

1878 BELL tr. *Gegenbaur's Comp. Anat.* 245 This indifferent condition of the organisation is developed along two distinct lines in the Pterygota. **1898** PACKARD *Textbk. Entomol.* 83 In the embryo of pterygote insects, an intermaxillary segment has not been yet detected.

‖**pteryla** (pt-, 'tɛrɪlə). *Ornith.* Pl. **-æ**. [mod.L. (Nitzsch 1833), f. Gr. πτερ-όν feather + ὕλη wood.] A definite clump, patch, or area of feathers, one of a number on the skin of a bird, separated by *apteria* or featherless spaces.

Of such patches or areas Nitzsch in his System of Pterylography (Halle 1840, Eng. tr. by Dallas 1867) recognized eight, viz. the spinal, ventral, neck-, wing-, tail-, shoulder-, femoral, and crural tracts, to which Prof. Newton adds the head-tract, and tract of the oil-gland. The distinctness of these varies greatly in different orders and groups of birds.

1867 tr. *Nitzsch's Pterylography* (Ray Soc.) 3 The feathered regions of the bodies of birds, to which I give the name of feather-tracts (*pterylæ*, Federnfluren). **1894** NEWTON *Dict. Birds* 744 Feathers..are generally restricted to well-defined patches or tracts, which in 1833 received from Nitzsch..the name of *pterylæ*..or 'feather-forests', in opposition to the *apteria*, or featherless spaces, which intervene.

pterylography (pt-, tɛrɪˈlɒgrəfɪ). *Ornith.* [f. PTERYLA + -GRAPHY.] The scientific description of, or a treatise on, the pterylosis of birds.

1867 *(title)* Nitzsch's Pterylography, translated from the German. **1870** ROLLESTON *Anim. Life* Introd. 49 The ulna carries the 'secondaries'..of pterylography.

Hence ˌ**pteryloˈgraphic, -ical** *adjs.*, of or pertaining to pterylography; descriptive of pterylæ; ˌ**pteryloˈgraphically** *adv.*, in respect of pterylography. So ˌ**pteryloˈlogical** *a.* [as if f. **pterylology*], of or pertaining to pterylosis.

1867 tr. *Nitzsch's Pterylography* (Ray Soc.) 43 The most important pterylographic characters of these [Diurnal Rapacious Birds] consist in the presence of an aftershaft on the contour-feathers. *Ibid.* 83 This group, although inferior to the preceding in extent, is nevertheless, much more variable pterylographically. **1896** NEWTON *Dict. Birds* Introd. 69 He [Dr. Cornay] also seems to have been aware of some pterylological differences exhibited in Birds.

pterylosis (pt-, tɛrɪˈləʊsɪs). *Ornith.* [f. PTERYLA: see -OSIS.] The arrangement or disposition of the pterylæ, or of the feathers, of birds.

1874 COUES *Birds N.W.* 590 Of the pterylosis it may be observed, after Nitzsch, that the general character is perfectly scolopacine. **1885** *Proc. Zool. Soc.* 175 The pterylosis of this Cuckoo is not widely different from that of *Cuculus.*

‖**ptilinum** (ˈptɪlɪnəm). *Entom.* [mod.L., ad. F. *ptiline* (J. B. Robineau-Desvoidy *Essai sur les Myodaires* (1830) i. 10), arbitrarily f. Gr. πτίλ-ον down, a plumelet.] A peculiar structure in some dipterous insects: see quots. Hence **ˈptilinal** *a.*

1853 F. WALKER *Insecta Britannica: Diptera* II. 2 The ptilinum is a soft membrane, which in many species, and especially in the newly-hatched flies, appears between the antennæ and the front. **1899** *Cambr. Nat. Hist.* VI. 442 About one-half of the Diptera possess a peculiar structure in the form of a head-vesicle called 'ptilinum'. In the fly emerging from the pupa this appears as a bladder-like expansion of the front of the head; being susceptible of great distension, it is useful in rupturing the hard shell in which the creature is then enclosed. In the mature fly, the ptilinum is completely introverted and can be found only by dissection. **1925** A. D. IMMS *Gen. Textbk. Entomol.* III. 593 The Ptilinum or frontal sac is a characteristic cephalic organ of Cyclorrhapha and its presence is indicated externally by the arched frontal or ptilinal suture. **1962** GORDON & LAVOIPIERRE *Entmol.* xxvii. 171 Having emerged from the puparium the insect pushes its way up through the soil to the surface by the alternate inflation and deflation of the ptilinum. **1969** R. F. CHAPMAN *Insects* xxii. 441 Once the fly has hardened the ptilinum is no longer eversible and the muscles associated with it degenerate. Its position is indicated in the mature fly by the ptilinal suture.

ptilo- (pt-, tɪləʊ), before a vowel **ptil-**, combining form of Gr. πτίλον a soft feather, a plumelet.

ˈptilocerque (-sɜːk) *Zool.* [Gr. κέρκος tail], an elephant shrew of the genus *Ptilocercus*, having a long tail with distichous hairs towards the end; the pen-tailed shrew. **ptiloˈgenesis**, the genesis or growth of feathers (*Syd. Soc. Lex.* 1895). **ˈptilolite** *Min.* [see -LITE], 'hydrous silicate of aluminum, calcium, and potassium, found in delicate tufts made up of short capillary crystals' (Chester). **ptilopædic** (-ˈpiːdɪk) *a. Ornith.* [Gr. παῖς, παιδ- child + -IC], of birds: hatched with a complete covering of down.

1895 *Funk's Standard Dict.*, *Ptilocerque. **1886** *Amer. Jrnl. Sc.* Ser. III. XXXII. 118 *Ptilolite, derived from πτίλον, down, in reference to the light, downy nature of its aggregates. **1887** *Min. Mag.* VII. 115 Ptilolite is gradually decomposed by strong sulphuric acid. **1884** COUES *Key N. Amer. Birds* (ed. 2) 88 Probably all præcocial birds are also *ptilopædic, and all psilopædic birds altricial, but..many altrices, as hawks and owls, [are] also ptilopædic. **1885** *Athenæum* 1 Aug. 146/2 The rails and cranes, the typical members of which are præcocial and ptilopædic.

‖**ptilosis**[1] (pt-, tɪˈləʊsɪs). *Path. Obs.* [a. Gr. πτίλωσις disease of the eyelids, f. πτίλος sore-eyed: see -OSIS.] A disease of the eyelids, attended with inflammation and loss of the eye-lashes (*Syd. Soc. Lex.*).

1684 tr. *Blancard's Phys. Dict.*, *Ptylosis*, when the Brims of the Eye-lids being grown thick, the Hairs of the Eye-brows fall off. **1799** HOOPER *Med. Dict.*, Ptilosis.

ptiˈlosis[2]. *Ornith. rare.* [f. Gr. πτίλ-ον soft feather, down + -OSIS.] Plumage; also, the arrangement of the feathers, = PTERYLOSIS.

1858 MAYNE *Expos. Lex.*, *Ptilosis*..term applied by Illiger to the assemblage of feathers or to the plumage of birds. **1872** COUES *Key N. Amer. Birds* 5 All a bird's feathers, of whatever kind and structure, taken together, constitute its *ptilosis* or Plumage.

ptisan (ˈtɪzən, tɪˈzæn), *sb.* Forms: α. 5 **thisan(e, tizanne, tysane,** 5–6 **tysan,** 6 **-ant(e,** 6–8 **tisan,** 6–9 **tisane,** 8 **tissane.** β. 6 **ptysan(e, ptisant,** 7 **ptizand, -anne, phtisan,** 8 **ptisen,** 8–9 **ptissan,** 9 **ptisanne,** 6–9 **ptisane,** 6– **ptisan.** [a. F. *tisane* (14th c. *tizanne*, 16th c. *ptisane*) = Pr. *tisana, tipsana*, Sp. and It. *tisana*, ad. L. *ptisana* (also in med.L. *tipsana*), a. Gr. πτισάνη peeled or pearl barley, also a drink made from this, f. πτίσσειν to peel, to winnow, to crush or bray as in a mortar.]

1. A palatable decoction of nourishing and slightly medicinal quality; originally a drink made of barley, barley-water (simple or with admixture of other ingredients); now often applied more widely.

α. **1398** TREVISA *Barth. De P.R.* XVII. cxv. (Bodl. MS.), Of barlich ischeled and isode in water is a medicinable drinke ymade þat phisicians clepen Thisan. *c* **1400** *Lanfranc's Cirurg.* 139 In þe v. day he took þikke tizanne [*v.r.* tysan]. *c* **1440** *Promp. Parv.* 494/2 Tysane, drynke, *ptisana.* **1567** TURBERV. *Epitaphs*, etc. 97 b, They will refuse the Tysants taste. **1596** DANETT tr. *Comines* (1614) 15 A little of the tysan the Earle had drunke of. **1709** MRS. MANLEY *Secret Mem.* I. 126 He could not confine himself to Wine and Water, or Tissanes. **1854** BADHAM *Halieut.* 119 Paul of Ægina advises that the patient quaff a light tisane.

β. **1533** ELYOT *Cast. Helthe* II. xxi. (1541) 34 b, Ptysane is none other than pure barley, braied in a morter, and sodden in water. **1544** PHAER *Regim. Life* (1553) G j b, Drynke a ptisane made of barley, lyquyryce, prunes, and the rotes of fenel. **1562** BULLEYN *Bulwark, Bk. Simples* 8 b, And of cleane Barly and puer Water, is made that excellente Water called Ptisant. **1612** *Enchir. Med.* II. 237 In the stead of wine, wee must vse Ptizand. **1643** J. STEER tr. *Exp. Chyrurg.* vii. 30 Let his drinke be phtisan. **1662** J. DAVIES tr. *Mandelslo's Trav.* 15 The benefit I had by the drinking of Ptizanne. **1699** GARTH *Dispens.* III. (1700) 36 Thrice happy were those Golden Days of old When dear as Burgundy, Ptisans were sold. **1772** T. PERCIVAL *Ess.* (1777) I. 327 He had drank about a pint of the ptisan. **1858** [see 2]. **1885** BURTON *Arab. Nts.* III. 94 The old woman ceased not to.. ply him with ptisanes and diet-drinks.

†**2.** Peeled or husked barley. *Obs. rare.*

[**1398** TREVISA *Barth. De P.R.* XVII. clxx. (Bodl. MS.), Tipsana..is barliche istampid in a morter & furste dried & scheled.] **1601** HOLLAND *Pliny* II. 33 Vnlesse it be taken with Ptisane, or husked Barly alone. **1858** MAYNE *Expos. Lex.*, *Ptisana*, barley pounded and made into balls; also, a drink made of farinaceous substances boiled in water and sweetened; a ptisan, tisane, more correctly, perhaps, ptissan.

3. *attrib.* and *Comb.*, as ***ptisan-broth, -vender.***

1590 BARROUGH *Meth. Physick* 228 Minister agaíne Ptisane broth. **1815** *Paris Chit-chat* (1816) I. 61 Narrow-brimmed hats, fit only for ptisan venders.

Hence **ˈptisan** *v. trans.*, to feed with ptisan; **ptiˈsanery** [Fr. *tisanerie*], the making of ptisan; the place in a hospital where ptisan is made.

1844 TUPPER *Twins* xxi, I am obliged to coddle her, and feed her, and ptisan her, like a sick baby. **1843** LE FEVRE *Life Trav. Phys.* I. I. vii. 147 He would not allow that anything French could be innocent, not even its ptisannery.

†**ptish** (ptɪʃ), *int.* and *sb. Obs.* = PISH!

1600 W. WATSON *Decacordon* (1602) 16 Sundry ptishes, face-makings, shaking of their heads, and diuerse verie disdainfull exclamations.

ptisic, -ick(e, -ike, -ique, obs. ff. PHTHISIC.

ptochocracy (pt-, təʊˈkɒkrəsɪ). [f. Gr. πτωχός poor, a beggar + -CRACY.] Government by beggars, the rule of paupers; a governing body consisting of the poor; *loosely*, the poor as a class.

1774 BURGH *Pol. Disquisitions* I. II. iv. 50 The British government..is neither absolute monarchy nor limited monarchy, nor aristocracy, nor democracy,..but may be called a ptochocracy (the reader will pardon a new word) or government of beggars. **1831** *Examiner* 140/2 Consistently the King has a Pension List for Charity to the Ptochocracy. **1878** GLADSTONE *Glean.* (1879) I. 182 To make its argument good, it should have shown the imminence of a ptochocracy.

ptochogony (pt-, təʊˈkɒgənɪ). [f. as prec. + -γονία begetting, generation.] The begetting or production of beggars.

1839 SYD. SMITH *Lett. to Archd. Singleton* iii. ¶21 The whole plan of the Bishop of London is a ptochogony—a generation of beggars. He purposes..to create a thousand livings of 130*l* per annum each. **1852** H. L. MANSEL *Let.* in *Oxford Univ. Commission Evid.* I. 20 It is..desirable that the dark as well as the bright side of academical ptochogony should be fully considered.

ptoˈchology. [f. as prec. + -LOGY.] The scientific study of pauperism, unemployment, etc.

1891 W. TUCKWELL in *Review of Churches* 15 Dec. 174 The parson..is, by vertue of his office, an adept in what Dean Mansel used to call ptochology, the science which estimates and classifies pauperage, mendicancy, unemploy.

Ptolemæan (tɒləˈmiːən), *a.* and *sb.* Also 7–8 **-mean.** [f. L. *Ptolemæ-us* (see PTOLEMAIC) + -AN.] = PTOLEMAIC *a.* 1 and *sb.*

1647 BOYLE *Let. to Hartlib* 8 Apr., Wks. 1744 I. Life 23 The dissenting opinions of the Ptolemeans, the Tychonians, the Copernicans. **1861** MAX MÜLLER *Sci. Lang.* i. 17 Although the Ptolemæan system was a wrong one, yet even from its eccentric point of view, laws were discovered determining the true movements of the heavenly bodies.

Ptoleˈmaian, *a.* [f. as next + -AN.] = next, A. 2.

1905 *Blackw. Mag.* May 629/1 [An] inscription of the Ptolemaian epoch.

Ptolemaic (tɒləˈmeɪɪk), *a.* and *sb.* [f. Gr. Πτολεμαῖ-ος (L. *Ptolemæus*) Ptolemy + -IC.]

A. *adj.* **1.** Of or pertaining to Ptolemy, a celebrated astronomer who lived at Alexandria in the second century A.D.

Ptolemaic system or ***theory***: the astronomical system or theory elaborated by Ptolemy in his Μαθηματικὴ σύνταξις (cf. ALMAGEST), in which the relative motions of the sun, moon, and planets were explained to take place around the earth, which was supposed to be stationary; it was, with modifications, the accepted theory till the time of Copernicus and Kepler.

1674 BOYLE *Excell. Theol.* I. v. 209 After the Ptolemaick number and order of the planets had past uncontradicted for very many ages. **1712** ADDISON *Spect.* No. 345 ¶3 The chief Points in the Ptolemaic and Copernican Hypothesis are described with great Conciseness and Perspicuity. **1886** SYMONDS *Renaiss. It.* (1898) VII. ix. 45 The doctrine of the Sphere..embraced the exposition of Ptolemaic astronomy.

2. Of or pertaining to the Ptolemies, the Macedonian Greek rulers of ancient Egypt from the death of Alexander the Great to Cleopatra.

1771 RAPER in *Phil. Trans.* LXI. 484 The Ptolemaic gold coins in the Pembroke collection. **1875** RENOUF *Egypt. Gram.* 65 Those of the Ptolemaic and Roman periods. **1904** R. C. JEBB *Bacchylides* (Proc. Brit. Acad.) 1 The MS. is a fine uncial, with traits of the Ptolemaic type.

B. *sb.* An adherent of the Ptolemaic theory (see A. 1); a Ptolemaist.

1751 HUME *Ess.* xii. (ed. 2) 251 A Copernican or Ptolemaic, who supports each his different System of Astronomy. **1906** *Hibbert Jrnl.* Apr. 594 There are left a few Ptolemaics who believe that the earth is the centre of the heavenly host.

Hence (all in reference to A. 1) †**Ptoleˈmaical** *a.* = A. 1; †**Ptoleˈmaid** *a.*, resembling the arrangement of spheres, etc. in the Ptolemaic theory; **Ptoleˈmaism**, the Ptolemaic principle; **Ptoleˈmaist**, one who holds the Ptolemaic theory.

1653 H. MORE *Antid. Ath.* II. ii. (1712) 40 The same Argument urged from the *Ptolemaical Hypothesis. **1649** G. DANIEL *Trinarch., Hen. V*, cclxxxiii, To involve the Stade Within his Sphære; a Structure *Ptolomaid. **1874** MASSON *Milton* (1877) I. 48 The *Ptolemaism of Milton's astronomical scheme. **1878** *N. Amer. Rev.* CXXVI. 163 Until the Copernicans have convinced the *Ptolemaists.

ptomaic (pt-, təʊˈmeɪɪk), *a.* [f. PTOMA(INE + -IC. The etymologically correct form would be *ptomatic*: cf. next.] Of or pertaining to ptomaïne.

1904 *Daily News* 18 June 3 Some time ago he was seriously ill through ptomaic poisoning.

ptomaine (pt-, ˈtəʊmeɪaɪn, ˈtəʊmeɪn). *Chem.* [ad. It. *ptomaina*, erroneously formed by Professor Selmi of Bologna, f. Gr. πτῶμα fallen body, corpse: see -INE[5]. As the Gr. combining stem is πτωματ-, the correct form of the word would be *ptomatine.*

Prof. Selmi's first paper in *Annali di Chimica* (1876) LXII. 165, announced the body as 'la *ptomaina* o prima alcaloide dei cadaveri'; but this was partly corrected in his work of 1878 to *ptomaina*; it is to be regretted that the full correction to *ptomatine* was not made at its reception into English, which would also have prevented the rise of the illiterate pronunciation (təʊˈmeɪn) like *domain.*—J.A.H.M.]

The generic name of certain alkaloid bodies found in putrefying animal and vegetable matter, some of which are very poisonous.

1880 *Year-bk. Pharmacy* 40 The identification of these alkaloidal substances, or *ptomaines*, is of great interest to toxicologists. **1881** *Pharmaceutical Jrnl.* 28 May 984/2 The discovery of Professor Selmi as to the formation of poisonous alkaloids, which he calls ptomaïnes, in the human body after death. **1884** *Athenæum* 26 Apr. 534/3 These 'cadaveric' alkaloids, or 'ptomaines' as they have also been called. **1891** *Lancet* 3 Oct. 752 The chemical ferments produced in the system, the albumoses or ptomaines which may exercise so disastrous an influence.

b. *attrib.*, as ***ptomaine absorption, poisoning.***

1893 *Westm. Gaz.* 27 June 5/3 All the medical witnesses agreed that death was due to ptomaine poisoning. **1897** *Allbutt's Syst. Med.* II. 215 Ptomaine erythemas, due to shell-fish, etc., may present considerable resemblance to small-pox initial rashes.

Hence **ˈptomained** *ppl. a.*, infected with ptomaine; **ptoˈmainic** *a.*, of or pertaining to ptomaine or the ptomaines (*Syd. Soc. Lex.* 1895). Also **ˈptomato-ˈatropine, ptomatropine,** *Chem.* [f. Gr. πτωματ- + ATROPINE], a ptomaine which resembles atropine in its physical action.

1898 G. W. STEEVENS *With Kitchener to Khartoum* xi. 94 We went to a Greek café and lunched on ptomained sardines. **1895** *Syd. Soc. Lex.*, *Ptomatropine.* **1899** CAGNEY *Jaksch's Clin. Diagn.* v. (ed. 4) 189 Mention should be made also of ptomato-atropin, a basic compound which has been discovered in the latter [i.e. putrid sausage].

‖**ptosis** (ˈptəʊsɪs). Pl. **ptoses** (-iːz). [a. Gr. πτῶσις falling, fall.] A falling, prolapsus: **a.** *spec.* Drooping of the upper eyelid from paralysis of the elevator muscle.

1743 tr. *Heister's Surg.* (1763) I. 390 Of Relaxation and Tumor of the Eye-lids, termed Phalangosis and Ptosis. **1807–26** S. COOPER *First Lines Surg.* (ed. 5) 310 Wounds of the lower part of the forehead or eyebrow, are sometimes followed by the disorder named *ptosis*, in which the upper eyelid hangs down. **1899** *Allbutt's Syst. Med.* VII. 681 Ptosis of the right upper eyelid appeared.

b. Prolapsus of any of the viscera or of the breasts.

1897 *Allbutt's Syst. Med.* III. 587 To discuss ptosis of the abdominal organs. **1905** *Brit. Med. Jrnl.* 26 Aug. *Epit. Curr. Med. Lit.* 34 The relative frequency and importance of ptosis of the various organs. **1909** *Amer. Jrnl. Med. Sci.* CXXXVII. 380 Ptoses of the splenic flexure and descending colon are rare. **1934** S. BECKETT *More Pricks than Kicks* 68 Man with weak bladder and tendency to ptosis of viscera. **1953** *Pageant* Aug. 68 About 4,000,000 young American women suffer in some degree from micromastia (immature breasts) and another 10,000,000 from ptosis (or collapse or sagging of the breasts). **1957** J. LAPIDES in J. G. Allen et al. *Surgery* xlviii. 1311/2 A number of operations have been devised and used for the fixation of the highly mobile kidney—renal ptosis. **1965** R. P. G. SANDON in R. J. V. Battle *Plastic Surg.* xiv. 319 Clothing tends to confine and flatten, rather than support correctly, such an enormous bosom, and with the years the relaxation of the skin allows an increasing element of ptosis.

Hence **ptotic** ('ptəʊtɪk) *a.*, pertaining to or affected with ptosis.

1890 in *Cent. Dict.* **1969** J. H. DEWEERD in Glenn & Boyce *Urologic Surg.* iv. 122/2 The hypermobile (ptotic) kidney.

ptyalagogue (pt-, 'taɪələgɒg). *Med.* [f. Gr. πτύαλ-ον spittle, saliva (f. πτύ-ειν to spit) + ἀγωγός leading, eliciting.] (See quots.)

[**1753** CHAMBERS *Cycl. Supp.*, *Ptyalagoga*, a word used by physicians to express such medicines as promote a copious discharge of the saliva.] **1842** in DUNGLISON *Med. Lex.* **1858** MAYNE *Expos. Lex.*, *Ptyalagogue*, applied to medicines which promote or increase the flow of saliva. **1895** *Syd. Soc. Lex.*, *Ptyalagogue*.. the same as Sialagogue.

Hence **ptyalagogic** (-'ɒdʒɪk) *a.*, of the nature of a ptyalagogue.

1890 in *Cent. Dict.* (mispr. *-ogogic*).

ptyalin (pt-, 'taɪəlɪn). *Physiol. Chem.* [f. Gr. πτύαλ-ον spittle, saliva + -IN[2].] An amylolytic ferment in saliva, discovered by Leuchs, 1831.

1845 G. E. DAY tr. *Simon's Anim. Chem.* I. 39 Ptyalin and pyin may be regarded as water-extracts of saliva and pus. **1872** HUXLEY *Phys.* vi. 141 The saliva.. contains a small quantity of animal matter, called Ptyalin. **1907** A. RAVENHILL *Pract. Hygiene* 188 The ptyalin (the active ferment in the saliva) of which the function is to convert insoluble starch into soluble sugar.

ptyalism (pt-, 'taɪəlɪz(ə)m). [ad. Gr. πτυαλισμός expectoration, f. πτυαλίζειν to expectorate, f. πτύαλον: see prec.] Excessive secretion or flow of saliva; salivation.

[**1681** tr. *Willis' Rem. Med. Wks.* Vocab., *Ptyalismus*, salivation, or a great flux of spitting.] **1684** tr. *Bonet's Merc. Compit.* x. 361 Mercury.. is a cause of the copious secretion of the Saliva, which is the cause of a Ptyalism. **1802** *Med. Jrnl.* VIII. 37 Harrassed by an almost incessant ptyalism. **1876** BARTHOLOW *Mat. Med.* (1879) 202 Moderate use of mercury, short of ptyalism.

So **'ptyalize** *v. trans.*, to induce ptyalism in, to salivate. **'ptyalose** *Chem.*, the sugar formed by the action of ptyalin on starch (*S.S. Lex.* 1895).

1875 H. C. WOOD *Therap.* (1879) 392 It is not necessary to ptyalize the patient severely.

†**'ptychode.** *Bot. Obs.* [f. Gr. πτυχώδης in folds or layers, f. πτυχή a fold + -ειδης = -form.] Hartig's name for a supposed membrane lining certain vegetable cells; in reality the contracted protoplasmic layer in contact with the cell-wall.

1849 *Ray Soc. Rep. & Pap. Bot.* 222 He was led to these researches by Hartig's investigations upon the structure of cells, and his assumption of their possessing a more internal membrane which lines their interior, and which he denominated a Ptychode.

ptychodont ('ptɪkəʊdɒnt). *Palæont.* [f. Gr. πτυχή fold + ὀδούς, ὀδοντ- tooth.] Having the crowns of the molar teeth folded, as in the fossil genus *Ptychodus*.

1890 in *Cent. Dict.*

ptygmatic (tɪg'mætɪk), *a. Geol.* [ad. Sw. *ptygmatisk* (J. J. Sederholm 1907, in *Bull. de la Commission Géol. de Finlande* XXIII. 89), f. Gr. πτύγμα, πτύγματ- folded matter: see -IC.] Applied to the highly sinuous and often discordant folding exhibited by the veins in some gneisses and migmatites, and to the veins themselves.

1907 J. J. SEDERHOLM in *Bull. de la Commission Géol. de Finlande* XXIII. 110 [*English summary of original Sw. article.*] The primary folding caused by melting, he designates as ptygmatic... These suggestions are made with every reservation. **1926** G. W. TYRRELL *Princ. Petrol.* xxi. 333 (*caption*) Ptygmatic folding of a quartz vein in amphibolite. **1952** *Geol. Mag.* LXXXIX. 1 The term 'ptygmatic' was originally coined by Sederholm in 1907 (p. 110) to describe 'the primary folding caused by melting' in gneisses and migmatites. The word.., as defined, would embrace most of the contortions, many of which are now included in the term 'flow fold', commonly seen in migmatite zones the world over... The term was later restricted by Sederholm (1926) to those tortuous quartzo-felspathic veins, which occur in areas of granitization. **1970** K. C. JACKSON *Textbk. Lithol.* vii. 420 (*caption*) Ptygmatic folding of a pegmatite dike in gneiss.

Hence **ptyg'matically** *adv.*, in a way characteristic of ptygmatic folds; also (as a back-formation) **'ptygma**, a ptygmatic fold.

1928 *Summary of Progr. Geol. Survey Gt. Brit. 1927* II. 72 Other observers of what are certainly ptygmatically folded veins have not accepted Sederholm's explanation. **1944** *Trans. R. Soc. Edin.* LXI. 228 The foliation (gneissic structure) of the host rock appears to conform to the plications of the 'ptygma'. **1960** *Rep. 21st Internat. Geol. Congr.* XIV. 138 It is concluded that ptygmas could have been formed as the result of development in a passive host or possibly, though improbably, as the result of magmatic flowage. **1971** *Scottish Jrnl. Geol.* VII. 316 Pre-D2 quartz veins are.. ptygmatically folded when at high angle to S2.

p-type ('piːtaɪp), *a. Physics.* [f. *P* (repr. *positive*) + TYPE *sb.*[1]] Applied to (a region in) a semiconductor in which electrical conduction is due chiefly to the movement of holes (rather than electrons). Opp. N-TYPE *a.*

1946 [see N-TYPE]. **1948** TORREY & WHITMAN *Crystal Rectifiers* iii. 49 A semiconductor that conducts principally by holes in the nearly filled band is referred to as a '*p*-type' semiconductor. *Ibid.*, The impurities added to silicon make it *p*-type. **1970** *New Scientist* 15 Oct. (Suppl.) 6/2 In a practical integrated circuit the triangular half of the rectifier is p-type material which is diffused into the silicon chip in a pattern similar to the wall plan for a house.

ptysmagogue ('ptɪzməgɒg). *Med. rare.* [f. Gr. πτύσμα spittle, expectoration.] = PTYALAGOGUE.

1730–6 BAILEY (folio), *Ptysmagogue*, a medicine which discharges spittle, whether it amounts quite to a salivation or not. **1858** in MAYNE *Expos. Lex.* **1895** in *Syd. Soc. Lex.*

‖**ptyxis** ('ptɪksɪs). *Bot.* [a. Gr. πτύξις folding.] (See quot.)

1880 GRAY *Struct. Bot.* (ed. 6) 132 *note*, *Ptyxis*.. is coming into use as a general term for the folding, etc., of single parts. *Ibid.* 133 The *Ptyxis* (or folding) of an individual leaf.. should be distinguished from the arrangement in the bud of the leaves of a circle or spiral in respect to each other.

pu, pu', Sc. forms of PULL.

pua, var. PUHA.

†**'puant**, *a. Obs. rare.* [a. F. *puant*, pres. pple. of *puer* formerly *puir*:—pop.L. *putīre* for L. *pūt-ēre* to stink.] Stinking. Hence †**'puantly** *adv.*

a **1529** SKELTON *Agst. Garnesche* III. 143 Your brethe yt ys so felle And so puauntely dothe smelle. **1621** T. WILLIAMSON tr. *Goulart's Wise Vieillard* 161 The bodies of rich-men.. are more puant and stinking then the bodies of poore men.

puarpure, variant of PUERPER *Obs.*

pub (pʌb), *sb. colloq.* [Shortened from PUBLIC *sb.* 4.] **1.** A public house, an inn.

1859 HOTTEN *Dict. Slang* 78 *Pub*, or *Public*, a public house. **1865** E. C. CLAYTON *Cruel Fortune* II. 155 The wealthy proprietress of a busy 'pub'. **1890** F. W. ROBINSON *Very Strange Family* 70 A barmaid from a Waterloo Road pub. **1893** K. MACKAY *Out Back* (ed. 2) II. v. 188 It's Molloy's fault... He got tanked at the pub last night. **1922** JOYCE *Ulysses* 70 Waiting outside pubs to bring da home. **1924** *Truth* (Sydney) 27 Apr. 6 *Pub*, hotel. **1936** M. ALLIS *Eng. Prelude* xxiii. 247 First comes the pub, the *Fox and Hounds*. **1946** *R.A.F. Jrnl.* May 175 There are German beer shops turned into typical English 'Pubs'. **1950** 'N. SHUTE' *Town like Alice* vi. 170 She was surprised at the rapidity of [the town's] growth. In 1928 it was about three houses and a pub. **1970** M. GREENER *Penguin Dict. Commerce* 268 A pub offering accommodation to casual customers will probably be a hotel within the definition of the Hotel Proprietors Act 1956 and the various Innkeepers Acts. **1980** 'D. KAVANAGH' *Duffy* ii. 36 They met at a drinkers' pub near Baker Street Station.

2. *attrib.* and *Comb.*, as ***pub-door, food, -friend, -goer, -grub, -keeper, -landlord, manager, meal, mirror, parlour, -singer***; ***pub-going, -running, -spieling*** vbl. sbs.; ***pub-hunting*** ppl. adj.; **pub-crawl**: see CRAWL *sb.*[1] b; hence as *v. intr.*; **pub-crawler**; **pub-crawling** *vbl. sb.* and *ppl. a.*; **pub-life**, the society of public houses; **pub lunch**, a lunch eaten in a pub; hence **pub-lunch** *v. intr.*, **pub-luncher**; **pub rock**, rock music of a type played in public houses; **pub-stiff** *N.Z. slang*, a look-out or sentinel acting on behalf of a licensee selling alcoholic drinks after closing-time; **pub theatre**, a public house at which theatrical performances take place; also, theatrical representation performed in a public house; **pub-time**, (*a*) the hour at which a public house opens or closes; (*b*) the time shown by a clock in a public house, with reference to the custom of advancing this slightly to bring forward closing-time.

1915 Pub-crawl [see CRAWL *sb.*[1] b]. **1937** *Times Lit. Suppl.* 27 Nov. 910/1 Mr. Lyons does not 'pub-crawl' as a writer in search of copy. **1959** [see CRAWL *sb.*[1] b]. **1972** J. SYMONS *Players & Game* xxiii. 182 He had taken a girl.. on a mild variety of pub crawl. **1974** *Canadian Mag.* (Toronto) 16 Mar. 2/3 Across Canada, kids aren't packing the discothèques; instead, they're pub-crawling. **1910** *Daily Chron.* 28 Jan. 4/4 These 'pub-crawlers' have captured the illiterate and the unthinking. **1976** J. R. L. ANDERSON *Redundancy Pay* ix. 145 You're turning me into quite a pub-crawler. **1919** 'W. N. P. BARBELLION' *Enjoying Life* 75 Drunken Barnabee's Journal.. is rhymed Latin verse.. describing the author's 'pub crawlings' up and down the country. **1921** F. B. YOUNG *Black Diamond* vii. 73, I bain't goin' to keep you in pub-crawling any longer. **1973** 'H. CARMICHAEL' *Candles for Dead* vi. 74 A pub-crawling reporter. **1980** I. MURDOCH *Nuns & Soldiers* i. 83 This sort of urban life suited Tim, pub-crawling, wandering, looking in shop-windows. **1960** T. HUGHES *Lupercal* 18 The lamp above the pub-door Wept yellow when he went out. **1977** *Times* 11 June 11/7 English people care more about pub food than they used to. **1959** J. CARY *Captive & Free* xviii. 85 His father had been a steady worker, but completely devoid of ambition; a man whose only interests were football, darts, his pub-friends. **1955** T. H. PEAR *Eng. Social Differences* vi. 160 Peter is primarily a pub-goer. *Ibid.* 161 The social differences which come out in pub-going. *Ibid.* 162 The new pub-going habit for girls and women is a genuine problem. **1978** *Country Life* 19 Oct. 1186/4 There are 'lounge bars' and 'singing bars' and many places advertising 'pub grub'. **1922** JOYCE *Ulysses* 599 He commented adversely on the desertion of Stephen by all his pubhunting *confrères* but one. **1925** W. DEEPING *Sorrell & Son* vi. 57 Our pub-keepers rarely visualize the atmosphere of a garden. **1980** D. FRANCIS *Reflex* vi. 67 The pub-keeper from the Sussex village where he lived. **1909** *Daily Chron.* 17 July 4/7 Mr. Lewis Harcourt's reference to 'the ground and the pub-landlord seeking to hold the common fort'. **1944** WYNDHAM LEWIS *Let.* 5 Jan. (1963) 374, I gather from Augustus that the pub-life of London is functioning as of yore. **1970** G. F. NEWMAN *Sir, You Bastard* v. 130 When he reported, Sneed had a pub lunch with the Governor. **1971** 'F. CLIFFORD' *Blind Side* II. iv. 113 He pub-lunched in Richmond. **1975** *Times* 8 Mar. 10/4 Cheapness is often the only virtue of the British pub lunch. **1971** *Times* 2 June 6/1 The sound of pub-lunchers arising merrily from below. **1977** P. COSGRAVE *Cheyney's Law* iv. 39 He waited, no longer the tweedy city stroller, pub luncher, book buyer. **1973** K. GILES *File on Death* v. 118, I got a letter asking if I had perhaps a vacancy for a pub manager. **1975** P. MCCUTCHAN *Very Big Bang* x. 96 He would.. snatch pub meals as and when he could. **1974** *Selfridges Bk. of Xmas* 80 Victorian style pub mirrors ..£18.75 each. **1977** J. WILSON *Making Hate* vii. 85 A reproduction Edwardian pub mirror. **1929** D. H. LAWRENCE *Pansies* 132 Little fleets.. that put to sea and boldly sink Armadas In a pub parlour, in literary London, on certain evenings. **1976** *Star* (Sheffield) 20 Nov., Pub-rock does a dying swan act at the weekend when Sheffield's most celebrated stronghold closes its doors to live entertainment. **1977** *Zigzag* Apr. 39/2 Joe was bored with singing pub rock standards. **1973** K. GILES *File on Death* v. 118, I own the local brewery... Pub-running has problems. **1975** *Radio Times* 3 Apr. 17 George Formby... His songs.. have passed.. into the repertoires of every comic, impressionist and pub-singer. **1900** H. LAWSON *Over Sliprails* 38 Jack Drew talked too straight in the paper, and in spite of his proprietors—about pub spieling and such things. **1946** F. SARGESON *That Summer* 63 The pub-stiff that was on the door told us to go upstairs. **1973** *Guardian* 23 Jan. 10/1 Pub theatres are in vogue for the first time since Shakespeare's day. **1976** *Alyn & Deeside Observer* 10 Dec. 11/5 As the pint is pulled downstairs, an audience is held upstairs by one of the best examples of Pub Theatre to be found in London. **1947** DYLAN THOMAS *Let.* 11 June (1966) 314 I'm used to working from after lunch until pub-time. **1968** L. MEYNELL *Death of Philanderer* x. 167 The clock behind the bar would be showing 'pub time', that is.. it would be at least five minutes fast.

pub, *v.* [f. prec. *sb.*] **a.** *int.* To frequent public houses. Also with *it*.

1889 JEROME *Three Men in Boat* ii, We decided that we would.. hotel it, and inn it, and pub. it.. when it was wet. **1950** *John o' London's* 24 Nov. 614/1 Pubbing through Edinburgh's Old Town and the Leith waterfront. **1960** L. COOPER *Accomplices* III. i. 152 We went pubbing together. **1972** S. CHANCE *Septimus & Minster Ghost* vii. 62 'Can't have you pubbing in your canonicals,' she said, going to the door and looking out into the alley.

b. *intr.* To own or manage a public house.

1936 M. FRANKLIN *All that Swagger* xiv. 130 The profits to be made from fools by pubbing could add to it.

pubarche (pjuː'bɑːkiː). *Med.* [f. L. *pūb-ēs* pubic hair, groin + Gr. ἀρχή beginning.] The first appearance of pubic hair; chiefly in ***premature pubarche***, the premature occurrence of this without other signs of sexual precocity.

1950 L. WILKINS *Diagn. & Treatm. Endocrine Disorders in Childh. & Adolescence* ix. 146/2 We would suggest for this condition the term 'premature pubarche' which does not attempt to define its etiology. **1974** N. D. BARNES et al. in M. M. Grumbach et al. *Control of Onset of Puberty* viii. 223 Premature pubarche or adrenarche, the isolated growth of sexual hair, is another form of precocious sexual development that may be neurogenically determined.

'pubbish, *a.* [f. PUB *sb.* + -ISH[1].] Of the nature or character of a public house.

1956 D. M. DAVIN *Sullen Bell* 56 You hardly ever use a pub, but like an old puritan you insist it must be as pubbish as possible. **1973** R. LUDLUM *Matlock Paper* ii. 13 The name of the country inn was the Cheshire Cat, and.. it was Englishy and pubbish.

'pubble, *a.* Now only *dial.* [Of obscure origin; cf. EFris. *pumpel*, LG. *pümpel* a fat burly person.] Fat, well filled, plump.

1566 DRANT *Horace, Sat.* ii. F ij b, Yf they bothe be dreste, The Pecocke, and the pubble hen, the Pecocke tasteth best. **1567** —— *Epist.* I. iv. D vij, Thou shalt fynde me fat, and wel fed, as pubble as may be. **1641** BEST *Farm. Bks.* (Surtees) 99 If the wheate bee a pubble, proude and well-skinned corne. **1691** RAY *N.C. Words* 56 *Pubble*, fat, full: usually spoken of corn, fruit and the like. **1855** ROBINSON *Whitby Gloss.* s.v., 'As pubble as a partridge', broad-breasted, stout.

'pubby, *a.* [f. PUB *sb.* + -Y[1].] = PUBBISH *a.*

1959 *Good Food Guide* 361 It retains a pleasant pubby atmosphere and there's a good, mildly chaotic restaurant upstairs. **1974** *Times* 5 Oct. 12/8 Balls Brothers wine bar in the Strand had a pubby atmosphere. **1976** *Eastern Daily Press* (Norwich) 16 Dec., In the first, pubs are made to look like anything but pubs, while the 'pubbier than pub' devotees prefer a severe environment.. echoing the style of the first urban public bars.

†**puber** ('pjuːbə(r)). *Obs.* [a. L. *pūber*, also *pūbēs*, *-er-em* adj., that has attained puberty, as sb. a youth, f. *pūbēs* PUBES.] A youth; one who is between the age of puberty and maturity.

c **1315** SHOREHAM I. 1742 Hy beþ icliped puberes, þat hys a word of lawe. **1545** *Records of Elgin* (New Spald. Cl. 1903) I. 86 Thomas Young, puber.

puberal ('pju:bərəl), *a.* [ad. late L. *pūberāl-is* (*Gloss. Cyril.* in Quicherat), adj. f. *pūber*: see prec. and -AL[1].] Of or at the age of puberty.

1836–7 SIR W. HAMILTON *Metaph.* (1870) I. App. 411 They are found in all puberal crania. **1876** tr. *von Ziemssen's Cycl. Med.* V. 483 The period of puberal development.

'puberate, *a. rare.* [f. L. *pūber* (see above) + -ATE[2].] = prec.

1880 MUIRHEAD tr. *Ulpian* viii. §5 Both males and females, and whether puberate or impuberate, may be adopted.

'pubertal, *a.* [irreg. f. next + -AL[1].] Of or pertaining to puberty.

1897 *Atlantic Monthly* Oct. 555 Until the beginning of the pubertal changes, growth is relatively very slow. **1972** *Clin. Endocrinol.* (1973) (B.M.A.) 99 Pubertal development lasts on average about three years in girls and four years in boys. **1976** *Times Lit. Suppl.* 2 Jan. 2/3 A pubertal woman is always potentially taboo [among gypsies] and is actually so after menstruation, childbirth and intercourse. **1979** J. BARNETT *Backfire is Hostile!* v. 49 Some rowdy youths cavorted in the rush and grope of pubertal ritual.

puberty ('pju:bətɪ). [ME. *puberte* = F. *puberté* (1474 in Hatz.-Darm.), ad. L. *pūbertās, -tāt-* the age of maturity, the signs of puberty, f. *pūber* or *pūbēs*: see PUBER.]

1. a. The state or condition of having become functionally capable of procreating offspring, which is characterized by various symptoms in each sex, as by the appearance of hair on the pubes, and on the face in the male.

In England the legal age of puberty is fourteen in boys and twelve in girls, but the actual time of development varies in different climates and environment and with different individuals.

1382 WYCLIF *Mal.* ii. 14 Bitwixe thee and the wijf of thi pubertee [*gloss*, that is, tyme of mariage]. **1398** TREVISA *Barth. De P.R.* VI. v. (Bodl. MS.), Er þei come to þe ȝere of puberte. **1549** *Compl. Scot.* iv. 29 Oure ȝong illustir princis be ane tendir pupil, ande nocht entrit in the aige of puberte. **1646** SIR T. BROWNE *Pseud. Ep.* 344 Though hee knew old age he was never acquainted with puberty, youth, or Infancy. **1774** GOLDSM. *Nat. Hist.* (1776) II. 68 When they arrive near the age of puberty. *a* **1862** BUCKLE *Misc. Wks.* (1872) I. 352 In towns, women reach puberty sooner than they do in the country.

b. *attrib.* Connected with the attainment of the age of puberty.

1908 *Athenæum* 11 Apr. 444/1 Puberty rites, which are found in full vigour notably in Australia. *Ibid.* 444/2 Dr. Webster supposes these societies to arise on the basis of the puberty institutions. **1924** A. LIPSCHÜTZ (*title*) The internal secretions of the sex glands: the problem of the 'puberty gland'. **1971** *Canad. Antiques Collector* Sept.–Oct. 4 Arapaho Painted Hide Puberty Robe 67 × 46 inches. **1978** *New York* 3 Apr. 32/2 Masks and helmets used in puberty rites of Sierra Leone and Liberia.

2. *transf.* Of plants: The state or stage of bearing flowers or fruit. *rare.*

1827 STEUART *Planter's G.* (1828) 454 All Trees have, I think, after they arrive at the age of puberty,.. more slender shoots at the extremities of the branches. **1837** *Penny Cycl.* IX. 224/2 We prevent the full flow of the sap.. and thus advance the age of puberty and bring on a fruit-bearing state.

puberulent (pju:'bɛr(j)ʊlənt), *a. Bot.* [f. L. *pūber* in the sense 'downy' + -ULENT, after *pulverulent*, etc.] Covered with down; pubescent. So **pu'berulous** *a.*

a **1864** GRAY cited in WEBSTER for *Puberulent. **1881** BAKER in *Jrnl. Linn. Soc.* XVIII. 278 A shrub.. with puberulent, white.. branchlets. **1870** HOOKER *Stud. Flora* 231 Cranberry.. peduncles capillary, erect, *puberulous. **1888** —— *Flora Brit. India* V. 625 Leaves.. puberulous or hoary beneath.

‖**pubes** ('pju:bi:z). [L. *pūbēs, -is* the pubic hair; the groin, private parts.]

1. The pubic hair.

c **1570** W. WAGER *The longer thou livest* 1572 (Brandl) In adolecnie when Pubes was springing. **1693** tr. *Blancard's Phys. Dict.* (ed. 2), *Pubes*, the Hair on the Privy Parts. **1706** in PHILLIPS.

2. The hypogastric region, which in the adult becomes covered with hair.

1682 T. GIBSON *Anat.* (1697) 7 The Pubes, which in the adult or ripe of age is covered with hair. **1840** G. V. ELLIS *Anat.* 484 The pyramidalis muscle is placed in the abdominal wall close above the pubes.

b. Erron. for *os pubis*, the pubic bone: = PUBIS 1.

1872 NICHOLSON *Palæont.* 304 The pelvic arch.. consists [on each side] of three pieces—the ilium, ischium, and pubes—which are usually anchylosed together.

c. Erron. pl. of PUBIS (in sense 1) for *ossa pubis*.

1841 RAMSBOTHAM *Obstetr. Med.* 29 In the female.. the rami of the ischia and pubes are smoother on their inner surface. **1872** MIVART *Elem. Anat.* 190 In Reptiles we find a pair of separate bones, usually called the pubes.

†**3.** = PUBERTY 1. *Obs.*

1637 T. MORTON *New Eng. Canaan* (1883) 142 After hee attaines unto the age which they call Pubes.

4. *Zool.* and *Bot.* = PUBESCENCE 2, 3.

1826 KIRBY & SP. *Entomol.* III. xxix. 58 The acquisition of certain organs, &c. as of teeth, pubes, feathers, &c. **1858** MAYNE *Expos. Lex., Pubes... Bot.,*.. a term for the kind of down on the leaves.. of certain plants: pubescence.

pubescence (pju:'bɛsəns). [a. F. *pubescence* (= med.L. *pūbēscentia* in Du Cange): see PUBESCENT and -ENCE.]

1. The fact or condition of arriving at puberty; also = PUBERTY 1.

1646 SIR T. BROWNE *Pseud. Ep.* IV. xii. 216 Solon divided it into ten Septenaries, because in every one thereof a man received some sensible mutation, in the first is Dedentition or falling of teeth: in the second Pubescence. **1822–34** *Good's Study Med.* (ed. 4) IV. 91 Young men when entering upon or emerging from pubescence.

2. *Bot.* The soft down which grows on the leaves and stems of many plants; the character or condition of being pubescent or downy.

1760 J. LEE *Introd. Bot.* III. xviii. (1765) 211 *Pubescence*.. is an Armature, by which Plants are defended from external Injuries. **1830** LINDLEY *Nat. Syst. Bot.* 151 Herbaceous plants,.. with a simple pubescence. **1870** HOOKER *Stud. Flora* 288 *Marrubium*... Hoary, pubescence almost woolly.

3. *Zool.* The soft down which occurs upon certain parts of various animals, esp. insects.

1826 KIRBY & SP. *Entomol.* IV. xliv. 203 In this disease when the animal [flesh-fly] is dead.. its almost invisible pubescence grows into long hairs. **1853** KANE *Grinnell Exp.* xxx. (1856) 261 The downy pubescence of the ears.

†**pu'bescency.** *Obs.* [ad. med.L. *pūbēscentia*: see prec. and -ENCY.] The quality or stage of being pubescent, puberty.

1658 SIR T. BROWNE *Gard. Cyrus* iii. 50 Maturation, from crude pubescency unto perfection. **1684** tr. *Bonet's Merc. Compit.* IV. 116 The Genuine Teeth, which first appear before Pubescency.

pubescent (pju:'bɛsənt), *a.* (*sb.*) [a. F. *pubescent* (1516 in Hatz.-Darm.), or ad. L. *pūbēscens, -ent-*, pres. pple. of *pūbēsc-ĕre* to become downy or hairy, to attain puberty, to ripen, flourish; inceptive verb f. *pūbēs* PUBES.]

1. Arriving or arrived at the age of puberty.

1646 SIR T. BROWNE *Pseud. Ep.* IV. xii. 210 That women are menstruant, and men pubescent, at the year of twice seven, is accounted a punctual truth. **1822–34** *Good's Study Med.* (ed. 4) IV. 86 Occurring, not only in pubescent, but even adult males.

2. *Bot.* and *Zool.* Having pubescence; covered with short soft hair; downy.

1760 J. LEE *Introd. Bot.* I. xiv. (1765) 37 *Pubescent*, downy. **1828** STARK *Elem. Nat. Hist.* II. 347 Antennæ filiform or setaceous; body pubescent. **1857** HENFREY *Bot.* §98 A pubescent surface is covered closely with short soft hairs.

B. *sb.* A youth at the age of puberty.

1894 G. S. HALL in *Forum* (U.S.) May 301 The young pubescent often shows signs of many insanities of intellect, will, and especially feeling.

pubic ('pju:bɪk), *a.* [f. PUBES + -IC.] **a.** Of, pertaining to, or connected with the pubes or pubis.

1831 R. KNOX *Cloquet's Anat.* 115 Forming one of the sides of the pubic arch. **1842** E. WILSON *Anat. Vade M.* 110 The posterior pubic ligament.. uniting the pubic bones posteriorly. **1872** MIVART *Elem. Anat.* 179 The pubis, or pubic bone, forms the inner part of the thigh-socket.

b. Employed to cover the pubes.

1940 A. UPFIELD *Bushranger of Skies* xi. 130 That Jack Johnson wore only the pubic tassel announced his non-employment by the station. **1959** S. H. COURTIER *Death in Dream Time* ii. 19 The bewildering display of aboriginal weapons and implements.. head-dresses and pubic bands.

pu'bigerous, *a. Anat.* [f. L. *pūbi-*, stem of PUBES + -GEROUS.] Bearing downy hairs.

1890 in *Cent. Dict.* **1895** in *Syd. Soc. Lex.*

pubio-, assumed combining form of PUBES (of which the L. stem is actually *pubi-*).

This appears to be the usual form in modern L. anatomical terms, as *pubio-femoralis, -prostaticus*, etc., whence also in the English equivalent forms *pubio-femoral* (so mod.F.), *pubio-ischiadic, -ischiatic, -prostatic, -sternal, -umbilical, -urethral.* But in Billings *Nat. Med. Dict.* 1890 only the corresponding forms in PUBO- are given as Eng., and in *Syd. Soc. Lex.* 1895 most of those in *pubio-* are referred to *pubo-*.

pubiotomy (pju:bɪ'ɒtəmɪ). *Surg.* [f. PUBIO- + -TOMY.] The operation of section through the *symphysis pubis*, esp. in obstetric practice.

1880 ALLBUTT & PLAYFAIR *Syst. Gynæcology* 634 It is beyond the scope of my article to deal with symphisiotomy, pelviotomy, and pubiotomy.

pubis ('pju:bɪs). [In sense 1 short for L. *os pūbis* the bone of the groin; in sense 2, variant of PUBES.]

1. That portion of the innominate bone which forms the anterior wall of the pelvis.

1597 A. M. tr. *Guillemeau's Fr. Chirurg.* 32 b/2 We.. place the Boxes on the bone Pubis in the flanckes. [**1693** tr. *Blancard's Phys. Dict.* (ed. 2), *Pubis os*,.. the share Bone. **1706** PHILLIPS s.v. *Coxæ Os*, In Infants it consists of three Bones, viz. Ilium, Ischium, and Os Pubis.] **1727–41** CHAMBERS *Cycl.* s.v. *Innominatum*, Os Innominatum.. composed of three bones; viz. the ilium, the pubis and the ischium, only connected by cartilages. **1854** OWEN *Skel. & Teeth* (1855) 61 The pubis and ischium on each side have coalesced with the ilium to form the lower boundary of the widely-perforated acetabulum.

2. Erroneously = PUBES 2.

1681 tr. *Willis' Rem. Med. Wks.* Vocab., *Pubis*, that part of the privy-parts, where the hair grows. **1800** *Med. Jrnl.* IV. 164 If I could succeed in bringing the occiput to the pubis. **1811** A. T. THOMSON *Lond. Disp.* (1818) 18 Applied to the pubis as a poultice.

puble, obs. variant of PEBBLE.

publes, -lesch, obs. forms of PUBLISH.

public ('pʌblɪk), *a.* (*sb.*) Forms: α. 5–6 **publyke,** 5–7 **-ike, -ique,** 6 **-icque, -ycke, -yque,** 6–7 **-icke,** *Sc.* **-icte,** 6–8 **-ick,** 7 **-iq,** 6– **public.** β. 5 **puplik,** 7 **-icke, -ique.** [ME. *publike, -ique*, a. F. *public* (1311 in Hatz.-Darm.), ad. L. *pūblicus*, in early L. *poplicus*, f. *poplus* (later *popul-us*) PEOPLE. (The change to *pūblicus* appears to have taken place under the influence of *pūbes*, in the sense 'adult men', 'male population'.)]

A. *adj.* In general, and in most of the senses, the opposite of PRIVATE.

The varieties of sense are numerous and pass into each other by many intermediate shades of meaning. The exact shade often depends upon the substantive qualified, and in some expressions more than one sense is vaguely present; in others the usage is traditional, and it is difficult to determine in what sense precisely the thing in question was originally called 'public'.

I. Pertaining to the people of a country or locality.

1. Of or pertaining to the people as a whole; that belongs to, affects, or concerns the community or nation; common, national, popular.

1484 Public administration [see ADMINISTRATION 1]. **1513** *Bradshaw's St. Werburge, An other Balade to auctour* 20 (E.E.T.S.) 201 One of thy clientes.. Hath chaunged newly, o mayde.. Thy legende latine to our language publique. **1563** WINȜET *Wks.* (S.T.S.) II. 21 To.. confound all, bayth priuat and publict, bayth hallowit and prophane. **1617** Public health [see HEALTH *sb.* 2 b]. **1632** SANDERSON *Serm.* Ep. Ded., Who.. can out of private wrongs worke publike good. **1657** HEYLIN *Hist. Ref.* I. ii. 23 The publique Liturgy in the vulgar tongue. **1673** J. RAY *Observations Journey Low-Countries* 163 He is entrusted with the management of public monies. **1676** in N. Brent *Sarpi's Hist. Councel of Trent* p. xiii, He was in the Publick Employment. **1687** A. LOVELL tr. *Thevenot's Trav.* I. 241 In the month of November there was.. at Caire.. a publick Rejoicing, because the Turks had taken two Castles in Hungary. **1721** *Mass. House of Representatives Jrnl.* (1922) III. 9 Acts have been Passed.. for Striking Bills of Credit, and Issuing out the same, in order to discharge their Publick Debts. **1727** in M. M. Verney *Verney Lett.* (1930) II. xxiv. 101 The main objection against him was his making up of the publick money in the South Sea. **1780** BENTHAM *Princ. Legisl.* xviii. §9 These may be termed public offences or offences against the State. **1781** in *Eng. Rep.* (1903) XXVIII. 1028 Treating it as a matter of public policy of the law, and similar to marriage brokage bonds, where, though the parties are private persons, the practice is publicly detrimental, [etc.]. **1785** J. WESLEY *Let.* 7 Apr. (1931) VII. 266, I beseech you.. to have no respect of persons.., in disposing of the Yearly Contribution and the Preacher's Fund or any other public money. **1787** M. CUTLER *Jrnl.* 21 July in *Life, Jrnls, & Corr.* (1888) I. iv. 127 Congress would pay more than four millions of the public debt. **1794** Public concern [see CONCERN *sb.* 6]. *c* **1799** *Ess. on Political Society* I. 59 To constitute the desiderated political system, is to constitute a permanent law for regulating the public administration. **1806** in *Documentary Hist. Amer. Industr. Society* (1910) III. 67 The newspaper called the *Aurora*, has teemed with false representations.. to poison the public mind. **1812** SIR H. DAVY *Chem. Philos.* 19 At this period there was no taste in the public mind to restrain vague imaginations. **1827** J. KENT *Commentaries on Amer. Law* II. IV. 222 Public corporations, are such as exist for public political purposes only, such as counties, cities, towns and villages. They are founded by the government, for public purposes, and the whole interest in them belongs to the public. **1846** *Penny Cycl.* Suppl. II. 457/2 It may be said that there are contracts which ought to be declared void for reasons of public policy, or, to use a more correct expression.., reasons of public utility. **1846** *Parl. Papers* I. 257 (*heading*) A bill for providing cemeteries, and promoting public health, in towns and populous districts. **1853** in *Eng. Rep.* (1901) X. 437 Public policy.. is that principle of the law which holds that no subject can lawfully do that which has a tendency to be injurious to the public, or against the public good. **1868** TROLLOPE *He knew he was Right* (1869) I. xxxviii. 300 The bias of the public mind. **1883** *Statutes at Large U.S.A.* XXII. 214 Any convict, lunatic, idiot, or any person unable to take care of himself or herself without becoming a public charge. **1887** *Polit. Sci. Q.* II. 212 Public administration is detailed and systematic execution of public law. **1889** G. B. SHAW *Fabian Ess. Socialism* 194 The Manchester School will urge.. the exemption of private enterprise from the competition of public enterprise. *Ibid.* 195 The superior prestige and permanence of public employment. **1894** Public eye [mentioned s.v. EYE *sb.*[1] 8]. **1904** *Whitaker's Almanac* 409/2 Public Record Office, Chancery Lane. Contains a collection of the National Records since 1100. *a* **1909** *Mod.* The event was celebrated by a public holiday. **1918** *Current Hist.* Aug. 277/2 The public debt of the.. United States.. At Most Recent Date [in millions of dollars] $15,008. **1919** A. M. TODD (*title*) Public ownership of railroads. **1928** *Britain's Industr. Future* (Liberal Industr. Inquiry) 63 In a modern community many services must be run by a Public Concern—meaning by this a form of organisation which.. is operated or regulated in the public interest. *Ibid.* 95 We propose.. a special class of Company to be designated Public Corporations... The distinction.. should depend.. mainly on their preponderant position in their own industry or trade. *Ibid.* 243 We stand, not for public ownership, but for popular ownership. **1928** J. BUCHAN *Runagates Club* x. 273 He had been returned to Parliament.. but he wasn't much in the public eye. **1937** *Times* 12 Jan. 13/6 Three years ago it was important to use public policy to increase investment. **1943** J. B. PRIESTLEY *Daylight on Saturday* xxxi. 245 A passionate defender of private enterprise (which he was careful always to contrast with..'State ownership' and never with public enterprise). **1943** W. H. Chase *Sourdough Pot* xix. 123 Some [gold miners] even became public charges with the passing of time. **1943** J. S. Huxley *TVA* ix. 69 Much curiosity has been aroused in the public mind. **1955** *Bull. Atomic Sci.* Apr. 112/3 Public employment does bring with it certain obligations beyond those required of citizens in private life. **1955** *Radio Times* 22 Apr. 15/2 It was a gramophone recording that first brought her before the public eye. **1970** E. Flores in I. L. Horowitz *Masses in Lat. Amer.* ix. 338 It is possible to substitute a cash deposit by Public Debt bonds. **1971** 'D. Halliday' *Dolly & Doctor Bird* i. 6 Public health is a doctor's concern. **1971** S. A. de Smith *Constitutional & Admin. Law* xxiv. 512 Decisions in public administration can be classified in various ways. **1971** P. Worsthorne *Socialist Myth* ix. 237 In a democracy..the expenditure of public money must be dependent on popular agreement. **1972** *Guardian* 24 Mar. 14/2 Ministers must.. keep open minds about public investment and public enterprise in the regions. **1973** I. M. Sinclair *Vienna Convention on Law of Treaties* v. 110 The gradual establishment in common law jurisdictions of the principle that certain types of contract are, by their very nature, injurious to society and therefore contrary to public policy. **1973** *Listener* 26 July 111/1 Mr Maudling said: 'I don't think Michael Foot has the slightest idea what he intends to do in this field of so-called public ownership extension.' **1975** C. Stuart *Reith Diaries* 66 The management of public corporations..was his particular field.

2. Phrases from 1.

a. In various phrases (mostly obsolete) rendering or suggested by L. *res publica*, as †***public state***, †***thing*** (also †***thing public***), the commonwealth or state; ***public good***, ***weal*** (also †***good*** or ***weal public***), ***public wealth***, the common or national good or well-being; †the commonwealth or state; also †***common public*** = common good. Cf. common *a.* 5 b.

1436 *Libel Eng. Policy* xi. in *Pol. Poems* (Rolls) II. 195 This was his laboure for the publique thinge. **1440** in *Wars Eng. in France* (Rolls) II. 445 The gode publique of youre royaumes. **1447** *Rolls of Parlt.* V. 137/1 Aynst alle vertue and ordre of welle puplike. **1470–85** Malory *Arthur* v. i. 160 The Emperour Lucyus..Dictatour or procurour of the publyke wele of Rome. **1475** *Bk. Noblesse* Title, The avauncyng and preferryng the comyn publique of the Royaumes of England and of Fraunce. **1483** *Grants Edw. V* (Camden) p. xliii, The fyrst institucion of the thynge public there made by Romulus. **1490** Caxton *Eneydos* vii. 33 He.. that for his partyculer wele wyll leue ye publike & comyn wele. **1538** Bale *Thre Lawes* 170 A great occasyon of peace and publyque welth. *a* **1628** F. Grevil *Inquis. Fame & Hon.* viii. Poems (1633) ii. 54 It therefore much concernes each publike State To hoyse these costlesse sayles up to the Skye. **1632** Sir T. Hawkins tr. *Mathieu's Unhappy Prosperitie* 180 The affaire..is of so great consequence, that..the weale-publike is either shaken, or confirmed. **1671** Milton *Samson* 867 To the public good Private respects must yield. **1757** Dyer *Fleece* ii. Poems (1761) 102 To the public weal Attentive none he [Jason] found.

b. ***public*** (formerly ***common***) ***act, bill, statute***: a parliamentary act or bill which affects the community at large; cf. private *a.* 7 b.

1678 Publick Bills [see private *a.* 7 b]. **1765** Blackstone *Comm.* I. Introd. iii. 85 Statutes are either general or special, public or private. A general or public act is an universal rule, that regards the whole community. **1863** H. Cox *Instit.* i. iv. 19 Of modern Acts of Parliament, the principal division is into *public* and *private*.

c. ***public office***: a building or set of buildings used for various departments of civic business, including the police office (q.v.), judicial, police, and coroner's courts, the meeting-place of the local authority, the departments of municipal officials, etc.

1792 *Act 32 Geo. III*, c. 53 §3 A certain Publick Office within the Liberty of Westminster known by the Name of The Public Office in Bow Street. **1826** *Hone's Every-Day Bk.* I. 768 On the 8th of June, 1825, a publican..was charged at the Public Office, Bow-street, by Mr. John Francis Panchaud, a foreigner. **1839** [see police court]. **1885** J. T. Bunce *Hist. Corp. Birmingham* II. 547 Formerly, and until the opening of the Council House, the Town Council met at the Public Office, and the Borough Surveyor's department was established there, as also were the offices for the police. **1891** *B'ham Daily Gaz.* 2 Mar. 7/8 Birmingham Public Office. First Court.—Saturday.

d. (†***the***) ***public opinion***: the opinion of the mass of the community: see opinion *sb.* 1 b.

e. ***public service***: service to the community, esp. under the direction of the government or other official agency; consideration of the common good; with *the* spec. = Civil Service; also *attrib.*

1570–6 Lambarde *Peramb. Kent* (1826) 7 So that they be well employed both in the publique service, and in their own particular. **1645** *Rec. Colony & Plantation New Haven* (1857) 168 The farmers that have butter and cheese were desired to keepe it in their hands, that in case the publicque service require it, they may be furnished. **1706** *House of Commons Jrnl.* 11 Dec. (1742–62) XV. 211/1 Resolved, That this House will receive no Petitions for any Sum of Money, relating to publick Service, but what is recommended from the Crown. **1709** [see service[1] 11]. **1818** *Ann. Reg. 1817*: *State Papers* 309/2 They are..not prepared at present to suggest to the House any alteration in *this* mode of conducting *this* important department of the public service. **1857** Dickens *Dorrit* II. xxviii. 557 It's like a limited game of cricket. A field of outsiders are always going in to bowl at the Public Service, and we block the balls. **1908** I. N. Stevens *Liberators* 187 The public service corporation had dictated the nomination of the entire Republican State and legislative ticket. **1921** *Daily Colonist* (Victoria, B.C.) 8 Apr. 2/3 John Mitchell, formerly of the public service, Ottawa, and now farming at Landsdowne, Ont., is mentioned as a likely Government candidate. **1921** C. W. Terry *Pract. Motor Body Building* xxxviii. 254 (*heading*) Public service vehicles. **1926** *Daily Chron.* 13 May 2/5 The Prince of Wales has been paying strictly private visits to public service depots in the London area. **1960** *Encounter* Jan. 42/2 Those public-service advertisements which enjoin us to sneeze into a handkerchief. **1960** *Road Traffic Act 8 & 9 Eliz. II* c. 16 §117 For the purposes of this Act a public service vehicle is a motor vehicle used for carrying passengers for hire or reward. **1972** *Guardian* 21 Nov. 3/2 The Civil Service ('Public Service' is the standard term here [in Canberra]). *a* **1974** R. Crossman *Diaries* (1975) I. 486 The special late-night programmes on the election put on by both commercial and public-service television. **1977** *Times* 2 Sept. 4/3 An independent Public Service Commission consisting of a Chairman and four other members. **1980** *Daily Tel.* 29 Feb. 16 A much broader look ought to be taken at the whole question of public service broadcasting and the way it is financed.

f. ***public menace, nuisance***, etc.: anyone or anything obnoxious or annoying to the community. See also sense 9 a below.

1638 Public nuisance [see nuisance 2 β]. **1877** Trollope *Amer. Senator* I. xxvii. 288 'What a very queer bird he is.' 'He is a public nuisance,—and so is the old lady who brought him here.' **1932** Kipling *Limits & Renewals* 293 She [*sc.* a sow] broke out again and again, till the local body..indicted Mr. Gravell once more as proprietor of a public nuisance. **1952** E. O'Neill *Moon for Misbegotten* iii. 149, I made such a public nuisance of myself that the conductor threatened if I didn't quit, he'd keep me locked in the drawing room. **1955** Public menace [see cricket *sb.*[2] 1 c]. **1965** *Listener* 7 Oct. 549/2 Regarded now..as Public Pest No. 1 among vertebrates.., what hell the life of wood-pigeons seems to be. **1977** *Time* 12 Dec. 41/1 Prosecutors saw Barnes as a public menace to put in prison.

g. ***public interest***, the common well-being. Also *attrib.* Also, ***public welfare***.

1678 Butler *Hudibras* iii. ii. 102 Both Parties joyn'd to do their best, To Damn the Publick Interest. **1730** Bolingbroke *Craftsman* (1731) VII. 22 No Man, who adheres to it, hath the least pretence left him to say that he pursues the publick Interest. **1858** Disraeli in *Hansard Commons* 27 Apr. 1822 Not..one who proposes a course which will conduce to the advantage of the public interest. **1858** M. Arnold *Merope* 119 Let us a union found..Bas'd on pure public welfare. **1901** *Edin. Rev.* Apr. 378 The chief trustee of public welfare is, in this country, Parliament, and with Parliament rests the responsibility of seeing that the interests of the whole community are not subordinated to those of any portions of it. **1934** G. B. Shaw *Too True to be Good* Pref. 15 They voluntarily lived holy lives and devoted themselves to the public welfare in obedience to the impulse of the Holy Ghost within them. **1955** Meyerson & Banfield (*title*) Politics, planning and the public interest. **1971** *Wall St. Jrnl.* 22 July w. 1/1 To work on coal miners' rights for a Washington public-interest law firm.

h. ***public law***: that part of the law pertaining to the state and its relationship with the person subject to it; (see also sense 9 a).

1773 J. Erskine *Inst. Law Scotl.* I. i. i. 9 The public law is that which hath more immediately in view the public weal, and the preservation and good order of society. **1923** W. J. Byrne *Dict. Eng. Law* 519/2 Public law is that part of the law which deals with the State, either by itself or in its relations with individuals. **1973** I. M. Sinclair *Vienna Convention on Law of Treaties* v. 110 The *jus publicum* was to be understood in a wide sense as embracing not only public law in the strict sense (that is to say, the law governing relations between individuals and the State) but also rules from which individuals were not permitted to depart by virtue of particular agreements. **1976** J. M. Kelly *Stud. Civil Judicature of Roman Republic* iii. 78 A second class obviously due for exclusion is that which can be broadly labelled 'public law'; legitimate subdivisions of this would be fiscal law, military law, and 'local government' or 'police' law.

i. ***public utility***: a service or supply, such as electricity, water, or transport, considered necessary to the community, usu. controlled by a (nationalized or private) monopoly and subject to public regulation. Also (with hyphen) *attrib.*

1903 R. T. Ely *Stud. Evolution Industr. Society* 225 The principal classes of these public utilities are water, light and transportation. **1915** *Political Q.* May 106 Now coal mining is a 'public-utility' industry. **1928** *Daily Chron.* 9 Aug. 7/2 Crops have been destroyed and communications and public utilities have been crippled. **1968** P. A. S. Taylor *Dict. Econ. Terms* (ed. 4) 88 *Public utility*, an industry, such as gas, electricity, water and transport facilities, which requires heavy and highly specialised initial investment of capital, on which the return is slow. **1976** H. Tracy *Death in Reserve* xvii. 129 Public utilities worked with the servicemen with an impressive coherence.

j. ***public sector***: that part of an economy, industry, etc., which is controlled by the state at any level of government. Usu. with *the*.

1952 [see private *a.* 7 j]. **1969** M. Ash *Who are Progressives Now?* i. v. 122 What we in the public sector miss above all is the sense of involvement of people with progressive ideas with the State system. **1972** *Guardian* 31 Jan. 13/5 Other public sector groups. **1976** F. Zweig *New Acquisitive Society* i. ii. 28 The public sector seems to be the most suitable object for pressure groups' claims. **1980** *Jrnl. R. Soc. Arts* Mar. 205/1 The public sector borrowing requirement would be reduced.

3. a. Done or made by or on behalf of the community as a whole; authorized by, acting for, or representing, the community. ***public defender*** (U.S.), a lawyer employed by the state who represents a defendant who is unable to pay for legal assistance, in criminal cases.

1560 Daus tr. *Sleidane's Comm.* 61 He should be constrained to stand to the publique judgement appointed by you. **1621** Bp. Mountagu *Diatribæ* 248 Those grand duties, and publique performances of Polity, or of Pietie. **1637** *Scotch Prayer Bk.*, *Communion* Rubric, For the decent furnishing of that Church, or the publike relief of their poore. **1676** in E. D. Neill *Virginia Carolorum* (1886) 361 For haveing upon specious preferences of publique works raised great unjust taxes [etc.]. **1676** Public servant [see servant *sb.* 2 e]. **1741** Richardson *Pamela* IV. xiii. 75 Poor Housekeepers, who..are asham'd to apply for publick Relief. **1796** H. Hunter tr. *St.-Pierre's Stud. Nat.* (1799) III. 515 To return to our public Assemblies... Nothing can be more inconsistent with the gravity and wisdom of a deliberative Assembly than acclamation. *c* **1810** W. Hickey *Mem.* (1918) II. xi. 146 The parties complaining were so unreasonable as to refuse any terms, whereby the progress of the public works was impeded. **1839–77** Public prosecutor [see prosecutor 3]. **1845** Public servant [see servant *sb.* 2 e]. **1869** *Bradshaw's Railway Manual* XXI. 95 Public Works Loan Commissioners. **1879–1902** Public prosecution [see prosecution 5 d]. **1884** B. Jerrold *At Home in Paris* II. xii. 185 That ready kindness of heart and chivalry towards the weak which pervade the 'Public Assistance' of the country. **1890** Ld. Esher in *Law Times Rep.* LXIII. 734/1 A public prosecution, ordered by an official of the Crown, for what was considered to be a public object. **1891** R. Wallace *Rural Econ. Austral. & N.Z.* xxxviii. 488 No public-works undertaking can be made economically to suit any purpose whatever when that purpose has only been named without being formulated or its details settled. **1918** *Policeman's Monthly* Oct. 9/2 (*caption*) A public defender needed. **1930** *Economist* 5 Apr. 767/1 The Public Assistance Committees through which the county councils and the town councils of county boroughs are henceforward to administer what will in future be called 'public assistance'. **1931** J. S. Huxley *What dare I Think?* iii. 87 A..method for exerting some control over population-growth would be to link it on to public relief. **1932** *N.Y. Times* 23 Mar. 15/1 The steps advocated [at the 1st Public Housing Conference] were..the presenting of questionnaires to candidates for the Legislature seeking to commit them on the question of public housing. **1937** *Statutes at Large U.S.A.* L. i. 887 The term 'public housing authority' means any..public body.. authorized to engage in the development or administration of low-rent housing or slum clearance. **1942** E. Paul *Narrow St.* xxii. 189 She is an ideal public servant, having all the minor ailments possible, a fiendish disposition, short stature and a healthy dislike for mankind. **1961** Webster s.v. Public *adj.* 1 c, Public expenditures. **1961** B. Crump *Hang on a Minute* 65 He was working in a Public Works road gang, clearing slips off roads and digging drains and things. **1964** Mrs. L. B. Johnson *White House Diary* 1 Aug. (1970) 187 He spoke, disheartened, of the enormous quantity of public housing in New York City. **1965** Seldon & Pennance *Everyman's Dict. Econ.* 45 One central fund from which all regular public expenditures should be paid. **1965** A. J. P. Taylor *Eng. Hist. 1914–1945* vi. 212 Far from welcoming any increase in public spending, let alone advocating it, Labour had inherited the radical view that money spent by the state was likely to be money spent incompetently and corruptly. **1971** *Archivum Linguisticum* II. 50 A working man..on public assistance. **1974** *State* (Columbia, S. Carolina) 15 Feb. 1-B/3 Pickens County Public Defender Joseph Board represented him while Thomas M. Greene.. represented the state. **1976** *Times* 21 May 1/5 The combined effects of the Government's public expenditure restraint and pay policies. **1976** *Birmingham Post* 16 Dec. 7/9 Two major hospital schemes in Dudley and Stafford, costing more than £20 million, may be delayed because of the public spending cuts. **1977** *N.Z. Herald* 8 Jan. 2-4/6 Until she breaks the seal and reads what was written in public servant scrawl 24 years ago, she cannot continue her search. **1977** *New Yorker* 27 June 85/3 Queens..has..only eighteen of the city's two hundred and forty-six public-housing projects. **1977** P. Johnson *Enemies of Society* v. 71 The new government public-relief system aggravated the evils it was designed to cure. **1977** G. Clark *World Prehist.* (ed. 3) ii. 75 Given the possibility of public works on an adequate scale, it was capable of producing food enough to support society at increasing levels of complexity.

b. In the ancient universities: Belonging to, made or authorized by, acting for or on behalf of, the whole university (as distinguished from the colleges or other constituents): as ***public disputation***, ***examination***, ***lecture***, ***schools***, ***hall***, ***theatre***, ***library***; ***public orator***, ***lecturer***, ***professor***, ***reader***, etc.

In some of these connexions, 'public' has given way to 'University', as *University Library*, *lecturer*, *professor*, *reader*, or to special designations as '*examination-schools*', *Bodleian Library*, *Sheldonian Theatre*, etc. In others the adj. is now often taken to mean 'open to all members of the university' or even 'open to the public generally', as in 4, or 'performed publicly' as in 5.

[**1522** *Camb. Univ. Stat.* (*Docmts. of Commission*, 1852, I. 431), Statuimus ordinamus et volumus ut unus aliquis orator publicus eligatur.] **1550** Udall tr. P. Martyr (*title*), A discourse or traictise of Petur Martyr..the publyque reader of diuinitee in the Uniuersitee of Oxford. **1614** in Willis & Clark *Cambridge* III. 35 There is an intention of erecting a new publique library in Cambridge in imitation of that of Oxford. [**1636** *Corpus Statut. Univers. Oxon.*, Tit. iii. §1 (1888) Cum..conducat ut Scholares non solum sub publico sed etiam sub privato regimine contineantur; Statutum est quod omnes Scholares..in aliquod Collegium vel Aulam admittantur. *Ibid.* Tit. iv, De Lectoribus Publicis. —— Tit. vi. i. §3 In Scholis Artium publicis Disputationes..habeantur. —— Tit. xvii. vii, De Publico Universitatis Oratore.] **1645** Public orator of the University [see orator 5]. **1656** Wood *Life* (O.H.S.) I. 205 Dr John Wilson, the public professor [of Music], the best at the lute in all England. **1731** *Ordinationes* in *Laudian Code* (1888) Appx. 320 The Public Librarian. *Ibid.*, The University Orator..to make a Speech in Commemoration of the Benefactors to the University in the Public Theatre once in the year. **1773** [J. Napleton] (*title*) Considerations on the public exercises for First and Second Degrees in the University of Oxford. **1810** *Oxf. Univ. Cal.* 56 The Public Examinations are held twice a year. *Ibid.*, A testimonial will be given him by one of the Public Examiners. **1814** Dyer *Hist. Univ. Camb.* I. 247 You enter the quadrangle that forms the public schools through the portico of the public library. **1862** *Oxf. Univ. Cal.* 134 The First Public Examination before the Moderators,..the Second Public

Examination before the Public Examiners. [So 1909.] **1900** *Cambr. Univ. Cal.* 683 Unless the Fellow hold the office of Professor, Public Orator, Registrary, or Librarian in the University.

4. a. That is open to, may be used by, or may or must be shared by, all members of the community; not restricted to the private use of any person or persons; generally accessible or available; generally levied (as a rate or tax). Also (in narrower sense), that may be used, enjoyed, shared, or competed for, by all persons legally or properly qualified.

Sometimes involving the sense, provided or supported at the public expense, and under public control: as in ***public elementary school***, and often in ***public baths, public library, public park***, and the like; ***public convenience***: see CONVENIENCE *sb.* 7 d. A thing may also be 'public' at once in senses 4 and 5, as ***public worship***, or in 1, 3, 4 and 5, as ***public meeting***. See also PUBLIC SCHOOL, in various senses.

1542 UDALL in *Lett. Lit. Men* (Camden) 6 Xenocrates.. readynge a publique lecture in philosophie. **1561** T. HOBY tr. *Castiglione's Courtyer* II. (1577) K iv b, To make great Theatres, and other publique buildings. **1606** SHAKS. *Ant. & Cl.* II. ii. 234, I saw her once Hop forty Paces through the publicke streete. **1611** CORYAT *Crudities* 290 There are reported to be in Venice.. twentie seven publique clocks. *Ibid.* 403 In an open court *sub dio* two publike bathes. **1613** PURCHAS *Pilgrimage* I. v. xvi. 453 They have their publike Meetings and Bankets in their Temples very often. **1617** MORYSON *Itin.* I. 77 Each Church hath a little market place ..and a publike Well. **1644** *Direct. Publ. Worship* Title-p., The Publique Worship of God. **1655** FULLER *Ch. Hist.* IV. i. §11 In publique assemblies, if the weaker party can so subsist as not to be conquered, it conquers in reputation. **1699** M. LISTER *Journey to Paris* 150, I never saw in all the Markets once Sprouts..nor in their publick Gardens any Reserves of old Stalks. **1705** *Boston News-Let.* 24 Sept. 2/1 We know not the certainty of any others besides those mentioned in the Publick Print. **1707** CHAMBERLAYNE *Pres. St. Eng.* III. xi. 386 A fair publick Library free for all Strangers in Term-time. **1718** in *Rep. Rec. Commissioners Boston* (1883) VIII. 129 The Projection of an Act for a Publick Market in Boston..Voted disallowed. **1738** W. STEPHENS *Jrnl.* 11 Feb. in *Colonial Rec. Georgia* (1906) IV. 80 Bailiff Parker and Mr. Hugh Anderson..took a Walk first to the publick Garden. **1762** in A. EARLE *Customs & Fashions in Old New England* (1893) 247 At the Public Room of the above Inn will be delivered a series of Moral Dialogues. **1763** J. BELL *Trav. from St. Petersburg* II. 54, I was present at the representation of a kind of farce in the publick street. **1777** Public print [see PRINT *sb.* 11]. **1781** Public street [see NUISANCE 2 c]. **1785** COWPER *Tirocinium* in *Poems* II. 334 And while on public nurs'ries they rely. **1793** SMEATON *Edystone L.* §59 His property was sold at public biddings. **1802** C. WILMOT *Let.* 16 May in *Irish Peer* (1920) 69 The most entertaining and pleasant day possible, at 'Bagatelle'... As it is a Publick garden, multitudes of people were parading about. **1804** R. SUTCLIFF *Jrnl.* 31 July in *Trav. N. Amer.* (1811) 42 This morning I was conducted.. to one of the Public Baths [in New York City]. **1819** *Sporting Mag.* IV. 211 There was a public road, right from our place to that of our 'salesman'. **1821–30** LD. COCKBURN *Mem.* vi. (1856) 346 We were..very angry, and had recourse to one of these new things called public meetings... It was held on the 2d of December 1817. **1822** J. C. LOUDON *Encycl. Gardening* 1186 Public Parks, or Equestrian Promenades, are valuable appendages to large cities. **1825** H. WILSON *Mem.* III. 38 We wanted to go to the play..but we had..no private box. I have never in my life, frequented the public boxes. **1832** in *Whig Almanac 1844* 38/1 Within a few years..restless men have thrown before the public their visionary plans for squandering the public domain. **1848** MRS. GASKELL *Mary Barton* I. i. 1 There are some fields near Manchester..through which runs a public footpath to a little village about two miles distant. **1850** *Eng. Jrnl. Educ.* IV. 434/2 A Public Nursery has recently been established in Nassau Street, Mary-le-Bone, for the purpose of receiving the children of the married industrious poor during the working-hours of the day. **1855** *Act 18 & 19 Vict.* c. 122 §3 In the construction of this Act..the following terms shall have the respective meanings herein-after assigned to them... 'Public building' shall mean every building used as a church, chapel, or other place of public worship; also every building used for purposes of public instruction; also every building used as a college, public hall, hospital, theatre, public concert room, public ball room, public lecture room, public exhibition room, or for any other public purposes. **1880** GEO. ELIOT *Let.* 6 June (1956) VII. 292 Your having learned the news of our marriage by the cable and public prints has always been a vexation to us. **1893** *McClure's Mag.* I. 394/2 There were even days when the Joneses questioned whether they were not running a public telephone, so often did the bell ring. **1898** E. HOWARD *Tomorrow* vii. 73 Their so-called 'public markets' ..are by no means public in the same full sense as are our public parks, libraries, water undertakings..which are carried on upon public property, by public officials, at the public expense, and solely with a view to the public advantage. **1903** Public park [see PARK *sb.* 2 b]. **1904** *Daily Chron.* 23 Jan. 5/2 On January 23, 1849, the first public baths in London, those at St. Martin's-in-the-Fields, were opened. **1908** Dec. 21 *Act 8 Edw. VII*, c. 66 §1 An act to prevent disturbance of Public Meetings...§2 This Act may be cited as the Public Meeting Act, 1908. **1910** *Bradshaw's Railway Guide* Apr. 1059/2 Private Hotel... Fine public rooms. **1910** W. J. LOCKE *Simon the Jester* xxii. 291, I..went in search of the nearest public telephone office. **1924** J. BUCHAN *Three Hostages* vi. 85, I went into a public telephone-booth. **1926** *Gloss. Terms Electr. Engin.* (Brit. Engin. Stand. Assoc.) 162 *Public call office* (*Pay station*, U.S.A.), a subscriber's station available for the use of the public on payment of a fee, which may be deposited in a coin box or paid to an attendant. **1927** W. B. YEATS *October Blast* 21 They hold their public meetings where Our most renownèd patriots stand. **1927** *Observer* 16 Oct. 11/4 Auto-electric advertising machines are about to be placed in 2,500 public telephone call boxes in London. **1928** D. L. SAYERS *Unpleasantness at Bellona Club* viii. 88 That phone-call.. was put through..from a public call-box. *Ibid.* 90 His call came from a public box. **1930** W. S. MAUGHAM *Cakes & Ale* xi. 136 He was rather fond of going down to the Bear and Key..and having a few beers in the public bar. **1932** KIPLING *Limits & Renewals* 386 Improved sanitary appliances and gratuitous public transport. **1933** *Radio Times* 14 Apr. 75/1 The war was newly over..and public clocks had resumed their forgotten chiming. **1933** E. WAUGH *Scoop* I. iii. 50 There was a dense crowd round the public lavatory. **1933** A. G. MACDONELL *England, their England* vii. 100 He covered the twenty yards to the public telephone box. **1943** J. S. HUXLEY *TVA* vii. 50 Over a quarter of the 40,000 square miles of the Southern Highlands is or will shortly be public domain, under either Federal or State ownership. **1952** M. LASKI *Village* xiii. 181 In these public streets, love was easiest spoken of when they talked of the children. **1961** E. WAUGH *Unconditional Surrender* I. i. 23 I'll drop you back at your office. Can't have you using public transport on your birthday. *Ibid.* III. ii. 230 Guy took to walking every afternoon in the public gardens. .. There were winding paths, specimen trees, statuary, a bandstand. **1962** J. BRAINE *Life at Top* x. 136 The Warley Council's plan for a new public baths. **1965** *Scotsman* 14 June 8 House contains 2 public rooms, 2 bedrooms, boxroom, scullery and bathroom. **1969** A. CORNELISEN *Torregreca* iv. 139 Our meeting is not entirely private... Our mutual understanding must become public property. **1971** H. CALVIN *Poison Chasers* vii. 83 Two of the security men..came into the public bar, and the rest of the customers..went into the lounge bar. **1971** D. LEES *Rainbow Conspiracy* ix. 134 All I had to look for was a broken stile with a Public Footpath sign. **1971** R. BUSBY *Deadlock* v. 74 A public telephone stood in one corner of the discreetly lit foyer. **1972** P. CLEIFE *Slick & Dead* I. iv. 37 The job of public lavatory attendant. **1973** A. MANN *Tiara* ix. 80 Available on the terrace was a row of public toilets. **1974** M. BIRMINGHAM *You can help Me* iii. 47 There was one caller from a public call-box..and another—not from a public box. **1974** R. C. DENNIS *Conversations with Corpse* xiii. 132 Nothing appeared in the public prints about the missing money. **1975** *Country Life* 2 Jan. 38/3 In 1963 Cypress was given to the City of Charleston as a public park. **1976** P. R. WHITE *Planning for Public Transport* ii. 31 We are concerned with public transport (which is taken to mean modes available for public use rather than any distinction based on ownership). **1977** *Listener* 30 June 861/3 After years of legal wrangles and bankruptcy, Jacques Tati has managed to get his films back into the public domain. **1977** W. MCILVANNEY *Laidlaw* xxii. 94 A pub which from the outside looked as inviting as a public toilet. **1978** 'D. RUTHERFORD' *Collision Course* 121 They paid admission to the Casino and ..strolled through the public rooms.

b. ***public education***, education at school, as opposed to being 'privately educated'; also education at a PUBLIC SCHOOL as distinguished from a private school.

1581 MULCASTER *Positions* xxxix. (1887) 183 Of priuate and publike education, with their generall goods and illes. **1797** GODWIN *Enquirer* I. vii. 59 Public education is best for ..a..healthful mind. **1835** ARNOLD *Let.* 15 Apr. in Stanley *Life* (1845) I. 421 Public education is the best where it answers... I should certainly advise anything rather than a private school of above thirty boys.

c. Professionally at the service of the public: as a tradesman, dealer, etc.

1825 *Greenhouse Comp.* I. 244 A public dealer can always afford to keep up a finer display of plants..than any private gentleman whatever. **1869** L. M. ALCOTT *Little Women* II. xi. 162 She excited the suspicions of public librarians by asking for works on prisons. **1972** C. DRUMMOND *Death at Bar* ii. 44 Dubious books submitted to their Members of Parliament by Watch Committees, Purity Leagues and Aldermen who had power over public librarians.

d. ***public woman***, † ***commoner***: a prostitute; = *common woman* (COMMON *a.* 6 b).

1585 T. WASHINGTON tr. *Nicholay's Voy.* II. xix. 56 b, [He] caused to be clothed two publique Turkish women, with very rich apparrell. **1604** SHAKS. *Oth.* IV. ii. 73 Oh, thou publicke Commoner. **1662** J. DAVIES tr. *Olearius' Voy. Ambass.* 287 To banish thence all the publick Women. **1892** E. REEVES *Homeward Bound* 194 The houses of the 'public women' (as they are still styled in modern places).

†**e.** ***public table*** = TABLE D'HÔTE. *Obs.*

1742 M. W. MONTAGU *Let.* 23 May (1966) II. 281 Nothing is cheaper than living in an Inn in a Country Town in France..25 sous for dinner and 30 for supper and lodging of those that eat at the public table. **1842** DICKENS *Let.* 4 Apr. (1974) III. 182 The public table, at this hotel and at the hotel opposite, has just now finished dinner. **1865** TROLLOPE *Can you forgive Her?* II. xxx. 234 At Lucerne they made no acquaintances... They did not even dine at the public table.

f. ***to go public***: of a privately-owned company, to seek a quotation on the stock exchange; also in trivial use (passing into sense 5) to reveal oneself, to come out into the open.

1965 H. I. ANSOFF *Corporate Strategy* (1968) iv. 62 Two major alternatives to this end [*sc.* of enhancing the liquidity of the firm's equity] are to 'go public', or to merge the firm with another large one. **1972** *Accountant* 5 Oct. 417/1 It.. disregarded the probability that the company would in the near future 'go public'. **1976** 'A. HALL' *Kobra Manifesto* xv. 211 The girl's fever..had either driven or panicked Kobra into the open and in seizing the Boeing they'd gone public. **1977** *Lebende Sprachen* XII. 158/2 This will see the Arabs go public with the new second stage of their economic strategy.

5. a. Open to general observation, sight, or cognizance; existing, done, or made in public; manifest; not concealed. Also of an agent: Acting in public.

a **1548** HALL *Chron., Rich. III* 28 b, Ther inwarde grudge could not refrayne but crye out in places publike, and also priuate. **1557** N. T. (Genev.) *Matt.* i. 19 A publike exemple of infamie. **1597** HOOKER *Eccl. Pol.* v. xix. §2 The Church, by her publike reading of the Booke of God, preacheth onely as a witnesse. **1641** BROME *Jov. Crew* II. i, Will you up to the hill-top of sports..? No, that will be too publique for our Recreation. **1709** STEELE *Tatler* No. 10 ¶7 The Count de Mellos..had made his Publick Entry into that City with much State. **1762** W. SMITH *Discourses Publ. Occasions* (ed. 2) App. 113 This attention to public speaking, which is begun here [in the College of Philadelphia] with the very rudiments of the mother-tongue, is continued down to the end. **1780** Public speaker [see SPEAKER 1 b]. **1825** T. MOORE *Mem. Life R. B. Sheridan* x. 322 And, in this great essential of public speaking, must be considered inferior to [etc.]. **1874** BLACKIE *Self-Cult.* 23 A certain awkwardness and difficulty in the public utterance of thought. **1905** G. B. SHAW *Let.* 27 Nov. (1972) 583, I do not know yet exactly how you get your effects, except that it is not in my rather rhetorical, public-speaker kind of way. **1931** *Economist* 28 Mar. 665/2 Mr. Morrison's final conclusion that the proper authority to be set up is a 'business Board' of five members, incorporating what he defined as 'an element of public accountability'. **1940** C. MILBURN *Diary* 25 Dec. (1979) 76 We..listened to our beloved King's speech... How bravely he overcomes the difficulties of public speaking. **1950** B. PYM *Some Tame Gazelle* xxi. 232 She was a confident public speaker and this afternoon's audience of parish women.. held no terrors for her. **1959** *Observer* 18 Oct. 24/7, I am sure she disapproved of the new euphemism: public accountability. **1965** *Mod. Law Rev.* XXVIII. v. 520 Judges ..had a near monopoly of the Chairmanships of Royal Commissions, indeed of public inquiries of every sort. **1965** *Times Lit. Suppl.* 25 Nov. 1059/1 The public-speaking Dr. Rosten points a neat moral. **1971** WRAITH & LAMB *Public Inquiries* i. 13 Public inquiries are constituted *ad hoc* to inquire into particular matters, and are for the most part concerned only to establish facts and to make recommendations. **1974** *Times* 17 Nov. 14/2 The important issue is that of public accountability. A body [*sc.* the BBC] which gets all its funds from the public ought to be obliged to answer any question from anyone about how the money is spent. **1975** *Oxf. Compan. Sports & Games* 1112/2 A wrestler at fault is given a warning and if he offends again he is given a public caution. *Ibid.* 1113/1 Should the same wrestler offend again he is given a second public warning. **1976** *Abingdon Herald* 9 Dec., With, it seemed, two men in the ring against him and only the whole crowd for him, Marino gave vent to justifiable retaliation and received the first public warning of the evening. **1979** *Jrnl. R. Soc. Arts* July 511/1 Mr. McWilliam knows all too well that digs at buildings in volumes so important can have a devastating effect at Public Inquiries, and can cause interesting buildings to fall victim to the destroyers.

†**b.** Easily seen, conspicuous, prominent. *Obs.*

1597 A. M. tr. *Guillemeau's Fr. Chirurg.* 29 b/2 The ninth [vein] is very publique, lyinge in the necke, and is called the Iugularis vayne.

†**c.** Of a person: That is before the public. *Obs.*

1650 HUBBERT *Pill Formality* 19 He is not so openly manifested to be wicked as the publike profane person. **1722** DE FOE *Col. Jack* (1840) 287, I was not so public here as to be very well known. **1727** P. WALKER *Life Cameron* in *Biog. Presb.* (1827) 294 Mr. George Barclay..was very publick at that Time, and had his Hand at many a good Turn.

d. Of a book, writing, etc.: (chiefly in phr. ***made public***) Made accessible to all; published; in print. ? *Obs.*, or merged in 5.

a **1641** BP. MOUNTAGU *Acts & Mon.* iii. (1642) 159 The Prophets, whose writings were publique, and extant amongst the Jews. **1657** AUSTEN *Fruit Trees* Ep. Ded., Your *Legacy of Husbandry* (and other pieces made publique by your means). **1716** HEARNE *Collect.* (O.H.S.) V. 264 Dr. South..hath many publick Works extant. **1777** ROBERTSON *Hist. Amer.* (1783) II. 451 The first of his dispatches has never been made public.

e. ***public address system***: a system comprising microphone, amplifier, and loudspeaker which enables speech or music to be projected to an assembly of people; so ***public-address equipment***.

1923 *Electrical Communication* I. IV. 46 Public address systems..developed for the purpose of extending the range of the voice of a speaker addressing an audience. **1950** *Engineering* 24 Nov. 392/2 Public-address equipment using magnetic tapes for announcing and recording..has been installed. **1972** *Police Rev.* 8 Dec. 1597/3 A public address system fitted to each vehicle. **1978** R. V. JONES *Most Secret War* xxi. 176 The effect would be rather like that which occurs in public address systems where the noise from the loudspeakers impinges on the original microphone, and is therefore picked up and relayed back to the loudspeakers again.

f. ***Public Lending Right***: the name given to authors' (and publishers') entitlement to a fee for books borrowed from public libraries.

1961 *Ann. Reg. 1960* 458 Sir Alan Herbert..celebrated his seventieth birthday by opening a campaign for what came to be known as the Public Lending Right. **1970** *Guardian* 6 Apr. 8/1 His..description on the ballot paper could well be..Ardent Advocate of Public Lending Right. .. Of the dust-gathering plan to give authors and publishers a bit of the royalty for the books we borrow from the public libraries. **1977** *Time Out* 17–23 June 14/1 Combined with the Public Lending Right, the author would be helped twice over, more sales and more loans.

g. ***public-access***: used *attrib.* to designate a form of television in which the general public can produce or contribute to programmes. *U.S.*

1972 *Listener* 6 July 1 Public-Access Television. **1976** *National Observer* (U.S.) 18 Dec. 1/1 All this appeared in recent weeks on a New York City 'public access' cable-TV channel that serves 85,000 families in Manhattan.

6. a. Of, pertaining to, or engaged in the affairs or service of the community; *esp.* of a person: occupying an official or professional position; also, holding a position of general influence or authority.

1571 CHILLESTER tr. *Chelidonius' Instit. Chr. Princes* Title-p., A Hystorie..very necessarie to be red not only of all Nobilitie and Gentlemen, but also of euerie publike person. **1611** CORYAT *Crudities* 205 The Duke sat about the publicke affaires with the other Senators. **1654** TRAPP *Comm. Ezra* i. 5 Men of publike places. **1673** J. RAY

Observations Journey Low-Countries 170 Those who assist the Commonwealth..have liberty granted to them to be present in this Council, and to understand the management of public affairs. **1783** JOHNSON in *Boswell* (1887) IV. 178 With how little real superiority of mind men can make an eminent figure in publick life. **1817** *Parl. Deb.* 10 July, The community at large, who knew Mr. Ponsonby only as a public man. **1822** *Sunday Times* 20 Oct. 1/3 (*heading*) Aspect of public affairs. **1861** EARL RUSSELL in *Times* 16 Oct., When I embarked in public life. **1901** *Westm. Gaz.* 11 Dec. 1/3 Public men are made for public affairs, not public affairs for public men. **1937** *Burlington Mag.* Feb. 94/2 The management of public affairs.

b. ***public notary, notary public***: see NOTARY *sb.*

7. Of or pertaining to a person in the capacity in which he comes in contact with the community, as opposed to his private capacity; official. Also *transf.*

1538 STARKEY *England* I. ii. 61 Both in the pryuate and publyke state of euery man. **1676** HOBBES *Iliad* I. 307 Two publick servants of the king were there. **1709** STEELE *Tatler* No. 10 ¶1 Effects..upon the publick and private Actions of Men. **1725** BUTLER *Serm.* v. 80 Every man is to be considered in two capacities, the private and publick. **1864** [see PRIVATE *a.* 6]. **1932** H. NICOLSON (*title*) Public faces. **1961** Public image [see IMAGE *sb.* 5 b]. **1962** *Listener* 1 Mar. 366/2 Finally, there is the question of Egypt's public face, the face which she presents to the world. **1967** M. ARGYLE *Psychol. Interpersonal Behaviour* ix. 154 There may be secondary aims [in an assessment interview], such as giving C [*sc.* the candidate] information about the job, or improving the public image of the employing organization. **1976** P. FERRIS *Detective* iii. 46 I'm not really on the board. .. I was only there today to report on our public image. **1977** C. STORR *Tales Psychiatrist's Couch* 8 Although she was still a difficult woman in her private relationships, she acquired a much easier public face.

8. Devoted or directed to the promotion of the general welfare; public-spirited, patriotic. Now chiefly in **b.** ***public spirit.***

1607 NORDEN *Surv. Dial.* v. 200 Some will be peruerse, and wilful, and hinder the best publike action that is. **1652** HOWELL *Giraffi's Rev. Naples* II. 78 Known to be a good Patriot, and of a publike soul. **1665** DRYDEN & HOWARD *Indian Queen* IV. i, Would it not breed Grief in your public heart to see her bleed? **1847** EMERSON *Repr. Men, Napoleon* Wks. (Bohn) I. 370 Napoleon had been the first man of the world, if his ends had been purely public.

b. 1654 WHITLOCK *Zootomia* 382 Private Persons with publike Spirits, are of a goodnesse Angelicall. **1691** T. H[ALE] *Acc. New Invent.* p. xix, Men of publick Spirits. **1712** STEELE *Spect.* No. 294 ¶1 The greatest Instances of publick Spirit the Age has produced. **1803** *Censor* Sept. 107, I am not influenced by motives of private revenge, but by a public spirit. **1836** SIR H. TAYLOR *Statesman* xxiii. 167 Discretion, knowledge of mankind, public spirit, a spirit of justice.

II. 9. With extended, international, or universal reference. **a.** Of or pertaining to the nations generally, or to the European, Christian, or civilized nations, regarded as a single community; general; international; esp. in ***public law*** (see also sense 2 h) Also freq. as ***public enemy***; now esp. (passing into sense 2 f above) in ***public enemy number one*** (orig. U.S.), the first named on a list of wanted criminals; the greatest threat to a community; also *transf.* and in extended use in similar phrases.

1560 DAUS tr. *Sleidane's Comm.* 304 A publique war was attempted against the Barbarians. **1581** HAMILTON *Cath. Traictise* in *Cath. Tractates* (S.T.S.) 103 Quhat vther nor the Romane kirk..be publict concilis hes condemnit all heretikes. **1665** BOYLE *Occas. Refl.* IV. xvii. (1848) 274 For almost all the publique Quarrels in Christendome. **1756** G. WHITEFIELD *Short Address* 9 We may as lawfully draw our swords, in order to defend ourselves against our common and public Enemy. **1792** BURKE *Pres. St. Affairs* Wks. 1826 VII. 99 In contradiction to the whole tenour of the publick law of Europe. **1842** ALISON *Hist. Europe* (1850) XIII. xcii. §68. 552 A declaration was..signed by all the powers.. which..proscribed Napoleon as a public enemy, with whom neither peace nor truce could be concluded. **1845** Public enemy [see ENEMY *sb.* 1]. **1849** MACAULAY *Hist. Eng.* i. I. 9 Races separated from each other by seas and mountains acknowledged..a common code of public law. **1931** *S. F. Call* (Mag.) 18 June 8 There are two people alive, at least, who love Al Capone—his wife and his kid. Public Enemy No. 1 is to them an idol. **1935** *Daily Mail* 23 Oct. 18/1 (Advt.), We all know who is Public Enemy No. 1 when it's time to get up! The 'Droops'. **1939** LD. CAMROSE in M. Gilbert *Winston S. Churchill* (1976) V. lii. 1081 Well, Winston was Public Enemy No 1 in Berlin, and Eden was the same in Italy. **1940** 'N. BLAKE' *Malice in Wonderland* II. ix. 123 The presence of a public enemy in our midst. **1958** *Listener* 17 July 75/1 Iraq..has been Public Enemy No. 1 to Egypt's propagandists. **1967** M. MURRAY *Ballad of Bonnie & Clyde* (song), 3 Bonnie and Clyde got to be public enemy number one—Running and hiding from ev'ry American lawman's gun. **1978** *Jrnl. R. Soc. Arts* CXXVI. 422/2 In some cities, the car has almost come to qualify for the title of public enemy number one. **1980** *Guardian* 19 Dec. 22/1 The fugitive Irishman..was 'a prominent member of the IRA and a public enemy'.

b. Of, pertaining, or common to the whole human race; = COMMON *a.* 1 b. *rare.*

1653 H. WHISTLER *Upshot Inf. Baptisme* 3 Whereby the guiltinesse of Adams sinne (as the publique Trustee for Man-kind) originally tainteth Children. **1697** DRYDEN *Virg. Georg.* I. 630 The Sun..In Iron Clouds conceal'd the Publick Light. **1858** HAWTHORNE *Fr. & It. Note-bks.* (1872) I. 44 Enjoying the public sunshine as if it were their own household fire.

III. 10. *Comb.*, as (from 8) ***public-hearted, public-minded*** (Webster 1828), adjs.; hence ***public-heartedness, public-mindedness; public-voiced*** adj. Also PUBLIC-SPIRITED.

1647 CLARENDON *Hist. Reb.* VI. §246 Their publick-heartedness, and joynt concernment in the good Cause. **1692** SOUTH *Serm.* (1697) I. 412 By the publick-mindedness of particular Persons. *a* **1706** EVELYN *Diary* an. 1691 (1955) V. 61 This church.., being beged by Dr. Tenison Rector of St. Martines, was set up by that publique minded, charitable & pious Doctor neere my sons dwelling Dover-streete. **1757** DYER *Fleece* II. Poems (1761) 105 Public-hearted Roe, Faithful, sagacious, active, patient, brave. **1976** *West Lancs. Even. Gaz.* 13 Dec. 6/5 A North Shore woman was particularly public-minded after buying some wrapping paper from a Cleveleys shop recently. She thought the paper might have been a fire hazard and took it round to Blackpool fire station for them to test it.

B. *sb.* (the adj. used absolutely or elliptically).

1. †**a.** The community or people as an organized body; the nation, the state; the commonwealth; the interest or well-being of the community; = L. *rēs pūblica.* Usually construed as singular. *Obs.*

1611 BIBLE *Transl. Pref.* 2 Whosoeuer attempteth any thing for the publike. **1611** B. JONSON *Catiline* v. vi, Hee's scarce a friend vnto the publike. **1640-1** *Kirkcudbr. War-Comm. Min. Bk.* (1855) 92 For the better furtherance of the service of the publict. **1673** RAY *Journ. Low C., Venice* 154 Though the public be not so rich as it hath been, yet will it soon recover itself. **1699** SHAFTESB. *Charac.* (1711) II. I. III. iii. 63 In a civil State or Publick, we see that a virtuous Administration..is of the highest service. **1764** BURN *Poor Laws* 209 Sustained, not at the expence of such parish or place, nor of the county,..but of the publick, to be paid out of some such rate as the land tax. **1769** BLACKSTONE *Comm.* IV. xi. 151 If both these points are against the defendant, the offence against the public is complete.

b. The community as an aggregate, but not in its organized capacity; hence, the members of the community.

In the latter sense now usually const. as plural.

1665 BOYLE *Occas. Refl.* Pref. (1848) 9 The favourable Reception that the public has hitherto vouchsafed to what has been presented it. **1711** STEELE *Spect.* No. 258 ¶2 Another Project which..will give the Publick an Equivalent to their full Content. **1781** COWPER *Let. to J. Newton* 5 Mar., One would wish, at first setting out, to catch the public by the ear, and hold them by it as fast as possible. **1796** BURKE *Regic. Peace* ii. Wks. VIII. 257 The publick is the theatre for mountebanks and impostors. **1808** *Times* 6 Feb., The Nobility, Gentry, and the Public, are respectfully informed, that [etc.]. **1821-30** LD. COCKBURN *Mem.* vi. (1856) 371 There was a feeble murmur against the ejection of what the few murmurers termed 'The Public'. **18..** E. JESSE *Notice at Hampton Court* in *Pall Mall G.* 9 Nov. (1891) 3/1 'The public is expected to protect what is intended for the public enjoyment.' **1883** *Law Times* 20 Oct. 408/1 The public and the Profession were alike urgent in calling for sweeping reforms.

†**c.** The world at large, mankind. Cf. the adj. 9 b. *Obs. rare.*

1699 SHAFTESB. *Charac.* (1711) II. I. II. iii. 30 The Mind ..readily discerns the Good and Ill towards the Species or Publick.

2. a. With *a* and *pl.* A particular section, group, or portion of a community, or of mankind.

1709 SHAFTESB. *Charac.* (1711) I. II. III. ii. 111 They.. enjoy the common Good and Interest of a more contracted Publick. **1794** PALEY *Evid.* I. i. (1817) 29 That general disbelief..which..prevailed amongst the intelligent part of the heathen public. **1815** W. H. IRELAND *Scribbleomania* 30 *note*, They would make no impression on a public accustomed to quartos of original poetry by the month. **1817** COLERIDGE *Biogr. Lit.* I. iii. 49 A shelf or two of Beauties, elegant Extracts and Anas, form nine-tenths of the reading of the reading public. **1843** RUSKIN *Arrows of Chace* (1880) I. 21 There is a separate public for every picture, and for every book. **1868** M. PATTISON *Academ. Org.* 3 The British public will not long ask this question without helping itself to the answer. **1884** *Manch. Exam.* 14 May 4/5 The outside public appear disposed to take Mr. C—— at his own valuation. **1894** M. G. TARDE in *Pop. Sci. Monthly* XLV. 458 While it is the most capricious of publics it is also the most sheeplike.

b. With preceding possessive. The particular section of society which is sympathetic to the person or thing indicated.

1921 H. CRANE *Let.* 19 Sept. (1965) 64, I am 'sold out' and will have to rush rhymes and rhythms together to supply my enthusiastic 'public' as fast as I can. **1952** GRANVILLE *Dict. Theatrical Terms* 145 My *public* will hate me in this part.

c. *Sociol.* A collective group regarded as sharing some cultural, social, or political interest but who as individuals do not necessarily have any contact with one another.

1927 J. DEWEY *Public & its Problems* ii. 39 There are associations which are too narrow and restricted in scope to give rise to a public, just as there are associations too isolated from one another to fall within the same public. **1933** F. H. ALLPORT *Institutional Behav.* v. 87 Since the public is no specific group of individuals, but is defined wholly by the range of the common interest in a particular transaction, there may be a separate public for every issue raised. We are compelled, therefore, to think of *various* publics. **1954** G. A. LUNDBERG et al. *Sociol.* xiii. 491 A great source of difficulty has been the varied and confused image of the term 'public'. Clearly one may belong to as many publics as one has interests. **1954** GERTH & MILLS *Character & Social Structure* xv. 435 Publics are composed of people who are not in face to face relation but who nevertheless display similar interests, or are exposed to similar, although more or less distant, stimuli. **1969** G. A. & A. G. THEODORSON *Mod. Dict. Sociol.* 324 Publics are usually large, physically separated, and often quite diverse... Publics have an impact through their voting, buying, noncooperation, financial contributions, letters to the editor, etc.

3. ***in public***: **a.** In a place, situation, condition, or state open to public view or access; openly, publicly: opposed to *in private*; so ***into public*** (*rare*). †Also, in or into a published form, in or into print (*obs.*).

c **1450** *Mirour Saluacioun* 916 Nor renne fro house to house to convers in publike [*gloss* in comon place]. **1611** SHAKS. *Wint. T.* II. i. 197 Follow vs, We are to speake in publique. **1642** ROGERS *Naaman* 156 Their helpes in both publique and private, being few. **1642** T. LECHFORD *Plain Dealing* To Rdr. (1867) 3, I have..presumed to enter into publique, for these reasons. **1662** GURNALL *Chr. in Arm.* verse 17. II. ix. (1669) 294/1 They read it at home, and hear it preacht powerfully in the publick. **1689** EVELYN *Let. to Pepys* 12 Aug., The roome where he us'd to eate and dine in publiq. **1727** SWIFT *Country Post* 2 Aug., Wks. 1755 III. I. 177 They having of late appeared very much in publick together. **1778** MISS BURNEY *Evelina* (1791) I. xxii. 119 She would never more take me into public. **1873** *Act 36 & 37 Vict.* c. 89 §13 The inquiry shall be held in public before an officer.

†**b.** In a public or collective capacity. *Obs.*

1653 HOLCROFT *Procopius, Persian Wars* I. 8 Bestowing many benefits upon their City in publique, and on particular men.

4. a. Short for PUBLIC HOUSE. *colloq.* Cf. PUB.

1709 *Churchw. Acc. St. Dunstan's, Canterb.*, For the Improvement of its [the newly-planted tree's] growth, aiournd to the publick and moistned it to the Root. **1799** SOUTHEY *Let. to T. Southey* 5 Jan., 'What, don't you keep a public?' **1824** SCOTT *Redgauntlet* ch. xv, He is a statesman, though he keeps a public. **1840** ARNOLD *Jrnl.* 23 July, in Stanley *Life* (1845) II. App. C. 426 Iron foundries and publics have no connexion with mere book literature. **1863-5** J. THOMSON *Sunday at Hampstead* I. ix, We can take our beer at a public. **1899** SIR A. WEST *Recoll.* I. ii. 67 There was a 'public' called the 'Half-Way House'.

b. *attrib.* Of the public house.

1756 WHITEFIELD *Life & Jrnls.* 3 My Mother..kept me in my tender Years from intermeddling in the least with the public Business. **1807** CRABBE *Parish Reg.* II. 124 He..Felt the poor purse, and sought the public door. **1844** DICKENS *Mart. Chuz.* xiii, I suppose it was something in the public line.

c. Short for 'public bar'. *colloq.*

1957 N. MARSH *Off with his Head* ii. 29 The bar-parlour at the Green Man..lay at right angles to the Public. **1969** M. DUFFY *Wounds* i. 19 The pints of beer she had to pull for the pensioners in the public. **1971** L. LAMB *Worse than Death* vii. 64 They had finished doing the bars, and..were having a cup of tea in the Public.

†**public**, *v. Obs. rare.* [ad. obs. F. *publicque-r* (in Godef.) or ad. L. *pūblic-āre*, f. *pūblic-us* PUBLIC.] *trans.* To make public, to publish.

1487 *Sc. Acts Jas. III* (1814) II. 179/1 That nane of þame tak apoune hand..to public or vse ouþer bullis or processis purchest or to be purchest. **1542** *Sc. Acts Mary* (1814) II. 424*/2 To publicte þis constitutioune. **1570** LEVINS *Manip.* 122/37 To publike, *publicare.*

†'**publical**, *a. Obs. rare*⁻¹. [f. as PUBLIC *a.* + -AL[1].] = PUBLIC *a.*

c **1440** *Alphabet of Tales* 248 þer suld all publicall honor and wurshup sese betwix þe fadur & þe son.

'**publically** (-ɪklɪ), *adv.* [f. PUBLIC *a.* + -AL[1] + -LY[2].] = PUBLICLY *adv.*

1920 E. SITWELL *Bath* i. 20 Goldsmith adds that 'the Masters, struck with such an uncommon instance of good nature, publically thanked him for his benevolence'. **1963** W. SELLARS *Sci., Perception, & Reality* 364 (Index), Publically observable. **1972** D. HOLBROOK *Pseudo-Revol.* viii. 140 Individuals leaping on to the stages of Danish sex clubs and publically copulating. **1974** GAGNON & SIMON *Sexual Conduct* ii. 56 The publically valued institution of marriage. **1977** *Grimsby Even. Tel.* 13 May 2/4 It was sometimes hard for parents to accept publically that their children had mental or physical difficulties.

publican ('pʌblɪkən), *sb.*[1] Forms: α. 3-4 **pupp-, puplicane, 4-5 -an.** β. 4 **publycan, 4-7 publicane, 5- publican.** [a. F. *publicain* (12th c. in Hatz.-Darm.), ad. L. *pūblicān-us* a farmer-general of the revenues, later a tax-gatherer, f. *pūblicum* the public revenue, neut. of *pūblic-us* PUBLIC. In the ME. form *puplican*, a. OF. *poplican*, a by-form influenced by *pople, puple*, PEOPLE *sb.*]

1. *Rom. Hist.* One who farmed the public taxes; hence, a tax-gatherer. (Chiefly in Scriptural quotations or allusions.)

α. *c* **1200** ORMIN 9295 Puplicaness comenn þær, Att himm to wurrþenn fullhtnedd. *a* **1225** *Ancr. R.* 328 Schrift schal beon edmed, ase þe Pupplicanes, & nout ase was þe Pharisewus. *c* **1380** WYCLIF *Serm.* Sel. Wks. I. 397 Whi etiþ your Maistir wiþ puplicans? *c* **1440** *York Myst.* xxv. 414 Of puplicans sen prince am I.

β. **1340** *Ayenb.* 175 þe farizeus..onworþede þane publycan. *c* **1386** CHAUCER *Pars. T.* ¶912 (Harl.) Such was þe confessioun of þe publican [so 3 texts; *Ellesm., Lansd., Seld.* Puplican, -e]. **1548** UDALL *Erasm. Par. Luke* iii. 12 Publicans, that is to saye, the customers and takers vp of tolles. **1596** SHAKS. *Merch. V.* I. iii. 42 How like a fawning publican he lookes. **1600** HOLLAND *Livy* xxv. i. 545 The captaine..had beene aforetime a Publicane or farmer of the citie reuenues. **1853** ROBERTSON *Serm.* Ser. II. 191 The publicans were outcasts among the Jews, because, having accepted the office under the Roman government of collecting the taxes imposed by Rome upon their brethren, they were regarded as traitors to the cause of Israel. **1855** J. H. NEWMAN *Callista* xvi. (1881) 181 A clerk..in the *Officium* of the society of publicans or collectors of *annona.*

b. *transf.* Any collector of toll, tribute, customs, or the like. Also *fig.*

1644 MILTON *Areop.* (Arb.) 64 Nothing writt'n but what passes through the custom-house of certain Publicans that have the tunaging and the poundaging of all free spok'n truth. **1650** JER. TAYLOR *Holy Living* II. v. §4. 122 We are not angry with Searchers and Publicans..; but when they break open trunks, and pierce vessels, and unrip packs, and open sealed letters. **1855** MACAULAY *Hist. Eng.* xi. III. 37 Outrages and exactions such as have, in every age, made the name of publican a proverb for all that is most hateful. **1893** *Westm. Gaz.* 25 Apr. 2/1 Next to Drink, the greatest Publicans of the British Exchequer are Death and Gambling on the Stock Exchange.

†**2.** *transf.* One who is regarded as 'a heathen man and a publican' (Matt. xviii. 17); one cut off from the church; an excommunicated person.

1303 R. BRUNNE *Handl. Synne* 11649 A publycan ys, yn oure sawe, A synful man, oute of þe lawe. *c* **1375** *Sc. Leg. Saints* x. (*Mathou*) 12 Quha in hopyne syne is tane, þe ewangell callis 'publicane'. *a* **1651** CALDERWOOD *Hist. Kirk* (Wodrow Soc.) II. 81 We, not one or two, but the whole church, must hold him as a publicane; that is, as one cutt off frome the bodie of Christ.

3. One who keeps a public house; a licensed victualler; a keeper of an ale-house or tavern.

1728 BAILEY, *Publican*,..also a Keeper of a publick House, a Victualler or Alehouse-keeper. **1744** N. SALMON *Pres. St. Universities* I. 416 It seems now to be the Business of most Publicans to propagate Vice and Disorder. **1817** W. SELWYN *Law Nisi Prius* II. 1033 An action by a publican, for beer sold. **1861** *Sat. Rev.* 23 Nov. 536 A profound politician in the eyes of a metropolitan publican. **1880** MCCARTHY *Own Times* IV. lxi. 354 A large proportion of the publicans carried on a respectable trade.

4. *attrib.* and *Comb.*, as ***publican*** †***lede*** (= race), ***sin***, ***state***, ***tenant***; ***publican-ridden*** adj.

a **1300** *Cursor M.* 13292 (Cott.) O puplicane lede was he, And als a man o gret pouste. *a* **1652** J. SMITH *Sel. Disc.* viii. 382 No extortioner, nor unjust, nor guilty of any publican-sins. **1685** BUNYAN *Pharisee & Publican* Wks. (1845) 103 Love..did cover with silence this his publican state. **1894** *Westm. Gaz.* 11 May 8/1 'A priest-ridden people is to be pitied, but a publican-ridden people is to be despised.' **1906** *Ibid.* 28 Mar. 2/1 To say..that the publican-tenant is in any sense a free agent is absurd.

Hence †ˈ**publican** *v. nonce-wd., trans.* to treat or regard as a publican. (Cf. Luke xviii. 10, 11.)

1648 C. WALKER *Hist. Independ.* I. 2 To Pharisee themselves, and Publican all the world besides [cf. PHARISEE *v.*].

ˈ**Publican**, *sb.*² *Eccl. Hist.* Forms: 5 **Popelican**, **-quan**, 7 **Poblican**, 6– **Publican**. [ME. *popelican*, a. OF. *popelican*, *publican*, ad. med.L. *Pop(e)licān-us*, *Publicān-us*, altered from med.Gr. *Παυλικιαν-ός* (*υ*=*v*) PAULICIAN, in allusion to, or by confusion with, L. *pūblicānus* PUBLICAN¹.]

A name applied to the Paulicians of the South of France in the 12th c.

[*a* **1225** RALPH OF COGGESHALLE *Chron.* (Rolls) 122 Temporibus Ludovici regis Franciæ, qui genuit regem Philippum, cum error quorumdam hæreticorum qui vulgo appellantur Publicani, per plures provincias Galliæ proserperet. *c* **1250** MATT. PARIS (*ad ann.* 1236), Gallice etiam dicuntur ab aliquibus Popelicani.] **1481** CAXTON *Godeffroy* xli. 80 Nygh by was a castel right strong, wherin alle the popeliquans of the lande were withdrawen. *Ibid.* lii. 94 And there was disputed ayenst this popelican. **1573** STOW *Ann.* (1592) 213 There came into England 30. Germanes,..who called themselues Publicans... They denyed matrimony, and the sacraments of baptisme, and the Lords supper, with other articles. **1855** MILMAN *Lat. Chr.* IX. viii. IV. 180 The Archbishops of Lyons and Narbonne.. sate in solemn judgment on some, it should seem, poor and ignorant men called Publicans.

Publicanism (ˈpʌblɪkənɪz(ə)m). [f. PUBLICAN¹ + -ISM.] The fact or profession of being a publican: in quot. 1903, antithetic to Pharisaism.

1638 W. SCLATER *Serm. Experimentall* 110 Amos his mean education; Matthew his Publicanisme; Paul his persecution. **1903** D. M'LEAN *Stud. Apostles* x. 145 We believe the utter hollowness of Pharisaism to have been a main cause of the revolt into Publicanism on the part of some Jews.

†ˈ**publicate**, *v. Obs.* [f. L. *pūblicāt-*, ppl. stem of *pūblicāre* to PUBLISH.] *trans.* To publish, make publicly known.

1540 in Hall *Chron., Hen. VIII* (1548) 246 b, Many other errors holden, saied, publicated and taught by hym. **1659** GAUDEN *Tears of Ch.* I. xiv. 115 Little sins in them [the Clergy], (if publicated) grow great by their scandall and contagion. **1745** FIELDING *True Patriot* No. 7 Wks. 1775 IX. 300, I have communicated my thoughts to you thereon, which you may suppress or publicate as you think meet. **1808** SOUTHEY *Lett.* (1856) II. 66 The 'Monthly Review' publicates me and Duppa as one D. Manuel.

publication (pʌblɪˈkeɪʃən). Also 5 **pupplicacion**. [ME. *publicacion*, a. OF. *publicacion* (14th c. in Hatz.-Darm.), in mod.F. *publication*, or ad. L. *pūblicātiōn-em*, n. of action f. *pūblicāre* to PUBLISH.] The action of publishing, or that which is published.

1. a. The action of making publicly known; public notification or announcement; promulgation.

1387 TREVISA *Higden* (Rolls) VII. 433 Anselme..demede þat Sodomytes schulde be accorsed every Sonday. But afterward he undede þat doynge, for publicacioun [HIGDEN *publicatio*] of vice. **1451** CAPGRAVE *Life St. Gilbert* (E.E.T.S.) 107, xj ȝer aftir his deth was no gret pupplicacion mad. **1553** *Reg. Privy Council Scot.* I. 140 To mak publicatioun and intimatioun heirof at the marcatt crossis. **1655** *Providence* (R.I.) *Rec.* (1893) II. 89 Ordred yᵗ ye Publication of mariage shall be vnder ye hand of a Magistrate set upon some eminent Tree in ye Towne streete. **1748** HARTLEY *Observ. Man* II. iv. 375 The Publication of the Gospel to us Gentiles. **1802–12** BENTHAM *Ration. Judic. Evid.* II. 577 Who could be allowed to speak of secret publication?

b. *spec.* in *Law.* Notification or communication to those concerned, or to a limited number regarded as representing the public. Cf. PUBLISH *v.* 1 b.

1590 SWINBURNE *Testaments* VI. xiii. 223 The Iudge may not..proceede to the publication of the testament, vnlesse there be lawfull proofe, or sufficient prescription for the testators death. **1656** BLOUNT *Glossogr.* s.v., In Chancery.. we say a cause is come to Publication, when the Plaintiff hath exhibited his Bill, the Defendant answered, and witnesses are examined. **1769** BLACKSTONE *Comm.* IV. xi. 150 The communication of a libel to any one person is a publication in the eye of the law. **1837** *Act 1 Vict.* c. 26 §13 Every will executed in manner hereinbefore required shall be valid without any other publication thereof. **1897** *Daily News* 21 Oct. 8/3 The Law of Libel... A man may tell his wife a thing, and that is not publication; or he may tell his next door neighbour, and that is.

2. a. The issuing, or offering to the public, of a book, map, engraving, photograph, piece of music, or other work of which copies are multiplied by writing, printing, or any other process; also, the work or business of producing and issuing copies of such works.

1576 FLEMING *Panopl. Epist.* 216 My bookes,..with the publication of which you charge me as blameable. **1665** BOYLE *Occas. Refl.* Pref. (1848) 29, I should not be destituted of a very just Excuse for the Publication of it [this Treatise]. **1786** COWPER *Let. to W. Churchey* 13 Dec. (in *Sotheby's Catal.* 29 Apr. (1897) 21), I know well that publication is necessary to give an edge to the poetical turn. **1870** DICKENS *E. Drood* iv, With an author's anxiety to rush into publication. **1902** *Daily Chron.* 3 Sept. 3/2 Some publishers think that to deposit the usual copies required by law at the Public Libraries constitutes publication.

b. A work published; a book or the like printed or otherwise produced and issued for public sale.

The first quotation may belong to 2.

1656 COWLEY *Poems* Pref., I have lost the Copy,..which makes me omit it in this publication. **1780** JOHNSON in *Boswell* (1848) 656/2 One instance..of a foreign publication in which mention is made of *l'illustre Lockman.* **1790** PALEY *Horæ Paul.* i. 7 They were originally separate publications. **1831** D. E. WILLIAMS *Life & Corr. Sir T. Lawrence* I. 141 Writers in the periodical publications of the day. **1846** MCCULLOCH *Acc. Brit. Empire* (1854) I. 751 The diffusion of books and periodical publications.

c. *attrib.*, as ***publication date***, ***day***.

1931 H. CRANE *Let.* 13 June (1965) 373 Will you tell me something about its publication date, etc. **1976** M. HINXMAN *End of Good Woman* xiii. 168 Sometimes I think it's a plot on the part of the publishers to make sure no one can salvage the books from the packing to review them in time for the publication date. **1888** 'MARK TWAIN' *Lett. to Publishers* (1967) 250 No notice should appear before publication-day. **1979** M. RUSSELL *Touchdown* I. 6, I felt an urge to demand how many previous stacks had melted away since publication day.

†**3.** The making of a thing public or common property; confiscation. (A Latinism.) *Obs. rare.*

1611 B. JONSON *Catiline* I. i, The rich men..proscrib'd And publication made of all their goods. **1650** JER. TAYLOR *Holy Living* IV. viii. 304 To redeem maydens from prostitution and publication of their bodies.

publicatory (ˈpʌblɪkeɪtərɪ, -ətərɪ), *a. rare.* [f. late L. *pūblicātor*, agent-n. f. *pūblicāre* to PUBLISH: see -ORY².] Of or pertaining to publication; intended for publication.

1702 *Parl. Orig. Rights Lower Ho. Convoc.* 32 A Mandate Publicatory of Archbishop Bancroft. **1830** *Fraser's Mag.* I. 131 Byron's Hours of Idleness was not without publicatory enticements.

publice, obs. Sc. var. of *publis*, PUBLISH.

public house. Also with hyphen.

1. A building belonging or open to the community at large; one provided for some public use or purpose; a public building. *Obs.* exc. with allusion to sense 2.

1574 HELLOWES *Gueuara's Fam. Ep.* (1577) 21 That he was the firste that inuented in Greece to haue publique or common houses founded at the charges of the common welth..where the sick might be cured, and the poore refreshed. **1617–20** [see PUBLIC SCHOOL 2]. *c* **1618** MORYSON *Itin.* (1903) 319 The publike house of the Citty, where this and all publike feasts are kept. **1708** J. CHAMBERLAYNE *St. Gt. Brit.* II. I. ii. (1737) 310 The Town of Glasgow have built a new Port, and named it Port-Glasgow, with a large Publick-House. **1903** *Westm. Gaz.* 4 Apr. 10/2 Lord Avebury..said there were now public-houses all over the country, not for the sale of beer, but for the use of books.

2. A house for the entertainment of any member of the community, in consideration of payment. **a.** An inn or hostelry providing accommodation (food and lodging, or light refreshments) for travellers or members of the general public; usually licensed for the supply of ale, wines, and spirits. Now commonly merged in b.

1669 WOOD *Life* 26 June (O.H.S.) II. 163 He was asham'd to go to a publick house [for his meals], because he was a senior master, and because his relations lived in Oxon. **1679** PRANCE *Narr. Pop. Plot* 12 Not beeing at home, but at a publique House hard by. **1711** STEELE *Spect.* No. 155 ¶2 Mr. Spectator, I Keep a Coffee-house...Good Mr. Spectator,..Say it is possible a Woman may be modest and yet keep a Publick-house. **1715** *Royal Proclam.* 5 Jan. in *Lond. Gaz.* No. 5292/2 Taverns, Chocolate Houses, Coffee Houses, or other Publick Houses. **1796** *Hist. Ned Evans* II. 151 Every night they were entertained by private families, there being no public-houses at so remote a distance. **1849** D. J. BROWNE *Amer. Poultry Yd.* (1855) 165 Fattening some of the earliest broods, in order to supply public houses, and such families as require turkeys early in the season.

b. In current restricted application: A house of which the principal business is the sale of alcoholic liquors to be consumed on the premises; a tavern.

1768 FOOTE *Devil on Two Sticks* II. (1778) 33 Step into the first publick-house to refresh you. **1812** COLERIDGE *Lett., to Southey* (1895) 598 A large public house frequented about one o'clock by the lower orders. **1824** MISS MITFORD *Village* Ser. I. (1863) 4 Lucky would it be for his wife and her eight children if there were no public-house in the land. **1882** *Encycl. Brit.* (ed. 9) XIV. 688/1 In nearly all countries the nature of the trade carried on in public-houses has subjected them to a much more rigorous police supervision than ordinary trades.

†**3.** A brothel. Cf. F. *maison publique*, Ger. *öffentliches Haus. Obs. rare*⁻¹.

1785 TRUSLER *Mod. Times* I. 87 Who never loses sight of her till she is picked up and taken to a public house.

4. *attrib.* and *Comb.*, as ***public-house club***, ***-keeper***, ***licence***, ***parlour***, ***score***, ***sign***, ***trust***, etc.

1704 in Trott *Laws Brit. Plant. Amer.* (1721) 256 No Publick House-keeper within this Province [New Jersey] shall suffer any Person or Persons to tipple and drink in his House on the Lord's Day. **1725** (*title*) The Publick-House-Keeper's Monitor. **1809** MALKIN *Gil Blas* I. ii. ¶3 The landlord was..overwhelming me with public-house civility. **1848** THACKERAY *Van. Fair* xxvi, They talked about them over their pints of beer at their public-house clubs. **1854** H. SPENCER in *Brit. Q. Rev.* July 143 Much as public-house scores are kept now. **1882** *Encycl. Brit.* (ed. 9) 690/1 [In Ireland] Public-house licences are generally held by shopkeepers. **1887** RUSKIN *Præterita* II. vi. 192 [He] wanted to promote himself to some honour or other in the public-house line. **1893** J. ASHBY STERRY *Naughty Girl* v, He would have..painted tea-trays and public-house signs.

publicist (ˈpʌblɪsɪst). [a. F. *publiciste* (1762 in *Dict. Acad.*), Ger. *publicist*, f. L. (*jus*) *public-um* public law: see -IST.]

1. One who is learned in 'public' or international law (PUBLIC *a.* 9); a writer on the law of nations.

1792 BURKE *Pres. St. Affairs* Wks. VII. 99 The two German courts seem to have as little consulted the publicists of Germany, as their own true interests. **1801** H. C. ROBINSON *Diary* (1869) I. v. 113 A distinguished publicist, to use the German term, the eminent political writer and statesman Friedrich Gentz. **1805** W. TAYLOR in *Ann. Rev.* III. 307 The cheapness of food is..justly considered by Vattel, and the publicists, as a chief purpose of political association. **1861** *N. Brit. Rev.* May 173 Plato was a publicist when he wrote the Laws and the Republic; Aristotle was a publicist when he wrote the Politics;.. Machiavel was a publicist in the Prince, Hobbes in the Leviathan, Montesquieu in the 'Esprit des Lois'. **1868** ROGERS *Pol. Econ.* x. (1876) 128 Problems which baffle the publicist and amaze the economist.

2. *loosely.* A writer on current public topics; a journalist who makes political matters his speciality.

1833 *Westm. Rev.* Jan. 195 We hear of editors, reporters, writers in newspapers, and sometimes 'publicists', a neological term; but the world..does not assign the definite meanings to these terms. **1863** S. EDWARDS *Polish Captivity* I. 78 Certain German publicists point with an air of triumph to the fact that Prussia has constructed a railroad from Posen to Breslau. **1874** GREEN *Short Hist.* x. §2. 752 The hacks of Grub Street were superseded by publicists of a high moral temper and literary excellence.

attrib. **1895** P. MILYOUKOV in *Athenæum* 6 July 25/3 The influence of the publicist polemics of the year.

3. A press or publicity agent.

1930 *Oxford Times* 4 Apr. 7/4 This is the experience of Sir Charles Higham, the famous publicist, who celebrated his 21st anniversary as an advertising agent in Fleet-street on Wednesday. **1942** *Sun* (Baltimore) 4 Nov. 9/4 Most of the testimony..was given by Paul H. De Kruff, bacteriologist and medical publicist. **1969** R. BLYTHE *Akenfield* ii. 60 Well-printed signs of expert publicist talents being employed to disseminate the new *caritas*. **1977** *Times* 12 Feb. 12/6 Mr William Camp's appointment as publicist of the railways... He and his company..will apparently become the overlords of BR publicity.

Hence **publiˈcistic** *a.*, of or pertaining to publicists. So ˈ**publicism**, the occupation or profession of a publicist; public journalism.

1827 CARLYLE *Germ. Rom.* III. 150 To divide his Biography, as Moser did his Publicistic Materials, into separate letter-boxes. **1875** POSTE *Gaius* I. Comm. (ed. 2) 127 The political or publicistic elements of *civitas*. **1885** *Society in London* 279 He has taken up publicism as he has taken up many other things. **1894** *Athenæum* 10 Nov. 634/2 Of publicistic and photographic accounts of Japan..we have more than enough.

publicitor (pʌˈblɪsɪtə(r)). *U.S.* [f. PUBLICIT(Y + -OR.] A press or publicity agent.

1936 *Daily News* (Chicago) 24 Apr. 30/4 But in this solicitous telephonery we detected the fine Italian hand of the publicitor. **1951** *Lincoln* (Nebraska) *Jrnl.* 8 Dec. 6 O—— ..who rose from the job of sports publicitor..was assailed by the Judge. **1955** *Sun* (Baltimore) 15 Dec. (B ed.) 25/5 'The fancy basketball is out unless we're way on top,' Rod

Hundley was saying. The publicitors call him Hot Rod. **1962** [see COOTIE *sb.*[2]].

publicity (pʌˈblɪsɪtɪ). [ad. F. *publicité* (*a* 1694 in Hatz.-Darm.), ad. med.L. *pūblicitās, -tātem*, f. L. *pūblic-us* PUBLIC.] **1. a.** The quality of being public; the condition or fact of being open to public observation or knowledge. **b.** *spec.* Public notice; the action or fact of making someone or something publicly known; the business of promotion or advertising; an action or object intended to attract public notice; material issued to publicize.

1791 HAMILTON tr. *Berthollet's Dyeing* I. Introd. 4 The sacrifices it makes by this publicity, are amply compensated by the advantages it derives from it. **1826** J. J. AUDUBON *Jrnl.* 16 Dec. (1897) I. 186 Mrs. Rathbone, Senior, refused me the pleasure of naming a bird after her, on account of the publicity, she said. *a* **1832** BENTHAM *Draught of Code* iv. Wks. 1843 IV. 316 Publicity is the very soul of justice. **1841** D'ISRAELI *Amen. Lit.* (1867) 611 The studious composed their works without any view to their publicity. **1842** DICKENS *Let.* 30 Apr. (1974) III. 222, I found the documents of which the inclosed are copies... You will see that they are signed by the first writers in England; and that their object..is *Publicity*. **1847** A. BRONTË *Agnes Grey* xiv. 222 If you add to it by giving publicity to this unfortunate affair, or naming it *at all*, you will find that I too can speak. **1851** *Times* 28 Oct. 5/1 We have reported his proceedings.. at greater length than any of the journals devoted to his cause, and we have thus secured to him all the publicity we had it in our power to bestow. **1869** ROGERS *Hist. Gleanings* I. 89 The only guarantee of public honour is publicity, for the only protection rogues have is secrecy. **1917** *Electric Railway Jrnl.* 6 Jan. 17/1 Continuous publicity of good work would have softened a public irritation in the day of trouble. **1936** *S.P.E. Tract* XLV. 185 The prejudice that many people feel against advertising is likely to be dispelled if they can be made to believe that it is no more than *publicity*. **1946** E. O'NEILL *Iceman Cometh* I. 38 Why, even at Harvard I discovered my father was well known by reputation, although that was some time before the District Attorney gave him so much unwelcome publicity. **1953** A. HUXLEY *Let.* 21 Dec. (1969) 692 Osmond sent me a copy... I have taken the liberty of forwarding it to Cass Canfield of Harpers, who may like to quote from it in his publicity. **1981** S. RADLEY *Chief Inspector's Daughter* ii. 17 'How come she's featured in a magazine, anyway?' 'Publicity. She's a romantic novelist.'

2. *attrib.* and *Comb.*, as ***publicity agent, boy, bureau, drive, expert, film, hand-out, hound, man, manager*** (so ***-manage*** vb. trans.), ***-monger, officer, omnibus, people, ramp, scheme, screen, section, stunt, value, woman, worker; publicity-hunting, -seeking*** vbl. sbs. and ppl. adjs.; ***publicity-loving*** ppl. adj.; ***publicity-conscious, -minded, -ridden*** adjs.; ***publicity-wise*** adv.

1911 J. C. LINCOLN *Cap'n Warren's Wards* xi. 180 He and his friends needed a representative on the press—a publicity agent, so to speak. **1922** R. G. COLLINGWOOD tr. *Croce's Aesthetic* II. vi. 244 Recognizing the great gifts of Meier as publicity-agent. **1955** W. GADDIS *Recognitions* I. v. 180 The publicity agent looks it over and signs her name to it. **1929** G. ADE *Let.* 8 Dec. (1973) 142 The publicity boys seemed to think it was a great joke to float these wild-eyed stories about my pursuing Dorothy Tennant, [etc.]. **1962** 'M. INNES' *Connoisseur's Case* iii. 33 Tourists sure to come along when the publicity boys do their stuff. **1907** U. SINCLAIR *Industr. Republic* 142 He had an army of experts to help him..skilful lobbyists, newspapers and publicity bureaus. **1959** F. NEWTON *Jazz Scene* v. 74 A publicity-conscious American impresario could advertise a plan to recruit an 'international' orchestra. **1977** H. INNES *Big Footprints* III. i. 217 He had agreed to our taking a camera... Extraordinary how publicity-conscious these men were. **1935** Publicity drive [see *copy-writer*]. **1915** *Truth* 4 Aug. 196/1 There are, as one publicity expert puts it, many shirkers doing remarkably well. **1969** *Morning Star* 25 Mar. 4 There has been an increase in short publicity films. **1973** *Screen* Spring/Summer 227 He [*sc.* A. Alexeieff]..made several commercials and publicity films. **1927** S. BENT *Ballyhoo* iii. 86 Washington is this country's premier city of publicity hand-outs. **1979** A. WILLIAMSON *Funeral March for Siegfried* x. 46 York..asked if they had a publicity hand-out on the singers in *The Ring*. **1928** Publicity hound [see HOUND *sb.*[1] 4 e]. **1936** 'J. TEY' *Shilling for Candles* vi. 62 And they say professional people are publicity hounds! **1971** 'E. LATHEN' *Longer the Thread* (1972) viii. 75 Annie was certainly no publicity hound. **1963** *Times Lit. Suppl.* 17 May 353/2 All the vices from publicity-hunting to jobbery. **1976** C. BERMANT *Coming Home* II. vii. 216 Lord Longford was.. regarded as a publicity-hunting fraud. **1938** *Amer. Speech* XIII. 59 A field of education that has suffered much from publicity- and money-loving quacks. **1907** J. C. LINCOLN *Old Home House* 37 You two can be proprietors and treasurers if you want to. But active manager and publicity man—that's yours cheerily, Peter Theodosius Brown! **1932** *Sunday Express* 3 July 9/1 Soon Hammerstein left me with his publicity man, a human talking machine. **1957** *Times Lit. Suppl.* 25 Oct. 638/2 No one, not even a modern film star hounded by his publicity man, has ever courted popular favour more devotedly than Louis Philippe. **1978** I. B. SINGER *Shosha* III. 50 What kind of publicity man will I make, anyway? **1952** L. DURRELL *Let.* 14 Nov. in *Spirit of Place* (1969) 114 My boss Eden whose much advertised tour was publicity-managed by little me. **1908** *Mod. Business* Aug. 86/2 *Publicity Manager.*—Can formulate and carry through an advertising campaign. **1931** 'G. TREVOR' *Murder at School* iii. 49 The rôle of 'writer-up' and general publicity manager. **1974** *Listener* 17 Jan. 66/2 Lady Glencora Palliser ..settles down to become..her husband's self-appointed publicity manager and hatchet-woman. **1962** *Observer* 11 Mar. 8/5 I'm a very publicity-minded chap. **1974** *Times* 28 Nov. 17/7 The poor image of universities..[is] emanating in large part from a publicity-minded student minority. **1951** N. MITFORD *Blessing* II. xi. 251 Charles-Edouard's heir was on the way to becoming a publicity-monger. **1962** *Economist* 15 Sept. 1017/1 The publicity-mongers of the various political parties. **1933** *Whitaker's Almanack* 284/2 Colonial Office... Publicity Officer, C. Becker-Platt..£666. **1966** 'H. MACDIARMID' *Company I've Kept* viii. 186, I..spent a year in Liverpool as Publicity officer for the Liverpool Organization. **1846** in *Daily Chron.* 19 Feb. (1903) 5/1 [Marriott..in the year 1846 registered as an article of utility an] improved publicity omnibus. **1932** *New Yorker* 14 May 44/2, I find..that all those competent publicity people in the shops around town can be counted on to call me up. **1933** DYLAN THOMAS *Let.* Oct. (1966) 31 Patriotism is a publicity ramp organised by holders of excess armament shares. **1961** *Times* 7 Jan. 9/7 A publicity-ridden world. **1907** *Instal. News* Sept. 4/1 The..fantastic publicity schemes now in vogue. **1911** R. D. SAUNDERS *Col. Todhunter* ix. 128 This amazing projection of himself..on the publicity 'screen' of a newspaper's front page appalled Colonel Todhunter. **1927** F. L. C. FLOUD *Ministry of Agric.* ii. 25 There is also a small publicity section for the issue of information to the Press. **1935** DYLAN THOMAS *Let.* July (1966) 159, I hope to have.. a little free love offstage from any publicity-seeking actresses I can find. **1939** 'N. BLAKE' *Smiler with Knife* v. 90 Charges of publicity-seeking. **1966** 'L. LANE' *ABZ of Scouse* Foreword., Be he a dollar-spending tourist or publicity-seeking politician. **1926** 'SAPPER' *Final Count* vii. 195 It was just an advertisement—an elaborate publicity stunt. **1972** P. DICKINSON *Lizard in Cup* xi. 176 The theft of the pictures ..being, as Nancy had hinted, a publicity stunt. **1922** FARJEON & HORSNELL *Advertising April* i. 19 The other woman. My successor. What's her name? What's her publicity value? **1978** J. PEARSON *Façades* viii. 149 Beaverbrook..knew the publicity value of controversy. **1958** *Punch* 1 Jan. 50/1 Publicitywise, Sabrina and the Duke of Bedford consolidated their respective resources. **1962** *Listener* 11 Jan. 102/2 Dr. Crick, who publicity-wise appeared the king-pin, was now announced as the colleague (or perhaps subordinate) of Dr. Brenner. **1958** A. HUXLEY *Let.* 22 June (1969) 851 There have been endless contretemps, including, as a last straw, the collapse of the publicity woman with, of all things, chickenpox. **1926** *Amer. Speech* I. 480/1 The public is worked on by a 'publicity worker', assisted sometimes by a person who has the 'technique' of describing 'personal interest' incidents.

publicize (ˈpʌblɪsaɪz), *v.* [f. PUBLIC *a.* (*sb.*) + -IZE.] *trans.* To bring to the notice of the public; to make generally known; to advertise.

1928 *Weekly Dispatch* 20 May 14/4 Nowadays the potential star has to be managed and publicised. **1938** M. BRINIG *May Flavin* iv. 363 In my present position it wouldn't do any good to publicize these things. **1943** J. S. HUXLEY *TVA* iv. 25 One of the original aims of the TVA, and one much publicized in its earlier years. **1967** N. FREELING *Strike Out* 78 I'm not in the habit of publicising my private life. **1976** *Guardian* 21 Apr. 6/1 The board does not adequately publicise itself.

Hence **publiciˈzation**; **ˈpublicized** *ppl. a.*, **ˈpublicizing** *vbl. sb.*

1932 *New Yorker* 11 June 40/1, I hear that all the.. manufacturers who aren't doing business intend to spend the Summer on that publicized isle [*sc.* Majorca]. **1956** A. H. COMPTON *Atomic Quest* 303 These much-publicized burns have had effects that are no more tragic than those resulting from other forms of modern weapons. **1958** *Jrnl. Amer. Water Works Assoc.* L. 1057/2 Of more value..will be accurate reporting—even publicizing—of the physical, chemical, and biological difference between the first water, the used supply, and the reclaimed water. **1966** 'H. MACDIARMID' *Company I've Kept* iv. 128 All the disgusting publicisation of our Scottish Queen Mother.

publicly (ˈpʌblɪklɪ), *adv.* [f. PUBLIC *a.* + -LY[2].] **1.** In a public manner; in the presence or with the knowledge of people generally; with publicity; in public; openly; without concealment.

1567 *Ælfric's Test. Antiquitie* Title-p., The auncient fayth ..here publikely preached, and also receaued in the Saxons tyme. **1569** in Dunlop *Confess.* (1722) II. 637 Thereunto war added secret Prayers publictlie made within the Houses. **1590** SHAKS. *Com. Err.* v. i. 130 Yet once againe proclaime it publikely. **1644** *Direct. Publ. Worship* 7 All the Canonicall Books of the Old and New Testament..shall be publiquely read in the vulgar Tongue. **1709** STEELE *Tatler* No. 6 ¶11 The Soldiers murmured publickly for Want of Pay. **1855** MACAULAY *Hist. Eng.* xix. IV. 379 Those books were not publicly exposed to sale.

2. By the public or community; by or with public or common action or consent; officially; collectively, as a community; also, †in a way common to all, commonly, generally, universally (*obs.*).

1585 T. WASHINGTON tr. *Nicholay's Voy.* III. xxii. 112 b, These Sacquas [water carriers]..are waged either publikely, or of som in particular. **1638** JUNIUS *Paint. Ancients* 142 The Athenians erected him such a one publiquely in the market place. *a* **1729** S. CLARKE *Serm.* (1734) III. 88 Able to be publickly beneficial to Mankind. **1902** *Westm. Gaz.* 15 Apr. 2/2 Provisions which will very largely close the door to all publicly-managed elementary schools. **1908** *Daily Chron.* 13 Apr. 4/4 Eventually no publicly-paid teacher would be allowed to give denominational teaching. **1928** *Britain's Industr. Future* (Liberal Industr. Inquiry) II. vi. 82 We hope that neither thought nor money will be spared to furnish this country with a publicly-owned system of electrical supply. **1969** *Listener* 28 Aug. 267/1 And can capitalism..achieve the rate of growth that planning in a really publicly-owned economy has achieved? *a* **1974** R. CROSSMAN *Diaries* (1976) II. 460 He was hoping to have a properly planned publicly-owned New Town like the others. **1980** *Daily Tel.* 16 Jan. 23/2 The first is a publicly-held corporation chartered by Congress.

publicness (ˈpʌblɪknɪs). Now *rare.* [f. as prec. + -NESS.] The quality or character of being public, in various senses; publicity, notoriety, openness; the fact of pertaining to or affecting the community as a whole; †devotedness to the public interest; †the condition of being commonly accepted, prevalence.

1605 A. WOTTON *Answ. Pop. Articles* 16 The truth of beleefe depends not vpon the publicknes of an exposition, but vpon the soundnesse thereof. **1641** W. HAKEWILL *Libertie of Subject* 137 The King may not exact money for passage in and out of his Court gates, because of the publikenesse of his Person. **1643** W. GREENHILL *Axe at Root* Ep. Ded., Publiquenesse of dangers calls for publiquenesse of spirits. **1662** BARGRAVE *Pope Alex. VII* (1867) 68 Pope Alexander VII. not enduring the publiqueness of this Cardinal's amours, sent him legate to Romania. **1676** TOWERSON *Decalogue* viii. 441 Differenc'd from each other by the publickness or privateness of the things taken away. **1748** RICHARDSON *Clarissa* (1811) III. xxix. 173 His objections as to the publicness of the place. **1828** WEBSTER s.v., The publicness of a sale. **1844** EMERSON *Lect., Yng. Amer.* Wks. (Bohn) II. 305 The timidity of our public opinion is our disease, or, shall I say, the publicness of opinion, the absence of private opinion. **1890** *Cent. Dict.* s.v., The publicness of a resort.

public office: see PUBLIC *a.* 2 c.

public opinion: see OPINION *sb.*

public relations. [RELATION *sb.* 6.] **a.** (The establishment or maintenance of) relations, esp. a good relationship, between an organization, firm, etc., and the general public; (also const. *sing.*) the art or practice of establishing or maintaining such good relations; *transf.*, a department or group with responsibility for relations with the public.

1807 T. JEFFERSON *Writings* (1854) III. 89 Questions calling for the notice of Congress, unless indeed they shall be superseded by a change in our public relations now awaiting the determination of others. **1913** *Electric Railway Jrnl.* 16 Oct. 829/1 Effective publicity to deal with questions of public relations and to consider the molding of public opinion by the presentation of real facts. **1917** *Ibid.* 6 Jan. 17/1 This adviser in public relations—for such a man should be far more than a mere publicity agent—should constantly study the temper of the public mind. **1933** *Planning* I. xiv. 5 Public relations may be defined as covering all the contacts between an official organisation and all other bodies with which it may have to deal, directly or indirectly, otherwise than through internal administrative channels. **1943** J. D'ARCY-DAWSON *Tunisian Battle* i. 21 Public Relations were now the possessors of six Simcas. **1945** *Manch. Guardian* 8 Aug. 4/6 The Central Insurance building, now headquarters of Public Relations in Italy. **1958** *Spectator* 8 Aug. 201/2 Some of our more 'enterprising' Cathedral cities have invented a new form of spiritual public relations, which is the Industrial Harvest Festival. **1961** *Observer* 19 Mar. 3/4 He..founded his own firm, first in public relations, then in advertising. *a* **1974** R. CROSSMAN *Diaries* (1976) II. 547 Wedgy is brilliant at public relations.

b. *attrib.*

1923 E. L. BERNAYS *Crystallizing Public Opinion* i. 12 To some the public relations counsel is known by the term 'propagandist'. **1929** [see HAND-OUT 2]. **1933** *Times* 2 Sept. 15/5 The post of Public Relations Officer in the Post Office is a new one. **1937** *Rep. Proc. 14th Conf. ASLIB* 72, I asked him if he could help me in finding a nice crisp definition of the duties of a Public Relations Officer. He replied, 'His principal function is interpreting his undertaking to the public and the public to his undertaking.' **1944** A. JACOB *Traveller's War* xii. 212 Publicity which verged ever so slightly upon the personal was regarded as improper by the Public Relations department. *Ibid.*, The Public Relations people had asked war correspondents to go slow on stories about Rommel because we had made him into quite a bogey man. **1956** in W. H. Whyte *Organization Man* (1957) I. iii. 26 Every practising public-relations man is an engineer too —a *social engineer*. **1958** M. ARGYLE *Relig. Behaviour* v. 54 There was an elaborate public relations campaign before the meetings, by posters and other publications, by a film, and via the churches. **1961** *Times* 10 Aug. 2/4 (Advt.), Public Relations Officer..experienced in Public Relations work, both with the press and within an organization. **1967** G. F. FIENNES *I tried to run Railway* vi. 67 Before the new time-tables I set out to do a public relations job. **1970** G. GREER *Female Eunuch* 151 The public relations experts seek to attract girls to nursing by calling it the most rewarding job in the world. **1976** *Church Times* 30 July 9/2 The public-relations officer improves 'image' but is reluctant to accept quantitative assessments of his own impressions of how much he has done so. **1977** *New Yorker* 19 Sept. 98/2 Mrs. Berner also hired the public-relations firm of Gurtman and Murtha to publicize the contest.

public school. A school which is public, in senses varying with time and place.

The Latin *publica schola* goes back under the Roman Empire to the fourth (and by implication, the first) century A.D., and also appears in the Capitula of Louis the Pious A.D. 829, in the sense of a school maintained at the public expense, national or local.

[**381** ST. JEROME *Interpr. Chron. Euseb.* ii. (A.D. 89), Quinctilianus ex Hispania Calaguritanus, qui primus Romae publicam scholam et salarium e fisco recepit, claruit. **829** *Capitula Hlodovici Pii* (Mon. Germ. Hist., Leges 37), Suggerimus ut morem paternum sequentes saltem in tribus congruentissimis imperii vestri locis scolæ publicæ fiant.]

1. a. In England, originally, A grammar-school founded or endowed for the use or benefit of the public, either generally, or of a particular locality, and carried on under some kind of public management or control; often contrasted with a 'private school' carried on at the risk and for the profit of its master or proprietors. In modern English use (chiefly from the 19th century), applied especially to such of the old endowed grammar-schools as have developed into large, fee-paying boarding-schools drawing pupils from all parts of the country and from abroad, and to other private schools established upon similar principles. Traditionally, pupils in the higher forms were prepared mainly for the universities and for public service and, though still true to some extent, this has in recent years become less of a determining characteristic of the public school. It is a general feature that order is maintained and discipline administered to a great extent by the elder pupils themselves: hence the prominent notion in such phrases as 'a public school education' or 'the public school ethos', which are today taken perhaps more broadly to connote the general qualities which the discipline and spirit of the public school are held to impart.

The Latin form appears in the 12th c., and is frequent from the 14th c. as applied to an endowed free grammar-school. The English form *public school* is known from 1580, and was no doubt used earlier. Down to the 18th c. it was very generally opposed to 'private school', and education in a 'public school' was also contrasted with education at home under a tutor The term was officially used in 1860 in the appointment of a Royal Commission, and in 1867 in 'An Act for the better government and extension of certain Public Schools'. As this act applied to the ancient endowed grammar-schools or colleges of Eton, Winchester, Westminster, Harrow, Rugby, Charterhouse, Shrewsbury, these have sometimes been spoken of as 'the Seven Public Schools'; but the name is generally used to include these and numerous other large schools, ancient and modern, of similar organization, which are not separated by any definite line from other endowed schools that depend upon a more local constituency.

[*c* **1180** *Hist. Bury St. Edmunds* (Rolls) I. 126 Hic ergo [Canutus rex] tam..benignus..fuisse memoratur ut per urbes et oppida publicas instituens scolas magistris deputatis..pueros..litteris tradidit imbuendos de ratione fiscali sumptibus constitutis. **1364** (Apr. 7) in *Vict. County Hist. Surrey* II. 155 Hugone de Kingston..pedagogo, ut informacioni et doctrine dictorum puerorum..in dicta villa intenderet, et scolas publicas gubernaret. **1437** (Feb. 23) in *Vict. County Hist. Lincoln* II. 430 [The Chapter] monuerunt pauperes clericos in persona Prepositi eorundem, quod adeant scolas publicas et addiscant effectualiter. **1558** (*a* Mar. 8) in Wilkins *Concilia* IV. 166 Qui in locis insignioribus publicas scholas salario publico vel privato tenent.]

1580 *Let. Privy Counc.* 18 June, in Strype *Life Grindal* 254 All such schoolmasters as have charge of children and do instruct them either in public schools or private houses. **1581** MULCASTER *Positions* xxxix. 186 In publicke schooles this swaruing in affection from the publicke choice in no case can be. **1604** *Act 1 Jas. I*, c. 4 §8 No person shall keepe any schoole..except it be in some publike or free Grammer Schoole, or in some such noblemans..or gentlemans..house as are not recusants. **1649** in *Perfect Diurnall* 26 Mar., That some Public Schools for the better education and principling of youth in virtue and justice would soberly be considered of and settled. **1663** (Dec. 4) in *Vict. County Hist. Bedford.* II. 165 Wee the Warden and Schollers of..New Colledge [Oxford] have..elected Mr John Allanson, clerke..to bee Schoolemaster of the publique free Grammer Schoole in..Bedford. **1673** ABP. OF ARMAGH in *Essex P.* (Camden) 113 An Account of the Publique Schooles within the Province of Ulster... There is a free schoole for the Diocesse of Meath, with a Salary according to the Act..of about 40*l.* p. ann. **1707** E. CHAMBERLAYNE *St. Eng.* 385 London. (*Heading*) Publick Schools and Colleges. The first is Westminster School.... St. Paul's School.... Merchant-Taylors School... Belonging to Christ's Hospital is another famous Grammar Free-School... That at Ratcliff was founded by Nicholas Gibson, Grocer of London. **1713** BERKELEY *Guard.* No. 62 ¶8, I regard our public schools and universities, not only as nurseries of men for the service of the church and state [etc.]. **1741** MIDDLETON *Cicero* Ded. 7 Your Lordship..by Your education in a public School and University, has learnt from Your earliest youth [etc.]. **1749** FIELDING *Tom Jones* III. v, This worthy man having observed the imperfect institution of our public schools, and the many vices which boys were there liable to learn, had resolved to educate his nephew, as well as the other lad..in his own house. **1760** FOOTE *Minor* I. i, He has run the gauntlet thro' a public school, where, at sixteen, he had practis'd more vices than he would otherwise have heard of at sixty. **1784** COWPER *Tiroc.* 372. **1820** *F. Westley's Catal.* 1 Dec., Elementary Publications recommended as Reward Books for Sunday and other Public Schools. **1828** ARNOLD *Let.* 14 Mar. in Stanley *Life*, I never ran down public schools in the lump, but grieved that their exceeding capabilities were not turned to better account. *a* **1832** CRABBE *Posth. Tales* xix. 223. **1839** W. LOVETT & J. COLLINS, etc. *Chartism*, To erect public halls or schools for the people throughout the kingdom. **1847** (*title*) Fagging: is it hopelessly inseparable from the discipline of a public school? **1848** MOBERLY *Winchester Serm.* II. Pref., What then..is a public school? and wherein does it essentially differ from a private one?.. A public school is one in which the government is administered, in greater or less degree, with the aid of the pupils themselves: a private school is one in which the government is altogether administered by masters. **1893** *Westm. Gaz.* 11 Feb. 4/2 Our Public Schools..(by which phrase we never mean real public schools like the Board schools at all, but merely schools for the upper and middle classes) are in their existing stage primarily great gymnasiums. **1899** A. F. LEACH *Hist. Winchester Coll.* ii, The only working definition of a Public School then is that it is an aristocratic or plutocratic school which is wholly or almost wholly a Boarding School, is under some form of more or less public control, and is ..'non-local':—a 'Boarding Academy for young Gentlemen', which draws its pupils from all parts of the Country, and is not a Private Adventure School.

b. *attrib.* and *Comb.* as ***public school accent, attitude, boy*** (hence ***-boyish*** adj.), ***code, English, girl, man, product, spirit, system, tie, training, type***, etc.; ***public school-bred, -educated*** adjs.; also appositive, as ***public-school-Oxford*** attrib.; also passing into *adj.*

c **1843** G. MOBERLY in Stanley *Arnold* (1845) I. iii. 191 Hardly to be found among public-school men. **1844** STANLEY *Ibid.* (1845) 112 The peculiarities which distinguish the English public school system from almost every other system of education in Europe. **1874** BURNAND *My time* xxiii. 205 He had not had a public-school training. **1899** KIPLING *Stalky* 164 Talking..of public-school spirit and the traditions of the ancient seat. **1901** *Athenæum* 27 July 121/1 The task of estimating public-school influence on the nation at large. **1914** 'I. HAY' *Lighter Side School Life* viii. 207 That is the Public School Attitude in a nutshell. *Ibid.* 220 We note a new factor in the composition of the Public School Type—the military factor. **1930** (*title*) The diary of a public school girl. **1930** E. WAUGH *Vile Bodies* x. 174 Knowledgeable young men with..old public-school ties. **1931** D. L. SAYERS *Five Red Herrings* v. 55 Waters.. spoke standard public-school English. **1933** *Granta* 26 Apr. 370/1 It is a movement for unemployed graduates and Public School boys. **1936** J. BUCHAN *Island of Sheep* I. ii. 21 The kind of son I had hoped for..was..the kind of public-school product you read about. *Ibid.* 22 Peter John..didn't care a rush for the public-school spirit. **1938** M. ALLINGHAM *Fashion in Shrouds* x. 162 'He's not *in* there,' said Jimmy, revealing a stammer and a public-school accent. **1943** M. SCHLAUCH *Gift of Tongues* 264 English writers themselves have sometimes jeered at certain details of 'public school-Oxford' speech as being affected. **1943** F. THOMPSON *Candleford Green* ii. 29 His highly-pitched, public-schoolboyish accent. **1946** P. BOTTOME *Lifeline* i. 10 He was an Eton master, and the Public School code..he believed in. **1952** KOESTLER *Arrow in Blue* xxviii. 263 Public School-bred Foreign Office diplomats like Guy Burgess and Donald MacLean. **1962** *Times* 27 Feb. 13/2 The public-schoolboyish professional Roman soldier. **1962** R. WILLIAMS *Britain in Sixties: Communications* v. 101 In fact 'public-school English'..cannot now become a common speech-form in the country as a whole: both because of the social distinctions now associated with its use, and because of the powerful influence of American speech-forms. **1966** J. CLEARY *High Commissioner* vii. 136 A veneer of public school accent had been laid over the gravel in his voice. **1967** *Listener* 30 Nov. 694/3 'The English public school-boy', the prototype of unimaginative disciplined conformity. **1971** HALSEY & TROW *Brit. Academics* xv. 421, 41 per cent of the public school educated teachers place themselves on the Left. **1973** 'D. JORDAN' *Nile Green* ii. 12 It's one of the curses of the English public school girl that she never believes in making the bed first thing in the morning. *a* **1974** R. CROSSMAN *Diaries* (1975) I. 131 While she is extremely tough in negotiation she is extremely public school when she's asked..to make a sacrifice in her departmental interests for the good of the nation or for the convenience of the Civil Service. **1975** J. I. M. STEWART *Gaudy* iii. 41 They were entirely English and very public-school. **1975** 'D. JORDAN' *Black Account* xx. 108 One of those public-school ties which carry important messages between all true Englishmen. **1978** CADOGAN & CRAIG *Women & Children First* v. 95 Eighteen-year-old Raleigh..dies still behaving in accordance with the public-school code.

†**2.** Formerly applied to the lecture-room or class of the professor of any faculty in a university or similar institution for advanced study or higher learning. *Obs.*

[**829**: see above]. **1582** ALLEN *Martyrd. Campion* (1908) 6 Thither [to Douai] he went where after a yere's great diligence and many exercises done booth in house and publike scholes, he proceeded bachilier of divinitie. *c* **1590** MARLOWE *Faust.* i. 88 I'll have them fill the public schools with silk, Wherewith the students shall be bravely clad. **1617–20** MORYSON *Itin.* (1903) 319 The publike schoole at Strasburg was not reputed an universitie yet gave the degrees of Bachelors and Masters of Artes, having a publike house for that purpose, and publike schooles where learned Professors did read. **1651** HOBBES *Leviath.* IV. xlvi. 370 That which is now called an University, is a Joyning together, and an Incorporation under one Government of many Publique Schools, in one and the same Town or City.

3. In Scotland, the Commonwealth and (former) colonial territories, and North America: A school provided at the public expense and managed by public authority for the use of the community of a defined district, as part of a system of public (and usually free) education. Occas. applied to schools in other countries.

The term has been used in New England and Pennsylvania from the 17th c., and has been adopted in all States of the American Union. An early synonym was 'free school', and a later one in some States, 'common school', which was subsequently however generally confined to a school of the lowest grade or 'public elementary school'. In Scotland, the name was made official by the Education Act of 1872: see quot. Scottish 'Public' Schools were by the Code of 1908 classed as *Primary*, *Intermediate*, and *Secondary*, a classification based solely on the extent of their curriculum. In some colonies the division was into First, Second, and Third Class Public Schools.

1644 *Acts of United* (New Engl.) *Colonies* (1859) 20 Prompt to extend their care for the good of publike Schooles. **1683** *Pennsylv. Frame of Govmt.* §10 The Governor and Provincial Council shall erect and order all public Schooles. **1711** (May 9) *Boston Town Records* VIII. 80 [To] be invested and laid out in some Real Estate for the use of the Publick Lattin School. **1785** (May 20) *Ordinance U.S. Congress*, There shall be reserved the lot No. 16 of every township for the maintenance of public schools within the said township. **1789** *Nova Scotia Mag.* I. 80/1 This seminary is erected in consequence of a law of this Province, intitled, 'An Act for establishing a public school, in the town of Halifax'. **1853** tr. *Siljeström's Educ. Instit. U.S.* 15 Public schools is the name given to all schools which are supported by the public, and which are therefore under public control. **1872** *Canadian Monthly* June 483/1 Public Schools..are distinguished from those which until recently were entitled Grammar Schools, and were intended to afford instruction in the elements of the classical languages as well as the mother tongue. **1873** *Pennsylv. Constit.* §10 The general assembly shall provide for the maintenance and support of a thorough and efficient system of public schools, wherein all the children of the commonwealth above the age of six years may be educated. **1894** G. H. MARTIN (*title*) Evolution of the Massachusetts Public School System. **1903** *Manual of Public Schools of Boston*, [Classified as] Normal, Latin, and High Schools, Grammar Schools, Primary Schools, [and] Kindergartens. **1968** *Globe & Mail* (Toronto) 17 Feb. 45 (Advt.), Not one street to cross to get to public school. **1976** D. HEFFRON *Crusty Crossed* xi. 79 In Big Point, there was nothing to fuss over. Only one school to go to until you passed grade eight. They called that kind of school a public school, which in England was the name for a private school which your parents have to pay quite a lot of money to send you to.

1872 *Act 35 & 36 Vict.* (Scotl.) c. 62 §25 Every school under the management of the school board of a parish shall be deemed a parish school, and every school under the management of the school board of a burgh shall be deemed a burgh school, and all such schools are hereby declared to be public schools within the meaning of this Act. *Ibid.* §26 There shall be provided for every parish and burgh a sufficient amount of accommodation in public schools available for all persons resident in such parish or burgh [etc.]. **1882** *Act 45 & 46 Vict.* c. 18 §1 This Act may be cited as the Public-Schools (Scotland) Teachers Act, 1882. **1908** *Scotch Education Code* §12 An Inspector or sub-Inspector may visit any public school, or any other school subject to inspection at any time without notice. **1909** *Let. to Editor*, In Scotland, apart from the official and legal use of the words 'public school', the term is now generally used in the sense of an elementary day school under a school board.

1901 'M. FRANKLIN' *My Brilliant Career* iii. 14 My parents received an intimation from the teacher of the public school..to the effect that the law demanded that they should send their children to school. **1904** *Cape of Good Hope C.S. List* 267 Public Schools. Course of Instruction... Class III. To include at least reading, writing, arithmetic, outlines of history and geography, and lessons on natural objects. *Ibid.* 268 (List of) The First Class Undenominational Public Schools. **1965** *Austral. Encycl.* VIII. 23/1 In Victoria (as in Tasmania) 'public school' generally carries its English meaning... In New South Wales..in 1892..'public school' then meant to most people 'State primary school'. **1972** *Mainichi Daily News* 7 Nov. 5/1 Students in Kanagawa Ken, both Japanese and foreign from public and private schools.

Hence **public-'schoolish** *a.*, characteristic or suggestive of a public school; **public-'schoolishness**; **public-'schooly** *a.* = PUBLIC-SCHOOLISH *a.*

1930 *Observer* 22 June 13 Mr Leslie Mitchell, as the simple Andy, is too public-schoolish in tone and manner. **1930** A. HUXLEY *Let.* 14 June (1969) 337 English literary criticism for the moment is all for being nice and gentlemanly and public-schooly. **1947** 'G. ORWELL' *Eng. People* 39 Many necessary abstract words..are rejected by the working class because they sound public-schoolish, 'tony' and effeminate. *a* **1960** E. M. FORSTER *Maurice* (1971) I. ix. 48 During the previous term he had reached an unusual level mentally, but the vac had pulled him back towards public-schoolishness.

ˌpublic-'spirited, *a.* Characterized by public spirit (PUBLIC *a.* 8 b); animated or prompted by zeal for the public good; directed to the common welfare.

1677 YARRANTON *Eng. Improv.* 157 There is one publick spirited Man lately come into that Countrey. **1712** STEELE *Spect.* No. 442 ¶3 Good or Ill-natur'd, Publick-spirited or Selfish. **1783** BURKE *Rep. Affairs Ind.* Wks. XI. 269 The act ..is not only disinterested, but generous, and publick-spirited. **1878** BOSW. SMITH *Carthage* 358 A new nobility of wealth, who..were not more farsighted or more public-spirited than their predecessors.

Hence **ˌpublic-'spiritedly** *adv.*, with public spirit; **ˌpublic-'spiritedness**.

1654 WHITLOCK *Zootomia* 382 The Spirit of Charity, the old Word for publike Spiritednesse. **1707** E. CHAMBERLAYNE *Pres. St. Eng.* I. (ed. 22) 50 Many eminent Qualifications, as Dexterity, Sagacity,..Publick spiritedness. **1847** WEBSTER, Public-spiritedly. **1860** MILL *Repr. Govt.* (1865) 72/1 The 'local' or 'middle class' examination for the degree of Associate, so laudably and public-spiritedly established by the Universities of Oxford and Cambridge. **1883** *Kendal Mercury & Times* 23 Nov. 5/1 The promptings of a noble public-spiritedness.

publish ('pʌblɪʃ), *v.* Forms: see below. [ME. *puplise, -ish, poplis*, etc., and *publisshe, publisce*, etc., f. OF. *puplier, poploiier*, (later) *publier*, ad. L. *pūblicāre* to make public, publish, confiscate, f. *pūblic-us* PUBLIC. The OF. *pup-, pop-* forms either represented a popular L. *poplicare* (cf. early L. *poplicus, poblicus* = *publicus*, and med.L. *pupplicare* in 15th c. eccles. documents), or were due to later influence of OF. *pople, peuple*, ad. L. *populus* PEOPLE. The normal Eng. repr. of OF. *publier* was PUBLY: cf. CARRY *v.* *Publish* may repr. an AF. **publir*, **puplir* (not found), but was app. due to imitation of verbs etymologically ending in *-ish* (-ISH²): cf. *astonish, distinguish, famish, vanquish*. The spelling *publice* may have been influenced by L. *publicāre*.]

A. Illustration of Forms.

α. 4–5 **puplis(e, -lissh(e, -lich(e, poplis, pupplis, -lisch(e, 4–6 -lish(e, 5 puplyssch, -llise, pupples, -lys(s)h(e, 6 puplice, -lyche.**

c **1330** R. BRUNNE *Chron.* (1810) 90 Þe folk that ascaped.. puplised it fulle wide. *c* **1380** WYCLIF *Sel. Wks.* I. 339 Men of þis world.. wolen haten hem þat puplisshen it. *Ibid.* III. 247 þus is heresye.. pupplischid in londis. **1382** —— *Matt.* i. 19 Joseph.. wolde not pupliche [**1388** puplische] hir. *c* **1400** *Cursor M.* 29540 (Cott. Galba) He þat poplist it furth. *c* **1400** *Rule St. Benet* 911 Als be þe apostil es pupplist. *Ibid.* 1953 So þat it be.. puplist. **1452** *Paston Lett.* I. 230 Hit is opunly puplysschid. **1484** *Certificate* in *Surtees Misc.* (1888) 41 To pupples and declare.. the treuth. **1509** *Sel. Cas. Crt. Star Chamber* (Selden Soc.) 200 That the abbot of Salop shuld puplice & openly say. *Ibid.* 201 Reportes thus puplished. **1530** in W. H. TURNER *Select. Rec. Oxford* (1880) 79 To be denownsyd and puplychyd.

β. 4-6 **publice, -lis(s)he, -lis(s)ch(e, 5 -lesch, -les(e, -lisce, 5-6 -lys(s)h(e, 6 -lis, 5- publish.**

1377 LANGL. *P. Pl.* B. XI. 101 No þinge þat is pryue publice [C. XIII. 38 publisshe] þow it neuere. *c* **1380** WYCLIF *Sel. Wks.* III. 445 Freris wold not here þis publischt. **1387** TREVISA *Higden* (Rolls) V. 147 þat were i-publesched [*v. rr.* puplisched, publesed] in þe Synod Nicena. *c* **1400** *Brut* 330 þis same Piers told & publissed þe trewþe. *c* **1450** *Prov.* in *Deutsch. Neuphil.* (1906) 55 Hyde and haue: publyssh & nouȝt haue. *c* **1460** G. ASHBY *Dicta Philos.* 66 Publisshing to his connyng your fauour. **1480** Publish [see B. 1 b]. **1509** FISHER *Fun. Serm. C'tess Richmond* Wks. (1876) 308 To publysshe the doctryne and fayth of cryste. *c* **1520** NISBET *N.T. in Scots, Acts* iv. 17 That it be na mare publisit in to the pepile. **1588** A. KING tr. *Canisius' Catech.* in *Cath. Tractates* (S.T.S.) 200 The Pandectis.. was publischeit be Iustiniane. **1588** in T. Morris *Provosts of Methven* (1875) 72 To be red and publicit. **1596** DALRYMPLE tr. *Leslie's Hist. Scot.* (S.T.S.) I. 38 Bot the truth of the mater is nocht publised.

B. Signification. To make public.

I. 1. a. *trans.* To make publicly or generally known; to declare or report openly or publicly; to announce; to tell or noise abroad; also, to propagate, disseminate (a creed or system).

c **1330** [see A. α]. **14..** *Cursor M.* 24731 (Fairf. MS.) Of þe concepcioun of our lauedi puplist bi an angel on þe see. **1568** GRAFTON *Chron.* II. 436 When this murder was published, all people cryed vnto God for vengeaunce. **1662** J. DAVIES tr. *Olearius' Voy. Ambass.* 219 At the very moment that the Sun came to the Equator, he publish'd the new year. **1782** MISS BURNEY *Cecilia* v. x, She now resolved to publish her resolution of going.. to St. James's-square. **1896** 'M. FIELD' *Attila* IV. 106 Do not publish Your shame, for your own sake.

b. *spec.* in *Law.* ***to publish one's will***: see quot. 1898. ***to publish a libel***: to communicate a libel to one or more persons.

1480 in *Bury Wills* (Camden) 59 Neuer wyllyng myne seyd mynde, wyll, and intent, so be me published, notified, and declared vpon the seyd ffeoffament, in any maner of wyse to be changyd. **1607** COWELL *Interpr.* s.v. *Libell*, A criminous report of any man cast abroad, or otherwise vnlawfully published in writing. **1649** in *Bury Wills* (Camden) 200, I doe publish and declare this to be my last will and testament. **1768** BLACKSTONE *Comm.* III. viii. 126 The defendent, on an indictment for publishing a libel, is not allowed to allege the truth of it by way of justification. **1897** *Encycl. Laws Eng.* s.v. *Defamation*, The plaintiff.. establishes a primâ facie case, as soon as he has proved that the defendant published to some third person actionable words. **1898** *Ibid.* s.v. *Publication*, Wills are said to be published when they are properly executed before witnesses.

†**c.** *refl.* To become known, to declare itself; cf. F. *se publier*. *Obs. rare*$^{-1}$.

1597 A. M. tr. *Guillemeau's Fr. Chirurg.* 3/2 All badde accidents publishe themselues at the full Moone, more then at other times.

2. a. *esp.* To announce in a formal or official manner; to pronounce (a judicial sentence), to promulgate (a law or edict); to proclaim. †***to publish war***, to declare war (*obs.*).

c **1380** WYCLIF *Wks.* (1880) 290 þei maken þe iuge erre and pupplische a sentence contrarie to trewþe. **1485** *Coventry Leet Bk.* 524 That ye doo publisshe this our Commaundement vnto all thinhabitantes of our said Citie. **1560** DAUS tr. *Sleidane's Comm.* 49 b, Such Ecclesiastical lawes as.., when they be ons published, shalbe obserued. **1759** ROBERTSON *Hist. Scot.* VII. Wks. 1813 I. 521 Meanwhile, she commanded the sentence against Mary to be published. **1874** GREEN *Short Hist.* iii. §3. 125 The Charter was published throughout the whole country.

b. To ask (the banns of marriage); also, to announce or put up the names of (persons intending marriage) (*obs.* exc. *U.S. dial.*).

1488 in *Prymer* (E.E.T.S.) Introd. 171 The Banys were asked & publisshed the xiij daye of Janyuer. **1572** tr. *Buchanan's Detectioun* F iij b, Theire sche taried with Bothwell, quhile the banes weir publishing. **1651** *Essex Antiquarian* (Mass.) VII. 45 Mr. Phillips of Rowley, having been published, writes to the General Court saying that there is no one [clergyman] to marry him. **1662** *Bk. Com. Prayer, Matrimony*, Saying after the accustomed manner: I publish the Banns of Marriage between M of ——, and N of ——. **1678** *Providence Rec.* (1894) V. 325 John Whipple junr., and Rebecah Scott widdoe.. were published in way of Marriage by a writting fixed upon a publick place in the sayd Towne. **1742** FIELDING *Jos. Andrews* IV. ii, It is my orders.. that you publish these banns no more. **1841** LYTTON *Nt. & Morn.* I. i, The Banns on her side will be published with equal privacy in a church near the Tower. **1886** P. STAPLETON *Major's Christmas* 124 Then say you will marry me, and we will be published to-day. **1975** *Budget* (Sugarcreek, Ohio) 20 Mar. 8/3 Published today in above district were Sam, son of Joe J. Yoders and Mary, daughter of Eli H. Weavers. Their wedding to be Saturday, April 5.

3. †**a.** To proclaim (a person) publicly as something, or in some capacity or connexion; also, (without compl.) to denounce, to 'show up'. *Obs.*

1382 [see A. α]. **1470** *Rolls of Parlt.* VI. 233/2 They have deserved to be puplysshed as fals Traytours. **1577** HANMER *Anc. Eccl. Hist.* (1619) 6 Our Saviour.. is published by an oath, Christ and Priest. **1611** SHAKS. *Wint. T.* II. i. 98 How will this grieue you,.. that You thus haue publish'd me? **1676** RAY *Corr.* (1848) 124 Mr. Oldenburgh hath published him as a considerable author. **1733** POPE *Hor. Sat.* II. i. 59 In this impartial glass, my Muse intends.. to.. Publish the present age.

†**b.** To bring under public observation or notice; to give public notice of. *Obs.*

1529 MORE *Dyaloge* III. Wks. 211/2 It were peraduenture a thinge not conuenient, after those witnesses published, to bring proues a freshe vpon the principall mater. **1647** N. BACON *Disc. Govt. Eng.* I. li. (1739) 89 Goods found shall be published by the Finder to the Neighbourhood. **1658** *Whole Duty Man* xiv. §11 While cursed Cham publisht and disclosed the nakedness of their father. **1709-10** STEELE *Tatler* No. 142 ¶7 [A diamond box] to be published on Monday which will cost Fourscore Guinea's.

c. To expose to public view. *rare.*

a **1860** ALB. SMITH *Lond. Med. Stud.* (1861) 73 Having arrived at the Hall, put your rings and chains in your pocket, and, if practicable, publish a pair of spectacles. **1885** W. W. STORY *Poems, Eng. Husb. to It. Wife* vii, I cannot, like Sarto, publish your face In every Madonna, Sibyl, and Saint.

4. a. *spec.* To issue or cause to be issued for sale to the public (copies of a book, writing, engraving, piece of music, or the like); said of an author, editor, or *spec.* of a professional publisher. Also *absol.* and by metonymy, with author, etc., as obj.

[*c* **1450** PECOCK *MS.* (in *Quaritch's Catal.* (1887) I. No. 54), That no person cristen.. after sufficient pupplisshing of this book to hem schulde have eny excusacioun for this that thei knowe not the lawe.. of her lord god.] **1529** MORE *Dyaloge* I. Pref., Wks. 106/1, I am now driuen.. to this thirde busynes of publishynge and puttynge my boke in printe my selfe. **1611** BIBLE *Transl. Pref.* 10 He could no sooner write any thing, but presently it was caught from him, and published, and he could not haue leaue to mend it. **1709-10** STEELE *Tatler* No. 115 ¶6, I shall here publish a short Letter which I have received from a Well-wisher. **1879** *Cassell's Techn. Educ.* IV. 33/1 Literary productions.. when they are circulated abroad and published with the author's consent they become common property. **1908** *Oxford Univ. Gaz.* No. 1255 (*Imprint.*) Printed by Horace Hart, M.A., Controller of the University Press, at his Office in the Press, in the Parish of St. Thomas; and published by him at the Depository, 116 High Street,.. in the City of Oxford. **1918** C. S. LEWIS *Let.* 27 Oct. (1966) 45 He [*sc.* Heinemann] told me that John Galsworthy (who publishes with them) had seen my MS. **1937** J. SQUIRE *Honeysuckle & Bee* 203 Lane.. seemed to publish almost all the exciting new authors. **1941** *Sphere* 6 Dec. 361/1 If a publisher chooses to publish you, your reward is almost certain. **1952** SACKVILLE-WEST & SHAWE-TAYLOR *Record Year* 213 It looks like a re-issue of the recording published by Decca during the war and since deleted. **1961** H. M. SILVER in *Webster* s.v., Pressure put on faculty members.. to publish as a condition of appointment or promotion. **1970** J. EARL *Tuners & Amplifiers* vi. 140 Test records are available for channel identification or recognition. Such a record is the excellent HFS69 published by the Haymarket Publishing Group. **1971** *Black Scholar* Dec. 23/2 Dr. Ladner is frequently published in professional journals.

b. To make generally accessible or available for acceptance or use; to place before or offer to the public, now *spec.* by the medium of a book, journal, or the like; to make generally available a description or illustration of (an archæological find, a work of art, etc.).

1638 JUNIUS *Paint. Ancients* 186 The old Artificers.. would not have their workes smoothered up in some private corners, so were they very careful in publishing them. **1771** LUCKOMBE *Hist. Print.* 5 Two Jewish Rabbins.. were the first who published the Hebrew character in separate types. **1803** *Med. Jrnl.* IX. 287 Mr. W. assures us that he will publish his medicine as soon as its efficacy is established. **1824** in *N. & Q.* 7th Ser. VI. 207/1 [A small bust of the Duke of York.. On the back are engraved the words] 'Published by T. Hamlet, Aug. 16, 1824'. **1842** GROVE *Corr. Phys. Forces* (1874) 63 The celebrated Leonard Euler had published a somewhat similar theory. **1931** *Oxf. Mag.* 18 June 888/2 H. R. Hall publishes an Egyptian axe in the British Museum. **1968** *Listener* 31 Oct. 580/2 (*caption*) Are you from the BBC? If so it is your duty to 'publish' an open-ended political statement I intend to deliver. **1973** *Oxf. Univ. Gaz.* CIII. Suppl. v. 8 We are grateful to Professor Ashmole, who will publish the head, for kindly consenting to its illustration in this report. **1975** *Times Lit. Suppl.* 10 Oct. 1196/3 The great bronze doors of medieval Europe.. are on the whole well known and fully published... Walter Cahn has now published, in *The Romanesque Wooden Doors of Auvergne*, a series of five sets of wooden doors, still extant though considerably damaged. **1976** *Nature* 1 Apr. 415/2 Unfortunately, we cannot know the V_P/V_S ratios in the decreasing stage, because of the scarcity of the data published by the Japan Meteorological Agency before 1950. **1978** *SLR Camera* Sept. 53/3, I wasn't quite sure what I was going to do with the films I shot on the way round but if I wanted to get any published I knew I had to get them back home while the race was still in progress. **1978** *Times Lit. Suppl.* 1 Dec. 1392/3 There are papyri in Greek and Latin (the Egyptian papyri are somewhere else entirely), ostraca (about 4,000 inscribed potsherds, of which only 300 have been published).

c. *intr.* in passive sense. To come into public circulation; to be published.

1928 *Public Opinion* 6 Apr. 325/1 The newspapers do not publish on Good Friday. **1972** *Evening Telegram* (St. John's, Newfoundland) 24 June 1/1 The Evening Telegram will publish Monday, June 26 which is being observed as Discovery Day in Newfoundland.

†**5. a.** *trans.* To people, populate (a country, etc.). **b.** *refl.* To propagate itself; to multiply, breed. *Obs.* (Cf. PEOPLISH *v.*)

c **1330** R. BRUNNE *Chron. Wace* (Rolls) 6485 (Petyt MS.) Forto puplise þe lond & tile. *c* **1374** CHAUCER *Boeth.* III. pr. xi. 77 (Camb. MS.) How gret is the diligence of nature, for alle thinges renouelen and pupllisen hem with seed I-multiplyed. *c* **1450** LOVELICH *Grail* xxxviii. 301 Forto pubplysche that Contre [Fr. *pour peupler la terre*]. **1577** HELLOWES *Gueuara's Chron.* 193 This temple [of Peace] in authoritie was most auncient,.. with priests most published, and in deuotion most esteemed.

II. †**6.** *trans.* To make public property, to confiscate (rendering L. *pūblicāre*). *Obs.*

1533 BELLENDEN *Livy* III. x. (S.T.S.) I. 287 Than was ane law made þat mont aventyne sall be publist and dividit amang þe pepill. *Ibid.* III. xix. II. 27 Baith þe gudis of appius claudius and Spu. Oppius war confiscate and publist be þe tribunis. **1560** DAUS tr. *Sleidane's Comm.* 457 His goodes also ought by the ciuile Magistrate to be published.

publishability (pʌblɪʃə'bɪlɪtɪ). [f. PUBLISHABLE *a.*: see -ILITY.] The quality of being publishable; suitability for publication.

1870 G. H. LEWES *Let.* 8 May in *Geo. Eliot Lett.* (1956) V. 94 When you have read them and decided as to their *publishability* in the Atlantic perhaps you will make me the channel of an offer. **1969** C. DERRICK *Reader's Report* 17 'Success'.. means for the most part mere publishability; we are not concerned with the heights. **1974** *Jrnl. Social Psychol.* XCIV. 302 The printed form of the report was rated significantly higher.. on the question of publishability than the two mimeographed forms.

publishable ('pʌblɪʃəb(ə)l), *a.* [f. PUBLISH *v.* + -ABLE.] That may be published or made public; liable to, fit for, or intended for publication.

1811 SOUTHEY *Lett.* (1856) II. 226 They.. would.. have been dead before that part of the correspondence was publishable, according to her will. **1820** *Blackw. Mag.* VII. 317 The two new cantos of Don Juan, which he says have been sent back to Lord Byron, to be softened into something like a publishable shape. **1891** *Longm. Mag.* July 326 It is not a publishable story.

published ('pʌblɪʃt), *ppl. a.* Also 7 -isht. [f. as prec. + -ED[1].]

1. Made generally known; publicly announced or declared; officially promulgated or proclaimed; of a book, etc., issued or offered to the public.

1605 SHAKS. *Lear* IV. vi. 236 Dar'st thou support a publish'd Traitor? **1644** MILTON *Areop.* (Arb.) 32 One of your publisht Orders. **1843** R. J. GRAVES *Syst. Clin. Med.* xi. 117 In my published lectures, I have endeavoured [etc.].

2. Exposed or exhibited to public view. *rare.*

1839 BAILEY *Festus* ix. (1852) 109 The published bosom and the crowning smile—The cup excessive. **1863** KINGLAKE *Crimea* (ed. 3) I. xiv. 245 The proffered Caesar and his long-prepared group of Captains—sitting published on the backs of real horses.

publisher ('pʌblɪʃə(r)). [f. as prec. + -ER[1].]

1. One who publishes or makes something public; one who declares, announces, or proclaims publicly. Now *rare.*

1453 in *Ep. Acad. Oxon.* (O.H.S.) I. 320 The first publisheris of the seide sclandirful noysyng. **1538** ELYOT, *Præco, onis*, a cryar, a publysshar of thynges. **1554** *Let. Q. Mary to Justices in Norfolk* in Burnet *Hist. Ref.* (1681) II. *Rec.* II. No. 14. 259 The Authors and Publishers of these vain Prophesies and untrue Bruits. **1646** H. LAWRENCE *Comm. Angells* 138 Preachers and publishers of peace. **1796** *Look at Home* 13 The Publisher of the Gospel of the Grace of God. **1878** NEWCOMB *Pop. Astron.* II. i. 106 The first publisher of a result or discovery, supposing such result or discovery to be honestly his own, now takes the place of the first inventor.

2. One who publishes a book or literary work: **a.** One who as author, or esp. as editor, gives it to the public; 'one who puts out a book into the world' (J.). Now *rare.*

1654 *Whitlock's Zootomia*, The Publisher [Sir John Birkenhead] to the Reader. **1657** RAWLEY *Bacon's Resuscitatio* (1661) 181 Written by his Lordship in Latin; and Englished by the Publisher. **1688** R. HOLME *Armoury* III. xv. (Roxb.) 25/1 Publisher, is one that causeth a booke to be printed after the death of the author. **1726** SWIFT *Gulliver*, The Publisher to the Reader. The author of these Travels, Mr. Lemuel Gulliver, is my ancient and intimate friend. **1775** JOHNSON *Journ. West. Isl.* Wks. 1816 VIII. 353, I have yet supposed no imposture but in the publisher.

b. *Comm.* One whose business is the issuing of books, newspapers, music, engravings, or the like, as the agent of the author or owner; one who undertakes the printing or production of copies of such works, and their distribution to the booksellers and other dealers, or to the public. (Without qualification generally understood to mean a *book-publisher* or (in the *U.S.*) also a newspaper proprietor.)

1740 DYCHE & PARDON, *Publisher*,.. among the Booksellers, is one that has his name put at the bottom of pamphlets, news-papers, &c. though the property is in another person, to whom he is accountable for the sale, &c. **1797** *Encycl. Brit.* (ed. 3) III. 392/1 Petty dealers, or venders of small ware, like our publishers. **1802** MONTEFIORE (*title*) The Law of Copyright, being a Compendium of Acts of Parliament and Adjudged Cases, relative to Authors, Publishers, Printers [etc.]. **1832** BABBAGE *Econ. Manuf.* xxxi. (ed. 3) 315 The Publisher, is a bookseller; he is, in fact, the author's agent. **1836** *Act 6 & 7 Will. IV*, c. 76 §20 Be it enacted, That the Printer, Publisher, or Proprietor of every Newspaper shall, within Twenty-eight Days after the last Day of every Calendar Month, pay or cause to be paid the Duty chargeable on all and every Advertisement.. contained in or published with such Newspaper. **1840** HOOD *Up Rhine* Introd. 1 On learning from my Publisher that in one short fortnight the whole impression of the present work had been taken off his hands. **1911** *Springfield* (Mass.) *Weekly Republican* 6 Apr. 11 Connecticut Publisher Dead. F. R. Swift, owner of the Bridgeport and Waterbury Herald, died last week. **1920** LD. NORTHCLIFFE *Let.* May in

W. F. Johnson *George Harvey* (1929) xxxvii. 383 Misunderstandings due to different meanings of the same words are among the basic difficulties of Anglo-American relations. Just now there is a discussion about the price of paper in which the use of the word 'publisher' for 'newspaper owner' confuses our people. **1949** *Manch. Guardian Weekly* 3 Nov. 2/2 Publishers and big advertising agencies in New York.. are laying off salesmen, art staff, and layout men. **1974** *Lebende Sprachen* XIX. 39/1 US publisher (of a newspaper)—BE (newspaper) proprietor. Zeitungsverleger (und besitzer).

3. One who puts anything into circulation; e.g. one who issues counterfeit paper money or the like; an 'utterer'. *rare.*

1828 in WEBSTER.

4. a. *attrib.* and *Comb.*, as *publisher dealer*, *-fighter*.

1897 *Q. Rev.* July 93 How many of the modern publisher-fighters would work a proud heart to death in paying off a colossal debt? **1902** *Daily Chron.* 19 Nov. 3/4 The French publisher-dealers of the [eighteenth] century.

b. publisher's (or **publishers'**) **binding**, a uniform binding provided for an edition of a book before it is offered for sale; **publisher's** (or **publishers'**) **cloth**, a publisher's binding in which cloth is used as the covering material.

1901 D. COCKERELL *Bookbinding* i. 20 For a permanent publisher's binding, something like that recommended for libraries.. is suggested. **1924** M. SADLEIR in *Bookman's Jrnl.* Feb. 154/1 It is obvious that no 'publisher's binding', in the accepted sense of lettered durability, was known [in the eighteenth century]. **1928** E. P. GOLDSCHMIDT *Gothic & Renaissance Bookbindings* I. 35 If the bindings with publishers' names or marks are 'original publishers' bindings'.. then surely all such bindings must contain books published by the man who signed the binding. **1974** R. MCLEAN *Victorian Publishers' Book-Bindings* 7 This is a picture book showing the richness of publishers' bindings principally in cloth or leather, produced in Britain during the nineteenth century. **1921** T. J. WISE *Bibliogr. Writings J. Conrad* (ed. 2) I. 44 If only collectors would refrain from purchasing copies of Conrad's books unless they are in the original publishers' cloth,.. their position would be perfectly safe. **1935** J. CARTER (*title*) Publisher's cloth: an outline history of publisher's binding in England 1820–1900. **1972** P. GASKELL *New Introd. Bibliogr.* 246 The more fanciful styles of publishers' cloth included gilt blocking over the whole area of the covers.

Hence *nonce-wds.* **'publisheress**, a female publisher; **'publishership**, the position or function of a publisher.

1851 *Fraser's Mag.* XLIV. 27 Authorship and publishership have become so identified in one common interest. **1888** *Bow Bells Weekly* 15 June 376/2 Mrs. Frank Leslie, the American publisher (or publisheress).

'publishing, *vbl. sb.* [f. as prec. + -ING[1].] The action of the vb. PUBLISH, in various senses.

1. = PUBLICATION 1.

c **1425** WYNTOUN *Cron.* v. 3828 Þat fully thretty dayis Sentens of ded or banyssynge Be haldyn in wryt but publissynge. *c* **1450** *Godstow Reg.* 401 Longe afore þe publisshyng or openyng of the statute aforsaid. **1561** T. NORTON *Calvin's Inst.* I. viii. §5. 17 In the very publishing of the law his face did shine. **1660** *Providence* (R.I.) *Rec.* (1893) II. 126 It being the first tyme of publishing [of banns]. **1752** FOOTE *Taste* II. Wks. 1799 I. 24 Will not the publishing of our crimes trumpet forth your folly?

2. *spec.* The action or business of issuing a book or books, etc.: see PUBLISHER 2 b; = PUBLICATION 2. Also *attrib.*

1580 HOLLYBAND *Treas. Fr. Tong, Publication de livres*, a publishing, or setting forth of bookes. **1667** *Phil. Trans.* II. 535 This Author.. promises the publishing of a Treatise about Insects. **1706** *License Q. Anne to Tonson*, He hath.. humbly besought Us to grant him Our Royal Privilege and Licence for the sole Printing and Publishing thereof for the Term of Fourteen Years. **1828** SCOTT *Let. to Mrs. Lockhart* 24 Oct. in *Life*, In book shops and publishing houses. **1862** R. H. NEWELL *Orpheus C. Kerr Papers* 1st Ser. 380, I'm agent for the great American publishing house of Rushem & Jinks. **1881** 'MARK TWAIN' *Lett. to Publishers* (1967) 143 A few days before Canadian publishing-date. **1885** *Athenæum* 26 Sept. 407/1 One of the mysteries which surround current French publishing. **1929** H. CRANE *Let.* 26 Feb. (1965) 339 A marvelous de luxe publishing establishment here. **1937** *Discovery* Mar. 80/1 A book recently published in Moscow by the Biological-Medical Publishing House. **1958** *New Statesman* 1 Feb. 136/3 Within a matter of months every single Yiddish theatre, publishing-house, magazine.. etc was closed down. **1978** *Maledicta* I. II. 327 By 'year' we mean the 'publishing year' which is not identical with the 'calendar year'.

† **'publishly**, *adv. Obs.* In 4–5 publis-, publesly, puplishily. Irregular form for PUBLICLY.

c **1400** *Sc. Trojan War* II. 1317 Thelamonyus publisly [*v.r.* publesly] Affermand þat he cruelly Of hys hondes suld thole þe ded. *c* **1468** in *Archæol.* (1846) XXXI. 329 Than the byshope shewid hyme and my ladye, bothe, the manner, and in hight wordes puplishilye fyaunced aither other.

publishment ('pʌblɪʃmənt). Now *rare.* [f. PUBLISH + -MENT.] The action of publishing; publication, proclamation, announcement; *esp.* in *U.S.*, publication of the banns of marriage.

1494 FABYAN *Chron.* VII. ccxxix. 259 Yᵉ Cardynall made sharpe processe agayn prestys, yᵗ noresshed cristen moyles, & rebuked them by open publysshement. **1611** SPEED *Hist. Gt. Brit.* IX. xx. (1623) 989 The before-said publishment of assurances at Pauls-Crosse. **1722** S. SEWALL *Diary* 14 Feb. (1882) III. 303 Went to James, and order'd our Publishment [i.e. of intended marriage]. **1750** *Acts & Laws Connecticut* 144 If any Person.. shall presume to Deface or pull down any Publishment set up in Writing, as aforesaid, before the expiration of eight Days,.. every such Person.. shall be Fined the Sum of Six Shillings. **1857** HOLLAND *Bay Path* xv, His fourteen days of publishment at last expired. **1887** in *Pall Mall G.* 30 Nov. 5/2, I.. must request the publishment of this letter in your next issue.

† **'publy**, *v. Obs.* Also 4 puple. [a. F. *publie-r*, ad. L. *pūblicāre*.] *trans.* To publish.

13.. *St. Gregory* 309 in Herrig's *Archiv* LVII. 63 Þo was hit pupled, & nouȝt ihud þat al þe eorldom was hire owe. **1489** CAXTON *Faytes of A.* II. vi. 101 He made hit to be cryed and publyed thrughe al his oost. *c* **1500** *Melusine* xix. 64 Whiche name within few dayes was so publyed, that it was knowen thrugh all the land.

pubo-, assumed combining form of L. *pūbēs* (of which the actual stem is *pūbi-*, and the modern L. and F. assumed form PUBIO-). The form *pubo-* is indefensible etymologically, but is recognized in Billings *Nat. Med. Dict.* 1890, and *Syd. Soc. Lex.* 1895, as the current English form in combinations having the sense 'Of or belonging to the pubes or os pubis, in conjunction with (some other part)'. Such are the adjs. **pubo-femoral**, belonging to the pubes and the femur (as in *pubo-femoral ligament*), **pubo-iliac, pubo-ischiatic** (as in *pubo-ischiatic bone*), **pubo-prostatic** (as in *pubo-prostatic ligaments*), **pubo-tibial, pubo-vesical**, belonging to the pubes and the bladder (as in *pubo-vesical ligaments, muscles*), etc.

1890 in BILLINGS *Nat. Med. Dict. Ibid., Pubo-ischiatic bone*,.. the combined ischium and [os] pubis (Henle). **1895** in *Syd. Soc. Lex.*

pubsy ('pʌbzɪ), *a. colloq.* [f. PUB *sb.* + -SY.] Characteristic or suggestive of a public house.

1966 *New Statesman* 30 Sept. 489/1 But the most attractive numbers are in that easy, pubsy English style which suggests Bud Flanagan, Tommy Steele and Julian Slade arm-in-arm, just strolling, lazily flexing their knees and getting nowhere. **1977** *Listener* 7 Apr. 447/3 Return briefly to the pubsy, Fitzrovian atmosphere of Lord Longford's.. party.

pucca, var. PUKKA.

‖**Puccinia** (pʌk'sɪnɪə). *Bot.* [Named after T. Puccini, an Italian anatomist.] A large genus of minute parasitic fungi, N.O. *Uredineæ*, the species of which are heterœcious. The best-known species, *P. graminis*, grows as an æcidium on the leaves of the barberry, and its spores produce the *Uredo* or rust on wheat, rye, oats, and grass.

1861 MISS PRATT *Flower. Pl.* II. 210 A small fungus, the Bramble *Puccinia*. **1875** BENNETT & DYER *Sachs' Bot.* 247 The second form of fruit [produced upon the leaves of Berberis] was at one time considered a distinct genus of Fungi, and described under the name of Æcidium; but this term is now only used to designate a particular form of fruit in the cycle of development of Puccinia.

Hence **'puccinoid** *a.*, allied in form to Puccinia.

1874 COOKE *Fungi* 201 The Æcidium which from the same disc produces the puccinoid resting spores.

Puccinian (pu:'tʃi:nɪən), *a.* [-AN.] Of, pertaining to, characteristic of, or resembling the works of the Italian operatic composer Giacomo Puccini (1858–1924).

1942 *Scrutiny* XI. 74 We have an exquisitely sensitive line which, the antithesis of Puccinian or Wagnerian hysteria, is almost French and Chausson-like in its delicacy. **1958** *Listener* 20 Nov. 850/3 The cardboard figures of Puccinian melodrama. **1962** *Times* 26 Jan. 16/4 He does not allow them much.. Puccinian nobility of soul. **1978** *Gramophone* Jan. 1289/2 On the Italian front, Tebaldi is dominant, giving good, cleanly sung, quite committed versions of several famous Puccinian passages.

So **Puccini'esque** *a.*, resembling the style of Puccini's works.

1927 *Sunday Express* 19 June 10/4 Yet Tom Burke has sung only once—in 'Rigoletto', which does not give him emotional scope, for he is a tenor of the voluptuously Pucciniesque type. **1961** *Times* 6 Dec. 17/6 As to Pucciniesque lyric passages, tender feelings are unmistakably clear when set to that kind of music.

puccoon (pʌ'ku:n). Forms: 7 **pohcoon, pochone, poughkone,** 7–8 *pl.* **pocones,** 8 **pochoon, pecoon, poccoon, puckoon,** 8– **puccoon.** The Virginian Indian name of a North American plant or plants yielding a red dye: originally, as it appears, of the red puccoon or blood-root, *Sanguinaria canadensis*, N.O. *Papaveraceæ*, and hoary puccoon, *Lithospermum canescens*, N.O. *Boraginaceæ*. Now applied also to the hairy puccoon, *L. hirsutum*, and yellow puccoon, *Hydrastia canadensis*, N.O. *Ranunculaceæ*, the root of which dyes yellow.

1612 CAPT. SMITH *Map Virginia* 13 *Pocones* is a small roote that groweth in the mountaines, which being dryed and beate in powder turneth red. *c* **1616** STRACHEY *Trav. Virginia* (1849) 64 Their heads and shoulders they paint oftennest, and those red, with the roote pochone. *Ibid.* 192 Poughkone, the red paint or die. **1705** BEVERLEY *Hist. Virginia* II. iv. (1722) 120 They have the Puccoon and Musquaspen, two Roots, with which the Indians use to paint themselves red. **1714** LAWSON *Hist. Carolina* 172 They sometimes use pecoon root, which is of a crimson color. **1836** *Backwoods of Canada* 243 The blood-root, sanguinaria, or puccoon, as it is termed by some of the native tribes. **1887** T. HEMPSTEAD in *Harper's Mag.* Apr. 677 Puccoon, and clematis with plumy locks.

puce (pju:s), *a.* (*sb.*) [a. F. *puce* sb.:—L. *pūlex, -icem* a flea; *couleur puce* flea-colour (17th c.).]

a. *attrib.* or as *adj.* (orig. *puce colour*): Of a flea-colour; purple brown, or brownish purple.

1787 BEST *Angling* (ed. 2) 83 Dip a feather in *aqua fortis*, put it on the ash,.. and it will make it a cinnamon, or rather a puce, or flea colour. **1791** HAMILTON tr. *Berthollet's Dyeing* I. I. I. ii. 32 Colours inclining to red on the one hand and black on the other, such as mordoré and puce colour. **1820** *Chron.* in *Ann. Reg.* 197/2 A rich twilled sarcenet pelisse, of a peuce colour. **1834** MRS. CARLYLE *Lett.* I. 10 The old black gown (which was dyed puce for me at Dumfries). **1893** J. ASHBY STERRY *Naughty Girl* ix. 79 His puce silk suit, his muslin cravat.

b. As *sb.* = puce colour.

1882 *Garden* 16 Sept. 260/1 Blooms of.. rich dark puce, suffused with maroon. **1897** *Daily News* 25 June 2/6 The mountains had all put on.. the purple puce of twilight. **1900** F. H. O'F. in *Lond. Let.* 26 Jan. 133/1 Varying shades.. from palest peach to deepest puce.

c. *Comb.* *puce-coloured*, adj.

1812 SIR H. DAVY *Chem. Philos.* 212 The puce-coloured oxide of lead. **1874** GARROD & BAXTER *Mat. Med.* 410 Cochineal yields when crushed a puce-coloured powder.

† **'pucelage.** *Obs.* Also 6 pusellage, 7 pucellage. [a. F. *pucelage* (12th c. in Hatz.-Darm.), *pucellage*: see PUCELLE and -AGE.] The state or condition of being a 'pucelle' or girl; maidenhood, virginity.

a **1536** *Calisto & Melib.* Bij, To inioy your yongh & pusellage. **1569** *Ane Tragedie* 70 in *Satir. Poems Reform.* x, He brocht agane with vs his pucelage. **1643** SIR T. BROWNE *Relig. Med.* I. §10 The tryall of the Pucellage and Virginity of women. **1783** *Char.* in *Ann. Reg.* 14/2 Their state of pucelage is denoted by their having rings.. on their wrists.

pucellas, erron. variant of PROCELLO.

pucelle. Forms: 5–9 pu'celle; 5–7 pucell, 5–6 pusell, 5 pusshell; 6–7 'pucel, 6 pusel, -elle, puzel, -ell, 'pussel, pussle, 7 pusil, pusle, puzzel, puzzle. [a. F. *pucelle* (pysɛl), OF. *pucele*, earlier *pulcele* (11th c.):—*pulcela, pulcella* (*c* 881 *Eulalia*):—late L. *pūlicella* (*a* 511 *Capitul. Chlodwig*, in Pertz IV. 5) a young girl; so Pr. *piucella, pieucela*, OCat. *punceyla*, OSp. *pun-, poncella*, OPg. *pucella* (from F.), Rhæt. *purscella*, It. *pulzella, pulsella*. With sense 2, cf. LG., EFris. *pussel* (? from F.) a dirty slovenly person, esp. woman, a slattern (Doornk.-Koolman).

For the origin, Diez suggested a late L. **pullicella*, dim. of med.L. *pulla* chicken, pullet, fem. of *pullus* young animal, chicken; the difficulty of which is that the Romanic form of *pulla* is *polla*, which ought to have given OF. **polcele*, F. **poucelle*. Gröber *Archiv Lat. Lex.* IV. 451 assumes a popular L. **pūellicella* (cf. *dominicella*), dim. of *pūella*, pop. L. for *puella* (*u* being lengthened as in *fuit, fuisset*, F. *fut*, †*fust, fut*). From **pūellicella*, the forms *pūlicella, pūlcel(l)a, pulcele, pucele, pucelle*, form a regular phonetic and graphic series for F. The late L. *pūlicella* might also be a dim. of L. *pūlex, pūlic-em* flea: but such a derivation is inconsistent with the sense.]

1. A girl, a maid. *Obs.* (exc. as Fr.).

c **1430** LYDG. *Commend. Our Lady* 54 Medecyne to mischeves, pucelle withouten pere. **1439** in *Archæologia* XXI. 36 In that other partie ys a pusell knelyng wᵗ a lambe. *c* **1489** CAXTON *Sonnes of Aymon* vi. 144 Whan the pucell vnderstode this worde she was right glad. *c* **1530** LD. BERNERS *Arth. Lyt. Bryt.* (1814) 494 A! gentil pusel! make good chere. **1534** MORE *Comf. agst. Trib.* II. xiv. (1573) 77 b, This Girle is a metely good pussel in a house, neuer idle, but euer occupied and busy. **1575** CHURCHYARD *Chippes* (1817) 147 Lyke pucell pure, a pearle in peace and warres. **1575** LANEHAM *Let.* (1871) 23 Three pretty puzels az bright az a breast of bacon. [**1814** BYRON in Moore *Life* (1830) I. 553 My passion can wait, till the *pucelle* is more harmonious.]

b. *spec.* The Maid of Orleans, Joan of Arc. *Obs.* exc. *Hist.*

(Usually mentioned as her French appellation: in 16th c. sometimes taken as her surname.)

[*c* **1431** HEN. VI in Monstrelet *Chron.* II. IV. cv. 442 Celle femme, qui se faisoit nommer Jehenne la Pucelle.] *c* **1450** *Brut* 439 The wicche of Fraunce that was callid th[e] 'Pusshell'. [*a* **1490** WILL. WORCESTER in *Wars Eng. in Fr.* (Rolls) II. II. 760 Quædam mulier, vocata Pucelle de Dieu, capta est ab Anglis. **1494** FABYAN *Chron.* VII. 641 To shewe vnto you somewhat of yᵉ mayden or pucell, which yᵉ Frenshmen named *La pucele de Dieu.*] *a* **1548** HALL *Chron.*, *Hen. VI* 109 Hauyng in his company Ione the Puzel, whom he vsed as an oracle. **1591** SHAKS. *1 Hen. VI*, I. ii. 110 Excellent Puzel, if thy name be so. *Ibid.* I. iv. 107 Puzel or Pussel, Dolphin or Dog-fish, Your hearts Ile stampe out with my Horses heeles. *Ibid.* III. ii. 38 Pucell that Witch, that damned Sorceresse. **1678** BUTLER *Hud.* III. *Lady's Answ.* 285 Or Joan de Pucel's braver name. **1874** GAIRDNER *Lancaster & York* vii. (1875) 133 The Pucelle.. threw herself into the town [of Compiègne].

†**2.** A drab, a slut, a courtesan. *Obs.*

[*c* **1520** *Marr. of London Stone* in Hazl. *E.P.P.* III. 161 Here begynneth the maryage of London Stone and the fayre pusell the bosse of Byllyngesgate.] **1583** STUBBES *Anat. Abus.* I. (1879) 78 Yee shall not haue any Gentlewoman almost, no, nor yet any droye or pussle in the Cuntrey, but they will carye in their hands nosegayes. **1607** tr. *Stephens' Apol. Herodot.* 98 (N.), Some filthy queans, especially our puzzles of Paris. **1617** MINSHEU *Ductor*, A *Pusle*, truill, or stinking wench. *a* **1700** B. E. *Dict. Cant. Crew*, *A dirty Quean*, a very Puzzel or Slut.

‖**puceron** (pysərɔ̃, pysrɔ̃). [F., deriv. of *puce* flea: cf. CHAPERON.] A plant-louse or aphis. (Applied by Tucker to some insects (Coleoptera or Heteroptera) which dart about on the surface of water; also, erroneously, by Hill to the *Podura* or spring-tail and its allies, *Collembola* of Lubbock.)

1752 J. HILL *Hist. Anim.* 20 *Podura*... This genus comprehends the Pucerons of Reaumur, and other of the French writers. **1768–74** TUCKER *Lt. of Nat.* (1834) I. 358 The little pucerons in water frisking nimbly about, as if delighted with their existence. **1840** HEREMAN *Gardener's Libr.* II. 171 Aphis Rosae, Rose Louse... Synonyms.—Brown Rose Louse.—Red puceron.

pucherite (ˈpuːxəraɪt). *Min.* [ad. G. *pucherit* (1871 Frenzel), after the Pucher mine in Saxony, where it was found.] Vanadate of bismuth found in brilliant reddish-brown crystals.

1872 DANA *Min.* App. i. 12 Named pucherite from the locality. **1892** *Ibid.* 755 Pucherite..in the closed tube decrepitates.

‖**puchero** (puˈtʃero). Also **puchera**. [a. Sp. *puchero*, *-a*.] **1.** A glazed earthenware cooking pot. Cf. OLLA[1] 1.

1841 BORROW *Zincali* II. III. App. 125 The puchero, or pan of glazed earth, in which bacon, beef, and garbanzos are stewed. **1846** R. FORD *Gatherings from Spain* x. 113 Most classes are equally satisfied with the Oriental earthenware *ollas*, *pucheros*, or pipkins.

2. A composite dish of beef or lamb, ham or bacon, and vegetables, cooked as a stew.

1841 [see GARBANZO]. **1903** CONRAD & HUEFFER *Romance* III. ii. 131 An old woman..cooked his food at an outside fire—his *puchero* and *tortillas*. **1923** *Glasgow Herald* 7 Nov. 6/3 The crop of garbanzo, of which is made the puchero that has superseded the olla of years ago. **1933** H. ALLEN *Anthony Adverse* VIII. lxi. 998 The puchero followed. Brought in separate dishes, it was finally combined into one on the diner's plate.

†**ˈpuchersum**, *a. Obs.* (?)

(The editor suggests 'devilish'; but *poker*, demon, is not found till 250 years later. *Pother*, *puther*, which might have given *puthersome*, 'troublesome, perplexing, difficult', is also much later.)

13.. *Cursor M.* 2182 (Cott.) Iapheth had suns seuen, Aparti puchersum to neuen [*Gött.* sinful for to neuen], Gomer, madan, iena, magog, Tubal, tiras, and mosog.

puck (pʌk), **pook** (pʊk), *sb.*[1] Forms: α. 1 **púca**, 3–4 (9 *Sc.*) **puke**, 4–7 **pouke**, 5 **powke**, 6 **pooke**, 9 **pook**, **pouk**. β. 6–7 **pucke**, 7– **puck**. γ. 9 *dial.* **poake**. [OE. *púca* = ON. *púki* a mischievous demon. Cf. W. *pwca*, *pwci*, Ir. *púca* (POOKA). Cf. POKER *sb.*[2], PUG *sb.*[2]

The ulterior history of the name and the question whether it was originally Teutonic or Celtic, is unsettled.]

An evil, malicious, or mischievous spirit or demon of popular superstition. **a.** Treated as a unique being, and in middle Eng. (*the pouke*) commonly identified with the biblical devil; from the 16th c. (with capital P) the name of a fancied mischievous or tricksy goblin or sprite, called also Robin Goodfellow and Hobgoblin. (In this last sense commonly *Puck*.)

α. *a* **1000** in Napier *O.E. Glosses* xxiii. 2 *Larbula* [i.e. *larvula*], puca. *c* **1275** *Sinners Beware* 120 in *O.E. Misc.* 76 Hwen deþ schal cume Al hit wurþ heom bi-nume, And he bitauht þe puke [*rime* bruke]. **13..** *St. Gregory* 243 in Herrig's *Archiv* LVII. 62 ȝeo mad þe croiz vppon his brest fforte hit saue fram þe pouke. **1362** LANGL. *P. Pl.* A. x. 62 Þenne haþ þe Pouke pouwer Sire *Princeps huius mundi*, Ouer suche Maner Men. *Ibid.* XI. 158 Nigromancye and perimancie þe pouke to Rise makeþ. **1377** *Ibid.* B. XIII. 161 Ne noither hete, ne haille, ne non helle pouke. *Ibid.* XVI. 264 Oute of þe poukes pondfolde no meynprise may vs fecche. **1595** SPENSER *Epithal.* 341 Ne let the Pouke, nor other euill sprights,.. Fray vs. **1757** W. THOMPSON *Hymn to May* xxxiii. 6 Ne let hobgoblin, ne the pouk, profane With shadowy glare the light.

β. **1590** SHAKS. *Mids. N.* II. i. 40 You are that shrew'd and knauish spirit Cal'd Robin Good-fellow. Are you not hee, That frights the maidens...? Those that Hobgoblin call you, and sweet Pucke, You do their worke, and they shall haue good lucke. *Ibid.* v. i. 438–42 As I am an honest Pucke ..We will make amends ere long: Else the Pucke a lyar call. .. And Robin shall restore amends. **1627** DRAYTON *Nymphidia* xxxvi, He meeteth Pucke, which most men call Hobgoblin. *Ibid.* xxxvii, This Puck seems but a dreaming dolt, Still walking like a ragged Colt, And oft out of a Bush doth bolt, Of purpose to deceive us. *a* **1635** CORBET *Iter Bor.* Poems (1647) 11 Turne your clokes Quoth he, for Pucke is busie in these Oakes:.. Then turne your Cloakes, for this is Fairie ground. **1637** B. JONSON *Sad Sheph.*, Persons of the play:.. Puck-hairy, or Robin-Goodfellow. *Ibid.* III. iv, O Puck, my Goblin! I have lost my belt. *c* **1745** (?) GRAY *Characters of Christcross row* Wks. 1884 I. 211 Pleased with his Pranks, the Pisgys call him Puck. **1831** RITSON *Fairy T.* 44 Puck, *alias* Robin Goodfellow, is the most active and extraordinary fellow of a fairy that we anywhere meet with. **1834** MARY HOWITT *Sk. Nat. Hist.*, *Monkey*, Monkey, little merry fellow,.. Full of fun, as Puck could be; Harlequin might learn of thee! **1864** LE FANU *Uncle Silas* II. vi. 88 And why the puck don't you let her out?

b. with *a* and *pl.* One of a class or number of such demons, goblins, or sprites.

c **1000** *Boulogne Glosses to Prudentius* in *Germania* N.S. XI. 388 *Uagantes demonas*, wandrigende pucan. **13..** *Coer de L.* 566, I wis, sere kyng, quod Ser Fouke, I wene that knyght was a pouke. *Ibid.* 4326 He is no man, he is a pouke. **1567** GOLDING *Ovid's Met.* IX. (1593) 229 The countrie where Chymæra that same pooke Hath goatish bodie, lyons head and breast, and dragons taile. **1614** *Sco. Venus* (1876) 34 And that they may perceive the heavens frown, The Poukes & Goblins pul the couerings down. **1621** BURTON *Anat. Mel.* I. ii. I. ii. (1624) 43 Those which Mizaldus cals *Ambulones*, that walke about midnight on great Heathes and desart places, which..draw men out of the way, and leade them all night a by way;..we commonly call them Pucks. **1824** J. MCCULLOCH *Highl. Scotl.* II. 350 They are here, water spirits, and pucks, and witches.

c. *transf.* A person having the character or habits attributed to Puck; in ME. a wicked man, a 'devil'; now, one given to mischievous tricks, esp. a mischievous child or youngster.

c **1412** HOCCLEVE *De Reg. Princ.* 1922 A deceyour..Good is a man eschewe swich a powke. **1852** MUNDY *Our Antipodes* (1857) 192 Sharp and intelligent, but terribly spoilt, nothing could be done..without the interposition of this little meddlesome Puck. **1901** *Westm. Gaz.* 10 July 1/3 How much longer is a political Puck to be allowed to play the very mischief with a national interest of such present magnitude?

d. Often entering into place-names.

946 in Birch *Cart. Sax.* II. 575 Þa land-ȝemæru þe sceotað dun to Pucan wylle. **11..** *Chron. Monast. de Bello* [Battle] (1846) 11 Per Puchehole usque at Westbece, juxta terram de Bodeham. **1312** *Close Roll* 5 *Edw. II* m. 3 in *Calr.* 426 Pukenhale [co. York]. **1906** KIPLING (*title*) Puck of Pook's Hill.

e. *Comb.* †**puck-bug**, a bugbear, a malignant spectre; **puckfoisted** *a.* (*dial.*), cheated by a demon, bewitched; **puck-led** *a.* (*dial.*): cf. PIXY-LED.

1582 STANYHURST *Æneis* III. (Arb.) 89 That night in forrest to vs pouke bugs [L. *immania monstra*] gastlye be tendred. **1852** ALLIES *Antiq. Worcestersh.* (ed. 2) 418 The peasantry in Alfric [Worcs.], and those parts, say that they are sometimes what they call Poake ledden; that is, that they are occasionally waylaid in the night by a mischievous sprite whom they call Poake. **1889** GISSING *Both of this Parish* I. xii. 246 To be a-puckledden by fancy. **1932** H. J. MASSINGHAM *Wold without End* App. 294 Here are a few of the Elizabethan words that were heard at the Globe more than three hundred years ago and are heard to-day in the inns between Chipping Campden and Stow-on-the-Wold ..'puckfoisted' for bewitched.

puck, *sb.*[2] [Origin uncertain: see Note below.] **1.** (Also *puck-bird*.) The nightjar or goatsucker.

1883 SAWYER *Sussex Nat. Hist.* ii. 8 The 'puck' would fly before her, and she did not dare to cross its path. **1885** SWAINSON *Prov. Names Birds* 97 In many places..it is considered that animals either become blind or are infected with disease after being sucked [by the nightjar]. The country-people in West Sussex call this complaint 'puck' or 'puckeridge'—perhaps from Puck, a malignant spirit—and the bird itself 'puck bird'.

2. A disease in cattle attributed to the nightjar.

1834 YOUATT *Cattle* 362 In some parts of Surrey, under the name of the *puck*, the fore-quarter, or the side, is the part mostly affected. **1879** DALZIEL *Diseases Dogs* (1892) 14 Anthrax,..a disease of cattle, known in the vernacular as ..'quarter ill', 'joint ill', 'hasty', 'puck', 'shoot of blood', &c.

[*Note. Puck*, *puck-bird*, and *puckeridge* are all rural names of the goatsucker or nightjar: it is not clear whether the two latter are compounds of *puck*, or whether this is itself short for one or other of them. As the bird is the object of much obloquy and even superstitious dread, it is quite possible that its name is derived from PUCK *sb.*[1], either as being 'Puck's bird', or itself a puck or demon-bird; but the composition and meaning of *puckeridge* then remain unexplained. The conjecture of some that the latter may be derived from PUCK *v.* to hit, strike, and *ridge*, OE. *hrycg* back, from the notion of its striking the backs of sheep and cattle and thus inflicting on them a fatal distemper (see PUCKERIDGE, quot. 1789) would app. withdraw the group from any connexion with PUCK *sb.*[1], except as a secondary association. But *-ridge* may be an oral corruption of some other word.]

puck (pʌk), *sb.*[3] [Origin obscure: cf. PUCK *v.*] *Sport.* **1.** A flat india-rubber disc used for a ball, in ice hockey or bandy.

1891 *Field* 7 Mar. 334/3 The ball (or 'puck', as it is called) is a flat piece of india-rubber, circular in shape, about two inches thick, and with a diameter of about four inches. The game is played with, usually, seven a-side, and no striking with the stick is allowed, only pushing the 'puck' along the ice. **1894** *Outing* (U.S.) XXIII. 409/2 These men handle the little innocent rubber puck as Paderewski handles the black keys of a piano. **1930** *Times* 20 Mar. 7/2 A little later.. Benchi put the puck over his body into the net. **1951** *Sport* 7–13 Jan. 16/2 His old speciality, taking the puck at full speed and boring through to the net, is working overtime. **1971** L. KOPPETT *N.Y. Times Guide Spectator Sports* i. 7 The scoring objective can be stated simply: in football to advance the ball across a goal line; in basketball, hockey, soccer or lacrosse, to get the ball (or puck) into a goal. **1974** *Cleveland* (Ohio) *Plain Dealer* 13 Oct. c. 1/2 Toronto jumped to a 2–0 lead in the first period when Featherstone streaked in for an unassisted goal at 1:35 and Dillon rammed the puck home at 18:48. **1978** *N.Y. Times* 30 Mar. D. 17/6 Wayne Dillon won the draw from Mike Kaszycki but pulled the puck back to an empty spot on the circle.

2. *attrib.* and *Comb.*, as *puck-dribbling*, *-handling*, *shot*; **puck carrier**, in ice hockey the player in possession of the puck during play; **puckchaser** *colloq.*, an ice-hockey player; so **puck-chasing** *vbl. sb.*; **puck crown**, ice-hockey championship; **puck pusher** *colloq.* = *puckchaser*; **puck sense**, natural skill in ice hockey; **puck shy**, of goalkeepers in ice hockey: afraid of being hit by a puck.

1957 *Maclean's Mag.* 28 Sept. 1/2 The top scorers in the League are the best puck carriers. **1921** *Daily Colonist* (Victoria, B.C.) 24 Mar. 11/3 Calgary puckchasers take all the honors. **1979** *Yale Alumni Mag.* Apr. CN 1 The continuing resurgence of puck-chasers and net-stuffers is to be applauded. **1950** *Sport* 24–30 Mar. 13/4 His family later moved to Fort William, in which town he did most of his puck chasing. **1955** *Penticton* (B.C.) *Herald* 17 Mar. 5/3 There is no doubt in my mind—the Vees will bring this puck crown back to Canada. **1974** *Globe & Mail* (Toronto) 28 Jan. s. 2/7 He also gave a few exhibitions of puck dribbling with his skates, the only NHL defenceman who has this unique skill. **1965** *Kingston* (Ontario) *Whig-Standard* 15 May 9/6 Flyers dominated the game with superior skating, checking, passing and puck-handling. **1897** *Medicine Hat* (Alberta) *News* 25 Feb. 1/5 We have a club which can hold its own with the puck pushers from almost anywhere. **1966** *Hockey News* (Montreal) 1 Jan. 13/2 An intangible part of Melnyk's all-round prowess is something called 'puck sense'. **1968** *Globe & Mail* (Toronto) 5 Feb. 17/3 He was lifted with three minutes to play in the second period when struck on the mask over the right eye by a puck shot at close range. **1965** *Ibid.* 29 Dec. 24/2, I think the new rule could cause a goalie to become puck shy.

puck (pʌk), *v.* Now only *dial.* (chiefly Ir.) [? f. root *puk-*: see POKE *v.*[1]] *trans.* To hit or strike; to butt.

[? *c* **1640** J. SMYTH *Lives Berkeleys* (1883) II. 12 Hee also would to the threshing of the cock, pucke with hens, blindfold, and the like.] **1861** CLAYTON *Frank O'Donnell* 57 The ball was struck here and there, often pucked up in the air, then let again before it reached the ground. **1870** KENNEDY *Fireside Stories Irel.* 37 (E.D.D.) The ram and the cow pucked her with their horns. **1922** JOYCE *Ulysses* 247 Myler Keogh, Dublin's pet lamb, will meet sergeantmajor Bennett, the Portobello bruiser... God, that'd be a good pucking match to see. *Ibid.* 313 The referee twice cautioned Pucking Percy for holding.

Hence **puck** *sb.*[4] (*dial.*), a stroke; a stroke at the ball in the Irish game of hurling; ˈ**pucking** *vbl. sb.* and *ppl. a.*

1900 *19th Cent.* XLVIII. 306 The rival hurlers..meet together in wild rivalry for a puck at the ever flying ball. **1906** SOMERVILLE & ROSS *Irish Yesterdays* 95, I gave William a puck in the chest. **1922** JOYCE *Ulysses* 247 One puck in the wind..would knock you into the middle of next week. **1934** J. O'HARA *Appointment in Samarra* (1935) iii. 80 What he should of done was give you a puck in the mouth when you threw the drink at him. **1961** 'F. O'BRIEN' *Hard Life* ii. 18 Many a good puck I had myself in the quondam days of my nonage. **1979** N. SMYTHE in E. Berman *Ten of Best Brit. Short Plays* 120 I'll give you a puck in the gob in short order, mate.

puck, *sb.*[5] Short for PUCKFIST 1, q.v.

puck, dial. var. POOK *sb.*, a haycock.

pucka, var. PUKKA.

puckarow, var. PUCKEROW.

‖**puckauly** (pʌˈkɔːlɪ). *Anglo-Ind.* Also 8 **buccaly**, 8–9 **puckally**, 9 **puckalie**, **pacauly**. [a. Hindī *pakhālī* a water-carrier, f. *pakhāl* a large water-skin.] A water-carrier; also, a water-skin.

1789 MUNRO *Narrative* xiii. 183 Another very necessary establishment..which is two *buccalies* to each company: these are two large leathern bags, for holding water, slung upon the back of a bullock. **1799** *Hull Advertiser* 21 Dec. 4/1 Black doctors, authorised Puckallys, Drummers. **1803** WELLINGTON in Gurw. *Desp.* (1844) I. 334 A puckalie from each corps of Native infantry in camp. **1803** PERCIVAL *Ceylon* v. 102 Water..brought by means of bullocks in leathern bags, called here puckally bags.

puckaun (ˈpʌkɔːn). *Anglo-Ir.* Also **puckawn**. [ad. Ir. *pocán*, a small male goat.] A billy goat.

a **1745** SWIFT *Irish Eloquence* in *Prose Wks.* (1957) IV. 279 His Cows..would hardly give a drop of Milk..For his herd had lost the Puckaun. **1870** P. KENNEDY *Fireside Stories of Ireland* 7 Bring me the giant's puckawn with the golden bells round his neck. **1913** J. STEPHENS *Here are Ladies* 287 Children will dance upon the slightest provocation, so also do lambs and goats; but policemen, and puckauns, and advertisement agents, and fish do not dance at all, and this is because they have hard hearts. **1953** S. BECKETT *Watt* iv. 246 Riley's puckaun again, said Mr Nolan, I can smell him from here.

[**puck-ball**, alleged syn. of PUFF-BALL 1, PUCKFIST 1: app. a misprint in Bailey's Folio.

[**1708** KERSEY, *Puck-fist* or *Puff-ball*, a kind of Mushroom full of Dust. So **1721–** BAILEY (octavo).] **1730** BAILEY (folio), *Puck-ball*, *Puck-fist*, a Kind of Mushroom full of Dust. **1755** JOHNSON, *Puckball* or *puckfist* (from *puck* the fairy, a fairy's ball). Hence in mod. Dicts.]

pucker (ˈpʌkə(r)), *sb.*[1] [f. PUCKER *v.*]

1. A ridge, wrinkle, or corrugation of the skin or other substance, or a number of small wrinkles running across and into one another; esp. one caused in sewing together two edges of cloth, etc., by keeping the one edge fuller than the other, or by drawing the thread too tightly, so as to make the seam shorter than the cloth on either side.

1744–50 W. ELLIS *Mod. Husbandm.* VI. III. 54 The Tasker does not make use of those sweeping horizontal Strokes..if he does, he will beat up the Straw in Puckers. **1773** JOHNSON, *Ruff*,..2. Any thing collected into puckers or corrugations. **1810** BENTHAM *Packing* (1821) 146 If, on the bed of roses..there be but a single leaf that has a pucker in it. **1836** MARRYAT *Midsh. Easy* x, The chin..was drawn in with unnatural seams and puckers. **1842** S. LOVER *Handy Andy* ii, His face..was screwed up to the scrutinising pucker. **1875** *Plain Needlework* 14 If this be done, even by one thread per stitch, a pucker must necessarily ensue.

2. *fig.* A state of agitation or excitement; a flutter, a fuss. *colloq.*

1741 RICHARDSON *Pamela* I. 164 Mrs. Jewkes..sat down by me, and seem'd in a great Pucker. **1801** MAR. EDGEWORTH *Angelina* iii, Pe not in a pet or a pucker! **1825** J. NEAL *Bro. Jonathan* I. 202 Edith was in tears; Jotham, powerless with amazement;—Miriam, in a 'plaguy pucker'. **1847** J. S. ROBB *Streaks of Squatter Life* i. 15 If I am delayed Gales and Seaton will be very angry, and Blair and Rives get in a pucker. **1883** J. PAYN *Thicker than Water* xiii, The few things that did not agitate Mrs. Sotheran, or, to use her own homely phrase, 'put her into a pucker'. **1888** HOWELLS *Annie Kilburn* xxix, I told William when we first missed her ..and he was in such a pucker about her..that [etc.].

3. *Comb.*, as ***pucker-mouthed*** adj.

1851 SCHOOLCRAFT *30 Yrs. Indian Tribes* 377 A tall, not portly, red-mouthed, and pucker-mouthed man.

pucker, *sb.*[2] *rare.* [f. PUCK *v.*] A boxer, a fighter.

1922 JOYCE *Ulysses* 247 The best pucker going for strength was Fitzsimons... But the best pucker for science was Jem Corbett before Fitzsimons knocked the stuffings out of him.

pucker (ˈpʌkə(r)), *v.* [Evidenced in the end of the 16th c., prob. earlier in colloquial use. The form is that of a frequentative: see -ER[5]. The root is prob. to be found in POKE *sb.*[1], *v.*[2] (*dial. pok, pock*), POCKET, the notion being that of forming small bag-like or purse-like gatherings; cf. PURSE *v.* in sense 'to wrinkle up', and F. *pocher, faire des poches* to bag, to pucker. Verbs of this class often shorten or obscure the original vowel: cf. *clutter, flutter, sputter, stutter*, etc.]

1. *intr.* To contract or gather into wrinkles, small folds, cockles, or bulges; to become drawn together into irregular wrinkles or corrugations; to cockle. Often with *up*.

1598 FLORIO, *Saccolare*, to pucker or gather or cockle as some stuffes doo being wet. **1602** MARSTON *Antonio's Rev.* III. ii, May I be numd with horror, and my vaines Pucker with sing'ing torture. **1670** SIR S. CROW in *12th Rep. Hist. MSS. Comm.* App. v. 15 The silke..beeing ill woven, will shrink and pucker. *a* **1845** HOOD *Two Peacocks of Bedfont* xxv, Ancient lips that puckered up in scorn. **1847** ALB. SMITH *Chr. Tadpole* xxvi. (1879) 235 His waistcoat..had a propensity to pucker up over his chest. **1883** *Hardwich's Photogr. Chem.* (ed. Taylor) 368 To ensure a hard film.. which will not pucker up.

2. *trans.* To draw together or contract into wrinkles, bulges, or fullnesses; to draw (the skin, lips, etc.) into ridges and furrows; to draw a seam too tight, so as to make the material bag on either side; to gather one side of (a seam) more fully than the other, either as a fault in sewing, or intentionally for some purpose. Often with *up*.

1616 J. CHAMBERLAIN in *Crt. & Times Jas. I* (1848) I. 423 The nether parts..are crumpled and puckered untowardly. **1639** R. YOUNG *Sin Stigmatized* 19 Hee fell downe and not being able to rise againe had his belly puckered together like a sachell, before the chamberlain could come to help him. **1712** BUDGELL *Spect.* No. 301 ¶9 An hideous Spectre,..his Skin puckered up in Wrinkles. **1792** A. YOUNG *Trav. France* 237 Their dress is very becoming; with jackets, the sleeves puckered and tied in puffs, with coloured ribbons. **1835–6** *Todd's Cycl. Anat.* I. 172/1 A continuation of the canal puckered up into numerous folds. **1876** MISS BRADDON *J. Haggard's Dau.* III. 62 Cynthia had finished her dozen of shirts, without a gusset set awry, a seam puckered, or one deviation from a right line. **1886** J. K. JEROME *Idle Thoughts* x. 116 Your pretty face will not be always puckered into wrinkles.

b. *absol.* To make puckers or bulges in sewing.

1862 FLORENCE WILFORD *Maiden of Our Day* 98 When she observed poor Fan's big stitches and tendency to pucker. **1881** MISS BRADDON *Asph.* II. 149, I get my thread entangled, and begin to pucker, and the whole business goes wrong.

c. *trans.* To form by puckering or gathering.

1753 in *Lond. Mag.* Sept. 396 Puff and pucker up knots on your arms and your toes; Make your petticoats short.

puckered (ˈpʌkəd), *ppl. a.* [f. prec. + -ED[1].] Drawn into puckers, wrinkles, or folds, as the skin, or as cloth, purposely or unintentionally, in sewing.

1611 COTGR., *Renfrongné*, furrowed, as an angrie brow; wrimpled, crumpled, puckered. **1755** JOHNSON, *Ruff*, a puckered linen ornament, formerly worn about the neck. **1796** A. C. BOWER *Diaries & Corr.* (1903) 163 My leilack bonnet I have had altered..; it is now made in what they call a puckered bonnet. **1818** *La Belle Assemblée* XVII. No. 108. 87/1 Innumerable rows of puckered muslin. **1870** MORRIS *Earthly Par.* II. III. 131 He heard the shipmen speaking low With anxious puckered brows.

†ˈ**puckerel.** *Obs.* Also 6 puckrel. [dim. of PUCK *sb.*[1] with suffix *-erel, -rel*: cf. *cockerel*.] A little puck or demon; an imp.

c **1580** JEFFERIE *Bugbears* III. iii. in *Archiv Stud. Neu. Spr.* (1897), Puckes, puckerels, hob howlard, bygorn and Robin Good-felow. **1593** G. GIFFORD *Dial. conc. Witches* (Percy Soc.) 9 She had three or foure impes, some call them puckrels, one like a grey cat, another like a weasel.

ˈ**puckerer.** *rare.* [f. PUCKER *v.* + -ER[1].] One who or that which puckers.

1775 in ASH. **1846** in WORCESTER; and in mod. Dicts.

puckeridge (ˈpʌkərɪdʒ). [Origin obscure: connected with *puck-bird*; see Note s.v. PUCK *sb.*[2]] A name of the nightjar; also, a disease of cattle attributed to the stroke or bite of the nightjar.

1789 G. WHITE *Selborne, Fern-Owl* (1875) 334 The country people have a notion that the fern-owl, or churn-owl, or eve-jarr, which they also call a puckeridge, is very injurious to weanling calves, by inflicting, as it strikes at them, the fatal distemper, known to cow-leeches by the name of puckeridge. **1885** [see PUCK *sb.*[2] 1].

puckering (ˈpʌkərɪŋ), *vbl. sb.* [f. PUCKER *v.* + -ING[1].] The action of the vb. PUCKER, or its result; a drawing together or gathering of cloth, the skin, etc., into wrinkles or irregular folds.

1611 FLORIO, *Crespatúra*, a puckring in any cloth or clothes. **1797** M. BAILLIE *Morb. Anat.* (1807) 98 Stricture from the Puckering of the inner Membrane of the Œsophagus. **1858** GLENNY *Gard. Every-day Bk.* 115/1 The flower should be circular, without puckering or frilling. **1870** *Eng. Mech.* 4 Mar. 615/3 How can zinc be laid..without puckering? **1875** *Plain Needlework* 14 Puckering in seaming is caused by the children holding the right elbow close to the right side.

puckering (ˈpʌkərɪŋ), *ppl. a.* [f. as prec. + -ING[2].] That puckers. (*trans.* and *intr.*)

1766 [ANSTEY] *Bath Guide* Epil. 287 Where oft, I ween, the Brewer's Cauldron flows With Elder's mawkish Juice, and puckering Sloes. **1889** *Anthony's Photogr. Bull.* II. 380 A double 'puckering string', such as our grandmothers used in their workbags. **1897** *Outing* (U.S.) XXX. 354/1 A puckering frown of ripples upon the pool.

pucker-needle: see PUCK-NEEDLE.

puckeroo (pʌkəˈruː), *a. N.Z. slang.* Also in various other phonetic spellings and with initial *b.* [ad. Maori *pakaru* broken; also vb., to break.] Useless, broken. Also as *v. trans.* (esp. in pa. pple.), to ruin.

[**1844** J. W. BARNICOAT *Jrnl.* (MS.) 160 Gideon [*sc.* a Maori] foreseeing the collision..shouted out Puikero! puikero! puikero! (broken).] **1885** *Short Sk. Life T. Hancock* ii. 19 [Maoris said] 'We will *pukeru* you!' 'Very well', I said, '*pukeru* me'. **1925** FRASER & GIBBONS *Soldier & Sailor Words* 220 *Pakaru*, broken; smashed. A Maori word, in use among the New Zealand Troops. **1941** BAKER *N.Z. Slang* v. 42 [By the 1890's] we had begun to *pukaroo* things, when we broke something, confused an issue, or ruined some plan of action. This is derived with extraordinary simplicity from the Maori *pakaru*, broken. **1943** *Amer. Speech* XVIII. 93 *Pukkaroo*, adjective.., (to make) worthless, useless—it could be used..of an engine that had broken down—..is perhaps from the Maori *pakaru*, to destroy. **1948** R. FINLAYSON *Tidal Creek* vii. 179 The surest way to buckeroo an axe. **1965** S. T. OLLIVIER *Petticoat Farm* i. 14, I come to see if you've got a spare shovel. Mine's puckerooed and I got a cow in the drain. **1970** *N.Z. Listener* 12 Oct. 12/1 Bad show, fighting. I puckerooed things properly last night.

puckerow (ˈpʌkərəʊ), *v. Army* and *Naut. slang.* Also **puckarow, puckero, puckerrow.** [ad. Hind. *pakṛo* imp. of *pakaṛnā* to seize.] *trans.* To seize, lay hold of. Also *intr.* or *absol.* (rare).

1866 G. O. TREVELYAN in *Fraser's Mag.* LXXIII. 390 Fanny, I am cutcha no longer. Surely you will allow a lover who is pucka to puckero. **1876** C. CHAPMAN *Sailor's Life at Sea* iv. 224 Now is the time; let us 'puckerrow' it. **1886** YULE & BURNELL *Hobson-Jobson* p. xix, Hindustani *verbs*..are habitually adopted into the quasi-English by converting the imperative into an infinitive. Thus..to *puckarow*. **1887** *Outing* July 331/1 Charley Wheeler were the lucky man as had 'puckerowd' poor Hans' dry-goods. **1899** F. T. BULLEN *Log of Sea-Waif* xvi. 194 So mechanically did they 'puckarow' those baskets, that often one would pass from the hatch to the gang way empty. **1907** M. ROBERTS *Flying Cloud* iii. 13 What with puckerowing cases, lashing tanks, and frapping stunsail-booms on the deck-house..there was enough to do. **1919** W. H. DOWNING *Digger Dial.* 59 *Puckero*, take; seize. **1931** W. KIRK in *Cabar Feidh* Sept. 389/2 Not all the legislators, robbing poor and rich to-day, can puckarow my talisman—the Badge of Cabar Feidh!

puckery (ˈpʌkərɪ), *a.* [f. PUCKER *sb.*[1] + -Y.]

1. Given to puckering; marked with puckers.

1830 *Massachusetts Spy* 10 Feb. 2/1, I didn't like the set of the shoulders, they were so dreadful puckery. **1858** CARLYLE *Fredk. Gt.* v. vi. (1872) II. 110 A..close-fisted old gentleman..with puckery much-inquiring eyes. *c* **1860** FARADAY *Forces Nat.* i. 42 The gold-leaf is puckery. **1888** F. M. CRAWFORD *With Immortals* I. iv. 81 A milliard of puckery, peppery, self-satisfied scientists.

2. That draws the mouth together; astringent.

1858 HAWTHORNE *Fr. & It. Note-Bks.* (1881) II. 180 These grapes are better than puckery cider apples. **1887** H. P. WELLS in *Harper's Mag.* Feb. 451 To the human palate it is dry, insipid, and puckery.

puckery (ˈpʌkərɪ), *sb. rare.* [PUCK *sb.*[1] + -ERY.] = PUCKISHNESS.

1877 G. MEREDITH *Let.* 24 June (1970) I. 545, I foresee the grin up to the ear tips of exulting Puckery.

puckery, obs. form of PUGGREE.

†**pucket.** *Obs. dial.* (See quots.)

1669 WORLIDGE *Syst. Agric.* (1681) 222 Gather them off in the Winter, taking away the Puckets which cleave about the Branches, and burning them. *Ibid.* 330 *Puckets*, nests of Caterpillars, or such like Vermine. **1674** RAY *S. & E.C. Words* 74 *Puckets*, nests of Caterpillars, *Suff.* **1787** in GROSE *Provinc. Gloss.* Suppl.

puckfist (ˈpʌkfɪst). Also 7 puc-, **pukfist, puckfoyst, 7–9 puckfoist.** See also *Eng. Dial. Dict.* [app. f. PUCK *sb.*[1] + FIST *sb.*[2] Cf. PUFF-FIST, -FOIST, which appears about the same date.]

1. The Puff-ball, *Lycoperdon Bovista.* Also abbreviated *puck.*

1601 B. JONSON *Poetaster* IV. v, I'll blow him into aire, when I meet him next: He dares not fight with a puck-fist. **1609** C. BUTLER *Fem. Mon.* x. (1623) T iij, Next vnto Brimstone [for smoking bees] is the smoake of Bunt or great Pucfists, Tuchwood, or Mushrums. **1766** *Complete Farmer* s.v. *Bee*, The narcotic, or stupefying fume, is made with the ..large mushroom, commonly known by the name bunt, puckfist, or frog-cheese. *Ibid.*, Cut off a piece of the puck, as large as a hen's egg, and fix it in the end of a small stick,.. which place so that the puck may hang near the middle of an empty hive. **1893** *S.E. Worc. Gloss.* s.v., I shud like a drap o' drink, fur I feels as dry as a puck-fyst.

2. A term of contempt for an empty braggart.

1599 B. JONSON *Ev. Man out of Hum.* I, To be enamour'd on this dusty turf, This clod, a whoreson puck-fist. **1605** *Tryall Chev.* IV. i. in Bullen *O. Pl.* III. 328 Giue me leaue to incounter this puckfist, and if I doe not make him cry *Peccavi* say Dicke Bowyer's a powdered Mackrell. **1637** SHIRLEY *Example* II. i, Lady, he is no man..A very puck-fist. *Jacinta.* What's that, I pray? *Vain.* A phantom, a mere phantom. **1821** SCOTT *Kenilw.* xviii, A base besognio, and a puckfist.

attrib. **1615** J. TAYLOR (Water P.) *Urania* xxiv. Wks. (1630) 3/2 Then loue him; else his puckfoist pompe abhorre.

†**3.** A close-fist, a niggard. (? an erroneous use.)

1608 R. MIDDLETON *Epigr.* (1840) 13 Old father pukfist knits his arteries, First strikes, then rails on Riot's villanies. **1630** B. JONSON *New Inn* III. ii, *Pierce.* A grazier's may —— *Fer.* O they are pinching puckfists! *Trun.* And suspicious.

puckish (ˈpʌkɪʃ), *a.* [f. PUCK *sb.*[1] + -ISH[1].] Of the nature of or characteristic of Puck; impish, mischievous, capricious. Hence ˈ**puckishly** *adv.*; ˈ**puckishness.**

1874 GREEN *Short Hist.* vii. §3. 365 Her delight..broke out in a thousand puckish freaks. **1891** G. MEREDITH *One of our Conq.* I. iv. 52 His Puckish fancy jack-o'-lanterning over it. **1900** *Academy* 28 Apr. 365/1 The jeering sea had puckishness enough to return upon its steps. **1972** *Daily Tel.* 20 Nov. 13/5 His feet could not reach the pedals... But when his fingers remained under control..he puckishly turned grace-notes and, in the Gigue, made the music swell imposingly. **1977** *N.Y. Rev. Bks.* 13 Oct. 14/4 Vice Chairman Tower adds puckishly, 'I might say further that the matter of assassinations might be viewed in a broader context of other options that might have been available.'

†**puckle,** *sb.*[1] *Obs.* [OE. *púcel*, f. *púca*, PUCK *sb.*[1] + *-el*, -LE I.] A kind of bugbear.

c **1000** *Boulogne Glosses to Prudentius* in *Germania* N.S. XI. 394/242 *Faunos*, wude wasan. *Priapos*, pucelas. *c* **1450** Poucle [see PUCK-NEEDLE]. **1584** R. SCOT *Discov. Witchcr.* VII. xv. 153 The hell waine, the fierdrake, the puckle, Tom thombe, hob gobblin,..and such other bugs. **1830** SCOTT *Demonol.* 180 That Phuca is a Celtic superstition from which the word Pook or Puckle was doubtless derived.

puckle (ˈpʌk(ə)l), *sb.*[2] *Sc.* [Local var. PICKLE *sb.*[2]] An indefinite amount, a few.

1877 G. STEWART *Shetland Fireside Tales* x. 78 A 'puckle o' oo' when da sheep wis rued. **1917** A. S. NEILL *Dominie Dismissed* vi. 86 Aw need hardly say onything aboot the object o' this concert, but it's to get a puckle bawbees to send oot a clean pair o' socks and maybe a clean sark to oor local sojers oot in France. **1930** *Aberdeen Univ. Rev.* XVII. 103 A hinna heard o' im for a gey puckle year an' A doot 'e maun be deid. **1968** E. BUCKLER *Ox Bells & Fireflies* xii. 165 The man with a small nest egg had saved up 'quite a puckle'.

pucklike (ˈpʌklaɪk), *a.* [f. PUCK *sb.*[1] + -LIKE.] Like, or in the manner of, Puck; cleverly mischievous, puckish, imp-like.

1845 DISRAELI *Sybil* II. xii, There was something of a Puck-like malignity in the temperament of Lord Marney. **1901** *Westm. Gaz.* 19 Feb. 2/1 In a delightful mood of Puck-like satire.

ˈ**puckling.** *nonce-wd.* [f. PUCK *sb.*[1] + -LING[1].] A little Puck.

1890 N. P. *To Sylvie* in *Life Lewis Carroll* (1898) 289 Though I still shall hold Thee, and that puckling sprite, thy brother, Dear.

ˈ**puck-ˌneedle.** [f. PUCK *sb.*[1] + NEEDLE.] A name for different weeds having needle-like or beaked fruit, as Shepherd's needle (*Scandix Pecten*), and Stork's-bill (*Erodium*). So **pucker-needle.**

[*c* **1450** *Alphita* (Anecd. Oxon.) 2 Acus muscata major, anglice pouclesnedele.] **1805** R. W. DICKSON *Pract. Agric.* I. 564 *Puck-needle* is a weed that is often abundant on such lands as are hard tilled. **1836** W. D. COOPER *Sussex Gloss.* 27 *Pookneedle*, Cocle, an injurious weed. **1853** *Ibid.* 67 *Pookneedle*, Cockle, or Shepherd's needle... The sharpened end of the seed vessel of the wild geranium, probably fairies' needle;..called *Beggar's needle* in Worcestershire. **1861** MISS PRATT *Flower. Pl.* III. 77 Common Shepherd's needle. .. These fruits are bright green..and sharp enough to merit the names applied to the plant of..Pucker-needle [etc.].

puckoon, variant of PUCCOON.

puckster (ˈpʌkstə(r)). *N. Amer. colloq.* [f. PUCK *sb.*[3] + -STER.] An ice-hockey player.

1939 *Kansas City Jrnl.* 5 Feb. 23 (*heading*) Greyhounds slaughter Tulsa Pucksters. **1941** *Sun* (Baltimore) 11 Feb. 14/7 (*heading*) Georgetown pucksters schedule five games. **1955** *Toronto Daily Star* 11 Apr. 18/5 Moncton Hawks, as optimistic a band of pucksters as ever came down the Allan Cup hockey trail. **1976** *Bangor* (Maine) *Daily News* 24 Aug. 20/3 U.S. pucksters face long odds.

pud (pʌd), *sb.*[1] [Of unknown origin. Cf. PAD *sb.*[3], also Du. *poot* paw.] A nursery word for the hand of a child or fore-foot of some animals.

1654 GAYTON *Pleas. Notes* I. iv. 14 Excoriation or fleaing the Podes [may be set as an equivalent] for giving leather to the Pudds. **1822** LAMB *Elia* Ser. I. *Distant Correspondents*, The Kangaroos..with those little short fore puds. **1865** *Cornh. Mag.* Mar. 296 The child's tiny white puds pat the jolly cheeks and pull the yellow beard. **1965** R. ERSKINE *Passion Flowers in Business* viii. 108, I saw him clutching your hot little puds. **1968** J. F. STRAKER *SIN & Johnny Inch* 165 How did they get their puds on you? More trickery?

pud (pʊd), *sb.*[2] Also **pudd**. Colloq. abbrev. of PUDDING *sb.* **1. a.** = PUDDING *sb.* 1, 2. Also as second element in *pock-pud* (see POKE-PUDDING). **b.** = PUDDING *sb.* 6 (now the usual sense). Also *transf.* and *fig.*

1706 in J. Watson *Choice Coll. Comic & Serious Scots Poems* I. 61, I leave my Liver, Puds and Tripes. **a 1776**, **1802**, etc. [see POKE-PUDDING 1, 2]. **1828** in P. Buchan *Anc. Ballads & Songs N. Scotl.* I. 261 Whan the puds war sodden. **1914** *Dialect Notes* IV. 164 *Pud*,..pudding. **1943** 'R. LLEWELLYN' *None but Lonely Heart* xli. 342 If you lot go to chokey, so do I, for harbouring. So we're all black-birds in the same old pud. **1951** J. B. PRIESTLEY *Festival at Farbridge* 47 These two have finished mopping up their horrible pink puds. **1955** M. EWER *No Abiding Place* i. 13 Soup, joint, two veg, pud and cheese. **1960** T. COOPER *Winter's Day* III. i. 164, I helped make the pudd. **1976** *Southern Even. Echo* (Southampton) 15 Nov. 10/2 Nostalgic and happy memories of our traditional Christmas 'Pud'.

2. *coarse slang.* = PUDDING 5 b. *to pull one's pud*: see PULL *v.* 20 i.

1939 JOYCE *Finnegans Wake* (1964) 445 There's a lot of lecit pleasure coming bangslanging your way, Miss Pinpernelly satin. For your own good, you understand, for the man who lifts his pud to a woman is saving the way for kindness. **1944** *Publ. Amer. Dial. Soc.* II. 35 *Pud*, *to pull the (his)*,..to masturbate... Boys and men. Common. **1972** R. A. WILSON *Playboy's Bk. Forbidden Words* 240 *Pud*, the penis; perhaps from *pudding* in *pull the pudding*. **1977** *Amer. Speech 1975* L. 54 *Pud*, 'penis'.

3. *fig.* = PUDDING *sb.* 7 b; *spec.* an easy college course. Also *attrib.* or as *adj.* *U.S.*

1938 *Amer. Speech* XIII. 6/2 *Pud*,..an easy job. **1963** *Ibid.* XXXVIII. 167 An easy college course..*pud* adj. **1967** S. B. FLEXNER in Wentworth & Flexner *Dict. Amer. Slang* Suppl. 700/1 *Pud*,..an easy course; a 'snap'... *Adj.* Easy to pass or make a good grade in, as a course or test. **1977** *Amer. Speech 1975* L. 64 *Pud*,..soft, easy. 'Do you know any pud courses?'

pud, pudde, varr. POOD, a Russian weight.

pudden, puddening: see PUDDING *sb.* and *v.*

pudder (ˈpʌdə(r)), *v.* *Obs.* or *dial.* [Of unknown origin: the quot. from *Ancren Riwle a* 1225 appears to contain the word, which otherwise is not known till near 1600. App. distinct from *pudder*, collateral form of POTHER *sb.* and *v.*]

1. *intr.* To poke or stir about with the hand or a stick; (of an animal) to poke or rout, with bill or snout; to dabble in water, mud, or dust.

[*a* **1225** *Ancr. R.* 214 [He] lið euer iðen asken, & fareð abuten asken & bisiliche stureð him..& bloweð þerinne, & ablent him sulf; padereð [*MS. T.* puðeres] & makeð þerinne figures of augrim.] **1591** SYLVESTER *Du Bartas* I. v. 175 Fishes..Some almost alwaies pudder in the mud Of sleepy Pools. **1601** HOLLAND *Pliny* x. lxxi. I. 306 Some peck and pluck it with their hookt bils, others pudder into their food with their broad nebs. **1611** COTGR., *Bourbetter*,..to paddle, or pudder, in the myre. **1639** T. DE GRAY *Compl. Horsem.* 153 He will not drinke much, but pudder long with his nose in the water. **1647** WARD *Simp. Cobler* (1843) 2 To pudder in the rubbish, and to raise dust in the eyes of more steady Repayrers.

2. *intr.* To go 'poking' *about*; to potter; to meddle and muddle, to dabble (*in*).

1624 BACON *Let. to Sir H. May*, You may perhaps think me partial to Potycaries, that have been ever puddering in physic all my life. **1643** T. GOODWIN *Trial Christian's Growth* II. ii. (1650) 69 Many..who have gone puddring on (as I may so speak) in the use of other meanes. *a* **1677** BARROW *Serm.* xxii. Wks. 1687 I. 307 We shall obtain vast benefit, much greater than we can hope to get by puddering in the designs or doings of others. **1863** COWDEN CLARKE *Shaks. Char.* xvii. 443 Listen to the natural talk of those carriers, puddering about with their lanterns.

Hence **ˈpuddering** *vbl. sb.* and *ppl. a.*, poking, pottering, muddling, meddling; †*puddering-pole*, a pole to poke with.

1603 HOLLAND *Plutarch's Mor.* 139 In other mens letters they keepe a puddering, they open and reade them. **1674** N. FAIRFAX *Bulk & Selv.* To Rdr., Leave to lay his eggs in his own nest, which is built beyond the reach of every mans puddering pole. **1811** LAMB *Notes Specimens fr. Fuller* Wks. (1895) 270 One feels the ashes of Wicliffe gliding away out of the reach of the Sumners, Commissaries, Officials, Proctors, Doctors and all the puddering rout of executioners of the impotent rage of the baffled Council.

pudder, *sb.* *rare*[−1], archaic or erroneous variant of PUDDLE *sb.*

1889 STEVENSON *Master of B.* iii, We found the body of a Christian..lying in a pudder of his blood.

pudder, obs. or dial. var. of POTHER *sb.* and *v.*

pudding (ˈpʊdɪŋ), *sb.* Forms: 3–4 poding, 4–6 podyng, (6 -ynge), puddyng; 5 podding, -yng, (6 -ynge); poodyng; puddingh; 5–6 puddynge; 6 pooding, pooddyng, *Sc.* puding; 6– pudding, (6 -inge, 6–9 *dial.* and *vulgar* pudden, -in, 8 puden). [ME. *poding*, *puddyng*: derivation uncertain: see Note below.]

I. 1. a. The stomach or one of the entrails of a pig, sheep, or other animal, stuffed with a mixture of minced meat, suet, oatmeal, seasoning, etc., boiled and kept till needed; a kind of sausage: for different varieties, see BLACK, HOG'S, WHITE PUDDING. Now chiefly *Sc.* and *dial.*

c **1305** *Land Cokayne* 59 Þe pinnes beþ fat podinges Rich met to princez and kinges. **1377** LANGL. *P. Pl.* B. XIII. 62 He eet many sondry metes, mortrewes and puddynges. *c* **1430** *Two Cookery-bks.* 42 Puddyng of purpaysse..putte þis in þe Gutte of þe purpays. *c* **1440** *Promp. Parv.* 220/2 Hagas, puddynge (*S.* hakkys, puddyngys). **1530** PALSGR. 259 Puddyng, *boudayn*. *Ibid.* 265 Sausedge a podyng. **1584** COGAN *Haven Health* cxlix. (1636) 146 Of the inward of beasts are made Puddings, which are best of an hog. **1592** NASHE *Four Lett. Confut.* (1593) 28 Euery thing hath an end, and a pudding hath two. **1615** MARKHAM *Eng. Housew.* (1660) 178 Pudding which is called the Haggas or Haggus, of whose goodnesse it is vain to boast. **1617** MORYSON *Itin.* III. II. iii. 81 In lower Germany they supply the meale with bacon and great dried puddings, which puddings are sauory and so pleasant. **1659** HOWELL *Proverbs, Lett. Advice*, There must be Suet as well as Oatmeal to make a Pudding. **1712** ADDISON *Spect.* No. 269 ¶8 He had sent a string of Hogs-puddings..to every poor Family in the Parish. **17..** '*Get up & bar the door*' vii, in Herd (1776), And first they ate the white puddings, And then they ate the black. *a* **1801** R. GALL *Elegy Pudding Lizzie* vii, The puddings, bairns, are just in season—They're newly made. **1819** *Sporting Mag.* V. 32 In Suffolk, black puddings made in guts are called links.

†**b.** A stuffing like the above, roasted within the body of the animal. *Obs.*

1596 SHAKS. *1 Hen. IV*, II. iv. 498 That rosted Manning Tree Oxe with the Pudding in his Belly. **1771** E. LONG *Trial of Dog 'Porter'* in *Hone's Every-day Bk.* II. 203 His worship had him [a hare] roasted, with a pudding in his belly.

2. (Chiefly *pl.*) The bowels, entrails, guts. Now *dial.* and *Sc.* [So OF. *bodeyn*, bowel, 14th c. in Godef.]

1444 *Coventry Leet Bk.* 208 Quod nullus deinceps lavet lez poodynges ad le condites sub consimili pena. **1530** LYNDESAY *Test. Papyngo* 1157 Tak thare, said he, the puddyngis, for thy parte. **1573** L. LLOYD *Marrow of Hist.* (1653) 245 The Fox..did bite and scratch the young man so sore, that his puddings gushed out of his side. **1597** LOWE *Chirurg.* (1634) 107 They [windy tumours] are sometimes in the..capacity betwixt the puddings and periton. **1796** PEGGE *Anonym.* (1809) 356 An antient monument in stone, of a Knight lying prostrate in armour, with what they call his puddings, or guts, twisted round his left arm, and hanging down to his belly. **1847** LE FANU *T. O'Brien* 255 Dar to touch me,—and I'll let the light into your puddens.

†**3. a.** ? Some kind of artificial light or firework. **b.** A kind of fuse for exploding a mine. (Cf. F. *boudin* and *saucisson* in Littré.) *Obs.*

1527 in Sharp *Cov. Myst.* (1825) 185 Payd to hym þat bayre þe podynges for bothe nyghts..vj d. **1549** *Ibid.*, Payd to þe boye þat bere þe podynges j d. **1691** *Treaty betw. Eng. & Denmark* in Magens *Insurances* (1755) II. 634 Under Contraband Goods are understood..Cannons, Muskets,..Granadoes, Puddings, Torches, Carriages for Ordnance.

4. *Naut.* **a.** A wreath of plaited cordage placed round the mast and yards of a ship as a support; a dolphin. **b.** A pad to prevent damage to the gunwale of a boat; a fender. **c.** The binding on rings, etc., to prevent the chafing of cables or hawsers. (So F. *boudin*.)

a **1625** *Nomencl. Navalis* (Harl. MS. 2301) lf. 59 b, *Puddings*, are Roapes nailde rounde to the Yarde-armes..close to the ende..to saue the Robbins from galling a sunder vpon yᵉ yards... Also the seruing of the Anchor with Roapes to saue the Clincke of the Cabill from galling against the Iron is called the Pudding of the Anchor. **1706** E. WARD *Wooden World Diss.* (1708) 80 Shew me the Gentleman, crys he, that can knot or splice, or make a Pudding as it should be. **1886** R. C. LESLIE *Sea-painter's Log* 149 The bow of such boats is protected by a large fixed fender, or 'pudding' of cocoa-nut-fibre rope.

5. *fig.* **a.** Applied to a stout thick-set person.

1789 E. BUTLER *Diary* 7 Oct. in G. H. Bell *Hamwood Papers* (1930) 231 A great fat pudding boy brought some. **1858** HAWTHORNE *Fr. & It. Note-Bks.* II. 31 What could possibly have stirred up this pudding of a woman? **1903** [see NON-SIGNIFICANT *a.*]. **1980** A. CORNELISEN *Flight from Torregreca* xi. 267 She is a sallow pudding of a child with a broad flat face.

b. *coarse slang.* The penis.

1719 T. D'URFEY *Wit & Mirth* III. 73, I made a request to prepare again, That I might continue in Love with the strain Of his Pudding. **1961**, **1970** [see PULL *v.* 20 i]. **1972** [see PUD *sb.*[2] 2].

c. *slang.* A fœtus; in phr. *a pudding in the oven* (and similar phrases), a child conceived but not yet born. Cf. BUN *sb.*[2] 1.

1937 PARTRIDGE *Dict. Slang* 665/1 *With a bellyful of marrow-pudding*,..pregnant. **1965** J. PORTER *Dover Two* vi. 75 'None of us ever suspected that she'd got a pudding in the oven.' 'She was going to have a baby?' asked Dover. **1966** 'L. LANE' *ABZ of Scouse* 112 *She's got a pudden in ther uvving*, she is pregnant.

II. 6. A preparation of food of a soft or moderately firm consistency, in which the ingredients, animal or vegetable, are either mingled in a farinaceous basis (chiefly of flour), or are enclosed in a farinaceous 'crust' (cf. DUMPLING), and cooked by boiling or steaming. Preparations of batter, milk and eggs, rice, sago, tapioca, and other farinaceous substances, suitably seasoned, and cooked by baking, are now also called puddings.

The earliest use (connecting this with 1) apparently implied the boiling of the composition in a bag or cloth (*pudding-bag* or *-cloth*), as is still often done; but the term has been extended to similar preparations otherwise boiled or steamed, and finally to things baked, so that its meaning and application are now rather indefinite.

a. with *a* and *pl.*, as an individual thing. Now usu. in British English, the sweet course following the main course of a meal, 'afters'.

1544 PHAER *Regim. Lyfe* (1545) 80 b, Take oyle of roses, crumes of bread, yolkes of egges, & cowes mylke, wyth a litle saffron, seeth them togyther a lytle as ye wolde make a pudding. **1589** RIDER *Bibl. Schol.* 1162 A pudding made of milke, cheese, and herbs, *moretum, herbosum moretum*. **1692** TRYON *Good House-w.* ix. 75 In Puddens it is usual to mix Flower, Eggs, Milk, Raisins or Currants, and sometimes both Spice, Suet, the Fat or Marrow of Flesh, and several other things. **1732** POPE *Ep. Bathurst* 346 One solid dish his week-day meal affords, An added pudding solemniz'd the Lord's. **1736–7** LD. CASTLEDURROW *Let. to Swift* 17 Jan., Your puddings..are the best sweet thing I ever eat. **1747** MRS. GLASSE *Cookery* vii. 70 In boiled Puddings, take great Care the Bag or Cloth be very clean... If you boil them in Wooden-bowls, or China-dishes, butter the Inside before you put in your Batter: And all baked Puddings, butter the Pan or Dish, before the Pudding is put in. **1755** JOHNSON, *Pudding*, a kind of food very variously compounded, but generally made of meal, milk, and eggs. **1851** *Rep. Juries Gt. Exhibition* (1852) 55 *United States.*—Maize-flour, commonly called..'corn-flour' in the U.S...is extensively used for puddings and other purposes in that country. **1909**, etc. [see AFTERS *sb. pl.*]. **1940** S. SPENDER *Backward Son* 12 At lunch there was fruit salad, his favourite pudding. **1954** *Good Housek. Cookery Bk.* (rev. ed.) II. 284 In this section will be found the recipes for suet and sponge puddings, and for some miscellaneous baked puddings. **1968** *New Society* 22 Aug. 266/2 Another course of a meal is called 'sweet' by the non-U... The U word for the course is pudding. **1974** E. AYRTON *Cookery of England* x. 430 Our grandfathers, even our fathers, expected a 'pudding' at least once a day, sometimes twice.

b. Without *a* or *pl.*, as name of the substance.

1670 EACHARD *Cont. Clergy* 87 Mr. Clerk's Lives of famous men,..such as Mr. Carter of Norwich, that used to eat such abundance of pudden. **1685** S. WESLEY *Maggots, Tobacco Pipe*, For that can best as you may quickly prove Settle the wit, as Pudding settles Love. **1716** POPE *Let. to Earl Burlington*, If you can dine upon a piece of beef, together with a slice of pudding. *a* **1721** PRIOR *Merry Andrew* 33 Mind neither good nor bad, nor right nor wrong, But eat your pudding, slave, and hold your tongue. **1876** G. MEREDITH *Beauch. Career* xviii, Our English pudding, a fortuitous concourse of all the sweets in the grocer's shop. *Mod.* Pudding is usually eaten after meat.

c. With defining word, expressing the essential ingredient, as ***apple-***, ***bread-***, ***fish-***, ***lemon-***, ***marrow-***, ***meat-***, ***milk-***, ***pease-***, ***plum-***, ***potato-***, ***rice-***, ***sago-***, ***steak-***, ***suet-pudding***, etc. Also ***Christmas pudding*** (CHRISTMAS 4), ***Sussex pudding***, ***Yorkshire pudding***. (See also these words.)

1616 [see MARROW *sb.*[1] 5]. **1711** [see PLUM PUDDING]. **1726** ARBUTHNOT *Diss. Dumpling* 6 The many sorts of Pudding he made, such as Plain Pudding, Plumb Pudding, Marrow Pudding, Oatmeal Pudding, Carrot Pudding, Saucesage Pudding, Bread Pudding, Flower Pudding, Suet Pudding. **1747** MRS. GLASSE *Cookery* vii. 68 Calf's-Foot Pudding. *Ibid.* 697 Stake-Pudding... Let your Stakes be..Beef or Mutton. **1769** MRS. RAFFALD *Eng. Housekpr.* (1778) 181 To make a Yorkshire Pudding to bake under Meat. **1825–9** MRS. SHERWOOD *Lady of Manor* IV. xxiv. 142 Their having a tansy pudding at Easter. **1862** MRS. H. WOOD *Mrs. Hallib.* II. iii, A delicious lemon pudding. **1883** *Harper's Mag.* Apr. 654/1 A Sussex pudding, or great boiled dumpling filled with meat instead of fruit.

d. Proverb. (See also PROOF *sb.* 4.)

1682 N. O. *Boileau's Lutrin* III. Argt. 23 The proof of th' Pudding's seen i' th' eating. **1790** WINDHAM *Speeches Parl.* 4 Mar. (1812) I. 189 Let us..apply to the British Constitution a homely adage,..—that 'the proof of the pudding is in the eating'. **1900** *Athenæum* 21 July 97/3 After all, the proof of a pudding is in the eating.

7. *fig.* **a.** Material reward or advantage: esp. in allit. antithesis to *praise*. (Without *a* or *pl.*)

1728 POPE *Dunc.* I. 54 Where, in nice balance, truth with gold she weighs, And solid pudding against empty praise. **1821** BYRON *Juan* III. lxxix, He turn'd, preferring pudding to *no* praise. **1843** CARLYLE *Past & Pr.* I. iv, Your own degree of worth or talent, is it..measurable by the conquest of praise or pudding it has brought you to?

b. *U.S. slang.* Something easy to accomplish.

1887 G. W. WALLING *Recoll. N.Y. Chief of Police* xix. 262 It was an 'inside' job from the start... In thieves' slang it was a 'pudding';..the vault, although apparently impregnable, was easy to enter, [etc.]. **1942** BERREY & VAN DEN BARK *Amer. Thes. Slang* §255/1 Something easy, ..*pudding*. **1974** *Guidelines to Volunteer Services* (N.Y. State Dept. Correctional Services) 42 *Puddin*, light action, easy.

8. *transf.* **a.** Anything of the consistency or appearance of a pudding (in sense 6).

1731 P. SHAW *Three Ess. Artif. Philos.* 61 Without the..danger of making what, in the Language of Distillers, is termed a Pudding. **1757** A. COOPER *Distiller* I. i. (1760) 5 Danger of coagulating the Malt, or what Distillers call, making a Pudding. **1902** CORNISH *Naturalist Thames* 92 The soaking rains have made a pudding, even of the pasture.

b. *spec.* (In recovering oil from waste suds.)

1884 W. S. B. McLAREN *Spinning* (ed. 2) 51 Tanks are prepared to receive the suds... The thicker portion at the bottom is..run into a filter-bed of sand and gravel, through which the..water gradually filters, leaving the solid and greasy matter behind. This is laid in cloths and called 'puddings', which are pressed in hydraulic or steam presses till all the oil is squeezed out.

c. *slang.* A pudding-shaped bomb.

1919 *Athenæum* 25 July 664/1 *Pudding, i.e.* our 60 lb. bomb.

9. *slang.* Poisoned or drugged liver, etc. used by burglars, dog-stealers, etc. to destroy dogs or render them insensible. (Cf. PUDDING *v.*[1], q. 1858.)

1887 HORSLEY *Jottings fr. Jail* i. 17 There was a great tyke lying in front of the door, so I pulled out a piece of pudding ..and threw it to him. **1891** *Daily News* 29 Jan. 7/1 He was found in possession of a dog collar and lead, a muzzle, and a quantity of prepared liver known as 'pudding'.

†**10.** = JACK-PUDDING. *Obs.*

c **1675** VILLIERS (Dk. Buckhm.) *Sat. Follies Age* Wks. (1752) 111 And play the pudding in a May-day farce. *a* **1680** BUTLER *Rem.* (1759) I. 163 No Pudding shall be suffer'd to be witty, Unless it be in order to raise Pity.

III. 11. *attrib.* and *Comb.* **a.** Of a pudding or puddings, as ***pudding course, -eater, -eating, -maker, -manufactory, -race*** (RACE *sb.*[2] 9); also ***pudding-like, pudding-shaped*** adjs. **b.** Used in the making or consumption of pudding, as ***pudding-book, -bowl, -cloth, -crock, -dish, fork, -mould, -pan, -plate, rice, -spoon, -stick.***

1865 *(title)* Massey and Son's Comprehensive *Pudding Book, containing above one thousand Recipes. *a* **1584** *Tom Thumbe* 89 in Hazl. *E.P.P.* II. 181 He sate vpon the *Pudding-Boule, the candle for to hold. **1895** KIPLING *2nd Jungle Bk.* (ed. Tauchn.) 177 Bylot's Island stands above the ice like a pudding-bowl wrong side up. **1845** E. ACTON *Mod. Cookery* xii. 255 The bird..wrapped in a thin *pudding-cloth, closely tied at both ends. **1868** M. JEWRY *Warne's Model Cookery* 482 A pudding-cloth must be kept very clean. **1971** *Country Life* 17 June 1537/2 He tried to do it with oddments of coloured knitting wools on a pudding cloth. **1948** 'J. TEY' *Franchise Affair* iv. 40 The gentle monologue went on, all through the *pudding course. **1495** *Will of Geffereys* (Somerset Ho.), *Podding crokke. **1829** LONGF. in *Life* (1891) I. 163 The Devil, dressed like a collier, with smutty face and *pudding-dish hat. **1726** ARBUTHNOT *Diss. Dumpling* 23 Let not Englishmen therefore be asham'd of the Name of *Pudding-Eaters. *Ibid.* 6 In the Esteem of this *Pudding-eating Monarch. **1896** *Woman's Life* 15 Aug. 368/1 If the *pudding-spoon and fork are grasped from beneath instead of from above, the awkward uplifting of the elbows will be avoided. **1914** JOYCE *Dubliners* 255 Freddy Malins beat time with his pudding-fork. **1540** PALSGR. *Acolastus* L iij, The pulters, cokes, *puddyng makers. **1726** ARBUTHNOT *Diss. Dumpling* 5 This John Brand, or Jack Pudding,..his Fame had reached France, whose King would have given the World to have had our Jack for his Pudding-Maker. **1874** LISLE CARR *Jud. Gwynne* I. iv. 116 If not in the way of your *pudding manufactory. **1904** *Daily Chron.* 19 July 8/5 Lining a *pudding-mould with thin slices of bread and butter. **1662** R. MATHEW *Unl. Alch.* §116. 190 In an old *pudding pan, or a frying-pan, keep them always stirring. **1844** DICKENS *Mart. Chuz.* ix, The *pudding-plates had been washed in a little tub. **1787** BURNS *To a Haggis* 2 Fair fa' your honest sonsie face, Great chieftain o' the *puddin-race! **1974** *Times* 10 Jan. 10/1 Long grain and short or round grain, often called '*pudding' rice. **1895** W. ROBINSON *Eng. Flower Garden* (ed. 4) v. 75 A great many delightful plants..in many cases are jammed into *pudding-shaped masses void of form or grace. **1976** *S. Wales Echo* 23 Nov., A pudding-shaped mound in Energlyn near Caerphilly. **1896** Pudding-spoon [see *pudding fork* above]. **1944** A. THIRKELL *Headmistress* iv. 73 Giving a final polish to the pudding spoons with a piece of washleather. **1973** J. WAINWRIGHT *Touch of Malice* 93 Harris..handled the gear-lever like a pudding-spoon. **17..** E. SMITH *Compl. Housew.* (1750) 183 Mix it with a broad *puddingstick; not with your hands. **1852** MRS. STOWE *Uncle Tom's Cabin* I. xviii. 298 Interrupting her meditations to give..a rap on the head to some of the young operators with the pudding-stick that lay by her side. **1878** B. F. TAYLOR *Between Gates* 109 You can get an idea of it by fancying a paddle or a pudding-stick turning into a fiddle.

c. Special Combs.: †**pudding-ale**, cheap ale, probably 'from its being thick like pudding' (Skeat); **pudding-ball** *Austral.* [ad. Aboriginal word], an edible marine fish resembling a mullet, perhaps the sea mullet, *Mugil cephalus*; **pudding basin**, a basin in which puddings are made; *transf.*, applied to a round hat, helmet, or hair-style; also *attrib.*; **pudding bree, broo,** *Sc.*, the water in which puddings (sense 1) have been boiled; **pudding-cake**: see quot.; †**pudding-cart**, an offal or refuse cart (cf. sense 2); **pudding chain** *Naut.* (see quot.); **pudding class** = next; **pudding club**: see CLUB *sb.* 14 c; **pudding-face**, a large fat face; hence **pudding-faced** *a.*; **pudding fender** = sense 4 b; †**pudding-filler** (from sense 2), one who lives to eat, a glutton; **pudding-fish**, = PUDDING-WIFE 2 (Hamilton *Dict. Terms* 1825); †**pudding-gut**, the entrail or skin used in making puddings (sense 1); **pudding-head**, a stupid person; hence **pudding-headed** *a.*; **pudding-heart**, soft-heart, coward; †**pudding-house**, (*a*) the stomach or belly (*vulgar*); (*b*) an offal house; **pudding-meat**, the meat stuffing for a pudding (sense 1); †**pudding-pack**, = *pudding-tobacco* below; **pudding-pipe**, the pod of an Indian tree, *Cassia fistula*, hence called ***pudding-pipe tree***; †**pudding-pit**, ? a pit into which offal is thrown; **pudding-poke**, the long-tailed tit, *Aegithalos caudatus*; **pudding-sleeve**, a large bulging sleeve drawn in at the wrist or above; also *attrib.*; hence **pudding-sleeved** *a.*; †**pudding-tobacco**, compressed tobacco, made in rolls resembling a pudding or sausage [cf. F. *boudin de tabac*]; **pudding-turnip**, a variety of turnip; **pudding way** = *pudding club* above; †**pudding-wright**, one who makes puddings. Also PUDDING-BAG, -GRASS, -PIE, etc.

1377 LANGL. *P. Pl.* B. v. 220 Peny ale and *podyng ale she poured togideres For laboreres and for low folke. **1847** J. D. LANG *Cooksland* iv. 96 The species of fish that are commonest in the Bay [*sc.* Moreton Bay] are mullet, bream, puddinba (a native word corrupted by the colonists into *pudding-ball)... The puddinba is like a mullet in shape, but larger, and very fat; it is esteemed a great delicacy. **1896** *Australasian* 28 Aug. 407/4 'Pudding-ball' is the name for a fish. **1945** BAKER *Austral. Lang.* xii. 214 Popular fish-names peculiar to the Australian include..puddingball, corrupted by the law of Hobson-Jobson from the aboriginal puddinba. **1861** MRS. BEETON *Bk. Househ. Managem.* xxvi. 611 *(caption)* *Pudding-basin. **1909** *Westm. Gaz.* 3 June 8/3 A grey straw hat of the inverted pudding-basin type. **1925** FRASER & GIBBONS *Soldier & Sailor Words* 231 *Pudding basin*, the British steel shrapnel helmet. (From its shape.) **1951** A. BARON *Rosie Hogarth* I. ii. 19 Each boy's hair close-cropped with a pudding-basin fringe. **1974** *Country Life* 28 Feb. 456/3 A male customer is looking for..shooting and fishing hats, saucy tweed pudding basins and tweed caps. **1977** B. PYM *Quartet in Autumn* i. 1 Now he..had adopted a medieval or pudding-basin style, rather like the American crew-cut of the forties and fifties. **17..** '*Get up & bar the Door*' ix. in Herd (1776) II. 160 What ails ye at the *pudding-broo, That boils into the pan? *Ibid.* x, Will ye kiss my wife before my een, And scald me wi' pudding bree? **1875** *Sussex Gloss.*, **Pudding-cake*, a composition of flour and water boiled; differing from a hard dick in shape only, being flat instead of round. **1562** in Strype *Stow's Surv.* (1754) II. v. xxi. 411/1 The *Pudding-Cart of the Shambles shall not go afore the Hour of Nine in the Night, or after the Hour of Five in the Morning. **1948** R. DE KERCHOVE *Internat. Maritime Dict.* 561/2 **Pudding chain*, short link chain occasionally used for running rigging. It runs well over sheaves and is easy to belay. It is used for jib halyards and sheets in small trading vessels, but has lately been generally replaced by flexible wire. **1969** E. GÉBLER *Shall I eat you Now?* 88 Girl soon comes..to announce she has a bun in the oven. I'm in the *pudding class. **1890** BARRÈRE & LELAND *Dict. Slang* II. 155/1 **Pudding club* (popular), a woman in the family way is said to be in the *pudding club.* **1978** L. DAVIDSON *Chelsea Murders* v. 28 'Was she in the pudding club?'..'Probably. They aren't saying.' **1748** RICHARDSON *Clarissa* (1811) IV. xlv. 297 Let me see what a mixture of grief and surprize may be beat up together in thy *puden-face. **1784** J. BARRY in *Lect. Paint* ii. (1848) 94 The hatchet or the pudding face. **1916** 'TAFFRAIL' *Pincher Martin* vii. 116 Orl right, old puddin'-face. Keep yer 'air on! **1950** G. BRENAN *Face of Spain* iv. 84 The Englishman, fresh from the dull hurry of London streets and from their sea of pudding faces. **1847** L. HUNT *Men, Women, & B.* I. ii. 23 Four boys going to school, very *pudding-faced. **1883** *Man. Seamanship for Boys' Training Ships R. Navy* (Admiralty) (1886) 186 *Pudding fenders are used in the Navy for large boats..and sometimes on lower yards, to take the chafe on the inside part of the quarter yard. **1961** F. H. BURGESS *Dict. Sailing* 164 *Pudding fender*, a fat enclosed bundle of old strands, etc., for use over the side of boats and yachts. **1500–20** DUNBAR *Poems* xiv. 69 Sic *pudding-fillaris, discending down from millaris, Within this land was nevir hard nor sene. **1598** FLORIO, *Scrizzótto*.., a reede that cookes vse to blow the *pudding guts before they fill them. **1851** H. MELVILLE *Moby Dick* III. xxii. 152 *Pudding-heads should never grant premises. **1893** 'MARK TWAIN' in *Century Mag.* Dec. 235/2 Perfect jackass—yes, and it ain't going too far to say he's a pudd'nhead. **1952** S. KAUFFMANN *Tightrope* xiv. 243 Why, you're not doing this at all badly, pudding head. **1978** P. G. WINSLOW *Coppergold* 153, I didn't tell Joss, no matter what that Yorkshire puddenhead thinks. **1726** ARBUTHNOT *Diss. Dumpling* 17 O wou'd..this little Attempt of Mine may stir up some *Pudding-headed Antiquary to dig his Way through all the mouldy Records of Antiquity. **1867** in Dickens *Lett., to Miss Hogarth* 16 Dec. (1893) 649 Surely it is time that the pudding-headed Dolby retired into the native gloom from which he has emerged. **1834** SIR H. TAYLOR *2nd Pt. Artevelde* III. i. 70 Go, *pudding-heart! Take thy huge offal and white liver hence. **1596** NASHE *Saffron Walden* P iv b, What a commotion there was in his entrayles or *pudding-house for want of food. **1609** ROWLANDS *Knaue of Clubbes* 24 His pudding-house at length began to swell. **1620** *Westward for Smelts* (Percy Soc.) 5 The pudding-house at Brooke's wharfe. **1777** BRAND *Pop. Antiq.* App. 355 A Kind of *Pudding-Meat, consisting of Blood, Suet, Groats, etc. *a* **1618** SYLVESTER *Tobacco Battered* 781 Impose so deep a Taxe On all these Ball, Leafe, Cane, and *Pudding-packs. **1597** GERARDE *Herbal* III. lxxvii. 1242 *Cassia fistula.* *Pudding Pipe tree... Cassia fistula..may also be Englished Pudding Pipe, because the cod or pipe is like a pudding. **1760** J. LEE *Introd. Bot.* App. 324 Pudding Pipe-tree, *Cassia.* **1866** *Treas. Bot.* 233. **1593** G. HARVEY *Pierce's Super.* 47 The person, that vnder his hand-writing hath stiled him..the bag-pudding of fooles, & the very *pudding-pittes of the wise, or honest. *a* **1825** FORBY *Voc. E. Anglia* 239 It [wren's-nest] is otherwise, and more descriptively at least, called a *pudding-poke's nest. **1848** *Zoologist* VI. 2186 The P[arus] caudatus is the 'pudding-poke'. **1708** SWIFT *Baucis & Philemon* 120 He sees..About each arm a *pudding-sleeve. **1720** HEARNE *Collect.* (O.H.S.) VII. 97 The Whiggs and the Enemies of the Universities, who all go in Pudding-sleeve Gowns. **1910** 'MEMBER OF ARISTOCRACY' *Manners & Rules of Good Society* xi. 85 Archbishops, bishops, and clergy should appear in full canonicals, that is black silk full- or *pudding-sleeve gowns, cassock and sash bands. **1939** M. B. PICKEN *Lang. Fashion* 136/3 *Pudding sleeve*,..full sleeve held in at wrist, or above. **1960** C. W. CUNNINGTON et al. *Dict. Eng. Costume* 172/1 *Pudding sleeve*,..a large loose sleeve, especially of a clergy-man's gown. **1599** B. JONSON *Cynthia's Rev.* II. i, He..never..prayes but for a pipe of *pudding tabacco. **1963** 'J. PRESCOT' *Case for Hearing* vi. 94 Getting a girl in the *pudding way isn't a crime. **1598** R. BERNARD tr. *Terence's Eunuch* II. ii, Cookes, *pudding-wrights.

Hence (*nonce-wds.*) **'puddingish** *a.*, of the nature of a pudding; **'puddingize** *v. trans.*, to make a pudding of; **'puddingless** *a.*, without pudding.

1866 R. BUCHANAN in *Academy* 15 June (1901) 506/1 Right stately sat Arnold..With *puddingish England serenely disgusted. **1726** ARBUTHNOT *Diss. Dumpling* 20 Physick is only a *Puddingizing or Cookery of Drugs. **1855** *Househ. Words* XII. 168 We went *puddingless that Christmas-day.

[*Note.* ME. *poding*, mod. *pudding*, and F. †*bodin, boudin*, have so many points in common that, but for the difficulties of form, they would at once be identified as the same word. They both appear first in the 13th century, had at first exactly the same sense (still retained in Sc.), and agree to a great extent in their transferred uses. Even the difference of form is not insuperable; *p* for Fr. or L. *b* occurs also in *purse*, L. *bursa*, F. *bourse*, and the existence of Eng. words in *pud-* (see below) might by a species of folk-etymology facilitate the substitution here; final *-in* might be identified with Eng. *-ing*; the interchange of *-ing* and *-in* is actually seen in the later *puddin, pudden.* The identity of the words, though highly probable, cannot however be held to be proved, and the matter is rendered more uncertain by the absence of any certain derivation of the Fr. Word. In the same sense, It. has or had *boldone* (Florio), and L. *botulus*; the former appears to be closely akin to F. *boudin*; with the latter connexion is more difficult, though to its stem *bot-* some would refer *boudin* and *bouder* to pout the lips. Leaving the Fr. aside, the origin of the Eng. word has been sought in a stem **pud-* to swell, bulge, inferred from rare OE. *puduc*, 'struma', wen, Westphal. dial. *puddek* lump, pudding, LG. *pudde-wurst* black-pudding, *puddig* thick, stumpy (Brem. Wbch.); cf. also Eng. dial. *pod*, Sc. *pud* belly, *poud* boil, ulcer, and PODGE, PUDGE; but it is not at all certain that the notion of swelling enters into the original sense. Mod.F. *pouding* (1754) and *poudingue*, mod.Du. *podding*, mod.LG. *pudding, pudden, buddin*, Ger. *pudding*, Da. *budding*, Sw. *pudding*, are all from the Eng. word in its current sense; the Irish *putog* and Gael. *putag* (in this sense) are also from Eng.]

pudding ('pʊdɪŋ), *v.* Also (*dial.* and *vulgar*) **pudden.** [f. prec. sb.]

1. *trans.* To supply or treat with pudding or a pudding-like substance.

? *a* **1600** I. T. *Grim, Collier Croydon* II. i, Now I talk of a Pudding,..I am old dog at it. Come Ione, let's away, I'le pudding you. **1858** LEWIS in Youatt *Dog* (N.Y.) v. 175 Thieves..are said to have a method of quieting the fiercest watch-dogs by throwing them a narcotic ball, which they call 'puddening the animal'. [See PUDDING *sb.* 9.] **1882** FREEMAN in Stephens *Life & Lett.* (1895) II. 264 So Mrs. Macmillan and her doctor..bathed me and dosed me and puddinged [*i.e.* poulticed] me behind and before.

2. *Naut.* To wrap with tow as a protection against chafing. See PUDDING *sb.* 4.

1711 W. SUTHERLAND *Shipbuild. Assist.* 162 To Pudden the Yards, to nail Pieces of old Rope round them, to preserve them from galling. **1833** MARRYAT *P. Simple* xiv, He was afraid to pudding an anchor on the fore-castle. **1886** R. C. LESLIE *Sea Painter's Log* 142 'Puddening the anchors',..or 'clapping a service on the cable'.

Hence **puddening** ('pʊd(ə)nɪŋ) *vbl. sb.*, *Naut.* etc.: see quots. and cf. PUDDING *sb.* 4.

1769 FALCONER *Dict. Marine* (1776) s.v. *Anchor*, The ring is..covered with a number of pieces of short rope,..called the puddening, and used to preserve the cable from being.. chafed by the iron. *Ibid.*, *Puddening*,..a thick wreath, or circle of cordage, tapering from the middle towards the ends, and fastened about the main-mast and fore-mast of a ship, to prevent their yards from falling down, when the ropes by which they are usually suspended are shot away in battle. **1866** W. HENDERSON *Folk Lore N. Counties* 12 Much importance attaches to the baby's first visit to another house, on which occasion it is expected that he should receive three things—an egg, salt and white bread or cake. Near Leeds this ceremony is called *Puddening.*

'pudding-bag. A bag in which a pudding is boiled. Also *transf.* and *fig.* Cf. *pudding-poke.*

c **1597** T. DELONEY *Jack of Newberie* (1619) iv. sig. G 3, The other maide..with the perfume in the pudding-bagge, flapt him about the face. **1626** in NARES (Halliw.), [A piece of Sail-cloth] about half a yard long, of the breadth of a pudding-bag. **1713** STEELE *Englishman* No. 40. 262 From the purple Bishop and his horned Mitre to the bare-legged Capuchin with his picked Pudding-bag. **1795** WOLCOTT (P. Pindar) *Pindariana* Wks. 1812 IV. 207 Turning, like Pudding-bags Men inside out. **1858** G. MEREDITH *Let.* 4 Jan. (1970) I. 32 It is a pudding-bag..a quiescent receptacle for Roast Beef, Punch, and mince Pies. **1881** DUFFIELD *Don Quix.* II. 538 The house of this lady is in a pudding-bag without any opening at the bottom. **1885** SWAINSON *Prov. Names Birds* 32 The penduline form of the nest [has] obtained for the bird [British Long-Tailed Titmouse] the names of..Poke pudding or Poke bag... Pudding bag (Norfolk). **1929** F. BOWEN *Sea Slang* 107 *Pudding bag*, a stocking pennant used as a vane. **1939** F. THOMPSON *Lark Rise* 238 They..yelled: Old Hardwick skags! Come..to pick up rags To mend their mothers' pudding-bags. **1943** W. W. GILL in *N. & Q.* 9 Oct. 232/1 *Pudding-bag*, blind alley. **1961** F. H. BURGESS *Dict. Sailing* 164 *Pudding bag*, a stocking or sleeve, used as a weather vane.

†**'pudding-grass.** *Obs.* exc. *Hist.* Pennyroyal, *Mentha pulegium.*

1538 TURNER *Libellus, Origanum*..est herba quam uulgus appellat Peny ryall, aut puddynge gyrse. **1562** —— *Herbal* II. 106 b, Puddyng grasse. **1629** PARKINSON *Paradisus* 477 Pennyroyall..vsed to be put into puddings,..and therefore in diuers places they know it by no other name then Pudding-grasse. **1760** J. LEE *Introd. Bot.* App. 324 Pudding-grass, *Mentha.* **1904** G. G. NILES *Bog-trotting for Orchids* x. 132 The Wild Pennyroyal of the ancients..was known in England, during 1500, as Podding-Grasse or Pudding-Grass. **1972** Y. LOVELOCK *Veg. Bk.* III. 336 It [*sc.* pennyroyal] was especially popular as a meat-stuffing, and was thus known as pudding grass or herb.

pudding-pie. A name for various forms of pastry; *esp.* a dough pudding containing meat, baked in a dish; a tart made with pie-crust and custard: see quot. 1829.

1593 *Bacchus Bountie* in *Harl. Misc.* (Malh.) II. 272 He brought with him a pudding pie, pretilie powdered with such hot spices as his countrie..doth afforde. **1632** MASSINGER *City Madam* IV. iv, Exchange wenches Coming from eating pudding-pies on a Sunday At Pimlico or Islington. **1663** BUTLER *Hud.* I. ii. 547 Some cry'd the Covenant instead Of Pudding-pies and Ginger-bread. *a* **1825** FORBY *Voc. E. Anglia, Pudding-pie*, a piece of meat plunged in batter and baked in a deep dish, thus partaking of the nature of both pudding and pie,..a 'toad in a hole'. **1829** HONE *Year-bk.* 361 The pudding-pies are from the size of a tea-cup to that of a small tea-saucer. They are flat.. made with a raised crust, to hold a small quantity of custard, with currants slightly sprinkled on the surface. *c* **1900** *Beeton's Every-day Cook. Bk.* 402/2 Folkestone Pudding-Pies.

b. *attrib.*, as ***pudding-pie man, woman.***

c **1680** *Roxb. Ball.* (1890) VII. 77 At every Corner, and in every street, This Pudding-pye-Woman be sure you oft shall meet. **1705** HEARNE *Collect.* 6 Dec. (O.H.S.) I. 117 A Pudding Pye man with whose Puddings..the first Founders of the Society were..pleas'd.

† **'pudding-prick.** *Obs.* A slender wooden skewer (see PRICK *sb.* 14) with which the ends of a gut containing a pudding were fastened. Often in similative phrase: see quots. 1562, 1611.

a **1518** SKELTON *Magnyf.* 2122 As hucksters they hucke and they stycke, And pynche at the payment of a poddynge prycke. *a* **1533** FRITH *Answ. More* (1548) I vj, Hys proue shall not be worth a podynge prycke. **1562** J. HEYWOOD *Epigr.* VI. xix, A pooddyng pricke is one, a mylpost is an other. **1611** COTGR. s.v. *Arbre*, (We say of one that hath squandered away great wealth) hee hath thwitten a mill-post to a pudding pricke.

'pudding-stone. A composite rock consisting of a mass of rounded pebbles cemented together by a siliceous matrix; conglomerate.

1753 CHAMBERS *Cycl. Suppl.* s.v. *Oculatus lapis*, What we call the pudding stone, a stone formed of a great number of pebbles, of a small size, immersed, and formerly bedded, in a flinty cement, little less hard than the stones themselves, [or] not at all so. **1774** STRANGE in *Phil. Trans.* LXV. 40 Confusedly concreted together, like a pudding stone. **1839** *Civil Eng. & Arch. Jrnl.* II. 434/1 Pudding stones differ from breccias, by being composed of rounded fragments, either of marble or hard stones.

b. *attrib.*, as ***pudding-stone marble, rock, stratum.***

1806 *Gazetteer Scotl.* (ed. 2) 295 The pudding-stone rocks near the village of Oban. **1839** URE *Dict. Arts* 799 Puddingstone marbles; a conglomerate of rounded pieces. **1894** MRS. DYAN *All in a Man's K.* (1899) 55 A mere rift between the great puddingstone rocks.

† **'pudding-time.** *Obs.* The time when pudding or puddings are to be had; hence *fig.*, a time when one is in luck; a favourable or useful time.

1546 J. HEYWOOD *Prov.* II. ix. (1867) 80 This geare comth euen in puddyng time rightlie. **1667** DRYDEN & DK. NEWCASTLE *Sir M. Mar-all* IV, Here he comes in pudding-time to resolve the question. **1716** ADDISON *Freeholder* No. 30 ¶4 The ordinary Salutation is, Sir, I am glad to see you, you are come in Pudding-time. *a* **1720** *Song, Vicar of Bray*, When George in pudding-time came o'er, And moderate men look'd big, sir. **1840** MARRYAT *Olla Podr., S.W. & by W. ¾ W.*, He came in pudding-time, and was invited to dinner.

'pudding-wife.

1. a. A woman who sells puddings or sausages. ? *Obs.* **b.** A professional or expert maker of puddings (sense 1: *Eng. Dial. Dict.*). Now *dial.*

1448 *Maldon, Essex, Court Rolls* Bundle 27 No. 1 b, Cristiana podyngwyf alias fisshwyf vendidit salmones fetidos in mercato. **15..** in Dugdale *Monast. Angl.* (1817) I. 443/2 Sche shall pay for a gown to her grome coke and her poding wief by the yere ij*s*. *a* **1680** BUTLER *Rem.* (1759) I. 217 When Pudding-Wives were launcht in cockquean Stools; For falling foul on Oyster-women's Schools.

2. The Florida blue-fish (*Platyglossus radiatus*); also called ***pudding-fish.***

1734 MORTIMER *Carolina & Bahamas* in *Phil. Trans.* XXXVIII. 317 The Pudding-Wife. Round the Eye spread seven blue Rays. **1876** GOODE *Fishes Bermudas* 17 *Turdus oculo radiato* (the Pudding-Wife) is a young specimen of *Chœrojulis radiatus.*

puddingy ('pʊdɪŋɪ), *a.* [f. PUDDING *sb.* + -Y.] Having the appearance, shape, or consistency of a pudding; pudding-like.

1709 *Rambl. Fuddle-Cups* 7 The Spark, in his Puddingy Robes. **1825** *New Monthly Mag.* XIV. 441 A face ruddy, plump and puddingy. **1888** R. S. SURTEES *Hillingdon Hall* 91 A roll puddingy white neckcloth replaced the sea-green silk one. **1898** *Daily News* 11 Mar. 3/1 Some soft, puddingy figure, stuffed with sawdust, with something faintly resembling a human face upon the..head.

puddle ('pʌd(ə)l), *sb.* Forms: 4–5 podel, (4 -elle, 5–6 -ell), 5 poþel, pothel, 5–7 puddel, (6 -elle, -il, 6–7 -ell), 6 poddell, podle, 6 *Sc.* pwdyll, 6–7 pudle; 6- puddle. [ME. *podel, puddel*, app. dim. from OE. *pudd* ditch, furrow (*puddas* 'sulcos' in Prudentius Gloss; cf. dial. *pudge, pudgell*), = G. dial. *pudel, pfudel* a puddle. W. *pwdel* is from Eng. Cf. next, also PLUD.]

1. a. A small body of standing water, foul with mud, etc. or with a muddy bottom, now always shallow, as those left in depressions of the ground in a road or footpath after rain; a small dirty pool. †Formerly in wider sense, including larger collections of water, as a pond, or a pit full or water, or even an extensive slough or swamp (quot. 1596).

c **1330** R. BRUNNE *Chron.* (1810) 54 He did Harald body do drawe vp also tite, & þorgh þe podels it drouh, þat foule were & deppest. *a* **1400** *Cath. Epist.* (MS. Douce 250) 2 *Pet.* ii. 22 (Paues 220) þe sowe þat wascheþ hyre in þe podel wiþ mukke al fyled. *c* **1440** *Promp. Parv.* 411/2 Poþel, slothe, or podel (*H.* pothel), *lacuna.* **1491** CAXTON *Vitas Patr.* (W. de W. 1495) I. clxiv. 173/1 A sowe dooth laye herself in a fowle puddel. *c* **1534** NISBET *N. Test. in Scots, Prol. Rom.* (S.T.S.) III. 347 That thou sulde returnne (as anne swynne) vnto thinne auld pwdyll agaynne. *a* **1548** HALL *Chron., Rich. III* 40 His younger sonne in a smal puddel was strangled & drouned. **1555** EDEN *Decades* 122 The vyllage it selfe, is in a maryshe, and in maner a standynge puddle. **1552** HULOET, Podle, or slowe. **1593** SHAKS. *Lucr.* 657 Thy sea within a puddels wombe is hersed, And not the puddle in thy sea dispersed. **1596** E. BARTON in Purchas *Pilgrims* (1625) II. VIII. x. 1359 They being intrenched..neere to a long puddle or moorish ground, of some foure miles long, in breadth some seuen or eight Rods. *a* **1632** G. HERBERT *Jacula Prudentum* Wks. (Rtldg.) 308 Every path hath a puddle. *a* **1660** *Contemp. Hist. Irel.* (Ir. Archæol. Soc.) II. 128 Preferringe the pudle before the pearle. **1742** H. BAKER *Microsc.* II. v. 90 Every Puddle can..present us with living Wonders. **1878** HUXLEY *Physiogr.* 136 A way-side puddle which receives the muddy drainage of the road.

b. *transf.* A small pool of any liquid (see also quot. 1726). Also (*colloq.*), a pool of evacuated urine; usu. in phr. ***to make a puddle***, with reference to a young child or pet animal (cf. ACCIDENT *sb.* 1 d).

1726 LEONI *Alberti's Archit.* I. 5/1 The Air for want of Motion will grow thick and muddy; such a Valley may..be call'd a Puddle, or Bog of Air. **1883** W. M. WILLIAMS in *Knowledge* 20 July 35/2 Pale slices of meat spread out in a little puddle of pale, watery liquid. **1968** J. LLOYD *Death at Roman Farm* i. 10 Are you sure she hasn't made a puddle? **1972** J. WILSON *Hide & Seek* vi. 107 Can I have a mop to wipe up Mary's puddle? **1977** M. UNDERWOOD *Murder with Malice* iii. 37 Why are you looking at me as if I'd just made a puddle on the floor?

c. Applied *fig.* and humorously to the sea, esp. the Atlantic Ocean; usu. in phr. ***this*** (etc.) ***side of the puddle.*** Cf. POND *sb.* 2.

1889 *Ally Sloper's Half Holiday* 6 July 214/2 There seems to be no end to the chaff which the downy dandies across the puddle have to bear. **1902** FARMER & HENLEY *Slang* V. 312 *The Puddle*,..the Atlantic Ocean... In Cornwall, the English Channel. **1978** *SLR Camera* Aug. 21/1 For many years the American company..have made fine enlarging frames (masking frames this side of the puddle) both for retail distribution and for exclusive use by Simmon-Emega.

d. *Rowing.* The circular, rippled, disturbance left in the water after the blade of an oar has been lifted from it at the end of a stroke.

1934 *Times* 17 Mar. 14/1 Holdsworth is rowing better than he has ever done before at No. 2. His puddle is worthy of a man a stone heavier. **1955** R. BANNISTER *First Four Minutes* iii. 39, I could see my oars were making some splendid 'puddles'.

e. A small pool of molten metal, esp. that formed during welding; a piece of metal solidified from a pool.

1935 C. G. BAINBRIDGE in *Symp. Welding Iron & Steel* (Iron & Steel Inst.) II. 14 A large rod melts slowly and cools the molten puddle, causing rapid solidification. **1942** J. A. MOYER *Welding* v. 43 As the torch flame moves away, the molten metal in the puddle solidifies and joins the two plates into one solid piece. **1958** *Man* LVIII. 64/1 The first flat celts were hammered out of natural copper, and then out of rough casts or puddles of it or of poor bronze, smooth on the lower side, rough and scabbed on the open side. **1975** BRAM & DOWNS *Manuf. Technol.* ii. 47 While one hand manipulates the torch to carry a puddle across the plate, the other adds the correct amount of filler rod.

2. a. *fig.* or in figurative allusion, esp. with reference to moral defilement, or to false doctrine, etc. regarded as polluting: cf. *sink.*

1533 MORE *Apol.* v. Wks. 854/2 The preacher stumbleth at the same stocke, and falleth into the same puddell that Tyndall didde. **1548** UDALL, etc. *Erasm. Par. Matt.* iii. 30 The puddle and synke of al myschiefe. **1695** LD. PRESTON *Boeth.* IV. 170 Dost thou see then in what a Puddle of Filth Impiety doth wallow. **1787** J. HOWIE *Plain Reasons for Dissent.* 179 Swimming down the impure puddle of Erastianism. **1865** CARLYLE *Fredk. Gt.* XX. vi. (1872) IX. 119 He stalks loftily through this puddle of a world, on terms of his own.

b. *fig.* A confused collection or heap; a state of confusion or embarrassment; a muddle, mess. Now only *colloq.* or *dial.*

1587 GOLDING *De Mornay* ix. (1592) 135 Seeing that in the middes of that Puddle of humors ech liuing wight hath a Soule dwelling. **1608** DEKKER *2nd Pt. Honest Wh.* Wks. 1873 II. 136, I am neuer out of one puddle or another. **1805** W. TAYLOR in *Monthly Mag.* XX. 123 This thoughtless jumble of terms, this confused puddle of phrases. **1871** CARLYLE in *Mrs. Carlyle's Lett.* (1883) II. 157 This drawing-room..without her would have been a puddle of wasteful failure.

3. Foul or muddy water such as is found in puddles (= *puddle water* in 6 a). Chiefly *fig.* or in figurative allusion: cf. 2. Now only *dial.*

1555 W. WATREMAN *Fardle Facions* II. iv. 137, I rather fansie..to folowe the founteines of the first Authours, then the brokes of abredgers, which often bring with them much puddle. **1597** A. M. tr. *Guillemeau's Fr. Chirurg.* 53 b/1 His drinck, foule and impure puddle, yea, & stinckinge water. **1681** CROWNE *Hen. VI*, IV. 64 Hard roots my only food, Foul puddle all my drink. **1791** BURKE *App. Whigs* Wks. VI. 96 When that monster was obliged to fly with his wife Sporus, and to drink puddle. **1835** LYTTON *Rienzi* VII. ii, One..of a great house; the least drop of whose blood was worth an ocean of plebeian puddle.

4. A preparation of clay, or of clay and sand, mixed with water and tempered, used as a water-tight covering for embankments, lining for canals, etc. Also called *puddling.*

1795 J. PHILLIPS *Hist. Inland Navig.* 365 *Puddle*, an article of great use in completing canals where the soil is leaky, or unfavourable for holding the water. **1838** SIMMS *Public Wks. Gt. Brit.* 29 Water..must be excluded..by a lining of puddle. **1861** SMILES *Engineers* I. 353 *note*, Puddle is formed by a mixture of well-tempered clay and sand reduced to a semi-fluid state, and rendered impervious to water by manual labour, as by working and chopping it about with spades.

attrib. **1839** *Civil Eng. & Arch. Jrnl.* II. 21/2 They are formed..with an upright 'puddle wall' in the centre. *Ibid.* 109/2 The want of a puddle lining. **1872** *Daily News* 13 July, The offices of the contractors..as well as the puddle waggons and working plant, were washed away.

5. *dial.* A muddler: a bungler.

[Eng. Dial. Dict. has 'One who is slow, dirty, inefficient, or unmethodical at work, a bungler, a muddler'.]

1782 MISS BURNEY *Cecilia* VII. v, I remember when I was quite a boy hearing her called a limping old puddle. **1835** CARLYLE *Jrnl.* 1 Jan. in Froude *C.'s Life in London* I. 18 A foot which a puddle of a maid scalded three weeks ago.

6. *attrib.* and *Comb.* (See also sense 4 and PUDDLE *v.* 7) **a.** *attrib.* or as *adj.* (in sense 1 or 3): Such as is found in puddles; dirty, muddy, thick, polluted: said esp. of water.

c **1380** WYCLIF *Serm.* Sel. Wks. II. 335 þei grutchiden aȝens þis water, and drunken podel water of þe canel. **1579–80** NORTH *Plutarch* (1676) 760 To see Antonius..so easily to drinke puddle water, and to eat wild Fruits and Roots. **1619** R. HARRIS *Drunkard's Cup* 12 Hee knowes how of puddle ale, to make a cup of English wine. **1642** J. EATON *Honey-c. Free Justif.* 374 As if one, to put away one spot in his face, should wash himself in puddle mire. **1835** LYTTON *Rienzi* I. iii, I would fain let their puddle-blood flow an hour or two longer. **1851** BORROW *Lavengro* xciv, I would consent to drink puddle-water.

b. *Comb.* as ***puddle-hole; puddle-deep, -like*** adjs.; † **Puddle dock**, † **Puddle wharf**, names of a place on the Thames at Blackfriars (see quots. 1598, 1720); **puddle-duck**, the domestic duck; **puddle-jumper** *U.S. slang*, a fast, highly-manœuvrable, means of transport (see quots.), esp. a small light aeroplane; hence **puddle-jumping** *ppl. a.*; **puddle-poet**, a contemptuous designation.

a **1637** B. JONSON *Discov., Ingeniorum discrimina* 5 They write a verse as smooth, as soft as cream... They are cream-bowl, or but *puddle-deep. **1633** ROWLEY *Match at Midn.* IV, To surprize her,..pop her in at *Puddle-dock, and carry her to Gravesend in a paire of oares. **1648** JENKYN *Blind Guide* i. 8 He seems to dip his pen, or rather his pia mater, in puddle-dock. **1681** T. FLATMAN *Heraclitus Ridens* No. 4 (1713) I. 25 To Libel, Calumniate, and throw Puddle-dock Wit in the Face of Superiors. **1720** STRYPE *Stow's Surv.* I. III. 229 On the Banks of the River Thames, are the Wharfs of Puddle Dock, used for a Laystall for the Soil of the Streets; and much frequented by Barges and Lighters, for taking the same away. **1877** *Scribner's Monthly* Nov. 6/1 Presently we heard a shrilly feeble whistle, precisely such as the young *puddle-duck of the barn-yard makes in his earliest vocal efforts. **1908** B. POTTER *Tale of Jemima Puddle-duck* 9 Listen to the story of Jemima Puddle-duck, who was annoyed because the farmer's wife would not let her hatch her own eggs. **1975** J. GORES *Hammett* (1976) xix. 132 Puddle ducks..and mud hens..skittered away. **1610** *Manchester Court Leet Rec.* (1885) II. 252 A *puddle hoale which he or his familie doth vse [as] a privye. **1833** *Boston, Lincoln*, etc. *Herald* 16 Apr. 4/2 Jane Hays..found drowned in a puddle-hole used for washing potatoes. **1932** *Daily Progress* (Charlottesville, Va.) 10 Oct. 9 (*caption*) Even the bicycles that these sisters use..seem to be related as they resemble each other almost as much as the owners. They are twins... They were on the way to classes on their '*puddle jumpers' when they halted for this picture. **1941** *Sun* (Baltimore) 23 Aug. 8/8 Only two power-boat tests are slated on today's program..but the 'puddle-jumpers' will take over complete control tomorrow. **1944** *Newsweek* 2 Oct. 31/2 A 'puddle jumper' observation plane with bazookas fixed on the wings dove down and knocked out two of the tanks. **1944** A. M. TAYLOR *Lang. of World War II* 161 *Puddle jumper*,..a nickname for Jeep. **1961** 'A. A. FAIR' *Stop at Red Light* (1962) viii. 127, I had to take a puddle-jumper with stops in Chicago, Denver and Salt Lake City. **1971** M. TAK *Truck Talk* 123 *Puddle jumper*, a lightweight truck. **1978** *Detroit Free Press* 16 Apr. (Parade Suppl.) 3/3 Any one..can call his plane an air ambulance even if it's just a 'puddle-jumper' without medical equipment. **1941** *Sun* (Baltimore) 2 Aug. 7/1 They are hoping to receive soon a long-promised consignment of three '*puddle-jumping' Vultee 049 planes in which they will be able to hop up and down from even the smallest corn field. **1655** FULLER *Ch. Hist.* I. iii. §1 It seems the *puddle-poet did hope that the jingling of his rhymes would drown the sound of his false quantity. **1598** STOW *Surv.* 297 Then is there..*Puddle Wharfe, a water gate into the Thames, where horses vse to be watered, and therfore being filed with their trampeling, and made puddle like,..it is (as I suppose) called Puddle Wharf.

puddle ('pʌd(ə)l), *v.* Forms: see prec.; also 7 poodle. [f. PUDDLE *sb.*; cf. Du. *poedelen*, LG., G. *pud(d)eln* to dabble or splash in water, also G. *butteln, buddeln* to dabble or paddle in mud, etc. F. *puddler*, G. *puddeln*, etc. to puddle (iron) are from Eng.]

1. a. *intr.* To dabble or poke about, esp. in mud or shallow water; to wallow in mire; to wade through puddles; *fig.* to busy oneself in an untidy or disorderly way; to 'muddle' or 'mess' about.

c **1440** *Promp. Parv.* 411/2 Poþelon, or pothelyn, or grubbyn yn the erthe. **1616** SURFL. & MARKH. *Country Farme* 78 The drosse of the Riddle or Searce must be cast about the edges of the Pond: and also within the same, to cause them to be pudling in the myre. **1846** THACKERAY *Cornhill to Cairo* v, Children..are playing and puddling about in the dirt everywhere. **1866** *Routledge's Ev. Boy's Ann.* 421 The little creatures pass half their day puddling about in the water in all the beauty of nakedness.

fig. **1591** BRUCE *Serm.* vi. M viij, Tha multitude..haue..gone to mumchances, mumries, & vnknawin language, wherein they pudled of befoir. **1633** *Fife Witch Trial* in *Statist. Acc. Scotl.* (1796) XVIII. App. 654 Let honest men puddle and work as they like. **1639** R. JUNIUS *Sin Stigmat.* Pref. (T.), I were very simple, if..I should poodle in a wasp's nest, and think to purchase ease by it! **1680** BUNYAN *Mr. Badman* To Rdr. (1905) 7, I know 'tis ill pudling in the Cockatrices den. **1768–74** TUCKER *Lt. Nat.* (1834) I. 115 We may puddle about for ever without getting up a drop of ink to write with. **1858** CARLYLE *Fredk. Gt.* II. viii. (1872) I. 100 Then they puddled considerably..in the general broils of the Reich. **1864** *Ibid.* XVI. v. VI. 171 He puddles about, at a great rate.

b. *trans.* To bring or get into some specified state by 'puddling'; in quots. *refl.*

1759 *Compl. Lett.-writer* (ed. 6) 224 Mrs. Langford..puddled herself into a minuet. **1862** CARLYLE *Fredk. Gt.* XIV. viii. (1872) V. 255 Men enough did puddle themselves to death on the clay roads.

2. *trans.* To bemire; to wet with mud or dirty water.

1535 LYNDESAY *Satyre* 4296 I fell into ane midding..As I was pudlit thair, God wait Bot with my club I maid debait. **1855** THACKERAY *Newcomes* viii, Tablecloths puddled with melted ice.

3. a. To make (water) muddy or dirty. Also *fig.*

1593 G. HARVEY *Pierce's Super.* **ij b, The other..shall neuer puddle or annoy the course of the cleere running water. **1698** FRYER *Acc. E. India & P.* 273 It was immediately puddled with the Mud of Heresy. **1870** ROSSETTI *Jenny* xxi, So the life-blood of this rose, Puddled with shameful knowledge, flows.

b. To muddle, confuse; to sully the purity or clearness of.

1604 SHAKS. *Oth.* III. iv. 143 Something sure of State,..Hath pudled his cleare Spirit. **1650** H. MORE *Observ.* in *Enthus. Tri.*, etc. (1656) 81 His phansie is pudled so and jumbled in the Limbus or Huddle of the Matter. **1847** TENNYSON *Princ.* III. 130 Such extremes, I told her, well might harm The woman's cause. 'Not more than now', she said, 'So puddled as it is with favouritism'.

4. a. To reduce the surface of the ground, earth, clay, etc., into mud or puddle, by trampling and 'poaching' it when wet; hence, *spec.* to knead and temper a mixture of wet clay and sand so as to form a plastic mass impervious to water, used for various purposes. See PUDDLE *sb.* 4.

1762 [see PUDDLING *vbl. sb.* 2]. **1796** *Trans. Soc. Arts* XIV. 239 The soil dug over and puddled as a base. **1805** R. W. DICKSON *Pract. Agric.* I. 157 Rendering the surface completely puddled, to use a term employed in ground works, and thereby to retain water equally with any clay. **1837** *Civil Eng. & Arch. Jrnl.* I. 1/1 The soil is then puddled round them. **1861** MUSGRAVE *By-roads* 24 This layer had been levelled to receive a stratum of clay, a yard in thickness, and firmly puddled. **1880** MISS BIRD *Japan* I. 85 The rice crop.. needs to be 'puddled' three times, *i.e.* for all the people to turn into the slush, and grub out all the weeds and tangled aquatic plants, which weave themselves from tuft to tuft, and puddle up the mud afresh round the roots.

b. To cover or line with puddle; to render water-tight by the application of puddle.

1810 in Southey *Comm.-pl. Bk.* IV. 391/2 Mr. Tuke..bequeathed..To seven of the oldest navigators, one guinea for *puddling* him up in his grave. **1844** STEPHENS *Bk. Farm* I. 179 It will be necessary to puddle the seams of the rock on that side of the well in which it dips downwards. **1850** *Beck's Florist* 235 If there is a small bog contrived in a shady corner, by puddling the bottom of a basin of stones with some tenacious clay. **1897** BAILEY *Princ. Fruit-growing* 246 Puddling the roots [of trees]..to be shipped any distance..consists in sousing the roots in a thin mud or paste of clay.

5. *Iron Manuf.* To stir about and turn over (molten iron) in a reverberatory furnace, so as to expel the carbon and convert it into malleable iron.

1798 [see PUDDLING *vbl. sb.* 3 b]. **1839** URE *Dict. Arts* 702 The fine metal obtained by the coke is puddled by a continuous operation, which calls for much care and skill. **1866** ROGERS *Agric. & Prices* I. xv. 253 This iron was..puddled in some rude fashion into blooms or masses weighing about a hundred.

6. *Gold-* and *Opal-mining.* To work (clayey or sticky wash-dirt) with water in a tub so as to separate the ore.

1853 E. CLACY *Lady's Visit Gold Diggings Austral.* vii. 114 This soil, from being so stiff, would require 'puddling', a work of which he did not seem to relish the anticipation. **1859** [see PUDDLING *vbl. sb.* 4]. **1864** ROGERS *New Rush* II. 26 There, in a row, the tub and cradle stands, The owner puddling with unchartered hands. **1869** *Routledge's Ev. Boy's Ann.* 597 These buckets were hoisted up..and their contents emptied into a big tub, where they were puddled. **1963** *Pix* 13 July 21 Machines are used to 'puddle' (separate and sieve) opal dirt. **1967** S. LLOYD *Lightning Ridge Bk.* (1968) i. 1 Opal dirt can be brought to the surface and examined or puddled.

7. *Comb.* (from sense 5: perh. orig. PUDDLED 4, cf. PUDDLING *vbl. sb.* 3 b): **puddle-ball**, a rounded mass of iron formed in puddling; **puddle-bar**, a flat bar formed by passing a *puddle-ball* between *puddle-rolls*; **puddle-steel**, steel made by puddling. Also, **puddle-roll**: see quot. 1858; **puddle-train**, a train of *puddle-rolls*.

1840 *Civil Eng. & Arch. Jrnl.* III. 104/2 Improvements in rolling puddle balls or other masses of iron. **1858** SIMMONDS *Dict. Trade, Puddle-rolls*, a pair of large heavy rollers with grooved surfaces, between which [puddled] iron is passed, to be flattened into bars. **1861** FAIRBAIRN *Iron* 108 In this state it is called a puddle-bar. **1863** P. BARRY *Dockyard Econ.* 234 Turning out 600 tons of malleable iron and puddle steel weekly.

puddled (ˈpʌd(ə)ld), *ppl. a.* [f. prec. + -ED[1].]

1. Rendered muddy or turbid by stirring, as water in a puddle; dirty, miry, foul. Also *fig.* (formerly sometimes, Muddled, confused, puzzled).

1559 MORWYNG *Evonym.* 17 Fill a great pot with the puddled water. **1590** SHAKS. *Com. Err.* v. i. 173 Great pailes of puddled myre. **1651** H. MORE *Second Lash* in *Enthus. Tri.*, etc. (1656) 221 The reeks and fumes of thy puddled brain. **1822** HAZLITT *Table-t.* Ser. II. i. (1869) 5 Spouting out torrents of puddled politics from his mouth. **1839** J. ROGERS *Antipopopr.* II. iv. §2. 172 Better go to the..pure original spring..than drink from puddled streams.

2. Turned into or filled with puddles.

1840 DICKENS *Barn. Rudge* xvi, One..let the fragment of his torch fall hissing on the puddled ground. **1867** BAKER *Nile Tribut.* iii. 67 All were wet from paddling through the puddled ground.

3. Converted into PUDDLE (*sb.* 4); covered or lined with puddled clay so as to be water-tight.

1796 *Trans. Soc. Arts* XIV. 240 Earth in this puddled state becomes so dense as to resist the impression of water, which can by no means penetrate it. **1861** SMILES *Engineers* I. 353 The canal..is confined within a puddled channel to prevent leakage. **1871** *Daily News* 21 Sept., A very considerable quantity of the puddled clay..had been removed.

4. *Iron Manuf.* Purified from carbon and rendered malleable by stirring up and turning over in a reverberatory furnace: see prec. 5, 7.

1838 SIMMS *Public Wks. Gt. Brit.* 49 The puddled ball to be put under the shingling hammer and rolled into rough bars, by some called 'puddled bars'. **1861** FAIRBAIRN *Iron* 179 The production of puddled steel.

puddler (ˈpʌdlə(r)). [f. PUDDLE *v.* + -ER[1].] One who puddles: chiefly in technical senses.

1. a. A workman employed in puddling iron.

1831 J. HOLLAND *Manuf. Metal* I. 84 When in this semi-fluid state the puddler introduces an iron rod. **1894** BOWKER in *Harper's Mag.* Jan. 420 The flame may be made oxidising, neutral, or reducing, at the will of the puddler.

b. An implement or machine for puddling iron.

1875 KNIGHT *Dict. Mech.* s.v., Mechanical puddlers have assumed two forms. 1. The Mechanical Rabble... 2. The rotary puddling-furnace. **1894** BOWKER in *Harper's Mag.* Jan. 421 The so-called 'puddlers' invented by Mr. Samuel Danks of Cincinnati.

2. One who works clay, etc. into puddle, or who covers or lines something with puddle: see PUDDLE *v.* 4.

1884 C. G. W. LOCK *Workshop Receipts* Ser. III. 251/1 This is smoothed over with 'puddlers' mine' which is a soft hematite made into a paste with water. **1899** *Daily News* 7 June 9/1 The puddlers, who must reach the clay, have had to go down as far as 63ft.

3. a. One engaged in puddling for gold or opals: see PUDDLE *v.* 6.

1859 *Adelong Mining Jrnl.* 15 July 6/3 A rather unpleasant case occurred on Monday, at Little Bendigo, between an European, and some Chinese puddlers. **1860** *Mining Surveyor's Rep.* (Mining Dept., Victoria) Aug. 214 A valuable piece of ground which could be advantageously worked by the puddlers. **1883** KEIGHLEY *Who are You* 55 The puddlers' horses are all at rest. **1890** 'R. BOLDREWOOD' *Col. Reformer* (1891) 285 He was not a miner, a speculator, a reefer, nor an engine-driver, a clerk, or puddler. **1967** S. LLOYD *Lightning Ridge Bk.* (1968) xiv. 99 Puddlers have ruined the whole Lightning Ridge Field.

b. A puddling machine.

1967 A. KALOKERINOS *In Search of Opal* ii. 19 Modern miners remove the..'pay dirt', in bulk..and spin it in a machine that sifts the dirt out and leaves the nobbies behind. .. These machines are called 'puddlers' and their variety is almost endless. **1971** J. S. GUNN *Opal Terminol.* 37 There are two dams..at which miners rent sites..where they operate power-driven wet puddlers capable of handling several tons of dirt in one operation.

puddler, dial. var. PODLER (young coal-fish).

puddling (ˈpʌdlɪŋ), *vbl. sb.* [f. PUDDLE *v.* + -ING[1].] The action of the verb PUDDLE; also *concr.* (see 2). **1.** *gen.*: see the verb, sense 1.

1758 MRS. DELANY in *Life & Corr.* (1861) III. 516 We are well after four hours' walking, wondering, and puddling.

2. The process of converting clay, etc. into puddle, or of lining or covering something with puddle to make it water-tight; also *concr.* = PUDDLE *sb.* 4. Also *attrib.*

1762 J. BRINDLEY in S. Hughes *Mem.* (Weale's Papers Civ. Engin. 1844 I. 47),[It is said that when in his evidence he was making frequent use of the expression] puddling, [some of the members were anxious to know what puddle really was]. **1796** *Trans. Soc. Arts* XIV. 238 The system of puddling in embankments made near to the sea. **1834–47** J. S. MACAULAY *Field Fortif.* (1851) 125 To construct the interior of the dam with well-tempered clay, called puddling. **1861** SMILES *Engineers* I. 353 So to work the new layer of puddling stuff as to unite it with the stratum immediately beneath.

3. a. The process of decarbonizing cast iron by stirring and turning it over continuously in a furnace, so as to render it malleable.

(The operation is described minutely by Dr. Beddoes in *Phil. Trans.* (1791) LXXXI. 173, but the word not used.) **1839** URE *Dict. Arts* 699 The second operation completes the first, and is called *puddling*. **1861** FAIRBAIRN *Iron* 9 In 1783–4, Mr Cort of Gosport introduced the processes of puddling and rolling. **1881** RAYMOND *Mining Gloss.* s.v., Silicon and phosphorus are also largely removed by puddling.

b. *attrib.*, as *puddling forge*, *furnace*, *process*, *roll* (= *puddle-roll*, PUDDLE *v.* 7).

1798 D. MUSHET in *Phil. Mag.* II. 14 One of the principal operations well known by the name of the Puddling Process. **1825** J. NICHOLSON *Operat. Mechanic* 334 When the cake of metal is broken into lumps of a convenient size, it is taken to the puddling furnace, where it is heated with coals, without the aid of an artificial blast. **1839** URE *Dict. Arts* 704 Cylinders..which serve to draw out the ball, called puddling rolls, or roughing rolls. **1862** *Edin. Rev.* CXVI. 226 Cinder is the refuse of the puddling forge.

4. In *Gold-* and *Opal-mining*: see PUDDLE *v.* 6. Also *attrib.* as *puddling machine*, *tub*.

1851 R. TESTER *Wombat Wallaby* 61, I spurred my little mare off, and in doing so she made a plunge, and very nearly bundled me and my mutton into the puddling tub. **1853** E. CLACY *Lady's Visit Gold Diggings Austral.* vii. 117 The great thing is, not to be afraid of over-work, for the better the puddling is, so much the more easy and profitable is the cradling. **1856** *16th Gen. Rep. Emigration Comm.* (Colonial Office) 26 'Puddling machines', which are contrivances for washing the soil by horse-power, appear to be numerous and valuable. **1859** CORNWALLIS *New World* I. 133 The cradle..proved very ineffectual in liberating it [the gold] from the stiff clay..which suggested the use of a puddling tub in its stead. **1890** 'R. BOLDREWOOD' *Miner's Right* v, The wash-dirt has to be..subjected to a puddling machine. **1966** J. HACKSTON *Father clears Out* 62 He was going to do something bigger this time, something better than the tin dish and the cradle—he'd borrow a puddling machine he knew of. **1971** J. S. GUNN *Opal Terminol.* 37 *Puddling tank*, large dam at which wet puddling takes place.

ˈ**puddling**, *ppl. a.* [f. as prec. + -ING[2].] That puddles, in various senses: see the verb. (In quots., a vague term of contempt: = MUDDLING, PIDDLING *ppl. adjs.*)

1764 FOOTE *Mayor of G.* II. Wks. 1799 I. 184 You paltry, puddling puppy. **1777** LADY SARAH LENNOX in *Life & Lett.* (1901) I. 260 At a little pudling bathing place of my brother's by the sea. **1803** MARY CHARLTON *Wife & Mistress* I. 105 Rescued..from the absurd and puddling management of its inconsistent mother.

† ˈ**puddlish**, *a. Obs.* [f. PUDDLE *sb.* + -ISH[1].] Partaking of the nature of a puddle; puddly.

1633 T. JAMES *Voy.* 24 Here the colour of the water changed; and was of a puddlelish and sandy red colour. *Ibid.*, Thick puddleish water.

puddly (ˈpʌdlɪ), *a.* Also 6–7 pudly, -lie, 7 pudley. [f. PUDDLE *sb.* + -Y.]

1. Having the quality of a puddle, or of 'puddle' (*sb.* 3); muddy, turbid, as water or other liquid; more generally, Foul, dirty. Now *rare* or *dial.*

1559 MORWYNG *Evonym.* 75 They will driue down the pudly matter to the bottom. **1600** SURFLET *Countrie Farme* IV. xvi. 650 In a pudlie and troubled water. **1734** SWIFT *Let. to Faulkener* Wks. 1841 II. 725/2 It is not sufficient to see a luminary like this now shining in a meridian lustre, but anon set for ever in a puddly cloud? **1861** CLAYTON *Frank O'Donnell* 69 O to see him tossing in the mud and his fine coat and cap all puddly.

2. Full of or abounding in puddles.

1857 HUGHES *Tom Brown* I. vii, Plashing in the cold puddly ruts. **1889** J. K. JEROME *Three Men* ii, You find a place..not quite so puddly as other places.

puddock, Sc. var. PADDOCK *sb.*[1], frog; obs. f. PADDOCK *sb.*[2], enclosure; dial. var. PUTTOCK[1].

puddy (ˈpʌdɪ), *a.* ? *dial.* [cf. PUD *sb.*[1], hand, paw; also *pud* Sc., belly.] 'Short, thick-set' (*Eng. Dial. Dict.*); stumpy; pudgy.

1842 ALB. SMITH in *Punch* II. 24 The olive branches..poking their little puddy fingers into the creams. **1849** —— *Pottleton Leg.* 283 One or two little girls had squeezed the keepsakes..so tightly in their little puddy hands. **1874** JEFFERIES *John Smith's Shanty* in *Toilers of Field* (1892) 196 Their red 'puddy' fists were fat. **1912** W. DEEPING *Sincerity* ii. 9 Her round, puddy, exquisitely complacent face looked out from between clay-coloured ringlets.

pudency (ˈpjuːdənsɪ). [ad. late L. *pudēntia*, f. *pudēns*, *-ēntem*, pr. pple. of *pud-ēre* to make or be ashamed: see -ENCY.] Susceptibility to the feeling of shame; modesty, bashfulness.

1611 SHAKS. *Cymb.* II. v. 11 She..did it with A pudencie so Rosie..That I thought her As chaste, as vn-Sunn'd Snow. **1794** C. PIGOT *Female Jockey Club* 4 Where Hypocrisy too often puts on the mask of pudency. **1860** EMERSON *Cond. Life, Consid.* Wks. (Bohn) II. 425 There is a pudency about friendship, as about love. **1902** GILDERSLEEVE in *Amer. Jrnl. Philol.* XXIII. 135 Unless we are taught to observe, we do not notice the pudencies of Homer.

pudendal (pjuːˈdɛndəl), *a.* [f. PUDEND-UM + -AL[1].] Of or pertaining to the pudenda; pudic.

1799 [see PUDICAL *a.*]. **1803** *Med. Jrnl.* IX. 395, I have never divided with it the pudendal artery. **1898** P. MANSON

Trop. Diseases xxix. 441 It [granuloma] is practically confined to the pudendal region.

pu'dendous, *a. rare.* ? *Obs.* [f. L. *pudend-us* (see next) + -OUS.] To be ashamed of; shameful.
1680 *Counterplots* 36 Disclosing those pudendous enormities which he had done. **1807** SYD. SMITH *Plymley's Lett.* ii. 29 A feeling laughable in a priestess, pudendous [1808 shameful] in a priest!

‖**pudendum** (pjuːˈdɛndəm). Usually in pl. **pudenda.** [L., neuter gerundive of *pudēre* to cause shame, ashame, lit. 'that of which one ought to be ashamed', used as sb., commonly in pl.] **a.** The privy parts; the external genital organs, esp. those of a woman.
[**1398** TREVISA *Barth. De P.R.* v. xlviii. (Bodl. MS.), Also for schame þese partyes hatte *pudenda* þe schamelich parties.] **1634** SIR T. HERBERT *Trav.* 15 She [Hottentot] will immediately pull by her flap, and discouer her pudenda. **1748** HARTLEY *Observ. Man* I. iv. 449 The original Sources of the Shame relating to the Pudenda are probably the Privacy requisite [etc.]. **1841** RAMSBOTHAM *Obstetr. Med.* (1855) 33 These parts, closing and surrounding the genital fissure, altogether constitute the pudendum. **1893** T. M. MADDEN *Clin. Gynæcol.* v. 59 The value [for pruritus] of a solution of cocaine freely brushed over the pudendum.. is unquestionable. **1922** A. G. MAGIAN *Sex Probl. Women* ii. 31 The Vulva, or Pudendum, includes—(1) The labia majora and minora bounding the pudendal cleft. (2) The mons veneris. (3) The vestibule, [etc.]. **1977** E. J. TRIMMER et al. *Visual Dict. Sex* (1978) v. 58 Sanskrit manuscripts show Indian women with shaved pudenda.
b. *fig.*
1938 S. BECKETT *Murphy* 47 Here are the pudenda of my psyche.

pudent (ˈpjuːdənt), *a. rare.* [f. L. *pudens, pudentem* pres. pple. of *pudēre* to make ashamed: cf. IMPUDENT.] Having or showing a sense of shame, esp. in regard to matters of a sexual nature; modest; delicate.
1908 G. B. SHAW in W. H. Davies *Autobiogr. Super-Tramp* p. vii, These pudent pages are unstained with the frightful language..of the fictitious proletarians of Mr. Rudyard Kipling and other genteel writers.

†**puder, puderer,** obs. ff. PEWTER, PEWTERER.
1507 *Knaresborough Wills* (Surtees) I. 1 Duas parapsides de puder. **1588** *Calr. Laing Charters* (1899) 289 [Twelve] patinarum *lie* puder plaittis. **1598** in Sharp *Cov. Myst.* (1825) 222 *note*, The plumers, puderers, glaciares, and paynters.

†**pudeswaie,** obs. form of PADUASOY.
1656 *Bk. Values* in Scobell *Acts & Ordin. Parl.* (1658) 474 Wrought Silks called..Pudeswaies.

‖**pudeur** (pydœr). [Fr.; see PUDOR.] A sense of shame or embarrassment, esp. in regard to matters of a sexual nature; bashfulness, modesty, constraint.
1937 WYNDHAM LEWIS *Let.* 21 Nov. (1963) 247 And why this strange *pudeur*? **1959** *Times* 22 Sept. 13/5 The choice of physical type in these figures with their sense of flaunted *pudeur*..acquires a close affinity with Italian Mannerism. **1961** *Spectator* 17 Feb. 221 There was a deep-seated *pudeur*, going back to a finely civilised upbringing in a Victorian working-class home. **1962** I. MURDOCH *Unofficial Rose* xxi. 201 She had in any case, with a sort of *pudeur*, arranged to be out of London. **1963** *Guardian* 15 June 4/7 Spencer's brother, Gilbert..could have given everyone a closer sense of the man than this editing and institutional pudeur. **1968** R. P. WARREN *Incarnations* (1970) 7 The peach has released the bough and at last Makes full confession, its *pudeur* Has departed. **1976** *Listener* 10 June 737/3 It is hard not to be goaded into guessing identities. Pudeur makes the reader bend over backwards to prevent this happening.

pudge[1] (pʌdʒ). *dial.* and *colloq.* Also *Sc.* poodge (pødʒ, pʏdʒ). [Origin obscure; app. to a certain extent identical with PODGE. Not known before 19th c. Connexion with Sc. *pud* belly, and with *pud-* in PUDDING has been conjectured; but the phonetic change would need explanation.] A short thick-set or fat person or animal; anything short and thick.
1808 JAMIESON, *Pudge*, any very small house, a hut, *Perths.* **1880** *Ibid.*, *Pudge* [ed. 1825 *Pudget*], (1) a term applied to a short, thick set animal or person; also, to a person who feeds well; (2) anything short and stout, or small and confined, as a house, a hut. **1892** E. L. WAKEMAN in *Columbus* (Ohio) *Dispatch* 28 July, The old town has always seemed to wish the glamor of immortality on its own account; for its wigged pudges of rulers, its wicked old slave traders. **1905** *Daily Chron.* 8 May 8/5 The tight shoe ages the face appallingly, the tight glove makes a shapeless 'pudge' of the hand.

pudge[2] (pʌdʒ). *dial.* [? Connected with OE. *pudd* furrow, ? ditch (see PUDDLE *sb.*). Cf. Sw. *puss* puddle, plash.] A puddle.
1820 CLARE *Rural Life* (ed. 3) 31 While countless swarms of dancing gnats Each water pudge surround. **1821** —— *Vill. Minstr.* II. 32 He whisk'd o'er the water-pudge flirting and airy. **1847–78** HALLIWELL, *Pudge*, a ditch or grip.

pudge, var. PADGE, PODGE *v.*

pudgily (ˈpʌdʒɪlɪ), *adv.* [f. PUDGY *a.*[1] + -LY[2].] In a pudgy manner.
1926 *Harper's Mag.* Feb. 351/1 One day she escorted the pudgily tottering six-weeks-old youngsters [*sc.* puppies] on a ramble over the lawn. **1978** R. BARNARD *Unruly Son* iii. 34 He remained pudgily sunk in the easy chair.

pudgy (ˈpʌdʒɪ), *a.*[1] [In form and sense a deriv. of PUDGE[1], and a doublet of PODGY, both forms being frequent in Thackeray, to whom the current use is app. largely due. If PUDSY, *pudsey* (1754) was the same word, it would be the earliest member of the group, which otherwise appears only in the 19th c.; but its connexion is doubtful.] Short and thick or fat.
1836 DICKENS *Sk. Boz, Our Parish* i, The vestry clerk..is a short, pudgy little man in black. **1837** THACKERAY *Ravenswing* i, Their fingers is always so very fat and pudgy. **1840** —— *Catherine* ii, A fat, pudgy pale-haired woman.. leaning on the Captain's arm. **1862** *Athenæum* 27 Sept. 403 A very short, pudgy omnibus.

pudgy (ˈpʌdʒɪ), *a.*[2] *dial.* [f. PUDGE[2] + -Y.] Muddy, miry.
1827 CLARE *Sheph. Cal.* 162 And litter'd straw in all the pudgy sloughs.

pudibund (ˈpjuːdɪbʌnd), *a. rare.* Also ‖**pudibond.** [ad. L. *pudibund-us* easily ashamed, bashful, modest, also shameful, f. *pudēre* to make or be ashamed; cf. F. *pudibond* (16th c. in Littré).] †**a.** That is a subject of shame; shameful. *Obs.* **b.** Modest, bashful, prudish. Also †**pudi'bundous** *a.*
1542 BOORDE *Dyetary* x. (1870) 253 And yf any man.. doth burne in the pudibunde places. **1656** BLOUNT *Glossogr.*, *Pudibund, Pudibundous*, shame-fac'd, bashful, modest, honest. **1888** *Sat. Rev.* 29 Dec. 785/2 To outrage the pudibund soul of their countryman. **1900** A. LANG in *Blackw. Mag.* Mar. 363/2 English literature became the most 'pudibund'..the world has ever known. *a* **1922** T. S. ELIOT *Waste Land Drafts* (1971) 103 Pudibund, in the clinging vine. **1923** G. SAINTSBURY *Second Scrap Bk.* iii. 25 My tutor in Scholarship was the late 'Johnny' King, an expert in his subject..and a very good fellow, but rather shy and extremely pudibund. *Ibid.* xxxviii. 269, I understand that Soviet education is not at all pudibund, and that the principles of parenthood are treated and illustrated in it with a fine 'candour'. **1930** D. B. WYNDHAM LEWIS *Stuffed Owl* p. ix, The illiterate, the semi-literate, the Babu,..the hearty but ill-equipped patriot, the pudibond yet urgent Sapphos of endless *Keepsakes* and *Lady's Magazines.*
Hence **pudi'bundity** (*pedantic*), **'pudibundness,** bashfulness, prudery.
1727 BAILEY vol. II, Pudibundness. **1888** *Sat. Rev.* 28 Jan. 100 Only the pudibundity of the Editor of this Review prevents us from at once vindicating..the Great F. B. **1893** *Ibid.* 4 Feb. 126/2 We cannot approve the editor's pudibundity in omitting a few 'indecent words'.

pudibundery (ˌpjuːdɪˈbʌndərɪ). Also ‖**pudibonderie.** [f. PUDIBUND *a.* + -ERY; cf. F. *pudibonderie.*] Bashfulness, prudery.
a **1913** F. ROLFE *Desire & Pursuit of Whole* (1934) xxii. 249 The pudibundery of Erastian peeping toms. **1915** T. BURKE *Nights in Town* 51 Everyday life is always disgusting to the funny little Bayswaterats, who are compact of timidity and pudibonderie. **1917** E. POUND *Let.* ? Jan. (1971) 107, I have only three quarrels with them: Their idiotic fuss over christianizing all poems they print, their concessions to local pudibundery, [etc.]. **1959** *Listener* 29 Oct. 744/1 This is not an isolated instance of *pudibonderie.*

pudic (ˈpjuːdɪk), *a.* (*sb.*) Also 5 -ique, -yke, 6 -ick, (*Sc.* -ict), 5–7 -ike. [a. F. *pudique* (14th c. in Hatz.-Darm.), ad. L. *pudīc-us* shamefaced, modest, chaste, f. *pud-ēre* to make or be ashamed.]
A. *adj.* **1.** Having a keen sense of shame; modest, chaste.
1490 CAXTON *Eneydos* vii. 32 To enterteyne hir pudeyque chastyte in perpetuall wydowhed. *Ibid.* ix. 36 To kepe thy pudyke chastyte vnhurte. *Ibid.* 37 Pudike. **1562** KNOX *Ressoning Crosraguell* (1563) Bij, An honest & pudick matron. **1581** N. BURNE *Disput.* in *Cath. Tractates* (S.T.S.) 172 Modest and pudict behauiour cumlie for vemen. **1610** TOFTE *Hon. Acad.* III. 141 Modest and pudike Cynthia. *a* **1913** F. ROLFE *Desire & Pursuit of Whole* (1934) 247 Water-babies (pudic, though incredibly tattered) wallow in every canal. **1974** *Times Lit. Suppl.* 22 Feb. 169/1 The instructive geographical screen fallen to reveal a pudic Lady Teazle.
2. *Anat.* = PUDENDAL.
1807–26 S. COOPER *First Lines Surg.* (ed. 5) 471 The external pudic branch of the femoral artery. **1863–76** CURLING *Dis. Rectum* 25 The pain..deeply seated in the pudic region.
B. *sb. Anat.* The pudic artery.
1827 *Lancet* 3 Nov. 195/2 There was not much bleeding from the divided external pudic. **1874** VAN BUREN *Dis. Genit. Org.* 3 The arteries come from the internal pudics.

†**'pudical,** *a.* and *sb. Obs.* [f. as prec. + -AL[1].]
A. *adj.* **a.** = PUDIC *a.* 1. **b.** = PUDIC *a.* 2.
1513 BRADSHAW *St. Werburge* II. 224 Blessed Werburge so glorious and pudicall. **1799** HOOPER *Med. Dict.*, *Pudical artery*, pudendal artery. A branch of the internal iliac.
B. *sb. Anat.* = PUDIC *sb.*
1803 *Edin. Rev.* I. 463 The origin and course of the external pudicals are more fully traced.

pudicity (pjuːˈdɪsɪtɪ). [ad. F. *pudicité* (1417 in Godef.), substituted for OF. *pudicicie* (13–15th c.), ad. L. *pudīcitia*, f. *pudīc-us*: see PUDIC.] Modesty, chastity.
1567 FENTON *Trag. Disc.* i. (1898) I. 47 Absolute experience of her undoubted pudicitie. **1645** PAGITT *Heresiogr.* (1647) 10 They broke the lawes of all pudicity and honesty. **1760–72** H. BROOKE *Fool of Qual.* (1809) IV. 109 Her pudicity awed me in the midst of transport. **1879** M. PATTISON *Milton* iii. 37 The pudicity of his behaviour and language covers a soul tremulous with emotion. **1931** C. MACKENZIE *Buttercups & Daisies* xxi. 274 Dodsworth in a turmoil of alarmed pudicity at the prospect of her bedroom being used as a thoroughfare called upon Ralph and Roger to stop their goings on at once. **1958** L. DURRELL *Balthazar* vi. 132 Yet it was accompanied by a delicacy, almost a pudicity, in his dealings with them.

†**'pudify,** *v. Obs. rare*$^{-0}$. [f. L. *pudē-re* to make or be ashamed + -FY: the L. form would have been *pudefacĕre*: cf. *patefacere, rubefacere.*]
1656 BLOUNT *Glossogr.*, *Pudify*, to make ashamed, to make to blush, to be ashamed.

pudisway, obs. form of PADUASOY.

†**'pudlay.** *Obs.* See quots.
1679 MOXON *Mech. Exerc.* ix. 171 *Pudlaies*, Pieces of Stuff [= timber] to do the Office of Hand-Spikes. **1703** T. N. *City & C. Purchaser* 230 *Pudlays*, Pieces of Stuff to do the Office of Leavers, or Hand-spikes.

'pudor (ˈpjuːdɔː(r)). Also 7 -ore, -our. [a. L. *pudor* shame, modesty, f. root of *pud-ēre* to make or be ashamed. So F. *pudeur* (16th c. in Hatz.).] Due sense of shame; bashfulness, modesty.
1623 COCKERAM, *Pudor*, shamefastnesse. **1639** G. DANIEL *Ecclus.* Induct. 12 The Muse..Has sung the beauties of devine Pudore: His second Love, the Darling of his Soule. **1659** RUSHW. *Hist. Coll.* I. 615 There is a Pudor in it, it was kept secret, some great Lords never knew it. **1686** AGLIONBY *Painting Illustr.* III. 121 An Air of Pudour and Sanctity that strikes the Spectator with Respect. **1922** JOYCE *Ulysses* 508 Woman undoing with sweet pudor her belt of rushrope. **1927** R. FRY *Flemish Art* i. 25 This tinge of sentimental feeling is very discreet. He never abandons himself. He has a certain shy pudor which is very attractive. **1966** *Times Lit. Suppl.* 3 Nov. 1012/4 Lawrence's..first head-on collision with the forces of British pudor.

pudsy (ˈpʌdzɪ), *a.* (*sb.*) Also 8 **pudsey.** [? Connected with PUD *sb.*[1] hand, paw. If related to *pudgy*, it is an earlier form.] Plump.
1754 RICHARDSON *Grandison* (1781) VII. xliii. 211 He.. took the little thing from me, kissed its forehead, its cheek, its lips, its little pudsey hands. **1774** T. HUTCHINSON *Diary* 27 Oct., I was determined..to kiss one of their little pudsey hands. **1831** FR. A. KEMBLE *Record Girlhood* (1878) II. 264 A fat, red, round, staring, pudsy thing! **1869** MRS. WHITNEY *Hitherto* v, His pudsy hands upon his dimpled knees.
B. *sb.* A term of endearment (primarily to a baby).
a **1756** MRS. HAYWOOD *Wife to Lett* III, Here, Pudsy, read this—Read, Pudsy, it's prettily turned.

‖**pudu** (ˈpudu). [Native Chilean name.] The venada, *Pudua humilis* or *Cervus pudu*, a very small species of deer, native to Chile.
1886 *List Anim. Zool. Soc.* (1896) 185. **1903** *Q. Rev.* Jan. 47 The tiny little pudu-deer of the Chilian Andes.

pue, obs. f. POOH, PEW *sb.*[1],[3], *v.*[1]; var. PEW *v.*[2]

pu-é, var. PWE.

pueblo (puːˈɛbləʊ, ˈpwɛbləʊ). Also with capital initial. [Sp., = people, population, town, village:—L. *popul-us* PEOPLE.]
1. A town or village in Spain or Spanish America; esp. a communal village or settlement of Indians. Also *attrib.*
In American Archæology applied to a communal or tribal dwelling of the aborigines of New Mexico, etc. ***Pueblo Indians***, self-governing Indians, dwelling in pueblos, in New Mexico and Arizona.
1818 *Amer. St. Papers, Foreign* (1834) IV. 307 There was in almost every valley a pueblo of peaceful and submissive Indians. **1844** J. GREGG *Commerce of Prairies* I. 132 About two thousand of the insurgent mob, including the Pueblo Indians, pitched their camp in the suburbs of the capital [*sc.* Santa Fé]. **1845** W. H. G. KINGSTON *Lusitanian Sk.* II. xxvii. 233 Pueblos scattered about in every direction shewed that the land was still the habitation of man. Near each pueblo were numerous horses and colts feeding. **1875** T. W. HIGGINSON *Hist. U.S.* ii. 10 The Pueblo Indians, in New Mexico,..seem to have a civilization of their own. **1879** H. GEORGE *Progr. & Pov.* VII. v. (1881) 346 Reduced to private ownership..as even the pueblo lands of San Francisco.. were reduced. **1891** C. ROBERTS *Adrift Amer.* 86 The Pueblos, or small walled towns that are scattered over this valley, are extremely picturesque. **1907** Pueblo Indian [see CREE *sb.* and *a.*]. **1923** D. H. LAWRENCE *Birds, Beasts & Flowers* 193 Across the pueblo river That dark old demon and I Thus say a few words to each other. **1949** *Nat. Geogr. Mag.* Dec. 783/2 Long-haired Pueblo Indians wrapped in cotton blankets exchange stare for stare with visiting easterners. **1957** T. VEBLEN *Theory of Leisure Class* 6 Some Pueblo communities. **1976** M. & G. GORDON *Ordeal* (1977) viii. 50 The Navajos were..quick to latch onto new ideas. From their next-door neighbours, the Pueblo people, they had borrowed sheep raising and weaving. **1979** *Arizona Daily Star* 5 Aug. (Advt. section) 21/7 This beautiful Territorial..features pueblo fireplace, exposed beams in family room.
2. Short for *Pueblo Indian*: see above.
1834 A. PIKE *Prose Sk. & Poems* 132 The Pueblos shall mount and prepare to pursue. **1844** J. GREGG *Commerce of Prairies* I. 268 Most of these Pueblos call themselves the descendants of Montezuma. **1850** G. A. MCCALL *Lett. fr. Frontiers* (1868) 497 The Pueblos were admitted to the rights of citizenship by the Mexican government under Iturbide. **1891** *Chambers' Encycl.* VIII. 482/1 The Pueblos ..are making steady progress in civilisation and education.

†**pu'ellarity.** *Obs. rare*$^{-0}$. [f. L. *puellār-is* girlish (f. *puella* a girl) + -ITY.] (See quot.) So

'puellile, pu'ellular *adjs.* (*nonce-wds.*), proper to little girls.

1623 COCKERAM, *Puellaritie*, girlishnesse. 1861 *Sat. Rev.* 3 Aug. 123 In many cases [they] are trivial and puellular, if we may be allowed to coin a much-needed feminine for puerile. 1891 *Guardian* 29 Apr. 682/2 [The tale] would be too puellile—may we coin a word?—for strictures, had not the writer challenged them by her introduction.

puer, obs. f. PURE *a.*, var. PURE *sb.* 5, PURE *v.* 1 b.

† **'puerice.** *Obs. rare.* [ad. L. *pueriti-a* boyhood, childhood, f. *puer* a boy, child; cf. obs. F. *puerice* (16th c.).] Boyhood, childhood.

1481 BOTONER *Tulle on Old Age* (Caxton) b iij, They can sey no reason how olde age entrith souner in the man after adolescence, no more than doeth adolescence aftir puerice, callid childhode. 1660 GAUDEN *Brownrig* 143 He drank in learning not..by drops, but as a sponge.., even in his puerice or minority.

puericulture ('pjuːərɪˌkʌltjʊə(r)). [ad. mod.F. *puériculture* (Littré), f. L. *puer* a child + *cultūra* CULTURE.] The rearing of children, as an art, or branch of sociology.

1901 *Brit. Med. Jrnl.* 6 Apr. 857/2 The defence of childhood (puericulture, suckling, weaning). 1904 *Daily News* 26 Sept. 6 France is..realising the enormous importance and the urgency of this question of 'puericulture', as the experts call it.

puerile ('pjuːəraɪl), *a.* (*sb.*) [ad. L. *puerīl-is* boyish, childish, f. *puer* a boy, child: see -ILE. Cf. F. *puéril, -ile* (15th c. in Hatz.-Darm.), perh. the immediate source.]

A. *adj.* **1.** Of, pertaining or proper to a boy or child; youthful, boyish, juvenile. Now *rare* exc. as in 2.

1661 K. W. *Conf. Charac.* To Rdr. (1860) 13 Let the.. reader mend what he sees amiss in these puerill exercises. *a* 1695 WOOD *Ath. Oxon.* (1721) II. 602 [Franciscus Junius] was..educated in puerile Learning at Leyden in Holland. 1784 COWPER *Tiroc.* 458 Our public hives of puerile resort. 1852 BLACKIE *Stud. Lang.* 7 There is no subject of puerile inculcation that more imperatively calls for a good teacher.

b. Of respiration: Characterized by the louder pulmonary murmur found in children, which in adults is usually a sign of disease.

1822-34 *Good's Study Med.* (ed. 4) II. 526 Distinguished by M. Laennec by the name of puerile or tracheal. 1834 J. FORBES *Laennec's Dis. Chest* (ed. 4) 289 Respiration was inaudible over the whole of the right side, but was puerile on the left. 1899 *Allbutt's Syst. Med.* VI. 131 Should the opposite lung be healthy and free to act, puerile breathing will probably be heard on that side.

2. (*Depreciative.*) Merely boyish or childish, juvenile; immature, trivial.

1685 *Remonstr. to Parl.* in Somers *Tracts* I. 211 Moved with an Itch of being in Print, they publish their own puerile Conceptions. 1751 EARL ORRERY *Remarks Swift* (1752) 78 They are trifling and I had almost said puerile. 1809-10 COLERIDGE *Friend* (1865) 196 It is mere puerile declamation. 1868 FARRAR *Seekers* Concl. (1875) 332 The puerile ostentation, which we have had to point out in Seneca.

B. *sb. pl.* (= L. *puerīlia*). Childish things, conditions, or productions.

1659 GAUDEN *Tears Ch.* I. i. 27 Which seek..to reduce ancient Churches, of long growth, of tall and manly stature, to their pueriles, their long coats and cradles. [1899 'ANTHONY HOPE' *King's Mirror* ii, A man's *puerilia* are to himself not altogether puerile; they are parcel of the complex explanation of his existent self.]

Hence **'puerilely** *adv.*, in a puerile fashion; **'puerileness**, = PUERILITY; **'puerilize** *v. trans.*, to make puerile.

1727 BAILEY vol. II, Puerilely..Puerileness. 1751 *Female Foundling* I. p. v, A Narration of Events which are visibly fictitious,..or puerilely extravagant. 1791 J. LEARMONT *Poems* 75 Puerileness of things And playful trifles held thee fast. 1887 *Harper's Mag.* Jan. 322 Its long-puerilized fancy will bear an endless repetition of them. 1894 *Westm. Gaz.* 22 Sept. 2/3 He..is puerilely grateful for the present of a wooden pipe.

puerility (pjuːə'rɪlɪtɪ). [a. F. *puérilité* (15th c. in Hatz.-Darm.), or ad. L. *puerīlitās, -tātem*, f. *puerīlis*: see prec.]

1. The condition of being a child; childhood; in *Civil Law*, the age between seven and fourteen.

1512 *Helyas* in Thoms *Prose Rom.* (1828) III. 34 Seinge the indigent puerylite of them. 1575 FENTON *Gold. Epist.* (1577) 259 Puerilitie, being the seconde age, continueth from seuen to fourteene years. 1646 SIR T. BROWNE *Pseud. Ep.* I. vii. 24 A Reserve of Puerilitie wee have not shaken off from Schoole. 1849 RUSKIN *Sev. Lamps* v. §3. 139 There would be hope if we could change palsy into puerility.

2. The quality of being puerile; (mere) childishness, triviality.

1576 FLEMING *Panopl. Epist.* 282 Who..playeth prankes of puerilitie and childishnesse. 1662 STILLINGFL. *Orig. Sacr.* III. iii. §1 In nothing did Epicurus more discover the weakness and puerility of his judgement. 1712 ADDISON *Spect.* No. 523 ⁋5 Downright Puerility, and unpardonable in a Poet that is past Sixteen. 1827 MACAULAY *Ess., Machiavelli* (1887) 45 That a shrewd statesman..should, at nearly sixty years of age, descend to such puerility is utterly inconceivable. 1907 *Academy* 16 Nov. 143/2 The puerility of this attempt is..astonishing.

b. With *a* and *pl.* An instance of childishness in behaviour, work, or speech; a thing that embodies or displays childishness. (In quot. 1779, juvenile productions.)

c 1450 *Mankind* 813 in *Macro Plays* 30 Ewyr to offend, & euer to aske mercy, þat ys a puerilite. 1692 DRYDEN *St. Euremont's Ess.* 363 Relaxing sometimes to very great Puerilities. 1712 ADDISON *Spect.* No. 279 ⁋5 Those trifling Points and Puerilities that are so often to be met with in Ovid. 1779 JOHNSON *L.P., Cowley* Wks. II. 7 Of the learned puerilities of Cowley there is no doubt, since a volume of his poems was..printed in his thirteenth year. 1830 SCOTT *Demonol.* iii. 116 The genius of Milton alone could discard all these vulgar puerilities. 1853 KANE *Grinnell Exp.* xxix. (1856) 245 Not a vermilion-daubed puerility, with a glory in Dutch leaf..but a good, genuine, hearty representative of English flesh and blood.

† **pu'erper**, *a. Obs. rare*$^{-1}$. In 5 *corruptly* puarpure. [ad. L. *puerper-us*: see next. Cf. OF. *puerpre* PUERPERY.] Parturient.

c 1450 *Mirour Saluacioun* 4978 Thi puarpure wombe childyng godson intacte and cloos.

puerperal (pjuː'ɜːpərəl), *a.* [f. L. *puerper-us* parturient, bringing forth children (f. *puer* a child + *-par-us* bringing forth) + -AL[1]. So F. *puerpéral* (1835 in *Dict. Acad.*).] Of, pertaining to, accompanying, or ensuing upon parturition. ***puerperal fever, sepsis***, etc., sepsis of the genital tract following parturition, or the fever associated with this.

1768 T. DENMAN (*title*) Essays on the Puerperal Fever, and on Puerperal Convulsions. 1791 COWPER *Iliad* XVI. 225 Ilithya, arbitress Of pangs puerperal. 1814 J. ARMSTRONG *Facts Rel. Fever called Puerperal* p. vii, Under the common term puerperal fever are comprehended, in the following work, both the ordinary peritoneal inflammation, and the low malignant fever, of lying-in women, and these are considered as modifications of the same disease. 1874 BUCKNILL & TUKE *Psych. Med.* (ed. 3) 350 The term Puerperal Insanity, Mania, or Madness, is by different writers employed in a restricted or a comprehensive use. 1876 W. S. PLAYFAIR *Sci. & Pract. Midwifery* II. v. v. 302 There is no subject in the whole range of obstetrics which has caused so much discussion and difference of opinion as that to which this chapter is devoted. Under the name of 'Puerperal Fever', the disease we have to consider has given rise to endless controversy. *Ibid.*, If this view be correct, the term 'puerperal fever', conveying the idea of a fever such as typhus or typhoid, must be acknowledged to be in itself misleading, and one that should be discarded. 1935 A. C. BECK *Obstetr. Pract.* xxxvi. 583 Puerperal infection is a wound infection in the birth passages. It often is referred to as puerperal fever, childbed fever, puerperal sepsis, or puerperal septicemia. 1955 *Sci. News Let.* 11 June 373/1 Puerperal sepsis, which is better known as childbed fever. 1974 GREENHILL & FRIEDMAN *Biol. Princ. & Mod. Pract. Obstetr.* lxx. 730/1 The term puerperal infection includes all the inflammatory processes which arise from bacterial invasion of the genital organs during labour or the puerperium. Other terms for this condition are puerperal sepsis, puerperal septicemia, puerperal fever and childbed fever. 1977 J. DONNISON *Midwives & Med. Men* v. 93 The deadly 'childbed' or 'puerperal' fever..regularly closed wards and contributed to maternal death rates as high as 28 per 1,000.

Hence **pu'erperally** *adv.* (in *Cent. Dict.*).

† **puer'perial**, *a.* (*sb.*) *Obs. rare.* [f. L. *puerperi-um* PUERPERY + -AL[1].] Of or pertaining to child-birth. **b.** As *sb.* (*pl.*) things or matters pertaining to child-birth.

1628 GAULE *Pract. The.* (1629) 116 What preparation for Puerperials? What ready helpe of a Midwife? 1648 BEAUMONT *Psyche* XIX. vi, With puerperial pain. 1710 T. FULLER *Pharm. Extemp.* 256 The Tulip..is a blessed.. Remedy for Puerperial After-Pains.

puerperium (p(ɪ)uːə'pɛrɪəm, -'piːrɪəm). *Med.* [L.: see PUERPERY.] The puerperal state or period; *spec.* the few weeks following delivery during which the mother's tissues return to their non-pregnant state.

1890 in BILLINGS *Med. Dict.* II. 410/1. 1894 GRANDIN & JARMAN *Obstetr. Surg.* viii. 164 Many such lacerations heal spontaneously, probably the vast majority if the course of the puerperium is aseptic. 1935 A. C. BECK *Obstetr. Pract.* xv. 232 The term puerperium is applied to the six or eight weeks following labor which are required for the involution of the maternal organism. 1977 *Lancet* Aug. 273/1 Early trials with a Lippes loop inserted in the first week of the puerperium resulted in a high and unacceptable expulsion-rate.

puerperous (pjuː'ɜːpərəs), *a. rare.* [f. as PUERPERAL + -OUS.] = PUERPER.

1656 BLOUNT *Glossogr.*, *Puerperous*, that beareth children, or causeth to bear and bring forth, or to be delivered of a child. 1658 in PHILLIPS.

pu'erpery. *rare.* Also in Lat. form **puer'perium.** [ad. L. *puerperi-um*, f. *puerper-us*: see PUERPERAL.] Child-birth; 'confinement'.

1602 FULBECKE *2nd Pt. Parall.* 60 As there is one conception of two twinnes, so there is one puerperie, though it bee finished at diuers times. 1652 J. MAYER *Comm. Prophets* 56 [They] make it plain that such a puerpery was to be expected. 1890 *Lancet* 5 Apr. 750/2 Illustrating the clinical history of nephritis in pregnancy and puerpery.

Puerto Rican (ˌpwɜːtəʊ 'riːkən), *sb.* and *a.* Also earlier **Porto Rican** (see note below), **Porto Riquenean.** [f. the name *Puerto* (or *Porto*) *Rico* + -AN.] **A.** *sb.* A native or inhabitant of Puerto Rico, an island in the Greater Antilles group of the West Indies, now a Commonwealth in association with the U.S.A. **B.** *adj.* Of or pertaining to Puerto Rico or its inhabitants.

The name was officially changed in 1932 from *Porto Rico* to *Puerto Rico*. The Commonwealth of Puerto Rico was established on 25 July 1952.

1858 J. T. O'NEIL *Mem. Island Porto Rico* in R. S. Fisher *Spanish West Indies* 152 The Porto Riqueneans..are generally indolent. 1898 R. T. HILL *Cuba & Porto Rico* xv. 146 The Cubans are fired with the spirit of progress and infected with American notions, while the Porto Ricans are plodding along in contentment. *Ibid.* xviii. 166 The Porto Rican Spaniards of the upper class..are the descendants of military men. 1898 *Times* 30 July 7/2 The American troops were received by the entire population.., the piers, balconies, roofs and streets being alive with Puertoricans [*sic*] representing every class. 1899 F. A. OBER *Puerto Rico* xii. 168 Scratch a Puerto Rican and you find a Spaniard underneath, so the language and home customs of Spain prevail here. *Ibid.* 171 The Puerto Rican home life..differs in no important particular from that of Spain and Mexico. 1907 J. H. MOORE *With Speaker Cannon through Tropics* ii. 38 Bright colors are affected by the Porto Rican women. 1926 K. MIXER *Porto Rico* vi. 102 Governor Towner has come to the Island under conditions which have given him an exceptional prestige with Porto Ricans. 1952 S. KAUFFMANN *Tightrope* xvi. 263 Jerry, the building's Puerto Rican shoe-shine boy was just finishing. 1956 'E. MCBAIN' *Cop Hater* (1958) iii. 29 Occasionally, a Puerto Rican wandered into *The Shamrock*. 1962 *Amer. Speech* XXXVII. 18 New York City..contains 80 percent of the Puerto Ricans of the entire United States. 1969 *Listener* 13 Mar. 332/1 On this particular campus, the provocative group was the black and Puerto Rican students' commune, so-called. 1972 D. DELMAN *Sudden Death* (1973) i. 15 It's exactly what that Puerto Rican hot dog would think is funny. 1978 *Language* LIV. 424 An example from Romance consonantism would be the uvular *r*, which is at present very widely distributed, from Brazilian Portuguese and Puerto Rican Spanish to French, north and central Italian, and even some speakers of Rumanian. 1979 *Tucson* (Arizona) *Citizen* 20 Sept. 10A/1 They would resort to violence again in the interest of Puerto Rican independence.

puet(t, pufellow, obs. ff. PEWIT, PEW-FELLOW.

puff (pʌf), *sb.* Forms: 3, 6 puf, 3-7 puffe, 6 pufe, *Sc.* pwf, 5- puff. [n. of action cognate with PUFF *v.* q.v.]

1. a. An act of puffing; a short impulsive blast of breath or wind; an abrupt emission of air, vapour, or smoke; a whiff. Also *fig.* †***by puffs*** (quot. 1579), by fits and starts, intermittently.

(A possible OE. instance of *pyf* has been suggested as the original reading in K. Ælfred's *Boeth.* xx. (1899) 47: Ac seo orsorhnes gæð scyrmælum swæðer windes [pyf]; where MS. B has *ðyf* = *pyf*, perh. for *pyf*. See Napier in *P.B. Beitr.* XXIV. 245 Note 1. Others would read *ðys* or *þys* = ON. *þyss* uproar, tumult.)

a 1255 *Ancr. R.* 122 Hwo nule þunchen þeonne wunder of an ancre þet a windes puf of a word auelleð? *Ibid.* 142 þes deofles puffes, þet beoð temptaciuns. *a* 1400 HYLTON *Scala Perf.* (W. de W.) II. xviii. (1507) P iv, A lityl puffe of wynde ..sholde soone caste hym downe. 1530 PALSGR. 259/1 Puffe of wynde, *boufflee*. 1579 TOMSON *Calvin's Serm. Tim.* 435/1 It is not inough for a man to teache by puffes, but he must frame himselfe neuer to bee wearie in taking paines to edifie the Church of God. 1582 STANYHURST *Æneis* II. (Arb.) 66 Eeche pipling puf doth amaze me. 1667 FLAVEL *Saint Indeed* (1754) 60 Like a candle blown out with a puff of breath. 1781 COWPER *Conversation* 245 The pipe, with solemn interposing puff, Makes half a sentence at a time enough. 1842 MACAULAY *Ess., Fredk. Gt.* (1887) 695 Between the puffs of the pipe. 1887 BOWEN *Virg. Æneid* III. 357 Canvases heave and swell with the puff of the South wind gale.

b. An act of puffing as an expression of contempt; a scornful gesture.

1585 STOW *Surv.* (1908) I. p. lxv, We aunswered it was by act of comon counsayle, whereat he made a pufe. 1598 DALLINGTON *Meth. Trav.* B iv, This is a better purchase then the Italian huffe of the shoulder, or the Dutch puffe with the pot, or the French apishnes, which many Trauellers bring home.

c. The sound of an abrupt or explosive emission of air, or the like.

1834 J. FORBES *Laennec's Dis. Chest* (ed. 4) 309 The phenomenon which I have termed the auricular puff, simple, or veiled, frequently accompanies the cavernous respiration and cough. 1856 KANE *Arct. Expl.* I. xxx. 411 [Walrus] rising at intervals through the ice in a body, and breaking it up with an explosive puff that might have been heard for miles. 1898 *Allbutt's Syst. Med.* V. 1021 This murmur..may be a short systolic 'puff' having a very limited area of audibility.

d. *concr.* A small quantity of vapour, smoke, or the like, emitted at one momentary blast; a whiff.

1839 tr. *Lamartine's Trav. East* 12/1 Giving to the wind the puffs of smoke from their pipes of red clay. 1858 LONGF. *M. Standish* v. 32 Suddenly from her side..Darted a puff of smoke, and floated seaward. 1869 PHILLIPS *Vesuv.* iv. 118 Puffs of vapour were rising at various points.

e. *slang* and *dial.* Breath, 'wind'.

1827 *Sporting Mag.* XXI. 137 Taking the puff out of most of the nags. 1863 W. C. BALDWIN *Afr. Hunting* ix. 387 Sustaining three more savage charges, the last..far from pleasant, as my horse had all the puff taken out of him.

f. *Criminals' slang* (orig. *U.S.*). Explosive powder or dynamite used for blowing open a safe.

1904 'No. 1500' *Life in Sing Sing* 251/1 *Puff*, explosive powder. 1926 J. BLACK *You can't Win* ix. 107, I always crush into these powder shacks for my 'puff'.

g. *colloq.* Life, span of existence; usu. in phr. ***in (all) one's puff*** and varr., in all one's life.

1921 [see CHEERIO *int.*]. **1922** JOYCE *Ulysses* 338 You never saw the like of it in all your born puff. **1929** WODEHOUSE *Mr. Mulliner Speaking* ix. 301 'Did you ever see a hat like that, Stinker?' 'Never in my puff,' replied his friend. **1938** —— *Code of Woosters* vii. 156 Did you ever in your puff see such a perfect perisher? **1960** K. MARTIN *Matter of Time* 165 That sort of thing's never happened to me in my puff. **1967** A. L. LLOYD *Folk Song in England* iv. 226 Hannah Snell.. served for years as a marine..took a public house in Wapping and wore trousers for the rest of her puff. **1972** 'A. ARMSTRONG' *One Jump Ahead* i. 9 Here's me actually going to dial nine-nine-nine! Never in all me puff would I've thought it!

2. a. A swelling caused by inflation or otherwise; a blister, tumour, protuberance, excrescence.

1538 ELYOT *Dict.*, *Hecta*,.. a lyttelle puffe, whiche riseth in breadde whanne it is baken. *Ibid.*, *Clauus*,.. also puffes growing in the stemmis of great trees. **1581** MULCASTER *Positions* xvii. (1887) 76 The vehement vpright wrastling.. taketh awaie fatnesse, puffes, and swellinges. **1676** MARVELL *Mr. Smirke* 21 Having thus plumed him of that puffe of Feathers, with which he buoy'd himself up in the Aire. **1715** LEONI *Palladio's Archit.* (1742) I. 5 The Iron to be without knots, puffs, or flaws. **1897** MARY KINGSLEY *W. Africa* 59 Men and women alike wear armlets, and in..the women.. you see puffs of flesh growing out from between them.

b. In costume, A rounded soft protuberant mass formed by gathering in the stuff at the edges and leaving it full in the middle as if inflated; now usu. with reference to the sleeves of a dress; = *puff sleeve*, sense 9 b below. Also, a similar mass formed of ribbons or small feathers, or by rolling in the ends of the hair on the head.

a **1601** ? MARSTON *Pasquil & Kath.* I. 124 Nor doe I enuie Polyphemian puffes, Swizars slopt greatnesse. **1606** *Sir G. Goosecappe* III. ii. in Bullen *O. Pl.* III. 52 See my wife.. Busied to starch her French purles, and her puffs. **1617** [see PUFFED *ppl. a.* 1 b]. **1666–7** PEPYS *Diary* 4 Feb., Mrs. Steward, very fine, with her locks done up with puffes, as my wife calls them. **1688** R. HOLME *Armoury* III. 98/1 Half Sleeves..are made..with Puffs, or ruffled in the turn-up. **1729** MRS. DELANY in *Life & Corr.* (1861) I. 244 Her lappets tied with puffs of scarlet ribbon. **1860** *Illustr. Lond. News* 26 May 510/2 Bonnets..with velvet flowers and delicious puffs, composed of a mass of small feathers. **1884** B. POTTER *Jrnl.* 2 Apr. (1966) 78 Tight long sleeves with puffs to put on over them. **1889** *Latest News* 5 Sept. 7 Puff of muslin, forming a panier. **1900** *Westm. Gaz.* 20 Sept. 3/2 The beautifully arranged forehead puff that almost all Parisians affect. **1908** L. M. MONTGOMERY *Anne of Green Gables* xi. 114 They all had puffed sleeves..it was awfully hard there among the others who had really truly puffs. **1968** J. IRONSIDE *Fashion Alphabet* 58 *Puff*, a short sleeve, gathered into the shoulder and into a band above the elbow.

c. A low padded seat or cushion; = POUF[1] 3.

1877 H. JAMES *American* xii. 195 Valentin was sitting on a puff. *Ibid.* 206 Then she gave a little push to the puff that stood near her, and by a glance at Newman seemed to indicate that she had placed it in position for him.

d. *Cytology.* A short swollen region of a polytene chromosome, active in RNA synthesis. Cf. PUFFED *ppl. a.* 1 d; PUFFING *vbl. sb.* 3 c.

1937 C. B. BRIDGES in *Cytologia* (Fujii Jubilee Vol.) II. 751 Sections 58E and F show another characteristic peculiarity—namely, they often are converted into a much swollen light-staining 'puff' in which the banding is very hard to see. **1957** *Proc. Nat. Acad. Sci.* XLIII. 964 The correlation between the secretory activity in certain cells and the appearance and disappearance of puffs at specific loci in these cells had led many authors to the hypothesis that the genes at the locus of the puff may be actively controlling the secretory process. **1966** *Proc. R. Soc.* B. CLXIV. 284 The two different kinds of 'puff': (1)..the multi-stranded true puffs, which occur only in giant chromosomes: and (2)..the single-stranded loop 'puff' of lampbrush chromosomes. **1974** *Cold Spring Harbor Symp. Quantitative Biol.* XXXVIII. 660/2 Puffs result from the accumulation of RNA and proteins at a band which is being transcribed.

3. a. A kind of fungus; = PUFF-BALL 1. *dial.*

1538 ELYOT *Dict.*, *Tuber*, a puffe growyng on the ground lyke a musherone or spunge. **1578** LYTE *Dodoens* III. i. 313 The rootes be round and swollen like to a Puffe or Turnep. **1601** HOLLAND *Pliny* II. 133 All the sort of those Puffes and Toadstooles. **1847–78** HALLIWELL, *Puff*, a puff-ball.

†**b.** Some kind of apple: also called PUFFIN[1] (sense 3).

1655 MOUFET & BENNET *Health's Impr.* (1746) 291 Apples be so divers of Form and Substance..; some consist more of Air than Water, as your Puffs called *Mala pulmonea*.

4. †**a.** An instrument like a small bellows, formerly used for blowing powder upon the hair. *Obs.* **b.** A small pad of down or other flossy substance, for applying powder to the hair or skin. More fully POWDER-PUFF.

1658 *Songs Costume* (Percy Soc.) 163 To eject powder in your hayre, Here is a pritty puff. **1712** STEELE *Spect.* No. 478 ⁋13 On the other [side], Powder Baggs, Puffs, Combs and Brushes. **1758** JOHNSON *Idler* No. 5 ⁋11 If the hair has lost its powder, a lady has a puff. **1822–34** *Good's Study Med.* (ed. 4) IV. 507 The pediculus pubis is best destroyed by calomel mixed with starch powder, and applied by means of a down puff. **1908** *Lady* 10 Dec. 1106/3 'Beauty Box' containing..one box of face powder, with swansdown puff, ..is sent post free.

†**c.** A small vessel for sprinkling scent. *Obs.*

1436 in *Test. Ebor.* (Surtees) II. 15 *note*, Unum puff argenti pro aqua rosarum spargenda.

5. A name for various kinds of very light pastry or confectionery; now *esp.* a piece of puff-paste (usually three-cornered), or a light porous cake, inclosing jam or the like; also, a light confection resembling a macaroon. In quot. 1908 = PUFF-PASTE. (So LG. *puffe*, *puffe-brodt*.)

1419 *Liber Albus* (Rolls) I. 353 Panis levis qui dicitur 'pouf'. **1769** MRS. RAFFALD *Eng. Housekpr.* (1778) 164 To make German Puffs. **1771** MRS. HAYWOOD *New Present* 195 Lemon Puffs..Chocolate Puffs..Ratafia Puffs. **1795** SOUTHEY *Lett. fr. Spain* (1808) II. 11 The hostess there had just made some puffs, and begged me to eat one. *a* **1845** HOOD *Sweets of Youth* 3, I used to revel in a pie, or puff. **1864** Jam-puffs [see JAM *sb.*[2] c]. **1908** *Westm. Gaz.* 15 Aug. 7/1 In pastry nothing is so heavy as puff that has failed.

6. *fig.* **a.** An inflated speech or piece of display; an empty or vain boast; vainglory or pride; vain show, showy adornment; inflation of style, bombast; brag, bluff. ? *Obs.*

1567 DRANT *Horace, Art Poetry* A iij, Put out no puffes, nor thwackyng words. **1631** R. H. *Arraignm. Whole Creature* xix. 331 The Idolatrous Philistins..all in their Puffe, and Iollity, swelling with pompe and pride. **1680** H. MORE *Apocal. Apoc.* 250 A blind puff of pride and vanity of Mind. **1747** W. HORSLEY *Fool* (1748) II. 166 It's all Puff, he has but a very indifferent Person. **1814** *Sporting Mag.* XLIII. 93 A real or pretended challenge..generally believed, how-ever, to be mere puff. **1819** SCOTT *Let. to Ld. Montagu* 3 Oct. in Lockhart *Life*, We gave our carriage such additional dignity as a pair of leaders could add, and went to meet him [Prince Leopold] in full puff. **1821** ARNOLD *Let.* 25 Apr. in Stanley *Life & Corr.* I. 65 Any thing like puff, or verbal ornament, I cannot bring myself to.

†**b.** Anything empty, vain, or unsubstantial; a 'thing of nought'. (Cf. *breath*.) *Obs.*

1580 BABINGTON *Exp. Lord's Prayer* (1596) 46 He careth not for the puffes of this world, birth, beautie, wealth or wit. **1583** GOLDING *Calvin on Deut.* cxciii. 1197 A man would haue thought, that all that euer had beene done in the person of Dauid had been but a puffe. **1606** SYLVESTER *Du Bartas* II. iv. III. *Magnif.* 336 Honour is but a puffe, Life but a vapour.

7. Undue or inflated praise or commendation, uttered or written in order to influence public estimation; an extravagantly laudatory advertisement or review of a book, a performer or performance, a tradesman's goods, or the like.

(In quot. 1602 the inflated praise of a flatterer.)

[**1602** MARSTON *Ant. & Mel.* IV. Wks. 1856 I. 46 Blowne up with the flattering puffes Of spungy sycophants.] **1732** *London Mag.* I. 81 Puff is a cant word for the applause that writers and Book-sellers give their own books &c. to promote their sale. **1742** CIBBER *Let. to Pope* 5, I am really driven to it (as the Puff in the Play-Bill says) At the Desire of several Persons of Quality. **1774** J. WESLEY *Let.* 8 Jan. (1931) VI. 66, I suppose Mr. Rivington's advertisement is only a puff, as the booksellers call it. **1774** GOLDSM. *Retal.* 110 The puff of a dunce, he mistook it for fame. **1779** SHERIDAN *Critic* I. ii. **1794** C. PIGOT *Female Jockey Club* 78 The amount..is consumed in paying newspaper puffs. **1822** J. ROBISON *Syst. Mechanical Philos.* II. 47 His encomiums ..are to a great degree extravagant, resembling more the puff of an advertising tradesman than the patriotic communications of a gentleman. **1827** SCOTT *Jrnl.* 13 Dec., My name would be only useful in the way of puff, for I really know nothing of the subject. **1889** RUSKIN *Præterita* III. iv. 159 The last puffs written for a morning concert. **1916** A. HUXLEY *Let.* 29 Dec. (1969) 118, I lighted in to-day's *Morning Post* on a little puff of myself, apropos of *Oxford Poetry*, '16. **1923** E. WALLACE *Captains of Souls* xlvii. 258 'Ambrose Sault was executed at Wechester Jail..Billet was the executioner.' The hangman always received his puff. **1960** *Punch* 16 Mar. 383/2 Students are advised to omit fine language, puffs for the product, or any form of cosy get-togetherness. **1974** S. CHITTY *Beast & Monk* III. iv. 229 In January 1864 Kingsley reviewed Volumes VII and VIII of Froude's *History of England*.., no doubt with a view to giving his brother-in-law a 'puff'.

8. Applied to a person. **a.** One who brags or behaves insolently, or who is puffed up or swollen with pride or vanity; a boaster, a braggart. *arch.*

1599 B. JONSON *Cynthia's Rev.* III. iii, The one a light voluptuous reueller, The other, a strange arrogating puffe, Both impudent and ignorant inough. *a* **1661** FULLER *Worthies, Norfolk* (1662) II. 253 John Fastolfe, Knight..the Stage hath been overbold with his memory, making him a Thrasonical Puff, and emblem of Mock-valour. **1850** WHIPPLE *Ess. & Rev.* (ed. 3) I. 392 The age groaned under a company of lewd, shallow-brained puffs, wretches who seemed to have sinned themselves into another kind of species.

†**b.** One who praises extravagantly or unduly, esp. from interested motives; a writer of puffs: = PUFFER 2. *Obs.*

1751 CHESTERF. *Lett.* 10 June (1774) III. 199 Lady Hervey, who is your puff and panegyrist, writes me word.. that you dance very genteelly. **1764** FOOTE *Patron* I. Wks. 1799 I. 337 The fellow has got a little in flesh, by being puff to the play-house this winter. **1789** SHERIDAN *Critic* I. i, [*Name of a character*] Mr. Puff, a gentleman well known in the theatrical world.

c. *slang.* A decoy in a gambling-house.

1731 *Gentl. Mag.* I. 25/1 Officers established in the most notorious Gaming-Houses... 5. Two Puffs, who have Money given 'em to decoy others to play. **1755** *Mem. Capt. P. Drake* II. x. 225, I..now and then ventured a Guinea at the other Banks in Earnest, to prevent any Suspicion of my being a Puff.

d. [See also POOF *sb.*[1]] An effeminate man; a male homosexual.

1902 FARMER & HENLEY *Slang* V. 313/1 *Puff*... 3 (tramps'), a sodomist. **1937** PARTRIDGE *Dict. Slang* 665/2 *Puff*,..a sodomist. **1961** P. WHITE *Riders in Chariot* xi. 414 It was that puf Mortimer would not let me alone. **1967** H. W. SUTHERLAND *Magnie* iv. 63 He'd be a puff boy, this Magnie, and God knows what entertainment he laid on for Arthur. **1974** P. WRIGHT *Lang. Brit. Industry* xi. 95 An infuriated spectator may shout at a plump, sleek referee, 'You nasty little ponce!' (or *puff*).

9. *attrib.* and *Comb.* (Some of these may be from the stem of PUFF *v.*) †**a.** *attrib.* or as *adj.* That is like a puff in senses 2–6. Puffed, inflated, swelling (*lit.* and *fig.*). *Obs.*

1472 in Swayne *Sarum Churchw. Acc.* (1896) 1, j pall of blew puffe feathers in manner of scaloppys. **1598** E. GILPIN *Skial.* i. (1878) 36 Like a Swartrutters hose his puffe thoughts swell, With yeastie ambition. **1598** MARSTON *Sco. Villanie* II. vii, Mean'st thou that wasted leg, puffe bumbast boot?

b. *Comb.*, as (sense 1) ***puff-roar***, ***-train***, ***-wind***; (sense 2 b) ***puff scarf***, ***sleeve***; ***puff-sleeved*** adj.; (sense 5) ***puff-tart***; (sense 7) ***puff-master***, ***merchant***, ***-purveyor***, ***-trap***, ***writer***, ***-writing***; †**puff-bagged** *a.*, wearing puffed 'bags' or breeches; **puff billiards**, a game resembling billiards, in which a ball is driven about on a table by puffs of air; **puff box**, a box to hold toilet-powder and a powder-puff; **puff-breeches**, puffed or inflated breeches; †**puff-cole**, a variety of cole or cabbage (see quot.); †**puff-doctrine**, vain or empty doctrine; **puff-fish**, a fish of either the *Tetrodontidæ* or *Diodontidæ*; also called, from their habit of inflating themselves with air, *globe-fish*, *swell-fish*, or *puffer*; in quot. a *Tetrodon*; **puff-leg**, a humming-bird of the genus *Eriocnemis*, having tufts of down upon the legs; **puff-netting** = *leaf-netting* (see LEAF *sb.*[1] 18); **puff-pig**, local name in Newfoundland for the porpoise (= *puffing-pig*, s.v. PUFFING *ppl. a.* 1); **puff pipe**, (*a*) a short pipe connected to a trap or valve in a drainage system in order to ventilate it; (*b*) on a vertical takeoff aircraft, a pipe out of which compressed air is blown in order to control attitude; **puff port**, on a hovercraft, a vent out of which compressed air is blown in order to control attitude; †**puff-ring**, (app.) a counterfeit ring made hollow instead of solid; **puff-shark**, a Californian species of dog-fish, *Catulus uter*; **puff-shouldered** *a.*, having puffs (sense 2 b) on the shoulders; **puff-stone**, local name for the soft porous marlstone of the Middle Lias; **puff-throated** *a.*, having a puffed or inflated throat; **puff-wig**, a puffed or full wig; †**puff-wing**, an inflated or prominent 'wing' or projection on the shoulder of a dress.

1653 URQUHART *Rabelais* II. ii, Great drops of water, such as fall from a *puff-bagged man in a top sweat. **1897** *Puff billiards [see INDOOR, IN-DOOR *a.* 1]. **1901** *Commercial Advertiser* (N.Y.) 11 May 12/5 Mrs. Hwfa Williams is said to have invented puff-billiards. **1953** P. L. Fermor *Violins of Saint-Jacques* 74 Usually some newly arrived acquisition from Paris occupied the centre of the room—a magic lantern, a kaleidoscope or..a game of puff-billiards. **1895** *Mongomery Ward Catal.* Spring–Summer 259/1 *Puff boxes, made of papier mache...$0.20. **1926–7** *Army & Navy Stores Catal.* 99 Puff Boxes. *c* **1843** CARLYLE *Hist. Sk. Jas. I & Chas. I* (1898) 260 The huge *puff-breeches of the time. **1620** VENNER *Via Recta* vii. 135 The top-leaues and heads of Cole that are but a little closed, which we commonly call *Puffe-cole. **1629** H. BURTON *Truth's Triumph* 11 This Pontifician *puffe-doctrine of preparatory workes. **1885** LADY BRASSEY *The Trades* 407 There were little *puff-fish, sometimes as round as a puff-ball, sometimes as flat as a pancake. **1874** WOOD *Nat. Hist.* 318 The Copper-bellied *Puff-leg... The 'puffs'..look like refined swan's down. **1762** *Harangues Celebr. Quack-Doctors* Ed. Let., To the Orator of Orators, and *Puff-Master-General of Lincoln's-Inn-Fields. **1951** R. CHANDLER *Let.* 6 July (1966) 143 *Puff merchants..will go on record over practically anything including the World Almanac, provided they get their names featured. **1882** *Puff Netting [see *leaf-netting* s.v. LEAF *sb.*[1] 18]. **1861** L. L. NOBLE *Icebergs* 91 At the mention of the *puff-pig, the local name for the common porpoise, we indulged ourselves in a childish laugh. **1894** A. J. WALLIS-TAYLER *Sanitary Arrangement of Dwelling-Houses* ix. 58 A *puff-pipe, about one inch in diameter, should be taken from the valve-box through the outer wall, and its free end be also fitted with a brass flap-valve. **1934** *Archit. Rev.* Jan. p. xliv, Puff pipes, always a doubtful practice, although admissable, under certain conditions, are..here abolished and the terminals of the vent pipes being fixed high above all openings to the building ensure a strong current of fresh air throughout the system. **1960** *Aeroplane* XCVIII. 572/1 (*diagram*) Pilot controls..attitude and yaw via 'puff-pipes'. **1965** J. L. NAYLER *Aviation* xiii. 188/2 Control in hovering flight was obtained by the 'puff-pipe' system first used in the *Flying Bedstead*. **1972** J. HASTINGS *Plumber's Compan.* 133 In Wiltshire the ornamental end of a puff pipe is a snake's mouth. **1967** *Jane's Surface Skimmer Systems 1967–68* 37/1 *Puff ports, to improve in particular low-speed yaw control, and segmented skirts will be incorporated. **1971** R. L. TRILLO *Marine Hovercraft Technol.* v. 93 Puff ports used on the Parkhouse Beckingham Hovercat to assist in directional control also provided rolling moment causing the craft to roll into a turn, thereby enhancing the comfort of the turning manoeuvre. **1908** *Athenæum* 11 Apr. 442/2 According to Hazlitt,..the rejected *puff-purveyor was none other than Charles Lamb. **1534** MORE *Comf. agst. Trib.* III. Wks. 1228/1 Like a *puffe rynge of Paris, holowe, lighte and counterfait in deede. **1592** GREENE *Upst. Courtier* G j b, Puffe ringes, and quaint conceits. **1582** STANYHURST *Æneis* II. (Arb.) 57 East, weast and Southwynd, with *pufroare mightelye ramping. **1880** *Amer. Mail Order Fashions in Americana Rev.* (1961) 32 New *puff-scarf, satin faced and lined. **1908** C. F. HOLDER *Big Game at Sea* 118 (Illustration), The *Puff Shark of California and Its Eggs.

1899 A. CONAN DOYLE *Duet* i. 7 A roomful of *puff-shouldered young ladies. **1894** B. POTTER *Jrnl.* (1966) 314, I had to take his arm in to dinner, not much encouraged by his scrutiny of my *puff-sleeves. **1975** G. HOWELL *In Vogue* 151/2 Little-girl dresses..with..full short skirts, tucks, smocking and puff sleeves. **1883** 'MARK TWAIN' *Life on Mississippi* xxxviii. 404 Grandpa and grandma..stiff, old-fashioned, high-collared, *puff-sleeved. **1969** *Observer* 21 Dec. 23/4 This smocked, puff-sleeved blouse. *c* **1640** J. SMYTH *Hundred of Berkeley* (1885) 175 In this towne [Dursley] is a rocke of a strange stone called a *Puffe stone. **1742** *De Foe's Tour Gt. Brit.* (ed. 3) II. 252 That soft, easy-to-be wrought Stone at Great Banington, called Puff-stone, prodigiously strong and lasting. **1829** *Glover's Hist. Derby* I. 100 Tufa, tophus, puff-stone or marl stone is a porous soft stone. **1906** *Westm. Gaz.* 4 Aug. 5/3 Before each man was a *puff tart and a glass of ginger-beer. **1863** BATES *Nat. Amazon* ii. (1864) 36 A species of *puff-throated manikin, a little bird which flies occasionally across the road. **1896** SWINBURNE *Let.* 29 May (1962) VI. 100 When the '*puff-train' did 'anything particularly startling or loud'. **1796** *Mod. Gulliver's Trav.* 172 News-paper, *puff-trap, yields supply of game. **1702** FARQUHAR *Inconstant* I. i, Here, sirrah, here's ten guineas for thee; get thyself a drugget suit and a *puff-wig, and so I dub thee Gentleman-Usher. **1582** STANYHURST *Æneis* II. (Arb.) 69 Much lyk to a *pufwynd, or nap that vannished hastlye. **1601** B. JONSON *Poetaster* IV. i, You shall see 'hem flock about you with their *puffe wings, and aske you, where you bought your lawne. **1870** T. A. BROWN *Hist. Amer. Stage* 21/2 In September he quit the business, and soon after obtained the situation of '*puff writer' for the Bowery Amphitheatre. **1807** SOUTHEY *Espriella's Lett.* III. 58 *Puff-writing is one of the strange trades in London.

puff (pʌf), *v.* Forms: 3–5 puffe(n, 4–7 poff(e, 5 pouff(e, 5–7 puffe, 7– puff. Pa. t. and pple. puffed (pʌft); 3, 6 pufte (*pa. t.*), 4 poffed, 6 poffte (*pa. pple.*), 5–9 puft. [ME. *puf* sb. and *puffen* vb. appear together in Ancren Riwle, early in 13th c., as well-established words, the verb implying an OE. **puffian*, existing beside the recorded form *pyffan* (imper. *pyf*, pa. t. *pyfte*):—OTeut. **puffôjan* and **puffjan*. (Or OE. *pyffan* might perh. itself give ME. *puffen* in the same way as OE. *kycgel* appears in Ancren R. as *cuggel*, later *cudgel*.) Of onomatopœic origin, representing the action and sound of emitting from the lips a puff of breath. Kindred forms, either from OTeut. or formed afresh, appear in MDu. *puffen* to puff, blow, early mod.Du. *pof* 'bucca, buccarum inflatio; bombus, flatus, sclopus' (Kilian); *pof* 'puff', *pofbal* 'ball blown or puffed up' (Hexham); *poffen*, 'flare, sufflare, buccas inflare; turgere, ampullari' (Kilian); 'to puf, blow, swell up, to boast, brag, vaunt' (Hexham).

Other senses of *puffen*, *poffen*, in LG. and Du., and thence in mod.Ger., Da., Sw., as to strike with an audible knock, to pop, thump, bang, crack, or simply to strike, and of the cogn. sb. in the corresponding sense of an audible blow, etc., may have been developed from the same original word, or may be later echoic formations expressive of sudden noise; cf. F. *pouf*, 'an exclamation expressing the noise of something falling', with derived vb. *pouffer*; also F. *soufflet*, from *souffler* to blow.]

1. a. *intr.* To blow with a short abrupt blast or blasts; to emit a puff of air or breath; to escape as a puff. ***to puff out, up***, to issue, arise in puffs.

[Cf. *c* **1000** in Napier *OE. Glosses* i. 1886, *Spirantis, i. sufflantis*, [*gl.*] piffendes. *Ibid.* 4931 *Exalauit*, ut apyfte. *Ibid.* xviii. 42 *Efflauit*, pyfte. *c* **1000** in *Techmer's Ztschr.* (1885) II. 121 Pyf on þinne scyte finger.] *a* **1225** *Ancr. R.* 124 Vor nouðer ne mei þe wind..fulen þine soule þauh hit puffe on þe, bute 3if þi sulf hit makie. *c* **1384** CHAUCER *H. Fame* III. 776 Eolus..toke his blake trumpe faste And gan to puffen and to blaste. **1576** FLEMING *Panopl. Epist.* 350 When the windes cease puffing. **1600** SHAKS. *A.Y.L.* III. v. 50 Like foggy South, puffing with winde and raine. **1656** TRAPP *Comm. Jas.* iv. 14 Thy breath is in thy nostrils, ever ready to puff out. **1841** BORROW *Zincali* I. xi. § 1. 53 The bellows puff until the coal is excited to a furious glow. **1865** BARING-GOULD *Werewolves* vii, The air puffing up off the blue twinkling Bay of Biscay.

b. (*a*) To breathe quick and hard, as when out of breath from running or other exertion; to breathe hard, pant violently; often, ***to puff and blow***; hence, to run or go with puffing or panting. Also (*b*) *trans.* with *out*: to utter breathlessly or with panting (quot. 1599); (*c*) *trans.* in *causal* sense: to cause to puff, to put out of breath (chiefly in *pa. pple.*: see PUFFED 3).

1377 LANGL. *P. Pl.* B. XIII. 87 He shal haue a penaunce in his paunche and puffe at ech a worde. **1581** MULCASTER *Positions* xxxiii. (1887) 119 To be hoat and chafe, to puffe and blow, to sweat. **1599** NASHE *Lenten Stuffe* (1871) 59 [He] came lazily waddling in, and puffed out, Pork, Pork, Pork. **1607** SHAKS. *Cor.* II. i. 230 Flamins Doe..puffe To winne a vulgar station. **1710** ADDISON *Tatler* No. 165 ¶ 4 Puffing and blowing as if..very much out of Breath. **1806–7** J. BERESFORD *Miseries Hum. Life* (1826) v. xvii, After toiling and puffing up to the very top of the building. **1898** *Allbutt's Syst. Med.* V. 955 They puff after trains.

c. To send forth puffs or whiffs of vapour or smoke, as a steam-engine, or a person smoking tobacco; to move *away*, *in*, *out*, with puffing, as a locomotive or steamboat.

1781 COWPER *Conversation* 248 The dozing sages drop the drowsy strain, Then pause and puff—and speak, and pause again. **1849** D. G. MITCHELL *Battle Summer* (1852) 222 The railway engines are puffing out of Paris. **1861** HUGHES *Tom Brown at Oxf.* iii, Sanders..puffed away at his cigar. **1870** MRS. RIDDELL *Austin Friars* i, Where the trains now go puffing in and out of Cannon Street Terminus. **1894** *Outing* (U.S.) XXIV. 372/2 A light rain was falling as the steamer puffed away from the South Stack Lighthouse.

d. Of a fungus: to discharge a cloud of spores suddenly.

1887 H. E. F. GARNSEY tr. *A. de Bary's Compar. Morphol. & Biol. Fungi* iii. 89 As long as the Fungus remains shut up in the damp atmosphere no amount of shaking will cause it to puff. **1953** C. T. INGOLD *Dispersal in Fungi* ii. 27 Once an apothecium has puffed it cannot, as a rule, be induced to do so again for a time.

†**2.** *intr.* To blow abruptly from the lips as an expression of contempt or scorn; to say 'pooh!' or the like; to speak or behave scornfully or insolently, to swagger. ***to puff at***, to express contempt of, to defy scornfully, to pooh-pooh. *Obs.*

c **1489** CAXTON *Sonnes of Aymon* i. 25 Yf ye hadde seen hym chaunge his colour, pouff, blowe, as a man cruell prowde and owterageouse. **1575** LANEHAM *Let.* (1871) 42 The King fumed,..Princes puft, Bar[o]nz blustered, Lordz began too loour. **1611** BIBLE *Ps.* x. 5 As for all his enemies, he puffeth at them. *c* **1620** Z. BOYD *Zion's Flowers* (1855) 137 Thus lye they low who did most proudly puff. **1677** OTWAY *Cheats of Scapin* II. i, One that frowns, puffs, and looks big at all Mankind.

3. a. *trans.* To drive, impel, or agitate by puffing; to blow *away*, *down*, *off*, *out*, *up*, etc. with a quick short blast; to emit (smoke, steam, etc.) in puffs.

a **1225** *Ancr. R.* 266 3if a miracle nere þet pufte adun þene deouel þet set on hire so ueste. **1377** LANGL. *P. Pl.* B. v. 16 Piries and plomtrees were puffed [C. VI. 119 poffed] to þe erthe. **1495** *Trevisa's Barth. De P.R.* XVI. lxxxi. (W. de W.) L viij b/1 Powder..hath that name for it is puft wyth þe wynde. **1567** DRANT *Horace, Epist.* II. i. G vj, That huffes it vp and puffes it downe. **1582** STANYHURST *Æneis* III. (Arb.) 74 In three days sayling wee shal too Candye be puffed. **1697** DRYDEN *Virg. Georg.* I. 623 When the clearing North will puff the Clouds away. **1720** GAY *Trivia* II. 191, I thirsty stand.., See them puff off the froth, and gulp amain. **1796** JANE AUSTEN *Pride & Prej.* xi, My feelings are not puffed about with every attempt to move them. **1867** TROLLOPE *Chron. Barset* xlvi, As he puffed the cigar-smoke out of his mouth. **1889** DOYLE *Micah Clarke* 138 Bullets which puffed up the white dust all around him.

†**b.** To blow short blasts (with mouth or bellows) upon (a fire) to make it burn up. *Obs.*

1610 B. JONSON *Alch.* II. i, That's his fire-drake, His lungs, his Zephyrus, he that puffes his coales. **1698** TUTCHIN *Whitehall in Fl.* iii, Embers... Which Fate puffs up unto a blaze. *a* **1763** SHENSTONE *Colemira* 52 She.. Foments the infant flame, and puffs it into life.

c. To blow *out*, extinguish with a puff.

1547 *Bk. Marchauntes* c ij b, Some poore foole..stycketh vp a candell vpon a pyller, and oure marchaunt anone snatcheth and puffeth it out. **1621** QUARLES *Argalus & P.* (1678) 51 This breath shall puff thee out. **1752** YOUNG *Brothers* I. i, Those That would make kings, and puff them out at pleasure. **1879** J. TODHUNTER *Alcestis* 104 Yet we go out, Like candles puffed, not willingly. We die.

d. To smoke (a tobacco-pipe or cigar) in intermittent puffs or whiffs.

1809 W. IRVING *Knickerb.* III. iii. (1820) 179 Here the old burgher would sit..puffing his pipe. **1861** GEO. ELIOT *Silas M.* vi, The farrier was puffing his pipe rather fiercely. **1875** H. JAMES *R. Hudson* i, Rowland..lighted a cigar and puffed it awhile in silence.

e. To apply powder with a powder-puff: with the powder, or the surface, as object. Also *absol.*

1838 D. JERROLD *Men of Character* (1851) 5 Job..tried to puff, but his unsteady hand..sent forth the powder above, below, about, but not upon the head. **1909** *Lady* 7 Jan. 34/3 Afterwards puff on a little rice powder. *Ibid.* 21 Jan. 116/1 The skin should then be puffed over with her Beauty Powder.

f. To drive or cause to move with puffing.

1903 *Smart Set* IX. 147/1 He puffed his automobile up the drive.

4. a. To cause (something) to swell by puffing or blowing air into it; to blow *out* or *up*; to inflate; to distend by inflation, or in any way, as by stuffing or padding, or, in costume, by bunching up the stuff in rounded masses.

1539 in *Vicary's Anat.* (1888) App. iii. 173 Apparelled in whyte Satten puffed out with crymson sarcenet. **1592** GREENE *Def. Conny Catch.* Wks. (Grosart) XI. 69 What say you to the Butcher..that hath pollicies to puffe vp his meate to please the eye? **1679** BLOUNT *Anc. Tenures* 11 He should dance, puff up his Cheeks, making therewith a sound. **1735** SOMERVILLE *Chase* III. 561 The Huntsman..puffs his Cheeks in vain. **1774** GOLDSM. *Nat. Hist.* (1776) VII. 152 This method of puffing itself up, is similar to that in pigeons, whose crops are sometimes greatly distended with air. **1899** *Allbutt's Syst. Med.* VII. 618 The cheeks..drawn in and puffed out by the respiratory movements.

b. *intr.* To swell *up* or become distended or swollen.

1725 *Bradley's Fam. Dict.* s.v. *Lemon*, Should the Lemon-Slips happen to puff or turn sower in the Vessels, wherein they are kept. *Ibid.* s.v. *Sweetmeats*, Wet Sweetmeats are.. subject to sour and puff, which proceeds from the moistness of the fruit. **1737** BRACKEN *Farriery Impr.* (1757) II. 238 They [wind-galls] will not rise and puff up. **1804** *Med. Jrnl.* XII. 119 When exposed..to a gradually increased fire, it [opium] begins to melt and to puff up.

c. *trans.* To adorn with puffs; to dress the hair in puffs. See PUFF *sb.* 2 b.

1891 SARAH J. DUNCAN *Amer. Girl in London* 293 The hairdresser..she puffed and curled me.

5. *fig.* **a.** To 'inflate' or cause to 'swell' with vanity, pride, ambition, or the like; to make vain, proud, or arrogant; to elate, exalt in mind; *rarely*, to cause to swell with anger, to enrage (quots. 1555, 1815). Usually with *up*; most commonly in pa. pple. ***puffed up***.

1526 TINDALE *Col.* ii. 18 Causlesse puft vppe with his fleshly mynde. **1535** COVERDALE *1 Cor.* viii. 2 Knowlege puffeth a man vp, but loue edifyeth. **1555** EDEN *Decades* 240 Kynge Iohn..was puffed vp with anger. **1634** HEYWOOD *Maidenhead Lost* II. Wks. 1874 IV. 122 There is no change of Fortune Can puffe me or deiect me. **1681** DRYDEN *Abs. & Achit.* I. 480 Not stain'd with cruelty, nor puft with pride. **1724** DE FOE *Mem. Cavalier* (1840) 257 Victory had not puffed him up. **1815** *Sporting Mag.* XLVI. 156 Being puffed up with rage, they commenced an attack on the temporary paling. **1863** E. V. NEALE *Anal. Th. & Nat.* 223 Its tendency is to puff men up with a persuasion of their own greatness.

†**b.** (with *up*.) To exalt unduly in position or authority. *Obs.*

1535 COVERDALE *Judg.* ix. 11 Shal I leaue my swetnes and my good frute, and go to be puft vp aboue the trees? **1612** BACON *Ess., Judicature* (Arb.) 456 Puffing a Court vp beyond her bounds for their own scrappes and aduantage. **1641** MILTON *Animadv.* xiii. 44 No more then a speciall endorsement could make to puffe up the foreman of a Jury.

6. a. To praise, extol, or commend in inflated or extravagant terms, usually from interested motives; *esp.* to advertise with exaggerated or falsified praise. Also with *off* (now *rare* or *obs.*).

1735 POPE *Prol. Sat.* 232 Full-blown Bufo, puff'd by ev'ry quill; Fed with soft Dedication all day long. **1749** CHESTERF. *Lett.* 27 Sept. (1775) II. 228 Sir Charles Williams has puffed you (as the mob call it) here extremely. **1750** *Ibid.* 12 Oct. (1774) III. 55 Where she will..puff you, if I may use so low a word. **1759** SARAH FIELDING *C'tess of Dellwyn* II. 283 The Captain proceeded..by puffing off himself. **1782** ELIZ. BLOWER *Geo. Bateman* II. 60 To puff his performances into notice. **1799** *Med. Jrnl.* II. 150 The only way a quack-medicine gets very celebrated, is, by its being constantly puffed off in advertisements. **1813** SCOTT *Fam. Lett.* 29 June, Each puffed the other in alternate compliments, which were mutually accepted. **1858** LD. ST. LEONARDS *Handy Bk. Prop. Law* ii. 7 You may falsely praise, or, as it is vulgarly termed, puff your property.

b. *absol.* (also with dependent clause). To tell or say to the praise of any one.

c **1750** W. STROUD *Mem.* 10 He wanted me to..puff for him (as he called it) that he had a large estate in Warwickshire. **1791** WOLCOTT (P. Pindar) *Ode to my Ass* x, I could say such things about myself—But God forbid that I should puff!

c. *intr.* To bid at an auction for the purpose of inflating or raising the price: cf. PUFFER 2 b, PUFFING *vbl. sb.* 4 b.

7. *Comb.*, as †**puff-loaf** *a.*, that 'puffs' loaves, i.e. causes them to swell up. (See also prec. 9 b.)

1577 STANYHURST *Descr. Irel.* iii. in *Holinshed* (1587) II. 23 The colerake sweeping of a pufloafe baker.

puff (pʌf), *int.* Also 6 poff. [Echoic. So also MDu. *puf*.] A representation of the act of blowing in puffs; also, of blowing abruptly from the lips; hence, an expression of contempt (cf. POOH).

c **1460** *Towneley Myst.* ii. 277 Puf! this smoke dos me mych shame. **1481** CAXTON *Reynard* xxvi. (Arb.) 59 Puf said the foxe,..be ye so sore aferd herof? **1606** *Sir G. Goosecappe* v. i. in Bullen *O. Pl.* III. 89 Puffe, is there not a feather in this ayre A man may challenge for her? *c* **1620** ROWLANDS *Paire of Spy Knaves* (Hunter. Cl.) 20 I'le teach thee..To take Tobacco like a Caualeere. Thus draw the vapor thorow your nose, and say, Puffe, it is gone, fuming the smoke away. **1620** *Swetnam Arraign'd* I. ii. A iv, Puffe, giue me some ayre, I am almost stifled, puffe, Oh, my sides! **1870** MISS BRIDGMAN *Ro. Lynne* I. iv. 55, 'I have found it so'—puff, puff [smoking a cigar].

ˈ**puff-adder.** [a. S. Afr. Du. *pof-adder*: see PUFF *v.*] **1.** A large and very venomous African viper (*Bitis* or *Clotho arietans*), which puffs out or inflates the upper part of its body when excited.

1789 W. PATERSON *Narr. Four Journeys Country of Hottentots* 164 The Puff Adder..has its name from blowing itself up to near a foot in circumference. **1824** BURCHELL *Trav.* I. 469 It is well known in the colony by the name of the *Pof-Adder* (Puff Adder). Its venom is said to be most fatal. **1834** PRINGLE *Afr. Sk.* viii. 279 The puff-adder..is a heavy..sluggish animal, very thick in proportion to its length. **1871** KINGSLEY *At Last* ii, But who will call the Puff Adder of the Cape..anything but ugly and horrible? **1896** *List Anim. Zool. Soc.* 643 *Bitis arietans*, Puff Adder. *Hab.* Africa and Arabia. **1915** *Chambers's Jrnl.* July 437/1 Perhaps the most loathsome of the snakes of Natal is the dreaded puff-adder. **1969** *Times* 15 Sept. (Uganda Suppl.) p. vi/8 Puff adders were sacred at Budo, so only Europeans could kill them. **1975** H. B. COTT *Looking at Animals* viii. 160 The difficulty is met by the application of patterns, such as those exhibited by African Rock Python, Gaboon Viper, Puff Adder.

2. *U.S.* The western hog-nosed snake, *Heterodon nasicus*, which belongs to the family Colubridæ but is not dangerous to man.

1882 *Amer. Naturalist* XVI. 566 Twice afterward I noticed this strange habit of the puff adders. **1897–8** 'MARK TWAIN' *Autobiogr.* (1924) I. 103 Snakes..liked to lie in it [*sc.* a road] and sun themselves; when they were rattlesnakes or puff-adders, we killed them. **1966** R. C. STEBBINS *Field Guide to Western Reptiles & Amphibians* x. 145 When disturbed it [*sc.* the western hog-nose snake] often spreads its head and neck and strikes with open mouth, hissing, but seldom biting. This behaviour has earned it the names 'puff adder', 'blow viper', and 'hissing adder'.

ˈpuffatory, *a. nonce-wd.* [f. PUFF *v.*, after such words as *laudatory*.] Having the quality of 'puffing', or of a 'puff': see PUFF *v.* 6, *sb.* 7.

1823 *Blackw. Mag.* XIV. 85 Used as a peg to hang a note-puffatory upon. **1854** G. GILFILLAN in Watson *Lett. & Jrnls.* (1892) 395 Authors are better of seeing all reviews, unless the helplessly puffatory or malignantly abusive.

ˈpuff-ball. [f. PUFF *sb.* (sense 3) or *v.* + BALL *sb.*[1]; so Du. *pof-bal*: see PUFF *v.*]

1. a. A fungus of the genus *Lycoperdon* or of some allied genus; so called from the ball-like shape of the ripe spore-case, and its emission of the spores in a cloud of fine powder when broken. (Some of the species are edible in an unripe state.)

1649 BLITHE *Eng. Improv. Impr.* (1653) 34 And filleth the Earth with Wind,..and makes it swell and rise like a Puf-ball. **1702** *Phil. Trans.* XXIII. 1364, I find the Dust of the ..Puff-Ball to be the minutest Powder that I ever saw. **1785** MARTYN *Rousseau's Bot.* xxxii. (1794) 502 Common Puff-ball is roundish, and discharges its dust by a torn aperture in the top. **1843** *Zoologist* I. 25 Intoxicating the bees..by filling the hive with the smoke of an ignited puff-ball. **1861** H. MACMILLAN *Footnotes fr. Page Nat.* 199 The giant puff-ball (*Bovista gigantea*)..increases from the size of a pea to that of a melon in a single night.

fig. **1826** PUSEY in Liddon, etc. *Life* (1893) I. iv. 87 [Writing from Berlin..he states that] Tholuck was initiated a few days since,..and that great puff-ball Marheineke delivered addresses in Latin. **1873** LELAND *Egypt. Sketch Bk.* 221 A poisonous puff-ball of pride.

b. *collect.* The powdery spores of a species of *Lycoperdon* used as a styptic.

1767 GOOCH *Treat. Wounds* I. 173 Over which..it will still be right to apply Puff-Ball,..or some such substance,.. to retard the fall of the eschar as long as possible.

2. = POWDER-PUFF 1 a; also *transf.* and *fig.*

1821–2 SWAINSON *Zool. Illustr.* II. Plate 99 The disproportionate size of the head [of the puff-bird] is rendered more conspicuous by the bird raising its feathers so as to appear not unlike a puff ball. **1860** *Macm. Mag.* Sept. 380/1 The puff-ball of the dandelion. **1872** *Routledge's Ev. Boy's Ann.* 396/1 The exquisite little white puff-balls of dogs.

3. *Naut. slang.* (See quot.)

1933 J. MASEFIELD *Bird of Dawning* 263 Bloody Bill China had bonnets on his courses and contrivances that he called puffballs in the roaches of his topsails. *Ibid.* 307 Puff-balls *or* Save-alls. Extra sails laced to the feet of square sails.

ˈpuff-bird. Any bird of the American family *Bucconidæ* or fissirostral barbets, so called from their habit of puffing out their feathers.

1821–2 SWAINSON *Zool. Illustr.* II. Plate 99 There is something very grotesque in the appearance of all the Puff birds. **1895** C. DIXON in *Fortn. Rev.* Apr. 144 The Bucconidæ or puff-birds with forty-three species.

puffed (pʌft), *ppl. a.* Formely also puft. [f. PUFF *v.*]

1. a. Blown up, inflated; distended by inflation.

1579 TOMSON *Calvin's Serm. Tim.* 38/2 It is as a blowen bladder, or a puffed thing, as ye tearme it here. **1598** FLORIO, *Fogliata*, a kinde of thin light puft paste meate made in Italie. **1616** SURFL. & MARKH. *Country Farme* 585 The last is that which is called puft paste, being of all other the most daintiest and pleasantest in taste. **1832** TENNYSON *Pal. Art* 63 Where with puffed cheek the belted hunter blew His wreathed buglehorn.

b. Swollen or distended in any way; stuffed or padded so as to swell out; gathered in so as to produce a soft swelling mass, as in costume.

1536 in *Archæologia* (1812) XVI. 24 There must be provided..a cast or puffed Ymage of a princesse apparailled in her Robes of Estate. **1591** SYLVESTER *Du Bartas* I. ii. 949 Thy huff'd, puff'd, painted, curl'd, purl'd wanton Pride. **1617** MORYSON *Itin.* III. 169 They weare great large puffed breeches, gathered close aboue the knees, and each puffe made of a diuers light colour. **1802** C. EDGEWORTH *Let.* 30 Oct. in C. Colvin *M. Edgeworth in France & Switzerland* (1979) 21, I always repeat..that puffed sleeves are *si ridicule* ..just like our mantua-maker. **1862** *Ladies' Gaz. Fashion* Jan. 8/1 Very small puffed under-sleeves. **1932** 'E. M. DELAFIELD' *Thank Heaven Fasting* III. iii. 278, I can remember a lovely pink evening dress you used to wear, with puffed sleeves. **1976** *National Trust* Autumn 25/1 (Advt.), *Ladies overblouses*..with V-cutaway pointed collar, cuffed and gently puffed sleeves.

c. Of cereal grain: expanded by means of high-pressure steam; used esp. in the names of breakfast foods.

1907 *Yesterday's Shopping* (1969) 11/2 *Breakfast Cereals* ..Quaker Puffed Rice—pkt. 0/5½. **1912** *Collier's* 21 Sept. 24/1 Prof. Anderson's process for Puffed Wheat and Puffed Rice requires a terrific heat. **1921** *Daily Colonist* (Victoria, B.C.) 23 Oct. 18/4 At I'Chang I saw the Chinese making puffed rice as for centuries past. **1930** B. S. BRONSON *Nutrition & Food Chem.* xvi. 372 Certain grains are sometimes subjected to a very high steam pressure which is suddenly released, expanding the grains and giving the various 'puffed' cereals. **1944** M. LASKI *Love on Supertax* i. 13 Would it be Puffed Rice or Shredded Wheat this morning? **1957** J. KERR *Please don't eat Daisies* (1958) 104 They all decide to make sandwiches of boiled egg and puffed wheat. **1972** *Sci. Amer.* Jan. 50/3 Most rats limited to exclusive diets of puffed rice, wheat flakes, shredded wheat and macaroni (all 'enriched') were barely able to hold their weaning weight (about 60 grams).

d. *Cytology.* Of part of a chromosome: see PUFF *sb.* 2 d. Cf. PUFFING *vbl. sb.* 3 c.

1938 *Genetics* XXIII. 159 In the giant chromosomes of *Sciarra ocellaris* Comst. certain particular regions appear greatly expanded or 'puffed'. **1965** J. D. EBERT *Interacting Syst. in Development* vi. 110 A given section of a chromosome may appear as a sharp band in most tissues, but as a diffuse 'puff' in one tissue. Or within the same tissue, a given section may be discrete at one time and 'puffed' at another. **1970** *Cold Spring Harbor Symp. Quantitative Biol.* XXXV. 534/1 At any particular stage in development only a subset of these sites is actually puffed and the pattern of puffs changes in a very regular and highly coordinated way as development proceeds.

2. *fig.* **a.** Inflated or swollen with vanity, pride, etc. Also ***puffed-up***: cf. PUFF *v.* 5.

1553 T. WILSON *Rhet.* 88 b, Puffed presumpcion, passeth not a poynct. **1628** FELTHAM *Resolves* II. [I.] lxviii, They are but puft minds, that bubble thus above Inferiours. **1748** THOMSON *Cast. Indol.* II. xxiii, Poor sons of puft-up Vanity, not Fame. **1818** COBBETT *Pol. Reg.* XXXIII. 317 The puffed-up agents of great English manufacturers.

b. Inflated or bombastic in language or style.

1587 FLEMING *Contn. Holinshed* III. 1363/2 With simplicitie of words, and not with puffed eloquence. **1847** L. HUNT *Men, Women & B.* II. i. 15 [He] has something of a puffed and uneasy pomp.

3. Put out of breath by exertion; 'blown'.

1813 MOORE *Post-bag* ii. 60 On his Lordship's entering puffed. **1847** TENNYSON *Princ.* IV. 246 Fleet I was of foot:.. behind I heard the puff'd pursuer. **1853** 'C. BEDE' *Verdant Green* xviii, You look rather puffed.

Hence **puffedness** (ˈpʌftnɪs); also **ˈpuffed-upness** (*nonce-wd.*).

1648–60 HEXHAM, *Bolsterachtigheydt*, Puffednesse, or Swolne up in the cheeks. **1887** *Chicago Advance* 14 July 447 A Quaker lady..gave a sermon in a single sentence 'Beware of puffedupness'.

puffer (ˈpʌfə(r)). [f. PUFF *v.* + -ER[1].] One who or that which puffs.

1. a. A person or thing that blows in short abrupt blasts, or emits puffs of smoke, steam, etc.: as a tobacco-smoker, a steam-engine or steamboat, etc. Also, *spec.* (chiefly *Sc.*) a small steamboat used for carrying cargo in coastal waters.

1629 ABP. HARSNETT *Rules Chigwell Sch.* in *Vict. Co. Hist., Essex* (1907) II. 544 [The Latin schoolmaster was to be] a man..of a grave behaviour, of a sober and honest conversation, no tipler nor Haunter of ale houses, no Puffer of Tobacco. **1664** COTTON *Scarron.* I. Wks. (1765) 9 Jove.. made him [Æolus] King of all the Puffers. **1801** in *Westm. Gaz.* 24 Dec. (1901) 10/2 [On Christmas Eve, 1801, the first load of passengers ever moved by the force of steam was conveyed by Trevithick's locomotive] 'Captain Dick's Puffer' [as it was called—through Camborne]. **1901** *Scotsman* 19 Dec. 5/4 One of the crew of the puffer had fallen overboard. **1922** *R. Cruising Club Jrnl.* *1921* 98 We got under way half an hour later, having been delayed by the puffer *Anna Bhan*, which had let go almost over our anchor. **1927** [see CHOO-CHOO]. **1946** J. IRVING *Royal Navalese* 139 *Puffer*, a heavily-built fishing-boat type of vessel, usually fitted with a single cylinder Diesel engine. **1959** *Times* 12 Dec. 9/7 Para Handy and his crew of three run a 'puffer' (a small cargo boat) between the towns and villages on the Firth of Clyde. **1968** 'D. HALLIDAY' *Dolly & Singing Bird* x. 112, I saw the anchor light of a big boat, a puffer. **1974** *Times* 7 Dec. 3/2 Mr Alan Pegler bought the majestic old LNER puffer [*sc.* the Flying Scotsman] in 1962. **1975** *Stornoway Gaz.* 5 July 1/9 A call for help was heard, stating that the puffer 'Lady Morven' had broken down and was drifting ashore in Loch Cuan.

b. Local name of various birds: see quots.

1773 *Gentl. Mag.* XLIII. 220/1 Among upwards of 160 species of birds, natives of or killed in England, are the following,..a kind of Puffer not described. **18..** ATKINSON *Prov. Names Birds*, Puffer, North England for Blue Tit-mouse, *Parus cærulea*. **1903** *Eng. Dial. Dict.*, *Puffer*..2. The little grebe, *Tachybaptes fluviatilis*. n[orth] Y[or]ks. *Yks. Weekly Post* (Dec. 31, 1898).

c. In full, ***puffer fish***. A carnivorous globe-fish that can swallow air to inflate itself, belonging to the family Tetraodontidæ, which includes about ninety species found in warm or temperate seas; also, a porcupine-fish belonging to the closely related tropical family Diodontidæ; cf. *puff-fish* s.v. PUFF *sb.* 9 b.

1814 S. L. MITCHELL *Fishes N.Y.* 473 Puffer... He is called in some places, toad-fish, because his back is mottled with yellow & dark. **1883** *Bull. U.S. Nat. Mus.* XXVII. 428 *Tetrodon nephelus*... Rough Swell-fish; Puffer; Blower; Swell Toad. Gulf of Mexico, abundant. **1884** G. B. GOODE *Fisheries U.S.: Nat. Hist. Aquatic Animals* I. III. 170 The Porcupine Fishes—Diodontidæ. Swell Fishes and Puffers. **1930** *Times Educ. Suppl.* 18 Oct. (Home & Classroom Section) p. ii/2 Puffer fish have the habit of inflating themselves with air, which they swallow. **1941** J. STEINBECK *Sea of Cortez* x. 77 Small spine-covered puffer fish..bloat themselves when they are attacked, erecting the spines. **1947** [see BLAASOP]. **1962** K. F. LAGLER et al. *Ichthyology* v. 151 A remarkable modification of the stomach exists in the puffers (Tetraodontidae) and porcupinefishes (Diodontidae) which can inflate themselves with water or air to assume often an almost globular shape. **1967–8** *Bahamas Handbk. & Businessmen's Ann.* (ed. 7) 456 Here and there.. the wader will find a solitary porcupine fish, also called puffers or blowfish. **1974** M. C. GERALD *Pharmacol.* i. 3 The ovaries of the pufferfish (an excellent source of tetrodotoxin, one of the most powerful poisons known to man).

d. A porpoise: cf. *puff-pig* (PUFF *sb.* 9 b), *puffing-pig* (PUFFING *ppl. a.* 1). *U.S.*

1884 G. B. GOODE *Fisheries U.S.: Nat. Hist. Aquatic Animals* I. I. 14 On the Atlantic coast occurs most abundantly the little Harbor Porpoise *Phocæna brachycion* Cope, known to the fishermen as 'Puffer', 'Snuffer', [etc.]. **1911** *Fisheries U.S. 1908* (U.S. Bur. Census Spec. Rep.) 314/1 Porpoise (*Phocæna communis*).—A cetacean found on the north Atlantic and north Pacific coasts, ascending rivers. It is known as 'harbor porpoise', 'herring-hog', 'puffer', [etc.].

e. A wheel-lock pistol.

1970 G. BOOTHROYD *Handgun* i. 16/2 The French makers equalled the Germans in ingenuity but..were able to combine with that ingenuity an elegance of form that is totally lacking in..the ball-butted Puffer, the German wheellock pistol. **1973** *Country Life* 29 Mar. 881 *Antique Firearms*..Saxon wheel-lock Puffer, dated 1590, length 23 inches. **1973** *Times* 22 May 18/3 A Nuremberg wheel-lock 'puffer' made £7,000.

f. A soft plastic container designed to blow powder on to the skin, etc., when squeezed; freq. *attrib.*, as ***puffer bottle***, ***pack***; also ***talc puffer***.

1971 *Homes & Gardens* Aug. 89/2 An insect powder in a puffer pack is convenient for this job. **1971** *Petticoat* 24 July 9/3 A must for your handbag is the..*Travel Trio* which contains a puffer talc. **1973** J. WOOD *North Beat* ii. 27 It's fine powder you get in a puffer bottle—puff it on your hair to make it look right grey. **1974** *Harpers & Queen* Sept. 50/1 Talc puffer 55 p. **1978** R. WESTALL *Devil on Road* viii. 52 I'll take..a puffer-bottle for the [cat's] ear-mites.

2. a. One who extols a person or thing in inflated terms, and usually for some interested reason; a writer of 'puffs' (see PUFF *sb.* 7).

c **1736** HOGARTH in A. Dobson *Life* iv. (1883) 33 What the puffers in books call *the great style of history-painting*. **1779** MME. D'ARBLAY *Diary* 12 Oct., He is..a prodigious puffer —now of his fortune, now of his family. *a* **1788** N. COTTON *Fable* Poems (1810) 25/1 Now, like the doctors of to day [He] Retains his puffers too in pay. **1883** S. C. HALL *Retrospect* I. 273 The gross devices resorted to by puffers of quack medicines.

b. A person employed by the vendor to bid at an auction for the purpose of 'inflating' or running up the price and inciting others to buy.

1760 C. JOHNSTON *Chrysal* (1822) III. 213 It is only slipping a puffer or two at them..and they may be raised to any price. **1818–19** LEIGH *New Pict. London* (1823) 101 (Mock Auctions) Associates, called puffers, are in waiting to raise the article beyond its value. **1867** *Act 30 & 31 Vict.* c. 48 §3 'Puffer' shall mean a person appointed to bid on the part of the owner. **1877** WILLIAMS *Real Prop.* 168 The sale of real estate by auction is now regulated by an act which renders invalid every such sale where a puffer is employed.

†**c.** A teacher who 'inflates' his pupils with superficial knowledge; a 'crammer'. *Obs.*

1786 CUMBERLAND *Observer* No. 28 I. 270 The Polishing Puffers.. who are endowed with the happy faculty of instilling arts and sciences into their disciples, like fixed air into a vapid menstruum.

3. Something that puffs up or inflates one with pride or the like. Cf. PUFF *v.* 5.

1789 J. BROWN *Sel. Rem.* (1807) 141 My knowledge but an accursed puffer up! A murderer of my soul!

4. A bucking-kier: see BUCKING *vbl. sb.*[1] and KIER. Also in comb. ***puffer-pipe***.

1875 KNIGHT *Dict. Mech.*, *Puffer*, a vat in which goods are boiled in an alkaline solution... *Puffer-pipe*, the vertical axial pipe in a kier in which cotton goods are washed during the bleaching process.

puffery (ˈpʌfərɪ). [f. PUFF *v.* or PUFFER: see -ERY. Cf. obs. Du. *pofferie* 'boasting, bragging, or vaunting' (Hexham).]

1. The practice of the 'puffer'; inflated laudation, esp. by way of advertisement. Now chiefly *U.S.*

1782 V. KNOX *Ess.* (1819) II. lxvi. 46 There would be no partial judgments, no puffery. **1831** CARLYLE *Sart. Res.* I. ii, An epoch when Puffery and Quackery have reached a height unexampled in the annals of mankind. **1893** *Times* 10 Feb. 10/2 No puffery and no trickery could beguile either the Bourses or the private investors. **1929** D. G. MACKAIL *How Amusing!* 518 The gossip-writers had all contributed their quota of unpaid puffery. **1963** D. OGILVY *Confessions Advertising Man* (1964) vi. 110 The reader finds it easier to believe the endorsement of a fellow consumer than the puffery of an anonymous copy-writer. **1966** *Daily Tel.* 3 Nov. 14/2 Richard Maney, Press agent to some 300 Broadway shows, and..a master of flamboyant puffery. **1970** *Observer* 1 Mar. 13/3 An American company selling weight reducing pills was prosecuted for misleading advertising. One of its defences was puffery. **1978** J. CARROLL *Mortal Friends* I. ii. 25 If you'll not be subject to the spiritual authority of the Church even on the day of your sacrament, don't blaspheme your martyred countrymen by such puffery.

2. Puffs collectively, frills or frilling of puffs: see PUFF *sb.* 2 b.

1860 *Illustr. Lond. News* 25 Feb. 198/1 All that hoops, powder, and puffery can do for them has been done. **1868** HOLME LEE *B. Godfrey* lx, The whiteness of her neck [was] veiled with white puffery of tulle. **1884** *Punch* 1 Mar. 100 In pufferies of all sizes dressed.

†**ˈpuff-fist, -foist.** *Obs. rare.* [f. PUFF *sb.* or *vb.* stem + FIST *sb.*[2], FOIST *sb.*[3], *crepitus*. Cf. PUCKFIST of same date.] = PUFF-BALL 1.

1597 GERARDE *Herbal* III. clxii. 1386 Puffes Fistes [*Index* Puffe Fistes], are commonly called in Latine *Lupi crepitus*, or Woolfes Fistes:..in English Puffes Fistes, and Fussebals in the north. **1634** WITHER *Emblemes* xxiii. 85 That uncleanly mushrum ball Which in some countries wee a Pufffoyst call.

puffick (ˈpʌfɪk), *a.* [Repr. colloq. and dial. pronunc. of PERFECT.] = PERFECT *a.* (esp. sense 5 d). So **ˈpufficklу** *adv.* = PERFECTLY *adv.*

1891 KIPLING *Many Inventions* (1893) 3 He knows pufficklу well where he is. **1907** E. NESBIT *Enchanted Castle* iv. 105 You aint allowed to arrest a chap on suspicion, even if you know pufficklу well who done the job. **1949** M. ALLINGHAM *More Work for Undertaker* xiv. 176 The chap.. was a puffick stranger. **1967** 'A. GILBERT' *Visitor* viii. 139

They'll ask..why you should take a chance like that for a puffick stranger. **1972** C. DRUMMOND *Death at Bar* ii. 61 She mimicked in Cockney, 'A puffick gentlemen I'm sure, dear.'

puffily ('pʌfɪlɪ), *adv.* [f. PUFFY *a.* + -LY[2].] In a puffy manner.

1882 CAULFIELD & SAWARD *Dict. Needlework* 415/1 When Petticoats are to be Quilted, the Runnings should be well indented and the satin or silk set up puffily. **1904** H. G. WELLS *Food of Gods* II. ii. 197 He did the rise over by the chalk-pit crest a little puffily. **1963** A. SMITH *Throw out Two Hands* xiv. 150 We could look back at the cloud... It was brooding over us no more, but clearly and puffily to one side. **1975** S. LAUDER *Killing Time on Corvo* i. 7 He looked puffily unhealthy. **1977** C. MCCULLOUGH *Thorn Birds* ii. 21 They paused.., the five bright heads haloed against a puffily clouded sky.

puffin[1] ('pʌfɪn). Forms: 4 poffoun, -in, (5 pophyn), 6 puffing, 4-7 puffyn, 7-8 puffen, 6- puffin. [ME. *poffin, pophyn*; in latinized form, pl. *poffones*; also *puffyn*. Origin unascertained: see Note below.]

1. a. A sea-bird of the genus *Fratercula*, of the family *Alcidæ* or Auks; *esp.* the common *F. arctica*, found abundantly on the coasts of the N. Atlantic, having a very large curiously-shaped furrowed and particoloured bill.

Formerly erroneously supposed by some to be wingless, and by others reckoned as a fish, its flesh having a fishy taste and being allowed to be eaten in Lent.

1337 *Caption of Seisin* (of Scilly) 5 May (Duchy of Cornwall), Ran[ulphus] de Albo Monastrio tenet Insulam de Sully et r[eddit] inde ad idem f[estu]m Di[midium] marce vel ccc poffouns. **1366** *Ministers' Acc.* Bundle 823 No. 22 (P.R.O.), Idem respondet de vs de poffon' hoc anno. **1367** *Ibid.*, Exitus chacee cuniculorum et Poffonum. *a* **1490** BOTONER *Itin.* (1778) 98 Insula Rascow..inculta cum cuniculis et avibus vocatis pophyns. **1502** *Acc. Ld. High. Treas. Scot.* II. 155 Item..to ane man of the laird of Cesnokkis that brocht puffingis to the King, xxviijs. *a* **1529** SKELTON *Ph. Sparowe* 454 The puffin and the tele Money they shall dele To poore folke at large. **1530** PALSGR. 259/1 Puffyn a fysshe lyke a teele. *a* **1552** LELAND *Itin.* VI. 65 Puffins, Birdes less then Dukkes having grey Fethers like Dukkes. **1602** CAREW *Cornwall* 35 b, The Puffyn..whose young ones are thence ferretted out, being exceeding fat, kept salted, and reputed for fish, as comming neerest thereto in their taste. **1655** MOUFET & BENNET *Health's Impr.* xviii. 166 Puffins, whom I may call the feathered fishes, are accounted even by the holy fatherhood of Cardinals to be no flesh but rather fish. **1678** PHILLIPS (ed. 4), *Puffin*, a sort of Coot or Seagull, supposed to be so called from its round belly; as it were swelling and puffing out. **1736** SHERIDAN *Let. to Swift* 12 May in *Swift's Corr.* (1768) IV. 159, I have twenty lambs..as plump as puffins. **1865** GOSSE *Land & Sea* (1874) 30 Known by the fishermen as sea parrots or coulternebs; but more generally designated in books as puffins.

b. Erroneously applied to a species of Shearwater (*Puffinus anglorum*, family *Procellariidæ*), found in the Isle of Man and the Scilly Islands.

1674 RAY *Collect. Words, Water Fowl* 94 The Puffin or Curviere: Puffinus Anglorum. This bird builds on a little Island called the calf of Man at the South End of the Isle of Man and also upon the Silly Islands, but is nothing such a thing as is described in Aldrovandus: for that is feather'd and can fly swiftly. **1678** —— *Willughby's Ornith.* 333 The Puffin of the Isle of Man, which I take to be the *Puffinus Anglorum.* **1688** R. HOLME *Armoury* II. 298/2 The Puffin of the Isle of Man, or the Mancks Puffin..is something less in body than a Tame Pigeon. **1884** *Yarrell's Brit. Birds* IV. 21 The Manx Shearwater is the commonest species of the genus in the British seas... It owes its trivial name to Willughby, who speaks of it as the Puffin of the Isle of Man.

c. Applied locally in Ireland to the Razor-bill.

1885 SWAINSON *Prov. Names Birds* 217 Razor bill (*Alca torda*)... Puffin (Antrim).

d. *attrib.* and *Comb.*, as ***puffin-cock, -hole***; **puffin-auk**, = sense a.

1796 CHARLOTTE SMITH *Marchmont* II. 199 The cries of the sand-piper, the puffin-awk; the screaming gull. **1901** *Wide World Mag.* VIII. 133/1 Absorbed in the pastime of probing puffin-holes in search of eggs. **1902** N. HOWARD *Kiartan* II. 32 Nay, they shall fight like puffin-cocks.

2. (With capital initial.) The proprietary name of a variety of children's paper-back book or series of books published by Longman Group Limited (see PENGUIN 2 c).

1947 *Trade Marks Jrnl.* 10 Sept. 535/2 Puffin 648,226. Printed publications, stationery, bookbinding materials, pens and pencils, but not including publications on puffins. Penguin Books Limited..Manufacturers and Publishers. —28th May, 1946. **1960** *Penguins Progress 1935–60* 54 Each month we publish fifteen to twenty books, varying from Penguin fiction..to Penguin Handbooks and Puffins. **1979** *Guardian* 29 Oct. 12/6 A list of leading children's writers who are not in Puffin would be a pretty short one.

3. (With capital initial.) The proprietary name of a make of duvet or continental quilt. Also ***Puffin Downlet.***

1959 *Trade Marks Jrnl.* 18 Feb. 206/2 Puffin... Filled bed coverings in the nature of quilts or eiderdowns. Arthur R. Davis and Company Limited,..Croydon, Surrey; manufacturers and merchants. **1970** 'R. CRAWFORD' *Kiss Boss Goodbye* II. viii. 107 Brenda was lying on her back on top of the Puffin Downlet. **1971** *Guardian* 29 Sept. 11/2 The cleaning of feather-filled continental quilts is a problem... One reader, taking her Puffin to..a well-known cleaners.. was met with the blankest confusion.

[*Note.* Suggestions as to the origin of the name *puffin* have mostly supposed some connexion with the verb or sb. *puff* or the adj. *puffy*. Thus it has been conjectured to refer to the 'puffy' or corpulent appearance of the bird (quot. 1678), or esp. to the plumpness of the young, formerly considered a delicacy (cf. the simile 'as plump as a puffin'); also to the soft downy clothing of the young (Prof. A. Newton). Others have sought an explanation in the remarkable 'puffed-out' beak, or in a puffing sound uttered by the bird or its young when seized. Caius (1570) expressly declares that the name is derived 'a naturali voce *pupin*'. But, as the ME. forms of the name are spelt *poff-*, and the earliest known association of the bird under this name was with Cornwall and Scilly, it is evident that these conjectures rest on insecure bases. The name may even have come from Cornwall, and its change to 'puff-' may be due to 'popular etymology' in English. The erroneous sense b, is due to Ray, who mistook young specimens of the shearwater from the Isle of Man for puffins, and applied to them the name *Puffinus anglorum* (applied by Gesner to the real puffin), which has unhappily been retained in ornithological nomenclature.]

†**'puffin**[2]. *Obs.* [app. f. PUFF *v.* or *sb.*: in sense 1, perh. with some notion of connexion with prec., which by 1600 was prob. popularly associated with puffing. The other senses appear to be more or less distinct formations from *puff*.]

1. Applied in contempt or reproach to a person puffed up with vanity or pride.

1610 B. JONSON *Alch.* III. iv, What shall we doe with this same Puffin [Dapper] here Now hee's o' the spit? **1631** BRATHWAIT *Whimzies, Neuter* 67 What will this puffin come to in time? **1661** *Sir H. Vane's Politics* 7 Before..that swoln Puffin rose to that growth and immense grandure.

2. Some kind of fish, also called *fork-fish*: see FORK *sb.* 16. Also ***puffin-fish.***

1598 FLORIO, *Bastango*,..a forke-fish, it is like a ray; some call it a puffin-fish. **1601** HOLLAND *Pliny* I. 261 The Puffen or Fork-fish..lieth in await..ready to strike the fishes that passe by with a sharpe rod or pricke that he hath. **1617** MINSHEU *Ductor*, A Puffen, or Forke-fish... Est enim furcatâ caudâ et aculeatâ, vt sagitta.

3. Name of a variety of apple: = PUFF *sb.* 3 b. Also ***puffin-apple.***

1589 RIDER *Bibl. Schol.* 47 A Puffin, otherwise called an 100. shillings, *Malum pulmoneum.* **1736** AINSWORTH *Lat. Dict.*, A puffin apple, *Malum pulmonium.* **1755** in JOHNSON.

4. = PUFF-BALL 1. *rare*[−0]. (? error.)

1755 JOHNSON, *Puffin*... 3. A kind of fungus filled with dust.

5. *pl.* ? Some inferior kind of meal or flour: see quot.

1587 J. HOOKER *Descr. Exeter* in Holinshed *Chron.* III. 1022/1 In this extremitie the bakers and housholders were driuen to seeke vp their old store of puffins and bran, wherewith they in times past were woont to make horssebread.

puffiness ('pʌfɪnɪs). [f. PUFFY + -NESS.] The quality or condition of being puffy.

1. Puffed-up or inflated condition (*lit.* and *fig.*).

1668 *H. More's Div. Dial.* I. To Rdr. A iij, The Levity and Puffiness of their Spirits has carried their conceptions.. above the levell of common Sense. *a* **1750** A. HILL (T.), Some of M. Voltaire's pieces are so swelled with this presumptuous puffiness. **1850** LEITCH tr. *C. O. Müller's Anc. Art* §204 (ed. 2) 193 A puffiness in the treatment of the folds is observable in the draperies. **1897** *Allbutt's Syst. Med.* IV. 321 The patient's attention is first attracted to the malady by the puffiness of the lower eyelids.

2. Inclination to puff or pant, short-windedness.

1813 *Examiner* 10 May 297/2 His breathing puffiness, and inarticulate enunciations.

puffinet ('pʌfɪnɛt). [f. PUFFIN[1] + -ET[1] *dimin.*] A local name of the Black Guillemot.

1678 RAY *Willughby's Ornith.* 326, I guess this..to be the same with the Puffinet of the Farn Islands, which they told us was of the bigness of a Dove. **1885** SWAINSON *Prov. Names Birds* 218 Black Guillemot... Puffinet (Farn Islands).

puffing ('pʌfɪŋ), *vbl. sb.* [f. PUFF *v.* + -ING[1].] The action of the verb PUFF: and derived senses.

1. a. The action of blowing in short blasts, panting as one out of breath, emitting puffs of steam, etc.

1398 TREVISA *Barth. De P.R.* x. v. (Tollem. MS.), A lytel puffynge of wynde quykeþ and tendeþ leye. **1548** PATTEN *Exped. Scot.* B ij b, So stepe be these bankes on eyther syde and depe.., that who goeth straight doune shalbe in daunger of tumbling, & the commer vp so sure of puffyng & payne. **1581** MULCASTER *Positions* xx. (1887) 84 To eager walking..encreaseth puffing and blowing. **1714** *Spect.* No. 558 ¶4 Another, after a great deal of puffing, threw down his Luggage. **1849** F. B. HEAD *Stokers & Pokers* iii. (1851) 41 The loud puffing of an engine announces the approach..of empty carriages.

b. The sudden discharge of a cloud of spores by a fungus.

1887 H. E. F. GARNSEY tr. *A. de Bary's Compar. Morphol. & Biol. Fungi* iii. 89 Many of the Discomycetes have the peculiar habit of 'puffing'.., of suddenly discharging a whole cloud of spores. **1953** C. T. INGOLD *Dispersal in Fungi* ii. 27 If a cup-fungus is picked and at once placed near the ear, puffing may occur and is then audible as a hissing sound. **1976** G. C. AINSWORTH *Introd. Hist. Mycol.* vii. 196 Micheli ..was also the first to record and illustrate the visible 'puffing' of spores from the ascocarps of discomycetes.

†**2.** *concr.* ? A powder-puff. *Obs. rare.*

1654 GAYTON *Pleas. Notes* III. vii. 112 [He] never went without a small Box of Powder, or dried Meale and his Puffings.

3. a. The action of distending something by blowing; blowing up, inflation. Also *fig.*

1495 *Trevisa's Barth. De P.R.* v. xlii. (W. de W.) k v/2 Puffynge and wyndynge of the guttes. **1530** PALSGR. 259/1 Puffyng up, *inflation.* **1593** [see b]. **1607** TOPSELL *Four-f. Beasts* (1658) 431 A Musk-cat..doth loosen and dissolve all thick puffings or windiness in the interior parts. **1688** R. HOLME *Armoury* III. 269/1 Thresh not Wheat but as you Eat it, for fear of Pufting and Fustiness.

b. The action of distending anything by stuffing or padding, or by gathering in; esp. in costume, the making of puffs (PUFF *sb.* 2 b); also *concr.* a puffed formation.

1593 NASHE *Christ's T.* (1613) 146 It is not..your floury iaggings, superfluous enterlacings, and puffings vp, that can any way offend God, but the puffing vp of your soules. *a* **1618** SYLVESTER *Hymn of Alms* 206 The puffing of his Periwig. **1824** MISS MITFORD *Village* Ser. I. 225 (*Mrs. Mosse*) A satin riband fastened in a peculiar bow, something between a bow and a puffing behind. **1896** A. H. BEAVAN *Marlbor. Ho.* ix. 162 A black sunshade, edged with a puffing of white chiffon.

c. *Cytology.* The occurrence or formation of puffs on a chromosome. Also *attrib.* Cf. PUFF *sb.* 2 d; PUFFED *ppl. a.* 1 d.

1938 *Genetics* XXIII. 159 Intermediate degrees of 'puffing' show the bands or discs in various stages of disruption. **1954** *Exper. Cell Res.* VI. 199 The 'lamp-brushes' show a considerable degree of lateral 'puffing' as judged from the fact that the immediately neighbouring branches of the chromosome are only half as thick. **1968** H. HARRIS *Nucleus & Cytoplasm* iv. 78 It has been contended that the pattern of puffing shows organ specificity, but the evidence for this does not seem to be at all conclusive. **1970** *Cold Spring Harbor Symp. Quantitative Biol.* XXXV. 534/1 Periods of greatest puffing activity are seen as the animals molt from one instar to the next and both events, molting and the initiation of a specific sequence of puffing, are primarily controlled by the same hormone,..ecdysone.

4. *fig.* **a.** The action of praising or extolling in inflated language for a purpose, esp. by way of advertisement; interested laudation or commendation.

1754 A. MURPHY *Gray's-Inn Jrnl.* No. 91 The above is not in the ordinary Way of puffing, but to promote the real Benefit of the Community. **1870** EMERSON *Soc. & Solit.*, *Success* Wks. (Bohn) III. 119 In this life of show, puffing, advertisement, and manufacture of public opinion.

b. Bidding at an auction for the purpose of inflating or raising the price.

1858 LD. ST. LEONARDS *Handy-Bk. Prop. Law* iv. 22 You may..appoint a person to bid for you at the sale, in order to prevent the estate from being sold at an undervalue. This is generally termed puffing.

attrib. **1901** *Times* 16 Nov. 14 By the Puffing Act, 1867, it is provided [etc.].

5. *attrib.* **puffing-hole** (see quot.); **puffing tube**, a blow-pipe.

1862 J. B. JUKES *Student's Man. Geol.* (ed. 2) II. x. 220 The sea sometimes gradually forms a passage for itself in the surface above, and if that be not too lofty, forms a 'blow-hole' or 'puffing-hole', through which spouts of foam and spray are occasionally ejected high into the air. **1883** DAY *Indian Fish* 68 (Fish. Exhib. Publ.) Malabar puffing tube, with darts used for killing fish.

'puffing, *ppl. a.* [f. as prec. + -ING[2].] That puffs: see the verb.

1. Blowing in puffs; panting violently; sending forth puffs of steam, etc. ***puffing-pig***, a name for a small species of porpoise (U.S.).

a **1618** SYLVESTER *Panaretus* 707 If the puffing gales Into the Deep transport her huffing sails. **1620** *Swetnam Arraign'd* (1880) 9 From whence comm'st thou in such a puffing heate? **1668** CHARLETON *Onomast.* 167 *Balæna Physeter*..the puffing, or spouting Whale. **1697** DRYDEN *Virg. Georg.* IV. 248 One brawny Smith the puffing Bellows plyes. **1845** J. COULTER *Adv. in Pacific* iii. 28 Shoals of a small kind of porpoise, commonly called puffing pigs.

b. ***Puffing Billy***, an affectionate name for a steam locomotive or train; also *transf.* and *attrib.*

The original 'Puffing Billy' was built by William Hedley in 1813.

1934 JOYCE *Let.* 25 Apr. (1966) III. 304, I prefer Puffing Billy to Swaggering Bob. **1963** A. LUBBOCK *Austral. Roundabout* 172 A 'Puffing Billy' engine, wood-fired, was dredging the silt. **1977** *Times* 19 Apr. 5/5 (*caption*) A replica of an early American 'Puffing Billy'..at the National Railway Museum, York.

2. Uttering scornful ejaculations; haughty in demeanour; swaggering. *Obs.* or *arch.*

1583 GREENE *Mamillia* Wks. (Grosart) II. 97 A cooling carde of misfortune to pluck down yᵉ puffing peate of prosperitie. **1687** T. BROWN *Saints in Uproar* Wks. 1730 I. 80 Thou huffing, puffing, sconce-building ruffian.

3. Becoming inflated or swollen; swelling up.

1661 BOYLE *Phys.-Chem. Ess. Salt-Petre* §8 Unless it chance, that the puffing matter do blow the coal too soon out of the crucible. **1856** KANE *Arct. Expl.* I. xx. 259 The willows are sappy and puffing.

†**4.** *fig.* Bombastic, 'swelling'. *Obs.*

1567 DRANT *Horace, Art Poetry* B vij, He that doth belch out puffinge rymes. *a* **1592** GREENE *Vision* Wks. (Grosart) XII. 203 The puffing glorie of the loftie still shadowing wanton conceipts.

†**5.** That puffs up; inspiring pride or arrogance; elating. *Obs.*

1598 E. GILPIN *Skial.* IV, Thee whom [Philosophy] hath taught to moderate Thy mounting thought, nor to be eleuate With puffingst fortunes. **1652** BENLOWES *Theoph.* XIII. vii, No puffing hopes, no shrinking fears them fright.

6. That praises extravagantly; putting forth 'puffs' or inflated commendations.

1768 GOLDSM. *Good-n. Man* Epil., As puffing quacks some caitiff wretch procure, To swear the pill, or drop, has wrought a cure. **1805** *Sporting Mag.* XXV. 187 Without the quackery of puffing advertisements.

Hence **'puffingly** *adv.*, with puffing.

1598 Florio, *Tremidamente*, swellingly, puffingly. **1611** Cotgr., *Bouffément*, puffingly. **1760–72** H. Brooke *Fool of Qual.* (1809) IV. 157 Dobson and his dame coming diffidently but puffingly up the avenue. **1905** *Blackw. Mag.* Jan. 98/2 A fat Turkish apothecary puffingly struggles up our ship's side.

puffinry (ˈpʌfɪnrɪ). [f. puffin[1] + -ry.] A place occupied by a breeding colony of puffins.

1954 Fisher & Lockley *Sea-Birds* iii. 64 There are seven separate puffin-slopes on St. Kilda each of which is larger than..even the largest puffinry in the..Shiant Isles. **1960** Williamson & Boyd *St. Kilda Summer* xi. 113 It [*sc.* Stac Lee, St. Kilda] has large guillemot and kittiwake colonies too, and Stac an Armin many razorbills and a big puffinry. **1974** *Country Life* 14 Feb. 290/2 Much the same is true of the other puffinries on the islands.

†**'puffkin.** *Obs. rare*⁻¹. In 7 pufkin. [f. puff *sb.* + -kin.] A little puff: applied to a light or flighty woman.

1638 Ford *Lady's Trial* iii. i, The best..are but flesh and blood, And now and then.., when the fit's come on 'em, Will prove themselves but flirts, and tirliry-pufkins.

'puffless, *a. rare.* [f. puff *sb.* + -less.]

1. Breathless, out of breath. *slang* and *dial.*

1882 J. Walker *Jaunt to Auld Reekie* 151 To sprachel puffless up to these heigh attics, O! what a task.

2. Of dress: Without puffs or fullness.

1899 *Daily News* 7 Oct. 8/5 Flat, high collars without stiff lining, puffless sleeves, and the slight fulness at the waist.

'pufflet. *nonce-wd.* [f. puff *sb.* + -let.] A very little puff or whiff.

1848 Lowell *Biglow P.* Poet. Wks. (1879) 206 The scarce discernible pufflet of smoke and dust is a revolution. **1883** *Daily News* 24 May, A pufflet or airy stream of..smoke.

'puff-,paste. [f. puff *sb.* or *vb.*-stem: cf. *puft paste* in puffed 1.] *Cookery.* A fine kind of flour paste, made very light and flaky by successive rollings and butterings.

1611 Cotgr., *Gasteau feuilleté*, a cake of puffe-past. **1611** Florio, *Fogliáta*, light-paste or puffe-paste [1598 puft paste]. **1615** Markham *Eng. Housew.* ii. ii. 65 For the making of puffe-past of the best kind, you shall take the finest wheat flowre [etc.]. **1633** Marmion *Antiquary* iv. i, An artificial hen made of puff-paste. **1747** Mrs. Glasse *Cookery* viii. 75 *Puff-Paste.* Take a quarter of a Peck of Flour, rub fine half a Pound of Butter, a little Salt,.. roll it up, and roll it out again; and so do nine or ten times, till you have rolled in a Pound and half of Butter. **1860** Tyndall *Glac.* i. 6, I followed up the observations..and had several practical lessons in the manufacture of puff-paste and other laminated confectionery.

b. *fig.* Applied to persons or things of a light, flimsy, or unsubstantial character.

1602 Marston *Ant. & Mel.* iii. Wks. 1856 I. 38 [*To a dandy*] Avoide, puffe paste, avoide. **1622** Mabbe tr. *Aleman's Guzman d' Alf.* ii. 169 Such store of this puffe-paste of vaine-glory had I swallowed downe my throat. **1673** Marvell *Reh. Transp.* II. 266 There is indeed material intellectual Puff-past; Pinners-hall has nothing like it. **1845** *Gentl. Mag.* i. 390/2 It is seldom that Guides..to what are called Watering-places..are anything more than *puff*-paste.

Hence **'puff-,pasted** *a.*, ? baked in or made of puff-paste; so also **'puff-'pastry**, fine pastry made with puff-paste; †**'puff-'pasty**, a 'pasty' or pie made of puff-paste.

a **1693** *Urquhart's Rabelais* iii. xxviii. 231 Puff-pasted cock. **1707** J. Stevens tr. *Quevedo, Knight's Epist.* iii, Could you find no body else to beg Puff Pasties of? **1853** Miss Sheppard *Ch. Auchester* xiv, Boiled custards, puff pastry, and our choicest preserves.

'puff-,puff. [Echoic: cf. puff *int.*] An imitation of the sound of repeated puffing by a steam-engine; hence, a nursery name for a locomotive, or a railway train.

1870 Miss Bridgman *Ro. Lynne* II. xiv. 307 With a puff-puff the train slowly passed out of Hampton Station. **1886** Ruskin *Præterita* I. iii. 87 In this present age,..people don't give their children toy bricks, but toy puff-puffs. **1889** P. H. Emerson *Eng. Idylls* 64 The stillness was broken only by the short sharp puff puff of the engines. **1894** H. Drummond *Ascent of Man* 214 The child who says *moo* for cow,..or *puff-puff* for train, is an authority on the origin of human speech.

puffy (ˈpʌfɪ), *a.* [f. puff *v.* or *sb.* + -y.]

1. a. Of wind: Blowing in puffs or short intermittent blasts, gusty; also, characterized by such wind. **b.** Of a person or animal: Easily caused to puff, or breathe quick and hard; short-winded. **c.** Of a sound: Dull, muffled.

1616 T. Adams *Soul's Sickness* Wks. 1861 I. 486 He lives at a high sail, that the puffy praises of his neighbours may blow him into the enchanted island, vainglory. **1799** J. Robertson *Agric. Perth* 222 The former gives them [horses] better wind; the latter renders them puffy. **1831** Brewster *Nat. Magic* ix. (1833) 220 The glass loses its power of ringing..and emits only a disagreeable and puffy sound. **1844** J. T. Hewlett *Parsons & W.* i, I am too puffy to enjoy hill-climbing. **1894** *Times* 25 July 11 A strong puffy off-shore wind was blowing.

2. a. Swollen or inclined to swell, by or as by puffing or inflation; turgid, tumid, puffed out; of persons, fat, corpulent: usually also implying soft, flabby, wanting in firmness.

1664 Power *Exp. Philos.* i. 12 House-Spiders..have a very puffy light body of an Oval figure. **1676** Wiseman *Chirurg. Treat.* i. xxvii. 143 Emphysema is a light puffy Tumour easily yielding to the pressure of your fingers. **1733** Tull *Horse-Hoeing Husb.* vi. 47 Puffy Land, which naturally swells up, instead of subsiding. **1828** Landor *Imag. Conv.* Wks. 1846 I. 340/2 The oriental train and puffy turban. **1865** Miss Braddon *Sir Jasper* xiv, Blanche Harding lounged in the downiest and puffiest chair by the fire in her spacious bedroom. **1874** Wood *Nat. Hist.* 278 The [owl's] round, puffy head, the little hooked beak just appearing from the downy plumage. **1899** *Westm. Gaz.* 6 Apr. 3/2 The shoulder deserted by the puffy sleeve.

b. Having the quality of puffing up, or causing to swell as if inflated. *rare*⁻¹.

1718 Rowe tr. *Lucan* ix. 1348 The puffy Poison spreads, and heaves around, Till all the Man is in the Monster drown'd.

3. *fig.* Having an empty or unsubstantial air of importance; puffed up, vain, swelling, inflated, turgid, bombastic. *rare.*

1599 Marston *Sco. Villanie, Lect. prorsus indignos*, Passe on ye vaine fantasticke troupe Of puffie youths. **1678** Cudworth *Intell. Syst.* i. iv. §18. 321 A puffy conceit and opinion of knowledge. **1679** Dryden *Troil. & Cress.* Pref., Ess. (Ker) I. 224 He distinguished not the blown puffy style from true sublimity. **1751** Lavington *Enthus. Meth. & Papists* iii. (1754) Pref., Puffy Pretensions to extraordinary Revelations. **1853–8** Hawthorne *Eng. Note-Bks.* (1879) II. 157 A rather puffy and consequential man.

4. *Comb.*, as ***puffy-bodied, -cheeked, -eyed, -faced, -looking*** adjs.; †**puffy-light** *v.* (*obs. nonce-wd.*) *trans.*, ? to give a puffy lightness to.

1610 W. Folkingham *Art of Survey* i. x. 28 Being.. intermedled by the plow with the soyle, it puffie-lights and party colours the same. **1851** *Fraser's Mag.* Mar. 360/2 A puffy-faced little man, with an overgrown body. **1859** Atkinson *Walks & Talks* (1892) 260 One of the puffy-bodied, pasty-faced Sunbury lads. **1922** H. Crane *Let.* 27 July (1965) 94 The Man Ray photo of J...is really not a good resemblance. The face is not so puffy-looking. **1926** V. Woolf *Writer's Diary* (1953) 89 In trotted a little puffy-cheeked cheerful old man [*sc.* Hardy]. **1929** *Sunday Dispatch* 20 Jan. 16/3 You watch the boy growing puffy-eyed and soft on his fast living. **1957** J. Kerouac *On Road* (1958) 170 Every-body looked like a broken-down movie extra, a withered starlet; disenchanted stuntmen,..puffy-eyed motel blondes..a lemon lot.

pufloafe: see puff *v.* 7.

†**puft.** *Obs.* [An early by-form of puff *sb.*: cf. tuft.] = puff *sb.*

1398 Trevisa *Barth. De P.R.* xvii. ii. (Tollem. MS.), With a stronge blaste, oþer a pufte of wynde. *c* **1450** *St. Cuthbert* (Surtees) 2648 All his [a spider's] webb A puft of wynde away reues. **1513** Douglas *Æneis* iv. xii. 122 With a puft of aynd, the lyfe furth went. **1615** Chapman *Odyss.* v. 65 With pace as speedy as a puft of wind. **1785, 1795** in *Eng. Dial. Dict.*

puft, *ppl. a.*: see puffed.

puftaloon (ˈpʌftəluːn). *Austral.* Also **pufftaloon, puftaloony, puffterlooner, puff de loon(ey),** etc. [Origin obscure; cf. puff *sb.* 5.] A small fried cake, spread with jam, sugar, or honey, and usu. eaten hot.

[**1853** Mossman & Banister *Australia* 126 'Leather-jackets'—an Australian bush term for a thin cake made of dough, and put into a pan to bake with some fat... The Americans indulge in this kind of bread, giving them the name of 'Puff ballooners'.] **1871** M. Clarke *His Natural Life* v. ii, in *Austral. Jrnl.* VI. 602/2 'Have a puffterlooner, Master Dick,' suggests Derwent Jack, 'or a bit o' sweetcake.' **1908** A. Gunn *We of Never Never* xiv. 189 The cooking lessons proceeded until the fine art of making 'puff de looneys'..had been mastered. **1935** *Bulletin* (Sydney) 27 Feb. 20/1 Camped in Tapalin Bend, River Murray, he was frying pufftaloons when a light shower caused the hot fat to jump and sting his hands and wrists. **1940** I. L. Idriess *Lightning Ridge* 82 Puftaloons are tasty though; fry them in fat, then smother them with treacle and swallow 'em while greasy. **1942** E. Langley *Pea Pickers* 296 She was making puftaloonies all the time we talked and in next to no time had a plate of them in front of us, with a hot cup of tea. **1964** T. Ronan *Packhorses & Pearling Boat* v. 140 A camp oven full of 'puff de loons' (fried scones to the uninitiated). **1970** P. White *Vivisector* i. 10 Mumma started telling all she had heard next door, with the kids stuffing on Mrs. Burt's cold puftaloons.

pufter, var. poofter.

pug (pʌg), *sb.*[1] Now only *dial.* [Origin unascertained. It occurs much earlier than pug *sb.*[2], and does not appear to be connected with it.]

1. The husks of any kind of small seed which are separated in cleaning it; the chaff of wheat or oats, the awns of barley, etc.; the refuse corn separated in winnowing.

c **1440** *Pallad. on Husb.* iii. 1079 Mast, chasteyn, yef hem [boars] pugges of thi corn [*orig.* vilia excrementa]. **1601** Holland *Pliny* xviii. vii. I. 562 The chaffe and pugs [*palea*] that come of Barly, is supposed to be as good as the best. *Ibid.* vi. 20 The best way to keep onions, is in corn chaf, and such like pugs. **1766** *Museum Rust.* VI. 338 Clean seed, cleared of the black husk, or pug, as we call it. **1854** Miss Baker *Northants. Gloss.*, *Pug*, the integument or chaff of small seeds, turnips, candy-tuft, &c.

2. The refuse from the cider-press. Hence **pug-drink,** water cider (Grose *Prov. Gloss.* 1787). *dial.*

1893 *Wilts. Gloss.*, *Pug*..the pulp of apples which have been pressed for cider.

pug (pʌg), *sb.*[2] [Of unknown origin and history; it is not certain that branches I and II belong to the same word. Exc. in sense 1, the earliest examples of which have *pugges* (? pl. used collectively), not known before 1600; but some senses may have been earlier in colloquial use.]

I. Applied to a person, etc.

†**1.** A term of endearment for a person (rarely an animal); also applied to a bauble or doll. *Obs.*

1566 Drant *Horace, Sat.* ii. iii. G iv, If in a couche, a fyne fleesde lambe a kinge shoulde cause to ryde, And geve it rayments neate and gay..And call it pugges and prety peate [*Rufam aut Pusillam appellet*]. **1578** Whetstone *2nd Pt. Promos & Cass.* i. iii, Nay, nay, sayes he (good pugges) no more of this. **1580** Sir G. Carey in J. H. Jeayes *Catal. Charters Berkeley Castle* (1892) 330 My sweete pugge,..thi absens will make the returne of thy swete cumpany the more welcum to me. **1602** Marston *Ant. & Mel.* ii. i, [To little boy] Hah Catzo, your master..cals for your diminutive attendance... Good pugge, give me some capon. **1602** —— *Antonio's Rev.* iii. iv, I have had foure husbands my selfe. The first, I called, sweet duck: the second, deare heart: the third, prettie pugge. **1611** Cotgr. s.v. *M'amie*, *Ma belle m'amie*, my prettie Pug (so fooles, hugging their bables, tearme them). *Ibid.*, *Marmouselle*, a little puppie, or pug to play with.

†**2.** A courtesan, mistress, harlot, punk. *Obs.* (Quot. 1600 apparently belongs here.)

1600 Sir R. Cecil *Lett.* 24 Sept. (Camden) 33 If you did ..remember the Lo. Admyrall and the Lord Threasurer with a couple of Pugges or some *vscough baugh* or some such toyes, it would shew that you do not neglect them, whoe, I protest, are to you wonderfull kynde. **1607** Dekker & Webster *Westw. Hoe* ii. ii. D.'s Wks. 1873 II. 307 The Lob has his Lasse,..the Westerne-man his Pug, the Seruing-man his Punke. **1611** Cotgr. s.v. *Gouge*, *Gouge* as *Vouge*,.. a Souldiors Pug, or Punke; a Whore that followes the Camp. *Ibid.*, *Saffrette*,..a flirt, queane, gixie, pug, punke. **1653** Urquhart *Rabelais* i. iii, He married Gargamelle,..a jolly pug [*orig.* *belle gouge*] and well mouthed wench. **1678** Dryden *Kind Keeper* Epil. 18 But all the female fry turn pugs, like mine. *a* **1700** B. E. *Dict. Cant. Crew*, *Pug*, *Pugnasty, a meer Pug*, a nasty Slut, a sorry Jade, of a Woman. **1708** T. Ward *Eng. Ref.* (1716) 16 Who ever knew a Royal Fancy Stoop thus to such a Pug as Nancy? **1719** D'Urfey *Pills* V. 83 If Miss prove peevish, and will not gee, Ne'er pine..at the wanton Pug.

†**3. a.** A bargeman. ***Western pugs***, men who navigated barges down the Thames to London: cf. *Western bargee* (quot. 1666 s.v. bargee). *Obs.*

1591 Lyly *Endym.* iv. ii, In a Westerne barge, when with a good winde and lustie pugges one may goe ten miles in two daies. **1592** Greene *Disput.* C j, Iack Rhoades, a reformed Man, and a Crosbite... I doubte the sandeyde Asse, will kicke like a Westerne Pugge: if I rubbe him on the gaule. **1603** Dekker *Wonderfull Yeare* F iij b, Euen the Westerne Pugs receiuing money there [in plague time], haue tyed it in a bag at the end of their barge, and trailed it through the Thames. **1611** W. Austin in *Coryat's Crudities* Panegyr. Verses, Slept in his clothes like Westerne Pugge Sans Monmouth Cap or gowne of Rugge.

†**b.** ? A ship's boy. *Obs.*

1598 W. Phillip *Linschoten* i. xcvi. 179 The officers and most of the sailers were on land, none but pugs [Du. *putgers*] and slaues being in the ships: for..wheresoeuer they anker, presently they goe all on land, and let the shippe lie with a boy or two in it. *a* **1680** Butler *Rem.* (1759) I. 77 [Ulysses] ty'd his deafen'd Sailors..to the Mast,..rather venture drowning, than to wrong The Sea-pugs chaste Ears with a bawdy Song.

4. In servants' vocabulary: An upper servant in a large establishment.

1847–78 Halliwell s.v., In large families, the under-servants call the upper ones *pugs*, and the housekeeper's room is known as *pugs'-hole*. **1860** *Athenæum* 17 Nov. 664 Servants have become a separate estate..with their own distinction of ranks, the 'Pugs' and the 'Tags'. *Mod. Newspr.*, The stillroom-maid, coming up to Pug's Parlour for orders.

II. An imp, a dwarf animal, etc.

[In 5, the word agrees completely in sense with puck *sb.*[1], but is not easily accounted for as a mere phonetic variant of that word; senses 6–12 do not occur with puck.]

†**5.** A small demon or imp; a sprite; Puck.

1616 B. Jonson *Devil an Ass* Dram. Pers., *Satan.* The great diuell. *Pvg.* The lesse diuell. **1635** Heywood *Hierarch.* ix. 574 Diuels in Sarmatia honored, Call'd *Kottri*, or *Kibaldi*; such as wee Pugs and Hob-goblins call. **1664** Butler *Hud.* ii. iii. 635 Agrippa kept a Stygian pug, I' th' garb and habit of a dog, That was his tutor. **1678** *Ibid.* iii. i. 1415 This is your Business, good Pug-Robin, And your Diversion, dull dry Bobbing T'entice Fanatics in the Dirt. [**1822** W. Irving *Braceb. Hall* (1823) II. 163 Those sprites which Heywood in his Hierarchie calls pugs or hobgoblins.]

6. a. A monkey, an ape. Also applied, like 'monkey', to a child. *Obs.* exc. *dial.*

1664 Power *Exp. Philos.* iii. 184 Pugs and Baboons may claim a Traduction from Adam as well as these. *c* **1733** D. Mallet *Cupid & Hymen* 102 Those Jack-puddings pug and parret. **1754** Richardson *Grandison* (1810) VII. xliii. 234 Take away the pug, said I, to the attendants... They rescued the still smiling babe. **1793** *Carlop Green* (1817) 132 Pugs, bears, and dancan' dogs, And raree-showers.

b. As *quasi*-proper name of an ape. (Cf. *Jacko.*)

1698 J. Crull *Muscovy* II. 322 The Monkey by chance came jumping out with them... Poor Pug was had before his betters. **1712** Addison *Spect.* No. 499 ¶4, I heard her call him dear Pugg, and found him to be her favourite monkey. **1815** *Zeluca* II. 218 Pug was on my shoulder. **1863** Robson *Tyneside Songs* 64 As regard poor pug aw've had my say.

7. Originally ***pug-dog***: A dwarf breed of dog, resembling a bull-dog in miniature; on account of its affectionate nature much kept as a pet.

Here there may be some connexion with sense 1: cf. quot. 1611[2] there.

a. [1731 Bailey, *Pug*, a Nickname for a Monkey, or Dog.] **1749** Garrick *Lethe* 22 A fine Lady..keeps a Pug-dog, and hates the Parsons. **1774** Goldsm. *Nat. Hist.* (1776) III. 290 Several others might be added, such as the pug-dog, the black breed, and the pointer. **1840** Barham *Ingol. Leg.* Ser. I. *Hand of Glory*, Then half arose..His little pug-dog with his little pug nose. **1851** D. Jerrold *St. Giles* ii. 11 You'll be thinking of keeping pug-dogs and parrots next.

b. **1789** Mrs. Piozzi *Journ. France* I. 148 The little pug dog or Dutch mastiff has quitted London for Padua, I perceive...Every carriage I meet here has a pug in it. **1798** *Sporting Mag.* XII. 7 Portrait of Dutch pugs. **1821** *Joseph the Book-Man* 133 My Lady, in her parlour snug, Is still delighted with her pug. **1876** *World* V. No. 119.4 A veritable pug of pugs, with large soft loving eyes.

8. a. A *quasi*-proper name for a fox; = reynard.

1809 Mar. Edgeworth *Absentee* viii, There is a dead silence till pug is well out of cover, and the whole pack well in. **1848** Kingsley *Yeast* i, Cunning old farmers rode off..to some well-known haunts of pug. **1858** R. S. Surtees *Ask Mamma* xv, Pug..turns tail, and is very soon in the rear of the hounds.

b. Also, in dialectal use, a *quasi*-proper name for a lamb, a hare, a squirrel, a ferret, a salmon.

See *Eng. Dial. Dict.*

9. a. *dial.* Applied to anything short and stumpy; a dwarf.

1837 J. F. Palmer *Dialogues Devon. Dial.* Gloss. 74 Pug..is used for anything short, thick and irregularly orbicular; thus Pug-faced, Pug-nosed [etc.]. **1903** in *Eng. Dial. Dict.*

b. A net or snood for tying up or holding a bun or knot of hair. Also *attrib.*

1927 *Blackw. Mag.* June 747/1 His hair tied in a knot in a little red cloth or pug, on the top of his head. **1967** E. B. Nickerson *Kayaks to Arctic* x. 92, I had been wearing my hair in a long braid but tonight I coiled and netted it in a pug. **1967** *Boston Globe* 21 May (Confidential Chat) 17/1 The old fashioned idea of a dark, gloomy building..with an old fashioned old lady with glasses and a pug hair-do for a librarian are far out these days.

10. Also ***pug-moth***: Collectors' name for geometrid moths of the genus *Eupithecia*.

1819 G. Samouelle *Entomol. Compend.* 363 *Geometra* [*Eupithecia* (Curtis)] *rufifasciata.* The red-barred Pug. *Ibid.* 406 *Geometra singulariata.* The grey Pug. *Ibid.* Index, Pug-moth, beautiful. **1832** Rennie *Conspect. Butterfl. & Moths* 132 The Beautiful Pug..the Green Pug..the Brass Pug [etc.: 33 species so named]. **1869** Newman *Brit. Moths* 116/2 The little moths which constitute the genus *Eupithecia*, or, as called by collectors, 'Pugs'.

11. In full ***pug-engine***: A small locomotive used chiefly for station or shunting purposes; a contractor's engine.

1880 W. Aitken *Rodgerson's Doug* Poems (1893) 156 No a shift of the waggons, or shunt with the pug. **1887** *Daily News* 28 Sept. 3/1 A pug engine was engaged shunting a number of waggons within the works when it exploded. **1901** *Daily Express* 28 Aug. 6/3 While twenty navvies were returning home on a pug engine..the engine overturned at a curve on the line and fell down the embankment.

†**12.** A short cloak worn by ladies about the middle of the eighteenth century (Planché). *Obs.*

(Doubtful sense: in quot. cited it may mean a pug-dog.)

1740 L. Whyte *Poems* 63 The Cape..now is grown a demi-cloke,..To keep the Hero warm and snug, As any lady's velvet.Pug.

III. 13. *attrib.* and *Comb.* (from II): see sense 9, and ***pug-bitch, -dog*** (sense 7), ***pug-engine*** (sense 11), ***pug-moth*** (sense 10); **pug-face**, a face compared to that of a monkey; a squat flat-nosed face; **pug-fox**, a small-sized, blunt-nosed variety of fox; **pug-peal**, a young grilse or salmon; **pug-slut**, the female of a pug-dog; **pug-trout**, a sea-trout. See also pug-nose, -nosed.

1916 E. Pound *Lustra* 111 Quite plump, with *pug-bitch features. **1897** *Dublin Rev.* Oct. 311 The natives grinning with delight at the sight of their *pug-faces in the mirror. **1907** *Westm. Gaz.* 9 Dec. 10/1 The importers have..brought over many *pug foxes, small-sized animals with too great a love for life underground ever to lead hounds far across country. **1861** *Act. 24 & 25 Vict.* c. 109 §4 All migratory fish of the genus salmon, whether known by the names..salmon..peal, herring peal, may peal, *pugg peal, ..or by any other local name. **1817** *Sporting Mag.* L. 137 My favourite dog, a small *pug-slut, about two years and a half old. **1865** Couch *Brit. Fishes* IV. 211 *Sea Trout.* Grey Trout... *Pugtrout.

Hence **'puglet**, a little pug (in quot., monkey); **'pugship**, the personality of a pug.

1681 T. Flatman *Heraclitus Ridens* No. 46 (1713) II. 45 As if he had sent the Lady Apess with a Puglet or two to have squeal'd and scream'd at us. **1818** *Sporting Mag.* II. 3 This sable livery of their pugships is not of long duration—it is merely an ornament of youth.

pug (pʌg), *sb.*^{3} [See pug *v.*^{2}; cf. also pug-mill.] Loam or clay comminuted, thoroughly mixed, kneaded, and prepared for brickmaking and other purposes. Also *transf.*: see quot. 1904.

1872 Mrs. Millet *Parsonage* iii. 55 The walls of the house were built of 'pug', which means simply well-pounded mud. **1876** S. Wood *Gd. Gardening* (ed. 2) 41 Form this compound into a very stout pug or mortar by chopping, treading, &c. **1904** Major A. Griffiths *50 Yrs. Public Service* xvii. 236 When by-and-by the 'kerf' thus formed was to be carried on to the 'pug', or raised platform from which the machine was fed, it was duly cut at the bottom of the heap... I could follow the 'kerf' to the 'pug'.

b. *Comb.* pug-mill, q.v.; **pug-cylinder**, the cylinder of a pug-mill. (These may be from pug *v.*^{2}) Also **pug-hole**: see quot.

1839 Ure *Dict. Arts* 187 There are boxes..upon each side of the pug cylinder containing sand. **1870** Symons *Life Draper* vii. 61 Bowden was a great brick-making place. Deep pits from which the clay had been excavated, known as 'pug holes' abounded in every direction.

‖**pug** (pʌg), *sb.*^{4} *Anglo-Ind.* [Hindī *pag* footprint.] The footprint of a beast. Also *Comb.*, as ***pug-mark***.

1865 *Daily Tel.* 12 Dec. 7/3 There are not many sensations worth getting up for so early..; but to see the first 'pug' of the tiger's track on the wet path is one of them. **1882** Floyer *Unexpl. Baluchistan* iv. 114 We with difficulty kept sight of the pugs of a camel which had preceded us. **1889** Baden-Powell *Pigsticking* 55 The goat has a square pug with blunt points to his toes. **1922** *Chambers's Jrnl.* Dec. 860/1, I found a good many pug-marks and from them I concluded that the man-eater was a smallish beast. **1946** J. Corbett *Man-Eaters of Kumaon* 8 Entering the ravine..I found the pug marks of a tiger in some fine earth..; these pug marks showed the animal to be a tigress, a little past her prime. **1974** *Country Life* 31 Oct. 1302/2 Tigers are elusive... We followed pug marks up hill and down ravine.

pug (pʌg), *sb.*^{5} *slang.* Abbrev. of pugilist. Hence **pug-glove**, a boxing-glove.

1858 A. Mayhew *Paved w. Gold* II. xii. 184 He was known by his brother pugs to be one of the gamest hands in the ring. **1888** 'R. Boldrewood' *Robbery under A.* xx, He was fond of talking about 'pugs' as he'd known intimate. **1924** J. Buchan *Three Hostages* v. 74 The man had been in the ring, and not so very long ago. I wondered at Medina's choice, for a pug is not the kind of servant I would choose myself. **1938** Dylan Thomas *Let.* 1 June (1966) 198 'Boxed' has the coffin and the pug-glove in it. **1961** *Lancet* 26 Aug. 447/2 It is well known that boxers, including fair-ground-booth pugs, can tolerate severe direct blows to the head. **1977** *Time* 19 Dec. 68/2 Hemingway had gone many rounds with pugs, and Journalist Paul Gallico once had his fillings loosened by Jack Dempsey.

pug (pʌg), *v.*^{1} Now only *dial.* [Origin obscure: perh. more than one word.]

1. *trans.* To pull, tug.

1575 *Appius & Virginia* in Hazl. *Dodsley* IV. 120 What tugging, what lugging, what pugging by the ear. **1717** Marchant *Diary* 30 Mar. in *Sussex Archæol. Coll.* (1873) XXV. 180 George pugg'd clover in the forenoon. **1790** Grose *Provinc. Gloss.* (ed. 2). **1819** W. Tennant *Papistry Storm'd* (1827) 211 Nae thing was prosperin' there and thrivin', But tirlin' roofs and rafter-rivin', And pullin' down and puggin'.

2. To dirty by overmuch handling.

1885 Sharland *Ways Devon. Village* iv. 55 To learn to handle things without pugging and pawing them.

pug (pʌg), *v.*^{2} [Origin obscure: cf. pug *sb.*^{3} and pug-mill.

If the group began with the vb., and sense 1 is properly put here, the word is prob. onomatopœic, expressing the action and accompanying dull heavy sound of pounding or ramming a stiff but yielding body such as clay.]

I. 1. *trans.* To poke, punch, strike.

1809 Wolcott (P. Pindar) *Middlesex Election* I. xxix, I'd quickly pug their guts.

II. 2. To temper (clay) for brickmaking, by kneading and working it into a soft and plastic condition, as in a pug-mill. Hence **pugged** (pʌgd), *ppl. a.*; **'pugging** *vbl. sb.*

Originally done by treading and stamping with the feet, which was prob. the original 'pugging': cf. Ure *Dict. Arts* (1839) 184 'The next step is to temper the clay, which is generally done by the treading of men or oxen. In the neighbourhood of London, however, this process is performed in a horse-mill. The kneading of the clay is..the most laborious but indispensable part of the whole business [of brick-making]... The more it is worked, the denser, more uniform, and more durable, the bricks which are made of it.'

1843 *Mech. Mag.* XXXIX. 193 The most useful properties of 'ciment', when well pugged or kneaded with the clay, was to hasten the drying, and to diminish the contraction. **1843** Parkes in *Jrnl. R. Agric. Soc.* IV. II. 374 It is requisite that the clay be well washed and sieved before pugging. **1843** *Civil Eng. & Arch. Jrnl.* VI. 348/1 The bricks were all burned in close kilns constructed with soft bricks set in pugged clay. **1884** C. G. W. Lock *Workshop Receipts* Ser. III. 105 The compound was pugged, moulded, and strongly pressed.

b. To trample or tread (ground) into a muddy and sticky mass, as is done by cattle near gates or drinking-places; to poach or *potch*.

1881 *Daily News* 4 June 5/5 The pugged and sticky sheep-folds could not be brought by plough and harrow into anything like suitable mould.

III. 3. To pack or fill up (a space) with pug, cement, etc.; *esp.* to pack the space under a floor with earth, old mortar, sawdust, or other substance to prevent the passage of sound: cf. pugging *sb.*

1823 [implied in pugging *sb.*]. **1870** *Eng. Mech.* 28 Jan. 488/1 Will any kind reader inform me of a material that will answer all the purposes of pugging floors? **1880** *Libr. Univ. Knowl.* (U.S.) V. 876 Wood, well pugged with cement, is strongly recommended by many architects..for girders and beams. **1906** *Pall Mall G.* 19 Mar. 2/3 Residents in semi-detached villas with the usual slender walls, or even in flats with the floors warranted duly 'pugged'.

4. To thrust, poke, or pack into a space. *dial.*

1854 Miss Baker *Northants. Gloss.* s.v., 'That small house is pugged in between two high ones.' 'The two families live pugging together.'

pug (pʌg), *v.*^{3} *Anglo-Ind.* [f. pug *sb.*^{4}] *trans.* To track by footprints. Hence **'pugging** *vbl. sb.*

1866 Newall *Eastern Hunters* 6 You never would take the trouble to learn pugging, though it is so essential an acquirement in wood craft. **1882** Floyer *Unexpl. Baluchistan* 18 To comment with considerable point on each false move the young man made in his pugging (tracking). **1889** Baden-Powell *Pigsticking* 57 We called up the head-man of the beat and asked him if he could pug... 'Of course I can pug. My work is pugging criminals.'

†**'puggard.** *Obs. rare*$^{-1}$. ? *Thieves' Cant.* [perh. f. pug *v.*^{1} + -ard.] A thief.

1611 Middleton *Roaring Girl* v. i, Cheaters, lifters, nips, foists, puggards, curbers.

puggaree, -ery, var. forms of puggree.

pugged (pʌgd), *a.* [f. pug *sb.*^{2} + -ed^2.] Formed like the nose of a pug-dog.

1847 H. Melville *Omoo* xx, With a viciously pugged nose.

pugged, *ppl. a.*: see pug *v.*^{2}

puggee, variant of puggy *sb.*^{2}

†**'puggered**, *ppl. a. Obs. rare*$^{-1}$. Perh. a variant of puckered.

1653 H. More *Antid. Ath.* II. xi. (1712) 73 Nor are we to cavil at the red pugger'd attire of the Turky, and the long Excrescency that hangs down over his Bill. **1706** Phillips, *Puggered*, as the red puggered Attire of the Turkey.

'pugginess^1. *dial.* [f. puggy *a.*^{2} + -ness.] Moistness from perspiration; clamminess.

1858 Mrs. Gatty *Aunt Judy's T.* ii. (1859) 26 Whenever ..some active exertion has brought a universal puggyness over the juvenile frame.

'pugginess^2. [f. puggy *a.*^{1} + -ness.] Squatness; stumpiness.

1910 H. G. Wells *Hist. Mr. Polly* vii. 227 Mr. Hinks..displayed a freckled fist of extraordinary size and pugginess ..to Mr. Polly's close inspection.

'pugging, *sb.* [f. pug *v.*^{2} 3 + -ing^1.] See quot. 1823, and pug *v.*^{2} 3.

1823 P. Nicholson *Pract. Build.* 392 *Pugging*, the materials composed of bricks and mortar, &c., introduced between the joists of floors, in order to prevent the communication of sound, or to deaden it in the interval from one story to another. **1884** Spon *Mechanic's Own Bk.* (1893) 341 A thick layer of old mortar or plaster, known as 'pugging'.

pugging, *vbl. sb.*: see pug *v.*^{2}, ^{3}.

†**'pugging**, *ppl. a. Obs. rare*$^{-1}$. Meaning uncertain.

Usually taken as = thieving, thievish; if so, it may be pr. pple. of pug *v.*^{1} as if = pulling down or off; cf. puggard. But some think it a mispr. for prigging. In Devonsh. dialect *pug-tooth* = eye-tooth (E.D.D.).

1611 Shaks. *Wint. T.* IV. iii. 7 The white sheete bleaching on the hedge,..Doth set my pugging tooth an edge, For a quart of Ale is a dish for a King.

'pugging screw. [pug *v.*^{2}] A screw for compressing peat, etc.

1862 *Fraser's Mag.* Nov. 634/2[Mr. Brunton's] process in subjecting freshly-dug peat to the action of a pugging screw, working in a conical case, the bottom of which is pierced by small holes.

puggish ('pʌgɪʃ), *a.* [f. pug *sb.*^{2} + -ish^1.] Resembling or characteristic of a pug, in various senses (as monkey, pug-dog), or a pug-nose.

1742 Richardson *Pamela* III. xxx. 197 The apes of imitation..were wont to hop and skip about, and play a thousand puggish Tricks. **1807–8** in *Spirit Pub. Jrnls.* XII. 10, I touch not what concerns their praise, Or wreathes their puggish pates with bays. **1826** Miss Mitford *Village* Ser. II. 308 (*Young Gipsy*) Nothing visible but their tails, (the one, the long puggish brush of which I have already made mention, the other a terrier-like stump). **1828** Scott *Diary* June in *Lockhart*, His son, a puggish boy, follows up the theme. *a* **1849** Poe *Wks.* (1864) I. 136 Doomed to perpetual contemplation of their noses—a view puggish and snubby.

'puggishness. [f. puggish *a.* + -ness.] The nature of or resemblance to a pug.

1924 W. J. Locke *Coming of Amos* ii. 13 There is a puggishness about her rebellious nose which would disqualify her in a competition of Classical Beauty.

puggle ('pʌg(ə)l), *v.* Chiefly *dial.* [Freq. from pug *v.*^{2} 1: see -le 3.] *trans.* To push or poke a stick or wire down (a hole, etc.) and work it about in order to clear the hole.

1863 *Trans. Essex Archæol. Soc.* II. 186 *Puggle*, to poke out, as to puggle the ashes, a drain, or anything that is encumbered with rubbish. **1899** *Let. to Rev. C. B. Mount*, The man gave me a wire and told me to puggle the pipe. I have puggled it several times, but the water does not come. **1905** *N. & Q.* 10th Ser. IV. 486/2 To get a rat or rabbit out of a hole by inserting a stick and working it about was to 'puggle'.

puggle, var. poggle *sb.* and *a.*

puggled, *a.*, var. poggled *a.*

puggly, var. poggle *sb.* and *a.*

puggree, puggaree (ˈpʌgriː, ˈpʌgəriː). Also 7 puckery, 8 pukree, 9 pugree, -aree, puggri, -gry, -gery, pagri. [a. Hind. *pagṛī* a turban.]

1. A light turban or head-covering worn by inhabitants of the Indian subcontinent.

1665 SIR T. HERBERT *Trav.* (1677) 140 Eastern People.. such.. as wear Turbans, Mandils, Dustars, and Puggarees. **1696** OVINGTON *Voy. Suratt* 314 With a Puggarie, or Turbant upon their Heads. **1698** FRYER *Acc. E. India & P.* 93 A Green Vest and Puckery (or Turbat). **1845** SIR W. NAPIER *Conq. Scinde* II. i. 224 The Mohamedan Belooch always obeys him who wears the Puggree. **1893** FORBES-MITCHELL *Remin. Gt. Mutiny* 287 The latter wore voluminous thick puggries round their heads. **1930** *Aberdeen Press & Jrnl.* 22 Apr. 5/2 He has no British officers and no uniform except a distinguishing kind of pagri (head-dress). **1930** *Punch* 1 Oct. 392/2 Mr Thompson should not allow this bee to find a permanent home in his *pagri*. **1974** 'B. MATHER' *White Dacoit* 18 Sowars straightened tunics and pagris.

2. A scarf of thin muslin or a silk veil wound round the crown of a sun-helmet or hat and falling down behind as a shade.

1859 DICKENS in *All Year Round* 30 July 332/1 A 'Puggery' is a long slip of white muslin which is bound round the hat and formed into a fantastic bow, with tails behind. **1866** *Cornh. Mag.* Dec. 741 A silk coat, a puggree, boots, and white cords, adorned the wealthier. **1885** *Times* 20 Feb. 6/1 Officers and men were attired in red serge tunics, .. sun helmets and puggarees. **1901** B. SHAW *Three Plays for Purit., Capt. Brassbound* I. 215 He wears the sun helmet and pagri, the neutral-tinted spectacles, and the white canvas Spanish sand shoes.

3. *attrib.*, as *puggree-cloth*.

1934 [see DRILL *sb.*[5]]. **1978** 'M. M. KAYE' *Far Pavilions* vi. 98 She slept soundly.. tied to him by a length of *pagri* (turban) cloth that prevented her from falling.

Hence **ˈpugg(a)reed** *a.*, covered with or wearing a puggree.

1881 MRS. C. PRAED *Policy & P.* I. 13 A broad-brimmed puggareed hat. **1900** *Daily News* 1 Aug. 3/1 A graceful wave of his green, puggareed soft slouch hat.

puggy (ˈpʌgɪ), *sb.*[1] [f. PUG *sb.*[2] + -Y.]

†**1.** A term of endearment used to women and children. See PUG *sb.*[2] 1. *Obs.*

1611 BEAUM. & FL. *Knt. Burn. Pestle* III. v, Begon, begon my juggy, my puggy, begon my love, my deere. **1719** D'URFEY *Pills* IV. 44 My Juggy, my Puggy, My Honey, my Bunny. **1721** BAILEY, *Puggy*, a soothing Word to a little Child, or a Paramour, as My little Puggy.

2. A monkey; = PUG *sb.*[2] 6. *Sc.*

1821 *Blackw. Mag.* Nov. 392/2 'See that wee body sittin' on the man's shouther'... 'That's a puggy, man'. **1897** C. M. CAMPBELL *Deilie Jock* i. 29 I've heard talk o' some missing link, atween men and puggies.

3. Quasi-proper name for a fox: = PUG *sb.*[2] 8.

1827 *Sporting Mag.* XXI. 134 Puggy, thinking it time to shift, got into a drain.

‖**puggy** (ˈpʌgɪ), *sb.*[2] *Anglo-Ind.* Also puggee. [Hindī *pagī*, f. *pag* PUG *sb.*[4]] A tracker.

1879 *Times of India* Overland Suppl. 12 May (Y.), Good puggies or trackers should be employed to follow the dacoits. **1883** LD. SALTOUN *Scraps* II. 258 The 'puggy' is one of a caste, who.. obtain the name from their skill in following foot-tracks, or 'pugs'. **1889** BADEN-POWELL *Pigsticking* 56 In pugging boars, the usual method is for four or five trackers or 'puggees' to start together.

puggy (ˈpʌgɪ), *a.*[1] [f. PUG *sb.*[2] + -Y.] Resembling the face or nose of a monkey or pug-dog; having such a face or nose; squat-faced; pug-nosed.

1722 RAMSAY *Three Bonnets* III. 78 'Tis gowd that maks some great men witty, And puggy lasses fair and pretty. **1893** STEVENSON *Catriona* 110 My affection for my King, God bless the puggy face of him, is under more control. **1904** *Daily Chron.* 12 Nov. 6/5 Its puggy little nose has quite a smashed-in appearance, and when the animal looked in a mirror it also must have noticed that, for it smiled an almost cynical smile.

puggy (ˈpʌgɪ), *a.*[2] *dial.* [f. *pug* vb. dial., to perspire (Halliwell).] Moist, clammy.

1814 *S. Pegge's Anecd. Eng. Lang., Suppl. Grose's Gloss.*, *Puggy*, moist, arising from gentle perspiration. A puggy hand. North. **1825** in BROCKETT *N.C. Gloss.* **1896** HARE *Story My Life* III. xv. 329, I remembered being sick as a child from the puggy smell of its hideous interior. It was just as puggy to day, but I was not sick.

pugh, obs. form of POOH.

pugil[1] (ˈpjuːdʒɪl). *arch.* [ad. L. *pugill-us* a handful, f. root *pug-* as in *pug-nus* fist.] Etymologically, A handful; but from the 17th century defined as 'as much as can be taken up between the thumb and the next two (or sometimes three) fingers'; a little handful or big pinch.

1576 BAKER *Jewell of Health* 237b, Gave a certain Phisition.. of this salt one lytle handfull or Pugill. **1626** BACON *Sylva* §17 Take Violets, and infuse a good Pugill of them in a Quart of Vineger. **1729** *Enquiry Causes Epid. Dis.* 42 Take of Roman Wormwood two Pugils (a Pugil is what two Fingers and a Thumb hold). **1747** WESLEY *Prim. Physic* (1765) 68 Add two Pugils of dry'd Elder Flowers. **1858** O. W. HOLMES *Aut. Breakf.-t.* iv, The old gentleman.. opened it [a snuff-box] and felt for the wonted pugil.

†**ˈpugil**[2]. *Obs. rare.* [a. L. *pugil* a boxer, f. root *pug-*: see prec.] One who fights with his fists; a boxer, pugilist.

1646 SIR T. BROWNE *Pseud. Ep.* IV. xi. 207 That which expresseth pugills, that is, men fit for combat and the exercise of the fist. *a* **1670** HACKET *Abp. Williams* I. §44 (1692) 37 He was no little one, but *Saginati corporis bellua*, as Curtius says of Dioxippus the Pugil.

Hence †**ˈpugilar** *a.*, pugilistic.

1636 SANDERSON *Serm. on Ps. xix.* 13 ¶37 So doth St. Pauls ὑπωπιάζω, 1 Cor. 9. which is an athletique pugilar word: as those that beat one another with their fists.

pugil[3] (ˈpjuːdʒɪl). *U.S. Mil.* [Prob. f. L. stem *pugil-*, as in PUGILISM, etc.] In full, *pugil stick*. A short pole with padded ends used as a substitute for a rifle and bayonet in military training. Also *attrib.* and *Comb.*, as *pugil bout*, *training*; *pugil-armed* adj.

1962 *Infantry* Nov.–Dec. 26/2 *Pugil training* was first adopted by the Marine Corps... The pugil stick is an oak staff, two inches in diameter, padded on both ends with polyfoam encased in canvas. This stick represents the rifle and is the same length as a rifle with bayonet fixed. *Ibid.* 26/3 The students engage in pugil bouts, applying all the movements taught in earlier periods with the rifle. *Ibid.* 28/3 Substitute pugil-armed students for dummies. **1964** A. N. HARDIN *Amer. Bayonet 1776–1964* 188 Modern U.S. Marine Corps practice virtually eliminates fencing bayonets by substituting the 'Pugil Stick' technique. **1967** *Britannica Bk. of Year 1966* 804/1 *Pugil or Pugil stick*, a padded club with large rounded ends used in bayonet practice by the military as a substitute for rifle with fixed bayonet. **1976** *Billings* (Montana) *Gaz.* 28 June 4-B/1 The first of three sergeants.. was accused of violating orders in the conduct of the.. pugil stick bouts in which the recruit was pounded into a coma.

ˈpugilant, *a. rare.* [ad. late L. *pugilāns, -āntem*, pres. pple. of *pugilārī* to box, f. *pugil*: see PUGIL[2].] Boxing, fighting.

1882 *Fraser's Mag.* XXVI. 432 Robert Grosseteste, pugilant, he, as well as literary; fighting his way to self-justification in stout English. **1932** J. JOYCE in *New Statesman* 27 Feb. 260/1 A pugilant gang theirs, per Bantry!

†**ˈpugilate.** *Obs. rare.* [ad. late L. *pugilātu-s* boxing, f. *pugilārī*: see prec. Cf. F. *pugilat, -illat* (1570 in Hatz.-Darm.).] Boxing.

1768 *Woman of Honor* III. 37 A pitiful complaisance,.. erected these black-guard battles into the dignity of the pugilate of the antients. **1817** *Sporting Mag.* L. 15 *note*, It seems as if this Gymnic exercise were more common in Palestine than the pugilate.

†**pugilation.** *Obs.* [ad. L. *pugilātiōn-em*, n. of action f. *pugilārī* to box.] Fighting with the fists, boxing.

1656 BLOUNT *Glossogr.*, *Pugillation*, the exercise of Champions, or of those that fight with fists. **1718** OZELL *Tournefort's Voy.* II. 108 Very skilful too at boxing, and at that kind of exercise which was called Pugilation.

pugilism (ˈpjuːdʒɪlɪz(ə)m). [f. L. *pugil* boxer, PUGIL[2] + -ISM.] The art or practice of fighting with fists; boxing. Also *fig.*

1791 HAMPSON *Mem. J. Wesley* III. 48 Pugilism and cock-fighting, and the rest. **1812** (*title*) Pancratia, or a History of Pugilism. **1877** TALMAGE *Serm.* 255 Men have made it the ring in which to display their ecclesiastical pugilism. **1882** MASSON in *Macm. Mag.* XLV. 250 Feats of strength, pedestrianism, and pugilism. **1890** *Spectator* 9 Aug., We do not find him hastening from the dinner-table to the diary, to enter up his last achievement in conversational pugilism. He leaves that to a Boswell.

pugilist (ˈpjuːdʒɪlɪst). [f. as prec. + -IST.] One who practises the art of boxing; a boxer, a fighter; *fig.* a vigorous controversialist.

1790 T. FEWTRELL (*title*) Boxing Reviewed... Comprehending a complete description of the Principal Pugilists. **1899** R. MUNRO *Preh. Scot.* vii. 238 One scene represents two pugilists with a crested helmet between them.

pugilistic (pjuːdʒɪˈlɪstɪk), *a.* (*sb.*) [f. prec. + -IC.] **a.** Of or pertaining to pugilists or pugilism.

1789 *Loiterer* 27 June 4 A tolerable Proficient in pugillistic Science. *a* **1790** J. H. BEATTIE *Dial. of Dead* III, in J. Beattie *Minstrel* (1799) II. 195 Some learned innovator.. clapping to it [*sc.* Latin *pugil*] part of a Greek termination, he made it *pugilist*; which.. gave rise to the adjectives *Pugilistic* and *Pugilistical*, as in this example,.. 'a.. pavilion at Newmarket for *Pugilistical* exhibitions'. **1811** *Sporting Mag.* XXXVII. 122 He reached the summit of pugilistic fame. **1855** THACKERAY *Newcomes* iv, He had been engaged.. in a pugilistic encounter.

b. as *sb.* A pugilist. *nonce-use.*

1827 SOUTHEY *Let. to G. C. Beaford* 10 June, What? will-we, nill-we, are we thrust Among the Calvinistics—The covenanted sons of schism, Rebellion's pugilistics.

So **pugiˈlistical** *a. rare*; hence **pugiˈlistically** *adv.*, in a pugilistic manner.

1840 HOOD *Kilmansegg, Her Misery* xvii, Pugilistical knocks, And fighting cocks. **1847** LYTTON *Lucretia* II. Prol. (1855) 142 Sure that it was a proper thing to resent pugilistically so discourteous a monosyllable. **1895** *Chamb. Jrnl.* XII. 758/1 They were most pugilistically inclined.

†**ˈpugillary.** *Obs.* [f. L. *pugillār* writing-tablet, f. *pugillār-is* adj. that can be held in the hand: see PUGIL[1] and -ARY[2].] A writing-tablet.

1758 *Phil. Trans.* L. 620 Many pugillaries, styles, and stands with ink in them.

Puginesque (ˌpjuːdʒɪˈnɛsk), *a.* [f. the name *Pugin* (see def.) + -ESQUE.] Of, pertaining to, or characteristic of the English architect A. W. N. Pugin (1812–1852) or his style of architecture; Gothic-revivalist. So **ˌPugiˈnesquery** [-ERY] *nonce-wd.*, matters related to Pugin or his architectural style.

1848 C. KINGSLEY *Yeast* v, in *Fraser's Mag.* XXXVIII. 286/1 When they talk Puginesquery, I stick my head on one side attentively, and 'think the more', like the lady's parrot. **1856** F. E. PAGET *Owlet of Owlstone Edge* 210 In her ambition to be Puginesque, she made her husband's chancel look as if it had been decked by a mad haberdasher. **1864** *Ecclesiologist* XXV. 345 The general idea is Puginesque, the style Middle-Pointed. **1904** A. C. BENSON *Let.* 5 Oct. in *Upton Lett.* (1905) 234 The roofs and towers of the big house —Puginesque Gothic, I must tell you—came in sight. **1907** E. GOSSE *Father & Son* xii. 339 My Father did not, indeed, forbid me to enter.. the stately Puginesque cathedral which Rome had just erected. **1961** E. WAUGH *Unconditional Surrender* II. iii. 72 The Catholic parish church is.. a Puginesque structure erected.. in the early 1860's. **1975** V. CUNNINGHAM *Everywhere spoken Against* iii. 86 The whole set of Puginesque-Arnoldian assumptions.

pugiˈoniform, *a. Bot.* [f. L. *pugiōn-em* dagger + -I)FORM.] Dagger-shaped.

1858 MAYNE *Expos. Lex.*, *Pugioniformis*.. pugioniform.

ˈpug-mill. [app. f. PUG *v.*[2] + MILL *sb.*[1]; but the vb. has not yet been found in this sense as early as *pug-mill*, so that the relation may be the reverse.] A machine for comminuting, thoroughly mixing, and working clay and other materials into a plastic state for making bricks and pottery; also, a similar machine for triturating ore, etc.

1824 *Mech. Mag.* No. 33. 78 The introduction of machines called pug-mills, into which the prepared earth is wheeled. **1825** J. NICHOLSON *Operat. Mechanic* 533 [The tread of men and oxen] has of late been superseded by the clay or pug mill, which is a very eligible, though simple machine. **1877** SPURGEON *Serm.* XXIII. 555 Like the brickmaker's blind horse which goes round and round his pug-mill. **1902** A. BENNETT *Anna of Five Towns* viii. 169 The press expelled the water, and the pug-mill expelled the air. **1930** *Industr. & Engin. Chem.* 20 Mar. 14/1 The machinery is.. simple in design and operation, including, in addition to the centrifuge, a 'pug mill' in which hot water and steam are used to wash the oil-impregnated sands. **1960** [see EXTRUDER 1]. **1980** M. FORSTER *Bride of Lowther Fell* xi. 168, I decided.. to ferret out a pug-mill.. together with a special plaster sink I would soon be needing.

pugnacious (pʌgˈneɪʃəs), *a.* [f. L. *pugnāx, -āci-* combative (f. *pugn-āre* to fight, f. *pugn-us* fist) + -OUS: see -ACIOUS.] Disposed to fight; given to fighting; quarrelsome; contentious.

1642 H. MORE *Song of Soul* IV. xiv, Plato affirms Idees; But Aristotle with his pugnacious race As idle figments stifly them denies. **1776** PENNANT *Zool.* (ed. 4) I. 328 [The whitethroat] A shy and wild bird..; seems of a pugnatious disposition. **1877** MRS. OLIPHANT *Makers Flor.* i. 10 These pugnacious Florentines, whose personal feuds and hatreds .. were infinitely more real and vivid.

Hence **pugˈnaciously** *adv.*, in a pugnacious manner; **pugˈnaciousness**, pugnacity.

1681 H. MORE *Exp. Dan.* iii. 64 The strength.. and pugnaciousness of the Ram well represent Cyrus and his Successours. **1829** PALMERSTON *Opinions & Policy* (1852) 102 If the nation is overflowing with so much pugnaciousness. **1847** WEBSTER, Pugnaciously. **1871** E. P. WHIPPLE *Success & its Conditions* 69 A politician weakly and amiably in the right is no match for [one] tenaciously and pugnaciously in the wrong. **1875** JOWETT *Plato* (ed. 2) III. 334 We valiantly and pugnaciously insist upon the verbal truth.

pugnacity (pʌgˈnæsɪtɪ). [ad. L. *pugnācitās*, f. *pugnāx*: see prec. So mod.F. *pugnacité* (rare).] The condition or character of being pugnacious; tendency or inclination to fight; quarrelsomeness.

1605 BACON *Adv. Learn.* II. viii. §4, I like better that entrie of truth which commeth peaceably.. then that which commeth with pugnacitie and contention. **1613** CAWDREY *Table Alph.* (ed. 3), *Pugnacitie*, striuing, or contending. **1846** GROTE *Greece* II. ii. II. 320 The turbulence and pugnacity of the heroic age. **1880** L. STEPHEN *Pope* v. 133 Bentley had provoked enemies by his intense pugnacity.

†**ˈpugnant**, *a.*[1] *Obs.* [ad. L. *pugnāns, -āntem*, pres. pple. of *pugn-āre* to fight.] Conflicting, hostile, opposed, repugnant.

1582 STANYHURST *Æneis* IV. (Arb.) 110 Thee fate's are pugnant, God, his ears quight stifned in hardnesse. **1645** USSHER *Body Div.* (1647) 228 Rites of Religion, which are pugnant to God's word. **1686** HORNECK *Crucif. Jesus* xix. 552 Governed by.. contrariety of pugnant humours.

Hence †**ˈpugnancy**, conflicting quality.

1660 BURNEY Κέρδ. Δῶρον (1661) 106, I so.. bear rule in these great Courts, that the Ballances of Justice are kept even, Prerogative and priviledge having no pugnancie.

†**ˈpugnant, -aunt**, *a.*[2] *Obs.* [An intermediate form between POIGNANT and PUNGENT. Cf. OF. *pongnant, puignant*, early variants of *poignant*, from *poindre, puindre, pugnre*:—L. *pungĕre* to pierce.] Piercing, poignant.

c **1400** *Rom. Rose* 1879 The God of Love an arowe took; Ful sharp it was and pugnaunt. **1529** MORE *Dyaloge* III. Wks. 224/2 Your wordes.. be somewhat pugnant and sharpe.

pugˈnastics, *sb. pl. nonce-wd.* [f. L. *pugn-us* fist, after *gymnastics*.] Pugilistic performances.

1830 H. ANGELO *Remin.* II. 65, I soon found my sisters, who were taken into a house during my pugnastics.

pug'natic, *a. rare*$^{-1}$. [irreg. f. L. *pugnus* (see prec.) after *dramatic*.] = next.
1818 *Blackw. Mag.* II. 439 On the 15th, while he employed the pugnatic method, he had a distinct pricking sensation in his thumbs.

'pugnatory, *a. rare*$^{-0}$. [ad. L. *pugnātōri-us*, f. *pugnātōr-em* fighter, f. *pugnāre* to fight: see -ORY[2].] Of or pertaining to a fighter or fighting.
1656 BLOUNT, *Pugnatory*, of or belonging to a fighter.

†**'pugne**, *v. Obs. rare.* [a. OF. *pugne-r* (1478 in Godef.), or ad. L. *pugn-āre*.] *intr.* To fight.
c **1400** *Laud Troy Bk.* 13347 Among Gregeis be-gan he [Troilus] pugne, That thei made many a lothely groyne.

pugniard, pugnicion, -ycion, pugnisshe, obs. forms of PONIARD, PUNITION, PUNISH.

pug nose, pug-nose ('pʌgnəʊz). [f. PUG *sb.*[2] 6 or 7 + NOSE *sb.*] A short nose with a wide base sloping upward; a short squat or snub nose.
1778 MISS BURNEY *Evelina* xxiii. (1791) I. 132 Perhaps, you may persuade her that her pug nose is all the fashion. **1826** DISRAELI *Viv. Grey* I. iv, A pallid wretch with a pug nose..and marked with the small-pox. **1840** [see PUG *sb.*[2] 7 a]. **1860** EMERSON *Cond. Life, Fate* Wks. (Bohn) II. 311 A squint, a pug-nose, mats of hair,..betray character.
Hence **pug-nosed** ('pʌg,nəʊzd) *a.*, having a short snub nose; whence **pug'nosedness**.
pug-nosed (pug-nose) eel, a deep-sea species of eel, *Simenchelys parasiticus*, found off the Newfoundland bank, having a short and blunt snout.
1834 *Oxf. Univ. Mag.* I. 39, I well remember Gibbon, a heavy pugnosed fellow. **1845** MAURICE *Mor. & Met. Philos.* (1850) I. VI. III. v. 186 It is obvious also that all notions of an ideal form of hollowness or of pugnosedness (we use Aristotle's favourite illustration) must be out of the question. **1888** GOODE *Amer. Fishes* 232 The Horse-fish.. was called by De Kay 'Blunt-nosed Shiner'...This name, sometimes varied to 'Pugnosed Shiner' [etc.].

pugnozzle ('pʌgnɒz(ə)l), *v. nonce-wd.* [f. PUG *sb.*[2] + NOZZLE *sb.* or *nozzle*, var. NUZZLE *v.*; cf. PUG NOSE.] *intr.* To move the upper lip and nostrils in the manner of a pug-dog.
1934 S. BECKETT *More Pricks than Kicks* 257 The wretched little wet rag of an upper lip, pugnozzling up and back in what you might call a kind of a duck or a cobra sneer to the nostrils.

†**'pugny**. *Sc. Obs. rare*$^{-1}$. [Variant of POYGNÉ, *punʒe*, OF. *poigniée*, L. *pugnāta*.] Fighting.
1456 SIR G. HAYE *Law Arms* (S.T.S.) 116 Suppos he pas to do sum pugny of were that be prouffitable to his lorde.

'pug-pile, *sb. Hydr. Engin.* [f. PUG *v.*[2] (? 4) + PILE *sb.*[1] 3. (But the sense of *pug* is not clear.)] One of a series of piles dovetailed into each other.
1882 OGILVIE (Annandale), *Pug-piles*, piles mortised into each other by a dovetail joint. They are also called *Dovetailed Piles*. **1886** in *Cassell's Encycl. Dict.*
So **'pug-'pile** *v. trans.*, to plank or line with pug-piles; hence **'pug-piling** *vbl. sb.*
1805 Z. ALLNUTT *Navig. Thames* 23 Sills at the bottom of the River to be pug-piled. **1823** P. NICHOLSON *Pract. Builder* 591 *Pug-piling*, dove-tailed or pile planking.

pugree, -ry, variants of PUGGREE.

Pugwash ('pʌgwɒʃ). The name of a village in Nova Scotia where in 1957 the first conference was held of scientists concerned to promote international responsibility in the peaceful uses of scientific discoveries, used *attrib.* of this and subsequent conferences, and also the movement which they generated, as ***Pugwash conference, group***, etc. Also *ellipt.*
1957 *N.Y. Times* 12 July 3/6 Asked if he and his Russian colleague came to the Pugwash meeting as independent scientists, Mr. Topchiev replied [etc.]. **1957** *Science* 2 Aug. 199/3 These men all signed the 'Pugwash Statement'. **1957** *Bull. Atomic Sci.* Sept. 244/2 The Pugwash discussion showed clearly that the most important unresolved disagreement among experts concerns not the radiation exposure caused by bomb tests..but the biological consequences likely to be produced by this exposure. **1958** *Washington Post* 15 Sept. 18/2 Pugwash conferences, so named because the first one took place at Pugwash, Nova Scotia, on the estate of American multimillionaire Cyrus Eaton. **1963** *Pugwash Newslet.* July 2 Since the Pugwash Newsletter is for private circulation only, it may provide a convenient medium for testing and impromptu..ideas. **1965** *New Statesman* 16 Apr. 601/1 He [*sc.* Albert Einstein] died 10 years ago on Sunday, two days after signing the great Russell-Einstein Manifesto which launched the Pugwash Movement of scientists (the 14th meeting took place in Venice this week). **1968** *Listener* 11 July 36/1 Pugwash..has set up a study group. **1972** *Guardian* 4 Sept. 10/6 Pugwash is this week spending much of its time discussing problems of developing nations. **1976** *Chronicle-Herald* (Halifax, Nova Scotia) 19 July 21/1 The banquet meeting of the Canadian and American Pugwash groups.

puh, puhn, obs. ff. POOH *int.*, POON *sb.*[1] (a tree).

puha ('pu:hɑ:). *N.Z.* Also **pua, puwha**. [Maori.] A sow-thistle belonging to the genus *Sonchus*, esp. *S. oleraceus*; the leaves of this plant used as a vegetable.
1843 E. DIEFFENBACH *Trav. N.Z.* II. III. 380 Pua—a sowthistle. **1868** W. COLENSO in *Trans. N.Z. Inst.* I. III. 37 The fresh gum-resin from the Kauri..was commonly chewed as a masticatory..mixed with the inspissated juice of the Puwha, or Sow-thistle. **1905** W. B. *Where White Man Treads* 177 All was ready for the contents of the haangi—pork, puha, and potatoes. **1947** *Coast to Coast 1946* 2 Flora Baker gathering puha outside the Bakers' pig-sty. **1963** *N.Z. Listener* 3 May 5/4 Around in the rank growth, the puha and rariki grew, despised by the Pakeha but loved by the true Maori. **1966** J. K. BAXTER *Pig Island Lett.* 6 Sea-eggs, puha, pork, and kumara. **1978** *Islands* (N.Z.) Aug. 12 Sometimes they bring food and cook it in my kitchen—mutton-bird with corn and *puha*—not my favourite dish, so greasy. **1978** P. GRACE *Mutuwhenua* ix. 53 He and his flat-mate had boiled mutton quite often but there wasn't any puha near their place so they had to use cabbage.

pui, var. POUI.

puind, obs. f. POIND.

puinde, obs. pret. of PING *v.*[1]

pui'nee, puiney, obs. ff. PUISNE.

puir, Sc. form of POOR, PURE.

puiranis, pureanis = poor ones, poor people.
1573 *Satir. Poems Reform.* xxxix. 371 Syne help the puiranis, as the cause recordis. **1581** *Ibid.* xliii. 50 Pureanis promouit that na man wald presume.

puirt-a-beul: see PORT-A-BEUL.

puirteith, -tith, Sc. var. POORTITH.

puisane, variant of PISANE *Obs.*

puisne ('pju:nɪ), *a.* and *sb.* Also 7 pui'nee, pu'nee, puiney, pusney, 7–8 puisny, 8 puisnee: see also PUNY. [a. OF. *puisne* (12–13th c. in Hatz.-Darm.), in mod.F. *puîné* (see PUNY), f. *puis*:—L. *postea*, or Romanic **postius, -um*, f. *post* after + *né*:—L. *nāt-us* born.]
A. *adj.* **1.** Born later; younger; junior (in appointment, etc.). Now only in legal use.
[**1315** *Rolls of Parlt.* I. 357/1 Monsr. Henri de Cobeham le puisne.] [**1579**: see PUNY *a.* 1.] **1613** CAWDREY *Table Alph.* (ed. 3), *Puiney*, younger borne. *a* **1618** SYLVESTER *Elegy on Marg. Wyts* 78 Under her Virgin-sway Her puisne Orphan-sisters to defray. **1705** in Hearne *Collect.* 30 Dec. (O.H.S.) I. 152 Being his Puisne Chancellor by 7 years. **1724** *Lond. Gaz.* No. 6307/3 The Poor Knights..began the Procession.., the Puisné going foremost.
b. Applied to an inferior or junior judge in the superior courts of common law: for the present official definition, see quot. 1877.
[*a* **1577, 1643**, etc.: see PUNY *a.* 1.] **1688** in Ellis *Orig. Lett.* Ser. II. IV. 136 Mr. Serjeant Stringer..is made puisné judge of the King's Bench. **1768** BLACKSTONE *Comm.* III. iv. 41 The judges of this court are at present four in number, one chief and three *puisnè* justices. **1852** MISS YONGE *Cameos* (1877) IV. v. 55 Sir John, though nearly ninety, still sat as senior puisne judge in the Court of King's Bench. **1877** *Act 40 & 41 Vict.* c. 9 §5 A puisne judge of the High Court of Justice means for the purposes of this Act a judge of the High Court other than the Lord Chancellor, the Lord Chief Justice of England, the Master of the Rolls, the Lord Chief Justice of the Common Pleas, and the Lord Chief Baron. **1882** SERJT. BALLANTINE *Exper.* xxx. 296 The puisne judges who have occupied the Bench during the last generation. **1907** *India List* 191 Puisne Judges of a High Court.
2. Later, more recent, of subsequent date. Now only in legal use.
[**1628**: see PUNY *a.* 2.] **1655** FULLER *Hist. Camb.* 63 No mention in this visitation of Gonvil Hall (the Pusnie House in Cambridge), as if so late and little, that the Commissioners did oversee it. *a* **1677** HALE *Prim. Orig. Man.* 124 There would upon such a Supposition follow an Eternity that had a beginning, an Eternity that was puisne to some other thing or some other Eternal. **1885** SIR R. BAGGALLAY in *Law Rep. 12 Q.B.* Div. 430 As regards the further advance they were incumbrancers puisne to the plaintiffs. **1889** SIR A. KEKEWICH in *Law Times* LXI. 71/2 Powers of sale are to be found in second and other puisne mortgagees.
†**3.** Small, insignificant, petty: now spelt PUNY.
1600 SHAKS. *A.Y.L.* III. iv. 46 As a puisny Tilter, yt spurs his horse but on one side. **1635** [GLAPTHORNE] *Lady Mother* III. ii. in Bullen *O. Pl.* II. 158 More cunning then to be ore reacht By puisne cosnage. **1756** C. LUCAS *Ess. Waters* III. 281 He..can not be dismayed at the puisnee threats..of the lesser factions. **1782** V. KNOX *Ess.* (1819) III. clii. 161 Frighten a puisne race of peers.
B. *sb.* †**1.** A junior; an inferior, an underling; a novice; = PUNY *sb. Obs.*
[**1548**, etc.: see PUNY *sb.*] **1598** E. GILPIN *Skial.* (1878) 40 Why thou young puisne art thou yet to learne, A harper from a shilling to discerne? **1601** B. JONSON *Poetaster* III. iv, To prey vpon pu'nees and honest citizens for socks, or buskins. **1616** —— *Epigr.* xcvi. *To J. Donne*, Let pui'nees', porters', players' praise delight. *c* **1640** [SHIRLEY] *Capt. Underwit* II. i. in Bullen *O. Pl.* II. 340 Preach to the puisnes of the Inne sobrietie. **1663** *Flagellum, or O. Cromwell* (1672) 29 Wherein Mr. Pym, Hambden, and other Puisnes with Cromwel, mainly busied themselves.
2. *spec.* A puisne judge: see A. 1 b.
[**1608**: see PUNY *sb.* 4 b.] **1810** BENTHAM *Packing* (1821) 169 In Pratt's time at least, viz. anno 1725, the Puisnes were not in the secret. **1907** *Cambr. Mod. Hist. Prospectus* 87 The Lord Chief Justices, the Chief Baron and five puisnes upheld the plea that no patent for sole printing restrained the rights of the University Press.
Hence **'puisneship**, the office and function of a puisne judge. Cf. PUNYSHIP.
1825 BENTHAM *Offic. Apt. Maximized, Observ. Peel's Sp.* (1830) 53 The thousands a year salaries of the minor and common law Chiefships, and Puisneships, and Masterships.

puissance ('pju:ɪsəns, pju:'ɪsəns, 'pwɪsəns). Now *arch.* exc. in sense 1 c. Forms: see below. [a. F. *puissance* (12th c. in Littré), f. *puissant*: see PUISSANT and -ANCE.
Not reckoning the final *e*, the Fr. is a disyllable (pwisɑ̃s); hence the historical pronunciation in Eng., exemplified from Lydgate to J. M. Neale, is (pwɪ'sɑ:ns), later ('pwɪsəns); but a trisyllabic (pu:ɪ'sɑ:ns), now ('pju:ɪsəns), appears in 16th c., esp. in Spenser, and is found in some later poets, and since 1790 has been favoured by the Dictionaries, although before Walker all orthoepists exc. Sheridan had approved of ('pwɪsəns) or (pju:'ɪsəns); the last is also used by some 19th c. poets. Shaks. and Tennyson have both ('pwɪsəns) and (pju:'ɪsəns); Milton always the former.]
A. Illustration of Forms.
5 **puiss-, pysauns, puysshaunce, peusawns**, 5–6 **puiss-, puyss-, puis-, puys-, pusaunce,** 6 **puissance, -auns, puissence, pusans,** *Sc.* **pusi-, puss-, pissance, piscence,** 6–7 **puisance,** 5– **puissance.**
1420 G. STOKES *Let. to Hen. V* in Ellis *Orig. Lett.* Ser. III. I. 70 The grete manhode myghtynesse and puissance. **1422** tr. *Secreta Secret., Priv. Priv.* 139 That his Pusaunce be not emblemyshit. **1447** BOKENHAM *Seyntys* (Roxb.) 60 Oure lorde god most of puysshaunce. **1449** J. METHAM *Amor & Cleopes* 302 Returnyd to Rome with hys oste & pysauns. **1503** DUNBAR *Thistle & Rose* 108 Beistis that bene of moir piscence. **1509** HAWES *Past. Pleas.* xxxiii. (Percy Soc.) 165 So great and huge of puysaunce. **1513** DOUGLAS *Æneis* VI. x. 79 The pissance quhilk in just battell, Slane in defence of thair kynd countre fell. **1519** *Interlude Four Elements* (Percy Soc.) 42 A lorde I am of gretter pusans. *a* **1548** HALL *Chron., Edw. IV* 192 b, Of puyssance sufficient to inuade, and likely to recouer the duchy of Guyen. **1563** WINȜET *Four Scoir Thre Quest.* §29 Wks. (S.T.S.) I. 94 Albeit he haif wit and pissance thairto. *a* **1600** MONTGOMERIE *Misc. Poems* xxv. 15 My pen thy princely pussance sall report. **1604** T. WRIGHT *Passions* v. §4. 215 Such is Loves puisance.
B. Signification.
1. a. Power, strength, force, might; influence.
1420, 1422 [see A]. *c* **1430** LYDG. *Min. Poems* (Percy Soc.) 25 Where been..Rome and Cartage, moost soverayn of puisaunce? *c* **1507** *Plumpton Corr.* (Camden) 202 She will helpe to promoote me to the uttermost of her puyssaunce. **1508** DUNBAR *Lament for Makaris* 33 He spairis no lord for his piscence, Na clerk for his intelligence. **1590** SPENSER *F.Q.* I. i. 3 To prove his puissance in battell brave. **1597** SHAKS. *2 Hen. IV*, II. iii. 52 O flye to Scotland, Till that the Nobles, and the armed Commons, Haue of their Puissance made a little taste. **1644** BULWER *Chiron.* 128 The puissance of the Right Hand proceeds from a veine *fine pari*. **1667** MILTON *P.L.* v. 864 Our puissance is our own, our own right hand Shall teach us highest deeds. *a* **1850** ROSSETTI *Dante & Circ.* I. (1874) 141 This stroke..From eyes of too much puïssance was shed. **1866** NEALE *Sequences & Hymns* 12 Ah! they little know the Puissance of the Cake of Barley Bread! **1868** LONGF. *Dante's Inf.* v. 36 There they blaspheme the puissance divine.
b. The persons in whom power is vested.
1871 R. ELLIS *Catullus* lxviii. 89 Now to revenge fair Helen, had Argos' chiefs, her puissance, Set them afield.
c. *Show-jumping*. A competition testing a horse's ability to jump large obstacles. Also *attrib.*
1951 M. P. ANSELL *Show Jumping* vi. 48 *Test* (*Puissance*). This competition is designed to test the horse's ability to jump large obstacles. **1952** R. S. SUMMERHAYS *Encycl. Horsemen* 218/2 *'Puissance' Jumping Competition*. In this all the straight fences in the course, with the exception of the first, are a minimum height of 4 ft. 7 in. (1 m. 40 cm.). The course usually consists of from six to eight fences, one of which is a double jump counting as one obstacle. **1954** P. SMYTHE *Jump for Joy* iv. 68, I lived for the week-ends, and many a lesson was passed in the haze of daydreams about jumping paddocks and over Puissance courses. **1959** *Times* 10 Aug. 5/6 It was the third triumph of the [Dublin Horse] show for Dundrum, who..shared first place in the *puissance* with Hollandia. **1974** *Country Life* 3 Jan. 9/2 Alcatraz, ridden by last year's puissance winner..attempted all three fences. **1975** *Oxf. Compan. Sports & Games* 281/1 The competition which tests jumping ability alone is known as a *Puissance*... There is no recourse to the clock, since the object is to test the horse over 'a limited number of large obstacles'.
†**2.** *concr.* **a.** An armed force. *Obs.*
1450 *Rolls of Parlt.* V. 177/1 If this puyssaunce come into this Reame. **1452** *Acts Privy Council* (1835) VI. 120 To have the leding..of oure saide puissance upon the see. *a* **1533** LD. BERNERS *Huon* lviii. 201 These two kynges fought one agaynst the other, pusaunce agaynst pusaunce. **1595** SHAKS. *John* III. i. 339 Cosen, goe draw our puissance together.
†**b.** A number, a crowd, a 'power' of people. *Obs.*
c **1450** *Cov. Myst.* xxvii. (Shaks. Soc.) 261 ȝe se weche peusawns of pepyl drawyth hym to, ffor the mervaylys that he hath wrowth. *c* **1502** in Grose *Antiq. Rep.* (1808) II. 286 *note*, In is solempnites was a great and a right pleasant puysauns of people.

†**'puissancy**. *Obs. rare.* [f. as prec. + -ANCY.] The quality of being powerful; power, potency.
1562 BULLEYN *Bulwark, Bk. Simples* 23 b, Some greater, and of more puissancie. **1607** TOPSELL *Four-f. Beasts* 312 Alexander..had neuer bin deliuered aliue, but for the puisancy of his horsse.

puissant ('pju:ɪsənt, pju:'ɪsənt, 'pwɪsənt), *a. arch.* Forms: 5–6 **puyss-, puissaunt(e,** 6 **puys-, pus-, -ant, -aunt, -a(u)nte,** *Sc.* **puss-, pissant,** 6–7 **puisant,** 6– **puissant.** [a. F. *puissant*, earlier *poissant*, also *possant*, *pussant*, *poussant* (Godef. *Compl.*):—Romanic type **possent-em*, pr. pple. of L. *posse* to be able, substituted for L. *potent-em*.

Some scholars explain the F. form in *puiss-* as influenced by the verbal forms *puis*, *puisse*: others suppose a Romanic **possient-em* for *possent-em*. The Fr. *puissant* is a disyllable (pwisɑ̃), as is also historically the Eng. (pwɪ'sɑːnt, 'pwɪsənt), from 15th c. to Matthew Arnold; so always in Sidney, Shaks., Drayton, and Milton, while Henry More, Shenstone, and others have (pjuː'ɪsənt), in 3 syllables; one or other of these was approved by all 18th c. orthoepists except Sheridan and Walker; these, following Spenser, give ('pjuːɪsənt), which is generally preferred by later dictionaries.]

Possessed of or wielding power; having great authority or influence; mighty, potent, powerful.

a **1450** *Knt. de la Tour* (1906) 12 A mighti and a puissant woman. *c* **1510** *Gesta Rom., Addit. Stories* i. 429 In Rome a puyssaunte Emperour. **1513** DOUGLAS *Æneis* v. Prol. 65 But quham na thing is worthy nor pissant. **1523** CROMWELL in Merriman *Life & Lett.* (1902) I. 37 Thys grete and puysant armaye. *a* **1533** LD. BERNERS *Huon* cxxxviii. 513 Yᵉ sowdan rode on a pusaunt horse, and Huon..folowed hym on the pusaunt mare. **1533** BELLENDEN *Livy* II. xvi. (S.T.S.) I. 156 Mare pussant þan afore. **1563** WINȜET *To Knox* Wks. (S.T.S.) I. 138 A pissant patroun of ȝour cause. **1568** GRAFTON *Chron.* II. 281 It was greate beautie to beholde theyr puyssant array. *a* **1586** SIDNEY *Arcadia* (1622) 85 Wise Counsellours, stout Captaines, puissant Kings. **1593** SHAKS. *3 Hen. VI*, II. i. 207 The Queene is comming with a puissant Hoast. **1598** DRAYTON *Heroic. Ep.* xvi. 28 Or who from France a puisant Armie brings? **1642** H. MORE *Song of Soul* II. iii. IV. xxxix, And with puissant stroke the head to bruize. **1663** BUTLER *Hud.* I. i. 351 His puissant Sword unto his side Near his undaunted heart was ty'd. **1750** SHENSTONE *Ode to Indolence* viii, And thou, puissant queen! be kind. **1867** M. ARNOLD *Bacchanalia* 63 The puissant crowned, the weak laid low.

Hence **'puissantness**, puissance, power. *rare*—¹.

1552 J. ASTLEY in *Ascham's Eng. Wks.* (1904) 123 Not by the puisantnes of others who were knowne to be his open enemyes.

puissantly (see prec.), *adv. arch.* [f. prec. + -LY².] In a puissant manner; with power, strength, or influence.

1475 *Bk. Noblesse* (Roxb.) 45 Whan youre nobille castelle and towne of Calix was beseigid..he puissauntly rescued it. **1523** LD. BERNERS *Froiss.* I. cccxxii. 500 To resyst pusantly agaynst his enemyes. **1592** WYRLEY *Armorie* 150 Puissantly the Frenchmen doth he daunt. **1658** J. WEBB *Cleopatra* VIII. II. 11 Who most puissantly served the Queen's resentment.

puit, -e, obs. forms of PEWIT, PUT.

puitternell, obs. Sc. variant of PETRONEL.

puja, pujah, variants of POOJAH.

‖**pujari** (puː'dʒɑːriː). Also poojari, pujaree. [Hindi, f. Skr. *pūjā* worship; cf. POOJAH, PUJA.] A Hindu priest.

1813 F. HAMILTON *Jrnl. Shahabad Survey* (1926) 129 The Pujaris who are making a good thing of the ghost have lately been disturbed by a..young Brahman. **1855** H. H. WILSON *Gloss. Judicial & Revenue Terms India* 396/1 At Benares, the *Pandá* officiates only on particular occasions, the duties of daily worship being performed by inferior priests or *Pujáris* in his employ. **1883** MONIER WILLIAMS *Relig. Thought & Life in India* ix. 249 Then the Pūjāri, or priest, takes the Bhūta sword and bell in his hands. **1907** B. M. CROKER *Company's Servant* xi. 108 Many baskets of rice were contributed..to the sacrificial pile. On this pile, a drove of buffaloes was killed by the Poojaris. **1967** SINGHA & MASSEY *Indian Dances* i. 33 Offerings of flowers and sweetmeats are placed at the base by the *pujarees* (worshippers). **1969** *Sunday Standard* (Bombay) 3 Aug. (Mag. Section) p. iv/3 Next week, Indran left the village, leaving the temple in charge of another poojari. **1969** *Enact* (Delhi) Nov. 10/3, I will not have any brahmins or *pujaris* up here, never,..any more than I will go to church for confession or have a mass said to save my soul. **1973** *Country Life* 11 Jan. 80/1 We..presented our credentials to the *pujari* (priest).

puka ('pʊkə). [Maori.] An evergreen New Zealand shrub or small tree, *Griselinia littoralis*, or *G. lucida*, a related, sometimes epiphytic, species, belonging to the family Cornaceæ and bearing leathery ovate leaves and panicles of tiny, greenish flowers followed by purple or black berries.

[**1853** J. D. HOOKER *Bot. Antarctic Voy.: Flora Novæ-Zelandiæ* I. 98 *Griselinia lucida*... Nat[ive] name, 'Poukater'.] **1889** T. KIRK *Forest Flora N.Z.* 67 Mr. Colenso informs me that the Native name 'puka' is correctly applied to this species [sc. *Griselinia lucida*] as well as to *Meryta Sinclairii*. **1970** M. E. FISHER et al. *Gardening with N.Z. Plants* I. 59 The puka is usually found perched high in the forks of some forest tree such as the rata.

2. A small evergreen tree, *Meryta sinclairii*, belonging to the family Araliaceæ, native to Australasia and the Pacific Islands, and bearing large glossy leaves and terminal panicles of greenish-white flowers followed by black berries. Also *attrib.*

1889 T. KIRK *Forest Flora N.Z.* 245 The Puka... This noble species is..restricted to a few individuals growing on one or two small islands near the northern extremity of the colony. **1951** *Post-Primary School Bull.* (Wellington, N.Z.) V. XII. 276 The puka (*Meryta sinclairii*)..has the largest leaves of any New Zealand tree. **1970** M. E. FISHER et al. *Gardening with N.Z. Plants* I. 78 The puka is a much branched, small tree from 12 to 20 feet in height... The leaves of this handsome tree are a beautiful glossy green, nine to 20 inches long and half as broad, usually with the broadest part near the apex. They are leathery and strongly veined and the margin is wavy.

pukaki, puka pu, varr. PUKEKO, PAKAPOO.

pukatea (pʊka'tea). *N.Z.* [Maori.] A tall forest tree, *Laurelia novæ-zelandiæ*, of the family Monimiaceæ, native to New Zealand, and distinguished by buttresses at the base of the trunk, pale bark, leathery, obovate leaves, and small clusters of tiny, yellowish flowers; also, the timber obtained from this tree.

1843 E. DIEFFENBACH *Trav. N.Z.* I. I. iii. 75 Another tree common in this part of the valley is the pukatea. **1868** W. COLENSO in *Trans. N.Z. Inst.* I. III. 51 From the aromatic leaves and bark of the Pukatea..a valuable essential oil might be extracted. **1882** W. D. HAY *Brighter Britain!* II. vi. 191 The Pukatea..is a tree of the second largest class. **1949** P. BUCK *Coming of Maori* III. vi. 426 Tree burial was resorted to in the thickly forested Urewera country. Natural hollow trees such as the *pukatea* were utilized when available. **1950** *N.Z. Jrnl. Agric.* June 602/3 The rata, pukatea, and titoki from which they [*sc.* the chairs] are made. **1966** *Encycl. N.Z.* II. 887/2 Pukatea grows to heights of over 120 ft.

†**puke**, *sb.*¹ *Obs.* Also 5–6 **pewke**, (5 **pewyke**), 6 **puck(e, pook(e, peuk.** [Late ME. *pewke*, *puke*, a. MDu. *puuc*, *puyck*, name of the best sort of woollen cloth (1420 in Verdam); in mod.Du. *puik* the best, the most excellent, the choice of anything, also as adj. 'excellent'; so LGer. *pük* (as in *püke ware* ware of superior quality, as cloth or linen), WFris. *puwck*, NFris. *pük*: ulterior origin unknown. Its use to designate a colour is found only in Eng. Not connected with F. *puce*.]

1. A superior kind of woollen cloth, of which gowns were made. Also *attrib.*

1466 *Mann. & Househ. Exp.* (Roxb.) 354 He axsethe for makenge of a longe gowne of pewke, ij.s. **1480** *Wardr. Acc. Edw. IV* (1830) 120, vj pair of hosen of puke. **1545** *Lanc. Wills* (Chetham Soc.) II. 63 A new gowne of ffrenche puke lyned withe saten. **1555** *Richmond Wills* (Surtees) 86 Item vj yards of black puck, xviijˢ. **1562** *Ibid.* 166 One gowne of fyne puke garded with veluett and furred with budge, xxvjˢ. viijᵈ. **1566** *Wills & Inv. N.C.* (Surtees) I. 257 In the Shopp. A sadd coller brod clothe iiij yerds xijˢ...a pooke viij yerds xliiijˢ. **1596** SHAKS. *1 Hen. IV*, II. iv. 78 Wilt thou rob this Leatherne Ierkin, Christall button..Puke stocking, Caddice garter? **1612** SHELTON *Quix.* I. i. (1620) 2 The rest and remnant thereof was spent on a Ierkin of fine Puke [orig. *sayo de velarte*].

2. A colour formerly used for woollen goods: as it was produced by galls and copperas, it must have been a bluish black or inky colour, but it is variously described: see quots. Also *attrib.*

Prob. originally the usual colour of the cloth (sense 1).

1530 PALSGR. 253/2 Pewke, a colour, *pers.* **1538** ELYOT, *Pullus*,..russette, sometyme blacke, but rather puke color, betwene russet & black. *c* **1550** *Disc. Common Weal Eng.* (1893) 82 Sume strange coullor or die as french puke. **1577** HARRISON *England* II. vii. (1877) I. 172 His coat, gowne, and cloake of browne, blue, or puke. **1598** FLORIO, *Pauonaccio cupo*, a deepe darke purple or puke colour. **1607** TOPSELL *Four-f. Beasts* 92 The colour of this Camell is for the most part browne or puke. **1615** MARKHAM *Eng. Housew.* II. v. (1660) 124 To dye wool of a puke colour, take Galls..and boyle your wool or your Cloth therein..halfe an hour: then take them up, and put in your Coperas into the same Liquor, then put in your wool again. **1725** *Bradley's Fam. Dict.* s.v. *Mixing colour*, If..you would needs have your Cloth of three Colours, as of two dark and one light, or contrary; supposing Crimson, Yellow or Puke.

puke (pjuːk), *sb.*² [f. PUKE *v.* (But the connexion of sense 3 is doubtful.)]

1. a. An act of vomiting, a vomit.

1737 BRACKEN *Farriery Impr.* (1756) I. 80 This [Pill] generally begins its Operation with a Puke of yellow slimy Matter. **1748** RICHARDSON *Clarissa* (1811) VII. lxi. 242 It gave him first a puke, then a fever. **1808** *Med. Jrnl.* XIX. 26 She..had two pukes, which might have been occasioned by increasing the squills to four grains.

b. Matter thrown up from the stomach; vomit. *coarse.*

1961 in WEBSTER. **1972** D. LEES *Zodiac* 109, I..choked back the puke that had rushed to my throat. **1975** *New Society* 4 Dec. 526/2 At the Black Raven, by Liverpool Street station,..there is a slight odour of puke and disinfectant.

2. An emetic, a vomit.

1743 *London & Country Brew.* III. (ed. 2) 226 Which Compound, one would think, more fit for a Puke, than a grateful, cordial, stomachic Bitter. **1775** ABIGAIL ADAMS in *Fam. Lett.* (1876) 95 Yesterday Patty was seized, and took a puke. *a* **1849** H. COLERIDGE *Poems* (1850) II. 332 He never once alludes to purge or puke.

3. *U.S.* **a.** *slang.* A disgusting person. **b.** *vulgar.* A nickname for a native of Missouri.

1835 A. A. PARKER *Trip to West & Texas* 87 The inhabitants..of Michigan are called *wolverines*,..of Missouri, *pukes.* **1838** HALIBURTON *Clockmaker* Ser. II. xix. 289 The suckers of Illinoy, the pukes of Missuri..and the corncrackers of Virginia. **1843** 'R. CARLTON' *New Purchase* II. 47 This Protestant assembly was a gathering of delegates principally from the land of Hoosiers..[with] a small chance of Pukes from beyond the father of floods. **1847** ROBB *Squatter Life* 152 Captain and all hands are a set of cowardly pukes. **1847** T. FORD *Hist. Illinois* (1854) ii. 68 The Illinoians..called the Missourians 'Pukes'... The lower lead mines in Missouri had sent up to the Galena country whole hoards of uncouth ruffians, from which it was inferred that Missouri had taken a 'Puke'. **1908** L. HOUCK *Hist. Missouri* III. xxiv. 36 'Hidalgos' the first residents of upper Louisiana and Missouri were called, until in the mouths of the vulgar the name of 'Pukes' was made current. **1944** [see MISSOURIAN *sb.* and *a.*].

4. *Comb.* **puke-weed** (*U.S.*), *Lobelia inflata*, employed as an emetic.

1853 in DUNGLISON *Med. Lex.*

puke (pjuːk), *v.* [Known first as used by Shaks. 1600; but the derivative *pukishness*, which implies an adj. **pukish*, and this a sb. or (?) vb. *puke*, is found of date 1581. Origin unknown.

It has been suggested that it might represent an earlier **spuke* (unrecorded), from the Indo-Eur. root *spu-*, *speu-* (whence OE. and OHG. *spîwan*, to spew, spit, L. *spuĕre*, etc.), which is app. also the origin of a mod.Flem. *spukken*, LG. *spucken* (whence mod.Ger. *spucken*) to spew, spit; but the late appearance of the English word and the absence of historical links make this a bare conjecture.]

1. *intr.* To eject food from the stomach; to vomit.

1600 SHAKS. *A.Y.L.* II. vii. 144 At first the Infant, Mewling, and puking in the Nurses armes. **1623** WEBSTER *Duchess of Malfi* II. i, Our duchess Is sick a-days, she pukes, her stomach seethes. **1691** SHADWELL *Scourers* I. Wks. 1720 IV. 311 You puk'd at the sight of her. **1735** POPE *Donne Sat.* IV. 153 As one of Woodward's patients, sick, and sore, I puke, I nauseate,—yet he thrusts in more. **1812** W. TENNANT *Anster F.* II. li, Their bench'd and gaudy boats, Wherein some joking and some puking sit. **1822–34** *Good's Study Med.* (ed. 4) I. 486 A most debilitating sickness supervened, with excessive efforts to puke.

2. *trans.* To eject by vomiting; to vomit.

1601 HOLLAND *Pliny* II. 102 It helpeth them that puke vp choler. **1655** CULPEPPER *Riverius* IX. vii. 265 Pewking forth a thin waterish Humor by Salivation. **1689** G. HARVEY *Curing Dis. by Expect.* iv. 19 They run no small risque of puiking their gross slimy Humours into their Lungs. **1799** M. UNDERWOOD *Treat. Dis. Children* (ed. 4) II. 243 After the child had puked-up a great quantity of meconium. **1841** CATLIN *N. Amer. Ind.* II. liv. 182 She is bleeding from her mouth, she is puking up all her blood.

3. To cause to vomit, to treat with an emetic.

1739 HUXHAM in *Phil. Trans.* XLI. 669, I then ordered him..Eight or Ten Grains of Turbith mineral, which scarce puked him. **1823** in *Spirit Pub. Jrnls.* 536 Inoculating for the chicken pox..and puking infant radicals.

puke, obs. and dial. form of PUCK.

pukeko ('puːkeko). *N.Z.* Also **pukaki.** [Maori.] The purple gallinule or swamp hen, *Porphyrio porphyrio* (formerly *P. melanotus*), belonging to the family Rallidæ and widely distributed in southern Europe, Africa, southern Asia, and Australasia.

1835 W. YATE *Acct. N.Z.* (ed. 2) ii. 62 *Pukeko*—A species of water-hen, the size of a well-grown capon. It..has very long red legs. **1845** E. J. WAKEFIELD *Adv. N.Z.* I. viii. 228 The *pukeko* is of a dark blue colour, and about as large as a pheasant. **1853** W. R. BRIDGES *Let.* 14 Nov. in *Richmond-Atkinson Papers* (1960) I. iii. 136, I amused myself with shooting wild duck and pukeko which are very abundant. **1874** A. BATHGATE *Colonial Experiences* vii. 85 In the swamps there is also the pukaki..or swamp-turkey, a bird which rises well and affords good sport. **1884** LADY MARTIN *Our Maoris* viii. 114 The place was populous with large black birds, called by the Maoris pu-ke-ko. They have a harsh cry like a corn-crake. **1921** H. GUTHRIE-SMITH *Tutira* xxii. 209 The Pukeko or Swamp-hen (*Porphyrio melanotus*) has..proved able to thrive better on dry ground than wet. **1930** L. G. D. ACLAND *Early Canterbury Runs* 1st Ser. vii 175 There were thousands and thousands of pukaki in the swamp. **1946** *Coast to Coast 1945* 110 Poachin' flappers in the swamp... Stringy pukekoes, too, when they're winged. **1957** J. FRAME *Owls do Cry* xviii. 74 Pukekos took long strides through the swamp. **1966** *Encycl. N.Z.* II. 888/1 Pukekos are not shot in any great numbers during their open season.

puker ('pjuːkə(r)). [f. PUKE *v.* + -ER¹.]

1. One who pukes or vomits.

1846 in WORCESTER.

†**2.** A medicine causing puking; an emetic. *Obs.*

1714 GARTH *Dispens.* III. 28 The Griper Senna, and the Puker Rue, The Sweetner Sassafras are added too.

pukeru, var. PUCKEROO *a.* and *v.*

Pukhto: see PASHTO, -TU *sb.* and *a.*

puking ('pjuːkɪŋ), *vbl. sb.* [f. PUKE *v.* + -ING¹.] The action of the vb. PUKE; vomiting. Also *attrib.* **puking fever** = *milk-sickness* (*Cent. Dict.* 1890).

1628 FORD *Lover's Mel.* II. ii, I feel a horrible puking myself. **1757** SMOLLETT *Reprisal* I. i, To be racked with perpetual puking. **1799** M. UNDERWOOD *Treat. Dis. Children* (ed. 4) I. 105 This spontaneous puking is not attended with any violence to the stomach.

puking ('pjuːkɪŋ), *ppl. a.* [f. as prec. + -ING².] That pukes; also *fig.*

1691 *Weesils* i. 4 If puking Conscience thus can make you squeak. **1730–46** THOMSON *Autumn* 534 No evasion sly, Nor sober shift is to the puking wretch Indulged apart. **1799** M. UNDERWOOD *Treat. Dis. Children* (ed. 4) I. 105 It is a saying with some experienced nurses, that a puking child is a thriving child. **1976** 'D. HALLIDAY' *Dolly & Nanny Bird* xv. 200 Order one of your puking friends to go below.

† **'pukish**, *a.*[1] *Obs. rare*⁻¹. [f. PUKE *sb.*[1] + -ISH[1].] Somewhat puke-coloured.

1566 DRANT *Horace, Sat.* viii. D viij b, Bare foote, hyr lockes about hyr heade, ytuckde in pukishe frocke [L. *nigra succinctam vadere palla*].

† **'pukish**, *a.*[2] *Obs. rare*⁻⁰. [See PUKE *v.*] Addicted to puking. Hence † **'pukishness**.

1581 MULCASTER *Positions* x. (1887) 56 Such, as be troubled with weaknesse, or pewkishnesse of stomacke.

‖**pukka** ('pʌkə), *a.* (*sb.*) *Anglo-Ind.* Also 7–9 pucka, 8- **pukka**, **pucker**, 9 **pakka**, **pucca**, **puckah**, **pukkha**. [a. Hindī *pakkā* (pʌkka:) cooked, ripe, mature; hence thorough, substantial, permanent: cf. CUTCHA. Sense c is the only sense used outside Anglo-Indian contexts.]

A. *adj.* **a.** Applied to the larger of two weights of the same name: Of full weight, full, good; also, genuine, thorough. †**b.** Strong, severe; malignant, as a fever. *Obs.* **c.** Sure, certain, reliable; thorough, out-and-out. Also in general use outside India in various extended senses. Of things: real, not sham; of information: factually correct; of persons: authentic, not pretended; proper or correct in behaviour, socially acceptable. Freq. in ***pukka sahib*** (cf. SAHIB 1 b), used with allusion to life in the former British Indian Empire. **d.** Permanent, esp. as an appointment. **e.** Permanent, as a building; solidly-built, of stone or brick and mortar.

a. 1698 FRYER *Acc. E. India & P.* 205 The Maund Pucka at Agra is double as much [as the Surat Maund]. **1803** WELLINGTON in Gurw. *Desp.* (1837) II. 43 It should be in sufficient quantities to give 72 pucca seers for each load. **1857** LD. LAWRENCE in Bosw. Smith *Life* (1883) II. i. 11 Your Lahore men have done nobly... Donald, Roberts, Mac, and Dick are all of them, *pucca* trumps. **1893** G. ALLEN *Scallywag* I. 44 That's a good word... Is it pucker English, I wonder.

b. 1765 MARTIN in *Phil. Trans.* LVII. 219 Malignant fevers,..here termed *pucker fevers*, meaning (in the natives language) strong fevers. **1774** BARKER *ibid.* LXV. 206 Pucker fevers. **1788** STOCKDALE *Indian Vocab.* (Y.), *Pucka*, a putrid fever.

c. 1776 *Trial of Nundocomar* 102/1 Maha Rajah said it was necessary to witness it to make it pukka. **1858** COL. KEITH YOUNG in *Diary & Corr.* (1902) App. D. 329 On receiving pucka information..that the Insurgents were at Singpore. **1894** *Scribner's Mag.* XV. 548/2 The Zinal-Rothhorn or 'Moming' is, to use an Anglo-Indian phrase, a 'puckah' mountain, which means that it is the real thing and not a sham. **1917** W. OWEN *Let.* 17 July (1967) 477 It was better paid than by a pukka Editor's best guineas. **1919** J. BUCHAN *Mr. Standfast* I. v. 113 My boy's at home, convalescing, and if he says you're *pukka*, I'll ask your pardon. **1924** E. M. FORSTER *Passage to India* I. iii. 26 Mrs. Turton..remarked that Mr. Fielding wasn't pukka, and had better marry Miss Quested, for she wasn't pukka. **1929** S. AUMONIER in *Mercury Story Bk.* 389 McLagan and Treadway were pukka soldiers of the old army. **1932** *Daily Express* 27 June 3/3 She wants also to play pukka golf. **1934** 'G. ORWELL' *Burmese Days* v. 88 The smell of pukka sahibdom. **1938** N. MARSH *Artists in Crime* xix. 280 Don't be so 'pukka sahib'. **1939** [see POONA]. **1942** T. RATTIGAN *Flare Path* I. 14 Pukka gen, sir. **1948** *Observer* 25 Apr. 2/1 Produced for the Government of Southern Rhodesia, that forty minute film..is one of many from British studios that are being specially commissioned to give straightforward information on important subjects—in fact 'pukka gen'. **1955** *Sci. Amer.* Feb. 116/3 The injunctions and other brawling seem now to have subsided, with general agreement that while Buh may not be a pukka sahib, he is a peerless climber. **1966** 'G. BLACK' *You want to die, Johnny?* v. 85, I just played pukka sahib greeting faithful old native servant. **1967** SINGHA & MASSEY *Indian Dances* xviii. 157 These barracks once the epitome of pukka British army tradition, for many years echoed all day to the sounds and rhythms of Indian music. **1971** *Daily Tel.* 19 Oct. 19 At one time hotels were classed with brothels in the minds of pukka brewers. **1973** C. MULLARD *Black Britain* III. vii. 75 A list of the reconstituted Board in 1968 showed all the new members, with the exception of two, to be pukka members of the white Establishment. **1973** *Times Lit. Suppl.* 30 Mar. 340/2 A small but pukkah group defending the last tatty remnants of colonial gentility. **1976** *Physics Bull.* Nov. 480/1 What it does show is a pucka trade union doing a proper trade union job. **1977** *Radio Times* 12–18 Nov. 15/1 The two genuinely brown faces in *It Ain't Half Hot Mum* belong to a Pakistani and a Bangla Deshi. He is the only pukka Indian in sight.

d. 1800 *Misc. Tracts* in *Asiatic Ann. Reg.* 160/1 Near it the Nurbudda springs from a small pucka-coond or well that furnishes a perennial stream. **1866** TREVELYAN in *Fraser's Mag.* LXXIII. 215 The Dawk Bungalow; or, Is his Appointment Pucka?

e. 1784 *Calcutta Gaz.* 22 Apr. (Y.), The House, cook-room, bottle-connah, godown, etc., are all pucka-built. **1811** MRS. SHERWOOD *Henry & Bearer* 2 A lady, who lived..in a large puckah house near the river. **1862** TORRENS *Trav. Tartary* 321 *Pucka* is an adjective, and when applied to a road, means it is a metalled one; when to a wall, that it is solid masonry. **1897** *Daily News* 17 June 5/7 At Dhubri all pakka buildings have been demolished.

B. *sb.* **a.** A weight or system of weights which is larger than 'cutcha'. **b.** A copper coin not now used; also ***pucka piece***. **c.** A building material of permanent nature, such as brick.

1727 A. HAMILTON *New Acc. E. Ind.* xxxiii. II. 9 Fort William was built..of Brick and Morter called Puckah, a Composition of Brick-dust, Lime, Malasses, and cut Hemp. *c* **1813** MRS. SHERWOOD *Ayah & Lady* i. 12 I'll make her a present of two puckah, to purchase cotton for a beginning.

pukree, obs. f. PUGGREE.

puku[1] ('pu:ku:). Also pookoo. [ad. Zulu *mpuku*.] A red water-buck or antelope (*Cobus vardoni*) found in southern Central Africa.

1881 [see LECHWE]. **1890** in *Cent. Dict.* **1893** SELOUS *Trav. S.E. Africa* 245, I saw three roan antelopes and a few pookoos (*Cobus vardoni*). **1894** LYDEKKER *Royal Nat. Hist.* II. 304 The puku is about the size of the pala, standing some 3 feet 3 inches at the shoulder. **1900** W. L. SCLATER *Mammals S. Afr.* I. 193 The flesh of the puku is stated by Selous to be even more nauseous and unpalatable than that of the common water-buck. **1946, 1972** [see LECHWE]. **1973** D. STEELE *Game Sanctuaries S. Afr.* 148 The puku is a medium-sized antelope, weighing up to 90 kilograms.

‖**puku**[2] ('pʊkʊ). *N.Z. colloq.* [Maori.] The stomach.

[**1905** W. B. *Where White Man Treads* 96 The Maori is pre-eminently gifted in the selection of suitable nomenclature... He meets a man... He looks him over... If he be massive in girth, what so delicate as reference thereto as 'Puku' (stomach)? **1918** C. H. WESTON *Three Years with New Zealanders* vi. 70 The Medical Officer.. injected the [anti-typhoid] serum in what the Maories call my *puku*.] **1941** BAKER *N.Z. Slang.* v. 42 By the 1890's..a stomach-ache became, with excellent alliterative effect, a *pain in the puku*. **1954** *Numbers* July 5 Let's stick to matters of the *puku*. **1958** M. K. JOSEPH *I'll soldier no More* ii. 50 Eat, Harry boy, eat; get some of this in your puku. **1966** G. W. TURNER *Eng. Lang. Austral. & N.Z.* viii. 170 The [Maori] words *potae* 'hat' and *puku* 'stomach' are still current, but North Island words mainly. **1971** *N.Z. Listener* 19 Apr. 57/1 He was too stonkered and crook in the puku to bother about it at the time. **1978** P. GRACE *Mutuwhenua* xx. 140 Your puku's getting in the way.

'puky, *a.* Also pukey. [f. PUKE *v.* + -Y.]

1. Inclined to puke or vomit; sickly. *rare.*

1864 G. MEREDITH *Sandra Belloni* xxxiii, He was rendered peaky and puky only by people supposing him so.

2. *fig.* Sick-making, disgusting. *colloq.*

1965 T. CAPOTE *In Cold Blood* (1966) i. 37 It was a puky idea. What the hell would they have thought? **1969** W. GARNER *Us or Them War* vi. 53 There'll be all sorts there, most of them pretty pukey and not really my thing.

pul (pu:l). Pl. puls, pooli, puli. [Pashto, a. Pers. *pūl*, f. Turk. *pul*; cf. Gr. φόλλις a small coin.] In Afghanistan, a monetary unit equivalent to one hundredth of an afghani; a coin of this value.

1927, 1934 [see AFGHANI]. **1941** *Whitaker's Almanack* 852/1 *Afghani* (of 100 *Puls*).

Pul, var. PEULH *sb.* and *a.*

pula ('pʊlə). Also † poola. [Tswana.] ‖ **1.** Rain. Freq. used as *int.*: in southern Africa, a traditional salute or expression of good luck.

1827 G. THOMPSON *Trav. & Adv. S. Afr.* I. 180 Mattebe ..waved the point [of his assagai] towards the heavens, when all called out 'Poola!' i.e. rain or a blessing. **1842** R. MOFFAT *Missionary Labours & Scenes S. Afr.* xxi. 350 The audience shouted, 'Pùla', (rain,) on which he sat down amidst a din of applause. **1934** in C. P. Swart *Africanderisms* (M.A. thesis, Univ. S Afr.) s.v., When Prince George.. uttered the traditional Basuto salute 'Pula' which means rain, a wave of enthusiasm swept the natives in the council chamber. **1974** *S. Afr. Panorama* Mar. 38/2 'Pula!' shouted the excited crowd of Bantu children.

2. The principal monetary unit of Botswana, consisting of one hundred thebe; a note of this value.

1976 *Eastern Province Herald* (S. Afr.) 23 Aug. 1 Botswana's new currency, the pula, will be introduced today. **1976** *Whitaker's Almanack 1977* 980 Botswana... Monetary unit... Pula.

Pulah, var. PEULH *sb.* and *a.*

pulamiting ('pju:lə,maɪtɪŋ), *ppl. a. dial.* [Prob. f. unrecorded *pulamite* vb. + -ING[2]; cf. PULE *v.* + MITE[2] 5.] Of a child or weak person: whining, whimpering. Also **'pula,miter** [-ER[1]], one who whines; a sniveller.

1913 D. H. LAWRENCE *Sons & Lovers* II. viii. 198 'Me!' exclaimed Morel—'me a good figure! I wor niver much more n'r a skeleton.' 'Man!' cried his wife, 'don't be such a pulamiter!' *a* **1930** —— in *Virginia Q. Rev.* (1941) XVII. Suppl. 43/1 You are a base, malingering pulamiting wretch.

pulane, Sc. var. POLAYN, *Obs.*, knee-armour.

pulao, var. PILAU.

pulas: see PALAS, E. Indian tree.

pulaski (pʊ'læskɪ). *U.S.* Also **Pulaski**. [The name of E. C. *Pulaski* (1866–1931), Amer. forest ranger, by whom the tool was designed.] A hatchet, of which the head forms an axe blade on one side and an adze on the other. Also *attrib.*

1924 *Frontier* Nov. 20, I saw Paul, his back bowed, his Pulaski swingin' like a flail. **1940** [see HOT SPOT 5 b]. **1946** *Trial & Timberline* June 91/1 Planting hoes, grub hoes, and Pulaski hoes had been provided by the rangers. **1948** *Highway Traveler* Aug. 37/1 Besides technical information on fighting fire with chemicals, or with axe and pulaski, smoke-jumpers are taught to bail out from a specially-constructed tower.

pulaskite (pʊ'læskaɪt). *Petrogr.* [See quot. 1891 and -ITE[1].] An alkali syenite containing a small proportion of nepheline.

1891 J. F. WILLIAMS in *Ann. Rep. Arkansas Geol. Survey 1890* II. iv. 56 Such a rock has not as yet been described and the writer suggests the name *pulaskite*—that of Pulaski county in which the city of Little Rock and Fourche Mountain are located—as a designation for this type of rock. **1962** W. T. HUANG *Petrology* iv. 129 In alkalic syenites the quartz-bearing type is nordmarkite..or simply quartz syenite... With a slight deficiency of silica, a little nepheline and sodalite may be present, leading to the formation of pulaskite... Other colored minerals found in pulaskite include aegirite-augite, barkevikite, or arfvedsonite.

pulaxe, pulce, obs. ff. POLE-AXE, PULSE.

† **pulch.** *Obs.* A kind of small fish: see quot.

1655 MOUFET & BENNET *Health's Impr.* xix. 180 Gulls, Guffs, Pulches, Chevins, and Millers thombs are a kind of jolt-headed Gudgins.

pulche, obs. f. POLISH *v.*; see also PULQUE.

pulchrify ('pʌlkrɪfaɪ), *v. nonce-wd.* [f. L. *pulcher*, *pulcer*, acc. *pulchr-um*, *pulcr-um* beautiful + -FY.] *trans.* To beautify, adorn, embellish.

1795 SOUTHEY *Lett. fr. Spain* i. (1797) 3 It was necessary that Senor Don Raimundo Aruspini should pulchrify his person. *Ibid.* viii. 96 [A hat] sent to be pulchrified by a hatter at Coruña.

pulchritude ('pʌlkrɪtju:d). Also 5–7 pulcri-, 6 pulc(h)ry-. [ad. L. *pulchri-*, *pulcritūdo*, f. *pulcher*, *pulcer* beautiful: see -TUDE.] Beauty.

Rare in British use since 17th c.; more used in U.S.

c **1400** *Beryn* 1109 Of som fair lusty lady, þat of pulcritude Were excellent al othir. **1432–50** tr. *Higden* (Rolls) II. 213 Equalite of complexion.., rectitude of stature, and pulcritude of figure. *a* **1548** HALL *Chron., Hen. VIII* 90 b, Your noble persone, so formed and figured in shape and stature with force and pulchritude. **1691** RAY *Creation* I. (1692) 94 There is great pulchritude and comliness of Proportion in the Leaves. **1737** WHISTON *Josephus, Agst. Apion* II. (1755) IV. 388 He represented God as..superior to all mortal conceptions in pulchritude. **1804** SOUTHEY *Lett.* (1856) I. 275 Both mother and grandmother cried out against me, notwithstanding my present pulchritude. **1897** *Outing* (U.S.) XXX. 468/2 Possessing little or no pulchritude.

b. With *a* and *pl.* A beauty.

1625 SHIRLEY *Love-Tricks* III. ii, To make ditties and ferses upon her mistress' beauties and pulchritudes. **1695** J. EDWARDS *Perfect. Script.* 583 It was thought to be a pulchritude in their stile.

So † **'pulchritudeness** (*erron.*) in same sense.

1547 BOORDE *Introd. Knowl.* i. (1870) 119 Suche a brydge of pulcritudnes, that in all the worlde there is none lyke. **1547** —— *Brev. Health* ccxcvii. 97 b, Beauty, fayrenes, or pulcritudines, the whiche is a deceyvable grace.

pulchritudinous (pʌlkrɪ'tju:dɪnəs), *a.* orig. *U.S.* [f. L. *pulc(h)ritūdin-*, *pulc(h)ritūdo* beauty + -OUS.] Beautiful, graceful, or fine in any way; morally excellent.

1912 L. J. VANCE *Destroying Angel* xv. 217, I love my love with a P because he's Perfectly Pulchritudinous and Possesses the Power of Pleasing. **1914** 'HIGH JINKS, JR.' *Choice Slang* 17 *Pulchritudinous pippen*, a pretty damsel. 'A peach.' **1925** *Times* 13 Dec. 11/6 In an American paper, in which the Yarmouth councillors were described as 'pulchritudinous',..the word actually meant moral excellence. **1949** *Chicago Tribune* 21 Feb. I. 28/5 By us the hippopotamus..Is never counted pulchritudinous. **1963** *Punch* 13 Feb. 246/1 Such nice, pulchritudinous girls! **1975** *Bookseller* 20–27 Dec. 2720/1 An ageing tycoon and a pulchritudinous blonde half his years but nearly equal to him in experience.

† **'pulchrous**, *a. Obs. rare.* In 5 pulcrious, 6 pulcruse. [f. L. *pulcher*, *pulchr-* beautiful + -OUS.] Beauteous, fair.

c **1475** *Partenay* 1263 The seffe child Ffromont..Inly wel formed, pulcrious of face. *c* **1540** BOORDE *The boke for to Lerne* A iij b, It..reioyseth a mannes harte to se..the pulcruse prospecte.

pulcrow: see *pull-crow* in PULL- 2.

† **pulder**, obs. Sc. f. PEWTER: cf. PUDER.

1573 *Reg. Privy Council Scot.* II. 269 Thre dosane of Flander pulder plaittis.

pulder, -ir, -re, obs. forms of POWDER.

puldron, obs. form of POULDRON.

pule (pju:l), *v.* Also 6 pewle, puil, peule. [In 16th c. also *pewle*, *peule*, perh. ad. F. *piaule-r* (16th c. *pioler* in Littré), dial. *piouler*, *piuler*, to cheep, chirp, whine = It. *pigolare*, Neap. *piolare* to cheep as a chicken; of echoic origin. But the Eng. may be merely parallel to the French.]

1. *intr.* To cry in a thin or weak voice, as a child; to whine, to cry in a querulous tone.

1534 MORE *Comf. agst. Trib.* II. xiv. Wks. 1182/2 Yet canne thys peuyshe gyrle neuer ceace whining and pulyng for fear. **1556** OLDE *Antichrist* 148 Ye soules that lye pewling in the paynles paynes of his pikepurce purgatoire. **1602** MARSTON *Ant. & Mel.* III. Wks. 1856 I. 41 We wring our selves into this wretched world, To pule, and weepe, exclaime, to curse and raile. **1633** FORD *Broken H.* v. ii, Wherefore should I pule, and, like a girl, Put finger in the eye? **1713** STEELE *Guardian* No. 151 ¶ 1 When he is puling for bohea tea and cream. **1877** MRS. FORRESTER *Mignon* I. 39 Don't come puling to me when it's too late.

2. To pipe plaintively, as a chicken, or the young of any animal; also said of the cry of the kite.

1598 FLORIO, *Vulpare*, to crie or pule like a kite. **1611** COTGR., *Pepier*, to peepe, cheepe, or pule, as a young bird in the neast. *Ibid.*, *Piauler*,.. to pule, or howle (as a young whelpe). **1631** R. H. *Arraignm. Whole Creature* v. 40 Hunger.. makes the Lyons roare,.. the Chicke chirpe, the Kite pule. **1725** *Bradley's Fam. Dict.* s.v. *Poultry*, In case she hears any one pule, she must presently see if the little Animal does not require some Help to get out of the Shell.

3. *trans.* To utter or say (something) in a whining or querulous tone.

1535 *Goodly Primer, Dirige* (1848) 232 We have.. piteously puled forth, a certain sort of psalms.. for the souls of our Christian brethren and sisters. **1594** DRAYTON *Idea* v. 6, I say, You Love, you peule me out a No. **1648** HERRICK *Hesper.*, *Temple* 43 A second [puppet priest] pules, 'Hence, hence profane'. **1812** W. TAYLOR in *Monthly Mag.* XXXIV. 235 In limbo pent it pules a curse.

†**4.** *intr.* To pine or waste away. Cf. PULING 2.

1607 TOPSELL *Four-f. Beasts* 214 All other kinde of Cattell when they are sicke consume and pule away by little and little, onely Goates perish suddenly.

pule, *sb.* [f. PULE *v.*] The action of puling; whining or plaintive utterance; a whine.

1893 F. ESPINASSE *Lit. Recoll.* ix. 367 The melancholy book.. made by Matthew Arnold the theme of some of his melodious pule.

pule, obs. f. PILLOW; Sc. var. POOL *sb.*[1]

puleal, -eol, variants of PULIOL.

†'**pulege.** *Herb. Obs.* Also 5 pulegye. [a. F. *pulège*, L. *pūlegium* (also *pūleium*), supposed to be f. *pūlex* flea.] The herb Pennyroyal: cf. PULIOL.

c **1400** tr. *Secreta Secret.*, *Gov. Lordsh.* 76 Tak.. þe rotys of Pulegye, þat ys pulyol. *c* **1410** *Master of Game* (MS. Digby 182) i, Whan þei pasture of .II. herbes, þat one is clepid Sorpol [? serpyl], and þat other puligin [*v. rr.* pulegium, puligium], þei be stronge and fastrennynge. **1599** A. M. tr. *Gabelhouer's Bk. Physicke* 364/2 Take Rue, Sentorye, Pulege, Agrimonye, Mintes.

puler ('pjuːlə(r)). [f. PULE *v.* + -ER[1].]

1. One who pules; a whining, weakly person.

1579–80 NORTH *Plutarch* (1895) III. 7 When they sawe other.. tenderly brought up like pulers. **1602** MIDDLETON *Blurt, Master-Constable* II. ii, Flaxen-haired men are such pulers, and such piddlers, and such chicken-hearts. **1662** R. CODRINGTON tr. *Ruggle's Ignoramus* v. ii, I am not such a puler as Mistress Katharine to be Sea-sick. **1832** *Blackw. Mag.* XXXI. 490 The puler at last has qualms.

†**2.** A young bird, a fledgeling. *Obs.*

1611 COTGR., *Pepieur*, a peeper, cheeper; puler. **1618** LATHAM *2nd Bk. Falconry* (1633) 56 To leaue her, and returne to the Eyas, Brancher, or Puler.

†'**puleray.** *Obs. rare*[−1]. ? Name of an obsolete fabric of silk or silk and worsted.

1719 [STEELE] *Spinster* 346 Many woollen stuffs, and stuffs mixed with silk, and even silks themselves are.. laid aside;.. some of them are quite lost, and thrown out of sale, such as brillants and pulerays, antherines and bombazines.

†**puleyn.** *Obs. rare.* Also 4–5 poleyne. [a. OF. *po(u)lain* (1280 in Godef.), transf. use of *poulain* colt.] A slide for lowering casks into a cellar; = PULLEY *sb.*[2]

[**1236** *Close Roll 21 Hen. III* m. 20 Ad iij pulinos faciendos ad discarocanda vina regis ibidem. **1313–14** *Calendar of Inq. post mortem* V. 265 [Rendering.. 2s. 9d. yearly at the castle of Norwich for a custom called] Pipe and Puleyn.] *c* **1357** *Durham Acc. Rolls* (Surtees) 560 Et Will'o de Stottesyete pro puleyns et aliis necessariis faciendis.. xiiij d. **1373** in Riley *Lond. Mem.* (1868) 369, 20 poleynes, 2 wyndyng poleys. *c* **1440** *Promp. Parv.* 407/2 Poleyne, *troclea.*

Pulfrich ('pʊlfrɪç). The name of Carl *Pulfrich* (1858–1927), German physicist, used *attrib.* and in the possessive with reference to an optical illusion first pointed out by him (see *Naturwissensch.* (1922) X. 553), in which a pendulum that is swinging in a plane perpendicular to the line of sight appears to describe ellipses when one eye is covered with a filter and the other is uncovered.

1925 *Brit. Jrnl. Ophthalm.* IX. 65 Men, getting on in years, who have been expert in games with a moving ball, find themselves unable to judge its position with their former accuracy... Pulfrich's phenomenon seems to give a probable explanation. **1941** S. H. BARTLEY *Vision* vii. 170 Pulfrich's stereoscopic pendulum is another example of a set of conditions which will induce the perception of movement of a kind not corresponding with the real movement of a physical object. **1966** R. L. GREGORY *Eye & Brain* vi. 78 The trading of temporal discrimination for sensitivity with dark adaptation is most elegantly, if somewhat indirectly, observed in a curious and dramatic phenomenon known as the Pulfrich Pendulum Effect. **1974** *Vision Res.* XIV. 184/2 The only thing that is important in producing a Pulfrich effect is the relative luminance of the objects which move across the retinae whether these be 'target' or 'background' or whether the subject fixates a stationary point or follows a moving object. **1980** *Sci. Amer.* May 134/2 According to most hypotheses about the Pulfrich illusion, the dark filter delays the perception of the visual signal at the retina of the covered eye.

puli ('puːlɪ). Pl. pulik. [Hungarian.] A black, grey, or white sheep-dog belonging to the breed so called, characterized by a long, thick coat having a corded appearance.

1936 *Amer. Kennel Gaz.* 1 Oct. 62/1 The Puli is used primarily as a sheep herding dog in the hill sections of Hungary. In appearance he has many points of resemblance to the Old English Sheepdog, but is much smaller and more active. **1948** L. BAUVALD in B. Vesey-Fitzgerald *Bk. Dog* II. 616 The Puli is probably one of the aboriginal dog races of the Magyars... Relatively few Pulik find their way to the exhibition bench. **1964** 'C. RICHARDS' *Gentle Assassin* (1965) i. 7 A puli, a Hungarian breed of dog. **1972** *Country Life* 10 Feb. 329/1 The Hungarian pulik—puli in the singular—are increasing numerically over here. **1973** *Times* 6 Aug. 26/7 Have a Hungarian Puli puppy.. small black sheepdogs with an unusual corded coat. **1978** *Times* 11 Feb. 2/4 The Hungarian puli, distinguished by its remarkable corded coat, had a class of its own [at Crufts] for the first time.

puliall, variant of PULIOL.

puli'carious, *a. nonce-wd.* [f. L. *pūlicāri-us* of or belonging to fleas, f. *pūlex*, *pūlic-em* flea; cf. *pūlicāria* (sc. *herba*) flea-bane: see -OUS.] Of the nature of a flea, of the flea kind.

1872 RUSKIN *Fors Clav.* xvii. 4 Has he multiplied himself into a host of pulicarious dragons—bug-dragons?

So †'**pulicary** *a. Obs.*

1657 TOMLINSON *Renou's Disp.* 358 Psyllium is a pulicary hearb so called from.. its seed.

pulicat(e, variant of PULLICATE.

pulicine ('pjuːlɪsaɪn), *a. rare.* [f. L. *pūlex*, *pūlic-em* flea + -INE[1].] Of or relating to fleas.

1656 BLOUNT *Glossogr.*, *Pulicine*, of or pertaining to a Flea. **1851** *Zoologist* IX. p. cxlv, My own pulicine experiences would excite some surprise.

†**pulick mountain, pulimountayn**, obs. ff. *poly-mountain* (POLY[1] c); cf. also PULIOL b.

1657 C. BECK *Univ. Charac.* K ij, Pulick mountain. **1562** TURNER *Herbal* II. 133 b, Serpillum that is in gardines is called for the moste parte in Englande creping thyme, and about Charde pulimountayn.

pulicous ('pjuːlɪkəs), *a. rare.* Also *erron.* pulicious. [ad. L. *pūlicōs-us*, f. *pūlex* flea: see -OUS.] Abounding in fleas; fleay.

1658 PHILLIPS, *Pulicous*, full of fleas. **1721–90** in BAILEY. **1843** LE FEVRE *Life Trav. Phys.* I. xviii, A pulicious fever, caused by lying upon an old leathern sofa, prevented me from closing my eyes. **1853** G. J. CAYLEY *Las Alforjas* I. 197 We slept in our clothes across a very pulicious mattress.

So '**pulicose** *a.*, infested with fleas, flea-bitten; *Path.* resembling flea-bites; **puli'cosity**, the condition of being infested with fleas.

1730 BAILEY (folio), **Pulicose*, abounding with or full of Fleas. [Hence in J., etc.] **1822–34** *Good's Study Med.* (ed. 4) II. 637 Pulicose or petechial spots were at one time supposed to be in every instance the result of debilitating and putrid fevers. *Ibid.* 638 Simple pulicose scurvy.—Exhibiting from the first a pulicose or flea-bite appearance. **1656** BLOUNT *Glossogr.*, **Pulicosity*, abundance of Fleas. **1809** *European Mag.* LX. 20 He could not get a wink of sleep.. from the extreme pulicosity of the beds.

puling ('pjuːlɪŋ), *vbl. sb.* [f. PULE *v.* + -ING[1].] The action of the verb PULE; whining, plaintive piping; a complaint.

1540 HYRDE tr. *Vives' Instr. Chr. Wom.* II. v. (1557) 83 The women will.. ofte complayne and vexe their housbandes, and angre them withe peuysshe puelynge. **1625** BACON *Ess.*, *Masques & Triumphs* (Arb.) 540 Let the Songs be Loud, and Cheerefull, and not Chirpings, or Pulings. **1855** THACKERAY *Newcomes* xxix, Be a man, Jack, and have no more of this puling.

†**b.** One who pules; a weakling. *Obs.*

1579–80 NORTH *Plutarch* (1895) I. 29 Catoes sonne.. was such a weake pulinge, that he could not away with much hardnesse.

puling ('pjuːlɪŋ), *ppl. a.* [f. PULE *v.* + -ING[2].]

1. Crying as a child, whining, feebly wailing; weakly querulous. Mostly *contemptuous.*

1529 MORE *Suppl. Soulys* Wks. 299/2 So much and in suche wise as we sely pore pewling sowles neither can deuise nor vtter. **1592** SHAKS. *Rom. & Jul.* III. v. 185 A wretched puling foole, A whining mammet. **1648** MILTON *Tenure Kings* (1650) 6 The unmaskuline Rhetorick of any puling Priest. **1781** COWPER *Expost.* 474 While yet thou [Britain] wast a grov'ling puling chit. **1857** W. COLLINS *Dead Secret* II. i, [She] is not one of the puling, sentimental sort.

†**2.** Pining, ailing, weakly, sickly. *Obs.*

1549 CHALONER *Erasm. on Folly* F j b, How weake and pewlyng his childhode. **1641** BROME *Joviall Crew* II. Wks. 1873 III. 382 As well as puling stomacks are made strong By eating against Appetite. *a* **1661** FULLER *Worthies* (1662) II. 126 Lean land will serve for puling pease and faint fetches. **1706** PHILLIPS, *Puling*, sickly, weakly, crazy.

Hence '**pulingly** *adv.*

1600 DEKKER *Gentle Craft* Wks. 1873 I. 42 Mistress, be rul'd by me, and do not speake so pulingly. *a* **1661** FULLER *Worthies, Wilts.* (1662) III. 146 An erected soul, disdaining pulingly to submit to an infamous death. **1904** C. L. MARSON *Folk Songs Somerset* I. p. xi, The so-called cultured people lament pulingly that we have been forgotten in the Divine Almonry.

†'**puliol.** *Herb. Obs.* Also 5 pylyol(e, -eol, 5–6 pulyol(e, 5–7 -ial(l, 6 -ioll, -iole, -yall, pilliall, 7 puleall. [a. OF. *puliol*, *poulieul*, *poliol* (14th c. in Godef.):—L. type **puleiolum*, dim. of *puleium*, *pulegium* pennyroyal (or ? ad. L. **poliolum*, dim. of *polium* POLY[1]). Cf. mod.F. *pouliot* (with different suffix) pennyroyal (Littré), also F. dial. *polieu*, *poulieu*, *pouillu* thyme (Godef.).]

The name of some aromatic herbs. **a.** (Also **puliol royal**) = PENNYROYAL, *Mentha Pulegium.* **b. puliol mountain**, perh. the same as *poly-mountain* (POLY[1] c); but sometimes identified with Wild Thyme, *Thymus Serpyllum*: cf. PELLAMOUNTAIN.

[Cf. **1450** *Alphita* 150/2 *Pulegium regale*, gliconeum idem, simile est calamento minori. *Pulegium ceruinum uel montanum*, serpillum, [herpillum] idem, minora habet folia quam alia. gallice puliol, anglice Brotheruurt... *Pulegium* quando simpliciter ponitur pro regale intelligitur. *Ibid.* 167/1 *Serpillum*.. gallice serpoul uel tymbre uel puliol. *Ibid.* 31/2 s.v. *Calamiten. Ibid.* 120/2 s.v. *Montanum serpillum.* **1597** GERARDE *Herbal* 672 Pennie royall [called] *Pulegium regale* for difference sake between it and wilde Time, which of some is called *Pulegium montanum.*]

a. [*c* **1265** *Voc. Names Plants* in Wr.-Wülcker 555/1 Chaudes herbes... *Pulegium*, *i.* puliol, *i.* hulwurt. *Ibid.* 557/20 *Origanum*, *i.* puliol real, *i.* wdeminte.] **14..** *Stockh. Med. MS.* I. 19 in *Anglia* XVIII. 295 Take eysyl & pulyole ryale And camomylle. *Ibid.* 35, viij [ounces] of puliol reall. **14..** *Voc.* in Wr.-Wülcker 601/25 *Pelegum*, *anglice* Pylyole. *c* **1440** *Promp. Parv.* 399/1 Pyleol ryal, *origonum.* **1486** *Bk. St. Albans* B ij b, Take puliall and garlek and stampe it wele togeder. *a* **1568** in *Bannatyne Poems* (Hunter. Cl.) 360 Sum bad hir tak erb pilliall. **1578** LYTE *Dodoens* II. lxv. 232 This herbe is called.. in English Penny Royal, Pulioll Royall. **1611** COTGR., *Pouliot*, Penniroyall, Pulial royall. **1706** [see b].

b. *c* **1440** *Promp. Parv.* 399/1 Pylyol mounteyne, herbe, *Pulegium.* *c* **1450** *M.E. Med. Bk.* (Heinrich) 104 Take puliol montayne, þat is to say hullewort and wasshe hit clene. **1542** BOORDE *Dyetary* xxvi. (1870) 289 These thynges folowynge doth purge Melancoly: quyckbeme,.. pulyall mountane. **1545** ELYOT *Dict.*, *Clinopodium*, the herbe whiche is called Puliole mountayne. **1657** C. BECK *Univ. Charac.* K ij, Puleall of the mountain. **1706** PHILLIPS, *Puliol*, or *Puliol-Mountain*, a sort of Herb; *Puliol-Royal*, the same as Penny-Royal.

pulisch(e, -ish(e, -ysh(e, obs. ff. POLISH *v.*

Pulitzer ('pjuːlɪtzə(r); in U.S. also 'pʊlɪtzə(r)). [Name of J. *Pulitzer* (1847–1911), Amer. journalist.] Designating any of several annual awards for distinguished work in journalism, letters, and music produced or published in the U.S. Also *ellipt.*

1918 *N.Y. Times* 3 June 9/7 The annual Pulitzer Prize of $1,000 for the best play written and produced by an American playwright in 1917.. awarded to Jesse Lynch Williams for his comedy, 'Why Marry?' **1934** [see CREATIVE *a.* 1 b]. **1941** B. SCHULBERG *What makes Sammy Run?* i. 20 Sammy was staring.. at George Opdyke, the three-time Pulitzer Prize winner. **1955** G. GREENE *Quiet American* I. iii. 38 Why, that account of Road 66.. that was worthy of the Pulitzer. **1962** *Publishers' Weekly* 26 Mar. 16 Pulitzer.. pronounced.. 'PULLitzer'—not, as so many people say, 'PEWLitzer'. **1971** R. A. CARTER *Manhattan Primitive* (1972) xiii. 121 The museum's sponsors—a famous concert musician, a film actress, and a Pulitzer Prize-winning novelist. **1972** R. LUDLUM *Osterman Weekend* iii. 52 You were quite successful as an investigative reporter... You were nominated for a Pulitzer, I believe. **1977** *Time* 31 Oct. 28/1 One.. led last year to a Pulitzer-prizewinning photograph of a woman and a little girl plummeting from a collapsed fire escape.

pulk[1] (pʌlk). Now *local.* Forms: α. 3–5 **polk**, 5 **polke**; β. 5–7 **pulke**, 7 **pulck**, 5– **pulk**. [ME. *polk*, app. dim. of OE. *pōl*, ME. *pōl(e* (in 15th c. also *pull*) POOL *sb.*[1] Cf. CHINK.] A small pool, especially of standing water; a small pond or water-pit; a shallow well or tank; a puddle, a plash; a small lake or 'broad'.

c **1300** *Havelok* 2685 On þe feld was neuere a polk [*rime* folk] þat it ne stod of blod so ful, þat þe strem ran intil þe hul. *c* **1320** *Sir Tristr.* 2886 Mine hors þe water vp brouȝt, Of o polk in þe way. *c* **1440** *Promp. Parv.* 408/1 Polke.. or pul yn a watur (*H.* pulk water, *P.* polke, or pulke water), *vortex.* **1642** ROGERS *Naaman* 842 It is easie for a woman to goe to a pond or pulke standing neare to her doore. **1674–91** RAY *N.C. Words* 56 A *Pulk*, a Hole of standing Water, is used also for a Slough or Plash of some depth. **1678** *Coll. Conn. Hist. Soc.* VI. 186 The Highway.. very chargeable to mayntayne by reason of swamps pulcks and Hoales that lye in the said Highway. *a* **1825** FORBY *Voc. E. Anglia*, *Pulk*, a hole full of mud, or a small muddy pond. Otherwise a *pulk-hole*, a shallow place containing water. **1883** G. C. DAVIES *Norfolk Broads* i. (1884) 7 In the little 'pulks' or miniature Broads, which everywhere open off the river, are lilies.. in dazzling abundance.

b. Comb. *pulk-hole.*

a **1825** [see above]. **1887** JESSOPP *Arcady* 55 The turf in the pulk hole or bog lands.

†**pulk**[2]. *north. dial. Obs.* A chest of drawers; a bureau.

1577 *Wills & Inv. N.C.* (Surtees) I. 415 A pulke of mazer xxvj[s] viij[d]. **1590** *Ibid.* II. 197 Myne uncle Barker's debt book, lyeinge in.. a dresser ther, the key whereof is in a pulke in the perlor. **1596** *Ibid.* 297 *note*, The standinge pulke in the hall.

‖**pulk**[3], **polk** (pʌlk, pɒlk). [a. F. *pulk*, a. Pol. *polk*, Russ. *polk*[ŭ] a regiment, an army.] A regiment of Cossacks. Also *transf.*

1791 *St. Papers* in *Ann. Reg.* 198/2 It is permitted to all citizens to serve in the army in any regiment or pulk. **1796** MORSE *Amer. Geog.* II. 302 Two pulks of cossacks, each pulk consisting of 500 men. **1848** THACKERAY *Contrib. to 'Punch'* Wks. 1886 XXIV. 195 Now charging a pulk of Chartists. **1861** W. H. RUSSELL in *Times* 22 Oct., A squadron of cavalry.. whose saddlery accoutrements.. and uniforms would not be tolerated in a polk of Cossacks of the Black Sea.

‖**pulka** ('pʌlkə). Also **pulkka**, *erron.* **pulkha**, **pulk**. [a. Finnish *pulkka*, Lapp. *pulkke*, (acc. to Friis, more purely) *bulkke*, *bulke*.] A Lapland travelling-sledge in shape like the front half of a boat, drawn by a single reindeer (see also quot. 1974). Also *attrib.*

1796 MORSE *Amer. Geog.* 35 Confined in one of those carriages or pulkhas. **1808** ELEANOR SLEATH *Bristol Heiress* I. 177 No rein-deer bids her pulkha fly. **1858** B. TAYLOR *North. Trav.* ix. 84 These pulks are shaped very much like a canoe; they are about five feet long, one foot deep, and eighteen inches wide, with a sharp bow and a square stern. You sit upright against the stern-board, with your legs stretched out in the bottom. **1881** DU CHAILLU *Land Midn. Sun* II. 79 Numerous pulkas.. were scattered around. **1885** S. TROMHOLT *Aurora Borealis* I. 108 The sleigh would capsize quicker than the Pulk. **1913** *Chambers's Jrnl.* Nov. 798/1 The Lapland sledge, or *pulk*, as it is called, is shaped something like a boat. **1952** *Ibid.* Jan. 33/2 In a trice he had put on her gay red-and-blue harness and fastened the traces to a pulkha, the canoe-like little sledge of north-east Lapland. **1960** G. TAYLOR *Mortlake* III. i. 130 A reindeer drawing a small boat-shaped sledge called a pulkka. **1964** *Punch* 25 Nov. p. xvii, This store's ski fashion wear includes the Ernst Engel collection, Canadian overboots, patterned Tyrol pullovers, Swedish pulka jackets, furry helmets. **1969** *Guardian* 31 July 3/4 All our equipment.. we pull behind us on pulka sledges.. made of wood. **1974** *Canad. Consumer* Feb. 11/1 A special accessory for family enjoyment is the Norwegian 'pulk' (sled) with a rigid harness for a man or dog to tow even babies along. The pulk.. is boatshaped, so that it will not tip on bumpy ground.

†**pull**, *sb.*[1] *Obs.* [OE. *pull*, found beside *pól*, POOL *sb.*[1] (q.v.); cf. also Welsh *pwll* in same sense: the relations between these forms are obscure. (The Sc. *pule*, *puil* (pyl) is = Eng. *pool*.)] A pool. (In the OE. example, a pool in a stream.) **b.** *Comb.* **pull-reed**, *dial.*: see *pool-reed*, POOL *sb.*[1] 3.

c **1075** *Grant by Offa* (*c* 779) in Birch *Cart. Sax.* I. 326 Of seʒes mere in þæs pulles heafod.. of ðorn brycge in þone pull, & æfter þam pulle in baka brycge.. in dodhæma pull, of þam pulle eft in Temede stream. **1199** *Rot. Chart.* (1837) 8/2 Terram de Hunfrideheved.. et partem polli que dicitur Kierkepolle. *a* **1300** *Joseph & Jacob* 18 Hi floten swiþe riued bi dich & bi pulle. *c* **1440** *Pallad. on Husb.* I. 1032 A sobur brook amydde or ellis a welle With pullis [L. *lacunis*] faire. **1847–78** HALLIWELL, *Pull-reed*, a long reed used for ceilings instead of laths. *Somerset.*

pull (pʊl), *sb.*[2] [f. PULL *v.*]

I. The act, action, or faculty of pulling.

1. a. An act of pulling or drawing towards oneself with force: a general term, including both a momentary pluck, wrench, or tug, and a continued exercise of force. Also *fig.*

c **1440** *Promp. Parv.* 416/1 Pul, or draȝte.., *tractus.* **1560** DAUS tr. *Sleidane's Comm.* 137 There were two hangemen ready and eche of them a payre of tonges read hote: at the three first pulles he helde his peace. **1609** S. W. *Marie Magd. Fun. Teares* 53 She beheld thy armes and legges racked with violent puls, thy hands and feet boared with nayles. **1681** FLAVEL *Meth. Grace* iv. 82 If the Lord draw not the soul, and that with an omnipotent pull, it can never come from itself to Christ. **1795** MRS. E. PARSONS *Myst. Warning* I. x. 178 He rang the bell... After waiting.. he was about to repeat the pull. **1875** HUXLEY & MARTIN *Elem. Biol.* viii. (1883) 77 There is a pull from above, and there is a push from below. **1883** GILMOUR *Mongols* 154 With a long pull, a strong pull, and a pull all together, round goes the wheel.

b. The force expended in pulling or drawing; pulling power or force (with or without the production of motion); draught, traction, strain; the force of attraction. Also *fig.*

1833 *Penny Cycl.* I. 505/1 If the stock [of an anchor] were very short, the pull of the cable would tend.. to drag the end of the stock along the bottom. **1837** WHEWELL *Hist. Induct. Sc.* II. i. §1 We may have pressure without motion, or dead pull. **1860** TYNDALL *Glac.* II. xvii. 319 The sides of the glacier are acted upon by an oblique pull towards the centre. **1863** —— *Heat* xiv. § 692 (1870) 480 The entire pull of the sun being then exerted upon it. **1900** *Engineering Mag.* XIX. 745/1 The amount of this magnetic pull may be very considerable.

c. The drawing or dragging of a weight; the exertion of carrying one's own weight up a steep ascent against the force of gravity. (Cf. 9.)

1841 MOTLEY *Corr.* (1889) I. iv. 70 The next night left.. for Königsberg, a long pull of fifty-eight hours in a diligence. **1861** SYMONDS in *Life* (1895) I. iv. 179 A stiff pull it was that brought us to the top. **1871** L. STEPHEN *Playgr. Eur.* (1894) vii. 158 The work had been simply a stiff pull against the collar. **1872** JENKINSON *Guide Eng. Lakes* (1879) 209 A good steady pull must necessarily land the tourist on the summit.

d. Paired with *push*: see PUSH *sb.*[1] 1 d.

2. Specific or technical uses of sense 1.

a. *Printing.* A pull of the bar of the hand-press (see PULL *v.* 14); hence, an impression taken, or a page or part of one printed, by this; now *spec.* a rough 'proof', taken without an overlay and the adjustments necessary for a finished impression.

first, second pull, the part of the forme printed at the first or second pull of the bar in the early presses, in which more than one impression of the platen was sometimes necessary to cover a large forme; so *forme of one pull*.

1683 MOXON *Mech. Exerc., Printing* 393 When a Form of one Pull comes to the Press. **1771** LUCKOMBE *Hist. Printing* 358 Having Pulled the First Pull,.. he turns the Rounce about again,.. and then Pulls his second Pull. **1787** *Printer's Gram.* 328 That which causes a Soft Pull is putting in pieces of felt or pasteboard.

1845 DICKENS *Let.* 1 Nov. (1977) IV. 423 The carriage.. is to call for a pull of the first part of the *Cricket*. **1885** J. COLEMAN in *Longm. Mag.* V. 500 Previous to its suppression, they gave me a 'pull' of it [*sc.* an article]. **1900** UPWARD *Eben Lobb* 41 Take away that pull and bring me a revise directly. There are five mistakes in one par of 'Talk'. **1909** H. HART in *Let.*, To a printer the difference between 'a pull' and a 'finished impression' is, that the one has no preliminary making-ready, and the other has.

b. A pull at the bridle in order to check a horse; *spec.* in *Racing*, a check dishonestly given to a horse in order to prevent its winning.

1737 BRACKEN *Farriery Impr.* (1757) II. 123 He will run thro' at the Speed he begins with, or nearly so, because every Horse.. requires to have a Pull. **1840** BLAINE *Encycl. Rur. Sports* §1258 The pull and hustle are effective bridle manipulations... The horse, which.. is so free.. a goer as on no occasion to require the pull and hustle, is the very one that will be benefited by it when running in. **1856** 'STONEHENGE' *Brit. Sports* II. II. ii. §2 (ed. 2) 381/2 It is easier to go into the saddling enclosure and select a winner of a steeplechase, barring accidents and pulls.

c. A pull at an oar; hence, a short spell at rowing; a passage or journey in a rowing-boat.

1793 SMEATON *Edystone L.* §283 We had a hard pull with our oars to get on board the buss. **1840** R. H. DANA *Bef. Mast* xxv, Whalemen make the best boats' crews in the world for a long pull. **1861** HUGHES *Tom Brown at Oxf.* vi, The college eight was to go down.. to the reaches.. for a good training pull. **1892** *Chamb. Jrnl.* 2 Apr. 221/2 The oarsman gave a lusty pull.

d. The act of pulling the trigger of a fire-arm; also, the force required to pull the trigger.

1888 RIDER HAGGARD *Col. Quaritch* xxxvi, He had never known the pull of a pistol to be so heavy before. **1892** GREENER *Breech-Loader* 186 As the angles given are similar to the action when pulling the trigger with the finger, it is necessary to know this when trying the pulls of guns. **1900** *Daily News* 5 Sept. 3/2 Armed with the Lee straight-pull rifle.

e. The act of drawing a card.

1715 LADY M. W. MONTAGU *Basset Table* 52 The Knave won Sonica,.. And, the next Pull, my Septleva I lose.

f. *Cricket.* A hit which brings a ball pitched to the off side round to leg. So in *Golf*, a hit which causes the ball to swerve in its flight towards the left (i.e. of a right-handed player).

1865 *Lillywhite's Guide to Cricketers* 135 A fast run-getter, little too fond of a pull. **1892** *Daily News* 29 June 2/7 The veteran E. M. Grace brought off some most alarming pulls. **1897** *Westm. Gaz.* 13 Aug. 3/2 The 'pull', which is simply an artistic method of placing the ball where the field is not. **1903** H. H. HILTON in Low *Concerning Golf* 66 When the wind is coming from the player's right the presence of a slight pull adds many yards to the length of a drive.

g. ***long pull*** (in public-house phraseology): the supply to a person of an amount of intoxicating liquor (usually beer) exceeding that for which he asks.

Understood to be so called from the extra pull given by the publican at the beer-pump (cf. sense 7).

1908 *Times* 3 Nov. 4/5 (Parl. Rept.) He [Mr. Asquith] would not say they [licensing bench] actually imposed conditions as to what was called the 'long pull', but they certainly had the power to do so. *Ibid.* 19 Nov. 6/5 (A member of committee) The licensing justices were to be empowered also to attach to the renewal of a licence a prohibition of what was known as 'the long pull'.

†**3. a.** A turn or bout at pulling each other in wrestling or any struggle; a trial of strength of body, will, determination, argument, etc.; a bout, a set-to; often in ***to stand*** or ***wrestle a pull***. *Obs.*

c **1330** R. BRUNNE *Chron. Wace* (Rolls) 1809 Þe firste pul so harde was set þat þeyr brestes to-gyder met... Ilk oþer pulled. *c* **1381** CHAUCER *Parl. Foules* 164 For manye a man that may nat stonde a pul It likyth hym at wrastelyng for to be. *c* **1400** *Laud Troy Bk.* 7996 Thei [Trojans] vnnethe stode hem a pul. *c* **1412** HOCCLEVE *De Reg. Princ.* 4480 At Auerice now haue here a pul. *Ibid.* 5232 Þer-with þis land hath wrastled many a pul. *a* **1568** *O wrechit Man* 39 in *Bannatyne Poems* (Hunter. Cl.) 210 Aganis his dynt thow may nocht stand ane pow. **1588** DRAKE in *Four C. Eng. Lett.* (1880) 32 We.. mynd with the Grace of God, to wressell a poull with him. **1747** RICHARDSON *Clarissa* (1749) II. xxxvi. 243 We have just now had another pull. Upon my word, she is excessively.. unpersuadable.

b. *fig.* A single effort or act likened to pulling; a 'go'.

1803 MARY CHARLTON *Wife & Mistress* II. 244 It's of no use my trying to get in more than a word at a pull,.. he would only stop me twenty times. **1871** 'M. LEGRAND' *Cambr. Freshm.* 54 The opportunity both desired of having the first 'pull' at their new master.

c. In fig. phr. ***to take a pull*** (***at, on, oneself***), to stop or check (oneself); to pull oneself together. *colloq.* (chiefly *Austral.*).

1890 BARRÈRE & LELAND *Dict. Slang* II. 155/2 *Pull* (society): to take a *pull* means to stop, check, put an end to. **1916** C. J. DENNIS *Songs Sentimental Bloke* i. 16, I tells meself some day I'll take a pull An' look eround fer some good, stiddy job. **1922** GALSWORTHY *Family Man* III. ii. 105 Take a pull, old man! Have a hot bath and go to bed. **1942** E. WAUGH *Put out more Flags* iii. 177 Suddenly she found herself weeping in earnest. Then she took a pull at herself. This wouldn't do at all. **1946** T. E. HAUGHEY *Railway Reminisc.* 21 Look here—, it's about time you took a pull. Just shake yourself up a bit quick. **1953** M. SCOTT *Breakfast at Six* xxiv. 202 She may be a wonderful friend, but she'll land you in gaol yet. For heaven's sake, take a pull. **1966** J. HACKSTON *Father clears Out* 110 Alf Hodgson talked so much about the Red Range Federal Capital Site Movement that people said he'd be standing for Parliament one of these days if he did not take a pull on himself.

4. a. The power or capacity of pulling instead of being pulled; advantage possessed by one party, course, or method over another; esp. in phrase ***to have a*** or ***the pull of, on, upon***, or ***over*** some one. ***the pull of the table***, in gambling games, the advantage possessed by the dealer or banker.

1584 R. SCOT *Discov. Witchcr.* v. vii. (1886) 82 They have a verie cold pull of this place, which is the speciall peece of scripture alledged of them. **1781** BURGOYNE *Ld. of Manor* III. i. 61 Oh, you'll have quite the pull of me in employment. **1812** J. H. VAUX *Flash Dict.*, *Pull*, an important advantage possessed by one party over another. **1855** THACKERAY *Newcomes* xli, That they may know what their chances are, and who naturally has the pull over them. **1890** HUXLEY in *Life* (1900) II. xv. 255, I think, on the whole, I have the pull of him. **1890** 'R. BOLDREWOOD' *Col. Reformer* (1891) 131 There's no particular pull in it. **1893** *Spectator* 10 June 767 Economy is the unquestionable 'pull' of vegetarianism.

b. *spec.* Personal or private influence capable of being employed to one's advantage. *colloq.* (chiefly *U.S.*).

1889 *Chr. Union* (N.Y.) 17 Jan. 68 The sole difference being that B had a 'pull' on the [excise] Board and A had none. **1894** STEAD *If Christ came to Chicago* 51, I have got a pull, and any one who has got a pull can do a great deal. **1897** in *Daily News* 28 May 6/4 Appointed to commissions because, to use an American expression, they had a political pull. *a* **1911** [see ISLAND *sb.* 1 d]. **1937** F. P. CROZIER *Men I Killed* vi. 109 Having been in France for so long and lacking the very necessary 'pull' in influential circles, we were unable to oust the family favourites at the War Office. **1940** [see BRACKET *sb.* 5 c]. **1978** J. KRANTZ *Scruples* ii. 57 His future in the giant corporation was assured in the long run through family pull, since he had, on his mother's side, as one said in slang, *du piston*.

5. A long or deep draught of liquor.

[Perh. in origin a different word: cf. PULL *v.* 12.]

1575 *Gamm. Gurton* v. ii, And when ye meete at one pot, he shall haue the first pull. **1707** J. STEVENS tr. *Quevedo's Com. Wks.* (1709) 510 He swallowed down both.. at two or three pulls. **1727** *Philip Quarll* 74 He calls for a Quart, and bids the Child take a hearty Pull. **1835–40** HALIBURTON *Clockm.* (1862) 319 Who's for a pull of grog? suppose we have a pull, gentlemen—a good pull, and a strong pull, and a pull altogether, eh! **1863** W. C. BALDWIN *Afr. Hunting* ix. 377 The oxen.. seemed to enjoy, not a little, a vigorous pull of good rain water. **1867** BAKER *Nile Tribut.* iv. (1872) 61 A long and deep pull at the water-skin.

6. = LAY *sb.*[7] 7 d. *slang.*

1969 FABIAN & BYRNE *Groupie* xxx. 219 'I'm not going to sleep with you.'.. 'Why not?' 'Because I'm not an easy pull.' **1973** M. AMIS *Rachel Papers* 33 A mental chant, *timor mortis conturbat me*, and I began on my clumsiest pull ever. *Ibid.* 37 It was so obviously me and my pull and Geoffrey and his pull getting together to plan a spotty removal to someone's house.

II. Concrete senses.

7. That part of a mechanism with which a pull is exerted; a handle or the like; often in *Comb.*, as ***beer-pull*** (the handle of a beer-pump), ***bell-pull***; also, an instrument or device for pulling.

1810 in G. Rose *Diaries* (1860) II. 438 She.. laid the pull of the bell over the end of the bed. **1823** in Cobbett *Rur. Rides* (1885) I. 344 There was a parlour, Aye, and a carpet and bell-pull too! **1864** Beer-pull [see BEER *sb.*[1] 4]. **1896** A. MORRISON *Child of the Jago* 43 The landlady hung hysterical on the beer-pulls in the bar. **1904** *Daily Chron.* 12 Apr. 3/5 'Pulls', too, may be procured; rubber pulls, threads, and tubes that run beneath the suave performer's clothes as the pipes and wires run invisibly under London.

†**8.** Some kind of draw-net. *Obs. rare*⁻¹.

c **1303** *Reg. Pal. Dunelm.* (Rolls) III. 40 Duæ sagenæ quæ vocantur 'Tol et Pul'.

9. A part of a road where more than ordinary effort is necessary; *esp.* a steep ascent. (Cf. 1 c.)

1798 CHARLOTTE SMITH *Yug. Philos.* IV. 130 This dairy woman was fain to get out to walk up this pull. **1812** SIR J. SINCLAIR *Syst. Husb. Scot.* I. 63 If the roads were without pulls, a greater weight might be taken. **1855** CHAMIER *My Travels* III. iv. 101 The.. track.. is a severe pull, and a most disagreeable, fagging one.

10. *Combinations*: see PULL-.

†**pull**, *sb.*[3] *Obs.* [a. F. *poule* fowl, orig. chicken:—late L. *pulla*, fem. of *pullus* young of any animal. Cf. PULLET.] A bird of the poultry kind, a fowl. In comb. ***pull-fowl***. Also ***pull-bill***, ***-roll*** (poultry-bill, -list).

1604 in *Househ. Ord.* (1790) 312 The giveing of allowance of all the Poultry in the Pull-Rowles, Pull-Bills.. and other particular Breivements of the Household. *a* **1688** J. WALLACE *Descr. Orkney* (1693) 16 Here is plenty both of wild and tame Fowls, Pull-Fowls, Hens, Dukes, Goose, &c.

pull (pʊl), *v.* Forms: 1 pullian, 4–5 pullen, -yn, 4–7 pulle, pul, 4– pull, (6 puyll, polle, poull; *Sc.* and *n. dial.* 5–8 pow, 8–9 pou, pu', 9 poo, poogh). [OE. *pullian* (with compound *a-pullian*), rare, and of uncertain etymology.

It has been compared with LG. *pûlen* to shell (peas, etc.), husk, decorticate, strip, pick, pluck, pinch, tear (*Bremisches Wbch.* III. 372), also *pülen*, *pülken*, MDu. *polen*, 'decorticare' (Kilian), EFris. (Saterland) *pûlje*, NFris. *püllin*, *pöle*: cf. MLG., LG. *pûle*, Du. *peul* husk, cod, shell. But there are great difficulties both of sense and form. If *pull* and *pluck* both went back to OTeut. a primitive connexion between them would be conceivable, but historical evidence of this is entirely wanting.

The OE. instances known show already three senses or uses; but all belong to the general notion of *pluck, snatch* (with fingers, claws, or beak), rather than to that of *draw with sustained force or effort*, as in modern use. The former is therefore assumed as the primary sense.]

I. In senses akin to *pluck*.

1. *trans.* To pluck or take away (anything) by force from where it grows or is set or attached;

= PLUCK *v.* 1. **a.** To pluck or draw out (feathers, hair, etc.). *Obs.* or *dial.*

[*c* **1000** *Sax. Leechd.* I. 362 ʒif þu nimest wulfes mearh and smyrest mid hraðe ða stowe þe þa hær beoð of apullud [*v.r.* -od] ne ʒeþafoð seo smyrung þæt hy eft wexen.] *c* **1386** CHAUCER *Manciple's T.* 200 To the Crowe he stirte and that anon And pulled hise white fetheres euerychon. *c* **1400** *26 Pol. Poems* xxvi. 10 Here federes were pulled, she myght nat fle. **1586** MARLOWE *1st Pt. Tamburl.* I. i, That Tamburlaine That..as I hear, doth mean to pull my plumes. **1591** SHAKS. *1 Hen. VI*, III. iii. 7 Wee'le pull his Plumes.

b. To pluck or draw up by the root (plants, e.g. turnips, carrots, flax). See also *pull up* (35 b).

c **1350** *Nom. Gall.-Angl.* 236 *Homme en gardeyn arace nauet*, M[an] in the ʒerde pullith nepus. **1523** FITZHERB. *Husb.* §146 How it [flax] shold be sowen, weded, pulled, repeyled, watred, wasshen, dryed, beten. **1613** PURCHAS *Pilgrimage* v. xii. (1614) 507 The herbe is..sowne as other herbs, in due time pulled and dried. **1785** BURNS *Halloween* ii, To burn their nits, an' pou their stocks [cabbages], An' haud their Halloween. **1846** J. BAXTER *Libr. Pract. Agric.* (ed. 4) II. 345 Their tops being of a darker green and stronger, which continued..until they [turnips] were pulled.

c. To pluck, gather, cull, pick (fruit, flowers, or leaves) from the trees or plants on which they grow. Now chiefly *Sc.* (*pu'*, *pou*, *pow*).

1340–70 *Alex. & Dind.* 128 þe sote-sauerende [sweet-savouring] frut sone to pulle. **1382** WYCLIF *Jer.* xxxi. 5 Thei shul not pulle grapes. *c* **1440** *Promp. Parv.* 405/2 Plukkyn, or pulle frute, *vellico, avello*. *c* **1450** LOVELICH *Grail* xliii. 398 To wheche Roser men gon..the flowres to pullen In gret hast. **1500–20** DUNBAR *Poems* lxi. 26 An ald ʒaid aver, Schott furth..to pull the claver. **1685** DRYDEN *Hor., Epode* ii. 30 He joys to pull the ripen'd pear. *c* **1710** CELIA FIENNES *Diary* (1888) 107 Hopp yards where they were at work pulling hopps. **1721** RAMSAY *Tea-t. Misc., Yng. Laird & Edin. Katy* iii, We'll pou the daisies on the green. **1724** —— *Royal Archers Shooting* viii, Haste to the garden then bedeen, The rose and laurel pow. **1794** LD. AUCKLAND *Corr.* (1862) III. 240, I pulled above 3000 peaches and nectarines. **1854** H. MILLER *Sch. & Schm.* vii. (1858) 136 We had delayed..until the better fruit had been pulled.

†**d.** To gather or collect (other produce). *Obs.*

1585 T. WASHINGTON tr. *Nicholay's Voy.* I. iv. 3 b, They pul from the said Sapins [fir trees] great abundance of rosin.

e. *intr.* To bear or admit of plucking or pulling.

1641 BEST *Farm. Bks.* (Surtees) 57 They [pease] pull the best when they are the most feltered togeather. **1778** [W. MARSHALL] *Minutes Agric.* 6 Sept. an. 1774, They [beans] may not pull so easily in dry weather.

f. *trans.* To extract (a tooth). *U.S.*

1880 'MARK TWAIN' *Tramp Abroad* xxiii. 222 A soldier was getting a tooth pulled in a tent. **1915** R. ADAIR *Pract. Oral Hygiene* (ed. 2) i. 8 Dr. —— used to pull teeth, but he has got to talking so much about clean mouths that he is losing some of his trade. **1927** M. R. REIDY *This Tooth Proposition* vi. 110 A long time ago, dentistry consisted mostly of pulling teeth and making plates. **1976** H. MACINNES *Agent in Place* xix. 202 It was like pulling teeth. But we did learn something important.

2. *trans.* **a.** *to pull caps*: to snatch or pull off one another's caps; hence, to scuffle, to quarrel: see CAP *sb.*[1] 9. So *to pull wigs*.

1778 MISS BURNEY *Evelina* (1791) II. xxxiv. 224 If either of you have any inclination to pull caps for the title of Miss Belmont, you must do it with all speed. **1785**, etc. [see CAP *sb.*[1] 9]. **1807–8** W. IRVING *Salmag.* vii. (1824) 120 A pair of Amazons pulling Caps. **1823** J. SIMPSON *Ricardo the Outlaw* II. 183 A man..for whom half the females of Paris were pulling caps. **1864** TREVELYAN *Compet. Wallah* (1866) 183 Twelve halls of justice might be provided—for the worst of which the judges at Westminster would pull wigs.

b. To snatch, steal, filch. *slang.*

1821 HAGGART *Life* (ed. 2) 63, I pulled a scout, and passed it to Graham. **1851** MAYHEW *Lond. Labour* I. 414/1 We lived by thieving, and I do still—by pulling flesh.

†**3. a.** *trans.* and *intr.* *Cards.* To draw a card from the pack; hence *fig.* *to pull for prime* (also *to pull prime*), to draw for a card or cards which will make the player 'prime'. (Cf. PLUCK *v.* 2 d, PRIME *sb.*[2] 9.) In last quot., to draw lots. *Obs.*

1593 DONNE *Sat.* ii. 86 Hee..spends as much tyme Wringing each Acre, as men pulling Prime. **1619** FLETCHER *Mons. Thomas* IV. ix, Faith Sir my rest is up, And what I now pull, shall no more afflict me Then if I plaid at span-counter. *a* **1625** —— *Woman's Prize* I. ii, My rest is up, wench, and I pull for that Will make me ever famous. **1633** G. HERBERT *Temple, Jordan* iii, Riddle who list, for me, and pull for Prime. *Ibid., Ch. Militant* 134 The world came both with hands and purses full To this great lotterie, and all would pull.

b. *trans.* To draw or to be assigned (a task or position); to carry out (a duty). *U.S.*

1894 *Lucky Bag* (U.S. Naval Acad. Yearbk.) 67 *Pull the sick list*,..to get on the sick list when not ill. **1941** KENDALL & YVONNE *Dict. Army & Navy Slang* 11/1 *To pull guard duty*, ..to do guard duty. For instance, 'I've got to pull K.P.' **1972** *Times* 13 Apr. 1/8, I feel that my life is more important than having to pull security on this place. **1976** *New Yorker* 15 Mar. 89/1 How come they got you pulling guard?

4. *intr.* To snatch or tear *at* something; *spec.* of a hawk: To tear or pluck at food; to feed by snatches.

1826 SIR J. S. SEBRIGHT *Observ. Hawking* 14 [The young hawk may be] allowed for a short time to pull upon a stump or pinion, from which he can get but little meat. **1852** R. F. BURTON *Falconry Valley Indus* vi. 65 Sometimes she is allowed to pull upon a stump. **1883** SALVIN & BRODRICK *Falconry Brit. Isles* Gloss., *Pull through the hood*, to eat through the aperture in the front of the hood. **1888** F. HUME *Mme. Midas* I. iii, The cattle..lingering..to pull at a particularly tempting tuft of bush grass growing in the moist ditches which ran along each side of the highway.

5. a. *trans.* By metathesis of object: To strip (a bird) of feathers, or †(a sheep or other beast) of wool or the like (*obs.*), by plucking; = PLUCK *v.* 5. Now *rare* or *dial.*

to pull a crow with another: see CROW *sb.*[1] 3 b.

c **1000** *Sax. Leechd.* III. 176 ʒif him þince þæt he sceap pulliʒe, ne biþ þæt god. *c* **1350** *Nom. Gall.-Angl.* 310 M[an] pyndith a gray gose..And pulluth [*deplume*] a coppid larke. **1390** GOWER *Conf.* I. 17 What Schep that is full of wulle Upon his back, thei [the shepherds] toose and pulle, Whil ther is eny thing to pile. *c* **1430** *Two Cookery-bks.* 9 Take smale byrdys, an pulle hem an drawe hem clene. *c* **1450** *Ibid.* 78 Ffesaunte rosted,..pull him dry. **1573–80** BARET *Alv.* P 838 To pull or plucke geese, *deplumare anseres*. **1597** LOWE *Chirurg.* (1634) 35 Take an olde Cocke and pull him quicke, bruse him well, and kill him. **1662** [see CROW *sb.*[1] 3 b]. **1727** *Philip Quarll* 17 One cast the Animal, and the other two pull'd the Fowls. **1851** *Beck's Florist* 19 [A labourer says] I'd pull a lot of sparrows, or maybe some blackbirds and thrushes, and then cut 'em down the back, and fill their bodies full of bread.

b. In *Tanning*, To remove the hair or wool from (hides or skins) with a pulling-knife; also, in *Hat-making*, To free (fur) from the long hairs.

1578–9 *Proclam. Q. Eliz.* 28 Feb., From Shroue Tuesday ..vntill the last day of June..no maner of person or persons ..shall pull or clippe, or cause to be pulled or clipped, any maner of wooll fell. **1902** *Brit. Med. Jrnl.* 15 Feb. 377/1 The fur..is then 'pulled'—that is, the long hairs or 'kemps' are removed with a curved knife, and sold to upholsterers.

6. †**a.** *fig.* (or in *fig. phrases*). To strip (a person) of his property or money; to fleece; to despoil, rob, plunder, cheat; = PLUCK *v.* 6. *to pull a finch, pigeon, plover*, etc., to fleece a simple or unsuspecting person: see the sbs. *Obs.*

c **1386** CHAUCER *Prol.* 654 And priuely a fynch eek koude he pulle. **1399** LANGL. *Rich. Redeles* II. 126 ʒe..plucked and pulled hem anon to þe skynnes. *c* **1400** *Rom. Rose* 5984 If I may grype a riche man, I shal so pulle him, if I can. *c* **1450** HOLLAND *Howlat* 972 ʒe princis..That pullis the pure ay. **1589** NASHE *Pasquil's Returne* Wks. (Grosart) I. 130 The same King Lewes..vrged with extreame necessitie.. beganne at the last to pull the Church himselfe. **1627** W. HAWKINS *Apollo Shroving* II. iv. 33 Hee's a yong fat gosling to pull. **1639** S. DU VERGER tr. *Camus' Admir. Events* 146 They pull pigeons in gaming houses.

b. To seize (someone's belongings); to recall or rescind (a document). Also *absol.*

1967 S. FAESSLER in *Atlantic Monthly* Apr. 107/1 One day a month was given over to repossessing merchandise from deadbeats. 'Today I am pulling,' he would say grimly. **1972** H. KEMELMAN *Monday the Rabbi took Off* xlv. 263 'They [*sc.* the police] pulled his passport, didn't they?' 'No... Officially they had just mislaid it.' **1973** R. HAYES *Hungarian Game* lii. 312 He had moved easily in dip circles until the.. State pulled his visa.

II. To draw with force; to move or try to move or remove by such action.

7. a. *trans.* To exert upon (anything) a force that tends to snatch, draw, or drag it away; to drag or tug at.

c **1000** *Epist. Alex. ad Aristot.* in *Anglia* IV. 152 þær eac cwoman hreaþemys..and þa on ure ondwlitan sperdon and us pulledon. *c* **1400** *Destr. Troy* 8295 þai..wold haue led the lord o-lyue to þe towne, But the stoure was so stithe & stedis so thicke, Thai pullid hym with pyne, but passid þai noght. **1573–80** BARET *Alv.* P 835 To pull, or plucke the haire, *vellico*. **1585** T. WASHINGTON tr. *Nicholay's Voy.* II. xxi, After they [the shampooers] haue well pulled and stretched your armes. **1871** TYNDALL *Fragm. Sci.* (1879) I. i. 6 The sun and the earth mutually pull each other. **1878** SPURGEON *Serm.* XXIV. 653, I shall pull your coat-tail. *Mod.* Don't pull my hair; you hurt me. He complains that another boy pulled his ears.

b. *to pull by the ear, nose, sleeve*, etc., orig. perh. to draw or move by pulling at these parts; subseq. to gain attention, or to inflict corporal chastisement or insult, by such means. Phr. *to pull one's coat*: (see quot. 1946) (*U.S. Blacks*).

13.. *E.E. Allit. P.* B. 1265 Pulden prestes by þe polle & plat of her hedes. **1570** T. NORTON tr. *Nowel's Catech.* (1853) 116 Such is our dulness and forgetfulness, that we must oft be taught and put in remembrance,..and, as it were pulled by the ear. **1677** HORNECK *Gt. Law Consid.* iv. (1704) 148 This would pull them by the sleeve, and bid them look on the covetous Gehazi. *a* **1688** W. CLAGETT 17 *Serm.* (1699) 330 Their consciences had pulled every one of them for it at certain times. **1712** STEELE *Spect.* No. 268 ¶2, I very civilly requested him to remove his Hand, for which he pulled me by the Nose. **1793** J. WILLIAMS *Life Ld. Barrymore* 79 Compelled to pull him by the tail. **1946** MEZZROW & WOLFE *Really Blues* 377/2 *Pull somebody's coat*, enlighten, tip somebody off. **1971** B. MALAMUD *Tenants* 55 The black..said: 'Lesser, I have to pull your coat about a certain matter.' **1972** T. KOCHMAN *Rappin' & Stylin' Out* 163 If someone is giving you information, he is 'pulling your coat'.

c. *to pull a bell*: to pull the bell-rope or handle in order to ring the bell; so *to pull a punkah* (i.e. its rope).

a **1815** in G. Rose *Diaries* (1860) II. 438 He put out his hand to pull the bell. **1883** F. M. CRAWFORD *Mr. Isaacs* i. 25, I was engaged to pull a punkah in the house of an English lawyer.

d. *to pull* (also *draw*) *one's leg*: see LEG 2. *to pull the long-bow*: see LONG-BOW 2. In imp. phr. *pull the other one*, (*it's got bells on it*) and varr., a statement of disbelief implying suspicion that 'one's leg is being pulled'.

1849 THACKERAY *Pendennis* xxx, What is it makes him pull the long bow in that wonderful manner? **1901** G. DOUGLAS *Ho. w. Green Shutters* 216 He had pulled his leg as far as he wanted it. **1905** *Athenæum* 22 July 122/3 We..suspect that some Irish harper was 'pulling the author's leg' when he gave it. **1966** D. FRANCIS *Flying Finish* v. 63 'They are English mares going to be mated with Italian sires,' explained Conker... 'Pull the other one, it's got bells on,' said the engineer. **1973** 'S. WOODS' *Enter Corpse* 112 'Believe it or not, neither Farrell nor I has the slightest interest in the gold...' 'Pull the other one!' said Nelson derisively. **1974** M. BUTTERWORTH *Man in Sopwith Camel* viii. 84 'Pull the other leg, it's got bells on!' she said. 'A bank's a bank, and you've got yourself charge of a bank for no other reason but to dip your fingers into the till.' **1975** D. BAGLEY *Snow Tiger* ix. 88 'She doesn't hold the mineral rights.' 'Pull the other one,' scoffed Eric. **1977** J. BINGHAM *Marriage Bureau Murders* xii. 146 Pull the other one, it's got bells on it. I saw it all... So don't give me that tripe.

e. *to pull the strings, wires*: see the sbs.

f. To draw or fire (a gun). Const. *on*. Also *absol.* *U.S.*

1854 J. F. COOPER *Deerslayer* I. iii. 54, I shall not pull upon a human mortal as steadily..as I pull upon a deer. **1883** 'MARK TWAIN' *Life on Mississippi* p. xxvi, When they happened to meet, they pulled and begun. **1895** *Century Mag.* June 282/1 He repeated it, and I struck him. He pulled a pistol on me. **1903** S. E. WHITE *Forest* x. 122 The birds had proved themselves most uncultivated and rude persons by hopping promptly into the trees... I had refused to pull pistol on them. **1926** J. BLACK *You can't Win* (1927) xiii. 182 He would have 'pulled' on us. **1952** *Sun* (Baltimore) 4 July 42/7 Dr. Brady and the would-be bandit were in a middle room..when a second man suddenly appeared and one of them pulled an automatic pistol. **1978** S. BRILL *Teamsters* ii. 70 They couldn't just pull a gun on Hoffa.

g. To stretch and draw (sugar candy, etc.) until it is ready to set. orig. *U.S.*

1842 W. T. THOMPSON in *Southern Miscellany* 10 Dec. 2/6 They's pullin lasses candy in the parlor. **1893** *Harper's Mag.* Feb. 442 He pulled candy with glee, but also with eager industry, covering platter after platter with his braided sticks. **1948** *Good Housek. Cookery Bk.* III. 637 Certain toffees..are pulled, which gives them a satiny, silvery look. Attractive effects are achieved by combining pulled and unpulled toffee before cutting it into cushions. The toffee should be pulled immediately it is cool enough to handle.

h. To strain (a muscle or tendon) by abnormal exertion.

1955 M. ALLINGHAM *Beckoning Lady* iii. 35, I pulled a tendon in my foot so I'm stuck at the desk. **1955** R. BANNISTER *First Four Minutes* 175 Until then I had never been able to understand how athletes pulled muscles. **1971** *Woman's Own* 27 Mar. 8/2, I think I pulled a muscle. **1976** P. HARCOURT *Dance for Diplomats* v. 51 'You're still limping.'.. 'I must have pulled a muscle.'

8. a. To draw, drag, or haul with force or effort towards oneself (or into some position so viewed or pictured); generally with an adv. or phrase expressing direction. For use with particular advbs., see senses 21–35.

a **1300** *Leg. Rood* (1871) 60 A caudron he let fulle Wiþ seþing oile vol Inouʒ and let him þer-Inne pulle. **1377** LANGL. *P. Pl.* B. II. 219 Tyl pardoneres haued pite and pulled hym in-to house. *a* **1425** *Cursor M.* 15837 (Trin.) And as þei to & fro him pulde: his body was stounde. **1562** *Child-Marriages* 99 As she was goynge for Turves, he.. pullid her to bed to hym. **1687** *New Hampshire Prov. Papers* (1867) I. 581, I did with much difficulty pull Wiggins off the deputy governor. **1687** A. LOVELL tr. *Thevenot's Trav.* I. 58 Holding a Handkerchief about their neck with both hands they pull it sometimes this way, and sometimes that way, as if they were out of their wits with Grief. **1848** THACKERAY *Van. Fair* xxx, He placidly pulled his nightcap over his ears. **1880** 'OUIDA' *Moths* I. 31 She had pulled her blonde perruque all awry in her vexation. **1898** ROWE, etc. *Rowing* (Badm. Libr.) 26 The oarsman [will] meet his oar. By this phrase is meant that he will pull his body to his oar at last instead of his oar to his body, thus very considerably shortening his stroke.

b. *to pull in* or *to pieces*, etc., to separate the parts of (anything) forcibly; to destroy, demolish; in *Bookbinding*, simply, *to pull*; also *fig.* to analyse and criticize unfavourably; = *pick to pieces* (PICK *v.*[1] 11). *to pull an old house on one's head*: see HOUSE *sb.*[1] 19.

1552 ELYOT *Dict.*, *Distraho*..to plucke or pull in peces. **1557** N. T. (Genev.) *Acts* xxiii. 10 The Captaine, fearing lest Paul should haue bene pulled in pieces of them, commanded the soldiers [etc.]. **1642** C. VERNON *Consid. Exch.* 88 Wary how they pull an old house upon their owne heads. **1703** ROWE *Fair Penit.* Ded., Public Conversations, where every body pulls and is pulled to pieces. **1790** BURKE *Fr. Rev.* 251 The complexional disposition of some of your guides to pull every thing in pieces. **1884** H. SMART *From Post to Finish* xx, But what cannot one pull to pieces? **1901** D. COCKERELL *Bookbinding* I. ii. 34 If the book should prove to be imperfect ..the owner should be communicated with, before it is pulled to pieces. This is very important, as imperfect books that have been 'pulled' are not returnable to the bookseller. **1931** A. ESDAILE *Student's Man. Bibliogr.* vi. 194 The book must be 'pulled', i.e. taken to pieces, first.

9. a. *intr.* To perform the action of pulling; to exert drawing, dragging, or tugging force. Often with *at* = sense 7. Also *fig.*

13.. *E.E. Allit. P.* B. 68 To see hem pulle in þe plow aproche me by-houez. *c* **1435** *Torr. Portugal* 1607 Sith he pullith at his croke, So fast in to the flesh it toke. **1500–20** DUNBAR *Poems* lxxii. 110 Than pane with passioun me opprest, And ever did Petie on me pow. **1694** *Acc. Sev. Late Voy.* II. (1711) 131 Notwithstanding that the Rope of its own accord doth pull or draw very hard. **1711** ADDISON *Spect.* No. 162 ¶3 When Ambition pulls one Way, Interest another, Inclination a third. **1726** SWIFT *Gulliver* I. v, Taking the knot in my hand, [I] began to pull; but not a ship would stir. **1815** J. SMITH *Panorama Sc. & Art* I. 405 The lever at which it [the spring of a watch] pulls is lengthened as it grows weaker. **1825** J. NICHOLSON *Operat. Mechanic* 179 In double-acting engines..the piston-rod forces upwards as well as pulls. **1825** BROCKETT *N.C. Gloss.* s.v.

Pou, 'Poo away me lads'. **1841** Lane *Arab. Nts.* I. ii. 78 He pulled, but could not draw it up. **1904** W. N. Harben *Georgians* 22 So you 'n the old man are still pullin' agin one another? *Mod.* You want a horse that pulls well.

b. *spec.* Of a horse: To strain (esp. habitually and persistently) against the bit.

1791 'G. Gambado' *Ann. Horsem.* ix. (1809) 106 My horse, who pulls like the devil, was off with me in a jiffey. **1840** Blaine *Encycl. Rur. Sports* § 1258 When the free-going horse is pulling somewhat harder than [his rider] thinks it prudent to indulge him in, he is checked by a steady and firm use of the bit. **1907** *Cavalry Training* (Gen. Staff War Office) iii. § 84 Many horses never pull unless they are going beyond a certain pace, when..they get so excited that they pull very hard or run away.

c. To struggle, wrestle; to exert oneself, work hard. Cf. pull *sb.*[2] 3. *rare.*

1676 Hobbes *Iliad* xvi. 106 The sweat ran down his limbs; nor could he well, Though mightily for breath he pull'd, respire. **1829** Thackeray *Let.* in *Pendennis* Introd., I have been pulling away at the Greek play and trigonometry.

d. Phr. ***pull devil, pull baker*** (†*parson*); ***pull dog, pull cat***, an incitement to effort in a contest between two persons or parties for the possession of something; hence as *sb.* denoting such a struggle; also *attrib.*

The origin of *pull devil, pull baker*, is unascertained.

1792 Wolcott (P. Pindar) *Odes to Kien Long* ii. 128 That most important contest then is o'er; Pull Dev'l, pull Parson, will be seen no more. [**1816** Scott *Old Mort.* xxxviii, Then my mither and her quarrelled, and pu'ed me twa ways at anes, .. like Punch and the Deevil rugging about the Baker at the fair.] **1828** Abernethy *Lect. Anat., Surg.*, etc. 276 It is such a regular pull-baker pull-devil concern, it is quite shocking. **1833** Marryat *P. Simple* x, 'Pull devil, pull baker!' cried the women. **1905** *Westm. Gaz.* 21 Mar. 2/1 In practice tariffs are determined by the pull-devil-pull-baker principle. **1907** *Daily Chron.* 22 Mar. 3/4 It's pull dog, pull cat wi' man and woman, ever since the days of the apple.

e. To move, go, go on, or proceed by pulling or by some exertion of force; cf. 29 d.

1877 M. Reynolds *Locom. Engine Driving* i. viii. (ed. 5) 131 The guard got up on the step of the engine, when they pulled gently down to the scene. **1891** Kipling *Light that Failed* (1900) 251 We'll pull out of this place, Bess, and get away as far as ever we can.

f. *transf.* Of the engine of a motor vehicle: to afford (adequate) propulsive force; hence, by metonymy, of the vehicle itself.

1902 C. S. Rolls in A. C. Harmsworth et al. *Motors* ix. 175 Motor will not 'pull' well or misses fire. **1933** J. Buchan *Prince of Captivity* iii. ii. 282 The driver stopped to examine his engine. 'She pulls badly, *mein Herr*,' he said. **1974** P. Wright *Lang. Brit. Industry* i. 24 Another transport term, *the bus* (or *car*) *won't pull*, is from the days of the horse and cart.

†**10. a.** *trans.* To take away forcibly or with difficulty; to tear off, to wrench away. *Obs.*

c **1400** *Destr. Troy* 7289 His pray [was] fro hym puld, & his pepull slayn. **1530** Rastell *Bk. Purgat.* iii. vii. 3 Than the soule [is] immedyatly pulled and separate from the body by naturall dethe. **1542–5** Brinklow *Lament.* (1874) 117 It is hyghe tyme to pull from them that wycked Mammon. **1603** Dekker *Grissil* (Shaks. Soc.) 10, I, that have..from my father Pull'd more than he could spare. **1616** R. C. *Times' Whistle* i. 322 Subtillie devisd'e only for private gaines, Which you pull from the simple as you list. **1625** Burges *Pers. Tithes* 11 To pull the poore mans bread out of his belly.

†**b.** *Arith.* To subtract. *Obs.*

1571 Digges *Pantom.* i. xiii. D iv b, If you haue made two stations, pull the lesse Quotient from the great. **1574** Bourne *Regiment for Sea* vii. (1577) 30 You must pul the heigth of the Equinoctiall from the Horizon.

11. *fig.* **a.** To draw or move by force or influence other than physical; to bring forcibly into or out of some state or condition. Now *rare* or *Obs.*

c **1400** *Destr. Troy* 10489 Parys full priuely sho pulled into councell. *c* **1483** H. Baradoun in *Pol. Rel. & L. Poems* (1903) 290 Anon ther is some obstacle or thyng That pullyth me thens, magre of my might. **1589** *Hay any Work* (1844) 71 To pull the pride of Gods enemy an ase lower. **1642** Rogers *Naaman* 38 When long-suffering hath spent it selfe in pulling them to repentance. **1676** Dryden *Aurengzebe* i. i, Thou should'st have pull'd the Secret from my Breast, Torn out the bearded Steel to give me Rest. **1725** Pope *Odyss.* xv. 349 Their wrongs and blasphemies ascend the sky, And pull descending vengeance from on high.

†**b.** To bring or draw (evil, calamity) *upon*. *Obs.* (superseded by draw *v.* 31).

1550 Crowley *Way to Wealth* B iv b, Bi pulling vpon your self that vengeaunce of God. **1621** Burton *Anat. Mel.* i. i. i. i. (1651) 2 Crying sins..which pull these several plagues ..upon our heads. **1662** Hibbert *Body Div.* i. 333 Sin pulls sickness upon us. **1690** W. Walker *Idiomat. Anglo-Lat.* 333 To pull mischief on one's pate.

c. *intr.* To exert influence or 'root' *for* (a person, etc.); to sympathize with, favour. Chiefly *N. Amer.*

1903 C. B. Gilbert in *Forum* (N.Y.) XXXV. 311 Such committees are exposed to all kinds..of influence..all pulling for this or that applicant. **1922** G. Ade *Let.* 22 Nov. (1973) 85 Tomorrow I go up to LaFayette to pull for Purdue against Indiana and I hope we may win at least one game. **1949** *National Geogr. Mag.* Sept. 321/1 I'm usually pulling for the Indians instead of the cowboys. **1968** *Globe & Mail* (Toronto) 17 Feb. 39 It sure helps to get this evidence that so many people at home are pulling for us. **1970** G. F. Newman *Sir, You Bastard* ii. 73 The Governor was pulling for him with the Divisional D[etective] C[hief] S[uperintendent].

d. *trans.* To attract (custom); to secure (patronage). Freq. *absol.*

1905 Calkins & Holden *Mod. Advertising* xi. 264 The advertiser likes to know which particular mediums pull best. **1929** L. F. Carr *America Challenged* 96 Both Republicans and Democrats have tried to pull the farmer vote by favoring legislation which the Populists had demanded. **1938** S. V. Benét *Thirteen O'Clock* iv. 234 I'd done some advertising copy for the firm that pulled. **1962** R. Stout *Gambit* (1963) iii. 36 She attracts. She pulls. **1974** S. Marcus *Minding Store* (1975) xi. 228 The booklets pulled fairly well, both in store response and through the mails. **1976** *Record Mirror* 3 Apr. 21/1 Brook Benton..can still regularly pull standing-room-only audiences for his live gigs.

e. *N.Z.* (See quot. 1933.)

1933 L. G. D. Acland in *Press* (Christchurch, N.Z.) 18 Nov. 15/7 *Pull*, a dog *pulls* sheep when he brings them towards his masters. **1935** G. L. Meredith *Adventuring in Maoriland* v. 47 [The dog] eventually 'pulled' the mob on the slope of a hill. **1938** R. Burdon *High Country* x. 107 The heading dog is silent and is used to 'pull' or bring sheep back to the shepherd.

f. To earn (a wage or salary). See also *pull down* (sense 25 f) and *pull in* (sense 26 b). *colloq.*

1937 'M. Innes' *Hamlet, Revenge!* ii. viii. 197 I'm twenty-two and pulling twelve pounds a week.

g. *coarse slang.* To pick up a partner (for sexual purposes); *spec.* to copulate with. So ***to pull a train***, to copulate successively with more than one partner.

1965 C. Brown *Manchild in Promised Land* i. 15 They thought that I was one of the guys who had pulled a train on their sister in the park the summer before. *Ibid.* iv. 112 If you gon pull a bitch, you can'[t] get excited and let her know that you want that pussy so bad you about to go crazy. **1965** *Sunday Express* 25 July 17/2 As a young man I could never pull (pick up) any birds of my own class. **1973** M. Amis *Rachel Papers* 23, I could easily pull the village idiotess, who in any case, one windless summer night, had wanked Geoffrey and me off through the school railings, simultaneously. **1973** Boyd & Parkes *Dark Number* vi. 69 Five years ago you did the big male-menopause bit, didn't you? Skulking off to Paris to prove you could still pull the birds. **1973** P. Cave *Speed Freaks* viii. 77 'Wanna pull a train for the movie?' Mucky asked Dodo, who was still unclothed. She shrugged resignedly. **1974** H. L. Foster *Ribbin'* iv. 148 To 'pull a train' is for a female to have consecutive sexual intercourse with numbers of males. The female pulling the train may do so voluntarily for financial remuneration, forcefully, or out of fear. *Ibid.* 149 Trains are pulled everywhere... Selby..described Tralala pulling endless trains in Brooklyn. **1976** P. Cave *High Flying Birds* iv. 47 She's certainly worth pulling... But I reckon you can forget it as long as she's got her mother with her.

12. a. To take a draught or drink of (liquor); to draw or suck (a draught of liquor) into the mouth; to drink from (a vessel); also ***to pull off***. Also *absol.*

[Perhaps orig. suggested by Du., LG. *pull-en*, EFris. *püll-en* to drink (esp. from a jug or bottle), to tipple, f. obs. Du. *pulle* (mod. *pul*), LG. *pulle*, EFris. *pülle*, *pül* a jug, stone bottle, held by continental etymologists to be a shortening of MDu. *ampulle* ampul; but evidently viewed in Eng. as a sense of the native vb.: cf. pull *sb.*[2] 5.]

1436 *Libel Eng. Policy* v. in *Pol. Poems* (Rolls) II. 169 That twoo Fflemmynges togedere wol undertake..or they rise onys, to drinke a barelle fulle, of gode berkyne: so sore they hale and pulle. *c* **1450** *Cov. Myst.* xiv. (Shaks. Soc.) 142 Syr, in good ffeyth oo draught I pulle. **1595** *Locrine* ii. ii. 147 This makes us work for company To pull the tankards cheerfully. **1608** Healey *Discov. New World* 59 Now so many stoopes must hee pull of, or else hee is held an vngratefull, vnmannerly fellow. **1751** R. Paltock *P. Wilkins* xxviii. (1883) 79/2, I set a bowl of punch before them..which they pulled off plentifully. **1820** J. H. Reynolds *Fancy* 22 Give us the keg, we'll pull a little Deady.

b. *intr.* To draw or suck *at* (a pipe, cigar, etc.). Also const. *on.*

1861 Dickens *Gt. Expect.* xv, Joe..pulled hard at his pipe. **1888** Rider Haggard *Col. Quaritch* v, He sat there.. and pulled at his empty pipe. **1897** T. De Leon *Novelette Trilogy* v. 44 He..strode rapidly homeward; pulling hard.. on the dead cigar between his lips.

c. *trans.* To draw (beer) from a keg, etc., by means of a pump or tap.

1969 *Sydney Morning Herald* 24 May 1/10 During Thursday's strike by hotel staff, the manager..pulled 17$\frac{1}{2}$ 18-gallon kegs from two taps between 10 a.m. and 10 p.m. **1975** M. Kenyon *Mr Big* v. 46 The muscled barmaid pulled pints.

13. *trans.* Uses implying an adv. †**a.** = *pull down* (25) (*obs.*). **b.** = *pull off* (27 a).

a. *a* **1607** Shaks. *Cor.* iii. ii. 1 Let them pull all about mine Eares, present me Death on the Wheele. *a* **1621** Fletcher *Isl. Princess* ii. i, I'le pull your courage, King. *a* **1623** —— *Wife for Month* v. iii, His ranke flesh shall be pull'd with daily fasting. **1655** *Nicholas Papers* (Camden) II. 158 These last fitts of discontent..have soe pulled the Queene that she may want strength to see another sommer.

b. **1888** Bryce *Amer. Commw.* II. App. 641 They pull their coats. The field is worked row by row and hill by hill.

III. In technical senses, with specific objects expressed or understood.

14. *trans. Printing.* In the old hand-press, To draw (the bar of the press) towards one, so as to press down the platen upon the sheet or forme; also *intr.* or *absol.* Hence, To print upon (a sheet) or from (a forme) in this way; to make or take (an impression, proof, or copy) by printing; to print off.

a. *trans.* **1683** Moxon *Mech. Exerc., Printing* xxiv. ¶ 7 Then..Running in the Carriage, [he] Pulls that Sheet. *Ibid.*, If the Impression of the last Pulled Side, stands within the Impression of the first Pulled Side. **1771** Luckombe *Hist. Printing* 336 He lays another sheet..upon the Tympan-sheet.., and Pulls these two sheets. Then he.. turns the other side of the Register-Sheet..and Pulls upon that the second side of the Register-sheet. *Ibid.* 357 The Press-man..Pulls the Bar towards him. **1876** Trevelyan *Macaulay* (1880) I. 172 The sheets had been pulled. **1881** *Times* 4 Jan. 3/6 The remainder of the bitumen film is removed and impressions are pulled from it like any other etched plate. **1882** J. Southward *Pract. Print.* (1884) 418 One of them pulls or works the [hand] press. **1900** *Pall Mall Mag.* Oct. 179 A few copies were pulled before the disaster occurred.

b. *intr.* or *absol.* **1653** Urquhart *Rabelais* i. li, He appointed them to pull at the Presses of his Printing-house, which he had set up. **1683** Moxon *Mech. Exerc., Printing* xxiv. ¶ 7 He..turns down the Frisket and Tympan on the Form..and Pulls as before. **1771** Luckombe *Hist. Printing* 365 His Companion that Pulls..casts his eye upon every single sheet.

15. a. *intr.* or *absol.* To pull an oar so as to move a boat; to row; to transport or convey oneself in a boat; to proceed by rowing.

1676 Shadwell *Virtuoso* ii. 20 Come along, pull away, Boys. Now, my choice Lads. **1697** Dampier *Voy. round World* (1699) 498 *Pull away*, an expression usual among English Seamen, when they are Rowing. **1748** *Anson's Voy.* ii. ix. 230 They exerted their utmost strength in pulling out to sea. **1855** Macaulay *Hist. Eng.* xx. IV. 511 He ordered his men to pull for the beach. **1859** Green *Oxf. Stud.* i. (O.H.S.) 17 Familiar to Oxford men pulling lazily on a summer's noon to Godstow. **1907** Griffith John *Voice fr. China* xi. 222 We pulled out and anchored in mid-stream.

b. *trans.* To pull (an oar or sculls); hence, to row, to propel (a boat) by rowing; to transport or convey in a boat by rowing.

to pull one's weight, to row with effect in proportion to one's weight; also *fig.*, to perform one's share of work, to take one's share of responsibility; also ***to pull weight***. ***to pull stroke***: see stroke *sb.*

1820 J. H. Reynolds *Fancy* (1906) 35 And oft on Sundays, scorning land,.. I've pulled a girl, with blister'd hand, And bleeding heart, through Chelsea Reach! **1835** Marryat *Jac. Faithf.* xxi, You know old deaf Stapleton, whose wherry we have so often pulled up and down the river? **1840** R. H. Dana *Bef. Mast* xiv. 36 The next day we pulled the agent ashore. **1854** Thackeray *Newcomes* xxx, Lady Kew still pulls stroke oar in our boat. **1865** Dickens *Mut. Fr.* i. i, The girl rowed, pulling a pair of sculls very easily. **1897** *Daily News* 10 Feb. 6/3 In boating phraseology, he 'pulled his weight'..; he was not a mere passenger. **1904** Kipling *Traffics & Discoveries* 278 They need a lot of working up before they can pull their weight in the boat. **1921** [see weight *sb.*[1] 10 c]. **1925** E. F. Norton *Fight for Everest: 1924* 98 No members of the climbing party pulled more weight in the team than these two by their unostentatious unselfish gruelling work. **1931** *Times* 27 Feb. 16/5 Referring to people in the administrative grade who did not 'pull their weight', Sir Alfred Woodgate said that assistant principals who had been twice passed over for promotion to principals were a menace to the office and should not be allowed to remain. **1948** M. Laski *Tory Heaven* x. 138 Lord Starveleigh asked him down to address the electors... We're all expected to pull our weight, you know. **1976** J. B. Hilton *Gamekeeper's Gallows* xii. 115 How long was he going to put up with me living off the fat of the land in his kitchen, not pulling my weight with his other servants?

c. Of a boat: (*a*) *intr.* with passive sense, to be pulled or rowed. (*b*) *trans.* ***to pull*** (*so many*) ***oars***, to be fitted for, or be rowed with (so many) oars.

1804 in Nicolas *Disp. Nelson* (1845) V. 496 She should be fitted so as to pull thirty-eight sweeps and two skulls. **1805** J. Smith in *Naval Chron.* XV. 75 The other [boat], from pulling heavy, not being able to get up. **1829** *Chron.* in *Ann. Reg.* 127/1 She pulls six oars. **1836** Marryat *Midsh. Easy* xiii, The boats pulled in shore.

16. *trans.* To arrest in the name of justice. Also, to make a raid on (a gambling house, etc.). *slang.* Cf. *pull up* (35 d) and *pull in* (sense 26 e).

1811 *Lex. Balatr.* s.v., To be pulled; to be arrested by a police officer. *c* **1811** in Farmer *Musa Pedestris* (1896) 77 He had twice been pull'd,..but got off by going to sea. **1871** *Figaro* 15 Apr. 5/2 The police 'pulled' every Keno establishment in the city. 'Pulling' is the slang for seizing the instruments, and arresting the players and proprietors. **1888** Rider Haggard *Col. Quaritch* xxxiv, He pulled me, and I was fined two pounds by the beak. **1907** J. Masefield *Tarpaulin Muster* 205 The police entered..and 'pulled the joint'—that is, they arrested and fined the proprietor. **1931** 'D. Stiff' *Milk & Honey Route* 189 He's pulled for a vag, his excuses won't do. 'Thirty days,' said the judge. **1950** Wodehouse *Nothing Serious* 244 Doom had come upon The Cedars... The joint had been pulled. **1970** G. F. Newman *Sir, You Bastard* 10 They..pulled drunks and bathed tramps, saw children across the road and directed traffic.

17. a. *Racing.* To hold in or check (a horse), *esp.* so as to cause it to lose in a race. Also *absol.* In quot. 1906 *fig.* to check, keep back.

c **1800** S. Chifney in H. H. Dixon *Post & Paddock* v. (1856) 84 The phrase at Newmarket is, that you should pull your horse to ease him in his running... He should be enticed to ease himself an inch at a time. **1861** Whyte Melville *Good for N.* xxviii, If you were there [at the Derby], you'll agree with me that Belphegor was pulled. **1888** Sir C. Russell in *Times* 26 June 4/4 If jockeys pulled horses in order to prevent them from winning. **1889** *Tablet* 6 July 11/2 Whether a jockey rides to win or has been bribed to pull. **1906** R. Kipling in *Westm. Gaz.* 20 Oct. 16/1 My point is that the books were 'pulled' simply and solely because they were not sold to the 'Times' on terms which would have enabled the 'Times' to undersell the booksellers.

b. *Boxing.* In phr. ***to pull one's punches***, to hold back or check one's blows. Also *fig.*, to use less force than one is capable of exerting, to be gentle or lenient, esp. in criticism or punishment.

1934 in WEBSTER. **1937** H. L. ICKES *Secret Diary* (1954) II. 88 He talked about the judiciary and he didn't pull his punches at any time, although neither was he in any degree personal. **1939** L. JACOBS *Rise of Amer. Film* 459 Either because Vidor 'pulled his punches' at the revolution or because..he was confused. **1947** *People* 22 June 5/3 Two of his boys recently fought for two solid hours—and no pulled punches—to provide a minute and a half's action in the actual film. **1955** A. L. ROWSE *Expansion Eliz. Eng.* 133 He charges Ormonde with..pulling his punches in pursuit of the rebels. **1957** D. J. ENRIGHT *Apothecary's Shop* 209 The fact—not a new one—that Eliot doesn't pull his punches. **1960** *Times* 4 Feb. 11/2 Lady Albemarle's committee have not pulled their punches. **1973** P. O'DONNELL *Silver Mistress* xi. 191 It was a demonstration match. The kicks, chops and punches were pulled at the last instant. **1977** *Time Out* 28 Jan.–3 Feb. 33/3 The film pulls all its political punches, settling instead for sentimental narrative.

18. *Cricket.* To strike (a ball) from the off to the leg side; also *transf.* with the bowler as obj. So in *Golf*, to drive a ball widely to the left. Also *absol.* = DRAW *v.* 14. Subsequently also used in *Baseball* (see quot. 1976).

1851 W. CLARK in W. Bolland *Cricket Notes* 143 Never try to pull a straight ball across you. **1884** *Lillywhite's Cricket Ann.* 122 His tendency to pull lost him his wicket more than once. **1892** *Daily News* 17 June 3/7 In trying to pull a ball, he was easily caught at mid-on. **1894** *Westm. Gaz.* 30 June 6/2 At 119 Briggs was bowled in attempting to pull Martin. **1897** RANJITSINHJI *Cricket* 156 There are players who can pull with great effect. **1899** *Westm. Gaz.* 25 Aug. 3/1 Errors of style which cause you to top, slice, or pull your strokes [at golf]. **1901** *Scotsman* 9 Sept. 4/7 At the fifth Vardon pulled his second under a fence. **1943** *Amer. Speech* XVIII. 105 If he can *pull* or *place* the ball he has a better chance of getting a hit. **1976** *Webster's Sports Dict.* 334/1 *Pull*,..[in baseball] to hit the ball to the field on the same side of the plate as the batter stands when he takes his normal position in the batter's box.

19. *Oil Industry.* To pull up or withdraw (casing, etc.) from a well.

1916 JOHNSON & HUNTLEY *Princ. Oil & Gas Production* xiv. 154 The hole in most cases gradually fills up at the bottom with cavings from the walls and sometimes from the roof of the oil sand. This makes it necessary to pull the tubing and clean the well. **1938** L. V. W. CLARK in A. E. Dunstan et al. *Sci. of Petroleum* I. ix. 434/2 In this position the string may be rotated as well as pulled or lowered. **1960** C. GATLIN *Petroleum Engin.* x. 170/1 A sudden decrease in penetration rate..may mean that the inner barrel is jammed or plugged and the assembly should be pulled for inspection. **1974** P. L. MOORE et al. *Drilling Practices Man.* xii. 308 If the well kicks when pulling the drill string, the formation fluid will enter the entire well bore below the drill string.

IV. Phrases. **20. a.** *to pull a face, faces*: to draw the countenance into a grimace, to distort the features: see FACE *sb.* 6 b; *to pull a* (*sanctimonious*, etc.) *face*, to put on an expression of the specified kind; *to pull a long face*: see LONG *a.*[1] 1 c.

1828 *Craven Gloss.* (ed. 2), *Pull-faces*, to distort the features. *a* **1845** HOOD *T. Trumpet* xxviii, Just suppose.. You see a great fellow a-pulling a face. —— *Ode to Rae Wilson* iv, No solemn sanctimonious face I pull. **1855** THACKERAY *Rose & Ring* vi, The Lord Chancellor..pulled a very long face because the prince could not be got to study the Paflagonian laws. **1877** MRS. FORRESTER *Mignon* I. 162 Don't pull sucht a long face.

b. *to pull foot*, also *to pull it*, to run away, to take to one's heels; to run with all one's might; see FOOT *sb.* 29. *to pull one's freight* (*U.S.*) to depart quickly. *colloq.*

1804 FESSENDEN *Yankee Doodle* Poems 96 She flew straight out of sight As fast as she could pull it. **1818** [see FOOT *sb.* 29]. **1833** M. SCOTT *Tom Cringle* xi. (1842) 251 The whole crew pulled foot as if Old Nick had held them in chase. **1876** *Whitby Gloss.*, *Pull feeat.* 'Thoo'l hae te pull feeat te owertak 'em'. **1895** F. REMINGTON *Pony Tracks* 252 The wily old fellow..had discreetly 'pulled his freight'. **1905** 'O. HENRY' in *Everybody's Mag.* XIII. 814/2 The Kid ..considered it not incompatible with his indisputable gameness to perform that judicious tractional act known as 'pulling his freight'. **1913** J. LONDON *Valley of Moon* II. xvii. 277, I guess we got a celebration comin', seein' as we're going to pull up stakes an' pull our freight from the old burg. **1926** in J. F. Dobie *Rainbow in Morning* (1965) 84 He pulled his freight in a hurry.

c. *to pull a boner* (etc.), to make a foolish mistake (BONER[2]). *U.S. slang.*

1913 [see BONER[2]]. **1926** *Scribner's Mag.* Sept. 246/1 The Washington newspaper correspondents are the pick of the land, and their dinners are not the softest spots in the lives of the speakers. It is no place to pull a bloomer. **1929** M. LIEF *Hangover* xv. 234, I pulled an awful boner when I was up in Newport last summer. *Ibid.*, That's nothing... I pulled a dumber thing than that once. **1967** *Boston Sunday Globe* 23 Apr. B 41/1 Apart from the shabby methods used by construction workers, who have been known to pull some boners, Moscovites are subjected to some truly baffling beauts from bumbling builders.

d. In various colloq. phrases denoting action or speech intended to deceive, shock, or amuse, as *to pull a fast one* (see FAST *a.* 11), *to pull a gag*, *to pull a trick*, etc.

1914 'HIGH JINKS, JR.' *Choice Slang* 17 *Pull a punk one* (*to*), to tell a poor joke. **1915** [see DOPE *sb.* 4]. **1922** G. ADE *Let.* 11 Oct. (1973) 83 The plot of the piece was that George and Frank both loved the same girl and Frank pulled a lot of dirty stuff and deceived the girl for a while but eventually virtue triumphed. **1929** M. LIEF *Hangover* xv. 235, I can tell you about the gag one of our better-known critics pulled in his review of Dillingham's new musical comedy. **1932** E. WALLACE *When Gangs came to London* xxiii. 232 'Fantastical,' suggested Jiggs. 'I'm getting quite used to the word. It's the one you pull when any hard-sense suggestion is made to you.' **1937** G. HEYER *They found him Dead* xiii. 260 Not that I think anyone would pull the same trick twice. **1940** WODEHOUSE *Eggs, Beans & Crumpets* 238 Your aunt.. has a right to early information about any rough stuff that is being pulled on the premises. **1957** H. ROOSENBURG *Walls came tumbling Down* ix. 208 Just be a little more careful about your company next time you pull a stunt like that. **1976** M. MACHLIN *Pipeline* xxviii. 333 For Christ sake, don't think about pulling any movie-type heroics. **1978** *Guardian Weekly* 2 Apr. 6/5 Many [U.S. coal] miners are now threatening to pull wildcat strikes.

e. *to pull a job, robbery* (etc.), to commit a crime, usu. theft. *colloq.* (chiefly *U.S.*).

1915 *Policeman's Monthly* Dec. 17/3 He replied that he had often noticed just before they were going to 'pull a job' his partner was happy. **1923** 'B. L. STANDISH' *Lego Lamb, Southpaw* viii. 58 Yet, by your own confession, you came over here to 'pull a job'. **1937** *Research Stud. State Coll. Washington* Mar. 19 Some boys think its an honor..to say.. that they pulled jobs with such and such gangsters. **1967** [see GRAFT *v.*[4]]. **1972** J. WAMBAUGH *Blue Knight* (1973) i. 28 A federal fugitive who..carried a gun and pulled stickups. **1973** E. BULLINS *Theme is Blackness* 160 Tootsie didn't work steady but we still ran together. Even pulled an occasional job. **1973** *Philadelphia Inquirer* (Today Suppl.) 7 Oct. 14/1, I even pulled three robberies in one night—two drugstores and a haberdashery. **1978** *Detroit Free Press* 5 Mar. B 1/1, I suggested we pull a robbery.

f. *to pull leather*, to grasp the saddle horn in order to avoid being thrown from a bucking horse (see also quot. 1933). *U.S.*

1916 *Daily Colonist* (Victoria, B.C.) 19 July 5/4 They [*sc.* bad horses] are still outlaws and..are guaranteed to send almost any rider to pulling leather. **1923** J. H. COOK *50 Yrs. Old Frontier* 16 He certainly made me 'pull leather', and I clung to his mane as well in order to keep in close touch with him. **1925** C. E. MULFORD *Cottonwood Gulch* v. 60, I'm pullin' leather, but I'm stickin' to the saddle. **1933** J. V. ALLEN *Cowboy Lore* III. 59/2 *Pulling leather*, holding on to the saddle with the hands while riding a bucking animal, prohibited by the rules of all contests and scorned by all real cowboys.

g. *to pull* (*one's*) *rank*, to employ (one's) superior status in exacting obedience, co-operation, or privilege. Also *to pull stripes* (etc.). orig. *U.S.*

1923 *Amer. Legion Weekly* 23 Feb. 18 Don't pull your rank on him, K.P. You were only a private yourself, once. **1926** *Amer. Speech* II. 62/2 Give him..officers who do not 'pull rank', and he is well content. **1958** V. CANNING *Dragon Tree* 90 He disliked pulling his rank to claim any personal privileges. **1958** M. K. JOSEPH *I'll soldier no More* xii. 242 Don't you pull your stripes on me, sarge. **1959** N. MAILER *Advts. for Myself* (1961) 228 Teddy pulled seniority and they gave him his way. **1976** H. MACINNES *Agent in Place* xiv. 148 'What if he refuses to go with them?' 'They'll be senior men, they'll pull rank.'

h. *to pull a* (proper name), to imitate, to behave in the manner of (the person named). *colloq.* (orig. *U.S.*).

1927 *New Republic* 9 Mar. 72/1 The following is a partial list of words denoting drunkenness now in common use in the United States... To pull a Daniel Boone. **1931** *Technol. Rev.* Nov. 67/1 *To pull a Lindbergh* means to do something heroic, but *to go Lindbergh* means to get the flying fever in a rather callow manner. **1935** WODEHOUSE *Luck of Bodkins* xiii. 133 He'll be much happier in the long run if he gets it into his bean that he can't pull a James Cagney on me every time he's a mite upset.

i. *to pull one's pud*(*ding*) or *wire*: to masturbate. *slang.*

1944 [see PUD *sb.*[3] 2]. **1961** PARTRIDGE *Dict. Slang* Suppl. 1101/2 *Pull one's pudding*,..may have originated *pull one's wire*. **1970** J. OSBORNE *Right Prospectus* 30 Remember what I said about sex. Keep away from the maids and pretty boys. As for pulling your wire, that's no occupation for a gentleman. **1970** W. SMITH *Gold Mine* xxvi. 61 Jesus... That was ugly. I felt like a peeping tom, watching someone, you know, pulling his pudding.

j. *to pull the rug* (*out*) *from under* (a person or thing), and varr., to weaken or unsettle (something) by an unexpected withdrawal of support or by some other action; to let down or betray (someone). *colloq.* (orig. *U.S.*).

1946 *Time* 23 Dec. 17/3 Strikes, for instance, would pull the rug out from under the best of prospects. **1948** *Sun* (Baltimore) 15 Dec. 8/3 Although both are reported to feel that United States commitments in western Europe preclude the 'bailing out' of Chiang's regime..they have chosen to say nothing that would 'pull the rug out' from under Chiang. **1952** *Manch. Guardian Weekly* 14 Aug. 3/2 What the President [*sc.* Truman] was talking about was his own part in clinching the nomination of Governor Stevenson. It entailed pulling the rug out from under Mr. Harriman. **1966** 'W. HAGGARD' *Power House* xvi. 179 James Mott had Victor's story... At the worst it could pull the carpet out. **1967** A. HUNTER *Gently Continental* ix. 132 The mat is pulled from under Shelton when he dares to assent to this point. **1973** *Physics Bull.* Feb. 75/2 Professor Jewkes.. proceeds to pull the rug from under many of the assumptions and arguments used to justify government support of 'high technologies'. **1974** W. GARNER *Big enough Wreath* xiii. 196 He did his last job for you... Not too successfully..which is another reason for pulling the rug from under. **1978** *Detroit Free Press* 2 Apr. C 12/2 When the rug was pulled out from under me in movies and television I went back to the theater.

k. Other phrases mentioned under senses.

pull caps, wigs: see sense 2; *p. a crow*, 5; *p. by the ear, the nose*, etc., 7 b; *p. a finch*, 6; *p. one's coat*, 7 b; *p. on one's head*, 8 b; *p. one's leg*, *p. the long bow*, 7 d; *p. the other one*, 7 d; *p. in or to pieces*, 8 b; *p. a pigeon, a plover*, 6; *p. for prime*, 3; *p. one's punches*, 17 b; *p. the strings, the wires*, 7 e; *p. a train*, 11 g; *p. one's weight*, 15 b.

V. With adverbs.

21. pull about. *trans.* To pull from side to side, this way and that way; *colloq.* to treat roughly, unceremoniously, or as a subject for arbitrary operations.

17.. *Cock Robin's Courtship*, In came the Cuckoo..He caught hold of Jenny, and pulled her about. *a* **1825** FORBY *Voc. E. Anglia*, *Pulling-time*, the evening of the fair-day when the wenches are pulled about. **1855** MACAULAY *Hist. Eng.* xviii. IV. 230 More than three years before, they had pulled him about and called him Hatchetface. **1865** W. WHITE *E. Eng.* II. 67 He's hevin' his place pull'd about. **1905** E. F. BENSON *Act in Backwater* xix, If there is one thing I dread, it is being pulled about by a professional man [i.e. a surgeon].

22. pull apart, asunder. *trans.* To separate by pulling.

1362 LANGL. *P. Pl.* A. VIII. 100 And Pers, for puire teone pollede hit a-sonder. **1545** ELYOT *Dict.*, *Distractio*, separacion, alienacion, or pullynge away, or a sunder. **1565** COOPER *Thesaurus*, *Distrahere cohærentia*, to pull a sunder or seperate thynges ioyned. **1796** C. MARSHALL *Garden.* v. (1813) 68 Either carefully pulled, or cut asunder with a sharp instrument; as the case may require.

23. pull away. a. *trans.* To pluck or snatch away; to withdraw or remove by force.

† *pull away the shoulder*, to turn away, turn a deaf ear. **1387** TREVISA *Higden* (Rolls) VII. 185 Þe grave i-pulled away, he spak to seint Cuthbert. **1430–40** LYDG. *Bochas* IV. vi. (1554) 104 Whan he gan away the mantel pul. *c* **1440** *Pallad. on Husb.* IV. 152 Pulle euery blacke away that thou may fynde. **1599** HAKLUYT *Voy.* II. 290 The Azamoglans, tribute children,..are collected from among the Christians, from whom..they are pulled away yeerely perforce. **1611** BIBLE *Zech.* vii. 11 They refused to hearken, and pulled away the shoulder. **1681** FLAVEL *Meth. Grace* ix. 187 If men ..pull away the shoulder from you, and will not be concerned about your troubles.

b. *intr.* (Cf. 15 and AWAY 7.)

c. Of a vehicle: to draw away, as *from* the kerb on starting. Also *absol.*

1955 H. KURNITZ *Invasion of Privacy* (1956) iv. 32 The grey convertible..pulled away from the curb. **1974** *Sunday Post* (Glasgow) 14 Apr. 6/2 As it [*sc.* a bus] pulled away I was horrified to see a man..pick up the old gents shopping bag and hurry away. **1976** 'P. B. YUILL' *Hazell & Menacing Jester* iv. 44 He was pulling away from the kerb before my reggie reached the upholstery.

24. pull back. a. See simple senses and BACK *adv.* **b.** *trans.* To draw or keep back (in space or in progress). **c.** To date further back. † **d.** To subtract. † **e.** To remove, withdraw.

1559 BP. SCOT in Strype *Ann. Ref.* (1709) I. App. vii. 12 Ther be two thinges that do..as it were, pull me backe from speaking. **1574** BOURNE *Regiment for Sea* xix. (1577) 51 You must pull backe so much from the poynt that the shippe hath sayled by, as the heygth of the pole doth shewe vnto you. **1610** WILLET *Hexapla Dan.* 298 Then must the beginning of Cyrus raigne be pulled back an 11. yeares. **1656** RIDGLEY *Pract. Physick* 217 The cause must be pulled back by opening the Liver Vein. **1701** STANHOPE tr. *Augustine's Medit.* ii. 6 The wickedness of my own heart dismays and pulls me back. *Mod.* He caught cold on the way home, which has pulled him back considerably.

f. *Sport.* To score (a goal) restoring, or serving towards restoring, level terms between two teams.

1976 *Northumberland Gaz.* 26 Nov. 20/6 Nicholson was on hand to score from the rebound. Annitsford pulled one back but Nicholson was then again on target with a magnificent shot. **1978** *Lochaber News* 31 Mar. 20/3 In the 60th minute Donald Murchison pulled one back. Five minutes later Mike MacPherson equalised.

25. pull down. a. See simple senses and DOWN *adv.*

[**1377** LANGL. *P. Pl.* B. XVI. 73, I prayed pieres to pulle adown an apple.] **1530** PALSGR. 669/1 Pull hym downe out of the tre. **1695** J. EDWARDS *Perfect. Script.* 554 That temporal punishment which the Corinthians pull'd down upon their heads. **1861** DICKENS *Gt. Expect.* xlvi, He should pull down the blind.

b. *trans.* To demolish, lay in ruins, destroy (a building).

1513 in G. P. Scrope *Castle Combe* (1852) 291 *note*, Saynd hye wold polle don the tyllys of my hos. **1560** DAUS tr. *Sleidane's Comm.* 219 The house should be pulled downe. **1560** BIBLE (Genev.) *Luke* xii. 18, I wil pul downe my barnes, and buylde greater. **1677** *Providence Rec.* (1895) VIII. 16 Such as haue set vp fences in ye Common..the Councell shall cause them to be pulled downe. **1712** HEARNE *Collect.* (O.H.S.) III. 294 This Day they began to pull down the Printing House by the Theater. **1891** *Law Rep.*, *Weekly Notes* 78/2 Desirous of pulling the house down and building a new one on its site.

c. To seize and bring to the ground; to overcome (a hunted animal).

1709 STEELE *Tatler* No. 76 ¶ 1 The last Stag that was pull'd down. **1886** HAWLEY SMART *Outsider* i, You weren't within half a field of the fair unknown when they pulled the fox down.

d. To lower or depress in health, spirits, size, strength, value, etc.; also, to 'bring low', to humble, humiliate. † *to pull down a side* = to pluck down a side: see PLUCK *v.* 3 b.

a **1586** SIDNEY *Ps.* xxxv. vi, I did pull down my self, fasting for such. **1607** *3rd Rep. Hist. MSS. Comm.* 53/2 They haue two tons of sassafras, which if thrown on the market..will pull down the price for a long time. **1636** MASSINGER *Gt. Dk. Florence* IV. ii, If I hold your card, I shall pull down the side, I am not good at the game. **1743** BLAIR *Grave* 260 A fit of common sickness pulls thee down With greater ease. **1822** COBBETT *Weekly Reg.* 9 Mar. 600 Paper-money pulls down the value of gold. **1890** *Spectator* 23 Aug., To pull down the average.

e. To depose or dethrone (a sovereign) violently; to overthrow (a government) by force.

1828 MACAULAY *Ess., Hallam* (1872) 71 In such times a sovereign like Louis the Fifteenth.. would have been pulled down before his misgovernment had lasted for a month. **1855** —— *Hist. Eng.* xiv. III. 442 One at least of the Apostles appears to have lived to see four Emperors pulled down in little more than a year. *Ibid.* xviii. IV. 163 That the author ..wished to pull down the existing government there could be little doubt.

f. To earn (money, esp. as a wage or salary). *slang.*

1917 S. LEWIS *Job* xiii. 192 Good job, too, assistant book-keeper, pulling down his little twenty-seven-fifty regular. **1919** WODEHOUSE *Damsel in Distress* xxi. 256 George pulls down in a good year, during the season—around five thousand dollars a week. **1922** [see BERRY *sb.*[1] 1 c]. **1933** D. L. SAYERS *Murder must Advertise* v. 78 'So you have become one of the world's workers.'.. 'Yes; I'm pulling down four solid quid a week.' **1968** *New Yorker* 9 Nov. 56 How much does your average cornettist pull down per year? **1976** N. THORNBURG *Cutter & Bone* i. 21 He..had been pulling down twenty-five thousand a year.

26. pull in. a. See simple senses and IN *adv. to pull in one's horns*: see HORN *sb.* 5 b.

b. *trans.* To get into one's possession. Cf. prec. sense.

1529 S. FISH *Supplic. Beggers* (1871) 2 Whate money pull they yn by probates of testamentes. **1841** *Punch* 17 July 6/2 I'm a boy in a school, with a bag of apples, which..I naturally sell at a penny a-piece, and so look forward to pulling in a considerable quantity of browns. **1973** *Scotsman* 13 Feb. 8/2 The Archbishop of York..pulls in £6000 a year.

†**c.** To withdraw from use or view. *Obs.*

1549 CHEKE *Hurt Sedit.* (1641) 5 You say, pull in the Scriptures, for we will haue no knowledge of Christ. **1622** FLETCHER *Sea Voy.* III. i, All my spirits..Pull in their powers, and give me up to destiny.

d. To rein in (one's horse); hence *fig.* Also *intr.* or *absol.* To check or bring oneself to a stop in any course.

1605 SHAKS. *Macb.* v. v. 42, I pull in Resolution, and begin To doubt th' Equiuocation of the Fiend. **1780** T. TWINING in *Recreat. & Stud.* (1882) 78, I must pull in, or my letter will never end. **1792** SOUTHEY *Lett.* (1856) I. 9, I pull in pretty sharply, and slowly descend. **1875** W. S. HAYWARD *Love agst. World* 11 Let us pull in a little, and take it quietly.

e. To arrest (a person); = sense 16.

1893 S. CRANE *Maggie* x. 89 'I'll tump 'im till he can't stand.'.. 'What's deh use! Yeh'll git pulled in!' **1923** E. RICE *Adding Machine* vi. 101 You read in the paper all the time about guys gettin' pulled in for annoyin' women. **1933** D. L. SAYERS *Murder must Advertise* ix. 162 We could pull him in any day, but he's not the real big noise. **1956** [see HEELED *ppl. a.* 2]. **1973** W. M. DUNCAN *Big Timer* xxiii. 159 If you hadn't come voluntarily, I'd have pulled you in.

f. *intr.* Of a locomotive train: to enter a station.

1905 D. G. PHILLIPS *Plum Tree* 91, I didn't know you till you took out your watch with the monogram on the back, just as we were pulling in. **1929** S. LEACOCK *Iron Man* 143 That's your train pulling in now.

g. *absol.* or *intr.* Of a driver: to drive a vehicle to the side of a road or off a road (for some specified purpose). Also of the vehicle itself.

1938 G. GREENE *Brighton Rock* III. iii. 122 Notices said: 'Pull in Here', 'Mazawattee tea', 'Genuine Antiques'. **1959** I. JEFFERIES *Thirteen Days* i. 13, I was forced to pull off the road on the way back... I would have pulled in thereabouts anyway. **1975** M. RUSSELL *Murder by Mile* viii. 81 Pulling in for a truck to pass, Hamilton sat tapping the wheel.

27. pull off. a. See simple senses and OFF *adv. to pull off one's hat*, etc., to uncover the head in salutation or reverence.

c **1000** [see sense 1]. *c* **1450** *M.E. Med. Bk.* (Heinrich) 92 Pul of þe croppes, and clippe hem wyþ a peyre sheris on smale peces. **1508** DUNBAR *Flyting* 157 Thow plukkis the pultre, and scho pullis off the pennis. **1586** A. DAY *Eng. Secretary* II. (1625) 83 Pull off my bootes and spurres. **1673** [R. LEIGH] *Transp. Reh.* 82 Every man has not the good fortune..to pull off his hatt and make a leg with an air. **1719** DE FOE *Crusoe* (1840) I. iv. 57, I pulled off my clothes. **1776** WITHERING *Brit. Plants* (1796) I. 259 Carefully and slowly pull off the petals. **1834** L. RITCHIE *Wand. by Seine* 42 They pulled off their hats to one another with great civility.

b. *Musketry. to pull off*, to pull the trigger so as to deflect the shot from its true aim.

c. *Sporting.* To win (a prize or contest); hence (*colloq.*) to secure (some benefit); to succeed in gaining or effecting (something).

1870 *Figaro* 9 Nov. 5/1 These sweepstakes, in which the commissioners are always to 'pull off' the money. **1883** MRS. E. KENNARD *Right Sort* v, Now and again..Jack Clinker managed to pull off some 'good thing' on the turf. **1887** BLACK *Sabina Zembra* 126 We haven't pulled it off this time, mother. **1902** ELIZ. L. BANKS *Newspaper Girl* 44 'I've got a fine thing for you, if you can pull it off!' **1918** *Policeman's News* 25 Feb. 3/2 Criminals can no longer dispose of loot in Reading without the sleuths having a pretty good insight as to who pulled off the job. **1923** H. G. WELLS *Men like Gods* I. i. 6 He was not really clever enough to pull such a thing off. **1968** *Times* 15 Oct. 16/8 Having succeeded in their earlier experiments, there seems no reason why they should not pull off another major 'first'. **1977** *Time* 15 Aug. 13/2 Both looked as if they had just pulled off some master stroke of détente.

d. To steal (something). Cf. sense 2 b. *slang.*

1883 [see LEATHER *sb.* 2 e (*a*)].

e. Usu. *refl.* To cause (a person) to ejaculate by masturbation. *coarse slang.*

1922 JOYCE *Ulysses* 745 How did we finish it off yes O yes I pulled him off into my handkerchief pretending not to be excited. **1961** PARTRIDGE *Dict. Slang* Suppl. 1236/1 *Pull oneself off*, (of the male) to masturbate: low: late C. 19–20. **1966** L. COHEN *Beautiful Losers* I. 4 Can an old scholar find love at last and stop having to pull himself off every night so he can get to sleep? **1971** 'V. X. SCOTT' *Surrogate Wife* 139 Spasms shook his entire body as I pulled him off.

f. *intr. Surfing.* To end a ride by bringing one's surfboard out of a wave. Cf. sense 29 g below.

1964 B. COOPER in P. L. Dixon *Men & Waves* (1966) 189, I can't really recall my first wave, but I'm sure I caught an edge and had to pull off. **1967** S. REID in J. Severson *Great Surfing* 22/2 If someone were sliding faster than you, you had to pull off.

28. pull on. a. See simple senses and ON *adv.*

†**b.** *trans.* To induce, promote, cause; *to pull on wine*, to provoke thirst. *Obs.*

a **1586** SIDNEY *Ps.* VI. vi, Age, pul'd on with paines, all freshness fretteth. **1592** NASHE *P. Penilesse* G iij, To haue some shooing horne to pull on your wine, as a rasher of the coles, or a redde herring. **1609** TOURNEUR *Fun. Poem Sir F. Vere* 282 Punishments that justly pull On death. **1657** R. LIGON *Barbadoes* 37 For a whetstone, to pull on a cup of wine, we have dryed Neats tongues. **1670** DRYDEN *2nd Pt. Conq. Granada* IV. iii, That crime thou knowest..Shall an unknown and greater crime pull on. **1814** SCOTT *Wav.* lx, Boots pulled on without stockings. **1894** DOYLE *Mem. S. Holmes* i. 7 He pulled on his large macintosh.

29. pull out. a. See simple senses and OUT *adv.*

1340 HAMPOLE *Pr. Consc.* 1914 Yf þat tre war tite pulled oute..with al þe rotes aboute. *a* **1400–50** *Alexander* 938 He prekis in-to þe palais to pull out þe quene. **1526** TINDALE *Luke* xiv. 5 Whiche of you shall haue an asse, or an oxe, fallen into a pitt, and will nott straight waye pull him out on the saboth daye? **1593** SHAKS. *2 Hen. VI.* IV. vii. 19 We are like to haue biting Statutes Vnlesse his teeth be pull'd out. **1642** J. EATON *Honey-c. Free Justif.* 206 The Dogge..will presently flie in ones face, and bee ready if he can to pull out ones throat. **1711** HEARNE *Collect.* 10 Mar. III. 133 He pull'd out a pen-knife & stabb'd Mr. Harley. **1742** P. FRANCIS tr. *Hor. Art Poetry* 626 He fell in on purpose, and ..Will hardly thank you if you pull him out.

†**b.** *trans.* To draw the lining out through slashes in (a sleeve or garment) so as to display it. Const. *with*, usually in the pa. pple. See PULLER 2, PULLING *vbl. sb.* 4. *Obs.*

1553 in J. C. Jeaffreson *Middlesex County Rec.* (1886) I. 14 Unum par calligarum de panno laneo pulled oute with sarsenett. **1558** in Feuillerat *Revels Q. Eliz.* (1908) 38 Undersleves of playne yellowe clothe of gowlde pulled oute under the armes with greene golde sarsenet. *a* **1603** *Q. Eliz. Wardr.* in *Leisure Ho.* (1884) 677/2 A pair of sleeves of gold, pulled out with lawn.

†**c.** To extend in length; to draw (a line). *rare.*

1571 DIGGES *Pantom.* I. xxxv. L ij, Pull out from the centre a right line to the like number of degrees.

d. *absol.* or *intr.* Of a locomotive engine or train: To move out of a station; to draw out; hence, of a person: To go away, take one's departure; cf. 9 e; to row out: see 15. Also, to withdraw from an undertaking, to 'get out'. orig. *U.S.* Also of a ship: to sail out of a harbour or port; of an aeroplane: to emerge from a dive; of a vehicle: to move outwards into another lane of traffic. Also of the driver, etc., or occupants of these means of transport.

1868 *Harper's Mag.* Feb. 293/1 Breakfast over we 'pulled out', for the next station. **1880** 'MARK TWAIN' *Tramp Abroad* xxviii. 287 We got under way..and pulled out for the summit again, with a fresh and vigorous step. **1884** *Missouri Republican* 24 Feb. (Farmer *Amer.*), He knows that if he keeps his money in the..business..he will lose it all, and so he has pulled out. **1887** F. FRANCIS *Saddle & Mocassin* viii. 146 For a minute or two they stood looking at one another, and then Doc 'pulled out'. **1891** C. ROBERTS *Adrift Amer.* 18 The train that was to take me on..was nearly ready to 'pull out', as the phrase goes in America. **1902** C. J. C. HYNE *Mr. Horrocks, Purser* 105 We pull out from here next Tuesday. **1917** 'CONTACT' *Airman's Outings* 46 We swerved violently, and they pulled out of their dive well away from us. **1938** G. GREENE *Brighton Rock* VII. ix. 349 A bus came upon them and pulled out just in time. **1942** T. RATTIGAN *Flare Path* I. 30, I put the old Wimpey into a dive and..pulled out only a few feet above his head. **1951** *Manch. Guardian Weekly* 15 Mar. 13/2 In the Far West, the San Francisco 'Chronicle' blanketed its whole page with the headline—'Wage board approved increase of 10 per cent —labour members pull out'. **1961** *Listener* 7 Dec. 962/1 Today they must choose—either to stay under an African government or to pull out..to face a new life. **1972** 'A. YORK' *Expurgator* I. iv. 59 The Mercedes was immediately in front of him. He pulled out, into the middle of the road, ..and saw the lorry coming at him. **1977** D. BAGLEY *Enemy* xx. 162 We can pull out and leave Ashton to sink or swim.. or we can get him out ourselves.

e. *colloq.* To extend oneself vigorously; to work hard. Cf. *to pull the stops out* s.v. STOP *sb.*[2]

1866 TROLLOPE *Belton Est.* III. x. 272 There's no getting people really to pull out in this country.

f. Of a drawer, etc.: to be capable of being pulled open.

1943 A. G. HATCHER in *Mod. Lang. Notes* LVIII. 12 Drawers *pull out*..easily.

g. *intr. Surfing.* (See quot. 1963.) Cf. *pull off* (sense 27 f above).

1963 *Surfing Yearbk.* 42/2 *Pull out*, ending a ride by getting your board out of a wave. There are many different ways of pulling out. **1964** J. SEVERSON *Mod. Surfing* xvii. 157 You may also have the opportunity of pulling out before reaching the section. **1968** D. KAHANAMOKU *World of Surfing* xiii. 127 You can also get wiped out when the wave begins to break in front of you. It's time to pull out of it and avoid an unwanted and unscheduled swim. **1971** *Studies in English* (Univ. Cape Town) Feb. 27 This is called being locked in, because in such a condition it is virtually impossible to pull-out.

30. pull over. a. See simple senses and OVER *adv.*

b. Of a driver: to bring a vehicle to the side of a road or street, or to some other place. Cf. sense 26 g above.

1930 *Morning Post* 12 June 5, I considered that I had not time to pull over to my near side. **1932** *Sun* (Baltimore) 24 Sept. 8/6 Notify him that you are actually about to pass. In most cases he will pull over for you. **1971** *It* 2–16 June 8/1 He's signaling me to pull over! **1972** D. DELMAN *Sudden Death* (1973) v. 135 The rain so heavy that..the wipers.. were unable to cope... 'Can't see too well,' I said. 'I better pull over.'

31. pull round. a. See simple senses and ROUND *adv.*

b. *intr.* To recover from sickness or fainting; to come round.

1891 R. BUCHANAN *Come, live with Me* II. xx. 253 The danger's over..and the little one is pulling round. **1896** *Pall Mall Mag.* Sept. 70 He thinks he's going to pull round again; but I'll bet on his not being alive this day week.

c. *trans.* To restore (a person) to health after sickness, etc.; to put into a healthier or better condition. Also *transf.*

1900 E. GREY *Outrageous Fortune* iv. 37 The attack of meningitis..was fortunately only slight, and the excellent nursing I received..served to quickly pull me round. **1928** *Sunday Express* 29 Apr. 20/1 In the second half Cardiff made a valiant attempt to pull the game round. **1955** A. L. ROWSE *Expansion Eliz. Eng.* 230 Smith had pulled the colony round at its lowest point. **1978** *Country Life* 27 July 236/3 'Twas my turn to need help. Denwood pulled me round.

32. pull through.

a. See simple senses and THROUGH *adv.*

b. *trans.* To get (a person) through a difficult, dangerous, or critical condition or situation; to bring (a thing) to a successful issue; to accomplish.

1856 READE *Never too late* li, Youth and a sound constitution began to pull him through. **1860** DICKENS *Uncomm. Trav.* viii, 'We shall pull him through, please God', said the Doctor. **1884** *Pall Mall G.* 16 Oct. 3/2 The work..is now in good hands, and will be pulled through.

c. *intr.* (? for *refl.*) To get through sickness, a trial, or an undertaking with effort or difficulty; to succeed in accomplishing or enduring something difficult or severe. Also with *through* prep.

1852 DICKENS *Bleak Ho.* xxxvii, Bless your heart,..I shall be all right. I shall pull through, my dear. **1856** READE *Never too late* xv, You pulled through it, and so will he. **1879** E. K. BATES *Egypt. Bonds* I. x. 233 She is very ill..but she may pull through after all. **1885** *Boston* (Mass.) *Jrnl.* 2 June 2/3 He is likely to pull through and pay a hundred cents on a dollar. **1891** KIPLING *Light that Failed* 172, I must pull through the business alone.

33. pull to. *trans.* To shut (a door, etc.) by drawing it towards oneself.

1898 [see TO *adv.* 4]. **1910** [see LISTEN *v.* 2 c]. **1922** JOYCE *Ulysses* 57 He pulled the halldoor to after him. **1946** W. DE LA MARE *Three Royal Monkeys* v. 67 He skipped out and pulled-to the door-flap behind him.

34. pull together.

a. *trans.* See sense 8 and TOGETHER. Also *transf.*

A rider is said to 'pull his horse together', when, by means of his legs and his reins, he makes it 'collect' or gather itself together.

1894 W. ARCHER in *World* 15 Aug. 25/1 The last act wants a great deal of working-up and pulling together. **1925** J. G. BRUCE in E. F. Norton *Fight for Everest: 1924* iii. 63 If the first party of porters could be pulled together again in twenty-four hours' time, they were then to be utilized to keep Camp III supplied from Camp II. **1952** *Listener* 31 Jan. 189/1 He has tried to pull together all that has been said and written about the political struggle between the western allies and Moscow. **1978** *Amer. N. & Q.* XVI. 142/1 A corpus of paintings not pulled together in any previous work.

b. *to pull oneself together*: to gather with an effort one's faculties or energies; to rouse or recover oneself; to rally. Also (non-*refl.*), to restore (a person) to a normal condition.

1872 *Punch* 29 June 269/1 The process of pulling myself together and picking myself up. **1878** BESANT & RICE *Celia's Arb.* xiii, I realized this in a moment, and pulled myself together with an effort. **1888** BRYCE *Amer. Commw.* III. xcvi. 349 It [the Republic] can pull itself together in moments of danger. **1906** W. S. MAUGHAM *Bishop's Apron* viii. 132 Now come and have tea... I know it'll pull you together.

c. *intr.* To act in unison; to work in harmony; to co-operate; also, to agree, 'get on' together.

1799 *Hist.* in *Ann. Reg.* 302/2 In the marine language of admiral Mitchel, they pulled heartily together. **1805** WORDSW. *Waggoner* I. 133 Ye pulled together with one mind. **1830** MARRYAT *King's Own* xiii, It was a ship's company which *pulled every way*, as the saying is, when there was nothing to demand union: but let..danger appear ..then they all *pulled together*. **1884** SIR R. BAGGALLAY in *Law Times Rep.* 14 June 467/2 Where tenants for life and trustees did not pull together, sales could not in such cases be effected.

35. pull up. a. See simple senses and UP *adv.*

c **1400** *Destr. Troy* 10858 And pull vp a port, let hom passe furthe. **1451** CAPGRAVE *Life St. Aug.* (E.E.T.S.) 13 þat same nyth þei pulled up sail & stole þe schip from hir. **1488** *Nottingham Rec.* III. 268 To pulhope pylys that was dryuen downe with flodys. **1766** G. WILLIAMS *Let.* in *G. Selwyn & Contemp.* (1843) II. 42 After he has pulled up his stockings. **1856** KANE *Arct. Expl.* II. xxvi. 264 One by one we pulled up the boats.

b. To drag out of the ground, or from where it is rooted or set, with the object of removal or destruction; to root out, demolish.

1382 WYCLIF *Jer.* i. 10, I haue set thee to dai vp.. that thou pulle vp, and destroȝe, and springe abrod, and waste. **1484** CAXTON *Fables of Æsop* I. xx, Whanne the flaxe was growen and pulled vp. **1532** *Act 23 Hen. VIII*, c. 18 The said fishgarthes, piles, stakes,..and other engines..to be auoyded, and pulled vp. **1668** *Plymouth Col. Rec.* (1857) VII. 143 Molesting him..in pulling vp his fence. **1765** A. DICKSON *Treat. Agric.* (ed. 2) 112 The weeds themselves must be pulled up by the root. **1860** BARTLETT *Dict. Amer.* 348 The allusion is to pulling up the stakes of a tent.

†**c.** To lift up, raise with an effort. ***to pull up one's head, pull oneself up***, to assume an erect attitude. Also, to pluck up, rouse up (one's heart, spirits, courage). *Obs.*

1390 GOWER *Conf.* I. 219 With that he pulleth up his hed And made riht a glad visage. *a* **1400–50** *Alexander* 2074 Þan pullis him vp þe proude kyng. *c* **1430** *Freemasonry* 606 Into the churche when thou dost gon, Pulle uppe thy herte to Crist, anon. **1460** *Lybeaus Disc.* 1178 Up he pullede hys herte. **1586** J. HOOKER *Hist. Irel.* in *Holinshed* II. 161/2 Now they pull vp their spirits. **1633** BP. HALL *Hard Texts, Joel* iii. 10 Let those that are weake and fearefull pull up their spirits. **1737** WHISTON *Josephus, Hist.* IV. vi. §1 The people..pulled up their courage for a while.

d. To cause to stop; to stop; to arrest, to apprehend; *esp.* to apprehend and take before a magistrate; hence, to reprimand, reprove, rebuke.

1623 in *Crt. & Times Jas. I* (1848) II. 392 A man, thinking nothing, pulled up his coach, and so made the horse start a little. **1800** in *Spirit Pub. Jrnls.* IV. 254 A few evenings since I had pulled him up on Hounslow Heath. **1812** J. H. VAUX *Flash Dict.*, *Pull* or *pull up*, to accost; stop; apprehend; or take into custody; as to pull up a *Jack*, is to stop a post-chaise on the highway. **1825** C. M. WESTMACOTT *Eng. Spy* I. 170 He was next day pulled up before the big wigs. **1836–9** DICKENS *Sk. Boz, Last Cab-driver*, [He] avowed his unalterable determination to 'pull up' the cab-man in the morning. **1864** M. CREIGHTON *Let.* 24 Aug. in *Life & Lett.* (1904) I. i. 12 Fellows won't stand being pulled up for breaking one school rule, when they know you break another. **1884** J. HALL *Chr. Home* 119 It is difficult..before the company, to 'pull up' a boy, or to lecture a girl.

e. To tighten (reins) by drawing them towards oneself; to bring (a horse) to a standstill by doing this; also *transf.* to check (a person) in any course of action, esp. a bad course.

1787 'G. GAMBADO' *Acad. Horsemen* (1809) 35 Of course you drop the reins entirely on that side, and pull them up sharp, with both hands, on the other. **1827** DISRAELI *Viv. Grey* VI. i, Two horsemen pulled up their steeds beneath a wide oak. **1874** MAHAFFY *Soc. Life Greece* x. 295 Socrates is at once pulled up if he whispers. **1892** ZANGWILL *Bow Mystery* 169 Well, I'll go slower; but pull me up if I forget to keep the brake on.

f. *absol.* Of a driver, etc.: To bring a horse or vehicle to a stop; also, of a horse or vehicle: To stop, come to a standstill.

1844 J. T. HEWLETT *Parsons & W.* lv, The coachman pulled up. **1847** MARRYAT *Childr. N. Forest* xxii, He pulled up at an inn. **1869** TOZER *Highl. Turkey* I. 314 [The horse] took fright, and galloped off... After he had gone about three-quarters of a mile, he pulled up, and one of the men was sent to secure him. **1874** BURNAND *My Time* x. 86 A carriage pulled up..close by the bridge.

g. *refl.* and *intr.* for *refl.* To check or stop oneself in any course of action.

1808 E. S. BARRETT *Miss-led General* 42 He pulled up now, surely?—No—played upon tick. **1861** HUGHES *Tom Brown at Oxf.* xliii, He pulled himself up short, in the fear lest he were going again to be false. **1883** LD. RANDOLPH CHURCHILL *Sp. Edinb.* 20 Dec., It is time, and high time, to pull up. Concede nothing more to Mr. Parnell.

h. *intr.* To advance one's position in a race or other contest. Also *transf.*

1893 *Outing* (U.S.) XXII. 155/1 At forty yards Harding invariably led by a yard or more, but from this onward Cary pulled up, passing him at about sixty yards. **1936** N. STREATFEILD *Ballet Shoes* xvii. 276 The death of King George in January cut the audiences down to about a quarter..and they never really pulled up again.

pull-, the stem of PULL *v.* (or PULL *sb.*[2]) in comb.

1. With advbs., forming sbs. or adjs., as ***pull-along***, ***-away***, ***-down***, ***-on***, ***-through***, ***-to***, (*a*) *sb.* the act of pulling in the direction specified; (*b*) *adj.* that pulls or is pulled in the direction specified; **pull-apart**, the action or result of being pulled in opposite directions so as to be ruptured; **pull-on**, a garment without fasteners that is pulled on; **pull-out**, withdrawal from an undertaking or affair; **pull-through**: see quot, 1891; **pull-to**, (*a*) in *Weaving* = *lay-cap* (see LAY *sb.*[8] 1 b); (*b*) see quot. 1899. Also PULL-BACK, -DOWN, -IN, -OFF, -OUT, -OVER, -UP, q.v.

1939–40 *Army & Navy Stores Catal.* 829/2 *Pull-along engine for child to ride in..25/-. **1967** *Punch* 6 Dec. p. xii, Buy beautifully made wooden pull-along toys for tiny children. **1951** *Special Publ. Soc. Econ. Paleontologists & Mineralogists* No. 2. 89 (*caption*) '*Pull-apart' developed in a laminated bed of clay lying on gravel bed and covered by silts. **1954** *Sun* (Baltimore) (B ed.) 6 Feb. 2/5 As the concrete sets these wires are tightened by special jacks, thus..getting rid of the pull-apart tendency in advance. **1971** *Nature* 2 July 21/1 Fig. 3 shows the initial opening of the proto-North Atlantic Ocean and the pull-apart of North and South America. **1899** MARY KINGSLEY *W. Africa* App. I. 446 Turning with an appealing look to the trader, he points out the bareness of the royal *pull-away boys. **1939** T. S. ELIOT *Old Possum's Pract. Cats* 17 Abandoning their sampans, and their *pullaways and junks, They battened down the hatches on the crew within their bunks. **1950** [see *last-resort* s.v. LAST *a.* C 2]. **1976** *Drive* May–June 90/2 A fuss-free pullaway from 20mph in top gear and an 11sec time from 30–50mph highlight the car's impressive flexibility. **1907** *Yesterday's Shopping* (1969) 172/1 Electric Indicator... *Pull-down Replacement, consisting of 1¼ yds. brass chain, pulley and ring. **1971** J. HENDERSON *Copperhead* (1972) vi. 76 There was a Leitz slide-projector..and.. a pull-down screen. **1978** *Daily Tel.* 24 Oct. 15/2 The pull-down compartment in the front holds six transparent pockets for credit cards. **1919** in C. W. Cunnington *Eng. Women's Clothing* (1952) v. 156 The vogue of the *pull-on is still predominant. **1921** *Glasgow Herald* 25 May 4/7 The turban ..does not hide all the hair as do the pull-on hat, the cloche, and other popular shapes. **1976** *Billings* (Montana) *Gaz.* 30 June 7-A/1 (Advt.), Debonair styling in delightful prints. Have yours in a V-neck pull-on with roll-up sleeves. **1978** *Detroit Free Press* 16 Apr. (*Detroit Suppl.*) 36 (Advt.), Pull-on pants in petite and average lengths, $15. **1891** *Pall Mall G.* 3 Feb. 2/3 Orders have been issued that a '*pull-through' is always to be used in future, this consisting of a piece of stout gimp or similar material with which the tow or rag for clearing the barrel is pulled through from breech to muzzle. How long will this 'pull through' last on service? **1906** *Blackw. Mag.* Apr. 533/2 Running a pull-through down the barrel of his rifle. **1875** KNIGHT *Dict. Mech.*, **Pull-to* (Weaving), the upper part of the lay, lathe, or batten, which is used to beat up the weft. Also called the lay-cap. **1899** H. C. HART in *Phil. Soc. Trans.* 11 The weed is dragged in to the beach as it floats near with a pull-to, a very long-handled, two-pronged fork with bent or hooked tines.

2. With sbs.: used *attrib.* in sense 'used by, for, or in pulling', = PULLING *vbl. sb.* 5; as ***pull-line***, ***-rod***, ***-trigger***, or 'for pulling, moved by pulling', as ***pull-engine***, ***-toy***; also **pull-bell**, a bell rung by a cord, as distinct from a handbell; **pull-boat**, a boat that is propelled by pulling a rope; also *U.S.*, a motorized flat-boat which draws logs over water; also *attrib.*; **pull-bone** *U.S.* = *wish-bone* s.v. WISH *sb.*[1] 4; **pull-cock**, a tap worked by pulling a handle or lever (Knight *Dict. Mech.* 1875); **pull-cord**, a cord which operates a mechanism when pulled (in quots. *attrib.*); **pull-crow**, †**pul-crow** *a.*, for pulling crows: cf. PULL *v.* 5; **pull-date** *N. Amer.*, the date stamped on a container of perishable goods indicating when it must be withdrawn as no longer suitable for sale; **pull-devil**, a bundle of fish-hooks fastened back to back, to be jerked through a shoal of fish (*Cent. Dict.* 1890); **pull-drive** = *pull-stroke*; **pull-hitter** *U.S. Baseball* (see quot. 1955); **pull-iron**, (*a*) in a horse-drawn car, the iron tongue by which the swingletree is attached to the car; (*b*) in a railway car, a bolt or lug to which the chain of a draught horse may be attached (*Cent. Dict.*); **pull-piece**, a string or wire by which a clock may be made to strike at will; **pull-stroke**, (*a*) PULL *sb.*[2] 2 f; (*b*) in other technical senses, a stroke (of an oar, etc.) effected by pulling towards oneself; **pull-switch**, a switch operated by means of a pull-cord; **pull-tab**, a device, usu. comprising a ring and short tongue of metal, by means of which a tin may be opened; also *attrib.*; **pull-tail**, **pull-tow** (*dial.*): see quots.

1552 *Inv. Ch. Goods* (Surtees No. 97) 53 One litle *puyll bell. **1919** R. MACAULAY *Three Days* 52 How a pull-bell clangs when it rings! **1883** G. H. BOUGHTON in *Harper's Mag.* Jan. 172/2 It is a treat to see a powerful young Dutchwoman handle a rope on a *pull-boat. **1903** *Sci. Amer.* 17 Oct. 276/3 In the cypress swamps of Louisiana there are employed what are known as pull-boats, an evolution from the plan of placing a hoisting engine upon a scow and snaking the logs out of the swamp... The endless-rope pull-boat engines have 44-inch winding drums. **1907** 'O. HENRY' *Trimmed Lamp* 136 In her mind she could hear the girls shrieking over a *pullbone. **1963** *Listener* 28 Feb. 399/1 It should be..fitted with either a *pull-cord switch or one outside the door. **1978** *Lancashire Life* Nov. 177/1 (Advt.), Mahogany Bracket clock—hour strike and pull-cord repeat. **1973** *Black Panther* 7 Apr. 14/2 What food manufacturer would be so foolhardy as to place his produce bearing a pack date alongside a competitor who uses a *pull date. **1977** *Daily Colonist* (Victoria, B.C.) 7 Aug. 2/4 All whipped butter..bearing the pull date of Sept. 12, 1977, or before is being recalled. **1905** *Athenæum* 18 Nov. 383/2 Like the hook-stroke and the *pull-drive, it is well illustrated here. **1907** *Daily Chron.* 8 Jan. 7/3 He played for runs. Most famous of all his strokes was his pull-drive. **1907** *Yesterday's Shopping* (1969) 1072/2 The *Pull Engine. With rubber composition tyres...each 16/3. **1937** *Philadelphia Record* 2 Sept. 17/1 Medwick hits to all fields. DiMaggio is mostly a *pull hitter. **1955** *Amer. Speech* XXX. 153 The term *pull hitter* denotes a hitter who pulls the ball (i.e., a right-handed hitter who hits to left field or a left-handed hitter who hits to right field). **1972** *N.Y. Times* 4 June v. 2/7 He is primarily a pull hitter to left and some teams stack defensive alignments against him. **1875** KNIGHT *Dict. Mech.*, **Pull-iron*, the piece at the hind end of the tongue of a street-car by which it is attached to the car. **1878** M. BROWNE *Pract. Taxidermy* ii. 25 There are..two unattached cords of some strength, called the *pull line and the forked line, which latter is attached..to the two staves nearest the bird catcher at the intersection of the top line. **1875** KNIGHT *Dict. Mech.*, **Pull-piece* (*Horology*), the wire or string..by pulling which the clock is made to strike. **1903** *Motor. Ann.* 296 Look for stretch in the *pull-rods, and wear off the braking surfaces. **1897** K. S. RANJITSINHJI *Jubilee Bk. Cricket* iii. 120 He.. applies a marvellous *pull-stroke to good-length balls just outside the off-stump. **1904** *Daily Chron.* 25 Aug. 7/3 Trott was run out through running a doubtful one off a pull stroke of his partner's that soared, only to be dropped by Blythe. **1968** J. ARNOLD *Shell Bk. Country Crafts* 74 All the 'work' of a cross-cut is done on the pull-stroke [of the saw], each man alternately pulling and releasing. **1969** *Publ. Amer. Dial. Soc.* LI. 10 *Pull stroke*,..a stroke whereby the kayakist leans far forward, thrusts the paddle into the water and with extreme exertion pulls the kayak forward. **1888** D. SALOMONS *Managem. Accumulators* (ed. 3) II. ii. 97 The Browett *pull switch is fixed near the cornice, and by pulling a cord, the light is put on; also turned off by a similar action. **1971** D. BAGLEY *Freedom Trap* vi. 130 The light switch in the bathroom was operated, as good building regulations insist, by a ceiling pull-switch from which a strong cord hung to a convenient hand level. **1965** *Economist* 5 June 1150/1 The successful development of *pull-tab tops for beer tins, so that they can be opened by hand rather than with an opener. **1978** J. UPDIKE *Coup* vi. 239 Take care..not to drop the pull-tab [on a can of soft drink], once removed, back into the can. **1891** T. HARDY *Tess* xliii, She..reclined on a heap of *pull-tails—the refuse after the straight straw had been drawn—thrown up at the further side of the barn. *a* **1825** FORBY *Voc. E. Anglia*, **Pull-tow, pull-tow-knots*, the coarse and knotty parts of the tow, which are carefully pulled out and thrown aside, before it is fit to be spun into yarn. **1946** *Sun* (Baltimore) 14 Dec. 14/6 Wagons and other *pull-toys should have rope handles. **1958** J. G. MACGREGOR *North-West of 16* v. 60, I was at the pull-toy stage. I went everywhere dragging behind me a fascinating collection of tin cans, bits of roots..all tied together with string. **1978** *Neiman, Marcus Christmas Bk.* 83 A purple cow pull toy, complete with the N-M brand. **1895** *Daily News* 17 July 2/1 The range officers began testing the *pull triggers for all who had made scores of 86 and upwards.

3. Forming phraseological combs. functioning either as sbs. or adjs., as **pull-and-push** *adj. phr.* = PUSH-AND-PULL *adj. phr.* b.

1950 *Railway Mag.* XCVI. 101 (*caption*) Dolgelly to Barmouth pull-and-push train approaching Barmouth Tunnel. **1959** H. ELLIS *Brit. Railway Hist.* II. II. i. 252 The Great Western and the South Western fought it [*sc.* the electric train] with steam rail motors and pull-and-push trains. **1968** *Railway Mag.* CXIV. 300/1 Pull-and-push trials on the G.N. main line..began in January.

pullable ('pʊləb(ə)l), *a.* [f. PULL *v.* + -ABLE.] Capable of being pulled.

1892 *Pall Mall G.* 26 Apr. 1/2 If he and his rivals were wooden crocks sent round by 'pullable' machinery.

‖**'pullace, -ase.** *Obs. rare*$^{-1}$. [app. an erron. variant of PULLEY (perh. founded on the pl. *pulleis*, influenced by *windas*, *windlass*).] A pulley.

1688 R. HOLME *Armoury* III. 107/2 *Pullases*, turning things on the top of the [weaving] Frame, by which with the help of the tradles the Spring-staves are raised up and down. *Ibid.* xviii. (Roxb.) 130/2 Drawing it [a battering ram] higher or letting it lower, by means of chaines and pullaces as it hung in it[s] carriage.

†**pu'llaile, -'ayle.** *Obs.* Forms: α. 4 **polyle**, 5 **-aile, -ayl(e, -ayll(e, -eyl**, 6 **polell**. β. 5 **pullaylle, -aille, -aile, -ayle.** [a. OF. *polaille* (13th c. in Godef.), *poulaille*, f. *poule* chicken, fowl (see PULL *sb.*[3]) + *-aille*, collective suffix:—L. *-ālia*: cf. Pr. *pollayllia*, It. *pollaglia*.] Poultry.

α. **13..** *E.E. Allit. P.* B. 57 My polyle þat is penne-fed & partrykes boþe. *c* **1412** HOCCLEVE *De Reg. Princ.* 979 (MS. R.) The kyte, That me byreve wolde my polaile [*v.r.* pullaille]. *c* **1430** LYDG. *Min. Poems* (Percy Soc.) 158 The sleihty fox smal polayl doth oppresse. **1481** CAXTON *Reynard* xii. (Arb.) 29 How goo your eyen so after the poleyl? **1527** ANDREW *Brunswyke's Distyll. Waters* I j b, The inwarde yelowe skynne of mawes of the polell.

β. *c* **1400** *Rom. Rose* 7045 With caleweys, or with pullaile, With coninges, or with fyn vitaille. **1481** BOTONER *Tulle on Old Age* (Caxton) F iv, Grete habondaunce..of..hennys capons and of othir pullaile. *a* **1483** *Liber Niger* in *Househ. Ord.* (1790) 17 The diverse kindes of pullayle, conyes, wild fowl & tame.

Pullak, var. POLACK *sb.* (*a.*)

†**pullan**, var. of POLAINE, a kind of sail-cloth.

1508 *Acc. Ld. High Treas. Scot.* IV. 46 Item, for vj^{m} j^{c} xl fut of sarris pullan and plank to the said schip and xiiij pece of barrotis; ilk fut xij deneris.

pull-and-push, pull-apart: see PULL-.

pullane, Sc. var. of POLAYN *Obs.*, knee-armour.

pullao, variant of PILAU.

†**pu'llarian**, *a. Obs. rare*$^{-1}$. [f. L. *pullāri-us* (f. *pull-us* young animal, chicken: see PULL *sb.*[3]) + -AN.] Of or pertaining to chickens or fowls (in quot. the sacred chickens used for divination).

1652 GAULE *Magastrom.* 330 Papyrius Cursor oppugning Aquilonia, the pullarian auspicator.

pullastrine (pʊ'læstraɪn), *a. Ornith.* [f. Zool. L. *pullastræ*, pl. of L. *pullastra* young hen, pullet (f. *pullus*: see prec. and -ASTER) + -INE[1].] Of or pertaining to the *Pullastræ*, a group of gallinaceous birds, comprising the Curassows, Mound-builders, and Pigeons (Lilljeborg 1866).

As proposed by Sundevall, 1836, *Pullastræ* included the Curassows, Lyre-bird, Plantain-eaters, and Pigeons.

1875 COPE *Check-list N. Amer. Batrachia* 56 Struthious, Pullastrine, and Clamatorial Birds. **1887** —— *Orig. Fittest* I. ii. 114 The Pullastrine birds are a generalized group.

So **pu'llastriform** *a.*, having the pullastrine form; resembling the *Pullastræ*.

1887 COPE *Orig. Fittest* I. ii. 122 Inferior in possessing.. Pullastriform and Struthious Birds.

†puˈllation. *Obs. rare*—⁰. [ad. L. *pullātio* hatching, f. *pull-us* young animal: see -ATION.]
1623 COCKERAM, *Pullation*, a hatching of chickins. So **1656** in BLOUNT *Glossogr.* **1658** in PHILLIPS.

pullayle, var. of PULLAILE *Obs.*

†puˈllayly. *Obs. rare.* Also 5 polaly. [a. OF. *pollalie* (1418 in Godef.), var. of *poulaille*, PULLAILE.] Poultry.
c **1440** *Promp. Parv.* 416/1 Pullayly, or pullay (*K.* pullery, *S.* pullayly, or pullayle), *altile, volatile.* **1466** *Paston Lett.* II. 269 For purveying of.. certain piggs and polaly.

ˈpull-ˌback. [f. phr. *to pull back*, PULL *v.* 24.]
1. a. The action or an act of pulling back.
1668 DRYDEN *Evening's Love* Epil. 14 In the French stoop, and the pull-back o' the arm. **1900** G. SWIFT *Somerley* 146 An occasional wrench and pull-back of the arms gave him considerable pain. **1903** A. MACLAREN *Last Leaves* ii. 21 There is very little conscious check or pull-back when we contemplate doing them again.
b. *spec.* An orderly withdrawal of military troops. Also *attrib.* orig. *U.S.*
1951 *Baltimore News-Post* 19 Mar. (Home Final 7th ed.) 1/2 Those who think the Red pullback is leading up to something don't put so much stock in the Red's abandonment of prepared defenses. **1953** *Sun* (Baltimore) 8 May B1/7 (*heading*) Reds continue Laos pullback. **1962** *Listener* 29 Nov. 896/2 *The New York Times* said the Chinese were now 'asking for border talks after a pull-back of troops that would still leave them in full possession of their main territorial objective'. **1971** *E. Afr. Standard* (Nairobi) 10 Apr. 2/7 He was working towards total American withdrawal and would step up the pull-back rate. **1974** *Times* 7 Jan. 4/1 (*heading*) Tel Aviv prepares pull-back offer. **1977** *Time* 10 Oct. 12/3 We had to get very deeply involved in pushing for a pullback and cease-fire.
c. *Cinematogr.* A shot in which the scene is observed to recede.
1957 MANVELL & HUNTLEY *Film Music* ii. 34 Long track, mostly in medium or medium-close shot, with one large pull-back during the market-place scene. **1959** W. S. SHARPS *Dict. Cinematogr.* 121/2 *Pull back*, the backward movement of a camera from a close to a long shot. **1977** *Listener* 5 May 590/1 Will Frayn appear next time.. on the end of a zoom-in or a pull back?
d. *Tap-dancing.* (See quot. 1957.)
1957 P. DRAPER in *Dance Mag.* May 60/3 A pull-back is a tap made by the front part of the foot striking the floor while the body is in the air moving backwards. **1975** *New Yorker* 7 July 26/3 The last bit to be recorded.. was a wonderful tap dance—a series of time steps, pullbacks, flaps.. and pickups done by Michael Bennett himself.
2. That which pulls back; that which opposes progress or action; a retarding influence; a check; = BACK-SET *sb.* 1, DRAWBACK *sb.* 4. (Very common in 17th c.) Now *colloq.* and *dial.*
a **1591** H. SMITH *Serm. on 1 Cor. ix.* 24, Wks. 1867 II. 98 Let us not fear all or any of our adversaries or pull-backs. **1604** HIERON *Wks.* I. 541 There are so many delayes, and so many pul-backs. **1662** PEPYS *Diary* 31 Dec., I fear when all is done I must be forced to maintain my father myself.. which will be a very great pull back to me in my fortune. **1710** SWIFT *Jrnl. to Stella* 21 Oct., Your disorders are a pull-back for your good qualities. **1742** RICHARDSON *Pamela* III. 354 Which (having expended much to relieve her) was a great Pull-back, as the good old Woman called it. **1854** MISS BAKER *Northants. Gloss.* s.v., 'He has had so many pull backs, he could not get on'.
3. A contrivance or attachment for pulling something back. **a.** See quot. 1703. **b.** A contrivance for pulling the fullness of a woman's skirt to the back, so as to make the front hang quite plain.
1703 T. N. *City & C. Purchaser* 100 Smiths in London ask'd me 6*d.* per Pound for Casements.., if they made them with Turn-bouts.. or Cock-spurs, and Pull backs at the Hind-side to pull them to with. **1885** 'TIC ROMA' *St. Peter & Cock* xvi. 210 She laid her scissors on the pull-back. **1890** *Standard* 10 Mar., As for the 'pull-back', it seems to be on the wane, not so much because it was a hindrance to progression, but because it did not suit more than a small minority of figures.

pull-bell to **pull-devil**: see PULL-.

pull-doo (ˈpʊlduː). *U.S.* The American coot.
1860 BARTLETT *Dict. Amer.*, *Pull-doo*, a small black duck found in the bays and inlets of the Gulf of Mexico... The word is probably a corruption of *poule d'eau*, i.e. water hen.

ˈpull-ˌdown. [f. phr. *to pull down*, PULL *v.* 25.]
1. The act of pulling down, or fact of being pulled down. Also *fig.* and *attrib.*
1588 R. BROWNE *New Years Guift* (1903) 34 Yet all theis were the pulldowne of Antichrist. *a* **1591** H. SMITH *Serm. 1 Pet. v.* 5 ¶5 Though he have many heart-breaks and pul-downs, and many times no countenance to shew it. **1938** N. STREATFEILD *Circus is Coming* viii. 129 Can't we see the pull-down? Hans says it's more exciting than the build-up. **1962** *Which?* Oct. 305/2 New exercises.. were added... Pull downs (pulling down a bar attached to pulleys and weights). **1965** M. STEWART *Airs above Ground* iv. 58 If this is the last performance, they'll start the pull-down [of the big top] the minute it's over. **1975** BRAM & DOWNS *Manuf. Technol.* vii. 204 (*heading*) Pull-down Broaching. *Ibid.* 205 An advantage of the pull-down method is that where the cutting pressure is evenly distributed around the axis of movement clamping need not be necessary.
2. a. In the organ, A wire which pulls down a pallet or valve when the key is depressed, thus admitting wind to the pipe.
1852 SEIDEL *Organ* 50 The lower part.. lying outside the great sound-board, is called the pull-down. **1876** HILES *Catech. Organ* v. (1878) 39 The pull-down [is] a small piece of wire connected with the tracker by another hook; and which by pulling the pallet down, or open, admits the wind to the pipes. **1881** C. A. EDWARDS *Organs* 49 Holes made.. to accurately fit the pull-down wires.
b. *Cinematogr.* (See quot. 1959.)
1953 [see *ghost-image* s.v. GHOST *sb.* 14 e]. **1959** W. S. SHARPS *Dict. Cinematogr.* 121/2 *Pull down*, the intermittent mechanism used to move film in a camera, projector or printer by engaging the film perforations.

pull-drive: see PULL-.

pulle, obs. f. POLE *sb.*[1]

pulled (pʊld), *ppl. a.* [f. PULL *v.* + -ED[1].]
1. a. Plucked (as feathers, fruit, flowers).
1495 *Act 11 Hen. VII*, c. 19 Bolsters and pillows made.. of scalded feders and drie pulled feders to gedre. **1903** KIPLING 5 *Nations* 40 To a couch of new-pulled hemlock.
b. Of wool. orig. *N. Amer.*
1904 J. M. MATTHEWS *Textile Fibres* ii. 24 There is a certain class of wool.. known in trade as *pulled wool*; this is obtained from the pelts of slaughtered sheep, and is usually removed from the skin by the action of time, the fibres being pulled out by the roots. **1921** *Daily Colonist* (Victoria, B.C.) 8 Oct. 15/2 The market for pulled wools continues dull. **1934** J. R. HIND *Woollen & Worsted Raw Materials* iii. 19 The removal of the wool is done by plucking or flipping the wool from the skins, which has given these wools the name of 'flipe' or 'slipe'. In the American wool trade, skin wool is known as 'pulled wool'. **1952** H. HAIGH *Work of Woolman* vii. 60 The class called 'English Pulled' or 'Scotch Pulled' includes many varieties of wool. **1963** E. M. POHLE in W. von Bergen *Wool Handbk.* (ed. 3) I. ix. 668 The domestic production of pulled wool in 1944 reached an all time high of 74 million pounds.
2. Denuded of feathers, etc., as a bird; plucked; stripped of wool or hair, as a skin or hide.
pulled fowl, fowl baked, then skinned and boned, and the flesh cut up and put into a rich white sauce.
c **1386** CHAUCER *Prol.* 177 He yaf nat of that text a pulled hen. **1508** KENNEDIE *Flyting w. Dunbar* 516 To suelly the in stede of a pullit hen. **1682** DRYDEN *Satyr* 190 So by old Plato man was once defin'd, Till a pull'd Cock that Notion undermin'd. **1897** *19th Cent.* Nov. 736 The other half is covered with pulled skins waiting to be taken into 'shop'.
3. a. Drawn; moved, extended, etc., by pulling.
pulled bread, irregular pieces pulled from the inside of a newly baked loaf, which are put into the oven again, and re-baked till crisp. ***pulled elbow***: see quot. 1902. ***pulled work*** (see quot.).
1896 *Allbutt's Syst. Med.* I. 402 Toast or 'pulled' bread or biscuits often well replace bread. **1902** *Brit. Med. Jrnl.* 12 Apr. *Epit. Curr. Lit.* 58 The abnormal condition known as 'pulled elbow'... supposed to be due to subluxation of the head of the radius. **1967** E. SHORT *Embroidery & Fabric Collage* ii. 48 *Pulled work.* For this holes are made without withdrawing threads from the ground fabric, but, as the name implies, by pulling and distorting the weave. *Ibid.* iii. 77 (*caption*) Detail of a tablecloth in pulled work, with a border of famous London buildings.
b. *Cricket* and *Golf.* See PULL *v.* 18.
1891 *Field* 7 Mar. 349/1 'Pulled' balls will invariably meet with punishment in some shape or form. **1897** *Blackw. Mag.* Sept. 387/1 Hoylake may exact a sterner punishment for a 'sliced' or 'pulled' ball.
4. (Also ***pulled down.***) Reduced in health and strength, or depressed in spirits; 'dragged'; fagged. Cf. PULL *v.* 25 d.
1616 W. BROWNE *Britannia's Pastorals* II. i. 14 In his flesh pull'd downe As hee had liu'd in a beleaguerd towne. **1801** NELSON *Let.* 2 May (in *Sotheby's Catal.* 15 June (1897) 20), I am dreadfully pulled down. **1831** MOORE *Mem.* (1854) VI. 224 Found him looking a good deal pulled. **1884** Q. VICTORIA *More Leaves* 334 His leg [is] now really fairly well, but he looks pulled. **1895** A. W. PINERO *Second Mrs. Tanqueray* 88 You look dreadfully pulled down. We poor women show illness so plainly in our faces.

pullein, obs. form of POLLAN.

pullen (ˈpʊlɪn). *Obs.* exc. *dial.* Forms: α. 4 pullan, 5 -layne, 6 -lain, -lyn, poullayne, 6–7 pulleyn, -e, -lein, -e, -lin, 7 -lyne, poulen, 8 *dial.* pulling, 6– pullen. β. 5 polayn, 6 -eyn, pol(l)ayne, polleine, -en. [Origin obscure; app. a. OF. *poulain, puleyn, polan* (12th c. in Hatz.-Darm.) young of any animal (:—pop. L. *pullān-us, -um*, deriv. of *pullus* young animal), identified in Eng. with *poullaille*, PULLAILE, poultry.]
1. Poultry; barn-door or domestic fowls; the flesh of these as food. Also *attrib.*, as ***pullen market.***
α. **1329** *Mem. Ripon* (Surtees) II. 102, xij pullan prec. 18*d.* *c* **1450** *Two Cookery-bks.* 67, v. disson pullayn for Gely. xij. dd. to roste. **1523** LD. BERNERS *Froiss.* I. ccccliii. 701 Mylke, chese, pulleyn, and other thynges. **1573** TUSSER *Husb.* (1878) 177 Where pullen vse nightly to pearch in the yard. **1591** NASHE *Prognost.* 10 Hennes, Capons, Geese, and other pullin. **1601** HOLLAND *Pliny* I. 220 To mingle hens or pullins dung especially with their meat. **1725** *Bradley's Fam. Dict.* s.v. *Turkey*, They are cur'd in the same manner as Pullen is. **1825** BROCKETT *N.C. Gloss.* s.v., The Pullen market in Newcastle. **1870** E. PEACOCK *Ralf Skirl.* II. 150 I'm not a goin' to hev' my pullen and lambs run'd away wi'.
β. **1486** *Bk. St. Albans* C ij b, Take whete.. and fede hennys or chykynnes therwith, and fede yowre hawke with thessame polayn. **1523** LD. BERNERS *Froiss.* I. xvi. 18 With right good chepe, as well of pollen, as of other vitailes. **1523** FITZHERB. *Husb.* §146 Gyue thy poleyn meate in the mornynge. **1549** CHEKE *Hurt Sedit.* (1569) H iij b, Diuers vermine destroye corne, kill Polleine.
2. Chickens collectively; young; rarely, a chicken; *fig.* a child. (Cf. OF. *polle* girl.)
1631 *Celestina* Prol. A vij, Your craven Kites presse upon our Pullen, insulting over them even in our own houses, and offring to take them even from under the hens wings. **1681** GREW *Musæum* I. IV. iii. 73 Whatever they [Puffins] eat in the day, they disgorge a good part of it in the night into the mouths of their Pullen. **1876** *Whitby Gloss.* s.v., 'Thoo little uneasy pullen', you tiresome child.

puller (ˈpʊlə(r)). [f. PULL *v.* + -ER[1].] One who or that which pulls, in various senses of PULL *v.*
1. a. One who plucks, draws, or drags (often with an adverb, as ***puller down, on, out***); a plucker, a drawer; a gatherer or reaper; a rower.
1382 WYCLIF *Isa.* l. 6 My bodi I ʒaf to the smyteres, and my chekes to the pulleris. **1593** SHAKS. *3 Hen. VI*, III. iii. 157 Proud setter vp, and puller downe of Kings. **1623** MIDDLETON *More Dissemblers* v. i, I was but a pumper, that is, a puller-on of gentlemen's pumps. **1844** J. T. HEWLETT *Parsons & W.* xv We were really good pullers [of oars]. **1849** *Jrnl. R. Agric. Soc.* X. I. 174 The pullers walk in the furrows, between the ridges. **1885** MRS. LYNN LINTON *Stabbed in Dark* iv, It was a heavy climb, even with the pullers and pushers.
b. In specific and technical applications: see quots. (Often with prefixed word indicating the thing pulled, as in *fur-puller* (FUR *sb.*[1] 10), *pole-puller* (POLE *sb.*[1] 5 c), etc.)
1683 MOXON *Mech. Exerc.*, *Printing* xxiv. ¶15 Though the Puller Lays on Sheets, Lays down the Frisket, Lays down the Tympans and Frisket, Runs in the Carriage, [etc.], Picks the Form, Takes off the Sheet, and Lays it on the Heap, yet all these Operations are in the general mingled and lost in the name of Pulling. **1861** *Illustr. Times* 5 Oct. 221 To each gang of [hop-]pickers there is appointed a pole-puller. **1890** *Pall Mall G.* 21 Aug. 7/1 Fur-pulling is hard and dirty work... At the best, the pullers can only earn 11*s.* or 12*s.* a week. **1892** GREENER *Breech-Loader* 258 A rotating trap which simply defies trickery on the part of the trap puller or his assistants. **1894** DOBSON *18th Cent. Vignettes* Ser. II. 198 He was his own puller, collater, sewer, forwarder, headbander, coverer, and finisher [in bookbinding]. **1898** *Daily News* 24 Sept. 10/6 Saw-mills.—Puller out for bench.
c. *Cricket.* A batsman who pulls (sense 18).
1911, 1972 [see HOOKER[1] 6 b].
2. An instrument or machine for pulling: see quots.; in quot. 1542–3 †***pullers out*** = *pullings-out* (PULLING *vbl. sb.* 4).
1542–3 *Privy Purse Exp. P'cess Mary* (1831) 96 A payr of wrought Sleves, & pullers out for an Italian gowne wrought. **1688** R. HOLME *Armoury* III. 425/2 The Volsella, or Puller, or Tweezers.. is an Instrument.. by which they take forth a peece of a bone which is corrupt and moueable. **1892** *Daily News* 28 June 5/3 The pullers are stated to be fixed at the end of the rows, in suchwise that each machine is pulling over 50 punkas.
3. A horse that pulls: see PULL *v.* 9 and 9 b.
1852 R. S. SURTEES *Sponge's Sp. Tour* (1893) 125 Mr. Wake rolled the thong of his whip round the stick, to be better able to encounter his puller. **1880** MISS BRADDON in *World* 14 Jan. 15 He's one of the best horses I ever rode, but a confounded puller. *Mod.* A capital draught-horse, a willing puller.
†4. *puller on*: a provocative of thirst: see *pull on*, PULL *v.* 28 b. *Obs.*
1608 HEALEY *Discov. New World* 68 A seruice of shooing-hornes.. of all sorts, salt-cakes, red-herrings, Anchoues, and Gammons of Bacon,.. and aboundance of such pullers on. [**1791–1823** D'ISRAELI *Cur. Lit.*, *Drink. Cust.*]
5. One who or that which attracts custom; *spec.* (*N. Amer.*), a person employed to solicit passers-by into a shop. Also ***puller-in.***
1894 J. L. FORD *Lit. Shop* ix. 132 The Jewish old-clothing quarter that lies close to the Five Points is near by. The 'pullers-in', as the sidewalk salesmen are termed in the vernacular of the trade, transact business with a ferocity that can be best likened to that of Siberian wolves. **1928** *Sunday Dispatch* 15 July 14/3 Next to the Prince of Wales, Shaw is the best box-office puller in the United States. **1944** *Sun* (Baltimore) 15 Jan. 6/7, I wonder whether radio announcers are descendants of the Gay street and Harrison street pullers-in and the tray men of Holliday and Baltimore streets (circa 1909)... They had to pass a law to stop the pullers-in. **1955** [see CHEESE-CAKE 2]. **1958** N. LEVINE *Canada made Me* ii. 57 The cheap clothing stores—with the pullers standing in the doorways like prostitutes. **1970** J. H. GRAY *Boy from Winnipeg* 199 Any country family that stopped to look at something in a window was doomed. The 'puller' would come out and sweet-talk them into the store.

†ˈpullery[1]. *Obs.* Forms: 5 pulare, 6 pullery, -rye, -rie, 7 pullary. [app. a. F. *poulerie* a place in which fowls are reared = POULTRY 2.] A place where fowls are reared; also, domestic fowls collectively; = POULTRY 2, 3.
1488 *Acta Dom. Conc.* (1839) 90/2, xviij pulare price of þe pece iij d. **1535** BP. GARDINER in *Chron. Calais* (Camden) 165 That such pullery and wylde-foule maye passe by Graveling as ye require. **1552** HULOET, Pultrye or pullerye feadynge at large, *pascilis, passalis. Ibid.*, Pullerye keper, *gallinarius.* **1592** NASHE *P. Penilesse* (1593) 30 b, They.. had in one night.. all the whole progenie of their Pullerie taken away. **1657** REEVE *God's Plea* 59 Thou art afraid of kites for thy pullary.

pullery[2] (ˈpʊlərɪ). *Tanning.* [f. PULL *v.* + -ERY.] The place in which wool, hair, and bristles are removed from hides.
1903 L. A. FLEMMING *Pract. Tanning* 1 The relations between the soaking process and the subsequent processes of the beamhouse or pullery, and the tannery are close. **1963** E. M. POHLE in W. von Bergen *Wool Handbk.* (ed. 3) I. ix.

668 The pulling is conducted in the pulleries which..are connected with the large slaughter-houses.

pullery, obs. form of PILLORY.

† **pulleson**, var. PELISSON *Obs.*, a fur gown.

1689 in *11th Rep. Hist. MSS. Comm.* App. VII. 109, 3 halberts and one pulleson with several old..twilled coats.

pullet ('pʊlɪt). Forms: *pl.* 4–5 **poletes, polettes, -ys**, 5 **poullettis, pulettis**, 6 **pullettes**; *sing.* 5–6 **poullet**, 6 **poulet**, 6– **pullet** (7 **pullit**). [a. F. *poulet* young fowl, chicken, dim. of *poule*. Cf. also F. *poulette* fem. young hen. The early instances, being pl., do not show whether the sing. was then *polet* or *polette*.]

1. A young (domestic) fowl, between the ages of chicken and mature fowl; but formerly often used more loosely; *spec.* and *techn.* a young hen from the time she begins to lay till the first moult, after which she is a full-grown hen or fowl.

1362 LANGL. *P. Pl.* A. VII. 267 'I haue no peny', quod pers, 'Poletes [*v. rr.* pulettis, pultys; B. VI. 282 poletes; C. IX. 304 polettes] to bugge'. *c* **1430** *Two Cookery-bks.* 38 Take Polettys y-rostyd, & hew hem. *c* **1483** CAXTON *Dialogues* 10 Goo into the pultrie, Bye poullettis, One poullet [Fr. *poulle*] & two chekens, But no capon Ne no cocke bringe not. **1530** PALSGR. 257/2 Poullet, *poulet, poucin*. **1577** B. GOOGE *Heresbach's Husb.* IV. (1586) 158 b, The yoong Pullets are better for laying then sitting. **1655** MOUFET & BENNET *Health's Impr.* (1746) 161 A Law, that nothing but Chickens or young Pullits fed in the Camp should be brought to him at his Meals. **1680** WOOD *Life* 18 May (O.H.S.) II. 486 Hailstones..as big as pullets' eggs. **1764** SMOLLETT *Trav.* xviii. (1766) I. 289 Chickens and pullets are extremely meagre. **1846** J. BAXTER *Libr. Pract. Agric.* (ed. 4) II. 217 Pullets commence laying before sitting-hens, as they do not moult the first year.

fig. *a* **1533** LD. BERNERS *Gold. Bk. M. Aurel.* Let. viii. (1535) 122 Ye that be auncyent teachynge vs, and we obedient, as olde fathers and yonge pullettes, beinge in the neste of the senate. **1823** 'J. BEE' *Slang* s.v. *Pullet*, in common life, a female barn-door fowl, which has not yet produced eggs. Young women are so denominated, occasionally. **1922** JOYCE *Ulysses* 224 Blazes Boylan looked into the cut of her blouse. A young pullet. **1941** J. SMILEY *Hash House Lingo* 44 *Pullet*, young woman.

2. Name of a bivalve mollusc, *Venerupis pullastra*, more fully ***pullet carpet-shell***. Cf. PALOURDE.

1803 G. MONTAGU *Testacea Britannica* I. 127 This species [*sc. Venus pullastra*]..is frequently eaten by the common people, and in some parts of Devonshire indiscriminately called *Pullers* or *Pullets*. **1890** in *Cent. Dict.* **1901** E. STEP *Shell Life* 136 The Pullet Carpet-shell (*T. pullastra*)... The colouring is in some specimens very suggestive of the plumage of a speckled hen, [whence] probably..the mollusk has got the name of Pullet, which is locally applied to it on parts of the Devon coast. *Ibid.* 137 The Banded, the Pullet, and the Cross-cut are used in different parts..as human food. **1974** S. P. DANCE *Encycl. Shells* 268/1 Pullet Carpet Shell. Very similar in shape, size and ornament to *V*[*enerupis*] *rhomboides*.

3. *attrib.* and *Comb.*, as ***pullet-broth***, † ***sperm***; **pullet disease** = *new wheat disease* s.v. NEW *a.* 10 b.

1598 SHAKS. *Merry W.* III. v. 32 *Bard.* With Egges, Sir? *Fal.* Simple of it selfe: Ile no Pullet-Sperme in my brewage. **1747** tr. *Astruc's Fevers* 176 He may use simple or emulsioned pullet-broth. **1941** JUNGHERR & LEVINE in *Amer. Jrnl. Vet. Res.* II. 267/2 The majority of the cases occur between the ages of 5 and 7 months..hence the appropriateness of the term 'pullet disease'. **1945** *Vet. Jrnl.* CI. 7 The exact course of the pullet disease syndrome is unknown. **1950** [see *blue comb* (*disease*) s.v. BLUE *a.* 13]. **1977** R. F. GORDON *Poultry Dis.* vii. 183 It is difficult to obtain an accurate estimate of the incidence of pullet disease today.

pullet, error in Phillips, etc. for PALLET *sb.*[2] 2.

† **pulle'tier.** *Rom. Antiq. Obs. rare.* [a. OF. *pouletier* poultry-keeper, poultry-dealer, f. *poulet* chicken.] The keeper of the sacred chickens observed for purposes of augury. Cf. PULLARIAN.

1600 HOLLAND *Livy* x. 382 The principall pulletier chaunced to be stricken with a Iavelin. **1601** —— *Pliny* x. xxi. I. 279 They that by their *tripudium solistimum* (*i.* their heartie feeding) observed by the pullitiers, shew good successe.

pulletrie, obs. form of POULTRY.

pulley ('pʊlɪ), *sb.*[1] Forms: see below. [ME. a. OF. *polie* (*c* 1150 in Godef. *Compl.*), mod.F. *poulie* = Genevese dial. *polie*, Prov. *polieja*, It. *puleggia*, Sp. *polea*, Pg. *polé*; also med.L. *polea*, *polegia*, orig. a neuter pl. of med.L. *polegium* (Prov. *poulejo*, obs. It. *puleggio*):—Romanic type **polidium*, prob.:—Gr. *πολίδιον little pivot or axis, dim. of πόλος POLE *sb.*[2] See G. Paris in *Romania* XXVII. 484. Cf. also MLG. *polleie*, *-eide*, *-eige*, *-ege*, *-eine*, a windlass, the wheel of a well (Lexer). The variant *polyve*, *polyff* may have been due to mistaken analogy with such words as *hastive*, HASTY, *jolif*, JOLLY, MASTIFF, *masty*, of which the two forms were used together in 14–15th c.

Others have suggested as the source Gr. *πωλίδιον, dim. of πῶλος a colt; cf. OF. *poulain* a colt, also = PULLEY *sb.*[2], and *poulier* a pully.]

A. Illustration of Forms.

α. 4–5 **poley, poyle**, *pl.* **poliees, poylleyes; polye, pole**, 5–6 **polley, polie**, 6 **polly**.

1324 *Acc. Exch., K.R.* Bd. 165 No. 2 lf. 17 b, Pro vij Haussers et aliis cordis ad poleys. *Ibid.* 20 In ij Ruellis seu Poleyis ereis. **1481** Polley [see B. 1]. **1485** *Naval Acc. Hen. VII* (1896) 36 Poleis with Stroppes. *Ibid.* 37 Poles of iij sheves and colkes of brasse. **1495** *Ibid.* 201 Polyes. **1495** *Ibid.* 204 Poliees with iiij colkes of Brasse. **1497** *Ibid.* 247 Snachepoylleyes & other smale poyles. **1548–77** VICARY *Anat.* vii. (1888) 49 Lyke vnto a Polly to drawe water with. **1594** R. ASHLEY tr. *Loys le Roy* 116 b, To the top of the masts were fastned polies with cordes.

β. 4–5 **puly**, 5 **pulie**, *pl.* **-eis; pouley, pwlly**, 5–9 **pully**, 6 **poolly, poully, -ie, powley**, *pl.* **pulleis**; *Sc.* **pillie**, *pl.* **-eis**; 6–7 **pullie, -ye**, 6–8 **pooly**, 7 **pullee**, *pl.* **-eies**; 6– **pulley**.

1396 *Mem. Ripon* (Surtees) III. 123 Et in ij trendelys..et mangnum puly, 10d. **1489** CAXTON *Faytes of A.* II. xxviii. 140 To euery ladder moost be ordeyned thre pouleyes. **1497** *Acc. Ld. High Treas. Scotl.* I. 358 For tua schyffis with xiij puleis. **1519** HORMAN *Vulg.* 139 Some fyll the boket with a rope slydyng in a pooly. **1528–9** *Rec. St. Mary at Hill* 347 Paide for a pully for the sacrament and for a roppe to the same. **1541** R. COPLAND *Guydon's Quest. Chirurg.* G ij, In forme of a poully. **1545** *Aberdeen Regr.* XIX. (Jam.), Tua pilleis pertening to the wobteris craft. **1551** RECORDE *Pathw. Knowl.* Pref., Their Compas, their Carde, their Pulleis, their Ankers, were founde by the skill of witty Geometers. **1568** *Ludlow Churchw. Acc.* (Camden) 130 To William, torner, for turnynge of the powleys. **1603** *Vestry Bks.* (Surtees) 281 For lainge of a geaste and makinge of the pullee. **1603–4** in Swayne *Sarum Churchw. Acc.* (1896) 154 A Candlestake and pullye, 13s. 4d. **1622** PEACHAM *Compl. Gent.* ix. (1634) 73 Pulleies and Cranes of all sorts. **1725** *Bradley's Fam. Dict.* s.v. *Plover*, A Pooly or Cord to carry it. **1825** J. NICHOLSON *Operat. Mechanic* 11 The pulley is the third mechanic power.

γ. 4–5 **polyve, -ive**, 6 **polyff**.

c **1386** CHAUCER *Sqr.'s T.* 176 Ther may no man out of the place it dryue For noon engyn of wyndas ne polyue [*v. rr.* poliue, palyue]. **1465** *Mann. & Househ. Exp.* (Roxb.) 201 Item [paid] for iij. grete polyves, ij.s. ? *a* **1500** *Debate Carpenters Tools* 155 in Hazl. *E.P.P.* I. 84 Than be-spake the polyff, With gret stronge wordes and styffe.

B. Signification.

1. a. One of the simple mechanical powers, consisting of a grooved wheel mounted in a block, so that a cord or the like may pass over it; used for changing the direction of power, esp. for raising weights by pulling downward. Also, a combination of such wheels in a BLOCK (*sb.* 5), or system of blocks in a TACKLE, by means of which the power is increased. ***fixed pulley***, a pulley the block of which is fixed. ***frame pulley***, a pulley in which the wheels or sheaves are fixed in a frame.

1324 [see A. α]. *c* **1386** [see A. γ]. **1426–7** *Durham Acc. Rolls* (Surtees) 465 Pro j puly pro feretro, xijd. **1481** CAXTON *Reynard* xxxiii. (Arb.) 96 The welle where the two bokettys henge by one corde rennyng thurgh one polley. **1485–6** *Naval Acc. Hen. VII* (1896) 45 Sengle poleis with Colkes of brasse. **1574** in Feuillerat *Revels Q. Eliz.* (1908) 240 Pulleyes for the Clowdes and curteynes. **1577** B. GOOGE *Heresbach's Husb.* I. (1586) 42 They haue a Pully..wher-with they hoyse vp the Corne to the very Rafters of the house. **1687** A. LOVELL tr. *Thevenot's Trav.* I. 170 A Basket which they let down by a Rope that runs in a Pully. **1839** G. BIRD *Nat. Philos.* 68 In the pulley, as in the lever, time is lost as power is gained.

† **b.** Used as an instrument of torture, or part of one. *Obs.*

1584 R. SCOT *Discov. Witchcr.* II. iii. (1886) 18 The complaint of anie one man of credit is sufficient to bring a poore woman to the racke or pullie. **1641** MILTON *Animadv.* 15 A little pulley would have stretch't your wise and charitable frame it may be three inches further. *a* **1711** KEN *Blandina* Poet. Wks. 1721 IV. 520 Then on the Rack the Saint they stretch, Her Limbs with Screws and Pulleys retch.

2. A wheel or drum fixed on a shaft and turned by a belt or the like for the application or transmission of power; usually used so as to increase speed or power.

With specific prefix, as ***brake-pulley*** (a wheel acting as a brake), ***driving-pulley***, etc.; also ***cone-pulley*** (CONE *sb.*[1] 16), ***dead pulley*** (DEAD *a.* 23), ***differential pulley*** (DIFFERENTIAL *a.* 4 b), ***fast pulley, fast and loose pulleys*** (FAST *a.* 11), ***grip pulley*** (GRIP *sb.*[1] 9), ***guide pulley*** (GUIDE *sb.* 14), ***loose pulley*** (LOOSE *a.* 9); also ***conical pulley*** = *cone-pulley*; ***crowning pulley***, a pulley-wheel with convex rim, which tends to keep the belt in place by centrifugal force; ***parting pulley, split pulley***, a pulley-wheel made in two parts for convenience in mounting.

1619 *Vestry Bks.* (Surtees) 174 P^d for mendinge the pullies for the bell ropes, viij d. **1688** R. HOLME *Armoury* III. 323/1 The Struck Wheel, or Pulley [of a Jack], that about which the Chain or Rope goes to turn the Broach about. **1835** URE *Philos. Manuf.* 50 They are apt to permit a slipping of the bands on the surface of the driving-drums or pulleys. **1873** J. RICHARDS *Wood-working Factories* 67 The brake pulley must always be placed on the slack side of the belt, where the bottom pulley is the driver. **1884** W. S. B. McLAREN *Spinning* (ed. 2) 164 The driving belt is first taken round a fixed pulley, round a guide pulley, the driving pulley, and finally round another guide pulley. **1902** *Daily Chron.* 29 Sept. 9/4 The cable cars..were stopped..owing to a grip-pulley breaking at the..cable station.

3. *fig.* from senses 1 and 2.

1581 N. BURNE *Disput.* 109 The Cauuinist maist bauld of al vil afferme..that ve be certane pilleis, or ingeynis ar liftit vp to heauin be ane incomprehensibil maner. **1607** WALKINGTON *Opt. Glass* 12 They are..pullies to draw on their..destenies. **1691** HARTCLIFFE *Virtues* 41 We must examine all the windings and Labyrinths of our whole Frame, and see, by what Pullies and Wheels all the operations of our Minds are performed. **1870** EMERSON *Soc. & Solit., Clubs* Wks. (Bohn) III. 93, I prize the mechanics of conversation. 'Tis pulley and lever and screw.

4. *Anat.* **a.** The grooved articulating surface of certain joints; a trochlea. **b.** A cartilaginous loop by which the direction of a tendon passing through it is changed.

5. *attrib.* and *Comb.*, as ***pulley-block***, ***-case***, ***-chain***, ***-cord***, ***-rope***, ***-shaft***, ***-shell***, ***-spoke***, ***-stand***, ***-twine***, ***-wheel***; also **pulley-box**, (*a*) a broad pulley-wheel, a drum or cylinder; (*b*) in the draw-loom, a frame containing the pulleys for guiding the tail-cords (Knight *Dict. Mech.* 1875); **pulley-check**, a contrivance which prevents the return of the cord through the block; **pulley-clutch**, (*a*) a clasping device for attaching a pulley-block to an overhead rafter or the like (Knight); (*b*) a clutch by which a loose pulley is connected with the shaft (Funk); **pulley-cone**, a cone grooved and rotating on its axis, forming a set of pulley-wheels of different sizes; **pulley-drum**, the block or shell in which the sheave or sheaves are mounted; **pulley-frame**: see quot.: also called *gallows-frame*; **pulley-gauge**, a tide-gauge in which a cord, having a float at one end and a weight at the other, runs over a wheel connected with the pointer; **pulley-mortise** = *chase-mortise*: see CHASE *sb.*[3] 7 and MORTISE *sb.* 2; hence **pulley-mortised** *a.*; **pulley-piece, stile**, one of the vertical side-pieces of a window sash-frame, in which the pulleys are pivoted; **pulley-sheave** (†*Sc.* **pillie-scheve**), the sheave or grooved roller over which a rope runs in a pulley-block; **pulley-stone**: see quot. 1859.

1825 J. NICHOLSON *Operat. Mechanic* 311 To the *pulley block V is hung the counterpoise W. **1862** *Catal. Internat. Exhib.* II. XXXI. 22 Wrought-Iron Pulley Block, with cast-brass or iron sheaves. **1839** URE *Dict. Arts* 364 Cords passing from this *pulley box..over guides,..communicate the motion..to the bobbins. **1844** STEPHENS *Bk. Farm* II. 293 The *pulley-case is moved in the slide. **1903** *Harvard Psychol. Stud.* I. 417 A disc..about 50c. in diameter, rotating on a vertical pivot, was driven by a *pulley-cone underneath mounted on the same spindle. **1851** GREENWELL *Coal-trade Terms Northumb. & Durh.* 40 **Pulley-frames*, the gearing above a pit, upon which the pulleys are supported. **1856** KANE *Arct. Expl.* I. xi. 117 Our tide-register was on board the vessel, a simple *pulley-gauge, arranged with a wheel and index. **1842** GWILT *Archit.* §2019 The lower tier of timbers..are either notched to them, or are what is called **pulley mortised* into them. **1827** *Fowler Corr.* 577 (MS.) Oak sills and *pulley-pieces. **1733** TULL *Horse-Hoeing Husb.* xiv. 192 A little Horse at the End of the *Pulley-Rope. **1835** URE *Philos. Manuf.* 51 In this way, the *pulley-shaft of the teagle would require too great a speed. **1566** *Inv. R. Wardr.* (1815) 169 (Jam.) Item, fyve *pillie schevis of braiss, ane of thame garnesit with irne. **1825** J. NICHOLSON *Operat. Mechanic* 593 The face of the *pulley-stile of every sash-frame ought to project about three-eighths of an inch beyond the edge of the brick-work. **1851** MANTELL *Petrifactions* i. §2. 84 The curious fossils called, in Derbyshire, Screw, or *Pulley-stones. **1859** PAGE *Handbk. Geol. Terms*, *Pulley-stones*, a familiar term for the hollow casts or moulds of the joints and stems of encrinites. **1373** in Riley *Lond. Mem.* (1868) 369, 2 wyndyng poleys, 2 skeynes de *poletwyne. **1677** PLOT *Oxfordsh.* 230 A *pully-wheel, fastened to the arbor or axis of the hand that points to the hour. **1956** G. TAYLOR *Silver* vii. 154 *Dish Rings*... The earliest type is shaped like a pulley-wheel. **1967** *Antiquaries Jrnl.* XLVII. 227 Globular flagon with moulded base-angle and pulley-wheel rim.

'**pulley**, *sb.*[2] [Alteration of PULEYN, a. F. *poulain*, in same sense (1280 in Godef.), transferred use of *poulain* colt; in form confused with PULLEY *sb.*[1]

In the same way the Promp. Parv. explains *poleyne* as '*troclea*', a pulley, and Godef. VI. 347 erroneously explains OF. *poulain* as 'poulie', which is corrected in the Compl.]

A kind of ladder used by brewers' draymen in lowering barrels into a cellar; also called a slide or skid, and in the north of England a gantry. Also *attrib.* as ***pulley-rope***.

1653 URQUHART *Rabelais* I. v. 26 It is a pully; by a pully-rope wine is let down into a cellar. **1901** *Law Jrnl. Rep.* LXX. *Chancery* 680/2 It was necessary to attach to the tailboard of the dray a slide, or what in the trade is called a pulley, down which the cask was slid.

'**pulley**, *v.* [f. PULLEY *sb.*[1]: cf. F. *poulier*.]

1. *trans.* To raise or hoist with or as with a pulley. Also *fig.*

1599 NASHE *Lenten Stuffe* 41 His hairie tuft, or louelocke he leaues on the top of his crowne, to be pulld vp, or pullied vp to heauen by. *c* **1645** HOWELL *Lett.* (1650) I. 24 A mine of white stone..is between a white clay and chalk at first, but being pullied up, with the open air it receives a crusty kind of hardness. **1660** R. COKE *Power & Subj.* 15 These of themselves are not sufficient to pully man up to eternal happiness.

2. To furnish or fit with a pulley; to use with or work by means of a pulley. Hence **pulleyed** ('pʊlɪd) *ppl. a.*

1767 JAGO *Edge-Hill* III. 526 Their heavy Sides th' inflated Bellows heave, Tugg'd by the pulley'd Line. **1865** E. BURRITT *Walk Land's End* 164 There is no..hydraulic contrivance nor pulleyed hoist to facilitate the ascent.

pulley-bone, var. PULLY-BONE.

'pulleyless, *a.* [f. PULLEY *sb.*[1] + -LESS.] Without a pulley or pulleys.

1843 THACKERAY *Irish Sk. Bk.* vii, Pulleyless windows and lockless doors.

pulleyn, var. *polen* (see POLEN WAX), PULLEN[1].

pulleyne (kind of cloth): see POLAINE *Obs.*

† **pulley-piece**[1]. *Obs.* [*Pulley* here is app. a corruption of POLAYN.] = GENOUILLERE I.

1611 COTGR., *Pompes*, armour, called Pullie-peeces, for the knees. **1688** R. HOLME *Armoury* III. xix. (Roxb.) 166/1 Pullie peeces or Pulley-pies, Armour for the Knees.

pulley-piece[2]: see PULLEY *sb.*[1] 5.

pull-hitter: see PULL-.

pullicate ('pʌlɪkət). Also 8 pullcat, 8–9 pulicat(e, 9 *dial.* pollicate. [From *Pulicat*, name of a town on the Madras coast, in Tamil *pala Vēlkādu* 'old Velkādu'.] **a.** A coloured handkerchief, originally made at Pulicat. **b.** Later (from *c* 1785), A material made in imitation of these, woven from dyed yarn; also = ***pullicate handkerchief***, a checked coloured handkerchief of this material. Also *attrib.*

a. [Cf. **1519** G. CORREA *Lendas da India* (1860) II. 567 Roupas pintadas e tecidas de côres que se fazem em Paleacate, que he costa de Choramandel. *Yule's transl.* Painted cloths and other coloured goods, such as are made in Paleacate, which is on the coast of Choromandel.] **1839** *Encycl. Brit.* (ed. 7) XVIII. 704/2 *Pullicat*... The inhabitants are principally manufacturers and fishermen, who manufactured the handkerchiefs that took their name from this town.

b. 1792 P. FRENEAU *Poems* (1809) I. 31 Hum-hums are here—and muslins—what you please—Bandanas, baftas, pullcats, India teas. **1794** *Statist. Acc. Scotl.* XII. 114 Manufactured pulicates of a very superior colour or cotton pulicate handkerchiefs. **1808** *Usef. Projects* in *Ann. Reg.* 131/2 For drying of dyed yarn and pullicates (a kind of coloured chequed cotton handkerchiefs) a higher temperature..is required. **1820** J. CLELAND *Rise & Progr. Glasgow* 95 The same year [1785] pullicate handkerchiefs were begun to be made. **1880** A. SOMERVILLE *Autobiog.* 59, I wrought all that day on his loom, finishing 16 napkins of a 10/100 pulicate. **1891** *Blackw. Mag.* Oct. 571 A pulicat or gingham weaver at St. Ninians. **1958** [see MONTEITH[2]].

'pull-in. [f. phr. *to pull in*: see PULL *v.* 26.]

1. The action of pulling anything in or towards one. Also *attrib.* or as *adj.*

1906 *Westm. Gaz.* 20 July 4/2 Then there is the pull-in [of the fish], the flash of the brilliant bit of rainbow leaping its life out on the deck. **1976** *Offshore Engineer* July 21/1 A flowline pull-in tool has been developed..to meet this problem. **1977** *Ibid.* Apr. 27/2 The port has a step-down diameter which provides a positive stop during pipe pull-in.

2. a. A café or refreshment stand in a lay-by. Also ***pull-in café***.

1938 G. GREENE *Brighton Rock* III. iii. 128 He didn't speak to her in the bus... The country unwound the other way: Mazawattee tea, antique dealers, pull-ins. *Ibid.* v. ii. 195 A window of Charlie's Pull-in Café. **1959** *Listener* 8 Oct. 593/3 At the pull-in where most of the play was enacted the café owners sometimes struck a slightly false note. **1973** J. WAINWRIGHT *Devil you Don't* 18 A blue and white sign warned five miles to the next service area... 'They'll be at the next pull-in.'

b. An entry, recess, or the like where a motor vehicle may pull in; a lay-by.

1954 E. HYAMS *Stories & Cream* 163 A sprawling public-house..in front of which was a vast pull-in for motor-coaches. **1972** M. GILBERT *Body of Girl* iv. 43 The site had not been designed as a garage, and..the pull-in in front was not as deep as it should have been. **1976** *Southern Even. Echo* (Southampton) 3 Nov. (Advt.), Required. Workshop,.. shop, suitable for antiques restoring. Main road. Good pull-in.

pulling ('pʊlɪŋ), *vbl. sb.* [f. PULL *v.* + -ING[1].] The action of PULL *v.* in various senses.

1. Plucking, picking, gathering.

1382 WYCLIF *Isa.* xlii. 24 Who ȝaf Jacob in to pulling awei [1388 rauyschyng], and Irael to wasteres? **1530** PALSGR. 259/1 Pullyng awaye, *abstraction.* **1577** B. GOOGE *Heresbach's Husb.* II. (1586) 84 With often digging, and pulling of the leaues. **1641** BEST *Farm. Bks.* (Surtees) 57 The best time for pulling of pease is in wette weather. **1857** RUSKIN *Pol. Econ. Art* i. (1868) 78 Holding his way in spite of pullings at his cloak and whisperings in his ear. **1868** *Rep. U.S. Commissioner Agric.* (1869) 261 It grows naturally in tufts or clumps, and is gathered by pulling. **1875** JAS. GRANT *One of the 600* ii, I fear there will be a great pulling of caps among the housemaids [see PULL *v.* 2 a].

2. Stripping of feathers, wool, etc.; plucking; the freeing of furs from long coarse hairs (in full *fur-pulling*: see FUR *sb.*[1] 10).

c **1440** *Promp. Parv.* 416/1 Pullynge, or plukkynge of fowle, *deplumacio.* **1578–9** *Proclam. Q. Eliz.* 18 Feb., The inordinate pulling of marchantable wooll fels. **1796** W. MARSHALL *W. England* II. 183 The whole [geese] are subjected to the operation of 'pulling'. **1897** *19th Cent.* Nov. 740 After the pulling (that is the removal of the longer and coarser hairs) the skins are again dried.

3. a. Drawing with force or effort.

c **1440** *Promp. Parv.* 416/1 Pullynge, or drawynge, *traccio, tractus.* **1562** in *Shropsh. Parish Docts.* (1903) 61 For polyng downe of the rode loft iii[s]. **1664** H. MORE *Myst. Iniq.* ii. 38 What forced pullings and drawings to make proper terms to stretch for the covering and palliating unproper actions. **1676** TOWERSON *Decalogue* 374 The pulling of death upon us with our own hands. *a* **1716** SOUTH *Serm.* (1744) IX. v. 139 He would make the rigours of the sabbath give way to the pulling of an ox or a sheep out of the ditch.

b. In various specific and technical uses: see quots., and senses of PULL *v.*

1676 MOXON *Print Lett.* 2 The pulling off at the Press. **1866** 'MARK TWAIN' *Lett. from Hawaii* (1967) 84 The arraigning of a ship's officers before the courts by the crew to answer for alleged cruelties practiced upon them on the high seas—such as the 'pulling' of captains and mates by the crews of the *Mercury*. **1869** BLAKE-HUMFREY *Eton Boating Bk.* (1875) 54 *note*, Silver Oars and Steerage [were given] to the winners of the Pulling. **1894** STEAD *If Christ came to Chicago* 371 The present system of arbitrary pulling is simply a regulation system under the mask of arbitrary arrest. **1899** W. G. GRACE in *Westm. Gaz.* 2 Aug. 2/1 They should be severely reprimanded if they show any tendency towards pulling [in cricket]. **1960** G. A. GLAISTER *Gloss. Bk.* 333/2 *Pulling*, the removal of the cover, boards, end papers, tapes, and any lining material which, with the softening of old glue and cutting of sewing threads, are necessary stages in the preparation of a book for rebinding. **1975** J. PIDGEON *Flame* ii. 24 Jack Daniels and the D.T.s liked the Jackoranda. They didn't care much for the cramped stage.. and the money was always lousy. But it was the best place they knew for pulling.

c. *Racing.* The dishonest checking of a horse.

1861 *Times* 31 Dec., The public 'pulling' of horses is too dangerous a precedent to be frequently resorted to. **1888** *Daily News* 30 June 5/1 He strenuously denied every allegation of pulling.

d. Of a horse: see PULL *v.* 9 b.

1907 *Cavalry Training* (*War Office*) iii. §84 The usual causes of pulling are:—Excitability, Pain, Fear, Freshness and want of work, Hard mouth, Bad breaking.

e. *N.Z.* (See quot.) Cf. PULL *v.* 11 e.

1947 P. NEWTON *Wayleggo* (1949) 154 The act of a heading dog bringing sheep back to his master is termed pulling.

4. That which is produced by pulling: see quots. † ***pullings-out***, rich linings drawn out for display, esp. through slashes in the sleeves of a garment: see PULL *v.*[1] 29 b (*obs.*).

1558 in Feuillerat *Revels Q. Eliz.* (1908) 23 After that agayne translated into lyninge pullinges oute. **1564** in Fairholt *Costume* Gloss. s.v., Two pullingsowte of blake cipers wrought with Venice gold. **1828** *Craven Gloss.* (ed. 2), *Poolins*, the fat which is stripped or pooled off the intestines of a slaughtered animal. **1863** BRIERLEY *Chron. Waverlow, Trevor Hall* iii. 50 Like a pokeful o' pooins ut they couldno' get a single eend eawt on.

5. *attrib.* and *Comb.*, as ***pulling-hook, -rope***; 'moved by oars, rowing-', as ***pulling boat, launch, pinnace***; also **pulling-bar** = DRAW-BAR 1; **pulling bone** *U.S.* = *wish bone* s.v. WISH *sb.*[1] 4; † **pulling clock**, a clock with weights pulling on a barrel; **pulling-jack**, a jack which acts by contraction instead of expansion; **pulling-knife**, a fleshing-knife (FLESHING *vbl. sb.* 7); **pulling power**, the ability to attract or persuade; **pulling-trees** (*dial.*): see quot.

1892 J. G. A. MEYER *Mod. Locomotive Constr.* 528 Fig. 850 shows the wrought-iron *pulling-bar which connects the tender to the engine. **1912** A. T. QUILLER-COUCH *Hocken & Hunken* p. xxiii, The penultimate race (randan *pulling-boats) was finishing amid banging of guns and bursts of music. **1975** *Country Life* 2 Jan. 23/2 The RNLI ..displays the former Whitby No. 2 lifeboat..the last pulling boat to have been in the service of the Institution. **1877** BARTLETT *Dict. Amer.* (ed. 4) 502 **Pulling-bone*, the common name in Maryland, Virginia, &c, for the yoke-like breast-bone of chickens, by pulling which till it breaks children and young ladies settle which will be the first married. **1733** BUDGELL *Bee* I. 37, I do give and devise to M[r]. John Mills..my *Pulling Clock in my Bed Chamber. **1573** TUSSER *Husb.* (1878) 36 A *pulling hooke handsome, for bushes and broome. **1805** R. W. DICKSON *Pract. Agric.* II. 752 The poles [are] drawn up by a tool for the purpose, which is termed a dog or pulling-hook. **1875** KNIGHT *Dict. Mech.*, **Pulling-jack*, a hydraulic device for lifting or pulling heavy weights. **1894** *Times* 7 July 7/5 The gun was afterwards put on board an ordinary *pulling pinnace. **1942** H. C. BAILEY *Dead Man's Shoes* i. 7 Posters..credited by the expert with much more *pulling power. **1966** N. NICOLSON in H. Nicolson *Diaries & Lett.* 66 Harold Nicolson's importance to Mosley, apart from the increasing pulling-power of his name, was his close connection with Beaverbrook. **1978** P. BAILEY *Leisure & Class in Victorian England* vii. 147 Enterprising publicans..abolished the refreshment check..relying on the pulling power of the entertainment. **1895** KIPLING in *Pall Mall G.* 25 Oct., She took the *pulling-rope, and stepped out boldly at the boy's side. **1895** *E. Anglian Gloss.*, **Pulling-trees*, the part [of a plough] to which the horses are attached.

'pulling, *ppl. a.* [See -ING[2].] That pulls.

1633 G. HERBERT *Temple, Familie* i, What do these loud complaints and pulling fears? **1894** DOYLE *Mem. S. Holmes* 29 Sometimes it is a pulling jockey. **1903** *Westm. Gaz.* 19 Mar. 6/3 The brew served by the handle-pulling damsel.

† **pullion**, obs. form of PILLION *sb.*[1], a saddle, etc., and of BULLION[4], trunk-hose.

1526 *Lanc. Wills* (Chetham Soc.) I. 13 To Elizabeth my doghtour my pullion of wolsted. **1681** COLVIL *Whigs Supplic.* (1751) 24 He wore a pair of pullion breeches.

pull-iron, -line: see PULL-.

pullisch, -ish, etc., obs. forms of POLISH *v.*

'pullisee, -shee. *Sc.* Also pilly-shee. [Either var. of *pulley-sheave* (PULLEY *sb.* 5), or the pl. *pullisees* may be for *pullases*, from PULLACE, -ASE.] A pulley.

1728 RAMSAY *To Starrat* 19 Pullisees Can lift on highest roofs the greatest trees. **1828** MOIR *Mansie Wauch* xix, Having fastened a kinch of ropes beneath her oxters, I let her slide down..by way of a pilly-shee.

Pullman ('pʊlmən). [From the name of the designer, George M. *Pullman* of Chicago.] **a.** In full, ***Pullman car*** (***saloon***): a railway carriage constructed and arranged as a saloon, and (usually) with special arrangements for use as a sleeping-car.

1872 W. F. BUTLER *Great Lone Land* iv. 57 One takes a Pullman..as one takes a Hansom, Pullman and sleeping-car have become synonymous terms. **1874** MISS KINGSLEY in *C. Kingsley's Life & Lett.* (1879) II. 319 On the 15th we left Omaha in the magnificent Pullman car which was our home for the next fortnight. **1875** *Midld. Railw. Co.'s Time Tables* April, On and after April 1 trains of the celebrated American Pullman Drawing Room and Sleeping Cars will be run between London (St. Pancras) and Liverpool (Central) station. **1876** *World* V. No. 112. 14 One may ask whether the Great Western might not be expected to have a Pullman attached. **1877** *Daily News* 21 Nov. 5/6, I was as glad to hire it as though I had obtained a Pullman saloon. **1878** F. WILLIAMS *Midl. Railway* 673. **1894** *Daily News* 5 Oct. 4/5 The locomotives, tenders, and all the front part of the train up to the Pullman were wrecked. **1951** N. MITFORD *Blessing* II. xii. 265 The Bunbury burglar was walking up the Pullman on his way..to the Trianon bar. **1972** *Daily Tel.* (Colour Suppl.) 28 Apr. 49 By the end of this decade, British Rail acknowledges,..the Manchester, the South Wales and the Bristol Pullmans..will have vanished. **1977** *Modern Railways* Dec. 476/2 The other Metro-Cammell Pullmans still mouldering away in sidings have apparently been abandoned so long that rehabilitation is now unacceptably expensive.

b. *attrib.*

1869 *Bradshaw's Railway Man.* XXI. 419 Pullman Palace Car Company Stock $72,300. **1873** *Forest & Stream* 28 Aug. 34/1 It was a close pack..the whole scene reminding one forcibly of a 'Pullman' sleeping car. **1885** S. BAXTER in *Harper's Mag.* Apr. 698/2 The traveller..goes to sleep in his Pullman berth. **1893** GUNTER *Miss Dividends* 54 The Pullman porter shouts to her to look out. **1896** in *Westm. Gaz.* 28 Nov. 2/3 The first Pullman trains were run in this country in 1875... I saw in the summer of that year the very first Pullman train running South through the Trent Valley. **1954** W. TUCKER *Wild Talent* (1955) v. 58 Ray Palmer slept soundly in the topmost Pullman bed. **1955** D. DAVIE *Brides of Reason* 28 While Pullman sleepers lulled your sleeping head. **1977** *Time* 18 Apr. 22/2 The cabin can accommodate eight passengers on comfortable Pullman seats.

c. *transf.* (Usu. with small initial.) A prefabricated unit of kitchen or bathroom fixtures, compact as in a railway carriage. Usu. *attrib.* Chiefly *U.S.*

[**1932** *New Yorker* 23 July 5/2 There are many people who ..would be glad to buy a Pullman section to install in their home.] **1967** 'L. EGAN' *Nameless Ones* iii. 37 A chipped but spotless pullman washstand. **1968** 'R. MACDONALD' *Instant Enemy* xxv. 155 It was what is called a studio apartment, consisting of one large room with a pullman kitchen. **1973** *Sunday Bull.* (Philadelphia) 7 Oct. (Parade Suppl.) F6 New double sink pullmans with bright colors are available, or, if you want to do-it-yourself, try separate wash basins. **1977** *Chicago Tribune* 2 Oct. I. 33/2 The apartments for the 16 families in the community consisted of two rooms and a Pullman kitchen.

Hence **'Pullmanize, Pullman-car** *vbs., intr.* to travel in a Pullman car. *nonce-wds.*

1882 SALA *Amer. Revis* (1885) 271 After three or four days' Pullmanising. **1892** *Pall Mall G.* 9 May 6/1 Caravanning..finds its parallel in America in Pullman-carring.

Pullo, var. PEULH *sb.* and *a.*

† **pullock**, obs. var. POLLACK, a fish.

1823 T. BOND *E. & W. Looe* 124 Young pullock and conger eels are taken with a rod and line.

pullock, var. PUT-LOG.

'pull-off, *sb.* and *a.* [PULL- 1.] **A.** *sb.* **1.** The fact or action of pulling off or of being pulled off, in various special applications.

1859 *Musketry Instr.* 17 It is erroneous to suppose that by loosening the sear or any other pin an easier or lighter pull off is obtained. **1904** *Westm. Gaz.* 9 Dec. 7/2 The Committee..were also agreed as to the drag pull-off recommended [for the rifle]. **1926** *Gloss. Terms Electr. Engin.* (Brit. Engin. Stand. Assoc.) 133 *Pull-off*, a metal fitting attached to an ear and used on curves for adjusting the position of a trolley-wire in a horizontal plane. **1950** *Richmond* (Va.) *News-Leader* 28 Jan. 1 Detailed on this maneuver chart are the Navy's plans for an all-out 'Operation Pull-Off' to free the U.S.S. Missouri from her Chesapeake Bay mudbank. **1953** R. KNOX *St. Paul's Gospel* i. 10 You might get the printer to give you a pull-off of that childish picture all in blue, with the yellows and the reds left out.

2. *spec.* in *Parachuting* (see quot. 1947). Also *attrib.*

1933 *National Geogr. Mag.* May 614 Heels over head at the 'pull off'... The officer climbed out on the lower wing to the outer strut and, holding on with one hand, pulled his rip cord. **1940** *War Illustr.* 26 Jan. 20/2 The 'pull-off' type is used only for training novices in the 'art' [of parachuting]. **1947** M. NEWNHAM *Prelude to Glory* iv. 14 The procedure.. was for the pupil..at a signal from the pilot [to] clamber along the lower wing... The pupil let go his hold on the strut, and willy-nilly he became a parachutist. This was known as the 'pull-off' method.

3. = LAY-BY *sb.* 1 c. Cf. PULL-IN 2 b.

1969 V. CANNING *Queen's Pawn* iv. 63 Gilpin..was waiting in a pull-off down the road with the Land-Rover. **1972** R. K. SMITH *Ransom* VI. 264 Just after the city line as you come down the parkway there's a pull-off—a parking area. **1975** V. CANNING *Kingsford Mark* x. 163 He..parked the car on a turfed pulloff.

B. *adj.* Designating that which may be pulled off or from which something may be pulled off.

1902 *Daily Chron.* 23 Dec. 3/5 A fine copy of Charles Lamb's 'Beauty and the Beast';..enclosed in a specially-printed paper pull-off case, on which is printed the title-page. **1962** *Sunday Express* 7 Jan. 13/6 A pull-off calendar still showed the date. **1973** *Daily Tel.* (Colour Suppl.) 11 May 38/1 Much of it comes in supermarket-style cans with pull-off tops.

pull-on: see PULL-.

pullony, obs. f. POLONY[2] (sausage).

pullorie, obs. f. PILLORY.

pullorum (pʊˈlɔːrəm). [mod.L., a. the specific epithet of *Bacterium pullorum* (L. F. Rettger 1909, in *Jrnl. Med. Res.* XXI. 117), f. gen. pl. of L. *pullus* young chick.] The specific epithet of *Bacterium pullorum* (now *Salmonella gallinarum*) used *attrib.* in **pullorum disease** to designate an acute, infectious, often fatal disease of young chicks, which is also known as bacillary white diarrhœa.

1929 *Bull. Mass. Agric. Exper. Station* XLVIII. 2 It was unanimously voted to accept the suggestion of Dr. Leo F. Rattger to change the name of Bacillary white diarrhea to 'pullorum disease'. **1930** M. A. JULL *Poultry Husbandry* xxvi. 411 The pullorum disease, which frequently causes such enormous losses among chicks, has been called 'bacillary white diarrhea'. **1960** *Farmer & Stockbreeder* 23 Feb. 124/1 Among these bacteria are the organisms responsible for respiratory diseases and pullorum disease. **1977** G. A. CULLEN et al. in R. F. Gordon *Poultry Dis.* i. 11 Outbreaks of pullorum disease in turkeys are rare in this country.

†ˈ**pullous,** *a. Obs. rare.* [f. L. *pullus* dark-coloured + -OUS.] Of a dark colour; blackish.

1698 B. ALLEN in *Phil. Trans.* XX. 377 The Body is of a Pullous Colour.

ˈ**pull-out,** *sb.* and *a.* Also as one word. [PULL- 1.] **A.** *sb.* **1.** The fact or action of pulling out; withdrawal from an undertaking or affair, *esp.* from military involvement or occupation.

1825 C. M. WESTMACOTT *Eng. Spy* II. 139 Something good for the pull out. **1944** *Daily Progress* (Charlottesville, Va.) 2 Oct. 9/5 A correspondent reported increasing signs of a pull-out..of tens of thousands of German troops. **1968** MRS. L. B. JOHNSON *White House Diary* 13 Apr. (1970) 664 Some of the headlines were easing up—'D.C. Curfew Off, Gradual Pull-Out of GI's Starts'. **1976** *Billings* (Montana) *Gaz.* 2 July 3-c/4 A weaker committee motion, specifying a one-year ban for a political pullout, was defeated by the same margin. **1976** P. HENISSART *Winter Quarry* v. 60 Most people think a missile pullout is overdue. **1977** P. THEROUX *Consul's File* 177, I inherited him [*sc.* a dog] in Saigon... I took him back to the States after the pull-out.

2. In various technical uses. **a.** *Aeronaut.* The transition from a dive or spin to normal flight.

1919 PIPPARD & PRITCHARD *Aeroplane Struct.* vi. 54 The combination of terminal velocity with a quick pull out is one which would break practically any aeroplane. **1932** *Discovery* Apr. 114/2 Individual records of 'pull-outs' from a dive have registered high accelerometer readings without the pilots experiencing ill effects. **1943** *Sun* (Baltimore) 20 July 3/2 All of the men were half dazed. They had been flung about the ship in its two dives and pullouts... The plane was under control, but barely so. **1962** F. I. ORDWAY et al. *Basic Astronautics* xii. 465 During World War II dive bomber pilots found they could minimize the effects of acceleration by..tightening muscles, and shouting during pullouts from dives.

b. *Surfing.* (See quot. 1967.)

1967 J. SEVERSON *Great Surfing* Gloss., *Pull-out*, steering the board over or through the back of the wave, as to end the ride. **1968** W. WARWICK *Surfriding in N.Z.* 13/1 To execute a pullout, guide your board to the top of the wave, then kick it into the wave. **1971** *Studies in English* (Univ. Cape Town) Feb. 27 Like the turn, the pull-out may be forehand or backhand.

3. A self-contained detachable section of a newspaper, magazine, etc. Also, = *fold-out* sb. s.v. FOLD *v.*[1] 10.

1952 *Conc. Oxf. Dict.* Add. *Pull-out*, page or plate in book that unfolds out from front edge of leaves to facilitate reference. **1955** *Sun* (Baltimore) 28 Oct. (B ed.) 26/4 TV Pull-Out... Have been meaning to write and tell you how wonderful is the new TV pull-out section of *The Sunday Sun.* **1971** S. E. MORISON *European Discovery Amer.: Northern Voy.* p. viii, The reproduction of old maps in a book presents typographical problems. Nobody likes a big pull-out; but if the size is too much reduced, one cannot read the names of places. **1971** *Woman's Own* 27 Mar. 21 Next week..8-page pull-out of dairy dishes. **1977** *Listener* 17 Mar. 332/2 A potential centre-page pull-out for..*Hustler* magazine.

B. *adj.* Designating that which may be pulled out (in various senses).

1881 *Daily News* 4 Aug. 5/2 First the box with a lid, then the cupboard with a door, then the perfected 'pull-out' drawer. **1929** 'R. CROMPTON' *William* iv. 86 They're frightened of the big roundabout—an' the pull-out toffee makes them sick. **1950** J. D. CARR *Below Suspicion* xii. 149 Dr. Bierce lowered himself on one of the pull-out seats facing them. **1955** [see sense 3 above]. **1966** *B.B.C. Handbk.* 79 The pull-out map..shows how..Soviet and Chinese broadcasters have exploited their geographical position. **1979** *Amat. Photographer* Feb. 62/1 The three cameras we're looking at this week..have pull-out or retracting lenses.

ˈ**pull-over.** [f. phr. *to pull over*: see PULL *v.*]

1. The action or an act of pulling over or from side to side; also *attrib.* or as *adj.* having the function of pulling over.

1894 *Westm. Gaz.* 10 Jan. 6/1 The overhead line is on one side of the street only, there are no cross or pull-over wires.

2. A gap in the coast sand-hills where vehicles can be pulled over to the beach; a cart-road over a sea-bank. *local* (Eastern counties).

1883 *Lincoln Chron.* 16 Mar., The sea swept over the pull-over at Sutton. *c* **1900** E. P[EACOCK] in *Eng. Dial. Dict.* s.v., There is a broad, but very heavy pull-over opposite the New Inn and Vine Hotels at Skegness.

3. *Hat-making.* A silk or felt cover or nap drawn over a hat body; also, a hat so made.

1875 in KNIGHT *Dict. Mech.*

4. (Usu. as one word.) Used *attrib.* or *absol.* to designate articles of clothing that are put on by drawing them over the head; *spec.* (chiefly in *absol.* use) a knitted or woven garment for the upper part of the body; a jumper or jersey.

1907 *Yesterday's Shopping* (1969) 320c/1 The 'Pullover' Storm Coat..is especially designed without any opening when in wear, and, being made without a rubber neck, entirely obviates any discomfort in pulling the garment on or off over the head. **1921** *Daily Colonist* (Victoria, B.C.) 6 Apr. 4/5 (Advt.), Another lot of these smart Wool Pull-Over Sweaters to sell at $2.98. **1925** *Westm. Gaz.* 28 Apr. 3 The vogue of the Pullover has supplanted the waistcoat for golf. **1930** *Daily Tel.* 9 Apr. 15/1 (Advt.), Attractive three-piece suit in tweedknit..designed with..new tuck-in pullover finely woven to tone with suit. **1940** GRAVES & HODGE *Long Week-End* iii. 42 Most women in 1919 were wearing jumpers, knitted by themselves as a relief from 'socks for soldiers'; and soon afterwards men, too, began to adopt them under the name of 'pull-over'. **1967** N. FREELING *Strike Out* 82 The young man was..darning the worn elbow of a pullover. **1977** *New Yorker* 10 Oct. 124/3 (Advt.), Pullover Dress. A most cozy dress in thick pure cotton flannel, brushed inside and out, long known for its wearing qualities.

Hence ˈ**pullovered** *a.*, wearing a pullover.

1926 *Daily Chron.* 13 May 2/2 'I'll be sorry to leave the old bus tonight,' said the plus foured pull-overed youth at the wheel of the 'General' yesterday afternoon. **1977** *Film & Television Technician* Jan. 10/3 (*caption*) Making whoopee at the fun-packed Animation Social..[were] pullovered Animation Section Chairman, Barry Merritt, Joe Telford and journal editor Roy Lockett.

pullow, obs. variant of PILAU.

pull-piece, -rod: see PULL-.

pulls (pʊlz), *sb. pl.*[1] *north. dial.* [app. = MDu., MFlem. *pöle, peule, puele, pole,* Du. *peul* husk, shell, pod.] The chaff or husks of rapeseed, pulse, or grain.

1788 W. MARSHALL *Yorksh.* II. 40 The seed is cured..in the chaff or pods—provincially, 'pulls'. *Ibid.* Gloss., *Pulls*, the shells or chaff of rape and other pulse. **1877** *Holderness Gloss.*, *Pulls*, the husks of oats.

pulls, *sb. pl.*[2] [f. PULL *v.*] Short straw which falls out when the straight straw is drawn; also called *pull-tails*: see PULL- 2; also, heads of corn broken off from the stalks in threshing.

1844 *Jrnl. R. Agric. Soc.* V. I. 268 The straw here weighed ..does not include the short and broken, which goes away in what is technically termed 'falls' or pulls. **1876** *Mid-Yorks. Gloss.*, *Pulls*, most usually applied to the heads of corn dispersed on a barn-floor, after thrashing.

pull-stroke to **pull-trigger:** see PULL-.

pullulant (ˈpʌljʊlənt), *a.* [ad. L. *pullulānt-em*, pr. pple. of *pullulāre*: see next.] Budding.

1889 *Scots Observer* 4 Jan., Certain pullulant *ébauches* of definition. **1907** *Daily Chron.* 8 Aug. 3/1 Where we find a pullulant world of new ambitions and brilliant promises.

pullulate (ˈpʌljʊleɪt), *v.* Also 7 -at. [f. L. *pullulāt-*, ppl. stem of *pullulāre* to sprout out, spring forth, spread, grow, increase, f. *pullul-us*, dim. of *pullus* young of any animal, chick.]

1. *intr.* **a.** Of a growing part, shoot, or bud: To come forth, sprout out, bud.

1619 H. HUTTON *Follies Anat.* (Percy Soc.) 50 Yet they, more urgent, whiles he would conceale, Like Hydra's heads did pullulate, renew. **1774** GOLDSM. *Nat. Hist.* I. 253 Beneath the bark of a tree they pullulate into branches. **1842** *Blackw. Mag.* LI. 723 Others whose pinions are but just beginning to pullulate. **1872** T. HINCKS in *Pop. Sci. Rev.* XI. 339 The sexual buds of the zoophyte..sometimes.. pullulate from a portion of the common substance.

b. Of a seed: To sprout, to germinate. Of a plant or animal: To send out shoots or buds, to propagate itself by budding; to breed, to multiply: now usually with the connotation of rapid increase.

1621 T. GRANGER *Exp. Eccles.* vii. 12. 175 The swellings and diseases of the body, whose root remaineth still within, and pullulateth againe after the same, or some other manner. **1657** W. MORICE *Coena quasi Κοινὴ* xi. 130 Seed doth not pullulate but after some little time. **1891** DU MAURIER *P. Ibbetson* 14 Those rampant, many-footed things that pullulate in damp and darkness under big flat stones.

c. *Path.* To put forth morbid growths.

1775 NOURSE in *Phil. Trans.* LXVI. 438 The surface of the intestines..began to pullulate, throwing up small grains of flesh from every point.

2. *intr. transf.* and *fig.* **a.** To be developed or produced as offspring, to spring up abundantly.

1657 FITZ-BRIAN *Gd. Old Cause dress'd in prim. Lustre* (1659) 6 Superstition..would in time have pullulated, and budded forth afresh. **1714** MANDEVILLE *Fab. Bees* (1733) I. 89 [They] may..see good spring up and pullulate from evil, as naturally as chickens do from eggs. **1890** *Times* 6 Oct., One of those lower forms of Christianity which pullulate so freely in the religious soil of the United States.

b. *intr.* To teem, to swarm.

1835 SOUTHEY *Doctor* xc. III. 153 The Egyptian mind seems always to have pullulated with superstition. **1883** W. H. RUSSELL in *19th Cent.* Sept. 490 As to the beggars, they pullulate in the place.

Hence ˈ**pullulating** *ppl. a.*, budding, sprouting.

1738 WARBURTON *Div. Legat.* II. vi. I. 277 Religious liberty which would have stifled this pullulating Evil in the Seed. **1819** G. S. FABER *Dispensations* (1823) I. 384 In our own evil days of rankly pullulating heresy and blasphemy. **1822–34** *Good's Study Med.* (ed. 4) I. 183 In the fresh pullulating grains of the glume.

pullulation (pʌljuːˈleɪʃən). [n. of action from PULLULATE *v.*: see -ATION.] The action of pullulating; sprouting, germination; generation, production. Also, the product of this; offspring, progeny.

1641 R. BROOKE *Eng. Episc.* II. vi. 87 Some of these Tenets ..have beene the base pullulations of spirits enslaved to false ends. **1653** H. MORE *Conject. Cabbal.* (1713) 29 The Generations or Pullulations of the Heavenly and Earthly Nature. *a* **1677** HALE *Prim. Orig. Man.* III. ii. 257 In some places..especially between the Tropicks, such a Pullulation of Men and Beasts may be supposed to be. **1890** E. JOHNSON *Rise Christendom* 123 Virtues then fructify; in their pullulation, purity of heart is acquired.

b. *spec.* in *Biol.* Generation or reproduction by budding; in *Path.*: see quot. 1897.

1822–34 *Good's Study Med.* (ed. 4) II. 22 Granulating pullulations..consist of exudations of coagulating lymph from the vessels. **1857** BERKELEY *Cryptog. Bot.* xiv. 23 The formation of a new cell by pullulation from the walls. **1897** *Syd. Soc. Lex.*, *Pullulation*, budding, or sprouting. Also, a morbid growth or sprouting of tissue.

ˈ**pull-up.** [f. vbl. phr. *to pull up*: see PULL *v.* 35 e.]

1. a. The act of pulling up a horse or vehicle; a sudden stop; hence *fig.*

1837 DICKENS *Pickw.* xxxiii. 344 That's rayther a sudden pull up, ain't it, Sammy? **1842** —— *Let.* 27 Feb. (1974) III. 92, I have so much to say that I could fill quires of paper, which renders this sudden pull-up the more provoking. **1854** MRS. GASKELL *North & S.* xviii, All his business plans had received a check, a sudden pull-up. **1883** FR. M. PEARD *Contrad.* xxxiv, Next they heard wheels, and the pull up at the door. **1950** A. HUXLEY *Let.* 6 Aug. (1969) 628 In the plain you and the child can walk abroad without having to take the car and without being fatigued by a pull up. **1980** 'M. INNES' *Going it Alone* xvii. 153 If they did a sudden pull up like that, it wouldn't be much good just driving on.

b. A lifting-up, encouragement.

1872 GEO. ELIOT *Middlem.* IV. VIII. 360 He told Mary that his happiness was half owing to Farebrother, who gave him a strong pull-up at the right moment. **1913** G. DE H. VAIZEY *College Girl* xxi. 291 Think of all that it means..if we can keep these men from drifting, and give them a pull-up in time!

2. A place for pulling up; a stopping-place for riders or drivers. Also *attrib.* Phr. ***a good pull-up for carmen,*** a roadside café; also in various *transf.* and allusive uses.

1887 *Advertisement*, This inn affords one of the most tempting positions for a pull-up house on the road. **1899** *Daily News* 27 May 4/1 A humble little coffee-shop, which is a good pull-up for carmen. **1902** *Daily Chron.* 30 Apr. 8/1 A favourite 'pull up' for cyclists. **1925** H. V. MORTON *Heart of London* 50 London's tea-shops are of many kinds, from the standardized shop to the good pull-up for millionaires constructed on the Paris plan. **1928** *Sunday Express* 29 Apr. 4/4 It was known in Hollywood as 'The Legs of Carmen', but your censor doubtless attended to that. The censor's office is usually a good pull-up for Carmen. **1935** A. J. CRONIN *Stars look Down* II. xx. 442 He went into a workman's coffee-house: *Good pull up for lorrys* was on the sign outside. **1952** M. ALLINGHAM *Tiger in Smoke* ix. 153 The pull-up on the corner opens at five... I want..to get a bit o' breakfast. **1965** [see DINER 2 b]. **1977** *Listener* 24 Mar. 382/2 Our mother..ran..a 'caff'—or what was then known as a good pull-up for car-men.

3. a. The fact or action of pulling something upwards; *spec.* in physical exercise, the action of pulling up the body by means of a bar or beam held by the hands.

1907 M. A. VON ARNIM *Fräulein Schmidt* lix. 255 'He only wants his wind,' said Vicki... 'It certainly was rather a long pull up,' said I. **1938** *Jrnl. R. Aeronaut. Soc.* XLII. 625 The manœuvres consisted of push-downs and pull-ups from level flight..and push-ups from inverted flight. **1946** J. E. Q. BARFORD *Climbing in Britain* iv. 63 The main types of holds are as follows:—A Straight Pull Up. This is a hold over which the fingers can curl as over the rung of a ladder. **1960** E. S. & W. J. HIGHAM *High Speed Rugby* 298 Pull-ups on beam, or other horizontal bar. **1971** A. A. MICHELE *You don't have to Ache* i. 21 Here are some things that you should not be doing:..Do not do push-ups or pull-ups.

b. *attrib.* or as *adj.* Designating that which may be pulled up.

1919 R. FRY *Let.* May (1972) II. 451, I live in a house which has..a real Victorian W.C. with a pull up plug. **1973** *Country Life* 26 July 260/2 The gear lever..is mounted on a floor console with the pull-up handbrake.

‖**pullus** (ˈpʊləs). Pl. pulli. [L., = young chick.] A young bird during the stage before it is fully grown or able to fly.

1774 G. White *Let.* 2 Sept. in *Selborne* (1789) I. xl. 100, I had been..comparing the tails of the male and female swallow, and this ere any young broods appeared; so that there was no danger of confounding the dams with their *pulli*. **1955** R. Spencer in *Brit. Birds* XLVIII. 468 Pull. (pullus)—nestling or chick not yet flying. **1964** A. L. Thomson *New Dict. Birds* 904/2 The bird is technically a 'pullus'..until it is full-grown and flying. *Ibid.*, After the pullus stage a bird is described as 'juvenile' while wearing its first plumage of true feathers.

pully-bone (ˈpʊlɪbəʊn). *U.S. dial.* Also **pulley-bone**. [f. PULL *v.* + -Y + BONE *sb.*] = *wish-bone* s.v. WISH *sb.*[1] 4. Cf. *pull-bone* s.v. PULL- 2 and *pulling-bone* s.v. PULLING *vbl. sb.* 5.

1939 B. K. Harris *Purslane* 148 The girls scrambled over the pulley-bone of the turkey. **1947** M. Henry *Misty of Chincotiague* xvi. 152 Somethin' told me to save the pully bone from that marsh hen. **1966** *Publ. Amer. Dial. Soc.* 1964 XLII. 22 *Pully-bone*, the wish-bone or furcula, of a chicken, often pulled after a meal, to determine who is to get married first. **1976** *Amer. Speech* 1973 XLVIII. 180 If we understand that there is a connection between the Southern mountains and coastal plains, the occurrence of *you-all*, *grea[z/s]y*, and *pulley bone* 'wishbone' in an area as far away as the Midwest becomes readily explainable.

pully-hauly (ˈpʊlɪˈhɔːlɪ), *a.* and *sb. colloq.* Also pulley-, -hawl(e)y, pull'e-haul'e. [f. PULL *v.* + HAUL *v.* + -Y.] **A.** *adj.* Consisting of, or characterized by, pulling and hauling. **B.** *sb.* The action or work of pulling and hauling.

a. 1820 *Sporting Mag.* VI. 192 It was a complete pully hawly contest on the part of Martin. **1854** Miss Baker *Northants. Gloss.* s.v., 'I hate such pully-hawly-wark'.

b. 1785 Grose *Dict. Vulg. Tongue* s.v., To have a game at pully hawly, to romp with women. **1877** *Q. Rev.* CXLII. 69 The ropes with which the old Norsemen played their favourite game of pully-hauly against one another. **1906** *Temple Bar Mag.* Jan. 57 There is the halliard-chanty, sung when the topsail or topgallant yards are being hoisted by pully-hauly or strength of arm.

Hence **pully-'haul** *v.*, to pull or haul with all one's strength; **,pully-'hauling** *vbl. sb.* (in quot. 1872 applied to unskilful bell-ringing).

1872 Ellacombe *Ch. Bells Devon*, etc. iii. 225 Hence it is, by way of ridicule, called 'Pully hauling'. **1880** *Daily Tel.* 30 Nov., Then commenced such a scrimmage for the mastery, such a pully-hauling and kicking of shins, as was remembered for months after. **1894** *Northumb. Gloss.*, *Pully-haal*, to pull by main force. **1899** Mary Kingsley *W. African Sk.* iii. 79 When the boys are pully-hauling [a tree] down the slope.

pullyn(e, obs. form of PULLEN[1].

pullysh(e, -ysshe, obs. forms of POLISH *v.*

†**pulme**. *Obs. rare.* [ad. L. *pulmo*.] The lungs.

1553 Udall tr. *Geminus' Anat.* A vj/1 Here foloweth of the Pulme, called of some, the Lightes and Lounges. **1578** Lyte *Dodoens* I. xviii. 27 Men say that it [Veronica] will heale all vlcers, inflammations and harmes of the Pulme or Lunges.

†**'pulment**. *Obs.* Also 4 polment. [ad. L. *pulment-um* sauce, condiment; food generally.]

1. Pottage.

c **1250** *Gen. & Ex.* 190 Esau fro felde cam, Saȝ ðis pulment, hunger him nam. **13..** *E.E. Allit. P.* B. 628 At þis ilke poynte sum polment to make. **1483** Caxton *Gold. Leg.* 45/1 [She] delyueryd to hym brede and the pulmente that she had boyled. **1514** Barclay *Cyt. & Uplondyshm.* 3 Sterynge the pulment Of peese or frument, a noble meete for lent.

2. A poultice or the like.

1599 A. M. tr. *Gabelhouer's Bk. Physicke* 256/1 Take pulverisatede Chalcke, put therto Vineger, and make therof a pulmente, spreade it on a cloth and apply it theron. *Ibid.* 256/2 Boyle Oatenmeale in Vineger, till that resemble a thicke pulmente, or pappe, and applye this thereon.

†**pulmen'tarious**, *a.* *Obs. rare*$^{-0}$. [f. L. *pulmentāri-s* of the nature of a relish + -OUS.]

1656 Blount *Glossogr.*, *Pulmentarious*, of or belonging to, or made with, Pottage or Gruel.

pulmo- (ˈpʌlməʊ), shortened from PULMONI-, combining form of L. *pulmo*, *pulmōn-em* lung; occurring in various terms of zoology, anatomy, etc., as ‖**pulmobranchiæ** (-ˈbræŋkiːː) *sb. pl.*, lung-sacs: see quots.; hence **pulmo'branchial**, **pulmo'branchiate** *adjs.*, having, or breathing by means of, pulmobranchiæ. **pulmo-'cardiac** *a.* [CARDIAC], pertaining to the (left) lung and heart (see quot.). **pulmo-cu'taneous** *a.* [CUTANEOUS], pertaining to or supplying the lungs and skin: applied to two main arterial trunks in the frog, from each of which arises a pulmonary and a cutaneous artery. **pulmo-'gastric** *a.*, pertaining to the (left) lung and stomach (see quot.). **pulmo'gasteropod**, **-'gastropod**, *a.* belonging to the *Pulmogaste'ropoda*, the pulmonate or air-breathing gastropods; *sb.* one of these. **'pulmograde** [after PLANTIGRADE, etc.], *a.* belonging to the *Pul'mograda*, a synonym of *Discophora* or jelly-fishes, so called from their swimming by alternate expansion and contraction of the body, resembling that of the lungs in breathing; *sb.* a pulmograde hydrozoon, a jelly-fish. **pulmo-he'patic** *a.* [HEPATIC], pertaining to the lung and liver (see quot.). **pul'mometer** [-METER], an instrument for measuring the capacity of the lungs, a spirometer; so **pul'mometry**, measurement of the capacity of the lungs, spirometry. **pulmo-'tracheate** *a.*, breathing by means of lung-sacs (or lung-books) as well as tracheal tubes, as the majority of spiders.

1875 Cambridge in *Encycl. Brit.* II. 272/2 Arachnids breathe by..**pulmo-branchiæ*, said to be a compound of the gill of fish and the lung of mammals. **1897** *Syd. Soc. Lex.*, *Pulmo-branchiæ*, the modified gills of certain animals (Arachnids, air-breathing Mollusca) adapted for air-breathing. **1890** *Cent. Dict.*, **Pulmobranchial*. **1897** *Syd. Soc. Lex.*, *Pulmo-branchial*. [**1841** *Penny Cycl.* XIX. 119 *Pulmobranchiata*, M. de Blainville's name for his first order of his second subclass of his *Malacozoa*.] **1841** T. R. Jones *Anim. Kingd.* 403 All the *pulmobranchiate Gasteropoda are not terrestrial; our fresh waters abound with various species that respire air by a similar contrivance. **1890** Billings *Nat. Med. Dict.*, **Pulmo-cardiac region*, portion of thorax where the heart is covered by a thin layer of lung. **1871** Huxley *Anat. Vert. Anim.* iv. 185 The hindermost, or *pulmo-cutaneous, passage ends in the pulmonary and the cutaneous arteries. **1875** Huxley & Martin *Elem. Biol.* (1877) 176 The apparently simple branches into which the *truncus arteriosus* divides, are, in fact, each made up of three separate trunks, the pulmo-cutaneous trunk behind, the aortic arch in the middle and the carotid trunk in front. **1890** Billings *Nat. Med. Dict.*, **Pulmo-gastric region*, region of thorax where an edge of the left lung lies over the stomach and spleen. **1842** Brande *Dict. Sci.* etc., **Pulmogrades*..the name of a tribe of Acalephans. **1843** Owen *Comp. Anat.*, *Invert.* 106. **1848** E. Forbes *Naked-eyed Medusæ* 75 The affinities of the Pulmograde Acalephæ. **1890** Billings *Nat. Med. Dict.*, **Pulmo-hepatic region*, region of thorax where an edge of lung covers the liver. **1814** E. Kentish (*title*) An account of Bathe..with the Description of a *Pulmo-meter, and Cases showing its utility in ascertaining the state of the Lungs in Diseases of the Chest. **1870** S. Gee *Auscult. & Percuss.* I. ii. (1893) 35 Instruments which have been invented for registering the respiratory movements and powers:..spirometers, pulmometers, pneumatometers, anapnographs. **1857** Dunglison *Med. Lex.* s.v. *Spirometer*, This mode of measurement has been called Spirometry, as it was formerly called *Pulmometry.

pulmonad (ˈpʌlmənæd), *adv.* *Anat.* [f. L. *pulmo*, *pulmōn-* lung + *-ad* as in DEXTRAD.] Towards or to the lungs.

1808 Barclay *Muscular Motions* 232 That which from the system carries the sanguineous fluid pulmonad, or towards the lungs; and that which from the lungs carries it systemad, or towards the system.

pulmonal (ˈpʌlmənəl), *a.* [ad. mod.L. *pulmōnāl-is* (irreg. for *pulmōnāris*), f. *pulmo*, *pulmōn-em* lung: see -AL[1].] = PULMONARY *a.*

1856-8 W. Clark *Van der Hoeven's Zool.* I. 571 Respiration in some tracheal, in others pulmonal. **1880** Günther *Fishes* 149 The lung has no pulmonal artery.

pulmonar (ˈpʌlmənə(r)), *a.* [f. L. type **pulmōnār-is*, f. *pulmo*, *-mōnem* lung: see -AR.] Having lungs or analogous organs; pulmonate; *spec.* belonging to the arachnid order *Pulmonaria*.

‖**Pulmonaria** (pʌlməʊˈnɛərɪə). *Bot.* [med.L. fem. (sc. *herba*) of L. *pulmōnāri-us* beneficial to the lungs, f. *pulmo*, *pulmōn-em* lung; so called from its assumed virtue in curing disease of the lungs, as supposed to be indicated by the spotted leaves resembling the lungs.] A genus of boraginaceous plants; lungwort.

The British species is *P. officinalis*, Bugloss Cowslip.

1578 Lyte *Dodoens* I. lxxxv. 125 This herbe is called of the Apothecaries..*Pulmonaria* and *Pulmonalis*, in Latine *Pulmonis herba*, that is to say Lungewurt, or the herbe for the lunges. **1753** Chambers *Cycl. Supp.* s.v., The common spotted pulmonaria, or..sage of Jerusalem, is esteemed an excellent medicine in many of the disorders of the lungs. **1785** Martyn *Rousseau's Bot.* xvi. (1794) 178 Gromwell, Pulmonaria, Cerinthe, and Viper's Bugloss, have the tube of the corolla naked. **1882** *Garden* 18 Mar. 173/2 The Pulmonarias are amongst our most interesting spring flowers.

†**pulmo'narious**, *a.* *Obs. rare*$^{-0}$. [f. as prec. + -OUS.] (See quot.)

1658 Phillips, *Pulmonarious*, diseased in the Lungs.

‖**pulmonarium** (pʌlməʊˈnɛərɪəm). *Entom.* Pl. -ia. [mod.L., neut. of L. *pulmōnārius*: see prec.] A membrane separating the ventral and dorsal parts of the abdomen in some insects, and containing the spiracles or respiratory openings.

1826 Kirby & Sp. *Entomol.* III. xxxvi. 713 If you examine the abdomen of the mole-cricket.., you will easily discover the true spiracles in the folds of the *pulmonarium*, which separates the back of that part from the belly.

pulmonary (ˈpʌlmənərɪ), *a.* (*sb.*) [ad. L. *pulmōnāri-us*, f. *pulmo*, *pulmōn-em* lung: see -ARY[1]. Cf. F. *pulmonaire*.]

1. Of, pertaining to, situated in, or connected with the lungs. (Chiefly *Anat.*)

pulmonary artery, the main artery, or each of its two branches (right and left), which conveys the blood from the heart to the lungs for aeration. ***p. circulation***, the course of the blood from the heart to the lungs and back to the heart, as distinguished from the general or *systemic* circulation. ***p. valves***, a name for the three semilunar valves at the entrance of the pulmonary artery. ***p. veins***, the veins which convey the aerated blood from the lungs to the heart.

1704 J. Harris *Lex. Techn.* I, *Pulmonary Vessels*, are those which carry the Blood from the Heart to the Lungs, and back again,..the Pulmonary Vein, and the Pulmonary Artery. **1779** *Phil. Trans.* LXIX. 351 A larger animal imparts a greater quantity of its pulmonary air to the inflammable air. **1826** Good *Bk. Nat.* (1834) I. 306 The blood is first received into the heart on the pulmonary side. **1848** Quain *Anat.* (ed. 5) 1149 Each bronchial tube..enters a distinct pulmonary lobule, within which it undergoes still further division, and at last ends in the small cellular recesses named the air cells or pulmonary cells.

b. Constituting a lung or lung-like organ; of the nature of a lung. ***pulmonary pouch, sac***, a lung-sac.

1834 *Penny Cycl.* II. 232/1 The external apertures of these, termed spiracles,..are transverse chinks, corresponding in number with the pulmonary pouches [in *Arachnida*]. **1872** Mivart *Elem. Anat.* 13 Respiration of air by pulmonary sacs is neither universal in man's sub-kingdom, nor unknown out of it.

c. Carried on by means of lungs.

1826 Kirby & Sp. *Entomol.* III. xxviii. 50 Yet their [birds'] respiration is perfectly pulmonary. **1869** Gillmore tr. *Figuier's Rept. & Birds* Introd. 5 To be succeeded by pulmonary respiration.

2. Occurring in or affecting the lungs (chiefly *Path.*); of or pertaining to disease of the lungs.

1727-41 Chambers *Cycl.*, Pulmonary consumption, or consumption of the lungs. **1793** Beddoes *Consumption* 139 Giving the pulmonary ulcers an opportunity to heal. **1836-41** Brande *Chem.* (ed. 5) 364 In some pulmonary complaints, the respiration of air slightly tainted by the admixture of chlorine has been resorted to as a stimulant. **1877** Roberts *Handbk. Med.* I. 17 The dusky or livid hue of some cardiac and pulmonary diseases.

b. Affected with or subject to lung-disease, esp. consumption; consumptive. Also *transf.* Of the quality associated with the consumptive.

1843 Thackeray *Jérôme Paturot*, Fond of inventing such suffering angels..pale, pious, pulmonary, crossed in love, of course. **1862** —— *Philip* ii, If you want a pulmonary romance, the present won't suit you. **1896** *Allbutt's Syst. Med.* I. 281 Inclined to regard the voyage..as unsuitable to the pulmonary invalid.

3. *Zool.* Having lungs, lung-sacs, or pulmonary organs; distinguished from *tracheary*, as ***pulmonary arachnids***; also, distinguished from *branchiate*, as ***pulmonary*** or pulmonate ***molluscs***.

1833 Doubleday in *Entomol. Mag.* I. 278 We could never separate the Pulmonary from the Trachean Arachnida, or Branchiferous from the Pulmonary Gasteropod Mollusca.

B. *sb.*

†**1.** = PULMONARIA. [Cf. F. *pulmonaire* (Cotgr.).]

1658 Phillips, *Pulmonary*, the herb Lungwort.

2. *Zool.* A pulmonary arachnidan, as a spider or a scorpion.

1835 Kirby *Hab. & Inst. Anim.* II. xix. 281 Latreille.. divides his Arachnidans into two Orders, *Pulmonaries*, or those that breathe by *gills*, and *Trachearies*, or those that breathe by *spiracles* in connection with *tracheæ*.

pulmonate (ˈpʌlmənət), *a.* (*sb.*) *Zool.* [ad. mod.L. *pulmōnāt-us*, f. *pulmo*, *-mōn-em* lung: see -ATE[2] 2. In F. *pulmoné*.] **A.** *adj.* Having lungs, as the higher vertebrates, or lung-like respiratory organs, as the orders *Pulmonata* of gastropod molluscs and *Pulmonaria* of arachnids. **B.** *sb.* A pulmonate mollusc (or, less usually, arachnid).

1842 Brande *Dict. Sci.* etc., *Pulmonates*, *Pulmonata*, the name of an order of Gastropodous Mollusks, including those which breathe air. **1862** Dana *Man. Geol.* III. 363 As late as the Carboniferous period there were only reptiles, insects, and pulmonate mollusks. **1883** E. R. Lankester in *Encycl. Brit.* XVI. 663/2 There is one genus of slug-like Pulmonates which frequent the sea-coast.

So (in same sense) **'pulmonated** *a.*

1841 T. R. Jones *Anim. Kingd.* 410 In the Snail and the generality of pulmonated Gasteropoda. *a* **1854** E. Forbes *Lit. Papers* I. (1855) 22 The absence of pulmonated vertebrata from the older formations should be expected.

pulmoni- (pʌlˈməʊnɪ), the full combining form of L. *pulmo*, *pulmōn-em* lung, as in **pulmoni'branchiate**, **pul'monigrade**, *adjs.* and *sbs.*: see *pulmobranchiate*, *pulmograde* under PULMO-.

1847 Webster, **Pulmonibranchiate*, having the branchiæ formed for breathing air... (A term applied to certain mollusks.) **1864** *Ibid.*, *Pulmonibranchiate*, one of an order of mollusks having the branchiæ formed for breathing air. **1846** Patterson *Zool.* 36 The term *pulmonigrades has been applied to these animals [gelatinous Medusæ].

‖**pulmonia** (pʌlˈməʊnɪə). *Path.* [mod.L., f. L. *pulmōn-em* lung. In F. *pulmonie*, in 16th c. *poulmonie*.] A name for disease of the lungs.

1844 W. Irving in *Life & Lett.* (1866) III. 320 In this state of mind she was attacked by measles and pulmonia. **1857** Dunglison *Med. Lex.*, *Pulmonia*, Phthisis pulmonalis, Pneumonia. **1858** Mayne *Expos. Lex.*, *Pulmonia*, old term the same as *Peripneumonia*.

†**pul'moniac**, *a.* *Obs.* *rare*⁻¹. [irreg. f. L. *pulmōn-em* lung, after words from Gr., as *cardiac, demoniac*.] = PULMONIC *a.* 3.

1657 TOMLINSON *Renou's Disp.* I. xiv. 28 Some Medicaments..corroborate some parts by a specifical virtue, as Cephalick..the head..Pulmoniack, Hepatick, the Lungs, Liver [etc.].

pulmonian (pʌl'məʊnɪən). *Zool.* [f. L. *pulmōn-em* lung + -IAN.] A pulmonate gastropod.

1839 *Penny Cycl.* XIV. 322/1, 1. Nudibranchians... 4. Pulmonians without an operculum... 5. Operculated Pulmonians.

pulmonic (pʌl'mɒnɪk), *a.* (*sb.*) [a. F. *pulmonique* (Paré 16th c.), f. as prec.: see -IC.]

A. *adj.* **1.** = PULMONARY *a.* 1.

1702 W. COWPER in *Phil. Trans.* XXIII. 1183 Liquors.. Injected into the Pulmonick Arteries pass to their Veins. **1794** SULLIVAN *View Nat.* I. 265 The pulmonic air..sent forth by respiration. **1799** J. BAILEY in *Med. Jrnl.* (1800) III. 128 The blood is propelled with less energy to the pulmonic system. **1854** BUSHNAN in *Orr's Circ. Sc.* I. *Org. Nat.* 63 This ventricle receives its blood partly from a systemic, partly from a pulmonic auricle.

2. = PULMONARY *a.* 2.

1661 [see PULMONICAL, quot. 1658]. **1666** G. HARVEY *Morb. Angl.* xxvi. (1672) 68 Pulmonique Consumption, or Consumption of the Lungs. **1725** CHEYNE *Health* i. §5 (1787) 9 Subject to nervous or pulmonick distempers. **1800** *Med. Jrnl.* IV. 292 Where pulmonic inflammation was dreaded. **1843** R. J. GRAVES *Syst. Clin. Med.* xiv. 151 For months together the pulmonic symptoms prevailed.

3. Remedial or curative in disease of the lungs; good for the lungs. ? *Obs.*

1694 SALMON *Bate's Dispens.* (1713) 187/2 Tincture of Guajacum, or Pock-wood..is Pulmonick, and profitable against Catarrhs.

4. *Phonetics.* Relating to the lungs as the initiator of the air stream used in the articulation of speech sounds.

1942 BLOCH & TRAGER *Outl. Linguistic Analysis* ii. 31 Stops with inner closure at the bottom of the lungs are called *pulmonic*. **1949** J. R. FIRTH in *Trans. Philol. Soc. 1948* 142 Types of sound which appear to crop up repeatedly in syllabic analysis..are..aitch or the pulmonic onset. **1959** [see GLOTTALIC *a.*]. **1975** F. R. PALMER in W. F. Bolton *Eng. Lang.* i. 17 Almost without exception the whole of the articulation of sounds in European languages is powered by air expelled from the lungs (it is 'pulmonic egressive').

B. *sb.* **1.** A remedy for disease of the lungs; a medicine good for the lungs. ? *Obs.*

1694 SALMON *Bate's Dispens.* (1713) 17/1 It is a good Pulmonick, profitable against the Phthisick, Consumption, Pining. **1710** T. FULLER *Pharm. Extemp.* 273 Our true Pulmonicks consist of such Particles as..cannot be.. assimulated by it [the blood].

2. A person subject to or affected with disease of the lungs; a consumptive person.

a **1735** ARBUTHNOT (T.), Pulmonicks are subject to consumptions, and the old to asthmas. **1893** *Edin. Even. Dispatch* 1 Apr. 2/2 Passing the winter at that recruiting ground for pulmonics—the Cape.

†**pul'monical**, *a.* *Obs.* [f. as prec. + -AL¹.] = prec. adj.

1597 A. M. tr. *Guillemeau's Fr. Chirurg.* 55 b/1 Autumne, enimye to all pulmonicalle woundes. **1599** —— tr. *Gabelhouer's Bk. Physicke* 105/1 [Recipe for] a Pulmonicall potione. **1658** R. WHITE tr. *Digby's Powd. Symp.* (1660) 40 Half of them who dye in London, dye of phthisicall and pulmonicall distempers [1661 cited by EVELYN *Fumifugium* I. 13 as 'pulmonic']. **1670** BLOUNT *Glossogr.* (ed. 3), *Pulmonical*, belonging to the Lungs or Lights.

pulmoniferous (pʌlməʊ'nɪfərəs), *a.* *Zool.* [f. L. *pulmōn-em* lung + -FEROUS.] Bearing or having lungs (or lung-like organs); pulmonate; *spec.* belonging to the group *Pulmonifera* (= *Pulmonata*) of gastropod molluscs.

1835–6 *Todd's Cycl. Anat.* I. 621/2 The pulmoniferous Mollusca. **1851–9** BRODERIP in *Man. Sci. Enq.* 400 The terrestrial or pulmoniferous Mollusca (land-shells).

b. Containing the lungs or lung-sacs.

1890 *Cent. Dict.* s.v., The pulmoniferous somites of an arachnidan.

So **pul'monifer**, a pulmoniferous gastropod.

pulmono-, irreg. combining form of L. *pulmo, -ōn-em* lung, sometimes used instead of PULMONI- or PULMO-, as in **pulmono'branchiate**, **-branchous** (-'bræŋkəs) *adjs.* = *pulmobranchiate*; **pulmono'gastropod** *a.* and *sb.* = *pulmogastropod* (*Cent. Dict.*): see PULMO-.

1824 J. E. GRAY in *Ann. Philos.* Aug. 107 On the Natural Arrangement of the Pulmonobranchous Mollusca. **1849** CRAIG, *Pulmonobranchiate*, belonging to the order Pulmonobranchiata. **1855** *Knight's Eng. Cycl., Nat. Hist.* III. 65 Affording a good character for dividing the Land Pulmonobranchous Mollusca into two families.

pulmotor ('pʌlməʊtə(r)). [f. PULMO- + L. *mōtor* that which moves.] An apparatus for automatically forcing air or oxygen into and out of the lungs when breathing has ceased or is weak. Also *attrib.* and *fig.*

Formerly a proprietary name in the U.S.

1912 J. W. PAUL *Use & Care Mine-Rescue Breathing Apparatus* (U.S. Bureau Mines: Miners' Circular No. 4) (rev. ed.) 25 The pulmotor is intended for use in the resuscitation of persons who have partly or wholly ceased to breathe as a result of inhaling irrespirable gases, of an electric shock, or of drowning. **1913** *Official Gaz.* (U.S. Patent Office) 24 June 1052/1 Dragerwerk..Lubeck, Germany..*Pulmotor*... Mechanical respiratory apparatus and devices for administering oxygen. Claims use since February, 1909. **1928** *Daily Express* 31 Dec. 12/4, I grabbed up my bag and the pulmotor, and was over here in a jiffy. **1940** *Economist* 6 Apr. 618/2 The third view is almost.. entirely mechanistic. It belongs in the pulmotor school of economics. **1951** W. KEES in *Furioso* Summer 35 Another fat woman In a dull green bathing suit Dives into the water and dies. The pulmotors glisten. **1974** S. SHELDON *Other Side of Midnight* vii. 180 She debated whether to stay in bed or call a pulmotor squad.

pulp (pʌlp), *sb.* [ad. L. *pulpa* the fleshy portion of the animal body; also, the pulp of fruit, the pith of wood: cf. F. *poulpe* (R. Estienne 1539), *polpe, pulpe* (Cotgr. 1611).] A soft, moist, homogeneous or formless substance or mass: in various applications.

1. The fleshy succulent part of a fruit; also, the soft pith in the interior of the stem of a plant.

1563 HYLL *Art Garden.* (1593) 154 Gourds without seeds, hauing onely but a soft pulpe within. **1578** LYTE *Dodoens* II. lxxxix. 269 The right Fenell hath round knottie stalkes.. filled with a certaine white pithe or light pulpe. **1605** TIMME *Quersit.* III. 179 Take the marrow or pulp of cassia. **1712** E. COOKE *Voy. S. Sea* 338 There is another Sort like a Curan, has a white Pulp. **1785** MARTYN *Rousseau's Bot.* vii. (1794) 74 *note*, The apple also has a firmer pulp. **1832** TENNYSON *Pal. Art* (ed. 1833) li, Ambrosial pulps and juices.

2. Any soft muscular or fleshy part of an animal body; the fleshy part of the limbs, hands, fingertips, etc.; the soft substance of internal parts of organs, as the spleen, the intervertebral disks, etc.; the soft nervous substance which fills the interior cavity of a tooth.

(This may have been the earliest sense in Eng., as in L.)

1611 COTGR., *Polpe*, the pulpe; brawne or fleshie part of the bodie. **1615** CROOKE *Body of Man* 815 These two together with the fourth doe make the pulpe or calfe of the Leg. **1685** BOYLE *Enq. Notion Nat.* 297 If..you carefully stop the upper Orifice with the Pulp of your Finger. **1713** STEELE *Guard.* No. 26 ¶6 It is not for me to celebrate the lovely height of her forehead, the soft pulp of her lips. **1835–6** *Todd's Cycl. Anat.* I. 311/2 There was a gelatinous pulp, analogous to the pulps which secrete teeth. **1848** CARPENTER *Anim. Phys.* 144 The matter composing this little body, which is termed the pulp, is gradually converted into the ivory of the tooth. **1858** O. W. HOLMES *Aut. Breakf.-t.* ix. (1883) 183 He..touched the..corner of his right eye with the pulp of his middle finger.

3. a. A soft formless mass; esp. of disintegrated organic matter, produced by moistening and trituration or by boiling.

1676 WORLIDGE *Cyder* (1691) 108 One end..may serve to contain the fruit, the other the vessels for the pulp. **1692** SIR T. P. BLOUNT *Ess.* 67 They boyl the bodies of their Dead, and afterwards pound them to a pulpe. **1792** *Trans. Soc. Arts* X. 145 Nine acres of the land..was almost an entire pulp. **1838** T. THOMSON *Chem. Org. Bodies* 839 A determinate quantity of potatoes was reduced with water to a pulp. **1853** KANE *Grinnell Exp.* xxxviii. (1856) 346 The trodden paths around our ship are in muddy pulp, adhering to the boots. **1868** *Rep. U.S. Commissioner Agric.* (1869) 161 Beet pulp for fattening cattle.

b. *spec.* The fibrous material, as linen, wood, etc., reduced to a soft uniform mass, from which paper is manufactured; paper-pulp.

1727–41 CHAMBERS *Cycl.* s.v. *Paper*, Paper is chiefly made among us of linen or hempen rags, beaten to a pulp in water. **1825** J. NICHOLSON *Operat. Mechanic* 377 The most eligible mode of adjusting the thickness of the paper would be by varying the proportion of the surface of the cylinder, which is covered with pulp. **1846** MᶜCULLOCH *Acc. Brit. Empire* (1854) I. 749 The first idea of a machine for converting pulp into paper, originated in France, the inventor being an ingenious workman of the name of Louis Robert. **1862** *Fraser's Mag.* Nov. 637 It is only necessary to put the wood into one end of the machine, and take out at the other the pulp ready for being converted into paper. **1902** *Westm. Gaz.* 27 May 9/3 Rags are no longer available in sufficient quantities for paper-making. Hence the resource to vegetable fibres such as wood-pulp... Experts regard the pulp re-made from old newspapers as about equal to calico pulp.

c. Ore pulverized and mixed with water, in which condition the dross is washed out; slimes. ***dry pulp***, dry crushed ore.

1837 J. T. SMITH tr. *Vicat's Mortars* 164 Each of these being hollowed in the middle like a funnel, received a fluid pulp, composed..of clay and water. **1872** RAYMOND *Statist. Mines & Mining* 137 The bullion, pulp, and tailings were tested by assay. **1877** *Ibid.* 24 Ten pans, holding 1 ton each of dry pulp.

4. *fig.* **a.** Appearance of pulpiness (of texture).

1801 FUSELI in *Lect. Paint.* ii. (1848) 383 The beauties of oil-colour, its glow, its juice, its richness, its pulp.

b. Something of a 'pulpy' character, without stability, strength, or 'backbone'.

1878 T. L. CUYLER *Pointed Papers* 164 The difference is clearly marked between the boy who has moral pluck and the boy who is mere pulp.

c. orig. *U.S.* Ephemeral literature, esp. (in derogatory use) that regarded as being of poor quality; popular or sensational writing generally. Freq. *attrib.*, as ***pulp artist, fiction, novel, writer***, etc. Also *ellipt.* = *pulp magazine* (sense 5 c below). Also *transf.*

1931 *Frontier* (Missoula, Montana) Nov. 82/1 Even should he fail to publish in the big magazines, and never graduate from the 'pulps', he can rise to as much as ten cents a word. **1945** [see GLOSSY *sb.* b]. **1945** R. CHANDLER *Let.* 24 Aug. (1966) 201 Marlowe just grew out of the pulps. He was no one person. **1951** WODEHOUSE *Old Reliable* ii. 32 Half the best known writers today started on the pulps. **1952** M. STEEN *Phoenix Rising* iii. 69 [He] picked up a handful of old pulps. **1966** *New Statesman* 15 July 104/3 There's only one well-known actor... The bulk of the others' experience comes from local rep, TV pulp and Shaftesbury Avenue trivia. **1972** D. E. WESTLAKE *Bank Shot* iv. 24 He'd discovered the pulps..when he was in high school. **1976** *National Observer* (U.S.) 3 July 17/1 When I started..the pulps were gasping their last.

attrib. **1936** Pulp writer [see ACE 2 d]. **1946** R. CHANDLER *Let.* 2 Oct. (1966) 24 We have a much better home than an out-of-work pulp writer has any right to expect. **1951** M. MCLUHAN *Mech. Bride* (1967) 151/1 Why aren't you interested in the private lives of the strippers and pulp artists who upholster our desert landscape? **1955** L. A. FIEDLER in D. Lodge *20th Cent. Lit. Crit.* (1972) 464 Wordless narrative: digests, pulp fiction, movies, picture magazines. **1958** *New Statesman* 6 Sept. 294/3 The wretched reader of pulp literature is encouraged to dream of sins and orgies he is forbidden to enact. **1959** *Listener* 30 July 176/3 The pulp novels of Mickey Spillane. **1965** *Ibid.* 27 May 788/1 Feelings should not run too high over sophisticated pulp literature. **1970** G. GREER *Female Eunuch* 164 The bored housewife.. intoning the otherwise very forgettable words of some pulp lovesong. **1975** J. MCCLURE *Snake* viii. 102 Constrictors.. are certainly not given to crushing anything to a bloody pulp. As pulp fiction would have it! **1976** *Listener* 29 July 122/2 Cody..met up with a pulp novelist..who proceeded to set Cody up as a regular frontier hero in a series of literary adventures. **1977** *Time Out* 17–23 June 35/3 Juicy pulp movie about the organisation's efforts to move in on the truck hi-jacking operataion run by Anna and her girls.

5. *attrib.* and *Comb.* **a.** esp. in technical terms referring (*a*) to the preparation of pulp for making paper (sense 3 b), as ***pulp-chest, factory, industry, -maker, -strainer, -ware***; ***pulp-making*** sb. and adj., ***pulp-made*** adj.; or (*b*) to the pulp of the teeth (sense 2), as ***pulp-cell, -fissure***, etc.; also ***pulp-assay*** (sense 3 c), ***pulp-hole, -pit***, etc. **b.** Special Comb.: **pulp-board**, a kind of millboard made directly from paper-pulp, instead of being made like pasteboard from paper; **pulp-boiler** = *pulp-digester*; **pulp-canal**, the pulp-cavity in the fang of a tooth; **pulp-capping**, the covering the soft interior of a tooth by artificial means; **pulp-cavity, -chamber**, the space in the interior of a tooth which contains the pulp; **pulp-digester**, a machine for reducing paper-stock and obtaining the fibre free from extraneous matter; **pulp-dresser, -engine, -grinder, -machine**, machines used in the preparation of paper-pulp; **pulp-meter**, an apparatus for measuring the amount of pulp required for a specified thickness of paper; **pulp-mill**, a mill in which wood is reduced to paper-pulp; also, a factory in which pulping is carried on; **pulp-nodule**, an excrescence of dentine in the pulp-cavity of a tooth; **pulp paper**, newsprint; paper of similar texture used for books or magazines; **pulp-stone**, (*a*) = *pulp-nodule*; (*b*) a stone used like a grindstone for reducing wood to pulp; **pulp-washer**, a machine for removing impurities from paper-pulp; **pulpwood**, wood suitable for making paper-pulp. **c.** (in sense 4 c) **pulp magazine**, a magazine devoted to popular or sensational literature; also (with hyphen) *attrib.*

1881 RAYMOND *Mining Gloss.*, **Pulp-assay*, the assay of samples taken from the pulp after or during crushing. **1882** *Rep. to Ho. Repr. Prec. Met. U.S.* 123 Pulp assays averaging about $130 per ton. **1904** *Let. to Editor fr. Jas. Spicer & Sons*, There are strawboards, made, (as the name implies) from straw, and *pulp boards, (white and coloured), various qualities, all made direct from the pulp. —— *Let. fr. J. Dickenson & Co.*, A Millboard is a Pulp Board of a dark color, made from old Rope, Bagging, etc., and also finished by mechanical pressure, without the aid of paste. **1845** OWEN *Odontography* II. Descr. Plates 16 The large central vascular or *pulp canals. **1875** *Dental Cosmos* XVII. 507 The success attending *pulp-capping. **1840** OWEN *Odontography* I. II. iv. 245 The *pulp-cavity in old teeth becomes occupied by a coarse bone. **1872** L. P. MEREDITH *Teeth* (1878) 54 Each [tooth] is supplied with blood vessels and nerves, which unite in a common *pulp chamber. **1853** URE *Dict. Arts* II. 350 A box..kept full of pulp from the *pulp-chest. **1893** *Westm. Gaz.* 2 Mar. 9/1 The Factory Inspectors..never see the *pulp-holes where all the bad jam and lemon-peel are thrown. **1858** GREENER *Gunnery* 387 From the *pulp-made cartridge paper. **1931** *Frontier* (Missoula, Montana) Nov. 83/1 We need some outlets for the work, with pay, of young and enthusiastic writers; something to keep them away from the '*pulp' and 'slick paper' magazines. **1934** *Sun* (Baltimore) 15 Mar. 21/1 He wrote 'Western' fiction for the 'pulp' magazines. **1937** A. HUXLEY *Ends & Means* xii. 191 Each month the pulp magazines offer to millions of readers their quota of true confessions, film fun, spicy detective stories, hot mysteries. *Ibid.* 207 Pulp-magazine stories are transcriptions of the commonest and easiest day-dreams. **1944** 'G. ORWELL' in *Horizon* Oct. 239 English imitations of the 'pulp magazine' do now exist. **1954** KOESTLER *Invisible Writing* III. xv. 186 We churned out a couple of detective stories for pulp magazines. **1968** E. A. MCCOURT *Saskatchewan* vii. 76 Farwell, as various stories attributed to him suggest, had a pulp-magazine mind. **1975** *Times Lit. Suppl.* 10 Oct. 1174/2 *The Continental Op* is the anonymous narrator of the stories which Dashiell Hammett wrote for the pulp magazine *Black Mask* during the 1920s. **1883** D. A. WELLS *Pract. Econ.* (1885) 107 Even the *pulp-makers..will find difficulty in marketing their pulp in the immediate future. **1901** *Daily Colonist* (Victoria, B.C.) 31 Oct. 3/2 It is therefore just as desirable that information should be compiled for their [*sc.* fishermen's] use as for the use of miners, lumbermen, pulp-makers or farmers. **1909** Pulp-maker [see *log-lumberer* s.v. LOG *sb.*[1] 9 b]. **1901** *Westm. Gaz.* 31 Oct. 2/1 Probably in the near future half the sawing-mills and paper- and *pulp-making mills which supply Europe will be transferred to Finland from Norway and Germany. **1853** URE *Dict. Arts* II. 350 The *pulp-meter which is driven in connection with the paper machine. **1898** *Daily News* 26 July 5/7 He has started *pulp mills and lumber mills, and he has made other valuable mineral finds. **1872** L. P. MEREDITH *Teeth* (1878) 132 It is a very hard matter to decide whether *pulp nodules exist or not. **1908** KIPLING *Lett. of Travel* (1920) 154 The advertising of Canadian papers,.. the brittle *pulp-paper, the machine-set type. **1931** *Times Lit. Suppl.* 9 July 542/3 The choice between writing for those pulp-paper magazines that pay by the word and the smooth-paper magazines that pay by the story. **1883** *Cassell's Fam. Mag.* Aug. 528/1 The [coffee-] bean falls over into a sieve below, and the skin is dragged behind the cylinder and escapes by a spout to the *pulp-pit. **1899** *Allbutt's Syst. Med.* VI. 742 Irregular calcification, with the formation of *pulp-stones, frequently leaves some living pulp. **1901** J. H. PRATT in *Mineral Resources of U.S.* 789 Pulpstones differ from grindstones in having a much broader face. **1957** *Encycl. Brit.* XVII. 232/2 Natural pulpstones are 27 to 36 in. wide by 54 in. or more in diameter. Artificial stones are 27 to 54 in. wide and 54 to 72 in. in diameter. **1885** *Rep. New Hampshire Forestry Comm.* 10 Telegraph-poles, *pulp-wood, bark, etc. **1900** *Montreal Witness* 13 Feb. 4/5 The tariff of dues on pulpwood. **1901** *Westm. Gaz.* 2 Apr. 6/2 The district.. contains a great pulpwood forest, besides 3,000,000,000 ft. of pinewood. **1928** R. S. TROUP *Silvicultural Syst.* xvii. 177 Where coniferous forests are grown solely for pulpwood or mining timber, the clear-cutting system with artificial regeneration is often the only one feasible. **1960** 'N. SHUTE' *Trustee from Toolroom* x. 284 The offcuts were turned into pulpwood for newsprint. **1974** *Globe & Mail* (Toronto) 28 Nov. 45/2 The spruce, which produced its first shoot a few weeks ago, is the first pulpwood tree anywhere to be grown in this way, according to scientists involved in the project.

pulp, *v.* [f. PULP *sb.*, in various senses.]

1. *trans.* To reduce to pulp or to a pulpy mass.

1662 [see PULPING]. **1683** TRYON *Way to Health* xv. (1697) 368 Conserve of Old-Red-Roses pulped. **1741** *Compl. Fam. Piece* I. ii. 122 Some love the Gooseberries only mashed, not pulped through a Sieve. **1875** *Encycl. Brit.* (ed. 9) I. 327/1 By pulping the roots and mixing them with a full allowance of chaff, every animal gets its fill. **1898** *Q. Rev.* Apr. 378 The whole work, of which 10,000 copies had been prepared, was seized by Savary and pulped.

†**2.** To make pulpy, give a pulpy appearance to.

1704 STEELE *Lying Lover* III, That [patch] so low on the Cheeks pulps the Flesh too much.

3. To remove the surrounding pulp from (coffee-beans, or the like).

1791 *Trans. Soc. Arts* VII. 180 The saving of time in pulping, peeling, picking it [coffee] clean. **1793** B. EDWARDS *West Ind.* II. v. iv. 295 The other mode is to pulp it [the coffee] immediately as it comes from the tree. **1894** [see PULPER 2].

4. *intr.* To become pulpy, to swell with juice.

1818 KEATS *Song, 'Hush, Hush! tread softly'*, My Isabel's eyes, and her lips pulp'd with bloom. *a* **1821** —— *Extracts fr. Opera*, A kiss should bud upon the tree of love, And pulp and ripen richer every hour. **1852** R. H. STODDARD *Poems* 32 The buried seed begins to pulp and swell In Earth's warm bosom.

Hence **pulped** (pʌlpt) *ppl. a.*, reduced to pulp.

1806 A. HUNTER *Culina* (ed. 3) 154 Put the soup into a stew-pan, with.. the pulped pease. **1890** *Farmer's Gaz.* 4 Jan. 1/1 Crushed oats and cake, mixed with pulped turnips, for a midday feed.

pul'paceous, *a. rare*[−1]. [f. L. *pulpa* pulp + -ACEOUS.] Of a pulpy consistency.

1853 KANE *Grinnell Exp.* xl. (1856) 363 Symmetrically embanked round with the pulpaceous material which he had excavated from the ice.

pulpal ('pʌlpəl), *a. Dentistry.* [f. PULP *sb.* + -AL[1].] Of or pertaining to the pulp of a tooth; *spec.* applied to that surface of a cavity which overlies the pulp.

1908 G. V. BLACK *Operative Dentistry* II. 6 That wall of a cavity which is to the occlusal of the pulp, and in a plane at right angles to the long axis of the tooth, is called the pulpal wall. **1925** *Dental Rec.* XLV. 627 It has been argued that grinding the enamel in preparation for the crown renders a tooth susceptible to thermal shock, with subsequent destruction of pulpal structures. **1953** J. R. SCHWARTZ *Inlays & Abutments* xiii. 142 The pulpal and axial walls should be flat and at right angles to one another. **1967** *Brit. Dental Jrnl.* CXXIII. 420/1 Pulpal involvement may be unavoidable if preparation for a jacket is undertaken.

†**'pulpament.** *Obs. rare.* Also in L. form, pl. **-a.** [ad. L. *pulpāmentum* the fleshy part or meat of animals, food prepared mainly from bits of meat, f. *pulpa* PULP *sb.*] **a.** A pulpy preparation of food; in *pl.* delicacies. **b.** A pulpified mass, as the chyle.

1599 B. JONSON *Ev. Man out of Hum.* v. vii, How now, monsieur Brisk? what! Friday night, and in affliction too, and yet your pulpamenta, your delicate morsels! **1699** *Phil. Trans.* XXI. 233 The grosser and more solid Parts.. dissolved into minuter Particles, so as to mix more equally with the fluid, and with that to make one Pulpament, or chylous Mass.

†**pulpa'toon.** *Obs.* [Cf. Sp. *pulpeton*, augm. of *pulpeta*, 'a slice of stuffed meat.'] A dish made of rabbits, fowls, etc., in a crust of forced meat.

1637 NABBES *Microcosm.* III. 109, I then send forth a fresh supply of Rabits, Pheasant, Kid, Partridge, Quaile,.. with a French troope of Pulpatoones, Mackaroones, Kickshawes, grand and excellent. **1728** E. SMITH *Compl. Housew.* 41 To make a Pulpatoon of Pigeons... Half roast six or eight Pigeons, and lay them in a Crust of Forc'd-meat..: Scrape a pound of Veal, and two Pounds of Marrow, and beat it together in a Stone Mortar.

pulpectomy (pʌl'pɛktəmɪ). *Dentistry.* [f. PULP *sb.* + -ECTOMY.] Surgical removal of the pulp of a tooth (usu. all of it: cf. PULPOTOMY).

1923 *Dental Items of Interest* XLV. 5 The remaining portion of a vital pulp following excision, or partial pulpectomy, will be destroyed. *Ibid.* 82 Operations upon the pulp are designated as 'Pulpotomy'. In case a portion of the pulp is excised and removed, the operation is termed 'Partial Pulpectomy'. The removal of the entire pulp is 'Pulpectomy'. **1924** F. E. HOGEBOOM *Pract. Pedodontia* v. 65 (*heading*) Pulpectomy and pulpotomy. *Ibid.*, Pulpectomy is the complete removal of the pulp. **1957** S. B. FINN *Clin. Pedodontics* xiv. 318 Pulpectomy may be complete or partial, depending on whether there is any vital tissue in the canal. **1976** ETTINGER & PINKHAM in A. J. Nowak *Dentistry for Handicapped Patient* xvi. 287/1 Pulpectomy with appropriate instrumentation and filling is a standard.. treatment for pulp pathology.

pulper ('pʌlpə(r)). [f. PULP *v.* + -ER[1].]

1. A machine for reducing fruit, straw, roots, paper-stock, etc. to pulp; a pulp-machine.

1862 *Times* 12 June, Reaping and grass-mowing machinery with root-slicers, pulpers, chaff-cutters. **1875** KNIGHT *Dict. Mech.* 1823/2 *Pulper*,.. a machine for reducing paper stock to pulp. **1890** *Farmer's Gaz.* 4 Jan. 1/1 Great saving can be effected by the use of the root pulper and chaff cutter.

2. A machine for removing the external pulp or rind from the coffee-bean.

1874 KNIGHT *Dict. Mech.* 584/1 The berries.. pass to the pulpers.. The pulper is a stout frame supporting a fly-wheel, shaft, and barrel. **1894** WALSH *Coffee* (Philad.) 92 There are times.. when it is impossible to pulp coffee; the pulpers may get out of repair.

3. A maker of or worker in paper-pulp.

1884 *Standard* 13 Mar. 5/2 [Articles] 'turned out' of a papier maché pulper's shop by hundreds of thousands.

‖**pulperia** (pulpe'ria). [Sp. Amer.] In Central and South America and the south-west U.S., a grocery or tavern.

1818 A. GILLESPIE *Gleanings & Remarks Buenos Ayres* viii. 91 At the intersected corners of almost every street in that capital, pulperias, or dram, and grocery shops, are established, that vend liquors, candles, and other articles. **1840** R. H. DANA *Two Yrs. before Mast* (1841) xxviii. 192 He ..came to the Pueblo de los Angelos... Here he went dead to leeward among the pulperías, gambling-rooms, &c. **1859** T. COCHRANE *Narr. Services in Liberation of Chili, Peru, & Brazil* I. x. 216 The two months' pay offered the other day could not now effect its purpose, as the whole—and more is due to the Pulperia keepers, to whose benefit, and not that of the seamen, it must have immediately accrued. **1871** H. M. & P. V. N. MYERS *Life under Tropics* iii. 21 We were forced by a sudden shower to seek shelter in a way-side pulperia. **1904** CONRAD *Nostromo* I. viii. 80 The horseman hammered with the butt of a heavy revolver at the doors of low pulperias. **1905** J. MASEFIELD *Mainsail Haul* 14 When Don Alfonso was in the pulperia (that's Spanish for grog-shop), he was a bluin' down that licker. **1936** *Times Lit. Suppl.* 29 Feb. 173/1 'Charlie the Gaucho' opens outside a *pulperia* on the Pampas. **1974** D. MEIRING *President Plan* ix. 74 The single *pulpería* which he had visited to buy food.

'pulpify, *v.* [f. PULP *sb.* + -FY.] *trans.* To reduce to a pulp or pulpy condition.

1871 HUXLEY *Anat. Vertebr. Anim.* viii. 381 These actions [of rumination] are repeated until the greater portion of the grass which has been cropped is pulpified. **1879** *St. George's Hosp. Rep.* IX. 291 Lower forearm much crushed and almost pulpified.

pulpily ('pʌlpɪlɪ), *adv.* [f. PULPY *a.* + -LY[2].] In a pulpy or flabby manner.

1879 W. COLLINS *Rogue's Life* vi, A smooth double chin resting pulpily on a white cravat.

'pulpiness. [f. as prec. + NESS.] The quality or state of being pulpy; softness, flabbiness.

1846 WORCESTER, Pulpiness. **1869** *Contemp. Rev.* XI. 357 Appreciating critics who write about its [a picture's] fruitiness, and juiciness, and pulpiness, and downiness, and peachiness. **1879** W. COLLINS *Rogue's Life* ix, There was a delicacy and propriety in the pulpiness of his fat white chin. **1901** *Weekly Reg.* 11 Oct. 442 This elasticity, or rather pulpiness, in regard to religion in boarding schools.

pulping ('pʌlpɪŋ), *vbl. sb.* [f. PULP *v.* + -ING[1].] The action of PULP *v.*; reduction to pulp. Also *attrib.*, as ***pulping-house, -machine, -mill, -sieve.***

1662 R. MATHEW *Unl. Alch.* §116. 192 Run it through a pulping Sive, and wash with clean water the still or the Lymbeck. **1793** B. EDWARDS *West Ind.* II. v. iv. 295 A pulping mill, consisting of a horizontal fluted roller, about eighteen inches long, and eight inches in diameter. **1825** *Gentl. Mag.* XCV. I. 215 After the coffee is gathered, it is taken to the pulping-mill. **1865** *Times* 15 Apr., Houses for thrashing, grinding, pulping, cooking. **1871** TYNDALL *Fragm. Sc.* (1879) I. xx. 485 Water agitated by the pulping-engine of a paper manufactory. **1875** *Encycl. Brit.* I. 327/1 A premium was offered for machines to perform this kind of work [*sc.* pulping of turnips and mangolds for cattle], under the somewhat inappropriate designation of 'pulping-machines'. **1883** *Cassell's Fam. Mag.* Aug. 527/2 The pulping-house and other necessary buildings have to be erected. **1909** *Chambers's Jrnl.* Aug. 518/1 From this pulping machine it passes to the centrifugal pump.

pulpit ('pʊlpɪt), *sb.* Also 4 pulput, 4–6 -pitte, -pite, 4–7 -pet, 5–7 -pitt, (5 pol(l)epyt, pulpytte, -pyte, 6 -pyt(t, -pette, -pete, poulpet, pilpett). [ad. L. *pulpit-um* (med.L. *pulpitrum*) a scaffold, platform, stage, in med.L. a pulpit in a church; cf. OF. *pulpate*, also *pepistre* (1357 in Godef. *Compl.*), *pulpistre, pupistre, pulpitre, poupitre*, mod.F. *pupitre*.]

1. In reference to ancient times: A scaffold, stage, or platform for public representations, speeches, or disputations. *Obs.* or *arch.*

1387 TREVISA *Higden* (Rolls) IV. 101 In þat hous poetes and gestoures uppon a pulpet rehersede poysees, gestes, and songes. **1535** COVERDALE *2 Chron.* vi. 13 Salomon had made a brasen pulpit [1611 scaffold],.. vpon the same stode he. **1556** WITHALS *Dict.* (1568) 62 b/1 A pulpit, *suggestus, podium.* **1586** T. B. *La Primaud. Fr. Acad.* I. 241 Herod Agrippa.. being gone up into the pulpit appointed for orations.. was suddenly strooken from heaven. **1601** SHAKS. *Jul. C.* III. i. 229 That I may Produce his body to the Market-place, And in the Pulpit as becomes a Friend, Speake in the Order of his Funerall. **1611** BIBLE *Neh.* viii. 4 And Ezra the scribe stood vpon a pulpit of wood [*marg. Heb.* towre of wood]. **1683** KENNETT tr. *Erasm. on Folly* 29 Demosthenes.. lost that credit in the Camp which he gained in the Pulpit.

2. a. A raised structure consisting of an enclosed platform, usually supplied with a desk, seat, and other accessories, from which the preacher in a church or chapel delivers the sermon, and in which in some denominations the officiating minister conducts the service. Hence, ***to occupy the pulpit***, to preach, or to conduct divine service.

(The earliest and also the usual sense in Eng.)

[*c* **1200** JOCELIN *Cronica* (Camden) 30 Unde et pulpitum jussit fieri in ecclesia et ad utilitatem audiencium et ad decorem ecclesie.] *c* **1330** R. BRUNNE *Chron.* (1810) 302 He stode vp in pulpite, þe office forto do. *c* **1386** CHAUCER *Sompn. T.* 574 With prechyng in the pulpit ther he stood. *c* **1425** *Voc.* in Wr.-Wülcker 649/20 *Hoc pulpitum*, polepyt. **14..** *Nom.* ibid. 719/28 *Hoc pulpitum*, a pollepyt. *c* **1440** *Gesta Rom.* lxxii. 391 (Add. MS.) Sone after come a persone into the pullpite, ande prechide. **1463** *Bury Wills* (Camden) 30 That my soule.. may be preyd fore in the pulpet on the Sunday. *c* **1520** NISBET *N. Test. in Scots* (S.T.S.) III. 275 The first lessoun at the first messe, quhilk is sungin in the pulpet. **1548–9** (Mar.) *Bk. Com. Prayer, Commination*, The prieste shal goe into the pulpitte and saye thus. **1582–8** *Hist. James VI* (1804) 291 A certaine minister, at his sermone in Glasgow, was pullit out of the pulpet, and buffittet be the Lord of Minto, for bakbytting and sclaundering. **1650** EVELYN *Diary* 4 Aug., In the afternoone [I] wander'd to divers churches, the pulpits full of novices and novelties. **1777** PRIESTLEY *Matt. & Spir.* (1782) I. Pref. 31 The doctrines publicly preached in the pulpits. **1866** G. MACDONALD *Ann. Q. Neighb.* i, Out of the pulpit I would be the same man I was in it. **1870** F. R. WILSON *Ch. Lindisf.* 111 In front of this low screen.. stands the oak pulpit.

b. In other than Christian places of worship.

1583 W. HARBORNE in Hakluyt *Voy.* (1599) II. I. 169 [Santa Sophia, Constantinople.] The pillers on both sides of the church are very costly and rich, their Pulpets seemely and handsome; two are common to preach in. **1718** LADY M. MONTAGU *Let. to C'tess of Bristol* 10 Apr., Mosque of Solyman... On one side is the pulpit, of white marble.

c. *fig.* The place from which anything of the nature of a sermon, as a moral lecture, is delivered.

a **1616** BEAUMONT *On Tombes in Westminster*, Thinke how many royall bones Sleep within these heap of stones;.. Where from pulpits seal'd with dust, They preach, 'In greatnesse is no trust'. **1665** BOYLE *Occas. Refl.*, *Occas. Medit.* IV. v, The whole World would be a Pulpit, every Creature turn a Preacher. **1868** LYNCH *Rivulet* CXLVI. i, A boat the pulpit whence He spake.

3. *transf.* **a.** The occupants of the pulpit, the preachers; Christian ministers or the Christian ministry as occupied with preaching.

1570 B. GOOGE *Pop. Kingd.* IV. (1880) 60 Do not the pulpettes of the Pope, perswade this martiall might? **1695** *Pol. Ballads* (1860) II. 50 The Bar, the Pulpit and the Press Nefariously combine To cry up an usurped pow'r And stamp it right divine. **1784** COWPER *Task* II. 332, I say the pulpit.. Must stand acknowledg'd, while the world shall stand, The most important and effectual guard, Support, and ornament of virtue's cause. **1854** EMERSON *Lett. & Soc. Aims, Eloquence* Wks. (Bohn) III. 187 We reckon the bar, the senate, journalism, and the pulpit peaceful professions; but you cannot escape the demand for courage in these. **1863** W. PHILLIPS *Speeches* xvi. 343 It is the duty of the pulpit to preach politics. **1882, 1901** [see PEW *sb.*[1] 2 c].

b. As title of a collection or periodically published series of sermons.

1823 —— (*title*) The Pulpit: a Collection of Sermons by eminent living Ministers. **18..** (*title*) The Christian World Pulpit. **18..** (*title*) The Metropolitan Tabernacle Pulpit.

4. Applied to other places elevated so as to give the occupant a conspicuous position, or enable him to direct or address others.

†**a.** An elevated royal pew or seat in a church.

? **1370** *Robt. Cicyle* 59 (Vernon MS.) Ye kyng to churche com ful riht.. And in his þouht a sleep him tok In his pulput as seiþ þe bok. **1485** *Rutland Papers* (Camden) 22 The King and the Quene.. shall retourne to their seages roiall and of estate, in the said pulpitt, wherin when thei are sett, the rulars of the quere shal begynne this postcommon, *Intellige* [etc.].

b. †The poop of a ship, from which directions were given (*obs.*); the harpooner's standing-place on a whaler or swordfishing vessel.

1513 DOUGLAS *Æneis* VIII. iii. 46 Eneas tho.. Maid ansuer from the pulpit of the schip [L. *puppi ab alta*]. **1888** GOODE *Amer. Fishes* 250 All vessels regularly engaged in this fishery are supplied with a special apparatus, called a 'rest' or 'pulpit', for the support of the harpooner as he stands on the bowsprit. **1927** G. BRADFORD *Gloss. Sea Terms* 135/1 *Pulpit*, the harpooning platform on the bowsprit of a sword-fishing vessel. **1959** W. R. BIRD *These are Maritimes* v. 132 We noted the 'pulpits' constructed far forward for the use of the man who throws the spear. **1972** E. STAEBLER *Cape Breton Harbour* i. 16 A bowsprit like a diving board with a metal sort of pulpit on the end of it.

c. An auctioneer's desk or platform. Now *local*.

1738 FIELDING *Hist. Reg.* II. Wks. 1784 III. 329 Why are you not at the auction? Mr. Hen has been in the pulpit this half-hour. **1777** SHERIDAN *Sch. Scand.* IV. i, Come, get to your pulpit, Mr. Auctioneer. **1798** *Hull Advertiser* 9 June 2/2 The Exchange and W. Bell's pulpit are at the service of every broker and auctioneer. **1889** *N.W. Linc. Gloss.* (ed. 2).

d. A small raised platform or room from which machinery can be observed and controlled.

1880 *Harper's Mag.* Dec. 62 Another shout, and the boy touches another lever in the gallery of levers, irreverently termed the 'pulpit'. **1903** *Electr. World & Engin.* 26 Dec. 1051/2 The operator of the hoisting motor stands in a pulpit above the floor. **1959** *Control* Feb. 97/3 The mill pulpit or control room.. is staffed by two rollermen and a member of the metallurgical department who keeps an eye on ingot quality. **1968** 'A. HAIG' *Sign on for Tokyo* 122 They were sitting in the 'pulpit', three of them, above the bars of the rolling mill.

e. The (pilot's, etc.) cockpit of an aeroplane. *R.A.F. slang.*

1933 D. GRINNELL-MILNE *Wind in Wires* I. ii. 96 The reason for its unofficial name—'The Pulpit'—was all too obvious. A little three-ply box projected from the front of the machine... The wretched man in this box had.. an unrestricted forward view. **1941** [see GREENHOUSE 3]. **1942** *Gen* 1 Sept. 14/1 A fighter pilot climbs into the 'pulpit' of his plane.

f. *Yachting.* (See quot. 1961). Also in other water craft.

1961 F. H. BURGESS *Dict. Sailing* 164 *Pulpit*, an elevated tubular metal guardrail set up at bow or stern. **1964** *Eng. Stud.* XLV. 23 A pulpit is a raised safety-rail in the bows of a yacht or motor cruiser. **1976** *Yachts & Yachting* 20 Aug. 382/3 (Advt.), Fast Week-ender, excellent condition.. two berths, pulpit, full foam buoyancy. **1977** *Mod. Boating* (Austral.) Jan. 110/1 Deck or even pulpit-mounted lights were often hidden from view.

5. *attrib.* and *Comb.* **a.** Of or belonging to a pulpit, as ***pulpit bible***, ***cushion***, ***door***, ***stair***, etc.

1631 WEEVER *Anc. Fun. Mon.* 49 A beaten-out pulpit cushion. **1641** *Rutland MSS.* (1905) IV. 531 Payd for the pulpet velvet and the velvet of the carving, *xli. xvjs.* **1848** G. STRUTHERS *Hist. Relief Ch.* v. in *United Presb. Fathers* 278 Mr. Boston heard the pulpit door open. **1900** CROCKETT *Fitting of Peats* i. in *Love Idylls* (1901) 5 The top of the shut pulpit Bible.

b. Of, pertaining to, or characteristic of the pulpit as the place of preaching, as ***pulpit eloquence***, ***key***, ***oratory***, ***service***, ***style***, ***thunder***, etc.

1609 *Ev. Woman in Hum.* I. i. in Bullen *O. Pl.* IV, Another in a rayling pulppet key Drawes through her nose the accent of her voice. **1649** MILTON *Eikon.* Pref., Wks. 1851 III. 334 The Prelats and thir fellow-teachers.. whose Pulpit-stuffe.. hath bin the Doctrin and perpetuall infusion of Servility and wretchedness to all thir hearers. *c* **1686** SOUTH *Serm., Prov. xxii.* 6 (1727) V. i. 31 Filled with Wind and Noise, empty Notions and Pulpit-tattle. **1751** J. BROWN *Shaftesb. Charac.* 33 In France, the applauded pulpit eloquence is of the enthusiastic.. species. **1895** J. J. RAVEN *Hist. Suffolk* 204 With caricature as well as pulpit-thunder he carried the war into the enemy's quarters.

c. Referring to the occupant of a pulpit (often uncomplimentary), as ***pulpit drone***, ***drum***, ***mountebank***, ***orator***, ***-thumper***, etc.

1546 J. HEYWOOD *Prov.* II. vii. (1566) I ij, Though this appeere a proper pulpet peece, Yet whan the fox preacheth, then beware your geese. **1649** G. DANIEL *Trinarch., Hen. V*, lxx, And Pulpit Drums awake the Iland round; All Boanerges. **1650** MILTON *Tenure Kings* (ed. 2) 47 That men may yet more fully know the difference between Protestant divines and these pulpit firebrands. **1673** [R. LEIGH] *Transp. Reh.* 11 Your weapons of offence.. you might have reserv'd for some of your pulpit-officers. **1682** T. FLATMAN *Heraclitus Ridens* No. 72 (1713) II. 191 How do they make one of these Pulpit-thumpers? **1705** HICKERINGILL *Priest-cr.* IV. (1721) 226 The Pulpit-prater (that has his Religion in his Tongue and Eyes, I mean, his Sermon-Notes). **1772** NUGENT tr. *Hist. Fr. Gerund* I. 564 Henceforth those Pulpit-Drones.. let not a braggart of a Frenchman praise. **1824** SOUTHEY *Bk. of Ch.* xiii. (1841) 230 Though he [Bp. Pecock] censured these pulpit-bawlers, as he called them. **1828** WEBSTER, *Pulpit-orator*, an eloquent preacher.

d. Special Combs.: **pulpit-cloth**, an ornamented cover of the reading-desk of a pulpit; **pulpit-cross**, a cross set up in a burying-ground or in a place where there was no church, from the steps or raised base of which sermons were often preached; a preaching-cross; †**pulpit-friar**, a preaching friar; **pulpit-glass**, a sand-glass placed on a pulpit to indicate the time to the preacher; †**pulpit-man**, a preacher; †**pulpit-prayer**, a prayer said in the pulpit (as distinguished from those read in the service); **pulpit-rail**, a rail on a ship's pulpit.

1552 in *Inv. Ch. Surrey* (1869) 44 One *pulpit clothe. **1711** ADDISON *Spect.* No. 112 ¶2 He has likewise given a handsome Pulpit-Cloth,.. at his own Expence. **1872** *Atlantic Monthly* Mar. 317 Fragments of richly colored altar-pieces, fine pulpit-cloths, and pieces of old carving. **1598** STOW *Surv.* (1603) 333 About the middest of this [Pauls] Churchyeard is a *Pulpit Crosse of timber, mounted vpon steppes of stone,.. in which are sermons preached.. euery Sundaye in the forenoone. **1555** EDEN *Decades* 165 Iohn Cacedus the *pulpitte fryer of the order of saynt Frances. **1907** *Daily Chron.* 4 Nov. 4/7 Probably the most modern *pulpit-glass in existence is that which adorns the pulpit of the Chapel Royal, Savoy. It is timed for eighteen minutes only, and was placed in the chapel in 1867. [Cf quots. 1591, 1852, s.v. HOUR-GLASS.] **1582** ALLEN *Martyrd. Father Campion* (1908) 8 Many Protestantes.. ever afterward contemned their vulgar *pulpit men in comparison of him. **1681** EVELYN *Diary* 5 Nov., Dr. Hooper.. is one of yᵉ first rank of pulpit men in the nation. **1684** BAXTER *Twelve Argts.* §20. 35 They have all that you have (*Pulpit Prayer and Sermon, and sometimes a Chapter). **1697** BURGHOPE *Disc. Relig. Assemb.* 92 Every pulpit-prayer made by a man's private spirit is valued much above the Common Prayer. **1958** S. A. GRAU *Hard Blue Sky* i. 42 Hector walked the full length of the boat and turning settled himself on the *pulpit rail. **1974** G. JENKINS *Bridge of Magpies* xv. 226 A light anti-aircraft gun platform.. surrounded by a rusty metal 'pulpit rail'.

Hence (mainly *nonce-words*) †**'pulpitable**, **'pulpital**, **'pulpitary**, **pul'pitic**, **pul'pitical** *adjs.*, connected with, appropriate to, or characteristic of the pulpit as the place of preaching; hence **pul'pitically** *adv.*, in a pulpitical manner; **'pulpitful**, enough to fill a pulpit; **'pulpitish** *a.*, resembling a pulpit performance or preaching; **'pulpitism**, a characteristic of language or style of preachers and sermons; **'pulpitless** *a.*, lacking a pulpit or a place as preacher; **'pulpitly** *adv.*, with regard to the pulpit or preaching; **pulpi'tolatry**, 'worship' of the pulpit or preaching.

1772 NUGENT tr. *Hist. Fr. Gerund* II. 84 This the exordium of my *pulpitable functions. *Ibid.* 511 The famous *pulpital performances of.. Friar Gerund. **1846** POE *Colton* Wks. 1864 III. 27 He converses fluently,.. but grandiloquently, and with a tone half tragical, half pulpital. **1784** J. BROWN *Hist. Brit. Ch.* (1820) I. 120 The *pulpitary contention between Popish and Protestant preachers was great. **1845** *Ecclesiologist* IV. 117 A slight poetical licence, a mere *pulpitic exaggeration. **1775** ASH, Suppl., *Pulpitical. **1885** CLARK RUSSELL *Strange Voy.* I. xvi. 229 Not a little impressed by the pulpitical twang and rattle of his north-country notes. **1751** CHESTERF. *Lett.* (1792) III. ccxlv. 123 To proceed then regularly and *pulpitically; I will first shew you, my beloved [etc.]. **1680** V. ALSOP *Mischief of Imposit.* xiii. 99 Whether he gave.. any encouragement.. to vomit up a whole *Pulpitful of Gall. **1847** WEBSTER, *Pulpitish. **1881** *Ch. Rev.* No. 589. 177 The common-places and *pulpitisms which have gone so far to make volumes of sermons odious. **1889** *Chicago Advance* 7 Feb., Some of them are *pulpitless, and some.. want a change of pulpit. **1872** H. W. BEECHER *Lect. Preaching* I. 24 As it is dangerous personally, so it is dangerous *pulpitly. **1853** *Ecclesiologist* XIV. 409 The *pulpitolatry of another arrangement is almost incredible.

'pulpit, *v.* [f. PULPIT *sb.*] **a.** *trans.* To provide with a pulpit, or place in the pulpit. **b.** *intr.* To officiate in the pulpit, to preach. Hence **'pulpited** *ppl. a.*, **'pulpiting** *vbl. sb.*

1529 MORE *Dyaloge* I. Wks. 151/1 Yet would thei long to be pulpeted. *c* **1540** *Old Ways* (1892) 39 Affter he had doone with his pulpitynge. **1653** MILTON *Hirelings* (1659) 84 It is not necessarie.. that Men should sit all thir life long at the feet of a pulpited Divine. **1729** BYROM *Jrnl. & Lit. Rem.* 19 Feb. (Chetham Soc.) I. II. 330 He said.. that he was in priest's orders, but.. that he had done with pulpiting. **1865** E. BURRITT *Walk Land's End* vi. 209 Mat and seat the rotunda..; pulpit at the central column of the great buildings such men as her preaching rolls may supply. **1867** O. W. HOLMES *Guard. Angel* xiii, The young girl sat under his tremendous pulpitings. **1904** *Edin. Rev.* July 147 Orderly, vulgarised, materialised, pulpited, prosperous England.

pulpitarian (pʊlpɪ'tɛərɪən), *sb.* (*a.*) [f. PULPIT *sb.* + *-arian*, as in *trinitarian*, etc.] A preacher, a pulpiteer; also, one who regards the pulpit or preaching as the chief feature of worship.

1654 WHITLOCK *Zootomia* 139 You may take away the Pewes, where all are Pulpitarians. *a* **1670** HACKET *Abp. Williams* I. (1692) 90 Directions, that had netled the aggrieved Pulpitarians. **1860** *Medical Times* 15 Sept. 266/1 Some of the most 'popular' of.. modern pulpitarians.

B. *adj.* Savouring of the pulpit; sermonical.

1887 *Daily News* 15 Oct. 3/6 Some fastidious critics may consider Dr. Bayne's style somewhat pulpitarian.

pulpiteer (pʊlpɪ'tɪə(r)), *sb.* [f. PULPIT *sb.* + -EER[1].] A preacher by profession; usually with contemptuous implication.

1642 HOWELL *Twelve Treat., True Inform.* (1661) 16 By the incitement of those fiery pulpiteers. **1679** *Answ. to Appeal fr. Country to City* 15 Against his Over-hot Church-men we'l set the Mechanique Pulpiteers and Tub preachers. **1738** NEAL *Hist. Purit.* IV. 464 The mouths of the High Church pulpiteers were encouraged to open as loud as possible. **1860** TENNYSON *Sea Dreams* 20 A heated pulpiteer, Not preaching simple Christ to simple men. **1861** TULLOCH *Eng. Purit.* i. 27 Travers.. seemed by far the more clever and successful pulpiteer.

Hence **pulpi'teer** *v. intr.*, to preach; chiefly in **pulpi'teering** *vbl. sb.* and *ppl. a.*

1812 *Religionism* 11 If your men a pulpiteering go. **1877** T. SINCLAIR *Mount* (1878) 48 A commonplace everyday pulpiteering king. **1883** *Spectator* 23 June 811 A thoughtful Scotchman who has no weakness for pulpiteering.

'pulpiter. [f. PULPIT *sb.* or *v.* + -ER[1].] A preacher, a PULPITEER.

1600 SHAKS. *A.Y.L.* III. ii. 163 O most gentle pulpiter [Spedding's emendation; *Folios* Iupiter], what tedious homilie of Loue haue you wearied your parishioners withall. **1681** HICKERINGILL *Vind. Naked Truth* II. 4 As some Pulpiters have also had. **1894** *Speaker* 2 June 613/1 The sanitary drain-maker does more for morals than the pulpiter.

pulpitis (pʌl'paɪtɪs). *Dentistry.* [f. PULP *sb.* + -ITIS.] Inflammation of the dental pulp.

1882 *Dental Rec.* II. 444 The tooth became sensitive upon percussion.. without signs of pulpitis. **1930** W. H. O. McGEHEE *Text-bk. Operative Dentistry* xxvi. 776 In the later stages of acute pulpitis, tenderness of the tooth to tapping may arise, from passage of the inflammatory area to the tissues of the apical space. **1977** CURL & PRUE in Boundy & Reynolds *Current Concepts Dental Hygiene* vii. 111 Chronic partial pulpitis will tend to be associated with pain.

'pulpitize, *v. nonce-wd.* [f. PULPIT *sb.* + -IZE.] **a.** *intr.* To pulpiteer, to preach. **b.** *trans.* To discuss or deal with in the pulpit. Hence **'pulpitizing** *vbl. sb.*

1651 BIGGS *New Disp.* §240 Cryed up even to pulpitising. **1798** COLERIDGE *Lett., to T. Poole* (1895) 18 Parson Warren did certainly *pulpitize* much better. **1875** *Contemp. Rev.* XXV. 798 The whole subject of how to encounter these enigmas.. must be popularised and pulpitised.

'pulpitry. [f. PULPIT *sb.* + -RY.] The work or service of the pulpit; preaching; the conventional talk of the pulpit; sermonizing.

1606 WARNER *Alb. Eng.* XV. xc. (1612) 389 For Fare And greater Ease than Studie them or Pulpetrie can spare. **1641** MILTON *Reform.* II. ¶1 To teach thus were meer pulpitry to them. **1861** K. H. DIGBY *Chapel St. John* (1863) 55 But perhaps you do not like pulpitry.

pulpitum ('pʊlpɪtəm). *Archit.* [L.: see PULPIT *sb.*] A stone screen separating the choir from the nave and freq. surmounted by a loft housing the organ.

1845 R. WILLIS tr. Gervase of Canterbury in *Archit. Hist. Canterbury Cathedral* iii. 37 A screen with a loft (*pulpitum*).. separated in a manner the aforesaid tower from the nave. **1908** F. BOND *Screens & Galleries Eng. Churches* iv. 159 The pulpitum differed from the rood screen in many ways. It formed the eastern barrier of the quire, and against the eastern face of it were placed the return stalls. *Ibid.*, The pulpitum always had a spacious loft above it, and carried the organ. **1923** *Trans. Scottish Ecclesiol. Soc.* VII. 101 As originally placed the painting took the shape of a boarded tympanum, occupying the entire space upward from the back of the pulpitum, or loft, to the roof. **1937** *Burlington Mag.* Mar. 128/2 The 'Master of the Naumburg Sculptures'.. was responsible.. for the sculptures on the pulpitum in Mainz Cathedral. **1966** J. FLEMING et al. *Penguin Dict. Archit.* 179/2 *Pulpitum*, a stone screen in a major church erected to shut off the choir from the nave. It could also be used as a backing for the return choir stalls.

pulpless ('pʌlplɪs), *a.* [-LESS.] Lacking pulp.

1778 LIGHTFOOT *Flora Scot.* I. 268 Barren Strawberry.. the fruit is dry and pulpless. **1875** *Dental Cosmos* XVII. 521 Ridiculous demands, such as for devitalization of pulps in pulpless teeth.

pulpose ('pʌlpəʊs), *a. rare*⁻⁰. [ad. L. *pulpōs-us* fleshy, f. *pulpa* PULP.] = PULPOUS.

1858 MAYNE *Expos. Lex.*, *Pulposus*.. of the consistence of pulp; having or full of pulp; pulpy: pulpose.

So †**pul'posity**, pulpousness. *Obs. rare*⁻⁰.

1721 BAILEY, *Pulposity*, fulness of Pulp, Substance, etc.

pulpotomy (pʌl'pɒtəmɪ). *Dentistry.* [f. PULP *sb.* + -O + -TOMY.] Surgical removal of the pulp of a tooth (usu. part of it only: cf. PULPECTOMY).

1923 [see PULPECTOMY]. **1924** F. E. HOGEBOOM *Pract. Pedodontia* v. 66 Pulpotomy means the partial removal of the pulp. **1957** S. B. FINN *Clin. Pedodontics* xiv. 318 Pulpotómies can be performed on teeth which have been exposed for as long as 72 hours. *Ibid.* 317 There are four courses of treatment open to the dentist: (1) pulp capping, (2) pulpotomy, (3) pulpectomy with or without apicoectomy, and (4) extraction of the tooth. **1976** ETTINGER & PINKHAM in A. J. Nowak *Dentistry for Handicapped Patient* xvi. 286/1 The contraindications to pulpotomies in the chronically ill patient are the same as for direct pulp capping.

pulpous ('pʌlpəs), *a.* [ad. L. *pulpōs-us* (see PULPOSE *a.*): cf. F. *poulpeux* (1539 R. Estienne in Hatz.-Darm.).] Of the nature of or consisting of pulp; resembling pulp; pulpy.

1601 HOLLAND *Pliny* I. 561 The leaues verily that this graine Rice doth beare, be pulpous and fleshy. **1660** INGELO *Bentiv. & Ur.* II. (1682) 119 A small mass of pulpous substance for the Brain. **1725** *Bradley's Fam. Dict.* s.v. *Pear Tree*, This flower is succeeded by a pulpous fruit. **1796** DE SERRA in *Phil. Trans.* LXXXVI. 503 A soft and pulpous matter, like that which is found in unripe antheræ. **1876** RUSKIN *Fors Clav.* lxix. 397 The special type of youthful blackguard.. more or less blackly pulpous and swollen.

Hence **'pulpousness** *rare*, pulpy consistency.

1727 in BAILEY vol. II.; whence **1755** in JOHNSON; and in mod. Dicts.

pulpwood: see PULP *sb.* 5 b.

pulpy ('pʌlpɪ), *a.* [f. PULP *sb.* + -Y.] **1.** Of the nature of, consisting of, or resembling pulp; soft, fleshy, succulent; also *fig.* flabby or (of literature) ephemeral, of poor quality, sensationalist: see PULP *sb.* 4 c.

1591 SYLVESTER *Du Bartas* I. iii. 860 Long'st thou for Butter? bite the poulpy part [of coco] And never better came to any Mart. **1694** J. RAY in *Lett. Lit. Men* (Camden) 200 The hard-bill'd [birds] touch not pulpy fruits. **1799** KIRWAN *Geol. Ess.* 330 Moist, pulpy, incoherent, argillaceous masses. **1800** tr. *Lagrange's Chem.* II. 417 The pulpy matter of the brain. **1843** CARLYLE *Past & Pr.* II. xvii, Some score or two of years ago all these were little red-coloured pulpy infants. **1863** GEO. ELIOT *Romola* xxxix, His mind was perhaps a little pulpy from that too exclusive diet. **1905** J. H. MCCARTHY *Dryad* 263 To make its way through ground as muddy and pulpy as a swamp. **1939** R. CHANDLER *Let.* 19 Feb. (1966) 195 *The Big Sleep* is very unequally written. There are scenes that are all right, but there are other scenes still much too pulpy. **1978** *Nature* 27 Apr. 786/1 Even the pulpiest science fiction includes this.

2. ***pulpy kidney (disease)***, a clostridial enterotoxæmia of sheep characterized by rapid postmortem degeneration of the kidneys.

1927 *N.Z. Jrnl. Agric.* XXXIV. 217 (*heading*) 'Pulpy kidney' disease of lambs. *Ibid.* 227 Out of a mob of 290 lambs twelve died, presumably from 'pulpy kidney'. **1938** tr. *F. Hutyra's Special Path. & Therapeutics Dis. Domestic Animals* (ed. 4) III. 14 In Australia.. an epizootic type of severe renal degeneration known as 'pulpy kidney disease' occurs..(the symptoms are paralysis and convulsions, and death occurs in 3 to 7 hours). **1953** *Cape Argus* 21 Mar. 7/3 Pulpy kidney disease is taking a heavy toll among sheep in the Lady Grey district. **1970** 'J. HERRIOT' *If only they could Talk* xxv. 149 The diseases which beset the lambs themselves—swayback, pulpy kidney, dysentery.

‖**pulque** ('pulke). [Sp. Amer. *pulque*, of uncertain origin.

According to F. X. Clavigero *Istoria antica del Mexico* 1780–81 (Eng. trans. 1787 I. 435), neither Sp. nor Mexican, but from Araucanian *pulcu*, the generic name for the intoxicating beverages used by the Indians. See J. Platt in N. & Q. 9th s. IX. 226 (1902), where other suggestions are also mentioned.]

a. A fermented drink made in Mexico and some parts of Central America from the sap of the agave or maguey (*Agave americana*).

1693 *Lond. Gaz.* No. 2848/1 The Viceroy Commanded, That the Indian Natives should not..consume any Mays in the making of a Drink common among them, called *Pulche*. **1796** MORSE *Amer. Geog.* I. 729 Pulque is the usual wine or beer of the Mexicans, made of the fermented juice of the Maguei. **1843** PRESCOTT *Mexico* I. v. (1850) I. 133 The older guests continued at table, sipping *pulque*, and gossiping about other times. **1900** *Speaker* 8 Sept. 619/2 The peon with money only bought pulque or gambled.

b. *attrib.* and *Comb.* as ***pulque alcohol, shop***; **pulque-brandy**, a strong intoxicating spirit distilled from pulque.

1836 C. A. GOODRICH *Universal Traveller* 139 But, unfortunately, in the lanes near the market are found numbers of pulque-shops (pulquerias). **1888** MRS. M. E. BLAKE & MRS. SULLIVAN *Mexico* 12 A corner cantine has its handful of quiet pulque-drinkers. **1910** *N.Y. Even. Post* 16 July (Sat. Suppl.) 3/2 All of the sweet savors of Araby combined could make slight headway against the reek of a pulque shop. **1931** H. CRANE *Let.* 21 Sept. (1965) 382 Straight pulque alcohol in each cup.

‖**pulqueria** (pulke'ria). [Sp. Amer.] In Mexico, a shop or tavern selling pulque.

1822 J. R. POINSETT *Diary* 28 Oct. in *Notes on Mexico* (1824) v. 49 They go to the pulqueria, and there dance, carouse, and get drunk on pulque and *vino mezcal*. **1847** G. A. F. RUXTON *Adventures Mexico & Rocky Mts.* vii. 43 After leaving the pulqueria, we visited..the dens where these people congregate for the night. **1914** C. J. C. HYNE *Firemen Hot* i. 2 By the time these [dollars] had been passed across the grimy counter of a pulqueria..they received [etc.]. **1922** *Outward Bound* Nov. 110/2 In the great pulquerias, or saloons..the gramophone is invariably to be found. **1934** S. E. WHITE *Folded Hills* 375 He can play his guitar and entertain the drunkards in the *pulquerias*.

pulsant ('pʌlsənt), *a. rare.* [ad. L. *pulsānt-em*, pr. pple. of *pulsāre*: see PULSATE *v.*] Pulsating.

1891 H. TUCKLEY *Under the Queen* 254 An atmosphere which is pulsant still with the mighty issues over which noble women have wept, and great men have bled, for a thousand years.

pulsar ('pʌlsɑː(r)). [f. *puls(ating st)ar*, after QUASAR.] **1.** *Astr.* A cosmic source of radio signals that pulsates with great regularity at intervals of the order of a second or less, and is believed to be a rapidly rotating neutron star. Also *fig.*

1968 *Daily Tel.* 5 Mar. 21/3 An entirely novel kind of star ..came to light on Aug. 6 last year and,..was referred to by astronomers as LGM (Little Green Men). Now..it is thought to be a novel type between a white dwarf and a neutron [*sic*]. The name Pulsar (Pulsating Star) is likely to be given to it... Dr. A. Hewish..told me yesterday: '..I am sure that today every radio telescope is looking at the Pulsars.' **1968** *Time* 26 Apr. 82 Under the careful scrutiny of increasing numbers of scientists around the world, astronomy's newest sensation—the pulsars—continued to beep away last week, confounding observers, with the breathtaking regularity of their signals. **1969** *New Yorker* 19 Apr. 55/1 A tough-looking astronomer, whose ideas stretch beyond the moon to quasars and pulsars. **1972** *Sci. Amer.* July 37/2 Although the pulsar in the Crab Nebula was first discovered at radio frequencies and was later studied visually, most of its energy is emitted in the X-ray range. **1973** L. M. BOSTON *Memory in House* xi. 132 Oscar is a pulsar, an output of concentrated energy. **1977** *Dædalus* Fall 45 Pulsars, that is, rotating neutron stars, have been detected in the Crab Nebula and in Vela X, a supernova remnant about ten times older than the Crab Nebula.

2. A kind of digital wrist-watch. (A proprietary name in the U.S.)

1970 *Daily Tel.* 14 May 13/7 Production is expected to begin next year, but at first pulsars will be sold in a limited edition at $1,500. **1971** *Official Gaz.* (U.S. Patent Office) 31 Aug. TM240/1 Hamilton Watch Co, Lancaster, Pa... *Pulsar* for watches... First use Apr. 27, 1970. **1977** R. E. HARRINGTON *Quintain* iii. 21 He flipped his wrist and the pulsar wristwatch winked on. **1979** G. SWARTHOUT *Skeletons* 69, I punched my Pulsar. Two minutes past nine p.m.

pulsatance (pʌl'seɪtəns). *Physics.* [f. PULSATE *v.* + -ANCE.] The angular frequency of a periodic motion, i.e. 2π times its actual frequency.

1919 A. CAMPBELL in *Proc. Physical Soc.* XXXI. 81 In English a name has not yet been found for $2\pi n$, where n represents frequency... I would suggest that it might be called 'pulsatance'. The termination 'ance' brings it into line with words like inductance and reactance. **1946** *Electronic Engin.* XVIII. 119 The displacement (D) at any point is a periodic time function of the form: $D = \psi \sin \omega t$ ..where ω is the pulsatance and ψ is the amplitude at any point in space. **1957** *Electronic & Radio Engineer* XXXIV. 145/2 Equation (22) represents a phase vibration of natural undamped pulsatance ωn and damping factor ζ.

pulsate (pʌl'seɪt, 'pʌlseɪt), *v.* [f. L. *pulsāt-*, ppl. stem of *pulsāre* to push, strike, beat, freq. of *pellĕre, puls-* to drive, strike, beat.]

1. *intr.* To expand and contract rhythmically, as the heart or an artery; to exhibit a pulse; to beat, throb. (Chiefly in scientific use.)

1794 E. DARWIN *Zoon.* I. x. 49 The heart of a viper or frog will continue to pulsate long after it is taken from the body. **1813** SIR H. DAVY *Agric. Chem.* (1814) 215 From the moment the heart begins to pulsate till it ceases to beat, the aeration of the blood is constant. **1899** *Allbutt's Syst. Med.* VII. 239 It has been asserted that the brain cannot pulsate in the closed cranium.

b. *fig.* or in figurative allusion, of life, feeling, etc.

1847 EMERSON *Poems, Saadi* vii, Leaves twinkle, flowers like persons be, And life pulsates in rock or tree. **1858** O. W. HOLMES *Aut. Breakf.-t.* iv, What strains and strophes of unwritten verse pulsate through my soul when I open a certain closet in the ancient house where I was born! **1883** *Schaff's Encycl. Relig. Knowl.* 2318 The Punic blood of his descent is visibly pulsating in his style.

2. *intr. gen.* To strike upon something with a rhythmical succession of strokes; to move with a regular alternating motion; to exhibit such a movement; to beat, vibrate, quiver, thrill.

1861 *Times* 22 Oct., The air pulsates with the flash of arms in the sunlight. **1867** LEWES *Hist. Philos.* (ed. 3) I. p. cii, The sensation excited..by that undulation pulsating on our tympanum. **1881** G. FORBES in *Nature* 18 Aug. 361/1 Dr. Bjerknes reproduces this experiment by causing two drums to pulsate in concord, the one above the other. **1884** H. SPENCER in *19th Cent.* Jan. 10 The spectroscope proves.. that molecules on the Earth pulsate in harmony with molecules in the stars.

3. *trans.* To agitate with a PULSATOR (sense 2).

1891 *Blackw. Mag.* Sept. 322 The stuff to be pulsated.

Hence **pul'sating** *vbl. sb.* (also *attrib.* in sense 3, as ***pulsating-pan***); **pul'sating** *ppl. a.*, that pulsates, exhibiting a pulsation or pulse; *spec.* of an electric current or voltage: flowing or acting in one direction but with a periodically varying strength.

1807–26 S. COOPER *First Lines Surg.* 247 An aneurism is generally a pulsating tumour, arising from a dilated, ruptured, or wounded artery, and filled with blood. **1880** GÜNTHER *Fishes* 312 Heart replaced by pulsating sinuses. **1891** *Blackw. Mag.* Sept. 322 We throw marked diamonds into the pulsating-pan, and we never fail to recover them. **1912** THIESS & JOY *Toll Telephone Practice* ii. 20 The pulsating current is used in signaling the exchange and the alternating current for calling the various subscribers on the line by means of the usual code rings. **1960** H. W. JACKSON *Introd. Electric Circuits* ix. 202 The tendency of inductance to oppose any change in current can be used to advantage in filtering or smoothing variations in load current that would otherwise occur when the load is fed from a d-c source.. which provides a pulsating emf.

pulsatile ('pʌlsətɪl, -aɪl), *a.* Also 6 -yle, 7 -il. [f. L. type **pulsātilis*, f. *pulsāre, pulsāt-*: see prec. and -ILE.]

1. *Anat.* and *Physiol.* Having the capacity or property of pulsating or throbbing, as the heart, an artery, a tumour, etc.; exhibiting pulsation.

†***pulsatile vein***, old name for an artery, *spec.* the aorta.

1541 R. COPLAND *Guydon's Quest. Chirurg.* Hjb, The braunche of the vayne pulsatyle that commeth fro the left syde. **1684** tr. *Bonet's Merc. Compit.* I. 11 You could no sooner press this Pulsatile Tumour with your Fingers, but [etc.]. **1858** H. SPENCER *Ess.* I. 332 Every heart is at first a mere pulsatile sac. **1872** MIVART *Elem. Anat.* x. (1873) 432 Such pulsatile structures are called lymphatic hearts.

b. Of, or characterized by, pulsation; pulsatory.

1684 J. P. tr. *Fambresarius' Art Physic* I. 64 Under the Pulsatil Actions are comprehended the Motions of the heart. **1728** NICHOLLS in *Phil. Trans.* XXXV. 444 Such a Tumor will rather have a pulsatile Dilatation, than a Pulsation, for its true Diagnostick. **1897** *Allbutt's Syst. Med.* IV. 647 Instances..of the common tendency towards 'pulsatile or rhythmic activity' manifested by all living matter.

2. Of a musical instrument: Played by striking or percussion; percussive: see PERCUSSION 2 c.

1769 *Mus. Dict.* 194 (T.) The rattle, among the ancients, is a musical instrument of the pulsatile kind. **1864** ENGEL *Mus. Anc. Nat.* 102 The Assyrians employed in their musical performances stringed, wind, and pulsatile instruments in combination. **1887** *Athenæum* 5 Nov. 612/3 The 'pulsatile instruments covered with skin' begin with the hymnal Mridanga, said to be invented by Brahma himself, and its modern form, the Bânya and Tabla.

Hence **pulsatility** (-'tɪlɪtɪ), the quality of being pulsatile (sense 1).

1835–6 *Todd's Cycl. Anat.* I. 243/1 The distinguishing characteristic of the third form of nævus is its pulsatility. *Ibid.* 460/2 A pulsatility scarcely inferior to that of an aneurism. **1930** *Amer. Jrnl. Physiol.* XCI. 716 The venous return to the chest must show a pulsatility which is nearly synchronous with the pulsatile outflow. **1977** *Lancet* 3 Sept. 490/2 They observed that the peak venous flow can be increased seven-fold, and its pulsatility thirty fold.

‖**pulsatilla** (pʌlsə'tɪlə). *Bot., Pharm.* Also anglicized 6 **pulsatill**, 7 **-il.** [med.L., dim. of *pulsāta* beaten, driven about; according to Linnæus *Philos. Botan.* 166 'from the beating of the flower by the wind': cf. the name ANEMONE.

Cf. also Pena & Lobel *Stirpium Adversaria Nova* (1570) 114 Pulsatilla, an Sylvestris Anemone. Huius comosi et tremuli seminum pappi quia huc atque illuc vel levissimo quoque flatu pultarentur, Pulsatillam barbari vocitarunt, Anemonemque.]

The Pasque-flower, a species of Anemone (*A. Pulsatilla*); in Tournefort, *c* 1700, a generic name; now in *Bot.* the name of a subgenus including this (then called *P. vulgaris*) and other species; also, in pharmacy, the extract or tincture of this plant.

[**1578** LYTE *Dodoens* III. lxxii. 420 Passe flower is called in Latine *Pulsatilla*.] **1597** GERARDE *Herbal* II. lxxiii. 309 In English Pasque flower..and after the Latin name Pulsatill. [**1706** PHILLIPS, *Pulsatilla*, a Plant call'd Pasque-Flower, the distilled Water of which is excellent for cleansing and curing Wounds.] **1876** tr. *von Ziemssen's Cycl. Med.* VI. 727 Bednar [has recommended] for some cases [of whooping-cough] the extract of pulsatilla. **1890** *Daily News* 7 Jan. 6/2 Take at the same time three drops of tincture of pulsatilla every half hour until relief is obtained. **1890** BILLINGS *Nat. Med. Dict.*, *Pulsatilla*, the herb of *Anemone Pulsatilla* and *A. pratensis*, and of *A. patens*, var. *Nuttalliana*, collected soon after flowering..; diaphoretic and emmenagogue.

pulsation (pʌl'seɪʃən). [ad. L. *pulsātiōn-em*, n. of action f. *pulsāre*: see PULSATE.]

I. The action, or an act, of pulsating or pulsing.

1. The movement of the pulse in a living animal body; rhythmic dilatation and contraction, as of the heart, an artery, etc.; beating, throbbing.

1541 R. COPLAND *Galyen's Terap.* 2 F ij b, Yf there be all redy vehement pulsacyon, in such wyse that there is no more hope of the curacyon of the sayd partyes. **1615** CROOKE *Body of Man* 859 This motion of the Arteries is called *pulsus* or pulsation..which is absolued by dilatation and contraction. **1664** POWER *Exp. Philos.* I. 9 In a greater Louse you might see this pulsation of her heart through her back also. **1804** ABERNETHY *Surg. Obs.* 229 The pulsation of the artery was not felt. **1876** BRISTOWE *The. & Pract. Med.* (1878) 501 Dilatation and pulsation of the larger veins.

b. with *pl.* A beat, throb (of the heart, an artery, etc.); = PULSE *sb.*[1] 1 c.

c **1645** HOWELL *Lett.* I. I. xxxvii, The Physitians hold, that in evry well dispos'd body, ther be above 4000 Pulsations evry hour. **1747** H. BROOKE *Fables, Female Seducers* Poems (1810) 413/2 Her frame with new pulsations thrill'd. **1834** J. FORBES *Laennec's Dis. Chest* (ed. 4) 659 The affection is distinguished by the pulsations of the heart appearing more audible in the back..than in the region of the heart itself.

c. *fig.* Cf. PULSE *sb.*[1] 2.

1765 STERNE *Tr. Shandy* VIII. xvi, It could neither give fire by pulsation, nor receive it by sympathy. **1848** H. ROGERS *Ess.* (1874) I. vi. 327 The pleasure..of beholding the pulsations, so to speak, of intellectual life. **1885** *Manch. Exam.* 15 Apr. 3/1 A little book..warm with the pulsation of individual thought.

2. *gen.* Rhythmical beating, vibration, or undulation: cf PULSE *sb.*[1] 4.

1658 J. ROWLAND *Moufet's Theat. Ins.* 1104 They [worms] move from place to place with a certain drawing and pulsation. **1850** TENNYSON *In Mem.* xii, As a dove.. Some dolorous message knit below The wild pulsation of her wings. **1870** EMERSON *Soc. & Solit., Art* Wks. (Bohn) III. 17 The pulsation of a stretched string or wire gives the ear the pleasure of sweet sound.

b. with *pl.* A beat, a vibration, an undulation; = PULSE *sb.*[1] 4 b.

1831 BREWSTER *Nat. Magic* ix. (1833) 243 A low continuous murmuring sound beneath his feet, which gradually changed into pulsations as it became louder. **1840** R. H. DANA *Bef. Mast* xviii. 52 No sound heard but the pulsations of the great Pacific! **1866** DK. ARGYLL *Reign Law* iii. (1867) 137 The pulsations of the wing in most birds are so rapid that they cannot be counted. **1878** HUXLEY *Physiogr.* xi. 171 In the open sea, the wave or pulsation is propagated, but the mass of the water..remains stationary.

II. 3. The action of striking, knocking, or beating; with *pl.* A stroke, knock, blow; in quot. 1891 one made by a pulsator (see PULSATOR 2).

1656 BLOUNT *Glossogr.*, *Pulsation*, a beating, striking, knocking or thumping. **1768** BLACKSTONE *Comm.* III. viii. 120 The Cornelian law *de injuriis* prohibited pulsation as well as verberation; distinguishing verberation, which was accompanied with pain, from pulsation, which was attended with none. **1891** *Blackw. Mag.* Sept. 322 A large flap of wood bestows a smart box on the ear,..on the surface of no. 2 pan. I estimated the number of these pulsations at 110 per minute.

Hence **pul'sational** *a.*, of, pertaining to, or characterized by pulsation; also **pul'sationally** *adv.*

1882 *Contemp. Rev.* Oct. 636 The striations seen athwart the tail..would be explained..as due to the observed pulsational manner in which the envelopes are raised. **1969** *Nature* 19 July 279/1 Despite the trend of recent evidence.. that radial pulsations may not be the source of variation in pulsars, the pulsational hypothesis has still not been disproved. *Ibid.* 280/1 Thermonuclear reactions are extremely effective in pulsationally destabilizing a degenerate star. **1976** *Ibid.* 15 Jan. 88/2 Periods decrease with increase of λ and of polytropic index *n*..for all different modes of oscillations (pulsational, transverse shear, and toroidal, modes).

pulsative ('pʌlsətɪv), *a.* Now *rare.* [f. ppl. stem of L. *pulsāre*: see PULSATE and -ATIVE.]

1. = PULSATILE 1, PULSATORY.

1398 TREVISA *Barth. De P.R.* v. lxi. (Bodl. MS.), þis veyne hatte pulsatif and is nedefulle to bringe quantite of blood and spurtes to þe lunges. *c* **1400** *Lanfranc's Cirurg.* 112 It is riȝtful þat an arterie schulde arise vpward from bynеþe, for þe blood þat is in him is sutil, & his meuynge is pulsatif. **1563** T. GALE *Antidot.* I. vi. 4 Great inflamations..doe induce payne, and pulsatiue dolour. **1668** CULPEPPER & COLE *Barthol. Anat.* Man. IV. xii. 348 A pulsative pain of the teeth. **1842** *Blackw. Mag.* LII. 786 Others..have laid bare to us the very pulsative heart of America.

†**2.** = PULSATILE 2. *Obs.*

1695 J. EDWARDS *Perfect. Script.* iv. 176 All other Musical Instruments..whether Pulsative or Pneumatick.

Hence **'pulsatively** *adv.* (in quot., with a blow or ? a series of blows).

1881 BLACKMORE *Christowell* xv, Handling him by the head, against the wall, pulsatively, [he] stirs up the muffled drum of his outer ear.

pulsator (pʌl'seɪtə(r), 'pʌlsətə(r)). [agent-n. in L. form from *pulsāre*: see PULSATE and -OR.]

1. One who or that which knocks or strikes: see quots.; in quot. 1753 the Death-watch. *rare.*

1656 BLOUNT *Glossogr.*, *Pulsator*, one that knocks or strikes. **1730–6** BAILEY (folio), *Pulsa'tor*, the plaintiff or actor. **1753** CHAMBERS *Cycl. Supp.*, *Pulsator*, a name given by some writers to that species of beetle, commonly known among us by the name of the death-watch. **1755** JOHNSON, *Pulsa'tor*, a striker, a beater. **1836** E. HOWARD *R. Reefer* xx, The pulsator, with pointed toe.., would make a progress in a direct line.

2. A machine, working on the principle of the jigger, for separating diamonds from the earth in which they are found.

1890 *Pall Mall G.* 13 Feb. 2/1 The residue of divers stones of divers sorts and sizes is then jogged about with more water in the 'pulsator'... The machine is a huge framework of graduated sieves and runlets. **1901** *Ibid.* 1 July 8/2 The finer material is graded by the screens of the trommel, and passes direct to the four compartments of a pulsator or jigger of the type used at Kimberley.

3. = PULSOMETER 2.

1884 KNIGHT *Dict. Mech.* Suppl., *Pulsator*, a name for the *Pulsometer*.

4. *Agric.* A device on a milking machine which releases the suction on the teat intermittently so as to simulate the sucking action of a calf.

1907 *Jrnl. R. Agric. Soc.* LXVIII. 133 By another flexible connection the pail communicates with a vacuum pipe, and an air exhaust, by which the pulsators are actuated. **1931** J. B. DAVIDSON *Agric. Machinery* xxxii. 339 The pulsator is an air valve so constructed as to alternate suction and release. **1950** *N.Z. Jrnl. Agric.* LXXX. 568/2 Efficient milking is not possible with leaking pulsators. **1970** R. JEFFRIES *Dead Man's Bluff* i. 12 The milk began to spurt into the glass jars... The rhythmic clicking of the pulsator, working off the vacuum line, gave him a conscious feeling of well-being.

pulsatory ('pʌlsətərɪ), *a.* [f. PULSATE: see -ORY².] Having the quality of pulsating; characterized by or of the nature of pulsation; acting or moving in intermittent pulses.

1613 WOTTON *Let. to Sir E. Bacon* 27 May, in *Reliq.* (1672) 418 These external evils do not so much trouble us, as an inward pungent and pulsatory ach within the skull. **1747** LANGRISH *Muscular Motion* iii. §129 in *Phil. Trans.* XLIV, Let us now..examine whether the nervous Æther is transmitted from the Brain to the Heart, in a pulsatory Manner, at equal Distances of Time. **1822–34** *Good's Study Med.* (ed. 4) I. 535 A pulsatory motion is always felt by the fingers when applied to a leaden water-pipe. **1878** G. B. PRESCOTT *Sp. Telephone* 206 A merely intermittent or pulsatory current.

b. = PULSATILE 1.

1802 *Med. Jrnl.* VIII. 4 A pulsatory swelling at the fore part of the elbow joint. **1868** DUNCAN tr. *Figuier's Insect World* Introd. 12 Malpighi and Swamerdam..discovered in different insects a pulsatory organ occupying the median line of the back, which appeared to them to be a heart.

pulsche, obs. form of POLISH *v.*

pulse (pʌls), *sb.*¹ Forms: α. 4–5 pous, pows, 4–6 pouce, 5 pouse, powce; β. 4–6 puls, 6 poulce, poulse, pulce, 5– pulse. [ME. *pous*, *pouce*, a. OF. *pous* (*c* 1175 in Godef. *Compl.*), *pousse*:—L. *pulsus* (*vēnārum*) the beating of the veins, f. *puls-*, ppl. stem of *pellĕre* to drive, beat; altered in mod.F. to *pouls*, and in late ME. to *pulse* after L.]

1. a. The 'beating', throbbing, or rhythmically recurrent dilatation of the arteries as the blood is propelled along them by the contractions of the heart in the living body; esp. as felt in arteries near the surface of the body, e.g. in the wrists and temples; usually in reference to its rate and character as indicating the person's state of health: often in phr. *to feel* (†*taste*) one's *pulse*. (A pulse also occurs exceptionally in the veins.)

Formerly sometimes construed erron. as a plural.

α. *c* **1330** R. BRUNNE *Chron. Wace* 9011 He tasted his pous, saw his vryn, He seide he knew his medycyn. **1340** HAMPOLE *Pr. Consc.* 822 His pouce es stille, with-outen styringes. *c* **1380** WYCLIF *Serm.* Sel. Wks. I. 151 A fisician lerneþ diligentli his signes, in veyne, in pows. *c* **1422** HOCCLEVE *Jonathas* 604 He sy hire vryne & eeke felte hir pous. **1470–85** MALORY *Arthur* XVII. xv. 712 They..felte his pouse to wyte whether there were ony lyf in hym. **1530** PALSGR. 257/1 Pouce of the arme, *povce*.

β. **1398** TREVISA *Barth. De P.R.* v. i. (Tollem. MS.), þe arteries takeþ þe spirite of þe herte, and bereþ forþe to make þe puls. **1483** *Cath. Angl.* 293/2 A Pulse, *pulsus*. **1530** PALSGR. 158 The poulce of a mannes arme. *Ibid.* 259/1 Pulce of mannes arme, *povx*. **1578** BANISTER *Hist. Man* VII. 95 Phisitions..take counsell at the pulse. **1590** SHAKS. *Com. Err.* IV. iv. 55 Giue me your hand, and let mee feele your pulse. **1773** T. PERCIVAL *Ess.* II. 65 In twenty minutes my pulse rose to 88. In half an hour they sunk to 82. **1876** FOSTER *Phys.* I. iv. (1879) 155 The average rate of the human pulse or heart-beat is 72 a minute.

b. *venous pulse*: see quot.

1897 *Syd. Soc. Lex.*, *P[ulse]*, *venous*, a term applied..1. To a pulse carried on from the arteries through the capillaries into the veins, *e.g.* in a secreting salivary gland. 2. To the backward propagation of a pulsation, *e.g.* in tricuspid regurgitation, when pulsation is seen in the great veins and the liver. 3. To variations of pressure in the great veins due to the movements of respiration.

c. Each successive beat or throb of the arteries, or of the heart. Usually in *pl.*

c **1430** *Pilgr. Lyf Manhode* II. xlvii. (1869) 94, I tastede his pouces, but..i fond nouht, in sinewe ne in condyt ne in veyne. **1566** PAINTER *Pal. Pleas.* I. 92 To take hede to the mutacion of his poulces. **1664** POWER *Exp. Philos.* I. 41 At every pulse of the Auricle you might see the bloud passe through this Channel into the heart [of the lamprey]. **1710** J. CLARKE *Rohault's Nat. Phil.* (1729) I. 193 If we will be at the Trouble to count how many Pulses of the Artery there are in the first twenty Vibrations. **1887** BOWEN *Æneid* II. 726, I, whose pulses stirred not at javelins showered in the fray.

d. As a vague or incidental measure of time.

1626 BACON *Sylva* §32 For the space of ten pulses. *Ibid.* §366 A Spoonfull of Spirit of Wine, a little heated, was taken, and it burnt as long as came to 116. Pulses.

†**e.** *concr.* The place where the pulse occurs or is felt; esp. in the wrist; also an artery or 'pulsating vein'. *Obs.*

c **1374** CHAUCER *Troylus* III. 1065 (1114) Þer-with his pous and pawmes of his hondes þei gan to frote. **1398** TREVISA *Barth. De P.R.* XVI. lxxxvii. (Tollem. MS.), The saphire keleþ moche in hete of brennynge feueres yf he is honged nyȝe þe pulses and þe veynes of þe herte [L. *juxta venas cordis pulsatiles*]. **1541** R. COPLAND *Guydon's Quest. Chirurg.* Q iv b, Wastyng of a brawne, and chyefly of a poulce, so that whan it is pynched it abydeth vpryght. **1614** W. B. *Philosopher's Banquet* (ed. 2) 16 The Artiries..are also called Pulses. **1623** COCKERAM, *Pulse*, a beating veine.

†**f.** Excessive or violent throbbing, palpitation.

1607 TOPSELL *Four-f. Beasts* (1658) 4 [It] strengthneth the heart, emboldneth it, and driveth away the pulse and pusillanimity thereof.

2. a. In various figurative or allusive uses, denoting life, vitality, energy, feeling, sentiment, tendency, drift, indication, etc.; with *pl.*, a throb or thrill of life, emotion, etc.

c **1540** [see b]. **1595** SHAKS. *John* IV. ii. 92 Thinke you I beare the Sheeres of destiny? Haue I commandement on the pulse of life? **1619** VISCT. DONCASTER in *Eng. & Germ.* (Camden) 201 Setting downe my observations upon the pulse of the affayres which I am neerer to feele. **1745** H. WALPOLE *Lett.* (1846) II. 91 All this will raise the pulse of the stocks. **1804** WORDSW. *'She was a phantom'* iii, And now I see with eye serene The very pulse of the machine. **1865** R. S. HAWKER *Prose Wks.* (1893) 43 Had this instrument [a barometer], the pulse of the storm, been preserved, the crew would have received warning of the..hurricane.

b. Phr. *to feel* (†*try*) *the pulse* (†*pulses*) *of* (*fig.*): to try to discover the sentiments, intentions, drift, etc., of; to 'sound'.

c **1540** tr. *Pol. Verg. Eng. Hist.* (Camden) I. 288 Godwinus, having no small confidence, after hee hadd once felte his pulses and perceaued his diet. **1639** S. DU VERGER tr. *Camus' Admir. Events* a iv, I have runne over some pieces of them, only as to feele their pulse, and informe my selfe of their language and Country. **1707** FREIND *Peterborow's Cond. Sp.* 263 With whom my Lord had occasion to talk and to feel his Pulse. **1869** SWINBURNE *Ess. & Stud.* 5 He only who has felt the pulse of an age can tell us how fast or slow its heart really beat towards evil or towards good.

c. Phr. *on the pulse* (and variants): through one's own experience (with allusion to Keats's use).

1818 KEATS *Let.* 3 May (1931) I. 154 Axioms in philosophy are not axioms until they are proved upon our pulses. We read fine things, but never feel them to the full until we have gone the same steps as the Author. **1970** *Guardian* 23 July 10/3 As I am one of his constituents, the appointment of Sir Robert Grant-Ferris..as Deputy Speaker..has made me feel 'on the pulse'..a frustrating anomaly of our parliamentary system. **1971** R. AP ROBERTS *Trollope* ii. 42 The problem of *The Warden* is—one might say—proved on our pulses. **1973** *Listener* 6 Dec. 798/3 The committed nationalism of, say, the 19th-century Russian composers, who had felt oppression on the pulse.

†**3.** A stroke, blow, impact; an attack, assault. (Cf. *impulse*, *repulse*, and PULSE *v.* 3 b.) *Obs.*

1587 FLEMING *Contn. Holinshed* III. 1024/1 The commons..ran all into the towne; and there ioine themselues togither to abide the pulse. **1677** GALE *Crt. Gentiles* II. IV. 309 Every bodie that is moved by an externe pulse is inanimate. *a* **1687** PETTY *Treat. Naval Philos.* I. ii, The quick and effectual pulse of the water upon the Rudder.

4. a. The rhythmical recurrence of strokes, vibrations, or undulations; beating, vibration.

1657 W. MORICE *Coena quasi Κοινή* xv. 218 Like the pulse of the flowing Sea. **1660** BOYLE *New Experim. Phys.-Mech.* xxvii. 208 So weak a pulse as that of the ballance of a Watch. **1665** HOOKE *Microgr.* xvi. 100 That there is such a fluid body..which is the *medium*, or Instrument, by which the pulse of Light is convey'd. **1850** TENNYSON *In Mem.* lxxxvii, The measured pulse of racing oars Among the willows. **1876** BLACKIE *Songs Relig. & Life* 157 Pulse of waters blithely beating, Wave advancing, wave retreating.

b. Each of a rhythmical succession of strokes or undulations; a single vibration or wave; a beat. In scientific use now *spec.* (*a*) a train of radio waves, sound waves, or the like, of very short duration; a short burst of radiated energy; (*b*) the more usual term for IMPULSE *sb.* 5.

1673 NEWTON in Rigaud *Corr. Sci. Men* (1841) II. 350 To suppose that there are but two figures, sizes, and degrees of velocity or force, of the ethereal corpuscles or pulses. **1704** —— *Optics* (1721) 326 The Vibrations or Pulses of this Medium..must be swifter than Light. **1756** BURKE *Subl. & B.* IV. xi, When the ear receives any simple sound, it is struck by a single pulse of the air, which makes the ear-drum and the other membranous parts vibrate. **1827** KEBLE *Chr. Y.*, *Evening* i, The last faint pulse of quivering light.

(*a*) **1905** S. R. BOTTONE *Radium* (ed. 2) iv. 74 A third kind of emanation is also produced by radium... Röntgen rays —ether vibrations—produced as a secondary phenomena by the sudden arrest of velocity of the electrons by the solid matter, producing a series of Stokesian 'pulses' or explosive ether waves, shot into space. **1906** *Nature* 29 Nov. 105/2 The signal produced by a spark discharge consists of a series of violent pulses each consisting of a short train of strongly damped vibrations of definite frequency. **1945** H. D. SMYTH *Gen. Acct. Devel. Atomic Energy Mil. Purposes* xii. 131 In this method a neutron source is modulated, i.e., the source is made to emit neutrons in short 'bursts' or 'pulses'. **1947** CROWTHER & WHIDDINGTON *Science at War* 16 Meanwhile the pulse flies on, reaches the aircraft, and is reflected back as an echo. **1969** *Times* 8 Jan. 12/1 Working from the measured length of the successive pulses of energy, it was possible to calculate that the stars concerned would have been as massive as the sun but rather smaller than the earth in size. **1978** *Sci. Amer.* Apr. 38/2 The bats and whales were before us, but now we humans make routine use of pulses of ultra-sound (or of microwave) to map the night or the depths.

(*b*) **1932** *Proc. Physical Soc.* XLIV. 77 A transformer.. translated the square-topped current pulsations into voltage pulses, alternately positive and negative, of very short duration. **1949** B. GROB *Basic Television* v. 63 The amplitude of the video signal is divided into two sections, the lower 75 per cent being devoted to the active camera signal while the upper 25 per cent is used for the synchronizing pulses. **1967** *Electronics* 6 Mar. 159/2 A simple change in d-c level cannot be used as a trigger because it locks up the flip-flop against further changes; a pulse is a must. **1975** D. G. FINK *Electronics Engineers' Handbk.* XVI. 6 In the field of radio-frequency interference ..the basic response curve of the receiver is defined in terms of its response to regularly repeated pulses... The area under the pulse must be a known constant which is a function of a limited number of circuit parameters.

c. *Pros.* and *Mus.* A beat or stress in the rhythm of a verse or piece of music.

1885 J. LECKY in *Philol. Soc. Proc.* p. v, Varieties of metre were caused (*a*) by altering the division and coalescence of pulses, as in passing from dactyl to anapest..(*b*) by altering the number of pulses into which the stress-group was divided (substitution of triplets in binary metre, and of duplets in ternary).

d. A temporary upward movement of magma through the earth's crust.

1964 *Nature* 13 June 1100/2 Difficulties with this concept have led petrologists..to postulate a pulse mechanism to explain such features as the magnetite layer near the top of the Main Norite Zone of the Bushveld Igneous Complex. **1970** *Ibid.* 25 July 365/1 A more restricted pulse (heave) of magma. **1977** A. HALLAM *Planet Earth* 68 Occasionally a new pulse of magma on its way to the surface breaks off fragments that emerge as xenoliths included in lava flows or ash falls.

5. *Biochem.* A period during which a culture of cells is supplied with an isotopically labelled substrate or substrates. Also *attrib.* Cf. PULSE *v.* 5.

1960 *Jrnl. Molecular Biol.* II. 308 Phage infection and the subsequent ^{32}P pulse experiment were performed at 28°C. **1961** *Nature* 13 May 580/1 The nascent protein can be labelled by a short pulse of $^{35}SO_4$. **1974** *Ibid.* 25 Jan. 243/1 If a long molecule is labelled at one end (as happens with a short pulse label) and then sheared, the labelled molecules will always appear to have lower molecular weights than the bulk material.

6. *attrib.* and *Comb.* (almost all in senses 1, 2 or 4 b). **a.** *attrib.*, as ***pulse amplitude***, ***-beat***, ***-beating***, ***height***, ***-place***, ***-rate***, ***repetition*** (or ***recurrence***) ***frequency*** (or ***rate***), ***-stroke***, ***-throb***, ***-tick***, ***train***, ***width***. **b.** Objective, etc., as ***pulse-feeling*** sb., adj., ***pulse-taking*** (*lit.* and *fig.*); ***pulse amplifier***, ***analyser***, ***compression***, ***counter***, ***generator***, ***transformer***; ***pulse-amplifying***, ***-counting***, ***-forming***, ***-generating***, ***-like***, ***-moving***, ***-quickening***, ***-shaping***, ***-stirring*** adjs. **c.** Special Combs.: **pulse amplitude modulation** *Telecommunications*, pulse modulation in which variations in the signal are represented by variations in the amplitude of the pulses; **pulse-breath** *Path.* (see quots.); **pulse code modulation** *Telecommunications*, pulse modulation in which the actual signal amplitude after each successive interval is approximated by the nearest in value of a set of permitted amplitudes, which is then represented by a short sequence of pulses in accordance with a binary code; **pulse column** = *pulsed column* s.v. PULSED *ppl. a.* a; **pulse curve** = *pulse-tracing*; **pulse duration modulation** *Telecommunications* = *pulse width modulation* below; **pulse frequency modulation** *Telecommunications*, pulse modulation in which variations in the signal are represented by variations in the frequency of occurrence of the pulses; **pulse-glass**, a glass tube with a bulb at each end, or at one end only, containing spirits of wine and rarified air, which when grasped by the hand exhibits a momentary ebullition, which is repeated at each beat of the pulse; **pulse jet** *Aeronaut.*, a type of jet engine in which combustion is intermittent, the ignition and expulsion of each charge of mixture causing the intake of a fresh charge; **pulse-'label** *v. trans. Biochem.*, to label the metabolites of (cells) by administering a pulse (sense 5); so **pulse-'labelled** *ppl. a.*, **pulse-'labelling** *vbl. sb.*; **pulse modulation** *Telecommunications*, modulation in which a series of initially identical, regularly recurring pulses is varied in some respect (as amplitude or timing) so as to represent the amplitude of the signal after successive short intervals of time; so **pulse-modulated** *a.*, **pulse modulator**; †**pulse-pad** *Obs. nonce-wd.* [PAD *sb.*[2] 3], humorous appellation for a medical man; **pulse position modulation** *Telecommunications*, pulse modulation in which variations in the signal are represented by variations in the time position of the pulses, relative to their unmodulated position; **pulse pressure** *Med.*, the difference between the maximum (systolic) and the minimum (diastolic) pressure of arterial blood; **pulse radar**, radar that transmits pulses rather than a continuous beam of radio energy; **pulse radiolysis**, radiolysis by means of a very short pulse of electrons or other ionizing radiation; **pulse repeater** *Electronics* (see quot. 1971); **pulse time modulation** *Telecommunications*, pulse position or pulse width modulation; so **pulse-time-modulated** *a.*; **pulse-tracing**, the curve traced by a sphygmograph, indicating the character of a pulse-wave; †**pulse-vein** *Obs.*, a 'vein' or blood-vessel in which there is a pulse, an artery; †**pulse-watch** *Obs.*, Floyer's name for a sand-glass used for estimating the rate and character of the pulse; **pulse-wave**: see quot. 1897; **pulse width modulation** *Telecommunications*, pulse modulation in which variations in the signal are represented by variations in the width (duration) of the pulses; **pulse-wise** *adv.*, discontinuously; a bit at a time.

1940 *Rev. Sci. Instruments* XI. 44/1 The use of ionization chambers in conjunction with *pulse amplifiers permits data to be taken much more rapidly. **1949** [see *pulse height* below]. **1962** SIMPSON & RICHARDS *Physical Princ. Junction Transistors* xv. 371 (*heading*) Video pulse-amplifier equivalent circuits. *Ibid.* viii. 182 This makes the point-contact transistor inherently unstable under certain conditions and makes possible the construction of simple *pulse-amplifying or trigger circuits. **1940** *Rev. Sci. Instruments* XI. 45/1 (*caption*) Wiring diagram of the *pulse amplitude selector. **1947** [see KICKSORTER]. **1947** *Bell Syst. Technical Jrnl.* XXVI. 396 When the pulses consist simply of short samples of the speech waves, their varying amplitudes directly represent the speech waves and the system is called pulse amplitude modulation or PAM. **1963** B. FOZARD *Instrumentation Nuclear Reactors* iv. 42 Discrimination against gamma rays is obtained by using a pulse amplitude discriminator in conjunction with the counter. **1972** Pulse amplitude modulation [see MODULATION 7]. **1947** *Pulse analyser [see KICKSORTER]. **1963** B. FOZARD *Instrumentation Nuclear Reactors* x. 123 In some applications it is required to determine the count rate of pulses of a particular amplitude or.. whose amplitudes lie in the band V and $V + \delta V$... Instruments known as pulse analysers are available which give the required result directly. **1841** EMERSON *Addr.*, *Method Nat.* Wks. (Bohn) II. 222 We do not take up a new book, or meet a new man, without a *pulse-beat of expectation. **1862** C. R. HALL in *Trans. Med.-Chirurg. Soc.* XLV. 167 By the term '*pulse-breath', I wish to signify..an audible pulsation communicated to the breath as it issues from the mouth by each beat of the heart. **1881** *Syd. Soc. Lex.*, *Breath, pulse*, a term applied to a pulsatile movement of the expired air in cases of phthisis, where there is a large cavity either close to the heart and the aorta, or separated from them only by indurated structures. **1947** *Pulse code modulation [see *PCM* s.v. P II]. **1967** *Times* 7 Feb. 9/3 The Post Office is to start work on the installation..of the world's first pulse code modulation exchange. This technique makes it possible for two ordinary telephone 'pairs' to carry 24 simultaneous conversations. **1976** *B.B.C. Handbk.* 71/2 Pulse Code Modulation is the system developed by BBC engineers for the distribution of high-quality stereophonic audio signals. **1954** R. STEPHENSON *Introd. Nuclear Engin.* ix. 333 The principal advantage of *pulse columns is their greater plate efficiency which permits a column of smaller height for a given separation. **1966** *New Scientist* 15 Sept. 609/1 By employing *pulse-compression radar techniques the designer can..produce a radar which has long range and yet gives good definition. **1975** D. G. FINK *Electronics Engineers' Handbk.* xxv. 74 Pulse compression is a technique in which a rectangular pulse containing phase modulation is transmitted. When the echo is received, the matched-filter output is a pulse of much shorter duration. **1809** MALKIN *Gil Blas* II. iv. ¶ 3 The little *pulse-counter set himself about reviewing the patient's situation. **1963** B. FOZARD *Instrumentation Nuclear Reactors* xiii. 166 Two scales.. indicate approximately (*a*) the current produced in a reactor instrumentation ionisation chamber..and (*b*) the pulse rate produced by a fission-type pulse counter. *Ibid.* viii. 74 *Pulse-counting systems are commonly used to measure radiation intensity in terms of count rate. **1890** BILLINGS *Nat. Med. Dict.*, **P[ulse] curve.* **1899** *Allbutt's Syst. Med.* VII. 239 *note*, The pulse curve is usually anacrotic. **1956** S. SEELY *Radio Electronics* xv. 439 In *pulse-duration modulation and pulse-position modulation..the signal/noise ratio is proportional to the bandwidth. **1975** Pulse duration modulation [see *pulse position modulation* below]. **1947** LEBACQZ & WHITE in L. N. Ridenour *Radar System Engin.* x. 376 A pulse transformer can be inserted between load and *pulse-forming network so that the network can be designed to use the available switching device most efficiently. **1950** *Pulse frequency modulation [see *communication(s) engineer* s.v. COMMUNICATION 12]. **1975** Pulse frequency modulation [see *pulse time modulation* below]. **1975** *Pulse-generating [see *pulse transformer* below]. **1931** *Proc. IRE* XXII. 911 (*caption*) Transmitter and *pulse generator with cathode ray oscillograph monitor. **1977** *Navy News* June 42 (Advt.), Ideally, applicants should be familiar with oscilloscopes, digital multimeters, pulse generators, frequency counters, etc. **1829** *Nat. Philos.* I. ix. 56 (Usef. Knowl. Soc.) The instrument called a *pulse-glass is a glass tube with a bulb at each end of the form represented. **1949** *Atomics* Sept. 57/1 When the gating instrument is in operation, random pulses from a Geiger counter are fed through the pulse amplifier to the *pulse height selector. **1952** *Proc. Physical Soc.* B. LXV. 320 An investigation of the pulse heights produced by alpha-particles in various scintillating crystals. **1957** *Economist* 30 Nov. 779/1 Because it sorts out electrical 'kicks' or impulses according to their amplitude—more than 16,000 of them in each of 100 channels..'kick sorter' is the technicians' colloquial name for a Pulse Height Analyser. **1962** F. I. ORDWAY et al. *Basic Astronautics* iv. 137 The pulse height distribution of the incident particles is obtained..by means of a sliding-channel, pulse-height analyzer. **1968** Pulse-height [see KICKSORTER]. **1946** F. HAMANN *Air Words* 43/1 **Pulse-jet*, a jet plane or motor that..operates in short bursts of power or impulses. **1949** *Aircraft Engin.* Mar. 71/3 No analysis will decide whether ram-jet or pulse-jet is the better —such questions are decided by service experience. **1966** *McGraw-Hill Encycl. Sci. & Technol.* XI. 95/2 In addition to their use on the German V-1 buzz-bomb, pulse jets have been used to propel radio controlled target drones and experimental helicopters. **1961** *Nature* 13 May 581 (*heading*) Unstable ribonucleic acid revealed by *pulse labelling of *Escherichia coli.* **1968** H. HARRIS *Nucleus & Cytoplasm* iii. 42 When the pulse-labelled cells were transferred to non-radioactive medium, radioactivity disappeared from the heterogeneous component and appeared in the ribosomal RNA. *Ibid.*, The pulse-labelling revealed a special class of RNA which was not ribosomal RNA or a precursor of ribosomal RNA. **1974** *Nature* 8 Nov. 168/1 Yeast protoplasts were pulse labelled for 30 min with H-adenine, then quickly cooled and lysed by osmotic shock. **1575** BANISTER *Chyrurg.* I. (1585) 6 The paine [of an abscess] is *pulslike beating mixt with pricking and some itching. **1943** *Gloss. Terms Telecommunication* (*B.S.I.*) 65 **Pulse-modulated waves*, recurrent wave-trains in which the duration of the trains is, in general, short compared with the time interval between them. **1962** *Science Survey* III. 279 They also respond to pulse-modulated sounds up to pulse repetition rates of about 800 cycles per sec. **1929** *Proc. IRE* XVII. 1787 It could not be predicted with certainty that the transmitter crystal would provide a suitably constant phase reference for comparison with the echoes, particularly because of the fact that its phase..might be shifted slightly by the *pulse modulation of the power amplifiers excited by the crystal circuit. **1945** *Electronics* Jan. 103/3 With pulse modulation, especially at very high carrier frequencies, problems of modulation at the transmitter are greatly simplified. **1975** D. G. FINK *Electronics Engineers' Handbk.* XIV. 28 All pulse modulation schemes require sampling analog signals, and some, such as pulse code modulation.., require the additional quantization of the analog signals. **1965** *Wireless World* July 18 (Advt.), EEV magnetrons, klystrons, *pulse modulators,..offer extreme reliability in quality marine electronics. **1706** BAYNARD in Sir J. Floyer *Hot & Cold Bath*, II. 202 These *Pulse-pads, these Bedside Banditti. **1644** G. PLATTES in *Hartlib's Legacy* (1655) 262 They say, that divers who were esteemed dead have been annointed with old Oyl in the five principal *pulse-places, and revived. **1945** *Electronic Industries* Dec. 82 (*heading*) *Pulse position modulation technic. **1975** D. G. FINK *Electronics Engineers' Handbk.* XIV. 34 In PTM the information is coded into the time parameter instead of, for instance, the amplitude... There are two basic types of PTM: pulse position modulation (PPM) and pulse width modulation (PWM), which is also known as pulse duration (PDM). **1904** J. ERLANGER in *Johns Hopkins Hosp. Rep.* XII. 93 The term '*pulse-pressure' is used in place of the phrase, oscillations of the pressure in the arteries produced by the beat of the heart. It is the difference between the maximum and minimum pressures. **1966** *Lancet* 24 Dec. 1387/1 Fig. 1 shows the mean responses of pulse-rate and pulse-pressure during the insulin-tolerance tests in the six men. **1949** D. G. C. LUCK *Frequency Modulated Radar* ix. 416 *Pulse radar is placed at a practical disadvantage, relatively to frequency-modulated radar, by the necessity of operating transmitters at very high peak-power levels. **1966** *McGraw-Hill Encycl. Sci. & Technol.* XI. 211/2 In pulse-radar systems the transmitter and receiver generally share a single antenna. [**1960** MCCARTHY & MACLACHLAN in *Trans. Faraday Soc.* LVI. 1187 The technique of pulsed radiolysis has not heretofore been applied to the transient measurement of rapid chemical reactions.] **1961** *Nucleonics* Oct. 54/1 *Pulse radiolysis has become feasible within the past few years through the availability of electron accelerators which deliver a very short pulse of high energy electrons of extremely high intensity. **1974** *Nature* 22 Nov. 323/1 On pulse radiolysis of nitrous oxide saturated solutions of either thymidine, cytidine, adenosine or guanosine..transient absorption spectra..attributable to the products of reactions of the hydroxyl radical, were observed. **1879** *St. George's Hosp. Rep.* IX. 799 The temperature had fallen to 99°; the *pulse-rate was 110. **1963** Pulse rate [see *pulse counter* above]. **1945** *Amer. Speech* XX. 310/1 *PRF*, *Pulse Recurrence Frequency. **1953** R. CHISHOLM *Cover of Darkness* xvii. 187 He listened patiently to discussions on megacycles, wave-lengths and pulse-recurrence frequencies. **1949** *Jrnl. R. Aeronaut. Soc.* LIII. 447/2 The Americans now used both words, defining a transponder as a *pulse repeater which received and transmitted on different wavelengths. **1971** *Gloss. Electrotechnical, Power Terms* (*B.S.I.*) III. i. 28 *Pulse repeater*, device for receiving pulses from one circuit and transmitting corresponding pulses into another circuit. **1948** L. B. ARGUIMBAU *Vacuum-Tube Circuits* xi. 560 Depending on the pulse height, the multivibrator will synchronize at one fifth, one fourth, or one third of the *pulse repetition rate. **1962** *Gloss. Terms Automatic Data Processing* (*B.S.I.*) 57 When the pulse repetition rate is independent of the interval of time over which it is measured it may be called the pulse repetition frequency. **1978** R. V. JONES *Most Secret War* xxiii. 193 If 40 kilometres were its maximum range, its pulse repetition rate should not exceed 3750 per second. **1963** B. FOZARD *Instrumentation Nuclear Reactors* ix. 105 Pulses from the counter are converted by means of an auxiliary *pulse-shaping (multivibrator) circuit into rectangular positive pulses of stable amplitude. **1971** J. H. SMITH *Digital Logic* v. 95 Flip flop *A* is used as a pulse shaping circuit and has no logical function to perform. **1832** MOTHERWELL *Poems* (1847) 86 Feel every *pulse-stroke thrill of good. **1950** *N.Y. Times* (City ed.) 20 Apr. 1/1 In the light of today's *pulse-taking, it appeared unlikely that the committee would agree on such an approach. **1977** *Proc. R. Soc. Med.* LXX. 425/1 We know that pulse-taking was an important ritual, especially among doctors who did not accept Harvey's discovery of the circulation of blood. **1855** BROWNING *Old Pict. in Florence* vi, One whom each fainter *pulse-tick pains. **1945** *Electronic Industries* Nov. 91/3 At the transmission end amplitude modulated speech signals are changed into *pulse time modulated signals by a tube similar to the cyclophone called the Cyclo-odos. **1944** *Electr. Communication* XXII. 92/1 The merits of another method of transmission applicable to telephony were considered by the Paris Laboratories of the International Telephone and Telegraph Corporation early in 1937... At the time the method was called *pulse 'time' modulation. **1975** D. G. FINK *Electronics Engineers' Handbk.* XIV. 28 The control applications [of pulse modulation] are usually confined to the use of pulse time modulation (PTM) and pulse frequency modulation (PFM), where on-off control power can be used to minimize device dissipation. **1896** *Allbutt's Syst. Med.* I. 314 This change is only maintained during the bath; after it the *pulse-tracing returns to its former standard. **1951** A. SHEINGOLD *Fund. Radio Communications* xx. 413 If the *pulse train is applied to a low-pass filter having an appropriate cutoff value, the signal may be separated from the higher-frequency pulse components. **1975** D. G. FINK *Electronics Engineers' Handbk.* XIV. 28 By interleaving a number of single-channel, low-duty-cycle pulse trains. **1945** *Electronic Industries* Sept. 222 **Pulse transformer*, a special transformer designed to have a frequency response suitable for passing a pulse without materially altering its shape. **1955** *Times* 12 July 2/5 (Advt.), Applicants should preferably be of honours degree standard, with interest in square-loop magnetic devices, ferro-resonant circuits, magnetic amplifiers, or pulse transformers. **1975** D. G. FINK *Electronics Engineers' Handbk.* VII. 18 Lower-power pulse transformers fall into two categories: those used for coupling or impedance matching similar to the high-power pulse transformers, and blocking oscillator transformers used in pulse-generating circuits. **1658** A. FOX *Würtz' Surg.* v. 353, I called for help, intreating them to cut the *pulse vein on my left temple. **1706** HEARNE *Collect.* 17 Dec., Sir Joh. Floyer [is printing] an Invention of a *Pulse-Watch wch being nicely set and adjusted to a Man's Constitution tels him when his Blood & that is out of order. **1707** FLOYER *Physic. Pulse-Watch* Pref., I caused a Pulse-Watch to be made which run 60 Seconds, and I placed it in a Box to be more easily carried, and by this I now feel Pulses. **1753** [see PULSILOGE]. **1851** CARPENTER *Man. Phys.* (ed. 2) 348 When the tonicity of the arteries is less than it should be, their walls yield too much to the *pulse-wave. **1897** *Syd. Soc. Lex.*, *P[ulse]-waves*, the component elements of the apparently simple movement of the pulsating artery, as detected by the sphygmograph. These are chiefly the summit wave, in which the line of ascent ends; the tidal or first secondary wave, due to the distension of the arteries; and the dicrotic or great secondary wave, produced probably by the aortic recoil. **1947** R. LEE *Electronic Transformers & Circuits* ix. 220 Common *pulse widths lie between 0·5 and 10 microseconds. **1978** *Nature* 23 Mar. 362/2 The digital nerves of the index finger were stimulated continuously at 3 times the threshold for perception (pulse width 50 μs, 50 shocks s^{-1}) through ring electrodes placed around the finger on either side of the distal interphalangeal joint. **1953** A. T. STARR *Radio & Radar Technique* i. 26 *Pulse Width Modulation does not correspond to any normally emitted C. W. system, but corresponds to phase modulations of the frequencies ωf, $2\omega f$,...each multiplied by the original low-frequency signal. **1978** *Gramophone* Apr. 1790/1 Sony offered the first class D (pulse width modulation) power amplifier utilizing VFETs and producing 180 watts per channel. **1909** W. JAMES *Pluralistic Universe* vii. 285 By us it [*sc.* reality] has to be taken *pulse-wise, for our span of consciousness is too short to grasp the larger collectivity of things except nominally and abstractly.

pulse (pʌls), *sb.*[2] Forms: (3 pols-, 4 pols', puls'), 5–7 puls, 6 poulse, poultz, *dial.* pousse, 7 powse, pulce, 8–9 *dial.* pouse, 6– pulse. [a. OF. *pols*, *pouls*, *pous* (Godef.), in mod.Norm. dial. *pouls*, in other dialects *poul*, *pou*:—L. *puls* pottage made of meal, pulse, etc. See also PULTS.]

1. The edible seeds of leguminous plants cultivated for food, as peas, beans, lentils, etc.

a. *collective singular*: sometimes const. as *pl.*

1297 [see PULSE-CORN]. **1355–6** *Abingdon Acc.* (Camden) 6 De j quarterio pols' vendito. **1388–9** *Ibid.* 53 Et de xij d. de puls' vendito. **1548** UDALL, etc. *Erasm. Par. Matt.* xiii. 77 Whiche of it selfe is lest among al pulse. **1591** SYLVESTER *Du Bartas* I. ii. 644 In Cods the Poulse, the Corn within the Ear. **1616** SURFL. & MARKH. *Country Farme* 570 Pulse (as we call them) that is.. such graine as is inclosed in coddes or huskes. **1694** WESTMACOTT *Script. Herb.* 22 Field Beans and Powse do feed horses. **1780** COWPER *Progr. Err.* 215 Daniel ate pulse by choice—example rare! *a* **1822** *Old Rime* in *Gentl. Mag.* XCII. I. 15/1 Thee eat thy pouse, and I will drink my beer. **1826** SOUTHEY in *Q. Rev.* XXXIII. 406 A soup composed merely of a few pulse. **1865** SIR T. SEATON *Cadet to Colonel* ix. 165 To search for and secure all grain, flour, pulse, and food of every description.

b. with *a* and *pl.* A kind or sort of such seeds.

1555 W. WATREMAN *Fardle Facions* I. v. 52 The priest may not loke vpon a beane, for that it is iudged an vncleane puls. **1604** E. G[RIMSTONE] *D'Acosta's Hist. Indies* VII. iv. 505 They sowed their land for bread and pulses, which they vsed. **1681** tr. *Belon's Myst. Physick* 47 All sorts of Milk-meats, Sauces, Pulces, Fruits. **1707** MORTIMER *Husb.* (1721) I. 141 There are several other Pulses or Seeds mentioned in many Authors. **1758** R. BROWN *Compl. Farmer* II. (1760) 86 The least of all pulses is the lentil.

2. a. *collective sing.* (sometimes const. as *pl.*) Plants yielding pulse; esculent leguminous plants.

1388–9 *Abingdon Acc.* (Camden) 53 Et de xij d. de stramine puls' vendito. **1542** UDALL *Erasm. Apoph.* 304 Deriued of the moste vsed Poultz called cicer. **1555** EDEN *Decades* 260 All kyndes of pulse, as beanes, peason, tares, and suche other. **1697** DRYDEN *Virg. Georg.* I. 110 Where Vetches, Pulse, and Tares have stood, And Stalks of Lupines grew. **1760–72** tr. *Juan & Ulloa's Voy.* (ed. 3) I. 123 Here are no pulse or pot-herbs of any kind. **1807** CRABBE *Parish Reg.* I. 141 High climb his pulse in many an even row. **1870** YEATS *Nat. Hist. Comm.* 48 Pulse grows everywhere.

b. *individual sing.* (with *pl.*) An esculent leguminous plant, or a species of such.

c **1440** *Pallad. on Husb.* VII. 55 For fodder now is tyme, and euery puls.

3. *attrib.* and *Comb.*, as ***pulse crop***, †*-shell* (*shale*), *-stick* (cf. *pea-stick*), ***tribe***; also PULSE-CORN.

a **1661** HOLYDAY *Juvenal, Sat.* xiv, A pulse-shale more I value, than the whole town's praise. **1785** MARTYN *Rousseau's Bot.* iii. (1794) 39 The leguminous or pulse tribe. **1830** *Kyle Farm Rep.* 35 in *Libr. Usef. Knowl., Husb.* III, A luxuriant pulse crop of itself fertilizes the soil. **1869** BLACKMORE *Lorna D.* vii, A hook and a bit of worm on it,.. or a blow-fly, hung from a hazel pulse-stick.

pulse (pʌls), *v.* Also 6 pulce. [ad. L. *pulsāre* to push, drive, strike, beat, freq. of *pellĕre* to drive, strike, beat. In sense 1 prob. in part from F. *pousser*, formerly *polser*, *poulser* (15th c. in Littré); in other senses more directly connected in use with PULSE *sb.*[1], and *pulsate*, *pulsation*, etc.]

†**1.** *trans.* To drive, impel; to drive *forth*, expel. *Obs.* (exc. as in 4).

1549 *Compl. Scot.* xv. 125 Necessite pulsis and constrenȝes me to cry on god. *Ibid.* xvi. 139 Ȝour ignorance, inconstance, ande inciuilite, pulcis ȝou to perpetrat intollerabil exactions. **1573** TWYNE *Æneid* x. (1584) Q v, Pulst forth through spite from princely throne [L. *Pulsus ob invidiam solio*]. **1586** *Reg. Privy Council Scot.* IV. 111 The Douglassis wes pulsit up to this be thame quha advanceit thameselffs to be farrest in his Hienes secreitis. **1666** J. SMITH *Old Age* (1752) 203 The heart.. doth.. cast it [the blood] forth, and pulse it to all, even the extremest parts.

2. a. *intr.* To beat, throb, as the heart, etc.: = PULSATE 1 (but now only in literary use).

1559, 1664 [see PULSING *ppl. a.*]. **1668** CULPEPPER & COLE *Barthol. Anat.* I. xxxvii. 82 For the Umbilical Arteries of a live Child being bound, as yet cleaving to the Mother.. they pulse between the Ligature and the Child. **1691** RAY *Creation* I. (1692) 35 The Heart, when separated wholly from the Body in some Animals, continues still to pulse for a considerable time. **1864** DUTTON COOK *Trials of Tredgolds* II. 118 The heart pulsed very, very feebly; his eyes were closed again. **1895** F. E. TROLLOPE *F. Trollope* I. i. 6 The warm blood pulsed beneath high-waisted gowns.

b. *fig.* or in figurative allusion, in reference to life, energy, influences, feelings, etc.: = PULSATE 1 b: cf. PULSE *sb.*[1] 2.

1818 KEATS *Endym.* I. 105 The mass Of nature's lives and wonders puls'd tenfold. **1874** GREEN *Short Hist.* v. §1. 216 The throb of hope and glory which pulsed at its outset.. died into inaction or despair. **1888** *Times* 26 June 9/5 The outward and sensible expression of the never-resting flow of thought, action, and feeling which pulses through it [London].

3. *intr.* **a.** *gen.* To perform or exhibit a rhythmic movement; to beat, vibrate, undulate: = PULSATE 2.

1851 CARLYLE *Sterling* II. i. (1872) 88 Playing and pulsing like sunshine or soft lightning. **1873** J. GEIKIE *Gt. Ice Age* iv. 41 The heat of the sun.. pulses through the great piles of ice that cumber the higher elevations of Alpine countries. **1883** *Harper's Mag.* June 117/1 The thermal water.. pulsed out of the cleft of the rock. **1904** M. HEWLETT *Queen's Quair* II. vii. 285 You could hear the regular galloping of a horse, pulsing in the dark like some muffled pendulum.

¶ **b.** To make recurrent sallies or attacks.

1851 CARLYLE *Sterling* I. iv. (1872) 30 His studies were.. pulsing out with impetuous irregularity now on this tract, now on that. **1865** —— *Fredk. Gt.* xx. v. (1872) IX. 89 Such charging and recharging, pulsing and repulsing, has there been. *Ibid.* vii. 146 Broglio, on the other hand, keeps violently pulsing out, round Ferdinand's flanks.

4. *trans.* To drive or send out in or by pulses or rhythmic beats.

1819 KEATS *Isabella* vi, The ruddy tide Stifled his voice, and pulsed resolve away. **1861** LOWELL *Washers of Shroud* ii, Pale fireflies pulsed within the meadow-mist Their halos, wavering thistledowns of light. **1876** MRS. WHITNEY *Sights & Ins.* II. iii. 371 Life is not dead, but living?.. coming down and out, always;.. pulsed into us, not set outside of us to grasp and define. **1954** R. STEPHENSON *Introd. Nuclear Engin.* ix. 332 One of the two liquid phases present is pulsed at the rate of about 60 pulses/min, each pulse causing the liquid in the column to oscillate over a distance of about 0·9 in. **1971** C. J. KING *Separation Processes* xiv. 740 The contents of either a packed column or a plate column can be pulsed by applying intermittent surges of pump pressure to the column. This pulsing promotes mass-transfer rates within the column. **1977** *Design Engin.* July 27/2 Energy in high power radar systems.. is pulsed through a magnetron in discrete 'pockets' to allow the returning echo to be related in time with the initial transmission.

5. *Biochem.* To subject (cells in culture) to a pulse of isotopically labelled substrate or substrates.

1960 *Jrnl. Molecular Biol.* II. 320 Uninfected cells were pulsed with ^{32}P under the same conditions and the purified soluble RNA was examined. **1975** *Nature* 14 Aug. 592/1 After various incubation periods the cells were pulsed for 1h with labelled amino acids or nucleosides, collected and macromolecular synthesis measured.

6. To apply a pulsed signal to.

1964 *Ann. N.Y. Acad. Sci.* CXV. 665 The.. 16 digital output lines.. can be pulsed individually by a special computer instruction. **1974** *Physics Bull.* June 257/1 The transmitter consists of a small loudspeaker pulsed by a capacitor discharge and the echoes are received by a small conventional microphone.

7. To modulate (a wave, beam, etc.) so that it becomes a series of pulses.

1969 *Sci. Jrnl.* Dec. 42/3 Semiconductor lasers whose output may be modulated up to 1 GHz by pulsing the pump current. **1971** *Nature* 26 Nov. 178/2 High-powered monochromatic beams of laser light.. may be modulated or pulsed in times as short as 10^{-11}s. **1975** D. G. FINK *Electronics Engineers' Handbk.* xiv. 28 In usual applications [of pulse modulation], subcarriers are pulsed, time-division-multiplexed, and then used to frequency-modulate a carrier.

†**'pulse-corn.** *Obs. rare.* Also 3 polscorn. [f. PULSE *sb.*[2] + CORN *sb.*[1]] = PULSE *sb.*[2] 1 a, 2 a.

1297 in Rogers *Agric. & Prices* (1866) II. 174/2 (Cheddington) Polscorn. **1558** WARDE tr. *Alexis' Secr.* 24 b, All sortes of pulse corne, as Pease, Beanes, Tares, and Fitches.

pulsed (pʌlst), *ppl. a.* [f. PULSE *v.* + -ED[1].]

a. Producing or involving pulses.

pulsed column: a tower for solvent extraction in which the natural countercurrent flow of the feed liquid and the solvent has mechanically superimposed on it a rapid reciprocating motion of small amplitude, in order to promote the extraction process.

1946 *Radar: Summary Rep. & Harp Project* (U.S. Nat. Defense Res. Comm., Div. 14) 143/1 Pulsed Doppler shift. **1949** *Jrnl. R. Aeronaut. Soc.* LIII. 439/1 A system employing secondary radar, i.e. a pulsed ground station working in conjunction with a responder, has been designed. **1958** *Engineering* 14 Feb. 205/3 The solvent and water solutions quickly separate after the mixing-contacting process, be this in a packed or pulsed countercurrent contactor column or a mixer-settler unit. **1972** *McGraw-Hill Yearbk. Sci. & Technol.* 268/1 Progress in the development of CW devices has spurred renewed interest in pulsed chemical lasers as.. sources of the very-high-energy pulses.. needed for plasma heating experiments. **1978** R. V. JONES *Most Secret War* ii. 16 In 1931 W. A. S. Butement and P. E. Pollard.. had devised and made a pulsed radio system on a wavelength of about 50 centimetres for detecting ships. **1978** *Nature* 23 Mar. 298/3 Because oxide fuel is highly radioactive, the process is carried out in pulsed columns (rather than mixer settlers) to minimise the contact time between the solvent and the dissolved acid fuel.

b. Consisting of pulses; in the form of pulses.

1949 *Jrnl. R. Aeronaut. Soc.* LIII. 438/1 (*heading*) Measurement of the density of the upper atmosphere by radar—pulsed violet or ultra-violet light. **1955** FRIEDMAN & WEISSKOPF in W. Pauli *Niels Bohr* 155 A pulsed initial neutron beam. **1957** F. HOYLE *Black Cloud* ix. 182 We ought to start sending pulsed messages on the one centimetre [wave-length]. **1971** *Nature* 16 Apr. 426/1 The X-rays from the hitherto unsurprising source Cygnus X-1 are pulsed at a rate of probably about 15 pulses per second.

pulseful ('pʌlsfʊl), *a. rare.* [f. PULSE *sb.*[1] + -FUL.] Full of pulses, pulsations, or throbbing.

a **1861** D. GRAY *Poet. Wks.* (1874) 193 The partridge cowers beside thy loamy flow In pulseful tremor.

pulseless ('pʌlslɪs), *a.* [f. as prec. + -LESS.]

1. Having or exhibiting no pulse or pulsation, as a body in which the heart has ceased to beat.

1748 RICHARDSON *Clarissa* (1810) VIII. xxiii. 100 While warm, though pulseless, we pressed each her hand with our lips. **1822** SHELLEY *Hellas* 142 His cold pale limbs and pulseless arteries. **1875** BEDFORD *Sailor's Pocket Bk.* viii. (ed. 2) 302 In shock the injured person lies pale, faint,.. almost pulseless.

2. *fig.* and *gen.* Devoid of life, energy, or movement; void of feeling, unfeeling, pitiless (quot. 1856); motionless; lifeless.

1856 AYTOUN *Bothwell* II. ix, There he stood, the pulseless man, The calculating lord. **1861** E. S. KENNEDY in *Peaks, Passes*, etc., Ser. II. I. 170 So often as she came, so often there floated on the pulseless air the gentle moan 'Mort Aratsch'. **1873** W. S. MAYO *Never Again* xxxii, Better than Joys of pale and pulseless Life, The agony of Strife.

Hence **'pulselessness**.

1853 DUNGLISON *Med. Lex.*, *Pulselessness*, asphyxia. **1889** *Sat. Rev.* 20 July 85/2 [He] points out the difference between the meanings of the terms asphyxia and apnoea, the former standing for pulselessness and the latter for breathlessness.

‖**pulsellum** (pʌl'sɛləm). *Zool.* Pl. **-a**. [mod.L., f. *puls-*, ppl. stem of *pellĕre* to drive, after FLAGELLUM.] A modified form of flagellum found in spermatozoa and certain infusorians, serving to propel the body through a liquid medium.

1880 KENT *Infusoria* I. 429 Among the free-swimming monoflagellate Infusoria as at present known, where the locomotive appendage without exception fulfils during natation the rôle of a tractellum, its recognition by such title in contradistinction to a propelling organ or pulsellum is uncalled for. **1885** E. R. LANKESTER in *Encycl. Brit.* XIX. 859/1 The flagellum of the Flagellata is totally distinct from the pulsellum of the Bacteria.

pulser ('pʌlsə(r)). [f. PULSE *sb.*[1] or *v.* + -ER[1].]

1. A device that generates electrical pulses.

1947 LEBACQZ & WHITE in L. N. Ridenour *Radar System Engin.* x. 373 Successful hard-tube pulsers have been made with power outputs up to 3 or 4 Mw. **1973** *Sci. Amer.* June 47/1 The resolution time, or fastest shutter time, of this type of gate is determined by the shortest duration provided by an electrical voltage pulser: about a nanosecond. **1978** *Ibid.* Mar. 58/3 The base houses.. a dial pulser to signal the required numbers to the central office and a bell to signal an incoming call to the subscriber.

2. A machine for producing mechanical pulsation in a liquid.

1954 R. STEPHENSON *Introd. Nuclear Engin.* ix. 334 Until satisfactory pulsers are developed.. it is doubtful that pulse columns will find any extensive use except for very special solvent extraction operations. **1963** J. H. PERRY *Chem. Engineers' Handbk.* (ed. 4) XXI. 33/1 The pipe connecting column and pulser may be of any length.., but high pressure drop in the transfer pipe contributes to cavitation difficulties.

pulshe, obs. form of POLISH *v.*

†**pulsidge.** *Obs.* Humorous blunder for PULSE.

1597 SHAKS. *2 Hen. IV*, II. iv. 25 You are in an excellent good temperalitie: your Pulsidge beates as extraordinarily, as heart would desire.

pul'sific, *a.* Now *rare.* [f. L. *puls-us* PULSE *sb.*[1] + -FIC.] Producing or causing the pulse or pulsation of the arteries; also, characterized by pulsation, pulsatory, throbbing.

1634 T. JOHNSON tr. *Parey's Chirurg.* VIII. xix. 314 Cruell symptomes doe follow, as pulsifique paine, a feaver, restlessnesse. *Ibid.* XX. vii. 772 The oppression of the vitall and pulsifick faculty by a cloud of grosse vapours. **1678** CUDWORTH *Intell. Syst.* I. iii. §17. 161 A pulsifick corporeal quality in the substance of the heart itself, is very unphilosophical and absurd. **1710** T. FULLER *Pharm. Extemp.* 425 The pulsific Motion of the Blood continually thrusting on. **1853** DUNGLISON *Med. Lex.*, *Pulsific*, that which causes or excites pulsation. **1897** in *Syd. Soc. Lex.*

†**'pulsiloge.** *Obs.* [ad. mod.L. *pulsilogium*, f. *puls-us* PULSE *sb.*[1], after *horologium*, HOROLOGE.] (See quots.)

[**1753** CHAMBER *Cycl. Supp.*, *Pulsilogium*, a name given by authors to a pulse-watch, or instrument to measure the celerity of the pulse.] **1812** *Edin. Rev.* XX. 185 Sanctorio.. applied the pendulum to determine the quickness of the pulse, forming what he called a *pulsiloge*, in which the string suspending a ball was gradually shortened, till its vibrations corresponded with the beats.

pulsimeter (pʌl'sɪmɪtə(r)). [f. L. *pulsus* PULSE *sb.*[1] + -METER. Cf. PULSOMETER.] An instrument for measuring the rate or force of the pulse. Also *attrib.*, as ***pulsimeter watch***.

1842 in DUNGLISON *Med. Lex.* **1894** *Brit. Med. Jrnl.* 26 May 1132/1 The advantages claimed for the 'Pulsimeter' watch are economy of time, accuracy of record, and the possibility of taking the pulse in the dark without any inconvenience to the patient.

'pulsing, *vbl. sb.* [f. PULSE *v.* + -ING[1].] The action of the vb. PULSE: rhythmical beating, throbbing, or flowing.

1839 BAILEY *Festus* xix. (1852) 281 Ceaseless as the pulsings of the blood. **1843** CARLYLE *Past & Pr.* III. xv, The pulsings of his own soul, if he have any soul, alone audible. **1894** CROCKETT *Raiders* 133, I could hear.. the pulsing of the sea. **1945** *Electronics* Jan. 105/1 The method of pulsing involved frequency-modulating the transmitter ± 75 kc by a continuous 170-cycle tone. **1971** [see PULSE *v.* 4].

'pulsing, *ppl. a.* [f. as prec. + -ING[2].] That beats, throbs, or flows with rhythmic cadence.

1559 MORWYNG *Evonym.* 359 This oyll anoynted vpon the pulsing veynes, where they appeare moste. **1664** POWER *Exp. Philos.* I. 4 If you divide the Bee.. near the necke, you shall.. see the heart beat most lively, which is a white pulsing vesicle. **1879** *Cassell's Techn. Educ.* IV. 250/2 The pulsing torrent rushes through the arteries.

pulsion ('pʌlʃən). Now *rare.* [ad. L. *pulsio*, *-ōn-em*, n. of action from *pell-ĕre*, *puls-* to drive, push.] The action of driving or pushing. In first quot., the beating of the pulse.

1634 T. JOHNSON tr. *Parey's Chirurg.* v. iii. (1678) 107 There may ensue.. a deadly interception of the pulsion of the brain. **1656** tr. *Hobbes' Elem. Philos.* (1839) 214 One

motion is pulsion or driving, another traction or drawing. Pulsion, when the movent makes the moved body go before it; and traction, when it makes it follow. **1731** S. HALES *Stat. Ess.* I. 111 If this great quantity [of sap] were carried up by pulsion or trusion. **1836–48** B. D. WALSH *Aristoph., Clouds* I. iv, Pulsion, and prension.
attrib. **1897** *Allbutt's Syst. Med.* III. 363 Acquired malformations [of the œsophagus]—Pressure pouches... pharyngeal pouches, pharyngoceles, pulsion diverticula.

pulsive (ˈpʌlsɪv), *a.* Now *rare*. [f. L. *puls-*, ppl. stem of *pell-ĕre* to drive, impel + -IVE.]
1. Having the quality of driving or impelling; constraining, compelling; impulsive; propulsive.
1602 MARSTON *Antonio's Rev.* IV. iii, What I here speake is forced from my lips By the pulsive straine of conscience. *a* **1687** PETTY *Treat. Naval Philos.* I. i. §85 The Tractive and Pulsive forces upon swimming Bodies. **188.** R. G. H[ILL] *Voices in Solitude* 83 The whirl of the wheels went on at length With the pulsive strain of their started strength.
† **2.** Beating or throbbing as the heart, etc. *Obs.*
1611 J. TAYLOR (Water P.) *Coriat's Commend.* Wks. II. 91/1 Such a straine That shall euen cracke my pulsiue pia mater In warbling thy renowne by land and water. **1630** —— *Descr. Eng. Poetry* ibid. 248/2 In end my pulsiue braine no Art affoords, To mint or stamp, or forge new coyned words.
3. Making a beating or throbbing sound.
1960 'W. HAGGARD' *Closed Circuit* x. 123 He knew a band, quite a small one, quiet and properly pulsive. **1969** G. MACBETH *War Quartet* 43 In wave On gathered wave of pulsive thumping, wings Grazed overhead.

pulsometer (pʌlˈsɒmɪtə(r)). [irreg. f. L. *pulsus* PULSE *sb.*[1] + -METER, after *barometer*, etc.]
1. = PULSIMETER.
1858 MAYNE *Expos. Lex., Pulsometrum*, term for an instrument for measuring or calculating the variations of the pulse: a pulsometer.
2. A name for a kind of steam-condensing vacuum-pump, with two chambers so arranged that the steam is condensed in, and the water admitted to each alternately: so called from the pulsatory action of the steam. Also ***pulsometer pump***. (Not being a *measuring* instrument, it is preferably called *pulsator*.)
1875 KNIGHT *Dict. Mech., Pulsometer*,.. a form of vacuum pump. **1881** *Mechanical World* 24 Dec. Advt., The Pulsometer Engineering Company Limited. **1891** *Daily News* 2 Sept. 3/1 The water is heated by means of a horizontal tubular boiler, a six-horse power engine, a centrifugal pump, and two pulsometer pumps. **1900** F. T. BULLEN *Idylls of Sea* 265 My heart worked like a pulsometer.

† **ˈpulsor.** *Obs. rare*$^{-1}$. [agent-n. from L. *pellĕre*, *puls-* to drive, impel: see -OR 2.] One who or that which drives or impels.
1666 J. SMITH *Old Age* (1676) 242 The great artery.. is to us the most apparent Pulsor; we can feel the blood to be forced along its Cavity.

pulsshe, obs. form of POLISH *v.*

pult, parallel form of PILT *v.* and *sb. Obs.*

pultaceous (pʌlˈteɪʃəs), *a.* [f. L. *puls, pult-em* pap, pottage + -ACEOUS.]
1. Of the nature or consistency of pap or of a poultice; soft, semi-fluid, pulpy.
1668 *Phil. Trans.* III. 751 He first denyeth, that the Testes are glandulous or pultaceous. **1738** STUART *ibid.* XL. 327 A soft white pultaceous Matter. **1835–6** *Todd's Cycl. Anat.* I. 71/1 In infancy the brain is extremely soft, almost pultaceous. **1896** *Allbutt's Syst. Med.* I. 403 Pultaceous or even solid food may be remarkably well borne.
2. Of the nature or class of pulse.
1762 tr. *Busching's Syst. Geog.* III. 667 Barley, peas and other pultaceous grain.

pultar, -er, etc., **pulterer, pult(e)rie**, obs. forms of POULTER, etc.

pultas, obs. or dial. form of POULTICE.

† **ˈpulter.** *Obs. rare*$^{-1}$.
In quot. prob. an error for *pultre*, POULTRY, fowls. (The whole passage is composed in the language of falconry, and some of the allusions are obscure.)
1399 LANGL. *Rich. Redeles* II. 165 But þe blernyed boynard þat his bagg stall, Where purraileis pulter was pynnyd ffull ofte, Made þe ffawcon to ffloter and fflussh ffor anger, That þe boy hadd be bounde þat þe bagge kepte.

pultes, -ess, -ice, obs. or dial. ff. POULTICE.

† **pulˈtifical**, *a. Obs. rare*$^{-0}$. [f. L. *puls, pult-em* pottage + -FIC + -AL[1].]
1656 BLOUNT *Glossogr., Pultifical*,.. wherewith Pottage, Pap, or such like meat is made.

pultis(e, -oss, pultre, pultron(e, -oon, -owne, obs. ff. POULTICE, POULTRY, POLTROON.

pultrusion (pʊl-, pʌlˈtruːʒən). [f. PUL(LING *vbl. sb.* + EX)TRUSION.] A process for making plastic articles reinforced with glass fibre in which long strands of the reinforcement, encased in liquid resin, are pulled through a heated die that shapes and cures the resin.
1964 OLEESKY & MOHR *Handbk. Reinforced Plastics* v. 324 (*caption*) 'Pultrusion' tank design. **1965** *Mod. Plastics Encycl. 1966* 632/2 Long lengths of reinforced plastics flat strip or sheet.. can be produced economically by the pultrusion process. **1968**, **1976** [see below].
Hence **pulˈtrude** *v. trans.*, to make by this process; **pulˈtruded** *ppl. a.*
1968 *6th Internat. Reinforced Plastics Conf.* (Brit. Plastics Federation) 6/1/1 The pull-trusion process is the oldest one of the technical processes nowadays used for a continuous production of glassfibre reinforced polyester articles... The percentage of pull-truded products made from glassfibre reinforced polyester has considerably increased. **1971** *Mod. Plastics Encycl. 1970–1* 592/3 Typical volume applications for pultruded products are electrical pole line hardware, ladders, fishing rods and corrosion-resistant structural shapes. **1976** *S9* (N.Y.) May/June 116/2 Plastigage Corporation.. has developed and perfected a new method to produce pultruded fiberglass rod ideal for OEM. **1976** *Reinforced Plastics* XX. 295/2 Another advantage of the pultrusion process is the ability to produce a number of similarly dimensioned products at the same time. Currently, the company are pultruding hollow section rods and solid rods at the same time. *Ibid.* 295/3 Early models of the Sky Stunter kite used aluminium tubing for the framework, but this has now been replaced with the pultruded components.

† **pults.** *Obs. rare.* [app. ad. med.L. *pultes* any victuals prepared by boiling (Du Cange), pl. of L. *puls, pultem* pap, pottage (see PULSE *sb.*[2]): cf. It. *pulta, polta* 'grewell, battre, or pap' (Florio).] Soft boiled food, pap, pottage.
c **1550** LLOYD *Treas. Health* S ij, Geue vnto the pacient.. two pennye weightes of bay beris made to pouder wyth a soft Egge or pults, without doubt the pacyent shalbe made hole.

‖ **pultun** (ˈpʌltʌn). *E. Ind.* Also pultan, -on, -oon. [Hindī *palṭan*, ad. Tamil and Telugu *paṭālan*, ad. Eng. *battalion* (the Eng. word having been first adopted in Southern India).] A regiment of infantry in India.
1800 WELLINGTON in Gurw. *Desp.* (1834) I. 21*, I.. shall probably destroy some campoos and pultans, which have been indiscreetly pushed across the Kistna. **1883** *Q. Rev.* Apr. 294 *Campos* and *pultuns* (battalions) under European adventurers. **1895** MRS. B. M. CROKER *Village Tales* (1896) 60, I know lots of Sahibs in a pultoon (i.e. regiment) at Bareilly.

‖ **pulu** (ˈpuːluː). [Hawaiian.] A fine yellowish silky vegetable wool obtained from the base of the leaf-stalks of the Hawaiian tree-ferns, *Cibotium menziesii*, *C. chamissoi*, and *C. glaucum*.
1833 W. TOLMIE *Jrnl.* 6 Apr. in *Physician & Fur Trader* (1963) 144 Met Madame Boki & retinue, her brows encircled with garlands of pulu. **1858** SIMMONDS *Dict. Trade, Pu-lu*, a species of brown thistle-down imported from the Sandwich islands, to mix with silk in the manufacture of hats. **1888** HILLEBRAND *Flora Hawai Is.* 546 The base of the leaf stalks is densely covered with a soft and glossy yellowish wool, which is used for stuffing mattresses and pillows, and under the name of pulu forms a regular article of export to California. **1917** *Nature* 20 Sept. 58/1 These plants [*sc.* Hawaiian tree ferns] produce at the base of the stipe a great ball of brownish-yellow wool called pulu by the natives, and used by them for stuffing pillows and mattresses.

† **puluere**, obs. f. PILLIVER, pillow-case, pillow.
c **1350** *Will. Palerne* 681 He wende ful witerly sche were in is armes; ac peter! it nas but is puluere.

‖ **pulut** (ˈpuːlʊt, puːluː). [Mal. (*padi*) *pulut* sticky (rice).] In Malaysia, glutinous rice.
1820 J. CRAWFURD *Hist. Indian Archipel.* I. IV. ii. 360 The most singular variety [of rice] is that called by the Malays *Pulut*.., the *Oryza glutinosa* of Rumphius. This is never used as bread, but commonly prepared as a sweetmeat. **1900** W. W. SKEAT *Malay Magic* 76 A special kind of glutinous rice called *pulut*.. is also very generally used for sacrificial banquets. **1972** A. AMIN tr. *Ahmad's No Harvest but Thorn* ii. 10 Our children love *pulut* in the mornings before school. With *pulut* the fullness lasts a long time. *Ibid.* xiv. 148 They would also separate the *Thai* rice from the *pulut* rice.

† **ˈpulver**, *sb. Obs.* [ad. L. *pulver-em* (nom. *pulvis*) powder, dust.] Powder, dust.
1502 ATKYNSON tr. *De Imitatione* III. ix. 204 Good lorde, I speke to the of my presumpcion, natwithstandinge that I am but puluer & asshes. **1535** STEWART *Cron. Scot.* (Rolls) II. 423 In puluer small gart birne thame euerie one. **1599** A. M. tr. *Gabelhouer's Bk. Physicke* 28/1 Mixe these prænominated pulvers.. addinge heerunto the Suger.
b. Pulver Wednesday = ASH-WEDNESDAY.
c **1454** AGNES PASTON in *P. Lett.* I. 270 Wretyn at Norwyche on Pulver Wedenesday.

† **ˈpulver**, *v. Obs.* [ad. L. *pulver-āre*, f. *pulver-*: see prec.] *trans.* To reduce to powder, to pulverize. Hence † **ˈpulvered** *ppl. a.*, † **ˈpulvering** *vbl. sb.*, sprinkling of ashes; ***pulvering day***, Ash Wednesday.
1621 G. SANDYS *Ovid's Met.* VII. (1626) 129 As pulvered flints [*ed.* 1632 lime of flints] infurnest under ground By sprinkled water fire conceive. **1754** T. GARDNER *Hist. Dunwich* 193 On pulvering Days, when Disposition of the said Lands was made, but not confirmed till St. Nicholas's Day. **1778** [implied in PULVERER].

pulverable (ˈpʌlvərəb(ə)l), *a.* [f. as prec. vb. + -ABLE.] Capable of being crushed or ground down to powder; pulverizable.
1657 *Physical Dict., Pulverable*, hard things (as oyster-shells) brought to pouder. **1680** BOYLE *Produc. Chem. Princ.* IV. 167 Some liquid substances afforded by wounded plants, that.. turned into consistent and pulverable bodies. **1789** NICHOLSON in *Phil. Trans.* LXXIX. 274 If a little mercury be added to melted zinc, it renders it easily pulverable. **1869** J. E. HALLIDAY in *Student* II. 228 Trap-rock,.. very soft and pulverable.

pulveraceous (pʌlvəˈreɪʃəs), *a. Bot.* and *Zool.* [f. L. *pulver-em* powder, dust + -ACEOUS.] Covered or sprinkled with powder; pulverulent.
1864 GRAY in WEBSTER.

† **pulverain.** *Obs.* [Corruption of Fr. *pulvérin* (*c* 1600 in Littré), = It. *polverino*, f. *polver*:—L. *pulverem* powder.] A powder-horn, esp. one for priming-powder.
1890 in *Cent. Dict.*

† **ˈpulveral**, *a. Obs. rare.* [f. L. *pulver-em* PULVER *sb.* + -AL[1].] In the state of powder.
1657 TOMLINSON *Renou's Disp.* 178 Solid.. or pulverall, which must be snuffed up.

† **ˈpulverate**, *v. Obs.* [f. L. *pulverāt-*, ppl. stem of *pulverāre* to powder: cf. PULVER *v.*] *trans.* To reduce to powder, to pulverize.
1615 G. SANDYS *Trav.* 65 They litter them in their owne dung, first dried in the Sunne and puluerated. **1657** TOMLINSON *Renou's Disp.* 60 Some cannot be so exactly pulverated by beating.

pulveration (pʌlvəˈreɪʃən). [ad. L. *pulveratiōn-em*, n. of action f. *pulverāre*: see prec.] Reduction to powder or dust; pulverization.
1623 COCKERAM, *Pulueration*, a beating into powder. **1733** TULL *Horse-Hoeing Husb.* v. 43 No further.. than the Hoe-Plow could turn it up, and help it in its Pulveration. **1866** C. W. HOSKYNS *Occas. Ess.* 103 The deep and perfect pulveration of the soil.

‖ **Pulveratores** (pʌlvəreɪˈtɔəriːz), *sb. pl. Ornith.* [mod.L., pl. of *pulverātor*, agent-n. from L. *pulverāre* to powder; in F. *pulvérateurs* (Buffon 1771).] Birds which habitually roll themselves in the dust, as the *Rasores*.

† **pulveratricious** (pʌlvərəˈtrɪʃəs), *a. Obs.* [f. mod.L. *pulverātrix*, *-trīc-em* (see next) + -IOUS.] Of, belonging to, or characteristic of birds that roll themselves in the dust.
1661 LOVELL *Hist. Anim. & Min.* Introd., Birds, which.. are pulveratricious and wild; as the Peacock, japonian, and turky. **1678** RAY *Willughby's Ornith.* III. ii. 371 The colour of the feathers.. comes near to that of pulveratricious birds. **1688** R. HOLME *Armoury* II. 313/1 Pulveratricious [is] an earthly kind of colour, mouse-colour. *Ibid.*, *Pulveratriceous*, covered with a dusty colour.

‖ **pulveratrix** (pʌlvəˈreɪtrɪks). *Ornith. rare.* Pl. -a'trices. [mod.L., fem. of *pulverātor*, agent-n. from *pulverāre* to powder (sc. *avis* bird); in F. *pulvératrice* (Littré).] A bird which cleanses itself by wallowing in dust.
Cf. Aristotle's κονιστικοί, *Hist. An.* 9. 49B, 10.
1770 G. WHITE *Selborne* 8 Oct., Ray remarks that birds of the *Gallinæ* order, as cocks and hens, partridges and pheasants, are *pulveratrices*, such as dust themselves... Common house-sparrows are great *pulveratrices*, being frequently seen grovelling and wallowing in dusty roads.

† **pulˈvereous**, *a. Obs. rare*$^{-0}$. [f. L. *pulvere-us* dusty (f. *pulver-em* powder, dust) + -OUS.]
1656 BLOUNT, *Pulvereous*, dusty, of dust, full of dust.

† **ˈpulverer.** *Obs. rare.* [f. PULVER *v.* + -ER[1].] A pulverizer, an instrument for pulverizing the soil.
1778 [W. MARSHALL] *Minutes Agric., Digest* 54 *note*, If used as a Pulverer and Compressor of fallows, this acting Bar ought to be set deeper.

pulverescence (pʌlvəˈrɛsəns). *Bot.* [f. as next + *-escence*: see -ENCE.] Incipient powderiness; tendency to become powdery.
1828 R. K. GREVILLE *Sc. Cryptog. Flora* VI. 338 Hoary, with a white pulverescence. **1858** MAYNE *Expos. Lex.*, *Pulverescentia*.. of a vegetable surface when covered with a kind of *farina*.. as in the *Chenopodium purpureum*: pulverescence. **1897** in *Syd. Soc. Lex.*

pulverescent (pʌlvəˈrɛsənt), *a.* [f. L. *pulver-em* dust + -ESCENT.] Tending to fall into powder; becoming powdery.
1805 MUSHET in *Phil. Trans.* XCV. 168 It was.. found to be very fine ore of iron in a pulverescent state.

pulverilentous, obs. f. PULVERULENTOUS.

pulverine (ˈpʌlvərɪn). Also -in. [Cf. It. *polverina* dust, fine powder.] Ashes of barilla.
1836 in SMART. **1858** SIMMONDS *Dict. Trade, Pulverine*, barilla ashes.

pulverizable (ˈpʌlvəraɪzəb(ə)l), *a.* [f. PULVERIZE *v.* + -ABLE. So F. *pulvérisable* (Littré).] Capable of being pulverized or reduced to powder.
1660 tr. *Paracelsus' Archidoxis* II. 60 Boil them until they are pulverisable. **1794** G. ADAMS *Nat. & Exp. Philos.* I. xi. 462 An earthy pulverizable matter. *c* **1865** J. WYLDE in *Circ. Sc.* I. 18/2 Tin becomes pulverisable.. at high temperatures.

† **'pulverizate**, *ppl. a. Obs.* [ad. *pulverizāt-us*, pa. pple. of late L. *pulverizāre* to PULVERIZE.] Pulverized, reduced to powder.

1471 RIPLEY *Comp. Alch.* XI. vi. in Ashm. (1652) 182 Lyke as Saffron when yt ys pulveryzate.

† **'pulverizate**, *v. Obs.* [f. ppl. stem of late L. *pulverizāre*: see prec.] *trans.* = PULVERIZE.

1597 A. M. tr. *Guillemeau's Fr. Chirurg.* 49 b/1 That all these Poulders be verye diminutlye pulverisated. **1599** —— tr. *Gabelhouer's Bk. Physicke* 1/2 Pulverisate it verye smalle. **1604–13** R. CAWDREY *Table Alph.*, *Puluerisated*, beaten or broken into dust, or powder.

pulverization (ˌpʌlvəraɪˈzeɪʃən). [n. of action f. late L. *pulverizāre* to pulverize: cf. F. *pulvérisation* (Oudin 1642).]

1. The action of pulverizing; reduction to the state of powder or dust.

[**1657** *Physical Dict.*, *Pulverication*, bringing to pouder.] **1658** PHILLIPS, *Pulverisation*, a breaking to dust, a reducing into powder. **1763** MILLS *Pract. Husb.* II. 197 Brought to that state of pulverization, in which alone plants can thrive well. **1846** J. BAXTER *Libr. Pract. Agric.* II. 64 Rains, alternate frosts, and thaws, greatly assist its pulverization.

b. *techn.* The separation (of a liquid) into minute particles, as spray.

1861 *N. Syd. Soc. Year-Bk. Med.* 207 Method of rendering Medicated Liquids Respirable by Pulverisation. **1863** *Ibid.* 421 Pulverization of liquids for Therapeutic Purposes.

c. *fig.* Crushing morally, reducing to nullity, utter demolition (of arguments, statements, etc.).

1873 MORLEY *Rousseau* II. i. 42 This criticism..marks a beginning of true democracy, as distinguished from the mere pulverisation of aristocracy. **1884** *Chr. World* 13 Mar. 192/5 The complete pulverisation of their case by the Minister whom they approached. **1897** *Windsor Mag.* Jan. 282/2 That the *Saturday Review* devote to your pulverisation two pages and a 'par'.

2. *concr.* A pulverized product or material.

1896 in *Columbus* (Ohio) *Dispatch* 18 Mar. 11/3 The pulverizations gradually find a place on the lowest levels of the ocean.

pulverizator (ˈpʌlvəraɪzeɪtə(r)). [Agent-noun from late L. *pulverizāre* to pulverize: so mod.F. *pulvérisateur* (Littré).] An instrument for reducing to powder; also, an apparatus for scattering powder or ejecting liquid in the form of spray.

1890 *Kew Bulletin* 191 It is mixed as a powder..and blown with 'pulverizators' on to the vine leaves. **1894** *Dublin Rev.* Oct. 433 There have been many patents taken out in Russia for injectors or pulverisators.

pulverize (ˈpʌlvəraɪz), *v.* [ad. late L. *pulverizāre*, or F. *pulvériser* (Paré 16th c.), †*polveriser* (14th c. in Hatz.-Darm.), f. L. *pulver-em*: see PULVER *sb.*]

1. *trans.* To reduce to powder or dust; to comminute, to triturate. Also *refl.*

1585 T. WASHINGTON tr. *Nicholay's Voy.* II. xxii. 60 b. A drugge..which being puluerised and tempered in water, they rubbe vppon..the bodye. **1605** SYLVESTER *Du Bartas* II. iii. III. *Law* 1142 The zealous Prophet with just fury mov'd..pulveriz'd their Idol. *c* **1790** IMISON *Sch. Art* II. 69 Let it dry, and then pulverize it. **1868** ROGERS *Pol. Econ.* xii. (1876) 154 Cultivable land must be pulverised and watered. **1869** J. MARTINEAU *Ess.* II. 235 The solid ground of life was pulverizing itself away.

b. *techn.* To divide (a liquid) into minute particles or spray.

1807 J. BARLOW *Columb.* VI. 230 Stroke after stroke with doubling force he plied, Foil'd the hoar Fiend and pulverized the tide.

2. *fig.* To demolish or destroy, to break down utterly; to 'smash'.

1631 MASSINGER *Believe as you List* I. ii, You shall..Feel really that we have iron hammers To pulverize rebellion. **1684** BAXTER *Twelve Argts.* Post. M ij, Between both which Truth and Peace is broken, and the Church pulverized. **1813** *Examiner* 17 May 313/1 Which, like a clap of thunder, has pulverized..chimerical hopes. **1864** J. H. NEWMAN *Apol.* iii. (1865) 117 The theory of the *Via Media* was absolutely pulverized. **1895** COL. MAURICE in *United Service Mag.* July 428 The four battalions..were..pulverised and driven helter-skelter partly among the defendants.

b. To dissipate in minute portions. *rare.*

1834 SIR W. HAMILTON *Discuss.* (1852) 373 The responsibility was so pulverized among a passing multitude of nameless individuals.

3. *intr.* To crumble or fall to dust; to become disintegrated. Also *fig.*

1801 *Farmer's Mag.* Apr. 147 If they are ploughed in November or December, the rains, snow, and frost, make them pulverize easily. **1860** EMERSON *Cond. Life, Worship* Wks. (Bohn) II. 394 The stern old faiths have all pulverized. **1866** LAWRENCE tr. *Cotta's Rocks Class.* (1878) 267 Sometimes these varieties [of limestone] pulverise to a crystalline sand.

4. *intr.* Of a bird: To roll in the dust; to take a dust-bath. *rare.*

1890 in *Cent. Dict.*

Hence **'pulverized** *ppl. a.*; **'pulverizing** *vbl. sb.* and *ppl. a.*

a **1693** *Urquhart's Rabelais* III. xxxiv. 288 That..pulverized Dose. **1727** DE FOE *Hist. Appar.* iv. (1840) 29 The man that lived there must be dried up sufficiently for pulverising. **1765** A. DICKSON *Treat. Agric.* (ed. 2) 363 Manures are found to enrich the best pulverised soil. **1832** CARLYLE *Misc.*, *Death Goethe* (1857) III. 110 The wrecks and pulverised rubbish of ancient things. **1832** *Planting* 37 (Libr. Usef. Knowl.) The pulverizing action of the sun and air. **1926** *Jrnl. Iron & Steel Inst.* CXIII. 507 The author continues his account of practice in the use of pulverised fuel, dealing with the efficiency of the method of powdered coal-firing as compared with other methods. **1950** *Engineering* 28 July 79/1 Where a high proportion of heat recovery was required in the air heater, pulverised-fuel firing was essential. **1976** *Horse & Hound* 10 Dec. 64/2 (Advt.), The latest in animal bedding... Made from pulverised wood—cheaper than straw.

pulverizer (ˈpʌlvəraɪzə(r)). [f. PULVERIZE *v.* + -ER[1].] One who or that which pulverizes; an instrument or machine that reduces to powder; also *techn.* one that reduces a liquid to spray.

1836 *Fraser's Mag.* XIII. 724 The high conservative, Fraser! the pulveriser of Voluntaryism, Radicalism, and Popery! **1847** *Illustr. Lond. News* 24 July 58/1 For the best subsoil pulveriser, £10. **1875** H. WALTON *Dis. Eye* 18 There are also spray-producing douches..absurdly named water pulverizers. **1888** *Pall Mall G.* 23 May 12/1 The crushing of the ores by the pulverizer. **1956** [see OF *prep.* 43 b]. **1967** *Punch* 6 Sept. 360/1 A small East Anglian local authority..would like to dump over 160,000 cubic yards of garbage in the four sidings... If they spend a further £30,000 on a pulveriser (which reduces all forms of household trash to a quarter of its collected volume and renders the result unattractive to flies and rodents) this novel dump should last them for sixteen years. **1971** P. GRESSWELL *Environment* 153 Giant pulverisers can shred a complete car to fist size fragments within seconds.

pulverous (ˈpʌlvərəs), *a.* [f. L. *pulver-em* dust + -OUS.] Powdery; dusty.

1778 [W. MARSHALL] *Minutes Agric.*, *Digest* 24 Soils..are stiff or light; that is, tenacious or pulverous. **1864** SALA in *Daily Tel.* 13 Oct., The trees and the herbage were powdered thick with pulverous particles.

pul'verulence. [f. as next, as if from a L. **pulverulentia*: see -ENCE.] Dustiness, powder.

1727 BAILEY vol. II, *Pulverulence*, dustiness. **1837** J. T. SMITH tr. *Vicat's Mortars* 131 This movement is obliged to be subdivided..into an infinite number of partial contractions, whence arises pulverulence.

pulverulent (pʌlˈvɛr(j)ʊlənt), *a.* [f. L. *pulverulent-us* dusty, f. *pulver-em* dust, powder: see -LENT. So mod.F. *pulvérulent* (1801 in Littré).]

1. Consisting of or having the form of powder or dust; powdery.

1656 BLOUNT *Glossogr.*, *Pulverulent*, dusty, of dust, full of dust. **1806** SAUNDERS *Mineral Waters* I. 20 The glutinous part of wheat flour, [which is] dry and pulverulent. **1830** LINDLEY *Nat. Syst. Bot.* 316 In Lycopodium..the pulverulent thecæ occupy the upper ends of the shoots. **1883** *Athenæum* 11 Aug. 183/2 The announcement by M. Spring that a pressure of 5,000 atmospheres caused pulverulent matters to aggregate into crystalline masses.

2. Covered with powder or dust; dusty; *spec.* in *Entom.* and *Bot.*

1744 AKENSIDE *Poet*, On shelves pulverulent, majestic stands His library. **1826** KIRBY & SP. *Entomol.* IV. xlvi. 275 *Pulverulent*,..covered with very minute powder-like scales. **1828** R. K. GREVILLE *Sc. Crypt. Flora* VI. 338 Perithecia..white and pulverulent.

3. Of very slight cohesion; crumbling to dust.

1794 SULLIVAN *View Nat.* I. 500 Calcareous stone is also found in the pulverulent form; and of this kind is chalk. **1811** PINKERTON *Petralogy* II. 381 Ashes, sand, and light pulverulent scoriæ. **1856** CARPENTER *Microsc.* 373 A thallus..which has no very defined limit, and which, in consequence of the very slight adhesion of its component cells, is said to be 'pulverulent'. **1882** GEIKIE *Text-bk. Geol.* II. II. iii. 91 A rock is said to be..pulverulent, when it readily falls to powder.

4. Pulverizing. *rare. erroneous.*

1864 RUSKIN *Arrows of Chace* (1880) I. 260 The pulverulent effect [on masses of stone] of original precipitation to glacier level from two or three thousand feet above.

5. Of birds: Characterized by or addicted to lying or rolling in the dust.

1828 in WEBSTER. **1869** GILLMORE tr. *Figuier's Rept. & Birds* v. 410 Partridges have, like the Quail, the pulverulent instinct.

Hence **pul'verulently** *adv.*, in a powdery or dusty manner. † **pulveru'lentous** *a.* (in quot. pulveri-), pulverulent. *Obs. rare.*

1640 PARKINSON *Theat. Bot.* 1594 We have many sorts [of myrrh].., great and small, fat and dry, pulverilentous like, pale and more red. **1821** W. P. C. BARTON *Flora N. Amer.* I. 113 Corolla pulverulently rough within.

pul'verulous, *a. rare.* [From *pulverulent*, with change of suffix.] = PULVERULENT.

1841 BRANDE *Chem.* (ed. 5) 219 About an ounce of the vitreous acid (not the opaque or pulverulous) should be dissolved in three ounces of the acid.

pulvil (ˈpʌlvɪl), *sb. arch.* Also 7 polvil, 8 pulville, -ile. [ad. It. *polviglio*: see PULVILIO.] Cosmetic or perfumed powder for powdering the wig or perfuming the person.

1691 *Islington Wells* 13 Saluted by the Fragrancy Of Powder de Orange, Jesmine, Pulvil, or something else. *a* **1693** *Urquhart's Rabelais* III. xlvi. 375 Great Ladies..with their..Polvil, Postillo's and Cosmeticks. **1700** FARQUHAR *Constant Couple* I. i, How many pound of Pulvil must the Fellow use in sweetening himself from the smell of Hops and Tobacco? *a* **1774** FERGUSSON *Burlesque Elegy* vi, The huge wig, in formal curls arrayed, With pulvile pregnant.

b. *transf.* Applied to snuff; also, any impalpable powder, as magnesia.

1806–7 J. BERESFORD *Miseries Hum. Life* XIX. *Farewell Snuff* i, The precious pulvil from Hibernia's shore. **1807** *Edin. Rev.* XI. 117 Adding but a little of the water at a time..and carefully and patiently rubbing it up with the refractory pulvil.

c. *attrib.* or *adj.* Of perfume; perfumed.

1690 *Songs Costume* (Percy Soc.) 187 To play at ombre, or basset, She a rich pulvil purse must get.

† **'pulvil**, *v. Obs.* [f. prec.] *trans.* To powder or perfume with pulvil. Hence † **'pulvilled** *ppl. a.*

1700 CONGREVE *Way of World* IV. i, Have you pulvill'd the Coachman and Postilion that they may not stink of the Stable when Sir Rowland comes by? *a* **1704** T. BROWN *Sat. agst. Woman* 100 The sooty negro, and the pulvill'd beau.

‖ **pulvilio, -villio** (pulˈviljo). *Obs.* exc. *Hist.* [a. It. *polviglio* fine or subtile powder, cosmetic powder, deriv. of *polve*, *polvere* powder.] = PULVIL.

1675 WYCHERLEY *Country Wife* IV. i, I have dressed you..and spent upon you ounces of essence and pulvillio. **1711** ADDISON *Spect.* No. 63 ⁋3 The Flowers perfumed the Air with Smells of Incense, Amber-greese, and Pulvillios. **1847** LYTTON *Lucretia* I. i, His vest of silk..showing a profusion of frill, slightly sprinkled with the pulvilio of his favourite martinique. **1892** LD. LYTTON *King Poppy* I. 235 The jewell'd box Wherein he carried his pulvilio.

attrib. **1676** WYCHERLEY *Plain Dealer* II. i, Since you have these two Pulvillio Boxes, these Essence Bottles [etc.]. **1901** GUY BOOTHBY *My Indian Queen* i, The multitude of patch and pulvillio boxes.

'pulvilized, *ppl. a.* [f. PULVIL *sb.* + -IZE + -ED.] Powdered and perfumed with pulvilio.

1788 BURNS *Let. P. Hill* Lett. (1887) 172 The pulvilised, feathered, pert coxcomb, is so disgustful in my nostril that my stomach turns.

pul'villar, *a.* [f. L. *pulvill-us* little cushion + -AR.] Of or pertaining to a pulvillus; cushion-like, pad-like.

1890 in *Cent. Dict.*

pulville, pulvillio: see PULVIL, PULVILIO.

‖ **pulvillus** (pʌlˈvɪləs). [L., contr. from *pulvīnul-us*, dim. of *pulvīnus* cushion.]

1. A little cushion; in *Surgery*, see quot. 1897.

[**1693** tr. *Blancard's Phys. Dict.* (ed. 2), *Pulvilli*, the same with *Splenia*.] **1706** PHILLIPS, *Pulvillus*, a little Pillow, or Cushion; also a Bolster us'd by Surgeons in dressing Wounds. **1897** *Syd. Soc. Lex.*, *Pulvillus*,..a small cushion or pillow. In Surgery..a small olive-shaped mass of lint used for plugging deep wounds.

2. *Entom.* A cushion-like process on the feet of an insect, by which it can adhere to a vertical surface as a wall, or in an inverted position to a ceiling or the like; a foot-cushion.

1826 KIRBY & SP. *Entomol.* III. xxxiii. 386 *Pulvilli*,..cushions of short hairs very closely set; or of membrane, capable of being inflated, or very soft; or of concave plates, which cover the underside, or their apex, of the four first joints of the Manus or Tarsus. *Ibid.* xxxv. 676 These organs are furnished with a sucker or *pulvillus*. **1835** KIRBY *Hab. & Inst. Anim.* II. xvii. 119 The pulvilli or foot cushions of flies. **1904** *Brit. Med. Jrnl.* 17 Sept. 666.

Hence **pul'villiform** *a. Entom.*, resembling a pulvillus, cushion-like.

pulvin, pulvino (ˈpʌlvɪn, pʌlˈviːnəʊ). *Archit.* [It. *pulvino* pillow.] A cushion cap, impost-block or dosseret.

1907 *Athenæum* 30 Mar. 389/2 The use of the pulvino to enable a thick wall above to be carried on the comparatively slender diameter of the classic column. **1910** G. McN. RUSHFORTH tr. *Rivoira's Lombardic Archit.* I. i. 8 The capitals..supported pulvins ('pulvini') or impost blocks, marked with crosses. *Ibid.* 12 From Ravenna and Naples the pulvin spread over Italy and beyond. *Ibid.* II. vi. 300 The corbel pulvins with rudely curled ends..are derived from the crutch-shaped pulvins, a Lombard creation of the Xth century. **1913** T. G. JACKSON *Byzantine & Romanesque Archit.* I. iv. 52 On the capital they placed a block of stone spreading upwards from the width of the column where it rested on the abacus, to the width of the wall above, and from the top of this stone they sprang their arch, of the full thickness of the wall. This dosseret, pulvino, or impost block is an entirely novel feature. *Ibid.* xi. 171 It is difficult to follow him in claiming the invention of the pulvino for Ravenna on the strength of its use in the church of S. Giov. Evangelista in 425; for he assigns the same date to the much more important Eski Djourna at Salonica where the pulvino is thoroughly developed. **1933** J. A. HAMILTON *Byzantine Archit. & Decoration* ii. 26 Constructive reasons led to the introduction of the impost (pulvino: dosseret) above the capital... The impost was a block, approximately of trapezoidal shape, often carved with a monogram, a cross, or some other device.

‖ **pulvinar** (pʌlˈvaɪnə(r)), *sb.* Also 6 -are. [a. L. *pulvīnar* a couch, orig. neuter *pulvīnāre* of *pulvīnāris* adj., f. *pulvīn-us* cushion, pillow.]

1. *Rom. Antiq.* A couch or cushioned seat of the gods; also, the cushioned seat in the circus.

1600 HOLLAND *Livy* V. lii. 213 In that one high feast and solemne dinner of Iupiter, can a Pulvinar be celebrated, or a sacred Table be spred and furnished in any place, but in the Capitoll? **1606** —— *Sueton.* 60 Himselfe beheld the Circeian Games..sometime out of the Pulvinar, sitting there with his wife onely and children. **1850** LEITCH tr. *C. O. Müller's Anc. Art* §290 (ed. 2) 323 The ornaments of the spina of the Roman Circus, among others the pulvinar.

2. *Surg.* A small pillow or cushion; sometimes, a medicated cushion or pad. ? *Obs.*

1599 A. M. tr. *Gabelhouer's Bk. Physicke* 53/2 But an hower therafter applye this little pulvinare on thy Eyes. **1811** *Hooper's Med. Dict., Pulvinar*.., a medicated cushion. **1897** in *Syd. Soc. Lex.*

3. *Anat.* The posterior inner tubercle of the optic thalamus.

1886 in *Cassell's Encycl. Dict.* **1890** H. Gray *Anat.* (ed. 12) 685 Its posterior extremity.. internally forms a well-marked prominence, the posterior tubercle or pulvinar. **1899** *Allbutt's Syst. Med.* VII. 337 A case of symmetrical softening of the pulvinar.

b. The cushion of fat by which the non-articular part of the acetabulum is filled up.

pulvinar (pʌl'vaɪnə(r)), *a.* [ad. L. *pulvīnār-is*: see prec.] Of or pertaining to a pulvinus.

1883 *Science* I. 179/1 The pulvinar parenchyma is composed in greater part of finely porous cells.

So **pulvi'narian** *a.* [f. L. *pulvīnāri-s* or *pulvīnāri-us* + -AN], cushion-like, pulvinated.

a **1886** Sir S. Ferguson *Ogham Inscript.* (1887) 31 The casts of these pulvinarian cope-stones..exhibit many imperfections.

pulvinate ('pʌlvɪnət), *a.* [ad. L. *pulvīnāt-us* made into or like a cushion, f. *pulvīn-us* cushion: see -ATE². In F. *pulviné*, Cotgr. 1611.] Pillowy, cushion-like, pulvinar; in *Bot.* and *Entom.*, cushion-shaped, swelling or bulging like a cushion.

1824 R. K. Greville *Flora Edin.* 235 *G[rimmia] pulvinata*, stems short, pulvinate. **1826** Kirby & Sp. *Entomol.* IV. xlvi. 328 *Pulvinate*, when in consequence of being depressed in one place, it seems to puff out in another. **1863** Berkeley *Brit. Mosses* Gloss., *Pulvinate*, forming cushion-like masses.

Hence **'pulvinately** *adv. Bot.*, in a pulvinate manner. Also **pulvi'nato-** comb. form, as ***pulvinato-echinulate*** adj., echinulate and partly pulvinate.

1890 *Cent. Dict.*, Pulvinately. **1846** Dana *Zooph.* (1848) 415 Surface pulvinato-echinulate.

pulvinated ('pʌlvɪneɪtɪd), *a.* [as prec. + -ED.]

1. *Arch.* Swelling or bulging; especially applied to a frieze having a convex face.

1773 J. Noorthouck *Hist. London* 598 It has the pulvinated or swelling freeze. **1817** Rickman *Archit.* (1848) 30 It was once the custom to work the Ionic frieze projecting like a torus... When thus formed it is called *pulvinated*. **1831** *Fraser's Mag.* IV. 281 The curvilinear, or pulvinated frieze occurs in not a single Grecian example. **1850** Leitch tr. *C. O. Müller's Anc. Art* §223 (ed. 2) 219 The shaft either diminished in a right line or pulvinated.

2. *Bot.* Having a pulvinus.

1880 C. & F. Darwin *Movem. Pl.* 113 With pulvinated leaves (i.e. those provided with a pulvinus) their periodical movements depend..on the cells of the pulvinus alternately expanding more quickly on one side than on the other.

3. *Entom.* = PULVINATE *a.*

1858 Mayne *Expos. Lex. Pulvinatus*...*Entomol.* Applied by Kirby to the prothorax when, being depressed at one point, it appears swoln out at another..: pulvinated.

pulviniform (pʌl'vɪnɪfɔːm), *a.* [ad. mod.L. *pulvīniform-is*, f. L. *pulvīn-us* cushion + -FORM. So mod.F. *pulviniforme*.] Cushion-shaped.

1858 Mayne *Expos. Lex.*, *Pulviniformis*,..pulviniform.

pulvinule ('pʌlvɪnjuːl). *Bot.* [ad. L. *pulvīnul-us*, dim. of *pulvīn-us* cushion, pillow, bank. (Also used in L. form.)]

1. One of a number of excrescences, sometimes like minute trees, rising from the thallus of lichens.

1858 Mayne *Expos. Lex.*, *Pulvinula*..term by Acharius for filaments,..often imitating small bushes or cushions, which are raised from the superior surface of the thallus of certain lichens, as the *Parmelia glomulifera*: a pulvinule.

2. A heap of naked spores.

1874 Cooke *Fungi* (1875) 39 There is great variability in the compactness of the spores in the sori, or pulvinules. *Ibid.* 144 The winter spores are in solid pulvinules.

3. = PULVINUS.

1928 E. Hughes-Gibb *Life-force in Plant World* vii. 153 Upon scratching or irritating the pulvinule of the terminal leaflet of either of these beans on its under-side, a downward movement very slowly begins. **1975** *Nature* 6 Mar. 69/2 We provide direct experimental evidence for cyclic changes in membrane properties in a circadian system from studies of the pulvinule cells at the base of the leaflets of clover.

‖**pulvinus** (pʌl'vaɪnəs). *Bot.* [L. *pulvīnus* cushion, pillow.] Any cushion-like swelling or expansion of a stem or petiole; *esp.* a protuberance or enlargement at the foot of the petiole of some leaves, when large, turgid, and contractile, forming a special organ for movement of the leaf.

1857 Henfrey *Bot.* §77 In woody Dicotyledons there is generally a little protuberance under the cicatrix, which is termed the *pulvinus*. **1880** C. & F. Darwin *Movem. Pl.* 112 The summit of the petiole is developed into a pulvinus, cushion, or joint (as this organ has been variously called), like that with which many leaves are provided. **1906** *Athenæum* 23 June 768/3 Mimosa..has in its pulvinus a structure which allows of the free play of the leaf.

'pulviplume. *Ornith.* [ad. mod.L. *pulviplūma*, f. L. *pulvi-s* dust + *plūma* plume, feather.] Powder-down.

1890 Coues *Field & Gen. Ornithol.* 129 Such plumulæ, from being always dusted over with dry scurfy exfoliation, are called *powder-down*... I call them *pulviplumes*.

†**pul'viscle.** *Obs. rare*⁻¹. [ad. L. *pulviscul-us*, *-um* small dust, dim. of *pulvis* dust.] A fine powder, a dust.

1599 A. M. tr. *Gabelhouer's Bk. Physicke* 62/1 Take Rue, Betonye [etc.]..make heerof a fine pulviscle, and use it with your meates.

‖**pulwar** ('pʌlwɑː(r)). *E. Ind.* Also **pulwaar, pulwah.** [Hindī *palwār*.] A light keelless native boat used on the rivers of Bengal, 'carrying some 12 to 15 tons' (Yule).

1765 Holwell *Hist. Events*, etc. I. 69 We observed a boat ..making for Patna: the commandant dispatched two light pulwaars after her. **1793** W. Hodges *Trav. India* 39 Besides this boat, a gentleman is usually attended by two others; a pulwah for the accommodation of the kitchen, and a smaller boat. **1798** S. Wilcocke in *Naval Chron.* (1799) II. 63 They have another kind of boats, which they call *pulwahs*. These are very long, low, and narrow... They are sculled instead of being rowed. **1860** C. Grant *Rural Life Bengal* 7 The Pulwar is a small description of native travelling boat, of neater build, and less rusticity of character.

†**pulwere,** obs. f. PILLIVER, pillow-case, pillow.

c **1350** *Will. Palerne* 672 He wend to haue lauȝt þat ladi loueli in armes; & clipte to him a pulwere.

puly ('pjuːlɪ), *a.* [f. PULE *v.* + -Y.] Given to puling; whining; sickly.

a **1688** Bunyan *Solomon's Temple Spiritualized* li. The church of Christ is of herself a very sickly puely thing. **1861** Sala in *Temple Bar Mag.* III. 25 The puly shabby piety which prompts some people..to be perpetually scrawling begging-letters to Heaven.

†**puly,** *Herb.*, var. of POLY¹. (Cf. PULIOL.)

1533 Elyot *Cast. Helthe* (1541) 60 Digestiues of fleume. Persely..Sinuy, Puly, Maioram, Peniroyall.

pulyal, -yol, var. PULIOL *Obs.*

†**pulypyk.** *Obs.* ? Some sort of pickaxe: cf. *pole-pike* s.v. POLE *sb.*¹ 5 c.

1360-61 *Durham Acc. Rolls* (Surtees) 562 In..uno pulypyk empt. pro minera de Heworth.

pulysh(e, obs. form of POLISH *v.*

pulza-oil ('pʊlzəɔɪl). A fixed oil obtained from the seeds of the Physic-nut (*Curcas purgans* or *Jatropha Curcas*), a native of Tropical America, but now generally cultivated in all tropical countries for the oil, which is used in medicine as a purgative, as well as for various domestic purposes.

1866 *Jrnl. Royal Soc. Arts* 17 Aug. 634/2 *Pulza Oil*.— Under this name, a considerable commerce is carried on in the Cape de Verd Islands, in the oil obtained from the seeds of the *Jatropha Curcas*, a euphorbiaceous plant... About 350,000 bushels of the seed are gathered and exported annually to Portugal, where the oil extracted is called purqueira oil, and is used principally for burning.

puma ('pjuːmə). [a. Sp. *puma* ('puma), a. Peruv. *puma*.] A large American feline quadruped, *Felis concolor*, also called COUGAR.

1777 Robertson *Hist. Amer.* IV. (1783) II. 17 The Puma and Jaguar, its [America's] fiercest beasts of prey, which Europeans have inaccurately denominated lions and tigers, possess neither the undaunted courage of the former, nor the ravenous cruelty of the latter. **1845** Darwin *Voy. Nat.* xii. (1879) 269 The Puma, or South American Lion, is not uncommon. **1898** C. F. Lummis *Mexico* xiv. 164 The proper name of the American lion to-day is Puma; and that is an Inca word that Pizarro found in the Fifteen-thirties among the Andes. The animal has a range 5000 miles long; but its Peruvian name..by now is accepted, not only in all Spanish countries, but wherever English is spoken.

Comb. **1897** Mrs. E. L. Voynich *Gadfly* (1904) 72/2 We had been wading a river on a puma-hunt.

b. The flesh of this animal.

1845 Darwin *Voy. Nat.* vi. (1852) 116 It turned out to be Puma; the meat is very white, and remarkably like veal in taste.

pumblenose, var. POMPELMOOSE *Obs.*, shaddock.

pumeise, -eyse, obs. ff. PUMICE.

pumel, -elle, obs. ff. POMMEL.

pumelo, var. POMELO.

‖**'pumex.** *Obs.* [L. *pūmex*.] = PUMICE *sb.*

1589 Greene *Tullies Loue* Wks. (Grosart) VII. 201 Seeke not sir to wring water out of the pumex. **1649** Roberts *Clavis Bibl.* 471 Expressions..so penetrating as might dissolve an heart as hard as Adamant into waters, and eyes as dry as Pumex into floods of tears. **1656** Ridgley *Pract. Physick* 319 A Pumex stone fired, and quenched twice in white wine. **1792** Mar. Riddell *Voy. Madeira* 42 There is no appearance of pumex nor vestiges of fire about it.

pumgarnade, -granad, etc., obs. ff. POMEGRANATE.

'pumicate, *v. rare.* [f. L. *pūmicāt-*, ppl. stem of *pūmicāre*, f. *pūmex*.] *trans.* To smooth with pumice. So †**pumi'cation.**

1623 Cockeram, *Pumicate*, to make smoothe. **1658** Phillips, *Pumication*, a making smooth with a Pumice-stone. **1925** *Chambers's Jrnl.* Nov. 704/2 When it is thoroughly 'pumicated' the coral is rinsed and put into a second bag.

pumice ('pʌmɪs), *sb.* Forms: see below. [ME. *pomis*, *-ys*, a. OF. *pomis* (*a* 1250 in Godef.), *pumis*, ad. late L. *pūmicem*, for cl. L. *pūmex*, *-icem*, It. *pomice*; a learned form for the popular F. *ponce*: see POUNCE *sb.*² In 16th c. gradually assimilated (*pomis*, *pomise*, *pomice*, *pumice*) to the Latin form; under the influence of which some now pronounce ('pjuːmɪs). (So in It., Florio has *pumice* as var. of *pomice*; Cotgr. *pumice* as syn. of *ponce*.) The β forms, *pumish* (*pomege*), were perh. due to Ital. influence; but cf. Eng. *-ish* in verbs for F. *-iss*. *Pumy*, *pummy*, prob. arose out of the reduction of *pumis stone* to *pumi-stone*. (The L. word had been taken into OE. in the form *pumic*; with this the ME. forms had no historical connexion.)]

A. Illustration of Forms.

α. 5-7 **pomys**; 5 **pomeys, -yce, pumys, -yce**; 6 **pomis, -aise, -ayse, -ice; pommes, -ice; pumise, -yse, -eise, -eyse**; 6-7 **pomise, pummise**; 7 **pumis**; 7-9 **pummice**; 6- **pumice.**

14.. *Voc.* in Wr.-Wülcker 606/12 *Pumex*, pomys. *c* **1440** *Promp. Parv.* 408/1 Pomeys, or pomyce, *pomex*. **1483** Pumys [see β]; Pomyce [see B. 1 b]. **1523** Pommes [see B. 1 c]. **1540** Palsgr. *Acolastus* S j b, That they be blowen out agayne lyght pomissis. *c* **1550** Lloyd *Treas. Health* ℭv, A pumyse made hote. **1552** Huloet, Pomaise for parchment, ..lyke a pomayse. **1579** Pommice [see B. 1 c]. **1581** J. Bell *Haddon's Answ. Osor.* 463 Being more narrowlye examined and vewed, was espyed to be a very pumeyse. **1591** Percivall *Sp. Dict.*, *Esponja*, a spunge, a pumise. **1591** Pumice [see B. 1 d]. **1607** Topsell *Four-f. Beasts* (1658) 104 A Pummise put in wine. *Ibid.* 318 White and crumbly like a Pomys. **1615** Pumis [see B. 1 a].

β. 5 **pumysch, -e, pomege**; 6 **poumysshe, pumishe**; 6-7 **pumish.**

1422-3 Pumysch [see B. 1 c]. *c* **1450** *Nom.* in Wr.-Wülcker 682/29 *Hic pumex*, pomege. **1483** *Cath. Angl.* 293/2 A Pumysche (*A.* Pvmys), *pumex*. **1530** Palsgr. 257/2 Poumysshe for a scryvenar, *pomys*. **1565** Cooper *Thesaurus* s.v. *Latebrosus*, A pumish full of little holes. **1658** tr. *Porta's Nat. Magic* xx. 407 It makes the bread extream dry, and like a pumish.

γ. 6 **pommie, -y, pummie, pumey, pumi (stone)**; 6-7 **pumie, -y**, 7 **pummy.**

1565 Golding *Ovid's Met.* III. (1575) 33 b, With flint and Pommy was it wallde by nature halfe about. **1567** *Ibid.* VIII. 105 The walles were made Of Pommy [**1593** pummie] hollowed diuersly and ragged Pebble stone. **1579** Spenser *Sheph. Cal.* Mar. 93 Pumie stones I..threwe: but..From bough to bough he lepped light, And oft the pumies latched. **1595** Peele *Anglorum Feriæ* 26 Thetis in her bower Of pumey and tralucent pebble-stones.

B. Signification.

1. a. A light kind of lava, usually consisting of obsidian made spongy or porous by the escape of steam or gas during the process of cooling.

14.., *c* **1440** [see A. α]. **1567** Maplet *Gr. Forest* A vij b, Of the seconde sort is the Pumeise [*printed* Pumelse] concrete of froth as Isidore witnesseth. **1615** G. Sandys *Trav.* 242 Much ground about it [Ætna] lies waste by meanes of the eiected pumis. **1796** Morse *Amer. Geog.* II. 164 Vast quantities of pumice or scoria of different kinds. **1813** Bakewell *Introd. Geol.* (1815) 331 The island of Lipari contains a mountain entirely formed of white pumice. **1854** F. C. Bakewell *Geol.* 86 Pumice is a well known volcanic product of a white colour, and so light that it swims upon water.

b. With *pl.* A piece or block of this substance.

c **1483** Caxton *Dialogues* 47/21 Goo fecche a pomyce And of the best papier, My penknyf, my sheris. **1501** *Acc. Ld. High Treas. Scot.* II. 63 For foure pumyses to him,..xij d. *c* **1550**, **1581**, **1607** [see A. α]. **1645** Evelyn *Diary* 7 Feb., In anno 1630, it [Vesuvius] burst out.., throwing out huge stones and fiery pumices. **1779** Hamilton in *Phil. Trans.* LXX. 82 This curious substance has the lightness of a pumice.

c. As a material used for smoothing or polishing (parchment, etc.), or removing stains; as an absorbent of ink, moisture, etc.; as proverbial for its dryness.

[*a* **1000** *Sax. Leechd.* II. 100 Of felle ascafen mid pumice.] **1422-3** *Durham Acc. Rolls* (Surtees) 619 Et in incausto, pumysch, cera rubea, empt. **1523** Fitzherb. *Husb.* §142 Penne, paper, ynke, parchment,..pommes,..thou remembre. **1579** Lyly *Euphues* (Arb.) 58 The greatest blot is taken off with the Pommice. **1580** *Ibid.* 374 If thou attempt agaie to wring water out of the Pommice. **1599** B. Jonson *Ev. Man out of Hum.* v. iv, Could the pummise but hold vp his eyes at other mens happines. **1665** South *Serm.*, *John* i. 11 (1718) III. 305 To oppress, beggar, and squeeze them as dry as a pumice. **1849** R. V. Dixon *Heat* I. 207 A U-shaped tube filled with sulphuric pumice..to prevent the vapour of the water in the aspirator reaching the desiccating tubes B and C. **1862** Merivale *Rom. Emp.* VI. liv. 229 *note*, A copy of one book..of Martial,..smoothed with pumice, and elegantly bound, was sold for 3*s.* 4*d.* **1871** R. Ellis *Catullus* i. 2 The new, the dainty volume,..fresh with ashy pumice. **1878** Huxley *Physiogr.* xii. (ed. 2) 193 The stone largely used for scouring paint under the name of pumice.

†**d.** *fig.* or *allusively*, esp. in reference to its qualities in c. *Obs.*

1591 GREENE *Farew. to Folly, Fr. Dante*, The pumice that defaceth memory,..Is but a stomach overcharged with meats. **1638** COWLEY *Loves Riddle* III. i, For I have Eyes of Pumice. *a* **1643** W. CARTWRIGHT *Ordinary* v. iii, I cannot weep, mine eyes are pumice. *a* **1658** CLEVELAND *On Rom. iv.* 25 Wks. (1677) 166 Marble can weep, whilest we are Pumices.

2. a. *attrib.* Consisting of or resembling pumice; †**pumice hoof**, a 'pumiced' hoof: see PUMICED 2. **b.** *Comb.*, as *pumice-like* adj., PUMICE-STONE, q.v.

1592 R. D. *Hypnerotomachia* 20b, The two..pillars of Porphyre..of a pumish or tawnie colour. **1624** CAPT. SMITH *Virginia* v. 169 A kinde of white hard substance..pumish-like and spungy. **1688** R. HOLME *Armoury* III. 89/1 Terms used..as to Horse-Shooing... Pomise, or Flat Hoofe. **1811** PINKERTON *Mod. Geogr., Bahama* (ed. 3) 665 The pumice lands soon imbibe the rain. **1845** DARWIN *Voy. Nat.* iv. (1879) 63 A firmly-cemented conglomerate of pumice pebbles. **1891** R. WALLACE *Rural Econ. Austral. & N.Z.* xv. 229 Pumice-topped land..covers unfortunately about thirty per cent. of the area of the North Island. **1950** *N.Z. Jrnl. Agric.* Jan. 17/3 In the north and north-west, where annual rainfall is over 50 in., the soils are classified as yellow brown pumice soils. They are light, fluffy pumice soils formed on volcanic ash. *Ibid.* Feb. 115/2 In its natural state the open pumice country, clothed in a tangled mass of manuha and manoao..looks barren and unattractive. *Ibid.*, The pumice lands of the central plateau area of the North Island consists of soils derived from volcanic-ash showers. **1965** S. T. OLLIVIER *Petticoat Farm* i. 1 Harry stood at the roadside and watched the white pumice dust rising between the bracken at each side of the road.

pumice ('pʌmɪs), *v.* Forms: see prec. [f. prec. sb.: cf. L. *pūmicāre* to smooth with pumice-stone, F. *poncer* POUNCE *v.*[3]] *trans.* To rub with pumice; to smooth, polish, trim, or clean by rubbing with pumice.

1483 *Cath. Angl.* 293/2 To Pumysche (*A.* Pumyce), *pumicare.* **1552** HULOET, Pomaisen or trimme parchment, *pumico.* **1591** PERCIVALL *Sp. Dict., Esponjar*, to sponge, to pumise. **1610** W. FOLKINGHAM *Art of Survey* II. vi. 58 Pounded Rossin both finely searced and lightly pummiced. **1647** R. STAPYLTON *Juvenal, Sat.* viii. 154 *note*, The Italians to this day have the fashion of pumicing their skin to get off the haire. **1797** *Trans. Soc. Arts* XV. 250 When dry to be pumiced over, so as to make the whole perfectly dry and smooth. **1873** E. SPON *Workshop Receipts* Ser. I. 393/2 The slab is then pumiced to reduce it to a level surface.

Hence **'pumicing** *vbl. sb.* (also *attrib.*).

1552 HULOET, Pomaysynge or trymmynge wyth pomaise, *pumigatio.* **1852** MORFIT *Tanning & Currying* (1853) 438 The leather..passes under the pumicing cylinders.

pumiced ('pʌmɪst), *ppl. a.* [f. prec. vb. + -ED[1].]

1. Rubbed smooth with pumice.

1552 HULOET, Pomaysed, *pumigatus.* **1846** LANDOR *Imag. Conv., Diogenes & Plato* Wks. I. 456/1 They who have pumiced faces and perfumed hair.

2. Applied to a horse's hoof that has become spongy on account of disease. Hence *transf.* of a horse-shoe adapted to such a hoof.

1688 R. HOLME *Armoury* III. 324/2 A flat or pomised shooe, having one side thick and the other thin,..is used for flat and pomised Hoofs. **1828** *Sporting Mag.* XXII. 349 With well-bred hunters, pumiced feet are, nineteen times in twenty, the effect of fever. **1861** WALSH & LUPTON *Horse* xxx. (1877) 542 The sole..is always either flatter than natural, or absolutely convex, and its horn is brittle and spongy, constituting what is termed the 'pumiced foot'.

pumiceous (pju:'mɪʃəs), *a.* [f. L. *pūmice-us* (f. *pūmex, -icem*) + -OUS.] Consisting of pumice; having the character or texture of pumice.

1676 H. MORE *Remarks* 10 If one side be pumiceous..and the other metalline, the metalline will gravitate on the pumiceous or spungie side. **1796** KIRWAN *Elem. Min.* (ed. 2) I. 416, I should..call them pumiceous mixtures. **1869** PHILLIPS *Vesuv.* ii. 35 Pompeii was overwhelmed with light-coloured pumiceous lapilli.

pumice-stone ('pʌmɪsstəʊn, 'pʌmɪstəʊn), *sb.* Forms: see below and PUMICE *sb.*

A. Illustration of Forms.

α. [1 pumicstan]; 7 pumick(e stone.

[*c* **1000** ÆLFRIC *Voc.* in Wr.-Wülcker 148/3 *Pumex*, pumicstan.] **1613** JACKSON *Creed* I. To Rdr. Ej, The Pumicke stones did flie about mens eares in the open fields. **1648** MACFARLANE *Geog. Collect.* (S.H.S.) II. 516 In this town ther ar aboundance of pumick stonis floating upon the water.

β. 6 pomise, pummyse stone, 7 pumis stone; 6– pumice-stone.

1576 BAKER *Jewell of Health* 4 What is it..than to desire wool from an Asses backe, or to wryng water out of a Pummyse stone? **1580** HOLLYBAND *Treas. Fr. Tong, Pierre ponce*, a pomise stone. **1590** Pumice stone [see B. d]. **1681** GREW *Musæum* III. I. vi. 321 An ash-colour'd Pumis Stone.

γ. 6 pumishe, 6–7 pumish stone.

1550 T. HOBY *Trav.* (1902) 52 Pumishe stones which are so light that they flee upp with the flame and so fall in the asshes. **1610** HOLLAND *Camden's Brit.* II. *Scot.* 24 A lighter body and spungeous..in maner of a pumish stone.

δ. 6 pumistone, pumy stone, 6–7 pumie, pummie, 7 pummy stone.

1578 BANISTER *Hist. Man* I. 2 The substance..spongie, not vnlike a thicke Pummie stone. **1579** Pumie stones [see B. a]. **1590** SPENSER *F.Q.* II. v. 30 A gentle streame, whose murmuring wave did play Emongst the pumy stones. **1615** CROOKE *Body of Man* 183 Like a fast sponge or a smooth pumie-stone. **1662** J. BARGRAVE *Pope Alex. VII* (1867) 123 Small cinders and pummy stones of Mont Aetna.

B. Signification.

a. A stone composed of pumice: = PUMICE 1 b.

1550 [see A. γ]. **1576** [see A. β]. **1579** SPENSER *Sheph. Cal.* Mar. 89 Tho pumie stones I hastly hent, And threwe: but nought availed. **1601** HOLLAND *Pliny* I. 567 By reason of..fistulous porosities therin, like a pumish stone. **1681** GREW *Musæum* I. i. 9 The Bones of a Humane Leg and Foot..in some places rarified like a Sponge or Pumice-Stone. **1767** HAMILTON in *Phil. Trans.* LVIII. 6 The pumice-stones, falling upon us like hail. **1836** W. IRVING *Astoria* (1849) 409 A plain..strewed with pumice stones and other volcanic reliques.

b. As a substance: = PUMICE *sb.* 1 a.

1598 SYLVESTER *Du Bartas* II. i. III. *Furies* 153 Repleat with Sulphur, Pitch and Pumy Stone. **1604** E. G[RIMSTONE] *D'Acosta's Hist. Indies* III. xxv. 197 Other thicke matter which dissolves into ashes, into pumice stone, or such like substance. **1794** SULLIVAN *View Nat.* II. 184 The fire was mixed with prodigious quantities of brimstone, sand, pumice-stone, and ashes. **1871** TYNDALL *Fragm. Sc.* (1879) I. v. 162 Filled with fragments of pumice-stone.

c. As a thing of use: = PUMICE *sb.* 1 c.

1573–80 BARET *Alv.* P 857 A Pumish stone vsed to make parchment smooth, *pumex.* **1601** HOLLAND *Pliny* I. 544 To slick, polish, & smooth them again with the pumy stone. **1662** PEPYS *Diary* 25 May, Trimming myself..with a pumice stone. **1873** SYMONDS *Grk. Poets* xi. 350 Scribes offer their pens and ink and pumice-stone to Hermes. **1879** *Cassell's Techn. Educ.* IV. 221/2 The body now receives a staining coat, after which it is well rubbed down with pumice-stone.

†**d.** *fig.*: cf. PUMICE *sb.* 1 d. *Obs.*

1583 GREENE *Mamillia* II. To Rdrs., Wks. (Grosart) II. 145 Although shee hath not the Pumistone of learning to pollish her words with superficiall eloquence. **1590** GREENE *Never too late* (1600) Title-p., Beeing a right Pumice stone, apt to race out idlenes with delight, and follie with admonition. **1622** DONNE *Serm., John xi.* 35 (1640) 160 To weep for other things, and not to weep for sin..this is a spunge dried up into a Pumice stone. **1647** OWEN *Death of D.* Wks. 1852 X. 333 Is not this rather a pumice-stone than a breast of consolation?

e. *attrib.*

1876 tr. *Wagner's Gen. Pathol.* (ed. 6) 319 The affected parts thereby assume..a pumice-stone consistency.

Hence **'pumice-stone** *v. trans.* = PUMICE *v.*

1851 *Ord. & Regul. R. Engineers* xix. 88 Putting up Lining Paper,..pumice-stoning,..and sizing. **1887** *Athenæum* 24 Dec. 867/1 The parchment..of a still more ancient MS. pumice-stoned to an even surface.

pumiciform ('pju:mɪsɪfɔ:m), *a. rare.* [ad. mod.L. *pūmiciform-is*, f. L. *pūmex, -icem*: see -FORM.] Having the form, appearance, or texture of pumice.

1858 MAYNE *Expos. Lex., Pumiciformis, Geol.* resembling pumice stone in appearance, as the *Lava pumiciformis*: pumiciform.

pumicite ('pʌmɪsaɪt). [f. PUMIC(E *sb.* + -ITE[1].] A volcanic ash like pumice in composition but occuring as powder or granules.

1916 E. H. BARBOUR in *Nebraska Geol. Survey* IV. 358 Pumicite has been variously called geyserite, volcanic dust, ..and the like... For all of these we have substituted the name pumicite, a self-explanatory term, which we have used for some years. **1949** J. A. BARR in *Industrial Minerals & Rocks* (ed. 2) xxxvi. 752 The principal use of pumicite is for concrete aggregate. **1965** G. J. WILLIAMS *Econ. Geol. N.Z.* xvi. 245/2 Other deposits at Takanini and Hurua [*read* Hunua] have been quoted as a source of diatomaceous material for fibrolite and light-weight concrete but Ritchie pointed out that this is pumicite with no diatoms. **1974** A. C. TENNISSEN *Nature of Earth Materials* vii. 394 Finely ground pumice and unground pumicite are used in general scouring powders... Other uses for unground pumicite and ground pumicite are..in insulation, as filter aids, as poultry litter, [etc.].

pumicose ('pju:mɪkəʊs), *a. rare.* [ad. L. *pūmicōs-us* (Pliny), like pumice, f. *pūmex, -icem*: see -OSE.] Of the nature or appearance of pumice.

1811 PINKERTON *Petralogy* I. 504 Fragments amorphous, blunt. Weight, pumicose. **1845** SIR W. HAMILTON *Metaph.* I. App. 435 A pumicose deposit.

†**'pumicous**, *a. Obs. rare.* [f. as prec.: see -OUS.] = prec.

1578 BANISTER *Hist. Man* I. 7b, This Pumicous substaunce, intersited betwene the sayd scales or crustes is the cause that some haue sayd, the scull to be condited and made of two walles.

†**'pumil**, *a. Obs. rare.* [ad. L. *pūmil-us*, *pūmil-is* dwarfish.] Dwarf, dwarfish, diminutive.

1776 *Evelyn's Sylva* 377 Which is a Pumil dwarf kind, with a smaller leaf slow of growth.

‖**pumilio, pumilo.** *Obs. rare.* Also pomilio. [L. *pūmiliō*, *pūmilō* a dwarf, f. *pūmilis*: see prec. Cf. obs. It. *pomilione* 'a Dwarfe or Pigmey' (Florio 1611).] A dwarf; a diminutive person, or plant.

1576 FLEMING *Panopl. Epist.* 237 *margin*, He was (belike) some Pomilio or litle dwarfe. **1776** *Evelyn's Sylva* 36 The warmer regions produce the tallest and goodliest trees and plants..far exceeding those of the same species, born in the cold North, so as what is a giant in the one, becomes a pumilo, and in comparison, but a shrubby dwarf in the other.

pumill, obs. f. POMMEL.

pumis, pumish, pummace, obs. ff. POMACE, PUMICE.

pummel, *sb.*, a parallel form of POMMEL *sb.*

pummel ('pʌm(ə)l), *v.* Also 6 pumble, poumle, poumile. [An alteration of POMMEL *v.*, in accordance with pronunciation now more usual.] **a.** *trans.* To beat or strike repeatedly, esp. with the fist; to pound, thump. Also *transf.* and *fig.* **b.** *intr.*

1548 UDALL *Erasm. Par. Luke* iii. 44 Thei turne him cleane out of his owne doores, and pumble hym about the pate. *Ibid.* xii. 118 Poumleyng and beating theym. *c* **1563** *Jack Jugler* in *Four Old Plays* (1848) 34 You would poumile him ioylile a-bout the pate. **1608** BEAUM. & FL. *Four Plays in One, Tri. Death* v, Your pate I would pummel. **1791** WOLCOTT (P. Pindar) *Ode to Ass* Wks. 1792 II. 401 Dragg'd, kick'd, and pummell'd, by a beggar's brat. **1837** DICKENS *Pickw.* xlv, A desire to pummel and wring the nose of the aforesaid Stiggins. **1878** E. C. G. MURRAY *Russians of To-day* 49 Mujicks continue to pummel one another, and to be pummelled by their superiors. **1927** *New Republic* 12 Oct. 208/2 Once the greater part of the population is pummeled night and morning in underground cattle-cars,..I shall be surprised if there is any energy left. **1972** *Newsweek* 10 Jan. 1/1 For five days U.S. Phantom jets and mammoth B-52 bombers pummeled North Vietnam in the heaviest raids since the 1968 bombing halt. **1977** *Chicago Tribune* 2 Oct. III. 16/6 The Carthage Redmen..went on to pummel the North Park Vikings 34–8. **1979** *Arizona Daily Star* 19 Apr. 1/1 Typhoon Cecil headed today for Japan after pummeling the Philippines.

b. 1833 MARRYAT *P. Simple* vi, 'You villain!'..cried he, pummelling at him as well as he could. **1842** S. LOVER *Handy Andy* iii, With Dick fastened on him, pummelling away most unmercifully.

Hence **'pummelled** *ppl. a.*, **'pummelling** *vbl. sb.*

1755 SMOLLETT *Quix.* (1803) I. 146 Our lot hath been nothing but cudgelling upon cudgelling, pummelling upon pummelling. **1887** TROLLOPE *What I remember* I. viii. 170, I..gave him as good a pummelling as my heart desired. **1902** *Daily Chron.* 6 May 7/2 The pampered and pummelled English boys who buy food and fury so dear.

pummelion, pummelnose, pummelo, -low: see POMMELION, POMPELMOOSE, POMELO.

†**pummet.** *Obs. rare*[−1]. [ad. F. *pommette*, in OF. *pumete* (12th c. in Hatz.-Darm.), a little ball, dim. of *pomme* apple: see -ETTE.] A ball used in the old game of troll-madam.

1572 J. JONES *Bathes Buckstone* 12 They [Ladies] may haue in the ende of a Benche, eleuen holes made, intoo the which to trowle pummetes, or Bowles of leade, bigge, little, or meane, or also, of Copper, Tynne, Woode, eyther vyolent or softe, after their owne discretion; the pastyme Troule in Madame is termed.

pummice, obs. f. POMACE, PUMICE.

pummy, pummyse: see POMMEY, PUMICE.

pump (pʌmp), *sb.*[1] Also 5–7 pompe, pumpe, (5–6 pomp, poompe, 6 poumpe): see also PLUMP *sb.*[2] [Late ME. *pumpe, pompe*, = early mod.Du. *pompe*, Du. *pomp*, LG. *pumpe, pump*, mod.Ger. *pumpe*; whence Da. *pompe*, Sw. *pump*; also Fr. *pompe*.

Machines for raising water were in ancient and mediæval use, but no trace of the name *pump* appears before the 15th c. This is, as yet, known first in Eng. *c* 1440, in the sense of a ship's pump, for pumping out the bilge-water, in which use it was quite common 1450–1500. In Du., LG., HG. not recorded in this sense before the 16th c.; in Fr. cited 1517 in Hatz.-Darm.; in Du. *a* 1556 in Verwijs & Verdam, in Ger. *c* 1550 (Hans Sachs in Grimm). Plantijn 1573 gives for Du. only the sense 'bilge', *de pomp des schips*, 'l'ossec de la navire, sentina', *pompen, wtpompen*, 'vuider l'ossec, sentinam expurgare'; but Kilian 1599 has *pompe* in sense both of a ship's pump, and a pump generally. In Du. dialects, *pompe* is found *a* 1463 in sense of a pipe or tube of wood or metal, or a stone conduit, for the conveyance of water under ground, a sense also found in Frisian, and in some Low German dialects. In view of these dates and various senses, it is not easy to form any inference as to the language in which the word arose; but the probability lies between English and Dutch (or Low German); in either case it was prob. first in nautical use. The primary sense seems to lie between that of 'pipe, tube', and an echoic formation from the sound of the plunger striking the water. In favour of the latter cf. the collateral form *plumpe*, PLUMP *sb.*[2], found as early as 1477, also LG. *plumpe* pump; and conversely Ger. *pump* the hollow sound of a blow, *pumpen* to make such a sound (Grimm), admittedly echoic. The Cat., Sp., Pg. *bomba* (pump), viewed by Diez as the source of the French, may have been derived from F. *pompe*, but is more prob. an independent though analogous echoic formation. The It. is *tromba*, orig. = trumpet, tube; but Venetian, and some other north It. dialects have *pompa* from Fr. or Ger.]

I. 1. a. A mechanical device, commonly consisting of a tube or cylinder in which a piston, sucker, or plunger is moved up and down by means of a rod, or rod and lever, so as to raise water by lifting, suction, or pressure, the movement of the water being regulated by a suitable arrangement of valves or clacks; from early times used on board ship to remove bilge-water; also, from 16th c., for raising water from mines, wells, etc.; now, a generic term for a great variety of machines and mechanical devices for the raising or moving of liquids, compressing or rarefying of gases, etc.

Pumps are variously qualified according to the principle of action, manner of construction, means of operating, purpose, etc., as *force, lift, lifting, suction pump*; *burr-*,

centrifugal, centripetal, chain-, double-acting, jigger-, oscillating, post-, rope, rotary, spiral pump; hand-, steam-pump; air-, beer-, bicycle-, bilge-, breast-, circulating, dental, donkey-, dredging, feed-, gas-, mining, oil-, petrol, pneumatic, saliva, stomach pump, etc.; for many of which see the specific words.

c **1440** *Promp. Parv.* 416/1 Pumpe of a schyppe, or oþer lyke, *hauritorium.* **1466** *Mann. & Househ. Exp.* (Roxb.) 205 For a pompe..for the spynas. **1485** *Naval Acc. Hen. VII* (1896) 41 Toppe sailes..j, pumps..ij. **1495** *Ibid.* 259 Poompes by the mayne meste j & by the mayne meson maste j. **1505** *Acc. Ld. High Treas. Scot.* III. 137 Item, payit for carying of tua treis quhilk suld be pompes to the schip. **1507** in Rogers *Agric. & Prices* (1882) III. 562/4 (Sion) 1 pompe. **1523** Fitzherb. *Surv.* 9 b, As the whele gothe..to blowe the bales or to dray any water lyke a pompe, as there be in Cornwall and dyuers other places. **1530** Palsgr. 256/2, 259/2 Pompe..Pumpe of a shyppe, *pompe.* **1626** Capt. Smith *Accid. Yng. Seamen* 11 The Pumpe, the pumpes-well, the pumpes brake, the pumpes can, the pumpes chaine, the spindle, the botes, the clap. *a* **1628** Preston *Breastpl. Love* (1631) 191 Their actions doe not come as water from a spring but as water from a pompe, that is forced and extorted. **1649** Bp. Reynolds *Serm. Hosea* v. 4 The putting of a little water into a Pumpe makes way to the drawing out of a great deale more. **1653** H. Cogan tr. *Pinto's Trav.* xli. (1663) 162 Cannons of Wood, made like unto the Pumps of Ships. **1688** The Bur-Pump, or Bildge-Pump [see burr-pump]. **1727–41** Chambers *Cycl.* s.v. *Pump*, The forcing Pump..acts by mere impulse or protrusion, and raises water to any height at pleasure. **1756** C. Lucas *Ess. Waters* I. 143 New river water and that of Couvent-garden pump. **1800** tr. *Lagrange's Chem.* II. 2 The mines..are kept free from water by means of pumps. **1810** E. D. Clarke *Trav. Russia* (1839) 122/1 All hands were called to the pumps, which were kept working continually. **1829** *Nat. Philos.* I. *Hydraulics* ii. 10 (Usef. Knowl. Soc.) Of pumps.. the simplest and most common is the ordinary lift, or Household Pump. **1835** Sir J. Ross *Narr. 2nd Voy.* vi. 85 To repair the feeding pump. **1887** *Pall Mall G.* 2 Nov. 11/1 The composition..is taken up by a little instrument called a 'pump', which afterwards throws it out in a compressed state. **1925** F. Scott Fitzgerald *Great Gatsby* iv. 81, I had a glimpse of Mrs. Wilson straining at the garage pump. **1972** [see *petrol station* s.v. petrol 3 b]. **1974** A. Price *Other Paths to Glory* ii. viii. 204 He helps with the odd jobs in the workshop and looks after the pumps.

fig. **1649** G. Daniel *Trinarch.* To Rdr. 54 The Pumpe of Witt beats faire and younge, And trills a Coppie. **1649** Howell *Pre-em. Parl.* 12 Put his hand to the pump, and stop the leaks of the great vessell of the State.

b. In figurative or allusive phrases.

1602 *2nd Pt. Return fr. Parnass.* v. iv. (Arb.) 70 When I arriue within the ile of Doggs, Don Phœbus I will make thee kisse the pumpe. *a* **1680** Butler *Descr. Holland* in *Rem.* (1759) I. 270 That always ply the Pump, and never think They can be safe, but at the Rate they stink. *a* **1754** Draught on Aldgate Pump [see draught *sb.* 35 b]. **1837** Dickens *Pickw.* ii, 'Put 'em under the pump', suggested a hot-pie man. [Cf. pump *v.* 4.] **1839** H. Ainsworth *Jack Sheppard* iii, If he don't tip the cole without more ado, give him a taste of the pump, that's all. **1860** J. Brown *Lett.* (1907) 137, I am very dull, somehow out of spirits and the pump off the fang. **1867** H. Kingsley *Silcote of Silcotes* xxxi, You might as well have argued with the pump. **1873** *Slang Dict.* 149 *Draft on Aldgate Pump*, an old mercantile phrase for a fictitious banknote or fraudulent bill.

c. As employed in medical treatment, esp. at a place where a mineral spring is used: cf. pump *v.* 4 b, pump-room, etc. †***dry-pump*** (*obs.*): see quot. 1631 and cf. pumping *vbl. sb.*

1631 Jorden *Nat. Baths* xvii. (1632) 135 Wee haue a Pump out of the hot Bath, which wee call the dry Pump, where one may sit in a chaire in his cloathes, and haue his head, or foot, or knee pumped. **1676** [see 3]. *c* **1710** Celia Fiennes *Diary* (1888) 13 (At Bath) The hot pumpe that persons are pumpt at for Lameness. **1758** (*title*) tr. Limbourg's Dissertation sur les Bains, etc., or A Dissertation on Baths of Simple Water by Immersion, the Pump and Vapour. **1758** J. S. *Le Dran's Observ. Surg.* (1771) 295, I advised the Patient to go to Bourbon to try the Hot Pump. **1804** *Med. Jrnl.* XII. 241 It should be had fresh from the pump, and then there cannot exist a doubt of its being superior in strength to the celebrated Tunbridge chalybeate. **1806** Dry Pump [see pumping *vbl. sb.* a]. *c* **1900** [see pump-room].

d. *transf.* Applied to the heart, the sucker or proboscis of an insect, the lachrymal glands (as shedding tears: cf. pump *v.* 6).

1796 H. Hunter tr. *St.-Pierre's Stud. Nat.* (1799) I. 295 A proboscis, which is at once an awl proper for piercing the flesh of animals, and a pump by which it sucks out their blood. **1825** Buckstone *Bear Hunters* i. ii, Your pumps have been at work—you've been crying, girl. **1832** Bryant *To Mosquito* xi, On well-filled skins..Fix thy light pump, and press thy freckled feet. **1885** A. W. Blyth in *Leisure Hour* Jan. 24/1 Parts of Bios sleep, but never the whole; the central pump ever goes. **1898** *Allbutt's Syst. Med.* V. 345 The action of the lymphatic pump depends upon the respiratory movements. **1899** *Ibid.* VII. 249 Whenever the power of the cardiac and respiratory pumps is not sufficient to raise the blood from the splanchnic area.

e. *Physiol.* A mechanism in living cells by which metabolic energy is utilized to cause specific kinds of ion to pass through the cell membrane in the direction opposite to that in which they would pass under ordinary diffusion.

1947 *Arch. Biochem.* XIV. 297 (*heading*) An osmotic diffusion pump. *Ibid.* 298 The essential unit of such a pump consists of the space between two membranes, in which a coupled chemical reaction, utilizing free energy supplied from outside, permits this unit to pump either solvent or dissolved solute into itself through one membrane and out through the other membrane, at a higher chemical potential than that from which it entered. **1964** A. White et al. *Princ. Biochem.* (ed. 3) xxxvii. 727 In the ascending limb of the hairpin-shaped loop of Henle an outwardly oriented sodium pump..operates while the same cells are relatively impermeable to water. **1965** *Nature* 4 Sept. 1099/1 Approximately three sodium ions are expelled for each molecule of ATP split by the pump. **1977** *Sci. Amer.* Aug. 117/3 The transfer of a phosphate group to such a protein could conceivably change the permeability of the membrane to ions,..for example by affecting the activity of an enzyme 'pump' that physically transports ions across the membrane.

†**2. a.** The 'well' or 'sink' of a ship where the bilge-water collects, and whence it is pumped out.

a **1533** Ld. Berners *Gold. Bk. M. Aurel.* (1546) K vj, The stynche of the pumpe in shippes. **1538** Elyot *Dict.*, *Sentina*, the pumpe of a shyp, a place where all fylthe is receyued. **1561** Eden *Arte Nauig.* Pref., The pompe of the shyppe if it be not auoyded is noyous to the shippe & all that are therein. **1577** Eden & Willes *Hist. Trav.* 290 The spyces are so corrupted by thinfection of the pompe and other filthinesse of the shyppes.

†**b.** *fig.* = 'sink'. *Obs.*

1536 Bellenden *Cron. Scot.* ii. xviii. (1821) I. 67 The tyrane Gillus, pump of every vice [orig. *tot malorum sentina*] is vincust. *Ibid.* II. 10 Uncouth lust, the pomp of all mischeif, amang the pepil. **1555** W. Watreman *Fardle Facions* ii. iv. 138 The king [drove out the Jews]..and they (as the poompe of all skuruines, not knowing wher to become) laye cowring vnder hedges.

†**c.** In the following perh. = Du. dial. and Fris. *pompe*, a pipe or conduit for conveying water. *Obs.*

(But the sense may be 1.)

1535–6 *Rec. St. Mary at Hill* 370 Paid..ffor a pompe yat lythe to brynge the water owt of y^e diche into y^e ponde.

II. [from the vb.]

3. An act of pumping; a stroke of a pump. Also *transf.*

1676 Wood *Life* 23 June (O.H.S.) II. 350, I went to the Bath for the recovery of my hearing... I received at the drie pump in the King's bath nine thousand two hundred and odd pumps on my head in about a fourtnight's time. **1698** W. King tr. *Sorbière's Journ. Lond.* 16 In an air Pump,..the Cat died after 16 Pumps. **1869** Blackmore *Lorna D.* ii, I came to my corner, when the round was over, with very hard pumps in my chest. **1900** *Westm. Gaz.* 28 May 2/1 Lying sideways..he hears the pump, pump, of his heart.

4. a. An attempt at extracting information from any one, by exhaustive or skilful questioning: cf. pump *v.* 7 b, 8 b. **b.** One who is clever at this.

1741 Richardson *Pamela* I. 204, I was the easier indeed; because, for all her Pumps, she gave no Hints of the Key [etc.]. **1900** *Daily News* 3 Apr. 5/5 Forbes had Scotch inquisitiveness. He was truly a pump. But when one was tired of being pumped, one could set him talking about events he had witnessed.

5. A representation of the action of or sound accompanying pumping.

1883 E. Thring *Theory & Pract. Teaching* v. 53 It is useless pumping on a kettle with the lid on. Pump, pump, pump. The pump-handle goes vigorously..but the kettle remains empty.

III. 6. *attrib.* and *Comb.* **a.** General: attributive, as ***pump gear, lift, machinery, pit, spout, station, stroke, work***; forming part of or belonging to a pump, esp. on board ship, as ***pump-bolt, -bore, -bucket*** (= bucket $sb.^1$ 2), ***-carling, -cheeks*** (= cheek *sb.* 13 d), ***-cistern, -clack*** (= clack *sb.* 5), ***-cylinder, -dale*** (= $dale^3$ 1), ***-foot, -leather, -nail, -piston, -plunger*** (= plunger 2 a), ***-shoe, -spindle, -switch, -tube, -valve***; used in making, working, etc. pumps, as ***pump-augur, -bit, -boat, -can, -log, -shaft, -trough***; objective, as ***pump-clip, -holder*** (of a pneumatic tyre pump), ***-maker, -making, -scraper, -sinker, -sinking***; also ***pump-driven, -like*** adjs. **b.** Special combs.: **pump action** *attrib.* (orig. *U.S.*), designating a type of repeating firearm (see quot. 1964 and cf. *pump gun* s.v. pump *v.* 16); also *absol.*; **pump attendant**, a garage hand who serves petrol; **pump-back**, a wooden casing over a chain-pump to receive the water when raised (Knight *Dict. Mech.* 1875); **pump-barrel**, the tube or cylinder of a pump; †**pump-bathing**, bathing in which the water is pumped on the body or part of it: cf. sense 1 c; **pump-bob**, the mechanism by which the motive power is applied to the action of the pump-rod at the top of the pump-shaft of a mine; **pump-borer**, †(*a*) a borer of tree-trunks for pump-barrels; (*b*) local name of the Spotted Woodpecker; **pump-box**, (*a*) the casing or cap of a pump; (*b*) the casing or box in a pump containing one of the valves; **pump-cart**, an irrigation cart carrying a pump; **pump-chain**, the chain holding the disks of a chain-pump; **pump-coat**, a canvas covering round a pump on the deck of a ship to prevent water getting through into the hold; **pump-head, -hood**: see quots.; **pump-hook**: see quot.; **pump-house**, (*a*) the pump-room of a spa; (*b*) a place in which pumps are made; (*c*) a pumping station; **pump island**, the part of a petrol station on which the pumps stand; **pump-kettle**, 'a convex perforated diaphragm placed at the bottom of a pump-tube to prevent the entrance of foreign matters; a strainer' (Knight); **pump-lug**, an appendage (cf. lug $sb.^2$ 3 a) on the cross-head of a locomotive by which the plunger of the feed-pump is worked; †**Pump Parliament**, a nickname for the Long or Pension Parliament of Charles II: see quot.; **pump-set, pumpset**, a complete pumping installation, comprising a pump, a source of power, and any necessary pipes, valves, filters, etc.; cf. *pumping set* s.v. pumping *vbl. sb.* d; **pump-spear, -staff**, a pump-rod; **pump-stock**, the body of a pump (Webster 1847); **pump-stopper** *Naut.*, a plug for stopping a pump-barrel; **pump-thunder**, a bird, the American bittern; the stake-driver; **pump-turbine** *Engin.*, a machine designed to operate as a pump running in one direction or a turbine running in the other; **pump-vale** = *pump-dale*. See also pump-brake, etc., and cf. verbal combinations in pump *v.* 16.

1912 *Collier's* 28 Sept. 30/1 (Advt.), The Marlin *Pump Action repeating rifle. **1964** H. L. Peterson *Encycl. Firearms* 249/2 *Pump action*, a popular term describing repeating firearms activated by a horizontally operating slide action. **1973** *Times* 1 Aug. 4/6 The Government decided..not to make self-loading rifles and pump-action shotguns prohibited weapons in its forthcoming Bill. **1977** *Field* 13 Jan. 44/1 (Advt.), A large selection of new and second-hand English weapons... Foreign side by sides, automatics, pump actions and single barrel guns. **1968** A. Binkley *What shall I Cry* 10 Harry was *pump attendant and not in charge of mechanics. **1972** *Times* 8 Sept. 21/5 The pump attendant's life of opening and shutting filler caps. **1835** Ure *Philos. Manuf.* 57 Cylindrical cavities for ..*pump-barrels. **1747** *Gentl. Mag.* XVII. 226/1 The ether ..being discharged therefrom as fast as received, like as the water is in *pump-bathing. **1878** *N. Amer. Rev.* CXXVII. 227, I brought to the assistance of her commanding officer two heavy *pump-boats. **1789** Falconer *Dict. Marine*, *Cheville de potence de pompe*, a long *pump-bolt. **1815** Burney *Falconer's Dict. M.*, *Pump-bolts*,..are two pieces of iron,..one serves to fasten the pump-spear to the brake, the other as a fulcrum for the brake to work upon. **1756** Blake in *Phil. Trans.* LI. 6 Without incurring the inconvenience of enlarging the *pump-bores. **1708** *Lond. Gaz.* No. 4487/3 A Wharf fronting the River of Thames,..called the *Pump-boarer's Wharf. **1848** *Zoologist* VI. 2191 The greater and lesser spotted woodpecker..are known by the most appropriate name of 'pump-borer'. **1697** Dampier *Voy. round World* (1699) 443 The two hollow sides were made big enough to contain a *Pump-box in the midst of them both. **1840** *Civil Eng. & Arch. Jrnl.* III. 41/1 The valves upon the *pump bucket. *a* **1625** *Nomencl. Navalis* (Harl. MS. 2301) lf. 60 b, *Ye *Pump-Can*, is the Cann which they drawe water in to poure in to the pumpes and this is a greate Can. **1867** Smyth *Sailor's Word-bk.*, **Pump-carlines*, the framing or partners on the upper deck, between which the pumps pass into the wells. **1839** Ure *Dict. Arts* 972 The water is drawn off in a spout to the nearest *pump-cistern. **1844** *Civil Engin. & Arch. Jrnl.* VII. 190/2 The common *pump clack, moving on a leather joint. **1907** *Yesterday's Shopping* (1969) 1060/3 Cooper's patent locking *pump clip. **1908** H. G. Wells *War in Air* ii. 52 Bert stared at these over the card of pump-clips in the pane in the door. **1825** J. Nicholson *Operat. Mechanic* 294 This tube is continued down to the *pump cylinder. **1871** Kingsley *At Last* viii, A rusty pump-cylinder gurgled, and clicked, and bubbled. *a* **1625** *Nomencl. Navalis* (Harl. MS. 2301) lf. 60 b, *Ye *Pump-dale* is as it were the Trough wherein the water doth run alongst the Deck out to the skupper holes. **1800**, *c* **1850** [see $dale^3$ 1]. **1815** Burney *Falconer's Dict. M.*, **Pump-gears*, any materials requisite for fitting or repairing the pump. **1875** Knight *Dict. Mech.*, **Pump-head*, an arrangement for causing all the water raised by a chain-pump to be directed into the discharge-spout instead of permitting a part to be thrown off by centrifugal force. **1908** *Daily Chron.* 6 June 8/3 The Lea-Francis [bicycle] carries the abolition of clips to the extent of brazing the *pump-holders to the down tube. **1815** Burney *Falconer's Dict. M.*, **Pump-hood*, a short semi-cylindrical frame of wood, serving to cover the upper wheel of a chain-pump. **1640** *Archives of Maryland* (1887) IV. 112 For a *pump-hook. **1702** in *Essex Inst. Hist. Coll.* (1906) XLII. 161 Inventory of ship... A pumpe Hooke. **1867** Smyth *Sailor's Word-bk.*, *Pump-hook*, an iron rod with an eye and a hook, used for drawing out the lower pump-box when requisite. **1742–9** J. Wood *Descr. Bath* (1765) II. iii. v. 269 The Conduits..three are enclosed within Rooms; the chief of which is, for its Eminence, stiled the *Pump House. **1801** R. Warner *Hist. Bath* v. v. 327 Building a pump-house or pump-room, in which the invalids might be supplied with water from a covered pump. **1863** P. Barry *Dockyard Econ.* 114 The Portsmouth pump-house.. supplied 1,236 feet of hand pumps. **1969** *Wall St. Jrnl.* 7 Oct. 19/1 We've seen crop after crop of dolts parade to the *pump island. **1974** *Petroleum Rev.* XXVIII. 706/3 Painted in BP or National livery will be the pump islands, canopies, shops, kiosks, [etc.]. **1805** R. W. Dickson *Pract. Agric.* I. 329 Expensive machinery of the *pump kind. **1497** *Naval Acc. Hen. VII* (1896) 322 Payed..for a pompe to the seid Ship—iijs. & for a Clampte iiijs. & a *pompe lether—iiij*d.* **1839** Ure *Dict. Arts* 972 Although from 20 to 30 fathoms be the common length of a *pump-lift, it sometimes becomes necessary to make it much longer. **1896** A. Morrison *Child of the Jago* 39 The sufferer's screams had a *pump-like regularity. **1857** Gen. P. Thompson *Audi Alt.* I. v. 16 That men in fine weather throw away their storm-sails, and heave overboard their *pump-machinery. [*a* **1490** Plump-maker: see plump $sb.^2$]. **1623** *Canterb. Marriage Licences* (MS.), John Poole of Canterbury, *pompemaker. **1825** Hone *Every-day Bk.* I. 1042 The worshipful company of pump-makers. **1534** *Acc. Ld. High Treas. Scotl.* VI. 235 For tua hundreth *pomp nale xv*d.* **1626** Capt. Smith *Accid. Yng. Seamen* 3 The Carpenter..is to haue the..pumpe-nailes, skupper-nailes, and leather. **1805** *State Papers & Publick Documents of U.S.* 2 Dec. (1814) I. 455 They robbed the brig of..all her candles, pump nails, locks, and gimblets. **1677** J. Verney 19 May in *V. Mem.* 469 The people about town call this the *Pump Parliament, alluding, as a little water put into a pump fetches up a good deal, so [etc.]. **1888** HASLUCK *Model Engin. Handybk.* (1900) 61 To give the *pump-plunger a travel of ⅝ in. **1875** KNIGHT *Dict. Mech.*, **Pump-scraper*, a round plate used for cleaning out the pump-barrel. *c* **1889** W. TATE *Princ. Mining adapted to S. Kensington Syllabus* xxi. 158 The thickness of *pump sets is calculated by the following formula. **1969** *Capital* (Calcutta) 27 Feb. 354/1 In 1967–68 alone, 250,000 pumpsets, 50,000 private tubewells and 1,000 large State tubewells were installed. **1974** *Petroleum Rev.* XXVIII. 704/1 A sea water injection pumpset. **1855** J. R. LEIFCHILD *Cornwall Mines* 36 Three summers were consumed in sinking the *pump shaft. **1534** in Rogers *Agric. & Prices* (1882) III. 569/2 (Richmond), 2 *pump shoes /4. **1827** G. DARLEY *Sylvia* 38 Uds my life! is their father a *pump-sinker? **1843** R. J. GRAVES *Syst. Clin. Med.* xxx. 418 In draining, *pump-sinking, and other similar occupations. **1702** in *Essex Inst. Hist. Coll.* (1906) XLII. 161 Inventory of ship..Two *pump Speares. **1789** FALCONER *Dict. Marine* G iv, The pump-spear..draws up the box, or piston, charged with the water. **1903** *Daily Chron.* 26 Sept. 6/1 We..punctured tyres six times, and sustained one half-hour's delay through a broken *pump spindle. **1867** 'T. LACKLAND' *Homespun* 321 He washes his ruddy face under the *pump-spout. **1888** *Harper's Bazaar* 22 Dec. 872/1 When he had filled his pail he took it carefully from the pump spout, and started back to the house. *a* **1600** '*Now, Gossop, I must neidis begon*' 25 in *Bannatyne Poems* (Hunter. Cl.) 1080 If she be laik it may be soon espyed, The *pompstaff and the maner holls will try it. **1877** RAYMOND *Statist. Mines & Mining* 164 The steam is conducted along the *pump-station from the main pipe to the pump. **1836** T. WICKSTEED in *Trans. Inst. Civ. Engin.* I. 118 The cylinder was 80 inches, the *pump stroke 9¾ feet. **1891** *Cent. Dict.*, *Stake-driver*, the American bittern..called from its cry.. pile-driver, *pump-thunder, thunder-pumper, etc. **1813** *Sporting Mag.* XLII. 212 Putting him into the *pump-trough, Straw came and pumped upon him. **1934** H. K. BARROWS *Water Power Engin.* (ed. 2) iii. 179 The Baldwin-Southwark Corporation..with the General Electric Company, have recently developed a combined *pump-turbine operated by a two-speed motor generator for such plants, model tests of which indicate relatively high efficiencies when acting as either a turbine or a pump. **1977** *Time* 17 Jan. (Advt., verso front cover), Bill has no idea that the six reversible pump-turbine generator-motors that now supply his area with low-cost electricity were made by Hitachi. *c* **1635** CAPT. N. BOTELER *Dial. Sea Services* (1685) 96 The *Pump-vale which is the Trough, wherein the Water that is pumped out runs along the Ship sides and so out of the Scoper holes. **1844** *Civil Eng. & Arch. Jrnl.* VII. 190/2 A model, showing the principal *pump valves used by mining engineers. **1858** SIMMONDS *Dict. Trade*, *Pump-valve*, the moveable interior part or lid of a pump. **1679–88** *Secr. Serv. Money Chas. & Jas.* (Camden) 112 For *pump work and water carriage in Hyde Park.

pump (pʌmp), *sb.*² Also 6 poumpe, pompe, 6–7 **pumpe.** [Of obscure origin; no word similar in form and sense has been found in other languages.

Suggestions have been offered of its identity with prec., and with POMP *sb.*, but without satisfactory grounds. The Ger. *pumpstiefel* and *pumphosen*, which have been compared, are so called from their tubular or pipe-like legs; and there does not appear in the early use of *pumps* any clear connexion with *pomp* or show. It may have been an echoic word, suggested by the dull flapping sound made by slippers, as distinct from the stamp of heavy shoes.]

a. A kind of light shoe, originally often of delicate material and colour, kept on the foot by its close fit, and having no fastening; a slipper for indoor wear; hence (in 17–18th c.) applied to a more substantial low-heeled shoe of this character, esp. one worn where freedom of movement was required, as by dancers, couriers, acrobats, duellists, etc.; now *spec.*, a light, low-heeled shoe, usually of patent leather and without fastening, worn with evening dress and for dancing, and regionally = PLIMSOLL 2; in North America, freq. = *court shoe* s.v. COURT *sb.*¹ 19. See also PINSON².

1555 W. WATREMAN *Fardle Facions* II. iii. 124 Their shoes are not fastened on with lachettes, but lyke a poumpe close aboute the foote. **1578** FLORIO *1st Fruites* 2 b, I wil buye me a payre of Pantofles and Pumpes. **1592** SHAKS. *Rom. & Jul.* II. iv. 66 Thy Pump..when the single sole of it is worne. **1598** FLORIO, *Scarpini*... Also dancing pumps or little shooes. **1599** B. JONSON *Ev. Man out of Hum.* IV. ii, The gallant'st courtiers kissing ladies' pumps. **1688** R. HOLME *Armoury* III. 14/2 Pumps are shooes with single soles and no heels. **1706** PHILLIPS (ed. Kersey), *Pumps*, a sort of Shooes without Heels us'd by Rope-dancers, Running Foot-men, &c. **1719** DE FOE *Crusoe* 172 They were not like our English Shoes..; being rather what we call Pumps, than Shoes. **1728** W. STARRAT *Epistle* 8 in Ramsay *Poems* (1877) II. 274 Well hap'd with bountith hose and twa-sol'd pumps. **1763** *Brit. Mag.* IV. 547 The flat-heel'd drudges now are thrown aside For the high pumps with toes of peeked pride. **1852** THACKERAY *Esmond* II. x, He was a very tall man, standing in his pumps six feet three inches. **1880** *Times* 21 Sept. 4/4 Slippers, called pumps, which have only one sole and no insole, are also sewed in the old-fashioned way. **1897** *Sears, Roebuck & Co. Catal.* 203/3 Men's gymnasium shoes... Men's low cut canvas pumps, canvas sole, [etc.]. **1908** *Ibid.* 813/2 A dainty pump of patent coltskin, much in favour with fashionable women. **1928** *T. Eaton & Co. Catal.* Spring & Summer, These smart, attractively-trimmed Pumps can be had in either Black Patent or Honey Beige-shade of leather. **1946** *Sun* (Baltimore) 2 Nov. 3 (Advt.), Two flattering styles to choose from—black suede anklet...and classic black suede sling pump—both mounted on black faille platforms. **1967** *Oxford Mag.* 10 Feb. 205/2 Informed by a girl that she has to wear pumps (court shoes) for her Convocation (degree ceremony) [in Canada]. **1968** J. IRONSIDE *Fashion Alphabet* 132 *Dancing shoes or pumps.* Usually worn by children, they have flat soles and elastic which goes criss-cross round the ankle. Very popular among smart nannies for their charges, especially in bronze leather. **1974** P. WRIGHT *Lang. Brit. Industry* ii. 28 For rubber-soled canvas shoes we have *pumps, plimsolls, gym-shoes* and *squeakers*. **1978** J. KRANTZ *Scruples* vii. 191 Wells Cope, wearing a Dorso sweater, pale beige twill trousers, and black velvet evening pumps embroidered in gold, sat with Harriet.

b. In Phrases (esp. in alliterative conjunction with *pantofle*: cf. PANTOFLE b). ***to keep toe in pump*** (*dial.*), to keep quiet or calm, not to get excited.

1589 R. HARVEY *Pl. Perc.* (1860) 23 One standing all vpon his pumps and pantables will be aboue a Shomaker. **1596** NASHE *Saffron Walden* Wks. (Grosart) III. 55 Not in the pantofles of his prosperitie..but in the single-soald pumpes of his aduersitie. **1607** BEAUMONT *Woman Hater* I. ii, To it shall be bidden..All pump and pantofle, foot-cloth riders. **1831–4** S. LOVER *Leg. Irel.* 172 So keep your tongue in your jaw, and your toe in your pump. **1863** TROLLOPE *Rachel Ray* xxiv, Keep your toe in your pump, and say nothing.

c. *attrib.*, as ***pump shoe, tie.***

1689 *Lond. Gaz.* No. 2484/4 Charles Russel, aged 14 years,..Woolen Stockins, Pitch'd and Tarr'd, Pump Shooes..; went away from his Master.., about 10 weeks since. **1904** *Daily Chron.* 5 May 8/4 The new pump tie is the generally accepted shoe.

pump (pʌmp), *v.* Also 6 pompe, poump, 6–7 pomp. [f. PUMP *sb.*¹; cf. Du. *pompen*, G. *pumpen*, F. *pomper*, etc.]

I. Literal senses.

1. *intr.* To work a pump (in early use, always a ship's pump); to raise or move water or other fluid by means of a pump.

1508 KENNEDIE *Flyting w. Dunbar* 463 Thow spewit, and kest out mony a lathly lomp, Fastar than all the marynaris coud pomp. **1530** PALSGR. 670/2 Pumpe a pace, for our shyppe leaketh. **1719** DE FOE *Crusoe* i. (1840) 12 The men ..told me that I..was as well able to pump as another. **1872** RAYMOND *Statist. Mines & Mining* 207 A good engine for hoisting and pumping is on the ground.

2. *trans.* To raise or remove (water or other fluid) by means of a pump. Chiefly with *out*, *up*.

1530 PALSGR. 670/2, I pumpe up water by a pompe. **1538** ELYOT *Dict.*, *Sentino*, to pumpe vp water out of a shyppe. **1653** BOGAN *Mirth Chr. Life* 560 Thou hast many a leake, and..a great deale of water in thee..pump it out at thine eyes, ere thy ship sink. **1742–9** J. WOOD *Descr. Bath* (1765) I. I. viii. 70 If the hot Waters are kept from the Air, and pumped up directly from the Spring. **1815** J. SMITH *Panorama Sc. & Art* II. 15 If this part of the apparatus be air-tight, the mercury may be pumped up into the tube. **1872** RAYMOND *Statist. Mines & Mining* 272 A 9-inch pipe through which they pump the water. *Mod.* To pump the air out of a receiver.

3. a. To free from water, etc. by means of a pump or pumps. Said simply in reference to a ship; of other things usually with extension, as ***to pump dry*** or ***empty***. Also, to free from air or other gas by means of a pump or pumps, to evacuate; also with *down* (cf. *pump up* in sense 5) or *out* (cf. *pump out* in sense 2); also *absol.*

c **1650** DENHAM *Old Age* 132 In a ship..some sweep the deck, some pump the hold. **1706** E. WARD *Wooden World Diss.* (1708) 34 Pumping a leaky Vessel. **1864** WEBSTER s.v., *To pump a ship*, to free it from water by means of a pump. **1890** *Ibid.* s.v., They pumped the well dry. **1923** *Phil. Mag.* XLVI. 724 The apparatus was pumped out and the residual gas removed as completely as possible. **1935** MILLER & FINK *Neon Signs* viii. 166 The average time required for pumping average lengths of tubing..is shown. **1936** *Physical Rev.* L. 250/1 The tube was opened up for three days, then pumped down. **1952** A. L. REIMANN *Vacuum Technique* ii. 27 Seal-off constrictions are commonly made with a diameter of 6 mm. for pumping water-cooled valves. **1955** KIRK & OTHMER *Encycl. Chem. Technol.* XIV. 547 The tube is sealed onto the manifold of a vacuum system which is capable of pumping down the tube to the order of 10^{-7} mm. of mercury. **1959** N. W. ROBINSON in A. S. D. Barrett *Progress in Vacuum Sci. & Technol.* 25/1 The advocates of oil pumps consider that the ability to pump down to 10^{-6}–10^{-7} mm. Hg without a refrigerant outweighs the disadvantage..of oil contamination. **1971** *Sci. Amer.* Aug. 114/1, I do not add the slurry until the system has been pumped to 10^{-2} torr. **1977** *Ibid.* Jan. 80/2 To measure bearing balls for exoelectron emission would call for..putting the ball in a vacuum chamber, pumping the chamber down and hoping that all this would not interfere with exoelectron emission.

b. ***to pump ship*** (also ***pumpship***), to urinate. *colloq.*

1788 GROSE *Dict. Vulgar T.* (ed. 2) s.v. *Pump*, To pump ship; to make water, and sometimes to vomit. *Sea phrase.* **1886** H. BAUMANN *Londinismen* 147/1 *To pump ship*, sein Wasser abschlagen. **1922** V. WOOLF *Let.* 22 Oct. (1976) II. 572 Its on a par with not pump shipping before your wife. **1938** J. CARY *Castle Corner* 163 The few passing guests who came now and then to smoke or to pumpship among the stacks. **1939** W. Z. FOSTER *Pages from Worker's Life* iv. 175 He excused himself from the room with the remark that he had 'to go and pump ship'. **1973** 'D. RUTHERFORD' *Kick Start* i. 12 A couple of men had come in to pump ship at the stand-up urinals.

4. To put (any one) under a stream of water from a pump: **a.** as a rough arbitrary punishment (in quot. 1838 *intr.* with *upon*); **b.** in medical treatment; cf. also PUMPING *vbl. sb.* ? *Obs.*

a. **1632** BROME *Northern Lasse* I. iv, A Divell in a most gentlewomanlike apparition. It had been well to have pumpd her. Is shee gone? **1642** *Ord. & Declar. both Ho., Lords Day* 8 They conveyed him to the pump and pumpt him. **1676** SHADWELL *Virtuoso* II. Wks. 1720 I. 345 Pump him soundly, impudent fellow! **1818** *Gentl. Mag.* LXXXVIII. II. 19/1 Publicly admonished for having been concerned in a riot, and in pumping a bailiff. **1838** D. JERROLD *Men of Char.* I. viii. 251 Warn't you once pumped upon?..Nor never in the Stone Jug?

b. **1631** [see PUMP *sb.*¹ 1 c]. **1631**, **1797**, **1840** [see PUMPING *vbl. sb.*]. **1758** MRS. DELANY in *Life & Corr.* (1861) III. 511 Advised him to go to the Bath to have his hip pumped.

5. ***to pump up***: to inflate (a pneumatic tyre, or the like) by pumping air into it.

c **1892** *colloq.* I must pump up my bicycle first. **1903** *Motor Ann.* 302 These tyres..are pumped up like an ordinary pneumatic.

II. Transferred and figurative senses.

6. a. To draw or force up or out, in a manner likened to the working of a pump; to move up, draw out, pour forth, or eject: said of the shedding of tears, the motion of the blood, the ejection of projectiles from a gun (especially a machine-gun), etc. Also freq., to force, inject, or pour (something) *into* (someone or something).

1604 DEKKER *1st Pt. Honest Wh.* xiii. Wks. 1873 II. 72 Sheel pumpe water from her eyes..in faster showers, Then Aprill when he raines downe flowers. **1796** H. HUNTER tr. *St.-Pierre's Stud. Nat.* (1799) I. 152 The waters, which the Sun is there incessantly pumping up. **1888** LEES & CLUTTERBUCK *Brit. Columbia* xxx, Unmindful of the rifle-shots which Cardie..would keep pumping at them [geese]. **1899** *Allbutt's Syst. Med.* VII. 614 The blood is then pumped [by the heart] into the soft brain tissue. **1901** ST. J. BRODRICK in *Daily Graphic* 14 Nov. 6/2 Undiluted censure has been pumped upon us for the burning of Boer houses. **1940** *War Illustr.* 12 Apr. 367/3 The other six Messerschmitts were circling round him pumping bullets into his 'plane as fast as they could work the guns. **1947** *Sun* (Baltimore) 15 Aug. 12/7 A gunman climbed on the running board of his car and pumped lead into him. **1953** *Times* 31 Oct. 2/7 The atomic energy production division..will be 'generating electrical power which would be pumped into the grid system within the next few years'. **1977** A. THWAITE *Portion for Foxes* 23 Made separate..By actions pumping fear into my blood. **1978** *Guardian Weekly* 29 Jan. 7/2 Moscow started pumping arms into Ethiopia.

b. *absol.* or *intr.*

1837 MARRYAT *Dog-fiend* ix, She vow'd she was so happy that she pump'd with both her eyes. **1899** *Daily News* 17 Nov. 7/5 Our men were exposed to fearful odds, especially with two quick-firers pumping at them. **1909** *Daily Chron.* 22 Sept. 9/5 My head aches. It pumps and pumps and I can't think.

7. a. *trans.* To subject (a person or thing) to a process likened to pumping, with the object of extracting something; to obtain something from by persistent effort; also, to drain, exhaust.

1610 B. JONSON *Alch.* IV. iii, You shall be emptied, Don; pumped, and drawne Drie, as they say. **1667** FLAVEL *Saint Indeed* (1754) 137 Others must pump their memories. **1825** SCOTT *Betrothed* Introd., The author, tired of pumping his own brains. **1881** W. B. JONES in *Macm. Mag.* XLIV. 128 The farm is clean pumped out of capital once in every generation.

b. *spec.* To subject (a person) to such a process in order to elicit information; to ply with questions in an artful or persistent manner.

1656 *St. Papers, Dom.* CXXX. 49 (P.R.O.), I know not what Mr Provost means by his directions to you; I have been pumping of him, but he..will tell me no more. **1659** *Clarke Papers* (Camden) IV. 300 Fleetwood sent Deane..to Sir Art. Haslewrigg to pumpe him. **1751** H. WALPOLE *Lett.* (1846) II. 398, I am going to pump Mr. Bentley for designs. **1886** BESANT *Childr. Gibeon* II. xxx, Pumping the old lady, who willingly told all she knew.

8. a. To extract, raise, or bring forth by means likened to the working of a pump, i.e. by persistent or factitious effort or art. Cf. PUMPED *ppl. a.* 1.

1663 BUTLER *Hud.* I. ii. 763 These words of Venom base Which thou hast from their native Place, Thy stomach, pump'd to fling on me. **1742** YOUNG *Night Th.* VIII. 1322 O how laborious is their Gaiety! They scarce can..Pump sad Laughter, till the Curtain falls. **1809** MALKIN *Gil Blas* VII. v. ¶6, I was no longer in a situation for him to pump anything out of me. **1905** *Westm. Gaz.* 26 Aug. 3/2 After a good deal of pumping-up of indignation we reach the climax of the argument.

b. To elicit (information, etc.) by such means. Const. *out of* a person.

1633 B. JONSON *Tale Tub* IV. iii, I'll stand aside whilst thou pump'st out of him His business. **1706** HEARNE *Collect.* 31 Jan. (O.H.S.) I. 174 The whole design..was..to pump and Fish some things out of them. **1852** R. S. SURTEES *Sponge's Sp. Tour* xiv, It..occurred to him, that he might pump something out of the servant about the family.

9. *intr.* To work or exert oneself in a way likened to pumping, to labour or strive: **a.** *for* the obtaining or gaining of something.

1633 MARMION *Antiquary* II. i, Not to feed you With further hopes, or pump for more excuses. *a* **1703** BURKITT *On N.T.* John v. 43 [They should] rest satisfied in the secret testimony and silent applause of their own consciences, without pumping for popular applause. **1844** THACKERAY *Crit. Rev.* Wks. 1886 XXIII. 213 In endeavouring to account for his admiration, the critic pumps for words in vain.

b. for the eliciting of information.

1669 W. SIMPSON *Hydrol. Chym.* 211 Expecting a.. lecture of their disease to be read thereon [on urine] which many physicians make a shift to do, pumping with a few considerable previous queries. *a* **1734** NORTH *Exam.* I. ii. §158 (1740) 119 So he goes on with his Friend Booth, pumping about this same Reward, but nothing, in certain, came out. **1847** DISRAELI *Tancred* II. ix, 'Well, are you in a hurry?' said Lord Eskdale, gaining time, and pumping.

c. *coarse slang.* To copulate. Also *trans.*, to copulate with (a woman).

1730 in Farmer *Merry Songs & Ballads* (1897) II. 204, I work'd at her Pump till the Sucker grew dry, And then I left pumping, a good Reason why. **1937** PARTRIDGE *Dict. Slang* 667/2 *Pump*, v., to coït with (a woman): low: C. 18–20;

ob[solescent]. **1971** R. K. SMITH *Ransom* v. 223 They began to pump on the soft seat... 'We never did it in no Caddy before,' he whispered. **1973** 'J. PATRICK' *Glasgow Gang Observed* xii. 108 Skidmarks had come by her name through the boys' practice of kicking her naked behind after they had 'pumped' her. **1976** G. V. HIGGINS *Judgement D. Hunter* xiv. 159 He told me Shanley's pumping Dottie Deininger... Fine-looking woman.

10. To work with action like that of the handle or piston of a pump: see quots. **a.** *trans.* In simple use. Also, to shake (a person's hand, or a person by the hand) vigorously.

1803 *Trans. Soc. Arts* XXI. 400 (*Clock-making*) The upper detent G being pumped off with the locking piece F, from the pins in the wheel A. **1912** MULFORD & CLAY *Buck Peters* i. 14 'Tex!.. When did you get here? Going to stay? .. You look white—sick?' 'City color..,' replied the other, still pumping the hand. 'I'm goin' to stay.' **1938** M. K. RAWLINGS *Yearling* xii. 123 They pumped hands in greeting. *a* **1951** 'J. HACKSTON' in Murdoch & Drake-Brockman *Austral. Short Stories* (1951) 230 He ebbed out looking swamped, with a big man pumping him up and down in a parting, very friendly handshake. **1958** J. COURAGE in *London Mag.* Dec. 26 He pumped my hand pleasantly. **1969** [see ETIC *a.*]. **1977** *Church Times* 14 Jan. 5/1 Clasping my hand, and pumping it up and down whilst looking intensely into my eyes.

b. *intr.*

1887 M. ROBERTS *West. Avernus* 241 A hand-car coming along.. with some section hands working it along by means of the lever, 'pumping', as it is commonly called. **1888** AMÉLIE RIVES *Quick or Dead* xx. (1889) 234 She found the organ unlocked, and thought she would see if she could get the sexton to pump for her. **1908** C. F. HOLDER *Big Game at Sea* vii. 118 This is known as 'pumping' from the up-and-down motion of the rod..; after some practice the motion is readily acquired, and the fish brought in with astonishing celerity. **1928** C. F. S. GAMBLE *Story N. Sea Air Station* xviii. 309 All submarines have a tendency to 'pump' in heavy seas, that is, they tend to move up and down in a vertical plane. **1938** M. K. RAWLINGS *Yearling* xiv. 148 The road under him was a treadmill. His legs pumped up and down, but he seemed to be passing the same trees and bushes again and again. **1976** *N.Y. Times Mag.* 12 Sept. 40/2 He [*sc.* a skateboard rider] pumped from cruise to speed, down the incline, faster until he felt almost weightless like a bird, spinning on wheels that really weren't there.

c. ***to pump iron***, to exercise with weights as a form of fitness training or body-building technique. Also *fig. colloq.* (orig. *U.S.*).

1972 C. GAINES *Stay Hungry* ii. 24, I just came up now to pump iron. **1976** *N.Y. Times* 8 May 12/5 Arnold Schwarzenegger.., believed by many to have the world's most perfect male body, was pumping iron the other day at the Mid-City Gym. **1982** S. BELLOW *Dean's December* x. 195 Even his throat has muscles, a pillar throat. I think he pumps iron. **1983** *Fortune* 12 Dec. 84/1 It just churned out minicomputers in the belief that the machines would sell on their merits... That strategy, known in the computer industry as pumping iron, worked spectacularly for two decades. **1986** *Times* 10 May 16/7 Pumping iron behind the Iron Curtain is a relatively new development.

11. *trans.* To work *up* as with a pump; to excite. Also *refl.* (Cf. 5.)

1791 F. BURNEY *Let.* 7 Nov. (1972) I. 77 She owns she found the greatest difficulty in *pumping up* decent expressions of concern. **1813** M. EDGEWORTH *Let.* 1 May (1971) 36, I could not pump up any enthusiasm for them.. I have no taste for these *hideous* old stones. **1844** THACKERAY *Contrib. to Punch, Punch in East* iii, I heard him roar out praises of, and pump himself up into enthusiasm for, certain Greek poetry.

12. To cause to pant violently for breath from excessive exertion; to put completely out of breath. Also with *out*. Usually in *passive*.

1858 [see PUMPED *ppl. a.* 2]. **1880** in Mrs. P. O'Donoghue *Ladies on Horseback* (1881) 317 A Mexican senora, whose favourite pace is a stretching gallop without cessation, until her steed is perfectly pumped out. **1887** H. D. TRAILL in *Macm. Mag.* July 177/1 Their patience, which is already showing manifest signs of distress, will be completely 'pumped' before long. **1899** F. V. KIRBY *Sport E.C. Africa* iii. 36 Although pumped after our climb, we hurried across the plateau.

13. *intr.* Of the mercury in a barometer: To rise and fall instantaneously in the tube as a result of sudden local alterations of pressure or of mechanical disturbance.

1875 BEDFORD *Sailor's Pocket Bk.* iv. (ed. 2) 79 *note*, Minute changes, unobservable.. owing to the pumping of the quicksilver, when the motion of the ship is violent. **1905** *Edin. Rev.* Jan. 230 When the wind rises in a typhoon, it blows in gusts and the mercury heaves in the barometer ('pumps' is the more usual expression).

14. *intr.* = HUNT *v.* 7 b.

1901 L. BELL *Electric Power Transmission* (ed. 3) vi. 227 Alternators in parallel are less likely to pump if they have solid poles. **1902** [see HUNT *v.* 7 b].

15. *Physics.* To raise (an atom or the like) *into* or into a higher energy state by irradiation, esp. so as to produce a population inversion and make the substance work as a laser; to excite (a substance or device) in this way. Cf. *optical pumping* s.v. OPTICAL *a.* 6.

1953 *Rev. Mod. Physics* XXV. 175/1 The vapor is illuminated with circularly polarized light.. to pump atoms from the ground state *a*, in which $m = -\frac{1}{2}$, into state *b*, in which $m = +\frac{1}{2}$. **1961** *Ann. Reg. 1960* 396 The method of 'pumping' the electrons into their excited state had also to be changed for a continuous method. **1973** *Sci. Amer.* June 52/3 Most substances can be pumped with just the fundamental and second-harmonic pulses emitted by these two lasers. **1973** *Physics Bull.* July 419/3 Perhaps the most important recent development has been the successful operation of the cw rhodamine 6G dye laser, pumped by an argon-ion laser. **1975** *Nature* 28 Aug. 695/2 Laser action over the range 2·5 to 2·9 μm was achieved using the F_A(II) centre in lithium-doped potassium chloride pumped by a krypton ion laser at 647·1 nm.

III. 16. *Comb.* **pump-** is used to qualify names of mechanical contrivances in which an essential part moves out and in, like the plunger of a force-pump, as ***pump-centre, -cylinder, -drill, jack, -screw, -spring***; **pump drill**, a primitive drill in which the shaft is rotated by sliding up and down a cross-piece to which is attached a cord that winds and unwinds about the shaft; **pump gun** orig. *N. Amer.*, a rifle having a tubular magazine and a sliding forearm; so ***pump-gunner***.

1884 F. J. BRITTEN *Watch & Clockm.* 83 Although the plate may be set true with the pump centre, it is liable to be drawn a little in fixing. *Ibid.* 216 [The] Pump Cylinder.. [is] a sliding telescopic gauge used by chronometer makers for taking heights. **1865** TYLOR *Early Hist. Man.* ix. 243 A curious little contrivance, known to English tool-makers as the 'pump-drill'. **1964** W. L. GOODMAN *Hist. Woodworking Tools* 180 Another primitive method still in use by.. natives of New Guinea is the pump drill,.. with a flywheel made of stone. **1974** P. W. BLANDFORD *Country Craft Tools* viii. 116 Pump drills were used by many craftsmen. **1906** *Daily Colonist* (Victoria, B.C.) 16 Jan. 10/5 He was using a Winchester pump gun, and in the operation of loading, the gun was fired, the charge striking the left foot. **1970** D. DODGE *Hatchetman* viii. 101 A guard with a pumpgun across his knees sat cross-legged on the floor. **1976** *Shooting Times & Country Mag.* 18–24 Nov., The 16-bore Model 12 is a durable weapon of reasonable weight, very easy to hit with (and to the pumpgunner, at least, having positively classical lines!). **1970** J. BLACKBURN *Land of Promise* v. 74, I had not bought Unzicker's small gasoline engine and pump jack at the sale. **1973** *Times* 1 Dec. 2/3 The Kimmeridge pump jack, familiarly known in the trade as a nodding donkey, seesaws steadily on. **1825** J. NICHOLSON *Operat. Mechanic* 497, M, the pump spring to the detent. **1901** *J. Black's Carp. & Build., Scaffolding* 52 Two sets of uprights are used, one set having pump screws and the other being provided with wedges.

pump, *int.* [Echoic.] A sound so represented; *adv.*, with this sound: see quot.

1897 *Westm. Gaz.* 8 June 2/1 A certain number [of bullets] with great regularity went pum—pum—pump into the earth-work.

ˈpumpable, *a.* [f. PUMP *v.* + -ABLE.] Capable of being pumped. Hence **pumpaˈbility**.

1881 W. WILLIAMS in *Knowledge* No. 5. 88 The pumpability of the air from the receiver shows that [etc.]. **1935** H. MOORE *Liquid Fuels* VI. i. 193 The pour-point test .. is only a rough guide in comparing the pumpability of different fuel oils at low temperatures. **1960** *Farmer & Stockbreeder* 12 Jan. 66/2 Agitators make the mass pumpable, through tractor-powered open-vane centrifugal pumps. **1970** *Sci. Jrnl.* Aug. 79/2 Traditional grouts are sand, lime or cement and sufficient water to make the mixture pumpable. **1973** *Nature* 9 Mar. 90/3 For centrifugal pumps with enclosed disk-type impellers there is likely to be a better pumpability with viscoelastic liquids. **1979** *Civil Engineering* Nov. 43/1 The bolt is installed and grouted by means of pumpable resin.

pumpage (ˈpʌmpɪdʒ). [f. PUMP *v.* + -AGE.] The work done at pumping, the quantity pumped.

1881 *Sci. Amer.* XLIV. 361 The pumpage for last year amounted to 21,120,792,786 gallons. **1893** *Columbus* (Ohio) *Dispatch* 6 Nov., The total average pumpage is given as 9,071,835 gallons.

pump-ball, obs. synonym of PUMPET, PUMPING-BALL: see the latter.

ˈpump-ˌbrake. The handle of a (ship's) pump, esp. one having a transverse bar for several persons to work at it; = BRAKE *sb.*[4] 1 b.

a **1625** *Nomencl. Navalis* (Harl. MS. 2301) lf. 60 b, *Ye Pump-brake* Is the handle theie pumpe by in the ordinary sort of pumpes. **1725** *Bradley's Fam. Dict.* s.v. *Pump*, The *Pump-Brake*, by which the People pump up Water. **1901** *Munsey's Mag.* XXV. 683/2 As the captain came on deck.. the cook struck him over the head with a pump brake, knocking him down.

ˈpump-down. Also **pumpdown.** [f. vbl. phr. *to pump down*: see PUMP *v.* 3.] The action or process of reducing the pressure of air or other gas inside an enclosed volume by pumping. Freq. *attrib.*

1948 *Rev. Sci. Instruments* XIX. 13/1 To obtain a conservative value for the 'pump-down' time, the pump speed.. is 0·37 liter per second. **1966** D. G. BRANDON *Mod. Techniques Metallogr.* 184 Preliminary pump-down can be performed with a liquid nitrogen-cooled sorption trap. **1971** *Sci. Amer.* Aug. 114/3 Gas will be liberated from the internal surfaces of the system during pumpdown. **1977** *Design Engin.* July 35/3 This greatly reduces pump-down time.

pumpe, obs. form of POMP, PUMP.

pumped (pʌmpt), *a.* [f. PUMP *sb.*[2] + -ED[2].] Wearing pumps; having pumps on.

1600 J. LANE *Tom Tel-troth* 325 Some dames are pumpt, because they liue in pompe, That with Herodias they might nimbly daunce, Some in their pantophels too stately stompe. **1828** *Blackw. Mag.* XXIV. 48 Splay feet [of a sailor] pumped and festooned on the instep with a bunch of ribbon. **1836–9** DICKENS *Sk. Boz, New Year*, As if we were duly dress-coated and pumped, and had just been announced at the drawing-room door.

pumped (pʌmpt), *ppl. a.* [f. PUMP *v.* + -ED[1].]

1. Obtained by pumping. ***pumped-up*** (*fig.*), raised by an effort likened to pumping; artificially worked up; laboured: cf. PUMP *v.* 8.

1792 MARY WOLLSTONECR. *Rights Wom.* v. 209 Lover-like phrases of pumped up passion. **1861** HUGHES *Tom Brown at Oxf.* xii, A basin of fresh pumped water. **1904** *Westm. Gaz.* 31 Oct. 6/2 The mob orator, with his sham indignation and pumped-up enthusiasm.

2. ***pumped-out*** (also ***pumped***), exhausted or out of breath with exertion; winded: cf. PUMP *v.* 12.

1858 R. S. SURTEES *Ask Mamma* liii, The first thing that attracted his attention was his own pumped-out steed.

3. ***pumped storage***, the pumping of water to a higher level when demand for electricity is low so that its return to the lower level can be used to generate hydro-electricity when demand is high. Freq. *attrib.*

1927 F. JOHNSTONE-TAYLOR *Water-Power Pract.* x. 163 A total of 450 h.p. being required, pumped storage was resorted to. **1964** *Times Rev. Industry* Jan. 73 A pumped storage scheme.. only requires the possibility of constructing two reasonably large storage basins at widely differing levels with a river or adequate rainfall to keep them filled. **1976** *National Observer* (U.S.) 12 June 5/1 In this ancient valley of the New River, American Electric Power Co... wants to build an $845 million pumped-storage project.. that would trap 42,100 acres of water behind two dams.

pumˈpee. *nonce-wd.* [f. PUMP *v.* + -EE[1] 2.] One who is pumped upon: see PUMP *v.* 4 a.

1834 [see PUMPER[1] 1].

pumpellyite (pʌmˈpɛlɪaɪt). *Min.* [f. the name of Raphael *Pumpelly* (1837–1923), U.S. geologist: see -ITE[1].] An iron- and magnesium-bearing hydrous calcium aluminosilicate, crystallographically similar to minerals of the epidote group, which occurs as colourless, greenish, or brown monoclinic crystals and is characteristic of certain low-grade metamorphic rocks.

1925 PALACHE & VASSAR in *Amer. Mineralogist* X. 412 For this mineral we propose the name of Pumpellyite for Raphael Pumpelly, the pioneer student of the detailed paragenesis of the minerals of this region. **1959** W. W. MOORHOUSE *Study of Rocks in Thin Section* vi. 170 The vesicles of basalts are filled with secondary minerals, of which the most typical are zeolites, carbonate, the silica minerals.., feldspar, epidote, pumpellyite, chlorite, and serpentinite. **1975** *Lithos* VIII. 72 The textures and crystal forms strongly suggest that the pumpellyite-quartz aggregates are reaction products which developed after equilibrium crystallization of the prehnite and chlorite. **1978** *Nature* 20 July 242/1 Prehnite and pumpellyite have been found in County Cavan, Ireland.

pumpelmousse, variant of POMPELMOOSE *Obs.*

pumper[1] (ˈpʌmpə(r)). [f. PUMP *v.* + -ER[1].]

1. a. One who or that which pumps or works a pump; *spec.* †(*a*) the official in charge of the pump-room (at a spa) (*obs.*); (*b*) one in charge of the pumping-machinery in a mine, etc.; a pumpman; (*c*) one engaged in a business in which pumping is the characteristic operation, e.g. ***brine-pumper***.

1660 BOYLE *New Exp. Phys. Mech.* x, The flame lasted about two minutes from the time the pumper began to draw out the air. **1723** *Lond. Gaz.* No. 6127/3 The Mayor.. of the City of Bath having appointed Carew Davis.. Pumper of all the Bath-waters. **1742–9** J. WOOD *Descr. Bath* (1765) I. II. xii. 224 The Pump House was immediately put under the Care of an Officer that bore the name of the Pumper. **1771** SMOLLETT *Humph. Cl.* 26 Apr., The pumper [at Bath], with his wife and servant, attend within a bar; and the glasses, of different sizes, stand ranged in order before them. **1834** *Blackw. Mag.* XXXV. 647 To have gone and assisted at the ceremony of immersion,—whether as pumper or pumpee, I should not have cared. **1904** *Daily Chron.* 18 Aug. 6/7 The accounts.. show that during the past year a rate of 2d. upon all brine pumpers realised £3,921.

b. An exertion, race, or the like which pumps or puts one out of breath. *colloq.*

1874 *Coursing Calendar* Spring 260 All the latter part of a pumper was in favour of Mr Mill's dog. **1879** H. DALZIEL *British Dogs* I. i. 23 Without this [*sc.* a good back] the dog [*sc.* a greyhound] could not endure the exhaustive process of the 'pumpers' he is submitted to.

2. *U.S.* An oil-well from which the oil is pumped up, as distinguished from a natural spring.

1890 in *Cent. Dict.*

3. *U.S.* A fire engine that carries the hose and pumps the water.

1915 *Fire & Water Engineering* 14 July 31/3 (*heading*) New Seagrave pumpers tested at Denver. **1919** *Ibid.* 16 July 140/3 Time was, when the motor pumper was still a novelty and many of the departments were still using the horse-drawn steamer to extinguish fires. **1934** W. C. PRYOR *Fire Engine Book* 32 He showed them a big pumper engine... 'Water power alone is not strong enough to throw the water high into the air.. so the pumper puts more pressure behind the water.' **1949** J. J. FLOHERTY *Fire Alarm* i. 9 Fire apparatus developed from the man-drawn hand pump to the powerful motorized pumper. **1975** *New Yorker* 10 Mar. 28/3 Pache showed us Aviation's current fire engine ('It's a 1951 Ward LaFrance pumper, and it carries five hundred and fifty gallons').

†**pumper**². *Obs. nonce-wd.* [f. PUMP *sb.*² + -ER¹.] (See quot.)

1623 MIDDLETON *More Dissemblers* v. i, I was but a pumper, that is, a puller-on of gentlemen's pumps.

‖**pumpernickel** (ˈpʊmpərnɪk(ə)l). [G., also †*pompernickel* (in use 1663); also (earlier) a lout, a booby. Origin uncertain.] Bread made (in Germany) from coarsely ground unbolted rye; wholemeal rye bread: associated esp. with Westphalia.

[The name was app. unknown in F. Moryson's time: cf. *Itin.* (1617) III. 50 That West-Phalians deuoure..browne bread (vulgarly *cranck broat*, that is, sicke bread).]

1756 NUGENT *Gr. Tour, Germ.* II. 80 Their bread is of the very coarsest kind, ill baked, and as black as a coal, for they never sift their flour. The people of the country call it *Pompernickel*. **1839** LONGF. *Hyperion* ii, The devil take you, and your Westphalian ham, and pumpernickel! **1906** *Blackw. Mag.* May 604/1 It [dhurra] makes a coarse but not unpleasant bread rather resembling pumpernickel.

†ˈ**pumpet, ˈpompet.** *Typogr. Obs.* Also 7 pompett. [a. obs. F. *pompette* a puff of ribbons, etc. in dress, = med.L. *pompeta* (1485 in Du Cange); also 'a pumple, or pimple on the nose, ..*pompette d'imprimeur*, a Printers Pumpet-ball' (Cotgr.). Ulterior origin uncertain; prob. connected with *pompon*, of which in some senses it was a synonym: cf. also PUMPING-BALL.]

Usually **pumpet-ball**: The ball, originally covered with sheep-skin, formerly used by printers for inking the type; an ink-ball. Cf. BALL *sb.*¹ 13. Also called *pump-ball, pumping-ball.*

[**1598**: cf. PUMPING-BALL.] **1611** COTGR., *Pompette d'imprimeur*, a Printers Pumpet-ball..wherewith he beates, or layes Inke on, the Formes. **1653** URQUHART *Rabelais* II. xii, If..they did not sacrifice the Printers pumpet-balls [Fr. *les pompettes*] at Moreb, with a new edge set upon them by text letters. **1661** BLOUNT *Glossogr.* (ed. 2), *Pumpet-bal.* **1875** KNIGHT *Dict. Mech.*, *Pompet*, a printer's inking-ball.

ˈ**pump-ˌhandle,** *sb.* **a.** The handle by which a pump, esp. the ordinary hand- or house-pump, is worked; also *transf.* (see quot. 1794).

1794 W. FELTON *Carriages* (1801) II. Gloss., *Pump* or *Plow Handles*, the long projecting timbers, on the hind part of the Carriages, on which the foot-board is placed. *Ibid.* I. 121. **1825** J. NICHOLSON *Operat. Mechanic* 252 The quantity of water raised by each stroke of the pump-handle is just as much as fills that part of the bore in which the piston works. **1852** R. S. SURTEES *Sponge's Sp. Tour* lxi, He ceased swinging [his]..arms to and fro like a pump-handle. **1883** [see PUMP *sb.*¹ 5].

b. *attrib.* Applied to movement resembling the working of the handle of a pump.

1820 *Sporting Mag.* VII. 108 The pump-handle shake [of hands] is the first which deserves notice. **1886** BESANT *Childr. Gibeon* I. ix, One after the other gave him her hand, which Sam accepted with a pump-handle movement. **1892** J. E. COX *Five Years in U.S. Army* 83 Performing the 'pump-handle act' with my right arm, I hastened away to obey orders. **1909** R. E. KNOWLES *Attic Guest* xv. 204 They nearly all shook hands in the high pump-handle fashion that was almost unknown in the South.

Hence ˈ**pump-handle** *v. trans.* (*colloq.*), to shake in greeting (a person's hand, or a person by the hand) as if working a pump-handle; to move (an arm, etc.) in such a manner; also *intr.*; ˈ**pump-handler**, a hand-shake of this nature.

1844 J. T. HEWLETT *Parsons & W.* xxi, Exchanged the salute for a most hearty old English pump-handler. **1858** R. S. SURTEES *Ask Mamma* xxxii, In an instant the four were..pump-handling each other's arms as if they were going into ecstasies. **1885** RIDER HAGGARD *K. Solomon's Mines* xx, He and Sir Henry were pump-handling away at each other.

ˈ**pumping,** *vbl. sb.* [f. PUMP *v.* + -ING¹.]

a. The action of the verb PUMP in various senses.

†*dry pumping*, pumping water on any particular part for curative purposes, without immersing the body. *Obs.*

1598 HAKLUYT *Voy.* I. 421 Notwithstanding their pumping with 3 pumps, heauing out water with buckets,..the shippe was halfe full of water ere the leake could be found and stopt. **1631** JORDEN *Nat. Bathes* xvii. (1632) 132 The vse [of Bath waters] is either generall to the whole body, as in bathing; or particular to some one part, as in bucketing or pumping. **1728** POPE *Dunc.* II. 154 And oh! (he cry'd) what street, what lane, but knows Our purgings, pumpings, blankettings, and blows? **1797** *Monthly Mag.* III. 509 To pour water on those who practised what we term medical pumping. **1806** *Guide to Watering Places* 27 Pumping in the King's and Queen's bath, 2*d.* each hundred strokes; at the dry pump, 4*d.* each hundred strokes. **1840** *Orig. Bath Guide* 39 An apartment..for *douching* or dry pumping, *i.e.* pumping on any particular part of the body. **1900** *Daily News* 18 Jan. 3/2 The harsher sound of the pumping of the Maxims, Hotchkiss,..and machine guns in general. *Ibid.* 27 July 8/5 Great Damage by Brine Pumping.

b. *fig.* See PUMP *v.* 7.

1635 A. STAFFORD *Fem. Glory* (1869) 91 Can Patience itselfe indure their tedious pumping for improper phrases. **1678** *Quack's Academy* 7 A Previous pumping, by apt and wary Questions. **1809** MALKIN *Gil Blas* I. xiii. ¶5, I got out of her, though by hard pumping, that Don Ambrosio's castle was but a short league from Ponte de Mula. **1881** W. S. GILBERT *Foggerty's Fairy* II, By a judicious course of pumping, I shall find out exactly how I'm situated.

c. *concr. pl.* Proceeds of pumping.

1800 *Hull Advertiser* 27 Sept. 2/1 For sale by the candle, ..7 casks olive pumpings.

d. *attrib.* and *Comb.*, as ***pumping-trough, -well***; esp. in reference to the machinery used in raising or moving water in mines, water-works, or sewage-systems, air in refrigerators, etc., as ***pumping-chamber, -engine, -plant, -shaft, -station***; **pumping set** = *pump-set* s.v. PUMP *sb.*¹ 6 b.

1739 LABELYE *Short Acc. Piers Westm. Bridge* 47 It may be drained dry..by Pumping, or other Engines. **1813** *Sporting Mag.* XLII. 213 The plaintiff was pulled out of the pumping-trough. **1838** *Civil Eng. & Arch. Jrnl.* I. 289/2 Being deprived of the pumping well and drain from Wapping. **1868** *Daily News* 31 July, All the sewage..has to be lifted, and for this purpose there are four pumping stations. *c* **1889** W. TATE *Princ. Mining adapted to Requirements of S. Kensington Syllabus* xlvi. 398 Pumping sets for lifting water to bank vary from 8 to 24 inches, and in extreme cases 36 inches in diameter. **1893** *Daily News* 5 July 5/7 The Wheatley seam..access to it is obtained from the pumping shaft by a cage. **1906** *Westm. Gaz.* 19 Apr. 5/3 He went to the pumping-room..to ask when the refrigerator would be started. **1926** *Power Engineer* XXI. 333 (*heading*) A turbine pumping set. **1957** T. G. HICKS *Pump Selection & Application* vii. 199 (*caption*) Fuel-oil pumping set fitted with 5 gpm 150-psi pumps and heaters. **1962** L. B. ESCRITT *Pumping Station Equipment & Design* iii. 27 Pumping sets are classed into horizontal-spindle and vertical-spindle types.

ˈ**pumping,** *ppl. a.* [f. as prec. + -ING².] That pumps; in quot. 1812, issuing as from a pump; in 1856, resembling the working of a pump.

1812 H. & J. SMITH *Rej. Addr.* ix, The firemen terrified are slow To bid the pumping torrent flow. **1856** A. R. WALLACE in *Ann. Nat. Hist.* July 27, A female Mias.. uttering at intervals a loud, pumping grunt.

†ˈ**pumping-ball.** *Obs.* [History obscure.

As obs. F. *pompette* was synonymous with *pompon*, it seems possible that *pumping-ball* was corrupted from **pompon-ball* = pumpet-ball.]

= PUMPET-*ball*; also called by Florio ***pump-ball.***

1598 FLORIO, *Tudice*, a printers inke bals, called pumping bals, wherewith they beat the letters in the forme lying vpon the presse. [**1611** a Printers inke-balles or pump-balles.]

So †ˈ**pumping-nail,** a nail used in fastening the leather on a printer's ink-ball, or 'pumping-ball' to the stock.

1683 MOXON *Mech. Exerc., Printing* xi. vi. ¶21 For Pelts or Leather, Ball-Nails or Pumping-Nails, Wool or Hair.. the Press-man generally eases the Master-Printer of the trouble of choosing. **1688** R. HOLME *Armoury* III. 301/1 Pumping Nails, with round Heads. [Cf. **1888** JACOBI *Printers' Vocab.* 6 Ball nails, tacks or clouts used for fastening on the coverings of the old ink-balls.]

pumpion, variant of POMPION, pumpkin.

pumpkin (ˈpʌm(p)kɪn). Also 7–9 pompkin, 8–9 pumkin, 9 (*U.S.*) punkin. [An altered form of *pumpion* (see POMPION), with the ending conformed to the suffix -KIN. In U.S. the *m* is often further assimilated to the *k*, the word being pronounced (ˈpʌŋkɪn), and sometimes spelt *punkin*, esp. in comb.]

1. a. The large fruit of a cucurbitaceous plant (*Cucurbita Pepo*), egg-shaped or nearly globular with flattened ends; widely cultivated for the fleshy edible layer next to the rind, which is used in cookery, esp. for pies, and as a food for cattle; in *U.S.* applied *spec.* to particular varieties in distinction from the *squash*.

[**1647** WARD *Simp. Cobler* 67 He would come over to us, to helpe recruite our pumpkin blasted braines.] **1670** D. DENTON *Descr. New York* (1845) 3 Tobacco, Hemp, Flax, Pumpkins, Melons, &c. **1706** PHILLIPS, *Pompion* or *Pumpkin*, a sort of Fruit of the nature of Melons. **1712** tr. *Pomet's Hist. Drugs* I. 155 Cotton-Seeds, made like those of Pumkins. **1833** L. RITCHIE *Wand. by Loire* 63 A single pumpkin could furnish a fortnight's pottage. **1852** CARLYLE *Misc. Ess., The Opera* VII. 127 A born nigger with mere appetite for pumpkin.

b. The plant producing this fruit; a trailing annual, growing often to a great length, having heart-shaped five-lobed leaves, and flowers of a deep yellow. Also called *pumpkin-vine*.

1698 FRYER *E. India & P.* 105 Planted with..Pompkins, Cucumbers, Gourds. **1729** *Dampier's Voy.* III. 455 *Great Pumkin*, its fruit striated, round, but somewhat flattish, mixt with white and red, but within yellow. **1877** A. B. EDWARDS *Up Nile* xvii. 463 A wall of enclosure overgrown with wild pumpkins.

2. *fig.* **a.** Applied contemptuously to the body or person; hence 'a stupid, self-important person' (*Funk's Stand. Dict.*). Cf. POMPION 3.

1830 GALT *Lawrie T.* II. i, But I ain't a pumpkin, the Squire he knows that. **1878** VILLARI *Life & Times Machiavelli* (1898) II. ix. 332, I wish to rid myself of this pumpkin of a body. **1885** R. BRIDGES *Nero* II. i, I'll let Rome know how pumpkin Claudius died [cf. *pumpkinification* below].

b. *U.S. slang.* A person or matter of importance; esp. in phrase ***some pumpkins*** (or ***punkins***).

1846 *Spirit of Times* 25 Apr. 97/1 The skins, Indian relics, etc. are 'some punkins' and no mistake. *a* **1848** RUXTON *Far West* 178 Afore I left the settlements I know'd a white gal, and she was some punkins. **1849** [see LAGNIAPPE]. **1852** BRISTED *Upper Ten Thousand* 216 We being punkins were of course among the invited. [*Note*] A slang expression of young New York for people of value and consequence. **1859** *Harper's New Monthly Mag.* Sept. 569/2 Gin'ral! you're *some* punkins! **1887** *Daily News* 10 Mar. 3/1 Driving..from Piccadilly to Hammersmith, he [H. W. Beecher] quaintly said: 'London is some pumkins, I tell you'—a profound Americanism, which is supposed to convey a wholly unutterable approbation and surprise. **1903** *McClure's Mag.* XXI. 330/1 He was some pumpkin both in politics and color, and the friend of me and Jones. **1913** J. LONDON *Valley of Moon* (1916) III. vii. 380 Say, friend, you're some punkins at a hundred yards dash, ain't you? **1930** E. POUND *XXX Cantos* xii. 54 Go to hell Apovitch, Chicago aint the whole punkin. **1975** *Publishers Weekly* 21 July 67/3 New England, where the Boston radio team of Eddie Andelman, Jim McCarthy and Mark Witkin is evidently considered some punkins.

3. A sea-cucumber. (Eastern U.S. *local*.)

1897 KIPLING *Captains Courageous* iv. 102 Stripping the sea-cucumbers that they called pumpkins.

4. *attrib.* and *Comb.*, as ***pumpkin butter, -chip*** (CHIP *sb.*¹ 2 b), ***-eater, ground, kind, patch, pudding, -shell, soup, -vine; pumpkin-coloured, orange, -purple, yellow*** adjs.; **pumpkin gourd** = sense 1; **pumpkin lantern,** a lantern made of the rind of a pumpkin hollowed out so as to be translucent; **pumpkin pie,** a pie of which pumpkin is a chief ingredient; in U.S. considered especially appropriate to Thanksgiving day; **pumpkin pine,** *U.S.*, a variety of the white pine, *Pinus strobus*; also, the timber from this tree.

1893 M. A. OWEN *Voodoo Tales* 6 The place of the vegetables was taken by..little jars of a villainous sweet compound of pumpkin stewed with watermelon-juice and known to all as '*punkin-butter'. **1862** T. W. HIGGINSON *Army Life* (1870) 21 Preserves made of *pumpkin-chips. **1873** 'SUSAN COOLIDGE' *What Katy did at Sch.* 12 She saw a big, *pumkin-coloured house. **1918** *N. & Q.* 12th Ser. IV. 189/1 Peter, Peter, *pumpkin-eater, Had a wife and couldn't keep her. Had another, didn't love her, Causing instantaneous bother. **1962** *Punch* 31 Oct. 648/1 Jake is the pumpkin eater of the title [of a novel]; he tries to put his wife in a pumpkin shell to keep her very well, as the old rhyme says, and it is this that precipitates the crisis. **1822** *Hortus Anglicus* II. 515 *Cucurbita Pepo*, Pompion, or *Pumpkin Gourd. **1799** WASHINGTON *Writ.* (1893) XIV. 223 The large lot..is to have oats sown on the potato and *pumpkin ground. **1745** POCOCKE *Descr. East* II. I. 181 A dish of the *pumkin kind, dressed after their way. **184.** LOWELL *Biglow P.* Ser. I. v, Something more than a *pumpkin-lantern is required to scare manifest and irretrievable Destiny out of her path. **1974** L. KOENIG *Little Girl* xix. 224 A waitress.. wearing a *pumpkin-orange uniform. **1935** Z. N. HURSTON *Mules & Men* I. iv. 99 Out dat door John come like a streak of lightning. All across de *punkin patch, thru de cotton over de pasture. **1654** E. JOHNSON *Wonder-working Providence of Sions Saviour in New England* 174 This poor Wilderness hath..quince tarts instead of their former *Pumpkin Pies. **1784** P. M. FRENEAU *Poems* (1786) 389 Systems they built on pumpkin pies, And prov'd that every thing went round. **1817** J. PALMER *Jrnl. Trav. U.S.* (1818) 241 Two dishes..peculiar to New England,..toast dipped in cream and pumpkin pie. **1844** WHITTIER *Pumpkin* 24 Ah! on Thanksgiving day..What calls back the past, like the rich Pumpkin pie? **1894** *Daily News* 29 Nov. 6/3 A very favourite dish, especially among the poorer classes of America, is pumpkin pie—pronounced 'punkin'. **1907** *St. Nicholas* May 615/2 Pumpkin pies and strawberry shortcake were also introduced to the French palate and found good. **1809** KENDALL *Trav.* III. 145 Of the white pine the lumberers distinguish two varieties, one of which they call *punkin pine... The name punkin (pompion) they employ on account of the softness and fine grain of the wood. **1851** J. S. SPRINGER *Forest Life & Forest Trees* 41 The pumpkin Pine is generally found on flat land and in ravines. **1907** *Springfield* (Mass.) *Weekly Republ.* 29 Aug. 15 The virgin white pine has practically disappeared from New England and huge 'pumpkin pines' four and five feet in diameter are now a matter of tradition. **1941** B. A. WILLIAMS *Strange Woman* vii. 576 It was an old pumpkin pine... It was better than six feet through, where I tackled it, about four feet from the ground. **1947** E. H. PAUL *Linden on Saugus Branch* 187 The solid old flooring of pumpkin pine, strewn with sawdust, rumbled and clicked beneath the tread of seamen's boots. **1951** E. M. GRAHAM *My Window looks down East* vii. 65 On the punkin pine bureau, which shines almost as golden as the heart I'd taken from the tree, were two bunches of flowers. **1805** *Indep. Chron.* 26 Dec. 3/1 Clams and oysters, succa-touch and *pumpkin puddings, turkies, ducks, [etc.]. **1841** A. M. MAXWELL *Run through U.S. during Autumn of 1840* I. 81 Real, genuine, Yankee, new England, pumpkin pudding. **1898** C. K. PAUL tr. *Huysman's En Route* ii. 27 Clad in robes of gamboge,..gooseberry-red, *pumpkin-purple and wine lees. **1837** HAWTHORNE *Twice-told T.* (1851) I. v. 81 Crop it [hair] forthwith, and that in the true *pumpkin-shell fashion. **1844** WHITTIER *Pumpkin* 32 Telling tales of the fairy who travelled like steam, In a pumpkin-shell coach, with two rats for her team! **1867** BAKER *Nile Tribut.* ix. (1872) 142 He had patches upon his cranium as bald as a pumpkin shell. **1884** *Cottage Hearth* Apr. 189/1 **Pumpkin Soup.* Cut the inside and edible part of the pumpkin into large dice. **1955** *Caribbean Q.* IV. II. 102 After the First Communion, there is a fete for each child, with toasts in vermouth, sheepshead and pumpkin soup. **1810** M. CUTLER *Jrnl.* 9 July (1888) II. 343 Saw the cactus grandiflora, or night-flowering cereus... The plant has a long stem, resembling a *pumpkin-vine, but no leaves. **1840** J. BUEL *Farmer's Comp.* 67 Weeds, potato and pumpkin vines, and other vegetable matters. **1909** F. B. CALHOUN *Miss Minerva & William Green Hill* xiii. 106 How's he going to sit under a pumpkin vine when he's inside of a whale? **1962** S. WYNTER *Hills of Hebron* iii. 42 Withered pumpkin vines..littered the earth. **1912** J. WEBSTER *Daddy-Long-Legs* 173 Mr. Weaver has painted his barn..a bright *pumpkin yellow.

Hence (*nonce-wds.*) ˈ**pumpkinish** *a.*, resembling or akin to a pumpkin; ˈ**pumpkinism,** ? pompous behaviour or language; **pumpˈkinity,** the nature or quality of a pumpkin (after *divinity*); also **pumpkinifi'cation** [suggested by the travesty (ascribed to Seneca) of the apotheosis of the Roman emperor Claudius Cæsar under the title of 'apocolocyntosis', Gr. ἀποκολοκύντωσις transformation into a pumpkin, f. κολοκύνθη pumpkin], **'pumpkinify** *v.*, **'pumpkinize** *v.*, to make a pumpkin of, dyslogistic terms for extravagant or absurdly uncritical glorification.

1856 MERIVALE *Rom. Emp.* V. l. 602 *note*, Seneca wrote a satire on the deification of Claudius to which he gave the name of *Apocolocyntosis* (or *pumpkinification). **1904** *Spectator* 15 Oct. 559/1 The writer..has..given us, not an apotheosis, but a pumpkinification of the Emperor William II. **1899** *Athenæum* 8 July 71/3 The unhappy Emperor Claudius, who has gone down to posterity as mercilessly '*pumpkinified' by Seneca. **1884** *Sat. Rev.* 6 Dec. 721/1 The phrases whereby the *pumpkinifier constructs his pumpkin. **1849** CARLYLE *Misc. Ess., Nigger Question* (1872) VII. 101 All this fruit..so far beyond the merely *pumpkinish and grossly terrene, lies in the West India lands. *a* **1835** MRS. HEMANS in H. F. Chorley *Mem.* (1837) II. 18 There will be an outpouring of spirit of *Pumpkinism upon me the moment I get back. **1856** MERIVALE *Rom. Emp.* V. l. 601 The senate decreed his divinity, Seneca translated it into *pumpkinity.

'pumpkin-head. *U.S. colloq.* **a.** A head having the hair cut short all round: see quot. 1781. **b.** A big head like a pumpkin. **c.** A person having a pumpkin-head (cf. *round-head*). **d.** A man with a head compared to a pumpkin, a stupid fellow, a dolt.

1781 S. PETERS *Hist. Connecticut* 195 Newhaven is celebrated for having given the name of pumkin-head to all the New-Englanders. It originated from the Blue Laws, which enjoin every male to have his hair cut round by a cap. When caps were not to be had, they substituted the hard shell of a pumkin, which being put on the head..the hair is cut by the shell all round the head. **1876** H. E. SCUDDER *Dwellers in Five-Sisters Court* v. 87 'Pumpkin head!' said the Doctor, more vigorously than politely. **1892** ZANGWILL *Childr. Ghetto* I. iii. 70 Children..with great pumpkin heads. **1898** H. FREDERIC *Deserter & Other Stories* 143 You can't raise a plug of [tobacco] in a whole regiment of 'em. Regular pumpkin-heads!

Hence **'pumpkin-,headed** *a.*, having a head compared to a pumpkin, stupid.

[**1607** WALKINGTON *Opt. Glass* 126 Like pumpion headed Solonists they looke.] **1835–40** HALIBURTON *Clockm.* (1862) 244 They ain't got two ideas to bless themselves with, the stupid, punkin-headed, consaited blockheads! **1939** WODEHOUSE *Uncle Fred* xvi. 234 You know that pumpkin-headed old man's views on class distinctions.

pumpkinification, etc.: see PUMPKIN.

'pumpkin-seed. **a.** The flattish oval seed of the pumpkin. **b.** A fresh-water fish of North America, *Lepomis gibbosus*, the sun-fish, pond-perch. **c.** Applied locally in *U.S.* to a yacht-built sailing-boat, and to a row-boat having the shape of a pumpkin seed.

1781 S. PETERS *Hist. Connecticut* 243 Maize..is planted in hillocks three feet apart, five kernels and two pumkin-seeds in a hillock. **1857** GRAY *First Lessons Bot.* (1866) 8 In the pumpkin-seed,..it is less than an eighth of an inch long. **1860** BARTLETT *Dict. Amer.*, *Pumpkin-Seed*,..common in fresh-water ponds and lakes. They are so called from their form. In the river St. Lawrence I have seen them from six to eight inches in length. **1862** LOWELL *Biglow P.* Poems 1890 II. 243 The bream, Whose on'y business is to head up-stream, (We call 'em punkin-seed). **1888** GOODE *Amer. Fishes* 64 The 'Pumpkin seed' and the perch are the first trophies of the boy angler.

pumple, obs. and dial. variant of PIMPLE.

1523 FITZHERB. *Surv.* xxx. (1539) 51 Except they haue many small pumples and springes about the rotes. **1601** SIR W. CORNWALLIS *Ess.* II. xlv. (1631) 252 Like a pumple the childes age of a sore. **1798** *Anti-Jacobin, New Morality* 296 Flaming cheek and pumple nose.

pumplemousse, -mus, -nose, var. POMPELMOOSE *Obs.*

'pumpless, *a.* [See -LESS.] Without a pump.

1899 *Daily News* 9 Nov. 8/1 The majority depend upon pumpless wells.

pump log. *U.S.* A hollowed log used in the construction of a pump or as a water-pipe. Also in *Comb.* as **pump-log borer** (see quot.).

1816 *N. Amer. Rev.* III. 429 He declared also, that the mill for grinding apples, which is an overshot and is fed by a pump log..would often stop during the day. **1858** D. K. BENNETT *Chronol. N. Carolina* 108 He had some men repairing pump-logs, through which water was carried from the mountain side to his hotel. **1879** F. R. STOCKTON *Rudder Grange* xvi. 235 He looked like he'd been drawn through a pump-log. **1965** E. TUNIS *Colonial Craftsmen* iii. 40 Such a one was the pump-log borer—his trade seems to have no generic name—who made wooden pumps and wooden pipes by boring holes lengthwise through logs.

'pumpman. Also **pumpsman.** A man who works a pump; *spec.* one who attends to the pumps in a coal or other mine.

1776 G. SEMPLE *Building in Water* 45 That subterraneous Water..never failed..to contribute greatly to the increase of the Pump-mens Labour. **1902** *Westm. Gaz.* 22 May 8/2 The Pennsylvania coal strikers threaten to call out the engineers and pump-men, which would result in the flooding of the mines. **1902** *Blackw. Mag.* Aug. 191/1 [He] speculates on which of his two pumpsmen will prove the weaker.

'pump-,priming, *vbl. sb.* orig. *U.S.* [f. the phr. *to prime a pump* (see PRIME *v.*[1] 4).] The stimulation of commerce or economy by means of investment; also *transf.* and *attrib.* or as *ppl. adj.*

1937 F. D. ROOSEVELT *Public Papers & Addresses* (1941) VI. 520 The things we had done, which at that time were largely a monetary and pump-priming policy.., had brought the expected result. **1938** *Sun* (Baltimore) 5 Jan. 1/7 (*heading*) Eccles urges pump-priming to end slump. *Ibid.* 18 Feb. 15/1 Farm products seemed most likely to benefit from the next 'pump-priming'. **1941** N. ALLEY *I Witness* xxxvi. 300, I spent a pump-priming week at Lisbon as the first step toward getting geared up for war coverage. **1950** *Ann. Reg. 1949* 161 Large development projects whose results would be out of all proportion to the 'pump-priming' required from U.N. **1960** *Guardian* 21 Oct. 24/6 The pump-priming period of the Welfare State. **1961** B. R. WILSON *Sects & Society* 9 The pump-priming activity of the revivalist to generate a distinctive form of religious expression. **1963** *Daily Tel.* 18 Jan. 12/2 To the financial purists, this appears as a bid for straightforward Keynesian pump-priming. Something of the sort is clearly required to stir the American economy out of its present sluggishness. **1978** M. PUZO *Fools Die* xxx. 351 He, Lieverman, would throw in the pump-priming cash, the development money.

Hence **'pump-,primer**, a financial grant or other action that stimulates economic enterprise.

1953 *Manch. Guardian Weekly* 13 Aug. 9/3 Sir Greville Maginness suggests that the grants will act as 'pump-primers' and encourage the more backward firms. **1962** *Times* 11 May 17/6 Expansion..could be effective as a pump-primer for the economy of the region. **1979** *Nature* 4 Jan. 7/3 Finance has been a constant anxiety, for the initial grants from the Wolfson Foundation and other funds were pump primers.

'pump-rod. A rod (ROD *sb.* 9 a) connecting the piston or plunger of a pump with the motive power; in mines a heavy iron or wooden beam or system of beams.

1825 J. NICHOLSON *Operat. Mechanic* 178 A pull at both ends of the beam, at the one end by the weight of the pump-rod. **1834–6** BARLOW in *Encycl. Metrop.* (1845) VIII. 101/1 The beam and pump-rods, sometimes weighing many tons. **1855** J. R. LEIFCHILD *Cornwall Mines* 192 The whole column of pumps in a shaft is worked by a single pump-rod.

'pump-room. A room or building where a pump is worked; *spec.* a place at a spa where the medicinal water is dispensed for drinking, etc.

The latter use arose at the King's Bath in Bath (England) where early in the 18th c. a building was erected for the shelter of the users (drinkers and bathers) of the water, which was supplied from the cisterns by pumping; the buildings were in course of time elaborated, features of the *Kursaal* being added; the name has been adopted and applied to buildings serving the same purpose at other spas.

[**1707** W. OLIVER *Pract. Diss. Bath-Waters* v. (1719) 68 The Inconveniencies [at Bath]..are much less, since the erecting a new Pump, and a convenient warm and dry Gallery to walk in.] **1742–9** J. WOOD *Descr. Bath* (1765) I. II. xi. 222 As the Passage on that Side the Bath was no more than nine Feet broad, the Corporation resolved [*c* 1704] to place the Pump Room over it. **1771** SMOLLETT *Humph. Cl.* 26 Apr. i, The pump-room which is crowded like a Welsh fair. **1797** *Encycl. Brit.* (ed. 3) III. 68/2 (Bath) At the King's bath is a handsome pump-room, where the gentlemen and ladies go in a morning to drink the waters. **1828** *Orig. Bath Guide* 26 The Great Pump-room is 60 feet long... In the centre of the south-side is the pump. **1838** *Murray's Handbk. N. Germ.* 407/2 Dr. Struve's establishment [at Dresden]..consists of baths and a pump-room. *c* **1900** *Guide Buxton* 12 The chalybeate water is also obtained at the Pump Room. At the western end of the Pump Room is the Public Pump, which is supplied from the same spring.

pumpship: see PUMP *v.* 3 b.

'pump-tree. A length of tree-trunk used as the body or stock of a hand-pump, or as a water-pipe; the stock, barrel, or cylinder of a pump.

1617 in Earwaker *Sandbach* (1890) 136 Item a Levill and a staffe vj[d]..pumptree v[s]. **1725** *Bradley's Fam. Dict.* s.v. *Pump*, The *Pump-Tree*, which is that Part that stands more above the Earth, or Top of the Well. **1829** R. STUART *Anecd. Steam Engines* I. 306 Employed..for boring the wooden pipes or pumptrees, used to convey water. **1842** *Civil Eng. & Arch. Jrnl.* V. 352/2 In Cornwall the cast iron pump-trees exposed to the action of mine water were very speedily destroyed.

'pump-water. Water obtained from below the surface of the soil by means of a pump, as distinguished from *rain-water*, *spring-water*, etc.

1663 BOYLE *Usef. Exp. Nat. Philos.* II. iv. 115 Very many Pump-waters will not bear Soap, as Rain-waters..will do. **1769** ELLIS in *Phil. Trans.* LIX. 142 Some I put into very hard pump-water. **1836–41** BRANDE *Chem.* (ed. 5) 169 The coldest pump-water that can be procured.

'pump-well. **a.** A casing or compartment in a ship in which the pumps work; the 'well' of a ship. **b.** A well having a pump combined with it; a receptacle in which water is collected to be removed by pumping.

a. [**1626** CAPT. SMITH *Accid. Yng. Seamen* 11 The Pumpe, the pumpes-well.] **1769** FALCONER *Dict. Marine* (1789), *Archipompe*, the pump-well. **1799** *Hull Advertiser* 28 Dec. 3/3 The unhappy man was found suspended in the pump-well of the ship.

b. 1812 SIR J. SINCLAIR *Syst. Husb. Scot.* I. 358 If a running stream cannot be obtained..a pump-well..may supply its place. **1824** MISS FERRIER *Inher.* viii, A nose like the handle of a pumpwell. **1882** *Rep. to Ho. Repr. on Prec. Metals of U.S.* 652 The rest..is..collected by pipes into the pump-well, whence it is pumped up back to the supply tanks, near the pans. **1885** R. L. & F. STEVENSON *Dynamiter* xiii. 197 A pump-well that ran poison.

pumy, pumyce, etc.: see PUMICE, -STONE.

pun (pʌn), *sb.*[1] Also 7–8 punn. [Appears first, with its cognate PUN *v.*[1], soon after 1660. Of unascertained origin: see Note below.]

a. The use of a word in such a way as to suggest two or more meanings or different associations, or the use of two or more words of the same or nearly the same sound with different meanings, so as to produce a humorous effect; a play on words.

1662 DRYDEN *Wild Gall.* I. i, A bare Clinch will serve the turn; a Carwichet, a Quarterquibble, or a Punn. **1670** EACHARD *Cont. Clergy* 37 Wits both ancient and modern.. that never..received their improvements by employing their time in puns and quibbles. **1673** *S'too him Bayes* 92 If this..be no quibble, but a pun. **1683** E. HOOKER *Pref. Pordage's Mystic Div.* 15 What of Whims and Shams, Punns and Flams, Stultiloquious Dialogs? **1711** ADDISON *Spect.* No. 61 ¶6 Having pursued the History of a Punn,..I shall here define it to be a Conceit arising from the use of two Words that agree in the Sound, but differ in the Sense. **1727** POPE, etc. *Art Sinking* x. 97 The Paronomasia or Pun, where a word, like the tongue of a jackdaw, speaks twice as much by being split. **1746** SMOLLETT *Reproof* 176 Debauch'd from sense, let doubtful meanings run The vague conundrum and the prurient pun. **1830** D'ISRAELI *Chas. I*, III. v. 74 Laud.. turned out Archy, the King's fool, for a pun [viz. for saying as grace 'Great praise be to God, and little Laud to the devil', or words to that effect]. **1870** L'ESTRANGE *Miss Mitford* I. v. 157 Even Shakespeare's magic is not proof against the artillery of puns.

b. *attrib.* and *Comb.*, as ***pun-hater***, ***-trap***; ***pun-abhorring***, ***-admiring***, ***-proof***, ***-provoking*** adjs.

1721–2 AMHERST *Terræ Fil.* No. 39. 204 It is no wonder that a punning monarch produced a race of punning and pun-admiring liege subjects. **1742** SHENSTONE *School-mistress* xi, The tufted basil, pun-provoking thyme. **1830** G. COLMAN *Br. Grins, Rem. Freshman* (1872) 448 The intolerant pun-hater. **1839** MORIARTY *Husband Hunter* III. 202 [He] frequently laid pun-traps and quibble-springes of which he took advantage. **1884** W. E. HENLEY in Ward *Eng. Poets* III. 230 A good and cheerful talker, whose piety was not always pun-proof.

Hence (*nonce-words*) **'punless** *a.*, void of puns; **'punkin** *rare*, **'punlet**, a little pun; **'punnage**, punning; **'punnic**, **'punnical** *adjs.*, of, pertaining to, or characterized by puns; **'punnigram** [after *epigram*], a punning saying or *mot*; **pu'nnology**, the subject or study of puns.

1866 H. JAMES in *Atlantic Monthly* XVII. 197/2 Blunt and I made atrocious puns. I believe, indeed, that Miss Blunt herself made one little *punkin, as I called it. **1716** SWIFT (folio broadsheet), God's Revenge against Punning... [Signed] 'the *Punless and Penyless J. Baker, Knight'. **1864** *Realm* 6 Apr. 8 Let our ingenious dramatists try their hands at a punless burlesque with some real fun and interest in it. **1819** COLERIDGE in *Lit. Rem.* (1836) II. 287 The *punlet, or pun-maggot, or pun intentional. *a* **1849** POE *Marginalia* Wks. 1864 III. 564 Such chapters of *punnage as Hood was in the daily practice of committing to paper. **1713** BIRCH *Guard.* No. 36 *heading*, What Rebuses exalt the *Punnic fame! **1721** AMHERST *Terræ Fil.* xxxix. (1754) 204 Punning is not intirely banish'd from the pulpit... Some persons have alledged..that this pun-ick art is of divine institution. **1780** R. GRAVES *Euphrosyne* II. 150 *Punnical. **1835** *Tait's Mag.* II. 420 Much that is merry and wise, punnical and entertaining. **1888** HUXLEY in *Life* (1900) II. xiii. 211 You.. have already made all possible epigrams and *punnigrams on the topic. *a* **1744** POPE (Jod.), He might have been better instructed in the Greek *punnology. **1826** *Examiner* 179/2 The extreme antiquity of some of the described incidents and punnology.

[Note. *Pun* was prob. one of the clipped words, such as *cit*, *mob*, *nob*, *snob*, which came into fashionable slang at or after the Restoration. Longer equivalents, found *a* 1676, were PUNNET and PUNDIGRION; the former app. a dim. of *pun*. It has been suggested that *pun* might originally be an abbreviation of It. *puntiglio*, small or fine point, formerly also a cavil or quibble ('cavillazione, sottigliezza nel ragionare, o nel disputare', *Vocab. Della Crusca*), a pun being akin to a quibble; and that *pundigrion* might perh. be a perversion, illiterate or humorous, of *puntiglio*. This appears not impossible, but nothing has been found in the early history of *pun*, or in the English uses of *punctilio*, to confirm the conjecture.]

pun, *sb.*[2] Also 8 punn. [Related to PUN *v.*[2]]

1. A layer or bed of clay to prevent leakage. ? *Obs.*

1795 J. PHILLIPS *Hist. Inland Navig.* 365 A bed (technically a *punn*) of clay, to prevent the water weeping through the arches.

2. A punner, a pounder, a rammer. *local.*

1905 J. T. MICKLETHWAITE *Let.* 15 Sept. (MS.), *Pun*, a sort of great pestle for beating mortar.

pun (pʌn), *v.*[1] [Goes with PUN *sb.*[1]]

1. *intr.* To make puns; to play on words.

1670 EACHARD *Cont. Clergy* 33 Whether or no punning, quibling, and that which they call joquing, and such other delicacies of wit..might not be very conveniently omitted? **1706** PHILLIPS (ed. 6), *Pun*, to quibble or play with words. **1727** SWIFT *God's Rev. agst. Punning* Wks. 1755 III. I. 171 One Samuel an Irishman, for his forward attempt to pun, was stunted in his stature. **1729** in Pope *Dunc.* I. 63 *note*, A great Critick formerly..declared He that would pun would pick a Pocket. **1817** COLERIDGE *Biog. Lit.* xxiii. (1819) 292

Edgar in Lear, who, in imitation of the gipsy incantations, puns on the old word *mair*, a hag. **1829** LYTTON *Devereux* I. iii, I punned and jested.

fig. **1698** FARQUHAR *Love & Bottle* II. ii, Here, here, master; how it [wine] puns and quibbles in the glass!

2. *trans.* To bring or drive by punning.

1711 ADDISON *Spect.* No. 61 ¶2 The Sermons of Bishop Andrews..are full of them [puns]. The Sinner was punned into Repentance. **1888** CRAWFORD *With Immortals* II. xii. 131 To be punned to death, sir, would be equally horrible.

pun, *v.*[2] [Early and dial. var. of POUND *v.*[1]]

1. *trans.* = POUND *v.*[1] in various senses.

1559–1903 [see POUND *v.*[1] 1 β, 2 β].

2. *spec.* (in technical use). To consolidate by pounding or ramming down (as earth or rubble, in setting poles, etc., or making a roadway); = POUND *v.*[1] 6.

1838 SIMMS *Public Wks. Gt. Brit.* 8 The materials shall be ..well punned, rammed and beaten down. **1876** PREECE & SIVEWRIGHT *Telegraphy* 196 Too much stress cannot be laid upon good sound punning. The earth, as it is thrown in, should be thoroughly well punned at every stage. **1879** *Cassell's Techn. Educ.* II. 95 The material used for the puddle..should be carefully punned in thin layers so as to secure that no vacuities are left in any part.

b. To work *up* to a proper consistency with a punner.

1825 W. PARSONS in *Fowler Corr.* (*priv. printed* 1907) 534 Barrow lime mortar and washed sand made through a fine riddle and punned up to a proper consistency, using as little water as possible. (**1907** *Note*, Well worked up with a 'pun', a wooden implement something like a great pestle.)

Hence **'punning** *vbl. sb.*; also in comb. **'punning-block**, a mechanical rammer.

1838 SIMMS *Public Wks. Gt. Brit.* 33 The operation of punning or packing performed, until the brickwork is complete. **1876** PREECE & SIVEWRIGHT *Telegraphy* 190 No matter how well the punning and ramming may be done after the pole is planted,..a considerable time will always elapse before the earth settles back to its former condition.

‖**puna** ('puːnə). [Peruvian, in sense 1.]

1. A high bleak plateau in the Peruvian Andes; *spec.* (with capital initial) the table-land lying between the two great chains of the Cordilleras at an elevation of more than 10,500 feet.

1613 PURCHAS *Pilgrimage* VIII. i. (1614) 721 There are other Deserts in Peru, called Punas, where the Ayre cutteth off mans life without feeling. **1745** P. THOMAS *Jrnl. Anson's Voy.* 93 *Vicunnas*,..breeding..in cold and desert-Places, which they call *Punas*. **1860** GOSSE *Romance Nat. Hist.* 50 It snuffs the thin air..in those loftier ridges which the Peruvians term *punas*, where the elements appear to have concentrated all their sternness. **1885** J. BALL in *Jrnl. Linn. Soc.* XXII. 6, I am inclined to place the lower limit of the Alpine zone on the *puna* at about 12,000 feet.

2. Difficulty of breathing arising from a too rarefied atmosphere; mountain sickness.

1842 DUNGLISON *Med. Lex.*, *Puna*, a sickness common in the elevated districts of S. America. **1845** DARWIN *Voy. Nat.* xv. (1873) 322 The short breathing from the rarified atmosphere is called by the Chilenos 'puna'. **1903** *Longm. Mag.* July 218 José..was suffering from puna.

3. *Comb.* **'Puna-,wind**, a cold dry wind which blows from the Cordilleras across the Puna.

1890 in *Cent. Dict.*

puna, punahlite, var. POON *sb.*[1], POONAHLITE.

pu'naise, pu'nese. *Obs.* exc. as Fr. Forms: α. 6– **punaise** (pjuː'neɪz); also 6 **punayse**, 6–8 **punese** (pjuː'niːz), 7–8 **puneze, punice**, 8 **punaize**. β. 6–8 **punie**, 7 **puny, -ee** ('pjuːnɪ). [a. F. *punaise* (pynɛz) a bed-bug, prop. fem. of the adj. *punais* stinking, fetid. The form *punee, punie* arose as a false singular of *punese*: cf. *cherry, Chinee*.] A bed-bug. Also, with defining words, applied to other noxious insects.

α. **1515** BARCLAY *Egloges* iii. (1570) Bvj/2 Make thee readye..For lise, for fleas, punaises, mise and rattes. **1569** J. SANFORD tr. *Agrippa's Van. Artes* 138 Gnates, puneses, flies. **1578** LYTE *Dodoens* III. lx. 402 The leaues..driueth away the stinking punayses. **1601** HOLLAND *Pliny* II. 356 The said punices ought to be lapped in a reddish clout of a carnation colour. **1669** DAVENANT *Man's the Master* II. i, They sleep so soundly that Puneses cannot wake 'em. **1678** BUTLER *Hud.* III. I. 437 His Flea, his Morpion, and Punese, H' had gotten for his proper ease. **1712** COOKE *Voy. S. Sea* 61 Nor..will it so much as suffer any Punaises, or Bugs..to live. **1815** KIRBY & SP. *Entomol.* iv. (1818) I. 142 On dissecting the brain of a woman there were found in it abundance of vermicles and punaises.

β. **1598** FLORIO, *Cimici*, a kinde of vermin in Italie that.. biteth sore, called punies or wall-lise. **1601** HOLLAND *Pliny* II. XXIX. iv, Punies or wall lice, the most ill-favored and filthie vermine of all other, and which we loth and abhorre at the verie naming of them. **1657** W. COLES *Adam in Eden* clxvi, Called a wall-louse or puny in English. **1681** GREW *Musæum* I. VII. ii. 171 The Great Winged Punee. *Cimex sylvestris alatus major*. **1725** BRADLEY *Fam. Dict.* s.v. *Rasberry bush*, The Strawberry-Bushes are infested with Field-Punies.

‖**punalua** (puna'lua). *Anthrop.* [Hawaiian.] A relationship term formerly denoting spouses who shared a wife or husband and used by L. H. Morgan in his theory of the evolution of kinship systems for a form of group marriage, assumed by him to have replaced promiscuity and preceded exogamy, in which wives' sisters and husbands' brothers were considered spouses. Hence **puna'luan** *a.*

..**1860** L. ANDREWS in L. H. Morgan *Anc. Society* (1877) III. iii. 427 The relationship of pŭnalŭa is rather amphibious [*sic*]. It arose from the fact that two or more brothers with their wives or two or more sisters with their husbands, were inclined to possess each other in common. **1877** L. H. MORGAN *Anc. Society* III. iii. 424 The Punaluan family has existed in Europe, Asia, and America within the historical period. *Ibid.* 428 All the sisters of his wife, own as well as collateral, are also his wives. But the husband of his wife's sister he calls *pŭnalŭa*, i.e., his intimate companion. **1889** C. S. WAKE *Marriage & Kinship* ii. 23 The *punaluan* group can, as will be shown hereafter, be accounted for satisfactorily without assuming the prior existence of the consanguine family. **1915** *Amer. Anthrop.* XVII. 223 He does attribute the change from the older Malayan to the later and more common Turanian form of the system to punaluan marriage as a predecessor of the institution of exogamy and to exogamy itself. **1922** B. MALINOWSKI in *Nature* 22 Apr. 502/2 Starting from promiscuity, mankind went through group marriage, then the so-called consanguineous family or Punalua, then polygamy. **1940** WEST & TORR tr. *Engels's Origin of Family* (1942) ii. 39 The American system of consanguinity..finds, down to the smallest details, its.. natural foundation in the punaluan family. *Ibid.* 42 The origin of the matriarchal gens could be derived directly from the punaluan family. **1970** K. MILLETT *Sexual Politics* II. iii. 111 A succession of sexual associations: promiscuity, group marriage, the consanguineous family, the Punalua. *Ibid.* 120 The first course of social change as Engels had charted it was from consanguine group marriage, to the Punaluan consanguine group.

punamu, var. POUNAMU.

Punan (pjuː'nɑːn). Also 9 **Panam**. [Native name.] A group of Dyak peoples inhabiting parts of Borneo, mostly living nomadically in interior jungles; a member of this people.

1838 J. BROOKE *Lett.* (1853) I. 25 The Panams, a race little better than monkeys, who live in trees, eat without cooking, are hunted by the other tribes, and would seem to exist in the lowest conceivable grade of humanity. **1876** *Encycl. Brit.* IV. 58/1 The fifth and lowest [branch of Dyaks] comprises the Manketans and Punans, who are still nomadic and ignorant of agriculture. **1927** *Brit. Weekly* 19 May 154/1 A Punan will never wantonly slay or attack a man of another tribe. **1960** *Spectator* 28 Oct. 662 The..elementary Punan, these..being nomadic forest hunters [of Borneo]. **1964** T. HARRISSON in Wang Gungwu *Malaysia* III. xi. 164 The nearest thing to the Malayan aborigine in Borneo is the nomadic Punan.

‖**punatoo** (pʌnə'tuː). [Sinhalese.] The preserved pulp of the fruit of the palmyra palm, used as food.

1858 in SIMMONDS *Dict. Trade*.

punay, variant of PUNYE *Obs.*

†**punce**, obs. var. POUNCE *sb.*[1] 4.

1660 HEXHAM *Dutch Dict.*, *Brytel*, a Punce to engrave with.

punce, dial. var. POUNCE *sb.*[1] and *v.*[1]; obs. f. PUNCH *sb.*[1] 2 c; var. PUNSE *Obs.*, var. PULSE *sb.*[1]

punch (pʌnʃ), *sb.*[1] Also 5–6 **punche**, 6 **ponche**. [app. a collateral form of POUNCE *sb.*[1], used in certain senses, chiefly related to uses of PUNCH *v.*[1]; or shortened from PUNCHEON[1], with which it is synonymous in nearly every sense.]

†**1.** A dagger; = PUNCHEON[1] 1. *Obs. rare.*

c **1460** *Play Sacram.* 474 (*Stage direction*, Here shalle yᵉ iiij Iewys pryk yᵉʳ daggeris in iiij quarters yᵘˢ sayng)..Wᵗ thys punche I shalle hym pryke.

2. a. An instrument or tool for pricking, piercing, perforating, or making a hole in anything; esp. for making holes or cutting out pieces of a particular shape; also for enlarging a hole already made, driving a bolt, etc. out of a hole (*starting punch*), or forcing a nail beneath the surface after it has been driven (*driving punch*). The name is also extended from the simple instrument to an appliance or machine of which it forms the essential part.

A punch may be actuated by percussion or by pressure; and, according to its purpose, the working end may be sharp, pointed, blunt, or hollow with a cutting edge; a punch for cutting out pieces of a particular shape may also impress a design upon these, and thus combine senses 2 and 3.

1505 *Nottingham Rec.* III. 100, j. hamer de ferro; j. punche. **1523** FITZHERB. *Husb.* §139 To graffe bytwene the barke and the tree..thou must haue made redy a ponche of harde wode with a stoppe and a tenaunt on the one syde. **1543** *Richmond Wills* (Surtees) 43 Item v ponchys, one ponce with a stame iijᵈ. **1546** LANGLEY *Pol. Verg. De Invent.* III. x. 77 The Squire the Lyne the Shaue the Pricker or Punche were diuysed by Theodor a Samian. **1570** LEVINS *Manip.* 189/1 A Punche, *punctorium, pugio*. **1703** MOXON *Mech. Exerc.* 6 Drills are used for the making such Holes as Punches will not conveniently serve for. *Ibid.* 11 You must then make a Steel Punch to the size and shape of the hole you are to strike,..place the point of the Punch where the hole must be, and with the Hand-hammer..punch the hole. **1831** J. HOLLAND *Manuf. Metal* I. 214 The punch used in cutting nails consists of a cube of steel. **1833** *Ibid.* II. 340 Far from becoming brittle, it will yield to the blows of the hammer and to the punch, which is used to enlarge the holes. **1839** URE *Dict. Arts* 660 In each of these apertures, there is a punch for the purpose of piercing the cards, slips, or pasteboards with holes. **1865** H. PHILLIPS *Amer. Paper Curr.* II. 27 Taking care to cut by a circular punch of an inch diameter, a hole in each bill. **1886** J. M. CAULFEILD *Seamanship Notes* 8, 2 Punches, 1 Starting, 1 Driving.

b. Often with a prefixed defining word indicating (*a*) the user or use, as *conductor's punch, cooper's punch, hand punch, pinking punch, pipe-slotting punch*; or (*b*) the substance punched or the nature of the hole or impression made, as BELT, *buttonhole, eyelet, leather, nail, paper, rail, sheet-metal, ticket-, wad-, wadding-punch*. (But any of these, or of the following, may, when its kind is known from the context, be called simply 'punch'.) Also **bell-punch**, a conductor's or ticket punch having a signal-bell which announces the punching of a ticket; **centre** or **centering-punch**: see CENTRE *sb.* 19; **cold-punch**, a punch used for perforating cold metal; **duplex punch**, (*a*) a punch having a counter die on the opposite jaw; (*b*) one whose force is derived from the rolling action of two levers on a common fulcrum; **gang punch**, a number of punches arranged in a single stock; **hollow punch**, a hollow circular chisel-edged punch used for cutting smooth holes in yielding material; **rasp punch**: see RASP *sb.*[1] 5; **ratchet punch**, a screw punching machine operated by a lever, pawl, and ratchet-wheel; **sheriff's punch**, an instrument formerly used by sheriffs in some ancient cities and boroughs for punching a mark on a freeman's copy or certificate of freedom at the time when he recorded his vote; **spring punch**, a punch which is drawn back after each stroke by means of a spring.

1703 MOXON *Mech. Exerc.* 22 Smiths call all Punches they use upon cold Iron, Cold-Punches. **1875** KNIGHT *Dict. Mech.*, The hollow punch is employed to make holes for rivets in leather..and on other occasions where a smooth, round hole is to be cut out of a yielding material. **1892** GREENER *Breech-Loader* 50 Deeply-cut furrows and meaningless scratches, put on by the dozen with a shading-punch. **1900** *Westm. Gaz.* 18 May 5/2 Upon entering the flesh the front of the bullet acts like a wadding-punch.

c. *Surgery.* Formerly a instrument used for extracting the stumps of teeth. (Also, in 8 **punce**.) In mod. use, an instrument for removing a small piece of tissue from a patient.

1742 *Edin. Med. Ess.* V. I. 461 The Punce has much better Effect in pushing from within outwards than in the common Way it is employ'd to thrust the Roots of Teeth from without inwards. **1842** DUNGLISON *Med. Lex.*, *Punch*, a surgical instrument, used for extracting the stumps of teeth. [**1859** S. D. GROSS *Syst. Surg.* II. xi. 631 With a large, sharp saddler's punch the whole of the diseased structures..are then removed.] **1887** *Amer. Jrnl. Med. Sci.* XCIV. 279 (*heading*) The cutaneous punch. **1897** *Syd. Soc. Lex.*, *Punch*,..name for a now obsolete form of dental elevator. **1915** A. MACLENNAN *Surg. Materials & their Uses* vi. 220 It is almost impossible to get punches to cut clean, and a certain amount of tearing out of the uncut tissue must be expected. **1937** C. G. DARLINGTON in S. C. Miller *Oral Diagnosis & Treatment Planning* xxix. 496 Tissue forceps,.. scissors, skin or biopsy punch, may be employed, depending on the type and location of the lesion. **1957** G. L. W. BONNEY in Rob & Smith *Operative Surg.* V. 250 The impactor punch is shaped at one end so as to fit on to the convex outer surface of the femur. **1978** *Nature* 9 Mar. 171/2 Skin biopsies were taken from the upper back of 21–39-yr-old male volunteers with an electric biopsy punch 3 mm in diameter.

3. A tool or machine for impressing a design or stamping a die upon or into some material; in *Coining* and *Die-sinking*, a hardened steel cameo for forming a die; in *Type-founding*, a steel die having a letter cut in relief on its face, for making the intaglio impression in the copper matrix from which types are cast; in *Plastic Art*, a rod, handle, or wheel-rim having a figure or pattern upon it in relief for impressing a design on clay or any plastic material.

1628 in H. Walpole *Vertue's Anecd. Paint.* (1786) II. 81 Patternes for the punches and stampes for his majesties coyne in the mynt. **1638** in *Dom. St. Papers* CCCLXXII. Nos. 13 & 14 Cutting the Punches and Matrices belonginge to the Castinge of one sorte of letters. **1683** PETTUS *Fleta Min.* I. (1686) 97 Number and Mark every piece..with a small iron or steel Punch. **1688** R. HOLME *Armoury* III. xxi. (Roxb.) 264/2 He [Punchard] beareth vert, a Punch, or Letter Punch, Argent... These are steele on the end whereof the letters are cut so that they are punched into the Matrice. **1822** BEWICK *Mem.* 59 Crests on silver and seals of various kinds, for which I made all the new steel punches and letters. **1853** HUMPHREYS *Coin-Coll. Man.* iii. (1876) 27 The idea of making the punch itself the vehicle of an ornamental design, as well as the die, marks another epoch in the art [of coinage]. **1880** GROVE *Dict. Mus.* II. 436/2 [In printing music] zinc has been of late used instead of pewter: the punches make a clearer impression. **1892** *Labour Commission* Gloss. No. 3 *Punch*, the top half of the prints in which bolsters [of knives] are made. **1904** *Athenæum* 21 May 656/2 A passage from the 42-line (Mazarin) Bible is closely imitated by types cast in leaden matrices produced by punches of hardened lead, obtained..from wooden punches.

4. A mason's chipping tool; = PUNCHEON[1] 2 b. ? *U.S.*

1875 in KNIGHT *Dict. Mech.*

5. a. A post supporting the roof in a coal-mine: cf. *punch-prop* in 7. **b.** See quot. 1875. Cf. PUNCHEON[1] 4.

1462 *Anct. Deed B.* 3217 (P.R.O.) Cum idem Willelmus.. dederit eisdem.. omnia ligna sua boscum et subboscum.. pro *punches* et *proppes* faciendis. **1875** KNIGHT *Dict. Mech.* 1833/1 *Punch 5 Carpentry.* Studding used to support a roof.

6. *Hydraulic Engin.* A lengthening block or extension piece placed on a pile that has been driven too low to be reached by the ram; a dolly.

Evidently derived from the *driving-punch* in sense 2.

1875 in KNIGHT *Dict. Mech.*

7. *attrib.* and *Comb.*, as ***punch-cutter, -holder, -operator, -projector, -receiver; punch-struck*** adj.; **punch biopsy** *Med.*, a biopsy in which a punch is used to remove tissue; **punch card** = *punched card* s.v. PUNCHED *ppl. a.* 2; **punch forceps** *Surg.*, a punch consisting of two hinged parts like a forceps; **punch graft**, a graft of tissue removed (usu. from the scalp) by means of a surgical punch; so **punch grafting** *vbl. sb.*; **punch-mark**, a mark punched on metal, a coin, etc.; **punch-marked** *a.*, of a coin: bearing a punch-mark; **punch-plate**, see quot.; **punch-press**, a press designed to drive a punch for shaping metal; **punch-prop**, † **-rod**: see quots.; **punch-ticket** *U.S.*, a railway or other ticket that has been punched.

1941 *Amer. Jrnl. Clin. Path.* XI. 519 We have.. performed *punch biopsies upon the livers of normal rabbits. **1955** TWISS & OPPENHEIM *Pract. Managem. Disorders of Liver, Pancreas, & Bilian, Tract* xiv. 260 Punch biopsy of the liver can be used successfully to make an etiologic distinction between the different forms of cirrhosis. **1976** *Lancet* 11 Dec. 1281/2 Some would not agree that punch biopsies should be routinely used on the face. **1945** J. VON NEUMANN in B. Randell *Origins Digital Computers* (1973) 355 These instructions must be given in some form which the device can sense: Punched into a system of *punchcards [etc.]. **1971** K. GOTTSCHALK in B. de Ferranti *Living with Computer* iv. 37 The punch cards embodying the program were deemed a manner of manufacture and not patentable. **1977** *New Yorker* 29 Aug. 41/2 The production by the computer of punch-card decks representing the processed data. **1789** (*title*) A Specimen of Printing Types... By William Colman, Regulator, And Richard Austin, *Punch-Cutter. **1818** *Gentl. Mag.* LXXXVIII. II. 595/1 Types.. can be obtained by means of punch-cutters and letter-founders. **1896** T. L. DE VINNE *Moxon's Mech. Exerc., Printing* 403 The leading punch-cutter of his time. **1870** *Brit. Jrnl. Dental Sci.* XIII. 497 A *punch forceps for punching holes in the backing for flat teeth, the peculiarity of which lay in the fact, that by a spring interposed between the jaws the plate was liberated from the punch directly the jaws of the forceps were opened. **1958** J. H. OTTY in Rob & Smith *Operative Surg.* VIII. XVIII. 93 The antrum is opened by removing a chip of bone wide enough to insert a Hajek's punch forceps, with which the opening is enlarged to the size desired. **1959** *Ann. N.Y. Acad. Sci.* LXXXIII. 465 Of a total of 284 *punch grafts, only one of the punch grafts failed to take. **1968** *Plastic & Reconstruction Surg.* XLII. 446 (*heading*) Use of hair-bearing punch-grafts for partial traumatic losses of the scalp. **1976** *Daily Tel.* (Colour Suppl.) 2 July 8/4 Punch grafts require umpteen sessions and are followed by 12-week intervals of frustration before anything grows. *Ibid.* 7/3 Most bald men retain a permanent expanse of hair at the back and sides, and *punch grafting has shown that this hair survives even when transplanted into bald areas of the head. **1839** URE *Dict. Arts* 660 This plate *g*, shown also in section, is called the *punch-holder. **1853** HUMPHREYS *Coin-Coll. Man.* ii. (1876) 18 The back has a *punch mark in four rough compartments. **1879** H. PHILLIPS *Notes Coins* 1 The earliest of all known coins exhibit on the reverse only a shapeless punch-mark. **1888** HASLUCK *Model Engin. Handybk.* (1900) 90 A hole drilled through the point of intersection of these two scratches and through centre punch-mark on opposite side, will be both at right angles to the axis of, and exactly diametrically across the piston-rod. **1910** HASTINGS *Encycl. Relig. & Ethics* III. 706/1 On account of this chief characteristic, the term '*punch-marked' is commonly applied to this currency. **1960** H. HAYWARD *Antique Coll.* 230/1 *Punch-marked coins*, flat, square silver coins of India of the last few centuries B.C. Surfaces covered with small punch marks of natural objects, animals and symbols, probably the marks of merchants and states guaranteeing the pieces. **1961** *Evening Standard* 17 July 16/1 (Advt.), Data Processing Department. British Wool Marketing Board—Bradford. Immediate vacancies... *Punch operators. **1968** *Brit. Med. Bull.* XXIV. 191/1 The data sheets are handed to a punch operator who types out the information on a keyboard which has a punch attachment. **1834–6** BARLOW in *Encycl. Metrop.* (1845) VIII. 334/2 This *punch plate.. prepared for making a single row of holes, has a number of holes drilled in it in one line, at such distances apart as are suitable to the nature of the work to be executed. **1911** W. J. KAUP *Machine Shop Practice* xviii. 180 Fig. 162 shows a typical modern *punch press. **1935** O. W. BOSTON *Engin. Shop Practice* II. vi. 332 A punch press.. is a gap or overhung type of fast, short-stroke press particularly suited for punching dies. **1976** *National Observer* (U.S.) 5 June 7/1 When Nelson Amsdill gets off work as a punch-press operator, he heads for the Veterans of Foreign Wars Post 6691. **1839** URE *Dict. Arts* 660 These wires are called the *punch-projectors. **1851** GREENWELL *Coal-trade Terms Northumb. & Durh.* 40 **Punch-prop*, a short prop, set upon a crowntree or balk, where it does not support the middle of the roof, on account of the place having fallen before the timber was set. Also, a short prop, about 14 or 15 inches long, placed by a hewer under his sump or back-end, when he is under apprehension of its dropping down before he has got it kirved sufficiently far. **1688** R. HOLME *Armoury* III. 88/2 **Punch-rod*, is [a] With or Wreathen stick turned about the Head of a fire punch, to hold it on to the hot Iron. **1900** H. HART *Cent. Typogr. Oxf.* 141 Each of these sets consists of 24 *punch-struck matrices for Greek Alphabets, of which I have only cast.. example types of the alphas and omegas. **1887** C. B. GEORGE *40 Years on Rail* xi. 227 Many cases have been reported where in *punch-tickets the bits of pasteboard punched out have been saved and carefully glued in the old places. **1890** *Harper's Mag.* May 908/1 A person.. who by many punch-tickets builds up the fortunes of the stockholders.

punch (pʌnʃ), *sb.*[2] [f. PUNCH *v.*[1]] **1. a.** An act of punching; a straight or thrusting blow, in mod. usage generally one delivered with the fist; also (*obs.* or *dial.*) a kick; cf. POUNCE *sb.*[1] 7.

1580 HOLLYBAND *Treas. Fr. Tong., Horion*, a blow, as *je te bailleray vn tel horion que, &c.* I will giue thee such a punch, that, &c. **1687** A. LOVELL tr. *Thevenot's Trav.* I. 75 No sooner had he let go his Foot, but he gave him a punch on the Belly. **1760–72** H. BROOKE *Fool of Qual.* (1809) II. 18 [He] aimed a punch at Harry's stomach. **1818** SCOTT *Hrt. Midl.* xiii, By a punch on the ribs [he] conveyed to Rory Bean it was his rider's pleasure that he should forthwith proceed homewards. **1820** BYRON *Morg. Mag.* lxiv, He gave him such a punch upon the head. **1840** HOOD *Up Rhine* 47, I couldn't help making a punch at the fellow's head.

b. *transf.* and *fig.* Forceful, vigorous, or effective quality in an activity or in anything spoken or written; vigour, weight, effectiveness. orig. *U.S.*

1911 E. FERBER *Dawn O'Hara* xvii. 254 It lacks that peculiar and convincing quality poetically known as the punch. **1914** 'I. HAY' *Knight on Wheels* xvii. 162 The two clerks and the office-boy carried out their duties with what is known in trans-atlantic business circles as 'a punch'. **1919** H. L. WILSON *Ma Pettengill* ii. 64 A gripping drama replete with punch. *Ibid.* 75, I believe he now admits frankly that he wrote most of the play, or at least wrote the punch into it. **1921** D. W. JOHNSON *Battlefields of World War* xii. 535 The attack lost its 'punch'. **1926** *Glasgow Herald* 1 Apr. 5 They lack for the most part the quality of 'punch' which we have come to regard nowadays as one of the principal essentials in a magazine story. **1933** G. ARTHUR *Septuagenarian's Scrap Book* 307 Within a few days French, Americans and British were beginning a forward movement with the necessary 'punch' behind them of which the recent enemy assaults had been devoid. **1947** *E. African Ann.* 1946–7 98/2 (Advt.), Are you satisfied your advertisements have the necessary punch to get their message across? **1955** *Sci. News Let.* 27 Aug. 134/2 Radioiodine loses its punch within weeks. **1968** *Globe & Mail* (Toronto) 13 Jan. 41/8 Oakland Raiders' coach John Rauch said yesterday his team.. has the punch to score against the defensively rugged Packers. **1976** *Oadby & Wigston* (Leics.) *Advertiser* 26 Aug. 16/3 Chances were created but there was just no punch up front.

2. Phr. ***to beat*** (someone) ***to the punch***: of a boxer, to land a blow before his opponent can strike him; also *transf.*, to anticipate or forestall someone in speech or action. ***to pull one's punches***: see PULL *v.* 17b; ***to roll with the punches***: see ROLL *v.*[2] 22f.

1923 H. C. WITWER *Fighting Blood* vii. 226, I beat Hanley to the punch.. and he went down on his haunches. **1965** *Listener* 1 July 6/1 The tracking station at Plumeur Bodou is the place that so exultantly beat Britain to the punch in getting the first pictures from America via the satellite Telstar. **1977** *Sunday Times* 3 July 28/3, I feel a batsman uses it as he thinks he will beat a fast bowler to the punch.

3. *attrib.* and *Comb.*, as ***punch-packed*** adj.; ***punch-packing*** ppl. adj.; **punch-bag**, a stuffed bag suspended at a suitable height on which boxers practise punching; **punch-pull** *v. intr.*, to 'pull one's punches', to refrain from striking as hard as one can, or from expressing oneself forcefully; so **punch-pulling** *vbl. sb.*

1889 A. C. GUNTER *That Frenchman!* 8 Sling from the ceiling a punch-bag such as prize-fighters train with. **1899** *Science Siftings* 25 Mar. 329/2 A fifteen-minute controversy with an active punch-bag. **1927** *Daily Express* 20 July 9/7 His trainer.. ordered Dempsey not to box, but to use the punch bag and to shadow box. **1973** D. FRANCIS *Slay-Ride* ii. 25, I.. woke at seven feeling like Henry Cooper's punchbag. **1963** *Times* 25 Apr. 15/1 The year's most punch-packed novel. **1936** *Variety* 17 June 26 (Advt.), The punch-packing short short stories of the screen. **1961** *New Statesman* 23 June 1010/3 The Bishop taught him how to punch-pull on all outstanding emotional issues. **1959** *Listener* 29 Jan. 224/2 There was some good photography.. and a conclusion in which there was no punch-pulling.

punch (pʌnʃ), *sb.*[3] (Also 7 punce, paunch.) [Origin uncertain; stated by Fryer, who travelled in Western India 1672–81, to be the Marāṭhi (and Hindī) word *pānch* (Skr. *pañchan*, Pers. *panj*) five, from its five ingredients, which may show an explanation then current in the East: but see Note below. The name is evidenced as early as 1632. Beside it, in 17th c., foreign writers have a name with a second element apparently representing *punch* (Du. *palepunts, -ponts*, Ger. *palepunz, -bunze*, Fr. *bolle-, bouleponge*), which is not explained by any eastern lang., but which appears to be an imperfect (perh. originally native) echo of the Eng. 'bowl o' punch', a phrase already very common in the 17th century. Mod.Du. *pons, punch*, Ger., Da., Sw. *punsch*, Fr. *punch*, in 18th c. *ponche*, Sp., Pg. *ponche*, are all from Eng. See Note below.]

1. a. A beverage now generally composed of wine or spirits mixed with hot water or milk and flavoured with sugar, lemons, and some spice or cordial; but varying greatly in composition with time and place. Usually qualified by the name of a principal constituent, as ***arrack, brandy, claret, gin, milk, rum, tea, whisky, wine punch.***

How to mix Drinks (New York, 1862) describes 68 kinds.

1632 (Sept. 28) R. ADDAMS *Let. to T. Colley, Merchant at Pattapoli* (Ind. Off. Rec. O.C. 1449), I am very glad you have so good compani to be with all as Mr. Cartwright, I hop you will keep a good house together and drincke punch by no allowanc. **1658** PHILLIPS, *Punch*, a kind of Indian drink [1696 (ed. 5) *adds* made of Lime-Juice, Brandy, and other Ingredients]. **1662** EVELYN *Diary* 16 Jan., I accompanied the Duke to an East India vessell that lay at Blackwall, where we had entertainment... Amongst other spirituous drinks, as punch, etc. they gave us [etc.]. **1665** R. HEAD *Eng. Rogue* I. lxxv, Going into China-row, (a street so called in Bantam) to drink Punce and tea. *Ibid.*, I never came ashore, but I drank very immoderately of *Punce, Rack, Tea*, &c. which was brought up in great China-Jugs holding at least two Quarts. **1672** W. HUGHES *Amer. Phys.* 34 Rum.. is ordinarily drank amongst the Planters, as well alone, as made into Punch. **1679** LOCKE in Fox Bourne *Life* (1876) I. viii. 426 *note*, Punch, a compounded drink, (to be had) on board some West India Ships. **1683** W. HEDGES *Diary in Bengal* 8 Oct., Our owne people and mariners.. are now very numerous and (by reason of Punch) every day give disturbance. **1683** TRYON *Way to Health* 192 Their [seafaring men's] drinking of that Liquor called Punch is also very Inimical to Health; For the Lime-Juice, which is one of the Ingredients.., is in its Nature, fierce, sharp and Astringent, apt to create griping Pains in the Belly. **1694** SALMON *Bate's Dispens.* (1713) 589/1 Make a pleasant and grateful sort of Punch.. with the following quantities. ℞ Fair Water: Brandy A. a Quart: choice pure Lime-juice a Pint: double refined Sugar lb j. mix and dissolve, and if you so please, add one Nutmeg grated. **1698** FRYER *Acc. E. India & P.* 157 At Nerule is made the best Arach or Nepa de Goa, with which the English on this Coast make that enervating Liquor called *Paunch* (which is Indostan for Five) from Five Ingredients. **1719** DE FOE *Crusoe* I. 9 We went the old way of all Sailors, the Punch was made, and I was made drunk with it. **1725** N. ROBINSON *Th. Physick* 216 Punch... The Ingredients are Brandy, Rack, or Rum, Water warm or cold, Lemon-juice, Sugar, and sometimes a little Milk is added, which denotes it Milk-Punch. **1739** ELTON in Hanway *Trav.* (1762) I. I. v. 15 We treated them with punch till our brandy was expended. **1811** R. FENTON *Tour Quest Genealogy* 13 Punch, whose basis was strong green tea, richly inspissated with jellies.

b. In phr. ***bowl of punch.***

1658 T. ALDWORTH *Let. to T. Davies* in *W. Hedges' Diary* (Hakl. Soc.) III. App. 194 Your Company, which wee haue often remembered in a bowle of the cleerest punch, hauing noe better Liquor. **1671** KIRKMAN *Eng. Rogue* III. xxii, We had good sport over a bowl of Punch. **1675** TEONGE *Diary* (1825) 4 [On board the Ship *Assistance*.] I.. dranke part of 3 boules of punch, (a liquor very strainge to me). **1685** J. DUNTON *Lett. fr. New-Eng.* (1867) 14 That which was the most esteem'd by every one was a large Bowl of Punch, a Liquor of that Noble and Divine Original that all the Gods and Goddesses.. contributed to its Composition. **1751** R. PALTOCK *P. Wilkins* (1884) II. i. 6, I set a bowl of punch before them, made with my treacle and sour ram's-horn juice. **1761** *Brit. Mag.* II. 462 The captain.. promising to regale him with a bowl of rum punch in the kitchen. **1837** DICKENS *Pickw.* xxx, A bowl of punch was carried up.. and a grand carouse held in honour of his safety.

β. Foreign adaptations app. of *bowl o' punch.*

[**1653** BOULLAYE-LE-GOUZ *Voy. & Obs.* 516 Bolleponge est vn mot Anglois, qui signifie vne boisson dont les Anglois vsent aux Indes faite de sucre, suc de limon, eau de vie, fleur de muscade, & biscuit rosty.] **1662** J. DAVIES tr. *Mandelslo's Trav.* 18 [In 1638 at Surat] every man was at liberty.. to drink *Palepuntz*, which is a kind of drink consisting of Aquavitæ, Rose-water, juice of Citrons and Sugar. **1671** H. O. tr. *Bernier's Relat. Voy. in 1604* in *Voy. & Trav.* (1745) II. 241 Since that they have taken care.. that their people shall not drink so much *Bouleponges*. **1676** WORLIDGE *Cyder* i. §6 *Pale-puntz*, here [England] vulgarly known by the name of Punch; a Drink.. very usual amongst those that frequent the Sea, where a Bowl of Punch is an usual Beverage. **1684** J. MORRISON tr. *Struys' Voy.* xxxvi, There are many Strangers who destroy themselvs with drinking of a Liquor much in use there, called *Palepunshen*, being compounded of Arak, Sugar, and Raisins. [**1687** A. LOVELL tr. *Thevenot's Trav.* II. 96 The Francks use a Beverage there [in Persia], which they call a Bowl of Punch, and is cooling [*orig.* (1682) Les Francs y usent d'un breuvage qu'ils appellent Bolponze, qui rafraîchit].]

†**2.** Applied in Barbados to a drink fermented from sugar. *Obs.*

1657 R. LIGON *Barbadoes* 32 [Besides strong drinks made from potatoes, cassavie, and plantine] Punch is a fourth sort: and of that I have drunke: it is made of water and sugar put together: which in tenne dayes standing will be very strong. **1660** in HOWELL *Lex. Tetraglotton.*

3. With *a* and *pl.* **a.** A bowl or drink of punch. **b.** A party at which punch is drunk.

1682 N. O. *Boileau's Lutrin* II. 156 Brontin.. Bethought himself, A Punch of Nappy Liquor In a Cold Winters Night was no false Latine. **1864** SALA in *Daily Tel.* 6 Apr., There was a committee-room, which.. had been converted into a bar, and there the consumption of rum-punches was enormous. **1871** *Daily News* 5 Jan., One battalion invites another to what they call a punch. **1888** *Scott. Leader* 26 Oct. 3 A 'punch' was given at Cherbourg on Wednesday night in honour of the officers of the Russian fleet. **1901** W. CHURCHILL *Rich. Carvel* i, He mixed a punch or a posset as well as any one in our colony.

4. *attrib.* and *Comb.*, as ***punch-club, -glass, -kettle, -ladle, -maker, -pot, -room.*** See also PUNCH-BOWL, etc.

1807 E. S. BARRETT *Rising Sun* III. 125 The Premier armed himself with the punch-ladle. **1815** *Edin. Rev.* XXV. 230 Frequents punch-clubs too frequently. **1822** SCOTT *Pirate* xvii, A house.. where the punch-kettle is never allowed to cool. **1827** DRAKE & MANSFIELD *Cincinnati in 1826* iii. 30 A spacious gallery, with commodious lobbies, punch room, etc. **1841** *Southern Lit. Messenger* VII. 764/1 If you won't go home with me, you can take me down to the punch-room. **1849** THACKERAY *Pendennis* v, Was it the punch, or the punch-maker who intoxicated him? **1960** *Times* 16 Apr. 9/3 A punch-pot measured about 9 in. across its globular body. **1971** *Canadian Antiques Collector* Feb. 16/1 The Museum collection contains..a large and rare punch-pot, the cover with an attractive lemon knop.

Hence (*nonce-words*) ˈ**punchery** [after *brewery*, etc.], a place where punch is prepared; ˈ**punchifier**, a punch-maker; ˈ**punchless** *a.*, without punch; ˈ**punchy** *a.*, of the nature of punch.

1825 *Blackw. Mag.* XVII. 119, I have..made it a standing order, that the punch be made in the *punchery. **1952** *John o' London's* 1 Aug. 724/3 The eighteenth century had a forerunner of our home cocktail bar. This was the Georgian punchery, a magnificent assembly of..bowls, spice dredgers, crystal bottles..and a..punch ladle. **1962** *Times* 20 Jan. 11/3 Well-stocked puncheries magnificently displaying colourful punch bowls. **1824** *Ibid.* XV. 706 Our youthful friend is a promising *punchifier. **1821** *Ibid.* X. 562 Breakfastless, milkless, tealess, soupless, *punchless. **1843** DICKENS *To Felton* 2 Mar. *Lett.* (1880) III. 47 A complication of *punchy smells.

[*Note.* As to the origin of the name *punch*, Yule thought that 'there is something of Indian idiom in the suggestion of Fryer'. But there are serious difficulties. The word for 'five' in the Indian vernaculars, Hindī, Guzarātī, Marāṭhi, etc., is *pānch* (in Anglo-Indian formerly spelt *paunch*), while the drink has uniformly been *punch*, and was by Fryer spelt *paunch* app. only to support the alleged derivation. The combining form of *pānch*, however, is *panch-* with short *ă* (= Eng. *ŭ* in *but*), as in Hindī *panchāmrit* a mixture of five substances, *panchbhodra* a sauce of five ingredients, *panchgāvya* the five products of the cow, etc.; and it has been suggested that *punch* may have been short for some such compound, as, in fact, *panchāyăt* 'a council of five' has been colloquially shortened to *panch*, PUNCH *sb.*[6] But the history of English pronunciation shows that *punch* was in the early 17th c. pronounced not with the *u* in *punt*, but with the *u* in *pull, put*, as it still is in the north of England, and was by Dr. Johnson ('Who's for Poonsh?': see PUNCH-BOWL quot. 1791); which is confirmed by the 17th c. foreign renderings *punts, puntz, punsch*, etc. Now *punch*, so pronounced, does not represent either *pānch* or *panch* in Indian languages; which makes its origin from that source improbable. Moreover, the number of ingredients does not seem to have been at any time so fixed as to give origin to a name; some early writers give four, some only three, some six; since Fryer's time it has been usual to say 'five', but the fifth has been very variously specified. As several early passages show that punch was especially a seaman's drink, the Rev. C. B. Mount has suggested that the name originated not in India, but on the way thither, and may have been a sailors' shortening of *puncheon*, as that to which sailors would look for their allowance of liquor. See *N. & Q.* 10th s. IV. 401, 18 Nov. 1905, and subseq. articles to 27 Jan. 1906.]

punch (pʌnʃ), *sb.*[4] and *a.* Now chiefly *dial.* [Of uncertain origin. No words certainly related are found outside English.

It has been suggested that it is short for PUNCHEON[2]; cf. Bav. dial. *punzon* a cask, also a short thick person or thing (Wedgwood); also that it is connected with BUNCH. But as Pepys, in quots. 1669 in PUNCHINELLO 2, and in A here, records the use of both *Punchinello* and *Punch* as appellations for a short and thick person or thing, it is highly probable that *Punch* in this sense, as well as in the next word, was in its origin short for PUNCHINELLO. As it is not certain whether the sb. or adj. was the original, the senses are here arranged chronologically, on the hypothesis that the adj. B was an attrib. use of the sb. A, and that an elliptical use of the adj. gave rise to the much later sb. C.]

A. *sb.* A name for a short fat man, or for anything short and thick. Cf. PUNCHINELLO 2. ? *Obs.*

1669 PEPYS *Diary* 30 Apr., Staying among poor people there in the ally, did hear them call their fat child Punch; which pleased me mightily, that word being become a word of common use for all that is thick and short. *a* **1700** B. E. *Dict. Cant. Crew, Punch*, a thick short Man. **1836** T. D. FOSBROKE in *Gentl. Mag.* Mar. 241/2 A juvenile figure of the best height, 5 f. 10 inch.; taller or shorter men being generally ill-made, knock-kneed, or Punches.

B. *adj.* Short and thick, stout. Now only *dial.*

Said esp. of horses, and so leading to use in C.

1679 *Lond. Gaz.* No. 1418/4 Taken away from two Grooms on Monday,..a little gray punch Stoned Horse, hath all his paces,..about 14 hands. **1680** *Ibid.* No. 1476/4 A strong punch Nag, with a star, trots all. **1702** *Ibid.* No. 3855/4 He is a short punch Man. **1728** CHAMBERS *Cycl.* s.v., In the Manage, a Punch Horse, is a well-set, well-knit Horse; short-back'd, and thick-shoulder'd, with a broad Neck, and well lined with Flesh. **1820** W. IRVING *Sketch Bk.* (1859) 195 Garrick..was..'a short punch man, very lively and bustling'. **1828** *Craven Gloss.* (ed. 2), *Punch*, short, fat.

C. *sb.* One of a breed of heavy draught horses (in full ***Suffolk Punches***), characterized by a short and very thick-set body and neck, and short legs.

1813 *Sporting Mag.* XLI. 37 The breed of horses, denominated Suffolk Punches. **1831** YOUATT *The Horse* 38 The Suffolk Punch, so called from his round punchy make. *Ibid.* 39 The Punch is not what he was. **1852** *P. Parley's Ann.* 261 Riding..not on hunters or blood mares, but on sturdy Suffolk punches.

Hence †**punch'd**, †ˈ**punching**, †ˈ**punchion** *adjs.*, of horses = PUNCH *a.*: see B. above. *Obs.*

1703 *Lond. Gaz.* No. 3881/4 A thick punching Horse between 5 and 6 years old. *Ibid.* No. 3959/4 A bright bay Nag,..short Punch'd, well Barrell'd. **1709** *Ibid.* No. 4523/4 Stoln..,a bright Bay Nag, near 14 hands high, a very strong Punchion Horse.

Punch (pʌnʃ), *sb.*[5] [Short for PUNCHINELLO.]

1. a. The name of the principal character, a grotesque hump-backed figure, in the puppet-show called Punch and Judy. (The name *Judy* for 'Punch's wife' appears to be later.) Also *attrib.* in ***Punch and Judy show***, etc.: see also 3; *ellipt.*, = ***Punch and Judy show***.

1709 STEELE *Tatler* No. 16 ¶2 When we came to Noah's Flood in the Show, Punch and his Wife were introduced dancing in the Ark. *Ibid.* No. 44 ¶5 He makes a prophane lewd Jester, whom he calls Punch, speak to the Dishonour of Isaac Bickerstaff. **1733** SWIFT *On Poetry* Wks. 1755 IV. I. 193 Some fam'd for numbers soft and smooth, By lovers spoke in punch's booth. *a* **1790** in Hone *Every Day Bk.* II. 504 Can't you see by my hunch, sir,..I am master Punch, sir. **1818** SCOTT *Br. Lamm.* i, Remaining behind the curtain unseen, like the ingenious manager of Punch and his wife Joan. **1825** C. M. WESTMACOTT *English Spy* II. 65 Old Punch with his Judy. **1828** [J. P. COLLIER] (*title*) Punch and Judy... Accompanied by the Dialogue of the Puppet-show [etc.]. **1841** C. FOX *Jrnl.* 18 Feb. (1972) 102 He..teaches us that Punch and Judy men, beggar children and daft old men are also of our species. **1857** C. KINGSLEY *Two Years Ago* I. p. xviii, Those poor idolaters, and their Punch and Judy plays. **1864** [see FAIR *sb.*[1] 1 a]. **1871** B. TAYLOR *Faust* (1875) I. i. 25 At the best a Punch and Judy play. **1876** BESANT & RICE *Gold. Butterfly* xi, There were picturesque beggars, Punch-and-Judy shows. **1886** C. E. PASCOE *London of To-day* xix. (ed. 3) 192 Ramsgate 'sands'..a rendezvous of Punch and Judy men, nigger minstrels, donkey-drivers, and the like.

b. In allusive phrases, e.g. ***as pleased, proud***, etc. ***as Punch***.

1813 MOORE *Let. to Lady Donegal* in *Diary* VIII. 137, I was (as the poet says) as pleased as Punch. **1818** —— *Fudge Fam. Paris* ii. 78 While Saxony's as pleased as Punch. *Ibid.* vi. 82 Give me the useful peaching Rat; Not things as mute as Punch, when bought. **1841** C. BRONTË *Let.* 4 May in C. K. Shorter *C. Brontë & her Circle* (1896) iii. 87 Mrs. White would be as proud as Punch to show it you. **1850** DICKENS *Dav. Copp.* li. 520, I am as proud as Punch to think that I once had the honor of being connected with your family. **1873** LOWELL *Lett.* (1894) II. 102, I am as pleased as Punch at the thought of having a kind of denizenship, if nothing more, at Oxford. **1888** G. B. SHAW *Let.* 20 Sept. (1965) I. 200 Headlam read out about all the gold and silver in the palace,..and the Bishop looked as proud as Punch of owning it all. **1889** GRETTON *Memory's Harkb.* 287, I was proud as Punch, for then I was trusted..to ride a journey by my own little self.

c. ***Punch's voice*** [F. *voix de Polichinelle*]: see quot.

1894 GOULD *Dict. Med.* etc. *Sci., Punch's Voice*, a peculiar bell-like, or ringing tone of voice, like that assumed by Punch in the Punch and Judy shows. It is sometimes heard among the insane, and has [etc.].

2. The title of a well-known comic weekly journal, published in London, of which 'Mr. Punch' is the assumed editor. Also *attrib.*

1841 (July 17) (*title*) Punch, or the London Charivari. **1856** WHYTE MELVILLE *Kate Cov.* viii, She with her knitting and I with the last Punch. **1856** *Men of the Time* 543 One of his younger brothers..is on the 'Punch' staff.

3. *Comb.*: **punch-man**, the owner or operator of a **punch-show**, or Punch and Judy show.

1861 MAYHEW *Lond. Labour* III. 47 'How are you getting on?' I might say to another Punchman. **1866** HOWELLS *Venet. Life* v, Little punch-shows on the Riva.

‖**punch** (pʌntʃ), *sb.*[6] *East Indies.* Short for PANCHAYAT; a council of five persons.

1862 BEVERIDGE *Hist. India* III. VIII. vii. 487 All real power was usurped by the army, who exercised it by means of delegates called punches. **1864** C. W. KING *Gnostics* 199 In our times, with the Sikhs, to hold a Punch, or council of five was the formal mode of deliberating. **1867** J. C. MARSHMAN *Mem. Havelock* (1890) IV. 145 Their movements were regulated by punches or councils of five.

punch *a.*: see PUNCH *sb.*[4]

punch (pʌnʃ), *v.*[1] Also 4–6 punche, 5–6 pounch, 6 ponch(e, 7 punsh, *Sc.* punsche. [app. a collateral form of POUNCE *v.*[1]; cf. the two forms *ponson* (or *punson*) and *punchon* in PUNCHEON[1]. Perhaps also regarded as a by-form of PUNGE *v.*]

I. † **1. a.** *trans.* To stab, prick, puncture with or as with a pointed instrument; = POUNCE *v.*[1] 6. *Obs.*

c **1440** *Promp. Parv.* 416/1 Punchyn, idem quod prykkyn. **1535** *Trevisa's Barth. De P.R.* IV. x. 31/2 A hote fume, that poncheth [*ed.* **1582** puncheth, L. *pungente*] and nyppeth the senowes of the stomake. **1621** MOLLE *Camerar. Liv. Libr.* V. vii. 346 That they might punch him with bodkins. **1664** POWER *Exp. Philos.* I. 2 A Proboscis..by which he [the flea] both punches the skin, and sucks the blood through it.

†**b.** *fig.* To pierce, prick (the heart, conscience, etc.). *Obs.*

a **1548** HALL *Chron., Hen. VII* 57 Euer punched, stimulated and pricked with the scrupulous stynges of domesticall sedicion and ciuile commocion. **1548** UDALL, etc. *Erasm. Par. Acts* ii. 13 The same sweorde..whose edge hath punched and stricken the Jewes hertes. **1602** MARSTON *Antonio's Rev.* I. v, Does thy hart With punching anguish spur thy galled ribs?

2. a. To poke or prod, esp. with a stick or other blunt implement. Now esp. in N. Amer. use, To drive cattle (by prodding them on). Also *absol.*

1382 WYCLIF *Ezek.* xxxiv. 21 For that that ȝe punchiden [1388 hurliden, Vulg. *impingebatis*] with sydis, and shuldris, and with ȝour hornis wynewiden alle seek beestis. **1542** UDALL *Erasm. Apoph.* I. cxxvii, Diogenes..beholding a young springal as he slept.., he pounched the same with his staffe. **1596** SPENSER *F.Q.* VI. ii. 22 Pounching me with the butt end of his speare. *c* **1611** CHAPMAN *Iliad* VI. 126 With a goad he punch'd each furious dame. **1691** LUTTRELL *Brief Rel.* (1857) II. 313, 2 other lords [were] puncht with the butt ends of muskets. **1833** J. A. ROEBUCK *Sp. Ho. Comm.* 13 June, The police..punched with their staves, women [etc.]. **1871** B. TAYLOR *Faust* (1875) I. ii. 40 He..with his elbow punched the maid. **1872** C. D. WARNER *Backlog Studies* 21 (U.S.) It is time to punch the backlog and put on a new forestick. **1885** *Nor' Wester* (Calgary, Alta.) 12 Feb. 3/2 It would pay the stockmen to keep men out during the winter to punch the cattle out of the brush during fine weather. **1886** KENDALL *Poems* 207 At punching oxen, you may guess There's nothing out can 'camp' him. **1890** *Stock Grower & Farmer* (Las Vegas, New Mexico) 21 June 4/1 J. O. Phillips ..will be initiated into the business of punching cattle. **1894** *Home Missionary* (N.Y.) June 68 In the end of each stick is a sharp iron spike, with which they punch the beasts and force them into the cars. Hence the cowboy is sometimes called the 'cow-puncher'. **1906** *McClure's Mag.* May 64/1 About ten year ago I got plumb sick of punchin' cows around my part of the country. **1910** W. M. RAINE *B. O'Connor* 30 We used to punch together on the Hashknife. **1923** 'B. M. BOWER' *Parowan Bonanza* xviii. 276 In that case ..you'd still be punchin' cows for your dad, most likely. **1946** F. D. DAVISON *Dusty* Forewd., Tailing tame old milkers into the farmyard,..punching stubborn bullocks through the mulga.

b. To put *out*, or stir *up* by punching or poking.

1863 COWDEN CLARKE *Shaks. Char.* vii. 189 To punch out the eyes of an adversary. **1867** F. H. LUDLOW *Brace of Boys* 275 They became galvanically active the moment they were punched up, and fell flat the moment the punching was remitted. **1872** HOWELLS *Wedd. Journ.* (1892) 281 A.. beadle..punched up a kneeling peasant.

3. a. To deliver a sharp blow or forward thrust at; *esp.* to strike with the closed fist; to beat, thump. Phr. ***to punch the ball***: to take exercise with the punching-ball. ***to punch out***: to knock out, to beat up (*U.S.*).

1530 PALSGR. 670/2, I punche, *je boulle, je pousse*... Whye punchest thou me with thy fyste on this facyon: *pour quoy me boulles tu, or pour quoy me pousses tu de ton poyng en ce poynt?* [Cf. *Ibid.* 472/2, I bunche, I beate, *je pousse*. He buncheth me and beateth me: *il me pousse et me bat*.] **1627** in Rushw. *Hist. Coll.* (1721) III. II. ii. App. 11 The Defendants.. kick'd and punch'd the Plaintiff's Wife. *a* **1690** G. FOX *Jrnl.* (1827) I. 166 They rudely haled me out, and struck and punched me. **1823** W. S. ROSE tr. *Ariosto* VI. lxv, Now grappl'd from behind, now punch'd before, He stands and plies the crowd with warfare sore. **1837** DICKENS *Pickw.* vi, A fourth was busily engaged in patting and punching the pillows..arranged for her support. *Ibid.* xix, [He] eased his mind by punching the head of the inventive youth. **1889** JESSOPP *Coming of Friars* v. 233 Punching their opponents on the nose. **1892** *Daily News* 14 Mar. 3/2 During the early morning walking and punching the ball occupied the attention of the crew. **1920** *Isis* 5 May 9/2 He will get runs, and in the getting of them the ball will be 'punched' very hard. **1929** W. FAULKNER *Sartoris* IV. 301 She put coal on it and punched it to a blaze. **1968** [see BUNT *sb.*[8] 2]. **1969** *New Yorker* 14 June 44/3 The orthodox way to hit a volley is to punch it, with a backswing so short that it begins in front of the player's body. **1971** *Current Slang* (Univ. S. Dakota) VI. 8 *Punch out*, to beat up; to fight physically. **1976** *National Observer* (U.S.) 12 June 19/2 Young blacks and Puerto Ricans..punched out Moonies who tried to restrain them. **1977** *Detroit Free Press* 11 Dec. 2-D/2 Abdul-Jabbar,.. broke his own hand punching out Milwaukee's Kent Benson in the season opener. **1977** RECHIN & PARKER *Crock* 48 One more smart remark about my nose and I'm punching you out.

b. To strike with the foot; to kick; = BUNCH *v.*[1] b. *north. dial.*

Cf. Sc. *punce*, to strike or thrust with the sole of the foot, not to kick with the toe: said of a person in bed, or a child in the lap; see POUNCE *v.*[1] 4.

1538 [see PUNCHING *vbl. sb.*]. **1781** J. HUTTON *Tour to Caves* (ed. 2) Gloss., *Punch*, to kick or strike with the foot. **1828** *Craven Gloss.* (ed. 2), *Punch*, to kick with the feet, not with the fist, as explained by Dr. Johnson. **1889** WESTALL *Birch Dene* II. ii. 15 If he ever comes to Birch Dene he'll get his shins punched.

c. ***to punch up***: to assault, beat up (cf. PUNCH-UP); also *fig.* in *Cinematogr.* (see quots. 1953, 1959).

1953 BERREY & VAN DEN BARK *Amer. Thes. Slang* (1954) §623a/8 Punch up one and fade it down, get the picture ready for fading up, as in an opening shot. **1959** W. S. SHARPS *Dict. Cinemat.* 121/2 *Punch up*. In acting, this is to add emphasis to a phrase or action. In filming, the term means to increase picture brightness, and in recording, to bring in a new sound, or to increase the volume or pitch of an existing sound. **1963** *Listener* 31 Jan. 202/1 The folknicks in Washington Square when they punch up the police of a Sunday afternoon.

d. ***to punch the*** or ***a clock***: to clock in or out; so ***to punch in***.

1927 *Sunday Express* 8 May 10 Costello flatly refused to 'punch the clock', and had definite ideas about what he would and would not do in connection with his art. **1943** J. B. PRIESTLEY *Daylight on Saturday* i. 2 What happens when you have shown your pass and punched the time-clock? **1944** G. FARWELL in *Coast to Coast 1943* 116 Yesterday I was late punching in. They'll be docking me. **1969** D. CLARK *Nobody's Perfect* iii. 103 We're soft-hearted in the way we treat our staff. Nobody has to punch a clock. **1978** S. BRILL *Teamsters* vii. 292 At the terminal Barkett punched in.

e. To press (a push-button); to operate, switch *on*, or tune *in* (a device) by doing this.

1954 W. TUCKER *Wild Talent* xiv. 211 The man punched the elevator button. **1971** 'R. MACDONALD' *Underground Man* x. 61, I punched on the car radio. It was tuned to a local station. **1972** M. KAYE *Lively Game of Death* (1974) vii. 40 Scott punched the intercom and asked to speak with Lasker. **1975** *Gramophone* Sept. 531/1 The user can also punch in any desired FM station frequency and scan for just stereo stations. **1977** *Guardian Weekly* 25 Sept. 19/2 The launch controller punched the destruction button and the rocket with its payload was automatically destroyed.

II. 4. a. To pierce or cut (anything) in the manner of a punch (see PUNCH *sb.*[1] 2) so as to make a hole or holes in or through it; to perforate or make holes in (a plate of metal, a sheet of cloth or paper, etc.). Cf. KEYPUNCH *v.* 1 a.

1594 SHAKS. *Rich. III*, v. iii. 125 My Annointed body By thee was punched full of holes. **1695** J. EDWARDS *Perfect. Script.* 248 To punch the lap of the ear, and to hang some ornament there. **1713** J. WARDER *True Amazons* (ed. 2) 126 A piece of Tin Plate punched full of Holes. **1846** GREENER *Sc. Gunnery* 271, 1-8th plate was easily punched by a charge of two and a half drachms coarse or three drachms fine. *a* **1909** *Mod.* A railway official came to punch our tickets. **1939** J. BERRYMAN in K. Amis *Spectrum* (1961) 167 With a rattle and a whir the calculators punched and sorted the cards. **1964** F. L. WESTWATER *Electronic Computers* vi. 98 The cards have to be punched by hand from information on original documents. **1971** *Daily Tel.* 3 May 2/6 It lights up a wall map, serves a memory bank, punches a tape for computer use and produces a copy in type for control room operators. **1974** J. BANNING *How I fooled World* ii. 13 When I..had to punch tape myself, the computer in London often rejected my copy.

b. With the hole or perforation as object.

1677 MOXON *Mech. Exerc.* i. 7 A piece of..Iron hath an hole punched a little way into it. *Ibid.* 12 With the Hand-hammer..punch the hole. **1832** BABBAGE *Econ. Manuf.* ii. (ed. 3) 22 The method of punching holes in iron plates. **1868** G. STEPHENS *Runic Mon.* I. 183 All these scorings would seem to have been puncht with a sharp tool. **1876** PREECE & SIVEWRIGHT *Telegraphy* 132 The messages are punched and transmitted in batches of five or six.

c. = KEYPUNCH *v.* 1 b (see quots.).

1864 C. BABBAGE *Passages from Life of Philosopher* viii. 119 The Tables to be used must..be computed and punched on cards by the machine. **1890** *Jrnl. Franklin Inst.* CXXIX. 301 In order to punch the individual records upon the cards, they are placed one by one in a suitable punching machine. **1900** *Daily News* 3 Aug. 4/6 The message is previously 'punched' out on a paper ribbon, and once the ribbon is placed on the transmitting machine the message reproduces itself at the receiving office at great speed on another ribbon there. **1901** H. McHUGH *John Henry* 79 I've just punched out a parcel of paragraphs which I shall turn in to Tommy. **1946** *N.Y. Times* 15 Feb. 16/3 When the problem is punched on the cards, they are dropped into a slot in a 'reader'. **1952** *Sci. Amer.* Sept. 112/3 The instructions..are punched in the paper tape by a special typewriter keyboard. **1968** *Brit. Med. Bull.* XXIV. 247/1 Use of the program achieves a very considerable saving in effort, which would be further enhanced if..observations of turnover diameter were punched directly on to tape at the time of measurement. **1971** H. LOVE in R. A. Wisbey *Computer in Lit. & Ling. Research* 51, I must not pass over his method of proofreading input, which is to have the text punched-up by two different operators and then use the computer to spot discrepancies.

d. To take *out* (a piece) by punching.

1827 FARADAY *Chem. Manip.* xv. 358 They are..punched out of boot or shoe leather. **1834–6** BARLOW in *Encycl. Metrop.* (1845) VIII. 333/2 In some cases the part punched out is the object in view, as in cutting the blanks for coin, buttons, &c. **1977** *Lancet* 26 Nov. 1140/2 Two 3 mm diameter discs are punched out from the filterpaper, one for testing and the other as a control.

5. *intr.* To penetrate, pierce, cut (as a punch).

1683 MOXON *Mech. Exerc., Printing* xiii. ¶1 To manage and command it while it is Punching into the Copper. **1865** *Athenæum* No. 1974. 270/3 In 'punching' through the armour of an ironclad.

6. *to punch out* (*Aeronaut.*): see quots. *slang.*

1968–70 *Current Slang* (Univ. S. Dakota) III–IV. 98 *Punch out, v.* To eject from an aircraft. **1974** *Sunday Times* 16 June 13/2 It never occurred to me to 'punch out' (eject).

punch, *v.*[2] *colloq. rare*⁻¹. [f. PUNCH *sb.*[3]] *intr.* To drink punch.

1804 COLERIDGE in *Lit. Rem.* (1836) II. 412, I dined and punched at Lamb's.

punch, *v.*[3], obs. form of PUNISH *v.*

ˈpunchable, *a.* [f. PUNCH *v.*[1] + -ABLE.] Capable of being punched: †*spec.* of coin.

(Act 7 & 8 Will. & M. c. 1 for improving the coinage enacted in §9 that hammered coins at the time in circulation and not damaged by clipping should be 'struck through.. with a solid Punch' before being passed further in circulation, as a means of preventing clipping: to this regulation the quots. refer.)

1696 *Lond. Gaz.* No. 3236/4 They will..take in Payment Old Hammer'd Money that is Punchable. **1696** LUTTRELL *Brief Rel.* (1857) IV. 60 An information against some goldsmiths in Lumbard street for offering clipt money not punchable since 4th of May. *a* **1700** B. E. *Dict. Cant. Crew, Punchable*, old passable Money.

punchayet, variant of PANCHAYAT.

ˈpunch-ball. [PUNCH *sb.*[2]] **1.** A stuffed or inflated ball suspended at a suitable height for practice punching by boxers. Also *fig.*

1901 *Humane Rev.* II. 218 There would be a large gymnasium with all sorts of appliances, *e.g.*, the punch-ball. **1910** *Cycling* 12 Jan. p. xxi/3 (Advt.), Punch-ball, 10s, cost double. **1927** *Daily Express* 22 June 17/5 He is developing his punch in secret, and..he has broken three punch-balls. **1932** *Pictorial Weekly* 12 Mar. 185/2 In the centre a player is using the punch-ball. **1963** *Times* 13 Mar. 12/5 The Home Office has always been something of a punchball for Mr. Sidney Silverman. **1973** M. AMIS *Rachel Papers* 13 Her buttocks, when she wore stretch-slacks, would dance behind her knees like punch-balls. **1977** *Time* 3 Oct. 50/2 Among the principals: the incomparable Lizzie, a daydreamy beautiful loser, 'punchball' for many lovers, whose flaws prove even more compelling than her easy virtue.

2. *U.S.* A ball-game (see quot. 1932).

1932 *Jrnl. Health & Physical Educ.* May 48/2 *Punch Ball.* .. The Youngstown, Ohio, playgrounds have promoted a new game... There are fifteen players on a side. A tightly blown rubber ball the size of a basketball is kicked, punched with the fist, or butted with the head as in soccer. **1935** C. F. WARE *Greenwich Village* v. 144 The district abounded in block teams..who played the ubiquitous game of punchball. **1976** *Washington Post* 28 July c6/3 Some of the games we played were called stickball and stoop baseball and punchball.

ˈpunch board. *N. Amer.* Also with hyphen and as one word. [PUNCH *sb.*[2]] **a.** A board perforated with holes containing slips of paper which are 'punched' out as a form of gambling, with the object of locating a winning slip.

1912 J. P. QUINN *Gambling & Gambling Devices* 231 (*caption*) Punch board. **1935** J. STEINBECK *Tortilla Flat* xvii. 315 Tito Ralph came in with a box of cigars he had won on a punch board. **1939** *Sun* (Baltimore) 12 Sept. 7/4 The worst form of petty gambling seems to be confined to punch boards. **1949** *Democrat* 15 Dec. 4/1 We would like to amend his paragraph to include punch boards. **1951** *Manch. Guardian Weekly* 15 Mar. 10/4 The sale of punch-boards (gambling machines) was running at about $100 millions a year. **1966** *Times* 28 Feb. (Canada Suppl.) p. x/4 Any dice game, three-card monte, punch board. **1978** *Rugby World* Apr. 50 (Advt.), Now available New Lakeland (tamper proof)..Football cards & Punchboards.

b. *fig.* A promiscuous woman.

1963 *Amer. Speech* XXXVIII. 173 A female who is dated because of her lax sexual habits..*punch*... The word *punch* may well be a shortened form of *punchboard*, which was recorded twice. **1970** G. GREER *Female Eunuch* 267 Girls who pride themselves on their monogamous instincts.. speak of the 'campus punchboard'. **1977** J. WAMBAUGH *Black Marble* (1978) iii. 23 There's one woman handler, named Wilma. A punchboard. What the hell, she's a little dumpy, but when you been looking at dogs all day.

ˈpunch-bowl. [f. PUNCH *sb.*[3] + BOWL *sb.*[1]]

1. A bowl in which the ingredients of punch are mixed, and from which it is served with a ladle.

1692 LUTTRELL *Brief Rel.* (1857) II. 624 Subscriptions are making in the city for a gold punch bowle of good value, to be presented to admirall Russell. **1716** B. CHURCH *Hist. Philip's War* (1865) I. 134 A Valley, in form of something shap'd like a Punch-bole. **1791** BOSWELL *Johnson* an. 1776, 23 Mar., Garrick sometimes used to take him [Johnson] off, squeezing a lemon into a punch-bowl, with uncouth gesticulations, looking round the company, and crying 'Who's for Poonsh?' **1881** BESANT & RICE *Chapl. of Fleet* I. viii, They..get what pleasure they can out of a punch-bowl.

2. *attrib.* Resembling a punch-bowl. Hence *sb.* (*a*) A round deep hollow between hills or in a hillside: cf. BOWL *sb.*[1] 3 c. †(*b*) A kind of wide river-boat.

1855 J. R. LEIFCHILD *Cornwall Mines* 27 The whole business is confined to the interior of the punch-bowl hollow. **1869** E. A. PARKES *Pract. Hygiene* (ed. 3) 289 Among hills, the unhealthy spots are enclosed valleys, punch-bowls. **1902** *Words of Eyewitness* 251 On the high ridges..more Boers,..scanning the punchbowl below them with field-glasses. **1870** DASENT *Annals* I. xii. 140 Then there was the water, and the funnies, cutters, wherries, punchbowls, and half-deckers that thronged the river daily.

punch'd, *a.* (of a horse): see PUNCH *sb.*[4]

ˈpunch-drunk, *a.* and *sb.* orig. *U.S.* [f. PUNCH *sb.*[2] + DRUNK *ppl. a.* and *sb.*[2]] **A.** *adj.* Of a boxer or one involved in physical fighting: dazed or stupefied from severe or continual punching; *spec.* exhibiting reduced muscular co-ordination, hesitant speech, slowness of thought, and other signs. Also *fig.*

1918 *Sat. Even. Post* 18 May 12/3 He was in the condition so aptly described as 'punch drunk'. **1927** *Daily Express* 29 July 1, I replied that in my opinion Moore was 'punch-drunk', that is to say that he had taken so much punishment that he could no longer feel it, and his nerves were practically gone. **1934** *Sun* (Baltimore) 2 Mar. 12/7, I am delegated to remind all who may be punch-drunk with winter that the famous Blizzard of Eighty-eight occurred on March 12. **1937** *Daily Mirror* 2 Mar. 12/4 Nowadays the Kid is punch-drunk. His limbs tremble and quiver like a man stricken with ague. His voice is so slurred that one cannot properly understand what he is saying. **1947** *Penguin New Writing* XXX. 126 A film which has been praised by critics who should certainly know better, unless they have themselves become punch-drunk with watching the hallucinated antics of the slap-happy puppets on the screen. **1952** C. DAY LEWIS tr. *Virgil's Aeneid* v. 105 So he called an end to the bout, saving the punch-drunk Dares From further punishment. **1954** J. STEINBECK *Sweet Thursday* 215 Doc's setting over there like he's punch-drunk. **1958** *Times Lit. Suppl.* 5 Sept. 497/3 In this punch-drunk civilization it is perverse to expect me to take seriously the horse itself, or indeed Mr. Kirkup's gracious swan, or Mr. Trypanis's seasick cock. **1959** N. MAILER *Advts. for Myself* (1961) 21, I seem to have turned into a slightly punch-drunk and ugly club fighter. **1974** 'A. GARVE' *File on Lester* xxxvi. 129 The papers are terrible this morning... I'm feeling punch drunk and hardly capable of rational thought. **1974** E. BRAWLEY *Rap* (1975) I. i. 31 You and me know he's so..punch-drunk he'd do anything anybody told him.

B. *sb.* One who is punch-drunk (usu. in literal use).

In quot. 1928 used as the name of the condition.

1928 *Jrnl. Amer. Med. Assoc.* 13 Oct. 1103/1 The early symptoms of punch drunk usually appear in the extremities. **1943** *Gen* 16 Jan. 30/2 Your out-and-out punch-drunk is harmless rather than homicidal. **1966** 'A. HALL' *Ninth Directive* viii. 78 He spoke with the dulled tone of a punch-drunk. **1969** *Daily Tel.* 13 Nov. 18 'Punch-drunks' are completely unknown in amateur boxing.

Hence **ˈpunch-drunkenness,** the condition of being punch-drunk.

1937 *Lit. Digest* 10 Apr. 40/1 The coincidence of boxers developing thickness of speech, unsteadiness of gait,..has prompted London's famed Guy's Hospital to initiate a special study of the cause and cure of punch drunkenness. **1939** J. BERRYMAN in *Astounding Sci. Fiction* May 51 Tiny bloodclots on the lining of the brain, whose pressure on delicate centers often caused them to manifest the symptoms of punch-drunkenness. **1941** *Lancet* 14 June 759/1 There is, however, that specific problem of boxing, 'punchdrunkenness'—the permanent damage due to repeated cerebral injury. **1959** *Daily Tel.* 27 June 7/5 There was 'plenty of evidence to show that punch-drunkenness is a very real hazard to boxers'. **1977** J. PORTER *Who the Heck is Sylvia?* xv. 144 A family which prided itself on never knowing when it was beaten and in which punch-drunkenness was practically an endemic disease.

punched (pʌnʃt), *ppl. a.* [f. PUNCH *v.*[1] + -ED[1].]

1. Of metal-work: Beaten, hammered, wrought; *repoussé*; = POUNCED *ppl. a.*[1] 1. *Obs.* exc. *Hist.*

1415 *Mandate of Hen. V to Corporation of York* in Drake *Eboracum* (1736) App. 17 Item 2 petitz ewers d'argent, d'orrez, l'une chased et l'autre pounched. **1488** *Acc. Ld. High Treas. Scot.* I. 85 Item, a cop with a couir ouregilt and punchit. **1861** W. R. WILDE *Catal. Antiq. R. Irish Acad.* 631 The details of the punched or hammered-up ornament.

2. a. Perforated or pierced with a punch. ***punched card***, a card in which a pattern of holes, punched in it in accordance with a prescribed code, represents information; similarly ***punched paper***, ***punched*** (***paper***) ***tape***; freq. *attrib.*; cf. *paper tape* s.v. PAPER *sb.* 12, *perforated tape* s.v. PERFORATED *ppl. a.* 1.

1876 PREECE & SIVEWRIGHT *Telegraphy* 122 The two lines of larger holes in the punched paper. **1885** *Electrician* 27 Nov. 57/1 The Wheatstone fast-speed transmitter.., by which one punched tape served for twenty or thirty different wires. **1890** *Jrnl. Franklin Inst.* CXXIX. 301 These punched record cards can easily be read and verified. **1903** *Daily Chron.* 18 July 8/4 Small punched holes, overcast with button-hole stitch. **1904** *Ibid.* 28 July 8/5 Broderie Anglaise, which we call punched or eyelet-hole embroidery. **1919** A. MACFARLANE *Lectures on Ten British Physicists* 79 To realize the first idea..he had recourse to the device of punched cards similar to those invented by Jacquard for the weaving loom. **1940** W. J. ECKERT *Punched Card Methods in Scientific Computation* 2 Tables of functions are constructed from their differences with great efficiency, either as printed tables or as a file of punched cards. **1948** *Electronics* Aug. 100/1 Approximate positions of the stars, already stored in a punched-card catalog, may be coupled to the servomechanism. **1959** *Engineering* 2 Jan. 5/3 The machine can operate from standard punched tape or can be plugged into a long distance teleprinter circuit. **1962** E. GODFREY *Retail Selling & Organ.* i. 6 Mechanized handling of goods, punched-card accounting systems and advertising direct to the consumer..involve costs which the smaller business cannot afford. **1963** *Listener* 21 Mar. 489/2 A computer.. which read a quarter of a million words of Greek prose, translated into its own punched-paper language. **1968** *Brit. Med. Bull.* XXIV. 191/1 The commonest way..of inserting data and program into a computer is via punched paper tape or punched cards. **1975** T. ALLBEURY *Special Collection* i. 5 In Central Intelligence Records they had thousands of simple punched cards..in May 1944. **1980** D. BLOODWORTH *Trapdoor* v. 24 The formidable batteries of punched-card systems and data banks.

b. *Bot.* = PERFORATED 1 c.

1793 MARTYN *Lang. Bot.*, *Punched* leaf.

3. ***punched out***: said of a wound with a defined edge.

1897 *Allbutt's Syst. Surg.* II. 616 Edges [of ulcer] punched out, perpendicular, irregular. **1898** HUTCHINSON in *Arch. Surg.* IX. No. 34. 129 He described the sore as 'punched out'. **1900** *Daily News* 19 Jan. 3/4 The wounds both of entrance and of exit [of Mauser bullets] were small, and presented a clean punched-out appearance.

puncheon[1] (ˈpʌnʃən). Forms: α. 4 **ponson**, 5 **-syon**, 6 **-sion**; 5 *Sc.* **pouncioun**, **pownsown**, 7 **pounceon**; 4–5, 7 **punson**, 5 **-soune**, **-sion**, 6 **-cion**. β. 4 **ponchong**, 5 **-choun**, 5–6 **-chon**, 6–7 **-chion**; 5 **pounchion**, 5–6 **-eon**, 6 **pownchion**; 5 *Sc.* **pwncheon**, 5–6 **punchion**, **-oun**, 5–8 **-chion**, 6 *Sc.* **-schion**, **-scheown**, 6–8 **-chin**, 7 **-tion**, **-ction**, 6– **puncheon**; **punchen**. [a. OF. *poinçon, poinchon* (13th c. in Godef.), *ponçon, ponchon, poinson*, mod.F. *poinçon*, a boring, graving, or stamping tool, an awl, punch, stamp; also, a king-post, a strut in a builder's centre, etc.; = Pr. *pounchoun*, Sp. *punzon*, Pg. *punção*, It. *punzone*, †*ponzone* a bodkin or any sharp-pointed thing, 'a pounce, a pouncer, a little stamp or printer's letter' (Florio): all masc.:—late L. or Com. Rom. **punctiōn-em*, a deriv. of *puncta* point, or late L. **punctiāre* (Sp. *punzar*, OSp. and Pg. *punçar*) to prick, punch, work with a punch. Generally held to be a distinct word from cl. L. *punctiōnem* fem., pricking, punction. Hence also Ger. *punzen, bunzen* a metal-worker's punch.]

I. Name of various pointed or piercing instruments. †**1.** A short piercing weapon; a dagger.

1375 BARBOUR *Bruce* I. 545 Syne in hys capitole wes he [Cæsar]..Slayne with a pu[n]soune rycht to the ded. *c* **1400** *Laud Troy Bk.* 9352 Some In his body bar a tronchoun, As it were put In with a ponchoun. *c* **1420** WYNTOUN *Chron.* IV. xxv. 2339 Þai stekyt hym [Cæsar]..Withe scharpe pvnsionnys [*v. rr.* pownsownys, etc.]. **1558** PHAER *Æneid.* VII. iv, Their..puncheons close in staues they beare. **1694** MOTTEUX *Rabelais* v. x. 45 Poinadoes, Skenes, Penknives, Puncheons.

2. a. A pointed tool for piercing; a bodkin. **b.** A marble-worker's tool, ? a mason's pointed chisel. Now *rare.* †**c.** A graving tool, a burin; = POUNCE *sb.*[1] 4 (*obs.*).

1367–8 *Durham Acc. Rolls* (Surtees) 571 In operacione iiij petr. et di. in calibem pro dictis secur., ponsones, chissels. *Ibid.* 574 Pro reparacione viij punsons cum calibe. **1397** *Priory of Finchale* (Surtees) p. cxix, Instrumenta operariorum. Item ij haks et j pyk... Item ij ponchong' cum j craw. *c* **1440** *Promp. Parv.* 416/2 Punchoun, *stimulus, punctorium.* **1496** *Naval Acc. Hen. VII* (1896) 174, iiij pounchions of Iron & Steele. *Ibid.* 215, iiij pownchions. **1576** BAKER *Jewell of Health* 121 b, Bored or stricken through with many strokes of a small punchin or small nayle. **1580** HOLLYBAND *Treas. Fr. Tong, Poinson de fer,* an yron bodkin or ponsion. **1596** LODGE *Marg. Amer.* 63 He with a punchion of steele in a table of white alablaster engraved this. **1658** tr. *Porta's Nat. Magic* III. viii. 74 Having first loosed the pith of either of them with a wooden puncheon. **1659** TORRIANO, *Buríno,* a graving-toole, a pounceon. **1660** *Act 12 Chas. II,* c. 4 (Bk. Rates), Punsons & Gravers for Goldsmithes. **1662** EVELYN *Chalcogr.* 4 Those who Carve with the cheezil, or work in Bosse with the Puntion, as our Statuaries do. **1714** *Fr. Bk. of Rates* 413 Swedish Ships..loaded with Awls, Punchins and such Tools. **1873** E. SPON *Workshop Receipts* Ser. I. 386/2 The pieces..are thickly grooved, bolstered with the puncheon.

3. An instrument for punching or stamping figures, letters, etc. on plate or other material; also, for making dies for coining and matrices for casting type; = PUNCH *sb.*[1] 3. Now *rare* or *Obs.*

1504 *Acc. Ld. High Treas. Scotl.* II. 222 For the cunȝe irnis and the punschionis for the samyn. **1562–3** *Reg. Privy Council Scot.* I. 227 The tursell..togidder with twa punscheownis, the ane berand the saidis letteris..and the uther berand the saidis crescentis and thirsell. **1594** R. ASHLEY tr. *Loys le Roy* 21 To make Characters for imprinting, it is requisite first to haue ponchions of steell, softned by the fire, on the which they graue with counter-ponchions hardned. **1604** in Devon *Iss. Exchequer Jas. I* 352 For making and graving certain punchеons for the shaping of his Majesty's picture upon the said pieces of largess. **1670** in Hart *Cent. Print. Oxf.* (1900) 163, I can furnish yᵉ Latin Matrices, but the Greek Punctions are not found together. **1677** in A. Ryland *Assay Gold & S.* 41 The Company of Goldsmiths have caused to be made..punchions of steell, and marks at the end of them, both great and small, of these several sorts following. **1718** J. CHAMBERLAYNE *St. Gt. Brit.* I. III. xi. 287 (Oxford, Clarendon Printing-House) An Office for the Letter-founder, furnished with Furnaces, Punchions, Matrices, Moulds [etc.]. **1780** *Newgate Cal.* V. 346 The puncheon makes the dye, and the counter-puncheon is the dye when it is made; the machines produced are puncheons, but not puncheons made at the Mint. **1818** *Gentl. Mag.* LXXXVIII. II. 330 The matrix and puncheon had not made his heart callous.

II. In building and carpentry.

4. A short upright piece of timber in a wooden framing which serves to stiffen one or more long timbers or to support or transmit a load; a supporting post; a post supporting the roof in a coal-mine; formerly also a door-post.

1466 in Willis & Clark *Cambridge* (1886) III. 93 With a purloyn on..the said sparres with punchions fro the bemes to bere the same. *c* **1470** HENRY *Wallace* IX. 1140 Mynouris sone thai gert perss throw the wall, Syn pounciouns fyryt, and to the ground kest all. **1519** HORMAN *Vulg.* 142 b, The dore felle of from the pouncheon, *fores cardini exciderunt.* **1617** in Willis & Clark *Cambridge* (1886) I 205 The particians shall bee maide with..punchions and studds of oake. **1703** T. N. *City & C. Purchaser* 7 Jambs, Posts, or Puncheons of Doors. **1710** J. HARRIS *Lex. Techn.* II, *Punchins,* in Architecture, are short pieces of Timber placed to support some considerable Weight: They commonly stand upright between the Posts... Those that stand on each side of a Door are called Door Punchins. **1729** DESAGULIERS in *Phil. Trans.* XXXVI. 204 The 7th Figure represents the Crane with the walking Wheel, the whole turning round upon the strong Post or Puncheon S. **1815** W. MARSHALL *Rev.* IV. 132 The principal appropriation of the Underwood is to Puncheons or Supporters for the Coal-Pits. **1825** J. NICHOLSON *Operat. Mechanic* 572 *Puncheons;* short transverse pieces of timber, fixed between two others for supporting them equally..sometimes called *studs.*

5. a. A piece of timber with one face roughly dressed, or a split trunk, used for flooring and rough building. *U.S.*

1804 in *Maryland Hist. Mag.* (1909) IV. 9 Houses or cabins..are generally made of heavy timber logs covered with split timbers called 'puncheons' which they pin to the rafters with wooden pins. **1807** P. GASS *Jrnl.* 61 A floor of puncheons or split plank were laid, and covered with grass and clay. **1855** W. SARGENT *Braddock's Exp.* 84 A roof of puncheons, rudely shaped with the broad-axe. **1892** *Review of Rev.* July 22/2 The cabin was an odd little structure, whose floor was of puncheon. **1946** C. RICHTER *Fields* 164 The puncheons had holes for seat legs.

b. A piece of timber used in building a railway track or a corduroy road. *N. Amer.*

1843 W. OLIVER *Eight Months Illinois* 236 Trees are split up into what are called puncheons, of three or four inches in thickness, which are laid down on the sleepers. **1955** R. HOBSON *Nothing too Good* xv. 165, I figure that all it will cost you is the axes, shovels, spikes for punchen, crow bars, [etc.].

III. 6. *attrib.* †**a.** Armed with a sharp point like a puncheon (sense 1), as ***puncheon pole, spear, staff.*** *Obs.* **b.** Made of puncheons (sense 5), as ***puncheon floor, stool,*** etc. (orig. *U.S.*).

a. *a* **1548** HALL *Chron., Hen. VIII* 82 Euery one in his hande a Punchion spere, wherewith..foyned and lashed alwayes one at another, two for two. **1577** Punchion staffe [see PUSH *sb.*[1] 3]. **1579–80** NORTH *Plutarch* (1676) 130 He did teach his Souldiers to carry long Javelins or Punchion-staves. **1600** HOLLAND *Livy* XXVII. xxviii. 650 Others from the turrets of the gate pelted the enemies with stones, and pushed at them with punchion poles [L. *sudibus*].

b. **1754** J. INNES *Let.* 27 Sept. in *Lett. to Washington* (1898) I. 48, I have erected a puntion Fort. **1784** G. WASHINGTON *Diary* 20 Sept. (1925) II. 294 A Logged dwelling house with a punchion roof. **1843** 'R. CARLTON' *New Purchase* xxi. 199 Adjoining the bureau was the puncheon table with its white oak legs. **1860** BARTLETT *Dict. Amer.* s.v., Split logs, with their faces a little smoothed with an axe or hatchet..laid upon sleepers, make a puncheon floor. **1891** *Scribner's Mag.* Sept. 316/2 The rude home of the plantation darky—a home with log walls, a puncheon floor. **1894** H. GARDENER *Unoff. Patriot* 99 Suddenly she swung her fat body about on the puncheon stool and gave a tremendous snort. **1940** W. FAULKNER *Hamlet* II. i. 110 The heatless lean-to room was his desert cell, the thin pallet bed on the puncheon floor the couch of stones on which he would lie. **1963** R. SYMONS *Many Trails* xiv. 145 The floor was of the puncheon type—that is, poplar poles laid across stringers and smoothed with an adze, with no attempt at nailing. **1972** E. WIGGINGTON *Foxfire Bk.* 33 Green chestnut was split into fence rails, puncheon floors, wide planking, [etc.].

c. puncheon iron = sense 3.

1503 *Acc. Ld. High Treas. Scotl.* II. 358 Ane hammyr, turcas, and othir punschioun irnis.

puncheon² (ˈpʌnʃən). Now *rare* exc. *Hist.* Forms: 5 **poncion, pwncion,** 6–8 **punchion,** (6 **ponchion, -cheon, punshion, -chon,** *Sc.* **pontioune, puncioune, -cheoun, -sion, -s(i)oun, -schioun, -tion,** 6–7 **punshon**), 8– **puncheon.** [a. OF. *ponçon* (13th c.), *poinchon* (13–14th c.), *ponchon, poinçon* (13–16th c.), also *ponson* (14th c.), *poinson* (14–16th c.) in Godef. The forms both in OF. and Eng. are identical with those of PUNCHEON¹; Italian also has *punzone* for both; but connexion of sense has not been found, and Fr. lexicographers treat them as separate words.] A large cask for liquids, fish, etc.; *spec.* one of a definite capacity, varying for different liquids and commodities.

As a liquid measure it varied from 72 (beer) to 120 (whisky) gallons.

1479 *Acc. Ld. High Treas. Scotl.* I. 134 Gevin..to John of Tyre to by a pwncion of wyne. **1503** *Ibid.* II. 384 For the fraucht..of ane pipe and ane punschioun brocht hame with stuf for the King. **1532** *Ibid.* VI. 156 For ane puncioune of wyne iiijl. vs. **1536** *Act 28 Hen. VIII,* c. 14 In the Parliament holden..in the first yere of the reign of Kyng Richarde the thirde..it was establisshed that..every tercyan or poncheon [of wine should contain] lxxxiiij galons. **1546** *Reg. Privy Council Scot.* I. 53 Ane pairt of the punsionis of the saidis wynis are full of salt watter. **1554** in R. G. Marsden *Sel. Pleas Crt. Adm.* (Selden) II. 61, xv tonne ij ponchions of wyne. **1571** DIGGES *Pantom.* III. xi. R iv, Sundrie kindes of wine vessels, as the tunne, the pipe, the punshion, hogsheads, buttes, barrels. **1572–3** *Reg. Privy Council Scot.* II. 190 Ane punsoun of talloun. **1576–7** *Ibid.* 603 Ane punsioun of salmond. **1593–4** *Exch. Rolls Scotl.* XXII. 401 Tua tunnis, tua puntionis, and twa bunnis of Inglis beir. **1596** DALRYMPLE tr. *Leslie's Hist. Scot.* (S.T.S.) II. 122 Andro Bartayne..slew sa mony piratis, that mony puncheounis full of thair powis he sent to Scotland, in gifte, to the king. **1670** NARBOROUGH *Jrnl.* in *Acc. Sev. Late Voy.* I. (1694) 45 As much Salt..as filled a Punchion. **1706** PHILLIPS s.v., Punchion..of Prunes from 10 to 12 Hundred Weight. **1833** MARRYAT *P. Simple* xxxii, She had a puncheon of otto of roses on board.

'puncheoned, *a.* [f. PUNCHEON¹ + -ED².] Covered or laid with puncheons (PUNCHEON¹ 5 a).

1843 'R. CARLTON' *New Purchase* xv. 109 And first, the puncheoned area was separated into two grand parts.

puncher (ˈpʌnʃə(r)). [f. PUNCH *v.*[1] + -ER¹.]

a. One who or that which punches, thumps, perforates, or stamps; an instrument for doing this.

1681 GREW *Musæum* I. v. i. 95 In the upper Jaw, five before; not Incisors, or Cutters, but thick Punchers. **1691** A. HAIG in J. Russell *Haigs* xi. (1881) 332 When the chartour came to the Great Seall it cost to the Chauncellour 12 lib., and to the punschearis 4 lib., and to the keaper of the seall four rex-dollars. **1762–71** H. WALPOLE *Vertue's Anecd. Paint.* II. 250 He was a rival..who used puncheons for his graving, which Johnson never did, calling Simon a puncher, not a graver. **1823** J. BADCOCK *Dom. Amusem.* 96 The puncher, a steel instrument. **1876** PREECE & SIVEWRIGHT *Telegraphy* 132 When a wire is kept going at its full speed two punchers, one adjuster or sender, and three writers, are employed. **1876** *Jrnl. Soc. Telegr. Engineers* V. 492 When one clerk considers a puncher quite workable, another declares it to be useless. **1880** *Scribner's Mag.* July 355 The very next puncher of our tickets. **1883** R. HALDANE *Workshop Receipts* Ser. II. 140/2 Puncher.—This instrument is used for beating or punching those articles which are too heavy to be taken in the hands and rubbed. **1904** *Daily Chron.* 16 Aug. 7/1 Palmer, a powerful 'puncher' of the over-tossed ball, made some splendid drives to the off. **1915** F. M. HUEFFER *Good Soldier* I. v. 73 Ready to lend you his cigar puncher. **1951** *Sport* 30 Mar.–5 Apr. 10/2 Both have reputations as punchers. *a* **1953** DYLAN THOMAS *Quite Early One Morning* (1954) 33 The clip of the chair-attendant's puncher. **1973** *Irish Times* 2 Mar. 3/3 They [*sc.* a hockey team] depend enormously on John Douglas to initiate their raids and have only one recognised 'puncher' in Tom Jenkinson.

b. *N. Amer.* Short for *cow-puncher*: cf. PUNCH *v.*[1] 2. Also *attrib.* in ***puncher-boy.***

1870 *Daily Territorial Enterprise* (Virginia City, Nevada) 17 Aug. 3/1 All the time the punchers are flying from ox to ox, plying their sticks right and left. **1894** *Harper's Mag.* Feb. 355 In the handling of these savage animals the punchers are brave to recklessness. **1905** S. E. WHITE *Rawhide* viii, The punchers in their daily rides gathered in the range ponies. **1910** in J. Lomax *Cowboy Songs* 96 But show me a man that sleeps more profound Than the big puncher-boy who stretches himself on the ground. **1912** S. A. WHITE *Wildcatters* 137 Ben had decked him out in puncher's garb. The lariot was correctly coiled at the saddle-horn. **1972** T. A. BULMAN *Kamloops Cattlemen* ii. 16 Tough as these old 'punchers' were, the years gradually took their toll.

punchery, punchifier: see PUNCH *sb.*[3]

'punch-house. [f. PUNCH *sb.*[3]: cf. *ale-house.*] A tavern where punch is supplied; *esp.* in India, an inn or tavern frequented by sailors.

1671–2 in Wheeler *Madras in Old Time* (1861) III. 423 It is..enorderd and declared hereby that no Victullar, Punch-house or other house of Entertainment shall be permitted to make stoppage at the pay day of their wages. **1697** *Ibid.* I. xiv. 320 Having in a Punch house upon a quarrel of words drawn his sword. **1727** A. HAMILTON *New Acc. E. Ind.* I. xxiv. 298 The English have Punch-houses, where the European Soldiers make Oblations to Bacchus. *a* **1805** A. CARLYLE *Autobiog.* (1861) 307 A company of seven or eight, all clergymen, supped at a punch-house in the Bow, kept by an old servant of his. **1859** J. W. PALMER *New & Old* 264 (Cassell's), Sailors, British and American, Malay and Lascar, [belong] to Flag Street, the quarter of punch-houses.

Punchine (ˈpʌntʃaɪn), *a. rare.* [f. PUNCH *sb.*[5] 2 + -INE¹.] Of or pertaining to the journal *Punch.*

1846 THACKERAY in *Punch* 8 Aug. 59/2 It was this braggart violence of soul that roused the Punchine wrath against Mr. O'Connell.

Punchinello (pʌn(t)ʃɪˈnɛləʊ). Forms: α. 7 **polichinello,** 7–9 **polichinelle,** 9 **policinello, pulc(h)inello.** β. 7 **puntionella, punchonello,** 7–8 **punch(i)anello,** 7–9 **punci-,** 8–9 **ponchi-,** 7– **punchinello.** γ. 7 **pugenello.** [In the form *polichinello,* app. ad. Neapolitan dial. *Polecenella* (whence also F. *Polichinelle,* 1680 in Hatz.-Darm.) name of a character of the puppet theatre; = It. *Pulcinella.* Origin uncertain. See Note below.]

1. Name of the principal character in a puppet-show of Italian origin, the prototype of Punch; hence applied to the show (and quot. 1666 in β, to the exhibitor); sometimes to a living performer.

[Cf. **1662** PEPYS *Diary* 8 Oct., The King, before whom the puppet plays I saw this summer in Covent-garden are acted this night.]

α. *a* **1666** PEPYS *Diary* 22 Aug., I with my wife..by coach to Moorefields, and there saw 'Polichinello', which pleases me mightily. **1668** *Ibid.* 2 May, [At the Duke of York's playhouse] A little boy, for a farce, do dance Polichinelli. **1668** *Ibid.* 31 Aug., Thence to the Fayre, and saw 'Polichinelle'. **1818** LADY MORGAN *Autobiog.* (1859) 195 Sanky went off without calling when he heard of a workbox and Polichinelle. **1827** DISRAELI *Viv. Grey* v. iv, A long grinning wooden figure, with great staring eyes, and the parrot nose of a pulcinello. **1880** WARREN *Book-plates* x. 110 Garnished about with festoons of roses, a branch of oak, mask and pulchinello, quiver and pan-pipe. **1897** *Q. Rev.* Oct. 331 They are simply Judy-puppets in the Policinello of conventionality.

β. **1666** *Overseers' Bks., St. Martins in-the-fields* 29 Mar., Rec. of Punchinello, yᵉ Italian popet-player, for his booth at Chareing Crosse £2 12 6. **1668** H. MORE *Div. Dial., Schol.* (1713) 570, I question not but the Quakers..would play the part of the Puppet or Punchinello in the Antelude of the Pageant. *a* **1680** BUTLER *Sat. on Imit. French* 101 And the worst Drols of Punchinellos Were much th' ingeniouser Fellows. **1683** *Norwich Crt. Bks.* 22 Dec. (1905) 173 Peter Dolman has leave to show a motion called his Majesty's Puntionella, at the Angel. **1709** *Rambl. Fuddle-Cups* 7 A Barthol'mew-Fair Punchanello. **1728** SWIFT *Mullinix & Tim.* Wks. 1755 III. II. 211 The world consists of puppet-shows; Where petulant conceited fellows Perform the part of Punchinelloes. **1797** MRS. RADCLIFFE *Italian* xxii, See signor, there is Punchinello. **1835** WILLIS *Pencillings* I. xx. 142 Puncinello squeaked and beat his mistress at every corner. [**1860** *Once a Week* 24 Mar. 281/1 (Stanf.) Harlequins, mysterious-looking dominoes, ponchinelli, and dresses of all periods.]

γ. **1667** DRYDEN *Sir Martin Mar-all* v. ii, *Rose.* I know no way so proper for you, as to turn Poet to Pugenello. **1668** SHADWELL *Sullen Lovers* v. 96 Enter a boy in the habit of Pugenello, and traverses the Stage.

2. *transf.* Applied to any person, animal, or thing, thought to resemble the puppet, esp. in being short and stout. Cf. PUNCH *sb.*[4]

1669 PEPYS *Diary* 20 Apr., Going away with extraordinary report of the proof of his gun, which, from the shortness and bigness, they do call Punchinello. **1683** TRYON *Way to Health* 478 We have no fatted Swine, fatted Oxen or Punchonello's amongst us: neither have we any of Pharoah's lean Kine. *a* **1769** JOHNSON in Boswell *Life* (Maxwell's Recollections), [Being told that Gilbert Cowper (who was short and very stout) called him the Caliban of literature] 'Well' [said he], 'I must dub him the Punchinello'. **1834** MARY HOWITT *Sk. Nat. Hist., Monkey,* Monkey, little merry fellow, Thou art Nature's Punchinello. *c* **1835** *Comic song, 'The great Mogul',* The great Mogul, as I've heard people say, Was a fat little Punchinello.

3. *attrib.*

Punchinello voice = *Punch's voice* (PUNCH *sb.*[5] 1 c).

1797 BURKE *Let. Mrs. Crewe* Corr. (1844) IV. 417 The shame and misfortune of our country would make one almost mad, if these punchinello statesmen did not sometimes come out to make us laugh. **1853** W. O.

MARKHAM tr. *Skoda's Auscult.* 283 The intensity of the râles ..; the punchinello voice accompanying the pectoriloquy.

[*Note.* There is every probability that the Eng. *polichinello* and F. *polichinelle* are derived from the Neapolitan word, and that *Punchinello*, although evidenced somewhat earlier, and actually given (prob. in error) as the name of the puppet-showman, was an English alteration. The Italian word is said in the *Vocabolario Napoletano* of 1789, to be a corruption of the name of a comedian *Puccio d'Aniello*, originally a peasant of Acerra, whose uncouth physiognomy is said to have served as the model for the mask of the character; another conjecture cites the name of one *Paulo Cinella*, said to have been a buffoon at Naples. Setting aside these legends or conjectures, it has been pointed out that It. *pulcinella* is dim. of *pulcina* chicken, and according to Quadrio and Barretti, cited by Pianigiani *Vocab. Etimol. della lingua Ital.*, 1907, in the Neapolitan dial. *pollecenella* is dim. of *pollecena*, the young of the turkey-cock, to the hooked bill of which the nose of the mask bears a resemblance.]

'punchiness. [f. PUNCHY *a.*[1]] Squatness.

1850 L. HUNT *Autobiog.* I. iii. 116 The other master .. was a short stout man, inclining to punchiness.

punching ('pʌnʃɪŋ), *vbl. sb.* [f. PUNCH *v.*[1] + -ING[1].] **a.** The action of the verb PUNCH in various senses; also, a marking produced by punching. Also, a piece of sheet metal cut out by a punch.

c **1440** *Promp. Parv.* 416/2 Punchynge, or bu(n)chynge (S. prykkynge), *stimulacio, trusio.* **1535** *Trevisa's Barth. De P.R.* VIII. xvii. 1236/2 Cause of hurtynge and of punchynge [L. *punctionis*; 1398 styngynge] of mans bodye. **1538** *Aberdeen Reg.* (Jam.), For the .. punching of him with his feytt in the wame. **1815** J. SMITH *Panorama Sc. & Art* I. 18 Punching is not applicable to cast iron, nor to small and deep, or very large, holes in any metal. **1892** *Daily News* 26 Oct. 2/1 A patent leather shoe is ornamented round the top with perforated punchings. **1903** *Electr. World & Engin.* 28 Mar. 532/2 The four-pole pieces are made of laminated steel punchings. **1947** R. LEE *Electronic Transformers & Circuits* iii. 75 There is always a certain amount of gap even with punchings stacked alternately in groups of 1. **1951** E. W. WORKMAN in P. Kemp *Electr. Engin.* III. 633/2 In the case of electrical transformers, generators and motors, sheet-steel punchings form a large proportion of the total works cost.

b. *attrib.* and *Comb.*; in names of tools used for making holes, as ***punching bear*** (= BEAR *sb.*[1] 7), ***iron, machine, nippers***, etc.; **punching-ball**, an inflated ball held in position by elastic bands or supported on a flexible rod, which is punched with the fists as an athletic exercise; so **punching bag** (also *fig.*), **block; punching match**, a boxing match, a fight; **punching press** = *punch-press* s.v. PUNCH *sb.*[1] 7; **punching room**, the cutting room in a glove manufactory; †**punching staff** = *puncheon-staff* (PUNCHEON[1] 6 a): a lance, a spear.

1889 *Cent. Dict.*, *Punching-bag. **1896** ADE *Artie* i. 4 Say, I like that church, and if they'll put in a punchin'-bag and a plunge they can have my game, I'll tell you those. **1897** *Outing* (U.S.) XXX. 182/2 Dumb-bells, .. traveling-rings and punching-bag, may be taken to develop different groups of muscles. **1911** *Boxing* IV. 456/2 Once again that old trial hope, Fred Drummond, was dragged from his stall to play the part of punching-bag. **1976** G. SIMS *End of Web* x. 72 Buchanan used him like a punching-bag, hitting him with every combination he knew. **1900** CONAN DOYLE *Green Flag*, etc. 118, I turned it into a gymnasium... You'll find all you want there: clubs, *punching ball, bars, dumb-bells, everything. **1875** KNIGHT *Dict. Mech.*, **Punching-bear*, a machine for making holes in sheet-metal, operated by simple lever power or by hydraulic pressure. **1594** T. NASHE *Unfort. Trav.* 87 Pritch-aule, spunge, blacking tub, and *punching yron. **1850** *Rep. U.S. Comm. Patents 1849* I. 185 My improved *punching machine. **1878** *Harper's Mag.* Apr. 645/2 The bar then goes to the punching-machine that .. bites a bar through the iron. **1962** F. T. DAY *Introd. Paper* viii. 87 Table mats and drip mats .. are often produced on a blanking-out or punching machine. **1809** *Sporting Mag.* XXXIII. 77 At the late *punching match. **1844** STEPHENS *Bk. Farm* III. 869 The markings are confined to the ears, and consist of .. holes made with *punching-nippers. *a* **1884** E. H. KNIGHT *Dict. Mech.* Suppl. 730/2 *Punching press. **1906** C. H. BENJAMIN *Mod. Amer. Machine Tools* x. 282 (*caption*) 60-inch punching press. **1562** J. SHUTE tr. *Cambini's Turk. Wars* 17 b, Manye layde holde of the Pikes and *punchinge staves of theyr enemies. **1590** BARWICK *Breefe Disc.* 2 b, For horsemen, a Launce, a punching staffe, Pistoll or mace.

'punching, *ppl. a.* [f. PUNCH *v.*[1] + -ING[2].] That punches: see the verb.

1602 [see PUNCH *v.*[1] 1 b]. **1683** MOXON *Mech. Exerc., Printing* xiii. ¶2 The Counter-Punch of A ought to be Forged Triangularly, especially towards the Punching End.

punching, punchion, *adjs.* (of a horse): see PUNCH *sb.*[4]

punchion, obs. f. PUNCHEON[1] and [2].

†**punchite,** obs. form of PANCHAYAT.

1827 D. JOHNSON *Ind. Field Sports* 141 Accustomed to decide their disputes by punchite.

punchless ('pʌnʃlɪs), *a.*[1] [f. PUNCH *sb.*[3] + -LESS.] Having no punch to drink.

1903 W. STEVENS *Let.* 26 July (1967) 64, I was looking forward to a cigarless, punchless weary life.

'punchless, *a.*[2] [f. PUNCH *sb.*[2] + -LESS.] Lacking a powerful punch; deficient as a boxer.

1950 J. DEMPSEY *Championship Fighting* ii. 11 Punchless performers who can win amateur or professional bouts on points.

'punch line. orig. *U.S.* Also with hyphen and as one word. [f. PUNCH *sb.*[2] + LINE *sb.*[2] 23.] Words or a sentence expressing the point of a joke, play, song, etc. Hence **punch-line** *v. intr.*

1921 *Variety* 25 Nov. 8/1 All of their sure-fire punch-lines went over. **1934** S. R. NELSON *All about Jazz* vii. 158 The gentlemen who write lyrics .. imagine the public hang on their doggerel—particularly the line known as the 'punch line'. **1937** *Dime Detective Mag.* Nov. 45/2 Go on .. give me the punch line. **1944** S. BELLOW *Dangling Man* 158 Yes, things change. *C'est la guerre. C'est la vie.* Good old punch lines. **1957** *Oxford Mail* 17 Oct. 1/2 It was Mr Dulles's punch-line and showed the Russians—and the American people—that President Eisenhower regards the Middle East crisis with great anxiety. **1959** *Time* 14 Sept. 44/2 'I'll kill myself..' said Benny. 'All right,' Truman punch-lined, 'I've got an undertaker friend.' **1961** B. WELLS *Day Earth caught Fire* vii. 107 'Wonder who writes his punchlines?' remarked Reynolds. **1971** *World Archaeology* III. 226 He [*sc.* V. G. Childe] was fond of dramatic punch-lines. **1977** *New Yorker* 27 June 67/1 Reaching the punch line, he erupted in laughter.

puncho, -chon, obs. ff. PONCHO, PUNCHEON.

'punch-up. *slang.* Also without hyphen and as one word. [f. PUNCH *v.*[1] + UP *adv.*[1]] A fight or brawl. Also *fig.*, a fierce or noisy argument.

1958 F. NORMAN *Bang to Rights* 28 The next morning after we had had this little punch up. **1960** H. PINTER *Caretaker* II. 36 Bloke saved me from a punch up. **1963** K. AMIS *One Fat Englishman* iii. 36 The fellow was earning a bigger and better punch-up, oral or physical, with every sentence he spoke. **1966** J. WAINWRIGHT *Evil Intent* 85 He's been responsible for more religious punch-ups than Judas himself. **1967** *New Scientist* 14 Dec. 673/1 Good old-fashioned punch-ups between the holders of rival theories, of the sort that so stimulated 19th century science, are sadly rare today. **1972** J. WILSON *Hide & Seek* viii. 151, I got six months .. all because you ruzzers stuck your noses into a private little punch up. **1976** *Daily Mirror* 11 Mar. 9/6 He was fired after an alleged punch-up with another worker. **1978** *Times Lit. Suppl.* 25 Aug. 944/3 Boxing and pub punch-ups were his main amusements.

punchy ('pʌnʃɪ), *a.*[1] [f. PUNCH *sb.*[4] + -Y.] Short and stout, thick-set, squat, stumpy.

1783 J. WOODFORDE *Diary* 10 Feb. (1926) II. 58 He bought .. a short dark Punchy Horse with a Hog main. **1791** 'G. GAMBADO' *Ann. Horsem.* viii. (1809) 102 If your horse is of the short punchy kind. **1810** *Sporting Mag.* XXXV. 40 The plaintiff being short and punchy. **1823** in *Spirit Pub. Jrnls.* 330 A beautiful punchy little pony.

punchy, *a.*[2]: see PUNCH *sb.*[3]

punchy ('pʌnʃɪ), *a.*[3] [f. PUNCH *sb.*[2] + -Y[1].] Full of punch or vigour.

1926 WHITEMAN & MCBRIDE *Jazz* ii. 41, I would direct a punchy number. **1930** *Observer* 19 Oct. 19 A punchy rhetorical speech on Free Trade. **1937** *Lit. Digest* 4 Dec. 30/3 The English language may some day be as colorful and punchy as it was in Elizabethan times. **1959** *Times Lit. Suppl.* 25 Sept. 545/5 (Advt.), In over a score of punchy entertaining chapters he delights readers. **1971** *Amateur Photographer* 3 Mar. 23/2 The 10-minute playlet with a punchy plot. **1977** *Time* 30 May 55/1 More gregarious than Woodcock, a punchier speaker, a hair more liberal, Fraser signals a change in style rather than substance.

'punchy, *a.*[4] *slang* (chiefly *U.S.*). [f. PUNCH *sb.*[2] or PUNCH-DRUNK *a.* and *sb.* + -Y[1].] = PUNCH-DRUNK *a.* Hence *transf.*, in a state of nervous tension or extreme fatigue. Also as *sb.* (*rare*).

1937 *Lit. Digest* 10 Apr. 39/2 'Slap-happy' or 'punchy' ex-fighters. **1937** E. HEMINGWAY *To have & have Not* III. xiv. 201 Shut up, slappy... You've got the old rale... You punchies make me sick. **1943** *Gen* 16 Jan. 30/1 He lives in a dream-world .. he is, as the boys put it, 'punchy'. **1950** E. B. WHITE *Let.* 12 Nov. (1976) 326 K and I are both pretty well, if a bit punchy. **1958** E. DUNDY *Dud Avocado* II. iii. 209, I am so punchy .. that I don't know whether I'm coming or going. **1970** K. PLATT *Pushbutton Butterfly* (1971) xiii. 149 I'm not coming at you because of what a punchy Hell's Angel tea-head told me. **1974** *Summerville* (S. Carolina) *Jrnl.* 24 Apr. 2/3 By the time the serviceman inserted a new tube, .. the kids were getting punchy from sitting before a gray screen, .. trying to imagine just what it was that the Roadrunner was doing to the wily Coyote. **1977** *Tennis World* Sept. 17/2 A player who breaks up on the court from nervousness is said to be 'punchy', 'gone cuckoo' or simply 'gone'.

punck, obs. form of PUNK *sb.*[1]

†**punct,** *sb. Obs.* Also 6 *Sc.* **punt.** [ad. L. *punct-um* point.] = POINT *sb.*[1] in various senses.

1. A dot, spot, speck: = POINT *sb.*[1] A. 2.

1398 TREVISA *Barth. De P.R.* XVI. lxviii. (Bodl. MS.), Marble purpurites .. is rodye wiþ punctis amonge. **1516** *Inv. Roy. Wardr.* (1815) 24 Ane saferon with punctis of gold.

2. A stop in punctuation: = POINT *sb.*[1] A. 3 a.

c **1620** A. HUME *Brit. Tongue* (1865) 34 The round punct concludes an assertion... The tailed punct concludes an interrogation.

3. *Sc.* **a.** An item, detail: = POINT *sb.*[1] A. 5. **b.** A particle, jot: = POINT *sb.*[1] A. 6.

1499 *Exch. Rolls Scotl.* XI. 393 The Punctis to be Inquirit at the Inqueist. **1563–4** *Reg. Privy Council Scot.* I. 263 The saidis Lordis ordinis Johne Johnestoun to insert thir puntis in the saidis bukis. *c* **1575** BALFOUR *Practicks* (1754) 172 He fulfillit not the punctis and clausis contenit in the said infeftment. **1653** R. SANDERS *Physiogn.* 270 Exact in the least punct of the measure thereof.

4. As a measure of time, or of the magnitude of an eclipse: = POINT *sb.*[1] A. 10, 11.

1398 TREVISA *Barth. De P.R.* IX. ix. lf. 94/1 (Bodl. MS.) A quadraunt conteyneþ sixe houres and an houre foure punctes, and a puncte ten momentes. **1561** EDEN *Arte Nauig.* II. viii. 35 For the quantitie of these Eclipses, the Astronomers deuide into .xii. equall partes, as well the Diameter of the Sunne as of the Moone. And these partes they call fyngers, punctes or prickes.

5. *Geom.* = POINT *sb.*[1] A. 18.

1639 NABBES *Encomium on Steeple at Worc.* Wks. 1887 II. 239 Infinite in shew As those small puncts, from whose concretion grow What else may be divided. **1653** R. SANDERS *Physiogn.* 273 As number [depends] on a unite, and a line upon a punct or point.

6. A moment, instant: = POINT *sb.*[1] A. 23.

1513 DOUGLAS *Æneis* XII. xiii. 29 Now is cum the extreme lattir punct. **1561** EDEN *Arte Nauig.* Pref., At the same instant & punct of time it maketh day in one place & nyght on the opposite parte. **1695** ALINGHAM *Geom. Epit.* 34 At the same punct of time.

†**punct,** *v. Obs. rare.* [Collateral form of POINT *v.*[1] and [2], after med.L. *punctāre.*]

1. *trans.* To appoint: = POINT *v.*[2] 2. *Sc.*

1473 *Rental Bk. Cupar-Angus* (1879) I. 169 With all vthyr condecionis as it is punctyt in Thomas Kantis tak.

2. To prick, pierce: = POINT *v.*[1] 1.

a **1548** HALL *Chron., Rich. III* 28 b, Her breste she puncted, her fayre here she tare.

puncta, pl. of PUNCTUM.

punctal ('pʌŋktəl), *a.* (*sb.*) *rare.* [In quot. *c* 1400, perh. an error for PUNCTUAL *a.* 1. In quot. 1897, rendering med.L. *punctālis* (Wyclif), f. *punct-um* point: see -AL[1].]

A. *adj.* †**a.** Of the nature of a point or puncture (*obs.*). **b.** Occupying a point in space.

c **1400** *Lanfranc's Cirurg.* 104 Make smale cauteries punctale, þat is to seie as smal as þe eende of a pricke, bitwene ech whirlebon of þe necke. **1897** M. DZIEWICKI *Wyclif's De Logica* III. (1899) p. xviii, If every punctal atom is and remains eternally the same, then the elements would remain in their compounds. *Ibid.* p. xxiii, His idea of the universe—one material being, made up of punctal atoms, filling all possible space.

B. †*sb.* A dot, speck, small spot. *Obs. rare.*

1688 J. CLAYTON in *Phil. Trans.* XVII. 990 The white Owl .. all the Feathers upon her Breast and Back being Snow-white, and tipp'd with a Punctal of Jet-black.

punctate ('pʌŋktət), *a.* [ad. mod.L. *punctāt-us*, f. L. *punct-um* point: see -ATE[2] 2. Cf. It. *puntato*, F. *pointé*.]

1. *Nat. Hist.* and *Path.* Marked or studded with points or dots; having minute rounded spots, or (esp.) depressions resembling punctures, scattered over the surface; of the nature of or characterized by such markings.

1760 J. LEE *Introd. Bot.* III. v. (1765) 183 *Punctate, dotted*; when it is besprinkled with hollow Points or Dots. **1826** KIRBY & SP. *Entomol.* IV. xlvi. 270 *Punctate*, beset with many points. **1847** J. HARDY in *Proc. Berw. Nat. Club* II. No. 5. 253 Elytra .. very thickly and finely punctate. **1889** J. M. DUNCAN *Clin. Lect. Dis. Wom.* ix. (ed. 4) 52 The mucous membrane .. has often a punctate appearance.

b. In advb. comb. with other adjs., as **'punctate-'scabrous**, scabrous with minute dots or points; **'punctate-'striate (-'striated)**, having striæ or streaks marked with dots, or formed of dots arranged in rows; **'punctate-'sulcate**, having furrows marked with dots. (Cf. PUNCTATO-.)

1833 G. R. WATERHOUSE in *Entomol. Mag.* I. 210 Elytra delicately punctate-striated. **1847** W. E. STEELE *Field Bot.* 196 Glumes .. slightly punctate-scabrous. **1854** WOODWARD *Mollusca* II. 181 Shell .. smooth or punctate-striate.

2. *Path.* Having or coming to a definite point.

1899 *Allbutt's Syst. Med.* VI. 390 The impulse [of an aneurysm] is rarely punctate.

†**3.** *Geom.* = PUNCTATED 1. *Obs.*

[**1704** NEWTON *Enumer. Linearum* (1711) 74 Punctatam, quæ conjugatam habet Ovalem infinite parvam id est punctum.] **1860** TALBOT tr. *Newton's Enumer.* 13 That which has an infinitely small conjugate oval, i.e. a conjugate point, the punctate hyperbola.

4. Having or ending in a point; pointed. *rare*[−0].

1828 WEBSTER, *Punctate, Punctated.* [1.] Pointed. **1847** —— *Punctate, Punctated.* 1. Pointed; ending in a point or points. Hence in later Dicts.

'punctated, *a.* [f. as prec. + -ED.]

†**1.** *Geom.* Having a conjugate point or acnode: see CONJUGATE *a.* 6 a. *Obs. rare.*

[**1704**: see prec. 3.] **1710** J. HARRIS *Lex. Techn.* II, *Punctated Hyperbola*, is an Hyperbola whose Oval Conjugate is infinitely small, that is, a *Point.* **1753** CHAMBERS *Cycl. Supp.*

2. = PUNCTATE 1.

1752 SIR J. HILL *Hist. Anim.* 544 The Cat-a-Mountain, .. with the upper spots virgated, the lower punctated. **1781–5** J. LATHAM *Hist. Birds* II. 541 Punctated Cuckow. **1869** G. LAWSON *Dis. Eye* (1874) 84 Small punctated opacities on the posterior surface of the cornea.

3. = PUNCTATE 4. *rare*[−0].

1775 ASH, *Punctated*, drawn into a point. **1828** [see PUNCTATE 4].

‖**punctatim** (pʌŋk'teɪtɪm), *adv. nonce-wd.* [L. in form, f. *punct-um* point, after *verbātim*. Cf. late L. *punctātim* briefly, concisely.] Point for point; = PUNCTUATIM b.

1816 *Q. Rev.* XV. 346 We shall give our extracts verbatim, literatim, and, if we may use the expression, punctatim.

punctation (pʌŋk'teɪʃən). [ad. L. type **punctātiōn-em*, n. of action from med.L. *punctāre* (It. *puntare*) to point.]

1. †**a.** = PUNCTUATION 3, 3 b. *Obs.*

1617 COLLINS *Def. Bp. Ely* II. x. 536 Let the Reader be carefull of reading these..words..with due punctation of them. **1748** J. MASON *Elocut.* 26 There is..so much Irregularity introduced, into the modern Method of Punctation, that it is become a very imperfect Rule to direct a just Pronunciation.

†**b.** *Heb. Gram.* The insertion of the vowel-points and accents; = POINTING *vbl. sb.* 2 b. *Obs.*

1642 CUDWORTH *Lord's Supper* 38 In the Hebrew the words..according to a severall Punctation..may be expounded severall ways. **1693** J. EDWARDS *Author. O. & N. Test.* 225 The true punctation of the proper Name.

2. *Nat. Hist.*, etc. The action of marking or fact of being marked with points or dots; the condition of being punctate; also *concr.* one of such dots, a series of such dots.

1852 DANA *Crust.* I. 154 Two minute punctations. **1872** NICHOLSON *Palæont.* 482 The woody fibres do not exhibit punctations. **1875** H. C. WOOD *Therap.* (1879) 242 It lacks the punctations of the rash of scarlet fever.

‖**3.** [repr. Ger. *punktation*.] A laying down of points; a stipulation; a contract or agreement.

1864 EDERSHEIM tr. *Kurtz's Ch. Hist.* III. 221 The Electors of Mayence, Triers, and Cologne, together with the Archbishop of Salzburg..assembled together in a spiritual congress at Ems (1786), and resolved upon the restoration of a German Roman Catholic National Church, independent of Rome, in the so-called Emser Punctation. **1890** *Q. Rev.* Oct. 332 The 'punctation of Olmutz' as it was called was signed 29 Nov. 1850.

punctato- (pʌŋk'teɪtəʊ), combining advb. form of mod.L. *punctātus*, with other adjs. = PUNCTATE 1 b; as **punc'tato-'striate, -'sulcate.**

1826 KIRBY & SP. *Entomol.* IV. xlvi. 303 The terms punctato-striate, or punctato-sulcate, signify that striæ or furrows are drawn with puncta in them.

punc'tator. *Heb. Gram.* [Agent-n. f. med.L. *punctāre* to point.] One who inserts the vowel (and other) points in writing; applied esp. to the Masoretes, who invented the points.

1723 MATHER *Vind. Bible* 294 The punctators used to point Scheva under Thau in the word Aschith.

punc'ticular, *a. rare.* [f. med. or mod.L. **puncticulum* a minute point + -AR.]

†**1.** Of the size or appearance of a small point or dot; extremely minute. *Obs.*

1658 SIR T. BROWNE *Gard. Cyrus* III. 51 Water in glasses, wherein a watchfull eye may..discover the puncticular Originals of Periwincles and Gnats.

2. Characterized by small dots or specks.

1858 MAYNE *Expos. Lex.*, *Puncticularis*, having small points; applied to fevers, etc.: puncticular.

So **punc'ticulate** *a.* = PUNCTULATE.

1890 in *Cent. Dict.*

punctiform ('pʌŋktɪfɔːm), *a. Nat. Hist.* and *Path.* [ad. L. type **punctiformis*, f. *punct-um* point: see -FORM.]

1. Having the form of a point, puncture, or dot.

1822 GOOD *Study Med.* I. 301 The female [thread-worm] has a small punctiform aperture a little below the head. **1856** W. L. LINDSAY *Pop. Hist. Brit. Lichens* 143 A small, black, punctiform Fungus.

2. Formed of, or presenting the appearance of, a number of points or dots; punctate: esp. in pathology, of eruptions, etc.

1839–47 *Todd's Cycl. Anat.* III. 601/2 These animals appear as a punctiform homogeneous mass. **1861** HAGEN *Syn. Neuropt. N. Amer.* 11 A band upon the middle and punctiform lines at the eyes. **1886** FAGGE & PYE-SMITH *Princ. Med.* I. 208 Instead of being punctiform [the rash of Scarlatina] may in rare cases consist of large, irregular, slightly raised maculæ.

punctigerous (pʌŋk'tɪdʒərəs), *a. Zool.* [f. L. *punct-um* point + *-ger-* bearing + -OUS.] Applied to the eyes of some molluscs, and other invertebrates: Consisting of mere eye-spots without a lens: opp. to *lentigerous*.

1883 E. R. LANKESTER in *Encycl. Brit.* XVI. 680/2 We have in one sub-class the extremes of the two lines of development of the Molluscan eye, those two lines being the punctigerous and the lentigerous.

punctiliar (pʌŋk'tɪlɪə(r)), *a.* [f. PUNCTILIO + -AR^1.] Of or pertaining to a point of time; = PUNCTUAL *a.* 5 e.

1906 J. H. MOULTON *Gram. N.T. Greek* I. vi. 109 The Aorist has a 'punctiliar' action, that is, it regards action as a *point*. [*note*] I venture to accept from a correspondent this new-coined word to represent the German *punktuell*, the English of which is preoccupied. **1944** E. A. NIDA *Morphol.* II. ix. 130 If an action is considered as a unit, occurring so to speak, at a 'point' of time, it may be considered 'punctiliar'. In such a case an action which takes place over a considerable extent of time may nevertheless be looked upon as a unitary action of a punctiliar nature. **1964** —— *Toward Sci. Transl.* ix. 199 As a description of the kind of action involved in the verb, aspect serves to differentiate a number of contrasts, of which some of the most common are: (1) complete vs. incomplete, (2) punctiliar vs. continuous, [etc.].

punctilio (pʌŋk'tɪlɪəʊ). Forms: α. 6–7 **puntilio,** 7 **-illo, -illio, -iglio.** β. 7 **punctiglio,** 7–8 **-illo, -illio,** 7– **punctilio.** [a. It. *puntiglio* and Sp. *puntillo*, dim. of *punto* point; = L. type **puncticulum*; later with *punct-* after Latin. Cf. F. *pointille* (ad. It.) *c* 1560.]

A. Illustration of Forms.

1596 HARINGTON *Metam. Ajax* Prol., Standing upon the puntilio of honour hauing been challenged. **1615** BRATHWAIT *Strappado* (1878) 61 *note*, Who stands on the puntiglio of his honour. **1626** T. H. *Caussin's Holy Crt.* 290 Animosityes, reuenges, quarrels, puntilloes. **1626**, etc. Punctilio [see B. 5]. **1630** EARL STRAFFORD in Slingsby *Diary* (1836) 324 Concerning that Punctillo. **1642** Puntillo's [see B. 4]. *a* **1648** LD. HERBERT *Hen. VIII* (1649) 207 As for the little cavills and punctiglios, concerning the receiving of Giovanni Joakim and the like. **1649** MILTON *Eikon.* xi. Wks. 1851 III. 420 With reason, conscience, honour, policy, or puntilios. **1659** *Gentl. Calling* v. §23. 423 [To] descend.. from their punctilioes. **1666** TEMPLE *Let. Godolphin* 1 Apr., Wks. 1757 I. 257 To lay by the puntiglio. **1709** O. DYKES *Eng. Prov. & Refl.* (ed. 2) 181 Tim'd according to the nice Punctillo's of nicking the Opportunity. **1792** *Anecd. W. Pitt* III. xxxviii. 28 The noble Lord talks of Spanish punctillios.

B. Signification.

†**1.** A small or fine point or mark, esp. one of those on a dial (with play on sense 5). *Obs. rare.*

1596 HARINGTON *Ulysses upon Ajax* C v b, He shall finde the Puntilio of his honour blunted. **1599** B. JONSON *Ev. Man out of Hum.* II. i. (1600) E j b, To the perfection of Complement (which is the dyall of the thought..) are requirde these three Proiects: the Gnomon, the Puntilios, and the Superficies: the Superficies is that we call Place; the Puntilios, Circumstance: and the Gnomon, Ceremonie.

†**2.** The highest point, acme, apex; a high projecting point or tip (sometimes with mixture of sense 4). *Obs. rare.*

1599 B. JONSON *Cynthia's Rev.* II. iii. (1601) D 3 b, He that is yet in..his Course..& hath not toucht the Puntillio or point of hopes. **1650** W. BROUGH *Sacr. Princ.* (1659) 1 A three-fold knowledge of religion..of pinacles or punctilio's, high and curious points in the building.

†**3.** A minute point of time, a moment, an instant; = POINT *sb.*^{1} A. 7. *Obs.*

1620 BP. J. KING *Serm. 24 Mar.* 23 Let no man..tye him to canonicall houres, atomes, and puntilio's of time, *tempus, tempus, statutum tempus.* **1659** *Unhappy Marksman* in *Harl. Misc.* (1809) IV. 4 In that punctilio of time wherein the bullets struck him..he is in an instant disanimated. **1679** C. NESSE *Antichrist* 235 To leave the pointing out of this punctilio of time to God only.

†**4.** A minute point, detail, or particular; a particle, whit, jot; a trifling point; a thing of no importance, a trifle. *Obs.* (exc. as in 5).

1642 FULLER *Holy & Prof. St.* IV. xvi. 323 He is zealous of the least puntillo's of his Masters honour. **1642** CHAS. I *Treaty at Oxford* Wks. 1662 II. 257 If every Punctilio must be forced to be sent forwards and backwards a hundred miles. **1796** BURKE *Regic. Peace* iii. Wks. VIII. 330 When one of the parties..will not..abate a single punctilio. **1815** J. ADAMS *Wks.* (1856) X. 131 We have never..lost any one punctilio of those rights or liberties.

5. a. A minute detail of action or conduct; a nice point of behaviour, ceremony, or honour; a small or petty formality. Formerly sometimes, A fine-drawn or fastidious objection, a scruple.

1599 [see 1]. **1626** J. PORY in Ellis *Orig. Lett.* Ser. I. III. 245 The Bishop stood upon his punctilios. **1638** FORD *Lady's Trial* I. ii, Guzman..observes the full punctilios of his nation. *a* **1680** BUTLER *Rem.* (1759) II. 50 He professes a mortal Hatred to Ceremonies, and yet has more Punctilios than a Jew. **1775** SHERIDAN *Duenna* I. ii, To trifle with me at such a juncture as this!—now to stand on punctilios! **1809–10** COLERIDGE *Friend* (1818) III. 248 In consequence of some punctilio, as to whose business it was to pay the compliment of the first call. **1836** H. ROGERS *J. Howe* ii. (1863) 17 He [Laud] was ready to visit the omission of the most trifling ecclesiastical punctilios with relentless severity.

b. (without *pl.*) Strict observance of or insistence upon minutiæ of action or conduct; petty formality in behaviour; punctiliousness.

1596, 1615 [see A]. **1676** D'URFEY *Mme. Fickle* I. i, My Lord was as unmannerly a Fellow as I ever saw... Ha, ha, ha—He a Noble man, and punctilio no better. **1709** STEELE *Tatler* No. 36 ¶2 [She] takes the Whole of this Life to consist in understanding Punctilio and Decorum. **1747** RICHARDSON *Clarissa* (1811) I. xxxvi. 271 People of birth stood a little too much on punctilio. **1820** W. IRVING *Sketch Bk., Spectre Bridegr.*, The preliminaries [of the marriage] had been conducted with proper punctilio. **1943** *R.A.F. Jrnl.* Aug. 22 All the matchless punctilio of an iron discipline coloured his daily round. **1978** J. UPDIKE *Coup* (1979) iv. 171 These noodly motifs the French had brought, along with military science, the metric system, and punctilio.

†**c.** (?) A punctilious person. *Obs. rare*$^{-1}$.

1603 HARSNET *Pop. Impost.* 47 A Male-content standing upon his worth like some of our high Puntilios scorned to sort himselfe with any of his ranke.

†**6.** A (or the) precise point or fact. *Obs. rare.*

1654 VILVAIN *Theol. Treat.* ii. 76 By their doctrin al depends on the peremptory punctilio of Gods..Decree. **1683** F. HODELSTON in *Lond. Gaz.* No. 1860/5 Treasonable Practices to a Punctillio of Rebellion, contriving the Murder of Your Person.

7. *attrib.* (or *adj.*) and *Comb.*

1660 MILTON *On Griffiths Serm.* Wks. 1851 V. 396 Should they who were left sitting, break up, or not dare enact aught ..for the punctilio wanting of a full number? **1702** VANBRUGH *False Friend* v. i, The injury's too great for a punctilio satisfaction. **1761** CHURCHILL *Rosciad* Poems (1769) I. 40 The nice punctilio-mongers of this age, The grand minute reformers of the stage.

Hence (*nonce-wds.*) **punc'tilionist,** one who is scrupulous about punctilios, a stickler about small points of behaviour or proceeding; **punc'tilioship,** punctilious performance (= sense 5 b).

1714 SAVAGE *Art of Prudence* 183 Punctilioship is tiresome. **1825** *New Monthly Mag.* XV. 200 A compliance.. which we could wish to see more frequent with other punctilionists of the drama.

punctili'osity. *rare.* [f. next: see -OSITY.] = PUNCTILIOUSNESS.

1858 MASSON *Milton* (1859) I. 454 A kind of sweet, modest punctiliosity is the virtue he strives to paint.

punctilious (pʌŋk'tɪlɪəs), *a.* Also 7 **puntillious,** 7–8 **punctillious.** [ad. F. *pointilleux, -euse*, f. *pointille*, ad. It. *puntiglio*: = mod.It. *puntiglioso*.] Attentive to punctilios; strictly observant of nice points or details of action or behaviour.

1634 ROWLEY *Noble Souldier* IV. i. in Bullen *O. Pl.* I. 307 His deeds were so Puntillious. **1653** H. COGAN *Pinto's Trav.* lxv. (1663) 263 These Jacas are the most punctillious.. Nation of the world. **1742** YOUNG *Nt. Th.* v. 425 On each punctilious pique of pride, Or gloom of humour. **1858** BUCKLE *Civiliz.* (1873) II. viii. 585 The punctilious honour of a Spanish gentleman has passed into a byeword. **1870** SWINBURNE *Ess. & Stud.* (1875) 225 The punctilious if not pedantic precision which has reformed the whole scheme of punctuation.

punc'tiliously, *adv.* [f. prec. + -LY^2.] In a punctilious manner; with precise or scrupulous attention to minute points of action or conduct.

1770 JOHNSON *False Alarm* Wks. (1787) X. 20, I have thus punctiliously and minutely pursued this disquisition. **1814** SCOTT *Wav.* lvi, Sternly and punctiliously greeting each other, like two duellists before they take their ground. **1849** MACAULAY *Hist. Eng.* vi. II. 10 So conspicuous an example of good faith punctiliously observed.

punc'tiliousness. [f. as prec. + -NESS.] The quality or character of being punctilious; scrupulous attentiveness to small points of conduct.

1685 *Gracian's Courtiers Orac.* 168 Punctiliousness is tiresome. There are whole Nations sick of that Nicety. **1838** MISS MAITLAND *Lett. fr. Madras* xxi. (1843) 218 He is a good man, but gives great offence by his punctiliousness about minor matters. **1882** FROUDE *Short Stud.* (1883) IV. II. vi. 252 They had their periods of outward repentance and ceremonial punctiliousness.

†**punc'tille.** *Obs. rare.* Also puntille. [ad. F. *pointille*: see PUNCTILIO; influenced by L. *punctum* and med.L. dim. *punctillum*.] = PUNCTILIO 5, 5 b.

1610 J. MORE in *Buccleuch MSS.* (Hist. MSS. Comm.) I. 87 It was a hard matter to give them contentment in such punctilles. *a* **1648** LD. HERBERT *Hen. VIII* (1649) 277 Their first meeting..was not without some of that Emulation and Puntille which is ordinary in their Sex.

†**'punction.** *Obs.* [ad. L. *punctiōn-em*, n. of action from *pungĕre, punct-* to prick. Cf. F. *ponction* (16th c. Calvin, Paré), Sp. *punzion*, It. *punzione*.] The action or an act of pricking or puncturing; a prick, a puncture. Also *fig.*

1543 TRAHERON *Vigo's Chirurg.* III. I. xv. 106 For the cure of synnowes hurte by punction. *a* **1548** HALL *Chron., Rich. III* 53 b, A punccion and pricke of hys synfull conscyence. **1677** W. HARRIS tr. *Lemery's Chym.* (ed. 3) 254 Its Emetick quality..can proceed from nothing but a punction made in the stomach. **1707** *Curios. in Husb. & Gard.* 99 The Punction of Plants, and the Pruning of Vines.

b. A pricking sensation.

1597 A. M. tr. *Guillemeau's Fr. Chirurg.* 48/1 With bitinge payn, with continuall punctions. **1607** TOPSELL *Four-f. Beasts* (1658) 202 Goats cheese also represseth all dolors and punctions. **1688** R. HOLME *Armoury* II. 387/2 A Punction, or Punctious feeling.

†**'punctious,** *a. Obs. rare*$^{-1}$. [f. prec.: see -OUS.] Of the nature of a 'punction'; pricking.

1688 [see prec. b].

punctist ('pʌŋktɪst). [f. L. *punctum* POINT + -IST.] One who holds the vowel-points in the Hebrew Scriptures to be authoritative.

1859 T. S. HENDERSON *Mem. E. Henderson* iii. 118 *note*, Mr. Henderson..had become a punctist before 1811,.. though he never went to the full-length of the writer above-mentioned, who vindicated even for the pause-accents 'the signature of a divine hand'.

puncti'uncle. *nonce-wd.* [ad. L. *punctiuncula*, dim. of *punctio*.] A very minute or trifling point.

1874 F. HALL in *N. Amer. Rev.* CXIX. 328 All the punctiuncles of the Quinquarticular Controversy.

†**'punctive,** *a. Obs. rare*$^{-1}$. [app. f. L. *punctum* point + -IVE.] In quot. app. Making straight for a point.

1612 R. DABORNE *Chr. turn'd Turke* I. i, Who like a ship vnman'd..doth seeme to make a course Direct and punctiue, till we see it dash Against some prouder Sylla.

puncto, obs. var. of PUNTO[1].

punctograph ('pʌŋktəgrɑːf, -græf). *Surg.* [ad. G. *punktograph*, f. L. *punct-um* point: see -GRAPH.] An instrument for ascertaining the precise position of a foreign body imbedded in the bodily tissues.

[**1901** *Lancet* 4 May 1292/1 For the surgical localisation of foreign bodies, such as bullets embedded in the tissues, he [Dr. Rosenthal of Munich] had, in conjunction with Surgeon-General Professor von Angerer, devised an instrument called the 'punktograph'.]

punctorious (pʌŋk'tɔərɪəs), *a. rare.* [f. L. **punctōri-us* (in *punctōrium* a piercing instrument) + -OUS.] Having the quality or property of pricking or puncturing. So †'**punctory** *a. Obs.*

1819 G. SAMOUELLE *Entomol. Compend.* 273 Sting not punctorious. **1661** LOVELL *Hist. Anim. & Min.* 432 Paine if punctory, is in the membranes; if pulsatorie in the arteries.

punctual ('pʌŋktjuːəl), *a.* (*sb.*) [ad. med.L. *punctuāl-is* (Grosseteste *c* 1210), f. L. *punctu-s* (*u-* stem) a pricking, a point: see -AL[1]. Cf. F. *ponctuel* (14th c. in Hatz.-Darm.).]

I. †**1.** *Surg.* **a.** Of the nature of a point or puncture: = PUNCTAL *a.* a. **b.** Used for making punctures, sharp-pointed, as a cautery or other surgical instrument. *Obs.*

c **1400** *Lanfranc's Cirurgie* 271 Sum men maken punctual cauterijs in þe maner of a cros vpon dindimum, & þan aftirward heliþ it vp. **1541** R. COPLAND *Guydon's Quest. Chirurg.* Piij, The fourth [cautery] is named punctuall, which hath the poynte sclendre and rounde. **1597** A. M. tr. *Guillemeau's Fr. Chirurg.* 20b/1 We may, in steade of the crooked lancet, vse our punctuall instrument.

II. 2. a. Of, pertaining to, or made by, a point or dot; of or belonging to punctuation.

1609 J. DOULAND *Ornith. Microl.* 54 If you finde two Semibreefe Rests after a perfect Breefe, it shall remaine perfect, vnlesse punctuall Diuision come betweene. **1818** COLERIDGE in *Encycl. Metrop.* (1845) I. Introd. §2 His days, months, and years, as the stops and punctual marks in the records of duties performed. **1904** T. HUTCHINSON in Shelley *Wks.* p. iv, Amongst the Editor's Notes at the end of the volume the reader will find lists of the punctual variations in the longer poems. **1930** *Bookman's Jrnl.* XVIII. xiv. (Second Supplement) 15 Both books have been entirely reset for this edition, and in addition to many minor alterations, mainly punctual, there is a new preface. **1931** *Times Lit. Suppl.* 16 Apr. 305/3 A punctual variation (which is also a misprint) between the publisher's imprint in the first two and in the third volume is not recorded.

b. *Geom.* Of or pertaining to a point: as ***punctual co-ordinates***, the co-ordinates of a point.

†**3. a.** Of the nature of or resembling a point or speck; small, minute (*lit.* and *fig.*). *Obs.*

1605 BACON *Adv. Learn.* I. iii. §8 Many may be well seene in the passages of governement and policie, which are to seeke in little and punctuall occasions. **1613** R. CAWDREY *Table Alph.* (ed. 3), *Punctuall*, small, or of no great force. **1639** FULLER *Holy War* III. xxiv. (1647) 154 The infinitenesse of punctual occurrences. **1667** MILTON *P.L.* VIII. 23 This Earth a spot, a graine, An Atom, with the Firmament compar'd And all her numberd Starrs, that seem to rowle Spaces incomprehensible . . meerly to officiate light Round this opacous Earth, this punctual spot.

†**b.** as *sb.* A minute point, a subtlety. *rare.*

1610 G. FLETCHER *Tri. over Death* xii, Let the . . schools these punctualls Of wills, all good, or bad, or neuter diss.

III. †**4. a.** Bearing directly on the point; to the point, to the purpose, apposite, apt. *Obs.*

1612 BACON *Charge touching Duels* Wks. 1879 I. 680/2 It is so punctual, and hath such reference and respect unto the received conceits. **1616** BULLOKAR *Eng. Expos.*, *Punctuall*, . . short, and direct to the purpose. **1629** PRYNNE *Ch. Eng.* 59 Nothing can be more full and punctuall to our present conclusion. **1642** ROGERS *Naaman* 347 If a man would compile a story . . for the demonstration of Providence, could he frame a more punctuall one?

b. Express, direct; explicit, definite. *arch.*

1615 T. ADAMS *Spir. Navig.* 33 The sea is full of monsters. Innumerable and almost incredible are the relations of Travellers in this punctuall demonstration. **1624** BP. MOUNTAGU *Gagg.* Pref. 5 Saint Augustine is punctuall . . that the severall Latine Translations in his time, could not be numbred. **1699** BENTLEY *Phal.* 179 A plain and punctual testimony. **1862** CARLYLE *Fredk. Gt.* XII. i. III. 169 The Polack King . . left his Dominions shared by punctual bequest among his five sons.

IV. 5. a. Exact in every point; precise, accurate. Now *rare* or *arch.*

1620 E. BLOUNT *Horæ Subs.* 536 If any do not find so punctual an agreement as hee expects. **1630** DAVENANT *Cruel Brother* IV. H2b, Be nimble then: and tell me punctuall truth. **1662** STILLINGFL. *Orig. Sacr.* II. vi. §8 Those predictions . . have had their punctuall accomplishment. **1752** SIR H. BEAUMONT *Crito* 5, I should as soon think of dissecting a Rainbow . . as of forming grave and punctual Notions of Beauty. **1852** SIR W. HAMILTON *Discuss. Philos.*, etc. 436 The punctual accuracy of our statement.

b. Of time or date: Exact or precise. Now *rare* or *arch.* Cf. 8.

1639 FULLER *Holy War* IV. ix. (1647) 183 About this time (though we find not the punctuall date thereof) happened the death of Reinoldus Fredericks. **1657** W. MORICE *Coena quasi Κοινὴ* II. 130 We doe not binde . . ourselves to a precise and punctual instant. **1710** WHEATLEY *Ch. of Eng. Man's Comp.* §23 As to the punctual time when the posture of kneeling [at Holy Communion] first began, it is hard to determine. **1826-7** DE QUINCEY *Lessing* Wks. 1859 XIII. 258 Nothing obliges the poet (like the painter) to concentrate his picture into one punctual instant of time.

c. Occurring at a precise point of time; exactly or aptly timed; timely. *rare.*

1611 SPEED *Hist. Gt. Brit.* IX. xx. (1623) 974 Sir William Stanley Lord Chamberlain to King Henry (by whose punctuall reuolt from K. Richard he had principally achieued the crown). **1816** WORDSW. *Ode Thanksgiving Day* i, Hail, orient Conqueror of gloomy Night! . . Whether thy punctual visitations smite The haughty towers where monarchs dwell; Or [etc.].

d. Of or belonging to a precise place. *rare.*

1805 WORDSW. *Prelude* VIII. 610 The human nature unto which I felt That I belonged . . Was not a punctual presence, but a spirit Diffused through time and space. **1843** DE QUINCEY *Ceylon* Wks. 1859 XII. 10 Whereas human nature has ever been prone to the superstition of local consecrations . . it is the usage of God to hallow such remembrances by removing . . all traces of their punctual identities.

e. *Gram.* Of action: occurring at a point in time; of aspect or tense: relating to an action or event that occurs at a point in time. Also as *sb.*, the punctual aspect or tense of a verb.

1914 L. BLOOMFIELD *Introd. Study Lang.* v. 145 The Slavic languages distinguish . . between . . durative and iterative . . action . . and . . punctual and terminative action. **1924** [see ASPECT *sb.* 9b]. **1933** L. BLOOMFIELD *Language* xvi. 272 The English categories of *aspect* distinguish between 'punctual' action (some grammarians call it perfective), envisaged as a unit, and 'durative' action . . which extends over a segment of time. **1956** J. GONDA *Character Indo-Europ. Moods* iv. 44 The pronounced preference for the aorist may be understood from the predilection for the punctual aspect in formulating prohibitions. **1962** —— *Aspectual Function of Ṛgvedic Present & Aorist* i. 19 The aorist . . . is considered 'punctual', whether the initial moment (δακρῦσαι 'burst into tears'), or the end (πεῖσαι 'to persuade, talk over') is indicated. **1971** *Archivum Linguisticum* II. 112 This means that the 'punctual meaning' and the other meanings traditionally thought of as the aorist's are, as far as the sigmatic aorist is concerned, simply another specialization, restricted to a limited dialectal field. *Ibid.* 113 Gonda makes some criticism of the general statement . . that VI class presents are 'punctuals', sometimes used to express punctual action, sometimes to describe actions indifferent to duration, but which sometimes can be thought of as punctual.

†**6.** Dealing with a matter point by point; minute, detailed, circumstantial. (Often with mixture of sense 5.) *Obs.*

1628 P. SMART (*title*) The Vanitie and Downe-fall of Svperstitiovs Popish Ceremonies, . . A Sermon . . containing not onely an Historical relation of all those severall Popish Ceremonies and practises . ., But likewise a punctual confutation of them. *c* **1645** HOWELL *Lett.* (1726) 40 A punctual relation of all the circumstances. **1772** NUGENT tr. *Hist. Fr. Gerund.* IV. v. 108 Having . . given a punctual topographical description of Anthony Zote's house.

V. 7. (Of persons, or their actions or attributes.) Attentive to, or insisting upon, points or details of conduct; punctilious.

a. Strictly or minutely observant of ceremony or convention; formal, ceremonious. *Obs.* or *arch.*

1609 [implied in PUNCTUALLY *adv.* 5]. **1618** WITHER *Motto Nec Curo* Juvenil. (1633) 560 Stand upon their points of honour so As if their Credit had an overthrow . . if in ought they misse Wherein the accomplisht Gallant punctuall is. **1626** MEADE in Ellis *Orig. Lett.* Ser. I. III. 220 It was one of the most punctual coronations since the Conquest. **1631** W. SALTONSTALL *Pict. Loq.* Dv, [He] gives his words such a punctuall stiffe pronunciation. **1702** *Eng. Theophrast.* 110 To have to do with a punctual, finical fop. **1725** C. PITT *Vida's Art Poetry* II. (1726) 39 So much on punctual niceties they stand. **1866** B. TAYLOR *Serapion* Poems 344 A hard cold man of punctual face.

b. Strictly or minutely observant of rule, principle, or obligation; attentive to duty; strict, precise, particular, scrupulous. Now *rare* or *arch.* exc. as implied in 8.

1598 [implied in PUNCTUALLY *adv.* 5]. **1625** BACON *Apophth.* §294 A gentleman that was punctual of his word. **1668** DRYDEN *Ess. Dram. Poesy* 44 We are not altogether so punctual as the French, in observing the lawes of Comedy. **1735** SOMERVILLE *Chase* II. 373 What these command, Those execute with Speed, and punctual Care. **1879** FROUDE *Cæsar* iv. 37 His punctual discharge of his duties.

c. Precise, accurate, exact, careful of details (in statement or action). *Obs.* or *arch.*

1620 SHELTON *Quix.* II. l. 332 Cid Hamete, the most punctuall Searcher of the very moats of this true History. **1636** POCKLINGTON *Sunday no Sabbath* (1637) 22 S. Nyssen is more punctuall and cleere: the Lords day (saith he) begins at cockcrowing. **1728** POPE *Dunc.*, *M. Scriblerus on Title* (1743) I. 39 *n.*, That accurate and punctual man of letters. **1845** CARLYLE *Cromwell* (1871) II. I. 190 *n.*, The punctual contemporaneous Collector has named him with his pen.

8. *spec.* Exactly observant of an appointed time; up to time, in good time; not late. (Also of actions.) The prevailing current sense.

In ***punctual to*** this sense is a contextual use of 7b.

1675 NEVILE tr. *Machiavelli's Marr. Belphegor* Wks. 527 He borrowed mony . . but . . he was not over-punctual to his day. **1694** CONGREVE *Double Dealer* v. x, *Mask.* Madam, you will be ready? *Cyn.* I will be punctual to the minute. *a* **1715** BURNET *Own Time* III. (1766) II. 41 He [Sir E. Godfrey] was a punctual man to good hours: so his servants were amazed when he did not come home. **1784** COWPER *Task* VI. 127 The undeviating and punctual sun. **1815** JANE AUSTEN *Emma* i, Every body was punctual, every body in their best looks. **1875** MRS. RANDOLPH *Wild Hyacinth* I. 54, I do wish you would be more punctual.

†'**punctualist.** *Obs. rare*$^{-1}$. [f. prec. + -IST.] One who discusses or treats of points of conduct or ceremony.

1641 MILTON *Ch. Govt.* II. i. Wks. 1851 III. 152 Bilson hath decipher'd us all the galanteries of Signore and Monsignore, and Monsieur as circumstantially as any punctualist of Casteel, Naples, or Fountain Bleau could have don.

punctuality (pʌŋktjuː'ælɪtɪ). [f. PUNCTUAL + -ITY. Cf. med.L. *punctuālitās* (Wyclif 1361); F. *ponctualité* (1629 in Hatz.-Darm.).]

I. The quality or character of being punctual (in various senses), or an instance of this.

1. a. Exactness, accuracy, precision; regularity; minuteness; preciseness; circumstantialness. Now *rare* or *arch.*

1620 SHELTON *Quix.* II. xlvii. 313 To recount with all the punctualitie, & truth that he vsually doth. **1631** MASSINGER *Emperor East* I. ii, I have . . With curious punctuality set down, To a hair's-breadth, how low a new-stamp'd courtier May vail to a country gentleman. **1750** JOHNSON *Rambler* No. 62 ¶9, I can relate, with great punctuality, the lives of all the last race of wits and beauties. **1846** TRENCH *Mirac.* v, St. Mark, with his usual punctuality, notes that they [the Gadarene swine] were 'about two thousand'.

†**b.** (with *a* and *pl.*) An instance of precision or accuracy; a small point, a nicety, a detail. *Obs.*

1661 FELL *Dr. Hammond* 95 His Memory, 'twas . . faithful to things and business, but unwillingly retaining the contexture and punctualities of words. **1701** GREW *Cosm. Sacra* IV. i. 140 Which Punctualities . . did not so much conduce to preserve the Text. **1714** MRS. MANLEY *Adv. Rivella* 12 She understands good Breeding to a Punctuality. *a* **1734** NORTH *Exam.* III. viii. §44, I kept no Journal. . . Therefore I am sensible that many Punctualities are here wanting.

c. *Gram.* The quality or character of being punctual (sense 5e); the punctual aspect of a verb.

1962 J. GONDA *Aspectual Function of Ṛgvedic Present & Aorist* i. 31 The basic notion of the opposition present stem: aorist stem in Greek is that of duration, the present being the marked term, the aorist which is the unmarked term sometimes being indifferent in respect to duration . . sometimes expressing punctuality. *Ibid.* 34 The fundamental idea of nondurativeness ('punctuality') in the aorist. **1971** *Archivum Linguisticum* II. 113 Both notions (non-duration and punctuality) became unified at a certain time, that is to say, their meanings became compatible, appearing alternatively according to context.

2. a. Formality, ceremoniousness; formal style: = PUNCTILIO 5b. *Obs.* or *arch.*

1629 MASSINGER *Picture* II. ii, The state were miserable if the Court had none Of her owne breede . . With forme and punctuallity to receiue Stranger Embassadours. **1742** AKENSIDE *Let. to Dyson* Poems (1845) 15 Those precisenesses of form and punctuality. **1755** JOHNSON *Let. to B. Langton* 6 May in *Boswell*, Your own elegance of manners, and punctuality of complaisance.

†**b.** (with *pl.*) = PUNCTILIO 5. *Obs.*

1641 EARL MONM. tr. *Biondi's Civil Warres* IV. 88 All punctuallities are vaine if unusefull, and foolish if harmfull. **1751** JOHNSON *Rambler* No. 112 ¶1 He that too long observes nice punctualities.

3. a. Precise observance of rule or obligation; strictness in the performance of duty; scrupulousness. Now *rare* or *arch.*

1640 HOWELL *Dodona's Gr.* 169 Those that . . hereafter should serve other Princes with that punctuality as Sophronio had done. **1689** D. GRANVILLE in *Surtees Misc.* (1858) 95, I did faithfully, and with as much punctuallity as I was able, discharge those trusts. **1748** *Anson's Voy.* III. x. 406 The resolution of the English at the fire, and their trustiness and punctuality elsewhere, was the general subject of conversation. **1863** A. BLOMFIELD *Mem. Bp. Blomfield* II. ix. 185 Scrupulous punctuality in all his engagements.

b. (with *pl.*) An instance of strictness in conduct; a point of duty or right. Now *rare* or *Obs.*

1639 LD. DIGBY, etc. *Lett. conc. Relig.* (1651) 74 There were so many circumstances that might tempt and lead them from the exact punctualities of a sincere conveyer. **1750** JOHNSON *Rambler* No. 70 ¶5 Ready to exact the utmost punctualities of right, and to consider every man that fails in any part of his duty, as without conscience. **1858** J. MARTINEAU *Stud. Chr.* 131 What . . must have been the feelings of the Hebrew, when told that all his punctualities had been thrown away?

4. Exact observance of an appointed time; the fact or habit of being in good time. (The prevailing current sense.)

1777 SHERIDAN *Sch. Scand.* IV. iii, *Joseph.* O, madam, punctuality is a species of constancy—a very unfashionable custom among ladies. **1849-50** W. IRVING *Mahomet* viii. (1853) 29 The troops . . summoned . . arrived at the appointed time with a punctuality recorded by the Arabian chroniclers as miraculous. **1880** MISS BRADDON *Just as I am* xlv, She is always a pattern of punctuality.

5. The character of a geometrical point; the fact of having position but no magnitude. *rare*$^{-1}$.

1881 G. S. HALL *German Cult.* 230 The very possibility of unspaciality or punctuality must be inferred as negative instances from indeterminate extension and movement.

II. 6. *pl.* Particulars or characteristics of punctuation. *nonce-use.*

1825 LAMB *Let. old Gentlem.* Wks. 1870 III. 306 He must be a thorough master of vernacular orthography, with an insight into the accentualities and punctualities of modern Saxon, or English.

punctually ('pʌŋktjuːəlɪ), *adv.* [f. PUNCTUAL + -LY².] In a punctual manner.

†**1.** By or as by pricking; in the way of puncture, or (*fig.*) of compunction. *Obs. rare.*

1631 R. BOLTON *Comf. Affl. Consc.* 134 'They were pricked in their heart'. *Marg.* The word in the originall signifieth to vexe, rent, and wound punctually. **1647** TRAPP *Comm. Acts* ii. 37 Punctually pricked and pierced.

†**2.** To the point, directly; explicitly, expressly; definitely, with direct aim, point-blank. *Obs.*

Quot. 1570 appears to belong here.

1570 BP. LESLEY *Let.* 15 Jan. in Robertson *Hist. Scot.* App. 67 For the retiring of her forces puntyvally for lack of aid. **1615** BYFIELD *Expos. Colos.* ii. 19 It is a most happy ability to speak punctually, directly to the point. **1638** ROUSE *Heav. Univ.* x. (1702) 152 Christ our Master punctually and expressly doth call for excellent Fruits of his Desciples. **1657** HAWKE *Killing is M.* Pref., This pestilent and perilous Libel, which punctually leveleth at the ruin and fate of his Highness. **1669** STURMY *Mariner's Mag.* v. xii. 68 Shooting punctually, Levill by a dispart 206. Paces.

3. Precisely, exactly, accurately, in every point or detail. *Obs.* or *arch.*

1604 E. G[RIMSTONE] *D'Acosta's Hist. Indies* VI. viii. 450 A kinde of writing with small stones, by meanes whereof, they learne punctually the words they desire to know by heart. **1678** CUDWORTH *Intell. Syst.* I. iv. §14. 240 The Question is so punctually stated..that there is no possibility of any subterfuge left. **1738** BIRCH *Milton* App., M.'s Wks. I. 69 Had the Memorandum been punctually dated. **1887** STEVENSON *Bks. which influenced me* Wks. 1895 III. 284 To understand that he is not punctually right, nor those from whom he differs absolutely wrong.

†**4.** Point by point; in detail; minutely, circumstantially. (Often with mixture of sense 3.)

1620 E. BLOUNT *Horæ Subs.* 533, I should now punctually search the seuerall Authors, and Inuenters of Lawes, amongst different Nations..but that would bee too long. **1649** MILTON *Eikon.* xx, This Chapter cannot punctually be answer'd without more repetitions than now can be excusable. **1679** *Hist. Jetzer* 31 The Papal Brief being read, and Jetzer Examined punctually of all his Confession. *a* **1741** CHALKLEY *Wks.* (1766) 26 He told me this Dream so punctually.

5. With careful attention to, or insistence upon, points or details of conduct; with strict observance of rule or obligation; strictly, scrupulously, carefully, punctiliously. Now *rare* exc. as in 6.

1598 BARRET *Theor. Warres* IV. i. 117 The other officers will more punctuallie performe their dutie. **1609** OVERBURY *St. France* (1626) 28 No men stand more punctually vpon their Honours in matter of Valour. **1719** DE FOE *Crusoe* (1840) II. xii. 251 The people..dealt very fairly and punctually with us in all their agreements and bargains. **1820** SOUTHEY *Wesley* II. 538 Never was resolution more punctually observed. **1859** LEWIN *Invas. Brit.* 78 Cæsar..found..that his orders for preparations had been punctually obeyed.

6. With strict observance of the appointed time; at the precise time. (Now the prevailing sense.)

In the early quots. contextual, the sense being really 3 or 5.

1647 CLARENDON *Hist. Reb.* IV. §161 All those..who were sent for, appeared punctually at the hour that was assigned them. **1691** RAY *Creation* I. (1692) 54 The Heavenly Bodies ..punctually come about in the same Periods to the hundredth part of a Minute. **1745** *De Foe's Eng. Tradesm.* ii. (1845) I. 18 [He] sends them up punctually by the time. **1896** SIR J. RIGBY in *Law Times Rep.* LXXIII. 614/2 If the instalments were not punctually paid, the building society would come down on the property. *Mod.* You can't expect the trains to arrive punctually on Christmas Eve.

'punctualness. Now *rare.* [f. as prec. + -NESS.] = PUNCTUALITY (in quots., in senses 1, 3).

1620 SHELTON *Quix.* II. xlviii. 318 That you may see the punctualnesse and good maners of my Husband. *a* **1652** J. SMITH *Sel. Disc.* VI. viii. (1821) 265, I will not here dispute the punctualness of these traditions..though I doubt not but the main scope of them is true. **1690** MARLBOROUGH in Wolseley *Life* (1894) II. 165 Nobody..shall with more punctuallness observe them [orders]. **1711** FELTON *On Classics* (1718) 94 The most Literal Translation of the Scriptures..is generally the best; and the same Punctualness which debaseth other Writings, preserveth the Spirit and Majesty of the Sacred Text.

†**'punctuary,** *a. Obs. rare*⁻¹. [ad. late or med.L. *punctuārius*, f. *punctu-s* pointing, point + -ARY.] Depending upon the Masoretic or other pointing of the Hebrew text of Scripture.

[**1575** SIXTUS SENENSIS *Biblioth. Sancta* I. 168/1 Στιγματική, sine Punctuaria exponendi Methodus]. **1657** W. MORICE *Cœna quasi Κοινή* II. 129, I perceive Sixtus Senensis ..was deceived, when telling us of a Stygmatical or punctuary interpretation of Scripture, he addes, that it is peculiar to the Hebrews.

punctuate ('pʌŋktjuːeɪt), *v.* [f. med.L. *punctuāre* (Du Cange) to prick, point, appoint, etc., whence It. *puntuare*, F. *ponctuer* (*c* 1500), f. L. *punctu-s* (*u*-stem) pointing, point.]

†**1.** *trans.* (?) To point out, note. *Obs. rare*⁻¹.

1634 W. TIRWHYT tr. *Balzac's Lett.* IV. ix. (vol. I) 331 You haue set such a luster upon that great City, and haue punctuated vnto me so many remarkeable things, and nouelties thereof, in the Letter you pleased to send me.

2. *Nat. Hist.* To mark with points or dots, esp. with small depressions resembling punctures. (? Usually in pa. pple.: see also PUNCTUATED 1, and PUNCTATE, -ED.) *rare.*

(?) **1818** R. P. KNIGHT *Symbolic Lang.* (1876) 105 A large white flower, the base and centre of which is..punctuated on the top with little..cavities, in which the seeds grow.

3. a. To insert the stops or punctuation-marks in (a sentence, etc.); to mark or divide with points or stops. Formerly *to point* (POINT *v.*¹ 3). Also *absol.*

1818 TODD, *To Punctuate*, to distinguish by pointing. **1841** [see PUNCTUATED 2]. **1848** *Where to Stop, and Why* 3 Some men punctuate according to vague ideas of sense [etc.]. **1884** P. ALLARDYCE *How to Punctuate* 52 All rhetorical questions are not thus punctuated. **1902** DE VINNE *Correct Compos.* 246 A knowledge of grammar is of great value in enabling a compositor to punctuate properly.

b. *fig.* †(*a*) To put a 'period' or stop to; to interrupt so as to bring to a close (*obs.*). (*b*) To interrupt at intervals (as a speech) by exclamations, etc.; to intersperse or 'dot' *with.*

1833 COLERIDGE *Table-t.* 29 June, I am glad you have come in to punctuate my discourse, which I fear has gone on for an hour without any stop at all. *c* **1865** E. DICKINSON *Poems* (1955) II. 731 A Flower's unobtrusive Face To punctuate the Wall. **1882** *Standard* 17 Mar. 3/1 That speech [Mr. Forster's] was..punctuated throughout with cries of 'Release the suspects'. **1892** ZANGWILL *Bow Mystery* 111 Mr. Gladstone's speech was an expansion of his postcard, punctuated by cheers. **1901** *Scotsman* 29 Oct. 9/4 The Miramar links are long and well punctuated with difficult hazards. **1941** *Penguin New Writing* II. 54 They communicated with each other in a low drone.., punctuated by an occasional deep-throated 'Ah!' **1966** C. M. BOWRA *Memories 1898–1939* v. 98 Roy Harrod.. punctuated his speeches with such phrases as 'I dare aver' or 'if you will permit the observation'. **1971** E. MAVOR *Ladies of Llangollen* ix. 159 Great delicacy had to be employed on both sides of a correspondence which was apt to be punctuated with small wounded silences, implied accusations followed by temporary reconciliations. **1977** *Times* 25 Nov. (Christmas Book Suppl.) p. xxxi/4 The novel is one of many nicely turned backward looks that have worthily punctuated the year.

4. To give point to; to emphasize, accentuate.

1883 TALMAGE in *Chr. Globe* 829/2 Telling the Custom House officer, 'There is nothing in that trunk but wearing apparel', and putting a 5 dol. gold piece in his hand to punctuate the statement. **1898** *Nat. Rev.* Dec. 501 To punctuate his perjury he added this remark.

'punctuate, *a. Nat. Hist.* = next, 1.

1890 in *Cent. Dict.*

'punctuated, *ppl. a.* [f. prec. vb. + -ED¹.]

1. Marked with, or composed of, dots; dotted: = PUNCTATE 1. (Chiefly *Nat. Hist.* and *Path.*)

1818 [see PUNCTUATE *v.* 2]. **1821–34** J. FORBES tr. *Laennec's Dis. Chest* (ed. 4) III. i. 393 The pleura in the state of acute inflammation presents a punctuated redness. **1893** TUCKEY *Amphioxus* 173 The mesoblastic somite boundaries indicated with punctuated lines.

2. Having the punctuation marks or stops inserted.

1841 *Penny Cycl.* XIX. 128/1 It must not be supposed that those [stops] which are usually inserted even in well punctuated books are sufficient [as a guide to reading].

‖**punctuatim** (pʌŋktjuː'eɪtɪm), *adv.* [mod.L., f. *punctu-s* point, after *verbatim*, *literatim*.]

a. 'Point for point'; with exact agreement in every point or detail; **b.** with exact correspondence of punctuation.

1623 T. POWELL *Attourn. Acad.* 166 The Originall must ..be so exactly set downe and drawn, that all the following Processe and proceeding, may be tyed to agree with it *punctuatim*. **1890** *Cent. Dict.* s.v., *Verbatim, literatim, et punctuatim*, word for word, letter for letter, and point for point.

punctuation (pʌŋktjuː'eɪʃən). [ad. med.L. *punctuātiōn-em*, n. of action from *punctuāre* to PUNCTUATE. Cf. F. *ponctuation* (1540 in Hatz.-D.).]

†**1.** The pointing of the psalms; the pause at the mediation. *Obs. rare.*

a **1539** in *Archaeologia* XLVII. 56 Your dyvyne seruice to be treateably song..with good pause and punctuation. **1782** BURNEY *Hist. Mus.* II. 18 *note*, The punctuation of the Psalms in the English Psalter, where a colon is constantly placed in the middle of a verse,..expresses this *Mediatio*, or breath-place.

2. The insertion of the vowel (and other) points in writing Hebrew and other Semitic languages (or those using a Semitic alphabet); the system of such points: = POINTING *vbl. sb.*¹ 2 b.

1659 BP. WALTON *Consid. Considered* 230 The punctuation of the Hebrew Text was an invention of the Masorites. *Ibid.* 272. **1838** *Penny Cycl.* XII. 93/1 It is now generally considered..that the whole system of punctuation was first introduced by the Masorites. **1870** J. F. SMITH *Ewald's Heb. Gram.* 37 There was formed gradually in the Massoretic schools..a set of reading signs..the so-called punctuation. **1880** *Encycl. Brit.* (ed. 9) XI. 600/1 A means of preserving not merely the consonants of this text but the exact punctuation and intonation of the synagogue.

3. a. The practice, art, method, or system of inserting points or 'stops' to aid the sense, in writing or printing; division of written or printed matter into sentences, clauses, etc. by means of points or stops. The ordinary sense.

1661 BOYLE *Style of Script.* Pref. (1675) 13 That there pass no mistakes of the punctuation. For..if the stops be omitted, or misplaced, it does..oftentimes quite spoil the sense. **1771** LUCKOMBE *Hist. Print.* 263 The expectation of a settled Punctuation is in vain, since no rules of prevailing authority have been yet established. **1824** L. MURRAY *Eng. Gram.* (ed. 5) I. 389 Punctuation is a modern art. The ancients were entirely unacquainted with the use of our commas, colons, &c. **1879** FARRAR *St. Paul* II. 248 *note*, On the punctuation of this..verse [Rom. ix. 5] a great controversy has arisen. **1895** W. A. COPINGER *Trans. Bibliogr. Soc.* II. ii. 113 As to punctuation..the *Lactantius*, printed at Subiaco in 1465, has a full point, colon, and note of interrogation.

b. *transf.* Observance, in reading or speaking, of the pauses, as indicated by the points or stops.

1807 ROBINSON *Archæol. Græca* V. xvi. 489 They were enjoined to pay the most scrupulous attention to punctuation... They often read the Fables of Æsop. **1863** MISS BRADDON *J. Marchmont* II. ii. 25 The good woman's talk..rambled on in an unintermitting stream, unbroken by much punctuation.

c. *fig.* The repeated occurrence or distribution (*of* something); something that makes repeated or regular interruptions or divisions.

1914 *Sat. Even. Post* 4 Apr. 12/1 The endless punctuation of ties led on and on until even the marshes rose and became level with the tracks. **1933** E. O'NEILL *Ah Wilderness!* I. 20 (*Stage direction*) The bang of firecrackers and torpedoes.. continues at intervals..sufficiently emphatic to form a disturbing punctuation to the conversation. **1970** H. BRAUN *Parish Churches* ix. 125 Vertical punctuation disciplines an elevation by sorting it out into orderly compartments and replacing confusion with a pleasant rhythm... Vertical punctuation is of course achieved by the pilasters, later becoming buttresses. Horizontal punctuation is primarily concerned with maintaining a sense of stability. **1977** *Times* 16 Apr. 14/4 It requires a considerable resistance to evidence not to see the Reformation, the Enlightenment, nineteenth-century liberalism and the current decline as stages in a continuous process rather than punctuations in an otherwise stable history.

†**4.** The action (or result) of marking by pricking or puncturing. *Obs. rare.*

1777 G. FORSTER *Voy. round World* I. 390 The punctuation which the natives call tattow.

5. *Nat. Hist.* = PUNCTATION 2.

1866 E. C. RYE *Brit. Beetles* 107 The elytra exhibit very coarse punctuation.

6. *attrib.*, as (sense 3) ***punctuation mark***.

1860 PRESCOTT *Elect. Telegr.* 88 Forty-one indications, corresponding to the letters in the alphabet, the numerals, and punctuation-marks.

Hence **punctu'ationist**, one who practises, studies, or treats of punctuation (sense 3).

1871 EARLE *Philol. Eng. Tongue* xii. 553 The line..may end in the middle of a phrase where the most lavish punctuationist could not bestow a comma.

punctuative ('pʌŋktjʊətɪv), *a.* [f. as PUNCTUATE *v.* + -IVE: see -ATIVE.] Of, pertaining to, or serving for punctuation (sense 3).

1855 J. RUSH *Philos. Hum. Voice* viii. (ed. 4) 154 The nature, or, if I may so call it, the punctuative intonation of this feeble cadence is such, that the ear allows a speaker either to pause after it, or to proceed in his discourse. **1874** M. COLLINS *Transmigr.* II. ii. 45 The note of interrogation is unknown in their punctuative system. **1883** *Q. Rev.* Jan. 187 The punctuative particles [in Corean]..giving in words the force of the comma, the colon, and the period.

punctuator ('pʌŋktjuːeɪtə(r)). [a. med.L. *punctuātor*, agent-n. f. *punctuāre* to PUNCTUATE.] One who punctuates.

1. *Heb. Gram.* = PUNCTATOR.

1659 BP. WALTON *Consid. Considered* 255 The word.. being without points was ambiguous, or capable of two significations, of which the one was followed by the translator, the other by the punctuators. **1880** W. ROBERTSON SMITH in *Encycl. Brit.* XI. 600/1 (*Hebrew Lang.*) The work of the punctuators was perhaps completed in the 7th century.

2. One who inserts the points or stops in writing or printing.

1846 WORCESTER, *Punctuator*, one who punctuates; punctuist. *S. Phelps.* **1885** *Sat. Rev.* 30 May 713/2 The sadly unintelligent punctuator of the *Times*.

†**'punctuist.** *Obs. rare.* [f. L. *punctu-s* pointing + -IST.] = prec.

1836 SMART, *Punctuist*, one skilled in punctuation. **1853** J. OWEN (of Thrussington) *Comm. Hebr.* App. 372 To connect 'forty years' with 'grieved', was the work of the Punctuists, and this mistake the Apostle corrected.

punctulate ('pʌŋktjʊlət), *a. Nat. Hist.* [ad. mod.L. *punctulāt-us*, f. *punctulum* (see PUNCTULE), after *punctum*, *punctāt-us*.] Marked or studded with punctules; minutely punctate.

1847 HARDY in *Proc. Berw. Nat. Club* II. No. 5. 237 Thorax quadrate, disk punctulate. **1870** HOOKER *Stud. Flora* 309 Fruit black, punctulate.

'punctulated (-leɪtɪd), *ppl. a.* [f. as prec. + -ED.]

†**a.** Consisting of small points or dots; dotted. *Obs.* **b.** *Nat. Hist.*, etc. = prec.

1685 H. MORE *Paralip. Prophet.* xxxi. 280 A perpetual *Porticus*, noted with three Lines, of which the middle is punctulated or made by points. *Ibid.* 281 The middle line, viz. that which is punctulated drawn through the midst of this walk. *a* **1728** WOODWARD *Nat. Hist. Fossils* (1729) I. 140 The Basis of this [stone] is flat and striated, the Ridges between the Striæ being punctulated. **1847** HARDY in *Proc. Berw. Nat. Club* II. No. 5. 242 Elytra..thickly, finely, and distinctly punctulated.

punctulation (pʌŋktjuːˈleɪʃən). *Nat. Hist.*, etc. [f. mod.L. *punctulāt-us* after prec. ppl. adj. + -ATION.] The condition of being punctulate; minute punctation; also *concr.* a number or mass of punctules.

1801 HERSCHEL in *Phil. Trans.* XCI. 292 The..darker coloured places in the punctulations. **1847** HARDY in *Proc. Berw. Nat. Club* II. No. 5. 244 The..less opacity of the elytra and abdomen, and the deeper and wider punctulation of the latter. **1858** GEIKIE *Hist. Boulder* vii. 119 Glossy scales ..ornamented with a very minute punctulation.

punctule (ˈpʌŋktjuːl). Also in Lat. form punctulum (ˈpʌŋktjʊləm), pl. -**a**. [ad. L. *punctulum*, dim. of *punctum* point.] A small point; *Nat. Hist.*, etc., a small punctum.

1640 WILKINS *New Planet* II. (1684) 82 What is this unto the vast frame of the whole Vniverse, but *punctulum*, such an insensible Point? **1837** WHEWELL *Hist. Induct. Sc.* I. v. iii. 405 And what is the earth and the ambient air with respect to the immensity of the universe? It is a point, a punctule.

‖**punctum** (ˈpʌŋktəm). Pl. puncta. [L. 'point', orig. neuter of *punctus*, pa. pple. of *pungĕre* to prick: cf. POINT *sb.*[1]]

†**1.** A point, in various figurative senses. *Obs.*

c **1590** GREENE *Fr. Bacon* ix. 33 Mongst the quadruplicitie Of elementall essence, *Terra* is but thought To be a *punctum* squared to the rest. *a* **1619** FOTHERBY *Atheom.* II. ix. §4 (1622) 298 God is that *Punctum*,..from whom, euery Creature..doth proceede;..and vnto whom, they bee destinated. *a* **1679** T. GOODWIN *Knowl. God* II. v, The punctum of which [assertion] lies in this, that in our Christ, God and man are become one person. **1683** KENNET tr. *Erasm. on Folly* 95 Which sentence is a Species of discrete Quantity, that has no permanent *punctum*.

†**2. a.** A (geometrical) point: = POINT *sb.*[1] A. 18.

1628 FELTHAM *Resolves* II. xxii, Like a Piramide, lessening it selfe by degrees, till it grows at last to a *punctum*, to a nothing. **1735** H. WALPOLE *Let. to R. West* 9 Nov., They plod on in the same eternal round, with their whole view confined to a punctum, *cujus nulla est pars*.

†**b.** A mere point of time, an instant: = POINT *sb.*[1] A. 7. *Obs.*

1682 BOYLE *2nd Pt. Contn. New Exp.* v. viii, I cast a flie into it, which died in one punctum of time.

†**3.** A chief or main point (see POINT *sb.*[1] A. 5), as opposed to *punctilio* (PUNCTILIO 4). *Obs.*

1651 BIGGS *New Disp.* Pref. 2 Though not the Punctilio's, yet the Puncta's the full points.

4. *Nat. Hist.* and *Path.* **a.** A minute rounded mark or visible object; a speck, dot; a minute rounded spot of colour, or of elevation or depression (esp. the latter), upon a surface: = POINT *sb.*[1] A. 2.

1665 NEEDHAM *Med. Medicinæ* 195 The least Creature that we can see without the help of Art, is a Mite, it resembling a little white *Punctum* or Point. **1808** *Med. Jrnl.* XIX. 164 The dark puncta of the petals and capsules afford this essential oil. **1826** KIRBY & SP. *Entomol.* III. xxxi. 245 In many of the hawkmoths..it [the skin of the pupa] is covered with impressed puncta. **1899** *Allbutt's Syst. Med.* VIII. 478 These papules..often disclose a central punctum.

b. ***punctum lachrymale***, pl. ***puncta lachrymālia*** (also ***lachrymal punctum***, or simply ***punctum***), the minute orifice of each of the two lachrymal canals at the corner of the eye. ***punctum saliens*** (cf. SALIENT *a.* 3), the first trace of the heart in an embryo, appearing as a pulsating point or speck; also *fig.*

For the origin of the latter cf. Aristotle *Hist. Anim.* VI. iii. τοῦτο δὲ τὸ σημεῖον πηδᾷ καὶ κινεῖται.

[**1651** HARVEY *De Generat. Animalium* 49 Apparet punctum sanguineum saliens, quod jam movetur (ait Aristoteles).]

1663 R. BOYLE *Consid. Usef. Nat. Philos.* II. i. 18 In Hen-eggs..you may observe the *Punctum saliens*, or Heart, to be ever and anon full of conspicuously red Blood. **1693** tr. *Blancard's Phys. Dict.* (ed. 2), *Lachrymale punctum*, an Hole made in the Bone of the Nose, by which the Matter that makes Tears, passes to the Nostrils. *Ibid.* s.v., In the growth of an Egg you see a little Speck or Cloud,..which growing gradually thicker, acquires a kind of slimy Matter, in the middle whereof you see first this *Punctum saliens* (a little Speck that seems to leap). **1780** BLIZARD in *Phil. Trans.* LXX. 243 The steel pipe was passed into the inferior punctum. **1812** *Edin. Rev.* July 169 To discover the origin of the *punctum saliens* in the incubated egg. **1814** M. BIRKBECK *Jrnl.* 18 Sept. in *Notes Journey through France* 83 Paris is the punctum saliens, the organ of political feeling; elsewhere political feeling is absorbed in the love of tranquillity. **1977** *Language* LIII. 56 The 'punctum saliens' is that it was the 'paradigmatic' alternation *u* ~ *o* which was felt to render the constituent structure opaque.

5. In mediæval music. **a.** (See quots.)

[**1879** HELMORE *Plainsong* 8 The Point (Punctum), having the value of a short note (*i.e.* a Semibreve).] **1901** H. E. WOOLDRIDGE *Oxf. Hist. Mus.* I. 116 The *punctum* or old grave accent, which signified a descending note, and the *virga* or old acute accent, which was used when the note ascended... The *virga* became the *longa*..and the *punctum* the *brevis*..of Discant. **1905** *Gram. Plainsong* 12 There are three forms of the single note: the square note or punctum, the tailed note, or virga, and the diamond.

b. A kind of inflexion used in singing collects, etc.

1853 DALE tr. *Baldeschi's Rom. Rite* 304 When the Prayer concludes with *Qui vivis* or *Qui tecum*, the Punctum only is used, as above in *Spiritus Sancte Deus*.

6. ***punctum indifferens*** (cf. INDIFFERENT *a.*[1] 8 a), a neutral point.

1923 A. T. QUILLER-COUCH *Shakespeare's Much Ado about Nothing* p. xv, Such a man is the Friar in this play; its steadying sane mind, its *punctum indifferens*. **1932** J. BUCHAN *Sir W. Scott* xiii. 342 This *punctum indifferens* is the peaceful anchorage of good sense from which we are able to watch with a balanced mind the storm outside. **1976** 'J. DAVEY' *Treasury Alarm* i. 11 Things may rearrange themselves around me just because I'm there—as a *punctum indifferens*.

7. *Palæogr.* A point used as a (weak) mark of punctuation in medieval manuscripts.

1952, 1975 [see PUNCTUS]. **1975** *Anglo-Saxon England* IV. 117 The poems in lyric metres are written across the page as prose, but each verse line is separated by at least a punctum (or greater punctuation if the syntax requires it). **1978** *N. & Q.* Oct. 396/1 Each octosyllabic couplet is written as one line, divided by a mid-line punctum.

†**punctuˈosity.** *Obs. rare*[−1]. [f. as if from a L. **punctuō-sus* or Eng. **punctuous* (cf. Sp. *puntuoso*) + -ITY.] = PUNCTUALITY I.

1733 *Shelton's Quix.* IV. vi. 43 (Dublin ed.) To recount with all the Punctuosity [*edd.* 1620, 1652, etc., punctualitie; Sp. *puntualidad*] and Truth that he usually doth.

puncturation (pʌŋktjʊəˈreɪʃən). [n. of action f. PUNCTURE *v.*: see -ATION.]

1. The action or operation of puncturing; in quot. 1733 in reference to a pricking sensation.

1733 CHEYNE *Eng. Malady* II. viii. §5 (1734) 197 Headachs either behind or over the Eyes, like a Puncturation. **1876** *Clin. Soc. Trans.* IX. 167 Mr. Squire, in place of the puncturation of Volckmann..prefers to scarify the skin with regular linear parallel incisions.

2. *Nat. Hist.* The condition of being punctured, pitted, or dotted; = PUNCTATION 2, PUNCTUATION 5.

1890 in *Cent. Dict.*

puncture (ˈpʌŋktjʊə(r)), *sb.* [ad. L. *punctūra* prick, puncture (Celsus), f. *punct-*, ppl. stem of *pungĕre* to prick: see -URE.]

1. a. An act, or the action, of pricking; a prick; perforation with a sharp-pointed instrument or object; in more recent use *spec.* an accidental perforation of a pneumatic tyre, as of a bicycle.

c **1400** *Lanfranc's Cirurg.* 16 If þat he be woundid in þe heed eiþer haue ony puncture of ony senewe. **1601** ? MARSTON *Pasquil & Kath.* III. 98 The pressure of my haires, or the puncture of my heart, stands at the seruice of your sollide perfections. **1646** SIR T. BROWNE *Pseud. Ep.* II. iii. 75 The Loadstone of Laurentius Guascus, wherewith.. whatsoever needles..were touched, the wounds and punctures made thereby, were never felt. **1765** *Chron.* in *Ann. Reg.* 157 The king of Denmark,..afflicted with a dropsical disorder, underwent..the operation of the puncture. **1846** LANDOR *Imag. Conv.* Ser. v. xxiii, A slight puncture will let out all the wind in the bladders. **1872** YEATS *Tech. Hist. Comm.* 153 The galls were the produce of the puncture of an insect. **1893** *Cycling* 28 Jan. 48/3 The specially thick outer cover renders burst or puncture practically impossible.

b. *fig.* A 'pricking'.

1660 JER. TAYLOR *Worthy Commun.* II. ii. 132 Although he feels no sensual punctures and natural sharpnesses of desire. **1780** S. J. PRATT *Emma Corbett* (ed. 4) III. 114 Henry felt the puncture of a want which even Emma could not accommodate.

†**c.** A sensation of pricking; a pricking pain. *Obs.*

1709 STEELE *Tatler* No. 36 ¶4 Our Africanus lives in the continual Puncture of aching Bones and poisoned Juices.

2. a. A mark, hole, or wound made by pricking.

1565 J. HALLE tr. *Lanfranc's Cirurg.* 4 If there be any Puncture in the sinewes. **1646** SIR T. BROWNE *Pseud. Ep.* v. xii. 251 The female Aspe hath foure, but the male two teeth, whereby it left this impression, or double puncture behinde it. **1777** G. FORSTER *Voy. round World* I. 391 His corpulence, his colour, and his punctures [tattoo-marks].. were very distinguishing marks of his rank. **1821** CRAIG in *Lect. Drawing* vii. 398 Making new scratches or punctures with the etching-needle. **1896** *Daily News* 27 June 8/4 The cyclist wrestling with a compound puncture and a refractory lamp.

†**b.** *Bot.* A prickly point on a surface. *Obs.*

1776 J. LEE *Introd. Bot.* Explan. Terms 385 *Scabrum*, rough, covered with rigid Punctures raised above the Surface.

c. *Zool.* A minute rounded pit or depression in a surface, as if made by pricking: cf. PUNCTUM 4.

1890 in *Cent. Dict.*

†**3.** The pricking part, the point. *Obs. rare*[−1].

1597 A. M. tr. *Guillemeau's Fr. Chirurg.* 17 b/2 A hollowe knife... The puncture or poyncte of the same.

4. *attrib.* and *Comb.* (chiefly in reference to pneumatic tyres, or to surgery). Also **puncture mark**, a mark made by a needle point, *esp.* in the injection of drugs.

1893 *Cycling* 15 July 445/3 The Puncture-Proof Pneumatic Company's trade-mark. *Ibid.* 448/2 By all means have puncture proof tubes. **1896** *Allbutt's Syst. Med.* I. 160 The study of puncture pyrexia [i.e. pyrexia produced by puncture of certain portions of the cerebral cortex]. **1904** *Brit. Med. Jrnl.* 20 Aug. 377 The puncture needle is then passed through the skin. **1907** *Daily Chron.* 12 Oct. 9/4 As an outcome of the plethora of cheap tyres attention has been re-directed towards puncture-preventing devices. **1927** D. L. SAYERS *Unnatural Death* xxiii. 274 Will you go down to the mortuary again and see if you can find any puncture mark on the body. **1935** A. CHRISTIE *Death in Clouds* ii. 23 There was a minute puncture mark on the side of her throat. **1957** D. DU MAURIER *Scapegoat* xxi. 280 The sleeve of her black wool coat fell back, showing the puncture marks between wrist and forearm. **1974** D. RAMSAY *No Cause to Kill* I. 13 She wasn't mainlining, but there's a mark on her arm that could be a puncture mark.

Hence **ˈpunctureless** *a.*, free from punctures; that cannot be punctured.

1890 *Cent. Dict.*, *Punctureless*, in *entom.*, without punctures; smooth. **1896** *Columbus* (Ohio) *Dispatch* 7 May 7/5 He rides a peculiar wheel with punctureless tyre.

ˈpuncture, *v.* [f. prec. sb.]

1. a. *trans.* To subject to puncture; to pierce with a sharp point; to prick; to perforate: esp. in *Surgery*. Also said of the instrument.

1699 GARTH *Dispens.* v. 350 With that he drew a lancet in his rage, To puncture the still supplicating sage. **1793** WELDON (*title*) On puncturing the bladder. **1807–26** S. COOPER *First Lines Surg.* (ed. 5) 112 When a large artery is only punctured, and not completely cut through. **1896** *Daily News* 4 Dec. 2/1, I punctured the tire within one mile of the start.

b. *spec.* To mark (the skin) with punctures; to tattoo.

1784 *Cook's Voy.* II. ix. 176 They differ in being of a darker colour, with a fiercer aspect, and differently punctured. **1848** LYTTON *Harold* VI. vi, His bare, brawny throat was punctured with sundry devices. **1859** J. C. CURTIS *Hist. Eng.* (1874) 5 All the Britons punctured their bodies.

c. *Nat. Hist.* To mark with spots or dots resembling punctures: chiefly in *pa. pple.*

1847 [see *puncturing* below]. **1860** HARTWIG *Sea & Wond.* vi. 82 The Narwal..is of a grey-white colour, punctured with many white spots.

d. *fig.* To 'prick'.

1896 *Nation* (N.Y.) 25 June 497/2 A few of the fallacies.. which Prof. Nicholson punctures. **1908** *Hibbert Jrnl.* Apr. 633 [He] may..touch [him]..with satire and even puncture him with epithet. **1927** *Scribner's Mag.* Apr. 450b/2 There is certain value in puncturing the Washington myth which the school histories used to teach. **1974** *Economist* 7 Sept. 16 It is time to puncture the continuing Greek accusation.

e. To punctuate or intersperse.

1899 C. M. M. SHELDON *His Brother's Keeper* xi. 249 The major..made a rattling speech, punctured with frequent amens and hallelujahs from the rest of the army.

2. To make (a hole, etc.) by pricking.

1831, 1865 [see PUNCTURED 2]. **1875** BENNETT & DYER *Sachs' Bot.* 701 If a hole is punctured by a fine needle in the bladder.

3. *pass.* and *intr.* or *absol.* To get a puncture: said of a pneumatic tyre, or *transf.* of the cycle or rider. *colloq.* Now *rare*.

1893 *Cycling* 15 Apr. 226/3 It was agreed that whoever punctured stood drinks round. *Ibid.* 1 July 401 I'm punctured! Have you got a repairing outfit? **1896** *Westm. Gaz.* 24 Apr. 3/2 During the last few years I have only punctured twice on the road. **1975** *Country Life* 4 Dec. 1529/2 Many cars suffered... Cowan punctured and spun.

Hence **ˈpuncturing** *vbl. sb.* (in quot., marking as with punctures, punctation), and *ppl. a.*

1847 HARDY in *Proc. Berw. Nat. Club* II. No. 5. 238 Variable..in the more or less frequent puncturing of the thorax. **1898** *Allbutt's Syst. Med.* V. 385 Keeping up a little pressure on the wound after the puncturing instrument has been withdrawn.

punctured (ˈpʌŋktjʊəd), *ppl. a.* [f. prec.]

1. Pricked, pierced, perforated. Also *fig.*

1672 R. VEEL *New Court Songs* 6 In vain the Surgeon does apply Soft Balsom to a punctur'd Heart. **1797** ABERNETHY *Surg. & Phys. Ess.* III. 97 One of the punctured places ulcerated. **1896** WELLS *Wheels Chance* ix. 62 Just then the other man in brown appeared..wheeling his punctured machine. **1898** BURR *Bicycle Repairing* ix. 135 To fix a burst casing and a punctured tire.

2. Made by puncturing; composed of punctures.

1807–26 S. COOPER *First Lines Surg.* (ed. 5) 401 A punctured wound, penetrating the side of the œsophagus. **1831** BREWSTER *Nat. Magic* iii. (1833) 43 The punctured pattern usually worked..round the edges of that garment [a shroud]. **1865** KINGSLEY *Herew.* i. *note*, William of Malmesbury, sub anno 1066..says that the English 'adorned their skins with punctured designs'. **1908** *Athenæum* 24 Oct. 516/3 The ornamentation of these beakers consists of small punctured dots arranged in parallel lines.

3. *Nat. Hist.* Marked with dots resembling punctures; punctate.

1860 [see PUNCTURE *v.* 1 c].

‖**punctus** (ˈpʌŋktəs, ˈpʊŋk-). *Palæogr.* [L., f. *pungere* to prick: cf. PUNCTUM.] A point, a punctuation mark. Freq. in phr. ***punctus elevatus*** (ɛləˈvɑːtəs), a raised point; ***punctus interrogativus*** (ɪntəˌrɒgəˈtiːvəs), a question mark; ***punctus versus*** (ˈvɜːsəs), a reversed point. See also quots.

1952 P. CLEMOES *Liturgical Influence on Punctuation in Late Old English & Early Middle English MSS* 4 *Punctus elevatus*, a symbol formed by combining *Punctum* and *Podatus*. It denoted the cadence with which a *Colon* ended, generally a gradual lowering of pitch followed by a return to the *Tuba* in one stage. *Ibid.* 5 *Punctus versus*, a symbol consisting of the *Punctum*. It denoted the cadence with which a *Periodus* ended. *Ibid.*, *Punctus interrogativus*, a symbol formed by combining *Punctum* and *Porrectus*. It denoted the cadence with which an interrogative sentence ended. **1954** D. WHITELOCK *Early Eng. MSS. in Facsimile* IV. 18/2 The usual mark of punctuation is the *punctus*, marking minor pauses as well as the end of sentences. *Ibid.*, A sign shaped like a semi-colon, the *punctus versus*, occurs. *Ibid.*, A mark like an inverted semi-colon, the *punctus elevatus*,..never marks the close of a period, but divides a main from a subordinate clause, or one subordinate clause from another. **1957** N. R. KER *Catal. MSS. containing Anglo-Saxon* p. xxxiv, The two marks, the dot and the ;, were reinforced at the end of the tenth century by a third mark, ;, which had been used hitherto only in Latin texts. It was known later in the Middle Ages as *punctus elevatus* and is often called now, inaccurately, the 'reversed semi-colon'. **1966** P. CLEMOES *Early Eng. MSS. in Facsimile* XIII. 24/1 Four marks are used, namely a simple point placed at about mid-height.. a *punctus elevatus*.. a *punctus versus*.. and a *punctus interrogativus*. **1971** P. J. LUCAS in *Archivum Linguisticum* II. 5 Notably absent are the *punctus elevatus* (or so-called 'inverted semicolon') and the *punctus interrogativus*... His [*sc.* Capgrave's] failure to use both the *punctus elevatus* and the *punctus interrogativus* probably indicates a movement away from liturgical (and formal rhetorical) influence. **1975** *Anglo-Saxon England* IV. 117 This [system of punctuation] consists of a hierarchy of punctum (.), punctus elevatus (:), punctus versus (;).. the punctus interrogativus (?) is also used.

pund, pundar, obs. ff. POIND, POINDER.

pund(e, -age, obs. or dial. ff. POUND, -AGE.

†**punde'lan.** *Sc. Obs. rare*⁻¹. Derivation and sense unknown: app. some kind of strong place.
1375 BARBOUR *Bruce* III. 159 Sekyrly now may ȝe se Be tane the starkest pundelan, That ewyr ȝour lyff-tyme ȝe saw tane.

punder, obs. f. PONDER, POUNDER.

pundfald, obs. Sc. form of PINFOLD.

†**pun'digrion.** *Obs. rare.* [app. related, either as earlier form or derivative, to PUN *sb.*[1], q.v.] A pun, a quibble.
1676 R. L'ESTRANGE *Counsellor Manner's Last Legacy* xvi. (1710) 23 Quibble, pun, punnet, pundigrion, of which fifteen will not make up one single jest. [Cf. *c* **1680–90** W. BLUNDELL in '*Cavalier's Note Book*' (1880) 185 Quibble, pun, punnet, pundigrion... I find these words in Counsellor Manners' last legacy, printed 1676.] **1812** SOUTHEY *Omniana* I. 103 Many.. will lose their friend rather than their jest, or their quibble, pun, punnet or pundigrion. **1820** —— *Wesley* I. 493 Thomas Adams had as honest a love of quips, quirks, puns, punnets, and pundigrions as Fuller the Worthy himself.

pundit ('pʌndɪt), *sb.* Also 7 **pendet**, 8 **pundeet**, 9 **pundet**, 9– **pandit**. [a. Hindī *paṇḍit*:—Skr. *paṇḍita* learned, skilled; as sb., a learned man. So Pg. *pandito*, *põdito* (16–17th c.), F. *pandit*, formerly *pandite*, *-decte*.] **a.** A learned Hindu; one versed in Sanskrit and in the philosophy, religion, and jurisprudence of India.
The *Pundit of the Supreme Court* (in India) was a Hindu Law-Officer, whose duty it was to advise the English Judges when needful on questions of Hindu Law. The office became extinct on the constitution of the 'High Court' in 1862. In Anglo-Indian use, *pundit* was applied also to a native Indian, trained in the use of instruments, and employed to survey regions beyond the British frontier and inaccessible to Europeans. 'The *Pundit* who brought so much fame on the title was the late Nain Singh, C.S.I.' (Yule.)
1672 H. O. tr. *Contn. Bernier's Emp. Mogol* III. 159 Their first study is of the Hanscrit, which is a Language.. not known but by the Pendets. **1698** FRYER *Acc. E. India & P.* 146 Into Places of Trust and Authority he puts only Brachmins, or their Substitutes, viz. Pundits.. for Physicians. **1783** JUSTAMOND tr. *Raynal's Hist. Indies* I. 60 The Pundits or Bramin lawyers, still speak the original language in which these ordinances were composed. **1792** T. MAURICE *Ind. Antiq.* I. Pref. 87 In an ancient Shaster.. translated by Colonel Dow's pundeet. **1837** MISS MAITLAND *Lett. fr. Madras* (1843) 86 Then there is the Pundit, or principal Hindoo law expounder—a Bramin. **1862** MAX MÜLLER *Chips* (1880) I. v. 119 All our great Sanskrit Scholars.. used to work.. with a Pandit at each elbow, instead of the grammar and dictionary. **1891** C. R. DAY *Music of S. India* v. 61 They.. were probably composed by some Telegu pandit at the court of Mysore. **1901** [see KASHMIRI *a.* and *sb.*]. **1953** *Encounter* Oct. 41/2 That this pandit (i.e. 'wise man') has become Prime Minister is one of the caprices of history. **1967** *Guardian* 26 Aug. 7/7 Having received choice jobs during the days of the Maharaja and the British Raj, the Pandits now resent the attempts to redress the balance in favour of.. the Moslems. **1971** *Illustr. Weekly India* 4 Apr. 19 After the hair is cut and the *puja* is performed by the *pandit*, the turban with the sehra is placed on the head of the child by the father.
b. *transf.* A learned expert or teacher.
1816 'QUIZ' *Grand Master* III. 73 For English pundets condescend Th' observatory to ascend. **1862** *Sat. Rev.* 15 Mar. 296 A point upon which the doctors of etiquette and the pundits of refinement will differ. **1896** SAINTSBURY *Hist. 19th Cent. Lit.* v. 213 Hallam.. an honoured pundit and champion of the Whig party. **1924** C. E. MONTAGUE *Right Place* xiv. 222 To say things and try to believe them, just because some aesthetic pundit or critical mandarin has said them before. **1938** R. HUGHES *In Hazard* ii. 37 First, this was developing into a true hurricane; and, second, it was not at all where it was thought by the pundits to be. **1941** C. H. WADDINGTON *Scientific Attitude* iv. 51 The architect who wished to build for a scientific and sceptical age had to.. find out what was left when scepticism had done its worst. The pundits would say that nothing was left. **1957** *Listener* 5 Sept. 338/1 The British Association.. is holding its 119th annual meeting... The pundits have gathered at Dublin. **1976** *Times* 30 Sept. 8/7 Though frowned upon by some pundits as out-of-date and middle-class, *Swallows and Amazons* and its many sequels remain immensely popular with children. **1977** J. I. M. STEWART *Madonna of Astrolabe* iii. 51 Here is what some pundit calls the phantom aesthetic state.
Hence **'punditly** adv. (*nonce-wd.*), in the manner of a pundit, in a learned way; **'punditship**, the position or office of a pundit; Hindu scholarship.
1868 G. STEPHENS *Runic Mon.* I. 94 Also punditly, theoretically, by a careful comparison of all the Staverows. **1873** F. HALL in *Scribner's Mag.* VI. 464 The shallowness of contemporary Punditship.

pundit ('pʌndɪt), *v. rare.* [f. prec.] *intr.* To make pronouncements like an expert. Also with quasi-obj.
1959 *Time* (Atlantic ed.) 19 Oct. 61 Huntley.. is.. inclined to take a panoramic view of the news, more inclined to pundit. **1967** *Punch* 4 Jan. 2/2 Take Alfie Hinds, currently punditing his head off as the BBC's escapological correspondent.

punditry ('pʌndɪtrɪ). [f. PUNDIT + -RY.] The characteristics of a pundit; opinions or actions befitting a pundit (sense b).
1926 T. M. HEALY in *Pioneer Ref. Spelling* Apr. 14, I.. decry the punditry of Civil Service Commissioners in making so-called orthography a test subject. **1930** *Times Lit. Suppl.* 13 Nov. 932/2 His latest book.. blends a good deal of punditry with its collectors' gossip. **1948** J. STEINBECK *Russ. Jrnl.* i. 3 News has become a matter of punditry. A man sitting at a desk in Washington or New York reads the cables and rearranges them to fit his own mental pattern and his by-line. **1958** *Oxford Mag.* 13 Feb. 278/1 All Oxford seemed to be there, with its focus in the ebullient punditry of Sir Isaiah Berlin. **1966** *Listener* 15 Sept. 397/3 It pounded and explored the whole subject of South Africa: past, present, future. Plenty of instant punditry. **1978** *Bull. Amer. Acad. Arts & Sci.* Jan. 22, I have caught him in a moment of punditry and while he was yielding to a weakness common to critics.

pundlar[1]. *local.* Also 7 **poundlar**, 7–9 **pundler**. [Altered form of ON. *pundari* steelyard, f. *pund* POUND *sb.*[1] (weight).] The name given in Orkney and Shetland to the steelyard or Danish balance with movable fulcrum.
1628 in G. Barry *Orkney Isl.* App. (1805) 473 That every pundlar be justed and made equal with the King's pundlar. **1693** WALLACE *Orkney* 93 *Pundler*, a Beam marked with the marks of their weight, which hath a stone on the one end, and a Hook at the other end for hinging up the Cassie [basket]. **1898** *Shetl. News* 26 Mar. (E.D.D.), From very early times it [the Bysmar] was with the Pundlar the universal steelyard, or weighing machine of Scandinavia.

pundlar[2], variant of POINDLAR *Sc. Obs.*

pundle ('pʌnd(ə)l). [Origin obscure: cf. *bundle*.]
†**1.** (See quots.) *Obs.* ? *dial.*
1706 PHILLIPS (ed. 6), *Pundle*, as 'She is a very Pundle', *i.e.* an ill shap'd and ill dress'd Creature. **1736** AINSWORTH *Eng.-Lat. Dict.*, *Pundle*, a short and fat woman. [Hence in Johnson and mod. Dicts.]
2. Local name for the wigeon. ? *Obs.*
[Cf. *pandle-whew*, s.v. PANDLE.]

pundler, var. POINDLAR *Sc. Obs.*, PUNDLAR[1].

‖**pundonor** (pundo'nor). [Sp. *pundonor*, contr. of *punto de honor* point of honour.]
a **1648** LD. HERBERT *Life* (1886) 205 The Spaniards do so much stand upon their pundonores. *a* **1648** —— *Hen. VIII* (1683) 234 And this was the end of the Cartels and Pundonnores betwixt these two great Princes. **1829** W. IRVING *Granada* I. xxxvi. 330 They stood not much upon the pundonor and high punctilio. **1932** E. HEMINGWAY *Death in Afternoon* xviii. 210 His.. body contains enough valour and pundonor to make a dozen bullfighters. **1967** MCCORMICK & MASCAREÑAS *Compl. Aficionado* ii. 45 That outcry was fascinating in its vehemence, for it had the false accents of him who protests too much; one is tempted to think that it could occur only in a land where *pundonor* is on every tongue. **1968** *Medium Ævum* XXXVII. 46 Nor do I think we have a right to assume that the sculptors followed epic pundonor so closely.

pundre, obs. form of PONDER, POUNDER.

pune, var. POON *sb.*[1], East Indian tree.

punee, pu'nee, puney, obs. ff. PUISNE, PUNY.

punee, punese, -eze, obs. ff. PUNAISE.

†**pung**, *sb.*[1] *Obs. rare.* [OE. *pung* = NFris. *pung*, MLG. *punge*, MDu. *pong*, *pungh*, LG., Du. dial. *pung*, Flem. *ponk*; OHG. **pfung*, *fung* (in *scazfung*); ON. *pungr* (Sw., Da. *pung*); Goth. *pugg-s* a purse; cf. also med.L. *punga*, med.Gr. πουγγή, πουγγίον a purse. See BUNG *sb.*[2], and SPUNG.] A purse.
c **725** *Corpus Gloss.* 391 *Cassidele*, pung. **13..** *K. Alis.* 1728, Y have the y-sent,.. with gold a litel punge [*so also Laud MS.*], For thow hast yeris yonge.

pung (pʌŋ), *sb.*[2] (*v.*[1]) *N. Amer.* [Shortened from *tom-pung*, or (?) *tow-pung*, corruptions of an Indian word akin to Chippeway *odābān*, *odābānak*, Montagnais *utāpān*, Abnaki *udaⁿbaⁿgan* 'instrument for drawing' or 'that on which something is drawn', the rude sledge on which Indians transport their goods. The same word in a northern Algonkin dialect has given the Canadian *tarbogin*, *tarbognay*, whence TOBOGGAN.
See Trumball in *Trans. Amer. Phil. Soc.* 1872, 25; Klein in *Herrig's Archiv.* 1876, LV. 455.]
a. A one-horse sleigh or sledge used in New England; also, a toboggan. (Loosely applied also to a two-horse sleigh.) Also *attrib.*
[**1798** *Dennie's Farmer's Museum*, Roxbury.. that famed town which sends to Boston Mart The gliding Tom Pung and the rattling cart.] **1840** LONGF. in *Life* (1891) I. 359, I drove on to Hartford, sitting on top of the mail-bags, which were piled in an uncovered pung. **1851** F. COOPER *Pioneers* i. 15 *note*, The 'pung', or 'tow-pung', which is driven with a pole. **1876** *Forest & Stream* 24 Aug. 33/2 The wheeler.. wound up by turning the pung upside down in a snowdrift. **1886** [see CLIP *v.*[2] 7]. **1908** L. M. MONTGOMERY *Anne of Green Gables* xix. 208 Her cousins are coming from Newbridge with a big pung sleigh. **1951** E. M. GRAHAM *My Window looks down East* iv. 31, I saw Carl Urlichson bringing home his fishing boat from the shore on sled runners drawn by a big Belgian horse... But I saw more than a boat on a pung. **1952** E. BUCKLER *Mountain & Valley* 171 The pung races on the lake. **1953** *N.Y. Times* 24 July 15/7 Carriages, buckboards and wagons were employed and pungs, sleds with box-like bodies, were popular.
b. (See quot.)
1901 *Scribner's Mag.* XXIX. 503/1 This old pung [here = boat: cf. PUNGY] 'll do to carry home fish in a pinch.
Hence **pung** *v. intr.*, to 'coast' on a sleigh, to toboggan.
1892 HOWELLS *Mercy* I. xii, A gait which.. exposed him to the ridicule of such small boys as observed his haste, in their intervals of punging... One who dropped from the runner of a sleigh.. jeered him for the awkwardness with which he floundered out of its way in the deep snow.

pung (pʌŋ), *v.*[2], *sb.*[3], and *int. Mah Jong.* [Chinese.] **A.** *vb. intr.* To take a discarded tile in order to complete a triplet of identical tiles. Also *trans.* **B.** *sb.* A set of three identical tiles; also, the action of the verb. **C.** *int.* The call made by the player performing this action. So **'punging** *vbl. sb.*
1922 R. E. LINDSELL *Ma-Cheuk or Mah-Jongg* 12 A useless domino.. is placed face upwards in the middle of the table, and can at once be claimed by any of the other three players who has already a pair or threes of that particular domino. This is called 'parking' or 'punging'. **1923** J. P. BABCOCK *Rules for Mah-Jongg* (ed. 2) ii. 15 Should a tile be discarded and any player have a pair (or three) of this same tile, even though out of his own turn, he may 'Pung', that is he says 'Pung' and takes this discarded tile, placing it with the pair (or three) from his own hand face up in front of him on the table... A Pung which completes a hand takes precedence over any other Pung. **1925** B. TRAVERS *Mischief* v. 86 Louise came in, all fatigued and heated from harbouring red dragons and punging her opponent's wind. **1934** *Neuphilologische Mitteilungen* XXXV. 132 Mah-jongg.. *pung* 'set of.. three identical tiles'. **1960** R. C. BELL *Board & Table Games* vi. 155 If any of the other three players holds two tiles identical with one just discarded, he may call 'Pung!' and take it out of the pool. Only the last discarded piece may be punged. **1964** E. N. WHITNEY *Mah Jong Handbk.* I. iii. 28 If you have a pair in your hand and *any* player discards an identical tile, you may declare 'pung' and claim the discarded tile instead of drawing from the wall. *Ibid.* 169 *Pung*, claiming a discard that completes a triplet. After punging, the player must meld his completed triplet.

pung, pungar, obs. ff. PUNK *sb.*[1], PUNGER.

punga, var. PONGA.

†**punge**, *v. Obs.* [ad. L. *pung-ĕre* to prick, puncture. Cf. *punȝe*, PUNYE *v.*]
1. *trans.* To prick, pierce; to push or drive with a pointed instrument, to goad.
c **1320** R. BRUNNE *Medit.* 567 Þey punged hym furþe þurgh euery slogh. **1362** LANGL. *P. Pl.* A. IX. 88 A pyk is in þe potent to punge a-doun þe wikkede. **1382** WYCLIF *Rev.* i. 7 Thei that pungeden [*gloss* or prickeden] him. **1570** FOXE *A. & M.* (ed. 2) I. 502/1 This byrde.. punged them with her beacke, plucked them by the skynne and fethers, and in all places hurted them.
2. To affect pungently; to cause to smart; to sting. Also *absol.*
1657 TOMLINSON *Renou's Disp.* 295 [A nettle] by the Greeks sometimes called *Cnide*, because it punges mordaciously. **1673** *Phil. Trans.* VIII. 7000 The smoak and soot of herbs and wood punge the eye.
Hence †**'punging** *vbl. sb.* and *ppl. a.*
a **1340** HAMPOLE *Psalter* xxi. 5 In spittynge buffetynge and pungynge with the thornes. **1670** MAYNWARING *Physician's Repos.* 90 Mixing alkalyes with acids, the acidity is destroyed, the punging quality is taken away.

punge, var. PUNJI.

pungence ('pʌndʒəns). *rare*⁻¹. [f. L. *pungent-em* PUNGENT: see -ENCE.] = next, 2.
1810 CRABBE *Borough* I. 86 Around the whole rise cloudy wreaths, and far Bear the warm pungence of o'er-boiling tar.

pungency ('pʌndʒənsɪ). [f. as prec.: see -ENCY.] The quality of being pungent.
1. The quality or property of pricking; the fact of having a sharp point or points. *rare.*
1656 BLOUNT *Glossogr.*, *Pungency*, a pricking, grieving or nipping. **1664** POWER *Exp. Philos.* I. 52 Oblong particles, angular and pointed, which may perchance exstimulate the Stomach, (by its netling pungency) like a heap of needles. **1732** ARBUTHNOT *Rules of Diet* in *Aliments*, etc. 407 Any Substance which by its Pungency can wound the Worms.
2. The quality of having a pungent smell or taste; such smell or taste itself; in more general sense, a stinging, irritant, or caustic property.
1676 GREW *Luctation Menstruums* I. § 11 The pungency of Ginger lyeth in a sulphureous and volatile Salt. **1774** GOLDSM. *Nat. Hist.* (1776) VI. 295 The violent pungency of

the slimy substance... If the smallest quantity but touch the skin..it burns it like hot oil. **1856** KANE *Arct. Expl.* I. xiv. 155 The air had a perceptible pungency upon inspiration. **1898** *Allbutt's Syst. Med.* V. 126 Carbonate of Ammonia should be..combined with syrup of tolu, liquorice or treacle, to soften its pungency.

b. *transf.* A stinging sensation, esp. of taste.

1792 WITHERING *Brit. Plants* (ed. 2) III. 295 [*Agaricus lactifluus*] abounding with white milky juice, at first mild, but at length leaving a slight pungency in the throat.

3. *fig.* in various senses (see PUNGENT 2, 3): Keenness; eagerness, intensity of desire or other feeling; intense painfulness, poignancy; severity, incisiveness, causticity; piquancy.

1649 JER. TAYLOR *Gt. Exemp.* Pref. §19 The pungency of forbidden lust is truely a thorne in the flesh. **1768** TUCKER *Lt. Nat.* (1834) II. 526 The pricks of conscience will.. stimulate our resolution..; and their repeated pungency will produce effects that could not have been worked by strength. **1800** *Charac.* in *Asiat. Ann. Reg.* 37/1 Camoens beheld it with a pungency of grief which [etc.]. *a* **1862** BUCKLE *Civiliz.* (1869) III. ii. 110 The large amount of truth contained in this bitter taunt increased its pungency.

pungent (ˈpʌndʒənt), *a.* (*sb.*) [ad. L. *pungent-em*, pr. pple. of *pung-ĕre* to pierce, prick; substituted for the earlier POIGNANT in many of its senses; cf. the intermediate PUGNA(U)NT².]

1. Pricking, piercing, sharp-pointed. Now only in *Nat. Hist.*, e.g. of leaves having stiff sharp points or prickles, or of a part or organ having a sharp point or serving for puncture.

1601 B. JONSON *Poetaster* II. i, Beneath it a blouddie Toe, betweene three Thornes pungent. **1606** CHAPMAN *Gentleman Usher* II. i, A Rush which now your heeles doe lie on here..Was whilome vsed for a pungent speare. **1750** tr. *Mem. R. Acad. Surg. Paris* I. 75 Cutting or pungent instruments. **1787** WITHERING *Brit. Plants* (ed. 2) I. 359 Terminating in a very sharp-pointed pungent leaf. **1880** GÜNTHER *Fishes* 563 The pectoral [fin] has a pungent spine.

2. *fig.* (of pain or grief). Sharp, keen, acute, poignant; causing or inflicting sharp pain; keenly painful or distressing.

1597 A. M. tr. *Guillemeau's Fr. Chirurg.* 48/2 The dolour not so pungent and sharp. **1684** T. HOCKIN *God's Decrees* 325 Intolerably pungent grief and sorrow. **1708** J. PHILIPS *Cyder* I. 5 With pungent Colic Pangs distress'd he'll roar. **1736** LEDIARD *Life Marlborough* I. 216 A very pungent Domestick Affliction. **1842** DUNGLISON *Med. Lex.* s.v., Pain is said to be pungent, when it seems as if a pointed instrument were being forced into the..part.

b. Of appetite or desire: Keen, eager; piercing. Now *rare* or *Obs.*

a **1710** BP. BULL *Serm.* ix. Wks. 1827 I. 226 To gratify a present pungent, languishing appetite. **1735** SOMERVILLE *Chase* III. 240 Hunger keen, and pungent Thirst of Blood. **1850** MRS. BROWNING *Vis. Poets* cxxxv, Burns, with pungent passionings Set in his eyes.

3. Keenly or strongly affecting the mind or feelings: with various shades of meaning (now usually with allusion to sense 4). †**a.** Pointed, telling, convincing. *Obs.*

1637–50 ROW *Hist. Kirk* (Wodrow Soc.) 194 Throw unwillingness to heare so pungent arguments, they were not insisted upon. **1661** PEPYS *Diary* 25 Aug., A very good and pungent sermon..discoursing the necessity of restitution. **1726** DE FOE *Hist. Devil* II. vii. (1840) 260 That which is still more pungent in the case.

b. Sharp in reproof, trenchant, severe; biting, caustic, incisive, acrimonious, sarcastic, satirical.

a **1661** FULLER *Worthies, Wilts.* (1840) III. 324 No author ..hath so pungent passages against the pride and covetousness of the court of Rome. **1693** DRYDEN *Disc. Satire* Ess. (ed. Ker) II. 100 Satire..consisting..chiefly in a sharp and pungent manner of speech. **1828** D'ISRAELI *Chas. I*, I. viii. 266 His conversations and his letters..seem to have been occasionally free and pungent. **1874** L. STEPHEN *Hours in Library* (1892) I. x. 363 A few pungent epigrams.

c. Exciting keen interest or curiosity; mentally stimulating; piquant.

1850 ROBERTSON *Serm.* Ser. III. ix. 118 Every amusement and all literature become more pungent. **1854** MRS. GASKELL *North & S.* xxiii, She was pungent, and had taste, and spirit, and flavour in her.

d. Exciting or stimulating to the senses. *rare.*

1879 G. ALLEN *Col. Sense* xii. 232 Red is the pungent and stimulative colour,..green is the restful and reparative colour.

4. Affecting the organs of smell or taste (or the skin, etc.) with a sensation resembling that produced by pricking; of the nature of such smell, taste, or sensation: penetrating and irritant.

1668 WILKINS *Real Char.* 92 Ground-pine..a small creeping plant..of a pungent sent. **1675** GREW *Disc. Tasts* iii. §11 *Cortex Winteranus*..is very Pungent upon the Tongue. **1742** SHENSTONE *Schoolmistr.* 102 Pungent radish, biting infant's tongue. **1800** tr. *Lagrange's Chem.* I. 103 A white vapour, exceedingly acrid and pungent. **1871** TYNDALL *Fragm. Sc.* (1879) I. ii. 36 Chlorine and sodium are elements, the former a pungent gas.

b. (*Path.*) Said of the fevered skin.

1822–34 *Good's Study Med.* (ed. 4) I. 722 If..the skin be still hotter..and more pungent to the touch. **1898** *Allbutt's Syst. Med.* V. 93 The skin [in pneumonia] is dry and pungent.

5. as *sb.* (or *absol.*) A pungent substance; an irritant, esp. of the nerves of taste.

1822–34 *Good's Study Med.* (ed. 4) III. 447 External and internal pungents. **1863** BATES *Nat. Amazon* iv. (1864) 85 Capsicum-pepper bushes..and lemon-trees; the one supplying the pungent, the other the acid, for sauce to..fish.

Hence **ˈpungently** *adv.*, in a pungent manner; with pungency; **ˈpungentness**, pungency (Bailey vol. II, 1727).

1842 S. LOVER *Handy Andy* ii, As you very properly and pungently remark, poor Egan is a spoon. *a* **1864** HAWTHORNE *Mother Rigby's Pipe* i, The pungently aromatic smoke. **1883** VILLARI *Machiavelli* IV. x. 207 His verses are ..often satirical and pungently vivacious.

punger (ˈpʌŋgə(r)). Now *dial.* Also 7 **pungar.** [Of uncertain origin: has been conjectured to represent, in some way, Gr. πάγουρ-ος, L. *pagūrus*, Fr. *pagure* (1552 in Hatz.-Darm.).] The large edible crab, *Cancer pagurus.*

1586 BRIGHT *Melanch.* vi. 28 The softer shel, or crustie are cray fish, the crab, the lobster, the punger. **1611** COTGR., *Carbasse*, the Crab-fish tearmed a Pungar. **1681** GREW *Musæum* I. v. iv. 120 The Claw of the Punger, or the Velvet-Crab, called Pagurus. **1820** T. MITCHELL *Aristoph., Com.* I. 215 Their food was young pungers. **1830** tr. *Aristoph., Knights* 76 They ate pungers instead of medic grass.

punȝe, Sc. var. POYGNÉ *Obs.*, fight, skirmish.

punȝet, var. POIGNET *Obs.*, a bracelet.

pungi, Hindu nose-flute: see POOGYE.

†**ˈpungitive**, *a. Obs.* [ad. med.L. *pungitīv-us* (Du Cange), irreg. f. L. *pung-ĕre* to prick, after *fugitīv-us*, etc., instead of the regular L. form **punctīv-us*, not found. So F. *pongitif*, 16th c. in Paré (Littré).] Having a pricking or stinging quality; sharp, keen, pungent.

c **1480** HENRYSON *Test. Cres.* 229 Angrie as ony Serpent vennemous, Richt pungitiue with wordis odious. **1501** DOUGLAS *Pal. Hon.* Prol. v, Thame to reserue fra rewmes pungitiue. **1586** FERNE *Blaz. Gentrie* 93 The pungitiue pricke of necessity. **1666** G. HARVEY *Morb. Angl.* iv. 48 Through their acidity they are rendred vellicating and pungitive. **1710** T. FULLER *Pharm. Extemp.* 133 It abounds with a smart pungitive, volatile Salt.

Hence †**ˈpungitively** *adv. Obs.*, in a stimulating manner.

1617 COLLINS *Def. Bp. Ely* II. ix. 400 The priest was to be possessed of a copy of the law, that he might obserue it punctually for his owne selfe. Not onely so, Sir, but pungitively for others.

pungle (ˈpʌŋg(ə)l), *v. U.S. colloq.* Also 9 **pongale, pungale.** [ad. Sp. *póngale* put it down, f. *poner* put, give.] *trans.* and *intr.* To contribute, hand over, or pay. Usu. with *down* or *up*.

1851 *Alta Californian* 19 July 2/3 A singular genius..was 'pongaling down' huge piles of gold at a monte table. **1854** *Pioneer* (San Francisco) Apr. 237 An additional slice of territory and its consequent classical influence upon our language, by the introduction of such precious words..as 'hombre',..'pungle', *et id omne genus.* **1857** *San Francisco Call* 6 Jan. 2/2 'Pungale down, gentlemen; come, pungale', as the vingt-et-un lady used to say. **1884** 'MARK TWAIN' *Huck. Finn* v. 33 'I'll ask him; and I'll make him pungle, too, or I'll know the reason why'... Next day he went to Judge Thatcher's and..tried to make him give up the money. **1910** E. S. FIELD *Sapphire Bracelet* xii. 141 I'll have him arrested, and then make him pungle up something handsome before I'll agree not to appear against him. **1959** A. K. LANG in *Alfred Hitchcock's Mystery Mag.* Feb. 71/1 The pusher couldn't pungle up Skreen's three hundred. **1975** J. GORES *Hammett* (1976) xix. 130 Hammett had coffee and pungled up the required fifty cents.

pungled (pʌŋg(ə)ld), *a. dial.* [Origin uncertain.] **a.** Shrivelled or shrunken, as grain.

1823 E. MOOR *Suffolk Wds.* 297 Wheat, from mildew, or other cause, not being plump grained, is said to be pungled —sometimes pingled. *a* **1825** FORBY *Voc. East Ang.*, *Pungled*, shrivelled and become tough; as winter fruit over-kept, but not turned rotten; also grain shrivelled with heat or disease. *a* **1856** T. W. HARRIS *Insects injur. to Veg.* (1862) 235 The *Thrips cerealium*,..sometimes infests wheat, in Europe, to a great extent... It is supposed to suck out the juices of the seed, thus causing the latter to shrink, and become what the English farmers call pungled.

b. Pinched, or pecuniarily embarrassed.

1881 MISS JACKSON *Shropsh. Word-Bk.*, *Pungled*, embarrassed in money matters. 'If Mr. —— had a large income he would not be so pungled as he is'.

pungy (ˈpʌŋ(g)ɪ). *U.S. local.* Also **pungo.** [Origin obscure: cf. PUNG *sb.*²] In Massachusetts, 'A small boat like a sharpey'; in Chesapeake Bay, A kind of fast-sailing schooner used in the oyster-trade; also, a canoe used in oyster-dredging. (*Cent. Dict.*) Also *attrib.*

1854 W. G. SIMMS *Southward Ho!* iii. 28 Their most innocent name is 'pungo'—a sort of schooner, hailing mostly from Manhattan and Massachusetts. *Ibid.*, For the better oysters..the 'pungos' pay three shillings. **1876** T. WESTCOTT *Centennial Portfolio* 32/2 There are models of fish-hatching houses, of fishing-rafts..and also of the oyster-catching material, vessels, pungys, canoes, drags, rafts, etc. **1880** G. A. TOWNSEND *T. Chesapeake* 29 They launched the pungy, not alone. **1884** *Forest & Stream* 24 Jan. 526/2 The model is of a round futtock with but little deadrise, with round stern, sharp, or what we call a pungy stern, but a sharp stern like that of a little canoe costs the least. **1891** W. K. BROOKS *Amer. Oyster Cult.* 166 The vast fleet of pungies and canoes. **1899** W. CHURCHILL *R. Carvel* xi, The big ship was already sliding in the water as I leaped into my pungy. **1938** 'J. DIGGES' *Bowleg Bill* 24 Next morning the whole harbor is cluttered up with dories, pungoes, and anything down to harness-casks. **1939** *Sun* (Baltimore) 4 Apr. 12/7 The pungy was a keel boat with no centreboard. **1941** M. V. BREWINGTON *Chesapeake Bay Bugeyes* 30 Not more than a dozen square stern, or 'pungy bugeyes', seem to have been built. *Ibid.* 34 Up to about 1908 many of the bugeyes were painted 'pungy style' with dark green bends, white rail and 'flesh' colored sides. *Ibid.* 46 The ordinary pungy rig, with sharply raking masts, round mastheads, iron rod cross-trees, upper and lower cap, and with the top-mast not fidded but resting in the lower cap. **1942** *Sun* (Baltimore) 28 Dec. 18/5 Several marine railways with tugs..pungies or bateaux. **1950** *Ibid.* 23 Aug. 20/5 The Old Pungy Wave, last of her type, has arrived safely in Detroit, which will be home to her for some while to come. **1967** L. S. TAWES *Coasting Captain* 4 In the fall of 1868 I left the farm and went dredging as cook on a pungy boat.

puniard, obs. form of PONIARD.

Punic (ˈpjuːnɪk), *a.* and *sb.* Also 5 **-yk**, 6 **-ik**, 7 **-ike, -icke, -ique, -icque**, 7–8 **-ick.** [ad. L. *Pūnicus*, earlier *Pœnicus*, f. *Pœnus* a Carthaginian; f. Gr. φοῖνιξ PHŒNICIAN, Carthaginian; also purple. Cf. F. *punique* (15th c. in Littré).]

A. *adj.* **1. a.** Belonging to Carthage; Carthaginian.

Punic Wars, the three wars between the Romans and Carthaginians waged between 264 and 146 B.C.

1533 BELLENDEN *Livy* I. viii. (S.T.S.) I. 46 Efter þe end of þe first punyk batall. **1601** HOLLAND *Pliny* I. 89 Our countreymen name it Tartessos, the Carthaginians Gadir [*margin* Or Gadiz], which in the Punicke language signifieth the number of seven. **1869** LECKY *Europ. Mor.* (1877) II. v. 302 Complete dissolution of Roman morals began shortly after the Punic wars. **1908** P. E. MORE in *Hibbert Jrnl.* Apr. 608 The Punic language was still spoken by the lower order.

b. †*Punic apple* (L. *Pūnicum mālum*, also absol. *Pūnicum*), the pomegranate; so †*Punic-tree*. *Punic wax*: see quot. 1848.

[*c* **1440**: see B. 1.] **1601** HOLLAND *Pliny* I. 398 The territorie of Carthage challengeth to it selfe the Punicke apple: some call it the Pomegranat. **1641** G. SANDYS *Paraphr. Song Sol.* IV. i, Thy Cheeks like Punicke Apples are. **1745** tr. *Columella's Husb.* x. 373 Soon as the punic-tree ..Itself shall with its bloody blossoms cloathe. **1848** WORNUM in *Lect. Paint.* 350 *note*, Punic wax (*cera Punica*) was..the common yellow wax, purified and bleached by being boiled three times in sea-water, with a small quantity of nitre... This wax was the Greek substitute for oil in painters' colours.

c. Having the character attributed by the Romans to the Carthaginians; treacherous, perfidious. ***Punic faith***: see FAITH *sb.* 11 b.

1600 HOLLAND *Livy* XXI. iv, Crueltie most savage and inhumane, falshood and trecherie more than Punicke. **1738** H. BROOKE *Tasso's Jerus. Del.* II. (1810) 376/1 Yes, yes, his faith attesting nations own; 'Tis Punic all, and to a proverb known! **1796** BURKE *Reg. Peace* i. Wks. VIII. 125 An invective against the ministry of Great Britain, their habitual frauds, their proverbial punick perfidy. **1853** W. STIRLING *Cloister Life Chas. V* 237 Astonished that a commander of so much experience should have put any trust in the Punic promises of a Moor.

†**2.** Purple; = PUNICEOUS. *Obs.*

1501 DOUGLAS *Pal. Hon.* I. xlvi, Purpour colour, punik and skarlote hewis. **1607** R. C[AREW] tr. *Estienne's World of W.* 296 A punick colour, that is, yellow drawing to a red.

B. *sb.* †**1.** = *Punic apple*: see A. 1 b. *rare.*

c **1440** *Pallad. on Husb.* III. 951 Graffyng is tassure In hem of euery fruit—punyk & serue.

†**2.** An inhabitant of Carthage, a Carthaginian.

1613 PURCHAS *Pilgrimage* (1614) 66 The Punikes called God, Bal, (from whence came those names Hannibal, Adherbal, and such like). **1696** BROOKHOUSE *Temple Open.* 13 The Punicks, the Sons of Cham, put in a Caveat.

3. The Carthaginian tongue, a Semitic language, an offshoot of Phœnician and allied to Hebrew.

1673 J. RAY *Observations Journey Low-Countries* 308 The language of the Natives [of Malta] is a corrupt Arabic or Moresco, introduced by the Saracens, the ancient language before their coming in probably having been Greek, with a mixture of Punick. **1813** *Q. Rev.* Oct. 269 The Maltese is immediately derived from the modern Arabic, without any intervention from the Punic. **1886** *Encycl. Brit.* XXI. 646/2 Plautus..inserts in the *Pœnulus* whole passages in Punic. **1971** S. E. MORISON *European Discovery Amer.: Northern Voy.* i. 11 Phoenician script is so simple that, as with the later Norse runes, it is easy for an overimaginative searcher to read Punic, like Runic, in natural grooves and scratches on rocks.

†**ˈPunical**, *a. Obs.* [f. as PUNIC *a.* + -AL¹.] = PUNIC *a.* In quot. 1606 = PUNIC *a.* 2.

Punical pome = Punic apple: see PUNIC *a.* 1 b.

c **1430** Punical pome [see POME *sb.*¹ 1]. **1432–50** tr. *Higden* (Rolls) IV. 21 From whiche tyme the batelles punicalle began to sprynge. **1559** MORWYNG *Evonym.* Pref., Put in wryting by men that used the Punicall or els the Arabicke tonge. **1606** BIRNIE *Kirk-Buriall* (1833) 10 Men ranking themselves under stately standerts and punicall pinsels displayed.

So †**ˈPunican** [cf. L. *Pūnicānus*] = PUNIC *sb.* 2.

1595 *Polimanteia*, etc., sign. Y, You who haue surpassed the false punicane, gaining that brand of trecherie which once was Carthage due.

punice, obs. f. PUNAISE (bed-bug), PUNISH.

punicean (pjuːˈnɪs-, -ˈnɪʃiːən), *a.* [f. L. *pūnice-us* (see next) + -AN.] = next: cf. PHŒNICEAN.

But in first quot. *fruit punicean* app. = *Punic apple.*

1866 J. B. ROSE tr. *Ovid's Met.* v. 142 Fruit punicean From bended bough with maiden hand [she] had ta'en And eaten seven grains. *Ibid.* VIII. 212 Nisus, who, midst his hairs of honoured grey, One only tress punicean had. *Ibid.* 398 Forth from the rock welled the punicean blood.

puniceous (pjuːˈnɪʃɪːəs), *a.* Also 8 *erron.* -ious. [f. L. *pūnice-us* Punic; also red, purple-coloured (f. *Pūnic-us* PUNIC, with suffix *-eus*) + -OUS.] Of a bright red, purplish-red, or reddish-yellow colour: cf. PHŒNICEOUS.

1730 BAILEY (folio), *Puniceous* (in Botan. Writ.) of a scarlet Colour. **1768** [W. DONALDSON] *Life Sir B. Sapskull* II. xxv. 212 To stimulate the flavour of the punicious fluid. **1890** *Cent. Dict.*, *Puniceous*, in *entom.*, purplish-red or crimson; having the color of a pomegranate.

punicin (ˈpjuːnɪsɪn). *Chem.* [See -IN[1].]

†**1.** [f. L. *pūnicum* pomegranate.] (See quots.)

1855 GARROD *Mat. Med.* 154 The root-bark [of the Granaceæ] contains .. tannin, and a principle called *Punicine* has also been detected. **1866** WATTS *Dict. Chem.* IV. 746 *Punicin*, an acrid uncrystallisable substance obtained from the bark of the pomegranate tree.

2. [f. L. *pūnicus* purple.] The colouring matter obtained from the purple whelk (PURPLE *sb.* 3); the purple of the ancients.

1879 SCHUNCK in *Jrnl. Chem. Soc.* XXXV. 595 This colouring matter [formed by insolation from the chromogen of the mollusc] .. is not identical with indirubin or any known member of the indigo group, and it being, as I think, a substance *sui generis*, I propose to call it *Punicin*.

punie, obs. form of PUNAISE, PUNY.

punily (ˈpjuːnɪlɪ), *adv.* [f. PUNY *a.* + -LY[2].] In a puny manner; weakly.

1775 H. WALPOLE *Let. to Conway* 22 Jan., Lord Rockingham, very punily, and the Duke of Richmond joined and supported the motion. **1827** W. KENNEDY *Fitful Fancies* 85 The narrow shell In which the creeping creature man Loves punily to dwell. **1906** BELLOC *Hills & Sea* 56 In Africa, where men build so squat and punily. **1942** W. FAULKNER *Go down, Moses* 193 That doomed wilderness whose edges were being constantly and punily gnawed at by men with plows and axes.

puniness (ˈpjuːnɪnɪs). Also 8 **punyness**. [f. PUNY *a.* + -NESS.] The state or quality of being puny; littleness and feebleness; pettiness.

1727 BAILEY vol. II, *Puniness*, Weakliness, Tenderness, Unthrivingness, spoken of Children. **1740** CHEYNE *Ess. Regimen* 66 The Frequency of nervous .. Distempers now, .. the Stuntedness, Punyness and Feebleness, so conspicuous among the better Sort. **1871** MORLEY *Carlyle* in *Crit. Misc.* Ser. I. (1878) 175 The same sense of the puniness of man in the centre of a cruel and frowning universe.

punish (ˈpʌnɪʃ), *v.* Forms: see below. [a. F. *puniss-*, extended stem (in *punisse*, *punissant*, etc.: see -ISH[2]) of F. *punir*:—L. *pūnīre* to punish, in earlier L. *pœnīre*, f. *pœna* = Gr. ποινή fine, penalty, requital, punishment, PAIN *sb.*[1]]

A. Illustration of Forms.

α. 4 puniss-en, -yss-en, punyes, punich, punyzsh, 4–5 punysch(e, punnishe, 4–6 punys(e, -yssh(e; 5 punice, -yce, -ych, -es(c)h, pugnysshe, *Sc.* pwnys, 5–6 punysh, 6 punnysch, punis, *Sc.* punise, -isse, -eise, -eish, -eis(s, -ische, -yss, pwnis, 6– punish (7 punnich).

1340 *Ayenb.* 148 Hou he ssel his broþer chasti .. oþer his seriont .. punissi. **1340** Ypunyssed [see B. 1 b]. *a* **1340** HAMPOLE *Psalter* iv. 6 A sorowful gast, punyschand þe self for synne. *Ibid.* xxvi. 14 Suffire me noght forto fall swa that thou punyes me in hell. *c* **1350** *Will. Palerne* 4068 Punichede at þe hardest. **1362** LANGL. *P. Pl.* A. III. 69 To punisschen [**1377** punyschen] on pillories .. Brewesters, Bakers. *c* **1375** Punyst [see B. 1]. *c* **1380** WYCLIF *Wks.* (1880) 425 [Thei] moten be punyȝshid. **1380** Punysshe [see B. 1 b]; punnishe [see B. 1 c]. *c* **1400** *Rom. Rose* 7235 Therfore god shal him punyce; But me ne rekketh of no vyce. **1460** *Paston Lett.* I. 525 My lord of York hath dyvers straunge commissions fro the Kyng .. to punych them by the fawtes to the Kyngs lawys. *c* **1470** HENRY *Wallace* VII. 1264 Wallace with force pwnyst [thaim] rygorusly. **1489** CAXTON *Faytes of A.* I. xv. 40 That suche men be pugnysshed. **1500–20** DUNBAR *Poems* lix. 22 Puness him for his deid culpabile. **1530** PALSGR. 670/2 That God punissheth them for their great vyce. *a* **1533** LD. BERNERS *Huon* lxxxiii. 257 For the whiche synnes he hath ben by me sore punyshyd. **1533** GAU *Richt Vay* 51 To punis al his inimis. **1538** STARKEY *England* I. iii. 90 And when hyt plesyth hym other wyse to punnysch vs, then we must lake. **1544** Punish [see B. 1]. **1562** Punisses [see B. 1 c]. **1563–7** BUCHANAN *Reform. St. Andros* Wks. (1892) 9 He sal punyss .. the writar. **1567** *Gude & Godlie B.* (S.T.S.) 191 Without God puneis thair cruell vice. **1582** J. HAMILTON *Cath. Traict. Epist.*, in *Cath. Tractates* (S.T.S.) 78 The leuing God puneisht thame. **1596** DALRYMPLE tr. *Leslie's Hist. Scot.* (S.T.S.) I. 127 To punise offenderis. **1612** PR. CHAS. in Ellis *Orig. Lett.* Ser. I. III. 104, I deserve to be punniched for my ill fortune.

β. 4 ponis, -esche, 4–5 -ysch(e, 5 -ysse, -ysshe, 5–6 ponysh, 6 poynysse.

c **1375** *XI Pains of Hell* 220 in *O.E. Misc.* 217 Vche cursid dede ponyschid truly. *c* **1380** WYCLIF *Sel. Wks.* III. 39, I schal al biþinke to ponesche hem wiþ eendelees peyne. *c* **1400** tr. *Secreta Secret.*, *Gov. Lordsh.* 57 To ponysse mysdoers and trespasours. *a* **1533** LD. BERNERS *Huon* l. 166 Therfore he hath ben ponyshyd. **1538** in W. A. J. Archbold *Somerset Relig. Ho.* (1892) 80 He lovethe vertew and wyll poynysse vyse.

γ. 4–5 punch, -e, punsch(e.

1340–70 *Alex. & Dind.* 747 ȝe schulle be punched & put in paine for euere. **1387** TREVISA *Higden* (Rolls) IV. 221 Punschynge of evel doers. *Ibid.* VIII. 315 For he schulde nouȝt be i-punsched by þe lawe. *c* **1440** *Promp. Parv.* 416/2 Punchyn, or chastysyn', .. *punio*, *castigo*. *c* **1450** *Cov. Myst.* viii. (Shaks. Soc.), *Joachim*. Punchyth me, Lorde, and spare my blyssyd wyff Anne. **1460** Punchid [see B. 1].

B. Signification.

1. a. *trans.* As an act of a superior or of public authority: To cause (an offender) to suffer for an offence; to subject to judicial chastisement as retribution or requital, or as a caution against further transgression; to inflict a penalty on.

1340, etc. [see A. α]. *c* **1375** *Sc. Leg. Saints* vi. (*Thomas*) 86 Bettir is þat þu For þis trespace be punyst nov, þan þar-fore þu be punyste sare, Quhare pardone sal be neuir mare. **1460** CAPGRAVE *Chron.* (Rolls) 162 Alle thoo malefactores were punchid with iii. maner peynis; for thei were first drawe, than hange, and last brent. **1526** *Pilgr. Perf.* (W. de W. 1531) 19 b, Crucifye and punysshe thy body with werkes of penaunce. **1544** tr. *Littleton's Tenures* (1574) 8 Tenant in taile after possibylity of yssue extinct shall never be punished of wast. **1651** HOBBES *Leviath.* II. xxvi. 144 'Tis against the Law of Nature, To punish the Innocent. **1754** RICHARDSON *Grandison* II. xxxi. 306 The violators of the social duties are frequently punished by the success of their own wishes. **1884** S. R. GARDINER *Hist. Eng.* IX. lxxxviii. 12 The King was not without hope that some legal means of punishing them might be found.

b. To requite or visit (an offence, etc.) with a penalty inflicted on the offender; to inflict a penalty for (something).

1340 *Ayenb.* 74 Al þet hit vint ine þe zaule of gelte of dede, of speche, of þoȝte .., al uorbernþ and clenzeþ and þer byeþ ypunyssed, and awreke. *c* **1380** WYCLIF *Wks.* (1880) 408 God may not forȝete þis trespas but punysshe it in his tyme. **1484** CAXTON *Fables of Æsop* II. Pref., The Athenyens .. wold haue demaunded a kynge for to punysshe alle the euyll. **1570** *Satir. Poems Reform.* xvii. 56 Throw him was .. Piracie puneist. **1769** BLACKSTONE *Comm.* IV. i. 7 It is clear, that the right of punishing crimes against the law of nature .. is in a state of mere nature vested in every individual. **1849** MACAULAY *Hist. Eng.* iv. I. 484 The spirit of the law .. was that no misdemeanour should be punished more severely than the most atrocious felonies.

c. *absol.* To inflict punishment.

c **1380** WYCLIF *Serm.* Sel. Wks. I. 40 Upon þe ferþe synne God ceessiþ never to punnishe. **1562** WINȜET *Cert. Tractatis* i. (S.T.S.) I. 8 God punissis oftymes in ye samyn thing quhairin man offendis. **1605** SHAKS. *Lear* III. iv. 16 But I will punish home. **1715** DE FOE *Fam. Instruct.* I. i. (1841) I. 9 God does not punish that way. *a* **1716** SOUTH *Serm.* (1744) X. vi. 180 To punish is properly an act of a superior to an inferior.

†**2. a.** To fine (a person). **b.** To exact (money due) *from* a person. *Obs.*

1572 HULOET, To punish, *pecunia multare*. **1591** HORSEY *Trav.* (Hakl. Soc. No. 18) App. 289 A desperate debte owinge by the chauncelere Shalkan .. was violently puneshed from him and payd the Companye. **1700** TYRRELL *Hist. Eng.* II. 819 He whose Dog .. shall be found Unlawed, shall be punished Three Shillings.

3. *transf.* To handle severely; to inflict heavy damage, injury, or loss on. Also *absol.*

In various slang, colloquial, or jocular uses: as, To inflict severe blows upon (an opponent in a boxing match); to thrash, belabour, maul; extended to handling severely in other forms of contest (e.g. football, cricket, boat-racing); also, jocularly, to make a heavy 'inroad' on (a stock of provisions, wine, etc.), to consume or diminish severely; to urge (a horse) by severe application of whip or spur; to abuse (a musical instrument) by playing it badly; in *dial.* or *colloquial* use, to cause pain or suffering to, to hurt; see *Eng. Dial. Dict.*

1801 *Sporting Mag.* XIX. 62/2 This desperate contest, comprising sixteen rounds, lasted twenty-one minutes, and we never witnessed a man more *punished* than Burk. **1807** R. SOUTHEY *Lett. from England* III. lxxi. 310 When the [boxing] champion .. comes off victor, after suffering much in the contest, he is said to be *much punished*. **1812** *Sporting Mag.* XXXIX. 22 He lost his science after he had been a good deal punished. *Ibid.* XLVIII. 187 In his prime no one could punish him. **1825** C. M. WESTMACOTT *Eng. Spy* I. 242 We .. drank freely—punished his claret. **1839** THACKERAY *Fatal Boots* xii, We punished her cellar too. **1844** DICKENS *Martin Chuzzlewit* xxxvi. 425 Tom, taking up his knife and fork again .. 'I shall punish the Boar's Head dreadfully.' **1848** THACKERAY *Van. Fair* liii, He punished my champagne. **1856** H. H. DIXON *Post & Paddock* xii. 209 If a foolish lad punishes his beaten horse unnecessarily. **1863** W. C. BALDWIN *Afr. Hunting* i. 16 They [*sc.* sjamboks] are very tough and supple .. and punish tremendously. **1864** *Sporting Mag.* XLV. 194 When the Eleven come to the wickets, how they punish the ball, and rapidly run-up a long score. **1882** *Garden* 3 June 384/3 Phlox divaricata is very pretty, but how the slugs and snails do punish it! **1883** *Daily Tel.* 15 May 2/7 The Oxonian's [bowling] was .. severely punished, both batsmen scoring a 3 hit off one over. **1891** W. G. GRACE *Cricket* xi. 312 It was a treat to watch him punish the bowling. **1896** DOYLE *Rodney Stone* xix, The smith, although he laughed at his own injuries, had none the less been severely punished. **1930** *Morning Post* 16 July 11/5 Chapman batted remarkably well. He refused to take any risk and yet punished the loose ball. **1934** DYLAN THOMAS in *Listener* 24 Oct. 691/2 Especially when the October wind With frosty fingers punishes my hair. *Ibid.*, Especially when the October wind .. With fist of turnips punishes the land. **1942** J. B. PRIESTLEY *Black-Out in Gretley* vii. 149 The bottle of brandy they'd punished was prominent on the little table. **1949** 'J. TEY' *Brat Farrar* iv. 34 Ungainly women in unseemly clothes punishing the saddles of broken-spirited horses. **1967** *Observer* 17 Dec. 1/1 An old man punishing a mandolin in Bond Street.

Hence **punished** (ˈpʌnɪʃt) *ppl. a.*

c **1806** SIR R. WILSON *Cape Gd. Hope* in *Life* (1862) I. App. ix. 375 It is also remarked .. that .. the backs of punished men require all the care and skill of the surgeon. **1866** S. B. JAMES *Duty & Doctr.* (1871) 32 Evil is personified in a punished Satan.

punishability (pʌnɪʃəˈbɪlɪtɪ). [f. next + -ITY. So mod.F. *punissabilité* (in Littré).] The quality or fact of being punishable; punishableness.

1868 BAIN *Ment. & Mor. Sci.* IV. xi. 404 Granting these two postulates, Punishability .. is amply vindicated. **1876** *Westm. Rev.* No. 98. 441 To inquire how the notion of Right and Wrong .. is linked to that of punishability.

punishable (ˈpʌnɪʃəb(ə)l), *a.* [f. PUNISH *v.* + -ABLE. Cf. F. *punissable* (14–15th c. in Hatz.-Darm.), perh. the immediate source.] Liable to punishment; capable of being punished.

a. Of a person.

1531 *Dial. on Laws Eng.* II. i, Tenauntes for terme of lyfe .. be punysshable of waste by the statute: .. but at the comon lawe before that statute they were nat punysshable. **1699** BURNET *39 Art.* x. (1700) 117 No man is accountable, rewardable or punishable, but for that in which he acts freely. **1749** FIELDING *Tom Jones* (1775) III. 94, I think it is a pity these hags are not punishable by law. **1874** SIDGWICK *Meth. Ethics* IV. iii. 408, I should be legally punishable if I omitted the act.

b. Of an offence: Entailing punishment.

1548 UDALL, etc. *Erasm. Par. Matt.* v. 24 b, Wherfore emonge the Jewes, onely periury is punyshable. **1632** MASSINGER *City Madam* I. i, 'Tis more punishable in our house Than *scandalum magnatum*. **1766** BLACKSTONE *Comm.* II. xviii. 278 It is not an offence punishable in a criminal way at the common law. **1846** MᶜCULLOCH *Acc. Brit. Empire* (1854) II. 637 An attempt was made to repress it, by treating it as a punishable offence. **1909** *Daily Chron.* 29 Nov. 3/1 If a punishable play is produced, the author and the lessee .. should be punished. **1959** *Daily Tel.* 31 Dec. 1/7 Confiscation of the latest issue of Reichsruf, weekly newspaper of the extreme Right-wing German Reich Party, and another party journal, .. was ordered by a Bielefeld court today. They were stated to have 'punishable contents'.

c. In sense 3 of the verb.

1910 *Blackw. Mag.* July 106/2 The punishable [ball] escaped scot-free.

Hence **ˈpunishableness**, the quality of being punishable; **ˈpunishably** *adv.*, in a punishable manner or to a punishable degree.

1727 BAILEY vol. II, *Punishableness*, Capableness or liableness to be punished. **1786** A. GIB *Sacr. Contempl.* 272 In respect of guilt or of punishableness. **1857** RUSKIN *Pol. Econ. Art* ii. (1868) 173 The guiltily and punishably poor. **1860** PUSEY *Min. Proph.*, *Amos* v. 20 The soul is a witness to its own deathlessness, its own accountableness, its own punishableness.

punisher (ˈpʌnɪʃə(r)). Forms: 4 **punysere**, 6 *Sc.* **punissar**, **-er**; 4 **punyscher**, **-are**, 4–6 **-yssher(e**, 6– **punisher**; 4 **punser**, **punscher**. [f. PUNISH *v.* + -ER[1]. Cf. F. *punisseur* (14th c.), in OF. *punissere*, which may be the source.] **a.** One who punishes, one who inflicts a penalty.

a **1340** HAMPOLE *Psalter* ix. 36 Noght trowand god punyscharе of synnes. *Ibid.* l. 5 Rightwise punysere of syn. **1387** TREVISA *Higden* (Rolls) VII. 23 Helper, punscher [*v.rr.* punser, punyscher] of trespas. **1552** ABP. HAMILTON *Catech.* (1884) 59 Ane rygorous punissar of our synnis. **1688** R. HOLME *Armoury* II. 17/2 A Punisher of Impiety. **1747** RICHARDSON *Clarissa* (1811) I. xlv. 353 Not to say anything about my poor sister—she is her own punisher. **1861** LYTTON *Str. Story* xxii, He received the blow, drew forth his school-boy knife, and stabbed the punisher.

b. *Boxing slang.* A hard hitter. Also *Cricket.*

1812 P. EGAN *Boxiana* 113 The *Lobster* had most powerful *claws*, and was a first-rate *punisher*. **1814** *Sporting Mag.* XLIV. 71 Smith was the heaviest man and a right-handed punisher. **1817** *Ibid.* L. 38 They are both active punishers, and a good battle is expected. **1832** MARRYAT *N. Forster* xlvii, A fine fellow!—a severe punisher. **1846** W. DENISON *Cricket: Sketches of Players* 12 If the bowling be at all loose, he is a powerful punisher.

c. *transf.* A thing that hits one hard; a heavy or severe task.

1827 *Sporting Mag.* XXI. 138, I had nearly fifty miles' road-work this day, which .. is a punisher.

punishing (ˈpʌnɪʃɪŋ), *vbl. sb.* [f. PUNISH *v.* + -ING[1].] The action of the vb. PUNISH; an instance of this; punishment.

c **1375** *XI Pains of Hell* 222 in *O.E. Misc.* 217 Þis schal be here ponyschyng. *c* **1375** *Sc. Leg. Saints* xxi. (*Clement*) 737 Fore-þi I thole þis punysing. *c* **1500** *Melusine* 2 The punysshinges of god ben as abysmes without bottom. **1630** EARL MANCH. in *Buccleuch MSS.* (Hist. MSS. Comm.) I. 271 The punishing of rogues and idle persons. **1659** MILTON *Civil Power* Wks. 1851 V. 317 He himself uses it to thir punishing. **1835** MARRYAT *Pirate* vi, You will see what effect your punishing may have upon him.

punishing (ˈpʌnɪʃɪŋ), *ppl. a.* [f. PUNISH *v.* + -ING[2].] **a.** That punishes; chastising, punitive.

a **1340** HAMPOLE *Psalter* xx. 8 Thi pouste punyesand be funden til all thi faas. **1624** T. GODWIN *Moses & Aaron* (1641) 114 That the punishing Angell might passe over them. **1659** HAMMOND *On Ps. ciii.* 9, 10 Par. 506 He takes off his punishing hand again.

b. *slang* or *colloq.* Hard-hitting.

1811 *Sporting Mag.* XXXVIII. 184/1 The punishing right hand of his adversary. **1820** J. H. REYNOLDS *Fancy* (1906) 69 With .. clenched hands, firm, and of punishing size. **1846** W. DENISON *Cricket: Sketches of Players* 15 As a batsman he has a good defence, and occasionally is found to be a punishing hitter. **1866** *Routledge's Ev. Boy's Ann.* 427 Some punishing hitter of the opposite side has come in. **1894** *Daily News* 24 May 5/4 An accomplished wicket-keeper .. and a punishing batsman. **1900** P. F. WARNER *Cricket in Many Climes* v. i. 178 Murray Bisset .. is a very sound and stylish bat with a good deal of wrist work, but is perhaps just a little short of punishing power.

c. Excessively severe and exhausting; scarcely tolerable.

1971 N. STACEY *Who Cares?* xiii. 216, I was still involved in a punishing fourteen-hours-a-day programme at Woolwich. **1973** A. ROSS *Dunfermline Affair* 180 He studied his *alter ego* almost every minute of every day for a punishing three years. **1975** *Nature* 6 Nov. 91/2 Barnes had considerable skill as a laboratory bench worker but little opportunity to exercise it in his later years because of the punishing load of advisory and administrative work that he willingly undertook. **1977** *Church Times* 14 Jan. 6/3 The OPEC countries.. have been giving real aid to some of the poorer countries which has more than equalled the punishing rise in the price of oil.

punisship, variant of PUNYSHIP *Obs.*

punishment (ˈpʌnɪʃmənt). Forms: see PUNISH *v.* [a. AF. *punisement* (13th c. in Britton) = OF. *punissement*, f. *punir* to PUNISH: see -MENT.]

1. a. The action of punishing or the fact of being punished; the infliction of a penalty in retribution for an offence; also, that which is inflicted as a penalty; a penalty imposed to ensure the application and enforcement of a law.

[**1292** BRITTON I. ix. §1 Aukun plus simple punisement, solum la manere del fet.] **1413** *Pilgr. Sowle* (Caxton 1483) IV. ix. 62 A wonder greuous thynge it semeth to me that.. he that hath mysdone shalle passe withoute punysshement. *c***1450** *Cov. Myst.* xi. (Shaks. Soc.) 108 His endles punchement may nevyr sees. **1482** *Monk of Evesham* (Arb.) 53 He was takyn.. to the vttermest peynys and ponissement of dethe. **1535** COVERDALE *Ps.* civ. 7 He is the Lorde oure God, whose punyshmentes are thorow out all the worlde. *c***1550** CHEKE *Matt.* xxiii. 29 How can ie flie from helles ponischment? **1631** MAY tr. *Barclay's Mirr. Mindes* I. 313 He desired that that Army.. should take punishment of him for deceiuing the King. **1690** LOCKE *Hum. Und.* II. xxviii. (1695) 192 We must, wherever we suppose a Law, suppose also some Reward or Punishment annexed to that Rule. **1736** BUTLER *Anal.* I. ii. Wks. 1874 I. 40 Divine punishment is what men chiefly object against, and are most unwilling to allow. **1817** W. SELWYN *Law Nisi Prius* (ed. 4) II. 817 The rule now laid down is, that it is the crime and not the punishment, which makes a man infamous. **1875** J. P. HOPPS *Princ. Relig.* x. (1878) 31 There are punishments that are inflicted from without, and punishments that naturally and of necessity grow out of offences.

b. *Psychol.* Pain, deprivation, or other unpleasant consequence imposed on or experienced by an organism responding incorrectly under specific conditions so that, through avoidance, the desired learning or behaviour becomes established. Cf. REWARD *sb.*[1] 4 f.

1907 R. M. YERKES *Dancing Mouse* vi. 99 In general, the method of punishment is more satisfactory than the method of reward, because it can be controlled to a greater extent. **1912** [see REWARD *sb.*[1] 4 f]. **1949** WOODWORTH & MARQUIS *Psychol.* xvi. 530 Punishment has two important effects. When the child gets a burn from a hot radiator he learns to *avoid* the radiator. When anyone in following a certain lead to his goal meets with punishment.. he tends to *shift to another lead.* **1953** B. F. SKINNER *Sci. & Hum. Behav.* xii. 185 In solving the problem of punishment we simply ask: What is the effect of withdrawing a positive reinforcer or presenting a negative. **1956** *Sci. Amer.* Oct 116/3 This finding contradicts the long-held theory that strong excitation in the brain means punishment. **1960** L. M. BAKER *Gen. Experim. Psychol.* xiii. 309 Punishment of undesired behavior soon led to escape activity and satisfactory conditioning in the dog. **1975** FISCHER & GOCHROS *Planned Behav. Change* iv. 54 No positive reinforcement whatsoever is provided for that behavior (as distinct from negative punishment). *Ibid.* 56 When.. there is a *decrease* in the probability that the behavior will occur, that stimulus is a negative reinforcer, and the operation is called positive punishment.

2. *slang* and *colloq.* **a.** Severe handling; belabouring, mauling; orig. that inflicted by a pugilist upon his opponent; extended to football, cricket, and other contests; pain, damage, or loss inflicted (without any retributive or judicial character) as in PUNISH *v.* 3; also *dial.* and *colloq.*, pain, suffering, misery: see *Eng. Dial. Dict.*

1811 *Sporting Mag.* XXXVIII. 140/1 Silverthorne, with timidity, arising no doubt from punishment in the first round, kept away from his adversary. **1829** P. EGAN *Boxiana* 2nd Ser. II. 97 Burns was not reduced by the punishment he received. **1846** W. DENISON *Cricket: Sketches of Players* 24 The batsman makes up his mind that he shall administer severe punishment. **1856** H. H. DIXON *Post & Paddock* xii. 209 The heavy punishment in which Clift and some of the old school delighted, is very much gone out. **1860** *Times* 18 Apr. 9/4 After these tremendous rounds Sayers still came up fresh, and showed not half the awful marks of punishment visible all over Heenan. **1862** THACKERAY *Adv. Philip* iv, Tom Sayers could not take punishment more gaily than they do. **1865** DICKENS *Mut. Fr.* III. iii, Stopping to examine his arms and hands, as if to see what punishment he has received in the Fight. **1882** *Daily Tel.* 19 May, The punishment Hill [the bowler] was receiving caused Bates to relieve him at 26. **1884** *St. James' Gaz.* 11 Dec. 10/1 He can ride horse or camel from early morning till late at night without showing punishment. **1885** LD. WOLSELEY in *Times* 22 Jan. 5/4 While severe punishment was being inflicted on enemy by all other parts of square. **1929** *Morning Post* 13 July 11/1 Too cautious play, during which loose stuff escaped punishment. **1930** *Daily Express* 6 Oct. 11/5 He took most of the punishment in the first round. **1949** 'J. TEY' *Brat Farrar* viii. 69 Now he looked stupid, like a boxer who is taking too much punishment.

b. Of materials, machinery, etc.: excessive use or rough handling.

1930 *Engineering* 11 Apr. 473/3 Steel from which a boiler tube is manufactured should have the following qualities:—It must be capable of withstanding severe punishment during manufacture and also when being rolled into a tube plate and belled. **1955** *Times* 17 May 18/3 Only the finest film-strength oils can withstand the punishment a tractor engine receives.

3. *attrib.* and *Comb.*

1844 *Regul. & Ord. Army* 120 All punishment drill is to be carried on in the Barrack-Yard or Drill-Ground. **1897** MRS. E. L. VOYNICH *Gadfly* (1904) 35/2 He remembered the 'punishment cell', and descended the ladder, shrugging his shoulders. **1905** *Macm. Mag.* Nov. 34 The rule that a punishment-book should be kept was established in the Navy. *Ibid.*, Croker.. told a young captain that the Admiralty did not like officers who had a long punishment-list. **1916** W. OWEN *Let.* 14 Mar. (1967) 385 Inspections, punishment parades, & more inspections. **1946** R. CAMPBELL *Talking Bronco* 16 Rather a punishment-parade For friend and enemy alike. **1958** J. TOWNSEND *Young Devils* vi. 54 In one year more than five hundred canings had been officially entered in the punishment book. **1968** L. BERG *Risinghill* 61 Risinghill, like every school, has a Punishment Book.

†punishworthy, *a. rare.* [irreg. f. PUNISH *v.* + WORTHY.] Deserving of punishment.

1621 LADY M. WROTH *Urania* 403 All of you.. merit punishment.., but you indeed most.. being the greatest, and therfore most vnfit to be ill, but ill beeing most punishworthy.

punition (pjuːˈnɪʃən). Now *rare.* Forms: 5- puni-, (5 pugny-), 5–6 puny-, (6 *Sc.* pwni-); 5–6 -cio(u)n, -cyon, -ssion, -ssyon, (5 -sshon), 6 -sion, etc., 6- -tion. [a. F. *punition* punishment (14th c. in Littré), ad. late L. *pūnītiōn-em*, n. of action from *pūnīre* to PUNISH.] The action of punishing; infliction of chastisement; punishment.

1425 *Rolls of Parlt.* IV. 276/1 The said merchantz, shall paie double the value of the Subsidee.. wyth outen any other punicion. *a***1450** *Knt. de la Tour* (1906) 98 God shewed her gret punissyon for her pride. **1471** CAXTON *Recuyell* (Sommer) 449 Why.. amendest the not.. for the pugnycion that thou hast suffred. **1513** DOUGLAS *Æneis* II. x. 23 Sair pwnitioun of Greikis dred scho. **1549** CROWLEY *Last Trumpet* 1576 Yet se if thou can cause him feare Goddes terrible punission. **1615** SIR E. HOBY *Curry-combe* iii. 109 The time after this life is for punition, not for purgation. **1657–83** EVELYN *Hist. Relig.* (1850) I. 85 Means for the punition of tyrants, and the vices of men. **1830** *Fraser's Mag.* II. 391 The doom of restitution and punition.

Hence **puˈnitional** *a.*, of, pertaining to or of the nature of punishment; whence **puˈnitionally** *adv.*

1824 BENTHAM *Mem.* Wks. 1843 X. 548 There should be no responsibility, punitional or compensational. **1826** —— in *Westm. Rev.* Oct. 494 Every lawyer.. might and should be made punitionally and compensationally responsible.

punitive (ˈpjuːnɪtɪv), *a.* [a. F. *punitif*, *-ive* (16th c. in Godef.), or ad. med.L. *pūnītīv-us* (Bonaventura *c* 1260), f. L. *pūnīt-*, ppl. stem of *pūnīre* to PUNISH: see -IVE.] Awarding, inflicting, or involving punishment; retributive, punitory. Also, in weakened sense: injurious in such a way as to have a deterrent effect.

In early quots. freq. with *justice*; since 1880, commonly of a military expedition or raid.

1624 BP. HALL *Serm. on Is. xxxii.* 17, Woe bee to them.. that, by the dam of their bribes, labour to stop the due course of punitive Iustice! **1695** J. EDWARDS *Perfect. Script.* 95 This punitive way of dealing with Achan. **1739** J. TRAPP *Right. over-much* (1758) 6 The utmost rigour of punitive justice. **1839** HALLAM *Hist. Lit.* IV. IV. iv. §2 ¶67 The legislative, punitive, and judiciary powers. **1881** *Times* 26 Sept. 5/1 Probably a punitive expedition will be undertaken next winter. **1897** *Lit. World* 22 Oct. 312/1 A British Punitive Expedition captured Benin City. **1959** *Listener* 23 July 154/2 The double, *over* the bid, continues to be punitive. **1959** *Spectator* 14 Aug. 188/1 Punitive box-office taxation. **1973** *Black Panther* 31 Mar. 4/3 Brother Cleophus has been in punitive segregation (lock-up) since the strike. *Ibid.* 20 Oct. 6/1 Punitive damages are assessed only when the judge believes that a defendant has acted deliberately and with malice. **1978** *Lancashire Life* Mar. 107/1 A situation could now develop whereby through punitive financial strategies the independent sector could be so reduced that eventually it could be held to be of no social significance.

Hence **ˈpunitively** *adv.*, by way of punishment; **ˈpunitiveness**, punitive quality.

1865 BUSHNELL *Vicar. Sacr.* II. i. (1868) 478 As if Christ were somehow punitively handled in our place. **1727** BAILEY vol. II, *Punitiveness*, punishing Nature or Quality. **1908** H. R. MACKINTOSH in *Hibbert Jrnl.* July 920 A similar inference as to the punitiveness of God.

punitory (ˈpjuːnɪtərɪ), *a.* [f. mod.L. type **pūnītōrius*, f. L. *pūnītor* a punisher: see -ORY[2].] Inflicting or involving punishment; = PUNITIVE.

1710 J. HARRIS *Lex. Techn.*, *Punitory Interest*, is a Term in the Civil Law, for such Interest of Money as is given for Delay, or Breach of Trust. **1768** TUCKER *Lt. Nat.* (1834) II. 43 Of avoidable evils.. some are prudential, such as labour, troubles, self-denials..; others punitory, which we draw upon ourselves by our ill conduct and wilful mismanagement. **1859** MILL *Liberty* v. 172 The preventive function of government.. is far more liable to be abused, to the prejudice of liberty, than the punitory function. **1880** *Times* 31 Jan., It had been originally intended that the punitory expedition should have started in October.

Punjab (ˈpʌndʒɑːb, -dʒɔːb). Also **Punjaub.** [Hindi *Panjāb*, f. Pers. *panj* five + *āb* water (see below).] The name of an extensive region of the Indian sub-continent, so called from its five rivers, now divided between India and Pakistan, used *attrib.* of its products. **Punjab head**: see quot. 1949.

1907 *Yesterday's Shopping* (1969) 205/2 Punjab Baskets. Nest of 6 baskets, complete—3/0. **1910** *Practitioner* Jan. 18 When a man begins to worry it is time for him to go home, and that applies if he suffers from the so-called Aden or Burma or Punjaub or Madras head. **1949** PARTRIDGE *Dict. Slang* (ed. 3) (Addenda) 1145/2 *Punjab head, have a*, to be forgetful; *Punjab head*, forgetfulness.

Punjabi, Panjabi (pʌnˈdʒɑːbɪ, -ˈdʒɔːbɪ), *sb.* and *a.* Also Penjabi, Punjabee, Punjaubee. [f. prec. + -I.] **A.** *sb.* **a.** The Indo-Aryan language spoken in the Punjab.

1801 *Asiatick Researches* VII. 230, I allude to the *Penjábí* and to the *Brij-bhákhá*. **1838** *Jrnl. Asiatic Soc. Bengal* VII. 711 The Sikhs.. carried their hatred.. to such an extent as to substitute a vocabulary for their native Punjábî. **1854** L. JANVIER *Dict. Panjábí Lang.* p. iv, The character here adopted, and ordinarily used in writing Panjábí, is that known as the *Gurmukhí*. **1862** R. G. LATHAM *Elem. Compar. Philol.* 219 The following.. gives a rough sketch of the grammatical character of the Punjabi. **1921** *Outward Bound* Feb. 74/1 They spoke only Punjabi, of which at that time I knew but three words. **1950** D. JONES *Phoneme* xvi. 84 Such a language as Panjabi which makes use of essential word-tones. **1964** S. K. CHATTERJI in D. Abercrombie et al. *Daniel Jones* 409 In a surrounding group of languages like Panjabi (or Eastern Panjabi), Hindki (Western Panjabi or Lahndi), ..and the Himalayan dialects.., we have these new substitutes for aspirates. **1979** *Trans. Philol. Soc.* 192 The very mixed character of the language of the *Adi Granth*.. should not be allowed to obscure the fact that these scriptures provide the best available evidence for Old Panjabi.

b. A native or inhabitant of the Punjab.

1846 *Hist. Punjab* I. ii. 36 In the plains, Patans.. are mixed with Jats and Cathis, who compose the bulk of the Punjabis, properly so called. **1878** G. SMITH *Life J. Wilson* xvii. 547 Nanuk, the herd-boy, was the Punjabee or Sikh. **1897** *Daily News* 21 Sept. 5/3 The brunt of the attack fell upon the portion of the camp which was held by the 5th Punjabis. **1969** *Hindu* (Weekly Mag.) 3 Aug. p. iii/1 One of the contributory factors enabling the average Punjabi to drink more milk than his counterpart in other States in the country. **1973** *Guardian* 16 Apr. 5/6 Punjabis are noted for their enterprise—and also for meanness.

B. *adj.* Of or pertaining to the Punjab.

1810 *Asiatick Researches* XI. 277 Nánac, according to *Penjábí* authors, admitted the *Hindú* doctrine of metempsychosis. **1812** W. CAREY *Gram. Punjabee Lang.* p. iv, The Punjabee language is confessedly of mixed origin. **1851** H. B. EDWARDES *Year on Punjab Frontier* I. 30 When all your fat Punjabee dogs are panting in vain after the hare. **1864** *Athenæum* 5 Nov. 597/1 To keep our regular troops.. at a strength more than sufficient to render utterly harmless all the turbulent elements of Punjaubee Society. **1886** MRS. EDWARDES *Mem. Sir H. B. Edwardes* II. 315 Before landing at Calcutta, a true Punjabee welcome met him. **1921** *Outward Bound* May 27/1 Ever since I was a boy.. these Punjabi lyrics have kept haunting me. **1948** A. TOYNBEE *Civilization on Trial* v. 88 The sonorous Panjabi names of stricken fields in the Anglo-Sikh wars. **1968** *Listener* 26 Dec. 844/3 Surely it's absurd to say.. that a child of a.. Punjabi family living in a Punjabi community, is just as much an English child as your children or mine. **1971** *Shankar's Weekly* (Delhi) 4 Apr. 4/1 It has been the vain task of the Punjabi elite of West Pakistan to hold down a section of Bengalis as their serfs.

‖**punji** (ˈpʌndʒɪ), *sb.* Also **panja, panji(e, punge.** [Origin unknown: prob. from a Tibeto-Burman language.] A sharpened (freq. poisoned) bamboo stake set in a camouflaged hole in the ground as a trap for enemy soldiers (or occas. for animals). Freq. *attrib.* in ***punji stake, stick.*** So **ˈpunji** *v. trans.*, to fortify with punji stakes; **ˈpunjied** *ppl. a.*

1872 E. DALTON *Descriptive Ethnol. Bengal* 11 They [*sc.* the Singphos] are skilled in fortifying naturally difficult positions, using freely the 'panja', a bamboo stake of different lengths sharpened at both ends and stuck in the ground. **1876** R. G. WOODTHORPE in H. L. Thuillier *Gen. Rep. Topogr. Surveys India 1874–5* 60 Two nasty panjied ditches to be crossed. *Ibid.* 61 Steep approaches, very thickly planted with 'panjees'. **1878** G. P. SANDERSON *Thirteen Years among Wild Beasts of India* xvii. 233 Until 1870 this distant abode of the British Lion [*sc.* Tura in the Garo Hills] was defended by a stockade.. whilst the neighbourhood was pleasantly *panjied*. The uninitiated may imagine that this *panjieing* is some ornamental arrangement of the grounds, so I must explain that panjies are.. a device for.. the discouragement, of visitors. They consist of bamboo spikes driven into the ground, almost level with the surface, the earth being scraped away round each so as to form a cup. Hundreds of these are laid in every direction; grass, falling leaves, &c., soon hide them; and if trodden upon they inflict fearful wounds. **1923** *Blackw. Mag.* May 580/2 We had warned the men against 'booby-traps'.. Only one man fell into one and got a *panjie*, luckily not poison-tipped, through his leg. **1927** *Ibid.* June 819/1 Others were planting sharp-pointed panjis in the undergrowth round the village to impale the enemy as they rush to the assault. **1950** J. H. WILLIAMS *Elephant Bill* iii. 47 The only effective fence against elephants is what is called the punge.. The punge fence, or trap, is made of.. sharpened and lightly roasted.. bamboo stakes of varying length. **1966** *Time* 4 Feb. 18 Children helped to fashion the village's huts and whittled vicious punji stakes of bamboo. **1969** I. KEMP *Brit. G.I. in Vietnam* iii. 50 Two casualties for evacuation; one had stepped on a *punji* stake, the other had stopped a sniper's bullet. **1973** R. HAYES *Hungarian Game*

xxxvi. 216 A workbench directly beneath the window. The thing was loaded with tools; it would be like jumping into a punji pit. **1977** *Time* 21 Nov. 8/1 Three camps in Thailand ..which have been set up for some of the thousands of refugees who have run the gauntlet of mines, snipers and *punji* stick booby traps along the frontier to reach freedom.

punk (pʌŋk), *sb.*[1] *Obs.* or *rare arch.* Forms: 6–7 **punck(e, 7 punke, punque, (pung), 7–9 punk.** [Appears *c* 1600; of unknown origin.] A prostitute, strumpet, harlot.

1596 LODGE *Incarn. Deuils* Wks. (Hunter. Soc.) IV. 69 He hath a Punck (as the pleasant Singer cals her). **1603** SHAKS. *Meas. for M.* v. i. 179 She may be a Puncke: for many of them, are neither Maid, Widow, nor Wife. **1607** MIDDLETON *Michaelm. Term* III. i. E ij b, I may grace her with the name of a Curtizan, a Backslider, a Prostitution, or such a Toy, but when all comes to al tis but a plaine Pung. **1785** WOLCOTT (P. Pindar) *Odes to R.A.'s* iii. Wks. 1812 I. 84 Like a poor pilloried Punk he bawled. **1894** GLADSTONE *Horace's Odes* I. xxxv. 25 The fickle herd, the perjured punk, Fall off. **1928** A. HUXLEY *Point Counter Point* xxix. 478 It amused him to hear the cast-off locutions of duchesses in the mouth of this ageing prostitute... The poor super-annuated punk was so gruesome.

Comb. **1610** B. JONSON *Alch.* IV. iii, This is a trauell'd punque-master. **1789** WOLCOTT (P. Pindar) *Expostul. Ode* xvi. Wks. II. 249 If Empresses will Punk-like kiss and drink.

Hence †**punk** *v. intr.*, to have to do with punks.

1719 D'URFEY *Pills* VI. 212 We scorn to Punk, or to be drunk.

†**punk**, *sb.*[2] *Obs. rare*$^{-1}$. [app. connected with PUNCH *sb.*[1] and *puncture*.] A punch.

1670 E. BROWN in *Phil. Trans.* V. 1198 They cut them out into round pieces with an Instrument like a Shomakers Punk.

punk (pʌŋk), *sb.*[3] Chiefly *U.S.* Also 8 **punck.** [Of obscure origin. For the senses cf. FUNK *sb.*[1] 2, SPUNK.

Perh. N. Amer. Indian: cf. PUNKIE *sb.* Some conjecture a clipt form of *spunk* 'touchwood, tinder' (in Stanyhurst 1582).]

1. a. Rotten wood, or a fungus growing on wood, used in a dry state for tinder; touchwood, amadou.

1705 R. BEVERLEY *Hist. & Present State Virginia* III. 49 Or else they take Punck, (which is a sort of a soft Touchwood, cut out of the knots of Oak or Hickory Trees, but the Hiccory affords the best). *c* **1707** J. CLAYTON *Virginia* in *Phil. Trans.* XLI. 149 As the East-Indians use Moxa [in blistering], so these burn with Punk, which is the inward Part of the Excrescence or Exuberance of an Oak. **1756** J. BARTRAM in Darlington *Mem.* (1849) 206 They [Indians].. shoot red-hot iron slugs, or punk, into the roof, and fire the house. **1792** J. BELKNAP *Hist. New Hampshire* III. 94 They [*sc.* the Indians] raised a blister by burning punk or touchwood on the skin. **1866** LINDLEY & MOORE *Treas. Bot.* II. 941/2 Punk. Touchwood or vegetable tinder. **1908** E. T. SETON *Two Little Sav.* III. viii. 321 Caleb worked on the hollow log... With the hatchet he cleared out all the punk and splinters inside. **1923** J. H. COOK *Fifty Years on Old Frontier* 15 Each man carries a flint and steel, together with a piece of punk. **1924** *Jrnl. Polynesian Soc.* XXXIII. 155 The Maori..carried live fire. To do so he procured..dry material of slow combustion... A kind of punk that grows on trees, [was] used for this purpose. **1936** M. FRANKLIN *All that Swagger* iii. 29 Should the fire die out, a greasy rag, ignited by firing it from the gun, could be applied to punk. **1956** *Te Ao Hou* (Wellington, N.Z.) July 24/2 Little has been recorded of this bracket fungus and its importance in the generation of fire and in carrying fire... In the Thames district..it was known as 'punk' to the early settlers, who learned of its use from the Maoris. **1965** *Austral. Encycl.* VII. 313/2 Such forest pathogens as *Fomes setulosus* and *Polyporus portentosus*..are often called brown punk and white punk respectively. **1972** *Science* 27 Oct. 395/2 In moxibustion only gentle warmth is allowed by the smoldering punk applied on the flesh. **1976** *Yankee* Apr. 107/1 *Wind Bird's* hull looked like a honeycomb with the intervening wood turned to punk.

b. *transf.* Something worthless; foolish or empty talk; nonsense, rubbish. *colloq.*

1869 J. M. HOPPIN *Office & Wk. Chr. Ministry* II. ii. 315 Better have the simplest..thoughts, clearly expressed, than what Carlyle calls 'phosphorescent punk and nothingness'. **1900** ADE *More Fables in Slang* (1902) 212 Well, if they are Right, then I must be Wrong, but to me it is Punk. **1927** D. L. SAYERS *Unnatural Death* xxi. 243 We..men stuff ourselves up with the idea that they're romantic and unemotional. All punk, my son. **1938** 'J. BELL' *Port of London Murders* ix. 164, I told him a lot of punk about..a secret process, but..he knew it was all my eye. **1958** 'A. GILBERT' *Death against Clock* viii. 109 After all, except for the kids, presents seem to me punk. **1970** 'D. HALLIDAY' *Dolly & Cookie Bird* v. 73, I told him what Celeste said about Capricorn and Scorpio, and he said, 'Honestly, Sarah. You don't believe all that punk?' **1973** in *Times* 30 May 5/5, I don't like the family Stein. There is Gert, there is Ep, there is Ein. Gert's writings are punk, Ep's statues are junk, Nor can anyone understand Ein.

c. Bread. ***punk and plaster***, bread and butter. *slang.*

1891 *Contemp. Rev.* Aug. 255 Bread is called 'punk' [by tramps]. **1899** 'J. FLYNT' *Tramping with Tramps* I. vi. 140 Coffee, a little meat, some potatoes, and 'punk an' plaster' (bread and butter). **1925** [see MUD *sb.*[1] 2 e]. **1961** R. P. HOBSON *Rancher takes Wife* ii. 45 Jack Lee..took a large slice of my bread, munched on it thoughtfully, and then pronounced it—'Good punk!' **1975** J. GORES *Hammett* (1976) i. 14 'Punk and plaster?' 'You bet.' The waiter picked up his tray... 'What's punk and plaster?' 'Bread and butter. Con talk.'

2. A composition that will smoulder when ignited, used to touch off fireworks.

1869 ALDRICH *Story of Bad Boy* 92 The smaller sort of fireworks, such as pin-wheels, serpents, double-headers, and punk warranted not to go out.

3. Chinese incense: cf. *joss-stick* (JOSS[1] 3).

1870 M. S. DE VERE *Americanisms* 157 A Chinese lady of rank in San Francisco walks attended by three maids of honor, bearing lighted sticks of punk highly perfumed. **1880** *Harper's Mag.* Dec. 73 Before the ancestral tablets..incense was consumed, punk or joss-sticks. **1890** *Boston* (Mass.) *Jrnl.* 10 May 5/8 The burning of innumerable sticks of bamboo punk, which sent forth a faint, sickening odor. **1953** H. MILLER *Plexus* II. viii. 12 The third night we burned Chinese punk and incense.

4. *slang.* **a.** [This sense may be influenced by PUNK *sb.*[1]] A passive male homosexual, a catamite; a tramp's young companion or 'gunsel'.

1904 'No. 1500' *Life in Sing Sing* 251/1 *Punk*,..a pervert. **1926** J. BLACK *You can't Win* (1927) x. 129 The 'punks', young bums, were sent for 'mickies', bottles of alcohol. **1927** [see GUNSEL 1]. **1950** [see *gay-cat* s.v. GAY *a.* 9]. **1973** B. BROADFOOT *Ten Lost Years* x. 137 They [*sc.* hoboes]'d pick up youngsters as, well—as their playthings. These kids were called punks. **1977** *New Yorker* 24 Oct. 64/3 The involuntary homosexuals tend to be good-looking young men..forced into becoming jailhouse 'punks' by older men serving long sentences.

b. A person of no account, a worthless fellow; a young hooligan or petty criminal. Also *gen.*, as a term of contempt or abuse.

1917 [see MUTT c]. **1928** M. C. SHARPE *Chicago May* xxxi. 287/1 *Punk*, apprentice thief. **1930** D. HAMMETT *Maltese Falcon* xviii. 216 We've absolutely got to give them a victim. .. Let's give them the punk... He actually did shoot both of them..didn't he? **1930** *Sat. Even. Post* 26 July 146/2 'Listen to me, you big punk!' he growled ominously. 'What do you think we are—a lot of fools?' **1933** E. HEMINGWAY *Winner take Nothing* 94 This fellow was just a punk..a nobody. **1939** C. R. COOPER *Designs in Scarlet* ii. 18 Punks like him—sixteen, seventeen, eighteen, nineteen years old. *Ibid.* iii. 37 'The punks', as youthful offenders are often called. **1940** *Sun* (Baltimore) 29 Mar. 17/4 This happens to be the Bomber's tenth defense. Most of them bums or punks? **1949** *Chicago Tribune* 10 Dec. 10 This punk must have robbed a bank or got paid off for settin' a forest fire! **1953** W. BURROUGHS *Junkie* iv. 50 Two young punks got off a train carrying a lush between them. **1959** H. NIELSEN *Fifth Caller* xiv. 207, I was a punk then... Fourteen years old and just a little punk... Then I began to fill out. I ain't a punk no more. **1963** T. PYNCHON *V.* vi. 145 There was nothing so special about the gang, punks are punks. **1964** V. S. NAIPAUL *Area of Darkness* ix. 245, I went back to the hotel. The telephone rang. 'Hallo, punk.' **1967** *Boston Sunday Herald* 30 Apr. I. 16/3 Berke has no sympathy for the 'punks' who act up in school, assault teachers or destroy property. **1976** 'D. HALLIDAY' *Dolly & Nanny Bird* ix. 113 Punks give their kids a punk childhood which leads to the next generation of punks. **1978** J. UPDIKE *Coup* vi. 246 'Uh—think you've come to the wrong place. Hasn't he?'..'You bet the punk has.'

c. In show business: a youth or novice; a young circus animal. Also *transf.*

1923 *N.Y. Times* 9 Sept. VII. 2/1 *Punk*, an amateur. **1926** *Amer. Speech* I. 282 *Punk*, a baby lion or other young animal. **1926** MAINES & GRANT *Wise-Crack Dict.* 12/1 *Punk*, child in show business. **1942** *Amer. Speech* XVII. 223/2 *Punk*, a boy or any young man not yet professionally dry behind the ears. **1971** *Islander* (Victoria, B.C.) 19 Dec. 6/2 At least 71, cantankerous Lizzie's trunk had been paralyzed as the result of once having overzealously disciplined a young elephant, or 'punk'.

d. Short for (*a*) PUNK ROCK; (*b*) PUNK-ROCKER. (Only these senses are widely current outside the United States.)

1974 *New Yorker* 20 May 142/3, I was getting a naïve kick out of watching a woman play rock-and-roll punk. **1976** *New Musical Express* 24 Jan. 20 He's strictly for white dopes high on punks. *Ibid.* 17 Apr. 43/1 Johnny Rotten..has the makings of a good punk. **1976** *Sunday Times* 28 Nov. 37/4 Johnny Rotten and the Sex Pistols are punks. They sing 'Anarchy in the UK.' *Ibid.* 37/5 Punk will fade. Its apologists are ludicrous. **1977** *Evening News* 27 Apr. 11/1 London's growing army of punks have developed a powerful animosity for teds... For the uninitiated, punks.. are the ones who match short, ragged hair with short ragged leather jackets. **1978** *Gramophone* May 1954/1 John Cale.. could be branded one of the original punks as a member of Velvet Underground. **1979** *Time* 30 July 76 The music on this record..is full of brash challenge, like the best punk.

5. Special Combinations. **a.** (In sense 1), as **punk-box**, a tinder-box; **punk-knot**, a protuberance in wood, indicating inward decay (*Funk's Stand. Dict.*); **punk-oak**, the water oak, *Quercus nigra*; **punk-wood** = sense 1.

1862 BURTON *Bk. Hunter* I. 46 As soon would you be tempted to pull out your meerschaum and *punk-box in a cathedral. **1920** *Bull. U.S. Dept. Agric.* No. 871. 20 The sporophores..which I find occasionally..on old *punk knots from which the original sporophores have fallen and are reviving. **1934** *Forestry* VIII. 155 One of the most characteristic and interesting symptoms of *Trametes pini* rot is the so-called punk knot, a mass of brownish friable substance that develops round embedded branch stubs. **1884** C. S. SARGENT *Rep. Forests N. Amer.* 152 *Quercus aquatica*... Possum Oak. *Punk Oak... Probably not used except as fuel. **1897** G. B. SUDWORTH *Nomencl. Arborescent Flora U.S.* 175 Common names [of the water oak] include.. Duck Oak, Possum Oak, Punk Oak. **1883** E. INGERSOLL in *Harper's Mag.* Feb. 427/2 She opened a flint-and-tinder box, and struck a spark into the *punk-wood. **1903** S. E. WHITE *Forest* 180 Sometimes a faint rounded shell..swelled above the level, to crumble to punkwood at the lightest touch of our feet.

b. (In sense 4), as ***punk band, critic, fan, hater, kid, style***; ***punk-related, -styled*** adjs. **punk chic** [after *radical chic* s.v. RADICAL *a.* 3 f], a fashionable style of design reflecting the unconventional aspects of a punk-rocker's dress or appearance; also in adj. use.

1976 *Melody Maker* 11 Sept. 37/6 Even in Britain there's a *punk band called the Suburban Studs. **1977** *Whig-Standard* (Kingston, Ont.) 15 July A1/2 Wherever they go punk bands bring violence. **1977** *Time* 11 July 49/1 Of late, *punk chic has even been taken up by a few high-fashion designers. **1977** *Sniffin' Glue* July 3 The sickest thing is the Zandra Rhodes 'punk chic' look. **1977** *Zigzag* Aug. 5/1, I dunno about fur coats but anyone who wears them Harpers and Queen punk chic outfits is in order for laying out. **1977** *Rolling Stone* 13 Jan. 20/3 Bangs and Meltzer usually know the difference but most of their followers and fellow *punk critics do not. **1977** *Whig-Standard* (Kingston, Ont.) 15 July A1/2 The *punk fans fight with other young groups. **1977** *Western Morning News* 1 Sept. 1/3 Mysterious posters ..have appeared all over Plymouth in the hope that punk fans will read between the lines. **1977** *Sounds* 1 Jan., Have these *Punk haters really thought about what they've heard? **1908** J. M. SULLIVAN *Criminal Slang* 17 **Punk kid*, a boy who begs and panhandles for yeggmen. **1935** *Amer. Speech* X. 19/2 *Punk kid*, an apprentice who works with any crook. **1939** C. R. COOPER *Designs in Scarlet* ii. 22 'We've got to kill 'em,' said a cop bluntly, 'or they'll kill us. Punk kids are dangerous.' **1939** R. CHANDLER *Big Sleep* xiv. 115 That punk kid?.. The kid that works at the store. **1954** *Cosmopolitan* June 87/2 Small time, a punk kid, am I? **1977** *New Yorker* 23 May 32/2 When you were a nobody, a punk kid just starting out, didn't anyone ever lend you a helping hand? **1977** *Ripped & Torn* VI. 3 There's only one restriction: *Punk*/**Punk related* stuff only, OK? **1977** *Sounds* 1 Jan., Ten concise memorable songs, in the pop, *punk style,..combine to form a dynamite package. **1977** *Ibid.*, Certain elements in what we did..created a taste for a certain kind of thing which meant that others could organise *punk styled bands.

punk (pʌŋk), *a.* orig. *U.S.* [f. PUNK *sb.*[3]]

1. Of timber: decayed; rotten, punky.

1902 S. E. WHITE *Blazed Trail* ii. 18 Supplies ran low unexpectedly; trees turned out 'punk'. **1904** —— *Blazed Trail Stories* iii. 49, I cull every log, big or little, punk or sound, that ain't sawed square.

2. *transf.* Devoid of worth or sense; poor in quality; disappointing; nonsensical; 'rotten'. *colloq.*

1896 ADE *Artie* iii. 23 And this crowd up there was purty-y-y punk. *Ibid.* xix. 178 They could n't be any punker'n they are now. **1916** E. WALLACE *Let.* 13 Nov. in M. Gilbert *Winston S. Churchill* (1972) III. Compan. II. 1582 K. J. wants you to do a punk interview with..Churchill. **1929** W. HEYLIGER *Builder of Dam* 4, I call this a punk way to spend an Easter vacation. **1943** *Amer. Speech* XVIII. 89 *Pretty punk* [in New Zealand] does some of the work performed in America by *lousy*. **1949** *Los Angeles Times* 21 May 6 This jail has about as punk, if not the punkest grub I ever packed away. **1972** *Maclean's Mag.* Mar. 48/2 When my uncle became mayor of Sherbrooke he spoke a pretty punk French.

3. *Comb.*, as **punk-ass** *a. slang* [ASS *sb.*[2]], of a person: worthless, good-for-nothing.

1972 J. WAMBAUGH *Blue Knight* (1973) vii. 102 A kid, a punk-ass kid, conned me. **1977** *Zigzag* Aug. 12/2 This period of court harassment..went on until July 25th, when I was locked up for good by punk-ass Colombo in Detroit.

punk (pʌŋk), *v. U.S. slang.* [f. PUNK *sb.*[3] 4 a.] *intr.* To back *out*; to withdraw one's support, to quit.

1920 E. POUND *Let.* 11 Sept. (1971) 157 You lay back, you let me have the whole stinking sweat of providing the mechanical means for letting through the new movement... Then you punk out, cursing me for not being in two places at once, and for 'seeing no alternative to my own groove'. **1956** 'E. MCBAIN' *Cop Hater* (1958) x. 92 We never punk out, but we never go lookin' for trouble, either. **1959** H. SALISBURY *Shook-Up Generation* iv. 65 The Chimp, unfortunately, has a tendency to 'punk out' when the fighting gets tough. **1972** C. H. FULLER in W. King *Black Short Story Anthol.* 145 Where was he? She couldn't believe he *punked out* and stayed away from school. **1977** *Zigzag* Aug. 12/1 Holzman punked out, even after he told us that he wouldn't change after all.

‖**punkah, punka** (ˈpʌŋkə), *sb. E. Indies.* Forms: 7 **punkaw, panhah, panha,** (8 *erron.* **punker, -ar**), 9 (**pankah, phoonka**), **punk-ha, punkah, punka.** [a. Hindī *pankhā* a fan, orig. a hand-fan:—Skr. *pakshaka* fan, f. *paksha* wing.]

1. 'A portable fan, generally made from the leaf of the palmyra' (Yule and Burnell).

In first quot. erron., an attendant who fans with a punkah.

a **1625** W. FINCH *Observ.* in Purchas *Pilgrims* IV. IV. vi. 439 The King sits in his chaire of State, accompanied with his Children and chiefe Vizier..no other without calling daring to goe vp to him, saue only two Punkaw's to gather wind. **1672** H. O. tr. *Bernier's Gt. Mogul* III. *Dehli & Agra* 4 Having a servant or two to fan one by turns, with their great Panhahs or Fans. **1800** *Misc. Tracts* in *Asiat. Ann. Reg.* 336/2 Over her head was held a punkar. **1828** *Asiat. Costumes* 45 The punk-ha, or fan, represented in the plate, is the leaf of the palmyra. **1834** [A. PRINSEP] *Baboo* II. viii. 140 Fair hands were gently waving a punkah over my face. **1903** G. W. FORREST *Cities of India* v. 132 Punkas and water were brought.

2. A large swinging fan made of cloth stretched on a rectangular frame, suspended from the ceiling or rafters, and worked by a cord so as to agitate and freshen the air in hot weather.

Mentioned under the Arabic name *khaish* or *mirwahat-al-khaish*, in 12th c., referred to 8th or 9th c.

1807 (Sept. 15) LD. MINTO in *Life & Lett.* (1880) 27 The punkah vibrates gently over my eyes. **1812** MAR. GRAHAM *Jrnl. Resid. India* 29 The punka (a large frame of wood covered with cloth)..is suspended over every table, and kept swinging, in order to freshen the air. **1842** *Civil Eng. & Arch. Jrnl.* V. 153/1 Strong brass hinge-hooks for punkahs. **1879** MRS. A. E. JAMES *Ind. Househ. Managem.* 41 The punkah is a straight board some two feet in width, and is put up diagonally across the centre of the room, hung from the ceiling or rafters by stout ropes: to this board is attached, by means of rings, a deep frill, or vallance, about eighteen inches in depth.

3. *attrib.* and *Comb.*, as ***punkah-board, -cord, -fan, -fringe, -puller, -pulling, -rope***; **punkah-coolie**, a native Indian servant who works a punkah; also **punkah-wallah** [cf. *competition-wallah*, s.v. COMPETITION 3]; whence **punkah-wallahing** (*nonce-wd.*), the occupation of a punkah-wallah.

1857 A. CASE *Let.* 6 Aug. in *Day by Day at Lucknow* (1858) v. 133 Last night..a shell burst close to our door, just behind the punkah wallah. **1859** LANG *Wand. India* 245 The idea of the poor men paying for punkah coolies! **1864** TREVELYAN *Compet. Wallah* (1866) 118 What well-regulated female can make dress an object in a society of a dozen people..; or music, when her audience consists of a Punkah-wallah and a Portuguese Ayah? **1870** J. W. KAYE *Sepoy War* v. ii. II. 273 There were..none to pull the punkah-ropes. **1879** MRS. A. E. JAMES *Ind. Househ. Managem.* 41 Punkah fringes, 20 R[upees]. *Ibid.*, The punkah boards and ropes are landlords' property. **1890** SARAH J. DUNCAN *Social Depart.* 259 He had never, in the whole course of his punkah-wallahing, been told to stop before. **1896** 'H. S. MERRIMAN' *Flotsam* x, The servant..resumed his place at the punkah-cord. **1899** CONRAD *Lord Jim* (1900) v. 39 The archway from the anteroom was crowded with punkah-pullers, sweepers, police peons, the coxswain and crew of the harbour steam-launch. **1904** *Brit. Med. Jrnl.* 17 Sept. 637 There is no class of native here to accept punkah-pulling as an occupation. **1959** *Listener* 13 Aug. 234/2 The Madras Government was still employing 714 'punkah-pullers'.

Hence **'punkah** *v.*, to fan with a punkah (*trans.* and *absol.*).

a **1625** W. FINCH *Observ.* in Purchas *Pilgrims* IV. IV. vi. 433 Portraitures of the King in state sitting amongst his women,..behind one punkawing, another holding his sword. **1859** LANG *Wand. India* 245 What would it cost to punkah the whole regiment during the hot season?

†punka'teero. *Obs. nonce-wd.* [f. PUNK *sb.*[1]; after such Sp. words as *mulatero* muleteer.] A purveyor of punks; a procurer, pander.

1602 MIDDLETON *Blurt* IV. i. F ij, Punckes, punkateeroes, nags, hags, I will ban.

†'punker. *Obs.* [f. PUNK *sb.*[1] or *v.* + -ER[1].] One who frequents the company of punks.

1736 ADDISON tr. *Petronius Arbiter* 87 He was a great Punker, and nothing that wore a Cap came amiss to him.

punker, obs. erron. f. PUNKAH.

†pun'ketto. *Obs. rare*$^{-1}$. [app. an arbitrary formation from *puncto*, PUNTO[1], with It. dim. ending *-etto*.] A minute point of behaviour.

1608 BEAUM. & FL. *Tri. Hon.* i, No more standing on your punctilios and punkettos of honour.

punk-fist, corruption of PUCKFIST, associated with PUNK *sb.*[3]

1890 in *Cent. Dict.*

punkie[1] ('pʌŋkɪ). *U.S. local.* Also **punk(e)y**. [See quot. 1794, and cf. Lenape, *ponk, punk*, light ashes, dust, powder, *pongus* sand-fly, *ponxu* full of sand-flies.] A minute fly or midge, common in some parts of the north-eastern States of America, which bites severely. Also *attrib.*

1769 R. SMITH *Tour Four Great Rivers* (1906) 42 We begin to be teazed with Muscetoes and little Gnats called here [*sc.* in New York] Punkies. [**1794** G. H. LOSKIEL *Mission Indians N. Amer.* III. 79 The most troublesome plague..especially in passing thro' the woods, was a kind of insect, called by the Indians *Ponk*, or Living Ashes.] **1876** *Forest & Stream* 13 July 368/2 Hands tingling from punkie bites. **1877** HALLOCK *Sportsman's Gaz.* 642 Sandy beaches or gravelly points are liable to swarm with midges or punkies. **1903** [see NO-SEE-EM]. **1933** F. H. CHELEY *Camping Out* 423 The 'punkeys' and 'midgets' can outstrip them [*sc.* mosquitoes] for ferocity and the painful character of the wound which they inflict. **1957** *Biol. Abstr.* XXXI. 1535/1 Punkies of the genus *Culicoides* are an important source of annoyance to personnel engaged in outdoor occupations over much of southern and central Alaska. **1962** GORDON & LAVOIPIERRE *Entomol. for Students of Med.* xxii. 148 Those members of the family Ceratopogonidae which suck blood are known to entomologists as 'biting midges', but in some parts of the world they are given local names, such as 'punkies'.

punkie[2] ('pʌŋkɪ). *W. Country dial.* [Perh. var. of PUNKIN, itself a var. of PUMPKIN + -IE.] A lantern made by setting a candle in a hollowed-out mangel or similar vegetable. **Punkie night** (see quots. 1931, 1960).

1931 *N. & Q.* 21 Nov. 372/2 At Hinton St. George, and in the neighbouring village of Lopen, mangolds, scooped out and fitted with candle ends to form lanterns, are known as 'punkies'. During the parade of punkies, the following lines are sung: 'Tis Punkie night to-night, 'Tis Punkie night to-night. Adam and Eve, they won't believe 'Tis Punkie night to-night. This is said to be a century-old custom.. based upon the fact that a party of men from Hinton and Lopen visited Chiselborough Fair..and did not return to their homes so early as promised. Their wives went in search of them, and the attractions of the fair..were so great that by the time they commenced the journey home, their lamps were innocent of oil, and improvised lanterns, made from mangold-wurzels..were utilised. 'Punkie Night' has been once more revived at Hinton St. George. *Ibid.* 26 Dec. 465/2 'Punkie night'..might be Oct. 31, the evening before All Saints' Day, which is very generally celebrated in America as Hallowe'en. **1959** I. & P. OPIE *Lore & Lang. Schoolch.* xii. 267 To children in south Somerset a punkie is a home-made mangel-wurzel lantern of more artistic manufacture than those commonly made elsewhere for Hallowe'en. **1960** *Guardian* 10 Nov. 10/2 In Somerset 'Punkie Night', during the third week in October, is a great occasion in the little village of Long Sutton... Punkies..are made from hollowed-out mangels to resemble a face. **1972** *Folklore* LXXXIII. 240 A punkie is a general term for a mangold, turnip or similar vegetable that has been hollowed out, a face marked through the skin, and a candle placed inside. *Ibid.*, Punkie Night was in early November.

punkin, U.S. dial. f. PUMPKIN.

punkin (little pun): see after PUN *sb.*[1]

†punkish, *a. Obs. rare*$^{-1}$. [f. PUNK *sb.*[1] + -ISH[1].] Resembling a punk; meretricious.

1616 T. ADAMS *Plain-Dealing* (1861) I. 28 These punkish outsides beguile the needy traveller... Such a house is like a painted whore; it hath a fair cheek, but rotten lungs.

†'punkling. *Obs. rare*$^{-1}$. [f. as prec. + -LING[1].] A little or young punk.

a **1623** FLETCHER *Love's Cure* II. i, Squiring puncks and puncklings up and down the city.

punk rock (pʌŋk rɒk). [f. PUNK *a.* 2 + ROCK *sb.*[3]] A loud, fast-moving style of rock music characterized by aggressive and deliberately outrageous lyrics and performance. Also *attrib.*

1971 D. MARSH in *Creem* May 43/3 He's [*sc.* Rudi Martinez is] doing the knee-drop, and the splits and every other James Brown move. He's the only one in punk-rock who's still got 'em and he's makin' a comeback. **1972** *Village Voice* 1 June 45/1 (*heading*) When punk rock met the Vietcong. **1973** *Fusion* Jan. 47 Punk rock top 20. **1975** *New Yorker* 26 May 6/2 On Tuesday, May 27, Manhattan Transfer returns and begins doing its thirties, forties, and fifties routines opposite Canadian punk-rock singer Lewis Furey. **1976** *New Musical Express* 21 Feb. 31/2 A quarter of spiky teenage misfits..playing 60's styled white punk rock. **1976** *Melody Maker* 14 Aug. 25/3 Now we have gone full circle. Critics groan: 'Bring back incompetent, illiterate punk-rock bands, and away with these boring old practising musicians!' **1977** *Gramophone* June 110/2 'Punk rock' groups (or 'new wave', as they are euphemistically called). **1979** *Fortune* 23 Apr. 59/2 At one extreme are hard rock, acid rock, and more recently punk rock—all characterized by the souped-up, violent sound of blaring electric guitars.

Hence **punk-'rocker**, one who plays or admires punk rock.

1976 *Sunday Times* 28 Nov. 37/3 Punk-rockers hate Mick Jagger (also, Led Zeppelin, Yes and Genesis) as much as they hate critics. **1977** *Sounds* 9 July 36/1, I cannot accept John Peel's suggestion that punk rockers are the only truly socialist representatives we have left. **1978** *Jrnl. R. Soc. Arts* CXXVI. 197/2 What a moral price has been paid in the name of fashion—unhealthy tight corsets, leopard-killing skin coats, the broken promise of false bosoms and the pierced faces of the punk-rockers.

punkster ('pʌŋkstə(r)). [f. PUNK *sb.*[3] 4 d + -STER.] = PUNK-ROCKER.

1976 *New Musical Express* 12 Feb. 20/1 From precocious Nazz punkster to It's-All-My-Own-Work wishful thinker and balladeer. **1977** *Oxford Times* (City ed.) 23 Sept. 6/1 An even more disturbing facet of the punksters—having the nose or cheeks pierced—does not seem to have caught on.

punky ('pʌŋkɪ), *a.* Chiefly *U.S.* [f. PUNK *sb.*[3] + -Y.] **a.** Containing, or of the nature of, punk or touchwood; of fire, smouldering.

1872 W. S. HUNTINGTON *Road-Master's Assistant* 117 A bridge may..have a small knot partially decayed, or 'punky', as it is termed. *a* **1876** H. BUSHNELL in *Life & Lett.* x. (1880) 209 The fire is punky and only smokes. **1880** *Northwest. Lumberman* 24 Jan., For punky knots the general rule is to allow the whole scale of the log for defects. *Ibid.*, A buyer should be allowed..one-half the scale of the punky log. **1903** [see PITCHPOLL, -POLE *v.* b]. **1955** *Sun* (Baltimore) 9 Aug. 16/8 All of the punky and weak wood was removed and a glass and resin putty applied to smooth out the sleek lines. **1958** *N.Z. Timber Jrnl.* Feb. 62/2 *Punky*, applied to wood showing signs of decay, or to soft spongy heartwood. **1959** E. COLLIER *Three against Wilderness* iii. 33 She was scurrying around..gathering punky chunks of wood for the smudge. **1968** C. HELMERICKS *Down Wild River North* II. xxiv. 386 We are seated..around a smudgy, punky fire.

b. *transf.* and *fig.* = PUNK *a.* 2.

1886 *Harper's Mag.* Dec. 105/2 George's mother's folks did have a kind of a punky spot somewhere in their heads. **1904** *N.Y. Times* 5 May 8 Written by another man Mr Austin would doubtless find these verses as amusing as the rest of us do—would appreciate their punky pretentiousness. **1926** F. RICKABY *Ballads* 63 Were you punky, were you hollow, You had been a lucky fellow. **1979** *Maclean's Mag.* 2 July 38/2 He doesn't expect to find his punky pubescents through conventional methods.

punky, var. PUNKIE.

punler, variant of POINDLAR *Sc. Obs.*

punless, punlet: see after PUN *sb.*[1]

'punnable, *a.* [f. PUN *v.*[1]] Capable of being punned upon; susceptible of puns.

1840 T. HOOK *Fitzherbert* I. xv, It was a punable word, but he could not make it tell. **1906** *Westm. Gaz.* 26 Sept. 2/1 The Browns, Whites, Blacks, Greens, Longs, Shorts, Smiths, Finches, and all the hosts who own punnable names.

punnage: see after PUN *sb.*[1]

punne, obs. form of *pun*, POUND *v.*[1]

punner[1] ('pʌnə(r)). Now *rare.* [f. PUN *v.*[1] + -ER[1].] One who makes puns; a punster.

1689 SHADWELL *Bury F.* I. i, A paltry old fashion'd wit and punner of the last age. **1691** WOOD *Ath. Oxon.* II. 561 Alsop ..hath been Quibler and Punner in ordinary to the dissenting party. **1710** SWIFT *Jrnl. to Stella* 1 Oct., The greatest punner of this town next myself.

punner[2] ('pʌnə(r)). [f. PUN *v.*[2]: a variant of POUNDER *sb.*[2]] One who or that which puns or rams earth, etc.; *spec.* a tool for ramming earth about a post or the like. Hence **punner-bar**, a punner and crow-bar combined.

1611 [see POUNDER *sb.*[2] 2]. **1876** PREECE & SIVEWRIGHT *Telegraphy* 193 The 'punner bar' should invariably accompany Marshall's borer. *Ibid.* 194 The upper end of this is tapered down to the form of a chisel, with the point tempered to deal with stones,..the lower end,..shaped like a punner, is employed for ramming and consolidating the soil around the pole. *Ibid.* 196 The hole [in which a pole is set] should not be hastily filled up, but ample time be given to the punners to do their share of the work.

†punnet[1]. *Obs. rare.* [app. a dim. of PUN *sb.*[1]] ? A little pun.

1676–1820 [see PUNDIGRION].

punnet[2] ('pʌnɪt). Also **punnit**. [Of obscure origin: perh. f. *pun*, dial. for POUND *sb.*[1] + ET.]

a. A small round shallow chip basket, used chiefly for fruit or vegetables. Less correctly = POTTLE[1] 2. Now also a container of other materials and shapes.

1822 LOUDON *Encycl. Gard.* Index, *Punnet*, a small flat basket from four to twelve inches in diameter, and one to two inches deep, formed of split wood or shavings of timber. **1849** ALB. SMITH *Pottleton Leg.* xxxix, Baskets of flowers —being punnets borrowed from the market-garden. **1884** *West. Daily Press* 29 May 3/7 The high and conical [bonnets]..suggest strawberry punnets turned upside down upon the head. **1906** *Spectator* 29 Sept. 437/1 Thin paper lining a frail punnet where Lay filberts woodland-brown. **1922** JOYCE *Ulysses* 289 Punnets of mushrooms. **1943** H. J. MASSINGHAM *Men of Earth* ii. 16 Some gave a pound for a punnet of strawberries, others a pound for a punnet of tomatoes. **1955** [see CHIP *sb.*[1] 4 b]. **1971** *Morning Star* 13 July 2 Whole families prepared to descend on the regimented lines of strawberries and fill thousands of punnets. **1975** *Times* 27 Nov. 13/7 A marvellous new filler..(80p a punnet), which claims to fill everything from plaster to concrete.

b. *Comb.*, as ***punnet-crowned, -shaped*** adjs.

1892 *Daily News* 29 Mar. 2/4 Some of the new hats have high, punnet-shaped crowns. *Ibid.* 4 July 9/2 Punnet-crowned bonnets were the principal wear.

Hence **'punneted** *ppl. a.*, packed in punnets.

1907 *Westm. Gaz.* 27 June 12/1 The Perth strawberry crops are heavy, and for the first time large quantities of punneted berries are to be sent down South.

punnic, -ical, punnigram: see PUN *sb.*[1]

punning ('pʌnɪŋ), *vbl. sb.*[1] [f. PUN *v.*[1] + -ING[1].] The making of puns.

1670 [see PUN *v.*[1] 1]. **1690** NORRIS *Refl. Cond. Hum. Life* (1691) 58 This great Mystery of Disputation is nothing else but a meer Tossing of Words backward and forward, sometimes without any meaning, which is Canting; and sometimes with more Meanings than one, which is Punning. **1711** ADDISON *Spect.* No. 61 ¶1 That [false wit] which consists in a Jingle of Words, and is comprehended under the general Name of Punning. **1719** SWIFT *Art of Punning* Wks. (1841) II. 413 Punning is a virtue that most effectually promotes the end of good fellowship, which is laughing. **1791** *Gentl. Mag.* 26/1 During the reigns of James and.. Charles, punning was the language of the Pulpit as well as of the Court. **1864** *Round Table* 18 June 12/1 Philadelphia has a world-wide reputation for punning. To be a Philadelphian is to be a born punster.

punning, *vbl. sb.*[2], stamping: see PUN *v.*[2]

punning ('pʌnɪŋ), *ppl. a.* [f. PUN *v.*[1] + -ING[2].] That puns or makes puns.

1683 DRYDEN & SOAME tr. *Boileau's Art of Poetry* II. *Epigram*, A Corporation of dull Punning Drolls. **1756–7** tr. *Keysler's Trav.* (1760) IV. 378 Such as have nothing to recommend them but a punning jingle of words. **1879** A. H. SAYCE in *Academy* 23 The Tyrrhenians, whom only a punning etymology made Tyrseni.

Hence **'punningly** *adv.*, in a punning manner; with a pun or play on words.

1791 *Gentl. Mag.* 32/2 Endemon punningly demands from what information Mr. Steevens has framed his dogmatic opinion. **1837** CARLYLE *Fr. Rev.* II. III. iii, The Plebeian 'Court of Cassation', as Camille might punningly name it, has done its work. **1893** *Times* 6 May 17/1 A picture punningly named 'Reflections'—shows a wide stretch of shore—with a donkey standing in the midst.

punnology: see after PUN *sb.*[1]

punny ('pʌnɪ), *a.* [f. PUN *sb.*[1] + -Y[1].] Consisting of, or characterized by, a pun or puns. Hence **'punnily** *adv.*

1961 WEBSTER, Punny. **1974** R. QUIRK *Linguist & Eng. Lang.* vii. 116 A confession, punnily derivative from Hannah More. **1976** *Glasgow Herald* 26 Nov. 5/7 Chris McClure..is known nowadays as Christian which provides the punny title of his impending album release, 'The First Christian'. **1977** *Time Out* 28 Jan.–3 Feb. 17/2 Risqué, funny and predictably punny. **1979** *Daily Tel.* 6 Feb. 15/6 (*caption*) 'I love ewe.' This funny punny card is one of a series of Valentine postcards done by cartoonist Haro.

punque, obs. form of PUNK *sb.*[1]

†**punquette.** *Obs. nonce-wd.* [f. *punque*, PUNK *sb.*[1]] ? A little or young punk. So †**punquetto.** (One of the forms may be a misprint.)

1599 B. JONSON *Cynthia's Rev.* II. i, To his Cocatrice or Punquetto, halfe a dozen Taffata gownes or Sattin Kirtles. **1610** —— *Alch.* II. i, You shall start vp yong Vice-royes, And haue your punques, and punquettes [*printed* punquettees].

punsch(e, obs. form of PUNCH *v.*[1]

punscheown, -ion, obs. ff. PUNCHEON[1].

†**punse.** *Sc. Obs. rare.* Also 6 punce. [Variant of PULSE *sb.*[1]; ? through association with *punse*, POUNCE *v.*, to beat.] = PULSE *sb.*[1]

a **1584** MONTGOMERIE *Cherrie & Slae* 274 My vaines with brangling like to brek—My punsis lap with pith. *Ibid.* 977 Thy punsis renuncis All kynd of quiet rest. *a* **1600** —— *Misc. Poems* xliv. 31, I quake for feir—my puncis lope.

punse, punss, obs. (Sc.) and dial. ff. POUNCE *sb.*[1] and *v.*[1]

punsh, punsh(i)on, -s(i)oun, -son, -soune, obs. ff. PUNCH *v.*[1], PUNCHEON[1] and [2].

punster ('pʌnstə(r)). [f. PUN *v.*[1] + -STER.] A professed maker of puns; one addicted to or skilled in punning. (In first quot., a quibbler.)

1700 CONGREVE *Way of World* v. i, To be a Theme for legal Punsters, and Quiblers by the Statute:..to discompose the gravity of the Bench. **1711** ADDISON *Spect.* No. 61 ¶2 That learned Monarch [James I] was himself a tolerable Punnster. **1855** MACAULAY *Hist. Eng.* xiv. III. 471 [Jane, the King's Professor of Divinity] was so unfortunate as to have a name which was an excellent mark for the learned punsters of his University. Several epigrams were written on the double-faced Janus. **1965** W. S. ALLEN *Vox Latina* 107 In the sixteenth century we find punsters identifying e.g. *habitaculum* with French *habit à cul long*. **1978** *Detroit Free Press* 16 Apr. 14C/1 The latest from the most outrageous living punster, bad jokester and molester of the language.

Hence '**punstress** (*nonce-wd.*), a female punster.

1825 SCOTT *Fam. Lett.* (1894) II. xxi. 279 Anne..is a decided punstress.

punt (pʌnt), *sb.*[1] [OE. *punt* (in 10–11th c. glossaries), ad. L. *ponto* a kind of Gallic transport (Caes. *B.C.* III. 29), also a floating bridge, a pontoon (Gellius *a* 175, Ausonius, Digest); in later sense referred to L. *pons, pontem* bridge. Cf. also MDu. *ponte*, Du. *pont* fem., 'ferry-boat, pontoon', MLG. *punte, punto*, LG. *pünte, pünto* ferry-boat, mud-boat, repr. the same L. word.

OE. *punt* was, from its vocalization, prob. an ancient word, representing a survival of the Latin word in Britain; but it may have been only in local use, in which also it seems to have continued during the ME. period, though no example has yet been noted. But *punt-boat* is found in the Maldon (Essex) Records of date 1500 as a current word, and it is noteworthy that the literary use begins with Phil. Holland, a native of that county, who in his translations uses it, evidently as a familiar term, to render various L. words, e.g. *linter, navis, ratis, alveus, arbor cavata*.]

1. a. A flat-bottomed shallow boat, broad and square at both ends; formerly used widely as a name for a raft, dug-out, river ferry-boat, float, lighter, etc.; also = PONTOON 2; now *spec.*, a boat of this kind propelled by means of a long pole thrust against the bottom of the river, or shallow water (see quot. 1892).

c **1000** *Ælfric's Voc.* in Wr.-Wülcker 166/2 *Pontonium*, punt. *c* **1050** *Suppl. Ælfric's Voc.* ibid. 181/31 *Pontonium*, flyte. *Caudex*, punt... *Trabaria*, anbyme scip. *a* **1100** *Voc.* ibid. 287/33 *Pontonium*, flyte. *Trabaria*, i. *caudex*, punt, *i. pontonium*.

1500, 1552 [in *pontebots*, etc.: see 3]. **1568** WITHALS *Dict.* 10 a/2 *Lintres sunt nauiculæ fluuiales, ex arbore cauata factæ*, as puntes or troughes be. **1600** HOLLAND *Livy* XXVI. ix. 589 Much ado he [Fulvius] had, for the great scarcitie of timber & wood, to make punts [*rates*] and boats for to set over his armie. **1603** —— *Plutarch's Mor.* 1294 She searched for them in a bote or punt made of papyr reed [ἐν βαριδι παπυρίνῃ]. **1615** J. R. *Trade's Incr.* in *Harl. Misc.* (Malh.) III. 308 Fishing, which now we use in crayers and punts. **1630** *R. Johnson's Kingd. & Commw.* 40 The Emperour (who yet had never greater vessell than a Punt or Yaugh upon the Danuby). **1725** DE FOE *Voy. round World* (1840) 322 One large float with sides to it, like a punt or ferry-boat. **1769** FALCONER *Dict. Marine* (1789) Fivb, Punts are a sort of oblong flat-bottomed boats..used by shipwrights and caulkers. **1789** PORTLOCK *Voy.* xi. 228 The carpenter, assisted by the cooper and three other hands, began to build a punt of twelve feet long, six feet wide, and about three feet deep. **1800** COLQUHOUN *Comm. Thames* i. 14 Lighters, Barges, and Punts employed in the trade of the river Thames. **1817** J. EVANS *Excurs. Windsor*, etc. 156 Procuring a boat, usually called a punt, and fixing it at some little distance from the shore, they fling their lines and quietly seize the finny prey. **1861** MUSGRAVE *By-roads* 28 The ships, so called, of Philippe de Valois' fleet were little else than punts of very great length, carrying one mast and a sail, but about fifteen hundred men. **1865** KINGSLEY *Herew.* xxi, A man cutting sedges in a punt in the lode. **1875** HELPS *Soc. Press.* xx. 289 It was a fine day, and we resolved to go out in a punt. **1892** *Row. Alm.* 206 (Rules for Punting, Thames Punting Club) A punt is a flat-bottomed craft without stem, keel, or stern-post, and the width at each end must be at least one-half of the width at the widest part.

b. [f. PUNT *v.*[2]] A push with a punt-pole.

1897 *Geogr. Jrnl.* IX. 12 Only practice enables one..to guide the raft by means of timely punts at the surrounding rocks with the pole with which one is armed.

†**2.** An ingot, shaped with two square ends like a punt. *Obs.*

1895 *Daily News* 28 Sept. 2/1 'Punts' [of silver].. weighing upwards of 4629 ounces, and of the value of about £700.

3. *attrib.* and *Comb.*: as ***punt-boat, -builder***; **punt-fisher**, one who fishes from a punt; so **punt-fishing**; **punt-gun**, a gun used for shooting water-fowl from a punt; so **punt-gunner, punt-gunning**; **punt-pole**, the long pole used in propelling a punt; **punt-shooter, -shooting** = *punt-gunner, -gunning*; **punt-stick** (*U.S.*) = *punt-pole*; **punt-well**, a well in a fishing-punt in which to deposit fish.

1500 *Maldon Crt.-rolls* (Bundle 59, No. 3), De Roberto Jacobbe pro custum. 11 *pontebots et pro bigis xii d. **1552** (Dec. 4) *Admir. Court, Libels*, Bundle 21, No. 64 (Valuation at Lowestoft) Finding there ffowr punte boots and a cocke bote..did..vallew the sayed puncte boote[s] and cocke bote at twelve pounds tenn shillings. **1849** J. FORBES *Phys. Holiday.* i. (1850) 3 He sins..worse than the *punt-fisher. **1816** COL. HAWKER *Instr. Sportsmen* (1824) 354 The barrel of a *punt-gun..should..be about seventy or eighty pounds weight. **1886** WALSINGHAM & GALLWEY *Shooting* (Badminton) II. 276 Double-barrelled Punt Gun; Bore 1½ in.; weight, 200 lbs.; length 9 ft. 6 in. **1892** C. R. B. BARRETT *Essex* 29 The punt-gun was hoisted out from the little cabin. **1958** L. DURRELL *Mountolive* xvi. 302 Time for the..tuning in of the long punt-guns. **1972** *Shooting Times & Country Mag.* 4 Mar. 21/2 A pair of fine Welney Wash punt guns. **1840** BLAINE *Encycl. Rur. Sports* §2754 Colonel Hawker was the first *punt gunner in Great Britain. **1956** C. WILLCOCK *Death at Flight* xv. 202 'Wire cartridges,' he said. 'Punt-gunners use these to get greater range.' **1971** *Country Life* 28 Oct. 1129/2 Famous alike as punt-gunner, eel-fisher, mole-catcher and skater. **1899** *Westm. Gaz.* 15 Dec. 2/2 A man needs to be uncommonly strong and hardy to pursue *punt-gunning without endangering his health. **1859** H. KINGSLEY *G. Hamlyn* xx. (1894) 165 Unable to reach the bottom with the spear she had used as a *punt-pole in the shallower water. **1897** *Daily News* 30 Aug. 5/1 *Punt sailing is becoming quite a popular pastime on the Upper Thames, so much so that a Thames Punt Sailing Club has been started. **1900** *Pall Mall G.* 25 Jan. 8/3 These *punt-shooters are not as a rule naturalists... Their object is to kill wild fowl for the market. **1816** COL. HAWKER *Instr. Sportsmen* (1824) 367 Those, who fancy *punt-shooting such a dangerous amusement. **1840** BLAINE *Encycl. Rur. Sports* §2754 (*heading*) Hampshire Coast Punt Shooting. **1905** W. E. GEIL *Yankee in Pigmy Land* xiii. 194 The crossing of the swift Semleki in native dugouts propelled by *punt sticks. **1901** *Pall Mall G.* 7 May 10/1 Anglers attribute the absence of trout in their baskets and *punt-wells to the cold winds.

punt (pʌnt), *sb.*[2] [ad. F. *ponte* (in both senses), 1718 in *Dict. Acad.*, or Sp. *punto* point.

The connexion of the two senses is obscure and disputed. Littré treats them as the same word, and refers both to Sp. *punto*. But Hatz.-Darm. treats the two senses as distinct words, taking *ponte* 'point' as ad. Sp. *punto*, but *ponte* 'the player against the bank' as a deriv. of *ponter*, PUNT *v.*[1], app. unconnected with *punto*, and of unknown origin. English writers have in general identified them.]

1. = PUNTER[1] 1.

1704 D'URFEY *Hell beyond Hell* 94 Th' Assembly meets, and on the board, Scatters, like Jove, the dazling hoard; Salutes the Punts with Bows and Dops. [**1794** *Sporting Mag.* IV. 44 Each ponte is furnished with a livret or book, containing a suit of thirteen cards.] **1850** [see sense 2].

2. In the game of faro: A point.

1850 *Bohn's Handbk. Games* 338 Terms used at Faro. *Ponte* or *Punt*, a Point. The punter or player.

punt, *sb.*[3] [Goes with PUNT *v.*[3]] An act of punting.

1. *Rugby Football.* A kick given to the ball dropped from the hands, before it reaches the ground. (Cf. DROP-KICK, PLACE-KICK.) Also in other varieties of football.

1845 *Rules Footb. Rugby School* §7 Kick out must not be from more than..twenty-five yards [out of goal] if a punt, drop, or knock on. **1857** HUGHES *Tom Brown* I. v. 109 The mysteries of 'off your side', 'drop kicks', 'punts', 'places', and the other intricacies of the great science of foot-ball. **1876** *World* (N.Y.) 19 Nov. 3/4 Princeton..now played all together on the ball, the captain himself being instrumental, with a good punt, in securing the second goal. **1881** *Laws Rugby Union* §28 A Fair Catch is a catch made direct from a kick or a throw forward, or a knock on by one of the opposite side, or from a punt out or a punt on. **1887** H. HALL *Tribune Bk. Open-Air Sports* 125 A goal may be won..by kicking the ball..over the cross-bar of the goal of the defence, except by a 'punt'. **1921** [see *fly-kick* s.v. FLY *sb.*[2] 8]. **1941** *Daily Progress* (Charlottesville, Va.) 14 Jan. 11 A player can elect to run back a punt from scrimmage if the ball is caught in the end zone. **1965** *Sun-Herald* (Sydney) 4 July 51 Denis Aitken won the long-distance kicking competition with a punt of 66¼ yards. **1975** *Times* 25 Aug. 9/8 A massive punt downfield from [goalkeeper] Parkes. **1979** *Arizona Daily Star* 5 Aug. 9/1 The Packers overtook the Chiefs with 12:57 remaining in the third quarter after Kansas City's Jimmy Edwards fumbled a Green Bay punt.

2. *transf.* An upward jerk. *rare.*

1897 KIPLING *Capt. Cour.* iv. 85 A grunt and squeal of the windlass; a yaw, a punt, and a kick, and the *We're Here* gathered herself together to repeat the motions.

3. *attrib.* and *Comb.* in sense 1, as ***punt return, returner***; **punt kick** = sense 1; hence **punt-kick** *v. intr.*

1876 *Sun* (N.Y.) 20 Nov. 3/1 A Harvard man redelivers the ball by a fine '*punt' kick. **1960** E. S. & W. J. HIGHAM *High Speed Rugby* ii. 27 Be sure you can punt-kick with either foot *accurately*. **1965** *Advertiser* (Adelaide) 17 July 25 Sturt back pocket player Brenton Adcock follows through with a long punt kick at training. **1961** J. S. SALAK *Dict. Amer. Sports* 345 *Punt return (football), a planned maneuver for running back a punted ball. **1967** *Boston Sunday Herald* 14 May II. 5/5 A kickoff and punt-return man. **1970** *Globe & Mail* (Toronto) 25 Sept. 31/7 A second injury to *punt returner Bryan De-Marchi.

punt, *sb.*[4] *Glass-making.* = PUNTY 1, PONTIL.

1832 G. R. PORTER *Porcelain & Gl.* 171 At this stage another implement, called a punt or pontil is brought into use. This is a solid iron rod of a cylindrical form smaller and lighter than the tube used for blowing.

punt, *sb.*[5] [cf. PUNTY 2.] The hollow at the bottom of a wine-bottle: = KICK *sb.*[2] 1.

1863 T. G. SHAW *Wine, Vine, & Cellar* xxiii. 363 To label each bottle..in large letters..on a piece of paper..gummed into the punt or hollow part of the bottom of the bottle.

punt, *sb.*[6] [f. PUNT *v.*[1] (perh. infl. by PUNT *sb.*[3]).] A bet, a gamble. Phr. ***to take a punt*** (Austral.), to take a chance or risk.

1965 J. O'GRADY *Aussie English* 71 To 'take a punt at' anything is the equivalent of to 'have a go'. **1969** *Sydney Morning Herald* 7 June 25/9 Melbourne.. selectors have 'taken a punt' in naming 20-year-old Russell Collingwood as centre half-forward. **1976** *Daily Tel.* 27 Mar. 2/3 People will still have a punt on Wimbledon. **1978** O. WHITE *Silent Reach* xxiv. 253 Blackness and silence. So take a punt... He ..eased the pencil torch out of his bag. **1979** *Ibid.* 29 Jan. 17/8 As a punt, or straightforward gamble with money that can be written off without hardship, there is some appeal in Carr Boyd Minerals.

punt (pʊnt), *sb.*[7] Also Punt. [Ir. = 'pound'.] The Irish monetary unit, until 1979 equivalent to £1 sterling. Also *Comb.*

1975 *Irish Times* 24 May 13/2 Do we devalue below sterling? Or do we stabilise our punt? Or maybe even attempt to revalue it upwards? **1978** *Observer* 17 Dec. 2/2 The Irish Government's decision to join the European Monetary System and break the link between Ireland's pound (now the punt) and Sterling came at the end of 10 days of hectic negotiations. **1979** *Ibid.* 8 Apr. 4/6 An advertisement in last Friday's *Derry Journal*..told readers: 'Punt holders are welcome in the North.'.. But when I was there last week the small shops in the..Bogside were taking three pence off the Punt, as the Irish pound is called, when one went to buy a packet of cigarettes.

punt (pʌnt), *v.*[1] [ad. F. *ponter*, in same sense (in *Dict. Acad.* 1718); according to Hatz.-Darm., of unknown origin. Cf. PUNT *sb.*[2]] **a.** *intr.* At certain card-games, as basset, faro, and baccarat: To lay a stake against the bank.

1706 [implied in PUNTER[1]]. **1712** ADDISON *Spect.* No. 323 ¶12 From Eleven at Night to Eight in the Morning Dream'd that I punted to Mr. Froth. **1715** LADY M. W. MONTAGU *Basset-table* 68 Wretch that I was! how often have I swore, When Winnall tallied, I would punt no more. **1738–9** *Act 12 Geo. II*, c. 28 §3 Every person..who shall.. play, set at, stake, or punt at..ace of hearts, pharaoh, basset, and hazard. **1855** THACKERAY *Newcomes* I. 360 Punting for half crowns at a neighbouring hall. **1881** BESANT & RICE *Chapl. of Fleet* II. xi, I shall punt low, and never lose more than a guinea a night.

b. *slang* and *colloq.* To bet upon a horse, etc.

1873 [implied in PUNTER[1] 2]. **1887** *Pall Mall G.* 13 Sept. 2/1 Resolving to punt, I selected a horse which was given as the favourite. **1898** *Referee* 4 Sept. 11/4 (Farmer) While Paul is punting with the outside book-makers.

c. ***to punt around***, in police slang: to patrol. Also as sb. in phr. ***to have a punt around***.

1970 P. LAURIE *Scotland Yard* 293 *Punt around, to*, to patrol. **1974** G. F. NEWMAN *Price* ii. 58 Thought I'd have a punt around, see who's about. **1977** P. MOYES *To kill a Coconut* vii. 99 To 'punt around' is to patrol.

Hence '**punting** *vbl. sb.*[1]; *spec.* in Football Pools.

1797 *Sporting Mag.* IX. 332 The information charged her with unlawfully playing, staking and punting at the game of Faro. **1855** THACKERAY *Newcomes* x, What must have been the venerable Queen Charlotte's mind when she heard..of his punting at gaming-tables? **1951** *Sport* 16–22 Mar. 22/2 My advice is to make sure that the system or method of punting you adopt is a good one.

punt, *v.*[2] [f. PUNT *sb.*[1]]

1. *trans.* To propel (a punt or other boat) by thrusting a pole against the bottom of the river, etc.; to propel or shove off, in the manner of a punt. Formerly called *poling*: see POLE *v.*[1] 6.

1816 SIR H. DOUGLAS *Milit. Bridges* 45 The pontoons are rowed or punted to their respective stations. **1863** DICEY *Federal St.* II. 116 She [*sc.* a raft] got aground, and had to be punted off with poles. **1885** *Athenæum* 16 May 637/1 A young lady standing in a boat, which she punts from bank to bank.

b. *intr.* or *absol.* To propel a punt, or any boat in the manner of a punt; = POLE *v.*[1] 6 b.

1846 LANDOR *Exam. Shaks.* Wks. II. 274 Will Shakespeare and another were sitting in the middle, the third punted. **1847** COL. HAWKER *Diary* (1893) II. 275, I.. punted up to a single goose..and killed him. **1865** LIVINGSTONE *Zambesi* iv. 100 Others are punting over the small intersecting streams.

2. *trans.* To convey in a punt, or by punting.

1853 'C. BEDE' *Verdant Green* I. ix, They had just been punted over the river. **1863** W. C. BALDWIN *Afr. Hunting* viii. 334 Two Makubas punted me several miles up the river.

Hence '**punting** *vbl. sb.*[2]; also *attrib.*

1865 LIVINGSTONE *Zambesi* xxi. 418 They preferred punting to paddling. **1870** *Daily News* 10 Oct., 50 years ago, when it was not the fashion to regard..the Nile as a punting and canoeing stream. **1875** HELPS *Soc. Press.* xx. 290 The punter, very nearly got upset, holding on stoutly to his punting-pole when it stuck in the mud. **1888** *Rowing Almanack* 189 Rules and Regulations for Punting, by the Thames Punting Club.

punt, *v.*^{3} [Goes with PUNT *sb.*^{3} History obscure: prob. in origin a dialect word.

In Northamptonsh., *punt* appears as a variant or modification of *bunt*, a word widely used in midland and southern dialects, from Cheshire to Kent, and Devon to E. Anglia, in the sense 'to push, butt, strike with the head, horns, or feet, to bump, raise, lift up'. Miss Baker's *Gloss. Northamptonsh. Words*, 1854, has *bunt* 'to kick or strike with the feet', *punt* 'to push with force, to raise by a push; to push with the head as a calf does a cow'. These words appear to be nasalized variations of BUTT and PUT (in its original sense), prob. of onomatopœic origin or modification.]

1. *Rugby Football.* **a.** *trans.* To kick (the ball), after dropping it from the hands, before it reaches the ground. Also *absol.* and in other varieties of football.

1845 *Rules Footb. Rugby School* §5 *Try at goal*... The ball when punted must be within, when caught without, the line of goal. **1885** *Daily News* 19 Feb. 2/8 Bowen secured [the ball] and punted it into touch in the home twenty-five. **1889** *Pauline* VIII. 36 From the scrummage..Houseman obtained the ball and..passed to Turner, who punted into touch. **1905** [see DROP *v.* 24 b]. **1961** *Dallas Morning News* 10 Oct. II. 1 He..punted once for 39 yards and caught one pass for 13 yards. **1967** *Sun-Herald* (Sydney) 16 Apr. 67 Ryan coolly punted the ball straight through the middle and Geelong had won by a point. **1972** G. GREEN *Great Moments in Sport: Soccer* xiii. 123 Gregg immediately punted the ball far down-field, well over the half-way line. **1974** *Plain Dealer* (Cleveland, Ohio) 26 Oct. 4-D/6 On their next offensive series, the Falcons were forced to punt.

b. To get (a goal) by punting: see PUNTED *ppl. a.*^{2}

2. To strike, hit, knock. *rare.*

1886 *Contemp. Rev.* Jan. 52 To see a stout Flamand of fifty or thereabouts solemnly punting, by the aid of a small tambourine, a minute india-rubber ball, to another burgher of similar aspect, which is the favourite way in which all ages and sexes take exercise on the *digue*. **1899** KIPLING *Stalky* 174 M'Turk's knee in the small of his back cannoned him into Stalky, who punted him back.

Hence **'punting** *vbl. sb.*^{3}

1893 *Daily News* 14 Dec. 2/6 Cambridge..got further towards the Oxford line by the aid of Neilson's punting. **1895** *Outing* (U.S.) XXVII. 250/1 This 'punting into touch' is a very favorite means of gaining ground. **1910** W. CAMP *Bk. of Foot-Ball* viii. 313 In punting, the ball is kicked with the instep and not with the toe. **1974** *Liverpool Echo* (Football ed.) 31 Aug. 3/3 His timing and immaculate positioning, together with his straight-backed, stiff-legged punting are..faithfully reproduced by Alec. **1979** *Tucson* (Arizona) *Citizen* 20 Sept. 11D/8 UA's Barry Kramer is second in punting with a 42·3 average.

‖**punta** ('punta). [It., lit. 'point'.] The narrow upper part of straw grown in Tuscany for plaiting. Also *attrib.*

1929 *Daily Express* 26 Jan. 5/2 Rough straws and picture hats are always popular... These are being shown of openwork tuscan or punta straw. **1968** J. IRONSIDE *Fashion Alphabet* 253 *Punta*, straw made of the upper part of the grain stalk.

'punt-a'bout. *Football.* [f. PUNT *v.*^{3} + ABOUT *adv.*] The kicking of a ball about for practice at odd times; also, a football used for this. Also *attrib.*

1845 *Rugby Misc.* 178 The impatience with which place-kicking is..regarded at punt-about. **1857** HUGHES *Tom Brown* I. v, 'Hurrah! here's the punt-about,—come along and try your hand at a kick'. The punt-about is the practice ball, which is just brought out and kicked about anyhow from one boy to another. **1917** KIPLING *Diversity of Creatures* 255 The 'tump-tump' of the puntabouts before the sides settled to games. **1924** —— *Debits & Credits* (1926) 97 An ancient, but air-tight puntabout-ball. **1963** *Times* 10 May 4/3 A puntabout at Twickenham..afforded an opportunity to bid godspeed..to England's Rugby football team.

‖**pun'tal.** *Obs.* Also 6 (*anglicized*) pointall. [a. Sp. *puntal*, f. *punto* point.] Properly, the name of a block-house on a point of sand at the entrance into the harbour of Cadiz; extended to a similar defensive work elsewhere; in Eng. usually plural, and treated as a common noun.

1587 *Spanish War* 1585–7 (Navy Records Soc. XI. 163) The White Lion being commanded..to ride as near to Puntales [*MS.* Pointall] as might be. **1702** *Lond. Gaz.* No. 3845/2 There were in Cadiz Bay 3 or 4 French Men of War.., who retired above the Puntals before the Entrance. **1725** DE FOE *Voy. round World* (1840) 197 To ride without the town of Callao, out of the command of the puntals or castles there. **1745** TINDAL *Contin. Rapin* III. xxvi. 569/1 The French men of war, and the gallies, that lay in the bay [of Cadiz], retired within the puntals.

punted ('pʌntɪd), *ppl. a.*^{1} [f. PUNT *sb.*^{1} and *v.*^{2} + -ED.] **a.** Frequented by punts. **b.** Propelled as, or conveyed in, a punt.

1847 ALB. SMITH in *Illustr. Lond. News* 12 June 374 Upon the punted Thames a fisher wight Is watching where his float is idly dangling. **1887** J. ASHBY STERRY *Lazy Minstrel* (1892) 23 And as the white sail passed along, A punted Poet sang this song!

'punted, *ppl. a.*^{2} *Football.* [f. PUNT *v.*^{3} + -ED^{1}.] Obtained by punting: see PUNT *v.*^{3} 1 b.

1864 *Field* 3 Dec. 386/3 The School claimed a 'punted' goal, which, by the rules of High House is not allowed to count.

puntee, variant of PUNTY 1.

puntel, var. PONTIL [cf. Sp. *puntel*].

1864 in WEBSTER s.v. *Pontee.*

Punt e Mes (punt e 'mɛs). Also **Punt e mes.** [It. (Piedmontese dial.), lit. 'point and a half'.] An Italian aperitif, made in Piedmont.

1956 C. G. BODE *Wines of Italy* x. 100 There are two kinds, Carpano 'Vermouth'—somewhat closer to the usual line of red vermouth, and Carpano 'Punt e Mes', with the bitter tang still more emphasized. **1959** W. JAMES *Word-bk. Wine* 152 *Punt e mes.* The Italian vermouth, of which one sees much in Italy but little elsewhere, is of the sweet type but with a pronounced bitter after-taste. **1965** *Harper's Bazaar* Jan. 45/1 A Negroni..equal parts of Campari, gin, and Punt e Mes. **1966** R. ARDREY *Territorial Imperative* (1967) vii. 265 You..take a table in the islet's little restaurant. You order a *Punt e Mes* or a second-rate omelet. **1974** *Times* 14 Mar. 9/6 (Advt.), *Vermouths & Aperitifs*.. Pimms..Punt e Mes..Cinzano.

punter^{1} ('pʌntə(r)). [f. PUNT *v.*^{1} + -ER^{1}.]

1. A player who 'punts' or plays against the bank at certain card-games: see PUNT *v.*^{1}

1706 PHILLIPS (ed. 6), *Punter*, a Term us'd at the Game of Cards call'd *Basset*. **1781** G. SELWYN *Diary* 22 June, I.. called in at Brooks's... Hare in the chair: the General chief Punter, who lost a 1000. **1850** *Bohn's Handbk. Games* (Faro) 335 The banker turns up the cards... The punter may at his option set any number of stakes..upon one or more cards chosen out of his livret [a suit of 13 cards, with four others called *Figures*]. **1891** HOFFMANN *Baccarat* 13 The player on his [the croupier's] right, who for the time being is dealer, or 'banker'. The other players are punters.

2. *transf.* A small professional backer of horses. Also, one who gambles in stocks and shares, or on football pools.

1873 in *Slang Dict.* **1884** *Graphic* 15 Nov. 507/2 Many 'punters' anxious to retrieve past losses. **1894** *Westm. Gaz.* 20 Feb. 6/1 The punter, having no longer the company's daily traffic returns..to play with. **1903** McNEILL *Egregious English* 185 Round it there has grown up a specious and parasitical finance which is rapidly transforming the English into a nation of punters. **1951** *Sport* 16–22 Mar. 22/2, I know of many punters who have decided to follow one system and then after a short losing spell switched to another system. **1976** *West Lancs. Evening Gaz.* 8 Dec. 1/7 A Great Eccleston punter has scooped £26,082 on the pools.

3. *slang.* A name for a member of various classes of criminal, esp. one who assists in the commission of a crime (see quots.).

1891 *Answers* 4 Apr. 338/1 Having filled the premises with pictures,..the auctioneer engages the assistance of what are known in the business as 'punters'. The 'punter'.. is the auctioneer's confederate, and it is his duty..to make sham bids. *Ibid.* 338/3 In addition to bidding, a 'punter' will often assist the auctioneer in cajoling the public. **1941** BAKER *N.Z. Slang* vi. 52 We have also acquired [this century] some underworld slang of our own:..*punter*, an assistant of a pickpocket who diverts the victim's attention while robbery is committed. **1973** 'J. PATRICK' *Glasgow Gang Observed* iii. 28 'Punter' was 'a normal man where you live who never gets caught', to whom you took stolen goods and traded them in for guns, 'blades', or money. *Ibid.* 29 They were the people who sold bottles of wine at extortionate prices on Sundays... The word was also generalized to mean a member of a 'team' or gang, as in the much used phrase 'Ya Cumbie punter'.

4. *slang.* The victim of a swindler or confidence trickster.

1934 P. ALLINGHAM *Cheapjack* xv. 187 But when the grafter decides that it is time for him to get the punter's money, he leans casually against the stall. *Ibid.* 320 *Punter*, a grafter's customer, client or victim. **1962** [see KITE *sb.* 4 c]. **1974** G. F. NEWMAN *Price* viii. 253 They were three card tricksters. Their patter never changed, but still punters stood for it.

5. *colloq.* A customer or client; a member of an audience or spectator; *spec.*, the client of a prostitute.

In some contexts almost synonymous with *person* (but depreciatory).

1965 *Sunday Times* (Colour Suppl.) 24 Oct. 66/3 There is plenty of irrational judgement about..but like all free-market operators, the traders have to concentrate it on people—on each other and on the 'punters' (dealer buyers). **1968** D. BRAITHWAITE *Fairground Architecture* iii. 60 Described by veteran showmen as 'a good oncer'—that is, a ride the *punters* would normally go on once—and once only—this must have been the least successful of his inventions. **1969** *Jeremy* I. III. 22/2 *Punter*, client. **1970** *Sunday Times* 15 Mar. 60/5, I [*sc.* a prostitute] always make the punter wear a rubber. **1975** *Ibid.* (Colour Suppl.) 23 Feb. 25/2 There's nuthin' but deid punters walkin' up and doon, wi' their beds under their airms. **1975** *Times* 20 Sept. 2/7 Their clients were known as 'punters' and the youths as 'rent boys'. Some boys, once corrupted, became male prostitutes. **1976** *Sunday Mail* (Glasgow) 28 Nov. 12 (*caption*) Ya eejit! Ah'm talkin' aboot thae punters inra Housa Lords..yir upper-crust. **1977** *Record Mirror* 7 May 17/2 The punters were well pleased. Some people even..said they preferred my sound, as far as I was concerned I played crap that night. **1977** *Drive* Sept.–Oct. 112/1 The more confused you are, the more likely you are to accept his offer. Because you are the punter. **1978** *Observer* 12 Feb. 3/5 Irene, a 19-year-old prostitute, was giving the glad eye to prospecting punters on the side streets of Chapeltown, Leeds. **1980** *Ibid.* 6 Apr. 33/3 Some of the punters [*contextually* pilgrims to Lourdes] were elderly and they were all tired.

'punter^{2}. [f. PUNT *v.*^{2} + -ER^{1}.] In earlier use, one who goes fishing or shooting in a punt; often = *punt-gunner*; later, one who punts or manages a punt.

1814 COL. HAWKER *Diary* (1893) I. 91 All over Poole harbour..according to report of punters..the same.. scarcity prevailed. **1886** WALSINGHAM & GALLWEY *Shooting* (Badm. Libr.) II. 243 The wildfowl shooter who uses a punt and swivel-gun is known as a 'punter' or 'puntsman'. **1906** *Daily News* 16 Sept. 6 Pangbourne, the sylvan haunt of the Thames angler, the summer retreat of the Saturday-to-Monday punter.

'punter^{3}. [f. PUNT *v.*^{3} + -ER^{1}.] In various forms of football, one who punts (cf. PUNT *v.*^{3} 1 a).

1890 in WEBSTER. **1910** W. CAMP *Bk. of Foot-Ball* viii. 314 Accuracy should be an aim of the punter as much as distance. **1956** V. JENKINS *Lions Rampant* iv. 58 Thus.., an enormous punter as well as goal-kicker, sent them back.. yards at a time. **1970** *Globe & Mail* (Toronto) 25 Sept. 31/7 Hamilton Tiger-Cats have signed University of Toronto punter and halfback Paul McKay. **1977** *New Yorker* 3 Oct. 111/1 Curry, up to now a demon punter, could not average better than twenty-nine yards a kick.

puntiglio, -ilio, etc., obs. ff. PUNCTILIO.

puntil, variant (in Dicts.) of PONTIL.

†**puntilion.** *Glass-making. Obs. rare*$^{-1}$. [ad. obs. It. *pontiglio*, *punteglio*: cf. PUNCTILIO.] = PONTIL, PUNTY 1.

1665 HOOKE *Microgr.* 42 Small..bubbles of glass..being crack'd off from the Puntilion whilst very hot.

‖**puntilla** (pun'tiʎa). Also (erron.) **puntillo.** [Sp., dim. of *punto* point.] In bull-fighting, a dagger used to give the *coup de grâce* to the bull.

1838 *Q. Rev.* LXI. 419 The butchers..are able infallibly to dart the 'puntilla' into the spine. **1924** E. HEMINGWAY *In Our Time* 23 One of the *cuadrilla* leaned out over his neck and killed him with the *puntillo.* **1932** [see MONOSABIO]. **1967** MCCORMICK & MASCAREÑAS *Compl. Aficionado* i. 21 The death of the bull at the butcher's *puntilla* was incidental to the central ritual.

Hence **puntillero** (punti'ʎero), an assistant at a bullring who uses the *puntilla*.

1910 *Encycl. Brit.* IV. 790/2 Should the bull need a *coup de grâce*, it is given by a *chulo*, named *puntilléro*, with a dagger which pierces the spinal marrow. **1923** W. J. LOCKE *Moordius & Co.* x. 144 An indistinguished member of the quadrilla, dignified by the sonorous title of puntillero, knelt down and with a poignard gave him [*sc.* the bull] the *coup de grâce*. **1970** A. FOWLES *Dupe Negative* xi. 152 On his faraway face had been the look a bull has the instant the *puntillero* strikes home.

punting, *vbl. sb.*: see PUNT *v.*^{1}, ^{2}, ^{3}.

puntion, obs. form of PUNCHEON^{2}.

puntist ('pʌntɪst). [f. PUNT *sb.*^{1} + -IST.] One who practises punting; = PUNTER^{2}.

1894 *Daily News* 1 Sept. 6/4 Our leading amateur lady puntist. **1904** *Daily Chron.* 9 July 7/6 The ever-increasing number of puntists to be seen afloat..on the Thames.

puntman ('pʌntmən). Pl. **-men.** [f. PUNT *sb.*^{1} + MAN *sb.*^{1}] = PUNTSMAN, PUNTER^{2}.

1863 in C. W. Hatfield *Hist. Notices Doncaster* (1866) I. 94 A puntman..stalking to a flock of wild-ducks in the twilight. **1894** *Daily News* 6 Dec. 5/2 In the early part of the eighteenth century a puntman named John Reeves, at Essex Stairs, near the Temple, gained a good living by taking anglers out in his boat.

punto^{1} ('pʌntəʊ). Also 6–8 (in senses 1–3) **puncto.** [a. It. or Sp. *punto*:—L. PUNCTUM.]

†**1.** A small point or detail; an atom, particle, jot; a moment, instant. (In first quot. with play on sense 3). *Obs.*

1598 B. JONSON *Ev. Man in Hum.* IV. vii, It must be done like lightning... 'Tis nothing, and't be not done in a—*punto*! **1623** ABP. WILLIAMS *Let. to Buckhm.* in Hacket *Life* (1692) I. 150 This..is expected to the utmost *punto.* **1706** E. WARD *Wooden World Diss.* (1708) 82 He will no more surpass one Puncto of Time.

†**2. a.** A small point of behaviour: = PUNCTILIO 5.

1591 *Garrard's Art Warre* 69 Amongst souldiers that stand much upon their Punctos. **1605** BACON *Adv. Learn.* II. xxiii. §3 Where that [reputacion] is not, it must be supplied by Puntos and Complementes. **1642** FULLER *Holy & Prof. St.* V. xiv, The Neapolitane Gentry, who stand so on the puntoes of their honour, that they preferre robbery before industry. **1726** SHELVOCKE *Voy. round World* 119 Every body..begged I would not put a meer puncto to orders in the balance against such a prospect. **1766** SMOLLETT *Trav.* xv. I. 249 Establishing a punto, founded in diametrical opposition to common sense and humanity.

b. Phr. ***in punto*** = in point (POINT *sb.*^{1} D 4 a).

1616 B. JONSON *Devil an Ass* IV. iv, And do they weare Cioppino's all? *Wit.* If they be drest in *punto*, Madame.

†**3.** *Fencing.* A stroke or thrust with the point of the sword or foil. ***punto dritto***, a direct thrust. ***punto riverso***, a back-handed thrust; also adverbially = in the position for such a thrust. *Obs.*

[**1595** SAVIOLO *Practise* I. K ij, Your dagger commaunding his Rapier, you maie giue him a *punta*, either *dritta*, or *riversa*.] **1596** LODGE *Incarn. Diuels* Wks. (Hunter. Soc.) IV. 23 His hat without a band, his hose vngartered, his Rapier *punto r'enverso*. **1598** SHAKS. *Merry W.* II. iii. 26. **1598** B. JONSON *Ev. Man. in Hum.* IV. vii, I would teach these nineteene, the speciall rules, as your *Punto*, your *Reuerso*, your *Stoccata*..till they could all play very neare, or altogether as well as my selfe. **1620** *Swetnam Arraign'd* I. ii, My rapier, swash... Ile put you to the Puncto presently. **1624** FORD *Sun's Darling* II. i, I'll drill you how to give the lie, and stab in the punto.

†**4.** A pricking pain: = PUNCTION b. *Obs.*

1617 COCKS *Diary* 8 Feb. (Hakl. Soc.) 235 Mr. Totton fell into an extreme payne of puntos (or stitches).

5. *Glass-making.* = PONTIL, PUNTY I.

1839 URE *Dict. Arts* 582 (*Glass-making*) Another workman now applies the end of a solid iron rod tipped with melted glass, called a *punto*, to the nipple or prominence.. and thus attaches it to the centre of the globe. *Ibid.*, An assistant nips it off from the *punto* with a pair of long iron shears, or cracks it off with a touch of cold iron.

†**6.** attrib. ***punto beard***, a pointed beard. *Obs.*

1659 SHIRLEY *Hon. & Mammon* I. ii, I can looke upon your buffe And punto beard.

7. *Lacework.* Used (= POINT *sb.*[1] 31) in phrases to denote various kinds of Italian lace and embroidery, as ***punto a maglia*** (mesh stitch); ***punto a rilievo*** (erron. *relievo*), (stitch in relief); ***punto in aria*** (stitch in the air), i.e. needlepoint lace used as a border; ***punto tagliato*** (cut-work); ***punto tirato*** (drawn-work).

1865 F. B. PALLISER *Hist. Lace* iv. 47 Punto tagliato.—Cut-work. *Ibid.*, Punto in aria.—Worked on a parchment pattern, the flowers connected by brides: in modern parlance, Guipure. *Ibid.*, Punto tagliato a fogliami.—The richest and most complicated of all points, executed like the former [sc. *punto in aria*], only with this difference, that all the outlines are in relief, formed by means of cottons placed inside to raise them. *Ibid.* 49 Punto a maglia quadra.—Lacis; square netting, the Modano of the Tuscans. **1865** Punto a rilievo [see *gros point* s.v. GROS *a.*]. **1881** C. C. HARRISON *Woman's Handiwork* I. 81 (*caption*) Old punto tirato, or Italian drawn-work. **1881** Punto a maglia [see DARNED *ppl. a.*[1] 2]. **1900** E. JACKSON *Hist. Hand-Made Lace* 192 *Punto a rilievo*, the Italian name for Venice Raised Point Lace. *Ibid.* 205 *Punto a Maglia.*—Lacis, or darned netting, much used for curtains and bed furniture. **1905** L. A. TEBBS (*title*) New lace embroidery (punto tagliato). **1953** M. POWYS *Lace & Lace-Making* iv. 9 *Embroidered linen*, Needlepoint, Italian, 16th century. Drawn thread work, with the pattern left in the linen. Punto Tirato e Tela Lasciato. The design typical of the period. *Ibid.* 11 *Gros point de Venise*, 17th century. Heavy raised Venetian Point. The grand effect is produced by the relief which gives the look of carved ivory and it is sometimes called 'Punto Tagliato a Fogliami', lace resembling cut or carved leaves. **1960** H. HAYWARD *Antique Coll.* 230/1 *Punto in aria embroidery*,..used to describe a very early form of lace, the cutwork fabric reduced to a strip supporting the needlepoint work. **1974** *Encycl. Brit. Micropædia* X. 386/3 From 1620 Venetian raised lace (in Italian *punto a relievo*, in French *gros point de Venise*) developed distinct from flat Venetian (*point plat de Venise*).

punto[2] ('pʊntəʊ). *Cards.* Also ponto ('pɒntəʊ). [a. Sp. *punto* point.] (See quots.)

1728 CHAMBERS *Cycl.* s.v. *Ombre*, If either of the red Suits be Trump, the Ace of that Suit, call'd *Punto*, [is] the fourth [trump]. **1781** *Gentl. Mag.* LI. 616 *Punto* is the Spanish Ace [in Quadrille]. **1861** *Macm. Mag.* Dec. 120 Fourth, if the trump suit be red, comes the ace of the trump suit, called *Ponto*; if black there is no Ponto. **1878** H. H. GIBBS *Ombre* 13 In Diamonds and Hearts, when trumps, the Ace takes rank before the King. It is called Punto (pronounced Poon'to) in Spanish and English. Quadrille players sometimes call it, corruptly, Ponto.

punto banco ('pʊntəʊ 'bæŋkəʊ). [In form answers to It. *punto* point, *puntare* to bet and *banco* bank: cf. also PUNT *sb.*[2] and BANCO *int.*] A gambling game resembling baccarat (see also quot. 1976[1]). Also *attrib.*

1973 'R. MACLEOD' *Burial in Portugal* vi. 116 The rows of tables..offering everything from roulette and boule to punto banco and blackjack. **1976** E. L. FIGGIS *Gamblers Handbk.* 125 Punto-Banco..is played entirely as a casino game at table with bases for 12 players, and spaces for the casino 'chips operator' between bases 6 and 7 and croupier between spaces 1 and 12. The actual banker and punter are both phantom inasmuch as all players must bet with the casino, not with each other. They may either bet 'Banco', that the phantom bank will win the coup, or 'Punto', that the phantom punter will win the coup. **1976** *Daily Record* (Glasgow) 23 Nov. 18/5 It has the biggest layout in Britain with 18 roulette, dice and punto banco tables all going under the plum-and-gold silk shades.

puntsman ('pʌntsmən). Pl. -men. [f. *punt's*, gen. of PUNT *sb.*[1] + MAN *sb.*[1]; cf. *batsman*, etc.] = PUNTER[2].

1881 GREENER *Gun* 531 It being the desire of puntsmen to pot as many birds as possible by one shot. **1882** JEFFERIES *Bevis* II. 30 The puntsman being too idle to bale till compelled, the space between the real and the false bottom was full of water. **1886** [see PUNTER[2]]. **1904** LD. ROSEBERY *Sp. at Glasgow* 5 Dec., In the history of every puntsman there comes a critical moment..when he has to make a decisive choice whether he will go overboard with the pole, or whether he will remain in the punt without the pole.

punty, ponty ('pʌntɪ). *Glass-making.* Forms: 7 ponte, 7–9 -ee, 9 punty, -ee, ponty. [app. ad. F. *pontil*: see PONTIL.]

1. An iron rod used in glass-blowing: see quots. Called also PUNT, PUNTO, POINTEL, PONTIL.

1662 MERRETT in App. to tr. *Neri's Art of Glass* 364 *Ponte* is the Iron to stick the Glass at the bottom for the more convenient fashioning the neck of it. *Ibid.* 365 *Tower* is the Iron on which they rest their Pontee when they scald the Glass. **1843** G. DODD *Days at Factories* 269 The whole was transferred from the tube to a rod called the 'punty'. **1869** *Routledge's Ev. Boy's Ann.* 483 A long iron rod called a ponty. **1876** BARFF *Glass & Silicates* 90 The workman sits during this operation in a seat with arms, laying the pontee on them. **1883** H. J. POWELL *Glass-Making* x. 56 The working rod or 'puntee'..is used for holding a vessel during the later stages of manipulation, by means of a seal of glass. **1890** W. J. GORDON *Foundry* 133 A lad standing ready with an iron-holder, called a 'punty', slips it on to the end of the bottle... Held by the punty the bottle is taken to the leader of the party.

2. A round hollow made on a glass object to remove the mark made in breaking it off the punty-rod; hence, a small circular or oval hollow made as an ornamentation on glass.

1884 KNIGHT *Dict. Mech.* Supp. s.v., A glass decanter.. is said to be cut in punties when the ornamentation consists of dots or cup-like depressions, usually circular but sometimes oval.

3. *Comb.*, as ***punty mark***; **punty-iron, -rod,** †**-stake**, see quots.; **punty-sticker**, a workman who sticks a quantity of melted glass on the punty.

1662 MERRETT in App. to tr. *Neri's Art of Glass* 364 *Pontee stake* is the Iron whereon the Servitors place the Irons from the Masters when they have knock'd off the broken pieces of Glass. **1839** URE *Dict Arts* 582 The workman having.. taken possession of the globe by its bottom or knobbed pole attached to his punty rod,..carries it to another circular opening, where he exposes it to the action of moderate flame. **1849** PELLATT *Glass Making* 101 Another workman then gathers upon a ponty-iron a small piece of Glass. **1890** *Cent. Dict.*, *Ponty-sticker.* **1909** JULIAN A. OSLER in *Let.* 3 Mar., To finish the glass neatly, a round hollow is made—not primarily as an ornament, but to remove the punty-mark.

puntyvally, obs. (Sc.) f. PUNCTUALLY (sense 2).

puny ('pju:nɪ), *a.* and *sb.* Also 6 puney, 6–7 punie, punye, 7 punay, punee. [Phonetic spelling of PUISNE, q.v.]

A. *adj.* †**1.** Junior; inferior in rank, subordinate: = PUISNE *a.* 1, 1 b. *Obs.*

a **1577** SIR T. SMITH *Commw. Eng.* (1609) 64 The officer before whom the Clerke is to take the essoyne, is the puny Justice in the common pleas. **1579** FULKE *Heskins' Parl.* 296 Appealing..from the lower house of punys Burgesses to the higher house of auncient Barons. **170.** in CELIA FIENNES *Diary* 278 The Lord High Steward askes ye Lords one by one beginning with the puny Lord, so to the highest. **1733** SWIFT *On Poetry* Wks. 1755 IV. I. 191 Put on the critick's brow, and sit At Wills' the puny judge of wit.

†**2.** Later, recent: = PUISNE *a.* 2. *Obs.*

1628 PRYNNE *Cens. Mr. Cozens* 29 Composed by some vaine and illiterate Monkes of punie times. **1648** —— *Plea for Lords* 373 No precedents of puny date within time of memory. **1651** N. BACON *Disc. Govt.* II. Pref. A 2 b, Knights, Citizens, and Burgesses of Parliament..were not knowne nor heard of till punier times than these.

†**3.** Raw, inexperienced; that is a novice or tyro.

1591 SHAKS. *1 Hen. VI*, IV. vii. 36 How the yong whelpe of Talbots raging wood, Did flesh his punie-sword in Frenchmens blood. **1602** HERRING tr. *Oberndoerffer's Anat.* A iij b, No Commander will prefer the punee and fresh-water Souldier before the auncient and well-disciplined Warriour. **1692** BENTLEY *Boyle Lect.* i. 21 These terrors may disturb some small pretenders and puny novices. **1712** W. ROGERS *Voy.* (1718) 244 Neither do I think it half so bad as these puny marriners tell us.

4. a. Of inferior size, force, or importance; minor; petty, weak, feeble; small, diminutive, tiny.

1593 SHAKS. *Rich. II*, III. ii. 86 Arme, arme my Name: a punie subiect strikes At thy great glory. **1596** —— *Merch. V.* III. iv. 74 And twentie of these punie lies Ile tell, That men shall sweare I haue discontinued schoole Aboue a twelue moneth. **1692** E. WALKER *Epictetus' Enchir.* viii, The puny loss shall not disturb your mind. **1791** BOSWELL *Johnson* an. 1739 (1831) I. 113 Some puny scribbler invidiously attempted to found upon it a charge of inconsistency. **1838** EMERSON *Addr., Lit. Ethics* Wks. (Bohn) II. 208 The great idea, and the puny execution. **1898** G. W. STEEVENS *With Kitchener to Khartum* 139 The River was punier than ever and the belt of bush thin.

b. esp. of human beings and animals: Of small growth and feeble vitality; undersized and weakly.

1604 SHAKS. *Oth.* v. ii. 244 Euery Punie whipster gets my Sword. **1647** TRAPP *Comm. 1 Tim.* v. 1 Lash him not with the scourge of the tongue, as a puny-boy. **1664** POWER *Exp. Philos.* 28 Muffet calls this Insect *Locustellum* or a puny-Locust. **1693** C. MATHER *Wond. Invis. World* (1862) 125 He was a very Puny Man, yet he had often done things beyond the strength of a Giant. **1742** YOUNG *Nt. Th.* IX. 2203 Each flow'r, each leaf, with its small people swarm'd, (Those puny vouchers of Omnipotence!). **1875** JOWETT *Plato, Rep.* Introd. (ed. 2) III. 39 They..did not wish to preserve useless lives, or raise up a puny offspring.

c. In bad condition or health; physically weak; ailing. *U.S. dial.*

1838 K. DE R. KENNEDY in N. E. Eliason *Tarheel Talk* (1956) 289, I found your dear Aunt Catherine in a very puny state, not entirely confined, but obliged to rest herself on the bed more or less every day. **1866** C. H. SMITH *Bill Arp* 170 Me and him like to have fit, and perhaps would, if I hadn't been puny. **1904** W. N. HARBEN *Georgians* xvii. 163 Little Minnie begun to fail; she got so puny she spit up ever'thing she ate. **1943** T. PRATT *Barefoot Mailman* i. 7 Don't you go making fun of sickness. Mister Dewey Durgan here has been puny the last few days and needs the best advice. **1947** *Publ. Amer. Dial. Soc.* VIII. 33/1 [S.W. Ohio] *Puny*, in poor health, thin, emaciated. **1979–80** *Verbatim* Winter 14/1 [In Missouri] *puny* was 'confined to bed', *poorly* meant 'chronically ill', and *bad sick* meant it was time to call the undertaker.

†**B.** *sb. Obs.*

1. One younger or more recent than another or others; a junior.

1565 JEWEL *Def. Apol.* (1611) 94 Therefore S. Augustine saith, Deus docuit Petrum per posteriorem Paulum... Thus God instructed Peter by Paul his punie, that was called after him. **1603** FLORIO *Montaigne* II. xii. (1632) 324 The eldest ..child shall succeed and inherit all; where nothing is reserved for Punies, but obedience. **1628** JACKSON *Creed* IX. xviii. §3 Much less did the ancient poets..borrow their fancies..from the Jewish rabbins, who were their punies.

2. A junior or recently admitted pupil or student in a school or university, or in the Inns of Court; a freshman. Also *fig.* or *allusively* (leading to sense 3).

1548 PATTEN *Exped. Scotl.* L vj Like y[e] play in Robin Cooks skole, whear bicaus the punies may lerne thei strike fewe strokes, but by assent & appointement. **1590** J. STOCKWOOD *Accidence* A j b, The Booke to the Punies and Petits of the Grammar Schoole. **1607** *Christmas Prince* (1816) 1 They whome they call Fresh-menn, Punies of the first yeare. **1673** *Lady's Call.* I. i. §19 As if vice now disdain'd to have any punies in its school.

3. A raw or inexperienced person; a novice, tyro.

1589 NASHE in Greene *Menaphon* Pref. (Arb.) 8 The idle vsage of our vnexperienst and illiterated punies. **1607** TOURNEUR *Rev. Trag.* I. iii, I see thou'rt but a puny in the subtill Mistery of a woman. **1638** CHILLINGW. *Relig. Prot.* I. iv. §23. 204 Punies in Logick, know that universall affirmatives are not simply converted. **1688** H. WHARTON *Enthus. Ch. Rome* 55 He was no puny in this Art.

4. a. An inferior, a subordinate; a person of small account. Now *rare. arch.*

1579 G. HARVEY *Letter-bk.* (Camden) 61 [To reap] displeasure of my worshipfullist dearist frendes... Contempte and disdayne of my punyes and underlings. **1626** C. MORE *Sir T. More* 2, I..who know my selfe a verie puney in comparison of so manie famous men. **1658** OSBORNE *Jas. I*, 23 The Swis, though owners of brave actions, are yet so farre their Punies in the learning of trade. **1711** *Countrey-Man's Let. to Curat* 4 Sacheverell Himself is but a puny for an oculist in comparison of him. **1922** JOYCE *Ulysses* 386 Thou chuff, thou puny, thou got in the peasestraw.

b. A junior judge; = PUISNE *sb.* 2.

1608 A. WILLET *Hexapla in Exod.* 526 That the punies and inferiour Iudges should deliuer their opinion first.

Hence (*nonce-wds.*) †'**puny** *v. trans.*, to make puny or insignificant, to dwarf; '**punyish** *a.*, somewhat puny; '**punyism**, puny character.

1649 CLEVELAND *Epitaph* ii, To puny the Records of time By one grand Gygantick Crime. **1832** WILSON in *Blackw. Mag.* XXXII. 865 Feeblish faces that must frown, punyish figures that must strut. **1791** PAINE *Rights of Man* (ed. 4) 70 The punyism of a senseless word like Duke, or Count, or Earl, has ceased to please.

puny, obs. form of PUNAISE, bed-bug.

punyard, obs. form of PONIARD.

†'**punye, punȝe**, *sb. Sc. Obs.* Also 4 poiné, punay. [a. F. *poignée*, in OF. also *puinnie, pugnie, puignie, -nee, puygnye*, etc. handful: = Pr. *ponhada*:—L. type **pugnāta*, f. L. *pugnus*, F. *poing* fist: see POIGNE and -ADE.] A handful of men (soldiers).

c **1330** *Arth. & Merl.* 3241 Þe kinges..seyd, gret schame hem was bifalle, Þat Arthour wiþ a litel punay Hadde ydriuen hem oway. *Ibid.* 5905 Michel wonder had Leodegan, Þat swiche a litel poine of man So fele in so litel þrawe So manliche had yslawe. **1513** DOUGLAS *Æneis* IX. viii. 129 Thai mycht on fors dissevyr that punȝe, Quhilk thaime assalȝeit thekyt with pavys hie.

punye, punȝe, -zie ('pʏnje), *v. Sc.* [ad. F. *poign-*, pres. stem of *poindre* to pierce: see POIN *v.*, PUNGE, and for the form cf. Sc. *cunȝe, cunȝie*, COIN.] *trans.* To prick, pierce; to spur.

c **1470** HENRY *Wallace* v. 606 The prent off luff him punȝeit at the last. *Ibid.* VII. 1198 The punȝeand hed the plattis persyt rycht. **1819** W. TENNANT *Papistry Storm'd* (1827) 164 His steed he punzied wi' his heel.

Hence '**punzie** *sb. Sc.*, a prick, a stab.

1819 W. TENNANT *Papistry Storm'd* 175 Strange! that ae punzie on the back Should sooner bring that carl to wrack.

punyness, variant of PUNINESS.

†'**punyship.** *Obs.* Also 6 punie-, 6–7 puni-. [f. PUNY + -SHIP.] The position, status, or character of a 'puny'; juniority; inferiority. Also with possessive as a mock title.

1581 MULCASTER *Positions* v. (1887) 32 Reading..must needes acknowledge and confesse her puniship to writing. **1599** NASHE *Lenten Stuffe* 51 In the punieship or nonage of Cerdicke Sandes, when the best houses and walles there were of mudde. **1624** BP. MOUNTAGU *Gagg* 18 Shall wee believe your Puniship or them? **1680** HICKERINGILL *Refl. Late Libel on Curse-ye-Meroz* 5 Undermining other mens good name, lest they should shine to eclipse and benight their twinckling Puny-ships.

puoy, variant of POY *sb.*[1] and [2].

puozzolana, variant of POZZOLANA.

pup (pʌp), *sb.*[1] Also 8 pupp. [Shortened form of PUPPY *sb.* Cf. PUP *v.*[1]

(Hence, *pup, puppy* are not parallel to *babe, baby, Tom, Tommy*, in which the form in -*y* is later and diminutive.)]

1. A young dog, a whelp, a young puppy. ***in pup, with pup***: (of a bitch) pregnant.

1773 *Gentl. Mag.* XLIII. 219 A Pupp with two mouths and one head. **1820** J. H. REYNOLDS *Fancy* (1906) 35 Farewell to bull, and stake, and pup. **1840** R. H. DANA *Bef. Mast* xxii. 66 A fine, promising pup, with four white paws. **1854** E. MAYHEW *Dogs* (1862) 195 To discover whether a bitch is in pup. **1873** E. A. FREEMAN *Let.* 21 Dec. in Stephens *Life* (1895) II. vii. 78 We have also a big Newfoundland pup growing up.

2. *fig.* and *transf.* **a.** Applied contemptuously to a person.

In quot. app. with some allusion to LIRIPOOP 2 (see also LURRY and POOP *sb.*[2]).

1589 R. HARVEY *Pl. Perc.* (1590) 16 Why haue you not taught some of those Puppes their lerrie? **1856** *Porter's Spirit of Times* 15 Nov. 172/3 There were three pups..a parcel of supercilious fellows, who, with a piece of glass stuck in their eye, survey the crowd as if contamination dwelt amongst them. **1870** J. K. MEDBERY *Men & Myst. Wall St.* 31 Down in the cock-pit the Commodore's 'pups', as the merciless, cacophonic 'street' argot denominates the broker friends of Vanderbilt, are making an ineffective rally.

b. A youthful or inexperienced person, a beginner; a young 'blood'. *colloq.* (chiefly *U.S.*).

1890 *Punch* 7 June 270/2 You ride very nicely indeed for a 'pup'. **1903** G. H. LORIMER *Lett. Self-Made Merchant* ix. 118 Chauncey's father was the whole village, barring the railroad station and the saloon, and, of course, Chauncey thought that he was something of a pup himself. **1903** A. H. LEWIS *Boss* vi. 48 'Here's a pup,' cried Big Kennedy, with his hand on my shoulder, 'I want you to look over.' **1938** *Amer. Speech* XIII. 228/1 The youngest intern..may be assigned to routine laboratory tests and called a *pup* or *junior*. **1948** F. BLAKE *Johnny Christmas* II. 70 A fresh pup breezin' in, cool as you please, and takin' over Bent's? **1977** *Transatlantic Rev.* LX. 36, I can remember my Daddy brought me down once when I was a young pup.

c. Also, ***Sopwith Pup***. A familiar name for the Sopwith Scout Tractor, a small, fast, aeroplane used for combative and instructional purposes in the war of 1914–18.

1917 *Jane's All World's Aircraft* 103b *Sopwith Scout Tractor.* Known as the 'Pup', and one of the fastest machines in the world... The 'Sopwith Pup' on active service has passed the 25,000 feet level with a Naval pilot. *a* **1918** J. T. B. MCCUDDEN *Five Years in R. Flying Corps* (1919) 181, I had taken charge of another machine for fighting instruction, this time a Sopwith Scout, vulgarly termed a 'Pup'. **1918** H. G. WELLS *Joan & Peter* xiii. 613 They [*sc.* air force officers] made a language for themselves an atrocious slang of facetious misnomers,..the machines were "buses' and 'camels' and 'pups'. **1928** C. F. S. GAMBLE *Story of North Sea Air Station* xiii. 211 A single-seater machine, the Pup, which was also a product of the Sopwith Aviation Company, passed into the Service during this year [*sc.* 1916]. **1977** J. CLEARY *High Road* i. 20 Pups, Camels.. even some Spads and Nieuports. *Ibid.* 21 What use was a Sopwith Pup to a couple intent on adding to the postwar baby boom?

d. A four-wheeled trailer drawn by a tractor, lorry, or other road vehicle. *U.S. slang.*

1951 *Amer. Speech* XXVI. 308/2 *Pup*, a narrow four-wheel trailer. They can be 'buttoned up' in tandem and will follow the tractor, just as puppies will follow their mother. **1960** *Newsweek* 20 June 91/1 Compact, 1½-ton 'pup' semi-trailers are hitched behind regularly scheduled intercity passenger buses. **1978** *Detroit Free Press* 14 Apr. 16D/2 On two of three trials earlier, without the modifications, the second tanker or 'pup' of the same truck bounced the wheels of its safety guard sharply against the ground.

3. Applied to the young of the fur seal. Also, the young of the sea lion or of rats or mice.

1815 *Sydney Gaz.* 22 Apr. 1/1 The *pups* or young seal were also indiscriminately slaughtered. **1824** A. EARLE *Jrnl. Residence Tristan d'Acunha* 30 Aug. in *Narr. Residence N.Z.* (1832) 354 We started off early for Elephant Bay to procure the skin of a [seal] pup, in order to convert it into caps... The pups were nearly all black. **1858** SIMMONDS *Dict. Trade*, *Pup*,..a young seal. **1886** F. H. H. GUILLEMARD *Cruise Marchesa* I. 196 The lamb-like bleat of a pup is audible above the rest. **1895** *Outing* (U.S.) XXVII. 23/2 An inexperienced hunter..started out to kill his first seal and in some way managed to steal a hood pup, without alarming its parents. **1937** *Discovery* May 140/2 Sea lions..resort to the island [*sc.* Lady Julia Percy Island] to breed, to raise their pups. **1944** E. C. WOOD in A. N. Worden *UFAW Handbk. Care & Managem. Lab. Animals* (1947) vi. 122 The individual pups [*sc.* young rats] are of low birth-weight. **1952** L. H. MATTHEWS *Brit. Mammals* ix. 266 The milk teeth of seal pups are shed or absorbed at a very early age. **1972** *Nature* 3 Nov. 21/2 The rats were under close observation... Mortality among offspring was very low.. only 1 dead pup out of 138 born. **1975** *Storktalk* (Ches. & N. Wales Branch of Nat. Childbirth Trust) Nov. 16 The female mouse lost 54% more pups than did control mice giving birth in the normal settings for mice. **1979** *Guardian* 14 Sept. 4/4 After failing to persuade the Canadian government to stop the killing of Harp seal pups in Newfoundland, the RSPCA is to campaign for a ban on the importation of Harp seal products.

4. (See quots.)

1898 W. B. HASKELL *Two Years in Klondike* 253 Every creek has its pups, and if any of them become of considerable importance they may have pups also. **1902** *Pop. Science Monthly* July 232 The principal streams [in the Klondike region] are known as creeks; the short steep tributaries which flow into them as 'gulches'; and the streamlets which feed these as 'pups'. **1904** ELIZ. ROBINS *Magn. North* xvi. 285 'That's the pup where my claim is'. 'The what?' 'Little creek; call 'em pups here [on the Yukon in Alaska]'. *Ibid.* xvii. 297 Above the pup, on the right, there's a bed of gravel. **1916** *Yukon Territory* (Canada Dept. Interior) I. iii. 27 On Hunker creek, below the mouth of Seventy Pup, practically all the gold occurred in a shattered porphyry bedrock. **1973** P. BERTON *Drifting Home* v. 69 The little pup creeks gurgling down through the thick forests.

5. Phrases. **a.** *to sell* (any one) ***a pup***, to swindle by selling something on its prospective value. Now usu. *fig.* and freq. *pass.*, e.g. *he was sold a pup*. Hence, ***to buy a pup***.

1901 *Daily Chron.* 4 May 5/2 There is a poetical phrase in our language, 'to sell a man a pup'. **1902** *Westm. Gaz.* 24 Nov. 6/2 The consensus of military opinion is..that Colonel Swayne's disaster was due to the native levies 'selling him a pup'. **1902** KIPLING in *Collier's Weekly* 6 Dec. 8/3, I wouldn't have sold old Van Zyl a pup like that..I must hunt him up and explain. **1927** W. DEEPING *Kitty* viii. 99 He was not the sort of man to advise a brother officer to buy a pup. **1930** W. S. MAUGHAM *Cakes & Ale* xiv. 165 The public has been sold a pup too often to take unnecessary chances. **1968** *Scottish Daily Mail* 9 Aug. 5/6 The Basset is the aircraft the RAF did not want in the first place. They were sold a pup, in more ways than one. **1978** A. RYAN in Hookway & Pettit *Action & Interpretation* 75 They may insist that..we worry incessantly about what price our virtues will fetch, and about whether we shall be sold a pup by others. **1978** *SLR Camera* Aug. 36/1 Letters have arrived on my desk from petrified owners..wanting to know more, terrified that they had bought a pup.

b. ***the night's*** (***only***) ***a pup***, the night is 'young' or not far advanced; 'it is still early'. Also, occas., ***the day's*** (***only***) ***a pup***. *Austral. colloq.*

1915 H. LAWSON *Coll. Prose* (1972) I. 913 The night was not even a pup yet—it was broad daylight, being Northern summer. **1921** K. S. PRICHARD *Black Opal* xii. 104 You're not taking her away yet, Michael? The night's a pup! **1928** 'BRENT OF BIN BIN' *Up Country* x. 167 The night is only a pup yet. **1934** T. WOOD *Cobbers* xi. 138 'What's the worry?' they say; 'the day's a pup.' **1947** K. TENNANT *Lost Haven* i. 28 'A man's got to get a bit of sleep.' 'Night's only a pup, hen,' Alec suggested, mildly. **1949** L. GLASSOP *Lucky Palmer* viii. 73 We'll get him in. The day's only a pup yet. **1968** G. DUTTON *Andy* xii. 198 'Are you thinking of driving out to Hangingstone to-night?' 'It's only forty miles and the night is a pup.'

6. *Comb.*, as ***pup-breeder***; ***pup-trained*** adj.; **pupfish**, a small killifish belonging to the genus *Cyprinodon*, esp. *C. macularius*, found in fresh or saline water in desert regions of California and Nevada; **pup joint** *Oil Industry*, a piece of drill pipe of less than the standard length; **pup-tent** orig. *U.S. Mil.*, a small tent or bivouac, a dog-tent; a shelter-tent, *spec.* one comprising two shelter-halves carried separately (see SHELTER *sb.* 3).

1905 THEODORA WILSON (*title*) Our Joshua,.. Octogenarian, Celebrity, and *Pup-Breeder, According to me, his Wife. **1958** *Copeia* 232/1 Ten live *pupfish were captured with a fine-mesh seine. **1973** *Daily Colonist* (Victoria, B.C.) 1 Apr. 9/8 The Owens pupfish survived for eons in a changing environment—from a vast inland lake to a string of shallow desert pools. **1976** P. B. MOYLE *Inland Fishes California* 251 Even the isolated and harmless pupfishes are being threatened by man's activities. **1937** *Amer. Speech* XII. 153/2 **Pup-joints*, short joint used to 'nipple out'. **1972** L. M. HARRIS *Introd. Deepwater Floating Drilling Operations* xii. 139 Adequate pup joints are necessary for final space out. Where 40-ft riser joints are selected, one pup joint each of 20-ft, 10-ft and 5-ft are needed. **1863** in *Ohio Archaeol. & Hist. Q.* (1929) XXXVIII. 651 About 10 a.m. we..pitched our *pup-tents. **1917** *Collier's Mag.* 21 Apr. 13 When a halt is reached, each pair of men set up their tent poles, stretch the line as a ridge, tie their canvas sheets together, and peg them down as a cover. The result is familiarly called a 'pup' tent. **1929** *T. Eaton & Co. Catal.* Spring & Summer 373/3 'Pup-Tent' For Boys... Just the thing you need during your holidays. .. Fitted with two uprights, guy ropes and pegs. **1953** K. TENNANT *Joyful Condemned* xiv. 123 They had equipped themselves for the camping holiday..: a pup-tent, blankets, a frying-pan. **1977** C. MCFADDEN *Serial* xxv. 56/1 Carol can't pick up any signals if you're a coupla boy scouts in a pup tent. **1928** KIPLING in *London Mag.* Dec. 693/2 The janitor's kitten had not been *pup-trained and leaped on the table, to make sure.

pup, *sb.*[2] *College slang.* Abbreviation of PUPIL, humorously associated with PUP *sb.*[1] Cf. CUB *sb.*[1] 3.

1871 'M. LEGRAND' *Cambr. Freshm.* 343 He rushed off exultant to his Coach, whom he discovered surrounded by 'pups'.

pup, *v.*[1] [Shortened f. PUPPY *v.*] *trans.* and *intr.* To bring forth pups, to litter. Hence **'pupping** *vbl. sb.*, also *attrib.*

1725 *Bradley's Fam. Dict.* s.v. *Dog*, If they are all over white; that is, pupp'd without any Spot upon them. **1787** HUNTER in *Phil. Trans.* LXXVII. 260 She pupped on the 24th of February 1787, and had six puppies. **1845** YOUATT *Dog* xiii, The pupping usually takes place from the sixty-second to the sixty-fourth day. **1877** F. WHYMPER *Sea* I. ii. 40 The seals were landing in the coast, it being the pupping season.

pup (pʌp), *int.* and *v.*[2] [Cf. *pup pup* in med.L., 8–9th c. (Du Cange).] Imitation of an inarticulate sound made with the lips; in quot. 1560 as a verb: = POOH, POOH-POOH.

1560 NEVILLE *Let. to Throgmorton* in Froude *Hist. Eng.* (1863) VII. iv. 294 The queen would pup with her lips: she would not marry a subject. **1599** MASSINGER, etc. *Old Law* III. ii, *Eugenia.* 'Slight! an you laugh too loud, we are all discovered. *Simonides.* Nay, an I should be hanged, I cannot leave it. Pup! there 'tis. (Bursts into a laugh.)

pup, obs. f. POOP *sb.*[1]; dial. f. POOP *v.*[1]

pupa ('pjuːpə). Pl. **-æ**. [mod.L. (Linnæus *Syst. Nat.* 1758 I. 340), a use of L. *pūpa* girl, doll. Cf. Ger., Da. *puppe*, Sw. *puppa*, Du. †*poppe*, *pop*, *popje*, doll, nymph, chrysalis, = Romanic *puppa* doll.]

1. a. An insect in the third and usually quiescent state (of complete metamorphosis), preceding that of the imago or perfect insect; a chrysalis.

1773 G. WHITE *Let.* 8 July in *Nat. Hist. Selborne* (1789) II. xv. 156 The black shining cases or skins of the *pupæ* of these insects [*sc.* forest-flies]. **1815** KIRBY & SP. *Entomol.* iii. I. 67 The states through which insects pass are four: the egg; the larva; the pupa; and the imago. **1849** H. MILLER *Footpr. Creat.* viii. 154 A mummy, in their apprehension, was simply a human pupa, waiting the period of its enlargement. **1868** DUNCAN tr. *Figuier's Insect World* i. 32 In another fortnight these pupæ become perfect insects. **1898** A. S. PACKARD *Textbk. Entomol.* III. 621 In some cases the obtected pupa remains within the loose envelope formed by the old larval skin. **1928** G. H. CARPENTER *Biol. Insects* vii. 172 The pupa..resembles the adult insect much more closely than the larva. **1932** RILEY & JOHANNSEN *Med. Entomol.* viii. 116 The pupae of mosquitoes and midges are quite active. **1964** V. WIGGLESWORTH *Life of Insects* vi. 94 Within the pupa a most complex development proceeds.

b. A stage in the development of some other invertebrates, as cirripeds, holothurians.

1877 HUXLEY *Anat. Inv. Anim.* vi. 298 Other important alterations take place, during the passage of the locomotive pupa into the fixed young Cirripede. **1900** E. R. LANKESTER *Treat. Zool.* iii. 5 When the Auricularia assumes a barrel shape, before changing into a Holothurian..the mouth has again passed up to the anterior pole, and the anus down to the posterior. This form is called the Pupa.

2. *Conch.* Name of a genus of pulmonate molluscs: a chrysalis-shell.

3. *attrib.* (See also PUPA-CASE.)

1788 G. WHITE *Let.* in *Nat. Hist. Selborne* (1789) II. xlvi. 252 All [the crickets] that I have seen at that season [*sc.* March] were in their pupa state. **1815** KIRBY & SP. *Entomol.* iii. I. 68 Linné has called it the *pupa* state, and an insect when under this form a *pupa*. **1851** CARPENTER *Man. Phys.* (ed. 2) 527 This is particularly the case in the Pupa state. **1862** *All Year Round* 13 Sept. 8 It assumes the pupa form, and is enclosed in a hard case, remaining motionless and to all appearance inanimate. **1898** A. S. PACKARD *Text-bk. Entomol.* III. 625 (*heading*) The pupa state.

Hence **'pupadom**, **'pupahood** (*nonce-wds.*), the condition of a pupa.

1893 E. A. BUTLER *Househ. Insects* 39 The grub..passes very rapidly through the resting-stage of pupadom. *Ibid.* 169 It would..be just as devoid of influence as if it had died in pupahood.

'pupa-case. [f. prec. + CASE *sb.*[2] 2b.] The horny case or sheath of a pupa or chrysalis.

1826 KIRBY & SP. *Entomol.* III. xxxi. 241 The wings.. remain attached to the puparium or pupa-case. **1841** T. R. JONES *Anim. Kingd.* xv. 300 The imprisoned dragon-fly splits its pupa-case along the back. **1895** MIALL *Aquatic Insects* 176 The pupa-cases are fixed to the rocks in clusters, which resemble small wasps' nests.

pupal ('pjuːpəl), *a.* [f. PUPA + -AL[1].] Of, pertaining to, or characteristic of a pupa; nymphal.

1866 DARWIN *Orig. Spec.* xiii. (ed. 4) 530 The caterpillar or maggot, and cocoon or pupal stages. **1877** HUXLEY *Anat. Inv. Anim.* vii. 449 A quiescent pupal condition is interposed between the active larval and the active imaginal states. **1907** *Athenæum* 22 June 764/2 For seventeen years the pupæ of this species [of locust] remain underneath the ground... This long subterranean vigil is not necessarily one of usual pupal inaction.

puparial (pjuː'pɛərɪəl), *a.* [f. PUPARIUM + -AL[1].] Of or pertaining to a puparium.

1904 *Brit. Med. Jrnl.* 17 Sept. 665 The duration of the puparial stage is from a fortnight to three weeks.

pupariate (pjuː'pɛərɪeɪt), *v.* [f. PUPARI(UM + -ATE[3].] *intr.* (See quot. 1973.)

1973 FRAENKEL & BHASKHARAN in *Ann. Entomol. Soc. Amer.* LXVI. 419/1 Formation of the puparium can be succinctly expressed by the term pupariation, with to pupariate as the appropriate verb. **1976** *Nature* 8 July 137/1 The posterior, which had pupariated, contained ovaries. **1978** *Ibid.* 20 Apr. 719/1 All the others were apparently full-term third instar larvae which had been produced normally and then had failed to pupariate.

pupariating (pjuː'pɛərɪeɪtɪŋ), *vbl. sb.* = next.

1939 METCALF & FLINT *Destructive & Useful Insects* (ed. 2) vi. 154 In the Diptera the formation of the motionless puparium may be called pupariating, to distinguish it from the shedding of the final larval skin, or true pupating.

pupariation (pjuːpɛərɪ'eɪʃən). [f. PUPARI(UM + -ATION.] (See quot. 1973.)

1973 FRAENKEL & BHASKHARAN in *Ann. Entomol. Soc. Amer.* LXVI. 418/2 Formation of the puparium in cyclorrhaphous flies occurs many hours before that of the pupa and should be consistently termed pupariation to distinguish it from the process of pupation. **1977** RICHARDS & DAVIES *Imms's Gen. Textbk. Entomol.* (ed. 10) I. xix. 367 The third-instar larva [of Cyclorrhaphan Diptera] eventually stops feeding and from then until the onset of puparium formation (pupariation) it may be referred to as the post-feeding larva. **1978** *Nature* 20 Apr. 720/1 In the larviparous tsetse fly, eggs hatch normally and development is not interfered with until the time of pupariation.

‖**puparium** (pjuː'pɛərɪəm). [mod.L., f. PUPA + -ARIUM, after *herbarium*, *vivarium*, etc.] The coarctate pupa of some Diptera and other insects, the case of which is formed by the last larval skin.

1815 KIRBY & SP. *Entomol.* iii. I. 71 The envelope of cased-nymphs, which is formed of the skin of the larva.. may be conveniently called the puparium. **1904** *Brit. Med.*

Jrnl. 17 Sept. 665 The puparium is a dark brown or black, cylindrical segmented body.

pupate ('pju:peɪt), *v.* [f. PUPA + -ATE[3] I.] *intr.* To become a pupa or chrysalis. Also *fig.*

1879 in WEBSTER Suppl. **1881** EL. A. ORMEROD *Man. Injurious Ins.* 15 Commonly they quit the leaves and pupate in the ground. **1902** *Q. Rev.* Apr. 394 If they lived long enough to pupate, the pupa perished. **1939** DUNCAN & PICKWELL *World of Insects* iv. 60 In its preparation to pupate, the swallowtail larva crawls to the underside of a stem. **1977** *Sci. Amer.* May 143/1 One fly larva, armed with antienzymes, feeds on the take and pupates cheerfully in the depths of the pitcher. **1979** *Times* 14 Nov. 12/7 The Parliamentary Labour Party, which has always lived on the edge of a metamorphosis into a cowardly rabble, has already begun to pupate, and will shortly complete the process.

pupation (pju:'peɪʃən). [n. of action f. prec.] The formation of the pupa.

1892 *Circular Board Agric.* (*Raspberry Moth*), When the time arrives for pupation, the caterpillar scoops out a hole in the pith of the canes..in which it turns to a chrysalis. **1893** E. A. BUTLER *Househ. Insects* 29 After several moults, the time for pupation arrives. **1905** V. L. KELLOGG *Amer. Insects* ii. 45 The larva, just before pupation, has spun a protecting silken cocoon about itself. **1932** RILEY & JOHANNSEN *Med. Entomol.* viii. 116 Just before pupation the larvae of many insects spin a cocoon. **1973** [see PUPARIATION].

†'**pup-barn.** *Obs. rare*[-1]. [app. f. MLG. *puppe, pup*, MDu., MFris. *poppe*, Du., Fris. *pop* doll (ad. L. *puppa, pūpa* girl, doll, puppet) + *barn* BAIRN.] ? A doll.

1483 *Cath. Angl.* 294/1 A Puppe barne (*v.r.* Pwbarne) *popa, pupa, pupula.*

†**pupe.** *Obs. rare.* [a. F. *pupe* pupa.] = PUPA I.

1842 BRANDE *Dict. Sci.*, etc., *Pupe*, the name of the oviform nymphs of Lepidopterous insects. *Ibid.*, *Pupa*, a genus of land snails, so called from the resemblance of the shell to the pupe, or chrysalis of an insect. [Hence in Dicts.]

pupelo (pju:'pi:ləʊ, 'pju:pɪləʊ). *U.S. local.* A name in New England for cider-brandy.

1806 *Salem Register* 7 Apr. 1/2 Do you not deny to the poor labourer..the common refreshment of a little toddy, and stint him with a glass of *pupelo*? **1851** S. JUDD *Margaret* I. vii, There were five distilleries for the manufacture of cider-brandy, or what was familiarly known as pupelo. *Ibid.* viii, They drink pupelo and rum.

pupiform ('pju:pɪfɔ:m), *a.* [ad. mod.L. *pūpiformis*, f. PUPA: see -FORM.]

1. Having the form or appearance of a pupa.

1897 *Naturalist* 75 The almost exactly pupiform [*printed* pupæform] shape of the typical *A*[*zeca*] *tridens.*

2. Resembling in shape a shell of the genus *Pupa.*

1854 WOODWARD *Mollusca* II. 166 *Cylindrella cylindrus*:.. shell cylindrical or pupiform, sometimes sinistral.

pupigenous (pju:'pɪdʒɪnəs), *a.* [f. L. *pūpa* + *-genous*, f. -GEN I + -OUS.] = PUPIPAROUS.

1890 in *Cent. Dict.*

pupigerous (pju:'pɪdʒərəs), *a.* [f. PUPA: see -GEROUS.] Of a larva: Forming a PUPARIUM; having the pupa enclosed within the last larval skin.

1884 *Stand. Nat. Hist.* II. 406 In the other group [of diptera], which are always pupigerous, the perfect insect escapes from the larval skin through a..circular opening.

pupil ('pju:pɪl), *sb.*[1] Forms: 4-6 pupille, 6 -yll, 6-7 -ill, puple, 7- pupil. [a. F. *pupille* masc. and fem. (14th c. in Godef.), ad. L. *pūpillus, pūpilla* orphan, ward, minor.]

1. An orphan who is a minor and hence a ward; in *Civil* and *Sc. Law*, a person below the age of puberty who is under the care of a guardian.

1382 WYCLIF *Jas.* i. 27 To visite pupilles [*gloss* that is, fadirles or modirles, or bothe], and widewes in her tribulacioun. **1487** *Sc. Acts Jas. III* (1814) II. 177/2 Acciouns & complaintis made be kirkmen wedowis orphanis & pupillis. **1530** PALSGR. 259/2 Puple within age, *pupille.* *a* **1548** HALL *Chron.*, *Edw. IV* 239 The French kyng.. claymed to haue the order and mariage of the yonge lady, as a pupille ward and orphane. **1615** SYLVESTER *Job Triumphant* xxiv, They pluck the Pupill from the tender Brest. **1754** HUME *Hist. Eng.* (1761) I. viii. 168 The chancellor..was the guardian of all such minors and pupils as were the king's tenants. **1869** *Act 32 & 33 Vict.* c. 116 §3 (Scotland) The judicial factor appointed to such pupil, minor, or lunatic.

2. One who is under a teacher or instructor; one who is taught by another; a scholar; a disciple.

1563 FOXE *A. & M.* 1543 There is but one in al thuniuersitie, that when he was a young man was my pupill. **1605** *Stow's Ann.* 1427 The Earle of Worcester and the Lord Zouche who had beene his puples when they were brought vp in Cambridge. **1700** WALLIS in *Collect.* (O.H.S.) I. 314 Every tutor with his pupills. **1812** SIR H. DAVY *Chem. Philos.* 6 This distinguished teacher..is said to have had a class of 2000 pupils. **1876** GRANT *Burgh Sch. Scot.* II. v. 161 The ordinance requiring the pupils of the grammar school of Glasgow to speak Latin only. **1891** E. PEACOCK *N. Brendon* I. 120 He took pupils to increase his income. **1894** FOWLER *Adamnan* Intr. p. 78 Laisren was a pupil of St. Columba.

3. *attrib.* and *Comb.* **a.** *appositive* (in sense 1): In the state of pupilage or nonage; under age, infant; also *fig.*

1611 SPEED *Hist. Gt. Brit.* IX. xxiv. §26 Francis the yong King was taken away by death, and another pupill King crowned, euen Charles his younger brother, and ninth of that name. *a* **1635** NAUNTON *Fragm. Reg.* (Arb.) 27 Espying his time fitting, and the Soveraignty in the hands of a pupil Prince. **1644** MILTON *Areop.* (Arb.) 57, I hate a pupil teacher, I endure not an instructer that comes to me under the wardship of an overseeing fist. **1659** TORRIANO, *Pupilla*, a pupil-woman. **1700** J. A. ASTRY tr. *Saavedra-Faxardo* II. 255 Fear was a necessary Tutor to this Pupil People. **1887** *Westm. Rev.* Sept. 103 The custody of his pupil children.

b. in sense 2, as ***pupil-master***; ***pupil-like*** adj. and adv.; **pupil power**: see POWER *sb.*[1] 4 f; **pupil-room** (at Eton), the room in which a tutor takes his pupils; also, the preparation and other work done there by a pupil; also, †the pupils' room in a barrister's chambers; **pupil-teacher** *a.*, designating the relation between pupils and teachers; *esp.* in phr. ***pupil-teacher ratio.*** See also PUPIL-MONGER, -TEACHER.

1593 SHAKS. *Rich. II*, v. i. 31 Wilt thou, Pupill-like, Take thy Correction mildly, kisse the Rodde? **1766** *Let.* in *Hist. Hawtrey Fam.* (190.) I, Mr. Norbury used to sleep in his pupil-room in a press-bed. **1849** THACKERAY *Pendennis* I. xxix. 285 In the pupil-room of Mr. Hodgeman, the special pleader,..six pupils were scribbling declarations. **1850** J. STRUTHERS *Life* in *Poet. Wks.* I. p. xxxvii, The pupil-master was a remarkably quiet man. *c* **1860** W. CORY *Lett. & Jrnls.* (1897) 577 He has done a good deal of extra work for me in pupil-room. **1899** A. LUBBOCK *Mem. Eton* i. 5 [He] was.. allowed to roast them [chestnuts] over the pupil-room fire while pupil-room was going on. **1958** J. TOWNSEND *Young Devils* vi. 47 How vitally important a good pupil-teacher, teacher-headteacher and teacher-environment relationship had been considered at my training college. **1960** *Where?* Winter 16 *Pupil-teacher ratio*, the number of pupils to a teacher in a school. **1974** *Times* 16 Jan. 13/1 The union knows that pupil teacher ratios are better in London than in some other parts of the country. **1978** C. HOOKWAY in Hookway & Pettit *Action & Interpretation* 40 There will be a network of pupil-teacher relations connecting them.

Hence (from sense 2) '**pupildom**, '**pupilhood**, the condition of a pupil; †'**pupiless**, a female pupil; '**pupilless** *a.*[1], without pupils.

a **1849** POE *E. B. Browning* Wks. 1864 III. 424 During the epoch of his *pupildom in that school. *a* **1785** T. POTTER *Moralist* II. 221 The *pupiless, the friend, the sensible and accomplished companion. **1854** E. FORBES *Opening Disc. in Nat. H. Chair* in Wilson & Geikie *Life* xv. (1861) 554 None who remained constant to the beautiful studies of his *pupilhood. **1865** DICKENS *Mut. Fr.* III. x, Sometimes accompanied by his hopeful pupil; oftener, *pupil-less.

pupil ('pju:pɪl), *sb.*[2] Also 6-7 -ill; and in L. form. [a. OF. *pupille* fem. (14th c. in Godef.) = It., Pr. *pupilla*, Sp. *pupila*; ad. L. *pūpilla* pupil of the eye, the same word as *pūpilla* female child (see prec.). Cf. BABY *sb.* 3.]

1. The circular opening (appearing as a black spot) in the centre of the iris of the eye, which expands or contracts in regulating the passage of light through it to the retina; the apple of the eye.

α. in Latin form.

[**1398** TREVISA *Barth. De P.R.* v. vii. (1495) 112 The blacke of theye..is callyd Pupilla in latyn for smalle ymages ben seen therin. *c* **1400** *Lanfranc's Cirurg.* 249 þe place þat is clepid pupilla, þat is þe poynt of þe i3e.]

1670 *Phil. Trans.* V. 1027 They contract much their pupilla or sight-hole of the Eye. **1718** J. CHAMBERLAYNE *Relig. Philos.* I. xii. §23 The Number of them [*sc.* rays] is much fewer than if they were immediately received in a greater Opening of the Pupilla without this hole.

β. in English form.

1567 MAPLET *Gr. Forest* 5 It [the Carbuncle] so warreth with the pupill or the eiesight, that it sheweth manifolde reflexions. **1646** SIR T. BROWNE *Pseud. Ep.* III. xx. 156 If beholding a candle we protrude either upward or downeward the pupill of one eye, the object will appeare double. **1685** BOYLE *Enq. Notion Nat.* vii. Wks. 1772 V. 232, I consider then that what is called the pupil or apple of the eye, is not (as it is known) a substantial part of the organ, but only a round hole or window made in the uvea, at which the modified beams of light enter, to fall upon the chrystalline humour. **1806** *Med. Jrnl.* XV. 388 The pupils of the eyes were much dilated. **1877** BLACK *Green Past.* ii, [Her eyes] were large and they had dark pupils.

2. *fig.* and *transf.*; in *Entom.* The dark central spot of an ocellus.

1599 DAVIES *Immort. Soul* 49 The Wit, the pupill of the soules clear eye. **1750** tr. *Leonardus' Mirr. Stones* 79 Beloculus is a white stone, having a black pupil. **1826** KIRBY & SP. *Entomol.* xlvi. IV. 286 *Ocellus*, an eye-like spot in the Wings of many Lepidoptera, consisting of annuli of different colours, inclosing a central spot or pupil.

3. *attrib.* and *Comb.*, as ***pupil change, contractor, dilator, reaction***; ***pupil-contracting, -dilating*** adjs.

1868 GARROD *Mat. Med.* (ed. 3) 415 Medicines which act upon the eyes... Pupil Dilators (Mydriatics)... Pupil Contractors (Myositics). **1899** *Allbutt's Syst. Med.* VI. 775 The course of the pupil-dilating fibres is more circuitous. *Ibid.* VII. 87 Optic atrophy, failure of pupil reaction. **1904** *Brit. Med. Jrnl.* 17 Dec. 1644 Such concomitant affections as muscular palsies and pupil changes.

Hence '**pupilless** *a.*[2], (of an eye) having no pupil.

a **1849** POE *Berenice* Wks. 1864 I. 442 The eyes were lifeless and lustreless, and seemingly pupilless. **1881** E. WARREN *Laughing Eyes* (1890) 81 The pupilless eyes of marble busts.

†**pupil** ('pju:pɪl), *v.* *Obs. rare.* Also 6 -ell. [f. PUPIL *sb.*[1]] *trans.* To treat as a pupil; to teach.

1599 PORTER *Angry Wom. Abingd.* (Percy Soc.) 28 Haue I seene thee Pupell such greene young things, and with thy counsell Tutor their wits? **1612** HEYWOOD *Apol. Actors* I. 30 It becomes my juniority rather to be pupil'd my selfe then to instruct others.

pupila'bility. *nonce-wd.* ? Pupillary nature.

In quot. with punning allusion to the pupils of the eyes.

1761 STERNE *Tr. Shandy* IV. i, What can he mean by the lambent pupilability of slow, low, dry chat, five notes below the natural tone..unless..the voice..forces the eyes to approach not only within six inches of each other—but to look into the pupils?

pupilage, pupillage ('pju:pɪlɪdʒ). [f. PUPIL *sb.*[1] or L. *pūpill-us* + -AGE.]

1. The condition of being a minor or ward; the period of this condition; nonage, minority.

1590 SPENSER *F.Q.* II. x. 64 By meanes whereof their uncle Vortigere Usurpt the crowne during their pupillage. **1690** LOCKE *Govt.* II. viii. §105 The Father..might thereby punish his transgressing Children even when they were Men, and out of their Pupilage. **1783** BURKE *Affairs India* Wks. XI. 258 A measure..professing to relieve the Nabob from a state of perpetual pupilage. **1877** E. R. CONDER *Bas. Faith* iii. 103 This protracted pupilage is needed by his moral nature.

b. *fig.* Said of the world, a country, etc.

1605 DANIEL *Queen's Arcadia* Wks. (1717) 183 They live as if still in the golden Age, When as the World was in its Pupillage. **1649** JER. TAYLOR *Gt. Exemp.* III. xiv, Moses Law, by which we were kept in pupillage and minority. **1777** ROBERTSON *Hist. Amer.* (1783) III. 269 Thus the colonies are kept in a state of perpetual pupillage. **1871** EARLE *Philol. Eng. Tongue* §329 The period when our language was in a state of pupillage.

2. The condition or position of being a pupil or scholar; pupilship.

a **1658** CLEVELAND *Gen. Poems* (1677) 61 Come all the Brats of this Expounding Age To whom the Spirit is in Pupilage. **1750** JOHNSON *Rambler* No. 87 ¶10 To raise themselves from pupillage by disputing the propositions of their teacher. **1846** J. BAXTER *Libr. Pract. Agric.* (ed. 4) I. p. ii, At the period of the Duke's pupillage at Westminster school, there were annual town-and-gown conflicts between the scholars and the boys of Tothill Fields. **1882** CARPENTER in *19th Cent.* Apr. 543 In the days of my medical pupillage the brewers' draymen were the terror of every hospital surgeon in London.

pupil age. [f. PUPIL *sb.*[1] I + AGE *sb.*; app. due to erron. analysis of prec.] The age during which one is a pupil; minority; nonage.

1596 SHAKS. *I Hen. IV*, II. iv. 106 Since the old dayes of goodman Adam, to the pupill age of this present twelue a clock at midnight. **1607** —— *Cor.* II. ii. 102 His Pupill age Man-entred thus, he waxed like a Sea. **1631** MASSINGER *Emperor East* II. i, Your pupill age is pass'd, and manly actions Are now expected from you. **1817** GODWIN *Mandeville* II. 92 You were..prepared at the pupil age of seventeen to play the part of a fox.

pupilar, -ary, -ate: see PUPILLAR, etc.

pupildom, -ess, -hood: see PUPIL *sb.*[1]

pupiled, pupilize: see PUPILLED, PUPILLIZE.

pupillage: see PUPILAGE.

pupillar, pupilar ('pju:pɪlə(r)), *a.*[1] [ad. L. *pūpillār-is* belonging to a pupil, orphan, or minor. Cf. F. *pupillaire.*] = PUPILLARY *a.*[1]

1832 *Blackw. Mag.* XXXI. 577 Charles I..estimated a House of Commons by its ancient standard, when—at best—in a pupilar and elementary state of transition. **1888** R. GARNETT *Emerson* ii. 56 The young schoolmaster..for a season retrograded into the pupilar condition.

'**pupillar,** '**pupilar,** *a.*[2] = PUPILLARY *a.*[2]

1887 A. M. BROWN *Anim. Alkaloids* 53 In injecting them hypodermically, they determined pupilar dilatation.

pupillarity, pupilarity (pju:pɪ'lærɪtɪ). *Civil* and *Sc. Law.* [a. F. *pupillarité* (14th c.), ad. med.L. **pūpillāritās*, f. L. *pūpillār-is* PUPILLAR *a.*[1]: see -ITY.] The state of being below the age of puberty; the period during which a person remains in this state.

1583-4 *Reg. Privy Council Scot.* III. 641 His tutour.. during the yeiris of his pupillaritie. **1609** SKENE *Reg. Maj.*, *Stat. Robt. I* 29 Be reason the heire is within age (within the yeares of pupillaritie). **1754** ERSKINE *Princ. Sc. Law* (1809) 83 The stages of life principally distinguished in law are, *pupillarity, puberty* or *minority*, and *majority*. A child is under pupillarity from the birth till fourteen years of age, if a male, and till twelve, if a female. **1818** SCOTT *Hrt. Midl.* v, 'Very true, gudewife,..we are *in loco parentis* to him during his years of pupillarity.' **1869** *Act 32 & 33 Vict.* c. 116 §7 (Scotland) Demand..intimated to the Grantor, whether of full age or in pupillarity or minority. **1880** MUIRHEAD *Gaius* I. §197 A minor who has passed the years of pupillarity shall have the assistance of a curator.

b. *loosely.* Childhood. *rare.*

1846 *Blackw. Mag.* LIX. 666 The deep-seated mischief of ..mispronunciation in a Cockney whose years of pupilarity have been passed on the spot of his birth.

pupillary, pupilary ('pju:pɪlərɪ), *a.*[1] [ad. F. *pupillaire* (1409 in Godef.), or L. *pūpillāris* PUPILLAR *a.*[1]] **a.** Of or pertaining to a person in pupillarity. **b.** Belonging to a pupil or scholar.

pupillary substitution (Rom. Law): nomination of a substitute to take on the death in pupillarity of an institute who had succeeded; in effect, a testament made by a father for his child living or posthumous, to take effect in the event of the latter dying under puberty and before he could make one for himself. (Muirhead *Inst. Gaius*, etc. 597.)

a. **1611** COTGR., *Pupilaire*, Pupillarie, of or belonging to a Pupill. **1756** NUGENT tr. *Montesquieu's Spir. Laws* I. XIX. xxiv. (1878) 329 The testator..may leave the vulgar substitution..and put the pupillary into a part of the testament, which cannot be opened till after a certain time. **1855** THACKERAY *Newcomes* lxv, Rosey was in a pupillary state..her duty was to obey the wishes of her dear Mamma. **1880** MUIRHEAD *Ulpian* xxiii. §8 A parent may make a pupillary substitution even to his disinherited children.

b. **1848** LOWELL *Biglow P.* Poems 1890 II. 2, I behold how those strains..bewitch the pupillary legs, nor leave to the pedagogic an entire self-control. **1868** M. PATTISON *Academ. Org.* iv 56 Scholarships and exhibitions are stipends enjoyed by students in the pupillary state.

'pupillary, 'pupilary, *a.*² [f. L. *pūpilla* PUPIL *sb.*² + -ARY: cf. prec. So mod.F. *pupillaire.*] Of or pertaining to the pupil of the eye.

1793 YOUNG in *Phil. Trans.* LXXXIII. 178 The lateral parts of the pupillary margin of the uvea. **1807** —— in *Med. Jrnl.* XVII. 405 A brownish grey, which is of the deepest colour in the Pupilary Ring. **1899** *Allbutt's Syst. Med.* VI. 836 The pupillary diameter is subject to a considerable range of variation.

pupillate ('pjuːpɪlət), *a. rare.* Also pupilate. [ad. mod.L. *pūpillāt-us*, f. *pūpilla* PUPIL *sb.*²: see -ATE² 2.] = PUPILLED.

1858 MAYNE *Expos. Lex.*, *Pūpillātus*, applied to the wings of birds and of butterflies when they present circular spots of divers colours, representing..an eye, and in the centre of which exists a black spot resembling a pupil: pupillate.

†**'pupillate,** *v. Obs. rare*⁻⁰. [f. L. *pūpillāre* + -ATE³.] *intr.* (See quot.) So †**pupi'llonian** [L. *pūpillōn-em*], one who cries like a peacock.

1623 COCKERAM, *Pupillate*, to cry like a Peacocke. **1600** NASHE *Summers last Will* Wks. (Grosart) VI. 132 This *Pupillonian* in the fooles coate shall haue a cast of martins, & a whiffe.

pupilled, pupiled ('pjuːpɪld), *a.* [f. PUPIL *sb.*² + -ED².] Having a central spot in the ocellus resembling a pupil; pupillate.

1819 G. SAMOUELLE *Entomol. Compend.* 421 *Noctua pupillata.* The pupilled Dart. **1895** A. G. BUTLER in *Proc. Zool. Soc.* 19 Mar. 254 Small ocelli..touched with black, and pupilled with blue.

pupilless: see PUPIL *sb.*¹, ².

pupillize, pupilize ('pjuːpɪlaɪz), *v.* [f. L. *pūpill-us* PUPIL *sb.*¹ + -IZE.] *intr.* and *trans.* To teach a pupil or pupils; to take pupils; to 'coach'. Hence **'pupillizing** *vbl. sb.* and *ppl. a.*

1822 J. POWER *Let. to J. Lynes* 17 Jan. in *Parr's Wks.* (1828) VIII. 634 He still continues at Clare Hall, and has been much engaged in pupillizing (as they call it at C.). **1844** J. T. HEWLETT *Parsons & W.* xiii, Private pupilising was in vogue at that period. **1856** J. H. NEWMAN *Callista* viii. 65, I am his bully, and shall pupilize him some day.

pupillography (pjuːpɪ'lɒgrəfɪ). [f. PUPIL *sb.*²: see -GRAPHY.] The recording and analysis of the movements and size of the pupils of the eyes.

1940 *Arch. Neurol. & Psychiatry* XLIV. 227 (*heading*) Pupillography: its significance in clinical neurology. **1958** *Arch. Ophthalm.* LIX. 358/2 The purpose of clinical pupillography is the detection and localization of pathological processes within the nervous centers and pathways of pupillary control. **1976** *Drive* May–June 20/1 In the late 1960s, Dr Yoss and his colleagues at the Mayo Clinic in Rochester, Minnesota, developed a technique, known as infra-red pupillography, for measuring loss of alertness.

Hence **pupillo'graphic** *a.*, **-'graphically** *adv.*; also **'pupillogram**, a record obtained in pupillography; **'pupillograph**, an apparatus used for pupillography.

1940 *Arch. Neurol. & Psychiatry* XLIV. 227 Lesions.. produce characteristic modifications of the pupillary movements and reflexes which are disclosed by pupillographic examination. *Ibid.* 228 Before the Argyll Robertson stage..there can be detected, pupillographically, a long evolution of seven well defined stages [of degeneration]. *Ibid.* 229 Pupillograms dealing with intra-ocular conditions, such as lesions of the macula and iris. **1958** *Arch. Ophthalmol.* LIX. 355/2 (*heading*) The electronic pupillograph. **1970** *Aerospace Med.* XLI. 1340/2 The pupillographic scanner measured the maximal horizontal diameter of the exposed portion of the pupils. *Ibid.* 1341/2 Three of the 32 well-rested pilots performed, pupillographically, in a less-than-perfect manner. *Ibid.* 1342/2 Data from his pupillogram are shown in Figure 5.

pupillometer (pjuːpɪ'lɒmɪtə(r)). Also (*rare*) pupilometer. [f. L. *pūpilla* PUPIL *sb.*² + -O)METER.] An instrument for measuring the size of the pupil of the eye.

1890 BILLINGS *Nat. Med. Dict.*, Pupillometer. **1920** *Jrnl. Optical Soc. Amer.* IV. 77 Various pupilometers have been suggested and used for determining the size of the pupil. **1975** L. S. SASIENI *Princ. & Pract. Optical Dispensing & Fitting* (ed. 3) iv. 105 The Pupillometer consists of two parallel tubes each containing a convex lens. **1975** *Sci. Amer.* Nov. 110/2 We have also been using an electronic pupillometer that scans the eye and automatically measures the diameter of the pupil while the experiment is in progress.

Hence ˌ**pupillo'metric** *a.*; ˌ**pupillo'metrics**, the study of psychological influences on the size of the pupil; **pupi'llometry**, the measurement of the pupil of the eye.

1899 *Nature* 18 May 72/1 Method for rapidly measuring the dimensions of small objects independently of their distance. Application to pupillometry and to laryngometry. **1968** E. H. HESS in F. M. Bass et al. *Appl. Sci. in Marketing Managem.* 431 Pupillometrics..is an area of psychological study that is based on our finding that the pupils..dilate when we see something pleasant or positive. **1968** F. J. VAN BORTEL in *Ibid.* 440 A new technique of pupillometric measurement. **1977** M. P. JANISSE *Pupillometry* iii. 35 The area of pupillometric research that is at once the most popular and the most controversial concerns interest and attitudes. **1980** D. BLOODWORTH *Trapdoor* xxv. 153 Pupillometrics—which means measuring the dilation of the pupil against ostensible emotions of the subject.

†**'pupil-ˌmonger.** *Obs.* [f. PUPIL *sb.*¹ + MONGER.] One who makes it his business to take pupils; *esp.* a tutor at Cambridge University.

a **1661** FULLER *Worthies, Northampt.* (1662) II. 291 He [J. Preston] was the greatest Pupil-monger in England in mans memory. *a* **1700** B. E. *Dict. Cant. Crew*, *Pupil-mongers*, tutors at the Universities, that have many Pupils, and make a Penny of them. **1773** W. COLE in Peacock *Stat. Cambridge* (1841) App. A. I My learned Friend, Mr. Farmer, Fellow and Pupilmonger of Emanuel College.

So †**'pupil-ˌmongering** *vbl. sb.*

1833 WORDSW. *Let.* 17 June in Chr. Wordsw. *Mem.* (1851) II. 264 You are at an age when the blossom of the mind are setting, to make fruit; and the practice of pupil-mongering is an absolute blight for this process.

pupilship ('pjuːpɪlʃɪp). [f. PUPIL *sb.*¹ + -SHIP.]

1. The condition or position of being a pupil.

1581 MARBECK *Bk. Notes* 616 The Church of Israel was vnder the lawe..vnto the time of Christ, when she waxed strong, and then hir pupilship ended. **1879** W. SENIOR *Trav. & Trout in Antipodes* (1880) 84 To-day you commence your pupilship to me. **1892** *Daily News* 2 Dec. 6/3 Time was when pupilship at this school was by nomination.

2. A fund for the education of a pupil: see quot.

1861 J. E. PHILIPPS *Mission. Pupils* 10 We require in addition to these missionary studentships, what I would call missionary pupilships—means for supporting and educating lads, in the time intervening between School and College.

pupil teacher ('pjuːpɪl'tiːtʃə(r)). A boy or girl preparing to be a teacher, who spent part of the period of preliminary education in employment as a teacher in an elementary school under the supervision of the head teacher, and concurrently received general education either from the head teacher or in some place of higher education.

The system was introduced into England from Holland in 1839–40, the pupil teachers being originally bound as apprentices, a plan which came to an end after 1870. The system underwent many changes; see *Memorandum on the history and prospects of the Pupil-Teacher system*, issued by the Board of Education in 1907. During the ensuing 30 years, it was gradually superseded (cf. *student teacher*).

1838 DR. KAY in *4th Ann. Rep. Poor Law Comm.* App. B. No. 3. 250 In the normal school at Haarlem..certain of the most intelligent scholars..were selected to be trained to the occupation of teachers... Those pupil teachers would constantly acquire a greater degree of skill and knowledge. **1846** *Min. Comm. Counc. Educ.* 21 Dec., To carry into execution the Minute of the Committee of Council on Education of the 25th day of August 1846, respecting the Apprenticeship of Pupil Teachers. [In the Minute of 25 Aug. called 'Apprentices'.] **1858** J. PAYN *Foster Brothers* x, The plan of pupil teachers was then in its infancy. **1861** M. ARNOLD *Pop. Educ. France* 108 Pupil-teachers—the sinews of English primary instruction, whose institution is the grand merit of our English State system, and its chief title to public respect. **1884** *Chr. World* 19 June 453/2 The pupil-teacher, as a rule, we fear, learns little and teaches less. **1907** [see b].

b. *attrib.*, as *pupil-teacher system*, etc.; **pupil-teacher centre**, a central institution where the pupil-teachers of a town or locality may receive their general education. (Introduced as '*Central Classes*' about 1874; much developed 1888–98.)

1897 *Daily News* 13 Jan. 5/3 A Committee to inquire into the working of the pupil-teacher system in England and Wales. **1902** *Westm. Gaz.* 14 Apr. 2/2 It should be noted that the London School Board have just had surcharged the cost of their pupil-teacher training-centres. **1906** *Daily Chron.* 29 Nov. 6/6 A compulsory subject..for pupil-teacher candidates. **1907** *Westm. Gaz.* 22 July 2/1 There are, at this moment, some 20,000 pupil-teachers, of the ages 16 to 18, attending institutions called pupil-teachers' centres. **1907** *Memo. on Pupil-Teacher syst.* §50 Obviously it would not be possible to drop the Pupil Teacher system as a source for the supply of adult teachers.

¶ 'Pupil teacher' in Milton: see PUPIL *sb.*¹ 3 a.

Hence **pupil-'teacherdom**, the body or institution of pupil-teachers; **pupil-'teachership**, the post or office of a pupil-teacher; **pupil-'teachery**, the work or position of a pupil-teacher.

1903 *Westm. Gaz.* 26 June 3/1 How can you complain about the teachers..now that we've opened *pupil-teacherdom to all alike? **1876** T. HARDY *Ethelberta* (1890) 122 If I could not get a *pupil-teachership in some London school..I could stay with you and be governess to Georgina and Myrtle. **1890** W. E. HENLEY *Views & Rev.* (1892) 132 Herself [George Eliot], too, has been variously described: as 'Apotheosis of *Pupil-Teachery'.

Pupin (pjuː'piːn). *Teleph.* The name of Michael I. *Pupin* (1858–1935), U.S. physicist born in Imperial Hungary, used *attrib.* or in the possessive to designate equipment, methods, and principles introduced by him, as **Pupin cable**, a telephone cable provided with loading coils at regular intervals so as to reduce attenuation and distortion of the signal; **Pupin coil** = *loading coil* s.v. LOADING *vbl. sb.* 7; **Pupin's law** (see quot. 1911). (No longer current.)

1900 *Amer. Jrnl. Sci.* CLX. 64 Pupin's interrupter may be modified to serve as an alternator in the following way. **1901** *Sci. Abstr.* IV. 1043 An intermittent direct current is produced by means of a Pupin interrupter. **1905** *Ibid.* B. VIII. 352 An adjacent insulator carries a vacuum lightning discharger contained in an ebonite case, to protect the Pupin coil from damage. **1908** *Ibid.* XI. 495 The range of transmission through a Pupin cable as compared with that through an open line having the same damping constant is smaller. **1911** J. A. FLEMING *Propagation of Electr. Currents* iv. 122 Pupin reduced the solution of the problem to a verbal statement, which may be called Pupin's Law, as follows: If there be a non-uniform cable line loaded with inductance coils at equal intervals, and if we consider the total inductance and resistance to be smoothly distributed along the line, then these two lines, the non-uniform and uniform lines, having the same total resistance and inductance, will be electrically equivalent for transmission purposes as long as one half of the distance between two adjacent coils expressed as a fraction of 2π taken as the wave length, is an angle so small that its sine has practically the same numerical value as that angle in circular measure. **1934** A. L. ALBERT *Electr. Communication* xi. 282 It remained for Pupin successfully to solve the difficult problem of loading... His method is known as the series or Pupin system of loading. **1955** P. R. BARDELL *Magnetic Materials in Electr. Industry* vii. 180 These coils are often referred to in the literature as 'Pupin' coils but are now usually known as 'Loading Coils'. **1958** [see next].

pupinized ('pjuːpɪnaɪzd), *ppl. a. Teleph.* [f. prec. + -IZE + -ED¹.] Of a telephone cable: provided with loading coils at regular intervals, so as to reduce attenuation and distortion of the signal. (No longer current.)

1910 *Electrician* 13 May 178/1 The attenuation coefficient determines the efficiency of any telephone circuit, and thus of a 'pupinised' circuit, so termed because it differs from an ordinary circuit by the introduction of inductance coils at definite points according to the formulæ of Prof. Pupin. **1913** *Sci. Abstr.* B. XVI. 152 (*heading*) Design of pupinised metallic and phantom circuits. **1933** *Jrnl. R. Aeronaut. Soc.* XXXVII. 463 Although great progress has been made in the construction of pupinised telephone cables, submarine telephony is still limited to relatively short distances, since intermediate amplifiers cannot be fitted. **1958** *New Scientist* 9 Oct. 990/3 Born..100 years ago on October 4, Pupin was to leave his name perpetuated in a million 'Pupin coils', used in telephone lines known as 'pupinised lines'.

‖**Pupipara** (pjuː'pɪpərə), *sb. pl. Entom.* [mod.L., neuter pl. of *pūpipar-us* bringing forth pupæ (f. *parĕre* to bring forth).] A division of *Diptera* in which the young are born in, or ready to pass into, the pupal state. Also called *Nymphipara.*

1874 LUBBOCK *Orig. & Met. Ins.* iii. 41 The case of the so-called Pupipara not constituting a true exception. **1878** BELL *Gegenbaur's Comp. Anat.* 259 The complete fusion of the ventral chord into one somewhat long knot, in the parasitic Pupipara.

Hence **pupiparous** (pjuː'pɪpərəs) *a.*, of or pertaining to the *Pupipara*; producing or bringing forth young already advanced to the pupal state.

1826 KIRBY & SP. *Entomol.* III. xxix. 65 *Pupiparous*, continuing in the matrix of the mother during the larva state, and coming forth in that of *pupa.* **1835**, **1844** [see NYMPHIPAROUS]. **1856** W. CLARK *Van der Hoeven's Zool.* I. 311 Pupiparous insects suck the blood of mammals and birds.

‖**Pupivora** (pjuː'pɪvərə), *sb. pl. Entom.* [mod.L. neuter pl. of *pūpivor-us* devouring pupæ.] A division of hymenopterous insects containing those, such as the Ichneumon flies, which deposit their eggs in the larvæ of other insects, chiefly *Lepidoptera*. Hence **'pupivore** [as in F.], a member of the *Pupivora*; **pupivorous** (pjuː'pɪvərəs) *a.*, of or pertaining to the *Pupivora*; devouring the pupæ of other insects; parasitic on pupæ.

The name *Pupivora* was introduced by Latreille 1806–9, as that of his second family of Hymenoptera. They correspond nearly to the *Entomophaga* of Westwood.

1836 SMART, Pupivorous. **1842** BRANDE *Dict. Sci.* etc., Pu'pivores, *Pupivora.*

puple, obs. form of PEOPLE, PUPIL *sb.*²

puplich(e, -is(e, -ish(e, etc., obs. ff. PUBLISH.

puplicke, -ik, -ique, obs. ff. PUBLIC.

pupoid ('pjuːpɔɪd), *a. Conch.* [f. PUPA + -OID.] = PUPIFORM 2; akin to the genus *Pupa.*

puppe: see PUP *sb.*¹ 2; obs. form of POOP *sb.*¹

puppet ('pʌpɪt), *sb.* Also 6 pupette, puppette, 6–8 puppit, 7 pupet. [A later form of POPPET, q.v., which has lost some senses and developed others, and has generally a more contemptuous connotation.]

1. A contemptuous term for a person (usually a woman): cf. POPPET *sb.* 1; but in sense app. associated with 2 or 3 below: a dressed up 'mere doll' or figure of a woman.

1586 A. DAY *Eng. Secretary* I. (1625) 69 If she be faire, then a spectacle to gaze on; if foule, then a simpring puppet to wonder on. **1601** DENT *Pathw. Heaven* (1831) 39 Is it not a shame, that women..should make themselves such pictures puppets and peacocks as they do? **1661** EVELYN *Tyrannus* 11 A Fregat newly rigg'd kept not half such a clatter in a storme, as this Puppets Streamers did when the Wind was in his Shrouds. **1828** SCOTT *F.M. Perth* xv, A pretender..to the favour of the scornful puppet [Catharine]. **1871** B. TAYLOR *Faust* (1875) I. vi. 102 But tell me now, ye cursèd puppets, Why do ye stir the porridge so?

2. a. A figure (usually small) representing a human being; a child's doll; = POPPET *sb.* 2. With quot. 1837, cf. POPPET *sb.* 2 b. *Obs.* or *arch.*

1562 TURNER *Herbal* II. 46 The rootes are..made like litle puppettes and mammettes which come to be sold in England in boxes. **1583** *Rates of Customs* D viij, Puppets or Babies for Children the groce *vis.* viij*d.* **1664** H. MORE *Myst. Iniq.* II. II. xxi, Having noted how Lactantius compared the Idols of the Heathen to the little Puppets that little Girls used to play with, and that the said Idols were but great Puppets for old Fools to play with. **1712** ADDISON *Spect.* No. 500 ¶3 The motherly airs of my little daughters when they are playing with their puppets. **1837** BARHAM *Ingol. Leg.* Ser. I. *Leech of Folkest.*, Where did you get this pretty doll ..? asked Susan, turning over the puppet. **1849** JAMES *Woodman* ii, I looked upon it as a sort of doll—a puppet.

†b. Contemptuously applied to an image or other material object which is worshipped; an idol; = POPPET *sb.* 2 c. Also *fig. Obs.*

1555 W. WATREMAN *Fardle Facions* II. x. 215 Thei [Tartars] make theim selues litle pupettes of silke or of felte, ..and do them muche reuerence. **1634** SIR T. HERBERT *Trav.* 56 At each end [of the tomb] was placed a Puppet or Pagod to protect it. **1664** [see 2]. **1809** COLERIDGE *Sibyll. Leaves, Tombless Epitaph*, The hollow puppets of a hollow age, Ever idolatrous, and changing ever Its worthless idols.

3. a. A small figure, human or animal, with jointed limbs, moved by means of strings or wires; *esp.* one of the figures in a puppet-show; a marionette; = POPPET *sb.* 3. Now also applied to a similar figure moved by rods, or to one in the form of a glove: see *glove puppet* s.v. GLOVE *sb.* 6, *rod puppet* s.v. ROD *sb.*[1] 12.

The original sense is now sometimes distinguished as *string puppet* s.v. STRING *sb.* 32.

1538 ELYOT *Dict.*, *Gesticulator*, he that playith with puppettes. **1591** SPENSER *M. Hubberd* 931 Like as a Puppit placed in a play, Whose part once past all men bid take away. **1602** SHAKS. *Ham.* III. ii. 257, I could interpret betweene you and your loue: if I could see the Puppets dallying. **1667** GALE *Crt. Gentiles* IV. 61 They are but as your *Automata*, those artificial Machines or Images called Puppits. **1712** ARBUTHNOT *John Bull* I. xii, You look like a puppet moved by clockwork! **1802** PALEY *Nat. Theol.* vii. (1819) 70 The adjustment of the wires and strings by which a puppet is moved. **1934** [see PUPPETEER]. **1958** *Oxf. Mag.* 6 Feb. 250/2 *The Water Babies* is said to be the first full-length play to have been performed in this country by puppets. **1967** *Oxf. Compan. Theatre* (ed. 3) 776/1 There are many different types of puppets, including the Hand- or Glove-Puppet, the Rod-Puppet, the Marionette, which are all rounded figures, and the flat puppets of the Shadow Show and the toy theatre.

b. *fig.* A person (usually one set up in a prominent position) whose acts, while ostensibly his own, are suggested and controlled by another; = POPPET *sb.* 3 b. Also, a country or state which is ostensibly independent but is actually under the control of some greater power. (Cf. 9 a, below.)

[**1550**: see POPPET *sb.* 3 b.] **1592** GREENE *Groat's W. Wit* (1621) E iv, Those Puppets..that speake from our mouths, those Anticks garnisht in our colours. **1622** BACON *Hen. VII* 25 To make the people see..that their Plantagenet was indeed but a puppit, or a Counterfeit. **1768** H. WALPOLE *Hist. Doubts* 81 He hoped by keeping the memory of Simnel's imposture, to discredit the true duke of York, as another puppet, when ever he should really appear. **1841** BROWNING *Pippa* Introd. 194 God's puppets, best and worst, Are we. **1867** FREEMAN *Norm. Conq.* I. iv. §3. 206 Charles remained for some while a puppet in the hands of Herbert. **1933** A. J. TOYNBEE *Survey Internat. Affairs* 452 In the wider field of international diplomatic negotiations over the Sino-Japanese dispute, the Japanese government deliberately gave formal recognition to their puppet in Manchuria. **1945** *Evening Standard* 20 Dec. 3 The role she [*sc.* Siam] played as a 'puppet' of the Japs in South-East Asia, made it essential that she should give restitution to the people who were harmed. **1976** *Survey* Summer–Autumn 18, I am not depressed about the large-scale non-fulfilment by the Russians (and their puppets) of the Helsinki agreements.

†c. A living personator in dramatic action; an actor in a pantomime. *Obs.*

a **1592** GREENE *Jas. IV* Induct., *Bohan.* What were those Puppits that hopt and skipt about me year whayle [= erewhile]? *Ober.* My subiects. **1605** SHAKS. *Lear* II. ii. 39 You come with Letters against the King, and take Vanitie the puppets part, against the Royaltie of her Father. *a* **1668** DAVENANT *Play-Ho. to Lett* I, All the dry old Fools of Bartholomew Fair are come to hire our house,..numberless Jack-puddings: the new motion men of Norwich, Op'ra-Puppets. [**1801** STRUTT *Sports & Past.* III. ii. §19 All the absurdities of the puppet-show, except the discourses, are retained in the pantomimes, the difference consisting principally in the substitution of living puppets for wooden ones.]

†4. A little dog; a whelp; = PUPPY 1, 2. *Obs.*

1607 R. C[AREW] tr. *Estienne's World of Wonders* 147 The great curres..the litle puppets. **1652** GAULE *Magastrom.* 336 She replied, Persa was dead; meaning her whelp or puppet. **1688** R. HOLME *Armoury* II. ix. 183/2 Whelpes, or Puppits, are..whelped blind.

†5. = POPPET *sb.* 4. *Obs.*

a **1619** FLETCHER *Wit without M.* II. ii, A maide makes conscience of halfe a Crowne a weeke for pinnes and puppits.

6. A lathe-head; = POPPET *sb.* 5.

1680 MOXON *Mech. Exerc.*, *Turning* I. 207 Then set your Puppets, and wedge them tight up. **1688** R. HOLME *Armoury* III. viii. 356/2 The Puppets, are the square peeces of wood..which have the..Iron Pinns in, upon which the work is turned. **1831** J. HOLLAND *Manuf. Metal* I. 208 Upon a strong table of wood..are fixed three cast-iron puppets or uprights.

†7. *Naut.* (See quot.) (Cf. POPPET *sb.* 6.)

1794 *Rigging & Seamanship* I. 8 *Screws*, bed or barrel, for raising the heads of large masts.., are made of elm, and consist of two puppets, a bed, and a sole: the puppets are four feet nine inches long, have their lower parts round.., and are cut with a screw; their..head, is larger, and is either eight-square or round.

†8. A pupa. (Employed to render Du. *popken.*)

1670 *Phil. Trans.* 2079 (Acct. of Swammerdam's *Hist. Insect. Generalis*, Utrecht, 1669) The manner how the Worms and Caterpillars turn into Puppets [Swammerdam 24, De maner op welke de Wurmen ende de Rupsen in Popkens veranderen]. **1753** CHAMBERS *Cycl. Supp.* s.v., Puppets..the name given by Swammerdam to the nymphæ of animals, which he distinguishes from the chrysalises by this simple name, calling these the *gilt puppets*, from their golden colour.

9. *attrib.* and *Comb.* **a.** Appositive (in senses 3 and 3 b): That is a puppet, *lit.* and *fig.*; managed by the will of another; so ***puppet administration, army, government, leader, régime, ruler, state, troops***.

a **1680** BUTLER *Rem.* (1759) II. 196 He is but a Puppet Saint, that moves he knows not how. **1715** ROWE *Lady J. Grey* IV. i, Their puppet queen reigns here. **1817** COLERIDGE *Biog. Lit.* xxiii. 286 She very much reminds us of those puppet-heroines, for whom the showman contrives to dialogue without any skill in ventriloquism. **1855** MACAULAY *Hist. Eng.* xiii. III. 299 Scotland would have been a smaller Poland, with a puppet sovereign, a turbulent diet, and an enslaved people. **1931** *Economist* 14 Nov. 892/2 At Mukden, the puppet Chinese Government set up by the Japanese military authorities is reported to have proclaimed its independence. **1934** C. LAMBERT *Music Ho!* III. 182 The gangster film or the comic strip would seem more suitable mediums in which to treat the self-appointed puppet leaders ..of the people. **1935** (*title*) The puppet state of 'Manchukuo'. **1937** E. SNOW *Red Star over China* 33 In 1935..the puppet régime of east Hopei was set up. **1938** *Ann. Reg.* 1937 267 The threat to Chinese sovereignty constituted by..the puppet administration set up by her in East Hopei. **1938** *Ibid.* 269 In December the Japanese set up two puppet Governments in North China. **1946** *News Chron.* 25 Feb. 1/1 Remnants of the Japanese forces in Manchuria, assisted by former puppet troops and Chinese reactionaries, were operating against the Red Army. **1947** *Sun* (Baltimore) 15 Aug. 12/8 We also have to ask ourselves whether strategically we can afford to let the Russians create another puppet state on the Asian mainland, just a few miles away from Japan. **1968** I. DEUTSCHER *Marxism in Our Time* (1972) 178 The support of the population permits them to make use of the jungle, while the Americans and their South Vietnamese puppet army cannot do this. **1971** *Standard* (Dar es Salaam) 7 Apr. 1/1 Those present [at the conference] were undecided about the relative merits of the Sihanouk Government and the American puppet regime. **1974** M. B. BROWN *Economics of Imperialism* xii. 299 After the tanks came massive economic support for the Soviet puppet government. **1980** *Times* 2 Jan. 9/2 Mr Babrak Karmal, the new puppet ruler of Afghanistan, appears to have been instructed to hold out a conciliatory hand to the rebels.

b. General attrib. uses and Combs. (chiefly in sense 3): 'of a puppet or puppets', as ***puppet-body, -drama, -fight, -land, -maker, -mover, -prompter, -stage, -string, -teacher, -theatre, -work; puppet-like*** adj. and adv.; **puppet-man, -master**, the manager of a puppet-show; also *fig.* Also PUPPET-SHOW, POPPET-VALVE, etc.

1870 G. MEREDITH *Odes Fr. Hist.* (1898) 62 What silly *puppet-bodies danced on strings. **1801** STRUTT *Sports & Past.* III. ii. §19 The subjects of the *puppet-dramas were formerly taken from some well-known and popular stories. **1827** *Blackw. Mag.* 265 The dolls threw stones behind them, and other dolls forthwith arose to people *puppetland. **1965** W. LAMB *Posture & Gesture* iii. 41 That the *puppet-like pin-up girl's beauty is only skin deep is often revealed the moment she opens her mouth. **1611** COTGR., *Poupetier*, a babe-maker, or *puppet-maker. **1731** SWIFT *Strephon & Chloe* 285 From yonder *puppet man inquire, Who wisely hides his wood and wire. **1630** B. JONSON *New Inn* V. v. (1631) 96 Fidlers, Rushers, *Puppet-masters, Juglers. **1965** M. ALLINGHAM *Mind Readers* ix. 97 Much more worrying was the question of the mind behind their experiments... Who was the puppet master? **1976** H. WILSON *Governance of Britain* 10 None of the prime ministers of my experience ..has been either a puppet or a puppet-master. **1745** FIELDING *Tom Jones* XII. vi, The landlady..fell foul on both her husband and the poor *puppet-mover. **1781** COWPER *Retirement* 312 With limbs of British oak and nerves of wire, And wit that *puppet-prompters might inspire. **1594** NASHE *Terrors of Night* Wks. (Grosart) III. 236 Comes some superfluous humour of ours..and erects a *puppet-stage, or some such ridiculous idle childish inuention. **1842** E. MIALL in *Nonconf.* II. 857 [The human understanding] is destined to higher ends than to be a sort of *puppet-string in the hands of state ecclesiastics. **1602** DEKKER *Satirom.* 93 Hold, silence, the *puppet-teacher speakes. **1871** B. TAYLOR *Faust* (1875) I. 224 The rude transportable *puppet theatres in which Goethe first saw Faust represented. *a* **1680** BUTLER *Rem.* (1759) I. 102 Th'are very Men, not Things That move by *Puppet-work and Springs.

Hence †**'puppet** *v.*, (*a*) *intr.* to play the puppet (sense 1 or 3 c); (*b*) *trans.* to dress like a puppet (? sense 1); **'puppetdom, 'puppethood, 'puppetism** (*nonce-wds.*), the condition of a puppet (sense 3 b); **pu'ppetical** *a.*, pertaining to a puppet.

c **1620** FLETCHER & MASSINGER *Trag. Barnavelt* II. ii, Good Ladies, no more Councells: This is no time to *puppet in. **1635** QUARLES *Embl.* V. viii. (1718) 277 Whom thy fond indulgence decks And puppets up in soft, in silken weeds. **1891** ELIZ. R. PENNELL in *Mary Wollstonecr.'s Rights Wom.* Introd. 23 Not to substitute for the old sham sensibility of *puppetdom the new sham sexlessness of emancipation. **1885** *Sat. Rev.* 19 Sept. 369/2 The dethronement or reduction to *puppethood of native dynasties. **1759** *Compl. Let.-writer* (ed. 6) 225 My Punch (to use a *puppetical expression). **1801** LD. CAMPBELL *Let.* Apr. in *Life & Corr.* (1881) I. 69 The intimacy between him [Addington] and Pitt continues as great as ever, and no doubt of his *puppetism any longer remains. **1818** COBBETT *Pol. Reg.* XXXIII. 120 It was then..that the idea of puppetism came into his mind.

'puppet-clack. [Cf. CLACK *sb.* 5.] = POPPET-VALVE.

1744 DESAGULIERS *Exper. Philos.* II. 472 If the Steam is stronger than you want, it may lift up the Valve, and go out. This is commonly call'd the *Puppet Clack.* **1829** R. STUART *Anecd. Steam Engines* I. 188 The return of the water is prevented by the usual means of a puppet-clack, or valve. **1844** *Civil Engin. & Arch. Jrnl.* VII. 275/2 Stop the engine, open the puppet clack, and fill the boiler.

puppeteer (pʌpɪ'tɪə(r)). [f. PUPPET *sb.* + -EER.] One who operates puppets; *spec.* one whose occupation is the creation, management, or exhibition of puppet-shows; also *fig.* (cf. PUPPET *sb.* 3 b).

1930 A. GERSTENBERG *Comedies All* 175 (*play-title*) The puppeteer. **1934** *Church Times* 30 Nov. 614/4 Every puppeteer has his own whimsies. Mr. William Simmonds.. makes as well as manipulates his own puppets. **1947** *Sun* (Baltimore) 14 Oct. 5/4 A cartoon in the Communist party newspaper *Pravda* today pictured the United States as a puppeteer manipulating votes of delegates in the United Nations. **1958** *Times* 10 July 4/5 The Rumanian and Polish puppeteers, at least, are set on their own underivative ways towards truly creative expression. **1969** A. R. PHILPOT *Dict. Puppetry* 8 The compiler of the Dictionary has had around forty years as a professional puppeteer, some twenty years as an instructor and nearly as long as editor of a puppetry magazine. **1972** M. SHEPPARD *Taman Indera* 69 A puppeteer and a group of musicians were maintained by many northern Malay rajas in the nineteenth century. **1979** *West Lancs. Even. Gaz.* 23 Nov. 25 (Advt.), Puppeteers available—International Cabaret Puppeteers, Scarborough.

puppet-head, variant of POPPET-HEAD.

'puppetish, *a. rare.* Also 6 popetish. [f. PUPPET *sb.* + -ISH[1].] Pertaining to or of the nature of a puppet. (Cf. PUPPET 2 b.)

1550 BALE *Image Both Ch.* II. H iv, Holye water makyng, for procession and sensinge wyth other Popetish gaudes. **1620** SHELTON *Quix.* II. xxvi. 174 He began to raine strokes vpon the Puppetish Moorisme, ouerthrowing some, and beheading others.

†**'puppetly**, *a. Obs. rare.* Also 6 popetly, puppitly. [f. as prec. + -LY[1].] = prec.

c **1550** BALE *K. Johan* (Camden) 17 You, Clargy,..With your latyne howrs, scimonyes, & popetly playes. **1576** FLEMING tr. *Caius' Dogs* in Arb. *Garner* III. 267 This puppitly and peasantly cur [the Spaniel gentle]. **1653** GAUDEN *Hierasp.* 448 Puppetly Idols lately consecrated to vulgar adoration.

'puppet-play, *sb.* Also 7 poppet-play.

1. A play or dramatic performance acted by means, or with the aid, of puppets; usually with dialogue spoken by a concealed person or persons.

1599 NASHE *Lenten Stuffe* Wks. (Grosart) V. 292 My inuectiue hath relation to such as count al Artes puppet-playes, and pretty rattles to please children, in comparison of their confused barbarous lawe. **1610** B. JONSON *Alch.* I. ii, And blow vp gamster, after gamster, As they doe crackers, in a puppet-play. **1633** R[OGERS] *Treat. Sacraments* I. 131 They make a mere apish Pageant and Poppet play of this Sacrament. **1712** ARBUTHNOT *John Bull* II. v, What he lost to sharpers, and spent upon country dances and puppet-plays. **1850** MARSDEN *Early Purit.* xii. 339 Every stage, every table, every puppet-play scoffed at the puritans.

2. The playing or acting of puppets.

1591 NASHE *Pref. Sidney's Astr. & Stella* in G. G. Smith *Eliz. Crit. Ess.* (1904) II. 223 Let not your surfeted sight, new come from such puppet play, think scorne to turn aside into this Theater of pleasure. **1849** WHITTIER *Calef in Boston* 21 Of your spectral puppet play I have traced the cunning wires.

Hence **'puppet-play** *v.* (*nonce-wd.*) *trans.*, to bring or drive by means of puppet-play or jugglery.

1649 *Trag. Massenello* 75 Do you not see yourselves puppet-plaid into a new war?

'puppet-ˌplayer. Also 6–8 poppet-. [f. PUPPET *sb.* + PLAYER[1].] **†a.** A performer in a pantomime (*obs.*). **b.** One who manages or exhibits a puppet-play.

1552 HULOET, Puppet plaier, *Circulator, Gesticulator.* **1644** EVELYN *Diary* 3 Feb., The Isle du Palais... The front looking on the greate bridge is possess'd by Mountebanks, Operators, and Puppet-players. *a* **1704** T. BROWN *Walk round Lond.*, *Presbyt. Meeting-Ho.* (1709) 14 The Wire in the Finger of the Poppet-Player. **1857** *Chamb. Jrnl.* VII. 124 Italy, the native land.. of modern puppetry, must.. at a very early period have sent her puppet-players abroad.

So **'puppet-ˌplaying**, the performance of puppet-plays.

puppetry ('pʌpɪtrɪ). Also 6 popatrye, popetry(e, -ie, 7 puppettry. [f. PUPPET + -RY.]

1. Mimic action or representation as of puppets; masquerade, mummery; false semblance, make-believe; artificial or unreal action; *spec.* applied to idolatrous or superstitious observances (in 16th c. often in form *popetry*, with play on *popery*).

1528 TINDALE *Obed. Chr. Man, Duty of Kings*, 53 b, Let not oure most holy father make them no moare dronken with vayne names, with cappes of mayntenaunce, and like babels, as it were popetry for children. **1530** —— *Answ. More* Wks. (1573) 256/1 No dumme popetrie or superstitious Mahometrie, but signes of the testament of God. **1549** LATIMER *Ploughers* (Arb.) 30 The Deuyl.. his office is to hinder religion.. to teach al kynde of popetrie. **1644** EVELYN *Diary* 24–5 Dec., The pupetry in the Church of the Minerva [in Rome], representing the Nativity. **1794** COLERIDGE *Relig. Musings* 233 Whoe'er Turn with mild sorrow from the victor's car And the low puppetry of thrones, to muse On that blest triumph. **1872** SWINBURNE *Ess. & Stud.* (1875) 55 Preconcerted pathos and puppetry of passion done to order.

2. Puppet-play; debased dramatic action.

1613 CHAPMAN *Rev. Bussy D'Ambois* I. C j b, Nay, we must now haue nothing brought on Stages, But puppetry, and pide ridiculous Antickes. **1651** BIGGS *New Disp.* §252 The pageantries and puppetries of Bartholmew Faire. **1857** [see PUPPET-PLAYER]. **1879** SWINBURNE *Stud. Shaks.* iii. (1895) 182 Remove [Iago].. and we have but the eternal and vulgar figures of jealousy and innocence, newly vamped and veneered and padded and patched up for the stalest purposes of puppetry.

†3. 'Get up' or dress as of a puppet. *Obs.*

1599 MARSTON *Sco. Villanie* III. viii. 216 Now doth the body led by senceless will.. Raue, talke idely as 'twere some deity Adorning female painted puppetry. **1638** FORD *Lady's Trial* II. i, With this language, Bold man of arms, shalt win upon her, doubt not, Beyond all silken puppetry.

4. Something compared to a puppet or set of puppets. **†a.** *pl.* False or pretended divinities. *Obs.*

1610 HEALEY *St. Aug. Citie of God* IV. ii. 157 The true God did vouchsafe them [the Romans] that increase of their Empire, when their own puppettries [*hii quos deos putant*] never did them a penyworth of good.

b. An unreal or artificial character in literary fiction; a set of such characters.

1822 LAMB *Elia* Ser. I. *Artif. Comedy Last Cent.*, What was it to you if that.. half-reality the husband was over-reached by the puppetry—or the thin thing.. was persuaded it was dying of a plethory? **1885** G. MEREDITH *Diana* i, A great modern writer.. groaned over his puppetry, that he dared not animate them.. with the fires of positive brain-stuff. **1898** *Westm. Gaz.* 29 Sept. 3/1 Fully furnished with the stage properties and puppetry of a Highland romance, but.. singularly destitute of romantic atmosphere and colour.

'puppet-show. Also 7 poppit-, 8 poppet-. [f. PUPPET *sb.* 3 + SHOW *sb.*] A show, display, or exhibition of puppets; *esp.* a dramatic performance with or of puppets; a puppet-play. Also *transf.* and *fig.*

1650 HUBBERT *Pill Formality* 138 The devil may buy his soul for a Poppit-shew. **1661** PEPYS *Diary* 7 Sept., Here was 'Bartholomew Fayre', with the puppet-showe, acted to-day. **1709** STEELE *Tatler* No. 16 ¶2 Prudentia.. had bespoke on the same Evening the Poppet-Show of The Creation of the World. **1774** J. HARROWER *Diary* in *Amer. Hist. Rev.* (1900) VI. 87 This night finishes the Puppet shows, roape dancings &c, which has continowed every night this week in town. **1795** tr. *C. P. Moritz's Travels* 88 Electricity happens at present to be the puppet-show of the English. **1807** *Salmagundi* XI. 262, I have seen that great political puppet-show—an Election. **1818** SCOTT *Let.* 10 Sept., I would much sooner write an opera for Punch's puppet-show. **1836** [see LOOKER *sb.* 1 b]. **1857** HAWTHORNE *Eng. Note-Bks.* (1870) II. 351, I.. saw a fair, with puppet-shows, booths of penny actors, merry-go-rounds, clowns, boxers. **1914** *Amer. Rev. of Reviews* Jan. 102/1 The puppet show does not flourish in our American cities. **1951** LAMBERT & MARX *Eng. Popular Art* i. 6 Bunyan's contemporaries.. could see their secular prototypes.. in pageants and puppet shows.

attrib. **1742** FIELDING *Miss Lucy in Town* (1762) 180 You must strip yourself of your poppet-shew dress. **1749** —— *Tom Jones* XII. vi, The puppet-show man ran out to punish his Merry Andrew.

Hence **'puppet-ˌshower, 'puppet-'showman**, a man who exhibits or manages a puppet-show.

1715 *Lond. Gaz.* No. 5329/3 Rope Dancers, Poppet Shewers. **1715** R. POWEL (*title*) Second tale of a tub: or the history of Robert Powel the Puppet-Show-Man. **1820** *Edin. Rev.* XXXIV. 278 The puppet-showman at a Venetian Carnival. **1855** HAWTHORNE *Eng. Note-bks.* (1870) I. 347 Tumblers, hand-organists, puppet-showmen,.. and all such vagrant mirth-makers.

puppet-valve: see POPPET-VALVE.

puppie-show, var. POPPY-SHOW.

†'puppify, *v. Obs. rare.* [f. PUPPY *sb.* + -FY.] *trans.* To make a puppy of; to befool.

1642 HOWELL *Twelve Treat.* (1661) 91 Never was there a poor people so purblinded and Puppified, if I may say so, as I finde them to be. **1660** —— *Parly of Beasts* 29 Never any who did fool and puppifie themselfs into such a perfect slavery and confusion.

†'puppily, *a. Obs.* [f. as prec. + -LY[1].] Characteristic of a puppy; puppy-like.

1682 T. FLATMAN *Heraclitus Ridens* No. 67 (1713) II. 168 He has found out a new Tory Popish-Plot upon his Puppily Courant; some body or other, if he don't lie, made his Printer tipsie. **1748** RICHARDSON *Clarissa* Wks. 1883 VI. 355 This impertinent heart is more troublesome to me than my conscience... I shall be obliged to hoarsen my voice and roughen my character, to keep up with its puppily dancings. **1795** R. CUMBERLAND *First Love* in *Brit. Theat.* XVIII. 46, I wish you would.. not insult my ears with that puppily word honour.

†'pupping, obs. var. PIPPIN[2] (early mod.Du. *puppingh*).

1617 MINSHEU *Ductor* 9783 A pupping-apple or Pippin.

pupplich(e, -is(e, -isch(e, obs. ff. PUBLISH.

†'pupprelle. *Obs. rare*[−1]. [f. next + -REL: cf. *cockerel, pickerel.*] A little puppy.

1583 STOCKER *Civ. Warres Lowe C.* III. 130 Gentlewomen were driuen to eate their little pupprelles, in whom before they took great pleasure.

puppy ('pʌpɪ), *sb.* Also 5–6 popi(e, 6 pup(p)ee, 6–7 puppie. [Corresponds in form, and, to a certain extent in sense, to F. *poupée* (in 13th c. *popee*, Littré) a doll, a woman likened to a doll as a dressed-up inanity, a lay figure used in dressmaking or as a butt in shooting; also, contextually, a plaything, hobby, toy (e.g. *il en fait sa poupée*), whence app. in Eng. 'a dog used as a plaything, a toy dog', a sense unknown to French. The *doll-* and *woman-* senses of F. *poupée* are usually represented in Eng. by PUPPET *sb.* 1, 2. But *puppet* and *puppy* are not always distinct; *puppet* (sense 4) was in early use synonymous with *puppy* (sense 1 or 2), and in dialects *puppy* is still widely used in the sense of *puppet*, esp. in *puppy-show* for *puppet-show*.

F. *poupée* has no cognate form in the other Romanic langs.; it appears to have been an anomalous French formation on the stem of Romanic *pupp-a* for L. *pūpa* girl, doll, puppet, but the use of L. and Rom. *-āta*, F. *-ée* in such a sense is apparently unparalleled.]

†1. A small dog used as a lady's pet or plaything; a toy dog. *Obs.*

1486 *Bk. St. Albans* f iv b, Smale ladies popis that beere a way the flees. **1519** HORMAN *Vulg.* 277 Lytel popies, that serueth for ladies, weere sumtyme bellis, sumtyme colers ful of prickis for theyr defence. **1542** UDALL *Erasm. Apoph.* I. cxl, Of doggues there ben diuerse sortes... There ben litle minxes, or pupees that ladies keepe in their chaumbers.. to playe withall. *Ibid.* II. xviii. 271 When he sawe in Roome straungiers carrye young puppees in their armes to plaie withall. **1576** FLEMING tr. *Caius' Eng. Dogs* S iii, Of the Spaniel gentle,.. Melitæus... These puppies the smaller they be, the more pleasure they prouoke. **1655** CAPEL *Tentations* 15 A foolish woman may in her foolish affection dote upon a puppy more than on her gold.

2. a. A young dog, a whelp.

1591 SHAKS. *Two Gent.* IV. iv. 3 One that I brought vp of a puppy: one that I sau'd from drowning, when three or foure of his blinde brothers and sisters went to it. **1598** —— *Merry W.* III. v. 11. *c* **1680** EARL DORSET *To Edw. Howard on his plays* 30 And though 'tis late if justice could be found, Thy plays, like blind-born puppies, should be drown'd. **1774** GOLDSM. *Nat. Hist.* (1776) III. 302 In less than a month the puppy begins to use all its senses. **1858** YOUATT *Dog* xiii. 348 A bitch that was often brought to my house was suckling a litter of puppies.

b. By extension, A young seal; cf. PUP *sb.*[1] 3. Also, the young of a shark; so *puppy shark*.

1890 in *Cent. Dict.* **1934** W. BEEBE *Half Mile Down* iv. 85, I saw five sharks milling around the foot of the ladder. Two were yard-long puppies. *Ibid.* 310 The uppermost one, about two feet in length, was a puppy shark. **1962** *Amer. Speech* XXXVII. 194 The name *puppy shark* may be applied to any small shark.

3. a. Applied to a person as a term of contempt; especially, in modern use, a vain, empty-headed, impertinent young man; a fop, a coxcomb.

In quot. *a* 1613 perh. = F. *poupée* a lay figure or dressed-up person.

1589 *Pappe w. Hatchet* in *Lyly's Wks.* (1902) III. 404 Pappe with an hatchet for such a puppie. **1597** G. HARVEY *Trimming Nashe* 1 To the polypragmaticall.. Puppie Thomas Nashe. *a* **1613** OVERBURY *A wife, &c.* (1638) 179 There is a confederacy between him and his clothes, to be made a puppy. *c* **1645** HOWELL *Lett.* (1650) IV. vii. 19 That opinion of a poor shallow-brain'd puppy, who [etc.]. **1710** SWIFT *Jrnl. to Stella* 14 Nov., Sir Richard Cox, they say, is sure of going over lord chancellor, who is as arrant a puppy as ever eat bread. **1738** —— *Pol. Conversat.* 110, I did a very foolish thing yesterday, and was a great Puppy for my Pains. **1748** CHESTERF. *Lett.* (1774) I. 342, I should be a most affected puppy if I did so. **1831** *Lincoln Herald* 17 June 3/6 There are only two classes amongst street smokers—namely puppies and blackguards. **1849** MISS MULOCK *Ogilvies* vi, A clever, sensible young man; has no conceit about him like the puppies of our day.

†b. Applied to a woman in sense of F. *poupée*: a (mere) doll. *Obs.*

1594 NASHE *Unfort. Trav.* 42 Who.. hath no wittie, but a clownish dull flegmatike puppie to his mistres.

†c. Applied to women in various figurative senses from 1 or 2. *Obs.*

1592 GREENE *Hee & Shee Conny-Catcher* Wks. (Grosart) X. 241 Holding such Maidens as were modest, fooles, and such as were not, as wilfully wanton as my selfe, puppies, ill brought vppe and without manners. **1602** *2nd Pt. Ret. fr. Parnass.* I. vi. 471 You light skirt starres.. By glomy light perke out your doutfull heads: But when Don Phœbus showes his flashing snout, You are skie puppies [*i.e.* lesser dog-stars] straight your light is out. *a* **1693** URQUHART *Rabelais* III. xxxiv, Other such like Queanish flurting Harlots.. and such like Puppies [Fr. *telles mastines*].

4. †a. = POPPET 2, PUPPET 2. *Obs.*

1659 TORRIANO *It.-Eng. Dict.*, *Pupa*.. a childs babby, puppy, or puppet to play withal.

b. A north and east country equivalent of PUPPET *sb.* 3; see *Eng. Dial. Dict.*

5. A white bowl or buoy used in the herring-fishery to mark the position of the net nearest the fishing-boat (*Cent. Dict.*).

6. *attrib.* and *Comb.*, as ***puppy-clumsiness***, ***-cup*** (see CUP *sb.* 2 b), ***-hunting***, ***-pertness***, ***-picture***, ***-play***, ***-stage***, ***stake***, ***style***; ***puppy-like***, ***-looking*** adjs.; **puppy-biscuit**, a finer kind of dog-biscuit; **puppy-drum**, a young or small-sized drum-fish; **puppy fat**, excessive fat in a child or adolescent causing a condition of plumpness which is freq. outgrown; **puppy-fish**, a name of the angel-fish, *Squatina Angelus*; **puppy foot** *U.S. slang* (see quots.); **puppy-god**, a puerile divinity; **puppy-headed** *a.*, stupid; **puppy-hole** *Eton slang*, a pupil-room; **puppy-love** (*contemptuous*): cf. *calf-love*; **puppy-peeping** *a.*, looking with half-closed eyes like a puppy; **† puppy-snatch**, a snare; **puppy-tooth**, a small dog-tooth or houndstooth check; **puppy walker**, one who takes hound-puppies to 'walk'; so ***puppy walking***; **puppy-water**, the urine of a puppy, formerly used as a cosmetic.

1895 F. ANSTEY *Lyre & Lancet* XI. 111 Ought a schipperke to have meat? Mine won't touch *puppy biscuits. **1845** YOUATT *Dog* i. 6 The characteristic *puppy-clumsiness of their limbs. *Ibid.* ii. 35 It seems.. to be agreed that no dog or bitch can qualify for a *puppy cup after two years of age. **1893** *Outing* (U.S.) XXII. 94/2 Small drum from eight to twelve inches in length are caught in set nets in the shoal waters of Pamlico Sound about Hatteras... They are called '*puppy-drum' by the natives. **1937** M. ALLINGHAM *Dancers in Mourning* x. 138 A large sulky youth in a black suit.. too small for his *puppy-fat body. **1940** M. DICKENS *Mariana* v. 152 You grew late, now you're getting your puppy-fat late. **1972** A. CHRISTIE *Elephants can Remember* xiii. 175 She was beautiful... Not when she was about thirteen or fourteen. She had a lot of puppy fat then. **1883** DAY *Fishes Gt. Brit.* II. 327 *Rhina squatina.* Names,—Angel-fish... Fiddle-fish, from its shape. *Puppy-fish. **1907** *Hoyle's Games* 410 **Puppy foot*, the ace of clubs. **1932** *Daily Progress* (Charlottesville, Va.) 26 Feb. 6/6 The ace of clubs is often called the puppyfoot. **1961** WEBSTER, *Puppyfoot*,.. a card of the club suit in a pack of playing cards. **1610** HEALEY *St. Aug. Citie of God* IV. xxxiv. 195 They.. were brought up without any of these *puppy-gods helpes [*sine tot diis puerilibus*]. **1597** SHAKS. *2 Hen. IV*, II. iv. 107 A tame Cheater, hee: you may stroake him as gently, as a *Puppie Greyhound. **1610** —— *Temp.* II. ii. 159, I shall laugh my selfe to death at this *puppi-headed Monster. **1912** G. FRANKAU *One of Us* I. 10 Idled in '*puppy-hole'. **1922** S. LESLIE *Oppidan* vi. 75 A list of lines due was hung in his *puppy-hole*. **1940** M. MARPLES *Public School Slang* 144 *Puppy-hole*,.. pupil-room, when boys work with their tutors. **1708** MRS. CENTLIVRE *Busie Body* II. ii, Let me catch you no more *Puppy-hunting about my Doors. **1839** KING LEOPOLD *Let. to Q. Vict.* in *Daily News* 10 Feb. (1899) 5/7 Without that *puppy-like affectation which is so often found with young gentlemen of rank. **1796** CHARLOTTE SMITH *Marchmont* III. 256 The *puppy-looking animal who came with her. **1834** W. A. CARUTHERS *Kentuckian in N.Y.* I. 175 Oh! it is nothing more than *puppy love! **1907** *Black Cat* June 4 He adored her with all the fatuous idolatry of puppy love. **1895** G. MEREDITH *Amazing Marriage* xvi, [A prize fighter] sat on the knee of a succouring seconder,.. *puppy-peeping, inconsolably comforted. **1795** WOLCOTT (P. Pindar) *Tales Hoy* Wks. 1812 IV. 390 With *puppy-pertness, pretty pleasant prig. **1692** J. SMYTH *Scarron., Travesty 2nd Bk. Virgil's Æneis* 10 So he by either means might catch Us Trojans in a *Puppy-snatch. **1856** 'STONEHENGE' *Brit. Sports* I. III. iv. §2. 174/2 Those who do not care for *puppy stakes. **1880** *Daily News* 12 Nov. 2/7 Four dogs are now left in for the Puppy Stakes. **1960** *Times* 22 Jan. 14/3 One [coat], particularly good, in black and white *puppy tooth silk. **1961** *Sunday Express* 26 Feb. 7/1 A trio of dark puppytooth checks. **1968** J. IRONSIDE *Fashion Alphabet* 218 *Hound's-tooth*, (in smaller versions—dog-tooth or puppy-tooth) is a variety of Broken check. **1887** *Field* 27 Aug. 362/2 The toast 'Success to fox-hunting, and the *puppy walkers of England'. **1900** *Daily News* 13 June 8/4 The events of the hunting man's year, beginning with *puppy-walking, the training of the hunter, and cub-hunting. **1687** SEDLEY *Bellam.* I. Wks. 1722 II. 93 You spend it him in Coach-hire, *Puppy-water and Paint, every day of your Life. **1730** SWIFT *Misc., Lady's Dressing Room*, With Puppy-water, Beauty's Help, Distill'd from Tripsey's darling Whelp.

Hence (*nonce-wds.*) **'puppycide**, the killing of a puppy or puppies; **'puppyess**, a female puppy (sense 3).

1791 *Bon Ton Mag.* Mar., Title-p. 2, 1. Portrait of a Modern Puppy. 2. Portrait of a Modern Puppeyess. **1865** *Pall Mall G.* 5 July 9/2 It is to be hoped that the crime of puppycide.. may be checked.

puppy ('pʌpɪ), *v.* [f. prec. sb.] *intr.* and *trans.* To bring forth puppies; to whelp, litter; to pup.

1589 GREENE *Menaphon* (Arb.) 83 Bitches that puppie in hast bring forth blind whelpes. **1601** HOLLAND *Pliny* II. 355 A young whelpe.. such an one as the bitch puppied the same morning. **1687** A. LOVELL tr. *Thevenot's Trav.* I. 51 A Bitch that had newly puppied. **1736** BAILEY (folio), *Pup*, to bring forth puppies, to puppy.

'puppy-dog. A child's word for PUPPY *sb.* 1, 2.
1595 SHAKS. *John* II. i. 460 Here's a large mouth.. That.. Talkes as familiarly of roaring Lyons, As maids of thirteene do of puppi-dogges. **1664** BUTLER *Hud.* II. III. 934 Of Monkeys, Puppy-Dogs, and Cats. **1702** S. PARKER tr. *Cicero's De Finibus* IV. 262 A Puppy-Dog, that's within a few Hours of the Age of Seeing, is as blind as another that's newly whelp'd. **1875** JOWETT *Plato* (ed. 2) III. 428 Like puppy-dogs, they delight to.. pull at all who come near them.

†**b.** ***puppy-dog water*** = *puppy-water* (PUPPY 6).
1663-4 PEPYS *Diary* 8 Mar., Up with some little discontent with my wife upon her saying that she had got and used some puppy-dog water, being put upon it by my Aunt Wight.. who hath a mind.. to get some for her ugly face.

puppydom ('pʌpɪdəm). [f. PUPPY *sb.* + -DOM.] **a.** = PUPPYHOOD. **b.** Puppies collectively.
1857 READE *White Lies* iii, The fate of this is to outgrow his puppydom, and be an average man. **1891** HANNAH LYNCH *G. Meredith* 5 The bites and barks of literary puppydom at his heels. **1894** *Westm. Gaz.* 29 Sept. 2/1 Mrs. B.. nurses them through all the troubles of puppydom to old age.

puppyhood ('pʌpɪhʊd). [f. as prec. + -HOOD.]
1. The state of being a puppy (sense 2); the early period of a dog's life.
1750 COVENTRY *Pompey Lit.* I. iii. (1785) 11/2 The puppyhood of little Pompey. **1848** J. MILLS *Life Foxhound* i, When I was at walk at the home of my puppyhood, the hospitable farm-house. **1881** G. ALLEN *Evolutionist at Large* 185 When a dog has once been brought up from puppyhood under a master.
2. The quality or character of a puppy (sense 3).
1849 C. BRONTE *Shirley* xiv, That six feet of puppyhood makes a perpetually recurring eclipse of our friendship.

puppyish ('pʌpɪɪʃ), *a.* [f. as prec. + -ISH[1].] Of the nature or character of a puppy (sense 2, 3).
1775 MME. D'ARBLAY *Early Diary, Let.* 14 Apr., He is conceited, self-sufficient, and puppyish. **1828** *Blackw. Mag.* XXIII. 34 Your stage fops are to be.. silly in stays, puppyish in pantaloons. **1852** F. E. SMEDLEY *Lewis Arundel* xl. 351 His whole demeanour *blasé* and puppyish in the extreme. **1925** F. SCOTT FITZGERALD *Great Gatsby* (1926) iii. 61 Girls were putting their heads on men's shoulders in a puppyish, convivial way. **1931** [see PAWING *vbl. sb.* and *ppl. a.*]. **1978** P. HARCOURT *Agents of Influence* ii. 45 'My daughter, Sally.'.. She was round, puppyish, charming.
Hence **'puppyishly** *adv.*; **'puppyishness.**
1817 H. C. B. CAMPBELL *Jrnl.* 10 Oct. in *Journey to Florence* (1951) 103 Mr Cornwall was puppieshly vulgar. **1941** *Scrutiny* X. 77 He becomes in short by an inevitable process Frank Churchill,.. a suspicion of the original puppyishness and lack of nice feeling still attached to his character. **1949** M. MEAD *Male & Female* iii. 67 There is.. much giggling puppyishness among boys.

puppyism ('pʌpɪɪz(ə)m). [f. as prec. + -ISM.] The character, style, or manners of a puppy (sense 3); impertinent conceit, affectation, 'side'.
1784 *New Spectator* No. 21. 6 There was a grand display of puppyism. The front boxes were much crowded with beardless young fellows. **1799** E. DU BOIS *Piece Family Biog.* II. 123 The affectation and puppyism of literature are less tolerable and more ridiculous than the puppyism of all other puppies in the world. **1862** THACKERAY *Adv. Philip* xl, What do you know of him, with his monstrous puppyism and arrogance?

pupsie, pupsy, a nursery or playful alteration of PUPPY: cf. *Betsy, popsy*.
1611 COTGR., *Chien de damoiselle*, a pupsie, little dogge.

pupton ('pʌptən). *Cookery.* Also †**poupeton.** [ad. F. *poulpeton, poupeton* (Littré 1718).] (See quots.)
1706 PHILLIPS, *Poupeton*... In *Cookery*, a Mess made in a Stew-pan, as it were a Pie, with thin slices of Bacon laid underneath; Pigeons, Quails, or other sorts of Fowl dress'd in a Ragoo in the middle; and a peculiar Farce or Dish of stuff'd Meat called *Godivoe* on the top; the whole to be bak'd between two gentle Fires. **1723** J. NOTT *Cook's & Confectioner's Dict.* sig. C2, *To make a Pupton of Apples.* Make the Apples into a Marmalade, with Sugar and Cinnamon; then add.. Eggs,.. grated Bread and some Butter; then form it as you please... Let it be bak'd in a slow Oven, and then turn it upside down, on a Plate, for a second Course. **1725** BRADLEY *Fam. Dict.* s.v., When.. you have made your Flesh Poupeton after the usual Manner, let two or three Handfuls of strain'd Pease be thrown into it, before it is cover'd with its Farce, and let all be inclosed with the Godivoe. **1747** H. GLASSE *Art of Cookery* ii. 45 A French Pupton of Pigeons. *Ibid.* ix. 83 To make a Pupton of Apples. Do them over a slow Fire... When it is quite thick.. let it stand till cool. Beat.. eggs, and stir in.. grated Bread, and.. Butter; then form it into what shape you please, and bake it. **1944** G. HEYER *Friday's Child* viii. 84 The dinner.. consisted of a broiled fowl.. followed by a pupton of pears. **1975** *TV Times* 31 May-6 June 54/2 *Pupton of rabbit*... Joint the rabbit... Simmer... Make the stuffing... Add the egg yolks, mushrooms and.. asparagus... Cover with.. bacon rashers... Bake.

pupunha (pʊ'pʊnjə). Also pupuña. [Pg., f. Tupi.] In full, ***pupunha palm.*** A South American palm tree, *Bactris* (or *Guilielma*) *gasipaes*, which has a spiny stem and yields edible red or yellow fruit about two inches long.
1853 A. R. WALLACE *Palms of Amazon* 10 His children are eating the agreeable red and yellow fruit of the Pupunha or peach palm. **1860** [see MURUMURU]. **1961** *Times* 13 May 9/7 Bananas, pupuña palms, pineapples and tobacco will grow. **1966** E. J. H. CORNER *Life of Palms* vii. 171 The fruits of the American pupunha.. are not eaten raw but roasted.

pur[1]. *dial.* Also 8 purr. [OE. in *pur lamb*, of uncertain origin.] **a.** A ram or wether lamb; also ***pur-lamb, pur-hog.*** **b.** *transf.* A male child, a boy.
c **1000** ÆLFRIC *Exod.* xii. 5 Nyme ælc mann an lamb.. þæt lamb sceal beon anwintre pur lamb clæne and unwemme. *a* **1722** LISLE *Husb.* Gloss., *Pur-lamb*, male lamb. **1787** GROSE *Provinc. Gloss.* s.v., In Dorsetshire a purr signifies a boy, also a male lamb. **1817** W. STEVENSON *Agric. Dorset* 411 Pur-lambs are sold to dealers, etc. from Somersetshire, and other districts, where breeding flocks are not so generally kept as in the upland parts of Dorsetshire. **1883** *Standard* 21 Apr. 5/8 The lambs.. are nearly all purs. **1888** ELWORTHY *W. Somerset Word-bk., Pur*, a male lamb... Seldom used in W. Som., but is the regular term in E. Som. and Dorset. *Ram* or *wether* is the common term in W.S.

†**pur**[2], **purr.** *Cards. Obs.* [Origin unascertained.] A name given to the knave or Jack in the game of post and pair (see POST *sb.*[4]). Also *attrib.* **pur-chop, pur-dog,** ? a card which would take the knave.
1592 LYLY *Midas* v. ii, Mine armes are all armarie, gules, sables, azure, or, vert, pur, post, pare, &c. **1616** B. JONSON *Masque Christmas*, Enter.. Post and Pair, with a pair-royal of aces in his hat; his garments all done ouer with Pairs and Purs. *Ibid.*, Post and Pair wants his pur-chops, and his pur dogs. *a* **1618** DAVIES *Wittes Pilgr.* Wks. 1878 II. 38/1 Some, hauing lost the double Pare and Post, Make their aduantage on the Purrs they haue: Whereby the Winners winnings all are lost, Although, at best the other's but a Knaue.

pur, obs. f. POOR, PORR, PURR, PURRE.

pur-, *prefix.* The usual AF. form of OF. *por-, pur-*, mod.F. *pour-*:—L. *pōr-, prō-*, prep. and prefix (see PRO- *prefix*[1]). The form in which this prefix came into early ME. through OF., still retained in numerous words as *purchase, purfle, purlieu, purloin, purport, purpose, purpresture, pursue, purvey*, and their derivatives, as well as in the earlier forms of some words in which it has been since altered to the L. form, as *promenade*, etc. See the individual words.

puraill, -rale, -rall, var. of PORAIL *Obs.*, poor people.

†**pura'lé, 'puralee.** *Old Law.* Forms: 3-4 purale, pouralee, 4 puralee, puraley, porale, 5 *Sc.* pureale, (*Hist.* 6-7 pur-, 6-8 pourallee, 7 purallie). [AF. *purale(e* (latinized *puralea*) = OF. *por-, puralee* a going through, f. OF. *por-, pur-, pouraler* to go through, traverse, f. *por-, pur-*:—L. *prō-*, forth; here interchanging with *par-*(:—L. *per-*) in OF. *paraler* to go through. Taken as AF. and ME. equivalent of L. *perambulātio*, PERAMBULATION, sense 3. (See also POURALLEE.)]
1. A perambulation made to determine the boundaries of a county, manor, parish, or district; *esp.* one made to ascertain the boundaries of a royal forest and to disafforest lands encroached upon by the crown.
[**1201-2** *Rotulus Cancell. ann. 3 Johan.* (1833) 49 Willelmus Ruff' reddit compotum de c.s. ne fieret puralea bosci de Waleshale. **1292** BRITTON II. xvii. §9 Et en mesme la manere soit fete puralee pur contek des parties. [*transl.* In the same manner perambulation shall be made in case of a difference between the parties. Cf. Bracton III. 402 Item cadit assisa in perambulationem propter incertitudinem, de consensu partium prædicto modo.] **1305** *Anc. Petit.* 13200 in *Mem. de Parl.* (Rolls) 9 La ou la purale fut fete par comaundement nostre seigneur le Roy en Ingelwode. **1305** *Ordinacio Foreste 33 Edw. I*, En droit de ceux qui terres & tenemenz sount deaforestez par la dite puralee, & qui demaundent davoir commun denz les boundes des forestes. **1323-4** *Tower Roll* (Manwood *L. Forest* xx. 134 b,), Ici comence le proces de la puraley de Winsor, fait en le Countie de Surrey. *c* **1330** *Ann. London*, an. 1306 in *Chron. Edw. I & II* (Rolls) I. 146 Super absolutione iuramenti domini regis Angliæ de foresta, quæ vulgariter et Anglice dicebatur *porale. Ibid.* an. 1310, *ib.* I. 175 Richerus de Reffham eligitur in maiorem... Fecit etiam cum suis aldermannis *la purale* in civitate.]
c **1330** R. BRUNNE *Chron.* (1810) 307 Þe erle for þam alle with luf bisouht þe kyng [Edw. I.].. Withoute any delay do mak þe purale Be a certeyn day, Sir, þat pray we þe. *Ibid.*, He suore on his fayth.. To mak þe purale, it suld not be delaied, With suilk men suld it be, þat þei suld hald þam paied. *Ibid.* 309 First þe nemnid alle þo, þe purale suld make, þat þorgh þe reame suld go, þe boundes forto stake. *Ibid.* 314, & for þe purale, set with certeyn bounde, þorgh þe lond suld be delaied no lengere stounde. **14..** *Ass. William* (an. 1184) in *Acts Parlt. Scot.* (1844) I. 379 Sua þat fra þin furth wyth breyff of pureale na wyth nayn oþir breyff he may tyn oþir al or part of þe sayd land bot gif it war throu a breyff of rycht. *a* **1634** COKE *Instit.* IV. lxxiii. *Courts Forest* (1797) 304 Some Letters Patents of the perambulations or purallies of forests made by king E. 3.. which we have seen.
2. From the middle of the 14th c., sometimes applied (in Law French) to the piece or tract of land between the wider bounds of a forest and the restricted bounds as fixed by perambulation, and thus passing into the sense of PURLIEU, q.v.
The exact history of this transfer of sense is not evidenced; it was prob. at first an incorrect popular use of the term; but it appears to have been already established before 1344 (when the L. *perambulatio* appears in the same sense), and thus within ten years of the date at which Robert of Brunne used *puralé* in the original sense. *English* examples have not yet been found before 1482, when the word evidently appears as PURLIEU; but *purallee, pourallee*, was used by Manwood and by other legal writers as identical with *purlieu*, and the form *purley* has come down from the 16th c. to modern times in the comb. *purleyman* as variant and spoken form of PURLIEU-MAN, q.v.
1344 *Inqt. conc. Whittlewood Forest* (*For. Proc. Tr. of Rec.*, No. 281, skin 7), Et quod R. le B. de S. est communis malefactor de uenacione domini regis effugans feras a foresta in perambulacionem, et sic effugatis feris facit stabilias inter forestam et perambulacionem. **1370** *Cartulary of Eynsham* (O.H.S.) II. 107 Quod quidam Thomas de Langeley.. fecit quandam perambulacionem citra forestam de Wychewode, elargando bundas predictas: et.. quod predictus hamelettus [Haneberghe] est infra les pural[ees] eiusdem foreste. **1372** *Rolls of Parlt.* II. 313/1 (46 Edw. III) Sur qoi supplie la dite Commune.. qe gentz de pays purront chaser le Purale sanz reez ou stableye faire, sanz estre attache, endite, ou empesche par Forester ou autre Ministre. **1377** *Ibid.* 368/1 (51 Edw. III), Item supplient.. qe nul homme soit empeche ne greve en temps a vener, par cause q'il ad chace ou chacera dedeinz le Poralee, ou aillours hors de le bounde du Forest. **1378** *Ibid.* III. 43/2 (2 Rich. II), Item supplient les Communes, q'ils puissent avoir lour Porales come y soloit avant ces heures, selonc le purport del Grande Chartre..; & qe Perambulation ent soit faite, com il fuist en temps du Roy Henry.
1598 MANWOOD *Lawes of Forest*: (*title-p.*) A Treatise declaring what Purallee is. *Ibid.* xx. §1. 127 Purlieu, or Pourallee, is a certain Territorie of ground adioining vnto the Forest.. which Territorie of ground was also once Forrest, and afterwards disafforrested againe by the perambulations made for the seuering of the new Forrestes from the old. **1726** C. KIRKHAM (*title*) Two Letters to a Friend, the First Shewing and Demonstrating by Law the Rights and Privileges of Pourallees or Free-Hey. [**1909**: see PURLIEU-MAN.]

‖**Purāna** (pʊ'rɑːnə). Forms: 7 poran(e, 9 pooraun, poorána, 8- purāna. [Skr. *purāṇá* belonging to former times, f. *purā* formerly. Cf. F. *pourana*, formerly *pouran, puran.*] One of a class of sacred poetical works in Sanskrit, containing the mythology of the Hindus. Also *attrib.*
1696 TOLAND *Christianity not Myst.* 31 To say it bears witness to itself, is equally to establish the Alcoran or the Poran. **1698** *Phil. Trans.* XX. 275 In which Language are written the Porane, or Sacred History. **1798** *Brit. Critic* XI. 120 From the numerous *puranas* and ancient *dramas* of India, many scattered rays of information are to be collected. **1889** J. M. ROBERTSON *Christ & Krishna* vii. 25 He disputes the point as to the early existence of literature of the Purāna order.
Hence **Pu'ranism**, the religious system taught in the Puranas.
1882 PIDGEON *Engineer's Holiday* II. 225 Buddhism has been replaced in India by Puranism, a religion based on an immense extension and perversion of the early Vedas.

Puranic (pʊ'rɑːnɪk), *a.* (*sb.*) Also pauranic, -ik (paʊ'rɑːnɪk), pooranic. [f. prec. + -IC. *Pauranic* follows the Skr. *paurāṇika.*] Of or pertaining to the Puranas.
1809 COLEBROOKE *Jains* in *Asiat. Res.* IX. 295 The Jainas, with whom the legendary story of their saints also seems to be engrafted on the Pauranic tales of the orthodox sect. **1869** MAX MÜLLER *Rig Veda* I. 244 In the epic and pauranic literature this Diti has grown into a definite person. **1889** J. M. ROBERTSON *Christ & Krishna* xii. 59 The Krishna Birth-Festival here departs from the Purânic legend.
b. *absol.* as *sb.* (*a*) A Puranic work or author. (*b*) A believer in the Puranas.
1808 WILFORD *Sacr. Isles* in *Asiat. Res.* VIII. 350, I shall give a few specimens.. in the very words of the Pauranics. **1878** G. SMITH *Life J. Wilson* iv. 103 Rama Chundra, formerly a Pooranik, would defend the Christian religion.

†**'Purantism.** Altered form of PURITANISM.
1602 WARNER *Alb. Eng.* x. liv. 242 It is but part of Maiestie, through Purantizme declynde.

purau ('puːraʊ). Also purao, puro(w). [Tahitian.] A small evergreen tree, *Hibiscus tiliaceus*, belonging to the family Malvaceæ, native to littoral regions of the tropics, and bearing pale yellow flowers fading to deep red; also, the light wood or the fibre produced by this tree; = MAHOE[1] 1 b. Also *attrib.*
1790 W. BLIGH *Narr. Mutiny on Bounty* 49 The trees that came within our knowledge were the manchineal and a species of purow. [**1865** B. SEEMANN *Flora Vitiensis* 18 *H*[*ibiscus*].. *tiliaceus*... Nomen vernac... Tahitiense, teste Solander, 'Purau'.] **1892** STEVENSON & OSBOURNE *Wrecker* 2 In the whole length of the single shoreside street, with its grateful shade of palms and green jungle of puraos, no moving figure could be seen. **1894** —— *Ebb-Tide* i. 2 At the far end of the town of Papeete, three such men were seated on the beach under a *purao*-tree. **1907** J. MASEFIELD *Tarpaulin Muster* iv. 68 Some said it was the leaf of the *puro* bush. **1933** *Jrnl. Polynesian Soc.* XLII. 306 The purau appears to be a native of most of the islands of the Pacific. **1952** R. FINLAYSON *Schooner came to Atia* v. 29 Where was he going there under the dark purau trees. **1959** L. M. NOBLE in A. H. McLintock *Descr. Atlas N.Z.* 82/2 The traditional rectangular hut with gable roof constructed of purau sticks and palm leaves is still common [in the Cook Islands].

puraventure, erron. var. of PERADVENTURE.

Purbeck ('pɜːbɛk). Name of a peninsula on the Dorsetshire coast; in full, Isle of Purbeck; used *attrib.* to designate the stone quarried there, or things made of this, and the geological formation there typically developed.

Purbeck beds *Geol.*, the three strata of the Purbeck series, reckoned as the uppermost members of the Oolite formation, or the lowest of the Wealden. **Purbeck marble**, the finer qualities of Purbeck stone, formerly much used in ornamental architecture. **Purbeck stone**, a hard limestone obtained from Purbeck, and used in building and paving.

[**1205** *Rot. Litt. Pat.* (1835) I. I. 53/2 Dedimus licenciam. .S. Cicestr̄ Episcopo quod possit ducere marmor suum de Purbicč. **1410** in Rogers *Agric. & Pr.* (1866) III. 401/3 Purbrick stone. **1598** STOW *Surv.* (1908) I. 272 The next yeare [1423, they gave] fifteene pound..to the saide pauement [of the Guildhall], with hard stone of Purbecke.] *a* **1691** BOYLE *Hist. Air* (1692) 207 A very experienced mason informed me that the Cathedral of Salisbury is made of Purbeck-stone, which in the air..will moulder away. **1812** *Monthly Mag.* I Dec. 396/1 The Purbeck strata are 410 feet. **1828** BAKEWELL *Introd. Geol.* (ed. 3) xii. 274 The Purbeck beds are by some geologists classed with the oolites. **1845** J. PHILLIPS in *Encycl. Metrop.* VI. 632/1 Columns, chimney-pieces, and other architectural uses for which the 'Purbeck marble' is celebrated. **1850** FORBES in *Mem. Geol. Surv., Org. Rem.* III. Pl. v. 3 New forms of marine Purbeck mollusca. **1850** *Ecclesiologist* XI. 113 A trefoil-headed niche with Purbeck angle-shafts.

b. *absol.* (*a*) = *Purbeck stone*; a Purbeck paving-stone. (*b*) Any one of the Purbeck strata.

1766 ENTICK *London* IV. 82 The floor is paved with Purbeck. **1771** LUCKOMBE *Hist. Print.* 319 The Press-Stone should be marble, though sometimes Master Printers make shift with purbeck. **1833** T. HOOK *Widow & Marquess* iv, Savile had been polishing the purbecks of Portland-place. **1871** LYELL *Elem. Geol.* xx. (1885) 286 Thick beds of chert occur in the Middle Purbeck. *Ibid.* 289 Between forty and fifty mandibles..have been found in the Purbecks.

Hence **Pur'beckian** *a.*, of or pertaining to the Isle of Purbeck, or to the Purbeck beds.

1885 GEIKIE *Text Bk. Geol.* (ed. 2) 788 Upper or Portland Oolites—Purbeckian, Portlandian, Kimmeridgian. *Ibid.* 799 The Purbeckian group has been divided into three sub-groups.

purblind ('pɜːblaɪnd), *a.* Forms: α. 3 **pur blind**, 4 **pure blynde**, 6 **pore**, **poure**, 6–7 **pore**, **poare**, **poore blind** (etc.), 8 **pur blind**. β. 6 **poore-blynd**, 6–7 **pur-blinde**, 7 **pore-**, **poare-**, **pure-blinde**, 7–8 **pur-blind**. γ. 3, 6–7 **purblinde**, 5–6 **purblynde**, 6–7 **purblynd**, 6– **purblind**; 6–7 **purreblind**; 6 **poore-**, **poureblind**, 6–7 **pourblind(e**; 6–8 **poreblind**, (6 **purblinde**, **purblynde**, 9 **perblind**). See also SPURBLIND. [In 13th c., and sometimes later, as two words, *pur*, *pure blind*, perh. *pure* adv. entirely, quite, or, as some suggest, OF. *pur-*, *pour-* intensive. But if this sense (which appears in the first quotation) was the original, it had come before 1400 to mean something less than blind, and was soon written as one word, the first element of which was in the 16th c. variously represented as *poor*, *pore*, *pour*.]

†**1.** Quite or totally blind. *Obs. rare.*

The sense appears certain in quot. 1297; in those of the 16th and 17th c. it is doubtful.

1297 R. GLOUC. (Rolls) 7713 Wo so bi king willames daye slou hert oþer hind Me ssolde pulte out boþe is eye & makye him pur blind. **1588** SHAKS. *L.L.L.* III. i. 181 This wimpled, whyning, purblinde waiward Boy,..don Cupid. **1592** —— *Rom. & Jul.* II. i. 12 Speake to my goship Venus one faire word, One Nickname for her purblind Sonne and her. **1615** BRATHWAIT *Strappado*, etc., *Love's Labyrinth* 63 But we by Cupids meanes, that pur blind boy, obtaine by death we could not earst enioy.

2. Of impaired or defective vision, in various senses: †**a.** Blind of one eye (*obs.*). **b.** Short-sighted, near-sighted. **c.** (Sometimes app.) Long-sighted, dim-sighted from age. **d.** Partially blind; almost blind; dim-sighted, generally, or without particularization.

a. 1382 WYCLIF *Exod.* xxi. 26 If eny man smyte the eye of his seruaunt, or of hondmayden, and make hem pure blynde [1388 makith hem oon iȝed; Vulg. *et luscos eos fecerit*; LXX καὶ ἐκτυφλώσῃ], he shal leeue hem free for the eye that he hath drawun out. *c* **1440** *Promp. Parv.* 416/2 Purblynde, *luscus*. **1617** MORYSON *Itin.* III. 16 The French haue a good Prouerbe, Entre les aueugles, les borgnes sont les Roys: Among the blinde, the pore blind are the Kings.

b. 1523 LD. BERNERS *Froiss.* I. lxi. 83 In the chase, sir Olphert of Guystels, was taken, for he was purblynde [orig. *car il auoit courte veue*]. **1601** HOLLAND *Pliny* II. 367 The dung..is singular good for those that be poreblind or short sighted. **1626** BACON *Sylva* §870 Pore-blinde Men..haue their Sight Stronger neare hand, than those that are not Poreblinde; And can Reade and Write smaller Letters. **1735–6** in *Swift's Lett.* 10 Feb. (1766) II. 227, I was in hopes you would have mended, like my purblind eyes, with old age. **1853** DUNGLISON *Med. Lex.*, *Purblind*, myopic.

c. *c* **1621** MOLLE *Camerar. Liv. Libr.* III. xvii. 202 Eies that are turned, that are poare-blind. **1794** G. ADAMS *Nat. & Exp. Philos.* II. xvii. 308 The apparent paradox of the pur-blind, or those who can scarcely see a small object at arm's length, yet discovering those that are very remote.

d. 1531 ELYOT *Gov.* III. iii, But a weighty or heuy cloke, freshely glitteringe in the eyen of them that be poreblynde. **1547** *Homilies* I. *Agst. Contention* II, It is more shame for hym that is whole blynd, to call hym blinkerd, that is but pore blynd. **1605** WILLET *Hexapla Gen.* 308 Her eyes..dull and heauie, which made her poore blind, or to looke a squint. **1621** T. WILLIAMSON tr. *Goulart's Wise Vieillard* 56 Some are borne starke blinde, and some purblinde. **1751** SMOLLETT *Per. Pickle* lxxiv. (1779) III. 13 Reconnoitering the company through a glass, for no other reason but because it was fashionable to be pur-blind. **1868** MISS BRADDON *Charlotte's Inher.* I. i, Old Nanon the cook, purblind, stone-deaf, and all but imbecile.

†**e.** Applied to the hare. *Obs.*

c **1280** *Names of Hare* in *Rel. Ant.* I. 133 He shal saien on oreisoun In þe worshipe of þe hare..þe brodlokere, þe bromkat, þe purblinde, þe fursecat. **1592** SHAKS. *Ven. & Ad.* 679 And when thou hast on foote the purblind hare, Marke the poore wretch.

f. *fig.* Of things: Dimly lighted.

1719 D'URFEY *Pills* III. 66 He was hir'd, To light the Purblind Skies. **1898** J. HOLLINGSHEAD *Gaiety Chron.* i. 17 Small..windows, blinking purblind at the busy..thoroughfare.

3. *fig.* Having imperfect perception or discernment; lacking or incapable of clear mental, moral, or spiritual vision; stupid, obtuse, dull.

1533 MORE *Answ. Poysoned Bk.* Wks. 1078/2 Maister Masker..is not..so pore blinde but that he seeth well in dede, that yᵉ meate which Christ speaketh of here, is our sauiour Christ himselfe. **1596** DRAYTON *Leg.* iv. 84 Which their dull purblind Ignorance not saw. **1629** PRYNNE *God no Impostor* 31 Mans darke, or purblinde carnall reason. **1660** W. SECKER *Nonsuch Prof.* 313 Man is such a pur-blind creature, that he cannot unerringly see a day before him. **1859** KINGSLEY *Misc.* (1860) I. 118 Foresight as short and as purblind as that of the British farmer.

purblind (pɜː'blaɪnd), *v.* [f. prec.: cf. *to blind*.] *trans.* To make purblind; to impair the sight of. Also *fig.* Hence **pur'blinded** *ppl. a.*

1572 R. H. tr. *Lauaterus' Ghostes* iv. 16 Poare blynded men whome the Greekes call Μύωπες. **1606** SHAKS. *Tr. & Cr.* I. ii. 31 A..purblinded Argus, all eyes and no sight. **1651** HOWELL *Venice* 175 This Signory..doth not admit the falshood of any interessed opinion to purblind Her own proper understanding. **1831** CARLYLE *Sart. Res.* III. iii, Were he not as has been said, purblinded by enchantment. **1874** W. JONES *N. Test. Illustr.* 595 The eagle..can, by frightening and purblinding the animal [chamois], make it leap the precipice.

'purblindly, *adv. rare.* [f. as next + -LY².] In a purblind manner.

1847 in WEBSTER, citing SCOTT. **1909** *Dundee Advertiser* 24 Feb. 6/2 To advance purblindly upon the problem..is to intensify the mischief.

'purblindness. [f. PURBLIND *a.* + -NESS.] The quality of being purblind (*lit.* and *fig.*).

1552 HULOET, Purblindnes, *Luscio*. **1577** B. GOOGE *Heresbach's Husb.* (1586) 903 [They] cure the dulnesse or purblindnesse of their eyes with the powder of wilde Marjoram. **1657** TOMLINSON *Renou's Disp.* 22 A thin plate of gold..cures bleared eyes, or purblindness. **1831** CARLYLE *Sart. Res.* III. x, The Professor's keen philosophic perspicacity is somewhat marred by a certain mixture of almost owlish purblindness. **1859** C. LYELL in *Darwin's Life & Lett.* (1887) II. 207 To believe the eye to have been brought to perfection, from a state of blindness or purblindness.

purcatorie, -y, obs. ff. PURGATORY.

purce, -er, obs. ff. PURSE, -ER.

purcelain(e, -lan(e, -line, -llan, etc., obs. ff. PORCELAIN, PURSLANE.

Purcellian (pɜː'sɛlɪən), *a.* and *sb.* [f. the name of Henry *Purcell* (*c* 1659–95), English composer + -IAN.] **A.** *adj.* Of, pertaining to, or characteristic of Purcell or his style of composition. **B.** *sb.* One who admires or imitates the style of Purcell.

1889 G. B. SHAW in *Star* 21 Feb. 4/3, I daresay many of the Bowegians thought that the unintentional quaintnesses of the amateurs in the orchestra were Purcellian antiquities. **1932** A. K. HOLLAND *Henry Purcell* II. i. 119 Liszt, whose songs, in their attention to immediate detail, are in the line of the Purcellian 'scena'. **1942** E. BLOM *Music in England* vi. 91 Only Turner and Croft, both doctors of music and both Purcellians, counted for a good deal, and may have influenced Handel. **1949** *Scrutiny* XVI. 78 The finest passages in the third Quartet seem to be recovering a more stable rhythmic norm, without any sacrifice of Purcellian and madrigalian intensity. **1959** *Listener* 4 June 972/1 There is some danger of mistaking for Purcellian influence on Handel what is really the influence of Lully on both. **1975** *Gramophone* Jan. 1379/2, I must also especially commend..the direction of that devoted Purcellian, Sir Michael Tippett. **1978** *Early Music* Oct. 577/2 Purcellian alto-clef tenors may have to adopt that term unless they relish some neologism like Rimsky's 'tenore altino'.

purceynt, var. PURCINCT *Obs.*

†**pur charite** [Anglo-Fr.], var. *par charity*: see PAR *prep.* I.

1393 LANGL. *P. Pl.* C. IX. 169 Ich praye þe..pur charite ..Awreke me of þese wastours.

purchasa'bility. [f. PURCHASABLE *a.*: see -ILITY.] Capability of being bought.

1904 F. LYNDE *Grafters* vii. 91 There isn't any doubt about his purchasability.

purchasable ('pɜːtʃɪsəb(ə)l), *a.* (*sb.*). Also **purchaseable**. [f. PURCHASE *v.* + -ABLE.] That may be purchased. †**a.** That may be obtained in any way; acquirable; procurable (*obs.*). **b.** Capable of being or liable to be bought for money. Also as *sb.*

1611 FLORIO, *Acquistéuole*, acquirable, purchasable. **1691** LOCKE *Lower. Interest* 43 Money being the Counter-ballance to all other Things purchasable by it. **1796** MORSE *Amer. Geog.* II. 371 (France) No public office is henceforth hereditary or purchaseable. **1848** MILL *Pol. Econ.* III. i. §2 I. 516 [The] exchange value of a thing,..the command which its possession gives over purchaseable commodities in general. **1879** S. HIGHLEY *Magic Lantern* in *Cassell's Techn. Educ.* IV. 234/1 The stock article of the shops..purchasable for about three guineas. **1957** L. MACNEICE *Visitations* 46 And from its branches muffled doves Drummed out the purchasable loves. **1966** *Listener* 17 Nov. 734/1 Much attention is given in this book to James Bond's exact social position and..to his use of purchasable objects. **1972** *Village Voice* (N.Y.) 1 June 13/4 Grocery stores tack on a 10-cent charge for the bag you carry your over-priced purchasables home in.

purchase ('pɜːtʃɪs, -əs), *sb.* Forms: α. 3 **porchas**, 5 **-ches**. β. 4 **pourchas**, **-chees**, 7 **-chace**. γ. 3–6 **purchas**, 4 *Sc.* **chass**, 4– **purchase**, (4–6 **-ches**, 4–7 **-chace**, 5 **-ches(s)e**, 5–7 **-chasse**, 6 **-chaz**). [ME., a. OF. *por-*, *pur-*, later *pourchas* masc. (12th c. in Hatz.-Darm.), f. *porchacier*, *por-*, *pur-*, *pourchassier* to PURCHASE. The 15th c. *purchace* is merely a graphic alteration of *purchas* (cf. *ace*, *ice*, *mice*), whence mod. *purchase* after the vb.; but the 17th c. *pourchace*, *purchasse*, were prob. influenced by F. *pourchasse*, OF. *porchace* fem., a parallel form to *porchas* masc.]

I. The act or action of purchasing.

†**1.** The action of hunting; the chase; the catching or seizing of prey; hence, seizing or taking forcibly or with violence; pillage, plunder, robbery, capture. *Obs.*

1297 R. GLOUC. (Rolls) 1745 So þat men of porchas come to him so gret route. **1390** GOWER *Conf.* II. 331 Forthi to maken his pourchas He [Covoitise, as a robber] lith awaitende on the pas. *c* **1480** HENRYSON *Mor. Fab.* 1946 Poems (S.T.S.) II. 145 Ane reuand wolf, that leuit vpoun purches On bestiall. **1596** Z. J. tr. *Lavardin's Scanderbeg* iii. 91 [The Turks] being scattered and dispersed..here and there about purchase and pillage. **16..** *Robin Hood* in Thoms *E.E. Prose Rom.* (1858) II. 110 Being overjoyed at the great purchase he had made. **1703** M. MARTIN *West. Isl. Scot.* 299 They [two eagles] commonly make their purchase in the adjacent isles and continent, and never take so much as a lamb or a hen from the place of their abode. **1725** DE FOE *Voy. round World* (1840) 216 We were bound now upon traffick, and not for purchase... They told us they were come into the South Seas for purchase, but that they had made little of it.

†**2. a.** Attempt or effort to obtain, procure, bring about, effect, or cause something; endeavour; attempted instigation; machination; contrivance, management. *Obs.*

13.. *Seuyn Sag.* (W.) 695 Yif thou him slest, bi hire purchas, On the falle swich a cas, As fel [etc.]. **1375** BARBOUR *Bruce* v. 534 The king, throu goddis grace, Gat hale vittering of his purchass. *c* **1407** LYDG. *Reson & Sens.* 2389 Alle pleyes be deuysed By his avys and his purchace. **1523** LD. BERNERS *Froiss.* I. xxxvii. 50 Desyryng them, that they wolde make no yuell purchase agaynst hym. *Ibid.* 375 Yᵉ Kynge of England made moche purchace to have the doughter of therle of F. to haue been married to his son Edward. *a* **1533** —— *Huon* cxliii. 533 His nephue and..his men, who were newly slayne by the purches of the abbot of Cluney.

†**b.** Hence, The actual bringing about or procurement of any deed or event. *Obs.*

1489 CAXTON *Blanchardyn* vii. 27 Ouer grete haste thou makest to the purchas of thy deth. **1513** BRADSHAW *St. Werburge* II. 1832 Diuers maydens louyng a chaste mynde From vilany ben saued by her purchase.

†**3. a.** The action or process of procuring, obtaining, or acquiring for oneself in any way; acquisition, gain, attainment. *Obs.*

1297 R. GLOUC. 12039 Sir henri of alemaine..Wende to þe court of rome, to make som purchas. **1303** R. BRUNNE *Handl. Synne* 6051 Yn alle ȝoure moste purchace Comþ ȝoure deþ sunnest yn place. *c* **1400** tr. *Secreta Secret.*, *Gov. Lordsh.* 53 It ys no purchas of no good lose, but of enuye. *c* **1440** *Promp. Parv.* 416/2 Purchase, *adquisicio*. **1502** *Ord. Crysten Men* (W. de W. 1506) I. iv. 45 Many faders & moders ben moche desyrous..to make purchases, & to gader goodes for the bodyes of theyr children. **1589** PUTTENHAM *Eng. Poesie* I. xviii. (Arb.) 53 No doubt the shepheards..trade [was] the first art of lawfull acquisition or purchase, for at those daies robbery was a manner of purchase.

†**b.** Concubinage. *Obs.*

[Cf. OF. *enfant, fils de porchas*, bastard child, 13th c.] *a* **1300** *Cursor M.* 26284 Bot he be yong o suilkin state þat he mai wijf forbere na-gate Oþer o spous or o purches. **1513** DOUGLAS *Æneis* IX. xi. 72 Son to the bustuus nobill Sarpedon, In purches get a Thebane wenche apon.

4. a. The action of making one's profit or gaining one's sustenance in any way; esp. of doing this in an irregular way, as by begging, or by shifts of any kind; shifting for oneself.

Quots. 1570, 1571 are obscure. To live *on one's purchase*, i.e. on what one can make in any way. To leave one *to his purchase*, i.e. to shift for himself, to his own resources. *Obs.* or *Sc.*

c **1386** CHAUCER *Prol.* 256 His purchas was wel bettre than his rente. *c* **1400** *Rom. Rose* 6840 To winne is alwey myn entent; My purchas is better than my rent. **1570** *Exuing Par. Reg.*, The 4 of Februarye was buryed one Fookes a pore man that cam to the towne of his purchase. **1571** *Boxford Par. Reg., Buryinges*, 3 Tho. Walle yᵗ wente of his purchase the xijth of Maye. **1710** RUDDIMAN in Douglas *Æneis* Gloss. s.v., He lives upon his purchase as well as others on their set rent. **1808** JAMIESON s.v., We still say, *He lives on his purchase*, of one who has no visible or fixed means of sustenance. **1816** SCOTT *Antiq.* xxiv, Dousterswivel's brow grew very dark at this proposal of leaving him to his 'ain purchase'. **1825** JAMIESON s.v., *To Live on one's Purchase*, to support oneself by expedients or shifts. It had originally signified living by depredation.

†**b.** A pursuit by which gain or livelihood is obtained; an occupation. *Obs.*

1588 T. Hickock tr. *Frederick's Voy.* 14 b, If euery Oyster had pearle in them, it [oyster-fishing] would be a very good purchase, but there is very many that haue no pearles in them. **1623–33** Fletcher & Shirley *Night Walker* I. i, Thou hast no Land, Stealing is thy own purchase. **1658** Slingsby *Father's Leg.* in *Diary* (1836) 208 It were very strange for them who practise that Trade long, to gain by the purchase.

5. *Law.* The acquirement of property by one's personal action, as distinct from inheritance. Also *fig.*

[**1292** Britton II. ii. §4 Purchaz pora estre en plusours maneres.] *c* **1460** Fortescue *Abs. & Lim. Monarchy* ix, The grete lordis off þe lande..by reason..off Mariages, purchasses, and oþer titles, shall often tymes growe to be gretter than thai be now. **1463** in *Somerset Med. Wills* (1901) 201 Euery creature that I haue hadde lande of..as well that which came by inheritaunce as by porches. **1523** Fitzherb. *Surv.* Prol., If the owner make a true pee degre or conueyaunce by discente or by purchace. **1544** tr. *Littleton's Tenures* (1574) 4 Purchase is called the possession of landes or tenementes that a man hath by his dede or by his agreemente. **1765** Blackstone *Comm.* I. iii. 215 These three princes therefore, king William, queen Mary, and queen Anne, did not take the crown by hereditary right or descent, but by way of donation or purchase, as the lawyers call it. **1848** Wharton *Law Lex, Purchase*,..an acquisition of land in any lawful manner, other than by descent, or the mere act of law, and includes escheat, occupancy, prescription, forfeiture, and alienation.

6. *spec.* **a.** Acquisition by payment of money or of some other valuable equivalent; buying. (Now the ordinary sense.)

[**1560** Bible *Jer.* xxxii. 8 Bye my field, I praie thee..: for the right of the possession is thine, and the purchase belongeth vnto thee.] **1611** *Ibid.* 11, I bought the field..and weighed him the money... So I tooke the euidence of the purchase. **1686** tr. *Chardin's Trav. Persia* 337 He would make his first Purchases of little Jewels. **1818** Cruise *Digest* (ed. 2) I. 459 To sell it, and to apply the money in the purchase of other lands. **1833** Ht. Martineau *Brooke Farm* ii, We turned into Miss Black's shop, where I wanted to make a purchase. **1888** Miss Braddon *Fatal Three* I. ii, She had only stopped her caprices and her purchases when the room would not hold another thing of beauty.

b. The action, practice, or system of buying commissions in the army; payment made for an appointment or promotion in the commissioned ranks.

The system was finally abolished in 1871.

1796 Stedman *Surinam* I. i. 4 An ensign's commission, presented me without purchase, in one of the Scots brigade regiments in the pay of Holland. **1837** *Penny Cycl.* VII. 400/2 In the navy, in the regiment of artillery, and in the corps of engineers and marines, the commissions are conferred without purchase. **1871** *Punch* 29 July 31/2 The Queen, by Royal Warrant, will put an end to all Purchase in the army.

c. ***compulsory purchase***, the enforced purchase of privately-owned land or property usu. by a local authority under statutory powers of compulsion. Freq. *attrib.* in ***compulsory purchase order***.

1869 *Bradshaw's Railway Man.* XXI. 40 Extra land, 10 acres; compulsory purchase, 2 years; completion of works, four years. **1932** *Act 22 & 23 Geo. V* c. 48 §25(2) They may ..be authorised to purchase that land compulsorily by means of an order (in this Act referred to as a 'compulsory purchase order'). **1962** J. Braine *Life at Top* x. 138 Hewley was the leader of the Labour group on the Council... And Hewley thought that the compulsory purchase wouldn't go through. *a* **1974** R. Crossman *Diaries* (1975) I. 67 Planning permissions and compulsory purchase orders. **1976** *S. Wales Echo* 26 Nov., Plans are in hand for compulsory purchase of 100 houses.

7. *fig.* Acquisition at the cost of something immaterial, as effort, suffering, or sacrifice.

1651 Hobbes *Leviath.* III. xxxii. 195 Our Senses and Experience..are the Talents,..to be..employed in the purchase of Justice, Peace, and true Religion. **1658** *Whole Duty Man* vii. §21 (1687) 65 They that pay thus dear for damnation well deserve to enjoy the purchace. **1711** Pope *Temp. Fame* 515 But if the purchase costs so dear a price, As soothing Folly or exalting Vice. **1758** S. Hayward *Serm.* 58 Has the Son of God..made a compleat purchase of all the blessings of salvation for us?

II. The produce of the action: that which is purchased or acquired.

†**8. a.** That which is obtained, gained, or acquired; gains, winnings, acquisitions; *esp.* that which is taken in the chase, in pillage, robbery, or thieving, or in war; the prey of an animal or hunter; spoil, booty, plunder; a prize; in later use, chiefly, a prize, or booty, taken by a privateer. Also *fig.*

1297 R. Glouc. (Rolls) 1738 Of willeuol men [he] him gaderede a gret route, & bi het hom god inou of porchas þat god hom sende. **13..** *Coer de L.* 3759 Geve off thy gold and off thy purchase To eerl, baroun, knyght, and servaunt off mace. *Ibid.* 6462 He gaff the ryche and the lowe, Off hys pourchas, good inowe. **1422** tr. *Secreta Secret., Priv. Priv.* 213 Y-temptid to geddyr mony or Purchas of the placis wyche he is sende to. **1594** Shaks. *Rich. III*, III. vii. 187 A Beautie-waining, and distressed Widow,..Made prize and purchase of his wanton Eye. **1610** B. Jonson *Alch.* IV. vii, Pack vp all the goods and purchase, That we can carry i' the two trunkes. **1666** *Lond. Gaz.* No. 106/2 A Dutch Caper.. having it seems been ten months at sea without meeting with any purchase. **1694** Luttrell *Brief Rel.* 1 Dec. (1857) III. 406, 36 of their privateers are laid up at St. Malloes, finding little purchace of late. **1721** De Foe *Col. Jack* (Bohn) 313 Several other jobs I told him of by which I made pretty good purchase. **1725** —— *Voy. round World* (1840) 3 To go anywhere that the advantage of trade, or hopes of purchase should guide us.

†**b.** An advantage gained or possessed. *Obs.*

c **1450** Capgrave *St. Kath.* II. 1333 Þerfor, madame, taketh heed her to, I pray, Lese not ȝour holde, lese not ȝour purchase, Lete mekenesse dwelle wyth swych a fresch may! *c* **1485** *E.E. Misc.* (Warton Club) 65 A best hath a mothe, but he spekkyt noȝt, Of God we have that fayre purches. **1698** Fryer *Acc. E. India & P.* 89 Jewellers..have made good Purchase by buying Jewels here, and carrying them into Europe to be Cut and Set, and returning sell them here.

†**c.** *spec.* A vessel falling to a pilot's turn to conduct; also, the sum earned as pilotage. *Obs. rare.*

1550 *Egerton MSS.* 2118 lf. 3 [If a ship wanting a pilot fire a gun when passing Dover, the pilot] who oweth the tourne may follow his purchase into the Downes & there shall not be denyed lett ne disturbed [by other pilots]. **1609** *Cinque Ports Crt. Loadmonage* ibid. lf. 35 The said John is to paye the one halfe of the purchase unto the fellowshipp of the Trinity House of Dover.

†**9.** Property acquired or obtained by one's own action or effort. *Obs.* (So in Anglo-L. and AF.)

c **1330** R. Brunne *Chron.* (1810) 86 We se alle day in place þing þat a man wynnes, It is told purchace, whedir he it hold or tuynnes. **1444** *Maldon, Essex* A. lf. 32 b, It shall be leefull to euery man that purchasith eny hous or londe with in the Burgh for to devyse his purchas.

10. The annual return or rent from land; in the phrase ***at so many years' purchase***, used in stating the price of land. Also *fig.*, in phrase ***not to be worth an hour's, a day's,*** (etc.) ***purchase***, not to be likely to last the length of time mentioned.

1584 Whetstone *Mirour for Mag.* 29 b, The most pernicious Broaker..he helpeth him to sell free land at fiue yeres purchase. **1625** Bacon *Ess., Usury* (Arb.) 545 Land purchased at Sixteene yeares Purchase, wil yeeld Six in the Hundred. **1667** Primatt *City & C. Build.* 21 A Lease for a single life is generally valued at seven years Purchase. *a* **1722** Fountainhall *Decis.* (1759) I. 11 The Earl was ordained to sell these lands at nine years purchase. **1833** Marryat *P. Simple* xxix, The doctor says that, with his short neck, his life is not worth two years' purchase. **1893** Forbes-Mitchell *Remin. Gt. Mutiny* 246 The life of General Walpole would not have been worth half an hour's purchase.

11. a. That which is purchased or bought.

1587 Harrison *Descr. Brit.* II. ix. (1877) I. 204 Now all the wealth of the land dooth flow vnto our common lawiers, of whome, some one hauing practised little aboue thirteene or fourteene yeares is able to buie a purchase of so manie 1000 pounds. **1603** Shaks. *Ham.* v. i. 117 A Lawyer... Will his Vouchers vouch him no more of his Purchases, and double ones too, then the length and breadth of a paire of Indentures? **1816** *Niles' Reg.* 3 June 334/2 The whole of that fine tract in Indiana territory, generally called Harrison's purchase, is now surveyed, and will be offered for sale. **1884** Pae Eustace *Outcast* 22 With a proud and swelling heart he entered in possession of his purchase.

b. *fig.*

1597 Hooker *Eccl. Pol.* v. lxxvii. §1 Are not soules the purchase of Jesus Christ? **1807** J. Barlow *Columb.* I. 53 Here lies the purchase, here the wretched spoil Of painful years and persevering toil. **1833** Chalmers *Const. Man* (1835) I. iii. 158 The precious fruit or purchase of each moral victory.

c. A (good, bad, dear, etc.) bargain. ? *Obs.*

1615 G. Sandys *Trav.* 17 Too deare a purchase for so short a breath. **1700** Dryden *Pal. & Arc.* I. 382 Who now but Arcite mourns his bitter fate, Finds his dear purchase, and repents too late? **1812** *Gen. Hist.* in *Ann. Reg.* 147 The total loss of the besiegers..amounted to upwards of 4850. This might perhaps be thought a dear purchase. **1857** Borrow *Romany Rye* vi, She could not pronounce her words,..so I thought she was no very high purchase.

†**12.** The price at which anything is or may be purchased or bought; purchase-money. Also *fig.*

a **1718** Penn *Maxims* Wks. 1726 I. 844 The Purchase [of this Treatise] is small. **1742** Young *Nt. Th.* v. 366 Insolvent worlds the purchase cannot pay.

III. [f. Purchase *v.* 7. Cf. also 8 b above.]

13. Hold or position for advantageously exerting or applying power; the advantage gained by the application of one of the mechanical powers; mechanical advantage, leverage, fulcrum.

1711 W. Sutherland *Shipbuild. Assist.* 26 Fix..the Post ..with such a regard always to the Weight, that the Purchase and Security may be an Overballance for it. **1776** G. Semple *Building in Water* 54 The further it goes the more Power it will gain, and thereby increase its own Purchase. **1793** Smeaton *Edystone L.* §253 The weight..was gaining more and more purchase upon the mast, as it heeled more outward. **1802** Paley *Nat. Theol.* xiii. §1 The head of an ox or a horse is a heavy weight, acting at the end of a long lever, consequently with a great purchase. **1832** G. Downes *Lett. Cont. Countries* I. 339 The streets of Florence, being flagged instead of paved, are..dangerous for riding—the horses having no purchase for their hoofs. **1860** Tyndall *Glac.* I. x. 66 If I could have calculated on a safe purchase for my foot. **1869** Boutell *Arms & Arm.* viii. 142 He might be enabled to bend his bow with a greater purchase. **1883** *Daily News* 29 Jan. 5/2 Unfilled door and window-spaces allowing entrance and purchase to the gale.

14. A device or appliance by means of which power may be brought to bear with advantage; any contrivance for increasing applied power; *esp. Naut.* such a device consisting of a rope, pulley, windlass, or the like.

1711 W. Sutherland *Shipbuild. Assist.* 37 That the Angles of the Purchase may be as obtuse as possible for the Facility of gaining the same with smaller Force. **1726** Shelvocke *Voy. round World* 241 When we came to make purchases to raise her again,..[we] found she did not hang so heavy. **1793** Smeaton *Edystone L.* 198 The compound purchase, called the Runner and Tackle. **1820** Scoresby *Acc. Arctic Reg.* II. 455 We had no other means of performing this singular evolution than by attaching purchases to the ice from the ship. **1899** F. T. Bullen *Log Sea-waif* 47 A derrick was rigged over the main-hatch with a double chain purchase attached.

15. *fig.* A 'hold', 'fulcrum', or position of advantage for accomplishing something; a means by which one's power or influence is increased.

1790 Burke *Fr. Rev.* 232 A politician, to do great things, looks for a power, what our workmen call a purchase; and if he finds that power, in politics as in mechanics, he cannot be at a loss to apply it. **1809** Knox & Jebb *Corr.* I. 547 This may give us a purchase, by which we may gain over people, from irreligion, to religion. **1853** Miall *Bases Belief* II. xvii. (1861) 97 They diminish the amount of evil to be contended with, and they provide a firmer purchase for the power which contends with it. **1868** Liddon *Serm. Spec. Occas.* vii. (1897) 150 The will has a subtle but strong purchase over the understanding in matters of belief.

IV. 16. *attrib.* and *Comb.*: in sense 6, as ***purchase-book, -deed, -making, -price, -sum***; in sense 6 b, as ***purchase officer, system***; in sense 13, as ***purchase-block*** (Block *sb.* 5), ***-fall*** (Fall *sb.*[1] 26), ***gear, power, -tackle***; also **purchase-land**, land acquired by purchase; **purchase tax**, a tax levied (between 1940 and 1973) on goods bought at a rate that was higher on luxuries than on more essential goods. See also Purchase-money.

1838 *Civil Eng. & Arch. Jrnl.* I. 148/2 With the assistance of double and single *purchase-blocks. *c* **1860** H. Stuart *Seaman's Catech.* 36 Purchase or shoulder blocks are used for masting, dismasting, or heaving down, or heaving off vessels on shore, or anything where immense strain is required. **1753** Chambers *Cycl. Supp.*, **Purchase-book*,.. the name given to a book..containing an account of all the purchases made. **1907** *Expositor* Dec. 498 The description of *purchase-deeds in the time of Jeremiah is suggestive of Babylonian usage. **1898** C. Bright *Submar. Telegraphs* iv. 150 Not only can the cable be cut in shallow water near the coast by any small steamer with *purchase gear that will raise an anchor, but [etc.]. **1485** in *Somerset Medieval Wills* (1901) 254, I bequethe to Henry, my sonne, all my *purchesse londes that I haue purchesed oute of the manor of Comtone. **1891** *Daily News* 5 Mar. 3/5 That they should re-open the whole question of purchase and the terms granted to *purchase officers. **1884** *Sword & Trowel* Feb. 49 Jesus paid the *purchase-price. **1898** *Westm. Gaz.* 30 Sept. 7/2 To issue 370,000 fully paid shares to the old company as purchase price for the undertaking. **1793** Smeaton *Edystone L.* §122 *note*, The term *Purchase-Tackle has of late years been applied to this kind of block. **1940** *Act 3 & 4 Geo. VI* c. 48 §18 A tax, to be called *purchase tax, shall be charged, ..on the wholesale value of all chargeable goods bought under chargeable purchases. **1940** *Manch. Guardian Weekly* 25 Oct. 293 The purchase tax came into operation on Monday [20 Oct.], amid some confusion and protest... The tax imposes $33\frac{1}{3}$ per cent on the wholesale value of luxury goods and $16\frac{2}{3}$ per cent on other more essential commodities. **1944** M. Laski *Love on Supertax* iv. 50 Add on the Purchase Tax and the increased Purchase Tax and Special Tax on Luxury Goods. **1947** J. Hayward *Prose Lit. since 1939* 10 The publishers..fought successfully to prevent the imposition of a purchase-tax on books. **1959** *Daily Tel.* 9 Apr. 1/7 The Trades Union Congress yesterday welcomed the Chancellor's cuts in purchase tax. **1972** *Times* 27 Jan. 14/1 Ribena..was held not to be a drug or medicine and therefore not exempt from purchase tax.

purchase ('pɜːtʃɪs, -əs), *v.* Forms: α. 3 porchas(s)i, -chasy, 3–4 -chacy, -i, -e(n, 3–6 -chase. β. 4 pourchase, 4–6 -chace, -chasse, 5 -chasshe, -chaas. γ. 3 purchaci, -chasy, 3–5 -chacen, 4–5 -chasen, 4 -chasce, -chaysse, -chaise, -chece, 4–6 -chas, -chass(e, -chess, 4–7 -ches, 4–8 -chace, 5 -chese, 4– purchase; (5 perchess). [ME. a. AF. *purchacer*, = OF. *por-, pur-, pourchacier, -chassier, -chasser* (11th c. in Hatz.-Darm.) to seek for, seek to obtain, procure, or bring about, f. *por, pur, pour*:—L. *prō* for + *chacier, chassier, chasser*:—pop. L. *captiāre* to catch, hunt, Chase; cf. It. *procacciare* to endeavour to get, to procure. (The ONF. dialect forms *porcachier*, and *por-, purcacier, pourkacier, pourkachier*, do not appear to be represented in Eng.)]

I. †**1. a.** *trans.* To try to procure or bring about; to contrive or devise (esp. something evil) *to* or *for* a person. *Obs.*

1297 R. Glouc. (Rolls) 9685 Þat hii ne ssolde purchasy non uvel þe king ne non of his. **1340** *Ayenb.* 8 He..þet deþ oþer porchaceþ ssame oþer harm to oþren. **1422** in E. Déprez *Études de diplomat. angl.* (1908) 37 Yat the saide Johan Moreau..ne purchase ne do no noyowse thyng..to owre seide rewme. **1481** Caxton *Godeffroy* 76 Wel they apperceyued certaynly that themperour pourchassed for them alle the euyl that he myght. **1483** —— *Cato* g j b, Whan they seken and purchasen the losse and the dethe of yonge chyldren. **1549** *Compl. Scot.* viii. 743e, vndir the culour of frendschip, purchessis my final exterminatione.

†**b.** With subordinate clause or infinitive. *Obs.*

1390 Gower *Conf.* III. 162 Wherof thou thenkest to deserve Thi princes thonk, and to pourchace Hou thou myht stonden in his grace. **1426** Lydg. *De Guil. Pilgr.* 4231 Wher thow..dist purchace Thy temptacioun to enchace. **1483** Caxton *Gold. Leg.* 408b/1, I shalle soo pourchaas to sette suche a clothe in thy lommes. **1523** LD. BERNERS *Froiss.* I. cxl. 168 Duke Johan of Brabant, purchased greatly that ye erle of Flaunders shulde haue his doughter in maryage. **1549** *Compl. Scot.* viii. 73 My mortal enemeis purchessis to raif my liberte.

†**2.** To exert oneself for the attainment of some object; to endeavour; to strive. *Obs.*

a. *refl.*

[= OF. *se porchacier* 's'efforcer, s'activer' (11th c.).]

[**1292** BRITTON v. xii. §3 Le tenaunt se purchace de amesurer la dowarie [*transl.* let the tenant proceed for admeasurement of the dower].] *c* **1330** R. BRUNNE *Chron. Wace* (Rolls) 7344 þey.. byddem go purchace þem best, To seke oþer lond & lede. *c* **1450** LOVELICH *Grail* li. 331 Pharans purchased him that ilke day.. that he hadde geten hym An Asse.

b. *intr.*

1481 CAXTON *Godeffroy* 191, I wote not how many poure pylgryms that wente pourchasshyng yf they myght fynde ony vytaylles in the countre. **1523** LD. BERNERS *Froiss.* I. cxlvii. 177 The Cardynall.. purchased somoche that a truse was taken bytwene ye kynges of Englande and of Fraunce. *a* **1533** —— *Huon* lxxxii. 253 He purchaseth for your deth. **1607** SHAKS. *Timon* III. ii. 52 That I shold Purchase.. for a little part, and vndo a great deale of Honour. **1674** EARL ESSEX *Let.* 17 Mar. (1770) 104 Mr. justice Jones purchased hard for it [to be made chief Justice].

†**3. a.** *trans.* To bring about, cause, effect, produce; to obtain, procure, manage. Const. *to* or *for* a person, or with dative. *Obs.*

c **1330** *Arth. & Merl.* 216 Nil Ich me nothing auentour, To purchas a fole gret honour. **1375** BARBOUR *Bruce* VII. 496 And went.. to hunt & play, Forto purchase thame venysoun. **1390** GOWER *Conf.* Prol. 129 The werre wol no pes purchace. *c* **1489** CAXTON *Sonnes of Aymon* ix. 232 None ought not to complayne my deth, sith that I have purchaced it myself. *a* **1533** LD. BERNERS *Huon* lxvii. 231 Ye haue founde here an yll brother, syn he hath purchased for you so moche yll. **1641** J. JACKSON *True Evang. T.* III. 176 As a Priest, he did earne, and purchace peace. **1678** SIR G. MACKENZIE *Crim. Laws Scot.* II. *Acts Convict.* (1699) 285 Accused, and pursued be vertue of Crimes purchast be him.

†**b.** *intr.* To arrange, make provision, provide. Const. *for. Obs.*

c **1386** CHAUCER *Man of Law's T.* 775 Ffor wynd and weder almyghty god purchace And brynge hire hoom. *c* **1430** LYDG. *Min. Poems* (Percy Soc.) 176 In every ffelaship so for thysilf purchace. **1483** CAXTON *G. de la Tour* lxxxiii, Lyke the lyonesse.. of all her faons she loueth best hym that best can purchace for hym self. **1523** LD. BERNERS *Froiss.* I. lxxii. 93, I trust I shall purchase for suche a capitayne, that ye shal be all reconforted.

II. †**4. a.** *trans.* To procure for oneself, acquire, obtain, get possession of; to gain. *Obs.*

[*a* **1135** *Leges Wilhelm. Conq.* (MS. *c* 1230) I. xiv, Li apelur jurra sur lui.. que pur haur nel fait ne pur auter chose, se pur sun dreit nun purchacer.] *c* **1290** *S. Eng. Leg.* I. 87/32 þat huy [Ursula] þe purchace clene maidenes: with þe to habbe in þi boure. **1297** R. GLOUC. (Rolls) 360 Corineus.. wende alond to honti.. Vor to porchassi hom mete. *c* **1330** R. BRUNNE *Chron. Wace* (Rolls) 14463 He purchased hym, þorow robberye, Men ynowe, & fair nauye. *c* **1386** CHAUCER *Pars. T.* ¶992 He hopeth for to lyue longe and for to purchacen muche richesse for his delit. *c* **1460** *Oseney Reg.* 38 All thynges þe which the church of Saynte Marye.. lawfully hath i-purchased [L. *adepta est*]. **1549** *Compl. Scot.* xii. 100 It sal be ane lang tyme or the romans can purches sa grit ane armye contrar ȝou. **1600** SURFLET *Countrie Farme* I. iv. 11 The water.. purchaseth from the lead an euill qualitie. **1630** *R. Johnson's Kingd. & Commw.* 314 If.. two or three united Cantons purchase any bootie by their peculiar Armes. **1703** M. MARTIN *Western Isles* 287 With these rude hooks, and a few sorry fishing lines, they purchas'd fish for their maintenance.

b. To obtain from a constituted authority (a mandatory or permissive instrument, as a brief, a licence, etc.); *spec.* in *Law, to purchase a writ,* to sue out, to obtain and issue a writ; hence, to commence an action. *Obs.* exc. *Hist.*

[**1292** BRITTON II. xvii. §4 Si le bref fust purchacé avaunt la disseisine.] *a* **1300** *Cursor M.* 19606 And þar-on purchest he þar breue For to seke.. Cristen men. *c* **1425** *Eng. Conq. Irel.* 6 Whan Macmorgh hade the kynges lettres thus y-purchasede. **1553** BECON *Reliques of Rome* (1563) 238 b, All thoe yt purchasen letters of any Lordes court. **1849** MACAULAY *Hist. Eng.* ii. I. 153 He could not alienate one acre without purchasing a licence. **1876** DIGBY *Real Prop.* v. §2. 222 *note,* 'Purchasing' a writ was the usual expression for commencing an action by suing out a writ, for which the usual fees must be paid, notwithstanding the provision of Magna Carta (c. 40), 'Nulli vendemus.. justitiam'.

†**c.** To gain, get to, reach (a port). *Obs. rare*⁻¹.

? **1587** R. TOMSON *Voy. W. Ind.* in Hakluyt *Voy.* (1589) 582 One of the shippes of our company.. went that night with the land: thinking in the morning to purchase the port of S. John de Vllua.

5. *spec.* **a.** *Law.* To acquire (property, esp. land) otherwise than by inheritance or descent; sometimes, to get by conquest in war. *Obs.* or *arch.*

[**1278** *Rolls of Parlt.* I. 10/2 Pur ceo qe la terre est de ancient demene le Roy u nul neste put purchaser par la commune ley.] **1303** [implied in PURCHASER 2]. *c* **1330** [see PURCHASED *ppl. a.* 1]. **1375** BARBOUR *Bruce* I. 433 Ga purches land quhar euir he may, For tharoff haffys he nane perfay. **1398** TREVISA *Barth. de P.R.* VI. xiv. (Bodl. MS.), þe fadir.. purchaseth lond and heritage for his children alwey [L. *acquirere.. non desistit*]. *c* **1425** *Eng. Conq. Irel.* 30 Al hys thoght & all hys wylle, was nyghte & day, wyth all hys myȝht to wend in-to Irland.. to do hym yn adventur, lond to purchace yn vnked land. **1435** *Rolls of Parlt.* IV. 487/1 The Manoirs, Londes,.. and Possessions, purchaced or amortised. **1503–4** *Act 19 Hen. VII,* c. 15 §4 Yf eny bondeman purches eny landes.. in fee symple. **1606** SHAKS. *Ant. & Cl.* I. iv. 14 His faults in him.. Hereditarie, Rather then purchaste. **1682** [see PURCHASED].

†**b.** *intr.* To acquire possessions; to become rich. *Obs.*

1340 HAMPOLE *Pr. Consc.* 1342 Swilk men purchaces and gaders fast, And fares als þis lyfe suld ay last. *c* **1386** CHAUCER *Prol.* 608 He [the Reve] koude bettre than his lord purchace; fful riche he was astored pryuely. **1390** GOWER *Conf.* II. 194 Riht so is Covoitise afaited To loke where he mai pourchace. **1623** WEBSTER *Devil's Law-case* IV. i, Were all of his mind, to entertain no suits But such they thought were honest, sure our lawyers Would not purchase half so fast. **1623–33** FLETCHER & SHIRLEY *Night-Walker* I. i, Why should that Scrivener.. Purchase perpetually, and I a rascal?

6. a. *trans.* To acquire by the payment of money or its equivalent; to buy. (Now the chief sense.)

1377 LANGL. *P. Pl.* B. XVII. 252 And purchace al þe pardoun of Pampiloun & Rome. **1393** *Ibid.* C. IV. 32 And porchace ȝow prouendres while ȝoure pans lasteþ. **14..** *Voc.* in Wr.-Wülcker 602/18 *Peronizo,* to purchase. **1611** BIBLE *Gen.* xxv. 10 The field which Abraham purchased of the sonnes of Heth. **1611** COTGR., *Acheter,* to buy, to purchase. *a* **1727** NEWTON *Chronol. Amended* v. (1728) 339 He that received money of the People for purchasing things for the Sacrifices. **1765** BLACKSTONE *Comm.* I. iv. 214 To buy wool for her majesty's use, to purchase oyl for her lamps. **1837** DICKENS *Pickw.* ii, 'We must purchase our tickets,' said Mr. Tupman.

b. *fig.* To obtain, acquire, or gain (something immaterial) at the cost or as the result of something figured as the price paid; *esp.* to acquire by toil, suffering, danger, or the like; to earn, win; to bring upon oneself, incur (mischief).

c **1400** tr. *Secreta Secret., Gov. Lordsh.* 51 He þat gyues his good to hem þat hauys no myster, he purchases no louynge þerof. *c* **1450** LOVELICH *Grail* xliii. 476 For be that deth he hym Ouercam, And purchaced lif to Every Cristen Man. **1456** *Paston Lett.* I. 405, I.. do purchasse malgre to remembre of evidenses lakkyng by negligence. **1521–2** *Wolsey* in Furnivall *Ballads fr. MSS.* I. 335 þat þou may purches hevyn to mede. **1548–77** VICARY *Anat.* Ep. Ded. (1888) 6 [They] purchased eternal prayse by their study and cunning in Phisicke and Surgery. **1680** OTWAY *Orphan* I. i, The Honours he has gain'd are justly his; He purchas'd them in War. **1709** STEELE & SWIFT *Tatler* No. 68 ¶4 He that commends himself, never purchases our Applause; nor he who bewails himself, our Pity. **1741** tr. *D'Argen's Chinese Lett.* xx. 141 At length they all perish'd, and made the Japonese purchase their Death by the Loss of 3000 of their Soldiers. **1778** MISS BURNEY *Evelina* (1791) II. xxx. 180 Dearly, indeed, do I purchase experience! **1871** FREEMAN *Norm. Conq.* IV. xviii. 183 The victory was purchased by the death of Rhiwallon.

c. With money or its equivalent as the subject.

1805 M. G. LEWIS *Bravo of Venice* II. vi. 214 Will ten thousand sequins purchase your departure from the republic? **1904** L. TRACY *King of Diamonds* iii. 35 An establishment where threehalfpence would purchase a cup of coffee and a 'doorstep'. **1916** G. B. SHAW *Androcles & Lion* p. xciv, Such pleasures as money can purchase are suppressed.

d. *absol.*

1850 T. S. ARTHUR *Golden Grains* 50 He purchased largely and had the goods forwarded before he left the city. **1904** R. M. WILLIAMSON *Bits from Bookshop* x. 77 The great public libraries where.. books are lent out for hire to those who wish to read but cannot purchase.

III. 7. *Naut.* To haul in, draw in (a rope or cable); *spec.* to haul up (the anchor) by means of the capstan; hence, to haul up, hoist, or raise (anything) by the aid of a mechanical power, as by the wheel-and-axle, pulley, or lever. Cf. PURCHASE *sb.* III.

From quot. *a* 1625 this appears to have arisen as a nautical use of sense 4, with the notion of 'gaining', applied at first to hauling in a rope with the two hands so as to 'gain' one portion after another, and to have been extended to hauling with the capstan, and so at length to the advantage gained by any mechanical power.

1567 *Admiralty Crt. Act* XII., 29 May, [Commission is awarded].. to recover, purchase, wey and bring to lande one sonken or wrecked shipp. *a* **1625** *Nomencl. Navalis* (Harl. MS. 2301) lf. 60 b, To Purchase Wee Call the gaining or Coming in of a Roape by our haling of it in with our handes, or heauing of it in at ye Capstaine or otherwise Purchasing; as the Capstaine doth purchase apace that is it drawes in the Cabell apace, or the Tackles doe purchase, and the Contrarie where wee cannot purchase with the Roape, Tackle, or the like Neate. **1627** CAPT. SMITH *Seaman's Gram.* I. xvi. (1692) 80. **1704** J. HARRIS *Lex. Techn.* I. **1711** W. SUTHERLAND *Shipbuild. Assist.* 141 Pendants of the Main and Foremast ought to be as big as the Shrowds, since they purchace a great Weight of Boats and Anchors. **1726** SHELVOCKE *Voy. round World* 180 In purchasing the anchor, the cable parted, and I lost it. **1768** J. BYRON *Narr. Patagonia* (ed. 2) 28 We were usually obliged to purchase such things as were within reach by means of large hooks fastened to poles. **1793** SMEATON *Edystone L.* §143 In this situation a strong hawser.. being passed under one of the arms of the anchor,.. the whole suspension was in that manner purchased. *Ibid., note,* A piece of strong timber overlaying the bows of a vessel, containing sheaves, or a roller for purchasing the anchor. **1835** MARRYAT *Jac. Faithf.* ii, Purchase the anchor I could not; I therefore slipped the cable. **1836** —— *Midsh. Easy* xxiv, After one or two attempts, he lowered down the steps and contrived to bump her [an old lady] on the first, from the first he purchased her on the second, and from the second he at last seated her at the door of the carriage.

purchased (ˈpɜːtʃɪst), *ppl. a.* [f. prec. + -ED¹.]

†**1.** Obtained by effort, entreaty, or the like; acquired, procured, gotten; of land, Acquired otherwise than by inheritance. Also *fig. Obs.*

c **1330** R. BRUNNE *Chron.* (1810) 87 Heritage þat lyues & leues to þe eldest sonne, Purchaced þing men gyues, woman weddyng to mone, Or tille a man is strange for his seruise oftsone. **1483** *Cath. Angl.* 294/1 Purchest (*A.* Purchessyde), *adeptus.* **1568** BIBLE (Bishop's) *Eph.* i. 14 Unto the redemption of the purchased possession. **1596** SHAKS. *Merch. V.* IV. i. 90 You haue among you many a purchast slaue. **1682** WARBURTON *Hist. Guernsey* (1822) 90 Purchased estates, acquêt or conquêt... Strictly, acquet is such as is purchased before marriage.

†**b.** Incurred by one's act or conduct. *Obs.*

1611 BEAUM. & FL. *Knt. Burn. Pestle* IV. iii, He is dead, Grief of your purchas'd anger broke his heart.

2. Bought with money or other equivalent.

1823 BYRON *Juan* XIII. lxxvi, An English autumn, though it hath no vines.. Hath yet a purchased choice of choicest wines. **1825** T. HOOK *Sayings* Ser. II. *Sutherl.* (Colburn) 44 Purchased roses decked her furrowed cheeks.

ˈpurchase-ˌmoney. The sum for which anything is or may be purchased. Also *fig.*

1720 *Rec. Early Hist. Boston* (1883) VIII. 146 The which purchace money to be Invested in Some Real Estate for the use of this Town. **1723** DUCHESS OF BUCKINGHAM *Let.* 1 Aug. in *Lett. to & from Henrietta, Countess of Suffolk* (1824) I. 115 Half the purchase-money, at least, will go to build him another [house] to his mind. *a* **1763** SHENSTONE *Wks.* (1764) II. 293, I would part with the purchase-money, for which I have less regard. **1818** COBBETT *Pol. Reg.* XXXIII. 57 The purchase money of farms is estimated upon the amount of rent. **1832** HART. MARTINEAU *Life in Wilds* ix, Labour is still the purchase-money of everything here. **1890** 'R. BOLDREWOOD' *Col. Reformer* (1891) 259 He.. retained the proceeds.. with which to pay off his purchase-money. **1892** M. A. JACKSON *Life & Lett. Gen. T. J. Jackson* viii. 114 He might be permitted to emancipate himself by a return of the purchase-money. **1961** NEW ENG. BIBLE *Acts* v. 2 He kept back part of the purchase-money. **1972** C. DRUMMOND *Death at Bar* ii. 47 Alwyn did not pay over the purchase money.

purchaser (ˈpɜːtʃɪsə(r)). Forms: 4 **purchasour,** 5 **-oure, -owre, purchesur,** 6 **-asser,** 6–8 **-asor,** 6– **purchaser.** [ME., a. AF. *purchasour,* = OF. *porchaceor,* later *pur-, pourchaseur,* agent-n. from *porchacier, pourchasser* to PURCHASE.]

†**1.** One who acquires or aims at acquiring possessions; one who 'feathers his nest'. *Obs.*

In quot. *c* 1386, many explain *purchasour* as 'conveyancer', which is possible; but cf. quot. 1591 and PURCHASE *v.* 5 b, quot. 1623–33.

1303 R. BRUNNE *Handl. Synne* 1105, Y se men þat purchasours are, þat coueyte catel with sorwe & kare. *c* **1386** CHAUCER *Prol.* 318 A Sergeant of the Lawe.. Of fees and robes hadde he many oon, So greet a purchasour was nowher noon; Al was fee symple to hym in effect; His purchasyng myghte nat been infect. *c* **1440** *Partonope* 6427, I haue lyued as a sowdyor A poure man but no purchasoure. **1591** GREENE *Disc. Coosnage* (1592) 11 Think you some lawyers coulde be such purchasers, if al their pleas were short, and their proceedinges iustice and conscience?

†**b.** One who procures or brings something about. *Obs. rare*⁻¹.

1653 WHITFIELD *Treat. Sinf. Men* vi. 25 Is he not the Author and purchasor of peace?

†**c.** *Mining.* See quot. 1747; cf. CAVER. *Obs.*

? **1556** in Pettus *Fodinæ Reg.* (1670) 95 That no Purchasors shall let or stop any Miners from any Wash-trough at any time. **1747** HOOSON *Miner's Dict.* s.v. *Mineral time,* Purcassers [are] Poor People that daily go to the Mines, with their Hammers, Bags, or Penny-wiskets, searching in the Deads that are daily drawn and tem'd on the Hillocks, for any Bits of Ore that they can find therein. *Ibid.,* Also Purchasers are all to go away from the Works when that time is expired.

2. *Law.* One who acquires land or property in any way other than by inheritance.

1303 R. BRUNNE *Handl. Synne* 9453 Also with purchasours ryȝt so hyt fareþ, Alle þat þey bygge, here eyrës bareþ. *c* **1540** in J. R. Boyle *Hedon* (1875) App. 71 Yf anye suche inherytor or purchessor absent them selfes [etc.]. **1642** tr. *Perkins' Prof. Bk.* viii. §539. 235 If husband and wife be joynt purchasers unto them and unto the heires of the husband of lands. **1766** BLACKSTONE *Comm.* II. xiv. 220 The first purchasor.. is he who first acquired the estate to his family, whether the same was transferred to him by sale, or by gift, or by any other method, except only that of descent. *Ibid.* xv. 241 If I give land freely to another, he is in the eye of the law a purchasor. **1833** *Act 3 & 4 Will. IV,* c. 106 § 1 (Act for Amendment of Law of Inheritance), The Words 'the Purchaser' shall mean the Person who last acquired the Land otherwise than by Descent, or than by any Escheat, Partition, or Inclosure.

3. One who purchases for money; a buyer.

1625 MASSINGER *New Way* II. i, I must have all men sellers, and I the only purchaser. **1712** ADDISON *Spect.* No. 511 ¶4 The Purchaser.. pays down her Price very chearfully. **1849** MACAULAY *Hist. Eng.* iii. I. 371 He was instantly discerned to be a fit purchaser of every thing that nobody else would buy. **1902** E. L. BANKS *Newsp. Girl* 129 Plenty of things are not for sale until a purchaser comes.

purchasing (ˈpɜːtʃɪsɪŋ), *vbl. sb.* [-ING¹.]

a. The action of the verb PURCHASE in various senses. In quot. 1747, the gathering of ore from the waste heap: cf. PURCHASER 1 c.

13.. *K. Alis.* 5197 In water and londe [is] his purchaceyng. Boþe hij eteth flesshe and fysshe. **1375** BARBOUR *Bruce* II. 579 And swa thar purchesyng maid thai. **1386** [see PURCHASER 1]. **1494** FABYAN *Chron.* VI. clxx. 164 As they wente in purchasynge of prayes. **1595** in Willis & Clark *Cambridge* (1886) II. 733 Monye.. for the purchasing of some competent landes. **1656** EARL MONM. tr. *Boccalini's Advts. fr. Parnass.* II. xxxvi. (1674) 188 The purchasing of Eternity to her name. **1747** HOOSON *Miner's Dict.* Sj, Sauntle [is] the first pee or bit of Ore that the Cavers find in a morning by Purchassing. **1800** in Picton *L'pool Munic. Rec.* (1886) II. 193 A fund..for the purchasing Potatoes.

b. *attrib.*, as ***purchasing agent, manager, officer, power, value***; **purchasing power parity** (see quots. 1918, 1939).

1921 *Daily Colonist* (Victoria, B.C.) 3 Apr. 1/2 G. W. Wooster, treasurer, and G. L. McNichol, *purchasing agent, two of the oldest employees of the company, have retired into private life. **1675** EARL ESSEX *Lett.* (1770) 221, I am not in a *purchasing condition. **1969** *Times* 2 May 34 (Advt.), **Purchasing Manager.* A large British Company in the chemical field requires a manager to establish and develop a new central section to be responsible for all research concerning materials, services and sources of supply. **1963** *B.S.I. News* Apr. 22/2 *Purchasing officers should make appropriate sample tests of goods received to ensure that they complied with the contract requirements. **1824** J. S. MILL in *Westm. Rev.* II. 42 Those commodities are also the measure of its *purchasing power. **1863** FAWCETT *Pol. Econ.* II. iv. (1876) 137 The cost of living is augmented, and wages possess less purchasing power. **1930** *Economist* 11 Jan. 78/2 Good chain-store sales this month indicate a satisfactory volume of purchasing power. **1979** *Bull. Amer. Acad. Arts & Sci.* Mar. 42 Those prices will rise, and in addition, wages and other prices will also tend to rise in order to maintain their original 'purchasing power'. **1918** G. CASSEL in *Economic Jrnl.* Dec. 413 At every moment the real parity between two countries is represented by this quotient between the purchasing power of the money in the one country and the other. I propose to call this parity '*the *purchasing power parity*'. **1939** I. DE VEGH *Pound Sterling* II. 75 This point of view, known as the purchasing power parity theory, rests fundamentally on the assumption that a change in the internal purchasing power of a currency will, under certain conditions, affect the merchandise balance of the country involved. **1965** SELDON & PENNANCE *Everyman's Dict. Econ.* 350 Purchasing power parity is.. only a partial explanation of exchange rates, although when other circumstances are generally stable it can give a rough guide to them. **1862** *Sat. Rev.* XIII. 640/1 If we could suddenly double the whole quantity of sovereigns and their equivalents in England, the *purchasing value of each coin would.. be reduced to exactly one half of its former amount.

purcholis, -ious, obs. forms of PORTCULLIS.

pur-chop: see PUR².

†**purcinct,** *sb. Obs.* Also 4 pursaunt, poursent, 4–5 purseynt, 5 -cynct. [a. AF. *purceynt(e* = OF. *porceinte*, sb. fem., *porceint*, sb. masc., from *porceindre*:—L. *prōcingĕre*, *prōcinctus*: see next and PROCINCT.] = PRECINCT *sb.*, PROCINCT *sb.*¹; compass.

[**1292** BRITTON VI. v. §3 Hors de la purceynte del Counté ne est nul tenu a receyvere somounse. **1304** *Year Bk. 32 Edw. I*, Trin. Term (Rolls) 261 Dens la purceynt de meisme le bois.] **13..** *E.E. Allit. P.* A. 1034 Vch pane of þat place [the new Jerusalem, *Rev.* xxi. 12] had þre ȝatez, So twelue in poursent I con asspye. [Some read *pourseut*, and explain as 'pursuit, sequence, order'.] **13..** *Ibid.* B. 1385 þe place, þat plyed þe pursaunt wyth-inne, Was longe & ful large. **1382** WYCLIF *2 Kings* xi. 8 3if eny man comme with in the purseynt of the temple, be he slayn. **1437** *Rolls of Parlt.* IV. 503/1 The suburbes and the Purseynt of ye same citee. **1495** *Act 11 Hen. VII*, c. 29 §1 Viewe of fraunciplegge within the purcynct of the seid Manoir.

†**purcinct, purseynt,** *ppl. a. Obs.* [a. OF. *porceint*, *-saint*(:—L. *prōcinctus*), pa. pple. of *porceindre*:—L. *prōcingĕre*: see PROCINCT.] Girt about, enclosed; = PRECINCT *ppl. a.*

1303 R. BRUNNE *Handl. Synne* 8914 Ne quest take of endytement Yn holy cherche, oþer ȝerde purseynt.

purcoloys, -culleis, obs. ff. PORTCULLIS.

purcy, purcyfant, obs. ff. PURSY, PURSUIVANT.

purdah ('pɜːdə). *E. Indies.* Also purda, pardah, parda (*erron.* purdow, purder). [a. Urdū and Pers. *pardah* veil, curtain.]

1. a. A curtain; *esp.* one serving to screen women from the sight of men or strangers. (See also quot. 1952.)

1800 *Misc. Tracts* in *Asiat. Ann. Reg.* 64/1 A purdow, or skreen, of a yellow kind of gauze, being dropt before the door. **1809** LD. VALENTIA *Trav.* I. 100 He led me to a small couch close to the purdah, and seated me on his right hand ..between his mother and himself, though she was invisible. **1844** KINGLAKE *Eöthen* i, They passed through no door, but only by the yielding folds of a purder. *a* **1858** D. WILSON in *Life* (1860) II. xv. 126 Purdahs or curtains of all colours hung from the crenated arches. **1898** C. P. STETSON *Women & Economics* iv. 66 Some air has come through the purdah's folds, some knowledge has filtered to her eager ears from the talk of men. **1927** *New Republic* 21 Sept. 127/2 Miss Mayo speaks as though the seclusion of women behind the *purdah* were universal throughout India. **1952** S. SELVON *Brighter Sun* i. 9 He didn't feel any sexual excitement... Even when he had looked at her face under the *purdah*—the white sheet thrown over them.

b. As typical of the seclusion of Indian women of rank; hence *fig.* the system of such seclusion.

1865 *Daily Tel.* 25 Nov. 8/6 As an Occidental, she will not like that tame bird's life inside the lattice cage and the pardah which Oriental wives must bear. **1893** W. S. BURRELL & EDITH E. CUTHELL *Indian Mem.* 23 The veil of the purdah hangs less heavily over Mahommedan than over Bengali women. **1905** *19th Cent.* Mar. 486 The purdah has been hardly any drawback to the women born with any talent for ruling. **1968** *Times* 6 Apr. (Pakistan Suppl.) p. vii/5 In Pakistan today the observance of purdah is, in the broadest terms, in inverse ratio to social status. **1971** R. RUSSELL tr. *Ahmad's Shore & Wave* iv. 39 She very rarely observed purdah and on the day in question was returning from school. **1975** *Language for Life* (Dept. Educ. & Sci.) xx. 293 Mothers may be at work all day, or live in purdah, or speak no English.

c. *transf.* Seclusion; (medical) isolation or quarantine; secrecy. Usu. in phrases ***in, into,*** (etc.), ***purdah***.

1928 J. GALSWORTHY *Swan Song* II. v. 143 The diagnosis of Kit's malady [*sc.* measles] was soon verified, and Fleur went into purdah. **1957** G. B. STERN *Seventy Times Seven* 182 He was supposed to be in purdah with Nicola and deeply occupied with those unspeakable Memoirs. **1958** *Times* 23 Oct. 15/5 The voluminous Dilke papers..had been kept in *purdah* by the family piety of the late Miss Tuckwell. **1963** *Times* 27 Feb. 10/5 Mr. Maudling, Chancellor of the Exchequer, from now on will be in purdah whenever questions touch upon the Budget. **1977** D. BAGLEY *Enemy* xxxix. 314 When I came out of purdah, but before I was discharged, I went to see her.

2. A striped cotton cloth, or other material, of which curtains are made.

1858 SIMMONDS *Dict. Trade*, *Purdah*, an Indian cotton cloth, with white and blue stripes, used for curtains, etc.

3. *attrib.* and *Comb.*, chiefly in reference to sense 1 b, as ***purdah girl, lady, walla*** [see WALLAH], ***woman; purdah costume, curtain, glass, party, system; purdah-like*** adj.

1847 MRS. SHERWOOD in *Life* xxi. (1854) 356 Amina was ..particularly dark for a purdah walla, or one, according to the Eastern custom, who is supposed always to sit behind a purdah, or curtain. **1894** S. S. THORBURN *Asiat. Neighbours* iv. 68 Of all his [Peter the Great's] social reforms, the greatest was the abolition of the purdah system for Russian ladies. **1902** *19th Cent.* Nov. 818 Purdah women are a comparatively small proportion of their sex. **1905** Purdah costume [see BURKA¹]. **1937** *Times* 13 Apr. p. xxxviii/1 In the first class compartment there are four special ventilators and purdah glass louvres above the side windows. **1955** *Times* 31 May 7/7 In Peshawar is the university and a college for women, where there are mixed debates with a *purdah* curtain dividing the sexes. **1971** R. RUSSELL tr. *Ahmad's Shore & Wave* x. 124 Let purdah girls play the men up. **1973** *New Society* 26 Apr. 198/3 A gilded door of purdah glass, which meant that Lady Jersey could see all of Lord Jersey approaching, while he could delight only in outline of her filmy silhouette. **1975** P. MASON in C. Allen *Plain Tales from Raj* 16 One formidable old lady..would fit in a purdah party for Indian ladies before her dinner party for the brigadier.

Hence **purdahed** ('pɜːdəd) *a.*, screened or secluded by a purdah; curtained; 'cloistered'.

1832 MRS. MEER ALI *Observ. Mussalmans India* I. xiv. 380 The hour is passed in lively dialogues with the several purdahed dames. **1949** L. DURRELL *Spirit of Place* (1969) 103 All the houses in the Turkish quarter have musharabaya trellis windows for purdah-ed girls. **1959** *Encounter* Sept. 33/1 Somewhat secluded (although not purdah-ed) women.

Purdey ('pɜːdɪ). The proprietary name of firearms and parts manufactured by the firm founded by James *Purdey* (1816–68).

1884 F. F. R. BURGESS *Sporting Fire-Arms for Bush & Jungle* viii. 85 For ordinary shot-guns, the Purdey bolt is a very good fastening. **1901** T. F. FREMANTLE *Bk. of Rifle* ii. 44 The Purdey was a four-grooved rifle, with an increasing twist. **1937** M. SHARP *Nutmeg Tree* ii. 17 At twelve the boy was to be given his father's old 20-bore, at eighteen the Purdey 12. **1961** C. WILLOCK *Death in Covert* ii. 31 Crumbe-Howard..was standing casually with a Purdey twelve-bore open. **1970** R. A. STEINDLER *Firearms Dict.* 185/1 *Purdey side lock*, perhaps the most famed & best of all side lock actions... The Purdey design differs in several important points from the standard side lock design... Even a well-used Purdey is considered a 'good buy'. **1974** *Trade Marks Jrnl.* 20 Mar. 468/1 *Purdey*... Guns, rifles and ammunition. James Purdey and Sons Ltd.,..London. **1976** *Shooting Times & Country Mag.* 9–15 Dec. 38/2 (Advt.), These weapons have the usual Purdey engraving with traces of original hardening colour.

pur-dog: see PUR².

pur'donian. Also -ion, -ium. [f. *Purdon*, name of the introducer.] Trade-name of a form of coal-scuttle.

1851 W. S. BURTON *Trade Catal., Lond. Internat. Exh.*, Purdonion. **1856** H. LOVERIDGE *Trade Catal.*, Purdonian. **1870** *Auction Catalogue* 29 Apr., A cocoanut mat, cinder sifter, japanned purdonium and scoop. **1901** *Ibid.*, An iron curb fender and oak coal purdonium with scoop and liner.

purdy ('pɜːdɪ), *a. rare.* Now *dial.* Surly, ill-humoured.

1668 SHADWELL *Sullen Lover* v, 'Slife, one shan't speak to you one of these days, you are grown so purdy. **1672** —— *Miser* IV, Why you saucy fellow you, what's to do with you? Ha, are you so purdy? *a* **1825** FORBY *Voc. E. Anglia*, *Purdy*, surly; ill-humoured; self-important.

pure (pjʊə(r)), *a.* (*sb.*, *adv.*) Forms: 3–5 pur, 4– pure. (Also 4 puȝr, por(e, 4 (6 *Sc.*) puyr(e, puir(e, 5 poure, 5–6 pewr(e, 9 pewer; 5–6, 9 puer, 6 peur.) [a. OF. *pur*, fem. *pure* (12th c. in Littré), = Pr. *pur*, Sp., It. *puro*:—L. *pūru-s* clean, clear, unmixed, pure, chaste, etc.]

A. *adj.* **I.** In physical sense.

1. a. Not mixed with anything else; free from admixture or adulteration; unmixed, unalloyed; often qualifying names of colours. **b.** *esp.* Not mixed with, or not having in or upon it, anything that defiles, corrupts, or impairs; unsullied, untainted, clean. **c.** Visibly or optically clear, spotless, stainless; in quots. 1481, 1652, clear, transparent. Rarely const. *from*.

(There is a wide range of sense here, but lines of division cannot well be drawn among the quotations, many of which unite more than one shade of meaning.)

1297 R. GLOUC. (Rolls) 184 So clene is al so þat lond & mannes blod so pur [*v.rr.* puir, pure]. *Ibid.* 3178 O cler leom wiþoute mo þer stod fram him wel pur. *c* **1300** *St. Brandan* 313 Caliz and cruetz, pur cler crestal. **13..** *E.E. Allit. P.* A. 227 So was hit clene & cler & pure, þat precios perle þer hit was pyȝt. **1362** LANGL. *P. Pl.* A. IV. 82 A present al of pure Red gold. **1398** TREVISA *Barth. De P.R.* XIII. ii. (Bodl. MS.), To make pitte water clene and pure. **1481** CAXTON *Myrr.* III. vi. 140 The mone is not so pure that the sonne may shyne.. thurgh her as thurgh an other sterre. **1590** SPENSER *F.Q.* II. vii. 15 At the well-head the purest streames arise. **1638** JUNIUS *Paint. Ancients* 42 To have his minde..like unto a pure, bright looking-glasse. **1652** GAULE *Magastrom.* 7 One reads them with the pure glass of Gods word: the other by his own false and fallacious perspicils. **1750** GRAY *Elegy* 53 Full many a gem of purest ray serene, The dark unfathom'd caves of ocean bear. **1784** COWPER *Task* II. 508 To filter off a crystal draught Pure from the lees. **1797** *Encycl. Brit.* (ed. 3) XVI. 33/1 There can be but one proper species of red;.. all other shades being adulterations of that pure colour, with yellow, brown, &c. **1800** tr. *Lagrange's Chem.* II. 308 If alcohol be re-distilled, and reduced to two-thirds, you will obtain it very pure. This is what is called Rectified Alcohol. **1804** J. GRAHAME *Sabbath* 42 The morning air pure from the city's smoke. **1839** URE *Dict. Arts* 414 A mixture of prussian blue and cochineal pink..in preference to a pure blue. **1853** W. GREGORY *Inorg. Chem.* (ed. 3) 74 In consequence of the great solvent power of water, it is never found pure in nature. **1860** TYNDALL *Glac.* I. xxv. 187 The snow was of the purest white.

†**d.** Intact, unbroken, perfect, entire. *Obs. rare.*

1607 TOPSELL *Four-f. Beasts* 716 Twenty of these hornes pure, and so many broken.

e. Of a musical sound or voice: Free from roughness, harshness, or discordant quality; smooth, clear: *spec.* in *Mus.* and *Acoustics*, said of tones that are perfectly in tune, i.e. whose vibration-ratios are mathematically exact, so as to give no beats: esp. as opp. to *tempered*. ***pure tone***, a tone composed of a single frequency and represented by a sine wave (earlier called a *simple tone*).

1872 F. JACOX *Aspects Authorship* iii. 44 The pure and most tuneful voice of Miss Clara Novello. **1873** HALE *In His Name* vi. 49 The voice was a perfectly clear and pure tenor. **1889** J. LECKY in Grove *Dict. Mus.* IV. 70/2 If..all the consonant intervals are made perfectly smooth and pure, so as to give no beats, the tuning is then called Just Intonation. **1902** *Encycl. Brit.* XXXI. 751/2 Considerable difference of opinion exists as to whether beats can blend so as to give a sensation of tone; but König, by using very pure tones of high pitch, appears to have settled the question. **1929** H. FLETCHER *Speech & Hearing* iv. 167 The masking effect of one pure tone by another was determined. **1961** *Lancet* 22 July 197/2 Pure-tone audiometry is only one item in a whole range of tests that are needed to build up a complete picture of the condition of a patient who has a hearing-loss. **1976** L. H. SCHAUDINISCHKY *Sound, Man & Building* i. 30 The beat grows progressively lower and vanishes altogether when $f_1 = f_2$. This gives rise to a method of extremely accurately determining the unknown frequency of a pure tone with the aid of the calibrated output of a sine-wave generator by simply listening in.

f. *Forestry.* Of a wood or plantation; consisting of trees of only one species.

1889 W. SCHLICH *Man. Forestry* I. II. iii. 177 Such woods may be composed of one species only, or they may contain a mixture of two or more species; in the former case they are called 'pure woods', and in the latter 'mixed woods'. **1927** *Forestry* I. 11 This century saw the return in an increasing degree to pure rather than mixed coniferous stands. **1948** *Misc. Publ. Univ. Michigan Mus. Zool.* LXVIII. 16 The creosote bush, usually in pure stands, covers great expanses of the broad desert basins. **1976** H. L. EDLIN *Nat. Hist. Trees* v. 64 The plantations just described are examples of more or less even-aged stands of a single species, also called a pure even-aged forest.

II. In non-physical or general sense.

2. a. Without foreign or extraneous admixture: free from anything not properly pertaining to it; simple, homogeneous, unmixed, unalloyed.

pure naturals: see NATURAL *sb.* 5.

1377 LANGL. *P. Pl.* B. XIII. 166 Þere nys neyther..Pope, ne patriarch þat puyre reson ne schal make þe meyster of alle þo men. **1487** in *Surrey Archæol. Soc. Collect.* III. 163, I Elizabeth Uvedale..in my pure widowhood make and ordain my will. **1614** PURCHAS *Pilgrimage* I. ix. (ed. 2) 47 In the time of Elisa or Dido, the Phænicean or Punike, which she carried into Africa, was pure Hebrew, as were also their letters. **1642** *Answ. Observ. agst. King* 23 'Tis Adams pure naturalls, impure nature that makes a Subject covet to be a King. **1724** A. COLLINS *Gr. Chr. Relig.* 81 The Sadducees profess'd to follow the pure text of Scripture, or to interpret it according to the literal sense. **1864** BOWEN *Logic* vi. (1870) 148, I know at once, or by Immediate Inference,—that is, by an act of Pure Thought. **1882** MINCHIN *Unipl. Kinemat.* 130 The strain at a point is said to be pure strain if the principal axes (axes of the strain ellipse) are not rotated by the strain.

b. In reference to descent or lineage: Of unmixed descent, pure-blooded. ***pure line*** [tr. G. *reine linie* (W. Johannsen *Erblichkeit in Populationen und in reinen Linien* (1903) 9)], an inbred line of descent; also *attrib.*, an individual belonging to such a line.

c **1475** *Rauf Coilȝear* 20 In point thay war to parische, thay proudest men and pure. **1568** GRAFTON *Chron.* II. 286 To people the towne with pure Englishe men. **1827** ROBERTS *Voy. Centr. Amer.* 137 He was an Indian of pure blood. **1853**

J. H. NEWMAN *Hist. Sk.* (1873) II. I. i. 24, I consider Attila to have been a pure Hun. **1866** G. MACDONALD *Ann. Q. Neighb.* xxvii, That horse..is very nearly a pure Arab. **1906** R. H. LOCK *Rec. Progess Study Variation* iv. 110 If we were to carry on this conception to the case of bisexual inheritance, we should find that the different pure lines would become crossed and confused together. **1926** J. S. HUXLEY *Ess. Pop. Sci.* ii. 22 Beans are self-fertilising; so that if, instead of treating the sample as a whole, he kept the beans produced from each plant separate, he could be sure of dealing with a hereditarily pure stock, or as it is usually called, a pure line. **1932** *Discovery* Oct. 320/2 In the cotton industry we have the magnificent succession of 'pure lines' particularly in the Egyptian cottons. **1947** *Ann. Rev. Microbiol.* I. 27 Ritz..later showed that an apparently inexhaustible succession of immunologically distinct variants may appear in a single animal. This work..is of especial interest since the strain of *T. brucei* used was a 'pure line' derived from a single trypanosome. **1958** SRB & OWEN *Gen. Genetics* xvi. 335 Selection within pure lines..is ineffective because it is biologically meaningless. **1965** 'LAUCHMONEN' *Old Thom's Harvest* i. 5 When I get my credit-bank money to buy pure-line seeds them ricefields gwine be planted again.

c. *Law.* Having no condition annexed; absolute, unconditional. ***pure alms***: cf. ALMOIGN 2.

[Cf. cl. L. *pūrus*, unconditional, absolute; med.L. *pūra (et perpetua) eleēmosyna* (a 1100), AF. *pure (et perpetuele) almoigne*; also F. *pur et simple* (Montesquieu 1747).]

1536–7 *Award. conc. St. Bartholomew's Hosp., Oxford* 3 Feb., The which said Hospital, King Edward the third.. gave and granted unto the predecessors of the said Provost and Scholars [of Oriel]..in free pure and perpetual alms. **1713** *Act 13 Anne*, c. 6 §8 To have and to hold the said Canonship or Prebend to the said Colwell Brickenden..and his Successors..in pure and perpetual Alms. **1818** COLEBROOKE *Obligations* 151 [If] one be conditional or deferred for a term, while the other is a pure and simple engagement. **1880** MUIRHEAD *Gaius* II. §244 Sabinus and Cassius think that a conditional legacy to him is valid, but not a pure one.

d. Of a subject of study or practice: Restricted to that which essentially belongs to it; not including its relations with kindred or connected subjects. (Often denoting the simply theoretical part of a subject, apart from its practical applications, as in ***pure mathematics***; opp. to APPLIED 2, MIXED 7.) Also said of a student or practitioner who confines himself to one particular subject or branch of a subject. Hence, with reference to the arts (chiefly music, painting, and poetry): used of an art in its absolute, essential, or most objective form; freq. in contrast to that which is representational, didactic, or commercial in intent. Also used of an artist whose work is of this sort.

1641 WILKINS *Math. Magick* I. ii. (1648) 12 Mathematicks ..is usually divided into pure and mixed; and though the pure doe handle only abstract quantity..that which is mixed doth consider the quantity of some particular determinate subject. **1750** JOHNSON *Rambler* No. 14 ¶5 The difference between pure science, which has to do only with ideas, and the application of its laws to the use of life. **1858** MAYNE *Expos. Lex.* s.v., In England..the profession is ostensibly divided into three distinct branches, viz. *pure* physicians, or those who profess to act only in medical cases; *pure* surgeons, or those who practise surgery alone; and surgeon-apothecaries, or general practitioners. **1883** *Encycl. Brit.* XV. 752/2 Pure Mechanism, or Applied Kinematics: being the theory of machines considered simply as modifying motion. **1901** A. C. BRADLEY *Poetry for Poetry's Sake* 28 Pure poetry is not the decoration of a preconceived and clearly defined matter: it springs from the creative impulse of a vague imaginative mass pressing for development and definition. **1903** R. B. CARTER *Doctors & Work* i. 4 A small number of operating, or so-called 'pure' surgeons. *a* **1909** *Mod.* He is a pure physicist; he does not know chemistry. **1914** [see ORPHIC *a.* (*sb.*)]. **1924** G. MOORE *Anthol. Pure Poetry* 34 If you approve of my definition of pure poetry, something that the poet creates outside of his own personality, we three might compile a book that would be a real advancement in the study of poetry—an anthology of pure poetry. **1926** H. READ *Reason & Romanticism* iii. 59 Pure poetry, Mr. Moore holds, is born of admiration of 'the only permanent world, the world of things'. **1927** *New Criterion* V. 10 Whither would the notion of 'pure art' lead us if pushed to its farthest logical extremity? To an art completely isolated from everything but its own laws of operation and the object to be created as such. **1929** E. WILSON *I thought of Daisy* iii. 183, I thought..of those other efforts, those efforts more characteristic of our time, which aimed, also, at an absolute beauty, at an art wholly independent of the appetites and agonies of men—paintings which represented nothing, 'pure poetry' devoid of ideas. **1934** C. LAMBERT *Music Ho!* III. 174 The recent invention by certain critics of a hitherto unknown art described as 'pure music' has resulted in the criticism of music becoming more and more detached from any form of life. **1935** W. STEVENS *Let.* 31 Oct. (1967) 288 There was a time when I liked the idea of images and images alone, or images and the music of verse together. I then believed in *pure poetry*, as it was called. **1941** 'G. ORWELL' in *Listener* 29 May 768/1 James Joyce, was..about as near to being a 'pure' artist as a writer can be. **1946** A. L. BACHARACH *Brit. Music of our Time* viii. 118 The superficial æstheticians who insist on the necessity of music being 'pure', the implication being that any music that has the remotest connection with 'literature' is necessarily impure, and therefore ineligible for admission into the musical heaven. **1954** C. S. LEWIS *Eng. Lit. in Sixteenth Cent.* I. i. 92 This minuet of conventions..enables the poem to remain recognizably occasional and yet at the same time to become almost 'pure' poetry. We celebrate the royal wedding..; yet equally, we wander in a world of beautiful forms and colours. **1955** *Times* 9 May 5/1 The exhibition would attract considerable attention and must help to break down the barrier which existed between commercial and pure art. **1959** D. COOKE *Lang. Mus.* v. 231 Mozart's Fortieth Symphony and Vaughan Williams's Sixth..would both appear to be 'pure' music, since we have no evidence that their composers ever imagined that they expressed anything at all. *Ibid.* 234 Our own age has retained the romantic period's conception of Mozart as a 'pure' composer, but adopted a different attitude. **1978** P. GRIFFITHS *Concise Hist. Mod. Music* iv. 47 His [*sc.* Debussy's] creative energies were directed..into works of pure music.

e. *Logic.* Of a proposition or syllogism: opp. to MODAL *a.* 4.

1697 tr. *Burgersdicius his Logic* I. xxviii. 112 A Pure Enunciation is that in which it is not express'd how the Parts cohere... Modal, in which it is. *Ibid.* II. xiv. 60 A Pure [Syllogism] is that which consists of Propositions pure... Modal either of one or both Modal. **1725** WATTS *Logic* II. ii. §4 When a proposition merely expresses that the predicate is connected with the subject, it is called a *pure proposition*; as, every true christian is an honest man: But when it includes also the way and manner wherein the predicate is connected with the subject, it is called a *modal proposition*; as, when I say, it is necessary that a true christian should be an honest man. **1827, 1870** [see MODAL *a.* 4].

f. *Gram.* (*a*) In Greek (*καθαρός*), of a vowel: Preceded by another vowel. Of the stem of a word: Ending in a vowel. Of a consonant (as *s*): Not accompanied by another consonant. (*b*) In Arabic, etc., of a syllable: Ending in a vowel, open.

1650 E. REEVE *Introd. Gr. Tongue* 24 Nounes ending in *δα*, *θα*, *ρα*, or pure *α*, do make the Genitive in *ας*. *Ibid.*, Adjectives in *ις*, having *ος* not pure [e.g. *εὔπατρις, ευπάτριδος*]. **1776** J. RICHARDSON *Arab. Gram.* v. 14 [Syllables] are divided into *pure* and *mixed*; the pure consisting only of one consonant and one vowel,..the mixed of two consonants joined by a vowel. **1818** BLOMFIELD tr. *Matthiæ's Gr. Gram.* I. 218 Verbs pure, whose final syllable *-ω* is preceded by a diphthong. **1870** E. ABBOTT tr. *Curtius' Gr. Gram.* I. vi. 57 In the formation of the acc. sing. of Masc. and Fem., the true vowel-nature of the stem declares itself, *πόλι-ν, πολύ-ν*; and the voc. sing...contains the pure vowel stem.

g. *Philos.* and *Psychol.* ***pure ego***: the essential, transcendental 'self' distinguished from the empirical 'self', esp. in phenomenological contexts.

1890 W. JAMES *Princ. Psychol.* I. x. 292 The constituents of the Self may be divided into two classes, those which make up respectively—(a) The material Self; (*b*) The social Self; (c) The spiritual Self; and (d) The pure Ego. *Ibid.* 296 By the Spiritual Self, so far as it belongs to the Empirical Me, I mean a man's inner or subjective being, his psychic faculties or dispositions, taken concretely; not the bare principle of personal Unity, or 'pure' Ego. **1925** *Mind* XXXIV. 320 In the second edition footnotes the reader of the Logical Studies learns that Husserl has changed his views on this crucial point, and has come to accept definitely ..Natorp's Pure Ego. **1931** W. R. B. GIBSON tr. *Husserl's Ideas* II. ii. 145 The thesis of my pure Ego and its personal life which is 'necessary' and plainly indubitable, thus stands opposed to the thesis of the world which is contingent. **1951** A. HUXLEY *Let.* 9 June (1969) 635 A deeper layer of 'Original Virtue', which is one of peace, illumination and insight, which seems to be on the fringes of the Pure Ego or Atman. **1961** G. W. ALLPORT *Devel. of Personality* vi. 129 Kant argued that..the knowing self is just there, a transcendental or pure ego. **1974** G. L. BRECKON tr. *de Muralt's Idea of Phenomenol.* §52. 328 The pure ego is therefore the subject of transcendental constitution, the ego pole of intentionality, the centre and point of departure of every intentional function.

h. *Biol.* ***pure culture***, a culture in which only one species or clone is present; also *attrib.*

1895 *Ann. Bot.* IX. 610 The method adopted by De Bary of cultivating each species separately for many generations —that of so-called 'pure cultures'—has been of inestimable value. **1930** *Forestry* IV. 66 It seemed possible..that pure culture experiments..might also yield some information.. on the origin of the mycorrhizal habit in trees. **1952** *New Biol.* XIII. 110 Pure-culture technique is a 'stock-in-trade' of the micro-biologist. **1973** G. D. BOWEN in Marks & Kozlowski *Ectomycorrhizae* v. 166 Many..of 27 mycorrhizal fungi in pure culture could use nitrate as the sole source of nitrogen.

3. a. Taken by itself, with nothing added; ... and nothing else; nothing but..., nothing besides ..., no more than...; mere, simple.

Often in phr. ***pure and simple***, following the sb. (cf. 2 c).

1297 R. GLOUC. (Rolls) 794 He isei þat he moste attenende Vor pur meseise vorfare. *c* **1375** *Sc. Leg. Saints* ii. (*Paulus*) 1026 For pure pytte & Ioy þai gret. *c* **1400** MAUNDEV. (Roxb.) xxxii. 144 Many ..diez for pure elde withouten sekeness. **1494** FABYAN *Chron.* v. cvii. 81 The .ii. sonnes of Mordred were constrayned of pure force to seche stronge holdes for theyr refuge. **1593** SHAKS. *2 Hen. VI*, II. i. 157 Alas Sir, we did it for pure need. **1639** FULLER *Holy War* IV. xix, Knowing no more how to sway a sceptre then a pure clown to manage a sword. **1724** A. COLLINS *Gr. Chr. Relig.* 79 This distinction is the pure invention of those who make the objection. **1860** GEO. ELIOT *Let.* 7 June (1954) III. 302 But the most ignorant journalist in England would hardly think of calling me a rival of Miss Mulock—a writer who is read only by novel readers, pure and simple, never by people of high culture. **1861** M. PATTISON *Ess.* (1889) I. 38 His delay in setting out was due to pure procrastination and dilatoriness. **1875** JOWETT *Plato* (ed. 2) I. 29 That of which we are speaking is knowledge pure and simple. **1954** C. S. LEWIS *Eng. Lit. in Sixteenth Cent.* 4 Even when hills are praised for not despising lowly plains we have still hardly reached the realm of metaphor pure and simple. **1977** *Lancs. Life* Nov. 58/3 They attract on a variety of levels: as toys or fun-things pure and simple, as tactile objects, [etc.].

b. In emphatic or intensive sense: Nothing short of..., absolute, sheer, thorough, utter, perfect, complete.

1297 R. GLOUC. (Rolls) 1917 He was..pur mesel þo & he bicom in is baptizinge hol of al is wo. *c* **1400** *Destr. Troy* 1817 Pelleus..sourdit into soure greme, And Priam reprouyt as a pure fole. **1472–3** *Rolls of Parlt.* VI. 36/1 Contynuyng alwey in his pure malice and envy. **1611** CHAPMAN *May-Day* v. Plays (1889) 303/1 His master hath such a pure belief in his wife, that he's apt to believe any good of her. **1794** GODWIN *Cal. Williams* 182, I believed that misery more pure than that which I now endured had never fallen to the lot of a human being. **1870** RUSKIN *Let.* in *Athenæum* 30 Sept. (1905) 428/3 Dickens was a pure modernist—a leader of the steam-whistle party *par excellence*. **1902** BUCHAN *Watcher by Threshold* 145 A lot of pure nonsense.

†**c.** That is the thing itself, not something else; true, real, genuine; very. *Obs.*

1297 R. GLOUC. (Rolls) 2308 He..sede he was purost eyr to be icrouned to kinge. *Ibid.* 8609 In a toun in barcssire.. out of þe erþe pur blod sprong ywis. **13..** *E.E. Allit. P.* B. 704 Wel nyȝe pure paradys moȝt preue no better. *c* **1386** CHAUCER *Knt.'s T.* 421 The pure fettres of his shynes grete Weren of his bittre salte teeres wete. *c* **1400** *Laud Troy Bk.* 6656 He..persed his Armure,..That it come to his fflesche pure. **1534** MORE *Comf. agst. Trib.* I. Wks. 1162/2 Til the pure panges of death pulled their heart fro their play.

III. Free from corruption or defilement.

4. Free from admixture of anything debasing or deteriorating; unadulterated, uncorrupted, uncontaminated; conforming accurately to a standard of quality or style; faultless, correct.

13.. *K. Alis.* 84 Thus he asaied the regiouns, That him cam for to asaile;—In puyr maner of bataile. **1390** GOWER *Conf.* II. 214 Mi ladi..is the pure hed and welle And Mirour and ensample of goode. **1526** TINDALE *Jas.* i. 27 Pure devocion and undefiled. **1540** PALSGR. *Acolastus* Ep. to King A iij b, In suche places of your realme as the pureste englyshe is spoken. **1617** MORYSON *Itin.* I. 182 At Geneua many French Gentlemen and Students comming thither.. did speake pure French. **1788** GIBBON *Decl. & F.* l. (1838) V. 21 The purest disciples of Zoroaster escaped from the contagion of idolatry. **1849** MACAULAY *Hist. Eng.* ii. I. 165 They had been oppressed, and oppression had kept them a pure body. **1882** PEBODY *Eng. Journalism* xvi. 124 His taste, if severe, was pure.

5. a. Free from moral defilement or corruption; of unblemished character or nature; unstained or untainted with evil; guiltless, innocent; guileless, sincere. Rarely const. †*of* (obs.), *from* (arch.). Often absol., ***the pure*** (*sc.* persons).

a **1340** HAMPOLE *Psalter* xxiii. 4 He..þat is pure in werkis and clen in thoghtis. **1481** CAXTON *Myrr.* I. xiv. 48 To saue his sowle whiche God hath lent to hym pure and clene to thende that he shold rendre it such agayn. **1526** TINDALE *Matt.* v. 8 Blessed are the pure in herte. *Ibid.*, *Acts* xx. 26, I am pure from the bloud of all men. *Ibid.*, *Titus* i. 15 Unto the pure are all thynges pure. **1667** MILTON *P.L.* VIII. 506 Nature her self, though pure of sinful thought. **1719** WATTS *Hymns* I. lxxxvi, How should the sons of Adam's race Be pure before their God? **1790** PALEY *Horæ Paul.* Concl., His morality is everywhere calm, pure, and rational. **1849** MACAULAY *Hist. Eng.* vii. II. 171 A friendship as warm and pure as any that ancient or modern history records. **1851** TENNYSON *To Queen* vii, Her court was pure; her life serene. **1855** MACAULAY *Hist. Eng.* xiii. III. 265 He protested..that his hands were pure from the blood of the persecuted Covenanters.

†**b.** Applied mockingly to Puritans; also to Quakers. *Obs.*

1598 MARSTON *Sco. Villanie* I. i, Lucia, new set thy ruffe; tut, thou art pure, Canst thou not lispe 'good brother', look demure? **1601** B. JONSON *Poetaster* IV. i, To helpe 'hem to some pure landresses, out of the citie. **1785** G. A. BELLAMY *Apology* II. 45 My mother, from being one of the pure ones, had changed her religion to that of a methodist.

6. Sexually undefiled; chaste.

c **1430** LYDG. *Min. Poems* (Percy Soc.) 8 Alle clad in white, in tokyn of clennes, Lyke pure virgines. **1588** A. KING tr. *Canisius' Catech.* in *Cath. Tractates* (S.T.S.) 209 That blissit Marie remaines still puir virgine. **1591** SHAKS. *1 Hen. VI*, v. iv. 83 And yet forsooth she is a Virgin pure. **1671** MILTON *P.R.* I. 134. **1771** tr. *Horstius' Parad. Soul* App. 21 Hail you, the Sea's bright Star, Who God's pure Mother are. **1904** *Hymns A. & M.* No. 55 A maiden pure and undefiled Is by the Spirit great with child.

7. Free from ceremonial defilement; fit for sacred service or use; 'clean'.

1611 BIBLE *Ezra* vi. 20 The Priestes and the Leuites were purified together, all of them were pure, and killed the Passeouer. **1613** PURCHAS *Pilgrimage* II. xvi. (1614) 199 His [a Jew's] wife hath prepared his dinner, pure meats purely dressed.

IV. 8. a. *slang* or *colloq.* (? orig. *ironical*). A general term of appreciation: Fine, excellent, capital, jolly, nice, splendid. Now *rare* or *Obs.*

1675 WYCHERLEY *Country Wife* III. i, I was quiet enough till my husband told me what pure lives the London ladies live abroad with their dancing, meeting and junketing. **1695** CONGREVE *Love for L.* v. ii, O I have pure news, I can tell you, pure news. *a* **1720** VANBRUGH *Journ. to London* I. ii, A slice of it [goose pie] before supper to-night would have been pure. **1734** MRS. DELANY in *Life & Corr.* (1861) I. 508 Well, is it not pure that we shall meet in a fortnight? **1747** GARRICK *Miss in her Teens* II, The door's double locked, and I have the key in my pocket. *Biddy.* That's pure. **1884** HENLEY & STEVENSON *Deacon Brodie* I. iii. Sc. 3 (1892) 35 O, such manners are pure, pure, pure!

b. In conjunction with another adj.: ***pure and*** ... = nice and..., fine and...; excellently, satisfactorily; thoroughly (= C. 1: cf. 2 above). Now *dial.* (See AND *conj.* 4.)

1742 FIELDING *Jos. Andrews* II. xiv, They [*sc.* hogs] were all pure and fat. **1788** CHARLOTTE SMITH *Emmeline* (1816) IV. 271 You would have been pure and happy to drive about in a one-horse chaise. **1769** ROMAINE *Let.* 27 Oct. (1795) xxvii. 122, I saw Lady H———, who was pure and well. **1865** *Let. to Editor*, In answer to the question 'How do you do?' in Cornwall..they say 'Pure and well, thank you'.

c. *dial.* Quite well, in good health: = PURELY 4 b.

1854 *N. & Q.* 1st Ser. IX. 527/1 The word pure is commonly used in Gloucestershire to express being in good health... 'I hope, Zur, the ladies be all pure.' **1900** *Eng. Dial. Dict.*

d. ***the pure quill***, the genuine article, the real thing. *N. Amer. dial.* or *colloq.*

1884 C. B. LEWIS *Sawed-off Sketches* 23 There's hairs of six different colors sticking in the splinters, and those blood stains are the pure quill. **1893** *N. & Q.* 23 Sept. 248/1 One of your correspondents..states that the expressions, 'the cheese', 'pick of the basket', &c., although now almost obsolete on this side of the Atlantic, are still to be heard in America. The expression 'the pure quill', having a similar meaning, I have often heard used in Canada and in the States. **1917** *Dialect Notes* IV. 327 That tobacco is the pure quill. **1935** H. DAVIS *Honey in Horn* xxi. 330 To prove that his product [*sc.* rattlesnake oil] was the pure quill, he also exhibited..a row of half-gallon fruit-jars, each containing one large live rattler. **1956** N. ALGREN *Walk on Wild Side* ii. 152 A pint of Bottled-in-the-Barn. They drank it down to the half-pint mark. 'That stuff is so good a feller can't hardly bite it off,' Dove told Luke. 'It's the pure quill.'

B. *sb.* (or *absol.*)

1. That which is pure; purity. *poet.*

a **1625** LODGE *Misc. Pieces* ii. Wks. 1883 IV, Her eies shrowd pitie, pietie, and pure. **1667** MILTON *P.L.* VIII. 627 Union of Pure with Pure. **1873** BROWNING *Red Cott. Nt.-cap* II. 735 How heaven's own pure may seem To blush. **1874** TENNYSON *Vivien* 35 The mask of pure Worn by this court. **1898** G. MEREDITH *Odes Fr. Hist.* 6 Earth's warrior Best To win Heaven's Pure.

†**2.** 'Pured' fur: see PURED 2, PUREE[1]. *Obs.*

1512 *Acc. Ld. High Treas. Scot.* IV. 215 For lyning of the said Tanne weluus goune within with puyr.

†**3.** A kept mistress. *Obs. slang.*

1688 SHADWELL *Sqr. Alsatia* II. i, Where's..the Blowing, that is to be my Natural, my Convenient, my Pure. *a* **1700** B. E. *Dict. Cant. Crew, Pure*, a Mistress. **1725** in *New Cant. Dict.*

4. A 'pure' physician or surgeon: see the adj., sense 2 d. *Med. colloq.*

1827 *Lancet* 15 Dec. 434/2 Do the Pures profess a kind of surgery in the abstract? **1843** SIR J. PAGET *Let.* 19 Dec. in *Mem.* vi. (1901) 148 The election of the pures in London was not I am told general. [*Note*, The 'pures' were the surgeons in consulting practice.]

5. [Cf. PURE *v.* 1 b.] *Tanning.* Dogs' dung or other substance used as an alkaline lye for steeping hides. Also in *Comb.* as ***pure-collector***, ***-finder***, ***-finding***. (Also spelt *pewer*, *puer.*)

1845 G. DODD *Brit. Manuf.* V. ix. 189 A solution called the 'pure' or the 'pewer' is prepared in a large vessel, and into this the skins are immersed. **1851** MAYHEW *Lond. Labour* II. 142 Dogs'-dung is called 'Pure', from its cleansing and purifying properties. *Ibid.*, The name of 'Pure-finders'..has been applied to the men engaged in collecting dogs'-dung from the..streets. *Ibid.*, There are about 30 tanyards..and these all have their regular Pure collectors. **1858** SIMMONDS *Dict. Trade, Puer*, a tanner's name for dogs' dung. *Ibid., Pure, Pewer.* **1946** *Thorpe's Dict. Appl. Chem.* (ed. 4) VII. 264/2 Modern artificial bates have replaced almost completely the older 'dung bate' or puer, an infusion of dog- or, less often, pigeon-dung.

6. A genuine person. *rare.*

1924 W. M. RAINE *Troubled Waters* xix. 201 You-all are losing a better man than Missie ever had. He's a pure, Mac is.

C. *adv.*

1. Absolutely, entirely, thoroughly, quite. Also, with verbs: just, simply; really, truly.

In early use from sense 3 b of the adj.; in 18th c. *slang* or *colloq.*, from sense 8 b; now *dial.* (esp *U.S.*).

1297 R. GLOUC. (Rolls) 1542 He bicom sone þer after pur gidy & wod. **1340** HAMPOLE *Pr. Consc.* 2499 He says 'our ille dedys er pur ille wroght, Bot our gud dedis pur gud er noght'. *c* **1394** *P. Pl. Crede* 170 Þe pris of a plouȝ-lond..To aparaile þat pyler were pure lytel. *c* **1491** CAXTON *Chast. Goddes Chyld.* 89 It is pure easy..to folow god and serue hym in tyme of tranquylite. **1560** DAUS tr. *Sleidane's Comm.* 37 This yere [1522] departed Reucline, a pure aged man [*ætate gravis*]. **1710** SWIFT *Jrnl. to Stella* 23 Sept., Ballygall will be a pure good place for air. **1750** *Let.* 29 May in *Mrs. Delany's Life & Corr.* (1861) II. 548 Your amiable and worthy sister is pure well. **1810** *Splendid Follies* I. 78 The course will be pure swampy in some parts. **1928** J. PETERKIN *Scarlet Sister Mary* iii. 27 My jaws pure leak water just to look at em. *Ibid.* 35 What you done pure cuts my heart-strings. **1932** W. FAULKNER *Light in August* (1933) xv. 332 He was pure crazy by now, standing on the corner and yelling at whoever would pass. **1937** *Frontier & Midland* Autumn 13/2 Hit was puore accidental and it was with a shotgun he was unloadin. **1942** W. FAULKNER in *Sat. Even. Post* 28 Mar. 38/3, I would pure cut a throat if it would bring you back to stay.

2. Purely, in various senses; simply, merely; rightly; chastely. *poet. rare.*

c **1460** G. ASHBY *Dicta Philos.* 590 A kynge shude be right besy and studious To gouerne his Roiaulme & his people pure. **1601** SHAKS. *Twel. N.* v. i. 86 For his sake, Did I expose my selfe (pure for his loue) Into the danger. **1602** —— *Ham.* III. iv. 158 O throw away the worser part of it, And liue the purer with the other halfe.

3. Qualifying an adj. of colour (chiefly *white*): Purely, with no admixture of any other colour.

(Not always clearly distinguishable from *pure* adj.: cf. a pure white rose: a rose whose colour is a pure white.)

1297 R. GLOUC. (Rolls) 182 So clene & vair & pur ȝwit among oþere men hii beþ. **1530** PALSGR. 259/2 Pure white sylke, *soye bissine.* **1611** SHAKS. *Wint. T.* III. iii. 22. *a* **1618** SYLVESTER *Spectacles* xxxiv, The Lily (first) pure-whitest Flow'r of any. **1853** W. GREGORY *Inorg. Chem.* (ed. 3) 256 Gold is distinguished by its pure yellow colour.

D. *Comb.*: **a.** parasynthetic, as ***pure-blooded*** (also *fig.*), ***-bosomed***, ***-coloured***, ***-eyed***, ***-hearted***, ***-mannered***, ***-minded***, ***-natured***, ***-sighted***, ***souled***, ***toned*** adjs.; ***pure-mindedness***; **pure-relational** *Linguistics* (see quots.); **pure-watered** *a.*, of unmarred brilliance (cf. WATER *sb.* 20). **b.** adverbial and complemental, as ***pure-bred*** (also *absol.* and *fig.*), ***-driven***, ***-living***, ***-washed***; **pure-breeding**, producing genetically similar progeny.

1850 L. H. GARRARD *Wah-To-Yah* vii. 109 The unfair horsetrader might have taken my scalp for presuming to dictate to him, a..*pure-blooded Cheyenne. **1886** C. SCOTT *Sheep-Farming* 157 Breeding pure-blooded rams for sale. **1892** W. JAMES in *Philos. Rev.* I. 149 They have quite as little [aptitude] as the pure-blooded philosophers have for discovering particular facts. **1903** *Rep. Kansas State Board Agric. 1901–02* II. 63 A quarter of a billion acres of grass, nurturing 10,000,000 head of cattle..can be doubled in value in a single decade, if only pure-blooded sires are used in all the cow herds during this time. **1868** *Rep. U.S. Commissioner Agric.* (1869) 10 Specimens of *pure-bred domestic fowls. **1903** *Biometrika* II. 171 Pure-bred mice usually are inbred. **1919** 'W. N. P. BARBELLION' *Jrnl. Disappointed Man* 179 If only I were pure-bred science or pure-bred art. **1923** D. H. LAWRENCE *Birds, Beasts & Flowers* 177 Sensitive mother Kangaroo. Her sensitive, long, pure-bred face, Her full antipodal eyes. **1927** HALDANE & HUXLEY *Animal Biol.* ii. 68 The original pure-bred rose-comb stock gives nothing but rose-combs. **1937** K. BLIXEN *Out of Africa* iii. 191 A stud-farm of purebreds. **1945** [see GRADE *sb.* 7]. **1976** *Sci. Amer.* Sept. 186/3 The object is merely to incorporate new traits into the heterogeneous population, not to create a purebred variety. **1976** *Cumberland News* 3 Dec. 15/3 In the live cattle section the pure-breds have made a come-back with a sharp rise in entries from 294 in 1975 to 318 this year. **1927** HALDANE & HUXLEY *Animal Biol.* ii. 69 We should get four *pure-breeding types in the second generation. **1964** D. MICHIE in G. H. Haggis et al. *Introd. Molecular Biol.* viii. 206 Griffith injected mice with living pneumococci of a pure-breeding strain lacking the polysaccharide capsule characteristic of most members of this species. **1634** MILTON *Comus* 213 O welcom *pure-ey'd Faith, white-handed Hope,..And thou unblemish't form of Chastity. **1832** J. G. WHITTIER in S. T. Pickard *Life & Lett. J. G. Whittier* (1894) I. iii. 108 Those who o'er our tarnished honor grieve..the *pure-hearted and the gifted. **1896** ABP. BENSON in *Nat. Church* Feb. 51/2 Pray we for a temperate, a *pure-living people. **1819** SHELLEY *Peter Bell* VI. xxxiv, The most sublime, religious, *Pure-minded poet. **1891** G. MEREDITH *One of our Conquerors* III. vii. 135 He might have put a reluctant faith in the *puremindedness of these aspirations, without reverting to her origin. **1855** BAGEHOT *Coll. Works* (1965) I. 319 They are emphatically *pure-natured and firm-natured. Instinctively casting aside the coarse temptations and crude excitements of a vulgar earth, [etc.]. **1913** J. MASEFIELD *Daffodil Fields* 12 Gentle she seemed, pure-natured, thoughtful, wise. **1921** E. SAPIR *Language* v. 107 **Pure Relational Concepts* (purely abstract): normally expressed by affixing non-radical elements to radical elements..or by their inner modification, by independent words, or by position; serve to relate the concrete elements of the proposition to each other, thus giving it definite syntactic form. *Ibid.* vi. 145 Languages that keep the syntactic relations pure and that do not possess the power to modify the significance of their radical elements by means of affixes or internal changes. We may call these *Pure-relational non-deriving languages* or, more tersely, *Simple Pure-relational languages.* These are the languages that cut most to the bone of linguistic expression. *Ibid.*, Languages that keep the syntactic relations pure and that also possess the power to modify the significance of their radical elements by means of affixes or internal changes. These are the *Pure-relational deriving languages* or *Complex Pure-relational languages.* **1944** R. A. HALL *Hungarian Gram.* (Language Monograph No. 21) 22 There are three fundamental types of suffixes which are added to substantives: derivational (the plural suffix), concrete-relational (the personal possessive suffixes, expressing ownership of the object denoted by the noun, on the part of the person indicated by the suffix), and pure-relational (twenty suffixes, including the accusative, whose addition gives the substantive adverbial function). **1945** *Language* XXI. 255 This analysis results in three pure-relational categories in Hungarian: case suffixes, suffixed postpositions, and free postpositions. The former two classes can be grouped together as pure-relational suffixes, to preserve both Hall's (originally Sapir's) term and class. **1963** N. N. POPPE *Tatar Manual* ii. 34 Pure-relational suffixes are added to the concrete-relational (possessive) suffixes... The pure-relational suffixes serve to denote the relations between an object and other objects or between an object and an action. The system of pure-relational forms is what is commonly called 'declension'. **1596** SPENSER *Hymn Heavenly Love* 276 All earthes glorie..[will] Seeme durt and drosse in thy *pure-sighted eye. **1910** F. M. FORD *Let.* 28 Oct. (1965) 45 When you—the unscrupulous villain and I, the *pure-souled Idealist join forces how *that* dovecote will flutter! **1923** F. L. PACKARD *Four Stragglers* II. vii. 220 A girl, high-minded, pure-souled. **1869** J. G. WHITTIER *Among Hills* 36 Through her his civic service shows A *purer-toned ambition; No double consciousness divides The man and politician. **1801** BLOOMFIELD *Rural T.* 86 On the *pure-wash'd sand. **1851** H. MELVILLE *Moby Dick* III. vii. 56 In the clear air of day,..the *pure-watered diamond drop will healthful glow. **1929** BLUNDEN *English Poems* (rev. ed.) 54 Here yet its fruit-trees shield love-nooks, Its well's pure-watered diamond.

c. pure-cone, -rod *attrib.*, having only cones, or rods, as photoreceptors; **pure food** *attrib.*, of or concerned with the maintenance and promotion of purity in food through the control of additives, avoidance of the use of chemical fertilizers, or the like; **pure-jet** *Aeronaut.*: usu. *attrib.*, denoting engines, aircraft, etc., in which all thrust is provided directly by reaction to the exhaust jet, without the assistance of fans or propellers; **pure-rod** *attrib.*: see *pure-cone* above.

1942 G. L. WALLS *Vertebrate Eye* iii. 73 Perfectly familiar to all is the increase of visual acuity with intensity... If we knew very accurately this relationship for pure-rod and *pure-cone animals, we would expect to find their curves of acuity-versus-intensity to be kinkless. **1962** *Science Survey* III. 243 One of the American ground squirrels, one of the few mammalian species known to have a pure-cone retina and to be strongly diurnal. **1970** *Jrnl. Marine Biol. Assoc. U.K.* L. 454 There is no evidence of summation in early development which is to be expected in a pure-cone retina. It is, however, surprising that there is also little evidence of summation in the two pure-rod eyes (leptocephalus and macrurid). **1894** *Jrnl. Franklin Inst.* Apr. 267 Senator Paddock, of Nebraska..after years of futile struggle, succeeded in having the Senate pass what is known as the *Pure Food Bill. **1913** *Collier's Weekly* 16 Aug. 24/2 The clubwomen of Idaho are banded together to have their State known as a pure-food State. **1923** WODEHOUSE *Inimitable Jeeves* xvi. 214, I was feeling more or less like something the Pure Food Committee had rejected. **1965** *Punch* 14 July p. xii/2 The *Four Seasons* is another of the popular pure-food centres. **1969** 'I. DRUMMOND' *Man with Tiny Head* xiv. 161 He was..a pure-food fanatic with a hatred of chemical fertilisers. **1946** *Jrnl. R. Aeronaut. Soc.* L. 360/2 The weight of a *pure jet engine, as compared with that of the aeroplane in which it had to be fitted..was small. **1959** *Daily Tel.* 2 Mar. 16/4 A pure-jet plane may evade interception. **1960** C. H. GIBBS-SMITH *Aeroplane* xvi. 127 Turboprop engines are ideal for commercial airliners whose operations take them too far from the optimum conditions of altitude and speed necessary for the economic use of the pure jet. **1969** *Jane's Freight Containers 1968–69* 415/1 By..1975, Lockheed will possess unrivalled knowledge of operating large, pure-jet freighters. **1942** *Pure-rod [see *pure-cone* above]. **1962** *Science Survey* III. 242 In 'pure-rod' eyes the retinal structure is always the limiting factor for visual acuity and in these eyes it is always poor. **1970** [see *pure-cone* above.]

pure, *v.* Also (sense 1 b) puer. [a. OF. *purer*:—L. *pūrāre* to purify (with religious rites), f. *pūrus* PURE.]

1. †**a.** *trans.* To make pure; to cleanse, purify, refine (*lit.* and *fig.*). *Obs.* exc. as in b.

c **1340** HAMPOLE *Prose Tr.* 16 Þat saule þat es purede in þe fyre of lufe of Godd. **13..** *E.E. Allit. P.* B. 1116 Þou may..pure þe with penaunce tyl þou a perle worþe. *c* **1400** MAUNDEV. (Roxb.) xxxiii. 149 Þe whilk pissemyres kepez bisily and pures þe gold and disseuerez þe fyne gold fra þe vnfyne. *c* **1460** G. ASHBY *Dicta Philos.* 90 Ye must pure youre selfe fyrst withoute blame. **1581** T. HOWELL *Deuises* (1879) 217 As fyre by heate the Golde doth fine and pure. **1608** MIDDLETON *Fam. Love* III. iii, If you be unclean..you may pure yourself. **1635** HEYWOOD *Hierarch.* v. 242 The Light, pur'd and refin'd.

b. *Tanning.* To cleanse (hides) by steeping them in a bate or alkaline lye. (Cf. PURE *sb.* 5.)

1845 G. DODD *Brit. Manuf.* V. ix. 190 After being 'pured' for some time, the skins are taken out and scraped well. **1883** *Workshop Receipts* Ser. II. 366/2 They [calf-skins] are then unhaired and fleshed in the usual manner, pured with a bate of dog's dung. **1907** *Camb. Mod. Hist. Prospectus* 100 Bating or puring as it is called, is a process by which all but a very small amount of the natural grease is removed from the skin. **1913** D. J. LAW in G. Martin *Industr. & Manuf. Chem.: Organic* XIX. 580 The goods are then 'puered', which operation consists in paddling in a weak warm infusion of fermented dog-dung.

†**2.** (?) *intr.* To become pure. *rare.*

c **1315** SHOREHAM *Poems* i. 67 And aldey he to senne falleþ, Her ne moȝe nauȝt pury Of serewnessche.

Hence **'puring** *vbl. sb.*

1897 [see GRAINERING *vbl. sb.*]. **1897** *Hide & Leather* 22 May 21/1 After puring, rinse well and work on flesh side. **1898** *Ibid.* 17 Dec. 25/2 The excrement used in puring should be as fresh as possible, hen manure being used for hides, pig manure for calfskin and dog's dung for goats. **1964** H. HODGES *Artifacts* xi. 150 This process of plumping, bating or puering, was essentially one of partial putrefaction. **1972** *Materials & Technol.* V. xii. 401 Puering and bating assist in the removal of short hairs, lime soaps, and cementing substances in the skin.

pure, obs. form of PORE *v.*, POOR.

pureanis, i.e. *pure anis*: see PUIRANIS.

pure-blind(e, obs. forms of PURBLIND.

pure blood, *sb.* and *a.* [f. PURE *a.* + BLOOD *sb.*]

A. *sb.* **1.** Unmixed inheritance or ancestry. Also *fig.*

1776 [see BLOOD *sb.* 8]. **1884** J. F. MAURICE *F. D. Maurice* II. ii. 62 A number of the political economists of pure blood, who were..the fiercest in opposition to co-operation. **1945** M. F. A. MONTAGU *Introd. Physical Anthropol.* vii. 201 The term 'blood-relationship'..enshrines the belief that all biological relationships are reflected in, and are to a large extent, determined by the character of the blood. Such terms as..'pure blood',..and 'good blood' further reflect that meaning. **1963** [see sense B]. **1971** *Biol. Abstr.* LII. 12246/2 Investigation on the possibility of improving important properties of Sjenica sheep by breeding in pure blood and crossing with Corriedale and Precoce.

2. An animal or breed of unmixed inheritance.

1882 *Harper's Mag.* May 895/1 The half and quarter breeds..seem to have..greater powers of resistance than the pure-bloods. **1894** *Rep. Vermont Board Agric.* XIV. 166 Having bred pure bloods for almost thirty years. **1903** *Rep. Kansas State Board Agric. 1901–2* II. 63 Fifty per cent. can be added to the value if pure-bloods only are used in the northern half of this territory.

B. *adj.* Also hyphened. Of unmixed inheritance or ancestry; pure-bred.

1860 *Trans. State Agric. Soc. Michigan* X. 355 The Durham cattle will keep as easy..as the pure blood, elegantly-constructed sprightly Devon. **1888** *Rep. Vermont Board Agric.* X. 49 Why don't you get some pure blood Holsteins? **1963** *English Studies* XLIV. 21 Only he and the other bears and the deer are pure-blood, and he is not so much distinguished from these other animals by his size and his age as he is representative of all pure blood, of all wildness before blood is mixed, of the wilderness itself. *Ibid.* 22 A pure-blood line Old Ben.

†**pured**, *ppl. a.* (*sb.*) *Obs.* Also 5 purid, -yd. [f. PURE *v.* + -ED[1].]

1. Purified, cleansed; refined.

13.. *Gaw. & Gr. Knt.* 633 Gawan was for gode knawen, & as golde pured. *c* **1400** MAUNDEV. (1839) xx. 217 Bordured alle aboute with pured Gold. *c* **1430** LYDG. *Min. Poems* (Percy Soc.) 173 Wedyde the cokkelle frome the puryd corne. **1509** HAWES *Past. Pleas.* xvii. Kj b, Mercury.. About the ayre castinge his pured lyght. **1513** *Bradshaw's St. Werburge, Balade to Auctour* (E.E.T.S.) 200 This delicious werke Thus surely sette by pured science.

2. Of fur: Trimmed or cut down so as to show one colour only. (Cf. PURE *a.* 1 a.)

pured gris or ***grey***, the grey fur of the back of the squirrel in winter, without any of the white of the belly. ***pured calabre, miniver***, the white belly part of these furs, with the dark or grey sides trimmed off. (Cf. also b, and PUREE *sb.*[1])

Beside pured miniver (*minutus varius puratus, menever puree*), the 14-16th c. records have also *m. v. dimidio puratus*, half-pured miniver, in which a narrow strip of the grey colour was left at the edges. (John Hodgkin.)

13.. *Gaw. & Gr. Knt.* 154 With pelure pured apert þe pane ful clene. *Ibid.* 1738 In a mery mantyle..furred ful fyne with fellez, wel pured. [**1363** *Rolls of Parlt.* II. 279 Et q'ils ne usent..Cloche, Mantel, ne Goune, fururez de menevoir purez.] *c* **1420** *Chron. Vilod.* cccxxxi, þe mantyl þ[t] was furuyd w[t] puryd gray. *c* **1450** *Brut* 434 Thanne was don on the Bisshop an abbite..of fyne Scarlet furrid with purid werke. **1463-4** *Rolls of Parlt.* V. 505 Their wyfes, may use and were the forseid Furres of Mattrones, Funes, Letyce, pured Grey, or pured Menyver. **1503** *Acc. Ld. High Treas. Scot.* II. 221 Payit to Pyeris Mainiryng, Maister of the Quenis wardrob, for vj tymir of pured calabar to the samyn, ilk tymir xxxiiijs. **1505** *Ibid.* III. 43 For xvj bakkis of pured gray; ilk pece xvjd.

b. *ellipt.* as *sb.* 'Pured' miniver: cf. PUREE *sb.*[1]

c **1435** *Chron. London* (1905) 95 Ther was putte vpon the bisshop a cardynall habyte off Skarlette furred with puredd. *c* **1450** *Ibid.* 131 A ffrerys coope of ffyne scarlett ffurred with puryd. *c* **1450** LOVELICH *Merlin* 4460 Jn the kynges tyme.. that aftyr the schal regnen in pured & palle.

pure D, puredee (ˈpjʊədiː), *a.* (and *adv.*) *U.S. dial.* [f. PURE *a.*: cf. D 3, DEE b.] Thoroughgoing, 'regular'. Also as *adv.*

1941 J. STREET *In my Father's House* ix. 148 I'm pow'ful fond of Woody. He's a pure D man. *Ibid.* xvi. 346 Mama has got pure D gumption. **1941** *Sat. Even. Post* 6 Dec. 110 It takes a pure D humdinger to hunt birds... If a dog's got pure D hoss sense and a fellow's got bat brains, he can train the dog to hunt birds. **1952** B. HARWIN *Home is Upriver* i. 8 Kip's lip curled at this slovenly practice, one which Pa had always called puredee shif'less. **1964** *Amer. Folk Music Occasional* I. 92 This State you can drink, this State you can't except pure-dee God-given water.

‖**puree, purray**, *sb.*[1] *Obs.* Also 4 purree, 5 purry. [a. AF. *purée*, for F. *puré*, pa. pple. of F. *purer*: see PURE *v.*] = PURED 2 b, i.e. pured or pure white miniver, the belly fur of the grey squirrel in winter, used in the furring of garments.

(In the London Letter Bks. in AF. form *puree*; in 15th c. Sc. as *puray, purray*.)

1351 *Lett. Bk. F. Lond.* lf. 208 Furree de Pellure come de meneueyr, Gris, Purree, Destranlyng, Popell' Desquirels, Bys des Conyns des leures. **1365** *Lett. Bk. G. Lond.* lf. 162 b, Item q' nul del mister entremelle ventres de calabre en furours de puree [in Lett. Bk. H. lf. 39 *in fururis puratis*] ne de menever ne de Bissh [tr. in Riley *Mem. Lond.* (1868) 329 No one of the trade shall mingle bellies of calabre with furs of puree, or of minever, or of bisshes]. **1429** *Sc. Acts Jas. I* (1814) II. 18 þat na man sal weir clathis of silk na furringis of mertrikis, funȝeis, puray, na grece, na nane oþir riche furring bot allanirly knychtis [etc.]. **1455** *Sc. Acts Jas. II* ibid. 43 The vþir lordis of parliament to haif ane mantill of rede rycht sa oppinnit befor and lynyt with silk or furryt with cristy gray, grece, or purray, togiddir with ane hude of the sammyn clath, and furryt as saide is.

purée (ˈpjʊəreɪ, ‖ pyre), *sb.*[2] Rarely in anglicized form ˈpury. [F. *purée* (*puree de pois* pea-soup, 1314 in Hatz.-Darm.), of uncertain and disputed origin.

Hatz.-Darm. take *purée* as the ppl. sb. from the OF. vb. *purer*, in sense 'to squeeze, press out'. Others would identify it with OF. *porée* (see PORRAY), from which it cannot always be separated in sense: cf. med.L. *purea, pureya*, as well as *porea* (1231 in Du Cange), in sense 'pea-soup'. See Scheler, Littré, Brachet.]

A kind of broth or soup made of vegetables, fruit, meat, or fish, boiled to a pulp and passed through a sieve. Also *fig.*

1707 J. MORTIMER *Whole Art of Husbandry* 593 This small Beveridge, or Cider Kin and Puree..is made for the common drinking of Servants, &c. supplying the place of Small-beer. **1723** J. NOTT *Cook's & Confectioner's Dict.* sig. D1, *Artichokes in Puree*..take them out of the Water, and make them into Puree; then strain them through a Sieve as you do Peas. *Ibid.* sig F8[v] Take a Quart of clung Peas, boil them..bruise them to a Mash..and strain the clear Puree. **1824** BYRON *Juan* xv. lxxi, Alas! I must leave undescribed the gibier, The salmi, the consommé, the *purée* [*rime* way]. **18..** —— *Let. to Bowles* Wks. (1846) 603/2 *note*, This stanza contains the *purée* of the whole philosophy of Epicurus. **1887** G. R. SIMS *Mary Jane's Mem.* 84 Mutton cutlets fried in cod liver oil with pury. **1896** *Allbutt's Syst. Med.* I. 392 Pounded fish may be cautiously given, pounded mutton or beef in purée. **1897** *Ibid.* II. 521 A purée of potato. **1929** A. BLACKWOOD *Dudley & Gilderoy* xvi. 183 Of flight and nuts, of hot sunshine, foliage, flowers, of numerous companions, of sex, age, nests and eggs—of all these his golden dreams formed a lovely *purée*. **1951** *Good Housek. Home Encycl.* 623/1 *Purée*, fruit, vegetable, meat or fish pounded or sieved into a finely divided pulp. The thickness of the purée depends on the amount of liquid present before sieving: a purée of cooked green peas and potatoes..is very stiff and can be piped for decoration.

purée (ˈpjʊəreɪ), *v.* [f. prec.] *trans.* To make into a purée. Also *fig.* Hence **ˈpuréed** *ppl. a.*

1934 WEBSTER, *Purée*.., to boil to a pulp and rub through a sieve. **1948** *Good Housek. Cookery Bk.* I. 55 *To purée*, to rub (vegetables and fruit) through a sieve [etc.]. **1951** *Good Housek. Home Encycl.* 251/1 Sieves are used..for puréeing foods. **1959** J. THURBER *Years with Ross* xiv. 223 He puréed his own peas. **1961** *Listener* 31 Aug. 331/2 A combined grinder-liquidizer..purées fruit and cooked vegetables, in seconds. **1963** HUME & DOWNES *Penguin Cordon Bleu Cookery* ix. 357 (*heading*) Puréed and Mousseline potatoes. **1973** *Daily Tel.* (Colour Suppl.) 9 Nov. 79/1 Purée the sugar, butter, powdered almonds and most of the cointreau in a blender to obtain a light and frothy cream. **1977** *Time* 21 Feb. 47/3 There are certain plays—and this is one of them—that can be called 'blender drama': puréed bits of other, better works.

purel(l, Sc. var. PORAIL *Obs.*, poor people.

purely (ˈpjʊəlɪ), *adv.* [f. PURE *a.* + -LY[2].] In a pure manner or degree: in various senses.

1. a. Without (physical) admixture, esp. of anything that stains or impairs; cleanly, clearly, spotlessly.

1509 HAWES *Past. Pleas.* xx. (Percy Soc.) 97 The fayre carbuncle, so ful of clerenes, That in thee truely dyd moost purely shyne. *c* **1600** DRAYTON *Elegy to Lady I.S.* 65 The Sunnes rayes..Bent on some obiect, which is purely white. **1824** MISS MITFORD *Village* Ser. I. (1863) 120 The purely grey rouleau..showed its mixture of black and white. **1864** TENNYSON *Aylmer's Field* 458 The soft river-breeze..on him breathed Far purelier in his rushings to and fro.

†**b.** So as to make pure or clean; so as to cleanse. *Obs.*

1576 BAKER *Jewell of Health* 232 b, Washe dilygentlye and purelie the bodie. **1611** BIBLE *Isa.* i. 25, I will..purely purge away thy drosse. **1669** WORLIDGE *Syst. Agric.* 27 It may be purely separated from its Husk by a Mill. **1683** MOXON *Mech. Exerc., Printing* xi. ¶ 15 These Ribs must be purely Smooth-fil'd and Pollish'd.

2. a. Without mixture of anything different (in non-physical or general sense); simply, merely; exclusively, solely; ...and nothing else: often implying 'entirely' (cf. b, and ENTIRELY 3).

c **1350** *Will. Palerne* 4219 We alle..neuer-more for no man mowe be deliuered..but purli þourh ȝour help. *c* **1380** WYCLIF *Wks.* (1880) 47 þat þei putte not glosis vnto þe reule ..but..sympliche and pureliche to seie & to write þe reule. *c* **1450** tr. *De Imitatione* II. v. 45 Lete no þyng be gret or hye or acceptable to þe, but purely god. **1552** HULOET, Purely, *liquido, mere, pure, puriter, Syncere.* **1662** J. DAVIES tr. *Mandelslo's Trav.* 5 Whether they had been..set there in the air purely for show. **1710** BERKELEY *Princ. Hum. Knowl.* §122 Reasonings and controversies purely verbal. **1883** GILMOUR *Mongols* xxxi. 362 The Government duty they have to perform seems to be purely formal. **1890** *Academy* 8 Nov. 415/2 There were..no children of origin purely Egyptian.

b. Of degree or extent: Absolutely, thoroughly, perfectly, completely, fully, utterly, entirely. Now *U.S. dial.*

1297 R. GLOUC. (Rolls) 1512 þe king louede is wif anon so purliche & so vaste þat al is herte onliche on hire on he caste. **1377** LANGL. *P. Pl.* B. XIII. 260 Ne [may] masse make pees amonges cristene peple, Tyl pruyde be purelich fordo. *c* **1400-50** *Alexander* 187 And þe province of Persee purely distruye. **1585** J. HILTON *Recant.* in Fuller *Ch. Hist.* (1655) x. vi. §27 The said Errours..I utterly abjure, forsake, and purely renounce. *a* **1656** HALES *Gold. Rem.* III. *Serm.*, etc. (1673) 44 A Gentleman..purely ignorant, yet greatly desirous to seem learned. **1938** M. K. RAWLINGS *Yearling* xiv. 140, I purely hate to think the Forresters has trapped 'em. **1952** B. HARWIN *Home is Upriver* xxi. 198 I'd purely like to see that old woman. She'd be glad. **1970** S. ELLIN *Bind* lvii. 285, I purely wish you wouldn't point that thing at me..there's all kinds of accidents can happen with a gun. **1975** J. F. BURKE *Death Trick* iv. 63 Managers of casbahs [i.e. hotels] like the Castlereagh purely loathe the sight of cops.

†**c.** Really, actually, truly, genuinely. *Obs.*

1297 R. GLOUC. (Rolls) 3323 Icholle make þi sulue..Abbe al þe fourme of þe erl as þou were purliche he. **1393** LANGL. *P. Pl.* C. XVI. 226 He haþ the power þat seynt peter hadde, He haþ pureliche þe pot with þe same salue.

d. *Law.* Without conditions, unconditionally.

1427 *Rolls of Parlt.* IV. 327/1 Y[e] open declaration.. subscribed pureli and simply. *a* **1661** FULLER *Worthies* (1662) I. 183 This his gift was a gift indeed, purely bestowed on the colledge, as loded with no detrimentall Conditions. **1880** MUIRHEAD *Gaius* III. §113 If I have stipulated purely, he may stipulate conditionally.

3. a. Without mixture of anything deteriorating or debasing; without blemish, corruption, baseness, or uncleanness; faultlessly; properly, rightly, correctly; guilelessly, innocently, chastely.

1526 *Pilgr. Perf.* (W. de W. 1531) 158 To behaue you purely, &..to apply yourselfe to labour in the seruyce of god. **1537** (*title*) The Byble, whych is all the holy Scripture: In whych are contayned the Olde and Newe Testament truelye and purely translated into Englishe by Thomas Matthewe. **1606** SHAKS. *Tr. & Cr.* IV. v. 169 Faith and troth, Strain'd purely from all hollow bias drawing. **1674** T. FLATMAN *To Mr. Faithorn* 6 One line speaks purelier Thee, than my best strain. **1823** BYRON *Juan* XIV. xcii, Or Germany, where people *purely* kiss.

b. So as to be ceremonially clean.

1613 [see PURE *a.* 7].

4. a. *slang* or *colloq.* Finely, excellently, capitally; nicely, satisfactorily, very well. Now *rare* or *Obs.*

1695 CONGREVE *Love for L.* II. ii, You can keep your countenance purely, you'd make an admirable player. **1712-13** SWIFT *Jrnl. to Stella* 1 Jan., Am I not purely handled between a couple of puppies? **1756** A. MURPHY *Apprentice* II. ii, That will do purely. *a* **1845** HOOD *Last Man* xxi, To see me so purely drest.

b. *dial.* Quite well, in good health. (Used predicatively like an adj.; cf. *well, ill, poorly*.)

1796 M. EDGEWORTH *Old Poz* in *Parent's Assistant* (ed. 2) 2nd Ser. II. 55 I'm glad to see your worship look so purely. **1809** —— *Absentee* xvi. (*Tales* 1825 X. 321), If the ladies' prayers are of any avail, you ought to be purely. **1828** *Craven Gloss.* (ed. 2) s.v., 'How's thy mam?' 'Purely, thank ye.' **1857** HUGHES *Tom Brown* I. ii, Well I never! you do look purely. **1859** THACKERAY *Virgin.* xxxiv, 'I hope the dear ladies are well, sir?' 'The ladies are purely.'

pureness (ˈpjʊənɪs). [f. PURE *a.* + -NESS.] The quality of being pure; purity.

1. Freedom from admixture; simplicity, homogeneity.

c **1485** *Digby Myst.* (1882) III. 322 þis soft metell led, nat of so gret puernesse. *a* **1618** RALEIGH (J.), An essence..of absolute pureness and simplicity. **1675** R. VAUGHAN *Coinage* 14 A proof of the pureness of the metal. **1695** LD. PRESTON *Boeth.* v. 240 His knowledg..remaineth in the Pureness & Simplicity of its Presence.

2. Freedom from defilement or blemish; cleanness; faultlessness, correctness.

1528 PAYNELL *Salerne's Regim.* O ij b, Many fynnes and skales betoken the purenes of the fyshes substance. *a* **1568** ASCHAM *Scholem.* II. (Arb.) 144 In all this good proprietie of wordes, and purenesse of phrases which be in Terence. *a* **1698** TEMPLE *Ess. A. & M. Learn.* Wks. 1760 I. 157 Great Pureness of Air, and Equality of Climate.

3. Freedom from moral blemish; innocence; sincerity; chastity.

1398 TREVISA *Barth. De P.R.* XIV. xxxv. (1495) 480 Mount Synay hyghte the mount of purenesse and of clennesse, for none myght come to the mount but those that were clene in bodi and in soule. **1526** TINDALE *2 Cor.* i. 12 With godly purenes. **1591** SPENSER *Daphn.* xxxv, She in purenesse heauen it self did pas. **1624** QUARLES *Sion's Sonn.* xv. 7 Virgin pureness. **1708** H. DODWELL *Nat. Mort. Hum. Souls* 149 To manage all Disputes..with..Pureness from Humane Passions. **1840** CLOUGH *Dipsychus* I. ii. 41 And thou, clear heaven, Look pureness back into me.

4. Ceremonial cleanness.

[Cf. quot. 1398 in 3]. **1607** *Schol. Disc. agst. Antichr.* I. ii. 78 Holy purenes from all communion with vncleane Gentiles. **1643** MILTON *Divorce* II. vi. Wks. 1851 IV. 77 Inflicting death..for the mark of a circumstantiall purenes omitted.

purete, -ty, obs. forms of PURITY.

‖**pur et simple** (pyr e sɛ̃pl), *a.* [Fr.] = *pure and simple* s.v. PURE *a.* 3 a (the more usual form).

1856 *Sat. Rev.* 5 Apr. 451/1 Mr. Disraeli fights for a Blue-book, *pur et simple*. **1864** BAGEHOT *Coll. Works* (1965) II. 300 Inherent eccentricity, oddity *pur et simple*, is *immiscible* in the great ocean of universal thought. **1871** LYTTON *Coming Race* xvi. 137 The great-grandfather was a magnificent specimen of the Batrachian genus, a Giant Frog, *pur et simple*. **1880** E. W. HAMILTON *Diary* 18 Nov. (1972) I. 77 Chamberlain..says that resort to such [extraordinary] powers *pur et simple* must entail his resignation.

Purex (ˈpjʊərɛks). [App. f. PUR(IFICATION + EX(TRACTION.] The name of an industrial process for separating the plutonium and uranium from spent uranium fuel by using tri-*n*-butyl phosphate as a solvent.

1956 *Proc. Internat. Conf. Peaceful Uses of Atomic Energy* IX. 471/1 A schematic chemical flowsheet for the Purex process is shown. **1976** *Sci. Amer.* Dec. 33/3 When the separated uranium and plutonium streams emerge from the Purex process, they contain only about a millionth as much radioactivity due to fission products as the feed material did.

purfle (ˈpɜːf(ə)l), *sb.* Forms: 4 porfyl, -fil, purf(i)el, 4-5 purfil(e, -fyle, 4-6 -fyl, 5-6 -fell, -full, 6 -ful, -fyll, -fele, -phell, 6- purfle. Also (in sense 2) 6 purflue; (in sense 3) 7 porfil(e, -phile, 7-8 pourfil. See also PROFILE. [a. OF. *porfil* (*c* 1215 in Godef.), later *pourfil* (1316, and 1611 in Cotgr. in sense 2), a border or edge; = Pr. *perfil*, Sp. *perfilo*, med.L. *perfilum*, It. *profilo*, PROFILE; prob. verbal sb. from *profilare, perfilāre*, etc.: see PURFLE *v.*]

1. A border; *esp.* a wrought or decorated border; the embroidered border or edge of a garment.

In ordinary use app. obs. after 1610; revived as an archaism in 19th c. (But cf. quot. *c* 1758 in PURFLE *v.* 1.)

13.. *E.E. Allit. P.* A. 216 Of precios perle in porfyl pyȝte. **1362** LANGL. *P. Pl.* A. IV. 102 Til..perneles porfyl [*v.rr.* purfil, purfyl] be put in heore whucche. *c* **1430** LYDG. *Min. Poems* (Percy Soc.) 57 A lewde wretche to were a skarlet gowne, Withe a blac lamb furre without purfile of sable. *c* **1440** *Promp. Parv.* 416/2 Purfyle of a clothe, *limbus*. *a* **1450** *Knt. de la Tour* (1906) 30 This astate that ye use of gret purfiles and slitte cotes. **1530** PALSGR. 259/2 Purfyll or hemme of a gowne, *bort*. *a* **1548** HALL *Chron., Hen. VIII* 2 b, The Trapper of his Horse, Damaske gold, with a depe purfell of Armyns. **1609** HOLLAND *Amm. Marcell.* XIV. vi. 10 Inner garments..beset with long jagges and purfles. **1610**

—— *Camden's Brit.* II. *Irel.* 148 They cast ouer these their mantells or shagge Rugges..with a deep fringed purfle. **1730** BAILEY, *Purfile*, a Sort of antient Trimming for Womens Gowns, made of Tinsel, Thread, &c., called also Bobbin-Work. **1813** HOGG *Queen's Wake* 292 Furnaced pillars..upright ranged in horrid array, With purfle of green o'er the darksome gray. **1821** JOANNA BAILLIE *Met. Leg., Lady G. Baillie* Concl., Betty's skill Leaves her in purfle, furbelow, or frill, No whit behind. **1894** *Athenæum* 5 May 571/2 The portrait of the gracious court lady in her ruff and purfles.

b. = PURFLING I c (as of a violin).

1706 PHILLIPS (ed. Kersey), *Purfle*... Also a kind of Ornamentation about the Edges of Musical Instruments, particularly of Viols, Violins, &c. **1905** HAWEIS *Old Violins* 125 He runs his purfle into his monogram with attendant flourishes.

†**2.** *Her.* A bordering line. *Obs.*

1562 LEIGH *Armorie* (1597) 90 b, This pale was giuen after it had a chiefe; because they were both of one colour, there goeth no purfle betweene. **1572** BOSSEWELL *Armorie* II. 27 That terme is so frequented, because two colors, or any mettal or colour, be gradately inferred one into the other, that no partition but onely the Purflue maie be seene betwene them.

†**3.** The contour or outline of anything; a representation of the outline; = PROFILE *sb.* 1, 3. *Obs.*

In this sense app. a new adoption from Fr., and there from It. Soon superseded by *profile*.

1601 HOLLAND *Pliny* XXXV. x. II. 535 Hee woon the prise and praise from them all in making up the pourfils and extenuities of his lineaments. **1610** GUILLIM *Heraldry* II. iii. 42 The naked and bare proportion of the outward lineaments thereof, or the outward Tract, Purfle, or shadow of a thing. *Ibid.*, The Portraicting out of any thing vmbrated, is nothing else but a sleight and single draught or Purfle, traced out with a Pensill. **1669** A. BROWNE *Ars Pict.* 83 Draw the lines of porphile (i.e. the outmost stroak) of a Face with lake and white.

†**b.** *in purfle*, as seen from one side; = *in profile* (PROFILE *sb.* 2). *Obs.*

1605 B. JONSON *Masque Blackness*, The backs of some were seen; some in purfle, or side; others in face. **1686** AGLIONBY *Painting Illustr.* 132 Cimabue his Picture is yet to be seen,..made in Porfil. *Ibid.* 268 All the left Side was seen in Porfile. **1706** PHILLIPS, *Pourfil*, (a Term in Painting) as A Face drawn in Pourfil, i.e. side-way; a Side-face.

purfle ('pɜːf(ə)l), *v.* Forms: 4–5 purfile, -fyle, 5 -fill, 5–6 -fell, -fyll, 5–7 -fel, 6 -fyl, -fulle, -phle, 6– purfle. Also 7 (sense 5) pourfil(l, pourfle. [a. OF. *porfiler* (1371 in Godef.), later *porphyler*, *pourfiler* to border, adorn the border of, adorn, = Pr., Sp. *perfilar*, It. *profilare*, med.L. *perfīlāre* (Du Cange), f. L. *prō* or *per* + *fīlum* thread: see PROFILE *v.*]

1. *trans.* To border; to decorate with a wrought or ornamental border; *esp.* to adorn (a robe) with a border of thread work or embroidery; to trim with gold or silver lace, pearls, fur, etc. *arch.*

c **1325** in *Rel. Ant.* II. 19 Hir wede, Purfiled with pellour doun to the teon. *c* **1386** CHAUCER *Prol.* 193, I seigh his sleues ypurfiled at the hond With grys. *c* **1460** *Wisdom* Stage Dir., in *Macro Plays* 36 A mayde, in a wyght clothe of golde ..purfyled with menyver. **1470–85** MALORY *Arthur* I. xxvii. 74 Kyng Ryons had purfyled a mantel with kynges berdes. *c* **1500** *Melusine* xxxv. 240 Robes of cloth of gold, & fourred with Ermynes, & purfylled all with precyous stones. **1502** *Privy Purse Exp. Eliz. of York* (1830) 83 Item for blake crewle to purfulle the rosys vjd. *a* **1548** HALL *Chron., Hen. VIII* 214 The knightes of the bath in uiolet gounes with hoddes purfeled with Miniuer lyke doctors. **1611** COTGR., *Pourfiler d'or*, to purfle, tinsell, or overcast with gold thread, etc. *a* **1625** FLETCHER *Woman's Prize* III. ii, Line the gown through with plush perfumed, and purfle All the sleeves down with pearl! *c* **1758** W. THOMPSON *Hymn to May* ix, A silken camus,..Purfled by Nature's hand! **1803** W. TAYLOR in *Ann. Rev.* I. 332 Like a garment embroidered in chenille, and purfled with beads, and spangles, and foil. **1840** H. AINSWORTH *Tower of Lond.* (1864) 4 The Bishop of Ely, who, in his character of lord high chancellor, wore a robe of scarlet, open before, and purfled with minever.

fig. **1607** *Lingua* IV. ii. in Hazl. *Dodsley* IX. 417 This [*Tragedus*] gorgeous-broider'd with rich sentences, That [*Comedus*] fair and purfled round with merriments.

†**b.** To work (a design) in embroidery. *Obs.*

1601 HOLLAND *Pliny* XIII. xi. I. 392 To weave and purfle letters in their cloths, after the manner of embroiderie.

c. *intr.* or *absol.* To do purfling; 'to hem a border' (*Cent. Dict.*).

†**2.** *trans.* To give to (leaves, flowers, etc.) a border or edge of a particular kind; to ornament with such a border; in *pa. pple.*, denoting the outline, contour, or distinctive colouring of the edge.

1562 BULLEYN *Bulwark, Bk. Simples* 49 b, Leaues.. purfled aboute with iagges, or small teeth like a sawe. **1578** LYTE *Dodoens* II. liii. 212 The great Tulpia, or rather Tulipa ..of colour very diuers.. and purfled about the edges or brimmes with yellowe, white, or red. **1640** PARKINSON *Theat. Bot.* IV. v. 428 Flower..consisting of five small pure white leaves, pointed at the ends, and sometimes a little purfled about the brims, and with a wash of purple.

3. In technical applications. †**a.** *Her.*, etc. To border or edge with a line of a different colour or tincture. (See also PURFLED *ppl. a.*[1] 2.) *Obs.*

1634 PEACHAM *Gentl. Exerc.* I. xxvi. 91 A faire blew deepned with lake, and purfled with liquid gold.

b. *Arch.*, etc. To ornament (the edge or ridge of any structure) *with* crockets, etc.: cf. PURFLED 3.

1849 ROCK *Ch. of Fathers* II. vi. 108 All the edges [of the mitre] were purfled with a border of exquisitely-wrought crockets in silver gilt. **1852** *Ibid.* III. i. 390 To this chest [shrine] the goldsmith..gave an architectural form: it had.. its tall crest purfled with knobs of sparkling jewels to run along the ridge of its steeply-pitched roof.

c. To adorn (the back or belly of a violin or other instrument) with a border of inlaid work: see PURFLER, PURFLING I c.

4. In vague or extended sense: To adorn, ornament, beautify.

c **1470** HENRYSON *Mor. Fab.* VIII., *Preach. Swallow* ix, Flouris..Quhilk..Phebus with his goldin bemis gent Hes purfellit and payntit plesandly. **1592** GREENE *Upst. Courtier* D ij, A nose, Autem nose, purphled pretiouslie with pearle and stone like a counterfait worke. **1615** CROOKE *Body of Man* 94 The close Meshes whereof, are purfled with curled veines. **1871** R. ELLIS *Catullus* i. 2 Who shall take thee, the new, the dainty volume, Purfled glossily, fresh with ashy pumice [*arida modo pumice expolitum*]?

†**5.** *trans.* To draw in profile, to outline; to draw. Also *absol.* or *intr.* *Obs.*

1601 HOLLAND *Pliny* XXXV. x. (1634) II. 539 Apelles..had no sooner pourfiled a little about the visage, but the king presently tooke knowledge there by of the partie that had played this pranke by him. *Ibid.* xii. 551 [She] used ordinarily to marke upon the wall the shaddow of her lovers face by candle light and to pourfill the same afterwards deeper, that so shee might enjoy his visage yet in his absence.

purfled ('pɜːf(ə)ld), *ppl. a.*[1] [f. prec. + -ED[1].]

1. Bordered; *esp.* having a decorative or ornamental border; bordered with embroidery, gold lace, fur, etc.; fringed; in vaguer use, embroidered, decorated. Also *fig.*

c **1470** *Compl. Christ* 284 in *Pol. Rel. & L. Poems* (1866) 178 What shalle than prophyte þi gowne purfylled? **1520** *Treat. Galaunt* 141 So many purfled garmentes furred with non sequitur With so many penyles purses hath no man sawe. **1600** HOLLAND *Livy* VII. i. 250 All of the Patritij, sitting like Consuls, with their purfled and pourpled long robes in yvorie chaires of estate. **1634** MILTON *Comus* 995 Flowers of more mingled hew Then her purfl'd scarf can shew. *a* **1717** PARNELL *Misc.* (1807) 30 The purfled border deck'd the floor with gold. **1870** ROSSETTI *Poems, Jenny* 117 But must your roses die, and those Their purfled buds that should unclose?

b. *transf.* Of a person: Decorated with purfling.

1362 LANGL. *P. Pl.* A. II. 9 Þenne was I war of a wommon wonderliche cloþed, Purfylet with pelure þe ricchest vppon eorþe. *a* **1450** *Knt. de la Tour* (1906) 30 Thus she shall be beter purfiled and furred thanne other ladies and gentill women. **1901** *Westm. Gaz.* 23 Oct. 2/1 The Austrian knights with mace and battle-axe, the plumed and purfled *Landvogts* from Bern.

†**c.** *transf.* Applied as a border. *Obs.*

1652 COLLIER in *Benlowes' Theoph.* Pref. Verses, But brighter Theophil behold, Whose Vest is wrought with purfled Gold.

†**2.** *Her.* Said of a charge having a bordering line, or a border or edging of another tincture: see also quot. 1868, and cf. PURFLEWE. *Obs.*

1562 LEIGH *Armorie* (1597) 91 The Fesse was first, & then the Cantone was giuen in rewarde. Being of one colour, they are not purfled. *Ibid.* 180 b, iii Cheuernes, Humettes, counterchanged, Purfled Argent. Ye cannot say bordured, because nothinge may be bordured, that is Humette w^t^in ye Escocheon. **1868** CUSSANS *Her.* (1882) 129 *Purfled*: when applied to a Mantle, implies that it is lined or guarded with fur; and when to Armour, that the studs and rims are of another metal.

3. *Arch.*, etc. (See quots.)

1823 P. NICHOLSON *Pract. Build.* Gloss. 591 *Purfled*, ornamented in a manner resembling drapery, embroidery, or lace-work. **1842–72** GWILT *Archit.* Gloss., *Purfled.* **1843** *Civil Eng. & Arch. Jrnl.* VI. 12 b, The tall and narrow south transept, with its..flying and attached buttresses, perforated parapets, and purfled pinnacles.

†**4.** *vaguely.* Variegated. *Obs.*

1602 CAREW *Cornwall* 110 b, So thou dost line the earth With purfeld streames of blew and white.

'**purfled**, *ppl. a.*[2] *Sc. rare.* 'Short-winded, esp. in consequence of being too lusty' (Jamieson 1808–24); plethoric.

1826 J. WILSON *Noct. Ambr.* Wks. 1855 I. 15 The language is out of condition—fat and fozy, thickwinded, purfled and plethoric.

purfler ('pɜːflə(r)). [f. PURFLE *v.* + -ER[1].] One who purfles; *spec.* one who inlays the ornamentation in violins.

1883 GROVE *Dict. Mus.* III. 53 The prince of purflers was Stradivarius.

†'**purflewe**, *a. Her. Obs.* Also 6 -ffleu, 7–8 -flew. [Obscurely f. PURFLE *v.* or *sb.*; app. orig. *purflewé.*] Having a bordure of a fur.

1562 LEIGH *Armorie* 190 b, The first is plaine,.. commonly called embordured... The vii is termed purffleu, which is, when that the bordure is occupied with anye of the nine furres afore rehersed. **1610** GUILLIM *Heraldry* I. v. (1611) 19 A bordure purflewe, Verrey. Note heere that this terme purflewe is common to all the furres before handled so often as they are vsed in bordures. **1725** *Bradley's Fam. Dict.* s.v. *Bordure*, If the Bordure consists of Ermins, Vairy or any of the Furs, the Term is, Purflew of Ermins.

So †'**purflewed** *ppl. a. Obs.*

1868 CUSSANS *Her.* (1882) 68 Armorists formerly used several distinctive terms in blazoning a charged Bordure, to signify the nature of such a charge: as *Enaluron*, if charged with Birds;..and *Purflewed*, if composed of a Fur. This method is now obsolete.

'**purfling**, *vbl. sb.* [f. PURFLE *v.* + -ING[1].]

1. Bordering, *esp.* the ornamenting of the edge or border of anything; also *concr.* ornamental bordering work, trimming, furring, fringing, etc.

1388 *Calverley Charters* (1904) 204 Pur j furrure de gray pur mesme la goune oue la perfulyng du mesme et la lynure du chaperon. **1483** *Wardr. Acc.* in *Antiq. Rep.* (1807) I. 45 To the furring of every harneys and purfiling of every sadell. ? *a* **1500** *Assembly of Ladies* 527 The coller and the vent, Lyk as ermyne is mad in purfeling. **1611** COTGR., *Pourfileure*, purfling; a purfling lace or work; baudkin-worke; tinselling. **1849** JAMES *Woodman* III. xii. 236 Especially where slashings and purffling..are out of symmetry. **1904** *Westm. Gaz.* 14 May 13/2 Where is the hood and the volupere, Wimple and coif with their purfilings?

b. *Arch.* The ornamentation of an edge or ridge: see PURFLE *v.* 3 b.

1849 ROCK *Ch. of Fathers* II. 106 A purfling of crockets in silver.

c. The inlaid bordering or marginal decoration with which the backs and bellies of violins and the like are often finished.

1848 J. BISHOP tr. *Otto's Violin* i. *note*, Some authors mention only two strips for the purfling, in which case the number of pieces would be reduced to 12. **1884** HAWEIS *Musical Life* I. 228 The purfling, more or less deeply embedded, emphasizes the outline of the violin. It is composed of three thin strips of wood, ebony, sometimes whalebone, the centre of two white strips. **1892** W. H. C[UMMINGS] in *Athenæum* 1 Oct. 457/3 A seventeenth century viol di gamba..remarkable for its beautiful 'purfling' of ebony and ivory.

attrib. **1908** MISS HARRADEN *Interplay* 265, I noticed how well he used the purfling chisel.

†**d.** *vaguely.* ? Decking, adornment. *Obs.*

1615 BRATHWAIT *Strappado* (1878) 150 Pritty-fac'd diuell ..that infects the heart, With painting, purfling and a face of Art. **1630** —— *Eng. Gentlem.* (1641) 60 To spend the whole Morne till the Mid-day in tricking, trimming, painting and purfling.

†**2.** *Her.* A border or contour line. *Obs.*

1610 GUILLIM *Heraldry* III. xi. 120 They be not incorporated one with another, but are diuidedly seuered by interposing the purflings. **1688** R. HOLME *Armoury* III. 148/2 Purfling, Hatching with a Pencill, as Herald Painters finish up their Work.

†**3.** Drawing in outline, outlining. Cf. PROFILE.

1601 HOLLAND *Pliny* II. 525 As for the Greeke writers,.. they all doe jointly agree in this, That the first pourtrait was nothing els but the bare pourfling and drawing onely the shaddow of a person.

purflue, obs. var. PURFLE *sb.* (sense 2).

'**purfly**, *a.* ? *Sc. rare.* = PURFLED *ppl. a.*[2]

1832 CARLYLE *Misc. Ess., Johnson* (1872) IV. 94 The purfly, sandblind lubber and blubber, with his open mouth, and face of bruised honeycomb; yet already dominant, imperial, irresistible! **1832** —— *Note Bk.* 18 Jan., in Froude *Life* (1882) II. 231 A very large, purfly, flabby man.

‖**purga** (pʊə'gɑː, 'pʊəgə). [Russ.] A blizzard of very fine snow in the U.S.S.R.

1889 L. F. GOWING *Five Thousand Miles in Sledge* v. 75 A *purga* was raging—one of those fierce snowstorms which visit with especial violence the eastern shores of Asiatic Russia. **1977** P. E. LYDOLPH *Geogr. U.S.S.R.* (ed. 3) xvii. 377/2 Most of the high winds at Barnaul are associated with cyclonic storms during winter that may produce strong blizzards, the so-called *buran* or *purga*. **1978** *Soviet Geogr.* XIX. 574 A *purga* is not just any snowstorm; it is a violent storm associated with an invasion of cold air.

†'**purgable**, *a. Obs. rare.* [ad. L. *purgābilis*, f. *purgāre* to PURGE: see -BLE. Cf. PURGEABLE.] Capable of being, or that has to be, purged.

1582 N. T. (Rhem.) *1 Cor.* iii. 13 *note*, Whosoever hath any impute matter of Venial sins or such other dettes to Gods iustice paiable & purgable, must into that fire.

†'**purgament.** *Obs.* [ad. L. *purgāment-um*, f. *purgāre* to cleanse, PURGE: see -MENT.]

1. That which is removed or rejected in the process of cleansing; *spec.* that which is excreted from an animal; excrement; filth, offscourings.

1597 J. KING *On Jonas* (1618) 295 In the..bowells of the fish,..where what nutriment hee [Jonah] had amiddest those purgaments and superfluities, the Lord knoweth. **1605** BACON *Adv. Learn.* II. ix. §5 For the humors, they are commonly passed ouer in Anatomies, as purgaments, whereas [etc.]. **1609** J. RAWLINSON *Fishermen* 38 The very paring, and filth, and purgament, and off-scouring of all things. **1676** HOBBES *Iliad* I. 298 And then Atrides th' army purify'd, And threw into the sea the purgament.

b. *transf.* An outgrowth; = EXCREMENT[2] 1.

1650 BULWER *Anthropomet.* ii. 48 These calumnies..that hairs are a Purgament of the body altogether unprofitable.

2. = PURGATION 1 b. *rare.*

1650 BULWER *Anthropomet.* xii. 131 The Beard..serves not for ornament..nor for a covering, nor for purgament.

3. That which purges; a purge, purgative. *rare*$^{-0}$.

1828 WEBSTER, *Purgament*, a cathartic. *Bacon.* [Prob. due to a misunderstanding of quot. 1605 in 1.]

†'**purgate**, *v. Obs. rare*$^{-1}$. [f. L. *purgāt-*, ppl. stem of *purgāre*: see PURGE *v.*[1] and -ATE[3] 5.] *trans.* To purge, purify.

1795 W. TAYLOR in *Monthly Rev.* XVIII. 122 It is by means of fear and pity that the passions are to be purgated.

purgation (pɜːˈgeɪʃən). Also 6 pour-; 4–6 -acion. [a. OF. *purgacion* (12th c. in Hatz.-Darm.), ad. L. *purgātiōn-em*, n. of action from *purgāre* to PURGE.] The action of purging.

1. The clearing away of impurities; the cleansing of anything from impure or extraneous matter; purification.

1412–20 LYDG. *Chron. Troy* II. 749 Þat it [*sc.* the river Xanthus] made a ful purgacioun Of al ordure & fylþes in þe toun. **1564** *Brief Exam.* ***** iv b, You woulde make a purgation of these thynges. **1612** WOODALL *Surg. Mate* Wks. (1653) 273 Purgation like to separation, is the clarification of impure liquor, having a thick sedement and spume by decoction. **1756** *Monitor* No. 74 II. 215 Such a total purgation of Augeas's stable..might possibly excite too great a noise. **1809** PINKNEY *Trav. France* 237 A century will pass before Lyons will recover itself from this Jacobin purgation.

b. *spec.* The discharge of waste matter from the body; excretion or evacuation; now only the evacuation of the bowels, esp. by means of a cathartic; the administration of cathartics; purging.

c **1375** *Sc. Leg. Saints* vi. (*Thomas*) 482 Alsa It is lyk to poycion men takis fore purgacione. *c* **1386** CHAUCER *Wife's Prol.* 120 Maade for purgacioun Of vryne. **1481** CAXTON *Myrr.* II. xx. 110 Other waters..the whiche..make grete purgacions to somme peple. *a* **1548** HALL *Chron., Hen. VIII* 194 b, For very feblenes of nature caused by purgacions and vomites. **1607** TOPSELL *Four-f. Beasts* 426 Purgations is defined by the Physitians, to be the emptiyng or voiding of superfluous humors, annoying the body with their evill quality. **1899** *Allbutt's Syst. Med.* VIII. 474 Promoting purgation and diuresis.

†**c.** Menstruation; *pl.* catamenia. In quot. 1555 applied to the lochia. *Obs.*

1555 EDEN *Decades* 208 When they are delyuered of theyr children, they go to the ryuer and washe them. Which doone, theyr bludde and purgation ceaseth immediatly. **1577** B. GOOGE *Heresbach's Husb.* IV. (1586) 190 b, The roote ..is good against..strangurie, and restraint of womens Purgations. **1645–52** BOATE *Irel. Nat. Hist.* (1860) 141 Among the women there are severall found, who do retain not only their customary purgations, but even their fruitfulness, above the age of fifty yeares. **1737** WHISTON *Josephus* I. xix. 30 Rachel..said that her natural purgation hindred her rising up.

2. Ceremonial or ritual cleansing from defilement or uncleanness; = PURIFICATION 3.

1382 WYCLIF *Luke* ii. 22 Aftir that the dayes of purgacioun of Marie weren fulfild, vp Moyses lawe. **14..** *Hymn to Virgin* in *Tundale's Vis.* (1843) 127 The dayes passed of thi purgacion To fullfyll the precept of the law. *a* **1711** KEN *Hymns Evang.* Poet. Wks. 1721 I. 63 The All-wise God.. Ordain'd Purgation Ritual, to show That nothing Clean cou'd from Uncleanness flow. **1769** BLACKSTONE *Comm.* IV. xiv. 187 Even the slaughter of enemies required a solemn purgation among the Jews.

3. Moral or spiritual cleansing; purification by the destruction or removal of sin, guilt, or any evil; freeing from moral defilement or corruption, from the taint of heresy, etc.; *spec.* in *R. C. Ch.*, the purification of the soul in PURGATORY.

1382 WYCLIF *Heb.* i. 3 The which..makynge purgacioun of synnes, sittith on the riȝthalf vp mageste in hiȝ thingis. *c* **1450** tr. *De Imitatione* III. xxxii. 101 A praier for purgacion of herte and hevenly wisdom. **1482** *Monk of Evesham* (Arb.) 64 A regyon where the soulys the whiche hadd done her purgacyon in purgatorye ioyfully restyd. **1504** ATKYNSON tr. *De Imitatione* I. xxiv. 174 The pourgacion therof [from sin] with the fyre of Pourgatory. **1598** BARCKLEY *Felic. Man* VI. (1603) 599 Hierocles saith that religion is the studie of wisdome, consisting in the purgation and perfection of life. **1682** NORRIS *Hierocles* 89 The former is effected by the purgation of Opinion. *a* **1703** BURKITT *On N.T., Luke* xi. 40 The inward purgation of their hearts and consciences from sin and uncleanness. **1838** PRESCOTT *Ferd. & Is.* (1846) I. vii. 325 The purgation of the land from heresy.

4. The action of clearing oneself from the accusation or suspicion of crime or guilt. *Obs.* exc. *Hist.*

canonical purgation (i.e. as prescribed by the canon law), the affirmation on oath of his innocence by the accused in a spiritual court, confirmed by the oaths of several of his peers. ***vulgar purgation***, a test by the ordeal of fire or water, or by wager of battle.

[*c* **1325** *Mirac. St. Willelmi* in *Hist. Ch. York* (Rolls) II. 542 Adjudicata fuit et purgatio ferri candentis, secundum consuetudinem regni.] ? *c* **1400** *Ploughman's Tale* 342 If a man be falsly famed, And wolde make purgacioun. **1494** FABYAN *Chron.* VI. ccx. (1516) 130 b/2 She [Queen Emma] was blyndefelde and lad vnto the place bytwene .ii. men, where yᵉ Iron laye glowynge hote, and passed the .ix. sharys vnhurte. Than at laste she sayd good Lorde, whan shall I come to the place of my purgacion? **1545** *Reg. Privy Council Scot.* I. 9 [To] mak his purgatioun of the suspicioun that tha have aganis him. **1600** SHAKS. *A.Y.L.* v. iv. 45 If any man doubt that, let him put mee to my purgation. **1611** —— *Wint. T.* III. ii. 7 We..Proceed in Iustice, which shall haue due course, Euen to the Guilt, or the Purgation. **1637** COWELL *Interpr.* s.v., Purgation is either Canonicall or vulgar. **1657** LD. STRICKLAND in *Burton's Diary* (1828) II. 149 [He] said indeed it was more than the Inquisition, which puts a man upon his own purgation. **1768** BLACKSTONE *Comm.* III. xxii. 342. **1788** PRIESTLEY *Lect. Hist.* v. xlviii. 361 The oath of purgation was substituted in the place of battle. **1868** FREEMAN *Norm. Conq.* II. App. H 695 If she [Queen Emma] will make a double purgation, if she will walk over four burning shares for herself, and five for the Bishop, her innocence shall be allowed.

†**5.** An agent or means of purging or cleansing.

a. An aperient medicine; a purgative. *Obs.*

14.. in *Rel. Ant.* I. 195 The body most purget ben..wyth summe gode purgacion That is of hot complexion. **1527** ANDREW *Brunswyke's Distyll. Waters* D j, After that they shall take a stronge purgacyon. **1542** J. HEYWOOD *Prov.* (1867) 33 Ye would..geue me a purgacion. But I am laxatiue inough. **1697** *Phil. Trans.* XIX. 403 She Recovered by Emetiques and Purgations.

†**b.** That which cleanses from sin or defilement, or from anything evil or noxious. *Obs.*

a **1533** FRITH *Answ. to Gardiner* Wks. (1573) 55 But our perfite purgation is the pure bloud of Christ. **1581** MULCASTER *Positions* xliii. 275 To giue schooles a purgation to voide them of some great inconueniences.

6. *attrib.*, as ***purgation-house***: see quot.

1642 DAVENANT *Unfort. Lovers* I. i. (1643) 4 The Lady.. was Arrested..by the Officers Of the Purgation house, and thither sent To suffer for unchastity. *Ibid.* 6 The new purgation house, where witnesses Have severally depos'd she was unchaste.

purgative (ˈpɜːgətɪv), *a.* and *sb.* [a. F. *purgatif, -ive* (14th c. in Hatz.-Darm.), ad. late L. *purgātīv-us* purgative, f. ppl. stem of L. *purgāre* to cleanse, PURGE: see -IVE, -ATIVE.]

A. *adj.* Having the quality of purging.

1. *Med.* Causing evacuation of the bowels; cathartic, aperient.

c **1400** tr. *Secreta Secret., Gov. Lordsh.* 96 Stryngthe digestyf, and purgatyf. **1538** ELYOT *Dict.*, *Catharctica*, purgatiue medicines. **1605** SHAKS. *Macb.* v. iii. 55 What Rubarb, Cyme, or what Purgatiue drugge Would scowre these English hence. **1631** JORDAN *Nat. Bathes* vii. (1669) 48 The purgative faculty of Medicines. **1732** ARBUTHNOT *Rules of Diet* in *Aliments*, etc. 248 The Juice of an unripe Cucumber is purgative. **1843** R. J. GRAVES *Syst. Clin. Med.* xxx. 416 A purgative pill was administered.

2. Cleansing or freeing from defilement, evil, sin, or guilt; †of or pertaining to purgatory (1605).

1605 BELL *Motives Romish Faith* 102 The great perplexitie of papistes, concerning this their purgatiue imagination. **1675** TRAHERNE *Chr. Ethics* 254 Among the vertues some are purgative, and some are perfective. **1856** R. A. VAUGHAN *Mystics* (1860) II. IX. ii. 128 A certain time-honoured division of the mystical process into Purgative, Illuminative, and Unitive. **1896** C. K. PAUL tr. *Huysmans' En Route* II. v. 240 This idea of a purgative life after death is so natural.. that all religions assume it.

B. *sb.* **1.** A cathartic or aperient medicine which provokes evacuation.

1626 BACON *Sylva* §491 Setting stronger poysons, or purgatives, by them. **1789** W. BUCHAN *Dom. Med.* (1790) 401 Small quantities of salt and water, or some other mild purgative. **1838** T. THOMSON *Chem. Org. Bodies* 433 We prefer cold drawn castor-oil as a purgative.

2. Any cleansing or purifying agent or means.

1701 DE FOE *True-born Eng.* I. 230 Civil Wars, the common Purgative Which always use to make the Nation thrive. **1712** ADDISON *Spect.* No. 507 ¶1 Plato has called Mathematical Demonstrations the Cathartics, or Purgatives of the Soul.

Hence **ˈpurgatively** *adv.*, **ˈpurgativeness**.

1847 WEBSTER, Purgatively. **1727** BAILEY vol. II, *Purgativeness*, purging, purifying, or cleansing Quality.

purˈgator. [a. late L. *purgātor* a cleanser, agent-n. from L. *purgāre* to PURGE. Cf. F. *purgateur* (16th c.).] A purifier.

1711 HICKES *Two Treat. Chr. Priesth.* (1847) II. 197 He.. is our great purgator in the primary and most principal sense of the word. **1933** K. MALONE *Deor* 15 He conceded the possibility that 'll. 31–34 may be a later insertion, made to give the whole a religious turn', but evidently had his doubts about yielding even these lines to the purgator.

purgatorial (pɜːgəˈtɔərɪəl), *a.* [f. late L. *purgātōri-us* or med.L. *purgātōri-um* (see PURGATORY *a.*, *sb.*) + -AL¹.] Of a spiritually cleansing or purifying quality; also, of, pertaining to, or of the nature of purgatory.

c **1450** *Mirour Saluacioun* 3026 So differences fire werldly fro thilk purgatoriale. **1632** LITHGOW *Trav.* x. 500 Now leauing Prodigalls to their Purgatoriall Postings. **1874** H. R. REYNOLDS *John Bapt.* IV. v. 258 If any class needed pungent, purgatorial test, the publicans required it. **1880** E. H. PLUMPTRE in *Dict. Chr. Biog.* II. 195/1 His [Augustine's] own view of a purgatorial punishment for the baptized.

purgatorian (pɜːgəˈtɔərɪən), *a.* and *sb. rare.* [f. med.L. *purgātōri-um* PURGATORY *sb.* + -AN.]

A. *adj.* Of, pertaining to, or relating to purgatory; purgatorial.

a **1624** CRAKANTHORP *Vigil. Dorm.* (1631) 314 Their Purgatorian fire, their five new-found proper Sacraments, condignity of workes, yea Supererogation, and an armie of like heresies. **1687** *Advise to Testholders* xi. in *Third Coll. Poems* (1689) 21/2 When all the Purgatorian flames have past. **1841** J. H. NEWMAN *Tract XC* 25 Another doctrine, purgatorian, but not Romish, is that said to be maintained by the Greeks at Florence.

B. *sb.* A believer in purgatory.

a **1550** *Image Ipocr.* IV. 191 in *Skelton's Wks.* (1843) II. 441 So be ther Sophrans,..Purgatorians, Chalomerians, And Ambrosians. **1772** (Mar.) JOHNSON in *Boswell*, We must either suppose that passage to be metaphorical, or hold, with many divines and all the Purgatorians, that departed souls do not all at once arrive at the utmost perfection. **1839** J. ROGERS *Antipapopr.* 272 Important to be upheld by the rigid purgatorian.

b. A soul in purgatory.

1607 R. C[AREW] tr. *Estienne's World of Wonders* 304 The soules of those poore Purgatorians..returned backe.

†**purgaˈtorious,** *a. Obs. rare*⁻¹. [f. as prec. + -OUS.] Belonging to or connected with purgatory.

1653 MILTON *Hirelings* Wks. (1851) 372 To som such purgatorious and superstitious Uses.

purgatory (ˈpɜːgətərɪ), *sb.* Forms: α. 3–7 purgatorie, 4–5 -tori, 5–6 -torye, 4– purgatory; (also 4 purcatorie, 4–6 -ory, 6 pourgatory). β. 4 purgatore, 4–6 -toire, 5 -tor. [ad. med.L. *purgātōri-um* (in St. Bernard *c* 1130, in sense 'a means of cleansing'), absol. use of neuter of *purgātōri-us* adj. cleansing, purifying, f. *purgāre* to cleanse, PURGE. Perh. immed. a. AF. *purgatorie* (Godef. *Compl.*) = OF. *purgatoire*, whence the β forms.]

1. a. A condition or place of spiritual purging and purification; *spec.* in Roman Catholic belief, a state 'in which souls who depart this life in the grace of God suffer for a time, because they still need to be cleansed from venial sins, or have still to pay the temporal punishment due to mortal sins, the guilt and the eternal punishment of which have been remitted' (*Cath. Dict.*).

a **1225** *Ancr. R.* 126 Anhonged, oðer ine purgatorie, oðer iðe pine of helle. *a* **1300** [see FIRE A. 1 c]. **1340** *Ayenb.* 73 Purgatorie þe ssel seawy hou god clenzeþ veniel zenne. **1362** LANGL. *P. Pl.* A. XI. 248, I shal punisshen in purcatory or in þe put of helle Eche man for his misdede. **1390** GOWER *Conf.* I. 207 The man which lith in purgatoire. *c* **1425** WYNTOUN *Chron.* v. xiv. 5510 Morys..askyt in his prayere þat he sulde noucht de befor þat her he tholit his purgator. **1426** LYDG. *De Guil. Pilgr.* 22876 Prayer abreggeth purgatory. **1526** *Pilgr. Perf.* (W. de W. 1531) 207 Aboue this lowest hell there is another hell called purgatory. **1534** in *Lett. Suppress. Monasteries* (Camden) 36 He wold proue purcatory by a certayne vers in the Saulter. **1562** *Articles of Religion* xxii, The Romish doctrine concerning purgatory..is a fond thing vainly inuented. **1626** BURTON *Anat. Mel.* III. iv. I. iii. (ed. 2) 522 Purgatory, Limbus Patrum, Infantum, and all that subterranean Geography. **1661** BLOUNT *Glossogr.* (ed. 2) s.v., The Council of Trent, Sect. 15. defines, that there is a Purgatory, and that the souls detained there, are benefitted by the prayers of the faithful. **1768** TUCKER *Lt. Nat.* (1834) II. 352 The doctrine of a purgatory seems innocent in itself, or, rather, salubrious..: it is only the absurd notion..of praying or buying souls out of purgatory, that renders it a heresy repugnant to reason, to religion, and to common sense. **1853** FABER *All for Jesus* 357 That the name of Purgatory was first authoritatively given to the Intermediate State in 1284 by Innocent IV. **1885** *Catholic Dict.* (ed. 3) 702/2 All the souls in Purgatory have died in the love of God, and are certain to enter heaven. **1898** A. G. MORTIMER *Cath. Faith & Practice* II. 352 The comparison of the differences between the Eastern and Western doctrines of Purgatory.. strongly inclines one to the Western view.

b. ***Saint Patrick's Purgatory***:

A name given to a cavern on an island in Lough Derg, Co. Donegal, where, according to legend, Christ appeared to St. Patrick and showed him a deep pit wherein whoever spent a day and a night could behold the torments of hell and the joys of heaven.

c **1290** *S. Eng. Leg.* I. 199/2 Seint paterik..makede ane put in Irlonde, þat seint patrike purgatorie is icleoped ȝeot. **1432–50** tr. *Higden* (Rolls) V. 305 The thrydde thynge of the Purgatory of Seynte Patrikke is ascribede to Seynte Patricke the secunde. **1703** *Irish Act 2 Anne* c. 6 §26 Whereas, the Superstitions of Popery are greatly increased and upheld by the pretended Sanctity..of a place called St. Patrick's Purgatory in the County of Donegall [etc.]. **1855** MILMAN *Lat. Chr.* XIV. ii. 430 The Purgatory of St. Patrick, the Purgatory of Owen Miles,..were among the most popular and widespread legends of the ages preceding Dante.

2. *fig.* **a.** Any condition, place, or thing having the characteristics ascribed to purgatory; a place or state of temporary suffering, expiation, etc.

c **1386** CHAUCER *Wife's Prol.* 489 By god in erthe I was his purgatorie For which I hope his soule be in glorie. **1490** CAXTON *How to Die* (1491) 7 The Infyrmyte tofore the deth is lyke as a purgatore. **1500–20** DUNBAR *Poems* xxv. 2 We that ar heir in hevins glory [at Court], To ȝow that ar in purgatory [at Stirling in distress]. **1642** FULLER *Holy & Prof. St.* I. vii. 19 Those who first called England the Purgatory of servants, sure did us much wrong. **1725** T. THOMAS in *Portland Papers* VI. (Hist. MSS. Comm.) 98 Half way to North Allerton is a very bad piece of road which goes by the name of Purgatory. **1756** FOOTE *Eng. fr. Paris* I. Wks. 1799 I. 105 And you really think Paris a kind of purgatory. **1807** W. IRVING in *Life & Lett.* (1864) I. 186 We have toiled through the purgatory of an election. **1880** 'OUIDA' *Moths* II. 199 The paradise of other women was her purgatory.

†**b.** That which purges from sin; an expiation.

1563–4 BECON *Jewel of Joy* Pref., We knew not Christ's most precious blood to be a sufficient purgatory for all our sins. **1639** N. N. tr. *Du Bosq's Compl. Woman* I. G j, Women are so late ere they fall to devotion, and take it ordinarily but as a Purgatory of the offences of their youth.

†**3.** A purgation, a cleaning out. *Obs. rare*⁻¹.

1596 NASHE *Saffron Walden* Wks. (Grosart) III. 75 The fire of Alchumie hath wrought such a purgation or purgatory in a great number of mens purses in England, that it hath clean fir'd them out of al they haue.

4. *U.S.* **a.** A cavern (cf. sense 1 b). **b.** A deep narrow gorge or ravine, with vertical or steep sides; also, a brook flowing through such a gorge. Usually as a place-name.

1766 M. CUTLER in *Life*, etc. (1888) I. 12 Hunted in Purgatory with Mr. Dean and Mr. Penniman [for botanical specimens] this afternoon, but found nothing. **1787** MORSE *Amer. Gazetteer, Sutton*, a township in Worcester co., Massachusetts... The cavern, commonly called Purgatory, is a natural curiosity. **1888** J. D. WHITNEY *Names & Places* 160 Along the coast of New England, and in the interior, narrow ravines with nearly perpendicular walls are called 'purgatories'. **1902** A. MATTHEWS *Purgatory River 1 note,* There are in New England several small brooks to which the name of Purgatory is given, either because they drain swamps, or flow through or near rock chasms which are called Purgatories.

c. A swamp, esp. one difficult to cross. Also *attrib. local U.S.*

1831 J. M. PECK *Guide for Emigrants* III. 308 In the low prairies near the Wabash, are swamps, called by the people *purgatories*, which are almost impassable in the wet season. **1834** —— *Gaz. Illinois* III. 172 The eastern part, towards the Wabash, contains some wet land and purgatory swamps.

5. A hole under a fire-place, covered with a grating through which the ashes may fall; also, the grating which covers it. *local.*

1841 C. H. HARTSHORNE *Salopia Antiqua* 537 *Purgatory*, the pit grate of a kitchen fire place; by falling through which the ashes become *purer*. **1866** MRS. H. WOOD *Elster's Folly* iii, The 'purgatory' in Mr. Jabez Gum's kitchen consisted of a hole, two feet square, under the hearth, covered with a grating, through which the ashes and the small cinders fell. **1874** —— *Mast. Greylands* xxiii, Sister Ann, in taking one of the irons from between the bars of the grate, let it fall with a crash upon the purgatory. **1897** R. M. GILCHRIST *Peakland Faggot* ii. 20 Et's onpossible, wi' them purgatories on th' harstone, to keep ashes fro' flyin.

6. *attrib.* and *Comb.*, as ***purgatory fire, legend, pain, -raker, suffering***, etc.; **purgatory hammer**, popular name of stone axes found in prehistoric graves in Ireland; **purgatory hole** (*local*) = sense 5.

c **1375** *Lay Folks Mass Bk.* (MS. B.) 472 Til alle in purgatory pyne, þis messe be mede & medicyne. *c* **1425** *St. Mary of Oignies* I. xii. in *Anglia* VIII. 148/18 She gat graunt ..at she shulde passe to paradys wiþ-outen purgatory peyne. **1553** BECON *Reliques of Rome* Wks. (1563) 198 Where thys place of Purgatorye is: none of oure purgatorye rakers or proctoures thereof is able to declare. **1596** NASHE *Lenten Stuffe* Wks. (Grosart) V. 247 The great yeare of Iubile in Edward the thirds time..three hundred thousand people romed to Rome for purgatorie pils and paternal veniall benedictions. **1692** BP. OF ELY *Answ. Touchstone* 27 Purgatory-fire; which..they have kindled already, and would have us believe Souls are now frying therein. **1851** D. WILSON *Preh. Ann. Scot.* vi. 135 The stone hammer.. popularly known in Scotland almost till the close of last century [as] the Purgatory Hammer. **1865** TYLOR *Early Hist. Man.* viii. 224 Purgatory Hammers, for the dead to knock with at the gates. **1895** [T. PINNOCK] *T. Brown's Black Country Ann.* (E.D.D.), What bad luck to drap yer weddin ring in the purgatory hole.

Hence **'purgatory** *v. trans. nonce-wd.*, to put into purgatory or a situation of pain.

1860 O. W. HOLMES *Elsie V.* xxi, Blanche Creamer..was purgatoried between the two old Doctors.

purgatory ('pɜːgətərɪ), *a.* [ad. post-cl. L. *purgātōri-us*, f. *purgātōr-em* cleanser: see PURGATOR and -ORY[2].] Having the quality of cleansing or purifying; = PURGATIVE *a.*; of or pertaining to purgation. ***purgatory prison*** = PURGATORY *sb.*

1377 LANGL. *P. Pl.* B. XVIII. 390 Thei shul be clensed clereliche & wasshen of her synnes In my prisoun purgatorie. *c* **1450** tr. *De Imitatione* I. xxiv. 33 þi sorowe is satisfactory and purgatory. **1579** W. WILKINSON *Confut. Familye of Loue* B iv, Clensing whiche he calleth Purgatorie. **1675** R. BURTHOGGE *Causa Dei* 21 Plutarch..tells us, that Infernal Punishments are Purgatory and Medicinal. **1790** BURKE *Fr. Rev.* Wks. V. 339 Every man who has served in an assembly is ineligible for two years after... This purgatory interval is not unfavourable to a faithless representative. *a* **1834** COLERIDGE *Aids Refl.* (1854) 256 *note*, Remorse is no Purgatory Angel.

purge (pɜːdʒ), *sb.* [f. PURGE *v.*[1], or (in sense 2) a. F. *purge* (14th c in Hatz.-Darm.) = It., Sp. *purga*. Sense 1 is not cited in Fr. before 1690.]

1. That which purges; *spec.* an aperient medicine, a purgative.

1563 HYLL *Art Garden.* (1593) 164 Rubarbe, Scamonie,.. and such like purges. **1641** HINDE *J. Bruen* xxxvii. 116 The Physitian that gave him a gentle purg so wisely, and the patient that took it so well. **1718** QUINCY *Compl. Disp.* 173 Vomits and Purges are so much alike in their Operations. **1822-34** *Good's Study Med.* IV. 301 The complaint was peculiarly obstinate and resisted the use of purges.

fig. **1602** *2nd Pt. Return fr. Parnass.* IV. v, Ben Ionson.. brought vp Horace giuing the Poets a pill, but our fellow Shakespeare hath giuen him a purge that made him beray his credit.

2. a. The act of purging; purgation; ridding of objectionable or hostile elements. In more recent use, the removal (from a political party, army, etc.) of persons regarded as undesirable. Also *transf.* and *attrib.*

1598 FLORIO, *Purga*, a purge, a purgation, a cleansing. **1655** FULLER *Ch. Hist.* II. ii. §38 The preparative for the purge of paganism out of the kingdom of Northumberland. **1893** S. R. GARDINER *Hist. Gt. Civil War* IV. lxviii. 272 The adoption of a purge in place of a dissolution [of Parliament]. **1933** H. G. WELLS *Shape of Things to Come* III. §6. 302 The eternal espionage, censorship and 'purges' of the G.P.U. **1935** *Sun* (Baltimore) 2 Nov. 2/6 Max Schachtman.. characterized the 'purge'..as a move to stifle every critical voice in the ranks of the A.F. of L. **1940** *Ann. Reg. 1939* 204 The Munich bomb..furnished a welcome pretext for a new purge on the model of June 30, 1934. **1946** A. HUXLEY *Let.* 27 Oct. (1969) 553 See the recent accounts of Russian purges of insufficiently patriotic and Marxist writers. **1957** R. N. C. HUNT *Guide to Communist Jargon* xii. 47 The statements elicited at the purge trials of the middle 'thirties. **1958** *New Statesman* 15 Feb. 186/3 In this he was supported by Ernst Wollweber, the second of the three victims of the new purge, who had been Minister of Security from 1953 until last autumn, and who is now accused of 'leniency towards the class enemy' in general and the Harich group in particular. **1969** L. HELLMAN *Unfinished Woman* vii. 80, I did not even know I was there in the middle of the ugliest purge period. **1970** G. F. NEWMAN *Sir, You Bastard* viii. 258 They liked nothing better than a sordid purge in an institution. **1974** *Guardian* 24 Jan. 3/1 The word 'purge', with its unhealthy overtones of Stalinism, is naturally frowned on in Yugoslavia... But..almost every party organisation has seen changes in its top leadership... As the purges have reached their climax..party members are being purged for indulging simply in 'factionalism'. **1976** *Survey* Summer-Autumn 127 The Chinese nation faces multiple crises. Deeply-rooted factionalism and a recent history of repeated purges contribute to the grave uncertainties of today. **1977** *New Yorker* 1 Aug. 50/3 To the extent that Coops politics were pro-Soviet politics, there was a falling away after every event like the purge trials or the Hitler-Stalin pact.

b. *spec.* ***Pride's Purge***, a name given in *Eng. Hist.* to the exclusion of those members of the Long Parliament who were suspected of Presbyterian and Royalist leanings, by Colonel Pride, on the 6th of December, 1648.

1730 OLDMIXON *Hist. Eng.* 354 Every act of the governing powers, from Prides Purge to the death of the King, is illegal. **1756** HUME *Hist. Eng.* (1841) V. 274 This invasion of the Parliament commonly passed under the name of Colonel Pride's Purge. **1893** S. R. GARDINER *Hist. Gt. Civil War* IV. lxviii. 273 One hundred and forty-three [members of Parliament] affected by Pride's Purge.

c. Removal of one fluid by flushing with another. Freq. *attrib.*

1958 J. B. GARDNER in H. W. Cremer *Chem. Engin. Practice* VI. 254 Since traces of acetylene are present in the atmosphere..it is necessary to take steps to prevent a dangerous accumulation occurring during continuous plant operation... Essentially two techniques—purging and adsorption—or a combination of them, are generally employed. In the first, a small bleed of liquid oxygen from the main bath is maintained to keep the acetylene concentration at a suitable low figure... Withdrawal of the liquid product itself in liquid oxygen plants constitutes a large purge and little difficulty is experienced on such units. **1960** V. B. GUTHRIE *Petroleum Products Handbk.* III. 38 The sweet natural-gas purge is preferable. **1970** [see *headset* s.v. HEAD *sb.*[1] 74]. **1976** *Offshore Platforms & Pipelining* 240/2 Oil then can be flushed from the lines by pumping through the surface manifold down the purge line.

3. *Comb.* (partly from the verb-stem): **purge-cock, -flax** = *purging cock, flax* (PURGING *ppl. a.* 2 b); †**purge-humors**, that which purges humours.

188. *Sci. Amer.* Supp. 8897 When it becomes necessary to empty the receiver, use is made of a *purge-cock. **1853** *N. & Q.* 1st Ser. VIII. 36/1 Mill Mountain or *Purge Flax. **1606** SYLVESTER *Du Bartas* II. iv. III. *Magnif.* 1053 Fasting,.. Quick healths preserver, curbing Cupids fits, Watchfull, *purge-humors, and refining wits.

purge (pɜːdʒ), *v.*[1] Forms: 3-4 puyrgi, 4 purgi, -gen, porgy, 4-5 purche, porge, 5 pur-, por-, poorgyn, powrg, 5-6 pourge, 4- purge. [a. OF. *purgier, -ger* (12th c. in Littré) = It. *purgare*, Pr., Sp., Pg. *purgar*:—L. *purgāre* to cleanse, in early L. *pūr-igāre*, f. *pūr-us* PURE (cf. *cast-īgāre, nāv-igāre*).]

A. Illustration of Forms.

c **1290** *Beket* 425 in *S. Eng. Leg.* I. 118 He ne miȝte him puyrgi nouȝt. **13..** *S. Eng. Leg.* (MS. Bodl. 779) in Herrig's *Archiv* LXXXII. 408/40 Hou ic myȝt I-porged be. *a* **1340** HAMPOLE *Psalter* xi. 7 Syluyre..purged seuenfald. **1387** TREVISA *Higden* (Rolls) IV. 459 He purchede and clensede þe covetise of his fadir. *a* **1400-50** *Stockh. Med. MS.* 122 A medicine for to porgyn þe stomak. **1422** tr. *Secreta Secret., Priv. Priv.* 240 Whan the stomake is purchet and clenset. **1434** MISYN *Mending of Life* v. 115 Fro all filth of mynde & body hym-self powrg. *c* **1440** *Promp. Parv.* 409/2 Poorgyn, or clensyn, *purgo*. **1460** CAPGRAVE *Chron.* 106 There the Pope porged himself of certeyn crymes. **1495** *Trevisa's Barth. De P.R.* II. viii. 36 That they maye..pourge theym that they may pourge other. **1577** B. GOOGE *Heresbach's Husb.* II. (1586) 65 Well picked and pourged.

B. Signification.

1. a. *trans.* To make physically pure or clean; to cleanse; to rid of whatever is impure or extraneous; to clear or free *of, from.*

a **1340** HAMPOLE *Psalter* xvi. 4 þe fournas þat purges metall. *a* **1400-50** *Stockh. Med. MS.* 145 A good watir to purgyn a mannys face of sprotys. **1473** *Rental Bk. Cupar-Angus* (1879) I. 167 To syft it and purge it [the seed] sa that al thing be put to profit. **1526** TINDALE *Matt.* iii. 12 He.. will pourge his floore. **1607** TOPSELL *Four-f. Beasts* (1658) 64 When Augea saw that his stable was purged by art, and not by labour. **1737** WHISTON *Josephus, Antiq.* III. x. §5 They purge the barley from the bran. **1780** A. YOUNG *Tour Irel.* I. 317 Purging the yarn, one halfpenny a hank. **1860** TYNDALL *Glac.* II. xxiv. 355 If water be thoroughly purged of its air.

†**b.** To prune (a tree); to snuff (a candle). *Obs.*

1526 TINDALE *John* xv. 2 Every braunche that beareth frute will he pourge [1611 he purgeth it, Gr. καθαίρει, L. *purgabit*] that it maye bringe moare frute. **1574** HELLOWES tr. *Guevara's Fam. Ep.* (1577) 73 Dresse the vines, purge the trees. **1608** WILLET *Hexapla Exod.* 591 Snuffers wherewith the lampe was purged. **1620** THOMAS *Lat. Dict., Averrunco,* to purge vines with a vinehooke.

†**c.** *humorously.* To clear or 'clean' out; to empty. *Obs.*

1604 HIERON *Preachers Plea* Wks. I. 493 [They] beguile the people and cozen them of their money, purging their purses and scouring their bags.

d. To rid of one fluid by flushing *with* another.

1960 V. B. GUTHRIE *Petroleum Products Handbk.* III. 37 The following precautions should be observed to prevent moisture from entering LP-Gas supplies... Purge new containers being put into service. **1962** W. SCHIRRA in *Into Orbit.* 51 In the final stages of descent, a snorkel opens automatically at about 20,000 feet, and brings in fresh, cool air from the outside which purges the hot suit and gives us our first whiff of the briny ocean. **1973** *Daily Tel.* 25 Oct. 1/5 The tank had been 'purged' 18 months ago with nitrogen to force out the remains of any gaseous contents.

2. a. To make figuratively or ideally pure or clean, to free from moral or spiritual defilement; to rid *of* or free *from* sin, guilt, fault, error, or evil of any kind; to rid of objectionable, alien, or extraneous elements or members. In recent use, to rid of persons regarded as politically undesirable; = PURIFY 2, 4.

a **1340** HAMPOLE *Psalter* xxii. 6 þou has purged my hert. **1415** HOCCLEVE *To Sir J. Oldcastle* 32 Ryse vp & pourge thee of thy trespas. *a* **1533** FRITH *Disput. Purgat.* III. Wks. (1573) 55 Yet was not Lazarus caried into purgatory to be purged of his sinnes. *a* **1582** BUCHANAN *Let. to Randolph* Wks. (1892) 58, I am besy wt our story of Scotland to purge it of sum Inglis lyis and Scottis vanite. **1602** MARSTON *Antonio's Rev.* v. vi, Let's cleanse our hands, Purge hearts of hatred. **1624** *More's Utopia* (title-p.), Translated from the Latin by Raphe Robinson,..newly corrected and purged of all Errors. **1798** *Anti-Jacobin, New Morality* 1 From mental mists to purge a nation's eyes. **1871** H. MONCRIEFF *Pract. Free Ch. Scot.* (1877) i. 15 The Kirk-session may revise or purge the [communion] roll at any period. **1873** EDITH THOMPSON *Hist. Eng.* xxxiii. ¶8 As the Parliament seemed likely to come to an agreement with him [Charles], it was 'purged',..more than a hundred members opposed to the army party were thus shut out. **1879** FROUDE *Cæsar* vii. 60 He insisted that the Senate must be purged of its corrupt members. **1885** S. COX *Expos.* ser. I. xiii. 157 A truth which will purge and raise the tone of our moral life. **1936** [see sense 3 a below]. **1942** [see JUDENREIN *a.*]. **1945** *Daily Express* 22 May 1 Tito's officials are still purging towns and villages of Italian Fascists and placing local committees in charge.

†**b.** To free from ceremonial uncleanness or defilement; = PURIFY 3. *Obs.*

1390 GOWER *Conf.* I. 77 Whan the Prestes wern dede, The temple of thilke horrible dede Thei thoghten purge. **1590** SPENSER *F.Q.* I. iii. 36 When mourning altars, purgd with enimies life, The black infernall Furies doen aslake. **1600** HOLLAND *Livy* XXI. xlvi. 419 Which straunge tokens being purged and cleered by an expiatorie sacrifice.

3. *transf.* **a.** To remove by some cleansing or purifying process or operation (*lit.* or *fig.*); to clear *away, off, out*; to expel or exclude; to void. In recent use, to remove (a person regarded as politically undesirable), freq. by drastic methods.

a **1340** HAMPOLE *Psalter* ix. 22 þat oure synnes swa be purged. **1340** *Ayenb.* 132 Bliþe he is huanne þet he may his [kueade humours] purgi and keste out. *c* **1386** CHAUCER *Wife's Prol.* 134 To purge vryne. **1526** TINDALE *1 Cor.* v. 7 Pourge [1560 (Genev.) Purge out] therfore the olde leven. **1568** BIBLE (Bishops') *Isa.* i. 25, I shal..purely purge away thy drosse. **1612** WOODALL *Surg. Mate* Wks. (1653) 4 Nature..will..help it self by purging the contused blood through the orifice. **1791** COWPER *Iliad* v. 150 From thine eye the darkness purge. **1873** EDITH THOMPSON *Hist. Eng.* xxxiv. ¶11 The Presbyterian members, who had been 'purged' out by Pride, again took their seats. **1875** JOWETT *Plato* (ed. 2) I. 312 To purge away the crime appears to him ..a duty. **1936** *Sun* (Baltimore) 11 Mar. 1/3 Reports that the AAA Adminstrator, who a year ago 'purged' the AAA of a number of its 'left wing' members..is himself being 'purged'. **1938** 'G. ORWELL' *Homage to Catalonia* xi. 224 The Russian Consul-General..has since been 'purged'. **1939** JOYCE *Finnegans Wake* 71 Purged out of Burke's. **1943** *New Statesman* 8 May 297 The sooner the more extreme elements in it are purged the better; it has throughout been a misfortune that an exiled Government here should contain members who would be more at ease collaborating against the U.S.S.R. **1958** *Spectator* 20 June 791/2 Saburov, now said to have been purged with a number of his supporters. **1974** [see PURGE *sb.* 2 a]. **1976** *Survey* Winter 162 Peterson was not immediately purged in 1935, but was sent to a military position in the Ukraine.

b. *intr.* for *refl.*

1805 SOUTHEY *Let. to C. W. W. Wynne* in *Life* (1850) II. 346 This sort of leaven soon purges off.

4. *Med.* **a.** Said of a medicine, or of one who administers it: To empty (the stomach, bowels, etc.); to deplete or relieve (the body or, now only, the bowels) by evacuation.

a **1400-50**, **1422** [see A]. [**1483** CAXTON *Cato* e viij b, Hit [mustard] purgeth and maketh clene the brayne.] **1613** PURCHAS *Pilgrimage* IX. xiv. (1614) 908 When they were to sacrifice, they purged themselues first,..and by vomit emptied their bodies. **1634** SIR T. HERBERT *Trav.* 210 Palmeto Wine..purges the belly and helpes obstructions. **1702** J. PURCELL *Cholick* (1714) 139 The next Day the Patient must be Purg'd, and a Paregorick given him that Night. **1804** ABERNETHY *Surg. Obs.* 175 On the second morning he was again purged. **1905** H. D. ROLLESTON *Dis. Liver* 262 Cheadle speaks of cases being 'purged to death'.

b. *refl.* and *intr.* (In quot. *c* 1645, to vomit.)

1484 CAXTON *Fables of Poge* x, He must nedes go purge hym. **1596** DANETT tr. *Comines* (1614) 213 Hee purged continually. *c* **1645** HOWELL *Lett.* (1650) I. 33, I did purge so violently at sea. **1684** BUNYAN *Pilgr.* II. 86 The Boy may do well again; but he must purge and Vomit. **1778** R. JAMES *Diss. Fevers* (ed. 8) 45 He awaked sick, vomited and purged considerably.

c. *absol.* To induce purgation; (of a drug) to act as a purge.

1606 HOLLAND *Sueton.* Annot. 27 The roote is that, whereof is made our sneesing powder. It purgeth extreemely by vomit. **1633** G. HERBERT *Temple, Rose* v, What is fairer then a rose? What is sweeter? yet it purgeth. **1707** FLOYER *Physic. Pulse-Watch* 285 In the quick and frequent Pulse we Purge little, because Purging accelerates the Pulse. **1811** A. T. THOMSON *Lond. Disp.* (1818) 190

Larger doses purge. **1875** H. C. Wood *Therap.* (1879) 446 Medicines which purge actively.

5. To clear (oneself or another, one's character, etc.) of a charge or suspicion of guilt; to establish the innocence of; to exculpate; *spec.* in *Law*, by assertion on oath, with the support of compurgators, or by wager of battle.

a. *refl.*

c **1290** *Beket* 423 in *S. Eng. Leg.* I. 118 I-loked him was to puyrgi him þoruȝ clergie, ȝif he miȝte. *c* **1440** *Jacob's Well* 67 Knowe þi synne to vs, ȝif þou be gylty, or ellys pourge þe þere-of lawfully. **1489** Caxton *Faytes of A.* iv. viii. 249 This man..offreth to deffende and purge himself by champ of batayile. **1555** Eden *Decades* 18 To purge him of such crimes as they shuld ley to his charge. **1647** Clarendon *Hist. Reb.* vi. §393 He so well purged himself, that he was again restored to his Office. *a* **1715** Burnet *Own Time* (1766) II. 26 They were required to purge them-selves by oath. **1878** Stubbs *Const. Hist.* III. xviii. 48 Archbishop Arundel had to purge himself from a like suspicion. **1888** Burgon *Lives 12 Gd. Men, Bp. Wilberforce* II. v. 15 Full opportunity [was] given him [Dr. Hampden] to purge himself of all suspicion of false doctrine.

b. *trans.*

c **1400** *Destr. Troy* 12640 He plesit the prince, & purgit his fame. *a* **1548** Hall *Chron., Rich. III* 42 Purgyng and declaryng his innocencie concernyng the murther of his nephewes. **1560** Daus tr. *Sleidane's Comm.* 62 Yet I speake not this to defende or pourge the Magistrates. **1577–87** Holinshed *Chron.* III. 1113/1 Wiat did purge me that I knew nothing of his stirre. **1678** *Trans. Crt. Spain* 101 That Reason ought to purge me from being the Author of the publick misery. **1768** Blackstone *Comm.* III. xxvii. 437 When facts..rest only in the knowledge of the party, a court of equity applies itself to his conscience, and purges him upon oath with regard to the truth of the transaction.

6. *Law.* **a.** To atone for (an offence, etc.) by expiation and submission, in order to gain relief from penalties; to 'wipe out' (the offence or sentence).

1681 Stair *Inst. Law Scot.* (1693) i. xiii. §14. 122 By payment at the Barr, it was allowed to be purged. **1687** *Assur. Abb. Lands* 196 That is only true where the Violence is not purged, but here the violence is purged by obtaining the Pope's Grant. **1766** Blackstone *Comm.* II. xxxi. 486 A plain direct act of bankruptcy once committed cannot be purged, or explained away by any subsequent conduct. **1818** Cruise *Digest* (ed. 2) I. 373 The Court said, that justification for heriot service on seisin of the ancestor, was an acceptance of the heir as tenant, and purged the forfeiture. **1894** *Daily News* 10 May 2/3 [The accused has] taken steps to purge the sentence of outlawry passed upon him in consequence of his non-appearance at the Justiciary Court, Edinburgh, for trial. **1897** *Encycl. Law* s.v. *Contempt of Court*, It is necessary for a person judged to be in contempt to clear or purge his contempt.

b. *Sc. Law.* To call upon (a witness) to clear himself by oath or affirmation of any implication of malice or interest before giving evidence; usually in passive *to be purged*.

1753 in *Stewart's Trial* App. 27 Katharine Maccoll, servant to the pannel,..being solemnly sworn,..purged of malice and partial council, and examined and interrogate, depones, That [etc.]. **1829** *Evans & Ruffy's Farmer's Jrnl.* 14 Sept. 294 The witnesses were sworn and purged according to the Scotch form. **1858** Polson *Law & L.* 97 Witnesses are brought into court upon a diligence, and before they can be examined, they must be purged.

7. *refl.* and *intr.* (also *pass.*). Of a liquid: To clear itself, to become or be made clear or pure by settlement or defecation. Also *fig.* ? *Obs.*

1681 Dryden *Abs. & Achit.* i. 38 Some warm excesses.. Were construed youth that purged by boiling o'er. **1726** Leoni *Alberti's Archit.* I. 5 b, Water not well purged, but heavy and ill-tasted. **1748** *Anson's Voy.* i. v. 45 After it [the water] has been in the cask a day or two it begins to purge itself. **1833** Lyell *Princ. Geol.* III. 309 Every current charged with sediment must purge itself in the first deep cavity which it traverses, as does a turbid river in a lake.

8. Combs. of the vb. stem: see purge *sb.* 3.

†**purge**, *v.*[2] *Obs. rare.* [app. for **porge*, ad. L. *porgĕre*, contr. form of *porrigĕre* to reach out, extend, put forth, f. *por-* = *prō* forth + *regĕre* to lead straight.] *intr.* To issue forth.

1398 Trevisa *Barth. De P.R.* v. lxi. (Bodl. MS.) 30 b/1 Þe veynes purgeþ oute of the lyuour as þe arteries and woosen out of þe herte and þe senewes oute of þe brayne. **1610** G. Fletcher *Christ's Tri.* i. xlii, Thear are but two wayes for this soule to haue, When parting from the body, forth it purges.

purgeable ('pɜːdʒəb(ə)l), *a.* [f. purge *v.*[1] + -able. Cf. purgable.] Capable of being purged.

1644 Digby *Nat. Bodies* xxxiv. §7. 292 When the Physitian giueth a purge, it worketh two thinges; the one is, to make some certaine humour more liquid and purgeable then the rest. **1678** in Fountainhall *Decis.* (1759) I. 10 The Lords declared that they will find that *mora* purgeable at the bar. **1802–12** Bentham *Ration. Judic. Evid.* (1827) V. 188 An interest not purgeable by release.

purged (pɜːdʒd), *ppl. a.* [f. purge *v.*[1] + -ed[1].]

1. Cleansed, clarified, purified; freed from impurity or defilement.

1486 *Bk. St. Albans* c vij, Take a quantyte of poorke..and porgede grece. **1501** Douglas *Pal. Hon.* i. Prol. 56 The purgit air with new engendrit heit. **1646** G. Daniel *Poems* Wks. 1878 I. 24 High, & purged Soules Leaue Time & Place, to dull earthporing fooles. **1788** V. Knox *Winter Even.* II. v. i. 107 They write not to the people, but to the purged ear of a few speculatists. **1836** Mrs. Browning *Poet's Vow* i. xviii, My purged, once human heart.

†**2.** Washed away (as sin). *Obs.*

? *a* **1500** *Chester Pl.* (E.E.T.S.) 433 That saved I hope fully to be For purged synnes that were in me.

purgee (pɜː'dʒiː). [f. purge *v.*[1] + -ee[1].] A person who is politically 'purged', expelled from an organization, or excluded from public life.

1938 *Kiplinger Washington Let.* (Kiplinger Washington Agency) 3 Sept. 4 Reelection of purgees will strengthen non-New Dealers in next Congress. **1958** *Economist* 1 Nov. 421/2 Mr Kishi, a former 'purgee' and suspected 'war criminal', became prime minister in February last year. **1963** *Probl. of Communism* July/Aug. p. x/1 Widow of two of Stalin's purgees, Grigori Sokolnikov and L. P. Serebriakov, Serebriakova herself spent a decade in prison.

†'**purgement.** *Obs. rare*[−1]. [a. OF. *purgement* (14th c. in Godef.), ad. L. *purgāmentum*: see purgament.] Purgation, purification.

1483 Caxton *Gold. Leg.* 442 b/1 Thys purgemente or wasshyng may sygnefye the purete and clennesse that the preest oughte to haue.

purger ('pɜːdʒə(r)). [f. purge *v.*[1] + -er[1].]

a. One who or that which purges (*lit.* and *fig.*). *spec.* One who carries out a political purge.

c **1460** *Wisdom* 966 in *Macro Plays* 67 Very contrycyon ..þat ys purger & clenser of synne. **1508** Fisher *7 Penit. Ps.* xxxviii. Wks. (1876) 72 Penaunce whiche is the very purger of synne. **1601** Shaks. *Jul. C.* ii. i. 180 We shall be call'd Purgers, not Murderers. **1615** Crooke *Body of Man* 138 Such men doe continually vomit choller, and are called.. purgers of choller vpward. *Ibid.*, Purgers of choller downward. **1641** S. Marshall *Fast Serm. bef. Ho. Com.* 40 Bee yee purgers and preservers of our Religion. **1907** A. Lang *Hist. Scot.* IV. ii. 35 The purgers of the Kirk were not subjected to the approval of the Privy Council. **1938** *Sun* (Baltimore) 20 June 3/2 (*heading*) Purgers reported purged in Ukraine as Soviet foes. *Ibid.* 25 Aug. 6/5 A number of Senator Tydings' admirers have been wondering who constitute the Maryland purgers.

†**b.** *spec.* A purgative, a cathartic. *Obs.*

1562 Turner *Baths* 10 Let the sicke purge him selfe with cassia fistula or suche..lenitiue or gentell purger. **1648** Winyard *Midsummer-Moon* 2 This purger is the only scammony, the rest somewhat milder simples. **1725** *Bradley's Fam. Dict.* s.v. *Gangrene*, Briony..being a great Purger it must be corrected.

†**c.** An expurgator of books. *Obs.*

1624 Gataker *Transubst.* 39 The Popish purgers authorised to maine and mangle Authors.

'**purgery.** [a. F. *purgerie* (1838 in Littré), f. *purger* to purge: see -ery.] (See quots.)

[**1858** Simmonds *Dict. Trade*, *Purgerie*, a bleaching or refining room for sugar.] **1864** in Webster. **1875** Knight *Dict. Mech.*, *Purgery*, the portion of a sugar-house where the sugar from the coolers is..allowed to drain off its molasses.

purging ('pɜːdʒɪŋ), *vbl. sb.* [f. purge *v.*[1] + -ing[1].] The action of the verb purge.

1. a. Purgation; cleansing, removal of impurities, faults, or errors.

1382 Wyclif *Num.* xix. 21 Eche that towchith the watris of purgynge, shal be vnclene vnto the euen. —— *2 Pet.* i. 9 Receyuynge forȝetingnes of the purgynge of his olde trespassis. *a* **1533** Frith *Disput. Purgatory* F vj, Wherfore shuld theyr inuencyon of purgatorye serue but to be a place of purgynge, punishment, and penaunce. **1553** Brende *Q. Curtius* 90 b, Therupon thei fel to weaping and purging of them selues. **1691** T. H[ale] *Acc. New Invent.* p. lx, Any other Engine for the purging the River of Thames from Obstructions. **1733** P. Lindsay *Interest Scot.* 165 The purging and washing of Yarn is now pretty well understood. **1867** Burton *Hist. Scot.* I. viii. 276 Purging of the lists of saints.

†**b.** *concr.* That which is washed away, or removed as refuse. *Obs.*

1398 Trevisa *Barth. De P.R.* xvii. cliv. (1495) 705 The codde of all manere of codware and pourgynge: wyth the whyche swyne ben fed. **1598** Grenewey *Tacitus' Ann.*, *Germanie* vi. (1622) 271 It lay as nought worth, like other purging of the sea.

c. Removal of political opponents.

1938 *Sun* (Baltimore) 27 Aug. 16/8 Four others marked for purging by the Washington group. **1940** E. Hemingway *For Whom Bell Tolls* xl. 398 Here it reports the purging of more of thy famous Russians. **1974** J. White tr. *Poulantzas's Fascism & Dictatorship* vii. v. 338 The judiciary..suffered least from purging after national socialism came to power.

d. = purge *sb.* 2 c.

1950 *Sun* (Baltimore) 3 Jan. 9/5 When..natural gas is allowed to flow into the line it will 'push the inert gas or oxygen-short-air ahead of it. This will be allowed to escape until tests indicate pure natural gas has completely filled the line,' an engineer explained. 'This process is called purging.' **1958** [see purge *sb.* 2 c]. **1973** J. G. Tweeddale *Materials Technol.* II. ii. 24 Various methods of removal can be used, such as reaction with a suitable flux, or by purging, in which an insoluble carrier-gas is bubbled through the liquid to create large surface areas at which the hydrogen can gather and be carried away. **1980** *New Scientist* 3 July 4/1 The purging of 57,000 curies of krypton from the containment building at TMI is an essential step in the $400 million clean-up operation.

2. *spec.* The excretion or evacuation of refuse matter, esp. (now always) from the bowels, generally by means of a purgative; = purgation 1 b.

1647 Cowley *Mistress, Counsel* i, Cordials of Pity give me now, For I too weak for Purgings grow. **1656** Ridgley *Pract. Physick* 122 Purging was continual with decoction of Mallows, Fennel,..Rheubarb, Senna, made like Claret. **1818–20** E. Thompson *Cullen's Nosol. Method* (ed. 3) 225 Vomiting and frequent purging of a bilious humour. **1896** *Allbutt's Syst. Med.* I. 908 Recurrent purging and vomiting.

3. Clearing from a charge or suspicion; exculpation; = purgation 4.

1726–31 Waldron *Descr. Isle of Man* (1865) 21 They are ..obliged to swear themselves innocent, or endure the shame and punishment... This they call purging.

4. *attrib.* and *Comb.*, as *purging day*, *faculty*, etc.; **purging-cock**, a cock for discharging sediment, dregs, or refuse from a steam-boiler, etc.; †**purging place**, (*a*) purgatory, (*b*) a privy.

1553 *Epit. on Gray* in Furnivall *Ballads fr. MSS.* I. 435 Nor fferynge ones the porgynge plase Devysed by the pope. **1577** Hellowes *Gueuara's Chron.* 29 He buylt in all streetes in Rome publique purging places. **1579–80** North *Plutarch, Romulus* (1595) 34 The feast of Lupercalia..on the vnfortunate daies of the moneth of Februarie, which are called the purging daies. **1617** Moryson *Itin.* iii. 21 Supping warm brothes, helps the purging faculty.

purging ('pɜːdʒɪŋ), *ppl. a.* [f. as prec. + -ing[2].] That purges.

1. Cleansing, purifying.

1598 Grenewey *Tacitus' Ann.* xii. ii. (1622) 157 That punishment and purging sacrifices of incest should bee sought. **1882** F. W. H. Myers *Renewal of Youth*, etc. 264 The purging sacrament of pain.

2. *spec.* That induces purgation of the alimentary canal; purgative, aperient, cathartic.

1562 Turner *Herbal* ii. 79 b, So haue the old autores gyuen vnto diuerse herbes a purgyng vertue. **1612** Woodall *Surg. Mate* Wks. (1653) 143 Let your purging Medicines be such as purge downward onely. **1696** Salmon *Fam. Dict.* 203 Purge with Mecoacan-Ale, or some such-like easie Purging-Ale. **1718** Quincy *Compl. Disp.* 235 Purging Waters.—There is no County scarce in England, but discovers some of these Springs. **1729** Woodward *Nat. Hist. Foss.* I. 73 A like flat Body..was found in sinking the Purging-Well at New-Cross, near Deptford. **1778** *Eng. Gazetteer* (ed. 2) s.v. *Richmond, Surry*,..On the ascent of the hill are wells of purging mineral water, to which a great deal of company resort. **1843** R. J. Graves *Syst. Clin. Med.* xxvii. 338 The purging mixture of Epsom salts.

b. In names of plants having purgative qualities: ***purging agaric***, a fungus, *Polyporus officinalis*; ***purging broom***, *Spartium purgans*; ***purging buckthorn***, *Rhamnus catharticus*; ***purging cassia***, *Cassia Fistula*; ***purging flax***, *Linum catharticum*; ***purging grain***, *Sesamum*; ***purging nut***, the seed of *Curcas purgans* (*Jatropha Curcas*) or Barbados nut; also, the seed of *Croton Tiglium*; ***purging thorn***, *Rhamnus catharticus*.

1822 *Hortus Anglicus* II. 223 *S[partium]. Purgans.* *Purging Broom. **1776** Withering *Brit. Plants* (1796) II. 256 *Purging Buckthorn. Woods and hedges near Norwich. **1778** Lightfoot *Flora Scotica* (1789) 174 *Linum catharticum*, *Purging-flax. *Anglis.* **1760** J. Lee *Introd. Bot.* App. 324 *Purging Grain, Oily, *Sesamum*. *Ibid.* 320 *Purging Nut, *Croton*. *Ibid.* 324 Purging Nut, *Jatropha*. **1836** J. M. Gully *Magendie's Formul.* (ed. 2) 151 It appears ..that the croton plant is the same which produces the seeds known in commerce as the Indian purging-nut. **1841** *Penny Cycl.* XX. 5/2 The Jatropha Curcas, or purging-nut of the Philippine Islands.

purgunnah, variant of pergunnah.

†'**purgy**, *a.* *Obs. rare*[−1]. [f. purge *sb.* or *v.* + -y.] Of purging quality; purgative.

1562 Turner *Herbal* ii. 79 Later writers haue founde..a purgy vertu in diuerse herbes.

‖**puri**[1] ('puːrɪ). [Indonesian.] An Indonesian palace.

1937 M. Covarrubias *Island of Bali* vi. 158 Women of the aristocracy..live restricted and secluded in the palace, the *puri*, usually going out only in groups to festivals. **1961** P. Kemp *Alms for Oblivion* viii. 129, I saw ahead..the carved gateway of the Rajah's *puri*, or palace. **1971** *Country Life* 17 June 1544/1 The puris or palaces of the nobility..are entered through elaborately sculptured split doorways.

‖**puri**[2] ('puːrɪ). [Hindi.] A small round cake of unleavened wheat-flour deep-fried in ghee or oil.

1952 J. Corbett *My India* v. 64 The wonderful occasion when they had been able to fill their bellies..with halwa and puris. **1960** R. P. Jhabvala *Householder* i. 79 'The puris were very good this morning,' he said sheepishly. **1971** *Shankar's Weekly* (Delhi) 11 Apr. 22/3 The Swamiji squatting before what appeared to be a veritable mountain of puris and curries. **1973** *Sat. Rev. World* (U.S.) 18 Dec. 48/2 An Indian baker..fries the bread, and it is called *puri*. **1976** *Punch* 11 Aug. 230/3 All those crowding an Indian confectionery shop and eating sweets, puris [etc.],..in typical Indian style were either Indians or Pakistanis.

†**purie.** *Obs.* [? early ad. F. *purée*, or var. of porray, *porrey*: cf. also Sc. *purry* pottage.] ? Broth or ? pottage.

? *a* **1500** *Chester Pl.* vii. 136 Nowe will I..pull out that I have in my poke, and a pigges foote from pudding purie.

†**puri'faction.** *Obs. rare.* Also purefaction. [irreg. f. purify: see petrifaction.] = next.

1652 Gaule *Magastrom.* i. §3·39 The ceremoniall emundations or purifactions which they prescribe. **1673** *Phil. Trans.* VIII. 6129 Of the Sea-waters capablenesse of Purefaction.

purification (ˌpjʊərɪfɪ'keɪʃən). [a. F. *purification* (12th c. in Hatz.-Darm.), or ad. L. *pūrificātiōn-*

em (Pliny), n. of action from *pūrificāre* to PURIFY.] The action or process of purifying.

1. Freeing from dirt or defilement; cleansing; separation of dross, dregs, refuse, or other debasing or deteriorating matter, so as to obtain the substance in a pure condition.

1598 FLORIO, *Purificatione*, a purification, a clensing, a scouring, a clearing. **1651** FRENCH *Distill.* i. 11 *Purification*, is a separation of any Liquor from its feces. **1661** BOYLE *Unsuccessfulness of Exp.* i. Wks. 1772 I. 327, I discerned a considerable difference in the operations of several kinds of salt-petre even after purification. **1802** *Med. Jrnl.* VIII. 465 He is minute in his directions for its purification and preparation. **1835** URE *Phil. Manuf.* 66 The art of the tallow-chandler. Purification of spermaceti.

b. *Eccl.* See quots., and cf. PURIFY 1 b.

1853 DALE tr. *Baldeschi's Ceremonial* 49 He..takes the purification and ablution as usual, cleanses the chalice.. with a purificator. **1885** *Cath. Dict.* (ed. 3) App., *Purification*, as distinct from ablution, is the pouring of wine into the chalice after the priest's communion, the wine being drunk by the priest. This purification is not of ancient date.

2. Ceremonial or ritual cleansing; freeing of a person or thing from uncleanness by appropriate rites; *spec.* the observances enjoined upon a woman after child-birth by the Jewish law; hence formerly applied to the churching of women.

c **1380** WYCLIF *Sel. Wks.* II. 147 A question was maad of Joones disciplis of purificacioun, þat men hadden of baptim. *c* **1440** *Gesta Rom.* lxiv. 276 (Harl. MS.) Þe lawe was þat tyme, that eche woman shuld go to chirche, in tyme of hire purificacion. *c* **1485** *Digby Myst.* (1882) I. 31 Our ladies purificacion that she made in the temple as the vsage was than. **1548-9** (Mar.) *Bk. Com. Prayer*, The Order of the Purificacion of weomen. **1579-80** NORTH *Plutarch, Romulus* (1595) 34 The feast of Lupercalia..is ordeined for a purification. **1789** BUCHAN *Dom. Med.* (1790) 103 The Mahometan, as well as the Jewish religion, enjoins various bathings, washings, and purifications. **1841** ELPHINSTONE *Hist. Ind.* I. I. iv. 83 More than half of one book of the [Brahminical] Code is filled with rules about purification.

b. ***the Purification of St. Mary*** (***of our Lady***, etc.), also simply ***the Purification***: a name in the Western Church for the festival (Feb. 2) of the Presentation of Christ in the Temple (see PRESENTATION 1) by the Virgin Mary on the completion of 'the days of her purification' (Luke ii. 22); also called CANDLEMAS.

1389 in *Eng. Gilds* (1870) 49 Þe secunde morspeche shal bene aftir þe Purificacioun of our leuedy. Þe thred, aftir þe feste of Phelip and iacob. **1444** *Paston Lett.* I. 50 Wretyn.. the Wednesday next to fore ye Fest of the Purificacion of Our Lady at London. *a* **1548** HALL *Chron., Hen. VIII* 22b, After the Purificacion of our Lady, the Kyng created Sir Charles Brandon Viscount Lisle. **1670** PETTUS *Fodinæ Reg.* 18 To hold from the Feast of the Purification next, for 40 years. **1880** F. MEYRICK in *Dict. Chr. Antiq.* II. 1140/2 The Purification... As first instituted, this was not a Festival of St. Mary, but of our Lord; and so it has always remained in the Eastern church.

c. *attrib.* **purification flower** (see quot.).

1866 *Aunt Judy's Mag.* I. 116 Annie asked about its [the snow-drop's] names, and she mentioned..'the morning star of flowers', 'fair maid of February', 'purification flower'.

3. Moral or spiritual cleansing; freeing from moral defilement or corruption; clearing from taint of guilt.

1660 JER. TAYLOR *Worthy Commun.* iii. 62 Water [in baptism] is the symbol of purification of the soul from sin. **1756-7** tr. *Keysler's Trav.* II. 131 A person who, for the purification of his soul, ought to remain in Purgatory a hundred thousand years. **1833** ALISON *Hist. Europe* (1849) I. ii. 50. 168 [Rousseau's essay] on the question 'Have the arts and sciences contributed to the corruption or purification of morals?' **1842** DICKENS *Amer. Notes* (1850) 34/1 To make his prison a place of purification and improvement, not of demoralisation and corruption.

4. Freeing from fault or blemish (in ideal or general sense); the action of clearing from debasing or corrupting elements.

1753 SMOLLETT *Ct. Fathom* i. (1784) 12/2 You..are one of those consummate connoisseurs, who, in their purifications, let humour evaporate, while they endeavour to preserve decorum. **1793** T. BEDDOES *Demonstr. Evid.* 132 The purification of the Greek grammar from a few of its absurdities. **1845** S. AUSTIN *Ranke's Hist. Ref.* III. 395 Zwingli demanded..the purification of the council from the ungodly. **1861** WRIGHT *Ess. Archæol.* II. xiv. 59 The invention of printing..contributed towards the final purification of the English language.

purificative (ˈpjʊərɪfɪkeɪtɪv), *a. rare.* [a. F. *purificatif, -ive* purificatory (14th c.), f. *purifer* to PURIFY: see -IVE.] = PURIFICATORY *a.*

1491 CAXTON *Vitas Patr.* (W. de W. 1495) I. i. 3 b/2 The body is puryfyed and wasshyd by the nytree whyche is a spece of Salte puryfycatyff. **1611** COTGR., *Purificatif*, purificatiue, purifying.

purificator (ˈpjʊərɪfɪkeɪtə(r)). [Agent-n. in L. form, f. L. *pūrificāre* to purify: see -OR. In sense 1 identified with PURIFICATORY *sb.*: see -OR 3.]

1. *Eccl.* A cloth used at communion for wiping the chalice and paten, and the fingers and lips of the celebrant.

1853 DALE tr. *Baldeschi's Ceremonial* 29 The Subdeacon cleanses the chalice with the purificator. **1890** *Ch. Times* 5 Sept. 844 The purificator, or napkin, used for cleansing the chalice and paten after the ablutions is laid on the chalice.

2. One who purifies: = PURIFIER 1; in quot., one who performs magical purifications. *rare.*

1866 FELTON *Anc. & Mod. Greece* I. II. vi. 414 The conjurers, purificators, mountebanks, and charlatans.

3. An apparatus for purifying gases or other substances: = PURIFIER 3. *rare.*

1898 H. R. HAWEIS in *Westm. Gaz.* 6 May 2/1 This admirable purificator receives all the vapours, gases, and impurities which escape from the first fire-chamber.

purificatory (ˈpjʊərɪfɪˌkeɪtərɪ), *sb.* [ad. med.L. *pūrificātōrium*, subst. use of neut. of late L. *pūrificātōrius*: see next and -ORY[1].] = prec. 1.

1670 BLOUNT *Glossogr.* (ed. 3), *Purificatory*, the little linen cloth with which the Priest wipes the Chalice. **1885** *Cath. Dict.* (ed. 3), *Mundatory* or Purificatory, a cloth of linen or hemp..used for cleansing the chalice.

ˈ**purificatory,** *a.* [ad. late L. *pūrificātōrius* adj. (*c* 375 in Ambrose) cleansing, f. ppl. stem of L. *pūrificāre* to PURIFY: see -ORY.] Having the quality of purifying; tending to purification.

1610 HEALEY *St. Aug. Citie of God* XXI. xvi. 856 If he be washed in the fountaine of regeneration..he is..freed from all paynes, eternall and purificatory. **1837** WHEWELL *Hist. Induct. Sc.* (1857) I. 220 His vertues are arranged as physical, moral, purificatory, theoretic, and theurgic. **1881** MONIER-WILLIAMS in *19th Cent.* Mar. 511 For use in purificatory ceremonies. **1882** WESTCOTT in *Dict. Chr. Biog.* (1887) IV. 139/2 A vast scheme of purificatory chastisement.

purified (ˈpjʊərɪfaɪd), *ppl. a.* [f. PURIFY + -ED[1].] Made pure; freed from admixture or defilement; cleansed: see the verb.

a **1515** DUNBAR *Poems* lxxxvi. 41 Hail, purifyet perle! **1623** WODROEPHE *Marrow Fr. Tongue* 325/2 This purifyed Gold is more estimed then the minerall. **1836** BRANDE *Chem.* 495 The specific gravity of purified coal-gas is liable to much variation. **1875** JOWETT *Plato* (ed. 2) V. 27 That purified religion..of which he speaks.

purifier (ˈpjʊərɪfaɪə(r)). [f. as prec. + -ER[1].]

1. A person who purifies (in various senses); a cleanser; a refiner.

1471 RIPLEY *Comp. Alch.* Pref. i. in Ashm. *Theat. Chem. Brit.* (1652) 121 O pitewouse puryfyer of Soules. **1611** BIBLE *Mal.* iii. 3 He shall sit as a refiner and purifier of siluer. **1775** ADAIR *Amer. Ind.* 91 The predicted Shilo, who is to be their purifier, king, prophet, and high-priest. **1826** [HALLAM] in *Edin. Rev.* XLIV. 5 *note*, One of the earliest purifiers of English style from pedantry. **1868** STANLEY *Westm. Abb.* 284 Addison the noblest purifier of English literature.

2. A thing that purifies (in various senses).

1660-2 JER. TAYLOR *Serm. Jas. ii.* 24 Faith is a great purger and purifier of the soul. **1793** BEDDOES *Lett. Darwin* 70 Oxygene air, which..deserves to be considered as the true sweetner or purifier of the blood. **1893** in Barrows *Parl. Relig.* II. 914 [Zoroastrianism] considers the sun as the greatest purifier.

3. An apparatus or contrivance for purifying; *spec.* **a.** An apparatus in which coal-gas is purified by passing it through or over lime or other substance; a gas-purifier. **b.** A separator to remove bran scales and flour from grits or middlings.

1834 *Encycl. Brit.* (ed. 7) X. 352/1 (Gas-light) A series of purifiers. **1836** BRANDE *Chem.* 495 The gaseous products [of coal]..are passed through or over hydrate of lime, or through a mixture of quicklime and water, in vessels called purifiers, by which the sulphuretted hydrogen and carbonic acid gases are absorbed. **1856** in *Orr's Circ. Sci., Pract. Chem.* 504 The gas is..made to pass through a set of vessels ..the purifiers. These contain milk of lime, or lime that has been recently slaked. In the former case it is named a wet-lime purifier, and in the latter a dry. **1884** *Bath Herald* 27 Dec. 6/4 [In a flour-mill] the most important machines are the 'purifiers'.

puriform (ˈpjʊərɪfɔːm), *a. Path.* [f. L. *pūs, pūr-*, PUS + -(I)FORM; cf. F. *puriforme.*] Having the form or character of pus; resembling pus.

1797 *Monthly Mag.* III. 153 Puriform effusion and exudation take place. **1822-34** *Good's Study Med.* I. 203 Muco-gelatinous matter, which..resembled thick milk or a puriform fluid. **1899** *Allbutt's Syst. Med.* VIII. 466 Vesications..whose contents may become sanguineous or puriform.

purify (ˈpjʊərɪfaɪ), *v.* Also 4 -yfie, 4-7 -ifie, 5 -efie, 5-6 -yfy(e; 6 *pa. pple.* (*Sc.*) purifit, -feit. [a. F. *purifi-er* (12th c.), ad. late L. *pūrificāre*, f. L. *pūr-us* pure: see -FY.]

I. *trans.* To make pure, in various senses.

1. To free from admixture of extraneous matter, esp. such as pollutes or deteriorates; to rid of (material) defilement or taint; to cleanse.

c **1440** *Promp. Parv.* 417/1 Puryfyyn, clensyn, or make clene. **1490** CAXTON *Eneydos* xv. 54 The ayer purifyeth and clenseth hym selfe for to receyue the Impressyons of influences of this god. **1508** KENNEDIE *Flyting w. Dunbar* 340, I..dulcely drank of eloquence the fontayne, Quhen it was purifit with frost, and flowit cleir. **1555** EDEN *Decades* 327 To purifie or pourge it [the metall] from drosse. **1651** HOBBES *Leviath.* III. xxxviii. 243 There used to be fires made ..to purifie the aire. **1697** DRYDEN *Virg. Georg.* IV. 541 Th' officious Nymphs,..With Waters..From earthly dregs his Body purifie. **1800** tr. *Lagrange's Chem.* 71 This sulphur may be purified..by washing it. **1837** GORING & PRITCHARD *Microgr.* 205 The mode of generating and purifying the oxygen gas. **1841** T. R. JONES *Anim. Kingd.* xxviii. 567 The air required for purifying the blood is, of course, continually changed.

b. *Eccl.* See quots. and cf. PURIFICATION 1 b.

1858 PURCHAS *Direct. Anglic.* 62 The Celebrant..first purifies the corporal..and then purifies the paten. **1876** SCUDAMORE *Not. Euch.* 806 In the Roman rite the Minister first 'pours into the Chalice a little wine for the Priest to purify himself'. **1885** *Cath. Dict.* (ed. 3) App. s.v. *Purification*, Innocent III...laid it down that the priest should always use wine to purify the chalice, and drink it, unless he was going to say another Mass.

2. To cleanse from moral or spiritual defilement; to rid of base motive or feeling; to free from taint of guilt or sin.

a **1300** *E.E. Psalter* l[i.] 8 Þou shalt purifie me, and y shal be made whyȝte vp snowe. *c* **1340** HAMPOLE *Prose Tr.* 14 When þe will and þe affeccyone es puryfiede and clensede fra all fleschely lustes. *c* **1422** HOCCLEVE *Learn to Die* 624 He shal be pourged cleene & purified, And disposid the glorie of god to see. **1526** *Pilgr. Perf.* (W. de W. 1531) 122 By this gyfte of goostly scyence, the tonge of man or woman is purifyed & fyled. **1611** BIBLE *1 John* iii. 3 Euery man that hath this hope in him, purifieth himselfe, euen as he is pure. **1729** LAW *Serious C.* xxi. 420 Purifying his heart all manner of ways, fearful of every error and defect in his life. **1872** MORLEY *Voltaire* (1886) 3 Each did much to..purify the spiritual self-respect of mankind.

3. To make ceremonially clean; to free from ceremonial uncleanness. Formerly *spec.* of the churching of women (mostly in *pass.*).

c **1330** R. BRUNNE *Chron.* (1810) 310 Þe quene Margerete with childe þan was sche,..þe kyng..went way, to se hir & hir barn, & with hir he soiorned, tille sho was purified. **1387** TREVISA *Higden* (Rolls) I. 101 No man durste neyhe [to Mount Sinai], but he were purified and i-made all clene. *c* **1440** *Promp. Parv.* 75/2 Chyrchyn, or puryfyen, *purifico*. **1548-9** (Mar.) *Bk. Com. Prayer, Purif. Weomen*, The woman that is purifyed, must offer her Crysome. **1671** MILTON *P.R.* I. 74 In the Consecrated stream..to wash off sin, and fit them so Purified to receive him pure. **1819** SCOTT *Ivanhoe* xxxviii, The holy places [have been] purified from pollution by the blood of those infidels who defiled them. **1853** J. H. NEWMAN *Hist. Sk.* (1873) II. I. iii. 138 Their priests washed and purified the altars where the Latin priests had said mass.

4. To free from blemish or corruption (in ideal or general sense); to clear of foreign or alien elements, esp. of anything that contaminates or debases.

a **1548** HALL *Chron., Hen. VII* 59 The kynge hauynge peace as well with foreyne princes,..as disburdened and purified of all domesticall sedicion. **1665** SPRAT *Hist. Roy. Soc.* I. 40 He saw the French Tongue abundantly purifi'd. **1845** S. AUSTIN *Ranke's Hist. Ref.* III. 373 The country communes determined (April, 1530) that these churches too should be purified. **1890** *Spectator* 27 Dec., The desire of the Russian Government to 'purify' Poland of Germans.

5. *Law.* To make (a contract or obligation) 'pure' by freeing it from conditions; also, to fulfil (a condition) so as to render the obligation 'pure': see PURE *a.* 2 c.

1590 SWINBURNE *Testaments* 133 If he die, then is the condition said to be purified or extant, and so thou art to bee admitted, otherwise not. *a* **1624** —— *Spousals* (1686) 130 Whether in this Case the conditional Contract be purified and made perfect Matrimony, is a Question. **1861** W. BELL *Dict. Law Scot.* s.v. *Obligation*, A conditional obligation, dependent on an event which may never happen, has no obligatory force until the condition be purified.

6. *transf.* with the thing removed as obj.: To cleanse or clear away. *rare.*

1399 GOWER *To Hen. IV*, 349 Al his lepre it hath so purified. **1760-72** H. BROOKE *Fool of Qual.* (1809) III. 2 He, who shineth in darkness, will..purify your pollutions.

II. 7. *intr.* for *refl.* To become pure.

1668 R. STEELE *Husbandman's Calling* ix. (1672) 237 Water, if it stand, it putrifies: if it run, it purifies. **1800** *Med. Jrnl.* III. 580 He does not put it in water to purify. **1805** SOUTHEY *Let. to C. W. W. Wynn* in *Life* (1850) II. 347 Send them to new settlements, and let the old ones purify. **1852** MANNING *Gr. Faith* i. 21 Of the intermediate state of departed souls, purifying for the kingdom of God.

ˈ**purifying,** *vbl. sb.* [f. prec. + -ING[1].] The action of the verb PURIFY; cleansing, purification.

1382 WYCLIF *Acts* xxi. 26 The fulfilling of dayes of purifiyng. **1526** TINDALE *John* iii. 25 There a rose a question betwene Jhons disciples and the iewes a bout purifiynge. **1581** SIDNEY *Apol. Poetrie* (Arb.) 29 This purifing of wit,.. which..we call learning. **1642** MILTON *Apol. Smect.* xi, Those ceremonies, those purifyings and offrings at the Altar. **1712** PRIDEAUX *Direct. Ch.-wardens* (ed. 4) 105 Without a long purifying in the Furnace of Affliction. **1823** J. BADCOCK *Dom. Amusem.* 25 Charcoal intended for purifying.

attrib. **1834** *Encycl. Brit.* (ed. 7) X. 352/1 The last step of the purifying process to which coal-gas is submitted. **1889** *Daily News* 11 Dec. 3/1 About 150 men were at work in one of the purifying sheds.

ˈ**purifying,** *ppl. a.* [f. as prec. + -ING[2].] That purifies; cleansing.

1597 A. M. tr. *Guillemeau's Fr. Chirurg.* 19/1 We must, with puryfyinge medicamentes, purifye that. **1660** T. GOUGE *Chr. Direct.* xxi. (1831) 137 A purifying disposition ..detests sin..and strives against it. **1801** SOUTHEY *Thalaba* XII. xxx, The sight Of Heaven may kindle in the penitent The strong and purifying fire of hope. **1834** *Encycl. Brit.* (ed. 7) X. 352/1 (Gas-light) Fresh portions of the purifying material are supplied.

‖**Purim** (ˈpjʊərɪm, ‖puːˈriːm). [Heb. *pūrīm*, pl. of *pūr*, a foreign word (perh. Assyrian or Persian) explained in Esther iii. 7, ix. 24, as = Heb. *gōrāl* lot.] A Jewish festival observed on the 14th and 15th of the month Adar, in commemoration of the defeat of Haman's plot to massacre the Jews: see Esther ix.

There are also several special or local Purims, in imitation of the original feast.

1382 WYCLIF *Esther* ix. 26 Fro that time these daȝis be clepid Furim [1388 Phurym], that is, of lotis, forthi that fur, that is, lot, in to a pot was put. **1535** COVERDALE *ibid.* 28 They are the dayes of Purim, which are not to be ouerslipte amonge the Iewes. **1676** HALE *Contempl.* I. 523 As if we might consign A Purim, or a Feast to celebrate Some Victory. **1908** *Daily News* 17 Mar. 4 In a Jewish Leap Year Adar is doubled and Purim falls in Adar the Second, which is the thirteenth month.

attrib. **1892** ZANGWILL *Childr. Ghetto* I. vii. 183, I must go to the Purim ball with him and Leah.

purine ('pjʊəriːn). *Phys. Chem.* Also *unsystematically* purin. [ad. Ger. *purin*, according to the inventor, Emil Fischer, 'combined from the L. words *pūrum* pure, and *ūricum* uric (acid)'. By the Chemical Society spelt *purine*, as a base: see -INE[5].] A white crystalline basic substance $C_5H_4N_4$, having a bicyclic structure consisting of fused imidazole and pyrimidine rings, which when oxidized forms uric acid ($C_5H_4N_4O_3$), and of which adenine, caffeine, xanthine, etc., are also derivatives, and known as ***the purines*** or members of the ***purine group***; *spec.* adenine or guanine, two substituted purines found in nucleic acids, etc. Freq. *attrib.*

(The group $C_5N_4H_4$ was so named by Fischer in 1884 as the source of derivatives then prepared and named by him, *methyl-purin* and *trichlor-methylpurin*; the substance itself was not isolated by him till 1898, 14 years after it had been named. See *Berichte d. deutsch. chem. Gesellsch.* XVII. 329 (1884), and XXXI. 2564 (1898).

1898 *Chem. News* 16 Dec. 304/1 (*heading*) Molecular transformation in the group of purines. **1899** *Jrnl. Chem. Soc.* LXXVI. I. 175 *Purine*,..is a readily soluble, well crystallised substance, which forms salts both with acids and with bases, and as regards its character in general falls naturally in the series uric acid, xanthine, hypoxanthine, purine. **1902** *Brit. Med. Jrnl.* No. 2163, 14 June 1461 Under the term 'purin' all the substances that contain the nucleus C_5N_4 may be included. *Ibid.*, The Estimation of Purin Bodies in food-stuffs... By the use of purin-free foods they ascertained the average amount of urinary purin in various individuals. **1921** *Spectator* 21 May 658/1 Purin bodies, precursors of uric acid, and purin-free diets have likewise had their day, although as inculcating abstemiousness the latter played a useful part. **1952** *Sci. News* XXIV. 43 The DNA isolated from different organs of the same animal species seems to be constant in composition with respect to the relative amounts of purine and pyrimidine bases but differs from samples obtained from other species. **1954** *New Biol.* XVI. 15 Nucleic acids appear to consist of alternate purine and pyrimidine nucleotides arranged in a chain. In desoxyribose nucleic acid the purine is either adenine or guanine. **1970** *Nature* 25 July 379/2 Naturally occurring cytokinins known so far have a purine nucleus as the essential moiety. **1973** R. G. KRUEGER et al. *Introd. Microbiol.* x. 307/2 Pairings between purines would distort the helix because of the large size of the molecules.

purinergic (pjʊəriː'nɜːdʒɪk), *a. Physiol.* [f. prec. + Gr. ἔργ-ον work + -IC.] Of a nerve-fibre: that liberates, and is stimulated by, a purine derivative.

1971 *Courier-Mail* (Brisbane) 16 Jan. 8/1 Professor Burnstock and colleagues..have just published a paper presenting evidence that this third type of autonomic nerve fibre acts by releasing..a purine nucleotide. Because of this they tentatively propose to call the nerves 'purinergic'. **1971** G. BURNSTOCK in *Nature* 22 Jan. 282/3 In the early 1960s powerful nerves were found to supply that gut which were neither cholinergic nor adrenergic... Evidence has recently been presented that the transmitter substance released from these nerves may be ATP or some related purine nucleotide. It would therefore seem reasonable..to propose that the new nerves be termed 'purinergic'. **1977** *Lancet* 19 Nov. 1065/2 Work on the non-adrenergic non-cholinergic (purinergic) system will probably shed more light on and possibly lead to more rational pharmacological approaches to the deranged internal sphincter.

‖**puriri** ('puːriri). [Native Maori name.]

1. A New Zealand forest tree, *Vitex lucens*, belonging to the family Verbenaceæ and bearing compound leaves and axillary clusters of red flowers; also, the hard, durable timber of this tree. Also *attrib.*

1835 W. YATE *Acct. of N.Z.* (ed. 2) ii. 43 Puriri (*Vitex littoralis*)—This tree, from its hardness and durability has been denominated the New-Zealand Oak. **1838** J. S. POLACK *N.Z.* II. 393 The Puriri..is a wood whose durability equals any of the timbers in the country. **1842** W. R. WADE *Journ. N. Zealand* 200 *note*, Puriri, misnamed *vitex littoralis*, as it is not found near the sea-coast. **1863** A. S. ATKINSON *Jrnl.* 29 Sept. in *Richmond-Atkinson Papers* (1960) II. 64 One [ball from a rifle] pitched.. in a very good line for me but stuck in a puriri log. **1886** *N. Zealand Herald* 1 June 2/2 The land is..finely sheltered by pretty clumps of puriri and other bush. **1910** L. COCKAYNE *N.Z. Plants* iii. 39 Birds also fertilise a few New Zealand plants, amongst others the puriri. **1952** *Landfall* VI. 31 The framework of this haystack cover stands on puriri uprights which though sunken into the ground are practically everlasting. **1959** *N.Z. Listener* 13 Mar. 5/4 These fascinating little owls had their nest in a clump of astelia in a puriri tree. **1973** ATKINSON & BELL in G. R. Williams *Nat. Hist. N.Z.* xv. 378/1 Large numbers of kohekohe, puriri, karaka and mahoe are also present.

2. *Comb.* **puriri moth**, a large green moth, *Hepialus* (or *Charagia*) *virescens*, of the family Hepialidæ, whose larvæ bore into the wood of the puriri and certain other trees.

1966 *Encycl. N.Z.* II. 590/1 The puriri or ghost moth is the largest native moth of New Zealand. **1971** *N.Z. Listener* 6 Sept. 17/1, I hoped I might be able to get a big green puriri moth on that soft and cloudy summer night.

purism ('pjʊərɪz(ə)m). [ad. F. *purisme*, f. *pur* PURE: see -ISM.] **1. a.** Scrupulous or exaggerated observance of, or insistence upon, purity or correctness, esp. in language or style.

1804 MITFORD *Inquiry* 392 Before we attempt to exercise on our language the spirit of what the French used to call purism. **1821** *Sporting Mag.* VIII. 236 The purism of modern times and your fastidious delicacy..would not allow me to give this story at full length. **1860** MARSH *Lect. Eng. Lang.* xxvii. 598 The spirit of nationality and linguistic purism..has..purged and renovated so many decayed and corrupted European languages. **1869** MISS BRADDON *Lady's Mile* 247 The strictest pureism in the ethics of costume. **1905** *Athenæum* 26 Aug. 269/2 The works and views of the writers on [French] grammar who upheld purism.

b. with *pl.* An instance of this; a scrupulously or excessively pure expression or principle.

1803 *Edin. Rev.* I. 254 The glory of illuminating his countrymen in purisms. **1844** *Blackw. Mag.* LVI. 144 The purisms of political delinquency had little share..in any remorse which Shah Soojah might ever feel.

2. *Art.* (With capital initial.) An early twentieth-century movement in painting arising out of a rejection of cubism and characterized by a return to the representation of recognizable objects with emphasis on purity of geometric form.

1931 A. OZENFANT *Foundations Mod. Art* p. xi, I have sought to formulate those tropisms which are most clearly apprehended. On them I base the art that derives from 'constants'. I call it 'Purism'. **1959** *Archit. Rev.* CXXV. 356/2 Jeanneret's contribution to Purism was curious. It is the work of a follower, but the pictures have greater presence than those they emulate. **1961** M. LEVY *Studio Dict. of Art Terms* 92 *Purism*, a movement in modern painting and sculpture, founded in 1918 by the painters, Amédée Ozenfant, Le Corbusier, and Brancusi. Purism was a reaction against the analytical spirit of Cubism and sought to remake, and thus purify, the world of objects, etc. **1973** *Times* 27 Nov. 12/5 For a time in the early twenties Servranckx worked in a style known as Purism, associated with Leger and Ozenfant, of simplified brightly coloured abstractions of machine forms.

‖**puris natu'ralibus.** [med.L.] = *in puris naturalibus* s.v. IN *Lat. prep.* 28.

1920 LD. F. HAMILTON *Vanished Pomps of Yesterday* (rev. ed.) ix. 307 Dick and I spent hours there swimming, and basking *puris naturalibus* on the rocks. **1974** *Listener* 17 Jan. 84/2 O the joy of being idle... With a bun and towel basking *Puris naturalibus.*

purist ('pjʊərɪst), *sb.* (and *a.*) [ad. F. *puriste* (1586, applied to the Puritans), f. *pur* PURE; or (sense 2) f. L. *pūr-us* PURE + -IST.]

1. One who aims at, affects, or insists on scrupulous or excessive purity, esp. in language or style; a stickler for purity or correctness.

1706 PHILLIPS (ed. 6), *Purist*, one that affects to speak or write neatly and properly. [**1751** CHESTERF. *Lett.* (1792) III. 185 English, in which you are certainly no *puriste*.] **1758** JORTIN *Erasmus* I. 443 Some Italian Purists, who scrupled to make use of any word or phrase, which was not to be found in Cicero. **1820** HAZLITT *Lect. Dram. Lit.* 143 The greatest purists (hypocrisy apart) are often free-livers. **1837–9** HALLAM *Hist. Lit.* (1847) III. 143 The use of quotations in a different language, which some purists in French style had in horror. **1842** *Murray's Hand-bk. N. Italy* 25/2 The cortile is a fine example of..the architecture which purists term *impure*—columns encircled by bands, story above story. **1866** FELTON *Anc. & Mod. Greece* II. II. ii. 275 The Macedonians were not acknowledged as genuine Greeks by the purists of Sparta and Athens. **1870** LOWELL *Lett., To C. E. Norton* 15 Oct. (1894) II. 74 As to words, I am something of a purist, though I like best the word that best says the thing.

2. One who maintained that the New Testament was written in pure Greek.

1835 MOSES STUART. **1907** *Expositor* Nov. 428 In the controversy of the Purists and Hebraists in the seventeenth century.

3. *Art.* (With capital initial.) An adherent of Purism (see PURISM 2).

1939 in WEBSTER Add. **1959** H. READ *Conc. Hist. Mod. Painting* vi. 215 Between the years 1920 and 1925 the Purists had a decisive influence on the development of abstract art throughout Europe and America. **1974** *Encycl. Brit. Micropædia* VIII. 309/3 There were many painters..who, like the Purists, were attracted to a machine-inspired aesthetic.

4. *attrib.* or as *adj.*

1939 in WEBSTER Add. **1945** KOESTLER *Yogi & Commissar* III. ii. 155 Not even the most purist critic could expect a sudden jump to total equalitarianism. **1959** H. READ *Conc. Hist. Mod. Painting* vi. 216 Nicholson began as a decorative painter of great charm, and then came under various 'purist' influences of which the most direct and powerful was that of Mondrian. **1961** R. B. LONG *Sentence & its Parts* 5 The sentences of spoken English are often poorly constructed —and this is not a purist judgement. **1965** W. S. ALLEN *Vox Latina* ii. 55 The purist reader would therefore be justified in reading the nominative plural forms *filii, di* as *filiī, dī* respectively. **1978** *Gramophone* Jan. 1307/3 Disc and cassette reproduce about equally well, though I suspect we would like both versions a lot better if a more purist recording technique were adopted.

Hence **pu'ristic, pu'ristical** *adjs.*, characteristic of a purist; characterized by purism.

a **1872** MAURICE (Ogilvie *Supp.*), Bentham's puristical wisdom. **1877** SYMONDS *Renaiss. in It., Reviv. Learn.* (1897) II. vii. 319 The imitation of the ancients grew more puristic and precise. **1880** VERN. LEE *Stud. Italy* I. 5 This national Italian drama, unnoticed by the puristic eighteenth century. **1882** *Athenæum* 15 Apr. 474/3 He complains..that the Persian language is flooded..by Arabic words and phrases; and the whole book is a practical illustration of his puristic theory. **1908** *Edinb. Rev.* Apr. 460 Her puristical vanity.

puritan ('pjʊərɪtən), *sb.* and *a.* Also **Puritan**, esp. in specific uses. [f. L. *pūr-us* pure, or *pūritās* PURIT-Y + -AN. Perh. formed in French or mod.Latin: cf. F. *puritain* (Ronsard 1564), mod.L. *pūritānī* (in Du Cange). The appellation appears to have been intended to suggest that of the *Καθαροί*, Catharans, or Catharists, assumed by the Novatian heretics, and thus to convey an odious imputation.]

A. *sb.*

1. a. *Hist.* A member of that party of English Protestants who regarded the reformation of the church under Elizabeth as incomplete, and called for its further 'purification' from what they considered to be unscriptural and corrupt forms and ceremonies retained from the unreformed church; subsequently, often applied to any who separated from the established church on points of ritual, polity, or doctrine, held by them to be at variance with 'pure' New Testament principles.

According to Stow (see quot. 15..) the name was (? originally) assumed by congregations of Anabaptists in London; but this is probably an error, for otherwise it appears in early use always as a term of reproach used by opponents, and resented by those to whom it was applied: see quot. from Fuller 1655. Its application changed with time and the course of events. Originally, it was applied to those within the Church of England who demanded further reformation, especially in the direction of Presbyterianism; afterwards, naturally, to the same party when they were separated from the Church, and became the anti-episcopal Presbyterians, Independents, or Baptists, and consequently to the typical 'Roundheads' of the Commonwealth period, whose puritanism was sometimes little more than political. In later times, the term has become historical, without any opprobrious connotation, and has even, from its association with *purity* and *pure*, come to be treated, by those who in opinion agree more or less with the early Puritans, as a name of honour.

[**15..** STOW in *Three 15th C. Chron.* (Camden) 143 About that tyme [1567] were many congregations of the Anabaptysts in London, who cawlyd themselvs Puritans or Unspottyd Lambs of the Lord.] **1572** J. JONES *Bathes of Bath* III. 24 Puritanes are they named, pure I wold they wer. *Ibid.* [see PRECISIAN]. **1572** [FIELD & WILCOX] *Admonition to Parlt.* Pref. A 1 b, They lincke in togither & slaunderously charge pore men..with greeuous faults, calling them Puritanes, worse than the Donatistes. **1572** WHITGIFT *Answ. to Admonition* 18 This name Puritane is very aptely giuen to these men, not bicause they be pure no more than were the Heretikes called *Cathari*, but bicause they think them selues to be *mundiores ceteris*, more pure than others, as *Cathari* did, and seperate them selues from all other Churches and congregations as spotted and defyled. **1573** T. CARTWRIGHT *Reply to Whitgift* 13 If you meane, that those are Puritanes or Catharans, which do set forth a true and perfect patern or platforme of reforming the church, then the marke of thys heresie reacheth vnto those, which made the booke of common prayer. **1573** G. HARVEY *Letter-bk.* (Camd.) 29 Alleging..that I had greatly commendid thos whitch men call præcisions and puritanes. **1589** *Hay, any Worke for Cooper* 25 The Ministers maintenance by tithe no Puritan denieth to be unlawful. For Martin.., you must understand, doth account no Brownist to be a Puritan. **1589** NASHE *Pasquil's Ret.* Wks. (Grosart) I. 94, I knowe they are commonly called Puritans, and not amisse... They take themselues to be pure, when they are filthy in Gods sight. **1601** SHAKS. *All's Well* I. iii. 98 Though honestie be no Puritan, yet it will doe no hurt, it will weare the Surplis of humilitie ouer the blacke-Gowne of a bigge heart. **1611** —— *Wint. T.* IV. iii. 46 The shearers (three-man song-men, all, and very good ones)..but one Puritan amongst them, and he sings Psalmes to horne-pipes. **1618** *King's Decl. conc. Sports* 6 (republ. 1633 10) Our pleasure likewise is, That the Bishop of that Diocesse take the like straight order with all the Puritans and Precisians..either constraining them to conforme themselues, or to leave the Countrey. *a* **1625** J. ROBINSON in Drysdale *Hist. Presbyt. in Eng.* (1889) 5 *note*, The Papists plant the ruling power of Christ in the Pope; the Protestants in the Bishops; the Puritans in the Presbytery; we [Independents] in the body of the Congregation of the multitude called the Church. **1641** MILTON *Reform. Ch. Disc.* I. 16 All those that found fault with the Decrees of the Convocation..strait were..branded with the Name of Puritans. **1655** FULLER *Ch. Hist.* IX. i. §66 The English Bishops..began..urging the Clergy..to subscribe to the Liturgie, Ceremonies, and Discipline of the Church, and such as refused..were branded with the odious name of Puritanes, a name which in this note first began in this year [1564]. *a* **1715** BURNET *Own Time* I. (1724) 17 The Puritans..put on external appearances of great strictness and gravity. They took more pains in their parishes than those who adhered to the bishops. **1732–8** NEAL (*title*) The History of the Puritans or Protestant Non-Conformists. *a* **1779** WARBURTON *Alliance betw. Ch. & St.* III. iii, Those prudent and honest men..gave it as their deliberate judgment, 'That the Puritans ought to conform, rather than make a schism: and that the church men ought to indulge the others' scruples, rather than hazard one'. **1825** MACAULAY *Ess., Milton* (1887) 23 The Puritans, the most remarkable body of men, perhaps, which the world has ever produced. **1830** COLERIDGE *Table-t.* 10 June, Is it not..an historical error to call the Puritans dissenters? Before St. Bartholomew's day they were essentially a part of the Church. **1845** JAMES *A. Neil* ii, His master was a rigid man, a Puritan of the most severe cast. **189.** BP. RYLE *Light fr. Old Times* (1903) 339 This saintly old Puritan [Baxter]. **1903** F. W. MAITLAND in *Camb. Mod. Hist.* II, xvi. 590 Those who strove for a worship purified from all taint of popery (and who therefore were known as 'Puritans') 'scrupled' the cap and gown.., and 'scrupled' the surplice.

b. *transf.* A member of any religious sect or party that advocates or aspires to special purity of doctrine or practice. (Cf. CATHARAN, CATHARIST.)

1577 HANMER *Anc. Eccl. Hist.* VI. xliii. (1663) 116 Novatus ..became himself the author and ringleader of his own hereticall sect, to wit, of such as through their swelling pride do call themselves Puritans. **1613** PURCHAS *Pilgrimage* IV. viii. (1614) 378 The Persians are a kinde of Catharists or Puritans in their impure Muhammedrie. **1637** GILLESPIE *Eng. Pop. Cerem.* II. v. 24 The old Waldenses..were also named by their adversaries, Cathares or Puritanes. **1655** FULLER *Ch. Hist.* IX. i. §67 We need not speak of the ancient Cathari or Primitive Puritans. **1709** J. JOHNSON *Clergym. Vade M.* II. 48 By the Puritans we are to understand the Novatians, who would not commune with the Catholic church under pretence that her communion was polluted. **1871** SIR W. W. HUNTER *Ind. Musalmans* 58 The Wahábis form..an advanced division of the Sunnis—the Puritans of Islám.

c. A member of any (non-religious) party or school who practises or advocates strict or extreme adherence to its principles; a purist.

1885 *Pall Mall G.* 20 May 1/1 The Crofters Holdings Bill has been received..very quietly by the Puritans of 'economic principle'.

2. Applied, chiefly in reproach or ridicule, to one who is, affects to be, or is accounted extremely strict, precise, or scrupulous in religion or morals.

The early Puritans were in many cases characterized by the prominence which they attached to personal religion, and by strictness and gravity of behaviour, with plainness of dress and manners; hence it was easy to look upon a 'puritan' as one who professed a higher standard of personal religion and morality than was usual.

1592 GREENE *Repentance* Wks. (Grosart) XII. 176 When I had discouered that I sorrowed for my wickednesse..they fell vpon me in ieasting manner, calling me Puritane and Presizian. **1611** RICH *Honest. Age* (Percy Soc.) 55 He that hath not for euery word an oath..they say hee is a puritan, a precise foole, not fitte to hold a gentleman company. **1655** FULLER *Ch. Hist.* IX. i. §67 (an. 1564) *Puritan* here was taken for the Opposers of the Hierarchie and Church-Service, as resenting of Superstition. But prophane mouths quickly improved this Nick-name, therewith on every occasion to abuse pious people. **1696** M. SYLVESTER *Life & Times Baxter* 32 When they had been called by that name awhile, the vicious Multitude of the Ungodly called all Puritans that were strict and serious in a Holy Life, were they ever so conformable! **1798** CHARLOTTE SMITH *Yng. Philos.* III. 26 Brought up among the strait-laced..puritans of the United States.

B. *adj.* **a.** Of, pertaining to, or characteristic of the Puritans; strict and scrupulous in religious observances. ***Puritan conscience***: a strict individual conscience requiring high standards; ***Puritan ethic***: the belief in the redemptive value of work. **b.** That is a Puritan. (In quot. 1607 satirically used as = hypocritical, dissembling.)

1589 *Marprel. Tr., Epit.* A ij, The Puritans are angrie with me, I meane the puritane preachers. **1607** TOURNEUR *Rev. Trag.* II. ii, I'll after him And..seeme to beare a part In all his ills, but with a Puritane heart. **1617** MORYSON *Itin.* III. 30 If a man would seeme (as I may say) a Puritan Papist,.. there is danger to fall into the suspition of an Hypocrite. **1638** LAUD *Diary* 29 Apr., There's a great concurrence between them [in Scotland] and the Puritan party in England. **1652** SANDERSON *Cases of Consc.* (1678) 192 To discover the weakness of the Puritan principles and tenents. **1806** in J. Thacher *Hist. Plymouth* (1832) 232 This is the 186th anniversary of the first landing of our puritan fathers. **1832** *Ibid.* 324 The venerable pastor of the pilgrims, and his puritan associates. **1840** DICKENS *Barn. Rudge* xxxvii, He was no less frugal in his repasts than in his Puritan attire. **1857** C. KINGSLEY *Let.* in *Life* (1879) II. 52, I am full of old Puritan blood. **1858** LONGF. *M. Standish* III. 40 Singing the hundredth Psalm, the grand old Puritan anthem. **1901** KIPLING *Let.* in C. Carrington *Rudyard Kipling* (1955) xiii. 318 Her Puritan conscience which she has inherited from her New England forbears still makes her take life too blame seriously. **1932** Q. D. LEAVIS *Fiction & Reading Public* II. ii. 97 (*heading*) The puritan conscience. **1972** C. WESTON *Poor, Poor Ophelia* (1973) v. 28 He beamed good cheer and the puritan ethic—*work for the night is falling*. **1975** *Listener* 16 Oct. 517/2 Hale White..did manage to write small, vigorous masterpieces of the puritan conscience trying to beat out a narrow path for itself. **1977** *Ibid.* 7 Apr. 434/1 The Puritan ethic..an ethic of discipline, work, responsibility.

c. ***Puritan spoon*** (see quot. 1960).

1956 G. TAYLOR *Silver* iv. 86 In the reign of Charles I the so-called Puritan spoon..began to appear. **1960** H. HAYWARD *Antique Coll.* 230/2 *Puritan spoon*, a mid-17th cent. spoon with flat stem, straight top edge and nearly oval bowl, the earliest form of English flat-stemmed spoon. **1971** *Country Life* 10 June (Suppl.) 58 (Advt.), Commonwealth 1659 Puritan Spoon.

Hence **'puritaness** (*nonce-wd.*), a female puritan; †**puri'tanian**, (-'nean) *a.* = PURITANICAL; Presbyterian; **'puritanly** *adv.*, in a puritan manner, towards Puritanism; †**puri,tano-'papist** *nonce-wd.*, a strict or austere papist, esp. a Jesuit.

1897 *Daily Tel.* 4 June 9/1 If our fair *Puritanesses press us much further. **1600** W. WATSON *Decacordon* (1602) 13 A blind conceit and opinion of their [Iesuits'] *puritanian holinesse. *Ibid.* 224 The Puritanean Consistorie, representing the ecclesiasticall state in Scotland. **1897** W. WALKER *Hist. Congregat. Ch. U.S.* 89 The see of London, the..most *Puritanly inclined. **1601** BP. W. BARLOW *Defence* 107 The *Puritano-papiste, Loyala.

puritanic (pjʊərɪ'tænɪk), *a.* [f. PURITAN + -IC; after *Satanic*, etc.] Of or pertaining to the Puritans, = PURITAN *a.* (now *rare*); having the character or manner of a puritan; = next.

1606 CHAPMAN *M. D'Olive* Plays 1873 I. 214 That nose of his (according to the Puritannick cut) hauing a narrow bridge. **1782** W. MASON *Eng. Gard.* IV. 34/622 Too dark a stole Was o'er Religion's decent features drawn By Puritanic zeal. **1794** *Mass. Mag.* (U.S.) May 288 When those venerable puritanic sages landed at Plymouth. **1828** D'ISRAELI *Chas. I*, I. iii. 35 The puritanic party..starting up among all ranks of society. **1830** FOSTER in *Life & Corr.* (1846) II. 157 A puritanic simplicity and unworldliness. **1882** SPURGEON *Treas. Dav.* Ps. xv. 5 The Puritanic divines are almost all of them against the taking of any interest upon money.

puritanical (pjʊərɪ'tænɪkəl), *a.* [f. as prec. + -ICAL.] Pertaining to or characteristic of the Puritans, or of puritans generally; having the character of a puritan; marked by the strictness, plainness, or other quality of puritans. (Chiefly in disparagement. In quot. 1882-3 used as = PURITAN *a.*)

1607 DEKKER & WEBSTER *Northw. Hoe* I. i, His wiues puritanicall coynesse. **1624** in Rymer *Fœdera* XVII. 616 Seditious Puritanical books and pamphlets, scandalous to our person or state, such as have been lately vented by some Puritanical spirits. *c* **1683** BURNET *Orig. Mem.* I. (1902) 71 The duke [of York] complained of this [insertion in the Bk. of Comm. Prayer] much to me as a puritanical thing. **1687** A. LOVELL tr. *Thevenot's Trav.* I. ej b, That Sect..was in Mahometanism the most Puritanical of all the Sects of the East. **1712** ADDISON *Spect.* No. 458 ¶6 Every Appearance of Devotion was looked upon as Puritannical. **1878** T. CUYLER *Pointed Papers* 162, I do not want to be thought queer or puritanical. **1879** L. STEPHEN *Hours in Library* III. 84 That Fielding in his hatred for humbug should have condemned purity as puritanical, is clearly lamentable. **1882-3** *Schaff's Encycl. Relig. Knowl.* 430/2 Pastor of a puritanical Calvinistic Congregation in..Boston.

Hence **puri'tanically** *adv.*, in a puritanical way; after the manner of the Puritans.

1607 DEKKER & WEBSTER *Northw. Hoe* III. D.'s Wks. 1873 III. 41 Shee would do it so puritannically, so secretly I meane, that no body should heare of it. **1706** HEARNE *Collect.* 9 Apr. (O.H.S.) I. 221 [He] was a little Puritannically inclin'd. **1847** LYTTON *Lucretia* II. xvii, The forehead, over which that stiff, harsh hair was so puritanically parted.

puritanism ('pjʊərɪtənɪz(ə)m). Also **Puritanism**, esp. in specific uses. [f. PURITAN + -ISM.]

1. The Puritan system; the doctrines and principles of the Puritans; Puritan opinion or practice.

1573 G. HARVEY *Letter-bk.* (Camden) 30 Let M. Phisician ..shew..that ever I have maintainid ani od point of puritanism, or præcisionism. **1601** ? MARSTON *Pasquil & Kath.* II. 220 Leaue praying for dead. 'Tis no good Caluianisme, Puritanisme. **1624** LAUD *Diary* 23 Dec., The same day I delivered my L. a little tract about Doctrinal Puritanism. **1661** PEPYS *Diary* 7 Sept., 'Bartholomew Fayre', with the puppet-showe,..which had not been [acted] these forty years (it being so satyricall against Puritanism). **1736** WARBURTON *Alliance Ch. & St.* III. iii, At one season it [the danger] might arise from Popery, at another from Puritanism. **1900** MORLEY *O. Cromwell* V. v. 409 Militant Puritanism was often only half-Christian. **1908** P. T. FORSYTH in *Contemp. Rev.* Feb. 159 Puritanism is the mother church of Western democracy.

b. *transf.* (Cf. PURITAN A. 1 b, c.)

1581 J. BELL *Haddon's Answ. Osor.* 132, I could wishe.. that we all could direct the course of our lyfe..accordyng to this Puritanisme of Osorius. **1870** RUSKIN *Lect. Art* iii. 73 This Puritanism in the worship of beauty, though sometimes weak, is always honourable and amiable.

2. Excessive (or affected) strictness or preciseness like that observed by or attributed to the Puritans; puritanical behaviour or principles; precisianism.

1592 NASHE *P. Penilesse* Wks. (Grosart) II. 100 Vnder hypocrisie [I comprehend] al Machiauilisme, puritanisme, & outward gloasing with a mans enemie. **1633** PRYNNE *Histriom.* I. ii. 25 Licentious Christians, who make their will and lusts their law, may deeme it Puritanisme, or brand it for ouerstrict precisenesse. **1831** *Blackw. Mag.* XXIX. 772 Scruples which grow out of excessive puritanism in style. **1832** G. DOWNES *Lett. Cont. Countries* I. 175 That moderate austerity..which may, without puritanism, be recommended.

puritanize ('pjʊərɪtənaɪz), *v.* [as prec. + -IZE.]

1. *intr.* (with *it*). To act the puritan; to practise, conform to, or affect puritanism.

1625 BP. MOUNTAGU *App. Cæsar* 270 He faine would puritanize it.

2. *trans.* To make puritan, imbue with puritanism.

1648 *Persecutio Undecima* 13 So generally peevish and puritanized were the people. **1838** HALLAM *Lit. Eur.* II. i. 55 *note*, Leicester succeeded in puritanizing, as Wood thought, the University. **1853** MISS YONGE *Heir of Redclyffe* iii, He has been puritanized till he is good for nothing.

Hence **'purita,nized**, **'purita,nizing** *ppl. adjs.*; also **'purita,nizer**, one who puritanizes.

1836 *New Monthly Mag.* XLVII. 99 St. Paul's was a puritanized prosaic imitation of St. Peter's. **1847** BP. WILBERFORCE *Let.* in Ashwell *Life* (1879) I. x. 408, I cannot effectually guard the purity of the faith..from dishonesty of subscription on the side of Romanizers, if I wink at a like sin on the side of Puritanizers. **1857** BADEN POWELL *Chr. without Judaism* 173 The continued struggle between the Puritanising and the Catholicising extremes of the Reformation. **1882** J. H. BLUNT *Ref. Ch. Eng.* II. 162 Cranmer and the Puritanizing party.

puritanly, etc.: see after PURITAN.

†**'Puritant.** *Obs. rare.* Alteration of PURITAN, after *Protestant*.

1604 HIERON *Popish Rime* Wks. I. 553 Many sundry sects ..The Caluinist, the Protestant, The Zwinglian, the Puritant. **1607** T. SPARKE *Brotherly Persuasion* 81 To burie and extinguish for euer the odious name of Puritants.

purity ('pjʊərɪtɪ). Forms: 3-6 **purete**, 4-5 **purte**, 4-6 **puryte**, 6 **purite**, **purety**, 6-7 **puritie**, 6- **purity**. [ME. *purte* (rare), a. OF. *purte* (12th c. in Hatz.-Darm.); but usually, from the beginning of 13th c. in a later F. form *purete*, mod.F. *pureté*, and at length more fully conformed, as *purite*, *-itie*, *-ity*, to L. *pūritās*, *-tātem* (f. *pūr-us* PURE: see -ITY). Cf. Pr. *purtat*, *-etat*, *-itat*, It. *purità*, Sp. *puridad*.] The quality or condition of being pure, in various senses.

1. In physical sense: The state of being unmixed; freedom from admixture of any foreign substance or matter; absence of any other ingredient; *esp.* freedom from matter that contaminates, defiles, corrupts, or debases; physical cleanness.

1526 *Pilgr. Perf.* (W. de W. 1531) 228 This corruptible body shall be indued with purite & incorupcyon. **1550** *Acts Privy Counc.* (1890) II. 430 French crownes..of the goodnes, purety, and waight, as they be currant in Fraunce. **1611** SHAKS. *Wint. T.* I. ii. 327 To..Sully the puritie and whitenesse of my Sheetes. **1727-46** THOMSON *Summer* 1267 This [bathing] is the purest exercise of health. .. Even from the body's purity the mind Receives a secret sympathetic aid. **1832** G. R. PORTER *Porcelain & Gl.* 164 To insure the absolute purity of the ingredients. **1860** TYNDALL *Glac.* I. xx. 138 Snow of perfect purity.

b. quasi-*concr.* Pure substance or part.

1460-70 *Bk. Quintessence* 5 þe purete of þe quinte essencie schal be sublymed aboue, & þe groste schal abide byneþe. *c* **1720** PRIOR *2nd Hymn Callimachus* 147 The nymphs.. from little urns Pour streams select, and purity of waters.

2. In non-physical or general sense: The state of being unmixed; freedom from any foreign or extraneous element, esp. from such as corrupt or debase; unalloyed or unadulterated condition; faultlessness, correctness.

1561 tr. *Calvin's 4 Godly Serm.* i. C iiij, To abolish al superstitions, y^t the true religion mai be set in her own puritie & holines. **1563** NOWELL in *Lett. Lit. Men* (Camden) 21 The purity of the Latine tongue. **1661** EVELYN *Diary* 10 Nov., He shew'd that the Church of England was for purity of doctrine..the most perfect under Heaven. **1700** DRYDEN *Fables* Pref., in *Ess.* (ed. Ker) II. 254 From Chaucer the purity of the English tongue began. **1704** NORRIS *Ideal World* II. iii. 182 The metaphysical purity..of thought is the immateriality..of its object. **1841** ELPHINSTONE *Hist. Ind.* I. i. 35 The daughters of such connections, if they go on marrying Bramins for seven generations, restore their progeny to the original purity of the sacerdotal class. **1875** FREEMAN *Venice* (1881) 257 The slight touch of *Renaissance* in some of the capitals..in no sort takes away from the general purity of the style.

3. Of persons, their faculties, actions, attributes, etc.: Freedom from moral corruption, from ceremonial or sexual uncleanness, or pollution; stainless condition or character; innocence, chastity, ceremonial cleanness. (The earliest sense in Eng.)

a **1225** *Ancr. R.* 4 All muwen & owen holden one riwle onont purete of heorte. **1340** *Ayenb.* 202 Þis chastete, þis clennesse, þis purte acseþ þet me loki þe herte uram euele þo3tes. **1426** LYDG. *De Guil. Pilgr.* 22985 Whanne it is songe off good entente, In clennesse and in purete. **1526** *Pilgr. Perf.* (W. de W. 1531) 145 b, Whan we be gyuen..to clennesse of vertue & purite of lyfe. **1598** SHAKS. *Merry W.* II. ii. 258, I could driue her then from the ward of her purity, her reputation, her marriage-vow. **1611** BIBLE *1 Tim.* v. 2 Intreate..The elder women as mothers, the yonger as sisters with all puritie. **1634** MILTON *Comus* 427 No savage fierce..Will dare to soyl her Virgin purity. *a* **1661** HOLYDAY (J.), Is it the purity of a linen vesture, which some so fear would defile the purity of the priest? **1729** LAW *Serious Call* vii. 109 Every thing about her resembles the purity of her soul. **1816** BYRON *Siege Cor.* xxi, 'Tis said the lion will turn and flee From a maid in the pride of her purity. **1827** HEBER *Hymn 'Holy, holy, holy'* iii, Perfect in power, in love, and purity. **1905** W. SANDAY *Crit. 4th Gosp.* IV. 120 The strictest ritualistic purity was required of those who took part in the feast.

b. quasi-*concr.* An embodiment of purity; a stainless being. *nonce-use.*

1602 MARSTON *Ant. & Mel.* I. Wks. 1856 I. 14 She comes: creations puritie, admir'd, Ador'd amazing raritie.

Purkinje (pɜː'kɪndʒiː) The name of a Bohemian physiologist (1787-1869), applied in the possessive to various phenomena and anatomical structures, as **Purkinje's cells**, large branching cells in the cortex of the brain; **Purkinje's fibres**, certain fibres in the ventricles of the heart, esp. in the fœtus; **Purkinje's figures**, visual figures produced by the shadows of the retinal blood-vessels cast by light (e.g. from a candle) entering the eye laterally; **Purkinje('s) phenomenon** or **shift** (also **phenomenon of Purkinje**), a decrease in the apparent brightness of light of long wavelength (e.g. red) compared with light of short wavelength (e.g. blue) when the degree of illumination falls; [described by Purkinje in *Mag. für die ges. Heilkunde* (1825) XX. 225]; **Purkinje's vesicle**: see PURKINJEAN *a.*

1869 HUXLEY *Phys.* ix. (ed. 3) 248 If you go into a dark room with a single.. candle, and.. allow the light to fall very obliquely into the eye, one of what are called Purkinje's figures is seen. This is a vision of a series of diverging, branched, red lines on a dark field. **1890** BILLINGS *Nat. Med. Dict.*, Purkinje's cells.. Purkinje's fibres.. Purkinje's figures.. Purkinje's vesicle. **1900** C. WEILAND tr. *M. Tscherning's Physiologic Optics* xvii. 260 A comparison of the brightness of two different colors is not easy,.. and the result depends besides on the phenomenon of Purkinje. **1910** M. GREENWOOD *Physiol. of Special Senses* xii. 101 A particular case of adaptation which is of much interest is 'Purkinje's Phenomenon'. **1949** H. C. WESTON *Sight, Light & Efficiency* i. 20 The 'Purkinje phenomenon'.. is familiar to everyone who has noted.. that when green leaves and red flowers are seen in twilight the green appears brighter compared with the red than is the case in full daylight. **1973** *Nature* 14 Dec. 380/1 The most familiar effect of the duality of human vision is the so-called 'Purkinje shift'.

Purkinjean (pɜːˈkɪndʒiːən), *a. Anat.* and *Phys.* Also erron. **-gian.** [f. PURKINJE + -AN.] Pertaining to or named after Purkinje: applied to various anatomical structures, etc., as the ***Purkinjean capsules*** in the cement of a tooth (see quot. 1854); ***Purkinjean vesicle***, the nucleus of the ovum, discovered by Purkinje in 1825, also called *germinal vesicle* or *Purkinje's vesicle*.

1835-6 *Todd's Cycl. Anat.* I. 785/1 During the last stage of its continuance in the ovary the vesicle of Purkinje disappears. **1836-9** *Ibid.* II. 452/1 The Purkinjean or germinal vesicle. **1854** OWEN *Skel. & Teeth* in *Orr's Circ. Sci., Org. Nat.* I. 292 (Elephant's grinders) The cells.. become confluent.., their primitive distinctness being indicated only by their persistent granular nuclei, which now form the radiated Purkingian capsules. **1890** BILLINGS *Nat. Med. Dict.*, Purkinje's vesicle.

purl (pɜːl), *sb.*[1] Forms: 6 pyrl(e, 6-9 purle, 7- purl (9, *in senses* 2, 5, *also* pearl: see PEARL *sb.*[4]). [In sense 1, app. orig. *pyrl(e*, f. *pyrl(e*, PIRL *v.* to twist ('I pyrle wyer of golde or syluer' Palsgr.). As to the other senses see Note below.]

I. 1. Thread or cord made of twisted gold or silver wire, used for bordering and embroidering. ***pearl purl***: see quot. 1882. ***silk purl***: see quot. 1899.

1535 *Rep. Dk. Rutland's Papers* (Hist. MSS. Comm.) IV. 277 For vj plightes of fyne lawne for sleves for the Quene with bandes of pyrles of golde, besides workinge the same by my Lady. *a* **1586** SIDNEY (Webster), A triumphant chariot made of carnation velvet, enriched with purl and pearl. **1600** in Nichols *Progr. Q. Eliz.* (1823) III. 502 One Frenche gowne of blacke vellat, with an edge of purle, and pipes of gold. **1611** COTGR., *Canetille*, (Gold, or siluer) Purle. [Cf. mod.F. *cannetille*,ribbon-wire, gold or silver thread, 'petite lame très-fine d'or ou d'argent tortillé' Littré.] **1621** in Elsing *Debates Ho. Lords* App. (1870) 141 They granted I should make purle upon condicion to be bound in 100li to give up an accompt of every parcell of gould and silver purle I should sell..; that through feare I was forced to condescend to seale the bond for not making any gold thread for this 2 yeares. **1797** *Boyer's Fr. Dict.*, *Cannetille*,.. purl or purfled gold or silver embroidery. **1882** CAULFEILD & SAWARD *Dict. Needlew.*, *Pearl-purl* is a gold cord of twisted wire, resembling a small row of beads strung closely together. Used for the edging of Bullion Embroidery. **1899** W. G. P. TOWNSEND *Embroidery* v. 82 (*Gold Threads*, etc.) *Bullion.*—The largest size of 'purl'... *Purl* may be either in gold or silver. It is made in a series of continuous rings rather like a corkscrew. *Ibid.* vi. 106 Purl is made of the finest gold wire twisted to form a round tube. *Ibid.*, *Silk purl* in a variety of colours is made (over wire)... It is worked in the same way as the gold. **1900** DAY & BUCKLE *Art Needlework* xxix. (1901) 245 Flat gold wire is known by the name of 'plate', and various twisted threads by the name of 'purl'. [See esp. the two works last quoted here.]

attrib. **1620** in *Naworth Househ. Bks.* (Surtees) 145 Two ounseis of gould and silver purle for making a perle drissing for Mrs. Marie. **1899** W. G. P. TOWNSEND *Embroidery* vi. 108 Horse-tail silk for purl embroidery should be well waxed.

2. Each of the minute loops or twists with a row of which the edges of lace, braid, ribbon, and the like, are ornamented (in Fr. *picot*); hence, collectively, a series or chain of such loops. In the machine-made lace trade, a twisted loop on the edge of a piece of lace, net, or braid; also, a similar twisted loop in the fabric (not on the edge) of lace. Hence laces and braids characterized by such loops are known as ***purl laces***, ***purl braids***, and elliptically as 'purls'. (Cf. also PEARL *sb.*[4])

1611 COTGR., *Canetille*, (Gold, or siluer) Purle; also, a small purle of needle-worke; or, a small edging (bone) lace. *Ibid.*, *Canetillé*, set, wrought, or inriched, with purle; also, edged with a small (needleworke) purle, or bone lace. **1688** MIEGE *Fr. Dict.* 11, Purl, *engrêlure petite bande à jour au bout de la dentelle.* **1706** PHILLIPS (ed. 6), *Purl*, a kind of edging for Bone-lace. *a* **1825** FORBY *Voc. E. Anglia*, *Purle*, a narrow list, border, fringe, or edging. **1865** *Patent Specif.* No. 801 These extra warp threads thereby become warp weft threads, and they also form the purls... Intermediate weft threads.. are caused to twist with the warp weft threads to produce combined twisted purl. To which the warp lacing threads attach the purls formed by the warp weft threads. **1867** W. FELKIN *Machine-Wrought Hosiery* 393 [A machine] producing, if wished, pearls either on one or both sides of the weaving edges. **1882** CAULFEILD & SAWARD *Dict. Needlework* 386/2 The loops that decorate the edges of Pillow Lace are called Pearls or Purls, and are made to any parts of the design that are disconnected in any way from the main body of the work. **1886** *Daily News* 13 Oct. 2/6 *Market Repts.*.. Business in Honiton braids and purls is far from being in a satisfactory condition. **1891** *Patent Specif.* No. 9483 A 'curl purl' is produced by the ordinary 'lap and press' process.

attrib. **1882** CAULFEILD & SAWARD *Dict. Needlework*, *Pearl-edge*, otherwise written Purl-edge. A narrow kind of thread edging made to be sewn upon lace as a finish to the edge; or projecting loops of silk at the sides of ribbons formed by making some of the threads of the weft protrude beyond the selvedge.

II. †**3.** 'The pleat or fold of a ruff or band' (Fairholt), as worn about 1600; a frill. *Obs.*

1593 NASHE *Christ's T.* 72 Your pinches, your purles, your floury iaggings. **1599** B. JONSON *Ev. Man out of Hum.* IV. iv, It graz'd on my shoulder, takes me away sixe purles of an Italian cut-worke band I wore. **1604** MIDDLETON *Father Hubburd's T.* in Bullen *O. Pl.* VIII. 91 Many puffs and purls lay in a miserable case for want of stiffening. **1631** T. POWELL *Tom All Trades* (1876) 173 For working in curious Italian purles, or French borders, it is not worth the while. **1632** MASSINGER & FIELD *Fatal Dowry* II. ii, My lord, one of the purls of your band is, without all discipline, fallen out of his rank. **1663** DAVENANT *Siege of Rhodes* I. Wks. (1672) 9 Our Powders and our Purls Are now out of fashion.

4. *transf.* **a.** A minute 'frilling' on the edge of a petal or leaf. **b.** A frill of feathers on the breast of some fancy varieties of pigeon.

1626 BACON *Sylva* §590 The jagging of pinks and gilly-flowers [is] like the inequality of oak leaves or vine leaves,.. but they seldom or never have any small purls. **1765** *Treat. Dom. Pigeons* 126 The feathers on the breast open, and reflect both ways, expanding itself something like a rose, which is called the purle by some, and by others the frill. *Ibid.* 127 The feathers on the breast (like that of the owl) open, and reflect both ways, standing out almost like a fringe, or the frill of a shirt; and the Bird is valued in proportion to the goodness of the frill or purle.

III. 5. *Knitting.* (Often *pearl.*) An inversion of the stitches, producing a ribbed appearance of the surface. (See PURL *v.*[1] 4.) Chiefly in *Comb.*, as ***purl-knitting***, ***-stitch***.

purl-edge, an edge made by 'taking off' the end stitches purl-wise; i.e. by turning the wires as in purl-stitch.

1825 JAMIESON, *Pearl*, the seam-stitch in a knitted stocking. *To cast up a pearl*, to cast up a stitch on the right side in place of the wrong; *Purl*, Teviotd[ale]. *Ibid.*, *Purl*, the seamstitch in a knitted stocking. *Ettr. For.* **1885** MISSES BRIETZCKE & ROOPER *Needlew. & Knitting* II. 99 In *purl* knitting the needle is put through the upper part of the stitch towards the lower... Purl knitting is also called seamed knitting. *Ribbed* knitting is when plain and purl knitting is worked alternately. *Ibid.*, Let them knit alternately 2 stitches plain and 2 purl. *Ibid.*, The purl stitches.

[*Note.* The various senses above have been treated together rather for convenience, as all relating to the decoration of apparel, than from any certainty that they are all uses of the same word. The derivation of sense 1 seems clear. That sense 2 had the same origin is possible, if the *twist* given to the minute loops was the characteristic. Or it may be that, as the purl edging of lace, etc. had a similar ornamental use to that of gold and silver purl, the name was extended from the one to the other; the possibility of this appears to be shown by Cotgrave's inclusion of both as meanings of F. *canetille*, in quot. 1611. The connexion of branches II. and III. is much more difficult to explain, and their inclusion must be considered as merely provisional; the latter may very well be a distinct word, and perhaps better spelt (as it often is) *pearl*. Minsheu in his *Ductor* suggested that *purle* was the same word as PURFLE, but this is historically as well as phonetically unlikely.]

purl (pɜːrl), *sb.*[2] Forms: 6-7 pirle, purle, 7 perle, 7- purl. See also PRILL *sb.*[2] [In earliest form *pirle*, mod. dial. *prill*: possibly connected with PIRL *v.* to whirl, twist; but certainly akin to PURL *v.*[2], and the Norse vb. there mentioned.]

†**1.** A small rill in which the particles of water are in a whirl of agitation. *Obs.*

α. *a* **1522** LELAND *Itin.* (1744-5) II. 79 Ther is a litle pirle of water. *Ibid.*, Thorowgh this wood rennith a pirle of water cumming out of an hil therby. **1584** *N. Riding Rec.* (1894) 231 They came nere a little becke or pirle of water called Slabecke. **1610** HOLLAND *Camden's Brit.* I. 666 Receiving sundry pirles to it and many a running rill.

β. *a* **1624** BP. M. SMITH *Serm.* (1632) 137 If the water at the well-head be corrupted, the streame, or perle running from the same, will not be wholesome.

γ. **1596** DRAYTON *Mortimer.* Q, Whose streame.. Which on the sparkling grauell runns in purles, As though the waues had been of siluer curles. **1650** JER. TAYLOR *Funeral Serm. C'tess of Carbery* 2 Watered with the purles flowing from the fountain of life. **1651** —— *Serm. for Year* xvi. 204 So have I seen the little purles of a spring sweat thorow the bottom of a bank, and intenerate the stubborn pavement.

2. The action or sound of purling as a rill.

1650 H. VAUGHAN *Silex Scint.*, *Idle Verse*, The Purles of youthful blood. **1850** J. STRUTHERS *Poet. Wks.* II. 251 How fraught with life the gentle purl is Of her sweet breath. **1876** T. HARDY *Ethelberta* (1890) 180 The pleasant lake, the purl of the weir, the rudimentary lawns, shrubberies, and avenue, had changed their character quite. **1886** —— *Mayor of Casterbr.* xxxviii, The purl of waters through the weirs.

purl (pɜːl), *sb.*[3] ? *Obs.* exc. *Hist.* Also 7 purle. [Origin unascertained (? related to prec.).]

a. Formerly, A liquor made by infusing wormwood or other bitter herbs in ale or beer. ***purl-royal***, a similar infusion of wormwood in wine. **b.** Later, A mixture of hot beer with gin (also called *dog's nose*), sometimes also with ginger and sugar: in repute as a morning draught.

1659-60 PEPYS *Diary* 19 Feb, To Mr. Harper's to drink a draft of Purle. **1707** MORTIMER *Husb.* (1721) II. 341 As grateful to the Stomach as the best Purl-Royal, or Wormwood Wine. **1712** ADDISON *Spect.* No. 317 Friday.. Twelve a-Clock... Drank a Glass of Purl to recover Appetite. *a* **1764** LLOYD *Fam. Epist.*, O Purl! all hail... Mum, Porter, Stingo, Mild and Stale. **1833** MARRYAT *P. Simple* x. The landlady made us some purl. **1865** DICKENS *Mut. Fr.* I. vi, For, it would seem that Purl must always be taken early. **1903** *Licensed Traders' Dict.*, *Purl*, hot beer with a glass of gin in it, re-christened 'dog nose' in later days.

c. *Comb.*: **purl-house**, a public house at which purl is sold and drunk (so **purl-boat**); **purl-man**, a man who sells purl.

1801 *Sporting Mag.* XIX. 126 The 'Jolly Gardeners' was stuck up at a Purl-house. **1851** MAYHEW *Lond. Labour* II. 93/2 The river beer-sellers, or purl-men, as they are more commonly called. **1902** A. MORRISON *Hole in Wall* 70 The men were purlmen.. selling liquor—hot beer chiefly, in the cold mornings—to the men on the colliers. *Ibid.* 102 The purl-boat swung round and shot off.

purl, *sb.*[4] *slang.* or *colloq.* [Goes with PURL *v.*[4], sense 3, of which (notwithstanding the want of earlier instances of the verb) it is prob. the derivative sb. naming the act.] An act of whirling, hurling, or pitching head-over-heels or head-foremost; a header or cropper in the hunting-field; a spill, a heavy fall; an overturn, upset, capsize.

1825 *Sporting Mag.* XV. 387 The purl was tremendous. **1829** *Ibid.* XXIV. 52 Mr. Tollemarsh got an awful purl over a gate. **1849** E. E. NAPIER *Excurs. S. Africa* II. 248 Spite of numerous tumbles.. I still kept ahead; but Piggy.. was soon close at my heels; and, at every purl I got, I fancied I felt his tusks. **1856** READE *Never too late* xxxviii, They [canoes] went a tremendous pace—with occasional stoppages when a purl occurred. **1861** G. MEREDITH *E. Harrington* xx, There's a purl: somebody's down.

purl, *sb.*[5] *Sc.* Also purle. A hard nodule of the dung of an animal, esp. of horse or sheep; also, 'dried cow-dung used for fuel' (Jam.).

1704 A. PITCAIRNE in Graham *Soc. Life Scot. in 18th C.* (1901) I. vi. 51 A handful of sheep's purles. **1799** *Prize Ess. Highl. Soc. Scot.* II. 218 (Jam.) The dung of the animal is excreted in small quantities, and in the form of small hard purls. **1825** JAMIESON s.v., The auld woman was gathering horse-purls.

purl, *sb.*[6] [Echoic, from the bird's cry; cf. PIRR *sb.*[2], PURRE *sb.*[1]] A local name of the tern.

1885 SWAINSON *Provinc. Names Birds* 202 Common Tern... Great purl (Norfolk). *Ibid.* 203 Little Tern... Small purl (Norfolk).

purl, *v.*[1] Also 6 pyrl(e, pirl(e. [f. *pyrle* PURL *sb.*[1]]

†**1.** *trans.* To embroider with gold or silver thread (PURL *sb.*[1] 1); to edge embroidered figures with gold or silver thread. Chiefly in *pa. pple.* and *ppl. a.*

1526 in *Inv. Goods Dk. Richmond* in *Camden Misc.* (1855) 14 Item, ij Copes of clothe of golde of damask paned with crymsen velvet pirled. **1527** *Inv. T. Cromwell's Goods* (Public Rec. Office), A purse of black vellet pyrled with golde threde. *a* **1548** HALL *Chron.*, *Hen. VIII* 73 b, Cloth of Tissue.. poudered with redde Roses purled with fine gold. **1587** FLEMING *Contn. Holinshed* III. 1947/2 The lord maior, recorder, and aldermen,.. who had crosses of veluet or satin pirled with gold. **1621** G. SANDYS *Ovid's Met.* x, A baldrick, purl'd with silver. *a* **1622** AINSWORTH *Annot. Ps.* xlv. 14 Purled workes or grounds, closures of gold, such as precious stones are set in. **1688** HOLME *Armory* IV. xii. (Roxb.) 504/1, 4 cushions of cloth of Gold Freezed and purled.

fig. **1622** FLETCHER *Sea Voy.* I. iii, Is thy skin whole? art thou not purl'd with scabs?

2. *absol.* To border or edge with or as with purls (PURL *sb.*[1] 2). Chiefly in **purled** *pa. pple.* and *ppl. a.*, ornamented with or as with an edging of minute twisted loops.

1766 W. GORDON *Gen. Counting-ho.* 430, 10 yards plain purled gauze. **1865** *Patent Specif.* No. 801 The manufacture in twist lace machinery of plain or ornamental fabrics having purled edges obtained from warp threads. *Ibid.*, As I am about to purl on the sides of this weaving, I must suppose that I have six carriages, the two outside ones being for the time being ordinary twisting or fabric carriages to which the warp lacing threads attach the purls formed by the warp weft threads.

†**3.** To pleat or frill like a ruff; to frill the edge of; also *transf.* Chiefly in *pa. pple.* and *ppl. a.*

1578 LYTE *Dodoens* I. xix. 29 Small, narrow, long and round, ragged or purled leaues. *Ibid.* xx. 31 The leaues.. be.. a little cut, or purlde about the edges. **1591** SYLVESTER *Du Bartas* I. ii. 59 Thy huff'd, puff'd, painted, curl'd purl'd wanton Pride. **1649** W. M. *Wand. Jew* (1857) 16 By his slash'd doublet, high galloshes, and Italian purld band [hee should be] a Frenchman. **1649** LOVELACE *Lucasta* 147 (T.) The officious wind her loose hayre curles, The dewe her happy linnen purles. *a* **1653** G. DANIEL *Idyll* 116 Wrought Pillow's bring Pownc'd Law, Stitched Common-wealth, and purled King.

4. *Knitting.* (*trans.* and *intr.*) To invert the stitches so as to produce a furrow or 'seam'. (See PURL *sb.*[1] 5.)

a **1825** FORBY *Voc. E. Anglia*, *Purle*, a term in knitting. It means an inversion of the stitches. The seams of stockings, the alternate ribs, and what are called the clocks, are purled. **1825** JAMIESON, *To Purl*, to form that stitch in knitting, or weaving stockings, which produces the hollow or fur. This is called the Purled or Purlin steek, and the stockings themselves Purled Stockings... It is to be observed, however, that *Purl* is merely a provincialism, *Pearl* being the common pronunciation of the S[cotch] term. **1885** MISSES BRIETZCKE & ROOPER *Needlework & Knitting* II. 99 As soon as the children can purl with ease. **1902** BARNES GRUNDY *Thames Camp* 299 Knitting her 'primrose edging', counting 'knit three, purl three'.

purl (pɜːl), *v.*[2] See also PIRL *v.* [Goes with PURL *sb.*[2]: cf. also Norw. *purla* (Aasen, Ross) to bubble up, gush out as water, Sw. dial. *porla* to purl, murmur, ripple, gurgle (Björkeman).]

1. *intr.* Of water, a brook, etc.: To flow with whirling motion of its particles, or twisting round small obstacles: often with reference to the murmuring sound of a rill.

a **1586** [see PURLING *ppl. a.*]. **1591** SYLVESTER *Du Bartas* I. iii. 81 From dry Rocks abundant Rivers purld. **1621** G. SANDYS *Ovid's Met.* xi, From the rock a spring With streames of Lethe softly murmuring, Purles on the pebbles, and invites repose. **1706** PHILLIPS (ed. 6), To *Purl*, to run with a murmuring Noise, as a Stream does. **1720** POPE *Iliad* XXI. 296 Swift o'er the rolling pebbles, down the hills, Louder and louder purl the falling rills. **1821** CLARE *Vill. Minstr.* I. 19 The gravel-paved brook..He often sat to see it purl along. **1830** TENNYSON *Ode to Memory* iv, The brook that loves To purl o'er matted cress and ribbed sand.

2. *transf.* Said of a stream of air, breath, wind, the sound of a wind instrument or a voice, etc.

1593 SHAKS. *Lucrece* 1407 From his lips did flie, Thin winding breath which purl'd vp to the skie. **1626**, **1863** [see PURLING *vbl. sb.*[2]]. **1648** HERRICK *Hesper.*, *Beucolick* iii, The soft, the sweet, the mellow note That gently purles from eithers Oat. **1847** *Whistle Binkie* (1890) II. 249 The saft wins pirlin through the trees.

b. *trans.* To utter with 'purling'.

1648 HERRICK *Hesper.*, *Ecl. betw. End. Porter & Lycidas H.* i, Tell me why Thy whilome merry Oate By thee doth so neglected lye And never purls a note.

purl, *v.*[3] Now *s.w. dial.* [Echoic.] *intr.* To purr, as a cat.

1698 FRYER *Acc. E. India & P.* 301 A Noise much the same as a Cat when she purls. **1866** 'NATHAN HOGG' (H. Baird) *New Ser. Poems Dev. Dial.* 71 Za zshore ez hur ole cat wid purdle, Ha wid'n du et in tother wurdle.

purl *v.*[4] [In sense 1, app. a (? dialectal) variant spelling of PIRL *v.* (sense 2), and thus in origin closely related to PURL *v.*[1], but with a different sense-development.]

1. *intr.* To revolve or whirl round rapidly, as a wheel; to spin round, as a peg-top, a whirligig, etc.; = PIRL *v.* 2.

1791–1808 (in form *pirl*): see PIRL *v.* 2. **1880** *Plain Hints Needlework* 104 In Wilts a shuttlecock is said to 'purl' when it spins in the air, after being thrown up in the air. **1881** *I. of Wight Words* (E.D.S.) s.v., He purled round like a top. **1903** *Eng. Dial. Dict.* s.v., [Warwicksh.] How that wheel goes purling round!

2. *intr.* To wheel *round* suddenly, as a horse.

1857 BORROW *Romany Rye* (1858) I. 360 All on a sudden a light glared upon the horse's face, who purled round in great terror, and flung me out of the saddle.

3. *trans.* and *intr.* To turn upside down, overturn, upset, capsize; to turn heels over head, turn a somersault. *dial.* and *colloq.*

1856 READE *Never too late* xxxviii, They [natives] commonly paddle in companies of three; so that whenever one is purled, the other two come on each side of him, each takes a hand, and..they reseat him in his cocked hat [canoe], which never sinks, only purls. **1874** 'S. BEAUCHAMP' *Grantly Grange*, II. xii. 267 A good pleached hedge will purl you like a wall; turn you right over..unless you slant it. *Ibid.* 268 (E.D.D.) He hit the fence, and then purled over.

†**purl**, *v.*[5] *Obs.* Variant of PROWL *v.*

c **1440** *Promp. Parv.* 415/1 Prollyn, as ratchys (or purlyn), *scrutor*. *Ibid.* 417/1 Purlyn, idem quod prollyn.

purl, var. PIRL *v.*, to twist, spin.

purled, *ppl. a.*: see PURL *v.*[1]

purleiw, -lew(e, -ley, obs. ff. PURLIEU.

purler ('pɜːlə(r)). *colloq.* [f. PURL *v.*[4] + -ER[1].]

1. A throw or blow that hurls any one headforemost; a knock-down blow; cf. PURL *sb.*[4] Also *fig.*

1867 'OUIDA' *Under Two Flags* I. iii. 47 In front of that Stand was an artificial bullfinch which promised to treat most of the field to a 'purler'. **1869** E. FARMER *Scrap Bk.* (ed. 6) 77 A 'purler' went Maxwell. **1878** JEFFERIES *Gamekeeper at H.* ix, Swung his gun round, and fetched him a purler on the back of his head. **1883** E. PENNELL-ELMHIRST *Cream Leicestersh.* 378 You were lucky if..you escaped the purler that stopped [his]..forward career. *a* **1903** H. S. MERRIMAN *Tomaso's Fortune*, etc. (1904) 154 It was precisely the attitude of one who has had a purler at football. **1921** H. G. PONTING *Gt. White South* 282 All went well till..on a very slippery surface I came an awful 'purler' on my shoulder. **1929** J. MASEFIELD *Hawbucks* 209 You seemed to go a fearful purler. **1962** *Spectator* 23 Nov. 830/3 Trevelyan's Indian career ended in a magnificent purler. **1976** *Church Times* 2 July 7/3 This is not just a..catalogue of classic military purlers (the Crimea, Kut, Cambrai, Singapore, Arnhem, etc.). **1976** *Horse & Hound* 3 Dec. 6/2 Even Up went a real purler at the last fence on the far side.

2. Also **pearler**. Something of surpassing excellence; a 'beauty'. orig. *N.Z.* and *Austral. slang*.

1941 BAKER *Dict. Austral. Slang* 57 *Purl, purler*, something excellent, outstandingly good. **1941** —— *N.Z. Slang* vi. 51 Expressions..in constant use by our youngsters ..swinjer pearler stunner snorter. **1965** *Telegraph* (Brisbane) 5 July 8 *Ripsnorter* (or pearler, bosker, boshter). **1966** *New Statesman* 7 Oct. 530/2 Bobby Charlton draws a couple of men and shoots that purler from 30 yards. **1973** *Listener* 8 Mar. 309/3, I hope the next goal he scores is an absolute purler. **1980** L. MANTELL *A Murder or Three* iii. 45 Never thought he'd ever get round to having any [children], then they produce a purler like that..a real little darling. **1980** *Weekend Australian* 16 Aug. 13 Flo's 35-minute speech was a pearler.

purley-man, variant of PURLIEU-MAN.

purlicue ('pɜːlɪkjuː), *sb. Sc.* Now *rare*. Also **parlicue, -lecue, -leycue, perlecue, -leque, -likew, pirlicue, -liecue, -liquey, purleycue**. [Origin and etymological form unascertained. See Note below.]

1. 'A dash or flourish at the end of a word in writing; a school-term, Aberd.' (Jamieson 1808.)

b. *pl.* 'Whims, particularities of conduct, trifling oddities, Angus.' (Jam. 1808.)

2. 'The peroration, or conclusion of a discourse; also used to denote the discourse itself, Strathmore, Roxb.' (Jam. 1825.)

3. See quot. 1825. (The practice is now obsolete.)

1825 JAMIESON, *Purlicue, Pirlicue, Parlicue*... The recapitulation made by the pastor of a congregation, of the heads of the discourses, which have been delivered by his assistants, on the Saturday preceding the dispensation of the sacrament of the Supper. *Scot. Orient.* pron[ounced] Pirlicue. Also, the exhortations which were wont to be given by him, on Monday, at what was called 'the close of the work', were thus denominated in other parts of S[cotland]. (I have been informed that the term has been sometimes extended to all the services on Monday.) **1886** STEVENSON *Kidnapped* xxiv, If you distaste the sermon, I doubt the pirliecue will please you as little. **1895** CROCKETT *Men of Moss-Hags* xxxvi, She would ware her life upon teaching them how to worship God properly, for that they were an ignorant wicked pack! A pirlicue which pleased them but little.

4. 'The space enclosed by the extended forefinger and thumb' (E.D.D.).

1825 BROCKETT *N.C. Gloss.* s.v., 'A spang and a purlicue' is a measure allowed in a certain game at marbles.

Hence '**purlicue** *v. trans.* and *intr.* (In the Presbyterian Churches): to give a résumé of the preceding sermons at the close of a sacrament season.

1825 JAMIESON, To *Purlicue, Pirlicue, Parlicue*. **1860** J. WILSON *Presbytery of Perth* 53 He kept up to the last the now all but obsolete custom of pirliecuing;..going up to the pulpit at the close of the service, and giving his people an abstract of the sermons preached by his assistants on Communion occasions, with any remarks thereon which he thought necessary. **1876** W. M. TAYLOR *Ministry of Word* 177 They have been content to 'say away' on the passage, or, to use an expressive, Scotch word, they have 'perlikewed' awhile. **1867** [JAS. HUNTER] *Remin. Quinquagenarian* (Annandale), At the close it was the custom of our minister to parleycue the addresses of the clergymen who had preceded him. **1896** H. M. B. REID *Cameronian Apostle* vi. 96 *note*, Dugald Williamson..was in his time reckoned the best purleycueing member of the Presbytery.

[*Note*. It is generally assumed that the last part of this curious word is *cue* or F. *queue* a tail; the first part has been conjecturally referred to F. *parler* 'to speak', *par la* 'by the', and *pour la* 'for the', each being supposed to yield a plausible sense. The word is not known before Jamieson; and it is noteworthy that in his Dictionary of 1808, he recognized only senses 1 and 1 b; although a Scottish clergyman, sense 3 was app. unknown to him both then and when he prepared his 8vo. ed. of 1818, and was added only in the Supplement of 1825.]

purlieu ('pɜːl(j)uː). Forms: 5 **purlewe**, 5–7 **purlew**, 6 **-liue**, 6–8 **-lue**, 7 **-lieue, -liew, -leiw; purly, -lie; pourlieu, -liew**; 8 **purleue, perlew**; 6– **purlieu**; also, *in comb.* 6 **purle, purley**. [Exemplified in 1482 in the form *purlew(e*, app. an erroneous alteration of *purley*, syncopated from *'puraley*, the natural Eng. spelling (cf. *alley, city, army*) in the 15th c. of AF. *puralé*, *-alée*, taken in its transferred sense (PURALÉ 2).

For the history of *puralé, -alee* (pura'leː) in English between *c* 1330 and 1482 written evidence is wanting; in Anglo-Fr. legal documents it continued to be written *puralé, poralee* (examples of which, of 1370–78, in the sense 'purlieu' appear under PURALÉ 2); but, as an English word, it would naturally become *puraley, puraly* ('pʊrəle, 'pʊrəlɪ), and easily be syncopated to *purley, purly*, as still seen in the 16th c. and later, esp. in the comb. *purleyman*, which shows that this was the pronunciation even after the spelling was changed. *Purlew* may have originated in a scribal error, or as a pseudo-etymological spelling, erroneously associating the word with *lew, leu*, LIEU, place; app. it did not appear in law Fr. till later, when it was prob. taken over from Eng., and Gallicized as *purlieu*: see quot. 1574[1].]

1. A piece or tract of land on the fringe or border of a forest; originally, one that, after having been (wrongly, as was thought) included within the bounds of the forest, was disafforested by a new perambulation, but still remained in some respects, especially as to the hunting or killing of game, subject to provisions of the Forest Laws.

1482 *Rolls of Parlt.* VI. 224/1 Within his Forest of Rokyngham, and other Forests, Chaces within his Reame of Englond, or Purlews of the same. *Ibid.*, To the likly destruction of the same Forest, Chaces and Purlewes. **1533** J. HEYWOOD *Play Weather* (1903) 414 Rangers and kepers of certayne places, As forests, parkes, purlews and chasys. **1570** B. GOOGE *Pop. Kingd.* II. (1880) 21 Large fieldes, with medowes fayre and townes and parks and purlues large. [**1574** in J. Dyer *Reports* (1592) 327 En le manor dun Fortescue de S. adjoynont al dit chace, come en le purlieu del chase..le libertie del purlieu remayna unextincted.] **1574** in *Hist. Fortescue Fam.* (1880) 322 The next day.. comes the boy that was wont to hunt that purliue. **1574** [see PURLIEU-MAN]. **1600** SHAKS. *A.Y.L.* IV. iii. 77 Pray you (if you know), Where in the Purlews of this Forrest, stands A sheep-coat, fenc'd about with Oliue-trees? **1616** BULLOKAR *Eng. Expos.*, *Purlue*, a place neere ioining to a Forrest, where it is lawfull for the owner of the ground to hunt, if he can dispend fortie shillings by the yeere of freeland. *a* **1634** COKE *Inst.* IV. lxxiii. *Courts Forests* (1648) 303 Purlieu containeth such grounds which H. 2. R. 1. or King John added to their ancient Forests over other mens grounds, and which were disafforested by force of the statute of *Carta de foresta*, cap. 1 and cap. 3, and the perambulations and grants thereupon. *Ibid.* 305 (2 R. 2 No. 48) The Commons made Petition that men might enjoy their purlieus freely [*orig. F.* q'ils puissent avoir lour Poralès], and that perambulations might be made as was in the time of King H[enry] 2. *c* **1645** HOWELL *Lett.* (1688) IV. xvi. 455 In Henry the third's time..ther was much Land disafforested, which hath bin call'd pourlieus ever since. **1665** J. WEBB *Stone-Heng* 126 How far did the Purlews of this Forrest extend? **1839** KEIGHTLEY *Hist. Eng.* I. 412 The King's officers were frequently attempting to recover the purlieus, or those lands adjoining the forests which had originally belonged to them, but had been disafforested by the charter of forests.

2. *transf.* and *fig.* A place where one has the right to range at large; a place where one is free to come and go, or which one habitually frequents; a haunt; one's bounds, limits, beat.

1643 SIR T. BROWNE *Relig. Med.* I. §51 Surely, though we place Hell under earth, the Devils walke and purlue is about it. *a* **1680** BUTLER *Rem.*, *Cat & Puss* 31 Wing'd with Passion, through his known Purlieu, Swift as an Arrow from a Bow, he flew. **1704** SWIFT *T. Tub* Pref., Wit has its walks and its purlieus, out of which it may not stray the breadth of an hair. **1744** *Mem. W. Stukeley* (Surtees) I. 368, I design to enter upon winter quarters, and travel chiefly the perlews of my garden. **1830** in Cobbett *Rur. Rides* (1885) II. 348 At the village of Hailstone, I got into the purlieu, as they call it in Hampshire, of a person well known in the Wen. **1884** BROWNING *Ferishtah*, *Bean-Stripe* 155 There's the palmaphis..and his world's the palm-frond,..An inch of green for cradle, pasture-ground, Purlieu and grave.

†**b.** Phrase. ***to hunt, follow one's game in purlieu, in the purlieus***, to pursue illicit love. *Obs.*

1611 BEAUM. & FL. *Philaster* IV. i, He Hunts too much in the Purlues, would he would leave off Poaching. *a* **1634** RANDOLPH *Muses Looking-glasse* IV. iii, To such as hunt in Purly; this is something With mine own Game reserv'd. **1690** DRYDEN *Amphitryon* I. i, He is weary of hunting in the spacious Forest of a Wife, and is following his Game *incognito*, in some little Purliew here at Thebes.

3. *pl.* **a.** *transf.* The parts about the border of any place; the outskirts. *arch.*

1650 FULLER *Pisgah* IV. iii. 44 It had some fertile intervalls, especially in the skirts, and purlews thereof, as about mount Horeb. **1667** MILTON *P.L.* II. 833 A place of bliss In the Pourlieues of Heav'n. **1712** BLACKMORE *Creation* (1786) 52 Venus, which in the purlieus of the sun Does now above him, now beneath him run. **1835** W. IRVING *Tour Prairies* xi, A wolf..was skulking about the purlieus of the camp. **1850** TENNYSON *In Mem.* lxxxviii. 12 They pleased him, fresh from brawling courts And dusty purlieus of the law.

b. *fig.* The region forming the outlying part of anything abstract. Cf. PALE *sb.*[1] 5. *arch.*

1647 WARD *Simp. Cobler* 7 Rather to live within the pale of Truth where they may bee quiet, than in the purlievs, where they are sure to bee hunted ever and anon. **1664** ETHEREDGE *Comical Rev.* I. iii, I walk within the purlieus of the law. **1712** STEELE *Spect.* No. 266 ¶4 To understand all the Purleues of this Game the better..I must venture my self, with my Friend Will. into the Haunts of Beauty and Gallantry.

4. An outlying district of a city or town, a suburb (*obs.*); also, the meaner streets about some main thoroughfare; a mean, squalid, or disreputable street or quarter. Also *attrib.*

1618 BOLTON *Florus* (1636) 79 Sicilia was now become a purleiw, or suburbe-province of the Roman State. *a* **1625** FLETCHER *Chances* I. vi, Sure he's gone home: I have beaten all the purlieus, But cannot bolt him. **1748** SMOLLETT *Rod. Rand.* xlix, Two tatterdemalions whom he had engaged.. about the purlieus of St. Giles's. *a* **1834** LAMB *Sir F. Dunstan* Misc. Wks. (1871) 390 A wretched shed in the most beggarly purlieu of Bethnal Green.

5. *attrib.* and *Comb.*, as † ***purlieu dinner*** (sense 4), **-*hunter***; **purlieu-wood**: see quot.

1621 BURTON *Anat. Mel.* I. ii. v. i, As a purly hunter, I haue hitherto beaten about the circuit of the forrest of this Microcosme. **1794** in Jas. Donaldson *Agric. Surv. Northampt.* 37 *Purlieu-woods* are those woods which are situate immediately in the vicinity of the forest. **1815** BYRON *Let.* Wks. (1899) III. 204 Murray has been cruelly cudgelled in his way home from a purlieu dinner, and robbed.

purlieu-man, † purley-man ('pɜːlɪmən). Also 6 **purle-**, 7 **purlie-man**. [f. prec. + MAN *sb.*[1]] The owner of freehold land within the purlieu of a forest; *spec.* see quot. 1607.

1574 SIR J. FORTESCUE in *S.P. Dom. Eliz.* XCII, No. 34 (cf. *Hist. Fortescue Fam.* (1880) 315), I answered that I wold not myselfe..hunt my groundes, nor yet suffre anie purlemen to hunte them at anie tyme. *Ibid.* 316 Neyther my selfe, nor anie purleymen shall hunte anie of my groundes. **1598** MANWOOD *Lawes Forest*, title-p., What a Purallee man may doe, how he may hunt and vse his owne Purallee. **1607** COWELL *Interpr.*, *Purlie man* is he that hath lands within the purlieu, and being able to dispend forty shillings by the yeare of freehold, is upon these two points licensed to hunt in his owne purlieu. *a* **1634** COKE *Inst.* IV. lxxiii. *Courts Forest* (1648) 304 Seeing the wilde Beasts doe belong to the purlieu man *ratione soli*, so long as they remain in his grounds, he may kill them, for the property *ratione soli* is in him. **1793–4** CHRISTIAN in *Blackstone's Comm.* II. xxvii. 419 *note*, If deer come out of the forest into the purlieu, the purlieu-man may hunt and kill them, provided he does it fairly and without forestalling. **1909** R. W. RAPER *Let. to Editor* 29 Mar., I am or claim to be a Purlieu man or Purley man: Having a little land and a Cottage in a Purlieu lying between the Bishop's Chase, Colwall, Herefordshire, and the Kings Chase, Worcestershire (Old Malvern Forest)... My Purlieu is so written, but always pronounced Purley.

purlin ('pɜːlɪn). *Carpentry.* Forms: 5 (perlion), purlyn, -lyon, 6 -lyne, 7 -lain, -linge, 7–9 purline, 8– -lin, (9 purling, perling); 5–7 purloyn(e, 8–9 -loin. [History unascertained; the forms suggest a Fr. origin, with the prefix *por-, pour-*, in AF. *pur-*.] A horizontal beam, usually one of two or more, which run along the length of a roof, resting upon the principal rafters (which they cross at right angles), and lending support to the common rafters or boards of the roof.

1447 *Tintinhull Churchw. Acc.* (Som. Rec. Soc.) 183 It. in perlionebus emptis ad idem opus. **1448–9** in Willis & Clark *Cambridge* (1886) II. 10 The principalles shalbe..x inch thik with a purlyn in the Middes from one principall to a nother. **1484** *Indenture Waynflete* in Parker *Gloss. Archit.* s.v., The lower doobyll purlyon pece..and the over purloyn for the seid floor. **1527** *Repairs at Drayton Manor* (Public Rec. Office), For sawynge of sparrs and syderasons and purlynes ij days. ij s. **1663** GERBIER *Counsel* 45 The Purlains for the Roof. *Ibid.* 72 Purloyns the same. *Ibid.* 73 The Purloynes the same. **1667** PRIMATT *City & C. Build.* 86 Four Purlines, being between eighteen and one and twenty foot long, and twelve and nine inches in thickness. **1714** S. SEWALL *Diary* 16 July, Split the principal Rafter next that end, to the purloin. **1864** in Brighton *Sir P. Wallis* (1892) 154 The purloins of the deck were about twelve feet long. **1881** *Mechanic* §1328 Common rafters..are notched slightly on the under side to fit over the purlins.

b. *attrib.*, as ***purlin piece, post, rafter.***

1484 *Indenture Waynflete* in Parker *Gloss. Archit.* s.v., The lower doobyll purlyon pece. **1875** KNIGHT *Dict. Mech.*, *Purlin-post*, a strut supporting a purlin. **1842** GWILT *Archit.* §2046 Purline rafters.

purlin: see PEARLING *sb.*, quot. *a* 1700.

'purling, *vbl. sb.*[1] [f. PURL *v.*[1] + -ING[1].]

†**1.** In sense 1 of the vb. *attrib.* as ***purling wire.***

1545 *Rates of Customs* C ij, Purlynge wyer the dossen pounde iiiis. **1579** J. JONES *Preserv. Bodie & Soule* I. x. 21 The Persian, Spanish, or Italian working of silks, as spinning, twisting, weuing sowing, imbroydring, aresing, counterfeyting, drawing, rasing, purling, buttoning, &c. *a* **1623** FLETCHER *Love's Cure* I. ii, If he live..to your years, shall he spend his time in pinning, painting, purling, and perfuming as you do?

2. *Knitting*: see sense 4 of the vb.

1880 *Plain knitting*, etc. 11 Purling or knitting back-wards should be the next step, as this is necessary for the completion of muffatees and stocking heels. **1902** BARNES GRUNDY *Thames Camp* 299 The knitting and purling may be made very easy.

'purling, *vbl. sb.*[2] [f. PURL *v.*[2] + -ING[1].] The action of PURL *v.*[2]: chiefly referring to the sound.

1598 FLORIO, *Sorgimento*, a rising..a mounting, a purling, a billowing. **1626** BACON *Sylva* §230 A pipe a little moistned on the inside,..maketh a more solemn sound, than if the pipe were dry: but yet with a sweet degree of sibilation or purling. **1665** HOOKE *Microgr.* 17 The purlings of Streams. **1863** MRS. OLIPHANT *Chron. Carl.* I. *Salem Ch.* vi, He..heard vaguely the polite purling of Masters's voice. **1891** —— *Jerusalem* II. ii. 258 The purling of the little river under the olive-trees.

'purling, *vbl. sb.*[3] [f. PURL *v.*[4] + -ING[1].] The fact of being capsized or thrown headlong.

1869 E. FARMER *Scrap Bk.* (ed. 6) 91 And with 'purling' and 'pumping' the field gets select.

'purling, *ppl. a.* [f. PURL *v.*[2] + -ING[2].] That purls, as a rivulet or stream; rippling, undulating; murmuring.

a **1586** SIDNEY *Astr. & Stella* xv. 1 Euery purling spring Which from the ribs of old Parnassus flowes. **1598** DRAYTON *Heroic. Ep.* xxii. 97 With ev'ry little perling breath that blowes. **1626** BACON *Sylva* §170 All instruments that have either returns, as trumpets; or flexions, as cornets; or are drawn up, and put from, as sackbuts; have a purling sound. **1631** CHAPMAN *Cæsar & Pompey* II. i. E 3 Exceeding calme, By reason of a purling winde that flyes Off from the shore each morning. **1655** VAUGHAN *Silex Scint.*, *Ps.* lxv, The fruitful flocks fill every dale, And purling corn doth cloath the vale. **1732** POPE *Ess. Man* I. 204 The whispering zephyr, and the purling rill. **1867** MISS YONGE *Six Cushions* xvi, The pathetic purling flow of talk. **1888** F. COWPER *Capt. of Wight* (1889) 293 The evening star flickered its glinting light across the purling water.

purloin (pɜː'lɔɪn), *v.* Forms: 5–6 perloyn(e, 5–7 purloyn(e, (5 pourloigne), 7 purloine, 6– purloin. [a. AF. *purloigner* = OF. *porloigner, -lognier, -lunier, purloigner, -luigner, -luinier*, later *pourloign(i)er, -longnier*, f. *por-, pur-*:—L. *prō-* + *loing, loin*:—L. *longe* far; hence, 'to put far off or far away, to put away, do away with'. The sense 'make away with, steal' appears to be of English development.

The OF. *por- purloigner* tended to be confused in use with *porlongier*, and the learned *prolonger*, representatives of L. *prōlongare* to PROLONG. In Eng. *prolong* is rarely found in the sense 'purloin', but the obs. PROLOYN *v.* combined the senses of both verbs.]

†**1.** *trans.* To put far away; to remove; to put away; to do away with; make of none effect. *Obs.*

c **1440** *York Myst.* xxx. 31 My duke doughty, demar of dampnacion, To princes and prelatis þat youre preceptis perloyned. *c* **1440** *Promp. Parv.* 394/2 Perloynyn, *idem quod* purloynyn. [*Ibid.* 417/1 Purlongyn, or prolongyn, or put fer a-wey, *prolongo, alieno.*] **1461** *Rolls of Parlt.* V. 494/1 The seid Enditementz and Presentementz been purloyned, embesiled and put away. **1660** R. COKE *Power & Subj.* 123 A Prince commands a Judge to execute the known Laws uprightly; he becomes corrupt, and sells, or otherwise purloyns judgment.

†**b.** To put out of the way, conceal. *Obs.*

1489 HEN. VII in *Epist. Acad. Oxon.* (O.H.S.) II. 559 The sayde bachelar hath..g[r]evously offendyd unto us in concellyng and pourloignyng þe sayde Thomas.

2. To make away with, misappropriate, or take dishonestly; to steal, esp. under circumstances which involve a breach of trust; to pilfer, filch.

1548 *Act 2 & 3 Edw. VI*, c. 2 §1 Yf any souldier..doe sell give awaie or willfullie purloyne or otherwise exchaunge alter or putt awaye anye horse. **1594** DRAYTON *Ideas* lviii, For feare that some their Treasure should purloyne. **1684** WOOD *Life* III. 103 A. W...made 2 such exact catalogues of his books that nothing could be purloyn'd thence. **1749** FIELDING *Tom Jones* VIII. xi, I took..an opportunity of purloining his key from his breeches-pocket. **1880** *Chamb. Jrnl.* CCII. 367 Epileptics have an irresistible impulse to purloin whatever they can secretly lay their hands upon.

b. *absol.* or *intr.* To commit petty theft.

1611 BIBLE *Tit.* ii. 10 Not purloynyng, but shewing all good fidelitie. *a* **1635** BP. CORBET *Poems* (1807) 28 Thence goes he to their present, And there he doth purloyne.

†**c.** *trans.* To steal from, to rob (a person). *Obs. rare.*

1571 CAMPION *Hist. Irel.* vi. (1633) 19 If neighbours and friends send their Catars to purloyne one another.

3. *transf.* and *fig.*

1593 SHAKS. *Lucr.* 1651 Euidence to sweare That my poore beautie had purloin'd his eyes. **1616** SURFL. & MARKH. *Country Farme* 653 If they [weeds] be suffered to grow vp, sucke, purloine, and carrie away the sap and substance of the earth. **1774** PENNANT *Tour Scot. in 1772*, I Galleries purloined from the first floor of each house. **1807** J. BARLOW *Columb.* I. 12 Slaves, kings, adventurers, envious of his name, Enjoy'd his labours, and purloin'd his fame. **1809** BYRON *Eng. Bards & Sc. Reviewers* 326 Lo! the Sabbath bard..Perverts the Prophets, and purloins the Psalms.

Hence **pur'loined** *ppl. a.*

1907 *Nation* 5 Oct. 13/1 Hermit crabs thrusting sharp nippers from the shelter of purloined whelk-shells.

purloin, variant of PURLIN.

purloiner (pɜː'lɔɪnə(r)). [f. PURLOIN *v.* + -ER[1].] One who purloins; a petty thief, a pilferer.

1585 ABP. SANDYS *Serm. on Jas.* iv. 8 (Parker Soc.) 135 Gleaners of other men's goods, and pillers, and purloiners. **1692** L'ESTRANGE *Fables* cxviii. 93 It may seem..Hard..to see Publique Purloyners..sit..upon the Lives of the Little Ones, that go to the Gallows. **1711** SWIFT *Examiner* No. 29 Wks. 1841 I. 325/1 Why these purloiners of the public cause such a clutter to be made about their reputations. **1791–1823** D'ISRAELI *Cur. Lit.*, *Literary filchers*, We have both forgers and purloiners..in the republic of letters. **1865** *Pall Mall G.* 6 Dec. 3 It is not only in nude statues that we English are for the most part mere prosaic purloiners from the antique.

pur'loining, *vbl. sb.* [f. as prec. + -ING[1].] The action of the verb PURLOIN; making away with; pilfering, filching.

1583 in *Yorksh. Archæol. Soc.* XVII. 256 For perloynynge of wreckes or goodes stolen upon the sea. **1622** F. MARKHAM *Bk. War* II. vi. 63 Hee is also to discouer all manner of thefts or purloynings (whether of victualls or other matter). *a* **1827** J. WHYTE *Serm. Doctr. & Pract. Subj.* xiii. (1831) 231 The allowable purloining of your earlier days.

pur'loining, *ppl. a.* [f. as prec. + -ING[2].] That purloins; pilfering, filching.

1576 FLEMING *Panopl. Epist.* 283 Thinking it safe from yᵉ purloyning robber. **1602** *2nd Pt. Return fr. Parnass.* I. iv. (Arb.) 17 Let vs run through all the lewd formes of lime-twig purloyning villanies.

purloyn(e, -lyn(e, -lyon, obs. ff. PURLIN.

purly, obs. form of PURLIEU.

†**purmein**, *v. Sc. Obs. rare.* [a. OF. *pourmene-r* (*-meine-*), earlier form of *promener*: see PROMENADE *v.*] *intr.* To walk about, take a walk.

1600 J. MELVILL *Diary* (Wodrow Soc.) 147 In privat conference purmeineing in the fields.

purmenade, -ado, obs. Sc. ff. PROMENADE.

purnancie, purnele, purnor: see PERNANCY, PARNEL, PERNOR.

puro- ('pjʊərəʊ), used as combining form from L. *pūs, pūr-* PUS, in a few pathological terms, instead of the more usual PYO- of Greek origin. **'puro-hepa'titis**, suppurative hepatitis. **'puro-lymph**, lymph containing pus-corpuscles, pyo-lymph. **ˌpuro-'mucous** *a.*, consisting of or containing both pus and mucus, muco-purulent.

1857 DUNGLISON, *Puro-hepatitis*.. *Puro-mucous*. **1869** G. LAWSON *Dis. Eye* (1874) 85 The iris at first appears hazy..; its surface then becomes partially or entirely coated with a film of puro-lymph. **1899** *Allbutt's Syst. Med.* VII. 497 There was greenish yellow puro-lymph along the vessels up to the vertex.

‖**puro** ('puro). [Sp., lit. 'pure'.] A cigar (in Spanish-speaking countries and south-west U.S.).

1841 J. L. STEPHENS *Incidents of Travel* I. 76, I offered for her choice a cigar and a puro. **1845** R. FORD *Hand-bk. Travellers Spain* ii. 194 Ferdinand VII.., when meditating a treacherous *coup*, would dismiss the unconscious victim with a royal *puron* [ed. 1846, *puro*]. **1963** W. MCGIVERN *Choice of Assassins* (1964) iii. 31 To talk..with his friends over sherry and *puros*.

puro, var. PURAU.

puromycin (pjʊərəʊ'maɪsɪn). *Biol.* and *Pharm.* [f. PUR(INE + -O + -MYCIN.] An antibiotic which is produced by the fungus *Streptomyces albo-niger* and is used esp. to treat sleeping sickness and amœbic dysentery.

1953 C. W. WALLER in *Jrnl. Amer. Chem. Soc.* LXXV. 2025/1 The new antibiotic, Puromycin, isolated from the mold *Streptomyces alboniger*, has been found to be active against certain bacteria and Trypanosomes. **1960** M. E. FLOREY *Clinical Applications of Antibiotics* IV. vi. 162 Puromycin..had the unique advantage of not only arresting the growth of trypanosomes but also of being able to kill them. **1968** W. HAYES *Genetics of Bacteria & their Viruses* (ed. 2) xii. 288 Puromycin has a close structural resemblance to the terminal amino-acyl adenosine of t-RNA and interferes with protein synthesis, both *in vivo* and *in vitro*, by inserting itself at ribosomal slot No. 2 [etc.]. **1978** *Bio Systems* X. 194/1 Puromycin is another commercially available antibiotic which, because of its toxicity, is not used therapeutically but rather as a research tool.

purow, var. PURAU.

pur'parley. *rare.* [app. alteration of POURPARLER after PARLEY.] = POURPARLER.

1904 M. HEWLETT *Queen's Quair* I. iv. 50 After some purparley, at a privy audience, he came to what he called 'close quarters'.

†**purpart.** *Law. Obs.* or *arch.* [= med.L. *prōpars, perpars* (in *Fleta*), *purpars* (1366) 'portio hæreditaria, seu divisio hæreditatis per partes' (Du Cange), f. *prō-* (OF. *por-, pur-*), or *per-* + *pars* part, portion: cf. *proportion.*] = PURPARTY.

1492 *Will Starky* (Somerset Ho.), Havendele or purpart. **1538** in Strype *Eccl. Mem.* (1721) I. App. xc. 250, I wyl that Margery my wyfe shal have one egal part to her own propre use, in name of her purpart. *a* **1625** SIR H. FINCH *Law* (1636) 335 There is a proviso, that euery one shall haue in her purpart, parcell of the lands holden in chiefe. **1790** *Dallas' Amer. Law Rep.* I. 354 The purparts of the valuation are not specified. **1818** CRUISE *Digest* (ed. 2) II. 511 If..the tenants or persons concerned, admitting the demandant's title parts and purparts, shall show to the Court an inequality in the partition.

Hence †**pur'parture** *Obs.*, in same sense.

1643 *Farington Papers* (Chetham Soc.) 99 Goods set out by the Collonells of this County for Mris ffarington of Wordet, purparture or fyft.

pur'party. *Law. arch.* Forms: 4 porpartie, 4–5 pour-, purpartie, 5 -ye, 6–8 purparty, 7– pourparty. [a. AF. *purpartie* (Britton 1292) = OF. *por-* (1255 in Godef., in med. Anglo-L. *purpartia, propartia*), f. *por- pour-*:—L. *prō-* for, forth, etc. + *partie* division, part: see PARTY; cf. prec.] A proportion, a share, esp. in an inheritance.

a **1325** *MS. Rawl.* B. 520 lf. 7 b, þe writ of nouele deseisine aut of purpartie. **1390** GOWER *Conf.* II. 184 That ech of hem as Heritage His porpartie hath underfonge. *Ibid.* 364 Pourpartie. **1495** *Act 11 Hen. VII*, c. 40 *Preamble*, The seid Manoris..were allotted to the purpartie and particion therof of the seid John Howard. **1596** BACON *Max. & Use Com. Law* I. xxiii, If three Coparceners be, and one of them alien her purparty. **1658** PHILLIPS, *To make Pour-party*, to sever the Lands that fall to partners, which before partition they held joyntly. **1793** H. WALPOLE *Let. to Miss M. Berry* 6 Oct., I am forced to eat all the game of your purparties, as well as my own thirds. **1856** *Bouvier's Law Dict.* (ed. 6) II. 405 To make purparty is to divide and sever the lands which fall to parceners. **1882** C. SWEET *Dict. Eng. Law* 659 Purparty is an old word for share or portion,..to hold land in purparty with a person is to hold it jointly with him. **1920** *Eng. Hist. Rev.* Jan. 30 To each co-heir was allotted, as a permanent pourparty, a definite manor or castle for a chief seat.

†**purpayne**, variant of PORT-PAIN *Obs.*

1513 W. DE WORDE *Bk. Keruynge* in *Babees Bk.* 270 Than knele on your knee tyll the purpayne passe eyght loues.

purpays(se, -pess, -peys, obs. ff. PORPOISE *sb.*

†**pur'pense**, *v. Obs.* Also 6 pour-. [a. OF. *purpenser* (11th c.) f. *pur-, pour-* (:—L. *prō* forth) + *penser* to think. Superseded in 16th c. by PREPENSE, so as to emphasize the notion of 'beforehand'.] *trans.* To think of, meditate or deliberate upon; to determine beforehand; to premeditate.

c1400 *Beryn* 2214 A Cachepoll..so was he ful ensensid How he hym wold engyne, as he had purpensid. 1450 *Rolls of Parlt.* V. 177/2 Purpensyng [in *Paston L.* I. 100 printed *prepensing*] that your said grete Ennemye and Adversarie Charles shuld conquere and gete by power and myght youre seid Reame of Fraunce. 1496 *Act 12 Hen. VII*, c. 7 James Grame..wilfully assentid and purpensed the murdre of oon Richard Tracy Gentilman, then his maister. 1512 *Helyas* in Thoms *Prose Rom.* (1828) III. 27 The said iniury (bi her commised and purpensed).

Hence †**pur'pensed** *ppl. a.* [after OF. *purpensé*], resolved, premeditated, planned, deliberate; esp. in *malice purpensed, purpensed malice*, the original form of *malice prepensed* or PREPENSE, q.v.

[a1170 *Laws Will. I*, i. §1 (Liebermann) 492 Autresi..de agwait purpensé [*v.rr.* purpensed, prepensed]. 1404 *Rolls of Parlt.* III. 541/1 Si soit trove qe ce soit fait par malice purpense.]

1436 *Rolls of Parlt.* IV. 498/1 William Pulle..in awayte lyggyng, by assaute purpensed,..the saide Isabell felonousely there than toke..and fro thens ledde. 1459 *Ibid.* V. 348/1 Contynuyng in their purpensed malicious and dampnable opynions. 1477 *Ibid.* VI. 193/1 Of the moost extreme purpensed malice. 1529 More *Dyaloge* III. Wks. 238/2 In such a wilfull purpensed haynous cruell dede. 1538 Fitzherb. *Just. Peas* 106b, Mourdour, by chaunce medley, and not of malyce pourpensed. 1548 Udall, etc. *Erasm. Par. Mark* iii. 30 A purpensed malice againste the goodnesse of God.

Also †**pur'pensedly**, †**pur'pensely** *adv.* = PREPENSELY.

1472-3 *Rolls of Parlt.* VI. 51/2 The yates of the same.. willfully and purpensely with fyere..[the Rioters] brent. 1496 *Act 12 Hen. VII*, c. 7 If any laie persone hereaftir purpensidly murder their Lord Maister or Sovereign immediate, that they hereaftir be not admytted to their Clergie.

†**'purpie**, *sb. Sc. Obs.* [a. OF. *porpié* (13th c. in Godef.), later *pourpié, pourpied*, altered from *polpié, poulpied*, ad. med.L. *pulliped-em*, acc. of *pulli pes* or *pes pulli* (i.e. colt's foot), in mediæval lists of plant-names a regular synonym of *portulaca*: see *Sinon. Barthol., Alphita.*] = PURSLANE.

1568 Skeyne *The Pest* (1860) 25 Latice, Cichorie, Purpie, Sourak. 1596 in *Analecta Scotica* II. 13 The seid of al sort of mawes, purpie, and sorrelis or sourochis. 1681 in *Thanes of Cawdor* (Spald. Club) 352 Purpie half ane unce.

'purpie, *a.* A Scottish variant of PURPLE.

1661 Lamont *Diary* 6 Aug. (1810) 173 He dyed of a purpie feaver. 1669 *Rec. Edin. Justic. Crt.* (1905) I She attended her brother who lay sick of a Purpie ffeuer. 1844 J. Lemon *Lays St. Mungo* 49 We laiggart a' our cheeks Wi' the bonnie purpie dye.

†**purpit**, obs. abbrev. PERPETUANA; cf. PERPET.

1727 Uring *Voy. & Trav.* 150 The goods they received was purpits, old sheets, caggs of tallow,..and powder.

†**'purpitle.** *Obs. rare.* Also 5 purpytyl, purpetill. [app. a metathesis of OF. *pulpitre*, med.L. *pulpitrum*, var. of *pulpitum*, staging, scaffolding, raised platform, PULPIT: cf. quot. in Du Cange 'magnum pulpitrum fieri in altum ex traverso dicte ecclesie, in quo sunt aliquando cantores ad Missam'.] A choir-screen or organ-screen.

1354 *Mem. Ripon* (Surtees) III. 91 In j clave cum una plate emp. pro hostio cameræ in le Purpitle, 8*d.* 1408 *Ibid.* 137 Pro j fundo in le purpytyl et pro hostio ibidem ad magnas organas, 18*d.* 1453 *Ibid.* 162 Rob. Wright operanti super le Purpetill dict[arum] organic[arum].

purple ('pɜːp(ə)l), *a.* and *sb.* Also 3 purpel, 4–5 purpul, 4–6 -pyl, 5 -pyll, 5–6 -pylle, -pull, -e, -pil(l. [ONorthumb. *purple*, early ME. *purpel, purpul*, altered from *purpre, purper* PURPUR, with *l* for *r* after preceding *r*, as in *marbre, marble*.

In the OE. *purpure*, ME. *purpre, purper*, PURPUR, the sb. use was the original, the adj. or attrib. use being later and derivative; but the form *purple, purpel*, appeared first in adj. or attrib. use, and only in the 15th c. supplanted *purpur* as the sb. But this adjective use of *purple* itself arose from the OE. sb.; the ONorthumb. *purple hræȝle* showing, like the *purpre reaf* of the Hatton Gospels, a weakened form either of the OE. genitive *purp(u)ran* 'of purple', or of the derivative adjective *purpuren*. See also PURPUR.]

A. *adj.*

1. a. Of the distinguishing colour of the dress of emperors, kings, etc.; = L. *purpureus*, Gr. πορφύρεος, in early use meaning crimson; hence, imperial, royal.

c975 *Rushw. Gosp.* John xix. 5 Eode forðon ðe hælend berende ðyrnenne beȝ & purple [*Lindisf. G.* purbple] hræȝle [*Ags. Gosp.* purpuren reaf, *Hatton Gosp.* purpre reaf; L. *purpureum vestimentum*]. a1225 *St. Marher.* xxvii, Ciclatoun ant purpel pal scaltou haue to wede. c1330 *King of Tars* 364 In cloth of riche purpel palle. c1430 Lydg. *Min. Poems* (Percy Soc.) 120 His purpul mantel his garnementis royalle. 1526 Tindale *John* xix. 2 They did put on hym a purple garment. 1791 Cowper *Odyss.* xxi. 144 Telemachus ..Cast off His purple cloak.

b. Of persons: Clad in purple; of imperial or royal rank. *poet.* or *rhet.*

a1704 T. Brown tr. *Æneas Sylvius' Death Lucretia* Wks. 1709 III. II. 88 Shou'd my passive Body be pregnant by the purple Villain. 1742 Gray *Adversity* 7 Purple tyrants vainly groan.

2. a. Of the colour described in B. 1, in its mediæval and modern acceptations.

1398 Trevisa *Barth. De P.R.* xvi. xciv. (1495) 585 Purpyl salt in Pathmos is so bryght and clere that ymages ben seen therin. 1466 in *Archæologia* (1887) L. I. 38, j hole vestment of rede purpyl silke. 1509 Hawes *Past. Pleas.* xxvi. (Percy Soc.) 115 Wyth purple colour the floures enhewed. 1560 Daus tr. *Sleidane's Comm.* 172b, He consecrated Anthony ..Cardinall of Medone, setting upon his head a purple hatte. 1573-80 Baret *Alv.* P 879 The Purple, or violet colour, *conchylium*. 1578 Lyte *Dodoens* I. xxxvii. 55 That [pimpernel] whiche beareth the purple floures [of Adonis]. 1696 J. Aubrey *Misc., Appar.* (1784) 117 This Stranger was in a purple-shag gown. 1776 Withering *Brit. Plants* I. 382 Lousewort..Blossoms purple, much slenderer than the calyx. 1792 S. Rogers *Pleas. Mem.* I. 71 When purple evening tinged the west. 1810 Scott *Lady of L.* III. v, Heath-bell with her purple bloom. 1826 Kirby & Sp. *Entomol.* xlvi. IV. 280 Purple... Equal parts of blue and red. a1839 Praed *Poems* (1864) I. 305 Beneath a purple canopy. 1879 O. N. Rood *Mod. Chromatics* ii. 28 In the prismatic spectrum and in our normal spectrum we found no representative of purple, or purplish tints. This sensation can not be produced by one set of waves alone, whatever their length may be: it needs the joint action of the red and violet waves, or the red and blue.

b. Preceded by an adj. or sb. indicating the shade of colour, as *amethyst, bluish, dahlia, dark, dun purple*, etc. (for other instances of which, see the first element). See also B. 1 d.

1629 Parkinson *Paradisus* 182 The three upright leaves are not so smoakie, yet of a dun purple colour. 1802 *Med. Jrnl.* VIII. 497 Her whole skin was always more or less of a bluish purple colour. 1859 Ruskin *Two Paths* v. 202 That lovely dark purple colour of our Welsh and Highland hills is owing, not to their distance merely, but to their rocks. 1882 *Garden* 1 Apr. 210/3 The varieties..sent are..rosy purple ..dark livid purple..deep rose purple..venous purple. 1906 *Daily Chron.* 15 Oct. 8/2 Made in dahlia-purple crêpe de chine.

c. Of this colour as being the hue of mourning (esp. royal or ecclesiastical mourning), or of penitence.

1466 in *Archæologia* (1887) L. I. 38 Item j nother purpyll chesebyll for gode fryday. 1493 *Petronilla* 119 With purple wede to the heuenly mancyon Hir soule went up the last day of may. 1542 in *Archæologia* (1887) L. I. 46 Item a vestement purpull silke for good frydaye. 1868 Marriott *Vest. Chr.* 174 The vestments..oftentimes..are purple, in times of fast, because of our mourning in respect of sin.

d. Used *poet.* to describe the colour of blood. (Properly said of the crimson venous blood, the colour of arterial blood being scarlet.) Hence, Bloody, blood-stained.

1590 Spenser *F.Q.* II. vi. 29 A large purple streame adowne their giambeux falles. *Ibid.* viii. 36 The red blood flowed fresh, That underneath his feet soone made a purple plesh. 1593 Shaks. *3 Hen. VI*, v. vi. 64 See how my sword weepes for the poore Kings death. O may such purple teares be alway shed From those that wish the downfall of our house. 1605 *1st Pt. Ieronimo* (1901) II. v, And by that slaue this purple act was done. 1710 Pope *Windsor For.* 417 There purple Vengeance bathed in gore retires. c1764 Gray *Owen* 33 Where he points his purple spear, Hasty, hasty Rout is there. 1805 Scott *Last Minstr.* I. x, When Mathouse-burn to Melrose ran All purple with their blood. 1819 Keats *Eve St. Agnes* xvi, A thought came like a full-blown rose, Flushing his brow, and in his pained heart Made purple riot.

3. a. *Rhetorically.* With reference to the qualities of this colour: bright-hued, brilliant, splendid, gaudy, gay; (of sin) deep-dyed, grave, heinous.

purple patch, passage, piece, a brilliant or ornate passage in a literary composition (after L. *purpureus pannus*, Hor. *De Arte Poet.* 15). So ***purple-patchery, patchwork***.

1598 Q. Eliz. *Horace* 20 (E.E.T.S.) 142 Oft to beginnings graue and shewes of great is sowed A purple pace, one or more for vewe. 1697 Dryden *Virg. Past.* II. 62 All the Glories of the Purple Spring. 1742 Gray *Ode Spring* 4 The rosy-bosom'd Hours..wake the purple year! 1756 C. Smart tr. *Horace* II. 379 One or two verses of purple patchwork, that may make a great shew. a1834 Coleridge in *Rev. de Litt. Comparée* (1927) VII. 253 Admirably reasoned as this Essay is, I yet regard it but as one of the rich Purple Patches of the Robe of Casuistry. 1872 Blackie *Lays Highl.* Introd. 51 Places once flaunting with purple prosperity. 1881 *Academy* 9 Apr. 256/2 A few of the purple patches scattered through the book may serve as a sample of the rest. 1895 E. Gosse in *Cent. Mag.* July 451/2 Emphasizing the purpler passages with lifted voice and gesticulating finger. 1905 H. A. Vachell *The Hill* vii. 147, I never said bridge was a purple sin. 1921 *Times Lit. Suppl.* 9 June 362/1 The back-talk between the Emperor and his Empress Nourmahal, in *Aurungzebe*, is admirable purple comedy. 1926 C. Connolly *Let.* 26 June in *Romantic Friendship* (1975) 145 He realises his epic to be but a collection of purple patches. 1941 Auden *New Year Let.* II. 37 And yet to show complete conviction, Requires the purpler kinds of diction. 1941 H. Haycraft *Murder for Pleasure* x. 216 The old, whipped-up underscoring and 'purple-patchery'. 1943 C. L. Wrenn *Word & Symbol* (1967) 139 An honoured place in English literature through Milton's 'purple passage'. 1975 V. Cunningham *Everywhere spoken Against* iii. 84 Arnold's famous purple patch about the last enchantments of the Middle Ages. 1975 *Language for Life* (Dept. Educ. & Sci.) xi. 164 Some teachers encourage children to strive for effect, to produce the purple patch, the stock response. 1975 C. N. Manlove *Mod. Fantasy* iii. 78 One [style] is 'purple' and highly emotive. 1977 *Gramophone* Sept. 507/3 One is grateful to be spared one of Wilde's purpler passages.

b. *colloq.* 'Gorgeous', 'splendid', 'royal'.

1894 *Pall Mall G.* 20 Dec. 3/2 Who should I see..having a purple time of it but Padishah and Potter. 1905 *Daily Chron.* 19 May 6/3 You had one purple moment in your life —a sackful of coins, and scrambling them among boys.

B. *sb.*

1. The name of a colour. **a.** Anciently, that of the dye obtained from species of gastropod molluscs (*Purpura* and *Murex*), commonly called ***Tyrian purple***, which was actually a crimson; **b.** in the Middle Ages applied vaguely to many shades of red; cf. PURPUR *sb.* 3; **c.** now applied to mixtures of red and blue in various proportions, usually containing also some black or white, or both, approaching on the one side to crimson and on the other to violet.

The various tints are frequently distinguished by the names of flowers, fruits, etc. in which they occur, as ***auricula, dahlia, heliotrope, plum, pomegranate, wine purple***; also by special names, as ***Indian, royal purple***; ***magenta, mauve, solferino***, etc.: see these words.

c1440 *Promp. Parv.* 417/1 Purpul, *purpura*. 1530 Palsgr. 321/2 Purpylle, *pourpre*. 1570 Levins *Manip.* 125/35 Purpil, *purpura, æ*. a1586 Sidney *Arcadia* v. (1598) 447 Not that purple which we now haue..but of the right Tyrian purple, which was nearest to a colour betwixt our murry and scarlet. 1614 Chapman in C. Brooke *Ghost Rich. III*, Poems (1872) 49 What does then Thy purple in graine, with these red-oker men? a1649 Drumm. of Hawth. *Mem. St.* Wks. (1711) 131 As the rose, at the fair appearing of the morning sun, displayeth and spreadeth her purples. 1720 Ozell *Vertot's Rom. Rep.* I. VII. 422 The first Prætor of Rome..was allowed the Prætexta, or Robe edged with Purple. 1774 Goldsm. *Nat. Hist.* (1776) V. 347 Their plumage is glossed with a rich purple. 1815 Byron *Destr. Sennacherib* i, His cohorts were gleaming in purple and gold. 1873 'Susan Coolidge' *What Katy Did at Sch.* xiii. 221 Painted in soft purples and grays. 1888 Rolleston & Jackson *Anim. Life* 474 In the genera *Purpura* and *Murex* the secretion [of the hypobranchial gland], at first colourless, changes in sunlight to a purple or violet, used as a dye by the ancients, and known as 'Tyrian purple'.

d. The Tyrian dye, or any pigment of the above-mentioned colours.

With many defining words, expressing the composition, source, inventor, etc., as ***alizarin, aniline, ethyl, madder, mineral, orchil*** or ***archil purple***; ***French, Indian, London purple***; ***Field's, Perkins's, regina purple***, etc. ***purple of Cassius*** (also *purple powder of Cassius* C. 2) = *gold-purple* (GOLD[1] 10); named after Andreas Cassius (died 1673).

1638-56 Cowley *Davideis* III. Note 26 The Purple of the Ancients was taken out of a kind of Shell-fish called Purpura. 1839 Ure *Dict. Arts, Purple of Cassius*, gold purple, is a vitrifiable pigment, which stains glass and porcelain of a beautiful red or purple hue. *Ibid., Purple of mollusca*, is a viscid liquor, secreted by certain shell-fish, the *Buccinum lapillus*, and others, which dyes wool, &c. of a purple colour, and is supposed to be the substance of the Tyrian dye. 1853 W. Gregory *Inorg. Chem.* (ed. 3) 220 With solutions of gold, salts of protoxide of tin produce a purple precipitate, the purple of Cassius.

e. ***visual purple***: see VISUAL *a.* and *sb.*

2. a. Purple cloth or clothing; a purple robe; = PURPUR *sb.* 1. ***purple and pall***: see PURPUR *sb.* 1.

Now only in imitations of Latin or Greek, or of biblical language.

c1460 *Towneley Myst.* x. 273 Marie wroght purpyll. 1526 *Pilgr. Perf.* (W. de W. 1531) 281b, The ryche gloton.. whiche was clothed in purpull & cloth of reynes. 1526 Tindale *Acts* xvi. 14 Lidia a seller off purple. 1579 Spenser *Sheph. Cal.* July 173 Yclad in purple and pall. 1648 Bp. Hall *Sel. Thoughts* §13 The rich glutton..clothed in purple and byss. 1850 S. Dobell *Roman* i. Poet. Wks. (1875) I. 8 She wraps the purple round her outraged breast. 1894 Gladstone *Horace, Odes* II. xviii, No well-born maidens, my poor doors within, Laconian purples spin.

b. As the distinguishing dress of emperors, kings, consuls, and chief magistrates; hence *fig.*; spec. ***the purple***, imperial, royal, or consular rank, power, or office. Also the colour of imperial and royal mourning.

c1440 Lydg. *Hors, Shepe, & G.* (Roxb.) 15 Of purpill rede was his riall clothing This agnus dei born of a pure virgine. 1553 Eden *Treat. Newe Ind.* Ded. (Arb.) 5 No lesse con-foundinge the order of thinges, than he whiche clotheth an ape in purple, and a king in sackecloth. 1609 Bible (Douay) *1 Esdras* iii. 2 King Darius made a great supper.. to al that weare purple, and to the praetors. 1610 Holland *Camden's Brit.* (1637) 271 Constantine..laid aside the Purple..[and] became a Priest. 1709 Pope *Ess. Crit.* 320 A vile conceit in pompous words express'd, Is like a clown in regal purple dress'd. 1736 Chandler *Hist. Persec.* 111 They worship not God, but the Purple. 1776 Gibbon *Decl. & F.* xiv. I. 400 As soon as Diocletian and Maximian had resigned the purple. 1869 Seeley *Lect. & Ess.* (1870) 67 The ablest generals are still frequently invested with the purple.

c. ***the purple***: in reference to the scarlet colour of the official dress of a cardinal; hence the rank, state, or office of a cardinal; the cardinalate.

1685 Burnet *Trav.* 8 Dec. (1686) 231 He retains the unaffected simplicity and humility of a Frier, amidst all the dignity of the Purple. 1695 *Lond. Gaz.* No. 3046/1 We are told that the present Duke of Modena..intends to quit the Purple, and to send back his Cardinals Cap to the Pope. 1786 W. Thomson *Watson's Philip III*, VI. (1839) 321 The necessity of exchanging the ease of former familiarity for those ceremonies of respect which were due to the purple... The presence of the cardinal was uneasy to him. 1898 Villari *Life & Times Machiav.* II. vi. 237 He was raised to the purple.

d. In phrase ***born, cradled in (the) purple***: said of a child of an imperial or royal reigning family; or by extension, of a noble or wealthy family, or of the highest or most privileged rank of any organization. (Commonly associated with sense 2; but, see, as to the origin, PORPHYROGENITE *a.*)

1790 Burke *Let. M. Dupont* in *Corr.* (1844) III. 161 He was born in purple, and of course was not made to a situation which would have tried a virtue most fully perfected. 1827 Hallam *Const. Hist.* (1876) II. x. 268 [Richard Cromwell] would probably have reigned as well as most of those who are born in the purple. 1876 Bancroft *Hist. U.S.* VI. lv. 438 The old Whig party reserved the highest places for those cradled in the purple. **1884** Labouchere in *Fortn. Rev.* Feb. 208 True Liberals who have not had the good fortune to be born in the Whig purple.

3. Any of the species of molluscs which yielded the Tyrian purple (see 1), or any allied species; in mod. use, a mollusc of the genus *Purpura*. Also called purple-fish.

The species which yielded the Tyrian dye are believed to have been *Murex brandaris*, *M. trunculus*, and *Purpura hæmostoma* (see *Proc. Royal Soc.* X. 579); but all species of *Murex* and *Purpura* secrete the fluid to some extent.

1580 Hollyband *Treas. Fr. Tong, Pourpre*,..a shell fish called a Purple. **1601** Holland *Pliny* I. 306 Purples also be caught by means of some stinking bait. **1682** Creech tr. *Lucretius* VI. 1072 The Purples blood gives Wool so deep a stain That we can never wash it out again. **1715** tr. *Pancirollus' Rerum Mem.* I. I. i. 5 The Tyrians, by taking away the Shells of the greater Purples, do come at that noble Juice. **1755** *Gentl. Mag.* XXV. 32 It belongs to yet another tribe, and is a Purple. **1901** Step *Shell Life* 254 The Purple (*Purpura lapillus*), commonly known as Dog-winkle, and in Ireland as Horse-winkle, is one of the commonest of marine snails.

4. † **a.** A purple or livid spot, botch, or pustule; also, the bubo of the plague (*obs.*). **b.** *pl.* A disease characterized by an eruption of purplish pustules; esp. purpura, but formerly often vaguely used.

c **1440** *Promp. Parv.* 417/1 Purplys, sorys, *morbuli purpurei dicuntur*. **1483** *Cath. Angl.* 294/2 A Purpylle, *papula*. *c* **1530** *Hickscorner* (1905) 146 God punisheth..with great sickness As pox, pestilence, purple and axes. **1533** Elyot *Cast. Helthe* (1541) 83 b, Whan they [children] waxe elder, than be they greved with kernelles,..swellynges under the chynne, and in England commonly purpyls, measels, and small pockes. **1638** R. Baker tr. *Balzac's Lett.* (vol. II.) 194, I am glad at heart to hear the Duke of Feria is dead of the Purples. **1660** Wood *Life* 3 Dec. (O.H.S.) I. 349 It is thought it is the spotted feaver or purples. **1755** Johnson, *Purples* (without a singular) spots of a livid red, which break out in malignant fevers. **1772** tr. *Life Lady Guion* II. 33 My daughter had the small-pox and the purples. **1866** A. Flint *Princ. Med.* 857 The term purpura, or the purples, denotes an affection characterized by a truly petechial eruption, or petechiæ.

c. ***purples***: swine fever.

1887 *Times* 1 Feb. 9/6 Swine fever..being known in different parts of Great Britain by the names of pig typhoid, pig distemper, purples, swine plague [etc.]. **1897** *Syd. Soc. Lex.*, *Purples*, a common name..for Swine fever.

d. ***purples***: a disease in wheat caused by *Vibrio tritici* (see quots.).

1808 *Ann. Agric.* XLV. 236 *Purples, the*, 'ear-cockle' in wheat. *Ess.* **1881** El. A. Ormerod *Injur. Insects* (1890) 104 'Cockle galls' or 'Purples' are the small roundish or distorted growths sometimes found in wheat which give to the ear an appearance much as if purplish or dark-coloured peppercorns had taken the place of wheat-grains.

5. A purple flower. ***long purples***: see long *a.*[1] 17 c.

1840 Browning *Sordello* v. 295 Plucking purples in Goito's moss. **1905** *Academy* 18 Nov. 1198/1, I took his bunch of purples, and I charmed his heart away.

6. With *the*, applied to blood: cf. A. 2 d.

1804 R. Couper *Poetry* II. 61 Tibb snyted Madge's muckle nizz, Till out the purple sprang.

7. a. = blueness 4. *rare.*

1930 D. H. Lawrence *Phoenix II* (1968) 489, I should show the public that here is a fine novel, apart from all 'purple' and all 'words'.

b. ***the purple***: purple passages; esp. in ***to sub the purple*** (Journalists' slang), to sub-edit purple passages.

1958 E. A. Robertson *Justice of Heart* iii. 33 A well-known outside contributor from whose copy he had, in his own words, 'subbed the purple'. *Ibid.* vi. 84 The 'subbing of the purple' was always a painful business for a journalist.

8. *slang.* **a.** = purple-heart 3. **b.** = LSD[2].

1968 C. Drummond *Death & Leaping Ladies* v. 112, I heard her on at the Doc..about some Purples to key them up but he hit the ceiling. **1971** E. E. Landy *Underground Dict.* 156 *Purple*, LSD.

C. Combinations and collocations.

I. Of the adjective.

1. General combinations: **a.** Parasynthetic, as ***purple-berried*** (having purple berries), ***-crested***, ***-crowned***, ***-eyed***, ***-faced***, ***-flowered***, ***-headed***, ***-hearted***, ***-hued***, ***-leaved***, ***-lidded***, ***-nosed***, ***-robed***, ***-skirted***, ***-spiked***, ***-spotted***, ***-tailed***, ***-tinged***, ***-tipped***, ***-topped***, ***-veined***, ***-vested***, ***-zoned***, etc. adjs.: freq. in specific names of animals and plants, e.g. ***purple-berried bay***, ***purple-tailed parakeet***. Hence such forms as **purple-back**, the purple-backed humming bird.

1430 Lydg. *St. Margarete* 25 This daysye with leves rede and white, Purpul-hewed. **1726** Pope tr. *Homer's Odyssey* IV. XIX. 263 A mantle purple-ting'd, and radiant vest. **1754** *Catesby's Nat. Hist. Carol.* I. 61 The Purple-berried Bay. **1759** Miller *Gard. Dict.* s.v. *Leaf*, The Cockscomb, the purple leaved Amaranth. *Ibid.* s.v. *Turnep*, The round red or purple topped turnip. **1781** Latham *Hist. Birds* I. 315 Purple-tailed Parrakeet. **1788** J. Woodforde *Diary* 8 July (1927) III. 36 To Mr. Aldridge for 6 Yards of purple spotted Cotton..0.12.0. **1822** *Hortus Angl.* II. 260 Purple-spiked Milk Vetch. *Ibid.* 333 Purple-eyed Succory Hawk Weed. **1841** Lever *C. O'Malley* lxxxviii, A large purple-faced old major. **1841** Bryant *Walk at Sunset* Wks. 44 Purple-skirted clouds curtain the crimson air. **1846** D. J. Browne *Trees Amer.* 22 *Magnolia purpurea*, The Purple-flowered Magnolia. **1862** J. G. Whittier in *Atlantic Monthly* Apr. 423 Purple-zoned, Wachuset laid His head against the West. **1868** M. Collins *Sweet Anne Page* I. 241 The golden-fruited and purple-berried leafage. **1881** O. Wilde *Poems* 208 Pansies close their purple-lidded eyes. *Ibid.* 215 White-shielded, purple-crested rode the Mede. **1887** R. B. Sharpe *Gould's Trochilidæ* Suppl. Pl. 38 *Zodalia Ortoni*. Quito Purpleback. **1908** E. J. Banfield *Confess. Beachcomber* I. iii. 96 Purple-crowned Fruit Pigeon, *Ptilopus superbus*. **1910** *Daily Chron.* 25 Mar. 6/5 The minute purple-hearted blossoms. **1913** Conrad *Chance* I. i. 8 He envied the purple-nosed old cab-drivers on the stand. **1921** G. Bell *Let.* 25 Nov. (1927) II. xxi. 627 Grassy hollows where a tiny spring would rise cradled in purple-flowered mint. **1952** A. G. L. Hellyer *Sanders's Encycl. Gardening* (ed. 22) 130 *C*[*orylus*]..*maxima*.., var. *atropurpurea*, purple-leaved. *Ibid.* 277 *L*[*ilium*]..*daliense*, white, purple-spotted. *Ibid.* 393 *P*[*opulus*]..*tremula*, 'Aspen',..with vars. *pendula*, 'Weeping Aspen', and *purpurea*, purple-tinged foliage. **1962** R. Page *Education of Gardener* x. 281, I used ..*Corylus maxima purpurea*, the purple-leaved hazel. **1971** *Country Life* 17 June 1521/3 The purple-leaved filbert, (*Corylus maxima purpurea*)..responds well to stooling.

b. Qualifying the names of other colours or shades, as ***purple-black***, ***-blue***, ***-brown***, ***-crimson***, ***-dark***, ***-green***, ***-grey***, ***-pink***, ***-rose***, ***-yellow*** adjs.; also as sbs. See also purple-red.

1587 *Mirr. Mag., Induct.* xi, At length appeared Clad in purple blacke Sweete Somnus. **1601** Holland *Pliny* I. 91 Shell fishes that yeeld the purple crimson colour. **1835–6** *Todd's Cycl. Anat.* I. 553/1 A..layer of a dark purple-brown pigment. **1845** J. R. Lowell in *Harbinger* 2 Aug. 122/3 Far away on Katahdin thou towerest, Purple-blue with the distance. **1856** Geo. Eliot in J. W. Cross *Life Geo. Eliot* (1885) I. vii. 401 The *Corallina officinalis*..with its purple-pink fronds. **1882** *Garden* 22 July 65/2 Varying in colour from a deep purple-rose to a delicate rose-pink. *Ibid.* 2 Sept. 207/3 Agaricus violaceus, a splendid purple-yellow, growing among dead leaves. **1897** *Allbutt's Syst. Med.* IV. 529 The surface of the spleen..is often found to be of a black or purple-green colour. **1897** Purple-brown [see *Italian earth*]. **1928** V. Woolf *Orlando* vi. 243 The wine-blue purple-dark hill. **1930** J. dos Passos *42nd Parallel* 147 Purplegray murk rose steadily. **1952** A. G. L. Hellyer *Sanders's Encycl. Gardening* (ed. 22) 93 *C*[*atasetum*]..*Rodigasianum*, flowers many, greenish, spotted purple-brown. **1957** Purple-blue [see dracocephalum]. **1960** Purple-black [see Carlsbad]. **1964** M. Hynes *Med. Bacteriol.* (ed. 8) 484 A colony subcultured on to the medium gives a purple-pink colour from NH_3 production in 2–8 hours.

c. Adverbial, as ***purple-beaming***, ***-dawning***, ***-dyeing***, ***-glowing***, ***-staining***, ***-streaming*** adjs.

1595 Daniel *Civ. War* II. cxxii, Riuers dide With purple streaming wounds of her owne rage. **1753** Chambers *Cycl. Supp.* s.v. *Trumpet-shell*, The purple-dying liquor of the *buccinum*. **1760** Fawkes tr. *Anacreon, Odes* lxiv. 4 Safely shroud Me in a purple-beaming Cloud. **1802** Bingley *Anim. Biog.* (1813) III. 465 The purple-staining whelk. **1898** *Month* Nov. 458 The purple-glowing heather.

2. a. Special collocations: **purple airway** [airway 2], a route reserved for an aircraft on which royalty is flying; **purple chamber**: see porphyrogenite, and cf. B. 2 d; **purple-coat**, a person dressed in a purple coat; cf. red-coat; so **purple-coated** *a.*; **purple copper (ore)** *Min.*, a native sulphide of copper and iron; = erubescite; **purple death** *slang*, a cheap Italian red wine; **purple fly**, a kind of anglers' artificial fly; **purple haze** *slang* = LSD[2]; **purple lake** [lake *sb.*[6]], a purple pigment; **purple-man**, an Irish party name for one who has reached a certain degree or rank in the 'Orange' system; cf. Orangeman; so **purple meeting**; **purple membrane**, a membrane found within the cell membrane of the bacterium *Halobacterium halobium*; **purple powder of Cassius**: see B. 1 d; **purple quartz**, the amethyst; also, a local name for fluorspar; **purple rash**, an eruption of purple pustules; **purple zone** = *purple airway*. See also purple fever.

1958 *Sunday Times* 30 Mar. 5/1 Now that the Duke of Edinburgh is doing a lot of flying, warnings about '*purple airway' are more frequently given to commercial pilots. Purple airway is a reserved track for a Royal flight. **1831** Scott *Ct. Robt.* iii, An imperial princess *porphyrogenita*, or born in the sacred *purple chamber itself. *Ibid.* xxi, You are a child of the purple chamber. **1644** Vicars *God in Mount* 200 The Lord Brooke his *Purple-coats..did most singular good service all this fight. **1906** *Westm. Gaz.* 3 July 1/3 The scarlet- or *purple-coated seminarists pause for breath. **1796** Kirwan *Elem. Min.* (ed. 2) II. 374 *Purple Copper Ore. **1881** Raymond *Gloss. Mining*, *Copper-ores*,..purple copper (variegated or peacock ore, bornite, sulphide of copper and iron). **1947** D. M. Davin *Gorse blooms Pale* 199 Everyone goes for the *purple death. **1799** G. Smith *Laboratory* II. 311 *Purple-fly. Dubbing, of purple wool, and a little bear's hair mixed [etc.]. **1967** J. Hendrix in *40 Greatest Songs* (1975) 28 *Purple haze is in my brain lately things don't seem the same. **1970** *Times* 24 Mar. 2/3 The American LSD..has been coming in..under such exotic names as..'purple haze', and 'blue cheer'. **1971** *Current Slang* (*Univ. S. Dakota*) VI. 9 *Purple haze*, LSD cut with methedrine. **1821** *London Mag.* Sept. 290/2 The *purple-lake-coloured stuffs. **1869** *Bradshaw's Railway Man.* XXI. 460/2 (Advt.), Reds..Crimson Lake—Scarlet and Purple ditto. **1934** H. Hiler *Notes on Technique of Painting* ii. 123 *Crimson lake, Purple lake*, etc., now usually made from alizarin... Also prepared from cochineal... Should be regarded as obsolete. **1830–3** W. Carleton *Traits & Stor. Irish Peasantry* Ser. II. (1843) I. 199, I am a true blue, sir, —a *purple man. **1836** *Fraser's Mag.* XIII. 393 The very names of 'Orange-man' and 'Purpleman' are beneath the real elevation of their high and noble cause. **1906** *Daily News* 10 Feb. 8/2 Injuries inflicted on the roadside..after a '*purple' meeting in the Bush Side Orange Hall. **1968** Stoeckenius & Kunau in *Jrnl. Cell Biol.* XXXVIII. 344/1 The purple band, henceforth called *purple membranes, contains considerably less RNA and slightly less lipid than the orange-red fraction. **1975** *Nature* 25 Dec. 766/2 *Halobacterium halobium* is indigenous to warm saline pools exposed to bright sunlight. Strains of this bacterium synthesise a purple pigment in the cell membrane (the 'purple membrane'). **1823** Ure *Dict. Chem.* 492/2 A plate of tin, immersed in a solution of gold, affords a purple powder, called the *purple powder of Cassius, which is used to paint in enamel. **1836** Brande *Man. Chem.* 1028 *note*, *Purple quartz or amethyst, is tinged with a little iron and manganese. **1896** *Cosmopolitan* XX. 450 The fluor-spar is locally known as 'purple quartz'. **1818–20** E. Thompson *Cullen's Nosol. Method.* (ed. 3) 326 Purpura; *Purple, or Scorbutic Rash. **1970** *Daily Tel.* 1 Aug. 1/2 'A *purple zone' was not in operation..because the Prince was flying only in the immediate area of Tangmere.

b. In names of species or varieties of animals characterized by a purple or purplish colouring, as ***purple grackle***, ***heron***, ***kaleege***, ***martin***, ***sandpiper***, ***sea-anemone***, ***urchin***, etc.; **purple bacterium** [ad. G. *purpurbacterium* (T. W. Engelmann 1888, in *Bot. Zeitung* 663)], any of a group of bacteria containing a purple photo-active pigment; **purple-bird**, **coot**, the purple gallinule of Europe: see porphyrio; **purple-bullfinch** = *purple-finch*; **purple crow**, one of several species of small glossy E. Indian crows, as *Corvusenca*, *C. orru*, and *C. violacea* (*Cent. Dict.*); **purple-egg**, a purple sea-urchin, as *Arbacia punctulata*; **purple-emperor**, a butterfly: see emperor 4; **purple finch**, a common American bird, *Carpodacus purpureus*: see finch 1 b; **purple gallinule**, (*a*) the swamp-hen, *Porphyrio porphyrio*, found in parts of Europe, southern Asia, Africa, and Australasia; cf. porphyrio; (*b*) a similar North American bird, *Porphyrula martinica*, which is smaller than the swamp-hen and has yellow legs instead of red ones; **purple heron**, a heron with greyish-blue plumage, *Ardea purpurea*, found in central and southern Europe, Africa, and parts of Asia; **purple martin**, a large North American swallow, *Progne subis*; **purple sandpiper**, a small wading bird, *Calidris maritima*, found in northern parts of Europe, North America, and Asia; **purple-shell**, (*a*) = B. 3; (*b*) an ocean snail of the genus *Ianthina*; **purple water-hen**, a water-hen of the genus *Porphyrio*; **purple whelk** = B. 3.

1900 A. C. Jones tr. *Fischer's Structure & Functions of Bacteria* 194/2 (Index), *Purple bacteria. **1912** W. H. Lang tr. *Strasburger's Textbk. Bot.* (ed. 4) II. i. 337 The Purple Bacteria, which develop in water with decomposing organic matter in the absence of oxygen and the presence of light, contain..a green and a red pigment. **1957** G. E. Hutchinson *Treat. Limnol.* I. xiii. 756 The second way in which hydrogen sulfide is oxidized in the hydrosphere is by the photosynthetic green and purple bacteria, of which the purple sulfur bacteria are best known. **1971** Berkeley & Campbell in Hawker & Linton *Micro-Organisms* v. 163 The phototactic behaviour of the purple bacterium Rhodospirillum rubrum..results from a response to lack of light. **1775** *Purple Emperor [see emperor *sb.* 4]. **1810** Crabbe *Borough* viii. 78 Above the sovereign oak a sovereign skims, The purple Emp'ror, strong in wing and limbs. **1754** *Catesby's Nat. Hist. Carol.* I. 41 The *Purple Finch. **1876** J. Burroughs *Winter Sunshine* I. 31 Those purple finches.. are they not stealing our berries? **1884** [see finch 1 b]. **1903** S. E. White *Forest* vii. 91 You will hear..purple finches or some of the pine sparrows warbling high and clear. **1971** *Islander* (Victoria, B.C.) 10 Oct 13/2 Purple finches nest every year in the trees beside our house. **1813** A. Wilson *Amer. Ornithol.* IX. 71 The *Purple Gallinule [was seen] in a thick swamp, a short distance from Savannah, Georgia. **1884** H. Seebohm *Hist. Brit. Birds* II. 562 The Purple Gallinule..is a resident in Algeria, Spain, and Italy. **1888** [see gallinule]. **1909** W. Verner *My Life among Wild Birds in Spain* II. i. 99, I have..been startled by the curious cry of the big Purple Gallinule. **1944** *Nat. Geogr. Mag.* June 694/1 There were Purple Gallinules, decked out in brilliant purple, green, sky-blue, red, and yellow. **1965** E. Richardson *Living Island* 92 [A] purple gallinule also stopped in these road-puddles after a foggy rain. **1782** Latham *Hist. Birds* II. 462 *Purple Grakle. **1886** *Pall Mall G.* 28 Apr. 11/2 Orioles, crows, blackbirds, purple-grackles, redwing blackbirds, bobolinks, and terns make very pretty ornaments. **1837** Gould *Birds Eur.* IV. Pl. 274 The food of the Purple *Heron consists of fish, frogs, mice, and insects. **1893** Purple heron [see heron 1 b]. **1905** Kelsall & Munn *Birds Hampshire & Isle of Wight* 198 Purple Heron. A very rare accidental visitor from Central and Southern Europe. **1971** *Country Life* 18 Feb. 356/2 The purple heron, once a common sight in the [Ebro] delta, has diminished considerably in recent years. **1743** M. Catesby *Nat. Hist. Carolina* II. p. xxvi, Land-Birds which breed and abide in Carolina in the Summer, and retire in Winter:..The yellow Titmouse. The *purple Martin. The humming Bird. **1808–14** [see martin[1] 1]. **1883** Newton in *Encycl. Brit.* XV. 581/2 The Purple Martin of America, *Hirundo* or *Progne purpurea*,..being such a favourite bird in Canada and in the United States. **1939** F. C. Lincoln *Migration Amer. Birds* 55 The Purple Martin is an early migrant. **1976** *National Observer* (U.S.) 29 May 12/2 We carefully watch certain species like the purple martins..and upland sandpipers, which are only now recovering from the 1972 fury of Hurricane Agnes. **1824** *Purple sandpiper [see sandpiper 1]. **1828** C. L. Bonaparte in *Ann. Lyceum Nat. Hist. N.Y.* II. 319 The Purple Sandpiper... Inhabits both continents on rocky shores only. **1837** Gould *Birds Eur.* IV. Pl. 334 The Purple Sandpiper. **1860** S. F. Baird *Birds N. Amer.* I. 717 The purple sandpiper..is frequently met with on the shores of the Atlantic. **1925** [see injury *sb.* 4]. **1940** H. F. Witherby et al. *Handbk. Brit. Birds* IV. 273 Though probably there is no wader which cannot swim well when necessary, Purple Sandpiper does so more habitually than most. **1978** C. HARRISON *Field Guide Nests N. Amer. Birds* 130 Purple Sandpiper... Breeds on the tundra. **1884** *Standard Nat. Hist.* I. 325 *Ianthina*, *purple shell, with the float supporting the eggs. **1855** P. H. GOSSE *Mar. Zool.* I. 61 The *Purple Urchin (*E[chinus] lividus*) excavates hollows for itself in limestone rock, in which it resides. **1893** NEWTON *Dict. Birds* 591 The genus *Porphyrio*, including the bird so named by classical writers, and perhaps a dozen other species often called Sultanas and *Purple Water-hens. **1681** GREW *Musæum* I. VI. i. 129 The *Purple-Wilk with long plated Spikes.

c. As a distinguishing prefix in names of species or varieties of plants having purple flowers, leaves, etc., as ***purple amaranth, beech, broomrape, camomile, cow-wheat, gromwell, groundsel, medick, melic, mullein, ragwort, spurge***, etc.; † **purple apple**, the genus *Anona*; **purple bottle**, a moss, *Splachnum ampullaceum*, from the reddish pitcher-shaped apophysis; **purple cone-flower**, a perennial herb belonging to the genus *Echinacea* of the family Compositæ, native to North America, and bearing flowers with a dark central disc and purplish rays; **purple grass**, (*a*) a garden variety of *Trifolium repens*: see quot. 1640; (*b*) *Medicago maculata*, Heart-clover or Spotted Clover (Deering *Catalog. Stirpium* 1738); **purple lily**, (*a*) = MARTAGON; (*b*) an Australian genus (*Patersonia*) of flag-like plants, bearing showy blue or purple flowers; native lily (Miller); **purple loosestrife**, a large perennial herb, *Lythrum salicaria*, belonging to the family Lythraceæ, widely distributed in temperate regions, and bearing purple flowers in clusters; **purple moor-grass**, a perennial grass with purplish panicles, *Molinia cærulea*, native to Europe and Asia; formerly called blue moor-grass; **purple osier**, a large shrub, *Salix purpurea*, belonging to the family Salicaceæ, native to Europe, North Africa, and central Asia, and distinguished by its purplish bark; **purple-tassels** = *purse-tassels* (PURSE *sb.* 11); **purple-velvet flower**, Love-lies-bleeding (*Amaranthus caudatus*); **purple willow** = *purple osier*; **purple-wood** = PURPLE-HEART, the timber of this; **purple-wort**, one of various plants of which the flowers, leaves, or stems are purple; as, a dark-leaved variety of *Trifolium repens*; also, *Comarum palustre*; **purple wreath**, a tropical American twining shrub (*Petræa volubilis*) bearing violet flowers (*Treas. Bot.*).

1788 LEE *Bot.* App., *Purple apple, *Annona*. **1866** *Treas. Bot.* 486/2 Ornamental varieties of the common Beech..as ..the *Purple Beech, with purple leaves. **1796** WITHERING *Brit. Plants* (ed. 3) III. 792 *S[plachnum] ampullaceum* ..*Purple Bottle-moss. **1848** A. GRAY *Man. Bot. Northern U.S.* 223 (*heading*) *Purple cone-flower. **1857** [see *cone-flower*]. **1900** L. H. BAILEY *Cycl. Amer. Hort.* II. 511/2 Purple Cone-flower. Four species of North American perennial herbs. **1939** *Nat. Geogr. Mag.* Aug. 220/2 Striking contrast is provided by some of the most brilliant flowers of the prairie notably..the purple coneflower, the butterfly milkweed,.. and the prickly pear. **1954** C. J. HYLANDER *Macmillan Wild Flower Bk.* 453 The conical receptacle which projects from the center of the Purple Coneflower bears disk-flowers which are purplish in colour. **1974** M. C. DAVIS *Near Woods* ii. 21 A purple cone flower..essentially is a large central disc and long ribbony rays. **1640** PARKINSON *Theat. Bot.* 1112 The *purple grasse spreadeth on the ground, the leaves are in some three in others foure or five on a stalke, of a sad greene colour, with a shadow of darke purple cast over them. **1578** LYTE *Dodoens* II. xliii. 201 The small *purple Lillie. *Ibid.* 202 The red purple Lillie.. Some call the greatest kinde *Martagon*. **1548**, **1633**, etc. *Purple loosestrife [see LOOSESTRIFE 1 b]. **1861** R. BENTLEY *Man. Bot.* II. iii. 538 *Lythrum Salicaria*, Purple Loosestrife, is a common British plant. **1977** *New Yorker* 5 Sept. 23/2 An impenetrable marsh of..purple loosestrife and other plants clogs the length of the channel. **1859** L. H. GRINDON *Manchester Flora* 439 *Purple Moor-grass... Everywhere on heaths and moors. **1928** M. A. JOHNSTONE *Plant Ecol.* viii. 93 Where water lodges even very plentifully the dominant grass is the purple moor-grass. **1979** R. GROUNDS *Ornamental Grasses* viii. 147/1 Purple moor grass... Deservedly one of the most popular garden grasses. **1870** J. D. HOOKER *Student's Flora Brit. Islands* 342 *S[alix] purpurea*... *Purple Osier. **1910** E. STEP *Wayside & Woodland Trees* 71 The Purple Osier gets its name from the red or purple bark which clothes the thin but tough twigs. **1958** R. D. MEIKLE *Brit. Trees & Shrubs* 196 *Salix purpurea*. .. Purple Osier. A loose spreading shrub..with slender yellowish or purple-tinged twigs. **1629** PARKINSON *Paradisus* 118 Called..the purple faire haired Iacinth..and ..of diuers Gentlewomen, *purple tassels. **1578** LYTE *Dodoens* II. xviii. 168 Called..in English floure Gentill ..*Purple veluet floure. **1776** W. WITHERING *Bot. Arrangement Veg. Gt. Brit.* 602 *Purple Willow. Leaves serrated; smooth; spear-shaped... Banks of rivers. **1838** J. C. LOUDON *Arboretum & Fruticetum Britannicum* III. 1490 *S[alix] purpurea*. The purple Willow. **1914** W. J. BEAN *Trees & Shrubs Hardy in Brit. Isles* II. 487 Purple Willow. A shrub with thin, graceful branches forming a loose-habited, spreading bush, 10 to 18 ft. high. **1960** *Oxf. Bk. Wild Flowers* 186/2 Purple Willow is locally common in fens, marshes, and on riverbanks. **1640** PARKINSON *Theatr. Bot.* Index 1743 *Purple wort or Purple grasse. **1736** AINSWORTH *Lat. Dict.* I. s.v. *Purple*, Purple wort, *Trifolium purpureum*.

II. Of the substantive.

3. General combinations: objective or obj. genitive, as ***purple-dyer, -seller, -wearer***; ***purple-producing*** adj.; instrumental, as ***purple-clad, -dusted, -dyed, -edged, -lined, -stained, -tinged***, etc. adjs.; locative, as ***purple-born*** adj.; † **purple-father**, a cardinal: cf. B. 2 c; **purple gland**, the gland in some gastropods which yields the purple dye.

1831 SCOTT *Ct. Robt.* xxxiv, The hero of many a victory, achieved, says the *purple-born [Anna Comnena], in..her history, sometimes by his arms and sometimes by his prudence. **1639** G. DANIEL *Ecclus.* xxxiii. 45 Heare me, O you *purple-Clad Magistrates, You civill Rulers. **1870** MORRIS *Earthly Par.* III. IV. 383 The *purple-dusted butterfly. **1581** PETTIE *Guazzo's Civ. Conv.* III. (1586) 125 b, Not perceiuing..her owne *purple died face. **1904** W. M. RAMSAY *Lett. to Seven Ch.* xxix. 421 The Jews..were organised in trade-guilds, the *purple-dyers, the carpet makers, and perhaps others. **1875** POSTE *Gaius* I. com. (ed. 2) 90 The *purple-edged praetexta was generally laid aside by boys along with the bulla aurea..on the first Liberalia,.. after the completion of their fourteenth year. **1615** BRATHWAIT *Strappado* (1878) 47 A purple sin..Since *purple-fathers oft-times go vnto it. **1888** ROLLESTON & JACKSON *Anim. Life* 483 **Purple gland* = hypobranchial gland of Purpura. **1819** KEATS *Lamia* II. 31 The *purple-lined palace of sweet sin. **1549** COVERDALE, etc. *Erasm. Par. Phil.* Argt. AA aj, In this citie was also Lydia the *purpleseller. **1819** KEATS *Ode Nightingale* ii, With ..*purple-stained mouth. **1726** POPE *Odyss.* XIX. 275 A mantle *purple-ting'd, and radiant vest. **1880** T. HODGKIN *Italy & Inv.* III. v. II. 426 The courtiers still contended for the smile of 'the *Purple-wearer'.

purple ('pɜːp(ə)l), *v.* [f. PURPLE *a.*]

1. *trans.* To make purple; to colour, stain, tinge, or dye with purple. Also *fig.*

1432–50 tr. *Higden* (Rolls) I. 41 In so moche that y schalle purpulle the mariantes [*margines purpurabo*] nye the hedes of þe gestes with a dowble ordre of yeres. *c* **1620** Z. BOYD *Zion's Flowers* (1855) 138 Blood did purple ov'r the grasse. **1667** MILTON *P.L.* VII. 30 Yet not alone, while thou Visit'st my slumbers Nightly, or when Morn Purples the East. **1783** JUSTAMOND tr. *Raynal's Hist. Indies* I. 395 Was it then to be reserved for this ignominy, that we purpled the seas with our blood? **1831** J. WILSON *Unimore* vi. 5 The heather bloom.. purples..The Moors and Mountains.

2. *intr.* To become purple.

1646, etc. [see PURPLING *ppl. a.*]. **1816** BYRON *Siege Cor.* i, The landmark to the double tide That purpling rolls on either side. **1885** MISS BRADDON *Wyllard's Weird* v, The heather was purpling on the hills. **1893** E. H. BARKER *Wand. Southern Waters* 87 It purpled and died away in grayness and mournful shadow.

Hence '**purpling** *vbl. sb.*

1860 FARRAR *Orig. Lang.* 125 The deep purpling of an agitated sea.

'**purple-ˌcoloured**, *a.* [f. PURPLE *sb.* + COLOURED, or parasynth. f. *purple colour* + -ED².] Of the colour of, or coloured with, purple.

1567 MAPLET *Gr. Forest* 1 b, It is Princes among those Gemes that be Purple coloured. **1592** SHAKS. *Ven. & Ad.* 1 The sunne with purple-colourd face, Had tane his last leaue of the weeping morne. **1800** HERSCHEL in *Phil. Trans.* XC. 526 The purple-coloured glass stops 993 rays of light. **1838** T. THOMSON *Chem. Org. Bodies* 466 At the bottom..we find a purple-coloured resin.

purpled ('pɜːp(ə)ld), *ppl. a.* Also 5 perpulid. [f. PURPLE *a.*, *sb.*, and *v.* + -ED: cf. L. *purpurātus*.] Coloured, stained, tinged, or dyed purple; hence, blood-stained, dyed with blood; clothed in purple. Also *fig.*

c **1400** *Apol. Loll.* 44 Not.. to be gilt bridils, peyntid sadels, ne siluern sporis, nor perpulid aray. **1561** DAUS tr. *Bullinger on Apoc.* (1573) 184 A Princely Senate of proude purpled Cardinals. **1595** SHAKS. *John* II. i. 322 All with purpled hands, Dide in the dying slaughter of their foes. **1712–14** POPE *Rape Lock* II. 2 Not with more glories in th' etherial plain, The Sun first rises o'er the purpled main. **1804** J. GRAHAME *Sabbath* (1839) 9/2 Oh England! England! wash thy purpled hands Of this foul sin. **1811** SHAW *Gen. Zool.* VIII. 201 Purpled Creeper. **1889** C. EDWARDES *Sardinia* 231 A cluster of bold purpled peaks.

† '**purple** '**fever**. *Obs.* An old name for PURPURA; but also applied vaguely to other fevers attended with purplish cutaneous eruptions.

1626 BACON *Sylva* §804 The Lesser Infections, of the small Pocks, Purple Feavers, Agues, in the summer Precedent, and hovering all winter, do portend a great Pestilence in the summer following. **1666** *Lond. Gaz.* No. 61/2 We are in..great fear of the Plague, several persons being lately dead of a very malignant Purple-Feavor. **1728–41** CHAMBERS *Cycl.* s.v. *Purple*, The *purple fever*..is a kind of plague, or a malignant fever discovering itself in eruptions on the skin like the bites of bugs or fleas, or like grains of millet, or the small-pox; whence it is sometimes also called the *spotted* and *miliary* fever. *Ibid.* s.v. *Fever*, Eruptive Fevers are..attended with cutaneous eruptions. Such are those of the small-pox, meazles, the petechial, the purple or scarlet fever, and the miliary fever. **1890** BILLINGS *Nat. Med. Dict.*, *Purple fever*, cerebro-spinal fever.

'**purple-fish.** Now *rare*. [f. PURPLE *sb.* + FISH *sb.*¹] A mollusc that yields a purple dye; = PURPLE *sb.* 3.

1591 PERCIVALL *Sp. Dict.*, *Bozina*, a trumpet,..a purple fish, *Buccina, purpura, murex*. **1601** CHESTER *Love's Mart.* lxxxii, The Purple-fish, whose liquor vsually, A violet colour on the cloth doth die. **1686** W. COLE *Purpura Ang.* (1689) 1 The Purple-Fish, which I found..on the Sea Coasts of Somerset-shire, and the shores of South-Wales opposite to it. **1820** W. TOOKE tr. *Lucian* I. 454 *note*, The murex, a species of shellfish, called also the purple-fish.

'**purple-heart.** Also as one word or two separate words. [f. PURPLE *a.* + HEART *sb.*]

1. a. A large tree of the genus *Peltogyne*, belonging to the family Leguminosæ and native to areas of tropical rain forest in Central and South America and the West Indies; also, the dark purplish-brown timber of this tree. Also *attrib.*

1796 STEDMAN *Surinam* II. 17 The purple-heart-tree grows sometimes to the height of fourscore feet..; the wood is of a beautiful purple colour. **1825** C. WATERTON *Wanderings in S. Amer.* 24 Wallaba, purple-heart,..and mora, are met with in vast abundance, far and near, towering up in majestic grandeur. **1845** LINDLEY *Veg. Kingd.* (1846) 550 The Purple Heart, a Guiana timber tree of great toughness, whose timber is found invaluable for resisting the shock of artillery discharges. **1902** G. S. BOULGER *Wood* I. v. 99 Hepplewhite and Sheraton employed Mahogany.. for small articles such as tea-caddies, whilst in the inlaid work of the period it was used..with other dark woods, such as Rosewood, Laburnum, and Purple-heart. **1924** RECORD & MELL *Timbers Trop. Amer.* II. 235 There is considerable variation in the size, abundance, and arrangement of the pores in different specimens of purpleheart. **1947** J. C. RICH *Materials & Methods of Sculpture* x. 285 Amaranth wood or Purpleheart is a rich, violet-colored, tropical hardwood imported from the Guianas. **1951** J. C. FENNESSY *Sonnet in Bottle* VI. i. 200 There were no tall trees, no soaring palms or smooth-stemmed purplehearts. **1951** *Archit. Rev.* CIX. 288 Floors are in polished purple-heart hardwood. **1956** *Handbk. of Hardwoods* (Forest Prod. Res. Lab.) 193 The different species of purpleheart vary in size at maturity. **1959** P. CAPON *Amongst those Missing* 215, I haven't noticed any purpleheart trees about. **1963** *Times* 26 Jan. 4/2 A nineteenth-century kingwood commode.., its sides inlaid with chrysanthemum branches in purpleheart, made £280. **1974** *Country Life* 30 May 1338/1 A second [chest], walnut with panels and banding in purple heart, ebony and ivory.

b. An evergreen tree of the genus *Copaifera*, belonging to the family Leguminosæ and native to tropical America or the West Indies.

1866 *Treas. Bot.* **1963** ROBERTSON & GOODING *Bot. for Caribbean* xxiii. 186 Purple-heart (*Copaifera pubiflora*).

2. *U.S.* (In form **Purple Heart**.) A decoration bestowed on a member of the armed services wounded in action. Also more fully, ***Purple Heart Award***.

A decoration consisting of a heart-shaped piece of purple cloth was instituted by George Washington in 1782, but later fell into disuse. The present bronze enamelled medal was instituted in 1932.

1932 *Army & Navy Jrnl.* 27 Feb. 602/4 Awards of the Purple Heart for acts or service performed prior to Feb. 22, 1932, will be confined to the following persons. **1948** E. E. CUMMINGS *Let.* 27 Aug. (1969) 185 The hyper-scientific climax of this hero (a prominent killer, holder of Silver Stars & Clusters & Purple Hearts galore)'s experience. **1974** *Sumter* (S. Carolina) *Daily Item* 23 Apr. 4A/4 He is a recipient of the Purple Heart Award and Army Commendation Medal. **1977** J. WAMBAUGH *Black Marble* (1978) ii. 15 Mason returned to Pasadena wearing a Bronze Star and a Purple Heart.

3. Usu. *pl.* A familiar term for tablets of the stimulant Drinamyl, so named because of their shape and colour. Also *attrib.*

1961 [see DRINAMYL]. **1962** *Daily Tel.* 31 Aug. 21/1 People involved in the investigation had already had 'purple heart' tablets prescribed for them by their own doctors. **1964** [see DEXAMPHETAMINE]. **1968** *Times* 30 Nov. 4/7 A mixture of the stimulant amphetamine and the depressant amylobarbitone... A similar mixture of drugs was popular a few years ago in the guise of 'purple hearts'. **1971** N. STACEY *Who Cares?* xvi. 276 They became more responsible, they took more interest in life, they stopped taking purple hearts and they settled down in their homes, their schools and their jobs. **1973** H. MILLER *Open City* xvi. 179 Drugs. Purple Hearts, amphetamines. The bloke was passing the stuff to kids.

'**purplely**, *adv.* [irreg. f. PURPLE *a.* + -LY².] In a purple manner, with purple. So '**purpleness**, the quality or condition of being purple.

c **1825** BEDDOES *Torrismond* I. i, The young lord..Like a young dragon on Hesperian berries Purplely fed, who dashes through the air. **1906** *Westm. Gaz.* 20 Apr. 2/1 Standing on an unsubstantial purpleness of the unwavering furrows, were a host of monoliths.

'**purple-**'**red.** **A.** *adj.* Red inclining to or tinged with purple. **B.** *sb.* A purple-red colour.

1578 LYTE *Dodoens* II. lxiv. 230 Wilde Tyme. The floures ..most commonly of a purple red colour. **1624** GATAKER *Transubst.* 67 The people are all died purplered in it with Christs blood. **1832** G. R. PORTER *Porcelain & Gl.* 271 Imparting to glass almost exquisite purple-red colour resembling the ruby. **1879** ROOD *Chromatics* xiv. 214 Every kind of pure red, from purple-red to orange-red.

'**purpling**, *ppl. a.* Chiefly *poetic.* [f. PURPLE *v.* + -ING².] Becoming purple.

1652 CRASHAW *Carmen Deo Nostro* 29 Th' Babe's bright face, the purpling Bud And Rosy dawn of the right Royall blood. **1652** —— *Mary Magd.* Wks. (1904) 261 The maiden gemme By the purpling vine put on. **1786** BURNS *To Mount. Daisy* ii, Upward-springing, blythe, to greet The purpling east. **1826** WORDSW. *Ode May Morning* i, From the purpling east departs The star that led the dawn.

purplish ('pɜːplɪʃ), *a.* [f. PURPLE *a.* + -ISH¹.] Somewhat purple; tinged with purple.

1562 TURNER *Herbal* II. 54 Mint..hath in yᵉ top of the stalkes a purplishe flour. **1608** TOPSELL *Serpents* (1658) 665 These Caterpillers are blackish-red, with spots or streaks going overthwart their sides, being half white, and half purpelish. **1800** tr. *Lagrange's Chem.* II. 137 If you put a piece of gold between two cards and expose it to a strong electric shock, you will obtain it in the state of a purplish oxide. **1886** *Century Mag.* XXXII. 274/1 The eggs..are greenish blue, with faint brown or purplish markings.

b. Qualifying adjs. and sbs. of colour.

1766 *Compl. Farmer* s.v. *Service-tree*, The branches, while young, have a purplish brown bark. **1828** SIR W. J. HOOKER *J. E. Smith's Eng. Flora* II. 14 Seed purplish-black. **1848** *Chambers' Inform. People* I. 368/1 Amethyst is a pure rock-crystal, of a purplish-violet colour. **1882** *Garden* 27 May 366/1 Spikes of purplish green flowers.

purply ('pɜːplɪ), *a.* [f. PURPLE *a.* or *sb.* + -Y.] Characterized by a purple colour or tint; purplish; also in *Comb.* as ***purply-brown, -gold, -grey.***

1725 *Bradley's Fam. Dict.* s.v. *May blossom*, That Part which is purply in the Flower..is good against the Squincy. **1842** G. DARLING in *Proc. Berw. Nat. Club* II. x. 4 He took Smelts of the salmon with their..dark purply fins. **1895** *Chamb. Jrnl.* XII. 774/1 The warmth of the soft sienna browns, and the rich purity of the purply grays.

purpoint, -pont, variants of POURPOINT.

purport ('pɜːpəʊt), *sb.* Also 5 purpurt. (See also PROPORT *sb.*[2]) [a. AF. = OF. *por-, purport* (13th c. in Godef.) produce, contents, f. *purporter*: see next. Formerly stressed *pur'port.*]

1. That which is conveyed or expressed, esp. by a formal document; bearing, tenor, import, effect; meaning, substance, sense.

[**1278** *Rolls of Parlt.* I. 10/1 Solum le purport de lur chartres.] **1455** *Ibid.* V. 306/2 Aftir the purportez and tenours of the same. **1466** in *Archæologia* (1887) L. I. 51 Our seyde graunt and lettres patentes accordyng to theffecte tenour and purport therof be and stond. **1495** *Stat. 11 Hen. VII*, c. 54 §2 Lettres patentes..[shall be] effectuell in the lawe aftir the tenures and purpurtis of the same. **1596** SPENSER *F.Q.* v. ix. 26 High over his head There written was the purport of his sin. **1602** SHAKS. *Ham.* II. i. 82 And with a looke so pitious in purport, As if he had been loosed out of hell. **1703** ROWE *Fair Penit.* II. ii. 578 To tell thee then the purport of my Thoughts. **1791** MRS. RADCLYFFE *Rom. Forest* viii, She resolved to acquaint Madame La Motte with the purport of the late conversation. **1881** JOWETT *Thucyd.* I. xxii, I endeavoured..to give the general purport of what was actually said.

†**b.** Outward bearing. *Obs. rare*[−1].

1590 SPENSER *F.Q.* III. i. 52 For shee her sexe under that straunge purport Did use to hide.

2. That which is intended to be done or effected by something; meaning, object, purpose, design, intention. Now *rare.*

1654 CROMWELL *Sp.* 4 Sept. (in *Carlyle*), What was the purport of it but to make the Tenant as liberal a fortune as the Landlord? **1751** EARL ORRERY *Remarks Swift* (1752) 133 Writings of that sort,..framed to serve particular views, fulfill the purport of their creation, and then perish. **1793** SMEATON *Edystone L.* §127 The whole purport of the present remaining season, was nothing more than cutting the rock to a shape..for the reception of any structure whatever. **1863** MARY HOWITT *F. Bremer's Greece* II. xiv. 95 The purport of our steamer's visit to these shores is to promote exchange of commodities and commerce.

purport (pɜː'pɔət, 'pɜːpət), *v.* Also 6 pour-. [a. AF. = OF. *pur-, porporter* (*c* 1160 in Godef.), later *pourporter* to embody, extend:—late pop. L. **prōportāre* to carry or bear forth; cf. med.L. *prōportāre* (*præ-, por-*) to extend (12th c. in Du Cange). OF. had also the variant *proporter*, whence the Sc. form PROPORT, q.v.]

1. *trans.* To have as its purport, bearing, or tenor; to convey to the mind; to bear as its meaning; to express, set forth, state; to mean, imply.

[**1300** *Lib. Custum.* I. 124, 28 Ed. I, Solom ceo qe lour chartre roiale le purporte.] **1528** GARDINER in Pocock *Rec. Ref.* I. xliv. 84 Like as our letters sent from Lyones..did purport. **1533** MORE *Debell. Salem* Wks. 955/1 This coniunccion, if, purporteth alway a doute. ?**1561** T. PRESTON *Cambyses* in Hazl. *Dodsley* IV. 173 Your grace's message came to me, Your will purporting forth. **1676** *Ancaster MSS.* (Hist. MSS. Comm. 1907) 458 [A silver cup] purporting a woman carrying a bucket on her head. **1693** *Mem. Cnt. Teckely* III. 2 The Declaration also purported, That from the 15th of February, those Malecontents..should find the Emperor's Commissioners at Presbourg. **1780** D. BRODHEAD in Sparks *Corr. Amer. Rev.* (1853) III. 120, I..inclose copies of letters.. purporting some of the above facts. **1858** MASSON *Milton* (1859) I. 5 It purports that some one from Oxfordshire.. applied to the College of Arms to have his title recognised.

b. Followed by *inf.* (of a picture, statue, document, book, or the like; rarely of a person): To profess or claim by its tenor. (Said without pronouncing as to the truth or validity of the claim.)

1790 PALEY *Horæ Paul.* i. 10 This epistle purports to be written after St. Paul had been at Corinth. **1808** COLEBROOKE *Vedas* in *Asiat. Res.* VIII. 377 A transcript of what purported to be a complete copy of the Védas. **1849** MACAULAY *Hist. Eng.* ii. I. 232 The Declaration which purported to give them entire freedom of conscience. **1879** TOURGEE *Fool's Err.* xxxiii. 220 A letter purporting to have been written by you. **1884** J. QUINCY *Figures of Past* 359 Jack Downing..who purported to accompany the presidential party and to chronicle its doings.

2. To mean, intend, purpose. *rare.*

1803 SOUTHEY *Let. to Coleridge* 3 Aug., After all, this is really nearer the actual design of what I purport by a bibliotheca than yours would be. **1814** —— *Roderick* x. 348 That even in the extremity of guilt No guilt he purported. **1817** HAZLITT *Char. Shaks.* (1838) 107 Where he alters the letters which Rosencrantz and Guildenstern are taking with them..purporting his death. **1872** ROBINSON *Bridge of Glass* II. II. iv. 47 What Matthew purports doing, I don't know.

Hence **purported** *ppl. a.*, professed, alleged.

1894 F. B. SHAWE in *Daily News* 19 June 6/2 Your readers will now be able to form an opinion as to the authenticity of this purported discovery.

pur'portedly, *adv.* [f. PURPORTED *ppl. a.* + -LY[2].] Allegedly, ostensibly.

1949 *Scrutiny* XVI. 10 The poem..was..Frere's ..*Prospectus and Specimen of an Intended National Work* purportedly written by the brothers Whistlecraft. **1957** J. HOLLANDER in N. Frye *Sound & Poetry* 76 Orsino's appetite at the start of the play is purportedly for Olivia. **1964** D. F. GALOUYE *Counterfeit World* xii. 105 The firm I purportedly represented. **1967** R. STEIN *Great Cars* 113/1 I've never driven one. But purportedly one of these hotter types would go from 0 to 100 in 17 seconds! **1976** *Daily Tel.* 1 Mar. 2/1 Cases of purportedly sterilised women becoming pregnant had recently become more common.

purportless ('pɜːpətlɪs), *a.* [See -LESS.] Having no purport; meaningless, objectless.

1816 SOUTHEY *Poet's Pilgr. Waterloo* II. xx, The central storms which shake the solid earth,..Are not more vague and purportless and blind, Than is the course of things among mankind! **1865** W. G. PALGRAVE *Arabia* I. i. 24 A fourth asks purportless or impertinent questions.

purpose ('pɜːpəs), *sb.* Forms: 3-6 porpos, (4 perpos, 6 porpose, -puse); 4-6 **pourpos,** (4-5 pourpoos, 5-7 -pose, 6 -poose); 4-7 **purpos,** (4-5 *Sc.* -poss, 5 -poos, -pas, -passe, 6 -post, *Sc.* -pois, -e, -pes), (4-5) 6- **purpose.** [a. AF. = OF. *porpos, purpos, pourpos* (12th c. in Godef.) (later *propos*, after L. *prōpositum*), f. *porposer* to PURPOSE. With the forms in *-e* cf. OF. *por-, purpose* = *purpos* in Godef. (See also PROPOSE *sb.*)]

I. Simple senses.

1. a. That which one sets before oneself as a thing to be done or attained; the object which one has in view.

to answer or ***serve one's purpose***, to be of use or service in effecting one's object, to do what one wants. † ***to put one beside his purpose***, to disappoint or defeat him in his aim (*obs.*). See also CROSS-PURPOSE 1.

c **1290** *S. Eng. Leg.* I. 362/8 And seide, 'mi porpos and mi wei: is noupe to ende i-brouȝt!' *c* **1300** *Exec. Sir S. Fraser* in *Pol. Songs* (Camden) 214 Al here purpos y-come hit ys to naht. *c* **1325** *Coer de Lion* 1367 Now frendes what is your perpos? **13..** *Cursor M.* 8402 (Gött.) Neyder i kepe to gabb ne glose, Bot say þe soth es my purpose. *c* **1384** CHAUCER *H. Fame* 377 Who-so to knowe hit hath purpos [*v.rr.* purpoos, purpose] Rede Virgile in Eneydos. **1390** GOWER *Conf.* III. 184 That he his pourpos myhte atteigne. *c* **1450** *Merlin* iii. 46, I..warned hym of Aungiers purpos. **1500-20** DUNBAR *Poems* lxvi. 27 Purpois dois change as wynd or rane. **1513** MOORE *Rich. III* 7 Oftner for ambition and to serve his purpose. **1526** TINDALE *Mark* vi. 26 For their sakes which sate att supper also he wolde not put her besyde her purpost. **1596** SHAKS. *Merch. V.* I. iii. 99 The diuell can cite Scripture for his purpose. **1782** MISS BURNEY *Cecilia* v. ii, It would be answering no purpose. **1842** TENNYSON *Locksley Hall* 137 Yet I doubt not thro' the ages one increasing purpose runs. **1857** MAURICE *Ep. St. John* i. 2 Either will serve our purpose.

†**b.** with vb. of motion implied (cf. PURPOSE *v.* 4). *Obs.*

1401 J. HANARD in Ellis *Orig. Lett.* Ser. II. I. 15 Oweyn was in porpos to Kedewelly..so Oweyn changed is purpos and rode to ȝens the Baron. **1590** SHAKS. *Mids. N.* IV. i. 166 My Lord, faire Helen told me of their stealth, Of this their purpose hither. **1596** —— *1 Hen. IV*, I. i. 102 A-while we must neglect Our holy purpose to Ierusalem.

2. a. Without *a* or *pl.* The action or fact of intending or meaning to do something; intention, resolution, determination.

c **1315** SHOREHAM i. 2040 Þay hy nolde by goud purpos Ine hare flesche werche. *c* **1400** *Destr. Troy* 2655 Persiueraunse of purpos may quit you to lure, Your landys to lose, & langur for euer. **1526** TINDALE *Acts* xi. 23 He..exhorted them all, thatt with purpose off hertt they wolde continually cleave vnto the lorde. **1604** SHAKS. *Oth.* IV. ii. 219 If thou hast.. purpose, Courage, and Valour. **1605** —— *Macb.* II. ii. 52 Infirme of purpose: Giue me the Daggers. **1742** YOUNG *Nt. Th.* II. 89 If nothing more than purpose in thy power; Thy purpose firm is equal to the deed. **1858** FROUDE *Hist. Eng.* III. xiii. 183 Honesty of purpose is no security for soundness of understanding. **1907** J. R. ILLINGWORTH *Doctr. Trinity* i. 10 No such thing as blind or unconscious purpose is conceivable.

†**b.** ***to take purpose***: to determine, resolve. *Sc.*

1375 BARBOUR *Bruce* I. 143 He..left purpos that he had tane. **1559-66** *Hist. Est. Scotl.* in *Wodrow Soc. Misc.* (1844) 78 Suddenly shee tooke purpose to pass to the Castle. *a* **1572** KNOX *Hist. Ref.* Wks. 1846 I. 230 Thei took purpose to devid thame selfis..and to go in sindrie partes.

3. The object for which anything is done or made, or for which it exists; the result or effect intended or sought; end, aim.

1390 GOWER *Conf.* II. 100 To this pourpos and to this ende This king is redy for to wende. **1523** LD. BERNERS *Froiss.* I. cxcv. 231 So he taryed on that purpose tyll the ryuer of Marne was lowe. **1563** WINȜET *Four Scoir Thre Quest.* (S.T.S.) I. 71 *marg.*, Wtheris tractatis for this porpose. **1611** BIBLE *Matt.* xxvi. 8 To what purpose is this waste? *a* **1680** BUTLER *Rem.* (1759) I. 3 This was the Purpose of their meeting. **1764** BURN *Poor Laws* 197 That the laws for relieving their distresses..have not answered their purposes. **1818** CRUISE *Digest* (ed. 2) IV. 334 In all feoffments and grants the word heirs is absolutely necessary for that purpose, and cannot be supplied by any other word whatever. **1863** *Q. Rev.* Apr. 488 He never sinks so nearly to the level of the ordinary sensation-novelist as when he is writing 'with a purpose'. **1874** *Cornh. Mag.* Aug. 192 His romances are not to be confused with 'the novel with a purpose' as familiar to the English reader. **1879** LUBBOCK *Sci. Lect.* ii. 52 Are these differences merely casual and accidental or have they a meaning and a purpose? **1900** F. H. STODDARD *Evol. Eng. Novel* v. 153 The novel of purpose. **1932** *Weekend Rev.* 19 Mar. 371/1 This is a pity; for though Isabel is a 'novel with a purpose', it is also, in a high degree, a work of imagination. [Cf. *purpose-novel* in 14.]

†**4. a.** That which one propounds; a proposition, question, or argument; a riddle; *pl.*, a game consisting of questions and answers (cf. CROSS-PURPOSE 2, CROSS-QUESTION *sb.* c). *Obs.*

a **1325** *Prose Psalter* xlviii [xlix]. 4 Y..shal open in þe sauter myn purpose [*aperiam propositionem meam*]. **1362** LANGL. *P. Pl.* A. IX. 115, I..putte forþ sum purpos to preuen his wittes. **1548** *Compl. Scot.* Prol. 13 It is the nature of ane man that hes..ane ripe ingyne, that euerye purpos ande questione is familiar tyl hym. **1556** T. HOBY tr. *Castiglione's Courtyer* I. (1561) A iv b, Manye tymes they fell into pourposes, as we nowe a dayes terme them. **1590** SPENSER *F.Q.* III. x. 8 Oft purposes, oft riddles, he devysd, And thousands like..With which he fed her fancy. **1611** COTGR., *Opinion*: Opinion..also, the prettie game which we call Purposes.

†**b.** Discourse, conversation: = F. *propos. Obs.*

a **1572** KNOX *Hist. Ref.* Wks. 1846 I. 137 He called for Johne Knox,..with whome he began to enter in purpose, 'that he weryed of the world:' for he perceaved that men begane to weary of God. **1587** GREENE *Tritam.* II. Wks. (Grosart) III. 128 He thought it very fit to passe away the morning with such profitable purposes. **1599** SHAKS. *Much Ado* III. i. 12 There will she hide her, To listen our purpose.

5. That which forms or ought to form the subject of discourse; the matter in hand; the point at issue. Now only in phr. ***to the purpose*** (formerly † ***to purpose***): see 12 a; ***from the purpose***, away from the point (*arch.*).

c **1386** CHAUCER *Man of Law's T.* 72 But now to purpos lat vs turne agayn. *c* **1450** HOLLAND *Howlat* 39 Tharfor in haist will I hens To the purposs. **1585** T. WASHINGTON tr. *Nicholay's Voy.* III. x. 90 It shall not be impertinent nor out of my purpose, if I do speak..of the kitchin of the great Turke. **1597** MORLEY *Introd. Mus.* 78 To talke of these proportions is in this place out of purpose. **1603** SHAKS. *Meas. for M.* II. i. 120 Come: you are a tedious foole: to the purpose. **1653** H. COGAN tr. *Pinto's Trav.* xxiv. 92 He answered him so far from the purpose..like a man that had lost his judgment. **1666** PEPYS *Diary* 3 Oct., J. Minnes.. said two or three words from the purpose, but to do hurt. **1703** MOXON *Mech. Exerc.* 32 For that I did not mention it there, I thought fit (since the Purpose required it) to do it here. **1706** PHILLIPS (ed. 6), *Purpose*,..subject Matter of Discourse. **1868** [see 12 a].

†**6.** Import, effect, meaning (of words); = PURPORT *sb.* 1; in phrase ***to this, that,*** etc. ***purpose.***

1606 SHAKS. *Tr. & Cr.* I. iii. 264 He bad me take a Trumpet, And to this purpose speake. **1611** BIBLE *Judith* xiii. 3 She spake to Bagoas according to the same purpose [1895 *R.V.* words]. **1712** ARBUTHNOT *John Bull* I. iv, There were several old contracts to that purpose. **1726** SWIFT *Gulliver* III. iv, With other common topics to the same purpose. **1789** BELSHAM *Ess.* I. 5 The advocates for philosophical liberty..reply to the following purpose:—'As all mankind' [etc.].

II. Phrases with prepositions.

7. a purpose, a-purpose (o' purpose) = *on purpose, of purpose.* (See A *prep.*[2] 2.) Now *dial.*

1530 A. BAYNTON in *Palsgr.* Introd. 11 He hath willyngly and a purpose..taken..the greattar paynes vpon him. **1648** GAGE *West Ind.* 24 Which had been brought a purpose from Mexico. **1694** R. L'ESTRANGE *Fables* cccclvii. (ed. 6) 496, I came..yesterday a-purpose to tell you the Story. **1876** MRS. G. L. BANKS *Manch. Man* xiv, 'An accident done a-purpose,' chimed in Mrs. Clowes.

†**8. for the purpose**: for instance, for example.

a **1704** R. L'ESTRANGE (J.), 'Tis common for double-dealers to be taken in their own snares, as, for the purpose, in the matter of power.

9. in purpose. a. ***to be in purpose***: to be minded or disposed, to intend (*to do* something). Also occas. ***to have in purpose.*** *arch.*

1340 *Ayenb.* 115 He is ine wylle and ine porpos uor to uoryeuene..yef me him misdeþ. *c* **1440** *Alphabet of Tales* 262 How he was in purpos to destroy hys roalm. **1517** TORKINGTON *Pilgr.* (1884) 47 The Sawdon was in porpuse to a removyd those pyllers. *a* **1626** BACON *New Atl.* (1627) 3 We were sometimes in purpose to turn back. **1630** EARL MANCH. in *Buccleuch MSS.* (Hist. MSS. Comm.) I. 271 We are in purpose to have a commission to send Councillors and Judges. **1856** J. H. NEWMAN *Off. Universities* I. 1, I have it in purpose to commit to paper..various thoughts of my own, seasonable, as I conceive.

†**b.** With the design, in order (*to do* something); = *on purpose*, 11 b. *Obs.*

c **1400** *Destr. Troy* 2643 If Parys..past into Grese, In purpas to pray or profet to gete. **1573** L. LLOYD *Marrow of Hist.* (1653) 213 Certain Souldiers came..in purpose to kill his master.

10. of purpose. a. (Also † ***out of purpose*** (obs.), ***of*** (***a***) ***set purpose.***) Purposely, designedly; = *on purpose*, 11 a. Now *rare* or *arch.*

1432 *Rolls of Parlt.* IV. 417 As wele with wynde dryven, as of purpos to come..to the saide Havenes. **1531** TINDALE *Exp. 1 John* ii. 1 (1573) 393 Whosoeuer sinneth of purpose after the knowledge of truth. **1560** DAUS tr. *Sleidane's Comm.* 24 b, Whiche was thought to be done of a set porpose. **1600** HOLLAND *Livy* x. xxvi. 371 A thousand horsemen of Capua, chosen out of purpose for that warre.

1611 Bible *Ruth* ii. 16 Let fall also some of the handfuls of purpose for her. **1741** Monro *Anat.* (ed. 3) Pref. 5, I..of Purpose omitted many. **1893** *Times* 22 Apr. (Leader), The whole of the arrangements..have been wrapped up, evidently of set purpose, in a cloud of ambiguities.

†**b.** With *inf.* or *that*: = *on purpose*, 11 b. *Obs.*

1535 Coverdale *1 Sam.* xviii. (*heading*), Saul geueth him his doughter of purpose, that the Philistynes mighte destroye him. **1589** Puttenham *Eng. Poesie* III. xxiv. (Arb.) 301 In gaming with a Prince it is decent to let him sometimes win of purpose, to keepe him pleasant. **1670** Baxter *Cure Ch.-Div.* 167 The Scripture is written in such words as men use, of purpose that they may understand it.

11. on purpose. a. (Also †*on set purpose*.) By design, as opposed to chance or accident; purposely, designedly, intentionally.

1590 Shaks. *Com. Err.* IV. iii. 92 Belike his wife..On purpose shut the doores against his way. **1690** W. Walker *Idiomat. Anglo-Lat.* Pref. 4 While one is looked for on set purpose many more will be gained..by-the-by. **1833** Ht. Martineau *Illustr. Pol. Econ.*, *Cinnamon & Pearls* i. 13 They had come out early on purpose. **1888** Rider Haggard *Col. Quaritch* xxx, 'He has been accidentally shot.' 'Who by?' 'Mrs. Quest.' 'Then she did it on purpose.'

b. With *inf.* or *that*: With the express purpose mentioned; in order *to do* something; with the particular design or aim *that*. Also with *for*, †*to*: Expressly for. So †*upon purpose*.

1599 Shaks. *Much Ado* II. iii. 41 How still the euening is, As husht on purpose to grace harmonie. **1635** R. Bolton *Comf. Affl. Consc.* v. 133 Upon purpose, that he may more solemly vow, and resolve. **1644** Milton *Areop.* (Arb.) 35 Treasur'd up on purpose to a life beyond life. **1702** Addison *Dial. Medals* Wks. 1736 III. 161 When there is a society pensioned and set apart on purpose for the designing of them. *a* **1713** Ellwood *Autobiog.* (1714) 166 [He] had thrust himself among our Friends,..on purpose to be sent to Prison with them. **1877** Spurgeon *Serm.* XXIII. 251, I may be placed where I am, on purpose that I may render essential help to the cause of God.

12. to (the) purpose. a. With relevancy to the subject or point at issue; (*to be*) *to the purpose*, (to be) pertinent, apposite, to the point. (See also 5.)

1384 Chaucer *L.G.W.* (*Dido*) 954 Of his auentourys..Tis nat to purpos for to speke of heyre. *c* **1386** —— *Clerk's T.* 517 He no word wol to that purpos seye. **1535** Coverdale *Job* xxxiv. 34 As for Iob he hath nether spoken to the purpose ner wysely. **1587** Fleming *Contn. Holinshed* III. 1949/1 She..receiued him with manie apt words and thanks, as was most to purpose. **1719** De Foe *Crusoe* (1840) II. iii. 58 I'll tell you a story to the purpose. **1868** Key *Philol. Ess.* 261 The examples..quoted by Bopp, are at first sight more to the purpose.

b. *to one's purpose*: useful or serviceable for one's purpose or ends.

[*c* **1386** Chaucer *Sqr.'s T.* 598 Whan it cam hym to purpos for to reste.] **1630** *R. Johnson's Kingd. & Commw.* A iij b, Tis to his purpose sometimes to deliver you the situation of the Countrey he discourses upon. **1668–9** Pepys *Diary* 10 Mar., Looking over the books there,..[I] did find several things to my purpose. **1716** Addison *Freeholder* No. 42 ¶7 Caesar's Observation upon our Fore-fathers is very much to our present purpose.

c. *to* (†*unto*) *purpose*, *to the purpose*, *to good*, *great*, *some*, *any*, etc. *purpose*: so as to secure the result or effect desired; with (a certain) effect; in an effective manner, effectively; *to little* or *no purpose*: with little or no effect or result; in vain. Also as adj. phr. predicatively.

c **1430** Lydg. *Min. Poems* (Percy Soc.) 46 Unto purpos by cleer experyence, Beute wol shewe, thogh hornys wer away. **1553** T. Wilson *Rhet.* (1580) 159 By an order we deuise, we ..frame our doynges to good purpose. **1560** Daus tr. *Sleidane's Comm.* 237 b, In hys opynion, a generall counsell shuld be to little porpos. **1579–80** North *Plutarch* (1595) 127 It was not the great multitude of ships..that could stand them to purpose, against noble harts. **1594** Hooker *Eccl. Pol.* Pref. iv. §6 Although it serve you to purpose with the ignorant and vulgar sort. **1611** Shaks. *Wint. T.* I. ii. 106 *Leo.* Hermione..thou neuer spoak'st To better purpose. *Her.*.. Why lo-you now; I haue spoke to th' purpose twice. **1611** Bible *Transl. Pref.* ¶6 These..were worthily and to great purpose compiled together by Origen. **1642** Fuller *Holy & Prof. St.* v. xiv. 411 Yet perchance he may get some almes of learning,..but nothing to purpose. **1677** Marvell *Season. Argum.*, etc., Wks. 1776 II. 562 He feathered his nest to some purpose. **1680** Burnet *Rochester* (1692) 132, I wrote a letter to the best purpose I could. **1718** *Free-thinker* No. 59. 25 His Letter may..be made Publick to Good Purpose. **1823** Scott *Peveril* iii, I prithee be plain, man,..or fetch some one who can speak to purpose. **1833** Ht. Martineau *Illustr. Pol. Econ.*, *T. Tyne* vii. 129, I used to insist on this.. but..to no purpose. **1886** Ruskin *Præterita* II. vii. 230 Another young draughtsman in Florence, who lessoned me to purpose.

†**d.** *to purpose that*: in order that; to the end that. *Obs. rare*[−1].

1582 N. Lichefield tr. *Castanheda's Conq. E. Ind.* I. vii. 17 This was done, to purpose, that uppon Sunday, they would heare Masse on lande,..and receiue the Sacrament.

†**e.** *to bring, come, fall to purpose*: to bring or reduce to effect. *to come to one purpose*, to have the same effect, to come to the same thing.

1375 Barbour *Bruce* III. 263 To stand agayne thar fayis mycht,..And ay think to cum to purpos. *c* **1491** *Chast. Goddes Chyld.* 2, I wyll shewe you..remedies with some other maters, that lightly wyll falle to purpose. **1551** R. Robinson tr. *More's Utop.* II. vi. (1895) 205 It maketh nothing to thys matter, whether yow saye that sickenes is a griefe, or that in sickenes is griefe; for all cummeth to one purpose. **1563** Shute *Archit.* C iv b, I haue begonne this order or rule, first with the Pedestale, (..Vitruuius.. beginneth first with the pillor, neuertheles they come to one purpose in the parfection).

13. from the purpose: see 5. **out of, unto, upon purpose**: see 10 a, 12 c, 11 b.

III. 14. *attrib.* and *Comb.* Simple attrib. = adj., 'done, made, etc., with a purpose or object', as *purpose-episode*, *-journey*, *-work*; obj. genitive, as *purpose-breaker*, *-changer*; instrumental, as *purpose-built*, *-designed*, *-directed*, *-made* adjs; †**purpose messenger**, a messenger sent on purpose or express; **purpose-novel**, a novel written with a specific purpose, e.g. to defend or attack some doctrine, custom, or the like.

1387–8 T. Usk *Test. Love* I. iii. (Skeat) l. 124 Wo is me that so many let-games, and *purpose-brekers ben maked wayters. **1959** *Times* 9 June 11/6 Local authorities have indeed made remarkable progress in..adapted houses and small *purpose-built homes. **1962** *Economist* 17 Mar. 980/2 New [bowling alley] centres will mostly be what has come to be known as 'purpose-built'. **1972** *Computers & Humanities* VII. 11 The need for a 'purpose built' command language is described in..'A Command Language for Text Processing'. **1977** *Modern Railways* Dec. 473/2 Rail movement of propylene in two weekly trainloads of purpose-built bogie tanks. **1595** Shaks. *John* ii. i. 567 With that same *purpose-changer, that slye diuel,..Commoditie. **1961** *Economist* 24 June 1347/2 Special trays adapted for fitting on to the arm of the '*purpose-designed' Bingo chair. **1971** J. Howlett in B. de Ferranti *Living with Computer* ii. 10 Purpose-designed experiment. **1975** *Language for Life* (Dept. Educ. & Sci.) xiii. 208 It would be wrong to assume that nothing can be done unless the spaces are purpose-designed. **1899** G. Tyrrell in *Month* May 497 Not in obedience to any *purpose-directed law. **1900** Stoddard *Evol. Eng. Novel* 188 It is not..the *purpose-episodes in the novels of Dickens that are the strongest pages. **1860** *Luck Ladysmede* (1862) I. 10 It was the abbot of Rivelsby who made a *purpose journey to Westminster. **1930** *Times Educ. Suppl.* 11 Jan. 11/4 In some places there are '*purpose-made' bricks. **1938** *Archit. Rev.* LXXXIV. 208 (*caption*) Ketton stone has been used for the stone dressings, the facing bricks being eleven inches wide and purpose-made. **1974** *Country Life* 21 Mar. 686/1 Wearable outfits, purpose-made for women who..like inconspicuous clothes. **1702** E. Lluyd *Let.* in E. Owen *Catal. MSS. relating to Wales* 506, I have been obliged to send *purpose messengers 60 or 70 miles for votes. **1809** Malkin *Gil Blas* IX. ii. (Rtldg.) 313 As Don Alphonso's patent was made out, I sent it by a purpose messenger. **1893** F. M. Crawford in *Forum* (N.Y.) XIV. 594 The *purpose-novel is an odious attempt to lecture people who hate lectures, to preach at people who prefer their own Church. **1900** Stoddard *Evol. Eng. Novel* 177 The direction of the *purpose-work of the hero.

purpose ('pɜːpəs), *v.* Forms: 4- **purpose**; also 4–5 **purpos**, 5 **purpoos**, **perpos(e**, 5–6 **pourpose**, 6 **porpose**; *pa. t.* 5 **purpast**, 6 **-pest**. [a. OF. *porposer*, *purposer*, also later *pourposer*, parallel forms of *proposer* (12th c. in Hatz.-Darm.) to propose, with *por-*, *pur-*, *pour-* for L. *prō-*. purpose is thus a doublet of propose.]

I. To put forth, propose, present.

†**1. a.** *trans.* To put forward for consideration, discussion, or treatment; to set forth, present to the mind of another; = propose *v.* 2. *Obs.*

[**1292** Britton II. xvii. §1 Issi qe les excepciouns al bref abatre soint purposez avaunt la excepcioun a la persone le pleyntif.] **1382** Wyclif *Deut.* xxx. 15 Bihold that to day I haue purposid in thi si3t lijf and good, and a3enward deth and yuel. *Ibid.*, *Judg.* xiv. 13 Purpos the problemes that we heren. **1413** *Pilgr. Sowle* (Caxton 1483) I. viii. To maken his compleynt, and purpoos his askynge. **1531** Elyot *Gov.* III. xxix, Merely purposynge to them some feigned question. **1633** Ford *Broken H.* I. iii, Mortality Creeps on the dung of earth, and cannot reach The riddles which are purposed by the gods.

†**b.** *absol.* or *intr.* To put forth remarks, questions, etc.; to discourse, converse, talk. Also with *it*. Cf. propose *v.* 5. *Obs.*

1590 Spenser *F.Q.* II. xii. 16 Whom overtaking, she in merry sort Them gan to bord, and purpose diversly. **1598** Marston *Satyres* I. 138 He that can purpose it in dainty rimes Can set his face, and with his eye can speake.

†**2.** To put forward for acceptance; to offer, proffer, present; = propose *v.* 3 a, c. *Obs. rare.*

1386 *Rolls of Parlt.* III. 225/1 (Anc. Pet. 997) Nichol Brembre wyth his upberers, purposed hym the yere next after Johan Northamptone Mair of the same Citee. **1563** Man *Musculus' Commonpl.* 287 This universall communion of the heavenly grace, whiche is porposed unto all [*mortalibus omnibus proposita*].

II. To set before *oneself* for accomplishment.

3. a. *trans.* To place before oneself as a thing to be done or attained; to form a purpose of doing (something); to design or resolve upon the performance of. Const. chiefly *inf.* (formerly with *for to*); also *that* and *clause*, *vbl. sb.*, and ordinary *sb.* Cf. propose *v.* 2 c, 4 b.

1382 Wyclif *Dan.* i. 8 Forsothe Danyel purposide in his herte, that he were not defoulid of the borde of the kyng. **1390** Gower *Conf.* Prol. I. 5 Thus I..Purpose forto wryte a bok. *c* **1391** Chaucer *Astrolabe* Prol. 1, I purpose to teche the a certein nombre of conclusiouns. *c* **1400** *Destr. Troy* 12296 Pirrus, full prest, þat purpost hom skathe. *c* **1470** Henry *Wallace* IX. 39 Off Kyrkcubre he purpost his passage; Semen he feyt. **1504** C'tess Richmond tr. *De Imitatione* IV. vii. 269 So often pourposynge many good thynges. **1508** Dunbar *Flyting* 77 Thow purpest for to vndo our Lordis cheif In Paislay, with ane poysone. **1596** Spenser *State Irel.* Wks. (Globe) 618/1 It is a capitall crime to devise or purpose the death of the King. **1623** Gouge *Serm. Extent God's Provid.* §10 A man may with himselfe plot and purpose this and that. **1758** Johnson *Idler* No. 12 ¶13 My friend purposes to open an office. **1850** Lynch *Theoph. Trin.* xi. 211 His mother purposed that he should be a preacher, and his own heart purposed it too. **1863** Fr. A. Kemble *Resid. Georgia* 16, I purpose..keeping a sort of journal. **1873** in Willis & Clark *Cambridge* (1886) II. 156 The Artists whom it is purposed to employ.

†**b.** *refl.* To determine, make up one's mind, resolve. Const. *inf.* Also *intr.*, to determine *upon*.

c **1400** *Three Kings Cologne* x. 38 Than þei ordeyned and purposed hem anoon with grete and riche 3iftes..to go seke and worschipp þe lord. *c* **1400** Maundev. (Roxb.) xix. 88 When any of þam purposez him to sla him self. *c* **1425** *Cast. Persev.* 132 in *Macro Plays* 81 þese parcellis in propyrtes we purpose us to playe þis day seuenenyt. ? **1507** *Communyc.* (W. de W.) A iij, Thou purposed the daye by daye To set my people in synnynge. **1574** tr. *Marlorat's Apocalips* xiii. 8 Euen from the beginning God purposed vppon thys sacrifice.

c. *passive.* To have as one's purpose; to be resolved or determined. (Cf. purposed *ppl. a.* 2.)

c **1400** *Destr. Troy* 1868, I am not purpast plainly his prayer to here. **1598** Hakluyt *Voy.* I. 70 The Emperour was purposed to send his ambassadors with vs. **1639** Fuller *Holy War* II. iii. (1647) 46 Peter Bishop of Aragnia in Italy was purposed here to lead his life. **1828** Scott *F.M. Perth* x, I am purposed instantly to return. **1869** Freeman *Norm. Conq.* III. xiii. §1. 263 The whole nation was..fully purposed that the next brood of Æthelings..should be.. Englishmen.

†**4.** *intr.*, *refl.*, and *pass.* ellipt. for *to purpose* or *be purposed to go*: To be bound *for* a place. *Obs.*

1467 Marg. Paston in *P. Lett.* II. 309, I shall purpose me thederward. **1473** Sir J. Paston *ibid.* III. 88 The Erle of Oxenford..is purposyd into Skotlond. **1581** Savile *Tacitus, Ann.* IV. xxxiii. (1604) 179 For Civilis also purposed thitherward. **1606** Shaks. *Ant. & Cl.* III. i. 35 He purposeth to Athens. **1632** W. Lithgow *Trav.* III. 92, I could get passage.., being purposed for Constantinople.

†**5.** *absol.* or *intr.* To have a purpose, plan, or design; esp. in the proverbial phrase ***Man purposes*** (now *proposes*), ***God disposes***: see dispose *v.* 7. (Cf. also propose *v.* 4 c, propone *v.* 5.) Also, To mean (well or ill) *to* any one. *Obs.*

c **1450** [see dispose *v.* 7]. **1530** Palsgr. 670/2 Man purposeth and God disposeth, *homme propose et Dieu dispose*. **1612** T. James *Corrupt. Scripture* III. 38 But homo proponit, Deus disponit: the Pope purposed, and God so disposed it. **1622** Fletcher & Massinger *Prophetess* IV. i, Nor did he e'er purpose To me but nobly. *c* **1634** [see dispose *v.* 7]. *a* **1656** Bp. Hall *Breathings Devout Soul* (1851) 164 Lord, it is from thee, that I purposed well.

6. *trans.* To design or intend for some purpose. Only in *pass.*: To be intended. Now *rare*.

1387–8 T. Usk *Test. Love* III. iv. (Skeat) l. 121 Hem that tofore werne purposed to be saintes. **1553** Ascham in *Lett. Lit. Men* (Camden) 14 My choise of quietnes is not purposed to lye in idleness. *a* **1568** —— *Scholem.* (title-p.), Specially purposed for the priuate brynging vp of youth in Ientlemen and Noble mens houses. **1581** Savile *Tacitus, Agricola* (1622) 200 [Domitian] sending a successor caused withall a bruit to be spred, that the prouince of Syria..was purposed vnto him. **1676** Wood *Jrnl.* in *Acc. Sev. Late Voy.* I. (1694) 152 Merchandize..such as was Reasonably purposed to Vend on the Coast of Tartaria. **1924** W. J. Locke *Coming of Amos* v. 53 What was the use of a stick purposed to beat neither beast nor man?

†**7.** To imagine to oneself, fancy, suppose: cf. propose *v.* 2 d. *Obs. rare*[−1].

1494 Fabyan *Chron.* VI. clxxxvi, Whan the Kynge had vnfolde the letter, and radde a parte therof, he smyled; wherof the lordes beynge ware, purposed the Kyng to haue receyued some iewellys or ioyous nouellys out of Englande.

¶**8.** *trans.* To place before, prefer.

(App. a literalism of translation.)

1502 *Ord. Crysten Men* (W. de W. 1506) II. x. K iij, By the vertue of prudence we purpose [Fr. *proposons*] the delytes spyrytuall vnto the temporalles and carnalles.

purpose, obs. form of porpoise *sb.*

'**purposed** (-əst), *ppl. a.* [f. purpose *v.* + -ed[1].]

1. a. Done or made of set purpose; intentional.

1456 Sir G. Haye *Law Arms* (S.T.S.) 84 Nocht be deliberacioun of purposit vertu. **1494** Fabyan *Chron.* v. cxvi. 91 That this chylde was slayne by poyson, or by some other purposyd malice. **1583** Stubbes *Anat. Abus.* (1882) II. 13 Although it be wilfull and purposed murther. **1605** Willet *Hexapla Gen.* 403 Much lesse was it a purposed lie. **1656–7** Burton *Diary* (1828) I. 333 To..make the people believe it was only a purposed plot to try men's spirits. **1865** Pusey *Truth Eng. Ch.* 31 There was..a purposed vagueness in the first edition.

b. Proposed to be done or attained; intended; aimed at.

1474 *Coventry Leet Bk.* 409 To serue vs, in the same oure viage & purposed enterprise. **1570** Dee *Math. Pref.* 15 The purposed, chief, and perfect vse of Geometrie. **1624** Capt. Smith *Virginia* 110 Prouiding pales, posts and railes, to impale his purposed new town. **1718** Rowe tr. *Lucan* IX. 564 Forc'd round and round, she quits her purpos'd Way. **1877** M. Arnold *Rugby Chapel*, We, we have chosen our path —Path to a clear-purposed goal.

2. Possessed with a purpose; having a settled object. (Cf. purpose *v.* 3 c.)

1530 Palsgr. 321/2 Purposed or full set upon a purpose, *resolu*. **1894** W. J. Dawson *Making Manhood* 39 The surrendered soul is the purposed soul.

Hence †'**purposedly** *adv.* = purposely 1.

1548 Record *Urin. Physick* Pref. 1, I will wittingly, and purposedly passe them over. *a* **1641** Bp. Mountagu *Acts & Mon.* 178 The Capitol being set on fire, whether casually, or purposedly, it was not knowne. **1796** *Hist.* in *Ann. Reg.* 6 The real motive was purposedly kept out of sight.

purposeful ('pɜːpəsfʊl), *a.* [f. PURPOSE *sb.* + -FUL.] Having a purpose or meaning; indicating purpose or plan; designed, intentional.

1853 RUSKIN *Stones Ven.* II. iii. §24. 43 The purposeful variation of width in the border.. admits of no dispute. **1871** TYLOR *Prim. Cult.* I. 290 A singularly perfect and purposeful cosmic myth. **1884** J. TAIT *Mind in Matter* 207 The framework of the earth by its purposeful conformation evinces control in its establishment.

b. Having a definite purpose in view.

1865 *Spectator* 19 Aug. 930 A collection of anecdotes.. unworthy of the purposeful nation [the Scotch]. **1880** *Cornhill Mag.* XLII. 649 He had been happy, and purposefull, and hard-working. **1905** J. B. FIRTH *Highways Derbysh.* xxx. 446 The smile.. upon her shrewd, purposeful face.

Hence **'purposefully** *adv.*; **'purposefulness**.

1859 RUSKIN *Two Paths* v. 240 It is much more pardonable to slay heedlessly than purposefully. **1899** CROCKETT *Black Douglas* xviii, Her feet pattering most purposefully along the flagged passages. **1873** HELPS *Anim. & Mast.* vi. (1879) 148 He must not fix his vanity upon the thing attempted, only his intention and his purposefulness. **1890** G. A. SMITH *Isaiah* II. 226 This intellectual sense of righteousness, as reasonableness or purposefulness.

purposeless ('pɜːpəslɪs), *a.* (*adv.*) [f. PURPOSE *sb.* + -LESS.] Devoid of purpose.

a. Done, made, or produced without purpose or design.

1552 HULOET, Purposeles, *absurdus*. Purposeles, or wythout purpose or reason, *absurde*. **1622** BP. HALL *Contempl. O.T.* XVI. *Death Absalom*, There are busie spirits that love to cary newes though thanklesse, though purposeless. *a* **1656** —— *Serm. on Eccl.* iii. 4 Wks. 1837 V. 552 Prayer is ever joined with fasting in all our humiliations; without which, the emptiness of our maws were but a vain and purposeless ceremony. **1835** SIR J. ROSS *Narr. 2nd Voy.* vi. 80 A purposeless waste of time.

b. Having no purposes, plans, or aims.

1868 *Daily News* 22 July, He looked limp and purposeless as a broken puppet. **1871** SMILES *Charac.* i. (1876) 12 Without a certain degree of practical efficient force.. life will be indefinite and purposeless.

Hence **'purposelessly** *adv.*, in a purposeless manner; aimlessly; **'purposelessness**, lack of purpose, object, or use; aimlessness, uselessness.

1859 *Chamb. Jrnl.* XI. 82 She was.. purposelessly unsympathetic. **1867** MISS BRADDON *Run to Earth* (1868) II. xiii. 221 [He] would.. lounge purposelessly about, sullen and gloomy. **1848** *Fraser's Mag.* XXXVII. 267 Repeating the same silly jingle of words with happy purposelessness. **1874–9** Purposelessness [see DYSTELEOLOGY].

'purpose-like, *a.* [f. PURPOSE *sb.* + -LIKE.]

1. Having the appearance of being efficient, fit, or suitable for a purpose. *Sc.*

1456 SIR G. HAYE *Law Arms* (S.T.S.) 302 Devisit and dytit, be wis clerkis, and men of counsale, and expert in the lawis, and purposlyke. **1782** SIR J. SINCLAIR *Observ. Scot. Dial.* 16 A purpose-like person.. a person seemingly well qualified for any particular business. **1816** SCOTT *Old Mort.* xxxviii, [She] should make a bed up for him at the house, mair purpose-like and comfortable than the like o' them could gie him. **1824** —— *St. Ronan's* xv, Mrs. Dods.. seeing what she called a decent, purpose-like body.

2. Having a definite purpose; purposed.

1604 BACON *Apol.* 60 [She] turned away from me with express and purpose-like discountenance. **1855** HT. MARTINEAU *Autobiog.* I. 315 In conversation no speaker could be more absolutely clear and purpose-like [than Browning].

purposely ('pɜːpəslɪ), *adv.* [f. PURPOSE *sb.* + -LY[2]: cf. PARTLY.]

1. Of set purpose; on purpose; by design; designedly; intentionally; deliberately.

1495 *Act 11 Hen. VII*, c. 17 It is ordyned.. that no man take any Eyre[r], Gossehauke [etc.] nor purposly drive them oute of their covertes. **1551** R. ROBINSON tr. *More's Utop.* II. v. (1895) 165 They gladly here also the yong men; yea and do purposly prouoke them to talke. *a* **1656** BP. HALL *Rem. Wks.* (1660) 123 A rude fellow spat purposely in his face. **1709** POPE *Ess. Crit.* 427 If the throng By chance go right, they [the learned] purposely go wrong. **1875** W. S. HAYWARD *Love Agst. World* 87 He had purposely waylaid her.

2. With the particular object specified; for the express purpose; on purpose; expressly.

1528 KNIGHT *Let. to Wolsey* MS. Cott. Vitell. B. x. 32 (cf. Pocock *Rec. Ref.* I. xxviii. 57) To enduce his holynes to send a legat purposly for hyt. **1588** SHAKS. *Tit. A.* III. ii. 73 As if it were the Moore, Come hither purposely to poyson me. **1694** LUTTRELL *Brief Rel.* (1857) III. 369 A fine new yatch.. built purposely for his majestie. **1787** MME. D'ARBLAY *Diary* 6 Jan., The Queen herself came also, purposely to see him. **1882** PITMAN *Mission L. Greece & Pal.* 175 He left Titus in Crete, purposely to ordain elders.

†**3.** To good purpose; effectively. *Obs.*

1560 DAUS tr. *Sleidane's Comm.* 416 To the intent the matter may the more easely and purposelye [orig. *facilius et majori cum fructu*] be broughte to passe.

purposer ('pɜːpəsə(r)). [f. PURPOSE *v.* + -ER[1].] One who purposes. †**a.** One who states a proposition or propounds a question or argument. *Obs. rare*[−1]. **b.** One who has a purpose; one who intends or plans anything.

1481 BOTONER *Tully on Old Age* (Caxton) I. ii. (R. Suppl.), How Caton was lerned in the lawe—a pleder and a purposer in the courtys. **1753** A. MURPHY *Gray's-Inn Jrnl.* No. 23 The bloody Purposer of determined Vengeance. **1841** ARNOLD *Lect. Mod. Hist.* Inaug. (1842) 5 Perhaps I ought not to press the word 'purpose'; because purpose implies consciousness in the purposer. **1884** *American* VIII. 344 The persistent determination of its purposers.

'purposing, *vbl. sb.* [f. PURPOSE *v.* + -ING[1].] The action of the verb PURPOSE; designing, planning; meaning, intention.

c **1400** *Sowdone Bab.* 326 Even as it was in purposynge, Right so was it aftir I-do. *c* **1450** LOVELICH *Grail* xlvii. 153 Thus, be here fals purposing,.. [they] beheveded On Aftyr Anothir, As wel the soster as the brother. **1534** MORE *Comf. agst. Trib.* II. Wks. 1199/2 In the shooting of this arowe of pryde, ther be diuers purposinges and apoyntinges.

'purposing, *ppl. a.* [f. as prec. + -ING[2].] That purposes; having a purpose; designing.

1387–8 T. USK *Test. Love* I. vi. (Skeat) l. 73 The rancoure of purposinge enuie. **1835** CHALMERS *Nat. Theol.* I. II. i. 223 A living and purposing agent who moulded the forms. **1836** J. GILBERT *Chr. Atonem.* iv. (1852) 92 Plainly the result of purposing will effecting its ends.

pur'positive, *a. rare.* [An alteration of next to assimilate the suffix to its etymological form as in *positive*.] = PURPOSIVE 2.

1890 B. KIDD in *Longm. Mag.* Sept. 506 The searching or feeling movements of the processes have a significantly purpositive effect.

purposive ('pɜːpəsɪv), *a.* [f. PURPOSE *sb.* or *vb.* + -IVE. (An anomalous form.)]

1. Characterized by being adapted to some purpose or end; serving or tending to serve some purpose in the constitution of things, esp. in the animal or vegetable economy.

1855 SIR J. PAGET in *Lett. Educ.* 240 Things that we call inorganic, when we would distinguish them from living organisms— are yet purposive, and mutually adapted to co-operate in the fulfilment of design. **1879** *Cornh. Mag.* June 717 Its final outcome will be a purposive structure,—that is to say, a structure specially adapted to its peculiar function. **1894** G. ALLEN in *Westm. Gaz.* 8 May 2/1 The stings of nettles are purposive, as stings. They act as protectors.

2. a. Acting or performed with conscious purpose or design.

1863 OWEN *Lect., Power of God* (1864) 5 Admiring the rare degree of constructive skill, foresight and purposive adaption, in many artificial machines. *Ibid.* 6 To exemplify the purposive or adaptive principle in creation. **1874** CARPENTER *Ment. Phys.* I. i. §19 (1879) 20 The most purely Volitional movements—those which are prompted by a distinct purposive effort. **1884** *Athenæum* 1 Mar. 283 In this work [Romanes 'Evolution in Animals'].. we have.. purposive intelligence distinctly opposed to natural selection.

b. Relating to conscious or unconscious purpose as reflected in human and animal behaviour or mental activity. Hence **'purposivism**, the theory that all human or animal activity is purposive; **'purposivist** *sb.* and *a.*

1884 W. C. COUPLAND tr. *von Hartmann's Philos. of Unconscious* I.B. v. 285 For us, who have already become acquainted with the purposive activity of the Unconscious.., there is here.. fresh support for our view. **1912** W. McDOUGALL *Psychol.* i. 29 If we make our notion of purposive activity or behaviour wide enough to include these phenomena of bodily organization in the animal kingdom, it must also include the similar purposes of plant growth. **1932** E. C. TOLMAN (*title*) Purposive behavior in animals and men. *Ibid.* i. 12 Behavior as behavior, that is, as molar, *is* purposive and *is* cognitive. *Ibid.* xxv. 423 Our psychology is a purposivism; but it is an objective, behavioristic purposivism, not a mentalistic one. **1936** J. KANTOR *Objective Psychol. of Gram.* v. 69 The second group of purposivists carry speech farther away from the individual than the first group. For them, speech is primarily an instrument for achieving social purposes. **1940** R. S. WOODWORTH *Psychol.* (ed. 12) xvii. 583 The purposivist school emphasizes the importance of striving and goal-seeking. **1947** G. MURPHY *Personality* vi. 125 (*heading*) Purposivism. **1953** J. STRACHEY tr. *Freud's Interpretation of Dreams* in *Compl. Wks.* V. 528 It can be shown that all that we can ever get rid of are purposive ideas that are *known* to us; as soon as we have done this, *unknown* —or.. 'unconscious'—purposive ideas take charge. **1962** H. CANTRIL in J. Scher *Theories of Mind* 339 It becomes increasingly clear that we must include in our consideration the purposive behavior of the organism of which mind is an aspect.

3. Of or pertaining to purpose.

1899 J. SMITH *Chr. Charac. as Soc. Power* 216 There is not a causal, but there is a purposive, connection here. **1905** *Outlook* 23 Sept. 390/1 The purposive aspect of Crabbe's writing.

4. Characterized by purpose and resolution.

1903 *Daily Chron.* 29 July 4/4 They are strong in mind and body, truthful and purposive, excellent leaders of the people of lower races. **1904** *Daily News* 10 Aug. 6 They have become aware of his practical talent,.. his lucidity, integrity, and calmly purposive steadfastness.

Hence **'purposively** *adv.*, in a purposive manner; purposely; **'purposiveness**, the quality or fact of being purposive.

1908 *Westm. Gaz.* 11 Dec. 2/1 Thus the subject community as a whole is definitely, even if not *purposively, shut out from the kind of political evolution which has gone and goes on in the dominant one. **1927** E. & C. PAUL tr. *Ludwig's Bismarck* II. vii. 192 Unless we were more intimately and purposively united with our other fellow countrymen. **1939** P. GORDON *New Archery* II. viii. 89 Never varying except purposively, to correct a mistake. **1949** WELLEK & WARREN *Theory of Lit.* xx. 298 Literary study within our universities.. must become purposively literary. **1965** *New Statesman* 10 Sept. 343/1 Ministers also speak purposively (this, currently, is a vogue adverb along Whitehall) about measures on rating and leasehold reform. **1973** H. KEMELMAN *Tuesday the Rabbi Saw Red* iii. 32 Dean Hanbury walked toward them purposively. **1876** E. R. LANKESTER tr. *Haeckel's Hist. Creat.* I. i. 19 [One] must necessarily come to the conclusion that this '*purposiveness' no more exists than the much-talked-of 'beneficence' of the Creator. **1876** BASTIAN in *Contemp. Rev.* Jan. 248 Its movements, instead of being wholly at random, show more and more signs of purposiveness. **1909** J. W. JENKINSON *Experim. Embryology* 286 Purposiveness.. is a characteristic of all organic functions and cannot be ignored. **1932** A. H. GARDINER *Theory of Speech & Lang.* iv. 181 The characteristic feature of the sentence, as opposed to mere unintelligible words, is its purposiveness. **1965** E. E. HARRIS *Found. of Metaphys. in Sci.* viii. 163 'Purposiveness' is the word that sums up these properties, but it is a word which precipitates controversy both as to its precise meaning and as to its legitimate applicability. **1974** G. SOMMERHOFF *Logic of Living Brain* ii. 23 The peculiar purposiveness found in living nature.

purpoure, -powr, -pre, obs. ff. PURPUR.

purpoynt, obs. form of POURPOINT.

†**pur'press**, *v. Sc. Law. Obs. rare.* [Another form of PURPRISE *v.*, app. influenced by *purpresture*.] *intr.* To commit purpresture; to encroach on another man's land, etc.

a **1575** in Balfour *Pract.* (1754) 444 Sic ane man, beand my tenent and vassal, purpressis and usurpis aganis me, that is his over-lord of sic landis, in sa far as he has causit eare, teill, and saw my landis of N., or has biggit upon thame in sic ane place.

†**purpressour**. *Obs. rare*[−1]. In 5 -ure. [In form an agent-n. from PURPRESS or F. *pourpresure* (see PURPRESTURE), but the sense in the quotation is peculiar.] Apparently, A person appointed to inquire into purpresture.

1477 *Surtees Misc.* (1888) 27 That the purpressures come in this day xiiij day, to gyf their presentment bilongyng to their office.

†**purprestor**. *Obs. Law.* [a. AF. *purprestour* one who encroaches, f. *purpresture* (see next), with agent-suffix *-our*, -OR.] (See quot. 1865.)

[**1292** BRITTON I. xix. §6 Et ceux qi serrount presentez deforceours et purprestours.] **1865** NICHOLS *Britton* II. 379 *Purprestour*, a purprestor, one who usurps or encroaches.

purpresture (pɜː'prɛstjʊə(r)). *Law.* Also (*erron.*) 6 -tour, 7 -tor; 7–8 pour-. [a. OF. *por-*, *pur-*, *pourpresture* (13th c.), altered from *por-*, *pourpresure*, f. *por-*, *pur-*, *pourprendre* to occupy, seize, usurp, appropriate, environ, enclose, encroach upon, etc., f. *por-*, *pour-* (:—L. *prō-*), here intensive + *prendre* (:—L. *præhendĕre*) to seize, take. Cf. med.L. *pur-*, *prōprestūra*, *purprisūra*, etc. (from Fr.), in Du Cange.] An illegal enclosure of or encroachment upon the land or property of another or (now only) of the public; as by an enclosure or building in royal, manorial, or common lands, or in the royal forests, an encroachment on a highway, public waterway, etc.

[*a* **1190** GLANVILLE *Tract. de Leg. Angl.* IX. xi. (1776) 521 De Purpresturis. **1292** BRITTON I. xix. §6 Et ausi soit enquis de totes maneres de purprestures fetes sur nous de terres et de fraunchises.] **1421** *Coventry Leet Bk.* 30 Allso we commaund.. þat no man make noo purpresture ne stoppyng with trees ne stones ne with no othur filthe in the forseid Ryver, up the peyn aforsaid. **1598** STOW *Surv.* x. (1603) 84 Purprestures, or enchrochmentes on the High-wayes, lanes, and common groundes, in and aboute this cittie. **1609** SKENE *Reg. Maj.* II. lxxiv. §1 Purpresture is, quhen ane man occupies vnjustlie anie thing against the King, as in the Kings domain.. or in stoppin the Kings publick wayis, or passages, as in waters turned fra the richt course. *a* **1634** COKE *Inst. IV*, lxxiii. *Courts of Forest* (1648) 291 To be quit of asserts, and purprestures. **1754** ERSKINE *Princ. Sc. Law* (1809) 176 Purpresture draws likewise a forfeiture of the whole feu after it, and is incurred by the vassal's encroaching upon any part of his superior's property. **1875** STUBBS *Const. Hist.* II. xiv. 36 note 2 To account for the essarts and purprestures made in the forests of Hampshire. **1879** E. ROBERTSON in *Encycl. Brit.* IX. 409/2 The offence of 'purpresture'.. was an encroachment on the forest rights, by building a house within the forest, and it made no difference whether the land belonged to the builder or not.

b. A payment or rent paid to a feudal superior for liberty to enclose land or erect any building upon it.

c **1384** *Charter Rich. II*, ciii. in Arnolde *Chron.* (1502) Dj b/2 Of alle maner custumes vsagis and ympesicions and also preprestures and other thinges what so they bee that fall with in the fraunches of the forsaid cite. *c* **1450** *Oseney Reg.* 29, I haue i-ȝefe to þe forsaide chanons.. in-to perpetuell almys, ffre and quite for all seruice and purpresture of here Gardeyne of Cudelynton. **1480** *Coventry Leet Bk.* 461 Be suffraunce of þe Meire & Comenalte, which be poynt of Charter & tyme out of mynde haue had profit of purprestures.

purpris, -ise, var. of POURPRISE *Obs.*

†**pur'prise**, *v. Sc. Obs.* [f. F. *por-*, *purprendre* (see PURPRESTURE, and cf. POURPRISE *v.*)] *intr.* To make a purpresture or illegal encroachment; *trans.* To enclose or encroach upon. Hence **purprising** = PURPRISION.

1480 *Acta Dom. Concil.* 74/2 Forfating of him.. of his tennandry of Wester Corswod.. for þe purprising apone þe said Schir Johne.. in þe raising & vptakin of þe malis of þe said landis. **1609** SKENE *Reg. Maj.* II. xxii. 159 He quha commits purpresture within the kings burgh, tines that quhilk he wrangouslie bigges, or purprises.

So † **purprise** *sb.* [cf. POURPRISE *sb.*], an illegal enclosure, an encroachment; = next.

1448 Perpriss [see next]. **1531** in Turner *Select. Rec. Oxford* 100 To enquere of the purpresture and purpryses wt other comen noysauns.

† **pur'prision.** *Sc. Law. Obs.* Also 6 **-prusioun.** [a. OF. *porprison* (in med.L. *porprension-em* occupation, usurpation), n. of action f. OF. *por-, purprendre*: see PURPRESTURE.] = PURPRESTURE.

1448 *Aberdeen Regr.* (1844) I. 401 Quhar thai find perpriss [to] merke it and put in writ and charge thame to reforme it within xi dais, and forberne vnder payne of perprisioune of the king. **1479** *Act. Audit.* 16 Oct. 91/1 The actioune.. aganis elizabeth nesbit..anent þe halding of a court of purprisione vppone þe landis of Raufburne wrangwisly haldin. **1497** *Reg. Privy Seal Scotl.* I. 17/1 Land.. pertenyng to the kingis hienes be ressoun of eschet be purprision apon his hienes. **1545** *Acc. Ld. H. Treas. Scot.* VIII. 384 To Barre, messinger, lettres of purprusioun upoun the laird of Glenkirk..chargeing them baith to compeir in Edinburght. **1600** *Sc. Acts Jas. VI* (1816) IV. 228/1.

purpur *Obs.*, **purpure** ('pɜːpjʊə(r)), *sb.* and *a. arch.* Forms: see below. [In OE. *purpure, -an* (weak fem.), ad. L. *purpura* sb. fem.; thence in early ME. *purpre*, coinciding with OF. *purpre* (*porpre*, later *pourpre* = Pr. *porpra, polpra*, It. *porpora*:—L. *purpura*, whence learned F. *purpure*); also in ME. *purper, purpur*, and in 14th c. *purpure*, orig. with *-e* otiose, but at length associated with the suffix -URE, which has attracted various endings, as in *moisture, pleasure, vulture*. Cf. OHG. *purpura*, ON. *purpuri*, Goth. *paurpaura, -pura*, all from L.; thence MHG., MLG., Du. *purper*, Ger., Da., Sw. *purpur*. L. *purpura* was an early ad. Gr. πορφύρα name of the shell-fish or whelk which yielded the Tyrian purple, hence the purple dye, and cloth dyed with it. The last is the earliest sense in Eng. (Cf. also PORPHYRY.)

OE. *purpure* was only a sb., the adj. or attrib. use being expressed by its genitive *purpuran*, or later by a deriv. adj. *purpuren*: cf. OHG. *purpurîn* in Otfrid. The wearing down of either of these gave the 12th c. *purpre* and ONorthumb. *purple*, as attrib. and, at length, adj. forms. A similar phenomenon appeared in OHG. in the tendency to treat the genitive *purpurûn* as an adj.]

A. Illustration of Forms.

α. 1 **purpure, -an, 2 purpre, -en.**

c **893** K. ÆLFRED *Oros.* VI. xxx. §3 Hie woldon..þa purpuran alecgan þa hie weredon. *c* **1000** *Ags. Gosp.* Mark xv. 17 Hi..scryddon hine mid purpuran [*c* **1160** *Hatton G.* purpren].

β. 3 *pl.* **purpras,** 3–6 **purpre,** 3–5 *pl.* **-es,** 4 **porpre,** 4–5 **pourpre.**

c **1205** LAY. 2368, & claðes inowe pælles & purpras [*c* **1275** purpres]. *Ibid.* 5928 þa palles & þa purpres. *a* **1225** *Juliana* 8 Wið purpre wið pal. **13..** *E.E. Allit. P.* B. 1568 Ful gaye in gounes of porpre. **1340** *Ayenb.* 229 Hi ham cloþeþ..mid pourpre and mid uayre robes. *c* **1440** *Gesta Rom.* xii. 38 (Harl. MS.) Y-clothid alle in purpre & bisse. **1483** CAXTON *Gold. Leg.* 169 b/1 In roobes of pourpre. **1605** [see B. II. 1].

γ. 4–5 **purper, -pir(e, porpere, 5 purpere, -pyr(e.**

a **1340** HAMPOLE *Psalter* xliv. 11 þis quene is atirid wiþ.. purpire. **13..** *Cursor M.* 25465 (Cott.), Ne purperpall, nee pride o pane. *c* **1385** CHAUCER *L.G.W.* 654 (Gg. 4. 27), Fleth ek the queen withal hire porpere [*v.rr.* purpre, purpyr, purpur] sayl. **1478** BOTONER *Itin.* (1778) 88 Cum tribus robis de purpyre. **1488** *Inv.* in *Tytler's Hist. Scot.* (1864) II. 393 Item a covering of variand purpir tarter.

δ. 4–7 **purpur,** (4 **-powr,** 4–5 **porpor,** 5–6 **purpour, -e, pourpour, -e,** 6 *Sc.* **purpoir).**

13.. *E.E. Allit. P.* B. 1743 þenne sone was danyel dubbed in ful dere porpor. **1382** WYCLIF *John* xix. 5 A clooth of purpur. *c* **1420** Purpour [see B. I. 1]. **1567** *Gude & Godlie B.* 40 Cled With purpour silk. **1649** ECLISTON tr. Behmen *Ep.* i. 29 Cloathed with Christs Purpur-Mantle.

ε. 4– **purpure.**

c **1375** *Sc. Leg. Saints* xxiii. (*VII Sleperis*) 192 þis gud emperoure [Theodosius]..putand a-way purpure & chare. ? *a* **1400** *Morte Arth.* 1288 Palaisez proudliche pyghte, þat palyd ware ryche, Of palle and of purpure. **1494–1894**: see B.

B. Signification.

I. *sb.* † **1.** Purple cloth or clothing; in earliest use, a purple robe or garment; *spec.* as the dress of an emperor or king; = PURPLE *sb.* 2. *Obs.*

purpur *(purple)* ***and pall,*** also † ***pall and purpur,*** a favourite alliterative collocation (see also in A.), which prob. arose when *pall*, OE. *pæll*, began to lose the spec. sense of 'purple cloth', and to be used in the more general sense of 'rich clothing': see PALL *sb.* 1. Cf. also the variation *purper pall*: quot. 13.. in A. γ.

c **893** K. ÆLFRED *Oros.* IV. iv. §4 Hit næs þeaw mid him þæt ænig oþer purpuran werede buton cyningum. *c* **1205** Pælles & purpras [see A. β]. *a* **1225** *Leg. Kath.* 1461 Ischrud & iprud ba wið pel & wið purpre. *c* **1330** R. BRUNNE *Chron. Wace* (Rolls) 4744 Desgysede in pourpre & bys. *c* **1375** [see A. ε]. **1382** WYCLIF *Luke* xvi. 19 Sum man was rich, and was clothid in purpur. *c* **1420** ? LYDG. *Assembly of Gods* 306 Clad all in purpur was she more & lesse. *c* **1420** *Anturs of Arth.* 443 With purpour and palle. **1494** FABYAN *Chron.* IV. lxiii. 42 This Caraucius had taken vpon hym to were the purpure. **1513** DOUGLAS *Æneis* I. xi. 14 Ourspred with carpetis of the fyne purpour. **1614** BARCLAY *Nepenthes* (Arb.) 116 When in a robe of purpure I wedded the metamorphosed Daphne.

† **2.** The mollusc whence the purple dye was obtained; = PURPLE *sb.* 3. *Obs.*

(The original sense of the word in Gr. and L.)

c **1374** CHAUCER *Boeth.* III. met. viii. (Camb. MS.) 64 Men ..knowen whych water habowndeth most of Rede purpre, þat is..of a manere shelle fysh with whych men dyen purpre.

† **3.** A deep crimson or scarlet colour; = PURPLE *sb.* 1. *Obs.*

c **1380** WYCLIF *Serm.* Sel. Wks. II. 125 So Jesus..baar a crowne of þornes, and cloiþ of purpur. **1489** CAXTON *Faytes of A.* IV. xvii. 280 Purpre that we calle red representeth the fire the moost noble of all iiii elementes. **1496** *Dives & Pauper* Comm. VIII. viii. 331/2 The chesyble betokeneth the cloth of purpure in whiche the knyghtes clothed hym in scorne.

b. *Her.* Purple as a colour or tincture; in engraving represented by diagonal lines from sinister to dexter.

1535 STEWART *Cron. Scot.* (1856) I. 585 With baneris braid, and standertis in the air, Palit with purpoir, plesand and preclair. **1562** LEIGH *Armorie* 17 b, The whiche colour in armes, is Purple, and is blazed by this word Purpure, which is a princelye colour. **1704** J. HARRIS *Lex. Techn.* I, *Purpure*, the Heralds Term for a Colour consisting of much Red and a little Black. **1894** *Parker's Gloss. Herald.*, *Purpure* ..this colour, as it is considered by some, but tincture as it is allowed to be by others, is found but rarely in early rolls of arms.

II. *adj.* † **1.** = PURPLE *a.* 2: often as the distinctive colour of imperial and royal dress; = PURPLE *a.* 1. *Obs.*

[*c* **1160** *Hatton Gosp.* John xix. 5 Purpre reaf [*Ags. Gosp.* purpuren reaf].]

13.. *E.E. Allit. P.* A. 1016 þe amatyst purpre with ynde blente. *c* **1375** *Sc. Leg. Saints* ix. (*Bertholom.*) 56 Sete with stanis of purpure hew. *c* **1470** HENRYSON *Mor. Fab., Preich. Swallow* 33 Thir Iolie flouris,..Sum grene, sum blew, sum purpour, quhyte & red. **1509–10** *Act 1 Hen. VIII*, c. 14 Sylke of Purpoure Colour. **1605** CAMDEN *Rem.* 84 Those birdes with purpre [edd. 1623–9 purple, 1657 purpure] neckes called Penelopes. *c* **1614** SIR W. MURE *Dido & Æneas* II. 19 With purpure blush, soone as the morne displayes Heaven's cristall gates.

† **b.** Qualifying another adj. of colour. *Obs.*

c **1470** HENRYSON *Mor. Fab., Lion & Mouse* Prol. v, His chemeis was of chambelet purpour broun. **1503** *Acc. Ld. H. Treas. Scot.* II. 209 For x elne wellus purpur violet.

2. *Her.* Of the colour called purpure: see I. 3 b.

1562 LEIGH *Armorie* (1597) 84 b, He beareth Purpure on a pale Sable, three imperial crownes, Or. **1799** *Naval Chron.* I. 393 Two eagles, purpure, beaked. **1864** BOUTELL *Her. Hist. & Pop.* (ed. 3) xiv. §1. 153 Sometimes blazoned purpure instead of gules.

‖ **purpura** ('pɜːpjʊərə). [L. *purpura* purple, ad. Gr. πορφύρα purple shell-fish, purple.]

1. *Path.* A disease due to a morbid state of the blood or blood-vessels, characterized by purple or livid spots scattered irregularly over the skin, with great debility and depression, and sometimes hæmorrhage.

Usually divided into ***purpura simplex***, the mild form, and ***p. hæmorrhagica*** or ***maligna***, the severer form. Formerly used more widely, with many defining words.

1753 CHAMBERS *Cycl. Suppl.* s.v. *Purpurea*, The going back of the eruptions in the white purpura is very often fatal. *Ibid.*, The red purpura, when the eruptions are struck back, is not attended with such sudden danger. **1799** *Med. Jrnl.* I. 234 The rash was succeeded by numerous livid spots, diffused over almost the whole body, and resembling those of the purpura, or the petechiæ sine febre, in their most dangerous form. **1858** MAYNE *Expos. Lex.*, *Purpura Hæmorrhagica*,..petechial fever. **1877** ROBERTS *Handbk. Med.* (ed. 3) I. 252 Purpura is due to a peculiar unhealthy condition of the blood and tissues.

2. *Zool.* A large genus of gastropods, including some of those which secrete the fluid whence the ancient purple dye was derived; a mollusc of this genus.

The common British and North Atlantic species is *P. lapillus*, which secretes a small quantity of the dye-liquid.

[**1686** W. COLE (*title*) Purpura Anglicana, being a Discovery of a Shell-fish Found on the Shores of the Severn, in which there is a Vein containing a Juice, giving the delicate and durable Tincture of the Antient, Rich, Tyrian Purple.] **1753** CHAMBERS *Cycl. Suppl.*, *Purpura*, It has been usual with most authors to confound together the genera of the murex and purpura. **1847** CARPENTER *Zool.* §924 The *Purpura*, a shell of comparatively small size,..very abundant..on our own coast.

purpuraceous (pɜːpjʊə'reɪʃəs), *a.* [f. L. *purpura* (see prec.) + -ACEOUS.]

1. Purple-coloured. (*Syd. Soc. Lex.* 1897.)

2. *Zool.* Of or pertaining to the *Purpuraceæ*, a family of gastropods of which *Purpura* is the typical genus.

1858 in MAYNE *Expos. Lex.*

So **purpu'racean** *a.* = prec. 2; *sb.* one of the *Purpuraceæ* (*Cent. Dict.*).

'purpuramide. *Chem.* = PURPUREIN.

† **'purpurare.** *Sc. rare*⁻¹. [ad. late L. *purpurāria* a female dyer in purple.] = PURPURESS.

c **1520** NISBET *Sc. N.T.*, *Acts* xvi. 14 A woman, Lydda be name, a purpurare [Vulg. *purpuraria*, WYCLIF purpuresse] of the citee of Thiathyrenis.

purpu'rascent, *a. Zool.* [ad. pres. pple. of L. *purpurascĕre* to become purple, f. *purpurāre*: see PURPURATE *v.*] Passing into purple.

1802 SHAW *Gen. Zool.* III. 549 Purpurascent Snake. *Coluber purpurascens*... Violaceous-green Snake, with a pale line on each side the abdomen.

purpurate ('pɜːpjʊərət), *sb. Chem.* [f. as PURPUR-IC + -ATE[1] 1 c.] A salt of purpuric acid.

1818 PROUT in *Phil. Trans.* CVIII. 423 On the supposition then, that it be named the *purpuric acid*, its compounds with different bases must be denominated *purpurates*. **1866** WATTS *Dict. Chem.* IV. 747 Purpurates are all distinguished by their splendid purple colour; many are gold-green by reflected light.

purpurate ('pɜːpjʊərət), *a.* Also 5–6 **purpurat.** [ad. L. *purpurāt-us*, pa. pple. of *purpurāre*: see next.]

1. Purple-coloured, purple; also, 'purpled', clothed in purple. Also *fig. Obs.* or *arch.*

c **1422** HOCCLEVE *Learn to Die, Joys Heaven* Min. Poems 214 The shynynges of martirs with purpurat corones of victorie. **1430–40** LYDG. *Bochas* VII. viii, Vitellius..Used a garment that was purpurate. **1513** DOUGLAS *Æneis* XII. Prol. 16 Aurora..In crammysin cled and granit violat, With sanguyne cape, the selvage purpurat. **1664** H. MORE *Myst. Iniq.* 280 His Senate of purpurate Cardinals.

† **b.** Born in the purple; of illustrious origin.

1669 *Address to hopeful yng. Gentry Eng.* Ep. Ded. A iv, Not their [the Nobles'] purpurate descent alone, but the unquestionable verity that the bloud is the vitals of the creature, warrants my assertion.

2. Of or pertaining to the disease *purpura*.

1846 in WORCESTER and in mod. Dicts.

† **'purpurate,** *v. Obs.* [f. ppl. stem of L. *purpurāre* to make purple, to clothe in purple, f. *purpura* PURPUR.] *trans.* To make purple, empurple. Hence † **'purpurated** *ppl. a.*

1642 G. EGLISHAM *Forerun. Rev.* 15 The concavities of his Liver greene, his stomach in some places a little purpurated with a blew clammy water. **1716** M. DAVIES *Athen. Brit.* II. 183 Those purpurated and elated Cardinals. **1804** *Miniature* No. 4 (1806) I. 57 Ode to Rainbow (*mock-sentimental*), Offspring of yonder ambient cloud, That purpurates the air.

purpure: see PURPUR.

purpureal (pɜː'pjʊəriːəl), *a.* Chiefly *poet.* [f. L. *purpure-us* (ad. Gr. πορφύρεος purple) + -AL[1].] Of purple colour; purple.

a **1712** W. KING *Art of Love* 1043 If by her the purpureal velvet's worn, Think that she rises like the blush of morn. **1814** WORDSW. *Laodamia* 106 Fields invested with purpureal gleams. **1831** MOIR in *Blackw. Mag.* XXX. 964 That purpureal dye Which gave the Tyrian loom such old renown. **1879** TRENCH *Poems* 221 Meadows with purpureal roses bright.

purpurean (pɜː'pjʊəriːən), *a. rare.* [f. as prec. + -AN.] = prec.

c **1615** SIR W. MURE *Sonn.* ix, Some ar transported wt pur[pur]eayn dyes, And some most value greene about ye light. **1656** BLOUNT *Glossogr.*, *Purpurean*, of purple, fair like purple, blewish. **1866** J. B. ROSE tr. *Ovid's Met.* 170 She twines the white and the purpurean threads.

† **'purpured,** *a. Obs.* [f. PURPUR + -ED[2].] Clothed in purple; coloured or dyed purple; empurpled; = PURPURATE *a.* 1; also as *pa. pple.*

1382 WYCLIF *1 Esdras* iv. 33 Thanne the king and the purprid men beheelden either in to other. **1398** TREVISA *Barth. De P.R.* XVIII. xli. (Br. Mus. Add. 27944 f. 284) þay [the Romans] halwede.. hors of dyuers colours and purpurede [*purpureos*] to þe reynbowe. **1557** GRIMALD in *Tottell's Misc.* (Arb.) 120 Now corpses hide the purpurde soyl with blood. **1557–75** *Diurnal of Occurr.* (Bann. Club) 68 Ane psalme buik, coverit with fyne purpurit veluot. **1610** G. FLETCHER *Christ's Vict.* II. ii, Euerie bush lay deepely purpured With violets.

purpureïn (pɜː'pjʊəriːɪn). *Chem.* [f. L. *purpure-us* (see PURPUREAL) + -IN; named after *orcein.*] A product of the action of ammonia on purpurin, which dyes a fine rose-red or amaranth-red. Also called *purpuramide*.

1863 STENHOUSE in *Proc. Royal Soc.* XIII. 145 This compound being in its mode of formation and physical properties very analogous to orceine, I have called it purpureine. **1866–8** WATTS *Dict. Chem.* IV. 749 Purpureïn or purpuramide is nearly insoluble in sulphide of carbon.

purpureo- (pɜː'pjʊəriːəʊ), combining form from L. *purpureus* adj. purple = PURPLE-; as ***purpureo-cobalt, -cobaltic*** adj.

1857 *Chem. Gaz.* XV. 188 The salts of purpureocobalt are often found among the direct products of the oxidation of ammoniacal solutions of cobalt. **1863** WATTS *Dict. Chem.* I. 1052 Pentammonio-cobaltic Salts..may be divided into two groups, the *Roseo-cobaltic salts*, which have a red colour, varying from brick to rose-red, and the *Purpureo-cobaltic salts*, which are purple, or violet-red. *Ibid.*, Purpureo-cobaltic chloride, $Co_2Cl_{3.5}NH_3$.

pur'pureous, *a. rare*⁻⁰. [f. L. *purpure-us* adj. purple + -OUS.] = PURPLE *a.* Hence **pur'pureously** *adv.*, purply, with purple colour.

1675 E. WILSON *Spadacrene Dunelm.* 54 As purpureously red as our genuine and best coloured Claret.

purpurescent (pɜːpjʊə'rɛsənt), *a.* [f. L. *purpura* purple + -ESCENT. (The L. was *purpurāscens*:

see PURPURASCENT.)] Inclining to or tinged with purple; turning purple.
1890 in *Cent. Dict.*

†**'purpuress.** *Obs.* Also 4 -iresse, 7 -urisse. [f. L. *purpura* purple + -ESS; transl. late L. *purpurāria.*] A female seller of purple.
1382 WYCLIF *Acts* xvi. 14 Lidda.., purpuresse of the citee of Tiatirens [*v.r.*, a purpiresse, either womman makinge purpur; **1611** a seller of purple]. **1647** TRAPP *Marrow Gd. Auth.* in *Comm. Ep.* 634 Paul cannot finde the purpurisse, nor Peter the Tanner.

purpuric (pɜː'pjʊərɪk), *a.* [f. L. *purpura* PURPLE + -IC: cf. F. *purpurique.*]
1. *Chem.* Applied to a hypothetical acid ($C_8H_5N_5O_6$), the salts of which are purple or red.
1818 PROUT in *Phil. Trans.* CVIII. 421, I shall..call this principle the purpuric acid, a name suggested by Dr. Wollaston, from its remarkable property of forming compounds with most bases of a red or purple colour. **1866** WATTS *Dict. Chem.* IV. 747 Purpuric acid has never been isolated, being decomposed when its salts are treated with a stronger acid.
2. *Path.* Of or pertaining to, or of the nature of purpura or purples; marked by a purple rash (as a disease). (*malignant*) ***purpuric fever***, cerebrospinal meningitis.
1839–47 *Todd's Cycl. Anat.* III. 56/2 The kidneys were found..with some purpuric..spots on their surface. **1853** KANE *Grinnell Exp.* xxxiv. (1856) 311 Purpuric extravasations appeared on his legs. **1880** M. MACKENZIE *Dis. Throat & Nose* I. 191 One patient labouring under a severe purpuric Small-pox. **1898** *Allbutt's Syst. Med.* V. 577.

purpuriferous (pɜːpjʊə'rɪfərəs), *a.* [f. L. *purpura* purple dye + -FEROUS: in F. *purpurifère.*] Producing purple; also *Zool.*, of or pertaining to the *Purpurifera*, a division of gastropods containing those which yield the purple dye.
1858 MAYNE *Expos. Lex.*, *Purpuriferus*,..applied by Lamarck to a Family (*Purpurifera*..) of the Trachelipoda ..: purpuriferous. **1870** ROCK *Text. Fabr.* vii. (1876) 75 The class mollusca and purpurifera family.

purpuriform ('pɜːpjʊərɪfɔːm), *a. Zool.* [f. mod.L. *Purpura* + -FORM.] = PURPUROID.

purpurigenous (pɜːpjʊə'rɪdʒɪnəs), *a.* [f. L. *purpura* purple dye + *-genus* or -GEN[1] + -OUS.] = PURPURIPAROUS; as in ***purpurigenous gland.***
1890 in *Cent. Dict.*

purpurin ('pɜːpjʊərɪn). *Chem.* Also (in commercial use) -ine. [f. L. *purpur-a* purple + -IN[1].] A red colouring matter, $C_{14}H_5O_2(OH)_3$, used in dyeing, orig. extracted from madder, hence called *madder-purple*; also prepared artificially by the oxidation of alizarin.
1839 URE *Dict. Arts* 785 Purpurine, the crude substance from which they profess to extract alizarine, is a richer dye than this pure substance itself. *c* **1865** J. WYLDE in *Circ. Sc.* I. 421/2 Other principles may be extracted from madder, such as purpurine, alizarine, xanthine. **1868** WATTS *Dict. Chem.* IV. 749 Purpurin.
b. *Path.* (See quots.)
1858 in MAYNE *Expos. Lex.* **1890** BILLINGS *Med. Dict.*, *Purpurin*, Prout's name for the red coloring matter found in the urine of some rheumatic patients. **1897** *Syd. Soc. Lex.*, *Purpurin*,..2. A red colouring-matter sometimes present in the urine, and supposed by some to be indicative of rheumatism or hepatic derangement.

†**'purpurine,** *a. Obs.* Forms: (1 purpuren), 3–4 purprin, 5 purperyn, 6 purpuryng, 8 purpurine. [OE. had *purpuren* adj., from *purpur*; ME. *purprin*, a. OF. *porprin*, *purprin* (12th c. in Godef.), mod.F. *purpurin* (15th c.), conformed to L. type **purpurīn-us*, f. *purpura* purple.] Of purple colour.
c **1000** ÆLFRIC *Voc.* in Wr.-Wülcker 151/24 *Clauus, uel purpura*, purpuren hrægel. *a* **1300** *Cursor M.* 16201 A purprin [*later texts* purpur(e] clath þai on him kest, And gain to pilate broght. *a* **1400–50** *Alexander* 4375 þe playne purperyn see full of prode fischis. **1530** PALSGR. 321/2 Purpuryng of the colour of purpyll, *purpurin.* **1718** OZELL tr. *Tournefort's Voy.* II. 369 This fruit is very thin upon bunches which are branch'd and purpurine.

purpuriparous (pɜːpjʊə'rɪpərəs), *a.* [f. L. *purpura* purple + -PAROUS.] Producing or secreting purple, as a gland of some gastropods; see PURPURA 2.
1883 E. R. LANKESTER in *Encycl. Brit.* XVI. 652/1 Adrectal purpuriparous gland.

†**purpurisse.** *Obs. rare*[−1]. [ad. L. *purpuriss-um* (Pliny).] A kind of red or purple colouring matter, used by the ancients.
1519 HORMAN *Vulg.* 169 They whyte theyr face..with cerusse: And theyr lyppis and ruddis with purpurisse.

‖**purpurissum** (pɜːpjʊə'rɪsəm). *Obs.* exc. *Hist.* [L.: see PURPURISSE.] = PURPURISSE.
1611 CORYAT *Crudities* 266 Thou maist easily discerne the effects of those famous apothecary drugs..*stibium, cerussa*, and *purpurissum.* For..the Cortezans..adulterate their faces..with one of these three. **1934** *Discovery* Nov. 323/2 From the artists' materials discovered at Pompeii Professor Pozzi was able to obtain a test-tube full of the mysterious colour *purpurissum*, the actual tincture of the murex used for the Roman purple dye twenty centuries ago.

purpurite ('pɜːpjʊəraɪt). *Min.* [f. L. *purpur-a* PURPLE *a.* and *sb.* + -ITE[1].] A phosphate of trivalent manganese and trivalent iron, $(Mn,Fe)PO_4$, occurring as red or purple orthorhombic crystals (sometimes altered to dark brown or black) and differing from heterosite in containing more manganese.
1905 GRATON & SCHALLER in *Amer. Jrnl. Sci.* CLXX. 146 Chemical analysis shows that the material is a new mineral, being a hydrous manganic ferric phosphate—the only manganic phosphate known. The most striking feature of this mineral is its purple or dark red color, and for this reason it has been named purpurite. **1951** [see HETEROSITE]. **1971** *Mineral. Abstr.* XXII. 226/1 A review of phosphate minerals from Brazilian pegmatites... The minerals described are..roscherite, purpurite, saléeite, [etc.].

†**'purpurize,** *v. Obs.* [f. L. *purpura* purple + -IZE.] *trans.* To make purple.
1632 J. HAYWARD tr. *Biondi's Eromena* 53 A shadow, purpurized under the obscuritie of veiles. **1650** FULLER *Pisgah* IV. vi. 99 So being scarlet purpurized, it might be termed by either, and both appellations.

purpurogallin (,pɜːpjʊərəʊ'gælɪn). *Chem.* [ad. F. *purpurogalline* (A. Girard 1869, in *Compt. Rend.* LXIX. 866), f. *purpurine* PURPURIN with inserted *-o* and *-gall* (f. *pyrogallique* PYROGALLIC *a.*): named after the unrelated purpurin by analogy with the preparation of that substance by oxidation of alizarin.] An orange-red crystalline dye, first prepared by mild oxidation of pyrogallol, which is now known to occur in some oak galls and is a tetrahydric phenol, $C_{11}H_8O_5$, consisting of fused tropolone and trihydroxybenzene rings.
1872 *Jrnl. Chem. Soc.* XXV. 703 Purpurogallin, the substance obtained by Girard..from pyrogallic acid by the action of silver nitrate, or of potassium permanganate and sulphuric acid, is the principal product of the oxidation effected by lead peroxide, hydrogen peroxide, [etc.]. **1919** *Ibid.* CXV. 1329 The investigation of the red colouring matter derived from the 'red pea gall' has..to some extent proved disappointing. It was found that dryophantin..was in no way allied either to the flavones or to the anthocyanins, but..consisted of purpurogallin and two molecules of dextrose. On the other hand, it must be mentioned that purpurogallin has not previously been found in nature. **1968** KIRK & OTHMER *Encycl. Chem. Technol.* (ed. 2) XVI. 191 Purpurogallin.., a red-brown to black mordant dye, results from electrolytic and other mild oxidations of pyrogallol.

purpuroid ('pɜːpjʊərɔɪd), *a. Zool.* [f. mod.L. *Purpura*, generic name + -OID.] Akin in form or structure to the genus *Purpura* of gastropod molluscs.
1890 in *Cent. Dict.*

purpurous ('pɜːpjʊərəs), *a. Path.* [f. PURPURA 1 + -OUS.] Of the nature of purpura.
1882 J. EDMUNDS in *Med. Temp. Jrnl.* LI. 112 If fresh vegetable juices are not regularly administered there arises a purpurous tendency.

purpyr, -e, obs. forms of PURPUR.

purr (pɜː(r)), *sb.*[1] Also 7 purre, 7–9 pur. [Cognate with PURR *v.*] An act of purring; the soft murmuring sound made by a cat or other animal when pleased; also, any similar sound.
1601 SHAKS. *All's Well* v. ii. 20 Heere is a purre of Fortunes sir, or of Fortunes Cat. **1801** WOLCOTT (P. Pindar) *Tears & Smiles* Wks. 1812 V. 70 The Cat amid the ashes purr'd, For purs to cats belong. **1849** *Sk. Nat. Hist.*, *Mammalia* IV. 146 [The] voice [of the acouchi] is a short, rather sharp, plaintive pur. **1872** DARWIN *Emotions* v. 129 The purr of satisfaction, which is made during both inspiration and expiration. **1898** *Daily News* 3 May 8/5 The heavier boom of the guns, and the cloth-tearing purr of the Maxims. **1971** G. EWART *Gavin Ewart Show* I. 12 At the lawn-mower's purr I stop for a moment. **1974** R. RENDELL *Face of Trespass* xviii. 168 The powerful purr of a Jaguar sports.

†**purr** (pɜː(r)), *sb.*[2] *Obs.* [Origin unascertained.] A small edible bivalve, *Tapes decussata*; also called PULLET. Also applied to allied species.
c **1711** PETIVER *Gazophyl.* VIII. lxxiii, Marbled Smyrna Purr... A beautiful Bivalve finely latticed and marbled. **1776** DA COSTA *Conchol.* 275 *Chamæ*, Purrs, or Gapers.

†**purr,** *sb.*[3] [Manx *purr* wild mountain boar (J. Kelly).] Name of a breed of wild pigs formerly found in the Isle of Man.
1861 WILSON & GEIKIE *Mem. E. Forbes* i. 30 The purrs, an odd-looking race of pigs, which are also dying out. **1890** A. W. MOORE *Surnames*, etc. *Isle of Man* 193 A curious breed of wild pigs, called purrs, which is now extinct.

purr, purre, ? *a. Obs.* or *dial.* [Of uncertain origin.] In **purre** (also 6 **pour,** 9 **poor**) **oats,** wild oats; so **purr barley**: see quots.
1578 LYTE *Dodoens* IV. xiii. 467 Also there is a barren Ote, of some called the purre Otes, of others wilde Otes. *Ibid.*, The Purwottes or wilde Otes. *Ibid.* xvi. 470 Pour Otes or wilde Otes, are in leaues and knottie strawes like vnto common Otes. **1847** HALLIW., *Purr-barley*, wild barley. **1888** ELWORTHY *W. Som. Gloss.*, *Poor oats*, wild oats. *Avena fatua.*

purr (pɜː(r)), *v.* Also 7–9 pur. [Echoic.]
1. a. *intr.* Of a cat or (occasionally) other feline beasts: To make a low continuous vibratory sound expressive of satisfaction or pleasure.
1620 SHELTON *Quix.* II. xlvi. 304 But the Cat, careless of these threats, purred, and held fast. **1769** G. WHITE *Selborne* xxii. (1789) 62 That its [goat-sucker's] notes are formed.. by the powers of the parts of its wind-pipe, formed for sound, just as cats pur. **1789** MRS. PIOZZI *Journ. France*, etc. II. 231 An English lady once made me observe, that a cat never purs when she is alone. **1872** DARWIN *Emotions* v. 129 The puma, cheetah, and ocelot likewise purr: it is said that the lion, jaguar, and leopard do not purr.
b. Said of other than feline animals.
1849 D. J. BROWNE *Amer. Poultry Yd.* (1855) 148 The young hens pur and leap. **1854** BADHAM *Halieut.* 172 How these fish manage to purr in the deep, and by means of what organ they communicate the sound to the external air, is wholly unknown. **1899** G. A. B. DEWAR in *Longm. Mag.* Dec. 155 A night-jar is still 'purring', as Tom Hughes expressed it, from a belt of trees.
2. *transf.* **a.** Of persons: To show satisfaction by low murmuring sounds, or by one's behaviour or attitude; also, to talk on in a quiet self-satisfied way.
1668 DRYDEN *Even. Love* II. i, We love to get our mistresses, and purr over them. **1789** WOLCOTT (P. Pindar) *Subj. Paint.* Wks. 1812 II. 204 The Doctor Who purring for preferment, slily mouses. **1858** O. W. HOLMES *Aut. Breakf.-t.* iii. 19, I never saw an author..that did not purr as audibly as a full-grown domestic cat..on having his fur smoothed in the right way by a skilful hand. **1889** T. A. TROLLOPE *What I remember* III. xxiii. 337 His audience purred with sympathetic tenderness.
b. Of things: To make a sound suggestive of the purring of a cat, as that caused by rapid vibrations, the boiling or bubbling of a liquid, a mechanical device, etc.
1657 R. LIGON *Barbadoes* 61 The huming Bird..never sitting, but purring with her wings, all the time she staies with the flower. **1747** HERVEY *Medit.* II. 51 He..blesses his good Fortune, if no frightful Sound purred at his Heels. **1852** MRS. STOWE *Uncle Tom's C.* xiii, Mary placed it [the kettle] over the stove, where it was soon purring and steaming. **1885** HOWELLS *Silas Lapham* xvi. 304 The soft-coal fire in the grate purred and flickered. [**1916** G. B. SHAW *Androcles & Lion* II. 42 The lion..purrs like a motor car.] **1922** JOYCE *Ulysses* 507 His lawn-mower begins to purr. **1962** L. DEIGHTON *Ipcress File* xxx. 190 Jay's Rolls purred along the Cromwell Road. **1974** P. WRIGHT *Lang. Brit. Industry* i. 16 Their engines *purr* or *tick over* sweetly. **1978** *Times* 3 Apr. 12/3 The white Cadillac purred to a halt.
3. *trans.* To utter or express by purring.
1740 MARY GRANVILLE *Autobiog.* (1861) II. 117 Jenny Tic purred out what consolation she could. *a* **1771** GRAY *Death Favourite Cat* ii, She [the cat] saw; and purr'd applause. **1897** RHOSCOMYL *White Rose Arno* 70 'You said he was not to be murdered', purred Chapel.

purr, *v.*[2], var. PORR *v. dial.*, to thrust, prod, etc.

purr, *int.* Also 6 pyr, purre, 9 *dial.* pur. A call to pigs, and to turkeys.
1549 LATIMER *3rd Serm. bef. Edw. VI* (Arb.) 98 They say in my contrye, when they cal theyr hogges to the swyne troughe. Come to thy myngle mangle, come pyr, come pyr. **1560** T. BECON *Displ. Popish Mass* Wks. (1560) III. 50 Ye tarry for no man; but, having a boye to help you say Masse, ye go to your myngle mangle, and never call purre to you. **1599** NASHE *Lenten Stuffe* Wks. (Grosart) V. 289 Some discourses of mine, which were a mingle mangle cum purre, and I knew not what to make of my selfe. **1879** MISS JACKSON *Shropsh. Word-bk.*, *Call-words to poultry*,.. Turkeys,..pur, pur, pur.

purr, var. PORR *sb.* (a thrust, etc.), PURRE[1], [2].

purra, var. PORO.

purray, variant of PUREE *sb.*[1]

purre[1] (pɜː(r)). Also 8–9 purr. [From the voice of the bird, whence also called *churre.* Cf. PIRR *sb.*[2], PIRR-MAW.] A local name of the Dunlin (*Tringa variabilis*), esp. in its winter plumage.
It is doubtful whether the name is historically connected with late OE. *pur* glossing Latin names of some birds.
[*c* **1000** *Ælfric's Voc.* in Wr.-Wülcker 116/41 *Bicoca*, hæferblæte, *uel* pur [? = snipe]. *a* **1100** *Ags. Voc.* ibid. 285/10 *Onagratulus*, raradumbla, þæt his pur [? = bittern].] **1611** COTGR., *Alouette de mer*, the little sea foule called, a Purre. **1678** RAY *Willughby's Ornith.* III. xiii. § 1 These Birds live about the Sea shores, and fly together in flocks. At Westchester they call them Purres. **1688** HOLME *Armoury* II. 279/2 In Chester we call..the Stint, or Junco..Purres; they fly together by the Sea and Water side, in great flocks. **1774** GOLDSM. *Nat. Hist.* (1862) II. VI. x. 190 Small birds of the crane kind,..the Dunlin, the Purre, and the Stint. **1837** R. DUNN *Ornith. Orkney & Shetl.* 88 In consequence of their change of plumage, they [dunlins] are considered to be a distinct species, and are then called the Purre or Stint.

†**purre**[2], **purr.** *Obs.* Also 7 pur. [Origin unascertained.] Water cider, ciderkin, perkin. (But see also quot. 1725.)
1669 WORLIDGE *Syst. Agric.* (1681) 142 The Feces..will not be lost, if you put it upon the Chaff, for then it meliorates your Pur, or Water-Cider, if you make any. **1676** —— *Cyder* (1691) 113 Your cider will then be the worse, and so will your purre or ciderkin. **1725** BRADLEY *Fam. Dict.* s.v., Ciderkin or Purre, a Drink for the meaner Sort of People. *Ibid.* s.v. *Seminary*, After having made any Cyder, Verjuice or Perry, they take the Must or Purr, which is the Substance

of the Fruit, after the Juice is press'd out. *c* **1791** [see PERKIN[2]].

purre, obs. form of PURR *sb.*[1], *a.*, *int.*

purre, purre-maw, dial. var. PIRR *sb.*[2], PIRR-MAW, the tern.

‖**purree** (ˈpʌriː). Also purrhee, piuri.

A yellow colouring matter imported from India and China, from which the pigment INDIAN *yellow* is prepared. It is essentially the magnesium salt of purreic or euxanthic acid: see below.

1852 *Fownes' Chem.* (ed. 4) 582 Purree, or Indian yellow, a body of unknown origin, used in water-colour painting, according to the researches of Stenhouse and Erdmann, is a compound of magnesia with a substance termed *purreic* or *euxanthic acid*. **1875** *Ure's Dict. Arts* III. 669 Purree..is said to be formed from the urine of camels, elephants, and buffaloes, after the animals have eaten the fruit of the mangosteen. **1890** *Kew Bulletin* 49 Piuri is a yellow dye used chiefly in painting walls of houses, doors, and railings.

Hence **puˈrreic** *a. Chem.*, in ***purreic acid***, an acid, $C_{19}H_{16}O_{10}$, obtained in pale yellow needles, which forms deep yellow compounds with the alkalis and earths. **purrenone** [-ONE a]: see quot. 1857.

1852 *Fownes' Chem.* (ed. 4) 582 Purreic acid [see above]. *Ibid.*, A neutral crystalline sublimate, purrenone or euxanthone. **1857** MILLER *Elem. Chem.* III. 518 When euxanthic acid is heated..a little above 212°, it melts, and a yellow sublimate of *purrenone* or *euxanthone* ($C_{40}H_{12}O_{12}$) is formed.

purree, obs. f. PUREE *sb.*[1]

†**purrell.** *Obs.* [Etymology unascertained; possibly = F. *burelle*, a barry stripe or barulet, in Heraldry.] A transverse stripe, or bar, made by one or several coloured weft threads, in a web of cloth (cf. LIST *sb.*[3] 4); ordered by Act 35 Eliz. c. 10 to be woven at the beginning and end of a piece, as evidence of its full length, and to prevent its subsequent fraudulent shortening.

14.. *Voc.* in Wr.-Wülcker 584/6 *Forago*, a lyste, or a purrel. [Cf. *Forago*, 'a dividing thread (in a web)', Lewis & Short; 'a thread inserted to distinguish a day's work', Riddle.] **1592** *Proclam.* 20 Jan., We also straightly charge and command all the said Weauers, that euery of them.. shall also shut one purrell through both the ends of the same [cloth], of some coloured yarne, euery such purrell to be three quarters of an inch breadth at the least. **1592–3** *Act 35 Eliz.* c. 10 §2 Eiche Weavor..shall also at eche end of everie of the same Kersies weave one Purrell likewise of coloured Yarne of the bredthe of Thre Quarters of an Ynche at the leaste.

purrer (ˈpɜːrə(r)). [f. PURR *v.* + -ER[1].] One who purrs, as a cat.

1826 *Blackw. Mag.* XX. 326/1 Invisible to every living soul..except Cyprus, our cat, a perpetual purrer. **1854** *Tait's Mag.* XXI. 561 The feline purrer of the hearth. **1972** *Village Voice* (N.Y.) 1 June 92/3 (Advt.), Adopt handsome male cat: 'Purry' Japanese Harlequin,..short silky fur, great purrer, playful.

purring (ˈpɜːrɪŋ), *vbl. sb.* [f. PURR *v.* + -ING[1].] The action of the verb PURR.

1653 H. MORE *Antid. Ath.* Scholia 162 The purring of catts. **1816** SHELLEY *Let. to Peacock* 17 July, Their hymns are the purring of kittens. **1888** ABP. BENSON in A. C. Benson *Life* (1899) II. 209 The night-jar fills up his [the nightingale's] intervals with the softest purring.

b. *attrib.* ***purring thrill, tremor, vibration***: a peculiar thrill (like that felt in a cat when purring), present in certain conditions of the heart and great vessels, as aneurysm, and valvular lesions.

1833 J. FORBES *Laennec's Dis. Chest* (1834) 657 These symptoms are still more marked, if the purring-thrill accompanies the bellows-sound. **1858** MAYNE *Expos. Lex.*, *Purring Tremor*. **1876** *Trans. Clinical Soc.* IX. 151 Marked pulsation being visible in the second, third and fourth left intercostal spaces, over which also a well-pronounced purring thrill was felt. **1876** tr. *Ziemssen's Cycl. Med.* VI. 127 In palpating the finger feels a purring vibration over the cardiac apex.

purring (ˈpɜːrɪŋ), *ppl. a.* [f. PURR *v.* + -ING[2].] That purrs: in various senses of the vb.

1699 POMFRET *Fortunate Complaint* 40, I would not change my chains For all the trophies purring Maevius gains. **1727** GAY *Fables* I. xxi. 18 She saw that, if his trade went on, The purring race must be undone. **1827** DARLEY *Sylvia* 17 His Hostess..Who at her purring wheel had been. **1874** L. STEPHEN *Hours in Library* (1892) I. x. 354 He mellowed down into an amiable purring old gentleman.

ˈ**purringly**, *adv.* [f. PURRING *ppl. a.* + -LY[2].] In a purring manner; while purring.

1907 *Westm. Gaz.* 25 May 6/2 Her tail is all unfolded and she walks purringly. **1925** *Glasgow Herald* 18 Aug. 8 Zizi.. would purringly allow herself to be stroked and fondled. **1939** JOYCE *Finnegans Wake* II. 234 Quite purringly excited. **1946** E. O'NEILL *Iceman Cometh* I. 56 (*Purringly*) Come now, Lieutenant, isn't it a fact that you're as guilty as hell? **1964** D. FRANCIS *Nerve* xvii. 217 Buttonhook [*sc.* a horse] was..neighing purringly in her throat when we opened her door.

purrock, obs. dial. form of PARROCK.

Purrow, var. PORO.

†ˈ**pursable**, *a. Obs. rare*[−1]. [f. PURSE *sb.* + -ABLE.] Possessed of money; financially able.

1610 NORDEN *Spec. Brit., Cornw.* (1728) 12 If a worke.. proue verie likely to be profitable, he that discoureth it associateth himselfe with some purs-able person to counterbeare the charge with equall profit.

‖**pur sang** (pyr sɑ̃). [ad. F. *pur-sang* thoroughbred animal, f. *pur* pure, *sang* blood.] Phr. used adjectivally (freq. following a *sb.*) or adverbially to mean: of the full blood, without admixture, through-and-through, genuine.

1864 G. A. SALA *Quite Alone* I. xii. 194 The Countess was a Frenchwoman, pur sang. **1868** *Sat. Rev.* 14 Mar. 340/2 It is only the old-fashioned sort, not girls of the period *pur sang*, that marry for love. **1911** J. WARD *Realm of Ends* xi. 225 To the speculative mind *pur sang* there is nothing satisfactory about such a view. **1934** C. LAMBERT *Music Ho!* III. 192 *Pur-sang* exoticism of the fruity Oscar Wilde order is indeed extinct. **1941** *Mind* L. 52 The subjective, *pur sang*, is that which is wholly dependent upon this or the other particular subject. **1947** D. MAHON *Studies in Seicento Art & Theory* I. 16 Many of Guercino's late pictures appear far from classic *pur sang* even by comparison with some contemporary work. **1958** *Listener* 24 July 133/3 A fusion of these two traditions, bearing in mind that they are not always found *pur sang* even at the beginning. **1961** 'W. HAGGARD' *Arena* xviii. 155 He wasn't a Lohmeyer but he was Lohmeyers *pur sang*. He'd despise a Sabin Scott. **1975** *Times Lit. Suppl.* 14 Feb. 162/2 It is in fact possible to be a sociologist *pur sang* and not a black (white, yellow, piebald, Scots, Croat, Methodist, Muslim, etc, etc) sociologist.

pursaunt, variant of PURCINCT *Obs.*

purse (pɜːs), *sb.* Forms: see below. [OE. and ME. *purs*, app. ad. late L. *bursa* purse (whence OF. *borse* (12th c.), F. *bourse*, Pr., It. *borsa*, Sp., Pg. *bolsa*); the later forms *pors, pours*, and those with final *e*, *porse, pourse, purse*, were evidently influenced by the Fr. word.

The initial *p* for *b* is not certainly explained: influence of OE. *pusa, posa*, ON. *posi* bag, has been suggested. As to the loss of the final vowel, if the word was taken as a strong feminine, it would naturally have the form *purs*, in oblique cases *purse*. L. *bursa* (*byrsa*), a. Gr. βύρσα hide, leather, appears in the grammarians Servius and Donatus *c* 385, and appears to be confined to glossaries before A.D. 600; it is glossed *corium*. For history see Körting s.v.]

A. Illustration of Forms.

α. 1, 3–6 purs, 3–4 pors, 4 pours.

a **1100** *Gloss Aldhelm* in Napier *OE. Glosses* (1900) 187/36 *Fiscus*, Purs *vel* Seod. *c* **1290** *S. Eng. Leg.* I. 62/293 þe pors al amti was and peni bi-lefte non. **1362** LANGL. *P. Pl.* A. v. 110 Lyk a leþerne pors lullede his chekes. **1390** GOWER *Conf.* I. 249 This Ring..Out of his Pours awey he dede. *Ibid.* II. 298 Bot crepe into mi purs ayein. *c* **1440** *Promp. Parv.* 417/1 Purs, or burs, *bursa*. **1562** J. HEYWOOD *Prov. & Epigr.* (1867) 10 Dooe ye after him that beareth the purs.

β. 3 (*in oblique case*), 4– purse, (4–6 porse, pourse, 5 porce, 5–7 purce, 6 pursse).

c **1250** *Lutel Soth Sermun* 39 in *O.E. Misc.* 188 Euer of þe purse þat seluer heo tulleþ. **1340** Porse [see B. 1]. **1387** TREVISA *Higden* (Rolls) I. 409 Seelde þey bereþ purse aboute. *c* **1440** Porce [see B. 8 b]. **1530** PALSGR. 657/1 Whyle I talked with the one of them, the other pyked my purce. **1545** *Rates of Customs* cij, Porses for chyldren. **1548** HALL *Chron., Hen. VII* 26 He lay..sore sicke of the fluxe of ye pursse. **1549** LATIMER *3rd Serm. bef. Edw. VI* (Arb.) 88 Had they a standynge at shooters hyll..to take a pourse? **1611** Purce-emptier [see B. 10].

B. Signification.

I. A money-bag or -receptacle and its contents.

1. a. A small pouch or bag of leather or other flexible material, used for carrying money on the person; originally a small bag drawn together at the mouth with a thong or strings, now of various shapes and fastened in various ways.

a **1100** [see A. α]. *a* **1225** *Ancr. R.* 168 Hit is beggares rihte uorte beren bagge on bac, & burgeises for to beren purses. *a* **1300** *Cursor M.* 15967 (Cott.) Moder, i haf my maister sald,..And in mi purs þe pris i bere. **1340** *Ayenb.* 53 Þanne ssolle we betuene þe porse and þe wombe of þe glotoune: habbe a uayr strif. Þe wombe zayþ 'ich wylle by uol'. Þe purs zayþ 'ich wylle by uol'. **1377** LANGL. *P. Pl.* B. XIII. 301 Pore of possessioun in purse and in coffre. *c* **1399** CHAUCER *Purse* 1 To yow my purse..Complayn I, for ye be my lady dere: I am so sory now that ye been lyght. *c* **1400** MAUNDEV. (Roxb.) xvi. 74 His purs full of gold. **1546** J. HEYWOOD *Prov.* (1867) 22 There is nothing in this worlde that agreeth wurs, Then dooeth a Ladies hert and a beggers purs. **1567** *Gude & Godlie B.* (S.T.S.) 195 Preistis, keip no gold, Siluer nor cunȝe in ȝour purs. **1604** SHAKS. *Oth.* I. iii. 345 Put Money in thy purse. **1630** B. JONSON *New Inn* I. i, A heavy purse makes a light heart. *a* **1694** TILLOTSON *Serm.* clxiv. (1743) IX. 389 He is an impudent villain in deed, that will venture to cut a purse in the presence of the judge. **1884** MISS BRADDON *Ishmael* iv, The kind old man opened his purse, and gave all its contents to his pupil.

fig. **1898** *Daily News* 13 Jan. 5/1 The rather hard saying [attributed to Bp. Stubbs] that London has always been the purse, seldom the head, never the heart of England.

b. *transf.* Something drawn together tightly like a purse: cf. PURSE *v.* 4.

1714 MANDEVILLE *Fab. Bees* (1729) II. iv. 170 We are forc'd to draw our Mouth into a Purse,..bite our Lips, or squeeze them close together.

2. a. A purse with its contents; hence *transf.* money, funds; esp. with qualifications, as ***a common purse***, funds possessed and shared by a number of people in common; ***a heavy*** or ***long purse***, wealth; ***a light purse***, poverty; ***the public purse***, the national treasury or wealth. ***privy purse***: see PRIVY *a.* 9.

c **1350** in *Eng. Gilds* 357 For commune profyȝt vp-on þe commune porse. *c* **1430** LYDG. *Min. Poems* (Percy Soc.) 49 My purs was falle in grete rerage. **1432–43** in *Cal. Proc. Chanc. Q. Eliz.* I. (1827) Introd. 23 He and other of his craft have made a comyn purce to wythstond us. *c* **1440** *Promp. Parv.* 275/2 Kyngys purs, or burs, *fiscus*. **1535** COVERDALE *Prov.* i. 14 Cast in thy lott amonge us, we shal haue all one purse. **1577** B. GOOGE *Heresbach's Husb.* I. (1586) 8, I build my house..according to my purse. **1598** SHAKS. *Merry W.* I. iii. 59 The report goes, she has all the rule of her husbands Purse. **1604** —— *Oth.* III. iii. 157 Who steales my purse, steales trash. **1624** *3rd Rep. Hist. MSS. Comm.* 34/1 Adversaries too potent in purse and friends for her to wage law with. **1640** *Ibid.* 81/2 To remain in France upon your own purse. **1652** J. WRIGHT tr. *Camus' Nat. Paradox* IX. 212 It was enough to let their Purses blood. **1748** RICHARDSON *Clarissa* IV. 87 If she make a private purse, which we are told by anti-matrimonialists, all wives love to do. **1771** *Junius Lett.* lix. (1820) 308 Let bounties be increased as far as the public purse can support them. **1868** FREEMAN *Norm. Conq.* II. vii. 124 It requires a very considerable political developement for a nation to feel that the power of the purse is the surest safe-guard of freedom.

b. Phrases (often in collocation with *person*): †***by*** or ***in the purse***, by fine (*obs.*); ***purse and person***, one's money and oneself; †***to be out of purse***, to be the loser, to be out of pocket (*obs.*).

13.. *K. Alis.* 1798 That he wol you bete, and chast. By the top, and by the purs. *c* **1386** CHAUCER *C.T.* Prol. 657 In his purs he sholde ypunysshed be. *a* **1552** LELAND *Itin.* IV. §3. 16 [He] was twise taken Prisoner, wherby he was much punished by the Purse. **1582** STANYHURST *Aeneis* II. (Arb.) 69 Thee yoonger Troians..Round to me dyd cluster, with purse and person. **1596** SHAKS. *Merch. V.* I. i. 138 My purse, my person, my extreamest meanes Lye all vnlock'd to your occasions. **1615** E. S. *Britain's Buss* in Arber *Garner* III. 635 The Owner and Adventurer of such a Buss shall not be out of purse. **1702** *Guide Constables* 8 Constables..which are out of purse for their charges. **1838** DICKENS *Nich. Nick.* x, You feel so keenly in your own purse and person the consequences of inattention to business. **1866** *Chamb. Jrnl.* 261 (Forest Laws) Where the offender could not pay in purse, he had to pay in person.

3. A sum of money collected as a present or the like; a sum subscribed as a prize for the winner in a race or other contest.

1650 R. STAPYLTON *Strada's Low-C. Warres* VII. 77 The same Merchants making a Purse..bought great store of Victuall, and therewith lading a Ship sent it to the Poore at Mechlin. **1699** BENTLEY *Phal.* xv. 496 His Friends made a Purse for him, when he was to travel to Ægypt. **1724** *Lond. Gaz.* No. 6292/2 No Horse..shall be admitted to Run for this Purse, that ever won the Value of 10 l. **1886** *Pall Mall G.* 20 Aug. 11/1 Few racing stables do pay their expenses in the money won in purses. **1891** *Sporting Life* 3 Apr. (Farmer), If any club or gentleman will give a purse for him to face the victorious one in the match referred to. **1903** *Daily Chron.* 31 Mar. 8/1 Payment of £500 per annum to [the] former mayor of the borough, [as] a mayoral purse to reimburse him for the expenses connected with the office. **1967** *Boston Globe* 5 Apr. 51/1 Race horse owners, irked at the New York state legislature for failing to approve the money necessary for increased purses, [etc.]. **1976** *Columbus* (Montana) *News* 27 May 2/5 The four-day tourney..will offer a 72-hole medal play with a $25,000 purse. **1976** *Scotsman* 24 Dec. 15/2 Valsecchi refused a £25,000 purse offered by British match-makers to stage the defence in England as he preferred not to give up the advantage of fighting at home.

4. A rendering of Arab., Pers., Turkish *kīsah, kīseh* 'purse', used in the Turkish empire for a definite sum of money.

the purse (***of silver***) was = 500 piastres; ***the purse of gold*** was = 10,000 piastres.

1686 *Lond. Gaz.* No. 2198/1 The Sultana [offers] 4000 Purses, of 500 Crowns each. **1687** A. LOVELL tr. *Thevenot's Trav.* I. 67 When they say a Purse, they understand five hundred Piastres, or fourty five thousand Aspres. **1753** HANWAY *Trav.* (1762) II. VIII. iii. 195 *note*, Garouche or purses, each of five hundred dollars of four shillings value. **1796** J. MORSE *Am. Geog.* II. 462 The public revenue amounts to 89955 purses, at 500 piastres each. **1880** E. SCHUYLER in *Macm. Mag.* Oct. 435/1 The sum of 15,000 purses (900,000*l.*) was paid to Russia as a war indemnity.

5. A fragment of live coal starting out of the fire with a report: regarded as a prognostic of good fortune.

(According to some, it is a 'purse' when it rings or rattles, a 'coffin' when it falls dead.)

1766 GOLDSM. *Vic. W.* x, The girls..had their omens,.. purses bounced from the fire, and true love-knots lurked in the bottom of every teacup. **1863** SALA *Purse or Coffin* 49 One of those red-hot cinders we call, from the ringing sound they make when cold, 'purses', and sometimes, from their odd, long shape, 'coffins'.

II. A bag or bag-like receptacle generally.

6. †**a.** A bag carried for any purpose; a wallet, scrip, pouch. *Obs.*

1377 LANGL. *P. Pl.* B. v. 311 'Hastow auȝte in þi purs any hote spices?' 'I haue peper and piones', quod she 'and a pounde of garlike'. **14..** *Tretyce* in *W. of Henley's Husb.* (1890) 50 Take heede to [the threshers] þat þey haue no poketes nor grete purses where as þey myght stelle and bere away your corne. **1466** in *Archæol.* (1887) L. I. 41 Item j lytill purse of yollowe and dyuers relekes within hyt. **1552–3** *Inv. Ch. Goods, Staff.* 88 A purce to bere the comunyon in. **1771** *Antiq. Sarisb.* 189 One chest containing relicks of the eleven thousand Virgins in four purses.

†**b.** *spec.* One of the official insignia of the Lord High Chancellor of England; = BURSE I.

1677 in *12th Rep. Hist. MSS. Comm.* App. v. 37 Some mischievous persons to dishonour my Lord Chancellour crept through a window of his house..and stole the mace and the two purses. **1901** [see PURSE-BEARER 2].

†**c.** The *sporan* of the Highland dress. *Obs.*

1779 *Ann. Reg.* 230 The mutiny..was occasioned by Lord Frederick Campbell's having purchased at London purses for his regiment, which constitute a part of the Highland dress, and..3*s.* 6*d.* was stopped from each man for his purse.

†**d.** *fig.* Cf. POCKET *sb.* 3 c. *Obs.*

c **1380** WYCLIF *Sel. Wks.* I. 308 What men þei [freris] shulden kille, oþer þer breþeren or aliens, þei holden ȝit in þeir purs. **1531** *Pilgr. Perf.* 117 b, Whiche..at theyr deth fyndeth nothynge but vanite in the purse of theyr conscyence.

e. A woman's handbag. *N. Amer.*

1955 W. GADDIS *Recognitions* I. ii. 77 A girl walking alone, swinging her purse. **1957** *New Yorker* 12 Jan. 32/2 Bernadett's purse hung over her arm. **1979** *Kingston* (Ont.) *Whig-Standard* 5 Apr. 24/3 The type of purse and the way you carry it can be enough to make purse snatchers or pickpockets think twice before choosing you as a victim.

7. *transf.* **a.** *Organ-building.* A small leather bag formerly used in connexion with the pull-downs which passed through the bottom board of the wind-chest, to prevent the escape of wind.

1852 SEIDEL *Organ* 28 To lead, instead of using the purse, the wire through the plates of steel or brass. **1881** W. E. DICKSON *Organ Build.* v. 66 This was formerly effected by 'purses' (French, *boursettes*), little leather bags, tied or otherwise attached to the pull-downs.

b. = COD *sb.*[1] 5; also a purse-net.

1879 HOLDSWORTH in *Encycl. Brit.* IX. 247/1 The body of the net tapers away to the entrance to the purse. **1893** J. WATSON *Conf. Poacher* 126 A rabbit goes rolling over and over, entangled in the purse.

8. a. Applied to various natural receptacles (in animals or plants) resembling a bag or pocket; e.g. a pouch, a marsupium, a cyst, an ovicapsule.

1528 PAYNEL *Salerne's Regim.* b iij b, The parte that gothe to the purse of the galle. **1613** PURCHAS *Pilgrimage* VIII. xiv. 816 With a naturall purse vnder her belly, wherein she putteth her young. **1634** T. JOHNSON *Parey's Chirurg.* III. x. (1678) 94 The Pericardium, or Purse of the Heart. **1721** BRADLEY *Philos. Acc. Wks. Nat.* 28 Stamina..terminated at their Tops by small Caps or Purses called Apices. **1769** PENNANT *Zool.* III. 63 The females [of the skate] begin to cast their *purses* as the fishermen call them (the bags in which the young are included). **1782** A. MONRO *Compar. Anat.* (ed. 3) 55 All fowls have..a..black triangular purse rising from the bottom of their eye just at the entry of the optic nerve. **1809** *Med. Jrnl.* XXI. 152 Each convolution is a kind of small purse or canal, closed externally by a double layer of cineritious and medullary matter.

b. *spec.* The scrotum.

c **1440** *Pallad. on Husb.* IV. 740 Knytte hym fast in his porce. **1569** R. ANDROSE tr. *Alexis' Secrets* IV. I. 29 To remedie the itche of the purse of the testicles. **1725** BRADLEY *Fam. Dict.* II. s.v. *Stoppage*, A Fomentation..which you are to apply to the Purse of the Beast.

†**9.** *Mining.* A small cavity filled with gold or other ore; = POCKET *sb.* 7 a. *Obs. rare.*

1604 E. G[RIMSTONE] *D'Acosta's Hist. Indies* IV. vi. 220 Mines of mettall..which were found as it were in purses, and not in fixed or continued veines.

III. *attrib.* and *Comb.*

10. a. Simple attrib., as ***purse clasp, -pocket, snap***; (sense 3) ***purse distribution, end, money, offer, winnings***; in sense 'that is like a purse, pursed up', as ***purse lip, mouth***; **b.** objective or obj. genitive, as ***purse-maker, -sewer***; esp. in colloq. and slang terms for a pickpocket or a swindler, as ***purse-catcher, -emptier, -lifter, -snatcher***; so ***purse-milking, -snatching*** adjs.; **c.** locative, similative, parasynth., etc., as ***purse-eyed*** (see 1782 in 8), ***purse-like, -lined, -lipped, -mad, -pinched, -shaped, -swollen*** adjs.

1602 T. FITZHERBERT *Apol.* 8 A *pursecatcher vpon the high-way, &..a common horse-stealer. **1968** *Globe & Mail* (Toronto) 13 Jan. 40/4 There would have to be a reduction of approximately 20 per cent in the aggregate *purse distribution. **1611** FLORIO, *Vuota-borse*, a nicke-name giuen to Lawyers or Phisicians, a *purce-emptier. **1886** *Pall Mall G.* 3 June 4/1 Worthy of ranking with Turpin, Paul Clifford, and the other celebrated purse-emptiers. **1928** *Sunday Express* 16 Dec. 21/1 A *purse end of £800 is more than Johnny need expect to receive in the States for his first fight. **1803** SHAW *Gen. Zool.* IV. 599 *Purse-eyed Mackrel, *Scomber Crumenophthalmus.* **1900** tr. Janssen *Hist. Germ. People* IV. 288 *Purse-lifters, loafers, depredators and thieves of all sorts. **1856** WOODWARD *Mollusca* 71 Body short, *purse-like. **1624** CAPT. SMITH *Virginia* Pref. 4 Thrust the beggar out of dores That is not *Purse-lyn'd. **1652** GAULE *Magastrom.* 185 A *purse lip [forespeaks] a scraping sneak; and a blabber lip, a nasty slut. **1629** —— *Holy Madn.* 324 Beetle-brow'd, *Purse-lip't. **1817** COLERIDGE *Biog. Lit.* 245 The Dane, whom he described as a fool, *purse-mad. **1630** *Canterbury Marr. Licences* (MS.), Mathew Holt of All Saints', Canterbury, *pursemaker. **1907** *Daily News* 22 Apr. 2 [He] had bought the purses from Hayes in the belief that he was a master pursemaker. **1621** BURTON *Anat. Mel.* I. ii. III. xv, Such a *purse-milking nation: Gown'd vultures, theeues, and a litigious rout Of coseners. **1898** *Kansas City Star* 19 Dec. 3/1 Bingen's share of the *purse money amounted to only $4,650. **1971** *Sunday Express* (Johannesburg) 28 Mar. 22/2 In Britain, many boxers sell batches of tickets to their followers instead of receiving purse money. **1855** TENNYSON *Maud* I. xviii, Maud with her sweet *purse-mouth when my father dangled the grapes. **1973** *Times* 16 Mar. 13/6 The long awaited return match between Bobby Arthur and John Stracey for the British welterweight title..is now up for *purse offers. **1603** J. DAVIES *Microcosmos* 14 *Purse-pinchèd and soule-pain'd. **1922** JOYCE *Ulysses* 430 Bloom pats..*pursepocket. **1905** *Daily Chron.* 21 Jan. 6/3 Mother keeps him by going out to work as a *purse-sewer. **1776** WITHERING *Brit. Plants* (1796) IV. 85 The fruit terminating, and *purse-shaped. **1902** MCNEILL *Egreg. Eng.* 160 Gang of daylight robbers, *purse-snatchers, watch-snatchers. **1906** WHITEING *Ring in New* 44 Two youths having been put away for a *purse-snatching case. **1823** *Coll. Poems* (ed. Joanna Baillie) 210 *Purse-swol'n neighbours. **1970** *Globe & Mail* (Toronto) 28 Sept. 20/4 In each of those starts he was carrying between 119 and 123 pounds because of his *purse winnings in South America.

11. Special Combinations: **purse-bag**, a handbag, often having a purse incorporated or attached; **purse-belt** = *money-belt* s.v. MONEY *sb.* 8; ˈ**purse-board**: see quot. and 7 a; **purse boat**, a large boat used in fishing with a purse-seine for menhaden, mackerel, etc.; ˈ**purse-ˌbouncer** (*slang*), a species of swindler; **purse-club**, a subscription club or guild; **purse-crab**, a crab of the genus *Birgus* living in burrows on the East Indian islands; **purse crew**, the crew of a purse-boat (*U.S.*); †**purse-cross**, a pecuniary loss or reverse; **purse davit**, a short strong davit attached to the gunwale and thwart of a purse-boat, to support the pursing blocks of a purse-seine; **purse-famine**, a scarcity of money; **purse gang** = *purse crew*; **purse-gill**, a marsipobranchiate fish; hence **purse-gilled** *a.* (*Cent. Dict.* 1890); **purse-girdle**, a girdle containing a receptacle for money, etc.; **purse-holder**, one who has charge or control of the funds of a society, party, nation, etc.; †ˈ**purse-ˈhood**, a hood drawn together at the neck like the mouth of a purse; † **purse-leech**, a person greedy for money; **purse-line** = *purse-rope*; †**purse-mulgent** *a.*, draining or 'milking' the purse; **purse-penance**, a fine; **purse-penny**, *Sc.*, a penny retained in the purse for luck; also *fig.*; **purse-rope**, the cord used to close up the mouth of a purse-seine; **purse silk**, silk thread used for knitting purses, and embroidering; **purse spider** = PURSE-WEB *spider*; **purse-sucker** = *purse-leech*; **purse-tassel**, (*a*) a purse-string; (*b*) the Tassel-hyacinth, *Muscari comosum*; **purse-trick**, a species of swindling trick; **purse twist** = *purse silk*; **purse-weight**, the weight or sinker of a purse-seine; **purse-wire**, †(*a*) ? wire used in making purses; (*b*) the wire which passes through a purse in an organ (see 7 a).

1907 *Yesterday's Shopping* (1969) 404/3 Roan leather 'Modern' *Purse Bag, with inside pocket for gold. **1914** G. B. SHAW *Fanny's First Play* III. 198 Putting down..her purse-bag. **1901** KIPLING *Kim* x. 263 A worn old *purse-belt embroidered with porcupine quill-patterns. **1943** *R.A.F. Jrnl.* Aug. 25 N.A.A.F.I. are producing those useful purse belts which you may wear under your jacket. **1852** SEIDEL *Organ* 50 That part of the bottom of the great sound-board, upon which these bags or purses are glued, is called the *purse-board. **1879** *U.S. Comm. Fish & Fisheries* V. 126 Besides these there are the 'purse' and 'mate' boats from which the seine is worked... The captain of the gang is in charge of the '*purse-boat'. **1911** *Oysterman & Fisherman* Sept. 25/2 Conant Brothers Company, Incorporated make a specialty of the construction of Purse boats, used so widely in purse net fishing along the coast. **1950** *Richmond* (Va.) *Times-Dispatch* (Mag. Sect.) 23 July 5/1 Next 'over the side' go powered purse boats, bearing the captain, seine-setters, other crewmen and a purse net. **1902** *Daily Chron.* 11 Apr. 9/1 Described as 'the king of *purse-bouncers'—people who practised the 'purse-trick'. **1790** J. WOODFORDE *Diary* 25 May (1927) III. 192 The *Purse-Club..came to my House this Morning with Cockades in their Hats. **1805** W. TAYLOR in *Ann. Rev.* III. 176 The guilds, or purse-clubs, of the different companies of tradesmen are not modern inventions, but of Syriac origin. **1713** PETIVER *Aquat. Anim. Amboinæ* i, *Cancer Crumenatus*... *Purse-Crab. **1589** WOTTON *Lett.* (1907) I. 233 Notwithstanding these *purse-crosses I find myself..able to carry the state of a gentleman with sufficiency. **1676** WYCHERLEY *Plain Dealer* III. i, Well, a plague and *purse-famine light on the law! **1559** *Knaresborough Wills* (Surtees) I. 83 My *purse gyrdell. **1864** CARLYLE *Fredk. Gt.* IV. 88 The two sea-powers as *purse-holders. **1609** C. BUTLER *Fem. Mon.* (1623) C ij, For the safeguard of your face..prouide a *purs-hood made of course boultering, to be drawn and knit about your collar. **1598** SYLVESTER *Du Bartas* I. iii. 1085 Proud *Purse-Leaches, Harpies of Westminster. **1648** *Brit. Bellman* in *Harl. Misc.* VII. 625 So long as you harpyes, you sucking purse-leeches, and your implements be our masters. **1628** VENNER *Baths of Bathe* 364 In like manner this *purse mulgent physician not long since dealt with a gentlewoman. **1610** BP. HALL *Apol. Brownists* xliii. Wks. (1629) 590 You send me to Sheet-penances and *Purse-penances. **1708** M. BRUCE *Good News* 38 If I had these three *purse-pennies, I wad think nothing to go thorow all the world with them. **1880** L. HIGGIN *Handbk. Embroidery* i. 6 (*heading*) *Purse silk is sometimes used for diapering, and..where a raised effect is required. **1671** MAYNWARING *Pract. Phys.* 62 Such that make a prey of Patients, and are *Purse-suckers. **1629** PARKINSON *Paradisus* 116 The whole stalke with the flowers vpon it, doth somewhat resemble a long *Purse tassel, and thereupon diuers Gentlewomen haue so named it. **1866** *Treas. Bot.*, Purse-tassels, *Muscari comosum.* **1907** *Daily Chron.* 14 Oct. 6/7 The boundless impertinence of the *purse-trick man. **1545** *Rates of Customs* C ij b, *Pursewyer the dossen pounde *vs.* **1852** SEIDEL *Organ* 50 The wire going through the purse is called the purse-wire.

purse (pɜːs), *v.* [f. PURSE *sb.*: cf. *to pocket.*]

1. *trans.* To put into one's purse; to pocket. Also with *up*. Now *rare.*

1303 R. BRUNNE *Handl. Synne* 6148 For shal y neuer, aftyr þys day, Purs pens, ȝyf þat y may. *c* **1400** *Plowmans T.* 178 Many be marchauntes of woll And to purs pennies wol come thrall. **1577** NORTHBROOKE *Dicing* (1843) 120 It is not lawfull to play for money, to wynne it, and purse it vp. **1634** MILTON *Comus* 642, I purs't it up, but little reck'ning made, Till now that this extremity compell'd. **1659** NOELL in *Burton's Diary* (1828) IV. 416, I never purse one penny of it. **1724** RAMSAY *Vision* xxiii, Sum thanes thair tennants pykt and squeist, And purst up all thair rent. **1810** CRABBE *Borough* xix. 177 I've not allow'd me time To purse the pieces.

†**2.** *fig.* In various senses: To pocket (an affront); to withdraw or keep back (a boast); to take possession of, shut up, confine. *Obs.*

c **1400** *Ywaine & Gaw.* 1277 His prowd wordes er now al purst, For, in fayth, ful ill he durst Anes luke opon that knyght, That he made bost with to fyght. **1570** G. BUCHANAN *Detect. Q. Mary* (1572) K iij, He [Darnley] was constrainit in silence to purse vp his passit iniuries. **1606** SHAKS. *Ant. & Cl.* II. ii. 192 When she first met Marke Anthony, she purst vp his heart vpon the Riuer of Sidnis. **1617** HIERON *Wks.* II. 314 A man is vtterly disgraced, if either he purse vp a disgrace, or else decline the fight when he is challenged. **1691** DRYDEN *King Arthur* III. ii, I am spell-caught by Philidel, And pursed within a net.

†**3.** *pass.* To be (well or ill) provided with money. *Obs.* (Cf. PURSED *ppl. a.* 2.)

c **1550** BALE *K. Iohan* (Camden) 71 With Iudas we love wele to be purste. **1614** J. COOKE *Greene's Tu quoque* D 4 b, *Purse.* The butcher and the baker then shall stay. *Spend.* They must till I am some what stronger purst. *a* **1652** BROME *City Wit* II. iii, How is she purs'd, Jack? is she strong that way?

4. a. *trans.* To contract, to draw together (the lips, brow, etc.) in wrinkles or puckers, suggesting the tightly drawn-in mouth of a purse. Often with *up*, *out*.

1604 SHAKS. *Oth.* III. iii. 113 Thou..didd'st contract, and purse thy brow together. **1668** CULPEPER & COLE *Barthol. Anat.* I. v. 9 If you cut a Muscle..it purses it self round and draws it self into it self like a ball. **1746** J. PARSONS *Hum. Physiog.* I. in *Phil. Trans.* XLIV. 14 Their Action is only to purse up the Mouth, as in whistling and blowing. **1839-47** TODD *Cycl. Anat.* III. 117/1, I have thus seen the superior aperture of the glottis..pursed up and closed. **1882** MISS BRADDON *Mount-Royal* I. viii, Lady Cumberbridge.. pursed her lips and elevated her eyebrows. **1896** O. SCHREINER *Story Afr. Farm* I. xii. 114 Pursing out his lips, and waving his hand, he solemnly addressed the boy.

b. *fig.* To collect, concentrate.

1809 MALKIN *Gil Blas* III. i. ¶6, I looked hard at my master..and pursed up all my penetration to remark upon the effect of my intelligence.

c. *intr.* and *absol.* To become wrinkled, to pucker.

1709 MRS. MANLEY *Secret Mem.* (1720) III. 285 Her Brows purs'd, she wrinkled her Forehead. **1748** RICHARDSON *Clarissa* V. viii. (1811) 106 The maiden fanned away, and primmed, and pursed. **1814** SOUTHEY *Roderick* VI. 183 His eyelids stiffened and pursed up.

5. *trans.* To close *up* like a purse. *rare.*

1823 LAMB *Elia* Ser. I. xxiii. *Decay Beggars*, Was this a story to purse up people's hearts, and pennies, against giving an alms to the blind?

†**6.** *intr.* To steal purses, to rob. *Obs.*

1592 LYLY *Galathea* I. iv. 229 The trade of pursing neare shal faile Until the hangman cryes *strike saile.* *a* **1616** BEAUMONT & FLETCHER *Scornf. Lady* I. i, I'll purse; if that raise me not, I'll bet at bowling-alleys.

7. *U.S. trans.* To draw a purse-seine into the shape of a bag so as to close it. Chiefly in *vbl. sb.* and *pr. pple.* Hence, ˈ**pursing** *vbl. sb.* (also attrib.) and *ppl. a.*, as **pursing-block, -gear, -line, -weight**, the block, etc., used in working a purse-seine.

c **1449** PECOCK *Repr.* v. xiv. 555 The forbering of the bare touche ther of [money] and the forbering of the pursing or bodili bering ther of. *a* **1624** BP. M. SMITH *Serm.* (1632) 270 Abigail..describeth the same safety by a metaphor of safe binding or safe pursing.

1883 *Pall Mall G.* 2 June, Supp., Her rowlocks, pursing-gear &c. are nickel-plated. **188.** *Bulletin U.S. Nat. Museum* (Knight *Dict. Mech.* Suppl.), The pursing weight varies from 100 to 150 pounds. **1890** *Cent. Dict.* s.v. *Purse-line*, the line by means of which a purse-seine is pursed.

ˈ**purse-ˌbearer.**

1. The bearer or carrier of a purse; one who has charge of the money of another or of a company; a treasurer, bursar.

c **1305** *Judas Iscariot* 114 in *E.E.P.* (1862) 110 Siþþe oure louerd him makede apostle: to fondi his mod And siþþe pursberer of his pans: to spene al his god. *c* **1475** *Voc.* in Wr.-Wülcker 804/39 *Hic naucherus*, a pursberer. **1598** *Ord. for Prayer* in *Liturg. Serv. Q. Eliz.* (1847) 681 D. Bagshaw, the Pope's Judas or purse-bearer. **1630** WADSWORTH *Pilgr.* vi. 58 The money which wee deliuered vnto him being our purse-bearer. **1840** THACKERAY *Pict. Rhapsody* Wks. 1900 XIII. 320 There is Mr. James Fraser, our employer, master, publisher, purse-bearer, and friend.

2. *spec.* The official who carries the Great Seal in front of the Lord Chancellor in a receptacle called 'purse' or 'burse'.

1688 LUTTRELL *Brief Rel.* I. (1857) 429 The lord chancellor hath turn'd out Mr. Harris, his pursebearer. **1705** HEARNE *Collect.* 28 Oct. (O.H.S.) I. 60 Mr. Wullaston made Purse-Bearer to the..Ld. Keeper. **1901** *Empire Rev.* I. 467 The Lord Chancellor..is preceded on his entry to the House by the Sergeant-at-Arms, bearing the Mace, the Purse-bearer carrying the Purse, which is supposed to contain the Great Seal, and his train is borne by a Trainbearer.

3. A pouched animal, a marsupial.

1851 BRODERIP *Note Bk. Naturalist* (1852) 161 The marsupiates, or purse-bearers.

So ˈ**purse-ˌbearing** *a.*, pouched, marsupiate.

† **ˈpurse-bound,** *a.* Keeping one's purse tightly closed; averse to spending money; stingy.

1656 HEYLIN *Surv. France* Ep. Rdr. b, Nor was I purse-bound when I had occasion to see any of those Rarities, Reliques, and matters of more true antiquity.

† **ˈpurse-ˌcarver.** *Obs.* = PURSE-CUTTER.

c **1380** WYCLIF *Sel. Wks.* III. 320 Most cursed of clipperis and purse-kerveris. **1387** TREVISA *Higden* (Rolls) VIII. 181 A purske[r]vere [*bursarum incisor*] in kuttinge of purses werþ i-cliȝt in his hondes. *c* **1440** *Promp. Parv.* 417/1 Purskeruare .., *bursida.*

ˈpurse-ˌcutter. A thief who cuts purses and abstracts their contents; a cutpurse.

c **1420** ? LYDG. *Assembly of Gods* 697 Tyburne coloppys, and pursekytters. *c* **1515** *Cocke Lorells B.* 11 Players, purse cutters, money baterers. **1690** [see PURSELESS]. **1881** BESANT & RICE *Chapl. of Fleet* 11, Footpads and purse-cutters no longer infest the streets.

So **ˈpurse-ˌcutting** *vbl. sb.*

1621 BP. SANDERSON *Serm. on 1 Cor. vii.* 24 §27 Such as live by Stealing, and Robbing, and Piracy, and Purse-cutting.

pursed (pɜːst), *ppl. a.* [f. PURSE *v.* + -ED.]

1. Drawn into close folds or wrinkles; drawn together, puckered. Usually with *up.*

1665 HOOKE *Microgr.* 148 The other.. was usually purs'd or wrinckled in the bending of the knee. **1833** HT. MARTINEAU *Fr. Wines & Pol.* i. 4 His large light blue eyes and pursed-up mouth. **1838** DICKENS *O. Twist* xvii, Mr. Brownlow looked apprehensively at Mr. Bumble's pursed-up countenance. **1891** S. BARING-GOULD *Troubadour Land* ii. 28 She sat scowling, with pursed lips. **1937** V. WOOLF *Years* 289 Maids.. with their inscrutable, pursed-up faces. **1955** P. LARKIN *Less Deceived* 34 Threading my pursed-up way across the park.

2. Supplied with money. (See also PURSE *v.* 3.)

1893 'A. HOPE' *Change of Air* xv, The unending talks with fellows like-minded and like-pursed.

purseful (ˈpɜːsfʊl). [f. PURSE *sb.* + -FUL.] As much as fills a purse.

c **1290** *S. Eng. Leg.* I. 62/283 A porsful of panes bi þe weie he fond. **1693** J. DRYDEN jun. in Dryden *Juvenal's Sat.* (1697) 364 Thy Teeth.. a Purseful of dear Gold, The last Remains of all thy Treasure, hold. **1846** MRS. GORE *Sk. Eng. Char.* (1852) 7 The unthrifty, who had flung about pursefulls of those bits of tin, began to hoard the new issue of the mint, as having more significance.

ˈpurse-ˌfull, *a. nonce-wd.* That has a full purse, opulent, wealthy.

1813 MAR. EDGEWORTH *Patron.* xix, Dr. Percy's next difficulty was how to supply the purse-full and purse-proud citizen with motive and occupation.

purselain, -lan, obs. ff. PORCELAIN, PURSLANE.

ˈpurseless, *a.* [f. PURSE *sb.* + -LESS.] Having no purse; without a purse.

1690 C. NESSE *O. & N. Test.* I. 346 The purseless traveller fears not the purse-cutter. **1867** R. PALMER *Life P. Howard* 3 As purseless, scripless and shoeless as the seventy-two disciples of Christ.

† **ˈpurse-ˌmaster.** Chiefly *Sc. Obs.* A purse-bearer, treasurer, bursar.

c **1440** *Jacob's Well* 43 Iudas.. was purs-mayster.. & receyvyd in-to þe purs all þe monye. *c* **1440** *Alph. Tales* 110 þis clerk.. went with hym, & he made hym his purs-maister. **1554** KNOX *Faythf. Admon.* C 7 b, Iudas was pursemaister with Christ Jesus. **1665** J. FRASER *Polichron.* (1905) 218 The year after he entered his pursemaster.

purse-net (ˈpɜːsnɛt).

1. A bag-shaped net, the mouth of which can be drawn together with cords; used especially for catching rabbits, also as a fishing net. Also *attrib.*

c **1400** *Master of Game* (MS. Digby 182) vii, Men taketh hem with houndes, with grehoundes, with heyes, and with pursnettes. **1576** TURBERV. *Venerie* 179 Set purse-nettes upon al the holes, or as many of them as you can finde. **1653** URQUHART *Rabelais* I. xl, I twist lines and weave purse-nets, wherein to catch coneys. **1766** *Compl. Farmer* s.v. *Rabbit,* The ferret is sent into a hole to force them out, and the purse-net, being spread over the hole, takes them, as they come out. **1883** F. DAY *Indian Fish* 15 There are purse-nets and bag-nets, some with, others without, pockets. **1911** [see *purse boat* s.v. PURSE *sb.* 11]. **1931** *Sun* (Baltimore) 29 Jan. 6/2 Fish that sold for approximately $1,000 was garnered.. by ten purse-net fishing boats. *Ibid.* 26 Feb. 5/6 Opponents of purse nets and buck net fishing in the Chesapeake Bay. **1971** *Stornoway Gaz.* 10 July 3/5 Over the past two weeks, a succession of large Norwegian pursers have been visiting the port, some to land purse nets for repairs. **1977** *Young's Sporting Appliances* (S. Young & Sons Ltd.) 4 Purse Net Line.. Purse Net Rings.

fig. **1611** MIDDLETON & DEKKER *Roaring Girl* IV. ii, We shopkeepers, when all's done, are sure to have 'em in our purse nets at length. **1675** V. ALSOP *Anti-sozzo* iii. 109 If he has not got us into such a Cramp and Purse-nett that we shall never escape without loss of Bag and Baggage.

†**2.** See quot. *Obs. slang.*

a **1700** B. E. *Dict. Cant. Crew, Pursenets,* goods taken upon Trust by young Unthrifts at treble the Value; also a little Purse.

3. *Comb.*: † **ˈpurse-net-fish,** a basket-fish.

1671 WINTHROP [see *net-fish,* NET *sb.*[1] 5].

Hence **ˈpurse-netting.**

1931 *Sun* (Baltimore) 13 Mar. 12/4 (*heading*) Mr. Denmead shows evils of purse netting. **1961** *Listener* 24 Aug. 269/1 The deadly purse-netting ships, with the aid of these depth-recorders, could pin-point the shoals at the exact depth when the fish were on spawning levels.

ˈpursepick. *rare.* = next: cf. PICKPURSE.

1508 DUNBAR *Flyting* 247 Herretyk, lunatyk, purspyk, carlingis pet. **15..** —— *Musing allone* 12 Every pelour and purspyk Sayis, Land war bettir warit on me. **1977** J. WAMBAUGH *Black Marble* (1978) vi. 76 Pigeon droppers, pursepicks, muggers. Don't walk the Boulevard at night.

† **ˈpurseˌpicker.** *Obs.* A thief who picks purses; a pickpocket. So † **ˈpurse-picking.**

1549 CHEKE *Hurt Sedit.* (1641) 41 They have all their life after an unsavory smack thereof, and smell still toward day-sleepers, pursse-pickers. **1571** BUCHANAN *Ane Admonitioun* Wks. (1892) 34 Sufferis.. purspykaris.. to exercise thift and reif as ane craft. *Ibid.* Dishonour.. to thevis in purspyking. **1622** J. TAYLOR (Water P.) *Thief* Wks. (1630) II. 121/1 He.. may rob the pot, Steale himself drunke, and be his owne Purspicker, And chimically turnes his coyne to liquor.

ˈpurse-pride. Pride of purse or wealth; the self-esteem or arrogance of the wealthy.

a **1656** BP. HALL *Sel. Th., Supernum.* iv. Wks. 1808 VI. 311 Even purse-pride is quarrellous, domineering over the humble neighbourhood. **1753** MURPHY *Gray's Inn Jrnl.* No. 62 The Insolence of Purse-pride. **1841** HOR. SMITH *Moneyed Man* I. iii. 55 The infection of vulgar purse-pride.

ˈpurse-proud, *a.* Proud of wealth; puffed up on account of one's wealth.

1681 HICKERINGILL *Black Non-Conf.* b, Having great Interest, and great Power, and withal, Purse-proud. **1745** *De Foe's Eng. Tradesman* xliii. (1841) II. 149, I think a purseproud tradesman one of the most troublesome and intolerable of all Men. **1781** COWPER *Hope* 18 The rich grow poor, the poor become purse-proud. **1838** LYTTON *Alice* III. ii, I.. could live happy in a garret, if this purse-proud England would but allow one to exist within one's income. **1930** L. G. D. ACLAND *Early Canterbury Runs* 1st Ser. v. 113 He was not in the least purse-proud or pompous, but always modest and unassuming. **1967** *Guardian* 27 June 8/3 One of Britain's biggest manufacturers of swimming pools.. claims to have captured 40 per cent of a purse-proud market.

purser (ˈpɜːsə(r)). Also 5 pursser, porser, pursor, 6 -our, 5–6 pursar, 5–7 purcer. [f. PURSE *sb.* + -ER[1]; cf. *miller, banker,* and F. *boursier,* med.L. *bursārius* BURSAR.]

†**1.** A maker of purses. *Obs.*

? **1475** in *Coventry Leet Bk.* 479 Joh. Smyth.. Taillour; Joh. Denton.. laborer..; Will. Banburgh.. purser. *c* **1481** CAXTON *Dialogues* 41/4 Lyon the pursser [F. *bourssier*] Hath pursses and pauteners. *c* **1515** *Cocke Lorells B.* 10 Sylke women, pursers, and garnysshers. **1638** BRATHWAIT *Barnabees Jrnl.* III. (1818) 107 Where be thy masters? fellows? scholers? bursers? O Stamford! to thy shame, they'r all turn'd pursers. [Referring to its defunct university.]

†**2. a.** An officer charged with managing money matters and keeping accounts; a purse-bearer, treasurer. *Obs.* in general sense.

c **1440** *York Myst.* xxvi. 136 [*Judas loq.*] Of his penys purser was I. **1483** *Cath. Angl.* 294/2 A Pursser, *bursarius.* **1530** PALSGR. 259/2 Purser, *boursier.* **1677** GILPIN *Demonol.* (1867) 444 Rich men are but God's pursers; they do but 'carry the bag', and what is put therein, for public uses. **1816** MUIR *Clydesd. Minstrelsy* 2 To rouse the clerk and purser wi' their sang.

b. The officer on board a ship who keeps the accounts, and usually has charge of the provisions. Also in the possessive in various combs. and phrases, as ***purser's crab*** (slang), a naval uniform boot; † ***purser's dip*** (see quot. 1867) *obs.*; ***purser's name,*** a false name under which, formerly, a man was entered on the books of a ship in the Royal Navy; ***a purser's shirt on a handspike,*** used as a type of the ill-fitting.

In the Royal Navy the purser was originally the commissariat officer of the ship, but not the paymaster of the crew (who were paid at the end of the voyage or commission). In 1825, by Act 6 Geo. IV, c. 18, a portion of the wages of the crew was permitted to be paid to them monthly, and the duty of making these payments was assigned to the purser, who in 1842 was officially designated 'Paymaster and Purser'. In 1852 the title was changed to 'Paymaster', and the officer's duties in regard to money transactions on board ship were largely extended. In modern passenger-ships, the purser is the head of the stewards' department, and has general superintendence of the passengers and their comfort and requirements, checks their tickets, issues those taken on board, etc.

1458 *Cal. Anc. Rec. Dublin* (1889) I. 300 All maysterys, owenerys, purserys of al maner schyppys. **1486** *Naval Acc. Hen. VII* (1896) 21 Also paid William Peny then Pursor of the same ship for the vittell of the said.. marriners for a weke. **1540** *Act 32 Hen. VIII,* c. 14 The owners maisters and pursers of Englyshe shyppes. **1627** CAPT. SMITH *Seaman's Gram.* viii. 34 A man of Warre hath onely a Purser. **1662** PEPYS *Diary* 29 Aug., I.. did begin to-night.. to look into the nature of a purser's account, and the business of victualling. **1704** J. HARRIS *Lex. Techn.* I, *Purser,* an Officer in a King's Ship, who receives her Victuals from the Victualler, and is to take care that it be in good Condition, and well laid up and stowed: His Office is also to keep a List of the Men and Boys belonging to the Ship, and to set down exactly the Days of each Man's admittance into Pay. **1748** ANSON *Voy.* II. ii. (ed. 4) 191 Our former Purser had neglected to take on board large quantities of several kinds of provisions. **1810** J. MOORE *Post-Captain* v. 23 There is nothing of him left but ribs and trucks. His coat fits him like a purser's shirt upon a handspike. **1821** P. EGAN *Life in London* II. v. 308 The greatest anxiety with most individuals .. is to appear what they are not; to copy some stylish *hero* for their *model,* but whose *dress* at most they merely *imitate,* and which generally fits them after the manner of a '*purser's shirt upon a handspike*'! **1828** *Night Watch* II. 82 Tom, when he was impressed into his Majesty's service, had taken the 'purser's name' literally '*un nom de guerre*' of Thomas Call, in which his warrant as boatswain was subsequently made out... Mr. Call's name, however, was in reality Thomas Whistle. **1829** MARRYAT *Naval Officer* I. viii. 231, I was down in one of the wings, reading by the light of a purser's dip—*vulgo,* a farthing candle. **1836** MARRYAT *Midsh. Easy* xxxviii, An old friend of his, a purser in the navy, who lived at Southsea. **1847** H. MELVILLE *Omoo* 232 Some, to be sure, had for the sake of formality, shipped under a feigned cognomen, or 'Purser's name'. **1852** Apr. 5 *Order in Council,* Paymasters and Pursers to be designated Paymasters of the Navy. **1858** SIMMONDS *Dict. Trade, Purser,* a kind of cabin steward or providore in a passenger ship. **1867** SMYTH *Sailor's Word-bk.* 550 *Purser's dip,* the smallest dip-candle. **1878** *Detroit Free Press* 12 Jan. (Suppl.) 2/5 It fits him like a purser's shirt on a handspike. **1913** T. T. JEANS *John Graham Sub-Lieutenant R.N.* 18 'Now for the purser's "crabs"!' the Model gurgled, when I'd.. produced a pair of service pattern boots. **1924** G. H. A. WILLIS *Royal Navy as I saw It* 83 Modern ships with wire hawsers instead of ropes, and iron decks and ladders, conduce to the wearing of shoes or 'purser's crabs'. **1927** P. RILEY *Memories* 89 Each mess being allowed a few small candles, known as 'Purser's dips', to last the week. **1970** P. O'BRIAN *Master & Commander* x. 264 'Mr. Dillon, who have we aboard that speaks Italian? John Baptist is an Italian.' 'And Abram Codpiece, sir—a purser's name.'

c. In Cornwall, The treasurer or cashier of a mine, esp. one worked on the cost-book principle.

1832 BABBAGE *Econ. Manuf.* xx. (ed. 3) 202 The Purser and Book-keeper manage the accounts. **1839** DE LA BECHE *Rep. Geol. Cornwall,* etc. xv. 566 In the generality of mines the purser is the chief officer. **1846** ADDISON *Law Contracts* I. i. §1 (1883) 103 In mining companies carried on on the cost-book principle.. the shareholders.. are not liable upon bills.. drawn.. by the purser.. of the company.

† **d.** ***purser-general,*** the head of a body of pursers, in a district, or department of service.

1633 G. GOSNELL *Let.* 4 July (Ind. Off. Rec. O.C. 1509), Mr. Turnour, Purser-Generall att Suratt, comends his love to you. **1657** T. MAYNARD in Thurloe *St. Papers* VI. 118 If somebody were joined with the purser-general by an order from his highness,.. there would be much money saved.

†**3.** One who steals or cuts purses; a cutpurse, a pickpocket. *Obs.*

1649 W. M. *Wand. Jew* (1857) 64 §3 All Executors that rob Orphans of their portions, are Theeves, and deserve more to be hanged then a Purser.

4. a. A ship using purse-nets. **b.** A fish caught in a purse-net.

1961 *Listener* 24 Aug. 269/1 The use of these pursers was forbidden in the cod waters of Lofoten. **1971** [see PURSE-NET 1]. **1973** *Stornoway Gaz.* 27 Jan. 1/1 The quality of the ring-net herring was mixed to very poor and soft, and the pursers very poor and soft.

Hence **ˈpursership,** the office of purser.

1600 DEKKER *Fortunatus* E 3 b, Ile haue the purse for a-yeere, you the Hat.. & when my pursourship ends, ile resigne, and cap you. **1864** in WEBSTER (citing TOTTEN); and in mod. Dicts.

purserette (ˌpɜːsəˈrɛt). [f. PURSER + -ETTE.] A female purser on a ship or other form of transport.

1959 *Times* 17 Mar. 4/4 Miss Suzette Pienaar, who has joined the Union-Castle Line to become an Afrikaans-speaking 'purserette'. **1960** *Aeroplane* XCVIII. 453/1 Inside of 707 is rather fun... The Purser (we note the big-ship touch) introduces us to the Purserette (we come ashore again rapidly). **1970** *New Scientist* 28 May 431/2 A new technique that British Rail is using to make uniforms for hovercraft purserettes—the low-flying equivalent of the air hostess. **1975** *Times* 19 Feb. 14/7 Of the 90,000 sea staff on British ships.. only a thousand or two are women and.. practically all are in 'female roles': nurses, stewardesses, purserettes.

ˈpurse-ring.

1. A ring, or one of the two sliding rings, closing a silk or leather purse.

1534 MORE *Comf. agst. Trib.* III. xiv. (1847) 236 Like a purse-ring of Paris, hollow, light and counterfeit indeed.

2. The ring of a purse-seine, through which the pursing line runs.

1890 in *Cent. Dict.*

purse-seine (ˈpɜːssein). A fishing-net or seine which may be pursed or drawn into the shape of a bag, used for catching shoal fish. Also *attrib.* ***purse-seine boat, fisherman, fishery, fishing, -net.***

1870 *Amer. Naturalist* IV. 515 Purse-seines are used to the best advantage in capturing [mackerel]. **1883** *Fish. Exh. Catal.* 196 Model of mackerel purse-seine. **1883** GOODE *Fish. Indust. U.S.* 66 There is.. reason to believe that our great purse-seine fisheries for menhaden and mackerel, though perhaps not causing a decrease in the numbers of the fish, have kept them farther from the shore. **1883** *Pall Mall G.* 1 Sept. 9/1 To enable our fishermen to see the practical working of the celebrated purse seine net, as used by the United States fishermen for the capture of mackerel, herring, and other fish usually caught by the drift net. **1884** *Bull. U.S. Nat. Museum* No. 27. 697 Purse-seine boat... This model represents the class of boats exclusively used in the mackerel purse-seine fisheries of New England. **1889** *Nature* XLI. 180/1 The purse-seine first came into general use in 1850. **1909** Purse-seine fishing [used s.v. PURSE-SEINER]. **1935** B. R. HUBBARD *Cradle of Storms* vi. 95 Floating canneries had been allowed to invade the False Pass area, and powerful purse-seine boats had come in with them. **1960** R. KIRKBRIDE *Innocent Abroad* x. 74 These purse-seine boats moved like cats' eyes over the water, luring shoals of fish with the beams of their kerosene pressure lamps. **1971** *Stornoway Gaz.* 7 Aug. 3/7 Its provisions apply to all nets, with the exception of purse-seine nets and ring nets, constructed to take fish while being towed or hauled through the sea by or from a fishing boat.

1971 *Country Life* 9 Dec. 1642/2 It was Gardenstown men who took over the first boat built specially for purse-seine fishing. **1975** *New Yorker* 22 Dec. 54/2 When the enormous purse seine (some three hundred fathoms long by eighty fathoms deep) is cast, the boat moves in a circle round a herring shoal, pulling the net into the shape of a pocket in a pool table. **1976** *Times* 14 Feb. 2/3 Huge nets, purse seine nets, that can trap up to 200 tons of fish in a single cast. **1976** *Quoddy Tides* (Eastport, Maine) 13 Aug. 2/1 Herring purse-seine fishermen in the Bay of Fundy have organized themselves with government assistance to change the purse-seine fishery from one based on fish meal to one based on food.

Hence **purse-seiner**, a vessel employed in purse-seine fishing; **'purse-seining**.

1890 in *Cent. Dict.* **1919** *Dialect Notes* V. 58 The purse-seiners are reaping a harvest here just now, lots of fish and a good price. Island Co. Times, Coupeville [Washington]. **1941** STEINBECK & RICKETTS *Sea of Cortez* i. 7 The purse-seiners of Monterey..are dependable work-boats. **1963** *Times* 25 Feb. (Canada Suppl.) p. ix/5 Present fishing methods are gill-netting, purse-seining and trolling. **1973** *Stornoway Gaz.* 27 Jan. 1/1 Last Wednesday's total of 7,612 crans from purse-seiners and pair trawlers was a record for the port of Stornoway. **1973** *Sunday Times* 10 June (Colour Suppl.) 44/4 The third and most controversial method is purse-seining—where a net is put round a school of tuna, the base is closed and the whole lot hauled on board. **1979** P. BENCHLEY *Island* i. 13 Commercial purse-seiners telling their wives when to expect them home.

'purse-string. Usually in *pl.*: The two threaded strings by drawing which the mouth of a purse is closed; hence in various *fig.* phrases, as ***to hold the purse-strings***, to control the expenditure of money; ***to tighten*** or ***loosen the purse-strings***, to be sparing, or generous, in spending money.

c **1412** HOCCLEVE *De Reg. Princ.* 4369 So haue I plukked at my purse strynges, And made hem often for to gape & gane. *c* **1530** *Wit & Folly* (Percy Soc.) XX. p. lx, I shall brynge them to heuen gate..And lede them thyther by purse strynges. **1630** DAVENANT *Cruel Brother* II. i, Those whom Fathers Purse-strings hoise up to honour. *a* **1659** BP. BROWNRIG *Serm.* (1674) I. v. 71 He endeavours to corrupt him..and so to tie the Holy Ghost to his Purs-strings. **1820** T. MITCHELL *Aristoph.* I. 239 Cleon now finds it necessary to open his purse-strings. **1849** COBDEN *Speeches* 20 The House of Commons..has to look after the purse-strings of the people. **1902** BRENAN *House Percy* II. ii. 58 Refusing to loosen his purse-strings any further.

b. *attrib.* That is drawn like a purse-string.

1905 *Brit. Med. Jrnl.* 1 July 15 The stump (of the appendix) being buried by a purse string suture of catgut.

† **'purset.** *Obs. rare*$^{-1}$. [f. PURSE *sb.* + -ET[1]. Cf. F. *boursette* (15th c.).] A small purse or bag.

1609 B. JONSON *Masque Queens*, 8 *Hag loq.*, The blood of the frog..I have been getting; and made of his skin A purset, to keep sir Cranion in.

† **'purse-,taker.** *Obs.* A highwayman or robber who deprived persons of their purses.

1611 COTGR., *Batre les chemins*, to belay the way, as purse-takers and boothalers doe. **1647** R. STAPYLTON *Juvenal* 147 Murdrers, mixt with pyrates, and purse-takers, Run-away slaves, hangmen, and coffin-makers. **1649** W. M. *Wand. Jew* (1857) 64 §2 A brave Purse-taker is the Great-Turke of Cavileroes, to such bastardly Handy-Crafts.

So † **'purse-,taking**.

1596 SHAKS. *1 Hen. IV*, I. ii. 115, I see a good amendment of life in thee: From Praying, to Purse-taking.

pursevant, -want, obs. Sc. ff. PURSUIVANT.

'purse-web. A (spider's) web of the form of a purse. *attrib.* **purse-web spider**, a spider of the genus *Atypus* which spins a close web against a tree; esp. the American species *A. abbatti*.

1888 McCOOK *Amer. Spiders* I. 325 The characteristic tube of the Purseweb spider is spun against the trunk of a tree, extending several inches above the surface of the ground and about an equal distance beneath it.

† **'pursewort.** *Obs.* An old name for the weed Shepherd's purse.

a **1450** *Alphita* 34/1 *Capsellula, herba sanguinaria,..bursa pastoris idem,..*pursewurt. *Ibid.* 81/1 Purs[e]-uu[o]rt.

pursey, purseynt, var. PURSY, PURCINCT.

† **'pursick,** *a.* and *sb. Obs.* [f. PURSIVE with suffix substitution: possibly influenced by SICK.]

A. *adj.* Of a horse: = PURSIVE, PURSY *a.*[1] 1.

1610 MARKHAM *Masterp.* I. xlviii. 99 Of the broken winded or Pursicke Horse. *Ibid.* ciii. 205 Looke he be not pursicke.

B. *sb.* Shortness of wind in a horse; pursiness.

1607 TOPSELL *Four-f. Beasts* (1658) 292 If it continue, it will either grow to the Pursick, or else break his winde altogether. *Ibid.* 293 Of the Pursick. This is a shortness of breath, and the Horse that is so diseased is called of the Italians, *Cavallo pulsivo*, or *Bolso*. **1688** R. HOLME *Armoury* II. 151/2 The shortness of Breath..[of a Horse], of some termed pur-sick.

Hence † **'pursickness**, pursiness.

1610 MARKHAM *Masterp.* II. clxxiii. 490 Dry figges..are good for pursicknesse, coughes, and diseases of the lungs.

'pursie. Sc. dim. of PURSE *sb.*: see -IE.

1785 BURNS *Jolly Beggars* Recit. iv, For mony a pursie she had hooked.

pursiness ('pɜːsɪnɪs). [f. PURSY *a.*[1] + -NESS.] The state or condition of being pursy; short-windedness, breathlessness, dyspnœa.

14.. *Nominale* in Wr.-Wülcker 708/37 (*Nomina morborum*) *Hec sinax, -cis*, pursenes. **1483** *Cath. Angl.* 294/2 A Pursynes, *cardia, cardiaca*. **1562** TURNER *Herbal* II. 123 Rue..is good..agaynst pursines & shortnes of breath. **1611** COTGR., *Pousse*, short wind, pursinesse. **1681** WORLIDGE *Dict. Rusticum* (1726) s.v., This Pursiness or shortness of Breath in Sheep is cur'd by cutting their Ears and changing their Pasture. **1834** *Good's Study Med.* (ed. 4) I. 464 Corpulent dyspnœa. Pursiness.

† **b.** Flatulence; internal stuffiness. *Obs.*

1607 TOPSELL *Four-f. Beasts* 649 [It] doth help the shortnesse of the breath, and ease the pursines of the stomacke. **1607** MARKHAM *Caval.* III. (1617) 20 As he is outwardly full of vnsound fatness, so hee is inwardly stuft with much glut and pursines.

pursing, *vbl. sb.* and *ppl. a.*: see PURSE *v.*

pursive ('pɜːsɪv), *a. arch.* Also 5–6 **-syf(e**, 6 **-sife**, **-cyfe**. [a. (?) AF. *porsif*, app. phonetic var. of OF. *polsif*, in Cotgr. *poulsif*, mod.F. *poussif* (L. type **pulsīv-um*), f. OF. *polser*, F. *pousser* in sense 'to breathe with labour or difficulty':—L. *pulsāre* to drive or agitate violently, freq. of *pellĕre* to drive. *Porsif* is given as Fr. in quot. 12.., and *pourcif* in Palsgr. 1530, but there is no evidence of its use in continental Fr., and the substitution of *r* for *l* was prob. English, perh. from some association with *purse*, which becomes evident in the later form PURSY.] Short-winded, broken-winded, asthmatic: originally said esp. of a horse.

(Cf. F. *cheval poussif*; *pousse* 'maladie des chevaux caractérisée par l'essoufflement, par le battement des flancs, et particulièrement par une interruption de l'inspiration'.)

[**12..** *Miracula S. de Montfort* (Camden) 68 Comitissa Gloverniæ habuit palefridum asmaticum, gall[ice] porsif'.] **1398** [see PIRRE]. **1530** PALSGR. 321/2 Purcyfe, shorte wynded or stuffed aboute the stomacke, *pourcif*. **1552** HULOET, Pursyfe manne, *anhelator, anhelus*. **1601** HOLLAND *Pliny* XX. xiii. II. 58 For the curing of foure footed beasts..broken winded and pursive. **1707** FLOYER *Phys. Pulse-Watch* 157 If my Pulse be 90, I am always Pursive, but 95 makes me Asthmatick. **1831–43** YOUATT *Horse* xii. 278 The pursive or broken-winded horse should not stand idle..a single day.

pursiveness ('pɜːsɪvnɪs). *arch.* [f. prec. + -NESS.] = PURSINESS.

1552 HULOET, Pursifenes, *dipsnœa*. **1601** HOLLAND *Pliny* II. (1634) 247 Hyssop is commended..for pursiuenesse and shortnesse of wind. **1602** MARKHAM *Caval.* v. (1617) 10 There is..pursivenes in the Pease and fulsomnes in the Beanes. **1754** J. BARTLETT *Farriery* 63 Distinguished in their symptoms from that pursiveness..we see in some horses.

purslaine, -lan(e, obs. ff. PORCELAIN.

purslane ('pɜːslən). Forms: α. 4–5 **purcelan(e**, 6 **-laine, -layne, -lline, -llyne, perseline, purselane**, 6–7 **-lain(e**, 7 **-lan, -lyn, purcellane**. β. 5 **porsulaigne, porceleyne**, 6 **-laine, -lene, -layn(e, -line, -llyne**, 6–7 **-lane**. γ. 5– **purslane**; also (5 **poslane**), 6 **purslayne, -lin, -land, pourslane**, 7 **purslan, -lein, pursslen**, 6–9 **purslain(e**. [a. OF. *porcelaine* (*a* 1300 in Godef.), *pourcelaine* (still in Cotgr.), = It. *porcellana* (Florio); identical in form with the Fr. and It. words for PORCELAIN, q.v., and app. altered, by assimilation to that word, from L. *porcil(l)āca*, used by Pliny for the more usual L. *portulāca* (which is taken in botany as the name of the genus).]

1. A low succulent herb, *Portulaca oleracea*, widely distributed throughout tropical and warmer temperate regions, used in salads, and sometimes as a pot-herb, or for pickling. Also called *common* or *garden purslane*. Formerly cultivated in English kitchen gardens, but now rarely met with.

α. *a* **1387** *Sinon. Barthol.* (Anecd. Oxon.) 34/1 *Portulaca*..purcelan. *c* **1400** *Lanfranc's Cyrurg.* 95 (Ashm. MS.) Wiþ ius of purcelane [*Add. MS.* poslane] or of sum oþere cold eerbe. **1563** HYLL *Art Garden.* (1593) 122 The Purselaine is much harmed by a long drooght. **1577** B. GOOGE *Heresbach's Husb.* I. (1586) 31 Leaues..not much vnlike to Purcelaine. **1590** SPENSER *Muiopotmos* 199 Fat Colworts, and comforting Perseline. **1620** J. MASON *New-found-land* (1887) 149 Of herbes there are likewise lettise, purselyn, etc. **1651** BIGGS *New Disp.* 36 ¶72 If Purselan or some other herbe were observed to do the like.

β. *a* **1450** *Alphita* (Anecd. Oxon.) 10/2 *Andrago,..portacla, portulaca idem*, g^e. et angl. porceleyne. *Ibid.* 149/2 *Portulaca uel portacla,..*porsulaigne. **1527** ANDREW *Brunswyke's Distyll. Waters* B iv, Water of porcelayn..is good for a person that spetteth blod. **1538** TURNER *Libellus, Portulaca,..*ab anglis Porcellyne dicitur. **1551** —— *Herbal* II. 103 Som vse porcellayn as a meat. **1561** HOLLYBUSH *Hom. Apoth.* 17 Let the same drincke water of Buglosse and Porcelene. **1597** GERARDE *Herbal* cxl. §2. 419 Called..in English Purslane and Porcelaine.

γ. *c* **1400** Poslane [see α]. *c* **1440** *Promp. Parv.* 417/1 Purslane, herbe, *portulaca*. **1530** PALSGR. 259 Purslayne.., *povrselayne*. **1533** ELYOT *Cast. Helthe* (1539) 23 b, Pourslane dothe mitigate the great heat in al the inward partes of the bodye. **1577** B. GOOGE *Heresbach's Husb.* (1586) 53 b, The Cucumber and the Gourd [come] the fifth daie, Purslin [is] longer ere it come. **1633** in *Naworth Househ. Bks.* 319 To Mrs. Orfeur's maide bringinge pursslen to my Ladie, ij^s. **1634** R. H. *Salernes Regim.* 145 To destroy Warts, nothing is better then to rubbe them with Purslaine. **1664** EVELYN *Kal. Hort.* 64 Sow also Lettuce, Purslan, Radish. **1693** —— *De la Quint. Compl. Gard.* II. 199 Purslain is one of the prettiest Plants in Kitchen-gardens, which is principally used in Sallets, and sometimes in Pottages. **1796** C. MARSHALL *Garden.* (1813) xvi. 272 Purslane is a low growing succulent herb. **1864** HAWTHORNE *S. Felton* (1883) 355 Rose ate her frugal dinner (consisting chiefly of purslain, and some other garden herbs). **1857** GRAY *First Less. Bot.* (1866) 15 Sometimes the embryo is coiled around the outside, in the form of a ring, as in the Purslane.

2. With qualification, denoting other species of *Portulaca*; also other plants similar in appearance or qualities to the Garden Purslane.

a. crimson-flowered purslane, *P. Thellussoni*; **red-flowered p.**, *P. splendens*; **yellow-flowered p.**, *P. aurea*. **b. black purslane** of N. America, *Euphorbia Preslii*; **horse-p.** of the West Indies, *Trianthema monogyna*; **milk-p.**, *Euphorbia maculata*; **mud-p.**, *Elatine americana*; **rock-p.**, the genus *Calandrinia*; **sea-p.**, *Atriplex portulacoides*, and *Arenaria peploides*; (of the West Indies), *Sesuvium Portulacastrum*; **Siberian p.**, *Claytonia sibirica*; **water-p.**, *Peplis Portula*, and *Isnardia palustris*; (of America), *Ludwigia palustris*; **winter-p.**, *Claytonia perfoliata*; **wild-p.**, *Euphorbia Peplis*.

1578 LYTE *Dodoens* V. xx. 575 Sea Purcelayne groweth vpon bankes..adioyning to the sea. *Ibid.* 575 The garden & wilde Purcelayne, do flower from after the moneth of June, vntill September. **1597** GERARDE *Herbal* cxl. ¶1. 418 There be diuers sortes or kindes of Purslane; one of the garden, and another wilde: and also two of the sea. **1678** PHILLIPS s.v., Besides the common sort there are two others, viz. The Sea Purslane, called *Halimus*, and the Water Purslane, called *Alsine*. **1760** J. LEE *Introd. Bot.* App. 324 Horse Purslane, *Trianthema*. *Ibid.*, Tree Sea Purslane, *Atriplex*. *Ibid.*, Water Purslane, *Peplis*. **1772–84** COOK *Voy.* (1790) V. 1844 A considerable quantity of wild purslain, long-wort, pease, &c. **1857** MISS PRATT *Flower. Pl.* I. 198 The Sea Purslane (*Arenaria peploides*). *Ibid.* IV. 277 *A*[*triplex*] *portulacoides* (Shrubby Orache, or Sea Purslane)..is a plant having a woody stem, and foliage of silvery whiteness, and much succulence.

3. *attrib.* and *Comb.*, as ***purslane leaf***, ***-leaved*** adj., *poultice*, *seed*, etc.; **purslane-moth**, a zygænid moth (*Copidryas gloveri*) of North America; **purslane sphinx**, an American moth (*Deilephila lineata*) which feeds upon the leaves of purslane, etc.; **purslane-tree**, † (*a*) ? the wild arbutus (after Gr. ἀνδράχνη purslane, also arbutus); (*b*) a South African shrub, *Portulacaria afra*; **purslane-worm**, the larva of the purslane moth, which feeds on wild purslane.

1855 DELAMER *Kitch. Gard.* (1860) 134 In proportion as the traveller approaches the German frontier, the more *purslane-leaves will he find in his vegetable soups. **1822** *Hortus Angl.* II. 15 *C. Halimifolius.* *Purslane-leaved Cistus. **1818** *Art Preserv. Feet* 50 A third ensures you a happy relief from *purslain poultices chopped up with vinegar. *c* **1550** LLOYD *Treas. Health* L vij, *Pursland sede..kylleth the wormes. **1664** EVELYN *Sylva* 61 An even Bed, which being made of fine earth, clap down with your Spade, as Gard'ners do for Purselain-seed. **1878** T. W. HARRIS *Insects Injur. Veget.* 638 *Purslane sphinx. **1604** B. JONSON *Cornwallis's Entertainm.* 60 Under yond' *purslane tree stood sometime my cradle. **1773** JOHNSON (ed. 4), *Purslan-tree*, a shrub proper to hedge with. **1794** T. TAYLOR *Pausanias's Descr. Greece* III. 48 In the temple of Promachos the remains of a purslain-tree are dedicated.

purslet ('pɜːslɪt). [f. PURSE *sb.* + -LET.] A small or tiny purse or bag.

1869 A. HUME *Brit. Antiq.* 94 Another purse..has two smaller purslets attached to it, and opening from the interior, like the thumb and little finger of a glove.

pursuable (pə'sjuːəb(ə)l), *a.* [f. PURSUE *v.* + -ABLE: cf. F. *poursuivable* (16th c. in Littré).] Capable of being pursued or prosecuted.

1611 COTGR., *Poursuivable*, pursuable. **1678** SIR G. MACKENZIE *Crim. Laws Scot.* I. xix. §14 (1699) 104 By the Common Law this was not pursuable. **1784** J. BARRY in *Lect. Paint.* v. (1848) 187 An infinity of resource for adjusting the composition;..and this is equally pursuable in the lights and darks, in the middle tint, and in the reflexes.

pursual (pə'sjuːəl). *rare.* [f. PURSUE *v.* + -AL[1].] The action or fact of pursuing; pursuance.

1814 SOUTHEY *Roderick* xiv. 117 The busy spirit, who, with powerful call Rousing Pelayo's people, led them on In quick pursual. **1878** VILLARI *Machiavelli* (1898) II. v. 216 [Their] constant pursual of certain wise maxims of government.

pursuance (pə'sjuːəns). Also 7 **pour-**, 7–8 **persuance**. [f. as PURSUANT: see -ANCE. Cf. OF. *pour-, prosuiance, poursivance* (Godef.).] The action, or fact, of pursuing, in various senses.

† **1.** The action of pursuing in order to catch or kill; chase: = PURSUIT 2. *Obs.*

1648 (Sept. 20) CROMWELL in Carlyle *Lett. & Sp.* (1871) II. 55 In pursuance of the remaining part of the enemy. *a* **1656** USSHER *Ann.* (1658) 243 Hoping..to make him desist from any further pursuance after them. **1693** *Mem. Cnt. Teckely* IV. 62 Altho' orders had been given for a speedy pursuance of them, they could overtake but some few.

2. The seeking after or aiming at something; endeavour to attain; search; = PURSUIT 6. (Now with *end*, *object*, or the like; formerly more widely.)

1640 BP. REYNOLDS *Passions* x. 84 The love of both which is then onely Regular, when it is..Humble in the manner of pursuance, without swelling and curiositie. **1648** MILTON *Tenure Kings* (1650) 43 In the pursuance of fame and dominion. *a* **1661** FULLER *Worthies, Yorks.* (1840) III. 421 He [Ripley]..studied twenty years together in pursuance of the Philosopher's stone. **1710** NORRIS *Chr. Prud.* viii. 391 As diligent in prosecuting our true and great End, as they are in the pursuance of their false and little ones. **1878** STEWART & TAIT *Unseen Univ.* ii. §50. 69 To start in pursuance of that object.

†**3.** The action or fact of following; that which follows or is consequent, a consequence. *Obs. rare.*

1596 BACON *Max. Com. Law* viii. (1630) 40 Any accessory before the fact is subiect to all the contingencies pregnant of the fact, if they bee pursuances of the same fact.

4. The action of following out (a process); following on with or continuance of something; continuation, prosecution.

1605 BACON *Adv. Learn.* II. x. §10 A man would thinke of the dayly visitations of the Phisitians, that there were a poursuance in the cure. **1638** CHILLINGW. *Relig. Prot.* I. Ep. Ded. 2 It is..nothing else, but a pursuance of, and a superstruction upon that blessed Doctrine. **1713** STEELE *Englishm.* No. 56. 363, I write to you in pursuance of my Letter which you printed on the Ninth. **1753** HOGARTH *Anal. Beauty* 7 A great assistance to us in the pursuance of our present enquiry. **1859** MISS CARY *Country Life* i. (1876) 29 In pursuance of some train of thought.

†**b.** That in which any process is continued; the course, sequence, sequel.

1645 MILTON *Colast.* Prose Wks. (1847) 220/1 What book hath he ever met with..maintaining either in the title, or in the whole pursuance, 'Divorce at pleasure'? **1704** NORRIS *Ideal World* II. vii. 330 The train and pursuance of our discourse requires that we should say [etc.].

5. The action of proceeding in accordance or compliance with a plan, direction, or order; prosecution, following out, carrying out. (The chief current sense.)

1660 *Trial Regic.* 46 In pursuance of that Order, I did receive, among other things [etc.]. **1672** *Essex Papers* (Camden) I. 35 We have publisht a proclamation in pursuance to his Majties Letter prohibiting all persons to commence any suits [etc.]. **1770** LANGHORNE *Plutarch* I. 35 He freely offered himself, in pursuance of some oracle, to be sacrificed. **1816** *Gentl. Mag.* LXXXVI. I. 553 General Chartrand has been shot at Lille, in pursuance of his sentence, for having joined Buonaparte. **1865** DICKENS *Mut. Fr.* IV. xii, When they reached London in pursuance of their little plan, they took coach and drove westward.

†**pur'suand**, *ppl. a.* (*sb.*) *Obs.* [f. PURSUE *v.* + -AND[1] suffix; prob. identified with *pursuant* from OF.] Pursuing, conformable; also quasi-*sb.*, one pursuing, a pursuer: = PURSUANT *sb.*

a **1300** *E.E. Psalter* xliii. [xliv.] 18 Fram þe voice of þe reproceand and þe oȝains spekand, fram þe face of þe enemy and of þe pursuand. *c* **1350** *Will. Palerne* 5028 Boþe kinges & quenes & oþer kud lordes, perteli in alle a-paraile pursewend. ? *a* **1600** *Rules* in Drake *Eboracum* (1736) I. vi. 196 That corn brought to the market be pursuand, i.e. as good beneath in the sack as above.

pursuant (pə'sju:ənt), *sb.* and *a.* Also 4 poursuiant. [ME. a. OF. *por-*, *poursuiant*, pr. pple. of *por-*, *poursuir*, also *-suivir*, mod.F. *poursuivre* to PURSUE, q.v. Subseq. conformed to AF. *pursuer* and *pursue* vb.]

A. *sb.* †**1.** One who prosecutes an action (at law); a suitor; a prosecutor. *Obs.*

1390 GOWER *Conf.* I. 167 These lovers..for that point which thei coveite Ben poursuiantz fro yeer to yere In loves Court. *Ibid.* 245 He, which was a poursuiant Worschipe of armes to atteigne. *c* **1470** HARDING *Chron.* CLVIII. ii, At whiche parliament the pursuantes theim bond, At his decree and iudgement to stond. **1542–3** *Act 34 & 35 Hen. VIII*, c. 27 §113 The pursuantes in euery suche writte of errour..do pay like fees therfore. *a* **1657** W. BRADFORD *Plymouth Plantations* 8 (1602–6) Vexed with apparators, and pursuants, and ye comissarie courts.

2. One who pursues; a pursuer. *rare.*

1924 W. J. LOCKE *Coming of Amos* xiii. 163 Amos..ran..followed also at a run by Hamilton, thereby giving..visitors..the impression of pick-pocket and pursuant. **1978** *Maledicta* 1977 I. 232 Little Bit's longtime pursuant and then casual lover.

B. *adj.* †**1.** Prosecuting (in a court of law). *Obs.*

1542–3 *Act 34 & 35 Hen. VIII*, c. 27 §77 At libertie of the partie pursuant.

2. a. With *to*, rarely *upon*: Following upon, consequent and conformable to; in accordance with. *Obs.* or merged in b.

1648 *Art. Peace* xiii. in *Milton's Wks.* (1851) II, That the Proceedings..shall be pursuant and according to his Majesties printed Book of Instructions. **1711** ADDISON *Spect.* No. 123 ¶4 They determined, pursuant to the Resolution they had taken.., to retire. **1818** CRUISE *Digest* (ed. 2) IV. 154 If..the fine is levied pursuant to the deed.

b. quasi-*adv.* = PURSUANTLY.

1675 OGILBY *Brit.* Introd. 1 Pursuant to our method..we have concluded it necessary. **1712–13** SWIFT *Let. to Mrs. Dingley* 4 Jan. Lett. (1767) I. 215 The bishop of Clogher and Dr. Pratt made me dine with them to-day at lord Mountjoy's, pursuant to an engagement which I had forgot. **1847** C. G. ADDISON *Law of Contracts* I. i. §1 (1883) 8 If the act has been performed pursuant to the previous request of the party making the promise. **1885** *Act 48 & 49 Vict.* c. 54 §15 Every monition..served on him pursuant to any of the provisions of the first-mentioned Act.

3. Going in pursuit; following after, pursuing.

1691 J. NORRIS *Practical Disc.* 347 Nothing but what is pursuant of the End for which he Created us. **1836** *Fraser's Mag.* XIV. 648 Whom varnished fiction vainly woos, Of stern reality pursuant. **1906** *Daily Chron.* 12 Mar. 3/4 There is..the landing of the noble lord, the pursuant lady,..and several other people, on an island.

pur'suantly, *adv.* [f. prec. + -LY[2].] In a way that is pursuant or consequent; accordantly. Const. *to.*

1531 *Dial. on Laws Eng.* II. lv. 153 b, It folowyth pursueantlye that yt belongyth to the lawe of man. **1675** J. HOWE *Living Temple* (1845) 167 We are here, pursuantly to the drift and design of the present discourse, to affirm a necessity. **1688** *Vox Cleri pro Rege* 31 Pursuantly.., 'It may be made appear, that [etc.]'. **1873** BROWNING *Red Cott. Nt.-cap* II. 872 Pursuantly, one morning—knock at door..broke startlingly On household slumber.

pursue (pə'sju:, -'sju:), *v.* Forms: see below. [ME. a. AF. *pursiwe-r*, *pursue-r* (also *pursu-re*) = OF. *porsievre*, *porsieure*, *-sivre*, *-suire*, etc. (see SUE *v.*), mod.F. *poursuivre* = Pr. *perseguir*, *persegre*, Sp. *perseguir* and *proseguir*, It. *proseguire* and *perseguire*:—L. *prosequĕre*, *-īre*, *persequĕre*, *-īre*, popular forms of *prōsequī* and *persequī*, compounds of *sequī* to follow, which to a great extent ran together in Romanic. In ME. the L. form of the prefix, *prō-*, was sometimes, and *per-* frequently, substituted.]

A. Illustration of Forms.

α. 3 **pursiwe(n**, 4–5 **-suwe**, **-sewe**, 4–6 **-sew**, 5 **-siewe**, **-syewe**, **-sywe**, **-suie**, **-suye**, **-su**, **-swe**; 4– **pursue**.

c **1290** *Beket* 945 in *S. Eng. Leg.* I. 133 Ȝwane..luþere men pursiweden me: louerd, min help þov beo! **1340** HAMPOLE *Pr. Consc.* 4450 Þan sal anticrist bygyn felly To pursue men thurgh tyrauntry. *c* **1375** *Cursor M.* 19618 (Fairf.) Saule saule..qui pursewes þou me. *a* **1400** Pursywed [see B. 11 b]. *c* **1400** *Destr. Troy* 1150 Pollux with his pupull pursu on the laste. **1412–20** LYDG. *Chron. Troy* (E.E.T.S.) 506/3889 Þat with al his myȝt My deth pursuwet[h]. *c* **1430** —— *Min. Poems* (Percy Soc.) 251 Heeryng this voys, after I shal purswe [*rime* remwe = remue]. **1449** *Rolls of Parlt.* V. 150/1 At the sute of him whiche in this cas will pursuye. **1470–85** MALORY *Arthur* Table II. v. 7 How Balyn was pursyewed. *a* **1533** LD. BERNERS *Huon* lix. 206 They were so hastyd and pursewyd.

β. 4 **poursuie**, 4–6 **-sewe**, 5 **-syewe**, **-sue**, **-su**.

1390 GOWER *Conf.* II. 117 Thei..lesen hope forto spede And stinten love to poursewe [*rime* hewe]. *Ibid.* [see B. 5 poursuie]. **1456** SIR G. HAYE *Law Arms* (S.T.S.) 119 To poursu bataill. **1485** CAXTON *Chas. Gt.* 150 Knowyng that he was poursyewed. **1487** HEN. VII in *Ep. Acad. Oxon.* (1898) II. 524 To be poursued unto us hereafter. **1596** SPENSER *F.Q.* IV. vii. 30 Whom seeing flie she speedily poursewed.

γ. 4–5 **porsewe**, **-sue**.

c **1350** *Will. Palerne* 2474 Al þe puple..þat him porsewed hadde. **1393** LANGL. *P. Pl.* C. XVIII. 167 And porsuede to haue be pope pryns of holychurche.

δ. ? 4 **persywe**, 5–7 **persew(e**, 5–8 **persue**, 6 **-seu**, **-schew**.

? *a* **1400** *Trevisa's Higden* (Rolls) V. 71 (MS. γ) Persywed. *c* **1400** *Apol. Loll.* 24 Wan men schal..persew ȝow. **1414** *Rolls of Parlt.* IV. 57/1 How that I persuede diverse billes. **1526** *Pilgr. Perf.* (W. de W. 1531) 18 To resyst and persewe the kynge. **1588** in *Lib. Offic. S. Andree* (Abbotsf.) 170 þat we nor nane..in our nayme sall perschew nor follow [etc.]. **1609** SKENE *Reg. Maj.* 22 To persew his clame. **1759** JOHNSON *Rasselas* xxx, Pekuah..entreated the princess not to persue so dreadful a purpose. *Ibid.* xxxii, Rasselas prepared to persue the robbers. **1779** Persued [see B. 10].

ε. 5 **prosew(e**.

1432–50 tr. *Higden* (Rolls) IV. 133 Anthiocus..prosewede [1387 TREVISA pursuede] Triphon.

B. Signification. **I.** Transitive uses.

1. To follow with hostility or enmity; to seek to injure (a person); to persecute; to harass, worry, torment. Now *rare* or *Obs.* exc. as implied in 2.

c **1290**, etc. [see A. α]. **1382** WYCLIF *Matth.* v. 11 Ȝee shulen be blessid, when men shulen curse ȝou, and shulen pursue ȝou. *Ibid.*, *Acts* ix. 4, 5 'Saul, Saul, what pursuest thou me?'..'I am Jhesu of Nazareth, whom thou pursuest'. **1526** *Pilgr. Perf.* (W. de W. 1531) 97 Loue your ennemyes, ..praye for them that persueth you. **1693** PEPYS in *Lett. Lit. Men* (Camden) 212 To pursue you in the matter of the Prints soe farr beyond what in good manners I..would have done. **1750** JOHNSON *Rambler* No. 79 ¶12 Those may justly be pursued as enemies to the community of nature. **1855** MILMAN *Lat. Chr.* (1864) V. IX. viii. 415 To expel, or to pursue to death, a large part..of their subjects.

†**b.** To avenge, to follow with punishment. *Obs.*

1570 *Satir. Poems Reform.* xxiii. 111 Thocht thair war nane his deith that wald persew, The michtie God he wald Reuenge his blude. **1603** SHAKS. *Meas. for M.* v. i. 109 That with such vehemency he should pursue Faults proper to himselfe. **1697** DRYDEN *Virg. Georg.* IV. 654 No vulgar God Pursues thy Crimes, nor with a common Rod.

2. To follow with intent to overtake and capture or kill; to chase, to hunt.

1377 LANGL. *P. Pl.* B. XII. 241 Þe pekok, and men pursue hym may nouȝte fleighe heighe; For þe traillyng of his taille. *c* **1400** MAUNDEV. (Roxb.) viii. 30 Kyng Pharao persued þam. **1560** BIBLE (Genev.) *Ps.* lxxi. 11 Pursue and take him, for there is none to deliuer him. **1697** DRYDEN *Virg. Georg.* III. 314 Boreas in his Race..with impetuous roar Pursues the foaming Surges to the Shoar. **1783** COWPER *Epitaph on Hare* 1 Here lies, whom hound did ne'er pursue, Nor swifter greyhound follow. **1874** GREEN *Short Hist.* VIII. vii, To rout their other wing of horse as it returned breathless from pursuing the Scots.

b. *fig.* Said of the action of things evil or hurtful.

1567 *Gude & Godlie B.* (S.T.S.) 79 Ay quhen temptatioun dois zow persew. **1613** SHAKS. *Hen. VIII*, IV. ii. 25 So went to bed; where eagerly his sicknesse Pursu'd him still. **1698** FRYER *Acc. E. India & P.* 261 The worst inconvenience that pursued us. **1842** BORROW *Bible in Spain* viii. 47 The cold still pursued me. **1895** SALMOND *Chr. Doctr. Immort.* VI. iii. 647 The penalties of a selfish life and wasted opportunity pursue one beyond death.

3. To prosecute in a court of law, to sue (a person). Chiefly *Sc.*

1580 *Rot. Scacc. Reg. Scot.* XXI. 548 Persewing the said Alexander for mair nor ten thousand pundis. **1643** *Declar. Com., Reb. Irel.* 58 The Lords of his Majesties Privy Councell have given order that Nithisdail and Aboyne be cited, and criminally pursued of high Treason. **1688** *Pennsylv. Archives* I. 102 All..such Person or Persons shall be pursued with the utmost Severities and the greatest Rigor. **1876** *World* V. 8 She cannot be pursued in Germany, for there she has committed no crime. **1893** *Dict. Nat. Biog.* XXXIII. 403 She 'pursued' him in the Scottish courts in November 1703 for the sum of 500 *l.*

4. To follow, as an attendant; to come after in order, or in time. Now *rare* or *Obs.*

c **1470** HENRY *Wallace* VI. 120 Schyr Jhon the Grayme,..To Laynrik come, gud Wallace to persew. **1606** SHAKS. *Ant. & Cl.* III. xii. 26 Fortune pursue thee. **1658** BRAMHALL *Consecr. Bps.* iii. 74 Here we see..how al things do pursue one another. **1700** DRYDEN *Meleager & Atalanta* 339 My son requires my death, and mine shall his pursue. **1755** GRAY *Progr. Poesy* 64 Her track, where'er the Goddess roves, Glory pursue, and generous Shame. **1789** W. GILPIN *Wye* (ed. 2) 119 Grand woody promontories, pursuing each other, all rich to profusion.

b. To follow the course of (in description, etc.); to trace. *poetic.* In quot. 1883 = FOLLOW *v.* 10.

1697 DRYDEN *Virg. Georg.* IV. 1 The Gifts of Heav'n my foll'wing Song pursues. **1712** ADDISON *Hymn*, '*When all thy mercies*' xi, Through every Period of my Life Thy Goodness I'll pursue. **1883** F. M. PEARD *Contrad.* vii, Said Lady Molyneux, pursuing them with her eye-glass.

5. To sue for, to seek after; to try to obtain or accomplish, to aim at.

1390 GOWER *Conf.* III. 154 In Rome, to poursuie his riht. *c* **1400** MAUNDEV. (Roxb.) xxxiv. 152 Oþer iles þare er, wha so wald pursue þam, by þe whilk men myght ga all aboute þe erthe. *c* **1440** *Jacob's Well* v. 29 Þat he may noȝt defendyn hym þere, ne pursewyn his ryȝt. **1538** STARKEY *England* I. i. 7 For euer that wych ys best ys not of al men..to be persuyd. **1594** KYD *Cornelia* III. iii. 83 He murdred Pompey that pursu'd his death. **1611** BIBLE *Ps.* xxxiv. 14 Seeke peace and pursue it. **1712** STEELE *Spect.* No. 462 ¶4 He pursued Pleasure more than Ambition. **1874** CARPENTER *Ment. Phys.* I. vii. (1879) 318 The mind instinctively pursues what is pleasurable.

†**b.** To make it one's aim or endeavour, to try (*to do* something). *Obs.*

1390 GOWER *Conf.* III. 82 Such Sorcerie..I schal eschuie, That so ne wol I noght poursuie Mi lust of love forto seche. *c* **1430** LYDG. *Min. Poems* (Percy Soc.) 67, I counsaile thow pursue all thy lyve To lyve in peas. *c* **1430** *Hymns Virg.* 62 Þi foote þou holde, And pursue for to passe þe beest. **1523** LD. BERNERS *Froiss.* I. ccxxix. 308 People and men of warre, that wolde pursue to go into Castell.

†**6.** To seek to reach or attain to, to make one's way to. *Obs.*

c **1470** HENRY *Wallace* VI. 190 Than Cartlane craggis thai persewit full fast. **1508** DUNBAR *Tua Mariit Wemen* 478 All my luffaris lele, my lugeing persewis. *a* **1520** —— *Poems* ix. 84 To keipe the festuall and the fasting day, The mess on Sonday, the parroche kirk persew. **1611** HEYWOOD *Gold. Age* II. i, Dianae's Cloyster I will next pursue. **1681** DRYDEN *Abs. & Achit.* 855 Here stop, my Muse..No Pinions can pursue Immortal height.

†**b.** To attack, assail, besiege. *Sc. Obs.*

c **1470** HENRY *Wallace* VIII. 498 Sotheroun marueld giff it suld be Wallace, With out souerance come to persew that place. **1547** *Reg. Privy Council Scot.* I. 81 Our auld ynemeis intendis to cum and persew the said house..to recover the samyn furth of the said lordis handis. **1583** *Ibid.* III. 567 A greit nowmer of wickit and seditious personis..persewit the houssis of the provest and ane of the baillies.

7. To follow (a path, way, course); to proceed along; = FOLLOW *v.* 1 b. Now chiefly *fig.* In quot. 1390, to go through in reading, to peruse.

1390 GOWER *Conf.* III. 46 For full enformacioun The Scole which Honorious Wrot, he poursuieth. **1638** JUNIUS *Paint. Ancients* 120 They could not choose but chearefully pursue the same way of Art. **1697** DRYDEN *Virg. Georg.* III. 449 We too far the pleasing Path pursue. **1709** STEELE *Tatler* No. 97 ¶2 To consider what Course of Life he ought to pursue. **1788** JEFFERSON *Writ.* (1859) II. 369, I..shall pursue the course of the Rhine as far as the roads will permit me. **1879** R. K. DOUGLAS *Confucianism* iii. 72 The Sage..pursues the heavenly way without the slightest deflection.

8. To proceed in compliance or accordance with; = FOLLOW *v.* 8. Now only with *method*, *plan*, *scheme*, *system*, and the like: see quots. 1817–79.

1426 LYDG. *De Guil. Pilgr.* 9039 Al hys desyrs thow pursues. ? **1656** BRAMHALL *Replic.* vi. 241 This is not to alter the Institutions..of generall Councells..but..to tread in their stepps, and to pursue their grounds. **1718** POPE *Iliad* XI. 192 The king's example all his Greeks pursue. **1748** SMOLLETT *Rod. Rand.* xiv, As we were going to pursue this advice. **1817** JAS. MILL *Brit. India* II. v. i. 315 The following scheme was invented and pursued. **1879** *Techn. Drawing* in *Cassell's Techn. Educ.* IV. 69/2 The same system is now to be pursued.

9. To follow up, carry on further, proceed with, continue (a course of action, etc. begun).

1456 SIR G. HAYE *Law Arms* (S.T.S.) 119 Nocht all men that pursewis bataill is nocht cled with that vertu of force. *c* **1586** C'TESS PEMBROKE *Ps.* (1823) cxv. iv, Israel pursue Thy trust in God. **1596** DALRYMPLE tr. *Leslie's Hist. Scot.* III. xxxvi. (S.T.S.) I. 191 Thay drew to pairties, and began to pe[r]sew the mater wt swordes. **1601** SHAKS. *Twel. N.* IV. ii. 76, I cannot pursue with any safety this sport [to] the vppeshot. **1668** DRYDEN *Evening's Love* IV. i, This is the Folly of a bleeding Gamester, who will obstinately pursue a losing Hand. **1736** LEDIARD *Life Marlborough* I. 99 The Earl was resolved to pursue this good Success. **1759** JOHNSON *Rasselas* xxv, The Princess persues her enquiry. **1796** JANE AUSTEN *Pride & Prej.* xxx, The subject was pursued no farther. **1802** E. FORSTER tr. *Arab. Nts.* (1815) II. 355 The brothers then pursued their journey.

b. *Law.* To carry on (an action); to lay (information); to present (a libel). Chiefly *Sc.* (Cf. 3 and 13 b.)

1478 *Acta Dom. Conc.* 3/1 Þe accioun and cause persewit be William of Cavers..on þe ta part again Andro broun.. one þe tother part. **1530–1** *Act 22 Hen. VIII*, c. 12 The moytee thereof to be to him that pursueth the informacion for the same. *c* **1750** *Interlocutor* in J. Louthian *Process* (ed. 2) 152 The Lords Justice-Clerk and Commissioners of Justiciary, having considered the Libel pursued at the Instance of *A. B.* of —— [etc.].

10. To follow as an occupation or profession; to carry on, practise; to make a pursuit of.

1523 LD. BERNERS *Froiss.* I. ccccxx. 735, I haue.. pursewed myne offyce, to the honoure of you and of your people. **1673** S. C. *Art of Complaisance* 25 When we enterprise any affair with hopes well conceived..we pursue it with all perseverance. **1779** *Gentl. Mag.* XLIX. 363 He persued..his studies, or his amusements without persecution, molestation or insult. **1851** HELPS *Comp. Solit.* i. (1874) 2 Others may pursue science or art.

II. Absolute and intransitive uses.

11. To go in chase or pursuit.

c **1350** *Will. Palerne* 2196 Þe puple þanne porsewed forþ & of here prey þei missed. **1390** GOWER *Conf.* III. 236 The womman fleth and he poursuieth. **1611** BIBLE *Prov.* xxviii. 1 The wicked flee when no man pursueth. **1755** GRAY *Progr. Poesy* 32 Now pursuing, now retreating, Now in circling troops. **1853** M. ARNOLD *Scholar Gypsy* xxii, Far on the forest-skirts, where none pursue.

b. *to pursue after*, to follow in pursuit, to chase; = sense 2. Also with *indirect passive*.

1377 LANGL. *P. Pl.* B. xix. 158 Peter..pursued after, Bothe iames & Iohan, Ihesu for to seke. ? *a* **1400** *Arthur* 574 Arthour on gret haste Pursywed after hym faste. **1560** BIBLE (Genev.) *Exod.* xiv. 9 And the Egyptians pursued after them. **1655** FULLER *Ch. Hist.* IX. vii. §15 Left to be pursued after by hunger and cold. **1760–72** H. BROOKE *Fool of Qual.* (1809) I. 66 To take every horse he had..and to pursue after the fugitives.

†**c.** *to pursue for*, to seek or 'hunt' after.

1412–20 LYDG. *Chron. Troy* I. 1892 Þei pursue ay for pluralite.

†**12.** To proceed with hostile intent against some one; with *on*, *upon*, *to*, to attack, assail. *Obs.*

13.. *E.E. Allit. P.* B. 1177 He pur-sued in to palastyn with proude men mony. *c* **1400** *Destr. Troy* 2773 To pursew On hom þat hir holdis, & vs harme dyd. *Ibid.* 4853 All þis wale pepull Are comyn to þis cost..And pursuyt to þis prouynse in purpos to venge Of harmys. *c* **1440** *Alphabet of Tales* 158 Þan þe Romans..wold suffre it no langer, & rase & pursewid opon hym, & drafe hym oute of þe cetie. **1480** CAXTON *Cron. Eng.* clxiv. 148 Kyng edward..ordeyned men to pursue vpon hym—and dauyd ferselich hym defended. *c* **1500** *New Not-b. Mayd* (Percy Soc.) 33 Yet yf that shrewe To hym pursue.

†**13.** To make one's suit; to sue, entreat. *Obs.*

1390 GOWER *Conf.* II. 13 For after that a man poursuieth To love, so fortune suieth. *c* **1400** *Destr. Troy* 11431 Þai.. chosyn Antenor..with the grekes to trete, And pursew for pes. **1414** BRAMPTON *Penit. Ps.* 25 To thi mercy I will pursewe, Wyth 'Ne reminiscaris, Domine!' *c* **1560** A. SCOTT *Poems* (S.T.S.) xi. 7 Ȝe may wᵗ honesty persew, Gif ȝe be constant, trest, & trew.

b. *spec.* To sue in a court of law; to make suit as plaintiff or pursuer. In later use chiefly *Sc.*

1377 LANGL. *P. Pl.* B. XVII. 302 For þere þat partye pursueth þe pele is so huge, þat þe kynge may do no mercy. **1389** *Eng. Gilds* 71 Yei shul pursu for her Catelle in qwat cowrte yat hem liste. *c* **1440** *Jacob's Well* 29 Wherby þe man is lettyd of his ryȝt, be-cause he may noȝt pursewe in holy cherch-lawe. *c* **1470** HARDING *Chron.* clviii. ii, That al Scottes, and other that were pursuyng Might there appere, their titles claimyng. *a* **1639** SPOTTISWOOD *Hist. Ch. Scot.* II. (1677) 55 If they should happen to die intestate, it was made lawful to their nearest kinsmen to call and pursue for the same. **1756** MRS. CALDERWOOD *Journey* (1842) 226 He was bred a papist, but his mother..set on the protestant heir to pursue for his estate.

†**14.** To follow as an attendant or supporter. *Obs.*

c **1470** HENRY *Wallace* IV. 197 He thaim comandyt ay next him to persew; For he thaim kend rycht hardye, wis and trew. *c* **1470** *Gol. & Gaw.* 1292 Heir I mak yow ane grant, ..Ay to your presence to persew, with al my seruice.

†**15.** To follow or come after in order. *Obs.*

1485 *Rolls of Parlt.* VI. 332/2 The Dede and Fyne, wherof the tenoure persueth. **1529** MORE *Dyaloge* IV. xvii. Wks. 284/2 Rewarde or punishement, pursuing vpon all our dooinges. **1688** HOLME *Armoury* I. i. 2 Lest..scandal do arise and effusion of blood do persue.

†**16.** To proceed continuously. In quot. *a* 1651, to go or come forth, issue. *Obs.*

1500–20 DUNBAR *Poems* lxiv. 6 In to ȝour garthe this day I did persew. *a* **1651** *Life Humphrey* in Fuller *Abel Rediv.* (1867) II. 92 Those weighty words which pleasantly pursued out of his mouth. **1652** LOVEDAY tr. *Calprenede's Cassandra* III. 189 But we pursued on our way, resigning our selves to the protection and guidance of the Gods.

17. To continue (to do or say something); to go on (speaking). Also with *on*.

1500–20 DUNBAR *Poems* xlvi. 12 Quhair did, vpone the tothair syd, persew A nychtingall, with suggurit notis new. **1583** T. WATSON *Centurie of Loue* (Arb.) 129 In the other two staffes following, the Authour pursueth on his matter. **1665** BOYLE *Occas. Refl.* IV. xi, But, (pursues Eusebius) this may supply us with another Reflection. **1718** HICKES & NELSON *J. Kettlewell* I. §33. 58 Notwithstanding this he persued on with all the Meekness of Wisdom. **1802** MAR. EDGEWORTH *Moral T.* (1816) I. iii. 17 'And I have buried the poor cat', pursued Forester: 'and I hope [etc.]'. **1837** WHEWELL *Hist. Induct. Sc.* I. ii. §2 'Something of this', he pursues, 'may be seen in language'.

Hence **pur'sued** *ppl. a.*, **pur'suing** *vbl. sb.* and *ppl. a.*; also **pur'suingly** *adv.*

1716 *Macfarlane's Geneal. Collect.* (1901) I. 136 He was obliged to give his bond for the *pursued Sum. **1742** J. WILLISON *Balm of Gilead* (1800) xv. 197 Pursued shelterless sinners hearken to Christ's voice. *c* **1380** WYCLIF *Serm.* Sel. Wks. I. 206 How hise martirs shulen do in tyme of her *pursuynge. *c* **1380** —— *Wks.* (1880) 138 Bi strong pursuynge to deþ of alle trewe men. **1651** G. W. tr. *Cowel's Inst.* 58 If a swarm of Bees forsake my hive, they are said to be mine so long as they continue in my sight and that the persuing of them becomes not impossible. **1864** LONGF. *Wind over Chimney* x, No endeavor is in vain; Its reward is in the doing, And the rapture of pursuing Is the prize the vanquished gain. **1603** KNOLLES *Hist. Turks* (1638) 282 As a wall against the *pursuing enemy. **1686** HORNECK *Crucif. Jesus* xviii. 520 The pursuing judgment of God. **1855** *Tait's Mag.* XXII. 422 Many women do love as eagerly..as *pursuingly—as Caroline Helstone is said to have done.

'pursue, *sb.* (in *draw pursue*, etc.): see PERSUE.

†**pur'suement.** *Obs. rare*⁻¹. [f. PURSUE *v.* + -MENT.] Pursuing; = PURSUIT 2.

1615 G. SANDYS *Trav.* 48 The seuerall vses, agreeing with their fights, their flights, or pursuements.

pursuer (pəˈsjuːə(r)). Forms: 4 pursuwer, -suere, 5 -suour, 5–6 persewar, -er, 6 perssouar, 4– pursuer. [f. PURSUE *v.* + -ER¹.] One who pursues. †**1.** A persecutor. *Obs.*

c **1380** WYCLIF *Wks.* (1880) 138 Þei ben manquelleris & pursueris of crist. **1382** —— *1 Tim.* i. 13, I first was a blasfeme, or dispiser of God, and pursuwer [**1388** pursuere], and ful of wrongis. **1513** DOUGLAS *Æneis* VI. ii. 22 Nor Juno, Troianis persewar expres, Sall nevir mair failȝe in ȝour contrary. **1545** JOYE *Exp. Dan.* i. 16 b, So cruel persewers of cryst in his members. **1642** ROGERS *Naaman* 106 Desperate opposites and pursuers of all grace, of Christ and Christians.

†**2.** = PURSUIVANT 1. *Obs. rare*⁻¹.

1384–5 *Durh. Acc. Rolls* (Surtees) 594, j pursuer de armes.

3. *Civil* and *Sc. Law.* A suitor; a plaintiff, a petitioner; a prosecutor.

c **1412** HOCCLEVE *De Reg. Princ.* 1534, Ful many swyche pursuours þere ben, þat for vs take, & ȝeue vs nat a myte. *c* **1470** HARDING *Chron.* clviii. i, Florence therle of Holand, and his compeers That claymed then the croune of Scotland ..as pursuers, Came to kyng Edward. **1503–4** *Act 19 Hen. VII*, c. 31 The demaundantes pleyntyffes or pursuers of the same accions. **1564–5** *Reg. Privy Council Scot.* I. 318 The saidis Gilbert Millar, persewar, and the said Johnne Hammiltoun comperand bayth personalie. **1708** J. CHAMBERLAYNE *St. Gt. Brit.* II. II. iv. (1737) 375 The Lord Advocate..is the Pursuer of all Capital Crimes before the Justiciary. **1875** JOWETT *Plato* (ed. 2) I. 317 What is your suit, Euthyphro? are you the pursuer or the defendant? **1880** MUIRHEAD *Gaius* IV. §37 There is the same fiction if he be either pursuer or defender in an action on the Aquilian law for wrongful damage to property.

†**4.** A besieger, an assailant. *Sc. Obs.* Cf. PURSUE *v.* 6 b.

a **1578** LINDESAY (Pitscottie) *Chron. Scot.* I. xxx. I. 143 The seige lastit langer nor the perssouaris expectatioun was. *Ibid.*, The persewaris war all maist tint in the lang seiging.

5. One who follows after or chases with intent to capture; in quot. 1824, a suitor, wooer.

1539 BIBLE (Great) *Josh.* ii. 16 Gett you into the mountayne, lest the pursuers mete you. **1596** DALRYMPLE tr. *Leslie's Hist. Scot.* (S.T.S.) I. 21 Quhill a persewar is following ony thing he wantis. **1728** MORGAN *Algiers* II. iv. 284 Above 40,000 died by the Weapons of their merciless Pursuers, the Spanish Cavalry. **1824** BYRON *Don Juan* XII. xxxvii, Sometimes they accept some long pursuer, Worn out with importunity. **1875** W. S. HAYWARD *Love agst. World* 14 The fox turns with savage fury on his pursuer.

6. One who pursues some object or aim.

1651 HOBBES *Leviath.* I. xiv. 70 A Generosity too rarely found to be presumed on, especially in the pursuers of Wealth. **1691** WOOD *Ath. Oxon.* I. 318, I [am] an eager pursuer of Truth. *a* **1745** SWIFT *Enq. Behav. Queen's Last Ministry* Wks. 1841 I. 499/1 Of his pleasures of which he had indeed been too great and criminal a pursuer.

pursuing, pursuingly: see PURSUE *v.*

pursuit (pəˈsjuːt). Forms: α. 4 pursut, 4–5 -suet, 4–6 -suyt(e, 4–7 -sute, 5 -suette, 5–6 -sewt, 5–7 -suite, 6 -suete, -syewte, 5– pursuit. β. 4 pourseut, 4–7 -suite, 7 -suyte. γ. (mainly *Sc.*) 6 persuit, -sut, -sewt, 6–7 -sute, -suit. [a. AF. *purseute*, *pursute*, OF. *por-*, *poursieute*, *poursuite* (1326 in Godef.), deriv. of *poursuivre*, after *suite* (:—pop. L. **sequita*) from *suivre*.] The action or an act of pursuing, in various senses.

I. †**1.** Persecution, annoyance, ill-treatment. *Obs.*

c **1380** WYCLIF *Wks.* (1880) 44 [To] haue mekenesse & pacience in pursuyt..and to loue hem þat pursuen vs. **1387** TREVISA *Higden* (Rolls) I. 195 His suster, þat fleiȝ þe malice and pursuet of here stepdame. **1425** *Rolls of Parlt.* IV. 304/2 Whiche þing shuld be to þe Merchantz..full grete hyndryng, and a poursuite infinite. **1629–39** SIR W. MURE *Ps.* cix. 31 Hee..The poore-man's right hand..from persute of such as wold Condemne his soule, setts free.

2. a. The action of pursuing, chasing, or following, with intent to overtake and catch or kill, a fleeing object, as a hunted animal or an enemy.

curve of pursuit: see CURVE *sb.* 1.

1412–20 LYDG. *Chron. Troy* I. 1783 So longe laste þe pursute and þe chas. *c* **1500** *Melusine* 135 The other that had be at the pursyewte & chaas of the paynemys. **1584** POWEL *Lloyd's Cambria* 81 The Danes fled as sheepe before him [Edmund Ironside], but he staied the Pursute by the wicked read of the traitor Edric. *a* **1680** BUTLER *Rem.* (1759) II. 454 He..makes his Escape, and flies beyond Persuit of Huon-cries. **1782** COWPER *Gilpin* 240 All and each that passed that way Did join in the pursuit. **1809** WELLINGTON in Gurw. *Disp.* IV. 565, I have been on the pursuit, or rather chace of Soult out of Portugal. **1890** S. LANE-POOLE *Barbary Corsairs* I. iv. 51 The Marquis gave hot pursuit.

b. *in pursuit* (*of*): said of the pursuer; *in pursuit* formerly sometimes of the pursued, = in flight.

1590 SHAKS. *Mids. N.* IV. i. 128 My hounds..Slow in pursuit. **1660** *Chas. II's Escape fr. Worcester* in *Select. fr. Harl. Misc.* (1793) 379 [He] enquired of his brother Yates, what news from Worcester? who told him, that the king was defeated, and in pursuit. **1681** FLAVEL *Meth. Grace* xiii. 270 Like children in pursuit of a painted butterfly. **1847** DE QUINCEY *Span. Milit. Nun* Wks. 1854 III. 59 In pursuit of some flying game, [they] had wandered far.

c. In track cycling, any of various kinds of competitive race (see quots. 1961 and 1975).

1938 *Encycl. Brit. Bk. of Year* 100/1, 2 miles team pursuit. **1961** F. C. AVIS *Sportsman's Gloss.* 146/2 *Australian pursuit*, a track race in which a number of riders, starting from different points on the track and equally spaced out, try to catch the rider in front, whereupon the rider caught drops out of the race. *Ibid.* 149/1 *British pursuit*, a track race between two teams starting at opposite sides of the track, the members of each team standing ready to ride a lap when the previous rider of the team has been round. *Ibid.* 162/1 *Italian pursuit*, a track race between two teams starting at opposite sides of the track, the riders being in file, and who one by one drop out of the race as the track is lapped; thus, the leader of the file rides one lap, the second two laps, and so on. **1975** *Oxf. Compan. Sports & Games* 237/1 *Individual pursuit*..Two riders take part in each race, starting from stations on opposite sides of the track and attempting to gain on each other. Victory goes to the first rider to reach his home station on completing the distance or, less often, to the rider who overtakes his opponent. *Ibid.*, *Team pursuit*, over 4 km., is between amateur teams of four riders. Each rider leads the team for one lap or half a lap, then swings up on the end banking and drops back to the end of the file. Thus, after another three laps or another lap and a half he finds himself leading the team once more.

†**3.** The action of suing or entreating; a suit, request, petition, instance. *Obs.*

c **1386** CHAUCER *Wife's T.* 34 Ffor which oppression was swich clamour And swich pursute vn-to the kyng Arthour. *c* **1400** *Destr. Troy* 8882 Syn I with prayer, ne with pursuet, preset not þeraftur. **1455** *Paston Lett.* I. 361 After long pursewts made to the Kyng and his conseill. **1503–4** *Act 19 Hen. VII*, c. 28 *Preamble*, Meny persones..made instaunte & diligente pursuyte..to his Highnesse. **1602** MARSTON *Antonio's Rev.* III. i, Thy Mellida is chaste; Onely to frustrate thy pursuite in love, Is blaz'd unchaste. **1701** SWIFT *Contests Nobles & Com.* Wks. 1755 II. I. 41 When a lover becomes satisfied by small compliances without further pursuits, then expect to find popular assemblies content with small concessions.

4. *Law.* An action at law; a suit; prosecution. In later use chiefly *Sc.*

[**1349–50** SIR T. GRENEVILLE in Bp. Grandison *Reg.* (1897) II. 1086 Par queux torceuouses pursutes..vous avetz este sovent grevez de cuer.] **1414** *Rolls of Parlt.* IV. 57/1 To graunte me duryng my pursuyte..to walken at large. **1512** *Act 4 Hen. VIII*, c. 14 *Preamble*, To have made pursuete of their severall atteynders to be reversed. **1575** in *3rd Rep. Hist. MSS. Comm.* 419/1 The lang trubill..the laird of Lekky hes sustinet be the persewt of the Erll of Menteithe. **1655** FULLER *Ch. Hist.* III. vi. §26 That pursuit for Tythes ought, and of ancient time did pertain to the spiritual Court. **1678** SIR G. MACKENZIE *Crim. Laws Scot.* I. xvii. §6 (1699) 89 Such a Criminal pursuit, as was intented. **1737** J. CHAMBERLAYNE *St. Gt. Brit.* II. II. iv. 375 The Lord Advocate..concurs in all Pursuits before Sovereign Courts for Breaches of the Peace. **1832** AUSTIN *Jurispr.* (1879) I. xvii. 417 It is often thought expedient to convert the offence into a crime. That is to say the pursuit of it is not left to the discretion of the injured party.

†**5.** Attack, assault, siege. *Sc. Obs.*

1508 DUNBAR *Gold. Targe* 182 Dissymilance scho bad go mak persute, At all powere to perse the Goldyn Targe. *a* **1578** LINDESAY (Pitscottie) *Chron. Scot.* (S.T.S.) I. 152 To be stout and deliegent in the persuit of the said castell. **1590** *Reg. Privy Council Scot.* IV. 533 For defens of the said burgh in tyme of foreyne persute. *a* **1670** SPALDING *Troub. Chas. I* (1850) I. 259 The toun of Edinbrughe..stellit cannonis on ilk ane of thir montis for persute of the castell.

II. **6. a.** The action of seeking, or striving to obtain, attain, or accomplish something; search; †endeavour, attempt (*to do* something).

1606 SHAKS. *Tr. & Cr.* II. ii. 142 Paris should ne're retract what he hath done, Nor faint in the pursuite. **1636** W. BOSWELL in *Lett. Lit. Men* (Camden) 152, I am in dayly poursuite of more [Medals]. **1700** DRYDEN *Pal. & Arc.* I. 294 One soul should both inspire, and neither prove His fellow's hindrance in pursuit of love. **1711** ADDISON *Spect.* No. 55 ¶2 An immoderate Pursuit after Wealth and Riches. **1836** J. H. NEWMAN *Par. Serm.* (ed. 2) II. xxviii. 395 You may hear men talk as if the pursuit of wealth was the business of life.

b. *transf.* The object aimed at; aim. ? *Obs.*

c **1592** MARLOWE *Jew of Malta* III. iii, Hard-hearted father,..Was this the pursuit of thy policy? *a* **1732** GAY *Fables* II. xi. 8 Be virtue then your first pursuit. **1742** GRAY *Propertius* II. 52 Be love my youth's pursuit, and science crown my Age.

7. The action of following or engaging in something, as a profession, business, recreation, etc.; that which one engages in or follows.

1529 WOLSEY in *Four C. Eng. Lett.* (1880) 10 That expedicion be usyd in my persuts, the delay wherof so replenyshyth my herte with hevynes. **1600** W. WATSON *Decacordon* (1602) 97 Yet ceassed they not to follow the pursuite of their impietie in persecuting his happie memorie. **1774** BURKE *Corr.* (1844) I. 489 Your constitution of mind is such, that you must have a pursuit. **1800** COLQUHOUN *Comm. Thames* Pref., Those..who follow Nautical Pursuits. **1862** SIR B. BRODIE *Psychol. Inq.* II. i. 2 In our daily pursuits we found much that served to illustrate our former speculations. **1874** GREEN *Short Hist.* ix. §1 (1882) 591 The pursuit of Physical Science became a passion.

†**8.** The pursuing or following out *of* a plan, design, etc. *Obs.* (replaced by PURSUANCE 4.).

a **1631** DONNE *Paradoxes* (1652) 68 Towards the pursuite of any worthy design. **1651** HOBBES *Leviath.* II. xxiv. 128 The doing of many things in pursuit of their Passions. **1655** tr. *Com. Hist. Francion* XII. 30 He made answer..in pursute of the Instructions which he had received.

†**9.** The action of going on with something already begun; a continuation, a sequel. *Obs.*

1650 EARL MONM. tr. *Senault's Man bec. Guilty* 103 We shall see all these truths in the pursuit of this discourse. **1668** OWEN *Exp. Heb.* (1790) I. 131 Unless we look on the words as a pursuit of the first promise. **1725** DE FOE *Voy. round World* (1840) 15, I return now to the pursuit of our voyage.

†**10.** Succession, sequence, serial order.

1605 BACON *Adv. Learn.* II. x. §10 It is order, poursuite, sequence, and interchange of application, which is mightie in nature. *Ibid.* xix. §1 That men may know in what order or pursuit to read.

III. 11. *attrib.* and *Comb.*, as ***pursuit force, party, squadron***; (sense 2c) ***pursuit cyclist, race***; **pursuit aeroplane, aircraft, airplane** (*U.S.*), **biplane, plane** = FIGHTER 3; **pursuit-flight** [repr. G. *reihen* sb. (E. Christoleit 1929, in *Beitr. Fortpflanzungsbiol. Vögel* V. 45)], a flight in which one or more male birds follow or attack a female.

1937 *Discovery* Sept. 277/2 The present type of *pursuit aeroplane weighs perhaps some 4500 lb. **1940** *Jrnl. R. Aeronaut. Soc.* XLIV. 485 A Curtiss YP-36 type pursuit aeroplane. **1931** *Flight* 25 Dec. 1265/1 The contracts placed with the Detroit Corp...include five Lockheed two-seater *pursuit aircraft of the type Y1P-24. **1928** CHATFIELD & TAYLOR *Airplane & its Engine* xv. 267 The *pursuit airplane is..purely an offensive type. **1920** H. WOODHOUSE *Textbk. Appl. Aeronaut. Engin.* iii. 93 The D.H.5 *Pursuit Biplane. **1970** *Soviet Weekly* 8 Aug. 14 In preparing for the world championship in England the Soviet *pursuit cyclists did a lot of road work. **1930** J. S. HUXLEY *Bird-Watching & Bird Behaviour* iii. 54 Almost immediately he will fly at her, she will fly off, and the two will turn and twist through the air in what may be called the *pursuit flight—a regular part of courtship in yellow-hammers and many other small birds. **1940** H. C. WITHERBY et al. *Handbk. Brit. Birds* III. 234 The pursuit-flights [of mallards]..have been discussed at length by German authors. **1954** D. A. BANNERMAN *Birds Brit. Isles* III. 376 Mr. Hartley describes tail-fanning by both sexes [of swallows] in pursuit flight. **1968** P. A. JOHNSGARD *Waterfowl* vi. 51 When the female is involved in incubating..these pursuit flights take a different form. **1945** *Diamond Track* (Army Board, N.Z.) 33/1 The *pursuit force opened out into desert formation. **1909** *Daily Chron.* 5 July 1/6 All available attendants were mustered as a *pursuit party. **1918** E. S. FARROW *Dict. Milit. Terms* 479 *Pursuit plane. **1932** *Flight* 17 Nov. 1099 (*caption*) A new Boeing pursuit plane. **1962** R. B. FULLER *Epic Poem on Industrialization* 1 Zooming aloft In a pursuit plane. **1908** T. A. COOK *Olympic Games* 188 *Pursuit Race Three laps (1·807 kilometres) Teams of four to start. First three to count in each heat. **1928** E. HEMINGWAY *Men without Women* 190 In a pursuit race, in bicycle racing, riders start at equal intervals to ride after one another. **1961** J. S. SALAK *Dict. Amer. Sports* 346 A pursuit race may have two or more contestants, who are started at equal distances behind and ahead of the nearest contestant or contestants so that the circuit of the track is divided equally by the starting points. A pursuit race may be run to a finish or for a specified distance. In either case the winner is he who has caught and passed all contestants or remaining contestants. **1976** 'A. HALL' *Kobra Manifesto* i. 13 He could be chased..by *pursuit squadrons of the Yugoslavian air arm.

†**pur'suite**, *v. Sc. Obs.* [In 6 *persuite* for *pursuite*, f. prec.: cf. PERSECUTE.] *trans.* To persecute: = PURSUE *v.* 1.

1563 WINȜET *Four Scoir Thre Quest.* (S.T.S.) I. 67 We ar ..iniustlie persuitit, with sa grete rigour, as we war heretikis or apostatis. *Ibid.* 95 King Saull..persuitand the said Dauid iniustlie to the deth.

†**pur'suiter.** *Obs.* Also 6 poursuter. [f. as prec. vb. + -ER[1], or f. *pursue, pursuit*, after *suitor*.] = PURSUER.

1542 PAGET *Let.* in *St. Papers Hen. VIII*, IX. 229 The poursuters here of these matyers..hath bene Deformes and thAdmiralles Secretarye. **1556** *Aurelio & Isab.* (1608) Bj, Love doth not equally love all his pursuiters.

pursuivant ('pɜːswɪvənt), *sb.* (*a.*) Forms: 4–5 purs(eu)aunt, 5–8 purseu-, -sevant, (5 -syaunt, 5–6 -cyvaunt, 6 -ceu-, -ceva(u)nt, -civant, -suiaunt, -siuant, -syvant, 6–7 -suyvant, 6–8 -sueuant, -vant, 7 -suvant, -sivant); 6– pursuivant, (7–8 pour-). Also *Sc.* 5 pursevand, -sewand, -ant, -sephant, -siwant, -syfant, -cyfant, 5–6 persevand. [ME. a. OF. *por-, pur-, poursivant*, etc., mod.F. *poursuivant*, pr. pple. of *porsivre, poursuivre* 'to pursue, follow after', also used subst., = follower, suitor, pursuivant-at-arms, etc.]

1. Formerly, A junior heraldic officer attendant on the heralds; also one attached to a particular nobleman. Now, an officer of the College of Arms, ranking below a Herald.

In the English College of Arms there are three Kings of Arms, six Heralds, and four Pursuivants, styled respectively: Rouge Croix, Bluemantle, Rouge Dragon, and Portcullis; in the court of the Lyon King of Arms in Scotland there are three Heralds, and three (down to 1867, six) Pursuivants: Carrick, Unicorn, and March (formerly Bute), formerly also Dingwall, Ormond, and Kintyre; in the court of the Ulster King of Arms in Ireland there are two Heralds and four Pursuivants: Athlone, and St. Patrick nos. 1, 2, and 3.

c **1384** CHAUCER *H. Fame* 1321 Pursevantes and herauldes That crien ryche folkes laudes. *c* **1440** *Promp. Parv.* 416/2 Purcyvawnte (*K.* purciwant). **1456** SIR G. HAYE *Law of Arms* (S.T.S.) 278 [He] has first tane sik a beste..to bere in his schelde..or in blasoun apon his heraulde or persevandis brest. *c* **1480** HENRYSON *Mor. Fab.* vi. *Father Wer* 49 Ane Unicorne..ane bill in breist he bure, Ane Pursephant semelie, I ȝow assure. **1556** *Chron. Gr. Friars* (Camden) 64 It was proclamyd opynly with the kynges shreffe and two harraldes and two pursevanttes and a trumpet. **1572–3** *Reg. Privy Council Scot.* II. 190 Johnne Calder, Bute Pursevant. **1583** *Rot. Scacc. Reg. Scot.* XXI. 560, I Robert Campbell, Carrik pursuevant..charged Maister Patrik Vaus..to content and pay. **1607** DEKKER & WEBSTER *Sir T. Wyatt* D.'s Wks. 1873 III. 85 Send for Heralds, call me Purseuants, Wher's the King at armes? **1766** ENTICK *London* IV. 27 The four pursuivants..are also created by the earl-marshal. **1866** *Chamb. Encycl.* VIII. 24/2 In ancient times, any great nobleman might institute his own pursuivant with his own hands and by his single authority. The Dukes of Norfolk had a pursuivant, called *Blanch-lyon*, from the white lion in their arms. **1902** *Westm. Gaz.* 24 May 10/1 He held the office of his Majesty's Unicorn Pursuivant for Scotland.

b. Also ***pursuivant at (of) arms.***

1532–3 *Act 24 Hen. VIII*, c. 13 Any henche man, heralde, or purcevant at armes. **1658** PHILLIPS s.v., The four Pursuivants at Arms are those that attend the Heralds, and are called Bluemantle, Rougecrosse, Rougedragon, and Percullis. **1805** SCOTT *Last Minstr.* IV. xxxii, The pursuivant-at-arms..Before the castle took his stand. **1806** A. DUNCAN *Nelson's Fun.* 19 Two Pursuivants at Arms, properly attired.

†**2.** A royal or state messenger with power to execute warrants; a warrant-officer. *Obs.*

In Scotland, the heraldic pursuivants usually served summonses of treason, thus connecting senses 1 and 2.

1503 *Priv. Purse Exp. Eliz. of York* (1830) 87 A purcevaunt belonging to my lord the Kinges Chambrelain. **1535** COVERDALE *Jer.* li. 31 One purseuaunt shal mete another, yee one poste shal come by another, to bringe the kinge of Babilon tydinges. **1569** *Nottingham Rec.* IV. 132 A pursyuant that brought the proclamasyon. **1600** HOLLAND *Livy* xxv. xli. 581 There was a speedie pursuivant or courrier sent throughout the battailons. **1603** OWEN *Pembrokeshire* vi. (1892) 50 These were sent for by lettres by a purcephant to make their repaire to the Counsell of the marches. **1628** tr. *Camden's Hist. Eliz.* IV. (1688) 526 Men, taking upon them the Authority and Badges of the Queen's Pursivants, rambled up and down all over England with counterfeit Warrants. **1641** MILTON *Reform.* II. Wks. 1851 III. 67 To let them still hale us, and worrey us with their band-dogs, and Pursivants. **1648** GAGE *West Ind.* 206, One of the State-Officers, a Pursevant. **1823** SCOTT *Peveril* vi, If he falls in with the pursuivant fellow who carries the warrant of the Privy Council.

†**b.** *transf.* and *fig.* = 'messenger'. *Obs.*

c **1530** tr. *Erasm. Serm. Child Jesus* (1901) 10 That great purseuaunt, Johan Baptist. *a* **1586** SIDNEY *Arcadia* I. x. 301 Her feet be Purseuants from Cupid sent, With whose fine steps all loues and ioyes conspire. **1631** DEKKER *Match Mee* v. Wks. 1873 IV. 212 Vnlesse he sent his Purseueant death for her.

3. A follower; an attendant. Also *fig.*

1513 DOUGLAS *Æneis* IX. x. 133 Ane Butes..That pursevant tofor and squyer had be To Troiane Anchyses, fader of Enee. **1845** LONGF. *To a Child* xiii, Fear, the pursuivant of Hope. **1854** CDL. WISEMAN *Fabiola* II. vi. 167 Proposed to be captain of a body of armed pursuivants picked out for their savageness and hatred of Christians. **1863** LONGF. *Wayside Inn* I. *Falcon of Ser Federigo* 130 The sole pursuivant of this poor knight. **1885–94** R. BRIDGES *Eros & Psyche* Oct. 17 But sleep, the gracious pursuivant of toil, Came swiftly down.

†**4.** A suitor (for a lady's hand). *Obs. rare.*

1523 SKELTON *Garl. Laurel*, Then to this lady and soverayne of this palace, Of pursevantis ther presid in with many a diverse tale.

†**B.** *adj.* Pursuing, prosecuting. *Obs. rare.*

a **1577** SIR T. SMITH *Commw. Eng.* (1609) 92 The party pursuiuant giueth good ensignes.

†**'pursuivant**, *v. Obs.* Forms: see prec. [f. prec.] *trans.* To send a pursuivant after; to pursue; to summon or arrest by a pursuivant. Also *fig.* Hence **'pursuivanting** *vbl. sb.*

1636 PRYNNE *Unbish. Tim.* Ded. (1661) 17 The late suspending,..pursevanting, vexing,..crushing of many learned..Ministers. **1639** FULLER *Holy War* IV. xxviii. 218 Their navie was pursuivanted after with a horrible tempest. *a* **1662** HEYLIN *Laud* (1668) 197 Divers of them had been pursevanted for Printing of orthodox Books. **1687** R. L'ESTRANGE *Brief Hist. Times* I. 84 Pursuivanting, Messengering, Sergeanting, Cooping-up, Squeezing, Rifling, Plundering, and Oppressing. **1716** M. DAVIES *Athen. Brit.* II. 199 He was pursevanted up to London.. and was committed Prisoner to the Fleet.

pursy ('pɜːsɪ), *a.*[1] Also 5 purcy, 6 poursye, porzy, 6–8 pursie, 7 purcie, 7–9 pursey. [Later form of *pursif* PURSIVE, with the ending *-if* reduced to *-i*, *-y* as in *hasty, jolly, tardy*, etc.]

1. Short-winded, asthmatic, puffy; = PURSIVE.

c **1440** *Promp. Parv.* 416/2 Purcy, in wynd drawynge, *cardiacus*. **1523** FITZHERB. *Husb.* §84 Pursy is a dysease in an horses bodye, and maketh hym to blowe shorte, and appereth at his nosethrilles, and commeth of colde. **1528** PAYNEL *Salerne's Regim.* D ij, We ought to take good hede.. that we make not our selfe poursye. **1573–80** BARET *Alv.* P 885 A pursie man, or that fetcheth his breath often, as it were almost windlesse. **1621** QUARLES *Argalus & P.* (1678) 89 Thy pamper'd Steeds are pursie, drive away. **1712** tr. *Pomet's Hist. Drugs* I. 51 Good Medicine to cure..short-winded or pursy Horses.

2. Fat, corpulent.

[Due to the close association of short-windedness with fatness, and of this with the notion of a swollen purse or bag, as in PURSY *a.*[2]]

1576 NEWTON *Lemnie's Complex.* (1633) 133 They that bee by nature very porzy and grosse, live as long as they that be slender bodied. **1607** WALKINGTON *Opt. Glass* i. (1664) 9 [He] was grown so pursie, that his fatness would not suffer him to fetch his breath. **1774** GOLDSM. *Nat. Hist.* xx. (1776) 76 The neck, thick and pursy, is joined to the head. **1820** W. IRVING *Sketch Bk., Christm. Day* §20 A short pursy man, stooping and labouring at a bass-viol, so as to show nothing but the top of a round bald head, like the egg of an ostrich. **1862** CARLYLE *Fredk. Gt.* XIV. i. (1865) V. 145 An elderly fat gentleman, pursy, scant of breath.

fig. **1602** SHAKS. *Ham.* III. iv. 153 In the fatnesse of this pursie times, Vertue it selfe, of Vice must pardon begge. **1654** TRAPP *Comm. Neh.* i. 9 (1657) II. 45 Our short legges and pursie hearts cannot hold out here.

pursy ('pɜːsɪ), *a.*[2] [f. PURSE *sb.* + -Y.]

1. a. Of cloth, the skin, etc.: Having puckers, puckered; drawn together like a purse-mouth.

1552 *Act 5 & 6 Edw. VI*, c. 6 §27 If..Cloth..prove either pursie, baudy, squally by Warp or Woof. **1613** J. MAY *Declar. Est. Clothing* v. 27 The mill leaues them shame-full in cockelles, baudes, pursey, narrower in some places than in other. **1835** WILLIS *Pencillings* II. xxi. 234 His heavy, oily black eyes twinkled in their pursy recesses. **1882** *Mrs. Raven's Tempt.* I. 4 Her pursy mouth softened.

b. Of clouds, ? Bagging, swollen; heavy.

1650 H. VAUGHAN *Silex Scint.*, *Dawning* 21 The pursie Clouds disband, and scatter, All expect some sudden matter.

2. Having a full purse; rich, wealthy; purse-proud.

1602 MANNINGHAM *Diary* (Camden) 48 One said, yong Mr. Leake was verry rich, and fatt, 'True', said B. Reid, 'pursy men are fatt for the most part'. **1839** *Times* 21 Sept., Their pursy pride has been signally humbled. **1856** EMERSON *Eng. Traits*, ix. *Cockayne* Wks. (Bohn) II. 64 The pursy man means by freedom the right to do as he pleases. **1905** *Daily Chron.* 29 Apr. 4/4 He is the precise antithesis of the conventional 'moneyed man'. A less 'pursey' man it would be impossible to imagine.

†**pur'taunte.** *Cards. Obs. rare.* Also **paire taunt.** [app. f. PAIR *sb.*[1] + F. *tant* so much, as much; i.e. scoring as much again as *pair-royal*. For reduction of *pair* to *pur-* cf. *peroyal* = PAIR-ROYAL.] In cribbage, Double pair-royal; four cards of the same denomination.

1688 R. HOLME *Armoury* III. xvi. (Roxb.) 72/1 Cribbidge. .. The Value of the cards is thus;..a paire Royall is 6, a double paire Royall or a purtaunte is 12. *Ibid.* 72/2 Noddy, and Cribbidge-Noddy... Each person has 3 cards and one turned up... They are thus markett,..a paire 4, paire Riall 12, a paire Taunt 24.

purte, obs. f. PURITY; obs. Sc. f. POVERTY.

purtenance ('pɜːtɪnəns). *arch.* Also 4 purteyn-, 4–6 purten-, purtynaunce, -ans, 5 pourtynans, 5–7 purtin-, portin-, portenaunce, -ance, -anse, 7 purt'nance (purtenants). [ME. a. AF. **purtinaunce*, with change of prefix, for OF. *parten-, pertinence* (cf. *purtinaunt*, 1278, in PERTINENT *a.* 1); thus an earlier form of PERTINENCE, corresp. in vocalization to APPURTENANCE, of which in later times it may have been taken as an aphetic form.] That which pertains or appertains, or forms an appendage, to that which is the principal thing; an APPURTENANCE.

†**1. a.** *Law.* That which pertains or is an appendage to a possession or estate. *Obs.*

c **1330** R. BRUNNE *Chron.* (1810) 251, I Jon Baliol þe Scottis King, I bicom þi man for Scotland þing, With alle þe purtenance þertille. **1432** *Rolls of Parlt.* IV. 396/2 The Maner of Helston, with the Bourgh of the same, with the purtenauncz. **1495** *Act 11 Hen. VII*, c. 62 §1 The Maner or Lordshippe of Huntingfield with the purtenauncis in the Countie of Kent. **1525** LD. BERNERS *Froiss.* II. cxcviii. (R.), That the duke of Lancastre shulde haue for euer..all the countrey of Acquitayne, with the purtenaunces.

†**b.** *fig.* and *gen.* = APPURTENANCE 2. *Obs.*

1362 LANGL. *P. Pl.* A. II. 71 To habben and to holden.. Wiþ þe purtinaunce of purgatorie in-to þe pyne of helle. *c* **1380** WYCLIF *Sel. Wks.* III. 128 Þo soule with his purtenaunses is better þen þo body. *c* **1449** PECOCK *Repr.* II. xiii. 226 The tabernacle, the temple, alle the vessellis and purtenauncis ther to weren clepid holi.

2. The 'inwards' of an animal; = PLUCK *sb.*[1] 6.

c **1440** *Promp. Parv.* 410/1 Portenaunce, of a thynge, *pertinencia, in plurali excidie*. **1530** PALSGR. 257/1 Portenaunce of a beest, *fressevre*. **1532–3** *Act 24 Hen. VIII*, c. 3 The heades, neckes, inwardes, purtynaunces, legges, nor feete, shall be counted no parte of the carcases. **1539** BIBLE (Great) *Exod.* xii. 8 Se that ye eate..therof..rost wt fire: the head, fete, & purtenance therof. [So **1611**; 1885 (R.V.) the inwards.] **1592** LYLY *Midas* I. ii, I will only handle the head and purtenance. **1662** J. WILSON *Cheats* v. i, To dream..Of a Calves head, and Purtenants [betokens] a Foreman, and his Fellows! **1760** STERNE *Tr. Shandy* III. xi, May he be damn'd in..his heart and purtenance, down to the very stomach! **1868** BROWNING *Ring & Bk.* v. 71 How she can dress and dish up—lordly dish Fit for a duke, lamb's head and purtenance.

purtract, -trai(c)t, -trayt, -e, obs. ff. PORTRAIT.

purtraie, -tray, -treie, -trey, -e, obs. ff. PORTRAY *v.*

purtraiture, -trato(w)re, -tra(y)ture, -tre(a)ture, etc., obs. ff. PORTRAITURE.

purtred, -tured, pa. pples. of PORTURE *v. Obs.*

purty ('pɜːtɪ), *a.* and *adv.*, repr. Irish and U.S. local pronunc. of PRETTY *a.* and PRETTY *adv.* Also (before a nasal consonant) **purt', purt** (*U.S.*).

1829 G. GRIFFIN *Collegians* II. xxiii. 177 Dhrinking away! Wisha, long life to you says I, if that's the way; a purty fruit the tree bears in you, says I. **1844** 'J. SLICK' *High Life in N.Y.* I. i. 1 Purty much alone. **1860** C. M. YONGE *Hopes & Fears* viii. 312 To be shure, an' it's not such a purty young lady as yourself that need be taking the trouble. **1898** J. D. BRAYSHAW *Slum Silhouettes* 50, I can hear you purty well. *a***1911** [see HON[3]]. **1922** JOYCE *Ulysses* 165 Three Purty Maids from School. **1926** J. BLACK *You can't Win* (1927) vi. 67 I'd take fifty cents of it purty pronto. **1938** R. E. BASS in B. A. Botkin *Treas. S. Folklore* (1949) III. i. 461 Them things was purt' nigh as handy as the eggs from them hens. **1946** *Amer. Speech* XXI. 98 *Purt nigh*, nearly. **1977** *Time Out* 28 Jan.–3 Feb. 17/3 Lawdy lawdy Miss Linda Lewis sings real purty. **1977** *Time* 17 Oct. 54/1 The frog-voiced, razor-witted Daumier of Dogpatch for purt' near 44 years casually told an assistant: 'You can stop cutting the paper. I'm not going to draw any more.'

purtye, obs. Sc. f. POVERTY.

purulage ('pjʊər(j)ʊlɪdʒ). *rare.* [From next, with change of suffix: see -AGE.] Applied to the contents of a liver abscess, in which there are other elements than purulent matter.

1898 P. MANSON *Trop. Diseases* xxiii. 363 Liver purulage has always a peculiar mawkish odour.

purulence ('pjʊər(j)ʊləns). [ad. post-cl. L. *pūrulentia*, f. *pūrulent-us* PURULENT: see -ENCE. So in Fr.] **a.** The fact of being purulent; the formation of pus; suppuration, festering. **b.** Purulent matter, pus.

1597 A. M. tr. *Guillemeau's Fr. Chirurg.* 4 b/1 The purulence, or matter, is not engendred the first daye. **1599** —— tr. *Gabelhouer's Bk. Physicke* 346/2 If the wounde will yeelde no purulence. **1755** JOHNSON *Dict.*, *Purulence, Purulency*, generation of pus or matter.

purulency ('pjʊər(j)ʊlənsɪ). [f. as prec.: see -ENCY.] The quality or state of being purulent.

1597 LOWE *Chirurg.* (1634) 175 If with these ulcers there be purulency and rottenness. **1661** LOVELL *Hist. Anim. & Min.* 115 The gall dropped into the eare with Womans milk, helps the purulencie thereof. **1732** ARBUTHNOT *Rules of Diet* iv. in *Aliments*, etc. (R.), Consumptions are induced by purulency in any of the other viscera. **1897** *Allbutt's Syst. Med.* II. 773 The nearest approach to purulency.

purulent ('pjʊər(j)ʊlənt), *a.* [ad. L. *pūrulent-us*, f. *pūs, pūr-* PUS: see -LENT. So in Fr.]

1. Consisting of, of the nature of, or resembling pus, or corrupt matter; also *gen.* corrupt, putrid (*rare*).

1597 A. M. tr. *Guillemeau's Fr. Chirurg.* 3/2 The purulent matter was suncke to the grownde off the wounde. **1684** T. BURNET *Th. Earth* II. 88 Streams and rivulets of sulphureous liquors, and purulent melted matter. **1713** SWIFT *Salamander* 53 Wks. 1755 III. II. 77 It spews a filthy froth Of matter purulent and white. **1815** KIRBY & SP. *Entomol.* xii. (1818) I. 387 Some of the Œstri regale themselves on a purulent secretion with which they are surrounded. **1880** W. MACCORMAC *Antisept. Surg.* 226 During the whole time was no purulent discharge.

b. *fig.*

1611 SPEED *Hist. Gt. Brit.* IX. xvi. 77 Lord Fauconbridge is sent to sound their affections, and to draw the purulent matter to an head. **1727** POPE, etc. *Art of Sinking* 75 A discharge of the peccant humour in exceeding purulent metre. **1836** *Fraser's Mag.* XIV. 506 Deal forth assertions purulent of slander.

2. Full of, forming, or discharging pus; suppurating, festering.

1615 CROOKE *Body of Man* 387 If any small braunch of these vesselles be broken the Lungs become purulent and yeeld matter vp in coughing. **1688** SOUTH *Serm.* Matt. xxii. 12 (1729) II. viii. 297 To probe and search a purulent old sore to the bottom. **1813** J. THOMSON *Lect. Inflam.* 443 The treatment of simple, purulent, or healthy ulcers.

b. Characterized by or accompanied with the formation of pus.

1834 J. FORBES *Laennec's Dis. Chest* (ed. 4) 185 Purulent infiltration. **1879** HARLAN *Eyesight* v. 56 Purulent ophthalmia is one of the most dangerous diseases to which the eye is subject.

Hence '**purulently** *adv.*, in a purulent manner; '**purulentness**, purulency.

1727 BAILEY vol. II, *Purulentness*, fulness of Matter or Corruption. *a***1834** COLERIDGE *Notes & Lect.* (1849) I. 137 He shall be allowed to abuse as much and as purulently as he likes. **1897** *Allbutt's Syst. Med.* III. 425 Surrounding the purulently infiltrated part.

purulo- ('pjʊər(j)ʊləʊ), combining form from assumed stem of L. *pūrul-entus* PURULENT.

1876 tr. *Wagner's Gen. Pathol.* (ed. 6) 285 The..purulent or purulo-fibrinous exudation. **1897** *Allbutt's Syst. Med.* II. 421 We recognise two forms of dysentery—the purulo-gangrenous and the fibrinous or pseudo-diphtheritic.

puruloid ('pjʊər(j)ʊlɔɪd), *a. Path.* [irreg. f. as prec. + -OID.] Resembling or having the appearance of purulent matter; pyoid.

1866 A. FLINT *Princ. Med.* (1880) 201 Presenting a purulent or puruloid appearance. **1880** BARWELL *Aneurism* 99 'Cribriform cavities' containing..puruloid matter.

Purum ('pʊrʊm). *Anthrop.* Pl. **Purum, Purums.** The name of a tribe of Mongoloid peoples living near the Indo-Burmese border, whose kinship system is characterized by matrilateral cross-cousin marriage; also *attrib.* or as *adj.*

1912 J. SHAKESPEAR *Lushei Kuki Clans* II. iii. 150 It is said that 'Pu rum' means 'hide from tiger', which connects them closely with the Lamgang legend. *Ibid.* 153 Among the.. Purum and Lamgang marriages must be made within the clan, but not within the family. **1945** T. DAS *Purums* 2 Terms of address used by male and female members of one sib in respect of the members of the remaining sibs also helped to form a correct idea about the ancient laws of Purum marriage. **1958** R. NEEDHAM in *Amer. Anthropologist* LX. 83 He also worked these out from Purum statements about who ought to marry whom. **1967** R. FOX *Kinship & Marriage* viii. 217 The picture of the Murngin then is of a 'Purum' type community with clans but with lineages as the operating units marrying asymmetrically. **1971** W. WILDER in R. Needham *Rethinking Kinship & Marriage* ix. 214 Some recent discussions..are about as far removed from Purum facts as it is possible to get and still call the material 'Purum'.

†**purvey** ('pɜːveɪ), *sb.* Also 6 **pervaie.** [f. next.]

1. The provision of a statute; = PURVIEW 1.

1553 *Act 1 Mary* Sess. II. c. 7 §1 Proclamations should have been made, according to the Purvey of the same Estatute. **1565** *Act 8 Eliz.* c. 8 §1 Promoters..have..taken away by Virtue and Purvey of the said Estatute from divers poor Men..their Horse.

2. An arrangement, provision. *rare*$^{-1}$.

*a***1535** MORE *How Sergeaunt wolde lerne*, etc. 70 in Hazl. *E.P.P.* III. 122 He made a good peruaie For euery whit by his owne wit, And tooke another waie.

3. The act of providing or supplying; that which is provided or supplied; *pl.* provisions.

1615 CHAPMAN *Odyss.* XVII. 216 Those that used to furnish that purvey. **1678** BUTLER *Hud.* III. III. 771 And when y' are furnish'd with all Purveys, I shall be ready, at your service.

4. A sum provided to meet current expenses: for specific use see quot. 1908. *local.*

1742 *Addingham* (Cumberld.) *Par. Bk.*, Collected by the Church Wardens..two Purveys thro the whole Parish 2[l] 7[s] 0[d]. **1794** W. HUTCHINSON *Hist. Cumberld.* I. 224 The rate assessed by purvey, about 30l. a year. **1838** *Addingham* (Cumberld.) *Par. Bk.*, 5 purvays Colected. **1839** *Ibid.*, 8 purvas Colected. **1908** C. C. HODGSON *Private Let.* 5 Nov., In this county [Cumberland], and it may be in others, the county rate used to be levied by 'purveys'. A Purvey was a sum of £100 and according as £100, £200 or £300 was required the Qr. Sessions ordered one, two, or three purveys to be levied. A certain sum was fixed against each Parish as its contribution to the purvey... This system was found in time to operate unfairly, and in 1810 a special Act of Parliament was obtained abolishing Purveys.

purvey (pə'veɪ), *v.* Forms: α. 3–4 **porvai(en, -vay(e;** 3–5 **-vei(en, -vey(e; purvei(en, -vey(en,** 3–6 **-vai(en,** 4–6 **-vaye,** 4–7 **-vei(e, -veye, -vay,** (4–5 *Sc.* **-way, -wey**), 5– **purvey,** (6–7 **-veigh, -veyghe;** 4–6 **pourveie, -vey(e;** 6 **poorvey**). (*Pa.t.* and *pple.* **purveyed:** in 5 *Sc.* **purvat, -vait, -voit, -ved, -vyde, -vyid.**) β. 4 **provei,** (*pa. pple.* **proveyd, -vyde**), 6 *Sc.* **provay,** *pa. pple.* **-uuait, -wyd.** γ. 4–5 **pervei(e, -vey(e.** (In all forms before 1620, *u* was commonly written for *v.*) [ME. a. AF. *por-, purveier, purveeir* = OF. *porveeir, -veoir, -veioir* (*je porveie, porvoie*), mod.F. *pourvoir*, = Pr. *provezir*, Cat. *provehir*, Sp. *proveer*, It. *provvidere*:—L. *prōvidēre* to PROVIDE, f. *pro-* for + *vidēre* to see. The forms in *pro-, per-*, were assimilated to the L. prepositions. In ME. often stressed '*purvey*.]

I. †**1.** *trans.* To foresee; = PROVIDE *v.* 1. *Obs.*

*a***1340** HAMPOLE *Psalter*, *Song Moses* 42 God gif thai.. puruayd thaire laste, that thai myght dye sikyrly. *c***1374** CHAUCER *Boeth.* v. pr. iii. 120 (Camb. MS.) It by-houeth nedes þat thinges þat ben to comyn ben yporueyid. *c***1374** —— *Troylus* IV. 1038 (1066) Þat god purueieth thynge þat is to come. **14..** *Voc.* in Wr.-Wülcker 605/36 *Provideo*, to purveye, or to see byfore.

†**b.** To see before or in front of one; to have in view. *Obs. rare*$^{-1}$.

*a***1340** HAMPOLE *Psalter* xv. 8, I poruayd god ay in my sight..i puruaid him ay in my syght.

II. †**2.** To see to, attend to (something) in advance; to order, arrange beforehand; to foreordain; to bring (something) about by previous planning; = PROVIDE *v.* 3. *Obs.*

[**1292** BRITTON I. v. §2 Qe il eynt tens de purveer lour respounse.] *a***1300** *Cursor M.* 8311 (Cott.) Þis wark..þou sal it puruai [*other texts*, deuise, ordaine] in þi thoght, Thoru salamon it sal be wroght. *c***1375** *Sc. Leg. Saints* xxvi. (*Nycholas*) 977 He gert purway..A mangery with glad chere. **1485** CAXTON *Paris & V.* 40, I shal pourueye somme Iewels and money for our necessyte. **1513** DOUGLAS *Æneis* x. ii. 54 To mak reddy for weyr, Purvay thar schippis, provyde armour and geyr. **1521** *Irish Act 13 Hen. VIII* in Bolton *Stat. Irel.* (1621) 73 According unto the statutes in that behalfe purveyed. *a***1548** HALL *Chron.*, *Hen. VI* 131 b, What vitale was purueyed for this greate enterprise.

†**b.** *absol.* or *intr. Obs.*

1387 TREVISA *Higden* (Rolls) VII. 115 After þis God schal purveie [L. *providebit Deus*]. **1470–85** MALORY *Arthur* I. xi. 51 To horsbak wente all the hoost, as Arthur had afore purueyed.

†**3.** *intr.* To take measures, arrange, or prepare beforehand. Const. *inf.* or *that.* Cf. PROVIDE *v.* 4.

*c***1330** R. BRUNNE *Chron.* (1810) 74 Þe Norreis [Northern people] purueied, to do him a despite. *c***1440** *Gesta Rom.* i. 2 (Harl. MS.) How þat his wif was a strompet, and which purveith in þat day that hire husbond shuld be ded. **1523** LD. BERNERS *Froiss.* I. vi. 5 Than the quene secretly dyd puruey to go in to Fraunce. *a***1533** —— *Gold. Bk. M. Aurel.* (1546) K v b, The good emperour pouruelyed, that all they of his palais shoulde depart. **1604** DRAYTON *Owle* 1187 In mercy, let thy mightinesse purvay, To ransome from this eminent Decay. **1612** —— *Poly-olb.* iii. 213 So nature hath puruai'd, that during all her raigne The Bathes their natiue power for euer shall retaine.

†**4.** *intr.* To make provision or adequate preparation for some event or action, or for the supply of something needed. Const. *for, of* (*against, to*). Cf. PROVIDE *v.* 2. *Obs.*

*c***1400** *Destr. Troy* 11700 Full prestly þe prest hase puruayet þerfore. *c***1430** *Syr Gener.* (Roxb.) 6788 But the maryner vp yede To purvey of that thei had nede. **1475** *Bk. Noblesse* (Roxb.) 75 That it may be purveied for by so dew meens that [etc.]. **1490** CAXTON *Eneydos* xxi. 77 Yf I had well thoughte to haue fallen in [this] inconuenyent..I wolde haue purueied therto. **1502** ARNOLDE *Chron.* (1811) 291 The Chaunceler..entendyng to puruey there ayenst. **1573–80** BARET *Alv.* P 889 To Purueigh for things necessarie. **1658** *Whole Duty Man* Pref. 3 'Tis forward to purvey for pleasures and delights for us.

III. 5. *trans.* To provide, furnish, supply (something); = PROVIDE *v.* 5. **a.** Const. †*to* a person, etc., or with dative. *Obs.* or *arch.*

*c***1290** *S. Eng. Leg.* I. 348/97 Heo poreuide hire riȝt feolonliche A poysun, strong i-nouȝ, For-to ȝiue þis ȝongue child to slen him. **1297** R. GLOUC. (Rolls) 1739 Þis false man ..poruelede hom gode ssipes & in to þe se wende. *c***1330** *Arth. & Merl.* 5566 Ther whiles the clerk Merlin Hem hadde y-puruaid a riche in. **1382** WYCLIF *Gen.* xxii. 8 God shal puruey to hym, my sone, the sacrifice. *c***1485** *E.E. Misc.* (Warton Cl.) 42 To purway the a plas In heywyn to dweylle. **1519** *Four Elements* in Hazl. *Dodsley* I. 25 Go, purvey us a dinner..Of all manner of dishes. **1820** SCOTT *Ivanhoe* xliii, Get thy wounds healed, purvey thee a better horse.

b. (*simply.*) Now in reference to articles of food, and as the act of a purveyor: cf. sense 9 and PURVEYOR 2.

13.. *Guy Warw.* (A.) 7921 (E.E.T.S.) 448 'Frende Youn', seyd þe king, 'Wiltow fiȝt for mi þing? Oþer y schal anoþer puruay.' **1382** WYCLIF *2 Cor.* viii. 21 We purueyen goode thingis, not oonli bifore God, but also bifore alle men. *c***1420** LYDG. *Assembly of Gods* 75 Wherfore a remedy puruey in hast. **1576** FLEMING *Panopl. Epist.* 228 Being prouident in purueying victuals for her nourishment. **1638** SIR R. COTTON *Abstr. Rec. Tower* 15 The late Queene, Anno 1567. caused by Warrant of privie Seale a great quantity of Beere to be purveyed, transported and sold to her owne use beyond the seas. **1784** COWPER *Tiroc.* 619 Such is all the mental food purvey'd. **1868** E. EDWARDS *Ralegh* I. xii. 234 The provisions..had been excellently purveyed under Ralegh's contract.

6. To furnish or supply (a person, etc.) *with* (†*of*) something; = PROVIDE *v.* 8. *arch.*

1297 R. GLOUC. (Rolls) 911 Þe kyng him porueide of poer inou. **13..** *Cursor M.* 25912 (Fairf.) Ilkan agh..puruay ham wiþ al þing fare. *c***1386** CHAUCER *Wife's Prol.* 591 But for þat I was purueyed of a make I wepte but smal and that I vndertake. *c***1400** MAUNDEV. (Roxb.) xiv. 62 Þare he refreschez him and puruays him of vitailes. **1446** in Willis & Clark *Cambridge* (1886) I. 339 Vnto such tyme as he be pourveyd of a place. **1508** KENNEDIE *Flyting w. Dunbar* 465 Had thai bene prouuait [*v.r.* prowydit] sa of schote of gvne ..but perile thay had past. **1590** SPENSER *F.Q.* II. iii. 15 Give no ods to your foes, but doe purvay Your selfe of sword before that bloody day. **1687** DRYDEN *Hind & P.* III. 940 His House with all convenience was purvey'd. **1843** JAMES *Forest Days* viii, Thence he went back to London, was purveyed with a spy [etc.].

†**b.** Const. *for* (a purpose, etc.). *Obs. rare.*

*c***1380** WYCLIF *Eng. Wks.* 386 Þat þe clergy was sufficyently purveyed for lyfelode. **1470–85** MALORY *Arthur* I. iii. 38 Merlin..said Syr ye must puruey yow for the nourisshyng of your child. *Ibid.* xxviii. 75 Thenne was he [Ryons] woode oute of mesure, and purveyed hym for a grete hoost.

†**7.** To furnish (a person, etc.) with what is necessary, to equip; = PROVIDE *v.* 7. *Obs.*

*c***1375** *Sc. Leg. Saints* xxxvii. (*Vincentius*) 77 Bot god þane purvoit þo þat he ferlyt quheyne þat cumyne mycht be. *c***1450** LOVELICH *Graal* xliv. 447 We scholen hem fynden most besy, And wers I-purveyed in Eche degre Thanne here Aftyr that they scholen be. *a***1548** HALL *Chron.*, *Edw. IV* 205 b, The erle hoped, and nothyng lesse mistrusted, then to be assured and purueyed in that place.

†**8.** *refl.* (and *pass.*). To prepare or equip oneself; to take measures, get ready (*to do* something, *for* some event); = PROVIDE *v.* 7 b. *Obs.*

*a***1330** *Syr Degarre* 481 A morewe the justes was i-set, The King him purueid wel the bet. *a***1352** MINOT *Poems* III. 14 He bad his men tham purvay, Withowten lenger delay. *c***1435** *Torr. Portugal* 2264 He purveyd hym anon, To wend over the see fome. **1493** *Festivall* (W. de W. 1515) 21 b, God sent hym [Pharaoh] a fayre warnynge to purvey hym before that sholde come after.

9. *intr.* (or *absol.* of sense 5 b). To furnish or procure material necessaries or the like; to act as purveyor (see PURVEYOR 2); *esp.* to make provision *for* a person, his needs, etc.; = PROVIDE *v.* 9. From 17th c. used chiefly or only of supplying victuals, and *fig.* from this.

c **1440** *Generydes* 5421, I will purvey for you another waye. **1480** CAXTON *Higden* VIII. ii. (Rolls) VIII. 525 By lycence of kyng Edward his fader he pourveyed for his ayde and helpe. **1514** *Test. Ebor.* (Surtees) V. 56 To th' entent that every of them may provyde and purvey for hymselff wᵗin the said halff year. **1667** MILTON *P.L.* IX. 1021, I [Adam] the praise Yeild thee, so well this day thou hast purvey'd. *a* **1711** KEN *Hymnotheo* Poet. Wks. 1721 III. 121 This for his lust insatiably purveys. **1872** YEATS *Growth Comm.* 838 Dantzic reaped great advantages in purveying for the troops during the Seven Years' war. **1888** GOODE *Amer. Fishes* 44 Frequented..by ten or twelve Connecticut smacks, which purvey for the New York market.

b. Const. *to. rare.*

c **1400** *Apol. Loll.* 55 Þe court of Rome..ordeyniþ.. traytors of þis world, þat it peruey to þe temporal lif of sum man. **1483** CAXTON *G. de la Tour* C vij b, A good ensample how God purueyeth to them that haue deuocion in hym. **1796** BURKE *Let. Noble Ld.* 4 Their turpitude purveys to their malice. **1878** B. TAYLOR *Deukalion* II. iii, Lute and lay espoused In adoration that purveys to sense.

pur'veyable, *a. rare.* [f. PURVEY *v.* + -ABLE.] †**a.** Provident, foreseeing, prudent. *Obs.* **b.** Procurable, obtainable.

c **1374** CHAUCER *Boeth.* III. met. ii. 53 (Camb. MS.) How þat nature..flitteth the gouernementz of thinges and by whyche lawes she purueyable [L. *provida*] kepith the grete world. **1542** UDALL *Erasm. Apoph.* II. xi. 286 b, And so, the physician abandoned, he tooke hym to meates purveiable.

purveyal (pəˈveɪəl). *rare*⁻¹. [f. PURVEY *v.* + -AL¹.] The action of purveying or supplying; purveyance, supply.

1887 *Hour Glass* June 181 What may be called the purveyal of lecturers was a task surrounded with difficulties.

purveyance (pəˈveɪəns). Forms: 3-4 (5) por-, 3-8 pour-, 3- pur-; 3-6 -vea(u)nce, (4 -ans), 3-6 -via(u)nce, (-ans), 4-6 -vya(u)nce, (-a(u)ns); 4 -veyonce, 4-6 -veya(u)nce, 4-7 -veia(u)nce, 5-6 -voyance, 5- purveyance, (6 -veigh-, -veygha(u)nce). Also 5 perveaunce, -viance; *Sc.* perwyans, pourwiance, purweans, -wians. (Bef. *c* 1620 commonly with *u* for *v.*) [ME. a. OF. *por-, purvea(u)nce*:—L. *prōvidēntia*: see PROVIDENCE. Subsequently conformed to the vb. *purveeir, pourvoir,* PURVEY, as F. *purvei-, pourvoyance*; in Eng., with shift of stress from *purve'ance, 'purviance,* to *pur'vei-, pur'veyance.*]

†**1.** Foresight; foreknowledge of and provision for the future; = PROVIDENCE 2. *Obs.*

1297 R. GLOUC. (Rolls) 9387 Fol hardi he is inou ac al wiþoute rede, Hastif wiþoute porveance. *a* **1340** HAMPOLE *Psalter* xciii. 8 Fulis withouten puruyaunce of þe toþer warld. **1340** *Ayenb.* 83 Wyþ-oute wyt and wyþ-oute poruevonce. *c* **1374** CHAUCER *Boeth.* v. vi. 83 (Camb. MS.) For which it nis nat yclepyd preuydence, but it sholde rather ben clepyd puruyaunce [*non prævidentia sed providentia potius dicitur*] þat byhooldeth from a-fer alle thinges. **1450-80** tr. *Secreta Secret.* 17 Thou maist with thi purveaunce and forsight helpe thi sugetis. **1567** *Test. Hen. Stewart* 130 in *Scot. Sat. Poems* I. 43 Quhair Venus anis gettis in hir guernance..Wisdome is exilit and prudent puruoyance. **1581** MULCASTER *Positions* xxxvii. (1887) 166 For youth..while it rometh without purueyaunce, makes marueilous a doe before it will die.

†**2.** The action of preparing, arranging, or ordaining; preparation, pre-arrangement; ordination, direction, government, management; = PROVIDENCE 1; PROVISION *sb.* 2. *Obs.*

a **1300** *Cursor M.* 11556 (Cott.) Qua herd euer ani slik Purueance sa ful of suike. *a* **1330** *Otuel* 666, & alle winter þe king of Fraunce, Lette maken his purueianse. **1432-50** tr. *Higden* (Rolls) IV. 241 He made perviaunce for meytes and drynkes and oþer thynges. **1465** *Paston Lett.* II. 200, I pray ..that ye will make such purveyaunce therfor that it may be to myn delyveraunce. *c* **1485** *Digby Myst.* (1882) III. 577 In-to þe sete I woll a-pere ffor my gestes to make porvyawns. *a* **1550** *Freiris of Berwik* 434 in *Dunbar's Poems* (S.T.S.) II. 299 He had witt of all hir purveance to. **1586** J. HOOKER *Hist. Irel.* in *Holinshed* II. 67/2 The citizens of Dublin.. made the best purueiance they could to defend their citie. **1607** WALKINGTON *Opt. Glass* xii. (1664) 132 The sweet sleepe of the senses, The fountain of sage Advice and good Purveyance.

†**3.** In full, *purveyance of God, divine purveyance*: = PROVIDENCE 3. *Obs.*

c **1386** CHAUCER *Frankl. T.* 137 Eterne god that thurgh thy purueiaunce Ledest the world by certein gouernaunce. **1390** GOWER *Conf.* Prol. I. 23 The hyhe almyhti pourveance, In whos eterne remembrance Fro ferst was every thing present. **1497** BP. ALCOK *Mons Perfect.* D ij 2 Dispeyred on the purueaunce of almyghty god how they sholde be fedde. **1513** BRADSHAW *St. Werburge* I. 1902 This yle of Ely by deuyne purueaunce With muddy waters is compased aboute. *a* **1555** PHILPOT *Exam. & W.* (Parker Soc.) 116 He was..born into this world by the divine purveyance.

†**4.** That which is ordained; an ordinance or statute, or a clause in one: cf. PROVISION *sb.* 8. In quot. 1632 = PURVIEW 1. *Obs.*

[**1261** *Patent 46 Hen. III* m. 19 in *Rymer's Fœdera* (1816) I. 411 Diuers ordeinemens, purveaunces, e establisemens fez a Oxinford.] **1297** R. GLOUC. (Rolls) 11007 So þat atte laste hii broȝte him þer to To makie a porueance amendement to do. Imad it was at Oxenford þut lond uor to seyte. *Ibid.* 11047 þe quene was ek biȝonde se & þe kinges breþeren al so, & euere þoȝte hou hii miȝte þe purueance vndo. *a* **1300** *Cursor M.* 11551 He made a purueance in hi, þat mani saccles suld it bij. **1433** *Rolls of Parlt.* IV. 439/1 Yhe yeerly moste renne in much gretter Dette, oo lesse than other purveance wer made. **1513** *Act 5 Hen. VIII*, c. 4 §2 Every Piece so calendred against the Ordinances and Purveyances aforesaid. **1632** *Womens Rights* 391 The count had recited the whole purueyance of the act.

5. The providing or furnishing (of some necessary), *esp.* the purveying or provision of victuals.

1387 TREVISA *Higden* (Rolls) VIII. 123 Me made grete purveaunce of vitailles for hym. *c* **1450** *St. Cuthbert* (Surtees) 1737 Of vitayles þai made na purueance. **1540** MORYSINE *Vives' Introd. Wysd.* B vj b, They are greatte and longe purviaunce for a lyttell and short lyfe. *a* **1548** HALL *Chron., Hen. V* 75 b, He made greate purveighance of all thynges necessary for the coronacion of his Quene. **1600** HOLLAND *Livy* XXII. 439 For purueyance of forage and fewell. **1788** PRIESTLEY *Lect. Hist.* IV. xxxi. 233 The way of collecting the rents, both in money and purveyances of victuals, &c. **1864** BURTON *Scot Abr.* I. iii. 119 All along the coast..there was busy baking of biscuits and purveyance of provender.

6. *spec.* The requisition and collection of provisions, etc., as a right or prerogative; *esp.* the right formerly appertaining to the crown of buying whatever was needed for the royal household at a price fixed by the PURVEYOR, and of exacting the use of horses and vehicles for the king's journeys.

1439 *Rolls of Parlt.* V. 32/2 Thabuse of the said purveaunce. **1475** *Bk. Noblesse* (Roxb.) 40 He rewardid fifty thousande sak wolle for perveaunce. **1483** CAXTON *Cato* d v b, Therfore she counceylled unto the kynge..that he sholde make pourueaunce and store of it. **1601** F. TATE *Househ. Ord. Edw. II*, §47 (1876) 29 A vallet of mestier purveiour of ale, which shal make the purveiance of ale. **1612** DAVIES *Why Ireland*, etc. (1787) 189 He established the composition of the Pale, in lieu of purveyance and sess of soldiers. **1668** E. CHAMBERLAYNE *Pres. St. Eng.* (1669) 113 The King by his Prerogative hath had at all times the Right of Purveyance or Pre-emption of all sorts of Victuals neer the Court. **1765** BLACKSTONE *Comm.* I. viii. 288 By degrees the powers of purveyance have declined, in foreign countries as well as our own. **1776** ADAM SMITH *W.N.* III. ii. I. 477 Great Britain is..the only monarchy in Europe where the oppression of purveyance has been entirely abolished. **1875** STUBBS *Const. Hist.* II. xvii. (1877) 538 The prerogative of purveyance included, besides the right of preemption of victuals, the compulsory use of horses and carts and even the enforcement of personal labour.

†**7.** That which is purveyed; a supply, stock, provision (of victuals, arms, or other necessaries). Cf. PROVIDENCE 1 b. *Obs.*

a **1300** *Cursor M.* 11677 Vr water purueance es gan. *c* **1386** CHAUCER *Frankl. T.* 176 A gardyn..In which that they hadde maad hir ordinance Of vitaille and of oother purueiance. *c* **1470** HENRY *Wallace* VIII. 1004 Breid, ayll and wyn, with othir purweans. **1523** LD. BERNERS *Froiss.* I. vi. 5 In a nother ship they had put all theyr purueyaunce. **1599** NASHE *Lenten Stuffe* 6 How Yarmouth..should..supply her inhabitants with plentifull purueyance of sustenance.

†**b.** An armed force fitted out; armament; array. *Obs. rare.*

c **1330** R. BRUNNE *Chron.* (1810) 125 The ȝere next on hand ȝede þe Kyng of France To þe holy land, with his purueiance. *c* **1400** *Laud Troy Bk.* 5734 He scholde with-oute distaunce Come with alle his puruyaunce, That were lefft with-Inne the walles.

Hence **pur'veyancer** *nonce-wd.*, purveyor.

1800 COLERIDGE *Piccolom.* II. xiv, Did the Duke make any of these provisos..when he gave you the office of army purveyancer?

†**pur'veyant,** *a. Obs. rare.* [f. PURVEY *v.* + -ANT.] Foreseeing, provident.

1422 tr. *Secreta Secret., Priv. Priv.* 138 A kynge..sholde be Purveyaunt and Pensyfe of thynges that may come aftyrwarde. *Ibid.* 234 Who-so hath the voice meene betwen grete and smale, he is wise, Purueyaunt, veritable.

purveyed (-ˈveɪd), *ppl. a.* [f. PURVEY *v.* + -ED¹.]

1. *ppl. adj.* †**a.** Pre-arranged, foreordained. †**b.** Equipped, prepared. **c.** Furnished, provided.

1390 GOWER *Conf.* III. 141 Practique..techeth hou and in what wise Thurgh hih pourveied ordinance A king schal sette in governance His Realme. **1435** *Rolls of Parlt.* IV. 491/1 Wherfore, like it to your purveyed discretions, to pray [etc.]. **1470-85** MALORY *Arthur* II. ix. 86 But syr are ye purueyed, said Merlyn, for to morne the hooste of Nero.. wille sette on yow. **1523** LD. BERNERS *Froiss.* I. xxxii. 146 We be nat as nowe purueyed to gyue you a full answere.

†**2.** *pa. pple. purveyed that*, provided that: see PROVIDED II. *Obs.*

1398 in Rymer *Fœdera* (1709) VIII. 61/1 Purvait that Heritages on bathe the Syds stand in the fourme and vertue as is compris'd within the Trewes. **1447** *Rolls of Parlt.* V. 135/1 Purveied also, that noo man havyng any Graunte of.. the King..of any Castels..bee stopped or prejudiced.

purveyer, purveyeress: see PURVEYOR.

pur'veying, *vbl. sb.* [f. PURVEY *v.* + -ING¹.] The action of the verb PURVEY.

†**1.** Foreseeing, foresight; providence, prudence.

c **1374** CHAUCER *Troylus* IV. 958 (986) If ther myght ben a variaunce To wrythen out fro goddes purueynge. **1382** WYCLIF *Prov.* x. 23 Wisdam forsothe is to a man purueing [1388 Wisdom is prudence to a man].

†**2.** Preparation, arrangement, management; = PURVEYANCE 2. *Obs.*

c **1430** *Syr Gener.* (Roxb.) 8170 Than he lete make purveing..Into Ynde to take werre on hond. **1644** MILTON *Areop.* 27 That which others have tak'n so strictly, and so unalterably into their own purveying.

3. The providing or procuring of supplies; foraging; = PURVEYANCE 5, 6.

1552 HULOET, Purueyghinge of corne or grayne, *frumentatio.* **1623** COCKERAM, *Lignation*, a hewing or purueying of wood. **1804** GILLESPIE in Duncan *Nelson* (1806) 220 The attention paid..to the victualling and purveying for the fleet. **1852** MISS YONGE *Cameos* (1877) I. xxviii. 235 His own household had neither wages, clothes, nor food, except what they obtained by purveying, in their case only a licence to rob.

pur'veying, *ppl. a.* [f. as prec. + -ING².] That purveys; that manages the provisioning.

1789 B. RUSH *Med. Enq.* 70 The union of the purveying and directing departments of hospitals in the same persons.

purveyor (pəˈveɪə(r)). Forms: see below. [a. AF. *purveür, -our*, = OF. *por-, pur-, pour-, proveor, -veour, -v(e)eur, -voieor* (13th c. in Godef.), in mod.F. *pourvoyeur*, agent-n. from OF. *porveeir*, mod.F. *pourvoir*: see PURVEY *v.* and -OR. The forms in *pro-* were assimilated to L. *prōvidēre*. Orig. stressed *purve'our*, whence *'purveour, 'purvior*; later conformed to *purvey* as *pur'veyor.*]

A. Illustration of Forms.

α. ¹ 4 **purveür, -vaour,** 4-5 **pur-, pourve'our.**

a **1300** *Cursor M.* 4607 (Cott.) Do gett þe a god purueur [*F.* puruaour, *G.* purueour]. *Ibid.* [see B. 1]. **1390** Pourveour [see B. 3]. **1448** Purueour [see B. 1].

α. ² 4 **porvey'our, purveyowr, -va(y)our,** 4-7 **-veyour, -e,** 5-7 **-veiour, -e, -veior,** (7 **pourveyour, -veyor),** 6- **pur'veyor.**

1340 *Ayenb.* 100 He ys uader, he is diȝtere and gouernour and poruevour to his mayne. *c* **1375** *Cursor M.* 4337 (Fairf.) Joseph þat noble puruayour. *a* **1430** *Ibid.* 11003 (Laud) Right was that the purveyoure Shuld come by-fore the Sauyoure. **1542** UDALL *Erasm. Apoph.* 287 Pompeius beeyng declared in woordes & in title the purveiour of corne. **1572** in Feuillerat *Revels Q. Eliz.* (1908) 164 As the purveior compounded. **1585** ABP. SANDYS *Serm. on Matt. xxi.* 12 §13 God is no purueyor for theeues and robbers. **1653** HOLCROFT *Procopius* II. 64 The Pourveyor of the expence of the army. **1658** PHILLIPS, *Pourveyour*,..an Officer of the King, or other great personage.

α. ³ 4-5 **'purvyour,** 5 **-viowre,** 5-6 **-viour,** 6 **vior,** *Sc.* **-vyar.**

1399 LANGL. *Rich. Redeles* IV. 13 To paie þe pore peple þat his puruyours toke, withoute preiere at a parlement. *c* **1440** *Promp. Parv.* 417/2 Purviowre, *provisor, procurator.* *a* **1548** HALL *Chron., Hen. VI* 161 Like a spedy purvior, whiche slacketh not tyme. **1569** *Nottingham Rec.* IV. 132 Gevyn.. to the Quen of Scottes purvyar ij s.

β. 4 **purvayer,** 5-7 **-veier, -veyer,** 7 **pur-, pourvoyer.**

c **1375** *Cursor M.* 13208 (Fairf.) For-þi is he calde cristis puruayer. *c* **1449** Purueier [see B. 2]. **1579-80** NORTH *Plutarch, Marius* (1895) III. 217 Purveyer for all necessarie provision. **1600** J. PORY tr. *Leo's Africa* II. 81 They haue certaine Caters and purueiers among them. **1666** J. DAVIES *Hist. Caribby Isles* 186 The Carribbians were as it were the Pourvoyers of the French. **1683** *Apol. Prot. France* iv. 27 His Purvoyer could find no room for him in the Castle.

γ. 4-5 **provyour, -wyour, -weour, -wour, -uour, -wor, -wer.**

1377 LANGL. *P. Pl.* B. XIX. 255 My prowor & my plowman Piers shal ben on erthe [*v.rr.* proweour, pourveour, prowyour]. **1393** C. XXII. 260 prowour, prouour]. **1387** Provyour [see B. 1]. *c* **1449** PECOCK *Repr.* IV. viii. 468 Crist.. oure beest prower ordeyned al that was best for us to haue.

B. Signification.

†**1.** One who makes preparation or prearrangement; a manager, director, steward. *Obs.*

a **1300** *Cursor M.* 4337 (Cott.) Joseph, þat was god purueur [*v.rr.* -uayour, -ueour] A dai he went in to þe bour. **1387** TREVISA *Higden* (Rolls) VIII. 147 As it were to þe comoun provyour of alle [L. *communi cunctorum provisori*]. **1448** HEN. VI in Willis & Clark *Cambridge* (1886) I. 378 For .ij. purueours either of theym at .vj.d. by day.

2. One who procures or supplies anything necessary, or something specified, *to* or *for* others.

In *commercial use*; One who makes it his business to provide or supply victuals, etc., esp. one who provides luncheons, dinners, etc., on a large scale or for a large number; also in such denominations as 'Purveyor to their Majesties', or 'to the Royal Household', 'Universal Purveyor', etc.

1340 [see A. α²]. *c* **1449** PECOCK *Repr.* 468 The wijsist purueier and tendirist louer. **1570-6** LAMBARDE *Peramb. Kent* (1826) 461 This man served the parson as Purveyour of his poultrie. **1635** QUARLES *Embl.* v. vi. 14 (1718) 269, I love the sea; she is my fellow-creature, My careful purveyor: she provides me store. **1725** DE FOE *Voy. round World* (1840) 312 The Spaniard..was their guide himself, and their purveyor also. **1815** W. H. IRELAND *Scribbleomania* 127 b, Mr. Allingham has not proved himself an indolent purveyor for the dramatic corps. **1875** JOWETT *Plato* (ed. 2) III. 240 A shoe-maker, or perhaps some other purveyor to our bodily wants. **1891** *Daily News* 15 July 3/3 Mr. Morton moved to reduce the vote by 50*l.* allowance to the purveyor of luncheons.

b. An official charged with the supply of requisites or of some necessary to a garrison, army, city, or the like; †in quots. 1787-91 an officer who provided timber for the navy (*obs.*).

1475 *Bk. Noblesse* (Roxb.) 68, I fynde by hys bokes of hys purveours how yn every castelle, forteresse, and cyte or towne he wolde hafe grete providence of vitaille. **1601** HOLLAND *Pliny* I. 175 To heare of the Treasurer and purveiour generall of the armie in Armenia. **1787** G. White *Selborne* i, The oaks of Temple and Blackmoor stand high in the estimation of purveyors, and have furnished much naval timber. **1791** Gilpin *Forest Scenery* II. 22 Besides these ancient officers of the forest, there is one of later institution. .. He is called the *purveyor*, and is appointed by the commissioner of the dock at Portsmouth. His business is to assign timber for the use of the navy. **1809** Wellington *Let.* 13 Dec. in Gurwood *Desp.* V. 365 The usual allowances, which the Purveyor General of the British Army will pay. **1868** E. Edwards *Ralegh* I. xii. 232 Both Essex and Ralegh acted as purveyors of the fleet. **1883** *Fortn. Rev.* July 122 The Purveyor-in-Chief was to furnish everything required for the hospital service.

3. A domestic officer who made purveyance of necessaries, lodging, transport, and the like for the sovereign (*king's* or *queen's purveyor*), or for some other great personage. Also *transf.* one who exacts supplies or contributions. Now *Hist.*

[**1360** *Act 36 Edw. III*, c. 2 Que le heignous noun de purveour soit chaunge & nome achatour.] **1390** Gower *Conf.* II. 194 He is overal A pourveour and an aspie. **1399** [see A. a³]. **14..** *Voc.* in Wr.-Wülcker 581/17 *Exactor*, a Puruyour. *c* **1440** *Jacob's Well* 189 As a purveyour goth beforn to takyn an jn for his mayster. *a* **1592** Greene *Jas. IV.* III. ii, I must needes haue your maisters horses... I am the Kings Purueyer, and I tell thee I will haue them. **1656** Blount *Glossogr.*, *Purveyor*, an Officer of the King or other great Personage, that provides Corn and other Victual for the house of him whose Officer he is. **1821** Scott *Kenilw.* xxv, The Queen's purveyors had been abroad, sweeping the farms and villages of those articles usually exacted during a royal Progress. **1875** Stubbs *Const. Hist.* II. xvi. 415 The hated name of purveyor was [1360] to be exchanged for that of buyer.

Hence **pur'veyoress**, a female purveyor.

1611 Cotgr., *Pourvoyeuse*, a Prouideresse, or Purueyeresse.

purview ('pɜːvjuː). Forms: 5 purveu, -vewe, 5–7 -vieu, 6 -vew, 7– purview. [a. AF. *por-*, *purveu*, *purview* provided = OF. *porveu* (= OIt. *proveduto*), in mod.F. *pourvu*, pa. pple. of *porveir*: see purvey). The word was used in the AF. statutes (*a*) in the phrase *purveu est* 'it is provided', to introduce that which is provided or enacted by the statute, and (*b*) in the phrase *purveu que* 'provided that', to introduce a special proviso, condition, or saving clause; hence as sb., the clause so introduced, the provision or proviso.

(*a*) **1275** *Act 3 Edw. I*, c. 1 Purveu est que nul y vengne manger, herbiger, ne gisir en meson de religion, al cust de la meson. *Ibid.*, Et est porveu que les poinz avaundiz lient ausi bien nos Conseillers, come autre gent.

(*b*) **1377** *Act 1 Rich. II*, c. 15 Purveue toutfoitz que les dites gentz de seint eglise ne se tiegnent deinz les eglises ou sanctuaries par fraude ou collusion. **1423** *Act 2 Hen. VI*, c. 11 Purveux toutfoitz que laverrement suit receu par nostre Sr le Roy que le Capitain est en plein vie.]

1. The body of a statute, following next after the preamble, and beginning with the words 'Be it enacted'; the enacting clauses; that which is provided or enacted by a statute; hence, the provision, scope, or intention of an act or bill.

1461 *Rolls of Parlt.* V. 468/1 Noo purvewe, provision, ne other thyng in this present Parlement made, .. in any wise be hurtyng .. vnto the Abbes and Convent aforeseid. **1533–4** *Act 25 Hen. VIII* c. 17 §11 Provyded also that yf any person or persones hereafter .. doo contrary to the purvew and remedy of this Acte. *a* **1677** Hale *Com. Law* III. (1716) 51 Many Times the Purview of an Act is larger than the Preamble or the Petition: and so 'tis here: For the Body of the Act prohibits all Appeals. **1706** Phillips (ed. 6) s.v., Thus a Statute is said to stand upon a Preamble and upon a Purview. **1850** Gladstone *Glean.* V. xlv. 200 We will assume then that the Statute intended .. to include in its purview all the circumstances of the consecration of Parker.

†**b.** A provisional clause; a proviso. *Obs.*

1442 *Petit. for Ld. Scrop* in *Rolls of Parlt.* V. 41, 42 Ensuyngly uppon which endosement was added a clause of Purveu, in this fourme that foloweth. Purveu toutz foitz, qe si trove soit a present [etc.]. **1455** *Rolls of Parlt.* V. 309/1 Soo alwey that Richard erle of Salisbury .. be not in eny wise by force or colour of this purvieu or exception hurt. **1755** Johnson, *Purview*, proviso, providing clause. [With quot. from Hale, *a* 1677 above.]

2. By extension, The scope or limits of any document, statement, scheme, subject, book, or the like; the purpose or intent; also, the range, sphere, or field of a person's labour or occupation.

1788 Madison *Federalist* (Webster 1828), In determining the extent of information required in the exercise of a particular authority, recourse must be had to the objects within the purview of that authority. **1811** Knox *Corr. w. Jebb* (1834) II. 30 Christianity .. takes mankind as it is, and, in its purview, leaves out nothing. **1881** J. G. Fitch *Lect. Teach.* (ed. 3) 38 If we seek to classify the objects of instruction, so far as they lie within the purview of a schoolteacher. **1884** J. Sharman *Hist. Swearing* i. 12 Questions that have influenced the mind of the writer in considering the purview of his book.

3. Influenced by view: Range of vision, physical or mental; outlook; range of experience or thought; contemplation, consideration.

1837 Richardson *Dict.*, *Purview*, the view forward: the forecast, the contemplation. **1859** Helps *Friends in C.* Ser. II. I. viii. 247 There is a delusion, too, in this width of purview. You see the extent of horizon, but do not make out the roads. **1875** Emerson *Lett. & Soc. Aims, Inspiration* ix. 222 A glimpse, a point of view that by its brightness excludes the purview, is granted, but no panorama. **1881** *Daily Tel.* 31 Jan., How was it that none of these facts seem to have come within the purview of her Majesty's Office of Works? **1904** S. J. Weyman *Abbess of Vlaye* xxii, In a twinkling she was hidden by the turn [of the road] from the purview of the castle.

†**purvision**, obs. variant of provision, influenced by purvey.

1583 Foxe *A. & M.* 2080 Letters .. from the Pallatine of Vilna and the Kyng of Poole offering them large curtesie. This puruison [*later edd.* puruision] vnlooked for, greatly reuiued theyr heauye spirites.

‖**purwanah, parwānah** (pɜː'wɑːnə). *East Ind.* Also 7 pher-, 8–9 per-; 7–8 -wanna, 8–9 -wannah, 9 -wanah, -wunah. [a. Urdū and Pers. *parwānah*, a royal patent or diploma, warrant, commission.] A letter of authority; an order, licence, pass.

1682 Sir W. Hedges *Diary* 10 Oct. (1887) I. 34 If we did not procure a Pherwanna from the Duan of Decca to excuse us from it. **1693** in J. T. Wheeler *Madras in Old T.* (1861) I. 281 (Y.), Egmore and Pursewaukum were lately granted us by the Nabob's purwannas. **1764** *Ann. Reg.* 191 The late perwannahs .. granting .. exemption of all duties .. shall be reversed. **1800** *Misc. Tracts* in *Asiat. Ann. Reg.* 250/2 My servant returned .. with the Rajah's acknowledgment of my letter, and a purwannah or pass through his dominions, written in the ancient Hindu character. **1849** E. B. Eastwick *Dry Leaves* 218 *note*, One of these officers .. signed a parwánah for a merchant to transport goods through Sindh to Cábul free of toll.

purwinkle, -wynkle, obs. ff. periwinkle².

pury, *a. Obs.*: see putry, rotten, putrid.

pus (pʌs). *Path.* Also 8 puss. [a. L. *pūs*, stem *pūr-*, viscous matter of a sore: cf. purulent.]

a. A yellowish-white, opaque, somewhat viscid matter, produced by suppuration; it consists of a colourless fluid in which white corpuscles are suspended.

1541 R. Copland *Galyen's Terap.* 2 F ij b, Hyppocrates .. teacheth vs that pus or suppuracyon is made wt some putrefaction. **1651** N. Biggs *New Disp.* 243 The Pus is materially produced of bloud. **1725** *Bradley's Fam. Dict.* s.v. *Ulcer*, A puss or corruption which retards the consolidating of the parts. **1813** J. Thomson *Lect. Inflam.* 123 The termination by suppuration is that process in animal bodies, by which the matter of sores or pus is formed. **1866** A. Flint *Princ. Med.* (1880) 240 Pus is opaque, less viscid than mucus, .. and in water sinks to the bottom.

fig. **1831** A. Fonblanque *Eng. under Seven Admin.* (1837) II. 105 A William infuses spirit of Reform, as a George .. would have infused pus of Boroughmongery.

b. *attrib.* and *Comb.*, as ***pus-cell***, ***-corpuscle***, ***-production***, ***-serum***; ***pus-containing***, ***-forming***, ***-like***, ***-producing***, ***-yellow*** adjs.

1845 Budd *Dis. Liver* ii. 58 It would seem, that cancer-cells, like pus-globules, usually, if not always, become arrested in the liver, and do not pass through to become the germs of cancerous tumors in other organs. *Ibid.* 89. **1873** Rolfe *Phys. Chem.* 169 The pus-corpuscles are spherical irregular bodies about $\frac{1}{2500}$ to $\frac{1}{3500}$ of an inch in diameter. **1873** T. H. Green *Introd. Pathol.* (ed. 2) 247 The extent of pus-formation will depend upon the severity of the inflammatory process. **1876** *Clin. Soc. Trans.* IX. 177 Discharge less in quantity and more pus-like. **1879** *St. George's Hosp. Rep.* IX. 432 Disintegrated pus-cells. **1899** *Allbutt's Syst. Med.* VII. 279 The pus cavity extended within two centimetres of the apex of the frontal gyrus. **1922** Joyce *Ulysses* 511 Virag .. claps .. on the wall a pusyellow flybill.

pusane, pusen, pusca, variants of pisane, posca (vinegar-water).

puschkinia (pʊʃ'kɪnɪə). [mod.L. (J. M. F. Adams 1805, in *Nova Acta Acad. Petropolitanæ* XIV. 164), f. the name of Apollos Mussin-*Puschkin* (d. 1805), Russian chemist and plant collector + -ia¹.] A small spring-flowering bulbous plant of the genus so called, belonging to the family Liliaceæ, and bearing spikes of blue or white cup-shaped flowers; also called the striped squill.

1820 *Curtis's Bot. Mag.* XLVIII. 2244 (*heading*) Squill-like Puschkinia. **1914** G. Jekyll *Colour Schemes for Flower Garden* (ed. 3) 6 The colour scheme begins with the pink of *Megasea ligulata* .. and later the blue-white of *Puschkinia*. **1925** A. J. MacSelf *Bulb Gardening* xi. 197 The flowers of Puschkinia are blue and white, arranged in a short close-set spike on a stalk only a few inches long. **1959** *Times* 22 Aug. 9/4 Most of the other small bulbs—muscari, chionodoxas, puschkinias—can be grown in-doors. **1974** H. G. W. Fogg *Compl. Handbk. Bulbs* vii. 122/2 As long as they are not forced, puschkinias can be grown indoors like crocuses.

puscle, puscull, pusel, -ell(e, obs. ff. pustule, pucelle.

†**pusesoun**, erron. obs. form of poison *sb.*

a **1330** *Roland & V.* 297 And of þe smoc of þat toun, Mani takeþ þer of pusesoun, And dyeþ in michel wo.

Puseyism ('pjuːzɪɪz(ə)m). [f. the name of Dr. E. B. Pusey, 1800–82, professor of Hebrew and Canon of Christ Church at Oxford + -ism.] A name given by opponents to the theological and ecclesiastical principles and doctrines of Dr. Pusey and those with whom he was associated in the 'Oxford Movement' for the revival of Catholic doctrine and observance in the Church of England which began about 1833; more formally and courteously called Tractarianism. Now little used.

Dr. Pusey's initials were appended to No. 18 (21 Dec. 1833, on Fasting) of the *Tracts for the Times*, and, of the ninety, seven were written by him. His academic and ecclesiastical position gave great weight to his support of the movement, and specially associated his name with it.

1838 Sterling in *Ess. & T.* I. (1848) cvii, Calvert .. an Oriel man, a contemporary and friend of Froude's, but quite opposed to Puseyism. **1840** Mrs. Car. Wilson *Listener in Oxford* vi. 171 The acquiescence .. in even the external peculiarities of Puseyism. **1843** Carlyle *Past & Pr.* II. xv. (1891) 101 O Heavens, what shall we say of Puseyism, in comparison to Twelfth-Century Catholicism? **1871** R. H. Hutton *Ess.* I. 424 Puseyism is very far from being at one in principle with Romanism. It is only a conservative movement towards ancient doctrine—while Romanism has a principle, a life, an idea of its own. **1893** Liddon, etc. *Life Pusey* II. 139 It was apparently during the year 1840 that the use of the word 'Puseyism' became widely popular.

So **'Puseyist** = Puseyite; also **Pusey'istic, Pusey'istical** *adjs.*, of or pertaining to the Puseyites or Puseyism. (All hostile terms.)

1849 *Eclectic Rev.* Jan. XXV. 27 Alloyed with .. general Puseyistical religious leaven. **1850** Mrs. Browning *Lett.* 13 Nov., Robert says it is as well to have the eyeteeth and the Puseyistical crisis over together. **1864** Webster, *Puseyistic*. **1870** Spurgeon *Treas. Dav.* Ps. xxxi. 6 More than Romanists and Puseyists deserve.

Puseyite ('pjuːzɪaɪt). [f. as prec. + -ite.]

a. A follower of Pusey; a supporter or promoter of the Oxford or Tractarian Movement: see prec.

1838 Whately in *Life* (1875) 163 Oxford .. has at present two-thirds of the steady reading men, Rabbinists, i.e. Puseyites. **1839** Ld. Blachford *Let.* 21 Jan., I heard the words 'Newmanite' and 'Puseyite' (a new and sonorous compound) from two passers-by. **1850** Disraeli *Let.* 16 Nov. in *Corr. w. Sister* (1886) 250 Riding the high Protestant horse, and making the poor devils of Puseyites the scape-goats.

b. *attrib.* or as *adj.*

1839 J. B. White *Let.* Aug. in *Life* (1845) III. x. 131 That association, called the *Puseyite* party, from which we have those very strange productions entitled *Tracts for the Times*. **1843** J. S. Mill *Let.* 23 Oct. in *Wks.* (1963) XIII. 603 The Puseyite review the British Critic .. almost exhausts language in admiration of me & my book. *a* **1847** J. B. White in Newman *Apol.* ii. (1904) 30/1 The most active and influential member of that association called the Puseyite party. **1851** Dickens *Househ. Wds.* Xmas No. 5 A spruce young Puseyite Curate.

Hence **Pusey'itical** *a.* = puseyistical.

1844 E. FitzGerald *Lett.* (1889) I. 139, I have exercised the children's minds greatly on the doctrine of Puseyitical reticence. **1845** *Bachelor Albany* (1848) 5 A man of much learning, eccentric habits, and Puseyitical opinions.

push (pʊʃ), *sb.*¹ Also 6 pussh(e, 6–7 pushe, 8 *Sc.* pouse. [f. push *v.*: cf. F. *pousse* (15th c.).]

I. 1. a. An act of pushing; a continued application of force or pressure to move a body away from the agent; a shove, thrust. In early quotations, A blow, stroke, knock (*obs.*).

1582 Stanyhurst *Æneis* II. (Arb.) 59 Pyrrhus with fast wroght twibbil in handling Downe beats with pealing thee doors... A broad gap yawning with theese great pusshes is opned. **1613** Purchas *Pilgrimage* II. x. (1614) 156 Here might you see the strong walls shaking and falling, with the pushes of the yron ramme. **1692** Dryden *Cleomenes* I. i, When his spacious hand Had rounded this huge ball of Earth and Seas To give it the first push, and see it roll Along the vast abyss. **1711** Addison *Spect.* No. 57 ¶3 She gives him a Push with her Hand in jest, and calls him an impudent Dog. *a* **1796** Burns *Answ. Ep. fr. Tailor* ii, I gi'e their wames a random pouse. **1841** Lane *Arab. Nts.* (Rtldg.) 66 Just at the edge of the well, he gave him a push and threw him into it. **1885** *Manch. Exam.* 28 Sept. 5/1 [It] is on the edge of a precipice, and .. it needs but a push to send it toppling into the gulf below.

b. *spec.* in *Billiards*. A stroke in which the ball is pushed instead of being struck with the cue, or in which the cue, the cue ball, and the object ball are all in contact at the time the stroke is made; also, in *Cricket* and *Golf*, a stroke in which the ball is pushed instead of being hit; a push-stroke.

1873 'Cavendish' & Bennett *Billiards* 309 Push strokes may be divided into the half-push and the push. **1888** R. H. Lyttelton in A. G. Steel et al. *Cricket* ii. 72 There is .. a good length ball on the legs to which this push can be usefully applied if the batsman .. cannot make use of the sweep to leg. **1893** *Daily News* 16 Mar. 5/5 He would .. prohibit what is called the 'push', and he would enact a rule by which the red ball on being put down from the billiard spot during a break should be placed on the pyramid spot. **1898** K. S. Ranjitsinhji *With Stoddart's Team* (ed. 4) xii. 233 [MacLaren] .. chiefly obtained his runs by his 'push' in the slips. **1921** G. R. C. Harris *Few Short Runs* iii. 58 [W. G. Grace] introduced what was then a novel stroke, .. viz., the push to leg with a straight bat off the straight ball. **1976** *Evening Post* (Nottingham) 14 Dec. 18/4 Both were caught by wicketkeeper Ved Raj off Lal's bowling, Fletcher playing an indeterminate defensive push.

c. *fig.* An exertion of influence to promote a person's advancement by one who is 'at his back'.

1655 Ld. Norwich *Let.* 1 June in *Nicholas Papers* (Camden) II. 318, I shall say much more to you .. concerning this pushe (give me leave soe to call it). For whoe is there yt now pusheth not for his interest? **1793** Capt. Bentinck in *Ld. Auckland's Corr.* (1862) III. 48 Your Lordship will judge whether in this you can give me a push.

1889 *Century* XXXVIII. 156 It is money or 'push' which secured the place that should have been awarded to merit.

d. Paired with ***pull***, esp. to convey the concept of a force.

1878 *Proc. R. Soc. Edin.* IX. 610 The ear does distinguish, as it were, between push and pull on the tympanum. **1932** ANDRADE & HUXLEY *Introd. to Science* iii. 63 Electric and magnetic forces act across perfect emptiness, as if with invisible pulls and pushes. **1966** L. BASFORD *Sci. of Movement* xii. 33/1 We usually think of a force as the push or pull needed to move something.

e. ***to give*** (a person) ***the push***, to eject (a person), to throw out; to dismiss, *esp.* from employment. *colloq.*

1899 C. ROOK *Hooligan Nights* ii. 23 He was employed as a chucker-out... His regular business..was 'giving mugs and other barmy sots the push out of pubs'. **1923** T. E. LAWRENCE *Let.* 23 Mar. (1938) 404 Nothing else showed up, after I got the push from the R.A.F. **1933** D. L. SAYERS *Murder must Advertise* ix. 158 He told me to string him along. And afterwards..to give him the push. **1957** W. CAMP *Prospects of Love* III. iii. 160 Mummy had her..to work here..but she was quite hopeless..and Mummy gave her the push. **1968** 'P. HOBSON' *Titty's Dead* xv. 155 His landlady's given him the push. **1976** S. BARSTOW *Right True End* III. xiv. 209 'Hedley Graham has started a month's notice.' 'You don't mean he's..?' 'Got the push? No. He gave Maurice Kendall his resignation on Friday.'

2. A thrust of a weapon, or of the horn of a beast. Also *fig.*

1577 HOLINSHED *Chron.* II. 1835/2 At the Tourney .xij. strokes, wyth the sword, three pushes with the punchion staffe. **1589** *Late Voy. Sp. & Port.* 27 Being charged by ours ..they stood..euen to the push of the pike, in which charge and at the push, Captaine Robert Piew was slaine. **1590** SPENSER *F.Q.* I. iii. 35 So great was the puissance of his push, That from his sadle quite he did him beare. **1641** MILTON *Animadv.* ii. Wks. 1851 III. 209 Repaire the Achelaian horne of your Dilemma how you can, against the next push. **1712** *Lond. Gaz.* No. 4966/2 He Attack'd the Enemy with push of Bayonet. **1849** JAMES *Woodman* iv, It was nothing but push and thrust. **1849** MACAULAY *Hist. Eng.* vii. II. 170 He..will not suffer them to go on a hunting party, where there would be risk of a push from a stag's horn. **1907** *Athenæum* 13 July 47/2 'All the fine pushes were caught in the wood,' or hide, of the shields.

†**3.** An attack, a vigorous onset. Also *fig. Obs.*

1563 GOLDING *Cæsar* III. xix. (1565) 77 They were not able to abyde one pushe [*unum impetum*] of us, but by and by tourned their backs. **1672** WYCHERLEY *Love in Wood* II. i, I will not stay the push. They come! **1677** EARL ORRERY *Art of War* 27 If the Push be vigorous, and the Resistance considerable. **1691** LUTTRELL *Brief Rel.* (1857) II. 264 The Irish army consisted of near 30,000 men, and 'twas beleiv'd would try one push. **1781** COWPER *Expost.* 706 The push And feeble onset of a pigmy rush. **1800** *Hist. Ind.* in *Asiat. Ann. Reg.* 24/2 The Major determined..to make one push at them, that their escape, at least, might be prevented.

4. a. An effort, a vigorous attempt; a turn, bout, 'go'; chiefly in phrases ***at one push, at the first push, to make a push*** (***at, for, to do*** something), ***upon the push***. Now *rare*.

1596 NASHE *Saffron Walden* Wks. (Grosart) III. 40 Many men that are able to pay their debts doo not..pay them presently at one push. **1641** MILTON *Reform.* I. Wks. 1851 III. 10 Exact Reformation is not perfited at the first push. **1721** PERRY *Daggenh. Breach* 80 A great Number of Hands ..wanting to make a Push as it was call'd, to turn the Tides out of the Levels. **1737** BRACKEN *Farriery Impr.* (1757) II. 168 All their Art cannot make a thick-winded Horse run as long Pushes as one with..a better Wind. **1746** CHESTERF. *Let.* 8 Feb., He [Demosthenes]..at last made his strong push at the passions of his hearers. **1815** JANE AUSTEN *Emma* ix, The consciousness of having made a push,—of having thrown a die. **1818** COBBETT *Pol. Reg.* XXXIII. 21 The Rump made a grand push to make over the City of Westminster to the Whigs.

b. A determined advance; a pushing forward; in phr. ***to make a push***. Const. *at* or *for*. Also, *spec.*, a military advance (first widely used in the latter stages of the war of 1914–18). Also *fig.*

1803 NELSON in Nicolas *Dispatches* (1845) V. 192, I wish I could know to a certainty where they are bound. I think.. they will make a push at Messina. **1828** SIR W. NAPIER *Penins. War* VI. iii. (Rtldg.) I. 282 Making a 'push' of 400 miles. **1849** MACAULAY *Hist. Eng.* v. I. 557 Argyle resolved to make a bold push for Glasgow. **1857** LIVINGSTONE *Trav.* iii. 64 We made a push for the lake. **1916** *Punch* 7 June 407 (*caption*) The far-reaching effect of the Russian push. **1916** F. M. FORD *Let.* 7 Sept. (1965) 75 The Big Push was too overwhelming for one to notice details; it was like an immense wave full of debris. **1918** J. M. GRIDER *War Birds* (1927) 260 Henry told us that there is going to be a big push shortly. Push? What's a push to us? That's for the Poor Bloody Infantry to worry over. We push twice a day, seven days in the week. **1929** E. W. SPRINGS *Above Bright Blue Sky* 69 I've shed many a tear over you. I heard that you were killed during the push in front of Amiens. **1935** *Sun* (Baltimore) 15 July 1/8 A marked push toward early completion of the Administration's 'must' program was expected. **1942** *R.A.F. Jrnl.* 30 May 33 The only original officer of the Wing who had been in the first push. **1964** *Wall St. Jrnl.* 5 Feb. 1 We're stepping up our drive on all fronts ..and that includes our whole Northern push on housing.. and voter registration. **1976** S. BARSTOW *Right True End* III. xiv. 223 They joined up together in gangs in that war—Pals —and in a big push they sometimes died together. **1978** *Time* 3 July 17/1 The top-priority items are the kind of antitank and antiaircraft weapons that could be used to repulse a Soviet push across the border.

c. *slang.* (See quot.)

1873 *Slang Dict.*, *Push*, a robbery or swindle. 'I'm in this push', the notice given by one magsman to another that he means to 'stand in'.

d. The act of selling drugs illicitly (cf. PUSH *v.* 13 c).

1973 J. WAINWRIGHT *High-Class Kill* 58 The push was made in one of the city's public parks. The main pusher was one of those men nobody ever really sees.

5. Pressure; *esp.* in *Building*, the thrust of an arch or the like.

1715 DESAGULIERS *Fires Impr.* 29 The Air that was in the Room..had been driven away up the Chimney, by the Push of the External Air. **1772** HUTTON *Bridges* 99 *Push*, of an arch, the same as drift, shoot, &c. **1807** —— *Course Math.* II. 269 The area of the triangular bank of earth is increased in the same proportion as its horizontal push is decreased. **1841** *Civil Eng. & Arch. Jrnl.* IV. 167/1 The 'push' is thrown upon the cast-iron abutting piece. **1897** *Allbutt's Syst. Med.* IV. 633 There is no forward push of the rib.

6. *fig.* The pressure of affairs or circumstances; the condition of being 'pushed'; a case or time of stress or urgency; a critical juncture, an extremity, a 'pinch'; esp. in phrases ***at*** (†***for***) ***a push***, in an emergency; ***to come, put, bring to the push***, i.e. to an extremity, hence to actual trial; cf. POINT *sb.*[1] 22 b. Sometimes fig. from 3.

1570–83 FOXE *A. & M.* 729/1 He..closely kept himselfe betweene both, till the pushe came that his helpe might serue at a pinch. **1599** SANDYS *Europæ Spec.* (1632) 202 To what a miserable push have they driven the World. **1644** in *11th Rep. Hist. MSS. Comm.* App. VII. 102 The extreame push of affaires that the associated Countyes are now put to. **1671** MILTON *P.R.* IV. 470 If thou..wilt prolong All to the push of Fate. **1691** WOOD *Ath. Oxon.* II. 22 Chillingworth ..was a subtile and quick Disputant, and would several times put the Kings Professor to a push. *a* **1700** B. E. *Dict. Cant. Crew*, *At a Push*, at a pinch or strait. **1764** *Mem. G. Psalmanazar* 187 Till it came to the solemn push. **1842** J. AITON *Domest. Econ.* (1857) 146 When a push comes, he procures additional hands to get the hay up, or the oats in, or the potatoes planted. **1883** S. C. HALL *Retrospect* I. 325 It was a hard push to make a newspaper pay.

7. Determined effort to get on; persevering energy; enterprise, esp. that which is inconsiderate of the rights of others.

1855 BAGEHOT *Lit. Stud.* (1879) I. 31 Like what is called 'push' in a practical man, Sydney Smith's style goes straight to its object. **1881** in Nodal & Milner *Lancs. Gloss.* (1882), *Push*, energy, determination. He'll never make nowt on it —he's no push in him. **1893** PEEL *Spen Valley* 56 The stolid indifference and want of push and enterprise which has characterised agriculturists.

II. Concrete senses.

8. a. A 'press' of people; a crowd, throng. Now *rare* exc. as in 9.

1718 C. HIGGIN *True Disc.* 13 He is a..thieves' watchman, that lies scouting..when and where there is a push, alias an accidental crowd of people. **1754** J. POULTER *Discov.* 30 In order to be out of the push or throng. **1830** MONCRIEFF *Hrt. London* II. 1 He's as quiet as a dummy-hunter [pickpocket] in a push by Houndsditch. **1866** G. MEREDITH *Vittoria* xxix, A great push of men emerged from one of the close courts. **1923** T. E. LAWRENCE *Let.* 21 May (1938) 422, I met your cousin once, at a push in London: had no proper talk of him. **1955** D. W. MAURER in *Publ. Amer. Dial. Soc.* XXIV. 174 A crowd is, to a pickpocket, a *tip*, a *press*, a *crush*, or a *push*... 'Three troupes is up against this push already.'

b. A moving school or shoal of fish. *dial.*

1876 ROBINSON *Whitby Gloss.*, *Skooal*, or *Push*, a shoal of fish pursuing their course.

9. *slang.* A 'crowd' or band of thieves; a gang of convicts at penal labour (Farmer); *esp.* in *Australia*, A gang of larrikins; hence, Any company or party; a 'crowd', 'set', 'lot'. Also *attrib.*

1884 DAVITT *Prison Diary* (1885) I. x. 95 The stocking-knitting party [in prison]..became known..as the 'upper ten push'. **1890** *Melbourne Argus* 26 July 4/3 'Doolan's push' were a party of larrikins working, or supposed to be working, in a potato paddock near by. **1893** *Sydney Morn. Her.* 26 June 8/7 Day by day the new 'push' has become more daring. From chaffing drunken men and insulting defenceless women, the company has taken to assault, to daylight robbery. **1898** E. E. MORRIS *Austral Eng.* s.v., Its use began with the larrikins, and spread, until now it often means clique, set, party, and even jocularly so far as 'the Government House Push'. **1901** J. FLYNT *World of Graft* 16, I like him, an' the push likes him, 'cause he gives us rope. **1902** *Blackw. Mag.* July 40/1, I was recruiting for my 'push' down in Durban. I used to go and get the fellows off the ships as they came in. **1903** R. BEDFORD *True Eyes & Whirlwind* xx. 127 The nightly push club assembled. **1911** [see NIT *sb.*[2] 1]. **1914** *Sat. Even. Post* 4 Apr. 12/2 'The whole push is hungry, Kid,' he said. 'I'm hungry.' **1926** KIPLING *Debits & Credits* 307 You're from Sydney, ain't you?.. I know how your push talk, well enough. **1927** [see MOB *sb.*[1] 5 b]. **1964** C. MACKENZIE *Life & Times* III. 182 Presently there burst into the room half a dozen of the rowing 'push'. **1967** *Sunday Mail Mag.* (Brisbane) 12 Nov. 3/1 Experts on push warfare in Sydney in the early 1870's rated The Rocks Push as the No. 1 team of larrikins in the city. **1973** *Nation Rev.* (Melbourne) 31 Aug. 1436/1 He was portrayed almost as another Keynes—or, at the very least, the intellectual peer of the Friedman-Galbraith-Samuelson push.

10. A flush of water. *dial.*

1886 COLE *S.W. Lincs. Gloss.*, *Push* (pronounced short, as Rush), a pool or puddle. The watter all stood in pushes. We'd such a push of watter agen our door, we had to let it off. **1894** *Daily News* 1 Nov. 3/5 The heavy push of water, which had long been looked forward to by anglers. **1895** *Ibid.* 7 Oct. 9/3 The heavy downpour in the early hours of yesterday morning ought to cause a 'push' of land water.

11. A contrivance or part which is pushed or simply pressed in order to operate a mechanism; a push-button.

1889 *Sci. Amer.* 18 May 313/1 The spring push, which was secured higher up on the door,..could be tampered with by patients so inclined. *c* **1890** F. E. POWELL *Electric Bells* 43 A push might be described as an automatic switch, as it is self-stopping when the pressure is removed. **1902** *Daily Chron.* 27 June 2/6 Push-tap valves..do not require a key, the driver simply having to press the push and the water runs off.

12. *attrib.* and *Comb.*: see PUSH-.

push (pʊʃ), *sb.*[2] *Obs.* exc. *dial.* Also 6 **poushe, powsh(e, pushe,** 6–7 **pussh(e.** [Origin obscure.

Possibly a use of PUSH *sb.*[1], with the sense 'something that pushes or is pushed out or up': But it occurs 30 years earlier than any of the known senses of that word, as well as with spellings not found there, though occurring in the verb; and it is difficult to separate it entirely from MDu. and MLG. *pûst*, mod.Du. *puist*, pimple, blister, E.Fris. *pûske* (dim. of **pûs*) pustule, pock, blister, and many related words, from an app. onomatopoeic stem *pûs-* or *pûst-* to inflate, swell up; coinciding also in form with the stem of L. *pust-ula*, *pus-ula*, blister, pimple, pustule. If the word entered Eng. from any source at an early date as *puss*, or *pousse*, it might share the phonetic history of F. *pousser*, and become *push*, like PUSH *v.*]

A pustule, pimple, boil.

1533 ELYOT *Cast. Helthe* III. vii. (1541) 59 b, Sometyme blacke poushes or boyles, with inflamation and moch peyne. **1542** UDALL *Erasm. Apoph.* 71 'Ἐξανθήματα, that is, litle pymples or pushes. **1547** BOORDE *Brev. Health* xxxv. 18 b, Asaphati is the greke worde. In Englyshe they be named whelkes or pushes the which be read. **1552** HULOET, Byle, botch, or powsh. *Ibid.*, Powshe, *Atheroma*, *Epinyctides*.. *Tubercula*..a little powshe. **1598** SYLVESTER *Du Bartas* II. i. III. *Furies* (1641) 98/2 The pining Phthisik fils them all with pushes Whence a slowe spowt of cor'sie matter gushes. **1665** G. HARVEY *Advice agst. Plague* 4 Risings like blisters, or small tumors and pushes, some red, others yellow. **1710** T. FULLER *Pharm. Extemp.* 422 Very useful for Pushes, Pimples, and Blemishes in the Face. **1822–24** *Good's Study Med.* (ed. 4) II. 41 In vernacular language, this species [a common phlegmon] is denominated a *push*. **1843** SIR T. WATSON *Princ. & Pract. Physic* II. 796 A very common.. pustular disease of the skin, usually called boil, in some parts of England a *push*, and by the learned *furunculus*.

†**push,** *int.* (*sb.*[3]). *Obs.* = PISH, TUSH, *int.*

1605 *Tryall Chev.* II. ii. in Bullen *Old Pl.* (1884) III. 294 Push! meet me. Ferdinand, I will. **1607** SHAKS. *Timon* III. vi. 119, 2, Know you the quality of Lord Timons fury? 3 Push, did you see my Cap? **1624** *Trag. Nero* I. ii. in Bullen *Old Pl.* (1882) I. 18 Push, it could not be like to this.

B. *sb.* An exclamation of 'push'; = PISH *sb.* ***to make a push at***, to treat with disdain.

1599 SHAKS. *Much Ado* V. i. 38 There was neuer yet Philosopher, That could endure the tooth-ake patiently, How euer they haue writ the stile of gods, And made a push at chance and sufferance.

push (pʊʃ), *v.* Forms: α. 4 ? **pusse,** *pa. t.* **puste;** 4–5 **posshe(n;** 5–6 **pusshe,** 6 **puszshe, pushe, powshe,** 7– **push.** β. 6–9 *Sc.* **pouss,** 7–9 *Sc.* **pouse,** 9 *dial.* **poose** (puːs), **powse** (paʊs). See also POSS *v.* [a. F. *pousser*, with palatalization of *s* (cf. *brush*, *cuish*, *quash*, with F. *brosse*, *cuisse*, *casser*); in OF. *polser*, *poulser* (:—L. *pulsāre*, freq. of *pellĕre* to drive, push, beat), which gradually supplanted *bouter*, in OF. to strike, thrust, push (see BUTT *v.*[1], and cf. sense 3 below), as in Eng. *push* has supplanted PUT *v.*[1] in its early senses 'thrust, butt'.]

I. Of physical action.

1. a. *trans.* To exert force upon or against (a body) so as to move it away; to move by such exertion of force; to shove, thrust, drive (the opposite of *to draw* or *pull*). In early use comprehending the force of impact as well as of pressure, but now spec. applied to the communication of force by pressure in contact.

a **1300** *K. Horn* (Harl. MS.) 1079 Horn þe wyket puste, þat hit open fluste. *c* **1400** *Rom. Rose* 4625, I..that was posshed in every side, That I nist where I might abyde. [Cf. *ibid.* 4479 s.v. POSS *v.* 1.] *c* **1440** *York Myst.* xlvi. 38 þei lusshed hym, þei lasshed hym, þei pusshed hym, þei passhed hym. **1562** ROWBOTHUM *Playe of Cheastes* E v, If he pushe his Paune one steppe more. **1601** SHAKS. *Jul. C.* V. v. 25 It is more worthy, to leape in our selues, Then tarry till they push vs. **1611** —— *Wint. T.* II. iii. 125 *Paul.* I pray you doe not push me, Ile be gone. **1755** JOHNSON s.v. *Push-pin*, A child's game in which pins are pushed alternately. **1833** *Manuf. Metal* (Cab. Cycl.) II. 269 Any one of them..being pushed the least degree too much or too little. **1852** MRS. STOWE *Uncle Tom's C.* xvii, The hindermost pushing the front ones faster than they would have gone of themselves. **1859** TENNYSON *Geraint & Enid* 1122 The door, Push'd from without, drave backward to the wall. **1893** *Labour Commission*, Glossary 65/2 The tram containing the coal is sometimes pushed by the boy, and sometimes pulled by a pony. *Mod.* The nurse was pushing the perambulator and met the gardener pushing a wheel-barrow. The gradient being steep, an additional locomotive is here put on behind to push the train.

b. with an adverb or advb. phrase, expressing the direction, or way, in which the thing is moved, e.g. ***to push back, down, in, out, onward, open***, etc. ***to push up daisies***: see DAISY *sb.* 1 c.

c **1450** in Aungier *Syon* (1840) 262 If any..schofte, pusche, or sperne any suster from her withe armes or scholders. **1530** PALSGR. 671/1 He pusshed me awaye as harde as he coulde..*il me rebouta*, or *me repulsa darriere luy tant quil peut.* **1611** SHAKS. *Wint. T.* II. iii. 73 Will you not push her out? **1611** BIBLE *Ps.* xliv. 5 Through thee will wee push downe our enemies. **1663** SIR G. MACKENZIE *Relig. Stoic* xiii. (1685) 126 The Rose being pous'd up by the salt nitre which makes it vegetative. **1791** MRS. RADCLIFFE *Rom. Forest* i, He was turning to go out when the man suddenly pushed him back, and he heard the door locked upon him. **1871** B. STEWART *Heat* § 131 As the liquid became heated its vapour pushed the mercury before it along the tube. **1897** *Allbutt's Syst. Med.* IV. 812 The mercury is pushed through the system much quicker than under ordinary circumstances. **1898** Watts-Dunton *Aylwin* I. i, She turned the key and pushed open the door.

fig. **1781** Cowper *Hope* 659 To parry and push by God's word With senseless noise. —— *Expost.* 690 The word of prophesy, those truths divine.. Are never long vouchsaf'd, if push'd aside With cold disgust or philosophic pride.

c. To drive or repulse by force of arms; to drive in the chase.

1634 Sir T. Herbert *Trav.* 27 The Mallabars pushing them [our skiffs] and throwing fire-balls at vs. **1709** *London Gaz.* 4585/2 They charged our Horse, and broke in upon us; we rallied, and pushed them. **1722** De Foe *Col. Jack* (1840) 238 After we had thus pushed the enemy's cavalry. **1735** Somerville *Chase* III. 492 The tenacious Crew Hang on the Track,.. And push him [the fox] many a League.

d. To move, throw forward, or advance (a force) against opposition or difficulty.

1748 *Anson's Voy.* II. xi. 254 He intended to have pusht two hundred of his men on shore in his boats. *Ibid.* xiv. 286 To hinder us from pushing our men on shore. **1800** Wellington in Gurw. *Desp.* (1834) I. 21 Some campoos and pultans, which have been indiscreetly pushed across the Kistna. **1879** Dixon *Windsor* II. xv. 158 Henry pushed his scouts along the road towards Windsor.

e. *absol.* To thrust others out (of one's way); to jostle, shove.

1735 Somerville *Chase* II. 236 Alternate they preside, and justling push To guide the dubious Scent. **1817** J. Scott *Paris Revisit.* (ed. 4) 13 Rather than pay three-pence to one of the men on the quays, they stumbled, and panted, and pushed, under a load which was heavier than it need to have been.

f. ***to push round the ale***, etc., ***to push the bottle***, to push the liquor from one to another in convivial drinking.

1788 J. Woodforde *Diary* 20 Aug. (1927) III. 44 Mr. Atthill being Chairman pushed the Bottle about pretty briskly. **1829** Lytton *Disowned* 7 Come, Mim, push round the ale. **1847** L. Hunt *Men, Women, & B.* II. iv. 55 Thomson could push the bottle like a regular *bon vivant*.

g. *trans.* or *absol.*, in *Billiards*. To make a push-stroke: see push *sb.*[1] 1 b. Also in *Cricket*.

1873 'Cavendish' & Bennett *Billiards* 314 To push, the cue must be placed all but touching the player's ball. **1893** *Cricket* 26 Oct. 442/1 Box.. has a style of getting off his ground when a ball is directed to his legs, with the intention of.. 'pushing' it to the 'leg'. **1920** D. J. Knight in P. F. Warner *Cricket* 34 If he [*sc.* the batsman] is pushing the ball away to long leg, he must face long leg. **1963** A. Ross *Australia 63* iii. 76 He moved quick enough up the wicket to Titmus, but having got there was content to push.

h. *absol.* ***push off***: Of a person in a boat (and *transf.* of the boat), To push oneself away from the bank or the like; to shove off; *fig.* (*slang* or *colloq.*), to begin a game, etc. Also, *fig.*, to depart, go away (freq. *imp.*). Also without *off* and ***to push along***. So ***to push out*** i.e. into the open water. Also, ***to push away*** i.e. from the shore.

1726 Swift *Gulliver* IV. x, Then, getting into my Canoo, I pushed off from Shore. **1740** *Proc. Sessions of Peace London & Middlesex* May 164/1 He.. heard somebody a cursing and swearing, and a Woman.. say, *d——n it, push off*, or *go off*. **1836** W. Irving *Astoria* III. 227 As M'Kenzie's canoes were about to push off. **1839** Thirlwall *Greece* IV. 119 The two Athenian galleys suddenly pushed out. **1865** J. Thomson *Sunday up River* v. ii, We push off from the bank. *a* **1909** *Mod.* We're all ready to play; push off! **1918** K. E. Harriman *Wine, Women & War* (1926) 39 Grand day to be pushing off for Bordeaux. **1923** Wodehouse *Inimitable Jeeves* xxii. 241 He helped himself absently to a handful of my cigars and pushed off. **1931** A. Christie *Sittaford Mystery* xxiii. 192, I shall be pushing along now. So long. **1947** Wodehouse *Full Moon* vii. 141 I'll be pushing along. **1949** J. B. Priestley *Delight* 231 This is my view, not yours. Push off! **1955** G. Freeman *Liberty Man* I. i. 21 Goodnight, Maur. I'll be pushin'. I've 'ad a day. **1964** R. Jeffries *Embarrassing Death* iii. 25 Bill finished his drink. 'I'd better be pushing.' **1973** E. Page *Fortnight by Sea* viii. 89 She must be quite certain to leave when the girl with the frizzy hair decided to push off. **1976** *National Observer* (U.S.) 26 June 16/4 A man in a small sailboat pushes away from the shore of the Atlantic and never is seen again.

i. (See quot.)

1867 Smyth *Sailor's Word-bk.*, *To Push*, to move a vessel by poles.

j. *intr.* To sit abaft an oar and propel a boat with forward strokes: as, to push down a stream.

k. ***to push*** (someone) ***around***, to move or cause (someone) to be moved roughly from place to place, to manhandle. Freq. *fig.* (orig. *U.S.*), to browbeat, bully, domineer over. Also, ***to push about***.

1923 H. C. Witwer in *Cosmopolitan* Aug. 45/2 Look at the pushing around he's getting because he hauled off and inherited a million. **1930** D. Runyon in *Liberty* 8 Nov. 24/1 After.. Johnny gets on the strong-arm squad, he never misses a chance to push Big Jule around. **1942** R. Chandler *High Window* iii. 29 If anybody tries to push Linda around, he'll have to push me around first. **1949** 'M. Innes' *Journeying Boy* i. 12 The father doted on the son, the son pushed the father around. **1963** D. Ballantyne in C. K. Stead *N.Z. Short Stories* (1966) 153 The Aussie.. has made it bloody clear he *won't* be pushed about. **1964** M. Argyle *Psychol. & Social Probl.* xiv. 177 Resistance to change on the part of industrial workers is reduced if they play some part in making the decision and its augmentation. Not only is the feeling of being pushed about avoided, but those concerned are able to set up the new social system to their satisfaction. **1973** 'J. Patrick' *Glasgow Gang Observed* xix. 170 The Glasgow gang boy feels that he is being pushed around, that he has no control over the social conditions which predetermine his future. **1974** N. Freeling *Dressing of Diamond* 93 Thought you could come and push me about. Not the first. But I'm still here. **1976** *National Observer* (U.S.) 26 June 6/2 America has pushed these people around too much, too long, and it's natural that they feel resentment and react violently.

l. Phr. ***to push*** (someone's) ***face in***, to punch (someone) on the nose. *slang*.

1930 'R. Crompton' *William—The Bad* ix. 228 I'll go and find the blighter and push his face in for him. I never heard of such beastly cheek!

m. Fig. phr. ***to push the boat out***, to be generous, *esp.* in paying for rounds of drinks. *slang* (orig. *Naut.*).

1937 J. Curtis *You're in Racket, Too* iii. 39 This bloke you're meeting up the Old Jacket and Vest to-night, let him push the boat out, the bastard. Surely he can pester for a tightener if you're hungry. **1946** J. Irving *Royal Navalese* 140 *Push the boat out, to*, a boatwork term used to imply paying for a 'round of drinks'. **1962** 'J. Le Carré' *Murder of Quality* i. 10 'Fielding's giving another dinner party tonight.' 'He's pushing the boat out these days.' **1977** B. Pym *Quartet in Autumn* x. 90 'Pushing the boat out, aren't you?' said Norman, with unusual jollity, as Ken topped up his glass.

n. Phr. ***when push comes to shove*** and varr., when action must back up threats; when the worst comes to the worst. *colloq.* (orig. *N. Amer.*)

1958 Murtagh & Harris *Cast First Stone* vii. 105 Some .. judges.. talk nice and polite... Then, when push comes to shove, they say 'Six months in the workhouse'. **1970** *Calgary* (Alberta) *Herald* 4 May 57/1 If push comes to shove, make good the threat. **1977** *National Observer* (U.S.) 22 Jan. 12/4 When—to use common parlance—push comes to shove, I have a great deal of faith in American youth. **1981** *Guardian* 10 Jan. 19/8 (*heading*) Push comes to shove.

2. a. *intr.* To thrust with a pointed weapon, stick, or the like (const. *at*); to tilt, fence; to use a spear, short sword, poniard, etc. *Obs.* or *arch.*

[**1362** Langl. *P. Pl.* A. vii. 96 Mi plouh-pote schal be my pyk and posshen atte Rootes, And helpe my coltre to kerue.] **1599** Shaks. *Hen. V*, II. i. 103 As manhood shal compound: push home. **1600** Holland *Livy* xxvii. xxviii. 650 Others.. pushed at them with punchion poles. **1698** Farquhar *Love & Bottle* II. ii, The Duke of Burgundy.. pushes the finest of any man in France. **1700** Dryden *Pal. & Arc.* III. 511 That none shall dare With shortned Sword to stab in closer War: ..Nor push with biting Point, but strike at length. **1791** Cowper *Iliad* IV. 383 Let the green In years.. Push with the lance. **1847** Tennyson *Princess* v. 522 But Arac rode him down: And Cyril seeing it, push'd against the Prince.

fig. *a* **1715** Burnet *Own Time* an. 1674 (1823) II. 57 When duke Lauderdale was hotly pushed at, he then promised.. that he would avoid all former errors. **1738** Neal *Hist. Purit.* IV. 577 A bold and forward man, who pushed at every thing that might ruin the Church.

†**b.** *trans.* To stab with a weapon; to 'strike'. Also *fig.* (cf. put *v.*[1] 3 b). *Obs.*

1694 *Martens' Voy. Spitzbergen* IV. in *Acc. Sev. Late Voy.* II. (1711) 160 For the most part they do not much mind where they launce or push them [whales]. **1728** Vanbrugh & Cib. *Prov. Husb.* IV. i, *Man.* Right! there you push'd him home.

3. *intr.* To thrust or butt with the horns: chiefly biblical. Also *trans.* = put *v.*[1] 1 b. Now *dial.*

1535 Coverdale *Exod.* xxi. 29 Yf the oxe haue bene vsed to push in tymes past. [So 1611; 1885 *R.V.* gore.] *Ibid.*, *2 Chron.* xviii. 10 With these [horns] shalt thou puszshe at the Syrians [**1611** push the Syrians], tyll thou brynge them to naughte. **1611** Bible *Exod.* xxi. 32 If the ox shall push [Coverdale gorre] a manservant or a maidservant. **1697** Dryden *Virg. Georg.* III. 343 They fence, they push, and pushing, loudly roar. **1888** E. Laws *Little Eng.* App. 421 *Push*, to butt like a cow.

4. *trans.* To thrust (a weapon); to thrust (a limb, organ, root, etc.) into some position; to put (anything) out in a projecting manner. ***to push a face***: see face *sb.* 7 b.

1692 *Diary Siege Lymerick* Pref. A ij b, With so poor a Handful to push so bold a Sword, and carry so intire a Victory. **1765** A. Dickson *Treat. Agric.* (ed. 2) 115 Some kinds of weeds push their roots very far down... If there are any stones in the land, they push their roots among the stones. **1778** Johnson *Let. to Mrs. Thrale* 15 Oct., I never could get anything from her but by pushing a face. **1894** R. Bridges *Feast of Bacchus* I. 376 What has he to do to push his nose into our affairs?

5. a. *trans.* To thrust *out*, stick *out* (an organ or part). Of a plant: To send forth (a shoot, runner, root); also, to put *forth* (fruit).

1614 D. Dyke *Myst. Self-Deceiv.* xxvii. 320 Some like Snailes push out their hornes till they be touched. **1768** Tucker *Lt. Nat.* (1834) II. 405 [To] manifest its vigour by continual efforts to push forth more fruit of good works. **1786** Abercrombie *Gard. Assist.* Feb. 32 In melon plants pushing runners: pinch off the end of the runners. **1849** *Florist* 252 To encourage the plants to push fresh roots.

b. *intr.* To stick out, project. Of a plant or stem: = put *v.*[1] 9.

1720 De Foe *Capt. Singleton* iii, A.. cape.. pushing out a long way into the sea. **1855** Browning *Childe Roland* xii, If there pushed any ragged thistle-stalk Above its mates, the head was chopped. **1858** Glenny *Gard. Every-day Bk.* 80/2 Those plants which are pushing strongly will do all the better if the ground is forked between them.

6. *intr.* To exert pressure upon something in the way described in 1.

1613 Shaks. *Hen. VIII*, v. iv. 16 We may as well push against Powles as stirre 'em. **1855** Tennyson *Brook* 83, I.. push'd at Philip's garden-gate. *Mod.* Do not push against me. The fence is weak; if you push against it it will give way. Push with all your might; all push at once!

7. a. *intr.* To make one's way with force or persistence (as against difficulty or opposition). With various adverbs and preps.; esp. ***to push on***, to press forward, to advance with continued effort. Also, ***to push along***.

1718 Rowe tr. *Lucan* VI. 269 Now push we on, disdain we now to fear, A thousand Wounds let ev'ry Bosom bear. **1768** Byron *Narr. Loss Wager* 122, I pushed into the next wigwam upon my hands and knees. **1804** Monson in Owen *Wellesley's Desp.* (1877) 526 The enemy pushed after and many were either killed or wounded. **1806** J. Beresford *Miseries Hum. Life* II. xi, Pushing through the very narrow path of a very long field of very high corn. **1850** Tennyson *In Mem.* liii, For fear divine Philosophy Should push beyond her mark. **1879** Froude *Cæsar* xiv. 222 Cæsar, after a short rest, pushed on and came under their walls. **1892** Gardiner *Stud. Hist. Eng.* 11 He pushed inland to the Kentish Stour. **1899** *Allbutt's Syst. Med.* VIII. 600 Both the horny and granular layers push downwards wherever they can. **1902** 'Mark Twain' in *Harper's Weekly* 6 Dec. 5/1 Push along, cabby, push along—no great lot of time to spare.

b. ***to push one's way***, to make one's way by thrusting obstacles or opponents aside.

1781 Cowper *Expost.* 17 Whom fiery suns.. Forbid in vain to push his daring way To darker climes. **1884** R. W. Church *Bacon* iii. 61 The shrewd and supple lawyers.. who unscrupulously pushed their way to preferment. *Mod.* He pushed his way to the front of the crowd.

II. Of action other than physical.

8. a. *intr.* To put forth vigorous effort or endeavour; to press, be urgent in request or persuasion; to aim *at* with endeavour to attain; to try or work strenuously *for*, press *for*; to seek actively, labour *after*.

1595 Daniel *Civ. Wars* I. xxv. 30 Glory won in great exploits his mind did elevate.. Which made him push at what his issue gate. **1601** in Moryson *Itin.* II. II. ii. (1617) 171 The King of Spaine meanes to make this place [Kinsale] the seate of the Warre.. [in order] to push for England. **1700** Congreve *Way of World* III. v, Will he be Importunate, Foible, and push? **1719** De Foe *Crusoe* (1840) II. xv. 319, I had no occasion to push at a winter journey of this kind. **1728** Ramsay *Gen. Mistake* 150 Macsomno pushes after praise. **1738** Neal *Hist. Purit.* IV. 88 While the Presbyterians were pushing for their Covenant uniformity. **1765** Sterne *Tr. Shandy* VII. xxviii, By pushing at something beyond that, I have brought myself into such a situation as [etc.]. **1844** G. Dodd *Textile Manuf.* i. 13 The manner in which the manufacturers 'pushed' for orders. **1975** *N.Y. Times* 10 Apr. 29/2 Former Governor Terry Sanford reportedly was one of the men pushing hardest for the primary repeal.

b. *trans.* To approach (a certain age). *colloq.*

1937 S. V. Benét in *Sat. Even. Post* 18 Sept. 42/4 I'd kind of like to beat out Ike Leavis... To hear him talk, you'd think nobody had ever pushed ninety before. **1953** R. Chandler *Long Good-Bye* xxiii. 148 When you're young.. you can absorb a lot of punishment. When you are pushing forty you don't snap back the same way. **1959** *Housewife* Oct. 134/2 Maria's a bit old... Pushing seventy, you know. **1962** *Woman's Own* 18 Aug. 16/1 All these women, either pushing 40, or looking back at it without too much regret, have been good box-office for years. **1976** *National Observer* (U.S.) 2 Oct. 12/5 Flicka is pushing 50, but she still wears her frosted hair shoulder length.

9. *trans.* To urge, press, incite, impel, drive (a person, etc.) *to do* something, or *to* (†*upon*) some course; to urge or egg *on*.

a **1578** Lindesay (Pitscottie) *Chron. Scot.* (S.T.S.) II. 95 His wickit and evill consall.. allurit him and puffit [*v.r.* poussit] him fast fordwart to fight witht Inglischemen. **1640** R. Baillie *Canterb. Self-convict.* 48 Nothing.. but that which conscience would pouse any man upon all hazards to avow. **1705** tr. *Bosman's Guinea* 332 Pushed on by the King of Ardra, he marched against the People of Fida. **1722** De Foe *Plague* (Rtldg.) 128 Apprehensions.. that desperation should push the People upon Tumults. **1730** A. Gordon *Maffei's Amphith.* 249 Then.. might the Wild-Beasts be seen pushed on to fight. **1761** Hume *Hist. Eng.* II. xxviii. 138 He pushed his master to seek an occasion of quarrel with that monarch. **1812** Joanna Baillie *Siege* III. ii, 'Tis a strange thing that women, who can't fight themselves, should so eagerly push us to the work. **1862** Goulburn *Pers. Relig.* IV. xi. (1873) 347 Shrinking from being pushed to greater lengths in Religion than we are prepared to go.

10. a. To impel (a horse, etc.) to greater speed; to urge *on*; *spec.* to urge (it) forward beyond its natural speed or endurance; also in reference to other animals, a steam-ship, etc. Also, with *along*.

1727 Boyer *Dict. Royal* 11, To push (or put) on a Horse, *Pousser, lancer, piquer un Cheval.* **1735** Somerville *Chase* III. 445 As I behold Each lovely nymph.. Push on the gen'rous steed. **1832** Standish *Maid of Jaen* 18 The steeds with urgent speed were push'd 'Till lost in distance all was hush'd. **1845** Mrs. S. C. Hall *Whiteboy* iv, The car-driver managed to push his poor starveling to a canter. **1907** *Daily Chron.* 14 Sept. 5/2 Mr. Cunard denied that there had been any effort whatever to push the vessel [the Lusitania]. **1911** H. B. Wright *Winning of Barbara Worth* xxix. 411 Give your horse a drink but don't wait to rest. You can push him from now on as hard as you like. **1962** *Which?* Oct. (Car Suppl.) 118/2 It was the back wheels which eventually broke away if the car was pushed too far. **1971** 'H. Calvin' *Poison Chasers* vii. 90 Dai was pushing the Land Rover all out, but it was still too slow for me. **1972** 'I. Drummond' *Frog in Moonflower* 18 The driver pushed the bus along... It was doing well over sixty now.

b. To force (a thing) into more intense action. Now *rare*.

1756 P. Browne *Jamaica* 41 Orpiment.. when pushed by a strong fire yields a great quantity of acrid volatile particles. **1797** *Encycl. Brit.* (ed. 3) IV. 603 By pushing the heat after the oil comes over. **1839** URE *Dict. Arts*, etc. 805 The fire, at first moderate, is pushed till the cucurbits are red hot.

c. *Bridge*. To try to force (an opponent) into a higher and more doubtful contract by overcalling him. Also *intr*.

1927 M. WORK *Contract Bridge* 149 *Push*, to overbid for the purpose of inducing the opponents to assume a losing contract. **1934** G. F. HERVEY *Mod. Contract Bridge* xxii. 247 If you know a player is determined to play every hand, you can 'push' much more successfully against him than against the player who knows when to leave off bidding and when to double. **1959** *Listener* 24 Dec. 1118/2 When East accepted the invitation to game he was pushed beyond game. **1980** *Guardian Weekly* 21 Dec. 23/5 West cunningly bid only 5S[pades] in the hope of being allowed to play in 6S when he was pushed there.

11. a. To press forward, prosecute, or follow up, press with vigour and insistence (some action or operation); to urge, press (a claim, etc.); also with advb. extension, esp. ***to push on***; ***to push it***, to press one's suit.

1611 SHAKS. *Wint. T.* II. i. 179 Camillo's flight..doth push-on this proceeding. **1701** W. WOTTON *Hist. Rome* iii. 52 Marcus was for pushing on his Blow. *a* **1720** SEWEL *Hist. Quakers* (1795) I. IV. 365 Since the churchmen pushed on so wicked a business. **1777** WATSON *Philip II* (1793) II. XIII. 136 If the Spanish commander..had pushed his operations with proper rigour, he must have made himself master of the town. **1827** *Examiner* 275/2 Such pupils..as chose to push their studies. **1842** S. LOVER *Handy Andy* ii, They say Tom's pushing it strong there. **1871** R. ELLIS *Catullus* lxiv. 85 So..Push'd he his onward journey to Minos' haughty dominion. **1952** *Sun* (Baltimore) 22 Mar. 6/4 Even if steelworkers push their productivity, a very large share of their production goes..into war materials. **1966** A. SACHS *Jail Diary* iii. 34 He only asked one question all the time, and did not even push that one. **1970** B. MATHER *Break in Line* v. 60 'Once is funny, twice is cheeky,' he grunted. 'Don't push things, boy.'

b. Phr. ***to push one's*** (†***a***) ***fortune***, to engage actively in making one's fortune. Cf. FORTUNE *sb*. 5.

1657 SIR W. MURE *Hist.* 251 A man wittie and hardie, fit for pouseing a fortoune in these times. **1697** DRYDEN *Virg. Georg.* Ded. (1721) I. 190 You push'd not your Fortune to rise in either. **1719** RAMSAY *3rd Answ. to Hamilton* xiv, We man to the bent, And pouse our fortune. **1749** SMOLLETT *Gil Blas* I. i, It is high time for a brisk lad of seventeen, like thee, to push thy fortune in the world. **1863** KINGLAKE *Crimea* (1876) I. xiii. 214 To glance at the operations of a small knot of middle-aged men who were pushing their fortunes in Paris. **1886** [see FORTUNE *sb*. 5].

c. To extend operations vigorously forward in space, or to more distant places.

1842 ALISON *Hist. Eur.* lxvi. §83 (1848) XIV. 285 The approaches were pushed with great rapidity. **1872** YEATS *Growth Comm.* 94 They pushed their trade to still more distant parts. **1884** *Manch. Exam.* 27 May 5/1 Hitherto Russia has been pushing her conquests in a region where there is no well-established authority and no clear boundaries.

d. ***to push one's luck***: see LUCK *sb*. 3.

e. Phr. ***to push it, things***, to cause (an action) to be rushed; to hurry, cut fine. *colloq.*

1967 H. DALMAS *Fowler Formula* iii. 31 [We] could have her by Christmas... It would be pushing things a little, but they said it could be done. **1971** 'F. CLIFFORD' *Blind Side* IV. iii. 165 Fourteen twenty-five?—or is that pushing it a bit?

12. To carry out (a matter, action, principle, etc.) to a farther point, or to the farthest limit. ***to push through***, to press or carry by force to a conclusion.

1713 ADDISON *Guard.* No. 137 ¶1, I think they have pushed this matter a little too far. **1779** *Mirror* No. 45 ¶7 He must push to excess every species of extravagant dissipation. **1839** J. YEOWELL *Anc. Brit. Ch.* i. (1847) 4 If we push our investigations to an earlier period. **1856** EMERSON *Eng. Traits, Cockayne* Wks. (Bohn) II. 64 Individual right is pushed to the uttermost bound compatible with public order. **1876** GREEN *Stray Stud.* 7 That peculiar temper.. which declines to push conclusions to extremes. **1888** BRYCE *Amer. Commw.* I. xxxii. 489 If it [*viz.* a measure] is not pressing, neither party..cares to take it up and push it through.

13. a. To advance or try to advance or promote; to urge or press the adoption, use, practice, sale, etc. of (a thing); to exert oneself for the advancement or promotion of (a person); also with *forward, on*. Also (now *obs.*?) with *off*.

1714 R. FIDDES *Pract. Disc.* II. 31 Journalists [are] employ'd to push and forward it. **1748** H. WALPOLE *Let. to Mann* 12 Jan., There is a transaction going on to send Sir Charles Williams to Turin; he has asked it, and it is pushed. **1758** JOHNSON *Let. to Burney* 8 Mar. in *Boswell*, Not that I mean to impose upon you the trouble of pushing them with more importunity than may seem proper. **1861** HUGHES *Tom Brown at Oxf.* i, Every one who had a son..whom he wanted to push forward in the world [etc.]. **1873** *Punch* 26 Apr. 178/2 Why do not the managers imitate another class of persons who push off drugs by means of puffing. **1888** *Pall Mall G.* 22 May 12/1 Pushing the sale of British goods. **1894** *Times* 28 Nov. 4/2 To correct your correspondent's misconception of the phrase 'pushing' a book. **1936** D. POWELL *Turn, Magic Wheel* II. 140 He saw a bad month ahead explaining to Dennis why his book was not being pushed. **1949** WODEHOUSE *Uncle Dynamite* xiv. 237 She was always complaining that her last publishers wouldn't push her books. **1977** *Jrnl. R. Soc. Arts* CXXV. 124/2, I think the improvement grants we have are fairly good. They need to be pushed more.

b. To press, force, or thrust (something) *on* or *upon* a person for attention, acceptance, or adoption.

1723 R. WODROW *Corr.* (1843) III. 99 They were not fond of having one that was in the family, and on that score pushed on them. **1869** J. MARTINEAU *Ess.* II. 91 Physicians are too apt to push their prescriptions upon the healthy. **1889** 'MARK TWAIN' *Yankee at Crt. K. Arthur* xx. (1905) 210 There was another fact, which he never pushed upon anybody unasked.

c. To peddle (drugs) illegally. Also *absol. slang* (orig. *U.S.*).

1938 *Amer. Speech* XIII. 190/1 *To push*, to peddle narcotics, especially as a sub-agent or small-time dealer. **1953** W. BURROUGHS *Junkie* ii. 33, I decided right then I would never push any more tea [*sc.* marijuana]. **1956** 'E. MCBAIN' *Pusher* (1959) 37 'How would I know..even if he was supplying himself and others besides?' 'Was he pushing?' **1959** J. OSBORNE *World of Paul Slickey* II. ix. 71 It will surely bug you when there is..no tea to push. **1968** B. TURNER *Sex Trap* xvi. 154 'Are you the man?.. You pushing or aren't you?' **1977** 'J. FRASER' *Hearts Ease in Death* xv. 171 Was Billy Nesbitt buying amphetamines.. and selling them to other kids? Was he, in fact, pushing drugs?

14. To press or bear hard upon (a person) in dealing with him, to put to straits; *esp.* in *passive*, To be hard pressed or put to straits, as by lack of time, means, etc.; often with *for*.

1761 HUME *Hist. Eng.* I. viii. 171 Henry laying hold of so plausible a pretence, resolved to push the clergy with regard to all their privileges. **1863** TROLLOPE *Small House at Allington* in *Cornh. Mag.* XVIII. 272 'They'll be very pushed about money,' said Mr. Boyce. **1867** J. R. BROWNE *Land of Thor* iii. 43 It is dreadful to see people so hard pushed to live. **1890** 'R. BOLDREWOOD' *Col. Reformer* (1891) 258 I'm a little pushed for time. **1893** RAYMOND *Gent. Upcott* ii, I'm a little pushed..and I thought perhaps you'd let me have a small matter of fifteen pound. **1946** *R.A.F. Jrnl.* May 170 He is occasionally a little pushed by the constant stream of callers. **1967** P. MOYES *Murder Fantastical* xiv. 209 Sorry we can't invite you to lunch, Tibbett, but what with the funeral and the Fête..Vi's a bit pushed. **1972** K. BENTON *Spy in Chancery* viii. 85 We think his boss may be pushing him. **1978** G. A. SHEEHAN *Running & Being* xii. 173 You frequently read that a runner would have done better if he only had someone to push him during a race.

Hence **pushed** (pʊʃt), *ppl. a.*; also *Comb.*, as ***pushed-back, -down, -up*** ppl. adjs.

1658 BP. REYNOLDS *Lord's Supper* xii, Would not God, in the Law, accept of any but pushed, and dissected, and burned sacrifices? **1878** *Q. Jrnl. Geol. Soc.* XXXIV. 566 Pushed-up mounds or long ridges of gravels..are a conspicuous feature along the shores of the Polar basin. **1922** JOYCE *Ulysses* 45 They wait, their pushedback chairs.. around a board of abandoned platters. **1948** P. WHITE *Aunt's Story* iv. 80 Theodora had gone. There was only the pushed-back furniture. **1962** *Listener* 5 Apr. 617/2 Mr Thomas has the commanding quality of a real *Heldentenor*, not a pushed-up baritone as are many Wagnerian tenors. **1969** *Jane's Freight Containers 1968–69* 286/1 The Rhône.. will be open to pushed convoys of 3,000 tons. **1971** D. E. WESTLAKE *I gave at the Office* (1972) 20 The pushed-down button for the line in use goes right on.

push-, the stem of PUSH *v.*, or PUSH *sb.*[1], in combination. **a.** General: in the senses (*a*) moved or actuated by a push, or by pushing, as ***push-bar, -basket, -boat, -net, -nipple, -pick, -plane, -tap***; (*b*) used for pushing, communicating a push, as ***push-pedal, -piece, -pole, -rod*** (also *attrib.*), ***-stick, -work***. (*c*) with advbs. forming sbs. and adjs., as ***push-along, -in, -on, -out*** (also PUSH-DOWN *sb.* and *a.*, etc.), indicating (*sb.*) the act of pushing in the direction specified; (*adj.*) that pushes or is pushed in the direction specified. **b.** Special Combs: **push-ball**, a game in which a very large ball is pushed by the hands and bodies of the players towards the opponents' goal; also *attrib.*; **push-barred** *a.*, (*Billiards*) in which a PUSH (1 b) is barred or forbidden; **push-battle**, a game; **push-bicycle, -cycle**, an ordinary bicycle, propelled by the rider, as distinguished from one driven by a motor; **push-bike** *colloq.*, a push-bicycle; hence as *v. intr.*, to ride a push-bicycle; also **push-biking** *vbl. sb.*; **push-board**, some parlour game: see quot.; **push-car**, (*a*) *U.S.* a hand-car; (*b*) *U.S.* a bogie car used to connect an engine with a train which is on a ferry-boat; (*c*) *U.S.* a plate-layers' trolley; (*d*) a perambulator; **push-cart**, (*a*) a hand-cart; also *attrib.*; (*b*) a perambulator; **push-chain** *Linguistics*, a sound shift in which one phoneme approaches a second and this in turn shifts so that their differentiation is maintained; also *attrib.*; **push-chair**, a small, wheeled, usu. folding chair in which a child can be pushed along; **push-cyclist**, a rider of a push-cycle; **push drive** *Cricket*, a drive (DRIVE *sb.* 1 d) in which the ball is pushed instead of struck; **push fit**, a fit which enables a part to be pushed into a hole by hand but does not allow free rotation; **push-foot** = *push-pedal*; **push-halfpenny**, a game in which coins are pushed over a mark on a level surface; shove-halfpenny; **push hold** *Mountaineering* = *pressure hold* s.v. PRESSURE *sb.* 10; **push-hole**, see quot.; **push-in**, (*a*) *U.S. slang*, a certainty; (*b*) *Hockey*, the act or action of pushing the ball into play from the side-line; (*c*) *Austral. slang* (see quot. 1979); **push money** *U.S. slang* = SPIFF *sb.*; **push moraine** *Physical Geogr.*, an arc-shaped moraine formed by an advancing or re-advancing glacier or ice-sheet which pushes material before it into low ridges; **push-out**, (*a*) *sb.*, one who is made to leave, esp. school; *slang*; (*b*) *adj.*, that pushes out; **push pass** *Sport*, a pass effected by pushing rather than hitting or kicking the ball; **push-penny** = *push-halfpenny*; **push-pit** *Naut.* [formed humorously after PULPIT *sb.* 4 f], a raised safety rail in the stern of a boat; **push plate**, a plate attached to a door by which it may be pushed open; **push-plough** = BREAST-PLOUGH; **push-process** *v. trans. Photogr. colloq.*, to develop (a film) in such a way as to increase or maximize its effective speed; so **push-processing** *vbl. sb.*; **push-shot** = *push-stroke*; **push-start** *v.*, to start (a motor vehicle or engine) by pushing (the vehicle), usu. after failure of normal procedures; also as *sb.* (*lit.* and *fig.*); **push-stroke**, in *Billiards, Cricket*, and *Golf* = PUSH *sb.* 1 b; **push-through**, (*a*) a narrow passage through a boundary wall, etc.; (*b*) an instrument for cleaning the bore of a rifle (cf. *pull-through* s.v. PULL- 1); (*c*) used *attrib.* to designate things in which one part is pushed through another; **push-towing** *vbl. sb.*, the propulsion of a line of connected unpowered barges by a powered one at each end; also *loosely* (see quot. 1959); so **push-tow**, a line of such vessels; also *attrib.* and as *v. trans.*

1977 *Grimsby Even. Tel.* 14 May 9/2 (Advt.), Pedigree *pushalong fur horse excellent condition, £4.50. **1898** *Encycl. Sport* II. 168/2 *Pushball was developed out of mere experiments into an organised game about the year 1895 by the Newtown Athletic Club near Boston U.S.A. The ball used is made after the same fashion as the ordinary round football used in the English Association game, but has a diameter of about 6 feet. **1895** *Funk's Stand. Dict.*, **Push-bar*, a bar that sustains a pushing stress. **1906** *Westm. Gaz.* 7 Feb. 8/1 Pointing to the extra push-bar exits and elaborate fire appliances. **1898** *Ibid.* 16 Apr. 7/2 A new *push-barred record of 679. **1956** *Harper's Mag.* May 20/2 She threads her *pushbasket along the alleys of the super market. **1898** B. GREGORY *Side Lights Confl. Meth.* 520 In our all-including games, like *push-battle. **1906** *Bazaar, Exch. & Mart* 16 Nov. (Suppl.) 2042/3 Exchange [motor-cycle]..for good make 25in *push bicycle and cash. **1908** *Daily Chron.* 21 Nov. 9/5 Spring forks, which are considered debatable points on a push bicycle, are now recognised as absolute essentials on the..motor cycle. **1913** 'I. HAY' *Happy-go-lucky* xiv. 180 Luckily I had the old *push-bike with me, and I managed to find my way down here. **1914** C. HOLME *Lonely Plough* xx. 236 Strenuous figures with bare knees and flapping overcoats push-biked past them. **1918** S. P. B. MAIS *Schoolmaster's Diary* xvi. 253, I 'push-biked' the eight miles into Lewes. **1920** *Isis* 3 Nov. 3/1 Self-advertisement, or the man who rides a push-bike with both hands in his trouser pockets. **1970** 'D. HALLIDAY' *Dolly & Cookie Bird* viii. 123 Derek..thought of a push-bike... He didn't want to be followed. **1926** *Punch* 8 Dec. 643/1 Music, Greek Plays, '*push-biking' tours—All figure in his pages. **1972** *Guardian* 22 Feb. 11/3 If you take to push-biking..you will need some pedal-pushers. **1906** *Daily Chron.* 10 Feb. 6/1 Playing a kind of bagatelle or *push-board. **1928** P. C. CHAMBLISS in J. Schoettle *Sailing Craft* 202 The patent stern affords means of fixing davits by which bugeyes may hoist their motor yawls or *push boats. **1967** *Guardian* 17 June 9/6 The pushboat picks them [*sc.* barges] up..loaded or unloaded. **1884** E. W. NYE *Baled Hay* 225 A section-crew ..riding down that mountain on a *push-car. **1922** JOYCE *Ulysses* 240 Edy..was rocking the chubby baby to and fro in the pushcar. **1893** E. KING *Joseph Zalmonah* ix. 105 Some hundreds of '*push-carts' like Ben Zion's were ranged within the narrow limits of Hester Street. **1897** F. MOSS *Amer. Metropolis* III. ix. 202 The visitor may stand at one point and see without moving..sidewalk merchants and push-cart vendors. **1899** MORROW *Bohem. Paris* 224 Street hawkers with their heavy push-carts. **1909** *Daily Chron.* 10 Dec. 5/4 She ran into the..street, and there found the push-cart, and saw the man hurrying away with the baby wrapped up in a travelling rug. **1921** *Daily Colonist* (Victoria, B.C.) 12 Oct. 16/3 (Advt.), Child's wicker push-cart, price $5. **1931** J. T. ADAMS *Epic of Amer.* xii. 346 Many of the other 'great' bankers..had the souls of pushcart peddlers. **1973** *Amer. Speech* 1969 XLIV. 265 All the level 3 stores operated on the supermarket plan with pushcarts and terminal checkout booths. **1952** A. MARTINET in *Word* VIII. 11 It may often be difficult to tell whether we have to do with a B→A→ chain, or drag-chain, or an A→C→ chain, or *push-chain. **1969** R. D. KING *Hist. Linguistics & Generative Gram.* viii. 194 If one rejects the gradualness of phonological change..and the notion that language abhors merger, push chains are deprived of their major source of plausibility. **1972** M. L. SAMUELS *Linguistic Evol.* iii. 31 If one phoneme shifts, others will also shift in such a way that the differentiation is preserved ('push-chain mechanism'), while others again will automatically increase their area of possible realisation by moving into the vacated space ('drag-chain mechanism'). **1977** *Language* LIII. 239 Graphemic change provides evidence for a push chain. **1921** *Sunday at Home* Feb. 257/2 Up the hill she struggled... She was throwing her weight against a small *push-chair with a carpet seat. **1963** *Times* 25 May 9/5 As the mothers come out of the shops they pop sweets into the mouths of the two-year-olds sitting in pushchairs. **1972** J. WILSON *Hide & Seek* i. 19 She hesitated, wondering whether to pop Jamie in his pushchair and go after them. **1905** *Daily Chron.* 1 June 3/6 Anyone who has tried it, knows that a motor-cycle is as comfortable as a '*push-cycle' over the same piece of road, at double the speed. **1931** D. L. SAYERS *Five Red Herrings* ii. 32 He had the body on the floor of the tonneau and on top of it he had a push-cycle, which has left tarry marks on the cushions. **1915** W. H. L. WATSON *Adventures Despatch Rider* v. 63 We stopped and questioned a 'civvy' *push-cyclist. **1927** *Daily Express* 27 Dec. 3/7 A push-cyclist.. writes to protest against being forced to show a red light behind. **1920** D. J. KNIGHT in P. F. Warner et al. *Cricket* (new ed.) 28 If the ball is not struck on the half-volley, but a little later, it [*sc.* the drive] becomes what is known as the *push drive, and is in fact the ordinary forward shot. **1918** D. T. HAMILTON *Gages, Gaging & Inspection* ii. 38 *Push fits.. are for shafts that are forced into a hole by hand and that would be free to rotate without seizing, but not free enough to rotate under anything but a very slow speed. **1960** *Practical Wireless* XXXVI. 330/1 A 2½in. length of steel knitting needle ground down to a push fit inside the nylon bearing. **1900** G. D. HISCOX *Horseless Vehicles* ii. 37 The movement.. was made by a *push-foot connection from a three-throw crank shaft. **1957** R. G. COLLOMB *Dict. Mountaineering* 122 *Push Hold. (*American.*) A pressure hold. **1976** D. CLARK *Dread & Water* v. 107 Zoom lens showing handholds—push hold, jug-handle, fingers clenched on a small hold. **1875** KNIGHT *Dict. Mech.*, *Push-hole (*Glass-making*), a hole in the flattening-furnace for annealing and flattening plate-glass. **1948** *Daily Progress* (Charlottesville, Va.) 22 July 11/1 The statement that William and Mary [College] is a *push-in for top honors in the Old Dominion is just a lot of wild talk. **1970** *Sunday Tel.* 9 Aug. 24/6 The push-in, the latest addition to the sporting glossary, makes its international debut.. today... The new rule.. becomes operative for British clubs at the start of the season. **1976** READ & WALKER *Advanced Hockey for Women* v. 119 Occasionally the opportunity may arise to send the ball directly to the middle of the field from a push-in. **1976** *Sunday Mail* (Brisbane) 7 Nov. 47/11 They then walk home —and are followed by the 'push-in' merchants, the teenage savages who push their victims into their apartments from behind, slam the door and then lace into them. **1979** *Courier-Mail* (Brisbane) 20 Jan. 18/6 *Push-ins*, mugging at the door. **1939** C. MORLEY *Kitty Foyle* (1940) xxx. 296, I was getting twenty-eight a week and my *push money extra. **1960** V. PACKARD *Waste Makers* (1961) xix. 231 The spiff or PM is the 'push money' offered as a reward for each item of the brand sold. **1890** T. C. CHAMBERLIN in *Bull. Geol. Soc. Amer.* I. 28. A glacier deposits material at its margin in three ways: (1) It pushes matter forward mechanically, ridging it at its edge, forming what may be termed *push moraines. **1913** *Zeitsch. für Gletscherkunde* VII. 310 Part of the glacier margin was bordered by a push moraine from 5 to 8 feet high. **1960** B. W. SPARKS *Geomorphology* xiii. 292 Push moraines are a specialised form of end moraine caused by a readvance of an ice sheet thrusting till, or some similar deposit, up into low ridges. **1979** J. RABASSA et al. in C. Schlüchter *Moraines & Varves* 68/2 In March 1977, the ice front had already advanced over the proximal part of the fluvioglacial plain.., bulldozing its upper sedimentary cover into a set of push-moraines. **1920** W. T. GRENFELL *Labrador Doctor* i. 7 The shrimp fishermen.. used *push-nets in the channels at low tide. **1976** *Weekend Echo* (Liverpool) 4/5 Dec. 9/8 (Advt.), Shrimp push nets for sale, £12.50. **1902** *Engin. Rev.* (N.Y.) May 15/2 The sections [of the boiler] are united by malleable iron *push-nipples coated with copper, and fitting accurately reamed holes in the sections. **1926–7** *Army & Navy Stores Catal.* 285/1 Massage Bath Shower and Shampoo Set complete, with large rubber *push-on unions. **1974** K. CLARK *Another Part of Wood* ii. 69 The old push-on variety [of pianola].. gave the executant much more control than the later one-piece model. **1970** *Britannica Bk. of Year 1969* 798/3 *Pushout, a student dropped from school for unsatisfactory performance. **1973** *Times* 17 Dec. 2 The growing number of girls who are becoming homeless are not 'drop-outs', as generally thought, but 'push-outs'. **1974** *Florida FL Reporter* XIII. 43/2 The 'push-out' rate of minority students is a national disgrace. **1977** *Design Engin.* July 73/2 They are easily installed by simply squeezing into punched or drilled holes in 1·5mm cold-rolled steel sheets, and resist pushout forces of 260lb. **1963** *Times* 25 Feb. 4/3 Their forwards.. used the *push-pass far too often on a surface which demanded hard hitting. **1977** *Time Out* 28 Jan.–3 Feb. 6 (Advt.), Push pass... There are at least 26 familiar football terms in this puzzle. **1907** *Westm. Gaz.* 9 Nov. 16/2 Multiple disc-clutch, *push-pedals, foot-accelerator. **1908** *Ibid.* 19 Mar. 4/2 The two push-pedals performing the usual functions of disconnecting the clutch and putting on the brake. **1872** B. JERROLD *London* xviii. 146 Benches where they are playing *push-penny. **1975** *Country Life* 11 Dec. 1677/4, I am.. looking for examples of the following regional inn sports: aunt sally (Oxfordshire).. push penny (Lincolnshire).. actually played in English pubs today. **1843** *Penny Cycl.* XXVII. 108/1 (Repeating Watch), P is the pendant-shank or *push-piece. **1884** F. J. BRITTEN *Watch & Clockm.* 132 For setting the hands a push piece.. is pressed with the thumb nail. **1964** *English Studies* XLV. 23 The pulpit is in the bows; a similar device at the stern has become known.. as a **push-pit*. **1976–7** *Sea Spray* (N.Z.) Dec./Jan. 90/1 (Advt.), It does not get chipped or rattle against the pushpit. **1928** V. G. CHILDE *Most Anc. East* iii. 54 A steep-ended scraper or *push-plane. **1977** G. CLARK *World Prehist.* (ed. 3) v. 214 Wood-working equipment, manifested most notably in heavy bifaces and picks and in high-backed push-planes. **1907** G. A. T. MIDDLETON *Mod. Buildings* VI. xiv. 112/2 The double bolts as supplied for swing doors are the proper pattern to use... They are actuated from the inside by a small *push plate. **1963** W. C. HUNTINGTON *Building Construction* (ed. 3) xv. 661 Push plates or door pulls are provided on the closing stile as required. **1686** PLOT *Staffordsh.* 115 The turf.. they cut in the Moorelands in the Spring time with an instrument call'd a *push-plow, being a sort of spade, shod somewhat in the form of an arrow. **1906** *Daily Chron.* 11 Aug. 5/5 *Push-pole, and the inevitable negotiation of the greasy pole. **1971** Push-pole [see KILHIG]. **1977** *Sat. Rev.* 23 July 3/2 (Advt.), The 200 [*sc.* 200 A.S.A film] can be '*push-processed' to 400 speed... Dealer can sell you a kit, including directions for 'push-processing'. **1979** *Amat. Photographer* 10 Jan. 90/1 All these fast films can be push-processed to produce even higher speeds. **1908** *Westm. Gaz.* 16 Jan. 4/2 The inlet-valves are.. placed immediately above the exhaust-valves, and actuated by rockers and vertical *push-rods. **1934** *Jrnl. R. Aeronaut. Soc.* XXXVIII. 191 Push rod valve mechanism for air-cooled engines.. has been almost universally adopted during the last few years. **1973** *Times* 18 Oct. 35/3 The Polski 125P saloon.. has the same body as the old Fiat 125 and a 1500cc push rod engine. **1909** P. A. VAILE *Modern Golf* v. 84 The *push-shot is a dead straight ball, one of the straightest when well played. **1925** *Country Life* 15 Aug. 244/2 The push shots or placing shots... You can steer and guide these strokes with tolerable accuracy. **1957** S. MOSS *In Track of Speed* xiv. 182 Mechanics rushed out and *push-started us. **1965** D. LODGE *Brit. Mus. is falling Down* vi. 107 He prepared to push-start his scooter. **1973** *Advocate-News* (Barbados) 29 June 3/3 (Advt.), Maybe you have an idea. And all it needs is a push-start to get it off the ground. **1977** *Daily Tel.* 12 Jan. 10/4 One of my minor objections to automatic transmissions is that they can't be push started. **1979** K. O'HARA *Searchers of Dead* viii. 80 Owen.. once gave me a push-start when my battery was flat. **1922** *Woodwork Machinery Reg.* in *Statutory Rules & Orders* (1923) 276 A suitable *push-stick shall be kept available for use at the bench of every circular saw which is fed by hand, to enable the work to be carried on without unnecessary risk. **1947** J. CHARLESWORTH *Law of Negligence* xviii. 388 Failure to use a 'push-stick'.. may amount to contributory negligence. **1873** *Push stroke [see PUSH *sb.*[1] 1 b]. **1884** W. COOK *Billiards* 64 In order to play the push stroke successfully, it is necessary to hold the cue [etc.]. **1901** *Daily News* 1 Feb. 8/7 When the Prince was holing a short put at the home green, he cautioned his Royal Highness against giving the ball a push stroke. **1904** *Westm. Gaz.* 31 May 3/1 Drives between the off-side fielders, and push-strokes between the bowler and mid-on, and past mid-on. **1902** *Daily Chron.* 27 June 2/6 To provide *push-tap valves to the several troughs in this borough. **1888** *Athenæum* 18 Feb. 217 The side pieces of a Derbyshire stile or '*push through' in the churchyard wall. **1920** G. BURRARD *Notes on Sporting Rifles* 68 Greener's 'push through' is an excellent invention for all ultra small bores. **1970** *Which?* Aug. 237/2 Slip-over threading points are better than push-through points. **1979** D. FRANCIS *Whip Hand* xvi. 195 The push-through switch on a table lamp. **1955** *Bull. Soc. Naval Architects & Marine Engineers* Feb. 12/1 Single-screw tugs have been *push-towing for many years. **1955** F. MARBURY *Push-Towing in Waves* (MS. thesis, Mass. Inst. Technol.) i. 1 The standard river pushtow cannot operate in waves. **1964** *Marine Engineering Log* July 59/1 The economy and flexibility of push-tow operations are gaining favor with Japanese maritime interests. **1970** *1st Internat. Tug Conf. 1969* 272/1 Petroleum barges could be push-towed. *Ibid.* 362/1 In 1957 the first real push-tow.. appeared on the Rhine. **1973** *Guardian* 22 Jan. 6/5 Push-tow craft.. are, basically, floating boxes which can carry 140 tons and be locked together in a procession of nine, operated by two tugs. **1974** *Encycl. Brit. Macropædia* III. 758/2 These assemblies of unpowered and individually unmanned barges are known, somewhat illogically, as push tows. **1955** F. MARBURY *Push-Towing in Waves* (MS. thesis, Mass. Inst. Technol.) vi. 22 The basic conclusion.. is that as far as these tests extend *pushtowing in waves is feasible. **1959** G. WALKER *Traffic & Transport in Nigeria* iii. 47 'Push-towing' has now become the accepted practice. Power craft have two barges lashed to the forequarters, a third being pushed ahead. **1972** *Daily Colonist* (Victoria, B.C.) 29 Mar. 40/5 The tugs are intended for use in.. push-towing of such barges in moderate sea conditions. **1884** F. J. BRITTEN *Watch & Clockm.* 36 The *pushwork for setting the hands.

'push-and-go, *sb. phr.* and *adj. phr.* Also push and go. [f. PUSH-: see GO *sb.* and *v.*] **A.** *sb. phr.* The ability to develop and prosecute a scheme vigorously (see quots.); enterprise, initiative, ambition.

[**1915** D. LLOYD GEORGE in *Hansard Commons* 9 Mar. 1277 We are on the look out for a good, strong business man with some go in him who will be able to push the thing through and be at the head of a Central Committee.] **1915** *Times* 10 Mar. 14/5 The Government should.. get a business man at the head of the organization. The Government were on the look-out for a good, strong business man with some push and go in him, who would be able to put the thing through. **1916** LD. FISHER *Let.* 26 Jan. in M. Gilbert *Winston S. Churchill* (1972) III. Compan. II. 1398, I said what was required was '*Push and Go*'! (NOT '*Wait and See*'!). **1959** F. M. G. WILLSON in *Polit. Stud.* VII. 224 Recruits from business, industry, and trade unions begin with Sir Eric Geddes, one of Lloyd George's men of 'push and go'.. graduating to the Cabinet as the first Minister of Transport in 1919.

B. *adj. phr.* **a.** Ambitious, enterprising, pushing.

1932 KIPLING *Limits & Renewals* 80 He is one of the push-and-go type.. the flower of the Higher Counter-jumpery.

b. Of a motorized toy etc.: having a mechanism that stores and releases the momentum generated by a preliminary push.

1958 *New Scientist* 9 Jan. 15 This novel type of shunting locomotive is a larger-scale version of a child's 'push-and-go' toy. **1959** *Oxf. Mail* 21 Jan. 6/3 The soft plastic trains and cars had their wheels removed very promptly and the push-and-go 'engines' soon fall out.

'push-and-pull, *adj. phr.* and *sb. phr.* Also push and pull. [f. PUSH-: see PULL *sb.*[2] and *v.* and cf. PUSH-PULL.] **A.** *adj. phr.* Involving pushes and pulls, esp. alternately. **a.** *gen.*

1914 H. CARRINGTON *Probl. Psychical Research* xii. 371 A straight push-and-pull action is easier to accomplish than the more detailed and complicated action of forming words and letters. **1949** KOESTLER *Insight & Outlook* xiii. 192 The mechanistic push-and-pull physics of the last century. **1960** *Times* 3 Oct. (Advt. Suppl.) p. ii/2 The Skid-Stac attachment.. consists of a load carrying plate and push-and-pull rack.

b. Designating (the operation of) a 'reversible' train, which may journey in either direction without having its engine turned about. Also, of the locomotive engine itself. See also *pull-and-push* s.v. PULL- 3.

1939 K. G. FENELON *Brit. Railways To-day* iii. 61 The most hopeful solution would appear to be the adoption of the push-and-pull type of train, which can be driven from either end, and which can take extra vehicles if required. **1955** C. J. ALLEN *Gt. Eastern Railway* vi. 66 The Edmonton & Cheshunt line.. was.. reopened, on March 1st, 1915, to serve some munition factories in the neighbourhood, and was worked by a two-coach 'push-and-pull' unit with 2-4-2 tank No. 1311. **1965** K. HOOLE in *Regional Hist. Railways Gt. Brit.* IV. xii. 219 Push-and-pull units, first used between Hartlepool and West Hartlepool in 1905, became a familiar sight throughout the system. **1975** G. BYE in G. W. Knight *Jackson Knight* v. i. 367 A much planned.. trip on the 'Tivvy Flyer', the push and pull train on the Tiverton and Bampton branch-line, was, alas, never made.

B. *sb. phr.* **a.** *U.S. Mil.* (See quot. 1929.) Also *attrib.*

1920 *Official Hist. 315th Infantry U.S.A.* 28 The greater part of the time was devoted to.. the 'push and pull' exercise. **1921** F. T. FLOYD *Company F Overseas* 37 These rides remind a soldier of that bit of army exercise popularly known as 'push and pull'. **1929** *Papers Mich. Acad. Sci., Arts & Lett.* X. 317 *Push and pull*,.. sighting and aiming drill.

b. *fig.* Tug of war.

1958 *Spectator* 4 July 19/3 The dramatic centre of the book is.. the push-and-pull between Yule and his devoted but mutinous daughter.

'push-button, *sb.* and *a.* Also pushbutton, push button. [f. PUSH- + BUTTON *sb.*] **A.** *sb.* A button that is pressed with the finger to effect some operation, usu. by closing or opening an electric circuit.

1878 G. B. PRESCOTT *Sp. Telephone* (1879) 376 The push button or key used in short circuits serves to close the latter in a very simple manner. **1901** *Munsey's Mag.* XXV. 367/2 The subscriber presses a push button, and the two numbers to be connected are 'rung up' simultaneously. **1912** L. WEAVER *House & its Equipment* 124 The multiple contact switch, which consists of a little board.. on which are arranged a number of push buttons. **1920** C. SANDBURG *Smoke & Steel* 218 She used to keep a houseful of girls in kimonos and three pushbuttons on the front door. **1935** *Times* 2 Feb. 9/5 Special signal lights will face pedestrians and push-buttons will be fitted to the posts. **1943** T. HORSLEY *Find, fix & Strike* 64 The range is point-blank... The pilot's thumb, already on the push-button on top of the throttle bar, jabs hard against the stop. **1957** *Railway Mag.* Mar. 159/2 The pantograph is raised by pressing the push-button in the driving trailer. **1976** *Gramophone* May 1835/1 Below the main controls are the following: sockets for stereo microphone and headphones, push-buttons for low filter, high filter,.. and power on-off.

B. *adj.* **1. a.** Operated or effected by pressing a push-button.

1916 *Inland Printer* LVII. 830/2 (*caption*) 'Push-button control'. **1936** *Discovery* Apr. 113/1 The diesel engine is started electrically and the push-button control for this purpose is mounted in the cab adjacent to the driving positions. **1943** *Gramophone* Dec. 107/1 The radio has 3 bands with push-button tuning. **1957** *Observer* 25 Aug. 11/1 It is no doubt true that guided missiles, nuclear warheads, flame-throwers, and push-button apparatus do not in the slightest invalidate the elementary military virtues of *esprit de corps* and self-discipline. **1957** *Amer. Speech* XXXII. 313 The following list of descriptive terms that appear on the aerosol containers of.. shaving creams... *push-button lather*. **1965** *Wireless World* July 8/2 (Advt.), Stereo Amplifier.. push-button selection. **1978** S. BRILL *Teamsters* iv. 127 He took his seat.. alongside a table bearing two separate push-button phones.

b. *push-button war(fare)*, warfare conducted by means of (nuclear) missiles launched by the press of a button.

[**1945** *Life* 20 Aug. 17/1 There may be devastating 'push-button' battles.] **1945** *Richmond* (Va.) *Times-Dispatch* 9 Nov. 6/2 (*heading*) 'Pushbutton' war seen by atom men. **1946** *Ibid.* 21 Feb. 12/6 The push-button warfare forecast for the future. **1948** *New Republic* 29 Nov. 15/3 The vision of the clean, fast, economical impersonal push-button war grows dim. **1955** T. H. PEAR *Eng. Social Differences* vi. 139 In what historical perspective can we see the changes which radio, television, faster-than-sound travel, push-button warfare.. and social medicine are causing in our social life? **1958** *Daily Tel.* 28 June 6/3 If you are thinking in terms of push-button warfare.

2. Characterized by the use of push-buttons, *spec.* implying technological advancement; fully automated or mechanized.

1946 *Birmingham* (Alabama) *News* 3 Feb. 1/3 The Army Air Forces came forth Saturday with a real push-button plane. **1955** G. FREEMAN *Liberty Man* I. iii. 39 One might have thought he was a ship's boy serving on a graceful old tea clipper, rather than an efficient piece of mechanism in a modern push-button navy. **1960** *Times* 12 Jan. 13/5 The married woman of the future will live in an increasingly push-button home. **1962** *Lancet* 19 May 1081/1 The push-button type of hospital, which already exists in some countries, is not the sort of place in which one would choose to be ill. **1973** *Times* 17 Oct. 14/4 If increased mechanization should be decided on.. engineering would.. offer a vastly increased number of 'push-button' jobs.

3. Easily obtainable, as at the press of a button; instant.

1947 *Sun* (Baltimore) 20 Mar. 2/1 Political rulers.. have regularly resorted to manufacturing money by one process or another. This measure is the latest of these attempts at 'push-button' money. **1967** *Listener* 22 June 821/3 Some part of the price we are paying for the alleged boon of push-button entertainment.. can already be discerned. **1972** [see JESUS 3 b].

'push-down, *sb.* and *a.* Also pushdown. [f. vbl. phr. *to push down*: see PUSH *v.* 1 b.] **A.** *sb. Aeronaut.* A manœuvre in which an aircraft in level flight loses altitude and resumes level flight.

1938 [see PULL-UP 3 a].

B. *adj.* **1.** *Computers* and *Linguistics.* Being or pertaining to a linear store or list that receives and loses items at one end only, the first to be removed on any occasion being always the last to have been added.

1961 *12th Symp. Appl. Math.* 104 These problems seem amenable to solution by the application of techniques based on the use of what some computer people have come to call a 'pushdown' store. **1963** N. Chomsky in R. D. Luce *Handbk. Math. Psychol.* II. 343 Evidently pushdown storage is an appropriate device for accepting (generating) languages..which have..nesting of units (phrases) within other units, that is, the kind of recursive property that..we called self-embedding. **1963** *IEEE Trans. Electronic Computers* XII. 872 A 'push-down' list is one that is manipulated in a last-in, first-out manner. **1967** D. G. Hays *Introd. Computational Linguistics* ii. 31 The importance of pushdown storage lies in the fact that it has exactly enough power to deal with context-free languages. **1972** R. Quirk et al. *Gram. Contemp. Eng.* xi. 736 The *wh*-element can be fronted from a position in a clause subordinate to the *wh*-clause (a pushdown *wh*-element); for example the informal: I don't remember *which shelf* he told me I was to fetch it from.

2. That may be or is designed to be pushed down.

1977 *Custom Car* Nov. 18/1 The Escort has sprouted chrome push-down bonnet catches.

pusher ('pʊʃə(r)). [f. push *v.* + -er[1].]

1. a. One who or that which pushes (*lit.* and *fig.*). Also in various technical uses.

1591 Percivall *Sp. Dict.*, *Corneador*, a pusher with the hornes. **1676** Wycherley *Pl. Dealer* v. i, The beggarly Pusher of his Fortune has all he has about him still only to shew. **1859** Sala *Tw. Round Clock* (1861) 135 The pushers of invalid perambulators. **1860** Emerson *Cond. Life* i. *Fate*, Everything is pusher or pushed: and matter and mind are in perpetual tilt and balance so. **1881** *Instr. Census Clerks* (1885) 87 Brickmaking: Clamp Process:..Pusher-out. *Ibid.* 89 Flattening Glass Making..Pusher. **1884** A. M. Mayer in *Sport in Amer. Woods* II. 751 Boats..with a broad stern in which was a roomy seat for the pusher to stand on while he plied his 'gaff'. This is the name given to the pushing-pole. **1885** [see puller 1]. **1895** *Nebraska State Jrnl.* 23 June 5/1 As a student he was known as a 'pusher'; a man who was first in his classes and first in all the doings of the college. **1909** *Daily Chron.* 12 Oct. 4/6 It is a very difficult matter for an agent to canvass in a legitimate manner, as these special 'pushers' have told such glowing yarns of 'increased bonuses and profits'. **1929** [see passer 3 d]. **1946** Wodehouse *Money in Bank* xix. 159 He was not without his dark suspicions of that big-hearted pusher of oil shares. **1954** *Sun* (Baltimore) 5 June 1/8 Perry had come to this city..to act as a 'pusher' of the stolen cash. **1973** *Amer. Speech 1969* XLIV. 259 *Pusher*, locomotive that helps to start a heavy train or to push a train up a grade.

†**b.** (See quots.) *Obs.*

a **1700** B. E. *Dict. Cant. Crew*, *Pushers*, Canary-birds new Flown that cannot Feed themselves. **1725** Bradley *Fam. Dict.* s.v. *Canary bird.*

c. A girl, a young woman; *spec.* a prostitute. *slang.*

1923 J. Manchon *Le Slang* 236 *Pusher*,..girl, une typesse, une gonzesse. **1936** J. Curtis *Gilt Kid* 116 Mr. Bloody Bedbug's up here having a good time with my pusher. **1944** A. Wykes in *Penguin New Writing* xix. 105 A pusher for me. I'm off the beer, but I could use a judy. **1971** B. W. Aldiss *Soldier Erect* 19 Nelson and his pusher took the chance to sneak away, and I managed to manoeuvre Sylvia as far as the kitchen.

d. One who peddles drugs illegally. *slang* (orig. *U.S.*).

1935 J. Hargan *Gloss. Prison Lang.* 6 *Pusher*, one who retails drugs. **1948** H. L. Mencken *Amer. Lang.* Suppl. II. 681 A marihuana smoker is a *viper*..and a peddler is a *pusher*. **1951** *N.Y. Times* 14 June 1/1 Encouraged by 'pushers' of narcotics who sometimes offered free samples to beginners. **1956** 'E. McBain' *Cop Hater* in *87th Precinct* (1959) 60 Junkies are easy to trace. Talk to a few pushers, zing, you're in. **1959** *Guardian* 3 Dec. 9/2 High-powered city detectives..looking for 'junkies' (drug-addicts) and 'pushers' (drug-peddlers). **1967** E. Wymark *As Good as Gold* ix. 140 People like Crane..were called 'pushers' and were usually addicts themselves. **1976** *Howard Jrnl.* XV. I. 46 Western loathing for temptation is vented..upon the scapegoats of the junkie and the pusher.

2. a. A part of a machine having or communicating a thrusting action; a machine having such parts.

1839 Ure *Dict. Arts* 261 A pusher now acts behind the staple, and drives it home into the leather. **1852** Seidel *Organ* 38 Between the two shanks a strong ledge, called the pusher, can be drawn. **1875** Knight *Dict. Mech.*, *Pusher*, a form of bobbin-net machine..having independent pushers to propel the bobbins and carriages from front to back. **1882** *Blackw. Mag.* Oct. 484 The bobbins were acted on separately by a 'pusher' or governor.

b. *Naut.* The seventh mast of a seven-masted schooner.

1902 *Boston Even. Transcript* 23 July 20/3 The name of the masts, by the way, are in order, fore, main, mizzen, spanker, jigger, driver, and pusher. **1909** *Shipping Illustr.* 25 Dec. 327/1 As is now well known, the sixth mast was denominated the driver and the seventh the pusher.

c. *Aeronaut.* An aircraft having an airscrew behind the main wings. Freq. *attrib.*

1913 *Flight* 7 June 613/2 The 'pusher', as this machine is familiarly called to distinguish it from a tractor biplane of the same make. **1915** [see nacelle 2 b]. **1918** Cowley & Levy *Aeronautics* i. 5 The pusher type is much less efficient as a flying machine than a tractor. **1922** *Encycl. Brit.* XXX. 20/2 The first biplanes..were of the 'propeller' type, colloquially 'pushers'; almost all monoplanes were 'tractors'. **1940** *Sun* (Baltimore) 23 Aug. 4/5 The new Nazi types are reported to be a 'pusher' fighter..and a medium bomber. **1955** *Sci. News Let.* 19 Feb. 114/1 Another small 'pusher' propeller mounted between the double tail assembly gives thrust for level flight. **1969** K. Munson *Pioneer Aircraft 1903–14* 104/2 Later in 1906 Blériot converted this machine into the Blériot IV, installing two Antoinettes driving pusher propellers. **1976** *National Observer* (U.S.) 25 Sept. 17/1 Kiceniuk's aerobike looks like some experimental light airplane. It has red wings..and a 6½-foot pusher propeller.

3. An implement, in profile resembling a rake, used by infants to push food on to a spoon or fork; also, a piece of bread used for this purpose.

1926–7 *Army & Navy Stores Catal.* 606/3 Child's silver spoon and food pusher, in case—18/-. **1937** Partridge *Dict. Slang* 671/1 *Pusher*,..a finger of bread used as a feeding-implement. **1939–40** *Army & Navy Stores Catal.* 578/1 Child's silver spoon and food pusher, in case. **1957** J. Kirkup *Only Child* v. 84 Among the cutlery were my own two personal pieces—a spoon and a 'pusher'; the latter was an inelegant little implement which I used to push food on to my spoon. **1959** *Sunday Times* 25 Oct. 20/3 The traditional pusher is..on the way out..dropped..in favour of the spoon alone. **1963** C. Mackenzie *Life & Times* I. 155 The pusher, a small piece of crust which one was always being adjured to use more carefully to assist the cut up meat on to one's fork.

4. A push-chair. *Austral. colloq.*

1953 A. Upfield *Murder must Wait* vii. 60 Several prams and pushers parked in an alcove. **1966** G. W. Turner *Eng. Lang. Austral. & N.Z.* viii. 180 What he calls a *pushchair*..or a friend from Adelaide [calls] a *pusher*. **1970** K. Giles *Death in Church* vi. 151 With her patent folding, plasticised pusher she intended taking the twins for a walk. **1979** *Verbatim* Summer 8/1 When a headline announces that *pushers* are to be allowed on Adelaide buses, the permission extends not to 'peddlers of drugs' but to 'a child's pushchair'.

5. *attrib.* and *Comb.*, as **pusher set**, a baby's spoon and pusher; **pusher-tug** (see quot. 1970).

1939–40 *Army & Navy Stores Catal.* 543/3 Baby spoon (loop) and *pusher set—Gift box 5/-. **1951** *Catal. Exhibits, South Bank Exhib., Festival of Britain* 125/1 Pusher set..Feeding set. **1970** *Guardian* 19 Sept. 18/5 A 'train' of three barges is propelled by a 300 hp twin-screw '*pusher-tug'. **1973** Hrůša & Coxon tr. *Kozák's Ships* 188/1 A new towing system..involves the pusher-tug pushing a group of closely connected barges.

'**pushery.** *nonce-wd.* [f. push *v.* + -ery; cf. *jobbery*, *puffery*, etc.] The practice of pushing.

1788 Twining *Let.* 20 Jan. in Mme. D'Arblay *Diary*, I actually asked for this dab of preferment; it is the first piece of pushery I ever was guilty of.

pushful ('pʊʃfʊl), *a.* [f. push *sb.* + -ful.] Full of 'push' (see push *sb.*[1] 7); active and energetic in prosecuting one's affairs; self-assertive; pushing; aggressively enterprising.

1896 Ch.-Just. Alvey (U.S.) in *Westm. Gaz.* 21 Jan. 5/2, I suppose Mr. Chamberlain, more than Lord Salisbury, is the present representative of that pushful spirit which makes England's attempts to advance her lines and extend her Empire on this continent a subject of national sensitiveness. **1896** *Gentlewoman* 23 May 692/3 The Pushful Woman. **1899** *Athenæum* 21 Oct. 550/2 A little pushful perhaps, and in danger of being a little vulgar. **1931** Wodehouse *If I were You* xiv. 163 What a pushful young devil you are. **1938** E. Waugh *Scoop* iii. 272 He must be a very pushful fellow, inviting himself here like this. **1970** *Rep. Comm. on University Press* (Univ. Oxford) 71 This more 'pushful' approach. **1974** 'W. Haggard' *Kinsmen* ix. 93 The tiresomely modern bishop..was pushful and very far to the Left.

Hence '**pushfully** *adv.*, '**pushfulness**: also *fig.*

1899 *Westm. Gaz.* 29 Nov. 2 It is little like pushfulness to rely in this way on someone's book. **1907** *Academy* 17 Aug. 800/1 Be pushful and your nose will obtrude on society pushfully. **1926** R. M. Caven *Gas & Gases* ii. 38 The great characteristic of a gas or vapour is its pushfulness: it is always pushing. *Ibid.* 39 The property of a gas which we have colloquially called its pushfulness..with more propriety we should call the expansive power. **1958** *Economist* 25 Oct. 297/2 Moscow and Peking have divided, by tacit agreement, their zones of interference: China in Asia, the Soviet Union in the Middle East and Africa. Even so, the pushfulness of the two has varied remarkably. **1968** *Listener* 29 Aug. 280/2 The Dick Whittington legend..with its twin themes of individual pushfulness and the escape from provincial stagnation.

pushiness ('pʊʃɪnɪs). **1.** *Philos.* [f. push *v.* + -y[1] + -ness.] A term used by A. N. Whitehead (1861–1947) for the property inherent in a material object which enables it to be apprehended and identified by touch (see quots.).

1920 A. N. Whitehead *Concept of Nature* ii. 43 We are left with spatio-temporal positions, and what I may term the 'pushiness' of the body. **1927** B. Russell *Outl. Philos.* x. 118 We must give up what Whitehead admirably calls the 'pushiness' of matter. **1944** E. Nagel in P. A. Schilpp *Philos. Bertrand Russell* 339 It seems to me grotesque to say that the 'pushiness' of matter can disappear as a consequence of a new analysis or redefinition of matter.

2. [f. pushy *a.* + -ness.] = pushfulness

1968 *Economist* 2 Mar. 10/2 Claims in areas of particular union pushiness—say, for engineering draughtsmen—should be looked at very carefully indeed. **1976** *Times Lit. Suppl.* 23 Jan. 79/1 She had a kind of insistent pushiness in the interests of her family that brooked no contradiction.

'**pushing,** *vbl. sb.* [f. push *v.* + -ing[1].] **a.** The action of the verb push in various senses.

1530 Palsgr. 259 Pusshyng, thrustyng, *rebovtement.* **1659** C. Noble *Mod. Answ. to Immod. Queries* To Rdr. 2 May we not take these bold disputes and questionings, as pushings at the feet of his present Highness? **1799** Han. More *Fem. Educ.* (ed. 4) I. 244 With the same earnest pushing on to continual progress. **1885** Miss C. F. Woolson in *Harper's Mag.* Feb. 471/2 With some pushing he made his way within. **1962** 'K. Orvis' *Damned & Destroyed* ix. 61 My boss don't go for guys that goof like that. So he bounced me fast. I'm through pushing. **1971** B. Malamud *Tenants* 148, I wouldn't want him to go back to numbers, or pushing, or anything like that. **1974** P. McCutchan *Call for Simon Shard* iv. 42 The body had contained no residue of heroin, so pushing was more likely to be the answer.

b. *attrib.* and *Comb.*, as *pushing-pole*; **pushing-jack**, a form of jack (Jack *sb.*[1] 10) for moving or pushing a heavy object, as a railway-truck or the like, a short distance; †**pushing-master**, a teacher of fencing; **pushing-net**, ? = pout-net; †**pushing-school**, see quot. *a* 1700.

1698 Farquhar *Love & Bottle* I. i, He appeared crowded about with a dancing-master, pushing-master, music-master, and all the throng of beau-makers. *Ibid.* II. ii, Sir, here comes the pushing-master. *a* **1700** B. E. *Dict. Cant. Crew*, *Pushing-School*, a Fencing School. **1883** *Fisheries Exhib. Catal.* 254 Two Bag Nets. Casting Net. Beach Net. .. Pushing Net. **1884** Pushing-pole [see pusher 1].

'**pushing,** *ppl. a.* [f. push *v.* + -ing[2].] That pushes. **a.** Thrusting, shoving, driving.

1693 T. Power in *Dryden's Juvenal* (1697) xii. 305 A Steer ..Forward he bounds his Rope's extended length, With pushing front. **1854** Chr. G. Rossetti *Poems* (1904) 182 With pushing horns and clawed and clutching hands.

b. *fig.* That pushes forward; active, energetic, enterprising, keen to do business; also, intrusively forward, self-assertive, officious.

1692 Dryden *St. Euremont's Ess.* Pref. 8 As for personal Courage, that of Augustus was not pushing. **1737** L. Clarke *Hist. Bible* I. (1740) I. 33 Nimrod, a bold and pushing man. **1755** Johnson, *Pushing*, enterprising, vigorous. **1765** C. Brietzcke *Diary* 8 Aug. in *N. & Q.* (1964) CCIX. 13/1 Said Nothing.., for fear he should think me pushing. **1864** Burton *Scot Abr.* I. iv. 167 A pushing rising family. **1884** *Birmingham Daily Post* 23 Feb. 3/3 Assurance..Pushing Man Wanted. **1966** *Listener* 27 Oct. 613/2 Lesser men might think him pushing or selfish or out for his own ends.

Hence '**pushingly** *adv.*, '**pushingness**.

1847 Webster, *Pushingly.* **1881** *Daily News* Leader 23 Mar., Avarice, ambition, and social pushingness.

pushmi-pullyu, pushme-pullyou ('pʊʃmiː 'pʊljuː). [f. phrs. *push me* and *pull you*: see push *v.* 1 a.] A fabulous creature resembling a llama, but with a head at both ends, invented by Hugh Lofting (1886–1947) in *Doctor Dolittle* (see quot. 1922); hence (with spelling rationalized), applied allusively to incoherent or ambivalent attitudes or policies.

Widely popularized by the film version of *Doctor Dolittle* (1967).

1922 H. Lofting *Doctor Dolittle* x. 92 Pushmi-pullyus are now extinct... They had no tail, but a head at each end, and sharp horns on each head... Only half of him slept at a time. The other head was always awake—and watching. **1964** *Daily Tel.* 5 May 16/2 With one hand it [*sc.* the Government] may give them incentives to get out of London. With the other, it already gives them incentives to stay where they are... The total effect of these push-me-pull-you policies must be conjectural. **1972** *Guardian* 11 Jan. 12/2 The Push-me Pull-you Bill. **1972** *Times* 28 Nov. 14/6 The [Labour] party's imitation of a Pushme-Pullyou over the European Parliament. **1974** *Economist* 21 Dec. 52/2 Wilsonologists are now trying to work out..whether his pushme-pullyou performance was due to..agnosticism on the common market..or..a shrewd eye on the polls. **1975** W. Percy *Message in Bottle* i. 19 Man's theory about himself doesn't work any more..because its parts are incoherent and go off in different directions like Dr. Doolittle's *pushmi-pullyu.* **1976** *Times Lit. Suppl.* 2 Apr. 399/3 Children likewise seem to need jabberwockies and pushmipullyous [*sic*] to help them learn the boundaries of the natural order.

pushmobile ('pʊʃməbiːl). *U.S.* [f. push *v.* + -mobile.] (See quots.) Also *attrib.*

1911 A. N. Hall *Handicraft for Handy Boys* xxiv. 364 A Pushmobile is a unique form of home-made wagon that has been developed from the simple wagons which the boys used to make for coasting, and for pushing from behind, when the automobile was unknown. It is patterned as nearly as possible after an automobile, and it is pushed by the mechanician, who runs behind, while the driver rides and attends to the steering. **1952** *Milwaukee* (Wisconsin) *Jrnl.* 31 May (Green Sheet) 2/2 (*heading*) Try it! An airplane pushmobile. *Ibid.*, In this pushmobile airplane illustration I have not shown dimensions, for no two boys would work this out alike. **1974** J. Heller *Something Happened* 545 We made push-mobile scooters out of ball-bearing roller skates.

'**push-off,** *sb.* (*a.*) [f. vbl. phr. *to push off*: see push *v.* 1 b.] **1. a.** The act of pushing a boat from the land; hence, an effective send-off in starting on any course.

1902 *Daily Chron.* 8 May 5/2 He was the right person to give a push-off to this newest venture of the Christian Social Union.

b. The, or an, action of pushing down with the foot so as to propel oneself into the air.

1949 Shurr & Yocom *Mod. Dance* v. 165 In the leap, the push-off from back foot onto the forward foot, gives impetus to the leap. **1960** E. S. & W. J. Higham *High Speed Rugby* iii. 38 The take-off is from the *right* foot and consists of a vigorous push-off, so that the *left* foot can take a fairly generous step diagonally to the left.

2. *attrib.* or as *adj.*, designating something that pushes off, *spec.* a powered frame or bar that pushes material from the tines of a buck-rake or the like; also *absol.*

1957 C. CULPIN *Farm Machinery* (ed. 5) x. 277 A hydraulically operated push-off device can be used in conjunction with a front-mounted buckrake, and this outfit is more suitable than the simpler tipping type for loading most types of vehicles. **1970** *Financial Times* 13 Apr. 8/6 A new twin-ram push off buckrake. *Ibid.*, The push-off assembly is moved forward by two hydraulic rams. **1976** *Billings* (Montana) *Gaz.* 5 July 9-c/4 (Advt.), Used F10 D loader with hay basket, steel teeth, push-off, manure fork & grapple fork.

pushover (ˈpʊʃəʊvə(r)). Also **push-over, push over.** [f. vbl. phr. *to push over*: see PUSH *v.* 1 b.]

1. Something easily accomplished or overcome: an easy task or victory; a 'cinch'. *slang* (orig. *U.S.*).

1906 *Outing* Jan. 461/2 To me it looks like a push-over. **1926** *Amer. Mercury* Dec. 465/2 The combination is a push-over on Loew's or any other time. **1927** *Vanity Fair* (N.Y.) Nov. 67/2 Among some of Conway's more famous expressions are:..'It's a push-over' (a 'cinch'; easy to accomplish); [etc.]. **1931** E. LINKLATER *Juan in Amer.* II. xiii. 147 Those Princeton guys have been boasting that this game's a pushover for them. **1943** *Amer. Speech* XVIII. 256 Americanisms which have wide currency in Australia:.. pushover, [etc.]. **1951** 'J. WYNDHAM' *Day of Triffids* vii. 133 If Brigham Young could bring it off in the middle of the nineteenth century, this ought to be a push-over. **1973** P. MALLOCH *Kickback* xxi. 133 About the security van... It's going to be hard to take... Eight years ago they were a push-over.

2. Someone who is easily pushed over or overcome. *slang* (orig. *U.S.*). **a.** *Boxing.* A mediocre fighter.

1926 *Variety* 29 Dec. 7/4 A push-over, which means a fighter with round heels along cauliflower alley, was, by the same token, a dame on rockers in another circle. **1958** C. WILLIAMS *Man in Motion* (1959) iii. 27 He was a long way from being a push-over. He was a little heavier than I am, and he could really punch.

b. A woman who makes little resistance to demands for sexual intercourse; an easy 'lay'.

1926 [see sense 2 a above]. **1929** E. WILSON *I thought of Daisy* i. 16 Oh, Myra Busch is a push-over!.. She's got round heels! **1936** [see CINCH *sb.* 2]. **1949** H. WADMAN *Life Sentence* II. i. 49 Then you came along with Lawrence—the dark reasons of the blood, and so on. Naturally I was a pushover for you. **1955** D. BARTON *Glorious Life* xlvi. 155 She was a pushover, hardly worth the elaborate build-up. **1978** M. PUZO *Fools Die* xlvi. 487 Why the hell shouldn't she be a pushover? Weren't men pushovers for girls who fucked everybody?

c. An easy victim.

1934 *Sun* (Baltimore) 3 May 12/7 The would-be cracksmen have come to regard a policeman as a natural push-over. **1941** W. STEVENS *Let.* 13 Jan. (1967) 385, I suppose Denmark was a push-over on account of the pastry they eat there. **1959** F. RICHARDS *Practise to Deceive* vii. 106 You tell me that I'm.. such a pushover—that a good-looking man can.. wrap me around his little finger? **1975** D. W. S. HUNT *On Spot* v. 83 Since then our overseas suppliers have never been quite sure that we are a push-over at any price they like to ask.

d. Const. *for*. One who is readily influenced by or susceptible to the attraction of something; a 'sucker'.

1944 H. CROOME *You've gone Astray* xii. 123 Are you quite advertisement-proof yourself?.. I'm not. I'm a pushover for Vanity. **1946** 'J. TEY' *Miss Pym Disposes* xviii. 184 I'm a push-over for passing plates. It must be the gigolo in me. **1956** S. ERTZ *Charmed Circle* 96 He was always trying new tooth pastes and was a 'pushover'.. for all the advertisements he saw. **1975** *New Yorker* 21 Apr. 139/1 This department, always an old pushover for a picture horse, picks Foolish Pleasure.

3. *Rugby Football.* The action whereby one side in a scrum pushes the ball over the opponents' goal line, esp. in *pushover try*.

1958 *Observer* 14 Dec. 24/2 A 'pushover' try by Blackheath.. was the only score in a game in which the players could be heard ploughing their way through the mud. **1959** *Ibid.* 15 Mar. 32/8 The Welsh pack wheeled.. to try a pushover. **1960** *Times* 7 Mar. 4/7 After 25 minutes came a genuine pushover. **1977** *Western Mail* (Cardiff) 5 Mar. (Rugby Suppl.) 4/3 J. J. Williams's disallowed try in that game, I felt, was only as dubious as the England push-over try, also disallowed.

push-pin (ˈpʊʃpɪn). [f. PUSH- + PIN *sb.*[1] See also PUT-PIN.] **1. a.** A child's game, in which each player pushes or fillips his pin with the object of crossing that of another player.

1588 SHAKS. *L.L.L.* IV. iii. 169 To see.. Nestor play at push-pin with the boyes, And Critticke Tymon laugh at idle toyes. **1645** WITHER *Vox Pacif.* 60 Conditions made By Boyes, or Girles, at Push-pin, or at Cat. **1648** HERRICK *Hesper, Love's Play at Push-pin*, Love and my selfe (beleeve me) on a day At childish Push-pin (for our sport) did play: I put, he pusht, and heedless of my skin Love prickt my finger with a golden pin. **1775** ASH, *Pushpin*, a child's play in which pins are pushed with an endeavour to cross them. **1825** BENTHAM *Ration. Rew.* 206 Prejudice apart, the game of push-pin is of equal value with the arts and sciences of music and poetry. **1906** *Fortn. Rev.* Aug. 350 It was poetry and not push-pin that comforted Mill when he fell into despondency.

b. *fig.* As the type of trivial or insignificant occupation; child's play, triviality.

1672 MARVELL *Reh. Transp.* I. 15 Our Authors Divinity might have gone to Push-Pin with the Bishop. **1788** COWPER *Let.* 21 Feb. in *Davey's Catal.* (1895) 20 Every-thing that we do is in reality important: though half that we do seems to be push-pin. **1820** *Examiner* No. 623. 191/2 This is the push-pin of literary reading.

c. *attrib.* passing into *adj.* in fig. sense.

1681 T. FLATMAN *Heraclitus Ridens* No. 39 (1713) I. 256 Come, let's hear a little of his Pushpin Labours. **1683** KENNETT tr. *Erasm. on Folly* 36 A meer childrens play and a worse than Push-pin diversion. **1780** COWPER *Table Talk* 547 Every effort ends in push-pin play.

2. Chiefly *U.S.* (See quot. 1961.)

1923 *Geyer's Stationer* 5 May 42 (Advt.), Extensive advertising has created big sales for Moore push-pins. Glass heads—steel points. **1926–7** *Army & Navy Stores Catal.* 448/2 Glass push pins... It is a steel point with a glass handle, and is surprisingly strong in wood and plaster.. easily inserted, and as easily withdrawn. **1942** *Amer. Cinematographer* Apr. 188/3 A story board is a large 4 × 8 foot piece of wallboard or celotex, on which the story sketches are pinned in rows with aluminium push-pins. **1961** WEBSTER, *Pushpin*, a steel point having a projecting glass or metal head for sticking into a wall or board and used chiefly as a picture hook or as an indicator on a map. **1974** C. C. WOODARD *Cable Television* vi. 138 A pushpin is stuck in the map at that location; and that pushpin's number is written in the Work Requested section.

push-pull (pʊʃˈpʊl), *a.*, *sb.*, and *adv.* [f. PUSH- + PULL *v.* or *sb.*[2]] **A.** *adj.* **1.** Characterized by, caused by, or being a forced reciprocating motion; responding to or exerting both pushes and pulls. Also *transf.* and *fig.*

push-pull train (see quot. 1966).

[**1894** *Phil. Mag.* XXXVIII. 301 They.. show that the 'push and pull' theory is capable of giving an adequate account of the action of the telephone.] **1929** *Prof. Paper Inst. P.O. Electr. Engineers* No. 124. 34 The frequency characteristics of a Western Electric.. 'push-pull' carbon transmitter [*sc.* a microphone]. **1934** [see MULTIPOLE *a.*]. **1940** *Chambers's Techn. Dict.* 687/2 *Push-pull microphone*, a carbon microphone in which two carbon-granule cells are mounted on either side of a stretched diaphragm, so that amplitude distortion arising in one is largely balanced out by the opposite phase amplitude distortion in the other. **1951** *Engineering* 10 Aug. 178/3 'Push-pull' fatigue tests on welded bridge members were continued. **1959** [see FACIA 2]. **1962** R. B. FULLER *Epic Poem on Industrialization* 50 Basic structural stability.. by segregated satisfaction of isolated articulating push-pull forces. **1963** *Times Rev. Industry* June 117/1 Fork Truck Attachments... Drum forks, brick handling forks, push-pull device. **1966** K. MÖLLER *Amer. & Brit. Railway English* 31 *Push-pull, reversible train*.. a type of locomotive-hauled suburban train fitted with driving control apparatus connected to the engine, at the rear end. **1971** *Engineering* Apr. 110/2 (Advt.), A responsive industrial control system taking care of loads from a few ounces to over 1000 lb through push-pull cables. **1972** *Modern Railways* Sept. 364 Instances continue to occur of Glasgow-Edinburgh push-pull trains being worked by single locomotives. **1972** *Science* 20 Oct. 311/3 Cyclic AMP and cyclic GMP function in opposite directions, that is, in a push-pull fashion to exert long-term control over neuronal excitability in the sympathetic ganglion. **1978** A. HUXLEY *Illustr. Hist. Gardening* iv. 119 The push-pull weeder hoe —with a flat oblong blade sharpened on both edges.

2. *Electronics.* Having or involving two matched valves or transistors that operate 180 degrees out of phase on identical alternating inputs, so that they conduct for alternate half-cycles and their combined output is the sum of each acting alone, making possible increased power without reduced efficiency.

1924 *Wireless World* 4 June 277/2 With the push-pull amplifier one may employ smaller and therefore less expensive valves. **1925** *Motor* 8 Dec. 980 B/1 The Push-pull Wireless Circuit. **1932** *Oxford Times* 23 Sept. 22/5 Some manufacturers stock 'pairs' of carefully matched valves for push-pull amplification. **1945** *Electronic Engin.* XVII. 431/2 A more satisfactory way of cancelling or reducing cathode self-bias distortion is to use push-pull stages with common self-bias. **1955** *Radio Times* 22 Apr. 30/1 Table radiogram with 6-watt 'push-pull' output. **1965** *Wireless World* July 329/2 Fig. 8 shows a push-pull 55 kc/s oscillator which provides erase and bias signals. **1970** J. SHEPHERD et al. *Higher Electr. Engin.* (ed. 2) xxiv. 778 The fact that both *p-n-p* and *n-p-n* transistors are available enables push-pull circuits to be designed without transformers... If a *p-n-p* and an *n-p-n* transistor are fed from the same drive, a given input swing will cause one transistor to conduct more while the other conducts less, giving a push-pull operation. **1974** HARVEY & BOHLMAN *Stereo F.M. Radio Handbk.* v. 127 The driver transistor TR_2 provides a common phase signal drive to the bases of the output pair but since they have complementary characteristics, the operation is in effect push-pull.

3. *Cinemat.* (See quot. 1973.)

1934 *Jrnl. Soc. Motion Picture Engin.* July 52 In addition to its inherent freedom from ground noise, the push-pull sound track has other advantages. **1938** *Encycl. Brit. Bk. Year* 498/1 Although not new in 1937, the use of push-pull sound recording increased considerably during the year. **1959** *B.S.I. News* Sept. 25 Sound records and scanning area of 35 mm double width push-pull sound prints (normal and offset centreline types). **1973** D. A. SPENCER *Focal Dict. Photogr. Technologies* 498 *Push-pull sound track*, optical sound track on a cine film divided into two equal parts which were exposed to light modulated in opposite phase.

B. *sb.* Chiefly *Electronics.* A push-pull arrangement or state; esp. in adv. phr. ***in push-pull***.

1929 *Exper. Wireless & Wireless Engineer* VI. 307/1 A pair of valves, (or banks of valves), working in opposite phase, commonly called 'Push-pull'. **1932** *Oxford Times* 23 Sept. 22/5 Push-pull gives the last stage a much greater power-handling capacity. **1943** *Electronic Engin.* XVI. 55/1 The advantages to be gained by the use of push-pull for deflection are so great that unbalanced time-bases are rarely employed in cathode-ray tube circuits. **1948** A. L. ALBERT *Radio Fund.* ix. 360 Radio-frequency power amplifiers often are operated in push-pull. **1962** A. NISBETT *Technique Sound Studio* 276 Movement of the stylus produces variations in the magnetic flux, which in turn generates a current in a coil (or in two coils situated on paths which are favoured alternately, and operate in push-pull). **1962** *Listener* 7 June 1006/2 One could not help speculating on the strange symbiosis or state of push-pull—call it what you like —which exists between him and his age. **1975** G. J. KING *Audio Handbk.* iv. 83 The output stages of hi-fi amplifiers employ two transistors in push-pull.

C. *adv. Electronics.* In a push-pull manner.

1947 R. LEE *Electronic Transformers & Circuits* v. 109 Operation may sometimes be improved by the use of two tubes connected push-pull. **1978** *Nature* 6 Apr. p. xxxiii/2 Errors existing between the DC reference and the detected signal are amplified and applied push-pull to a transverse field electro-optic light modulator.

push-push (ˈpʌʃpʌʃ). [f. PUSH *v.*] (See quots.)

1907 *Westm. Gaz.* 13 Dec. 12/1 The only means of conveyance for travellers in this delightful part of India has been the 'push-push',.. resembling a bathing-machine, which is impelled by relays of coolies. **1921** *United Free Church Miss. Rec.* June 187/2 All rode wherever they went, or stayed at home, if they did not care to hire the 'push-push', an unwieldy machine like a long bathing-coach on four wheels, and drawn and shoved by eight or ten men.

Pushtoo, -tu, *sb.* and *a.* Formerly usual spellings of PASHTO *sb.* and *a.*

Pushtun, var. PAKHTUN *sb.* and *a.*

'push-up, *sb.* and *a.* Also **pushup, push up.** [f. vbl. phr. *to push up*: see PUSH *v.* 1 b.]

A. *sb.* = PRESS-UP; also, an exercise on parallel bars in which the body is supported by the bent forearms and raised by straightening the arms. Also *attrib.* Chiefly *U.S.*

1906 *Amer. Mag.* LXIII. 139/1 First they put him on the parallel bars and beseeched him to do many push-ups, prodding him gently to further exertion when he showed signs of fatigue. **1943** *Sun* (Baltimore) 16 June 8/6 Ten pushups and work details are standard punishments for other minor offences. **1952** J. STEINBECK *East of Eden* xlvi. 516 William C. Bunt died right on the armory floor in the middle of a push-up. His heart couldn't take it. **1958** *Times* 26 Feb. 8/4 Half the boys examined could not do a single push up. **1968** M. RICHLER *Cocksure* vii. 44 Tomasso.. did push-ups on his office carpet every morning. **1973** *Black Panther* 24 Mar. 6/2 Sometimes they make you remain in a push-up position on your knuckles until your knuckles begin to bleed. **1978** S. BRILL *Teamsters* iii. 107 Twenty push-ups.. was all the exercise a busy union leader should have time for.

2. The act or process of picking a pocket in which the victim's arm is pushed away from his pocket by an accomplice; also *attrib.*, as ***push-up man, mob.*** *Austral. slang.*

1919 V. MARSHALL *World of Living Dead* 69 He acts as chief amongst his 'push-up' and 'break' men, associates skilled in their way, but unpossessed of his dexterity. **1938** F. D. SHARPE *Sharpe of Flying Squad* i. 15 Pick-pockets are known as 'Wizzers' or 'The Push Up Mob'. *Ibid.* 332 *Push Up (The)*, picking pockets.

3. A muskrat's resting-place, formed by pushing up vegetation through a hole in the ice. *N. Amer.*

1936 K. CONIBEAR *North Land Footprints* 254 There's no danger of catching her [*sc.* a fox] either; she didn't go near the push-up. **1956** H. S. M. KEMP *Northern Trader* (1957) iv. 57 He indicated.. the little 'pushup' wherein the muskrat would come to sun himself on the warmer days. **1959** E. COLLIER *Three against Wilderness* xxviii. 297 The ice should be sound enough for us to get onto it afoot to start staking the muskrat push-ups.

B. *adj.* **1.** That pushes or may be pushed up.

1963 *N.Y. Times* 17 Nov. 12 This slipon coverall.. in deftly cut cotton with.. push-up sleeves. **1966** A. E. LINDOP *I start Counting* iv. 71 The big push-up windows. **1972** D. LEES *Zodiac* 145 A door that.. had one of those push-up bars like the emergency door of a cinema. **1977** *Detroit Free Press* 11 Dec. 6-c/2 (Advt.), Seamless push-up bra with underwire, removable padding.

2. *Computers.* (See quots. 1966, 1977.) Cf. PUSH-DOWN *a.* 1.

1966 C. J. SIPPL *Computer Dict.* 149/2 *Push-up list*, a list of items where the first item is entered at the end of the list, and the other items maintain their same relative positions in the list. **1969** P. B. JORDAIN *Condensed Computer Encycl.* 406 The pushup-list concept is used whenever there is a queue of approximately equal-priority requests that are waiting to be serviced. **1977** P. QUITTNER *Problems, Programs* 375 *Pushup list*, a list that is constructed and maintained so that the next item to be retrieved and removed is the oldest item still in the list, that is first in, first out (FIFO).

push-wainling (ˌpʊʃweɪnlɪŋ). *nonce-wd.* Also **pushwainling.** [f. PUSH- + WAIN *sb.*[1] + -LING *suffix*[1] 2.] A perambulator.

1878 W. BARNES *Outl. Eng. Speech-Craft* 72 *Perambulator* (the child's carriage), push-wainling. **1908** A. C. SWINBURNE *Let.* 22 Jan. (1962) VI. 211, I met.. a fair friend ..who beamed.. from the depth of her pushwainling (I hope you never use the barbaric word 'perambulator'?)... The happy term 'pushwainling' for a baby's coach of state is what makes him [*sc.* W. Barnes] immortal in my eyes. **1962** *Listener* 16 Aug. 257/1 He [*sc.* W. Barnes] was also a philologist, the kind that.. advocates such coinages as 'two-horned rede-ship' (dilemma) and 'pushwainling' (perambulator).

pushy (ˈpʊʃɪ), *a. colloq.* (orig. *U.S.*). [f. PUSH *sb.*[1] or *v.* + -Y[1].] Unpleasantly forward or self-assertive; aggressive.

1936 M. MITCHELL *Gone with Wind* viii. 142 It [*sc.* Atlanta] had nothing whatever to recommend it—only its railroads and a bunch of mighty pushy people... Restless, energetic people from the older sections of Georgia. **1959** T.

Griffith *Waist-High Culture* xi. 148 The more talented.. can be counted on to disqualify themselves further by seeming too pushy. **1963** M. Beadle *These Ruins are Inhabited* xii. 187 A retired-colonel type.. would.. turn and glare because you were being pushy. **1969** *New Yorker* 14 June 44/2 His speaking style.. sounds pushy. If I'm in a bad mood, it bugs me. **1971** *Nature* 20 Aug. 510/2 Is it.. that pushy polytechnics will in future be encouraged to usurp the position of the weaker universities in the academic pecking order? **1972** M. Babson *Murder on Show* vi. 71, I don't mean to be *pushy*... I just thought one had a duty as a citizen. **1979** *N.Y. Rev. Bks.* 25 Oct. 49/1 He faced the rise to autonomous power during the war of pushy new groups—generals, industrial managers, the secret police. **1980** *Times* 29 Feb. 13 The poor dancers gibber earnestly through its minimal dance content, pushy violence and unmotivated antics.

pusill ('pju:sɪl), *a.* and *sb.*[1] *rare.* [ad. L. *pusillus* very small; cf. F. *pusil* feeble (16th c.).]

†**A.** *adj.* Small, insignificant, petty. *Obs.*

1623 Cockeram, *Pusill*, small. **1640** G. Watts tr. *Bacon's Adv. Learn.* iv. iii. §3 To be enquired, by what efforts such a pusill and a thin-soft aire should put in motion such solid and hard bodies.

B. *sb.* †**1.** A variety of pear. *Obs.*

1615 Brathwait *Strappado* (1878) 170 Heere the Plum, the Damsen there The Pusill, and the Katherins peare.

2. A little or weak one, a child. *rare*$^{-1}$.

1884 Blackmore *Tommy Upm.* v, He has not doubted to encounter.. the foes of the pusill committed to his charge.

Hence †'**pusillage** *Obs.*, littleness, smallness, insignificance; '**pusilling** *rare*$^{-1}$ [cf. *weakling*], a small person, a dwarf.

1610 W. Folkingham *Art of Survey* Author to Wk. 8 Thy abortiue Limbes I rather chose In close concealement from this captious Age To smoother, ay, than rashly thus t'expose.. thy Pusilage. **1891** Atkinson *Last of Giant-Killers* 107 Stand out of the way, you pusilling of a dwarf, you.

†**pusill**, *sb.*[2], obs. var. of pucelle.

c **1610** B. Jonson *To Fletcher on Faithf. Shepherdess*, Lady, or Pusill, that wears mask or fan. **1624** Middleton *Game at Chess* i. i. 282 To invite the like obedience In other pusills by our meek example.

†'**pusilla,nime**, *a. Obs.* [a. F. *pusillanime* or ad. L. *pusillanimis*.] = pusillanimous.

1570 Foxe *A. & M.* 1128/2 It were farre from reason, to thinke that he which hetherto for his estate hath liued in such abundance, should be so pusillanime. **1577** Patericke tr. *Gentillet* (1602) 46 We discover our selves.. to be of a pusillanime, base, and feeble heart.

pusillanimity (,pju:sɪlæ'nɪmɪtɪ). Also 4-5 **pusillamite**, 5 **-animite**. [a. F. *pusillanimité* (14th c. in Godef., *pusillamité* 14th c. in Gower, *Mirour de l'omme*), ad. eccl. L. *pusillanimitās* (4th c.), f. *pusillanimis*: see next.] The quality or character of being pusillanimous; lack of courage or fortitude; pettiness of spirit; cowardliness, timidity.

1390 Gower *Conf.* III. 210 Bot it is Pusillamite, Which every Prince scholde flee. *Ibid.* II. 12, 25. *c* **1425** *Orolog. Sapient.* i. in *Anglia* X. 334/27 So þat sumtyme for þe pusillanimite and febelnesse of spiryte he wote neyþer wheþene hit comeþ or wheder hit goþ. **1534** More *Comf. agst. Trib.* ii. xiii. **1597** Shaks. *2 Hen. IV*, iv. iii. 114 The Blood: which.. left the Liuer white, and pale; which is the Badge of Pusillanimitie, and Cowardize. *a* **1653** Binning *Serm.* (1845) 529 It is a great weakness and pusillanimity to be soon angry. **1776** Mickle tr. *Camoens' Lusiad.* vii. 313 *note*, The.. pusillanimity with which they have long submitted to the oppressions of a few Arabs. **1855** Milman *Lat. Chr.* xiv. vii. (1864) IX. 251 The shame of Germany at the pusillanimity of Louis of Bavaria wrought more strongly on German pride.

pusillanimous (pju:sɪ'lænɪməs), *a.* [f. eccl. L. *pusillanimis* (in Itala *a* 150, rendering Gr. ὀλιγόψῡχος) f. *pusillus* very small, petty + *animus* soul, mind + -ous. Cf. F. *pusillanime*.]

1. Lacking in courage and strength of mind; faint-hearted, mean-spirited, cowardly.

1586 B. Young *Guazzo's Civ. Conv.* iv. 194 A scoffe is the reward of shamefast and pusillanimous persons. **1642** Milton *Apol. Smect.* Wks. 1851 III. 296 Where didst thou learne to be so agueish, so pusillanimous? **1769** Robertson *Chas. V*, vii. Wks. (1831) 576/2 An indignity which no prince, how inconsiderable or pusillanimous soever, could tamely endure. **1840** Carlyle *Heroes* iii, Nature.. remains to the bad, to the selfish and the pusillanimous forever a sealed book.

2. Of qualities, actions, etc.: Proceeding from or manifesting a want of courage.

c **1611** Chapman *Iliad* i. Com., Who can deny, that there are teares of manlinesse and magnanimity, as well as womanish and pusillanimous? **1698** W. Chilcot *Evil Thoughts* ix. (1851) 110 What a cowardly and pusillanimous disowning of his power and goodness! **1797** Mrs. Radcliffe *Italian* xxiv, You are now anxious to form excuses to yourself for a conduct so pusillanimous. **1882** Farrar *Early Chr.* I. 76 [Nero's] end, perhaps the meanest and most pusillanimous which has ever been recorded.

Hence **pusi'llanimously** *adv.*; **pusi'llanimousness** = pusillanimity.

1638 Sir T. Herbert *Trav.* (ed. 2) 91 The rebells *pusillanimously opposing that new torrent of destruction, gaze awhile. **1788** Gibbon *Decl. & F.* xl. IV. 87 He [John of Cappadocia] pusillanimously fled to the sanctuary of the church. **1871** Meredith *H. Richmond* xxxii, I was tormented by the delusion that I had behaved pusillanimously. **1727** Bailey vol. II, **Pusillanimousness*, want of Courage. **1889** J. Pearson in *Our Day* (U.S.) Sept., A veritable pusillanimousness had taken possession of that part of the people that really wanted the law enforced.

†**pu'sillity.** *Obs.* [ad. post-cl. L. *pusillitās*, f. *pusill-us* little, petty.] Littleness, pettiness.

a **1619** Fotherby *Atheom.* Pref. (1622) 18 Mans most contemptible pusillitie & baseness. **1661** Feltham *Resolves* ii. xxxiii, Without lessening God to the Pusillity of Man.

†**pusk.** *Obs.* [ad. obs. F. *posque*.] = posca.

c **1440** *Pallad. on Husb.* iv. 526 Suspence in rewle, hem kepe with pusk condite, Ypuld in myddis of a day serene.

pusle, pusley: see pucelle, pussley.

pusney, pusoun, obs. ff. puisne, poison.

puss (pʊs), *sb.*[1] Also 6-7 pus, pusse. [A word common to several Teutonic langs., usually as a call-name for the cat (rarely becoming as in Eng. a synonym of 'cat'): cf. Du. *poes*, LG. *puus*, *puus-katte*, *puus-man*, Sw. dial. *pus*, *katte-pus*, Norw. *puse*, *puus*; also, Lith. *puž*, *puiž*, Ir. and Gael. *pus*. Etymology unknown: perh. originally merely a call to attract a cat.]

1. a. A conventional proper name of a cat; usually, a call-name.

a **1530** Heywood *Johan & Tyb* (Brandl) 590, I haue sene the day that pus my cat Hath had in a yere kytlyns eyghtene. **1565** *K. Daryus* (ibid.) 181, I can fere the knaues with my grannams Cat. Pusse pusse, where art thou? **1568** *Jacob & Esau* ii. iv. in Hazlitt *Dodsley* II. 223 Esau left not so much [of the pottage] as a lick for puss, our cat. **1591** Percivall *Sp. Dict.*, *Miça*, the terme to call a cat, as we saie 'pusse'. **1648** Herrick *Hesper.*, *His Age* 89 Fore-telling.. weather by our aches... True Calenders, as Pusses eare Washt o're, to tell what change is neare. **1712** E. Cooke *Voy. S. Sea* 214 The Spaniards, when they call them, say Miz, as we do Puss. **1841** S. Warren *Ten Thousand a Year* xxxvi, 'Poor puss!' he exclaimed, stroking her.

b. Hence a nursery synonym or pet-name for 'cat'. Now mostly superseded by pussy.

1605 Chapman, etc. *Eastw. Hoe* iv. i, When the famous fable of Whittington and his pusse shal be forgotten. **1694** Motteux *Rabelais* iv. xvii. (1737) 71 The Bite of a She Puss [F. *chatte*].. was the Cause of his Death. **1744-5** Mrs. Delany in *Life & Corr.* (1862) 342 Have I told you of a pretty tortoiseshell puss I have? *c* **1840** W. E. Forster in Reid *Life* (1888) I. v. 135 A most delightful black kitten..; a most refined, graceful, intellectual, amusing puss.

2. Applied to other animals. **a.** A hare. In recent use only as a quasi-proper name.

1668 Etheredge *She would if she could* iv. ii, If a leveret be better meat than an old puss. **1703** Farquhar *Inconstant* iii. ii, Ah sir, that one who has follow'd the game so long.. shou'd let a Mungril Cur chop in, and run away with the Puss. **1709** O. Dykes *Eng. Prov. & Refl.* (ed. 2) 289 Makes a Hare of the one, and a Hound of the other, and only takes Puss's Part, to set the Dog after her. **1747** *Gentl. Mag.* 536 Now Puss in circling mazes flies. What glorious peals of musick rise! **1858** R. S. Surtees *Ask Mamma* xxxviii, After scudding up the hill, puss stopped to listen and ascertain the quality of her pursuers.

b. As quasi-proper name for a tiger.

1837 *Heath's Bk. Beauty* 156 Puss—a remarkably fine animal.. had fastened on the trunk of Falkiner's elephant.

3. Applied to a girl or woman; †**a.** Formerly, as a term of contempt or reproach (*obs.*); **b.** in current use, playfully, as a familiar term of endearment, often connoting slyness.

1608 Dekker *2nd Pt. Honest Wh.* i. Wks. 1873 II. 111 This wench (your new Wife).. This Shee-cat will haue more liues then your last Pusse had. **1610** B. Jonson *Alch.* v. iii, The bawdy Doctor, and the cosening Captaine, And Pvs my suster. **1663** Pepys *Diary* 6 Aug., His wife, an ugly pusse, but brought him money. **1732** Fielding *Mod. Husb.* iv. iv, I think her an ugly, ungenteel, squinting, flirting, impudent, odious, dirty puss. **1753** *School of Man* 95 The ingratitude, the villainy, says he, of the little Puss. **1846** Dickens *Battle of Life* i, 'Somebody's birth-day, Puss', replied the Doctor. **1861** T. A. Trollope *La Beata* I. v. 102 To think that the little puss should defend herself so coolly. **1881** Besant & Rice *Ch. Fleet* ii. ix, They could not have believed their daughter so sly and deceitful a puss.

c. int. **puss, puss**: used to imply that the person addressed is a 'cat' (see cat *sb.*[1] 2 a).

1926 H. Nicolson *Let.* 14 May in J. Lees-Milne *Harold Nicolson* (1980) xi. 235 The man was merely a prig.. he would look very foolish.. in Gordon Square (Puss, puss, puss). **1936** A. Christie *Murder in Mesopotamia* vi. 47 'We've been so very worried about dear Mrs. Leidner, haven't we, Louise?'.. 'Puss, puss,' I thought to myself. **1948** D. Ballantyne *Cunninghams* xviii. 95 'Stuck-up, if you ask me,' Joy said. 'Puss puss,' Ralph said. **1954** 'M. Cost' *Invitation from Minerva* 75 'Your cinema career was short-lived anyway.' 'Puss-puss,' she warned.

4. Short for puss-moth.

1819 G. Samouelle *Entomol. Compend.* 431 *Cerura Vinula*. The Puss.

5. Puss in the corner: a game played by children, of whom one stands in the centre and tries to capture one of the 'dens' or 'bases' as the others change places; also, in a more elaborate form, a sailors' game in the British Navy; also called **Puss, Puss**.

1709 W. King *Useful Trans. in Philos.* v. 43 The English Plays have barbarous sounding Names, as.. Puss in a Corner.. and the like. **1714** Pope *Mart. Scriblerus* i. v, I will permit my son to play at Apodidascinda, which can be no other than our Puss in a corner. **1738** *Gentl. Mag.* VIII. 81 The favourite one was Puss in the Corner... In this play, four Boys or Girls post themselves at the four corners of the room and the fifth in the middle, who keeps himself on the watch to slip into one of the corner places when the present possessors are endeavouring to supplant one another. **1864** Knight *Passages Work. Life* I. i. 34 The King.. caught Fanny Burney playing at puss-in-the-corner. **1866** *Daily Tel.* 8 Feb. 4/4 The necessities which frequently compel a Premier to make the reorganisation of his Cabinet a game of Puss-in-the-Corner. **1926** 'R. Crompton' *William—the Conqueror* xiii. 240 Now, what shall we play at first?.. Puss in the Corner? **1969** I. & P. Opie *Children's Games* vi. 207 The fun of 'Puss in the Corner' is that the players themselves negotiate when they are going to run; its disadvantage is that it is normally for five players, no more and no less. *Ibid.*, Names: 'Puss in the Corner' and 'Puss, Puss' (both common).

6. = pussy *sb.* 6. *coarse slang.*

Quot. 1664 may not exemplify this meaning, claimed for it by Farmer and Henley.

1664 Cotton *Scarronides* 107 Æneas, here's a Health to thee, To Pusse and to good company. And he that will not do, as I do, Proclaims himself no friend to Dido. **1902** Farmer & Henley *Slang* V. 333/1 *Puss*... The female *pudendum*.. also *pussy* and *pussy-cat*. **1935** in A. W. Read *Lexical Evidence from Folk Epigr. in W.N. Amer.* 71 She may (not?) be a cat trader's daughter, but she's got some puss. **1978** I. M. Gaskin *Spiritual Midwifery* (rev. ed.) i. 32 'Vagina' is the medical term, a Latin word, but I prefer to use 'puss' because it sounds friendlier. *Ibid.* 76 A loose mouth makes for a loose puss which makes the baby come out easier.

7. *attrib.* and *Comb.*, as ***puss-house***, ***-purr***; ***puss-faced***, ***puss-like*** adjs.; **puss boot, shoe** *Jamaica* (see quots. 1961 and 1970); **puss-gentleman**, a gentleman perfumed with civet (cf. *cat* = *civet-cat*, cat *sb.*[1] 4).

1942 L. Bennett *Jamaica Dialect Verses* 36 She.. Put awn wan tear-up frack Shove har foot eena wan ole *puss boot An go. **1961** F. G. Cassidy *Jamaica Talk* vi. 114 Tennis shoes with rubber soles and canvas tops are widely known in Jamaica as *puss boots* or *puss shoes*. **1970** *Country Life* 26 Feb. 510/3 We [in Jamaica] say 'puss boots' for plimsolls. **1883** Besant *Let Nothing You Dismay* ii, No poor *puss-faced swab to fear fair fighting. **1781** Cowper *Conversat.* 284, I cannot talk with civit in the room, A fine *puss-gentleman that's all perfume. **1869** J. S. Mill *Let.* 16 Jan. (1910) II. 177 Among the other additions there is a *puss-house. **1873** Leland *Egypt. Sketch Bk.* 59 The cobras are *puss-like in their habits, and like petting. **1935** T. S. Eliot *Murder in Cathedral* i. 43 *Puss-purr of leopard, footfall of padding bear.

puss (pʊs), *sb.*[2] *dial.* and *slang* (chiefly *Ir.* and *U.S.*). [a. Ir. *pus* lip, mouth.] A (discontented, pouting) mouth; a sour or ugly face; the mouth or face (considered as the object of a blow).

1890 D. A. Simmons *Words & Phr. Armagh & S. Donegal* in *Eng. Dial. Dict.* (1903) IV. 653/2 He has an ugly puss. **1891** J. Maitland *Amer. Dict. Slang* 213 *Puss* (P[rize] R[ing]), the mouth. **1898** G. Bartram *White-Headed Boy* 40 Say I'm the besht man, or I'll break your puss. **1910** P. W. Joyce *Eng. as we speak it in Ireland* 309 'He had a puss on him', i.e. he looked sour or displeased—with lips contracted. **1911** C. B. Chrysler *White Slavery* viii. 67 She gets 'a slam in the puss' (slugged, struck in the face). **1932** J. T. Farrell *Young Lonigan* iii. 111 He twisted his lips in sneers, screwed up his puss. **1936** 'F. O'Connor' *Bones of Contention* 210 Are you a dummy or what to be standing there with that idioty bloody smile on your puss? **1953** [see belt *sb.*[4]]. **1961** C. McCullers *Clock without Hands* iv. 81 When you looked at the picture I didn't like the look on your puss. **1971** A. Burgess *MF* xiii. 149 You can get her to keep quiet about it, threaten her with a sock on the puss and that. **1973** 'J. Patrick' *Glasgow Gang Observed* v. 49 Ah don't fancy the look o' his puss. Go ower an' stab him fur me. **1978** *Guardian* 2 Apr. 18/3 On the air, Frost's pasty puss looked like Nixon's with the air let out of it.

puss, *v. rare.* [f. puss *sb.*[1]] *intr.* To move or act like a cat, silently and stealthily.

a **1953** Dylan Thomas *Adventures Skin Trade* (1955) 101 They pussed and spied around the room, unaware of their dancing.

puss, obs. form of pus.

'**puss-cat.** = pussy-cat.

1565 *K. Daryus* (Brandl) 304 He shall go play with my mothers pussecat. **1598** Florio, *Micia*, a pusse-kat, a kitlin. **1604** W. Terilo *Fr. Bacon's Proph.* 171 in Hazl. *E.P.P.* IV. 274 The Pus-Cat and the Dogge, For safegard from the stealth Of Rats, and Mise, and Wolfe, and Foxe. **1915** J. Galsworthy *Bit o' Love* i. 19 Old puss-cat! **1957** [see hep-cat].

'**puss-,clover.** *U.S.* The hare's-foot clover, *Trifolium arvense*: so named from its silky heads.

1890 in *Cent. Dict.*

pussel, pussle, obs. forms of pucelle.

pussens ('pʊsɪnz), playful elaboration of puss *sb.*[1]

1922 Joyce *Ulysses* 55 Milk for the pussens, he said.

pusser ('pʌsə(r)), repr. naut. pronunc. of purser (sense 2 b). Also *attrib.* and in the possessive, as issued by, or characteristic of, a naval purser (cf. purser 2 b).

1903 [see matlo(w)]. **1916** 'Taffrail' *Pincher Martin* ii. 13 The articles comprising Martin's kit, even down to his 'pusser's dagger' or seaman's knife. **1925** Fraser & Gibbons *Soldier & Sailor Words* 232 *Pusser's crabs*, seamen's boots. (Navy—lower-deck.) *Ibid.*, *Pusser's dip*, a candle. **1929** F. Bowen *Sea Slang* 107 *Pusser's grins*, sneers. **1943** Baker *Dict. Austral. Slang* (ed. 3) 62 *Pusser*, that which conforms to Naval regulations, e.g., 'pusser's cow', tinned milk; 'pusser's duck', a naval seaplane; 'pusser's waggon', a warship; 'pusser's rig', naval clothes. (R.A.N. slang.) **1944** J. Mallalieu *Very Ordinary Seaman* 90 All the discomfort of a small ship and the pusser routine of a big one. **1948** Partridge *Dict. Forces' Slang* 149 *Pusser's duck*, a Supermarine 'Walrus' flying-boat. *Ibid.*, *Pusser's issue*, clothing, tobacco, food, etc., provided by the Admiralty.

1964 J. HALE *Grudge Fight* iv. 69 'Hot water,' he said, 'plenty of pussers soap—and elbow grease, got it?' *Ibid.* vi. 91 A pair of pusser's long pants. **1973** *Daily Colonist* (Victoria, B.C.) 29 Aug. 2/2 Then, of course, there was Navy pusser rum—not to be confused with any other make of rum. **1977** *Navy News* June 6/3 And dancing was in pusser's shoes on planks of wood laid on the grass. **1977** *Ibid.* Aug. 18/4 Pusser's rum, obtained commercially in Gibraltar, was poured from wicker-work covered jars.

'pussful. *Ir. nonce-wd.* [f. PUSS *sb.*[2] + -FUL.] Something to fill a person's (discontented) mouth.

1922 JOYCE *Ulysses* 197 The drouthy clerics do be fainting for a pussful.

pussivanting ('pʊsɪˌvæntɪŋ), *ppl. a.* and *vbl. sb. S.W. dial.* Also **puzzivanting**. [Corruption of PURSUIVANT *sb.* (*a.*) or *v.*] Causing a disturbance, intruding, meddling, fussing.

1880 COURTNEY & COUCH *Gloss. Words Cornwall* 45/2 *Pussivanting*, part., fussing; meddling. In the latter part of the seventeenth century the *Poursuivants* came into the county to search out all those entitled to bear arms. **1888** 'Q' *Troy Town* xvii. 203 'This 'ere pussivantin' may be relievin' to the mind, but I'm darned ef et can be good for shoe-leather.' (Note: in the Fifteenth Century, so high was the spirit of the Trojan sea-captains,..that King Edward IV sent poursuivant after poursuivant to threaten his displeasure. The messengers had their ears slit for their pains; and 'poursuivanting' or 'pussivanting' survives as a term for ineffective bustle.) **1915** GALSWORTHY *Bit o' Love* I. 17 There's puzzivantin' folk as'll set an' gossip the feathers off an angel.

pussley, -ly ('pʌslɪ). Also **pusley**. A corruption of PURSLANE, common in U.S.

1861 N. A. WOODS *Pr. Wales in Canada & U.S.* 309 The instant the land is ploughed a weed called 'Pussley' makes its appearance... This, when boiled, is a most delicious and wholesome vegetable, the leaves being like spinach, and the branches in taste resembling sea-kale. In prairie settlements pussley is always a standing dish. **1870** C. D. WARNER *Summer in Gard.* (1886) 150, I doubt if any one has raised more 'pusley' this year than I have. **1888** *Amer. Nat.* XXII. 778 To select the most offensive among the worst weeds.. among the annuals, especially in gardens, the purslane or 'pusley' perhaps takes the lead.

'puss-moth. [f. PUSS *sb.*[1] + MOTH: see quot. 1806.] A large European bombycid moth, *Cerura* (*Dicranura*) *vinula*, having the fore-wings of a whitish or light grey colour with darker markings and spots.

1806 SHAW *Gen. Zool.* VI. 228 This moth [*Phalæna Vinula*], from its unusually downy appearance, has obtained the popular title of the Puss Moth. **1817** KIRBY & SP. *Entomol.* xxi. (1818) II. xxii. 289 The caterpillar of the puss-moth..and some others, instead of the anal prolegs, have two tails or horns. **1869** NEWMAN *Brit. Moths* 216 When the caterpillars of the Puss-moth are about..to form their cocoons, the whole ground colour changes to a dull brown. **1881** EL. A. ORMEROD *Injur. Insects* (1890) 266.

pusso-, combining form of PUSS *sb.*[1], in humorous nonce-words: **pusso'maniac**, one with a mania for cats; **pu'ssophilist**, a lover of cats.

1890 *Sat. Rev.* 19 July 76/1 His master..is the reverse of a pussomaniac. **1891** *Athenæum* 22 Aug. 252/3 Cat lovers—pussophilists as J. S. Mill used to call them.

†'pussock. *Obs. rare.* [f. PUSS *sb.*[1] + -OCK.] A term for an old maid; an 'old tabby'.

1622 MABBE tr. *Aleman's Guzman D'Alf.* I. 26, I haue knowne since some old Maids Pussockes in comparison of her [my Mother] of greater yeeres and lesse Handsomnesse, that would call themselues..Girles and little pretty Maidens.

pussoun, obs. Sc. and dial. form of POISON.

'puss-tail. [f. PUSS *sb.*[1] + TAIL.] A popular name in U.S. for a common grass of the genus *Setaria* or Bristle-grass, in England sometimes called Foxtail.

1890 in *Cent. Dict.*

pussy ('pʊsɪ), *sb.* Also 6–8 -ie, 8 -ey; *Sc.* **poussie, poosie**. [f. PUSS *sb.*[1] + -Y dim. suffix.]

1. A cat: used much in the same way as PUSS *sb.*[1], but more as a common noun and less as a call-word.

1726 MRS. DELANY in *Life & Corr.* (1862) 124 My new pussey is..white,..with black spots. **1821** CLARE *Vill. Minstr., Sorrows Fav. Cat* vi, Ah mice, rejoice!..'Tis yours to triumph, mine's the woe, Now pussy's dead. **1870** E. PEACOCK *Ralf Skirl* III. 144 A saucer of milk put on the rug for pussy. **1889** J. K. JEROME *Idle Thoughts* 119 He strokes the cat quite gently, and calls it 'poor pussy'.

2. a. Used as a proper name for the hare: cf. PUSS *sb.*[1] 2. Also (*Austral.*), a rabbit.

1715 T. CAVE *Let.* 26 Oct. in M. M. Verney *Verney Lett. of 18th Cent.* (1930) I. xvii. 342 The Dog is very young and has seen but few Pussies, but..I doubt not of his having Appear'd a profess'd enemy to your Hares by this Time. **1785** BURNS *1st Ep. J. Lepraik* 3 Paitricks scraichan loud at e'en, And morning Poosie [*v.r.* poussie] whiddan seen. **1790** —— *Tam o' Shanter* 195 As open pussie's mortal foes, When, pop! she starts before their noses. **1821** CLARE *Vill. Minstr., Autumn* xxxii, Poor pussy through the stubble flies. **1841** J. T. HEWLETT *Parish Clerk* II. 15 Away went pussy for her home. **1941** BAKER *Dict. Austral. Slang* 58 *Pussy*, a rabbit.

b. A humorous name for a tiger: cf. PUSS *sb.*[1] 2 b.

1873 *Routledge's Yng. Gentl. Mag.* 535, I should have liked to have potted a pussy, particularly such a blood-thirsty brute as this one seems to be.

3. a. Applied to a girl or woman: cf. PUSS *sb.*[1] 3. Also, a finicky, old-maidish, or effeminate boy or man; a homosexual.

1583 STUBBES *Anat. Abus.* (1877) I. 97 You shall haue euery sawcy boy..to catch vp a woman & marie her... So he haue his pretie pussie to huggle withall, it forceth not. **1852** MRS. STOWE *Uncle Tom's C.* xvi, 'What do you think, pussy?' said her father to Eva. **1870** DICKENS *E. Drood* ii, I'd Pussy you, young man, if I was Pussy, as you call her. **1925** S. LEWIS *Martin Arrowsmith* vi. 65 You ought to hear some of the docs that are the sweetest old pussies with their patients—the way they bawl out the nurses. **1932** A. CHRISTIE *Thirteen Problems* xi. 193 '*The dame de compagnie*, you described, I think, as a pussy, Mrs. Bantry?' 'I didn't mean a *cat*, you know,' said Mrs. Bantry. 'It's quite different. Just a big soft white purry person. Always very sweet.' **1941** —— *N or M?* iii. 38 Old boarding-house pussies. Nothing to do but gossip and knit. **1942** BERREY & VAN DEN BARK *Amer. Thes. Slang* §405/2 *Pussy*, an effeminate boy. **1952** M. TRIPP *Faith is Windsock* iv. 73 'Your rear gunner is a hit with the ladies.' 'Jake knows how to make the pussies purr; it's an old Jamaican custom.' *a* **1957** J. CARY *Captive & Free* (1959) x. 50 Some of those old pussies, especially the males, are just longing to put you in a corner. **1958** L. DURRELL *Mountolive* viii. 157 'I first met Henry James in a brothel in Algiers. He had a naked houri on each knee.' 'Henry James was a pussy, I think.'

b. A person who lives in another's house as an inmate; a 'house-cat'.

1904 MARIE CORELLI *God's Good Man* xxi, I shall invite Roxmouth and his tame pussy, Mr. Marius Longford.

4. a. In childish speech applied to something soft and furry, as a fur necklet, a willow or hazel catkin, etc.

1858 *Zoologist* XVI. 5858 Little children call their warm neck-comforters by the name of 'pussies'. **1882** *Garden* 4 Feb. 77/1 These catkins, 'pussies', and 'lambs'-tails', as the country people call them.

b. *Criminals' slang.* A fur garment.

1937 'D. HUME' *Halfway to Horror* 4 Those who steal furs handle them as 'pussies'. **1960** *Observer* 25 Jan. 5/2 If it was tom or pussies (furs) it was probably one of the big buyers. **1972** J. WAINWRIGHT *Night is Time to Die* 129 The coat... Ten to one, a fur coat, and there was always somebody ready to lift a pussy. **1973** 'B. GRAEME' *Two & Two make Five* vii. 66 From one house they stole every piece of Regency silver ..from another..they restricted themselves to jewellery, toms and pussies.

5. ***pussy-wants-a-corner***, an American name for *puss in the corner*: see PUSS *sb.*[1] 5.

1897 GEN. H. PORTER *Campaigning w. Grant* in *Cent. Mag.* Jan. 349/2 [The manœuvres] now became more like the play of *pussy-wants-a-corner*.

6. The female pudendum. Hence, sexual intercourse; women considered sexually. ***to eat pussy***, of a man: to engage in sexual intercourse or cunnilingus. *coarse slang.*

1879–80 *Pearl* (1970) 268 Her legs are wide open showing the red lips and clitoris of her pussy. **1913** L. STRACHEY *Ermyntrude & Esmeralda* (1969) ii. 12 I'm also sure that it's got something to do with the thing between our legs that I always call my Pussy. **1922** F. HARRIS *My Life & Loves* I. iii. 61 By thinking of Lucille and her soft, hot, hairy 'pussy', I grew randy again. **1940** C. MCCULLERS *Heart is Lonely Hunter* I. iii. 37 She crossed over to the opposite wall and wrote a very bad word—*pussy*. **1959** N. MAILER *Advts. for Myself* (1961) 98 This is the magical evil of the big city, but he is wary of being taken in: 'I come to see pussy..and I ain't seen pussy yet.' **1962** J. BALDWIN *Another Country* I. i. 63 You wouldn't be putting that white prick in no more black pussy. **1965** 'A. HALL' *Berlin Memorandum* xi. 105 You go to town on the tits and pussy, symbolising carnality till it moans. **1967** M. MCCLURE *Freewheelin Frank* i. 8 When we talk about eating pussy we make it sound as dirty and vulgar as possible. **1973** A. POWELL *Temporary Kings* v. 258 Louis's stuffed a charming little cushion with hair snipped from the pussies of ladies he's had. **1976** J. O'CONNOR *Eleventh Commandment* v. 70 He killed about five prostitutes, cut them to pieces and stuffed various objects up their pussies. **1978** J. KRANTZ *Scruples* ii. 21 There was nothing, he had discovered, like flying a girl away for a weekend to insure as much pussy as you could eat. **1979** *Maclean's Mag.* 12 Mar. 25/3 As one blonde in a black leather coat bluntly replied, 'I sell pussy, not opinions.'

7. a. *attrib.* or as *adj.* Soft and furry like a cat: cf. 4. Also *fig.* Cf. also sense 3.

1842 *Amer. Pioneer* I. 182, I walked up very carelessly among the soldiers..and concluded they could never fight with us. They appeared to me to be too pussy. **1863** KINGSLEY *Water Bab.* v. (1886) 236 She was the most nice, soft,..pussy, cuddly, delicious creature who ever nursed a baby. *Ibid.* 241 Little boys..who have kind pussy mammas to cuddle them. **1930** D. L. SAYERS *Strong Poison* xvi. 197 Mrs. Pegler, a very *stout, pussy* old lady with a *long tongue* (!)

b. *Comb.*, as ***pussy-baudrons*** (*Sc.*); **pussy bow** = *pussy-cat bow*; **pussy four-corners** = *puss in the corner* s.v. PUSS *sb.*[1] 5; **pussy hair** *slang*, a woman's pubic hair; **pussy-hoisting** *slang*, stealing fur garments; **pussy mob** *slang*, a gang of fur thieves; **pussy palm**, = PALM *sb.*[1] 4 and PUSSY-WILLOW; **pussy posse** *U.S. slang* (see quot. 1963); **pussy power** (see quots.); **pussy-talk**, feminine gossip; **pussy-whip** *v. trans.* (slang), = HEN-PECK *v.*

1894 CROCKETT *Raiders* 52 Innocent as *pussy-bawdrons thinking on the cream-jug. **1972** *Times* 28 July 10/1 His satin faconne shirts tie in a neat *pussy bow. **1922** JOYCE *Ulysses* 477 He plays *pussy fourcorners with ragged boys and girls. **1972** R. D. ABRAHAMS in T. Kochman *Rappin' & Stylin' Out* 231 When the pepper tree begin to bear It burn off all of Jennifer' *pussy hair. **1975** R. H. RIMMER *Premar Experiments* I. 68 The wild disarray of your pussy hair beneath your panties. **1962** PARKER & ALLERTON *Courage of his Convictions* i. 82 Then I got three years for *pussy-hoisting from a warehouse in the City. **1967** M. PROCTER *Exercise Hoodwink* xiii. 91 He became the wheel man of a '*pussy' mob... The Flying Squad caught him with a car load of stolen furs. **1936** N. STREATFEILD *Ballet Shoes* ix. 134 The catkins and *pussy palm showed there would not be much more winter. **1978** *Guardian Weekly* 26 Mar. 19/1 They used to start coming in April like the returning swallows and house martins. Then they arrived for the daffodils and pussy palm. **1963** R. I. MCDAVID *Mencken's Amer. Lang.* xi. 730 **Pussy posse*, the vice squad. **1973** *Times* 22 Mar. 8/7 The police do their best. They have special teams of detectives (known as pussy posses) who mount drives against the girls. **1970** G. GREER *Female Eunuch* 126 Women in America are reported to be manipulating their menfolk by *pussy-power, which is wheedling and caressing, instead of challenging. **1970** *New York* 16 Nov. 48/1 Her specialty at political meetings was the Pussy Power speech. With it Elaine Brown originated the concept that a woman's function is to use her body to entice men into the Panther Party. **1937** AUDEN & MACNEICE *Lett. from Iceland* xii. 161 It looks like a week of *pussy-talk. **1963** *Amer. Speech* XXXVIII. 173 One informant noted that a male..is said to be **pussy whipped*, a term one of the authors recalls having heard in the Navy in 1956. **1973** C. & R. MILNER *Black Players* vi. 161 White men (and square Blacks) are thought to be 'pussy-whipped' by their wives. **1978** J. KRANTZ *Scruples* viii. 230 Some men are pussy whipped from the day they are born, some have it happen to them later in life, some never.

pussy ('pʊsɪ), *v.* [f. the sb.] *intr.* (With advbs.) To behave or move like a cat (see also quot. 1973).

1943 K. TENNANT *Ride on Stranger* xi. 134 Buzz off, Pop. You don't want to be pussying around. **1952** C. ARMSTRONG *Black-Eyed Stranger* ii. 17 He came pussying up. **1973** 'J. PATRICK' *Glasgow Gang Observed* 235 *Pussyin' aroun'*, playing about, mostly used in a sexual context.

pussy ('pʌsɪ), *a.*[1] [f. PUS *sb.* + -Y.] Full of pus.

18.. *Med. News* LIII. 695 The most pussy gland ruptured during extrication.

pussy ('pʌsɪ), *a.*[2], **pussel** ('pʌsəl), *a.* Also **pussle, puzzle.** Chiefly U.S. dial. corruptions of PURSY *a.*[1] Mainly in **pussy-, pussel-gutted** *adjs.*, corpulent, obese; also **pussy-, pussel-gut**, a corpulent stomach; (*pl.*) a fat person (see also quot. 1976[1]); hence **pussel-gut** *v. trans.* (*nonce*), to render obese.

1844 'J. SLICK' *High Life in N.Y.* II. 89 As..pussy as a turkey-gobbler. *Ibid.* 92 As pussy and pompous as a prize pig jest afore killing time. **1886** F. T. ELWORTHY *W. Somerset Word-bk.* 598 What a *pussy* old fuller th'old Zaddler White's a-come; I can min' un when he used to go a-courtin, a slim young spark. **1892** S. HEWETT *Peasant Speech Devon* 115 'Er's drefful pussy tü-day, an can't walk vast nur var. **1906** *Dialect Notes* III. 152 *Pussy-gutted*, adj., corpulent. 'He's terrible *pussy-gutted*.' **1907** *Ibid.* 197 *Pussy* .., adj., corpulent. 'He didn't use to be so *pussy*.' **1909** *Ibid.* 361 *Pussle-gutted*, adj., same as *pussy-gutted*. *Ibid.*, *Pussy-gutted, adj.*, corpulent, having a large abdomen. Often used as a term of contempt. 'You low-lifed, *pussy-gutted* scounderl.' *Ibid.* 402 *Pussy guts, n. phr.*, a corpulent man. 'See that old *pussy guts*.' **1933** M. K. RAWLINGS *South Moon Under* xiii. 133 Sort o' pussle-gutted, eh? **1935** W. FAULKNER *As I lay Dying* 10 You pussel-gutted bastard. *Ibid.* 35 He has pussel-gutted himself eating cold greens. **1942** Z. N. HURSTON *Dust Tracks on Road* viii. 143 Goat-bellied, puzzle-gutted,..knock-kneed..so-and-so. **1946** *Amer. Speech* XXI. 99 A *body* who has gained weight enough to show signs of obesity is said to be *fleshy* or *pussy* (pursy). **1949** 'J. NELSON' *Backwoods Teacher* ix. 88 A lantern-jawed ol' varmint with a big golden watch chain acrost his ol' pussy-gut. **1959** W. FAULKNER *Mansion* 55 Old pussel-gutted Hampton that could be fetched along to look at anything, even a murder, once somebody remembered he was Sheriff. **1976** C. S. BROWN *Gloss. Faulkner's South* 157 In northern Florida, the pot-bellied little mosquito-fish, or gambusia, is called the pusselgut. **1976** *N.Y. Times Mag.* 10 Oct. 111/2 All watched over by a savage God, by the dead and by pussel-gutted deputies.

'pussy-cat. 1. A nursery word for a cat.

1805 *Songs for Nursery* 40 Pussy cat, pussy cat, where have you been I've been to London to see the queen. **1837** MARRYAT *Olla Podr.* xl, The term pussy cat may be considered tautological. **1844** 'J. SLICK' *High Life in N.Y.* I. 154 As affectionate as a pussy cat. **1871** E. LEAR *Nonsense Songs, Stories, Bot. & Alphabets*, The Owl and the Pussy-cat went to sea In a beautiful pea-green boat. **1933** [see *baby-talk* s.v. BABY *sb.* B. 1 d]. **1955** *Sci. News Let.* 26 Mar. 203/1 For better-fed pussycats, add to their diet a good dash of personal attention and a heaping tablespoonful of affection.

2. A willow or hazel catkin: cf. PUSSY *sb.* 4.

1850 C. M. YONGE *Henrietta's Wish* xv. 216 The silver 'pussycats' on the withy. **1861** S. THOMSON *Wild Fl.* III. (ed. 4) 169 Every boy knows the 'pussy-cats' of the willow. **1889** E. PEACOCK *Gloss. Words Manley & Corringham, Lincolnshire* (ed. 2) 421 *Pussy-cat*.., the catkins of the willow.

3. Applied to a person (cf. PUSS *sb.*[1] 3, PUSSY *sb.* 3); now esp. one who is attractive, amiable, or submissive.

1859 J. A. SYMONDS *Let.* Apr. (1967) I. 184 Dalrymple's brother is going to be married to the Lady Edith Dalhousie: I wrote a solemn letter of congratulae [*sic*] to the old pussey cat! **1864** *Realm* 6 Apr. 1 What a purblind old pussy-cat, instead of the light and agile kitten we imagined was tripping before us! **1881** E. J. WORBOISE *Sissie* ix, 'What a wild pussy-cat she is!' said her father, looking fondly at her, as she dashed abruptly from his side. **1955** *Amer. Speech* XXX. 119 *Pussy cat*, a pilot who is overcautious, fearful, or reluctant. **1959** *Times* 17 Aug. 12/7 Ronder, a sly pussy-cat of a man, able to scratch as well as purr. **1964** L. NKOSI *Rhythm of Violence* 25 Jimmy: (*to Mary*) Don't worry pussycat! **1973** E. JONG *Fear of Flying* 89 'Some men claim to be afraid of me.' Adrian laughed. 'You're a sweetheart,' he said, 'a pussy-cat—as you Americans say.' **1975** P. G. WINSLOW *Death of Angel* iv. 104 He can be a dear, but he's also one of the chief pussycats of the psychic world. **1976** C. DEXTER *Last seen Wearing* v. 36 The secret sex-life of a glamorous Hollywood pussycat. **1978** G. VIDAL *Kalki* i. 7, I was the one who paid the alimony... Women wrote me ugly letters. I was not apparently, a pussycat.

4. Cattiness, spitefulness. *rare*.

1911 W. J. LOCKE *Glory of Clementina Wing* xxiv. 361 Let us have a straight talk like sensible women, and put the pussy-cat aside.

5. *Comb.*, as ***pussy-cat-like*** adj.; **pussy-cat bow**, a soft, floppy bow.

1964 *Sunday Express* 2 Feb. 18/3 For dressy occasions a *pussycat bow..under a high, round jacket collar. **1967** [see GENTIAN 2 b]. **1977** J. BINGHAM *Marriage Bureau Murders* ii. 21 Her white silk blouse, with the pussy cat bow tied at the neck, lent a touch of femininity. **1881** J. E. H. THOMSON *Upland Tarn* 26 Her noiseless *pussy-cat-like ways.

ˈpussyfoot, *sb.* [f. PUSSY *sb.* + FOOT *sb.*]

1. One who moves stealthily or warily.

1914 JACKSON & HELLYER *Vocab. Criminal Slang* 68 *Pussy foot*... A detective. **1916** *Dialect Notes* IV. 279 *Pussy-foot, v.i.* To be sly, intriguing, or underhand. 'That girl goes pussy-footing around.' Also *n.* 'She's a regular pussy-foot.' **1977** 'E. CRISPIN' *Glimpses of Moon* xii. 257 Grateful that the creature [*sc.* a cat] was in both senses a pussyfoot, Fen drank some champagne.

2. [f. the nickname 'Pussyfoot' of an American supporter of Prohibition, W. E. Johnson (1862–1945), given to him on account of his stealthy methods when a magistrate.] An advocate or supporter of prohibition; a teetotaller. Also allusively.

1919 *Punch* 23 July 86 *Gloomy Policeman*. 'You've had enough. Better go home.' *Reveller*... 'Shurr-up—Pussy-foot!' **1920** 'SAPPER' *Bull-Dog Drummond* vi. 146 We are all confirmed Pussy-foots, and have been consuming non-alcoholic beer. **1921** T. BURKE *Outer Circle* 169 The tea arrived, a viscid, leathery fluid of Pussyfoot vintage. **1922** LD. RIDDELL *Some Things that Matter* ii. 28 Mrs. A., a 'pussyfoot', with an ardent desire to interfere with other people's habits. **1946** G. MILLAR *Horned Pigeon* x. 137 There was the heavy drinker... And there was the pussy-foot who said 'poison'.

3. *attrib.* or as *adj.* **a.** Teetotal; without alcohol; non-alcoholic. **b.** Soft; easy.

1923 D. H. LAWRENCE *Birds, Beasts & Flowers* 15 Even the word Marsala will smack of preciosity Soon in the pussy-foot West. **1940** DYLAN THOMAS *Portrait of Artist as Young Dog* 217 He'd be knocking back nips without a thought that on the sands at home his friend was alone and pussyfoot at six o'clock. **1973** D. MILLER *Chinese Jade Affair* xvii. 156, I was trying to deflect the inevitable course of the evening with a 'Pussy-foot' cocktail. **1974** *Country Life* 17 Oct. 1108 Covering 38 laps of the circuit..ensured this was no genteel pussyfoot operation.

So **pussy-footed** *a.*, having a light step; elusive; evasive; **pussy-ˈfootedness**; **ˈpussyfootism**, teetotalism, advocacy or enforcement of prohibition.

1893 *Scribner's Mag.* Nov. 653 Men who were beginning to walk pussy-footed and shy at shadows. **1919** *N.Y. Times* 7 Jan. 4/6 The Republican Party..was evidently in imminent danger of taking a 'pussy-footed' position on the war. **1923** *Daily Mail* 23 July 7 In Tudor England people sang the music they liked, and read the books they liked. They had real freedom, and there was no pussy-footism. **1924** D. S. BARRY *Forty Years in Washington* v. 106 Ingalls once said of Senator William B. Allison that he was so pussy-footed he could walk from New York to San Francisco on the keys of a piano and never strike a note. **1926** 'A. BERKELEY' *Wychford Poisoning Case* vii. 78 They reached the Man of Kent and ordered the night-caps to which their position as residents entitled them, in defiance of the dictates of a maternal government, pussy-footism and all the other futilities which order our lives for us in these days. **1931** *Times Lit. Suppl.* 10 Sept. 685/1 He was pussyfooted and quick to spring. **1957** *Times* 10 May 13/4 This letter may sound cautious, perhaps pussy-footed, almost priggish... We must tread softly. **1964** *Daily Tel.* 9 Mar. 14/2 There is nothing pussy-footed about this economic strategy... It is a bold mixture of more competition and more responsibility. **1966** *Economist* 30 Apr. 450/1 Politically here is confirmation..of the essential caution, not to say pussy-footedness, of the Wilson Government. **1980** *Jrnl. R. Soc. Arts* Mar. 181/2 Aesthetics is a pussy-footed way of referring to beauty.

ˈpussyfoot, *v.* [f. as prec.] **1.** *intr.* To tread softly or lightly to avoid being noticed; to proceed warily; to conceal one's opinions or plans; to behave evasively or timidly. Also with *it*.

1903 *Atlanta Constitution* 20 Mar. 3 Vice President Charles Warren Fairbanks is pussy-footing it around Washington. **1916** [see PUSSYFOOT *sb.* 1]. **1918** C. SANDBURG *Cornhuskers* 73 Who pussyfoots from desk to desk with a speaking forefinger? **1928** *Observer* 5 Feb. 18/1 While most papers are still 'pussy-footing' on the Presidency they called their editors together and afterwards announced a unanimous decision. **1931** E. THOMPSON *Farewell to India* 203 Trying to coax a horse to wait while I pussy-footed up to him. **1934** D. L. SAYERS *Nine Tailors* III. ii. 286 When I got out through the porch, I had to pussyfoot pretty gently over that beastly creaking gravel. **1949** *Time* 9 May 25/2 The ones who pussy-footed, side-stepped, straddled, carried water on both shoulders and compromised were left at home. **1951** E. PAUL *Springtime in Paris* viii. 155, I saw you pussyfooting around the exhibition. **1973** *Times* 16 Oct. 6/6 A Labour Government should not 'pussyfoot around' with reform of the Official Secrets Act but scrap it. **1975** B. WOOD *Killing Gift* (1976) IV. i. 129 Why do you pussy-foot, captain?.. Why not just say it—you think Jennifer Gilbert killed him. **1977** *Jrnl. R. Soc. Arts* CXXV. 626/1 We have 'pussy-footed' round this issue of profit for years. **1980** *Brit. Med. Jrnl.* 29 Mar. 937/1 It is time someone was honest enough to stop pussyfooting about.

2. [f. PUSSYFOOT *sb.* 2.] *trans.* To render teetotal; to impose prohibition on. *rare*.

1921 [implied in PUSSYFOOTING *vbl. sb.*].

So **ˈpussyfooting** *vbl. sb.* and *ppl. a.*

1921 *Q. Rev.* Jan. 100 The tyranny that would ensue from the Pussy-footing of Canada is too horrible to contemplate. **1928** *Collier's* 29 Dec. 38/1 The wrappings which..the pussy-footing politicians impose upon a candidate. **1956** G. P. KURATH in A. Dundes *Mother Wit* (1973) 107/2 Certain qualities seem to predominate... These are whole-bodied movements,..dynamics from pussy footing to violent acrobatics, rhythmic complexity. **1974** J. CLEARY *Peter's Pence* vi. 187 Authority had been given to the pussyfooting amateur..and nothing had gone right. **1976** *Times* 16 Feb. 8/7 In the face of political dogma, 'pussy-footing' and ill-informed decision making, is Mr Laker downhearted? **1977** *Time* 8 Aug. 1/1 To hell with what timid, pussy-footing diplomats think!

ˈpussyfooter. [f. PUSSYFOOT *v.* and *sb.* + -ER[1].] **a.** One who pussyfoots (in any sense of the verb). **b.** An advocate or supporter of prohibition.

1927 *Sat. Even. Post* 24 Dec. 9/1 A good politician is a natural-born pussy-footer. **1928** *Daily Express* 28 Dec. 8/3 The pussyfooters..have given a weary and blasé world a new game to play. **1932** *N.Y. Times* 20 May 10/4 The conditions which are attached to its operation make plain its insincerity. It is, therefore, on that very account beginning to attract the favorable attention of the trimmers and the pussyfooters. **1946** S. H. HOLBROOK *Lost Men Amer. Hist.* 160 The appeasers and pussyfooters of 1850 also provided that any territories that might come into the Union later could do so with or without slavery.

ˈpussy-ˌwillow. orig. *U.S.* A popular name for several species of willow or their soft, fluffy catkins, which appear before the leaves; esp., in North America, the glaucous willow, *Salix discolor*, and, in Great Britain, the goat willow, *Salix caprea*.

1869 J. G. FULLER *Flower Gatherers* 52 The aments appear before the leaves, and are covered with hairs so soft and silken that children often call them Pussy-Willows. **1878** MRS. STOWE *Poganuc People* xvii. 182 Then the pussy-willows threw out their soft catkins. **1884** ROE *Nat. Ser. Story* vi, He pressed through them to look for..pussy willows. **1893** DARTNELL & GODDARD *Gloss. Words used in Wiltshire* 126 Pussy-willow. *Salix*. **1897** W. D. HOWELLS *Landlord at Lion's Head* 364 He begged her to let him keep one switch of the pussy-willows. **1924** A. D. SEDGWICK *Little French Girl* II. i. 103 Sometimes it [*sc.* Alix's skin] was grey, like pussy-willow. **1939** F. THOMPSON *Lark Rise* i. 1 There were violets under the hedges and pussy-willows out beside the brook. **1949** *Lisle* (Illinois) *Eagle* 31 Mar. 5/4 The spring motif decoration of jonquils and pussy willows..gave a gay and festive setting. **1958** R. D. MEIKLE *Brit. Trees & Shrubs* 198 In recent years the childish 'Pussy Willow' has tended to replace these older names [of 'Palm' and 'Goat Willow']. **1969** *Canadian Antiques Collector* Aug. 20/1 Pussywillows are arranged in one of a collection of..sugar bowls. **1976** *Burnham-on-Sea Gaz.* 20 Apr. 12/9 All [the congregation] carried branches of pussy willow which had been cut locally for the occasion [*sc.* Palm Sunday].

†**pust, puyst.** *Obs.* [In quot. 1527 a. Du. *puist*, MDu. *pûst*; in quot. 1677 perh. a misreading of *push*.] A pustule; = PUSH *sb.*[2]

1527 ANDREW *Brunswyke's Distyll. Waters* L iv, Good for scabbes, puystes, and other impostumyng on the body. **1677** LADY CHAWORTH in *12th Rep. Hist. MSS. Comm.* App. v. 43 The..nurse keepers..laid ceres to a pust under the arme which drive the malignity of it to the heart.

pustle, obs. form of PUSTULE. Hence †**pustled** *a. Obs. rare*[−1] = PUSTULATE.

1627 P. FLETCHER *Locusts* II. xxviii, Her hands with scabbes array'd, Her pust'led skin with ulcer'd excrements.

pustulant (ˈpʌstjʊlənt), *a.* and *sb.* [ad. late L. *pustulānt-em*, pr. pple. of *pustulāre* to PUSTULATE.] **a.** *adj.* Giving rise to the formation of pustules (*Syd. Soc. Lex.* 1897). **b.** *sb.* An irritant affecting the skin and causing pustulation, as a solution of silver nitrate, croton oil, etc.

1871 GARROD *Mat. Med.* 417 The pustulants induce deeper action, and are sometimes of greater value than vesicants.

pustular (ˈpʌstjʊlə(r)), *a.* [ad. mod.L. *pustulār-is*, f. *pustula* PUSTULE: see -AR.]

1. Of, pertaining to, of the nature of pustules; characterized by pustules.

1739 HUXHAM in *Phil. Trans.* XLI. 669 The pustular and leprous Eruptions increased daily. **1800** WOODVILLE in *Med. Jrnl.* IV. 256, I differ in opinion from Dr. Jenner in not imputing the pustular eruptions..to any adulteration of the vaccine matter employed in the inoculations. **1818–20** E. THOMPSON *Cullen's Nosol. Method.* (ed. 3) 329 The five genera of pustular diseases. **1876** BRISTOWE *The. & Pract. Med.* (1878) 572 Petechial or pustular rashes.

2. *Bot.* and *Zool.* Having low glandular excrescences like blisters or pustules.

1776 WITHERING *Brit. Plants* (1796) IV. 393 *Sphæria fraxinea* [Fungus]. Black; roundish, convex, dotted... Nearly sitting, pustular.

pustulate (ˈpʌstjʊlət), *a.* [ad. late L. *pustulāt-us*, pa. pple. of *pustulāre*: see next.] Furnished with, or having pustules; pustulous, pustular.

(In quot. 1607, perh. an error for *pustulant*.)

1607 TOPSELL *Four-f. Beasts* 615 If the worme bee cut asunder in the wound, there issueth out of her such a venemous pustulate matter, that poysoneth the wound. **1846** DANA *Zooph.* (1848) 126 The smooth exterior sometimes graduates into the pustulate. **1852** —— *Crust.* I. 90 Surface seriately pustulate, and pustules setigerous.

pustulate (ˈpʌstjʊleɪt), *v.* [f. ppl. stem of late L. *pustulāre*, trans. and intr., f. *pustula* PUSTULE.] **a.** *trans.* To form into pustules. **b.** *intr.* To break out into or form pustules.

1732 STACKHOUSE *Hist. Bible* III. iv. (1749) 364/2 Besides the blains pustulated to afflict his [Job's] body, the devil.. instigated his wife to grieve his mind. **1898** P. MANSON *Trop. Diseases* xxxvii. 560 Sometimes the little vesicles [of prickly heat] may pustulate.

pustulation (pʌstjʊˈleɪʃən). [ad. late L. *pustulātiōn-em*, n. of action from *pustulāre*: see prec.] The action of pustulating; formation of pustules; sometimes, also, blistering.

1875 H. C. WOOD *Therap.* (1879) 155 Peculiar burning or tingling pain, which is very shortly followed by pustulation. **1876** BARTHOLOW *Mat. Med.* (1879) 540 The pustulation of the chest with croton-oil or tartar-emetic ointment is rarely if ever justifiable. **1899** *Allbutt's Syst. Med.* VIII. 610 It is often necessary to await the healing of the pustulation. *Ibid.* 870 The slightest appearance of pustulation or blistering should be..treated on antiseptic lines.

pustulatous (pʌstjʊˈleɪtəs), *a.* [f. PUSTULATE *a.* + -OUS.] = PUSTULATE *a.* ***pustulatous moss***: see quots.

1856 W. LAUDER LINDSAY *Pop. Hist. Brit. Lichens* 91 The 'Mosses' [i.e. crustaceous or foliaceous dye-lichens] are irregularly designated, the specific name in some being due ..to their physical characters, as 'Tartareous or Pustulatous moss'. *Ibid.* 177 *Umbilicaria pustulata*..is largely imported by the London orchill-makers..under the commercial designation of Pustulatous Moss.

pustule (ˈpʌstjuːl). Also 6 puscull, -cle; 6–8 pustle, 7 pustel. [ad. L. *pustula* blister, pimple, pustule. Cf. F. *pustule* (13–14th c.).]

1. A small conical or rounded elevation of the cuticle, with erosion of the cutis, inflammatory at the base and containing pus; a pimple; formerly, sometimes, a blister.

1398 TREVISA *Barth. De P.R.* VII. lxi. (1495) 276 Pustules ben callyd gaderynges of postumes and superfluyte in the vtter partyes of the body. *c* **1400** *Lanfranc's Cirurgie* 190 Cossi ben litil pustulis & harde þat ben engendrid in þe face, & principali aboute þe nose. **1578** LYTE *Dodoens* III. xxviii. 354 The same..cureth the sores and pustules of the gummes. **1718** QUINCY *Compl. Disp.* 91 Of manifest Service in ripening the Small Pox, where the Pustules rise with a pellucid Humour. **1876** BRISTOWE *The. & Pract. Med.* (1878) 168 The pustules of discrete small-pox are always larger than those of the other variety.

a **1529** SKELTON *Elynour Rummyng* 555 Wythe here and there a puscull Lyke a scabbyd muscull. **1600** F. WALKER *Sp. Mandeville* 41 With the continuall moystnes, they engender & bring forth certaine Puscles like Mushromps. **1612** WOODALL *Surg. Mate* Wks. (1653) 32 To cool and heal any moist pustles. **1643** J. STEER tr. *Exp. Chyrurg.* vii. 27 Pustels or blisters are raised. **1742** *Lond. & Country Brew.* I. (ed. 4) 46 It will there raise little Pustles or Blisters.

b. ***malignant pustule***, the carbuncular disease produced by the anthrax bacillus; = ANTHRAX 2.

[**1543** TRAHERON *Vigo's Chirurg.* II. xix. 29 Anthrax is a malygne pustle.] **1864** E. A. PARKES *Pract. Hygiene* 158 Anthrax (malignant pustule, carbuncular fever). **1872** T. BRYANT *Pract. Surg.* 443 Anthrax of the lips has nothing in common with malignant pustule.

2. a. *Bot.* A small wart or swelling, natural or caused by parasitic influences. **b.** *Zool.* A warty excrescence of the skin, as in the toad; a pimple.

1776 WITHERING *Brit. Plants* (1796) IV. 392 *Sphæria maxima* [Fungus]. Large, thick, black, marked above with pustules. **1807** VANCOUVER *Agric. Devon* (1813) 433 On the leaves of pears..and gooseberry trees, it exhibits itself at first in small yellow pustules, increasing in size until they effloresce in clusters of various shapes. **1869** GILLMORE tr. *Figuier's Rept. & Birds* i. 25 Toads, in colour are usually of a livid grey, spotted with brown and yellow, and disfigured by a number of pustules or warts.

3. *transf.* An eruptive swelling of the ground.

1849 MURCHISON *Siluria* xvi. 404 These subaërial volcanos..are nothing more than superficial pustules. **1861** E. T. HOLLAND in *Peaks, Passes & Glac.* Ser. II. I. 95 Steaming excrescences of clay. The approach..is over beds of sand and clay, out of which they rise in variegated blotches and pustules of blue, white, red, and yellow.

4. *Comb.*, as ***pustule-like*** adj.

1815 KIRBY & SP. *Entomol.* iv. (1818) I. 87 They are produced in the flesh in small pustule-like tumours. **1845** *Florist's Jrnl.* 37 Peculiar to this plant is the property of producing pale pustule-like callosities on the branches.

pustuliform (ˈpʌstjʊlɪfɔːm), *a.* *Bot.* and *Zool.* [ad. mod.L. *pustuliform-is*, f. *pustula* PUSTULE + -FORM.] Having the form of a pustule.

1846 DANA *Zooph.* (1848) 654 The pustuliform verrucæ are rounded and unequal.

ˌpustulocruˈstaceous, *a.* [f. *pustulo-*, combining form of L. *pustula* pustule + CRUSTACEOUS.] Covered with a pustulous crust or scab.

1890 in *Cent. Dict.* **1897** in *Syd. Soc. Lex.*

ˈ**pustulose**, *a.* [ad. post-cl. L. *pustulōs-us*, f. *pustula* pustule: see -OSE.] = next.

1882 J. T. CARRINGTON in *Zoologist* Mar. 107 *Portunus tuberculatus* is distinguished by its tubercular pustulose carapace.

pustulous (ˈpʌstjʊləs), *a.* [ad. L. *pustulōsus*: see prec. and -OUS. Cf. F. *pustuleux* (1549 in Godef.), perh. the immediate source.] Abounding in or characterized by pustules; pustular.

1543 TRAHERON *Vigo's Chirurg.* v. i. 161 Anoynt the pustulous place wyth a lyniment folowing. **1658** PHILLIPS, *Pustulous*, full of Pustules, *i.* blisters, blaines, or wheales. **1799** *Med. Jrnl.* II. 352 A prescription 'for the great pustulous eruption and its degrees'. **1804** *Ibid.* XII. 536 That the pustulous disease produced in the vaccine patients in the Small-pox Hospital was the small pox, I can safely aver. **1846** DANA *Zooph.* 707 Surface either smooth or somewhat pustulous. **1852** —— *Crust.* I. 109 Carapax.. tubercular or pustulous above.

puszta (ˈpʊstə). Also **pussta, puzta.** [Hungarian = plain, steppe, waste.] The flat treeless country of Hungary; a plain in Hungary.

1842 F. W. FABER *Styrian Lake* 324 The hailstorms with white oars across the putzas [*sic*] roam. **1852** T. Ross tr. *Humboldt's Trav.* II. xvii. 86 The widely extended pastures, which reach in every direction to the horizon, are called in the country, *Puszta.* **1896** *Daily News* 9 June 7/6 Only a nation of horsemen who have the Pussta to practise upon could turn out such a number of first-class horses. **1927** *Daily Express* 14 Dec. 9/1 They are the Chicos, as the 'cowboys' are called, and the Pusztas, or prairies, are to be found only a few hours' journey from Budapest. **1947** M. R. SHACKLETON *Europe* v. xxvii. 334 South-east of Kecskemét the soil is impregnated with salts and there is a large area of *puszta* (= 'waste'), known as the Bugác steppe. **1972** *Guardian* 4 Nov. 14/4 The Great Hungarian Plain... Pleasant to lunch here, serenaded by Hungarian Gipsy bands as you eat your puszta steak. **1973** *Country Life* 11 Jan. 74/1 There can be few areas of Europe that are flatter.. than the great plains, the *puszta*, of Hungary.

put (pʊt), *sb.*[1] Also 5–8 **putt** (see also next). [f. PUT *v.*[1]] An act of putting, in various senses.

1. An act of thrusting or pushing; a thrust; a push, a shove. Also *fig.* (with quot. 1748 cf. PUT *v.*[1] 3 b). *Obs.* exc. *dial.* = BUTT *sb.*[9]

c **1430** *Syr Gener.* (Roxb.) 4588 In his sadle he held him still, And smote Darel with so goodewill In middes of the sheld ful butt That Darel fell doun with that putt. **1508** DUNBAR *Tua Mariit Wemen* 231 A tender peronall, that myght na put thole. *a* **1572** KNOX *Hist. Ref.* (1644) 117 When it begins at us, God knows.. who shall bide the next put. *a* **1598** ROLLOCK *Sel. Wks.* (Wodrow Soc.) II. 511 He will come and give them a putt, with sharpness and mercy. **1633** RUTHERFORD *Lett.* (1862) I. 104 To help you to bear your burden, and to come in behind you, and give you and your burdens a put up the mountain. **1748** RICHARDSON *Clarissa* Wks. 1811 IV. 316 The dear creature.. wanted to instruct me how to answer the Captain's home put. **1869** E. FARMER *Scrap. Bk.* (ed. 6) 60 The pig made a put at the closed.. door. **1974** B. BROPHY in *New Statesman* 28 June 929/1 The jacket, an unsuccessful but not dishonourable put at the manner of Magritte.

2. The act of casting a heavy stone or weight overhand, as a trial of strength; a throw, a cast. (In this sense pronounced (pʌt) in Sc., and identified with PUT, PUTT *sb.*[2])

c **1300** *Havelok* 1055 Þe chaunpiouns þat put sowen, Shuldreden he ilc oþer, and lowen. *c* **1340** *Hymns Virg.*, etc. 73 Þe put of þe stoon þou maist not reche, To litil myȝte is in þi sleue. **1889** *Boy's Own Paper* 7 Sept. 780/2 After each put has been marked the ground is smoothed over. *Ibid.*, I noticed.. the puts on several occasions knocked out the pegs of previous marks.

3. In phr. ***forced put***: see FORCE-PUT.

The precise sense of *put* in this phrase is obscure.

4. In *Stock-jobbing* and *Speculation*: The option of delivering a specified amount of a particular stock or produce at a certain price within a specified time: see OPTION *sb.* 4, and cf. PUT *v.*[1] 10 h.

1717 MRS. CENTLIVRE *Bold Stroke for Wife* IV. i, Are you a bull or a bear to-day, Abraham? *3rd Stockbroker.* A bull faith; but I have a good putt for next week. **1825** C. M. WESTMACOTT *Eng. Spy* II. 139 For the call or put. *a* **1860** C. FENN *Eng. & For. Funds* (1883) 127 A 'Put' is an option of delivering stock at a certain time, the price and date being fixed at the time the option-money is given. **1893** BITHELL *Counting-H. Dict.* s.v. *Options*, When money is paid for the option of buying at a given price, the operation is called 'giving for the call'. When it is paid for the option of selling, it is called 'giving for the put'. Sometimes both operations are combined, and then it is called 'giving for the put and call'.

5. *attrib.*, as ***put option***.

1881 *Guide Oper. Stocks* 15 A Put Option should be obtained when a decline in the market is expected to take place. **1961** *Daily Mail* 18 Sept. 13/4 In the past three weeks 'put' options (where a fall in the shares is expected) have been an outstanding feature of the option market. **1977** *Private Eye* 4 Mar. 17/1 One suggestion was that some of the shares had come from Jim himself as a result of a 'put' option held on him personally by former lieutenant Herbert Despard.

put, putt (pʌt), *sb.*[2] [A differentiated pronunciation of prec.; of Scotch origin.]

1. *Sc.* = prec., sense 2.

2. *Golf.* (orig. *Sc.*) An act of 'putting': see PUT *v.*[2] 3; a gentle stroke given to the ball so as to make it roll along the putting-green, with the purpose of getting it into the hole.

1743 MATHIESON *Goff* in *Poems on Golf* (1867) 58 With putt well directed plump into the hole. **1857** *Chambers's Inform. for People* 694/1 One who can gain a full stroke on his opponent between two far-distant holes, frequently loses his advantage by missing a 'put' within a yard of the hole! **1863** in R. Clark *Golf* (1875) 137 The first hole was halved.. Drumwhalloch holin' a lang putt. **1901** *Scotsman* 9 Sept. 4/7 On the next green he got down his putt from a distance of.. twenty yards.

3. *fig.* in phr. ***to make one's putt good*** (*Sc.*), to succeed in one's attempt, gain what one aims at.

1661 RUTHERFORD in *Life* (1881) 28 Fearing I should not make my putt good. **1822** GALT *Steam-Boat* ix. (1850) 230 The mistress.. made her putt good, and the satin dress was obligated to be sent to her. **1824** MACTAGGART *Gallovid. Encycl.* 389 A man is said to have made his *putt gude*, when he obtains what his ambition panted for.

put, putt (pʌt), *sb.*[3] *Obs.* or *arch.* [app. f. PUT *v.*[1]: cf. sense 22 d; but the history is not clear.]

An old game at cards for two, three, or four players, somewhat resembling Nap, three cards being dealt to each player; the score at this game.

1680 COTTON *Compl. Gamester* (ed. 2) xv. 92 Putt is the ordinary rooking Game of every place. *Ibid.*, If you play at two-handed Putt (or if you please you may play at three hands) the best Putt-Card deals. *Ibid.* 93 Five up or a Putt is commonly the Game. **1711** E. WARD *Vulgus Brit.* IX. 99 Where day by day they us'd to sot, At All-fours, Cribidge, or at Put. **1725** YOUNG *Univ. Pass.* IV, *To Sir S. Compton* 30 Since Apes can roast the choice castanian nut; Since Steeds of genius are expert at Put. *c* **1778** in F. Moore *Songs & Ball. Amer. Rev.* (1856) 192 Jack, thinking of cribbage, all fours, or of put, With a dextrous hand, he did shuffle and cut. **1851** MAYHEW *Lond. Labour* I. 267/1 He had heard an old tailor say that in his youth..'put' was a common public-house game. **1887** BESANT *The World went* xxiv, Bess.. could play All-fours, Put, Snip-snap-snorum.

b. Comb. ***putt-card***, a card used in this game.

1680 COTTON *Compl. Gamester* (ed. 2) xv. 93 The best Putt-Cards are first the Tray, next the Deuce, then the Ace. **1711** J. PUCKLE *Club* 21 *note*, Bending one, to know where to cut a good Putt-card. *Ibid.* 23 Marking Putt-cards on the edge with the nail as they come to hand.

put (pʌt), *sb.*[4] *Obs.* or *arch.* (*slang* or *colloq.*) Also **putt.** [Arose in 17th c. slang; origin unascertained.] A stupid man, silly fellow, blockhead, 'duffer'; ***country put***, a lout, a bumpkin.

1688 SHADWELL *Sqr. Alsatia* I. i, O fy, cousin; a company of Putts, meer Putts! *a* **1700** B. E. *Dict. Cant. Crew*, *Country-Put*, a silly, shallow-pated Fellow. **1710** *Tatler* No. 230 ¶7 The Third Refinement.. consists in the Choice of certain Words invented by some pretty Fellows, such as *Banter*, *Bamboozle*, *Country Put* and *Kidney*. **1721–2** AMHERST *Terræ Fil.* No. 46. 247 They were metamorphosed into compleat smarts, and damn'd the old country putts, their fathers. **1753** *Adventurer* No. 100 ¶2 Peculiarities which would have denominated me a Green Horn, or in other words, a country put very green. **1802** in *Spirit Pub. Jrnls.* VI. 215 The buck, who scorns the city puts, And thinks all rich men noodles. **1823** *New Monthly Mag.* VIII. 92 The footmen of the House of Lords.. keep clear of the borough-mongers and country puts of the lower house. **1859** THACKERAY *Virgin.* xliv, Look at that old putt in the chair: did you ever see such an old quiz? **1886** F. HARRISON *Ess.* 168 What droll puts the citizens seem in it all!

put (pʊt), *v.*[1] Pa. t. and pa. pple. **put** (pʊt). Forms: see below. [Late OE. *putian* (? *pūtian*), represented *c* 1050 by the vbl. sb. *putung* (? *pūt-*), PUTTING; thence early ME. *pūten* and ? *puten*, later *putten*, *putt*, *put*. Beside this, late OE. had *potian* (11th c.), ME. *pōten* (see POTE *v.*), and *potten*; also, OE. *pȳtan* (repr. by *pýtan út* in the OE. Chron., MS. F. (12th c.), anno 796, and *út ápȳtan*, put out, thrust out, Numbers xvi. 14), which app. gave southern ME. *puiten*, *puyte* (= *pūte*), and may even have been the source of the late ME. *pytten*, *pitten*, *pyt*, *pit*. Prof. Sievers thinks that the stem-vowel in OE. *pȳtan* (:—**pūtjan*) was certainly long, and in *putian* probably so, and suggests that the ME. shortening of the vowel was carried over from the pa. t. and pa. pple. *pytte*, *putte* from *pȳt-te*, *pūt-te*. The normal conjugation was pa. t. *put-te*, now *put* (cf. *cut*), in ME. and early mod.Eng. also *puttede*, *putted*; pa. pple. ME. *yput*, *iputte* and *putt*, now *put*, also in 14–16th c. *putted*. But in Sc. and north Eng. dialects, *put* (or rather its northern form *pyt*, *pit*), has been from the 15–16th c. conjugated as a strong vb., with pa. t. *pat*, pa. pple. *putten* or *pitten* (also in Eng. dialects *potten*); and perhaps the southern *ipitte* also arose out of **ipitten*. With these compare the northern inflexion of HIT, *hat*, *hutten* or *hitten*. The variant *pot*, *pott*, occurs as an existing dialect form, besides surviving in a differentiated form and sense as POTE. The differentiated vb. PUT[2], PUTT (pʌt), used in golf, and in Sc. also in 'putting the stone', is conjugated *putt*, *putted*, *putted*, and is thus quite distinct in Sc. from *pit*, *pat*, *putten*, as well as from the ordinary Eng. *put*, *put*, *put*.

For the earlier history evidence is wanting, but the various forms appear to be parallel formations from a stem *pŭt-*, *pot-*, whence app. also Da. *putte* to put, put in; but this appears in Kalkar only from the 17th c. Rietz gives a southern Swedish *putta* (with variants *pötta*, *potta*) in two senses: (1) = slå, stöta, knuffa til lindrigt (to strike, knock or push gently); (2) = sticka undan, ställa bort, 'putta i lomman' (to put out of the way (or conceal), put away, 'put in the pocket'). The Welsh *pwtio* and Gaelic *put* are from Eng. ME. had also a vb. *pulten*, *pilten* (see PILT), which was synonymous with *put*, and even occurs as a variant reading in 15th c. MSS., but could not be formally related. It became obs. (at least in the senses in question) before 1500. In the sense 'strike with the head or horns', ME. *putten* was in early use synonymous with *butten*, BUTT *v.*[1], by which it has been superseded in literary English; but some dialects retain *put* in this sense.]

A. Illustration of Forms and Inflexions.

I. From OE. *pŭtian*, ME. *pŭte-n*, *putt-en*, mod. *put*.

1. *Inf.* and *Present tense.* 1 ***putian, 2–4 pute(n, 2–5 putten, 3–6 pute, 4–6** (also 7–9 in special senses: see PUT *v.*[2]) **putt; 5** (–6 *Sc.*) **pwt, 6** *Sc.* **powt; 4– put.**

c **1050** *Rule of Chrodegang* 99 Þurh deofles putunge.. an belæd. *c* **1175** Puttest [see B. 1]. *c* **1220** *Bestiary* 669 A ȝungling raðe to him luteð, his snute him under puteð. **1382** WYCLIF *John* xv. 13 That ony man putte his soule for his frendis. *a* **1400** *R. Brunne's Chron. Wace* (Petyt MS.) 8880 Now makes assay, To putte þis stones doun [*Lamb. MS.* potte þe stones] if ȝe may. **14..** LYDG. *Lyke thyr Audience* 30 in *Pol. Rel. & L. Poems* (1903) 48 Thy lyfe to putt in morgage. **1479** J. PASTON in *P. Lett.* III. 265, I must pwt me in God, for her must I be for a season. **1528** in *Exch. Rolls Scot.* XV. 584 Tak the rentall of Fyf fra the Arsdan and powt in thes berar and his wyf. **1533** GAU *Richt Vay* 12 Thay quhilk.. pwtis noth al thair traist.. in hime. **1671** H. M. tr. *Erasm. Colloq.* 236 Thou indeed puttest me hard to it.

2. *Past tense.* α. **3–6 putte,** (4 **pudt,** 5 **pute**), **5–7 putt; 4– put.**

c **1205** LAY. 18092 He smat hine uuenen þat hæued.. And þat sweord putte in his muð. *a* **1300** Put [see B. 16 b]. **13..** Pudt, putte, put [see B. 1, 25]. *c* **1470** HENRY *Wallace* III. 101 The worthi Scottis.. putt thair hors thaim fra. *c* **1477** CAXTON *Jason* Yb, Peleus and his neuewe putte hem to poynte in armes. **1785** Put [see B. 1 d].

β. 4 **puttede, -ide, 5 -id, -yd, 6** *Sc.* **puttit, 6– putted** (see PUT *v.*[2]).

1382 WYCLIF *Luke* i. 66 And alle men that herden puttedyn in her herte. **1388** —— *Matt.* xxvii. 29 And thei foldiden a coroun of thornes, and putten [*v.r.* (*c* **1390–1420**) puttiden] on his heed. *c* **1449**, **14..** Puttid, -yd [see B. 10 d, 25]. **1520** NISBET *Sc. N.T.*, *Acts* xxviii. 10 (S.T.S.) III. 124 Quhilkis.. puttit [**1388** WYCLIF puttiden] quhat thingis war necessarie. **1575** LANEHAM *Let.* (1871) 28 Than putted he in his hostes hande other . v . thousande guldens.

3. *Past pple.* α. **4 y-put, i-put(te, pute, 4–7 putte, putt, 4– put.**

13.. *Cursor M.* 1258 (Cott.) Quen we war put o paradis. *c* **1340** HAMPOLE *Pr. Consc.* 6135 To be putt til pastur strayt. **1377** LANGL. *P. Pl.* B. XIV. 207 Þere þe pore is put bihynde [**1393** C. XVII. 50 yput, *v.r.* putte]. **1387** TREVISA *Higden* (Rolls) VII. 9 His feet þat he hadde with i-putte [*v.r.* yput] seint Odo his tombe. **1483** *Cath. Angl.* 295/2 Putte oute, *expulsus.* **1606** G. W[OODCOCKE] *Lives Emperors* in *Hist. Ivstine* G g 4 His corpes was.. putte into the sepulchre. **16..** SIR. W. MURE *Sonn.* xii. Wks. (S.T.S.) I. 58 Thy epitaph sall then be putt in prent. **1839** MARRYAT *Phant. Ship* xii, We might have put the royals on her.

β. **4–5 putted, 5 putet, puttid, -yd.** See also PUT *v.*[2]

1340 HAMPOLE *Pr. Consc.* 2055 Þus sal þai.. be putted til endeles pyne. *c* **1450** *Mirour Saluacioun* 3063 The folk.. in to the lake hadde puttid Daniel. **1495** *Trevisa's Barth. de P.R.* VI. ii. (W. de W.) 187 He is putet [*MSS.* iput, iputte, put] asyde and buryed.

II. From OE. *potian*, ME. *pote*, *poote*, *potte*, mod. dial *pot*.

1. *Present.* α. 1 **potian, 4–5 poten, 6 pote, poote.**

c **1000** Potedon [see POTE *v.* 1]. **1382** WYCLIF *Prov.* xix. 18 To the slaȝter.. of hym ne poote [*Vulg.* ne ponas] thou thi soule. —— *Isa.* lv. 2 Whi poote ȝee vp siluer not in loeues? —— *Mark* v. 10 He preide hym.. that he shulde nat put [*v.r.* poten] hym out of the cuntreie. **1435–1530** [see POTE *v.* 1].

β. **4–5 potte(n, pot, pott.**

c **1330** R. BRUNNE *Chron. Wace* (Rolls) 8885 Ropes to drawe, tres to potte, þey schouued, þey þriste, þey stode o strot. *c* **1385** CHAUCER *L.G.W.* 909 To pottyn [*v.rr.* putten, puten] hire in swich an aventure. **1387** TREVISA *Higden* (Rolls) III. 183 Þey potteþ þeire lif [MS. γ a potteþ here lyf] for wommen. *Ibid.* 313 Þat he wolde putte [MS. γ potte] of þe fevere by deeþ. *Ibid.* 333 To putte [MS. γ pot] of alle manere lett of his speche. *c* **1425** *Cast. Persev.* 1131 in *Macro Plays* 111 Speke þi neybour mekyl schame; pot on hem sum fals fame. *c* **1450** LOVELICH *Grail* xlii. 348 But ȝif ȝe potten þerto Consaille. *c* **1485** *Digby Myst.* III, *Mary Magd.* 1554 Pott don þe pryd of mamentes violatt!

2. *Past tense.* **4–5 potte, 5, 9** *dial.* **pot.**

1387 TREVISA *Higden* (Rolls) VI. 51 Þe senatoures.. putte [MS. γ potte] hym.. out of his kyngdom. *a* **1417** in *Cal. Proc. Chanc. Q. Eliz.* (1827) I. Introd. 13 Wheche Johan.. pot my land to ferme. **1881** J. SARGUSSON *Joe Scoap's Jurneh* 16 (Cumbld. Gloss.), T' girt injin screamt, an off we pot.

3. *Past pple.* **4–5, 9** *dial.* **pot, 5 poot.**

1387 TREVISA *Higden* (Rolls) III. 187 After þat Tarquinius was put [MS. γ pot] out of Rome. **1480** *Newcastle Merch. Vent.* (Surtees) I. 2 At the mony of the said fines.. be poot in the said box. **1878** *Cumbld. Gloss.*, *Pot*, *Pat*, has put, did put.

III. From OE. *pȳtan*, ME. *puite*, *puyt(e.*

Present. 1 **pýtan, 4 puite, puyt(e.**

11.. *OE. Chron.* an. 796 (MS. F) Ceolwulf.. let him pytan ut his eaȝan & ceorfan of his handa. *c* **1330** *Spec. Gy*

Warw. 923 þin almesse þu shalt forþ puite [*rime* luite]. **1362** LANGL. *P. Pl.* A. VI. 100 And puiteþ forþ pruide to preisen þi-seluen. *Ibid.* XI. 42 And puyteþ forþ presumpciun. *a* **1400** *Minor Poems fr. Vernon MS.* 598/527 Auyse þe wel in þi þouȝt, Puyt þi strengþe in-to prou.

IV. From ME. *pytte(n, pitte(n, pyt*, mod. dial. *pyt, pit*. (With *putte* and *pitte*, cf. *cutte* and *kitte*: CUT *v.*)

1. *Present.* Now only *north. dial.* and *Sc.* 4–5 **pitt**, 5 **pyt**, 7 **pitte**, 6– **pit**.

c **1400** *Wyclif's Bible* Luke xii. 25 Who of ȝou.. may adde [*v.r.* pitt] o cubite to his stature? *c* **1420** *Liber Cocorum* (1862) 33 In erþyne pot þou shalt hit pyt [*rime* hit]. **1588** A. KING tr. *Canisius' Catech.* I. viij, Pitting sic men in thair kallendar for sanctes. **1641** BEST *Farm. Bks.* (Surtees) 32 Hammer to pitte the strickle with to make it keepe. **1786** BURNS *Twa Dogs* 69 What poor cot-folk pit their painch in. **1816** SCOTT *Antiq.* xxxviii, If we didna pit hand til 't oursell. **1865** G. MACDONALD *A. Forbes* 2, I jist dinna like to pit the lid ower him.

2. *Past tense.* α. 4 **pitte**; 9 *Sc.* **pit** (in E.D.D.).

1390 GOWER *Conf.* III. 369 As he pitte forth his hond Upon my body, wher I lay.

β. 6– *Sc.* and *north. dial.* **pat**.

1533 GAU *Richt Vay* 48 The halie spreit.. the quilk.. pat in thaime the luiff of god. **1549** [see B. 10]. *c* **1650** in Sir R. Gordon *Hist. Earls of Sutherl.* (1813) 242 The messingers.. pat them all in such a fray. **1787** BURNS *Death & Dr. Hornbook* vi, Something.. That pat me in an eerie swither. **1878** *Cumbld. Gloss.*, *Pat*,.. did put.

3. *Past pple.* α. 4–5 **ipit, ypitte** (4 ? **pett**), 5–6 *Sc.* **pit**.

[**13..** *K. Alis.* 7495 þou art ful of þewes pett.] *a* **1400** *Pol. Rel. & L. Poems* (1903) 268 Hou þi fairnisse is bi-spit, Hou þi swetnisse is i-betin and ipit. *c* **1400** *Wyclif's Bible* Luke xii. 19 Thou hast many goodis kept [*v.r.* pit vp]. *c* **1440** *Palladius on Husb.* I. 1119 With brymstoon resolute ypitte [*rime* slitte]. **1501** *Acc. Ld. High Treas. Scot.* II. 128 Ane masoun in Faukland that wes pit fra the werk.

β. 5, 7–9 *Sc.* and *north. dial.* **putten**, (5 **-yn**), 9 **pitten, potten** (in Eng. Dial. Dict.).

c **1400** *Destr. Troy* 11434 Braunches.. of bright Olyue.. puttyn O lofte. *c* **1450** *Merlin* I. 18 As touchynge this that is putten on my moder. ? *a* **1700** *Edom o' Gordon* iii. in Child *Ballads* (1889) III. 430 She had nae sooner busket her sell Nor putten on her gown. **1804** R. ANDERSON *Cumbld. Ball.* 113 A chubby-feac'd angel o' top on't they've putten. **1827** T. WILSON *Pitman's Pay* I. 52 (Northumbld. Gloss.) Aa've hewed and putten twee and twenty. **1876** *Whitby Gloss.*, *Putten*, put or placed.

B. Signification.

I. To thrust, push, and allied senses, in which the application of force is expressed.

†**1. a.** *trans.* To thrust, push (with or without resulting change of position), to shove; to knock. *Obs.*

In literary use after the 16th c. the sense 'thrust' occurs in contexts which make it indistinguishable from sense 10.

c **1175** *Lamb. Hom.* 15 ȝif þu me puttest in þet eȝe, ic þin alswa, dunt a-ȝein dunt. *c* **1205** LAY. 30780 þe an hine putte hiderward, and þe oðer hine putte ȝeondward. **13..** *Cursor M.* 12292 (Gött.) Leue sun, me say, queþer þu pudt [*Cott.* putte] þe child or nai? **13..** *Minor Poems fr. Vernon MS.* xxxvii. 359 ȝif eny mon a-gult aȝeynes þe, Smyteþ or elles puiteþ þe. *c* **1440** *Promp. Parv.* 417/2 Puttyn, or schowwyn, ..*impello, trudo, pello*.

b. To butt with the head or horns. Now *n. dial.*

c **1430** *Pilgr. Lyf Manhode* I. xv. (1869) 10, j shulde putte and hustle þe yuel folk with myne hornes. **1523** FITZHERB. *Husb.* §70 The beastes with theyr hornes wyll put bothe horses and the shepe, and gore them in theyr bellyes. **1828** *Craven Gloss.* (ed. 2), *Put*, to push with the horns.

†**c.** *fig.* To urge, incite, instigate. *Obs.* See PUTTING *vbl. sb.*¹ 1 b.

†**d.** *absol.* or *intr.* To deal a thrust or blow, to give a push or knock; to push, knock (*at, on*, etc.). Now *north. dial.* To butt.

c **1330** R. BRUNNE *Chron. Wace* (Rolls) 8890 When þey ofte hadde put & þryst & ilk man do what hym do lyst. *c* **1375** *Cursor M.* 11817 (Fairf.) þe parlesi puttis in his side [*Trin.* smoot his oon side]. **1398** TREVISA *Barth. De P.R.* VI. iv. (Tollem. MS.), When þe body.. fongeþ soule, and lyf, and begynneþ to meue it selfe, and sprawle and putteþ with feet and hondis [orig. *manibus et pedibus calcitrare*]. *c* **1425** *Seven Sag.* (P.) 1357 The wyf fonde the dore faste,.. Scho pute at the dore in hye. *c* **1450** *St. Cuthbert* (Surtees) 6250 With' his croche on him he putt. **1504** *Sel. Cases Crt. Star Chamber* (Selden) 212 [Men on boats] with hookis & sparris of iron.. puttith at the seid Brigge & greetly Fretith lowsith.. & castyth downe the stones. **1684** [MERITON] *Yorksh. Dial.* 12 (E.D.S.) Whaugh, Mother, how she rowts! Ise varra Arfe, Shee'l put, and rive my good Prunella Scarfe. **1785** HUTTON *Bran New Wark* 17 They say she yance hed horns and put furiously.

†**e.** *intr. fig.* To make a push, to exert oneself.

1616 B. JONSON *Devil an Ass* I. i. (1905) 7 Stay i' your place ..and put not Beyond the spheare of your actiuity. **1619** FLETCHER *False One* IV. iii, If it be possible That an arch-villain may ever be recover'd, This penitent rascal will put hard.

2. a. *trans.* To propel (a stone or weight) mainly by the swing of the body from the right hand raised and placed close to the shoulder: as an athletic exercise. Usually in phr. ***putting the stone*** (***shot, weight***). See also PUT, PUTT *v.*² 2.

c **1300** *Havelok* 1044 For neuere yete ne saw he or Putten þe stone, or þanne þor. *a* **1518** SKELTON *Magnyf.* 406 They haue made me here to put the stone. **1653** URQUHART *Rabelais* I. xxiii. (1737) I. 223 He did cast the dart, throw the bar, put the stone. **1724, 1816** [see PUT *v.*² 2]. **1862** SMILES *Engineers* III. 25 Lifting heavy weights, throwing the hammer and putting the stone. **1884** H. C. BUNNER in *Harper's Mag.* Jan. 304/1 The Scottish-Americans will teach you to put the shot. **1889** *Boy's Own Paper* 7 Sept. 780/1 The same plan can be adopted for both putting the weight and the broad jump.

b. *intr.* Also *to put at* (or *with*) *the stone*.

For the later Sc. absolute use of this, see PUT *v.*² 2 b.

c **1300** *Havelok* 1033 Hwo so mithe putten þore Biforn a-noþer, an inch or more.. He was for a kempe told. *Ibid.* 1051 þat heui ston, þat he sholde puten wiþe. *c* **1440** CAPGRAVE *St. Kath.* I. 763 As well in wrestyllyng as puttyng at þe ston. **1535** COVERDALE *2 Macc.* iv. 14 To leape, to daunce, & to put at yᵉ stone.

3. a. *trans.* To thrust or plunge (a weapon) †*home*, or *into* a body; to drive or send a missile *through*. Phr. ***to put a*** (***one's***) ***knife into***, to stab; ***to put a bullet through***, to shoot.

Now felt as a euphemistic use of sense 10.

c **1205** [see A. I. 2]. **1382** WYCLIF *John* xix. 37 Thei schulen se in to whom they piȝten [*v.rr.* putteden, putten; Vulg. *transfixerunt*] thorw. *a* **1425** *Cursor M.* 16838 (Trin.) þe iewes made him þourȝe his side to put hit [a spear] sone anone. **1590** *Reg. Privy Counc. Scotl.* IV. 486 Threitnyt to put twa bullettis throw his heid. **1604** SHAKS. *Oth.* V. i. 2 Weare thy good Rapier bare, and put it home. **1700** T. BROWN *Amusem. Ser. & Com.* 51 Mistresses, as a Man would desire to put his Knife into. **1894** [see KNIFE *sb.* 1 b].

†**b.** *fig.* (Cf. HOME-THRUST.)

1603 BEN JONSON *Sejanus* II. ii, That trick was well put home; and had succeeded too, But that [etc.]. **1657** SANDERSON *Serm.* (1674) I. 1 Their hypocrisie he putteth home to them. **1719** DE FOE *Crusoe* (1840) II. xii. 257, I should.. find an opportunity to put it home to them.

4. *Coal-mining.* To propel (a tram or barrow of coal), orig. by pushing behind; now also by means of a pony, a stationary engine, etc. (Cf. PUTTER *sb.*¹ 6.) Also *absol.*

1708 J. C. *Compl. Collier* 36 These Persons.. put or pull away the full Curves of Coals. *Ibid.* 39 [see CORF 2]. **1770–4** A. HUNTER *Georg. Ess.* (1804) II. 159 They are employed.. in putting or drawing the coals. **1812** [see PUTTER *sb.*¹ 6]. **1851** GREENWELL *Coal-trade Terms Northumb. & Durh.* 7 The average day's work of a barrow-man,.. when putting alone,.. is equal.. to.. 3.0580 tons pushed a distance of one mile. **1883** GRESLEY *Gloss. Coal Mining*, *Put*, to haul coal, etc. underground.

†**5. a.** To drive; to send by force or command. ***to put again***: to drive back, repel. *Obs.*

1375 BARBOUR *Bruce* XII. 355 And how at thai war put agane And part of thair gud men wes slane. *Ibid.* XVII. 396 The defendouris.. can thame payne Till put thair fais fors agane. **1382** WYCLIF *Ecclus.* xiii. 13 Be thou not to gredi, lest thou be put aȝeen [Vulg. *ne impingaris*]. *c* **1394** *P. Pl. Crede* 308 Paul primus heremita put vs him-selue Awey into wildernes þe werlde to dispisen. *c* **1400** *Destr. Troy* 1796 Fro Priam full prist put am I hider, As a messynger made at þis mene tyme. *a* **1533** LD. BERNERS *Huon* lx. 210 He hath.. chasyd & put fro him all noble men.

b. *Naut.* Of the wind or a storm: To drive or cast (a ship) on or from shore, to sea, etc. ? *Obs.*

1569 SIR J. HAWKINS *2nd Voy.* (Hakl. Soc.) III. 515 The ordinary Brise taking us,.. put us, the 24th [June] from the shoare. **1579–80** NORTH *Plutarch, Romulus* (1595) 20 Certaine Troians, which.. were by windes put to the Thvscane shore. **1612** DABORNE *Chr. turned Turke* B 2 b, Nay, then we are put from shore. **1780** YOUNG *Tour Irel.* I. 229 One.. on her voyage was put ashore at Black Sod.

6. *trans.* To launch (persons, a boat, a fleet, etc.).

1470–85 MALORY *Arthur* I. xxviii. 75 All were put in a ship to the see. **1639, 1892** [see *put off* 45 n (*c*)]. **1877** MISS YONGE *Cameos* Ser. III. xv. 132 He put a fleet to sea.

†**7.** *refl.* To embark on a sea voyage (*to, into,* or *in the sea, to sail*); = 8 a. *Obs.*

1375 BARBOUR *Bruce* IV. 441 In hy thai put thame to the se, And rowit fast with all thare mayn. *c* **1425** *Eng. Conq. Irel.* (1896) 134 He put hym to saylle at Melyford. **1456** SIR G. HAYE *Law Arms* (S.T.S.) 39 Thai put thame in the see, and thocht to passe in Lombardye. *c* **1500** *Melusine* xxiv. 178 They were in nombre six knightes and þeire companye, which putte them in to the see.

8. *Naut. intr.* To set out, set forth, proceed, take one's course (to sea, into harbour, etc.).

See also *put back*, 40 f; *put forth*, 43 k; *put in*, 45 f; *put off*, 46 n; *put out*, 48 j; *put over*, 50 e; *put to*, 53 e.

1590 SHAKS. *Com. Err.* V. i. 21 My honest friend, Who but for staying on our Controuersie, Had hoisted saile, and put to sea to day. **1595** MAYNARDE *Drake's Voy.* (Hakl. Soc.) 7 We putting for the shore of the Canaries.. found a great seege. *c* **1595** CAPT. WYATT *R. Dudley's Voy. W. Ind.* (Hakl. Soc.) 42 Insteed of goinge to the ilande of Trinidado, putt into a bay of the maine. **1612** DEKKER *If it be not good* Wks. 1873 III. 312 Thou putst into a Sea, thou canst not sound. **1748** *Anson's Voy.* III. viii. 379 With a view of preventing them from putting before the wind. **1838** THIRLWALL *Greece* IV. xxviii. 57 Clearchus.. after having put into Delos for shelter, returned to Miletus. **1890** *Temple Bar Mag.* June 180 He stepped into a fishing-boat and put to land. **1899** *Westm. Gaz.* 5 Oct. 5/1 *Erin*.. was among the first vessels to put down the bay this morning.

b. *intr.* To set out; to start; to pass, make one's way. *Obs.* exc. *U.S. colloq.*, to make off, be off, 'clear out'. Cf. *put off* 46 n (*b*), *put out* 47 j (*c*).

c **1400** *Destr. Troy* 8987 Deffibus drogh furth.., Then Paris with prise put next after. *a* **1518** SKELTON *Magnyf.* 1330 Foly hath a rome, I say, in euery route; To put where he lyst, Foly hath fre chace. **1839** MARRYAT *Diary Amer.* Ser. I. II. 231 Clear out, quit, and put—all mean 'be off'. 'Captain, now, you hush or put'. **1897** *Outing* (U.S.) XXX. 176/1 The pair.. glanced apprehensively at me, then they put for home like a tandem team.

c. *intr.* Of a stream, etc.: To make its way, to flow (*into* or *out of* a larger piece of water). *U.S.* Also of sap: to flow (in some direction). *Obs.*

1615 W. LAWSON *Country Housew. Gard.* 37 Where you take any thing away, the sap the next summer will be putting. *a* **1626** BACON *Sylva* §616 In the fibrous [roots], the sap delighteth more in the earth, and therefore putteth down-ward. **1773** P. V. FITHIAN *Jrnl.* (1900) 56 From his house we see the Potowmack, and a fine River putting from it. **1807** P. GASS *Jrnl.* 172 A small river which puts into a large bay on the south side of the Columbia. **1810** F. CUMING *Sk. Tour Western Country* xiii. 97 The creek.. puts in from the Virginia side. **1903** A. ADAMS *Log of Cowboy* 347 The trail on leaving the river led up Many Berries, one of the tributaries of the Yellowstone putting in from the north side.

9. *intr.* Of a plant: To shoot out or grow; to send forth shoots or sprouts; to sprout, bud; cf. *put forth* (43 g). Now *dial.*

1615 W. LAWSON *Country Housew. Gard.* (1626) 29 Some [graffes].. keeping proud and greene, will not put till the second yeere. *a* **1626** BACON *Sylva* §653 The roots of trees do some of them put downwards deep into the ground. **1848** *Jrnl. R. Agric. Soc.* IX. II. 367 The one arm.. still shows life, and puts into leaf, and produces acorns. **1893–4** *Northumbld. Gloss.*, *Put*, to vegetate, as when a plant begins to show the first sign of buds. 'Aa see its aall reet; it's puttin'.

II. To move (a thing or person) physically into or out of some place or local position.

A weakening of the sense 'thrust' or 'push', with elimination of the notion of dynamic force; which is, however, often still traceable in senses 10 and 10 b.

10. a. *trans.* To move (a thing) so as to place it in some situation (with reference to the result rather than the process); to cause to get into or be in some place or position expressed or implied (see also the phrases with preps. and advs., 31–56); to place, lay, set.

The most general word for this sense, which cannot be so simply expressed by any other word or phrase, and which is more or less implied, literally or metaphorically, in nearly all the other senses that are still in use. The original notion of 'thrust', 'set or insert with some force' is still traceable in some contexts, esp. when followed by *into* or *in*.

c **1175** *Lamb. Hom.* 53 þis faȝe folc.. speket alse feire bi-foren heore euencristene alse heo heom walde in to heore bosme puten. *a* **1225** *Ancr. R.* 116 Nout one monglinde honden, auh puten honden utward. *a* **1300** *Cursor M.* 4762 (Cott.) Soruful war þai.. þat had noght to put in þair mouth. *Ibid.* 15797 In þe forel þou pute þi suerd. **1382** WYCLIF *Matt.* iii. 10 For now the axe is putt [**1388** put] to the rote of the tree. *c* **1400** MAUNDEV. (1839) xxii. 235 Putteth ȝoure honde vpon ȝoure hede. **1434** *E.E. Wills* (1882) 102/10 A litel cofur to putte in his smale thynges. **1549** *Compl. Scot.* Ep. 5 The duc of guise.. pat ane garnison of tua thousand men vitht in the toune of sanct quintyne. **1576** FLEMING *Panopl. Epist.* 370 As he was putting the pot to his lips ready to drinke. **1623** B. JONSON *On Portrait Shaks.*, This Figure, that thou here seest put, It was for gentle Shakespeare cut. **1699** T. BROWN in R. L'Estrange *Erasm. Colloq.* (1725) 336 Put your Hand to your Heart and tell me fairly. *a* **1756** ELIZA HEYWOOD *New Present* (1771) 43 Put about an ounce of butter into a frying-pan. **1760** FOOTE *Minor* II. Wks. 1799 I. 269 Bread, greens, potatoes, and a leg of mutton, A better sure a table ne'er was put on. **1818** in Willis & Clark *Cambridge* (1886) I. 573 Putting some ornamental Clumps of Trees or Shrubs to break the line. **1843** R. J. GRAVES *Syst. Clin. Med.* xxxi. 422 The patient.. had an issue put into the top of the head. **1844** R. M. BEVERLEY *Ch. Eng. Exam.* (ed. 2) 150 When they are thus put on the rails.. the train will go forward. **1855** MACAULAY *Hist. Eng.* xvii. IV. 37 A sealed packet was put into his hands. **1865** RUSKIN *Sesame* I. §35 You have put a railroad bridge over the fall of Schaffhausen. **1872** GEO. ELIOT *Middlem.* viii, Somebody put a drop under a magnifying glass. **1883** *Daily Tel.* 15 May 2/7 Mr. Cave put his next ball to leg for 2. *Mod.* He put the key in his pocket.

b. To remove, dismiss, expel, send away; to turn away, or divert *from*. *Obs.* or *arch.* Also ***to put.. off***: to divert from, cause to give up. So *to put* BESIDE, BESIDES (B. 4 c), and BY (A. 16 c).

The original notion of 'thrust' or 'push' is often traceable; see also *put away* (39), *put off* (46), *put out* (48).

13.. *Cursor M.* 29355 Fra sacrament þai sal be put bot þai repent. *c* **1400** *Destr. Troy* 267 Fortune.. will put hym fro purpos þat he presys after. *c* **1430** *Hymns Virg.* 93 He puttiþ his hauke fro his fist. *a* **1450** *Knt. de la Tour* (1906) 93 To putte a good man from his right. **1470–85** MALORY *Arthur* X. lxxi. 537 Ye putte me from my worship now. **1539** BIBLE (Great) *Ps.* xliii. 2 Why hast thou put thee from me? **1590** SIR J. SMYTH *Disc. Weapons* Ded. viij b, Vppon the occasion of anie battaile, to put their horses from them. **1618** FLETCHER *Loyal Subject* V. ii, Rashly I thought her false, and put her from me. **1732** NEAL *Hist. Purit.* I. 118 Princess Elizabeth.. was led in by the Traitor's gate; her own servants being put from her. **1862** *Temple Bar Mag.* VI. 331 Don't be put off this by any consideration of weight or expense. **1883** MRS. F. MANN *Parish Hilby* xix, She could not put from her some feeling of pride.

c. To place (an article of apparel or an ornament) *on, upon* (also †*off*) the body. See also *put on, put off* (47 c, 46 d).

1382 WYCLIF *2 Kings* xi. 12 He brouȝt forthe the sone of the kyng, and putte vpon hym a dyademe. **1422** tr. *Secreta Secret., Priv. Priv.* 200 He.. Put of hym his clothis and hym clothyd in Sake. **1484** CAXTON *Fables of Æsop* II. xv, None ought to were and putte on hym the gowne of other. **1560** DAUS tr. *Sleidane's Comm.* 25 He putteth also a rynge on his Fynger. *Ibid.* 43 a, He hath put vpon him an albe and a Vestement. **1611** BIBLE *Luke* xv. 22 Bring foorth the best robe, and put it on him, and put a ring on his hand, and shooes on his feete.

d. *spec.* To place upon or affix *to* a writing or document (a title, seal, signature, name, etc.).

c **1449** PECOCK *Repr.* V. ii, Whenne to a certein book which y have mad y puttid this name, The rule of Cristen religioun. **1762** *North Briton* No. 12 To bring the name into contempt by putting it to two insipid tragedies. **1776** *Trial of Nundocomar* 22/2 He put his seal to letters. **1864** J. H. NEWMAN *Apol.* iv. (1904) 132/1 To this number.. I also put my initials. *Mod.* It seems to be in his handwriting, but he hasn't put his name to it. Put a tick against the names you know. Put a cross against the name of the candidate you approve.

e. To harness (a draught animal) *to* a vehicle; to place *in* the shafts of a cart, etc.

1565 COOPER *Thesaurus* s.v. *Iungo*, To couple or put horses in the carte... To put lions to draw the chariote... To put the horses to the carte. **1716** *Lond. Gaz.* No. 5461/2 The Ammunition-Waggons should have the Horses put to them. **1815** MRS. PILKINGTON *Celebrity* II. 29 Whilst fresh horses were putting [= being put] to his chariot. **1847** MARRYAT *Childr. N. Forest* v, He..put Billy [the pony] in the cart to draw him home.

f. To introduce (a male animal *to* a female, or *vice versa*) for breeding. Also const. *ellipt.*

1523 FITZHERB. *Husb.* §37 What tyme of the yere the rammes shulde be put to the ewes. **1577** B. GOOGE *Heresbach's Husb.* III. (1586) 126b, Neither must you put him to a yoong mare. **1607** TOPSELL *Four-f. Beasts* (1658) 88 If two males be put to one female, they fight fiercely. **1758** R. BROWN *Compl. Farmer* (1759) 21 They are put to the bull about July. **1819** KEATS *Let.* 22 Sept. in G. G. Williamson *Keats Mem. Vol.* (1921) 120 Chowder died long ago—Mrs. H. laments that the last time they *put him* (*i.e.* to breed) he didn't take. **1864** *Jrnl. R. Agric. Soc.* XXV. I. 221 The mares ..if put to a good thoroughbred horse would produce good hunters.

g. To convey (a person, etc.) across a river, etc.; to transport; to set down on the other side.

a **1649** WINTHROP *New Eng.* (1825) I. 184 Cattle..which came late, and could not be put over the river, lived very well all the winter without any hay. **1891** C. ROBERTS *Adrift Amer.* 204, I went to the ferryman and told him if he would put me across that..I would pay him when I came back again. **1893** SELOUS *Trav. S.E. Africa* 61 He at once agreed to put me across the river in one of his large boats.

h. *Stock-jobbing.* To deliver (stock or produce) at a specified price within a specified time: cf. PUT *sb.*[1] 4.

1814 *Stock Exchange Laid Open* Gloss., *Put their Bears*, selling to put more to it, if the seller choose on a certain day at the same price. **1885** *Daily News* 13 Mar. 2/1 Those who desire to buy the option of 'putting'—i.e. delivering—Russian stock on the present basis of prices during the next six weeks. **1895** *Westm. Gaz.* 9 Nov. 6/1 If his tone with regard to the political outlook is favourable operators will 'call' the stock; if otherwise, they hope to be able to 'put' it.

i. with abstract obj., in various shades of meaning: see quots. (See also the phrases mentioned under 57.)

c **1374** CHAUCER *Compl. Mars* 229 He that wroght her.. That put suche beaute in her face That made me coueten and purchace. *a* **1425** *Cursor M.* 3563 (Trin.) Whenne þat he bicomeþ olde Vnwelde putt at him a pulle. **1594** SHAKS. *Rich. III*, I. iii. 131 Let me put in your mindes, if you forget, What you haue beene ere this, and what you are. **1598** [see LIFE *sb.* 4]. **1707** FREIND *Peterborow's Cond. Sp.* 219 Your Excellencies..conduct..has..put new lives into the Ministers. **1812** CHALMERS *Jrnl.* 12 Mar. in *Life* (1851) I. 277, I..am greatly struck with the quantity of business which he [Doddridge] put through his hands. **1889** F. BARRETT *Under Strange Mask* II. xiv. 78 The thing had been put before her in such vivid reality.

III. To place or bring (a thing or person) in or into some relation, or into some condition, state, mode, or form.

* *Where the notion of motion in space is subordinated to that of relation.*

11. a. To place (a thing or person) *in* or *into* the hands or power of, *in* or *under* the care of a person; †formerly also *in, to, unto* the person; †to commit or entrust *to* a person, to be dealt with, protected, etc. Often *refl.*

c **1375** *Cursor M.* 20795 (Fairf.) Putte al in him þat is of miȝt. *Ibid.* 25353 For-þi putte al in goddis hande. **1399** LANGL. *Rich. Redeles* Prol. 78, I put me in his power. *a* **1400–50** *Alexander* 2861 Let ane dryue to Dary & bede him dryffe sone, Or put him to my powere. **1429** in *10th Rep. Hist. MSS. Comm.* App. v. 330 The said William putt him to grace. *c* **1440** *Alphabet of Tales* 207 All þe gudis att he had, he putt þaim vnto þe bisshopp. **1470–85** MALORY *Arthur* XIX. v. 778 Now I put me holy in to your grace. **1553** *Respublica* II. ii. 507 Will ye putte yourselfe nowe wholye into my handes? **1583** GOLDING *Calvin on Deut.* xv. 90 Let vs put ourselues to his protection. **1588** ALLEN *Admon.* 38 A prince that was put to him for an ostage. **1662** GERBIER *Princ.* 26 Builders put their design to Master-Workmen by the Great, or have it Wrought by the Day. **1843** R. J. GRAVES *Syst. Clin. Med.* xxix. 366 A very fine healthy young man put himself under my care for chancre. **1882** R. G. WILBERFORCE *Life Bp. Wilberf.* III. xv. 424 He wished 'to put himself in my hands' for our journey to Holmbury.

†b. To commit (a person) *to* another for the purpose of being educated or trained in a business; to place with; to apprentice *to*. *Obs.*

1632 BROME *Crt. Beggar* I. i, To put you to some Tellers Clearke to teach you Ambo-dexterity in telling money. **1716–20** *Lett. fr. Mist's Jrnl.* (1722) I. 184 Tom was put Clerk to an Attorney in the Temple. **1772** JOHNSON 5 Apr. in *Boswell*, I would not put a boy to him, whom I intended for a man of learning.

12. To place, set, or cause to be in some place or position, in a general or figurative sense, or when the name of a thing or place stands for its purpose, as ***to put*** a person ***to bed, to school, in ward, in prison, to put*** a thing ***to sale, on the market, on the stage***, etc.

1387 TREVISA *Higden* (Rolls) VIII. 323 Þe Kyng of Engelond..was i-putte in ward, in þe castel of Kelynsworþe. **1416** *Satir. Proclam.* in *Pol. Rel. & L.P.* 13 For my curtesie I was put to the Soudenys house & was made vssher of halle. *c* **1440** *Promp. Parv.* 417/2 Puttyn a thynge to syllyn. *a* **1450** *Knt. de la Tour* (1906) 117 Yong women, maydenes, shulde be putte vnto scole to lerne vertuous thinges of the scripture. **1560** DAUS tr. *Sleidane's Comm.* 453 To put the kinges sonne or his brother in to the possession of Scotlande. **1561** WINȜET *Cert. Tractates* i. Wks. (S.T.S.) I. 7 Putand in the place of godly ministeris.. dum doggis. **1620** E. BLOUNT *Horæ Subs.* 106 That haue not been by any casualtie, or accident put behinde hand in the world. **1635** R. N. *Camden's Hist. Eliz.* III. 374 His goods were put to port sale. **1698** FRYER *Acc. E. India & P.* 122 Having others put over their heads. **1850** J. H. NEWMAN *Serm. Var. Occas.* xii. (1881) 229 He was ever putting himself in the background. **1879** M. J. GUEST *Lect. Hist. Eng.* xxviii. 283 The landlords even strongly objected to their serfs putting their children to school. **1897** *Tit-Bits* 4 Dec. 172/2 If..some new patent is being put on the market, it is an opportunity that our traveller will not miss.

13. To place with or in, by way of addition; to add. Const. *to* (†*unto*), *in*. **a.** with material obj.

c **1430** *Two Cookery-bks.* 32 Take halfe a dosyn Chykonys ..þen putte þer-to a gode gobet of freysshe Beef. *Ibid.* 40 Þen put pouder Pepir, & þrow it þer-on. **1703** *Art & Myst. Vintners* 33 Put thereto a gallon of Milk. *Ibid.* 61 Then take 8 gallons of Soot and put to it. **1764** ELIZ. MOXON *Eng. Housew.* (ed. 9) 82 Take twelve eggs, beat them well, put to them a pint of cream. *a* **1849** E. ELLIOTT *More Verse & Prose* I. 21 Said Death to Pol Sly, 'Put no rum in thy tea'. **1891** *Gd. Words* Aug. 532/2 They put water to their wine.

b. with immaterial obj.

1382 WYCLIF *Rev.* xxii. 18 If ony man shal put to to thes [Vulg. *apposuerit ad hæc*], God shal putte vpon him [*apponet super illum*] the plages writun in this book. **1535** COVERDALE *Ecclus.* xviii. 6 There maye nothinge be taken from them, nothinge maye be put vnto them. **1623** LISLE *Ælfric on O. & N. Test.* Pref. 4 The invention of a thing..is very hard and rare: yet easie is it for a man to eeke and put somewhat thereto.

14. To place, insert, or enter (a name or an item) in a list, account, or table. Now more usually (esp. in certain connexions) ***put down*** (see 42 i).

1513–25 in Ellis *Orig. Lett.* (K. O.), Put me in his wylle. **1611** SHAKS. *Wint. T.* IV. iii. 131 Let me be vnrold, and my name put in the booke of Vertue. **1611** BIBLE *1 Chron.* xxvii. 24 Neither was the number put in the account of the Chronicles of King Dauid. **1687** SETTLE *Refl. Dryden* 27 The poorest Servitour in the University would tell him that putting so much upon a mans name, had signified placing so much to his account. **1692** WASHINGTON tr. *Milton's Def. Pop.* M.'s Wks. 1738 I. 535 Assure your selves, you are like to be put in the black List. **1735** J. HUGHES tr. *Fontenelle's Dial.* II. i. (ed. 3) 62 They could not all be put into a Panegyrick, but into a Satyr they might. **1828** *J. H. Moore's Pract. Navig.* (ed. 20) 138 Those are generally put in a table, against the names of their respective places in an alphabetical order.

** *Where there is no notion of physical motion.*

15. To place (a thing or person) in a scale of estimation or a classification; to allot a place to in thought, opinion, or statement; †also, to regard or suppose (a thing) to be (so-and-so) (*obs.*).

to put..at: to estimate or price at (a certain value). † ***to put at no reverence***: to hold in no esteem. † ***to put before***: to give the precedence to; so † ***to put behind***.

1377 LANGL. *P. Pl.* B. XIV. 207 Þe riche is reuerenced by resoun of his richchesse, þere þe pore is put behynde. *c* **1380** WYCLIF *Serm.* Sel. Wks. I. 390 Matheu..takiþ two bigynneris, Daviþ and Abraham;..Daviþ was putt bifore for worshipe and acordaunce, alȝif Abraham was bifore. *c* **1380** —— *Wks.* (1880) 31 No man owiþ to putt by-hynde goddis biddynge and þe byddynge of a synful man bifore. *c* **1400** *Destr. Troy* 4874, I put not vnpossible yon place for to take. *c* **1400** *Three Kings Cologne* 134 Þe bodyes and þe Reliqes of .iij. holy kyngis were put at [*v.r.* had in] no reuerence. **1660** BARROW *Euclid* v. xiv. 103 If A be put equall to C, then C.B::eA. Bf::C.D.g. **1803** [see INCOME-TAX]. **1846** *Jrnl. R. Agric. Soc.* VII. II. 288 The rental of this field is put too high at 50s. **1857** RUSKIN *Pol. Econ. Art* Add. No. 8 §5 There are three weighty matters of the law—justice, mercy, and truth; and of these the Teacher puts truth last... But men put, in all their efforts, truth first. **1865** —— *Sesame* i. §5 Whether you think I am putting the motives of popular action too low. **1890** *Lippincott's Mag.* Jan. 79 A circulation which a competent authority puts at three millions.

16. a. To convert or change *into* something else (*obs.*); *esp.* to translate or render *into* another language or form of expression.

c **1400** MAUNDEV. (1839) Prol. 5, I haue put this boke out of latyn into frensch, and translated it aȝen out of frensch into englyssch. **1607** TOPSELL *Four-f. Beasts* (1658) 487 If a man would change any part of his Horses hair, as..take away the black hairs and put them into white. **1742** FIELDING *Jos. Andrews* III. iii, We..put our small fortune [invested in effects]..into money. **1743** EMERSON *Fluxions* 129 Put these Equations into Fluxions. **1893** LIDDON, etc., *Life Pusey* I. i. 32, 'I never knew', Keble once said, 'how Pindar might be put into English until I heard Pusey construe him in his examination'.

b. To express (something) *in* spoken or written words; to turn *into* speech or writing, or *into* some particular form of speech or writing.

a **1300** *Sat. People Kildare* xi. in *E.E.P.* (1862) 154 Sleiȝ he was..þat þis lore put in writte. *c* **1369** CHAUCER *Dethe Blaunche* 54 Fables That..other poetes put in ryme. **1542** SIR. N. UYLLAGON *Lam. & Pit. Treat.* Addr. in *Harl. Misc.* (Malh.) I, Put in writing the ordre and estate of my voyage. **1668–9** PEPYS *Diary* 14 Feb., I do purpose to put in writing that which shall make the Treasurers ashamed. **1879** M. J. GUEST *Lect. Hist. Eng.* xix. 185 Henry's principal plans.. were put into writing. *Ibid.* xxii. 218 Thoughts which they did not know how to put into words.

c. To express or state (in a particular way).

1699 BENTLEY *Phal.* xv. 481 Was ever any Declamator's Theme so extravagantly put? **1729** BUTLER *Serm. Forgiven. Injuries* Wks. 1874 II. 116 This natural notion of equity the son of Sirach has put in the strongest way. **1836** MARRYAT *Japhet* lxxiii, This new feature of the case, so aptly put by the old lawyer. **1867** *Gd. Words* 597/2 The French have such a brilliant, graceful, and ingenious way of 'putting things'. **1881** SAINTSBURY *Dryden* i. 13 One thing..I have never seen fairly put as accounting for the complete royalization of nearly the whole people. **1883** *Harper's Mag.* Oct. 751/2 This was putting it strong. **1889** F. PIGOT *Str. Journ.* 301 He heard a good story well put.

17. To assign or attribute one thing to another in some relation.

a. To assign or set (a quality, meaning, value, price) *on, upon, to* (†*in*) a thing.

c **1380** WYCLIF *Wks.* (1880) 3 It is a fendis pride a synful creature to putte defautte in þe ordynaunce of crist. **1519** *Four Elem.* in Hazl. *Dodsley* I. 24 For physic putteth this reason thereto. **1530** [see FAULT *sb.* 7a]. **1608** WILLET *Hexapla Exod.* 338 Our Sauiour reproueth the Pharisees for washing of their hands..because they put holinesse therein. **1657** EARL MONM. tr. *Paruta's Pol. Disc.* 79 That high esteem which is deservedly put upon the Roman Affairs. **1668** PEPYS *Diary* 25 Nov., I do see that he do continue to put a value on my advice. *a* **1708** BP. BEVERIDGE *Thes. Theol.* (1710) II. 155 Putting the best construction upon all men's words and actions. **1711** ADDISON *Spect.* No. 1 ¶2 That was the Interpretation which the Neighbourhood put upon it. **1871** FREEMAN *Norm. Conq.* IV. xvii. §2. 31 This too we need not doubt, at least in the sense which the great Survey enables us to put upon it. **1885** *Law Rep.* 29 *Chanc. Div.* 463 A gloss is put upon these documents which they will not bear. **1890** *Temple Bar Mag.* Aug. 493 Watteau sometimes put ridiculously low prices upon his work.

b. To assign or ascribe (a thing) to something else as cause, reason, or basis; to regard or represent as based upon or arising from; to base, found, rest *upon*.

1722 DE FOE *Plague* (1754) 222, I reflect upon no Man for putting the Reason of those Things upon the immediate Hand of God. **1729** BUTLER *Serm.* Wks. 1874 II. 155 A plain rule of life..has..put the principle of virtue upon the love of our neighbour. **1818** CRUISE *Digest* (ed. 2) V. 597 It was said generally, and was not put upon any custom. **1864** J. H. NEWMAN *Apol.* ii. (1904) 29/2, I would have no dealings with my brother, and I put my conduct upon a syllogism. **1884** SIR J. STEPHEN in *Law Rep.* 12 *Q.B. Div.* 282, I wish to put my judgment on the plain and broad ground already stated.

18. To apply *to* a use or purpose.

c **1400** MAUNDEV. (1839) Prol. 3 The comoun peple, þat wolde putte here bodyes and here catell, for to conquere oure heritage. **1483** CAXTON *G. de la Tour* H iij b, To put remedye therto. **1568** GRAFTON *Chron.* II. 263 They put all their goodes vnto the Englishmens pleasures. **1604** E. G[RIMSTONE] *D'Acosta's Hist. Indies* VI. xv. 463 The Indians tilled and put to profite the Inguas lands. **1628** EARLE *Microcosm.* xiv. (Arb.) 35 No man puts his Braine to more vse than hee. **1671** MILTON *Samson* 37 O glorious strength Put to the labour of a Beast. *a* **1700** LOCKE (J.) The great difference in the notions of mankind is from the different use they put their faculties to. **1847** MARRYAT *Childr. N. Forest* viii, To what uses are they to be put?

19. To set mentally or conceptually *in the place of* (something else); to substitute (one thing) *for* another, in thought or expression.

1483 *Cath. Angl.* 295/2 To Putte a thinge for a noder, *reciprocare*. **1560** BIBLE (Genev.) *Isa.* v. 20 Which put darknes for light, and light for darkenesse. **1631** GOUGE *God's Arrows* I. §47. 83 Figuratively..a speciall put for the generall, it signifieth the pestilence. **1659** SIR A. A. COOPER in *Burton's Diary* (1828) IV. 284 It is clearly a putting others in their place, and is setting up a thing that is quite contrary. **1715** tr. *Pancirollus' Rerum Mem.* I. 2 In Pliny, Purple is often put for the Chief Magistrate. **1865** RUSKIN *Sesame* i. §25 Putting ourselves always in the author's place. **1870** READE (*title*) Put yourself in his place.

20. a. To establish or introduce and bring to bear (a state, condition, relation, or alteration) *in, on,* or *to* an existing thing, action, or state of things. Chiefly, now only, in special phrases.

† ***to put (no) doubt*** (obs.): to raise or 'make' (no) doubt. † ***to put order to*** (obs.): to take measures for (cf. *to take order* s.v. ORDER *sb.* 14). ***to put an end, stop, period to***: to bring to an end, to stop, to cause to cease: see the sbs. So ***to put a check, stopper, veto on*** (= to check, stop, or forbid), and similar phrases. colloq. phr. ***to put paid to***: to deal finally or effectually with (a person); to terminate (aspirations, hopes, etc.); to eliminate or put an end to (something).

1382 WYCLIF *Gen.* iii. 15 Enemyte I shal put bitwix thee and the woman. *c* **1420** ? LYDG. *Assembly of Gods* 761 They hym comfortyd & bad hym put no dowte, Hys vttyr enemy Vyce to ouerthrow. **1485** CAXTON *Chas. Gt.* III. I. xiv. 227 After that he had put and sette good estate..in spayne. **1526** TINDALE *Acts* xv. 9 And he putt no difference betwene them and vs. **1556** *Aurelio & Isab.* (1608) Lj, He ordennede, soddainely that..one put ordre to the deathe of his doughter. **1592** *Sc. Acts Jas. VI* (1597) c. 114 To put ordour to all maters and causes Ecclesiasticall. **1601** [see PERIOD *sb.* 5]. **1647** [see END *sb.* 22 c]. **1712** ADDISON *Spect.* No. 403 ¶10 This Intelligence put a Stop to my Travels. **1760** *Impostors Detected* I. iii. I. 14 [This] put a sudden damp to their zeal. **1807–8** SYD. SMITH *Plymley's Lett.* Wks. 1859 II. 137/2 Infamous and damnable laws..which have been put an end to by him. **1855** MACAULAY *Hist. Eng.* xii. III. 213 To solicit the Lords to put some check on the violence of the Commons. **1889** H. D. TRAILL *Strafford* viii. 101 These indecencies were speedily put a stop to. **1891** T. HARDY *Tess* xxxvi, 'What were you thinking of doing?' he enquired. 'Of putting an end to myself'. **1919** *Boy's Own Ann.* XLI. 457/2 She [*sc.* a destroyer]..was about to proceed to sea on her mission of 'putting paid' to U-boats. **1931** T. R. G. LYELL *Slang* 606 You can put paid to any friendship that ever existed between him and me. **1951** J. B. PRIESTLEY *Festival at Farbridge* II. iii. 344, I thought one time Tanhead might ha' swung 'em, but Commodore put paid to him all right. **1955** 'E. C. R. LORAC' *Ask Policeman* v. 54 He and his premises..were put paid to by a land mine. **1957** J. BRAINE *Room at Top* xvi. 144, I wanted to put paid to Communism once and for all. **1959** *Listener* 30 July 183/3 The translator's deficiencies put paid to the book altogether. **1971** G. HOUSEHOLD *Doom's Caravan* ii. 40 The return journey..put paid to my only pair of formal trousers. **1976** *Economist* 13

Mar. 13/2 [That choice] would also probably put paid to any hopes of fully reintegrating France into the Nato alliance.

b. To place, repose (trust, confidence, etc.) *in* (†*to*).

1475 *Bk. Noblesse* (Roxb.) 25 Over grete favoure and trust put to youre adversaries. **1526** *Pilgr. Perf.* (W. de W. 1531) 5 b, Puttynge theyr trust onely in spirituall or heuenly thynges. **1529** MORE *Dyaloge* I. Wks. 121/1 Those nygromancers..that put theyr confydence in the roundell and cercle on the grounde. **1535** COVERDALE *Ps.* cxlv[i.] 3 Put not youre trust in prynces. **1847** MARRYAT *Childr. N. Forest* xvii, Of course I put implicit confidence in you. **1888** G. R. GISSING *Nether World* (1889) III. v. 94 He put no faith in Sidney's assertion.

21. a. To commit (the fate of something) *to* a risk or hazard; to stake *on, upon.*

1611 SHAKS. *Cymb.* I. iv. 133 Would I had put my Estate, and my Neighbors on th' approbation of what I haue spoke. **16..** BACON (J.), They durst not put it to a battle at sea, and set up their rest wholly upon the land enterprize. **1641** J. JACKSON *True Evang. T.* III. 190 So farre as my interest in Religion goeth..I shall willingly put it wholly upon this issue. **1700** DRYDEN *Ovid's Met.* I. 239 When our universal state Was put to hazard. **1711** in *10th Rep. Hist. MSS. Comm.* App. v. 129 The resolution had been taken of putting all upon a battle. **1781** *Hist. Eur.* in *Ann. Reg.* 53/2 [It] obliged him, at no small hazard, to put all at the issue. **1885** *Manch. Even. News* 17 June 2/4 A Frenchman who had patriotically put his money on Reluisant.

b. To invest or venture (one's money) in.

1604 MOUFET *Will* in *Health's Impr.* (1746) Life 27, I give thirtie Shillings, to be put into a Ringe. **1737** [S. BERINGTON] *G. de Lucca's Mem.* (1738) 29 He put what was left, together with my little Stock, into that unfortunate Bottom. **1890** *Harper's Mag.* July 184/2 The poor people had put their substance into purchases of land.

c. *refl.* ***to put oneself on*** or ***upon***: to entrust or commit oneself to the ruling or verdict of.

1660- [see COUNTRY 7]. **1712** ARBUTHNOT *John Bull* App. iii, So Jack resolved; but he had done more wisely to have put himself upon the trial of his country. *a* **1715** BURNET *Own Time* an. 1682 (1823) II. 330 The king being now resolved to live on his revenue, without putting himself on a parliament, he was forced on a great reduction of expenses. **1869** W. LONGMAN *Hist. Edw. III*, I. ii. 39 Thomas de Berkeley, accused..'put himself on his country', and was consequently tried by a jury of twelve men.

*** *Where a thing* (*usually non-material*) *is put in some relation to a person* (*or agent*).

22. To propose to or place before a person for consideration or answer; to propound (a question, supposition, etc.); †in first quot., to address *to* a person (*obs.*). ***put*** (***the***) ***case***: see CASE *sb.*[1] 12. See also *put forth* (43 c), *put forward* (44 c).

Used with indirect (dative) and direct obj. in ***to put one a question.***

c **1300** in Wright *Lyric P.* xvi. 53 To love y putte pleyntes mo. *c* **1440** *Jacob's Well* xxvi. 174 But I putte þis cas; þou art contryte & sory in herte for þi synne [etc.]. *a* **1548** HALL *Chron., Edw. V* 9 Put the case that we neither loued her nor her kynne, yet there were no cause why [etc.]. **1681** H. MORE *Exp. Dan.* 85 The Queen..put hard and weighty questions to him. **1827** ROBERTS *Voy. Centr. Amer.* 267 Whatever others assert who may have put the question. **1888** G. GISSING *Life's Morn.* II. ix. 73 He did not put to himself the plain alternative. **1888** FARJEON *Miser Farebrother* xvii, You are putting a riddle to me. **1892** *Harper's Mag.* Dec. 24/1 He put me too hard a question.

b. *spec.* To submit (a point for decision) formally to the vote of an assembly.

1683 *Col. Rec. Pennsylv.* I. 57 The question was putt whether the Ballott should be used in all cases? **1689** T. R. *View Govt. Europe* 14 The Counsel..put it to the Vote who shall be their General. **1700-15** [see PREVIOUS 2 c]. **1792-3** GIBBON *Autobiog.* (1896) 15 On the question being put, it was carried without a division. **1830** *Examiner* 778/1 The resolution was put and carried. **1888** 'R. BOLDREWOOD' *Robbery under Arms* xlv, Let us put it to the vote.

c. ***to put it***: to present or submit a question, statement, etc. *to* a person for consideration or by way of appeal.

1747 RICHARDSON *Clarissa* I. vi. 33 My aunt Hervey has put it to my mother, whether it were not best [etc.]. **1825** *New Monthly Mag.* XVI. 35 B—— put it to me if I should like to see Spenser as well as Chaucer. **1889** *Repent. P. Wentworth* I. ix. 183, I appeal to you; I put it to you to be frank with yourself. *Mod.* (Counsel cross-examining) 'I put it to you that you were not there at the time.'

†**d.** *Cards.* (*intr.*) In the game of PUT (*sb.*[3]): app. To put it to the other player whether he will play out the hand; to challenge one's antagonist. (Also spelt *putt.*) *Obs.*

1680 COTTON *Compl. Gamester* (ed. 2) xv. 93 The eldest [hand] if he hath a good Game, and thinks it better than his Adversaries, puts to him, if the other will not or dare not see him, he then wins one, but if he will see him they play it out. *Ibid.* 96 Who would not put at such Cards?

23. To impose (something) *on, upon* (†*to*, †*unto*) a person, etc.

a. as a burden, charge, or obligation.

c **1380** *Antecrist* in Todd *Three Treat. Wyclif* (1851) 134 þei putten grete penaunce unto men þere Cristis charge is liȝt. **1382** WYCLIF *1 Kings* xii. 4 Thi fader putte [**1388** puttide] to vs moost hard ȝok. *Ibid. 2 Kings* xviii. 14 Al that thou puttist on to me, I schale beren. **1426** in *Surtees Misc.* (1890) 10 þe charge..þat is put vnto me. **1508** KENNEDIE *Flyting w. Dunbar* 254 Put I nocht sylence to the, schiphird knaif? **1550** *Reg. Privy Council Scot.* I. 87 To putt inhibitioun to the capitanis. **1568** [see IMPOST *sb.*[1] 1]. **1583** GOLDING *Calvin on Deut.* vii. 39 When God hath..giuen vs the vpper hand of all assaultes that could be put vnto vs. **1724** DE FOE *Mem. Cavalier* (1840) 7 We were very sensible of the obligation he had put upon us. **1735** LD. LYTTELTON *Lett. Persian* xxxi, The constraint that was put upon him. **1740** J. CLARKE *Educ. Youth* (ed. 3) 84, I have..declared myself against putting any more Grammar upon Boys. **1891** *Sat. Rev.* 10 Oct. 427/1 Heavy dues were put on cattle.

b. as an indignity, insult, censure, etc.

c **1380** WYCLIF *Sel. Wks.* III. 347 We mai not pynche at þis lawe þat God himsilf ordeynede first, but ȝif we putten blasphemye on God þat he ordeynede folily. **1536** *Primer Eng. & Lat.* 85 b, Smytynge the..and many other greuous paynes puttynge to the. **1633** BP. HALL *Hard Texts* Mal. i. 8 Will they..not..think that you put a scorne upon them? **1687** BURNET *Repl. Varillas* 21 A severe censure I had put on his works. **1707** NORRIS *Treat. Humility* v. 204 Putting indignities upon one another. **1796** BURNEY *Mem. Metastasio* III. 332 The contempt which lyric poets put upon instrumental music. **1870** J. E. T. ROGERS *Hist. Gleanings* Ser. II. 121 One humiliation after another would be put on the unhappy king.

c. as something unwelcome or unpleasant; sometimes, to saddle a person with. Now *rare* or *Obs.*

Used occas. with favourable application (quot. 1718).

1633 BP. HALL *Hard Texts* Rom. vii. 8 Sinne had not had such force to put itself upon us. **1668** PEPYS *Diary* 23 Dec., Sir D. Gauden is mightily troubled at Pen's being put upon him, by the Duke of York. **1718** POPE *Iliad* XVI. 466 *note*, We have Virtue put upon us by Surprize, and are pleas'd to find a thing where we should never have look'd to meet with it. **1727** SWIFT *Art Polit. Lying* Wks. 1751 VI. 179 There wants nothing to be put upon the publick, but a false Author, or a false Cause. **1752** CHESTERF. *Lett.* (1792) IV. 1 She put herself upon him for a saint. **1825** *New Monthly Mag.* XVI. 418 Putting upon you gifts of no real value.

d. something false or delusive, as a deception or trick.

1601 SHAKS. *All's Well* IV. v. 63 If I put any trickes vpon em. **1616** B. JONSON *Devil an Ass* III. iii, You ha' there now Some Bristo-stone, or Cornish counterfeit You'ld put vpon vs. **1650, 1823** [see CHEAT *sb.*[1] 4 b]. **1688** BURNET *Lett. St. Italy* 115 They see such gross Deceptions put upon the World. **1853** HAWTHORNE *Tanglewood T.* (Chandos ed.) 252 C. suspected..that he was putting a joke upon him.

e. ***to put the ass*** or ***fool upon***: to impose the name or character of ass or fool upon; to call or account an ass or fool. ? *Obs.* (See also FOOL *sb.*[1] 3.)

1617 MORYSON *Itin.* III. 50 If any German will put the Asse vpon another cunningly, he will say, that the other was neuer in Silesia. **1654** GATAKER *Disc. Apol.* 40 Who merrily in familiar discourse was pleased to put the fool upon me for it. **1760-72** H. BROOKE *Fool of Qual.* (1809) III. 144 The public..have put the fool on me from my birth.

f. *absol.* ***to put upon***: †(*a*) to play a trick upon, befool, impose upon (*obs.*); (*b*) to impose unfair or excessive tasks upon; to exact over-much from; to oppress, victimize. Chiefly in indirect passive.

1693 CONGREVE *Old Bach.* III. viii, Sir Joseph has found out your trick, and does not care to be put upon. **1742** FIELDING *Jos. Andrews* III. vii, [He] advised him not to carry the jest too far, for he would not endure being put upon. **1857** KINGSLEY *Two Y. Ago* I. ii. 54 'I should not have fancied Miss Harvey the sort of person to set up herself in defiance of me'. 'The more reason, Sir, if you'll forgive me, for your not putting upon her'. **1862** *Temple Bar Mag.* VI. 158 Sharp little women, who evidently could not be 'put upon'. **1890** MRS. H. WOOD *Ho. Halliwell* II. iii. 58 You remember..how she used to put upon me.

24. To lay the blame of (something) *on* or *upon*; to lay (crime or fault) to a person's charge, tax with; to charge *against*, impute *to*.

c **1380** WYCLIF *Sel. Wks.* III. 174 þou puttes here on Crist consense of mayntenynge of þefte. **1382** —— *Acts* xxv. 7 Jewis stooden aboute him..puttinge aȝens [him] manye and greuouse causis. **1387** TREVISA *Higden* (Rolls) V. 15 þat Cristene men schulde nouȝt be dampned wiþ oute trespass i-put aȝenst hem, and i-previd. *a* **1400** *Relig. Pieces fr. Thornton MS.* 40 þe Jewes..put appone hym þat he had saide blasefeme. *c* **1450** tr. *De Imitatione* III. xxi. 89 He dide me gret harme, & puttid þinges up on me þat I neuere þouȝte. **1456** SIR G. HAYE *Law Arms* (S.T.S.) 74 Tharfore suld men be wele avisit, or thai put crime till a man. **1502** *Ord. Crysten Men* (W. de W. 1506) I. iii. 30 The whiche delyuerest Susanne from the infamye y[t] of wronge unto her was put. **1530** PALSGR. 671/2 You put upon me that I have hurte hym. **1605** SHAKS. *Macb.* I. vii. 70 What cannot you and I performe vpon Th' vnguarded Duncan? What not put vpon His spungie Officers? **1702** STEELE *Grief A-la-Mode* v. i, I'll try you for his Murder, which I find you'd put on me, thou hellish Engine! **1904** WEYMAN *Abb. Vlaye* iv, Because it [the mishap] was within a league of his castle, you put it on him?

**** *Where a person* (*or thing*) *is put to some condition, suffering, or action.*

25. a. To place *in*, bring *into*, or reduce (a person or thing) *to* some state or condition; as, ***to put at ease, at rest; to put in doubt, fear,*** † ***hope, mind, remembrance, trust; to put in*** (or ***into,*** occas. †***to***) ***action, adventure, communication, competition, execution, force, motion, order,*** † ***peace, play, possession, one's power, practice, print, readiness,*** † ***respite, shape,*** † ***suspense, tune, use,*** † ***work,*** etc.; ***to put on one's guard, on one's honour, on one's oath, on record,*** † ***to life, to rights, to silence, to sleep, in the wrong,*** etc.: see also the sbs.

Also in U.S. dial. phr. ***to put*** (someone) ***in the dozen***(s), to force (someone) to 'play the dozens' (cf. PLAY *v.* 16 e); *spec.* to insult (a person) by referring to his mother in a derogatory way.

13.. *Cursor M.* 2425 (Gött.) Qui put þu vs in were, þat said þi wijf þi sister were? *c* **1374** CHAUCER *Anel. & Arc.* 275 To..putte yowe in sclaundre nowe and blame. *c* **1386** —— *Frankl. T.* 767 A lewed man in this That he wol putte his wyf in Iupartie. **14..** *Gosp. Nicodemus* (A.) 54 He..puttyd to lyfe þat ded lay. **1433** *Rolls of Parlt.* IV. 424/1 Desiryng to be putte in certainete of certain Articles. **1526** TINDALE *2 Tim.* ii. 14 Of these thynges put them in remembraunce. **1539** BIBLE (Great) *Ps.* ix. 20 Put them in feare. **1559** W. CUNNINGHAM *Cosmogr. Glasse* 30 This rule will I put in practise. **1585** T. WASHINGTON tr. *Nicholay's Voy.* II. v. 34 b, We had putte our gallies in order, with theyr flagges, banners [etc.]. **1676** HOBBES *Iliad* I. 389 Put Jove in mind of this. **1688** HOLME *Armoury* III. 51/2 The Lords..are not like a Jury, put upon their Oaths, but do it upon their Honor. *a* **1715** BURNET *Own Time* an. 1685 (1823) II. 463 She was put upon the secret, and spoke of it to no person alive but to her confessor. **1719** DE FOE *Crusoe* (1840) I. i. 6 This put my mother into a great passion. **1847** MARRYAT *Childr. N. Forest* xvi, You have put me under an obligation which I never can repay. **1866** W. COLLINS *Armadale* III. xiv, It was decided that the servants should be put on board wages. **1892** SIR N. LINDLEY in *Law Rep. 2 Q.B.D.* 540 The person deputed..to receive the proposal and to put it into shape. **1939** J. DOLLARD in *American Imago* Nov. 8 Herbert had been put in the Dozens by another boy in the following manner: the boy said, 'Your mama needs a bath.' **1941** W. A. PERCY *Lanterns on Levee* xxiii. 301 'Some fool nigger puts you in the dozen.'.. 'What's putting you in the dozen?' 'That's sho nuff bad talk.' 'Like what?' 'Well,' said Ford, modest and hesitant, 'that's talking about your mommer.' **1973** A. DUNDES *Mother Wit* 299 To be 'put in the dozens' is to be put in a bad or losing position. **1974** H. L. FOSTER *Ribbin'* v. 226 If a teacher is attempting to really stop the dozens playing, just..holding your elbow, could be considered as putting another boy in the dozens.

b. With complement: To cause to be or become something; to make, render so-and-so: †(*a*) with sb.; (*b*) with adj. (usually ***to put right*** or ***wrong***).

In Wyclif a freq. literalism of translation fr. Lat. *ponere*.

1377 LANGL. *P. Pl.* B. XI. 61 Pouerte pursued me and put me lowe. *c* **1380** WYCLIF *Sel. Wks.* III. 363 þat men..putte þe pope here heierste iuge. **1382** —— *Lam.* iii. 11 He putte me desolat [Vulg. *posuit me desolatam*]. **1651** *Life Musculus* in Fuller *Abel Rediv.* (1867) I. 303 Musculus was put void of his church. **1790** A. WILSON *Pack*, To think how aft I'm putten wud. **1835** J. H. NEWMAN *Lett.* (1891) II. 138 He and Keble both being away puts everything wrong. **1885** *Law Times* 30 May 74/2 All that the tenants complained of could undoubtedly have been put right..in a very few hours. **1892** H. R. MILL *Realm Nat.* ii. 20 The least mistake..would put the calculation all wrong. *Mod.* Haven't you put the clock fast?

26. a. To subject (a person, etc.) *to* the suffering or endurance of something; as, ***to put to*** †***pain,*** † ***pine, punishment, torture; to put to death, destruction, execution,*** † ***mischief; to put to*** †***finance,*** †***fine, ransom; to put to charge, expense, loss, straits, trouble; to put to*** †***judgement,*** (***the***) ***proof, test, touch, trial; to put to the halter, the horn, the rack, the sword; to put to confusion, rebuke, shame; to put to the worse*** or ***worst,*** etc.; ***to put upon one's trial,*** etc.: see also the sbs.

a **1300** *Cursor M.* 10072 (Cott.) þa[t] he ne him put til hel pin. **1399** LANGL. *Rich. Redeles* II. 87 Whane þe pore pleyned that put were to wrongis. *c* **1400** *Destr. Troy* 8852 All the pepull to pyne put, and dethe at oure lust? *c* **1470** HENRY *Wallace* x. 722 Ye se the Scottis puttis feill to confusioun. **1523** LD. BERNERS *Froiss.* I. xv. 15 The kyng..was deposed..and certayne of his counsellours..put to distruction. **1535** COVERDALE *Matt.* xxiv. 9 Then shal they put you to trouble. **1542-3** *Act 34 & 35 Hen. VIII*, c. 26 §32 No..persone..for Murther or Felony, shallbe put to his fyne. **1611** BIBLE *Heb.* vi. 6 They crucifie..the Sonne of God afresh, and put him to an open shame. **1678** BUTLER *Hud.* III. i. 1148 Soon as they had him at their mercy, They put him to the cudgel fiercely. **1749** FIELDING *Tom Jones* VIII. viii, She had put herself to the expense of a long hood. **1832** SOUTHEY *Hist. Penins. War* III. xliii. 606 Foy..put the defenders to the bayonet without distinction. **1891** *Sat. Rev.* 24 Jan. 99/1 Most of the insect and worm feeders are put to sore straits.

b. *spec.* To subject (a piece of ground) to the plough, or to the raising of a particular crop. Const. *to, into, under* the crop, etc. Also const. *down to.* Cf. 18.

1845 *Jrnl. R. Agric. Soc.* VI. II. 423 The field..was put into potatoes. *Ibid.* 524, I put the ground..under early potatoes. **1847** *Ibid.* VIII. I. 112 It is stocked with cattle or put under the plough. **1861** *Ibid.* XXII. II. 294 The oat-stubbles being put to winter vetches. *Ibid.*, The land can be put to wheat. **1960** R. WILLIAMS *Border Country* I. ii. 58 He was able to rent two strips of garden..and these he put down one to gooseberries and currants, the other to potatoes.

27. a. To set (a person or animal) to do something, or upon some course of action. †Formerly sometimes with the notion of inciting, urging, or persuading. (*a*) with infin. or *to*.

1377 LANGL. *P. Pl.* B. XIV. 289 Selden is any pore yput to punysshen any peple. **1393** *Ibid.* C. VIII. 191 In alle kynne craftes..he putte me to lerne. **1530** *Act 22 Hen. VIII*, c. 4 To the great hurte of the Kynges true Subjectes puttynge their Childe to be prentyse. *a* **1533** LD. BERNERS *Huon* xl. 132 She to be put to your doughter to teche hyr to speake..the language of frenche. **1625** BURGES *Pers. Tithes* 21 How can they aduise, and put their Minister to sue Husbandmen for Tithes? **1737** BRACKEN *Farriery Impr.* (1757) II. 50 If we did..put Horses to perform Things which Nature never designed them for. **1844** *Jrnl. R. Agric. Soc.* V. I. 54 Horses..are put to work at three years old. **1889** PHILIPS & WILLS *Sybil Ross's Marr.* xx, I suppose they'll put me to herd the swine.

(*b*) with *on, upon.*

1605 SHAKS. *Lear* II. i. 101 'Tis they haue put him on the old mans death. **1645** T. COLEMAN *Serm. bef. Ho. Comm.* 30 July 14 His folly might put him on the same way of resistance. **1662** H. MORE *Philos. Writ.* Pref. Gen. §6 He can neither hit upon a right sense of things himself..or rightly pursue it, when he is put upon it by another. **1674** RAY *Coll. Words* Ded. P. Courthope, You were the first that Contributed to it, and indeed the Person that put me upon it. **1748** *Anson's Voy.* III. ix. 396 The strong addiction..to lucre often..puts them on defrauding the authority that protects them. **1885** *Law Times Rep.* LIII. 467/2 He had notice of facts which ought to have put him on inquiry. **1890**

Chamb. Jrnl. 13 Sept. 580/2 The disappointment..might..put them upon some wild scheme.

(*c*) ***to put*** (a person) ***through it***: to impose a severe test on (a person); to subject (a person) to an ordeal or trying experience.

1872 G. P. BURNHAM *Mem. U.S. Secret Service* p. vii, *Put 'em through*, subjecting persons to a thorough searching ordeal. **1922** A. A. MILNE *Red House Mystery* vi. 50 Everybody else is bundled off except me, and I get put through it by that inspector as if I knew all about it. **1923** WODEHOUSE *Inimitable Jeeves* iv. 48 Aunt Agatha..was putting the last of the bandits through it in the voice she usually reserves for snubbing waiters in restaurants. **1935** *Discovery* Oct. 311/2 The work of the pupils whom he 'put through it'. **1940** H. G. WELLS *Babes in Darkling Wood* I. ii. 59, I am afraid we have put you through it, rather. **1959** P. MCCUTCHAN *Storm South* xii. 179 Evidently she'd been put through it in the interval, for she was crying bitterly. *a* **1976** A. CHRISTIE *Autobiogr.* (1977) VIII. ii. 380 Mad as a hatter. .. My goodness, he must have put you through it now and again!

b. *refl.* To set oneself *to*; to set about an action or course of action, etc.; to betake or apply oneself *to*. *arch.* or *dial.*

1362 LANGL. *P. Pl.* A. Prol. 20 Summe putten hem to þe plouȝ and pleiden hem ful seldene. *c* **1400** *Destr. Troy* Prol. 33 Sum poyetis full prist þat put hom þerto. *a* **1400–50** *Alexander* 1483 Ilka bodi þat in þe burȝe lengis, Putt þam to prayris & penaunce enduris. **1470–85** MALORY *Arthur* V. viii. 174 Alle the Romaynes with all their hoost put them to flyght. *c* **1511** *1st Eng. Bk. Amer.* (Arb.) Introd. 33/2 Whan the Vnicorne hath put hym to rest at a tree. **1853** HAWTHORNE *Tanglewood T.* (Chandos ed.) 256 Looking as queerly as cows generally do, while putting themselves to their speed. **1865** BUSHNELL *Vicar. Sacr.* II. i. (1866) 96 Christ put Himself to His works of healing for this purpose.

c. To set to learn, study, or practise. Const. *to*, †*on*, †*upon* (something).

1389 R. WIMBELDON *Serm. Luke xvi. 2* (1584) A viij, Why, I pray you, doe men put their sonnes to the Ciuill Law. *c* **1430** *Freemasonry* 30 Thys onest craft he putte hem to. **1610** WILLET *Hexapla Dan.* 23 They which are put to learning must not be *non proficientes*. **1633** BP. HALL *Hard Texts* Hos. x. 11, I will put Ephraim to the saddle, Judah to the plow. *a* **1687** PETTY *Pol. Arith.* (1690) 113 Since the generality of Gentlemen, and some Noblemen, do put their younger sons to Merchandize. **1740** J. CLARKE *Educ. Youth* (ed. 3) 58 This Custom of putting Boys upon the Greek Tongue, before they understand any Thing of the Latin. *Ibid.* 63 They are..put upon Versifying.

d. To direct or urge (a horse) towards something, esp. an obstacle to be cleared; also, to cause (a horse) to perform a particular pace, a leap, etc.: const. *to*, *at*, etc. ***to put through***: to cause (a horse) to perform (a particular movement); *transf.* to cause (a person) to go through an exercise, course of study, etc. Also (chiefly *N. Amer.*) ***to put*** (a person) ***through*** (a school, college, etc.): to pay the cost of educating (a person); also const. *ellipt.*

1589 R. HARVEY *Pl. Perc.* (1590) 4 A Rancke rider hath put his horse to a hedge, and lay in the ditch. **1766** [see PACE *sb.*[1] 6]. **1823** BYRON *Juan* XII. xxxix, Which puts my Pegasus to these grave paces. **1833** *Regul. Instr. Cavalry* I. 38 The Major..will put the regiment through the 'Manual' and 'Platoon Exercise'. *Ibid.* 84 He [a horse] may be put to the leap. **1847** MARRYAT *Childr. N. Forest* viii, Edward put the pony to a trot. **1861** DICKENS *Gt. Expect.* ix, Mr. Pumblechook then put me through my pence-table. **1861** *Temple Bar Mag.* II. 406 He was not put through a course of searching educational inquiries. **1886** RUSKIN *Præterita* I. viii. 258 My father had himself put me through the two first books of Livy. **1891** 'ANNIE THOMAS' *That Affair* II. ii. 23 She..puts the cob up the hill. **1908** L. M. MONTGOMERY *Anne of Green Gables* xxx. 338 I'd love to be a teacher. But ..Mr. Andrews says it cost him one hundred and fifty dollars to put Prissy through. **1943** *Deb. House of Commons* (Canada) 4 Feb. 161/2 Voluntary committees should be set up throughout Canada to pick out..boys and girls with a view to seeing that they are put through university. **1949** *Manch. Guardian Weekly* 27 Jan. 13/2 He..put himself through Emory College.

e. To set (cattle) to feed upon; to restrict (a person) to a diet or regimen of. Const. *to*, *on*, *upon*.

1620 MARKHAM *Farew. Husb.* xxii. (1668) 125 In the month of December, put your sheep and swine to the pease Reeks, and fat them for the..market. **1840** *Jrnl. R. Agric. Soc.* I. III. 315, I..changed the food, and put the sheep on bran and oats. **1845** *Ibid.* VI. II. 364 All my ewes were put to turnips. **1849** MACAULAY *Hist. Eng.* v. I. 585 To put the garrison on rations of horse flesh. **1888** *Times* 21 June 10/3 He was put upon bread and water. **1904** *Brit. Med. Jrnl.* 17 Sept. 649, I put her on red medulla tabloids.

28. a. To force or drive (a person, etc.) to the performance of some action, e.g. of making a choice, playing a certain card; as,

to put to flight, to the run, to one's jumps, plunges, shifts, trumps, etc.: see also the sbs.

1425 *Rolls of Parlt.* IV. 271/2 Such possession..ought not to be..affermed, ne putte my seid Lord..to his action. **1483** CAXTON *G. de la Tour* D vij b, God dyde putt her to reason askynge to her why she had trespaced his commaundement. **1559** AYLMER *Harborowe* L ij b, Englande was put to a sore plunge through hir wylfulnes. **1563** *Homilies* II. *Prayer* 111, Salomon beyng put to his choyse. **1651** H. L'ESTRANGE *Smectymnuus-mastix* 27 When Smectymnuus are put to instance they can onely tell us, that [etc.]. **1667** MILTON *P.L.* IV. 386 Thank him who puts me loath to this revenge. **1722** WOLLASTON *Relig. Nat.* ix. 207 If at the end of their course they were put to their option, whether [etc.].

†**b.** Const. *inf.* To oblige, compel, force, require, call upon *to do* something. *Obs.* or *arch.*

1603 SHAKS. *Meas. for M.* I. i. 5 Since I am put to know, that [etc.]. **1611** —— *Cymb.* II. iii. 110 You put me to forget a Ladies manners By being so verball. **1635** SIR H. BLOUNT *Voy. Levant* (1637) 102, I have divers times beene put to defend myselfe with my knife. **1651** *Life Father Sarpi* (1676) 22 The Father was never put to provide for himself while he was under the care of this good old man. **1654** BRAMHALL *Just Vind.* v. (1661) 97 Men are not put to prove negatives. **1741** RICHARDSON *Pamela* II. 305 He..is reckon'd a great Master of his Sword. God grant he may never be put to use it! **1831** SCOTT *Ct. Robt.* vii, Put me not..to dishonour myself by striking thee with this weapon.

c. ***to put*** (a person) ***to it***. (*a*) To force, urge, challenge, or call upon (him) to do what is indicated by the context. Chiefly in *passive*.

1581 PETTIE *Guazzo's Civ. Conv.* I. (1586) A vj, A pleasant Gentleman (who could haue spoken sufficientlie, if he had bene put to it). **1607** J. NORDEN *Surv. Dial.* II. 38 When they are put to it, they come far short of some principall pointes required. *c* **1620** Z. BOYD *Zion's Flowers* (1855) 146 I'le put him to 't, before the play be plaide. **1707** NORRIS *Treat. Humility* vi. 245 Pride is no more put to't to obey, than humility is to govern. **1868** MISS BRADDON *Dead Sea Fr.* xviii, There is nothing a man of the world can't do when he's put to it.

(*b*) *spec.* To force (one) to do one's utmost; to reduce to straits; to drive to extremities; to hamper or embarrass. Now always in the passive and usually with an adv. of degree, as ***hard, sore(ly), sadly, greatly put to it***.

1603 SHAKS. *Meas. for M.* III. ii. 101 Lord Angelo Dukes it well in his absence: he puts transgression too 't. **1641** J. SHUTE *Sarah & Hagar* (1649) 179, I know this is difficult, and puts a man to it. **1650** W. BROUGH *Sacr. Princ.* (1659) 286 Thou didst pose heaven it self and put God to it. **1684** BUNYAN *Pilgr.* II. 66 *margin* The Hill puts the Pilgrims to it. **1699** SWIFT *Ballads* Wks. 1755 III. II. 63 [He] was sorely put to't in the midst of a verse, Because he could find no word to come pat in. **1719** DE FOE *Crusoe* I. 138, I was sadly put to it for a Scythe or a Sickle to cut it down. **1825** *New Monthly Mag.* XVI. 575 You see how we are put to it. **1865** DICKENS *Mut. Fr.* IV. xiii, We were hard put to it..to get it done in so short a time.

***** ***to put a thing***: in pregnant senses of L. *pōnĕre*.

†**29.** To posit, suppose, assume. With obj. cl. (= ***put case*** in 22) or simple obj. *Obs.*

c **1386** CHAUCER *Melib.* ¶ 511 But lat vs now putte that ye haue leue to venge yow. **1620** T. GRANGER *Div. Logike* 95 And one being put, the other is put. **1626** W. FENNER *Hidden Manna* (1652) 74 Put that Christ did not dye for them. **1654** Z. COKE *Logick* 7 An End in Arts not conjectural ..must be put when the means are put.

†**30. a.** To lay down (one's life) *for*, or *on behalf of*. *Obs.*

(A Latinism: *animam suam ponere pro...*)

c **1380** WYCLIF *Sel. Wks.* III. 363 Crist..puttide his lyf for his sheep. [Cf. Vulg. John x. 15 *Animam meam pono pro ovibus meis.*] **1387** TREVISA *Higden* (Rolls) III. 183 Whanne Kynges comeþ to strengþe þey putteþ [*v.r.* potteþ] þeire lif for wommen [Higden, *animas pro mulieribus exponunt*]. *c* **1440** *Gesta Rom.* xciii. 423 (Add. MS.) If the housbond be myghty and good, he oweth to deffende here, and putt his life for here life. *c* **1449** PECOCK *Repr.* III. viii. 323 Redi forto putte her lijfis for witnessing of trouthe.

†**b.** To 'lay down'; to state, assert, affirm, declare as a fact. *Obs.*

c **1400** *Destr. Troy* 1016 As poyetis han put, plainly þo two Were getyn by a gode on a grete lady. **1483** CAXTON *Gold. Leg.* 29 b/1 Saynt Bernard putteth iiii maners of love. **1529** MORE *Dyaloge* II. Wks. 183/2 Y[e] holders of y[t] oppinion do put, y[t] no man maye for all y[t] take vpon him to preache or medle as priest, til he be chosen by the congregacion. **1530** TINDALE *Answ. More* IV. ii. Wks. (1573) 324/2 The true faith putteth the resurrection, which we be warned to looke for euery houre. **1607** SHAKS. *Timon* V. i. 196 As common bruite doth put it.

†**c.** To lay down as a rule or law; to ordain. (With *obj. cl.*) *Obs.*

c **1465** *Eng. Chron.* (Camden) 105 And forthermore ordeyneth, putteth and stabylyssheth..that all statutys ordenaunces [etc.]. **1678** *Min. Bar. Crt. Stitchill* (1905) 83 Therefor the Judge..putts inacts and decernes for futur trouble in tyme cummeng that every persons grasse [etc.].

IV. In combination or construction of the intransitive use with prepositions.

31. put at ——. *intr.* To strike at, proceed against, take measures against; to attack; to prosecute. [*fig.* from 1 d.] *Sc.* With *indirect passive*.

1547 *Reg. Privy Council Scot.* I. 69 The autorite to putt at thame baith in thair personis, landis, and gudis, quhill tha cum to obedience. *a* **1572** KNOX *Hist. Ref.* Wks. (Wodrow Soc.) I. 284 Gif the authoritie wald putt at me and my house, according to civile and cannon laws. *a* **1578** LINDESAY (Pitscottie) *Chron. Scot.* (S.T.S.) I. 322 The Douglassis pat sair at the Lord Lyndsay. **1583** *Reg. Privy Council Scot.* III. 599 Thay ar persewit and put at for the said publict act. **1616** SIR C. MOUNTAGU in *Buccleuch MSS.* (Hist. MSS. Comm.) I. 248 Sir Robert Rich puts hard at them for the extent of his land. **1866** GREGOR *Banffsh. Gloss.*, *Pit-at*, to dun; as 'the banker's beginnin' t'pit-at him for the bill'. [**1907** A. LANG *Hist. Scot.* IV. iii. 73 Argyle advised Carstares that Simon should not be put at for this.]

†**32. put for** ——. *intr.* **a.** To make an attempt or effort to obtain; to try for; to strive to do or attain. *Obs.* Cf. ***push for***, PUSH *v.* 8.

1596 NASHE *Saffron Walden* 139 Let them..looke after it, or the man in the Moone put for it. **1596** DRAYTON *Leg.* i. 587 Henry againe doth hotly put for all. **1613** DANIEL *Hist. Eng.* I. (1621) 5 Many..were proclaimed Cæsars and put for the whole empire. **1646** FULLER *Good Th.* etc., *Wounded Consc.* (1841) 279 Now Satan being no less cunning..will put hard for our souls. **1676** C. HATTON in *H. Corr.* (1878) 122 Some of my Ld Treasurer's creatures..put for S[r]. John Ernley[’s] place, as commissioner of y[e] Navy. **1739** *Encour. Sea-f. People* 39 The Superbe putting for it to lay the Admiral aboard, fell on his Weather Quarter.

†**b. *put fair for***: to 'bid fair' for; to be in a fair way of attaining. *Obs.*

1595 MAYNARDE *Drake's Voy.* (Hakl. Soc.) 7 Had wee lanced under the forte at our first cominge to anchor, wee had put fayre to bee possessors of the towne. *a* **1677** HALE *Prim. Orig. Man.* 135 Those Nations whose Historians put fair for the greatest Antiquity, are the Romans [etc.].

†**c.** To make for, argue for. *Obs.*

1624 BP. MOUNTAGU *Gagg* 52 It would put for Hebrew or Syriacke, their mother tongue.

put out of: see 49. **put upon**: see 23 f.

V. Combined with adverbs, forming the equivalents of compound verbs in other languages.

†**33. a. put aback.** *trans.* = ***put back***, 40 a, b. *Obs.*

c **1380** WYCLIF *Wks.* (1880) 332 It semeþ þat antecrist bi þis puttiþ cristis ordynaunce aback. **1450** *Rolls of Parlt.* V. 181/2 True maters..were hyndred and put abakke. **1484** CAXTON *Fables of Æsop* IV. viii, The men of trouthe ben set alowe and put aback. **1530** PALSGR. 671/2 To put a backe from promocyon. *a* **1557** *Diurn. Occur.* (1833) 34 The saidis personis..was put abak be the lordis Ruthven, [etc.].

34. put about.

a. See simple senses and ABOUT.

1382 WYCLIF *Mark* xv. 36 Fillinge a sponge with vynegre, and puttinge aboute [Vulg. *circumponens*] to a reede. **1766** AMORY *Buncle* (1825) III. 78 The bottle after dinner I put about pretty quick. **1768** LADY M. COKE *Jrnl.* 28 Aug., That Strange Girl that you remember was used to put her-self about upon the Stage, almost all her Cloaths off.

b. *Naut. trans.* To lay or place (a sailing vessel) on the opposite tack. Also *transf.* to cause (a horse, a body of men, etc.) to turn round so as to face in another direction.

1771 SMOLLETT *Humph. Cl.* 8 Aug. i, Every time the vessel was put about, we shipped a sea. **1832** *Prop. Regul. Instr. Cavalry* III. 83 The..wing is..to be put about by Threes. **1842** MARRYAT *Percival K.* xix, The Stella was then put about, and the other broadside given. **1865** KINGSLEY *Herew.* xxi, Put your horses' heads about and ride for Spalding.

c. *Naut. absol.* or *intr.* To turn on to the other tack; to go about. Also *transf.*

1748 *Anson's Voy.* III. v. 342 The proas..run from one of these Islands to the other and back again..without ever putting about. **1823** SCORESBY *Jrnl. Whale Fish.* 338 The main interests of my voyage obliged me to put about, and return to the northward. **1842** J. WILSON *Chr. North* (1857) I. 251 Down with the helm, and let us put about.

d. *trans.* To circulate, publish (a statement).

1781 MME. D'ARBLAY *Diary* May (1842) II. 34 Is it what she [Mrs. Thrale] put about in the morning? **1851** J. H. NEWMAN *Cath. in Eng.* 313 This has been put about as a discovery. **1881** MRS. LYNN LINTON *My Love* II. v. 102 Who has put this lie about?

e. To trouble; to put to inconvenience, embarrass; to distress. (Orig. and still chiefly *Sc.* and *north. dial.*) Cf. ***put out***, 48 f (*b*), (*c*), (*d*).

1825 JAMIESON, *To Put about*, to subject to inconvenience or difficulty;..as, 'I was sair put about to get that siller'. **1843** F. E. PAGET *Warden of Berkingholt* 149 You see I don't let a thoughtless word put me about, and you must'na neither. **1857** LIVINGSTONE *Trav.* Introd. 6, I would not have been much put about, though my offer had been rejected. **1866** READE *G. Gaunt* (ed. 2) II. 297 Oh, don't put yourself about for me. **1890** DOYLE *Capt. 'Polestar', Little Sq. Box* 152 What's put you about, Hammond? You look as white as a sheet.

†**35. put abroad.** *trans.* To spread abroad, unfurl, display. *Obs.*

1615 CHAPMAN *Odyss.* I. 68 When in him shall be..the prime Of youth's spring put abroad. **1628** DIGBY *Voy. Medit.* (Camden) 3 To giue notice..by putting abroad his flag. **1669** STURMY *Mariner's Mag.* I. ii. 19 She puts aboard [**1683** abroad] her Waste-clothes; she will fight us.

36. put across.

a. ***to put it across*** (a person): (*a*) to visit with retribution or punishment; to get even with.

1915 E. WALLACE *Man who bought London* iv. 39 He won't half put it across you people. **1918** 'D. VALENTINE' *Man with Clubfoot* xxi. 309 When you..put it across 'der Stelze'..you settled a long outstanding account we had against him. **1923** M. ARLEN *These Charming People* 238 There was something —well, indecent, in talking about a man dead nine years or more as though he were alive and still wanting to 'put it across' Antony at every turn. **1928** *Daily Mail* 6 Aug. 14/6 You are a master of mob tactics, but we will put it across you yet. **1929** WODEHOUSE *Mr. Mulliner Speaking* iv. 129 It was his intention to..confront his erring man-servant and put it across him in no uncertain manner. **1936** —— *Laughing Gas* xvi. 179, I was glad that I had put it across him. My pride was involved. There are some remarks which one does not forgive. **1978** *Rugby World* Apr. 38/2 Meyer was a sports nut who enjoyed nothing more than seeing his pupils put it across the golden youth of Eton and Winchester.

(*b*) to impose upon; to deceive, to delude; to convince by deceit.

1919 E. P. OPPENHEIM *Strange Case J. Thew* II. vi. 235 'Well,' she exclaimed, 'he does put it across you, doesn't he?' **1923** H. C. BAILEY *Mr. Fortune's Practice* i. 25, I say, you have put it across us in the Dean case. **1927** *Observer* 27 Mar. 6/4 It would be difficult for a greedy, hysterical, shameless, half-insane revivalist..to 'put it across' ever-increasing audiences. **1928** *Daily Express* 26 May 13/4 How Mother Cuckoo manages to 'put it across' certain inoffensive countryside birds. **1934** D. L. SAYERS *Nine Tailors* 63, I hope our friend doesn't put anything across the good Rector. **1936** A. L. ROWSE *Mr. Keynes & Labour Movement* 19 They succeeded in putting it across large sections of the middle classes that Labour's economics meant financial ruin. **1959** D. EDEN *Sleeping Bride* xiv. 117 Don't Let

Blandina put it across you. She isn't as ill as she pretends to be.

b. To make acceptable or effective; to convey the significance of. Cf. ACROSS *prep.* 2 b.

1922 S. ANDERSON in R. L. White *S. Anderson/G. Stein* (1972) 15 The author had done a thing we Americans call 'putting something across'—the meaning being that she had, by a strange freakish performance, managed to attract attention to herself. **1923** H. CRANE *Let.* 13 Apr. (1965) 131 This 'new consciousness' is something that takes a long while to 'put across'. **1927** M. DIVER *But Yesterday* II. xxiii. 263 The Exchange reported, 'No answer.' She was out—naturally; very busy putting it across! **1935** [see *copy-writer* s.v. COPY *sb.* C]. **1938** E. BOWEN *Death of Heart* II. iv. 247 Supposing she had a wish to be put across, who could do this for her better than Eddie could? **1943** W. S. CHURCHILL *Second World War* (1951) IV. 839 We must be ready with our plans in the Eastern Mediterranean, and put it hard across Turkey to come in with us. **1943** J. S. HUXLEY *TVA* 129 The TVA was managing to put across a good deal of its plan. **1945** MENCKEN *Amer. Lang.* Suppl. I. 449 He [*sc.* C. T. Onions in 1936] noted that *to put it across, to get it across*, and *to put it over* were already 'firmly domiciled' in England. .. They really got their vogue in the United States as baseball terms. **1959** *Times Lit. Suppl.* 9 Jan. 15/3 Many readers, however, dazzled by Mr Graves's gifts as a prose entertainer, by his ability to put across Third Programme material with a Light Programme zing, may not give the poems the attention they deserve. **1970** 'D. HALLIDAY' *Dolly & Cookie Bird* ii. 11 If you don't put yourself across, who'll do it for you? **1977** *Wandsworth Borough News* 7 Oct. 5/1 'Help police fight crime by helping yourself'— that is the message the police are trying to put across to the public.

c. *Baseball.* To pitch (a ball) directly over home plate.

1936 MENCKEN *Amer. Lang.* (ed. 4) 191 The history of baseball terms also deserves to be investigated, for many of them have entered the common speech of the country, *e.g.*.. *to put it* (or *one*) *across* (or *over*). **1943** *Amer. Speech* XVIII. 106 If the pitcher throws a straight ball with good control, he is said.. to *put it over*, to *put it across*, or to *put it right in there*. If he has speed, he may.. *put over a fast one*.

put again: see 5. **put apart** = *put aside*, 37 a.

37. put aside.

a. See simple senses and ASIDE.

1398 TREVISA *Barth. De P.R.* VI. ii. (Br. Mus. Add. 27944 f. 67 b/2) He hatte sepultus iburied . for he is iput aside iburyed vndir þerþe. **1535** COVERDALE *Susanna* 51 Put these two asyde one from another.

b. To lay aside out of use, etc.; = *put away*, 39 e; also to bury = 39 f (*d*).

1872 BLACK *Adv. Phaeton* ii, She told him he must put aside his uniform while in England. **1891** *Law Rep.* Weekly Notes 80/1 The salesman, seeing that the meat was bad, did not expose it for sale, but put it aside. **1892** TENNYSON *Charity* xiii, They put him aside for ever, and after a week .. a widow came to my door.

38. put asunder. *trans.* To separate.

1526 TINDALE *Matt.* xix. 6 Let not man therfore put asunder, that which god hath cuppled togedder. **1530** [see 54 b]. **1611** COTGR., *Separer*, to separate, sever, part,.. put asunder.

39. put away.

a. See simple senses and AWAY.

a **1300** *Cursor M.* 5700 (Cott.) He put þe hirdes all a-wai. **1398** TREVISA *Barth. De P.R.* XVI. lxii. (Br. Mus. Add. 27944 f. 202/2) The magnas draweþ to iren in o cornere and putteþ it away in anoþer corner. **1530** PALSGR. 671/2, I dyd put hym awaye as harde as I coulde. **1592** SHAKS. *Rom. & Jul.* II. iv. 209 Two may keepe counsell putting one away. **1639** S. DU VERGER tr. *Camus' Admir. Events* 9 Vexing this little creature, by threatning to put her away from the Prince. **1867** SMYTH *Sailor's Word-bk.* s.v. *Veer*, The head of the vessel is put away from the wind. **1890** *Blackw. Mag.* July 29/1, I had.. put away the picture in despair.

b. *trans.* To send away, dismiss, get rid of; to reject; *spec.* to divorce. Somewhat *arch.*

c **1380** WYCLIF *Sel. Wks.* III. 361 Þei semen alle Anti-cristis proctours to putte awey Cristis ordenaunce. **1387** TREVISA *Higden* (Rolls) V. 269 Þe kyng putte away his laweful wif. *c* **1440** *Promp. Parv.* 417/2 Puttyn a-wey, or refusyn, *repudio, refuto.* **1526** TINDALE *Matt.* xix. 9 Whosoever putteth awaye his wyfe (except hit be for fornicacion) and maryeth another, breaketh wedlocke. *a* **1533** LD. BERNERS *Huon* xliii. 143 Put awaye thy dyspleasure and perdon me. **1599** *Aycliffe Reg.* in Sir C. Sharp *Chron. Mirab.* (1841) 36 A publycke admonition.. for all maysters and dames to put away such servants.. as wyll not usually come to churche. **1816** BYRON *Pris. Chillon* vii, He loathed and put away his food. **1890** *Univ. Rev.* 15 June 204 That is the last vanity that man learns to put away.

†**c.** To drive away, dispel; to do away with, abolish, put an end to. *Obs.*

a **1349** HAMPOLE *Comm. Love to God* Wks. 1896 I. 70 It.. puttes a-wey wykked dredes & vices, & clenses þe thoght. *c* **1400** *Brut* 300 Philip of Valeys.. cast & purposed.. to put awey þe sege. *a* **1450** MYRC *Festial* 49 The ensens he brent to put away þe stench of þe stabull þer scho lay. **1495** *Act 11 Hen. VII*, c. 2 §5 It [shall] be laufull to ij of the Justices.. to rejecte and put awey comen ale selling in Tounes. **1559** MORWYNG *Evonym.* 108 It putteth awaye cleane the Canker. **1873** MRS. OLIPHANT *Innocent* xxviii, Ask God to put it away out of your mind.

†**d.** To part with, dispose of, sell; = *put off*, 46 j.

1574 in *Exch. Rolls Scotl.* XX. 467 To sell.. and put away his landis, heretagis [etc.]. **1607** *Stat.* in *Hist. Wakefield Gram. Sch.* (1892) 61 To sell give or putt away anye part of the landes. *a* **1649** WINTHROP *New Eng.* (1825) II. 348 He took two skins and a half.. which he carried to Mr. Cutting's ship, and put it away there for twenty-four shillings.

e. To put (out of one's hands or immediate use) into a receptacle for safe keeping; to stow away; also, to lay by for future use (money, etc.); = *put by*, 41 g.

1843 *Jrnl. R. Agric. Soc.* IV. II. 398 The fruit should be.. carefully put away in bins. **1861** DICKENS *Gt. Expect.* xxxix, I've put away money, only for you to spend. **1890** *Illustr. Lond. News* 13 Sept. 330/1 Searching for the spectacles he had put away overnight. **1891** *Murray's Mag.* Mar. 373 She had put away her books, writing materials [etc.].

f. *slang* or *colloq.* (*a*) To consume as food or drink, take into the stomach.

1878 BESANT & RICE *Celia's Arb.* xlviii, I never saw a man put away such an enormous quantity of provisions at one time. **1889** DOYLE *Micah Clarke* xvi, He could put away more spruce beer than you would care to pay for. **1924** [see BUFFY *a.*[2]]. **1958** *Punch* 8 Oct. 469/1 The object of a wine-tasting is not to put the stuff away but to assess the relative values of a varied assortment of bottles. **1969** G. GREENE *Trav. with my Aunt* I. viii. 76 Between us we can probably put away half a bottle of vodka. **1976** R. HILL *Another Death in Venice* I. i. 6 You look well enough.. but you don't deserve to, not the way you were putting it away.

(*b*) To put in jail, to imprison; to commit to an old people's home; to confine to a mental institution.

1872 G. P. BURNHAM *Mem. U.S. Secret Service* p. vii, *Put away* sent to the State Prison, after conviction. **1883** *Daily Tel.* 4 Aug. 2/1 Having been 'put away' since the previous October.. and only just now released. **1938** N. MARSH *Death in White Tie* xvi. 179 She became hopelessly insane. .. He arranged to have her put away. **1952** *Sun* (Baltimore) 2 June 14/3 There is less social pressure on people to make a place for grandparents at home, less feeling that it would be disgraceful to have them put away. **1971** S. PHILLIPS *Death in Sheep's Clothing* v. 48 The mother is nearly frantic now, she is always afraid 'they' are going to 'put him away'. **1973** W. M. DUNCAN *Big Timer* xxi. 138 He was an inspector then. He put me away. **1974** P. M. HUBBARD *Thirsty Evil* iv. 40, I said, 'But can it go on? Won't they have to—?' 'Put him away? I suppose so, if he gets worse.'

(*c*) To put in pawn, to pawn.

1887 *Daily News* 22 Oct. 3/3 They have clothes and household effects.. which, if need be, they can 'put away' during the winter. **1909** GALSWORTHY *Silver Box* I. iii. 32 *Mrs. Jones.* We've not got a home, sir. Of course we've been obliged to put away most of our things. *Barthwick.* Put your things away! You mean to—to—er—to pawn them? *Mrs. Jones.* Yes, sir, to put them away. **1926** MAINES & GRANT *Wise-Crack Dict.* 12/1 *Putting away his ice*, pawning his diamond.

(*d*) To put in the grave, to bury. Also, to kill.

1588 GREENE *Pandosto* f. A4[v], Deuising with himself a long time how he might best put away Egistus without suspition of treacherous murder, hee concluded at last to poyson him. **1847** A. BRONTË *Agnes Grey* p. xiv, A reward, I should have greatly valued,.. were he [*sc.* a dog] not now in danger of being 'put away'. **1896** MRS. H. WARD *Sir G. Tressady* 148 It's three weeks now sen they put him away. **1920** E. WALLACE *Daffodil Mystery* viii. 70 If I could only put her away for it! **1932** E. WAUGH *Black Mischief* viii. 311 The dogs had long been rounded up and painlessly put away. **1971** E. LEMARCHAND *Death on Doomsday* ix. 137 I'd like to see old Peplow put away decently. **1974** M. BUTTERWORTH *Man in Sopwith Camel* xiii. 165 What kinda guy puts a buddy away for three lousy dollars?

g. *slang.* To inform against, 'give away', betray.

1890 *Melbourne Argus* 2 Aug. 4/3 It's all right, mate; I won't put you away. **1891** N. GOULD *Double Event* 184, I had an idea you put me away over the Derby.

40. put back.

†**a.** *trans.* To thrust or force back, repulse; to refuse, reject. *Obs.*

c **1450** *Merlin* xxv. 460 Thourgh his prowesse thei were putte bakke and chaced to the town. **1530** PALSGR. 671/1 He had thought to take orders at this tyme, but he was put backe. **1535** COVERDALE *2 Esdras* iii. 16 As for Iacob thou didest chose him and put backe Esau. **1599** ? SHAKS. *Pass. Pilgr.* 334 Be thou no slack To proffer, though she put thee back.

b. To reduce to a lower position or condition; to retard, or check the advance of; †to revoke (*obs.*).

1535 COVERDALE *Hos.* iv. 17 Their dronckennesse hath put them backe, & brought them to whordome. **1616** in *10th Rep. Hist. MSS. Comm.* App. v. 468 All subsidies and saulf conducts.. whatsoever shalbe put back and extinguished. **1626** BACON *Sylva* §354 An ouerdrie nourishment in child-hood putteth back stature. **1892** *Field* 7 May 695/1 Their one mistake.. should not have.. put them back to second place.

c. To move (the hands of a clock) back to an earlier position; to set back; also *fig.*

a **1745** SWIFT *Adv. Servants, Cook* §28 When you find that you cannot get dinner ready at the time appointed, put the clock back. **1881** MRS. LYNN LINTON *My Love* III. ix. 157 She had put back her age ten years at the least. **1889** — *Thro' Long Night* I. xvii, Nor tears nor prayer can.. put back the hand of time.

d. To prevent from coming on at the time appointed or expected; to defer; = *put off*, 46 c.

1885 J. PAYN *Luck Darrells* III. xlii. 184, I have taken upon myself to put the dinner back for an hour. **1890** T. F. TOUT *Hist. Eng. fr. 1689*, 189 The defeat of the former at Novara put back the unity of Italy.

e. To restore to its former place or position.

1816 SCOTT *Antiq.* xxv, I'll pit back the pick and shule whar I got them. *Mod.* When you've done with the book, please put it back on the shelf.

f. *intr. Naut.* To reverse one's course; to return to the port which one has left. (Cf. sense 8.)

1771 SMOLLETT *Humph. Cl.* 8 Aug. i, My aunt desired her brother to order the boatman to put back to Kinghorn. **1859** CORNWALLIS *Panorama New World* I. Introd. 6 The latter vessel.. having a few days previously been compelled to 'put back', owing to.. having sprung a leak. **1892** *Chamb. Jrnl.* 27 Feb. 136/2 The *Kate*.. put back to Salcombe.

g. *trans.* With personal object: to cost. *colloq.*

1909 *Dialect Notes* III. 402 'How much did that put you back?' 'Six dollars.' **1958** B. RUCK *Third Love Lucky* iv. 31 It puts you back five shillings for a quarter of an hour.

h. To return or 'plough back' (money, etc.). Cf. PLOUGH *v.* 9 g.

1930 *Economist* 19 July 112/2 In view of Mr. Snowden's recent refusal to consider abatement of income tax on company reserves employed for re-equipment.. the recent tendency to reduce the proportion of earnings 'put back' is significant. **1931** *Ibid.* 11 July 59/1 The percentage 'put back into the business' during the past twelve months, 15·7 per cent., compares unfavourably with the figure of 18·6 per cent. ascertained for the twelve months ended June 30, 1930.

41. put by. (See also BY *prep.*, *adv.* B. 2.)

a. *trans.* To thrust or set aside (*lit* and *fig.*); to reject; to neglect, let alone; †to leave out, except (quot. 1594); †to give up, desist from.

c **1440** *Alphabet of Tales* 448 He wexid so fond on hur.. and evur sho putt hym bye. **1500–20** DUNBAR *Poems* xxx. 30 Cum on thairfoir annone, All sircumstance put by and excusationis. **1538** BALE *Thre Lawes* 1716 Shal thys baggage put by the word of God? **1594** NASHE *Christ's T.* (ed. 2) To Rdr., Euen of the meanest and basest.. I desire to bee thought fauorably of, onely the blould of the Harueys put by. **1601** SHAKS. *Jul. C.* I. ii. 221 A Crowne.. being offer'd him, he put it by with the backe of his hand. **1604** —— *Oth.* II. iii. 172 For Christian shame, put by this barbarous Brawle. **1750** CHESTERF. *Lett.* (1792) III. 24 He will be discouraged, put by, or trampled on. **1865** RUSKIN *Sesame* ii. §90 There is no putting by that crown; queens you must always be.

b. To turn aside, ward off, divert, avert (a blow, or *fig.* a calamity, etc.). Also *absol.* ? *Obs.*

c **1530** LD. BERNERS *Arth. Lit. Brit.* 271 He stept asyde, and well and warely put the stroke by. **1647** W. BROWNE *Polex.* II. 104 Almanzor.. charg'd him with so much vigour .. that he scarce gave him leasure to put by, or avenge himselfe. **1682** FLAVEL *Fear* 10 An imminent.. evil, which we see not how to escape or put by. **1753** RICHARDSON *Grandison* I. xxvii. 195, I was aware of his thrust, and put it by. **1809** MALKIN *Gil Blas* III. vii. ¶10, I had the good fortune to put by all his thrusts.

c. To turn aside, evade (a question, argument, etc.); to put off (a person) with an excuse or evasion: = *put off*, 46 g.

1618 HALES *Gold. Rem.* II. (1673) 42 When they were prest with any reason they could not put by. **1688** BURNET *Lett. St. Italy* 114 The Pope put it by in some general Answers. **1779** *Sylph* I. 241 How long will they remain satisfied with being repeatedly put by with empty promises? **1842** TENNYSON *Day-dream, The Revival* iv, The chancellor.. smiling, put the question by. **1878** R. H. HUTTON *Scott* xv. 159 The medical men.. tried to make him give up his novel-writing. But he smiled and put them by.

†**d.** To prevent (a person) *from* attaining or carrying out something; to divert *from*. *Obs.*

a **1586** SIDNEY *Arcadia* (1622) 38 Which put by their young cosin from that expectation. **1609** DANIEL *Civ. Wars* VI. xi, Put by from this, the Duke of Yorke dessynes Another course to bring his hopes about. **1724** DE FOE *Mem. Cavalier* (1840) 25 Considering.. whether they should march to the relief of Casal, but the chimera of the Germans put them by. **1806** R. CUMBERLAND *Mem.* (1807) II. 177 The well-considered remonstrances of some of his nearest friends.. put him by from his resolve.

†**e.** To drive out, dislodge (an enemy). *Obs.*

1604 EDMONDS *Observ. Cæsar's Comm.* II. 84 Cæsar went out of his campe.. put by the garrison [*deiecto praesidio*], and possessed himselfe of the place.

†**f.** To remove, dispel; to rid one of. *Obs.*

1643 TRAPP *Comm., Gen.* iv. 14 This makes.. others [call] for other of the Devills anodynes to put by the pangs of their wounded spirits. **1701** GREW *Cosm. Sacra* II. vi. 61 A Fright alone hath put by an Ague-fit, And mitigated a Fit of the Gout.

g. To lay aside (something out of use); to stow away; to lay by, save (esp. money) for future use.

1795 J. WOODFORDE *Diary* 31 July (1929) IV. 216 We had it [*sc.* the pork] taken up and put by for them against another Day. **1802** MAR. EDGEWORTH *Moral T.* (1816) I. xvii. 142 A slate, which.. the little girl had put by very carefully. **1840** DICKENS *Old C. Shop* xx, The old gentleman had put by a little money that nobody knew of. **1862** MRS. H. WOOD *Mrs. Hallib.* II. v, They had better wait a few years.. until they shall have put by something. **1890** *Illustr. Lond. News* 9 Aug. 170/1 Herbs and roots and apples put by for the winter.

42. put down.

a. See simple senses and DOWN *adv.* *to put one's foot down*: see FOOT *sb.* 28.

1483 *Cath. Angl.* 295/1 To Putte downe, *calare*.., *commergere, deponere, deprimere.* **1599** B. JONSON *Cynthia's Rev.* v. iv, As buckets are put downe into a well. **1795** J. WOODFORDE *Diary* 29 June (1929) IV. 210 We were put down at the White Hart in Stall Street. **1841** DICKENS *Let.* 2 May (1969) III. 276 'Mind Coachman' as the old ladies say 'you take me as fur as ever you go, and don't you put me down till you come to the very end of the journey.' **1879** F. W. ROBINSON *Coward Consc.* II. vi, Whereabouts.. do you want me to put you down? **1887** BARING-GOULD *Gaverocks* xviii, She put down her needlework. **1897** HOWELLS *Landl. Lion's Head* 142 The new rooms were left.. uncarpeted; there were thin rugs put down. **1933** [see NITWIT]. **1981** R. BARNARD *Mother's Boys* iv. 48 This ruddy cough. It's the climate... They shouldn't have put people down in this climate.

b. *trans.* To put an end to by force or authority, to suppress, repress, crush; †to bring into disuse, abolish (*obs.*).

1303 R. BRUNNE *Handl. Synne* 818 But, he [the Pope] may, þurgh no resun, þe sunday puttyn vp no dowun. **1340** HAMPOLE *Pr. Consc.* 4084 Alle haly kyrk sal be put don. **1526** *Pilgr. Perf.* (W. de W. 1531) 12 b, This gyfte suppresseth & putteth downe all carnalytees. **1603** SHAKS. *Meas. for M.* III. ii. 111 It is impossible to extirpe it quite, Frier, till eating and drinking be put downe. **1636** SHERLEY in Bradford *Plymouth Plantation* (1856) 345 Here is no trading, carriors from most places put downe. **1777** SHERIDAN *Sch. Scand.* II. ii, Sir Peter is such an enemy to scandal, I believe he would have it put down by parliament. **1855** MACAULAY *Hist. Eng.* xvii. IV. 65 Putting down a riot. **1873** H. SPENCER *Stud. Sociol.* vi. 121 The determination to put down opposition. **1891** *Law Times* XCI. 32/2 Putting down the fraudulent devices by means of which the pockets of..investors are..picked.

c. To depose from office, authority, or dignity; to dethrone, degrade. Somewhat *arch.*

1382 WYCLIF *Luke* i. 52 He puttide doun myȝty men fro seete. *c* **1400** *Brut* 247 His fader was in warde in þe castel of Kenylworþ, and eke was put doun of his realte. *c* **1460** FORTESCUE *Abs. & Lim. Mon.* ix. (1885) 129 Hyldericus kyng off Ffraunce..was putt doune by Pepyne son of Carollus Marcellus. **1593** SHAKS. *2 Hen. VI*, IV. ii. 38 Inspired with the spirit of putting down Kings and Princes. **1879** M. J. GUEST *Lect. Hist. Eng.* xlvii. 477 Judges..were almost tools of the king, who could set them up and put them down at his pleasure.

d. To lower the presumption, pride, or self-esteem of; to 'take down'; to snub; to refute, put to silence. Now more usually, to disparage, to criticize forcefully, to humiliate.

a **1400** *Relig. Pieces fr. Thornton MS.* 28 Þe toþer es tribulacyone, to putt hym downe with many scharpnes. **1588** SHAKS. *L.L.L.* IV. i. 143 Lord, Lord, how the Ladies and I haue put him downe. **1600** ROWLANDS *Lett. Humours Blood* iv. 65, I scorne..To let a Bowe-bell Cockney put me downe. **1831** MACAULAY *Ess., Johnson* (1887) 181 With what stately contempt she put down his impertinence. **1888** KNOX LITTLE *Child Stafferton* xiv, The peremptoriness with which Lady Dorothy put him down. **1923** G. M. TREVELYAN *Manin & Venetian Revolution* vi. 112 The principal speaker was Avesani, an eloquent and able lawyer who at once put Palffy down when he tried to speak in a tone of authority. **1958** *Amer. Speech* XXXIII. 225 When someone *puts* you *down* he criticizes you unfavorably, he *fluffs* you. **1961** RIGNEY & SMITH *Real Bohemia* p. xvi, *Put down, to*, to humiliate, or tell off, or part company with someone. **1969** *Down Beat* 20 Mar. 31/3 It became fashionable to put him down as too much of a showman and not enough of a jazzman. **1972** D. DELMAN *Week to Kill* 86 So why did you put him down that way, in front of me? **1972** W. LABOV *Language in Inner City* viii. 350 Sounding is only one of the many ways of putting someone down. **1977** MILLER & SWIFT *Words & Women* p. x, We ourselves had for years been innocently using the words and grammatical forms that put our own sex down.

†**e.** To overthrow, subdue, defeat (a person, an enemy). *Obs.* (merged in 'suppress' in b).

c **1400** *Destr. Troy* 6672 This Celidis, forsothe, fought with a speire, Polidamas to put doun, & his pride felle. **1616** R. C. *Times' Whistle* v. 1886 We shall put downe all that dare contest With vs. **1616** B. JONSON *Devil an Ass* I. i. 93 To mount vp on a joynt-stoole, with a Iewes-trumpe, To put downe Cokeley. **1847** MARRYAT *Childr. N. Forest* vi, The Levellers had opposed Cromwell, and he had put them down with the other troops.

†**f.** To lower in estimation; to excel, surpass, 'beat', etc., by comparison. *Obs.*

1592 NASHE *P. Penilesse* (ed. 2) 14 Ready to..die for griefe if he be put downe in brauery neuer so litle. **1621** BURTON *Anat. Mel.* III. ii. III. iii. (1651) 477 Lucullus ward-rope is put downe by our ordinary Citizens. **1678** BUNYAN *Pilgr.* Apol. 134 Holy Writ, Which for its Stile, and Phrase puts down all Wit. **1713** C'TESS WINCHELSEA *Misc. Poems* 209 Her Rooms, anew at ev'ry Christ'ning drest, Put down the Court, and vex the City-Guest. **1754** RICHARDSON *Grandison* V. x. 56 Your brother is indeed enough to put all other men down.

g. To make away with, put to death, kill.

1560 ROLLAND *Crt. Venus* I. 535 Lufe..slais the saull, and puttis the bodie down. **1589** *Par. Reg.* in Brand *Hist. Newcastle* (1789) I. 674 Alice Stokoe..did put downe her-self in her maisters house in her own belt. ? *a* **1800** *Queen's Marie* xv. in Scott *Minstrel. Scot. Bord.*, Little wist Marie Hamilton..That she was ga'en to Edinburgh town And a' to be put down. **1827** *Blackw. Mag.* XXI. 446 Word came that Eppy Telefer had 'put down' herself over night, and was found hanging dead in her own little cottage at day-break. **1899** H. D. RAWNSLEY *Life & Nat. Engl. Lakes* 173 A dog that shows signs of worrying [sheep] is 'put down' at once. **1936** W. HOLTBY *South Riding* IV. v. 253 Best have him [*sc.* a dog] put down, mercifully. **1942** G. KERSH *Nine Lives Bill Nelson* vii. 41 You could of put Bill down with a Humane Killer. **1958** *Times* 20 Nov. 3/1 An unwanted husband is as easily 'put down' as any other domestic pet. **1971** *Daily Tel.* 19 Aug. 3/6 Kim was ordered to be put down last year after he had bitten two people. **1977** *Guernsey Weekly Press* 21 July 4/7 One of the Jersey police dogs which entertained the large crowd at the recent open day of the local force at Les Vauxbelets has had to be put down.

h. To cease to keep up (something expensive); to stop the expense of, give up the use of.

1807 SOUTHEY *Espriella's Lett.* III. 120 In vain does he put down the carriage, dismiss the footman, and block up windows. **1888** MRS. LYNN LINTON *Thro' Long Night* II. vi, Since they had put down their carriage,..she had been able to go about so little.

i. To set down in writing, write down; to enter in a written account, list, etc.

(In first quot., ? to state in writing, or ? to lay down.)

1579 W. WILKINSON *Confut. Familye of Loue* 26 b, Dauid George first put downe the principles of this sect. **1824** *Examiner* 397/2 Mr. Bolton put down his name for 20*ol.* **1826** *New Monthly Mag.* XVI. 480, I have put you down in my will for a ring. **18..** MRS. CAMERON *Little Dog Flora* 5 They talked to each other in the way I shall put down. **1879** M. PATTISON *Milton* iv. 47 Milton consented to put down his thoughts on paper. **1885** G. ALLEN *Babylon* x, She was going to put herself down at a registry office. **1890** *Graphic* 9 Aug. 143/2 [Amendments] had been put down by members of the Opposition.

j. *fig.* To account or reckon; to estimate *as, at*; to take *for*; to count or attribute *to*.

1791 J. WOODFORDE *Diary* 14 Oct. (1927) III. 306, I dont know that I ever eat a better Hare tho' we had put it down for an old one by skinning it. **1847** MARRYAT *Childr. N. Forest* ix, I should have put you down for eighteen or nineteen at least. **1883** MRS. F. MANN *Par. Hilby* xvii. 205 It was put down to his credit that he never complained. **1886** MRS. C. PRAED *Miss Jacobsen* iv, She mentally put him down at thirty-five. *Ibid.* v, Don't put it all down to pure Christian good feeling. **1890** *Chamb. Jrnl.* 7 June 358/1, I should.. have put him down as a Yankee but for his accent.

k. To sink (a shaft, pit, etc.).

1875 R. F. MARTIN tr. *Havrez' Winding Mach.* 1 We found that we ought to put down an entirely fresh drawing pit. **1883** *Century Mag.* July 325/2 The searcher for brine put down a hole four hundred feet, and, instead of salt water, it discharged vast quantities of petroleum or..Seneca Oil.

l. In technical sporting use: (*a*) To cause (a fish) to swim low down; (*b*) To cause (a pointer or setter) to lie down.

1891 *Longm. Mag.* Feb. 389 The descent of the mist ..'puts down' the trout and prevents them from feeding. **1892** *Field* 7 May 695/3 Doon, who was put down by hand, moved a little as the gun was fired.

m. *Cricket.* (*a*) To hit (a wicket), dislodging a bail. (*b*) With a batsman as subject: to stop or strike (a difficult delivery) without attempting to score. (*c*) With a bowler as subject: to deliver (a ball). (*d*) With a member of the fielding side as subject: to drop a catch.

17.. *Laws of Cricket* in Grace *Cricket* (1891) 14 He that runs for yᵉ Wicket that is put down is out. **1816** W. LAMBERT *Cricketer's Guide* (ed. 6) iii. 39 If the Striker should move of his ground, with an intention to run, he [*sc.* the wicket-keeper] must then do his best endeavour to put down the Wicket, which is called *stumping out.* **1841** in *Cricket Q.* (1967) V. I. 13 *Put down,..to put down a ball* or *the bowling*. .. Dean putting the bowling down. **1860** *Baily's Monthly Mag.* Oct. 41 With rare patience did he stop at home and skilfully put down the slows, rarely even attempting to hit them. **1893** R. DAFT *Kings of Cricket* xv. 260, I have often seen little men put down with ease a bumping ball which many taller men would let hit their fingers. **1906** A. E. KNIGHT *Compl. Cricketer* iv. 150 When bowlers or wicket-keepers neglect this precaution [of keeping behind the wicket], it may happen that the throw forces them back upon the wicket which they are unable to legitimately put down. **1924** A. C. MACLAREN *Cricket Old & New* xiv. 140 On sticky wickets I should doubt if he [*sc.* J. T. Hearne] ever put down a bad ball. **1955** I. PEEBLES *Ashes* vii. 67 At 26 he had another bit of luck when Hole put him down at first slip.

n. *U.S.* To preserve (food).

1843 *Knickerbocker* XXI. 436 Daniel Gilbert's property.. cut up very handsomely, (to borrow the common figure upon such occasions, derived from the putting down of pork for the winter). **1881** S. O. JEWETT *Country By-Ways* 40 He's put down a kag of excellent beef. **1889** R. T. COOKE *Steadfast* xxi. 229 Who'll put down my pork and beef as Almiry did?

o. *Aeronaut.* To land (an aircraft or spacecraft). Also *intr.* (with the craft or the pilot as subject).

1933 C. K. STEWART *Speech of Amer. Airman* (Univ. of Akron thesis) 85 *Put down*, to land. **1939** *War Pictorial* 6 Oct. 7/3 Orders are to 'put down' the machine on the two-acre landing-deck of a naval aircraft-carrier. **1946** *Sun* (Baltimore) 21 Dec. 17/1 The badly damaged C-47 landed at Phillips Field, while the Eastern Airliner put down at Washington. **1958** 'N. SHUTE' *Rainbow & Rose* i. 14 They put her [*sc.* a freighter] down at Launceston and taxied in. **1972** T. LILLEY *K Section* xl. 183 Can you get a chopper.. to bring in the District Commissioner?..It can put down on the padang in front of the police station. **1976** 'L. BLACK' *Healthy Way to Die* ii. 17 The helicopter put down, the engine cut, the rotors gradually slowed. **1976** *New Scientist* 24 June 683/1 If there are no hitches the Viking lander should put him down early on 5 July.

p. *Jazz.* To establish (a rhythm or a style); to play or perform. Chiefly *U.S.*

1944 D. BURLEY *Orig. Handbk. Harlem Jive* 145 *Put down*, say, perform, describe, do. **1952** B. ULANOV *Hist. Jazz in Amer.* (1958) vi. 67 He put down a good walking beat. **1953** *Down Beat* 11 Feb. 16/3 Those old masters have really put something down, and it'll be a long, long time before those basic sounds change. **1968** *Ibid.* 7 Mar. 19/3 But the *tenor* saxophonists..reasoned that Coleman had been away from the source too long to know the hot licks that Harlem was putting down now.

q. *U.S. slang.* To reject or abandon.

1953 D. WALLOP *Night Light* xii. 135 You really ought to put school down and play full-time. **1959** L. LIPTON *Holy Barbarians* 102, I put that scene [*sc.* domesticity] down when I got divorced. **1964** *Amer. Folk Music Occasional* I. 62 My mother was the mother of all those kids and my father look like he wanted to put her down, leave her. **1966** E. LIEBOW *Behavior & Values of Street-corner Negro Men* (Ph.D. thesis, Catholic Univ.) v. 111 Richard..once 'put down' a woman of thirty or so, foregoing the pleasures of her automobile as well, because 'She's too old'.

r. To replace (the receiver of a telephone), usu. abruptly, in the course of a call; to 'hang up' (the telephone) *on* someone. Freq. in phr. ***to put the phone down.***

1966 A. E. LINDOP *I start Counting* xxi. 263 He picked up Leonie's telephone..and got through to our flat... When he put down the phone he picked up Leonie. **1970** 'M. CARROLL' *Bait* v. 67 He put the phone down on me before I could say a word. **1972** T. LILLEY *K Section* xl. 187 'You know where I am now; keep in touch.' Carter put the phone down. **1975** C. FREMLIN *Long Shadow* iv. 33, I was..so startled, and shocked. I..just put the phone down. **1979** K. M. PEYTON *Marion's Angels* v. 77 Geoff put down the receiver and explained gloomily to Marion what was expected of them.

s. To put (a child) to bed.

1968 C. ARMSTRONG *Balloon Man* i. 5 Johnny bounced out of his healthy three-and-a-half-year-old sleep at 6 a.m. The trouble was she had to put him down so early. **1971** D. DEVINE *Dead Trouble* iv. 33 Sarah Caine was putting Timmy down for his afternoon nap when the telephone rang. **1978** P. NIESEWAND *Underground Connection* 152 'Is the baby asleep?' 'I think so. She went off very quickly when I put her down.'

43. put forth.

a. *trans.* To stretch forth, stretch out, extend (the hand or other member of the body, or a thing held in the hand). Now *rare* or *arch.*

1362 LANGL. *P. Pl.* A. VI. 28 'Peter!' quod a Plouȝ-mon and putte forþ his hed. **1398** TREVISA *Barth. De P.R.* VI. vii. (Br. Mus. Add. 27944 f. 70) The modir..puttiþ and profreþ forþ þe brest to bede þe child. **14..** HOCCLEVE *Mother of God* 33 Thyn hand foorth putte & helpe my distresse. **1535** COVERDALE *1 Sam.* xiv. 27 He put forth his staff that he had in his hande. **1610** HOLLAND *Camden's Brit.* (1637) 244 A little rivelet..that putteth forth his head neere unto the Castle De Vies. **1712–4** POPE *Rape Lock* III. 57 The hoary Majesty of Spades appears, Puts forth one manly leg. **1848** THACKERAY *Van. Fair* xxxi, 'You are very unwell', the visitor said, putting forth her hand to take Amelia's.

b. To set forth; †to expose for sale (*obs.*); *fig.* to display, exhibit.

1362 LANGL. *P. Pl.* A. XI. 42 Þanne telleþ þei of þe Trinite hou two slowen þe þridde..And puyteþ forþ presumpciun to preue þe soþe. **1382** WYCLIF *Ezek.* xxvii. 17 Thei.. puttiden forth in thi fayris bawm, and hony, and oyle. **1667** MILTON *P.L.* I. 641 His Regal State Put forth at full, but still his strength conceal'd. **1878** BROWNING *La Saisiaz* 45 Light by light puts forth Geneva.

c. To set forth in words, propound, state, assert; †in quot. 1535, to utter (*obs.*).

1362 LANGL. *P. Pl.* A. IX. 115 To putte forþ sum purpos to preuen his wittes. **1382** WYCLIF *Matt.* xiii. 24 Another parable Jhesus putte forth [Vulg. *proposuit*] to hem. **1388** —— *Judg.* xiv. 12 Y schal putte forth [**1611** put forth] to you a probleme. **1480** CAXTON *Chron. Eng.* ccxxv. 230 The kynges nedes were put forth and promoted as touchyng the kyngdom of Fraunce. **1535** COVERDALE *Iob* x. 1 Now will I put forth my wordes. **1857** BUCKLE *Civiliz.* I. vii. 336 Such were the opinions put forth by Sir Thomas Browne. **1884** *Brit. Q. Rev.* Apr. 352 The Theory put forth by our brethren in the United States.

†**d.** To thrust, push, or send into view or prominence, out of concealment, retirement, or privacy; to put out to service, etc.; in quot. 1482, to expose *to* something; *refl.* to push or put oneself forward, come forward; to offer oneself. *Obs.*

1377 LANGL. *P. Pl.* B. XVIII. 40 Tho put hym forth a piloure bifor pilat, & seyde [etc.]. **1482** *Monk of Evesham* (Arb.) 36 There we sawe..men and women..put forth to the gretnes of dyuers and inenarrabulle peynes. **1530** PALSGR. 672/2 Let hym alone, he can put forthe hym selfe as well as any man in this courte. **1557** *Order of Hospitalls* C viii, The Thresorer..shall put forth any of the children of this Howse to service. **1667** MILTON *P.L.* VII. 171 Though I uncircumscrib'd my self retire, And put not forth my goodness. **1679–88** *Secr. Serv. Money* (Camden) 97 To Margaret Marshall, bounty..to put her children forth apprentices.

e. To put in operation, to bring into play; to exert (one's strength), lift up (one's voice); also † ***to put it forth***, and †*refl.* to exert oneself (*obs.*).

c **1400** *Master of Game* (MS. Digby 182) xxxiii, If þe hunters here þat þe houndes renne wele and putte it lustely forth. *c* **1420** ? LYDG. *Assembly of Gods* 963 Put the forthe boldly to ouerthrow Vertew. **1470–85** MALORY *Arthur* x. lxxiv. 544 Whanne sire Tristram wold put forth his strengthe and his manhode. **1535** COVERDALE *Prov.* viii. 1 Doth not wysdome crie? doth not vnderstondinge put forth hir voice? **1605** BACON *Adv. Learn.* I. viii. §3 When Virgil putteth himself forth to attribute to Augustus Cæsar the best of human honours. **1674** PLAYFORD *Skill Mus.* I. ii. 42 A good way of putting forth the Voice gracefully. **1722** WOLLASTON *Relig. Nat.* iv. 64 If men would be serious, and put forth themselves. **1849** MACAULAY *Hist. Eng.* iv. I. 434 It was to no purpose, however, that the good Bishop now put forth all his eloquence. **1892** *Harper's Mag.* June 81/1 They put forth their best pace.

f. To issue, publish, put in circulation.

1551 R. ROBINSON tr. *More's Utop.* To P. Giles (1895) 8 If he be mynded to publyshe and put forth his owne labours. **1669** in Sir J. Picton *L'pool Munic. Rec.* (1883) I. 313 Puttinge forth halfe-penys without the townes lycense. **1826** *Examiner* 11/2 'John'..is about to put forth a new daily Morning Paper. **1849** MACAULAY *Hist. Eng.* iv. I. 455 Jeffreys..advised James to put forth an edict declaring it to be his majesty's will and pleasure that the customs should continue to be paid. **1876** F. G. FLEAY *Shaks. Man.* II. ix. 242, I put forth in the year 1874 a chronological table of Shakespeare's plays.

g. (*a*) Of a plant: To send out (buds or leaves). Also *intr.* or *absol.*: To shoot, sprout, burst forth into bud, leaf, or blossom. Sometimes, of an animal: To produce (feathers, etc.); †also, to develop (a morbid growth).

1530 PALSGR. 672/1 This eglantyne tre putteth forthe the very tymely. *Ibid.*, This peare tre putteth forthe all redye. **1599** SHAKS. *Hen. V*, V. ii. 44 Her Hedges..Put forth disorder'd Twigs. **1626** BACON *Sylva* §407 The standard [rose-tree] did put forth a fair green leaf... It is likely that if it had been in the spring time, it would have put forth with greater strength. **1667** MILTON *P.L.* VII. 310 Let th' Earth Put forth the verdant Grass. **1737** BRACKEN *Farriery Impr.* (1757) II. 215 A Two year old Colt, that put forth a Bog-Spavin. **1865** TENNYSON *On Mourner* iii, The beech and lime Put forth and feel a gladder clime. **1884** BROWNING *Ferishtah, Family* 77, I may put forth angel's plumage.

(*b*) *intr.* for *refl.* Of buds, leaves, etc.: To sprout out, shoot out, come out.

1592 SHAKS. *Ven. & Ad.* 416 Who plucks the bud before one leafe put forth? **1658** SIR T. BROWNE *Gard. Cyrus* iii, In Acornes, Almonds,..the germ puts forth at the remotest part of the pulp. **1682** CREECH *Lucretius* (1683) 146 When flowers put forth, and budding branches shoot. **1924** R.

MACAULAY *Orphan Island* xx. 262 Like some lovely fruit that puts forth, ripens, and tumbles, over-mellow, to the ground.

†**h.** (*a*) *trans.* To thrust out; = *put out*, 48 b; (*b*) to put out (the eyes); (*c*) to extinguish (fire or light): = *put out*, 48 b (*b*), e (*b*). *Obs.*

1526 TINDALE *Matt.* ix. 25 As sone as the people were put forthe a dores [**1611** put foorth]. **1530** PALSGR. 672/2, I shall put hym forthe at all adventures, put hym in afterwarde who wyll. *a* **1547** in J. R. Boyle *Hedon* (1875) App. 88 All them that putethe furthe anye mens or womens ees. **1621** BRATHWAIT *Nat. Embassie* (1877) 31 [Phineus] put forth the eyes of his children had by his first wife. **1631** WEEVER *Fun. Mon.* 493 By the negligence of a Scholler forgetting to put forth the Lights of this Chappell..[it was] burnt to ashes.

†**i.** To turn out, dismiss from possession, fellowship, or service; to discharge, expel. *Obs.*

1545 in J. S. Leadam *Sel. Cas. Crt. Requests* (1898) 81 They [tenants] were dryuen to take copies of the Abbot for feare of puttyng forthe. **1564** HAWARD *Eutropius* VIII. xxiii, Certain legions..he dismiste & put forthe of wages. **1589** [see PUTTING *vbl. sb.*[1] 9]. **1597** BEARD *Theatre God's Judgem.* (1612) 445 He put him forth of pay, & tooke his horse from him by force.

†**j.** To lay out (money) to profit: cf. *put out*, 48 m (*b*). *Obs.*

1599 B. JONSON *Ev. Man out of Hum.* II. i, I am determined to put forth some five thousand pound, to be paid me five for one, upon the return of myself, my wife, and my dog from the Turk's court. *c* **1600** SHAKS. *Sonn.* cxxxiv, Thou vsurer that put'st forth all to vse.

k. *intr.* To set out, start on one's way, esp. to sea; to make one's way forward. (Cf. *put out*, 48 j.) Now somewhat *arch.*

1590 SHAKS. *Com. Err.* III. ii. 155 If any Barke put forth, come to the Mart, Where I will walke till thou returne to me. **1623** BINGHAM *Xenophon* 18 Cyrus putting forth a little before the rest, viewed both Armies at a good distance. *a* **1648** LD. HERBERT *Hen. VIII* (1683) 241 Hugo de Moncada..puts forth with a few Galleys. **1821** SHELLEY *Time* 9 Who shall put forth on thee, Unfathomable Sea? **1843** WORDSW. *Grace Darling* 50 Together they put forth, Father and Child! Each grasps an oar.

44. put forward.

†**a.** *trans.* To cause to 'go forward' or make progress; to further, advance. *Obs.*

1635 CROMWELL *Let.* 11 Jan., in *Carlyle* (1873) I. 77 It only remains now that He who first moved you to this, put you forward in the continuance thereof. **1793** SMEATON *Edystone L.* §288 Being wanted at Plymouth, to put forward the work of..the lantern.

b. To push into view or prominence, to make conspicuous; = *put forth*, 43 d. Also *refl.*

1611 BIBLE *Acts* xix. 33 And they drew Alexander out of the multitude, the Iewes putting [TINDALE, etc., thrustyng] him forward. **17..** SWIFT (J.), When men and women are mixed and well chosen, and put their best qualities forward, there may be any intercourse of civility and good will. **1849** [see FORWARD *adv.* 5]. **1886** AD. SERGEANT *No Saint* xi, People don't like to put themselves forward. **1888** MRS. LYNN LINTON *Thro' Long Night* I. ii, He wanted him..to put himself forward and make a dash.

c. To advance for consideration or acceptance; to propound, advance, urge; to set forth, allege; to represent *as*: see FORWARD *adv.* 5.

1855 MACAULAY *Hist. Eng.* xvi. III. 678 The Duke put forward a claim which..might have been fatal to the expedition. **1872** BLACK *Adv. Phaeton* xx, The girl put forward all manner of entreaties in vain. **1885** *Manch. Guard.* 20 July 5/5 Showing the groundlessness of the argument put forward by the Economist. **1885** *Law Rep.* 14 *Q.B. Div.* 792 A spurious child whom she puts forward as the child of her husband. **1889** H. D. TRAILL *Strafford* iv. 32 Several theories..have been put forward to account for Wentworth's apostasy.

d. *intr.* To press forward, advance, hasten on; to put oneself forward, come forward. ? *Obs.*

1599 MASSINGER, etc. *Old Law* IV. ii, Put forward, man! thou art most sure to have me. **1633** BP. HALL *Hard Texts* 1 Cor. ix. 24. 217 Many make a profession and put forward to an holy conversation. **1745** FIELDING *Tom Jones* XII. xii, Jones put forwards as fast as he could, notwithstanding all these Hints and Cautions, and poor Partridge was obliged to follow. **1815** JANE AUSTEN *Emma* xix, Always putting forward to prevent Harriet's being obliged to say a word.

45. put in. (Cf. INPUT *v.*)

a. (*a*) *trans.* To thrust into or place within a receptacle or containing space; to insert, introduce: see simple senses and IN *adv.*

a **1300** *Cursor M.* 5823 (Cott.) He put his hand in, fair in hele, And vte he drogh it als mesel. *c* **1400** *Lanfranc's Cirurgie* 151 To fulfille þe wounde wiþ hoote oile of rosis & to putte in a tente. *c* **1450** *Merlin* xv. 236 Thei putt in fier, and brent hem ther-ynne. *a* **1533** LD. BERNERS *Huon* xl. 130 When ther shypp was garnysshed, they put in theyr horses and ther armure. **1605** SHAKS. *Macb.* IV. i. 43 And now about the Cauldron sing,..In chanting all that you put in. **1614** B. JONSON *Barth. Fair* IV. vi, Come put in his legge in the middle roundell. **1859** TENNYSON *Vivien* 329 A Gardener putting in a graff. **1887** BARING-GOULD *Gaverocks* xii, The old gentleman puts in his head at the door.

spec. (*b*) To put (a letter) in the post.

1711 SWIFT *Jrnl. to Stella* 15 Dec., I put in my letter this evening myself. **1814** *Owen's New Bk. Roads* 191 Letters and Packets..are..to pay, at the Office where they are put in, the full postage to London.

(*c*) To put into the ground (seed or plants); to sow or plant.

1805 DICKSON *Pract. Agric.* I. 474 Drills..for putting in bean, pea, and turnip crops. **1845** *Jrnl. R. Agric. Soc.* VI. II. 425 Oats..are put in with the grass seeds in one ploughing.

(*d*) To place (a horse) between the shafts; to harness to a vehicle. Cf. *put to*, 53 c (*c*).

1840 DICKENS *Barn. Rudge* xxi, The horse was accordingly put in, and the chaise brought round. **1891** *Strand Mag.* Jan. 90/2 Tell them to put the horses in at once.

b. To install in or appoint to an office or position; sometimes with mixture of literal sense, as ***to put in a caretaker, a bailiff***; so ***to put in a distress, an execution.*** Also *spec.* in *Cricket*, (*a*) to send (a member of one's team) in as batsman; (*b*) To cause (a team, usu. the opposing one) to take first innings.

1387 TREVISA *Higden* (Rolls) IV. 7 Whanne Odo was dede þis Elsinus..gat slyliche a maundmente of þe kyng, and was i-put in at Caunterbury. **1596** SHAKS. *3 Hen. VI*, II. ii. 92 You..Haue caus'd him by new Act of Parliament, To blot out me, and put his owne Sonne in. **1745** POCOCKE *Descr. East* II. I. IV. viii. 267 The archbishop is put in by the patriarch of Constantinople. **1823** *Lady's Mag.* July 390/2 David Willis, who, injudiciously put in first..was bowled out, without a stroke, from actual nervousness. **1829** *Examiner* 716/2 The conduct of Mr. Mores, in putting in an execution under these circumstances. **1833** NYREN *Yng. Cricketer's Tutor* 118 Whenever a man is put out, and if the bowling have become loose, put in a resolute hard hitter. **1836** [see DISTRESS *sb.* 3]. **1836** *New Sporting Mag.* Oct. 360 Eton having won the toss, put Winchester in. **1859** *All Year Round* 23 July 305/2 The town won the toss for innings, and put their men in first. **1887** BARING-GOULD *Gaverocks* xxii, She..had to put in a couple, as caretakers, at so much per week. **1888** A. G. STEEL in Steel & Lyttelton *Cricket* iv. 200 It is as well not to put in two hard-hitters together if possible, as it often tends to make one hit against the other. **1900** P. F. WARNER *Cricket in Many Climes* 212 Lord Hawke, on winning the toss, put the other side in. **1976** J. SNOW *Cricket Rebel* 78 It was to be his [*sc.* Mike Denness's] last as captain, after putting the Australians in and then losing the match.

c. To present, or formally tender, as in a law court (a document, evidence, a plea, a claim, surety, BAIL, an APPEARANCE, etc.).

1459 *Paston Lett.* I. 499 There be many and diverse particuler billes put inne. **1557** in W. H. Turner *Select. Rec. Oxford* (1880) 265 Putyng yn suffycyent suirty for the payment. **1601** SHAKS. *All's Well* v. iii. 286 *Kin.* To prison with her... *Dia.* Ile put in baile my liedge. **1654** *Clarke Papers* (Camden) III. 11 The Court ordered him a coppie thereof, and 14 dayes time to putt in his answere. **1742** FIELDING *Jos. Andrews* IV. ii, If they have put in the bans, I desire you will publish them no more without my orders. **1781** D. WILLIAMS tr. *Voltaire's Dram. Wks.* II. 281 Colette may put in a claim. **1862** *Temple Bar Mag.* VI. 335 Gray hair No. 19 has just put in an appearance. **1888** *Times* 19 Apr. 12/3, I received..a letter from Mr. T. M. Kelly... (Letter put in.) **1891** *Law Times Rep.* LXIII. 733/1 At the trial..the plaintiff..put in an information sworn by the defendant.

d. *intr.* To make a claim, plea, or offer: (*a*) to present or advance one's own claim, to apply *for*; to offer oneself as a candidate, to enter *for*, bid *for*; †to claim or profess to be, to set up *for* (*obs.*); (*b*) to interpose on behalf of some one or something, to plead or intercede *for* (quot. 1603).

1603 SHAKS. *Meas. for M.* I. ii. 103 They had gon down to, but that a wise Burger put in for them. **1607** —— *Timon* III. iv. 85 *Lucil.* Put in now, Titus. *Tit.* My Lord, heere is my Bill. **1622** FLETCHER & MASSINGER *Span. Curate* I. i, A Woman..whose all-excelling Forme Disdaines comparison with any She That puts in for a fair one. **1627** USSHER *Lett.* (1686) 376 Many most unfit Persons are now putting in for that place. **1712–3** STEELE *Guard.* No. 6 ¶5 He puts in for the Queen's plate every year. **1741** MIDDLETON *Cicero* I. vi. 530 Clodius was putting in at the same time for the Prætorship. **1892** *Sat. Rev.* 16 July 65/1 Opposition without mercy to every Minister who puts in for re-election.

e. *trans.* To drive in, cause or compel to go in: (*a*) *Naut.* (a ship) into a port or haven; (*b*) *Falconry*, (the game) into covert. Cf. 5.

1615 CHAPMAN *Odyss.* (J.), Whom stormes put in there, are with stay embrac't. **1795** NELSON *Let. to McArthur* 25 July, in *Pearson's Catal.* No. 9 (1886) 29 The Agamemnon is put in here by bad weather. **1826** SIR J. S. SEBRIGHT *Observ. Hawking* (1828) 25 If the bird is put in, the second may be in the right style, as the hawk will then have time to get up to his pitch. **1852** BURTON *Falconry Valley Indus* viii. 78 They compare..her conduct, after she has 'put in' her quarry, to a cat's. [*Footnote*] To 'put in' the quarry is to drive it into a bush.

f. *intr.* To go in, enter:

spec. (*a*) *Naut.* to enter a port or harbour, esp. by turning aside from the regular course for shelter, provisions, repairs, etc.; (*b*) to make a call at a house for entertainment, or on a chance visit (now *rare* or *obs.*); (*c*) to fly into covert for safety, as a bird pursued by a hawk. In quot. 1612, to join, unite *with.*

1598 W. PHILLIP *Linschoten.* I. i, Lisbone, where some of our Fleet put in, and left vs. **1604** SHAKS. *Oth.* II. i. 65 *Cassio.* How now? Who ha's put in? *Gent.* 'Tis one Iago. **1612** DRAYTON *Poly-olb.* xi. 99 When Peever with the helpe of Pickmere, make apace To put-in with those streames. **1667–8** PEPYS *Diary* 16 Feb., Mr. Holliard put in, and dined with my wife and me. **1719** DE FOE *Crusoe* (1840) I. x. 168 Here I put in. **1883** SALVIN & BRODRICK *Falconry Brit. Isles* Gloss. 152 The place..where the quarry has 'put in'.

g. *trans.* To interpose (a blow, shot, etc.; a word or remark; also with the actual words as obj., usually preceding); to intervene with; to get in (a word). ***to put in one's oar***: see OAR *sb.* 5 a. Also ***to put in the leather*** = ***to put the boot in*** s.v. BOOT *sb.*[3] 1 b.

16.. DIGBY (J.), A nimble fencer will put in a thrust so quick, that the foil will be in your bosom, when you thought it a yard off. **1693** *Humours Town* 30 A Man can no more put in a word with you, than with..some of our Coffee-House Holders-forth. **1722** DE FOE *Plague* (1756) 145 At last the Seaman put in a Hint that determin'd it. **1821** BYRON *Juan* IV. xlix, The third..took The blows upon his cutlass, and then put His own well in. **1837** DICKENS *Pickw.* lii, My father..complicates the whole concern by puttin' his oar in. **1849** MACAULAY *Hist. Eng.* iv. I. 493 Wallop sate down; and Baxter himself attempted to put in a word. **1862** MRS. H. WOOD *Channings* I. xi. 157 'Gently, Tom!' put in Mr. Channing. **1889** C. LARKING *Everything agst. her* III. v. 97 You may depend upon my putting in a word for you whenever I can. **1943** J. PHELAN *Lett. from Big House* ii. 30 Almost before he reached the ground the party piled on him. Some punched and cursed, others..'put in the leather'. **1952** M. ALLINGHAM *Tiger in Smoke* iii. 57 Someone has been 'putting in the leather'... That was done with a boot.

h. *intr.* or *absol.* To intervene.

1614 B. JONSON *Barth. Fair* Induct., He has..kick'd me three or four times..for but offering to put in with my experience. **1656** EARL MONM. tr. *Boccalini's Advts. fr. Parnass.* I. xc. (1674) 122 Unless your Majesty put in betwixt my misery, and my Creditors rage. *a* **1713** ELLWOOD *Autobiog.* (1714) 254 [A Man] of a Temper so throughly Peaceable, that he had not hitherto put in at all. **1855** *Harper's Mag.* Oct. 602/1 The unfortunate victim hollowed out, 'Oh, Moses, if you have any love for your brother, *put in*, and divide this fight!' **1901** W. N. HARBEN *Westerfelt* 290 You wus tellin' me..'at the lan'an' house wus in yore name an' her'n, an' 'at I had no right to put in.

i. *trans.* To furnish in addition, to 'throw in'; to insert as an addition or supplement.

1632 MASSINGER *City Madam* II. ii, These are arts Would not misbecome you, tho' you should put-in Obedience and duty. **1643** [ANGIER] *Lanc. Vall. Achor* 7 But when God put the work into their hands, he put in skill. *a* **1708** [see 48 e (*a*)]. **1858** MRS. LYNN LINTON *Thro' Long Night* II. v, He..put in an untrained bass to her well-taught soprano. **1890** T. F. TOUT *Hist. Eng. fr. 1689*, 209 The Lords put in amendments which the Commons would not accept. **1891** MRS. L. ADAMS *Bonnie Kate* i, As though a painter had touched them with a brush fresh from 'putting in' a sunset.

j. To contribute as one's share of work or duty; to perform (a piece of work, etc.) as part of a whole, or in the midst of other occupations.

1890 *Standard* 14 Feb. 2/8 The Dark Blues resumed work yesterday..and put in some useful practice. **1891** *Gd. Words* May 338/2 He had to..'put in' his term of military service. **1892** *Pict. World* 9 Apr. 670/2 Nothing could induce that man to put in more than four chapels a week. *a* **1909** *Mod.* I may be able to put in an hour's work in the evening. **1972** J. AIKEN *Butterfly Picnic* i. 9 The hours I have put in hanging about for her on station platforms.

k. *colloq.* To pass, spend, use up (a portion or period of time), usually by means of some occupation.

1863 C. B. GIBSON *Life among Convicts* II. viii. 105 A man with a sentence of twelve years, no matter how exemplary his conduct, must put in nine years. **1882** STEVENSON *Fam. Stud. Men & B.* 308 If he had to wait for a dish of poached eggs, he must put in the time by playing on the flageolet. **1889** 'MARK TWAIN' *Yankee at Crt. K. Arthur* xliii, I couldn't do anything with the letters after I had written them. But it put in the time. **1892** *Field* 10 Dec. 893/1 They ..'put in' the summer at some fashionable resort.

l. To inform against; to 'frame'; to secure the conviction of (a person); to send to prison. Also *transf. slang.*

1922 A. WRIGHT *Colt from Country* 153 'I might have a chance with the girl again.' 'After what you did to put her in?' laughed the detective. 'I like your hide.' **1951** S. MACKENZIE *Dead Men Rising* I. 52 Nothing would give me greater pleasure than to put you in, only that's about the one thing I've never done in my life. **1958** D. NILAND *Call me when Cross turns Over* vii. 174 Don't put me in. Don't try to hang anything on me. **1966** P. COWAN *Seed* iv. 106, I suppose when they make you a prefect you'll put us in.

m. To let in (the clutch of a motor vehicle).

1928 J. GALSWORTHY *Swan Song* III. iv. 246 'This is where I put in my clutch,' she said, 'as they say in the 'bloods'!' **1943** A. RANSOME *Picts & Martyrs* xvii. 167 He put in his clutch and drove off. **1976** 'E. MCBAIN' *Guns* (1977) vii. 174 Colley puts in the clutch and manipulates the gear shift.

46. put off.

a. See simple senses and OFF *adv.*

[**1825**: implied in PUT-OFF 3.] **1891** C. ROBERTS *Adrift Amer.* viii. 125 Where..conductors and brakesmen..have nothing to do but hunt for dead-beats and put them off [i.e. off the train]. *Mod.* To save time, I had them put me off [from the steamer] at Gravesend. We took him in our boat and put him off at Godstow.

†**b.** *trans.* To drive off, repulse, repel; to dispel, drive away. *Obs.*

c **1374** CHAUCER *Boeth.* I. pr. iv. 8 (Camb. MS.) How ofte ek haue I put of or cast owt [orig. *dejeci*] hym..of þe wronges [etc.]. **1375** BARBOUR *Bruce* VII. 369 He ves sa fortravalit To put of thame that hym assalit. *c* **1400** *Destr. Troy* 8582 Telamon..þe Troiens pursuet; Paris hym put of, & preset hym sore. **1512** *Act 4 Hen. VIII*, c. 1 §1 To put theym of at theire landyng. **1627** CAPT. SMITH *Seaman's Gram.* xiii. 61 If we be put off, charge them with all your great and small shot.

c. To postpone to a later time; to defer. Also *absol.*

1398 TREVISA *Barth. De P.R.* II. ii. (Brit. Mus. Add. 27944 f. 12 b), [Angels] doþ his hestes..in an instant and puttiþ nouȝt of for to a morwe. **1530** PALSGR. 673/2 It is put of for this tyme. **1583** STUBBES *Anat. Abus.* (1882) II. 9 Farre from delaieng, or putting of poore mens causes. **1664** DRYDEN *Rival Ladies* I. ii, All things are now in Readiness, and must not Be put off. **1699** BENTLEY *Phal.* Pref. 105, I am oblig'd to put off the Others to another opportunity. **1748** *Anson's Voy.* II. xi. 254 The departure of the galeon was put off. **1889** MRS. R. JOCELYN *Distracting Guest* II. xv. 227, I shall assuredly put our wedding off.

d. (*a*) To remove or take off (clothes, or other things worn); to doff; to divest oneself (rarely another) of. (The opposite of *put on*, 47 c.)

1470–85 MALORY *Arthur* VII. xxx. 261 He put syr Gawayne to the werse, for he put of his helme. **1530** PALSGR. 673/2 Put of his bridell and gyve hym a locke of haye. **1535**

COVERDALE *Song Sol.* v. 3, I haue put off my cote, how can I do it on agayne? **1698** J. CRULL *Muscovy* 152 Their Way of Saluting is by putting off their Caps. **1771** SMOLLETT *Humph. Cl.* 4 July i. §10 Should he be so weak or ill as to require a servant to put off and on his clothes. **1891** *Eng. Illustr. Mag.* Jan. 281 The hawthorn put off her bridal veil.

(*b*) *fig.* To divest oneself of (a character, habit, or manner).

1526 TINDALE *Col.* iii. 9 Ye have put off the olde man with his workes, and have putt on the nue. **1649** MILTON *Eikon.* vi. ¶9 Putting off the courtier, he now puts on the philosopher. **1713** [see f]. **1889** *Repent. P. Wentworth* I. iv. 59 She met him very kindly... Certainly she had put off the scornful princess for the day.

e. To 'put out of the way', make away with, kill. *Obs.* exc. *dial.*

1456 SIR G. HAYE *Law Arms* (S.T.S.) 158 It war than spedefull that sik a man war put off for the better. **1868** ATKINSON *Cleveland Gloss.* s.v., Hev ye heared at au'd Mally at t' work'us has putten herself off?

†**f.** To dismiss, put away: (*a*) from one's mind or thought; (*b*) from one's service or employment. *Obs.*

c **1400** *Destr. Troy* 2664 Hedis to þat, And puttis of þat purpos: let paris not wend. *Ibid.* 11416 To put of þat purpos he paynet him sore. **1613** SHAKS. *Hen. VIII*, I. ii. 32 The Clothiers all not able to maintaine The many to them longing, haue put off The Spinsters, Carders, Fullers, Weauers. *a* **1713** ELLWOOD *Autobiog.* (1714) 58 Having put off his Husbandry, he had put off with it most of his Servants.

g. To dismiss or get rid of (as an importunate person or demand) by evasion or the like; to baffle or balk of his desire by giving something inferior or less acceptable (const. *with*).

Sometimes with mixture of sense c: to dismiss till a later time, bid to wait.

1568 GRAFTON *Chron.* II. 141 The king put them of for that Season, and warned them to sue him about Mighelmas. **1630** SANDERSON *Serm. on Prov. xxiv.* 10 §8 Let no man think to put off this duty with the Lawyers question,—But who is my neighbour? **1718** *Free-thinker* No. 16 ¶2 You may put them off with Shells, and Pebbles, or any Trumpery. **1846** JERROLD *Mrs. Caudle's Lect.* xv, Of course you've some story to put me off with. **1869** J. MARTINEAU *Ess.* II. 2 Psychology has been put off with complimentary acknowledgments.

h. To divert *from* one's purpose; to hinder, debar; to dissuade *from* doing something. Now usually (without const.), to hinder (a person) from performing some act by diverting his attention. Also, to cause (someone) to be mistaken.

1616 B. JONSON *Devil an Ass* I. iv, Nor can his mirth, With whom I make 'hem, put me off. **1642** *Perkins' Prof. Bk.* x. §646. 276 This exception shall not put off the grauntee of the piscarie in the same poole. **1662** J. DAVIES tr. *Olearius' Voy. Ambass.* 276 We could not by any means put off the second Brother out of an Humour [that] had taken him to accompany us. **1890** FENN *Double Knot* II. vi. 114 Millet was put off from resuming the subject. **1918** A. BENNETT *Pretty Lady* xxii. 146 'That's not *you*, Frankie!' said the Major with a start of recognition... 'Yes, sir,' said Molder. .. 'It was the red hat put me off,' the Major explained.

i. To pass, spend, get through (time). *Obs.* or *dial.*

1637 RUTHERFORD *Lett.* (1862) I. 376, I am here, Sir, putting off a part of my inch of time. *a* **1704** T. BROWN *Dial. Dead, Reas. Oaths* Wks. 1711 IV. 95 But what will serve the turn full as well, to put off half an Hour or so of Conversation. **1824** SCOTT *St. Ronan's* xxxvii, I am as stupid as he, to put off my time in speaking to such an old cabbage-stock. **1850** *Tait's Mag.* XVII. 727/2, I have purposely put off time, in order that if anybody was coming forward they might have an opportunity.

j. To dispose or get rid of (a commodity) by sale; to make to 'go off', to sell (? now *dial.* and *slang*); †to dispose of (a woman) in marriage.

1639 S. DU VERGER tr. *Camus' Admir. Events* 308 The middlemost called Callinice, which was likeliest to be put off, remained in the world to expect when her beauty.. would purchase her a husband. **1654** HOWELL *Let. to Sir E. Spencer* 24 Jan., Of all Dowries exceeding £100 there should be two out of every cent deducted, for putting off hard-favour'd and poor Maids. **1655** GURNALL *Chr. in Arm.* xlv[i.] §1 (1669) 404/1 As if it were of little more importance to marry a child, than it is to put off a horse or cow at a fair. **1705** tr. *Bosman's Guinea* 390 He may put off every Pipe for the worth of Twopence. **1864** *Jrnl. R. Agric. Soc.* XXV. II. 295 As to oxen, I put off two lots in the year, one from the grass and the other from the yards.

k. To dispose of deceptively or fraudulently; to pass off for what it is not; to palm off (?*obs.*); to impose unwarrantably, foist *upon* some one.

1653 H. MORE *Antid. Ath.* III. i. §4 To sophisticate metals, and then put them off for true Gold and Silver. **1740** CHESTERF. *Lett.* (1792) I. 187 A plagiary is a man who steals other people's thoughts and puts them off for his own. **1780** *Newgate Cal.* V. 79 Great part of this counterfeit money was put off at country-fairs. **1892** *Harper's Mag.* LXXXIV. 243/2 Do you think it was quite right.. to put him off on your uncle, if you didn't like him yourself?

†**l.** To set off; to make attractive, as food, etc.

1700 WALLIS in *Collect.* (O.H.S.) I. 326 Riding the great horse.. is the expedient for putting-off the great house to good advantage. **1758** *Descr. Thames* 234 A Mackrel, dressed as soon as taken,.. requires no Goosberries or rich Sauce to put it off.

†**m.** *Farriery.* To discharge, pass. *Obs.*

1737 BRACKEN *Farriery Impr.* (1757) II. 84 Low Feeding ..causes a Horse to put off his Meat before it has been sufficiently acted upon by the Stomach. *Ibid.* 103.

n. (*a*) *intr. Naut.* To leave the land; to set out or start on a voyage; also, to leave a ship, as a boat. (*b*) *intr.* To depart, leave a place, make off. *rare*, ? now only *U.S.* (cf. 8 b). (*c*) *trans.* To push off, send off (a boat) from the land, or from a ship. (= *put out*, 48 j.)

(*a*) **1582** N. LICHEFIELD tr. *Castanheda's Conq. E. Ind.* I. lxxix. 162 They did shoote such abundance of arrows..y[t] they made our men put off. **1606** SHAKS. *Ant. & Cl.* II. vii. 78 Let me cut the Cable, And when we are put off, fall to their throates. **1629** J. COLE *Of Death* 90 When the ship is putting off. **1725** DE FOE *Voy. round World* (1840) 66 A boat put off from one of the ships. **1748** *Anson's Voy.* II. iii. 153 The six, who.. remained in the barge, put off with her to sea. **1890** S. LANE-POOLE *Barbary Corsairs* I. ix. 98 In the summer.. Barbarossa put off to sea.

(*b*) **1858** *Nat. Intelligencer* 22 July (Bartlett) Over fifteen thousand persons have deserted their homes in California, and put off by every means of conveyance for Fraser's river.

(*c*) **1639** WINTHROP *New Eng.* (1825) I. 312 He caused the boatsmen to put off the boat. **1892** *Black & White* 2 Jan. 25/2 It was too rough to put a boat off.

o. *slang* or *colloq.* = *put out* (48 f (*c*)). Now usu., to offend, to disconcert; to cause (a person) to lose interest in or enthusiasm for something.

1909 *Spectator* 12 June 927/1 People.. forget that a horse can be 'put off' as easily as a man. **1909** F. BARCLAY *Rosary* ix. 77, I am so afraid of her putting Dal off. He is so fastidious. **1928** *Observer* 19 Feb. 6/3 The prefatory note, with its apparently exaggerated claim, rather put me off. **1932** 'E. M. DELAFIELD' *Thank Heaven Fasting* I. ii. 34 A man is very quickly put off, if he thinks that a girl hasn't even taken the trouble to remember what he looks like. **1949** D. SMITH *I capture Castle* ix. 134 He'll end by putting them off us. **1973** L. MEYNELL *Thirteen Trumpeters* v. 80 I'm in grave danger of becoming virtuous. To see those acres of fat Germanic flesh spread out by the pool is enough to put me off for life.

47. put on.

* **a.** *lit.* To place on or upon something; to superimpose: see simple senses and ON *adv.*: often with special implication, e.g. to put (a cooking-vessel) on the fire, (a play) on the stage, (a card) on another card already played; also, to fix or attach (a part) to some structure.

1711 *Milit. & Sea. Dict.* (ed. 4), The putting on of the Rudder is call'd, Hanging of it. **18..** *Nursery Rime*, Polly, put the kettle on, We'll all have tea. **1828** *Sporting Mag.* XXIII. 33 His head is not well put on. **1885** J. PAYN *Luck Darrells* II. xxiii. 137 It is possible.. to get a through carriage put on at St. Pancras. **1889** F. C. PHILIPS *Ainslie's Courtship* II. vi. 63 A gorgeous spectacular piece.. put on with a reckless disregard of expense. **1924** A. HUXLEY *Let.* 29 Apr. (1969) 229 Playfair, who is producing it for the 300 club performance, seems to think that it will make a very good entertainment and has some hopes of getting it put on for a run. **1941** L. A. G. STRONG *Bay* 192 A couple of new plays that some amateurs were putting on. **1977** A. MORICE *Scared to Death* i. 7 Presumably, if his play is any good, this David Winter would have put it on anyway?

b. *trans.* To impose or inflict as a burden or charge. In quot. 1588, ? to 'lay on as a blow' (Schmidt). *to put it on*, to add to the price, to overcharge.

1382 WYCLIF *1 Kings* xii. 4 The moost greuous 30k that he hath putte on to vs. **1588** SHAKS. *L.L.L.* IV. i. 116 Finely put on indeede. **1879** M. J. GUEST *Lect. Hist. Eng.* xxi. 210 The fines were not fixed sums; the king could put on just what he liked. **1891** *Daily Tel.* 16 Jan. 5/3 If any 'brother' comes out with profane language we put on a nominal fine. *Mod. colloq.* Half-a-crown for that job! They know how to put it on!

c. (*a*) To place (apparel or an ornament) upon one's person; to don; to clothe oneself (or another) with. Also *fig.* in scriptural language (cf. d); of a plant, to 'clothe itself' with (leaves or blossoms).

c **1440** *Alphabet of Tales* 226 He did on his maister clothyng, & putt on his ryng on hys fynger. **1526** TINDALE *Rom.* xiii. 14 Put ye on the lorde Jesus Christ [Gr. ἐνδύσασθε]. *Ibid.*, *Ephes.* vi. 11 Put on the armour of god. **1628** EARLE *Microcosm.* xx. (Arb.) 41 Hee has not put on the quaint Garbe of the Age. **1782** MISS BURNEY *Cecilia* VI. v, Pray put on your hat. **1846** MRS. MURCER *Seasons* I. 8 You must ask Ann to put you on a great coat. **1878** T. HARDY *Ret. Native* VI. iv, Mrs. Venn has got up, and is going away to put on her things. **1883** MRS. F. MANN *Parish Hilby* xv, The wife had washed him up and put him on a clean jacket.

†(*b*) *absol.* To put on one's hat, to 'be covered'; also, to put on one's clothes, dress oneself (*Sc.*). *Obs.*

1611 CHAPMAN *May Day* II. i. Plays 1873 II. 344 *Tem.* When your yong man came to me: I pray let him put on, vnlesse it be for your pleasure. *Leo.* He.. can endure the cold well enough bare-headed. **1636** MASSINGER *Gt. Dk. Florence* I. i, Nay, pray you, guardian, and good sir, put on. **1788** SHIRREFS *Jamie & Bess* II. ii, I thank you Branky, what's the news in town? Pit on, pit on; How's Simon? ? *a* **1800** *Queen's Marie* xii. in Scott *Minstr. Scot. Bord.*, O slowly, slowly raise she up, And slowly put she on.

d. *fig.* To take upon oneself, adopt, assume (a character or quality, real or feigned).

1526 TINDALE *Col.* iii. 10 [see 46 d (*b*)]. *a* **1548** HALL *Chron., Hen. V* 33 This kyng.. determined with hymself to put on the shape of a new man. **1592** KYD *Sol. & Pers.* I. iii, In Italy I put my Knighthood on. **1600** SHAKS. *A.Y.L.* v. iv. 187 The Duke hath put on a Religious life. **1781** D. WILLIAMS tr. *Voltaire's Dram. Wks.* II. 113 A young stripling.. who puts on airs of gravity. **1809** MALKIN *Gil Blas* XII. i. ¶8 Whim.. determined her to put on the stranger, and receive my compliments with.. coldness. **1890** *Harper's Mag.* June 20/1 The streets had put on their holiday look.

e. In mod. emphatic use: To assume deceptively or falsely; to affect, feign, pretend. *to put it on*, to pretend to something in excess of the fact. Also, to impose on, to take advantage of; to puzzle or deceive intentionally. *colloq.*

1621 [see PUT-ON *ppl. a.* 2.] **1682** DRYDEN *Dk. Guise* III. i, 'Twas all put on that I might hear and rave. **1806** LADY JERNINGHAM in *J. Lett.* (1896) I. 270 The first days the Duke supposed the illness a little Put on. **1888** RIDER HAGGARD *Col. Quaritch* x, I wonder if he puts it on or if he deceives himself. **1891** *Pict. World* 8 Aug. 166/1 That voice is put on. *a* **1909** *Mod.* He is not so tired as all that; he is putting it on. The horse is putting it on with him; he knows the man can't ride. **1949** D. SMITH *I capture Castle* xiv. 290 'We shall be ashamed of our callousness if father really is going off his head.' 'He isn't—he's putting it on or something.' **1958** *Times* 12 Nov. 3/3 Miss Mollie Sugden's wife has got into the habit of 'putting on' her husband because the husband .. rather enjoys being 'put on'. **1958** *Amer. Speech* XXXIII. 225 When a hipster *puts* someone *on* he is pulling his leg (perhaps putting him on a stage to be laughed at). **1960** WILLMOTT & YOUNG *Family & Class in London Suburb* x. 111 'Some of the parents at the school seem to put it on a bit,' said Mr. Prior, a bank manager whose children go to a local preparatory school, 'you do get a bit of the old blue-blooded attitude among them.' **1964** H. E. F. DONOHUE *Conversations with Nelson Algren* xi. 272 She's putting me on and I'm putting her on, and she marvels at her good fortune in meeting me, I'll marvel at my good fortune in meeting her. **1966** T. PYNCHON *Crying of Lot 49* vi. 167 Has it ever occurred to you, Oedipa, that somebody's putting you on? That this is all a hoax? **1967** 'G. BAGBY' *Corpse Candle* (1968) x. 133 Greg was forever putting people on... He'd do it just for fun. The poetry was his way of putting the English faculty on. **1977** *Sci. Amer.* Dec. 17/3 Persi's brief description of the Rockwell prediction method was so outlandish that I assumed he was putting me on.

f. To add, make an addition of. (*a*) To develop additional (flesh or weight). Also, *to put it on*. (*b*) To add (so much) to the charge or price.

1850 *Jrnl. R. Agric. Soc.* XI. II. 580 [They] put on no meat until they were put up to feed. **1897** *Allbutt's Syst. Med.* IV. 4 The woman returned.. in a state of robust health, having put on a stone in weight. **1900** MARIE CORELLI *Boy* ii, I can never take sugar. I put on flesh directly. *a* **1909** *Mod. colloq.* How much have they put on to the price? **1933** E. HEMINGWAY *Winner take Nothing* (1934) 35 It's terrible.. the way I put it on. **1967** A. DIMENT *Dolly Dolly Spy* vii. 98 She had put on a lot of weight... I could see her checking herself off against Veronica—who has definitely been putting it on. **1971** 'J. J. MARRIC' *Gideon's Art* i. 11 'You both take sugar?'.. 'Not for me,' Slater said, slapping his rounded belly. 'I'm putting it on again.'

(*c*) To add (runs, a goal) to the score at cricket, football, etc.

1868 *Baily's Mag.* Sept. 246 The last wicket fell for 689, six players thus putting on nearly as many hundred runs. **1882** *Daily Tel.* 24 June, Five wickets were at this point disposed of for 258 runs. Of these Giffen had put on 43. **1891** *Standard* 6 Nov. 6/5 After crossing over the visitors could only put on one more goal. **1921** *Glasgow Herald* 17 Oct. 13/7 In the second half P. R. Johnstone scored, and afterwards G. A. Able put on another for Stepps. **1975** [see OUTFIELD *sb.* 3 a]. **1977** *World of Cricket Monthly* June 32/1 Haroon and Imran put on 34.

(*d*) Of a taxi-driver: to join (the end of a rank).

1930 A. ARMSTRONG *Taxi* xii. 164 'Putting on' is the taxi man's expression for coming on at the end of the rank. A driver will say he 'put on sixth cab at the so-and-so', meaning he came on the so-and-so rank when there were only five other cabs there. **1939** H. HODGE *Cab, Sir?* 22, I decide to put on a hotel rank.

g. To lay, stake, bet (a sum of money).

[**1849** THACKERAY *Pendennis* lxii, Altamont put the pot on at the Derby, and won a good bit of money. *Ibid.* 'I put on the pot, sir'. 'You did what?' 'I laid my money on'.] **1890** *Standard* 21 July 4/4 The Defendant 'put on' for her 10*l.* upon Oberon for the Lincolnshire Handicap.

** †**h.** To urge onward, encourage; to incite, impel (*lit.* and *fig.*); to promote (a state of things).

1602 SHAKS. *Ham.* v. ii. 408 He was likely, had he beene put on To haue prou'd most royally. **1605** —— *Lear* I. iv. 227 That you protect this course, and put it on By your allowance. **1642** J. SHUTE *Sarah & Hagar* (1649) 170 They haue put them on to the shedding of blood. **1689** G. BULKELEY in *Andros Tracts* II. 86 Tis onely.. my reall desire of the Common good which puts me on.

i. *intr.* To go faster, go ahead; to push on, hasten onward; to go on, proceed. ?*Obs.*

c **1611** CHAPMAN *Iliad* VIII. 217 When none, though many kings put on [orig. πολλῶν περ ἐόντων], could make his vaunt. **1653** in *Nicholas Papers* (Camden) II. 12, I am clearly of opinion he will now very speedily put on to make himself or some other.. to be elected K. **1655** GURNALL *Chr. in Arm.* iii. §3 (1669) 252/2 No stop nor halt in their way, but ever putting on. **1746** in G. Sheldon *Hist. Deerfield, Mass.* (1895) I. 548, I came up with Othniel Taylor, on horseback, and ordered him to put on faster. **1811** W. TAYLOR in *Monthly Mag.* XXXI. 447 If she walks, put on; if she puts on, run.

j. *trans.* To push forward (the hands of a clock, the time) so as to make it appear later. Also in fig. allusion.

1865 G. MEREDITH *Rhoda Fleming* xl, My belief, sir, is the clerks at Mortimer and Pennycuick's put on the time. **1885** C. H. EDEN *G. Donnington* i, Heigh-oh, I wish some good fairy would put the clock on. **1891** F. W. ROBINSON *Her Love & His Life* v. i, We can afford to put on the hands of the clock a few more weeks.

*** **k.** To bring into action or operation; to cause to act; to apply; to exert. With various objects, as a screw, brake, or other part of mechanism; steam, gas; force, pressure; pace, speed, etc.; often implying increase of force or velocity. Also in fig. applications: see PRESSURE *sb.*, SCREW, STEAM, etc.

1748 RICHARDSON *Clarissa* (1811) VIII. xlii. 171 When we were within five miles of Harlowe-place, I put on a hand gallop. **1863** W. C. BALDWIN *Afr. Hunting* vii. 238 They [giraffes] do not put on the steam until you get within about sixty [yards of them]. **1867** *Gd. Words* 68/2 Now and then he even put on 'a spurt', as rowers say. **1889** G. ALLEN *Tents of Shem* III. xxxviii. 62 The driver put on the brake quick and hard. **1889** J. MASTERMAN *Scotts of Bestminster* vii, Ann would soon make me bankrupt if I didn't put on the screw occasionally. **1894** BLACKMORE *Perlycross* xvii, He put on a fine turn of speed, and rang the bell. **1897** [see PRESSURE *sb.* 7].

l. (*a*) To set or appoint (a person) to some work or occupation, or to do something; in *Cricket*, to set (a person) on to bowl; to set or appoint (a train, steamer, etc.) to make regular journeys or voyages; to lay (a hound) on the scent.

1836 *New Sporting Mag.* XI. 360 Mr. Paterson's bowling was again very reasonably put on. **1859** *All Year Round* I. 306/1 They put on bowler after bowler, .. but they could not get us out. **1867** TROLLOPE *Chron. Barset* (1869) II. xxx. 354 They say he's not very good at talking English, but put him on in Greek and he never stops. **1889** F. PIGOT *Strangest Journ. my Life* 142 He put on good masters in subjects of which he only had a smattering himself. **1890** *Graphic* 11 Oct. 410/1 The Pacific Railway are putting on a line of powerful vessels to the East. **1891** *Standard* 12 Mar. 3/3 It was only when the day was well advanced that men were put on to clean it up. **1897** 'TIVOLI' (H. W. Bleakley) *Short Innings* vi. 95 'I can't bowl slows', expostulated Tuckett. 'Then put someone else on', returned the inexorable senior.

(*b*) In slang phr. *to put it on* (a person), to charge to (someone else).

1895 *People* 6 Jan. 16/5 Arter all the brass .. was nearly all gone, Selby says, 'I'll go round to the Mug agin, and put it on him (make him pay) for another bit.' **1944** L. GLASSOP *We were Rats* i. 6 I'll have a pint at the Royal tomorrer and put it on the blonde.

(*c*) *colloq.* To draw the attention of or introduce (a person) *to* a particular person or thing.

1895 *N.Y. Dramatic News* 12 Oct. 5/3 Mr. Jack is always a newspaper man's friend, and only too pleased to put one on 'to a good thing' in the shape of news. **1901** O. WISTER in *Lippincott's Monthly Mag.* Aug. 199 We're awfully obliged for the way you are putting us on to this. **1902** H. G. WELLS *Let.* 2 Sept. in H. Wilson *Arnold Bennett & H. G. Wells* (1960) 83 Accept I pray you my warmest thanks. And also for putting me on to that quite brilliantly done and (as Dr. Robⁿ Nicoll would say) most unpleasant book, *Le Journal d'une Femme de Chambre.* **1924** A. CHRISTIE *Poirot Investigates* vii. 165 A friend of mine in the City put me on to a very good thing, and .. I have money to burn. **1926** H. J. LASKI *Let.* 21 Feb. in *Holmes-Laski Lett.* (1953) II. 833 He also put me on to a new American life of Godwin. **1949** A. CHRISTIE *Crooked House* xii. 93, I could put you on to a couple of the tame psychiatrists who do jobs for us. **1977** C. MCCARRY *Secret Lovers* iii. 33 He put us on to some people who turned out to be .. useful.

48. put out. (Cf. OUT-PUT *v.*)

* **a.** See simple senses and OUT *adv.* 1–6.

1530 PALSGR. 675/2, I wene he be deed, he putteth out no breathe. **1693** LYDE *Retaking 'Friends Adventure'* 4 He .. then put out French Colours and fired a Gun, whereby we knew he was a Frenchman. **1831** FR. A. KEMBLE *Jrnl.* in *Rec. Girlhood* (1878) III. 68 Having put out my dresses for my favourite Portia for to-night. **1879** 'CAVENDISH' *Card Ess., Clay's Decis.*, etc. 69 He put out four cards and took in the stock.

b. (*a*) To thrust, drive, or send out of a place; to expel, eject, turn out; †to discharge (*obs.*).

a **1300** *Cursor M.* 943 (Cott.) He put him oute .. Vnto þe werld þar he was made. **1388** WYCLIF *Matt.* ix. 25 Whanne the folc was put out, he wente in, and helde hir hond. *c* **1400** *Lanfranc's Cirurg.* II. vii. 169 To helpe putte out þe fecis & wijnd & vrine. **1483** *Cath. Angl.* 295/2 To Putte oute, *depellere.* **1526** TINDALE *Mark* v. 40 Then he put them all out .. and entred in. **1875** JOWETT *Plato* (ed. 2) I. 132 He is .. put out by the constables.

(*b*) To destroy the sight of, to blind (an eye), either by literally gouging it out, or by burning or other means. (See OUT *adv.* 4.) Also *fig.*

11 .. [see A. III]. *a* **1300** *Cursor M.* 21451 (Cott.) His eien first put vte i sal. **1485** CAXTON *Chas. Gt.* 194, I shal .. also put out thyn eyen. **1595** SHAKS. *John* IV. i. 56 Will you put out mine eyes? .. *Hub.* I haue sworne to do it: And with hot Irons must I burne them out. **1671** MILTON *Samson* 33 Betray'd, Captiv'd, and both my Eyes put out. **1937** C. CARMER *Hurricane's Children* 105 He wore waistcoats that would put your eyes out.

†(*c*) To expel, dismiss, put away. *Obs.*

c **1380** WYCLIF *Sel. Wks.* II. 129 By þis word he puttide out slouþe, whanne he preiede his God. **1502** *Ord. Crysten Men* (W. de W. 1506) I. iii. C vj, Hym [the man chylde] lyketh to put out all thy fraudes and decepcyons.

(*d*) To put out of joint; to dislocate. (OUT *adv.* 19.)

1780 J. WOODFORDE *Diary* 15 July (1924) I. 289 John had a fall lately .. and put out his shoulder bone, being a little merry. *c* **1820** MRS. SHERWOOD *Penny Tract* 8 (Houlston's Juv. Tr.) Francis .. had the misfortune to put out his ancle. **1890** *Blackw. Mag.* CXLVIII. 567/2 He put out his shoulder in one of the most dangerous deadlocks.

c. To remove or turn out of office, dignity, possession, etc.; to depose, dismiss. (See OUT *adv.* 4 b.) Now *rare* or *arch.*, exc. in sense 'to put out of play', in games, athletic contests, or the like; *esp.* in *Cricket*, to cause (a batsman) to be 'out' (OUT *adv.* 4 c, 19 c); in *Baseball*, to cause (a batter or runner) to be 'out'; in *Boxing*, to knock out.

1387 TREVISA *Higden* (Rolls) II. 403 Pelias .. dredde lest Iason .. wolde werre in his londes and putte hym out. *c* **1420** *Brut* 345 He deposid & put out the Mayre of London. **1530** PALSGR. 675/1 He was baylyffe of the towne, but the lorde hath put hym out. **1694** EVELYN *Diary* 22 Nov., The same day .. that Abp. Sancroft was put out. **1735** in Waghorn *Cricket Scores* (1899) 9 Upon London's second innings four of them were put out before they headed the county. **1744** J. LOVE *Cricket* III. (1754) Argt., Bryan is put out by Kips. **1818** CRUISE *Digest* (ed. 2) II. 77 If a man puts out his lessee for years, or disseises his lessee for life. **1845** in *Appleton's Ann. Cycl.* XXV. 77/2 A runner can not be put out in making one base, when a balk is made by the pitcher. **1890** *Field* 24 May 776/2 Although nearly put out .. in the fifth round, his steady shooting eventually enabled him to win. **1890** *St. Nicholas Mag.* Aug. 830/2 So easily fielded as to result in putting out the batsman. **1910** J. DRISCOLL *Ringcraft* iii. 84, I have .. not infrequently put opponents 'out' with a blow on the neck. **1912** C. MATHEWSON *Pitching in a Pinch* 107 Snodgrass was put out trying to get to third base.

d. To extinguish, do away with, put an end to, destroy, abolish. Now only in slang use, to kill (a person). (Perh. a *fig.* use of sense e (*b*).)

1398 TREVISA *Barth. De P.R.* XVIII. xxiii. (Bodl. MS.), His [goottes] galle putteþ oute dymnes of yȝen. **1580** SIDNEY *Ps.* IX. iii, Their renoune .. Thou dost put out. *c* **1650** FULLER *Life H. Smith* S.'s Wks. 1866 I. 7 Those who .. bury their talents in the ground, putting them out, because they will not put them out, extinguishing their abilities because they will not employ them. **1826** SOUTHEY *Vind. Eccl. Angl.* 180 An odour which put out the former perfume. **1890** *Field* 24 May 776/3 A sharp left-hander put out Mr. Ellis's chance. **1917** W. OWEN *Let.* 25 Apr. (1967) 452 For twelve days we lay in holes, where at any moment a shell might put us out. **1935** E. WALLACE *Mouthpiece* xvii. 225 That's the offer the gentleman made—five hundred quid to put you out and keep me mouth shut. **1975** 'E. LATHEN' *By Hook or by Crook* xii. 114 The minute his stomach started acting up, he would've been yelling for the cops. He had to be put out fast.

e. †(*a*) To strike out or delete (a writing, drawing, etc.); to expunge, erase, efface. *Obs.*

1530 PALSGR. 675/1 There was a writynge upon his grave, but the weather hath put it out. *Ibid.*, Here was a horse properly paynted, but all his heed is put out. **1535** COVERDALE *Ps.* l[i]. 9 Turne thy face fro my synnes, and put out all my myszdedes. **1568** GRAFTON *Chron.* II. 103 He sent to the foure Bishops agaıne, that they should put out that poynt of restitution. **1610** WILLET *Hexapla Dan.* 356 When he portraiteth the picture he putteth out the first lines [= outlines]. *a* **1708** BEVERIDGE *Thes. Theol.* (1710) II. 312 The Constantinopolitan Bishops put *a patre* into the Creed, the Western Churches *filioque* ..; Leo III put it out, and Nicolaus put it in again, and so arose the schism.

(*b*) To extinguish (fire or light, or a burning or luminous body). (See OUT *adv.* 6, 22 a.)

1526 *Pilgr. Perf.* (W. de W. 1531) 40 No wynde ne rayne coude quenche it ne put it out. **1530** PALSGR. 675/1 Rake up the fyre and put out the candell. **1671** GREW *Anat. Plants* Ep. Ded., It is your Glory, that you like not so to shine, as to put out the least Star. **1709** STEELE *Tatler* No. 58 ¶1 All my idle Flames are extinguish'd, as you may observe, ordinary Fires are often put out by the Sunshine. **1846** *Jrnl. R. Agric. Soc.* VII. II. 546 Water was used to put the fire out. **1889** AD. SERGEANT *Esther Denison* I. x, A draught from the door put out the candles.

f. (With person as obj.) (OUT *adv.* 5, 20.) †(*a*) To baffle, foil, defeat. *Obs. rare.*

1485 CAXTON *Chas. Gt.* 218 He beyng put out alle fro hys purpose, toke leue of the kyng.

(*b*) To cause to lose one's self-possession; to disconcert, discompose, confuse, embarrass.

1588 SHAKS. *L.L.L.* V. ii. 102 Euer and anon they made a doubt, Presence maiesticall would put him out. **1834** J. H. NEWMAN *Let. to R. F. Wilson* 15 June, You must not be at all surprised or put out at feeling the difficulties you describe. *a* **1849** POE *Diddling* Wks. 1864 IV. 268 He is never seduced into a flurry. He is never put out. **1886** MRS. C. PRAED *Miss Jacobsen* II. xiii. 203 You are so cool and composed, and nothing puts you out.

(*c*) To disconcert, disturb, or 'upset' (any one) in the course of his action, speech, calculation, etc.; to interrupt or distract (an actor, orator, reciter, musician, or performer), so as to cause him to lose the 'thread' of his subject: see OUT *adv.* 5, 20.

1673 WYCHERLEY *Gentl. Dancing-Master* IV. i, My aunt is here, and she will put me out: you know I cannot dance before her. **1831** FR. A. KEMBLE *Jrnl.* in *Rec. Girlhood* (1878) III. 53 They put us out terribly in one scene by forgetting the bench on which I have to sit down. **1890** *Sat. Rev.* 9 Aug. 165/1 The bill-brokers .. are therefore put out in their calculations. *Mod.* I had learned my speech carefully, but she put me out by giggling.

(*d*) To cause to lose one's equanimity; to distress, 'upset' (mentally); in mod. use, to put out of temper, annoy, irritate, vex.

1822 LAMB *Let. to Wordsworth* 20 Mar., Deaths overset one, and put one out long after the recent grief. **1861** HUGHES *Tom Brown at Oxf.* xxvi, He was a little put out for a moment, but then recovered himself. **1871** MRS. H. WOOD *Dene Hollow* xxx, Sir Dene [was] .. thoroughly put out with the captain. **1876** DORAN *'Mann' & Manners* I. Introd. 10 Mr. Fane was a very particular person, and was very easily put out.

(*e*) To put any one out of his way; to put to inconvenience.

1861 T. HUGHES *Tom Brown at Oxford* III. xvi. 290 Don't you lose heart because he won't put himself out for you. **1880** J. PAYN *Confid. Agent* I. 154 Stephen .. was not the man to 'put himself out'— that is to say, to make the least sacrifice of independence.

** **g.** (*a*) †To utter, pronounce, give forth (words, the voice). *Obs.* (*b*) To vent (in words, etc.). *rare.*

c **1340** *E.E. Psalter* xliv[v.] 1 Myn hert put out gode worde. **1486** *Bk. St. Albans* e v b, The first woorde to the houndis that the hunt shall owt pit Is at the kenell doore when he openys it. **1888** S. TYTLER *Blackhall Ghosts* II. xix. 120 All his anger was put out on poor me.

h. To put in exercise, exert; = *put forth*, 43 e.

1483 *Cath. Angl.* 295/2 To Putt out voce or strenght. **1592** SHAKS. *Rom. & Jul.* IV. v. 124 Pray you put vp your Dagger, and put out your wit. **1659** GUTHRIE *Chr. Gt. Interest* II. iv. (1724) 171 Unless a Man .. put out Faith in Christ Jesus .. he cannot be saved. **1856** *Titan Mag.* July 4/1 I'm not putting out my strength. **1890** *Temple Bar Mag.* July 302 When she puts herself out to please.

i. To publish, issue, put in circulation; = *put forth*, 43 f. Also, to broadcast.

1529 MORE *Dyaloge* III. Wks. 223/1 Tyndal hath put out in hys own name another booke entitled Mammona. **1621** BURTON *Anat. Mel.* II. ii. IV. (1651) 280 To peruse those books of Cities, put out by Braunus, and Hogenbergius. **1697** C. LESLIE *Snake in Grass* (ed. 2) 141 There is a Primmer put out for the Quaker Children, by W. Smith. **1702** ADDISON *Dial. Medals* iii. Misc. Wks. 1736 III. 163 He put out a Coin, that on the reverse of it had a ship tossed on the waves to represent the Church. **1709** HEARNE *Collect.* (O.H.S.) II. 279 To put out a new Edition. **1879** MISS YONGE *Cameos* Ser. IV. xiv. 150 Injunctions were put out this winter .. against carrying candles on Candlemas Day. **1938** H. NICOLSON *Diary* 20 Feb. (1966) 323 On the late news it is put out that Eden has resigned. **1965** G. MELLY *Owning Up* xi. 135 His version of 'Rock Island Line' .. was put out as a single and rose to be top of the Hit Parade. **1966** *Listener* 13 Jan. 78/1 Earlier this year Midland Region and Anne Owen put out .. an unusually direct and perceptive investigation of present-day standards of honesty. **1978** *Times* 26 July 4/2 The BBC says that whatever it films and tapes it is entitled to put out.

j. (*a*) *Naut.* To send or take (a vessel) out to sea. *rare.* (*b*) *intr.* To go out to sea; to set out on a voyage. (Said of a vessel, or person.) (*c*) *intr.* To depart, make off, go away; to set out. (Chiefly *U.S.*) (= *put off*, 46 n.)

1590 SHAKS. *Com. Err.* III. ii. 190 If any ship put out, then straight away. **1610** —— *Temp.* V. i. 225 As when We first put out to Sea. **1814** CARY *Dante, Paradise* II. 14 Through the deep brine ye fearless may put out Your vessel. **1835** *Niles' Reg.* 22 Aug. 436 Apprehending judge Lynch's law, he put out in a hurry. He was pursued and caught. **1842** MACAULAY *Lays, Armada* 11 Many a light fishing boat put out to pry along the coast. **1856** G. D. BREWERTON *War in Kansas* 42 We 'put out' in search of fire and a shelter. **1889** TENNYSON *Crossing the Bar* i, And may there be no moaning of the bar, When I put out to sea.

k. (*a*) To stretch forth, extend, protrude (the hand or other member of the body); to extend from within an enclosing space; to cause to stick out or project; to display, exhibit, hang out (also *fig.*).

1535 COVERDALE *Gen.* xxxviii. 28 The one put out his hande. **1585** T. WASHINGTON tr. *Nicholay's Voy.* II. xi. 46 b, The port, at the entring wherof were put out all the flags .. of our gallies. **1607** SHAKS. *Timon* IV. ii. 28 Let each take some: Nay put out all your hands. **1687** A. LOVELL tr. *Thevenot's Trav.* I. 14 When he had put out the Colours of St. Mark, we shewed ours. **1889** F. M. CRAWFORD *Greifenstein* I. vii. 203 Putting out his hand to prevent the act. **1905** —— *Soprano* v, As if he were going to feel her pulse, and tell her to put out her tongue.

(*b*) *intr.* Of a river or natural formation: to extend or stretch (in relation to a specified point). *U.S.* See also sense 8 c.

1755 *N. Jersey Archives* XIX. 532 One Mile from Shrewsbury River, and about three Quarters of a Mile from a good Landing that puts out of said River. **1840** C. F. HOFFMAN *Greyslaer* I. 116 A ledge of bald rock to the left yonder .. puts out from the ridge. **1878** J. H. BEADLE *Western Wilds* 311 Commenced the ascent of the Buckskin, a low range of partially-wooded hills, putting out across the plateau nearly to the Colorado.

l. = *put forth*, 43 g. Also *absol.* Now *rare.*

1626 BACON *Sylva* §653 They forsake their first root, and put out another more towards the top of the earth. **1688** BURNET *Lett. St. Italy* 138 The Trees had not yet put out their Leaves. **1737** BRACKEN *Farriery Impr.* (1756) I. 259 If the Sore seem to put out fungous or spungy Flesh. **1856** *Titan Mag.* Aug. 161/2 Roses .. too sickly to put out their flowers.

absol. **1807** P. GASS *Jrnl.* 227 The grass and plants here are just putting out.

m. (*a*) To place (a person) away from home under the care of some one, or in some employment; to turn out (a beast) to graze or feed; to plant out (seedlings, young plants); to send out (a domestic pet) for exercise, etc.

1602 MARSTON *Antonio's Rev.* IV. iv, As some weake breasted dame Giveth her infant, puts it out to nurse. **1639** *Rec. Dedham, Mass.* (1892) III. 65 Every Swyne that shalbe put out at liberty shalbe well and sufficiently Ringed. **1778** *Eng. Gazetteer* (ed. 2) s.v. *Bromsgrove*, A charity school for teaching, cloathing, and putting out 12 boys apprentices. **1851** MRS. GASKELL *Let.* 7 Apr. (1966) 149 We are sowing very few annuals this year .. & relying on putting out the greenhouse things for a summer show. **1852** *Jrnl. R. Agric. Soc.* XIII. I. 25 In the morning she [cow] was put out to grass. **1869** W. LONGMAN *Hist. Edw. III*, I. xix. 343 Their children were often put out to wet nurse with the native Irish. **1892** *Field* 17 Sept. 442/2 To raise plants from seed, and .. [have] a vigorous healthy stock to put out annually. **1917** D. CANFIELD *Understood Betsy* ii. 46 'Mother, did you put Shep out?' **1925** WODEHOUSE *Carry On, Jeeves!* ii. 40 When he has put the cat out and locked up the office for the night, he just relapses into a state of coma. **1974** *Listener* 10 Oct. 462/1 The BBC's nightly *Campaign Report* .. at an hour when most voters are putting the cat out. **1977** 'E. CRISPIN' *Glimpses of Moon* viii. 128, I was snug in bed ... And then .. I remembered .. that I ought to have put Sal out ... She barks rather a lot.

(*b*) To lend (money) at interest, or lay it out to profit; to invest; also *fig.* to employ to advantage. Also (*U.S.*), To expend, lay out.

1611 BIBLE *Ps.* xv. 5 He that putteth not out his money to vsury. **1616** B. JONSON *Devil an Ass* III. iv, With purpose, yet, to put him out I hope To his best vse? *c* **1650** [see d].

1690 E. GEE *Jesuit's Mem.* 230 The said Dowry.. is put out to Rent, and assurance given for it. **1781** D. WILLIAMS tr. *Voltaire's Dram. Wks.* II. 248 Employing it to do good is to put it out to the highest interest. **1884** *Boston* (Mass.) *Jrnl.* 13 Sept., If the opposing candidate did not have a rich father-in-law, who will put out money freely. **1893** *Nat. Observ.* 5 Aug. 290/1 The pound was put out to multiply itself.

(*c*) To give (work) to be done off the premises, or by some one not in one's regular employment. Also, to place (articles) for collection by tradesmen.

1653 R. VERNEY *Let.* in M. M. Verney *Mem.* (1894) III. iv. 112, I will keepe but one woeman kind, who must wash my small Linnen (bed & board linnen shall bee put out). **1680** MOXON *Mech. Exerc.* xiii. 226 Being.. unaccommodated of a Lathe of my own, I intended to put them out to be Turned. **1834** *New Monthly Mag.* XLII. 117 The farmer has availed himself of the power.. to put out, as it is termed, the reaping of his wheat. **1846** *Jrnl. R. Agric. Soc.* VII. I. 124 To let or put out the job at a certain rate per acre. **1873** A. J. MUNBY *Diary* 18 Feb. in D. Hudson *Munby* (1972) 322, I should like very well to clean his boots.. and I said to Tarrant 'If you put 'em out I'll clean 'em with pleasure, along with mine.' **1884** MRS. G. L. BANKS *Sybilla*, etc. III. 49 Mrs. Price did not put out her washing. *a* **1909** *Mod.* All work is done on the premises; nothing put out. **1975** 'D. JORDAN' *Black Account* v. 33 It was late; Sue was in her kimono and putting out milk bottles.

n. *intr.* Of a woman: to offer oneself for sexual intercourse. Also const. *for* (a man). *slang.*

1947 *Horizon* Sept. 202 'Maybe all the whores'll be puttin' out free on New Year's!' Muggleston shouted. **1961** J. HELLER *Catch-22* xiii. 131 The beautiful.. countess and her beautiful.. daughter-in-law, both of whom would put out only for Nately, who was too shy to want them, and for Aarfy, who was too stuffy to take them and tried to dissuade them from ever putting out for anyone but their husbands. **1975** D. LODGE *Changing Places* vi. 232 If she won't put out the men will accuse her of being bourgeois and uptight. **1977** I. SHAW *Beggarman, Thief* III. i. 178 Sometimes those plain-looking little dolls are powerhouses when it comes to putting out. **1978** M. PUZO *Fools Die* vi. 80 He was especially challenged if a girl had a reputation for only putting out for guys she really liked.

49. put out of. (See OUT OF *sb.*)

a. *trans.* To remove or expel from (a place, or a status conceived as a place). *Obs.* or *arch.*

a **1300** *Cursor M.* 3047 (Cott.) Oute of þe hus was pute agar, Hir sun a-pon hir bak sco bar. *c* **1380** WYCLIF *Sel. Wks.* III. 361 þei puttiden men out of chirche, and persueden hem in Cristis tyme. **1483** CAXTON *G. de la Tour* F vij b, God.. made her to become lepre in soo moche that she was put oute of the town. **1530** PALSGR. 675/2 And I were as you, I wolde put my selfe out of the waye for a whyle. **1611** BIBLE *John* xvi. 2 They shall put you out of the Synagogues. **1768** STERNE *Sent. Journ.*, *Remise Door* iii, It will oblige you to have a third horse, which will put twenty livres out of your pocket. **1779** G. KEATE *Sk. Nat.* (ed. 2) II. 92 The new India silk handkerchief.. which.. he had forgot to put out of his pocket.

†**b.** To expel or dismiss from the possession or occupation of property, office, etc.; to do out of. *Obs.*

a **1300** *Cursor M.* 7340 þai wit-in a tuel-moth stage War put vte o þair heritage. **13..** *Seuyn Sag.* (W.) 1206 Thai sschal.. Put the out of thi kinges sete. **1442** *Rolls of Parlt.* V. 45/1 Robbed.. and put oute of his lande and godys. **1526** TINDALE *Luke* xvi. 4 When I am put out of my stewardshippe. **1530** PALSGR. 675/2 All the crewe that was at Guynes is put out of wages. **1678** WANLEY *Wond. Lit. World* v. i. §102. 468/2 The King.. of Bohemia.. is proscribed and put out of his Electorship. *a* **1715** BURNET *Own Time* an. 1679 (1823) II. 232[The Duke of York] moved that the duke of Monmouth should be put out of all command.

c. To expel from one's thoughts, memory, etc.

a **1225** *Ancr. R.* 92 þet heo pute euerich worldlich þing.. ut of hire heorte. *c* **1374** CHAUCER *Boeth.* I. pr. vi. 15 (Camb. MS.) Thou.. by-weptest þat oonly men weren put owt of the cure of god. **1470–85** MALORY *Arthur* x. xxvii. 457 He putte all that oute of his thoughte. **1535** [see REMEMBRANCE 1]. *a* **1548** HALL *Chron.*, *Rich. III* 29 b, To obliterate and put oute of memorie that note of infamie. **1816** [see HEAD *sb.*[1] 59].

d. To remove, liberate, or extricate from a condition of.

to put out of misery or ***pain*** (euphem.), to dispatch or kill a wounded or suffering person or animal; also, to put an end to a state of mental suspense (by an unfavourable decision), to let one know the worst.

c **1480** *Pol. Poems* (Rolls) II. 287 To be put owt of dystress. *a* **1533** LD. BERNERS *Huon* xlvi. 154 His grete youthe put hym out of his sorow. **1792** J. WOODFORDE *Diary* 16 May (1927) III. 351 My poor old Horse, Punch.. was shot by Ben this Morning to put him out of his Misery. **1855** C. KINGSLEY *Westward Ho!* III. xii. 353 Writhing in his great horror, he called to Cary to kill him and put him out of his misery. **1911** *Maclean's Mag.* Oct. 286/1 Get the gun, for God's sake, an' put me out of my misery. **1923** G. ATHERTON *Black Oxen* xxvi. 145 Tell them all about it... Put them out of their misery. **1957** D. ROBINS *Noble One* v. 59 Then I'll *have* to stalk him and put him out of his misery. **1975** A. CHRISTIE *Curtain* xi. 113 We were talking of euthanasia... 'Does the person most concerned ever wish to 'put himself out of his misery', as we say?'

e. To remove from the region or sphere of; to cause to be out of the condition of.

to put out of joint: see JOINT *sb.* 2.

1530 PALSGR. 675/2 To put you out of doute it is so in dede. **1560** DAUS tr. *Sleidane's Comm.* 235 To put the matter out of doubt. *a* **1586** [see JOINT *sb.* 2]. **1659–60** PEPYS *Diary* 9 Mar., I made a promise.. to drink no strong drink this week, for I find that it puts me quite out of order. **1686** [see PATIENCE *sb.* 1 f]. **1742** H. WALPOLE *Let. to Mann* 10 Mar., I will not work you up into a fright, only to have the pleasure of putting you out of it. **1855** MACAULAY *Hist. Eng.* xvi. III. 685 The English Commons had sometimes put him out of temper. **1884** *Manch. Exam.* 15 May 5/4 The opposition of the Board of Trade.. put that out of the question.

50. put over.

a. *trans. Falconry.* Of a hawk: To pass (the food) on from the 'gorge' or crop to the stomach; to swallow. Also *transf.* and *fig.* ? *Obs.*

1486 *Bk. St. Albans* a vij, An hawke puttith ouer when she remeuith the mete from hir goorge in to hir bowillis. **1575** TURBERV. *Falconrie* 332 Sometimes.. a hawke cannot well indew nor put over his meate. *a* **1656** BP. HALL *Sel. Th.* §66 Death did but taste of Him, could not devour him, much less put him over. [**1880** *Jamieson's Sc. Dict.* s.v., Tak some milk to put owre your bite.]

b. To defer, postpone: = *put off*, 46 c. (Cf. *carry over*, *hold over*.)

1528 HEN. VIII in Burnet *Hist. Ref.* II. Rec. xix, [If you] do thus delay, protract and put over the accomplishment of the Kings so instant desire. **1618** HALES *Gold. Rem.* II. (1673) 16 Both these questions were put over to the next Session. **1655** *Nicholas Papers* (Camden) II. 210, I heard last weeke the day was putt over till Wensday last. **1828** WEBSTER, *To put over*.. (2) To defer; to postpone. The court put over the cause to the next term. **1871** 'MARK TWAIN' *Lett. to Publishers* (1967) 55 If you can without fail issue the book on the 15th of May—putting the Sketch book over till another time. **1926** J. BLACK *You can't Win* xxii. 343 We went to court again the next day, but were put over twenty-four hours on the plea of the police that witnesses were on their way from Canada. **1978** H. KEMELMAN *Thursday the Rabbi walked Out* (1979) xxx. 145 The only thing to do is to put it over for a week.

c. To get over; *esp.* to get through (time); *absol.*, to get over the time, 'get along'. Now *dial.*

1593 *Pass. Morrice* (1876) 79 Which bad beginning was carelesly put ouer with the conceiued ioy of his presence. **1679** BURNET *Hist. Ref.* (1865) I. 541 To engage him in discourse, and so put over the time. **1823** J. WILSON *Trials Marg. Lyndsay* iv. 11/2 The stranger offered.. money; but she.. said they could all put over very well till their father was set free. **1851** CARLYLE *Sterling* II. iv. (1872) 118 There.. he might put over the rigorous period of this present year.

d. To convey or take across or to the other side; to transport: see OVER *adv.* 5.

c **1595** CAPT. WYATT *R. Dudley's Voy. W. Ind.* (Hakl. Soc.) 36 To give them a faire gale to putt them over to the maine. **1610** HOLLAND *Camden's Brit.* (1637) 49 By swimming they put the horses over. **1890** CLARK RUSSELL *Ocean Trag.* II. xvi. 71 The helm was put over and the yacht's head fell off.

e. *intr. Naut.* To sail or go across, to cross.

1617 ABP. ABBOT *Descr. World* (1634) 283 Carthagena, a City in the maineland, to which he put over. *a* **1656** USSHER *Ann.* vi. (1658) 391 He put over from thence to Phocaea.

†**f.** *trans.* To hand over, to refer. *Obs. rare.*

1595 SHAKS. *K. John* I. i. 62 For the certaine knowledge of that truth, I put you o're to heauen, and to my mother.

†**g.** To transfer, make over. *Obs.*

a **1641** BP. MOUNTAGU *Acts & Mon.* vii. (1642) 432 To put over their wealth and possession unto their friends. *a* **1649** WINTHROP *New Eng.* (1825) I. 381 It were good he.. paid his sister her £100 which he promised when I put over his land to him.

h. To knock over (with a shot). *colloq.*

1859 H. KINGSLEY *G. Hamlyn* xxxvii, That pistol.. I've put over a parrot at twenty yards with it.

i. ***to put it (all) over (on)***, to excel or surpass (in a particular enterprise); to defeat or trounce.

1898 F. P. DUNNE *Mr. Dooley in Peace & War* (1899) 172 I've seen.. Fitz beat Corbett; an', if I live to cillybrate me goold-watch-an'-chain jubilee, I may see some wan put it all over Fitz. **1905** J. LONDON *Let.* 24 June (1966) 175 If Hillquit.. didn't put it all over Bierce—I'll quit thinking at all. **1944** *Living off Land* viii. 155 So far as bushcraft is concerned, he [*sc.* the Aboriginal] could put it all over you. **1973** *Time Out* 2 Mar. 15/2 The teachers.. only had time for the Thomas boys; we were treated like shit. So we started throwing our weight around, we put it over on them.

j. To make acceptable or effective; to convey or communicate; to present convincingly; = *to put across* (sense 36 b above).

1912 R. A. FOLEY in *Mag. Maker* Dec. 8 He saw his opportunity and he 'put it over'. **1914** G. ATHERTON *Perch of Devil* II. 298 You don't go into any business.. and put it over without running the risk of being shot. **1928** *Daily Express* 18 Apr. 11/2 Is it true that you wanted a star name to put the play over? *Ibid.* 11 July 9/3 On the screen you.. are fascinated by the extraordinary way in which he 'puts himself over'. **1929** J. B. PRIESTLEY *Good Companions* II. i. 252 He's a find. Works hard, got personality, puts it over all the time. **1931** F. L. ALLEN *Only Yesterday* viii. 213 The president emeritus of Harvard had had no professional talent to put over his funeral in a big way. **1935** *Motion Picture* Nov. 6/2 Clark Gable plays one of those powerful, he-men rôles in which he glories. And he puts it over with a bang! **1958** *Times* 1 Sept. 3/6 About Mr. Presley's ability to 'put over' a song in his own particular way there can be no two opinions. **1966** *Listener* 17 Mar. 380/2, I did not know how to select what I wanted to do or really put over emotion. **1978** D. MURPHY *Place Apart* iii. 59 They blamed 'that Paisley'... They agreed with his anti-ecumenism.. but they didn't like the way he put it over.

k. To impose (something false or deceptive) *on* a person; to best or upstage (someone); to achieve by deceit.

1912 J. SANDILANDS *Western Canad. Dict.*, *Put one over on* him, catching him with the latest puzzling by-word or smart saying... A Winnipeg newspaper recently put up the heading, 'Put one over on Bernard Shaw'. **1914** 'HIGH JINKS, JR.' *Choice Slang* 17 *Put one over, to*: to beat by strategy, 'to hornswoggle'. **1916** H. L. WILSON *Somewhere in Red Gap* i. 19 Funny, the way the little man tried to put it over on us, letting on he was just puzzled—not really bothered, as he plainly was. **1923** R. D. PAINE *Comrades of Rolling Ocean* viii. 130 Who calls it a crime to put one over on the Custom House flatties? **1928** A. S. W. ROSENBACH *Books & Bidders* 117 One of the greatest hoaxes ever planned was put over by a French forger. **1945** C. WILLIAMS *All Hallows' Eve* 35 A fellow who's put it over all America and bits of England is likely to know where he is. **1958** *People* 4 May 8/3, I cannot see her letting any of the Italian or French sex-pots put one over on her. **1967** *Listener* 5 Jan. 37/1 Christmas, after all, is essentially an 'old' festival (however much Batman may seem to have put one over on Santa Claus this year). **1972** WODEHOUSE *Pearls, Girls, & Monty Bodkin* x. 150 It's low. It isn't done. You can't do the dirty on a business competitor just to stop him from putting it over on you in a business deal. **1976** *Church Times* 30 July 7/2 She may have been fleeced in Florence, robbed in Ravenna, grossly overcharged in Ostia..; but *Baedeker* at least has not tried to put one over on her. **1979** *Jrnl. R. Soc. Arts* CXXVII. 650/1 We are not appearing to put something over on the public.

l. *Baseball.* = *put across* (sense 36 c above).

1936, **1943** [see sense 36 c above].

51. put there.

In imp. phr. ***put it*** (or ***her***, etc.) ***there***: shake hands! *colloq.* (orig. *U.S.*).

1898 R. HUGHES *Lakerim Athletic Club* i. 3 'Put her there, Punk; you're a white man!' Tug had to exclaim; and the two captains shook hands. **1915** A. CONAN DOYLE *Valley of Fear* II. i. 154 'Put it there,' he said. A hand-grip passed between the two. **1925** *New Yorker* 20 June 14/1 Well, I'll be damned. Glad ta see ya. Put it there. **1931** O. NASH *Hard Lines* 50 Put it there, Mr. Linthicum, put it there! **1947** WODEHOUSE *Full Moon* vii. 168 'I'm engaged!'... 'Well, I'm dashed,' said Freddie. 'Put it there, pardner.' So beaming was his smile, so cordial his handshake, that Tipton found his last doubts removed. **1970** *Private Eye* 13 Mar. 16 Glad to meetcha! Put it there!

52. put through.

†**a.** *trans.* (?) To get through, traverse, penetrate, cross. (Cf. 3.)

1708 J. C. *Compl. Collier* (1845) 21 Quick-Sands (if not to thick) are often put through by Deals or Timber.

b. To cause to pass through any process; to carry (successfully) through; to carry out, bring to a finish; to get done with. orig. *U.S.*

1852 MRS. STOWE *Uncle Tom's C.* xxxi, I rayther think she's sickly, but I shall put her through for what she's worth. She may last a year or two. **1888** BRYCE *Amer. Commw.* II. II. xliv. 163 Becoming accomplices in the jobs or 'steals' which these members were 'putting through'. **1891** *Longm. Mag.* Aug. 379 Taking prompt action.. to 'put through' a certain nefarious design. **1929** T. H. BURNHAM *Engineering Econ.* xv. 199 Rush orders are difficult to put through, even in well-organized works. **1966** 'J. HACKSTON' *Father clears Out* 54 Put through a second lot of tailings, but not from the same place.

c. In literal sense, as To put a telegram or telephonic call through between points; to place a person in telephonic connexion with another through one or more exchanges.

1891 F. C. ALLSOP *Telephones* vi. 98 In an exchange system any of the stations wishing to communicate with any other must first ring up the central station, and request to be 'put through' to the other station. **1916** 'BOYD CABLE' *Action Front* 86 Ask to be put through to the inquiry office. **1928** D. L. SAYERS *Unpleasantness at Bellona Club* viii. 59 That phone-call you asked me to trace.. was put through.. from a public call-box. **1949** A. CHRISTIE *Crooked House* xvii. 139 He lifted the receiver—listened and then said: 'Put her through.' **1973** J. M. WHITE *Garden Game* 182, I found the number and dialled Whitehall... I was put through to the Home Office.

d. *Econ.* (See quot. 1959.)

1959 *Economist* 21 Mar. 1099/1 Where the market is narrow, as it can be for example in rubber and tea shares, the jobbing system may not work either smoothly or perfectly. The brokers in these shares then find it convenient to 'marry' the buying and selling orders. The normal practice has been for such a deal to be 'put through' a jobber at a very small turn for him... The stock exchange council.. has now proposed a change in the rules governing these 'put through' deals. **1978** *Times* 17 Nov. 21/8 The principle of the put-through deal involves the broker finding a buyer for a large line of stock which one of his clients has on offer. The jobber then puts the shares through his books at a mutually agreed price but does not necessarily make such a good turn on it as he would if he was buying them from the broker and selling them on himself.

53. put to.

†**a.** *trans.* To add (actually or mentally). Also *absol.* Cf. 13. *Obs.*

1382 WYCLIF *Matt.* vi. 27 Who of ȝou thenkinge may putte to [Vulg. *adjicere*] to his stature oo cubite? *c* **1460** Ros tr. *Belle Dame sans Mercy* 500, I may not put to, nor take away. **1502** *Ord. Crysten Men* (W. de W. 1506) II. xvi. 124 Besyde the .x. commaundementes of god.. holy chyrche hath put to fyue. **1577** HANMER *Anc. Eccl. Hist.* (1619) 70 Pulling away some things, and putting to other some. **1605** BACON *Adv. Learn.* II. xiii. §7 When he cometh to a particular he shall have nothing to do, but to put to names, and, times, and places.

b. (*a*) To exert, apply, put forth. ***to put to one's hand***: to set to work at something; to render assistance. Now *rare* or *arch.*

1382 WYCLIF *Gen.* xix. 10 The men putten to hoonde, and brouȝten into hem Loth. *c* **1450** *Merlin* iv. 70 Ye must put to grete besynesse to take the Duke. **1588** PARKE tr. *Mendoza's Hist. China* 134 Putting to their diligence and industrie. **1603** KNOLLES *Hist. Turks* (1621) 1115 Where-unto also Clement.. put to his helping hand. **1674** RAY *N.C. Words* 173 That so all Parties concerned may put to their fires at the same time. **1888** BRYCE *Amer. Commw.* III. lxxviii. 33 People think of the government as a great machine which will go on, whether they put their hand to or not.

†(*b*) *intr.* for *refl.*, or *absol.* To go to work, 'set to'. *Obs.*

1611 SHAKS. *Wint. T.* I. ii. 277 [She] deserues a Name As ranke as any Flax-Wench, that puts to Before her troth-plight.

†c. (*a*) *trans.* To attach, affix, 'set to' (as a seal or signature to a document). *Obs.*

1415 HEN. V in Madox *Form. Angl.* (1702) 16 Wee have, to these Vowes afore written, putto our seallᴇs. *c* **1450** *Godstow Reg.* 145 Both partyes maade hit stronge by puttyng to þere seelys, euerych to oþer. **1552–3** *Inv. Ch. Goods, Staffs.* in *Ann. Lichfield* (1863) IV. 2 In wittenes wherof..we..to thes presents interchaungeabli have putto our handes. **1609** BIBLE (Douay) *1 Kings* vii. 36 They semed not to be engraven, but put to round about.

(*b*) To place (a male animal) with a female for breeding. Cf. 10 f. ? *Obs.*

1523 FITZHERB. *Husb.* §37 Euery man maye not put to theyr rammes all at one tyme.

(*c*) To attach (a horse, etc.) to a vehicle (cf. 10 e); *transf.* (an engine) to a train.

1768 STERNE *Sent. Journ., Montriul* iv, I..bid him..get the horses put to. **1815** JANE AUSTEN *Emma* xxvi, You know how impossible my father would deem it that James should put to for such a purpose. **1841** LYTTON *Nt. & Morn.* I. i, Tell the post-boy to put-to the horses immediately. **1862** *Temple Bar Mag.* V. 142 A Scotch engine was being put to at Berwick.

d. To shut. Now *arch.* and *dial.*

c **1440** *Gesta Rom.* xxiii. 82 (Harl. MS.) Anon he put to the dore ayen. **1535** COVERDALE *Judg.* iii. 23 Ehud gat him out at the backe dore, & put to [1611 shut] yᵉ dore after him, and lockte it. **1775** R. CUMBERLAND *Choleric Man* v. iii, I'll put the shutters to. **1828** *Examiner* 588/1 Shut the door and put to the window shutters. **1903** *Eng. Dial. Dict., Put to the door, put the door to.* [Many localities: Scotland to Huntingdon and Devon].

e. *Naut. intr.* To put in to shore; to turn in, take shelter.

1797 F. BAILY *Jrnl. Tour N. Amer.* (1856) 195 We pushed off..and after going about twenty miles, were obliged to put-to on account of the wind. **1807** P. GASS *Jrnl.* 163 We put to at a branch of fresh water, under high cliffs.

f. *pass.* To be reduced to straits; = *to be put to it*: see 28 c (*b*).

1791 J. WOODFORDE *Diary* 8 Aug. (1927) III. 291 We were rather put to for a Dinner in so short a time how-ever we did our best and gave them some Beans and Bacon, mince Veal, Neck of Mutton [etc.]. **1803** *Pic Nic* No. 6 (1806) I. 221 He is,..like myself, hard put to at times for a little money. **1886** T. HARDY *Mayor Casterbr.* iv, We must needs be put-to for want of a wholesome crust. **1889** M. GRAY *Reproach Annesley* II. ii, Terble hard putt to they be to beat out the time.

54. put together. a. See simple senses and TOGETHER.

c **1440** *Promp. Parv.* 417/2 Put to-geder, but not onyd, *contiguus.* **1690** LOCKE *Hum. Und.* I. ii. 9 Upon the first Occasion that shall make him put together those Ideas in his Mind and observe whether they agree or disagree.

b. *trans.* To combine, unite (parts) into a whole; to join, e.g. in marriage.

c **1440** [see a]. **1530** PALSGR. 671/2 Sythe they be ones put togyther by the lawes of holy churche, I wyll never put them asonder. **1651** H. MORE *Second Lash* in *Enthus. Tri.*, etc. (1656) 218 It is you that have put things together so ill-favouredly. **1687** ABP. WAKE *Prep. for Death* 10 That those few directions I have here put together, may be as truly useful to you. **1793** SMEATON *Edystone L.* §271 Every thing was ready in the yard for putting together.

†**c.** *refl.* To join, combine, unite. *Obs. rare.*

1556 *Aurelio & Isab.* (1608) P v, The Quene and the ladies put them againe together for to geve Affranio a very bitter sopper.

d. To form (a whole) by combination of parts; to construct, compile, compose, compound.

1530 PALSGR. 676/1 He can spell, but he can nat put to gyther. **1638** JUNIUS *Paint. Ancients* 18 Our mind putteth the whole figure out of those visible parts together. **1825** *New Monthly Mag.* XV. 212/2 This figure can be taken to pieces and put together with the greatest ease. **1862** *Temple Bar Mag.* VI. 404, I put together some account of a series of incidents. **1889** FR. A. KEMBLE *Far Away & Long Ago* xii, His figure was ill put together.

e. To combine mentally; to add or reckon together, to sum; often in *pa. pple.*, taken or considered together, in a body, collectively.

to put this and that together: to consider two facts or circumstances together and draw a conclusion from them. So *to put two and two together*: see TWO.

1622 MABBE tr. *Aleman's Guzman d' Alf.* II. 195 All this put together..was nothing, being compared with her retirednesse of life. **1707** J. STEVENS tr. *Quevedo's Com. Wks.* (1709) 351 Put that and that together. **1748** RICHARDSON *Clarissa* vii. (1810) 70 All these things put together, excited their curiosity. **1861** *Temple Bar Mag.* I. 468 He knew more than all the old school put together. **1865** DICKENS *Mut. Fr.* III. xv, He puts this and that together.

f. *Cricket.* To make up, 'compile', as a 'score'.

1890 *Field* 31 May 784/3 Webbe and O'Brien..put together thirty-nine runs for the third wicket. *Ibid.* 21 June 919/2 The largest score they have ever put together in a first-class engagement.

55. put under.

a. *trans.* To kill or bury (a person).

1879 R. A. STERNDALE *Afghan Knife* II. vii. 75, I wanted to see your bonny face once more, in case these blackguards put me under. **1958** C. WATSON *Coffin, scarcely Used* iii. 27 There'll be some pressure to have him put under without any unseemly inquiries.

b. To render unconscious by means of an anaesthetic or by hypnosis.

1962 L. PAYNE *Too Small for his Shoes* v. 94 Given him something to put him under. Be right as rain. **1963** E. LANHAM *Monkey on Chain* xiv. 207 He put Dora under and learned conclusively that she went down to Bleecker Street. **1971** P. O'DONNELL *Impossible Virgin* xii. 235 'Is Willie going to give the ether?' 'Yes. I'll put her under myself.'

56. put up.

* **a.** (*a*) *trans.* To put into a higher position; to raise; to lift: see simple senses and UP *adv.*, also the sbs. BACK, HAIR, SHUTTER, etc.

a **1300** *Cursor M.* 5833 (Cott.) þe water o þe flum þou ta And put it vp apon þe land. *a* **1400** *Sir Beues* 3040 Beues wiste wel and sede, Put vp a pensell, lest Saber vs drede. *a* **1500** *MS. Ashm.* 344 lf. 19 (Chess) And must he nedis put vp his pon & mated in c. **1503** DUNBAR *Thistle & Rose* 54 The purpour sone..Throw goldin skyis putting vp his heid. **1605** SHAKS. *Macb.* IV. ii. 78 Why then (alas) Do I put vp that womanly defence? **1662** J. DAVIES tr. *Olearius' Voy. Ambass.* 75 Married Women put up their hair within their Caps or Coifs. **1861** HUGHES *Tom Brown at Oxf.* ix, There were others sneering..and that puts a fellow's back up. **1889** M. GRAY *Reproach Annesley* V. i, Shopkeepers had hastily put up their shutters. **1897** FLOR. MONTGOMERY *Tony* (1898) 17 You will put up the windows in the tunnels, won't you?

spec. (*b*) To fix up for public view, to post up.

Hence, of a cricketer: To score (so many runs); orig. to have them put up on the scoring board.

1833 *Act 3 & 4 Will. IV*, c. 46 §113 Such rules..shall..be put up, either in print or in writing, on such place..as the..council shall think proper. **1860** *Baily's Mag.* I. 428 Grundy put up 11 and 16. **1890** *Globe* 7 June 1/4 He put up notices requesting visitors to leave the plants alone.

(*c*) To set up or mount (a person, esp. a jockey) on horseback; to employ as a jockey.

1848 TROLLOPE *Kellys & O'Kellys* II. ii. 46 Brien was saddled..and Pat was put up. **1888** *Times* 26 June 4/5 Would they put up a jockey they believed to be dishonest? **1893** *Illustr. Sporting & Dram. News* 15 Apr. 183/1 Some trainers believe in putting up stable boys instead of jockeys. **1953** E. COXHEAD *Midlanders* i. 32 Don't suppose you've yet been on horseback, miss? We'll put you up and see how you like it.

(*d*) To put or bring (a play, etc.) on the stage for performance. Cf. *put on*, 47 a.

1838 DICKENS *Let.* Nov. (1965) I. 465, I don't know what they put up at the Theatre for that night. **1852** *Punch* 11 Dec. 257/1 The entertainments this week have been of a slight and desultory character, the management being..glad to 'put up' anything they could get. **1890** F. BARRETT *Between Life & Death* II. xxvi. 148 A new spectacle was..put up for rehearsal after Christmas. **1891** *New Rev.* Dec. 506 A manager..may 'put up' the 'Midsummer Night's Dream'.

(*e*) In imp. phr. ***put them*** (or *'em*) ***up***: (i) a challenge to raise the fists before a fight; (ii) a command to raise the hands above the head. *colloq.*

1923 E. WALLACE *Captains of Souls* xliv. 240 I'm going to give you the damnedest lacing you ever had..put 'em up! **1937** PARTRIDGE *Dict. Slang* 672/1 *Put 'em up!*, raise your arms!: from ca. 1860... Put up your fists!..late C. 19–20.

(*f*) To place (a military or other decoration) on one's uniform or other clothes.

1959 M. GILBERT *Blood & Judgement* xiv. 147 He could easily have put up a medal ribbon he wasn't entitled to. **1961** E. WAUGH *Unconditional Surrender* 5 He had been trained in the first batch of temporary officers..had twice put up captain's stars and twice removed them; their scars were plainly visible on his shoulder straps.

b. (*a*) *Hunting.* To cause (game) to rise from cover; to rouse, start.

? *c* **1475** *Hunt. Hare* 112, Y wylle ryde and putt her vp. **1575** TURBERV. *Falconrie* 131 Let him which hath the Hearoner (that is the make Hawke) put up the Hearon. **1629** H. BURTON *Truth's Triumph* 308 A spaniell..puts vp many a foule. **1711** ADDISON *Spect.* No. 131 §2 In Town,..I..put up such a Variety of odd Creatures, that they foil the Scent. **1805** SOUTHEY *Lett.* (1856) I. 345 Camp is in good health, and put up a hare. **1890** *Longm. Mag.* June 222 We put up a couple of tigers.

(*b*) *intr.* for *refl.* To rise: (in *Angling*) of a fish.

1600 SURFLET *Countrie Farme* II. liv, When as the sappe putteth vp and commeth to the barke. **1890** *Field* 31 May 799/1 The trout that put up here and there were after a tiny speck of midge-like character.

c. *trans.* To cause to spring up or grow; of a beast, to develop or 'cut' (a tooth).

1626 BACON *Sylva* §549 It is reported, that hartshorn shaven, or in small pieces, mixed with dung and watered, putteth up mushrooms. **1854** *Jrnl. R. Agric. Soc.* XV. II. 321 These teeth are put up when the calf is six months old.

d. *Cricket.* To hit (a ball) so that it rises high.

1845 W. DENISON *Cricketer's Compan.* p. ix, Had the chances from the ball being put up been taken advantage of. **1890** *Field* 31 May 790/2 Holden next put a ball up to long-on.

e. To 'raise' (a shout). *rare.*

1892 *Quiver* Mar. 359/1 They put up a great shout of admiration.

f. To raise in amount.

1890 *Harper's Mag.* Oct. 758/1 His governor..had quite lately put his allowance up a hundred pounds. **1892** *Sat. Rev.* 26 Nov. 617/2 Making preparations to put up the price still higher.

g. *colloq.* To show, exhibit (a game, play). ***to put up an appearance*** (*north. dial.* and *Sc.*), to make one's appearance. Also ***to put up a fight***, to acquit oneself well in a contest (also *fig.*).

1832 HT. MARTINEAU *Tales Pol. Econ.* II. IV, *Demerara* i. 10 A few of the sluggards who had not put up their appearance at the proper hour. **1892** *Field* 30 Jan. 133/3 Pettitt put up a good game..but it was not severe enough for the English champion. **1897** *Outing* (U.S.) XXX. 431/1 Able to put up a game at golf that the youngster will find hard to beat. **1919** H. CRANE *Let.* 7 Mar. (1965) 13 Mrs. Brooks is afflicted with consumption against which she is doubtless putting up a strenuous Scientific fight. **1928** —— *Let.* 27 Mar. (1965) 320, I put up quite a fight, but neither of us were in much condition.

** **h.** †(*a*) To send or hand up to a superior for consideration; to present (a petition, etc.). *Obs.*

1362 LANGL. *P. Pl.* A. IV. 34 þene Pees com to parlement and put vp a Bille, Hou þat Wrong aȝeyn his wille his wyf hedde I-take. **1439** *Rolls of Parlt.* V. 9/1 In a Petition putte up to the Kyng. **1530** PALSGR. 676/1, I wyll put up a complaynt agaynst the. **1589** *Pasquil's Ret.* C iij b, The reuerend Elders of Martinisme had neuer put vppe any Billes of endightment against her the last Parliament.

(*b*) To offer (prayer or worship) to God or a divine being 'on high'; to present a petition to any exalted personage.

1641 [see PUTTING *vbl. sb.*¹ 9]. **1709** STRYPE *Ann. Ref.* I. xlvi. 502 Our church..put up prayers to God in the behalf of it. **1757** HUME *Ess., Nat. Hist. Relig.* §4 (1788) II. 377 The Lacedemonians..always during war, put up their petitions very early in the morning, in order to be beforehand with their enemies. **1848** THACKERAY *Van. Fair* lix, The coarse tyrant..to whom she had been forced to put up petitions for time, when the rent was overdue. **1889** F. C. PHILIPS *Ainslie's Courtsh.* xiii, Prayers for fine weather were put up. **1889** DOYLE *Micah Clarke* xxv, At dinner I heard him put up thanks for what he was to receive.

i. To bring (a person) up before a magistrate; to bring into court on some charge; to accuse formally.

c **1440** *Alphabet of Tales* 121 On a tyme he was ferd to be putt vp at þe sene [*in synodo accusari*]. **1526** TINDALE *Matt.* x. 19 When they put you vp, take no thought howe or what ye shall speake. **1541** in Foxe *A. & M.* (1563) II. 1194/2 All these were put up for railing against the Sacramentes and Ceremonies. **1912** GALSWORTHY *Justice* II, in *Plays* II. 59 *Judge.* Call the next case. *Clerk of Assize.* (To a warder) Put up John Booley. **1949** F. SARGESON *I saw in my Dream* 75 Anyhow he'd been sacked and put up for it, and he'd only got six months probation. **1960** 'M. UNDERWOOD' *Cause of Death* xii. 152 The clerk of the court..said in a loud clear voice, 'Put up David Lucas.' **1964** J. PRESCOTT *Case for Court* ix. 175 Mr. Rose asked for the Sorensens to be put up at once so that the Chief Constable might make his application... The two accused were brought up into the dock. **1976** *Howard Jrnl.* XV. I. 42 There are a number of minor errors:..On p. 20 the prisoner is sitting in the dock before he has been put up.

j. (*a*) To propose for election or adoption. Also, to propose for an honour or award.

1573 G. HARVEY *Letter-bk.* (Camden) 2 Sinc mi grace amongst the rest was put up in the hous. *Ibid.* 3. **1682** *Enq. Elect. Sheriffs* 31 [They] both put up and Voted for Sir Humphrey Nicolson, and Mr. Box. **1692** R. L'ESTRANGE *Fables* cxvi, The Beasts Met in Councel to Chuse a King. There were Several Put up. **1840** LYTTON *Money* (ed. 4) I. 30 Shall I put you up at the clubs? *a* **1859** MACAULAY in *Encycl. Brit.* (1885) XIX. 137/1 Soon after this debate Pitt's name was put up by Fox at Brookes's. **1967** N. MARSH *Death at Dolphin* vi. 154 We'll put you up for the Police Medal. **1971** J. R. L. ANDERSON *Reckoning in Ice* vii. 143 He was..a sailor, and I'd put him up for the Mariners. We met at the club occasionally.

(*b*) *intr.* for *refl.* To offer oneself for election; to stand as a candidate.

1705 HEARNE *Collect.* 20 Dec., He..modestly declin'd it. The like did also Dr. Hudson, who was desir'd by divers to put up. **1890** DOYLE *Firm Girdlestone* xviii, He put up at Murphytown in the Conservative interest.

(*c*) *fig.* To 'set up' *for*, offer (to do something).

1892 *Quiver* Sept. 872/2, I am not master enough of the occult sciences to put up for defending Dan's character as a charmer. **1969** 'R. GORDON' *Facts of Life* 140, I spend all my time putting up for jobs. In the last six months, I've been to Liverpool, Exeter, Oxford, and York.

(*d*) *trans.* (with mixture of lit. sense): To bring forward (a person) to stand up and speak.

1889 DOYLE *Micah Clarke* xxxv, What use to put a witness up, when he was shouted down..and threatened by the Chief Justice? **1890** *Blackw. Mag.* CXLVIII. 597/1 He was the only speaker the Conservatives could put up..to answer or criticise Mr. Gladstone.

k. To send or hand in (a communication) to be published in a church in the course of the service; esp. in reference to banns; also, to publish (banns).

1685 S. SEWALL *Diary* 26 Mar., I put up a note to pray for the Indians. **1830** *Examiner* 396/2, I then went and put up the banns. **1842** MARRYATT *Perc. Keene* xxxii, We are to be put up in church next Sunday, and it takes three Sundays. **1892** *Cornh. Mag.* July 46 Their banns had been put up in the East End parish.

l. To offer for sale by auction, or for competition.

1706 *Lond. Gaz.* No. 4287/3 The Buyer to pay down 2 Guineas each Lot, or to be put up again. **1856** *Leisure Hour* V. 279/2 The lot was put up again, to be knocked down for six and threepence. **1892** *Chamb. Jrnl.* 3 Dec. 773/2 Oughtn't the post..to have been put up for public competition? **1899** GOLDW. SMITH *United Kingd.* I. 108 He [Richard I] put everything up to sale.

m. †(*a*) *intr.* ? To advance *to*, approach; or ? to make up *to*, address oneself *to* a person (*obs.*). (*b*) *trans.* To submit (a question, etc.) *to* a person: cf. 22, 22 b.

? **1728** SWIFT *Discovery* 17 Wks. 1755 IV. I. 298 With this he put up to my lord, The courtiers kept their distance due. **1906** *Harper's Mag.* June 68/1 When he finally put it up to me what I would do,—'It would depend', I answered, 'on what it was the woman has done'. **1909** P. A. VAILE *Mod. Golf* xvi. 211, I am directing my manufacturers' energies to producing the exact amount of marking required [on a golf ball]... I should not have troubled with it had it not been 'put up to me', as the American would say. **1913** F. H. BURNETT *T. Tembarom* xxiv. 306 'Oh, well, I just put it up to them.'..'You mean that you made them feel that they alone were responsible.' **1924** GALSWORTHY *White Monkey* I. viii. 58 I'll put it up to Mr. Desert; if he speaks for you, perhaps it may move Mr. Danby.

***** n.** (*a*) To place in a receptacle for safe keeping; to stow away; to put into a bag, pocket, box, or the like; to lay aside out of use, put by (somewhat *arch.*); to lay up in store, lay by for future use (now *rare* or *obs.*); to pack up, do up, make up into a parcel, or place in small vessels or receptacles so as to be kept ready for use.

to put up one's pipes: see PIPE *sb.*[1] 1 e. (Cf. *put away*, 39 e; *put by*, 41 g.)

c **1368** CHAUCER *Compl. Pite* 54, I haue put my compleynt vp agayne, ffor to my foos my bille I dar not shewe. **1382** WYCLIF *Luke* xii. 19 Soule, thou hast many goodis kept [*v.r.* put vp] in to ful manye 3eeris. **1588** SHAKS. *L.L.L.* IV. i. 109 Thou hast mistaken his letter.. Here, sweete, put up this. **1637** GATAKER *Serm., On 1 Tim. vi.* 6, I. 134 They might not pocket or put up ought to carry away with them. **1651** FRENCH. *Distill.* v. 125 Put it up in bottles. **1825** *New Monthly Mag.* XV. 406/1 It will keep sweet a very long time put up in good flour barrels. **1883** MRS. F. MANN *Parish Hilby* iv, If you aren't for any more whist,..we may as well put up the cards. **1889** F. BARRETT *Under Str. Mask* II. xiv. 76, I took the money..and put it up in the pocket-book. **1892** *Field* 21 May 778/1 The housekeeper..had put us up plenty of edibles and drinkables. **1916** *Daily Colonist* (Victoria, B.C.) 2 July 4/5 Sidney women, under Mrs. Wheeler, have started putting up jam for the boys at the front. **1924** T. S. P. STRANGEWAYS *Technique of Tissue Culture* 39 To put up the cultures take the tissues or organs which have been set aside for cultivation and cut up into suitably sized fragments. *Ibid.* 73 If more cultures are desired, put them up in a similar way. **1951** [see MID *a.*, *sb.*[1], and *adv.* 1 c]. **1954** J. R. R. TOLKIEN *Fellowship of Ring* I. iv. 107 He produced a large basket from under the seat... 'Mrs. Maggot put this up for Mr. Baggins, with her compliments.' **1970** *Nature* 19 Dec. 1139/2 When either bone marrow or circulating blood cells from humans, mice or rats are put up in culture in a freshly made medium containing calf serum, few if any colonies of haematopoietic cells grow. **1971** R. THOMAS *Backup Men* v. 34 He's helping me put up some marmalade.

(*b*) To put into the sheath, to sheathe (a sword); also *absol.* to sheathe one's sword (cf. DRAW *v.* 33 b). Also *fig. arch.*

c **1470** *Golagros & Gaw.* 1123 Thai..Put up thair brandis sa braid, burly and bair. **1526** TINDALE *John* xviii. 11 Put vppe thy swearde into the sheath [Gk. βάλε, Vulg. *mitte*]. **1592** SHAKS. *Rom. & Jul.* I. i. 72, I do but keepe the peace, put vp thy Sword. **1602** MIDDLETON *Blurt Master Constable* v. ii, *Font.* I'm arm'd: let him come in... *Imp.* Goe, goe, put vp. **1608** DOD & CLEAVER *Expos. Prov.* 164 To be wary how we carry our tongues, that they be safely put up from doing of hurt, and never unsheathed. **1775** SHERIDAN *Rivals* v. iii, Put up, Jack, put up..—how came you in a duel? **1826** SCOTT *Woodst.* xxv, None shall fight duellos here... Put up, both of you.

(*c*) To shut up, enclose (a beast for fattening, a meadow for hay).

1607 TOPSELL *Four-f. Beasts* (1658) 517 They put up a Hog to fatting. **1799** WASHINGTON *Writ.* (1893) XIV. 225 Before the period arrives for putting them up as porkers. **1854** *Jrnl. R. Agric. Soc.* XV. II. 401 The stall beasts are.. put up in sheds in October. **1892** J. C. BLOMFIELD *Hist. Heyford* 2 'Ings', or meadows put up for hay.

(*d*) To settle (any one) to rest or repose; to settle (a patient) in bed.

1800 *Med. Jrnl.* III. 36, I just applied simple dressing,.. putting him up in blankets, with no hope of his recovery. **1860–6** FLOR. NIGHTINGALE *Nursing* 39 Everything you do in a patient's room, after he is 'put up' for the night, increases tenfold the risk of his having a bad night.

(*e*) To deposit, stake (a sum of money); to pay up. Also *absol.* orig. *U.S.*

1865 'MARK TWAIN' in *N.Y. Sat. Press* 18 Nov. 249/2 And so the feller..put up his forty dollars along with Smiley's. **1884** *Boston* (Mass.) *Jrnl.* 16 Aug., A wealthy Bostonian yesterday wagered $1000, and put-up the money, that Mr. Blaine's majority in New York State would exceed 40,000. **1891** C. ROBERTS *Adrift Amer.* 126, I will pick you up if you choose to put up a couple of dollars.

(*f*) In imp. phr. *put up or shut up*: defend yourself or be silent. *colloq.* (chiefly *U.S.*).

1878 F. H. HART *Sazerac Lying Club* 167 'P.U. or S.U.' means put up or shut up, doesn't it? **1884** *National Police Gaz.* (U.S.) 26 Apr. 1 (*caption*) Put up, shut up, or get! **1889** 'MARK TWAIN' *Connecticut Yankee* xl. 512 This was a plain case of 'put up, or shut up'. **1952** *Manch. Guardian Weekly* 1 May 3/4 The old alternatives will be revived: put up or shut up—get out or get on to the Yalu and beyond. **1976** *Billings* (Montana) *Gaz.* 17 June 6-c/1 It wasn't a case of put up or shut up because the money was voted as a sincere effort to clean up the mess.

o. (*a*) To lodge and entertain (man or beast).

1766 GOLDSM. *Vic. W.* xxii, The hired horse that we rode was to be put up that night at the inn. **1828** *Blackw. Mag.* XXIII. 375 Mr. Hunt..was 'put up' in the ground-floor of his Lordship's house. **1867** TROLLOPE *Chron. Barset* xx, Mr. Robarts went to the inn, put up his horse, and then.. sauntered back up the street. **1890** 'R. BOLDREWOOD' *Col. Reformer* (1891) 129 Can you put us up for the night?

(*b*) *intr.* for *refl.* or *pass.* To take up one's lodging, to 'stop' (at an inn, etc.).

1727 *Philip Quarll* (1816) 32 We put up at the first cottage. **1753** *Scots Mag.* Oct. 483/1 The inns where their waggons put up. **1840** DICKENS *Barn. Rudge* xxxv, Let's either go on to London, sir, or put up at once. **1884** D. C. MURRAY in *Graphic* Xmas No. 5/3 Would it not be better..to put up here for the night?

p. *fig.* †(*a*) *trans.* To 'pocket', submit to, endure, suffer quietly, patiently, or tamely (an affront or injury); 'to pass unrevenged' (J.). *Obs.* (now displaced by *put up with*: see (*b*)).

1573 G. HARVEY *Letter-bk.* (Camden) 48 All this I put up quietly. **1600** W. WATSON *Decacordon* (1602) 91 Abuses.. which, with honour, he can neuer put vp at their hands. **1604** SHAKS. *Oth.* IV. ii. 181. **1628** EARLE *Microcosm.* lv. (Arb.) 79 He can put vp any iniury sooner then this. **1752** FIELDING *Amelia* IX. iii, He who would put up an arrest, would put up a slap in the face. **1832** *Philol. Museum* I. 477 The ridicule which the minister..might put up from his jocose friend.

(*b*) *to put up with*: to submit to (an injury), 'to suffer without resentment' (J., 1765): = (*a*); in wider sense, To bear, endure, tolerate, do with (anything inconvenient or disagreeable); 'to take without dissatisfaction' (T., 1818).

1755 P. SUPPLE in *Connoisseur* No. 100. 605 All these indignities I very patiently put up with. **1761** COLMAN *Genius* No. 9 in *Prose on Sev. Occas.* (1787) I. 90 This loss.. would have been the least, and most easily to be put up with. **1839** DE QUINCEY *Casuistry Rom. Meals* Wks. 1854 III. 280 Whether Pope ever put up with four o'clock dinners again, I have vainly sought to fathom. **1887** JESSOPP *Arcady* viii. 235 [An] organ grinder..hunted out of London streets, where they will not put up with him.

****** q.** *trans. to put* (a person) *up to* (*colloq.*): (*a*) To make conversant with or aware of; to inform of, instruct in (something, originally some artifice or expedient).

1812 J. H. VAUX *Flash Dict.* s.v., To suggest to another, the means of committing a depredation,..is termed, putting him up to it. **1824** *Hist. Gaming*, etc. 18 Those who had been 'put up' to the secrets, or made acquainted with the manner of doing the flats. **1828** *Examiner* 589/1, I want you to put the people at the inn up to my not coming. **1891** *Cornh. Mag.* Oct. 357 He put me up to one or two things worth knowing.

(*b*) To stir up, instigate, incite, induce, persuade (*to* some action, etc., or *to do* something).

1824 in G. T. Curtis *D. Webster* (1870) I. 266 'You find it hard work enough this morning, I think', said Mr. Webster. 'Yes, Sir', said the boatman, 'it puts a man up to all he knows, I assure you'. **1849** E. FITZGERALD *Lett.* (1889) I. 193 You must not believe however that it is only chance which puts me up to this exertion. **1889** M. GRAY *Reproach Annesley* IV. i, Always putting them up to mischief. **1892** *Gd. Words* Sept. 584/1 He put me up to try to get into Harris's secrets.

(*c*) Sense (*b*) used without following *to* and adjunct: to annoy, to vex (a person).

1930 H. G. WELLS *Autocracy of Mr. Parham* IV. i. 266 This cheap Mussolini at Westminster is putting us up some! **1960** T. MCLEAN *Kings of Rugby* xi. 160 Hill's protest was more likely to restore the true spirit of the game than..some other method of retaliation by the Canterbury men who believed that they were being put up.

******* r.** To erect, set up (a building or other structure); to construct, build.

1699 M. LISTER *Journey to Paris* 25 There are an infinite number of Busto's of the Grand Monarque every where put up by the Common People. **1818** in Willis & Clark *Cambridge* (1886) I. 573 The making a Bridge and putting up the Gates at the end of that walk. **1857–8** SEARS *Athan.* xii. 102 A building which..God put up carpenter-fashion. **1873** H. SPENCER *Stud. Sociol.* xi. 287 Here are lighthouses we have put up to prevent shipwrecks. **1879** TROLLOPE *Thackeray* i. 58 A bust to his memory was put up in Westminster Abbey.

s. To make up or compose by union of individuals or parts; *spec.* in *Angling*, to make up or construct (an artificial fly).

1892 *Harper's Mag.* May 870/1 Prussia, together with the remaining states, puts up sixteen army corps. **1892** *Field* 17 Sept. 454/1 When putting up a new fly, the wings, hackle, and body are painted over with the paraffin. *Ibid.* 10 Dec. 901/2 Our guest put up a cast of midges.

t. *fig.* To concoct or plan in combination with others; to prearrange, preconcert (a robbery, or any iniquitous or underhand piece of work). Orig. and chiefly *Thieves' slang*: see also PUT-UP *ppl. a.* 1.

1810–38 [see PUT-UP *ppl. a.* 1]. **1856** *Leisure Hour* V. 542/2 Her account..affords a good example of the style of 'putting up' a house robbery. **1892** *Illustr. Sporting & Dram. News* 13 Aug. 790/1 Barclay put up a job to ruin old Overton.

u. To judge, regard, or assess (a person, situation, etc.) in a particular way. *U.S.*

1877 'MARK TWAIN' in *Atlantic Monthly* Nov. 590/1 Would you like to have me explain that thing to you?.. Now, this is the way I put it up. **1880** —— *Tramp Abroad* xx. 192 'Didn't I put you up right?' 'Oh, yes.' 'Sho! I spotted you for *my* kind the minute I heard your clack.' **1895** *Century Mag.* Sept. 674/2 And Jack says to himself, 'Well, ..I done what I could! What is to be will be.' That's about the way I put it up.

VI. 57. In numerous idiomatic, proverbial, and other phrases, as *to put to the* BLUSH, *to the* PUSH; *to put in one's* POCKET, *in* REQUISITION, *into* (*out of*) *one's* HEAD, *into one's* MOUTH, *out of* COUNTENANCE, *out of* COURT, *out of* JOINT, *out of the* WAY; *to put the* BOOT in, *the* CHANGE *upon*, *a* (*good*, etc.) FACE *upon*, *the* FEAR of God *into*, *one's* FOOT *in it*, *too fine a point upon it* (POINT *sb.*[1] B. 1 d), *a person's* POT *on*, *one's* SHOULDER *to*, SPURS *to*; *to put a* BONE *in any one's hood*, *the* CART *before the horse*, *the finger in the* EYE, *one's best* FOOT *foremost*, *one's* NOSE *out of joint*, *one's hand to the* PLOUGH, *pen to* PAPER, *a* SPOKE *in one's wheel*, *the* WIND *up* (a person), etc., for which see the sbs.; *to put next to* (NEXT *a.* 13 c); *not to put it past someone* (PAST *prep.* 3 b); *to put* (*one*) *wise* (*to*) (WISE *a.* 3 b (*b*)).

put, putt (pʌt), *v.*[2] Pa. t. and pa. pple. putted ('pʌtɪd). [The same word as prec., used in particular senses differentiated by pronunciation and by the use of the regular weak conjugation.

This is not merely the Sc. pronunciation of PUT *v.*[1], which in Sc. is conjugated *pit, pat, putten* or *pitten*; while this is *putt, puttit, puttit*, and in current use felt as a distinct verb. But the regular weak conjugation formerly occurred in Eng. with senses belonging to PUT *v.*[1]]

† **1.** *intr.* To push, shove, butt; = PUT *v.*[1] 1 d. *to put on*: to push gently, nudge. *Sc. Obs.*

1513 DOUGLAS *Æneis* IX. x. 91 The beste..Can allreddy wyth hornis fuyn and put. **1583** *Leg. Bp. St. Androis* 477 How everie wyfe on vther puttis, Bidding the bischop pay for his guttis. **1630** RUTHERFORD *Lett.* (1862) I. vii. 54 It were time for us, by prayer, to put upon our master-pilot Jesus, and to cry, 'Master, save us: we perish'. **1637–50** Row *Hist. Kirk* (Wodrow Soc.) 47 He sent one who, putting on me, awakened me. **1768** ROSS *Helenore* 38 (Jam.), I putted o' you for to set you free.

2. *trans.* To throw or hurl (a stone or weight) from the shoulder, as an athletic exercise; = PUT *v.*[1] 2. *Sc.*

[*c* **1300–**: see PUT *v.*[1] 2.] **1724** RAMSAY *Gentle Sheph.* II. iv, When thou ran, or wrestled, or putted the stane. **1816** SCOTT *Antiq.* xxix, Auld Edie, that kens the rules of a' country games better than ony man that ever drave a bowl, or threw an axle-tree, or putted a stane. **1816** —— *Old Mort.* iv, Would the bumpkins but wrestle, or pitch the bar, or putt the stone.

b. *intr.* = PUT *v.*[1] 2 b.

[*c* **1300–1535**: see PUT *v.*[1] 2 b.] ? *a* **1800** *Rose the Red & White Lilly* xviii. in Scott *Minstr. Scot. Bord.*, O it fell anes, upon a time, They putted at the stane. **1820** [see PUTTER *sb.*[2] 1]. *Mod. Sc.* Let's try who can putt farthest!

3. *Golf.* To strike the ball gently and carefully (with the PUTTER), so as to make it roll along the surface of the PUTTING-*green*, with the object of getting it into the hole. Usually *intr.*; also *trans.* with the ball as obj. *orig. Sc.*

1743 [implied in PUTTER *sb.*[2] 2 a]. **1833** G. F. CARNEGIE *Golfiana* in R. Clark *Golf* (1875) 150 Well he plays the spoon and iron, but He fails a little when he comes to putt. **1857** *Golfer's Man.* in *Chambers's Inform. for People* 696/1 Some golfers put almost exclusively with a metal club, an iron or cleek. **1892** *English Illustr. Mag.* X. 59 It seems a little matter..to drive your ball up in one and 'put' into the hole in two more. **1894** *Times* 16 June 16/1 He..approached with his iron with great effect, and putted in most deadly style.

put (pʊt), *ppl. a.* Also 7 *Sc.* putt. [pa. pple. of PUT *v.*[1]] Place, set, appointed, etc.: see PUT *v.*[1] Usually with an adverb, as **put-aside** (in quot. *absol.*); **put-away** (PUT *v.* 38 e); **put-down** (42: in quot., degraded, 42 c); **put-off** (46: in quots., †cast away, abject (*obs.*); deferred, postponed, 46 c); **put-out** (48: in quots., 48 f (*d*), m (*c*)); **put-together** (54: in quots. 54 d); **put-upon** (23 f (*b*)); also *absol.* as *sb. to stay put*: see STAY *v.*[1] 6 b. See also PUT-ON, PUT-UP *ppl. adjs.*

1868 YATES *Rock Ahead* I. viii, The *put-aside and rejected of Gilbert Lloyd. **1891** KIPLING *Light that Failed* (1900) 261 It was this *put-away treasure that he was trying to find. **1860** GEN. P. THOMPSON *Audi Alt. Part.* III. cxliii. 126 It ought to be asked in parliament, if parliament was not a *put-down thing and a plaything of the minister. **1636** B. JONSON *Discov., Princeps*, I am a wretch and *put of man, if I doe not reverence and honour him. **1871** MRS. H. WOOD *Dene Hollow* xxxix, A put-off wedding sometimes brings ill-luck. **1899** F. V. KIRBY *Sport E.C. Afr.* xi. 118 Grunting in a *put-out sort of way. **1907** *Westm. Gaz.* 24 Oct. 10/3 The put-out work of some West End tailors. **1950** in E. C. Richards *Diary of E. R. Chudleigh* 23 Such a '*put-together' mob of wild cattle required at least six to eight experienced stockmen. **1957** J. KEROUAC *On Road* (1958) 21 Country boys in a put-together jalopy. **1970** *Times* 2 June 8/2 The essential of the put together look which stays put is a belt. **1920** *Quill* (N.Y.) Nov. 12 Lulu is the ideal poor relation of fiction, the *put-upon slavey. **1966** M. KELLY *Dead Corse* iv. 53 Those who follow unquestioning, docile, simple... The put-upon. **1976** *Listener* 6 May 586/2 Juliet Mills was very good as Cady's put-upon wife. **1980** G. MITCHELL *Uncoffin'd Clay* iii. 32 Having to cook..a sensitive charwoman would regard as victimisation or, in her parlance, a put-upon.

put, obs. f. PIT *sb.*[1], PITH; var. PUTT *sb.*[1]

put- (pʊt), the stem of PUT *v.*[1] in combination with adverbs, forming sbs. derived from adverbial combinations of the verb (see PUT *v.*[1] V.): as **put-away** *Lawn Tennis* and *Rackets* = KILL *sb.* 2 c; also *attrib.*; **put-back**, an act of putting back, or something that puts back; a set-back; **put-by**, an act of putting by or setting aside; **put-down**, (*a*) an act of putting (a person) down, a snub; also *attrib.*; (*b*) *attrib.*, with reference to the act of alighting from a vehicle; † **put-forth**, an act of putting forth, or ? one who puts forth; in quot. an imposture, pretence, or ? an impostor, pretender; **put-in**, (*a*) *U.S. colloq.*, one's turn to speak, one's affair; (*b*) the act of putting the ball into a scrum in rugby football; **put-out**, (*a*) an act of putting out (in quot., of putting a player 'out' at baseball); (*b*) *U.S.*, an annoyance or inconvenience (? *obs.*); **put-through**, (*a*) a measure of the number of persons or objects which have been put through a process; (*b*) *Econ.*, a financial transaction in which a broker arranges the sale and the purchase of shares simultaneously; also *attrib.* **put-up**, a place to 'put up' in, a lodging, 'quarters'. Also rarely with a preposition, as **put-upon**, an act of 'putting upon' any one, or fact of being 'put upon' (see PUT *v.*[1] 23 f); an imposition. See also PUT-OFF *sb.*, PUT-ON *sb.*

1969 *New Yorker* 14 June 75/1 He intercepts, and sends a light and graceful *putaway past Graebner, down the line. **1977** *Ibid.* 25 July 70/2 Connors.. also carried off the next three games on the strength of some fine, deep approaches and remarkable put-away volleys. *a* **1697** J. AUBREY *Lives, Hobbes* (1898) I. 333 For ten yeares together his thoughts were.. chiefly intent on his 'De Cive', and.. his 'Leviathan', which was a great *putt-back to his mathematicall improvement. **1913** D. H. LAWRENCE *Love Poems* p. lviii, An' mind... Ye slip not on the slippery ridge Of the thawin' snow, or it'll be A long put-back to your gran' marriage. **1549** LATIMER *Serm. Ploughers* (Arb.) 36 There be so manie put offes, so many *put byes, so many respectes, and considerations of worldly wisedome. **1549** [see PUT-OFF 1]. **1628** FELTHAM *Resolves* Ser. II. lvi. (1647) 175 The cast of the eye, and the put-by of the turning hand. **1962** J. BALDWIN *Another Country* II. iv. 335 Flattery will get you nowhere, son. Or is that a subtle *put-down? **1968** *Punch* 23 Oct. 593/2 Michael Denison sustains an appropriately truculent pout and Dulcie Gray delivers tart and catty put-downs with relish. **1972** G. LYALL *Blame the Dead* xiv. 100 He'd picked me up at the put-down place for Euston station. .. It's a one-way underground street. **1973** *N.Y. Times* 18 Feb. 1. 24/1 He [*sc.* Trudeau] doesn't rise to bait—with choice epithets and that put-down Gallic shrug of his. **1974** S. ALSOP *Stay of Execution* II. 160 He [*sc.* Dean Acheson] detested silliness, and he was justly famous for his put-downs—when he put down a fool, the fool was left in no doubt that he was a fool. **1976** *National Observer* (U.S.) 20 Mar. 14/2 The woman whom former Attorney General John Mitchell immortalized with his famous putdown, 'Katie Graham's gonna get her tit caught in a big fat wringer', is hardly the 'bitch bringing down Presidents'. **1977** MILLER & SWIFT *Words & Women* vi. 100 Some speakers and writers use Ms. only as a put-down. **1581** MULCASTER *Positions* xxxix. 205 Learning empouerished in purses, though replenished in *putfurthes by such interceptours. **1853** 'MARK TWAIN' in *Hannibal* (Missouri) *Jrnl.* 25 May 3/1 Never speak when it's not your '*put-in'. **1903** W. N. HARBEN *Abner Daniel* xxxv. 301 This ain't no put-in o' mine, gracious knows. I hain't got nothin', an' I don't expect to lose or gain by what is done. **1962** *Times* 11 Jan. 4/3 The Navy came out better in the matter of put-ins against the head. **1975** *Sunday Tel.* 2 Mar. 30/1 He may have lost confidence as the game developed after being penalised four times for a crooked put-in. **1833** J. NEAL *Down-Easters* I. vi. 83, I shouldn't think twould be any *put-out to you to take somebody else. **1843** A. S. STEPHENS *High Life N.Y.* ii. 32 Don't be uneasy about the trouble, it won't be no put out to Captain Doolittle. **1885** *California Athlete* 19 Dec. 5/1 He assisted yesterday in fourteen put outs. **1891** N. CRANE *Baseball* vi. 44 An 'assist' is given to every player who handles the ball in assisting a put-out or other play of the kind. **1896** KNOWLES & MORTON *Baseball* 83 Every base that was run was ticked off.. and every 'put-out' and every 'assist' was shown on the painted plan. **1904** R. H. BARBOUR *School & College Sports* 200 *Put-out*, a play by which a batsman or a base-runner is retired. **1972** *Evening Telegram* (St. John's, Newfoundland) 24 June 21/8 He.. led the league's shortstops in fielding percentage, putouts, assists and double plays. **1958** *Punch* 8 Jan. 84/1 He.. gave me the acreage, cost, cubic capacity and passenger *put-through. **1959** [see *put through* s.v. PUT *v.*[1] 52 d]. **1968** *Economist* 4 May 64/1 Even in the leaders trading is often very narrow, and the resulting prices (on the basis of which an increasing amount of shunting and 'put throughs' now go on) are not struck on the total volume of trading. **1973** *Daily Tel.* 7 June 21 Trading on the Paris Bourse traditionally has consisted either of very big 'put-throughs' or of small deals for private individuals. **1891** *Longm. Mag.* Oct. 564 We must get a *put-up at Queen's Gate. **1889** J. K. JEROME *Three Men in Boat* iv, The presence of your husband's cheeses in her house she would.. regard as a '*put upon'.

‖**puta** ('puta). *slang.* [Sp.] A whore, a slut.

1967 MCCORMICK & MASCAREÑAS *Compl. Aficionado* iii. 72 You must be like a young priest—do not go near the *putas*, and keep away from all women as long as you can. **1968–70** *Current Slang* (Univ. S. Dakota) III–IV. 99 *Puta*, a promiscuous girl. **1969** E. BISHOP *Compl. Poems* 207 Under the false-almond tree's Leathery leaves, a childish *puta* Dances. **1971** L. GRIBBLE *Alias the Victim* vii. 121 You tricky bitch of a *puta*.

†**putage.** *Obs.* [a. OF. *putage* (Godef.), f. *pute* harlot, PUTE + -AGE.] Fornication on the part of a woman; whoredom. (Cf. PUTERY.)

1480 CAXTON *Ovid's Met.* XII. iii, Yt pleseth me better that men saye that Helayne is a good wyf than she had doon putage. **1670** BLOUNT *Law Dict.*, *Putage*, fornicatio ex parte fœminæ. **1706** in PHILLIPS (ed. Kersey).

†**pu'taile, -'tayle.** *Obs.* [In form = OF. *putaille* (Godef.) a body of harlots, a harlotry; but the sense appears to be that of PEDAILE, q.v.] Rabble; (?) foot-soldiers.

13.. *Coer de L.* 1286 They slowe knyghtes and gret putayle Off Sarezynys that mys-belevyd. *Ibid.* 4291 Folk of armes.. fyffty thousent With other smal putayle, That ther com into the batayle. *c* **1450** *Merlin* xiii. 192 The saisnes.. were well x ml. of horse-men, with-oute the putaile that ronne vp and down and robbed the peple.

†**putain.** *Obs.* Also 4 -aine, (-eyn), 4–5 -ayn, 6 -ane, 7 pewtene. [a. OF. *putain*:—late popular L. **puttānem*, acc. of *putta*:—L. *pūtida* stinking, disgusting. (See Schwan *Gram. Altfr.* ed. 2, §341, 352.)] A whore, a prostitute, a strumpet.

Fitz-a-putain (Anglo-Fr.) = whoreson: see FITZ.

a **1300**, etc. [see FITZ]. *c* **1380** WYCLIF *Serm.* Sel. Wks. II. 27 Puplicans and puteyns trowiden to him. **1560** ROLLAND *Seven Sag.* Prol. iii, Ane prydfull pure Putane, At quhais wordis men wald tak small disdane. **1603** *Philotus* lxxxiii, Fals pewtene, hes scho playit that sport, Hes scho me handlit in this sort?

‖**putamen** (pjuː'teɪmɪn). [L. *putāmen* that which falls off in pruning or trimming, husk, shell, f. *putāre* to prune.]

1. *Bot.* The endocarp of a fruit when hard and woody, as the 'stone' of a plum, etc.; rarely applied to the shell of a nut.

1830 LINDLEY *Nat. Syst. Bot.* 84 Fruit a drupe, with the putamen sometimes separating spontaneously from the sarcocarp. **1885** GOODALL *Physiol. Bot.* (1892) 176 A fragment of the hard shell of a nut or of the putamen of a drupe.

2. *Anat.* The outer zone or segment of the extra-ventricular portion of the grey matter of the brain (*nucleus lenticularis*).

1890 in BILLINGS *Nat. Med. Dict.* **1899** *Allbutt's Syst. Med.* VII. 334 [Certain lesions] in the lenticular nucleus in its outer segment or putamen.

3. The tough membrane or skin which lines the inside of the shell of an egg.

1890 in *Cent. Dict.* **1897** in *Syd. Soc. Lex.*

putaminous (pjuː'tæmɪnəs), *a. rare.* [f. L. *putāmen* (*-min-*) + -OUS.] Of the nature of or pertaining to shell, husk, or putamen.

1597 A. M. tr. *Guillemeau's Fr. Chirurg.* 26 b/2 Some putaminous substance chaunced to be theron [the teeth] hardened. **1660** HICKERINGILL *Jamaica* (1661) 28 The outward crust, or putaminous husk, being broken, appears full of little kernells, or nuts. Also in mod. Dicts.

ˌ**put-and-'call.** *Econ.* (See quot. 1905.) Also *attrib.*

1892 *Congress Rec.* 6 June App. 448/1 Members of exchanges do not deal in '*puts and calls*'. **1893** [see PUT *sb.*[1] 4.] **1905** F. BOWER *Dict. Econ. Terms* 133 *Put and call*, on the Stock Exchange it is a common practice to arrange to buy or sell a certain number of shares at option at a fixed price within a specified time. The arrangement may be (1) to buy shares, known as the 'Call', (2) to sell shares, the 'Put', or (3) to buy or sell at option, called the 'Put and Call'. **1929** *Sun* (Baltimore) 26 June 1/6 She started business for herself, dealing in options, or in Wall Street slang the 'put and call' or 'put and take' brokerage business. **1962** S. STRAND *Marketing Dict.* 599 Put and call contracts are written for 30, 60 or 90 days, or longer. **1973** *N.Y. Law Jrnl.* 4 Sept. 7/5 (Advt.), Lawyers, their clients and those involved in the put and call trading process.. need to have up-to-date knowledge on the nature of these investments. **1975** G. V. HIGGINS *City on Hill* ix. 216 He.. bought silver futures, puts and calls, I think.

ˌ**put-and-'take.** **1.** A gambling game played with a six-sided top. Also *transf.*, the top with which the game is played. Also *attrib.* and *fig.*

1922 *Daily Mail* 5 Jan. 5/4 (*heading*) Put and take in court. *Ibid.*, For playing Put and Take in a recreation ground a youth was charged under the Gaming Act at Hull yesterday. **1922** *Vet. Jrnl.* XXVIII. 105 A rough-haired fox-terrier dog, 'Jazz',.. was brought to me with the history that a brass 'Put and Take' top, 'put' on the hearthrug, had been 'taken' up and swallowed by him. **1940** GRAVES & HODGE *Long Week-End* viii. 132 In 1922 the craze was for a simple gambling device known as 'Put and Take'.. a small six-sided top which players.. spun in turn. **1960** R. C. BELL *Board & Table Games* v. 146 Put and Take. Each player.. spins a six sided teetotum and obeys the instructions on the face falling uppermost. **1970** *Guardian* 9 Dec. 1/5 The deadly game of put-and-take brought on by the electricity generating workers' work-to-rule. **1972** *Observer* 3 Sept. 32/1 Each juror was issued with two bronze tokens with a shaft through the middle, rather like a put-and-take.

2. *Econ.* = PUT-AND-CALL.

1929 [see PUT-AND-CALL].

3. The stocking of streams and lakes with fish for anglers to catch. Usu. *attrib.*

1943 *Sun* (Baltimore) 26 Jan. 6/3 (*heading*) Put-and-take fishing planned by W. Virginia. *Ibid.*, The revision would take the form of stocking a much larger number of legal size trout on a 'put-and-take' basis in rivers and creeks which are not year-around trout streams. **1973** *Country Life* 21 June 1804/1 The rainbow trout is.. the ideal stock fish for enclosed waters.. where fishing is increasingly on a 'put and take' basis. **1974** *Ibid.* 26 Sept. 831/3 The cultivation of sizeable trout which are stocked makes Traws a sort of put-and-take fishery unlike most put-and-take places.

†**putanie.** *Obs.* [Cf. It. *puttana*.] = PUTAIN (for which the instances may be misprints).

1566 *Pasquine in Traunce* 28 Some are called Celestines,.. other Carmilitanes, and some Putanies also. *Ibid.*, *note*, Putanies be those Nunes that we call the greene Friers on strawbery banke.

'**putanism.** *rare.* [f. PUTAIN + -ISM: cf. F. *putanisme*, It. *puttanismo*.] (See quot.)

1696 PHILLIPS, *Putanism*, the Trade and Living of a Whore. **1721** in BAILEY, and in later Dicts. **1922** P. NIELSEN *Black Man's Place in S. Afr.* 57 Immorality is rife amongst Natives.., but neither can putanism amongst the whites be denied.

†**pu'tation.** *Obs.* [ad. L. *putātiōn-em*, n. of action from *putāre* to cleanse, prune, reckon, consider, think.]

1. The pruning or trimming of trees.

c **1440** *Pallad. on Husb.* XII. 50 Putacioun autumnal celebrate Is now in vyne & tre ther nys no coold. **1623** COCKERAM, *Putation*, a lopping of trees.

2. The action of considering or reckoning; supposition, estimation.

1658 PHILLIPS, *Putation*,.. a thinking, reputing, or esteeming. **1670** BAXTER *Life Faith* III. viii. 322 It is not possible.. by any putation, estimation, or misjudging whatsoever.

Hence †**pu'tationary** *a.*, based on hypothesis or theory, suppositional; †**pu'tationer**, a theorizer.

1657 G. STARKEY *Helmont's Vind.* 86 An insufferable task for an old Putationer. **1658** —— *Pyrotechny* III. ii, A lazie person, or a conceited Putationer. **1669** W. SIMPSON *Hydrol. Chym.* 207 In a putationary and consequently deceitful philosophy.

†**puta'titious,** *a. Obs.* [f. L. *putāt-us*, thought, supposed, pa. pple. of *putāre* to think: see prec. and -ITIOUS[1].] Of a supposed, reputed, or imaginary sort.

1660 tr. *Paracelsus' Archidoxis* II. 50 An inhibition might be imposed on such putatitious, imaginary Physicians. **1671** J. WEBSTER *Metallogr.* xxix. 380 The putatitious transmutation of Iron doth otherwise not happen. **1674** R. GODFREY *Inj. & Ab. Physic* 145, I found neither Truth nor Knowledge in my Putatitious Doctrine.

Hence †**puta'titiously** *adv.*, supposedly, reputedly, in reckoning merely.

1660 H. MORE *Myst. Godl.* VIII. iv. 375 Even as Christ was righteous, who was not putatitiously and imaginarily righteous, but really so indeed.

putative ('pjuːtətɪv), *a.* [a. F. *putatif* (14–15th c. in Hatz.-Darm.), or ad. late L. *putātīv-us* (Tertullian *c* 200), f. *putāt-us*: see prec. and -IVE.] That is such by supposition or by repute; commonly thought or deemed; reputed, supposed.

putative marriage, in *Canon law*, a marriage which though legally invalid was contracted in good faith by at least one of the parties.

1432–50 tr. *Higden* (Rolls) III. 331 Philippus,.. fader putatiue of the noble conquerour Alexander. **1539** *Test. Ebor.* (Surtees) VI. 92 John Beilbie, my sone putative. *a* **1548** HALL *Chron.*, *Edw. IV* 196 Of al hys other putatyue (I dare not say fayned) frendes.. he had bene clerely abandoned. **1577** tr. *Bullinger's Decades* (1592) 688 Neither is the Scripture it selfe ashamed, to call Marie.. not the putatiue or supposed, but the true and naturall mother. **1681** FLAVEL *Meth. Grace* vi. 130 Let their blasphemous mouths call it in derision putative righteousness, (*i.e.*) a mere fancied or conceited righteousness; yet we know assuredly Christ's righteousness is imputed to us, and that in the way of faith. **1765** BLACKSTONE *Comm.* I. xvi. 458 If such putative father, or lewd mother, run away from the parish, the overseers.. may seize their rents, goods, and chattels, in order to bring up the said bastard child. **1858** SEARS *Athan.* II. xi. 240 He [Christ] imparts not a putative, but a subjective, righteousness to the believer.

1811 (Febr.) LD. MEADOWBANK in *Brymner v. Riddell* (Ct. of Session), Here there was a putative marriage, acknowledged by all the friends of both parties, and by the general admission.. of the legality of that marriage. **1825** RT. BELL (*title*) Report of a case of legitimacy under a putative marriage [Brymner v. Riddell] tried.. 1811. **1876** P. FRASER *Husb. & Wife Law Scotl.* (ed. 2) I. 152 The children born of such a putative marriage are, by the law of Scotland legitimate, though the marriage be null.

Hence '**putatively** *adv.*, in a putative way or manner; supposedly, reputedly.

1716 M. DAVIES *Athen. Brit.* II. 220 He subjoin'd also that Christ did not really suffer, but only Putatively in people's Fancies. **1851** P. COLQUHOUN *Rom. Civ. Law* II. §1078 Putatively married persons have the same privilege. **1903** MCNEILL *Egregious English* 109 Mr. Davidson is a Scot, and Mr. Yeats, putatively at any rate, an Irishman.

†'**putatory,** *a. Obs. rare*⁻⁰. [ad. late L. *putātōrius*, f. *putāre* to prune.] (See quot.)

1656 BLOUNT *Glossogr.*, *Putatory*, of or belonging to cutting, dressing or pruining of Trees.

†**put-bone.** ? The knuckle-bone or astragalus.

1664 E. BROWNE in *Sir T. Browne's Wks.* (1836) I. 45 Mr. Osborne sent my father a calf, whereof I observed the knee joynt, and the neat articulation of the put bone, which was here very perfect. I dissected another bull's heart. *Ibid.* 48 In a putbone the unfortunate casts are outward, the fortunate inward.

put-card: see PUT *sb.*[3]

†'**put-case.** *Obs.* [f. the phrase *put case*: PUT *v.*[1] 22.]

1. The act of putting a case; a supposition or hypothesis.

1565 JEWEL *Def. Apol.* IV. ix. §3 What a foolishe putcase, and what a fond wishe if that is, to saie, What if a Pirate inuade the Arke of Noe? **1577** tr. *Bullinger's Decades* (1592) 282 They with their innumerable perchances and put-cases do make the treatise of restitution so tedious.

2. A person skilled in putting cases; one who states or argues hypothetical cases.

a **1734** NORTH *Lives, Ld. Guildford* I. 20 He used to say that no man could be a good lawyer that was not a put-case.

putchamin, early form of PERSIMMON.

putcheon, var. PUTCHER.

putcher ('pʌtʃə(r)). *local.* Also **putcheon.** [The same as *putchen, -eon, -in*, recorded in the Eng. Dial. Dict. from Shropsh., Worcester, Warwick, Gloucestersh., in sense 'eel-basket, wicker eel-trap'. Origin unknown. Cf. PUTT *sb.*[2]] A conical basket or wicker trap for catching salmon (see quot. 1885).

1873 *Act 36 & 37 Vic.* c. 71 §21 (1) Licenses for fishing weirs, fishing mill dams, putts, putchers, fixed nets, and other fixed instruments or devices. **1883** *Fisheries Exhib. Catal.* 51 Models of Salmon Nets.. Weirs with fish-passes ..Putchers, [etc.]. **1884** *Daily News* 1 Sept. 6/7 In the [Severn] estuary large hauls were made with the nets and putchers in July and August. **1885** *Daily Tel.* 18 Aug., Putchers..are funnel-shaped baskets of wicker-work set at right angles to the shore, into which the salmon press themselves in trying to press through, and are unable to return. **1898** *Birmingham Daily Post* 16 Dec. 8/6 Heavy catches of eels in 'putcheons'. **1945** J. MOORE *Portrait of Elmbury* iv. 147 Jim also earned £4 by selling eel-putcheons which he'd made out of withies. **1968** J. ARNOLD *Shell Bk. Country Crafts* 258 Salmon traps, putchers or putcheons, are quite different in structure. *Ibid.* 260 The putcheons are arranged in a stout, permanent framework, forming a 'barrage' extending for scores of yards across the Severn grounds.

‖**putchuk, putchock** ('pʌtʃək). Also 7 pochok, 8–9 putchick, 9 patchuk. [Dukhnī or Southern Hindustānī *pachak*; origin doubtful: widely prevalent as a trade name.] The root of the plant *Aplotaxis auriculata* (*Aucklandia Costus* of Falconer), a native of Kashmīr, exported to China and other Eastern countries, and used as a medicine and for making the Chinese joss-sticks.

(*native*) ***green putchuk***, a name for the root of the Chinese *Aristolochia recurvilabra*, used in medicine.

[**1588** T. HICKOCK tr. *C. Frederick's Voy.* 5 Aboundaunce of Opioum, Assa Fetida, Puchio, with many other sorts of drugs.] **1617** R. COCKS *Diary* (Hakl. Soc.) I. 294, 5 hampers pochok. **1704** in C. Lockyer *Trade Ind.* (1711) 77 Putchuck or Costus dulcis. **1727** A. HAMILTON *New Acc. E. Ind.* I. xi. 126 Nothing of it is usefull but the Root, called Putchock, or Radix dulcis. **1802** CAPT. ELMORE *Brit. Mariners Direct.* 129 Putchick, shark fins, olibanum. **1845** STOCQUELER *Handbk. Brit. India* (1854) 34 Bombay..supplies..grain, oils, putchock, seeds, tobacco, and soap, from the northern coast. **1858** SIMMONDS *Dict. Trade Prod.*, Putchuk.

†**pute**, *sb. rare*$^{-1}$. [a. F. *pute* = Pr., Sp. *puta*, It. *putta*, late pop. L. *pŭtta*:—L. *pūtida* stinking: cf. PUTAIN.] A whore, strumpet, prostitute.

c **1380** WYCLIF *Serm.* Sel. Wks. I. 293 þei ben foule putis.

pute (pju:t), *a.* Now *rare* or *arch.* [ad. L. *putus* clean, pure, used in the phrase *purus* (*ac*) *putus* = *purissimus*.] In phrases ***pure pute, pure and pute***, pure, clean, mere.

c **1619** BP. HALL *Via Media* §5 Arminius..acknowledges faith to be the pure pute gift of God. **1657** SANDERSON *Serm.* Pref. §24 A pure pute Christian. *a* **1734** NORTH *Exam.* II. iv. §49 (1740) 256 Dangerfield had the Honour to be a single Discoverer of a pure and pute Sham-plot, Name and Thing. **1906** R. KIPLING *Puck of Pook's Hill, Hal o' Draft* 240 Only you and I chance to be pure pute asses.

pute, obs. form of PIT *sb.*[1]

puteal ('pju:tiːəl), *sb. Rom. Antiq.* [a. L. *puteal*, (*-āle*), orig. neuter of *puteālis*: see next.] The stone curb surrounding the mouth of a well.

[**1832** GELL *Pompeiana* II. xiii. 27 A marble mouth or *puteale*.] **1850** LEITCH tr. *C. O. Müller's Anc. Art* (ed. 2) §379 *note*, The Capitoline puteal has adopted a younger figure of Hermes. **1862** E. FALKENER *Ephesus* I. iv. 63 Vestiges of a circular building, the small size of which renders it probable that it formed a puteal.

†'**puteal**, *a. Obs. rare.* [ad. L. *puteālis*, f. *puteus* pit, well.] Of or pertaining to a well or pit.

1656 BLOUNT *Glossogr.*, *Puteal*, of or belonging to a pit or well. **1657** TOMLINSON *Renou's Disp.* 219 The best water, therefore, is fontane, fluvial, and puteal water.

puteanic (pju:tiː'ænɪk), *a. Chem.* [f. L. *puteān-us* pertaining to a well (f. *puteus* well) + -IC.] In ***puteanic acid***: see quot.

[**1834** HAENLE in *Kastner's Archiv*, Nurnberg, XXVI. 399 Ich bezeichne sie daher..mit dem Namen Brunnensäure (*Acidum puteanum*).] **1838** T. THOMSON *Chem. Org. Bodies* 156 Puteanic acid..discovered, in 1835, by M. Haenlé, apothecary at Lahr, in the ochre which deposits abundantly in the wells of that neighbourhood... It is a resinous-looking body, transparent when in thin crusts, having a strong lustre, and a brown colour. It has no smell.

puten, error for PETUN, q.v., quot. 1600–14.

puter, obs. form of PEWTER.

†'**putery.** *Obs.* Also 4 putrie, 4–5 -erie, 5 putrye, -ree, -erye. [a. OF. *put(e)rie* whoredom, f. *pute*: see PUTE *sb.*: -ERY[1].] Unchastity (properly in a woman); harlotry, prostitution.

c **1380** WYCLIF *Wks.* (1880) 10 þes pharisees geten hem moo holderis vp for here putrie þan for here trewe prechyng. *c* **1386** CHAUCER *Pars. T.* ¶812 What seye we eek of Putours þat lyuen by the horrible synne of putrie, and constreyne wommen to yelden to hem a certeyn rente of hire bodily puterie? *c* **1440** *York Myst.* xxiv. 30 We haue hir tane with putry playne. **1483** CAXTON *G. de la Tour* lj, In puterye and in synne mortalle or dedely he [the deuylle] hath grete power.

putfalle, obs. form of PITFALL.

†**put-gallary, putt-**, var. of POT-GALLERY, *Obs.*

1658 *Lease* in *N. & Q.* 10th Ser. (1908) IX. 212/2, 4 Putt Gallaries, or shedds, built over the mill stream upon the wharfe thereof, in Paris Garden.

†**put-gally.** *Obs.* Also 6 putt-. [ad. Du. and Fl. *put-galg* a bascule to raise water from a well, in Hexham *put-galge* 'a swipe to drawe up water out of a well', in Kilian *put-galghe*, 'tollenon, pertica putealis'; f. *put* well, pit + *galge*, gallows, post of a draw-well.] A bascule or lever fixed on a high fulcrum and having a counterpoise on the handle, by means of which water is lifted from a well or pit; a swipe or sweep.

1584–5 *Indenture 27 Eliz.* in *N. & Q.* 8th Ser. (1894) V. 348/2 With free egresse and regresse thorowe the same waye, and with free accesse, egresse and regresse to the Putt gally, findinge wherewith to drawe and carrye the same water aweye, And together also withe like accesse egresse and regresse to the litle well there. **1611** COTGR., *Bascule*, a swipe, scoope, or put-gally to draw vp water withall.

†**puther**[1], obs. form of PEWTER.

1562 in J. R. Boyle *Hedon* (1875) App. 206 A litle brasse pott, two puther dublers, two dishes of puther.

puther[2], obs. and dial. form of POTHER.

puthery: see POTHERY *a.*

putid ('pju:tɪd), *a.* Now *rare.* [ad. L. *pūtid-us* stinking, foul, f. *pūtē-re* to stink: see -ID[1].]

†**1.** Stinking, rotten, putrid. *Obs.*

1659 GAUDEN *Slight Healers* (1660) 21 Some putid or corrupt humors in the body.

2. *fig.* Foul, base; morally or intellectually 'rotten' or worthless. (Often merely a term of contempt or execration.)

1580 FULKE *Dang. Rock* xviii. Wks. (Parker Soc.) II. 391 O putid and absurd slanders! **1635–56** COWLEY *Davideis* I. Notes, Wks. (1669) 28 Made up..by the putid officiousness of some Grammarians. **1681** BAXTER *Answ. Dodwell* iv. 28 A chain of forgeries or putid falshoods. *a* **1734** NORTH *Exam.* III. vii. §70 (1740) 556 He hath..framed so putid a Libel upon his Lordship. **1818** J. C. HOBHOUSE *Hist. Illustr.* (ed. 2) 216 To reject this narration as a putid fable.

Hence **pu'tidity** [ad. med.L. *pūtiditās*, *c* 1150 in Thomas *Thesaur.*], '**putidness**, the quality of being putid, rottenness; '**putidly** *adv.*

1659 GAUDEN *Tears Ch.* II. xvi. 199 High-tasted sawces.. applied to tainted meats, to make their putidness less perceptible. **1864** WEBSTER, Putidity, Putidness. **1897** *Sat. Rev.* 7 May 552/2 What we most feebly and putidly nowadays call a lady-doctor.

putlog, putlock ('pʌtlɒg, -lɒk), *sb.* [The form *putlock* appears to have been the earlier; derivation obscure; ? from *put*, pa. pple. of PUT *v.*[1]]

One of the short horizontal timbers of a scaffolding, on which the scaffold-boards rest; one end is inserted at right angles in a hole left in the wall for that purpose (*putlog-hole*), the other being supported by the ledger.

α. **1645** *Docum. St. Paul's* (Camden) 143, Putlocks for scaffolding 3763. **1688** R. HOLME *Armoury* III. 262/1 Putlocks, pieces of Spar put into the Sides of the Wall to lay Boards on for the Bricklayer to stand and work up high Walls. **1727–41** CHAMBERS *Cycl.*, *Putlogs*, or *Putlocks*, in building. **1823** P. NICHOLSON *Pract. Build.* 591 Putlogs or Putlocks; in scaffolding, the transverse pieces, at right angles to the wall. **1866** *Standard* 12 June 7/2 The putlock..came away, and a bricklayer..was precipitated from a considerable height to the ground.

β. **1703** MOXON *Mech. Exerc.* 251 *Putlogs*..pieces of Timber, or short Poles, about 7 Foot long. **1862** E. FALKENER *Ephesus* iv. 85 The walls are for the most part disfigured by small square holes (like those left by putlogs). **1901** *J. Black's Carp. & Build.*, *Scaffold.* 89 Scaffold poles, putlogs, and boards are rented..most largely to builders.

b. *Comb.* **putlog-, putlock-hole**, one of a series of small square holes left in the brickwork or stonework of a wall to receive the ends of the putlogs.

1757 SMEATON in *Phil. Trans.* I. 202 Putlock-holes for the scaffolding. **1878** MCVITTIE *Christ Ch. Cathedral* 61 Small holes were found running through the wall at different heights, resembling putlock holes.

Hence '**putlog** *v. trans.*, to insert in the manner of a putlog.

1908 *N. & Q.* 10th Ser. VII. 483/1 A beam putlogged into the north and south walls.

put-off (pʊt'ɒf, -ɔː-), *sb.* Pl. put-offs. [f. the verbal phrase *put off* (PUT *v.* 46).] An act of putting off, in various senses.

1. An act of dismissing a question, argument, etc., or the person propounding it, by evasion or the like; a pretext for not doing something, or for deferring it till later (cf. 2); an evasion, a shift.

1549 LATIMER *3rd Serm. bef. Edw. VI* (Arb.) 79 Nowe they haue theyr shyftes, and theyr putofs sainge, we maye not go before a lawe, we maye breake no order. **1549** E. BECKE *Bible* (Matthew's) Prol., Then should neyther Goddes cause nor poore mans matters haue so many putoffes, so many put byes & delayes. *a* **1704** T. BROWN *Dial. Dead, Friendship* Wks. 1711 IV. 59 He..repay'd my past Services with..base Put-offs. **1823** BENTHAM *Not Paul* 42 Promises, put-offs, evasions— and, after all, no performance. **1886** STEVENSON *Kidnapped* xxii, I think I would have asked farther, but Alan gave me the put-off. 'I am rather wearied', he said.

2. An act of deferring or postponing something; postponement, delay, procrastination; a putting a person off to a later time.

1623 R. CARPENTER *Conscionable Christian* 28 Instantly, as the occasion is giuen, without put-offs to aftertimes, or any tedious protraction. ? **1625** JAS. I in *Waller's Poems* (1711) p. ix, No Put-offs, my Lord, answer me presently. **1759** FRANKLIN *Ess.* Wks. 1840 III. 425 What the governor's set-off could not effect, was to be reattempted by this put-off. **1827** MOORE *Mem.* (1854) V. 157 Expecting..to receive a put-off from Lady Holland for the evening.

3. *lit.* A putting off or setting down a person from a vehicle or a vessel, esp. a boat. *rare.*

1825 HONE *Every-day Bk.* I. 603 This delay..is occasioned by 'laying to' for 'put offs' of single persons and parties, in Thames wherries.

put-off, *ppl. a.*: see PUT *ppl. a.*

put-on (pʊtɒn; stress var.), *ppl. a.* [pa. pple. of *to put on*: see PUT *v.* 47.]

1. Placed upon the person, as clothing.

1894 MISS BROUGHTON *Beginner* xii, The Russian net of her accurately put-on veil.

b. *transf.* of the person: Clothed, dressed (with qualifying adv., as *well* or *ill*). *Sc.* and *north. dial.*

1815 SCOTT *Guy M.* l, I'm no just that weel put on. **1887** MABEL WETHERAL *Two North-Country Maids* xxiii, It changes lassies when they look so trim, and well put on. **1896** BARRIE *Marg. Ogilvy* ix. (1897) 167 The first thing I want to know about her is whether she was good-looking, and the second how she was put on.

2. *fig.* Assumed, affected, feigned, pretended.

1621 FLETCHER *Wildgoose Chase* III. i, With such a reverend put-on Reservation Which could not miss. **1775** MME. D'ARBLAY *Early Diary* 28 Feb., He assumed no manner of superiority; nor yet..affected a certain put-on equality. **1884** CHURCH *Bacon* iii. 58 The put on and worldly life.

'**put-on**, *sb.* Chiefly *N. Amer.* [PUT-: cf. PUT *v.* 47 e.] A deception, a ruse, a hoax.

1937 PARTRIDGE *Dict. Slang.* 672/2 *Put-on*, a deception, subterfuge, excuse..from ca. 1860. **1949** H. HORNSBY *Lonesome Valley* xxiv. 316 He knew there was no put-on; that she was not talking just to make him feel better. **1967** *New Yorker* 24 June 34/3 What was once an occasional surprise tactic—called 'joshing' around the turn of the century and 'kidding' since the twenties—has been refined into the very basis of a new mode of communication. In all its permutations, this phenomenon is known as the 'put-on'. It occupies a fuzzy territory between simple leg-pulling and elaborate practical joke. **1968** 'E. MCBAIN' *Fuzz* ix. 140 Meyer thought the call was a put-on, nobody had a name like Carlyle Butterford. **1970** *Globe & Mail* (Toronto) 28 Sept. 8/7 (Advt.), Wool carpet excellence is assured by the Woolmark label. Protecting you from a put-on. **1973** *Sat. Rev. Society* (U.S.) May 76/3 A wild mishmash of put-on, fantasy, and cultivated lunacy. **1975** *New Yorker* 17 Nov. 125/1 There is no hint of satire here—or, to be fair, of put-on. **1977** *Time* 4 Apr. 44/2 Much of the tone of such writing is personal, confessional, full of macho bellicosity and show-biz put-on.

‖**putonghua** (pu:tʊŋhwɑ:). Also pu-, p'ut'ung-hua. [Chinese *pǔtōnghuà*, f. *pǔtōng* common + *huà* spoken language.] The standard spoken language now in general use throughout the People's Republic of China, based on the northern dialects, esp. that of Peking. Cf. KUO-YÜ.

1950 J. DE FRANCIS *Nationalism & Lang. Reform in China* v. 94 He expressed his views..in the following statement: ' ..China now has a *p'u-t'ung hua* (common language) which can serve as a general standard.' **1968** P. KRATOCHVÍL *Chinese Lang. Today* v. 164 This concept of the so-called *pǔtōnghuà* 'Common Language' is largely based on the latter stage of *guóyǔ* (the two terms *guóyǔ* and *pǔtōnghuà* are now almost synonymous). **1971** R. NEWNHAM *About Chinese* 75 The Communists took up the ['spoken language'] of the older 'literary revolutionists', renaming it *pǔtōnghuà* or 'common speech'. The inspiration became firmly social. Pǔtōnghuà is now what the West generally thinks of when it speaks of 'Mandarin'... It is adopted by all the communications media in China (the phrase 'national language' is not heard), while in print it is virtually standard. **1973** T. R. TREGEAR *Chinese* vi. 124 The *pai hua* has had a profound influence since today it forms the basis of *p'u t'ung hua*, 'usual words' now in universal use throughout the land. **1976** W. H. CANAWAY *Willow-Pattern War* xv. 156 He spoke enough *pu-t'ung hua*, the Common Chinese, for Shao to give him instructions before we left. **1978** *Nagel's Encycl.-Guide: China* 68 A common spoken language, now known as *putonghua* (Common Language) was imposed throughout China.

†'**putor.** *Obs. rare.* [a. L. *pūtor* stench, f. *pūtēre* to stink.] (See quot.)

1656 BLOUNT *Glossogr.*, *Putor*, a stink or ill savor.

†**putour.** *Obs.* [app. AF. *putour*, collateral form of OF. *putier* PUTYER.] A whoremonger; a pimp; a fornicator.

c **1386** [see PUTERY]. **1393** LANGL. *P. Pl.* C. VII. 172 Lady, to þy leue sone lowte for me nouthe, That he haue pyte on me putour [*v.r.* putrour] of hus pure grace and mercy.

put-out, *sb.* and *ppl. a.*: see PUT-, PUT *ppl. a.*

†'**put-pin.** *Obs.* [f. PUT *v.*[1] + PIN.] = PUSH-PIN.

1592 NASHE *Foure Lett. Confut.* (1593) 52, I will play at put-pinne with thee for all that thou art woorth. **1658** J. HARRINGTON *Prerog. Pop. Govt.* I. ix. (1700) 269 His Put-pin is pretty: The Emperor puts Power into the hands of the Electors; and the King of Poland puts Power into the hands of the Gentlemen. **1665** GLANVILL *Scepsis Sci.* xxiii. 178 He ..will not leave the Throne to play with Beggars at Put-pin, or be fond of Tops and Cherry-stones.

put-put ('pʌtpʌt), *sb.* orig. *N. Amer.* Also **putt-putt.** [Echoic.] A muffled explosive sound characteristic of an internal-combustion engine. Also applied to objects which make such a sound, as a machine-gun, a motorized boat or bicycle, etc. Also *attrib.*

1905 *Rudder* Feb. 61/2 Already the class of small launches, of which the converted [St. Lawrence] skiffs form the majority, has achieved the distinction of a special title, of unknown origin, but of universal use; 'put-put', or more briefly, 'put'. The words themselves are now almost as common to the ear as the familiar voice of the two-cycle motor which called them into being. **1929** M. A. GILL *Underworld Slang* 9/2 *Put-put*, machine gun. **1930** J. P. BURKE in *Amer. Mercury* Dec. 457/1 *Putt-putt*, an out-board motorboat used in liquor running. 'A sneaker's no good. Water's too shallow. Got to use a putt-putt.' **1959** P. CAPON *Amongst Those Missing* 165 The others could hear it now, a quick-fire 'put-put-put' like a distant motor-bike. **1964** E. A. NIDA *Toward Sci. Transl.* iii. 31 An onomatopoeic expression, such as *putt-putt* or *choo-choo*, is presumably an imitation of the very sound made by the object in question. **1965** S. T. OLLIVIER *Petticoat Farm* iv. 46 A roar of laughter drowned the put-put of the engine. **1967** *Guardian* 28 Dec. 5/3 The little put-put boat which carries passengers ashore. **1968** *Sunday Mail Mag.* (Brisbane) 15 Sept. 4/2 Anchored right in the middle was a small, old putt-putt type launch. **1974** J. MITCHELL *Death & Bright Water* xii. 134 [He] listened to the putt putt of the two-stroke as he rode back to Kronis. **1977** *Time* 19 Dec. 13/2 Does he really think the new cruise missile is no better than Hitler's high-flying, inaccurate put-put? **1978** M. Z. LEWIN *Silent Salesman* xv. 80 The cop..got on his putt-putt, and went away.

put-put ('pʌtpʌt), *v.* orig. *N. Amer.* Also **putt-putt.** [Echoic.] *intr.* To make an intermittent explosive sound characteristic of an internal-combustion engine. To move, making such a noise. Also quasi-*trans.* Also *fig.* Hence **put(t)-putting** *vbl. sb.*

1905 *Outing* July 389/1 In and out between them trim little launches go *put-putting*. **1939** A. KEITH *Land below Wind* vii. 113 The motor put-puts back a horrid petrol odour. **1955** 'D. CORY' *Phoenix Sings* v. 82 A peculiar put-*put*-put-*put*... The put-*putting* noise was increasing... I made out the shape of a great sailing-barge..its tiny donkey-engine chugging away. **1958** *Spectator* 4 July 12/2 The diesel engine put-put-puts its warm gargle. **1961** J. C. LILLY *Man & Dolphin* xi. 153 A dolphin..naturally uses other sounds to convey and receive 'meaning':..putt-putting and whistles for exchanges with other dolphins. *Ibid.* 158 Lizzie [*sc.* a dolphin], near the hydrophone, putt-putted. **1973** 'D. JORDAN' *Nile Green* xliii. 220 The helicopter..came in fast over the desert, the put-putting loud overhead. **1974** R. JEFFRIES *Mistakenly in Mallorca* viii. 78 Old Morley keeps boasting about how he putt-putts all his money out of England.

putred, obs. erron. form of PUTRID.

† **'putrede.** *Obs. rare.* Also **-ride.** [ad. L. *putrēdo*: see below.] Rotting, putridity.

c **1400** *Lanfranc's Cirurg.* 86 If þat þe membre be drie..& þei han greet putride [MS. B. putrede] & rotschipe.

† **pu'tredinal,** *a. Obs.* Also 7 putri-. [a. F. *putrédinal* (16th c. in Godef.), f. late L. *putrēdo, -inem*: see PUTREDO and -AL[1].] Proceeding from or characterized by putrefaction.

1574 J. JONES *Nat. Beginning Grow. Things* 18 It is the naturall heate, become putredinall or rotten. **1666** G. HARVEY *Morb. Angl.* xv. 178 Lice..engendred out of their clammy sweat, by a putredinal heat that attends them.

† **pu'tredinous,** *a. Obs.* [ad. F. *putrédineux* (Cotgr. 1611), f. as prec.: see -OUS.] = prec.; also *fig.* filthy, abominable.

1641 BURGES *Serm. bef. Ho. Com.* 5 Nov. 60 All putredinous vermine of bold Schismaticks and frantick Sectaries glory in her ashes. **1708** *Brit. Apollo* No. 35. 3/2 From Putredinous Humours this ill doth proceed. **1711** G. CARY *Phys. Phylactick* 209 Most Putredinous Sectaries.

‖ **putredo** (pjuː'triːdəʊ). *Obs.* [Late L. *putrēdo* rottenness, putridity, f. *putrēre* to rot: cf. *torpēdo* f. *torpēre*.] Putrefaction; *spec.* in *Path.*, hospital gangrene (*Syd. Soc. Lex.*).

1704 F. FULLER *Med. Gymn.* (1718) 161 Accounting for things by Occult Qualities, Putredo's and the like.

putrefacient (pjuːtrɪ'feɪʃ(ɪ)ənt), *a.* (*sb.*) [ad. L. *putrefacient-em*, pres. pple. of *putrefacĕre* to make rotten: see next.] = PUTREFACTIVE.

1883 *American* VI. 173 One of which is..a putrefacient poison. **188.** *Alienist & Neurol.* IX. 363 Putrefacient action on the blood and tissues after the lapse of some hours.

B. *sb.* A putrefactive agent or substance.

1890 in *Cent. Dict.*

† **putre'fact,** *v. Obs.* Also 7 putri-. [f. L. *putrefact-*, ppl. stem of *putrefacĕre* to make rotten, f. *putrēre* to be rotten (f. *puter, putr-* rotten) + *facĕre* to make.] *trans.* To make rotten, to putrefy.

1597 A. M. tr. *Guillemeau's Fr. Chirurg.* 33 b/2 To prevente the same [bone] to be..putrefacted and corrupted.

Hence † **putre'facted** *ppl. a.*, putrefied; † **putre'factible** *a.*, capable of putrefaction; putrescible.

1602 MARSTON *Antonio's Rev.* IV. iv, Vermine bred of putrifacted slime. **1634** PEACHAM *Gentl. Exerc.* I. xviii. 60 Grosse and putrefacted vapours, that issue from the eyes. **1651** BIGGS *New Disp.* § 287 As often as any putrefactible or cadaverizable thing is ingested in the stomack.

putrefaction (pjuːtrɪ'fækʃən). Forms: 5–9 (*erron.*) putri-, 6 putry-, 5– putre-; 5 -faccio(u)n, -faccyon, -factioun, 6– -faction. [a. OF. *putrefaction* (14th c. in Littré), or ad. L. *putrefactiōn-em*, n. of action f. *putrefacĕre*: see prec.]

1. The action or process of putrefying; the decomposition of animal and vegetable substances, with its attendant unwholesome loathsomeness of smell and appearance; rotting, corruption.

In quot. 1432–50, applied to a corrupting pestilence.

1432–50 tr. *Higden* (Rolls) V. 339 A grete dragon, thro the pestilente putrefaccion of whom moche peple diede in the cite. **1533** ELYOT *Cast. Helthe* III. xv. (1541) 72 b, It shal be necessary for them..to be circumspecte in eatyng meate y^t^ shortly will receiue putrifaction. **1661** J. CHILDREY *Brit. Baconica* 55 Heat and moisture are the greater disposers to putrifaction. **1789** W. BUCHAN *Dom. Med.* (1790) 63 Animal substances have a constant tendency to putrefaction. **1833** MARRYAT *P. Simple* xxx, The body is never allowed to remain many hours unburied in the tropical climates, where putrefaction is so rapid. **1875** HUXLEY & MARTIN *Elem. Biol.* (1883) 26 All the forms of putrefaction which are undergone by animal and vegetable matters are fermentations set up by Bacteria of different kinds.

b. Decomposition of tissues or fluids in a living body, as in ulceration, suppuration, or gangrene.

c **1400** *Lanfranc's Cirurg.* 51 þe which quytture schulde corrupte þilke lyme [= limb] & brynge him to putrifaccioun [*v.r.* putrefactioun]. **1460–70** *Bk. Quintessence* 21 Alle philosophoris seyn þat þe feuere contynuele is gendrid of putrifaccioun of blood and of corrupcioun of humouris in it. **1579** LANGHAM *Gard. Health* (1633) 403 Mirrhe preserueth from putrifaction, both the intrals and all outward sores, wounds, and vlcers. **1605** BACON *Adv. Learn.* I. vi. § 9 That putrefaction is more contagious before maturitie than after. **1756** GRAY *Let. to Wharton* 25 Mar., I maintain that one sick rich patient has more of pestilence and putrefaction about him than a whole ward of sick poor. **1806** *Med. Jrnl.* XV. 492 It is attended with great debility, and there is frequently a great tendency to putrefaction and mortification.

† **2.** In reference to inorganic matter, esp. in *Alchemy*: The disintegration or decomposition of a substance by chemical or other action; also, the oxidation or corrosion of metals, etc. *Obs.*

1471 RIPLEY *Comp. Alch.* v. iii. in Ashm. *Theat. Chem. Brit.* (1652) 148 And Putrefaccyon may thus defyned be After Philosophers sayings it ys of Bodyes the fleyng, And in our compound a dyuysyon of thyngs thre. **1610** B. JONSON *Alch.* II. v, Name the vexations, and the martyrizations of Mettalls... Sir, Putrefaction, Solution, Ablution, Sublimation [etc.]. **1626** BACON *Sylva* § 291 Metals give Orient and Fine colours in Dissolutions..likewise in their Putrefactions or Rusts. **1671** J. WEBSTER *Metallogr.* viii. 128 A certain metallick body..that is of an easie solution and putrefaction.

3. *concr.* Decomposed or putrid matter.

1605 BACON *Adv. Learn.* I. vi. § 11 The mosse vppon the wall, which is but a rudiment betweene putrefaction, and an hearbe. **1634** SIR T. HERBERT *Trav.* 39 In the midst is a hole, discending to the bottome, which receiues that putrefaction and vncleannesse, issuing from the melting bodies, which are laid there naked..exposed to the sunnes fiery rage. **1692** BENTLEY *Boyle Lect.* iv. 134 They would readily [deposit their eggs] in all Putrefaction, even in a mucilage of bruised spiders.

4. *fig.* Moral corruption and decay.

a **1631** DONNE *Select.* (1840) 164 We bring elements of our own; earth of covetousness, water of unsteadfastness, air of putrefaction, and fire of licentiousness. **1750** JOHNSON *Rambler* No. 47 ¶ 14 Sorrow..is the putrefaction of stagnant life, and is remedied by exercise and motion. **1871** TYNDALL *Fragm. Sci.* (1879) II. ix. 148 Rome, and the other cities of the Empire, had fallen into moral putrefaction. **1907** *Edin. Rev.* Jan. 22, It is thanks to heretics that orthodoxy has been kept from putrefaction.

Hence † **putre'factious (putri-)** *a. Obs.*, of the nature of, or full of putrefaction; putrefying, putrid.

1609 W. M. *Man in Moone* D iij, Your complexion..shall be of a saffron colour; your cheekes, thinne; your nosethrils putrifactious;..your breath, noysome. **1616** R. C. *Times' Whistle* v. 2178 Drunkennesse, whose putrefactious slime Darkens the splendour of our common wealth.

putrefactive (pjuːtrɪ'fæktɪv), *a.* (*sb.*) Also 6–7 putri-. [a. F. *putréfactif, -ive* (14th c. in Littré), f. L. *putrefact-*: see PUTREFACT and -IVE.]

1. Causing or inducing putrefaction; putrefying.

1545 ELYOT *Dict.* H h vj b/1, *Septicus*,..putrifactife, or corrosife. **1601** HOLLAND *Pliny* XXVIII. ix. II. 321 Their bloud is corrosiue by nature, and putrifactiue. **1610** MARKHAM *Masterp.* II. clvi. 460 The medicines are either corrosiue, putrifactiue, or caustick. **1744** BERKELEY *Siris* § 69 Where the obstruction is attended with a putrefactive alkali. **1830** M. DONOVAN *Dom. Econ.* I. 99 The existence of some putrefactive ferment. **1899** *Allbutt's Syst. Med.* VI. 165 Putrid softening is due to the invasion of putrefactive bacteria.

2. Of, pertaining to, produced or characterized by putrefaction; indicative of putrefaction. ***putrefactive fermentation***, putrefaction scientifically viewed as a species of fermentation.

1646 SIR T. BROWNE *Pseud. Ep.* II. vi. 95 Making putrifactive generations correspondent unto seminal productions..when the Oxe corrupteth into Bees, or the Horses into hornets. **1676** WISEMAN *Chirurg. Treat.* (J.), If the bone be corrupted, the putrefactive smell will discover it. **1758** REID tr. *Macquer's Chem.* I. 111 The third generates an alkaline salt;..this last sort takes the name of the Putrid or Putrefactive Fermentation. **1815** KIRBY & SP. *Entomol.* iv. (1818) I. 87 The authors..had mistaken for lice some other species of insects, which are not unfrequently found in putrefactive sores. **1838** *Penny Cycl.* X. 237/2 Fermentation is of three kinds: the vinous, producing alcohol; the acetous, yielding vinegar; and the putrefactive, of which the products are very variable and usually fetid.

† **3.** Undergoing or subject to putrefaction; putrefying; corruptible. *Obs.*

1610 MARKHAM *Masterp.* II. clxxiii. 487 It cleanseth al putrifactiue humors. **1661** FELTHAM *Resolves* II. xvii. Wks. (1677) 194 If momentary and putrefactive man can undiscerned and unburthen'd bear so much about him.

† **B.** *sb.* A substance which causes putrefaction; a putrefactive agent. *Obs.*

1610 MARKHAM *Masterp.* II. clvi. 461 The corrosiues are weaker then the putrifactiues, and the putrifactiues are weaker then the caustickes.

Hence **putre'factiveness**, the quality of being putrefactive.

1864 in WEBSTER.

† **putre'factory,** *a. Obs. rare.* Also putri-. [f. as prec. + -ORY[2].] = PUTREFACTIVE *a.*

1650 BULWER *Anthropomet.* 251 Their way is, to cut a man in pieces, and then put him into a Putrifactory Vessel.

putrefiable ('pjuːtrɪfaɪəb(ə)l), *a.* [f. PUTREFY + -ABLE.] Capable of being putrefied; putrescible.

1883 W. T. BELFIELD *Relat. Micro-Org. to Disease* 60 For absorption of putrefiable materials. **1884** *19th Cent.* Feb. 325 Some epidemic agent..which converts putrefiable impurities into a specific poison.

putrefied ('pjuːtrɪfaɪd), *ppl. a.* [f. PUTREFY + -ED[1].] **1.** Rendered putrid; rotten.

1526 *Pilgr. Perf.* (W. de W. 1531) 202 b, Many other beestes and wormes be gendred of the erth onely, or other putrefyed matter. *a* **1640** J. BALL *Answ. to Canne* II. (1642) 55 As rotten and putrified stuffe to be cast out. **1724** R. WELTON *Chr. Faith & Pract.* 359 Their hearts are filthy and corrupt like those putrefied carcasses. **1765** A. DICKSON *Treat. Agric.* (ed. 2) 370 The dung..is still to be considered as vegetables in a putrefied state.

¶ **2.** *U.S. dial.* A malapropism for 'petrified'.

1848 G. F. RUXTON in *Blackw. Mag.* June 714/2 'I've seen a putrefied forest.' 'La, Mister Harris, a what?' 'A putrefied forest, marm.' *Ibid.* 715/1 'I shows him the piece I chipped out of the tree, and he called it a putrefaction too; and so, marm, if that wasn't a putrefied peraira, what was it?' **1896** 'MARK TWAIN' in *Harper's Mag.* Sept. 536/2 Jubiter..was just fairly putrefied with astonishment.

putrefier ('pjuːtrɪfaɪə(r)). [f. PUTREFY + -ER[1].] A putrefying agent. Also *fig.*

1651 BIGGS *New Disp.* § 118 Putrefyers of the blood. **1883** *Workshop Receipts* Ser. II. 196/2 A series of experiments upon putrefiers and antiseptics. **1895** *Voice* (N.Y.) 9 May 5/4 Who are the putrefiers of society to-day?

putrefy ('pjuːtrɪfaɪ), *v.* Also 5–6 putry-, 6–9 putrify. [a. F. *putréfi-er*, ad. L. *putrefacĕre* (see PUTREFACT), with the ending *-fy*, as if from a L. **putrificāre* (whence the spelling *putrify*): see PUTRIFICATION and -FY.]

1. *trans.* To render putrid; to cause to rot or decay with a fetid smell. Now *rare.*

1432–50 tr. *Higden* (Rolls) V. 117 This Galerius..hade the partes interialle of his breste and exterialle putrefiede [*putrefacto pectore*] and corrupte so soore..that [etc.]. **1528** ROY *Rede me* Epist. (Arb.) 25 For one rotten apple lytell and lytell putrifieth an whole heape. **1591** SHAKS. *1 Hen. VI*, IV. vii. 90 They would but stinke, and putrifie the ayre. **1659** PEARSON *Creed* iv. (1662) 242 The bodies were often left upon the Crosse till the sun and rain had putrified and consumed them. **1784** COWPER *Task* II. 184 God..bids a plague Kindle a fiery boil upon the skin, And putrefy the breath of blooming health. **1863** *Intell. Observ.* IV. 103 (tr. *Pasteur's Researches*) Let us putrefy lactate of lime sheltered from air.

† **b.** *Alchemy* and *Old Chem.* To decompose chemically; to subject to any decomposing or destructive process, e.g. to oxidize. *Obs.*

1471 RIPLEY *Comp. Alch.* v. li. in Ashm. *Theat. Chem. Brit.* (1652) 160, I have the tought How thou the Bodys must Putrefy. **1651** FRENCH *Distill.* i. 14 Things are sooner putrefied in cloudy weather then in faire. *Ibid.* v. 118 Putrefie them together in Balneo the space of three dayes.

† **c.** *fig.* To corrupt morally or socially; to destroy the purity or soundness of; to render corrupt. *Obs.*

1538 BALE *Thre Lawes* 1927 We charge you no more thys lawe to putryfye. **1593** G. HARVEY *Pierce's Super.* in G. G. Smith *Eliz. Crit. Ess.* (1904) II. 260 Out vpon ranke and lothsome ribaldry that putrifieth where it should purify. **1685** BAXTER *Paraphr. N.T.* Matt. v. 13 The World is putrified with the corruption of all sin.

2. *intr.* To become putrid; to decay with an offensive smell; to decompose, rot, 'go bad'.

1412–20 LYDG. *Chron. Troy* III. xxviii, Aboue the grounde if the body lye That by all reason it must putryfye. **1539** ELYOT *Cast. Helthe* 37 Suche is the nature of hony, that it suffreth not the bodies to putrifie. **1692** BENTLEY *Boyle Lect.* iv. 134 He suffer'd those things to putrefy in Hermetically sealed glasses. **1774** GOLDSM. *Nat. Hist.* (1776) I. 314 In the cold arctic regions, animal substances, during their winter, are never known to putrefy. **1838** THOMSON *Chem. Org. Bodies* 1010 Albumen and fibrin putrefy very quickly.

b. Of the tissues or fluids in a living body: To become putrid or gangrenous; to fester, suppurate.
c **1500** [see PUTREFYING *vbl. sb.*]. **1540–54** CROKE *Ps.* (Percy Soc.) 11 Myne old sores do breake out agayn, And are corrupte and putrefie. **1660** R. COKE *Power & Subj.* 170 No Physitian can rightly cure any disease or wound until the venemous matter which putrifies inwardly be drawn out. **1871** TYNDALL *Fragm. Sci.* (1879) I. v. 176 The blood would putrefy and become fetid.

c. *fig.* To become corrupt or decay, morally, socially, or in any non-physical sense.
1526 TINDALE *1 Pet.* i. 4 An inheritaunce immortall and vndefiled, and that putrifieth not. **1597** HOOKER *Eccl. Pol.* v. lxxvi. §4 The name of vnrighteous persons shall putrifie. **1675** TRAHERNE *Chr. Ethics* 29 Raising up some persons thereby to be like salt among corrupted men, least all should putrifie and perish. **1720** T. BOSTON *Hum. Nat. Fourfold St.* (1797) 114 We putrified in Adam as our root.

putrefying (ˈpjuːtrɪfaɪɪŋ), *vbl. sb.* [-ING[1].] The action of the verb PUTREFY; putrefaction.
1471 RIPLEY *Comp. Alch.* III. xvi. in Ashm. *Theat. Chem. Brit.* (1652) 143 And hete of Askys and balnys for putrifying. *c* **1500** *Melusine* xxiii. 157 The venym that was within the wounde caused grete putrefyeng & rotyng of his flesshe.

ˈputrefying, *ppl. a.* [-ING[2].] That putrefies.
a. *intr.* Undergoing putrefaction; rotting. Also *fig.*
1611 BIBLE *Isa.* i. 6 Wounds, and bruises, and putrifying sores. **1746–7** HERVEY *Medit.* (1818) 157 Alas! a mass of putrefying clay. **1839** DARWIN *Voy. Beagle* xi. 231 The ground is concealed by a mass of slowly putrefying vegetable matter. **1896** *Allbutt's Syst. Med.* II. 789 These 'putrefactive' bacteria are..present..in putrefying liquids.
b. *trans.* = PUTREFACTIVE *a.* 1. *rare.*
1758 J. S. *Le Dran's Observ. Surg.* (1771) 298 From a continual Use of putrefying Medicines.

†**ˈputrer.** *Obs. rare.* [f. *putrie*, PUTERY + -ER[1].] A whoremonger; a fornicator.
c **1393** [see PUTOUR]. ? **14..** in Arnolde *Chron.* (1811) 90 Ye shall enquyre yf there bee putrer comon hasurdur contrary mayntener of quarels..or other comon mysdoers be dwellyng wythin the warde.

putrescence (pjuːˈtrɛsəns). [f. L. *putrēscent-em* PUTRESCENT: see -ENCE. Cf. F. *putrescence* (18th c. in Littré).] The action or process of rotting or becoming putrid; incipient or advancing rottenness.
1646 SIR T. BROWNE *Pseud. Ep.* IV. x. 202 They prevent ..putrescence of humors. **1783** JOHNSON *Let. to Mrs. Thrale* 22 Sept., You would not have me for fear of pain perish in putrescence. **1800** *Phil. Trans.* XC. 165 As soon as a great degree of putrescence has taken place, the luminous property of the fishes is destroyed. **1802** *Trans. Soc. Arts* XX. 213 Having always a putrescence *per se*, or tendency to putrify. **1861** WYNTER *Soc. Bees* 197 (*Preserved Meats*) How did this putrescence arise?
b. *concr.* Putrescent or rotting matter.
1843 CARLYLE *Past & Pr.* III. x, Nameless masses of putrescence, useful only for turnip-manure. **1898** *Westm. Gaz.* 29 Aug. 2/3 The sanitary inspector described one of the lots as 'perished, diseased, and rotten'... Is the only penalty..the carting away of the putrescence and the burying of it at the bottom of the sea?
c. *fig.*; esp. Moral rottenness or corruption.
1840 CARLYLE *Heroes, Luther*, The European World was asking him: Am I to sink ever lower into falsehood, stagnant putrescence, loathsome accursed death? **1865** RUSKIN *Arrows of Chace* (1880) II. 141 A putrescence through the constitution of the people is indicated by this galled place.

putrescency (pjuːˈtrɛsənsɪ). [f. as prec. + -ENCY.] The state or condition of being putrescent.
1756 C. LUCAS *Ess. Waters* III. 151 This..corrects the putrescency, blunts the acidity. **1794** SULLIVAN *View Nat.* I. 148 When these bodies are only at the commencement of putrescency. **1837** M. DONOVAN *Dom. Econ.* II. 33 Putrescency is no blemish, in the opinion of many nations. .. The inhabitants of Terra del Fuego find the putrid flesh of the whale and seal quite agreeable.

putrescent (pjuːˈtrɛsənt), *a.* [ad. L. *putrēscent-em*, pr. pple. of *putrēsc-ĕre* to grow rotten, inceptive of *putrēre* to be rotten. Cf. F. *putrescent* (16th c. in Godef.).]
1. Becoming putrid; in process of putrefaction.
1732 ARBUTHNOT *Rules of Diet* in *Aliments* 257 The State of a putrescent Alkali. **1818–20** E. THOMPSON *Cullen's Nosol. Method.* (ed. 3) 240 Scorbutus. In cold countries occurring after living on putrescent, salted animal food. **1834** *Brit. Husb.* I. 225 Putrescent manures..all animal and vegetable substances which can be reduced through decomposition, fermentation, and putrefaction, into such a state as will render them fit to assist the melioration of the land. **1881** TYNDALL *Floating Matter Air* 67 Bacteria were numerous in the exposed tubes, and soon afterwards all three of them became thickly muddy and putrescent.
2. Of, pertaining to, or accompanying putrescence.
1775 SIR E. BARRY *Obs. Wines Ancients* 10 Stronger Wines are more apt to degenerate..into a vapid, ropy, and at length a putrescent state. **1849–52** *Todd's Cycl. Anat.* IV. 862/1 We find game, in a putrescent state, eaten as a luxury.
fig. **1876** BLACKIE *Songs Relig. & Life* 40 He saw God's features, in the dim putrescent light Of his own sick imaginings.

putrescible (pjuːˈtrɛsɪb(ə)l), *a.* [f. L. *putrēsc-ĕre* to grow rotten + -IBLE. Cf. F. *putrescible* (14th c. in Godef.), and PUTRIBLE.] Liable to rot or become putrid; subject to putrefaction.
1797 PEARSON in *Phil. Trans.* LXXXVIII. 28 It does not appear to be putrescible, nor form a viscid solution with water. **1815** MILLARD *Time's Telesc.* (1825) 87 The white cabbage is the most putrescible. **1878** TYNDALL in *19th Century* Mar. 505 The substances after having been superheated remain putrescible, though they do not putrefy.
Hence **putresciˈbility** [cf. F. *putrescibilité* (Littré)], the quality of being putrescible.
1800 HATCHETT in *Phil. Trans.* XC. 393, I..suspect, that strong..muscular fibre..is not of easy putrescibility. **1881** TYNDALL *Floating Matter Air* 101 The putrescibility of pheasant..was exceeded by that of snipe, partridge, and plover.

putrescine (pjuːˈtrɛsaɪn). *Physiol. Chem.* Also erron. -in. [f. as prec. + -INE[5].] One of the ptomaines or cadaveric alkaloids: see quots.
1887 A. M. BROWN *Anim. Alkaloids* 36 Putrescine $C^4H^{12}N^2$.—Like the preceding ptomaines is obtained from the flesh of the mammifera and herring brines. It is a limpid, slightly oily liquid, the odour of which resembles that of sperm. **1896** *Allbutt's Syst. Med.* I. 588 Brieger..has isolated and named a number of these ptomaines, such as putrescine, cadaverine, neurine, &c. **1897** *Ibid.* II. 788 Some [alkaloids] such as cadaverine, putrescine, and choline are but slightly poisonous. **1899** CAGNEY *Jaksch's Clin. Diagn.* v. (ed. 4) 188 These observers..established the identity of Brieger's putrescin with tetramethylendiamine.

†**ˈputrible,** *a. Obs. rare.* [ad. late L. *putribilis* corruptible, f. *putrēre* to rot: see -IBLE.] Liable to become putrid; = PUTRESCIBLE.
1620 VENNER *Via Recta* vi. 97 Olives..breed a putrible and vnwholsome nourishment. *Ibid.* vii. 122 They..fill the body with crude and putrible humours.

putrid (ˈpjuːtrɪd), *a.* (In 6–7 *erron.* putred.) [a. L. *putrid-us* rotten, f. *putrēre* to rot, f. *puter* rotten. Cf. F. *putride* (14th c. in Godef.).]
1. Of organic bodies or substances: In a state of decomposition; rotten.
1598 MARSTON *Sco. Villanie* I. Proem. (1599) 171 Quake guzzell dogs, that liue on putred slime, Skud from the lashes of my yerking rime. **1692** BENTLEY *Boyle Lect.* iv. 133 [He] made innumerable trials with the putrid Flesh of all sorts of Beasts and Fowls. **1750** tr. *Leonardus' Mirr. Stones* 83 Coral cleanses putrid sores. **1774** GOLDSM. *Nat. Hist.* (1776) I. 234 Stagnant sea-water, like fresh, soon grows putrid. **1777** PRIESTLEY *Matt. & Spir.* (1782) I. x. 130 Only vegetable and animal substances ever become properly putrid and offensive. **1862** BURTON *Bk. Hunter* 350 Glad to appease their hunger on putrid horse-flesh.
2. a. Pertaining to, causing, proceeding from, accompanying, or infected with putrefaction; foul.
1610 HEALEY *Vive's Comm. St. Aug. Citie of God* x. xi. 377 Whole heauen (perforce) shall see thy putred hew. **1612** DRAYTON *Poly-olb.* xviii. 50 From her there yet proceeds unwholesome putrid air. *c* **1750** SHENSTONE *Elegies* xviii. 24 Avoid the putrid moisture of the mead. **1813** SHELLEY *Q. Mab* IV. 87 Their bones Bleaching unburied in the putrid blast. **1898** *Allbutt's Syst. Med.* V. 351 Symptoms which are called typhoid or putrid, and which are indicative of septic infection of the whole body.
b. *putrid fever*, a name for typhus fever; pythogenic fever; *putrid sore throat*, gangrenous pharyngitis; sometimes applied to diphtheria.
[*a* **1412** LYDG. *Two Merch.* 295 And putrida is causyd gladly thus.] **1651** FRENCH *Distill.* iii. 64 Spirit of Salt is very good in Feavers putrid. **1771** *Gentl. Mag.* XLI. 471/2 Mr. Poole, his wife, daughter and mother, who all died a few days ago of a putrid sore throat. **1774** PENNANT *Tour Scot. in 1772*, 305 Putrid fever, the epidemic of the coasts, originating from unwholesome food. **1822–34** *Good's Study Med.* (ed. 4) I. 682 The diseases called the putrid fever, and putrid sore throat are but of late date.
3. *fig.* (*a*) Morally, socially, or politically corrupt; æsthetically abominable. (*b*) Corrupting, noxious, noisome. (*c*) Used as a mere intensive: dreadful, awful, appalling. *colloq.*
[**1602** MARSTON *Antonio's Rev.* I. iv, Yon putred ulcer of my roiall bloode.] **1628** FELTHAM *Resolves* I. xii. Wks. (1677) 18 The sedulous Bee..working that to honey which the putri'd Spider would convert to poyson. **1649** MILTON *Eikon.* xxvii, Teaching to his Son all those putrid and pernicious documents, both of State and Religion. **1766** C. O'CONOR *Dissert. Hist. Scot.* 64 Quoting and ridiculing also, Some putrid Lines which he ascribes to Irish Bards. **1883** 'MARK TWAIN' *Life on Mississippi* ii. 37 La Salle drew from these simple children of the forest acknowledgments of fealty to Louis the Putrid, over the water. **1893** *Scotsman* 28 June 6 In respect to electoral morality Pontefract is putrid. **1898** *Windsor Mag.* Dec. 40/1 You're an ass—a putrid ass. **1902** S. J. COTES *Those Delightful Americans* 104 Last night at billiards you first said your luck was 'rotten', and then you got excited and declared it was 'putrid'. **1913** 'I. HAY' *Right Stuff* p. vi, He seems to have perfectly putrid notions about some things. **1931** D. L. SAYERS *Five Red Herrings* iv. 45 Some putrid fool sliced a ball..and got me slap-bang in the eye.
†**4.** Of soil (rendering L. *putris* in Vergil): Loose, crumbling, friable, mellow. *Obs.*
1635–56 COWLEY *Davideis* IV. 708 Here with sharp neighs the warlike Horses sound; And with proud prancings beat the putrid ground [*putrem quatit ungula campum*]. **1697** DRYDEN *Virg. Georg.* II. 281 Fat crumbling Earth [*putris glæba*] is fitter for the Plough, Putrid and loose above, and black below. **1780** A. YOUNG *Tour Irel.* (Nat. Libr. ed.) 161 A mellow, putrid, friable loam.

Hence **ˈputridly** *adv.*, in a putrid manner; **ˈputridness**, putrid condition, rottenness.
1889 J. M. DUNCAN *Clin. Lect. Dis. Women* x. (ed. 4) 60 A putridly decomposing bit of decidua, or of placental tissue. **1669** W. SIMPSON *Hydrol. Chym.* 371 To begin to undergo a putridness. **1698** FRYER *Acc. E. India & P.* 68 An Infecundity in the Earth, and a Putridness in the Air. **1903** *Daily Record & Mail* 2 June 4 The excuse made..was that the stores had revealed a tendency to putridness.

putridity (pjuːˈtrɪdɪtɪ). Also 7–8 *erron.* **putredity.** [f. as prec. + -ITY; cf. med.L. *putriditās* (*c* 1150 in Thomas *Thesaur. Nov. Lat.*), F. *putridité* (1794 in Hatz.-Darm.).]
1. The quality or condition of being putrid or rotten; rottenness; loathsome decay.
a **1639** BURTON *Anat. Mel.* I. iii. II. iv. (1651) 202 The whole malady proceeds from that inflammation, putredity, black smoky vapours. **1777** G. FORSTER *Voy. round World* I. 92 The degree of freshness or of putridity. **1801** *Med. Jrnl.* V. 145 A true typhus, with symptoms of putridity. **1866** BRIGHT *Sp., Reform* 16 Oct. (1876) 380 General corruption and putridity are the destruction of most bodies which they affect. **1898** *Allbutt's Syst. Med.* V. 34 According to some bacteriologists putridity is mainly due to the influence of micro-organisms.
b. *fig.* Moral or metaphorical rottenness.
1823 SOUTHEY *Lett.* 31 Oct. (1856) III. 408 Not against the principle of the government..but against the stagnation and putridity. **1873** 'OUIDA' *Pascarel* I. 8 We—whose whole year-long course is one Dance of Death over the putridity of our pleasures. **1877** J. D. CHAMBERS *Div. Worship* 183 The emblem of purity and preservation from putridity.
2. *concr.* Putrid matter.
1790 CATH. M. GRAHAM *Lett. Educ.* 356 As we find the Deity has made putridity agreeable and wholesome to several of the animals, he might have made it so to all. **1799** J. ROBERTSON *Agric. Perth* 448 The smoke and putridities, which taint the air of large cities. **1859** DARWIN *Orig. Spec.* vi. (1860) 197 The naked skin on the head of a vulture is considered as a direct adaptation for wallowing in putridity.

putrifaction, obs. form of PUTREFACTION.

†**puˈtrificat,** *pa. pple. Obs.* [ad. L. type **putrificāt-us*, pa. pple. of **putrificāre*: see next.] Putrefied, become putrid.
1471 RIPLEY *Comp. Alch.* VI. xxx. in Ashm. *Theat. Chem. Brit.* (1652) 168 The Bodys be Putryfycat.

†**putrifiˈcation.** *Obs.* [n. of action f. L. type **putrificāre*, f. **putrific-us*, f. L. *putri-s* rotten: substituted for the actual L. *putrefacĕre* to make to rot: see PUTREFY.] = PUTREFACTION.
1548 R. CROWLEY *Confut. Shaxton* D vij b, Seynge..that the putrification muste nedes be in a bodye, and that the qualities be no bodyes. **1608** WILLET *Hexapla Exod.* 245 The manna..kept without any putrification vntill the sabbath. **1612** T. TAYLOR *Comm. Titus* i. 16 (1619) 321 Like the graues full of putrification and rottennes.

ˈputriform, *a. rare.* [f. L. *putri-s* rotten + -FORM.] Of putrid form or appearance.
1872 L. P. MEREDITH *Teeth* (1878) 72 It is also subject to other changes which render it liable to putrefy with rapidity. This is noticed in bilious, albuminous and putriform saliva.

putrify: see PUTREFY.

putrilage (ˈpjuːtrɪlɪdʒ). Also 7 *erron.* putre-. [ad. L. *putrilāgo, -lāginem* rottenness, f. *puter, putri-s* rotten: cf. *cartilage*. So in mod.F. (Littré).] Putrid matter.
1657 TOMLINSON *Renou's Disp.* 485 Roots and herbs cocted to putrelage. **1669** W. SIMPSON *Hydrol. Chym.* 201 The other humours..are forthwith transmuted into a slimy putrilage. **1756** P. BROWNE *Jamaica* p. ccclxxvii, These [insects] were for a long time considered as the mere productions of filth and putrilage. **1874** GARROD & BAXTER *Mat. Med.* (1880) 257 The septic fever produced artificially in dogs by the injection of putrilage into their veins.

putrilaginous (pjuːtrɪˈlædʒɪnəs), *a.* (Also 7 *erron.* putre-.) [f. L. *putrilāgin-em* (see prec.) + -OUS: perh. through F. *putrilagineux* (16th c. in Littré).] Of the nature or character of putrilage.
1597 A. M. tr. *Guillemeau's Fr. Chirurg.* 33/1 First, the corrupted bone waxeth fattye, then blacke or put[r]ilaginous, that is, corroded. **1620** VENNER *Via Recta* vii. 129 They..expectorate the putrilaginous matter. **1669** W. SIMPSON *Hydrol. Chym.* 99 A putrelaginous corrupt matter. **1853** *Fraser's Mag.* XLVIII. 694 The oil began to run apace from the putrilaginous mass.

†**ˈputrilency.** *Obs. rare.* [f. L. *puter, putris* rotten + -ENCY, after a type **putrilentia*: cf. *pestilentia* pestilence, f. *pestis* plague.] = PUTRILAGE.
1657 TOMLINSON *Renou's Disp.* 200 Softened stalks cocted to a putrilency.

†**ˈputritude.** *Obs.* Also 7 putre-. [ad. L. type **putritūdo*, f. *puter, putri-s* rotten: see -TUDE.] The quality or condition of being putrid; putridity.
1612 WOODALL *Surg. Mate* Wks. (1653) 76 Coperas.. keepeth the flesh moist and from putritude. **1657** TOMLINSON *Renou's Disp.* 160 That they may be long conserved without putretude and marcour. **1688** R. HOLME *Armoury* III. 446/1 Putrifaction is the resolution of a naturall Putritude to make it more excellent.

†**ˈputriture.** *Obs. rare.* [f. assumed ppl. stem *putrit-* of L. *putrēre* + -URE; cf. F. *pourriture*,

OF. *purreture*, f. **pourrir*:—L. *putrīre* for *putrēre* to rot.] Rotting; rottenness; putrefaction.

1569 STOCKER tr. *Diod. Sic.* II. xliv. 100 It [asphalt] is very excellent..to preserue dead bodies from..putriture. **1579–80** NORTH *Plutarch, Sylla* (1898) III. 313 The chaunging of his flesh into this putriture wanne it straight againe.

†**putry, pury,** *a. Obs. rare*[−1]. [Form and etymology uncertain.

Putry, if correct, was app. ad. L. *puter, -tris, -tre*, rotten, decaying, putrid; *pury*, if correct, may have been ad. F. *pourri* rotten, decomposed.]

Rotten, decomposed, formed by decomposition.

1602 MARSTON *Antonio's Rev.* III. iii. (Wks. 1633) Hjb, Howle not thou putry [ed. 1602 pury] mould, groane not yee graues!

putrye: see PUTERY *Obs.*

‖**putsch** (putʃ). [Swiss G., orig. knock, thrust, blow.]

a. A revolutionary attempt.

1920 *Times* 3 June 15/5 The possibility of a *Putsch* continues to exercise the minds of all parties. **1922** *Q. Rev.* Jan. 125 King Charles has made his second attempt to ascend the Hungarian Throne. In the circumstances outlined above it was doomed to failure. So was Louis Napoleon's second *coup d' état*—*Putsch* is the modern word—at Boulogne. **1930** *Economist* 4 Oct. 612/2 The officers were charged with conspiring..to secure the neutrality of the Reichwehr in the event of another 'Putsch' by the revolutionaries of the Right. **1945** A. J. P. TAYLOR *Course of German Hist.* xi. 192 No one who took part in the *putsch* was punished. **1950** [see BLANQUISM]. **1968** A. COATES *Myself a Mandarin* i. 5 Since the end of the Second World War the population [of Hong Kong] had topped the million mark, and the place was thus technically already overcrowded when the communist *putsch* began. **1975** *N.Y. Times* 29 Nov. 27/2 Allende, of course, is gone—a suicide in September 1973 when the current President, Gen. Augusto Pinochet Ugarte, seized power in a bloody putsch. **1981** *Listener* 1 Jan. 12/2 The greatest achievement had been to keep the [Ghanaian] army putsch a secret.

b. *colloq.* Any sudden vigorous effort or campaign.

1938 A. CAMPBELL *Flying Blind* xi. 89 He grasped it firmly, and flexing his muscles prepared a putsch. **1940** C. T. CARR in *Mod. Lang. Rev.* XXXV. 71 *Putsch*, a coup d'état... The word was apparently borrowed round about 1920 and is now quite common in English newspapers.. spreading to English slang in the non-political significance of a 'push forward'. **1953** M. MCCARTHY *Groves of Academe* x. 215 Criticism..has been reduced to a minimum... No poet of any real merit has been excluded... You..are too impatient. You want to make a *putsch* for the sake of tighter control, more daring methods of promotion, but violence is unnecessary. **1970** *New Scientist* 30 July 221/2 The present step-by-step attack on brucellosis is much more likely to succeed than a premature *putsch*. **1973** *Observer* 14 Jan. 29/6 Apart from a much-needed putsch on our chimneys and exhaust pipes there is little more that the public health departments can do to increase the level of our good health.

Hence **'putsching** *vbl. sb.*; **'putschism**, the advocacy of a *putsch* or of the violence associated with a *putsch*; **'putschist**, an advocate of or participant in a *putsch*; also *attrib.* or as *adj.*

1898 A. P. ATTERBURY tr. *Sombart's Socialism 19th Cent.* iv. 73 Putschism..is the fanatical tendency towards street struggle, faith in the barricade. *Ibid.* v. 113 The Putschists, Clubists, and Blanquists were utopists, who through conspiracies and street riots would through all time control economic development. **1923** *Glasgow Herald* 26 Oct. 9 The Separatist 'Putschists' have succeeded in maintaining their position. **1937** E. SNOW *Red Star over China* IV. v. 167 P'eng Pai..formed a Soviet, which, following a policy of putschism, was soon destroyed. **1940** K. MANNHEIM *Ideology & Utopia* 125 The ideology of 'putschist' groups led by intellectuals. **1954** P. TOYNBEE *Friends Apart* v. 65 The Communist Party..would have regarded it as a piece of futile 'diversionism', 'putschist' and disorganised. **1966** 'HAN SUYIN' *Mortal Flower* I. iv. 128 The practice of shooting deserters and of inflicting corporal punishment, both of which smack of putschism. **1968** *Economist* 1 June 44/1 Mr Cecil King has gone the same way that he came in—by a boardroom putsch. Seventeen years ago it was Mr King who did the putsching. **1974** J. WHITE tr. *Poulantzas's Fascism & Dictatorship* IV. ii. 169, 1921. A series of 'putschist' attempts in Prussia by the KPD. *Ibid.*, The Comintern, at its Third Congress, passed a severe judgment on this 'putschism'. **1975** *New Left Rev.* Nov.–Dec. 66 When the putschists struck at Nicosia in July 1974, only a few EDEK members were armed and ready to resist. **1979** *China Now* Mar./Apr. 24/2 The essentially putschist character of both Lin Biao and the Four.

putt[1] (pʌt). *local.* Also 6 putte, 9 put. [Variant of BUTT *sb.*[13]: cf. also POT *sb.*[1] 5.] A small cart used on a farm, esp. for manure: = BUTT *sb.*[13] Also *attrib.* Hence **'puttful.**

1508 *Pilton Churchw. Acc.* (Som. Rec. Soc.) 56 It. a putteful of erth..iij[d]. **1766** WILLY in *Compl. Farmer* s.v. *Turnep*, I pulled them [turnips] before Christmas, and had fifteen putt loads. **1850** *Jrnl. R. Agric. Soc.* XI. II. 739 A low single-horse cart like a large wheelbarrow, called a three-wheel put, is common in the [Somerset] hills. **1888** ELWORTHY *W. Som. Wds.*, *Putt*,..a heavy, broad-wheeled tipping cart, for manure. This is the 'fine' form of what is known as a *butt* or dung-*butt*. I never heard a labourer say *putt*.

putt[2] (pʌt). *local.* Also 7 putte. [Variant of BUTT *sb.*[12]: cf. also POT *sb.*[1] 5 b.] A basket-trap for catching fish: cf. PUTCHER.

1610 GUILLIM *Heraldry* IV. xi. (1611) 219 The skill of fishing..sometimes with nets, and sometimes with Ginnes, with puttes, Wheels, &c. *a* **1676** HALE *De Jure Maris* I. vi. in Hargrave *Law Tracts* (1787) I. 35 They had..granted these fishing-places,..at their several manors, by the names of rocks, weares, staches, boraches, putts. **1688** R. HOLME *Armoury* II. xvi. (Roxb.) 79/2. **1873** [see PUTCHER]. **1883** *Fisheries Exhib. Catal.* (ed. 4) 125 Putts..are used..for taking salmon, shrimps, and various kinds of fish.

†**putt**[3], Sc. var. POOT *sb.*[1], POULT, young bird.

1600 *Sc. Acts Jas. VI* (1814) 236 (Jam.) Be ressone of the great slauchter of thair puttis and youngeanes.

putt, var. form of PUT *sb.*[2], [3], [4], *v.*[2]

putt, obs. form, or variant, of PUT *sb.*[1] and *v.*[1]; obs. form of PIT *sb.*[1]

puttargo, obs. variant of BOTARGO, a relish.

‖**puttee** ('pʌtiː). Also **putti, puttie, putty.** [Hindī *paṭṭī* band, bandage; cf. Skr. *paṭṭa* strip of cloth, bandage.] A long strip of cloth wound spirally round the leg from the ankle to the knee, worn as a protection and support to the leg by sportsmen, soldiers, etc. Also *attrib.*

[**1875** F. DREW *Jummoo & Kashmir Territ.* 175 Leggings of a peculiar sort, a bandage about six inches wide and four yards long... This, which is called 'patāwa', is a much-cherished article of dress, and without doubt is a very good thing for mountain work.] **1886** GUILLEMARD *Cruise Marchesa* II. 193 The perspiring sportsman can now..recover his breath and shake the gravel out of his putties. **1894** *Westm. Gaz.* 7 Apr. 2/3, I would infinitely prefer the 'puttie', or long, light serge or flannel bandage wrapped tightly round the leg. **1900** *Daily Mail* 3 Dec. 4/6 To protect the legs [of the dog] from the strong needles of the thick gorse, he was provided with puttees. **1900** *Times* 24 Dec. (Yule), The Puttee leggings are excellent for peace or war, on foot or on horseback.

Hence **'putteed, puttied** *a.*, clothed in or wearing puttees.

1900 *Daily News* 10 Apr. 2/4 One [soldier] with his puttied legs kicking aimlessly over the side, was singing. **1929** E. BOWEN *Last September* xii. 141 The last they saw of him was a putteed leg.

putter ('putə(r)), *sb.*[1] [f. PUT *v.*[1] + -ER[1].] A person or thing that puts, in various senses.

1. A beast that pushes or butts with the head or horns: cf. PUT *v.*[1] I. *Obs.* exc. *dial.* ('pʌtə(r)).

1382 WYCLIF *Exod.* xxi. 29 If an oxe be an hornputter fro ȝisterday and the thridde day hens. **1388** *Ibid.* 36 The oxe was a puttere. **1825** JAMIESON, *Putter*...2. An animal that butts with the head or horns.

2. One who or that which puts (in current senses of the vb., *lit.* and *fig.*); one who or that which places or sets; one who propounds a question, etc. Also with extension, as ***putter to death, to flight***, etc.: see also 8.

c **1425** *Cursor M.* 3744 (Trin.) Skilful is iacob his nome þat is to say in riȝt langage Putter out of heritage. *a* **1515** DUNBAR *Poems* lxxxv. 29 Haill,..puttar to flicht Of fendis in battale! **1581** SAVILE *Tacitus, Hist.* III. lxxiii. 160 Euery man was a commaunder, and no man a putter in execution. **1587** GOLDING *De Mornay* xxxii. 509 The putters of Iesus and of his disciples to death. *a* **1704** R. L'ESTRANGE (J.), The most wretched sort of people are dreamers upon events and putters of cases. **1821** LAMB *Elia, Mackery End*, The putter of the said question. **1847** L. HUNT *Men, Women & B., Lying* (1876) 133 O love of truth!..putter of security into the heart.

†**3.** 'Prob., the horn or erector of the *cheffroun* or head-dress' (*Jamieson's Dict.* 1880). *Obs.*

1516 *Inv. R. Wardr.* (1815) 27 Item, ane cheffroun with ane putter with settis of perle siclik send to the quene in Ingland.

†**4.** An instrument for crimping a ruff; also called ***putting-stick*** or ***poting-stick*** (see POTE *v.*).

1583 STUBBES *Anat. Abus.* II. (1882) 36 This instrument [must] be heated in the fire, the better to stiffen the ruffe... And if you would know the name of this goodly toole, forsooth the deuill hath giuen it to name a putter, or else a putting sticke. [**1602**: see POOTER *sb.*]

†**5.** See quot. and cf. PUTTERLING. *Obs. rare.*

a **1670** SPALDING *Troub. Chas. I* (1850) I. 297 He had about 800 men..and six puttaris or schort peices of ordinans.

6. *Coal-mining.* A man or boy employed in 'putting' or propelling the trams or barrows of coal from the workings; a haulier; orig. one who pushed the tram or barrow from behind: see PUT *v.*[1] 4. Also *attrib.*, as ***putter-boy, lad.***

1708 J. C. *Compl. Collier* (1848) 36 Barrow-Men, or Coal-Putters..put or pull away the full Corves of Coals. **1812** J. HODGSON in J. Raine *Mem.* (1857) I. 97 This work was done by putters and barrow-men, the latter pulling before, and the former putting or thrusting behind. **1880** *Daily News* 17 Sept. 6/3 Two putter lads were found jammed against some broken tubs. **1893** *Labour Commission* Gloss. s.v., The tram containing the coal is sometimes pushed by the boy, and sometimes pulled by a pony, hence the terms *hand-putters* and *pony-putters*.

†**7.** See quot. *Obs.* [Perh. a different word.]

1807 SIR R. WILSON in *Life* (1862) II. viii. 374 The road ..being made of putters or young trees.

8. With adverbs, forming compound agent-nouns corresponding to adverbial combinations of PUT *v.*[1] (branch V.): as ***putter away, back, forth, forward, in, together***; **putter down,** (*a*) one who puts something down, in various senses (see PUT *v.*[1] 42); (*b*) *spec.* = *putter off* (*b*); **putter off,** †(*a*) one who shoots off or discharges a missile (*obs.*); (*b*) one who passes off something fraudulently (? *obs.*); (*c*) one who defers or postpones; **putter on,** †(*a*) one who urges on, an instigator, inciter; (*b*) one who puts something on, or affixes it to, something else, *esp.* a workman employed in doing this in various manufactures, etc.; **putter out,** (*a*) one who extinguishes; (*b*) one who deposits or lends money at interest; (*c*) one who puts an animal out to graze or feed; (*d*) see quot. 1865; **putter up,** (*a*) one who puts something up, in various senses (see PUT *v.*[1] 56); (*b*) *spec.* one who prearranges a robbery or other criminal proceeding (*slang*).

1552 HULOET, *Putter awaye, *expulsor.* *Putter backe, *repulsor.* **1701** STANHOPE *St. Aug. Medit.* (1720) ix. 22 Come, thou *putter down of the proud and teacher of the Meek. **1869** TROLLOPE *He was right* xxxv, A republican, a putter-down of the Church, a hater of the Throne. **1906** *P.T.O.* 16 June 16/2 Three men as a rule take an active part in a forgery—the 'putter-up', the capitalist who finds the necessary funds; the 'blacksmith', the actual forger; and the 'putter-down', who actually presents the forged document and obtains the money. **1926** *Clues* Nov. 162/1 *Putter-down*, the party who passes forged checks for the real forger. **1824** *Examiner* 724/2 The fabricators and *putters-forth of such 'Narratives'. **1886** *Eng. Hist. Rev.* I. 746 William Squire, the putter-forth of the 'Squire Papers', was before their issue concerned in two hoaxes. **1632** BROME *Novella* v. i, The Chambermayde, a kind of *putter-forwards, Sir, to the businesse. **1881** *Instr. Census Clerks* (1885) 97 Bolt Making: ..*Putter-in. **1615** CHAPMAN *Odyss.* XVIII. 379 Troy traines vp approued sonnes In deeds of armes: braue *putters off of shaftes. *a* **1700** B. E. *Dict. Cant. Crew, Queere-cole-fencer*, a Receiver and putter off [of] false Money. **1803** in *Spirit Pub. Jrnls.* VII. 227 *note*, Fabius is the patron saint of delayers and putters-off. **1611** SHAKS. *Wint. T.* II. i. 141 You are abus'd, and by some *putter on, That will be damn'd for't. **1613** —— *Hen. VIII*, I. ii. 24 My good Lord Cardinall, they vent reproches Most bitterly on you, as putter on Of these exactions. **1864** A. MCKAY *Hist. Kilmarnock* (ed. 4) 254 He was a putter-on in a printwork. *a* **1586** SIDNEY *Arcadia* (1622) 470 O know him, and become not the *putters out of the worlds light. **1610** SHAKS. *Temp.* III. iii. 48 Men Whose heads stood in their brests? which now we finde Each putter out of fiue for one, will bring vs Good warrant of. [Cf. quot. s.v. PUT *v.*[1] 43j.] **1639** *Rec. Dedham, Mass.* (1892) III. 65 After the sayd owner or putter out of ye same Swyne shall haue knoweledge therof. **1795** J. AIKIN *Manchester* 239 A number of hands are also employed by the putters-out on account of the merchants in Manchester. **1865** BRIERLEY *Irkdale* I. 125, I succeeded in obtaining a situation as putterout to a firm in Manchester. *Ibid. note*, Putterout is a term applied to the person who gives out the work to handloom weavers. **1767** *Misc.* in *Ann. Reg.* 220/1 Many a *putter together of long and short verse in Latin. **1881** *Instr. Census Clerks* 45 Scissors Putter Together. **1812** J. H. VAUX *Flash Dict.*, **Putter up*, the projector or planner of a put-up affair, as a servant in a gentleman's family, who proposes to a gang of housebreakers the robbery of his master's house. **1859** SALA *Tw. round Clock* (1861) 137 The chief swineherd and I were friends. He was my 'putter-up' at skittles. **1881** *Instr. Census Clerks* (1885) 75 Hosiery Manufacture:.. Putter-up. *Ibid.* 76 Boot and Shoe Making:..Putter-up. *Ibid.* 88 China, Porcelain, Manufacture:..Putter-up. **1891** *Pall Mall G.* 15 Sept. 2/3 [The bull] is..a beast of burden, or a putter-up of flesh for the benefit of the Madrid butchers. **1929** C. HUMPHREYS *Great Pearl Robbery* i. 12 The police knew that Grizard was the 'putter-up'. **1975** M. CRICHTON *Great Train Robbery* ii. 18 Edward Pierce.. accumulated sufficient capital to finance large-scale criminal operations, thus becoming what was called 'a putter-up'.

putter ('pʌtə(r); in sense 1 also 'putə(r)), *sb.*[2] [f. PUT, PUTT *v.*[2] + -ER[1].]

1. One who 'puts' or throws a heavy stone or other weight: see PUT *v.*[1] 2, *v.*[2] 2. Chiefly *Sc.*

1820 HOGG *Wint. Even. T.* I. 265 'Thou's naething of a putter', said Meg,..; 'an thou saw my billy Rwob put, he wad send it till here'. **1884** H. C. BUNNER in *Harper's Mag.* Jan. 303/1 The champion..putter of the ponderous weight. **1898** *Allbutt's Syst. Med.* V. 915 Sprint-runners, putters of weights, wrestlers and the like.

2. *Golf.* **a.** A club used in 'putting': cf. PUT *v.*[2] 3. ***driving putter***: see quot. 1881 and DRIVING *vbl. sb.* 3 b.

1743 MATHIESON *Goff* in *Poems on Golf* (1867) 59 Let each social soul Drink to the putter, the balls, and the hole. **1805** FORSYTH *Beauties Scotl.* I. 84 The putter is used where a short stroke is intended. **1833** G. F. CARNEGIE *Golfiana* in R. Clark *Golf* (1875) 151, I see Mount-Melville stand Erect, his driving putter in his hand. **1857** *Chambers's Inform. People* 693/2 The putter..is a short-shafted, stiff club, with a large, flattish head, and square face; it is used when the ball arrives within close proximity to the hole. **1877** MAR. M. GRANT *Sun-Maid* ix, The 'putter' has expelled the mallet. **1881** FORGAN *Golfer's Handbk.* 11 The two varieties of Putters are used for very different purposes. They are the most 'upright' fellows in the set... The 'Green Putter'..is employed on the putting-green... One function of the Driving-Putter..is to force a ball out of long grass... The Driving-Putter is fast falling into disuse.

b. A player who 'puts' (well or ill).

1857 *Chambers's Inform. People* 694/1 To be a good putter, is what all golfers aim at, and comparatively few ever attain. **1895** W. T. LINSKILL *Golf* (ed. 3) 21 A player who is a really good putter is often more than a match for the longest driver.

putter ('pʌtə(r)), *sb.*[3] [Echoic. Cf. PUT-PUT *sb.*] A muffled explosive sound characteristic of an internal-combustion engine, as an outboard motor, etc. Also applied to an engine or vehicle which makes such a sound.

1942 'N. SHUTE' *Pied Piper* 224 There was a fishing-boat . . coming in from the sea; faintly they heard the putter of an engine. **1948** G. GREENE *Heart of Matter* II. I. ii. 118 Across the river the tinkering in the launch went on: the sharp crack of a chisel, the clank of metal, and then again the spasmodic putter. **1964** J. MASTERS *Trial at Monomoy* ii. 56 The putter of the marine diesels and the slap and sigh of the sea. **1969** *Listener* 12 June 814/1 We heard the first putter of outboard motors that, by mid-morning, become the background noise of the region. **1975** *Islander* (Victoria, B.C.) 27 July 7/1 We had a small open boat with an inboard engine. This 'putter' would provide slow but reliable transportation. **1979** R. LAIDLAW *Lion is Rampant* xiv. 111, I could hear the putter of farm machinery.

putter ('pʌtə(r)), *v.*[1] *Obs.* exc. *dial.* [An onomatopœic word, akin to *patter* and *mutter*. Cf. the parallel Sw. *puttra* to mutter.] *intr.* To mutter; to grumble.

1611 COTGR., *Brimboter*, mumble, putter, mutter, grumble, or babble vnto himselfe. *c* **1903** J. H. in *Eng. Dial. Dict.* (Norf.) s.v. *Puter*, She putters all day long.

'putter, *v.*[2] orig. *U.S.* [var. of POTTER *v.*: cf. PUDDER.] = POTTER *v.* 4 and 5. Hence **'putterer**, **'puttering** *vbl. sb.* and *ppl. a.*, **'putteringly** *adv.*

1878 L. M. ALCOTT *Under Lilacs* xii. 130 Ben infinitely preferred to watch ants and bugs . . rather than 'putter' over plants with long names. **1878** L. C. BELL in *Wide Awake* Jan. 24/1 Every morning in the midst of his chores, Max found time for a long, hovering, puttering visit. *Ibid.*, Max likes to 'putter' with the housework, too. **1882** *Century* XXV. 202 The aged grandfather of this group was usually absent after wood, or else puttering near the fire-place. **1887** *Harper's Mag.* Aug. 479 So wanderingly, putteringly benevolent are some of his letters. **1894** MRS. ALDEN in *Chicago Advance* 27 Dec. 448/3 If you two girls would stop your everlasting puttering over paint and embroidery, and do something. **1895** SARAH M. H. GARDNER *Quaker Idyls* v. 85 He was a hard-workin' kind of a putterer. **1897** KIPLING *Captains Courageous* iii. 82 But it's a putterin' job all the same. **1907** J. M. SYNGE *Let.* 3 June (1971) 153 Yesterday we puttered about, and today we are going for another long expedition. **1925** R. FROST *Let.* 20 June (1964) 174, I am free to putter my days out without even writing any more. **1925** J. G. MACLEOD in *Oxf. Poetry* 26 His still moving body Like a strange motor-boat propelled by nothing puttered round The headland. **1931** D. L. SAYERS *Five Red Herrings* xxiv. 278 He would be the one person who might habitually see Campbell having breakfast and puttering about the house. **1952** *Arena* (N.Z.) XXXI. 5 Real man of mystery he was these days. Puttering round the whare at all hours. **1960** M. K. JOSEPH *I'll Soldier no More* 150 Tired, they putter slowly back to billets. **1977** G. DURRELL *Golden Bats & Pink Pigeons* v. 121 The Box fish puttered to and fro like some weird, orange boat.

putter ('pʌtə(r)), *v.*[3] [Echoic. Cf. PUT-PUT *v.*] *intr.* To make an intermittent explosive sound characteristic of an internal-combustion engine; to move, making such a sound. Hence **'puttering** *vbl. sb.* and *ppl. a.*

1937 M. LANE *At Last Island* ix. 270 The boat puttered and back-fired out of the harbour. **1947** J. STEINBECK *Wayward Bus* 197 The rain had diminished so that there was only a faint puttering on the roof. **1956** J. MASTERS *Bugles & Tiger* i. 31 A groaning truck . . backfired and puttered steadily down the road to the plains. **1958** *Times* 7 July 9/4 The mower must depend on human exertion and not be of the petrol-puttering kind. **1971** P. CRAMPTON tr. *Heyerdahl's Ra Expeditions* vii. 163 Our first hesitant moves were now being followed by excited journalists and experienced old salts on board the puttering vessels which circled about us. **1975** *New Yorker* 28 Apr. 98/3 They [*sc.* Hanoians] rent rowing shells or go for a ride in the motorboats that putter back and forth between its islands.

†**'putterling.** *Obs. rare*$^{-1}$. [f. PUTTER *sb.*[1] + -LING[1].] See quot.; ? = PUTTER *sb.*[1] 5, or a smaller form of it.

a **1670** SPALDING *Troub. Chas. I* (1850) II. 353 They war weill furneschit . . With pistollis, puterlinges, and vther armes.

‖**putti**, pl. of PUTTO.

puttie, puttied: see PUTTEE, PUTTY *sb.* and *v.*

puttier: see PUTTY *v.*

†**puttine.** *Obs. rare*$^{-1}$. [ad. It. *puttin-o* little boy, dim. of *putto* boy.] = PUTTO.

1612 PEACHAM *Graphice* 117 Captive Fame is drawn as a Lady in a long black Robe painted with *Puttines*, or little Images with black wings, a Trumpet in her hand.

putting ('pʊtɪŋ), *vbl. sb.*[1] Also 1 putung, 4 pottyng. [f. OE. **putian*, PUT *v.*[1] + -ING[1].] The action of the verb PUT, in various senses.

1. a. Pushing, shoving, thrusting. *Obs.* exc. *dial.*

c **1330** R. BRUNNE *Chron. Wace* (Rolls) 8891 And left þer pottyng many on, ȝit stirede þey nought þe leste ston. *a* **1340** HAMPOLE *Psalter* xii. 5, I sett noght by þaire stirynge na mare þan a geaunte dos at þe puttynge of a waik man. **14..** *R. Glouc.'s Chron.* (Rolls) 4313 þer was pultinge & ssouinge [*MS. β.* puttynge & schowynge] & stroc mony on. *c* **1440** *Promp. Parv.* 418/1 Puttynge, or schowynge, *pulsus.*

†**b.** *fig.* Instigation, incitement; urging, driving.

c **1050** *Rule of Chrodegang* (E.E.T.S.) 99 Hation þæt þurh deofles putunge wæs an belæd, & lufian þæt þurh Godes godnysse gesceapon wæs. *a* **1340** HAMPOLE *Psalter* xxxv. 12 þe hand of þe synful, þat is, þe puttynge of þe fende, stire me not till syn. **1599** H. HOLLAND *Wks. R. Greenham* 2 He thought all afflictions to be puttings of him to God from slothfulnes.

†**c.** Driving out, expulsion, emission. *Obs.*

1398 TREVISA *Barth. De P.R.* VII. xxix. (Bodl. MS.), þe pacient trauaileþ . . muche in drawing and putting of breeþ.

2. Sprouting, germination.

1615 W. LAWSON *Country Housew. Gard.* (1626) 20 The growth of the Tree, couering of wounds, putting of buds. *Ibid.* 29 The first shew of putting is no sure signe of growth.

3. *Coal-mining.* The pushing or propelling of the trams or barrows of coal: see PUT *v.*[1] 4.

1867 W. W. SMYTH *Coal & Coal-mining* 150 The more the actual present workings are hampered by lowness and want of room, the higher will be the expenses of putting, &c. **1894** *Times* 11 Oct. 4/6 From putting, the lad, now recognized as a full-grown and properly-trained miner, passes to hewing.

4. *Naut.* The action of setting out or taking one's course (to sea, into harbour, etc.).

1590 NASHE *Pasquil's Apol.* I. Wks. (Grosart) I. 247 This is euen at the first putting into harbour, to cast away the Shyp. **1748** *Anson's Voy.* III. iii. 328 The day of their putting to sea.

5. Placing, laying, setting, etc.: see PUT *v.*[1] 10, 13.

c **1440** *Promp. Parv.* 418/1 Puttynge, or leyynge, *posicio, collocacio.* **1665** SIR T. HERBERT *Trav.* (1677) 39 At his [a corpse's] putting into the Sea the Captain of our Ship honoured his Funeral with the rending clamour of four Culverins. **1707** MORTIMER *Husb.* (1721) II. 338 The time of putting of your Spirits into your Cyder. **1847** L. HUNT *Men, Women, & B.* I. vi. 109 We . . were earnest only in the putting of cakes.

6. In various general and figurative senses: see PUT *v.*[1] 10 i, 11, 12, 15–28.

148. WRIOTHESLEY *Chron.* (Camden) I. 87 With the image of his puttinge to death. **1613** SIR T. LAKE in *Buccleuch MSS.* (Hist. MSS. Comm.) I. 149 At their first putting into the world. **1884** tr. *Lotze's Metaph.* 32 It is by this act of putting that there is constituted the very intelligible though not further analysable idea of an objectivity which can be ascribed only to that which is, not to nothing.

†**7.** *Cards.* In the game of 'put' or 'putt': see PUT *v.*[1] 22 e. *Obs.*

1680 COTTON *Compl. Gamester* (ed. 2) xv. 93 Sometimes they play without putting, and then the winner is he that wins most tricks. *Ibid.*, He that once hath the confidence to putt on bad Cards cannot recall his putting.

8. The exercise of throwing a heavy stone or weight from the shoulder: see PUT *v.*[1] 2. In *Sc.* ('pʌtɪŋ).

c **1300** *Havelok* 1042 Hauelok stod, and lokede þer-til; And of puttingge he was ful wil. *Ibid.* 2324 Wrastling with laddes, putting of ston. *c* **1440** [see PUT *v.*[1] 2 b]. **1871** L. STEPHEN *Playgr. Eur.* (1894) ii. 47 There is wrestling and putting of weights and dancing on holidays.

9. With adverbs, expressing the action of the adverbial combinations s.v. PUT *v.*[1] V.: as ***putting away, back, by, down, forth, in, off, on, out, to, together, up*** (in various senses general and technical: see under the verb).

1382 WYCLIF 1 *Pet.* iii. 21 The *puttinge awey of flesch of filthis. **1659** LD. LAMBERT in *Burton's Diary* (1828) IV. 473 It is not a putting it away but taking it in. **1892** *Temple Bar Mag.* Dec. 580 Tired and heated with final packings and puttings away. **1530** PALSGR. 259/2 *Puttyng backe, *repulce.* **1398** TREVISA *Barth. De P.R.* II. ii. (1495) 28 A myrrour of euerlastyng durynge without ony *puttyng betwene. **1580** HOLLYBAND *Treas. Fr. Tong.*, *Interposement*, a putting or setting betwene. **1601** SHAKS. *Jul. C.* I. ii. 231 At euery *putting by, mine honest Neighbors showted. **1530** TINDALE *Pract. Prel. Expos. & Notes* (Parker Soc.) II. 334 Concerning the Cardinal's *putting down, I consider many things. **1598** SHAKS. *Merry W.* II. i. 30 I'le Exhibit a Bill in the Parliament for the putting downe of men. **1495** *Trevisa's Barth. De P.R.* XVIII. xcv. 841 The serpent crepyth wyth preuy *puttynges forthe of scales. **1589** *Acts Privy Counc.* (1898) XVII. 353 His putting furth of their Society without anie just cause should be noe prejudice unto him. **1847** BUSHNELL *Chr. Nurt.* II. ii. (1861) 261 Their every putting forth has a lying character. **1599** MINSHEU *Span. Gram.* 78 With a certaine disdaine and *putting-from with the hand. **1483** *Rolls of Parlt.* VI. 249/1 After the retourne or *puttyng in of any suche Offices. **1574** tr. *Marlorat's Apocalips* 18 This putting in of the Sunday in sted of the Sabbat day. **1668–9** PEPYS *Diary* 19 Feb., I did propose to him my putting in to serve in Parliament. **1867** RUSKIN *Time & Tide* ix. §44 (1904) 53, I write you my letter straightforward, and let you see all my scratchings out and puttings in. **1580** HOLLYBAND *Treas. Fr. Tong*, *Delay*, a delay, a *putting off. *c* **1680** W. MOUNTAGU in *Buccleuch MSS.* (Hist. MSS. Comm.) I. 332 The putting off of the motion. **1803** in *Spirit Pub. Jrnls.* VII. 229 Wilt thou never yet have done With puttings-off eternal? **1842** MANNING *Serm.*, *Obedience* (1848) I. 136 What a putting off of this lower life shall there be at that day! **1603** SHAKS. *Meas. for M.* IV. ii. 120 Lord Angelo . . awakens mee With this vnwonted *putting on. **1663** BUTLER *Hud.* I. I. 914 Honour is, like a Widow, won With brisk Attempt and putting on. **1860** TRENCH *Serm. Westm. Abb.* i. 7 A putting on of the armour of light. **1930** A. ARMSTRONG *Taxi* xii. 163 'Putting on' is the taxi man's expression for coming on at the end of the rank. **1968** *Listener* 31 Oct. 566/1 They acknowledged their debt to McLuhan and paraded his definition of modern myths—the putting on of an audience and its environment. *c* **1440** *Alphabet of Tales* 288 A [= on] payn of *puttyng oute of bothe his een. **1613–39** I. JONES in Leoni *Palladio's Archit.* (1742) I. 72 The putting out of the Landing-place of the Stairs farther than the Range of the Rooms. **1630** EARL MANCH. in *Buccleuch MSS.* (Hist. MSS. Comm.) I. 271 The putting out of apprentices. **1947** S. C. ADAMS in A. Dundes *Mother Wit* (1973) 519 The younger generation are largely indifferent either as to the necessity of joining the church, or, if they are already members, as to the 'putting out' of the church. *c* **1450** *Godstow Reg.* 197 He strengthed hyt with þe *puttynge to of hys seele. **1579** J. LOUD in Strype *Eccl. Mem.* (1721) I. li. 388 At the first putting to of the fire. **1856** 'STONEHENGE' *Brit. Rural Sports* 545/2 Putting-to is managed very differently, according to whether the horse is going in shafts or with a pole. **1890** 'R. BOLDREWOOD' *Col. Reformer* (1891) 187 The volunteers who had assisted at the ticklish business of putting to. **1626** BACON *Sylva* §821 In the first *putting up it cooleth in little portions. **1641** MILTON *Animadvers.* ii. 18 The putting up of our Praiers. *c* **1806** D. WORDSWORTH *Jrnl.* (1941) I. 258 She did not much encourage us to go, because . . it was a long way, 'and there was no putting-up for the like of us'. **1834** M'CULLOCH *Dict. Comm.* 1082 Employed . . in embroidering, mending, bleaching, dyeing, . . putting-up, &c. **1907** J. G. MILLAIS *Newfoundland* iv. 76 During the month of September the big stags keep to themselves in various 'putting up' spots . . near the lakes and rivers. **1909** *Daily Chron.* 16 June 1/2 It was the biggest fight he had ever undertaken, but he was going to win it . . or if he did not win he was going to give the other side a rare 'putting up'. **1914** *Chambers's Jrnl.* Aug. 536/1 Herrings cause similar bubbles, which fishermen call 'putting up'.

10. *attrib.* and *Comb.*: **putting-road**, a road along which coal is 'put' (see sense 3) in a mine; also **putting-stick**, = PUTTER *sb.*[1] 4, *poting-stick* (see POTE *v.*).

1887 P. M'NEILL *Blawearie* 21 [The pit] has been stopped for some years, not because the '*putting roads' had become too far, or too heavy for the putters; . . but because the seam had become utterly flooded with water. **1583** *Putting sticke [see PUTTER *sb.*[1] 4].

putting ('pʌtɪŋ), *vbl. sb.*[2] [f. PUT, PUTT *v.*[2]]

1. *Golf.* The action of striking the ball with the putter in order to get it into the hole.

1805 FORSYTH *Beauties Scotl.* I. 84 The art . . of so proportioning the force and direction of the stroke, or putting as it is called, that the ball may with few strokes be driven into the hole. **1857** *Chambers's Inform. People* 695/1 It is only by careful judgment that nicety in putting is arrived at. **1892** *Eng. Illustr. Mag.* X. 58 All golf . . is divided into three parts—driving, iron play, and putting.

b. *Comb.* **putting cleek**, a cleek used in putting; **putting course** *poet.* = *putting green*; **'putting-green**, (*a*) the part of the ground, usually kept smooth and clear of obstacles, around each hole; (*b*) a miniature golf course; **putting-hole**: where the ball is 'putted'; **putting-iron**, an iron putter (PUTTER *sb.*[2] 2 a).

1881 FORGAN *Golfer's Handbk.* 13 The '*Putting Cleek' . . is employed on the putting-green, but is a very treacherous weapon. **1905** VARDON *Compl. Golfer* 146 Whether it is a plain gun-metal instrument, a crooked-necked affair, a putting cleek, an ordinary aluminium, [or] a wooden putter. **1945** J. BETJEMAN *Coll. Poems* (1958) 116 Over the *putting-course rashes were seen Of pink and of yellow among the burnt green. **1966** —— *High & Low* 62, I will not go to Finsbury Park The putting course to see. **1841** *Links o' Innerleven* iii. in *Poems on Golf* (1867) 61 Yet oft upon the *putting-green He'll rest to gaze upon the scene That lies round Innerleven. **1857** *Chambers's Inform. People* 695/1 Your ball . . lies on the sward, or 'putting-green', within a dozen yards from the hole. **1977** *Evening Post* (Nottingham) 27 Jan. 14/1 (Advt.), Local amenities bowls, tennis, putting green, paddling pool. **1906** *Westm. Gaz.* 3 Nov. 3/1 Finding nothing to reward them in that, they [jackdaws] left it, to visit the *putting-hole of the clock-golf. **1857** *Chambers's Inform. People* 695/1 Should you be advised to substitute a *putting-iron for the *bonâ-fide* tool, shun the advice, and stick to the putter.

2. = prec. 8, which in Sc. is ('pʌtɪŋ).

putting ('pʊtɪŋ), *ppl. a.* [f. PUT *v.*[1] + -ING[2].] That puts: see the verb. Usually with adverbs, as †**putting-forth**, putting oneself forward, self-assertive, presumptuous (*obs.*); **putting-off**, disconcerting, off-putting, repellent; cf. *off-putting* ppl. adj. s.v. OFF-PUT; **putting-on**, employed in placing something on something else (in manufactures, etc.).

1621 BP. MOUNTAGU *Diatribæ* 28 Whatsoever we are we doe not vaunt: nor φανητιᾶν [*mispr.* φαινετιᾶν], as many putting-forth fellowes use to doe. **1642** ROGERS *Naaman* 128 What is so selfe putting forth, as an handmaid affecting the place of her mistresse? **1839** *Guide to Trade, Printer* 40 Putting-on Boys. **1928** M. ARLEN *Lily Christine* vi. 86 The idea of anyone living . . her life 'bravely' . . is, to tell the truth, slightly embarrassing—'putting-off', the phrase is. **1932** S. GIBBONS *Cold Comfort Farm* i. 9 'Would it impress them with my efficiency?' 'No. . . It would be *too* putting-off.' **1945** C. WILLIAMS *All Hallows' Eve* 184 She was very putting-off, and only said: 'Pray, nurse, do not interfere.' **1959** *Sunday Times* 22 Mar. 24/5 The first act was so putting-off that I should not have been much surprised if many viewers had accepted the B.B.C.'s invitation to 'Follow The Fleet', with Fred Astaire and Ginger Rogers, on the other channel.

putting-stone ('pʊtɪŋ-, *Sc.* 'pʌtɪŋstəʊn). [f. PUTTING *vbl. sb.*[1] 8.] A heavy stone used in the athletic exercise of putting.

17.. POPE (J.), In some parts of Scotland, stones . . are laid at the gates of great houses, which they call putting stones, for trials of strength. **1771** PENNANT *Tour Scot. in 1769*, 214 Antient sports of the Highlanders . . retained are, throwing the putting-stone, or stone of strength (*Cloch neart*), as they call it, which occasions an emulation who can throw a weighty one the farthest. **1863** W. C. BALDWIN *Afr. Hunting* 221 Played quoits . . and got through the time with the putting-stone.

†**puttish** ('pʌtɪʃ), *a. Obs.* [f. PUT *sb.*[4] + -ISH[1].] Of the character of a 'put': see PUT *sb.*[4]

1738 *Gentl. Mag.* VIII. 157/2 The rural squire, that puttish spark, Shines signal by the barber's mark.

‖**putto** ('putto). Pl. **putti** ('putti), also 7 puti. [It. *putto*, pl. *putti*, boy, lad, stripling, ad. L. *putus* boy, child.] A representation of a child, nude or in swaddling bands, used in art, esp. in Italy in the 15th–17th c.

1644 Evelyn *Diary* 17 Nov., That stupendous canopy of Corinthian brasse [in St. Peter's]; it consists of 4 wreath'd columns..incircl'd with vines, on which hang little puti, birds and bees. **1649** —— *Ibid.* 7 Sept., The staire-case and the ornaments of Putti about it. **1894** B. Berenson in *Nation* (N.Y.) 30 Aug. 157/2 It was his passion..for the expression of the joyful feeling that led Correggio to seize every chance to paint putti. **1914** C. F. Bell *Drawings by Old Masters in Christ Church* 44 Fiammingo, François du Quesnoy, *attributed to*... A nude putto playing with a goat. **1931** B. Berenson *Ital. Pictures of Renaissance* 109 Bramantino (*Bartolommeo Suardi*)... Milan... 16. Fresco: Putto under Vine. **1968** *Listener* 22 Aug. 247/1 The omission in Poussin's painting of anything corresponding to the *putto* in the Bordone leads to a strange placing of the left leg. **1973** *Daily Tel.* 13 Feb. 13/6 On one side are two coats of arms in Baroque mantling held together by ribbons in the hand of a flying putto.

puttock[1] (ˈpʌtək). *Obs.* exc. *dial.* Also 5 **puttok(e, potok, 5–7 puttocke,** 9 *dial.* **puttick, puddock.** [Found early in the 15th c. Origin uncertain; the ending seems to be the dim. -ock, OE. *-oc, -uc*, as in *bullock, hillock*.

The stem has been conjectured to be the *putt- of OE. *pyttel*, pittel, a name applied to the same birds, of which the ulterior etymology is obscure. Some have suggested derivation from L. *būteo* buzzard, or a kind of hawk, which might have given an OE. **bȳta*, and perh. a dim. **byttoc*.]

A bird of prey; usually applied to the Kite or Glede (*Milvus ictinus* or *regalis*); sometimes to the Common Buzzard (*Buteo vulgaris*).

Also, according to Swainson (*Prov. Names Brit. Birds*), sometimes incorrectly applied to the Marsh Harrier or Moor Buzzard, *Circus æruginosus*.

?*c***1400** Lydg. *Æsop's Fab.* iii. 81 The hound..Witnesse tweyne brought in jugement, The wolf and the puttok. *c***1400** *Plowman's Tale* 1338 Gledes and bosardes weren hem by; Whyt molles and puttockes token hir place. *c***1440** *Gesta Rom.* li. 370 (Add. MS.) The puttok come flyeng, and houyd ouer the henne and hire briddes. *c***1475** *Pict. Voc.* in Wr.-Wülcker 762/5 *Hic milvus*, a potok. **1496** *Dives & Paup.* (W. de W.) i. xlvi. 87/2 Yf the kyte or the puttoke flee ouer the waye afore them. **1575** Gascoigne *To D. Dine*, A puttocke set on pearch Fast by a falcons side Will quickly shew it selfe a kight. **1668** Charleton *Onomast.* 65 *Accipiter Milvus regalis*..the long-winged Kite, or Puttock. **1678** Ray *Willughby's Ornith.* ii. viii. §2 Of the common Buzzard or Puttock, called in Latine *Buteo*. **1817** J. Mayer *Sportsman's Direct.* (ed. 2) 184 The Grey Bob-tailed Buzzard or Puttock. **1827** Clare *Sheph. Cal.* 87 A shrilly noise of puddocks' feeble wail. **1881** *Standard* 2 Mar. 5 The kite, or glead, or puttock, is almost extinct.

†**b.** *fig.* Applied opprobriously to a person, as having some attribute of the kite (e.g. ignobleness, greed): cf. hawk *sb.*[1] 3; *esp.* (from the kite's preying on chickens) a catchpole. *Obs.*

1605 *Tryall Chev.* ii. i. in Bullen *O. Pl.* (1884) III. 290 Peter, dost see this sword?.. Whorson puttock, no garbage serve you but this? have at you. **1611** Dekker *Roar. Girle* ii. iii, *Adam.* Who comes yonder? *S. Dauy.* They looke like puttocks, these should be they. **1631** Chapman *Cæsar & Pompey* i. i. Plays 1873 III. 128 And such a flocke of Puttocks follow Cæsar. **1867** Smyth *Sailor's Word-bk.*, *Puttock*, a cormorant, a greedy fellow.

c. *Comb.*, as ***puttock-grey, -hued, -like*** adjs.

1447 *Crt.-Roll Gt. Waltham Manor, Essex* 26 July, Unus equus *puttokhewed* provenit de extranea infra istud dominium. **1620** Melton *Astrolog.* 14 The clawes of the Puttock-like Catch-poles. **1685** *Lond. Gaz.* No. 2092/4 Stolen.., a large strong grey Gelding,..a kind of Puttock grey, low in flesh. **1720** *Ibid.* No. 5854/3 Stolen,..a Puttock coloured Horse.

†**puttock**[2]. *Naut. Obs.* [Origin obscure: see below.] The original name of the small or short shrouds connecting the lower shrouds with the top; also, where there is a top gallant mast, the similar set connecting the topmast shrouds with the top-gallant top. After 1700 usually called **puttock shrouds**, and now *futtock-shrouds*, from an erroneous confusion of the word with futtock in the latter half of the 18th c.

*a***1625** *Nomencl. Navalis* (Harl. MS. 2301) 100 *Puttocks*, are the small Shrowdes which goo from the Shrowdes of the Main, Fore and Missen masts and also to the Topmast shrowdes, if the Topmast have a topp gallant topp, the use whereof is to goo of the shrowdes into the Topp, for when the shrowdes come neare upp to the mast they fall in so much that otherwise they could not gett into the Topp from them. The Puttocks goo..above to a plate of Iron or to a Deadman-eie to which the Lanniers of the Topmast [MS. Foremast] Shrowdes doe come. **1627** Capt. Smith *Seaman's Gram.* v. 19 The top-Masts shrouds..are fastened with Lanniers and dead mens eyes to the Puttocks or plats of iron belonging to them, aloft ouer the head of the Mast. *Ibid.* 20 [as in *Nomencl. Nav.*]. *c***1635** Capt. N. Boteler *Dial. Sea Services* [as in *Nomencl. Nav.*]. **1658** in Phillips. **1704** J. Harris *Lex. Techn.* I, *Puttocks or Puttock Shrowds* [as in *Nomencl. Nav.*]. **1711** W. Sutherland *Shipbuild. Assist.* 113 The Puttock Shrowds binding the main Shrowds and Top-mast Shrowds together. **1748** *Anson's Voy.* i. viii. 81 One of the..dead-eyes was broke, as was also a main-shroud and puttock-shroud. [**1769** Falconer *Mar. Dict.* s.v. *Shrouds*, The topmast-shrouds are extended from the topmast-heads to the edges of the tops... The lower deadeye..is fitted with an iron band, called the foothook-plate, which passes through a hole in the edge of the top and communicates with a rope called the foothook-shroud, whose lower end is attached to the shrouds of the lower mast.] **1815** Burney *Falconer's Dict. M.*, *Puttock* or *Foot-hook Plates*..are narrow plates of iron attached to the dead-eyes of the topmast shrouds. **1867** Smyth *Sailor's Word-bk.*, *Puttock-shrouds*, synonymous with *futtock*; a word in use, but not warranted.

fig. **1751** Smollett *Per. Pic.* lxxiii, Expressing his hope that..he should be able to surmount the puttock-shrouds of despair, and get aloft to the cross-trees of God's good favour.

[*Note.* The form *puttock* was regularly used down to 1750 at least; but after that date it appears to have been, from similarity of sound, confused with futtock, the name of the middle timbers of the ship's frame, with which the *puttocks* had no manner of connexion. Hence in Falconer's *Marine Dict.* 1769, and app. in all later works, *puttock* is replaced by *futtock*; in the combinations given in futtock 2, *futtock hole, hoop, plate, rigging, shroud, staff, stave* belong to this erroneous substitution of *futtock* for *puttock*. As *futtock* was perh. orig. *foot-hook*, it has been suggested that *puttock* was = *pothook* (of which a form *pottock* occurs in 1707): but nothing in the sense appears to confirm this suggestion. Some allusive use of puttock[1] has also been conjectured. More probable is a connexion with Du. *putting*, applied in 1673 to the chains of the main shrouds, while *mars-putting* in 1702 renders F. *gambes de hune*, the puttock-shrouds. Cf. EFris. *pütting* (pl. *-s, -en*), Ger. *putting* or *pütting* (*-s, -en*), Da. *pytting* (*-er*), Sw. *pütting*, the iron links or chains by which the shrouds of the masts are secured to the ship's sides, the chains of the dead-eye; Ger. *putting-taue*, Da. *pytting vanter*, Sw. *püttingsvant* = 'puttock-shrouds'. But the source of *putting* or *pütting* is unknown.]

puttock[3] (ˈpʌtək). Chiefly *north. dial.* Now *Obs.* or *rare.* [Derivation unascertained.] A make-weight; chiefly in comb. ***puttock-candle***.

1674 Ray *N.C. Words* (1691) 56 A Puttock-Candle: the least in the Pound, put in to make weight. **1787** Grose *Provinc. Gloss.*, Puttock-candle. **1876** Robinson *Whitby Gloss.*, *Puttocks, Inses*, or *Mak-weights*, small portions..put into the scale to make up the required weight. **1887** Parish & Shaw *Kentish Gloss.*, *Puttock-candle*, the smallest candle in a pound, put in to make the weight.

‖**puttony** (ˈputoɲ). Pl. **puttonys.** [Hungarian; cf. Hung. *puttonyos* holding as much as goes into one *puttony* (e.g. *öt puttonyos tokaji* five-basket Tokay).] In Hungary, a basket or dosser made of wooden staves or wickerwork used to transfer grapes from the vineyard to the wine-press.

1958 A. L. Simon *Dict. Wines* 156/1 They [*sc.* over-ripe grapes] are gathered in wooden vessels known as *puttony*, holding about 25 quarts... When the label on the bottle records '1 puttony', it means that about 10 per cent of the grapes used were *trockenbeeren*..; if '3 puttony', the proportion was 30 per cent. **1959** W. James *Word-Bk. of Wine* 190 Pickers carry a small container called a puttony, into which they put selected overripe berries..; the number of full puttonyos mixed with the ripe but not overripe grapes in the fermentation cask determines the richness of the wine, the range being from one to five (and occasionally six) puttonyos. **1967** A. Lichine *Encycl. Wines & Spirits* 426/2 The collar label on every bottle of Tokaji Aszu will state: 3 Puttonos, 4 Puttonos, etc.—the export agency simplifies the spelling by removing the 'y'. *Ibid.* 522/2 The buckets or *puttonys* of raisin-dry, concentrated grapes added to the fermentation..are shown on each bottle of the vatting. *Ibid.* 523/1 The overripe, dried, shrivelled berries, picked separately and put into the little *puttony* pails, are worked in a trough... Alcoholic content and other characteristics of course vary with the *puttonys* content. **1972** *Guardian* 26 Jan. 9/5 In theory there can be a Tokay of 6 puttonyos; but in practice only the five turns up.

‖**puttoo** (ˈpʌtuː). *East Indies.* [a. Hindī (Panjābī and allied langs.) *paṭṭū*, a. Old Kashmīrī *paṭu*, allied to Skr. *paṭa* woven stuff, cloth.] A fabric made of the coarse refuse hair of the Cashmere goat. Also *attrib.*

1857 Col. Keith Young *Diary, Siege of Delhi* (1902) 110 A puttoo coat and equally warm continuations, as Seymour calls them. **1858** Simmonds *Dict. Trade*, *Puttoo*, a coarse thick fabric made of the refuse wool and long hair from the shawl goat, *Capra changra*. **1893** *Baily's Mag.* Oct. 263/2 A coat (Norfolk jacket style) and loose knickerbockers of puttoo.

putt-putt, var. put-put *sb.* and *v.*

putty (ˈpʌtɪ), *sb.* Also 7 **puttey, -ie, -ee,** 8–9 *Sc.* **potty.** [a. F. *potée* (12th c. in Hatz.-Darm.), used in senses 1, 5a, b, below; orig. a potful, or the contents of a pot, f. *pot* pot *sb.*[1]]

1. A powder of calcined tin (amorphous stannic oxide), or of calcined tin and lead, used for polishing glass or metals; distinctively called ***jewellers' putty***, also ***putty of tin, putty powder***. (So F. *potée*.)

1663 Boyle *Exp. Hist. Colours* ii. xiii, The common putty, that is sold and used so much in shops, instead of being, as it is pretended and ought to be, only the calx of tin, is by the artificers that make it, to save the charge of tin, made..but of half tin and half lead, if not far more lead than tin. **1670** Flamsteed in Rigaud *Corr. Sci. Men* (1841) II. 93, I intend to grind with ordinary sand fine dressed, and polish first with chalk, after with putty. **1763** W. Lewis *Comm. Phil. Techn.* 58 Fine powder, called putty prepared by calcining a mixture of lead and tin. **1839** Ure *Dict. Arts* 1241 When [tin is] heated to redness, with free access of air, it absorbs oxygen with rapidity, and changes first into a pulverulent gray protoxide, and by longer ignition, into a yellow-white powder, called putty of tin.

2. A fine mortar or cement made of lime and water without sand; distinctively called ***plasterers' putty*** or 'fine stuff'.

1633 Gerard *Somerset* (1900) 131 With them putte was soft dyett, which name wee still conserve in a wett and liquid morter for cementing stones together by Masons called Puttey. **1641** Best *Farm. Bks.* (Surtees) 138 To mingle water and lime, and not to temper it too thicke, but to make it thinne like unto puttie. **1759** Colebrooke in *Phil. Trans.* LI. 47 What the bricklayers call fine stuff, or putty. *Note*, Putty is lime slacked, and, while warm, dissolved in water, and strained through a sieve. **1825** J. Nicholson *Operat. Mechanic* 612 A thin and smooth coat spread over it, consisting of lime only, or, as the workmen call it, *putty*, or set. **1881** Young *Ev. Man His Own Mechanic* §1201 The mortar used for the white lines [in pointing] is what is technically called 'putty', that is to say, plasterer's putty, and not glazier's putty.

3. a. A cement composed of powdered whiting made into a stiff paste with raw linseed oil or occasionally other ingredients, used in fixing panes of glass, and for making up inequalities in woodwork, etc. before painting; distinctively, ***glaziers' putty***.

1706 Phillips (ed. 6), *Putty*,..also a kind of Composition that Painters made use of to stop up Holes in Wood, &c. **1727–41** Chambers *Cycl.*, *Putty*, in its popular sense, denotes a cinericious kind of paste, compounded of whiting and linseed-oil beaten together to the consistence of a tough dough. **1815** J. Smith *Panorama Sc. & Art* I. 258 The nails are driven in a little below the surface of these boards, and the cavity is filled with glazier's putty. *Ibid.* 221 A mixture of oil-putty. **1875** Knight *Dict. Mech.* s.v., Some trades employ glue-putty, in which hot melted glue is substituted for the oil.

b. Phr. ***up to putty***, worthless, useless. *Austral. colloq.*

1916 *Anzac Bk.* 32/1 A man's got a chance to hit back there, but down 'ere it's up to putty. **1953** D. Stivens *Gambling Ghost* 24 'I don't hear anything, Cabbage-tree,' said Thunderclap. 'Your hearing's up to putty,' said Cabbage-tree. **1965** *Telegraph* (Brisbane) 5 July 8/5 *Up to putty*, no good.

c. Used *fig.* to designate one who is easily influenced or malleable. Freq. in colloq. phr. ***to be (like) putty in*** (someone's) ***hands***.

1924 H. Crane *Let.* 3 Feb. (1965) 173, I was quite exemplary of both sides of my family in not being made of any putty—knowing what I want to do, and sticking it out. **1946** W. S. Maugham *Then & Now* ii. 3 You are infatuated with the man. You're like putty in his hands. **1979** D. Kyle *Green River High* vii. 90, I was putty in her hands... The arguments *were* very attractive.

†**4.** *Med.* Lead-plaster, diachylon. *Obs. rare*[−1].

1828 *Lancet* 28 June 388/1 Plaster, or *putty*, is a composition of oil and oxide of lead..it is sometimes called *lead plaster*.

5. In various transferred senses.

(a. and b. are senses of F. *potée*; they are given in Ogilvie's *Imperial Dict.* 1882, but have not been found in English or Scottish use.)

†**a.** *Pottery.* Glaze or glazing-slip for earthenware. †**b.** *Foundry.* The 'loam' of which moulds are made; a mixture of clay, horse-dung, and sand.

c. (*slang* or *colloq.*) Sticky mud at the bottom of a body of water.

1883 G. C. Davies *Norfolk Broads & Rivers* i. 5 All the other Broads have bottoms of black mud..so soft that a yacht's anchor will not hold in it, so that large blocks of iron ballast are used instead, which will not drag through the 'putty,' as the mud is locally called. **1890** P. H. Emerson *Wild Life* 60 My punt..may stick in the putty. **1902** *Work. Men's Coll. Jrnl.* VII. 367 The tide was running down..and the quant had to be used a good deal, the yacht sticking 'on the putty' more than once. **1961** P. Moyes *Sunken Sailor* ii. 33 My adorable wife has put us on the putty. On a falling tide.

d. As the name of a colour, esp. in dress-materials: A light shade of yellowish grey; in full ***putty-colour***.

1886 *Daily News* 16 Mar. 6/3 Another pretty colour with an ugly name is that called 'putty'. It is really a very sweet tone of grey with a touch of fawn in it. **1915** *T. Eaton & Co. Catal.* Spring & Summer Suppl. 1/2 Natty tailored Suit... In light Putty (Tan) shade only. **1926–7** *Army & Navy Stores Catal.* 698/1 *Hose*..Botany Wool, in Black, Grey, Tan, Nigger, Putty, Beige, Nude.

e. A former type of golf ball made of some material other than gutta-percha.

1891 R. Forgan *Golfer's Handbk.* 39 The 'putty' being the popular name for the 'Eclipse'. **1900** A. E. T. Watson *Young Sportsman* 293 Several kinds of composition balls, known generically as 'putties' in contradistinction to the 'gutties' or gutta-percha balls..have failed to take the place of those made of the raw material.

f. *Naut.* (See quots.)

1946 J. Irving *Royal Navalese* 141 *Putty*, the ship's painter. **1961** F. H. Burgess *Dict. Sailing* 165 *Putty*,..a ship's painter.

6. *attrib.* and *Comb.*, as ***putty bed, beige, colour*** (hence ***putty-coloured*** adj.), ***face, grey, joint, mark, shade, state, white***; also ***putty-cool, -faced, -like, -looking, -stopped*** adjs.; **putty-blower**, a blow-tube for shooting pellets of putty (sense 3); **putty-cement**, = sense 2; **putty-eye**, a pigeon's eye having a thick fleshy cere; **putty-head** *U.S.*, a stupid person; **putty-headed** *a.*, stupid, softhearted; **putty-hearted** *a.*, lacking in courage, cowardly; **putty-knife**, a knife with a blunt flexible spatulate blade for spreading putty (sense 3); **putty medal** *jocular*, a worthless reward for insignificant service or achievement (cf. medal *sb.* 2 b); **putty-powder**, = sense 1; **putty-root**, a rare N. American orchid (*Aplectrum hyemale*), the corm of which contains a glutinous matter sometimes used as a cement; **putty-shooter** = *putty-blower*; **putty-work**, decorative work executed in a putty-like composition which hardens after it is moulded.

1902 *How to make Things* 33/2 [In bird-stuffing] the insertion of the artificial eyes, in a *putty bed, follows the operation of pinning the wings to the body. **1969** *Sears Catal.* Spring/Summer 10 *Putty beige. **1862** R. H. NEWELL *Orpheus C. Kerr Papers* 1st Ser. 156 [The muskets] are inferior to the *putty-blowers of our innocent childhood. **1878** B. HARTE *Man on Beach* 96 The boot-black drew a tin putty-blower from his pocket, and took unerring aim. **1825** J. NICHOLSON *Operat. Mechanic* 538 *Putty cement will stand longer than most stones. **1933** *Burlington Mag.* Sept. 122/1 The olive-grey celadon glaze has the same peculiar tint, with a slight suggestion of *putty colour. **1979** 'G. BLACK' *Night Run from Java* iii. 32 Banana palms..bleached to a kind of putty colour. **1889** *Daily News* 4 Dec. 5/6 The Baroness..wore *putty-coloured silk with trimmings of handsome gold and fawn embroidery. **1906** H. BEGBIE *Priest* ii. 8 At one end was a great spread of folding doors putty coloured. **1970** R. LOWELL *Notebk.* 69 Our bedroom, putty-gray and *putty-cool. **1927** M. SINCLAIR *Hist. A. Waring* xvii. 88 Charlie, in spite of his *putty face, was handsome in a heavy way. **1931** W. FAULKNER *Sanctuary* vii. 68 'Yes, putty-face!' the woman cried. **1969** *Putty-grey [see *putty-cool* above]. **1856** M. J. HOLMES *L. Rivers* 370 He got so engaged about the darned 'liquor law', and the *putty-heads that made it, that he'd no idee 'twas so late. **1873** 'MARK TWAIN' *Gilded Age* xliii. 393 In a word, the great *putty-headed public loves to 'gush'. **1885** R. L. STEVENSON *Prince Otto* II. i, A springless, *putty-hearted, cowering coward. **1838** *Civ. Eng. & Arch. Jrnl.* I. 330/1 A fine brick ..to be..laid in what is called a close *putty joint. **1858** SIMMONDS *Dict. Trade*, *Putty-Knife,..used by glaziers and painters, to spread putty. **1901** *J. Black's Carp. & Build., Usef. Recipes* 51 Take a sharp-edged putty-knife..and cut the paint off as low as you can without scratching the glass. **1865** *Daily Tel.* 3 Nov. 5/4 Leaving a huge *putty-like cake of clay at the bottom. **1849–52** *Todd's Cycl. Anat.* IV. 1009/1 The *putty-looking chalky matter often observed in the lungs. **1898** R. E. F. COHEN in W. A. Morgan '*House*' *on Sport* 378 Not even the proverbial *putty medal or a memento of any sort was awarded to the man who upheld the honour of his University by beating his rival in the water. **1958** M. KELLY *Christmas Egg* (1965) iii. 195 'You know what you'll be given for all this?'..'A putty medal. Sooner have a cheque.' **1972** *Guardian* 12 Sept. 15/7 Putty medal blues... The Americans are busy mounting a major public inquest on their showing at Munich and on the Olympic Games. **1832** G. R. PORTER *Porcelain & Gl.* x. 245 The outer surface being then covered with washed *putty powder, which is a combination of the oxides of tin and lead. **1868** WATTS *Dict. Chem.* V. 817 Amorphous stannic oxide.. is hard, and is therefore used for polishing stone and glass, and for sharpening and polishing steel, etc. The oxide used for this purpose is called *putty-powder*; it is sometimes a mixture of the oxides of tin and lead. **1895** *Oracle Encycl.* I. 598/2 The artist..next develops the figure with very delicate tools of steel wire..finally polishing with putty powder. **1857** HENFREY *Bot.* 411 *Aplectrum hyemale*, the North American *Putty-root, is used for making a cement for china. **1930** *Daily Express* 6 Oct. 11/6 (Advt.), The Barry 'militaire' (in fashionable *putty-shade). **1896** D. C. BEARD *Amer. Boy's Bk. of Sport* xxxiii. 395 When people depend for their dinner or personal safety upon a '*putty-shooter' you may be sure that they learn to shoot with great accuracy. **1881** YOUNG *Ev. Man his own Mechanic* §161 They could not be *putty-stopped well enough. **1971** *Guardian* 20 July 9/3 Caramel..and *putty-white make the season's signature combination.

putty ('pʌtɪ), *v.* [f. prec. sb.] *trans.* To cover or smear with putty; to fix, mend, or join with putty; to fill up (a hole, woodwork, etc.) with putty.

1734 CURTEIS in *Phil. Trans.* XXXVIII. 267, I..stopt the Holes at the Bottoms with Corks; and..puttyed the Corks, that no Water could filtrate through them. **1771** J. ADAMS *Diary* 4 June, A glass mug broken to pieces and puttied together again. **1879** *Encycl. Carriage Build.* in *Cassell's Techn. Educ.* IV. 221/2 Any joints..are carefully puttied up with oil putty.

Hence '**puttied** *ppl. a.*, '**puttying** *vbl. sb.*; also '**puttier**, one who putties, a glazier.

1775 JEFFERSON *Writ.* (1892) I. 450 To detain them about a month to harden the puttying. **1860** THACKERAY *Lovel* ii, Cracked old houses where the painters and plumbers and puttyers are always at work. **1892** *Photogr. Ann.* II. 39 Fix the lens..and focus on a large sheet of puttied or ground glass.

put-up ('pʊt ʌp), *ppl. a.* [pa. pple. of *to put up*: see PUT *v.*[1] 56.]

1. (orig. *Thieves' slang.*) Arranged or concocted beforehand, as a burglary, by conspiracy with other persons, as servants in the house; preconcerted, planned in an underhand manner: see PUT *v.*[1] 56 t. Often in phr. ***a put-up job***. Also *absol.* as *sb.*

1810 *Ann. Reg.* 296 The police officers are of opinion, that the robbery of the above cathedral is what is called, in the slang language, *a put-up robbery*. **1838** DICKENS *O. Twist* xix, At least it can't be a put-up job, as we expected. *Ibid.* xxxi, We call it a put-up robbery,..when the servants is in it. **1893** G. J. GOSCHEN in *Westm. Gaz.* 6 Dec. 3/1 Your acceptance of one amendment is part and parcel of your rejection of the other. It is a put-up job. **1903** *Outing* XLII. 660/2 'Why, man,' he exclaimed, 'it's a graft—a dirty put-up game. Can't you see it?' **1923** H. G. WELLS *Men like Gods* I. ii. 19 The whole of this business is, as they say nowadays, a put-up thing. **1936** J. CURTIS *Gilt Kid* xv. 148 He would believe that it was a put-up. **1941** [see LINE *sb.*[2] 13 g]. **1974** N. FREELING *Dressing of Diamond* 213 There's going to be a lot saying it's a put-up job.

2. a. Rarely in other senses of *put up*, as 'a put-up statue' (PUT *v.*[1] 56 r), 'a put-up candidate' (56 j), 'put-up drugs' (56 n), 'put-up goods' (56 l).

1846 DICKENS *Pictures from Italy* 124 An English lady.. who always carries..a put-up parasol. **1897** G. B. SHAW *Let.* 26 Mar. (1965) 738 He sends Felix to bid for fashionable put-up plays.

b. *transf.* ***put-up price***, the up-set price at or above which something will be sold at an auction (see PUT *v.*[1] 56 l).

1895 *Daily News* 17 Aug. 5/3 The put-up prices are very low.

put-up, *sb.*: see PUT-.

put-'up-able-with, *a. rare.* [f. phr. *to put up with*: see PUT *v.*[1] 56 p (*b*) + -ABLE.] That may be put up with; tolerable.

1812 M. EDGEWORTH *Tales of Fashionable Life* VI. 37 The accommodations, and everything of that nature, now is vastly put-up-able with!

†'**puture**, '**pulture**. *Obs.* [a. AF. *puture* = ONF. *pulture* (Ph. de Thaun *Best.* 294), OF. *peuture*, *poture*, *pouture* (Godef.), food, nourishment, mod.F. dial. *pouture*, *peuture* food for horses, cattle, or pigs:—late L. type *pultūra*, in med.L. also *putūra* (Du Cange), supposed to be an irreg. deriv. of *puls*, *pultem* pap, porridge.] Food for man or beast; *esp.* in Forest Law, that meat and drink for themselves and their attendants, and food for their horses, hawks, and hounds, claimed by the foresters from every one within the bounds of the forest, and sometimes by other officers on an official circuit; also *ellipt.* the custom of giving or the right of demanding such entertainment.

In the ME. period common in the L. form *putura*, in Latin records; rare as an English word.

[*c* **1280** *Placita Coronæ* (1818) 219 Bene cogn[oscitur] quod forestarii sui capiunt puturam de omnibus et singulis tenentibus terras..infra metas chacearum suarum. **1343** *Placita apud Preston* 17 *Edw. III* (Blount), Johannes de Radecliffe..clamat unam Puturam in Prioratu de Penwortham..pro se et Ministris, equis, et garcionibus suis, per unum diem et duas noctes, de tribus septimanis in tres septimanas, *viz.* de victualibus, ut in esculentis, et poculentis. **1390–91** *Earl Derby's Exp.* (Camden) 64 Pro putura pulletrie. *Ibid.* 96 Pro xxx multonibus..et pro putura eorundem.] **1601** F. TATE *Househ. Ord. Edw. II*, §57 (1876) 44 He shal take for each doges puture j[d]. ob. a day. *Ibid.* §59. 45 He shal have for each doges puture ob. a daye. [*a* **1634** COKE *Inst.* IV. lxxiii. *Courts Forest* (1797) 308 And after they claimed the same for all victuals for themselves, their servants, horses, and dogs, which was called *putura*. **1670** BLOUNT *Law Dict.*, *Putura*.] **1881** W. BEAMONT *Acc. Frodsham* v. 31 Puture was the right to exact food and lodging for the lord's peace officers whenever they were making an official circuit through the district.

‖**putwary** (pʌt'wɑːrɪ), **patwari** (pæt'wɑːrɪ). *East Ind.* Also -**war**(**r**)**ee**. [Hindī *paṭwārī*, f. *paṭṭā*: cf. POTTAH.] A village registrar or accountant under a zemindar.

1801 R. PATTON *Asiat. Mon.* 118 Officers who have been denominated *canongoes* and *putwaries*. The canongoe was the principal, and the putwary the subsidiary officer, in the department of control. **1819** F. HAMILTON *Acct. Kingdom Nepal* II. i. 155 A Patwari or clerk..has one-half ana on the rupee of rent. **1858** SIMMONDS *Dict. Trade*, *Putwarree*, a registrar or collector under an Indian zemindar, or land-holder. **1873** E. BALFOUR *Cycl. India* (ed. 2) IV. 457/2 *Patwari*.., a village accountant, responsible for keeping the accounts of the village, noticing changes in the list of proprietors, [etc.]. **1907** *19th Cent.* Nov. 714 As village putwaris they have almost the monopoly. **1913** J. H. MORRISON *On Trail of Pioneers* xiii. 60 The headman of the village is the patél, and, assisting him, is the patwari or village clerk, usually a Brahmin, who keeps a record of the village lands. **1931** E. A. H. BLUNT *Caste System N. India* xi. 222 The numerous class of *patwaris* (keepers of the village revenue records) consists almost entirely of Kayasthas: and as the *patwari* has a bad name for chicanery, the better class Kayasthas affect to despise this occupation. **1948** 'P. WOODRUFF' *Whatever Dies* 180 The patwari, who is the local representative of the government and looks after some sixty or eighty villages. **1958** O. LEWIS *Village Life N. India* iii. 95 The plots were never..officially registered, because the *patwari* [sic] wanted 30 rupees for the registration, which the villagers refused to pay.

†'**putyer**. *Obs.* Also 5 **puttyer**. [a. OF. *putier*: cf. *pute* (13th c. in Littré): see PUTE *sb.*] A whoremonger; = PUTOUR.

1480 CAXTON *Ovid's Met.* XII. iii, Ha what comyth this wenche here wyth this putyer in this contree? **1483** —— *Cato* e v b, Somme ben kynges or dukes and the other are puttyers and ryght wycked and euyl.

'**put-you-up**. Also **Put-u-up**. [f. phr. *to put up*: see PUT *v.*[1] 56 o (*a*).] A sofa or settee which can be converted into a bed. Also *attrib.*

The form *Put-u-up* is a proprietary term.

1924 *Trade Marks Jrnl.* 20 Aug. 1898 Put-u-up... Settees convertible into bedsteads. Greaves & Thomas,..London, ..manufacturers. **1948** G. V. GALWEY *Lift & Drop* viii. 206 He did have a 'Put-u-up' in the office for firewatching. **1966** M. CRONIN *Jump Gun* iv. 45, I found some blankets, wrestled with the put-u-up and coaxed it into some semblance to a couch. **1966** A. E. LINDOP *I start Counting* i. 14 The sofa was one of those big double-bed Put-U-Ups. **1973** *Country Gentlemen's Mag.* Mar. 180/2 (*heading*) Fitted cabin trunk..ideal service cadet or world rover, £12. Or exchange settee Put-u-Up bed. **1973** *Country Life* 22 Mar. 753/1 A sofa bedstead (an early form of put-you-up). **1978** *Morecambe Guardian* 14 Mar. 9/2 Besides traditional beds, there are the convertible put-you-up types which are essential when space is short.

putz (pʊts, pʌts). *U.S.* [a. G. *putz* decorations, ornaments.] **1.** *dial.* In Pennsylvanian Dutch homes, a representation of the Nativity scene traditionally placed under a Christmas tree.

1902 *N.Y. Times Mag.* 14 Dec. 15/2 Only the chosen few can afford to have a really impressive 'putz' which fills half a room, and represents a landscape in miniature... This more elaborate '*putz*' requires not only money for its erection, but artistic handiwork. **1926** *Ladies' Home Jrnl.* Dec. 82/2 The putz is simply the pictured story of the Nativity, built near or at the base of the Christmas tree. **1938** A. HARK *Hex Marks Spot* 186 Everybody's curious to see what kind of putz everybody else has this year, so they go around visiting. **1970** L. M. FEINSILVER *Taste of Yiddish* i. 44 In Pennsylvania, Jews who know Yiddish are often startled during the Christmas season by ads inviting the public to some company's 'putz'... This German word for decoration means, in Pennsylvania Dutch, a Nativity scene.

2. *slang.* [Yiddish.] **a.** The penis.

1934 H. MILLER *Tropic of Cancer* (1935) 34 [She] ought to have better sense than be tripped up by every guy with a big putz who happens to come along. **1968** L. ROSTEN *Joys of Yiddish* 298 *Putz*, rhymes with 'nuts'. Literally, *putz* is vulgar slang for 'penis'... *Putz* is not to be used lightly, or when women or children are around. It is more offensive than *shmuck*;..*putz* has a pejorative ambience. **1969** P. ROTH *Portnoy's Complaint* 101 He simply cannot—*will* not —control the fires in his putz, the fevers in his brain.

b. A fool, a simpleton; an objectionable person.

1964 W. MARKFIELD *To Early Grave* (1965) vii. 127 What I think is—you're a *putz*. *P, U, T, Z!* **1966** 'E. V. CUNNINGHAM' *Helen* (1967) v. 66 'What are you telling me? That you fell for her—love at first sight?' 'Don't be a putz. I run a gambling house. I don't fall in love.' **1975** A. BERGMAN *Hollywood & Le Vine* (1976) v. 56 He understood life's mysteries and tragedies, this gold-plated putz. **1975** *Publishers Weekly* 21 July 60/1 Leaving their 'putz' of a son Harry home to nurse his ulcers. **1978** J. KRANTZ *Scruples* i. 6 'You,' she said, enunciating clearly, 'are a putz, a schmekel, a schmuck, a schlong, and a shvantz. And a WASP putz, at that.'

‖**Putzfrau** ('pʊtsfraʊ). [Ger.] A charwoman.

1927 J. JOYCE *Let.* 25 July (1966) III. 162 Mrs. Purefoy is not a Putzfrau. **1977** *Time* 8 Aug. 22/3 Says one Greek *Putzfrau* (charwoman): 'I know the West Germans wish us to hell.'

‖**puukko** ('puːkko). Also **puuko**. Pl. **puukot**. [Finn.] A type of knife used in Finland.

1952 *Chambers's Jrnl.* Jan. 37/1 He fumbled desperately for his sharp-bladed 'puukko', expecting to be set upon forthwith by a snarling fury. **1959** A. GLYN *I can take it All* ii. 36 His knife, his puukko, a large weapon with a plain handle and a double-edge blade in an embossed leather scabbard. **1964** C. GAVIN *Fortress* xi. 188 A red braided belt from which swung..the Finnish knife, the *puuko*, in its heavy leather sheath. **1964** G. LYALL *Most Dangerous Game* iii. 24, I caught the glint of *puukot*, those nasty little hook-ended Finnish knives. *Ibid.*, The first *puukko* merchant dodged.

puwang, **puwha**, varr. PAWANG, PUHA.

puwe, **puwit**, obs. forms of PEW, PEWIT.

‖**puy** (pwiː). [F. *puy*, in OF. *pui*, *poi* hill, mount, hillock:—L. *podium* elevation, height, in med. (Franco-) L. *podium*, *pogium* hill, peak.] A small volcanic cone; *spec.* one of those in Auvergne, France; also, in *Geol.*, generalized.

1858 G. P. SCROPE *Geol. Centr. France* 180 Among the puys of the Monts Dome we are enabled..to trace almost every stream of lava to the crater which marks the spot of its emission. **1878** HUXLEY *Physiogr.* 203 There the traveller may see hundreds of volcanic cones, known locally as 'puys'. **1880** DAWKINS *Early Man* iv. 74 Clusters of small lateral cones or puys sprang up on their flank, like those on Mount Etna.

puy, variant of POY *sb.*[1], a punt-pole.

puy-: see PUI-.

puya ('puːjə). Also **puza**. [mod.L. (G. I. Molina *Saggio della Storia Naturale del Chile* (1782) 160), a. Amer. Sp., f. Sp. *puya* goad.] A herbaceous or woody plant of the genus so called, sometimes as large as a small tree, belonging to the family Bromeliaceæ, native to dry regions of the Andes, and distinguished by rosettes of spiny leaves and blue or yellow flowers borne singly or in large panicles or racemes.

1809 tr. *J. I. Molina's Geogr., Nat. & Civil Hist. Chili* I. iii. 130 The trunk of the *puya*..is used for cork throughout Chili. **1847** *Curtis's Bot. Mag.* LXXIII. 4309 (*heading*) Altenstein's Puya; gigantic variety. **1885** *Pall Mall Gaz.* 11 Mar. 11/1 We mounted over rocks and more dust for some 2,000 feet, among puzas and succulent and prickly plants. **1902** *Westm. Gaz.* 23 May 12/1 The blue Puya is known to frequenters of Kew by the beautiful picture of it painted by Miss North in Chili. **1920** *Nature* 8 Apr. 160/2 On a sandstone plateau [in Bolivia]..was growing the gigantic 'Puya'. **1963** W. BLUNT *Of Flowers & Village* 240 The Chilean puyas, if it is true that they are fertilized by hummingbirds, are exceptions. **1974** T. MORRISON *Land above Clouds* 149 The tallest flower spikes in the world grow from solitary stands of a giant bromeliad, the Puya.

puynt, obs. form of POINT *sb.*[1] and *v.*[1]

puyste, variant of PUST *Obs.*, pustule.

puyt(e, obs. form of PUT *v.*[1]

puzel, puzzel, puzzle, obs. ff. PUCELLE.

puzzivanting, var. PUSSIVANTING *ppl. a.* and *vbl. sb.*

puzzle ('pʌz(ə)l), *sb.* Also 7 pusle. [Goes with PUZZLE *v.*, q.v.]

1. The state of being puzzled or bewildered; bewilderment; confusion; perplexity how to act or decide.

1607–12 BACON *Ess., Great Place* (Arb.) 280 While they are in the pusle of businesse, they haue noe tyme to tend theire health, either of body, or minde. **1628** FELTHAM *Resolves* II. xxviii. [I. xxvii], Beyond them wee meete with nothing but the puzzle of the soul, and the dazle of the minds dimme eyes. **1697** J. SERGEANT *Solid Philos.* 59 Later Philosophers were at a great puzzle about it. **1736** BUTLER *Anal.* I. vi. Wks. 1874 I. 112 The puzzle and obscurity, which must unavoidably arise from arguing upon so absurd a supposition as that of universal Necessity. **1767** G. WHITE *Selborne* x, Linnæus seems to be in a puzzle about his *mus amphibius*. **1873** M. ARNOLD *Lit. & Dogma* (1876) 139 The result would be..utter puzzle and bewilderment.

2. A puzzling or perplexing question; a poser, 'problem', 'enigma'.

1655 H. MORE *Antid. Ath.* App. xi. §9 To the last puzzle propounded, whether these Archei [or seminal forms] be so many sprigs of the common soul of the world, or particular subsistences of themselves; there is no great inconvenience in acknowledging that it may be either way. **1760** GRAY *Wks.* (1884) I. 306 About the painting I have a great puzzle in my head between Vertue, Mr. D'Urry, and Bishop Tanner. **1823** LAMB *Elia, Poor Relations*, He is a puzzle to the servants, who are fearful of being too obsequious, or not civil enough, to him. **1856** KANE *Arct. Expl.* I. xxix. 397 It is a puzzle of some interest where they have retreated to.

3. a. Something contrived or made for the purpose of puzzling, or exercising one's ingenuity and patience; a toy or problem of this kind.

1814 SCOTT *Wav.* lxv, He looked not unlike that ingenious puzzle, called *a reel in a bottle*, the marvel of children, (and of some grown people too, myself for one,) who can neither comprehend the mystery how it has got in or how it is to be taken out. **1858** SIMMONDS *Dict. Trade, Puzzles*, various articles of turnery ware and carving; dissecting maps, and pictures for children. **1859** TENNYSON *Vivien* 652 Like a puzzle chest in chest. **1872** ELLACOMBE *Ch. Bells Devon* Suppl. ix. 269 At p. 34 of *Devonshire Bells*, I have mentioned where some ABC puzzles are to be found. **1895** (*title*) The Puzzle Box. Containing six distinct puzzles.

b. ***Chinese puzzle***: one of the ingenious puzzles made by the Chinese, in which the problem is to fit together the dissected pieces of a geometrical or other figure, to disentangle interlocked rings, to remove a string from an object without untying it, etc., etc. The name was app. first applied to the dissected square called *tangram*. Hence, *fig.* Any specially intricate puzzle or problem.

c **1815** [Pamphlet, *Brit. Mus.* No. 15,257 d. 18, containing upwards of 330 figures, formed out of the seven pieces of the 'tangram'] (*title*) A Grand Eastern Puzzle. The following Chinese puzzle is recommended to the Nobility, Gentry, and others, being superior to any hitherto invented for the amusement of the Juvenile World. **1844** *Juv. Missionary Mag. L.M.S.* I. 90 A real Chinese Puzzle.—Young people are fond of puzzles, and have often puzzled for hours over bits of wood called Chinese Puzzles, to very little purpose. **1859** MRS. GATTY *Aunt Judy's Tales* 60 Putting Chinese puzzles together into stupid patterns. **1874** S. W. WILLIAMS *Syllabic Dict. Chinese Lang.* 987 [*Ch'i ch'iao t'u*] The Chinese puzzle of seven pieces, the tangram. **1895** *Gentl. Mag.* vol. 278, p. 279 The Chinese religion may be said to be a Chinese puzzle. **1906** *Times* 1 Feb. (*Article*) Faulty Legislation: A statute is by this process converted into a sort of Chinese puzzle.

c. Short for PUZZLE-PEG.

1845 YOUATT *Dog* v. 113 There was the puzzle and the check-collar [as a punishment] for killing other dogs.

4. *attrib.* and *Comb.*: attrib., 'of a puzzle', or appositive, 'that is or involves a puzzle', as ***puzzle-card, -map, -picture, -poetry, -question, -solving, -thing, -word, -work***; in names of various mechanical contrivances presenting a puzzle or operated by some trick, as ***puzzle-cup, -jug, -locket, -piece*** (hence ***puzzle-piecing***), ***-ring, puzzlewise*** adj. and adv.; **puzzle-box**, a puzzle in the form of a box; *spec.* in *Psychol.*, a box with no obvious connection between its door and the opening device, designed to test the learning abilities of an animal in trying to release itself; also *attrib.* **puzzle-lock**: see quot.; **puzzle-path, puzzle-walk**, a maze (MAZE *sb.* 4). Cf. also PUZZLE *v.* 5.

1866 TROLLOPE *Claverings* in *Cornh. Mag.* XIII. 396 Another girl..was engaged with a *puzzle-box. **1908** M. F. WASHBURN *Animal Mind* x. 232 The dropping off of useless movements is further illustrated in those experiments where animals are required to work some kind of mechanism. This may be called briefly the puzzle-box method. **1921** R. S. WOODWORTH *Psychol.* (1922) xiii. 308 (*caption*) A puzzle box. The animal must here reach his paw out between the bars and raise the latch, *L.* **1966** H. C. LINDGREN et al. *Psychol.* iv. 105/1 Guthrie and Horton..have used the behavior of a cat trying to escape from a puzzle box as a basis for demonstrating this concept of learning. **1970** E. R. GUTHRIE in W. S. Sahakian *Psychol. of Learning* iii. 58 An account of the behavior of cats in a puzzle-box is here offered, with the hope that he [*sc.* the reader] will begin to see himself..in a multitude of puzzle-box situations. **1853** *Puzzle-card [see *conversation card*]. **1882** *Hamilton Sale Catal.* No. 806 A two-handled *puzzle-cup painted with flowers. **1878** *Puzzle-jug [see CAUGHLEY]. **1960** R. G. HAGGAR *Conc. Encycl. Continental Pott. & Porc.* 375/1 The potter, Cornelis Hendricksz (born 1566), is stated to have made surprise jugs or puzzle jugs at Haarlem. **1980** R. RUBENS *Cosway Miniature* ii. 13 Bonnie's greatest love was old china..Regency-striped saucers and Swansea lustre frogs and puzzle jugs. **1834–6** BARLOW in *Encycl. Metrop.* (1845) VIII. 316/2 The *puzzle or combination lock. **1882** SIR E. BECKETT in *Encycl. Brit.* XIV. 746 It used to be supposed that locks which could only be opened by setting a number of rings or disks to a particular combination of letters could not possibly be opened by anybody who was not in possession of the secret; and hence they were also called puzzle-locks. **1891** *Daily News* 23 Feb. 5/5 Mr. T. had just been explaining to Mr. D. the secret of how to open a certain *puzzle locket. **1870** *Food Jrnl.* Nov. 533 The arrangement of the different collections and classes reminding one of a *puzzle-map well shaken in a bag. **1886** KIPLING *Lispeth* in *Plain Tales from Hills* (1888) 5 There was an old puzzle-map of the World... She used to put it together. **1906** B. L. TAYLOR *Extra Dry* 73 (*caption*) *Puzzle picture. Find the man who is paying for the drinks. **1929** W. FAULKNER *Sartoris* II. vi. 151 Pieces of a patient puzzle-picture. **1978** *Country Life* 21 Sept. 850/4 Roy Strong.. treated Yeames's *And when did you last see your father?* as a puzzle picture which 'leaves us to fill in what has gone before ..in a highly tantalizing way'. **1879** *Spectator* 6 Sept. 1134/2 We maintain that anything like a final reliance on anatomical *puzzle-piecing and dissection, on the part of the artist, would be a perfect illustration..of the instructive fable of the goose which was anatomised for the sake of her golden eggs. **1883** SIMCOX *Hist. Lat. Lit.* II. 447 The natural interest of Ennodius lay in the direction of *puzzle poetry. **1908** *Daily Chron.* 2 Apr. 4/7 The General Knowledge inquiry..has a tendency to produce the, rather unfair, *puzzle-question. **1877** W. JONES *Finger-ring* 321 Some curious specimens of linked or '*puzzle-rings'. **1974** J. GARDNER *Corner Men* v. 36 Long slim fingers and a Greek puzzle ring. **1781** J. WOODFORDE *Diary* 16 Mar. (1924) I. 304 To 7 pieces of wood, a *Puzzle thing, pd o. o. 6. **1914** W. J. LOCKE *Fortunate Youth* xii. 163 Paul stood ruminating *puzzlewise on the audacious behest. **1950** *Mind* LIX. 174 No doubt all this sounds stale and naïve to puzzle-wise professional philosophers. **1900** *Daily News* 6 Dec. 4/4 Another *puzzle word competition was described at the North London Police-court. **1834** *Tait's Mag.* I. 543/1 It is all *puzzle-work that to me.

puzzle ('pʌz(ə)l), *v.* Forms: 6–7 pusle, puzzell, 7 puzel, pussell, 7–8 puzzel, puzle, 7– puzzle. [Appears in the end of the 16th c.; the cognate PUZZLE *sb.* is not known till somewhat later (*a* 1612), and appears from its sense to have been a derivative from the verb. Their etymology is obscure: see Note below.]

1. *trans.* †**a.** *orig.* To cause (any one) to be at a loss what to do or how to turn; to embarrass with difficulties; to put to a non-plus; to perplex, bewilder, confound: said of circumstances, material obstacles, etc. *Obs.*

(The quotations in brackets show transition to the modern sense c.)

[*a* **1380**: see POSELET.] *c* **1595** CAPT. WYATT *R. Dudley's Voy. W. Ind.* (Hakl. Soc.) 41 The passage verie troublesome by reason of whole trunckes and bodies of trees lyinge cross the mouth of that narrow ryver, over which men weare forced to carrie the bote upon theire shoulders by maine strength. And whilst wee weare theare pusled..Baltizar.. dropped overborde with his companion and sodenlie gott into the thicketts. *Ibid.*, Here will I leave our Captaine and his companie pusled in the bote and returne to speake of our conceipts aborde the shipp. **1601** SHAKS. *Twel. N.* IV. ii. 48 Thou art more puzel'd then the Ægyptians in their fogge. **1638** SIR T. HERBERT *Trav.* (ed. 2) 34 [Certain signs] assured us we were neere the shoare (the last storme had puzled us). **1653** HOLCROFT *Procopius, Goth. Wars* IV. xiv. 144 Their ships stood jumbled together like so many baskets ..and thus puzzelling one another, they were the cheifest cause of the Enemies victory. **1735** SOMERVILLE *Chase* III. 188 The panting Throng In their own Footsteps puzzled, foil'd, and lost.

[**1598** BARRET *Theor. Warres* I. i. 6 Then commeth he to cast them into a ring..now there is he puzzelled. **1639** N. N. tr. *Du Bosq's Compl. Woman* II. 19 So many great personages were pusled in a great uncertainty. **1641** BROME *Jov. Crew* III. Wks. 1873 III. 405, I am pussell'd in the choice. **1697** DAMPIER *Voy. round World* (1699) 105 A large green Turtle, with her weight and struggling, will puzzle two Men to turn her. **1732** BERKELEY *Alciphr.* IV. §2 This sort of arguments ..may perhaps puzzle, but never will convince me.]

b. To perplex or bewilder (the brain, mind, understanding, will, wit): in late use passing into c.

1602 SHAKS. *Ham.* III. i. 80 (Qo. 1) A hope of something after death? Which pusles the braine and doth confound the sence. **1604** *Ibid.* (Qo. 2), The dread of something after death..Puzels the will. **1662** STILLINGFL. *Orig. Sacr.* III. i. §7 They do far more puzzle our understandings than when we conceive them to be in God. **1666** SANCROFT *Lex Ignea* 29 All our Wit was puzzeld, and all our Industry tir'd out. **1754** SHERLOCK *Disc.* (1759) I. i. 42 Reveal Mysteries merely to puzzle the Minds of Men. **1831** *Society* I. 152 Fanny was puzzling her brain to think where she had heard the name before.

c. To perplex, put to a non-plus, or embarrass mentally, as or by a difficult problem or question; to pose. The current sense.

a **1634** RANDOLPH *Muse's Looking-gl.* III. iv. (R.), I very much fear there be some languages That would go near to puzzle me. **1664** H. MORE *Myst. Iniq.* I. xv. 54 It would puzzle men to conceive a way of expression of sufficient honour..for such a wonder-working Priesthood. **1668** —— *Div. Dial.* (J.), A very shrewd disputant in those points is dexterous in puzzling others. *c* **1680** BEVERIDGE *Serm.* (1729) I. 273, I know these words have much puzzled interpreters. **1771** *Junius' Lett.* lxi. 319 He did it with a view to puzzle them with some perplexing questions. **1787** BURNS *Let. to Moore* 2 Aug., I..used..to puzzle Calvinism with so much heat and indiscretion, that I raised a hue and cry of heresy against me. **1807–8** W. IRVING *Salmag.* (1824) 14 Poor Will Honeycomb..even with his half century of experience, would have been puzzled to point out the humours of a lady by her prevailing colours. **1853** KANE *Grinnell Exp.* xxix. (1856) 247 The disconsolate little cupola, with its flag of red bunting..may puzzle conjectures for our English brethren. **1870** EMERSON *Soc. & Solit., Eloquence* Wks. (Bohn) III. 35 Like a schoolmaster puzzled by a hard sum. **1875** JOWETT *Plato* (ed. 2) IV. 407 Men are annoyed at what puzzles them. **1891** E. PEACOCK *N. Brendon* I. 162 The question has always puzzled me.

d. *refl.* To bewilder or perplex oneself; to exercise oneself with difficult problems.

1691 HARTCLIFFE *Virtues* Pref. 37 We are apt to puzzle our selves with obscure Marks of Grace and doubtful Signs of our good State. **1725** DE FOE *Voy. round World* (1840) 316 After they had puzzled themselves here..two or three days. **1875** JOWETT *Plato* (ed. 2) I. 405 When he was young he had puzzled himself with physics. **1883** A. ROBERTS *O.T. Revis.* iii. 48 Many readers have doubtless puzzled themselves with the two different forms of the same word.

2. *intr.* (? for *refl.*) To be at a loss how to act or decide; to be bewildered; to be perplexed for a solution; to ponder perplexedly; to exercise oneself with the solution of a puzzle. Const. *about*, *over*, *upon*.

1605 CAMDEN *Rem.* 93, I my selfe..have pored and pusled vpon many an old Record. **1611** COTGR., *Metagraboulizer*, to dunce vpon, to puzzle, or (too much) beat the braines about. **1690** tr. *Five Lett. Inspiration* 115 Contradictions which the Divines..have not been able to reconcile, after puzling about it above three thousand Years. **1742** WARBURTON *Rem. Tillard* Wks. 1811 XI. 180 Our Advocate, ..puzzling on between his true and false Gods, hangs, like a false teacher as he is, between heaven and earth. **1803** BEDDOES *Hygëia* IX. 205, I dare say they would puzzle long before guessing what pattern I mean to propose to them. **1833** *Sporting Mag.* Jan. 210 Whenever the dog puzzles over the scent.

b. To search in a bewildered or perplexed way; to fumble, grope *for* something; to get *through* by perplexed searching.

1817 H. T. COLEBROOKE *Algebra*, etc. 27 Which dull smatterers in algebra labor to excruciate, puzzling for it in the six-fold method of discovery there taught. **1818** SCOTT *Hrt. Midl.* i, Are you puzzling in your pockets to seek your only memorial among old play-bills? **1853** KANE *Grinnell Exp.* (1856) V. xlvii. 437 After puzzling through the floes, we reached a large berg. **1884** *St. James' Gaz.* 17 Oct. 6/1 The dogs are puzzling about for a bird or a rabbit in cover.

3. *trans.* To make puzzling; to complicate, involve, entangle (some matter or subject); to put into confusion, mix up, confound; to confuse or muddle (drawing). Now *rare*.

1647 CLARENDON *Hist. Reb.* II. §76 His parts were most prevalent in puzzling and perplexing that discourse he meant to cross. **1650** W. BROUGH *Sacr. Princ.* (1659) 63 Let me think Thou art the judg, that I may not..pervert or puzzle right. **1713** ADDISON *Cato* I. i, The ways of Heaven are dark and intricate, Puzzled in mazes. **1892** *Harper's Mag.* Oct. 702/2 He [an artist] is never obliged to resort to trick or device, or to employ meretricious effects. He never has to 'puzzle' bad or doubtful drawing.

4. ***to puzzle out***: to make out by the exercise of ingenuity and patience.

1781 COWPER *Charity* 473 While the clerk just puzzles out the psalm. **1863** HAWTHORNE *Our Old Home* (1879) 221 The inscriptions..were not sufficiently legible to induce us to puzzle them out. **1889** *Century Mag.* XXXVIII. 190 The bloodhound..can puzzle out a cold scent under the most adverse conditions.

5. Combinations of the verb-stem: **'puzzle-brain**, (*a*) *adj.*, that puzzles the brain, brain-puzzling; (*b*) *sb.*, one who puzzles his brain about a subject; **'puzzle-cap**, that which puzzles the cap or the head; a cap (*fig.*) which bespeaks a puzzled head; **'puzzle-ˌmonkey**, a familiar name of the Chilean tree *Araucaria imbricata*, from the difficulty which a monkey would have in climbing it (also called *monkey-puzzle*); **'puzzle-text**, one who makes a puzzle of a scripture text; **'puzzle-wit** *a.*, that puzzles or would puzzle one's wit. Cf. also PUZZLE *sb.* 4.

1870 THORNBURY *Tour Eng.* I. v. 108 After all these *puzzle-brain theories, the result is..no great enlargement of knowledge. **1873** BLACKIE *Self-Cult.* 60 They are mostly crotchet-mongers and puzzle-brains. **1889** GRETTAN *Memory's Harkb.* 231 Another *puzzle-cap to me with regard to the hunting-field. *Ibid.* 275 This entirely put the puzzle-cap upon him as to my actual whereabouts. **1883** MRS. RIDDELL *Haunted River* i, A garden..adorned probably by a *puzzle-monkey and a stone vase. **1885** *Pall Mall G.* 11 Mar. 11/1 To see and paint the old forests of Araucaria imbricata, known in England as the puzzle-monkey tree, rather unreasonably, as there are no monkeys here to puzzle. **1837** *Gambler's Dream* I. 269 The petticoat *puzzletext curtsied to her young master and retired. **1861** WHYTE MELVILLE *Mkt. Harb.* xviii, What is called a 'monogram'—a thing not unlike the *puzzle-wit lock on a gate.

[*Note.* For the etymology of *puzzle* the first question is the relation of the sb. and vb. The vb. has been held to be derived from the sb., and the latter viewed as an aphetic form of APPOSAL or OPPOSAL. But the chronology of the words, and still more the consideration of their sense-history, seem to make it clear that the verb came first, and that the sb. was its derivative. In the light of this, the vb. has been referred to POSE *v.*[2], as a diminutive (or other derivative formation), as in *suck*, *suckle*. This is phonetically possible: cf. *nuzzle* from *nose*. But there are serious difficulties in the signification. Of the earlier sense of *puzzle*, as seen in the examples under 1 a above, no trace appears in the original sense of *pose* and *appose* 'to examine by putting questions', and it is only the derivative senses 2 of *pose* and 1 c of *puzzle* that come into contact. Thus their relation seems to be that of two words originally distinct, which (as in some other cases) have subsequently attracted each other. *Puzzle* was possibly the same verb of which the pa. pple. POSELET occurs late in the 14th c., app. in the sense 'bewildered, confused, confounded', and which, riming with *hoselet*, i.e. *hūselet*, HOUSLED, was prob. pronounced ('puːzəlɛt), which would regularly give by 1600 ('pʊzlɛd), later ('pʌzlɛd). The non-appearance of the verb during the intervening 200 years might be owing to its being one of the colloquial words which came into literary use in the 16th c. This is however conjectural and, even if true, leaves the ulterior derivation still to seek. (A verb of similar form appears in late OE. *puslian* 'to pick out best pieces of food' (Sweet), = Du. *peuzelen* to pick, to piddle, LG. *pöseln*, *pusseln*, Norw. *pusla*; but it is difficult to see in its sense any connexion with that of 'puzzle'.)]

puzzle'ation. *nonce-wd.* [f. prec. + -ATION.] Puzzled condition; state of perplexity.

1773 FOOTE *Bankrupt* III. Wks. 1799 II. 133 They have got the old gentleman into such puzzleation, that I don't believe he knows what he wishes himself.

puzzle-brain, -cap: see PUZZLE *v.* 5.

puzzled ('pʌz(ə)ld), *ppl. a.* [f. PUZZLE *v.* + -ED[1].] **a.** Of a person, the mind, head, etc.: Nonplussed, bewildered, confused; perplexed to find a solution. **b.** Of a thing: Made puzzling; involved, complicated, intricate; †tangled (*obs.*).

1651 HOBBES *Leviath.* I. iv. 17 Coyned by Schoole-men, and pusled Philosophers. **1656–9** *Burton's Diary* (1828) III. 130 *note*, If there were any, it was but a puzzled nomination, and that very dark and imperfect. *a* **1694** TILLOTSON *Serm.* (1742) III. 167 Like a puzzled lump of silk, so that the man cannot draw out a thought to any length. **1784** COWPER *Task* III. 145 They disentangle from the puzzled skein, In which obscurity has wrapp'd them up, The threads of politic and shrewd design. **1790** BURKE *Fr. Rev.* 297 Their puzzled situation, under two sovereigns, over neither of whom they have any influence. **1865** TROLLOPE *Belton Est.* xxiv, There came across his face a puzzled, dubious look.

Hence **'puzzledly** *adv.*, **'puzzledness.**

1655 H. MORE *Antid. Ath.* App. iii. Summ. (1662) 6 Several instances of the puzzledness of Phansy in the firm conclusions of Sense, and of Reason. **1870** MISS BROUGHTON *Red as Rose* I. 182 Her eyes..meet his, looking at her curiously, interestedly, puzzledly. **1935** *Theology* XXXI. 152 The first thing which strikes a simple reader is the apparent puzzledness of the accounts in the three Gospels. **1951** D. KNIGHT *Turning On* (1967) 144 He peered at Mazurin puzzledly. 'Is that what you're for?' **1964** *Economist* 10 Oct. 114/1 They puzzledly ask what the issues ..really are. **1975** J. GRADY *Shadow of Condor* (1976) xvi. 251 Captain Roe looked at his executive officer puzzledly.

puzzledom ('pʌz(ə)ldəm). [f. PUZZLE *sb.* + -DOM.] The realm of puzzle; the state of being puzzled; perplexity, bewilderment.

1748 RICHARDSON *Clarissa* lxxiv. (1810) VI. 377, I was resolved to travel with him into the land of puzzledom. **1851** SOUTHEY *Comm.-pl. Bk.* IV. 577 Placing the reader in puzzledom. **1874** LISLE CARR *Jud. Gwynne* iii, He could not make out in the depths of his puzzledom what had gone wrong.

'puzzle-,headed, *a.* [f. PUZZLE *sb.*, or put for *puzzled* + HEAD *sb.*[1] + -ED[2].] Having a puzzled head; having confused ideas.

a **1784** JOHNSON in *Boswell*, Mattaire..seems to have been a puzzle-headed man, with a large share of scholarship, but with little geometry or logick in his head. **1855** MACAULAY *Hist. Eng.* xx. IV. 465 He [Harley] was really a dull puzzle-headed man. **1906** *Outlook* 14 July 40/1 A singularly puzzle-headed sentimentalism.

Hence **puzzle'headedness**; so also **'puzzle-head**, a puzzle-headed person.

1874 LISLE CARR *Jud. Gwynne* v, To survey the flames with open eyes of dull puzzleheadedness. *a* **1884** M. PATTISON *Mem.* v. (1885) 167 This anomaly can only be accounted for by a certain puzzle-headedness on the part of the Professor. **1888** MRS. H. WARD *R. Elsmere* xli, 'They don't see it in that light themselves'... 'No,..because most men are puzzleheads'.

puzzlement ('pʌz(ə)lmənt). [f. PUZZLE *v.* + -MENT.] The fact or condition of being puzzled; perplexity, bewilderment, confusion.

1822 MOORE *Mem.* (1853) III. 350 Four invitations to dinner on my list to-day, but, owing to some puzzlement about Holland House, lost all. **1833** *Blackw. Mag.* XXXIII. 839 His mind between the two must be in a queer puzzlement. **1874** RUSKIN *Hortus Inclusus* (1887) 8 The puzzlement I have had to force that sentence into grammar! **1880** MCCARTHY *Own Time* IV. lxv. 472 To avoid the possibility of any historical misunderstanding or puzzlement hereafter.

b. Anything that puzzles; a puzzle.

1842 G. S. FABER *Prov. Lett.* (1844) I. 78 In short, Dr. Todd's ingenious puzzlement works altogether upon the false principle, that no more than four horns came up. **1881** *Spectator* 29 Oct. 1368 A puzzlement for some of the wisest antiquarian heads of Europe. **1893** *N. & Q.* 8th Ser. IV. 313/2 Examiners in our own day are not always innocent of similar sprightly puzzlements.

puzzle-monkey: see PUZZLE *v.* 5.

'puzzle-pate. [f. PUZZLE *v.* + PATE[1].] One who puzzles his pate; one who is puzzle-headed.

1775 T. MORTIMER *Ev. Man his own Broker* 88 *note*, Two or three puzzlepates said I had too much Divinity. **1864** A. LEIGHTON *Myst. Leg. Edinburgh* (1886) 220 A great scheme of philosophy which attracts those puzzle-pates who are much given to the habit of ultimate thinking.

So **'puzzle-,pated** *a.*, puzzle-headed; hence **,puzzle-'patedness.**

1795 G. WAKEFIELD *Reply 2nd Pt. Paine* 12 This said Thomas Paine..shews himself but a puzzle-pated fellow. **1799** MRS. J. WEST *Tale of Times* II. 251 Monteith really has a very good heart, which excuses a little accidental puzzle-patedness. **1867** TROLLOPE *Chron. Barset* xix, He was very ignorant,—puzzle-pated as you may call it.

'puzzle-peg. [f. PUZZLE *sb.* or *v.* + PEG *sb.*[1]] A piece of wood, about a foot in length, pointed at one end and flattened towards the other, fastened to the lower jaw of a dog so that the pointed end projects a few inches in front, and prevents him from putting his nose close to the ground.

1819 *Sporting Mag.* IV. 264 The principal use of the puzzle-peg, appears to be that of worrying and fretting the animal to no purpose. **1870** 'STONEHENGE' *Brit. Sports* I. I. iii. §7. 56 By the constant use of this puzzle-peg..the dog loses, by habit, the tendency to stoop.

b. *fig.* A puzzling subject, a puzzle.

1845 *Zoologist* III. 947 This last insect, to use the term of its late..describer, has always been a 'puzzle-peg'.

puzzler ('pʌzlə(r)). [f. PUZZLE *v.* + -ER[1].] One who or that which puzzles; also, one who occupies himself with puzzles.

a **1652** BROME *Elegy on Schoolm.*, Hebrew the general puzzler of old heads. **1654** VILVAIN *Epit. Ess.* Pref. 4 No marvel if many of the Puzlers here be not so wel planed..or perfected as is expected. **1762** J. H. STEVENSON *Crazy Tales* 93 Lawyers..these puzzlers and confounders..who embroil and complicate what should be simple. **1872** (*title*) The Puzzler's Manual, or monthly journal of enigmatical amusements. **1872** O. W. HOLMES *Poet Breakf.-t.* ix, My question..seems to me to be a puzzler.

puzzle-text, -wit: see PUZZLE *v.* 5.

'puzzling, *vbl. sb.* [f. PUZZLE *v.* + -ING[1].] The action of the verb PUZZLE in its various senses.

1598 BARRET *Theor. Warres* I. 6 He will neuer ranke them aright without helpe: and (God knoweth) with what puzzeling and toyle. **1874** BLACKIE *Self-cult.* 28 You can find out for yourself by a little puzzling why the three angles of a triangle..must be equal to two right angles. **1907** *Athenæum* 1 June 662/1 The puzzling of the Russians by rumour that the turning-flank-march of the Japanese was first by the Russian left, then by the Russian right.

'puzzling, *ppl. a.* [f. PUZZLE *v.* + -ING[2].]

1. Bewildering, confusing, perplexing; that puzzles one to solve or answer.

1666 BOYLE *Orig. Forms & Qual.* i. Wks. 1772 III. 50 A more puzzling question it may be to some. **1705** BERKELEY *Comm.-pl. Bk.* Wks. 1871 IV. 428 The grand puzzling question, whether I sleep or wake? **1712** J. JAMES tr. *Le Blond's Gardening* 60 The various Turnings..of this Labyrinth, render it extremely intricate and puzzling. **1855** KINGSLEY *Heroes, Argonauts* 176 This is a puzzling matter. **1872** JENKINSON *Guide Eng. Lakes* (1879) 204 The summit of the mountain is most puzzling and dangerous.

2. Bewildering oneself; laboriously trying to puzzle something out.

1692 R. L'ESTRANGE *Fables* liii, The Servant, says he, is a Puzzling Fool that heeds nothing. **1735** SOMERVILLE *Chase* II. 202 The puzzling Pack unravel Wile by Wile, Maze within Maze. **1871** BLACKIE *Four Phases* i. 96 Certain precise and puzzling minds.

Hence **'puzzlingly** *adv.*, in a way that puzzles one; **'puzzlingness.**

1727 BAILEY vol. II, *Puzzlingness*, perplexedness, embarrassing Quality. **1881** M. A. LEWIS *Two Pretty G.* III. 87 A puzzlingly unamiable trait in her friend's character. **1894** *Naturalist* 58 Shade-grown forms..puzzlingly simulated the orange-flowered Plancheon's furze.

puzzlist ('pʌzlɪst). *U.S.* [f. PUZZLE *sb.* + -IST.] One who devises puzzles.

1961 *Times Lit. Suppl.* 24 Feb. 127/1 Readers in this country are unlikely to accept 'ticktack toe' for 'noughts and crosses' or speak of their favourite composer as a 'puzzlist'. **1970** *Sci. Amer.* Feb. 112/3 This cryptarithm (or alphametic, as many puzzlists prefer to call them) is an old one of unknown origin. **1971** *Ibid.* Oct. 106/3 Let us combine the rules of the two rival puzzlists by allowing both steps and hops, as in Halma.

puzzolan, -ana, -ane, -ano, puzzuolana, etc., varr. POZZOLANA.

pwdyll, pwf, pwir, pwr, pwyr, pwll, pwn, pwnt, pwnȝhe, pwt, pwynd, etc., obs. Sc. forms of PUDDLE, PUFF, POOR, POOL, PUN, POINT, POYGNÉ, POYNYE, PUT, POIND, etc.

‖**pwe** (pwe). [Burmese.] Also **poi, pooay, pu-é.** A Burmese festival which includes drama, dancing, sports, or other entertainments.

1861 *Chambers's Encycl.* II. 443/1 A *pooay*, or theatrical representation, is a very favourite amusement. **1876** *Encycl. Brit.* IV. 556/1 The historical books are then read, as well as the *Pu-és* or dramatic productions. **1878** A. FYTCHE *Burma* II. i. 21 It is a strange and curious sight to see the large crowds of Burmese assembled for the night to witness the performance of a *pooay*, or play. **1884** T. H. LEWIN *Fly on Wheel* vii. 213 The night after my arrival at Cox's Bazaar, I was invited to attend a Burmese 'poi', or dramatic representation. **1905** *Statesman* (Calcutta) 23 Aug. 5/3 What the Chief Judge had to decide was whether a foot race fell within the definition of a 'pwe'. A 'pwe' ordinarily means a puppet show or other theatrical or dramatical performance, or a native cart, pony, boat or water race held for the public entertainment. **1908** *Athenæum* 29 July 254/3 A story with a Burmese Pwe dancer for heroine. **1929** F. T. JESSE *Lacquer Lady* I. xii. 88 Each of the Princes..has his own pandal erected and has pwès acted for seven days. **1934** 'G. ORWELL' *Burmese Days* viii. 128 No one with eyes in his head could resist a pwe-dance. *Ibid.* 129 They're having a pwe—that's a kind of Burmese play; a cross between a historical drama and a revue. *Ibid.* 134 The pwe girl began dancing again. **1936** F. RICHARDS *Old-Soldier Sahib* xix. 323 The Burmese were having a *pooay*, a festival which lasted seven days and was entirely devoted to gambling and enjoyment. **1971** *Nat. Geographic* Mar. 349/1 Burmese still obey, as seen by their enthusiasm for the *pwe*, a marathon of drama, singing, dancing, and joke telling. **1974** P. GORE-BOOTH *With Great Truth & Respect* 205 It was one of the famous Burmese *Pwes* in the open and it went on all night.

py, var. PEE *sb.*[1] *Obs.*, kind of coat; obs. f. PIE.

‖**pya** ('piːa). [Burmese.] A Burmese monetary unit, the hundredth part of a *kyat*; a coin of this value.

1952 [see KYAT]. **1962** B. FERGUSSON *Return to Burma* x. 201, I grudge the fare!.. I'd rather have the money! Twenty *pyas*!.. I could do with twenty *pyas*. **1971** *Whitaker's Almanac 1972* 984 Burma..Coins... *Pyas* 50, 25, 10, 5, 1. **1975** P. THEROUX *Great Railway Bazaar* xvii. 181 A Burmese with a telescope urged me to have a look. I paid my fee of 25 pyas (five cents).

pya, variant of PIA[2].

‖**pyæmia** (paɪ'iːmɪə). *Path.* Also **pyemia**, and less correctly **pyohæmia.** [mod.L., f. Gr. πύ-ον pus, matter + αἷμα blood: see quot. 1880.] A condition of blood-poisoning accompanied by fever, caused by the presence in the blood of pathogenic bacteria and their toxic products, and characterized by the formation of multiple pus-foci in different parts of the body; septicæmia.

1857 DUNGLISON *Med. Dict.*, *Pyæmia*, pyohæmia. **1871** TYNDALL *Fragm. Sc.* (1879) I. v. 156 Hospital wards where death was rampant from pyæmia. **1876** BRISTOWE *The. & Pract. Med.* (1878) 264 Pyæmia occurring after parturition constitutes one of the most common and fatal forms of so-called 'puerperal fever'. **1876** GROSS *Dis. Bladder* 267 Pyemia is most liable to occur in broken-down persons. **1880** FLINT *Princ. Med.* (ed. 5) 85 As the name denotes, pyaemia originally was supposed to be due to the entrance of pus into the blood. The disease is no longer attributed to the direct absorption, by the blood, of pus-corpuscles.

pyæmic (paɪ'iːmɪk), *a.* [f. prec. + -IC.] Of, pertaining to, or of the nature of pyæmia; affected with pyæmia.

1859 J. Y. SIMPSON in *Nat. Encycl.* I. 149 The dangers of pyæmic poisoning. **1869** E. A. PARKES *Pract. Hygiene* (ed. 3) 123 Almost complete exposure of pyæmic patients to the open air. **1876** BRISTOWE *The. & Pract. Med.* (1878) 270 The feebleness of the pyæmic pulse is remarkable.

‖**pyal** ('paɪəl), *a.* *E. Indies.* Also **pyall, pial.** [South Indian ad. Pg. *poyal* a jossing block or mounting stone, deriv. of Pg. and Sp. *poyo* a bench by the door:—L. *podium* raised place: see PODIUM.] 'A raised platform on which people sit, usually under the veranda, or on either side of the door of the house' (Yule). Also *attrib.* **pyal school.**

1873 E. C. GOVER in *Ind. Antiq.* II. 52 (heading) Pyal Schools in Madras. **1896** *Indian Mag. & Rev.* Jan. 39 Every village has its self-supporting pyall school, where boys and girls are taught simple lessons. **1898** *Mission Herald* (Boston) Apr. 153 In front of an earthen pial where I might sit.

pyan, pyany, obs. forms of PEONY.

pyanit, pyannet, -ot, obs. forms of PIANNET.

‖**pyarthrosis** (paɪɑː'θrəʊsɪs). *Path.* [mod.L., f. Gr. πύ-ον pus + ἄρθρωσις jointing.] The formation of pus in a joint; suppurative arthritis.

1858 in MAYNE *Expos. Lex.* **1890** in BILLINGS *Nat. Med. Dict.* **1897** in *Syd. Soc. Lex.*

pyaster, obs. f. PIASTRE.

pyat, var. PIET, magpie, etc.

pybald, obs. f. PIEBALD.

pybble, pyble, obs. forms of PEBBLE.

Pybuthrin (paɪ'buːθrɪn). Also **pybuthrin.** [Blend of PYRETHRIN and *butoxide* (f. BUT(YL + OXIDE *sb.*).] A proprietary name for an insecticide compounded of pyrethrins and piperonyl butoxide.

1951 *Trade Marks Jrnl.* 3 Jan. 5/2 *Pybuthrin*... Chemical substances used for veterinary and sanitary purposes, insecticides, fungicides and preparations for destroying vermin. Cooper, McDougall & Robertson Limited.. Manufacturers and Merchants. **1958** *Times* 7 July 2/7 The simplest way of dealing with them [*sc.* red mites], and with lice at the same time, is to spray the birds while at roost.. with a fine sprayer containing pybuthrin. **1971** *Homes & Gardens* Aug. 89/1 A spray containing pybuthrin for rapid effect and chlordane for persistence will control ants in house or garden for a period of two to three months outside and up to a year indoors.

pycar(d, variants of PICARD *Obs.*, a sailing boat.

pycche, pych(e, pyccle, pyce, pychar, -er, obs. forms of PITCH, PICKLE, PICE, PITCHER.

pyche (paɪtʃ). *n. dial.* Also 6 **piche,** 8–9 **poich,** 9 **pytch.** [? Phonetic variant of *pike*: cf. PIKE *sb.*[2] 2.] A bee-hive.

1570 LEVINS *Manip.* 115/29 Piche, *corbiculus.* **1775** J. WATSON *Hist. Halifax* 544 *Poich,* an Hive to take bees in after they have swarmed. **1828** *Craven Gloss.* (ed. 2), *Pyche,* a bee-hive. **1882** *Lanc. Gloss.*, *Pytch,* a hive for bees.

pychel, obs. form of PIGHTLE, a small field.

pycht, obs. Sc. pa. pple. of PITCH *v.*[1]

pyck, pyckage, obs. ff. PIQUE *sb.*[1], PITCH *sb.*[1], PICKAGE.

pyckard, pycker, var. ff. PICARD *Obs.*

pycke, pyckerylle, pyclet, obs. ff. PIKE, PICK, PICKEREL, PIKELET.

pycnaspideæ, pycnaster: see PYCNO-.

pycnic, var. PYKNIC.

pycnid, -ide. *Bot.* [mod.F. *pycnide*] = next.

1867 J. HOGG *Microsc.* (ed. 6) II. i. 305. **1900** B. D. JACKSON *Gloss. Bot. Terms,* Pycnid, Pycnide, Pycnidium.

‖**pycnidium** (pɪk'nɪdɪəm). *Bot.* Pl. **-ia.** [mod.L., f. Gr. πυκνός thick, dense + dim. suff. -ίδιον.] The special receptacle in certain ascomycetous fungi in which the stylospores are produced.

1857 BERKELEY *Cryptog. Bot.* §280 In *Erysiphe* the pycnidia appear frequently to arise from the transformation of one of the joints of the moniliform threads. **1882** VINES *Sachs' Bot.* 308. **1887** GARNSEY *De Bary's Comp. Morph. & Biol. Fungi* 225 Receptacles resembling perithecia..have been termed by Tulaine *pycnidia,* and the spores or gonidia formed in them *stylospores.* **1938** G. M. SMITH *Cryptogamic Bot.* I. xii. 416 If the fertile layer lies in a cup- or flask-shaped cavity that is open from the beginning, the cavity and the surrounding tissue constitute a pycnidium. **1966** K. TUBAKI in Ainsworth & Sussmann *Fungi* II. iv. 127 Simple or branched sporophores may line a hollow flask-shaped fruit body, the pycnidium.

Hence **pyc'nidial** *a.*, of or pertaining to a pycnidium; **pyc'nidiophore** [-PHORE], a compound sporophore bearing pycnidia; **pyc'nidiospore** [Gr. σπόρος seed], a stylospore developed inside a pycnidium.

1880 C. E. BESSEY *Bot.* xvii. 294 The cavities are called pycnidia, and the small bodies pycnidiospores. **1890** in *Cent. Dict.* **1923** *Nature* 21 Apr. 553/1 The hyphomycete stage [of *Polythrincium Trifolii*] is followed by a pycnidial stage. **1971** P. H. B. TALBOT *Princ. Fungal Taxon.* x. 146 Most of the pycnidial Deuteromycotina have slimy spores. **1977** *Lancet* 26 Mar. 672/2 Various pycnidial fungi related to the *Phoma* sp. isolated produce the mycotoxin responsible for lupinosis in sheep and cattle.

‖**'pycnis.** *Bot.* Pl. **pycnides.** [mod.L.] A rare synonym of PYCNIDIUM.

pycnite ('pɪknaɪt). *Min.* [mod. (Haüy 1801) f. Gr. πυκν-ός thick, dense + -ITE[1].] A variety of topaz occurring in columnar aggregations.

1802 BOURNON in *Phil. Trans.* XCII. 321 The stone called *schorlartiger beryl* by Werner (the *pycnite* of the Abbé Hauy). **1866** LAWRENCE tr. *Cotta's Rocks Class.* (1878) 31 Pycnite is a fibrous variety of topaz.

pycnium ('pɪknɪəm). *Bot.* Pl. **pycnia.** [mod.L., f. Gr. πυκνός thick.] In rust fungi of the order Uredinales, a fruit-body resembling a pycnidium. So **'pycnial** *a.*, of or pertaining to a pycnium; **'pycniospore,** a spore from a pycnium.

1905 J. C. ARTHUR in *Bot. Gaz.* XXXIX. 221 For the sorus of the initial stage [of uredineal fungi], usually..called spermogonium, pycnidium, etc., I propose pycnium..; derivatives pycnial, pycniospores, etc. **1926** *Mycologia* XVIII. 90 The inefficient sori (pycnia) are present or absent in both macrocyclic and microcyclic rusts. **1929** J. C. ARTHUR et al. *Plant Rusts* i. 6 The pycnia produce pycniospores. **1937** Pycnial [see ÆCIUM]. **1937** *Nature* 8 May 800/2 Pycniospores..were present in the nectar. **1946** K. S. CHESTER *Nature & Prevention of Cereal Rusts* v. 49 The pycnia occur on both leaf surfaces. **1976** G. C. AINSWORTH *Introd. Hist. Mycol.* v. 132 Isolated monosporidial infections gave rise to pycnia which produced pycniospores and nectar but no aecia developed as they frequently did when two or more pycnial pustules were adjacent to one another.

pycno- (pɪknəʊ), bef. a vowel **pycn-,** combining form of Gr. πυκνό-ς 'thick, dense', forming various terms. (Occasionally spelt *pykno-*; erron. *picno-*.) ‖**pycna'spideæ** *Ornith.* [Gr. ἀσπίς, ἀσπιδ- shield], in Sundevall's classification, a cohort of scutelliplantar passerine birds, having the planta or back of the tarsus studded with small irregular scales or plates; hence **pycna'spidean** *a.*, belonging to the *Pycnaspideæ*; **pyc'naster** [Gr. ἀστήρ star], a kind of sponge spicule; **pycno'chlorite** *Min.* [ad. G. *pyknochlorit* (J. Fromme 1903, in *Min. und Petrogr. Mitt.* XXII. 70)], a chlorite, $(Mg,Fe^{2+},Al)_6(Si,Al)_4O_{10}(OH)_8$, having the same silicon content as clinochlore (2·8–3·1 atoms per formula unit) but more iron (1·5–3 atoms); **'pycnocline** *Physical Geogr.*, a thin layer separating water of different densities; **pycnoco'nidium** *Bot.* [CONIDIUM] = PYCNOSPORE; **'pycnodont** *Ichthyol.* [Gr. ὀδούς, ὀδοντ- tooth], *a.* pertaining to or having the characteristics of the *Pycnodontidæ*, an extinct family of ganoid fishes typified by the genus *Pycnodus*, so called from the obtuse teeth on the palate and sides of the jaw; *sb.* a pycnodont fish; so **pycno'dontoid** *a.* and *sb.*; **'pycnogon** = *pycnogonid*; **pyc'nogonid** *Zool.* [f. mod.L. class name *Pycnogonida*, f. generic name *Pycnogonum* (M. T. Brünnich *Entomologia* (1764) 84), f. Gr. γόνυ knee], a marine arthropod of the group *Pycnogonida*, somewhat intermediate between *Crustacea* and *Arachnida*, typified by the parasitic genus *Pyc'nogonum*; a sea-spider; also *attrib.*; ‖,**pycnogo'nidium** *Bot.* [GONIDIUM] = PYCNOSPORE; **pyc'nogonoid** *Zool.* [-OID] *a.*, resembling or belonging to the *Pycnogonida*; *sb.* a pycnogonid; ,**pycnohy'drometer**: see quot.; **pyc'nometer** [-METER], a specific gravity flask; see GRAVITY 4d.; ‖,**pycnome'tochia** (-'ɒkɪə) *Gram.* [Gr. μετοχή participle], the close connexion or frequent use of participles or participial phrases; polymetochia; so ,**pycnome'tochic** (-'ɒkɪk) *a.*, containing or using many participles; **pycno'metric** *a.*, involving or employing a pycnometer; hence **pycno'metrically** *adv.*; **pycno'morphic** *a.*, *Biol.* [Gr. μορφή shape, form], exhibiting dense formation or structure; †**pycno'morphous** *a.* *Cytology* [ad. G. *pyknomorph* (F. Nissl in *Neurol. Centralblatt* (1894) XIII. 683, (1895) XIV. 70), f. Gr. μορφή form, shape], characterized by much darkly staining matter; **pycno'notine** *a.*, *Ornith.* [Gr. νῶτος back], belonging to a sub-family of passerine birds, *Pycnonotinæ*, the bulbuls or rock-thrushes, typified by the genus *Pycnonōtus*; **'pycnospore** *Bot.* [Gr. σπόρος seed], = PYCNIDIOSPORE; also = *pycniospore* s.v. PYCNIUM.

1899 EVANS *Birds* in *Cambr. Nat. Hist.* IX. 479 The metatarsus scutellated in front, and usually covered with small round scales behind (**pycnaspidean*) is especially strong in Pyroderus and Rupicola. **1888** SOLLAS in *Challenger Rep.* XXV. p. lxiv, **Pycnaster*, a minute aster with short conical strongylate actines. This..might be regarded as a variety of the chiaster. **1903** *Mineral. Mag.* XIII. 375 *Pyknochlorite... A greyish-green, compact chlorite occurring in a quartz and calcite vein in the gabbro of the Radauthal, Harz. It has the same general formula.. as clinochlore, but differs from this in containing much more ferrous iron and in its compact (πυκνός) texture. **1960** *Amer. Mineralogist* XLV. 797 The co-existing chlorite occurs in fairly large pale green crystals and shows the typical anomalous interference colors. Its analysis shows it to be fairly rich in Mg and Al, and following the classification of Hey (1954) it may be termed a pycnochlorite, with Fe (total): (Fe + Mg) = 0·273 and Si 2·83, on the basis of 14 oxygens (anhydrous). **1973** *Nature* 2 Mar. 28/1 Microscopic studies reveal that the metamorphic boundary involves the replacement by quartz and a chlorite mineral of fixed composition (pycnochlorite). **1978** *Ibid.* 20 July 243/1 Chlorites occurring as matrix in greywacke and amygdule fillings and groundmass replacement in spilite are either pycnochlorite or diabantite. **1957** G. E. HUTCHINSON *Treat. Limnol.* I. v. 282 When a wind blows over a thick layer of water lying over a second layer of greater density, not only will the surface level be raised at the lee end but the *pycnocline, or plane separating the two layers of different density, will be tilted in the opposite direction. **1967** *Oceanogr. & Marine Biol.* V. 278 Changes in the sinking rate ..are well substantiated... In pycnoclines a retardation of passive organisms is frequent, sometimes associated with a synthesis of pigments. **1976** *Nature* 2 Sept. 8/1 Over large areas of the present-day ocean, a permanent density discontinuity (pycnocline) arises as a consequence of the latitudinal variation in the intensity of incident radiation from the Sun. **1836** BUCKLAND *Geol. & Min.* I. 281 The habits of the family of *Pycnodonts appear to have been omnivorous. **1862** DANA *Man. Geol.* 526 The Pycnodont group is now extinct. **1927** *Proc. Imper. Acad. Japan* III. 610 (*title*) Notes on some *pycnogons living semi-parasitic on holothurians. **1935** T. H. SAVORY *Arachnida* xvi. 172 Ever since the first pycnogon was described..the problem of their affinities has been debated. **1959** A. C. HARDY *Open Sea* II. v. 100 Sea-slugs, ascidians, sea-spiders (pycnogons) and spider-crabs, starfish and brittlestars—all these, and more, may be in just one haul. **1877** W. THOMSON *Voy. Challenger* II. 349 The *Pycnogonida..attained an enormous size in cold Arctic and Antarctic water. **1881** *Times* 6 Jan. 4/6 We are promised very shortly similar volumes..on the Pycnogonids or nobody-crabs, on the seaweeds, and on certain groups of worms. **1935** T. H. SAVORY *Arachnida* xvi. 172 The Pycnogonid crawls about, extremely slowly. **1973** P. E. KING *Pycnogonids* i. 7 The pycnogonid body is considerably reduced. *Ibid.* 8 The pycnogonids have a wide geographical and bathymetric range. **1852** DANA *Crust.* II. 1383 Of this last class are nearly all the Entomostraca, and with them the *Pycnogonoids. **1884** KNIGHT *Dict. Mech.* Suppl., **Picnohydrometer*, a combination of the picnometer and hydrometer... Described in *Scientific American*, xxxiv. 340. **1858** THUDICHUM *Urine* 33 The weight of the urine required to fill the *pycnometer is then ascertained. **1881** *Nature* XXIV. 294 The specific gravity bottle or pyknometer. **1925** *Arch. Internal Med.* XXXV. 133 Specific gravity determinations were made by the *pyknometric method. **1938** *Trans. Faraday Soc.* XXXIV. 1214 (*heading*) Pyknometric studies on chemical equilibrium. **1934** *Jrnl. Chem. Soc.* 498 The samples of water obtained by combustion were carefully distilled..and their densities were measured *pyknometrically. **1976** *Nature* 3 June 438/3 There is a reasonable agreement between X-ray and pycnometrically determined densities in the minerals of the oldest rocks. **1900** *Lancet* 30 June 1849/2 The cell shows a distinct *pyknomorphic condition. **1899** L. F. BARKER *New Syst. Constituent Neurones* xi. 123 Nissl consequently designates the extremely darkly stained cells as *pyknomorphous cells, or cells in which the stainable portions are arranged relatively most closely. **1903** *Med. Chron.* XXXIX. 19 The stained, chromophile, or tigroid substance of nerve cells is regarded as nutritional substance. When it is abundant the cell is described as being in a pyknomorphous condition. **1887** H. E. F. GARNSEY tr. *Ade Bary's Compar. Morphol. & Biol. Fungi* v. 246 Pycnidia: receptacles..producing gonidia which are known as *pycnospores. **1898** tr. *Strasburger's Text-bk. Bot.* (1903) 352 Conidia..termed pycnospores or pycnoconidia. **1938** G. M. SMITH *Cryptogamic Bot.* I. xii. 416 In addition to forming conidia or pycnospores, a mycelium may also form large thick-walled spores.

pycnosis, var. PYKNOSIS.

pycnostyle ('pɪknəʊstaɪl), *a.* and *sb.* *Arch.* [ad. L. *pycnostȳlos* (Vitruvius), a. Gr. πυκνόστῡλος, f. πυκνός dense + στῦλος column.] **a.** *adj.* Having close intercolumniation; having the space between the columns equal to one diameter and a half of a column. **b.** *sb.* A building having such intercolumniation.

[**1563** SHUTE *Archit.* Fjb, Picnostylos whose..pillers standeth distant from echeother a Diameter, & a halfe or .2. at ye furdest.] **1697** EVELYN *Acc. Archit.* Misc. Wks. (1825) 391 The rest [of the columns]..plac'd as the pycnostyle closer to one another. **1823** P. NICHOLSON *Pract. Build.* 466. **1837** *Penny Cycl.* IX. 315/2 Within the court the colonnades were pycnostyle. **1849** FREEMAN *Archit.* 319 The wide intercolumniations of the later Grecian edifices probably came nearer to the primitive model than the old Doric pycnostyle.

pycnotic, var. PYKNOTIC.

pycos(s, pycows, pycoys(e, obs. ff. PICKAXE.

pyctes, pyctoure, -ure: see PICT *sb.*, PICTURE.

py'd, pyde, pydgion, obs. ff. PIED, PIGEON.

pye, obs. f. or var. of PIE *sb.* and *v.* (in quot. 1547 = PIE *sb.*[3] 2); var. PEE *sb.*[1], *Obs.*, a coat.

1536 *Acc. Ld. High Treas. Scotl.* (1905) VI. 257 Deliverit ..to be ane ryding pye and ane pair of hois to the Kingis Grace. **1547** in *35th Dep. Kpr.'s Rep.* (1874) 195 A pye of all the names of such Balives as been to accompte pro anno regni regis Edwardi sexti primo.

pyeannet, obs. f. PIANNET.

pyebald, pyed-ball, obs. ff. PIEBALD.

pyece, pyed, obs. ff. PIECE, PIED.

pyedema, variant of PYŒDEMA.

pye-dog, pie-dog ('paɪdɒg). orig. *Anglo-Ind.* Also **pi-dog,** and shortened **pye.** [f. Anglo-Ind. *pye, paë,* Hindī *pāhī* outsider.] An ownerless dog, a PARIAH-*dog*.

1864 *Daily Tel.* 9 Aug., In India..pariahs, or 'pye-dogs' as they are called, wander all the land over ownerless. **1884** KIPLING *Departmental Ditties* (1886) (ed. 2) 52 Glare down old Hecate..And bid the pie-dog yell. **1886** YULE & BURNELL *Hobson-Jobson, Pye,* a familiar designation among British soldiers and young officers for a Paria-dog. **1904** *Brit. Med. Jrnl.* 17 Sept. 665 In the corner of the hut was the usual small fire and a sleeping pye-dog. **1920** *Blackw. Mag.* Oct. 525/2 Later still at night..would come droves of pi-dogs sweeping..through the compound. **1924** *Blackw. Mag.* Sept. 355/1 The men of Bokkos and their dogs—the sorriest-looking pie-dogs in all Africa..go forth to get what they can. In a poor lot these Bokkos pies are the poorest. **1927** *Daily Express* 30 May 7/5 They were hounds running with a good cry, not pi-dogs barking. **1940** F. STARK *Winter in Arabia* 107 The Saint who is buried in the tomb below has pye-dogs who slink in to him at night. **1954** M. K. WILSON tr. *Lorenz's Man Meets Dog* i. 14 There are lots of localities in the near East where Pie dogs and golden jackals abound, yet never intermingle. **1959** *Times* 12 June 14/6 A mangy pi-dog shared his humble abode. **1972** 'M. RENAULT' *Persian Boy* xxii. 287 It was so quiet, you could hear..the pi-dogs bickering. **1977** *Times* 25 June 15/5, I tied red, white and blue ribbons round the neck of my pye-dog. **1978** J. UPDIKE *Coup* (1979) i. 29 His woman whispered to me that he was a rascal without a tribe, who had never had so much as a pet pi-dog to his name.

pyeenock (paɪ'iːnɒk), dial. var. of PEONY.

1911 D. H. LAWRENCE *White Peacock* II. ix. 354 There's a fine show of pyeenocks this year.

†**pye'large.** *Obs. rare.* [Corrupt ad. F. *pelarge*, ad. Gr. πελαργός stork.] A stork.

1484 CAXTON *Fables of Æsop* VI. ix. C j b, The ix fable is of the labourer and of the pyelarge... Amonge a grete meyny of ghees and cranes he took a pyelarge.

‖**pyelitis** (paɪɪ'laɪtɪs). *Path.* [mod.L., f. Gr. πύελος trough, pan, taken in sense 'pelvis' + -ITIS.] Inflammation of the mucous membrane of the pelvis of the kidney.

1842 in DUNGLISON *Med. Dict.* 1847–9 *Todd's Cycl. Anat.* IV. 81/2 Renal calculi.. produce such atrophy of the kidney with pyelitis. 1878 T. BRYANT *Pract. Surg.* (1879) II. 50. 1897 *Allbutt's Syst. Med.* IV. 444 If there is calculous pyelitis.. nephrotomy and extraction of the stone are the necessary measures.

Hence **pyelitic** (-'ɪtɪk) *a.*, of, relating to, or of the nature of pyelitis.

1865–85 W. ROBERTS *Urin. & Ren. Dis.* III. v. (ed. 4) 521 Existence of a pyelitic tumour.

pyell, obs. form of PILE *sb.*[4]

pyelo- (paɪɪləʊ), combining form from Gr. πύελος trough, taken in sense 'pelvis'; in pathological and other terms, as ‖**pyelocy'stitis**, pyelitis accompanied by cystitis (Billings *Nat. Med. Dict.* 1890); **'pyelogram**, an X-ray photograph showing the pelvis of the kidney; †**'pyelograph**, a pyelogram; hence **pye'lography** [ad. G. *pyelographie* (Voelcker & Lichtenberg 1906, in *Münchener med. Wochenschr.* 16 Jan. 105)]; **pyeloli'thotomy**, the removal of a renal calculus by incision into the pelvis of the kidney (*Syd. Soc. Lex.* 1897); **pye'lometer**, = PELVIMETER (Dunglison *Med. Dict.* 1844); ‖**pyelone'phritis**, 'inflammation of the kidney and of the pelvis and calices' (ibid. 1842); hence **pyelone'phritic** *a.*; **'pyeloplasty** *Surg.*, a plastic operation on the pelvis of the kidneys.

1923 R. KNOX *Radiogr. & Radio-Therapeutics* (ed. 4) I. facing p. 388 (*captions*) *Pyelogram—dilated pelvis with kinking of the ureter... Pyelogram of a normal kidney. 1952 M. E. FLOREY *Clin. Appl. Antibiotics* xvii. 507, 25 days after the operation a pyelogram revealed no abnormalities. 1980 *Brit. Med. Jrnl.* 29 Mar. 930/1 We in Britain do not feel that intravenous pyelograms are necessary before every hysterectomy. 1913 *Jrnl. Amer. Med. Assoc.* 18 Jan. 184/2 A *pyelograph is taken while the fluid is being injected and the pelvis or the ureter is kept as full as possible at the time the exposure is being made. 1914 *N.Y. Med. Jrnl.* XCIX. 1057/2 Doctor Furniss, in making pyelographs, had until recently been injecting argyrol or collargol with a syringe. 1906 *Jrnl. Amer. Med. Assoc.* 14 Apr. 1149/2 *Pyelography.—Voelcker and Lichtenberg have coined this term for radiography of the kidney and ureter after these structures have been filled with a solution of a silver salt. 1975 *Daily Colonist* (Victoria, B.C.) 23 Dec. 2/1 In pyelography, a contrast medium, the 'dye', is injected intravenously. 1890 *Cent. Dict.*, *Pyelonephritic. 1866 A. FLINT *Princ. Med.* (1880) 895 Suppurative nephritis.. called.., when there is coincident inflammation of the renal pelvis, *pyelo-nephritis. 1913 C. H. CHETWOOD *Practice of Urol.* xxxi. 587 (*heading*) *Pyeloplasty (Fenger's operation). 1976 *Lancet* 20 Nov. 1109/2 The boy with a horseshoe kidney had a pyeloplasty and 1 of the boys with obstructed congenital megaureter had a reimplantation.

pyement, pyemia, var. PIMENT *Obs.*, PYÆMIA.

pyep, pyepowder, pyere, pyerre, pyerrerye, obs. forms or variants of PEEP *v.*[1], PIEPOWDER, PEER *sb.*, PIER *sb.*[2], PIERRERIE.

pyet, var. PIET; obs. Sc. f. PIED.

pyetous, var. PIETOUS *Obs.*

pyf, pyfle, obs. or dial. var. PITH, PIFFLE.

pyg, obs. f. PIG.

pygal ('paɪgəl), *a.* (*sb.*) *Zool.* [f. Gr. πυγή rump + -AL[1].] Of or pertaining to the rump or hinder quarters of an animal.

1838 *Penny Cycl.* XI. 469/1 Pygal callosities large. 1854 OWEN *Skel. & Teeth* in *Orr's Circ. Sc.* I. *Org. Nat.* 217 [In the tortoise] the ninth, tenth, and pygal plates, with the marginal plates of the carapace, do not coalesce with any parts of the endo-skeleton.

b. *sb.* (Short for *pygal plate* or *shield.*) The posterior median plate of the carapace of a turtle.

1890 in *Cent. Dict.* 1896 LYDEKKER *Roy. Nat. Hist.* V. 45 In front the series is completed by a large nuchal plate, while behind it terminates in one or two pygals.

pygarg ('paɪgɑːg). Forms: 4 **phigarg**, (**figarde**), 6 **pygarge**, 7 **pygargue**, **pigarge**, 7– **pygarg**. Also in L. form **pygargus** (4 **pigargus**). [ad. L. *pȳgarg-us* (Pliny), a. Gr. πύγαργος lit. 'white-rump', applied to a kind of antelope, a white-tailed eagle, and a sandpiper; f. πυγή rump + ἀργός white.]

1. A kind of antelope mentioned by Herodotus and Pliny: by some supposed to be the addax.

In the LXX and Vulgate, whence in Wyclif, Douay, and Bible of 1611, used to render Heb. *dīshōn.*

1382 WYCLIF *Deut.* xiv. 5 This is the beest that ȝe owen to eete; oxe, and sheep, and.. phigarg [1388, figarde; 1609 (Douay), pygargue; 1611 and R.V., Pygarg]. 1572 BOSSEWELL *Armorie* II. 56b, The fielde is Veneris, a Pygarge, of the Sunne. This is an horne beaste, like a Goate bucke, but yet greater, and lesse then the Harte. 1706 PHILLIPS (ed. 6), *Pygargus*, a wild Beast like a Fallow Deer, so call'd because its back Parts are white.

2. (In L. form.) The osprey or sea-eagle.

1398 TREVISA *Barth. De P.R.* XVIII. lxxxv. (Bodl. MS.) 282/2 Hugucione seiþ þat pigargus is a litel lowe brid. 1587 HARRISON *England* III. v. (1878) II. 32 Of hawkes and rauenous foules... Neither haue we the pygargus or gripe. 1752 SIR J. HILL *Hist. Anim.* 331 The pygargus, the falco.. with the tailfeathers white and black at the end.

pygeon, pygg(e, obs. ff. PIGEON, PIG.

pygges nye, pyggysny, var. PIGSNEY *Obs.*

pyght, pyȝt, pyghtell, pyghtur, obs. forms of PIGHT, PIGHTLE, PICTURE.

‖**pygidium** (paɪ'dʒɪdɪəm, paɪ'gɪdɪəm). *Zool.* [mod.L., f. Gr. πυγή rump + dim. suff. -ίδιον.] The posterior part of the body in certain invertebrates, chiefly insects, crustaceans, and worms, when forming a distinct segment or division; the caudal or pygal segment.

1849 MURCHISON *Siluria* App. L. 545 *Pygidium*, or tail of some minute entomostraca. 1862 DANA *Man. Geol.* 188 *note*, The posterior [segment of a trilobite] when shield-shaped and combining two or more segments [is] the pygidium. 1872 NICHOLSON *Palæont.* 161 The crust exhibits three regions.—1, a cephalic shield; 2, a variable number of movable 'body-rings' or thoracic segments; and 3, a caudal shield or pygidium. 1899 D. SHARP in *Cambr. Nat. Hist.* VI. 187 The last of such exposed dorsal plates [in Beetles] is termed pygidium.

Hence **py'gidial** *a.*, of or pertaining to the pygidium.

1877 HUXLEY *Anat. Inv. Anim.* v. 234 The hindermost segment of the body.. divided at the end into two supports for the pygidial cirri.

†**pygist.** *Obs. rare*—[0]. [f. Gr. πυγή rump + -IST; cf. Gr. πυγίζειν, *pædicāre.*]

1623 COCKERAM, *Pygist*, one that useth buggerie.

pyglyng, var. PICKLING *Obs.*, kind of cloth.

†**'pygmachy.** *Obs. rare*—[0]. [ad. Gr. πυγμαχία boxing, f. πύξ (stem πυγ-) with clenched fist, or πυγμή fist + μάχη fight.] Boxing.

1656 BLOUNT *Glossogr.*, *Pygmachy*, a fighting with Hurlbats or Clubs. 1658 in PHILLIPS.

pygmæan, -mean (pɪg'miːən), *sb.* and *a.* Also 6– **pig-**. [f. L. *pygmæus* (see PYGMY) + -AN.]

†**A.** *sb.* = PYGMY *sb.* 1. *Obs.*

1555 EDEN *Decades* 85, I nowe compare a Pigmean or a dwarfte to a giant. 1559 W. CUNNINGHAM *Cosmogr. Glasse* 191 Ther are also Pygmeans (men but a cubite in height) which riding on Goates and Rammes, do kepe warre with Cranes. 1594 BLUNDEVIL *Exerc.* v. xii. (1636) 558 They are meere lyes that are wont to be told of the Pigmeans. 1601 HOLLAND *Pliny* VII. ii. I. 156 Aristotle writeth, That these Pygmæans liue in hollow caues & holes under the ground.

B. *adj.* Of or pertaining to the pygmies; of the nature or size of a pygmy; diminutive, dwarfish.

1667 MILTON *P.L.* I. 780 Now less then smallest Dwarfs, in narrow room Throng numberless, like that Pigmean Race Beyond the Indian mount. 1676 HOBBES *Iliad* III. (1677) 37 Or like the cranes, when from the north they fly, The army of pygmæan men to charge. 1735 SOMERVILLE *Chase* III. 139 The tall, plump, brawny Youth Curses his cumbrous Bulk; and envies now The short Pygmean Race. 1904 *Speaker* 21 May 173/1 The expenditure of Japan.. has been on a pigmean scale compared with that of Russia.

Pygmalion (pɪg'meɪlɪən). The name of a play by George Bernard Shaw (1856–1950), used quasi-advb. in ***not Pygmalion likely***, a joc. euphemism for the phrase 'not bloody likely' which occurs in Act III of the play (see BLOODY *adv.* 2, quot. 1914) and was the occasion of a public sensation at the time of the first London production in 1914. Also used *attrib.* of utterances regarded as mildly shocking.

1949 PARTRIDGE *Dict. Slang* (ed. 3) Add. 1121/1 *Not Pygmalion likely!* Not at all likely; certainly not! 1960 *Guardian* 8 Mar. 7/2 (*heading*) Not Pygmalion likely. 1960 *Times* 28 Apr. 14/5 Mr. S. M. Nutley.. said: 'The trouble really began when Alderman Mrs. K. Sheridan was speaking about the council fleecing tenants and used a pygmalion word.' 1964 N. SQUIRE *Bidding at Bridge* 185 So we *pass*? Not pygmalion likely! 1967 G. FALLON *Rendezvous in Rio* xiii. 106 'Are you thinking of joining in?' 'Not Pygmalion likely,' Bland returned brusquely. 1967 A. WILSON *No Laughing Matter* II. 96 You bloody bird! No, no, Mouse, Mr Polly and I were just talking Pygmalion talk! 1976 *Times* 18 Mar. 11/5 My immediate reaction was to say, 'Not Pygmalion likely'.

Pygmalionism (pɪg'meɪlɪənɪz(ə)m). *Psychol.* Also **pygmalionism.** [f. *Pygmalion* a character in Greek mythology + -ISM. According to Ovid (*Metam.* x. 243–97), Pygmalion was a King of Cyprus who made a statue of a beautiful woman and loved it so deeply that Aphrodite gave life to it.] The condition of loving a statue, image, or inanimate object; love for an object of one's own making.

1905 H. ELLIS *Stud. Psychol. Sex* IV. 188 Pygmalionism, or falling in love with statues, is a rare form of erotomania founded on the sense of vision and closely related to the allurement of beauty. 1923 —— *Dance of Life* vii. 328 We find records of Pygmalionism and allied perversities in Lucian. 1940 HINSIE & SHATZKY *Psychiatric Dict.* 453/1 *Pygmalionism*,.. the condition of falling in love with a creation of one's own. 1946 'M. INNES' *From London Far* III. iv. 201 'Did you ever happen to hear of something called Pygmalionism?' '.. It's a fancy name for iconolagnia'. 1954 H. T. F. RHODES *Satanic Mass* vi. 52 After the kiss, accounts agree that the priestess offered herself to the God by an act of pygmalionism. 1966 J. COHEN *Human Robots* iv. 66 We may infer that the Greeks, who had a highly developed visual sense, were inclined to *Pygmalionism. Ibid.*, We may regard *Pygmalionism* as a manifestation of a more general tendency to excitement induced by a partner's passivity.

†**'pygman.** *Obs.* Also 5 **pigmen.** [a. OF. *pigmain, pigman* (Godef.).] = PYGMY *sb.* 1.

c 1400 MAUNDEV. (Roxb.) xxii. 103 þe land of þe Pigmens [Fr. *pigmeinez*], whilk er men of litill stature. 1481 CAXTON *Myrr.* II. v. 69 Peple that ben horned, and ar but ii cubits hye... This peple is callyd pygmans.

pygment, obs. form of PIGMENT *sb.*

pygmoid ('pɪgmɔɪd), *a.* [f. PYGMY *sb.* + -OID.] Resembling a pygmy; having (some of) the characteristics of a pygmy. Also as *sb.*

1933 R. G. AUSTIN tr. O. Menghin in *Antiquity* VII. 242 Mr Clark is perfectly correct in stating (p. 12) that I connect the Mughem men with the Grimaldi and Bushman types, treating them as pygmoid (not as pygmies). 1958 *Listener* 2 Oct. 507/1 The majority of these little people whom you see outside the forests in the north-east [*sc.* of the Congo] are not pygmies. They are pygmoids, the offspring of a liaison between a pygmy and a normal-sized Negro. 1965 E. E. EVANS-PRITCHARD *Theories Primitive Relig.* v. 102 The Pygmies and Pygmoids of Africa and Asia. 1976 EVELETH & TANNER *Worldwide Variation in Human Growth* vii. 190 In New Guinea where one encounters numerous short-statured populations there can be no clear separation of pygmoid groups. 1977 P. JOHNSON *Enemies of Society* xvii. 226 The Veddas, a pygmoid people of primeval hunters living in the interior of Ceylon.

pygmy, pigmy ('pɪgmɪ), *sb.* and *a.* Forms: 4–7 **pigmey** (4–6 *pl.* **-eis**), 5 *pl.* **pigmez**, 5–7 **pygmey** (*pl.* 5–6 **-eis**, **-eyes**, 7 **-eys**), **pygme**, 6 **pigmay**, **-mé**, 6–7 **pigmie**, 7 **pigmee**, **pygmie**, 6– **pigmy**, 8– **pygmy**. *β.* 5 **pygmew**, 5–6 **pigmew**. [In *α* form, ad. L. *pygmæ-us*, a. Gr. πυγμαῖ-ος adj. dwarfish, sb. a dwarf, a pygmy, f. πυγμή a measure of length from the elbow to the knuckles, also the fist (the pl. *pigmeis* in Wyclif being directly ad. L. *pygmæi*); cf. F. *pygmée*, Rabelais. In the *β* form, *pygmew*, ad. med.L. *pygmeu-s*, L. *pygmæus*, cf. *Andrew*, †*Grew*, *Hebrew*, *Jew*, *Matthew*, †*Pharisew*, also OF. *pigmeau* (Godef.), *pimeau* (14th c. in Hatz.-Darm.).]

A. *sb.*

1. a. One of a race (or several races) of people of very small size, mentioned in ancient history and tradition as inhabiting parts of Ethiopia or India; in later times generally supposed to be fabulous. (*b*) One of a group of very short people inhabiting equatorial Africa, who were first encountered by Europeans in the last quarter of the 19th c., and who may be the Πυγμαῖοι of Homer and Herodotus.

1382 WYCLIF *Ezek.* xxvii. 11 Pigmeis that weren in thi touris hangiden her arewgirdlis in thi wallis bi cumpas. 1398 TREVISA *Barth. De P.R.* XV. cxx. (1495) 534 Pigmea is a countree in Ynde towarde the eest in mountaynes afore the ocean. Therin dwelled the Pigmeis: men lytyll of body: vneth two cubytes longe, they gendre in the fourth yere and aege in the seuenth. Thyse.. fyghte wyth cranes and destroyen theyr nestes, and breke theyr egges, that theyr enmyes be not multyplyed. *c* 1400 MAUNDEV. (Roxb.) xxii. 100 þai er sumwhat mare þan pigmez [*MS. C.* pygmeyes; Fr. *pigmeiz*]. *c* 1440 *Promp. Parv.* 395/2 Pygmew [*S.* pygme], *pigmeus*. *c* 1520 L. ANDREW *Noble Lyfe* H ij b, Pigmeis be men & women, & but one cubite longe, dwellinge in the mountaynes of ynde. They be full growen at their third yere, & at their seuen yere they be olde. 1599 SHAKS. *Much Ado* II. i. 278, I will.. fetch you a hayre off the great Chams beard: doe you any embassage to the Pigmies. 1675 J. BARNES *Gerania* 21 Eucompsus had by this time pretty well confirmed us all in the opinion, that these were Pygmies. 1696 PHILLIPS (ed. 5), *Pigmy*, a sort of People, if there be any such, said to be not above a Cubit high. 1711 ADDISON *Spect.* No. 31 ¶2 That part of India which is said to be inhabited by the Pigmies. 1796 BURKE *Regic. Peace* iv. Wks. 1808 IX. 42 That the battle of Marignan was the battle of the Giants, that all the rest.. were those of the Cranes and Pygmies. 1887 H. M. STANLEY *Darkest Africa* (1890) I. 251 A march of nine and a half miles on the 9th of November took us to a Pigmies' camp. 1898 G. BURROWS *Land of Pigmies* viii. 176 The term Akka, by which the Pigmies are known.

†**b.** Formerly applied to the chimpanzee and other anthropoid apes as the assumed originals of the pygmies of ancient story. *Obs.*

1699 E. TYSON *Ourang-outang* 1 That the Pygmies of the Antients were a sort of Apes, and not of Humane Race, I shall endeavour to prove in the following Essay... A Puny Race of Mankind, call'd to this day, *Homo Sylvestris*, The Wild Man: Orang Outang, or a Man of the Woods. 1774 GOLDSM. *Nat. Hist.* (1862) I. VII. i. 491 The Troglodyte of Bontius, the Drill of Purchas, and the Pigmy of Tyson, have all received this general name—oran outang, or wild man of the woods. 1778 CAMPER in *Phil. Trans.* LXIX. 144 As the celebrated Dr. Tyson had found the organ of voice so similar to that of men in his Pigmy. 1863 HUXLEY *Man's Place Nat.* I. 8 This 'Pygmie', Tyson tells us, 'was brought from Angola';.. sufficient to prove his 'Pygmie' to be a young chimpanzee.

2. a. *gen.* A person of very small stature; a dwarf.

1520 in *Archæologia* LIII. 17 A case of wode covered w^t sylver..havyng a man and a woman called pygmeis. **1532** MORE *Confut. Tindale* Wks. 731/2 As very a manne is he that hath little stature, as hee that hathe a greate, and a Pigmay as a Geaunt. **1640** J. STOUGHTON *Def. & Distrib. Div.*, etc. ii. 67 Though a Gyant be taller then a Pygme, yet a Pygme upon his shoulders hath advantage of him. **1711** ADDISON *Spect.* No. 98 ¶2 A Woman, who was but a Pygmy without her Head-dress, appear'd like a Colossus upon putting it on. **1820** KEATS *Hyperion* I. 28 By her in stature the tall Amazon Had stood a pigmy's height.

b. *fig.* A person (or something personified) of very small importance, or having some specified quality in a very small degree. (Cf. GIANT A. 3.)

1592 KYD *Sol. & Pers.* II. ii. 91 Ile send some Crane to combate with the Pigmew. **1682** SIR T. BROWNE *Chr. Mor.* III. §14 Though Giants in Wealth and Dignity, we are but Dwarfs and Pygmies in Humanity. **1760** DODD *Hymn Gd.-Nature* Poems (1767) 6 We stood Mere pigmies on the strand. **1860** READE *Cloister & H.* lxxiv, These are heathen arts, and we but pigmies at them. **1888** BRYCE *Amer. Commw.* I. viii. 110 They were intellectual pigmies beside the real leaders of that generation—Clay, Calhoun, and Webster.

c. *transf.* A thing that is very small of its kind.

1838 T. THOMSON *Chem. Org. Bodies* 967 The plant.. does not cease to vegetate, but it continues always a mere pigmy. **1849** H. MILLER *Footpr. Creat.* x. (1874) 181 They took their place..among the pigmies and abortions of creation. **1880** HAUGHTON *Phys. Geog.* ii. 49 Venus contains mountain ridges upwards of 25 miles in height, in comparison with which our giant Himalayas would appear like pygmies. **1905** *Westm. Gaz.* 1 Mar. 12/1 Since the application of the dry process to photography..the detection of these planetary pigmies [asteroids] has been rendered much easier.

3. An elf, puck, pixy.

1611 COTGR., *Pigmée*, a Pigmey, dwarfe,..elfe, twattle. **1646** SIR T. BROWNE *Pseud. Ep.* IV. xi, The Pygmies of Paracelsus, that is, his non-Adamicall men, or middle natures betwixt men and spirits. **1774–6** J. BRYANT *Mythol.* II. 350 The Greek and Roman Poets reduced the character of this Deity [Eros] to that of a wanton mischievous pigmy. **1830** SCOTT *Demonol.* iv. 123 All tribes of Celtic origin assigned to..these silvan pigmies, more social habits. **1855** LONGF. *Hiaw.* XVIII. 7 They the fairies, and the pigmies, Plotted and conspired against him.

B. *adj.*

1. Of or pertaining to the race of pygmies: see A. 1. (Partly attrib. use of the sb.)

a **1661** HOLYDAY *Juvenal* xiii. 240 The pygmie-warriour runs to fight In his dwarf-armour. **1704–5** POPE *Jan. & May* 461 Their pigmy king, and little fairy queen, In circling dances gamboll'd on the green. **1749** COLLINS *Ode, Pop. Superstit. Highl.* 143 In whose small vaults a pigmy-folk is found. **1870** BRYANT *Homer* I. III. 80 Bring fearful battle to the pigmy race, Bloodshed and death.

2. a. Of persons and animals: Of very small size or stature, dwarf.

1591 SYLVESTER *Du Bartas* I. v. 76 As a rare Painter draws ..Here a huge Cyclop, there a Pigmé Elf. **1592** NASHE *P. Penilesse* Wks. (Grosart) II. 65 Thou great baboune, thou Pigmie Braggart, thou Pamph[l]eter of nothing but peans. **1645** EVELYN *Diary* 22–24 May, A pigmy sort of spaniels. **1735** SOMERVILLE *Chase* I. 261 The pigmy Brood in ev'ry Furrow swims. **1823** SCOTT *Peveril* xxxiii, 'You have him before you, young man', said the pigmy tenant of the cell, with an air of dignity. **1837** HAWTHORNE *Twice-told T.* (1851) II. x. 153 The old showman..stirred up the souls of the pygmy people with one of the quickest tunes in the music book.

b. *gen.* Very small, diminutive, tiny. In *Nat. Hist.* often used in the names of species of animals that are very small of their kind. Also *fig.*

1595 SHAKS. *John* v. ii. 135 Prepar'd To whip this dwarfish warre, this Pigmy Armes From out the circle of his Territories. *a* **1678** MARVELL in *Casquet of Lit.* (1873) I. 309/2 An arrow hurtel'd ere so high..Goes but a pigmy length. **1763** CHURCHILL *Epist. to W. Hogarth* 438 Bid the Deep Hush at thy pigmy voice her waves to sleep. **1771** PENNANT *Syn. Quadr.* 98 Pygmy Ape. **1781** LATHAM *Hist. Birds* I. 256 Pygmy Parrakeet. **1803–6** WORDSW. *Ode Intim. Immort.* vii, A six years' Darling of a pigmy size. **1830** *Edin. Encycl.* XIII. 399/2 *P[ithecus] sylvanus.* The Pigmy ape inhabits Africa, the East Indies, and Ceylon,..and, when standing on its hinder legs, measures about two feet in height. **1893** LYDEKKER *Horns & Hoofs* 358 The smallest of all the pigs is, however, the pigmy hog (*Sus salvaninus*). **1898** *Daily News* 16 Aug. 6/2 The pigmy shrew..which really is the smallest mammal we have, and the least but one in all Europe.

C. *Comb.* as ***pygmy-cup***, **-*folk***, **-*minded*** adjs.; **pygmy-flint** *Archæol.*, a type of microlith; **pygmy-weed**, an annual weed, *Tillæa simplex*, an inch or two high, found in the eastern United States.

1936 *Proc. Prehist. Soc.* II. 223 The urns comprise two food-vessels, a *pigmy-cup and an encrusted urn. **1963** H. N. SAVORY in Foster & Alcock *Culture & Environment* iii. 43 The Breach Farm barrow, with its dry-stone wall kerb and its fine biconical Pygmy Cup. **1907** T. R. HOLMES *Anc. Britain* 82 Of all stone implements the most curious are the tiny objects which are known as '*pygmy flints'. **1930** F. ELGEE *Early Man in N.E. Yorkshire* v. 31 The pygmy-flint men lived by hunting and fishing. **1963** *Field Archaeol.* (Ordnance Survey) (ed. 4) 8 Various palæolithic objects like hand-axes and choppers, microliths ('pygmy' flints), arrow and lance heads. **1788** W. COLLINS *Ode on Pop. Superstitions Highlands of Scotl.* 18 In..small vaults a *pigmy-folk is found. **1835** PUSEY in Liddon *Life* (1893) I. xiii. 320 One point in the plan did strike me as less *pigmy-minded.

Hence (*nonce-wds.*) **'pygmy**, **'pigmy** *v. trans.*, to make a pygmy of, to reduce to insignificance, to dwarf; **'pygmydom**, the realm of pygmies; **'pygmyhood**, **'pygmyism**, **'pygmyship**, the condition, position, or character of a pygmy.

1658 SAM. AUSTIN *Naps Parnass.* E ij, Stand off thou Poetaster from the Press, Who *pygmi'st Martyrs with thy dwarf-like verse. **1828** *Blackw. Mag.* XXIII. 598 They were pigmied to nothing in such a lordly neighbourhood. **1909** *Church Times* 23 July 120/3 This great..church towers high above everything. It pigmies the parish church. **1892** BOOTH-TUCKER *Catherine Booth* lxxvii. II. 162 Lilliputian nobodies from the land of *pigmydom strutted out. **1892** SWINBURNE *Stud. Prose & Poetry* (1894) 231 What we do not understand, we declare, from the height of our *pigmyhood, to be useless. **1837** BP. INGLIS *Let.* in E. Churton *Mem. J. Watson* (1861) II. 99 Do not laugh at our *pigmyism. **1862** *Temple Bar Mag.* V. 288 His *pigmyship.

pygo- (paɪgəʊ), repr. Gr. πυγο-, combining form of πυγή rump, used in the formation of zoological terms. **pygo'branchiate** [Gr. βράγχια gills] *a.*, belonging to the *Pygobranchia*, a group of gastropods having the gills arranged round the anus; so **pygo'branchious** *a.* **pygo'melian** [Gr. μέλος limb] *a.*, pertaining to or connected with a ***py'gomelus***, a monster having a supernumerary limb behind or between the normal posterior pair; *sb.* a pygomelian animal. **'pygopage** [ad. mod.L. *pȳgopagus*, f. Gr. πάγος that which is fixed or firmly set, f. πήγνυναι to fix, fasten], a monster consisting of twins united in the region of the buttocks; so **py'gopagous** *a.* **py'gopagus** = *pygopage* [a. F. *pygopage* (I. G. St.-Hilaire 1830, in *Ann. des Sci. nat.* XX. 338)]. **'pygopod** [Gr. πούς, ποδ- foot], (*a*) *adj.* of or pertaining to the *Pygopodes*, an order of aquatic birds, including the auks, grebes, and loons, having the legs set very far back; (*b*) *adj.* of or belonging to the genus *Pygopus* or family *Pygopodidæ* of Australian lizards having rudimentary hind legs; *sb.* a lizard of this family; hence **py'gopodous** *a.* **'pygostyle** [Gr. στῦλος column], the vomer or triangular plate formed of the fused caudal vertebræ, which supports the tail-feathers in most birds; hence **'pygostyled** *a.*, furnished with or forming a pygostyle.

1858 MAYNE *Expos. Lex.*, *Pygobranchius*,..applied by Gray to an order (*Pygobranchia*) of the *Gasteropodophora*..; *pygobranchious. **1894** BATESON *Variation* 401 *note*, *Pygomelian geese are often recorded. **1891** *Amer. Nat.* Oct. 894 The case of Rosa-Josepha is not entirely analogous and comparable to the two other *pygopages. **1895** *Teratologia* II. 274 Several of the *pygopagous twins of whom there are scientific records, survived birth and lived for a number of years. **1902** *Brit. Med. Jrnl.* 5 Apr. 850 Pygopagous twins..united together in the region of the nates and having each its own pelvis. **1866** *Trans. Med. Soc. State of N.Y.* XXIV. 224 The symmetrical *pygopagus is exceedingly rare. **1903** J. W. WILLIAMS *Obstetrics* xxxix. 680 Ischiopagi and pygopagi, as a rule, call for complicated and difficult manœuvres before delivery can be effected. **1959** *Jrnl. Chronic Dis.* X. 84 A wooden carving from the Solomon Islands suggests conjoined twins of the pygopagus type with the union of the bodies and heads and the extremities shortened by achondroplasia. **1836** *Buck's Handbk. Med. Sc.* II. 226 The heat of such homothermous animals as the whale, the seal, the walrus, and the *pygopodous birds. **1875** W. K. PARKER in *Encycl. Brit.* III. 719/2 A ploughshare-shaped bone or *pygostyle. **1899** EVANS *Birds* in *Cambr. Nat. Hist.* IX. 47 The tail [of Hesperornis] was fairly long and broad, but had no pygostyle. **1884** COUES *Key N. Amer. Birds* 238 Tail short (as to its vertebræ, which are *pygostyled).

pygrall, pygsnye, pygymast, pygyn: see PEGRALL, PIGSNEY, PEGGYMAST, PIGEON.

†**pygyn**, obs. form of PIGGIN.

1334 *Black Bk. Denbigh* lf. 429 Reddendo domino per annum vj vasa et pygyn butiri.

†**py hy**, *int. Obs.* A representation of laughter; cf. TEE-HEE.

1589 *Hav any Work* (1844) 10, I cannot but laugh, *py hy hy hy.* **1589** *Martins Months Minde* Nashe's Wks. (Grosart) I. 198 Ha, he, tse, tse, py, hy, see fortunes wheeles, So how, Mad Martin hath turnde vp his heeles.

pyic ('paɪɪk), *a. rare*⁻⁰. [f. Gr. πύ-ον pus + -IC.] Of or pertaining to pus; purulent.

1858 in MAYNE *Expos. Lex.*

pyin ('paɪɪn). *Phys. Chem.* [f. as prec. + -IN¹.] An albuminoid substance found in pus.

1845 TODD & BOWMAN *Phys. Anat.* I. 51 It is..stated, that the element which may be obtained from the young cells of areolar tissue is pyine. **1866–8** WATTS *Dict. Chem.* IV. 752 Pyin closely resembles mucin. **1873** RALFE *Phys. Chem.* 39 Pyin can be obtained by agitating recently drawn pus with a 10 per cent. solution of sodium chloride.

†**'pying**, *vbl. sb. Obs.* [f. implied *pie vb. (f. PIE *sb.*³) + -ING¹.] The alphabetical indexing of rolls and records: see PIE *sb.*³ 2.

1658 *Practick Part Law* (ed. 5) 283 The keepers of the files of Declarations Hath for the filing, pying, and shewing the files of every Clerke for every Terme, 2s.

pyinkado ('pjɪŋkədəʊ, pɪ'ɪŋk-). Also †**pingadoo**, **pyengadu**, **py(i)ngado**, **pynkado**, [Burmese.] The heavy timber of the tree *Xylia xylocarpa* (formerly *X. dolabriformis*), which belongs to the family Leguminosæ and is native to Burma and parts of India; also, the tree itself. Also *attrib.*

1832 W. ROXBURGH et al. *Flora Indica* II. 543 It [sc. *Minosa xylocarpa*] is called Pingadoo in Pegu, where it is used for knees, crooked timbers, &c. in ship building. **1875** T. LASLETT *Timber & Timber Trees* xxi. 129 The Pyengadu, or Iron-wood tree,..is a species of Acacia, of straight growth, found in the Burmese forests. **1885** W. T. OLDREAVE in Rattray & Mill *Forestry & Forest Products* xii. 381 Pynkado..is said to be a species of acacia. **1896** W. R. FISHER in W. Schlich *Man. Forestry* V. I. ii. 117 In London ..doubtless Pyngado..and other heavy Indian woods might be used with advantage [for wooden paving]. **1902** G. S. BOULGER *Wood* I. v. 92 Pynkado or Pyengadu..is the Ironwood of Pegu. **1934** 'G. ORWELL' *Burmese Days* 69 At the edge of the stream there was a huge dead pyinkado tree festooned with spidery orchids. **1940** *Archit. Rev.* LXXXVII. 47 For the remainder of the building sound-proofing floors are used finished with 3 in. pyinkado strips. **1951** *Dict. Gardening* (R. Hort. Soc.) IV. 2295/1 Pyingado.. is extremely hard, heavy, strong, and durable. **1956** *Handbk. of Hardwoods* (Forest Prod. Res. Lab.) 194 Pyinkado grows to a height of 100–120 ft. *Ibid.* 195 Pyinkado is unsuitable for plywood manufacture because of its weight. **1971** F. H. TITMUSS *Commerc. Timbers of World* (ed. 4) 263 Pyinkado is a difficult timber to work.

pyione, obs. form of PEONY.

pyjamas, pajamas (pə'dʒɑːməz, formerly paɪ'dʒɑːməz), *sb. pl.* Also 9 **peijammahs**, **pie-**, **pyjamahs**. [a. Pers. and Urdū *pāē* (*pāy*) *jāmah*, f. Pers. *pāē*, *pāy* foot, leg + *jāmah* clothing, garment. In Persian, a sb. singular; in Eng. made plural with *-s*, after *breeches*, *drawers*, *trousers*, etc. *pyjamas* is now standard in the U.K., *pajamas* in the U.S.] **a.** Loose drawers or trousers, usually of silk or cotton, tied round the waist, worn by both sexes in Turkey, Iran, India, etc., and adopted by Europeans in those countries, especially for night wear; hence applied outside Asia (orig. in trade use) to a sleeping suit of loose trousers and jacket. In extended use, applied to a similar day-time or evening garment worn by women (see also *beach-pyjamas* s.v. BEACH *sb.* 4, *palazzo pyjamas* s.v. PALAZZO 3). Also (*occas.*) *sing.*, as *pyjama.*

1800 *Misc. Tracts* in *Asiat. Ann. Reg.* 342/2 Memorandum relative to Tippoo Sultaun's wardrobe... 3d, pai jamahs, or drawers. *Ibid.*, Pai Jamahs. **1834** MEDWIN *Angler in Wales* I. 188 In a pair of 'pigammahs' and a shirt. **1839** THACKERAY *Major Gahagan* iii, I stripped him of his.. peijammahs. **1840** E. E. NAPIER *Scenes & Sports For. Lands* II. v. 156 Equipped in our broad straw hats, shirts, light silk or muslin 'piejamahs'. **1845** STOCQUELER *Handbk. Brit. India* (1854) 108 He usually undresses, puts on his pajamas (the loose Turkish trouser). **1859** LANG *Wand. India* 360 Pyjamahs of red silk trimmed with gold lace. **1878** E. S. BRIDGES *Diary* 6 Sept. in *Round World in Six Months* (1879) iii. 37, I relinquished my English *chemise de nuit* and took to pyjamas—bedclothes are not used at this time of year [in Japan]. **1886** *Girl's Own Paper* 23 Oct. 59/1 The pattern for this month..is a combination nightgown, or lady's 'pyjama'. **1893** EARL DUNMORE *Pamirs* I. 277 They wore the usual short blue silk cloak and loose white pyjamas. **1897** [see *sleeping-suit* s.v. SLEEPING *vbl. sb.* 2 b]. **1903** *Smart Set* IX. 122/1 I'd as lief be seen in my pajamas. **1932** *Barker's Spring Catal.* This ideal pyjama is made of a very soft washing cotton. **1932** *Boston Even. Transcript* 6 Aug. 1 Clad in pajamas and admitting to police that she was returning home from a party, Mary Callahan, twenty four..was arrested at seven o'clock this morning. **1936** A. CHRISTIE *ABC Murders* xvi. 120 Girls passed him..in summery frocks and pyjamas and shorts. **1968** J. IRONSIDE *Fashion Alphabet* 62 *Pyjamas*, blouse or shirt and wide-legged trousers worn for lounging or for beach wear—introduced by Chanel in the late 1920s. **1976** *Washington Post* 19 Apr. A12/4 (Advt.), Pre-school boys' pajamas reduced. **1978** *Neiman-Marcus Christmas Bk.* 32 The ambient glow of soft panne velvet for party pajamas.

b. *attrib.* and *Comb.* (in sing. form), as ***pyjama-clothes***, ***coat***, ***cord***, ***dress***, ***jacket***, ***leg***, ***pants***, ***suit***, ***top***, ***trousers***; ***pyjama-clad***, **-*legged***, **-*like*** adjs.; **pyjama bottom**, the bottom half of a suit of pyjamas, pyjama trousers; usu. *pl.*; **pyjama case**, a bag or other container in which pyjamas can be kept when not being worn; **pyjama party**, a party at which those present are dressed in pyjamas; also **pyjama-and-bottle-party**.

1928 *Sunday Dispatch* 5 Aug. 15/2 Mention was made of the splendid work of Mrs. X—— Y—— for her *pyjama-and-bottle party. **1959** R. CONDON *Manchurian Candidate* (1960) i. 10 The..movie actor..had opened the door of the hotel suite wearing only *pyjama bottoms. **1972** J. WAINWRIGHT *Requiem for Loser* iii. 48 He..stepped out of his pyjama bottoms and began dressing himself. **1973** *Black World* Oct. 55/1 None of the kids had on a complete outfit of clothes: some were in a pajama top—or a bottom. **1925** 'R. CROMPTON' *Still—William* ix. 164 Thrusting his..paper fleet into his *pyjama case. **1976** W. J. BURLEY *Wycliffe & Schoolgirls* viii. 151 Lying on it [*sc.* the bed] was a pyjama case in the shape of a dog with 'Jane' embroidered across it. **1904** *Daily Chron.* 27 Apr. 6/4 The spectacle presented by the learned counsel..and the officials of the court, arranged in front of the *pyjama-clad judge. **1921** R. MACAULAY *Dangerous Ages* i. 2 Her slight, straight, pyjama-clad body. **1976** 'L. BLACK' *Healthy Way to Die* iv. 38 The pyjama-clad legs dangling inside the silken dressing-gown. **1939** AUDEN & ISHERWOOD *Journey to War* 43 The Cantonese, in their light *pyjama-clothes. **1916** M. DIVER *Desmond's Daughter* II. v. 71 A Punjab Cavalryman in a turban and silk *pyjama coat. **1978** C. STORR *Winter's End* v. 68 She wore a blue and white striped pyjama coat. **1917** E. FENWICK *Diary* 18 Feb.

in *Elsie Fenwick in Flanders* (1981) 143 He tried to hang himself with his *pyjama cord. **1972** *Times* 28 July 10/1 Top coats with pyjama cord belts. **1967** *Guardian* 2 Nov. 7/6 For luscious evening attire..a *pyjama dress in hot pink and orange. **1891** E. Dowson *Let.* 1 July (1967) 206, I am more elaborately vested, in a *Pyjama jacket. **1976** C. Dexter *Last seen Wearing* xxxviii. 261 The top button of the pyjama jacket already undone. **1933** A. Thirkell *High Rising* ii. 48 Tony, by now in what he called his *pyjama-legs, executed a dance of joy. **1977** *Transatlantic Rev.* lx. 145 The water isn't as cold as I figured, but when the bottom of my pajama-leg gets wet, I get a little nauseous. **1960** *Pyjama-legged [see culotte 2]. **1960** Koestler *Lotus & Robot* i. i. 41 Another table in the Mascot's dining-room was occupied by an Egyptian gentleman in a *pyjama-like attire. **1956** 'E. McBain' *Cop Hater* (1958) iv. 38 He was wearing *pajama pants and nothing else. **1980** G. Lord *Fortress* i. 7 She pulled down her pyjama pants. **1910** *Westm. Gaz.* 13 Apr. 5/3 A *pyjama party held a couple of days ago at the residence of Mrs. Edwin Avon, a well-known member of Chicago society. **1928** A. Waugh *Nor Many Waters* ii. 36 They'd thought of making a dressing-gown and pyjama party of it, so you can guess what it'll be like from that. **1933** Dylan Thomas *Let.* (1966) 67 It sounds as though you'd invited me to a pyjama party. **1978** S. Sheldon *Bloodline* xii. 157 They had often invited Elizabeth to their pajama parties. **1883** C. Bell tr. *Haeckel's Visit to Ceylon* xx. 329 The rest of our attire consisted of that particularly light and airy white flannel garment, known throughout India as a *pajama suit. **1897** Hughes *Medit. Fever* v. 188 It has the disadvantage over the pyjama suit of being more difficult to change. **1973** 'G. Black' *Bitter Tea* iii. 41 She was.. wearing the kind of pyjama suit some women go shopping in [in Malaysia]. **1949** N. Mitford *Love in Cold Climate* i. vi. 66 Lady Montdore..in bed..wearing what appeared to be a man's striped *pyjama top under a feathered wrap. **1976** C. Dexter *Last seen Wearing* xxxiii. 225 She..fastened all but the top button of her pyjama top. **1900** G. Swift *Somerley* 42 To make your *pyjama-trousers look like trunk-hose. **1932** D. C. Minter *Mod. Needlecraft* 146/2 For pyjama trousers cut straight down. **1975** W. J. Burley *Wycliffe & Pea-Green Boat* i. i. 10 A tall, skinny young man in pyjama trousers.

Hence **py'jamaed** *a.*, clad in pyjamas. Also **pyjama'd**.

1883 *World* 28 Nov. 18/2 Ten pyjamahed and betowelled unfortunates are standing..outside. **1890** *Westm. Gaz.* 6 Sept. 2/3 A stranger who strolled into (say) the Lord Chief Justice's Court, pyjama-ed and not ashamed. **1922** F. Hamilton *P. J. the Secret Service Boy* i. 47 Mr. Davenant sleepily extended a pyjama'd arm. **1929** D. Hammett *Dain Curse* (1930) xvi. 182, I..let in Jack Santos, pajamaed, bathrobed, and slippered. **1959** D. Campbell *Evening under Lamplight* 47 Pyjama'd figures were clambering..into the shadowy bedroom. **1959** P. McCutchan *Storm South* ix. 124 Her pyjama-ed legs. **1974** 'D. Meiring' *President Plan* xvii. 158 She knew where he slept... A light went on and.. he was there, pyjamaed.

pyjams, pyjies ('paɪ-), colloq. abbrevs. of pyjamas, pajamas *sb. pl.* Also **pygies** and (redupl.) **pyjimjams**.

1926 D. L. Sayers *Clouds of Witness* iv. 99 Why do girls wear such mimsy little pyjimjams in this damn cold climate? **1929** P. Sturges *Strictly Dishonorable* ii. 139 Now go and get the pygies and things. **1937** Partridge *Dict. Slang* 674/2 *Pyjams*, abbr[eviation of] *pyjamas*. **1960** J. Betjeman *Summoned by Bells* vii. 66 House-slippers, sponge-bag, pyjams. **1962** J. Braine *Life at Top* i. 8 But Daddy has to earn pennies..for pyjies and frocks.

pyjon, obs. form of pigeon.

pyk, -e, pykke, obs. ff. *pick*, north. f. pitch *sb.*[1]

pyk, pykage, pykar, pykarelle, obs. ff. pick, pike, pickage, picard, piker[1], pickerel[1].

pykas, -ax, pykeax(e, pykeis, pykes, obs. ff. pickaxe.

pyke, obs. f. peck *v.*[1], pick *v.*[1], pike, pique.

pykefork, obs. f. pickfork.

pykeled, var. pickled *ppl. a.*[2] *Obs.*, speckled.

pyker, pykerel, -elle, pykery, obs. ff. picard, piker[1], pickerel[1], pickery.

†**pykestole, -olle.** *Obs.* [Origin unascertained.] Name of a play or sport formerly engaged in at Ripon on Easter Monday.

1439 *Mem. Ripon* (Surtees) III. 235 Et in pane et cerevisio emptis pro ludentibus le Pykestolle in crastino Paschæ..1*d.* **1447** *Ibid.* 240 Et in solucione facta xv ministris ludentibus in crastino festi Paschæ..15*d.* Et in pane et cervis. emptis pro le Pykestole ludentibus eodem die, 1½*d.*

pykfork, pykid, pyking, pykit, obs. ff. pickfork, piked, picking, picked, piked.

pykk, -e, pykkert, pykkyll, pykle, -let, obs. ff. pick, picard, pightle, pickle, pikelet.

pyknic ('pɪknɪk), *a.* Also **pycnic**. [f. Gr. πυκνός thick, close-packed + -ic.] In Kretschmer's theory of human physical and corresponding temperamental types, designating a stocky physique with a rounded body and head, thickset trunk, and a tendency to fat, usu. accompanied by a cycloid temperament; also *absol.*, a person belonging to this type. Cf. asthenic *a.* b; athletic *a.* 3; leptosomic *a.* Phr. *pyknic practical joke* (see quot. 1964).

1925 W. J. H. Sprott tr. *Kretschmer's Physique & Character* i. ii. 29 The pyknic type..is characterised by the pronounced peripheral development of the body cavities (head, breast, and stomach), and a tendency to..fat about the trunk. *Ibid.*, The pyknics tend emphatically to a covering of fat. **1940** W. H. Sheldon *Varieties of Human Physique* (1963) iii. 32 Much of the confusion associated with Kretschmer's terminology arises from the fact that his term 'pyknic' actually applies to a physique combining endomorphy and mesomorphy. **1942** —— *Varieties of Temperament* iv. 109 The mother was a PPJ (pyknic practical joke). She was slim-waisted and active.., but after the first pregnancy she came into her full endomorphic blossom. **1958** A. R. Radcliffe-Brown *Method in Social Anthropol.* i. iv. 103 Psychiatry affords an example of a 'special psychology', as do attempts to define psychological 'types'—..pycnic, asthenic. **1960** J. Comas *Man. Physical Anthropol.* vi. 340 A well-developed thorax predominates over the shoulders in the pyknic type. **1964** L. J. Bischof *Interpreting Personality Theories* (1970) xi. 431 *Pyknic practical joke* (PPJ).., the PPJ refers to a person who has a muscular mesomorphic body in adolescence but in later life balloons out into obesity to become an endomorph. **1971** J. Z. Young *Introd. Study Man.* xxxix. 576 Kretschmer.. found that his pyknics tended to be what Jung called extroverted. **1975** A. Ferraro in S. Arieti *Amer. Handbk. Psychiatry* (ed. 2) IV. 103/1 Badia found that the megalosplanchnic type of Viola, or pycnic type of Kretschmer, discloses a tendency to chronic changes in the blood vessels of the heart.

pykno-: for words beginning thus see also pycno-.

pyknolepsy ('pɪknəʊlɛpsɪ). *Med.* [ad. G. *pyknolepsie* (Schröder: see *Monatsschr. für Psychiatrie und Neurol.* (1916) XL. 281), f. Gr. πυκνός thick, crowded, after *narkolepsie* narcolepsy.] An epileptic condition in which brief attacks similar to petit mal occur many times in a day. Hence **pykno'leptic** *a.*

1922 *Q. Cumulative Index Current Med. Lit. 1921* 533/2 (*heading*) Pyknolepsy. **1924** *Brain* XLVII. 98 Pyknolepsy, in spite of its long duration and the great frequency of the attacks, does not impede mental development nor give rise to psychical defects. *Ibid.*, Of the many that have been used the name pyknolepsy is recommended for use by English writers... It allows us to coin a handy adjective, 'pyknoleptic', by analogy with epileptic. **1952** F. A. Elliott et al. *Clin. Neurol.* vii. 133 In pyknolepsy, the attacks cease with puberty and may not recur. **1972** P. H. Hoch *Differential Diagnosis in Clin. Psychiatry* iii. xiii. 395 Grand mal, petit mal,..or other subgroup forms..such as the narcoleptic, pyknoleptic and so forth—have a special metabolic formula of their nervous system. **1975** S. Arieti *Amer. Handbk. Psychiatry* (ed. 2) IV. xiii. 320/2 The incidence of absence attacks varies from very few, often in the morning, to a great many, up to 100 or more per day ('pyknolepsy').

pyknosis (pɪk'nəʊsɪs). *Cytology.* Also **pycnosis**. [f. Gr. πυκν-ός close, compact + -osis.] The contraction of a dying cell, or of its nuclear material, into a densely staining mass or masses.

1900 Dorland *Med. Dict.* 552/1 *Pyknosis*, a thickening; especially degeneration of a cell in which the proto-plasmic substance becomes more dense and the size of the cell smaller. **1926** *Arch. Neurol. & Psychiatry* XVI. 135 In general there is a progressive shrinking and pyknosis of the nucleus. **1946** [see hyperchromatosis 2]. **1950** A. W. Ham *Histol.* v. 60 The changes that occur in nuclei as, or after, individual cells die in the living body are of three sorts. The commonest one is called pycnosis; this consists of a shrinkage of the nuclear material into a homogeneous hyperchromatic mass. **1972** *Physics Bull.* Mar. 147/1 The biological end points that will be studied include glycogen accumulation, nerve cell pyknosis, nerve cell injury or loss and glial reaction. **1978** *Nature* 25 May 306/2 In minced muscle grafts sarcoplasmic structure was rapidly lost, and most muscle nuclei seemed to undergo pyknosis, fragmentation and lysis.

pyknotic (pɪk'nɒtɪk), *a.* Also **pyc-**. [ad. Gr. πυκνωτικός, f. πυκνόειν to condense.] **1.** Pertaining or relating to condensation: applied to a theory of the formation of matter.

1900 tr. *Haeckel's Riddle Univ.* 222 In fundamental opposition to the theory of vibration, or the kinetic theory of substance, we have the modern 'theory of condensation', or the pyknotic theory of substance. It is most ably established in the suggestive work of J. C. Vogt on The Nature of Electricity and Magnetism on the Basis of a Simplified Conception of Substance (1891). **1904** R. Christie in *Contemp. Rev.* Apr. 504 The pyknotic theory of substance differs from the kinetic theory, we are informed, in so far as the centres of condensation of the primitive ether are endowed with sensation and will.

2. *Cytology.* Displaying pyknosis.

1910 in *Lippincott's New Med. Dict.* 798/1. **1926** *Arch. Neurol. & Psychiatry* XVI. 134 This change..was characterized by pyknotic shrinking of the nuclei and an increase in cytoplasm. **1936** J. Krafka *Textbk. Histol.* i. 3 In old senescent cells a pycnotic nucleus is produced by a condensation of chromatin to the extent that no ground substance shows. **1957** C. P. Swanson *Cytol. & Cytogenetics* ii. 34 The pycnotic state..persists into interphase to form what were formerly called pro-chromosomes. **1974** *Nature* 11 Oct. 509/1 Within 3 h of furosemide administration..single cell necrosis with pyknotic hepatocytes showing eosinophilic degeneration was..occasionally present.

pykois(e, -oys, pykrelle, pykrie, -ry(e, pykulle, -yl, pyl, obs. ff. pickaxe, pickerel, pickery, pickle, pile *sb.*, pill *sb.* and *v.*

py korry (paɪ 'kɒrɪ), *int. N.Z. slang.* [Maori corruption of *by golly*.] = *by golly* s.v. golly *int.*

1938 R. D. Finlayson *Brown Man's Burden* 32 'Py korry, that right!' Wi admitted to himself. **1941** Baker *N.Z. Slang* ix. 71 There is..not much to distinguish the authenticity of an expression like *py korry*! (by God) from one like *rekureihana* (regulation) except that the former is colloquial. **1943** J. A. W. Bennett in *Amer. Speech* XVIII. 94 The Maori treatment of certain English words is conventionally indicated by such spellings as *plurry* and *py korry* for 'bloody' and 'by golly'. **1961** J. Reid *Kiwi Laughs* 12, I have steered clear in this selection of the 'Py korry, Hori' type of alleged Maori humour. **1966** G. W. Turner *Eng. Lang. Austral. & N.Z.* x. 200 Maori English interlarded with *plurry* and sentences like 'Py korry, that the nice baby, eh?' belongs to the language of journalists rather than the language of Maoris.

pykrete ('paɪkriːt). Also **Pykrete**. [f. the name of G. N. *Pyke* (1894–1948), an Englishman involved in Combined Operations (where pykrete was invented) during the war of 1939–45 + conc)rete *a.* and *sb.*] A frozen mixture of ice and wood pulp or sawdust.

1948 *Jrnl. Glaciol.* I. 96 In February 1943 the..outlook was suddenly transformed by the discovery that the inclusion of a small percentage of wood pulp improved the mechanical properties of ice in a spectacular manner. The discovery was made by Mark and Hohenstein, working at the Brooklyn Polytechnic. In view of the similarity to concrete and in honour of the originator of the bergship project, the frozen wood pulp was given the code name of pykrete (Pyke's concrete). *Ibid.* Pykrete..was ductile and could even be machined on a lathe. *Ibid.* 104 As a protection against explosives pykrete is weight for weight as good as concrete. **1960** *New Scientist* 28 Apr. 1081/3 The aircraft carrier project showed that the engineering properties of ice are greatly improved by 'alloying' it with sawdust (to make 'pykrete'). **1966** *Ibid.* 3 Feb. 284/3 Just as the Eskimo had learned to stiffen and toughen ice by freezing moss into it, so Pykrete owed its strength to fibres of cellulose that blocked the spread of cracks.

‖**pyla** ('paɪlə). *Anat.* Pl. **pylæ**. [mod.L., ad. Gr. πύλη a gate.] Each of the openings forming a communication between the cavities of the optic lobes of the brain and the iter.

1890 in *Cent. Dict.* **1897** in *Syd. Soc. Lex.*

pylagore ('pɪləgɔə(r)). *Gr. Antiq.* Also in Gr. form **pylagoras**. [ad. Gr. Πυλαγόρας, f. Πύλαι, Thermopylæ (the older place of assembly of the Pythian Amphictyony) + ἀγορά assembly.] The title of one of the two deputies sent by each constituent tribe to the Amphictyonic Council.

1753 Chambers *Cycl. Supp.*, Pylagore. **1822** T. Mitchell *Aristoph.*, *Com.* II. 76 Every Grecian state..sent to its meetings two deputies, one of whom bore the name of Pylagore, the other the appellation of Hieromnemon. **1835** Thirlwall *Greece* I. x. 380 At Athens three pylagores were annually elected. **1846** Grote *Greece* ii. ii. II. 325 Æschines, himself a Pylagore sent to Delphi by Athens.

‖**pylangium** (paɪlæn'dʒaɪəm). *Anat.* [mod.L., f. Gr. πύλη gate + ἀγγεῖον vessel.] The undivided portion of the arterial trunk next the ventricle in the lower vertebrates.

1875 Huxley in *Encycl. Brit.* I. 763/1 *Pylangium* and *synangium*, together, are the equivalents of that portion of the heart which lies between the ventricle and the anterior wall of the pericardium. **1900** *Nature* 16 Aug. 365/1 Figures of the frog's heart, which, as regards the detailed structure of the pylangium..are wholly unconventional.

Hence **py'langial** *a.*, of or pertaining to the pylangium.

pylar ('paɪlə(r)), *a. Biol. rare.* [f. Gr. πύλη (see pyla) + -ar.] Pertaining to a pyla or pyle.

1890 in *Cent. Dict.*

pylar, -ard, -aster, obs. ff. pillar, pilaster.

pylche, pylcherd, obs. ff. pilch, pilchard.

pylcraft(e, obs. variant of pilcrow.

pyle (paɪl). *Biol. rare.* [ad. Gr. πύλη gate.] A small orifice, a pore; generally used in combination, as in micropyle.

1890 *Cent. Dict.* cites Coues.

pyle, obs. f. peel *sb.*[2], pile, pill, pillow.

pyle-, bef. a vowel **pyl-**, ad. Gr. πύλη gate, orifice, applied to the portal vein; irreg. used as combining form instead of the regular *pylo-*. **pylemphraxis** (paɪlɛm'fræksɪs) [Gr. ἔμφραξις stoppage, obstruction], obstruction of the portal vein (Mayne 1858). **pylephlebitis** (ˌpaɪlɪflɪ'baɪtɪs) [phlebitis], inflammation of the portal vein; hence **pylephle'bitic** *a.* **pylethrombosis** (paɪlɪθrɒm'bəʊsɪs), thrombosis of the portal vein.

1899 *Allbutt's Syst. Med.* VI. 439 *Pylephlebitic abscesses in the liver. **1858** Mayne *Expos. Lex.*, *Pylophlebitis. **1880** R. C. Drysdale in *Med. Temp. Jrnl.* Oct. 8, Cases of pylephlebitis of adhesive type due to alcohol. **1900** Billings *Nat. Med. Dict.*, *Pylethrombosis. **1905** H. D. Rolleston *Dis. Liver* 64 To diagnose pylethrombosis.

pyleol ryal, pennyroyal: see PULIOL.

pyler(e, pylery, obs. ff. PILLAR, PILLORY.

pylet, pylewer, obs. ff. PELLET *sb.*[2], PILLIVER.

pylfer, pylfry, obs. ff. PILFER, PILFERY.

pylgreme, -grime, -grym(e, obs. ff. PILGRIM.

Pylian (ˈpiːlɪən, ˈpaɪ-), *sb.* and *a.* [f. Gr. πύλος, L. *Pylos* Pylos: see -IAN.] **A.** *sb.* A native or inhabitant of the Homeric town of Pylos in the southern Peloponnese, traditionally regarded as the birthplace of Nestor and the name of his dynasty, and usually identified with Messenian Pylos at the northern end of Navarino Bay. Hence, by extension, a native or inhabitant of the territory ruled by Nestor or his dynasty. **B.** *adj.* Of or pertaining to Pylos or its inhabitants.

1611 CHAPMAN *Homer's Iliads* II. 28 The Pylians and their townes. ? **1614** —— tr. *Homer's Odysses* III. 32 Soone they reacht the Pylian throngs and seates, Where Nestor with his sonnes sate. *Ibid.*, When the Pylians saw These strangers come: in thrust did all men draw About their entrie. **1725** POPE in *Homer's Odyssey* I. 142 This was a very solemn sacrifice of the Pylians. **1846** G. GROTE *Hist. Greece* II. I. xviii. 16 The Pylians, together with the great heroic family of Nêleus and his son Nestôr, who preside over them, give place to the Dorian establishment of Messênia, and retire to Athens, where their leader Melanthus becomes king. **1934** A. TOYNBEE *Study of Hist.* I. 403 In the Homeric epic, Pylos is not called 'Minyan' as Orchomenos is, nor are the Pylians called 'Minyae'. *Ibid.*, The Greek inhabitants of..the *ci-devant* Pylian domain. **1965** *Language* XLI. 315 Scribes who use different orthographies may have come from different localities within the Pylian territory.

pylie, pylion, pyliwe, obs. forms of PILY *a.*[2], PILLION, PILLOW.

pyll, pyllar, -er, pyllary, pyllaster, obs. ff. PILE, PILL, PILLAR, PILLER, PILLORY, PILASTER.

pylle, pyllery, obs. ff. PILE, PILL, PILLORY.

†**pylletori, -ory**, obs. forms of PELLITORY.

1562 TURNER *Herbal* II. 107 b, The other new kynde of pylletori. *Ibid.*, Pylletoris is good for the tuth ach.

pyllory(e, pyllow(e, pyllyon, obs. forms of PILLORY, PILLOW, PILLION.

pylon (ˈpaɪlɒn). *Arch.* [a. Gr. πυλών a gateway, f. πύλη gate.] **1. a.** A gateway, a gate-tower; *spec.* in recent use, the monumental gateway to an Egyptian temple, usually formed by two truncated pyramidal towers connected by a lower architectural member containing the gate.

1850 LEITCH tr. *C. O. Müller's Anc. Art* §220 (ed. 2) 217 The principal structures begin with a pylon, that is, pyramidal double towers or wings (Strabo's ptera) which flank the gateway. **1862** FAIRHOLT *Up Nile* (1863) 406 A square panel in the entry of the great pylon records the visit of the French General Desait and his myrmidons in 1799. **1893** BUDGE *Mummy* 33 The names of the places conquered by Thothmes were inscribed..on some of the pylons at Karnak.

transf. **1903** *Daily Chron.* 20 May 4/1 At each end of the bridge [over the Thames at Vauxhall], according to the design, there were two 'pylons'... The Bridges Committee recommended that these pylons should be omitted. **1930** *Morning Post* 9 Aug. 11, 200 men have been employed excavating granite for the facing of the bridge piers and pylons. **1974** *Sci. Amer.* Nov. 145/1 The Bayonne bridge lacks the huge pylons of Sydney Harbor, which contain the thrust visually as well as in Newtonian fact.

fig. **1905** W. SANDAY *Crit. Fourth Gosp.* vi. 185 The pylon of the Fourth Gospel is of course the prologue.

b. *attrib.* and *Comb.*, as ***pylon-shaped*** adj.

1890 RIDER HAGGARD & A. LANG *World's Desire* II. i, There on the pylon brow stood..Hathor's self. **1904** BUDGE *Guide 3rd & 4th Egypt. Rooms Brit. Mus.* 70 Head-rest on a support, with a pylon-shaped opening in it.

2. *Aeronaut.* Also †**pylone** [F. *pylône*]. **a.** A tall structure used to mark out the course round which aeroplanes fly (or, formerly, in launching them); also, by extension, a structure round which cars drive on a race-track.

1909 *Flight* 13 Mar. 143/1 The machine is brought to earth conveniently close to the pylone. **1909** *Westm. Gaz.* 16 Oct. 9/3 After a successful round of the course his aeroplane came to earth near the second pylon on the south side. **1913** A. E. BERRIMAN *Aviation* Pl. facing p. 38 (*caption*) The lower picture illustrates a similar machine banking while turning about one of the pylones at the Hendon Aerodrome. **1970** *Pop. Mechanics* Oct. 106/1, I still had the third and best run to make. A pylon was placed in the centre of the pad. Instructions were to hit the brakes as before and *steer around the pylon*, brakes full on! **1977** *Sci. Amer.* Oct. 74/3 The craft had to take off unassisted from level ground in a wind of 10 miles per hour or less, fly in a figure-eight pattern around two pylons half a mile apart and pass over a 10-foot hurdle at the start and finish.

b. A post on some early aircraft to which wires for supporting or warping the wing were attached; also, in modern aircraft, a pillar that projects from a wing or fuselage to support an engine, rotor, weapon, or the like.

1912 *Aero* Aug. 236/1 The machine bears..a resemblance to a torpedo boat on account of its squat 'funnels', which are ..the..pylons carrying the wing bracing wires. **1919** PIPPARD & PRITCHARD *Aeroplane Structures* xi. 142 The pylon bracing..comes into operation (1) In high speed flight. (2) In landing. *Ibid.*, The vertical components of the loads in the pylon wires AD, CD throw an extra load in the interplane strut BE. **1955** LIPTROT & WOODS *Rotorcraft* iii. 20 The rear-end ring [of the fuselage] carries the pylon on which is mounted the tail rotor. **1959** *Times* 26 Feb. 10/6 On the Boeing 707-120..the engines are mounted separately on pylons beneath the wings. **1969** K. MUNSON *Pioneer Aircraft 1903–14* 106/1 As flown for the first time at Issy on 23 January 1909, it had a 30 h.p. R.E.P. engine.., and a small kite-shaped fin was fixed above the wing-warping pylons. **1979** *Daily Tel.* 29 May 1/4 The airline said it believes the attachments of the engine pylon to the wings of its aircraft are sound.

3. *Surg.* A temporary, unjointed, artificial leg.

1920 *Lancet* 14 Feb. 373/2, I will endeavour to illustrate the most important details in the manufacture of a thigh pylon. **1945** THOMAS & HADDAN *Amputation Prosthesis* ii. 49 It is the opinion of many that the most effective and rapid shrinkage and adaptation of the stump takes place with the use of a pylon or a temporary prosthesis. **1971** P. J. R. NICHOLS *Rehabil. Severely Disabled* II. iii. 107 Many elderly patients fitted with a satisfactory pylon are reluctant to exchange it for a definitive limb, which is heavier and 'more difficult' to use.

4. a. A tall structure erected as a support; *spec.* a lattice-work metal tower for overhead electricity lines.

1923 E. SHANKS *Richest Man* iii. 52 Half a mile up the mountain, a cable, a thin black line, traversed the crystal air, borne up on pylons. **1930** AUDEN *Poems* 67 Pylons fallen or subsiding, trailing dead high-tension wires. **1942** J. LEES-MILNE *Ancestral Voices* (1975) 51 This unconfined, Thames estuary is rather exciting, sprinkled as it is with drifting pylons, factory chimneys and distant gasometers. **1966** J. BETJEMAN *High & Low* 67 Encase your legs in nylons, Bestride your hills with pylons O age without a soul. **1971** *Nature* 12 Nov. 62/3 A commercial application of the hovertrain would operate on pylons spaced up to 150 foot apart and 25 to 30 foot off the ground. **1972** R. ADAMS *Watership Down* xviii. 104 They had heard the unnatural humming of a pylon in the summer air. **1977** *Times* 19 Jan. 14/2 The North-Western Electricity Board were understandably forbidden to string wires on over-head pylons up the valley.

b. Used *attrib.* to designate those poets of the nineteen-thirties (chiefly Auden, Day Lewis, MacNeice, and Spender) who used industrial scenes and imagery as themes of their poetry.

Spender's poem 'The Pylons' was published in 1933.

[**1935** H. A. MASON in *Scrutiny* III. 405 In *Vienna* Spender appears very clumsily dressed in the robes of Eliot (chiefly *Ash Wednesday*) the 'pylon' imagery and possible other borrowed garments.] **1951** H. SERGEANT *Tradition in Making of Mod. Poetry* I. iii. 44 His [*sc.* Wilfrid Gibson's] method of recording factual details of the industrial background to many of his poems furnishes a parallel with that of the 'pylon' school of the thirties. **1957** R. HOGGART *W. H. Auden* 14 His first links were made with others who were to become writers and publicists in what has variously been called the Thirties Group, the Pylon School and the Auden Group. **1958** *Listener* 4 Dec. 924/2 The trouble with most of the 'Pylon Poets'—with the honourable exception of W. H. Auden—is that to them industry was still too much of a new thing. **1961** *Ibid.* 24 Aug. 284/1 After Eliot..there appeared Auden and Spender and the 'pylon' school of the nineteen-thirties. **1973** *Commentary* Dec. 53/2 After the withering of 30's illusions it became fashionable to laugh at 'Pylon' poetry.

5. *U.S.* A small pillar or column, used to accommodate a sign or signal.

1934 *Sun* (Baltimore) 10 Oct. 7/1 A proposal to replace the safety pylons with an overhead signal light, with pedestrians waiting on the sidewalk until ready to board a street car, was made yesterday. **1977** *Washington Post* 24 Mar. D.C. 5 Officials have recommended changes in the station that include an end to total dependence upon station names lettered sideways on upright pylons located along the station platforms, requiring passengers to crane their necks to read them.

pyloric (paɪˈlɒrɪk), *a.* (*sb.*) *Anat.* [f. PYLORUS + -IC.] **A.** *adj.* Of or pertaining to the pylorus.

1807 HOME in *Phil. Trans.* XCVII. 145 Two cavities; one large, which I shall call the cardiac portion, the other small, which I shall call the pyloric. **1851** WOODWARD *Mollusca* (1856) 29 The pyloric orifice is on the posterior dorsal side. **1859** HUXLEY *Oceanic Hydrozoa* 9 A pyloric valve. **1875** HUXLEY & MARTIN *Elem. Biol.* (1883) 131 These unite with a cross-piece, the 'pyloric' ossicle, which arches over the roof of the pyloric division of the stomach. **1900** S. & W. S. FENWICK *Ulcer of Stomach & Duodenum* I. ii. 41 Pyloric stenosis is a frequent result of gastric ulcer. **1970** H. M. SPIRO *Clin. Gastroenterol.* xvi. 272/1 The characteristic physical finding of pyloric stenosis is the succession splash. Shaking the patient's abdomen or grasping the stomach through the abdomen and shaking it will elicit a loud gurgling sound.

B. *sb.* (*pl.*) The pyloric glands.

1885 *Field* 26 Dec. 896/1 When ascending into fresh water with their ova nearly ready for extrusion, their pylorics are loaded with fat.

pyloro- (paɪˈlɔːrəʊ), before a vowel pylor-, stem of Gr. πυλωρός (see next); a formative element in various pathological and surgical terms. **pyloˈrectomy** [ECTOMY], excision of the pylorus. **pyˈloroˌplasty** [see -PLASTY], plastic surgery of the pylorus. ‖**pyˌloroˈscirrhus**, scirrhus of the pylorus. **pyˈlorospasm**, spasm of the pylorus.

1895 MORISON in *Lancet* 16 Feb. (*title*) A successful case of Pyloroplasty. **1898** J. C. HEMMETER *Dis. Stomach* III. ix. 643 (*heading*) Pyloric spasm (pylorospasm, cramp, convulsion, spasm of the pylorus). *Ibid.* 644 Under narcosis the pylorospasm relaxes. **1900** *Brit. Med. Jrnl.* No. 2040 257 Of his last 11 cases..2 were pylorectomies. **1960** JONES & GUMMER *Clin. Gastroenterol.* xix. 564 Pylorospasm, so frequently invoked as a cause of symptoms in peptic ulcer, gall-bladder disease, and chronic appendicitis, has been considered as a possible cause [of hypertrophic pyloric stenosis] but without any convincing evidence in its support.

‖**pylorus** (paɪˈlɔːrəs). *Anat.* [Late L. *pylōrus* the lower orifice of the stomach (Cæl. Aurel. 5th c.), a. Gr. πυλωρός, πυλουρός gatekeeper, porter, f. πύλη gate + οὖρος watcher, warder.] The opening from the stomach into the duodenum, which is guarded by a strong sphincter muscle; also, that part of the stomach where it is situated.

1615 CROOKE *Body of Man* III. v. (1631) 105 The guts are continued with the stomack at the right Orifice called the Pylorus. **1767** GOOCH *Treat. Wounds* I. 394 Its superior orifice, called also the cardiac, is on the left, and the inferior or pylorus, on the right side of this organ. **1808** BARCLAY *Muscular Motions* 543 The pylorus opens into the intestine. **1875** C. C. BLAKE *Zool.* 198 At the pylorus there is an annular membranous valve, near which the gall-duct opens.

b. An analogous part in invertebrates; e.g. the posterior opening of the stomach in insects; also, the valvular structure which separates the gastric from the somatic cavity in the siphonophorous hydrozoans (the *pyloric valve* of Huxley).

1826 KIRBY & SP. *Entomol.* IV. xl. 99 The stomach... At its posterior end it terminates in the pylorus, a fleshy ring or sphincter formed of annular muscular fibres.

pylot, -ott(e, pylote, obs. ff. PILOT, PELLET[1].

pylour, -owre, pylowe, -lu, -lwe, pylt(e, pylwere, pylyol, pylyon, obs. ff. PILLAR, PILLER, PILLOW, PILT, PILLIVER, PULIOL, PILLION.

pym-, pyn- were, for the sake of greater legibility, usually written by ME. scribes instead of *pim-*, *pin-*; for all such forms not found here, see the corresponding words in PIM-, PIN-.

pymander, pymentarie, -ye, pyn, obs. ff. POMANDER, PIGMENTARY, PIN, PINE.

pynacle (Caxton), erron. f. PIACLE, expiation.

pyncheon, pyncon, obs. ff. PINSON[1] and [2].

pynd(e, obs. pa. t. and pple. of PIN *v.*, PINE *v.*; var. of PIND *v. Obs.*, to impound.

pyndare, -er(e, pyndfold(e, obs. ff. PINDER, PINFOLD.

pyne, obs. f. PEEN *v.* (to beat thin), PIN, PINE.

pyneable, obs. f. PINE-APPLE.

†**pyne doublet.** *Sc. Obs.* [First element is obscure; cf. *py-* or *pee-doublet*, PEE *sb.*[1]] Supposed to be the same as JACK *sb.*[2] 1 b, a quilted and sometimes iron-plated doublet or coat of fence.

1713 EARL CROMERTY *Hist. Acc. Conspir. Earl Gowry* 61 Mr Alexander [Ruthven] being almost on his Knees, had his Hand upon His Majesty's Face and Mouth; and his Majesty seeing the Deponent, cry'd, Fy! strike him laigh, because he has a Pyne Doublet upon him. **1849** JAS. GRANT *Kirkaldy of Gr.* iv. 35 A breastplate, a jack or pyne doublet were usual parts of everyday attire.

pyneon, obs. f. PINION.

†ˈ**pynepeny.** *Obs.* [f. (?) PINE *v.* + PENNY; cf. PINCHPENNY.] A niggard.

c **1412** HOCCLEVE *De Reg. Princ.* 4095 Thow pynepeny [*v.r.* pynchepeny], ther ay mot þou slepe!

pyne pig. *Sc.* [First element uncertain (? the same as in prec.); the second is PIG *sb.*[2]] A pot or an earthenware vessel (or sometimes one of tin or other material) for the keeping of money; a savings box. (Cf. *penny-pig* s.v. PENNY *sb.* 12.)

1488 [see PIG *sb.*[2]]. **1825** JAMIESON, *Pyne Pig*, a vessel used for keeping money. **1881** J. LONGMUIR in *Mod. Scot. Poets* II. 45 [Why] keep your Savings' pyne-pig toom o' white or yellow?

pynesse, -ice, obs. ff. PINNACE.

pynn-: see PINN-, PIN-.

pynok, pyno(u)n(e, pyno(u)r, -owr, obs. ff. PINNOCK[1], PENNON, PINION, PINER[1].

pynot, dial. f. PIANNET.

pynote, obs. f. PINE-NUT.

pynsal, pynsell, -il, obs. ff. PENCEL, PENCIL.

pynsen, -son, -soun, var. PINSON[1] and [2] *Obs.*

pynshe, pynsor(e)s, -sours, obs. ff. PINCH, PINCERS.

pynstal, obs. f. *pine-stall* (PINE *sb.*[1] 6).

pyntche, pynt(e, pyntil, -ul, etc., obs. ff. PINCH, PAINT *v.*[1], PINT[1], PINTLE.

pynun, pynyo(u)n, obs. ff. PINION, PENNON.

pyo- (paɪəʊ), before a vowel **py-**, repr. Gr. πυο-, combining form of πύον pus; used to form medical and pathological terms. **pyo'coccal** *a.* [Gr. κόκκος grain], pertaining to the ‖**pyo'coccus**, a microbe or coccus causing suppuration. ‖**pyo'cœlia** [Gr. κοιλία cavity], the presence of pus in the abdominal cavity (Dunglison 1853). **py'octanin(e** [Gr. κτείνειν to kill], name given to methyl violet from its alleged power of checking suppuration. **pyo'cyanine** (also **-in**) [CYANIN], a blue colouring matter, 5-methyl-9-oxo-5, 9-dihydrophenazine, $C_{13}H_{10}N_2O$, obtained from blue or lead-coloured pus; so **pyocy'anic** *a.* **'pyocyst**, an encysted collection of pus, esp. in the lung. **pyo'derma**, pyodermia; **pyo'dermic** *a.* [DERMIC], of or pertaining to ‖**pyo'dermia**, a purulent state of the skin. ‖**pyodi'athesis**, a purulent diathesis. ‖**pyœ'dema** [ŒDEMA], œdema caused by purulent infiltration (Dunglison 1853). **pyo'genesis**, the formation of pus, suppuration; so **pyoge'netic, pyo'genic** *adjs.*, of or pertaining to pyogenesis; producing pus. †**pyo'hæmia**, = PYÆMIA (Dunglison 1842); hence †**pyo'hæmic** *a.* = PYÆMIC (*Syd. Soc. Lex.* 1897). **pyohæmo'thorax**, presence of pus and blood in the pleural cavities. **'pyolymph**, lymph containing pus corpuscles. ‖**pyometra** (-'miːtrə) [Gr. μήτρα womb]: see quot. **pyone'phritis** [NEPHRITIS], suppurative inflammation of the kidney; hence **pyone'phritic** *a.* ‖**pyone'phrosis** [Gr. νεφρός kidney: see -OSIS], the presence of pus in the kidney; hence **pyone'phrotic** *a.* ‖**pyoperi'cardium**, the presence or a collection of pus in the pericardium. ‖**pyoph'thalmia**, production of pus in the eye (Dunglison 1853). ‖**pyopneumoperi'cardium** [PNEUMOPERICARDIUM], the presence of pus together with air or gas in the pericardium. ‖**pyopneumo'thorax** [PNEUMOTHORAX], the presence of pus and air in the pleural cavities; = PNEUMOPYOTHORAX. ‖**py'optysis** [Gr. πτύσις spitting], expectoration of pus (Dunglison 1842). ‖**pyo'rrhœa** [Gr. ῥοία flux], (also, *U.S.*, -rrhea) discharge of pus; also, *spec.* (in full ***pyorrhœa** alveolaris*) a purulent inflammation of the tissues surrounding the teeth that results in shrinkage of the gums and loosening of the teeth. ‖**pyo'salpinx** [Gr. σάλπιγξ a tube], the presence of pus in the Fallopian tube. ‖**pyosepti'cæmia**, pyæmia together with septicæmia; hence **pyosepti'cæmic** *a.* ‖**pyo'thorax** [THORAX], collection of pus in the pleural cavities. **pyo'xanthin, pyo'xanthose** [Gr. ξανθός yellow], a yellow colouring matter found with pyocyanin in blue suppuration.

1896 *Allbutt's Syst. Med.* I. 726 Potent also against the *pyococcal infections. **1897** *Ibid.* III. 715 Due to the *pyococci contained in the sputum they swallow. **1890** *Lancet* 11 Oct. 783/2 [He] has tried *pyoktanin, the new aniline antiseptic, in several cases of suppurative ear disease. **1891** *Standard* 2 Feb. 5/2 Experiments with solutions of methyl violet, also called pyoctanine, a new pigment manufactured at Darmstadt. **1901** W. OSLER *Princ. & Pract. Med.* (ed. 4) 163 The *pyocyanic disease..is an extremely interesting form of infection with bacillus pyocyaneus. **1860** *Chem. News* II. 119/1 M. Fordos has..succeeded in extracting..blue matter to which he gives the name of *pyocyanine. **1866-8** WATTS *Dict. Chem.* IV. 752 Pyocyanin crystallises in needles or in rectangular flakes. **1873** RALFE *Phys. Chem.* 40 A blue colour is often noticed on the dry bandages and linen which have been in contact with pus; this is due to pyo-cyanin. **1947** *Sci. News* V. 90 Many bacteria in presence of certain organic substances, which they activate, reduce a molecule such as pyocyanine to its colourless leuco form. **1949** H. W. FLOREY et al. *Antibiotics* I. xii. 549 Pyocyanine, a substance which is now recognized to be bactericidal and to which pyocyanase probably owes some of its activity... This is the blue pigment to which 'blue pus', characteristic of infection by *Ps[eudomonas] pyocyanea*, owes its name. **1957** G. A. SWAN in Swan & Felton *Phenazines* x. 176 Pyocyanine, the first phenazine compound discovered in nature. **1976** *Ann. Rev. Microbiol.* XXX. 247 The purified enzyme contains FAD, which functions when pyocyanine is the electron donor. [**1853** DUNGLISON *Med. Lex.*, **Pyocystis*, vomica.] **1858** MAYNE *Expos. Lex.*, *Pyocystis*, term for a cyst of pus, especially in the lung; a *vomica*: a pyocyst. **1930** *Arch. Dermatol. & Syphilol.* XXI. 151 The case was presented simply as *pyoderma. **1930** *Ibid.* XXII. 655 The term 'pyoderma' denotes a purulent infection of the skin due to pyogenic organisms, ordinarily staphylococci. **1936** *Ibid.* XXXIII. 811 Pyodermas and ulcerations of the skin have been described under various names. **1974** PASSMORE & ROBSON *Compan. Med. Stud.* III. xix. 102/2 A rare skin lesion which is almost specific for ulcerative colitis and Crohn's disease is pyoderma gangrenosum; intra-epidermal bulla form and contain clear fluid which soon becomes milky and frankly purulent, but is sterile. **1899** *Allbutt's Syst. Med.* VIII. 911 Certain other clinical forms of *pyodermia have received special names. *Ibid.* 918 Impetiginous and other *pyodermic disorders. **1858** MAYNE *Expos. Lex.*, **Pyodiathesis*. **1847** *Todd's Cycl. Anat.* IV. 116 The true doctrine of *Pyogenesis is a modification of that of 'secretion'. **1896** *Allbutt's Syst. Med.* I. 55 *note*, Pyogenesis must not be confounded with inflammation. **1858** MAYNE *Expos. Lex.*, *Pyogeneticus*,..*pyogenetic. **1896** *Allbutt's Syst. Med.* I. 70 The pyogenetic inflammation. **1897** *Ibid.* II. 86 Pyogenetic bacteria are as a rule present in varying numbers. **1839-47** *Todd's Cycl. Anat.* III. 754/2 *note*, The *pyogenic membrane..lines the cavity of an abscess. **1861** *N. Syd. Soc. Year-bk. Med.* 137 On the Pyogenic or Suppurative Diathesis. **1896** *Allbutt's Syst. Med.* I. 73 Conditions of great virulence of the pyogenic microbes. **1890** *Cent. Dict.*, *Pyohemothorax; *Pyolymph. **1893** W. R. GOWERS *Dis. Nerv. Syst.* (ed. 2) II. 333 If a scalpel is passed over the surface, it removes a little pyo-lymph. **1860** TANNER *Pregnancy* iii. 181 The collection..of pus—*pyometra—in the [uterus]. **1876** BRISTOWE *The. & Pract. Med.* (1878) 831 The cholesterine was traced to a *pyonephritic cyst. **1897** *Allbutt's Syst. Med.* IV. 308 Abscess of the kidney, with or without perinephritic abscess, and pyelitis, leading to *pyonephrosis. **1885** W. ROBERTS *Urin. & Renal Dis.* III. v. (ed. 4) 514 Contracted from the pressure of a *pyonephrotic tumour. **1853** DUNGLISON, **Pyopericardia*, a collection of pus in the pericardium. **1898** *Allbutt's Syst. Med.* V. 125 Successful cases of draining the pyo-pericardium have been published. *Ibid.* 776 Pyopericardium is occasionally acute in its manifestations. **1878** tr. *Von Ziemssen's Cycl. Med.* VIII. 124 *Pyopneumopericardium has thus far been observed only a few times. **1898** *Allbutt's Syst. Med.* V. 214 In a few recorded cases a pulmonary cavity has perforated the pericardium and produced pyopneumopericardium. **1894** *Lancet* 3 Nov. 1033 The right side of the chest gave the physical signs of a *pyopneumothorax. **1897** *Allbutt's Syst. Med.* III. 537 Pyopneumothorax or gangrene of the lung. **1811** HOOPER *Dict.*, **Pyorrhœa*, a purulent discharge from the belly. **1875** *Dental Cosmos* XVII. 278 Your correspondent..while not very definite in his descriptions, is sufficiently so to indicate the disease as 'pyorrhoea alveolaris' of the French writers. **1878** tr. *von Ziemssen's Cycl. Med.* VIII. 777 The treatment of chronic pyorrhœa. **1921** *Daily Colonist* (Victoria, B.C.) 25 Mar. 7/6 (Advt.), Be suspicious of any tenderness or bleeding of the gums. This is usually the first stage of Pyorrhea—an insidious disease of the gums that destroys the teeth. **1975** J. SYMONS *Three Pipe Problem* xii. 93 The brick and mortar shaking loose like teeth with pyorrhoea. **1878** tr. *von Ziemssen's Cycl. Med.* X. 345 The accumulation of pus in the tube—*pyosalpinx—may even lead to ulceration of the mucous membrane. **1897** *Allbutt's Syst. Med.* IV. 132 Other symptoms significant of a general *pyosepticæmic infection of the system are present. **1853** MARKHAM *Skoda's Auscult.* 319 Effusions of blood, or pus—Hæmothorax—*Pyothorax—into the pleural cavity. **1876** tr. *von Ziemssen's Cycl. Med.* IV. 611 Purulent pleuritis (pyothorax, empyema). **1873** RALFE *Phys. Chem.* 40 Minute yellow crystals of *pyoxanthin. **1866-8** WATTS *Dict. Chem.* IV. 752 After the separation of the pyocyanin, the chloroform retains in solution a yellow substance called *pyoxanthose.

pyocyanase (paɪəʊ'saɪəneɪz). *Med.* [a. G. *pyocyanase* (Emmerich & Löw 1899, in *Zeitschr. f. Hygiene u. Infektionskrankheiten* XXXI. 10), f. mod.L. *pyocyan-eus* (f. Gr. πύο-ν pus + κυάνεος dark blue), former specific epithet of the source bacterium + *-ase* -ASE.] An antibiotic preparation, orig. thought to be an enzyme, which was obtained from cultures of the bacterium *Pseudomonas aeruginosus* and was formerly used to treat a number of infections, esp. diphtheria.

1900 *Jrnl. Chem. Soc.* LXXVIII. II. 159 Thus pyocyanase, the enzyme of *Bacillus pyocyaneus*, destroys the deadly effect of the diphtheria toxin. **1908** *Lancet* 21 Mar. 899/1 If pyocyanase came in contact with leucocytes, their plasma was dissolved so that the granules and the nuclei only remained and these were..immobilised. **1949** H. W. FLOREY et al. *Antibiotics* I. i. 24 After 1914 the mention of pyocyanase for clinical use almost entirely disappeared from the literature. **1969** *Listener* 5 June 781/1 The experiments of Florey and Chain on pyocyanase..went to show that pyocyanase was a complicated mixture of substances, all equally poisonous to microbes and to mice.

pyoid ('paɪɔɪd), *a.* [ad. Gr. πυοειδής like pus, f. πύ-ον pus: see -OID.] Of the nature of or resembling pus; purulent.

1853 DUNGLISON *Med. Lex.* s.v., Pyoid corpuscles or globules. **1875** H. WALTON *Dis. Eye* 136 The cells are converted into pus, or pyoid cells. **1897** *Allbutt's Syst. Med.* II. 514 Soft, greasy, pyoid material.

pyoine, pyon(e, -onie, etc., obs. ff. PEONY.

pyonar, -eer, -er, -ier, obs. ff. PIONEER.

pyone, obs. f. PEON.

pyoning: see PION *v. Obs.*

‖**pyosis** (paɪ'əʊsɪs). *Path.* [mod.L., a. Gr. πύωσις.] Formation of pus, suppuration.

c **1693** tr. *Blancard's Phys. Dict.* (ed. 2), *Pyosis*, a Collection of Pus in any part of the Body. **1706** in PHILLIPS (ed. 6). **1842** in DUNGLISON. **1897** *Syd. Soc. Lex.*, *Pyosis*, the process of pus-formation.

pyot, pyot(t)y, a magpie: see PIET.

†**pype,** obs. f. PEEP *sb.*[2], *v.*[2], PIP, PIPE.

c **1470** HENRYSON *Mor. Fab.* IX. (*Wolf & Fox*) xxvi, It is ane side of salmond, as it wair, And callour, pypand like ane pertrik ee.

pyp-grass ('paɪp,grɑːs, -æ-). [app. f. Du. *pijp*, formerly *pyp* pipe + GRASS.] A tall-growing South African species of grass, *Ehrharta gigantea*.

1854 P. L. SIMMONDS in *Pharmac. Jrnl.* XIII. 421 Something must be sown with the berry [of the Myrica] to screen its shoot... Pyp grass seed should..be prepared for the purpose. **1880** *S. Africa* (Silver & Co.), Of indigenous grasses which may be usefully employed to arrest drifting sands none are better than the Pyp grass.

pypkin, obs. form of PIPKIN.

pypoudre, pypowder, etc., var. PIEPOWDER.

pyppe, obs. f. PIP, PIPE.

pyppen, pypyn(e, obs. ff. PIPPIN.

pypple, obs. f. PEBBLE, PIPPLE.

pypryge, obs. f. PIPPERIDGE.

pyquoys, obs. f. PICKAXE.

pyr, variant of PURR *int.* (call to pigs).

pyracanth ('paɪərəkænθ), ‖**pyracantha** (paɪərə'kænθə). Also 8 **pyracanthe, piracanthy,** 9 **pyracanthus.** [ad. L. *pyracantha*, a. Gr. πυράκανθα, name of an unidentified shrub or plant, casually mentioned (but not described) by Dioscorides (I. xviii); applied by 16th c. botanists to the shrub here noted, and adopted by Linnæus as its specific name. See Note below.]

An evergreen thorny shrub, *Cratægus Pyracantha*, a native of southern Europe, bearing clusters of white flowers and scarlet berries; in England often trained against walls as an ornamental shrub; also called Christ's, Egyptian, or Evergreen Thorn.

1664 EVELYN *Sylva* xx. ¶9 Some Pyracanths which I have removed to a Northern dripping shade. **1705** tr. *Cowley's Plants* Wks. 1711 III. 458 Phyllyrea here and Pyracantha rise, Whose Beauty only gratifies the Eyes. **1775** R. GOUGH in Nichols *Lit. Anecd. 18th C.* (1814) VIII. 614, I can talk only of..Pyracanthas and Syringas. **1855** MRS. GASKELL *North & S.* vi, The long low parsonage house half-covered with China-roses and pyracanthus. **1878** T. HARDY *Return Native* II. v, A huge pyracanth now darkened the greater portion [of a house-front].

b. *attrib.* and *Comb.*, as ***pyracantha seed***; ***pyracantha-leaved*** adj.; **pyracanth-medlar**, the pyracanth (reckoned as a species of *Mespilus*).

1825 *Greenhouse Comp.* II. 83 *Celastrus Pyracanthus*, pyracantha-leaved Staff-tree, a low tree also from the Cape. **1834** MARY HOWITT *Sk. Nat. Hist.*, *Old-fashioned Winter* 66 And the finches in their need Picked the pyracantha seed. **1842** J. B. FRASER *Mesopot. & Assyria* xv. 353 On the flanks of forests..there appear..*Mespilus Pyracantha*... Pyracanth medlar [etc.].

Hence **pyra'canthine** *a.* [-INE[1]], of or belonging to the pyracanth.

1880 BLACKMORE *Mary Anerley* III. 255 Lips as red as pyracanthine berries.

[*Note.* The numerous Latin versions of Dioscorides left πυράκανθα unidentified, and merely latinized as *pyracantha*. According to Lobel *Adversaria* 438 (1576), this was derived from L. *pyrus* pear + Gr. ἄκανθα thorn, from the resemblance of the leaves to those of the wild pear ('arbusta cui facies et folium Pyrastri..propter foliorum similitudinem nonnulli Pyracantham vocant'). But this hybrid origin was, of course, impossible for the Greek word, and the name has been commonly taken as meaning 'fire-thorn', f. πῦρ fire + ἄκανθα thorn, and considered to be appropriate to the modern pyracanth, from its profusion of scarlet or flame-coloured berries. For the identity of this with the πυράκανθα of Dioscorides there is no other evidence.]

pyracid, variant form of PYRO-ACID.

pyracie, -acy(e, obsolete forms of PIRACY.

pyrage, obs. erron. form of PIROGUE.

pyral ('paɪərəl), *a. rare.* [f. L. *pyra* PYRE + -AL[1].] Of or pertaining to a pyre.

1658 SIR T. BROWNE *Hydriot.* iv. 57 After the pyrall combustion. *Ibid.* 61 More inflammable, and unctuously constituted for the better pyrall combustion. **1888** *Science* XII. 40 In connection with each house..was what the explorer calls a pyral mound. On this the bodies and effects of the dead were consigned to fire.

‖**pyralis** ('pɪrəlɪs). Pl. **pyralides** (pɪ'rælɪdiːz). Also (in sense 1) in anglicized form (from Fr.) **pyralide.** [ad. Gr. πυραλίς a winged insect supposed to live in fire, f. πῦρ fire; also a. obs. F. *pyralide* 'a fire-fly or worme bred in the fire' (Cotgr.).]

†**1.** A fabulous fly supposed to live in or be generated by fire. *Obs.*

1588 GREENE *Planetom. Venus Trag.* Wks. (Grosart) V. 60 As the flie Pyralis cannot liue out of the flame. *a* **1600** MONTGOMERIE *Misc. Poems* xvii. 41 His pain wes lyk the pyralide, A beist in birning that does breid. **1684** *Contempl. State Man* II. vii. (1699) 212 Place us in the Light and Bright One [i.e. flame] of thy Love; where like Pyralides and sacred Salamanders we shall live happy without Pain or Torment.

2. *Entom.* [mod.L., Schrank 1801.] A genus of moths typical of the family *Pyralidæ*. So **'pyralid**, *a.* resembling or belonging to the

Pyralidæ; *sb*. a moth of this family; **pyra'lideous** *a*. = PYRALID *a*.; **py'ralidiform** *a*., resembling the *Pyralidæ* in form or structure; **py'ralidine** *a*. = PYRALID *a*.

1859 STAINTON *Man. Brit. Butterfl. & Moths* II. 124 The Pyralidina are divided into two main groups:—1. The Pyralideous group. 2. The Crambideous group. The Pyralideous group is further divided into two main sections: 1. The Deltoides. 2. The Pyralites. **1903** *Westm. Gaz.* 9 Oct. 12/2 In some of the vineyards .. in France .. great havoc has been wrought by the pyralis.

pyrallolite: see PYRO- 2.

†**'pyrame**. *Obs. rare*. Also 4–5 **piram, -e**, 7 **piramee**. [Shortened from L. *pȳramis* PYRAMID, perh. by taking *piramis*, *pirames* as a pl.]

1. Applied by Trevisa to the cone or pencil of rays entering the eye from any object; see PYRAMID *sb*. 2.

1398 TREVISA *Barth. De P.R.* III. xvii. (Harl. MS.) lf. 14 b/2 [Al þe lynes þat ben y-drawe from alle þe partyes of þe þing þat is i-seon, he makeþ a piramis [L. *faciunt piramidem*] in schape as a top [*Tollemache MS.* trompe], & þe poynt þerof is in þe blak of þe eyȝe]. *Ibid.* 15/1 þerfor nedes yt nedeþ to have a piram [*ed.* 1495 pyrame] a schelde oþer a toppe of liȝt, & al þe piramis þo poyntes be in þe eyȝen & þe brode endes in þe þinges þat ben i-seyen. *Ibid.* (Add. MS.), Whanne þe liknes of þe þing comeþ to þe siȝt upon þese pirames [*ed.* 1495 piramis], þenne þe liknes of liȝt & colour passiþ by þe smale curtiles & humoures of þe eiȝe.

2. A pyramid, spire, or steeple: see PYRAMID 3.

1604 HIERON *Papists Rime Answ.* Wks. 1620 I. 574 Well may the heathen people boast Of piramees & churches cost.

†**py'ramical**, *a*. *Obs*. [irreg. f. L. *pȳramis*, a. Gr. πυραμίς PYRAMID + -ICAL. The etymological form is PYRAMIDICAL.] = PYRAMIDAL *a*.

1633 P. FLETCHER *Purple Isl.* IV. xvii, That Great All, This His work's glory, made pyramicall. **1656** W. COLES *Art of Simpling* 167 Of a pyramical Figure, and not unlike to a Pine Apple.

pyramid ('pɪrəmɪd), *sb*. Forms: see below. [Originally in form *'pir-*, *'pyramis*, pl. *pir-*, *py'ramides* (pɪ'ræmɪdiːz), later *py'ramids*, a. L. *pȳramis* (med.L. also *pīramis*), pl. *pȳramidēs*, a. Gr. πυραμίς, pl. πυραμίδες (perh. of Egyptian origin, but anciently explained by some as a deriv. of πῦρ, πυρ- fire, by others as f. πυρός wheat, grain, as if a granary). The later form *'pyr-*, *'piramide*, *'pyramid* was app. after F. *pyramide* (in 12th c. *piramide*, Hatz.-Darm.). The pl. *pyramisis*, *pyramidies*, and sing. *pyr-*, *pyramidis*, *-es*, were popular or illiterate analogical formations.]

A. Illustration of Forms.

α. 4–7 **'piramis**, 6–8 **'pyramis**; *pl*. (4 syll.) 6–7 **pi'ramides, py'ramides**; (7 **py'ramidis, py'ramisis**, 8 **pi'ramidies**); also (3 syll.) 6–7 **py'ramides** (*e* mute), **py'ramids**.

The 3-syll. plurals *py'ramides* (*e* mute), *py'ramids*, retained the stress of *py'rami-des*; but it is only in verse that they can be distinguished from the 3-syll. *'pyra-mides*, *'pyra-mids*, with stress on first syllable, in *β*.

1398 Piramis [see PYRAME 1]. **1555**, **1586** Pyramides, piramides [see B. 1]. **1570**, **1651** Pyramis [see B. 2, 4]. **1589** PUTTENHAM *Eng. Poesie* II. xi. (Arb.) 105 The Spire or taper, called piramis. **1606** SHAKS. *Ant. & Cl.* II. vii. 40 *Lepidus*, I haue heard the Ptolomies Pyramisis are very goodly things. *Ibid.* v. ii. 61 Rather make My Countries high pyramides my Gibbet. **1619** *Pasquil's Palin.* xxxviii, To cast your tall Piramides to ground. **1662** GERBIER *Princ.* 30 His Figures and Statues Colosses, his Pyramidis like those of Ægypt. *c* **1710** CELIA FIENNES *Diary* (1888) 78 Two piramidies full of pipes spouting water. **1716** HEARNE *Collect.* V. 256 The Church hath a Pyramis or Spire.

1591 SPENSER *Ruins Rome* ii, Greece will the olde Ephesian buildings blaze, And Nylus nurslings their Pyramides faire. **1595** —— *Sonn.* iii, Their huge Pyramids, which do heauen threat. **1611** BEAUM. & FL. *Philaster* v. iii, Make it rich .. Like the Pyramides: lay on epitaphs.

β. 6–7 **pyramide, piramide**, 7 **piramid**, 7– **pyramid**; *pl*. 7 **'pir-, 'pyramides, 'piramids, 'pyramyds**, 7– **'pyramids**.

1597 A. M. tr. *Guillemeau's Fr. Chirurg.* p. xv. b/1 The Pyramide which passeth cleane through the Trepane. *Ibid.* 7 b/1 The poynt a piramide of a Trepane. **1605** SHAKS. *Macb.* IV. i. 57 (1623) Though Pallaces, and Pyramids do slope Their heads to their Foundations. **1606** —— *Ant. & Cl.* II. vii. 21 They take the flow o'th'Nyle By certaine scales i'th'Pyramid. **1632** W. LYNNESAY in Lithgow *Trav.* B iij, Memphis, in parch'd Ægypts soyle: Flank'd with old Piramides, and melting Nyle. **1638–56** COWLEY *Davideis* I. 752 Numbers which still encrease more high and wide From One, the root of their turn'd Pyramide. *a* **1649** DRUMM. OF HAWTH. *Poems* Wks. (1711) 10 My heart a living pyramide I raise. **1649** G. DANIEL *Trinarch., Hen. IV* cccxxxvi, Th' intent Stood, a true Piramid, in Government. **1667** MILTON *P.L.* II. 1013 Satan .. Springs upward like a Pyramid of fire, Into the wilde Expanse. **1823** BYRON *Juan* VIII. cxxxvii, Guessing at what shall happily be hid As the real purpose of a pyramid.

γ. *sing*. 6–7 **piramidis**, 7 **pyr-, piramides**; *pl*. 6 **piramidesses**.

1595 in *Rep. Hist. MSS. Comm., Var. Coll.* III. Introd. 38 The free mazons finishing .. four of the topstones for the piramidesses. *Ibid.*, The base and spire of a piramidis. **1600** W. WATSON *Decacordon* Pref. (1602) A ij b, He also was cast off from the highest Pyramides of fortunes wheele. **1603** KNOLLES *Hist. Turks* (1621) 306 A certaine tower built like a piramidis. **1642** VICARS *God in Mount* (title-p.), A Panegyrick Piramides, erected to the everlasting high honour of England's God.

B. Signification.

1. A monumental structure built of stone or the like, with a polygonal (usually square) base, and sloping sides meeting at an apex; *orig*. and *esp*. one of the ancient structures of this kind in Egypt. Also ***Great Pyramid***, the pyramid of the fourth-dynasty pharaoh Cheops at Giza; freq. used (usu. *attrib*.) with reference to its supposed mystical powers. (***Great***) ***Pyramid prophecy***, the prediction of events of worldwide importance, based on a belief in the occult significance of the internal measurements of the Great Pyramid; pyramidology.

1555 EDEN *Decades* Pref. (Arb.) 49 The hugious heapes of stones of the Pyramides of Egypt. **1586** T. FORSTER *Pilgr. Mecca* in Hakluyt *Voy.* (1599) II. I. 201 Without the Citie, sixe miles higher into the land, are to be seene neere vnto the riuer diuerse Piramides, among which are three marueilous great, and very artificially wrought. **1611** BEAUM. & FL. *Philaster* IV. iv, Place me, some god, upon a Piramis, Higher than hills of earth. **1615** G. SANDYS *Trav.* 129 Cheops, a King of Ægypt, & the builder of this *pyramis*. **1711** ADDISON *Spect.* No. 1 ¶4, I made a Voyage to Grand Cairo, on purpose to take the Measure of a Pyramid. **1802** E. A. KENDAL tr. *Denon's Trav. in Upper & Lower Egypt* I. 102 Herodotus relates that he was informed the great pyramid was the tomb of Chæops. **1813** SHELLEY *Q. Mab* II. 129 Nile shall pursue his changeless way: Those pyramids shall fall. **1816** BYRON *Ch. Har.* III. lvi, By Coblentz .. There is a small and simple pyramid; .. Beneath its base are heroes' ashes hid. **1842** GWILT *Archit.* (1876) 48 The great pyramid of Cholula, the largest and most sacred temple in Mexico. **1843** PRESCOTT *Mexico* IV. vii. (1864) 253 [A Mexican *teocalli*] A stone building on the usual pyramidal basis; and the ascent was by a flight of steep steps on one of the faces of the pyramid. **1859** J. TAYLOR *Great Pyramid* p. vi, I have confined my observations to the Great Pyramid alone. **1877** A. B. EDWARDS *Up Nile* i. 19 The Great Pyramid .. towers close above one's head. **1937** E. GILL *Let.* 7 July (1947) 389, I did go and see the great Pyramid! and went up & into its middle! Nought but exclamation marks will convey to you its amazing & marvellous mad grandeur! **1948** A. CHRISTIE *Taken at Flood* I. iv. 36 Did you read the book on the Pyramid prophecies I sent you? .. Really explains everything. **1958** L. DURRELL *Balthazar* vi. 150 It gave me the respite I needed to have a go at his heart. It was silent as the Great Pyramid. **1960** M. BOUISSON *Magic* 288 The case of the Great Pyramid prophecy for the date of 20 August 1953 seems to us .. inexplicable. **1961** E. WAUGH *Unconditional Surrender* II. v. 145 His objections .. were .. occult, being in someway based on the dimensions of the Great Pyramid. **1972** *Guardian* 5 Oct. 17/6 Innumerable errors of the Shakespeare cypher and Great Pyramid Prophecy variety. **1976** *Listener* 19 Feb. 199/1 Books on ESP, UFOs, the mystic powers of the Great Pyramid .. are .. strong runners in the publishing stakes.

2. a. The form of a pyramid; in *Geom.* a solid figure bounded by plane surfaces, of which one (the base) is a polygon of any number of sides, and the other surfaces triangles having as bases the sides of the polygon, and meeting at a point (the vertex) outside the plane of the polygon.

Formerly sometimes extended to include the CONE, which differs in having a circular (or other curved) base, and a continuous curved surface between the base and the apex.

1398 Piramis [see PYRAME 1]. **1570** BILLINGSLEY *Euclid* II. def. x. 314 A Pyramis is a solide figure contained vnder many playne superficieces set vpon one playne superficies, and gathered together to one point. **1603** HOLLAND *Plutarch's Mor.* 1322 The shadow of the earth being round, groweth point-wise or sharp at the end, in maner of a cone or pyramis. **1620–55** I. JONES *Stone-Heng* (1725) 70 That Fire hath the Form of a Pyramis is evident. **1672** TEMPLE *Ess. Govt.* Wks. 1731 I. 105 The Rules of Architecture, .. teach us that the Pyramid is of all Figures the firmest. **1795** HUTTON *Dict. Math.* s.v., A cone is a round Pyramid, or one having an infinite number of sides... The *axis* of the Pyramid, is the line drawn from the vertex to the centre of the base. When this axis is perpendicular to the base, the Pyramid is said to be a *right* one; otherwise it is *oblique*. **1875** BENNETT & DYER *Sachs' Bot.* 367 The apical cell has .. the form of an inverted triangular pyramid.

†**b.** Erroneously used for the vertex or point of a pyramid or similar figure. (Cf. CONE *sb*.[1] 15.)

1649 JER. TAYLOR *Gt. Exemp.* I. ii. §21 A great Body of Light transmitting his rayes through a narrow hollownesse does by that small Pyramis represent all the parts of the magnitude. *Ibid.* v. §6 The rayes of light passing through the thin air, end in a small and undiscerned pyramis.

†**3.** *Arch.* Any structure of pyramidal form, as a spire, pinnacle, obelisk, etc. Also applied to a gable. (Cf. PEDIMENT 1.) *Obs.* exc. as in 1.

[*c* **1440** *Promp. Parv.* 397 Pykewalle (or gabyl), *Murus Conalis, piramis, vel piramidalis*.]

a **1552** LELAND *Itin.* (1710) I. 77 Ther be 3 great old Toures with pyramides on them. **1595** [see A. *γ*]. **1600** HOLLAND *Livy, Martianus' Topogr. Rome* VIII. xi. 1401 There stood a Pyramis or steeple in times past, under which they say P. Scipio Africanus lay enterred. **1610** —— *Camden's Brit.* (1637) 585 [Lichfield Cathedral Church] doth mount on high with three pyramids or spires of stone. **1625** T. BROWNE in Darcie *Ann. Q. Eliz.* I. 82 A most rare Piramide of the Cathedrall Church of Saint Paul, in London, was strucken .. with fire from heaven. **1630** MILTON *On Shakespear* 4 What needs my Shakespear .. that his hallow'd reliques should be hid Under a Star-ypointing Pyramid? **1632** in E. P. Jupp *Carpenters' Co.* (1887) 302 The Carpenters .. have allwaies vsed to have the Cutting of .. ballesters, hauces, tafferrells, pendants and piramides. **1634** in Willis & Clark *Cambridge* (1886) II. 699 The piramides upon the little gable ends. **1687** A. LOVELL tr. *Thevenot's Trav.* II. 60, I could observe .. a square Minaret that spires into a Pyramid. *c* **1710**, **1716** [see A. *α*].

4. a. Any material thing or object of pyramidal form; a number of things arranged or heaped up in this form, a pyramidal pile.

1570 DEE *Mathemat. Preface* 29 Make of Copper plates, .. a foursquare vpright Pyramis, or a Cone. **1597** [see A. *β*]. **1634** SIR T. HERBERT *Trav.* 4 The top of this Peake or Pyramide [Teneriffe] .. seldome without Snow. **1651** STANLEY *Poems* 77 Or when one flame twined with another is They both ascend in one bright pyramis. **1727** SWIFT *Gulliver, Pref. Let.* §3 Smithfield blazing with pyramids of law-books. **1756–7** tr. *Keysler's Trav.* (1760) I. 425 On each side of the altar, stands a pyramid of bones. **1831** BREWSTER *Nat. Magic* x. (1833) 257 Among the remarkable exhibitions of mechanical strength and dexterity, we may enumerate that of supporting pyramids of men. **1886** C. E. PASCOE *London of To-day* xvi. (ed. 3) 137 Horse-chestnuts with massive pyramids of white blossom.

b. *Gardening.* Applied (orig. *attrib*., hence also *simply*) to a tree, esp. a fruit-tree, trained in a pyramidal form. So ***pyramid-trained*** adj., ***-training***.

[**1646** EVELYN *Diary* Apr.–June, At the entrance of this garden growes the goodliest cypresse I fancy in Europ, cut in pyramid.] **1712** BYROM *Jrnl. & Lit. Rem.* (1854) I. I. 17 The pyramid yew trees are set in the nursery. **1882** *Garden* 14 Jan. 19/3 Long lines of pyramid Apples and Pears. **1887** NICHOLSON *Dict. Gard.* III. 47/1 Pyramid training is largely practised with Pear-trees... Pyramids may be procured worked either on the Pear stock or on the Quince. **1890** *Farmer's Gaz.* 4 Jan. 7/1 A pyramid trained tree consists essentially of an upright stem, and as many side branches as can be .. trained without overcrowding.

5. *fig.* or *allusively* (from prec. senses).

1593 DRAYTON *Past.* IV. vi, He that to worlds pyramides will build On those great heroes .. Should have a pen. **1600** [see A. *γ*]. *a* **1628** F. GREVILLE *Sidney* (1652) 129 An unsteddy and sharp pointed Pyramis of power. **1670** COTTON *Espernon* II. VII. 313 The most glorious Act of his life, .. which .. ought to be plac'd on the highest Pyramis of his Fame. **1826** DISRAELI *Viv. Grey* II. i, The apex of the pyramid of his ambition was at length visible. **1882** FARRAR *Early Chr.* II. 488 To me the whole theory looks like an inverted pyramid of inference tottering about upon its extremely narrow apex.

b. *Finance.* A structure of financial control achieved by a small initial investment; *spec.* in *Stock Exchange*, (*a*) a series of increases in stock acquired from the increased value of stocks already held; (*b*) a system by which a controlling interest in a holding company leads to control of a series of companies and their subsidiaries. orig. *U.S.*

1911 in WEBSTER. **1932** *New Yorker* 14 May 22/1 The bankers who were setting up the biggest financial pyramids of yesterday are replaced by other steel-nerved bankers today. **1971** *Financial Mail* (Johannesburg) 26 Feb. 701/1 A further development came in 1969 when, at the height of the boom, an investment pyramid, Bivec, was floated. It had a 50 per cent interest in BBH and also controlled the properties of both Berzack and Illman. *Ibid.* 703/3 For the cautious investor seeking soundness, the yields are tempting, with the pyramid the more attractive and accessible share.

c. *U.S.* A form of lottery in which each participant recruits two or more further participants. Also *attrib.*

1949 *Washington Post* 22 Mar. 1/6 All night long people would call me up to ask how the pyramids work. *Ibid.* 11/1 He personally believes pyramid clubs are illegal and violate the State lottery laws. **1955** *Britannica Bk. of Year* 489/2 The gullibility of some members of the public gave notoriety to the *Pyramid-Party*, a new version of the old chain-letter game, in which the individual, by paying an initial subscription and by recruiting two new members for the scheme, hoped eventually to reach the top of the 'pyramid', a position which would (theoretically) involve a considerable monetary profit.

d. *attrib.* Used to designate: (*a*) a system of profit involving extensive subcontracting of work; (*b*) a sales market in which each buyer secures the participation of further buyers. See also sense 10 below.

1964 *Daily Tel.* 1 Apr. 24/5 Douglas sub-contracted the work to another firm, made only a plastic cover itself and then charged on the basis of the total cost. The Senate report .. was on public hearings in 1962 into 'pyramid' profits of this type. **1970** *Toronto Daily Star* 24 Sept. 12/1 Pyramid sales is a system whereby goods are sold, often at an inflated price, but a reduction in price is offered to purchasers who supply the names of others who buy the product. **1972** *Observer* 5 Nov. 13/2 Pyramid distributors .. can and may make more money by recruiting other people to sell products. **1973** *Daily Tel.* 1 Feb. 3 Scotland Yard detectives have obtained a warrant for the arrest of .. an American businessman who controls Koscot Interplanetary (U.K.), a pyramid firm selling cosmetics.

6. *Cryst.* A set of faces belonging to a single crystallographic form and, if symmetrically developed, meeting in a point; also, a form consisting of two such sets of faces on opposite sides of a common base.

1748 SIR J. HILL *Fossils* 154 Crystal .. consisting .. of eighteen sides, dispos'd in order of an hexangular column, terminated by an hexangular pyramid at each end. **1800** tr. *Lagrange's Chem.* I. 190 A salt, under the form of a solid with eighteen sides, terminated at each extremity by a pyramid of six faces. **1836–41** BRANDE *Chem.* (ed. 5) 663 Large right rectangular prisms, terminated by a four-sided pyramid. **1878** GURNEY *Crystallogr.* 51 A group of triangular faces meeting in one point is called a pyramid. **1895** STORY-MASKELYNE *Crystallogr.* §201 The terms proto- and deutero-pyramid have been applied by various writers somewhat ambiguously to the diplo-pyramidal figures, or, in crystallographic language, pyramids, which have been here termed isosceles octahedra.

7. *Anat.* Applied to various parts or structures of more or less pyramidal form; *spec.* (*a*) a mass of longitudinal nerve-fibres on each side of the medulla oblongata (some of which cross from one side to the other in the ***decussation of the pyramids***); (*b*) each of the conical-shaped masses (distinctively called MALPIGHIAN *pyramids*) constituting the medullary substance of the kidney, projecting, and opening at the apices by papillæ, into the pelvis of the kidney; (*c*) see quot. 1842.

1805 *Med. Jrnl.* XIV. 329 The most important..pair of nerves is what was hitherto called the pyramids, this fascicle of nerves is the origin of the cerebrum, or the *hemispherii cerebri.* **1842** DUNGLISON *Med. Dict.*, *Pyramid*, a small, bony projection in the cavity of the tympanum, which is excavated to lodge the muscle of the stapes. **1869** HUXLEY *Phys.* v. (ed. 3) 124 Into this [*pelvis* of the kidney], sundry conical elevations, called the *Pyramids*, project; their summits present multitudes of minute openings—the final terminations of the *tubuli. Ibid.* xi. 303 At the lower and front part of the medulla oblongata, these [efferent impulses]..cross over; and the white fibres which convey them are seen passing obliquely from left to right and from right to left in what is called the *decussation of the anterior pyramids.* **1881** BEHNKE *Mechanism Hum. Voice* (ed. 2) 36 The remaining two cartilages [of the larynx]..are the Pyramids, so called because of their shape. **1890** BILLINGS *Nat. Med. Dict.* s.v., *P*[*yramid*] *of cerebellum*, lobule of inferior surface of vermis of cerebellum... *P-s. of Ferrein... P. of thyroid gland... P. of tympanum*, a small bony eminence in the tympanum, behind the fenestra ovalis, enclosing the stapedius muscle. **1899** *Allbutt's Syst. Med.* VII. 355 Paralysis of the limbs and tongue.., due to softening in the left olive and pyramid.

8. a. *loosely.* A plane figure suggesting the profile of a pyramid; a triangular or cuneiform figure or formation, as a wedge-shaped body of men; a poem the successive lines of which increase or decrease in length; etc. *spec.* Formations of men or pieces in sports and games. (Cf. the sense 'gable' in 3.)

1589 PUTTENHAM *Eng. Poesie* II. xi. (Arb.) 108 Of the Spire or Taper called Pyramis... In metrifying his base can not well be larger then a meetre of six,..neare the toppe [of the Pyramis] there wilbe roome litle inough for a meetre of two sillables, and sometimes of one to finish the point. ?**1650** *Don Bellianis* 194 The Emperor gathering his men in form of Pyramids. **1658** SIR T. BROWNE *Gard. Cyrus* ii. 10 In Chesse-boards and Tables we yet finde Pyramids and Squares. *a* **1680** BUTLER *Rem.* (1759) II. 120 As for Altars and Pyramids in Poetry, he [Benlows] has out-done all Men that Way; for he has made a Gridiron, and a Frying-Pan in Verse. **1869** TOZER *Highl. Turkey* I. 104 When the sun rose, the shadow of the peak was projected over sea and land..in a distinctly marked pyramid. **1899** A. H. QUINN *Pennsylvania Stories* 25 It was Penn's ball. The pyramid started with the cheers of ten thousand back of it. **1948** C. DAY LEWIS *Otterbury Incident* iv. 39 Peter..who is super at gym.,..began a routine of tumbling, pyramids, etc. **1969** R. C. BELL *Board & Table Games* II. iii. 58 (*caption*) Initial position of pieces in 'Pyramid'. **1973** *Guardian* 28 Mar. 15/2 There was nothing new about one line [bingo] games or games such as the 'pyramid' and the 'sandwich'.

b. *Billiards. pl.* A game played (usually) with fifteen coloured balls arranged in a triangle, and one cue-ball: see quot. 1850, and *pyramid-spot*.

1850 *Bohn's Handbk. Games* 554 Pyramid.—This game.. can be played with any number of balls,..but the usual number is sixteen, viz. fifteen coloured, and one white... The fifteen coloured balls are placed on the table in the form of a triangle: the first, or point, being on the winning spot. **1864** *Daily Tel.* 1 June, I had played at pyramids by myself in the deserted billiard-room of the hotel.

†**9.** *pl.* (in form *piramides*). Name of some textile fabric: see quot. *c* 1605. *Obs.*

c **1605** *Allegations of Worsted Weavers* (B.M. Add. MS. 12504 art. 64), This Cloath [a Say] hath continewed his name and fashion till this day; but now lately by putting the same into coullours and twistering one thridd of one coullour with another of another coullour, beinge made narrowe, yt is now called Piramides. **1640** in Entick *London* (1766) II. 178 Piramides or Maramuffe, the piece, narrow.

10. *attrib.* and *Comb.*, as ***pyramid-builder***, ***-building*** (also *fig.*); ***-fashion***; ***pyramid-like***, ***-shaped***, adjs.; (*spec.* with ref. to the supposed mystical powers of pyramids: cf. sense 1 above) ***pyramid energy***, ***freak***, ***power***; **pyramid-rest** (*Billiards*), a cue-rest the head of which is arched so as to allow it to be placed over a ball which would otherwise be in the way; **pyramid-selling** *vbl. sb.*, the selling of goods by a pyramid system (see sense 5 d (*b*) above); also ***pyramid-sell*** vb. trans.; **pyramid-shell**, a gastropod shell of the family *Pyramidellidæ*; **pyramid-spot**, the spot on a billiard table where the apex of the pyramid is placed, between the centre and the top spot; **pyramid-text**, any ancient Egyptian text found in the Pyramids; **pyramid-wise** *adv.*, in the manner or form of a pyramid, pyramidally. (See also 4 b.)

1877 W. R. COOPER *Egypt. Obelisks* iii. (1878) 13 Deified *pyramid builders of the Vth dynasty. **1961** L. MUMFORD *City in Hist.* v. 152 All this..was *pyramid-building, both in the Egyptian and later Keynesian sense of the words. **1973** C. SAGAN *Cosmic Connection* ix. 67 Harold Urey has perceptively referred to the space program as a kind of contemporary pyramid-building. **1976** *National Observer* (U.S.) 30 Oct. 17/1 (Advt.), Discover *pyramid energy... Send $7.50..for this 3" × 5" Pyramid Energy Generator. **1613** PURCHAS *Pilgrimage* VIII. xii. 670 A mount of earth and stone fiftie fadome long every way, built *Pyramide-fashion. **1977** *Undercurrents* June–July 19/3 The Book of Revelation has remained a happy hunting ground for Jehovah's Witnesses, UFO and *Pyramid freaks, and amateur apocalyptics of all denominations. **1838** *Lett. fr. Madras* (1843) 133 This gateway is the *pyramid-like building that one sees outside. *a* **1618** SYLVESTER *Wood-mans Bear* xliv, Like a pale *Pyramid pillar. **1976** *Globe & Mail* (Toronto) 24 Apr. 1/1 A book entitled Psychic Discoveries Behind the Iron Curtain says that Russia has been into *pyramid power for a long time. *Ibid.* 1/2 Mrs Kelly isn't prepared to say whether it was pyramid power or whether the pyramid created a psychological effect that led to Casey's release from headaches. **1821** BYRON *Sardan.* v. i. 65 Regal halls of *pyramid proportions. **1873** BENNETT & 'CAVENDISH' *Billiards* 28 The *pyramid or spider-rest is cut out at the bottom. **1975** D. BLOODWORTH *Clients of Omega* xiv. 135 Why have you been *pyramid-selling confidential information on the side to all and sundry? **1972** *Daily Tel.* 30 Mar. 3/1 A company whose cosmetic business is said to involve '*pyramid selling'—a system whereby a franchiser sells to others the right to market goods—was banned in the High Court yesterday from operating its bank account. **1973** D. FRANCIS *Slay-Ride* iv. 51 Always full of get-rich-quick schemes..I even heard him on about pyramid selling once. **1942** PARSONS & STALLARD *Dis. Eye* (ed. 10) xxxii. 657 A *pyramid-shaped gauze dressing, with its apex against the wound is firmly applied. **1976** *Billings* (Montana) *Gaz.* 7 July 1-B/1 Green-uniformed troops..patrolled the pyramid-shaped twin buildings where Olympic teams are living. **1873** BENNETT & 'CAVENDISH' *Billiards* 83 Place the red again six inches nearer the *pyramid spot. **1894** MAHAFFY in *19th Cent.* XXXVI. 270 The study of the *Pyramid-texts, the documents of the Old Empire. **1600** FAIRFAX *Tasso* XV. xxxiv, Whose top *Pyramide-wise did pointed shew High, narrow, sharp, the sides yet more outspred. *a* **1722** LISLE *Husb.* (1757) 494 The haycocks..are made with a broad bottom and sharp top, pyramidwise.

Hence (*nonce-wd.*) ˌ**pyramiˈdaire** [after *millionaire*], a person to whom a pyramid is erected as a monument.

1875 EMERSON *Lett. & Soc. Aims* xi. *Immortality*, Every palace was a door to a pyramid; a king or rich man was a pyramidaire.

ˈ**pyramid**, *v.* [f. the sb.] **1.** *intr.* Of a group in a painting: to be disposed in a form suggesting a pyramid, i.e. symmetrically about a central figure in an elevated position.

1845 *Blackw. Mag.* LVIII. 418 It contributes to the goodness of the picture..if by means of it [the light] the groups pyramid and unite well. *Note*, Fuseli objects that the principal figures and chief action in the *Raising of Lazarus*.. are crowded into a corner. He would have had them 'pyramid'.

2. *trans. Finance.* **a.** To accumulate (assets); *spec.* in *Stock Exchange*, to build up (stock) from the proceeds of a series of advantageous sales. Also *absol.*

1901 G. H. LORIMER *Lett. Self-Made Merchant* (1903) v. 64 He'd invent a system for speculating in wheat and go on pyramiding his purchases till he'd made the best that Cheops did look like a five-cent plate of ice cream. **1927** P. MARKS *Lord of Himself* ii. 23 He pyramided his winnings and piled gold on gold..and finally saw himself a millionaire three times over. **1961** 'E. LATHEN' *Banking on Death* (1962) xiv. 113 He started pyramiding; put up twenty dollars and got the banks to lend him eighty to a hundred dollars. **1976** *National Observer* (U.S.) 13 Mar. 3/4 (Advt.), And if you are older than 30, it is true that you do not have as long a period of time to pyramid your savings.

b. To set up (a company) as part of a pyramid (see sense 5 b (*b*) of the sb.).

1942 E. PAUL *Narrow St.* xxiv. 212 With the money Stavisky borrowed he floated several companies and sold stock, pyramiding one concern upon the other until he had a finger in practically every financial pie in France. **1955** A. S. LINK *Amer. Epoch* II. xiv. 312 The promoter might pyramid one holding company on top of another almost indefinitely.

3. To distribute (assets or costs), esp. to pass on (costs) by means of a pyramid (sense 5 d (*a*)) of subcontracted work.

1933 *Sun* (Baltimore) 19 Aug. 1/6 Cotton manufacturers are attempting to make abnormal profits by pyramiding their labor costs and the processing tax. **1973** *Time* 25 June 86/2 Southwestern pyramids its commissions to reward the chain of students and executives above the salesman for each sale.

4. *fig.* To arrange in the form of a pyramid; *gen.*, to pile up.

1945 L. MUMFORD in *Archit. Rev.* XCVII. 6/1 Centres like New York, which continue to pyramid their mistakes, will descend with Gadarene swiftness into the abyss. **1948** J. STEINBECK *Russ. Jrnl.* iii. 41 The canned goods are piled in mountains, the champagne and wine from Georgia are pyramided. **1964** GOULD & KOLB *Dict. Social Sci.* 287/1 Power may be pyramided as in the army or relatively evenly divided as in fellowships. **1976** *National Observer* (U.S.) 10 Apr. 21/1 He will pinch powdery tobacco between his thumb and forefinger, pyramid it on the back of his opposite hand, bring it to his nostrils, and sniff.

5. *intr.* To become rich; to acquire greatly increased value or wealth. Also with *up*.

1960 I. JEFFERIES *Dignity & Purity* vii. 134 There is something about the spectacle of..Gobbo pyramiding up on property—houses, flats and so on, that the ordinary person needs must have—that I don't quite like. **1962** K. ORVIS *Damned & Destroyed* ii. 21 The same ounce of heroin ..has pyramided in black-market value.

Hence ˈ**pyramided** *ppl. a.*, ˈ**pyramiding** *vbl. sb.* and *ppl. a.*

1930 J. R. AIKEN *Eng. Present & Past* IV. xi. 226 In the words *uppermost*, *furthermost*, *innermost*, *hindermost*, and several others like them, we have the comparative degree combined with the doubly superlative *most*,..causing a triple pyramiding of inflections. **1933** *Sun* (Baltimore) 19 Aug. 1/1 Couzens said he 'knew of no other city in the whole world where there was such an orgy of pyramiding of corporations and the fixing of fictitious values and earnings'. **1941** *Ibid.* 25 Mar. 14/3 Because the projects are in the jurisdictions of differing metal trades unions, the unhappy welders have had to pay tribute not to just one union, not to just one local of one union, but to many metal trades unions and to many locals of metal trades unions. It is this pyramiding of initiation, membership and 'permit' fees on the welders that Mr. Hillman tried to stop. **1951** M. MCLUHAN *Mech. Bride* (1967) 128/1 Production for use? Yes. But for the briefest possible use consistent with the rigging of the market for the pyramiding of profits. **1957** D. L. BOLINGER in *Publ. Amer. Dial. Soc.* XXVIII. 18 Imputations..share the characteristic of the larger class of pyramided Qs to which they belong and may be inverted with little or no change of meaning. *Ibid.* 21 How—why Qs with *that* and their pyramiding are discussed. **1958** *Times* 22 Nov. 7/7 The pyramiding of prosperity, American style, poised more and more on the expanding leisure of a consumers' State. **1967** *Economist* 17 June 1248/4 There is strong feeling against companies..which retain control of an empire with the minimum of capital through 'pyramiding'. **1976** G. W. MCKENZIE *Econ. Euro-Currency System* vi. 78 It is possible that euro-banks may place their dollar assets with other euro-banks. This raises the possibility of a 'pyramiding' chain of inter-bank deposits being created. **1977** *Time* Feb. 33/1 Winter stress can be aggravated by the thought of pyramiding fuel bills.

pyramidal (pɪˈræmɪdəl), *a.* (*sb.*) [ad. med.L. *pȳramidālis* (Du Cange): see PYRAMID *sb.* and -AL[1]. Cf. F. *pyramidal* (1507 in Hatz.-Darm.).]

1. Of or pertaining to a pyramid; sloping, as an edge or face of a pyramid. *rare.*

1571 DIGGES *Pantom.* III. viii. R j b, The Pyramidall side HB. **1597** R. WRAG *Voy. Constantinople* in Hakluyt *Voy.* (1599) II. I. 308 Two hils rising in a piramidall forme. **1762–71** H. WALPOLE *Vertue's Anecd. Paint.* (1786) II. 90 Some were made of glass in a pyramidal shape. **1857** J. G. WILKINSON *Egypt. Pharaohs* 151 The pyramidal, or sloping, line was intended to insure the durability of a wall.

2. a. Of the nature or shape of a pyramid; resembling a pyramid.

1599 T. M[OUFET] *Silkwormes* 45 A Pyramidall and most steepe hil. **1634** SIR T. HERBERT *Trav.* 61 High Pyramidall Cypresse-trees. **1678** CUDWORTH *Intell. Syst.* I. i. 53 Plato.. would compound the Earth of Cubical, and Fire of Pyramidal Atoms, and the like. **1784** COWPER *Task* VI. 159 The Lilac various in array,..With purple spikes pyramidal. **1816** SHELLEY *Let.* 22 July, Pr. Wks. 1888 I. 349 Conical and pyramidal crystallizations. **1874** MOTLEY *Barneveld* II. xxi. 385 One tall pyramidal gable of ancient grey brickwork. *fig.* **1641** MILTON *Ch. Govt.* vi. Wks. 1851 III. 128 Prelaty if she will seek to close up divisions in the Church, must be forc't to dissolve and unmake her own pyramidal figure. **1872** MINTO *Eng. Prose Lit.* II. v. 368 That the most stable government is the pyramidal,—that rests on the widest basis of popular confidence.

b. *fig.* In journalistic use (after F. *pyramidal*): Astonishingly huge, colossal.

[**1827** C'TESS GRANVILLE *Lett.* (1894) I. 432 Madame de Montjoie has just told me that Miss Foote's success is *pyramidale.*] **1902** *Westm. Gaz.* 16 Aug. 3/2 The pyramidal ignorance of the average Englishman concerning the great Republic and her institutions.

3. Specific technical applications.

a. *Anat.* Applied to certain structures of more or less pyramid-like form, esp. to certain muscles in the abdomen, and in the nose (both often denoted by the L. *pyramidalis* used absol., sc. *musculus*). Also, Pertaining to or connected with the pyramids of the medulla oblongata, as in ***pyramidal tract***, a tract of motor nerve-fibres in the spinal cord. Also *Path.* applied to a form of cataract in which the capsule of the crystalline lens is opaque and prominent at its centre.

[**1693** tr. *Blancard's Phys. Dict.* (ed. 2) s.v., Muscles of the Nostrils and of the Abdomen called Pyramidales, or of a Pyramidical Figure.] **1725** *Bradley's Fam. Dict.* s.v. *Nose*, The Nostrils are dilated by six Muscles, three on each Side, viz. the pyramidal, oblique Ascendant or Myrtiformis, and the oblique descendant. **1872** DARWIN *Emotions* vii. 190 The pyramidal muscle serves to draw down the skin of the forehead between the eyebrows, together with their inner extremities. **1879** CALDERWOOD *Mind & Br.* ii. 26 The most important of the cells are known as pyramidal. **1899** *Allbutt's Syst. Med.* VII. 732 Sclerosis of the pyramidal tracts.

b. *Cryst.* Used in senses 1 and 2; also applied to the TETRAGONAL system, of which the square pyramid is a characteristic form.

1789 J. K[EIR] *1st Pt. Dict. Chem.* 69/1 A brown salt, which..forms white, pyramidal crystals. **1828** STARK *Elem. Nat. Hist.* II. 482 Fundamental forms of minerals... The Pyramidal, in which the crystals assume the form of an isosceles four-sided pyramid. **1851** RICHARDSON *Geol.* v. 97 The Pyramidal includes the octohedron with a square base, and the right square prism.

c. Applied to particular species of plants having the flowers in a pyramid-like spike or cluster (often translating the specific name *pyramidalis*); also to fishes or other animals having the body or some part of a pyramid-like form. ***pyramidal orchid*** or ***orchis***, an orchid, *Anacamptis pyramidalis*, which is native to Europe and North Africa, and bears dense spikes of deep pink flowers.

1778 W. HUDSON *Flora Anglica* (ed. 2) II. 383 Pyramidal Orchis. **1796** C. MARSHALL *Gardening* xix. (1798) 355

Saxifrage plants are usually potted to move into the house.. as indeed the pyramidal in particular should be. **1804** SHAW *Gen. Zool.* V. 390 Pyramidal Sucker. *Ibid.* 425 Pyramidal Trunk-fish. **1858** A. IRVINE *Illustr. Handbk. Brit. Plants* 316 Pyramidal Orchis... Flowers in a very dense, short, ovate spike, of a beautiful rose colour. **1882** *Garden* 11 Feb. 89/1 Other native Orchises, such as..the Pyramidal Orchis.., live and flower in a garden, but do not increase or improve. **1951** V. S. SUMMERHAYES *Wild Orchids Brit.* iii. 51 The pyramidal orchid is a very beautiful example of perfect adjustment to pollination by butterflies and moths. **1977** M. ALLAN *Darwin & his Flowers* xi. 198 The Pyramidal Orchid ..has its parts arranged very differently from *Orchis mascula.*

4. a. *Arith.* Applied to the several series of numbers, each beginning with unity, obtained by continued summation of the several series of POLYGONAL numbers; so called because each of these numbers, represented (e.g.) by balls, can be arranged according to a certain rule in the form of the corresponding pyramid (on a triangular, square, or polygonal base).

Thus the series of *triangular* numbers, 1, 3, 6, 10, 15, 21 ..gives, by summation of successive terms, the series of *triangular pyramidal* numbers 1, 4, 10, 20, 35, 56... Similarly from the series of square, pentagonal, etc. numbers are obtained corresponding series of pyramidal numbers. The pyramidal numbers constitute the second (sometimes called the *third*) order of figurate numbers: see FIGURATE *ppl. a.* 3 b. The term was formerly extended (with ordinal numeral) to the succeeding orders of figurate numbers, each obtained similarly from the preceding by continued summation: see 1795 in b. (In quot. 1674 erroneously used.)

1674 JEAKE *Arith.* (1696) 663 Six is called the first Pyramidal Number; for the Units therein may be so placed, as to represent a Pyramis. **1795** HUTTON *Math. Dict.*, *Pyramidal Numbers*, are the sums of polygonal numbers, collected after the same manner as the polygonal numbers themselves are found from arithmetical progressions. **1806** —— *Course Math.* I. 224 Column c contains the sum of the triangular numbers, that is, the shot contained in a triangular pile, commonly called pyramidal numbers.

b. (as *sb.*) A pyramidal number.

1706 W. JONES *Syn. Palmar. Matheseos* 165 Pyramidals having their Names from their Number of Sides. **1795** HUTTON *Math. Dict.* s.v. *Pyramidal Numbers*, These are particularly called First Pyramidals. The sums of First Pyramidals are called Second Pyramidals;..and so on. Particularly, those arising from triangular numbers, are called Prime Triangular Pyramidals.

5. *Comb.*, as ***pyramidal-shaped***, adj.

1859 W. S. COLEMAN *Woodlands* (1866) 108 The Yew forms a pyramidal-shaped tree. **1868** *Rep. U.S. Commissioner Agric.* (1869) 202 A weeping, pyramidal-shaped plant.

Hence **py'ramidalist** = PYRAMIDIST; *spec.* one who holds certain theories or beliefs about the pyramids of Egypt. So **py'ramidalism**, the body of theories or beliefs held by pyramidalists.

1877 PROCTOR *Myths & Marvels Astron.* 52 The facts most confidently urged by pyramidalists in support of their views. **1882** —— *Gt. Pyramid* i. 11 Taylor, Smyth, and the Pyramidalists generally, consider this sufficient to prove that the pyramid was erected for some purpose connected with religion.

pyramidally (pɪ'ræmɪdəlɪ), *adv.* [f. PYRAMIDAL + -LY².] In a pyramidal manner; in the form of a pyramid.

1561 EDEN *Arte of Nauig.* II. viii. 34 The shadowe of the ..earth is piramidallye sharpe. **1575** LANEHAM *Let.* (1871) 50 Vpon a base a too foot square, & hy,..a square pilaster rizing pyramidally of a fyfteen foote hy. **1671** GREW *Anat. Plants* ii. §9 They stand both together pyramidally. **1778** PRYCE *Min. Cornub.* 84 Rising pyramidally..at least five hundred and forty feet above the sea. **1890** *Farmer's Gaz.* 4 Jan. 7/1 The shoots of a pyramidally trained tree.

†**b.** *fig.* in allusion to the embalmed bodies of the dead preserved in the pyramids: After the manner of a mummy. *Obs.*

1646 SIR T. BROWNE *Pseud. Ep.* VII. xiii. 366 A man may be happy without the apprehension thereof: surely in that sence he is pyramidally happy. **1658** —— *Hydriot.* v. 72 But to subsist in bones, and be but Pyramidally extant, is a fallacy in duration.

c. *fig.* Hugely, colossally: cf. PYRAMIDAL 2 b.

1891 *Sat. Rev.* 28 Feb. 275/1 So pyramidally ignorant is the British newspaper-man.

pyramidate (pɪ'ræmɪdət), *a. rare.* [ad. late L. *pȳramidāt-us*, f. *pȳramid-em*: see -ATE² 2.] Fashioned as a pyramid; = PYRAMIDAL 2.

1584 R. SCOT *Discov. Witchcr.* XIII. xix. 258 Experiments may be seene in diverse sorts of [perspective] glasses; as in the hollowe, the plaine, the embossed, the columnarie, the pyramidate or piked, the turbinall, the bounched. **1826** KIRBY & SP. *Entomol.* xlvi. IV. 289 *Pyramidate Fascia*,..a band which juts out into an angle on one side.

So **py'ramidated** *a.*, formed with pyramids, or into a pyramid.

1805–17 R. JAMESON *Char. Min.* (ed. 3) 196 A crystal is named pyramidated, when the primitive form is a prism, and has a pyramid on each extremity. **1903** *Nature* 1 Oct. 530/2 Some of the pyramidated summits among the South American volcanoes.

pyramides, pl. of *pyramis*: see PYRAMID.

pyramidia, pl. of PYRAMIDION.

pyramidic (pɪrə'mɪdɪk), *a. rare.* [f. PYRAMID + -IC; perh. after Gr. πυραμιδικός.] Of, like, or proper to a pyramid; heaped up, or lofty and massive, like a pyramid.

1743 SHENSTONE *Elegies* xix. 50 Their gold in pyramidic plenty pil'd. **1821** BYRON *Juan* v. lxxxvii, The enormous gate which rose O'er them in almost pyramidic pride.

pyramidical (pɪrə'mɪdɪkəl), *a.* Now *rare.* [f. as prec. + -AL¹.] = PYRAMIDAL; in quot. 1628, enduring like a pyramid: cf. MONUMENTAL 4.

1621 BURTON *Anat. Mel.* I. i. II. iv. (1651) 18 [The heart] of a pyramidical forme, and not much unlike to a Pine-apple. **1628** FELTHAM *Resolves* II. lxxv, Though the Athenians demolished his Statues, yet they could not extinguish his more pyramidicall vertues. **1693** [see PYRAMIDAL 3 a]. **1743** *Lond. & Country Brew.* IV. (ed. 2) 322 They set six or eight Waggon Loads of Coal in a pyramidical Heap. **1867** BAKER *Nile Tribut.* xv. (1872) 270 The pyramidical hill beneath which I had fixed our camp. **1895** *Westm. Gaz.* 16 Aug. 8/2 After the Switchback and the Great Wheel comes the Pyramidical Railway, which is being erected at the Devil's Dyke, near Brighton... The idea is to build a tower of varying height, round which a spiral track will carry a car from the top to the bottom.

pyramidically (pɪrə'mɪdɪkəlɪ), *adv.* [f. prec. + -LY².] In a pyramidical manner or form; pyramidally. (In quot. 1886 = PYRAMIDALLY c.)

1697 LUTTRELL *Brief Rel.* 28 Oct. (1857) IV. 298 A very noble bonefire..consisting of about 140 pitcht barrels, placed pyramidically on 7 scaffolds. **1871** NESBITT *Catal. Slade Coll. Glass* 70 Pyramidically-clipped trees. **1886** D. C. MURRAY *First Pers. Singular* xxiii, She is terribly rich. Awfully, colossally, pyramidically rich.

So **pyra'midicalness** (Bailey vol. II, 1727).

‖**pyramidion** (pɪrə'mɪdɪɒn). Pl. **-ia**, **-ions**. [mod.L., a. Gr. type *πυραμίδιον, dim. of πυραμίς PYRAMID. Cf. F. *pyramidion* (Littré).] A small pyramid; *spec.* in *Arch.*, the pointed pyramidal portion forming the apex of an obelisk.

1840 BONOMI in *Trans. Roy. Soc. Lit.* (1843) Ser. II. I. 161 The height of the pyramidion should be about a tenth of the whole length. **1850** J. LEITCH tr. *C. O. Müller's Anc. Art* §224 Four-sided pillars on a low base, which diminish upwards and end in a pyramidion, usually of granite. **1877** W. R. COOPER *Egypt. Obelisks* i. (1878) 2 Its apex is abruptly terminated by a small pyramidion, whose faces are inclined at about an angle of sixty degrees.

b. *Cryst.* Used by Story-Maskelyne in naming figures formed from other solid figures by constructing a small pyramid upon each face of the original.

1895 STORY-MASKELYNE *Crystallogr.* §167 Holo-symmetrical forms of this [the cubic] system:..2. The triakis-octahedron or the octahedrid pyramidion...4. The tetrakis-hexahedron or the cube-pyramidion..: the term pyramidion being employed in the case of forms in which a pyramidion or small pyramid composed of similar isosceles triangles surmounts every face of a simpler figure..: such a figure is then an isoscelohedron. *Ibid.* §172 The figure presents the aspect of a cube each face of which is surmounted by an obtuse pyramid, and it may, on this account, be termed the cube pyramidion.

pyramidist ('pɪrəmɪdɪst, pɪ'ræm-). [See -IST.] One who investigates or is specially versed in the structure and history of the Egyptian pyramids.

1874 P. SMYTH *Our Inher. in Gt. Pyramid* v. xxi. 41 A scientific pyramidist..confines himself to stating..that the Great Pyramid was erected in the times of the Fourth Dynasty. **1883** PROCTOR *Great Pyramid* App. A. 187 The length of the earth's polar axis is assumed by pyramidists to be 500,000,000 pyramid inches.

'pyramidize, *v.* [f. PYRAMID *sb.* + -IZE.] *intr.* To form a pyramid; to converge towards a summit or apex: cf. PYRAMID *v.* Hence **'pyramidizing** *vbl. sb.* and *ppl. a.*

a **1831** T. HOPE *Hist. Ess. Archit.* (1840) I. xi. 388 The gradual contraction and pyramidizing, as they rose higher, of the indispensable arches, and buttresses, and pinnacles and roofs. **1850** INKERSLEY *Roman & Pointed Archit. in France* 325 A very graceful pyramidising composition of two distinct portions.

py'ramido-, combining form from Gr. πυραμίς, πυραμιδ-, PYRAMID, as in **py,ramido-a'ttenuate** *a.*, pyramidally attenuated; †**py,ramido-pris'matic** *a.*, of a form due to a combination of pyramid and prism.

1821 R. JAMESON *Man. Mineral.* 165 Pyramido-Prismatic Augite. **1846** DANA *Zooph.* (1848) 478 Summit branchlets .., arcuate and pyramido-attenuate.

†**,pyrami'dography** (also in L. form **py,ramido'graphia**). *Obs.* [f. prec. + -GRAPHY.] A description of, or dissertation on, the pyramids.

1646 GREAVES (*title*) Pyramidographia: or a description of the Pyramids of Egypt. **1656** BLOUNT *Glossogr.*, *Pyramidography.* **1671** *Phil. Trans.* VI. 2091 By whom the Pyramidographia, the Roman Foot and Denarius are.. traced out.

pyramidoid (pɪ'ræmɪdɔɪd). *Geom. rare.* [ad. mod.L. *pȳramidoīdes* (sc. *schēma*): see PYRAMID and -OID.] A solid figure in form approaching a pyramid, but of which the edges that meet or intersect at the vertex are curves, instead of straight lines as in a pyramid; as the ***parabolic pyramidoid***, in which the vertical sections through the edges are parabolas instead of triangles.

[**1655** J. WALLIS *De Sectionibus Conicis* Prop. IX, De Conoide et Pyramidoide Parabolico. *Ibid.* XIV, De Elliptico Pyramidoide et Conoide. **1656** —— *Arithmetica Infinitorum* Prop. iv, Item, Pyramidoides vel Conoides Parabolicum.. ad Prisma vel Cylindrum (super æquali base æquealtum) est ut 1 ad 2.] **1704** J. HARRIS *Lex. Techn.* I, *Parabolick Pyramidoid*..so named by Dr. Wallis from its Genesis, or Formation. **1795** HUTTON *Math. Dict.* s.v. *Parabola.*

¶ Erroneously identified with a *parabolic spindle.*

1710 J. HARRIS *Lex. Techn.* (ed. 2) II. s.v.; thence **1727** in BAILEY vol. II, and **1730** *folio*; **1839** *Encycl. Brit.* XVIII. 746/2; and some recent Dicts.

So **pyrami'doidal** *a.*, (*a*) Of or pertaining to a pyramidoid. (*b*) Of the general figure of a pyramid upon a base of any shape.

1807 T. YOUNG *Nat. Philos.* II. 20 All pyramidoidal solids are equal to one third of the circumscribing prismatic or cylindroidal solids of the same height.

,pyrami'dology. [f. PYRAMIDO- + -LOGY.] The study of or theories about the mathematical or occult significance of the measurements of the Great Pyramid. Hence **,pyramido'logical**; **pyrami'dologist.**

1924 DAVIDSON & ALDERSMITH *Great Pyramid* I. p. xi, The reader..will probably have realised that Pyramidology, for over sixty years, has consisted of intuitions, and theories based on these intuitions. **1948** 'N. SHUTE' *No Highway* i. 4 'Call yourself a scientist, and you don't know pyramidology!'.. 'Well, I don't. What is it?' 'It's all about the Great Pyramid, in Egypt. Prophecies, and all that sort of thing.' **1954** A. HUXLEY *Let.* 12 Dec. (1969) 719 What may be called the Baconian-pyramidological-cryptographic-spiritualist-theosophical syndrome afflicts a large percentage of the human race. **1964** *Listener* 23 July 117/2 Taylor..believed that he had found various mathematical truths in its [*sc.* the Great Pyramid's] measurements which showed him that the Egyptian priests knew most..of the secrets of the universe... Taylor was, therefore, the founder [1859] of the cult of pyramidology. **1972** *Guardian* 5 Oct. 17/7 Some comfort for would-be biological pyramidologists —cycles are real. **1974** *Nature* 2 Aug. 448/1 Somewhere about here one crosses the transitional zone between statistics and pyramidology. *Ibid.*, Like the pyramidologists he clearly believes that man should be very alert to the hidden meanings buried in the depths of what appear to be fairly straight forward objects or events.

pyramidon¹ (pɪ'ræmɪdɒn). [f. PYRAMID, after *accordion*, *harmonicon*, etc.] A pedal organ-stop having wooden pipes in the form of an inverted pyramid, and producing very deep tones.

1876 HILES *Catech. Organ* ix. (1878) 63 Pyramidon, a Pedal stop of 16 or 32 feet-tone. **1881** C. A. EDWARDS *Organs* 156 [The] Pyramidon has been mentioned in some works, but it was found impracticable to make this stop answer throughout the entire scale, and it therefore is abandoned.

Pyramidon² (pɪ'ræmɪdɒn). *Pharm.* Also **pyr-**, **-one** (-əʊn). [a. G. *pyramidon* (W. Filehne 1896, in *Berliner klin. Wochenschr.* XXXIII. 1061), f. *pyrazolon* PYRAZOLONE with inserted *amid-* (see AMIDO-).] A white crystalline solid used as an anti-pyretic and analgesic; 4-dimethyl-amino-1, 5-dimethyl-1-phenylpyrazolin-3-one, $C_{13}H_{17}H_3O$.

Formerly a proprietary term in Britain, and still registered as one in the U.S.

1898 *Jrnl. Chem. Soc.* LXXIV. II. 656 Dimethylamidophenyldimethylpyrazolone, or pyramidone, prepared by Filehne and Spiro, and recommended by them as a substitute for antipyrin..yields bluish-violet colours when oxidised by ferric chloride, nitric and nitrous acids, and the halogens. **1898** *Official Gaz.* (U.S. Patent Office) 6 Dec. 1582/2 Remedy for certain named disease. Farberwerke, vormals Meister, Lucius & Brüning, Höchst-on-the-Main, Germany... *Pyramidon*... Used since December, 1896. **1903** *Brit. Med. Jrnl. Suppl.: Weekly Epitome of Current Med. Lit.* 21 Nov. 79/3 Having heard a good account of pyramidon he proceeded to employ it in a case which he and the nurse were able to observe very closely. **1908** A. BENNETT *Jrnl.* 14 Dec. (1932) I. 300, I..saw a chemist make me a cachet of pyramidon. **1925** W. GERHARDIE *Polyglots* xlix. 358 She took pyramidon for her head, and aspirin for her cold. **1942** *R.A.F. Jrnl.* 30 May 35 A German industrialist in 1942 testified that in the Rhineland it was almost impossible to buy soothing drugs, like pyramidon, any more.

†**pyramidy.** *Obs. rare.* ? Illiterate form of PYRAMID (from pl. *piramidies* in PYRAMID A. *α*), used *attrib.*; or ? derived adj. = PYRAMIDAL.

1627 SPEED *England, Scot.* i. §15 A Well, whose trickling drops turne (in Piramidy-wise) into hard stone. *c* **1710** CELIA FIENNES *Diary* (1888) 33 Manborn hills..are in a Pirramidy fashion on yᵉ top. *Ibid.* 179 With four pirramidy spires on Each Corner.

pyramis: earliest form of PYRAMID, q.v.

pyramoid ('pɪrəmɔɪd). *Geom. rare*⁻⁰. [ad. Gr. πυραμοειδής pyramid-shaped, f. πυραμίς PYRAMID: see -OID.] = PYRAMIDOID (Webster 1864). So **pyra'moidal** *a.* = PYRAMIDOIDAL b.

1883 HEDDLE in *Encycl. Brit.* XVI. 354/2 Producing..in the hexagonal system 'pyramoidal' and 'gyroidal' forms.

pyran ('paɪəræn). *Chem.* Also **-ane** (-eɪn). [f. PYR(ONE + -AN, -ANE.] **a.** A heterocyclic compound, C_5H_6O, having a doubly unsaturated six-membered ring consisting of five carbon atoms and one oxygen atom; two isomers (differing in the positions of the double bonds) are possible, only one of which, $CH_2CH:CH\cdot CH:CH\cdot O$ (*γ-pyran*), has been isolated, as a colourless, unstable oil. **b.** Any derivative of either isomer containing a pyran ring. Freq. *attrib.*, as **pyran ring**, a ring (which may be saturated) of five carbon atoms and one oxygen atom.

[**1901** *Jrnl. Chem. Soc.* LXXX. I. 559 7-Hydroxy-2-phenyl-4-methylbenzopyran.] **1904** *Ibid.* LXXXVI. I. 816 (*heading*) Properties of oxygen in the pyran ring. **1927** *Ibid.* 3139 The normal sugars are thus seen to be representatives of the parent form indicated by pyran and the labile or γ-sugars have as their parent substance furan. **1952** K. VENKATARAMAN *Chem. Synthetic Dyes* II. xxiv. 742 The γ-pyran ring..occurs in the anthocyanins, the red, violet and blue coloring matters of flowers and fruits. **1953** FRUTON & SIMMONDS *Gen. Biochem.* xvii. 374 The ring in the cyclic form of glucose is related to the heterocyclic compound pyrane. **1962** *Jrnl. Amer. Chem. Soc.* LXXXIV. 2453/1 γ-Pyran is extremely unstable at room temperature, particularly when exposed to air. **1965** KICE & MARVELL *Mod. Princ. Org. Chem.* xix. 360 The two double bonds can be conjugated or unconjugated, and two types of pyran rings are known. *Ibid.*, Like enol ethers in general these rings are unstable, and α-pyran itself is unknown.

pyranometer (paɪərəˈnɒmɪtə(r)). [See quot. 1916 and -METER.] An instrument for measuring the amount of radiation incident from the entire sky on a horizontal surface.

1916 ABBOT & ALDRICH in *Smithsonian Misc. Coll.* LXVI. No. 7. 2 The name Pyranometer, selected for the instrument we have devised, is taken from Greek words (πῦρ, fire; ἀνά, up; μέτρον, a measure) signifying that which measures heat above. The name was chosen with reference to the fact that the instrument is designed to measure the energy of radiation to or from a complete hemisphere lying above the measuring surface. **1967** *Jrnl. Appl. Meteorol.* VI. 688 (*heading*) An integrating pyranometer for climatological observer stations and mesoscale networks. **1973** *Nature* 16 Feb. 448/2 These data were obtained by subtracting the solar radiation measured by a temperature compensated Eppley pyranometer from the mean hemispherical all-wave radiation obtained from three Fritschen-type net radiometers converted to hemispherical operation.

pyranose (ˈpaɪər-, ˈpɪrənəʊz). *Chem.* [f. PYRAN + -OSE[2].] A structure containing a saturated pyran ring, frequently assumed by sugars; a sugar having this structure. Freq. *attrib.*

1927 GOODYEAR & HAWORTH in *Jrnl. Chem. Soc.* 3141 On the basis of the conclusions now reached, the formula (A) must be accepted as a general representation of a normal sugar, which might be described as a pyranose. **1953** FRUTON & SIMMONDS *Gen. Biochem.* xvii. 380 Another important hexose found in nature is..fructose... The open-chain form..is in equilibrium with the corresponding pyranose and furanose forms; in solutions of the free sugar, the pyranose form predominates. **1957**, **1963** [see FURANOSE]. **1971** *Nature* 26 Nov. 220/1 The anomers α -and β-D-mannose differ structurally only in that H and OH at the C_1 atom of the pyranose ring are interchanged.

pyranoside (paɪər-, pɪˈrænəsaɪd). *Chem.* [f. prec. + -IDE.] Any glycoside in the pyranose form.

1932 *Jrnl. Chem. Soc.* 2254 Usually the product is also contaminated with small amounts of the corresponding pyranosides. **1934**, **1966** [see FURANOSIDE]. **1970** R. W. MCGILVERY *Biochem.* xxviii. 715 Furanosides and pyranosides can be distinguished by the number of moles of periodate consumed in their oxidation.

pyrantimonite, **pyrargillite**, **pyrargyrite**: see PYRO- 2.

pyrate, **pyratic**, etc.: see PIRATE, etc.

† **pyraugue**, obs. form of PIROGUE.

1725 SLOANE *Jamaica* II. 129 Pyraugues made of [Cedar].

‖ **pyˈrausta.** *Obs. rare.* [L. (Pliny = *pyralis*), ad. Gr. πυραύστης a moth that gets singed in the flame; in obs. F. *pirauste* (Cotgr. 1611).] A fabulous insect supposed to live in fire.

1591 SYLVESTER *Du Bartas* I. vi. 1121 So of the fire in burning furnace springs The fly Pyrausta with the flaming wings. **1706** PHILLIPS (ed. 6), *Pyrausta* or *Pyrogonus*, the Fire-Fly or Salamander-Fly; an Insect.

pyrauxite: see PYRO- 2.

pyrazinamide (paɪər-, pɪrəˈzɪnəmaɪd). *Pharm.* [f. PYRAZINE + AMIDE.] A white crystalline powder, pyrazine-2-carboxamide, $CH:N\cdot CH:CH\cdot N:C\cdot CONH_2$, which is used in the treatment of tuberculosis, usu. in conjunction with other drugs.

1952 *Amer. Rev. Tuberculosis* LXV. 515 The antituberculous activity of pyrazinamide..in mice lies between that of streptomycin and that of PAS. **1961** *Lancet* 2 Sept. 533/2 With 1 g. of streptomycin daily on six days a week..and 1–1·5 g. of pyrazinamide in a single daily dose by mouth, 32..of the 57 patients..attained bacteriological quiescence by the end of the year. **1974** R. M. KIRK et al. *Surgery* ii. 29/2 Ethionamide, pyrazinamide, viomycin and capreomycin may be used in the treatment of tuberculosis when it proves resistant to the usual combination of streptomycin, INAH, and PAS.

pyrazine (ˈpaɪər-, ˈpɪrəzɪn). *Chem.* [ad. G. *pyrazin* (A. T. Mason 1887, at suggestion of V. Merz, in *Ber. d. Deut. Chem. Ges.* XX. 267). f. *pyridin* PYRIDINE with inserted *az-* (see AZO-).] A weakly basic white crystalline solid, $CH:N\cdot CH:CH\cdot N:CH$; any substituted derivative of this.

[**1887** *Jrnl. Chem. Soc.* LII. I. 493 Xylenedihydropyrazine.] **1888** *Proc. Chem. Soc.* IV. 107 The author [*sc.* Mason] adopts Widman's nomenclature..: the 'Ketines'.., 'Pyrazines'.., 'Aldines'.., and all compounds containing a ring of four carbon-atoms and two nitrogen-atoms in para-position are now termed Paradiazines, or Piazines. **1926** H. G. RULE tr. *J. Schmidt's Text-bk. Org. Chem.* III. viii. 699 Pyrazine itself is produced by the condensation of amino-acetaldehyde or amino-acetal. It..has an odour of heliotrope. **1967** M. H. PALMER *Struct. & Reactions Heterocyclic Compounds* iii. 89 Pyrazines are readily prepared by the self-condensation of α-aminoketones. **1970** *Acta Crystallographica* B. XXVI. 979/1 Pyrazine..and $Cu(NO_3)_2$ form an anhydrous crystalline complex with a 1:1 pyrazine to $Cu(NO_3)_2$ ratio.

pyrazole (ˈpaɪər-, ˈpɪrəzəʊl). *Chem.* [ad. G. *pyrazol* (L. Knorr 1885, in *Ber. d. Deut. Chem. Ges.* XVIII. 311). f. *pyrrol* PYRROLE with inserted *az-* (see AZO-).] A weakly basic white crystalline solid, $CH:CH\cdot CH:N\cdot NH$; any substituted derivative of this.

1887 *Jrnl. Chem. Soc.* LII. II. 665 In order to examine whether the formation of pyrazoline-derivatives from phenylhydrazine and acids of the acrylic series is analogous to the formation of pyrazole-derivatives from unsaturated ketones, cinnamyl hydrazine was prepared and its products of decomposition investigated. **1926** H. G. RULE tr. *J. Schmidt's Text-bk. Org. Chem.* III. iii. 566 Pyrazole differs strongly from pyrrole in its remarkable stability and more definitely basic character. **1938** C. D. HURD in H. Gilman *Org. Chem.* I. vii. 679 β-Diketones and β-keto esters give rise to..pyrazoles with hydrazines. **1968** [see PYRAZOLONE]. **1970** *New Scientist* 5 Mar. 447/1 By dosing rats heavily with pyrazole, a compound that inhibits alcohol dehydrogenase, Krebs and his group have shown that quite high levels of alcohol can build up in the bloodstream if not removed.

pyrazoline (paɪər-, pɪˈræzəlɪn). *Chem.* [ad. G. *pyrazolin* (L. Knorr 1887, in *Ann. d. Chem.* CCXXXVIII. 144): see prec. and -INE[5].] Any of three isomeric compounds, $C_3H_6N_2$, which are dihydro derivatives of pyrazole; *spec.* $CH_2\cdot CH_2\cdot CH:N\cdot NH$ (*2-pyrazoline*), a colourless basic liquid, the only one of the three so far prepared; also, any substituted derivative of any of these compounds.

1887 [see PYRAZOLE]. **1938** R. C. FUSON in H. Gilman *Org. Chem.* I. i. 30 Pyrazolines are unstable toward heat and decompose to give cyclopropane derivatives. **1961** G. M. BADGER *Chem. Heterocyclic Compounds* v. 223 Pyrazolines are much less stable than the corresponding pyrazoles and are attacked by oxidizing agents. **1967** C. H. JARBOE in R. H. Wiley *Pyrazoles* vi. 177 Examples of each of the three tautomeric pyrazoline structures..are well known, 2-pyrazoline being by far the most common. **1968** [see PYRAZOLONE].

pyrazolone (paɪər-, pɪˈræzələʊn). *Chem.* [ad. G. *pyrazolon* (L. Knorr 1887, in *Ann. d. Chem.* CCXXXVIII. 145): see PYRAZOLE and -ONE.] Any keto derivative of a pyrazoline; *spec.* $NH\cdot N:CH\cdot CH_2\cdot CO$ (*5-pyrazolone*), a weakly acidic white crystalline solid; also, any of their substituted derivatives, several of which on coupling with diazo compounds give rise to commercially important dyestuffs.

1887 *Jrnl. Chem. Soc.* LII. 601 Many of the compounds obtained by the action of ethyl acetoacetate and its derivatives on the primary aromatic hydrazines have already been described by the author as quinizines... The author [*sc.* Knorr] now regards these substances as pyrazolones. **1926** H. G. RULE tr. *J. Schmidt's Text-bk. Org. Chem.* III. iii. 566 The oxygen of pyrazolones may also be removed by heating..with phosphorus oxychloride, when chloro-derivatives are formed. **1961** G. M. BADGER *Chem. Heterocyclic Compounds* v. 226 Theoretically, there are three types of..pyrazolone, but only derivatives of 3-pyrazolone and of 5-pyrazolone are known. **1968** *Kirk-Othmer Encycl. Chem. Technol.* (ed. 2) XVI. 763 Neither pyrazoles nor pyrazolines have found extensive uses, but pyrazolones have been widely utilized as fabric dyes and pigments, as food coloring agents, in color photography, as photographic developing agents, and as pharmaceuticals. **1977** *Lancet* 23 Apr. 905/1 Reversible agranulocytosis has also been described with pyrazolone derivatives (such as phenylbutazone).

pyre (paɪə(r)). [ad. L. *pyra*, a. Gr. πυρά a hearth, a place where fire is kindled, the place of a funeral fire, a funeral pile.] A pile or heap of combustible material, esp. wood; usually, a funeral pile for burning a dead body: see PILE *sb.*[3] 3 d.

1658 BROWNE *Hydriot.*, Ep. Ded., When the Funeral Pyre was out, and the last Valediction over, Men took a lasting Adieu of their Interred Friends. **1712–14** POPE *Rape Lock* II. 41 With tender Billet-doux he lights the pyre. **1715** —— *Iliad* I. 72 For nine long nights through all the dusky air The pyres thick-flaming shot a dismal glare. **1810** SOUTHEY *Kehama* I. xiv, Then hand in hand the victim band Roll in the dance around the funeral pyre. **1871** R. ELLIS *Catullus* xxxix. 4 Near the pyre they mourn Where weeps a mother o'er the lost, the kind one son.

attrib. **1848** HAMILTON *Sabbath* iv. 100 The fabled Phoenix was only reborn amidst its pyre-nest of incense.

pyre, obs. f. PEAR, PEER, PIER *sb.*; var. PIRE *v.*

pyˈrectic, *a.* [a. Gr. πυρεκτικ-ός feverish, f. πυρέσσ-ειν to be feverish: cf. PYRETIC.] Of, pertaining to, or affected with fever, feverish.

1822–34 *Good's Study Med.* (ed. 4) I. 153 Thus shell-fish ..will sometimes excite great uneasiness with pyrectic heat. *Ibid.* IV. 291 The thirst and general irritation and pyrectic symptoms increase.

† **pyree.** *Obs. rare.* [a. F. *pyrée* (Littré), f. Gr. πῦρ fire: cf. πυρεῖον a pan for coals.] The altar of fire in the religion of the ancient Persians.

1638 SIR T. HERBERT *Trav.* (ed. 2) 186 Albors..infamous in the Pyreë or Temple of Idolatrous Fyre, which has never gone out for fifty Ages. *Ibid.* 277 The Pyree he incinerated, and made other common fire be commixt with that they boasted they had from heaven.

† **ˈPyren**, *a. Obs. rare.* [f. L. *Pȳrēnē*, Gr. Πυρήνη the Pyrenees.] = PYRENEAN *a.*

1613 HEYWOOD *Braz. Age* I. Wks. 1874 III. 179 White as the garden lilly, pyren snow, Or rocks of Christall. **1647** R. STAPYLTON *Juvenal* x. 183 He, to his Moores..o're the Pyren mountains jaunts.

‖ **pyreˈnæmia.** *Path.* [mod.L. f. Gr. πυρήν fruit-stone, nucleus + αἷμα blood + -IA.] The presence of nucleated red corpuscles in the blood.

1890 in BILLINGS *Nat. Med. Dict.* **1897** in *Syd. Soc. Lex.*

Hence **pyreˈnæmatous** *a.*, having nucleated red blood corpuscles.

1890 in *Cent. Dict.*

‖ **pyreˈnarium.** *Bot.* [mod.L. f. *pȳrēna* PYRENE[1] + -ARIUM.] A drupaceous pome: i.e. a pome containing pyrenes or 'stones', as those of the medlar and hawthorn.

1890 in *Cent. Dict.*

pyrene[1] (ˈpaɪəriːn). *Bot.* Also in L. form **pyˈrena**, pl. **-æ**. [ad. mod.L. *pȳrēna*, f. Gr. πυρήν fruit-stone.] The stone of a fruit; *esp.* one of those in a drupaceous pome.

1837 KEITH *Bot. Lex.* s.v., If a putamen is composed of several cells, each cell takes the name of pyrena, as in *Cornus*. **1880** GRAY *Struct. Bot.* vii. §2. 296 The pyrenæ or stony inner portion of such carpels when drupaceous or composing a drupe of 2 or more stones. **1882** OGILVIE, Pyrene.

pyrene[2] (ˈpaɪəriːn). *Chem.* (Also 9 **pyren.**) [f. Gr. πῦρ fire + -ENE.] A solid hydrocarbon ($C_{16}H_{10}$) obtained from the dry distillation of coal, crystallizing in microscopic laminæ.

1839 R. D. THOMSON in *Brit. Ann.* 356 Pyren, was prepared from the last process by taking the ether which was employed for the purification of the chrysen, mixing it [etc.]. *Ibid.*, Nitrate of pyrenase; nitric acid forms with pyren a thick oily substance, which is purified by boiling with water and alcohol. **1857** MILLER *Elem. Chem.*, *Org.* III. 552 Pyrene is soluble in hot ether, and may be separated from chrysene by means of this solvent, which at a low temperature deposits it in microscopic rhomboidal plates... This hydrocarbon appears to have been first observed by Laurent. **1877** WATTS *Fownes' Chem.* II. 592 Pyrene $C_{16}H_{10}$ and Chrysene are contained in the portion of coal-tar boiling above 360° (boiling point of anthracene).

b. *Comb.* as *pyrene-ketone*, *-quinone*, etc.

1895 MUIR & MORLEY *Watts' Dict. Chem.* III. 350.

Hence **pyˈrenic** *a.*, of, belonging to, or derived from pyrene, as *pyrenic acid*, $C_{16}H_8O_5$, forming pale yellow plates.

Pyrenean (pɪrəˈniːən), *a.* and *sb.* Also 6– -aean; -eean, 7 Perennean, Pirenean. [ad. F. *Pyrénéen*, or f. L. *Pȳrēnæ-us* (f. *Pȳrēnē*, a. Gr. Πυρήνη, name of the daughter of Bebryx, beloved of Hercules, said to be buried on these mountains) + -AN.]

A. *adj.* **a.** Of or belonging to the Pyrenees.

1865 [see *hair-net* s.v. HAIR *sb.* 10]. **1892** C. M. YONGE *Old Woman's Outlook* 50 The gorgeous Pyrenean anemone, brilliant scarlet with a black or purple centre. **1895** *Army & Navy Co-op. Soc. Price List* 1089/1 (*caption*) Dressing Jacket, Pyrenean Wool, with girdle. **1925** G. JEKYLL *Colour Schemes for Flower Garden* (ed. 6) i. 2 Some groups of the pale early Pyrenean Daffodil gleam level on the ground. **1931** *Times Lit. Suppl.* 21 May 399/3 General Beatson..is already known to the reading public as the author of three monographs on Wellington's operations in the Pyrenean area. **1936** A. W. CLAPHAM *Romanesque Archit.* vi. 132 It is curious that the XP monogram maintained its place in the Pyrenean countries well into the twelfth century. **1966** M. R. D. FOOT *SOE in France* vii. 155 This donnish figure made some highly unacademic contacts with the Pyrenean smugglers.

b. Pyrenean (mountain or **†guard) dog**, a large, heavily built, white dog of the breed so called, often with grey or brown markings on the head, distinguished by a thick, shaggy, double coat; **Pyrenean sheepdog**, a small, fawn or grey, long-coated sheepdog, often with white markings, belonging to the French breed so called; also = *Pyrenean mountain dog* above; **Pyrenean wolfhound** = *Pyrenean mountain dog* above.

1851 H. MAYHEW *London Labour* I. 358/2 The collars most in demand are brass. One man pointed out to me the merits of his stock, which he retailed from 6d each..to 3s—for collars seemingly big enough for Pyrenean sheep dogs. **1865** M. EYRE *Lady's Walks in S. France* xiv. 168 The Pyrenean sheep-dogs equal the largest Newfoundland in size. They are very sagacious and tractable, and usually snow-white. **1871** Pyrenean wolf-hound [see WOLF-HOUND]. **1885** C. M. YONGE *Two Sides of Shield* I. iv. 40 There's Basto, the big Pyrenean dog. **1894** R. B. LEE *Hist. & Descr. Mod. Dogs Gt. Brit. & Ireland (Non-Sporting Division)* iv. 107 The so-called Pyrenean guard dog we often see on our show benches, is a dog some one hundred and twenty pounds weight and more. **1922** R. LEIGHTON *Compl. Bk. Dog* v. 62 The beautiful white-coated Pyrenean Dog is also essentially a Mastiff. **1927** E. C. ASH *Dogs* II. IX. ii. 589 There is..the remarkable similarity of the St. Bernard of about that time to the Pyrenean sheep-dog 'Cabbas', the property of her Majesty Queen Victoria. **1931** A. C. SMITH *About our Dogs* xxiii. 364 So great was my admiration of the Pyrenean Mountain Dogs..that it is rather difficult for me to write with becoming restraint. **1945** C. L. B. HUBBARD *Observer's Bk. Dogs* 184 Pyrenean Sheepdog... This is quite a distinct race from the Pyrenean Mountain Dog,..being much smaller and seldom used for guard work. **1964** *Vogue* 15 Apr. 90 A great heap of Pyrenean mountain dog called Addo de Fontenoy. **1978** *Times* 11 Feb. 2/4 Those shaggy dogs masquerading as overcoats called Pyrenean mountain dogs.

B. *sb.* **a.** A native of the Pyrenees. †**b.** *pl.* The Pyrenees.

1592 *Survay of France* To Rdr., The Pyrenæan mountaines towardes Spaine. **1595** SHAKS. *John* I. i. 201 Talking of the Alpes and Appenines, The Perennean and the riuer Poe. **1656** BLOUNT *Glossogr.*, Pyrenæan Mountains. **1693** MORDEN *Geogr. Rect.* (ed. 3) 178 The Province of Artois..united to the Crown of France by the Pyrenæan Treaty [between France and Spain, 1659]. **1768** EARL MALMESBURY *Diaries & Corr.* I. 35 At fifteen posts from Bayonne you discover the Pyreneans. **1779** H. SWINBURNE *Trav. through Spain* viii. 58 The prospect is..grand..bounded by the mountains of Roussillon. The true Pyreneans appear only through some breaks in that chain. **1802** PINKERTON *Mod. Geog.* I. 275 The Pyrenean chain. *a* **1861** A. H. CLOUGH *Poems* (1862) 245 My Pyrenean Verses will you hear. **1906** *Daily Chron.* 10 Sept. 8/5 Long circular capes in Pyrenean wool fabrics.

c. A Pyrenean mountain dog or sheepdog.

1922 R. LEIGHTON *Compl. Bk. Dog* v. 62 The Pyrenean has the same massive body. **1931** A. C. SMITH *About our Dogs* xxiii. 364 The biggest of the Pyreneans are taller than Newfoundlands. **1950** A. C. SMITH *Dogs since 1900* xii. 272 The Pyreneans..have temperaments that make them most pleasing companions. **1971** F. HAMILTON *World Encycl. Dogs* 73 The Pyrenean is the smallest [French sheepdog]. **1976** *Drive* July-Aug. 31/2 Mischka..is the Wilsons' fifth Pyrenean.

Pyrenees (pɪrəˈniːz), *sb. pl.* Also 7 **Pyrenes, Pir-, Pyreneys, Pirhenese.** [a. F. *Pyrénées*, ad. L. *Pȳrēnæī* (sc. *montes*): see prec.] Name of the range of mountains separating France and Spain.

[**1555** EDEN *Decades* Pref. (Arb.) 53 In the mountaines named Pyrinei th[e] inhabitantes burnt vp the wooddes.] **1632** LITHGOW *Trav.* x. 440 The South Pendicles of the high Pirhenese. *c* **1645** HOWELL *Lett.* (1650) I. 27 These parts of the Pyreneys that border upon the Mediterranean are never without Theeves. **1693** MORDEN *Geogr. Rect.* (ed. 3) 206 Extending from the Pyrenes..Southwards. **1797** *Encycl. Brit.* (ed. 3) XV. 683/2 Pyrenean Mountains, or Pyrenees. **1837** ALISON *Hist. Europe* VI. xlix. 510 Napoleon..felt with Louis XIV, that it was necessary there should be no longer any Pyrenees.

†**b.** *attrib.* (in sing. form **Pyrenee, -ey**). *Obs.*

1608 TOPSELL *Serpents* 598 A Serpent in the Pireney Mountains. *c* **1645** HOWELL *Lett.* (1650) I. 27, I pass'd between som of the Pyreney Hills.

pyreneite (pɪrəˈniːaɪt). *Min.* Also **-aïte.** [ad. Ger. *pyreneit* (Werner 1812), f. as prec.: see -ITE[1].] A variety of iron-lime garnet, greyish-black and of semi-metallic lustre.

1821 URE *Dict. Chem.*, *Pyreneite*..occurs in primitive limestone, in the Pic of Eres-Lids, near Bareges, in the French Pyrenees. **1854** DANA *Syst. Min.* (ed. 4) II. 192. **1866–8** WATTS *Dict. Chem.* IV. 754 Pyrenaite.

pyrenic: see PYRENE[2].

pyrenin (paɪˈriːnɪn). *Phys. Chem.* [f. as PYRENE[1] + -IN[1].] Schwartz's name for the substance composing the nucleolus of a cell.

1890 in *Cent. Dict.* **1897** in *Syd. Soc. Lex.*

‖**pyrenium** (paɪˈriːnɪəm). *Bot.* [mod.L., ad. Gr. πυρήνιον, dim. of πυρήν: see PYRENE[1].] The hypothecium of a nucleiform or angiocarpous apothecium, i.e. that of an angiocarpous lichen.

1866 *Treas. Bot.*, *Pyrenium*, either the receptacle or perithecium of certain fungals. **1882** J. M. CROMBIE in *Encycl. Brit.* XIV. 554/2 (Lichens) When the pyrenium quite covers the nucleus it is said to be entire.

pyrenocarp (paɪˈriːnəʊkɑːp). *Bot.* [f. Gr. πυρήν (see PYRENE[1]) + καρπός fruit.] **a.** 'Any drupaceous fruit' (*Cent. Dict.*). **b.** = PERITHECIUM.

1889 BENNETT & MURRAY *Cryptog. Bot.* 355 The *Pyrenomycetes*, with pyrenocarps or peritheces (hymenia within flask-shaped bodies open at the neck).

Hence **pyreno'carpous** *a.*, resembling, pertaining to, or having a pyrenocarp.

1871 LEIGHTON *Lichen-flora* 36 Apothecia pyrenocarpous verrucarioid.

pyre'nodeous, *a. Bot.* = next, A. So **py'renodine** *a.*

1871 LEIGHTON *Lichen-flora* 4 Apothecia pyrenodine. *Ibid.* 36 Apothecia pyrenodeous.

pyrenoid (paɪˈriːnɔɪd), *a.* and *sb.* [f. Gr. πυρήν (see PYRENE[1]): see -OID.]

A. *adj.* Resembling in form the stone of a fruit: see quots. *rare*⁻⁰.

[**1693** tr. *Blancard's Phys. Dict.* (ed. 2), *Pyrenoides processus*, the Tooth of the second Vertebra.] **1858** MAYNE *Expos. Lex.*, *Pyrenoides*,..pyrenoid. **1897** *Syd. Soc. Lex.*, *Pyrenoid*, kernel-shaped. *Anat.* Epithet formerly applied to the odontoid process of the axis vertebra.

B. *sb.* A small colourless proteid body, resembling a nucleus, found in certain algæ and protozoa.

1883 *Science* I. 148/2 Schmitz finds in the chromatophors of many algæ more or less spherical bodies to which he gives the name of pyrenoids. **1895** OLIVER tr. *Kerner's Nat. Hist. Plants* II. 629 The exact part played by the pyrenoid is very obscure, but there can be no doubt that it influences in some way the formation or deposition of starch by the protoplasm. **1901** G. N. CALKINS *Protozoa* 117 Chromatophores in which one or more deeply staining bodies—the *pyrenoids*—may be found.

‖**pyrenomycetes** (paɪˌriːnəʊmaɪˈsiːtiːz), *sb. pl. Bot.* [mod.L. *Pȳrēnomycētēs*, f. as prec. + μύκης, pl. μύκητες mushroom.] An order of ascomycetous fungi, characterized by the asci being formed in flask-shaped receptacles or perithecia. So **pyˌrenomy'cetous** *a.*, belonging to or of the nature of the *Pyrenomycetes*.

1874 COOKE *Fungi* 56 The hard, or carbonaceous Ascomycetes, sometimes called the Pyrenomycetes. **1882** J. M. CROMBIE in *Encycl. Brit.* XIV. 559/1 (Lichens) Distinguishing them from certain pyrenomycetous fungi.

pyrenous (paɪˈriːnəs), *a. Bot. rare*⁻⁰. [f. as PYRENE[1] + -OUS.] Containing pyrenes or 'stones'; chiefly in comb. with a numeral.

1858 MAYNE *Expos. Lex.*, *Pyrenodes*, having or full of fruit-stones: pyrenous. **1890** *Cent. Dict.*, *Pyrenous*, in *bot.*, containing pyrenes: used only in composition with a numeral: as *2-pyrenous*, *5-pyrenous*, etc.

†**'pyrergy.** *Obs. nonce-wd.* [f. Gr. πῦρ, πυρ- fire + ἔργον work; properly **pyrurgy*: cf. PYRURGIAN.] Working in or with fire.

1651 NOAH BIGGS *New Dispens.* 220 ⁋ 297 She can perfect nothing without Pyrergy.

pyretætiology: see PYRETO-.

pyrethrin (paɪˈriːθrɪn). [a. G. *pyrethrin* (Staudinger & Ruzicka 1924, in *Helvetica Chimica Acta* VII. 181): see PYRETHRUM and -IN[1].] Any of a class of insecticidal terpenoid esters which are obtained from flower heads of *Chrysanthemum cinerariæfolium* and related species, or have been synthesized; *spec.* either of two such compounds (*pyrethrins* I and II) which are the major active principles of pyrethrum powder.

1924 *Chem. Abstr.* XVIII. 1819 A mixt. of the semicarbazones..of pyrethrin I..and pyrethrin II. *Ibid.* 2135 Myrcene and N_2CHCO_2Et give 31% of an acid, $C_{12}H_{18}O_2$, which yields a very slightly active pyrethrin. **1934** *Discovery* Sept. 251/2 Although the difference between pyrethrin I and II is of chemical and biological importance, their action is sufficiently similar for it to be disregarded in practical work. **1951** H. H. SHEPARD *Chem. & Action Insecticides* viii. 146 The pyrethrin content is higher in flowers produced in cool mountain valleys than where the mean temperature is high. *Ibid.* 150 The pyrethrins and cinerins, together referred to generally as pyrethrins, are chemically unstable. **1971** *Inside Kenya Today* Mar. 43/2 Pyrethrin-based insecticides have proved patently safe. **1971** *Nature* 15 Oct. 441/1 Six esters are found in the pyrethrum of which the most important and plentiful are known as pyrethrins I and II.

pyrethrine (paɪˈrɛθraɪn). *Chem.* Also 9 **-in.** [ad. F. *pyrétrine* (Parisel, 1833): see PYRETHRUM and -INE[5].] The substance to which the sialagogic action of pyrethrum root is due; it appears, when pure, to be a white crystalline alkaloid. Hence **py'rethric** *a.*, in *pyrethric acid*, a substance obtained by the action of potassium hydroxide on pyrethrine.

1838 THOMSON *Organic Bodies* 815 To the acrid substance M. Parisel has given the name of pyrethrin. But it appears..that it is not a simple vegetable principle as he supposed, but a compound of two oils and a resin. **1881** WATTS *Dict. Chem.* VIII. 1699 s.v. *Pyrethrum*, R. Buchheim, by evaporating to dryness the alcoholic extract of *Radix pyrethri*, and exhausting the residue with ether, obtained a crystalline substance, *pyrethrin*, which melted at the heat of the body, and was resolved by alcoholic potash into pyrethric acid and piperidine. **1895** DUNSTAN & GARNETT in *Jrnl. Chem. Soc.* LXVII. 101 We propose provisionally to name it *pellitorine*. It is very probable that it is the same substance as that isolated..by Buchheim, in 1876, and named by him *pyrethrine*.

pyrethroid (paɪˈriːθrɔɪd). *Chem.* [f. as PYRETHRIN + -OID.] Any substance possessing the terpenoid structure and insecticidal properties characteristic of the pyrethrins.

1954 *Analytical Chem.* XXVI. 604/1 In recent attempts to estimate small quantities of pyrethrins in flour which had been stored in pyrethrum-treated cotton bags..the extraction..was found to be difficult and there were apparent limitations in the accuracy of the analysis of pyrethroids. **1956** *Nature* 25 Feb. 357/2 It has now also been established that the pyrethroids undergo detoxification in the adult housefly. **1971** *Ibid.* 15 Oct. 441/2 Organochlorine and organophosphorus insecticides, many of which tend to break down less quickly than the pyrethroids. **1977** *Protecting World's Crops* (Shell Internat. Petroleum Co.) 2 Insecticides fall into four main categories: chlorinated hydrocarbons, organo-phosphorus, carbamates and synthetic pyrethroids.

‖**pyrethrum** (paɪˈrɛθrəm, -ˈiːθrəm). Also 6–7 (from Fr.) **pyrethre.** [L. *pyrethrum*, *-on* (Pliny) = sense 1, a. Gr. πύρεθρον feverfew: cf. πυρετός fever. In F. *pyrèthre*, in OF. *piretre* (13th c. in Hatz.-Darm.). Cf. PELLETER, PELLITORY.]

1. Originally, The name of the plant *Anacyclus Pyrethrum*, N.O. *Compositæ*, also called Pellitory of Spain, a native of Barbary, Arabia, and Syria, having a pungent root (*radix pyrethri*) used in medicine. Now so called only in pharmacy.

1562 TURNER *Herbal* II. 107 b, Pyrethrum..hath a stalk & leues like vnto fenell. **1578** LYTE *Dodoens* III. xix. 342 The roote of Pyrethre is hoate and dry in the thirde degree. **1583** *Rates of Customs* D vij, Piretheum [*sic*] the pounde iii *d.* **1607** TOPSELL *Four-f. Beasts* 350 To provoke him to neese, by blowing Pepper and Pyrethre beaten to powder, up into his nostrils. **1799** G. SMITH *Laboratory* II. 422 Take pyrethrum (wild or bastard pellitory) boil it in strong vinegar, so as to prevent the steam from having any vent. **1858** MAYNE *Expos. Lex.*, *Pyrethrum*, The pharmacopœial name for the root of the plant *Anthemis pyrethrum*, or..*Anacyclus pyrethrum*, or pellitory of Spain.

2. a. [Adopted as a generic name in A. Haller *Enumeratio Methodica Stirpium Helvetiæ* (1742) II. 720.] A composite plant of the genus formerly so called, now included in the genus *Chrysanthemum* or the subgenus *Tanacetum*.

As a current florists' name, usually applied to *Pyrethrum* (or *Chrysanthemum*) *roseum*, now grown in many colours, single and double, in summer-gardens in England; also to *P. parthenifolium aureum*, a free-growing hardy dwarf annual or biennial, extensively used for carpet-bedding and edging, having white flowers with yellow disks. Both species are natives of the Caucasus, Armenia, and Persia, and were introduced into England *c* 1803.

1882 *Garden* 13 May 322/3 There seems to be a growing taste for single-flowered Pyrethrums. **1907** *Outlook* 9 Nov. 596/1 New sorts..which combine the virtues of the pyrethrum and daisy with the peculiar quality of the chrysanthemum. **1939** A. CUMMING *Hardy Chrysanthemums* ii. 27 Efforts of the writer to cross this species with the garden chrysanthemum have been unsuccessful, which may indicate..that it is a true pyrethrum. **1951** *Dict. Gardening* (R. Hort. Soc.) I. 469/1 The forms [of chrysanthemum] most widely grown are varieties of *C. morifolium*..and of *C. roseum*, generally known in gardens as Pyrethrums. **1964** G. B. SCHALLER *Year of Gorilla* (1965) iv. 86 Many Europeans have settled in the rift mountains. There they grow tea and white-flowered pyrethrum, used in making insect powder. **1976** *Hortus Third* (L. H. Bailey Hortorium) 267/1 Feverfews. These are forms of *C*[*hrysanthemum*] *Parthenium*, sometimes known as pyrethrum. *Ibid.*, Pyrethrums. These are derived from *C. coccineum*, and bloom in late spring and summer.

b. In full, ***pyrethrum powder***: an insecticide made of the powdered flower-heads of *Chrysanthemum* (or *Tanacetum*) *cinerariifolium* or *C. coccineum*.

1876 DUHRING *Dis. Skin* 599 The best preventives against bugs in beds are corrosive sublimate [and] pyrethrum powder. **1888** *Insect Life* I. 145 Pyrethrum powder was freely used. **1902** *Chambers's Jrnl.* 22 Feb. 191/1 A house where a case of fever had occurred would be fumigated with burning pyrethrum, contiguous dwellings being treated in the same manner. [**1905** *Westm. Gaz.* 15 Apr. 2/3 Another product [of Montenegro] is the 'pyrethrum' flower, which is dried and exported to Italy..for use as insect-powder.] **1955** *Sci. News Let.* 10 Sept. 169/2 Pyrethrum is harmless to human beings and animals, but fatal to flies. **1964** *Which?* Apr. 115/1 The risk is reduced by using..short-lived insecticides, such as derris or pyrethrum. **1978** C. JEFFREY in V. H. Heywood *Flowering Plants of World* 268/3 *Tanacetum cinerariifolium* is the main commercial source of natural pyrethrum, used as an insecticide.

pyretic (paɪər-, pɪˈrɛtɪk), *a.* and *sb.* [ad. mod.L. *pyretic-us*, f. Gr. πυρετ-ός fever: see -IC. Cf. Gr. πυρεκτικός PYRECTIC.]

A. *adj.* **1.** Of or pertaining to fever; producing feverish symptoms; tending to raise the bodily temperature.

1858 MAYNE *Expos. Lex.*, *Pyreticus*, of or belonging to fever: pyretic. **1875** H. C. WOOD *Therap.* (1879) 650 Whenever the bodily temperature falls below normal, pyretic treatment is demanded. **1894** BLACKMORE *Perlycross* xiii, If..pyretic action does not supervene, we shall save her life.

2. Used for the cure of fever, antipyretic.

1868 *Pharm. Jrnl.* Ser. II. IX. 347 An effervescing preparation, called..'Pyretic Salts', and also..'Effervescing Pyretic Saline'.

B. *sb.* A remedy for fever; a febrifuge, an antipyretic. *rare*⁻⁰.

[**1693** tr. *Blancard's Phys. Dict.* (ed. 2), *Pyretica*, Medicines that cure Fevers.] **1728** CHAMBERS *Cycl.*, *Pyretics*, medicines good against Fevers. **1836** in SMART.

pyreto- (ˈpaɪər-, ˈpɪrɪtəʊ), before a vowel **pyret-**, combining form of Gr. πυρετός fever, entering into a few scientific terms. **pyretæti'ology** [ÆTIOLOGY], the ætiology of fevers (Mayne *Expos. Lex.* 1858). ‖**,pyretoge'nesia, -'genesis** [Gr. γένεσις production], the production of fever (ibid.). **pyretoge'netic, pyre'togenous** *adjs.*, breeding or producing fever. **pyre'tography** [-GRAPHY], a description of fevers (Mayne). **pyre'tology** [mod.L. *pyretologia* (R. Morton 1692): see -LOGY], the branch of medical science which treats of fevers.

1899 *Allbutt's Syst. Med.* VI. 253 The absorption of *pyretogenetic substances. **1885–8** FAGGE & PYE-SMITH *Princ. Med.* I. 44 The '*pyretogenous' material in symptomatic fever. **1799** HOOPER *Med. Dict.*, **Pyretology*, a discourse or doctrine on fevers. **1898** P. MANSON *Trop. Diseases* xiii. 214 The study of the pyretology of the tropics.

pyretoid ('paɪər-, 'pɪrɪtɔɪd), *a.* [f. Gr. πυρετ-ός fever + -OID.] Resembling or simulating fever.

1899 *Allbutt's Syst. Med.* VIII. 461 Pseudo-pyretic, or pyretoid erythemata. *Ibid.* 464 A number of erythrodermias which are pyretoid.

pyrewinkes: see PILLIWINKS.

Pyrex ('paɪərɛks). Also **pyrex**. [Invented word. Cf. the following quot.: **1957** *Amer. Speech* XXXII. 290 The assistant secretary of the [Corning Glass] company wrote me as follows: The word *pyrex* is a purely arbitrary word which was devised in 1915 as a trade-mark for products manufactured and sold by Corning Glass Works... We had a number of prior trade-marks ending in the letters *ex*. One of the first commercial products to be sold under the new mark was a pie plate and in the interests of euphonism the letter *r* was inserted between *pie* and *ex* and the whole thing condensed to *pyrex*.]

The proprietary name of a hard, heat-resistant, borosilicate glass. Freq. *attrib.*

1915 *Amer. Cookery* Aug.–Sept. 159 (Advt.), Pyrex ('fire-glass') Glass Dishes for Baking. *Ibid.*, Pyrex is a new-process glass, fire-proofed to withstand the heat of the hottest oven. **1916** *Official Gaz.* (U.S. Patent Office) 1 Aug. 245/1 Corning Glass Works, Corning, N.Y. Filed July 10, 1915 *Pyrex*... Glass. Claims use since May 20, 1915. **1917** *Trade Marks Jrnl.* 10 Jan. 30 *Pyrex*... All goods included in Class 15. Corning Glass Works.. New York, U.S.A... 11th October 1916. **1927** *Glasgow Herald* 1 July 10 Housewives no longer use iron pots and pans. Their kitchenettes are bright with aluminium and pyrex ware. **1932** AUDEN in *Rev. Eng. Stud.* (1978) Aug. 295 Tea was served, Poured by the secretary from a pyrex teapot. **1932** *Discovery* June 199/2 The door itself is fitted with a Pyrex glass window for inspection of the flame. **1958** *Times Lit. Suppl.* 7 Feb. 70/2 Fashionable art critics' jargon which attributes organic qualities to Mr Moore's bronzes or Mr Frank Lloyd Wright's pillars of Pyrex glass. **1961** R. M. DASHWOOD *Provincial Daughter* 107 Odd pieces of Cornish Ware, Pyrex, Willow pattern. **1976** 'Z. STONE' *Modigliani Scandal* IV. iv. 178 Moore took out his false teeth..and dropped them in a Pyrex beaker.

‖**pyrexia** (paɪər-, pɪ'rɛksɪə). *Path.* Pl. **-iæ**. Also anglicized **'pyrexy**. [mod.L., f. Gr. πύρεξις, f. πυρέσσειν (see PYRECTIC). So F. *pyrexie*.] Febrile disease; fever.

1769 W. CULLEN *Nosol. Method.* Init. Synopsis, Class I. Pyrexiæ. Order i. Febres. **1776** —— *First Lines* I. §6 Wks. 1827 I. 479 Pyrexiae, or febrile diseases..beginning with some degree of cold shivering, they shew some increase of heat. **1822–34** *Good's Study Med.* (ed. 4) I. 36 There is heat, thirst, and other concomitants of pyrexy. **1897** *Daily News* 26 Mar. 3/1 On Saturday there was moderate pyrexia, with loss of appetite and intestinal irritation.

Hence **py'rexial, py'rexic, py'rexical** *adjs.*, of, pertaining to, or characterized by pyrexia; febrile.

1846 WORCESTER, *Pyrexical*, relating to fever; febrile. **1847** WEBSTER, *Pyrexial*, relating to fevers. **1876** HARLEY *Mat. Med.* 141 A pleasant drink in pyrexial conditions. **1897** *Allbutt's Syst. Med.* II. 144 During the pyrexial stage. **1890** *Cent. Dict.*, *Pyrexic*, same as *pyrexial*.

pyrgocephalic (,pɜːgəʊsɪ'fælɪk), *a.* [f. Gr. πύργο-ς tower + κεφαλή head + -IC, after *brachycephalic*, etc.] 'Tower-headed', an epithet descriptive of a form of skull having a highly arched vertex. So **pyrgo'cephaly** (-'sɛfəlɪ), the condition of being pyrgocephalic.

1878 BARTLEY tr. *Topinard's Anthrop.* v. 176 Pyrgocephalic, elevated skull. **1897** *Syd. Soc. Lex.*, *Pyrgocephaly*.

pyr'goidal, *a.* *rare*–⁰. [f. Gr. πυργο-ειδής, πυργώδης tower-like (f. πύργος tower: see -OID) + -AL[1].] Tower-shaped; consisting of a prism having a pyramid of corresponding base on one of its ends. (Cf. PYRAMIDATED.)

1890 in *Cent. Dict.*

pyr'gologist. *nonce wd.* [f. Gr. πύργος tower, after *geologist*, etc.] One versed in the structure and history of towers.

1877 *Athenæum* 18 Aug. 218 Those who had the advantage..of hearing what fell from the lips of the great 'castellan' and pyrgologist.

pyrgom ('pɜːgɒm). *Min.* [ad. (by Breithaupt 1830) Gr. πύργωμα, that which is furnished with towers, a fenced city, f. πύργος tower; 'alluding to the grouping of its crystals', Chester.] An aluminous variety of pyroxene allied to sahlite: = FASSAITE b.

1836 T. THOMSON *Min., Geol.*, etc. I. 190.

†**pyrgo'polinize**, *v. Obs. nonce-wd.* [irreg. f. L. *Pyrgopolinīcēs*, name of a swaggering soldier in the 'Miles Gloriosus' of Plautus, f. Gr. πύργος tower + πόλις city + -νικης conquering: see -IZE.] *intr.* To swagger, hector.

1605 G. POWEL *Refut. Epist. Puritan-Papist* To Rdr. 3 His Maiestie need not feare these pyrgopolinizing Champions, for all their desperate threats and big lookes.

pyrheliometer (pɜːhiːlɪ'ɒmɪtə(r)). [f. Gr. πῦρ fire + ἥλιος sun + -METER.] An instrument for measuring the amount of heat given off by the sun, by allowing the rays to fall perpendicularly for a given time upon water or mercury in a blackened closed shallow cylindrical vessel, and observing the consequent rise of temperature in the liquid.

1863 TYNDALL *Heat* xiii. 391 The radiation from the pyrheliometer is often intercepted, when no cloud is seen. **1871** B. STEWART *Heat* §398 Instruments for measuring the intensity of the sun's radiant heat have been devised by Herschel and Pouillet. The instrument of the latter he calls a *pyrheliometer*. **1883** *Science* I. 254/1 The new method of deducing the solar constant from pyrheliometer observations at the earth's surface.

Hence **pyrhelio'metric** *a.*, of, pertaining to, or conducted by a pyrheliometer, as *pyrheliometric experiments*.

1890 in *Cent. Dict.*

Pyribenzamine (pɪrɪ'bɛnzəmiːn). *Pharm.* [f. PYRI(DINE + BENZ(O- + AMINE.] A proprietary name in the U.S. for the antihistamine tripelennamine hydrochloride.

1946 *Proc. Soc. Exper. Biol. & Med.* LXII. 65/1 B-dimethylaminoethyl benzhydryl ether (Benadryl) and pyridil-N'-benzyl-N-dimethylethylenediamine (Pyribenzamine)..have proven effective in histamine, and anaphylactic shock and in the management of some allergic conditions in man. **1946** *Official Gaz.* (U.S. Patent Office) 27 Aug. 511/1 Ciba Pharmaceutical Products, Inc., Summit, N.J... *Pyribenzamine* for preparation indicated for use in allergic conditions. Claims use since July 12, 1945. **1962** F. J. FERGUSON *Drug Therapy* xliv. 346 Recommended agents are promethazine, or Phenergan (if marked sedation is desired), tripelennamine, or Pyribenzamine (for lesser degree of sedation), and phenindamine (Thephorin). **1974** M. C. GERALD *Pharmacol.* ii. 30 Antihistamines such as tripelennamine (Pyribenzamine) do not cure allergies, but they do prevent the agonist, histamine, from initiating an allergic response.

pyridazine (pɪ'rɪdəziːn). *Chem.* [f. PYR(O- + -ID[4] + AZINE.] The weakly basic colourless liquid $C_4H_4N_2$, 1,2-diazine; also, any derivative of this.

1895 *Jrnl. Chem. Soc.* LXVIII. 301 When it is heated.. with 5 per cent. hydrochloric acid at 200°, it yields pyridazine. **1926** H. G. RULE tr. *Schmidt's Text-bk. Org. Chem.* VIII. i. 697 Pyridazines can often be prepared by the oxidation of their dihydro-derivatives. **1975** R. F. BROWN *Org. Chem.* xxviii. 902 The three isomeric diazines are 1,2-diazabenzene (pyridazine), 1,3-diazabenzene (pyrimidine), and 1,4-diazabenzene (pyrazine).

pyridine ('pɪrɪdiːn). *Chem.* [f. Gr. πῦρ, πυρ- fire + -ID[4] + -INE[5].] **a.** A colourless volatile liquid alkaloid (C_5H_5N) of offensive odour and poisonous quality, produced in the dry distillation of bone-oil and other bituminous matter. The inhalation of its vapour was said to be beneficial in asthma, etc.

pyridine bases, the series of alkaloids, of composition $C_nH_{2n-5}N$, of which pyridine is the lowest member, and picoline, lutidine, collidine, parvoline, etc., other examples.

1851 T. ANDERSON in *Trans. Roy. Soc. Edin.* (1853) XX. 253 The first of these [pyrrol bases], to which I give the name of pyridine. **1866** WATTS *Dict. Chem.* IV. 755 Pyridine is a colourless mobile liquid, having a most powerful and peculiar odour closely resembling that of picoline, and, like that alkaloid, causing a bitter taste in the mouth and back of the throat. **1881** *Ibid.* 3rd Suppl. 1699 Pyridine may be regarded as benzine having one of its CH groups replaced by nitrogen. **1888** *Daily News* 26 June, 7/7 The latest practice adopted by the German Government,..is that of mingling with the [methylated] spirit 'pyridine', an essence which gives the 'peculiarly offensive and characteristic odour' to a refuse of the gas-works which the men call 'devil water'.

b. *Comb.* as *pyridine-carboxylic acid*, a name for picolinic and nicotinic acids. **pyridine nucleotide**, either of the two oxidizing co-enzymes di- and triphosphopyridine nucleotide (co-enzymes I and II); (sometimes with added *di-* or *triphosphate* respectively).

[**1936** *Chem. Abstr.* XXX. 8262 Cozymase is an adenine-pyridine-nucleotide, which is a H-transporter because the pyridine changes to dihydropyridine.] **1937** *Proc. R. Soc.* B. CXXII. 355 The question then arose whether or not the action of pyridine nucleotide triphosphate was specific and if it could be replaced by pyridine nucleotide diphosphate. *Ibid.* 359 The two pyridine nucleotides were active as 'V' factor, the limit of the activity of pyridine nucleotide triphosphate being about 1/600,000,000. **1951** WHITBY & HYNES *Med. Bacteriol.* (ed. 5) xvi. 282 The V factor is the di- or tri-phosphate of pyridine nucleotide, coenzymes that act as intermediate hydrogen receptors in cytochrome and other respiratory mechanisms. **1966** S. P. COLOWICK et al. in Florkin & Stotz *Comprehensive Biochem.* XIV. i. 4 The pyridine nucleotides are thus concerned in virtually all biosynthetic and degradative processes involving oxidation-reduction steps.

Hence **py'ridic** *a.*, of or related to pyridine; *pyridic group* or *series*, the series of pyridine bases: see above; **'pyridone** = oxy-pyridine, C_5H_5NO; **'pyridyl**, the radical C_5H_4N of pyridine.

1887 A. M. BROWN *Anim. Alkaloids* Introd. 11 Those.. which are constantly present in prolonged putrefactive fermentations, belong to the pyridic and hydropyridic series; they do not differ widely from the poisonous bases of hemlock and tobacco. *Ibid.* 93 A base which seems to belong to the pyridic group.

pyridostigmine (,pɪrɪdəʊ'stɪgmiːn). *Pharm.* [ad. G. *pyridostigmin*: see PYRIDINE and *neostigmine* s.v. NEO- 1 b.] The ion $(CH_3)_2N{\cdot}CO{\cdot}O{\cdot}C_6H_4N^+CH_3$ or its bromide derivative, a whitish crystalline powder similar in action to neostigmine but weaker and longer-acting and giving rise to fewer side-effects.

1953 *Jrnl. Amer. Med. Assoc.* 12 Sept. 175/1 Since 1948, a pyridine homologue of neostigmine (Pyridostigmine), was given a therapeutic trial in 23 patients with myasthenia gravis associated with pseudoparalysis. Results of animal experiments..showed that Pyridostigmine is five times less toxic than neostigmine. **1961** D. DUNLOP et al. *Textbk. Med. Treatm.* (ed. 8) 875 Myasthenia Gravis... The drug which is most generally useful is pyridostigmine bromide, B.P.C. (Mestinon)... Pyridostigmine gives a very satisfactory smooth control with few parasympathomimetic side-effects, and the long action without sudden withdrawal effects makes it particularly suitable for treatment during the night. **1980** *Sci. Amer.* Apr. 38/2 Reversible inhibitors of acetylcholinesterase such as pyridostigmine (administered by means of pills swallowed a short time before nerve-gas exposure) may improve the prognosis.

pyridoxal (pɪrɪ'dɒksæl). *Biochem.* [f. as next + -AL[2].] One of the forms of vitamin B_6 (derived from pyridoxine by oxidation of the 4-hydroxymethyl group to aldehyde), which usu. occurs in mammals as the phosphate ester and is a co-enzyme in a number of metabolic processes, notably transamination. Cf. PYRIDOXINE.

1944 E. E. SNELL in *Jrnl. Biol. Chem.* CLIV. 313 (*caption*) Pyridoxal. *Ibid.*, When pyridoxamine or pyridoxal is used as a standard of comparison with *S[treptococcus] lactis*, values for the 'B₆' content of natural materials are obtained similar to those indicated by yeast assay, instead of the absurdly high values obtained against a pyridoxine standard. **1955** *Sci. News Let.* 1 Oct. 211/1 The cancer cells..need these seven vitamins: choline, folic acid, nicotinamide, pantothenate, pyridoxal, riboflavin and thiamine. **1966** E. R. M. KAY *Biochem.* xxiii. 302 Transamination reactions appear to involve a transfer of the amino group to the pyridoxal, forming pyridoxamine and a keto acid. **1970** [see PYRIDOXAMINE]. **1974** *Nature* 9 Aug. 502/2 Pyridoxine, the major dietary form of vitamin B_6, is rapidly converted in the body to pyridoxal phosphate.., the coenzyme form.

pyridoxamine (pɪrɪ'dɒksəmiːn). *Biochem.* [f. as next + AMINE.] One of the active forms of vitamin B_6 (related to pyridoxine by replacement of the 4-hydroxymethyl group by an aminomethyl group), which is usu. present in mammals as the phosphate ester and is a co-enzyme in protein metabolism. Cf. PYRIDOXINE.

1944 E. E. SNELL in *Jrnl. Biol. Chem.* CLIV. 315 (*caption*) Pyridoxamine. **1944** [see PYRIDOXAL]. **1950** *Thorpe's Dict. Appl. Chem.* (ed. 4) X. 316/2 Schlenk and Fisher..working with the glutamic-aspartic transaminase system from pig-heart, have suggested that the reversible interconversion of pyridoxal and pyridoxamine in the prosthetic group forms the basis of the enzyme system. **1961** [see PYRIDOXINE]. **1966** [see PYRIDOXAL]. **1968** J. MARKS *Vitamins in Health & Dis.* 94/2 The B_6 group are rapidly converted in the body into the co-enzymes pyridoxal phosphate and pyridoxamine phosphate... These co-enzymes play an essential role in protein metabolism. **1970** R. W. MCGILVERY *Biochem.* vi. 120 The substituted pyridine ring of pyridoxal phosphate.. cannot be synthesized by vertebrates, and its dietary precursors are lumped together as vitamin B_6, which includes pyridoxal, pyridoxamine, and the corresponding alcohol, pyridoxine.

pyridoxic (pɪrɪ'dɒksɪk), *a.* *Biochem.* [f. as next + -IC.] *pyridoxic acid* (more explicitly *4-pyridoxic acid*), an inactive oxidized derivative of pyridoxine (the 4-hydroxymethyl group having been oxidized to carboxyl), which is the form in which excess vitamin B_6 is usu. excreted.

1944 HUFF & PERLZWEIG in *Jrnl. Biol. Chem.* CLV. 355 A fluorescent compound appearing in urine after the ingestion of pyridoxine was isolated and identified as 2-methyl-3-hydroxy-4-carboxy-5-hydroxymethylpyridine (4-pyridoxic acid). **1950** W. SHIVE in R. J. Williams et al. *Biochem. of B Vitamins* D. viii. 657 Pyridoxic acid is the chief metabolic product of either pyridoxine, pyridoxal or pyridoxamine. **1968** BAKER & FRANK *Clinical Vitaminol.* vii. 79 In subjects on a normal diet, pyridoxic acid excretion accounted for only about half the intake of vitamin B_6.

pyridoxine (pɪrɪ'dɒksiːn, -ɪn). *Biochem.* Also **-in**. [f. PYRIDINE with inserted OX- 1.] One of the three common forms of vitamin B_6, a colourless, weakly basic, crystalline solid which occurs esp. in cereals, liver oils, and yeast, is also manufactured commercially, and is readily interconverted inside the body to the other forms of the vitamin, pyridoxal and pyridoxamine, with which it usu. occurs; 3-hydroxy-4,5-di(hydroxymethyl)-2-methyl-pyridine, $C_8H_{11}NO_3$; = ADERMIN.

1939 [see ADERMIN]. **1941** *Science* 5 Dec. 545/2 *In vitro* experiments with pyridoxine..failed to demonstrate the presence of the unknown substance. **1948** *New Biol.* IV. 24 Roots of a hybrid [tomato] are apparently able to synthesise pyridoxine and nicotinamide better than the roots of its parents. **1961** *Lancet* 16 Sept. 623/1 Pyridoxine deficiency induced by these drugs is an alternative mechanism invoked to explain the liver damage, and Coursin..found low levels of circulating pyridoxal and pyridoxamine in a patient showing iproniazid toxicity. **1970** L. J. HARRIS in J. Needham *Chem. of Life* vi. 164 In 1934, a second component of the vitamin B_2 complex, at first called vitamin B_6..and now generally known as pyridoxin, was identified. **1972** *Materials & Technol.* V. xix. 679 Pyridoxine hydrochloride is produced commercially by synthesis... It is used in multi-vitamin preparations and in larger quantities to counteract drug effects. **1974** M. C. GERALD *Pharmacol.* x. 182 Deficiencies of pyridoxine (vitamin B6) and niacin cause convulsions in infants and pellagra, respectively.

Now also called **pyri'doxol** [-OL].

1959 *Recueil des Travaux Chimiques des Pays-Bas* LXXVIII. 226 (*heading*) An improved synthesis of vitamin B_6 (pyridoxol). [*Note*] The name pyridoxol was proposed at the 17th IUPAC congress at Stockholm in 1953. **1966** MAHLER & CORDES *Biol. Chem.* viii. 341 Numerous nutritional studies..have established that a deficiency of pyridoxol (pyridoxine)..results in many lesions in protein metabolism. **1973** ZEFFREN & HALL *Stud. Enzyme Mechanisms* viii. 157 The nutritional factor vitamin B_6 was known in 1934 to be involved in protein metabolism. Chemical studies showed that its structure was 3-hydroxy-4,5-di(hydroxymethyl)-2-methylpyridine.., called pyridoxol.

pyrie, variant of PERRY[1] *Obs.*, a pear-tree; obs. form of PIRRIE, a squall.

pyriform ('paɪərɪ-, 'pɪrɪfɔːm), *a.* Also piri-. [ad. mod.L. *pyriformis*, f. *pyrum*, erron. med.L. spelling of *pirum* pear + -FORM.] **a.** Of the shape of a pear, pear-shaped; obconic; differing from *oviform* in having a slight stricture at or near the narrow end.

1741 MONRO *Anat. Nerves* (ed. 3) 77 The *Receptaculum Chyli*..is a..somewhat pyriform Bag. **1757** JOHNSTONE in *Phil. Trans.* L. 546 This calculus..was of a pyriform shape. **1863** *Wand. W. Africa* II. 36 The fruit..is a pyriform pod with crimson skin enclosing black brown seeds. **1913** *Cunningham's Text-bk. Anat.* (ed. 4) 164 The apertura piriformis [*ed.* 3 (1909): pyriformis].., which lies below and in part between the orbits, is of variable shape and size—usually piriform [*ed.* 3: pyriform], it tends to be long and narrow in Europeans. **1928** V. G. CHILDE *Most Anc. East* v. 117 The piriform mace has a very long history in Babylonia. **1932** *Times Lit. Suppl.* 20 Oct. 743/1 His performances on the putting green with an archaic piriform wooden putter were marked by a deadly accuracy. **1948** A. BRODAL *Neurol. Anat.* x. 327 The olfactory fibres ultimately transmitting olfactory impulses to the cerebral cortex are those passing to the piriform lobe. **1948, 1962** [see PALÆOPALLIUM]. **1971** *Country Life* 15 July 184/1 Shapes of fashionable cruet glass followed those of silver. Castors were at first pyriform. **1973** M. CROWELL *Greener Pastures* 167 Birds like the murre..lay triangular, or pyriform, eggs that roll in tight circles. **1973** *Nature* 3 Aug. 314/2 A small snout with a small piriform aperture projected from a broad and very flat face.

b. *Anat.* Denoting a muscle of the hip. Usually in L. form *pyriformis*, also *absol.* (sc. *musculus*).

1704 J. HARRIS *Lex. Techn.* I, *Pyriformis, seu Iliacus Externus*, is a Muscle of the Thigh. **1841** RAMSBOTHAM *Obstetr. Med.* (1855) 4 The sciatic and pudic nerves, and the pyriform muscle. **1872** MIVART *Elem. Anat.* 301 The Pyriformis arises from the front of the sacrum. **1897** *Allbutt's Syst. Med.* IV. 859 The anterior wall of the pyriform sinus.

c. In comb. with another adj. expressing form.

1821 W. P. C. BARTON *Flora N. Amer.* I. 117 Root pyriform-bulbous. *Ibid.* 118 Germ pyriform-triangular.

So **'pyriformed** *a. rare*, = prec.

1874 *Archæol. Assoc. Jrnl.* Dec. 433 Both spoons are of the sixteenth century... The pyriformed bowl is stamped with the maker's mark, a rose.

pyrimethamine (pɪrɪ'mɛθəmiːn). *Pharm.* [f. PYRIM(IDINE + ETH(YL + AMINE.] A white crystalline solid, 2,4-diamino-5-*p*-chloro-phenyl-6-ethylpyrimidine, $C_{12}H_{13}N_4Cl$, which is given orally for the prophylaxis and suppression of malaria.

1953 *Brit. Med. Jrnl.* 31 Jan. 253/1 Pyrimethamine..is the latest of the new synthetic anti-malarial drugs to be tested by us... This compound is produced by Burroughs Wellcome & Co. under the trade name 'daraprim'. **1961** *New Scientist* 20 Apr. 120/1 Pyrimethamine resistance has appeared in some districts in East Africa. **1966** *Lancet* 24 Dec. 1382/1 The combination of dapsone to shorten the red-blood-cell life-span and pyrimethamine to inhibit erythropoiesis has now been used successfully on five patients with secondary polycythæmia. **1976** *Ibid.* 4 Dec. 1257/1 When a dose of 25 mg weekly is taken for malarial prophylaxis, pyrimethamine is unlikely to produce adverse hæmatological effects except in those actually or potentially folate deficient.

pyrimidine (pɪ'rɪmɪdiːn, paɪər-). *Chem.* Also †-in. [ad. G. *pyrimidin* (A. Pinner 1885, in *Ber. d. Deut. Chem. Ges.* XVIII. 760) f. *pyridin* PYRIDINE with inserted *-im* (f. *imid* IMIDE).] A colourless, crystalline basic solid, CH:N·CH:N·CH:CH; any substituted derivative containing this ring structure, *spec.* cytosine, thymine, or uracil, pyrimidines found in nucleic acids, etc. Freq. *attrib.*

1885 *Jrnl. Chem. Soc.* XLVIII. II. 751 The author substitutes the formula $R\cdot C\left\langle\begin{matrix}N\cdot C(OH)\\ N{:}CMe\end{matrix}\right\rangle CH$ for that previously assigned, terming the nucleus pyrimidine. **1886** *Ibid.* L. 45 The author has tried to prepare the corresponding pyrimidines from various amidines. **1899** *Ibid.* LXXVI. I. 639 Pyrimidine..melts at 20–22°..; it has a penetrating, stupefying odour. **1924** *Nature* 12 Apr. 524/1 In these bodies [sc. the nucleic acids] a carbohydrate group is associated with a phosphoric acid group and also with a purin or pyrimidin base. **1947** *Sci. News* IV. 109 The I.C.I. men started on something quite different: the pyrimidine ring, an assemblage of atoms found in uric acid, in the chromosomes of the nucleus of living cells, and widely in all living things. **1952, 1954** [see PURINE]. **1960** *New Biol.* XXXI. 40 The two pyrimidines, which are smaller molecules than the purines, are named thymine and cytosine. **1962** D. J. BROWN *Pyrimidines* iv. 116 Until recently, pyrimidine was an exceedingly rare substance, but several good methods of preparation have now made it readily available in quantity. **1976** *Ann. Rev. Microbiol.* XXX. 92 Other auxotrophs such as those requiring amino acids, purines, and pyrimidines do not assume a colonial or semicolonial growth habit if the biochemical supplement in the medium is limiting.

pyritaceous (paɪər-, pɪrɪ'teɪʃəs), *a. rare.* [f. PYRITES + -ACEOUS.] Of the nature of or containing pyrites.

1794 SULLIVAN *View Nat.* I. 448 Sprinkled with yellow, bright pyritaceous specks or streaks. **1796** KIRWAN *Elem. Min.* (ed. 2) I. 104 Pyritaceous limestone gives a grey powder, is not magnetic..detonates with nitre.

pyrite ('paɪəraɪt). Also 6 **pyrit**, 6–7 **pirrite**. [f. L. *pyrītēs*: see next. In F. *pyrite* (12th c.).]

†**1.** In early use (often *pyrit(e stone* = Gr. πυρίτης λίθος) = PYRITES 1; fire-stone. Later, in general sense of PYRITES 2. *Obs.*

1567 MAPLET *Gr. Forest* 17 b, The Pirrite must with easie hand..enholden be. **1588** GREENE *Perimedes* Wks. (Grosart) VII. 62 Resembling the Pyrite stone. **1589** —— *Tullies Love* ibid. 107 A Pyrit stone, which handled softly is as colde as ice, but pressed betweene the fingers burneth as fire. **1590** —— *Never too late* (1600) 34 Like the pyrit stone, that is, fire without, and frost within. **1688** R. HOLME *Armoury* II. 41/2 The Pirrite is a kind of stone yellow. **1791** E. DARWIN *Bot. Gard.* I. ii. 350 Hence sable Coal his massy couch extends And stars of gold the sparkling Pyrite blends.

2. *Min.* Native disulphide of iron (FeS_2), crystallizing in isometric forms, esp. in cubes and pyritohedra: one of the forms of *iron pyrites* (next, 2).

1868 DANA *Min.* 63 The pyrite of most gold regions is auriferous. Pyrite occurs abundantly in rocks of all ages, from the oldest crystalline to the most recent alluvial deposits. **1896** CHESTER *Dict. Names Min.* s.v., Pyrite..is now only applied to the disulphide of iron which crystallizes in isometric forms.

‖**pyrites** (pɪ'raɪtiːz). Pl. (rare) †**py'ritæ**. Also 6 **pirrites**. [L. *pyrītēs* (Pliny) fire-stone, flint, pyrites, a. Gr. πυρίτης 'of or in fire' (f. πῦρ fire), πυρίτης (sc. λίθος) 'a mineral which strikes fire, the copper pyrites of mineralogists' (L. & Sc.).

1668 CHARLETON *Onomast.* 301 Pyrites (ita dictus, vel quod ex eo ignis excutiatur; vel quod ignei sit coloris) Arabibus Marcasita et Zeq nigrum.]

†**1.** In early use, vaguely, a 'fire-stone' or mineral capable of being used for striking fire. *Obs.*

Formerly the subject of fabulous statements.

1588 GREENE *Alcida* Wks. (Grosart) IX. 45 As the stone Pyrites once set on fire burneth in the water. **1610** HEALEY *St. Aug. Citie of God* XXI. v. (1620) 788 The Persian Pyrites pressed hard in the hand burneth it, whereupon it hath the name. **1706** PHILLIPS (ed. 6), *Pyritis*, a precious Stone, which burns the Fingers, if one holds it hard. **1750** *Leonardus' Mirr. Stones* 220 In a large Sense, all Stones that strike Fire may be called Pyrites. **1796** KIRWAN *Elem. Min.* (ed. 2) II. 75 Pyrites is a name antiently given to any Metallic compound that gave fire with steel, exhaling at the same time, a Sulphurious or Arsenical smell.

2. In modern use: Either of the two common sulphides of iron (FeS_2), pyrite and marcasite, also called distinctively ***iron pyrites***; also, the double sulphide of copper and iron ($Cu_2S.Fe_2S_3$), chalcopyrite or ***copper pyrites***.

Used also generically to include many related sulphides and arsenides of iron, cobalt, nickel, etc., or of iron with another metal; e.g. **arsenical p.**, including Leucopyrite $FeAs_2$, and Mispickel $FeAs_2$. FeS_2; **capillary p.**, native sulphide of nickel = MILLERITE[2]; **magnetic p.**, Fe_7S_8 = PYRRHOTITE; **spear p.**, **white iron p.**, varieties of MARCASITE; **tin p.**, $Cu_2S(SnS_3.Fe_2S_3)$; **variegated p.**, $FeS.2Cu_2S$, = ERUBESCITE. Also COBALT, COCKSCOMB, HEPATIC *Pyrites*.

[**1555** EDEN *Decades* 133 *margin*, These colers or floures are cauled Marchesites, Pyrites.] **1567** MAPLET *Gr. Forest* 17 b, Pirrites is a kinde of stone, yealow, like to the fire his flame. **1601** HOLLAND *Pliny* II. 588 There is another fire stone going vnder the name of Pyrites or Marcasin, that resembleth brasse ore in the mine. **1694** SLARE in *Phil. Trans.* XVIII. 218 He..engrossed all the Pyrites or Copperas-stone to himself. **1748** SIR J. HILL *Hist. Fossils* 615 The most common of all the species of striated Pyritæ. **1794** SULLIVAN *View Nat.* I. 381 The heated Bath waters..owe their origin to the contact of common water with pyritæ, whose composition is iron, sulphur, and the vitriolic principle. **1839** DARWIN *Voy. Nat.* xii. (1852) 260 The Chilian miners were so convinced that copper pyrites contained not a particle of copper, that [etc.]. **1870** YEATS *Nat. Hist. Comm.* 354 Pyrites sometimes contains gold, and it is then called auriferous pyrites. **1880** DAWKINS *Early Man* x. 358 Fire was obtained in the Bronze age by striking a flint flake against a piece of iron pyrites. **1886** *Encycl. Brit.* XX. 128/2 By modern mineralogists the term 'pyrites' has been extended to a number of metallic sulphides, and it is..now used rather as a group-name than as the specific designation of a mineral.

attrib. and *Comb.* **1864** *Jrnl. Chem. Soc.* XVII. 118 The flue-dust of Pyrites-burners. **1896** *Daily News* 15 Aug. 11/1 Pyrites lodes..carrying over an ounce of gold to the ton, are now being opened up.

pyritic (paɪə-, pɪ'rɪtɪk), *a.* [f. PYRIT-ES + -IC.] Of or pertaining to pyrites, containing or resembling pyrites. *spec.* applied to a process for smelting sulphide copper ores with pyrites so that oxidation of the latter produces all the necessary heat.

1802 HOWARD in *Phil. Trans.* XCII. 179 Bright shining spiculæ, of a metallic or pyritic nature. **1813** BAKEWELL *Introd. Geol.* (1815) 104 Yorkshire slate..is sometimes covered with thin pyritic configurations resembling trees, hence called 'dendritical'. **1892** *Pall Mall G.* 5 May 2/1 The deep levels..where the ore becomes pyritic. **1897** HUNTINGTON & MCMILLAN *Metals* (new ed.) 331 This is the process known as pyritic smelting, and there is some prospect that it may take a prominent position in the metallurgy of copper, although at present it is mainly employed in the extraction of gold and silver from complex ores. **1926** D. M. LIDDELL *Handbk. Nonferrous Metallurgy* II. xxvii. 944 There are three distinct processes in blast-furnace smelting: (1) The reduction process... The blast oxidizes the carbon of the coke and but little of the sulphur in the ore... (2) The pyritic process, in which raw massive sulphides are smelted in a highly oxidizing atmosphere without the addition of carbonaceous fuel... (3) The partial- or semipyritic process. *Ibid.* 945 The essential requirements for pyritic smelting are siliceous material which is high in free silica, and heavy pyrite ore... The pyrite ore not only furnishes the heat for the operation, but also the sulphur for the matte required. **1974** D. AVERY *Not on Queen Victoria's Birthday* xiv. 280 'Pyritic smelting', developed by Lawrence Austin and Robert Sticht at [*sic*] Montana between 1887 and 1896 and introduced at Mount Lyell in Tasmania in the latter year,..provided a means of producing much cheaper copper.

pyritical (paɪə-, pɪ'rɪtɪkəl), *a.* [f. as prec. + -AL[1]: see -ICAL.] = prec.

1756 P. BROWNE *Jamaica* 58 A green copper ore in a pyritical matrix. **1789** J. WILLIAMS *Min. Kingd.* I. 419 The pyritical or marcasitical yellow copper ores. **1845** J. PHILLIPS *Geol.* in *Encycl. Metrop.* VI. 673/1 Striped loam and plastic clay, containing a few pyritical casts of shells.

pyritiferous (paɪər-, pɪrɪ'tɪfərəs), *a.* [f. PYRITES + -FEROUS.] Yielding pyrites.

1828–32 in WEBSTER. **1847–8** H. MILLER *First Impr.* xii. (1857) 188 Here it trickles..through a pyritiferous shale. **1877** RAYMOND *Statist. Mines & Mining* 391 All the siliceous pyritiferous ores are selected for this purpose.

pyritify (paɪə-, pɪ'rɪtɪfaɪ), *v.* [f. PYRITES, after *petrify*.] *trans.* = PYRITIZE. So **pyritifi'cation** = PYRITIZATION.

1757 tr. *Henckel's Pyritol.* 94 Nature finds materials..as grounds and foundations for a pyritification. **1851** MANTELL *Petrifactions* i. §2. 27 fig., Stem of a young plant, pyritified.

†**pyritish**, *a. Obs. rare.* [f. PYRITE or PYRITES + -ISH[1].] Resembling that of pyrite or pyrites.

1756 C. LUCAS *Ess. Waters* II. 133 A pyritish smell arises about the well.

pyritize ('paɪər-, 'pɪrɪtaɪz), *v.* [f. PYRIT-ES + -IZE.] *trans.* To convert into pyrites (as wood by replacement of the original substance by iron pyrites); to impregnate with pyrites. Hence **'pyritized** *ppl. a.*; also **pyriti'zation**, conversion into pyrites.

1805 CHENEVIX in *Phil. Trans.* XCV. 115 Professor Lampadius, in distilling some pyritized wood,..obtained the same substance. **1839** MURCHISON *Silur. Syst.* I. xxvi. 334, I use the term *pyritized* in reference to these altered rocks in contact with the trap which contain numerous and large crystals of iron pyrites. **1889** *Q. Jrnl. Geol. Soc.* Feb. 124 Rarity of fossil Radiolaria... Their pyritization would tend to their ready destruction.

pyrito- (pɪ'raɪtəʊ, 'paɪərɪtəʊ), combining form of PYRITES, occurring in a few scientific terms. **pyrito-bi'tuminous** *a.*, containing pyrites and bitumen. **pyritohedron** (-'hiːdrən, 'hɛdrən), pl. **-hedra**, *Cryst.* [Gr. ἕδρα side, after *tetrahedron*, etc.], a form of pentagonal dodecahedron, or solid contained by twelve pentagons, common in crystals of pyrite; hence **pyrito'hedral** *a.*, pertaining to or of the form of a pyritohedron. **pyri'tology** [ad. mod.L. *pyritologia*: see -LOGY], a treatise on, or the study of, pyrites.

1796 KIRWAN *Elem. Min.* (ed. 2) II. 17 The Ores in which Allum owes its origin to the decomposition of Pyrites... 1st. The purely pyritous... 2d. The *Pyrito Bituminous. **1868** DANA *Min.* 62 Pyrite. Isometric; *pyritohedral... The cube..most common; the *pyritohedron..and related forms..very common. Cubic faces often striated. **1895** STORY-MASKELYNE *Crystallogr.* §190. 229 A remarkable combination of pyritohedron and octahedron is a not uncommon form of pyrites and cobaltite... The eight faces of the octahedron are equilateral triangles, and the twelve faces of the pyritohedron assume also a triangular form. [**1725** J. F. HENCKEL (*title*) *Pyritologia, oder Kiesz Historie. **1757** (*title*) Pyritologia, or a History of the Pyrites.] **1828–32** WEBSTER, *Pyritology*, a discourse or treatise on pyrites.

pyritoid (pɪˈraɪtɔɪd), *a.* [f. PYRIT-ES + -OID.] Resembling or allied to pyrites.

1895 STORY-MASKELYNE *Crystallogr.* vii. §190 Pyro-electricity . . has no place in the case of the pyritoid minerals. *Ibid.*, Of the different pentagonohedra known on the pyritoid minerals the only one that is self-existent is the 'pyritohedron'.

pyritose (ˈpaɪər-, ˈpɪrɪtəʊs), *a.* [f. PYRIT-ES + -OSE: cf. next.] = next.

1758 REID tr. *Macquer's Chym.* I. 382 When the ore to be smelted is pyritose and refractory, it may be roasted at first with a much stronger degree of fire than is used for ores that are fusible. **1842** *Mechanic's Mag.* XXXVI. 294 In Great Britain, where sulphate of iron from refuse pyritose coal and gypsum may be had almost for nothing.

pyritous (ˈpaɪərɪtəs, pɪˈraɪtəs), *a.* [f. PYRIT-ES + -OUS; in F. *pyriteux.*] Of, of the nature of, or containing pyrites; characterizing, or characterized by the presence of, pyrites.

1756 C. LUCAS *Ess. Waters* II. 180 More or less of the pyritous smell is generally perceptible. **1794** SULLIVAN *View Nat.* II. 112 All pit coal is more or less pyritous. **1839** URE *Dict. Arts* 337 Pyritous Copper; Kupferkies; a metallic looking substance, of a bronze-yellow colour. **1852** TH. ROSS *Humboldt's Trav.* I. vi. 235 Ravines, of which the pyritous strata have borne for ages the imposing names of 'Minas de oro!' **1881** BODDY *Hist. Salt* iv. 34 Those sulphates so prevalent in the . . pyritous beds of the Lias.

†**ˈpyrity**, *a. Obs.* [f. PYRITE + -Y.] Containing pyrite or pyrites.

1757 tr. *Henckel's Pyritol.* 175 Small or poor ores, which are commonly quartzy, mock-leady, and pyrity. *Ibid.* 302 Neither pyrity nor vitriolic.

pyrk(e, obs. forms of PERK *sb.*[1] and *v.*[1]

pyrl(e, obs. forms of PIRL, PURL *sb.*[1] and *v.*[1]

pyro (ˈpaɪərəʊ). *Photogr.* Abbreviation of PYROGALLIC *acid* or PYROGALLOL, extensively used as a developing agent. Often *attrib.* and in *Comb.*, as in *pyro-developer*, *-solution*, etc.

1879 *Cassell's Techn. Educ.* III. 294 The proper developing agent for collodio-bromide plates is . . known as the alkaline pyro-developer. **1885** C. G. W. LOCK *Workshop Receipts* Ser. IV. 376/2 Take enough of the pyro solution in your developing tray to well cover the plate. **1892** *Photogr. Ann.* II. 44 Pyro and other photo chemicals are violent poisons. **1893** *Brit. Jrnl. Photogr.* XL. 747 Pyro is used in conjunction with sodium sulphate. **1905** *Westm. Gaz.* 5 Aug. 14/2 One of the chief merits of the pyro-developed negative.

b. *Comb.*, indicating a mixture of pyrogallic acid with another substance, as a developer: e.g. *pyro-ammonia*, *-lime*, *-metol*, *-potash*, *-soda*; **pyro-carbonate**, pyrogallic acid with carbonate of soda.

1885 C. G. W. LOCK *Workshop Receipts* Ser. IV. 357/1 The pyro-lime developer becomes violet and brown in use. **1890** *Anthony's Photogr. Bull.* III. 108 Now a word about developers. I have tried them all. . . Ferrous oxalate pyro-soda, pyro-potash, hydroquinone, etc. *Ibid.* 312, I have developed a good many dozens of exposures, and with pyro-ammonia or pyro-carbonate I have not yet got an unevenly developed film. **1907** *Westm. Gaz.* 2 Mar. 18/2 A green-brown or brown-black colour, such as is given by a pyro-metol developer or pyro-soda not too heavily dosed with sulphite.

pyro- (paɪərəʊ, pɪrəʊ), before a vowel or *h* sometimes **pyr-** (but more freq. *pyro-*), repr. Gr. πυρο-, combining form of πῦρ fire, forming the first element in many terms belonging to various arts and sciences. (The second element is properly of Greek, but sometimes of Latin or English origin.)

1. In various terms, chiefly scientific or technical, in the sense Of, relating to, done with, caused or produced by fire.

pyroˈcellulose, a form of nitrocellulose containing slightly less nitrogen than gun-cotton (see quots.); **ˈpyroclast** *Geol.*, a pyroclastic rock fragment; **pyroˈclastic** *a. Geol.* [Gr. κλαστός broken: cf. CLASTIC], consisting of fragments broken through the action of volcanic fire, or comminuted in the process of eruption; also as *sb.*, a pyroclastic rock or rock fragment; **ˈpyrocone**, a cone of flame, as in the blow-pipe flame; **ˌpyro-enˈgraver**, an artist who practises PYROGRAVURE or poker-work; **pyrognomic** (-ˈgnɒmɪk, ˈgnəʊmɪk) *a.* [Gr. γνώμη means of knowing, mark, token]: see quot.; **pyrognostic** (-ˈgnɒstɪk) *a. Min.* [Gr. γνωστικός pertaining to knowledge: after *diagnostic*, *prognostic*, etc.], applied to, or relating to, those characters of a mineral that are ascertained by means of the flame of a blow-pipe or of a Bunsen burner; so **pyroˈgnostics** *sb. pl.*, pyrognostic characters, or the branch of mineralogy that deals with them; †**pyˈromachy**, *Obs. nonce-wd.* [cf. Gr. πυρομαχεῖν to contend with fire], fighting with fire; **pyromagˈnetic** *a.*, applied to a dynamo invented by Edison, the working of which depends on the diminution of the magnetization of iron with increase of temperature; more widely, pertaining to or exhibiting pyromagnetism; **pyroˈmagnetism** [ad. G. *pyromagnetismus* (W. Voigt 1901, in *Nachrichten v.d. K. Ges. d. Wissensch. zu Göttingen* (*Math.-phys. Klasse*) I. 1)], magnetism that is dependent on the temperature of the material; **pyroˈmania**, insanity characterized by an impulse to set things on fire, incendiary mania; so **pyroˈmaniac** *sb.*, one affected with pyromania; *adj.*, pertaining to or affected with pyromania; also **pyromaˈniacal** *a.*; **pyroˈmanic** *a.*, of or relating to pyromania; **pyroˈmetallurgy**, metallurgy in which high temperatures are employed for the extraction of metals; hence **ˌpyrometaˈllurgical** *a.*, **pyroˈmetallurgist**; **ˌpyrometaˈmorphism** *Geol.*, metamorphism resulting from the action of heat; so **ˌpyrometaˈmorphic** *a.*, of, pertaining to, or characterized by pyrometamorphism; **pyroˈmorphous** *a. Min.* [Gr. μορφή form], having the property of crystallizing after fusion by heat (cf. *pyromorphite* in 2); **pyroˈnaphtha**, an illuminant made from the waste products of the distillation of Baku petroleum; †**pyronomics** (-ˈnɒmɪks), †**pyˈronomy** (-ˈrɒnəmɪ) [? after *economics*, *economy*], the phenomena and laws of the action of fire or heat; **pyrophanous** (paɪˈrɒfənəs) *a. Min.* [Gr. -φανης appearing; cf. *diaphanous*], having the property of becoming transparent or translucent when heated (cf. *pyrophane* in 2); ‖**pyroˈphobia** *Path.* [see -PHOBIA], 'morbid dread of fire' (Billings *Nat. Med. Dict.* 1890); **ˈpyrophone** (-fəʊn) [Gr. φωνή voice, sound], a musical instrument devised by Kastner, having a series of glass tubes each containing two hydrogen flames burning close together, which by pressing down a key are caused to separate, and then produce a sound; **pyroˈpuncture** *Surg.*, 'puncturing with red-hot needles' (Billings); a puncture so made; **ˈpyroscope** [see -SCOPE], an instrument invented by Leslie, *c* 1825, for measuring the intensity of radiant heat, consisting of a differential thermometer having one bulb covered with silver; **pyroˈsilver**, a trade name for electro-plated goods in which the silver is 'burnt in', i.e. fixed more firmly by means of heat; **pyrosophy** (-ˈrɒsəfɪ) [Gr. σοφία wisdom], 'the knowledge of the nature and properties of fire or heat' (Mayne *Expos. Lex.*); **ˈpyrosphere** *Geol.* = BARYSPHERE; **ˈpyrostat** [Gr. στατός standing: cf. *heliostat*, *thermostat*], 'an automatic draft-regulator for chimneys, smoke-pipes, and smokestacks' (*Cent. Dict.*); **pyroˈstereotype**, a printing plate in relief cast from an intaglio burnt in a wooden block by means of a blade, or of steel plugs, heated by a gas-flame; used esp. for printing music; also, short for *pyrostereotype process* (Knight *Dict. Mech.* 1875–84); **pyroˈsynthesis**, synthesis by the action of heat; hence **pyrosynˈthetic** *a.*; †**pyrotheˈology**, the part of natural theology which is founded on the laws and phenomena of fire; **pyrothonide** (-ˈrɒθəʊnaɪd) [Gr. ὀθόνη linen, sail-cloth], an empyreumatic oil, formerly used in medicine, obtained by burning linen, hemp, or cotton in a closed vessel.

1906 E. M. WEAVER *Notes Military Explosives* iv. 123 *Pyrocellulose, a soluble nitrocellulose of so called definite percentage of N(12·4), corresponding to the molecular formula, $C_{30}H_{38}(NO_2)_{12}O_{25}$, claimed to have been produced by Mendeléef; it possesses just sufficient content of O to burn all of the C to CO, the H to H_2O. **1920** O. W. WILLCOX in A. Rogers *Industr. Chem.* (ed. 3) xlvi. 1076 Nitrocellulose of from 12·50 to 12·70 per cent of nitrogen is called pyrocellulose, or simply pyro, and is the material from which smokeless powder for cannon is made. **1951** KIRK & OTHMER *Encycl. Chem. Technol.* VI. 36 Various types or grades of nitrocellulose are characterized by their nitrogen contents and the following names are used: pyroxylin, 8–12% nitrogen; pyrocellulose, 12·6 ± 0·1% nitrogen; guncotton, 13·3 ± 0·1% nitrogen. **1974** *Encycl. Brit. Macropædia* VII. 87/1 It was . . the most important type of smokeless powder used by the Allies in World War I. It was made from a nitrocotton of relatively low nitrogen content, called pyrocellulose, because that type is quite soluble in ether-alcohol. **1920** A. HOLMES *Nomencl. Petrol.* 193 *Pyroclasts, a general term for fragmental deposits of volcanic ejectamenta. **1934** *Bull. Amer. Assoc. Petroleum Geologists* XVIII. 1573 The bentonite beds in the basal McLure shale represent purer beds of originally vitric pyroclasts. **1944** A. HOLMES *Princ. Physical Geol.* xx. 443 The great clouds of gases, vapours, and pyroclasts that are the most conspicuous feature of explosive eruptions may be luminous or dark. **1972** *Nature* 21 Jan. 157/1 This eruption was extremely violent: an estimated 1·4 km³ of pyroclast flow and fall was emitted. **1887** J. J. H. TEALL in *Geol. Mag.* Decade III. IV. 493, I venture to suggest that . . we should distinguish between the three types of clastic rocks at present recognized by using the terms epiclastic, cataclastic, and *pyroclastic. . . *Pyroclastic*—Fragmental rocks of volcanic origin. The same terms may be applied to the structures which characterize the rocks in question. **1888** RUTLEY *Rock-Forming Min.* 124 Breccias and tuffs, whether of pyroclastic origin or not. **1897** GEIKIE *Anc. Volcanoes Gt. Brit.* I. 14 All kinds of pyroclastic detritus discharged from volcanic vents. **1903** *Bull. U.S. Geol. Survey* No. 213. 73 The gravels of Slate Creek contain . . a certain proportion of material derived from the older quartzites, pyroclastics, and granite intrusives occurring on the south side of its lower valley. **1939** W. H. TWENHOFEL *Princ. Sedimentation* viii. 291 The coarse-grained pyroclastics fall near the places of expulsion. **1976** P. FRANCIS *Volcanoes* iv. 127 All volcanic rocks . . may turn up either as lavas or pyroclastics. *Ibid.* v. 158 Pumice is the best-known of all pyroclastic . . rocks. **1880** W. A. ROSS in *Nature* XXI. 275/1 The blue *pyrocone produced by the blowpipe from an ordinary gas-burner. **1897** *Daily News* 27 Mar. 6/7 Henri Guénard, the eminent draughtsman, painter, aquafortist, *pyro-engraver, and engraver in colours. **1882** OGILVIE (Annandale), *Pyrognomic, applied to certain minerals which, when heated to a certain degree, exhibit a glow of incandescence, probably arising from a new disposition of their molecules. **1849** DANA *Geol.* iii. (1850) 207 *note*, *Pyrognostic Characters.—In an open tube gives off a small quantity of water. **1851** RICHARDSON *Geol.* v. 76 Bromel, a French mineralogist, . . being the first who classified mineral substances according to their pyrognostic qualities. **1593** G. HARVEY *Pierces Super.* Wks. (Grosart) II. 66, I looke for Agrippas dreadfull *Pyromachy: for Cardans multiplied matter, that shall delude the force of the Canon. **1887** *Times* 9 Sept. 14/5 The *pyro-magnetic dynamo will allow of the waste heat being utilized for other purposes. **1901** Pyromagnetic [see *piezomagnetic* adj. s.v. PIEZO-]. **1931** S. R. WILLIAMS *Magn. Phenomena* v. 164 A pyromagnetic crystal must show a magnetic moment at room temperature. **1975** *Jrnl. Appl. Physics* XLVI. 2250/1 The low-frequency pyromagnetic effect has been used to study the behavior of a ferromagnetic material both in the low-temperature region as well as near its Curie temperature. **1901** *Pyromagnetism [see *piezomagnetism* s.v. PIEZO-]. **1956** *Soviet Physics: JETP* III. 436/2 Recently the opinion has been expressed that pyromagnetism, piezomagnetism, etc., are impossible. **1973** *Jrnl. Appl. Physics* XLIV. 424/1 Another interesting application of pyromagnetism revealed by the present study is the possibility of verifying, or determining, the relationships between crystalline anisotropy constants and the magnetization near the critical point. **1842** DUNGLISON *Med. Dict.*, *Pyromania. **1847** tr. *von Feuchtersleben's Med. Psychol.* (Syd. Soc.) 293 An irresistible impulse to incendiarism (pyromania). **1867** MAUDSLEY *Physiol. Mind* 273 Instances of . . homicidal monomania, kleptomania, pyromania, and suicidal monomania. **1895** Pyromania [see ONOMATOMANIA b]. **1937** *Times* 7 Oct. 11/2 Mr. A. Lawson-Walton . . said that there was no evidence of spite . . , and it seemed that the accused had a kind of pyromania and delighted in making fires. **1887** *Amer. Jrnl. Psychol.* I. 191 *Pyromaniacs rarely incriminate themselves. **1897** *Westm. Gaz.* 2 Apr. 7/2 A dangerous pyromaniac has been discovered in Brooklyn . . [who] has set over twenty tenements on fire . . simply for the pleasure of seeing them burn. **1929** W. S. SADLER *Mind at Mischief* x. 141 We have the same condition in the case of certain types of pyromaniacs. **1967** *Listener* 6 Apr. 466/2 Jeanne Moreau lends to the role . . more credibility than was apparent in her full-length portrayal of the pyromaniac school-mistress. **1972** G. W. KISKER *Disorganized Personality* (ed. 2) viii. 260/1 The defiance is usually aimed at the police in their role of father image. Pyromaniacs of this type go about setting fires indiscriminately. **1873** G. H. LEWES *Probl. Life & Mind* 1st Ser. I. 234 Phases which manifest homicidal, kleptomaniacal, and *pyromaniacal instincts. **1926** J. I. SUTTIE tr. *Ferenczi's Further Contrib. Theory & Technique Psycho-Anal.* xxxi. 258 There were quite a number [of cases] in which incendiaries set fire to their *beds*, as though to indicate the . . enuristic primitive source of their *pyromanic character trait. **1968** G. JONES *Hist. Vikings* I. ii. 52 According to *Ynglinga Saga*, this pyromanic imbecility cost the Ynglings their realm of Uppsala. **1917** E. OBERG *Machinery's Encycl.* II. 204/2 There are three methods by means of which copper may be obtained from its ores: 1. By the *pyro-metallurgical or dry method. **1971** *Daily Tel.* 29 Apr. 25 (Advt.), Applicants should have . . a strong pyrometallurgical background and a minimum of 3 years' smelting or related development experience. **1960** *Times* 6 Apr. 3/1 (Advt.), Applications are invited . . for appointment to the posts of *Pyrometallurgist, [etc.]. **1974** *Daily Tel.* 2 May 23 (Advt.), The Pyrometallurgist will work in the Smelter, which has an annual production capacity of approximately 84,000 tonnes of copper. **1909** WEBSTER, *Pyrometallurgy. **1957** *New Scientist* 26 Sept. 20/1 Pyrometallurgy, the study of metals in the molten state, may find an application in the treatment of metals which are 'hot' in the sense of being highly radioactive. **1973** R. D. PEHLKE *Unit Processes of Extractive Metallurgy* i. 5 Following the mining and concentration of minerals, their extraction is accomplished by application of chemical metallurgy in one of the three areas of extractive metallurgy: pyrometallurgy, hydrometallurgy, or electrometallurgy. **1879** RUTLEY *Stud. Rocks* xii. 208 Commonly called metamorphic action, but which might more properly be designated *pyro-metamorphic action. *Ibid.*, *Pyro-metamorphism, by which rocks originally stratified . . come to be subsequently acted on by heat, and so transformed into what are commonly called the metamorphic rocks. **1847** WEBSTER, *Pyromorphous, in mineralogy, having the property of crystallization by fire. **1834** *Tait's Mag.* I. 39 *Pyronomics, hydrostatics, phrenology, . . and other crabbed sciences. **1601** GILL *Treat. Trinitie* Wks. (1635) 220 They which understand the rules of *Pyronomie, know what I say. **1858** MAYNE *Expos. Lex.*, *Pyronomia*, term for the doctrine of the nature and use of fire: pyronomy. **1836** SMART, *Pyrophanous, rendered transparent by heat. **1882** *Nature* XXVI. 304/1 This phenomenon, which Kastner called the interference of flames, was the . . starting-point of Kastner's *Pyrophone or Flame-Organ, which he patented in 1873. **1828** WEBSTER, *Pyroscope. **1832** *Nat. Philos.* II. *Therm. & Pyrom.* iv. 44 (U.K.S.) When one ball of the differential thermometer is smoothly covered with thick silver leaf, or inclosed in a polished sphere of silver, and the other ball is naked, it forms the pyroscope. **1883** *Fisheries Exhib. Catal.* 78 Neal's Patent *Pyro-Silver Cutlery. **1832** L. HUNT *Sir R. Esher* (1850) 244, I would willingly elude the experiment, and take the wings of the ancient *pyrosophy. **1846** J. C. BROWN tr. *Arbousset's Narr.* xxi. (1852) 309 Who can tell all the ingredients which may enter into the product of a pyrosophy so new? **1900** *Geogr. Jrnl.* XV. 88 A coloured diagram showing an ideal section of the Earth on the hypothesis that within the solid lithosphere lies a *pyrosphere of intensely high temperature. **1963** D. W. & E. E. HUMPHRIES tr. *Termier's Erosion & Sedimentation* i. 1 Glyptogenesis is the process of sculpturing of the lithosphere through the agency of the atmosphere, hydrosphere, biosphere and pyrosphere. **1947** *Bull. Geol. Soc. Amer.* LVIII. 1232 (*heading*) *Pyrosyntheses of telluride minerals. **1955** *Jrnl. Amer. Chem. Soc.* LXXVII. 1048/2 (*heading*) Pyrosynthesis of aspartic acid and alanine from citric acid cycle intermediates. **1961** *Amer. Mineralogist* XLVI. 823 Differential thermal pyrosynthesis may be considered a modification of differential thermal analysis which allows investigation under closed system conditions. A record is obtained of thermal reactions which occur during synthesis by heating elemental constituents to the fusion point. **1956** *Amer. Scientist* XLIV. 357 *Pyrosynthetic experiments. **1755** tr. *Pontoppidan's Nat. Hist.* Pref. 7 That circumstantial examination..which hath been undertaken and executed by Fabricius, in his *pyro- and hydro-theology. **1857** DUNGLISON *Med. Lex.*, **Pyrothonide*.

2. In names of minerals and rocks, usually indicating some property exhibited or alteration produced by the action of fire or heat; sometimes denoting a fiery red or yellow colour. **pyrallolite** (-ˈræləʊlaɪt) [Gr. ἄλλος other; Nordenskiöld 1820, in Ger.: see -LITE], an altered form of pyroxene, usually of a whitish or green colour, which changes colour when heated; †**pyˈrantimonite**, obs. synonym of KERMESITE; **pyrargillite** (-ˈrɑːdʒɪlaɪt) [Gr. ἄργιλλος clay; Nordenskiöld 1833, in Ger.], an alteration product of iolite, which has a clayey smell when heated; **pyrargyrite** (-ˈrɑːdʒɪraɪt) [Gr. ἄργυρον silver; Glöcker 1831, in Ger.], a dark red silver ore, a native sulphide of silver and antimony; †**pyˈrauxite**, obs. synonym of *pyrophyllite*; **pyroaurite** (-ˈrɔːraɪt) [L. *aurum* gold; Igelström 1865, in Sw.], hydrate of magnesium and iron, which has a golden-yellow colour when heated; **pyroˈbelonite** *Min.* [ad. G. *pyrobelonit* (G. Flink 1919, in *Geol. Föreningens i Stockholm Förhandl.* XLI. 436), f. Gr. βελόνη needle], a basic vanadate of manganese and lead, $MnPb(VO_4)(OH)$, occurring as red, transparent, needle-shaped crystals; **pyroˈbitumen**, any of a class of native hydrocarbons that differ from the bitumens proper in being relatively hard, infusible, and insoluble in organic solvents; hence **ˌpyrobiˈtuminous** *a.*; **ˈpyrochlore** (-klɔə(r)) [Gr. χλωρός greenish-yellow; Wöhler 1826, in Ger.], a niobo-titanate of calcium, cerium, and other bases, occurring in octahedral crystals of a brown colour, becoming greenish-yellow when strongly heated; also, any of a group of minerals that includes pyrochlore, microlite, betafite, and obruchevite, the members of which have the general formula $A_2B_2O_6(O,OH,F)$, where A may be sodium, potassium, calcium, cerium, or certain other elements, and B may be niobium, tantalum, titanium, or certain other elements; freq. *attrib.* in *pyrochlore group*; **pyrochroite** (-ˈkrəʊaɪt) [Gr. χροιά colour; Igelström 1864, in Ger.], a pearly-white foliated hydrate of manganese, which becomes coloured when heated; †**pyroˈchrotite**, obs. synonym of *pyrostilpnite*; **pyˈroclasite** [Gr. κλάσις fracture], **pyroˈguanite** [GUANO], names given to hard guano; **ˈpyrolite** [-LITE], †(*a*) an artificial rock (see quot. 1848) (*obs.*); (*b*) a mixture proposed as the primitive material of the earth's upper mantle (see quots. 1962, 1975); **pyˈromelane** [Gr. μέλας black; C. U. Shepard 1856, 'because it turns black when heated', Chester *Names Min.*], a reddish mineral (prob. titanite), found in the gold sands of N. Carolina; **pyroˈmeline** [Gr. μήλινος yellow; Kobell 1852, in Ger.], hydrous sulphate of nickel, pale yellow or greenish white; **pyˈromeride** [Gr. μέρ-ος part], a granitoid rock containing felspathic spherules thickly disseminated (Watts *Dict. Chem.*); **pyroˈmorphite** [Gr. μορφή form; Hausmann 1813, in Ger.], chlorophosphate of lead, occurring in green, yellow, or brown crystals; so called because the globule produced by melting assumes a crystalline form on cooling; †**ˈpyrophane** (-feɪn) [Gr. -φανης appearing], a variety of opal which absorbs melted wax, and consequently becomes translucent when heated (cf. HYDROPHANE); also sometimes = FIRE-*opal*; **pyˈrophanite** [Gr. φανός bright; A. Hamberg 1890], titanate of manganese found in brilliant red crystals and scales; **pyrophillite**, var. *pyrophyllite*; **pyrophyllite** (-ˈfɪlaɪt) [Gr. φύλλον leaf; R. Hermann 1829, in Ger.], a hydrous silicate of aluminium, occurring in foliated masses which exfoliate when heated; **pyrophysalite** (-ˈfɪsəlaɪt) [Gr. φυσαλλίς bubble; Berzelius 1806, in Sw.], a coarse, nearly opaque variety of topaz, which swells up when heated; **pyroˈpissite** [Gr. πίσσα pitch; Kenngott 1853, in Ger.], a greyish-brown earthy friable substance, consisting of a mixture of hydrocarbons, which when heated melts into a mass resembling pitch; **pyroˈretin** [Gr. ῥητίνη resin; Reuss 1854], a resin occurring in masses in brown coal, in the vicinity of basaltic dykes, in Bohemia; hence **pyroˈretinite**, 'the part of pyroretin which dissolves in hot alcohol and deposits in cooling' (Chester *Names Min.*); **pyˈrorthite** [ORTHITE; Berzelius 1818] an impure mineral resembling orthite, but containing carbonaceous matter, and hence burning when strongly heated; **ˈpyroschist** (-ʃɪst), a highly bituminous schist or shale, which burns or yields inflammable gas when heated; **pyrosclerite** (-ˈsklɪəraɪt) [Gr. σκληρός hard; Kobell 1834, in Ger.], a green mineral allied to the chlorites, forming seams in serpentine: so called 'because a fragment becomes very hard when heated before the blow-pipe' (Chester *Names Min.*); **pyrosiderite**: see PYRRHOSIDERITE; **pyrosmalite** (-ˈrɒzməlaɪt) [orig. (in Ger.) *pirodmalit* (Hausmann 1808), f. Gr. ὀδμαλέος stinking; altered by Karsten 1808, after Gr. ὀσμή smell], a chlorosilicate of iron and manganese, occurring in dark green or brown crystals, which when heated give off an odour of chlorine; †**pyroˈstibite**, obs. synonym of KERMESITE; **pyroˈstilpnite** [Gr. στιλπνός shining; Dana 1868], a sulphantimonide of silver, occurring in minute bright red crystals; also called *fire-blende*; †**pyroˈtechnite**, obs. synonym of THENARDITE.

1822 CLEAVELAND *Min.* (ed. 2) I. 426 **Pyrallolite*, this new mineral occurs both massive, and in crystals... This mineral..has received its name..in allusion to its changes of color from white to dark, and from dark to white, before the blowpipe. **1837** DANA *Min.* 256 Pyrallolite. Tersilicate of Magnesia. **1866–8** WATTS *Dict. Chem.* IV. 753 *Pyrallolite*, name of a series of decomposition-products of augite and occasionally of hornblende, consisting mainly of magnesian hydrosilicates. They blacken when heated, then burn white if in contact with the air. **1834** *Amer. Jrnl. Sc.* July 387 **Pyrargillite*. **1841** *Penny Cycl.* XIX. 153/1 *Pyrargillite* occurs in four-sided prisms, with bevelled edges and massive. **1849** NICOL *Min.* 500 Dark *pyrargyrite or antimonial silver-blende. **1866–8** WATTS *Dict. Chem.* IV. 753 Pyrargyrite. Dark-red silver ore. Ruby silver.. occurring in rhombohedral crystals. **1868** DANA *Min.* (ed. 5) 179 *Pyroaurite... Perfectly soluble in muriatic acid. **1920** *Chem. Abstr.* XIV. 1097 (*heading*) *Pyrobelonite, a new lead-manganese vanadate from Långbanshyttan. **1969** *Canad. Mineralogist* X. 117 The specimen..was Harvard 94831 from the type locality, Långban, Sweden. It consists largely of massive to well-crystallized hausmannite in contact with, and cut by, calcite. The pyrobelonite occurs as very fine grains with a few small crystals (commonly < 100 μ in largest dimension) primarily in the hausmannite. **1903** C. RICHARDSON in *Science* 13 Mar. 420/1 The evidence thus obtained has been carefully analyzed, and the following classification of the native bitumens deduced: Gas... Petroleum... Maltha. Solid Bitumens... *Pyrobitumens: Practically insoluble in chloroform or heavy petroleum hydrocarbons. **1951** K. K. LANDES *Petroleum Geol.* iv. 127 The solid hydrocarbons may be subdivided into four main groups: petroleum bitumens, pyrobitumens, disseminated bitumens, and oxygen-bearing bitumens. **1965** Pyrobitumen [see IMPSONITE]. **1918** H. ABRAHAM *Asphalts & Allied Substances* xi. 149 They [*sc.* pyrobitumens] are grouped into five classes, viz.: elaterite, wurtzilite, albertite, impsonite, and asphaltic *pyrobituminous shales. **1937** *Bull. Amer. Assoc. Petroleum Geologists* XXI. 122 Regardless of the possible economic value of the Brazilian algal deposits and other pyrobituminous sediments, those now forming in fresh-water ponds and the related geologically young deposits have great scientific interest. **1830** *Amer. Jrnl. Sc.* XVIII. 392 *Pyrochlore from Norway in zircon syenite. **1866** LAWRENCE tr. *Cotta's Rocks Class.* (1878) 39 Pyrochlore occurs as an accessory in granite and syenite. **1906** J. P. IDDINGS *Rock Minerals* II. 464 Pyrochlore group. Pyrochlore, $RNb_2O_6.R(Ti,Th)O_3.NaF$. Koppite, $R_2Nb_2O_7.\frac{1}{2}NaF$. Microlite, $Ca_2Ta_2O_7$.pt. **1941** *Amer. Mineralogist* XXVI. 504 A study of the available analyses of pyrochlore shows that both cerium and titanium are invariably present in appreciable amounts and must therefore be regarded as essential constituents. *Ibid.* 505 Koppite... Winchell (1933) describes this mineral as 'a pyrochlore containing K' while Brandenberger (1931) states that koppite should be regarded as an iron-columbium pyrochlore. **1959** [see PANDAITE]. **1977** *Amer. Mineralogist* LXII. 404/1 The pyrochlore group comprises those multiple cubic oxides having the following characteristics: (*a*) essential amounts of niobium, tantalum, and titanium, either individually or in combination (*b*) the space group *Fd3m*, (*c*) the pyrochlore structure as defined by Gaertner (1930) and Brandenberger (1931), and (*d*) the general formula $A_{2-m}B_2O_6(O,OH,F)_{1-n}\cdot pH_2O$... The recommended subgroups are: Pyrochlore Subgroup in which Nb + Ta > 2 Ti and Nb > Ta. [Etc.] **1868** DANA *Min.* (ed. 5) 177 *Pyrochroite... Occurs in veins, 1 to 2 lines broad. **1856** C. U. SHEPARD in *Amer. Jrnl. Sci. & Arts* Ser. II. XXII. 97 The altered guano is composed..of two mineral species, which I have called *pyroclasite and glaubapatite. *Ibid.* 96 *Pyro-guanite minerals. The three following species occur at Mong's Island. **1848** *Mining Jrnl.* 4 Nov. 521/1 Mr. Twining's object is to form, by chemical means, a comprehensive series of petreous substances which he proposes to designate..*pyrolite or artificial lava, as.. being of igneous origin. **1962** A. E. RINGWOOD in *Jrnl. Geophysical Res.* LXVII. 860/1 Immediately below the M discontinuity, the mantle consists dominantly of dunite and peridotite... This zone passes downward..into the primitive 'pyrolite'. [*Note*] Peridotite is an unsatisfactory name for the hypothetical primitive mantle material, chemically equivalent to 1 part basalt plus 4 parts of dunite. Since a rock of this composition would crystallize dominantly as a mixture of olivine and pyroxene, the name 'pyrolite' is suggested. **1975** *Sci. Amer.* Mar. 56/1 Assigning an appropriate chemistry to the residual peridotite, one arrives at the hypothetical composition of the upper mantle. Pyrolite (pyroxene-olivine rock) is the name given to one of these hypothetical peridotites. **1856** C. U. SHEPARD in *Amer. Jrnl. Sci. & Arts* Ser. II. XXII. 96 *Pyromelane. Found in crystalline grains of the size of kernels of Indian corn. **1866–8** WATTS *Dict. Chem.* IV. 762 **Pyromeline*. **1866** LAWRENCE tr. *Cotta's Rocks Class.* 218 *Pyromeride..in addition to the usual quartz crystals, contains balls of felsite. **1814** ALLAN *Min. Nomencl.* 29 Brown and green lead ore ..*pyromorphit. **1842** BRANDE *Dict. Sci.*, etc., *Pyromorphite*, native phosphate of lead. **1794** KIRWAN *Min.* (ed. 2) I. 291 It is said that some *pyrophanes are found in Armenia which are transparent while exposed to the sun, and opake at night. **1946** J. R. PARTINGTON *Gen. & Inorganic Chem.* xviii. 506 Montmorillonite shows the same X-ray pattern as *pyrophillite, which occurs crystalline in slates. **1975** TINDALL & THORNHILL *Blandford Rock & Mineral Guide* II. 96 This structure can extend indefinitely in a two-dimensional network or 'sheet'; it is found, for example, in the mineral pyrophillite, $Al_2Si_4O_{10}(OH)_2$. **1830** *Edin. Philos. Jrnl.* VIII. 183 The name *pyrophyllite is given to it on account of its exfoliation on exposure to heat. **1862** DANA *Man. Geol.* §67. 62 Pyrophyllite, a mineral resembling talc in appearance and soapy feel. **1808** *Nicholson's Jrnl.* XIX. 33 Mineralogical Description..of a Stone, called *Pyrophysalite. **1866** BRANDE & COX *Dict. Sci.*, etc., s.v. *Mineralogy* 531/2 *Pyropissite. **1868** DANA *Min.* (ed. 5) 344 **Pyroretinite*, part of *Pyroretin of Reuss. **1881** *Jrnl. Chem. Soc.* XL. 359 Four resins belonging to the retinite group., viz., Pyroretin, Reussinite, Leucopetrite, and Euosinite. **1828** WEBSTER s.v., *Pyrorthite is in black plates, thin and almost parallel. **1866** LAWRENCE tr. *Cotta's Rocks Class.* (1878) 330 *Pyroschist is..very bituminous and..dark-brown or black-coloured argillaceous shale. **1862** DANA *Man. Geol.* §8. 82 They [nickel and chrome] occur also in the *pyrosclerite and Williamsite of Chester Co. Pa. **1896** CHESTER *Dict. Names Min.*, *Pyrosclerite*,..a micaceous mineral, one of the uncertain alteration products classed with vermiculite. **1816** R. JAMESON *Syst. Min.* (ed. 2) III. 311 *Pyrosmalite or native Muriate of Iron. **1852** SHEPARD *Min.* (ed. 3) 160 Pyrosmalite..heated in a tube yields water. **1868** DANA *Min.* (ed. 5) 93 *Pyrostilpnite... Fireblende... Lustre pearly-adamantine. Color hyacinth-red.

3. In Chemistry, *pyro-* is prefixed to the name of a substance or to an adjective forming part thereof, in order to name a new substance formed by destructive distillation or other application of heat.

Names thus formed appeared first in the *Méthode de Nomenclature Chimique* of De Morveau, Lavoisier, etc. 1787. Many of the substances originally so called have subsequently received other names.

a. Prefixed to the adj. denominating an acid (†sometimes an ether or spirit), to form the name of a new acid, etc. The substances properly so denominated were themselves mostly acids, but sometimes anhydrides or other derivatives. †**pyro-aˈcetic acid** = *pyroligneous acid* s.v. PYROLIGNEOUS *a.*; †**pyro-acetic ether** or **spirit**, early name of ACETONE. **pyro-aliˈzaric acid**, $C_8H_4O_3$ = *phthalic anhydride* s.v. PHTHALIC *a.* **pyro-arˈsenic acid**, $H_4As_2O_7$, an acid produced by the action of heat on arsenic acid expelling H_2O. **pyrocamˈphretic acid**, $C_{10}H_{14}O_4$. **pyrocateˈchuic acid** = *pyrocatechin*: see b. †**pyroˈcitric** = CITRACONIC. †**pyrocoˈmenic** = PYROMECONIC. **pyroˈfellic** = *pyrolithofellic*. †**pyroˈglucic acid** = *pyrodextrin*: see b. †**pyroguaiˈacic acid** = GUAIACOL. †**pyroˈkinic acid** = QUINIDE. †**pyroˈleic** = SEBACIC. †**pyroˈlithic** = *pyro-uric*, CYANURIC. **pyrolithoˈfellic acid**, $C_{20}H_{34}O_3$: see quot. **pyroliˈvilic acid** [OLIVIL], $C_{20}H_{26}O_5$. †**pyro-ˈmalic** = MALEIC. **pyroˈmaric acid**: see quot. 1866–8. **pyromeˈllitic acid**, $C_{10}H_6O_8$. **pyroˈpectic acid**: see quot. **pyrophosˈphamic acid**, $P_2NH_5O_6$. **pyroˈphosphate**, a salt or ester, or the anion, of pyrophosphoric acid; a group or linkage formed from two condensed phosphate groups. **pyrophosˈphoric acid**, $H_4P_2O_7$, a tetrabasic acid, produced as a glass-like solid, by the action of heat on phosphoric acid. **pyroraˈcemic acid** = PYRUVIC ACID. †**pyroˈsorbic** = *pyromalic*, MALEIC. **pyrosulˈphuric acid**, $H_2S_2O_7 = (HSO_3)_2 + O$: see quots. **pyroteˈrebic acid**, $C_6H_{10}O_2$; also called *hexenoic acid*. **pyro-ˈuric** = CYANURIC. Also in the names of salts of these acids, as **pyroarsenate**, **-citrate**, **-phosphamate**, **-sulphate**, etc. See also PYROGALLIC, PYROMECONIC, PYROMUCIC, PYROTARTARIC, PYRUVIC.

1815 HENRY *Elem. Chem.* (ed. 7) II. 281 The peculiar fluid, which Derosne has termed *pyro-acetic ether, but to which Mr. Chenevix is of opinion, the less definite name of pyro-acetic spirit will be better adapted. **1859** FOWNES *Man. Chem.* (ed. 7) 396 Acetone: pyroacetic spirit... A peculiar inflammable volatile liquid, designated by the above names.

1868 *Nat. Encycl.* I. 115 A..volatile inflammable fluid called pyro-acetic spirit. **1876** *Mat. Med.* (ed. 6) 296 *Pyroarsenate of soda, isomorphous with the pyrophosphate of that base. **1882** *Encycl. Brit.* XIV. 91/2 The methylated gallic ether or *pyrocatechuic acid. **1838** T. THOMSON *Chem. Org. Bodies* 62 Dumas subjected the pyrocitric acid in *pyrocitrate of lead to an ultimate analysis by means of oxide of copper. **1810–26** HENRY *Elem. Chem.* II. 216 **Pyro-citric Acid.* M. Lassaigne has given this name to an acid, produced by the destructive distillation of citric acid. **1838** T. THOMSON *Chem. Org. Bodies* 338 Of pyrocitric and pyrotartaric ethers. **1863–8** WATTS *Dict. Chem.* I. 992 Citraconic acid (Pyrocitric acid), $C_5H_6O_4$. (Lassaigne, 1882.) **1873** WATTS *Fownes' Chem.* 739 *Pyrocomenic acid is a weak acid. **1873** RALFE *Phys. Chem.* 59 Submitted to dry distillation, lithofellic acid loses 1 atom of water and is converted into *pyrofellic acid. **1843** *Chem. Gaz.* 1 Dec. 725 *Pyroguaiacic Acid obtained by the Distillation of Guaiacum Resin. **1858** MAYNE *Expos. Lex.*, **Pyrokinate*,.. a combination of pyrokinic acid with a salifiable base. **1832** *Encycl. Brit.* VI. 430/1 *Pyrokinic acid is formed when kinic acid is distilled in a retort. **1836** SMART, **Pyrolithic*, an epithet applied to an acid obtained from uric acid. **1897** *Syd. Soc. Lex.*, *Pyrolithic acid*, the same as Pyro-uric acid. **1866–8** WATTS *Dict. Chem.* IV. 760 **Pyrolithofellic acid*,..an acid oil produced by the dry distillation of lithofellic acid, the chief constituent of some kinds of oriental bezoar. **1847** WEBSTER, **Pyromalate* [citing URE]. **1810–26** HENRY *Elem. Chem.* II. 225 When malic acid is heated out of the contact of air, it sublimes, and the sublimed crystals possess characters differing from those of the original acid. When thus altered, it has been called **pyromalic acid.* **1865–8** WATTS *Dict. Chem.* III. 784 Maleic Acid. (Pyromalic acid, Pyrosorbic acid.) **1857** MILLER *Elem. Chem.* III. 501 *Pyromaric acid. **1866–8** WATTS *Dict. Chem.* IV. 760 Pyromaric acid.. obtained by subjecting pimaric acid to dry distillation. **1882** *Jrnl. Chem. Soc.* XLII. 850 Crystals of ammonium *pyromellate. *Ibid.* 851 *Pyromellic acid. **1851** *Chem. Gaz.* 15 Sept. 341 A new acid, to which he [Erdmann] has given the name of *pyromellitic acid. **1866–8** WATTS *Dict. Chem.* IV. 369 When pectin..is heated to 200°, water and carbonic anhydride are evolved, and *pyropectic acid remains in the form of a black substance, insoluble in water, but soluble in alkaline liquids... Frémy deduces the formula $C_{14}H_{18}O_9$. *Ibid.* 766 *Pyrophosphamate of Ammonium is obtained as a gummy mass. **1864** *Jrnl. Chem. Soc.* XVII. 237 It seems preferable to adopt the names given by Laurent... These are *pyrophosphamic and pyrophosphodiamic acids. **1866–8** WATTS *Dict. Chem.* IV. 766 Laurent (1850) suggested that these acids were amic acids derived from pyrophosphoric acid, the first being *pyrophosphamic acid*, $P_2NH_5O_6$, and the second *pyrophosphodiamic* acid, $P_2N_2H_6O_5$, and these formulæ have been confirmed by the more recent analyses. **1836–41** BRANDE *Chem.* (ed. 5) 492 Phosphoric acid, after it has been exposed for some time to heat, yields, when saturated with bases, salts possessed of certain peculiarities, which have hence been termed *pyrophosphates. **1866–8** WATTS *Dict. Chem.* IV. 537 Intermediate between ortho- and meta-phosphates there are at least three distinct classes of salts, the most important of which are *pyrophosphates* or *paraphosphates*. **1869** ROSCOE *Elem. Chem.* 159 If common sodium phosphate be heated to redness, water is driven off, sodium pyrophosphate remains. **1912** E. FEILMANN tr. *Molinari's Inorg. Chem.* 348 The pyrophosphates..give a precipitate with copper salts, which is soluble in excess of pyrophosphate. **1950** N. V. SIDGWICK *Chem. Elements* I. 746 Ethyl pyrophosphate $Et_4P_2O_7$ can be made from the silver salt and ethyl iodide. **1957** G. E. HUTCHINSON *Treat. Limnol.* I. xii. 728 Though pyrophosphate plays an important role inside the organism, it is easily hydrolyzed and only orthophosphate is likely to be of importance in the environment. **1970** AMBROSE & EASTY *Cell Biol.* vii. 248 There is another type of reaction, catalysed by enzymes known as phosphorylases, in which a sugar phosphate reacts with another sugar to form a disaccharide and inorganic pyrophosphate. **1832** *Encycl. Brit.* VI. 380/1 Mr. Clarke..called the newly modified acid *pyrophosphoric acid. **1850** DAUBENY *Atom. The.* x. 334. **1866–8** WATTS *Dict. Chem.* IV. 539 Pyrophosphoric acid is converted into metaphosphoric acid when heated to redness, and into orthophosphoric acid when boiled with water. **1837** R. D. THOMSON in *Brit. Ann.* 339 *Pyroracemic acid. **1866–8** WATTS *Dict. Chem.* IV. 770 Pyroracemic acid is a liquid having a faint yellowish colour, smelling like acetic acid. **1894** MUIR & MORLEY *Watts' Dict. Chem.* IV. 363 Pyroracemic or Pyruvic acid, $C_3H_4O_3$ = $CH_3.CO.CO_2H$. **1865–8** *Pyrosorbic: see *pyromalic.* **1894** MUIR & MORLEY *Watts' Dict. Chem.* IV. 582 Potassium *pyrosulphate, $K_2S_2O_7$, is formed by heating K_2SO_4 with half its weight of H_2SO_4 till acid ceases to come off at an incipient red heat. **1872** *Jrnl. Chem. Soc.* XXV. 669 Proofs that sulphuric and *pyrosulphuric acids are really distinct compounds. **1875** WATTS *Dict. Chem.* VII. 1140 Disulphuric, Pyrosulphuric, or Anhydrosulphuric Acid; Nordhausen Sulphuric Acid. **1866–8** WATTS *Dict. Chem.* IV. 776 **Pyroterebic Acid*..belonging to the acrylic series..is a liquid boiling at 210°, and smelling of butyric acid. *Ibid.*, **Pyroterebrate of silver*, $C_6H_9AgO_2$, crystallises with difficulty, and blackens on exposure to light. **1810–26** HENRY *Elem. Chem.* II. 413 The liquid, when filtered and evaporated, yielded small white needles which were pure *pyro-uric acid. **1836–41** BRANDE *Chem.* (ed. 5) 564 Cyanuric Acid... Scheele first described this acid under the name of *pyrouric acid.*

b. Prefixed to a sb. (Now often superseded by other names.)

†**pyro'benzoline** = LOPHINE, $C_{21}H_{16}N_2$. **pyrocatechin** (paɪrəʊ'kætɪtʃɪn), also called *catechol*, *pyro-catechuic acid*, and *oxyphenic acid*, $C_6H_6O_2$, produced by the dry distillation of catechu, kino, and other substances, forming broad white strongly shining laminæ, and rhombic or small rectangular prisms. **pyro'catechol** = CATECHOL, *pyrocatechin* s.v. PYRO- 3 b. **'pyrocoll** [Gr. κόλλα glue]: see quot. **pyro'dextrin**, a product of the action of a high temperature upon starch. **pyro'glycerin**, diglycerin = $C_3H_5(OH)_2.O.C_3H_5(OH)_2$. **pyro'glycide**, diglycide, $C_3H_5(OH).O_2.C_3H_5(OH)$. **pyro'guaiacin**, a crystalline substance, $C_{18}H_{18}O_3$, produced by the dry distillation of gum guaiacum. † **pyro'quinol** = HYDROQUINONE. †**pyro'stearin**: see quot. See also PYROXANTHIN, -XANTHOGEN, and PYROXYLIN.

1857 MILLER *Elem. Chem.* III. 263 *Pyrobenzoline (lophine). *Ibid.* 349 Catechin..yields a crystallizable substance termed *pyrocatechin, or oxyphenic acid. **1878** KINGZETT *Anim. Chem.* 236 Pyrocatechin was discovered in human urine by Müller and Ebstein. **1897** *Allbutts' Syst. Med.* IV. 555 Mühlmann has put forward the view that the symptoms of Addison's disease are due to chronic poisoning with pyrocatechin. **1890** *Proc. Chem. Soc.* VI. 90 The very high price of *pyrocatechol renders it desirable to discover improved methods of preparing it. **1932** I. D. GARARD *Introd. Org. Chem.* xiv. 199 Pyrocatechol is used as a photographic developer. **1956** *Nature* 28 Jan. 184/2 Copper cyanide, though it accelerates considerably the rate of autoxidation of pyrocatechol.., is not very superior to cupric ions alone as regards catalytic activity on pigment formation from pyrocatechol. **1881** *Jrnl. Chem. Soc.* XL. 295 The authors propose to call it *pyrocoll, because of its mode of formation from gelatin. **1894** MUIR & MORLEY *Watts' Dict. Chem.* IV. 359 Pyrocoll, $C_{10}H_6N_2O_2$, a product of the distillation of gelatin when free from fat but containing albumen, casein or gluten. **1858** *Chem. Gaz.* 1 May 178 *Pyrodextrine..is precipitated by baryta. **1866–8** WATTS *Dict. Chem.* IV. 758 Pyrodextrin is a solid, brown, friable mass, shining and tough when moist. Inodorous and tasteless... [It] dissolves readily in water, forming a brown adhesive gum. **1861** *Chem. News* III. 111/2 *Pyroglycerine oxidises phosphorus, potassium, and copper. **1864–72** WATTS *Dict. Chem.* II. 894 The hypothetical body glycide, $C_3H_6O_2$..is the alcohol of the glycidic ethers, and is related to glycerin in the same manner as *pyroglycide to pyroglycerin. **1866–8** *Ibid.* IV. 771 **Pyrostearin*, the name applied by Berzelius to the less fusible portion of the distillate obtained by distilling empyreumatic oils with water.

c. Also in the derivative names of certain hydrocarbon compounds and groups: **'pyrazine** [AZO- + -INE], a ring-group; **'pyrazole** [AZO- + L. *oleum* oil], a compound; hence ***pyrazoleblue***, a dye substance ($C_{20}H_{16}N_4O_2$).

1895 MUIR & MORLEY *Watts' Dict. Chem.* III. 349.

pyro-acetic to **-arsenic**: see PYRO- 3 a.

pyro-acid ('paɪrəʊ'æsɪd). *Chem.* Also 9 †**pyracid**. An acid formed from another acid by dry or destructive distillation: see PYRO- 3.

1835–6 *Todd's Cycl. Anat.* I. 47/1 The other animal acids ..are artificially produced... Such as the..animal pyroacids. **1838** T. THOMSON *Chem. Org. Bodies* 11 Sometimes the saturating power of a vegetable acid is not altered by converting it into a pyroacid. **1866–8** [see PYROGEN b].

pyro-aurite, etc.: see PYRO- 2.

†**pyro'ballogy.** *Obs.* [Altered from PYROBOLOGY, after Gr. βάλλειν, to throw.] The study of the art of casting fire, i.e. of artillery.

1738 [see PYROBOLOGY, quot. 1728]. **1759** STERNE *Tr. Shandy* II. iii, He was enabled, by the help of..Gobesius's military architecture and pyroballogy, translated from the Flemish, to form his discourse with passable perspicuity.

pyrobelonite to **-bitumen**: see PYRO- 2, 3 b.

†**pyro'bolic**, *a. Obs. rare*[−1]. [f. PYRO- + Gr. βολή a throw + -IC.] (See quot.)

(Perh. due to a misunderstanding of *parabolic.*)

1688 R. HOLME *Armoury* III. xiv. (Roxb.) 12/1 A pyrobolick Mirrour is such a Glass that casts forth fire in a moment of tyme by the suns heat.

†**pyro'bolical**, *a. Obs.* [f. as prec. + -AL[1].] Relating to the art of casting fire, i.e. ? to artillery, or ? to fireworks. So †**py'robolist** [F. *pyroboliste*, Ger. *pyroballist*], one who makes or manages artillery or fireworks; †**pyro'bology** [F. *pyrobologie*, 18th c.], †**py'roboly**, the art of making or managing fireworks, pyrotechny.

1728 CHAMBERS *Cycl.* s.v. *Pyrotechny*, Some call Pyrotechny by the name Artillery;..Others chuse to call it Pyrobology [*ed.* 1738 *adds* or rather pyroballogy], *q.d.* the Art of Missile Fires. **1729** SHELVOCKE *Artillery* III. 165 To fire several Pyrobolical Machines, which are used upon Rejoicing Occasions. *Ibid.* 169 Nothing..that may be of Use to the diligent and expert Pyrobolist. **1732** *Hist. Litteraria* III. 110 He called together the most expert of the Fire-workers and Pyrobolists. *Ibid.* IV. 114 If the Chinese have been so ancient in the Mystery of Pyroboly and Pyrotechnics.

pyro-camphretic, etc.: see PYRO- 1, 2, 3 a, b.

pyro-carbonate: see PYRO b.

pyrocellulose: see PYRO- 1.

Pyroceram ('paɪərəʊsɛ,ræm). Also **pyroceram**. [f. PYRO- + CERAM(IC *a.* (*sb.*).] A proprietary term in the U.S. for a type of strong, heat-resistant glass which has been heat-treated so that it consists entirely of microscopic crystalline domains.

1957 *New Scientist* 23 May 27/1 The name of this fabulous stuff, which Dr. Stookey invented, is pyroceram. It is harder than flint, light as aluminium, stronger (in ratio to its weight) than stainless steel. *Ibid.* 28/2 The Corning Glass Works has at least a thousand different formulæ for pyrocerams. **1957** *Amer. Ceramic Soc. Bull.* XXXVI. 279/1 Pyroceram is melted and formed like glass, but with a formula containing one or more nucleating agents. **1958** *Official Gaz.* (U.S. Patent Office) 20 May TM 75/1 Corning Glass Works... *Pyroceram*... First use Feb. 7, 1957. **1965** *New Scientist* 4 Nov. 341/1 Housewives who can afford to pay for..coffee pots made of pyroceram are by now accustomed to being told that 'this is the material used in American rocket noses'. **1968** *McGraw-Hill Yearbk. Sci. & Technol.* 38/2 Controlled devitrification to give glass-ceramics or Pyrocerams depends upon the availability of adequate nuclei.

pyro-'chemical, *a. rare.* [f. med. or early mod.L. *pyrochymia*, *-icus*, in F. *pyrochimie*, *-chimique*: see PYRO- 1 and CHEMICAL.] Pertaining to the chemical action of fire. Hence **pyro-'chemically** *adv.*, by the chemical action of fire.

1839 G. ROBERTS *Dict. Geol.*, Pyro-chemically formed.. through the instrumentality of fire, as crystals of prismatic felspar on the walls of a furnace in which copper slate and ore have been melted.

pyrochlore, **-clast(ic**: see PYRO- 2, 1.

pyrodin (paɪ'rəʊdɪn). *Med.* [f. Gr. πυρώδης like fire + -IN[1].] A crystalline substance consisting essentially of acetyl-phenyl-hydrazine, $C_6H_5N_2H_2(C_2H_3O)$, used as an antipyretic.

1890 BILLINGS *Nat. Med. Dict.*, *Pyrodine.* **1897** *Syd. Soc. Lex.*, *Pyrodin.* **1899** CAGNEY *Jaksch's Clin. Diagn.* (ed. 4) 352 Observed in cases of poisoning by naphthol, carbolic acid, pyrodin, and chinin.

,pyro-e'lectric, *a. Min.* Also **pyroelectric**. [PYRO- 1.] Applied to certain crystals which on being heated become electrically polar, i.e. exhibit positive and negative electricity at opposite ends (the effects being reversed while cooling). Also applied to the effect exhibited by such crystals and to devices employing it. Hence **,pyro-elec'tricity**, the property of being pyro-electric.

1834 in *Encycl. Brit.* VIII. 595/1 Pyro-electricity. **1853** *Pharm. Jrnl.* XIII. 112 The crystals..are..pyroelectric. **1864–72** WATTS *Dict. Chem.* II. 411 In Crystals:—Pyro-electricity. **1871** B. STEWART *Heat* §167 Haüy was the first to remark that those crystals are pyroelectric which are deficient in symmetry. **1895** [see PYRITOID]. **1899** O. LODGE *Mod. Views Electr.* §63 (heading) Pyro-electricity. **1902** H. A. MIERS *Mineralogy* 480 The pyro-electric property [of tourmaline], which was first observed at the beginning of the eighteenth century,..can be very easily shown by means of Kundt's dusting method. **1922** GLAZEBROOK *Dict. Appl. Physics* II. 598/1 The existence of a true pyro-electric effect has been questioned by several investigators. **1973** *Physics Bull.* Mar. 161/2 The flame monitor uses two telescopes, each containing either a photoelectric or pyroelectric cell, to pinpoint and monitor a particular flame. **1979** 'R. CASSILIS' *Arrow of God* III. v. 60 Beneath a layer of Wordsworth we packed..half a dozen pyroelectric-vidicon cameras.

pyro-engraver, **-fellic**: see PYRO- 1, 3 a.

pyroet, **pyrog**, obs. ff. PIROUETTE, PIROGUE.

1707 *Curios. in Husb. & Gard.* 206 The Savages.. transport Plants in their Pyrogs.

pyrogallic (,paɪərəʊ'gælɪk), *a. Chem.* [f. PYRO- 3 + GALLIC *a.*[2]] Produced from gallic acid by the action of heat: in ***pyrogallic acid***, an acid substance, $C_6H_6O_3$ (strictly a trihydric phenol, $C_6H_3(OH)_3$, hence systematically named *pyrogallol*), which crystallizes in long flat colourless prisms, soluble in water; much used as a reducing agent in photography (see PYRO) and otherwise. Hence ***pyrogallic developer***, etc.

1836 BRANDE *Man. Chem.* (ed. 4) 933 Pyrogallic acid has been analyzed by Berzelius under the name of gallic acid. **1838** T. THOMSON *Chem. Org. Bodies* 86 Braconnot.. showed that when gallic acid is sublimed, it is converted into a substance possessing quite different properties... He therefore gave it the name of pyrogallic acid. **1856** E. A. HADOW in *Orr's Circ. Sci.*, *Pract. Chem.* 194 After the pyrogallic solution has apparently done its utmost. **1861** *Photogr. News Alm.* in *Circ. Sc.* (*c* 1865) I. 160/1 There are two methods of development; with pyrogallic acid and with gallic acid. **1869** ROSCOE *Elem. Chem.* 417 On heating, gallic acid splits up into carbon dioxide and pyro-gallic acid or trihydroxyl benzol. **1878** ABNEY *Photogr.* (1881) 103 A pyrogallic-acid developer.

Hence **pyro'gallate**, a salt of pyrogallic acid; **pyro'gallein**, a product of the action of air on an ammoniacal solution of pyrogallic acid; †**pyro'gallin** (*rare*), **pyro'gallol**, synonyms of pyrogallic acid.

1836 BRANDE *Man. Chem.* (ed. 4) 933 Ammonia, soda, and potassa, form soluble *pyrogallates. **1878** ABNEY *Photogr.* (1881) 98 The alkaline pyrogallates have..an affinity for the halogens. **1866–8** WATTS *Dict. Chem.* IV. 758 *Pyro-galleïn, an uncrystallisable product. **1876** HARLEY *Mat. Med.* (ed. 6) 422 Heated to 410°, gallic acid is..converted into *pyro-gallin and carbonic anhydride. **1876** *Encycl. Brit.* V. 564/2 Trihydric phenols comprising..pyrogallic acid (or *pyrogallol). **1899** *Allbutt's Syst. Med.* VIII. 580 The remedies..found most useful are tar, chrysarobin, and pyrogallol.

pyrogen ('paɪərədʒɛn). [f. PYRO- + -GEN; lit. 'fire-producer', or 'fire-produced'.] A term proposed in various senses. †**a.** A name for electricity considered as a material substance; the 'electric fluid'. *rare.* †**b.** (See quot. 1866–8.) *rare.* **c.** A substance which, when introduced into the blood, produces fever; a pyrogenetic agent.

a. **1858** MAYNE *Expos. Lex.*, *Pyrogen*, a term proposed for electricity considered as a material substance possessing weight. **1864** in WEBSTER.
b. **1866–8** WATTS *Dict. Chem.* IV. 759 *Pyrogen*, a name applied by Dumas to pyro-acids and other products of the action of heat on organic bodies.
c. **1896** *Allbutt's Syst. Med.* I. 157 In 1875 I prepared a substance, which I ventured to call pyrogen, from putrid extract of flesh. **1955** *Times* 30 Aug. 4/3 We have now reached the stage where bacterial pyrogens in pure form can, with advantage, replace the older materials and methods for producing a general stimulation of the defence mechanisms of the body. **1957** *New Scientist* 12 Dec. 25/1 Rabbits, too, played their part..in pyrogen tests, to ensure the safety of injectable solutions. **1961** M. HYNES *Med. Bacteriol.* (ed. 7) iii. 28 Fluids for parenteral use must be pyrogen-free as well as sterile. **1973** *Nature* 16 Nov. 162/2 It is not known whether the malarial parasite produces a pyrogen, like bacteria, or whether the malarial fever results from destruction of red blood cells.

pyrogeneous, erron. form of PYROGENOUS.

‖**pyro'genesis.** [f. PYRO- 1 + GENESIS.] The generation of fire or heat.

1858 in MAYNE *Expos. Lex.* **1890** in *Cent. Dict.*

pyrogenetic (ˌpaɪərəʊdʒɪ'nɛtɪk), *a.* [f. PYRO- 1 + -GENETIC.] **1. a.** Having the property of producing heat, esp. in the body; thermogenetic. **b.** Having the property of producing fever.

1858 MAYNE *Expos. Lex.*, Pyrogenetic. **1875** tr. *von Ziemssen's Cycl. Med.* I. 255 What the chemical natures of these pyrogenetic processes may be, we have never learnt. **1885** *Buck's Ref. Handbk. Med. Sc.* II. 226 Not the least curious phenomenon of the pyrogenetic mechanism is the influence that increases the resistance to cold. **1896** *Allbutt's Syst. Med.* I. 155 Artificial fever produced by the introduction of pyrogenetic substances.

2. *Petrol.* Of a mineral: crystallizing from a magma at a high temperature.

1920 A. HOLMES *Nomencl. Petrol.* 193 *Pyrogenetic minerals*, a term applied to the primary magmatic minerals of igneous rocks, excluding those due to pneumatolytic, hydrothermal, and thermodynamic processes... The solidification of a magma may constitute a continuous process beginning with indubitable pyrogenetic minerals, and yet finishing with a well-defined hydrothermal series of minerals. **1923** *Mineral. Mag.* XX. 146 In the granites, tourmaline, muscovite, and topaz..behave as pyrogenetic minerals and commence to crystallize at an early stage but.. their crystallization continued to a late stage in the consolidation of the rock. **1950** F. H. HATCH et al. *Petrol. Igneous Rocks* (ed. 10) iii. 163 The separation of these pyrogenetic minerals leaves the liquid relatively enriched in H_2O and various other components of low atomic and molecular weights. **1954** H. WILLIAMS et al. *Petrogr.* i. 9 The first minerals to form from magma are usually anhydrous... Such minerals are called pyrogenetic.

pyrogenic (-'dʒɛnɪk), *a.* [f. as PYROGEN + -IC.] †**1.** *Geol.* = PYROGENOUS 1 a. *Obs. rare.*

1853 TH. ROSS *Humboldt's Trav.* III. xxxii. 370 The ancient pyrogenic rocks which I found near Parapara. **1904** A. W. GRABAU in *Amer. Geologist* XXXIII. 230 Returning now to the..chemically deposited rocks, we may readily distinguish four groups... The first..includes the well recognized Igneous rocks, to which the term *pyrogenic* is applicable.

†**2.** *Chem.* Name for a supposed peculiar acid, now identified with formic acid. *Obs.*

1864–72 WATTS *Dict. Chem.* II. 684 Tünnermann (Pogg. Ann. xv. 307) thought that he had discovered two peculiar acids, to which he gave the names of *pyrogenic* and *amylenic acids*.

3. *Phys.* and *Path.* = PYROGENETIC b.

1877 ROBERTS *Handbk. Med.* (ed. 3) I. 80 Dr. Burdon-Sanderson found..that by injecting certain fluids—which he terms 'pyrogenic'—..fever could be excited. **1896** *Allbutt's Syst. Med.* I. 157 The pyrogenic substance was perhaps a body analogous to the unformed ferments.

4. *Chem.* Caused by the application of heat.

1887 *Jrnl. Chem. Soc.* LII. I. 572 (*heading*) Pyrogenic reactions. **1912** *Ibid.* CI. II. 1453 One of the authors was engaged in examining the pyrogenic decomposition of American turpentine with the object of obtaining isoprene in quantity. **1920** *Ibid.* CXVIII. I. 589 (*heading*) Pyrogenic acetylene condensations.

pyrogenicity (ˌpaɪrəʊdʒɪ'nɪsɪtɪ). [f. prec. + -ITY.] The property of producing fever; freq. *attrib.*

1956 *Nature* 17 Mar. 497/1 The procedure..to be used in toxicity, pyrogenicity and sterility tests. **1973** *Ibid.* 16 Nov. 162/2 We took advantage of this differential sensitivity to test the pyrogenicity and nature of malarial parasites. **1977** *Lancet* 2 July 47/2 Intravenous pyrogenicity tests in rabbits were negative.

pyrogenous (-'rɒdʒɪnəs), *a.* Erron. -geneous. [f. as PYROGEN + -OUS.]

1. Produced by fire or heat. **a.** *Geol.* Of rocks: = IGNEOUS *a.* 2. **b.** *Chem.* Applied to a substance produced by the combustion of another substance.

1839 G. ROBERTS *Dict. Geol.*, *Pyrogenous*,..produced by the agency of fire. **1845** J. PHILLIPS *Geol.* in *Encycl. Metrop.* VI. 760/1 The phenomena of pyrogenous rocks. **1858** MAYNE *Expos. Lex.*, *Pyrogeneus*,..pyrogeneous. Applied by Berzelius to empyreumatic oils and resins, i.e. those produced by distillation of organic substances.

2. Producing fire, heat, or fever: = PYROGENETIC.

1890 *Cent. Dict.* s.v., Pyrogenous action in the blood. **1897** *Syd. Soc. Lex.*, *Pyrogenous*... 2. *Med.* Fever-producing, pyrogenetic.

pyroglucic to **-gnostics**: see PYRO- 1, 3 a, b.

py'rography. [f. PYRO- 1 + -GRAPHY.] †**1.** A description of fire-arms. *Obs.*

1684 tr. *Agrippa's Van. Arts* xxii. 67 The several varieties of Guns and Fire-vomiting Engines, of which lately my self have written a..Treatise, Entituled *Pyrographie*.

2. a. A method of wood-carving by means of heated metallic plates or cylinders in relief, by which the design is burned into the substance of the wood (Knight *Dict. Mech.* 1875).

b. The art of making drawings or designs on wood, bone, etc. by means of a heated metallic point: = POKER-WORK.

1891 MRS. MAUDE *Pyrography* iii. 43 Bone and Ivory form very delicate grounds for Pyrography in small work. **1895** MRS. STEVENS in *Proc. 14th Convent. Teach. Deaf* 366 The 'Legend of Sleepy Hollow', done in pyrography on the wood-work of a fire-place.

So **'pyrograph** *v. intr.*, to practise pyrography or poker-work; **py'rographer, py'rographist**, one who practises or is skilled in pyrography; **pyro'graphic** *a.*, pertaining to, done by, or using pyrography; **pyrogravure** (ˌpaɪərəʊgrə'vjʊə(r)) = PYROGRAPHY 2 b, poker-work.

1891 MRS. MAUDE *Pyrography* iv. 56 The general tones of the animal to be *Pyrographed. *Ibid.* v. 80 Pyrographed frames for sepia drawings. **1811** JOS. SMITH in *Fowler Corr.* (1906) 204 To send you the *Pyrographic Picture you ordered of me. **1895** MRS. STEVENS in *Proc. 14th Convent. Teach. Deaf* 366 Some very fine specimens of pyrographic work. **1891** MRS. MAUDE *Pyrography* ii. 28 A very clever lady *Pyrographist. **1888** *Sci. Amer.* 9 June 353 *Pyrogravure is a new method of engraving in black, reddish brown, bister, etc., by the use of a red hot metallic point. **1901** *N. Amer. Rev. Adv.* Feb. 2 This panel and the rest of the wood-work are in pyrogravure.

pyroguaiacic to **-kinic**: see PYRO- 2, 3 a, b.

pyrogue, obs. form of PIROGUE.

pyroheliometer: = PYRHELIOMETER.

‖**pyrola** ('pɪrələ). *Bot.* Also 7 **pirola**; and in anglicized form, 6 **pyrole**, 7 **pyrol**. [med. or mod.L. dim. of *pyrus*, med.L. for *pirus* pear-tree; in F. *pirole*. So called from the resemblance of the leaves to those of the pear-tree.] A genus of plants, type of the N.O *Pyrolaceæ*, often viewed as a sub-order of the *Ericaceæ*, consisting of smooth herbs, with running underground stems, evergreen usually entire and rounded leaves, and simple racemes of flowers; several of the species are known as *wintergreen*.

Formerly including some allied plants now removed to other genera, as *Moneses grandiflora* (*Pyrola uniflora*) and *Chimaphila* (*Pyrola*) *umbellata*.

1578 LYTE *Dodoens* I. xcii. 134 Pyrola groweth in shadowy places, and moyst wooddes. *Ibid.* 135 Greene Pyrole is also good to be layde vpon woundes, vlcers, & burnings. **1651** DAVENANT *Gondibert* II. VII. iii, New wounds..such..As balm nor juice of pyrol never heals. **1672** JOSSELYN *New Eng. Rarities* 67 Pirola, or Winter Green, that kind which grows with us in England is common in New-England, but there is another plant which I judge to be a kind of Pirola, and proper to this Country. **1834** MARY HOWITT *Sk. Nat. Hist.*, *The Garden* xii, I found within another wood The rare Pyrola blowing.

Hence **pyrolaceous** (-'eɪʃəs) *a.*, belonging to the *Pyrolaceæ* (Mayne *Expos. Lex.*, 1858).

pyrolatry (paɪ'rɒlətrɪ). [f. PYRO- + Gr. λατρεία service, worship: cf. IDOLATRY.] The worship of fire, fire-worship.

1669 GALE *Crt. Gentiles* I. II. ix. 144 Their Pyrolatrie, or fire-worship, which they learnt from the Chaldeans. **1839** MOORE *Hist. Irel.* I. ii. 26 The Pyrolatry, or Fire-worship, of the early Irish. **1891** MAX MÜLLER *Phys. Relig.* 241 Anything like pyrolatry or worship of fire, as a mere element, is foreign to the character of the Greeks.

Hence **py'rolater (-or)**, [cf. IDOLATER], a fire-worshipper.

1801 SOUTHEY *Thalaba* VIII. *note*, The fires..having too near an analogy to the religion of the pyrolators.

pyroleter (paɪ'rɒlɪtə(r)). [f. Gr. πῦρ fire + ὀλετήρ destroyer.] An apparatus for extinguishing fire, consisting of a double pump by which solutions of hydrochloric acid and sodium bicarbonate are mixed in a cylinder, and the carbonic acid generated by the reaction is projected upon the fire.

1878 *Ure's Dict.* IV. 712 The pyroleter is a small double pump worked by hand, which sucks up from tubes on either side muriatic acid and a solution of carbonate of soda.

pyroligneous (paɪərəʊ'lɪgnɪːəs), *a.* [a. F. *pyroligneux* (De Morveau and Lavoisier, 1787), f. PYRO- + L. *lignum* wood.] Produced by the action of fire or heat upon wood. ***pyroligneous acid***: a crude acetic acid (wood vinegar) obtained by the destructive distillation of wood. So ***pyroligneous alcohol, ether, spirit***, methyl alcohol.

[**1787** DE MORVEAU, LAVOISIER, etc. *Nomencl.* 150 Noms nouveaux: *Acide pyro-ligneux.* Esprit acide empyreumatique du bois.] *c* **1790** tr. *De Morveau's*, etc., *Table Chem. Nom.* (*Encycl. Brit.* (ed. 3) IV. 598) 21 Pyroligneous acid. Spirit of wood. **1810–26** HENRY *Elem. Chem.* I. 336 Liquid products of value are collected,..an impure vinegar called pyroligneous acid. **1822** P. TAYLOR in *Philos. Mag.* 31 Oct. 316 This spirit, which, from its greater resemblance to æther than to any other substance, I have called pyroligneous æther. **1861** *Photogr. News* 3 May 211/2 Pyroligneous Spirit, known also as pyroxylic spirit, wood alcohol, and wood naphtha. **1873** E. SPON *Workshop Receipts* Ser. I. 64/1 Some turpentine being drawn from green trees abound[s] with a pyroligneous acid. **1876** HARLEY *Mat. Med.* (ed. 6) 336 Pyroligneous æther or wood naphtha,—a fluid quite distinct from mineral naphtha, which is a simple hydrocarbon.

So †**pyro'lignic**, †**pyro'lignous** *adjs.* in same sense; **pyro'lignate**, †**pyro'lignite** [so in Fr.; see -ITE[1] 4 b], a salt of pyroligneous acid, an impure or crude acetate.

1823 J. BADCOCK *Dom. Amusem.* 22 Acetate of Lime. Sometimes termed *Pyrolignate of Lime. *a* **1799** J. BLACK *Lect. Elem. Chem.* (1803) II. 374 An acid now called *pyrolignic (pyro-xylic). **1805** NISBET *Dict. Chem.*, *Table Nomencl.* i. 359 *Pyrolignic radical*, basis of acid distilled from birch and other woods. [**1787** DE MORVEAU, LAVOISIER, etc. *Nomencl.* 208 *Pyro-lignite de chaux, etc.] *c* **1790** tr. *De Morveau's*, etc., *Tabl. Chem. Nom.* (*Encycl. Brit.* (ed. 3) IV. 598) 21 Pyro-lignite of lime, Pyrolignite of zinc, etc. **1839** URE *Dict. Arts* 223 The pyrolignite of iron called iron liquor in this country, is the only mordant used in calico-printing for black, violet, puce, and brown colours. **1790** KERR tr. *Lavoisier's Elem. Chem.* 260 The Combinations of *Pyrolignous Acid with the Salifiable Bases. **1823** J. BADCOCK *Dom. Amusem.* 21 Pyrolignous acid, about twice the strength of vinegar..possesses a dull, acidulous, offensive smack.

pyroline, *Chem.*, var. of PYRROLINE.

pyrolite: see PYRO- 2.

pyrolithic to **pyrolivilic:** see PYRO- 3 a.

pyrology (paɪ'rɒlədʒɪ). *rare.* [ad. mod.L. *pyrologia*: see PYRO- 1 and -LOGY.] The science or study of fire or heat; now *spec.* that branch of chemistry which deals with the application of fire to chemical analysis, etc.

[**1669** R. WITTIE (*title*) Pyrologia Mimica; or an Answer to Hydrologia Chymica of W. Simpson..In Defence of Scarborough-Spaw. **1692** D. BOTTONI (*title*) Pyrologia Topographica, id est, de Igni dissertatio, juxta loca, cum eorum descriptionibus.] **1731** *Hist. Litteraria* III. 348 The Discoveries made by the modern Philosophers in Pneumaticks, Hydrology, Pyrology, &c. **1797** W. OKELY (*title*) Pyrology; or the Connection between Natural and Moral Philosophy. **1875** W. A. ROSS (*title*) Pyrology or Fire Chemistry.

Hence **pyro'logical** *a.*, pertaining to or involving pyrology; **py'rologist**, one versed in pyrology.

a **1799** BLACK is cited by Webster (1828) for *Pyrologist*. **1881** W. A. ROSS in *Knowledge* No. 7. 137 The young 'pyrologist', or blowpipe chemist. **1881** *Eng. Mechanic* 27 May 284/1 Even with his pyrological methods, he would have difficulty in determining the carbonic acid in a pinch of soot. **1883** *Ibid.* 20 July (*title*) Easy Lessons in Blowpipe Analysis and Pyrological Mineralogy.

pyrolusite (paɪərəʊ'l(j)uːsaɪt). *Min.* [ad. Ger. *pyrolusit* (Haidinger 1827), f. Gr. πυρο- (PYRO-) + λοῦσ-ις washing + -ITE[1]: from its use, when heated, for discharging colour from glass.] Native dioxide of manganese, MnO_2, a common ore of black or dark-grey colour and metallic lustre.

1828 *Edin. Jrnl. Sc.* IX. 304 An account of pyrolusite or prismatic manganese ore. **1839** DE LA BECHE *Rep. Geol. Cornwall*, etc. xv. 610 Pyrolusite, or grey and black ore, containing from 70 to 99 per cent. of peroxide of manganese. **1868** DANA *Min.* (ed. 5) 166 Pyrolusite parts with its oxygen at a red heat, and is extensively employed for discharging the brown and green tints of glass. Hence..whimsically entitled by the French *le savon des verriers*.

pyrolyse ('paɪərəʊlaɪz), *v.* Also -lyze, -lize (both chiefly *U.S.*), -lise. [f. PYROLYSIS, after *hydrolysis, hydrolyse*.] **1.** *intr.* To undergo pyrolysis. Const. *to*.

1929 C. D. HURD *Pyrolysis of Carbon Compounds* ii. 12 Who would predict that the groupings $\equiv C-CH_2OH$ and $=N-CH_2OH$ pyrolyze differently? **1938** *Jrnl. Amer. Chem. Soc.* LX. 2420/1 Phenyl acetate pyrolyzed smoothly into ketone and phenol. **1970** *Sci. Jrnl.* May 68 (Advt.), The Pye range of liquid chromatographs is capable of detecting all organic compounds which vaporise or pyrolyse at temperatures up to 700°C. **1974** *Physics Bull.* Feb. 56/2 The fuel, in approaching the flame in the absence of oxygen, tends to pyrolyse to soot and other products of incomplete combustion. **1977** *Engin. Materials & Design* Aug. 26/2 On exposure to high temperatures the resin binder may undergo some further cross-linking... There-after, the surface layer of resin begins to pyrolise.

2. *trans.* To decompose by heating; *loosely*, to cause to undergo any chemical change by heating.

1932 *Jrnl. Amer. Chem. Soc.* LIV. 3632 Hydroanisamide was pyrolyzed and found to yield no compound which corresponded in composition to trimethoxylophine. **1959** *Times Rev. Industry* Dec. 18/1 Chlorodifluoromethane. This substance is a gas..which, on pyrolizing at about 800 deg. C., forms tetrafluoroethylene. **1973** *Nature* 23 Mar. 232/2 The results of pyrolysing 50 mg portions of the lunar samples indicated that carbon was present in the gases. **1976** *Amer. Scientist* LXIV. 625/1 The second sample was pyrolized first at 350°C to attempt to drive off most of the water and increase sensitivity to organics.

Hence **'pyrolysed** *ppl. a.*; also **'pyrolysable** *a.*, capable of being pyrolysed; **py'rolysate** [after *distillate*, *filtrate*, etc.], a product of pyrolysis.

1934 NASH & HOWES *Princ. Motor Fuel Prep. & Appl.* x. 496 T. S. Wheeler and I.C.I. Ltd., have suggested the removal of hydrogen from pyrolyzed gas before it is passed to a second stage. **1953** D. H. R. BARTON in E. H. Rodd *Chem. Carbon Compounds* II B. xvi. 755 The acid fraction of the pyrolysate..on dehydrogenation..gave 1:2-dimethylnaphthalene..and the anhydride. **1961** *Flight* LXXIX. 836/2 Modern finishing schemes for the internal and external surfaces of military and civil aircraft must supply protection against moisture condensation, heat, pyrolised ester lubricants, hydraulic fluids, etc. **1972** *Sci. Amer.* Oct. 83/2 The lunar samples contained less than one p.p.m. of volatile and pyrolyzable organic matter. **1976** *Ibid.* Mar. 41/3 Clusters of benzene rings, as in pyrene, benzopyrene and perylene, are..commonly found in pyrolysates. **1977** *Nature* 10 Feb. 493/3 Molecular analysis of the surface dust by pyrolysis-gas chromatography-mass spectrometry..show that it is virtually free of all pyrolysable carbon compounds.

pyrolysis (paɪ'rɒlɪsɪs). [f. PYRO- + -LYSIS.] Decomposition of a substance by the action of heat; *loosely*, any chemical change produced by heating.

1890 BILLINGS *Med. Dict.* II. 420/1 *Pyrolysis*, dry distillation, decomposing by heat. **1928** W. A. GRUSE *Petroleum & its Products* ix. 164 The growth of the petroleum industry, and of the gas-making processes using petroleum, prompted a number of interesting theoretical researches on low-temperature, and particularly on high-temperature, pyrolysis. [*Note*] The use of this word was suggested in 1918 by W. A. Hamor. **1928** *Fuel in Sci. & Pract.* VII. 539/2 Benzene has been found to be an important product of pyrolysis of methane between 875.. and 1,100 deg. Cent. **1943** *Endeavour* Jan. 27/2 In 1924–25 Kennaway succeeded in producing carcinogenic tars by the pyrolysis of petroleum, skin, hair, yeast and cholesterol. **1954** *Chem. & Industry* 13 Nov. 1418/1 It is possible that the presence of the polycyclic hydrocarbons..is due to the pyrolysis of acetylene which is known to occur in cigarette smoke. **1968** A. A. BAKER *Unsaturation in Org. Chem.* ii. 20 Modern investigations on the pyrolysis of carbon compounds have shown that when ethyl alcohol is passed through a glass tube at 610°–630°C, the yield of ethylene is only about 9 per cent. **1975** *New Scientist* 7 Aug. 315/2 Gas evolved by pyrolysis from any organic material will pass to a detector to check for the presence of carbon-14. **1977** *Nat. Westminster Bank Q. Rev.* Aug. 68 Another promising possibility is the use of Pyrolysis which involves the heating of the refuse in the absence of air in order to produce gas, liquid and char which can all be used as fuel.

pyrolytic (paɪrəʊ'lɪtɪk), *a.* Also -litic. [f. PYROLYSIS: see -LYTIC.] Of, involving, or produced by pyrolysis; ***pyrolytic carbon*** or ***graphite***, a strong, heat-resistant, highly-ordered form of graphite deposited as a vapour from products of hydrocarbon pyrolysis and used esp. in rocket-engine nozzles and as a coating in missile nose-cones, etc.

1909 in *Cent. Dict.* Suppl. **1922** B. T. BROOKS *Chem. Non-Benzenoid Hydrocarbons* i. 36 It is..readily understood that small differences of operating temperature may cause very great difference in the character of the pyrolytic products. **1936** *Chem. Abstr.* XXX. 6176 Some general laws of pyrolytic reactions..are proved thermodynamically. **1946** *Electronic Engin.* XVIII. 66 A new component..for use in electrical communications equipment..is the pyrolytic or cracked carbon resistor. **1961** *Aeroplane* C. 70/1 The big change in the graphite situation of recent years has been the development of a new type of product deposited from the vapour and termed pyrolytic graphite. This is distinguished from the so-called conventional graphite by having a highly oriented structure, and by a higher density. **1966** *Economist* 20 Aug. 754/2 New fuels, pellets rolled and coated in pyrolytic carbon..have overcome a good deal of the radio-active contamination problem. **1970** *Daily Tel.* 22 Jan. 18 Makers of the coloured pipes said the bowls were made of 'pyrolitic graphite', a very hard substance used in the making of nose-cones for missiles. **1972** DEPUY & CHAPMAN *Molec. Reactions & Photochem.* ii. Enol ethers are readily converted to ketones under pyrolytic conditions. **1976** *National Observer* (U.S.) 4 Sept. 3/3 Another test with the pyrolitic release experiment, which looks for evidence that carbon dioxide is being taken up by something in the soil (perhaps life), confirmed the instrument's earlier findings.

Hence **pyro'lytically** *adv.*, by pyrolysis.

1956 *Amer. Scientist* XLIV. 356 This reaction was not highly reproducible pyrolytically. **1975** *Nature* 5 June 474/1 We have studied the influence of high temperature on the tensile fracture strengths of pyrolytically deposited silicon carbide fibres.

pyromachy to **-malic**: see PYRO- 1, 3 a.

pyromancy ('paɪrəʊmænsɪ, 'pɪrəʊ-). Now *rare*. Forms: 4 **piromance, -aunce,** (**perimancie**), 5–6 **piromancy,** (5 **-cye,** 6 **-cie**), 5– **pyromancy,** (5 **-cye,** 6–7 **-cie,** 7 **-ty**). [a. OF. *piromance, pyromancie* (14th c. in Godef. *Compl.*), ad. late L. *pyromantīa*, a. Gr. πυρομαντεία: see PYRO- and -MANCY.] Divination by fire, or by signs derived from fire.

1362 LANGL. *P. Pl.* A. xi. 158 Nigromancye and perimancie. **1390** GOWER *Conf.* III. 45 The craft..That Geomancie cleped is,..And of the flod his Ydromance, And of the fyr the Piromance. *c* **1400** [see HYDROMANCY]. **1496** *Dives & Paup.* (W. de W.) I. xxxvi. 77/1 Pyromancye, that is wytche-crafte done in the fyre. *c* **1590** GREENE *Fr. Bacon* ii. 15 Thou art read in Magicks mystery, In Piromancy, to diuine by flames. **1630** J. TAYLOR (Water P.) *Water Cormorant* Wks. III. 12/2 By Fire he hath the skill of Pyromanty. **1855** SMEDLEY *Occult Sc.* 292 Pyromancy, by which conjectures were made from the motions of the sacrificial flame.

So **'pyromancer**, one who divines by fire; **pyro'mantic** *a.*, pertaining to or practising pyromancy; †*sb.* = *pyromancer*.

c **1400** *Apol. Loll.* 96 Þus are callid..piromauncers þat wirkun bi þe fire. *c* **1590** GREENE *Fr. Bacon* ix. 71 The Pyromanticke Genij. **1608** DAY *Law Trickes* IV. ii, Skill in pyromantique rules. **1638** SIR T. HERBERT *Trav.* (ed. 2) 215 Many Witches, Sorcerers, Inchanters, Hydro and Pyromantiques, and other Diaboliques.

pyromania to **-maric**: see PYRO- 1, 3 a.

pyrome'conic, *a. Chem.* [f. PYRO- 3 + MECONIC.] In ***pyromeconic acid***, a crystalline bitter acid, $C_5H_4O_3$, occurring in large transparent tables; it is obtained by the dry distillation of meconic or of comenic acid. Hence **pyro'meconate**, a salt of this acid.

1836 BRANDE *Man. Chem.* (ed. 4) 1023 Pyromeconic Acid. This acid is among the products of the destructive distillation of the meconic acid; it is a crystalline sublimate, which fuses at a temperature of about 250°. *Ibid.* The neutral pyromeconeate of lead. **1838** T. THOMSON *Chem. Org. Bodies* 82 Pyromeconic acid..was first examined by Robiquet in 1832. **1866–8** WATTS *Dict. Chem.* IV. 761 With bromine water it yields bromopyromeconic acid ($C_5H_3BrO_3$)... Chloride of iodine converts it into iodopyromeconic acid ($C_5H_3IO_3$).

†**'pyromel.** *Obs.* [f. PYRO- + L. *-mel* honey.] An old name for treacle.

1897 in *Syd. Soc. Lex.*

pyromelane to **-metamorphism**: see PYRO-.

pyrometer (paɪ'rɒmɪtə(r)). [f. PYRO- + -METER.] † **a.** *orig.* An instrument for measuring the expansion of solid bodies under the influence of heat. *Obs.* **b.** Any instrument for measuring high temperatures, usually those higher than can be measured by the mercurial thermometer.

Such instruments have been made on a variety of principles, depending on the expansion, contraction, or fusion of solids, the radiation, conduction, etc. of heat, the production of electrical or chemical action, etc.

1749 *Gentl. Mag.* XIX. 361/2 The Draught of an accurate Pyrometer or Instrument to measure the Extension or Contraction, of Metal, or other Rods,..invented by Mr. Withurst of Derby. **1793** W. & S. JONES *Catal. Optical*, etc. *Instr.* 8 Pyrometers, shewing the expansion of metals. **1796** KIRWAN *Elem. Min.* (ed. 2) I. Pref. 10, I..examined..their fusibility in various degrees of heat by the help of Mr. Wedgewood's pyrometer. **1812** SIR H. DAVY *Chem. Philos.* 73 Clay contracts considerably in dimensions by a very intense heat, and on the measure of its contractions the pyrometer of Wedgwood is founded. **1906** *Westm. Gaz.* 16 July 4/2 Special furnaces which are controlled by the assistance of electrical pyrometers. **1907** *Athenæum* 18 May 609/3 A modification of Prof. Féry's radiation pyrometer, which in principle consists of receiving in a concave mirror the total radiation of a hot plate.

Hence **pyro'metric, pyro'metrical** *adjs.*, pertaining to a pyrometer or to pyrometry; of the nature of, or measurable by, a pyrometer; formerly said of effects due to the expansive power of great heat; ***pyrometric cone***: (see quots.); **pyro'metrically** *adv.*, in the manner of, or by means of, a pyrometer; **py'rometry**, the measurement of very high temperatures.

1800 tr. *Lagrange's Chem.* I. 20 This pyrometer [Wedgewood's] consists of two parts, one of which, called the Gage, serves to measure the degrees of diminution or contraction: the other consists of small cylinders of clay, called *Pyro-metric Pieces. **1837** HERSCHEL in Babbage *Bridgew. Treat.* App. I. 237 The elevation of strata by pyrometric expansion of the subjacent columns of rock. **1839** URE *Dict. Arts* 1016 Pyrometric balls of red clay, coated with a very fusible lead enamel, are employed in the English potteries to ascertain the temperature of the glaze kilns. **1947** J. C. RICH *Materials & Methods of Sculpture* ii. 46 Pyrometric cones..are used to determine and thereby control the firing temperatures of the kiln. **1964** H. HODGES *Artifacts* i. 40 Today potters use small cones of clay—pyrometric cones—which melt below the maturing point of the wares being fired. **1977** *Western Living* (Vancouver) Apr. 25/3 The way you tell the temperature..is with pyrometric cones which are little triangular objects made of different combinations of ceramic materials. **1791** *Phil. Trans.* LXXXI. 107 The substances employed..must have been influenced in their length by *pyrometrical and hygrometrical effects. **1834–6** BARLOW in *Encycl. Metrop.* (1845) VIII. 460/2 *Pyrometrical beads*, technically called *trials*,..are made in the form of small hoops, of Egyptian black clay. **1865** MISS METEYARD *Wedgwood* II. 160 Thos. and John Wedgwood..about 1740 introduced what they termed pyrometrical beads..formed of prepared clay. **1778** *Phil. Trans.* LXVIII. 419 (heading) An Essay on *Pyrometry and Arcometry. *Ibid.* 421 The occasion which led me to Pyrometry. **1830** HERSCHEL *Stud. Nat. Phil.* 319 The dilatation of bodies by heat forms the subject of.. pyrometry. **1897** ROSE in *Mining Jrnl.* 30 Jan. 143/3 Pyrometry and the testing..of alloys continue to receive much attention.

pyromorphite, -morphous: see PYRO- 2, 1.

pyromucic (paɪrəʊ'mju:sɪk), *a. Chem.* [f. PYRO- 3 + MUCIC: cf. F. *pyromucique* substituted for *pyromuqueux* (De Morveau and Lavoisier 1787).] In ***pyromucic acid***, an acid, $C_5H_4O_3$, metameric with pyromeconic acid, produced by the dry distillation of mucic acid, and occurring in white glistening scales or needles. So ***pyromucic alcohol, chloride, ether***, etc.

1794 G. PEARSON tr. *De Morveau*, etc. *Table Chem. Nom.* 22 Radical Pyro-mucic. **1819** J. G. CHILDREN *Chem. Anal.* 284 Pyromucic acid has been lately discovered by M. Hontou Labillardière. **1836–41** BRANDE *Chem.* (ed. 5) 1072 When mucic acid is subjected to destructive distillation it yields..pyromucic acid.

Hence **pyro'mucamide**, an amide of pyromucic acid, $C_5H_5NO_2$; ***dipyromucamide***, $C_5H_6N_2O$; **pyro'mucate**, a salt of pyromucic acid; **pyro'mucyl**, the radical $C_5H_3O_2$ of pyromucic acid; also †**pyromucous** *a.* = *pyromucic*, †**pyromucite** = *pyromucate*.

1790 KERR tr. *Lavoisier's Elem. Chem.* 263 Table of the Combinations of Pyro-mucous Acid with the Salifiable Bases. *Ibid.* 260 Pyro-mucite of lime. **1819** J. G. CHILDREN *Chem. Anal.* 284 Pyromucate of barya is composed of acid 57.7 barya 42.2. **1847** *Chem. Gaz.* V. 85 Pyro-mucamide differs essentially from this body. **1866–8** WATTS *Dict. Chem.* IV. 763 The pyromucates of the alkali-metals are.. difficult to crystallise. *Ibid.* 765 Dipyromucamide forms white, shining laminæ, easily soluble in alcohol and ether, less soluble in water. **1881** *Jrnl. Chem. Soc.* XL. 715 Ethylamine pyromucate when distilled with phosphorus pentachloride yields pyromucyl chloride.

pyronaphtha to **pyronomy**: see PYRO- 1.

pyrone ('paɪrəʊn). *Chem.* [ad. G. *pyron* (Haitinger & Lieben 1885, in *Sitzungsber. d. österreichischen Akad. d. Wissensch. in Wien* XCI. (Abt. II.) 923): see PYRO- and -ONE.] Either of two unsaturated heterocyclic compounds, $C_5H_4O_2$, which are mono-keto derivatives of the pyrans; *spec.* CH:CH·O·CH:CH·CO (γ- or 1, 4-*pyrone*), a colourless, basic, crystalline solid; also, any heterocyclic ketone or lactone containing the ring structure characteristic of either isomer. Freq. *attrib.*, as ***pyrone ring***.

1891 *Jrnl. Chem. Soc.* LX. I. 458 The pyrone is almost insoluble in water or alkalis. *Ibid.* II. 939 The conversion of α-pyrone into pyridine derivatives. **1913** T. H. POPE tr. *Molinari's Org. Chem.* 626 Chelidonic acid,..which is found in celandine, loses CO_2 giving comanic acid and pyrone. **1938** G. H. RICHTER *Textbk. Org. Chem.* xxxi. 659 The pyrones are interesting also because the hetero oxygen atom is basic forming oxonium salts with strong acids. **1962** K. VENKATARAMAN in T. A. Geissman *Chem. Flavonoid Compounds* iv. 94 Isoflavones undergo hydrolysis with opening of the pyrone ring under mild conditions of alkali treatment. **1963** L. F. & M. FIESER *Topics in Org. Chem.* ii. 103 α-Pyrone has the properties expected of a doubly unsaturated δ-lactone. *Ibid.* 104 Representative natural γ-pyrones are kojic acid, formed by bacterial fermentation of carbohydrates; maltol, isolated from the bark of the larch tree; and yangonin, from the roots of the kava shrub. **1972** J. M. TEDDER et al. *Basic Org. Chem.* IV. iii. 139 The reactivity of the carbonyl group is reduced so much by the conjugation..that the α-pyrone ring is much more stable towards alkali than the unsubstituted coumarin.

pyronin ('paɪrənɪn). *Chem.* and *Biol.* Also **ine** (-i:n), and with capital initial. [a. G. *pyronin* (trade name), prob. f. *pyro-* PYRO- + *-in* -IN[1], -INE[5] with inserted *n*.] Any of a class of synthetic red xanthene dyes employed chiefly as microscopic stains; now *esp.* either of two such dyes, called ***pyronin G*** or ***Y*** and ***pyronin B***.

1895 *Jrnl. Chem. Soc.* LXVIII. I. 47 Formaldehydetetramethylamidofluorimum chloride, the zinc double salt of which is known commercially as pyronine. **1906** *Practitioner* Nov. 666 Stained with pyronin and methyl green, the nuclei were large, rounded, pale, and contained chromatin in 'lumps'. **1952** K. VENKATARAMAN *Chem. Synthetic Dyes* II. xxiv. 745 Pyronines are obtained by condensing *m*-dialkylaminophenols with formaldehyde in presence of concentrated sulfuric acid, and oxidizing the xanthene derivative. **1957** *Nature* 31 Aug. 440/1 Both the nucleolus and the puffs stain bright red with pyronin. **1960** E. GURR *Encycl. Microscopic Stains* 340 Pyronin B..is in fairly frequent use in bacteriology and in animal and plant histology. *Ibid.* 341 Pyronin Y finds its chief application.. in conjunction with methyl green for demonstrating nucleic acids. **1960** *New Biol.* XXXI. 99 Their cytoplasm is unusually strongly stained by dyes, such as pyronine, which specifically combine with ribonucleic acid. **1974** H. C. COOK *Man. Histol. Demonstration Techniques* ii. 43 For better results the pyronin should be of 'Y' or 'G' type in preference to the 'B' variety.

pyrope ('paɪrəʊp). Forms: 4 **pirope,** 7 **pirop,** 7–9 **pyrop,** 9 **pyrope;** also in Lat. form 6 **pi'ropus,** 7–9 **py'ropus,** (*pl.* -i). [a. OF. *pirope* (13th c. in Godef.), ad. L. *pyrōpus* gold-bronze, also a kind of gem, a. Gr. πυρωπός gold-bronze, lit. 'fiery-eyed', f. πῦρ, πυρ- fire + ὤψ eye, face.]

1. In early use applied vaguely to a red or fiery gem, as ruby or carbuncle. Also *attrib.*

13.. *K. Alis.* 5682 Jacynkte, Piropes, Crisolites. **1553** EDEN *Treat. Newe Ind.* (Arb.) 14 *Piropi* (whiche are a kind of Rubies or Carbuncles). **1602** CAMPION *Eng. Poesie* vii. in G. G. Smith *Eliz. Crit. Ess.* (1904) II. 345 The glossy Pirop faines to blaze, But toucht cold appeares, and an earthy stone. **1625** LISLE *Du Bartas, Noe* 154 Two pyrops are her eyes Or flaming carbuncles. **1795** SOUTHEY *Joan of Arc* II. 84 Rubies and amethysts..With the gay topaz,..and the emerald's hue, And bright pyropus. **1948** R. GRAVES *Coll. Poems, 1914–1947* 237 He carved his law on tables of sapphirus, Jerusalem shines with his pyrope gates.

2. *Min.* Applied by Werner, 1803 (*Pyrop*), to the Bohemian garnet or fire-garnet, a deep-red gem. Also ***pyrope garnet***.

1804 *Edin. Rev.* III. 301 The pyrop, which has lately exfoliated from the class of garnets, has no difference but superior beauty. **1805–17** R. JAMESON *Char. Min.* (ed. 3) 91 Precious garnet, pyrope and iron-sand. **1840** BROWNING *Sordello* VI. 411 Cool citrine-crystals, fierce pyropus-stone. **1868** DANA *Min.* (ed. 5) 267 The original pyrope is the kind containing chrome. **1888** RUTLEY *Rock-Forming Min.* 112 Pyrope, or magnesia-alumina garnet. **1959** *Times* 31 Oct. 9/5 Four..types of garnets interest the collector..the red varieties pyrope and almondine being the most popular... Carbuncles are the large oval red pyrope garnets which were cut *en cabochon*. **1976** *Nature* 8 Apr. 517/2 In the Elie Ness vent, high pressure pyroxenes and pyrope garnets indicate rapid elevation from depths in excess of 60 km. **1977** A. HALLAM *Planet Earth* 34/3 It is likely that the mantle consists dominantly of magnesian olivine,..together with smaller amounts of enstatite.., diopside.., pyrope garnet ($Mg_3Al_2Si_3O_{12}$) and perhaps some phlogopite mica.

pyropectic to **pyrophone**: see PYRO-.

pyrophore (ˈpaɪərəfɔə(r)). *rare.* [a. F. *pyrophore* (1762 in *Dict. Acad.*), ad. mod.L. *pyrophorus*.]

1. = PYROPHORUS 1; also applied to a substance which takes fire on contact with water.

1884 KNIGHT *Dict. Mech.* Supp., *Pyrophore*..a body which has the faculty of inflaming by contact with air or water.

‖**2.** [prop. Fr.] A fire-fly of the genus *Pyrophorus*: see PYROPHORUS 2.

1885 *B'ham Weekly Post* 26 Dec. 1/4 These insects had been brought from Mexico, where they are to be found in the forests. Their scientific name is the pyrophore.

pyrophoric (-ˈfɒrɪk), *a.* [f. next + -IC.] Of, pertaining to, or of the nature of a pyrophorus; having the property of taking fire on exposure to air. ***pyrophoric alloy***, an alloy (usu. of iron and cerium) that emits sparks when scratched or struck with a file or the like. Also **pyrophorous** (-ˈɒfərəs), *a.*

1828 WEBSTER, *Pyrophorous*, pertaining to or resembling pyrophorus. **1836** BRANDE *Man. Chem.* (ed. 4) 1119 A residue..which burns like tinder when heated, and at a high temperature is pyrophoric. **1866–8** WATTS *Dict. Chem.* IV. 766 The pyrophoric character is exhibited by all the more easily oxidable metals. **1876** HARLEY *Mat. Med.* (ed. 6) 247 At a higher temperature this is completely decomposed, leaving a pyrophoric mixture of lead and carbon. **1906** C. A. VON WELSBACH *U.S. Patent 837,017* What I claim is—1. A pyrophoric alloy, containing cerium alloyed with iron; substantially as and for the purposes described. **1950** *Thorpe's Dict. Appl. Chem.* (ed. 4) X. 328/2 The pyrophoric alloy, in the form of a small rod, is generally pressed firmly against a hard steel wheel with a roughened surface. The shower of sparks produced on rapidly rotating the wheel is projected on to a cotton wick impregnated with..lighter fluid.

‖**pyrophorus** (paɪˈrɒfərəs). Pl. -i (-aɪ). [mod.L., ad. Gr. πυροφόρος fire-bearing.]

1. *Chem.* Any substance capable (esp. in a finely divided state) of taking fire spontaneously on exposure to air. In early use applied *spec.* to ***Homberg's pyrophorus***, a substance made by heating alum with lamp-black, starch, sugar, or flour.

1778 M. CUTLER in *Life*, etc. (1888) II. 204 That these acids may produce such appearances is probable from the easy experiment of Pyrophorus. **1798** *Monthly Mag.* Jan. 20/1 There is a particular composition, known to chemists by the name of pyrophorus, because it possesses the property of being liable to spontaneous inflammation in the open air. It was composed by Homberg. **1842** PARNELL *Chem. Anal.* (1845) 345 The metallic cobalt thus obtained acts as a pyrophorus when it comes in contact with the air. *c* **1860** FARADAY *Forces Nat.* iv. 199 *note*, Lead Pyrophorous ..is a tartrate of lead which has been heated in a glass tube to dull redness as long as vapours are emitted.

2. (With capital initial.) *Entom.* A genus of beetles (named by Illiger, 1809) of the family *Elateridæ* (see ELATER[1] 2), found in tropical and subtropical America, containing the most brilliantly luminous 'fire-flies'.

pyrophosphamic, -phoric: see PYRO- 3 a.

pyrophosphatase (paɪrəʊˈfɒsfəteɪz, -s). *Biochem.* [f. *pyrophosphate* s.v. PYRO- 3 a + -ASE.] Any enzyme which hydrolyses pyrophosphate esters or ions, or pyrophosphoric acid; ***inorganic pyrophosphatase***, an enzyme capable of hydrolysing the free acid or its ions, liberating orthophosphate.

1928 H. D. KAY in *Biochem. Jrnl.* XXII. 1446 Both kidney extract and takadiastase..contain, therefore, a pyrophosphatase. *Ibid.* 1448 Pyrophosphatase is widely distributed in mammalian tissues. **1951** *Jrnl. Biol. Chem.* CXCII. 87 Bauer..found that autolysates of slowly dried bottom yeast were a rich source of inorganic pyrophosphatase. **1970** R. W. MCGILVERY *Biochem.* xi. 209 The inorganic pyrophosphate..is in turn hydrolyzed by the ubiquitous inorganic pyrophosphatase with an additional liberation of free energy. **1976** *Soil Biol. & Biochem.* VIII. 391/1 An assay procedure for soil pyrophosphatase activity.

pyro-photograph (ˌpaɪərəʊˈfəʊtəgrɑːf, -æ-). [f. PYRO- 1 + PHOTOGRAPH.] A photographic picture burnt in on glass or porcelain. Hence **pyro-photoˈgraphic** *a.*, of, pertaining to, or of the nature of a pyro-photograph, or of pyro-photography. **pyro-phoˈtography**, a process in which heat is used to fix a photographic picture.

1869 *Photogr. Jrnl.* 15 Oct. 136 Pyro-photography, or fire-proof photography, is the production of transparent glass photographs by means of fusible pigments, the latter being attached to a film rendered sensitive to the action of light. *Ibid.*, The pigments of the pyro-photographic pictures. *Ibid.* 137 It is this almost incredibly delicate graduation of hygroscopic power, imparted to the film by exposure..to light, that is utilized for the production of pyro-photographs. **1875** H. VOGEL *Chem. Light* xiv. 213 We shall see..that there are other means of producing such pyro-photographs. *Ibid.* xv. 257 Section ix.—Pyro-Photography with Salts of Chromium.

pyrophyllite to **pyrosilver**: see PYRO-.

pyropus, L. form of PYROPE; var. PEROPUS *Obs.*

‖**pyrosis** (paɪˈrəʊsɪs). *Path.* [mod.L., a. Gr. πύρωσις setting on fire, burning, f. πυροῦν to set on fire.] An affection characterized by a burning sensation in the stomach and œsophagus, with eructation of watery fluid; water-brash.

1789 CULLEN *Mat. Med.* II. 248 The pyrosis, frequent in this country under the name of the Water-brash. **1843** R. J. GRAVES *Syst. Clin. Med.* Introd. Lect. 32 The preparation of bismuth used in pyrosis. **1847** E. J. SEYMOUR *Severe Dis.* I. 9 The next morbid condition of the stomach is what is called pyrosis or water-brash.

pyrosmalite: see PYRO- 2.

pyrosome (ˈpaɪərəʊsəʊm). *Zool.* [ad. mod.L. *Pyrosōma* (also in Eng. use), f. Gr. πῦρ fire (PYRO-) + σῶμα body.] An animal of the genus *Pyrosōma*, consisting of highly phosphorescent compound ascidians, the individuals being united into a free-swimming colony in the form of a hollow cylinder closed at one end.

1812 tr. *Peron's Voy. S. Lands* in *Pinkerton's Voy.* XI. 760 What..of those Pyrosomes shaped like an enormous finger of a glove..which cover the sea with their innumerable hosts? **1834** *Lancet* 20 Sept. 1013/2 Compound tunicata, as the pyrosoma and the botryllus. **1856** WOODWARD *Mollusca* III. 344 The Pyrosomes are often gregarious in vast numbers. **1883** C. F. HOLDER in *Harper's Mag.* Jan. 187/2 The most glorious fire bodies of the sea, the salpa and pyrosoma, the latter a pelagic aggregation of individuals, forming a hollow cylinder, closed at one end, from five inches to five feet in length.

pyrosophy to **-synthetic**: see PYRO-.

pyrotartaric (ˌpaɪərəʊtɑːˈtærɪk), *a.* *Chem.* [f. PYRO- 3 a + TARTARIC: cf. F. *pyrotartarique*, substituted for *pyrotartareux* (De Morveau and Lavoisier 1787).] In ***pyrotartaric acid***, $C_5H_8O_4$, a colourless crystalline substance, obtained by the dry distillation of tartaric acid. So ***pyrotartaric anhydride***, $C_5H_6O_3$; ***pyrotartaric ether***, etc.

1794 G. PEARSON tr. *De Morveau*, etc. *Table Chem. Nom.* 15 Basis of Pyro-tartaric Acid. **1815** HENRY *Elem. Chem.* (ed. 7) II. 208 From the experiments of Fourcroy and Vauquelin, it appears that the pyrotartaric acid is a peculiar species. **1819** J. G. CHILDREN *Chem. Anal.* 280 Pyrotartaric acid..is solid, extremely acid to the taste, and reddens vegetable blues strongly. **1866** ODLING *Anim. Chem.* 36 Diatomic Fatty Acid Series: $C_5H_8O_4$ Pyrotartric.

Hence **pyroˈtartranil**, $C_{11}H_{11}NO_2$, formed by heating aniline with the acid; **pyrotartraˈnilic acid**, $C_{11}H_{13}NO_3$ (hence **pyrotarˈtranilate**, a salt of this); **pyroˈtartrate**, a salt of pyrotartaric acid; **pyroˈtartrimide**, the imide of this acid; and other derivatives. Also †**pyro-ˈtartarous, -tarˈtareous** *a.* = *pyrotartaric*; †**pyroˈtartarite, -ˈtartrite** = *pyrotartrate*.

1790 KERR tr. *Lavoisier's Elem. Chem.* 261 The name of Pyro-tartarous acid is given to a dilute empyreumatic acid obtained from purified acidulous tartarite of potash by distillation in a naked fire. *c* **1790** tr. *De Morveau's*, etc. *Table Chem. Nom.* (*Encycl. Brit.* (ed. 3) IV. 598) Pyro-tartareous acid. *Ibid.*, Pyro-tartarite of lime. **1805** NISBET *Dict. Chem.*, *Table Nomencl.* i, Pyrotartareous, Pyrotartrites. **1817** T. THOMSON *Chem.* (ed. 5) II. 150 The French chemists..distinguished them by the names of *tartarous* and *pyrotartarous* acids; which were afterwards changed into those of *tartaric* and *pyrotartaric* acids. **1836** BRANDE *Man. Chem.* (ed. 4) 990 The pyrotartrates of ammonia, potassa,..and lime, are very soluble. **1856** *Jrnl. Chem. Soc.* VIII. 172 Pyrotartanil. *Ibid.* 173 Pyrotartanilic acid is a very stable though rather weak acid. *Ibid.*, Pyrotartanilate of ammonia. **1866–8** WATTS *Dict. Chem.* IV. 775 Pyrotartranil ..is easily soluble in..aqueous alkalis, by which when heated it is converted into pyrotartranilic acid. *Ibid.*, Pyrotartrimide forms small needles or hexagonal plates belonging to the trimetric system.

pyrote, obs. form of PIRATE.

pyroˈtechnian. *rare*⁻⁰. [f. PYROTECHNY + -AN.] = PYROTECHNIST.

1731 BAILEY vol. II, *Pyrotechnian, Pyrotechnician*, a maker of fire works, one skill'd in Pyrotechny.

pyrotechnic (paɪərəʊˈtɛknɪk), *a.* and *sb.* [f. Gr. πυρο-, PYRO- + τεχνικ-ός, f. τέχνη art; or f. PYROTECHNY + -IC.]

A. *adj.* Pertaining to pyrotechny.

†**1.** Of or pertaining to the use of fire in chemistry, metallurgy, or gunnery. *Obs.*

1704 J. HARRIS *Lex. Techn.* I, *Pyrotechnick-Art*, is the Art of Chymistry, so called..because Fire is the chief Instrument the Chymist makes use of in the separating..the purer Substances of mixt Bodies. **1731** BAILEY vol. II, *Pyrotechnick, Pyrotechnical*, of or pertaining to Pyrotechny [1736 (folio) *adds* or the art of gunnery].

2. a. Of or pertaining to fireworks, or the art of making or managing them; of the nature of a firework. Also more widely, capable of being ignited for technical or military purposes.

1825 C. M. WESTMACOTT *Eng. Spy* I. 64 The pyrotechnic artiste. **1837** SIR F. PALGRAVE *Merch. & Friar* Ded. (1844) 11 The pyrotechnic cases in which the powder is to be contained. **1869** H. AINSWORTH *Hilary St. Ives* II. xviii, The glories of extinct Vauxhall pale the modern pyrotechnic displays. **1873** *Board of Trade Notice* in Bedford *Sailor's Pocket Bk.* iii. (1875) 68 The Pyrotechnic Light, commonly known as a Blue Light, every 15 minutes. **1919** H. B. FABER *Military Pyrotechnics* I. I. v. 45 In the latter part of the eighteenth century and the beginning of the nineteenth, there was great activity on the part of those enthusiastic over pyrotechnic devices as war instruments. **1922** A. ST. H. BROCK *Pyrotechnics* iii. 13 Pyrotechnic compositions and gunpowder are inextricably mixed together in early European records. **1953** KIRK & OTHMER *Encycl. Chem. Technol.* XI. 324 In addition to illuminating and signal compositions there are many other types of pyrotechnic compositions such as smoke, incendiary, whistle, dark-fire, tracer, and igniter compositions. **1970** *Guardian* 18 Apr. 1/1 The astronauts fired the pyro-technic bolts that connect the command ship and the service module. **1974** *Encycl. Brit. Micropædia* VII. 186/2 Napalm is also employed in formulating a pyrotechnic gel containing gasoline.., powdered magnesium, and sodium nitrate.

b. *fig.* Resembling or suggesting fireworks; esp. said of a brilliant or sensational display of wit, rhetoric, etc.

1849 MISS MULOCK *Ogilvies* xxiv, Sending forth his bon-mots in a perfect shower of scintillations, so that his conversation became quite a pyrotechnic display. **1897** 'IAN MACLAREN' (J. Watson) *Bonnie Brier Bush, Dr. Old School* iv. 133 This was considered to be rather a pyrotechnic display of Elspeth's superior memory than a serious statement.

B. *sb.* **1.** = PYROTECHNIST. *rare.*

1817 *Blackw. Mag.* I. 470 Like the fiery wheel of some skilful Pyrotechnic.

2. *pl.* **pyrotechnics. a.** = PYROTECHNY 1, 3.

1729 SHELVOCKE *Artillery* III. 169 The whole Excellence ..of Pyrotechnics doth not consist in the Construction of Rockets. **1834** DE QUINCEY *Autob. Sk.* Wks. 1853 I. 41 All subjects..from the Thirty-nine Articles..down to pyrotechnics, legerdemain..thaumaturgy and necromancy.

b. A display of fireworks; also *transf.* of lightning; in quot. 1840, the juggler's trick of pretending to eat fire.

1840 BARHAM *Ingol. Leg.* Ser. I. *Leech Folkest.*, He was eating fire!..the attention of the multitude was absorbed by the pyrotechnics of Mr. Merryman. **1850** B. TAYLOR *Eldorado* i. (1862) 10 Broad scarlet flashes of lightning, surpassing any celestial pyrotechnics I ever witnessed. **1861** N. A. WOODS *Pr. Wales in Canada* 108 The long deferred fireworks for the people came off at last. The pyrotechnics were very fine. **1884** ROE *Nat. Ser. Story* ix, A great black cloud..was the background for the electric pyrotechnics.

c. *fig.* Brilliant displays. (Cf. A. 2 b.)

1901 *Spectator* 17 Aug. 220/1 Orchestral pyrotechnics can be infinitely more exciting. **1905** *Daily Chron.* 16 Aug. 3/1 An Edinburgh graduate, in the period illuminated there by the kindling pyrotechnics of Professor Blackie. **1921** F. SCOTT FITZGERALD *Let.* a 12 Dec. (1964) 150 The cruel Hebrew God, against whom such writers as even Mark Twain..have delivered violent pyrotechnics from time to time. **1970** S. SCHOENBAUM *Shakespeare's Lives* VII. x. 686 Such pyrotechnics of rationalization must be a Baconian's envy. **1977** *Rolling Stone* 7 Apr. 44/2 No emotional pyrotechnics for him, just calm, deathly calm.

3. A device or material which can be ignited to produce light, smoke, or noise, e.g. for purposes of display or illumination.

1919 H. B. FABER *Military Pyrotechnics* I. 7 The art of manufacturing military pyrotechnics. **1948** W. HAYNES *Amer. Chem. Industry* IV. ix. 130 When demand shrank to peacetime uses, chiefly in matchheads and pyrotechnics.., European manufacturers..began cutting prices. **1953** KIRK & OTHMER *Encycl. Chem. Technol.* XI. 332 Commercial pyrotechnics mainly having to do with *sound* include cannon crackers..and trick cigars. **1957** *Spaceflight* I. 51/2 A Fifth-of-November rocket or catherine wheel is a pyrotechnic, and modified forms of these have been used to ignite liquid propellant rockets. **1964** F. G. W. & M. G. JONES *Pests of Field Crops* xvi. 355 Smokes are made by combusting a mixture of pesticide and a suitable pyrotechnic. **1972** *Materials & Technol.* IV. xix. 732 The chemical reactivity of the ingredients and their particle size have very significant effects on the ignition characteristics and burning rates of pyrotechnics.

pyroˈtechnical, *a.* [f. as prec. + -AL[1].]

†**1.** = PYROTECHNIC A. 1. *Obs.*

1610 HEALEY *St. Aug. Citie of God* 169 The warlike artes were Minerva's charge, the pyrotecknicall, or such as worke in fire,..Vulcans. **1753** *Chambers' Cycl. Supp.*, *Ball*, in the military and pyrotechnical arts, is a composition..of the combustible kinds, serving to burn and destroy, give light, smoak, stench, or the like. **1800** T. GREEN *Diary L. Lit.* (1810) 233 Count Rumford, with all his pyrotechnical devices.

2. = PYROTECHNIC A. 2.

1755 JOHNSON, *Pyrotechnical*, engaged or skilful in fireworks. **1765** R. JONES *Fireworks* vi. 254 A variety of pyrotechnical representations. **1801** STRUTT *Sports & Past.* IV. iii. 334 Some of the actors concerned in the pyrotechnical shows. **1862** M. HOPKINS *Hawaii* 99 The pyrotechnical display created..the greatest astonishment.

b. *fig.* = PYROTECHNIC A. 2b.

1825 *Eng. Life* I. 194 All the warmth of her nature was exhausted by her manner: there was a sort of pyrotechnical blaze, without any real heat. **1898** *Chicago Advance* 17 Feb. 211/2 The hysterical and pyrotechnical fashion of the French.

Hence **pyro'technically** *adv.*, in a pyrotechnical manner; by means of fireworks; *fig.* like fireworks.

1867 E. DOWDEN *Contemp. Rev.* VI. 51 He can mention 1789 without exploding pyrotechnically. **1883** *Daily News* 11 Sept. 3/1 Gala nights with Chinese lanterns and 'the mouse ran up the clock' done pyrotechnically.

pyrotech'nician. *rare.* [f. PYROTECHNIC + -IAN, after *mechanician, physician*, etc.] One skilled in pyrotechny; a maker of gunpowder, etc., or of fireworks (= next).

1729 SHELVOCKE *Artillery* III. 169 To consult able Pyrotechnicians. **1731** [see PYROTECHNIAN]. **1979** F. MORTON *Nervous Splendour* (1980) xxx. 316 Pyrotechnicians labored ..for Easter Sunday: a symphonic fireworks.

pyrotechnist (paɪərəʊ'tɛknɪst). [f. next + -IST: cf. *botanist*, etc.] One employed or skilled in pyrotechny; a maker or displayer of fireworks.

a **1791** STEEVENS in Boswell *Johnson* (1888) IV. 325 The authour of *The Rambler*..may be considered, on this occasion, as the ringleader of a successful riot, though not as a skilful pyrotechnist. **1855** MACAULAY *Hist. Eng.* xxi. IV. 613 The whole skill of the pyrotechnists..was employed to produce a display of fireworks which might vie with any that had been seen in the gardens of Versailles. **1858** T. R. JONES *Aquarian Nat.* 47 The azure, gold, and silver rain of the pyrotechnist.

b. *fig.* (Cf. PYROTECHNIC A. 2b.)

1826 SCOTT *Diary* 2 Mar., The bankers will be persuaded that it is a squib which may burn their own fingers, and will curse the poor pyrotechnist that compounded it. **1879** G. MACDONALD *Sir Gibbie* III. x. 164 To hear the new preacher, the pyrotechnist of human logic and eloquence.

pyrotechnite: see PYRO- 2.

pyrotechny ('paɪərəʊtɛknɪ). [a. F. *pyrotechnie* (1556 in Hatz.-Darm.) or mod.L. *pyrotechnia* (also formerly in English use), f. Gr. πυρο- PYRO- + τέχνη art.] The art of employing fire: with various connotations.

†**1.** (*military pyrotechny.*) The manufacture and use of gunpowder, bombs, fire-arms, etc. *Obs.*

1579 DIGGES *Stratiot.* title-p., Whereto he hath also adioyned certaine Questions of great Ordinaunce, resolued in his other Treatise of Pyrotechny and great Artillerie, hereafter to be published. **1591** —— *Pantom.* (ed. 2) 176 Certaine Diffinitions, taken out of my thirde Booke of Pyrotechnie Militarie, and great Artillerie. **1646** SIR T. BROWNE *Pseud. Ep.* II. v. 89 Some as Beringuccio in his Pyrotechny affirmeth, have promised to make it red. **1696**, **1728** [see 2].

†**2.** The use of fire in chemical operations or in metallurgy. *Obs.*

1592 DEE *Compend. Rehears.* vii. (Chetham Soc. Misc. I) 30 My three laboratories serving for Pyrotechnia. **1651** BIGGS *New Disp.* §80 Mechanick experiments of Pyrotechny. **1696** PHILLIPS (ed. 5) s.v., Military Pyrotechny teaches the Art of making all sorts of Fire-Arms: Chymical Pyrotechny teaches the Art of managing Fire in Chymical Operations. **1728** CHAMBERS *Cycl.* s.v., Pyrotechny is of two kinds, Military, and Chymical... Some reckon a third kind ..viz. the Art of fusing, refining, and preparing Metals.

3. The making and managing of fireworks for scenic display, for military use, or as signals, etc.

1635 J. BABINGTON (*title*) Pyrotechnia or a discourse of Artificiall Fireworkes for Pleasure, in which the true grounds of yͤ Art are plainely and perspicuously laid downe. **1741** CHAMBERS *Cycl.* s.v. *Rocket*, In pyrotechny, an artificial fire-work. **1835** BURNES *Trav. Bokhara* (ed. 2) I. 176 All the fireworkers of Lahore seemed to be exerting their talents in pyrotechny. **1864** MOORE *Brit. Ferns* 94 The powdery spores [of *Lycopodium*]..are highly inflammable, and used in pyrotechny under the name of vegetable brimstone.

b. *fig.* (Cf. PYROTECHNIC A. 2b, B. 2c.)

1845 *Blackw. Mag.* LVIII. 328 [They] make such a noise in the world..with artificial volcanoes and puerile pyrotechny of all kinds. **1855** E. L. YOUMANS in *N.Y. Tribune* 23 Oct., Brilliant coruscations of thought, and a blaze of imaginative pyrotechny. **1856** R. A. VAUGHAN *Mystics* (1860) I. 277 A notable example of mystical pyrotechny.

'pyrotect. *nonce-wd.* [After *architect*.] A maker of fireworks, a pyrotechnist.

1851 LANDOR *Popery* 53 The premises of many a pyrotect have been blown up into the air, together with his crackers and serpents, and wheels and rockets.

Pyrotenax (paɪrəʊ'tɛnæks). *Electr.* Also **pyrotenax.** A proprietary name for a make of robust, heat-resistant copper-sheathed cable with magnesia insulation.

1937 *Nature* 20 Nov. 887/2 'Pyrotenax' cable has a copper conductor, magnesia insulation, and copper sheath. **1949** *Trade Marks Jrnl.* 2 Feb. 95/2 Pyrotenax... Terminal plates and boxes for electric cables. Pyrotenax Limited, Hedgeley Road, Hebburn-on-Tyne.., Manufacturers. **1958** MOLLOY & SAY *Electr. Engineer's Ref. Bk.* (ed. 9) xxx. 84 Tailor-made lengths of Pyrotenax cables, tested at 2,000 V. after water immersion. **1958** *Oxf. Univ. Gaz.* 7 Mar. 694/1 At the same time this part of the Library was rewired with pyrotenax. **1960** *Official Gaz.* (U.S. Patent Office) 17 May TM115/2 Societe Alsacienne de Constructions Mecaniques [*sic*], Paris... *Pyrotenax*. Owner of French Reg. No. 2,373, dated June 28, 1952... For electrical conductors, [etc.].

pyroterebic to **pyrothonide:** see PYRO-.

†**py'rotic,** *a.* and *sb. Med. Obs.* [ad. mod.L. *pyrōtic-us*, a. Gr. πυρωτικός burning, f. πυροῦν to burn.] = CAUSTIC A. 1, B. 1.

1634 T. JOHNSON *Parey's Chirurg.* xxvi. xviii. (1678) 640 That medicine is said to be Pyrotick or Caustick, which by its acrimony and biting..burns and consumes the skin and flesh. **1684** tr. *Bonet's Merc. Compit.* vi. 205 Not unlike the impression of an actual Pyrotick. **1728** CHAMBERS *Cycl.*, *Pyrotics*,..remedies either actually, or potentially hot; and which, accordingly, will burn the Flesh, and raise an Eschar. **1858** MAYNE *Expos. Lex.*, *Pyroticus*,..having power to burn; caustic: pyrotic.

pyro-uric: see PYRO- 3a.

pyroxanthin (paɪərɒk'sænθɪn). *Chem.* [f. PYRO- 3b + Gr. ξανθ-ός yellow + -IN[1].] A yellow crystalline substance, $C_{15}H_{12}O_3$, contained in crude wood-spirit, and produced by the action of potash on one of the constituents of the heavy oil of wood-tar.

1838 R. D. THOMSON in *Brit. Ann.* 331 Eblanin or pyroxanthin. **1866-8** WATTS *Dict. Chem.* IV. 776 Pyroxanthin crystallises in long yellow needles.

Hence **pyro'xanthogen** *Chem.*, the constituent of wood-tar from which pyroxanthin is supposed to be formed (Watts *Dict. Chem.* 1866-8).

pyroxene ('paɪərɒksiːn). *Min.* [f. Gr. πῦρ, πυρο- fire + ξένος stranger: so named by Haüy 1796, because he thought it 'a stranger in the domain of fire' or alien to igneous rocks.] A species including a large variety of minerals, all bisilicates of lime with one or more of various other bases, most usually magnesia and iron oxide, but also manganese, potash, soda, and zinc, or two or more of these. In mod. use, any of a group of silicates characterized by the presence of single chains of SiO_4 tetrahedra and prismatic cleavages at nearly 90 degrees, the general formula of which is approximately $XY(SiO_3)_2$.

Often identified with AUGITE, q.v.; but, according to Dana, *pyroxene* 'is properly the name of the species, while *augite* is only entitled to be used for one of its varieties'.

1800 *Philos. Mag.* VII. 254 He [Vauquelin] has analysed the pyroxene of Ætna. **1811** PINKERTON *Petral.* II. 475 Few fragments of augite or pyroxene. **1833** LYELL *Princ. Geol.* III. Gloss. 63 The modern Lavas of Vesuvius are characterised by a large proportion of augite (or pyroxene). **1862** [see PYROXENITE]. **1875** DAWSON *Dawn of Life* ii. 28 Pyroxene rock or pyrallolite. *Ibid.* v. 108 White pyroxene, an anhydrous silicate of lime and magnesia. **1888** J. P. IDDINGS tr. *Rosenbusch's Microsc. Physiogr. Rock-Making Minerals* 202 The orthorhombic pyroxenes become transparent in various colors, according to the position of the section and to the iron percentage. **1906** J. P. IDDINGS *Rock Minerals* II. 286 (*heading*) Pyroxene group. *Ibid.*, The triclinic pyroxenes are less closely related to the other forms, and are less frequently met with as rock-making minerals. **1959** *Dana's Man. Mineral.* (ed. 17) 434 The pyroxenes crystallize at higher temperatures than their amphibole analogues and hence are generally formed earlier in a cooling igneous magma. **1966** W. A. DEER et al. *Introd. Rock-Forming Minerals* II. 99 The pyroxene group includes both orthorhombic and monoclinic minerals. The orthorhombic sub-group consists essentially of the compositional series $MgSiO_3FeSiO_3$ while the monoclinic sub-group includes members having a wide range of chemical composition. *Ibid.*, The general formula of the pyroxene group may be expressed $X_{1-p}Y_{1+p}Z_2O_6$ where X = Ca,Na; Y = Mg,Fe^{+2},Mn,Li,Ni,Al,Fe^{+3},Cr,Ti; Z = Si,Al. **1975** D. SHELLEY *Man. Optical Mineral.* vii. 143 Most pyroxenes form rather stumpy prismatic crystals, though occasionally, as in the case of aegirine, the crystals are more elongate. **1978** *Sci. Amer.* Apr. 125/2 Peridotite..is composed mainly of olivine and another silicate mineral, pyroxene.

Hence **pyroxenic** (-'ɛnɪk) *a.*, pertaining to, having the character of, consisting of, or containing pyroxene; **pyroxenite** (-'ɒksɛnaɪt), also **-yte** [see -ITE[1] 2b], a metamorphic rock consisting chiefly of pyroxene; **pyroxe'nitic** *a.*, of or pertaining to pyroxenite.

1828 WEBSTER, **Pyroxenic*, pertaining to pyroxene, or partaking of its qualities. **1830** LYELL *Princ. Geol.* I. 328 Violent explosions, like those which, in 1822, launched from Vesuvius a mass of pyroxenic lava, of many tons weight, to the distance of three miles. **1893** *Nation* (N.Y.) 27 July 71/1 Bunsen's Theory of pyroxenic and trachytic magmas forms the starting-point for all theories for the differentiation of magmas. **1862** DANA *Man. Geol.* §8. 78 *Pyroxenite... Coarse or fine granular pyroxene rock, consisting of granular pyroxene of a grayish green or brown color. **1868** —— *Min.* (ed. 5) 220 *Pyroxenyte* is a metamorphic rock consisting mainly of compact pyroxene of the Sahlite section. **1933** R. A. DALY *Igneous Rocks & Depths of Earth* ix. 189 The speeds of seismic waves cannot be said to demonstrate a peridotitic or *pyroxenitic layer between the 40-kilometer and 60-kilometer levels. **1979** *Nature* 5 Apr. 545/1 Gorgona is one of the rare places in the world where young pyroxenitic komatiites exhibiting typical quenched spinifex textures..occur.

pyroxenoid (paɪ'rɒksənɔɪd). *Min.* [f. prec. + -OID.] Any of a small group of triclinic silicates formerly classed as pyroxenes but now differentiated from them on structural grounds.

1937 H. BERMAN in *Amer. Mineralogist* XXII. 389 The so-called 'triclinic pyroxenes' are not included here in the pyroxenes because the writer believes they are more properly considered as a separate group, with no isomorphous relations to any of the pyroxene minerals, and with physical and chemical properties clearly differing from those of the pyroxenes. To these pyroxene-like minerals we here give the name pyroxenoids. **1942** ROGERS & KERR *Optical Mineral.* (ed. 2) II. 275 Pyroxenoids include rhodonite, bustamite, pectolite, and wollastonite. **1966** J. SINKANKAS *Mineral.* II. 487 The pyroxenoids are species whose chemical compositions resemble the pyroxenes, but [whose] crystal structures differ slightly but importantly in the way the chains are linked and arranged. **1977** A. HALLAM *Planet Earth* 136 Rhodonite is closely similar in structure to the pyroxene group (for this reason it is sometimes called a pyroxenoid).

pyroxferroite (paɪrɒks'fɛrəʊaɪt). *Min.* [f. FERRO- + -ITE[1], after next.] A yellow pyroxenoid, $Fe_6Ca(SiO_3)_7$, that has been found on the moon and is an iron-rich analogue of pyroxmangite.

1970 E. C. T. CHAO et al. in *Proc. Apollo 11 Lunar Sci. Conf.* I. 65 Pyroxferroite was first recognized by the LSPET (1969) as an unidentified yellow mineral that seemed to be concentrated in vuggy areas of the Type B rock. *Ibid.* 75 Lindsley (1967) recently synthesized pyroxferroite of composition $Ca_{0.15}Fe_{0.85}SiO_3$ at pressures from 10 to 17·5 kbar and temperatures from 1130 to 1250°C. **1973** SORRELL & SANDSTROM *Rocks & Minerals of World* 60 The major lunar minerals are calcic plagioclase..and pyroxene... Common are olivine..and pyroxferroite, $CaFe_6(SiO_3)_7$, a new mineral similar to the pyroxenes.

pyroxmangite (paɪərɒks'mæŋgaɪt). *Min.* [f. PYROX(ENE + MANG(ANESE + -ITE[1].] A manganese- and iron-containing pyroxenoid, $(Mn,Fe)SiO_3$.

1913 FORD & BRADLEY in *Amer. Jrnl. Sci.* CLXXXVI. 169 (*heading*) Pyroxmangite, a new member of the pyroxene group and its alteration product, skemmatite. **1937** *Amer. Mineralogist* XXII. 720 The discovery of a further occurrence of pyroxmangite among the Lewisian rocks of Scotland has provided additional data on this interesting mineral. *Ibid.*, The pyroxmangite forms an important constituent of a manganiferous schist interbedded with a series of para-gneisses... Pyroxmangite in this rock occurs in pink grains of $\frac{1}{2}$–$\frac{3}{4}$ mm. average grain size. Exceptionally grains up to 5 mm. diameter may appear as porphyroblasts. **1963** W. A. DEER et al. *Rock-Forming Minerals* II. 201 Pyroxmangite is a mineral of metamorphic or metasomatic rocks, being found typically in manganese-rich assemblages in association with spessartine garnet, tephroite,..or rhodochrosite. **1970** *New Scientist* 15 Jan. 94/2 Some 68 elements forming minerals familiar to geologists were sorted out of the lunar soil and rock, along with three new minerals. They..were identified as a titanium-chromium spinel, a ferro-pseudobrookite and a pyroxmangite.

pyroxyle (paɪ'rɒksɪl). *Chem.* Also erron. **-ile.** [a. F. *pyroxyle*, f. Gr. πυρ(ο- PYRO- + ξύλον wood (Pelouze, 1846; *Comptes Rendus* 23, 893).] = PYROXYLIN: chiefly as the Fr. name of gun-cotton.

1847 [see PYROXYLIN 2]. **1870** *Echo* 8 Nov., A chemical manufactory at Grenelle blew to pieces, with four men, who were making pyroxile for the Government. **1881** tr. *Verne's Myst. Isl.* III. 55 Our guns would bear..the expansion of the pyroxile gas. **1900** *Westm. Gaz.* 31 Aug. 4/3 The heavy rains ..hindered the pyroxyle from acting as the conspirators designed.

pyroxylic (paɪərɒk'sɪlɪk), *a. Chem.* Also erron. **-ilic.** [f. as prec. + -IC.] Obtained from wood by means of fire, i.e. by dry distillation; chiefly in ***pyroxylic spirit***, an early name for methyl alcohol (CH_4O), also called *wood-spirit*.

a **1799** [see PYROLIGNIC]. **1824** *Ann. Philos.* July 69 Pyroxylic spirit..is obtained during the rectification of pyrolignous acid. **1838** T. THOMSON *Chem. Org. Bodies* 346 When wood is distilled for the purpose of obtaining acetic acid, the pyroxylic spirit is formed, and found in the aqueous liquid which comes over. **1857** MILLER *Elem. Chem.* III. 125 Methylic Alcohol, Methylic Hydrate, Wood Spirit, or Pyroxylic Spirit.—This alcohol..was first observed by Taylor in 1812 amongst the products of the destructive distillation of wood. **1874** GARROD & BAXTER *Mat. Med.* (1880) 175 Creasote..is also obtained from oil of tar, or pyroxylic oil, and is contained in the smoke from wood.

pyroxylin (paɪ'rɒksɪlɪn). *Chem.* Also improp. **-ine.** [In 1, f. PYRO- + Gr. ξύλ-ον wood + -IN[1]; in 2, ad. F. *pyroxyline* (Pelouze 1846), f. as PYROXYLE + *ine*, -IN[1].]

†**1.** = PYROXANTHIN. *Obs.*

1839 URE *Dict. Arts* 1053 Pyroxiline is a name which I have ventured to give to a substance detected by Mr. Scanlan..and..called by him Eblanin [cf. *pyroxanthin*, quot. 1838].

2. Any one of the class of explosive compounds, including gun-cotton, produced by treating vegetable fibre with nitric acid, or with a mixture of nitric and sulphuric acids; chemically, they are nitrates of cellulose, $(C_6H_{10}O_5)_n$, in which a varying number of OH groups are replaced by ONO_2 groups. Thus, gun-cotton is *cellulose trinitrate* $\{C_6H_7(NO_3)_3O_2\}_n$. A solution of soluble pyroxylin forms COLLODION.

1847 DANA in WEBSTER, *Pyroxyline, Pyroxyle*, a term embracing gun-cotton and all other explosive substances which are obtained by immersing vegetable fibre in nitric acid, or a mixture of sulphuric and nitric acid, and then suffering it to dry. **1866–8** WATTS *Dict. Chem.* IV. 777 The term 'pyroxylin' is sometimes applied especially to the more highly nitrated compounds; but it is much better to use this term as a generic name for all the substitution-compounds formed by the action of nitric acid on cellulose, and to designate as 'gun-cotton' the most highly nitrated compound, trinitrocellulose,.. the only one adapted for use in gunnery. **1883** *Hardwich's Photogr. Chem.* (ed. Taylor) 80 Photographic Pyroxyline is prepared with hot acids, heat being found remarkably to modify the products. *Ibid.* 158 In preparing a Pyroxyline for fluid and adhesive Collodion.

pyrozone (ˈpaɪərəzəʊn). *Pharm.* [f. PYRO- + OZONE.] An antiseptic substance containing three parts of hydrogen peroxide in a hundred parts of water.

1897 in *Syd. Soc. Lex.*

† **pyrre**, obs. form of PIRR *sb.*[1], a fit of temper or pettish humour.

1581 MULCASTER *Positions* xliii. 280 One displeased parent will do more harme vpon a head, if he take a pyrre at some toy, neuer conferring with any, but with his owne cholere, then a thousand of the thankfullest will euer do good.

pyrré, variant of PERRIE *Obs.*, jewellery.

pyrrey, obs. form of PERRY[2], pear-cider.

pyrrhic (ˈpɪrɪk), *sb.*[1] and *a.*[1] *Greek Antiq.* Forms: 6–7 pir(r)hicke, 7–8 pyrrhick, 8 pyrric(k, 8– pyrrhic. [ad. L. *pyrrhicha* or Gr. πυρρίχη a dance in armour, said to have been so named from one Πύρριχος the inventor; prop. an adj. qualifying ὄρχησις dance. Perh. through F. *pyrrique* (14th c. in Hatz.-Darm.).]

A. *sb.* The war-dance of the ancient Greeks, in which the motions of actual warfare were gone through, in armour, to a musical accompaniment.

1597–8 BP. HALL *Sat.* VI. i. 266 Or dance a sober pirrhicke in the field. **1776** BURNEY *Hist. Mus.* (1789) I. vi. 67 Proper for military dances called Pyrrhics in which the dancers are armed. **1906** *19th Cent.* Mar. 450 In Sparta.. all who were above five years of age learnt the Pyrrhic.

B. *adj.* Epithet of this dance; of or pertaining to this dance.

1630 B. JONSON *New Inn* I. iii, Do they not still Learn there.. The Pyrrhic gestures, both to dance and spring In armour, to be active in the wars? **1632** HEYWOOD *Iron Age* III. i. Wks. 1874 III. 306 Musicke strike A pirhicke straine. **1748** CHESTERF. *Lett.* 11 Oct. II. xxxix, I now plainly see the prelude to the pyrrick dance in the north, which I have long foretold. **1815** ELPHINSTONE *Acc. Caubul* (1842) II. 81 Their amusements are listening to songs.. and dancing a sort of Pyrrhic dance, in which they go through some warlike attitudes, and leap about, flourishing their swords. **1821** BYRON *Juan* III. lxxxvi. x (*Isles of Greece*), You have the Pyrrhic dance as yet: Where is the Pyrrhic phalanx gone?

So †ˈ**pyrrhical** *a. Obs. rare* = B.; ˈ**pyrrhicist** [ad. Gr. πυρριχιστής], a dancer of the pyrrhic.

1698 FRYER *Acc. E. India & P.* 109 Dancing in such Antick Dances as resemble the Pyrrhical Saltation. **1842** SMITH *Dict. Grk. & Rom. Antiq.* s.v. *Saltatio*, Three Pyrrhicists, two of whom.. are engaged in the dance.

pyrrhic (ˈpɪrɪk), *sb.*[2] and *a.*[2] *Prosody.* Forms: 7–8 pyrrhick, 7– pyrrhic, 9 pyrr(h)ich. [ad. L. *pyrrhichius*, a. Gr. πυρρίχιος of or pertaining to the πυρρίχη or Pyrrhic (dance); as sb., short for *pes pyrrhichius*, ποὺς πυρρίχιος pyrrhic foot, a metrical foot used in the war-song: see prec.]

A. *sb.* A metrical foot in ancient Greek and Latin verse, consisting of two short syllables. Sometimes applied to a group of two unstressed syllables in modern accentual verse: see quots.

1626 B. JONSON *Staple of N.* IV. iv, His Hyper, and his Brachy-Catalecticks, His Pyrrhicks, Epitrites and Choriambicks. **1749** J. MASON *Numbers in Poet. Comp.* 43 A Pyrrhic may possess any Place of the Verse except the last. But wherever it is, it gives a brisk Movement to the Measure. **1824** L. MURRAY *Eng. Gram.* (ed. 5) I. IV. ii. 372 A Pyrrhic has both the words or syllables unaccented: as, 'ŏn thĕ tall tree'. **1871** ROBY *Lat. Gram.* I. xii. §289 Of words ending in ă or ŏ a pyrrich or dactyl is rarely elided before a short syllable, except (1) in proper names; or (2) in first foot [etc.]. **1886** MAYOR *Eng. Metre* ii. 31 They intended to vary the ordinary rhythm by introducing an accentual pyrrhic. **1907** ORMOND *English Metrists* 175 A trochee he [Ruskin] prefers to name choreus, keeping the former term for what most writers call pyrric or dibrach.

B. *adj.* Consisting of two short syllables; composed of or pertaining to pyrrhics.

1749 J. MASON *Numb. Poet. Comp.* 16, I have exemplified the Pyrrhic, which contains two short Times, by two short Monosyllables, because every Word of two Syllables hath in the Pronunciation an Accent upon one of them, and in English Metre every accented Syllable is long; and therefore no English Word of two Syllables can properly exemplify a Pyrrhic Foot, which consists of two short ones.

Pyrrhic (ˈpɪrɪk), *a.*[3] [ad. Gr. πυρρικός, f. Πυρρός, L. *Pyrrhus*, name of a king of Epirus.] Of, pertaining to, or like that of Pyrrhus.

Pyrrhic victory, a victory gained at too great a cost; in allusion to the exclamation attributed to Pyrrhus after the battle of Asculum in Apulia (in which he routed the Romans, but with the loss of the flower of his army), 'One more such victory and we are lost'.

1885 *Daily Tel.* 17 Dec., Although its acceptance might secure for the moment the triumph of a party division, it would be indeed a Pyrrhic victory.

‖**pyrrhichius** (pɪˈrɪkɪəs). *Pros.* Forms: 6 pirr-, 6–8 pyrrichius, 7 -ychius, 8- pyrrhichius. The Latin form of PYRRHIC *sb.*[2]

1586 W. WEBBE *Eng. Poetrie* (Arb.) 69 Two short [syllables] called *Pyrrichius* as ◡◡ *hyther.* **1589** PUTTENHAM *Eng. Poesie* II. xiii. (Arb.) 133 For your foote *pirrichius* or of two short silables ye haue these words [*mănĭe*] [*mŏnĕy*] [*pĕnĭe*] [*sĭlĭe*] and others of that constitution or the like. **1702** ADDISON *Dial. Medals* Wks. 1730 I. 429 'My barber has often combed my head in dactyls and spondees... Nay', says he, 'I have known him sometimes run even into pyrrhichius's and anapæstus's'. **1818** HALLAM *Mid. Ages* ix. I. (1868) 589 *Hodie* is used as a pyrrhichius.

pyrrhite (ˈpɪraɪt). *Min.* [Named in Ger. 1840, f. Gr. πυρρός reddish + -ITE[1].] A rare mineral, occurring in minute orange-yellow octahedral crystals: see quots.

1844 DANA *Min.* (ed. 2), *Pyrrhite*,.. Primary form the regular octahedron. **1866–8** WATTS *Dict. Chem.* IV. 783 *Pyrrhite*, is the name given by G. Rose to a mineral occurring at Mursinsk in the Ural, in small orange-yellow octahedrons. **1896** CHESTER *Dict. Names Min.*, *Pyrrhite*, small, orange-red, octahedral crystals, not fully examined. Probably a columbate near pyrochlore.

pyrrho-arsenite (pɪrəʊˈɑːsənaɪt). *Min.* [Named 1886, f. Gr. πυρρός reddish + ARSENITE.] An orange-red variety of BERZELIITE.

1890 in *Cent. Dict.* **1896** in CHESTER *Dict. Names Min.*

‖**pyrrhocorax** (pɪˈrɒkəræks). *Ornith.* [L. *pyrrhocorax* (Pliny), a. Gr. πυρροκόραξ a red-beaked crow, f. πυρρός reddish + κόραξ crow.] A genus of crows, typical of the subfamily *Pyrrhocoracinæ*; the choughs; sometimes confined to the Alpine Chough, *P. alpinus*. Hence **pyrrhoˈcoracine** *a.*

1706 PHILLIPS (ed. 6), *Pyrrhocorax*, the Cornish Chough, a Bird having a red Bill. **1871** KINGSLEY *At Last* vi, It feeds on very hard fruits, as the Nutcracker and the Pyrrhocorax.

pyrrholite (ˈpɪrəlaɪt). *Min.* [Named 1862 (in Fr.), f. Gr. πυρρός reddish + -LITE.] An altered anorthite similar to polyargite.

1868 DANA *Min.* (ed. 5) 480 The name Pyrrholite has been given to a reddish lamellar mineral from Tunaberg [Sweden], which is very similar to polyargite.

Pyrrhonian (pɪˈrəʊnɪən), *a.* and *sb.* Also 7 -ien, 8 -ean. [a. F. *pyrrhonien* (Rabelais, 16th c.), f. L. *pyrrhōnius, -eus* adj. and sb. (f. *Pyrrho*, Gr. Πύρρων, name of a sceptic philosopher of Elis: see definition s.v. PYRRHONISM): see -AN.]

A. *adj.* = PYRRHONIC *a.*

1651 BIGGS *New Disp.* §159 The most pyrrhonian incredulity may be evinced. **1678** MANTON *Serm.* xiv. Wks. 1871 II. 321 The Pyrrhonian conceit that the whole world is but a fantasy. **1751** HUME *Ess. Hum. Underst.* (ed. 2) xii. III. 254 The natural Result of the Pyrrhonian Doubts and Scruples. **1908** *Hibbert Jrnl.* Apr. 586 The form of consolation offered us by the Pyrrhonian writers of the day.

B. *sb.* = PYRRHONIST.

1638 CHILLINGW. *Relig. Prot.* I. vi. §38. 356 If he be a true Aristotelian, or Platonist, or Pyrrhonian, or Epicurean. **1683** DRYDEN *Life Plutarch* in *Pl.'s Lives* (1700) I. 18 The Pyrrhonians.. who bring all certainty in Question. **1751** HUME *Ess. Hum. Underst.* (ed. 2) xii. II. 252 A Pyrrhonian cannot propose that his Philosophy will have any constant Influence on the Mind. **1900** *Q. Rev.* Oct. 432 If one has the misfortune not to be a Christian, it is wise to be a Pyrrhonian.

Pyrrhonic (pɪˈrɒnɪk), *sb.* and *a.* Also 6 Pironik. [f. Gr. Πύρρων (see prec.) + -IC.] **a.** *sb.* = PYRRHONIST. **b.** *adj.* Of or pertaining to the sceptic philosopher Pyrrho, or to his doctrines (see next); purely sceptical.

1593 NASHE *Christ's T.* (1613) 120 They followe the Pironiks, whose position and opinion it is, that there is not hel or misery but opinion. **1668** M. CASAUBON *Treat. Spirits* (1672) 155, I am no Sceptick or Pyrrhonick. **1725** WATTS *Logic* II. ii. §7 After these arose the sect of Pyrrhonics. **1831** I. TAYLOR *Pref. Ess. to Edwards' Freed. Will* 32 Such doctrines as the Pyrrhonic or the Stoic.. have a claim to be listened to. **1892** *Nation* (N.Y.) 13 Oct. 275/1 The inquiring, pyrrhonic spirit of the age is fatal to presumptions of this sort.

Pyrrhonism (ˈpɪrənɪz(ə)m). Also 8 pyrro-. [f. as prec. + -ISM. In F. *pyrrhonisme* (Pascal, 17th c.).] A system of sceptic philosophy taught by Pyrrho of Elis (*c* 300 B.C.), founder of the first school of Greek sceptic philosophy; the doctrine of the impossibility of attaining certainty of knowledge; absolute or universal scepticism; hence *generally*, scepticism, incredulity, philosophic doubt.

1670 BLOUNT *Glossogr.* (ed. 3), *Pyrrhonism*, the Doctrine or tenets of Pyrrho. **1711** SHAFTESB. *Charac.*, *Moralists* III. i, You,.. tho you disown philosophy, are yet so true a Proselyte to Pyrrhonism. **1768** TUCKER *Lt. Nat.* (1834) I. 116 Driven into arrant pyrrhonism, as being wholly uncertain whether we know anything or not. **1863** F. JACOX in *Bentley's Misc.* LIV. 241 Another noble lord.. avows his disposition to extend his pyrrhonism.. to historical facts themselves. **1893** J. B. BROWN *Stoics & Saints* 12 A misinterpretation of the Socratic method was at the root of Pyrrhonism. **1899** S. L. WILSON *Theol. Mod. Lit.* 359 To lapse into the unreasoning pyrrhonism which would treat all history in the light of 'a laborious deception skilfully concocted'.

Pyrrhonist (ˈpɪrənɪst). [f. as prec. + -IST.] A follower or disciple of Pyrrho; a professor of Pyrrhonism; one who doubts everything; a sceptic.

1598 MARSTON *Sco. Villanie* I. i. B viii, Fye Gallus, what, a skeptick Pyrrhomist? **1797** *Encycl. Brit.* (ed. 3) I. 49/2 The distinguishing tenet of the Pyrrhonists was their asserting an absolute acatalepsy in regard to every thing. **1893** LIDDON, etc. *Life Pusey* (1894) I. ii. 45 Now he.. was too much of a Pyrrhonist to think that any opinions, even when entirely negative, were certainly true.

Hence **Pyrrhoˈnistic** *a. rare*, of the nature of a Pyrrhonist or of Pyrrhonism.

1886 SWINBURNE *Misc.* 146 Disciples of a radically and essentially Pyrrhonistic system of theosophy.

pyrrhonize (ˈpɪrənaɪz), *v. rare.* [f. as prec. + -IZE.] **a.** *intr.* To practise Pyrrhonism; to doubt of everything. **b.** *trans.* To treat or transform sceptically.

1603 FLORIO *Montaigne* II. xii. (1632) 322 It had beene to Pyrrhonize a thousand yeares agoe, had any man gone about to make a question of the art of Cosmography. **1838** SIR J. STEPHEN *Eccl. Biog.* (1850) II. 145 Any half-believing, half-rejecting, interpreter, who has pyrrhonised them into a series of myths.

pyrrhosiderite (-saɪˈdɪəraɪt, -ˈsɪdəraɪt). *Min.* Also (erron.) **pyrosiderite**. [ad. Ger. *pyrrhosiderit* (Ullmann *a* 1813), f. Gr. πυρρός reddish + σίδηρος iron + -ITE[1].] A synonym of GOETHITE.

1830 J. H. BROOKE in *Encycl. Metrop.* (1845) VI. 495/1 Goethite; Pyrosiderite; Iron Froth. **1836** T. THOMSON *Min., Geol.* etc. I. 439 Pyrosiderite. **1854** DANA *Syst. Min.* (ed. 4) II. 129 Pyrrhosiderite. **1868** *Ibid.* (ed. 5) 170 In thin scale-like or tabular crystals, usually attached by one edge. Such is the original Göthite (Pyrrhosiderite) of Siegen.

pyrrhotine (ˈpɪrətaɪn). *Min.* [Named 1835 f. Gr. πυρρότης redness + -INE[5].] = PYRRHOTITE.

1849 J. NICOL *Min.* 452 *Pyrrhotine*, Breithaupt; magnetic iron pyrites. **1881** *Metal World* No. 21. 323 The ore of the Gap Mine is.. a nickeliferous pyrrhotine,.. and is extremely difficult to work.

pyrrhotite (ˈpɪrətaɪt). *Min.* [Altered by Dana, 1868, from prec.: see -ITE[1] 2 b.] A widely distributed magnetic sulphide of iron, occurring massive and amorphous, having a granular structure, and a colour between bronze and copper-red.

1868 DANA *Min.* (ed. 5) 59 The niccoliferous Pyrrhotite is the one that affords most of the nickel of commerce. **1900** in *Daily News* 25 July 2/1 The first cross-cut which had entered a body of solid pyrrhotite 11ft., was continued until it had passed through the vein, here 27ft. 5in. wide.

pyrrhous (ˈpɪrəs), *a. rare.* [f. Gr. πυρρός reddish + -OUS.] Reddish.

1890 in *Cent. Dict.*

pyrrhuline (ˈpɪr(j)ʊlaɪn), *a. Ornith.* [f. mod.L. *Pyrrhula*, generic name + -INE[1].] Of or pertaining to the genus *Pyrrhula* or to the subfamily *Pyrrhulinæ*, the bullfinches.

1890 in *Cent. Dict.*

pyrrie, -y(e: see PERRY[1], [2], PIRRIE.

pyrrole (ˈpɪrəʊl). *Chem.* Also -ol, pyrrhol. [f. Gr. πυρρός reddish + L. *oleum* oil.] **a.** A feebly basic, colourless transparent liquid, C_4H_5N, contained in bone-oil and coal-tar, having an odour like chloroform. Also, any derivative of this containing a pyrrole ring.

1835 F. F. RUNGE in *R. D. & T. Thomson's Rec. Gen. Sc.* I. 48 Pyrrol (red oil) in a pure state is a gaseous body possessing the odour of turnips. **1842** *E. Turner's Elem. Chem.* (ed. 7) 1180 Runge has described under the names of carbolic acid,.. pyrrole, and cyanol,.. compounds derived from coal tar. **1902** *Jrnl. Chem. Soc.* LXXXII. I. 54 Better yields of pyrroline are obtained by reducing pyrroles with zinc and hydrochloric acid than by using zinc and acetic acid. **1926** H. G. RULE tr. *J. Schmidt's Text-bk. Org. Chem.* 521 Pyrroles are aromatic in character and possess points in common with both phenols and aromatic amines. **1954** *New Biol.* XVI. 33 The tendency of the related pyrroles to combine with metal atoms to form highly coloured reactive compounds, such as hydrogenase and cytochrome, and probably later chlorophyll and haemin, points the way to the evolution of enzyme systems and photosynthesis. **1972** J. M. TEDDER et al. *Basic Org. Chem.* IV. ix. 454 On reduction with hydriodic acid haem yields eight comparatively simple pyrroles.

b. *attrib.* and *Comb.*, as **pyrrole base**, any of a series of bases containing a pyrrole ring; **pyrrole nucleus, ring**, a doubly unsaturated ring of four carbon atoms and one nitrogen atom; **pyrrole red**: see quot. 1877.

1851 T. ANDERSON in *Trans. Roy. Soc. Edin.* (1853) XX. 249 A series of bases..which I designate provisionally by the name of pyrrol bases. **1875** WATTS *Dict. Chem.* VII. 1035 Pyrrol-bases appear to be present, together with bases of the pyridine series, in tobacco-smoke. **1877** —— *Fownes' Chem.* II. 375 By heating an acid solution of pyrrol, a red, flaky substance, pyrrol-red, is produced, containing $C_{12}H_{14}N_2O$. **1913** BLOXAM & LEWIS *Bloxam's Chem.* (ed. 10) 782 The metals are not present as bases, but as integral parts of the complex molecules, probably exercising their subsidiary valencies, and uniting a number of pyrrol nuclei. **1926** H. G. RULE tr. *J. Schmidt's Text-bk. Org. Chem.* 523 This oxidation has recently been recognised as a valuable means of determining the orientation of substituents in the pyrrole nucleus, and also for detecting the presence of a pyrrole ring in substances of unknown constitution. **1970** R. W. McGILVERY *Biochem.* xxi. 494 The basic unit of porphyrins is the pyrrole ring, with four of these linked to form the large porphyrin ring.

Hence **py'rrolic** *a.*

1909 in *Cent. Dict.* Suppl. **1912** *Chem. Abstr.* VI. 2749 Pyrrolic α-, β- and γ-diketones. **1955** *Endeavour* July 135/2 (*caption*) Porphobilinogen, the simplest pyrrolic substance known to be a precursor of haem and porphyrins. **1972** J. M. TEDDER et al. *Basic Org. Chem.* IV. ix. 464 The blood-red, tripyrrole microbial pigment, prodigiosin, provides an example of the biogenesis of pyrrolic compounds.

pyrrolidine (pɪ'rɒlɪdiːn). *Chem.* [ad. G. *pyrrolidin* (Ciamician & Magnaghi 1885, in *Ber. d. Deut. Chem. Ges.* XVIII. 2080): see PYRROLE and -IDINE.] A saturated heterocyclic compound, $(CH_2)_4NH$, which is a colourless, pungent, strongly basic liquid obtained esp. by catalytic reduction of pyrrole; any substituted derivative of this. Freq. *attrib.*, as **pyrrolidine nucleus, ring,** a saturated ring of four carbon atoms and one nitrogen.

1885 *Jrnl. Chem. Soc.* XLVIII. II. 1243 Pyrrolidine.. C_4NH_9, is obtained with other products from hydropyrroline in the above reaction; it shows great similarity in properties to piperidine, hence the name given to it. **1926** H. G. RULE tr. *J. Schmidt's Text-bk. Org. Chem.* 532 Certain important degradation products of the *coca* and *atropa* alkaloids have been identified as carboxylic acids of pyrrolidine. **1956** I. L. FINAR *Org. Chem.* II. xiv. 531 The presence of this pyrrolidine nucleus also accounts for the formation of pyrrole when nicotine zincichloride is distilled. **1963** T. ROBINSON *Org. Constituents of Higher Plants* xii. 256 Leete..using 1, 4-labelled putrescine fed to tobacco found that it was an efficient precursor of the pyrrolidine ring in nicotine. **1976** STREITWIESER & HEATHCOCK *Introd. Org. Chem.* xxxv. 1065 Pyrrolidine and piperidine are typical secondary amines.

pyrrolidone (pɪ'rɒlɪdəʊn). *Chem.* [ad. G. *pyrrolidon* (J. Tafel 1889, in *Ber. d. Deut. Chem. Ges.* XXII. 1861): see prec. and -ONE.] Either of two isomeric mono-keto derivatives of pyrrolidine; *esp.* $\underbrace{NH{\cdot}(CH_2)_3{\cdot}CO}$ (*2-pyrrolidone*), a colourless crystalline solid with weakly basic properties; any substituted derivative of either isomer.

[**1889** *Jrnl. Chem. Soc.* LVI. 961 Methylpyrrolidone.] *Ibid.* 1211 The first product..is very unstable, condensation immediately taking place, with formation of a derivative of pyrrolidone. **1926** H. G. RULE tr. *J. Schmidt's Text-bk. Org. Chem.* 517 The 2-keto-derivative of pyrrolidine is commonly known as 'pyrrolidone'. *Ibid.* 520 Since succinimides are readily prepared in quantity, this process also renders the pyrrolidones easy of access. **1951** I. L. FINAR *Org. Chem.* I. xvi. 309 When reduced with sodium and ethanol, succinimide forms pyrrolidine,..and when reduced electrolytically, it forms pyrrolidone. *Ibid.* xxx. 617, 2-Pyrrolidone is the lactam..of γ-aminobutyric acid. **1975** GUTSCHE & PASTO *Fund. Org. Chem.* xxvii. 817 The reaction between pyrrolidone and acetylene in the presence of potassium hydroxide to yield N-vinylpyrrolidone.

pyrroline ('pɪrəliːn). *Chem.* [f. PYRROLE + -INE[5], as an alkaloid.] †**a.** = PYRROLE. *Obs.*

1881 WATTS *Dict. Chem.* VIII. II. 1728 *Pyrroline* (commonly called *Pyrrol*), C_4H_5N = NH:CH·CH:CH·CH. *Ibid.* 1729 Pyrroline..is a perfectly colourless, highly dispersive liquid, which, when quite pure, remains colourless for several days. **1895** MUIR & MORLEY *ibid.* IV. 366/2.

b. Formerly also -in. A partially reduced derivative of pyrrole having the formula C_4H_7N, of which three isomers are possible; *esp.* $\underbrace{HN{\cdot}CH_2{\cdot}CH{:}CH{\cdot}CH_2}$ (*3-pyrroline*), a colourless, basic liquid obtained by reduction of pyrrole with nascent hydrogen; also a substituted derivative of any of these compounds. [Named in Ger. as *pyrrolin* (Ciamician & Dennstedt 1883, in *Ber. d. Deut. Chem. Ges.* XVI. 1539).]

1884 ROSCOE & SCHORLEMMER *Treat. Chem.* III. II. 610 Pyrrol unites with nascent hydrogen, forming pyrrolin, $C_4H_6(NH)$, an oily liquid that boils at 90°–91°, and acts as a strong base. **1902** [see PYRROLE a]. **1926** H. G. RULE tr. *J. Schmidt's Text-bk. Org. Chem.* 517 Dihydro-pyrroles are known as pyrrolines, and the completely reduced tetrahydro-pyrroles as pyrrolidines. **1961** G. M. BADGER *Chem. Heterocyclic Compounds* ii. 17, 3-Pyrrolines have been isomerized to the corresponding 1-pyrrolines by heating with Raney nickel. *Ibid.* 18, 2-Pyrrolines have been poorly characterized. **1972** J. M. TEDDER et al. *Basic Org. Chem.* IV. ix. 463 Another group of tetrapyrrolic macrocyclic compounds found in nature are the corrins which are made up of four partially reduced pyrrole (pyrroline and pyrrolidine) rings.

pyrrolizidine (ˌpɪrə'lɪzɪdiːn). *Chem.* [ad. G. *pyrrolizidin* (G. Menschikoff 1936, in *Ber. d. Deut. Chem. Ges.* LXIX. 1802), f. *pyrrolidin* PYRROLIDINE with inserted *-iz* (ult. f. *azo-* AZO-) after *chinolizin* quinolizine, an analogous compound containing six-membered rings.] A colourless basic liquid, $C_7H_{13}N$, which has a structure consisting of two fused pyrrolidine rings sharing a carbon and a nitrogen atom; any derivative of this. Freq. *attrib.*, as **pyrrolizidine alkaloid,** any of a large class of toxic alkaloids based on this structure which occur widely in plants, esp. in the genera *Senecio*, *Crotalaria*, and *Heliotropium*.

[**1936** *Chem. Abstr.* XXX. 6379 A satd. tertiary base $C_8H_{15}N$..for which is proposed the name 2-methylpyrrolizidine.] **1939** *Ibid.* XXXIII. 5850 P[relog] and H[eimbach] have found a method of preparing the hitherto unknown pyrrolizidine (I)... The free I is a water-sol. oil of basic odor, b.p. 148°. **1950** *Thorpe's Dict. Appl. Chem.* (ed. 4) X. 710/2 All Senecio and related alkaloids are esters of a cyclic amino-alcohol of pyrrolizidine type with aliphatic or alicyclic acids. **1968** *New Scientist* 20 June 619/2 Many pyrrolizidine alkaloids..not only exert their effects as liver poisons but may also produce lung damage. **1975** K. NAKANISHI et al. *Natural Products Chem.* II. x. 299 Recent studies on the metabolism of the alkaloids have shown that it is not the pyrrolizidine alkaloids themselves, but their pyrrole derivatives, formed as metabolites, which exhibit toxicity.

pyruline ('pɪrjʊlaɪn), *a.* *Zool.* [f. mod.L. *Pyrula*, generic name (f. L. *pirum, pyrum* pear) + -INE[1].] Related to the gastropod genus *Pyrula* or subfamily *Pyrulinæ*, having a pear-shaped shell, the pear-shells or fig-shells. So **'pyrulid** *sb.*, a gastropod of the family *Pyrulidæ*; **'pyruloid** *a.*, resembling the *Pyrulidæ* in general form.

†**py'rurgian.** *Obs. nonce-wd.* [f. Gr. πυρο- fire, after *chirurgian*, CHIRURGEON: cf. Gr. πυροεργής working in fire.] One who treats wounds, etc. with caustic applications.

1684 *Bonet's Merc. Compit.* I. 34 Above all things Hippocrates his Golden Rule is to be observed by our Pyrurgian.

pyruric, var. PYRO-URIC = CYANURIC.

‖**pyrus** ('paɪərəs). *Bot.* [med. and mod.L. erroneous spelling of L. *pirus* pear-tree. Adopted by Linnæus (*Hortus Cliffortianus* (1737) 189) as a generic name.] A small tree of the genus so called, belonging to the family Rosaceæ and widely cultivated for the sake of its blossom or its fruit, the pear; also, a tree or shrub once included in this genus and now in a separate one, esp. the japonica (*Chænomeles* species) or the rowan (*Sorbus* species).

1849 THOREAU *Week Concord Riv.* 92 The shad make their appearance early in May, at the same time with the blossoms of the pyrus, one of the most conspicuous early flowers. **1894** *Daily News* 26 Mar. 4/7 Garden borders, bright with belts of daffodil, with sheets of crocus white and blue, with scarlet pyrus all ablaze against the whitewashed wall. **1897** MRS. E. L. VOYNICH *Gadfly* (1904) 87/1 The blossoming pyrus japonica that hung over the garden wall looked dark in the fading light. **1904** FARRER *Garden Asia* 42 The intense and glowing rubies of the creeping pyrus. **1914** W. J. BEAN *Trees & Shrubs Hardy in Brit. Isles* II. 269 All the Pyruses like a loamy soil. **1930** F. K. WARD *Plant Hunting on Edge of World* vi. 120 As for the Pyrus, its numerous clusters of reddened berries presently turned snow white.

pyruvate (paɪ'ruːveɪt). *Biochem.* [f. PYRUV(IC *a.* + -ATE[4].] **1.** A salt or ester, or the anion, of pyruvic acid; *loosely*, denoting either anions or the acid itself.

1855 H. WATTS tr. *Gmelin's Hand-bk. Chem.* IX. 419 The Pyruvates are prepared by saturating the dilute acid with the base. **1905** *Jrnl. Chem. Soc.* LXXXVIII. I. 572 Butyroin.. yields a pyruvate which boils at 134–138° under 12 mm. pressure. **1946** *Nature* 7 Sept. 350/1 Pyruvate accumulates in the blood of thiamin-deficient animals. **1955** *Sci. Amer.* Jan. 76/2 They [*sc.* Rickettsiæ] also proved capable of oxidizing slowly two other substances, pyruvate and succinate, which, like glutamic acid, are oxidized by most animal and plant tissues. **1970** AMBROSE & EASTY *Cell Biol.* vi. 183 Two molecules of pyruvate are finally produced. *Ibid.*, Normally, muscle respires aerobically, oxidizing pyruvate via the Krebs cycle.., but during violent exercise oxygen cannot reach the tissues fast enough. In this case muscles obtain extra energy by reduction of pyruvic acid to lactic acid. **1970** *New Scientist* 23 Apr. 168/1 Glycolysis is the process which oxidizes carbohydrates to pyruvate, ready to enter the citric acid cycle and be burnt up completely. **1976** *Ann. Rev. Microbiol.* XXX. 157 Pyruvate in polysaccharides of *R. trifolii*, *R. meliloti*, *R. radicicolum*, and Pn 27 functions as a major determinant in serological specificity.

2. Special Comb.: **pyruvate kinase,** any enzyme which catalyses the transfer of a phosphate group between adenosine triphosphate and pyruvic acid; **pyruvate oxidase** = *pyruvic oxidase*.

1951 S. P. COLOWICK in Sumner & Myrbäck *Enzymes* II. I. xlvi. 123 'Creatine kinase', 'pyruvate kinase' and '3-phosphoglycerate kinase' will refer to the respective enzymes which catalyze the reversible reaction of ATP with these substrates. **1970** *New Scientist* 23 Apr. 168/2 The enzyme pyruvate kinase..is slightly different in liver and kidney from that in other tissues. **1959** *Jrnl. Vitaminol.* V. 94 Recently, further attempts were made to elucidate whether vitamin B_{12} activates the pyruvate oxidase system in B_{12}-deficient rats. **1970** AMBROSE & EASTY *Cell Biol.* vi. 188 Pyruvate..is first converted to acetyl-coenzyme A by combination with coenzyme A. (Catalysed by pyruvate oxidase.)

pyruvic (paɪ'ruːvɪk), *a.* *Chem.* [ad. mod.L. *pyruvicus*, in *acidum pyruvicum* pyruvic acid (J. J. Berzelius 1835, in *Ann. der Physik u. Chem.* XXXVI. 5), f. PYR(O- 3 a + L. *uva* grape + -IC.] In *pyruvic acid*, $C_3H_4O_3$ = $CH_3.CO.CO_2H$, also called *pyroracemic acid*, produced by the dry distillation of racemic or tartaric acid; a liquid smelling like acetic acid, and boiling at about 165° C. The acid occurs widely in living organisms as an intermediate in many metabolic processes, notably glycolysis. So *pyruvic alcohol* = acetyl carbinol, $CH_3.CO.CH_2OH$; *pyruvic aldehyde* = methyl glycoxal, $CH_3.CO.CHO$; *pyruvic kinase* = *pyruvate kinase*; *pyruvic oxidase*, any enzyme or enzyme complex which catalyses the oxidation of pyruvic acid.

1838 T. THOMSON *Chem. Org. Bodies* 65 Pyruvic acid is a yellowish, somewhat thick liquid. **1857** MILLER *Elem. Chem.* III. 332 A new acid termed pyruvic or pyroracemic acid. **1873** WATTS *Fownes' Chem.* 707 Ordinary lactic acid is also produced..by the action of nascent hydrogen on pyruvic acid. **1927** M. BODANSKY *Introd. Physiol. Chem.* ix. 226 There is..no convincing evidence that physiologically lactic acid is converted into pyruvic acid, although the change is known to occur *in vitro* under the influence of hydrogen peroxide. **1941** *Adv. Enzymol.* I. 147 Even the pyruvic acid oxidase of *Bacterium Delbrueckii*..might be called a composite thiamin enzyme as it contains flavin adenine nucleotide besides thiamin pyrophosphate, both of which are possibly bound to the same protein. **1945** *Jrnl. Biol. Chem.* CLIX. 543 The pyruvic oxidases of *Proteus vulgaris* and *Escherichia coli* do not appear to require inorganic phosphate for activity. **1951** *Sci. News* XXII. 80 An illuminated preparation of spinach chloroplasts can reduce carbon dioxide plus pyruvic acid to malic acid. **1951** SUMNER & MYRBÄCK *Enzymes* II. II. 1433/1 (Index), Pyruvic kinase. **1962** S. G. WALEY in A. Pirie *Lens Metabolism Rel. Cataract* 357 Thiamine (as the pyrophosphate) is the coenzyme in the decarboxylation of the α-keto acids, pyruvic acid and α-ketogluric acid. **1963** CONN & STUMPF *Outl. Biochem.* xi. 201 The conversion of pyruvate to acetyl-CoA is catalyzed by the enzyme complex known as pyruvic oxidase. **1967** BATSAKIS & BRIERE *Interpretive Enzymol.* xii. 242 Pyruvic kinase deficiency leads directly to an impairment of ATP synthesis. **1970** [see PYRUVATE 1]. **1971** C. J. GRAY *Enzyme-Catalysed Reactions* vii. 291 Porcine pyruvic oxidase catalysed the synthesis of α-acetolactate from pyruvate and the hydroxyethylthiamine pyrophosphate.

Also **py'ruvin,** or *glycide pyruvate*, $C_6H_8O_4$, a white crystalline substance obtained by distilling glycerin with tartaric acid.

1872 *Jrnl. Chem. Soc.* XXV. 400 When glycerin is heated in a retort with tartaric acid, crystals of pyruvin are formed in the neck of the receiver.

pyrwykes: see PILLIWINKS.

pyrwynke, obs. f. PERIWINKLE[1], the plant.

pyry, pyrye: see PERRY[1], PIRRIE.

pys, obs. f. PISS.

pysan, obs. pl. of PEASE *sb.*

pysan(e, var. PISANE *Obs.*, breast-armour.

pysangh, pysauns, obs. ff. PISANG, PUISSANCE.

pysche, pyse, obs. ff. PISS.

pyse, obs. f. PEASE *sb.*, PICE.

pysell, obs. f. PIZZLE.

pysemer, pysmar, pysmere, etc., obs. ff. PISMIRE.

†**pys'matic,** *a.* *Obs. rare*$^{-1}$. [ad. Gr. πυσματικός, f. πύσμα question.] Interrogatory.

1652 URQUHART *Jewel* Wks. (1834) 292 Dialogismes, displaying their interrogatory part with communicatively pysmatick and sustentative flourishes.

pyss(e, obs. ff. PIECE, PISS.

pyssan(e, var. PISANE *Obs.*, breast-armour.

pyssell, pyssemere, pyssmowre, obs. ff. PIZZLE, PISMIRE.

pystace, obs. f. PISTACHIO.

pystel, pystell, -il(l, -le, etc., obs. ff. PESTLE, PISTLE.

pystelade: see PASTELADE.

pystiller, pystolet, -ett(e, var. PISTLER, PISTOLET *Obs.*

pyt, pytagru, -rwe, obs. ff. PIT, PUT *v.*, PEDIGREE *sb.*

pytaille, var. PEDAILE *Obs.*, foot-soldiery.

pytch(e, pytcher, obs. ff. PITCH, PITCHER.

Pytchley (ˈpaɪtʃlɪ). The name of a village in Northamptonshire, used *attrib.* and *ellipt.* to denote a famous hunt centred there. *Pytchley (riding) coat* (see quots. 1907, 1963).

1866 J. BLACKWOOD *Let.* 26 Apr. in *Geo. Eliot Lett.* (1956) IV. 245, I enjoyed her..laughing at his French accent... It is like the House of Commons..laughing at Bright for talking of the *Pittchley*. **1867** 'OUIDA' *Under Two Flags* I. iv. 74 It lay in the Melton country, and was equally well placed for Pytchley, Quorn, and Belvoir. **1907** *Yesterday's Shopping* (1969) 323/1 Pytchley Riding Coat. Full Skirt to cover saddle. **1919** J. BUCHAN *Mr Standfast* xiv. 257 He used to hunt with the Pytchley. **1935** *Encycl. Sports* 294/1 About 1750, the modern system of hunting was introduced in the Quorn country by Meynell and by Lord Spencer in the Pytchley Hunt. **1955** M. ALLINGHAM *Beckoning Lady* ii. 16 Two seasons with the Pytchley foxhounds. **1963** BLOODGOOD & SANTINI *Horseman's Dict.* 157 *Pytchley coat* (More usually called *Shadbelly*, *Swallow tail* or *Cutaway*), tight-fitting, Regency, double-breasted hunting coat (either scarlet or black) worn with a double-breasted buff waistcoat and named after its originators, the thrusters, or hard riding members of the Pytchley Hunt, England. **1969** A. HORSBRUGH-PORTER in A. S. C. Ross *What are U?* 51 It would be tedious to delve into the date which constituted the name of 'the shires', denoting the Pytchley, Quorn, Belvoir, Fernie and Cottesmore Hunts.

pyte, obs. var. *pight*, pa. t. of PITCH *v.*[1]

pyte, pytee, pytell, obs. ff. PITY, PIGHTLE.

pyteous, -evous, -ewous, etc., obs. ff. PITEOUS.

pyth, obs. f. PITH; obs. pa. t. of PITCH *v.*[1]

Pythagorean (pɪθægəˈriːən, paɪ-), *a.* and *sb.* Also 6 **Pyˈthagoran**, 6–7 **Pythaˈgorian**. [f. L. *Pȳthagorē-us, -ī-us*, a. Gr. *Πυθαγόρειος*, f. proper name *Πυθαγόρας* Pythagoras + -AN.

At first spelt and pronounced *Pythaˈgorian*; the spelling was changed *c* 1600–34, but the pronunciation was still used by Cowley and Dryden. Bailey 1731 (vol. II) has *Pythaˈgorean*, in 1736 (folio) *Pythagoˈrean*.]

A. *adj.* Of or pertaining to Pythagoras, an ancient Greek philosopher and mathematician of Samos (6th c. B.C.), or to his system or school.

In early quots. often with allusion to the belief in the transmigration of souls, attributed to Pythagoras (whence the *transf.* use in b); sometimes to the consequent practice of his school of abstaining from animal flesh as food.

Pythagorean bean: see quot. 1858, and cf. BEAN *sb.* 4. ***Pythagorean comma***: see COMMA 3. ***Pythagorean letter***, the Greek *Y*, used by P. as a symbol of the two divergent paths of virtue and of vice. ***Pythagorean lyre***, a lyre of eight strings said to have been invented by Pythagoras. ***Pythagorean proposition*** or ***theorem***, the 47th of the 1st book of Euclid, namely, that the square on the hypotenuse of a right-angled triangle is equal to the sum of the squares on the other two sides: said to have been discovered by Pythagoras. ***Pythagorean scale***, a scale of musical notes (nearly corresponding to the modern diatonic scale) attributed to Pythagoras: hence applied to the intervals of this scale, as ***Pythagorean semitone, third***, etc. ***Pythagorean system*** (of Astronomy): see quot. 1704.

1579–80 NORTH *Plutarch, Dion* (1896) vi. 143 Archytas the Pythagorian Philosopher. **1602** MARSTON *Antonio's Rev.* III. ii, If Pythagorian Axiomes be true, Of spirits transmigration. **1649** OGILBY tr. *Virg. Georg.* IV. (1684) 116 *note*, Upon this Pythagorean Opinion, 'That Bees derive from a Celestial strain'. **1693** DRYDEN *Juvenal's Sat.* iii. 373 There, love the Fork, thy Garden cultivate, And give thy frugal Frinds a Pythagorean Treat. **1694** HOLDER *Harmony* (1731) 116 The Pythagoreans, not using Tone Minor, but two equal Tones Major, in a Fourth, were forced to take a lesser Interval for the Hemitone; which is call'd their Limma, or Pythagorean Hemitone. **1704** J. HARRIS *Lex. Techn.* I, *Pythagorean System*, is the same with the Copernican,..being maintained by Pythagoras and his Followers, and therefore is the most ancient of any. **1785** REID *Intell. Powers* IV. ii, The Platonic system of ideas..was the invention of the Pythagorean school. **1822** T. TAYLOR *Apuleius* I. 322 Desirous of imitating the Pythagorean abstinence and chastity. **1858** BAIRD *Cycl. Nat. Sci.* s.v. *Nelumbiaceæ*, The 'faba Ægyptiaca', the Pythagorean bean, ..is supposed by many to be the celebrated lotus of antiquity. **1878** W. H. STONE *Sci. Basis Music* v. 52 The third of the Greek scale was made by four fifths taken upwards, and is still called a Pythagorean third.

b. *transf.* Metamorphosed, transformed.

a **1667** COWLEY *Verses, on Chair made fr. Sir F. Drake's Ship*, This Pythagorean Ship (for it may claim Without presumption so deserv'd a Name, By knowledge once, and transformation now).

B. *sb.* A disciple or follower of Pythagoras.

1550 W. LYNNE *Carion's Cron.* 37 The Pythagorians taughte their doctrines priuatly amonge themselues. **1598–9** MARSTON *Sat.* I. iii, Giue him his fiddle once againe Or he's more mute then a Pythagoran. *a* **1612** SIR J. HARINGTON *Epigr.* I. lxviii, An use there was among some Pythagoreans, If we give credit to the best Historians, How they..Did keep a wondrous strict and sparing diet. **1737** WHISTON *Josephus* (1812) II. xv. x. 368 These men [Essenes] live the same kind of life as do those whom the Greeks call Pythagoreans. **1876** BANCROFT *Hist. U.S.* I. i. 5 Nearly three centuries before the Christian era, Aristotle following the lessons of the Pythagoreans, had taught that the earth is a sphere.

b. *transf.* or *allusively*. A person whose doctrine or practice agrees with that attributed to Pythagoras.

1599 NASHE *Lenten Stuffe* 31 The Rhomish rotten Pithagoreans or Carthusian friers, that mumpe on nothing but fishe. **1709–10** STEELE *Tatler* No. 134 ¶ 1 This ancient Pythagorean, who has as much Honesty as any Man living, but good Nature to an Excess. **1817–18** COBBETT *Resid. U.S.* (1822) 207 Nor have even the Pythagoreans a much better battery against us. Sir Richard Phillips..does, indeed, eat neither flesh, fish, nor fowl... But..his shoes and breeches and gloves are made of the skins of animals.

Hence **Pythagoˈreanism**, the Pythagorean philosophy; **Pythagoˈreanize** *v. intr.*, = PYTHAGORIZE *v.* 1 (*Cent. Dict.* 1890); **Pythagoˈreanly** *adv.*, in a Pythagorean manner.

1727 BAILEY vol. II, **Pythagoreanism*, the Doctrine or Principles of the Pythagoreans. **1865** *Sat. Rev.* 4 Nov. 577 There is, by the way, a slight sniff of Pythagoreanism about the phrase 'appreciative numbers'. **1596** NASHE *Saffron Walden* Ep. Ded., I will tutour thee so *Pythagoreanly how to husband them in al companies.

Pythagoric (pɪθəˈgɒrɪk, paɪ-), *a.* (*sb.*) Now *rare.* [ad. L. *Pȳthagoric-us*, a. Gr. *Πυθαγορικός*, f. *Πυθαγόρας*: see prec. So F. *pythagorique* (Rabelais, 16th c.).] = PYTHAGOREAN *a.*

1653 H. MORE *Conject. Cabbal.* (1713) 38 It may be a question, whether in that Pythagorick Oath. *Οὐ μὰ τὸν*, &c. they did not swear by God. *a* **1704** T. BROWN tr. *Æneas Sylvius' Lett.* lxxxii, With more than Pythagorick Silence, you pass your melancholy Hours. **1746** FRANCIS tr. *Horace, Ep.* II. i. 70 Ennius..Forgets his Promise, now secure of Fame, And heeds no more his Pythagoric Dream. **1881** SHORTHOUSE *J. Inglesant* xvii, An ethereal sort of body—to use the Pythagoric phrase.

†**B.** *sb.* = PYTHAGOREAN *sb. Obs. rare.*

1652 GAULE *Magastrom.* xxvi, That..which the Pythagoricks did assert. **1678** CUDWORTH *Intell. Syst.* I. i. 22 An Ancient Opinion..delivered down by some.. Pythagoricks.

†**Pythaˈgorical**, *a. Obs.* [f. as prec. + -AL[1]: see -ICAL.] = PYTHAGORIC *a.* In quot. 1608 *allusively* (cf. PYTHAGOREAN A. b).

1570 DEE *Math. Pref.* ☛iiij b, The Pythagoricall, and Platonicall perfect scholer..may (like the Bee) gather, hereby, both wax and hony. **1608** MIDDLETON *Trick to Catch Old One* IV. v, Pythagorical rascal!..Ay, he changes his cloak when he meets a sergeant. **1638** RAWLEY tr. *Bacon's Life & Death* (1650) 19 Apollonius Tyaneus..In his Dyet Pythagoricall; A great Traveller; Much Renowned. **1696** EDWARDS *Demonstr. Exist. & Provid. God* I. 68 The Pythagorical Musick of the spheres.

Pythaˈgorically, *adv. rare.* [f. prec. + -LY[2].] In a Pythagorical manner; like a Pythagorean, or according to Pythagorean doctrine.

1609 BP. W. BARLOW *Answ. Nameless Cath.* 198 Pythagorically peremptorie without yeelding reason. **1683** J. BARNARD *True Life Heylyn* 23 The Soul of St. Augustine (say the Schools) was Pythagorically transfused into the corps of Aquin.

Pythagorician (pɪθægəˈrɪʃən, paɪ-). Now *rare.* [f. PYTHAGORIC + -IAN: cf. *arithmetician, logician*, etc. So F. *Pythagoricien* (Voltaire, 1768), perh. the immediate source.] = PYTHAGOREAN *sb.*

1752 HUME *Ess. & Treat., Rise Arts & Sc.* (1768) 71 Those sects of Stoics and Epicureans, Platonists and Pythagoricians could never regain any credit. **1768–74** TUCKER *Lt. Nat.* (1834) I. 334 Plato and the Pythagoricians asserted the eternity of ideas and forms. **1844** *Fraser's Mag.* XXX. 336/1 The symbols of the Pythagoricians.

†**Pythaˈgoricism**. [f. as prec. + -ISM.] = next.

1656 BLOUNT *Glossogr.*, *Pythagoricism*, the Tenets, or opinion of Pythagoras.

Pyˈthagorism. ? *Obs.* [ad. Gr. *Πυθαγορισμός*, f. *Πυθαγορίζειν* to PYTHAGORIZE.] The principles and practice of Pythagoras; Pythagoreanism.

1653 H. MORE *Conject. Cabbal.* (1713) 156 Though Platonism be derived from Pythagorism, yet it has left out the Theory of the Earth's Motion. **1662** —— *Philos. Wks.* Pref. Gen. ¶5 To make for the discovering that Pythagorisme had relation to the Text of Moses.

Pyˈthagorist. ? *Obs.* [ad. Gr. *Πυθαγοριστής*, f. *Πυθαγορίζειν*: see prec.] One who follows the principles or practice of Pythagoras; a Pythagorean.

1576 FLEMING *Panopl. Epist.* 223 *margin*, Declare your selfe to be a right Pythagorist. **1652** GAULE *Magastrom.* xxvi, The sortilegious Pythagorist will suppute for me unlucky numbers. **1786** POLWHELE tr. *Theocritus' Idyllia*, etc. II. 28 The absurd mortifications of the Pythagorists.

†**Pyˈthagorite**. *Obs. rare*[−1]. [f. *Pythagor-as* + -ITE[1].] A disciple of Pythagoras.

1660 STANLEY *Hist. Philos.* IX. *Pythagoras* xvi. (1687) 503/2 Calling upon this account, some Pythagoreans (those of the System), some Pythagorites (those of the Homacoeion [*ὁμακοεῖον* the school of Pythagoras]).

pythagorize (pɪˈθægəraɪz, paɪ-), *v.* [ad. Gr. *πυθαγορίζειν* to be a disciple of Pythagoras; L. *pȳthagorissāre* to imitate Pythagoras. Cf. F. *pythagoriser* (Cholieres 1587) in sense 1.]

1. *intr.* To follow Pythagoras; to speculate after the manner of Pythagoras.

1610 HEALEY *Vives' Comm. St. Aug. Citie of God* x. xxx. (1620) 381 Plato Pythagorizing held that the Soules after death passed into other bodies. **1666** BP. S. PARKER *Free & Impart. Censure* (1667) 48 The latter Platonists..especially those of them that did most Pythagorize.

†**2.** To pass by transmigration. *Obs. nonce-use.*

1651 BIGGS *New Disp.* 184 Peradventure the Shop of choler from the very thresh-hold of life hath Pythagorized into the private ware-house of the head.

†**3.** *trans.* To change (one person or thing) into another as by transmigration of souls. *Obs.*

1631 J. DONE *Polydoron* 211 If our godlesse dainty Gallants were but so Pythagorized, how they would wish they had lived better. **1721** RAMSAY *Morn. Interview* 253 O happiest of herbs! who would not be Pythagoriz'd into the form of thee, And with high transports act the part of tea!

Hence **pyˈthagorizing** *ppl. a.*; also **pyˈthagoˌrizer**, one who Pythagorizes, or follows the doctrine or practice of Pythagoras.

1677 GALE *Crt. Gentiles* II. III. 19 These Pythagorising Gnostics..were professed enemies to Pietie. **1875** LIGHTFOOT *Comm. Col.* 146 Satirised..as 'pythagorizers', in other words as total abstainers and vegetarians.

‖**Pythia** (ˈpɪθɪə, ˈpaɪ-). [a. Gr. *Πυθία* (sc. *ἱέρεια*) the priestess of Pythian Apollo at Delphi, fem. of *Πύθιος* adj. Delphic, f. *Πυθώ*, a place-name (see PYTHIAN). In F. *Pythie* (Rabelais).]

1. *Gr. Antiq.* The priestess of Apollo at Delphi, who delivered the oracles.

1842 L. SCHMITZ in Smith *Dict. Gr. & Rom. Antiq.* 668/2 When Greece was in its most flourishing state,..there were always two Pythias who took their seat on the tripod alternately. *Ibid.* 669/2 Over this chasm there stood a high tripod, on which the Pythia..took her seat whenever the oracle was to be consulted. *Ibid.* 671/1 In the days of Plutarch one Pythia was, as of old, sufficient to do all the work. **1844** MRS. BROWNING *Dead Pan* xxx, Pythia staggered, feeling o'er her Her lost god's forsaking look.

2. *Zool.* A genus of gastropod molluscs.

Pythiad (ˈpɪθɪæd, ˈpaɪ-). [a. Gr. *Πυθιάς, Πυθιαδ-*, f. *Πύθια*, pl. (sc. *ἱερά*) the Pythian games.] The period between two celebrations of the Pythian games. (Cf. OLYMPIAD.)

1842 L. SCHMITZ in Smith *Dict. Gr. & Rom. Antiq.* 811/1 The chariot-race with four horses was not introduced till the second Pythiad. *Ibid.* 811/2 A Pythiad..ever since the time that it was used as an aera, comprehended a space of four years, commencing with the third year of every Olympiad.

pythiˈambic, *a.* (*sb.*) *Ancient Pros.* [ad. mod.L. *pythiambic-us*, f. *Pȳthius* Pythian (versus *Pȳthius* hexameter verse) + *iambicus* IAMBIC.] The epithet or name of an episynthetic or composite metre consisting of a dactylic hexameter (Pythian verse) followed by an iambic colon.

There are two varieties according as the hexameter is followed (1) by an iambic dimeter, as in Horace *Epod.* 14 and 15; (2) by an iambic trimeter, as in *Epod.* 16.

1832 PEMBLE *Horatii Opera* p. xii, The First Pythiambic is a couplet consisting of the common Dactylic Hexameter and an Iambic Quaternarius... The Second Pythiambic is a couplet of the Dactylic Hexameter and Iambic Senarius. **1877–94** GILDERSLEEVE *Lat. Gram.* 489. **1877** WICKHAM *Horace* I. 385.

Pythian (ˈpɪθɪən, ˈpaɪ-), *a.* (*sb.*) [f. L. *Pȳthi-us* (a. Gr. *Πύθιος* of Delphi, or the Delphic Apollo) + -AN.

Πύθιος is now generally held to have been derived from *Πυθώ* or *Πυθών*, the older name of Delphi and the surrounding region; but it was in ancient times connected with the legend of the *πύθων* or monstrous snake said to have been slain there by Apollo: see PYTHON[1].]

Of or pertaining to Delphi, or to the oracle and priestess of Apollo there; also, of or pertaining to the games held near Delphi.

Pythian Apollo, Apollo in his legendary and oracular connexion with Delphi. ***Pythian games***, one of the four national festivals of the Greeks, held near Delphi. ***Pythian meter*** or ***verse*** (L. *versus Pythius*), the dactylic hexameter; said to be so called either from its use in the Pythian oracles, or from the first song of triumph to Apollo on his victory over the Python.

1603 Pythian games [see PYTHIC]. **1655** STANLEY *Hist. Philos.* III. *Socrates* v. (1687) 75/1 The Pythian Oracle. **1660** *Ibid.* IX. *Pythagoras* xiii. 502/1 To Discourse..in the Temple of Pythian Apollo to the Boys. **1667** [see PYTHON[1] 1]. **1797** HOLCROFT *Stolberg's Trav.* (ed. 2) II. lxiii. 430 Pindar mentions this victory in his first Pythian hymn. **1807** ROBINSON *Archæol. Græca* III. xxii, The Pythian Games were celebrated in honor of Apollo near Delphi..The most common opinion is that Apollo himself was the author of them after he had overcome Python, a serpent or cruel tyrant. **1842** L. SCHMITZ in Smith *Dict. Gr. & Rom. Antiq.* s.v. *Pythia*, Previous to Ol[ympiad] 48 the Pythian games.. had been celebrated at the end of every eighth year, but [after Ol. 48. 3] they were held at the end of every fourth year. **1879** P. BROOKS *Influence Jesus* iv. 268 The self-excitement of the Pythian damsel on her tripod. **1884** J. TAIT *Mind in Matter* (1892) 255 The Pythian deliverances became very intermittent after the birth of Christ, and ceased finally in the time of the Apostles.

B. *sb.* A native or inhabitant of Delphi; *spec.* the Delphic priestess; hence, one who is ecstatic or frenzied like the priestess; also, an appellation of the Delphic Apollo; hence *transf.*

1598 MARSTON *Sco. Villanie* II. vi. (1599) 201 But when I saw him read my fustian, And heard him sweare I was a Pythian. **1821** SHELLEY *Adonais* xxviii, How they fled, When like Apollo, from his golden bow, The Pythian of the age one arrow sped And smiled! **1844** MRS. BROWNING *Vis. Poets* clxxvi, If poets on the tripod must Writhe like the Pythian to make just Their oracles and merit trust. **1860** RUSKIN *Mod. Paint.* V. IX. xi. §10. 327 That Contest of Apollo with the Python..the victor deity..took his great name from it..the Pythian.

Pythic ('pɪθɪk), *a.* [ad. L. *Pȳthic-us*, Gr. *Πυθικός*, f. *Πυθώ* or *Πύθων*: see prec.] = PYTHIAN *a.*

1603 HOLLAND *Plutarch* Explan. Wds., Pythick or Pythian games, were celebrated to the honour of Apollo Pythius, neere the city Delphos, with great solemnity. **1746** FRANCIS tr. *Horace, Art Poetry* 559 A Youth..Who sings the Pythic Song. **1860** E. FALKENER *Dædalus, Anc. Art* ii. 61 Conquerors in the Olympic and Pythic games.

b. Like or of the nature of the Pythian priestess; ecstatic, phrenetic.

1837 CARLYLE *Fr. Rev.* I. IV. i, Count..d'Aintrigues..rises into furor almost Pythic. **1850** MASSON *Ess., Wordsw.* (1856) 386 There was no tremendousness, nothing of the Pythic, in the nature of Wordsworth.

pythogenic (paɪθəʊ'dʒɛnɪk), *a.* [f. Gr. *πύθειν* to rot + *-γεν-* producing + -IC.] Generated by or from corruption or filth; esp. in ***pythogenic fever***, a name for typhoid or enteric fever.

1862 C. MURCHISON *Contin. Fevers Gr. Brit.* iv. 385 Pythogenic or Enteric Fever. *Ibid.* 388 These considerations induced me to suggest a few years ago, the name Pythogenic Fever derived from what I endeavoured to show was the cause of the fever. **1881** TYNDALL *Floating Matter Air* i. 15 It was..no problematical pythogenic gas—that killed the worms, but a definite organism. **1898** P. MANSON *Trop. Diseases* x. 179 Malta fever—a disease probably of pythogenic origin.

So **pytho'genesis**, production or generation by or from filth; **pythoge'netic** *a.* = PYTHOGENIC.

1882 OGILVIE, Pythogenesis. **1896** *Allbutt's Syst. Med.* I. 792 The pythogenetic theory of Murchison..became untenable.

python[1] ('paɪθən, 'pɪθən). [a. L. *Pȳthōn*, a. Gr. *Πυθων*, name of the serpent fabled to have been slain near Delphi by Apollo. So F. *python*.

The Gr. word is supposed to have been connected in some way with *Πυθώ* or *Πύθων*, the ancient name of the locality; and both, according to some, with *πύθειν* to rot, *πύθεσθαι* to be rotten, because the serpent was said to have rotted there. According to one form of the legend, the oracle originally belonged to or was guarded by the serpent, and, on the extermination of the latter, became the oracle of Apollo.]

1. *Gr. Mythol.* (With capital initial.) The huge serpent or monster fabled to have been slain near Delphi by Apollo; hence *poet.* any monster or pestilential scourge.

1590 PEELE *Polyhymnia* Wks. (1861) 571 Entering the lists, like Titan arm'd with fire When in the queachy plot Python he slew. **1603** HOLLAND *Plutarch* Explanation of Words, Apollo Pythius..who tooke that name of Python there slaine by him and lying putrified. **1667** MILTON *P.L.* x. 531 [Satan] Now Dragon grown, larger then whom the Sun Ingenderd in the Pythian Vale on slime, Huge Python. **1757** AKENSIDE *Pl. Imag.* I. (Ald.) 94 The laurel boughs That crown'd young Phœbus for the Python slain. **1851** C. L. SMITH *Tasso* IV. v, Hydras hiss, and Pythons whistling wail.

2. *Zool.* A genus of large non-venomous snakes inhabiting the tropical regions of the Old World, which kill their prey by constriction; the rock-snakes; popularly, any large snake which crushes its prey; loosely including the BOAS of tropical America, etc., ***diamond python***: see quot. 1896.

1836 *Penny Cycl.* V. 19/2 The murderous power and voracity of the Indian boas or Pythons. **1841** *Ibid.* XIX. 176/1 The size to which the Pythons grow is fully equal to that attained by the Boæ. **1847** CARPENTER *Zool.* §508 The true Boas are restricted to America; the name of Python being given to the large Serpents of Africa and India. **1865** LIVINGSTONE *Zambesi* iv. 89 Two pythons were observed coiled together among the branches of a large tree. **1896** *List Anim. Zool. Soc.* 605 *Python spilotes*,..Diamond-Python. *Hab.* Australia.

3. *Comb.* as ***python-like*** adj., ***python-slayer***, ***-steak***, ***-stretch***.

1874 GEO. ELIOT *Coll. Breakf. P.* 320 As Python-slayer of the present age. **1898** C. REYNOLDS in *Wide World Mag.* Oct. 93/1 The boy is knocked over by a blow from his [a conger's] python-like head. **1923** D. H. LAWRENCE *Birds, Beasts & Flowers* 177 The great muscular python-stretch of her tail. **1953** R. CAMPBELL *Mamba's Precipice* ii. 26 He and Nyali had had python-steak for supper.

python[2] ('paɪθən, 'pɪθən). Also 7 pithon(e. [ad. late L. *pȳthō*, *-ōnem* (Vulg.) or late Gr. *πύθων* (New Test.), a familiar spirit, the demon possessing a soothsayer; in pl. *πύθωνες* persons speaking by professed divine inspiration, ventriloquists (Plutarch). In Gr. the same word in form as prec., but the sematology is not clear; in sense obviously related to *πύθιος*, *Πυθία* PYTHIA, and their derivatives.] A familiar or possessing spirit; also, one possessed by such a spirit and acting as its mouthpiece.

1603 HOLLAND *Plutarch's Mor.* 1327 Those spirits speaking within the bellies of possessed folkes, such as in old time they called Engastrimithi [= ventriloquists],..and be now termed Pythons, entred into the bodies of Prophets. **1609** BIBLE (Douay) *Deut.* xviii. 11 Neither let there be a sorcerer, nor inchanter, nor that consulteth with pithone, or diviners [Vulg. *nec qui pythones consulat*, LXX *ἐγγαστρίμυθος*, WYCLIF 1388 hem that han a feend spekynge in the wombe]. *Ibid.*, *Isa.* xix. 3 They shal aske their idols, and their diviners, and Pythons, and Southsayers [Vulg. *pythones et ariolos*, LXX *τοὺς ἐκ τῆς γῆς φωνοῦντας, και τοὺς ἐγγαστριμύθους*]. *Ibid.* Index II, Saul... In distresse he consulted a Pithon spirite. **1611** BIBLE *Acts* xvi. 16 A certaine Damosell possessed with a spirit of diuination [*marg. or*, of Python; **1881** R. V. *marg. or*, a spirit, a Python: Gr. *πνεῦμα Πύθωνα* (*v.r.* -*ος*), Vulg. *spiritum pythonem*]. **1678** PHILLIPS (ed. 4), *Python*..also a familiar or prophesying Spirit, or one possessed with it. **1880** W. E. SCUDAMORE in Smith & Cheetham *Dict. Chr. Antiq.* s.v. *Python*, The attributes of the demon and the serpent were interchanged... The python slain by Apollo at Delphi was thought to have inspired the oracle before the god took his place... Hence..both in Jewish and Christian antiquity the name of python was given to prophesying spirits.

python[3] ('paɪθən). *Mil.* [A code name.] Leave granted at the end of the 1939–45 war to members of the British forces who had served a long period overseas. Also *attrib.*, as ***python leave***.

1945 L. DURRELL *Spirit of Place* (1969) 82, I took down a pomegranate..and tried to send it to her with a friend on python. **1945** *Punch* 22 Aug. 166/1 Naturally they are all either due for Python or their Age and Service Groups, and the last few days we have suffered from a constant round of farewell parties. **1949** D. E. STEVENSON *Vittoria Cottage* xiv. 95 When men come home from FARELF after doing their three years they say they are *coming home on Python*... FARELF..means Far Eastern Land Forces. **1959** I. JEFFERIES *Thirteen Days* iii. 37 Your python must be coming up soon. **1969** A. G. THOMAS in L. Durrell *Spirit of Place* 82 Under Python leave any soldier who had been in the Middle East for more than four years was granted one month at home with his family and then three months in some unit in Britain. **1976** R. LEWIN *Slim* xv. 252 *Python*, the scheme for repatriation of men who had served a minimum of three years and four months in the Far East.

† **'pythoner.** *Obs. rare.* In 5 phitoner. [f. **phiton*, PYTHON[2], or f. OF. *phitonie* art of divination + -ER[1]: cf. PYTHONESS.] A soothsayer, a diviner.

c **1400** *Apol. Loll.* 92 If þey sey to ȝow, seek of Phitoneris and of diuineris, þat gnasten wiþ þer teþ in her chauntingis. *Ibid.* 95 Enchauntors are þoo þat in callun fendis to ken hem þingis... And swilk we callen phitoners.

Pythonesque (paɪθə'nɛsk), *a.* [-ESQUE.] Of, pertaining to, or characteristic of *Monty Python's Flying Circus*, a popular British television comedy series of the 1970s, noted esp. for its absurdist or surrealistic humour.

1975 *Guardian* 18 Oct. 8/1 A range of comic methods that stretches from Pythonesque funny walks..to comedy of manners. **1977** *Time Out* 17 June 9/1 It veered from the Pythonesque, mostly due to the presence of the Cleese-like Julian Hough, to the twee. **1979** *Listener* 28 June 873/2 It is doubtful if anyone looked up a dictionary for a definition of 'python', but it is certain that future compilers of dictionaries are going to have to append a new meaning to 'Pythonesque', for the word is now common English usage on both sides of the Atlantic... It describes a set of events that are more than bizarre, yet less than surreal. **1986** *Financial Times* 28 Feb. 19/1 Everything from classically timed slapstick scenes to Pythonesque non sequiturs.

pythoness (paɪ-, 'pɪθənɛs). Forms: *α.* 4–6 phiton-, 5 phyton-, phetonesse, (fetonass), 5–6 phitones, phetonysse, 7 phytonisse. *β.* 6–7 pythonisse, 7 python-, pithonesse, 6– pythoness. [a. OF. *phitonise* (13th c. in Godef. *Compl.*), ad. med.L. *phitonissa* (Du Cange); later F. *pythonisse*, ad. late L. PYTHONISSA, q.v.]

A woman supposed, or professing, to have a 'familiar spirit', and to utter his words; a woman having the power of divination or soothsaying; a witch. In the early examples, applied (after the Vulgate) to the witch of Endor (*1 Sam.* xxviii. 7): cf. also PYTHONISSA. In quot. 1823 applied to the Delphic Pythia.

1375 BARBOUR *Bruce* IV. 753 That quhilom did the Phitones [*MS. C* fetonass; *ed.* 1616 Pithonesse] That..Rasit, throu hyr mekill slycht, Samuell sperit als tit. *c* **1384** CHAUCER *H. Fame* 1261 Iugelours, Magiciens and tregetours And Phitonesses [*Bodl. MS.* Phytonessys, *Caxt.*, *Th.* phetonysses] charmeresses. **1513** DOUGLAS *Æneis* I. Prol. 212 Lyke as the spreit of Samuell, I ges, Rasit to King Saul was by the Phitones. **1587** GOLDING *De Mornay* xv. (1592) 245 In a Pythonesse or in a possessed person. **1649** JER. TAYLOR *Gt. Exemp.* III. xiv. 23 Asking counsel of a Pythonisse. **1702** ECHARD *Eccl. Hist.* (1710) 287 They were often followed by a Pythoness, a maid servant actuated by a spirit of divination [cf. Acts xvi. 16]. **1808** RANKEN *Hist. France* IV. i. 49 He employed the abbot..to consult a famous Pythoness or witch of these times. **1823** BYRON *Juan* VI. cvii, She stood a moment as a Pythoness Stands on her tripod. **1835** MISS SEDGWICK *Linwoods* (1873) I. 20 The pythoness Effie turned her art to good account.

pythonic (paɪ-, pɪ'θɒnɪk), *a.*[1] [ad. L. *pȳthōnic-us*, a. Gr. *πυθωνικός* prophetic, f. *Πύθων* PYTHON[2]. Cf. OF. *phitonique* in same sense.] Of or pertaining to divination; prophetic, oracular.

1658 BROMHALL *Treat. Specters* I. 70 They sought counsel of them that prophesie of future things, by a Pythonick or divellish spirit. **1825** T. M. HARRIS *Nat. Hist. Bible* s.v. *Asp*, A young woman [Acts xvi. 16] who had *a pythonic spirit*. **1906** G. G. COULTON *St. Francis to Dante* 82 Which was as much as to consult a pythonic spirit.

pythonic (paɪ-, pɪ'θɒnɪk), *a.*[2] [f. PYTHON[1] + -IC.] Of, pertaining to, or resembling (*a*) the python of mythology, or (*b*) the pythons of natural history; python-like, monstrous, huge.

1860 C. SANGSTER *Hesperus*, etc. 85 Wrestling with some Pythonic wrongs. **18..** *Science* VII. 242 (Cent.) A new species of reptile..almost pythonic in structure. **1903** *Blackw. Mag.* Apr. 504/1 Huge wooden sheds and pythonic iron pipes.

py'thonical, *a.* Now *rare.* [f. as PYTHONIC *a.*[1] + -AL[1]: see -ICAL.] = PYTHONIC *a.*[1]

1582 N.T. (Rhem.) *Acts* xvi. 16 A certaine wenche hauing a Pythónical spirit. **1609** BIBLE (Douay) *Lev.* xx. 27 Man or woman, in whom is a pithonical or divining spirite..they shal stone them. *Ibid.* *1 Kings* xxviii. 7 There is a woman that hath a pithonical spirite in Endor [Vulg. *est mulier pythonem habens in Endor*]. *a* **1872** J. D. AYLWARD in *Ess. Relig. & Lit.* Ser. III. (1874) 71 Revealing in his natural character the makings of an ecstatic saint, or of a pythonical medium.

pythonid ('paɪθənɪd). *Zool.* [f. PYTHON[1] + -ID.] A snake of the family *Phythonidæ* or Pythons.

1895 in *Funk's Stand. Dict.*

So **'pythoniform** *a.*, of the form or structure of the pythons; **'pythonine** *a.*, of or belonging to the subfamily *Pythoninæ*, typified by the genus *Python*.

1890 in *Cent. Dict.*

'pythonism. *rare.* [f. PYTHON[2] + -ISM.] Intercourse with or possession by a pythonic spirit; occult power thence derived; divination.

1662 STILLINGFL. *Orig. Sacr.* II. vi. §16. 202 This is much like what another of their Doctors sayes,..that Elisha his raising the child to life, and curing Naamans leprosie [etc.]..might all come to pass by the influence of the stars, or by Pythonisme. **1670** BLOUNT *Glossogr.* (ed. 3), *Pythonism*, the art of prophecying by a divelish spirit.

‖ **pytho'nissa.** Now *rare.* Forms: 4–5 phitonissa, -yssa, 5–7 -essa, 6 phætonissa, 7- pythonissa. [Late L. *pȳthōnissa* (Vulgate), med.L. *phitonissa* (Du Cange), fem. of *pȳthō* PYTHON[2].] = PYTHONESS. (Often treated as proper name of the witch of Endor.)

[Cf. *Vulg.* 1 Chron x. 13 Eo quod..insuper etiam pythonissam consuluerit: LXX *ἐν τῷ ἐγγαστριμύθῳ*.]

c **1386** CHAUCER *Friar's T.* 210 Speke as renably..As to the Phitonissa [*v. rr.* -yssa, -essa] dide Samuel. **1586** *Tri. Trophes* 73 in Bond *Lyly's Wks.* (1902) III. 430 In Phætonissa schoole, at Endor they were taught. **1608** MIDDLETON *Fam. Love* III. iv, What heauenly breath of Phitonessaes powre (That rays'd the dead corpes of her friend to life). **1625** BACON *Ess., Of Prophecies* (Arb.) 535 Saith the Pythonissa to Saul; To Morrow thou and thy sonne shall be with me. **1825** *Ann. Reg.* 216/2 The oracles of the humble Pythonissa [Mme. Krudener] were declared seditious.

† **'pythonist.** *Obs.* Also 6 phitonist, 7 pithonist. [f. PYTHON[2] + -IST.] One who professes to be possessed with, and to speak by the inspiration of, a familiar spirit; a soothsayer; a conjurer; a deceiving ventriloquist.

1584 R. SCOT *Discov. Witchcr.* VII. ii. 104 How the lewd practise of the Pythonist of Westwell came to light. **1591** SPARRY tr. *Cattan's Geomancie* Ep. Ded. Aij, The professions of the Phitonists, Sorcerers, Soothsaiers, Wissardes. **1601** DEACON & WALKER *Spirits & Divels* 126 That was cunningly deliuered by the Witch alone in her cell, she being a cunning Ventriloquist, as all Pythonistes are. **1682** N. O. *Boileau's Lutrin* IV. 100 His belly swell'd like Sybils raptur'd Priest, With hollow sounding noise like Pythonist.

'pythonize, *v. nonce-wd.* [f. as prec. + -IZE. Cf. med.L. *pȳthōnizāre* (Du Cange).] *intr.* To act as a python, to soothsay.

1852–5 LYTTON in *Life*, etc. (1883) I. 99, I might have been a much smaller [man] if the poor maniac had never pythonised of my future.

pythonoid (paɪ'θəʊnɔɪd), *a.* and *sb.* *Zool.* [f. PYTHON[1] 2 + -OID.] **a.** *adj.* Having the form or characters of a python; belonging to the sub-order *Pythonoidea* (the peropodous snakes), including the families *Pythonidæ*, *Boidæ*, and *Charinidæ*. **b.** *sb.* A snake of this division. Hence **pytho'noidean**, a pythonoid.

1890 in *Cent. Dict.*

pythonomorph (paɪ'θəʊnəʊmɔːf). *Palæont.* [ad. mod.L. *Pȳthōnomorpha* pl., f. PYTHON[1] 2 + Gr. *μορφή* form.] One of the *Pythonomorpha*, a division of extinct reptiles allied to the existing *Pythonoidea*; a MOSASAURIAN. So **pythono'morphic**, **pythono'morphous** *adjs.*, belonging to or having the characters of a pythonomorph.

1880 NICHOLSON *Zoology* (ed. 6) 558 To regard the *Mosasauridae* (= the *Pythonomorpha* of Cope [1875–8]) as an extinct group of the *Lacertilia*. **1887** HEILPRIN *Distrib. Anim.* 327 Whether or not they are..descendants of the lacertilian pythonomorphs..still remains to be determined. **1887** GÜNTHER in *Encycl. Brit.* XXII. 189/1 The former [order, Ophidians] is probably merely a specialized descendant of the latter [Lacertilians] or of the pythonomorphous reptiles, or perhaps of both. **1890** *Cent. Dict.*, Pythonomorphic. **1907** *Westm. Gaz.* 21 July 12/2 The latest fossil skeleton discovered in Wyoming is one of the pythonomorphic saurians.

pythy, obs. form of PITHY.

pytis, -os, -ous(e, pytoyable, obs. ff. PITEOUS, PITIABLE.

pytt(e, pyttel, obs. ff. PIT, PITTEL.

pytte, pyttye, obs. ff. PITY.

pytter-pattour, pytyr-patyr, obs. ff. PITTER-PATTER.

pytthe, obs. f. PITH.

pytuose, -ouse, obs. var. PITEOUS.

pytyable, pytye, pytyows, obs. ff. PITIABLE, PITY, PITEOUS.

pyuria (paɪ'ʊərɪə). *Path.* [f. PYO- + -URIA.] Discharge of pus with the urine.

1811 HOOPER *Med. Dict., Pyoturia, Pyuria*, a mucous or purulent urine. **1818–20** E. THOMPSON *Cullen's Nosol. Method.* (ed. 3) 302 Local diseases... Of the Secretions and Excretions..81 Pyuria. **1897** *Allbutt's Syst. Med.* II. 1141 The hydatid may suppurate and then burst into the pelvis and cause pyuria.

pyx (pɪks), *sb.* Also 5–7 **pixe, pyxe**, (5–6 **pixt**, 6 **pixte, pyxk**), 5–9 **pix**. See also PYXIS. [ad. L. *pyxis*, a. Gr. πυξίς a box, f. πύξος box-tree.

The specific senses 2 and 3 were the earliest in Eng.; the general sense 'box' being late and only literary. Cf. PYXIS.]

1. A box; a coffer; a vase. *rare.*

1604 R. CAWDREY *Table Alph.* (1613), *Pyxe*, a boxe. **1661** BLOUNT *Glossogr.* (ed. 2), *Pyx* (*pyxis*) a box, properly made of Box-tree. **1840** BROWNING *Sordello* I. 588 Some pyx to screen The full-grown pest, some lid to shut upon The goblin. **1885–94** R. BRIDGES *Eros & Psyche* Jan. ix, 'This box', and in her hands she took a pyx Square-cut, of dark obsidian's rarest green, 'Take'.

2. *Eccl.* The vessel in which the host or consecrated bread of the sacrament is reserved.

?*c* **1400** MAUNDEV. (Roxb.) xi. 41 When þe preste passez by vs with þe pyxe [*over an erasure*; *Cott. MS.* as wee don to Corpus domini; Fr. *contre Corpus Domini*]. **1432–50** tr. *Higden* (Rolls) VII. 491 The pix [TREVISA, box] in whom the sacramente was contenede, brekynge the chene, did falle, whiche was a pronosticacion contrary to the victory of the kynge [Stephen]. **1482** *Will Marg. Paston* in *P. Lett.* III. 287 Item, I bequeth to Margery Paston..my pixt of silver with ij. silver cruettes and my massebook. **1550** BALE *Eng. Votaries* II. cxix, They tell of kynge Steuen, that..the pixte fell out of hys tabernacle, at his coronacyon. **1554** *Yatton Churchw. Acc.* (Som. Rec. Soc.) 166 For tassells for ye pyxk. **1589** WARNER *Alb. Eng.* v. xxii a. (1612) 115 We kisse the Pix, we creepe the Crosse, our Beades we ouerrunne. **1605–6** *Act 3 Jas. I*, c. 5 §15 Any Altar Pix Beades Pictures or suche like Popish Reliques. **1756–7** tr. *Keysler's Trav.* (1760) I. 325 The pyx in which the host is kept, is made of lapis lazuli. **1850** MRS. JAMESON *Leg. Monast. Ord.* 286 Clara..took from the altar the pix of ivory and silver which contained the Host. **1903** J. H. MATTHEWS *Mass & Folklore* iv. 63 A dove-shaped pyx of precious metal, suspended over the altar by a chain from the roof.

fig. *a* **1861** MRS. BROWNING *Bianca* xii, She lied,..And spat into my love's pure pyx The rank saliva of her soul.

3. At the Royal Mint, London, the box or chest in which specimen gold and silver coins are deposited to be tested at the ***trial of the pyx***, i.e. the final official trial of the purity and weight of the coins, now conducted annually by a jury of the Goldsmiths' Company, under the direction of the King's Remembrancer.

1598 STOWE *Surv.* (1603) 55 To receyue them with an account, what summe had been coyned, and also their Pix, or Boxe of Assay. *a* **1637** B. JONSON *Underwoods, Misc. Poems* xxii, For gouerning the pix, A say-master hath studied all the tricks Of fineness and alloy. *a* **1661** FULLER *Worthies* (1840) I. 311 This solemn weighing, by a word of art, they called the pix. **1745** LEAKE *Nummi Brit. Hist.* (ed. 2) 105 The trial or assay of the pix was established, as a check upon the master of the mint. **1789** *Chron.* in *Ann. Reg.* 230/2 Tuesday was held a trial of the pix of moneys coined at the Mint in the Tower of London. **1808** R. RUDING in *Archæol.* XVI. 165 The earliest notice of the pix which I have met with in any modern foreign mint is in the reign of Philip VI of France. **1870** *Act 33 & 34 Vict.* c. 10 §12 A trial of the pyx shall be held at least once in every year in which coins have been issued from the Mint. **1871** (29 June) *Order in Council*, To make regulations respecting the trial of the Pyx. **1900** *Times* 5 July 7/3 The jurors' being [this year] called upon to examine not only the Pyx of the Mint of London, but that of the branch Mint of Perth, Western Australia, as well. **1901** (30 Jan.) (*title*) Trial of the Pyx Order in Council, 1901. *Ibid.* §4 The coins to be set apart for the trial of the Pyx shall consist, in the case of gold coins, of one from every two thousand pieces ready for issue, instead of one from each journey weight as provided by 'the Trial of the Pyx Order in Council, 1871'.

†**4.** The mariner's compass, = PYXIS 3: cf. BOX *sb.*[2] 15 a. *Obs. rare.*

1686 GOAD *Celest. Bodies* I. xii. 61, I see not that Natural Knowledge requires so exact a Pyx as Navigation useth. *c* **1710** BENTLEY in Hearne *Collect.* (O.H.S.) II. 460 Truth mix'd with error, shade with rays, Like Whiston, wanting pyx or stars, In ocean wide or sinks or strays.

5. *Anat.* The acetabulum; = PYXIS 2.

1864 in WEBSTER.

6. *attrib.* and *Comb.*, as, in sense 2, ***pyx-canopy***; **pyx-cloth, -kerchief, -veil**, a cloth used to veil the pyx; in sense 3, ***pyx-box, -chest***; **pyx-dinner, -feast**, an entertainment on the occasion of the trial of the pyx.

1833 R. MUSHET in *Encycl. Brit.* (ed. 7) VII. 53/1 The other piece is ensealed in a packet, and put into a box, called a *pix box,..there to remain until the final trial of the pix by jury before the king. **1867** *Chamb. Jrnl.* XXXVIII. 107 There were two hundred and sixty three pyxes or deposits of gold coin in the Mint pyx-box. **1908** *Athenæum* 12 Sept. 21/3 A 'sacrament-house', which is supposed to have formerly swung as a kind of gigantic *pyx-canopy over the high altar. **1901** *Daily Chron.* 2 July 7/1 The *Pyx chest is brought to the hall and opened in the presence of a jury of goldsmiths, who examine the coins in regard to their number, weight, and fineness. **1496–7** *Rec. St. Mary at Hill* 31 Item, a *pyx clothe for the hight auter, of Siper frenged with gold. **1876** ROCK *Text. Fabr.* 108 To make this pyx-cloth a piece of thick linen, about two feet square, was chosen. **1900** *Times* 5 July 7/3 The Goldsmiths' Company entertained in the evening all the officers engaged on the trial, together with the jurors and numerous other guests..at a banquet known as the '*Pyx Dinner'. **1697** LUTTRELL *Brief Rel.* 13 July (1857) IV. 251 Thursday next will be the *pix feast at Westminster, there being a jury of goldsmiths sworn to try all our money coyned in the Tower this last year.

pyx (pɪks), *v.* [f. prec. sb.] *trans.* To place in a pyx. **a.** To reserve (the host) in a pyx. **b.** To deposit (specimen coins) in the pyx (PYX *sb.* 3); hence, To test (coin) by weight and assay. Hence **pyxed** (pɪkst) *ppl. a.*, **'pyxing** *vbl. sb.*

a. **1546** BALE *First Exam. Anne Askewe* D ij, In al the xij. hondred yeares afore that was it neyther boxed nor pixed, honoured nor sensed unyuersallye. **1563** FOXE *A. & M.* x. Pref. 890/2 Christ ordeined the supper to be a taking matter: ..our masse men make it a matter not of taking, but of gasing, peping, pixing, boxing [etc.].

b. **1561** in *Rep. Comm. Roy. Mint* (1849) App. 22 After that the pyxed moneys is tolde by the teller. **1833** R. MUSHET in *Encycl. Brit.* (ed. 7) VII. 52/2 This money..is carried to the mint office to undergo inspection, and to be pixed. **1866** *St. James' Mag.* Jan. 203 The finished and perfect coins are put up in bags of a given weight, ready for the final process of pyxing.

pyxidate ('pɪksɪdeɪt), *a. Bot.* [ad. mod.L. *pyxidāt-us*, f. *pyxis, pyxidem* box: see -ATE[2] 2.] Having the form of a pyxis or pyxidium: opening, as a capsule, with a transverse slit; also, bearing pyxidia. Also, in same sense, **'pyxidated** *a.*

1753 CHAMBERS *Cycl. Supp.* s.v. *Heath-moss*, These [varieties of cup-mosses] are but very lightly pixidated, and the first of the two scarce distinguishably so. **1858** MAYNE *Expos. Lex., Pyxidatus*, having the form of a little box, as *Scyphorus pyxidatus*: pyxidate. **1897** in *Syd. Soc. Lex.*

‖**pyxidium** (pɪk'sɪdɪəm). *Bot.* Pl. **pyxidia**. [mod.L., ad. Gr. πυξίδιον, dim. of πυξίς a box: see PYX.] A capsule opening by transverse dehiscence, so that the top comes off like the lid of a box.

1832 *Encycl. Brit.* (ed. 7) V. 42/1 When a capsule opens transversely, it is called a pyxidium. **1847** W. E. STEELE *Field Bot.* 123 Pimpernel... Fruit a pyxidium. **1857** HENFREY *Elem. Bot.* 143 The *Pyxidium* is a one- or more-celled, many-seeded fruit, the upper part of which falls off like a lid by circumscissile dehiscence.

pyxie ('pɪksɪ). *U.S.* Also **pixy**. [Abbrev. of mod.L. *Pyxidanthera* (A. Michaux *Flora Boreali-Americana* (1803) I. 152), f. Gr. πυξίδ-ιον box + ἀνθηρά, fem. of ἀνθηρός flowery.] In full, ***pyxie moss***. A small, prostrate, evergreen shrub, *Pyxidanthera barbulata*, belonging to the family Diapensiaceæ, native to limited areas of New Jersey and the Carolinas, and bearing tiny white flowers; also called the pine-barren beauty (see PINEBARREN b).

1882 *Harper's Mag.* June 65 Among her [*sc.* Nature's] treasures is the delicate pyxie..a little prostrate trailing evergreen. **1892** *Amer. Folk-Lore* V. 100 *Pyxidanthera barbulata*, pyxie moss. **1916** J. W. HARSHBERGER *Vegetation New Jersey Pine-Barrens* xvi. 240 The flowering-moss, or pyxie, is usually a prostrate or creeping plant. **1925** *Scribner's Mag.* July 35/1 Innumerable clusters of oval-leaved *Diapensia lapponica* in rounded clumps like red pin-cushions (closely resembling what is called pixy-moss). **1951** E. W. TEALE *North with Spring* xxviii. 276 If we had been a few weeks earlier, we would have found..the pyxie of the pine barrens, the matted, mosslike flowering plant. *Ibid.*, One year, on the 31st of March,..I came upon a dense mass of pyxie moss,..across which a host of tiny waxy-white flowers were scattered. **1973** ROBICHAUD & BELL *Vegetation New Jersey* xii. 217 The most commonly known of these [pine-barren plants] include the turkey-beard, pyxie moss, goat's-rue, [etc.].

‖**pyxis** ('pɪksɪs). Also 5, 8 **pixis**. Pl. **pyxides** ('pɪksɪdiːz). [L. *pyxis*: see PYX.]

1. A small box or vase; a casket; = PYX 1, 2.

[**1390** *Earl Derby's Exp.* (Camden) 222 Item pro j pixide et tunder, fyryren et broches, j duc. xx s.] **1536** *Regr. Riches* in *Antiq. Sarisb.* (1771) 190 Divers Pyxides of Ivory with clasps and without them, of silver, with many holy relicks. **1842** J. YATES in *Smith's Dict. Gr. & Rom. Antiq.* 812/2 Nero deposited his beard in a valuable pyxis, when he shaved for the first time. **1897** *Syd. Soc. Lex., Pyxis*, a small box for holding salves, medicines, etc. **1907** *Edin. Rev.* Apr. 470 In ivory there is a cylindrical pyxis, pagan work of about the fourth century.

2. *Anat.* The acetabulum or socket of the hip-bone, into which the head of the thigh-bone is inserted.

c **1400** *Lanfranc's Cirurg.* 176 Eueri of hem haþ a box þat is clepid pixis, haunche & vertebrum sit þeron. **1693** tr. *Blancard's Phys. Dict.* (ed. 2), *Pyxis*, the Cavity of the Hip-bone, which is called *Acetabulum*. **1854–67** C. A. HARRIS *Dict. Med. Terminol., Pyxis*,..also, the acetabulum.

3. (In full ***pyxis nautica***.) The mariner's compass. Also, the name of one of the southern constellations, often considered as part of Argo.

1686 GOAD *Celest. Bodies* I. xii. 61, I had not the accomodation of the Pyxis, nor any Horizontal Plate divided into more points of the Compass. **1841** *Penny Cycl.* XIX. 177/2 *Pyxis nautica* (the Mariner's Compass), a southern constellation of Lacaille, placed in Argo.

4. *Bot.* **a.** = PYXIDIUM. †**b.** The theca of a moss. *Obs.* **c.** A cup-like dilatation of the podetium in lichens, having shields on its edge.

1845 LINDLEY *Sch. Bot.* i. (1858) 17 The *pyxis*, which throws off a cap, as in the Henbane. **1880** GRAY *Struct. Bot.* vii. §2. 293 A Pyxis or Pyxidium is a dry fruit which opens by a circular line, cutting off the upper part as a lid.

5. *Zool.* **a.** A genus of land-tortoises, having as the only known species *Pyxis arachnoides* (Gray) of Madagascar and Mauritius. **b.** A genus of coleopterous insects, containing about 8 species (Dejean, 1834). †**c.** A synonym of *Productus*, a genus of Brachiopods (Chemnitz, 1784).

pyynte, pyzel(l, obs. ff. PINT[1], PIZZLE.

Q

Q (kjuː), the seventeenth letter of the modern and the sixteenth of the ancient Roman alphabet, was in the latter an adoption of the ϙ (*κόππα*, *koppa*) of some of the early Greek alphabets. The Phœnician letter from which this was derived had the forms Ϙ, Φ, ϟ, and was used as the sign for the deeper or more guttural of the two *k*-sounds which exist in the Semitic tongues (Hebrew ק, Arabic ق). Though this sound had no real equivalent in Greek, ϙ is found in early inscriptions, e.g. as the initial of *Κόρινθος* Corinth, but was not accepted as a letter of the Athenian alphabet, being retained only as a numerical symbol = 90. In Latin, however, Q was regularly employed, in combination with V, in representing the double sound (kw) which arose partly from the labialized velar guttural, as in *quis*, *quattuor*, and partly from a palatal *k* followed by the labial semi-vowel, as in *equus*. In the Romanic tongues this Latin combination was either retained with its original value, or in certain cases (esp. in Fr.) was modified to a simple *k*-sound. In the former case the spelling with *qu-* has commonly been retained, even where the sound has at a later period been reduced to (k).

The Latin *qu-* might naturally have been adopted in OE. orthography to represent the Common Teutonic initial combination *kw-* (for which Wulfila employed the special sign **u**); but though *qu-* is found in the earliest glosses and occas. in the Rushworth gospels, the ordinary OE. symbol for the sound was *cw-* (in early use also *cu-*). After the Conquest *qu-* was again introduced, though at first sparingly employed; *quarterne* appears in the Laud MS. of the OE. Chron., an. 1137, the *Lambeth Hom.* have *quic*, *quiken* (but *cweð*, *cwiðe*), and Ormin has *quarrterrne* once, though regularly using *cw-* except in *quaþþrigan*. In the 13th c. the usage varies in different MSS., and sometimes even in the same text. The earlier version of Layamon has regularly *qu-*, the later *cw-*; the *Leg. St. Kath.* and *Jul.* have *cw-*, but *qu-* in *quoð*; and the *Ancren Riwle* usually *cw-*, even in French words, but also *qu-*, esp. in French words. In *Gen. & Exod.* there is no *cw-*, only *qu-* or *quu-* being used. By the end of the 13th c. *cw-* was entirely discontinued, and *qu-* (or its variants *qv-*, *qw-*) was the established spelling for all cases of the sound (kw), whether of English, French, or Latin origin. The author of the *Ayenbite*, however, also writes *ku-*, and this, as well as *kw-*, is occas. found in other MSS. of the 14–15th c.

In certain dialects of ME., however, the combination *qu-* (*quu-*, *qv-*, *qw-*) was not confined to words in which it represented OE. *cw-* or Romanic *qu-*, but also took the place of ordinary ME. *wh-* (OE. *hw-*), as in *quan*, *quat*, *qvele*, *qwelpe* = when, what, wheel, whelp. The earliest occurrence of these spellings is in *Gen. & Exod.*, where they are exclusively employed; in later use they are characteristically northern, and are found as late as 1570, Levins having *quilome*, *quip* = whilome, whip. In the 14–15th c. the combinations *qh-* and *qhw-* are similarly employed in MSS. written in the NE. midlands. Scottish scribes preferred *quh-* (*qvh-*, *qwh-*), which is also, though more rarely, used in northern English MSS.; this orthography survived till the 17th c., and is defended by A. Hume (*Orthogr. Brit. Tongue* 18) as a more correct method of representing the sound than *wh-*. On the other hand *wh-* was freq. written by northern scribes in the 14–15th c. in place of *qu-*, as *whik*, *wheme*, *white* = quick, queme, quite; and alliteration of original *qu-* with *wh-* is not infrequent in some poems, as the *Wars of Alexander*, *Destr. Troy*, and *Morte Arthure*. The pron. implied by this is still current in the northern and north-midland counties (not in Scotland): see esp. the words QUAINT, QUEME, QUEY, QUICK.

In certain words of French origin, *qu-* varies with *c-* in ME. and early mod.E. As in OF., this is most common when *oi* or *ui* follows: see the forms given under *coif*, *coil*, *coin* (*quoin*), *coyn*, *quoit*, *cuirass*, *cuir-bouilli*, *cuisse*, *cushion*, *custron*, and *quaint*. More rarely *que-* replaces original *co-* or *cu-*, as in *quengeoun* congeoun, *quenger* conjure, *quenquest* conquest, *queral* coral, *querch* curch, *quesing* cousin, *questrel* custrel; with these cf. the Norman *quemander*, *quemencher*, *quemodité*, *quemun*, etc. (Godef. and Moisy). In a few cases the *qu-* forms survive in western dial., as *querd* cord, *quile* coil, *quine* coin, *quirt* court. A similar variation of *c* and *q* in native words is rare, but *quo-* is sometimes found for *co-*, as in *quod* cod, *quodgel* cudgel, *quore* core, *quorn* corn: see also QUEEST, QUITCH *sb.*[1] and COUCH *sb.*[2], QUID *sb.*[3]

In ordinary mod.Engl. words Q is employed only in the combination *qu*, whether this is initial as in *quake*, *quality*, medial as in *equal*, *sequence*, or forming a final consonant (k) as in *cheque*, *pique*, *grotesque*. There is, however, a tendency among scholars to use Q by itself to transliterate the Semitic *kōph*, writing, e.g., *Qabbala*, *Qaraite*, *Qurán* for *Cabbala*, *Karaite*, *Koran*.

I. 1. Illustrations of the use of the letter.

c **1000** Ælfric *Gram.* iii. (Z.) 6, *h* and *k* ȝeendiað on *a* æfter rihte. *q* ȝeendað on *u*. **1530** Palsgr. 9 Whan *v* followeth *q* in a frenche worde..than shall *u* be left unsounded. *a* **1637** B. Jonson *Eng. Gram.* iv, The English Saxons knew not this halting *Q*, with her waiting-woman *u* after her. **1727–41** Chambers *Cycl.* s.v., Many grammarians, in imitation of the Greeks, banish the *Q*, as a superfluous letter. **1797** *Encycl. Brit.* (ed. 3) 724/2 The q is never sounded alone, but in conjunction with u..and never ends any English word. **1872** Morris *Eng. Accid.* 61 From this table of consonants we have omitted..*q*, because this is equivalent to *kw*.

b. *attrib.* Used *spec.* to designate one of the two main groups of languages which developed from Common Celtic, so called because its distinctive phonological features include the retention of IE. *q^u, as ***Q-Celt***, a speaker of ***Q-Celtic***. Cf. *P-Celtic* s.v. P I. 1.

1891, **1913** [see P I. 1]. **1944** J. Whatmough *ΚΕΛΤΙΚΑ* 49 The possibility that traces of *q*-Keltic may lurk hidden in the magico-medical formularies of Marcellus of Bordeaux. **1962** T. C. Lethbridge *Witches* vi. 72 This adds to the evidence which suggests that the Iceni were 'Q' Celts, speaking a form of Gaelic. **1972** [see P I. 1].

2. Used to denote serial order, as 'Q Battery', 'Section Q', etc., or as a symbol of some thing or person, a point in a diagram, etc. ***Q-boat***, ***Q-ship***, an armed and camouflaged merchantman used as a decoy or to destroy submarines; also *ellipt.*; cf. DECOY *sb.*[2] 6, *mystery ship* s.v. MYSTERY[1] 13. Hence ***Q car***, a disguised police car.

1920 *Blackw. Mag.* Mar. 325/1 They had complied with the regulations that dictated that no uniform must be shown abroad sailing 'Q's'. **1918** *Army & Navy Gaz.* 10 Aug. 501/1 Among the anti-submarine measures initiated and encouraged by Mr. Churchill and Lord Fisher were the 'Q' boats, the mystery attaching to which has now been dispelled by Sir Eric Geddes... The 'Q' boat may be briefly defined as a decoy. **1976** R. Moore *Dubai* iv. 51 We're talking about making your dhow into a high-speed Q-boat. **1937** *Times* 13 Apr. p. xxvii/2 Among the cars used by the London police are a number to which the name 'Q' is applied... If inside a small and unimpressive body there is an engine that will develop the highest speed attainable by the most powerful vehicle the 'Q' car is complete. **1961** *Guardian* 29 Sept. 2/3 Three men jumped out of a badly-damaged car, which crashed into the side of a lorry..and in turn was rammed by a police 'Q' car. **1976** L. Henderson *Major Enquiry* xiv. 88 She..doubled back..to the waiting Q car. The watch was being kept by Sheehan and Milton. **1919** *Boy's Own Paper* July 458/1 One of the finest examples of coolness, discipline, and good organisation in the history of Q-ships. **1946** *Daily Tel.* 15 May 5/4 After his experience with two British 'Q' ships, the 10,000 ton Kolchak..and the motor vessel Alfred Jones,..which nearly led to his destruction in 1941, he thought U-boat captains perfectly justified in not attempting rescue work after torpedoing ships. **1972** J. Broome *Convoy is to Scatter* I. 25 The Q-ship's lure-power lay in her half-sunken appearance appealing to the U-boat captain for his coup-de-grâce.

†**3.** ***q in the corner***, ? = puss in the corner. *Obs.*

1782 Miss Burney *Cecilia* I. 41, I will either hide or seek with any boy in the parish; and for a Q in the corner, there is none more celebrated.

4. Used with reference to its shape, *spec.* in *Skating*. Also *attrib.*

1852 G. Anderson *Art of Skating* vi. 73 The Q Figure. Start with a curve on the outside forwards, then change the edge to inside forwards, and finish with a circle outside backwards, all on the one foot, without setting down the other. **1935** *Encycl. Sports* 559/2 A difficult but beautiful figure called the Q... The figure bears a pretty distinct resemblance to the letter.

5. Repr. clipped pronunc. of 'thank you'; = KEW.

1925 Wodehouse *Sam the Sudden* ii. 13 The conductor presented himself, punch in hand. 'Fez, pliz.' 'Valley Fields,' said Kay. 'Q,' said the conductor. **1956** J. Latimer *Sinners & Shrouds* xxiii. 181 'Son of a bitch!' 'I beg your pardon?' 'I beg yours.' 'Q.'

II. Abbreviations.

1. Of Latin words or phrases. †**a.** **Q**, (in mediæval notation) = 500; **q.**, **qu.** = QUASI, as if; **q.** = *quadrans* farthing. *Obs.* **b.** †**q.d.** = *quasi dictum* 'as if said', *quasi dicat* 'as if one should say', etc.; †**q.e.** = *quod est* 'which is'; **q.v.** = *quod vide* 'which see'. †**c.** From the language of medical prescriptions: **q.d.s.** = *quater in die sumendus* 'to be taken four times a day'; **q.i.d.** = *quater in die* 'four times a day'; **q.l.** = *quantum libet*; **q.pl.** = *quantum placet* 'as much as one pleases'; **q.s.** = QUANTUM SUFFICIT; **q.v.** = *quantum vis* 'as much as you wish'. **d.** Formulæ placed at the end of mathematical problems, etc.: **Q.E.D.**, **Q.E.F.**, **Q.E.I.**, = *quod erat demonstrandum* (also as *sb. phr.*), *faciendum*, *inveniendum*, 'which was to be demonstrated, done, found'.

1542 Recorde *Gr. Artes* (1575) 29, q a farthing the iiij part of a penny. **1631** Weever *Anc. Fun. Mon.* 240 Worth 1412*l.* 4*s.* 7*d.* ob. q. **1658** Phillips, *Alfreton* q. *Alfred's* Town. *a* **1662** J. Symcotts in *Publ. Beds. Hist. Rec. Soc.* (1951) XXXI. 101 For the shaking of the hands: Take rosemary bruised q.s. and apply it to the wrists. **1678** Phillips (ed. 4), *Bangle-eared* (*qu.* Bendle-eared). **1710** *Lond. Gaz.* No. 4706/2 The Ballance..amounting to 71019*l.* 1*s.* 5*d.* 2*q.* has been..credited to the Publick. **1721** Bailey, *Gossip*, of *God*, and *Syb*,..a Kinsman, *q.d.* Kindred in God. **1722** Quincy *Phys. Dict.* 69/2, *q.s.* A sufficient Quantity. **1760** L. Sterne *Tr. Shandy* II. xix. 168 If..people can walk about and do their business without brains,—then certes the soul does not inhabit there. Q.E.D. **1818** Moore *Fudge Fam. Paris* ii. 127 The argument's quite new, you see, And proves exactly Q.E.D. **1848** Mrs. Gaskell *M. Barton* (1882) 86/2 [My thoughts] don't follow each other like the Q.E.D. of a Proposition. **1932** *Times Lit. Suppl.* 7 Jan. 1/3 Matisse, with his frugal presentation of purely aesthetic values to a purely aesthetic appetite, appears to be the Q.E.D. of French painting as looked at in perspective. **1955** R. J. Schwartz *Compl. Dict. Abbrev.* 149/1 *q i d*, four times a day (*quater in die*—Latin). **1960** Laurence & Moulton *Clin. Pharmacol.* 454 q.d.s., quater in die sumendus, four times a day (q.i.d. and q.q.h are sometimes used). **1975** J. Mitchell *Smear Job* xviii. 159 He hates himself... He drinks. Q.E.D. **1977** *Lancet* 20 Aug. 376/1 Two subjects who inhaled 400 µg salbutamol q.i.d. from the start. **1978** *Jrnl. R. Soc. Med.* LXXI. 464/2 Abbreviations such as bds and qds will not be understood by foreign readers.

2. Of English words or phrases. **a.** **Q.** = Quartermaster, Quartermaster-General or -Sergeant; also *attrib.* or as *adj.*, and *ellipt.* for the Quartermaster's or Quartermaster-General's Department; **Q.** = QUARTO 2; **Q.** = Queen; **Q.**, **q.** = query, question; **q.** (in a ship's log) = squalls; †**q.** = quod, QUOTH. *Sc. Obs.* **b.** **Q and A**, question and answer (esp. *attrib.*); **Q.B.** = Queen's Bench; **Q.B.I.** (*R.A.F. slang*), quite bloody impossible, (applied to flying conditions); also *ellipt.*; **Q.C.** = Queen's Counsel (hence **Q.C.-dom**); **QCD**, quantum chromodynamics; **QED**, quantum electrodynamics; **QF.**, **q.f.**, quick-firing; also *ellipt.*, a quick-firing gun; **Q.I.**, quartz-iodine; **Q.M.** = Quartermaster; also *attrib.*; **Q.M.G.** = Quartermaster-General; **Q.M.S.**, Quartermaster-Sergeant; **QS** [? f. *quadraphonic-stereophonic*: cf. *SQ* s.v. S 4 a], a designation (proprietary in the U.S.) of audio equipment used with reference to a system of quadraphonic recording and reproduction; **QSO**, quasi-stellar object (i.e. a quasar); **QSS**, quasi-stellar source (of radio waves); **Q.T.**, **q.t.** = quiet *slang*. **c.** †**qd.** = quod, QUOTH. *Obs.*; **qr.** = quarter, quire; **qt.** = quart, quantity; **qu.** = query.

1916 G. Frankau *Poetical Wks.*, (1923) I. 223 And the Boche shells; and '*Q.' still issues bromo. *Ibid.* 227 No more I'll turn the mordant line till 'Q' clerks blush incarnadine. **1918** *Punch* 2 Jan. 15/2 Military experts will tell you that this is a 'Q.' war, meaning thereby that the Quartermaster-General's department is the one which matters. **1919** W. S. Churchill in M. Gilbert *Winston S. Churchill* (1977) IV. Compan. I. 456 Another inroad on 'Q' should it seems to me be made by transferring all discipline to the Adjutant General. **1930** H. Belloc *Wolsey* v. 126 It was certainly he who did all the 'Q' work, to him all the letters were addressed; he gave the orders, bought provisions, organised transport, [etc.]. **1942** W. S. Churchill *Second World War* (1951) IV. I. xx. 311 The arrangements for bringing off the wounded would alone open up a vista of Q problems. **1976** D. Clark *Dread & Water* v. 119 A well-run army Q store. **1871** H. H. Furness in *New Variorum Ed. Shakespeare* I. p.

ix, I have very seldom noted the *variæ lectiones* of the First Quarto... When referred to in the textual notes it is designated as (*Q_1). **1936** *Times Lit. Suppl.* 23 May 440/2 The stage directions of the stolen Q1 and of the authoritative Q2 were not contradictory. **1964** F. Bowers *Bibliogr. & Textual Crit.* v. iv. 157 If Q is a memorially reconstructed 'bad quarto'.., its reading derives ultimately from the prompt-book. **1625** Bacon *Ess., Prophecies* (Arb.) 536 The *Q. Mother.. caused the King her Husbands Natiuitie to be calculated. **1568** *Bann. MS.* in *Poems A. Scott* (S.T.S.) iii. 18 ffinis *q. Alex^r. Scott. *Ibid.* xviii 52, q. Scott off þe Mr. of Erskyn. **1954** W. R. & F. K. Simpson *Hockshop* v. 127 We stalled until we could get the police into the *Q. and A. contest. **1976** B. Bova *Multiple Man* (1977) i. 14 McMurtie wanted.. to know if I'd planned a Q and A session after the speech. **1938** *Times* 3 Mar. 7/3 Instructions.. as to height and position to be kept when flying in controlled areas during '*Q.B.I.' conditions. **1942** *Tee Emm* (Air Ministry) II. 69 So now you fly in Q.B.I. *Ibid.* 143 He waited for some Q.B.I. And rushed aloft, the beam to try. **1870** A. J. Munby *Diary* 14 May (1972) 284 Came Vernon Lushington *Q.C., and I did greet him friendly. **1887** L. George *Let.* 25 Feb. (1973) 18 A Q.C. of high standing. **1892** Mrs. Clifford *Aunt Anne* II. 293 She is sister of an eminent Q.C. **1865** *Cornh. Mag.* Aug. 144 The hard struggle was over, the comparative table-land of *Q.C.-dom gained. **1976** *QCD [see *quantum chromodynamics* s.v. quantum 7a]. **1979** *Nature* 1 Feb. 349/3 The one essential difference between QED and QCD is that whereas there is but one type of electrical charge in QED, the colour charge has three independent varieties. *c* **1525** *Douglas' Æneis* (Small) IV. 231 *Qd. Gawinus Douglas. **1969** *Physics Bull.* June 223/2 The energy splitting between the $2S_{\frac{1}{2}}$ and $2P_{\frac{1}{2}}$ states of the hydrogen atom—the Lamb shift—.. arises entirely from higher order effects in *qed. **1975** *McGraw-Hill Yearbk. Sci. & Technol.* 115/1 The detection of positrons from overcritical electric fields would constitute an important test of QED. **1890** G. S. Clarke *Fortification* Pl. xxviii, Balance pillar mounting for 4·7-inch *Q.F. gun. **1902** *Encycl. Brit.* XXXI. 347/2 Endeavouring.. to produce a more powerful gun than the then existing Q.F. **1915** Kipling *Fringes of Fleet* 1 They gave her Government coal to burn And a Q.F. gun at bow and stern. **1972** D. Dakin *Unification of Greece* xi. 157 The Greek government ordered 144 7·5 mm Q.F. Schneider-Canet mountain guns. **1976** *Yorkshire Evening Press* 9 Dec. 21/1 (Advt.), Escort Mexico, 'K' reg. 60,000 miles. *Q.I. headlamps, inertia belts. **1977** J. Hedgecoe *Photographer's Handbk.* 34 Q.I. lamps generate considerable heat, and must be ventilated. **1916** *Wipers Times* 12 Feb. (1918) 11/1 Obtainable from all *Q.M. stores. **1933** M. Lowry *Ultramarine* i. 49 It's good of you to ask me in, Q.M., thanks. **1907** *Field Service Pocket Bk.* viii. 160 *Q.M.G. (Maj.-Gen.). **1918** in M. Gilbert *Winston S. Churchill* (1977) IV. Compan. i. 367 As regards the latter the General Staff will inform QMG of our requirements and he will take up the matter with you. **1977** 'D. MacNeil' *Wolf in Fold* xvi. 165 I'm not leaving all those tents... Just think, the trouble there'd be with the QMG's department! **1916** *Anzac Bk.* 65, I am a *Q.M.S... We have a Quartermaster, but of course, I do all the work. **1969** V. de S. Pinto *City that Shone* ix. 207 A genial horsy character called Bob Duffield, the Q.M.S. and myself. **1971** S. Hill *Strange Meeting* ii. 157 The day I went to the village to see the Q.M.S. **1734** Ward *Young Math. Guide* (ed. 6) 90 A Grocer bought 3 c. 1 *qr. 14 lb. Weight of Cloves. **1972** *Wireless World* Feb. 55/2 A way of avoiding the mislocalization.. in the simple matrix technique has been adopted by Sansui in their *QS system. **1975** *Official Gaz.* (U.S. Patent Office) 8 Apr. TM123/1 Sansui Electric Company Limited,.. Tokyo, Japan. Filed Dec. 13, 1972. *QS*... For disc-type music recordings... First use Oct. 23, 1970; in commerce Sept. 19, 1972. **1975** G. J. King *Audio Handbk.* vii. 167 Image error results when a basic QS decoder is used to play an SQ record. *Ibid.* 168 SQ records also yield good stereo.., but QS records are less objectively accommodating in this respect. **1964** *New Scientist* 13 Aug. 393/3 The objects known variously as superstars, quasars, quasi-stellar objects or (for short) *QSO's continue to cause intense interest among astronomers. **1973** *Nature* 23 Nov. 205/1 Although it is the majority view that QSO redshifts are cosmological in origin and related to distance by Hubble's law, several workers have proposed that QSOs may be more local objects. **1977** J. Narlikar *Struct. Universe* iii. 87 In looking for new QSOs, the astronomer picks upon starlike objects showing a marked ultraviolet radiation excess. **1965** Sandage & Wyndham in *Astrophysical Jrnl.* CXLI. 328 To the present time there have been positive identifications of nine quasi-stellar radio sources (hereinafter called '*QSS'). **1973** QSS [see quasi-stellar *a.*]. **1711** *Lond. Gaz.* No. 4845/4, 4 Bales *qt. each 3 c. of Coffee. **1884** G. Moore *Mummer's Wife* (1887) 99 It will be possible to have one spree on the strict *q.t. **1910** A. Bennett *Clayhanger* ii. xxi. 315 Mind you this is strictly q.t.! Nobody knows a word about it, nobody! **1922** Joyce *Ulysses* 610 Sailing under false colours after having boxed the compass on the strict q.t. somewhere. **1972** *New Yorker* 17 June 24/1 (*caption*) This is strictly on the q.t., Senator.

III. As a symbol. **1.** *Q* or *q* in *Physics* represents electric charge. [f. the initial letter of *quantity*.]

1846 W. Thomson in *Cambr. & Dublin Math. Jrnl.* I. 91 Denoting by *Q, Q'* the quantities of electricity constituting the charges before, and *q, q'* after contact, we shall have [etc.]. **1879** *Encycl. Brit.* VIII. 22/1 The law of electric force between two quantities *q* and *q'* now becomes Force = qq'/d^2. **1938** G. P. Harnwell *Princ. Electr. & Magn.* i. 11 F is the force in dynes exerted by the charge q_1 on the charge q_2. **1973** L. J. Tassie *Physics of Elem. Particles* xix. 40 The antiparticle of a particle of charge *Q* and baryon number *B*, has charge − *Q* and baryon number − *B*.

2. *Theol.* [Prob. abbrev. of G. *quelle* source.] The symbol used to denote the hypothetical source of the passages shared by the gospels of Matthew and Luke, and not found in that of Mark.

1901 J. Moffatt *Historical New Testament* 266 It is still hotly disputed.. whether Matthew had access to any sources besides Q and Mark. **1920** *Jrnl. Theol. Stud.* XXI. 286 'Real Aramaism may be allowed ungrudgingly in those parts of the New Testament which are virtually translated from Aramaic oral or written sources', i.e. Mark and Q. **1935** R. H. Lightfoot *Hist. & Interpretation in Gospels* ii. 27 Dr. Armitage Robinson.. maintained.. that he himself was the first to use the symbol... In the 'nineties of the last century, he was in the habit.. of alluding to St. Mark's gospel as P (reminiscences of St. Peter), and to the presumed sayings-document as Q, simply because Q was the next letter after P in the alphabet. **1955** A. M. Farrer in D. E. Nineham *Stud. in Gospels* 56 We can conceive well enough how St. Luke could have both read St. Matthew's book as it stands, and written the gospel he has left us. Then at one stroke the question is erased to which the Q hypothesis supplied an answer. **1965** J. H. Roberts *Q Document* i. 33 The Q document is a hypothetical document invented by German biblical historians in the 1800s to explain a gap in our knowledge of the early Christian Era... They called this document the *quelle* or 'source' document. Later this was shortened to 'Q'. **1978** F. Neirynck in *Ephemerides Theologicae Lovanienses* LIV. 123 It seems to be a fair conclusion that he [*sc.* J. Weiss] substituted Q (= *Quelle*) for Λ (= Λόγια).

3. Also *Q factor*. The ratio of the reactance of an inductor or capacitor to its electrical resistance; more widely, a parameter of any oscillatory system representing the degree to which it is undamped, equal to 2π times the ratio of the mean total energy of the system to the energy that must be supplied each cycle to sustain the oscillations. So **Q-meter**, an instrument for measuring the *Q* of a component.

1931 *Proc. IRE* XIX. 874 Let $Q = \omega_r L/R$. **1932** F. E. Terman *Radio Engin.* ii. 39 Tubing.. has.. a better current distribution.. than does either flat- or edgewise-wound strip and hence has a better *Q* in proportion to the amount of conductor material employed. **1933** K. Henney *Radio Engin. Handbk.* vi. 109 For a coil, $Q = \omega L/R$. For a condenser, $Q = 1/\omega RC$. **1938** *Admiralty Handbk. Wireless Telegr.* II. §F 19 Good coils often have a Q of the order of 100. **1943** F. E. Terman *Radio Engineers' Handbk.* xiii. 916 *Q* meters are frequently used to measure reactance and resistance (or conductance) of choke coils, dielectrics, etc., by the substitution method. **1943** *Electronic Engin.* XVI. 33/3 The two crystals were operated at 'Q' values of 20,000 and 5,000. **1948** P. M. Morse *Vibration & Sound* (ed. 2) ii. 25 Another method of expressing this is in terms of the '*Q* of the system', where $Q = (\omega_o m/R_m)$ is the number of cycles required for the amplitude of motion to reduce to $(1/e^\pi)$ of its original value. **1965** *Wireless World* July 338/1 A technique .. which had resulted in inductors with good Q factors of 50 to 80. *Ibid.* Aug. 413/1 A Q-meter can be used to establish the effective series resistance. **1971** [see *quality factor* s.v. quality *sb.* 13]. **1975** D. G. Fink *Electronics Engineers' Handbk.* xi. 13 By lowering the *Q* of the optical cavity, the laser cannot oscillate, and a large inverted population builds up. When the *Q* is restored, a single 'giant pulse'.. is generated.

4. *Psychol.* Used in factor analysis to designate personality testing methods used to obtain correlations between the persons tested, by requiring each subject to rate in order those personality traits that seem most applicable to himself. Usu. as *Q-sort, -technique*.

1935 G. H. Thomson in *Brit. Jrnl. Psychol.* July 75 Then we have $Y'\ Y = Q$.. where *Q* is a *p*-square matrix of *q*-correlations, each correlation being between *two persons*, not between two tests. **1936** W. Stephenson in *Ibid.* Apr. 345 Following Prof. G. H. Thomson's suggestion, I shall use *Q* as the sign for correlations between persons, so distinguishing them from correlations such as r_{12} between two tests... It is convenient to designate all previous factor analysis as *r* technique, and this new inverted form as *Q* technique. **1952** R. B. Cattell *Factor Analysis* vii. 93 He [*sc.* Stephenson] has particularly urged a method in which each subject writes down a set of traits or questionnaire-like statements about himself in order of their *significance* for his own personality (*Q-sort*). **1954** A. Anastasi *Psychol. Testing* xx. 543 This approach.. bears a certain resemblance to the procedure proposed by Stephenson in his 'Q-sort' technique. **1967** M. Argyle *Psychol. Interpersonal Behaviour* vii. 118 The so-called 'Q-sort' in which subjects are asked to place a series of statements on cards in order, with the cards which apply most to themselves at the top. **1972** *Jrnl. Social Psychol.* LXXXVIII. 84 The Q-sort variant known as the own-categories technique was used.

5. A unit of energy equal to 10^{18} British thermal units (very nearly 10^{21} joules).

1952 *Resources for Freedom* (President's Materials Policy Commission, U.S.) IV. xv. 213/1 In the first 18½ centuries of this era, the total input to the energy system of the world was about 6Q, equivalent to some 225 billion short tons of bituminous coal. [*Note*] 1·0Q = 1·0 × 10^{18} B.t.u. **1971** *Nature* 29 Oct. 593/1 The present annual energy consumption rate of the world is 0·2Q. **1978** *Jrnl. R. Soc. Arts* CXXVI. 605/2 The earth and its atmosphere intercepts some 5200 Q of solar energy each year, one Q representing one million, million, million British Thermal Units.

q, obs. form of cue *sb.*²; see also qu.

qabab, var. kebab.

‖**qadi, qadhi, qazi**, varr. cadi.

1885 T. P. Hughes *Dict. Islam* 255/1 It becomes a Muslim not to covet the appointment of Qāẓī. **1899** *Folk-Lore* X. 409 So strict a Musalman as one must presume a Qazi to be. **1906** F. A. Klein *Relig. of Islam* iv. 201 He appoints the Qâdi or judge, whose office and duty is to examine law-suits. **1918** G. Bell *Let.* 6 Mar. (1927) II. xvii. 448, I sat in a row with the Qadhi, the Mudir of Church Lands.., the Judge of Appeal and so on and so on. **1955** G. E. von Grunebaum *Islam* i. 11 The canon-law judge, the qâḍî, will find himself unable to take care effectively of all contingencies. **1959** *Listener* 19 Nov. 888/1 Subsequent legislation provides for a similar *qadi*'s court at Kombo St. Mary. **1971** *Illustr. Weekly India* 4 Apr. 47/1 The imperative that the law must be enforced by a Muslim *qazi* became meaningless in British India. **1977** *Times* 21 Nov. 7/3 At the service, a *qadi* read a sermon in which he said abandoning Jerusalem was like abandoning Mecca.

qaimaqam, var. kaimakam.

qanat, var. kanat.

qanon, qanun, varr. kanoon.

‖**qasida** (ka'siːda). Also 9 **kaszyde; kasida(h, quasida.** [Arab. *ḳaṣīda*.] An Arabic or Persian panegyric or elegiac poem or ode, usu. having a tripartite structure.

1819 J. L. Burckhardt *Trav. Nubia* 354 Like the eastern Arabs, they celebrate the praises of their warriors in the Kaszyde. **1842** McG. de Slane in Ibn Khallikan *Biogr. Dict.* I. p. xxxiii, The opinion held in the schools that the ancient *kasîdas* were masterpieces of art contributed also to the perversion of good taste; their plan and ideas were servilely copied, and it was by refinement of expression alone that writers could display their talent. **1885** *Encycl. Brit.* XVIII. 656/1 Those principal forms of poetry now used in common by all Mohammedan nations—the forms of the *ḳaṣída* (the encomiastic, elegiac, or satirical poem), the *ghazal* or ode [etc.]. **1903** C. Huart *Hist. Arabic Lit.* ii. 10 According to the ancient rules.. the author of a *qaṣîda* must begin by a reference to the forsaken camping-grounds. Next he must lament, and pray his comrades to halt, while he calls up the memory of the dwellers who had departed. **1907** R. A. Nicholson *Lit. Hist. Arabs* iii. 76 This fashion centres in the *Qaṣída*, or Ode, the only form, or rather the only finished type of poetry that existed in what.. may be called the classical period of Arabic literature. **1927** F. Krenkow in T. Houtsma et al. *Encycl. of Islam* II. 796/1 An Arabic (or Persian etc.) ḳaṣīda is a very artificial composition; the same rhyme has to run through the whole of the verses, however long the poem may be. *Ibid.* 796/2 The form of the ḳaṣīda has survived to modern times and I have specimens by poets still living where we find.. a description of a desert-ride by persons who live in Cairo and travel by railway. **1934** *Times Lit. Suppl.* 27 Sept. 641/2 The four main types of Persian poetical composition are still.. the *qasida*, the *ghazal*, the *masnavi* and the *ruba'iy*. **1940** F. Stark *Winter in Arabia* 45 Iuslim last night brought a singer of Qasidas. **1958** L. Durrell *Balthazar* iv. 82 He was delighted to hear some music and listened with emotion to the wild *quasidas* that the old man sang. **1964** *Listener* 25 June 1036/1 This translation .. from the Spanish of an Arabic-Andalusian *qasida* fragment from eleventh-century Toledo epitomizes one aspect of this breath of fresh air from the east which began to revivify the poetry of southern Europe. **1971** G. Household *Doom's Caravan* iii. 158 My translation of Shakespeare's sonnets into kasidahs.

qat, var. kat.

Qatabanian (ˌkætə'beɪnɪən), *a.* and *sb.* Also **Catabanian, Kata-, Qatha-.** [f. *Qatabān* (see below) + -ian.] **A.** *adj.* Of or pertaining to the kingdom of Qatabān in south Arabia, or its ancient Semitic dialect or language. **B.** *sb.* A native or inhabitant of Qatabān; the Qatabanian language. Also **Qata'banic** *a.*

1926 A. Musil *Northern Heǵâz* 310 It is named after the Catabanian, Esbonitan, and Scenitan Arabs. **1934, 1936** [see Minæan *sb.* and *a.*]. **1939** L. H. Gray *Foundations of Lang.* 364 *South Arabic* is known only from inscriptions (Minaean, Sabaean, Qathabānian, and Ḥaḍramautian) ranging, perhaps, from the eighth century B.C. to the sixth A.D., and by.. modern dialects. **1948** D. Diringer *Alphabet* II. ii. 225 The Qatabanian kingdom, with its capital at Tamna'. *Ibid.* 226 The South Arabian inscriptions.. are generally divided into five groups: The Minaean.. the Sabaean.. the Himyaritic.. the Qatabanic and the Hadhramautic. **1951** W. F. Albright in H. H. Rowley *Old Testament & Mod. Study* (1961) 9 The most archaic South-Arabic dialect, Qatabanian, shows uses of enclitic *m* more closely parallel to Proto-Sinaitic as deciphered by the writer than does any other Semitic tongue. **1959** A. F. L. Beeston *Qahtan* i. 8 *N* is the twelfth letter of the Qatabanian alphabet. *Ibid.* 12 And when the overseer of šmr announces that he desires Qatabanians to make (trading) journeys among the tribes,.. then Qatabanians may trade on their own account with the tribes. **1971** B. Doe *Southern Arabia* i. 22 It is possible to note that the languages of the Minaeans, Sabaeans, Qatabanians and Ḥaḍramaut were similar but with differing dialects. *Ibid.* ii. 70 The Qatabanian kingdom was for centuries a neighbour south-west of Saba', and the capital city was Timna', now also known as Hajar Quḥlan (Koḥlān) in the Wadi Baihān. **1973** A. K. Irvine in D. J. Wiseman *Peoples Old Testament Times* xii. 299 The apparent relationships of the South Arabian languages may suggest that while Minaean, Qatabanian, and Ḥaḍrami could have a north-eastern origin, Sabaean came rather from Central or North Arabia.

Qatari (kə'tɑːrɪ, ‖ gaʼtɑri), *sb.* and *a.* [f. *Qatar* (see below) + -i.] **A.** *sb.* A native or inhabitant of the state of Qatar in the Persian Gulf; also *Comb.*, as ***Qatari-born*** adj. **B.** *adj.* Of or pertaining to Qatar.

1959 R. Hay *Persian Gulf States* 110 The Ruler's Courts exercise jurisdiction over Qataris. **1960** *Geogr. Jrnl.* CXXVI. 447 The transcription used in this article is a conventional one, with a few exceptions which show the Qatari pronunciation of certain consonants, vowels and diphthongs. **1964** *Ann. Reg. 1963* 316 New regulations controlling foreign investment laid down that any foreign firms engaging in commerce or industry.. must have Qatari partners holding at least 51 per cent of the capital. **1970** *Guardian* 10 Apr. 11/7 Qatar is regarded.. as a protégé of Saudi Arabia, a point some Qataris indignantly deny. **1976** *Times* 3 Sept. (Qatar Suppl.) p. i/1 Qatari-born civil servants occupy many of the top-level posts. *Ibid.* p. i/7 Western expatriates as well as Qataris indisputably live well, usually employing a domestic servant or nanny... All educated Qataris speak English as their second langauge. **1978** *Financial Times* 22 Feb. 20/2 A further licence has been granted to a group of Qatari nationals to start a thirteenth bank, but it is not known when, or whether, this bank will commence business. **1979** R. S. ZAHLAN *Creation of Qatar* 118 For the next thirty years, no indication of the number of Qataris is available.

Qazaq, var. KAZAKH.

qazi: see QADI.

qere, Qᵉre, varr. KERI.

Q fever ('kjuː ˌfiːvə(r)). [f. the initial letter of QUERY *sb.*[1] + FEVER *sb.*[1]] A disease caused by the rickettsia *Coxiella burnetii* that is variable in symptoms and often resembles influenza.

1937 E. H. DERRICK in *Med. Jrnl. Australia* 21 Aug. 282/1 The suspicion arose and gradually grew into a conviction that we were here dealing with a type of fever which had not been previously described. It became necessary to give it a name, and 'Q' fever was chosen to denote it until fuller knowledge should allow a better name. **1947** *Ann. Rev. Microbiol.* I. 342 The serological diagnosis of Q fever is at present the only satisfactory one for routine work, since the clinical picture is such that Q fever may be confused with a number of other diseases. **1964** E. H. DERRICK in *Queensland's Health* Dec. 11/2 'X' is a recognised term for an unknown quantity. But Australia already had an 'X disease', now known as Murray valley encephalitis. However, the rest of the alphabet was open. Query also signified the unknown. 'Q (for query) fever' it became. *Ibid.*, Many have wrongly assumed that the 'Q' stands for Queensland. **1978** *Jrnl. R. Soc. Med.* LXXI. 765 There appear to have been no further military outbreaks of Q fever until the Cyprus epidemic of 1974.

qhat, qheche, qhom, qhwom, qhythsontyd, obs. ff. WHAT, WHICH, WHOM, WHITSUNTIDE.

‖**qi** (tʃi). Also ch'i, Qi, etc. [Chin. *qì* air, breath.] The physical life-force postulated by certain Chinese philosophers; the material principle.

1850 *Chinese Repository* XIX. 370 The following short expression of the doctrine of the Yih King is that in which probably all the literati would agree. It is from the 49th section of Chú-fútsz's entire works. 'All things.. come only from the Great Extreme (*t'ái kih*). The Great Extreme is the primordial substance (*k'í*) which, moving along, divided and made two *k'í*; that which in itself has motion is the *Yang*, and that which had rest,.. is the *Yin*.' **1917** S. COULING *Encycl. Sinica* 436/2 The nature of man consists of this *Li*, or the Ethical Principle... In its essence it is absolutely pure and good, but seeing that it is inseparable from the material element *Ch'i*.. it is from Man's birth to a greater or less extent impeded and tainted. **1958** W. WILLETTS *Chinese Art* II. vii. 586 Corresponding to this formal cause of each existence was its material cause, *ch'i*. **1964** K. K. S. CH'EN *Buddhism in China* xiv. 395 Chang Tsai (1020–1077) put forward a metaphysical system based on the theory that ch'i, ether or matter, existed at the beginning of the world. He held that ch'i consolidated itself into things at the beginning, and that things dissolved into ch'i in the end. **1971** F. MANN *Acupuncture* vi. 57 To the ancients the cornerstone of the theory of acupuncture, the concept whereby they explained its effects and action, was Qi, the energy of life. **1972** *Which?* Feb. 49/2 The energy of life (called Ch'i) flows along various 'meridians' in the body, and acupuncturists believe that if needles are inserted at.. points along these meridians.. the flow of energy in the body can be corrected. **1973** *Lancet* 14 July 58/1 They are not connected to internal organs, and Qi or anything else cannot flow along them. **1978** *Nature* 26 Oct 697/1 Arguably the most original Letter so far is a report of some experimental results on the physical basis of the traditional *yunqi* therapy—the curing of disorders through the passing of *qi* (pneuma) from doctor to patient without bodily contact.

Qiana (kɪ'ɑːnə). Chiefly *U.S.* Also **qiana**. [Invented word.] A proprietary name in the U.S. for nylon.

1968 *Official Gaz.* (U.S. Patent Office) 3 Sept. TM25/1 Qiana. For Yarns of Man Made Fibers.. First use May 15, 1968... E. I. du Pont de Nemours and Company. **1969** *Science Year* 274/1 Qiana is said to have color, clarity, and luster equal to or better than most luxurious silks. **1971** *New Yorker* 10 July 69 The commendable and reasonable sedate bathing suits produced by Edith Lances of sea-blue Qiana, which is a man-made silk. **1975** *Times* 13 May 12/4 Washable qiana jersey dress... Approx. £39.50. **1977** *Monitor* (McAllen, Texas) 26 June 1C/2 The mother of the bride wore a pale blue gown of Qiana with a fitted long-sleeved jacket. **1979** *Farmington* (New Mexico) *Daily Times* 27 May 3A/5 (Advt.), Give him his favorite Qiana shirt.

qibla(h, var. KIBLAH.

qibli, var. GIBLI.

‖**qiviut** ('kɪvɪət). [Eskimo.] The underwool of the arctic musk-ox; fibre made from this.

1965 *Sci. News Let.* 12 June 370/1 Many woolen manufacturers are enthusiastic about the principal product of the musk ox, its underwool, which the Eskimos call 'qiviut'. The fiber is similar to that of cashmere but about twice as long and half as thick. **1968** *Beaver* Winter 37/2 Eskimos call him [*sc.* the musk-ox] 'umingmak', the bearded one, and have long known his wonderful underwool as qiviut, a fibre far warmer than the silken down of the northern grey goose. **1972** *Guardian* 26 June 12/7 Collection of qiviut begins at the end of April. Bulls yield 6lb, and cows 5lb. **1979** R. FIENNES *Hell on Ice* viii. 125 The early explorers shot many musk-oxen. They took the soft wool that lies beneath the long brown hair. This *qiviut* was valuable to the Eskimo.

Q-'spoiling, *vbl. sb. Physics.* [f. Q III. 3 + SPOILING *vbl. sb.*[1]] = Q-SWITCHING *vbl. sb.* So **Q-'spoil** *v. trans.*, **Q-'spoiled** *ppl. a.*

1963 *New Scientist* 24 Oct. 201/2 A technique known as 'Q-spoiling' is used to store the laser's energy and liberate it in brief but tremendous bursts. **1966** *Appl. Physics Lett.* IX. 285 A technique involving the use of a magnetic field in 'Q'-spoiling a ruby laser cooled to 77°K is discussed. **1970** *Physics Bull.* Mar. 116/2 By temporarily 'Q-spoiling' the laser resonator by inserting a Kerr cell shutter between the high reflectivity mirror and the ruby laser rod, the energy storage capacity of the ruby was increased above the level at which relaxation oscillation would normally begin. *Ibid.*, By 1965 powers of 10^9 W in pulses of duration ~ 10 ns were produced by following the *Q*-spoiled oscillator with a series of ruby amplifiers. **1975** D. G. FINK *Electronics Engineers' Handbk.* XI. 13 The typical output of an optical laser consists of a series of spikes occurring during the major portion of the time that the laser is pumped... Q switching (Q spoiling) is a means of obtaining all the energy in a single spike of very high peak power.

Q-switch ('kjuːswɪtʃ), *sb. Physics.* Also **q-switch**. [f. Q III. 3 + SWITCH *sb.*] A means of suddenly increasing or decreasing the *Q* of a laser by effectively unblocking or blocking the optical path to one of the mirrors.

1963 *Jrnl. Appl. Physics* XXXIV. 1000/2 (*heading*) Faraday effect as Q-switch for ruby laser. *Ibid.*, The Q-switch.. was placed between the ruby and the separated end mirror. **1966** *New Scientist* 20 Oct. 93 Q-switches are employed to obtain a very powerful pulsed output from a laser by allowing the laser to store up energy; when it reaches a maximum the blockage is quickly removed, and an intense pulse of radiation is emitted. **1973** *Jrnl. Appl. Physics* XLIV. 4067/1 The oscillation of the laser with the cavity closed is sensed by a fast photodiode whose output signal opens the electro-optical Q switch. **1979** *Nature* 5 July p. vii/2 A compact pulsed ruby laser, that incorporates a q-switch.

So **Q-'switching** *vbl. sb.*, the process of pumping a laser that has a low *Q*, and so cannot oscillate, and then suddenly increasing the *Q* so that the stored energy is released in a single pulse of very high power; **Q-switch** *v. trans.*, to subject (a laser) to this process; **Q-'switched** *ppl. a.*

1963 *Jrnl. Appl. Physics* XXXIV. 1000/2 We wish to report the successful application of the Faraday effect (magneto-optic shutter) as a Q-switching technique for a ruby laser. *Ibid.* 3407/1 (*heading*) Q-switched $CaWO_4$: Nd^{3+} laser. *Ibid.*, A $CaWO_4$:Nd^{3+} laser was successfully Q-switched. **1965** *Wireless World* July 351/3 The ruby laser is Q-switched by a rotating prism. **1968** *McGraw-Hill Yearbk. Sci. & Technol.* 223 Saturable absorbers have recently been used very successfully to Q-switch ruby and neodymium-doped lasers. **1968** *New Scientist* 24 Oct. 205/1 Q-switching is a technique for producing giant laser pulses by preventing lasing action until a large amount of energy has been pumped into the atoms responsible. **1970** *Sci. Amer.* Mar. 41 They used the 104-inch telescope to transmit and detect pulses of 50-nanosecond duration produced by a 'Q-switched' (short-pulse) ruby laser. **1974** *Physics Bull.* Jan. 13/1 A four stage Q switched ruby laser is used to fire a pulse every three seconds, with a pulse length of a few tens of nanoseconds and an output energy of about 3 J.

†**qu, q**, var. of CUE *sb.*[1], half-a-farthing. *Obs.*

c **1440**, **1617** [see CUE]. **1594** LYLY *Moth. Bomb.* in *Old Pl.* (1814) I. 264 [To Halfpenny] Rather pray there be no fall of money for then wilt thou go for a q. **1597** *1st Pt. Return fr. Parnass.* I. i. 434 Adew single beare and three qus of breade. **1674** JEAKE *Arith.* (1696) 77 Some.. divide the Farthing into 2 Ques, the Q into 2 Cees.

‖**qua** (kweɪ, kwɑː), *adv.* Also **quà, quâ**. [L., the abl. sing. fem. of *qui* who.] In so far as; in the capacity of.

1647 WARD *Simp. Cobler* 56 Every man was as good a man as your Selfe, *qua* man. **1649** *Bounds Publ. Obed.* (1650) 90 The Apostle commands Wives to submit to their Husbands, surely *quà* Husbands, not *quà* men. **1776** *Claim Roy Rada Churn* 17/1 (Stanf.) A body corporate, *quà* corporate, cannot make an affidavit. **1885** *Manch. Exam.* 4 Apr. 4/6 Their censures are not directed against the Church *quà* Church, but against the Church *quâ* Establishment.

†**qua**, *sb.* abbrev. of L. *quadrans* farthing; cf. QUADRANT *sb.*[1] 2 b. *Obs.*

1631 WEEVER *Anc. Fun. Mon.* 766 It was valued at.. three pounds foure shillings, pennie, halfe penny qua.

qua, obs. northern form of WHO.

Qua, var. KWA.

quaa, variant of QUAW, bog. *Sc.*

quaake, obs. var. of QUACK *v.*[2]

Quaalude ('kwɑːl(j)uːd). *Pharm.* A proprietary name for methaqualone; also, a tablet of this.

1966 *Official Gaz.* (U.S. Patent Office) 12 Apr. TM72/1 William H. Rorer, Inc., Fort Washington, Pa... *Quaalude*. For Sedative-hypnotic tablets. First use Aug. 5, 1965. **1967** H. BECKMAN *Dilemmas in Drug Therapy* 186/2 As 'newer' hypnotics I list the following:.. methaqualone (Quaalude), 150 mg. at bedtime. **1968** *Trade Marks Jrnl.* 4 Dec. 2107/2 *Quāālude*... Sedative-hypnotic pharmaceutical preparations. William H. Rorer, Inc... Fort Washington. **1974** *Saturday Night* (Toronto) July 21/2 A quick trip to an interior bedroom, a little Quaalude to relax, a little coke to get the performing ego's motor humming and you were ready to face down King Kong. **1977** *Rolling Stone* 13 Jan. 31/1 A doctor had prescribed the chalky white Quaaludes to help her sleep at night. **1979** *Guardian* 9 Jan. 5/8 Quaalude (Mandrax in Britain).. has a reputation as an aphrodisiac and is one of the fastest rising drugs of abuse in the U.S.

†**quab**, *sb.*[1] *Obs. rare.* Also 7 quabbe, 8 quobb(e. [a. MDu. (and MLG.) *quabbe* (Du. *kwab*, *kwabbe*, (L)G. *quabbe*, Da. *kvabbe*, Sw. *qvabba*), burbot or eelpout, goby, tadpole; var. of *quappe*, OLG. *quappa*.]

1. a. A sea-slug (see HOLOTHURIAN *sb.*). **b.** An eelpout or burbot. **c.** (See QUABLING.)

1617 MINSHEU *Ductor*, A Quabbe, a kinde of fish ..*Holothuria*. *Ibid.*, ..A Quabbe, or Eele-powt.. *Mustela fluviatilis*. **1748** *Phil. Trans.* XLV. 174 An extraordinary Fish in that Country [Russia], called the Quab, which is reported to be first a Tadpole, then a Frog, and at last a Fish. **1799** W. TOOKE *View Russian Emp.* III. 113 Quobbs are likewise in the Irtysh in surprising numbers.

2. *fig.* A crude or shapeless thing.

1628 FORD *Lover's Mel.* III. iii, I will show your highness A trifle of mine own brain.. a scholar's fancy, A quab; 'tis nothing else, a very quab.

quab, *sb.*[2] *Obs.* exc. *dial.* Also 7 **quabbe**; *dial.* **quob**. [= Du. *kwabbe* a boggy place; cf. MLG. *quabbel* slime, and see QUAG.] A marshy spot, a bog. Cf. QUABMIRE.

1617 MINSHEU *Ductor*, A Quabbe, or quagmire. *a* **1656** USSHER *Ann.* VI. (1658) 596 Defended by the Mæotis and those quabs. **1847** HALLIWELL, *Quob*, a quicksand or bog. *West.* **1879** MISS JACKSON *Shropsh. Word-bk.*, *Quob*, a marshy spot in a field; a quagmire.

quab, *v. Obs.* exc. *dial.* Also *dial.* **quob**. [var. of QUAP *v.*; cf. G. *quabbeln* in same sense.] *intr.* To beat, throb, quiver. Hence **quabbing** *ppl. a.*

1663 *Flagellum, or O. Cromwell* (1672) 123 A dangerous impostume [*printed* -ure] of ambition, whose quabbing, beating pains gaue them no rest. **1863** BARNES *Dorset Gloss.*, *Quob*, to quiver, like jelly. **1881** *Leicester Gloss.*, *Quob*, to throb.

qua-bird ('kwɑːbɜːd). *U.S.* Also 8 **quaw-**. [f. *qua*, imitative of its note + BIRD *sb.*] The Night Heron of North America, *Nycticorax nævius* or *Gardeni*.

1789–96 MORSE *Amer. Geog.* I. 212 Quaw-bird or Frog Catcher. **1835** *Penny Cycl.* IV. 471 The Night Heron or Qua Bird.. is found in both the old and new world. **1890** E. GOSSE *Life P. H. Gosse* 115 Thompson's Point, the former residence of the night-heron or qua-bird.

†'**quabling**. *Obs. rare*$^{-1}$. [f. QUAB *sb.*[1] + -LING.] A goby or gudgeon.

1617 MINSHEU *Ductor*, A Quabling, or little Quabbe, ..*gobio*.

quabmire. *Obs.* exc. *dial.* Also *dial.* **quob-**. [f. QUAB *sb.*[2] or *v.*, but found earlier.] A quagmire.

1597 BROUGHTON *Ep. Nobil. Eng.* Wks. 570 Oversights, which for a dry causie bring us to quabmyres. **1841** HARTSHORNE *Salop. Antiq.* Gloss. 539 *Quobmire*, a quagmire.

quacha, obs. form of QUAGGA.

†'**quacham**. *Obs. rare*$^{-1}$. (?)

1515 BARCLAY *Egloges* iv. (1570) C. iv. b/2 We other Shepherdes.. Of common sortes, leane, ragged and rent, Fed with rude frowise, with quacham, or with crudd.

quacia, obs. form of QUASSIA.

quack (kwæk), *sb.*[1] Also 7 **quacke**. [Abbrev. of QUACKSALVER.]

1. a. An ignorant pretender to medical or surgical skill; one who boasts to have a knowledge of wonderful remedies; an empiric or impostor in medicine. = CHARLATAN 2.

1659 T. PECKE *Parnassi Puerp.* 145 Sir Quack his Patient told, nothing could cure The stubborn Feaver. **1683** KENNETT tr. *Erasm. on Folly* 47 All these hard named fellows cannot make So great a figure as a single Quacke. **1722** DE FOE *Plague* (1754) 36 Running after Quacks and Mountebanks.. for Medicines and Remedies. **1783** CRABBE *Village* I, A potent quack, long versed in human ills, Who first insults the victim whom he kills. **1809** W. IRVING *Knickerb.* (1861) 127 He who has once been under the hands of a quack, is for ever after prone to dabble in drugs. **1880** BEALE *Slight Ailm.* 22 Persons would be easily influenced by what the quack says.

b. *slang* (orig. *Austral.* and *N.Z.*). A doctor (with no implication that he is unqualified); also in *Mil.* use, a medical officer.

1919 W. H. DOWNING *Digger Dial.* 40 *Quack*, a medical officer. *c* **1926** 'MIXER' *Transport Workers' Song Bk.* 43 And ask me if I want a 'sub'. For to take me to the 'quack'. **1943** *Coast to Coast* 1942 29 Might be he lose his leg if we don't get him across right away to the quack. **1945** C. H. WARD-JACKSON *Piece of Cake* (ed. 2) 51 *Quack*, medical officer. **1960** J. IGGULDEN *Storms of Summer* 169 I'll get the quack at the Bush Hospital to have a look at it in the morning. **1962** GRANVILLE *Dict. Sailors' Slang* 93/1 *Quack, the*, medical officer. Jocular. **1976** D. IRELAND *Glass Canoe* 136, I go along to this quack and he says Get back to the surf and get some green vegetables into you.

2. *transf.* One who professes a knowledge or skill concerning subjects of which he is ignorant. = CHARLATAN 3.

1638 FORD *Fancies* III. i, There he sits.. The very quack [*eds.* quaik, quake] of fashions. **1710** STEELE *Tatler* No. 195 ¶2 Rules for knowing the Quacks in both Professions [Law and Physic]. **1782** COWPER *Progr. Err.* 474 Church quacks, with passions under no command, Who fill the world with doctrines contraband. **1864** BURTON *Scot Abr.* I. v. 249 There is scarcely an instance of a lord rector having been a clamorous quack or a canting fanatic.

3. *attrib.* and *Comb.*, as *quack-advertisement*, *-bill*, *-bookseller*, *-doctor*, *-medicine*, etc.; also *quack-adoring*, *-ridden* adjs.

1653 H. More *Antid. Ath.* III. ix. §2 (*Schol.*) Principles that no..pert Saucy Quack-Theologist can any way enervate. **1695** tr. *Colbatch's New Lt. Chirurg. Put out* Title-p., The Base Imposture of his Quack Medicines. *a* **1704** T. Brown *Table Talk* in *Coll. Poems* (1705) 130 A Chymist.. put out a Quack-Bill. **1707** Hearne *Collect.* (O.H.S.) II. 65 Mr. Bolton..now a quack-Physitian in London. **1751** Warburton *Pope's Wks.* IV. 18 The bills of Quack-Doctors and Quack-Booksellers being usually pasted together on the same posts. **1785** *Europ. Mag.* VIII. 469 A dialogue between the doctor and his clerk satirizes quack advertisements. **1839** Carlyle *Chartism* v. 138 Europe lay pining,..quack-ridden, hag-ridden. **1855** Browning *Bp. Blougram* 366 Quack-nonsense about crowns, And..The vague idea of setting things to rights. **1874** Helps *Soc. Press.* ii. 26 A puffing, advertising, quack-adoring world.

quack (kwæk), *sb.*[2] [Imitative: cf. Du. *kwak*, G. *quack*, Sw. *qvack* (of ducks or frogs), Icel. *kvak* twittering of birds. See also quake *int.*] The harsh cry characteristic of a duck; a sound resembling, or imitating this. **b.** *humorously.* A duck.

1839 *Lett. fr. Madras* (1843) 290 Showing his teeth, and uttering a loud quack! **1869** Blackmore *Lorna D.* x, He gave me a look from his one little eye..and then a loud quack to second it. *a* **1897** *Bird o' Freedom* (Barrère & Leland), I send her herewith a couple of quacks. **1901** A. R. Conder *Seal Silence* 211 The voice of the footman rose high above the general quack of conversation.

† **quack**, *sb.*[3] *Obs. rare.* In 5 quakke, 6 quacke. [Imitative: cf. quackle *v.*[1] and LG. *quakken* to moan, groan.] A state of hoarseness or croaking in the throat.

c **1386** Chaucer *Reeve's T.* 232 He yexeth, and he speketh thurgh the nose As he were on the quakke, or on the pose. **1577** Harrison *England* II. xxii. (1877) I. 338 The smoke.. was reputed a far better medicine to keepe the goodman and his familie from the quacke or pose.

quack (kwæk), *sb.*[4] *U.S.* [var. of quick *sb.*[2]] Couch-grass, *Agropyron repens*, a European grass with creeping roots, widely naturalized elsewhere. Cf. quick *sb.*[2]

1833 L. C. Beck *Bot. N. & Middle States* 416 A troublesome weed. Couch Grass. Quack. **1872** *Rep. Vermont Board Agric.* I. 289 He who sets out to subdue a piece of quack must resolve on no half-way measures. **1909** *N.Y. Even. Post* (semi-weekly ed.) 11 Mar. 5 In conquering the quack he did the one thing that could have enabled him to get a crop from that unfertilized soil. **1930** *Times Educ. Suppl.* 31 May 248/1 It [*sc.* couchgrass] has a good many names: squitch, scutch, quack..are all in use. **1948** H. A. Jacobs *We chose Country* 189 The big garden across the road, where we fought quack instead of weeds, really established us.

2. *Comb.* **quack-grass** = prec. sense.

1822 A. Eaton *Man. Bot.* (ed. 3) 404 *Triticum repens*, wheat-grass, couch-grass, quack-grass... Very troublesome in fertile soil, and useful in barren sand. **1839** J. Buel *Farmer's Compan.* xiv. 151 One of our neighbours has been enabled completely to eradicate quack-grass in his Indian corn. **1884** G. Vasey *Agric. Grasses U.S.* 108 Quack grass. .. There has been a good deal of discussion relative to this grass, some pronouncing it one of the vilest of weeds. **1949** *This Week Mag.* 17 Sept. 2/2 The quackgrass and the sassafras is getting the best of him. **1970** *Daily Progress* (Charlottesville, Va.) 24 May 4/2 Burning robs the topsoil of its fertility..and actually increases the growth of quackgrass, weeds, and other unwanted, troublesome, perennial plants.

quack (kwæk), *v.*[1] [f. quack *sb.*[1]]

1. *intr.* To play the quack. **a.** To pretend to have medical knowledge; to dabble ignorantly in medicine. **b.** To talk pretentiously and ignorantly, like a quack. †Also with *of*.

1628 Venner *Baths of Bathe* (1650) 362 In quacking for Patients he is so kind and free of his service. **1678** Butler *Hud.* III. i. 330 To quack of universal cures. *Ibid.* 364 A Virtuoso, able To smatter, quack, and cant, and dabble. **1722** De Foe *Plague* (Rtldg.) 45 Ignorant Fellows; quacking and tampering in Physick. **1756** C. Lucas *Ess. Waters* I. Pref., Enlighten then their understandings..and who then will venture to quack, or be quacked? **1876** G. Meredith *Beauch. Career* III. ii. 29 A wiseacre who went quacking about the country, expecting to upset the order of things.

2. *trans.* To advertise, puff, or palm off with fraudulent and boastful pretensions, as a quack-medicine or means of cure. †Also with *forth*. † *to quack titles*: to invent new titles for old books in order to make them sell.

1651 Biggs *New Disp.* Pref. 9 To be Quacked forth in Bartholmew-Fayr. **1651** Cleveland *Poems* 33 Could I (in Sir Emp'ricks tone) Speak pills in phrase, and quack destruction. **1715** Mrs. Centlivre *Gotham Elect.* I, My third Son is a bookseller..he has an admirable knack at quacking Titles. **1727** Bradley *Fam. Dict.* s.v. *Gill ale*, A notorious Imposition, which is quack'd upon the World..to be a great Restorative and Curer of Consumptions. **1830** *Examiner* 610/2 The Politician must be quacked, paragraphed,..and coteried into notoriety.

3. To treat after the fashion of a quack; to administer quack medicines to; to seek to remedy or put right by empirical or ignorant treatment. Also with *up*.

1746 H. Walpole *Lett. to Mann* (1833) II. 124 If he has any skill in quacking madmen, his art may perhaps be of service now. **1757** Eliz. Griffith *Lett. Henry & Frances* (1767) I. 84, I am..as 'hoarse as bondage'. I shall there-fore stay here to-night, and quack myself. **1778** *Sketches for Tabernacle Frames* 17 For quacking Souls you cannot be attack'd. **1810** Bentham *Packing* (1821) 144 Epitaph on a Valetudinarian, who quacked himself to death. **1820** Col. Hawker *Diary* (1893) I. 195, I tried with bricks, baskets and everything..to quack up one of them [defective chimneys]. *a* **1876** Ht. Martineau *Autobiog.* (1877) I. 147 The less its condition is quacked..the better for the mind's health. **1925** *Scribner's Mag.* Oct. 385/1 Time..has not obliterated the love of being quacked.

Hence **quacked** *ppl. a.*

a **1876** Ht. Martineau *Autobiog.* (1877) II. 461 Such exhortations are too low for even the..quacked morality of a time of theological suspense.

quack (kwæk), *v.*[2] Also 8 quaake. [Imitative: cf. Du. *kwakken*, G. *quacken* to croak, quack. Older variants are quackle, quake, queck, q.v.]

1. *intr.* Of a duck: To utter its characteristic note. Also with cognate obj.

1617 Minsheu *Ductor*, To Quacke as a ducke,..*coaxare*. *a* **1712** W. King (J.), Wild ducks quack where grasshoppers did sing. **1727** Bailey vol. II, *Quacking* [*ed.* 1731 *Quaaking*], making a Noise, as ducks do. **1755** Johnson, *Quack*... This word is often written *quaake*, to represent the sound better. **1815** [see quacking *vbl. sb.*[2]]. **1862** G. Kearley *Links in Chain* ix. (1863) 222 [The duck] no sooner recognized the aviary..than he quacked vehemently. **1869** Blackmore *Lorna D.* x, There were thirteen ducks..and..they all quacked very movingly. **1893** Earl Dunmore *Pamirs* I. 185 They [some ducks]..quacked the quack of derision at us.

b. Of a raven or frog: To croak. *rare.*

1727 Boyer *Anglo-Fr. Dict.*, To Quack (*or* to croak, as Ravens do), *croasser*. **1892** Tennyson *Foresters* II. ii. 97 My frog that used to quack When I vaulted on his back.

2. *transf.* To make a harsh sound like the note of a duck; to make a noisy outcry.

a **1624** Bp. M. Smith *Serm.* (1632) 136 An example to all busie-bodyes, that will dare..to quacke against their betters. **1894** Hall Caine *Manxman* 265 He puffed till his lips quacked, though the pipe gave out no smoke.

quack, quack-belly, -breech, -myre, quacker: see quake *v.*[1], quaker.

quacker ('kwækə(r)). *colloq.* [f. quack *v.*[2] + -er.] One that quacks; a duck. Also *fig.*

1846 *Swell's Night Guide* 75 Jest pipe her—she turns her ogles up like a croaking quacker (dying duck). **1965** *New Statesman* 18 June 980/2 The noisiest quackers have now felt a wind of deflation beginning to stir about the world and have fallen silent. **1978** *Times* 23 Feb. 16/4 Though ducks are plentiful along the Thames..two dozen quackers were brought along.

quackery[1] ('kwækərɪ). [f. quack *sb.*[1] + -ery.] The characteristic practices or methods of a quack; charlatanry.

1709–11 J. Spinke (*title*) Quackery Unmask'd. **1717** Lady M. W. Montagu *Let. to Abbé Conti* 1 Apr., I know you Condemn the quackery..as much as you revere the.. truths, in which we both agree. **1798** *Trans. Soc. Arts* XVI. 190 All the nostrums offered..are mere quackery. **1840** Carlyle *Heroes* (1858) 187 Quackery and dupery do abound; in religions..they have fearfully abounded. **1874** Mahaffy *Soc. Life Greece* ix. 273 The old quackery of charms and incantations. **1885** *Contemp. Rev.* June 908 Theosophy [is]..one of the least interesting of spiritual quackeries.

quackery[2] ('kwækərɪ). *nonce-wd.* [f. quack *v.*[2] + -ery.] The quacking of a number of ducks.

1828 J. Wilson in *Blackw. Mag.* XXIV. 293 A sort of low, thick, gurling,..nor unmusical quackery. **1831** *Ibid.* XXX. 966 The quackery of a startled storm of wild ducks.

quackhood ('kwækhʊd). [f. quack *sb.*[1] + -hood.] = quackery[1].

1843 Carlyle *Past & Pr.* III. xiii, To worship new and ever-new forms of Quackhood.

quacking ('kwækɪŋ), *vbl. sb.*[1] [f. quack *v.*[1] + -ing[1].] The action or practice of playing the quack; ignorant dabbling in medicine.

1652 Wadsworth tr. *Colmenero's Treat. Chocolate* Introd. Verses. Leave Quacking; and Enucleate The vertues of Chocolate. **1664** Evelyn *Sylva* 34 Quacking is not my trade: I speak only here as a plain Husband-man. **1702** De Foe *Mock Mourners* in *Misc.* (1703) 46 All other Remedies ..Are Tampering and Quacking with the State. **1733** Cheyne *Eng. Malady* III. Introd. (1734) 265 The Medicines I have only hinted at to prevent the Quacking of Patients themselves. **1827** J. W. Croker in *C. Papers* 7 Aug. (1884), They found..the patient so reduced by..alternate quacking and indulgence.

attrib. **1682** S. Pordage *Medal Rev.* 210 Some State-Physicians..on thee..would try some quacking trick.

quacking ('kwækɪŋ), *vbl. sb.*[2] [f. quack *v.*[2] + -ing[1].] The uttering of the harsh sound denoted by the vb.

1815 W. H. Ireland *Scribbleomania* 1 The sage waddling goose, Whose quacking you'll own is the very repeater Of my famous Muse. **1880** Mackenzie *Dis. Throat & Nose* I. 491 The barking of a dog or the quacking of a duck. **1892** Baring-Gould *Trag. Cæsars* I. 218 Being incommoded by the quacking of frogs he ordered them to be silent.

quacking ('kwækɪŋ), *ppl. a.*[1] [f. quack *v.*[1] + -ing[2].] That acts or practises as a quack.

1628 Venner *Baths of Bathe* (1650) 357 To..reject the counsell of any quacking Physician. **1722** De Foe *Plague* (1754) 39 These quacking sort of Fellows rais'd great Gains out of the miserable People. **1843** Le Fevre *Life Trav. Phys.* II. I. xiv. 31 A more quacking race..does not exist, and they are always swallowing some kind of medicine.

quacking ('kwækɪŋ), *ppl. a.*[2] [f. quack *v.*[2] + -ing[2].] That quacks or makes a sound as a duck.

1620 Dekker *Villanies Disc.* xvii, *A Quacking cheate*, a Ducke. **1898** R. Hichens *The Londoners* 82 The quacking voice hurled out these last three words with impressive emphasis.

quackish ('kwækɪʃ), *a.* [f. quack *sb.*[1] + -ish.] Of the nature of a quack or quackery.

1732 *Hist. Litteraria* III. 558 To complete his quackish Farce [he] spread printed Bills all over Paris. **1790** Burke *Fr. Rev.* 198 All the arts of quackish parade. **1800** *Monthly Mag.* XIII. 131 Regular, not quackish innovating practitioners. **1865** *Sat. Rev.* Nov. 570 Another.. confounds preaching the Gospel with a quackish interpretation of prophecies.

Hence **'quackishly** *adv.*

1816 J. Gilchrist *Philos. Etym.* 119 Do not let them.. quackishly boast of new light and great discovery.

quackism ('kwækɪz(ə)m). [f. quack *sb.*[1] + -ism.] Quackery, charlatanism.

1720–21 *Lett. Mist's Jrnl.* (1722) II. 22, I understand that is exploded as Quackism by the Judicious. **1762** Lloyd *St. James's Mag.* I. iv, Others, in the true spirit of Quackism, circulate their intentions by handbills. **1833** Carlyle *Misc. Ess., Cagliostro* (1899) 274 What unmeasured masses of Quackism were set fire to.

quackle ('kwæk(ə)l), *v.*[1] *Obs.* exc. *dial.* [Imitative: cf. quack *sb.*[3]] *trans.* and *intr.* To choke.

1622 S. Ward *Woe to Drunkards* (1627) 22 The drinke or something in the cup quackled him, stucke so in his throat, that..[it] strangled him presently. **1655** Gurnall *Chr. in Arm.* I. (1665) 72 God knowes, thou art almost quackled with thy teares. **1806** Bloomfield *Wild Flowers* Poems (1845) 221 Some quack'ling cried, 'let go your hold'; The farmers held the faster. **1865** *Standard* 19 Sept., The verb 'to quackle' is used in Suffolk in reference to suffocation, when caused by 'drink going the wrong way', or by smoke. **1895** Rye *Gloss. E. Anglia*, s.v. 'My cough quackles me'. 'He fanged her by the throat and nearly quackled her'.

quackle ('kwæk(ə)l), *v.*[2] [In form a deriv. of quack *v.*[2], but found earlier.] *intr.* To quack, as a duck. Hence **'quackling** *vbl. sb.* and *ppl. a.*

1564–78 Bulleyn *Dial. agst. Pest.* (1888) 64 Vpon a tyme when quacklyng Duckes did speake and caklyng hennes could talke. **1825** Hone *Every-day Bk.* I. 534 The loud.. quackling of ducks..is a sign of rain. **1837** Carlyle *Fr. Rev.* II. I. i, Simple ducks..quackle for crumbs from young royal fingers. **1865** Mrs. Whitney *Gayworthys* I. 11 Underneath ..splashed and quackled the ducks.

quackmire, variant of quakemire.

quack-quack ('kwæk'kwæk). [Imitative: see quack *sb.*[2]] An imitation of the note of a duck; a nursery name for a duck.

1865 Dickens *Mut. Fr.* III. xv, Mew says the cat, Quack-quack says the duck. **1869** Ouida *Puck* xxxviii. (1873) 491 [They] could not themselves tell for their lives..a canvas-back duck from a quack-quack of the gutter. **1889** Mivart *Truth* 226 'Quack-quack' and 'gee-gee' are just as good abstract universal terms as 'duck' and 'horse'.

Hence **quack-quacking** *vbl. sb.*

1824 Carlyle tr. *Wilhelm Meister* (1864) II. 257 As the duck on the pond..to the future quack-quacking and gibble-gabbling of his life.

quacksalver ('kwæksælvə(r)). Also 6–7 quack(e)-, 7 quaksaluer. [a. early mod.Du. (16th c.) *quacksalver* (Kilian; mod.Du. *kwakzalver*), whence also G. *quacksalber*, Sw. *qvacksalfvare*: the second element is f. *salf*, *zalf* salve, ointment, and the first is commonly regarded as the stem of *quacken* (mod.Du. *kwakken*) to quack.

On this view a quacksalver is one who 'quacks' or boasts about the virtues of his salves; it has however been suggested that *quack-* or *kwak-* may mean 'to work in a feeble bungling fashion' (Franck).]

1. An ignorant person who pretends to a knowledge of medicine or of wonderful remedies: = quack *sb.*[1] 1.

Very common in 17th c.; in later times largely superseded by the abbreviation quack *sb.*[1]

1579 Gosson *Sch. Abuse* (Arb.) 53 A quacke-saluers Budget of filthy receites. **1605** B. Jonson *Volpone* II. ii, They are quack-saluers, Fellowes, that liue by senting oyles, and drugs. **1658** Rowland tr. *Moufet's Theatr. Ins.* 1074 One accidental rash cure of a disease..makes a Quacksalver a great Physician. **1719** D'Urfey *Pills* (1872) IV. 87 Come you Quack-salvers that do kill Sometimes a Patient by your skill. **1856** Vaughan *Mystics* (1860) II. VIII. ix. 98 What a gulf between the high personage our romance imagines and ..that shuffling quacksalver which our matter-of-fact research discovers.

attrib. *a* **1670** Hacket *Cent. Serm.* (1675) 544 St. Peter had no such Quacksalver tricks in Divinity.

2. *transf.* = quack 2.

1611 W. Baker *Panegyr. Verses* in *Coryat's Crudities*, The Anatomie dissection or cutting up of that great Quack-salver of words Mr. Thomas Coryate our British Mercurie. **1889** Swinburne *Stud. B. Jonson* 43 Brother Zeal-of-the-land is no vulgar impostor, no mere religious quacksalver.

Hence **quacksalverism**, † **-salvery**, quackery.

1617 Minsheu *Ductor*, Quacksaluerie. **1864** Carlyle *Fredk. Gt.* IV. 392 Sublime quacksalverism.

† **quacksalving** ('kwæksælvɪŋ), *ppl. a. Obs.* [f. **quacksalve* vb. (inferred from quacksalver) + -ing[2].] Quackish.

1. Of things: Belonging to, or characteristic of, a quacksalver.

1608 Middleton *Mad World* II. vi, Any quacksalving terms will serve for this purpose. *a* **1691** Bp. Croft in *Somers Tracts* (ed. Scott) VII. 290 Generals and particulars, the *quid*, the *quale*, the *quantum*, and such-like quack-salving forms.

2. Of persons: Resembling, acting like, a quack.

1608 DEKKER *Lanth. & Cand.* k. Quack-saluing Empericks. **1620** MELTON *Astrolog.* 18 If you should kill three hundred, you would still remain but a Quack-salving Physician. **1622** MASSINGER & DEKKER *Virg. Mart.* IV. i, Quacksalving, cheating mountebanks! **1649** C. WALKER *Hist. Independ.* II. 207 A Quack-salving Doctor of Phisick.

Hence †**quacksalvingly** *adv.*, in the manner of a quack. *Obs.*

1652 GAULE *Magastrom.* 105 An experiment in physick or medicine, sc., brought to effect, many times, empirically, quacksalvingly, ignorantly.

†'**quackster.** *Obs. rare*⁻¹. [f. QUACK *v.*[1] + -STER.] A quack, quacksalver.

1709 *Brit. Apollo* II. No. 44. 3/1 The Quackster..with Death signs our Quietus.

quacky ('kwækɪ), *a.*[1] [f. QUACK *sb.*[1] + -Y[1].] Inclined to quackery.

1836 *Southern Lit. Messenger* II. 327 The critical department of this work..is in our opinion decidedly quacky. **1846** POE *Criticism* Wks. 1864 III. 23 Who although a little quacky per se has..a whole legion of active quacks at his control.

quacky ('kwækɪ), *a.*[2] [f. QUACK *sb.*[2] + -Y[1].] Of voices: Having the harsh quality characteristic of the cry of a duck. Hence '**quackiness**.

1895 *Forum* (N.Y.) June 502 Our women's voices are.. hardened..into an habitual 'quacky' or metallic quality... 'Quackiness' and shrillness prevail less in the Southern States than in the Northern and Western.

quad (kwɒd), *sb.*[1], abbrev. (orig. in Oxford slang) of QUADRANGLE *sb.* 2.

1820 in *Brasenose Ale* 8 When first thy Quad, O Brasenose, sprung from earth. **1827** *Sporting Mag.* XXI. 70 Mr. Protheroe once met me in 'Quad' during the frost. **1861** HUGHES *Tom Brown at Oxf.* i, The rooms ain't half so large or good in the inner quad. **1884** *Pall Mall G.* 24 Jan. 3/2 Pump Court—the dreariest of all the Temple quads.

quad (kwɒd), *sb.*[2], abbrev. of QUADRAT *sb.* 2.

1880 in WEBSTER Suppl. **1884** *Western Morn. News* 17 July 4/6 A quad is a compositor's instrument for the filling up of blanks. **1884** TUER (*title*) Quads within Quads, for Authors, Editors, and Devils. **1884** *Pall Mall G.* 1 Aug. 4/2 'Quads' in the present case are a trade term applicable to printers' jokes.

quad (kwɒd), *sb.*[3], abbrev. of QUADRUPLET.

1896 *Daily News* 2 June 9/2 Stocks was paced by five triplets and a quad. **1897** *Whitaker's Alm.* 641/2 A quad team did a flying quarter in 24·6 secs. **1951** M. ABERCROMBIE et al. *Dict. Biol.* 182 An armadillo (*Dasypodus*) always has identical quads from a single ovum. **1974** *Publishers Weekly* 26 Aug. 302/3 The good sports books seem to come in quads or pairs: four Babe Ruth books, two on [etc.]. **1975** *Nature* 3 Apr. 379/2 If the same pairs, triples, quads.., of references are observed in a number of articles, there is an implied consensus of opinion. **1978** *Daily Tel.* 4 Dec. 2/6 A five-year-old Friesian cow has given birth to quads. **1979** *Daily Tel.* 16 Nov. 3/4 Quads were born by Caesarean operation at St. Mary's Hospital, Paddington.

quad (kwɒd), *sb.*[4], abbrev. of QUADRUPED 1 b.

1894 ASTLEY *Fifty Years Life* I. 97 He was mounted on a sorry old quad. *Ibid.* II. 88, I stuck to my quad and rode into the paddock.

quad, *sb.*[5]: see QUAD *a.*[1]

quad (kwɒd), *sb.*[6] *Teleph.* [Abbrev. of QUADRUPLEX *a.* and *sb.*] A group of four insulated conductors twisted together, the conductors usu. forming two circuits. Also *attrib.* or as *adj.*, as ***quad cable***.

1922 *Bell Syst. Techn. Jrnl.* I. 72 The cable is of quadded construction, that is, the wires are first wrapped with dry paper for insulation and twisted into pairs and then two pairs are twisted into what is called a quad. **1940** *Chambers's Techn. Dict.* 691/1 *Quad* (or *star-quad*) *cable*, lead-covered cable in which the unit group is four paper-insulated conductors twisted together, opposite conductors forming the go and return circuits of a four-wire channel respectively. **1941** A. E. KNOWLTON *Stand. Handbk. Electr. Engineers* (ed. 7) xxii. 2075 A quad is formed by twisting together two individual pairs,..in the same manner that each pair is formed. **1958** J. R. G. SMITH *Elem. Telecommunications Pract.* v. 72 The quads are then made up in the number of layers required for the size of the cable.

quad (kwɒd), *sb.*[7] [Abbrev. of QUADRILATERAL *a.* and *sb.*] **1.** *Naut.* A four-sided jib used on racing yachts. Also *attrib.*

1937 *Sun* (Baltimore) 4 Aug. 14/1 Endeavour's board of strategy had ordered a new quadrilateral Genoa jib made of synthetic silk and similar to the big 'quad' which has proved so effective in Ranger's windward work. **1937** *Yachting Monthly* LXIII. 376/1 Both yachts broke out their Genoa jibs, but whereas Ranger's was a double-clewed sail, or 'quad', that aboard the challenger was somewhat smaller. *Ibid.* 378/1 Vanderbilt sprang his own choice in head rigs and set a wonderful quad Genoa. **1938** *Britannica Bk. of Year* 712/1 A feature of 'Ranger's' rig was the efficient use of quadrilateral jibs and particularly of a large 'quad' Genoa jib made of rayon.

2. *Radio.* An aerial in the form of a square or rectangle broken in the middle of one side. Freq. *attrib.*

1961 *Amateur Radio Handbk.* (ed. 3) xiii. 385/2 A quad aerial is practicable for 14 Mc/s but it is, of course, a one-band aerial; however, 21 and 28 Mc/s quads can be nested instead inside a 14 Mc/s structure without serious interference. **1962** *Flight Internat.* LXXXI. 596/1 A quad-helix aerial could be seen... It is one of 52 Cubic installations furnished for acquisition, telemetry and communications for manned orbital flights. **1976** PERKOWSKI & STRAL *Joy of CB* xi. 125 Even greater directionality is achieved with a stacked quad consisting of four elements.

quad, *sb.*[8]: see QUAD *a.*[2]

quad (kwɒd), *sb.*[9] [Abbrev. of QUADRILLION.] A unit of energy equal to 10^{15} British thermal units (very nearly 10^{18} joules).

1974 *Newsweek* 7 Oct. 84/2 The current standard energy forecast is that U.S. demand will double in the next ten years to nearly 145 'quads' (or quadrillion BTU's). **1976** *Sci. Amer.* Jan. 21/2 Without any new initiatives the need for imported oil will rise steadily from about 12 quads at present to more than 60 in the year 2000. **1976** *National Observer* (U.S.) 17 Apr. 8/3 The nation's energy consumption in 1974 was about 73 quads. **1980** *Nature* 10 Apr. 501/2 The first assumes a level of energy consumption in the US of 71 quads, equal to estimates of consumption in 1975 when the study was started.

quad (kwɒd), *a.*[1] and *sb.*[5], abbrev. of QUADRUPLE *a.* and *sb.* **A.** *adj.*

1888 in JACOBI *Printers' Vocab.* **1891** *Star* 12 Nov. 1/1 Printing Plant, including..quad crown perfecting machine, quad demy and double demy machines. **1961** *Times* 30 Oct. (Brit. Posters Suppl.) p. iii/6 Posters ranging from quad-crown to crown-folio. **1967** *Electronics* 6 Mar. 158/1 One manufacturer..offers a 'quad 2-input OR gate' that actually has three 2-input AND gates and one 3-input AND gate feeding into a NOR gate. **1972** G. V. HIGGINS *Friends E. Coyle* xviii. 106 Eddie Coyle drove the old Sedan de Ville cautiously, the quad headlights on high beam. **1972** *Country Life* 10 Feb. 341/2 Asked what brought her to the forecourt apart from the imminent need for petrol, she replied unhesitatingly: 'Quad stamps and promotion offers.' **1973** D. ROBINSON *Rotten with Honour* 176 How much should I ask him for it?.. I'll try two-fifty and maybe throw in quad stamps. **1974** *Sunday Times* 16 June 29/6 Their time of 4 min 49·80 sec...was only 20 seconds slower than Eton's record in the eights, clearly indicating the potential speed of quad scullers.

B. *sb.*[5] Also **Quad**. A vehicle with four-wheel drive; *spec.* (see quot. 1948). orig. *U.S.*

1919 'I. HAY' *Last Million* xiv. 224 Smaller vehicles of American design, known as 'Quads'. These possess the unusual feature of a drive upon either axle. **1941** *Illustr. London News* 24 May 657/2 The third drawing shows 'Quads', powerfully mechanised units, which haul and guide the new guns into position and out. **1948** PARTRIDGE *Dict. Forces' Slang* 150 *Quad*, a four-wheel drive, gun-towing vehicle. **1961** W. VAUGHAN-THOMAS *Anzio* vi. 122 The Recce Regiment cars were trying to tuck themselves behind the walls as shelter for the night, a Quad, towing an anti-tank gun, was vainly trying to do the same thing.

quad (kwɒd), *a.*[2] and *sb.*[8] **A.** *adj.* Abbrev. of QUADRAPHONIC *a.*

1970 *Sat. Rev.* (U.S.) 27 June 56/1 Their new Quadraphonic Processor is an add-on bringing true (and quite well simulated) quad sound to two-channel systems. **1972** *Observer* (Colour Suppl.) 22 Oct. 56/4 The manufacturers have been to great pains to make their quad equipment 'compatible'. **1976** *Washington Post* 19 Apr. c8/4 (Advt.), 'Jesus Christ Superstar' 7:30, 9:30. Shown in quad sound and Big Screen Projection. **1977** *Listener* 20 Oct. 507/3 With quad transmissions now a regular feature of Radio 3, the argument that the BBC cannot afford to extend stereo coverage seems a little thin. **1980** *Broadcast* 7 July 8/3 A 17-year-old 2" quad VTR machine.

B. *sb.*[8] Abbrev. of QUADRAPHONY.

1971 *Esquire* Nov. 228/2 The necessity of making quad compatible with mono and stereo recordings and broadcasts is probably going to necessitate the use of some system that matrixes the four channels down to one. **1974** *Radio Times* 27 June 5/1 Quad adds a depth and perspective to radio that is missing in stereo. **1975** *Time Out* 15 Aug. 49/3 They give a live electronic concert (in quad) of music by little-known younger composers.

quad (kwɒd), *v.*[1], abbrev. of QUADRUPLEX *v.* Hence '**quadded** *ppl. a.*, '**quadding** *vbl. sb.*

1886 *Pall Mall G.* 26 Aug. 11/1 Some lines are 'quadded' or quadruplexed. **1914** H. PENDER *Amer. Handbk. Electr. Engineers* 1355 *Quadded* or *phantomed cable*,..a cable adapted for the use of phantom circuits. **1922** [see QUAD *sb.*[6]]. **1962** *Engineering* 16 Feb. 245/1 Once insulated, the conductor wires are either twisted into pairs or 'quadded' in groups of four. *Ibid.* 245/2 After twisting or quadding each conductor wire is given a 'ring through' test with a bell and battery.

quad (kwɒd), *v.*[2] *Printing.* [f. QUAD *sb.*[2]] To insert quadrats in (a line of type); to fill with quadrats. Also ***to quad out***.

1888 in JACOBI *Printers' Vocab.*

quad, var. QUOD *sb.*, prison; QUED(E *a.*, bad.

quad, obs. form of QUOTH *v.*

†**quade**, *v. Obs. rare*⁻¹. [? f. *quade*, var. of QUED(E *a.*, bad.] ? To destroy, deface.

1565 J. HALLE *Hist. Expost.* 34 If thou in chirurgerye, Alone wylte walke and wade; Thine errores will thy worke confounde, And all thine honoure quade.

†'**quader**, *v. Obs. rare.* Also 5–6 quadr-. [ad. L. *quadrāre*: see QUADRATE *v.*, and cf. F. *cadrer*, *quadrer* (16th c.).] **a.** *trans.* To square (a number). **b.** *trans.* and *intr.* = QUADRATE *v.* 3.

c **1430** *Art of Nombryng* (E.E.T.S.) 16 [A given number] to be quadrede. **1588** KYD *Househ. Philos.* Wks. (1901) 269 In the quadering and making euen of the enteries with the expences. **1593** —— in *Fortn. Rev.* (1899) LXV. 220 Nor wold indeed the forme of devyne praiers vsed duelie in his Lordship's house have quadred with such reprobates. **1620** SHELTON *Quix.* II. IV. vii. 91 The *X* doth not quader well with him because it sounds harshly.

quadern, a square: see QUADRAN *sb.*[1]

quadle, obs. variant of CODDLE *v.*[1], to boil.

1633 HART *Diet of Diseased* I. xvii. 66 Raw Apples before they be ripe, if used, are best quadled. **1649** G. DANIEL *Trinarch.* To Rdr. 105 Thus wee sett you out Perboyled Kinges and Quadled Crownes.

quadling, obs. variant of CODLING[2].

1584 COGAN *Haven Health* c. (1612) 87 Rawe Apples and Quadlings. **1609** C. BUTLER *Fem. Mon.* (1634) 173 Let them boil till they be as tender as Quadlings.

†**quadmire.** *Obs. rare*⁻¹. = QUAGMIRE, q.v.

1609 BIBLE (Douay) *Ps.* lxviii. *comm.*, I am as one intangled with quickesand or quadmyre in the bottom of a great water.

‖**quadra** ('kwɒdrə). *Arch.* [L. *quadra* a square, used by Vitruvius in sense 1.]

1. a. The plinth or socle of a podium. **b.** A platband or fillet, *esp.* that above or below the scotia in the Ionic base.

1664 EVELYN tr. *Freart's Archit.* 131 Pilæ, and their Quadra's or Tables..were employ'd for Inscriptions. **1842–76** in GWILT *Archit.* (Hence in recent dicts.)

2. A square border or frame round a bas-relief, panel, etc.; also, loosely, a border or frame of any form.

1727–41 in CHAMBERS *Cycl.* **1842–76** in GWILT *Archit.* (Hence in recent Dicts.)

quadra-, occas. erron. form of QUADRI-.

quadrable ('kwɒdrəb(ə)l), *a. Math.* Also 8 -ible. [ad. L. type **quadrābilis*, f. *quadrāre* to square: see QUADRATE *v.* and -ABLE.] Capable of being represented by an equivalent square, or of being expressed in a finite number of algebraic terms.

1695 WALLIS in *Phil. Trans.* XIX. 111 The Spaces in the Cycloid, which are perfectly Quadrable. **1743** EMERSON *Fluxions* 196 Here the Curve is not quadrible in this Form. **1798** *Phil. Trans.* LXXXVIII. 260 The areas of any parabolic segments..are geometrically quadrable. **1872** LOOMIS *Calculus* vi. 253 When the area limited by a curve can be expressed in a finite number of algebraic terms, the surface is said to be quadrable.

Hence **quadra'bility**, the quality or condition of being quadrable.

1743 EMERSON *Fluxions* 194 In Curves of more Terms, there are several Conditions requisite to their exact Quadrability.

quadragenarian (ˌkwɒdrədʒɪ'nɛərɪən), *a.* and *sb.* Also *erron.* quadri-. [f. L. *quadrāgēnāri-us* (f. *quadrāgēnī* distrib. of *quadrāgintā* forty) + -AN.]

a. *adj.* Forty years old. **b.** *sb.* A person forty years of age.

1839 *Fraser's Mag.* XX. 752 The quadrigenarians may reasonably object, that as Lord Byron only lived to seven-and-thirty, he could not be a competent judge on this matter. **1892** STEVENSON *Vailima Lett.* xix. (1895) 184 A stalwart well-oiled quadragenarian. **1897** *Sat. Rev.* 20 Feb. 195/2 Quadrigenarian critics.

So ˌ**quadrage'narious** *a.*

1656 BLOUNT *Glossogr.*, *Quadragenarious*, of or belonging to forty years. **1719** BOYER *Fr.-Eng. Dict.*, *Quadragenaire*, quadragenarious, forty years old. **1895** *Harper's Weekly Mag.* Feb. 337/2 One of these plumply mellow quadrigenarious bodies.

†**quadragene.** *Obs. rare.* [ad. med.L. *quadrāgēna*, neut. of *quadrāgēnī* forty each, forty.] An indulgence for forty days.

1664 JER. TAYLOR *Dissuas. Popery* ii. §4 You have.. purchased your self so many Quadragenes or Lents of pardon; that is, you have bought off the penances of so many times forty days.

‖**Quadragesima** (kwɒdrə'dʒɛsɪmə). *Eccl.* [med.L., fem. (sc. *dies* day) of L. *quadrāgēsimus* fortieth, f. *quadrāgintā* forty; hence also It., Pg. *quadragesima* (Sp. *cuad-*), F. *quadragésime* (1487).

The popular Romanic forms are It. *quaresima*, Pg. *quaresma*, Sp. *cuaresma*, OF. *quaresme*, *caresme*, F. *carême*; cf. also Ir. *corghas*, *cairghios*, Gael. *carghus*, W. *garawys* from pop.Lat. **quarages-ima*.]

†**a.** The forty days of Lent. *Obs.* **b.** (Also ***Quadragesima Sunday***.) The first Sunday in Lent.

[**1398** TREVISA *Barth. De P.R.* IX. xxx. (1495) 364 Lente highte Quadragesima.] **1604** *Bk. Com. Prayer* Tables, Quadragesima, before Easter, vi weekes. **1617** MINSHEU *Ductor*, Quadragesima Sunday, or the first Sunday in Lent. *Ibid.*, Quadragesima is the first Sunday in Lent. **1662** *Bk. Com. Prayer* Tables, Quadragesima, six weeks before Easter. **1662** GUNNING *Lent Fast* 167 A Quadragesima all call'd it. **1665** EVELYN *Corr.* 9 Feb. (1872) III. 151, I have always esteemed abstinence *a tanto* beyond the fulfilling of periods and quadragesimas. **1794** W. TINDAL *Evesham* 34 He was on Quadragesima Sunday confirmed Abbot.

quadragesimal (kwɒdrə'dʒɛsɪməl), *a.* and *sb.* Also 7 quadrigess-. [ad. late L. *quadrāgēsimāl-is*:

see prec. and -AL¹. Cf. F. *quadragésimal* (15–16th c.).]

A. *adj.* **1.** Of a fast (*esp.* that of Lent): Lasting for forty days.

1654 HAMMOND *Answ. Animadv. Ignat.* ii. §2. 38 The Quadrigessimal Fast was observed in the Church to commemorate both these. **1725** tr. *Dupin's Eccl. Hist. 17th C.* I. v. 171 The Quadragesimal Fast was also regarded as Penance. **1844** W. H. MILL *Serm. Tempt. Christ* i. 12 That quadragesimal Fast and retirement of our Lord. **1855** —— *Applic. Panth. Princ.* (1861) 111 The retirement and quadragesimal fast of Elijah.

2. Belonging or appropriate to the period of Lent; Lenten.

1629 MABBE tr. *Fonseca's Dev. Contempl.* title-p., Two and Fortie Sermons upon all yᵉ Quadragesimall Gospells. **1691** WOOD *Ath. Oxon.* II. 359 Quadragesimal Disputations were publickly performed in the Schools. **1727–41** CHAMBERS *Cycl.* s.v. *Quadragesima*, Hence some monks are said to lead a quadragesimal life; or to live on quadragesimal food all the year. **1882** J. W. LEGG *Hist. Liturg. Colours* III. 40 The colour of the Quadragesimal ornaments.

fig. a **1643** W. CARTWRIGHT *Ordinary* III. v. in Hazl. *Dodsley* XII. 268 But quadragesimal wits, and fancies lean As ember weeks.

3. Consisting of forty.

1662 GUNNING *Lent Fast* 50 The Quadragesimal number not constituted of men, but consecrated from God.

† **B.** *sb.* **a.** A fast, properly one of forty days. **b.** A set of forty. **c.** A Lent sermon. **d.** *pl.* Lent offerings (see quot. 1721). *Obs.*

1660 JER. TAYLOR *Duct. Dubit.* III. IV. Rule xiii. §17 It is no wonder..that all the set and stationary fasts of the Primitive Christians were called Quadragesimals. *Ibid.* §18 A quadragesimal of hours is as proper as a quadragesimal of days. **1691** tr. *Emilianne's Frauds Romish Monks* 284 They who print their Quadragesimals and their Advent Sermons, ..never print the Second part of them. **1721** BAILEY, *Quadragesimals*, Mid-Lent contributions, Offerings made by People to their Mother Church on Mid-Lent Sunday.

‖ **quadragesi'malia.** *rare.* [neut. pl. of late L. *quadrāgēsimālis*: see prec.] = prec. B. d.

1727–41 in CHAMBERS *Cycl.* **1876** *Prayer-book Interleaved* 103 Taking Quadragesimalia or Lent-offerings.

† **quadragesimarian.** *Obs.* *rare*⁻¹. [f. QUADRAGESIMA.] An observer of Lent.

1655 FULLER *Ch. Hist.* II. vii. §74 Otherwise it is suspicious that the Quartadecimans were no good Quadragesimarians.

† **Quadragesime, -gesme.** *Obs. rare.* [ad. L. *quadrāgēsim-a*: see above.] = QUADRAGESIMA.

c **1440** *Gesta Rom.* I. lxii. 266 (Harl. MS.) A goode cristyn man that wele blessidly hath fast all the quadragesme. **1612** R. SHELDON *Serm. St. Martin's* 5 To proportion my discourse to the season, when we all are..making a Quadragesime, or fortieth, as a parasceue of Christ his death and passion. **1612** SELDEN *Illustr. Drayton's Poly-olb.* XI. 207 Wks. 1876 II. 91 You will lose therein forty days, and the common name of Quadragesime.

,quadragin'tesimal, *a.* *rare*⁻¹. [For QUADRAGESIMAL, after L. *quadrāgintā*.] Forty-fold; having forty parts.

1789 BURNEY *Hist. Mus.* III. i. 75 Twelve bars of universal chorus in quadragintesimal harmony.

quadra'gintireme. *rare*⁻¹. [f. L. *quadrāgintā* forty: cf. *quadrireme*, etc.] (See quot.)

1799 CHARNOCK in *Naval Chron.* I. 132 Quadragintiremes, or vessels..described as having forty ranks..of oars.

quadrain, a square: see QUADRAN *sb.*¹

quadrain, obs. variant of QUATRAIN.

quadral ('kwɒdrəl), *a.* *rare*⁻¹. [f. QUADR(I)- + -AL¹.] By four, into four parts.

1891 W. TUCKWELL *Tongues in Trees* 146 They held to the quadral division of time, distributing the day-night into four, eight or sixteen parts.

† **'quadran,** *sb.* (and *a.*). *Obs.* Forms: 6 quadron, 6–7 quadrain, 7 quadran, -ren, quadern. [Alteration of QUADRANT *sb.*², with dropping of the *-t* and assimilation to other endings.]

1. A square.

1591 HARINGTON *Orl. Fur.* VI. lxxi, These ornaments.. All are enrich't with stones of great estate,..In parted quadrons. **1595** B. BARNES *Spir. Sonn.* lxxxiii, Bright soldiours muster up..Raungde into quadraines and triumphant rings. **1648** GAGE *West Ind.* xii. (1655) 51 In the midst of this Quadern stood a mount of earth and stone square likewise. **1653** R. SANDERS *Physiogn.* 153, I erected this Figure, and thereupon made certain Quadrains and Resolutions, that my Friends might understand the significations of the said Figure.

2. *attrib.* or *adj.* Square.

1598 SYLVESTER *Du Bartas* II. i. IV. *Handie-Crafts* 206 Sixteen fair Trees..Whose equall front in quadran form prospected. **1611** SPEED *Theat. Gt. Brit.* xxxvii. (1614) 73/1 In a long Quadren-wise the wals doe incompasse the citie.

quadran, obs. var. QUADRANT *sb.*¹ (sense 3), QUATRAIN.

quadrangle ('kwɒdræŋg(ə)l), *sb.* [a. F. *quadrangle* (13th c.), ad. late L. *quadrangulum*, neut. of *quadrangulus* (see next), f. *quadr-* QUADRI- + *angulus* ANGLE. The stressing *qua'drangle*, which appears in some of the quots., is given by Bailey, Ash, and Sheridan, and is still the constant Sc. use.]

1. a. *Geom.* A figure having four angles and therefore four sides.

In *mod. Geom.* a quadrangle is regarded as a figure formed by four points (vertices), three of which are not in the same straight line, and by the six straight lines which join the four points two by two. (Cf. QUADRILATERAL.) In ordinary use the term commonly denotes a square or other rectangular figure: cf. quot. 1884 and senses 2 and 3.

c **1430** *Art of Nombryng* (E.E.T.S.) 14 ffor dyvisioun write by vnytes, hathe .4. sides even as a quadrangille. **1471** RIPLEY *Comp. Alch.* Ep. iv. in Ashm. (1652) 112 Of the Quadrangle make ye a Figure round. **1551** RECORDE *Pathw. Knowl.* I. *Defin.*, Thus haue I done with trianguled figures, and nowe foloweth quadrangles. **1653** R. SANDERS *Physiogn.* 58 The Quadrangle is between the Table-line, the middle natural, that of the Sun, and that of Saturn, when there are four angles. **1869** DUNKIN *Midn. Sky* 141 Eight stars forming two similar quadrangles. **1884** tr. *Lotze's Logic* 130 Nothing is commoner than for a person who speaks of a quadrangle to mean really a parallelogram or often even a square.

b. *Palmistry.* (See quot. 1883.)

1883 FRITH & HERON-ALLEN *Chiromancy* 138 The Quadrangle is that part of the human hand comprised between the line of the Head and the line of the Heart and between the line of Fate and the line of Apollo. **1895** H. FRITH *Pract. Palmistry* III. i. 121 The Quadrangle is an extremely important space, for upon its width and general appearance the mind and the disposition of the man or woman may be estimated and 'reckoned up'. **1934** C. DE SAINT-GERMAIN *Study of Palmistry* IV. 313/1 A cross in the Quadrangle touching the Line of Heart—Influence of the opposite sex on the subject... A cross in the Quadrangle touching the Line of Head—The subject will exert in the matters of love or friendship more influence on the other person than the said person will exert on him. **1952** J. MALCOLM *Frith's Pract. Palmistry* (rev. ed.) xviii. 112 The Quadrangle should be regular and wide in the centre, and it should expand at both ends. This indicates good health, honesty and trustworthiness. **1971** *Cheiro Bk. of Fate & Fortune* xli. 122 When the quadrangle is abnormally wide in its entire length, it denotes want of order in the brain, carelessness of thought and ideas, an unconventional nature, and one imprudent in every way.

2. A square or rectangular space or court, the sides of which are entirely or mainly occupied by parts of a large building, as a college, palace, etc. (See also QUAD *sb.*¹, and cf. QUADRANT *sb.*²)

1593 SHAKS. *2 Hen. VI*, I. iii. 156 My choller being ouer-blowne, With walking once about the Quadrangle. **1642** *Caval. Adv. Majesty* 7 Our men..went in at the back Gate opposite to Oriall Colledge, and through Canterbury quadrangle. **1764** HARMER *Observ.* XI. iii. 103 These quadrangles or courts are paved..with marble. **1828** SCOTT *F.M. Perth* x, A lofty vaulted entrance led through this eastern front into the quadrangle. **1877** W. THOMSON *Voy. Challenger* I. ii. 112 We passed through an archway into a large quadrangle.

3. a. A rectangular building or block of buildings; a building containing a quadrangle.

1620 T. PEYTON *Paradise* in Farr. *S.P. Jas. I* (1848) 179 Like a quadrangle seated on a hill With twelue braue gates. **1645** EVELYN *Mem.* (1857) I. 217 They [the Schools] are fairly built in quadrangle, with cloisters beneath. **1712** AMHERST *Terræ Fil.* No. 5 (1754) 24, I would not have them set their minds too much upon new quadrangles, and empty libraries, and spacious halls. **1846** MCCULLOCH *Acc. Brit. Empire* (1854) II. 383 The buildings of Trinity College [Dublin]..consist of three quadrangles. **1870** F. R. WILSON *Ch. Lindisf.* 64 Beadwell [has] an additional quadrangle of houses.

b. A square block (in quot., an iceberg).

1853 KANE *Grinnell Exp.* xlix. (1856) 461 A second quadrangle stood out from the shore at the same rate.

4. *Comb.*, (? of the adj.) as ***quadrangle-wise*** adv.

1582 N.T. (Rhem.) *Rev.* xxi. 16 The citie is situated quadrangle-wise. a **1604** HANMER *Chron. Ireland* (1633) 189 The walles foure square, or quadrangle wise.

† **quadrangle,** *a.* *Obs.* [ad. L. *quadrangulus* four-cornered: see prec. and cf. obs. F. *quadrangle* (Godef.).] **a.** = QUADRANGULAR. **b.** *Astron.* = QUADRATE *a.* 2.

1562 BULLEYN *Bk. Simples* 47 b, The garden Madder, with quadrangle stalks. **1575** T. ROGERS *Sec. Coming Christ* 39/2 The Greeke letter χ rather betokeneth the quadrangle figure. **1601** HOLLAND *Pliny* I. 13 In the quadrangle aspect of the Sun she [the Moon] appeareth diuided in halfe: in the triangle she is well neere inuironed.

quadrangled ('kwɒdræŋg(ə)ld, kwə'drænŋg(ə)ld), *a.* [f. as prec. + -ED².]

1. = QUADRANGULAR. Now *rare* or *Obs.*

1552 in HULOET. **1570** BILLINGSLEY *Euclid* I. xxxii. 42 The angles of euery quadrangled figure are equall to 4 right angles. **1620** DEKKER *Dreame* (1860) 30 Those quadrangled haile-stones, which..Kill teemes and plowmen. **1674** JEAKE *Arith.* (1696) 175 The other Species of Quadrangled Figures are an Oblong..and a Rhomboide. **1800** J. HURDIS *Favourite Village* 155 The quadrangled tube Into a pipe monotonous converts.

2. Furnished with a quadrangle.

1880 SIR J. B. PHEAR *Aryan Village* 86 There will be the brick-built, quadrangled house.

quadrangular (kwə'dræŋgjʊlə(r)), *a.* [ad. late L. *quadrangulāris* (Boethius), f. *quadrangulum*: see QUADRANGLE and -AR, and cf. F. *quadrangulaire* (1542).] Shaped like a quadrangle; having four angles; of four-cornered base or section.

1592 G. HARVEY *Pierce's Super.* (1593) 20 The Ægyptian Mercury..his Image in Athens was quadrangular. **1607** TOPSELL *Four-f. Beasts* (1658) 250 A company of Horses set like a Tower in a Quadrangular form in a field, was called Pergus. **1611** CORYAT *Crudities* 169 It hath a prety quadrangular Court adjoyning to it. **1671** *Phil. Trans.* VI. 2216 It was a very dark Spot almost of a quadrangular form. **1776** GIBBON *Decl. & F.* xiii. I. 396 The form was quadrangular, flanked with sixteen towers. **1784** COWPER *Task* IV. 217 With spots quadrangular of diamond form. **1849** GROTE *Greece* II. lviii. VII. 227 The lower part was left as a quadrangular pillar. **1882** MISS BRADDON *Mt. Royal* III. iii. 47 The little quadrangular garden.

Comb. **1656** HEYLIN *Surv. France* 74 A house built quadrangular wise. **1854** *Poultry Chron.* I. 431 It is a spacious, quadrangular-shaped house, built of a greyish stone.

Hence **qua'drangularly** *adv.*, in the manner of a quadrangle; with four corners. **qua'drangularness,** the state or fact of being quadrangular (Bailey, vol. II, 1727).

1708 OZELL tr. *Boileau's Lutrin* II. (1730) 125 An inverted Cone..Sharp pointed, and quadrangularly long. **1875** H. C. WOOD *Therap.* (1879) 322 Quadrangularly prismatic crystals.

† **qua'drangulate,** *a.* *Obs. rare.* [ad. late L. *quadrangulāt-us* (Tertull., Vulg.); see QUADRANGLE *sb.* and -ATE².] Made quadrangular; squared.

1592 R. D. *Hypnerotomachia* 5 b, The pointed quadrangulate Corner stones. **1599** R. LINCHE *Fount. Anc. Fict.* H iv, A certaine squared and quadrangulate circle.

Hence † **qua'drangulateness,** the state or condition of having four corners. *Obs. rare.*

1597 A. M. tr. *Guillemeau's Fr. Chirurg.* 53/2 Through the quadrangulatenes therof it cutteth..al that wheron it glaunceth.

† **quadranguled,** *a.* *Obs. rare*⁻¹. [cf. prec.] = QUADRANGLED.

1592 R. D. *Hypnerotomachia* 4 b, Hir charmes and quadranguled plaints. [A mistranslation].

quadrant ('kwɒdrənt), *sb.*¹ Also 5–6 -ent, 7 -an. [ad. L. *quadrans, quadrant-* fourth part, quarter (*spec.* of an as, an acre, a foot, a pound, a sextarius, a day; cf. the senses below), f. *quadr-* four; see QUADRI-.]

† **1.** A quarter of a day; six hours. *Obs.*

1398 TREVISA *Barth. De P.R.* IX. ix. (1495) 354 A day conteynyth foure quadrantes, and a quadrant conteynyth syxe houres. a **1628** SIR J. BEAUMONT *End his Majesty's 1st Yeare* (R.), The sunne, who in his annuall circle takes A daye's full quadrant from th' ensuing yeere. **1646** SIR T. BROWNE *Pseud. Ep.* 219 The intercalation of one day every fourth yeare, allowed for this quadrant, or 6 houres super-numerary.

† **2. a.** The fourth part of a Roman as. *Obs.*

1533 BELLENDEN *Livy* III. vii. (1901) 270 Ilk man went to Valerius hous, and left ane quadrent in it, to caus him be the more richely buryit. **1601** HOLLAND *Pliny* II. 518 A small piece of brasse coin, although it be no more than a Quadrant. **1655** MOUFET & BENNET *Health's Improv.* 191 They were highly esteemed, being sold every Dishfull for fourscore Quadrants.

b. A farthing. (So med.L. *quadrans*, AF. *quadrant*.) *Obs.*

1609 SKENE *Reg. Maj.* 123 b (*Burgh Lawes* c. 40), Hee.. sall giue ane quadrant (farding). *Ibid.* 26 b (*Burgh Lawes* c. 66), The maister..sall haue ane pennie for his Ouen; the twa servants ane pennie, and the boy ane quadrant.

c. *attrib.* in contemptuous sense. *Obs.*

1589 NASHE *Ded.* to *Greene's Menaphon* (Arb.) 8 Our quadrant Crepundios, that spit *ergo* in the mouth of euerie one they meete.

† **3.** The fourth part of a sextarius or Roman pint. *Obs. rare.*

1601 HOLLAND *Pliny* I. 267 One of their shels ordinarily would containe 80 measures called Quadrants. **1688** R. HOLME *Armoury* III. 339/1 Gill or Quadran, is 4 to a pint.

4. a. A quarter of a circle or circular body, viz. (*a*) an arc of a circle, forming one fourth of the circumference; (*b*) one fourth of the area of a circle, contained within two radii at right angles.

1571 DIGGES *Pantom.* I. B iv, A Quadrant is the fourth part of a Circle, included with two Semidiameters. **1625** N. CARPENTER *Geog. Del.* I. vi. (1635) 123 A circle is diuided into foure quadrants. **1660** BARROW *Euclid* VI. 33 *cor.* As the arch *BC* is to four quadrants, that is, the whole circumference. **1694** HOLDER *Disc. Trine* (J.), In each quadrant of the circle of the ecliptick. **1727–41** CHAMBERS *Cycl.* s.v. *Quarter-round*, Any projecting moulding, whose contour is a perfect quadrant. **1812** WOODHOUSE *Astron.* i. 6 *PQ, Pq* [are] quadrants containing 90 degrees. **1843** PORTLOCK *Geol.* 682 In each quadrant of the kiln, there is an opening. **1869** DUNKIN *Midn. Sky* 74 The north-western quadrant of the sky. **1900** *Brit. Med. Jrnl.* (No. 2046) 622 An insignificant nebula in the lower-inner quadrant of the left cornea.

b. A thing having the form of a quarter-circle. ***quadrant of altitude***, a graduated strip of brass on an artificial globe, fixed at one end to some point of the meridian, round which it revolves, and extending round one fourth of the circumference.

1638 CHILMEAD tr. *Hues' Treat. Globes* (1889) 33 Then fasten the quadrant of Altitude to the Vertical point. **1726** tr. *Gregory's Astron.* I. 269 With the Quadrant of Altitude, find that Point of the Ecliptic which is elevated 12 Degrees above the Western Part of the Horizon. **1816** J. SMITH *Panorama Sc. & Art* II. 717 A sliding piece N, (much like the nut of the quadrant of altitude belonging to a common globe). **1825** J. NICHOLSON *Operat. Mechanic* 114 The inclined shaft ..working in the toothed quadrant Z, elevates or depresses the sluice. **1888** JACOBI *Printers' Vocab.* 107 *Quadrant*, a small crescent-shaped piece of iron or steel used for the movement of the vibrating roller on a platen machine.

(i) *Naut.* A metal frame, shaped as the quadrant or sector of a circle, that is fixed to the rudder head or stock and to which the steering ropes or chains are attached.

1885 H. PAASCH *From Keel to Truck* 32/1 *Tiller..quadrant*, barre de gouvernail en quadrant. Quadrant als Ruderpinne. **1894** *Ibid.* (ed. 2) 223 Steering-quadrant. **1923** *Glasgow Herald* 3 Feb. 8/7 The modern helm, or its equivalent, the quadrant, is placed out-board. **1961** *Lloyd's Register of Shipping: Rules & Regs. Construction Steel Ships* 57/1 Tillers and quadrants are to be shrunk on or bolted to the rudder head. **1976** *Oxf. Compan. Ships & Sea* 731/2 It is by means of the quadrant, with the assistance of a steering engine, that force is applied to turn the rudder.

(ii) (See quot. 1940.)

1885 H. PAASCH *From Keel to Truck* 80/1 *Quadrant, reversing*, secteur de changement de marche. Umsteuerungs-Quadrant. **1940** *Chambers's Techn. Dict.* 691/1 *Quadrant*, a slotted segmental guide through which an adjusting lever (e.g. a reversing lever) works. It is provided with means for locating the lever in any desired angular position. **1959** *Weekly Times* (Melbourne) 30 Sept. 1 (Advt.), At your fingertips is the 'automatic brain' of your Ferguson [tractor]—the amazingly simple control quadrant that gives you complete 4-way work control. Without moving your hand more than six inches, you can raise and lower implements or hold them rigidly in any position. **1971** 'D. RUTHERFORD' *Clear the Fast Lane* 46 He took the sharp curve..snicking the gearbox quadrant into second. **1977** *R.A.F. News* 8–21 June 11/2 In such foggy conditions..quadrant operators would be unable to sight and pinpoint the bomb and rocket hit points.

c. A quarter of a sphere or spherical body.

1882 VINES tr. *Sachs' Bot.* 300 In each of the four quadrants [of a cell] a third division takes place.

d. (Freq. with capital initial.) A street or part of a street curved in a quarter-circle; *spec.* the eastern end of Regent Street adjoining Piccadilly Circus in London.

1822 S. LEIGH *New Picture of London* (new ed.) vi. 289 Quadrant, extending from Piccadilly to Glasshouse-street, ornamented by handsome colonnades supported by about 140 cast-iron pillars. **1847** THACKERAY *Van. Fair* (1848) xxxviii. 348 The bearded savages..who..scowl at you..in the Quadrant arcades. **1875** A. E. HOUSMAN *Let.* 9 Jan. (1971) 6 The Quadrant, Regent Street, and Pall Mall are the finest streets. **1885** *List of Subscribers, Brighton* (South of Eng. Telephone Co.) 3 Farringdon B.—5, North-street-quadrant. **1974** F. SELWYN *Cracksman on Velvet* II. 131 The wagon rumbled the length of Nash's elegant quadrant. **1974** J. GARDNER *Return of Moriarty* 131 They were in a house near Regent Street, near the Quadrant.

5. An instrument, properly having the form of a graduated quarter-circle, used for making angular measurements, *esp.* for taking altitudes in astronomy and navigation.

Various kinds of quadrants (some being improperly so called) have been employed for different purposes, but are now to a great extent superseded by more perfect instruments. The distinctive names are derived either from the inventors (as *Adams's, Coles's, Collins's, Davis's, Godfrey's* or *Hadley's, Gunter's, Sutton's quadrant*), from those by whom it is used (as *gunner's, surveyor's quadrant*), or from some property, use, etc., of the instrument (as *horodictical, mural, sinical quadrant*).

a **1400** in Halliwell *Rara Mathematica* (1841) 58 Til..þe threde whereon þe plumbe henges falle vpon þe mydel lyne of þe quadrant, þat es to say þe 45 degre. *a* **1400–50** *Alexander* 129 Quadrentis [*MS.* In adrentis] corven all of quyte siluyre. **1555** EDEN *Decades* 245 With my quadrant and Astrolabie instrumentes of Astronomie. **1627** CAPT. SMITH *Seaman's Gram.* xiv. 68 The Gunners quadrant is to leuell a Peece or mount her to any randon. **1638** CHILMEAD tr. *Hues' Treat. Globes* (1889) 102 Observe the Meridian Altitude of the Sunne with the crosse staffe, quadrant, or other like instrument. **1696** PHILLIPS (ed. 5), *David's* [1706 *Davis's*] *Quadrant*, an Instrument us'd by Seamen, wherewith they observe the height of the Sun with their Backs toward it. **1774** M. MACKENZIE *Maritime Surv.* 10 With a Theodolite, or Hadley's Quadrant..take the Angles YXA, YXB, YXC. **1848** DICKENS *Dombey* iv, The stock in trade of this old gentleman comprised..sextants, and quadrants. **1897** F. T. BULLEN *Cruise Cachalot* 100 Anything..more out of date than his 'hog-yoke', or quadrant, I have never seen.

6. *attrib.* and *Comb.*, as ***quadrant cell, lever***; ***quadrant-like, -shaped*** adjs.; **quadrant-compass**, a carpenter's compass with an arc to which one leg may be screwed (Knight *Dict. Mech.* 1875); **quadrant electrometer**, an electrometer in which the index moves through a quarter of a circle; **quadrant method** *Archæol.*, a method of dividing up a site to be excavated (see quot. 1954); **quadrant steam-engine**, an engine in which the piston oscillates through a sector of a circle, instead of sliding along a cylinder (Knight *Dict. Mech.*).

1777 T. CAVALLO *Compl. Treat. Electr.* III. iii. 161 Fig 7th. represents Mr. Henly's quadrant electrometer. **1816** J. SMITH *Panorama Sc. & Art* II. 247 This conductor should be furnished with a quadrant electrometer. **1833** J. HOLLAND *Manuf. Metal* II. 278 The principle [of Strutt's lock]..consists in a number of quadrant levers. **1874** MICKLETHWAITE *Mod. Par. Churches* 163 The mediæval quadrant-shaped cope-chests. **1884** BOWER & SCOTT *De Bary's Phaner.* 20 Each quadrant cell is again divided into two unequal parts. **1897** *Outing* (U.S.) XXIX. 525/1 The quadrant-like part of the shutter. [**1930** A. E. VAN GIFFEN *Die Bauart der Einzelgräber* 7 Bei den Hügeluntersuchungen wird von mir mit Vorliebe nach der sog. Quadrantenmethode..vorgegangen. Ich verwendete sie zuerst..im Jahre 1916.] **1939** G. CLARK *Archæol. & Society* iv. 97 For dealing with round barrows with internal structures of timber Dr A. E. van Giffen of Groningen has evolved what he terms the 'quadrant method'. **1954** M. WHEELER *Archaeol. from Earth* viii. 95 It is known as *quartering* or the *quadrant method*. The mound is marked out into four quarters by two strings, laid preferably to the cardinal points of the compass and over the approximate centre. Opposite quarters are then excavated in turn, a balk 1½–3 feet wide being left between each quadrant in such a fashion as to give a complete transverse section across the mound in both directions. **1967** L. DE PAOR *Archæol.* ii. 49 The 'quadrant method'..is much used in the excavation of circular barrows and other small mounds... It will be observed that one of the objects of the method is to preserve to the last moment two full cross-sections.

†**quadrant**, *sb.*[2] *Obs.* [App. an alteration of QUADRAT or QUADRATE *sb.*[1], through assoc. with prec. See also QUADRAN *sb.*]

1. = QUADRANGLE *sb.* 2, 3.

1443 in Willis & Clark *Cambridge* (1886) I. 389 Werkemen and labor' dryving the berne in to the quadrant of the College. **1537** in W. H. Turner *Select. Rec. Oxford* 143 The abbot send for me,..he beyng under the ellme in the quadrant. **1582** STANYHURST *Æneis* IV. (Arb.) 118 Dido affrighted..Too the inner quadrant runneth. **1631** WEEVER *Anc. Fun. Mon.* 412 A faire large Chappell on the East side of the Quadrant. **1655** FULLER *Hist. Camb.* v. §29 The present quadrant of the Schools.

2. A square; a square thing or piece (also *fig.*): a square picture.

1474 CAXTON *Chesse* 140 The kyng..is sette in the iiij quadrante or poynt of theschequer. **1563–87** FOXE *A. & M.* (1596) 587 Since the time they did receiue the catholicke faith of our Lord Jesus Christ, as a most perfect quadrant. **1601** HOLLAND *Pliny* II. 440 The quadrants or square cantons of the old Tuny fish, burnt to a cole..are thought to be good for the tooth-ach. **1651** *Life Father Sarpi* (1676) 22 A portable quadrant of Christ in the Garden.

b. One side of a square. (Cf. QUADRATURE 2.)

1577–87 HOLINSHED *Chron.* III. 856/2 A palace, the which was quadrant, and euerie quadrant of the same palace was three hundred and twentie eight foot long.

quadrant, *sb.*[3]: see QUADRATE *sb.*[3]

†**'quadrant**, *a. Obs.* [ad. L. *quadrant-em*, pres. pple. of *quadrāre* to square: in sense 1 perh. an alteration of *quadrat* QUADRATE *a.* (cf. prec. and QUADRAN 2).]

1. Square; of a square form.

1509 HAWES *Past. Pleas.* III. (Percy Soc.) 15 The craggy rocke, whiche quadrant did appeare. **1535** R. LAYTON *Let. to Cromwell* 12 Sept. in Wood *Ann.* 62 Wee found all the great Quadrant Court [of New College] full of the leaves of Dunce. **1577–87** [see prec. 2 b]. **1591** GARRARD *Art Warre* 161 Taking from the quotient yᵉ roote of the quadrant number. **1601** BP. W. BARLOW *Defence* 105 The quadrant stones of Salomons building. **1603** T. M. *Progr. Jas. I* in Arb. *Garner* VIII. 501 A goodly edifice of free stone, built in quadrant manner. **1618** *Barnevelt's Apol.* E b, The truth resembles, right, the right Cubes figure;..Whose quadrant flatness neuer doth disfigure.

b. *Astron.* = QUADRATE *a.* 2.

The form in this case may be due to association with QUADRANT *sb.*[1] 4.

1594 BLUNDEVIL *Exerc.* VII. x. (1636) 662 Characters..Whereof the first signifieth a conjunction..the fourth a quadrant aspect.

2. Agreeing, consonant, or conformable (*to* or *with*). Cf. QUADRATE *a.* 4. (So obs. F. *quadrant.*)

1536 *St. Papers Hen. VIII*, I. 521 Perceyving that your opinion and advise is quadrant with the same; We haue sent..a pardon to our Cousin. **1598** YONG *Diana* 241 To do the contrarie..were..not quadrant to that, which is expected at your hands. **1720** WELTON *Suffer. Son of God* II. xx. 567 Thou art content with the Sincerity and Uprightness of my Inclinations, tho' they should not be so exactly Conformable and Quadrant to Thine Own.

quadrantal (kwɒ'dræntəl), *a.*[1] [ad. L. *quadrantālis*: see QUADRANT *sb.*[1] and -AL[1].]

a. Having the shape of, consisting of, connected with, a quadrant or quarter-circle; esp. ***quadrantal arc*** (**† *arch***).

1678 HOBBES *Decam.* ad fin., Wks. 1845 VII. 180 A straight line equal to the quadrantal arc BLD. **1703** T. N. *City & C. Purchaser* 14 A Quadrantal Casement, rising from its Plain. **1797** HELLINS in *Phil. Trans.* LXXXVIII. 529 The length of a quadrantal arch of the circle. **1867** G. BARRY *Sir C. Barry* iv. 116 The central building with quadrantal corridors. **1871** B. STEWART *Heat* (ed. 2) §71 A quadrantal arc of a meridian on the earth's surface. **1914** *Trans. Ophthalm. Soc.* XXXIV. 209 Uncomplicated quadrantal unrecognised hemianopsia. **1918** *Arch. Ophthalm.* XLVII. 126 Early homonymous upper quadrantal defects in Stage I.

b. ***quadrantal deviation, error, triangle*** (see quots.).

1706 PHILLIPS (ed. Kersey), *Quadrantal Triangle*, a Spherick Triangle, that has at least a Quadrant for one of its Sides, and one Angle Right. **1788** HERSCHEL in *Phil. Trans.* LXXVIII. 374 We may resolve the quadrantal triangle *q c n.* **1857** WHEWELL *Hist. Induct. Sc.* (ed. 3) III. 528 The magnetic effect of the iron in a ship may be regarded as producing two kinds of deviation [of a ship's compass]..a 'polar-magnet deviation',..and a quadrantal deviation, which changes from positive to negative as the keel turns from quadrant to quadrant. **1865** *Q. Rev.* 358 The quadrantal error which depends only on the position of the horizontal soft iron of the ship.

†**qua'drantal**, *a.*[2] *Obs. rare.* [f. QUADRANT *sb.*[2] + -AL[1].] **a.** Square; having a square base. **b.** *Astron.* = QUADRANT *a.* 1 b.

1665 J. GADBURY *Lond. Deliv. Predicted* i. 4 The Conjunctional, Opposite, or Quadrantal Rays of Jupiter. **1690** LEYBOURN *Curs. Math.* 317 Let *ABCDE* be a Quadrantal Pyramis, (for a Pyramis is denominated from the number of the equal Sides of the Base thereof, as here four..).

†**qua'drantal**, *a.*[3] *Obs. rare*[−0]. [ad. L. *quadrantāl-is* of a quarter-foot, f. *quadrant-* QUADRANT *sb.*[1]] (See quot.)

1656 BLOUNT *Glossogr.*, *Quadrantal*..used Adjectively..four fingers thick, or three inches.

quadrantanopia (ˌkwɒdræntə'nəʊpɪə). *Ophthalm.* [mod.L., f. QUADRANT *sb.*[1] + Gr. ἀν- priv. + -ωπια sight.] A quadrantic loss of perception in an eye.

1942 I. S. TASSMAN *Eye Manifestations of Internal Dis.* iii. 75 The quadrantanopias affecting both fields may be homonymous, bitemporal, or binasal, inferior, superior, or crossed. **1964** S. DUKE-ELDER *Parsons' Dis. Eye* (ed. 14) xxiv. 358 Rare cases of homonymous quadrantanopia have been reported, in which corresponding quadrants of each field—the upper or lower half of one temporal, and the upper or lower half of the other nasal—have been lost. **1979** *Internat. Rehabilit. Med.* I. 53/1 The presence of a hemianopia or quadrantanopia was assessed by a confrontation method and confirmed by peripheral perimetry.

quadrantanopsia (ˌkwɒdræntə'nɒpsɪə). *Ophthalm.* [mod.L., f. as prec. + Gr. ὄψις sight.] = prec.

1910 *Lippincott's New Med. Dict.* 802/1 *Quadrantanopsia*, a sector defect of the eye with blindness limited to a portion of the visual field and due to cortical disease. **1947** F. H. ADLER *Gifford's Textbk. Ophthalm.* (ed. 4) iv. 46 The result of a lesion in this region [*sc.* Meyer's loop] is to produce an isolated quadrantanopsia. **1964** D. O. HARRINGTON *Visual Fields* (ed. 2) vii. 134 The quadrantanopsia [ed. 1: -opia] is truly congruous..in a patient with a cortical lesion. **1977** TATE & LYNN *Princ. Quantitative Perimetry* i. 44 Testing of both eyes assures that the pattern is not a pair of right and left homonymous quadrantanopsias.

quadrantic (kwɒ'dræntɪk), *a. Ophthalm.* [f. QUADRANT *sb.*[1] + -IC.] Involving the upper or lower part of one side of the visual field.

1914 *Trans. Ophthalm. Soc.* XXXIV. 212 Lower quadrantic right hemianopsia of four years standing. **1938** W. S. DUKE-ELDER *Textbk. Ophthalm.* II. xxix. 1228 If the sector defect is bounded by vertical and horizontal radii, the defect is called quadrantic anopia. **1976** *Lancet* 6 Nov. 1007/1 Neurological signs are absent—with the occasional exception of an isolated sixth-nerve palsy or an inferior-nasal quadrantic visual-field defect.

quadrantid (kwə'dræntɪd). [f. L. *quadrant-* stem of *quadrans* + -ID.] One of a shower of meteors falling on Jan. 2 and 3, and having its radiant point in the constellation *Quadrans muralis.* (Usu. in *pl.*)

1876 G. F. CHAMBERS *Astron.* 799.

quadrantile, *a. rare*[−1]. [f. QUADRANT *sb.*[1] + -ILE.] = QUADRANTAL *a.* 1.

1797 *Encycl. Brit.* (ed. 3) II. 585/2 On this pin are two moveable collets..to which are fixed the quadrantile wires.

†**'quadrantly**, *adv. Obs. rare.* [f. QUADRANT *a.* + -LY[2].] Squarely; in a square form. ***to multiply quadrantly***, to square.

1538 LELAND *Itin.* III. 33 In the midle of the Toun..is a House buildid quadrantly. **1581** STYWARD *Mart. Discipl.* II. 108 An order to imbattell 12. C men quadrantlie at the sodaine. **1594** BLUNDEVIL *Exerc.* I. xxvi. (1636) 62 You must multiply the said 4 in it selfe Quadrantly, which maketh 16.

quadrapertite, obs. form of QUADRIPARTITE.

quadraphonic (kwɒdrə'fɒbɪk), *a.* and *sb.* Also quadro-, quadri-. [f. QUADRA-, QUADRO-, QUADRI- + PHONIC *a.* (*sb.*)] **A.** *adj.* Produced by or pertaining to a system of sound recording and reproduction that employs four signal sources, two or more channels, and four loudspeakers, these being placed so that the original front-to-back sound distribution may be reproduced as well as the side-to-side one of stereophony.

1969 *High Fidelity* Sept. 63/1 The four channels might be used for double ping-pong effects — perhaps a quadriphonic version of 'Switched on Bach'. **1970** [see QUAD *a.*[2]]. **1971** *Sci. Amer.* Aug. 13/3 One of my main interests..is music — from rock to Bach preferably in live concert or quadrophonic sound. **1972** *Sat. Rev.* (U.S.) 25 Mar. 34/2 The quadrophonic sound proves very satisfactory on stereo equipment. **1974** *Radio Times* 27 June 55/3 Raymond Raikes talks about the quadraphonic experimental broadcast which can be heard at 12.5. **1975** D. G. FINK *Electronic Engineers' Handbk.* XIX. 81 Figure 19-147 summarizes the track and playback head locations for open-reel, eight-track cartridge and cassette tapes for both stereo and quadriphonic operation. **1975** *Jrnl. Audio Engin. Soc.* XXIII. 3/1 These presentations were made through each of the three basic types of quadraphonic system under test, namely, 4-4-4, 4-3-4, and 4-2-4. **1975** G. J. KING *Audio Handbk.* vii. 168 All 'quadraphonic' records will play through a stereo system with varying degrees of accuracy. **1977** *Times* 13 Apr. 1/8 Quadraphonic broadcasts — radio in the round — are to be transmitted for an experimental period of 12 months by the BBC. **1977** *Time* 19 Sept. 56/2 At the starting gun in Rhode Island Sound this week, thousands of people will be watching in everything from little outboards to palatial cruisers with bars and quadraphonic sound systems. **1978** *Daily Tel.* 22 Feb. 16/6 (Advt.), BMW 528...Aluminium sports wheels. Quadraphonic radio and cassette player.

B. *sb* = QUADRAPHONY.

1972 *Esquire* June 55/3 (Advt.), Should you wait until quadraphonic is perfected? **1977** *Homes & Gardens* Nov. 161 Quadraphonic was boosted..when the BBC developed

Matrix II, a new method of mixing and encoding quadraphonic signals.

Hence **quadra'phonically** *adv.*, in a quadraphonic way; by means of quadraphony.

1970 *High Fidelity Mag.* Nov. 76/2 In classical music recorded quadriphonically the two front channels serve the same use as the left and right channels of conventional stereo. **1973** [see MATRIX 6 e]. **1976** *Gramophone* Mar. 1441/2 The hall sound and orchestral layout were beautifully conveyed quadraphonically.

quadraphonics (kwɒdrə'fɒnɪks), *sb. pl.* (usu. const. as sing.). Also **quadro-**, **quadri-**. [f. prec.: see -IC 2.] = QUADRAPHONY.

1970 *High Fidelity Mag.* Nov. 76/2 (*heading*) The quadriphonics sweepstakes. **1972** *Observer* (Colour Suppl.) 22 Oct. 55/2 How could one have been taken in for so long by stereo which merely made you a member of a concert audience when quadraphonics elevate you to a member of the orchestra? **1974** H. W. HELLYER *Stereo Sound* ix. 182 Quadrophonics purports to give us back that lost illusion of reality by supplying the lost ambience. **1976** *Which?* May 99/1 One purpose of quadrophonics is to recreate this ambience properly.

quadraphony (kwɒ'drɒfənɪ). Also **quadro-**, **quadri-**. [f. as prec.: see -Y³.] Quadraphonic reproduction; the use of quadraphonic techniques.

1969 *High Fidelity* Sept. 3 Has quadriphony finally arrived? **1970** *Ibid.* Jan. 38/2 With musical material emanating from all four corners of the room, we found that visitors stood every which way to listen. Perhaps the most descriptive terminology for these two techniques, therefore, would be polarized and unpolarized quadriphony, respectively. **1972** *Daily Tel.* 20 Jan. 4 (Advt.), Where stereophony ends quadraphony begins. **1973** *B.B.C. Handbk. 1974* 74/1 Quadrophony involves four sound channels leading to four loudspeakers, normally placed in the four corners of a room. **1974** *Radio Times* 27 June 55/3 With your front two speakers bringing you Radio 2 on VHF Stereo.., and another Stereo Receiver driving your two back speakers and tuned to Radio 3 on VHF Stereo.., you will be able to hear this programme in Quadraphony. **1975** G. J. KING *Audio Handbk.* ix. 211 For quadraphony or four-channel stereo four microphones are required. **1976** *Sci. Amer.* Sept. 144/1 (Advt.), Lowest effective stylus mass (0·39 mg) in quadriphony.

quadraplegic, var. QUADRIPLEGIC *a.* and *sb.*

quadrasonic (kwɒdrə'sɒnɪk), *a.* Also **quadro-**, **quadri-**. [f. QUADRA-, QUADRO-, QUADRI- + SONIC *a.*] = QUADRAPHONIC *a.*

1970 *Time* 28 Sept. 73/2 Davis is looking forward to Columbia's further development of quadrisonic sound, a kind of double-stereo system that was introduced on tapes last year by Vanguard. **1970** *Rolling Stone* 12 Nov. 40/5 Phillips of Holland..has shown some very promising four-channel tapes and cassette machines, called a 'quadrosonic' system. **1971** *Hi-Fi Sound* Feb. 66/2 A compact system with good bookshelf speakers..can be quadrasonic if you like. **1973** *New Yorker* 24 Sept. 113/1 Be a part of New York's newest disco... Appreciate the elite atmosphere of total quadrasonic sound.

quadrat ('kwɒdrət). Also 8 **quadrate**. [var. of QUADRATE *sb.*¹, in special senses.]

†**1. a.** An instrument formerly used for measuring altitudes or distances, consisting of a square plate with two graduated sides, sights, etc. *Obs.*

a **1400** in Halliwell *Rara Mathematica* (1841) 65 When ..þou wolde mesure þe heght..make a quadrat..þat es to sey a table even foure square of wode or brasse. **1617** MINSHEU *Ductor*, A Quadrat, or Geometricall instrument, whereby the distance and height of a place is knowne afarre off by looking thorow a certaine little hole therein,..*dioptra*.

b. Two graduated sides of a square, marked in the rectangular corner of a quadrant to facilitate its use. *Obs.*

a **1400** in Halliwell *Rara Mathematica* (1841) 59 þe quadrat..whilk es descryvede..in þe quadrant has tuo sides. **1706** PHILLIPS (ed. Kersey), *Quadrate* and *Line of Shadows* (on a Quadrant) is a line of natural Tangents. **1727-41** CHAMBERS *Cycl.*, *Quadrat*..called also *geometrical square*, and *line of shadows*, is an additional member on the face of the common Gunter's and Sutton's quadrants.

2. *Printing.* A small block of metal, lower than the face of the type, used by printers for spacing; abbrev. QUAD *sb.*²

1683 MOXON *Mech. Exerc.*, *Printing* xxii. ¶5 If his Title.. make three or more Lines, he Indents the first with an m Quadrat. **1727-41** CHAMBERS *Cycl.* s.v., There are quadrats of divers sizes, as m quadrats, n quadrats, &c. which are respectively of the dimensions of such letters. **1824** J. JOHNSON *Typogr.* II. iii. 65 An m-quadrat is the square of the letter to whatever fount it may belong; an n-quadrat is half that size. **1843** *Penny Cycl.* XXV. 455/1 Larger quadrats, equal in body to two, three, or four m's.

attrib. and *Comb.* **1683** MOXON *Mech. Exerc.*, *Printing* viii, Head sticks..are Quadrat high. **1894** *Amer. Dict. Printing* s.v., To throw all the pi and broken letter..into the quadrat box.

3. *Ecology.* Each of a set of small measured plots of land, formerly usu. one metre squares, used in studying the local distribution of plants and animals. Also *transf.* (see quot. 1960).

1905 F. E. CLEMENTS *Res. Methods Ecol.* iv. 161 Vegetation exhibits both development and structure, and is, in consequence, open to exact methods of inquiry. In the search for feasible methods, it was quickly seen that the quadrat, first used for determining the abundance of species, furnished the key to the problem. *Ibid.* 164 The unit size of quadrat is the meter, and when the term is used without qualification, it refers to the meter quadrat. **1922** *Ecology* III. 158 He does not say whether the quadrats as counted were contiguous or scattered. **1939** CLEMENTS & SHELFORD *Bio-Ecol.* v. 196 Cross checking rendered possible by his use of four methods, viz: trapping, censuses, hare transects, and quadrats of droppings. **1950** *Jrnl. Ecol.* XXXVIII. 108 There has thus grown up in botanical ecology a study of the distribution of species in 'quadrats' or small samples of fixed area (usually 1 sq. m. or less) in which only the presence or absence of particular species is recorded and not its numbers. **1960** *New Phytologist* LIX. 1 In the point quadrat method of vegetational analysis..thin needles are passed vertically through grassland..and the number of contacts between needles and foliage is recorded. **1974** *Nature* 25 Oct. 713/2 It is difficult to estimate the number of snails in natural populations since they move around too slowly for ordinary capture-recapture methods, and their patchy distibution makes quadrat or transect counts unreliable.

quadrat, obs. form of QUADRATE.

†**'quadratary**, *a.* *Obs.* *rare*⁻¹. [ad. L. *quadrātāri-us*: see QUADRATE *sb.*¹ and -ARY¹.] Relating to a square.

1690 LEYBOURN *Curs. Math.* 328 The Proportions Cubatory and Quadratary, in relation to a Sphere's.. Periphery.

quadrate ('kwɒdreɪt), *sb.*¹ Also 6-8 **quadrat**. [ad. L. *quadrāt-um* sb., neut. sing. of *quadrātus* QUADRATE *a.*¹: cf. QUADRANT *sb.*² and QUADRAT.]

†**1.** A square; a square area or space; also, a rectangle or rectangular space. *Obs.*

1471 SIR J. PASTON in *P. Lett.* III. 17 What brede eche towr takythe within iche corner off the quadrate ovyrthwert the dorys. **1483** [see QUADRATE *a.* 1]. **1551** RECORDE *Pathw. Knowl.* I. xxi, When any two quadrates be set forth, howe to make a squire about the one quadrate, whiche shall be equall to the other quadrate. **1598** BARRET *Theor. Warres* III. ii. 46 A Quadrat of ground will bee of men two times and one third more broade then long. **1658** SIR T. BROWNE *Gard. Cyrus* 45 The Labyrinth of Crete, built upon a long quadrate, containing five large squares. **1667** MILTON *P.L.* VI. 62 The Powers Militant, That stood for Heav'n, in mighty Quadrate joyn'd. **1680** T. LAWSON *Mite Treas.* 33 Their.. Cone, Cylinder, Parallelogram, Quadrat [etc.].

†**b.** A square number, the square *of* a number.

1590 RECORDE, etc. *Gr. Artes* (1640) 575 That number is called a Quadrate, which is made by the multiplication of two equal numbers. **1646** SIR T. BROWNE *Pseud. Ep.* 217 The life of man, whose Period..he placed in the Quadrate of 9. or 9. times 9. that is, 81.

†**c.** A group of four things. = QUATERNION 1.

1637 SALTONSTALL *Eusebius' Life Constantine* 139 By the number of twice two, hee invented the quadrate of the foure Elements.

2. A square or rectangular plate or block. *rare.*

1647 H. MORE *Song of Soul* I. II. cxliii, A leaden Quadrate swayes hard on that part That's fit for burdens. **1799** W. TOOKE *View Russian Emp.* I. 50 It was constructed of huge quadrats of ice hewn in the manner of free-stone. **1821** LAMB *Elia* Ser. I. *Old Benchers I.T.*, His person was a quadrate, his step massy and elephantine.

†**3.** *Astron.* **a.** Quadrate aspect; quadrature. *Obs.*

1665-6 *Phil. Trans.* I. 5 This Comet..Having been in Quadrat with the Sun it should still descend. **1686** GOAD *Celest. Bodies* I. vi. 22 The Moon, on the day of the Last Quadrate decreasing, makes as high a Water, sometimes higher than at the first in the Increase. **1695** CONGREVE *Love for L.* II. v, Can judge..of sextiles, quadrates, trines and oppositions.

†**b.** A right angle. *Obs.* *rare*⁻¹.

1686 GOAD *Celest. Bodies* I. vi. 18 In the one the Moon is conjoin'd with the Sun in diameter-line making no Angle, in the Other making a Quadrate, the utmost distance from the Conjunction and Opposition.

4. *Anat.* **a.** The quadrate bone. **b.** A quadrate muscle.

1872 MIVART *Anat.* 121 Other bones, the lowest of which is termed the Quadrate. **1878** [see QUADRATO- 2]. **1883** MARTIN & MOALE *Vertebr. Dissect.* II. 103 The quadrates, projecting ventrally and forward and bearing the articular facets for the mandible.

†**quadrate**, *sb.*² *Obs.* Also **quadrat**. [App. an alteration of QUADRANT *sb.*¹, through assoc. with prec., or through misreading of *quadrāt* = *quadrant*.]

1. A quarter; *spec.* of a circle. = QUADRANT *sb.*¹ 4.

1551 RECORDE *Pathw. Knowl.* I. Defin., The quarter of a circle, named a quadrate. **1604** R. CAWDREY *Table Alph.*, *Quadrate*, a quarter.

2. = QUADRANT 5.

1551 RECORDE *Pathw. Knowl.* II. Pref., The arte of Measuryng by the quadrate geometricall, and the disorders committed in vsyng the same. *Ibid.*, A newe quadrate newely inuented by the author hereof. **1559** W. CUNNINGHAM *Cosmogr. Glasse* 163 The use of the shipmans quadrat, whose inventor was worthy D. Gemma. *Ibid.* 164 The hier part of the Quadrate.

†**quadrate**, *sb.*³ *Her.* *Obs.* Also 5 **quadrant**, 5-6 **quadrat**. [Prob. identical with one or other of the prec. sbs., but the precise origin is not clear.] (See quots. 1486.)

1486 *Bk. St. Albans, Her.* B iij, In blasyng of armys be ix. quadrattis that is to say v. quadrate finiall and iiij. Royall. *Ibid.* B iv, Quadrat is calde in armys whan the felde is set with sum tokyn of armys. **1572** BOSSEWELL *Armorie* II. 77 b, The Crosse thus charged, is called of olde Heraultes, the first quadrate royall. **1586** FERNE *Blaz. Gentrie* 206-209.

quadrate ('kwɒdrət), *a.* Also 5-7 **quadrat**. [ad. L. *quadrāt-us*, pa. pple. of *quadrāre* to square: see QUADRATE *v.*]

1. Square, rectangular. Now *rare.*

1398 TREVISA *Barth. De P.R.* XIX. cxviii. (1495) 922 Quadrate shape and square is moost stedfaste and stable. **1483** CAXTON *Gold. Leg.* 332 b/2 For whanne euery beest was quadrate as we may ymagyne In a quadrate ben foure corners and euery corner was a penne. **1538** LELAND *Itin.* III. 44 A strong Castel quadrate having at eche corner a great Round Tower. **1560** ROLLAND *Crt. Venus* I. 139 Tabletis of gold, bayth quadrate als & round. **1593** NORDEN *Spec. Brit.*, *M'sex* I. 35 The form of the building is quadrate. **1813** T. BUSBY *Lucretius* II. iv. 437 And circular appears the quadrate pile. **1866** HUXLEY *Preh. Rem. Caithn.* 137 The quadrate pelvis is that which is compressed..so that the brim is almost quadrangular. **1880** BASTIAN *Brain* 77 These two pairs of ganglia..are combined into one quadrate mass in Hyalea.

Comb. **1610** GUILLIM *Heraldry* II. vii. (1660) 85 This is termed Quarter pierced, quasi, Quadrate pierced, for that the piercing is square as a Trencher.

†**b.** *Math.* Of numbers or roots. = SQUARE. *Obs.*

c **1430** *Art Nombryng* (E.E.T.S.) 14, .4. is the first nombre quadrat, and 2. is his rote. **1571** DIGGES *Pantom.* I. xxv. Hj, These two ioyned together make 43600, whose Quadrate roote being about 208 pace 3 foote is the Hypothenusall line *AC*. **1611** SPEED *Hist. Gt. Brit.* IX. viii. §31. 552 The Rings Roundnesse must remember the King of Eternitie; the Quadrat number of Constancy. **1646** SIR T. BROWNE *Pseud. Ep.* 215 Consisting of square and quadrate numbers [viz. 49 and 81]. **1655-60** STANLEY *Hist. Phil.* (1687) 527/2 The Tetrad..being quadrate..is divided into Equals.

c. *Anat.* in the distinctive names of certain parts of the body having an approximately square shape.

quadrate bone, a special bone in the head of birds and reptiles, by which the lower jaw is articulated to the skull. *quadrate muscle*, the name of several muscles, esp. the *quadratus lumborum* (of the loins), *q. femoris* (of the thigh), and *q. pronator* (in the forearm): see QUADRATUS.

1856-8 W. CLARK *Van der Hoeven's Zool.* II. 334 The quadrate bone of birds is..divided above into two arms.

†**2.** *Astron.* = QUARTILE *a.* *Obs.*

This use of *quadrate* is due to the fact that the lines joining four equidistant points on a circle form a square; hence also the sign for 'quartile aspect' is □, as that for 'trine' is Δ. Cf. QUADRATURE 4.

1552 HULOET, Quadrate aspecte of the planettes. **1594** BLUNDEVIL *Exerc.* IV. pr. 43 (1636) 501 And they [two Planets] are said..to be in a quadrat aspect when they are distant one from another, by three signes. **1601** HOLLAND *Pliny* I. 12 The planet of Mars..maketh station but in quadrate aspect: as for Iupiter, in triangle aspect. **1685** BOYLE *Enq. Notion Nat.* v. 126 At some time She and the Sun should have a Trine, or a Quadrate Aspect.

†**3.** *fig.* Complete, perfect. *Obs.*

1608 J. KING *Serm. St. Mary's* 7 There yet remaineth a fourth point to make vp a quadrate and perfitt honor of the King. *c* **1645** HOWELL *Lett.* VI. (1650) 253 The Moralist tells us that a quadrat solid wise man should..be still the same. **1679** HARBY *Key Script.* II. 45 That future quadrate Righteousness of Gospel-Promise.

†**4.** Conformable, corresponding (*to* or *with*). Cf. QUADRANT *a.* 2. *Obs.*

a **1657** R. LOVEDAY *Lett.* (1663) 68 To construe me right, and believe my meaning quadrate to my words. **1674** S. VINCENT *Yng. Gallant's Acad.* 99 His word and his meaning are quadrate, and never shake hands and part. **1720** WELTON *Suffer. Son of God* I. vi. 112 Whose State of Life is Quadrate and Concentrick with the Low and Humble Poverty of their Redeemer.

5. *Her.* *cross quadrate*, a cross which expands into a square at the junction of the arms.

1780 EDMONDSON *Compl. Body Heraldry* I. [See of] *Litchfield.* Per pale gu. and ar. a cross potent quadrat. **1797** *Encycl. Brit.* (ed. 3) VIII. 452/1.

quadrate ('kwɒdreɪt), *v.* Also 7-9 (6 *Sc. pa. pple.*) **quadrat**. [f. L. *quadrāt-*, ppl. stem of *quadrāre* to square.]

1. *trans.* To make (a thing) square. *rare.*

1560 ROLLAND *Crt. Venus* II. 586 With subtill wark it was sa roborat Properlie alswa with kirnalis weill quadrat. **1798** in *Spirit Publ. Jrnls.* (1799) II. 151 The winding stream quadrated into fishponds. **1841** *Penny Cycl.* XIX. 197/2 The materials..are there quadrated or formed into rectangular blocks.

b. *Math.* To square (a circle, etc.). *rare.*

c **1645** HOWELL *Lett.* (1650) I. 26 The hardest things in the world were; To quadrate a circle, to find out the philosopher's stone. **1838-9** HALLAM *Hist. Lit.* III. III. viii. §9 399 It had long been acknowledged by the best geometers impossible to quadrate by a direct process any curve surface.

†**2.** To square (a number or amount). *Obs.* *rare*⁻¹.

1613 JACKSON *Creed* II. §III. iv. 388 The Pharisees..did as it were quadrate the measure of Proselytes sinnes; multiplying Gentilisme by Pharisaisme.

3. *intr.* To square, agree, correspond, conform *with* (rarely *to*).

1610 GUILLIM *Heraldry* VI. v. (1611) 265 This forme of Helmet..doth best quadrate with the dignity of a Knight. **1671** *True Nonconf.* 18 That it exactly quadrates to the case of our Controversie is apparent. **1720** WELTON *Suffer. Son of God* I. xi. 273 When their Lives Quadrate with their Doctrine, their Words Become of weight. **1794** PALEY *Evid.* II. i. (1817) 10 The description..quadrates with no part of the Jewish history with which we are acquainted. **1876** J. PARKER *Paracl.* II. xviii. 325 He had to make a creed which would quadrate with his immorality.

b. Without const.: To be fitting, suitable, or consistent. Also of two things: To harmonize with each other. Now *rare*.

1664 EVELYN *Sylva* (1776) 516 The same arguments do not Quadrate in trees. **1718** *Freethinker* No. 44 ¶7 The Compliment..of comparing a Beauty to a Star, will now quadrate in every Respect. **1791** E. DARWIN *Bot. Gard.* II. Interl. 84 The similies of Homer..do not quadrate, or go upon all fours. **1833** CHALMERS *Const. Man* (1835) I. vi. 256 That the natural..and the legal or political..should quadrate as much as possible.

c. *trans.* To make conformable (*to*). *rare.*

1669 WORLIDGE *Syst. Agric.* (1681) 296 Therefore I desire all such that expect any success to their Observations, that they quadrate the Rules to the places where they live. **1817** T. L. PEACOCK *Melincourt* xxv, He quadrates his practice as nearly as he can to his theory.

4. *Artillery.* **a.** *trans.* To adjust (a gun) on its carriage (see quots.). **b.** *intr.* Of a gun: To lie properly on the carriage.

1706 PHILLIPS (ed. Kersey) s.v., In Gunnery, to quadrate or square a Piece, is to see whether it be duly plac'd, or well pois'd on the Carriage and Wheels. **1800** *Naval Chron.* IV. 53 A gun quadrates, or hangs well in her carriage. **1867** SMYTH *Sailor's Word-bk.*, *Quadrate*, to trim a gun on its carriage and its trucks, to adjust it for firing on a level range.

5. In *pa. pple.*: Placed in quadrate aspect.

1829 POE *Poems, Al Aaraf* (1859) 192 What time the moon is quadrated in heaven.

'quadrated, *ppl. a.* [f. prec. + -ED[1].] **a.** Made square, squared. ? *Obs.* **b.** Quartered. *rare*$^{-1}$.

a. 1578 BANISTER *Hist. Man* VIII. 109 A nerue..is at length implanted to the quadrated or foure squared Muscle. **1727-41** CHAMBERS *Cycl.* s.v. *Printing*, Little quadrated pieces of metal, called quotations.

b. 1810 MOOR *Hindu Pantheon* 249 The quadrated lozenge, on the breast and in the palm of this image, is also unaccounted for, and singular.

†**quadrateness.** *Obs. rare*$^{-1}$. Squareness.

1599 A. M. tr. *Gabelhouer's Bk. Physicke* 112/1 Malleate.. with the broadest hammers..till it be about thre quart. in the quadratnes therof.

quadratic (kwə'drætɪk), *a.* and *sb.* [ad. L. type **quadrātic-us*: see QUADRATE *sb.*[1] and -IC, and cf. F. *quadratique*.]

A. *adj.* **1. a.** Square. *rare.*

1656 in BLOUNT *Glossogr.* **1876** tr. *Wagner's Gen. Pathol.* 115 They first assume the quadratic form at a distance of one metre behind the head. **1884** BOWER & SCOTT *De Bary's Phaner.* 107 One epidermal cell which appears in surface view rounded and quadratic.

b. *Cryst.* Of square section through the lateral or secondary axes; characterized by this form.

1871 ROSCOE *Elem. Chem.* 215 On boiling this solution the salt is formed, and may be crystallized in quadratic prisms. **1875** BENNETT & DYER tr. *Sachs' Bot.* 66 The calcium oxalate..crystallises in the quadratic system.

2. *Math.* Involving the second and no higher power of an unknown quantity or of a variable; esp. in ***quadratic equation***: see EQUATION 6. Also ***quadratic form*** (see FORM *sb.* 5 d); ***quadratic programming***, a technique analogous to linear programming but dealing with a quadratic rather than a linear objective function.

1668 WILKINS *Real Char.* II. vii. 181 Those Algebraical notions of Absolute, Lineary, Quadratic, Cubic. **1690** LEYBOURN *Curs. Math.* 337 All Quadratick Aequations of this kind..have two Roots. **1706** W. JONES *Syn. Palmar. Matheseos* 128 All Quadratic Equations are reducible to one of these Forms. **1806** HUTTON *Course Math.* I. 247 A simple quadratic equation, is that which involves the square of the unknown quantity only. **1859** [see FORM *sb.* 5 d]. **1885** WATSON & BURBURY *Math. The. Electr. & Magn.* I. 169 If we express every *e* in terms of the potentials by means of equations..*E* will be a quadratic function of the potentials. **1896** *Bull. Amer. Math. Soc.* III. 100 The general theory of quadratic forms is not taken up. **1965** C. H. SPRINGER et al. *Adv. Methods & Models* viii. 232 *Quadratic Programing*—a name given to a problem which looks much like a linear program, except the objective function is of second degree, i.e., contains squared terms in it. **1968** E. T. COPSON *Metric Spaces* ix. 141 This space was first studied by David Hilbert in his work on quadratic forms in infinitely many variables. **1974** ADBY & DEMPSTER *Introd. Optimization Methods* v. 153 Although this is an effective strategy for quadratic programming, it can multiply unnecessary function evaluations for general *f*.

B. *sb.* **a.** A quadratic equation. **b.** *pl.* The branch of algebra dealing with quadratic equations.

1684 BAKER *Geometr. Key* Title-p., Of linears, qvadratics, cubics [etc.]. **1690** LEYBOURN *Curs. Math.* 337 The three sorts of Mixed Aequations above expressed, are all that can happen in Quadraticks. **1727-41** CHAMBERS *Cycl.* s.v., There are several methods of extracting the roots of adfected quadratics. **1827** HUTTON *Course Math.* I. 256 *note*, Cubic equations, when occurring in pairs, may usually be reduced to quadratics, by extermination. *a* **1839** PRAED *Poems* (1864) II. 41 By turns, as Thought or Pleasure wills, Quadratics struggle with quadrilles. **1870** [see ADFECTED].

qua'dratical, *a.* Now *rare.* [f. as prec. + -AL[1].] = QUADRATIC *a.*

1674 JEAKE *Arith.* (1696) 645 The Quotient shall be squaredly Quadratical. **1690** LEYBOURN *Curs. Math.* 343 To receive as many Cubical Points, as the Co-efficient doth Quadratical. **1880** GILBERT *Pirates Penzance*, I understand equations, both the simple and quadratical.

Hence **qua'dratically** *adv.*

1891 in *Cent. Dict.* **1928** *Physical Rev.* XXXI. 74 Such an equation has no quadratically integrable solution. **1955** *Rev. Sci. Instruments* XXVI. 116/1 The mode separation varies quadratically as the limit is approached. **1974** ADBY & DEMPSTER *Introd. Optimization Methods* iv. 90 A quadratically terminating method..which makes use of conjugate gradient vectors..has been utilized in procedures for constrained optimization because of its modest memory requirements. **1979** *Sci. Amer.* May 32/3 This implies that in the past the storehouse has grown quadratically with time, as Engels said, not linearly, as Rescher argues.

quadrato- (kwə'dreɪtəʊ), mod. comb. form of L. *quadrātus* or *quadrātum*, QUADRATE *a.* or *sb.*[1]; used in some scientific terms.

†**1.** *Math.* **quadrato-cubic** *a.*, of the fifth power or degree. **quadrato-quadrat(e,** the fourth power. **quadrato-quadratic, -quadratical** *adjs.*, of the fourth power; biquadratic. *Obs.*

1662 HOBBES *Seven Prob.* Wks. 1845 VII. 67 There be some numbers called plane..others *quadrato-cubic. **1787** WARING in *Phil. Trans.* LXXVII. 81 Biquadratic and quadrato-cubic equations. **1684** T. BAKER *Geometr. Key* d. 2 The *quadrato-quadrat of *x*, x^4. **1728** CLARKE in *Phil. Trans.* XXXV. 387 The Cube, or the quadrato-quadrate, or any other Power. **1674** PETTY *Disc. Dupl. Proportion* 45 To have like Vessels..equally strong, the Timber of which they consist must be *Quadrato-quadratic. **1677** BAKER in Rigaud *Corr. Sci. Men* (1841) II. 18 The geometrical constructions of all cubic, and quadrato-quadratic equations. **1668** BARROW *ibid.* 63 When the equations are *quadrato-quadratical.

2. *Zool.* Connected with or pertaining to the quadrate together with some other bone, as **qua,drato-'jugal** *a.* and *sb.* (see quot. 1878), **-man'dibular, -(meta)'pterygoid, -squa'mosal** *adjs.* (see the second element).

1870 ROLLESTON *Anim. Life* 18 The quadratojugal rod. **1878** BELL *Gegenbaur's Comp. Anat.* 462 In Birds the quadrato-jugal is a slender piece of bone, which arises from the side of the mandibular joint of the quadrate. **1888** ROLLESTON & JACKSON *Anim. Life* 338 The quadrate or in Teleostei..the quadrato-metapterygoid.

3. *Cryst.* **,quadratocta'hedron,** an eight-sided crystal of square section through the secondary axes.

1884 BOWER & SCOTT *De Bary's Phaner.* 137 The fundamental form of the crystals belonging to the quadratic system is the quadratoctahedron.

quadratrix (kwə'dreɪtrɪks). Pl. **quadratrices.** [mod.L., fem. agent-n. from *quadrāre* to QUADRATE; cf. F. *quadratrice* (17th c.).] A curve used in the process of squaring other curves.

1656 tr. *Hobbes' Elem. Philos.* (1839) 316 The ancient geometricians..who made use of the quadratrix for the finding out of a strait line equal to the arch of a circle. **1727-41** CHAMBERS *Cycl.* s.v., The most eminent of these *quadratrices* are, that of Dinostrates [etc.]. **1816** tr. *Lacroix's Diff. & Int. Calculus* 662 The Quadratrix, a curve formerly celebrated for its apparent connection with the quadrature of the circle. **1898** tr. H. Schubert *Math. Essays* 124 The solution of the quadrature of the circle founded on the construction of the quadratrix.

quadrature ('kwɒdrətjʊə(r)). [ad. L. *quadrātūra* a square, the act of squaring: see QUADRATE *v.* and -URE. Cf. F. *quadrature* (1529).]

†**1.** Square shape, squareness. *Obs*

1563 FOXE *A. & M.* (1596) 1670 The maruellous quadrature of the same, I take to signifie the vniuersal agreement in the same. **1600** HOLLAND *Livy* XXV. xxiii. 565 One of the Romans..counted the stones..and made estimate to himselfe of their quadrature and proportion. **1653** R. SANDERS *Physiogn.* 60 When the Quadrangle is broad, and well-proportioned in its quadrature. **1667** MILTON *P.L.* x. 380 Parted by th' Empyreal bounds, His Quadrature, from thy Orbicular World.

†**2.** One side of a square. *Obs. rare*$^{-1}$.

1553 EDEN *Treat. Newe Ind.* (Arb.) 25 Euery quadrature or syde of the wall hath in it thre principal portes or gates.

3. *Math.* **a.** The action or process of squaring; *spec.* the expression of an area bounded by a curve, esp. a circle, by means of an equivalent square. More widely, the calculation of the area bounded by, or lying under, a curve.

1596 NASHE *Saffron Walden* 22 As much time..as a man might haue found out the quadrature of the circle in. **1652** BENLOWES *Theoph.* XI. xxxvii, As hard to find thy cure As circles puzling Quadrature. **1664** *Phil. Trans.* I. 15 A method for the Quadrature of Parabola's of all degrees. **1743** EMERSON *Fluxions* p. iii, Drawing Tangents to Curves, finding their Curvatures, their Lengths, and Quadratures. **1829** MRQ. ANGLESEA *Let.* 28 Feb. in *Lady Morgan's Mem.* (1862) II. 278, I am as incapable of making a rhyme as of effecting the quadrature of the circle. **1881** ROUTLEDGE *Science* ii. 36 The attention which the problem of the quadrature of the circle has attracted. **1911** E. B. WILSON *Adv. Calculus* xi. 313 It is therefore customary to restrict the application of the term 'area' to such simple closed curves as have $l_u = 0$, and to say that the quadrature of such curves is possible, but that the quadrature of curves for which $l_u \neq 0$ is impossible. **1942** H. M. BACON *Differential & Integral Calculus* i. 3 The desire was to find a *square* equal in area to the area bounded by the given curve (in this case, a circle). For this reason the problem has been called the problem of quadrature. *Ibid.* xiv. 410 The definite integral, which solves the problem of quadrature mentioned in Chap. I, suggests the notation for integrals, the $\int$ being a conventionalized form of 'S' for 'sum'. **1968** FOX & MAYERS *Computing Methods* ix. 170 Apart from the rare possibility of being able to perform the quadrature by expressing the indefinite integral in closed form.., we have various general methods and some special methods.

†**b.** (See quot.) *Obs.*

1727-41 CHAMBERS *Cycl.*, *Quadrature-lines*, or *lines of Quadrature*, are two lines frequently placed on Gunter's sector. [Description follows.]

4. *Astron.* †**a.** One of the four cardinal points. *Obs. rare*$^{-1}$. (See note on QUADRATE *a.* 2.)

1601 HOLLAND *Pliny* I. 37 When this concurrence [of the planets with the sun] is about the quadratures of the heaven. [L. *circa quadrata mundi*.]

b. One of the two points (in space or time) at which the moon is 90° distant from the sun, or midway between the points of conjunction and opposition.

1685 BOYLE *Enq. Notion Nat.* vii. 256 When the Moon is in Opposition to the Sun..that Part of Her Body which respects the Earth, is more Enlightned than at the New Moon, or at either of the Quadratures. **1726** tr. *Gregory's Astron.* I. 126 The Passage of the Body *L* from the Quadratures to the Syzygies. **1774** GOLDSM. *Nat. Hist.* (1862) I. 91 The tides are greatest in the syzygies and least in the quadratures. **1867-77** G. F. CHAMBERS *Astron.* I. ii. (ed. 3) 39 After starting from conjunction with the Sun it successively reaches its Eastern quadrature [etc.].

c. The position of one heavenly body relative to another when they are 90° apart, *esp.* of the moon to the sun when at the quadratures (see prec.). †Also ***quadrature aspect***.

1591 SPARRY tr. *Cattan's Geomancie* (1599) 185 The Quadrature Aspect is from the first to the fourth, or from the first to the tenth. **1797** *Encycl. Brit.* (ed. 3) II. 508/2 Thus the sun and moon,..or any two planets, may be in conjunction, opposition, or quadrature. **1812** WOODHOUSE *Astron.* vii. 44 The Sun is said to be in quadrature with a star, or planet, when the difference of their longitudes is 90° or 270°. **1854** BREWSTER *More Worlds* xvi. 236 The rays reflected from them when the planets are in quadrature.

†**d.** *Her.* ***in quadrature***, at intervals of a quarter-circle. *Obs.*

1766 PORNY *Heraldry* (1787) 188 A circular Wreath, Pearl and Diamond [= Argent and Sable] with four Hawk's Bells joined thereto in quadrature Topaz [= Or].

e. *Electr.* A phase difference of 90 degrees. Usu. *attrib.* or in phr. ***in quadrature (with)***.

1889 T. H. BLAKESLEY *Alternating Currents of Electr.* (ed. 2) xiii. 117 The only induction in the secondary coil is derived from the core, and is, therefore, as regards phase, in quadrature with the magnetization. **1892** S. P. THOMPSON *Dynamo-Electric Machinery* (ed. 4) xxii. 628 The waves of self-induced electromotive-force will lag exactly a quarter-period behind those of the current, or will be 'in quadrature' with them. **1940** *Chambers's Techn. Dict.* 691/2 *Quadrature transformer*, a transformer designed so that the secondary e.m.f. is 90° displaced from the primary e.m.f. *Ibid.* 705/1 *Reactive component*, the term now preferred for the component of the vector representing an alternating quantity which is in quadrature (at 90°) with some reference vector... Also called quadrature component. **1944** *Electronic Engin.* XVII. 58/2 The only unusual section is the reactance modulator or quadrature tube, so called because the anode circuit is back-coupled to the grid..in such a way as to cause a 90-degree phase difference between grid and anode voltages. **1967** *Electronics* 6 Mar. 120/2 The current in these resistors is in quadrature with the current in A_3's input resistor. **1974** HARVEY & BOHLMAN *Stereo F.M. Radio Handbk.* iv. 65 The normal signal is again divided by 2 to give a 19kHz quadrature signal for feeding back along the phase-lock loop.

†**5.** A division into four parts (? cf. QUADRATE *sb.*[2]). *Obs. rare*$^{-1}$.

1578 LYTE *Dodoens* VI. lxxix. 759 Foure straight lines running alongst the young shutes or branches, the which do make a quadrature, or a diuision of the said young branches into foure square partes or cliftes.

‖**quadratus** (kwə'dreɪtəs). *Anat.* [L.: see QUADRATE *sb.*[1] and *a.*] A quadrate muscle. ***quadratus femoris, lumborum***, etc. (see QUADRATE *a.* 1 c).

1727-41 CHAMBERS *Cycl.*, *Quadratus*..a name applied to several muscles, in respect of their square figure; as the palmaris, and pronators. **1756** WINSLOW *Anat.* (ed. 4) I. 211 A tendon..inserted between the Gemelli and Quadratus. **1843** J. G. WILKINSON *Swedenborg's Anim. Kingd.* I. ii. 60 Some of the before mentioned muscles: these are the triangulares and quadratus. **1870** ROLLESTON *Anim. Life* 3 The two psoas muscles and the quadratus lumborum.

quadreble, var. QUATREBLE, quadruple.

quadred, pa. pple. of QUADER *v. Obs.*

quadrefoil, obs. form of QUATREFOIL.

quadrein, obs. variant of QUATRAIN.

†**quadrel.** *Obs.* Also 7 -ell. [ad. It. *quadrello* (med.L. *quadrellus*, OF. *quarrel*, F. *carreau*) square stone or brick, dim. of *quadro* a square: cf. QUARREL *sb.*[1]] A square block, esp. of brick, and *spec.* of a kind of brick used in Italy (see quot. 1703). Also *attrib.*

1686 PLOT *Staffordsh.* 358 Their Quadrells of peat, are made into that fashion by the spade that cutts them. **1688** R. HOLME *Armoury* III. 457/1 A Quadrell Wall, that is a wall of Artificiall Stone, as Brick, Tyle, etc. **1703** T. N. *City & C. Purchaser* 232 Quadrels, a sort of artificial Stones..made of a chalky, whitish and pliable Earth, and dry'd in the Shade. **1715** LEONI *Palladio's Archit.* (1742) I. 80 A sort of Bricks larger than Quadrels, or common ones.

quadren, square: see QUADRAN.

quadrennial (kwə'drɛnɪəl), *a.* and *sb.* Also (correctly) quadriennial, (7 -ennal). [ad. L. type **quadrienniāl-is*, *-ennāl-is*: see QUADRENNIUM and -AL[1], and cf. F. *quatriennal*.]

A. *adj.* **1.** Occurring every fourth year.

1701 W. Wotton *Hist. Rome, Marcus* iii. 46 Their Accounts of Time were reckoned by the Quadriennial Returns of the Grand Games. **1847** Grote *Greece* II. xxviii. IV. 92 Peisistratus..first added the quadrennial or greater Panathenæa to the ancient annual or lesser Panathenæa. **1880** *Times* 27 Sept. 8/1 The Archbishop of Canterbury..continuing his quadrennial visitation of his diocese. **1884** *Sat. Rev.* 7 June 745/2 Its statutes only demanded quadrennial residence.

2. Lasting for four years.

1656 Blount *Glossogr.*, *Quadriennial*, of four years. **1727** Bailey, vol. II, *Quadrennial*, of the Space of four Years. **1881** *Daily News* 11 Mar. 6/2 Biennial Budgets and quadrennial Parliaments.

B. *sb.* †**a.** A period of four years. *Obs. rare*$^{-1}$. **b.** An event happening every four years. **c.** A fourth anniversary, or its celebration (*Cent. Dict.*).

a **1646** J. Gregory *Posthuma, De Æris et Epochis* (1650) 163 The Egyptians called everie daie in the year by the Name of som God..and everie year of their Lustrums or Quadriennals in like manner. **1856** *Sat. Rev.* 8 Nov. 625/2 The great quadrennial—the Presidential election—is the 'Derby Day' of America.

Hence **qua'drennially** *adv.*, every fourth year.

1796 Morse *Amer. Geog.* I. 626 The senate [of Virginia] chosen quadrennially. **1932** H. G. Wells *Work, Wealth & Happiness of Mankind* xii. 599 It could go to the country triennially or quadrennially for new blood and the elimination of persons who had become unpopular. **1972** *Publishers' Weekly* 24 Jan. 62/3 Campaign biographies are quadrennially the cream cheese of publishing.

‖**quadrennium** (kwə'drɛnɪəm). Also (correctly) **quadriennium.** [a. L. *quadriennium*, f. *quadri-* QUADRI- + *annus* year.] A period of four years; *spec.* in *Sc. Law* (see quot. 1823).

1823 Crabb, *Quadriennium utile*,..the term of four years allowed..to a minor after his majority, during which he may by suit, or action, endeavour to annul any deed granted to his prejudice during his minority. **1857** G. Oliver *Coll. Hist. Cath. Relig. Cornwall* 482 Francis Watmough..is known to have filled several quadrienniums before his death. **1876** Fox Bourne *Locke* I. ii. 52 In taking his bachelor's degree..Locke abridged the old quadrennium..by one term.

quadri- ('kwɒdrɪ), a first element used in combs. with the sense 'having, consisting of, connected with, etc. four (things specified)'. The L. *quadri-* was so employed in a few words during the classical period, as in the sbs. *quadriduum*, *quadriennium*, *quadrirēmis*, *quadrivium*, the adjs. *quadrifidus*, *quadrijugus*, and the pple. *quadripartītus*. In the post-classical and later language such compounds are much more numerous, esp. adj. forms, as *quadriangulus*, *-ennis*, *-formis*, *-gamus*, *-laterus*, etc. (See also QUADRU-.)

The earliest examples in English are *quadrangle*, *quadripartite*, *quadrivial*, which are as old as the 15th c.; others, as *quadrifid*, *quadriform*, *quadrilateral*, *quadrireme* were introduced later, esp. in the 17th c. By far the greater number of *quadri-* compounds, however, belong to the language of modern science, the employment of the prefix in popular words being much rarer than that of *bi-* and *tri-*. A considerable number of those given in the following lists are self-explanatory, and in these cases the definition is omitted.

I. Adjectives with the sense 'having or consisting of four —', 'characterized by the number four', as **a. quadri'basic** *Chem.*, applied to certain acids containing four atoms of displaceable hydrogen (Webster, 1864); **ˌquadricen'tennial**, consisting of, connected with, a period of four centuries (*Cent. Dict.* 1891); **quadri'farious** [L. *-farius*], fourfold, having four parts; **quadri'focal**, having four foci (*Cent. Dict.*); **quadri'frontal** [L. *-frons*], having four faces; **quadri'gabled**; **quadri'jugal** [L. *-jugus*], four-horsed, belonging to a four-horse chariot; **quadri'libral** [L. *lībris*], containing four pounds; **quadri'lingual** [late L. *-linguis*], using, written in, etc., four languages; **qua'drimanous** = QUADRUMANOUS; †**quadrimood** (see quot.); **quadri'nomial, -'nomical, -'nominal**, consisting of four (algebraic) terms; **qua'driparous** *Ornith.*, laying only four eggs; **quadri'paschal**, including four passovers (cf. BIPASCHAL, *tripaschal* s.v. TRI- 1); **quadri'planar**; **qua'driplicate(d)**, having four folds or pleats (Craig, 1848); **quadrisy'llabic(al)**, †**-'syllable**, **-'syllabous** [late L. *-syllabus*].

1977 *Times* 19 Apr. 14/6 The three-year *quadricentennial celebrations [in California] of Sir Francis Drake's voyage round the world. *a* **1745** Swift *To George-Nim-Dan-Dean Esq.* Wks. 1841 I. 762 Hail human compound *quadrifarious..Invincible as wight Briareus. *a* **1859** De Quincey *Posth. Wks.* (1891) I. 235 All the quadrifarious virtue of the scholastic ethics. **1886** *Academy* 25 Apr. 288/1 The famous *Quadrifrontal Roman Arch [at Tripoli]. **1892** A. Heales *Archit. Ch. Denmark* 69 On the north is a staircase, the angles are of brick; *quadrigabled. **1819** H. Busk *Vestriad* IV. 636 Aurora's neighing steeds..draw on her *quadrijugal car. **1674** Jeake *Arith.* (1696) 91 Some mention a Triple Choenix, as Bilibral, *Quadrilibral, and Quinquelibral. **1876** Birch *Rede Lect. Egypt* 41 A *quadrilingual stele at Suez, in Egyptian hieroglyphs, Persian, Median, and Babylonian cuneiform. **1962** Quadrilingual [see FRANCOPHONE *sb.* and *a.*]. **1969** *Internat. Herald Tribune* 6 Nov. 14/2 (Advt.), Young American, excellent education U.S.A.-Europe, Ph.D. quadri-lingual, well traveled,..seeks unparalleled + challenging position. **1609** Douland *Ornith. Microl.* 18 Diapente..is the leaping of one Voyce to another by a fift, consisting of three Tones, and a semitone..Therefore Pontifex cals it the *Quadrimoode Interuall. **1727** Bailey vol. II, *Quadrinomial*,..consisting of four Denominations or Names. **1866–99** W. R. Hamilton *Elem. Quatern.* (ed. 2) I. 245 The principal use which we shall here make of the standard quadrinomial form. **1883** *Quadripaschal [see *tripaschal* s.v. TRI- I. 1]. **1908** J. Hastings *Dict. Christ* II. 185/1 The *long period* theory..holds that there were four Passovers in the ministry, and is hence called the *quadripaschal* theory. **1882** Salmon *Anal. Geom. 3 Dimens.* (ed. 4) 23 We shall use these *quadriplanar coordinates, whenever..our equations can be materially simplified. **1883** *Contemp. Rev.* Dec. 938 The old absurdity of reading everything possible into *quadrisyllabic feet. **1656** Blount *Glossogr.*, **Quadrisyllable*,..that hath four syllables. **1678** Phillips (ed. 4), *List Barbarous Words*, **Quadrisyllabous*, consisting of four syllables.

b. *Bot.* and *Zool.*, as **quadri'alate**, having four alæ or wing-like processes (*Syd. Soc. Lex.* 1897); **quadri'annulate**, having or consisting of four rings; **quadriar'ticulate(d)**, having four joints; **quadri'capsular, -'capsulate**; **quadri'carinate**, having four carinæ or keel-shaped lines, *spec.* of an orthopterous insect (*Cent. Dict.* 1891); **quadri'cellular**; **quadri'ciliate**, having four cilia or hairs; **quadri'cipital**, having four heads or points of origin, as the quadriceps muscle; **'quadricorn**, having four horns (*ibid.*); so **-cornous** (Blount *Glossogr.* 1656); **quadri'costate**, having four costæ or ribs; **quadricoty'ledonous**, having two deeply divided (and thus apparently four) cotyledons; **ˌquadricre'scentic, -toid**, having four crescents; of teeth: having four crescentic folds; **quadri'cuspid, -'cuspidate**, of teeth: having four cusps or points; **quadri'digitate**, having four digits or similar divisions; **quadri'foliate**, consisting of four leaves; also = **quadri'foliolate**, of a compound leaf: having four leaflets growing from the same point; **quadri'furcate(d)**, having four forks or branches; **quadri'geminal, -ous**, belonging to the *corpora quadrigemina* at the base of the brain; also = **quadri'geminate**, formed of four similar parts, fourfold; **quadri'glandular**; **quadri'hilate** (see quot.); **quadri'jugate, -'jugous**, of a leaf: having four pairs of leaflets (Martyn, 1793); **quadri'laminar, -ate**; **quadri'lobate, -lobed**; **quadri'locular, -ate**, having four compartments; **quadri'membral**; **quadri'nodal**; **quadri'nucleate**; **quadri'pennate**, having four wings (Worcester, 1846); †**quadri'phyllous** (see quot.); **quadri'pinnate**, having four pinnæ or side leaflets; **quadri'polar**, having four poles or centres of division in a cell; **quadri'pulmonary**, of spiders: having two pairs of pulmonary sacs (*Cent. Dict.*); **quadri'radiate** (see quot.); **quadri'septate**, having four septa or dissepiments; **quadri'serial**, arranged in four series or rows; **quadri'setose**, having four setæ or bristles (*Cent. Dict.*); **quadri'spiral**; †**quadrisulc** [late L. *-sulcus*], **quadri'sulcate(d)**, having four grooves or furrows, having a four-parted hoof; **quadritu'bercular, -tu'berculate**; **'quadrivalve, -'valvular**; **quadri'voltine** [It. *volta* time, turn], (of a silkworm moth) producing four broods in a year; also as *sb.*

1856–8 W. Clark *Van der Hoeven's Zool.* I. 321 Abdomen *quadriannulate, oval. **1826** Kirby & Sp. *Entomol.* IV. 325 *Quadriarticulate. **1834** McMurtrie *Cuvier's Anim. Kingd.* 361 The Insects..are remarkable..for their short *quadriarticulated tarsi. **1731** Bailey vol. II, **Quadricapsular*,..having a seed pod divided into four partitions. **1857** Berkeley *Cryptog. Bot.* 163 The biciliate spores..do not arise..from the same tissue as the *quadriciliate. **1854** Owen *Skel. & Teeth* in *Circ. Sc.*, *Organ. Nat.* I. 299 The three true molars are *quadricuspid. **1839–47** Todd *Cycl. Anat.* III. 264/2 The three *quadricuspidate grinders of the upper jaw. **1858** Mayne *Expos. Lex.*, *Quadridigitatus*,..applied to a leaf, the petiole of which terminates in four folioles..*quadridigitate. **1866** *Treas. Bot.* 947/1 **Quadrifoliate*. **1884** Bower & Scott *De Bary's Phaner.* 341 The leaves..are ranged in alternating, usually quadrifoliate whorls. **1777** Pennant *Zool.* IV. 7 Cr. with a *quadri-furcated snout. **1839–47** Todd *Cycl. Anat.* III. 686/1 The *quadrigeminal bodies rest upon two processes of fibrous matter. **1856** Todd & Bowman *Phys. Anat.* II. 39 From the quadrigeminal tubercles to the chiasma. **1866** *Treas. Bot.* 947/1 **Quadrihilate*, having four apertures, as is the case in certain kinds of pollen. **1819** *Pantologia* X, **Quadrilobate leaf*. **1839–47** Todd *Cycl. Anat.* III. 607/2 These cords..encircle the œsophagus above which they develope a quadrilobate ganglion. **1775** Jenkinson tr. *Linnæus Brit. Plants* 255 **Quadrilocular*. **1835** Lindley *Introd. Bot.* (1839) I. 176 The anther could not originally be quadrilocular, because it opens by two fissures only. **1956** *New Biol.* XXI. 93 At last the little *quadrinucleate amoeba breaks free as a whole. **1973** *Nature* 3 Aug. 293/1 Of these multinucleate compartments 88% were binucleate, 9% were trinucleate, and 3% were quadrinucleate. **1731** Bailey vol. II, **Quadriphyllous*,..Plants whose flowers have [four] leaves or petals. **1881** *Gard. Chron.* XVI. 685 The fronds are *quadripinnate in the lower and more compound portions. **1867** J. Hogg *Microsc.* II. ii. 400 Some Smyrna sponges, and species of Geodia, have four rays—*quadriradiate. **1887** W. Phillips *Brit. Discomycetes* 149 Pallid; cups clavate, substipitate; margin incurved; sporidia..long, *quadriseptate. **1839** Johnston in *Proc. Berw. Nat. Club* I. No. 7. 199 Suckers of the..tentacula *quadriserial. **1693** *Phil. Trans.* XVII. 934 Musk he takes to be..secreted in its proper Cystis near the Navil of a *Quadrisulc Animal like a Deer. **1775** Jenkinson tr. *Linnæus Brit. Plants* 255 **Quadrisulcated*. **1856–8** W. Clark *Van der Hoeven's Zool.* II. 753 The two other true molars *quadrituberculate. **1785** Martyn *Rousseau's Bot.* xvi. 199 The capsule is *quadrivalve [*ed.* 1794 quadrivalvular] or opens into four parts. **1875** H. C. Wood *Therap.* (1879) 268 Readily distinguished by its..quadrivalve spinescent capsules. **1762** Russell in *Phil. Trans.* LII. 556 What appeared to be the mouth, was situated a little below the apex, and was *quadrivalvular. **1888** *Quadrivoltine [see BIVOLTINE *a.*]. **1969** R. F. Chapman *Insects* xxxv. 719 In *Bombyx mori*..univoltine, bivoltine and quadrivoltine strains are known.

II. Sbs., vbs., and advs., chiefly from adjs. in I: **a. quadricen'tennial**, a four hundredth anniversary; **quadriceps** (extensor) [cf. BICEPS], a large muscle of the leg, having four heads; **'quadrichord** [late L. *-chordum*] = TETRACHORD; **'quadricorn**, an animal with four horns or antennæ (Brande *Dict. Sci.* 1842); **'quadriˌcycle**, a four-wheeled cycle; also **quadracycle**; **quadri'fariously** *adv.*, in a fourfold manner; **'quadrifoil** = QUATREFOIL; **ˌquadrifur'cation**, a division into four branches; **qua'drigamist** [L. *-gamus*], one four times married; **'quadrilogue**, an account by four persons; a dialogue between four; **qua'drilogy**, a tetralogy; **quadri'paresis** *Med.*, paresis of both arms and both legs; hence **quadripa'retic** *a.*; **quadri'pennate**, a four-winged insect (Brande, 1842); **quadri'porticus**, a colonnade or peristyle round a quadrangular building or space; **ˌquadrisacra'mentalist, -sacramen'tarian**, a name applied to some 16th c. German reformers who held Baptism, the Eucharist, Confession and Orders to be sacraments (Blunt *Dict. Sects* 1874); **'quadrisect** *v.*, to divide into four equal parts; hence **quadri'section**; **quadri'sulcate**, a four-toed animal (Brande, 1842); **quadri'syllable**, a word of four syllables; **qua'drivalence**, the power of an atom or radical to combine with four univalent atoms; **quadri'valency** = *quadrivalence*; **'quadrivalve**, a plant with a quadrivalvular seed-pod; an instrument, *esp.* a speculum, with four valves; †**qua'drivirate**, a union of four men.

1882 *Standard* 23 Aug. 5/1 To celebrate their *quadricentennial with a banquet. **1840** G. V. Ellis *Anat.* 636 They separate the *quadriceps extensor muscle from the others. **1585** T. Washington tr. *Nicholay's Voy.* II. ix. 42 Terpandre the famous Musition, which joined the seventh string to the *quadricord. **1728** R. North *Mem. Music* (1846) 34 That these might augment the voice is certain, but then they must be tuned to the quadrichord. **1884** *Cycl. Tour. Club Gaz.* Mar. 86/1 A *quadricycle of the form of the Coventry. **1963** Bird & Hutton-Stott *Veteran Motor Car* 90 Between about 1898 and 1908 more than 100 different makes of bicycle, tricycle, quadricycle, tricar, fore-car and light car proper..were powered by De Dion Bouton engines. **1972** *Sci. Amer.* May 104/3 By the second half of 1891..the Peugeot quadricycle..had covered the 1,200 kilometers (745 miles) from Paris to Brest and back to Paris in 10 days. **1979** *Time* 8 Jan. 80/3 Accordingly, Wilson is proposing a two-seat lunar vehicle or quadracycle, made of lightweight metals. **1822** T. Taylor *Apuleius, On God of Socrates* 300 There are four most known elements, nature being as it were *quadrifariously separated into large parts. **1845** Ld. Campbell *Chancellors* (1857) I. xiii. 198 The scholar..stuffs his volume with firstling violets, roses, and *quadrifoils. **1884** Blackmore *Tommy Upm.* II. 316 A convenient *quadrifurcation. **1656** Blount *Glossogr.*, **Quadrigamist*. **1865** *Pall Mall G.* 10 Feb. 5/2 The swindler bigamist or quadrigamist, we forget the precise number of his marriages. *a* **1556** Cranmer *Wks.* (Parker Soc.) I. 66 Your wise dialogue, or *quadrilogue, between the curious questioner, the foolish answerer, your wise catholic man standing by, and the mediator. **1570–6** Lambarde *Peramb. Kent* (1826) 358 The Quadriloge of Beckets life. *a* **1656** Ussher in Gutch *Coll. Cur.* I. 46 Thomas Becket (as we read in the Quadrilogue, or Quadripartite History of his Life). **1865** *Athenæum* No. 1950. 355/3 His *quadrilogy of Nibelungen operas. **1956** *Jrnl. Neurol., Neurosurg. & Psychiatry* XIX. 170/2 The patient had a *quadriparesis, complete in the left leg and more marked in the left arm than the right. **1977** *Lancet* 27 Aug. 461/1 By discharge on day 32 he was fully mobile with only a residual spastic quadriparesis. **1956** *Jrnl. Neurol., Neurosurg. & Psychiatry* XIX. 163/1 The patients remained *quadriparetic and almost totally unresponsive from the time of the accident. **1849** Freeman *Archit.* 276 The form of Amru's mosque..being a mere *quadriporticus round an open space. **1865** C. R. Weld *Last Winter Rome* 97 Among the most remarkable features of this building..are the Atrium and quadriporticus. **1809** Cavendish in *Phil. Trans.* XCIX. 227 in *quadrisecting, the error of the middle point = 2ε. **1673** Wallis in Rigaud *Corr. Sci. Men* (1841) II. 571 We find, by the *quadrisection of an arch or angle, a biquadratic equation of four roots. **1809** Cavendish in *Phil. Trans.*

XCIX. 227 In the method of continued bisection, the two opposite points must be found by quadrisection. **1706** PHILLIPS (ed. Kersey), **Quadrisyllable*, a Word made up of four Syllables. **1827** HARE *Guesses* Ser. I. (1873) 109 Our dignity will not condescend to enter into any thing short of a quadrisyllable. **1884** TRAILL in *Macm. Mag.* Oct. 444/1, I will end the sentence with ignoramus.. a quadrisyllable. **1932** *Nature* 19 Nov. 756/2 The *quadrivalency of carbon. **1937** A. FINDLAY *Hundred Yrs. of Chem.* ii. 40 The theory of molecular constitution.. rested on two main postulates, the quadrivalency of the carbon.. and the capacity of the carbon atoms for mutual linking. **1731** BAILEY vol. II, **Quadrivalves*,.. those Plants whose seed pods open in four valves or partitions. **1872** F. G. THOMAS *Dis. Women* (ed. 3) 76 Of valvular specula the bivalve of Ricord.. and the quadrivalve of Charrière have long been popular. **1654** GAYTON *Pleas. Notes* IV. xvii. 258 This blood-lesse victory, over a *Quadrivirate of Mummers.

b. *Math.* Chiefly in sense 'quadric', 'of the second degree or order', as **'quadricone, -co'variant, -de'rivative, quadrin'variant**; also **quadri'nomial**, an expression consisting of four terms.

1856 A. CAYLEY *Wks.* (1889) II. 272 No. 9 is the *quadricovariant, or Hessian. **1706** W. JONES *Syn. Palmar. Matheseos* 171 To raise any.. *Quadri-nomial.. to any given Power. **1827** HUTTON *Course Math.* I. 167 When the compound quantity consists of two terms, it is called a Binomial,.. when of four terms a Quadrinomial. **1856** A. CAYLEY *Wks.* (1889) II. 271 No. 1 is the quadric itself; no. 2 is the *quadrinvariant. **1884** W. R. W. ROBERTS in *Hermathena* X. 182 Functions.. expressed by the quadrinvariants of the quantics [etc.].

c. *Chem.* In the names of chemical compounds, denoting the presence of four atoms or equivalents of an element or radical in a compound, as ***quadrioxalate, -phosphate, -stearate, -sulphide***. Now superseded by TETRA-.

1836–41 BRANDE *Chem.* (ed. 5) 1067 Then ether would be a compound of 1 atom of *quadrihydrocarbon and 1 of water. **1826** HENRY *Elem. Chem.* I. 591 *Quadriphosphate of lime. **1836–41** BRANDE *Chem.* (ed. 5) 685 The phosphoric glass.. is considered by Dr. Thomson as a definite compound, which he has termed quadriphosphate of lime. **1849** D. CAMPBELL *Inorg. Chem.* 299 *Quadrisulphide of molybdenum, MoS_4. **1897** *Allbutt's Syst. Med.* IV. 293 It [uric acid] is present in the urine in the form of a *quadriurate.

quadri-, occas. erron. form of QUADRU-.

quadrible, obs. variant of QUADRABLE *a.*

quadrible, variant of QUATREBLE *a.* and *v.*

quadric ('kwɒdrɪk), *a.* and *sb. Math.* [ad. L. type **quadric-us*, f. *quadra* square: see -IC.]

A. *adj.* Of the second degree. (Used in solid geometry, and where the variables are more than two.)

1858 A. CAYLEY *Wks.* (1889) II. 497 The case of any quadric function of *n* variables. **1865** *Athenæum* No. 1950. 352/2 Quadric Inversion. **1884** A. S. HART in *Hermathena* X. 164 Such curves.. can be traced on a quadric surface. *Ibid.* 166 Two of the given equations will represent quadric cones.

B. *sb.* A quantic or surface of the second degree.

1856 A. CAYLEY *Wks.* (1889) II. 271 The tables Nos. 1 and 2 are the covariants of a binary quadric. **1881** MAXWELL *Electr. & Magn.* I. 215 A variable parameter, which we shall distinguish by a suffix for the species of quadric. **1884** A. S. HART in *Hermathena* X. 164 There are many such [twisted algebraic] curves which do not lie on any quadric.

quadridentate (kwɒdrɪ'dɛnteɪt), *a.* [f. QUADRI- + L. *dentātus* (see DENTATE *a.*).]

1. *Bot.* and *Zool.* Having four serrations or indentations.

1760 J. LEE *Introd. Bot.* I. xv. (1765) 39 Quadridentate, split into four segments. **1828** STARK *Elem. Nat. Hist.* II. 159 Body covered with a reddish down,.. front quadridentate.

2. *Chem.* Of a ligand: forming four separate bonds. Of a complex: formed by such a ligand.

1925 MORGAN & SMITH in *Jrnl. Chem. Soc.* CXXVII. 2031 We have now succeeded in identifying a group capable of quadruple attachment to metallic atoms, this being the first known case of a quadridentate group in co-ordination complexes. **1937** *Chem. Rev.* XXI. 98 Probably the first synthetic quadridentate compounds.. were the copper and bivalent platinum compounds of ethylene bisthioglycolic acid. **1956** R. W. PARRY in J. C. Bailar *Chem. Coordination Compounds* v. 239 The base is a quadridentate molecule in which the four nitrogen atoms can be expected to occupy the corners of a tetrahedron. **1972** M. L. TOBE *Inorg. Reaction Mechanisms* vi. 70 (*caption*) Trigonal bipyramidal complex of a 'tripod' quadridentate ligand showing how the trigonal symmetry of the ligand forces the configuration in the complex.

quadriennial, -ium: see QUADRENNIAL, -IUM.

quadrifid ('kwɒdrɪfɪd), *a.* (*sb.*) Also 7 quadrifide. [ad. L. *quadrifid-us*, f. QUADRI- + *fid-* root of *findĕre* to cleave. Cf. mod.F. *quadrifide*.] Cleft into four divisions or lobes.

1661 LOVELL *Hist. Anim. & Min.* 109 Claws like a Cow; but quadrifide. **1766** PENNANT *Zool.* (1769) III. 320 The tail is naturally bifid, but in many is trifid, and in some even quadrifid. **1830** LINDLEY *Nat. Syst. Bot.* 52 Distinguished by.. the quadrifid calyx. **1875** DARWIN *Insectiv. Pl.* xiv. 326 The quadrifid processes on the outer parts of the lobes.

b. *absol.* as *sb.* A quadrifid process.

1875 DARWIN *Insectiv. Pl.* xiv. 326 On the broad outer surfaces of the lobes where the quadrifids are situated.

quadriform ('kwɒdrɪfɔːm), *a.*[1] [ad. late L. *quadriformis*: see QUADRI- and -FORM. Cf. obs. F. *quadriforme*.] Having four forms or aspects.

1668 H. MORE *Div. Dial.* v. x. (1713) 440 This quadriform aspect of the Cherubims. **1850** NEALE *Med. Hymns* (1867) 109 Quadriform His Acts, which writing They produce before our eyes. **1858** MAYNE *Expos. Lex.*, *Quadriformis*,.. applied to a crystal which presents the combination of four distinct forms.. quadriform. **1874** *Supernat. Relig.* II. III. ii. 476 Quadriform is the Gospel, and quadriform the course of the Lord.

'quadriform, *a.*[2] *rare*. [f. L. **quadri-* comb. form of *quadra* square + -FORM.] Square-shaped. †Also *fig.*: Perfect (cf. QUADRATE *a.* 3).

1679 HARBY *Key Script.* II. 34 It principally intends.. that true quadriform Righteousness of Gospel-Promise. **1888** *Pall Mall G.* 6 July 10/1 On the extreme end of the scabbard is a large quadriform mace head.

‖**quadriga** (kwə'draɪgə). [L.; later sing. form for pl. *quadrigæ* contr. of *quadrijugæ*, f. *quadri-* QUADRI- + *jugum* yoke. Cf. F. *quadrige* (17th c.), and see QUATHRIGAN.]

1. A chariot drawn by four horses harnessed abreast; esp. as represented in sculpture or on coins.

1727–41 CHAMBERS *Cycl.* s.v., On the reverses of medals we frequently see Victory, or the emperor, in a *quadriga*, holding the reins of the horses. **1850** LEITCH tr. *C. O. Müller's Anc. Art* (ed. 2) 452 Apollo.. guides a quadriga, in which he is carrying off a lofty and noble female form. **1884** *Chr. World* 14 Aug. 612/5 A quadriga in bronze carrying a figure of Victory.

2. A form of surgical bandage for the sternum and ribs. ? *Obs.*

1743 HEISTER *Surgery* (1768) II. III. iv. 371 The Generality of Surgeons make use of a peculiar and stronger Bandage for this purpose, which they call the *Quadriga* or *Cataphracta*. [Hence in CHAMBERS *Cycl.* Suppl. (App.), and some later dicts.]

Hence † **quadri'garious** *a.*, 'of or belonging to a Charriot-man' (Blount *Glossogr.* 1656).

† **quadrigate**, *a.* (*sb.*) *Obs. rare*. [ad. L. *quadrigāt-us*: see prec.] Of a coin: Stamped with the figure of a quadriga. **b.** *sb.* A coin so stamped.

1600 HOLLAND *Livy* XXII. lii. 464 To pay 300 quadrigate pieces of siluer. *Ibid.* liv. 465 *note*, A Quadrigate.. is a piece of siluer coyne among the Romanes, the same that Denarius: called so of Quadriga.

† **quadrilater**, *a.* *Obs. rare*. [ad. late L. *quadrilater-us*, f. *quadri-* QUADRI- + *later-* stem of *latus* side. Cf. F. *quadrilatère* (*a* 1554).] = next.

1570 BILLINGSLEY *Euclid* I. xxi. 31 Wherefore this present figure.. is a quadrilater triangle. **1571** DIGGES *Pantom.* II. xvii. O ij b, The figure signified by the quadrilater superficies ABGF.

quadrilateral (kwɒdrɪ'lætərəl), *a.* and *sb.* Also 7 quadrilaterall. [ad. L. type **quadrilaterālis*, f. *quadrilater-us* + -AL[1]. See prec. and cf. F. *quadrilatéral*.]

A. *adj.* **a.** Four-sided; having a four-sided base or section.

1656 STANLEY *Hist. Philos.* v. (1701) 162/2 The Altar.. was no longer a Cube, but.. a quadrilateral Pillar. **1674** tr. *Scheffer's Lapland* xvi. 83 The whole form seems to be like a quadrilaterall house. **1718** QUINCY *Compl. Disp.* 33 In common Salt we plainly discover Quadrilateral Pyramids, with square Bases. **1836–41** BRANDE *Chem.* (ed. 5) 1125 Carbazotate of Potassa crystallizes in long yellow quadrilateral needles. **1876** DUHRING *Dis. Skin* 38 Nails are rounded or quadrilateral bodies.

b. *Bot.* Of a stem: (see quot.).

1875 BENNETT & DYER *Sachs' Bot.* 184 The principal sections of all the leaves.. may lie in two planes, crossing one another at right angles, when the shoot is quadrilateral.

B. *sb.* **a.** A figure bounded by four straight lines; a space or area having four sides.

In *mod. Geom.* A figure formed by four straight lines, no three of which pass through the same point, and by the six points (vertices) forming the intersections of these lines, taken two by two (Cf. QUADRANGLE).

1650 T. RUDD *Euclide* 45 To forme a.. Quadrilaterall, about which a circle may be circumscribed. **1827** HUTTON *Course Math.* I. 282 A Diagonal is a line joining any two opposite angles of a quadrilateral. **1866** R. A. PROCTOR *Handbk. Stars* 16 The intermediate figures are quadrilaterals of varying form. **1893** E. H. BARKER *Wanderings by Southern Waters* 301 Four.. towers occupying the angles of a small quadrilateral.

b. The space lying between, and defended by, four fortresses; *spec.* that in North Italy formed by the fortresses of Mantua, Verona, Peschiera, and Legnano.

1859 *Times* 1 July 8/5 Such fortresses as compose the famous 'Quadrilateral'. **1866** *Sat. Rev.* 21 July 66/1 The Quadrilateral and Venice still remain in the hands of the Austrians. **1870** *Pall Mall G.* 2 Sept. 2 He has four fortresses around him.. but upon twelve square miles of territory.. he cannot play at quadrilaterals.

fig. **1888** LD. ROSEBERY in *Daily News* 20 Feb. 5/5 Am overjoyed.. that Edinburgh is once more the quadrilateral of Liberalism.

c. *Eccl.* The four essential principles of Anglicanism, orig. enunciated in 1870 and approved by the Lambeth Conference of 1888 as a basis for the reunion of the Christian Church. Freq. ***Lambeth Quadrilateral***. (Transf. use of sense b.)

1870 W. R. HUNTINGTON *Church-Idea* vii. 157 1st. The Holy Scriptures as the Word of God. 2d. The Primitive Creeds as the Rule of Faith. 3d. The two Sacraments ordained by Christ Himself. 4th. The Episcopate as the key-stone of Governmental Unity. These four points, like the four famous fortresses of Lombardy, make the 'Quadrilateral' of pure Anglicanism. **1902** [see LAMBETH 1]. **1925** J. W. SUTER *Life & Lett. William Reed Huntington* vii. 162 It might, with some reason, be maintained that Dr. Huntington's chief claim to lasting fame was his invention and promulgation of the Quadrilateral... It was in a sermon preached at Worcester [Mass.], January 30, 1870, that he for the first time set forth the term. **1944** W. TEMPLE *Church Looks Forward* ii. 14 The Lambeth Conference has repeatedly offered as a basis of negotiation the famous Quadrilateral. **1954** ROUSE & NEILL *Hist. Ecumenical Movement* v. 250 When Huntington had boiled Anglicanism down to its irreducible minimum, there remained his basis for a united Church—a platform later to be known as the 'Chicago-Lambeth Quadrilateral'... The House of Bishops at the General Convention of 1886 [at Chicago] finally adopted his 'Quadrilateral' and it was reaffirmed in slightly modified form by the Lambeth Conference of 1888. **1957** *Oxf. Dict. Chr. Ch.* 781/2 Lambeth Quadrilateral... The text of the Articles is as follows: A. The Holy Scriptures of the Old and New Testaments,.. as being the rule and ultimate standard of faith. B. The Apostles' Creed.. and the Nicene Creed... C. The two Sacraments ordained by Christ Himself—Baptism and the Supper of the Lord... D. The Historic Episcopate, locally adapted.

Hence **quadri'lateralness**, 'the property of having four sides' (Bailey, vol. II, 1727).

quadriliteral (kwɒdrɪ'lɪtərəl), *a.* and *sb.* [f. QUADRI- + LITERAL.]

A. *adj.* Consisting of four letters; *spec.* of Semitic roots which have four consonants instead of the usual three (see *triliteral*).

1771 W. JONES *Zool. Eth.* 102 It must be deemed a quadriliteral word, and as such compounded of a double radix. **1793** T. BEDDOES *Math. Evid.* 133 They assume triliteral and quadriliteral as well as biliteral roots. **1837** PHILLIPS *Syriac Gramm.* 96 Quadriliteral verbs. **1869** B. DAVIES tr. *Gesenius' Hebrew Gram.* 86 Such lengthened forms.. are not regarded as quadriliteral.

B. *sb.* A word of four letters: a (Semitic) root containing four consonants.

1787 SIR W. JONES *Disc. Arabs* Wks. 1799 I. 40 If we suppose ten thousand of them [Arabic roots] (without reckoning *quadriliterals*) to exist [etc.]. **1839** PAULI *Anal. Hebr.* xxviii. 205 The so-called Quadri- and Quinti- literals are compounds [etc.]. **1864** PUSEY *Lect. Daniel* 566 On the principle of reducing the words to quadriliterals. **1874** SAYCE *Compar. Philol.* ii. 78 Quadriliterals.. for the most part have extended a vowel into a liquid.

quadrilla, var. CUADRILLA.

1921 E. E. CUMMINGS *Let.* 22 Apr. (1969) 75 Gentlemen in cockades.. come out again heading a procession of quadrillas, bandilleros, and espadas, all of whom bow. The bull is admitted: the quadrillas—each matador has his own group—try him with cloaks. **1923** W. J. LOCKE *Moordius & Co.* x. 140 The proud procession of the quadrillas, matadors, banderilleros, picadores.

quadrille (see next), *sb.*[1] Also 8 quadrill. [a. F. *quadrille* (1725); referred by Littré to It. *quadriglio* of the same meaning, but by Hatz.-Darm. said to be ad. Sp. *cuartillo*, the form in F. being due to association with *quadrille*, Sp. *cuadrilla* (see next).] A card-game played by four persons with forty cards, the eights, nines, and tens of the ordinary pack being discarded. †Also *pl.*

Quadrille began to take the place of ombre as the fashionable card game about 1726, and was in turn superseded by whist.

1726 in *Suffolk Corr.* (1824) I. 257 Sir T. Coke [etc.].. made a party at quadrille... The game being new, drew many spectators. **1727** SWIFT *On a Woman's Mind* Misc. 1735 V. 113 Improving hourly in her Skill, To cheat and wrangle at Quadrille. **1768** in *Priv. Lett. Ld. Malmesbury* I. 161, I preferred a sober game of quadrilles with Miss Chudleigh. **1789** MRS. PIOZZI *Journ. France*, etc. I. 22 The petty pleasures of sixpenny quadrille. **1823** LAMB *Elia* (1860) 51 Quadrille, she has often told me, was her first love, but whist had engaged her maturer esteem. **1861** T. L. PEACOCK *Gryll Gr.* xxiii. 198 Amongst the winter evening's amusements were two forms of quadrille: the old-fashioned game of cards, and the more recently fashionable dance.

attrib. **1731** FIELDING *Mod. Husb.* I. ii, Bring the Quadrille book hither; see whether I am engaged. **1732** GAY *Distr. Wife* IV, Lady Rampant depends upon your ladyship to make up her quadrille party. **1843** LEFEVRE *Life Trav. Phys.* II. I. xiv. 44 The old Countess sat down to the quadrille table with three other ladies.

quadrille (kwə'drɪl, kwə-, kə-), *sb.*[2] [a. F. *quadrille* (Cotgr. 1611), ad. Sp. *cuadrilla*, Pg. *quadrilha*, It. *quadriglia*, a band, troop, company, 'a Squadron containing 25 (or fewer) Souldiers' (Cotgr.), app. f. *cuadra*, *quadra* square; cf. Sp. *escuadra*, It. *squadra*, *squadrone* SQUADRON.]

1. One of four groups of horsemen taking part in a tournament or carousel, each being distinguished by special costume or colours.

1738 G. SMITH *Curious Relat.* II. 389 The first Quadrille, led on by their Chief, the Duke of Weissenfels. **1766** *Chron.* in *Ann. Reg.* 118/1 The four quadrilles representing four different nations. **1777** J. CARTER *King Zayde* in Evans *O.B.*

(1784) III. xviii. 182 Two of the four quadrilles,.. Take lances in their hands.

transf. **1821** SCOTT *Kenilw.* xxxvii, The four quadrilles of masquers.. drew up in their several ranks.

2. A square dance, of French origin, usually performed by four couples, and containing five sections or figures, each of which is a complete dance in itself. Also called 'a set of quadrilles'.

1773 MRS. HARRIS in *Priv. Lett. Ld. Malmesbury* I. 269 A few evenings ago some company were rehearsing quadrilles at Mrs. Hobart's in St. James' Square. **1823** BYRON *Juan* XI. lxx, Dissolving in the waltz.. Or proudlier prancing with mercurial skill Where Science marshals forth her own quadrille. **1833** HT. MARTINEAU *Loom & Lugger* II. iv. 64 A twang of the fiddle called her up for her first quadrille. **1862** GRONOW *Remin.* 44, I recollect the persons who formed the first quadrille that was ever danced at Almack's were Lady Jersey [etc.].

attrib. and *Comb.* **1818** LADY MORGAN *Autobiog.* (1859) 36 There was some pretty quadrille-dancing. **1829** LYTTON *Devereux* II. viii, I disappointed her in not searching for her at every drum and quadrille-party.

b. A piece of music to which a quadrille may be danced.

qua'drille, *sb.*[3] *rare*$^{-1}$. [? ad. It. *quadrello* pack-needle, assimilated to prec.] A square needle.

1818 *Art Preserv. Feet* 68 Scratching it with the point of the quadrille or squared bodkin.

† **qua'drille,** *v.*[1] *Obs. rare*$^{-1}$. [f. QUADRILLE *sb.*[1]] *intr.* To play at the game of quadrille.

1734 MRS. DELANY *Lett. to Mrs. A. Granville* 508 They quadrilled after dinner till ten, and I dozed by them.. losing at cards infallibly lulls me to sleep.

quadrille (kwə'drɪl, kwə-, kə-), *v.*[2] [f. QUADRILLE *sb.*[2]] *intr.* To dance quadrilles. Also quasi- *trans.* with cognate obj., and *trans.* in *nonce-use.* Also *transf.*

1828 *Light & Shade* II. 195 His uses are.. to quadrille with young [ladies]. **1831** MOORE *Summer Fête*, These gay things, born but to quadrille, The circle of their doom fulfil. **18..** —— *Country Dance & Quad.* xxvii, Men.. Quadrilled on one side into fops, And drilled on t'other into slaves! **1841** MOTLEY *Corr.* (1889) I. iv. 93, I waltzed one waltz, and quadrilled one quadrille, but it was hard work. **1903** LD. R. GOWER *Rec. & Reminisc.* 59 Teaching us how to quadrille and how to valse. **1905** W. H. HUNT *Pre-Raphaelitism* I. ii. 24, I.. rejoiced with the happy birds quadrilling around the sentinel trees.

Hence **qua'driller; qua'drilling** *vbl. sb.*

1820 *Blackw. Mag.* VII. 521 Her husband was formerly one of the gayest.. quadrillers, waltzers [etc.]. **1820** PRAED *County Ball* 399 Upon our waltzing and quadrilling. **1840** LADY C. BURY *Hist. of Flirt* i, They were the most indefatigable of quadrillers. **1853** READE *Chr. Johnstone* 99 Dancing reels, with heart and soul, is not quadrilling.

‖ **quadrillé** (kadrije), *a.* (and *sb.*) Also quadrille. [F.; f. *quadrille* a small square, ad. Sp. *cuadrillo* QUADREL.] = next. Also *ellipt.* as *sb.*

1884 *Cassell's Fam. Mag.* Apr. 313/1 The new lace is called 'quadrillé'. It has large square meshes [etc.]. **1895** *Montgomery Ward Catal.* Spring & Summer 38/3 Red leather vest pocket memorandum... 40 leaves.. quadrille ruling. **1907** *Yesterday's Shopping* (1969) 354/2 *Manuscript and Account Books.* Ruled either with Feint lines, Cash Column, or Quadrille. **1926** *Paper Terminol.* (Spalding & Hodge, Ltd.) ii. 22 *Quadrille*, paper ruled on the surface or in watermark with a multitude of small squares. Used by draughtsmen, diary makers, and for foreign correspondence. **1960** R. G. HAGGAR *Conc. Encycl. Continental Pott. & Porc.* 375/1 *Quadrillé*, a diapered ground pattern with quatrefoils and squares much favoured at Chantilly, painted in blue third quarter of the eighteenth century. **1969** R. MAYER *Dict. Art Terms & Techniques* 320/1 *Quadrille paper*, paper faintly ruled with small squares. Also, paper so patterned with a water-mark or a plate finish. **1978** *E & A Office Equipment Catal.* 122/1 Memo Pads... Quadrille 5 mm.

quadrilled (kwə'drɪld), *a.* [ad. F. *quadrillé*: see prec.] Marked with squares; having a pattern composed of small squares.

1835 *Court Mag.* VI. p. xvii/2 The prettiest of these is the quadrilled gros de Naples, with a white ground, and a flower in each square. **1899** *B'ham Weekly Post* 2 Sept. 20/3 The second [tie] is of red silk quadrilled with black.

quadrillion (kwə'drɪljən). [a. F. *quadrillion* (16th c.), f. *quadri-* + *(m)illion*: see BILLION.]

a. In Great Britain originally: The fourth power of a million, represented by 1 followed by twenty-four ciphers. **b.** In U.S. (and increasingly in Great Britain): The fifth power of a thousand, or 1 followed by fifteen ciphers.

1674 JEAKE *Arith.* (1696) 14 Others.. call the twenty-fifth place Quadrillion. **1706** W. JONES *Syn. Palmar. Matheseos* 8 Then the 4th point from Units stands under Quadrillions. **1795–8** T. MAURICE *Hindostan* (1820) I. I. iv. 142 Two quadrillions.. of lunar years. **1891** *Pall Mall G.* 4 Mar. 3/2, I wonder how many quadrillions, quintillions, sextillions there are of them [locusts]. **1975** *Offshore* Sept. 246/2 Southern areas of the North Sea off the northeast coast of England produced a record 129 quadrillion BTU's last year. **1976** *Sci. Amer.* Jan. 21/1 The ERDA projections are expressed in terms of quads, or quadrillions (10^{15}) of British thermal units (B.t.u.). **1977** *Ibid.* Apr. 71/1 When *n* is 31, the total number of possible binary trees is 14,544,636,039,226,909, and each of these 14 quadrillion trees will be optimum for some set of assumed frequencies for the 31 words.

Hence **qua,drillio'naire** (after MILLIONAIRE), one who possesses a quadrillion of the standard unit of money in any country. **qua'drillionth** *a.*, the ordinal numeral corresponding to quadrillion; *sb.*, a quadrillionth part (*Funk's Stand. Dict.* 1893).

a **1876** M. COLLINS *Pen Sketches* (1879) I. 172 A millionaire (we shall soon have billionaires, trillionaires, quadrillionaires). **1882** SALA *Amer. Revis.* (1885) 174 Silver-mine millionnaires and Wall-street quadrillionnaires. **1976** *New Yorker* 3 May 30/3 Further advances.. should make it possible to record even faster chemical reactions—reactions that take place in femtoseconds, or quadrillionths of a second.

quadrimanous, obs. var. QUADRUMANOUS.

† **qua'drimular,** *a. Obs. rare*$^{-1}$. [f. L. *quadrīmus* (f. *quadri-* + *hiem-s* winter) + -ULAR.] Lasting for four years.

1664 H. MORE *Synopsis Proph.* 341 This quadrimular antichrist shall not onely over-run Christendom, but subdue the Grand Signior.

quadrin, variant of QUADRINE[1].

quadrinate ('kwɒdrɪnət), *a. Bot.* [f. QUADRI- on anal. of BINATE.] Having four leaflets; quadrifoliate.

1870 BENTLEY *Bot.* 164.

† **quadrine**[1]. *Obs. rare.* Also -in. [a. obs. F. *quadrin* (It. *quadrino*), var. of *quatrin* QUATRINE.] A small copper coin; a farthing.

1557 N.T. (Genev.) *Mark* xii. 42 And there came a certayne poore wydow, and she threw in two mytes which make a quadrin. **1579–80** NORTH *Plutarch* 722 (R.) One of her paramours sent her a purse full of quadrines (which are little pieces of copper money) instead of silver.

† **quadrine**[2]. *Obs. rare*$^{-1}$. [For QUADRAN or QUADRANT, on anal. of TRINE.] Quartile aspect.

1628 WITHER *Brit. Rememb.* v. 1050 In Sextile, or in Quadrine, or in Trine.

† **quadringe'narious,** *a. Obs. rare*$^{-0}$. [ad. L. *quadringēnāri-us*, f. *quadringēnī* four hundred each.] 'That contains four hundred' (Blount *Glossogr.* 1656).

quadripartite (kwɒdrɪ'pɑːtaɪt), *a.* and *sb.* Also 7 -partit; 6 quadri-, 6–7 quadrapertite; 6–8 quadrupartite, (6 -pertite). [ad. L. *quadripartīt-us*, f. *quadri-* QUADRI- + pa. pple. of *partīrī* to divide, PART.]

A. *adj.* **1.** Divided into, or consisting of, four parts. Now chiefly in *Bot.*, *Zool.*, and *Arch.*

quadripartite vault, one divided into four converging compartments; so ***quadriparte groining***.

1432–50 tr. *Higden* (Rolls) III. 111 That kynge Nabugodonosor hade a dreame of a quadripartite ymage. **1570** LEVINS *Manip.* 151/43 Quadripartite, *quadripartitus*. **1612** SELDEN *Illustr. Drayton's Poly-olb.* IV. 215 Wks. 1876 I. 115 Frederic III's institution of the quadripartite Society of S. George's shield. **1768–74** TUCKER *Lt. Nat.* (1834) II. 464 The quadripartite discourse upon Phil. ii. 6. **1849** FREEMAN *Archit.* 246 The aisles of large churches are almost always covered with plain quadripartite vaulting. **1875** BENNETT & DYER tr. *Sachs' Bot.* 584 The tubular receptacle .. is even quadripartite, corresponding to the four perianth-leaves and to the four stamens.

b. *spec.* Of a contract, indenture, etc.: Drawn up in four corresponding parts, one for each party.

1527 *Lanc. & Chesh. Wills* (Chetham Soc. 1854) 33 A declaracion of my will mynde and testament quadripertite therunto annexed. **1592** WEST *1st Pt. Symbol.* §47 These deedes indented are not only bypartite.. but also may be made.. quadrupartite. **1650** *Bury Wills* (Camden) 224 As in the said indenture quadrapertite fully appeareth. **1874** MACRAY in *4th Rep. Hist. MSS. Comm.* 461/1 Extract from the will of Hugh Falstolf.. made in the form of a quadripartite indenture.

2. Divided among or shared by four persons or parties.

1594 LYLY *Moth. Bomb.* III. ii, They commit the matter to our quadripartite wit. **1741** RICHARDSON *Pamela* (1824) I. lxxvii. 434 Your reconciliation is now effected; a friendship quadrupartite is commenced. **1835** *Blackw. Mag.* XXXVII. 44 They.. formed a quadripartite alliance.

3. ***quadripartite division*** (†*distinction*), division into four parts, classes, etc.; *spec.* in *Eccl.* a four-fold division of tithes (see quot. 1855).

1614 SELDEN *Titles Hon.* 383 The quadripartit distinction of Ciuilians which they haue. **1650** FULLER *Pisgah* I. iv. 10 Making a quadripartite division of good wine. **1727** T. JENKINS tr. *Father Paul's Eccl. Benef.* (1736) 28 The Quadripartite division came to be arbitrary. **1855** MILMAN *Lat. Chr.* (1864) II. III. vii. 116 *note*, The quadripartite division, to the bishop, the clergy, the fabric and services of the church, and the poor, generally prevailed in the West. **1882–3** SCHAFF *Encycl. Relig. Knowl.* I. 724 The quadripartite division of theology, into exegetical, dogmatical, historical, and practical theology.

B. *sb.* The Tetrabiblos of Ptolemy.

1477 NORTON *Ord. Alch.* i. in Ashm. (1652) 21 In his Quadripartite made of Astrologie, Of Physique, and of this Arte of Alkimy, And also of Magique naturall. **1559** W. CUNINGHAM *Cosmogr. Glasse* 133 Ptolomæus maketh mention of them in his quadripartite. **1822** J. M. ASHMAND (*title*) Ptolemy's Tetrabiblos or Quadripartite, being Four Books of the Influence of the Stars.

Hence **quadri'partitely** *adv.*, into four parts. Also † **quadri'partite** *v.*, to divide into four.

1552 HULOET, Quadripartitlye. **1656** W. D. tr. *Comenius' Gate Lat. Unl.* 177 The year [is divided] quadripartitely into Spring, Summer, Autumn, Winter. **1709–29** V. MANDEY *Syst. Math., Arith.* 3 Division.. Its kinds are, Halving or Bipartiting,.. Quadripartiting, &c.

quadripartition (ˌkwɒdrɪpɑː'tɪʃən). Also 7 quadru-. [ad. L. *quadripartītio* (Varro): see prec. and PARTITION.] Division into or by four.

1650 FULLER *Pisgah* II. viii. §3 The quadripartition of the Greek empire into four parts. **1690** LEYBOURN *Curs. Math.* 144 The.. Rules.. of Logarithms, whereby.. the Square Root [is] extracted by Bipartition.. the Biquadrate Root by Quadrupartition, &c. **1886** *Contemp. Rev.* Oct. 528 This convenient quadri-partition of the month.

quadriphonic, -phony, -plane, varr. QUADRAPHONIC *a.*, QUADRAPHONY, QUADRUPLANE.

quadriplegia (kwɒdrɪ'pliːdʒ(ɪ)ə). *Path.* [mod.L., f. QUADRI- + PARA)PLEGIA.] Paralysis of both arms and both legs.

1921 *Brain* XLIV. 428 To elicit nociceptive reactions of the upper or lower limbs in our cases of hemiplegia and quadriplegia potentially painful stimuli were usually necessary. **1948** *Brit. Med. Jrnl.* 14 Feb. 289/2 A man aged 56 suffered damage to his cervical cord.. following a blow. The resultant spastic quadriplegia was thought to be due to a haematomyelia. **1974** LUCKMANN & SORENSEN *Med.-Surg. Nursing* xxxviii. 444/1 Quadriplegia is the same as paraplegia except that the level of injury to the spinal cord is cervical and thus the upper extremities are affected as well as the lower extremities.

quadriplegic (kwɒdrɪ'pliːdʒɪk), *a.* and *sb. Med.* Also **quadra-, quadru-.** [f. prec. + -IC.] **A.** *adj.* Suffering from quadriplegia. **B.** *sb.* A quadriplegic person.

1921 *Brain* XLIV. 438 Three of the quadriplegic patients .. showed extensive reflex reactions involving the trunk and limbs. **1961** WEBSTER, Quadriplegic, *n.* **1962** *Lancet* 6 Jan. 3/1 The patient emerging from stupor was at first mute and quadriplegic. **1965** *Listener* 27 May 772/2 Young girls.. both of whom, as a result of their injuries, became quadriplegics, that is they became permanently paralysed from the neck downwards. **1969** *Age* (Melbourne) 24 May 5/6 A Geelong man who became a quadraplegic following a car accident in October 1967, was awarded damages of $100,000 yesterday. **1971** *Daily Tel.* 25 May 3/7 He was left a quadruplegic and will spend the rest of his days in a wheelchair. **1971** *Rand Daily Mail* 4 Sept. 13/4 The youth injured his spine in the accident and was totally paralysed from the neck down. Like all quadriplegics, he is tied to a wheelchair existence for life. **1974** PASSMORE & ROBSON *Compan. Med. Stud.* III. liv. 4/1 The quadriplegic patient presents greater problems than those of the paraplegic with regard to rehabilitation and resettlement. **1975** 'M. FONTEYN' *Autobiogr.* II. x. 241 It was a long time before I realized what everyone else knew perfectly well—that Tito was incapacitated and probably a quadruplegic for life. **1980** *Times* 8 Feb. 4/7 He is a quadriplegic after having sustained multiple injuries in a fall.

quadriplex, var. QUADRUPLEX *a.* 3.

quadripole ('kwɒdrɪpəʊl). [ad. F. *quadripôle* (L. J. Collet 1926, in *Ann. des Postes, Télégraphes et Téléphones* XV. 939): see QUADRI- and POLE *sb.*[2]] **1.** *Electr.* A network or device having one pair of input terminals and one pair of output terminals; *esp.* one that is passive.

1928 *Sci. Abstr.* B. XXXI. 103 The author considers the quadripole, its.. velocity of propagation, characteristic impedance and reflection properties. The amplifying valve is considered as an example of a quadripole. **1935** G. P. HARNWELL *Princ. Electr. & Magn.* iv. 115 In order to effect such a transfer [of power] a device with two pairs of terminals must be used. The transfer circuit itself generally contains no source of power and hence is known as a passive quadripole. **1952** *Electronic Engin.* XXIV. 264/1 The method of dealing with the steady state analysis of passive quadripoles in terms of the matrix of the linear transformation expressed by the network equations was introduced by Strecker and Feldtkeller in 1929. **1955** [see EIGEN-]. **1962** *Newnes Conc. Encycl. Electr. Engin.* 629/2 A quadripole may be designed with dissipative elements as an attenuator, or with reactive elements as a filter.

2. Var. QUADRUPOLE.

quadrireme ('kwɒdrɪriːm), *a.* and *sb.* [ad. L. *quadrirēm-is*, f. *quadri-* QUADRI- + *rēmus* oar.]

A. *adj.* Of ancient ships: Having four banks of oars.

1600 HOLLAND *Livy* XXXVII. xxiii. 957 Now of the Rhodians there were 32 quadrireme Gallies and 4 other triremes besides. **1697** POTTER *Antiq. Greece* III. xiv. (1715) 134 Trireme, quadrireme, and quinquereme Gallies, which exceeded one another by a Bank of Oars. [Hence in Robinson *Archæol. Græca* IV. xiii. (1807) 387.]

B. *sb.* A vessel having four banks of oars.

a **1656** USSHER *Ann.* (1658) 286 There were often sea fights.. between the Triremes, and the Quadriremes. **1656** in BLOUNT *Glossogr.* **1799** CHARNOCK in *Naval Chron.* I. 132 Ancient galleys, called Triremes, Quadriremes, Quinquiremes. **1852** GROTE *Greece* II. lxxxii. (1856) X. 667 Dionysius or his naval architects now struck out the plan of building.. quadriremes or quinqueremes, instead of triremes.

quadrisonic, var. QUADRASONIC *a.*

quadrivalent (see below), *a.* and *sb.* [f. QUADRI- + L. *valēnt-em*, pres. pple. of *valēre* to be worth.] **A.** *adj.* **1.** *Chem.* (kwɒdrɪ'veɪlənt).

Having a valency of four; capable of combining with four univalent atoms.

1865 A. W. HOFMANN in *Chem. News* 13 Oct. 176/1 The nitrogen and carbon atoms, respectively trivalent and quadrivalent, are provided with three and four arms, indicating the three and four combining units respectively distinguishing these atoms. **1869** *Eng. Mech.* 12 Nov. 198/3 The elements are classified as..tetratomic or quadrivalent, having four attractions. **1880** CLEMINSHAW *Wurtz' Atom. The.* 283 Carbon is quadrivalent and oxygen bivalent. **1922** A. D. UDDEN tr. *Bohr's Theory of Spectra* III. iii. 109 While an element like titanium in the fourth period already shows a marked tendency to occur with various valencies, on the other hand an element like zirconium is still quadri-valent like carbon in the second period and silicon in the third. **1964** J. W. LINNETT *Electronic Struct. Molecules* ii. 30 The carbon atom..is, of course, quadrivalent. **1978** *Sci. Amer.* Feb. 58/2 Cerium, alone among the trivalent rare earths, can be oxidized to the relatively insoluble quadrivalent state.

2. *Cytology.* (kwɒ'drɪvələnt). Applied to a meiotic structure composed of four wholly or partly homologous chromosomes joined together.

Less common than the corresp. sb. (see B. 2).

1898 *Zool. Jahrb.* (Abt. für Anat.) XII. 44 Frequently also in the loose spirem are found quadrivalent chromosomes with a constriction about the middle. **1929** *Jrnl. Genetics* XXI. 18 The hyacinths offered an opportunity for the comparative study in the same cell of the structure and behaviour of bivalent, trivalent and quadrivalent chromosomes of distinct types.

B. *sb.* **1.** *Chem.* A quadrivalent element. *rare*⁻¹.

1880 CLEMINSHAW *Wurtz' Atom. The.* 211 Carbon is therefore a quadrivalent.

2. *Cytology.* (kwɒ'drɪvələnt). A quadrivalent group of chromosomes.

1923 *Proc. Nat. Acad. Sci.* IX. 109 In one quarter and more of the pollen-mother-cells this regular distribution does not occur with regard to all of the 12 quadrivalents. **1946** [see MICROSPOROGENESIS]. **1952** [see BIVALENT *a.* 2]. **1975** *Nature* 17 Apr. 595/2 A sister plant which was a monosomic ($2n = 41$)..formed some trivalents, quadrivalents.., pentavalents and hexavalents, in addition to bivalents.

quadrivial (kwə'drɪvɪəl), *a.* and *sb.* Forms: 5 quadrivialle, -vall, 5–6 quatrivial, quadryuyall(e, 7 quadruviall. [ad. med.L. *quadriviālis*: see QUADRIVIUM, and -AL¹. Cf. OF. *quadruvial* (Godef.).]

A. *adj.* **1.** Having four roads or ways meeting in a point. Of roads: Leading in four directions.

a **1490** BOTONER *Itin.* (Nasmith 1778) 177 Wythynne the yate iiii quadryvyalle weyes. *a* **1637** B. JONSON *To Inigo Marquis* He [may] draw a forum with quadrivial streets. **1862** THOREAU *Excurs.* (1863) 171 A trivial or quadrivial place. **1890** O. CRAWFURD *Round the Calendar in Portugal* 303 Passing one day through the quadrivial square that lies beneath the clerigos tower.

2. Belonging to the QUADRIVIUM. Also *transf.*

c **1420** *Pallad. on Husb.* Proem 76 The philosophre..thus prompt to profre Vche art quadriuial. **1481** BOTONER *Tulle on Old Age* (Caxton), Light sciences called trivals, as be grammar, logyk, and rethorik in comparison of the quadrivall sciences. *c* **1495** *The Epitaffe*, etc. in *Skelton's Wks.* (1843) II. 390 Frendely him fostered quatriuial aliaunce. **1886** S. S. LAWRIE *Rise & Constit. Universities* 61 Practically under the name of dialectic, logic was a quadrivial study. **1912** *Encycl. Relig. & Ethics* V. 172/2 The 'trivial' arts were Grammar, Rhetoric, and Dialectics... The 'quadrivial' arts were Geometry, Arithmetic, Astronomy, and Music. **1949** *Author* Winter 40/2 A quadrivial passion for theology and literature, horses and international peace. **1964** C. S. LEWIS *Discarded Image* vii. 196 The four Quadrivial Arts must here be summarily dismissed.

†**3.** Quadrilateral. *Obs. rare.*

1540 BOORDE *The boke for to Lerne* B iij, Deuyde the lodgynges by the cyrcuyte of the quadryuyall courte. *Ibid.*, If there be an vtter courte made, make it quadryuyall with howses of easementes.

B. *sb.* †**1.** A group of four. *Obs. rare*⁻¹.

1432–50 tr. *Higden* (Rolls) I. 5 The triuialle of the vertues theologicalle and quadriuialle [L. *quadrivium*] of the cardinalle vertues.

2. *pl.* The four sciences constituting the QUADRIVIUM. Now only *Hist.*

1522 SKELTON *Why not to Court* 511 A poore maister of arte..had lytell parte Of the quatriuials Nor yet of triuials. **1577** HARRISON *England* II. iii. (1877) I. 78 The quadriuials ..(I meane arethmetike, musike, geometrie, and astronomie). *a* **1656** HALES *Gold. Rem.* (1688) 357 Trivials and Quadrivials as old clerks were wont to name them. **1716** M. DAVIES *Athen. Brit.* II. 92 Edward Seymour..was educated in Trivials, and partly in Quadrivials in Oxon. **1886** BRODRICK *Hist. Univ. Oxford* 64 These seven sciences were no other than the old Trivials and Quadrivials.

quadrivious (kwə'drɪvɪəs), *a. rare.* [cf. prec. and -OUS.] Going in four directions.

1860 READE *Cloister & H.* III. 34 Denys..pretended to shoot them all dead: they fled quadrivious, shrieking.

‖**quadrivium** (kwə'drɪvɪəm). [L. (f. *quadri-* QUADRI- + *via* way), a place where four ways meet; in late L., the four branches of mathematics (Boethius).] In the Middle Ages, the higher division of the seven liberal arts, comprising the mathematical sciences (arithmetic, geometry, astronomy, and music).

1804 RANKIN *Hist. France* III. IV. 308 Arithmetic, music, geometry, and astronomy formed Quadrivium. **1842** MRS. BROWNING *Grk. Chr. Poets* (1863) 123 The trivium and quadrivium of the schools. **1872** LOWELL *Dante* Pr. Wks. 1890 IV. 124 There can be no doubt that he went through the trivium..and the quadrivium..of the then ordinary university course.

‖**quadro**, *sb.*¹ *Obs. rare*⁻¹. [It. *quadro*, a square, a picture.] ? A square of tapestry.

a **1711** KEN *Edmund* Poet. Wks. 1721 II. 273 Her Palace was with glorious Quadro's lin'd, Made by her Virgins, by herself design'd.

quadro ('kwɒdrəʊ), *a.* and *sb.*² Colloq. abbrev. of QUADRAPHONY, QUADRAPHONIC *a.* Cf. QUAD *a.*² and *sb.*⁸

1972 *Guardian* 28 July 13 The critics say that the real reason for quadro is pure commercial pressure to sell more records. **1976** *Which?* May 99/1 It's possible to use quadro to create a totally new listening experience by getting the sounds to surround you completely. **1977** *Gramophone* Aug. 357/1 This will necessitate the introduction of decks equipped with two heads to accommodate both stereo and quadro-tapes.

quadro-. A less correct form of QUADRI-.

†**qua'drobulary**, *a. Obs. rare*⁻¹. App. = 'fourfold', with suggestion of TRIOBOLAR(Y *a.*

1647 WARD *Simp. Cobler* 48 There is a quadrobulary saying, which passes current in the Westerne World [etc.].

†**quadrohydrate.** *Chem. Obs.* A compound containing four times as much water as a simple hydrate.

1825 T. THOMSON *1st Princ. Chem.* II. 303 Berzelius considers it as a compound of 3 atoms carbonate of magnesia and of 1 atom of quadrohydrate.

quadron, a square: see QUADRAN *sb.*

quadroon (kwə'dru:n). Forms: α. 8 quarteron, (9 -oon), quatron, 8–9 -eron, 9 -roon. β. 8 quaderoon, 9 quadroon. [ad. Sp. *cuarteron* (hence F. *quarteron*), f. *cuarto* fourth, quarter; the mod. form may be due to assoc. with other words in *quadr-*.]

1. a. One who is the offspring of a white person and a mulatto; one who has a quarter of Negro blood. **b.** *rarely.* One who is fourth in descent from a Negro, one of the parents in each generation being white.

In early Sp. use chiefly applied to the offspring of a white and a mestizo, or half-breed Indian. When it is used to denote one who is fourth in descent from a Negro, the previous stage is called a *terceron*: see the transl. of Juan and Ulloa's *Voyage* (1772) I. 30, and cf. QUINTROON.

α. **1707** SLOANE *Jamaica* I. p. xlvi, The inhabitants of Jamaica are for the most part Europeans..who are the Masters, and Indians, Negros, Mulatos, Alcatrazes, Mestises, Quarterons, &c. who are the Slaves. **1793** JEFFERSON *Writ.* (1859) IV. 98 Castaing is described as a small dark mulatto, and La Chaise as a Quateron. **1819** W. LAWRENCE *Lect. Physiol. Zool.* 295 Europeans and Tercerons produce Quarterons or Quadroons. **1837** CARLYLE *Fr. Rev.* II. v. iv, Your pale-white Creoles..and your yellow Quarteroons. **1840** R. H. DANA *Bef. Mast* xiii. 29 The least drop of Spanish blood, if it be only of quatroon or octoon.

β. **1796** STEDMAN *Surinam* I. 296 The Samboe dark, and the Mulatto brown, The Mæsti fair, the well-limbed Quaderoon. **1819** [see α]. **1833** MARRYAT *P. Simple* (1863) 228 The progeny of a white and a negro is a mulatto, or half and half—of a white and mulatto, a quadroon, or one quarter black. **1880** OUIDA *Moths* I. 178 That brute goes with a quadroon to a restaurant.

Comb. **1860** O. W. HOLMES *Elsie V.* xxi. (1891) 292 How could he ever come to fancy such a quadroon-looking thing as that?

c. *transf.* Applied to the offspring resulting from similar admixture of blood in the case of other races, or from crossing in the case of animals or plants.

1811 SOUTHEY in *Q. Rev.* VI. 346 Whether a man were a half-new Christian, or a quateron, or a half-quateron..the Hebrew leaven was in the blood. **1879** tr. *De Quatrefages Hum. Spec.* 72 Koelreuter artificially fertilised hybrid flowers..and thus obtained a vegetable quadroon. **1892** *Daily News* 17 June 5/3 The offspring of these crosses [of rabbits] did not in any instance produce a 'quadroon'.

2. *attrib.* or as *adj.* ***quadroon ball***; ***quadroon black***, the offspring of a pure Negro and a quadroon (*Syd. Soc. Lex.* 1897).

1748 *Earthquake Peru* iii. 240 Quatron Indians, born of Whites and Mestizos. *Ibid.*, Quatron Negroes, born of Whites and Mulattos. **1796** STEDMAN *Surinam* I. vi. 126 A young and beautiful Quadroon girl. *Ibid.* II. xviii. 56 A female quaderoon slave. **1805** J. F. WATSON in *Amer. Pioneer* (1843) II. 236 These colored women have..their weekly balls, (called quartroon balls) at which none but white gentlemen attend. **1849** MACAULAY *Hist. Eng.* I. i. 14 A marriage between a white planter and a quadroon girl. **1880** G. W. CABLE *Grandissimes* iii. 19, I saw the same old man, at a quadroon ball a few years ago. **1893** F. C. SELOUS *Trav. S.E. Africa* 60 A pretty..mulatto, or rather quadroon girl. **1948** *Chicago Tribune* (Grafic Mag.) 8 Feb. 18/3 Most notorious of the carnival affairs, was the Quadroon ball, given by the young men of the town for their mistresses and friends.

quadrophonic, -phony, -sonic, varr. QUADRAPHONIC *a.*, QUADRAPHONY, QUADRASONIC *a.*

quadroxalate (kwə'drɒksələt). *Chem.* [f. QUADR(I)- + OXALATE *sb.*] A compound containing four equivalents of oxalic acid; esp. ***quadroxalate of potash.***

1808 WOLLASTON in *Phil. Trans.* XCVIII. 101 The quadroxalate as 1 and 2, or 2 particles potash with 4, acid. **1850** DAUBENY *Atom. The.* iii. (ed. 2) 112 Binoxalate of potass is a compound of 2 of acid and of 1 of base; quadroxalate of 4 of the former to 1 of the latter. **1876** HARLEY *Mat. Med.* (ed. 6) 316 Quadroxalate of Potash, erroneously called 'Salt of Lemons'.

qua'droxide. *Chem.* [f. as prec. + OXIDE.] = TETROXIDE.

1860 WORCESTER cites Graham.

quadru- ('kwɒdru:), a variant of QUADRI-; in L. restricted to a few formations in which the second element begins with *p*, as *quadrupēs*, *quadruplex*, *quadruplus*, and their derivatives. Apart from words based on these L. forms, mod. Eng. has *quadru-* only in *quadrumanous* etc. (after *quadruped*), but a few other examples are found in 16–17th c., as **quadrucorn**, a four-horned animal; **quadrulapse**, a fourth lapse or fall; **quadrupart(ed)** = QUADRIPARTITE *a.* Also **quadru-pawed** *nonce-wd.*, having four paws.

1575 SIR T. GRESHAM in *Wills Doctors' Comm.* (Camden) 64 The said indenture quadrupartted dated the saide xxth day of Maie. **1600** W. WATSON *Decacordon* (1602) 203 The quadrupart monarchie began in Babylon vnder Nabuchodonosor. **1607** TOPSELL *Four-f. Beasts* (1658) 546 The Oryx..which Aristotle and Pliny call a unicorn, Aelianus a quadrucorn. **1663** in Cramond *Annals of Banff* (1893) II. 43 Helen Morrison is ordained to appear..in Sackcloth, it being a quadrulapse. **1685** *Rec. Dingwall Presb.* (Sc. Hist. Soc.) 357 [A] quadrulapse in fornication. **1828** STERLING *Ess.* etc. (1848) II. 35 A quadru-pawed monster.

‖**Quadrumana** (kwə'dru:mənə), *sb. pl. Zool.* [neut. pl. (sc. *animālia*) of mod.L. *quadrumanus* four-handed, f. *quadru-* QUADRU- + *manus* hand. Cf. BIMANA.] An order of mammals, including monkeys, apes, baboons, and lemurs, of which the hind as well as the fore feet have an opposable digit, so that they can be used as hands.

1819 W. LAWRENCE *Lect. Physiol. Zool.* 175 The crania of all the quadrumana..are distinguished from the human skull by the comparative size..of the jaws. **1833** SIR C. BELL *Hand* (1834) 18 If we describe the hand as [etc.]..we embrace in the definition the extremities of the quadrumana or monkeys. **1863** LYELL *Antiq. Man* xix. 375 Those species of the anthropoid quadrumana which are most akin to him [man] in structure. **1882** OWEN in *Longm. Mag.* I. 67 This tooth..is the last of the permanent set of teeth to be fully developed in the Quadrumana.

quadrumanal (kwə'dru:mənəl), *a.* [f. prec. + -AL¹.] = QUADRUMANOUS.

1871 *Daily News* 17 Mar., The habitation of our quadrumanal relatives. **1882** OWEN in *Longm. Mag.* I. 67 The lowest..variety of the Bimanal order differs from the Quadrumanal one in the order of appearance..of the second or 'permanent' set [of teeth].

quadrumane ('kwɒdru:meɪn), *a.* and *sb.* Also **quadruman** (-mæn). [a. F. *quadrumane* (Buffon): see QUADRUMANA, and next.]

A. *adj.* = QUADRUMANOUS.

1835 KIRBY *Hab. & Inst. Anim.* II. xvii. 213 Cuvier's second Order of Mammalians, which he names Quadrumane or four-handed. **1864** *Spectator* No. 1875. 650 The lemurine—and consequently quadrumane..affinities of Chiromys. **1867** H. BUSHNELL *Moral Uses Dark Things* 303 What now shall we say of these quadruman people?

B. *sb.* One of the QUADRUMANA.

1828 in WEBSTER. **1835** KIRBY *Hab. & Inst. Anim.* I. ii. 71 What Zoologists call the Quadrumanes, or Four-handed beasts. **1856** W. CLARK tr. *Van der Hoeven's Zool.* II. 605 The Quadrumanes and Ruminants. **1882** OWEN in *Longm. Mag.* I. 66 Points of approximation in cranial and dental structure of the highest Quadrumane to the lowest Bimane.

quadrumanous (kwə'dru:mənəs), *a.* Also 8 quadri-. [f. mod.L. *quadruman-us* (see QUADRUMANA) + -OUS.] Belonging to the order of QUADRUMANA; four-handed.

[**1699** TYSON *Orang-Out.* 91 Our Pygmie is..tho' a Biped, yet of the Quadrumanus-kind. *Ibid.* 94 The Orang-Outang ..being Quadrumanus, like the Ape-kind.] **1819** W. LAWRENCE *Lect. Physiol. Zool.* 128 All the simiæ, and the lemurs likewise, are quadrumanous. **1830** LYELL *Princ. Geol.* I. 152 Not a single bone of a quadrumanous animal has ever yet been discovered in a fossil state. **1860** EMERSON *Cond. Life, Fate* Wks. (Bohn) II. 317 He betrays his relation to what is below him—small-brained, fishy, quadrumanous quadruped. **1874** WOOD *Nat. Hist.* 2 The Quadrumanous, or Four-handed animals, are familiarly known by the titles of Apes, Baboons, and Monkeys.

b. Ape-like (in destructiveness).

1790 BURKE *Fr. Rev.* Wks. V. 308 At this malicious game they display the whole of their quadrumanous activity.

qua'drumvirate (kwɒ'drʌmvɪrət). [for *quattuorvirate, on anal. of *duum-*, *triumvirate*.] A union of four men. So †**qua'drumvir**, one of four men.

1752 FIELDING *Covent Gard. Jrnl.* 21 Mar., This quadrumvirate..called themselves 'The Wits'. **1790** *Bystander* 38 A quadrumvirate appeared almost at the same time. *Ibid.*, Taking a seat as a quadrumvir. **1923** *Contemp. Rev.* Feb. 151 He [*sc.* Mussolini] formed a quadrumvirate .. to whom he entrusted full powers. **1955** *Times* 3 May 11/3 He is the third to go of the quadrumvirate who for much of the post-war period held the leadership of the

Trades Union Congress largely in their hands. **1958** P. KEMP *No Colours or Crest* viii. 155 Colonel Fiqri Dine,.. one of the original quadrumvirate of chiefs that had helped Zog in his early days of power. **1974** *Times Lit. Suppl.* 29 Mar. 315/3 Osler..one of the remarkable quadrumvirate who established the Johns Hopkins Medical School.

[**quadrune.** Error perhaps founded on a mistaken form of *Quadersandstein*, 'the German term for certain soft sandstones of the Chalk formation' (Page).

1832 WEBSTER, *Quadrune*, a gritstone with a calcarious cement. **1860** WORCESTER [citing MAUNDER]. Hence in *Cassell's Encycl. Dict.*, Funk's *Standard Dict.*]

quadrupartite, -pertite, obs. variants of QUADRIPARTITE.

quadruped ('kwɒdru:pɛd), *sb.* (*a.*) Also 7–8 -pede. [ad. L. *quadrupēs, -ped-is*, four-footed, a four-footed beast, f. *quadru-* QUADRU- + *pēs* foot.]

1. An animal which has four feet. (Usually confined to mammals, and excluding four-footed reptiles.)

1646 SIR T. BROWNE *Pseud. Ep.* 104 Quadrupedes, Volatills and Fishes..have distinct and prominent organs of motion, legs, wings, and fins. **1664** POWER *Exp. Philos.* I. 2 The knees or flexure of his fore legs forwards (as in most quadrupeds). **1728** MORGAN *Algiers* I. ii. 21 Quadrupedes of the Serpentine Breed. **1774** GOLDSM. *Nat. Hist.* (1776) II. 105 The arms of men but very little resemble the fore feet of quadrupedes. **1833** J. RENNIE *Alph. Angling* 25 In quadrupeds, the ear is nearly as large in the young as in the full grown animal. **1846** MCCULLOCH *Acc. Brit. Empire* (1854) I. 123 The fishes, upon which nearly all the aquatic quadrupeds almost entirely subsist.

Comb. **1870** LUBBOCK *Orig. Civiliz.* vi. (1875) 258 If..we compare..serpent worship with quadruped-worship..we shall find that it has no exceptionally wide area.

b. Applied *spec.* to the horse: cf. QUAD *sb.*[4]

1660 BOND *Scut. Reg.* 7 Even I..can hardly restrain the unbridled fierceness of the Quadrupedes. **1755** YOUNG *Centaur* vi. Wks. 1757 IV. 253 Others, with Swift..look on the noble quadrupede as superior to the man. **1868** G. DUFF *Pol. Surv.* 220 The long straggling line of soldiers..with their quadrupeds and baggage.

2. *attrib.* or as *adj.* Four-footed.

1741 WATTS *Improv. Mind.* I. xvi. §2 (1) The cockney, travelling into the country, is surprised at many actions of the quadruped and winged animals. **1784** COWPER *Task* VI. 622 Learn we might, if not too proud to stoop To quadruped instructors. **1834** CAUNTER *Orient. Ann.* vi. 65 This herd of quadruped giants was only at a short distance from us. **1848** CARPENTER *Anim. Phys.* 68 The Mammalia are for the most part quadruped.

b. Belonging to, connected with, or appropriate to four-footed animals.

a **1835** MCCULLOCH *Attributes* (1843) II. 21 The Kangaroo labours under an invention which is an infringement upon the general simple and effectual one for quadruped motion. **1847** EMERSON *Repr. Men, Montaigne* Wks. (Bohn) I. 346, I do not press the scepticism of the materialist. I know the quadruped opinion will not prevail.

3. A verse of four feet. *rare*$^{-1}$.

1800 W. TAYLOR in Robberds *Mem.* I. 328 The French.. make no difference between an anapaestic quadruped and a six-foot iambic.

Hence (or directly from stem of L. *quadrupēs*) **qua'drupedan, †quadrupeded, †quadru'pedial, †-'pedian, quadru'pedic, quadru'pedical** *adjs.* = QUADRUPEDAL. **'quadrupedism,** the fact of being a quadruped. **qua'drupedous** *a.*, quadrupedal (Bailey Vol. II, 1731).

1806 *Edin. Rev.* IX. 37 The human character may undergo strange mutations from *quadrupedan sympathy. **1542** BOORDE *Dyetary* xvi. (1870) 272 So great murren or syckenes to any *quadrypedyd beste. **1709** *Brit. Apollo* II. No. 64. 2/2 Quadrupeded Brutes. **1700** MOXON *Math. Dict.* 136 **Quadrupedial Signs.* **1647** *App. Almanak for 1386*, 74 Aries, Taurus, Leo, Sagittarius, and Capricorn, are called bestial or *quadrupedian signes, having representation of four-footed creatures. **1888** *Daily News* 26 June 9/1 The episcopal bacon which..roams, *quadrupedic, among the potato beds. **1824** DIBDIN *Libr. Comp.* 681 Devoured or mutilated by (apparently) some hungry *quadrupedical animal. **1834–43** SOUTHEY *Doctor* cxcix. (1862) 530 Among the Mahometans also, *quadrupedism is not considered an obstacle to a certain kind of canonisation.

quadrupedal (kwə'dru:pɪdəl), *a.* and *sb.* Also 7 quadrupedall. [ad. late L. *quadrupedālis* (Bæda), f. *quadrupēs*: see prec. and -AL[1]. Cf. obs. F. *quadrupedal* (Godef.).]

A. *adj.* **1.** Of animals: Four-footed; using all four feet for walking or running; *transf.*, of a person: on hands and knees. Also *transf.* of things.

1620 VENNER *Via Recta* iii. 54 It [veal] is of an excellent.. nutriture..exceeding all quadrupedall creatures. **1715** *Hist. Reg.* (1724) Chron. Diary 57 Even the Quadrupedal Animals were strangely terrify'd. **1821–5** BARHAM in *Life & Lett.* I. ii. 80 According as he found them more or less intelligent than his quadrupedal companion. **1854** [see BIPEDAL *a.* 2]. **1864–5** WOOD *Homes without H.* i. (1868) 6 Shafts through which the quadrupedal miner ejects the materials which it has scooped out. **1869** BROWNING *Ring & Bk.* VIII. 510 Beasts quadrupedal, mammiferous, Do credit to their beasthood. **1881** *Harper's Mag.* Oct. 696 Two forces riding quadrupedal stools. **1897** *Proc. R. Soc.* LX. 412 The posture assumed suggests the taking of a forward step in quadrupedal progression. **1914** CHESTERTON *Wisdom of Father Brown* x. 249 Seeing him thus quadrupedal in the grass, the priest raised his eyebrows rather sadly. **1971** *Nature* 12 Mar. 86/1 The four gaits [of the kangaroo] identified were a slow progression, a walk, a quadrupedal bound and a bipedal hop.

2. Of, belonging, or appropriate to, a quadruped.

quadrupedal signs, zodiacal signs named after quadrupeds (PHILLIPS 1696; cf. *quadrupedian* above, and BESTIAL 1).

1747 *Gentl. Mag.* XVII. 480 Worms of various kinds are bred in animal bodies, quadrupedal as well as human. **1850** H. MILLER *Footpr. Creat.* viii. (1874) 149 The round ligament in the head of the quadrupedal thigh-bone. **1875** *Lyell's Princ. Geol.* II. III. xxxiv. 261 The natural tendency in man to resume the quadrupedal state. **1971** *Nature* 30 Apr. 577/1 Those early or middle Miocene dryopithecines ..have been dubbed 'dental apes'—primates which apparently combined a hominoid dentition with limbs which retained a more primitive quadrupedal monkey-like morphology.

†3. 'Four foot long' (Phillips 1678). *Obs.*$^{-0}$

†B. *sb.* A quadruped. *Obs. rare.*

1643 NETHERSOLE *Parables refl. on Times* 12 The Eagle, the King of Volatills,..the Lyon, King of Quadrupedals. **1660** HOWELL *Parly of Beasts* 11 My bloud..I confess to be the coldest of any Quadrupedals.

Hence **quadru'pedally** *adv.*

1847 W. J. BRODERIP *Zool. Recreations* II. 179 Ask the zoologists, and one will tell you that the jackal..is the impure source of all that is quadrupedally good and amiable. **1952** RIESEN & KINDER *Postural Devel. Infant Chimpanzees* vi. 46 (*table*) Creeps (quadrupedally for chimpanzees). **1976** *Nature* 29 Jan. 305/2 At these speeds the mice either 'trotted' with the hind legs moving independently or 'galloped' quadrupedally with the hind legs moving together.

qua'drupedant, *a.* and *sb. rare.* [ad. L. *quadrupedans* adj. and sb., f. *quadrupes* QUADRUPED.] **a.** *adj.* Quadrupedal. **b.** *sb.* A horse.

1656 BLOUNT *Glossogr.*, *Quadrupedant*,..that goeth on four feet. **1870** J. ORTON *Andes & Amazons* iv. (1876) 79 The huge nails which enter into the hoofs of the quadrupedants.

So **†quadrupedant** *v.*, to use the four feet. **†quadrupedate** *v.*, *intr.* to act as a quadruped; *trans.* to convert into a quadruped. **quadrupe'dation,** stamping with the four feet.

1792 *Bar. Munchausen's Trav.* xxix. 130 At which, *quadrupedanting, plunged the steed. **1623** COCKERAM, **Quadrupedate*, to goe on foure legs. **1629** T. ADAMS *England's Sickness* in *Wks.* 306 We were..quadrupedated with an earthly, stooping, groueling couetousnesse. **1862** G. MACDONALD *D. Elginbrod* III. xvi, A carriage and pair pulled sharply up at the door, with more than the usual amount of *quadrupedation.

quadruplane ('kwɒdru:pleɪn). Also quadri-. [f. QUADRU- + PLANE *sb.*[3]] An aeroplane having four sets of wings, one above another.

1909 A. BERGET *Conquest of Air* 141 Naturally we can make triplanes or quadriplanes, but one must not proceed too far in this direction. **1909** *Times* 17 Aug. 10/5 Major Baden-Powell will attempt a flight with his quadruplane. **1919** *Jane's All World's Aircraft* 60 a (*caption*) Experimental Armstrong-Whitworths.—Two of the F.K. 10 Type Quadruplanes. **1937** *Times* 5 Oct. 9/3 He [*sc.* Major Baden-Powell] made two aeroplanes, one with swivelling propellers to obtain direct lift, and the other a kind of quadruplane.

†quadruplate, *v. Obs. rare.* Also 5 quatriplate. [f. ppl. stem of L. *quadruplāre*: see QUADRUPLE and -ATE[3].] To multiply by four.

1486 *Bk. St. Albans, Her.* E vij, Ther be certan nobull men the wich bere theys tractis triplatit..and sum bere hit quatriplatit. **1571** DIGGES *Pantom.* I. xi. D iij, Then quadruplate the distance. **1611** COTGR., *Quadrupler*..to quadruplate, or make foure times as much. **1656** in BLOUNT *Glossogr.*

So **†quadruplate** *ppl. a.*, quadruple. *Obs.*

c **1470** HENRYSON *Orph. & Eur.* 228 Thair leirit he tonis.. As duplare, triplare, and..the quadruplait.

†quadruplator. *Obs.* [a. L. *quadruplātor*, (1) a public informer, (2) one who multiplies by four (see prec.). The exact origin of sense 1 is not certain, though there is probably some connexion with *quadruplum* a fourfold penalty.]

a. A public informer. **b.** One who restores fourfold.

1624 SANDERSON *Serm.* I. 109 Our prouling informers, like those old sycophants in Athens, or the quadruplators in Rome. *Ibid.* 114 Zacheus..imposed upon himself..a fourfold restitution... Here was a right quadruplator indeed; and in the best sence. **1647** TRAPP *Comm. Matt.* viii. 32 A cunning fetch of an old quadruplator.

So **†quadruplation,** multiplying by four. *Obs.*

1557 RECORDE *Whetst.* N n iv b, That must be doen by that quadriplation as you taught before. **1658** in PHILLIPS.

quadruple ('kwɒdru:p(ə)l), *a.*, *sb.*, and *adv.* Also 6 quadriple, 8 quadruble. [a. F. *quadruple* (13th c., OF. also *quadruble*), ad. L. *quadruplus*, f. *quadru-* QUADRU- + *-plus* as in *duplus* DOUBLE. An earlier form in Eng. was QUATREBLE, q.v. The stressing *qua'druple* (see quots. *a* 1745 and 1820 in A) is usual in Sc.]

A. *adj.* **a.** Fourfold; consisting of four parts; four times as great or as many as. Const. *of*, *to*, or without prep.

1557 [see b]. **1594** HOOKER *Eccl. Pol.* III. x. §3 A law that ..doth punish thieves with a quadruple restitution. **1628** MEAD in Ellis *Orig. Lett.* Ser. I. III. 268 The quadruple strength which they have prepared against our fleet. *a* **1648** LD. HERBERT *Hen. VIII* (1683) 9 [A sum] quadruple to so much in this age. *a* **1745** SWIFT *To George-Nim-Dan-Dean, Esq.* (R.), How I joy to see thee wander..In circling mazes, smooth and supple, And ending in a clink quadruple. **1807** HUTTON *Course Math.* II. 269 To receive light and heat quadruple to that of the earth. **1820** KEATS *Hyperion* II. 146 A quadruple wrath Unhinges the poor world. **1825** MACAULAY *Ess., Machiavelli* (1887) 34 When the value of silver was more than quadruple of what it now is. **1884** BOWER & SCOTT *De Bary's Phaner. & Ferns* 576 Single, triple, or quadruple concentric series of narrow elements.

b. In various special applications.

quadruple algebra, algebra in which four independent units are used. ***quadruple counterpoint***, four-part counterpoint in which the parts may be interchanged without breaking the rules of counterpoint. ***quadruple expansion***, the use of four stages of expansion in a compound steam engine, the same steam expanding successively in four cylinders; usu. *attrib.* ***quadruple pistole*** = sb. 2b. †***quadruple proportion*** = quadruple ratio. ***quadruple quaver***, a hemidemisemiquaver. ***quadruple ratio***, the ratio of four to one. ***quadruple rhythm, time***, in *Mus.*, rhythm or time having four beats in a measure.

1557 RECORDE *Whetst.* B j b, If it containe it .4. tymes, then is it [the proportion] quadrupla, or quadruple. *Ibid.* C j, Proportion..Doble, Triple, Quadriple. **1727** CHAMBERS *Cycl.*, *Pistole*..has its augmentations, and diminutions; which are *quadruple pistoles*, *double pistoles*, and *half pistoles*. **1869** OUSELEY *Counterp.* xvii. 134 Triple and quadruple counterpoints..consist of three or four melodies so interwoven that any of them may become a correct bass to the others. **1885** R. SENNETT *Marine Steam Engine* (ed. 2) i. 23 In some few cases, in which steam of 150 to 180 lbs. has been used, quadruple expansion engines have been fitted,.. but there is not sufficient evidence yet to show that the additional complication thus introduced is compensated for by any marked gain in economy. **1894** J. J. ASTOR *Journey in Other Worlds* iv. 48 The electricity generated by..slow-moving quadruple-expansion steam engines, provides the power required to run our electric ships. **1898** J. HAMMOND *Let.* 22 Dec., Hamilton's Quaternions is a quadruple algebra, the 4 independent units being his i, j, k, and the unit of quantity. **1919** *Jane's Fighting Ships* 260/2 Kashima.. machinery: 2 sets 4 cylinder vertical quadruple expansion. **1952** FOX & MCBIRNIE *Marine Steam Engines & Turbines* vii. 137 The quadruple-expansion engine is not now so common as formerly, and modern practice appears to favour the triple-expansion engine with fairly high initial superheat.

c. *Hist.* ***quadruple alliance***, an alliance of four powers, *esp.* that of Britain, France, Germany and Holland in 1718, and of Britain, France, Spain and Portugal in 1834.

1735 H. WALPOLE *Corr.* (1820) I. 3, I believe you will guess there is no quadruple alliance. **1825** JEFFERSON *Autobiog.* Wks. 1859 I. 76 She [France] secretly engaged, also, in negotiations with Russia, Austria, and Spain, to form a quadruple alliance. **1872** FREEMAN *Gen. Sketch* xv. §2 (1874) 304 France, England, and the United Provinces presently joined the Emperor in the Quadruple Alliance against Spain.

fig. **1787** BURNS *Let. to Miss Chalmers* 12 Dec., Misfortune, bodily constitution, hell, and myself, have formed a 'quadruple alliance' to guarantee the other.

d. Applied to printing-papers which are four times the usual size, as ***quadruple crown, -demy, -foolscap***, etc. Cf. QUAD *a.*[1]

B. *sb.* **1.** Anything fourfold; a sum or quantity four times as great as another.

1609 DOULAND *Ornith. Microl.* 61 Now if we place these Triples..in the vpper ranke we shall produce Quadruples. **1640–1** *Kirkcudbr. War-Comm. Min. Bk.* (1855) 149 The quadruple of the pryce of the inch of the best sort of schoes. **1822** J. FLINT *Lett. Amer.* 309, I believe, if he had laid them [the damages] at quadruple, the jury would have given him every cent.

2. *spec.* **†a.** A tooth having a quadruple root. *Obs.* **†b.** A coin of the value of four pistoles (so in French; cf. A. b, quot. 1727). *Obs.* **†c.** A fourfold fine. *Obs.* **d.** A printing machine which prints four copies at once.

1541 R. COPLAND *Guydon's Quest. Chirurg.*, Two donales two quadruples .viij. molares and two cassalles. **1655** tr. *Com. Hist. Francion* XII. 20 See here his Quadruples which I never touched before. **1673** DRYDEN *Amboyna* II. i, No transitory Sum, three hundred Quadruples in your own Country Gold. **1682** *Lond. Gaz.* No. 1784/4 A considerable Sum of Money was stolen, among which were several Quadruples, or Four-Pistol-Pieces. **1695** *Sc. Acts Will. III*, c. 55 (1822) IX. 453/1 Incurring the Quadruples appoynted by the said Act by way of penalty. **1890** W. J. GORDON *Foundry* 203 It was Mr. Lloyd who had the first of these new Quadruples at work on a London daily newspaper.

C. *adv.* in *Comb.* In a fourfold manner.

1840 DICKENS *Barn. Rudge* xli, Places of distrust and cruelty, and restraint, they would have left quadruple-locked for ever. **1884** *Health Exhib. Catal.* 62/1 Blundell's Patent Duplex (quadruple acting) portable Fire Engines.

quadruple ('kwɒdru:p(ə)l), *v.* Also 6 quadriple, 7 -ruble. [ad. F. *quadrupler* (1404) or L. *quadrupl-āre*, f. *quadrupl-us*: see prec.]

1. *trans.* To make four times as great or as many as before; to multiply by four.

1375 BARBOUR *Bruce* XVIII. 30 He suld fecht that day, Thouch Tryplit or quadruplit war thai. **1557** RECORDE *Whetst.* F iij, Therfore I doe quadriple .195. and it maketh .780. *c* **1611** CHAPMAN *Iliad* I. 129 Yet we all, all losse thou sufferst thus, Will treble; quadruple in gaine. **1642** HOWELL *For. Trav.* (Arb.) 87 Double the howers above twelve in the longest solstitiall day, and the product will shew the climat, quadruble them 'twill shew the parallell. **1792** A. YOUNG *Trav. France* 439, I am confident..that the mass of human wretchedness is quadrupled by their influence. **1882** PEBODY *Eng. Journalism* xxiii. 178 The Press, by reporting the speeches of these men, quadrupled their power in Parliament. **1883** *Stubbs' Mercantile Circular* 8 Nov. 982/2 The import of raw cotton.. has more than quadrupled itself in two years.

2. To amount to four times as many as.

1832 LEWIS *Use & Ab. Pol. Terms* xi. 92 The number of females.. probably more than quadrupled that of the male governors.

3. *intr.* (for *refl.*) To grow to four times the former number, amount, or size.

1776 ADAM SMITH *W.N.* II. ii. (1869) I. 296 The trade of Scotland has more than quadrupled since the first erection of the two publick banks at Scotland. **1833** HT. MARTINEAU *Cinnamon & Pearls* v. 97 The exports.. have quadrupled since the relaxation of the monopoly. **1882** PEBODY *Eng. Journalism* xix. 145 Mr. Levy reduced the price of the paper. .. The circulation doubled, trebled, quadrupled.

Hence **'quadrupled** *ppl. a.* = QUADRUPLE *a.*

1607 TOPSELL *Four-f. Beasts* (1658) 99 The Harts of Briletum and Ibarne, have their reins quadrupled or four-fold. **1865** MANSFIELD *Salts* 465 A quadrupled salt with a single molecule of adjunct.

quadruplegic, var. QUADRIPLEGIC *a.* and *sb.*

quadrupler (kwɒ'dru:plər). [f. QUADRUPLE *v.* + -ER[1].] A device that makes something four times as great.

1941 MILLMAN & SEELY *Electronics* xii. 416 The circuit.. can be extended from a doubler to a quadrupler by adding two tubes and two condensers. **1946** *Nature* 5 Oct. 477/1 During the years 1929–32 they developed together the voltage quadrupler steady potential generator of 600 kilovolts. **1947** L. B. YOUNG in C. G. Montgomery *Technique Microwave Measurem.* vi. 368 The crystal-oscillator frequency is multiplied to 5 Mc/sec by means of a push-push quadrupler.

quadruplet ('kwɒdrʊplɛt). [f. QUADRUPLE + -ET[1]; after *triplet.*]

1. *pl.* Four children born at a birth.

1787 GARTHSHORE in *Phil. Trans.* LXXVII. 355 These are the only cases of quadruplets.. he had ever heard of as born in Scotland. **1836–9** TODD *Cycl. Anat.* II. 736/1 An instance of quadruplets consisting of three boys and a girl. **1898** *Daily News* 15 Apr. 5/2 Huller ventured on the assertion.. that quadruplets were born once in 20,000 cases.

2. a. Any combination of four things or parts united or working together, *esp.* four combined springs (Knight *Dict. Mech.* Suppl.).

1852 DE MORGAN in Graves *Life Hamilton* (1889) III. 338 We have then an harmonic quadruplet and sextuplet, and we might have octuplets, &c.

b. *Mus.* A group of four notes to be played in the time of three of the same value.

1873 H. C. BANISTER *Music* 13 Other irregularities.. such as four notes for three, termed a Quadruplet. **1938** *Oxf. Compan. Mus.* p. xlviii (*heading*) Irregular rhythmic groupings (duplets, triplets, quadruplets, etc.). **1946** P. HINDEMITH *Elem. Training for Musicians* ix. 117 The names of these newly established values are: duplets, triplets, quadruplets, and so forth up to decuplets... Some of these terms are so awkward (linguistically) that they are hardly ever used.

3. A bicycle for four riders. Cf. QUAD *sb.*[3] Also *attrib.*

1895 *Daily News* 27 July 5/3 Professional riders on tandems, triplets, and quadruplets. **1897** *Whitaker's Alm.* 641/2 A quadruplet team covered a flying quarter in 25.2 secs.

quadruplex ('kwɒdrʊplɛks), *a.* and *sb.* [a. L. *quadruplex* fourfold, f. QUADRU- + *plic-*, to fold.]

A. *adj.* **1.** *Electric Telegraphy.* Applied to a system by which four messages can be sent over one wire at the same time.

1875 KNIGHT *Dict. Mech.* 1842/1 *Quadruplex Telegraph.* **1879** G. PRESCOTT *Sp. Telephone* p. iii, In 1874 Edison invented a quadruplex system for the simultaneous transmission of four communications over the same conductor. **1881** LUBBOCK *Pres. Addr. Brit. Assoc.* in *Nature* No. 618. 411 Duplex and quadruplex telegraphy, one of the most striking achievements of modern telegraphy.

2. *Engineering.* Applied to an engine in which the expansion of the steam is used four times in cylinders of increasing diameter.

1896 *Westm. Gaz.* 8 May 10/2 A steamer, fitted with five-crank quadruplex engines.

3. *Genetics.* Also **quadri-**. Of a tetraploid individual: having the dominant allele at some particular locus represented four times.

1923 [see DUPLEX *a.* 1 e]. **1932** SANSOME & PHILP *Rec. Adv. Plant Genetics* v. 182 There are five possible types of zygote in the tetraploid, quadruplex SSSS, triple SSSs, duplex SSss, simplex Ssss and nulliplex ssss. **1963** [see NULLIPLEX *a.*].

B. *sb.* A telegraphic instrument by means of which four simultaneous messages can be sent over the same wire.

Hence **'quadruplex** *v.*, to make (a telegraph circuit, etc.) quadruplex. Cf. QUAD *v.*

1887 *Brit. Merc. Gaz.* 15 June 43/2 The multiplication of wires soon attracted attention to methods of duplexing and quadruplexing the circuits. **1889** *Times* (weekly ed.) 29 Mar. 5/2 If the line is already duplexed.. the addition of the phonophore will quadruplex it.

quadruplicate (kwə'dru:plɪkət), *a.* and *sb.* [ad. L. *quadruplicāt-us*, pa. pple. of *quadruplicāre* to quadruple, f. *quadruplex*: see prec.]

A. *adj.* **1.** Fourfold; four times repeated. ***quadruplicate proportion, ratio***, the proportion or ratio of fourth powers in relation to that of the radical quantities.

1657 HOBBES *Absurd Geom.* Wks. 1845 VII. 378 An infinite row of Arithmetically proportionals, in proportion quadruplicate. **1794** G. ADAMS *Nat. & Exp. Philos.* III. xxxi. 269 The efforts tending to destroy the adhesion of beams from their gravity only, increase in the quadruplicate ratio of their lengths. **1816** PLAYFAIR *Nat. Phil.* II. 169 The same [probability] is increased in a quadruplicate ratio, from considering the phenomena of all these four superior planets.

2. Forming four exactly corresponding copies.

1807 PIKE *Sources Mississ.* III. App. (1810) 72, I have directed the formula for you to sign of four corresponding quadruplicate receipts.

B. *sb.* **1.** ***in quadruplicate***: In four exactly corresponding copies or transcripts.

1790 W. HASTINGS *Let. to Boswell* 2 Dec. in *B.'s Johnson* an. 1781 Of these [letters], one which was written in quadruplicate.. has already been made publick. **1900** *Rules* (25 Oct.) *under Money-Lenders Act* vi, The order shall be signed in quadruplicate by the permanent Secretary. *fig.* **1886** KIPLING *Departm. Ditties*, etc. (1899) 47 Four times Cupid's debtor I—Bankrupt in quadruplicate.

2. *pl.* Four things exactly alike; *esp.* four exactly corresponding copies of a document.

1883 SIR C. S. C. BOWEN in *Law Rep. 11 Q. Bench Div.* 342 The.. conveniences which merchants.. believed to be afforded by the system of triplicates or quadruplicates.

quadruplicate (kwə'dru:plɪkeɪt), *v.* [f. ppl. stem of L. *quadruplicāre*: see prec.]

1. *trans.* To multiply by four; to make four times as many or as great; to quadruple.

1661 in BLOUNT *Glossogr.* (ed. 2). **1674** JEAKE *Arith.* (1696) 56 Or else duplicate,.. quadruplicate, &c. the Fraction according to the given Integer. **1694** SALMON *Bate's Dispens.* (1713) 327/2 Sometimes the Proportion is to be quadruplicated. **1861** *Under the Spell* III. 220 Prices 'were "quadruplicated",' the demand for places being great. **1888** G. W. CABLE in *Amer. Missionary* Apr. 90 If you knew the national value of this work,.. you would quadruplicate it before the year is out.

2. To make or provide in quadruplicate; to provide four (things) exactly alike.

1879 G. MEREDITH *Egoist* III. iii. 64 We are in danger of duplicating and triplicating and quadruplicating [wedding presents].

Hence **qua'druplicating** *vbl. sb.* (Ash *Suppl.* 1775).

quadruplication (kwə,dru:plɪ'keɪʃən). [ad. L. *quadruplicātiōn-em*, n. of action from *quadruplicāre* to make fourfold: see prec.]

1. The action or process of making fourfold, of multiplying by four; also, the result of this; a thing folded four times.

1578 BANISTER *Hist. Man* v. 78 It [the vein] is admitted into the quadruplication of Dura mater. **1611** COTGR., *Quadruplication*, a quadruplication. **1616** in BULLOKAR *Eng. Expos.* [Hence in COCKERAM, BLOUNT, etc.] **1674** JEAKE *Arith.* (1696) 24 Quadruplication.. is to double the Duplication. **1839** ALISON *Europe* (1849–50) VII. xli. §15. 19 Twenty-eight years; the well-known period of the quadruplication of the Sum at compound interest of five per cent.

2. *Civil* and *Canon Law.* A pleading on the part of the defendant, corresponding to the rebutter at common law. Cf. QUADRUPLY *sb.*

1651 W. G. tr. *Cowel's Inst.* 243 After a Triplication [follows] a Quadruplication. **1726** AYLIFFE *Parergon* 251 Quad[r]uplications, which the Defendant propounds to the Plaintiffs Triplications.

qua'druplicature. [f. QUADRUPLICATE *v.* + -URE.] = prec., sense 1.

1891 in *Cent. Dict.*

quadruplicity (kwɒdru:'plɪsɪtɪ) [ad. L. *quadruplicitās*, n. of quality f. *quadruplex*: see QUADRUPLEX and -ITY.] Fourfold nature; the condition of being fourfold, or of forming a set of four.

c **1590** GREENE *Fr. Bacon* ix. 31 The quadruplicity Of elemental essence. **1593** NORDEN *Spec. Brit., M'sex* I. 44 King Canutus the Dane,.. in regard of his quadruplicitie of kingdomes, esteemed himselfe more then a man mortall. **1664** POWER *Exp. Philos.* 37 Dr. Brown.. hath ranked this conceit of the eyes of a snail (and especially their quadruplicity) amongst the vulgar errors. **1825** S. T. COLERIDGE *Aids Reflect.* App. C. (1858) I. 395 The universal quadruplicity, or four elemental forms of power. **1890** J. H. STIRLING *Gifford Lect.* iii. 41 The origin of the term [final causes] lies in the Aristotelian quadruplicity of causes as such.

†**quadruplify**, *v. Obs. rare*[−1]. [f. L. *quadruplus* QUADRUPLE + -(I)FY.] = QUADRUPLE *v.*

1578 BANISTER *Hist. Man* VIII. 99 In the hynder part of the head these Membranes are Quadruplified.

quadrupling ('kwɒdru:plɪŋ), *vbl. sb.* [f. QUADRUPLE *v.* + -ING[1].] The action of the vb.

1694 *Phil. Trans.* XVIII. 70 The doubling, trebling, quadrupling, &c. of Rations is performed by squaring, cubing, biquadrating, &c. of the terms. **1885** *Pall Mall G.* 27 Mar. 1/1 Supplemented, say, by the quadrupling of our field artillery.

†**'quadruply**, *sb. Sc. Law. Obs. rare.* [ad. obs. F. *quadruplique* (16th c. in Littré *Suppl.*); cf. DUPLY.] = QUADRUPLICATION 2.

1695 *Sc. Acts Will. III*, c. 6 (1822) IX. 365/2 The Clerks writing of the Defences, Duplyes, Triplyes, Quadruplyes, and so furth for the defender and pursuer. **1762** (*title*) Quadruplies for.. R. Graham.. J. Bakie [etc.] to the triplies for P. Honeymoon [etc.], Feb. 10. **1820** [see DUPLY b].

quadruply ('kwɒdru:plɪ), *adv.* [f. QUADRUPLE *a.* + -LY[2].] Four times; in a fourfold degree or manner.

1726 SWIFT *Gulliver* I. vi, The innocent person is quadruply recompensed.. for the danger he underwent. **1793** T. TAYLOR *Orat. Julian* p. lxvi, Thy orb quadruply intersects these worlds. **1857** GEO. ELIOT *Ess.* (1884) 4 The poet's [Young's] father was quadruply clerical, being at once rector, prebendary, court chaplain, and dean.

quadrupole ('kwɒdru:pəʊl), *sb.* and *a. Physics.* Also quadri-. [ad. Du. *quadrupool*: see QUADRU-, QUADRI-, and POLE *sb.*[2]] **A.** *sb.* **a.** A multipole of order $l = 2$ (cf. MULTIPOLE *sb.*). Usu. *attrib.*

1922 *Proc. Sect. Sci. K. Akad. Wetensch. Amsterdam* XXIII. 939 Assuming the molecules to act on each other as electric quadrupoles with constant quadrupole moment.. Burgers has calculated the quadrupole moment of the hydrogen molecule. **1927** *Proc. Cambr. Philos. Soc.* XXIII. 930 A method of calculating the probability of switches due to radiation by the quadripole moment seems to be supplied by Dirac's recent theory of the interaction between matter and radiation. **1932** *Proc. R. Soc.* A. CXXXVIII. 666 Assuming for the field of the nucleus the field of a quadripole, instead of that of a dipole. **1957** [see DIPOLE 1]. **1957** *Sci. News* XLIII. 87 There is an electrical property of nuclei.. called the quadrupole moment, which is a measure of the departure of the nucleus from a spherical to an ellipoidal shape. **1970** G. K. WOODGATE *Elem. Atomic Struct.* iii. 50 Pure quadrupole radiation arises when two parts of the charge distribution are oscillating like dipoles out of phase so that the dipole contribution vanishes.

b. An arrangement of four magnetic (or electric) poles, of alternate polarity, pointing at the same volume of space (used to focus beams of sub-atomic particles).

1954 *Rev. Sci. Instruments* XXV. 289/2 The introduction of the quadrupoles Q_1 and Q_2 introduces both vertical and horizontal focusing effects for a given energy. **1961** D. LUCKEY in D. M. Ritson *Techniques High Energy Physics* ix. 429 A single quadrupole can be used to obtain vertical focusing in a broad-range uniform-field spectrometer. **1969** *IEEE Trans. Nucl. Sci.* XVI. 728/2 Work on the dipole magnetic circuits as well as on cryogenic temperature iron core quadrupoles and sextupoles has continued. **1976** *McGraw-Hill Yearbk. Sci. & Technol.* 387/2 Even when dipoles or quadrupoles are to be operated at flux densities considerably above 2 T,.. addition of iron shields around the windings has important advantages.

B. *adj.* Having or pertaining to two pairs of magnetic (or electric) poles.

1955 *Rev. Sci. Instruments* XXVI. 220/1 A second possibility.. is to use a succession of electric or magnetic quadrupole lenses. **1960** *Ann. Rev. Nucl. Sci.* X. 163 A single quadrupole magnet has a focusing action for motion in one plane (either horizontal or vertical) and a defocusing action in the other plane. However, two or more quadrupole magnets may be used to give a net focusing action in both planes. **1976** *McGraw-Hill Yearbk. Sci. & Technol.* 387/1 Usually, uniform or quadrupole fields are required over considerable distances along the beam path. **1979** *Sci. Amer.* May 64/3 The ZGS lacks the quadrupole and sextupole magnets that are employed for focusing in many other accelerators.

Hence **quadru'polar** *a.*

1950 *Physical Rev.* LXXIX. 698/1 A situation in which any quadrupolar splitting of the nuclear resonance in a magnetic field is small compared to the magnetic resonance frequency itself. **1959** G. TROUP *Masers* ii. 28 This statement can be generalized, because the dipole moment may be electric or magnetic; or the moment may be of higher order, quadrupolar, for example. **1972** *Science* 26 May 903/3 The author directly proceeds to describe the effects due to quadrupolar and hyperfine interactions between electrons and nuclei.

quadruviall, obs. form of QUADRIVIAL.

quadrypedyd: see after QUADRUPED.

quadundrum, obs. variant of CONUNDRUM.

‖**'quædam.** *Obs. rare.* [L., fem. sing. and pl. of *quidam* some one, QUIDAM.] A woman, female (in disparaging sense). Also as *pl.*

a **1670** HACKET *Abp. Williams* I. (1692) 35 Vain attire, wherein wanton Quædams in those days came to.. excess. *Ibid.* II. 128 He.. settles in Bugden-House for three Summers with a Seraglia of Quædam.

quaem, obs. form of QUALM *sb.*

quaer, obs. form of QUIRE *sb.*, WHERE *adv.*

‖**quære** ('kwɪəri:), *v. imper.* and *sb.* Also 6–9 quere, (7 queer, quire). [L., imper. of *quærĕre* (med.L. *querere*) to ask, inquire. Now usually in anglicized form, QUERY.]

1. *v. imper.* Introducing a question or subject of inquiry: Ask, inquire; hence, 'one may ask', 'it is a question' (*whether*, etc.).

1535 tr. *Littleton's Nat. Brev.* 18 b (Stanf.) Quere the dyuersite. **1548** STAUNFORD *Kinges Prerog.* (1567) 54 b, But *quere* whether his highnes may bee brought in possession in those cases by a clayme or not. **1602** CAREW *Cornwall* 135 Notwithstanding, quære, whether a causlesse ambition.. turned not rather Golunt into Gallant. **1705** HEARNE *Collect.* 17 Dec. (O.H.S.) I. 131 Quaere more about this. **1774** J. ADAMS in *Fam. Lett.* (1876) 3 David Sewall.. has no ambition nor avarice, they say (however, *quaere*). **1823** J. BADCOCK *Dom. Amusem.* 52 *Quere*, whether the natural influence of light and heat occasions this apparent coincidence. **1860** O'DONOVAN *Three Fragm.* 126 *Quære*, is *Conung* an Hibernicized form of the Teutonic.. *koenung*, king?

2. *sb.* A question, QUERY.
1589 WARNER *Alb. Eng.* VI. xxx. (1612) 150 Thy bad doth passe by probate, but a Quere is for mee. **1619** H. HUTTON *Follies Anat.* (Percy Soc.) 54 It would be thought a quære at the beste. **1646** SIR T. BROWNE *Pseud. Ep.* 282 The greater Quere is, when he will come again, and yet indeed it is no Quere at all. **1736** SWIFT *Let. to Pope* 25 Mar., I wondered a little at your quaere who Cheselden was? **1856** LEVER *Martins of Cro' M.* 254 'The quere itself is its own reply' said I. **1863** A. J. HORWOOD *Yearbks. 30 & 31 Edw. I* Pref. 26 *note*, This appears to answer Mr. Booth's quaere..as to the reason for the tender of the demy-mark.

Hence † **quære, quere** *v.*, to query. *Obs.*
1627 W. SCLATER *Exp. 2 Thess.* (1629) 131 It might be quæred. **1663** *Aron-Cimn.* 101 He quæres what it is that renders a people blessed. **1681** T. FLATMAN *Heraclitus Ridens* No. 23 (1713) I. 153 Nay, let 'em consider of it; and let us Quere about the matter. **1756** H. WALPOLE *Corr.* (1837) III. 137 Should not one quere whether he had not those proofs in his hands antecedent to the cabinet?

quæree, -rie, quærent, obs. ff. QUERY, QUERENT.

† **'quæritate,** *v. Obs. rare*$^{-1}$. [f. ppl. stem of L. *quæritāre*, freq. of *quærĕre* to ask, inquire.] *trans.* To inquire or search into.
1657 TOMLINSON *Renou's Disp.* 387 Apothecaryes quæritate its Medicinall use, which Mithridates knew.

quæry, obs. form of QUERY.

† **quæsite,** anglicized f. QUÆSITUM. *Obs. rare*$^{-1}$.
1655 OUGHTRED in Rigaud *Corr. Sci. Men* (1841) I. 83 Your fourth quæsite is, why the equation whereby it is solved is the very same in both?

‖ **quæsitum** (kwiːˈsaɪtəm). Pl. quæsita. [L., neut. sing. of *quæsīt-us*, pa. pple. of *quærĕre* to seek: see QUESITED.] That which is sought for; an object of search; the answer to a problem.
1748 HARTLEY *Observ. Man* I. Introd., So as to proceed intirely from the Data to the Quæsita, from things known to such as are unknown. **1830** HERSCHEL *Stud. Nat. Phil.* II. vi. (1851) 176 A series of careful and exact measures in every different state of the datum and quæsitum. **1864** BOWEN *Logic* viii. 229 In the Analytic order the Conclusion would be more properly called the Quaesitum.

quæstor (ˈkwiːstə(r)). *Rom. Antiq.* Also 4–7 questor. [a. L. *quæstor*, agent-n. from *quærĕre* to seek, inquire.]
1. a. One of a number of Roman officials who had charge of the public revenue and expenditure, acting as treasurers of state, paymasters of the troops, etc. **b.** In early times: A public prosecutor in certain criminal cases.
1387 TREVISA *Higden* (Rolls) IV. 49 Caton þe questor brouȝte hym [Ennius] to Rome. Questor is he þat gadreþ tribut to Rome, and þe domesman was somtyme i-cleped questor. **1577** HELLOWES *Gueuara's Chron.* 80 Adrian was made Questor, that is to say, he had charge to prouide victuals and furniture for the campe. **1641** 'SMECTYMNUUS' *Answ.* §12 (1653) 45 Tiberius granted a Questors dignitie unto a Bishop for his eloquence. **1781** GIBBON *Decl. & F.* xvii. II. 53 In the course of nine centuries, the office of quæstor had experienced a very singular revolution. **1838** ARNOLD *Hist. Rome* I. 339 The two quæstors who judged in cases of blood, were also chosen from the patricians.
transf. and *fig.* **1850** S. DOBELL *The Roman* v. Poet. Wks. (1875) 63, I, her [Pity's] quæstor, Claim tribute from you. A few tears will pay it. **1863** TREVELYAN *Compet. Wallah* (1866) 124 Our modern quæstors are every whit as grasping and venal as the satellites of Verres and Dolabella.
2. The chief financial officer, the Treasurer, of the University of St. Andrews and, formerly, of other universities, esp. in Scotland.
1673 J. RAY *Observations Journey Low-Countries* 85 This Senate chuses..a Quaestor, who gathers up the University Revenue and Rents [at Heidelberg]. **1754** *Session Papers* 5 Mar. 12 In effect the Quaestor of the Library, Quaestor of the University, Aerarii universitatis quaestor, falls to be deemed as one and the same Thing. **1920** H. SCOTT *Fasti Ecclesiæ Scoticanæ* III. 123/1 He was Quaestor [*sc.* collector of revenues] of the Univ. of Glasgow in 1577. **1946** R. G. CANT *Univ. St. Andrews* 109 [The Senatus] authorised the conferring of degrees, it administered the university finances, controlled the common Library, and appointed the common officers, such as the Librarian, the Quaestor, and the Archbeadle. **1966** *Times* 17 June 3/2 (Advt.), Applications are invited for the post of an additional Assistant Quaestor in the University, in the Quaestor & Factor's department, St. Andrews.

quæstor, variant of QUESTOR *sb.*[1]

quæstorial (kwiːˈstɔːrɪəl), *a.* [f. L. *quæstōri-us* + -AL[1].] Of or pertaining to a quæstor or his position in the state.
1862 MERIVALE *Rom. Emp.* l. (1865) VI. 197 Narcissus had received the quaestorial ornaments as the reward of his services. **1868** FARRAR *Seekers* I. v. (1875) 67 Men of consular and quaestorial parentage.
So **quæ'storian** *a.*
a **1641** BP. MOUNTAGU *Acts & Mon.* (1642) 335 Consular, Prætorian, Questorian or Equestrian officers. **1879** LEWIS & SHORT *Latin Dict.* 1503/1 *Quaestōrĭus*,..of or belonging to a quæstor, quæstorian. **1976** *Classical Q.* XXVI. 99 Under the Republic the *calles* of Italy were..a quaestorian *provincia*. *Ibid.* 106 At some point in the second century the occasional quaestorian *provinciae* of the *calles* and the *aquae* were devised.

quæstorship (ˈkwiːstəʃɪp). [f. QUÆSTOR + -SHIP.] The office of quæstor.
1570 LEVINS *Manip.* 141/5 Yᵉ Questorship, *quæstura*. **1581** SAVILE *Tacitus, Agricola* (1622) 186 After his Questorship till he [Agricola] was created Tribune of the people. *c* **1650** DENHAM *Of Old Age* 94, I, five years after, at Tarentum wan The Quæstorship. **1834** LYTTON *Pompeii* I. iv, Your petty thirst for fasces and quæstorships. **1871** SEELEY *Livy* I. Introd. 90 Of all the great magistracies, the quaestorship was the lowest in dignity.
So † **'quæstory** (in 6 questorie). *Obs. rare*$^{-1}$.
1533 BELLENDEN *Livy* IV. (1822) 382 The small pepill had sic victorie, that thay belevit the questorie nocht to be the end of this honoure.

quæstuary (ˈkwiːstjuːərɪ), *a.* and *sb.* Also 7 quest-. [ad. L. *quæstuāri-us*, f. *quæstus* gain: see -ARY. Cf. obs. F. *questuaire* (Godef.).]
A. *adj.* Connected or concerned with gain; money-making.
1594 R. ASHLEY tr. *Loys le Roy* 125 If they be poore, they applie themselues to questuarie, or gainfull arts; whereby to haue meanes to liue. **1646** SIR T. BROWNE *Pseud. Ep.* 137 Although lapidaries, and questuary enquirers affirme it, yet the Writers of Mineralls..are of another beliefe. **1694** R. L'ESTRANGE *Fables* 454 The Lawyers, the Divines, and all quæstuary professions. *a* **1864** FERRIER *Grk. Philos.* (1866) I. xii. 352 This..may be termed the quæstuary class,..this being the end which they aim at.
† **B.** *sb.* One who seeks for gain; *spec.* = QUESTOR *sb.* 1. *Obs.*
1614 BP. HALL *No Peace with Rome* §12 Not giuen by the popes, but lewdly deuised by some of his base questuaries for an aduantage. **1664** JER. TAYLOR *Dissuas. Popery* ii. §3 Gerson and Dominicus à Soto are asham'd of these prodigious indulgences, and suppose that the Pope's Quæstuaries onely did procure them.

† **quæsture.** *Obs. rare*$^{-1}$. In 7 questure. [ad. L. *quæstūra*.] = QUÆSTORSHIP.
1673 S. C. *Art of Complaisance* 96 A great many Noble persons who stood in competition for the Questure.

† **quafer,** *v. Obs. rare*$^{-1}$. [Onomatopœic.] (See quot.).
1693 CLAYTON in *Phil. Trans.* XVII. 990 A Duck has larger Nerves that come into their Bills than Geese or any other Bird that I have seen and therefore quafer and grope out their Meat the most. [Copied as *quaffer* by Derham *Physico-Theol.* IV. xi. 192, and Bell *On the Hand* 150.]

quaff (kwɑːf, -æ-), *sb.* [f. QUAFF *v.*] An act of quaffing, or the liquor quaffed; a deep draught.
1579 TOMSON *Calvin's Serm. Tim.* 512/2 They thinke that a sermon costeth no more then a quaffe wil them. **1594** GREENE & LODGE *Looking Gl.* G.'s Wks. (Rtldg.) 141 Now Alvida begins her quaff, And drinks a full carouse unto her King. **1627–77** FELTHAM *Resolves* I. lxxxiv. 129 Proteas gaue him a quaff of two gallons. **1889** G. GISSING *Nether World* I. v. 97 Each guest having taken a quaff of ale.

quaff (kwɑːf, -æ-), *v.* Also 6 quaft, quaf, 6–7 quaffe. [Of obscure origin; prob. onomatopœic (cf. QUAFER and QUASS *v.*).
The date and history of the word are against any connection with *quaff*, var. of QUAICH, which has been suggested as the source. (Vigfusson's ON. *kveyfa* 'to quaff' is an error, the correct form being *kneyfa*). The precise relationship of the earliest form *quaft* to Palsgrave's QUAUGHT and Sc. WAUCHT is obscure.]
1. *intr.* To drink deeply; to take a long draught; also, to drink repeatedly in this manner. Const. *of* (†*in*).
1529 MORE *Suppl. Soulys* Wks. 331/2 The dregges of olde poysoned heresies in whiche they fell a quaftinge with the deuill. **1547** BOORDE *Introd. Knowl.* ix. (1870) 149 In Holand..many of the men..wyll quaf tyl they ben dronk. **1577** RHODES *Bk. Nurture* in *Babees Bk.* 77 Eate softly, and drinke manerly, take heede you doe not quaffe. **1628** PRYNNE *Cens. Cozens* 47 Poyson must alwayes be administred in golden Challices, else none wille quaffe. **1645** QUARLES *Sol. Recant.* iii. 35 To day we feast, and quaffe in frolique Bowles; To morrow fast. **1757** SMOLLETT *Reprisal* II. xv, We laugh, and we quaff, and we banter. **1830** LYTTON *P. Clifford* iv, She had that day quaffed more copiously of the bowl than usual. **1876** BROWNING *Epilogue to Pacchiarotto*, Have faith, give thanks, but—quaff.
2. *trans.* To drink (liquor) copiously or in a large draught.
1555–8 PHAER *Æneid* III. G iv, Wyne in plenty great they quaff. **1648** HERRICK *Hesper.*, *Lyrick to Mirth*, Let us sit and quaffe our wine. **1768** BEATTIE *Minstr.* I. xliv, Merry swains, who quaff the nut-brown ale. **1820** W. IRVING *Sketch Bk.* I. 74 They quaffed the liquor in profound silence. **1878** *Masque Poets* 31 Now with back-flung head she quaffs The odorous white Mareotic wine.
fig. **1613** HEYWOOD *Braz. Age* Wks. 1874 III. 216 I'le rather at some banquet poyson him, And quaffe to him his death. **1674** MILTON *P.L.* v. 638 (ed. 2) They drink, and in communion sweet Quaff immortalitie and joy. **1820** LANDOR *Heroic Idylls, Thrasymedes & Eunoe* 38 Let my lips quaff purity From thy fair open brow.
b. With advbs. as *down, off, out, round, up*. (Cf. DRINK *v.*)
1596 SHAKS. *Tam. Shr.* III. ii. 174 Hee calls for wine.. quaft off the Muscadell. **1633** P. FLETCHER *Purple Isl.* I. xxvii, Oh let them in their gold quaffe dropsies down. **1635–56** COWLEY *Davideis* II. 593 In helmets they quaff round the welcome flood.
3. To drain (a cup, etc.) in a copious draught or draughts. Also with *off, out, up*.
1523 [COVERDALE] *Old God & New* (1534) O iij, To quaft of two cannes or tankardes of wine. **1607** DEKKER *Wh. Babylon* Wks. 1873 II. 198, I quaffe full bowles of strong enchanting wines. **1633** BP. HALL *Occas. Medit.* (1851) 152 Why do not I..quaff up that bitter cup of affliction. **1748** THOMSON *Cast. Indol.* viii, As one who quaffs Some potent wine-cup. **1831** SCOTT *Cast. Dang.* vii, Your cup, filled with right good wine, I have just now quaffed off. **1868** FITZGERALD tr. *Omar* xliii. (1899) 98 And proffering his Cup, invites your Soul Forth to your Lips to quaff it.
4. To drive *away*, to bring *down to* or *into* (a certain state), by copious drinking. *rare.*
1714 *Love's Relief* in *Steele's Poet. Misc.* 42 Be brisk and gay, And quaff this sneaking Form away. **1821** BYRON *Sardan.* I. ii. 442 When..I have quaff'd me down to their abasement. **1847** J. WILSON *Chr. North* (1857) I. 147 The room in which he quaffs, guzzles, and smokes himself into stupidity.

quaff, obs. var. QUAICH; see also QUAYF(E.

quaffer (ˈkwɑːfə(r), -æ-), *sb.* [f. QUAFF *v.* + -ER[1].] One that quaffs or drinks deeply.
1520 WHITINTON *Vulg.* (1527) 13b, He is a quaffer namely of swete wyne. **1579** G. HARVEY *Letter-bk.* (Camden) 82 A company of honest good fellowes, and reasnable honeste quaffers. *a* **1624** BP. M. SMITH *Serm.* (1632) 278 What a grief it was to Novellus Torquatus..that his sonne was such a quaffer. **1822** *Blackw. Mag.* XI. 346 Pouring it out and calling so lustily for quaffers.

quaffer, *v.*: see QUAFER.

quaffing (ˈkwɑːfɪŋ, -æ-), *vbl. sb.* [f. QUAFF *v.* + -ING[1].] The action of the vb.; copious drinking.
1532 MORE *Confut. Tindale* Wks. 687/2 By bibbing, & sipping, & quaffing. **1579** GOSSON *Sch. Abuse* (Arb.) 34 We haue robbed Greece of Gluttonie..and Dutchland of quaffing. **1664** MRQ. WORC. in Dircks *Life* xviii. (1865) 325 Frivolous discourse tending to quarrels and quaffing. **1812** COMBE *Dr. Syntax, Picturesque Tour* XII, The Doctor talk'd nor ceased his quaffing. **1830** M. DONOVAN *Dom. Econ.* I. 39 The unremitted quaffing of wine.
attrib. **1587** TURBERV. *Trag. T.* (1837) 144 A quaffing cup, Wherein he tooke delight To bouse at boorde. *a* **1638** MEDE *Wks.* (1672) 123 Causing the Vessels of God's House to be made his Quaffing-bowls. **1701** C. WOLLEY *Jrnl. New York* (1860) 35 Their quaffing liquors are Rum-Punch and Brandy-punch.

quaffing (ˈkwɑːfɪŋ, -æ-), *ppl. a.* [f. as prec. + -ING[2].] That quaffs. Hence **'quaffingly** *adv.*
a **1693** MOTTEUX *Rabelais* III. xxxi. 255 The Lubbardly quaffing Monks. **1843** *Tait's Mag.* X. 275 At evening empty a bottle or two, Quaffingly, quaffingly.

† **quaff-tide.** *Obs.* The season for drinking.
1582 STANYHURST *Æneis* IV. (Arb.) 105 Bacchus third yeers feasting, when quaftyde aproacheth.

† **'quaffy,** *a. Obs.* Of the nature of quaffing.
1582 STANYHURST *Æneis* I. (Arb.) 24 Theyre panch with venison they franck and quaffye carousing.

quaft, obs. variant of QUAFF *v.*

quag (kwæg, kwɒg), *sb.* Also 6, 8 quage, 7 quagg(e. [Related to QUAG *v.*; cf. QUAB, QUAW, and see QUAGMIRE.] **a.** A marshy or boggy spot, *esp.* one covered with a layer of turf which shakes or yields when walked on. Also *transf.* and *fig.*
1589 IVE *Fortif.* 16 Where you finde quicke sands, quages, and such like. **1657** HOWELL *Londinop.* 342 Moorfields, which in former times, was but a fenny quagge, or moore. *a* **1677** BARROW *Serm.* Wks. 1716 III. 143 The latter walk upon a bottomless Quag into which unawares they may slump. **1784** COWPER *Tiroc.* 253 We keep the road, Crooked or straight, through quags or thorny dells. **1842** I. TAYLOR *Anc. Christianity* II. VIII. 480 Thoughtless thousands of the people are thus beguiled into the filthiest quags of 'abominable idolatry'. **1883** BESANT *All in a Garden fair* I. ii. (1885) 19 There are pools in the forest..there are marshy places and quags. **1888** *Ch. Times* 27 Jan. 68/3 All who are trying to find a way out of the Vatican quag, without turning Protestants. **1904** *Daily Chron.* 18 May 3/4 Her clothes were a quag of blood.
b. *attrib.* and *Comb.*, as *quag-brain, -kind, -water*.
1719 D'URFEY *Pills* (1872) II. 244 Tho' Law and Justice were of slender growth Within his quag Brain. **1772** WALKER in *Phil. Trans.* LXII. 124 It was mostly of the quag kind, which is a sort of moss covered at top with a turf of heath and coarse aquatic grasses. *a* **1870** D. G. ROSSETTI *Poems* (1870) 252, I..fouled my feet in quag-water.

quag (kwæg), *v.*[1] *Obs.* exc. *dial.* [Onomatopœic: cf. *wag, swag*. Some dialects have also *quaggle* corresp. to *waggle*.] *intr.* To shake; said of something soft or flabby.
1611 COTGR., *Brimbaler*,..to shake, swag, or quag, as a great dug, or th' vnsound flesh of a foggie person. **1616–61** HOLYDAY *Persius* 337 That To him a strutting panch may quagge with fat. **1623** tr. *Favine's Theat. Hon.* v. i. 35 The earth being uncertaine and quagging. **1881** BLACKMORE *Christowell* xlviii, Many a poor head will ache, and many a poor belly quag, if it is so bad as they tell me.

quag, *v.*[2] *rare*$^{-1}$. [f. QUAG *sb.*] *trans.* To submerge or fix in a quag.
1673 MARVELL *Reh. Transp.* II. Wks. 1776 II. 502 Unfortunately..you sink deeper and quag yourself in your Roman Empire.

quagga (ˈkwægə, ˈkwɒgə). Also 8–9 quacha, 9 -ccha, kwagga, quagger. [South African. The earliest authorities give it as a Hottentot word, writing it *quacha* (Juncker, 1710), *quaiha* (Kolbe, 1719, prob. a misprint), or *quagga* (Sparrman, 1783), but it is now current in Xhosa in the form *iqwara*, with clicking *q* and guttural *r*. (J. Platt, in *Athenæum*, 19 May, 1901).] **a.** A South African equine quadruped (*Equus* or *Hippotigris Quagga*), related to the ass and zebra, but less fully striped than the latter. **b.** Burchell's zebra.

The true quagga is believed to have been exterminated about 1873.

1785 G. FORSTER tr. *Sparrman's Voy. Cape G.H.* I. 223 One of the animals called quaggas by the Hottentots and colonists. 1797 *Encycl. Brit.* (ed. 3) VI. 713 The quacha, or quagga. 1815 SIR J. BARROW *Travels* 320 The Qua-cha, which was long thought to be the female Zebra, is now known to be of a species entirely different. 1815 *Times* 25 July 1/4 To be Sold..Two beautiful Animals of the Zebra species, called Quaggers; they are perfectly docile..being two of the handsomest ever imported to this country. 1834 PRINGLE *Afr. Sk.* viii. 274 The poor quagga..is a timid animal with a gait and figure much resembling those of an ass. 1839 DARWIN *Jrnl. Beagle* v. 100 Two zebras, and the quaccha, two gnus, and several antelopes. 1859 —— *Orig. Spec.* v. (1873) 128 The quagga, though so plainly barred like a zebra over the body, is without bars on the legs. 1899 *Pall Mall Gaz.* 21 Nov. 2/1 It [*sc.* Cape Colony] was the great home of the brown quagga. ('Kwokka'..is the proper pronunciation of the name of the old friend of my childhood's natural history.) 1937 *Nature* 25 Dec. 1079/2 The blaauwbok..and the quagga have already vanished. 1966 E. PALMER *Plains of Camdeboo* viii. 141 Of all our vanished creatures we mourn these quaggas most of all. 1974 *Nature* 11 Oct. 468/2 The last quagga died in the Amsterdam Zoo in 1883, but it is thought that this one had outlived by several years the wild quagga in South Africa.

attrib. 1899 *Q. Rev.* Oct. 412 The quagga hybrid was less striped than many dun-coloured horses.

quaggy ('kwægɪ, 'kwɒgɪ), *a.* [f. QUAG *sb.* or *v.*[1] + -Y.]

1. Of ground: That shakes under the foot; full of quags; boggy, soft. Also of streams: Flowing through boggy soil.

1610 HOLLAND *Camden's Brit.* I. 499 Certaine uneven and quaggie miry plots. *a* 1756 COLLINS *Ode Superst. Highl.* 59 O'er the watery strath or quaggy moss. 1814 SCOTT *Wav.* xvi, The path..was rough, broken, and in many places quaggy and unsound. 1867 MORRIS *Jason* XI. 188 A plain..with quaggy brooks cleft through. 1956 PETERSON & FISHER *Wild Amer.* xxxiii. 356 The banks..were aproned by mud—quaggy and adhesive. 1969 P. DICKINSON *Pride of Heroes* 98 Putting his foot into a quaggy area, which sent..stinking inky ooze between shoe and sock.

2. Of things, esp. of the body or flesh: Soft, yielding, flabby. Also of persons in respect of their flesh, and *fig.*

?16.. *Time's Storehouse* 26 (L.) Heate and travaile are yrkesome to the Gaules' quaggy bodies. 1611 COTGR., *Mollasse*, quaggie, swagging [etc.]. 1694 MOTTEUX *Rabelais* IV. ix. (1737) 37 A female called *Pear*..said to be quaggy and flabby. 1748 RICHARDSON *Clarissa* (1811) VIII. 158 Behold her, then, spreading the whole troubled bed with her huge quaggy carcase. 1806–7 J. BERESFORD *Miseries Hum. Life* (1826) VI. 120 O the quaggy rascal!..I'd have given him a little bone to his fat. 1822–34 *Good's Stud. Med.* (ed. 4) II. 680 The cells [of dead bone] being filled with a corrupt sanies or spongy caruncles, so that the whole assumes a quaggy appearance. 1851 H. MELVILLE *Whale* xxv. 125 A mature man who uses hair-oil..has probably got a quaggy spot on him. 1968 G. JONES *Hist. Vikings* II. iv. 139 Alas, Einar's late-acquired nickname [*sc.* Thambarskelfir] has nothing to do with..a bowstring; it refers to his pendulous and quaggy belly.

Comb. 1721 RAMSAY *Tartana* 343 May she turn quaggy fat.

Hence **'quagginess**, quaggy condition.

1653 GATAKER *Vind. Annot. Jer.* 85 Considering the unsoundnesse and qagginesse of their [Astrologers'] grounds. 1940 *Chambers's Techn. Dict.* 692/1 *Quagginess*, a term used to indicate the defective condition of timber having shakes at the heart of the log.

quaȝte, obs. pa. t. of QUETCH *v.*

quagmire ('kwægmaɪə(r), 'kwɒg-). [app. f. QUAG *sb.* or *v.*[1] (but evidenced a little earlier) + MIRE. Numerous synonyms, with a first element of similar form, were in use in the 16th and 17th cents., as *qua-*, *quab-*, *quad-*, *quake-*, *qual-*, *quave-*, *quawmire*, which will be found in their alphabetical places: cf. also *bog-*, *gog-* and *wagmire*. The precise relationship of these to each other is not clear: all, or most, may be independent attempts to express the same idea (cf. etym. note to QUAKE *v.*).]

1. A piece of wet and boggy ground, too soft to sustain the weight of men or the larger animals; a quaking bog; a fen, marsh.

1579–80 NORTH *Plutarch* (1676) 530 There was a certain quagmire before him, that ran with a swift running stream. 1610 ROWLANDS *Martin Mark-all* 26 They come to bogs and quagmyres, much like to them in Ireland. 1665 *Surv. Aff. Netherl.* 120 [Holland is] the greatest Bogg of Europe, and Quagmire of Christendom. 1756 C. LUCAS *Ess. Waters* II. 131 The quagmire being pierced..is found no where above two feet deep. 1838 PRESCOTT *Ferd. & Is.* (1846) III. xiv. 121 The excessive rains..had converted the whole country into a mere quagmire. 1882 OUIDA *Maremma* I. 47 To reach the mountain crest without sinking miserably in a quagmire.

Comb. 1611 COTGR., *Mollasse*,..quagmire-like.

2. *transf.* and *fig.* **a.** Anything soft, flabby, or yielding.

1635 QUARLES *Embl.* I. xii. (1718) 50 Thy flesh a trembling bog, a quagmire full of humours. *a* 1704 T. BROWN *Praise Poverty* Wks. 1730 I. 100 The rich are corpulent, drown'd in foggy quagmires of fat and dropsy. 1822–34 *Good's Study Med.* (ed. 4) IV. 488 The indurated patches seem, in some cases, to be fixed upon a quagmire of offensive fluid.

b. A position or situation from which extrication is difficult.

1775 SHERIDAN *Rivals* III. iv, I have followed Cupid's Jack-a-lantern, and find myself in a quagmire at last. 1851 BRIGHT *Sp., Eccl. Titles Bill* 12 May, The noble Lord..is in a quagmire, and he knows it well. 1873 HAMERTON *Intell. Life* v. ii. (1875) 178 Many a fine intellect has been driven into the deep quagmire.

Hence **'quagmire** *v.*, in *pass.* to be sunk or stuck in a quagmire; also *fig.* † **'quagmirist**, one who makes a quagmire of himself. **'quagmiry** *a.*, of the nature of a quagmire; boggy.

1637 WINTHROP *New Eng.* (1825) I. 233 A most hideous swamp, so thick with bushes and so quagmiry [etc.]. 1655 R. YOUNGE *Agst. Drunkards* 4 These drunken drones, these gut-mongers, these Quagmirists. 1701 *Laconics* 120 (L.) When a reader has been quagmired in a dull heavy book. 1846 LANDOR *Imag. Conv.* Wks. II. 42 A man is never quagmired till he stops.

†**quagswag**, *v. Obs. rare*$^{-1}$. [f. QUAG and SWAG, both used by Cotgr. in rendering F. *brimbaler*.] *intr.* To shake to and fro.

1653 URQUHART *Rabelais* II. xi. 78 Advised her not to put her selfe into the hazard of quagswagging in the Lee.

quahaug, quahog (kwə'hɔːg, 'kwɔːhɒg). *U.S.* Also **quau-, quohog, cohog.** [Narraganset Indian, given by Roger Williams as *poquauhock*: *-k* or *-g* is the plural ending in Algonquian tongues.] The common round clam (*Venus mercenaria*) of the Atlantic coast of North America: = HEN *sb.* 6.

[1643 R. WILLIAMS *Key Lang. Amer.* 107 Poquauhock, this the English call Hens, a little thick shel-fish, which the Indians wade deepe and dive for.] 1753 *Southampton* (N.Y.) *Rec.* (1878) III. 6 The Trustees shall have the care of the Fishery of Quogue. 1781 S. PETERS *Gen. Hist. Connecticut* 262 The oysters, clams, quauhogs, lobsters, crabs, and fish, are innumerable. 1788 M. CUTLER in *Life, Jrnls., & Corr.* (1888) I. 416 Went into the water; found a great number of clam cohog shells. 1815 *Topogr. & Hist. Wareham* in *Coll. Mass. Hist. Soc.* (1846) 2nd Ser. IV. 289 The quahaug clam is common. 1851 MELVILLE *Whale* xiv. 70 They first caught crabs and quohogs in the sand. 1870 *Amer. Naturalist* III. 354 Fragments of Quahaug valves..are quite abundant. 1872 SCHELE DE VERE *Americanisms* 29 The more costly beads [in wampum] came from the largest shells of the Quahaug or Cohog. 1881 *Scribner's Mag.* XXII. 656/1 So seemingly impregnable a victim [of the star-fish] as the quahaug. 1882 *Standard* 26 Sept. 2/1 In every hotel bill of fare the clam or quahog..figures in a variety of shapes. 1934 E. REYNARD *Narrow Land* v. 249 He handed over his Old Woman's recipe for quahaug fritters. 1949 R. J. SIM *Pages from Past* 66 The quahog, or hardshell clam, is deservedly the most famous of all. 1960 S. PLATH *Colossus* 24 The gritted wave leaps The seawall and drops onto a bier Of quahog chips. 1967 *Boston Sunday Herald Mag.* 26 Mar. 11/1 Anybody who uses potatoes in quahog pie is no Cape Codder. 1977 *Time* 4 July 37/1 On the Fourth, New Englanders will be flocking to Clam Shacks for rolls stuffed with batter-fried whole quahogs or steamers.

Hence as *v. intr.*, to dig or collect quahaugs; **qua'hauging** *vbl. sb.*

1905 J. C. LINCOLN *Partners of Tide* iv. 76 How's the quahaugin' nowadays? 1949 K. KNIGHT *Bass Derby Murder* 122, I was down to the pond quahoggin', all afternoon.

quahis, obs. f. WHOSE.

quahte, obs. pa. t. of QUETCH *v.*

quai (keɪ, ‖ke). [Fr.: see QUAY *sb.*] **1.** A public way constructed on the quay or embankment of a stretch of navigable water, usu. having buildings along the land side; *spec.* such a street on either bank of the Seine in Paris.

1870 [see KIOSK 2]. 1873 BROWNING *Red Cotton Night-Cap Country* II. 89 One whose father's house upon the Quai Neighboured the very house where that Voltaire Died mad and raving. 1927 C. CONNOLLY *Let.* 11 Feb. in *Romantic Friendship* (1975) 251 The solidarity of this town [*sc.* Bordeaux] with its respectable houses and cobbled quais. 1949 E. POUND *Pisan Cantos* lxxxi. 110 And at first disappointed with shoddy The bare ram-shackle quais. 1954 I. MURDOCH *Under Net* xiv. 191 The cloudless light drew a wash of colour along the grey façades of the *quais*. 1963 V. GIELGUD *Goggle-Box Affair* xi. 103 The *quais* and the cafés of the Left Bank in spring. 1977 *Time* 28 Nov. 31/3 The canal that once passed along the quai has been replaced by a Métro station.

2. *ellipt.* for QUAI D'ORSAY.

1960 N. MITFORD *Don't tell Alfred* iv. 47 They know absolutely everything you do..what impression Alfred makes at the Quai..and so on. 1973 H. TREVELYAN *Diplomatic Channels* i. 20 During General de Gaulle's later years, French diplomats who received their instructions from the Quai were handicapped, since the Quai often did not know what policy the General was pursuing through his inner circle.

quai, variant of QUAY.

quaich, quaigh (kweɪx). *Sc.* Forms: α. 7–8 **quech**, 7, 9 **queich**, 8– **quegh**, 9 **quaigh, quaich, (quoich).** β. 8 **quaff, queff, coif.** [a. Gael. *cuach* cup, OIr. *cúach*, prob. ad. L. *caucus* (Gr. καῦκα), whence also W. *cawg*. The β-forms are peculiar, as there is no general tendency in Sc. to substitute *f* for *ch*.] A kind of shallow drinking-cup formerly common in Scotland, usually made of small wooden staves hooped together and having two ears or handles, but sometimes fitted with a silver rim, or even made entirely of that metal. Also in extended use: a drinking vessel or trophy of similar design.

α. 1673 *Acc. Bk. Sir J. Foulis* (1894) 14 A quech weighting 18 unce and 10 drop. 1697 *Inv.* in *Scott. N. & Q.* (1900) Dec. 90/2 Three round queichs without luggs. 1715 PENNECUIK *Descr. Tweeddale*, etc. II. 71 A great Quech, which they were made to Drink out of. 1808 SCOTT *Marm.* III. xxvi, The quaighs were deep, the liquor strong. 1849 MRS. CARLYLE *Lett.* II. 61 Passing a cooper's shop..I stept in and bought two little quaighs. 1884 Q. VICTORIA *More Leaves* 142 A silver quaich out of which Prince Charles Edward had drunk. 1971 *Timber Trades Jrnl.* 14 Aug. 54/3 Play in the morning will be for the Brownlee trophy against bogey under handicap and for the Granton quaich for the best net score. 1975 *Listener* 5 June 728/2, I drink a ceremonial draught from an immense, lacquered quaich [at Koriyama, Japan]. 1976 D. MARLOWE *Nightshade* iii. 44 Lapotre had arrived accompanied by a tall negro... He was a *houngan*, a voodoo priest... Lapotre stopped before a woman..carrying a souvenir (a mahogany quaich).

attrib. 1703 *Inv.* in *Scott. N. & Q.* (1900) Dec. 90/2 A big quech cup with three lugs.

β. 1711 RAMSAY *On Maggy Johnstoun* ix, Sae brawly did a pease-scon toast Biz i' the queff. *c* 1730 BURT *Lett. N. Scotl.* (1818) I. 157 It is often drank..out of a cap, or coif as they call it; this is a woodden dish [etc.]. 1771 SMOLLETT *Humph. Cl.* 3 Sept., The spirits were drunk out of a silver quaff.

quaid, var. QUED *a.*; see also QUAY *v.*

Quai d'Orsay (ke dɔrsɛ). The name of a *quai* (see QUAI) in Paris, used by metonymy for the French Ministry of Foreign Affairs, which is situated there. Also *attrib.*

1922 W. S. MAUGHAM *On Chinese Screen* xix. 74 He represented certain important French interests in China and was said to have more power at the Quai d'Orsay than the minister himself. 1927 N. WAINWRIGHT tr. *Dekobra's Madonna of Sleeping Cars* xii. 167 The Quai d'Orsay would register a formal protest. 1933 G. ARTHUR *Septuagenarian's Scrap Bk.* 33 The Foreign Office and the Quai d'Orsay must have put their cards on the table with quite amazing confidence in one another's goodwill. 1940 H. G. WELLS *New World Order* §11. 151 The Germans..have to get on with collectivisation..and they cannot give themselves to that if they are artificially divided up and disorganised by some old-fashioned Quai d'Orsay scheme. 1958 L. DURRELL *Mountolive* viii. 158 Your Quai d'Orsay people shock me. 1969 B. WEIL *Dossier IX* viii. 63 Asher chuckled. 'I suppose the Quai d'Orsay felt it was going to be caught with its knickers down again!' 1975 C. MOTT-RADCLYFFE *Foreign Body in Eye* vii. 138 Preliminary negotiations had taken place in Paris for several weeks between Sir Maurice Peterson from the Foreign Office, and St Quentin from the Quai d'Orsay.

quaier, obs. f. QUIRE.

quaies kateah, var. QUAISS KITIR *int.*

quaife, -ff(e, obs. Sc. ff. COIF.

quai hai, var. QUI-HY.

quaik, obs. Sc. f. QUAKE *v.*; var. Sc. *quhaik*, WHAIK.

quail (kweɪl), *sb.* Forms: 4 **quaille**, 4–5 **quaylle**, 4–6 **quayle**, 4–7 **quaile**, 5 **qwayle, qwyle**, 6 **quale**, *Sc.* **qua(i)lȝe**, (7 **-ȝie**), 6– **quail.** [a. OF. *quaille* (F. *caille*) = Prov. *calha*, It. *quaglia*, OSp. *coalla*, med.L. *qualia*, *qualea* and *quaquila*, *quacula*; the source is prob. Teutonic, cf. MDu., MLG. *quackele* (Du. *kwakkel*) and OHG. *quatala*, of imitative origin.]

1. A migratory bird allied to the partridge (family *Perdicidæ*), found in the Old World and Australia; *esp.* the European species, *Coturnix communis* or *dactylisonans*, the flesh of which is much esteemed for the table.

The Australian quails are chiefly hemipods (*Turnix*), esp. the painted quail, *T. varius*, or *Hemipodius melinatus*. The single New Zealand species (*Coturnix Novæ-Zelandiæ*) is now extinct.

13.. *E.E. Allit. P.* B. 1084, I stod as stylle as dased quayle. *c* 1386 CHAUCER *Clerk's T.* 1150 Thou shalt make him couche as doth a quaille. 1444 *Pol. Poems* (Rolls) II. 219 Geyn Phebus uprist syngen wyl the quaylle. 1535 COVERDALE *Exod.* xvi. 13 At euen the quayles came vp. —— *Ps.* civ. 40 At their desyre, there came quales. 1555 W. WATREMAN *Fardle Facions* I. v. 53 Quaill, and mallard, are not but for the richer sorte. 1601 SIR W. CORNWALLIS *Ess.* II. (1631) 284 The fighting game at Quailes was Anthonies overthrowe. 1684 OTWAY *Atheist* I. i, Do you dispise your own Manna..and long after Quails? 1727–46 THOMSON *Summer* 1657 While the quail clamours for his running mate. 1774 GOLDSM. *Nat. Hist.* (1776) V. 212 The quail is by all known to be a bird of passage. 1846 STOKES *Disc. Australia* II. vii. 259 It is known to the colonists as the Painted Quail. 1870 MORRIS *Earthly Par.* III. IV. 296 Close within the long grass lies the quail.

2. *dial.* **a.** The corn-crake. (First quot. dub.)

c 1470 HENRYSON *Mor. Fab.* VIII. (*Preach. Swallow*) xxiii, The quailȝe craikand in the corne. 1881 *Leicest. Gloss.*, *Quail*, the land-rail or corn-crake.

b. The small spotted water-hen.

1766 PENNANT *Brit. Zool.* (1768) II. 504 In Lincolnshire it is known by the name of quail.

3. One of several American gallinaceous birds resembling the European quail, *esp.* the Virginian quail or colin (*Ortyx virginianus*), and the Californian or crested quail (*Lophortyx californicus*).

1817–8 COBBETT *Resid. U.S.* (1822) 43, Chickens..as big as American Partridges (misnamed quails). 1840 *Penny Cycl.* XVII. 440 *Ortyx Virginianus*,..the Quail of the inhabitants of New England, the Partridge of the

Pennsylvanians. **1861** G. F. Berkeley *Sportsm. W. Prairies* xi. 185 A brace of what the Americans call quail.

†**4.** *fig.* A courtesan. *Obs.* (So F. *caille coiffée*.)

An allusion to the supposed amorous disposition of the bird: see the passages cited by Nares.

1606 Shaks. *Tr. & Cr.* v. i. 57 Heere's Agamemnon,.. one that loues Quails. **1694** Motteux *Rabelais* iv. Prol. (1737) 83 Several coated Quails, and lac'd Mutton.

5. *U.S. slang.* A girl, a young woman.

1859 *Yale Lit. Mag.* XXIV. 291 (Th.), [The Freshman] heareth of 'Quails', he dresseth himself in fine linen, he seeketh to flirt with ye 'quails'. **1901** *Dialect Notes* II. 146 *Quail*, a young lady student at co-educational institution. Wesleyan Univ. **1904** *Hartford* (Connecticut) *Courant* 4 Oct. 1 Because she was hazed by the young women students at Wesleyan, one 'quail', as the boys call them, who was a freshman here last year did not return to Wesleyan this fall. **1935** J. Hargan *Gloss. Prison Lang.* 6 *Quail*, a girl. **1935** A. J. Pollock *Underworld Speaks* 93/1 *Quail*, an attractive girl, not of age. **1947** *Time* 6 Oct. 68/1 A less active sport is 'piping the flock', when Cal males watch Cal 'quails' preening in the sun on the steps of Wheeler Hall. **1970** *Women Speaking* Apr. 5/1 For any woman..man has a strange conglomeration of terms:..quail, squab, [etc.].

6. *attrib.* and *Comb.*, as ***quail-bagger***, ***-bagging***, ***-basket***, ***-feeding***, ***-fight***, ***-fighter***, ***-fighting***, ***-net***, ***-pit***, ***-potage***, ***-shot***, ***-time***, ***-track***, ***-trap***, etc.; ***quail-surfeited*** adj.; **quail-call** = quail-pipe; **quail-dove**, a dove of the West Indies and Florida (*Starnœnas cyanocephalus*); **quail-hawk**, a New Zealand species of falcon; **quail-pigeon**, a pigeon of the genus *Geophaps*; **quail-snipe**, a South American plover of the genus *Thinocorys*. Also quail-pipe.

1879 *Harper's Mag.* Oct. 703 The..advice offered by a circle of *quail-baggers and other by-standers. *Ibid.*, The conclusion that a *quail-bagging expedition was regarded as an event of considerable importance. **1598** Florio, *Quagliere*,..a *quaile basket. **1822** D. Booth *Analyt. Dict.* i. 99 A Quailpipe or *Quailcall. **1884** *Encycl. Brit.* XX. 147/1 In old days they were taken in England in a net, attracted thereto by means of a Quail call. **1820** T. Mitchell *Aristoph.* I. p. lxiii, When a mania took place in Athens..for *quail-feeding or philosophy. **1581** Mulcaster *Positions* xviii. (1887) 78 Cokfights and *quaile-fightes. **1836-48** B. D. Walsh *Aristoph., Acharnians* i. iv. *note*, The Athenians..were great cock-fighters and *quail-fighters. **1776** Goldsm. *Nat. Hist.* (1790) V. 214 *Quailfighting was a favourite amusement among the Athenians. **1873** Buller *Birds N. Zeal.* (1888) I. 217 The *Quail-Hawk exhibits great perseverance in pursuit of its prey. **1598** Florio, *Quagliera*, a *quaile-net. **1879** Mrs. A. E. James *Ind. Househ. Managem.* 56 Quails..kept in your own *quail-pit and well fed. **1725** Bradley *Fam. Dict.* s.v. *Quail*, You may also have a *Quail-Potage in the Form of an Oil. **1865** 'Mark Twain' in *N.Y. Saturday Press* 18 Nov. 249/2 He got the frog out..and filled him full of *quail-shot. **1649** G. Daniel *Trinarch., Hen. V*, cxxv, And hang a Nose to Leekes, *Quaile-Surfetted. **1897** *Outing* XXX. 94/2 Ever since last *quail-time I have been casting rather dubious glances at a certain old gun. **1842** *Yale Lit. Mag.* VIII. 96, I can't always decipher *quail tracks. **1855** *Trans. Mich. Agric. Soc.* VI. 495 One acre of quail track corn planted on muck land. **1807** *Salmagundi* 1 Oct. 312 He was particularly adroit in making our *quail-traps. **1845** Quail-trap [see *fishing-light* s.v. fishing *vbl. sb.*[1] 5 a].

quail (kweɪl), *v.*[1] Forms: 5–6 quayll, 5–7 quayle, (5 whayle), quaile, 6–7 quale, 7 quaille, 6– quail. See also queal. [Of uncertain origin. The early spelling and rimes prove a ME. *quailen* (with diphthongal *ai*), for which there is no obvious source. Phonology, sense, and date are against any connexion with early ME. *quelen* quele.

In literary use the word is very common from about 1520 to 1650, after which it practically disappears until its revival, app. by Scott, in the early part of the 19th c.]

I. *intr.*

1. Of material things, as persons, plants, etc.: To decline from a natural or flourishing condition; to fail or give way; to fade, wither, etc. *Obs.* exc. *dial.*

c **1440** Capgrave *Life St. Kath.* iv. 1775 Ewery thyng.. that maketh resistens Ageyn nature, ful soone wil it quayle. *c* **1460** G. Ashby *Dicta Philos.* 1071 Better were a thing never to [be] had Than in handes to quaile & to be badde. **1568** T. Howell *Arb. Amitie* (1879) 24 Length of time, causeth man and beast to quaile. **1579** Spenser *Sheph. Cal.* Nov. 91 The braunch once dead, the budde eke needes must quaile. **1602** J. Rhodes *Answ. Rom. Rhyme, Sp. touch. Heretics*, Christ's word..that heauen and earth should quaile, Before his word one iote should faile. *a* **1796** Pegge *Derbicisms* (E.D.S.), *Quail*, to grow ill. **1825** Brockett *N.C. Gloss.*, *Quail*, to fail, to fall sick, to faint. **1879** Miss Jackson *Shropsh. Word-bk.*, *Quail*, to languish; to fail; to fall sick. **1880** *W. Cornw. Gloss.* s.v., *Quail*, to wither;..'These flowers soon quail'.

2. Of immaterial things.

a. Of an action, undertaking, state of things, etc.: To fail, break down, come to nothing. *Obs.* In mod. use (transf. from 3): To give way, yield *to* or *before*.

c **1440** Capgrave *Life St. Kath.* iv. 1019 Whan moost nede is, his resons will quayll [*v.r.* whayle]. **1523** *St. Papers Hen. VIII*, VI. 197 Thei fynally concludyd..ther shold lack 2 or 3 voyces, wherby the election shold quayle. **1570** B. Googe *Pop. Kingd.* ii. 23 b, They toyle and moyle least that his state by talke of tongue should quaile. **1600** Holland *Livy* v. xxi. 194 After great massaker and execution committed, the fight began to quaile. **1611** Speed *Hist. Gt. Brit.* ix. ix. §23. 585 The Kings Ambassadours returne out of France, without hauing effected that which they went about, so that the whole enterprize quailed.

1810 Scott *Lady of L.* ii. xxv, Roderick Dhu's renown ..[should] quail to that of Malcolm Græme. **1857** Maurice *Mor. & Met. Philos.* III. iv. §9. 117 The name of William himself quailed before that of Abelard.

b. Of courage, †hope, †faith, etc.: To fail, give way, become faint or feeble.

1557 Pole in Strype *Eccl. Mem.* (1721) III. App. lxviii. 246 The faythe of the sacraments began to quayle in so many hartes. *a* **1577** Gascoigne *Flowers* Wks. 1869 I. 43 Since courage quayles, and commes behind, Go sleepe. **1606** Bryskett *Civ. Life* 89 If..the hope began to quaile, forthwith courage failed withall. **1642** Rogers *Naaman* 408, I perceiue your zeale quales shrewdly in this Laodicean age. **1835** Thirlwall *Greece* I. vi. 212 Perils, which make the courage of the hardiest quail.

3. Of persons: To lose heart, be cowed or discouraged; to give way through fear (*to* or *before* a formidable person or thing).

1555 in Strype *Eccl. Mem.* (1721) III. App. xliii. 122 He made them this faithful promise to the intent that they should not quaile. **1577-87** Holinshed *Chron.* III. 1212/1 The comming forward of these forces caused the rebels..to quaile in courage. **1604** T. Wright *Passions* i. vi. 23 Braggers..vaunt much at the beginning, but quaile commonly in the middle of the fray. **1618** Bolton *Florus* (1636) 222 All the Lords quailing, and Appuleius tyrannizing. **1813** Byron *Giaour* xxxv, I have not quail'd to danger's brow. **1874** Green *Short Hist.* iii. §5. 137 The Earl of Chester..who had risen in armed rebellion, quailed before the march of Hubert.

b. Of the heart or spirit; also of the eyes.

1563 *Homilies* ii. *Repentance* i. (1859) 531 Mens hearts do quail and faint, if they once perceive that they travail in vaine. **1600** Holland *Livy* xxxvi. ix. 924 Seeing many of the defendants..hurt and wounded, their hearts began to quaile. **1611** Shaks. *Cymb.* v. v. 149 Thy daughter For whom my heart drops blood, and my false spirits Quaile to remember. **1837** W. Irving *Capt. Bonneville* II. 225 [They] felt their hearts quailing under their multiplied hardships. **1841** Borrow *Zincali* I. i. 26 Their sharp eyes quailed quickly before his savage glances. **1892** J. Tait *Mind in Matter* (ed. 3) 249 In Gethsemane, the brave spirit of Jesus quailed.

II. *trans.*

†**4.** To affect injuriously, to spoil, impair; to overpower, destroy, put an end to. *Obs.* **a.** a thing.

1551 Gardiner *Explic. Cath. Faith, Of the Presence* 60 The truthe of that place hindreth and qualeth in maner all the booke. **1604** T. Wright *Climact. Years* 11 Nature in the meane time is strengthened with good foods, and the humour either purged or quailed with phisicke. **1655** H. Vaughan *Silex Scint.* ii. *Time's Book* iv, As some meek night-piece which day quails To candle light unveils. **1669** Boyle *Cont. New Exp.* ii. (1682) 66 The Apricocks were flaccid or quailed as if they had been dry or withered.

absol. **1590** Shaks. *Mids. N.D.* v. i. 292 O Fates!..Cut thred and thrum, Quaile, crush, conclude, and quell.

b. an action, state, quality, feeling, etc.

1532 More *Confut. Barnes* viii. Wks. 805/2 If he belieue saynt Austine..than is his owne fond ymaginacion quayled. **1551** R. Robinson tr. *More's Utop.* Ep. Cecil (1895) 20 Mine old good wil and hartye affection towardes you is not..at all quayled and diminished. **1577** Hanmer *Anc. Eccl. Hist.* (1619) 75 Quailing the chearefulnesse of others. **1628** Venner *Baths of Bathe* (1650) 350 The taking of cold drink doth suddenly quaile the heat. **1654** tr. *Martini's Conq. China* 5 Their antient..warlike Spirit, which the pleasures ..of that Country had quailed and tamed.

5. To daunt or cow (a person), to bring into subjection by fear; to cause to quail.

1526 *Pilgr. Perf.* (W. de W. 1531) 126 b, Some power of the soule shall quayle & trouble them. **1569** Golding *Heminge's Post.* 22 Paul was not quayled with the hugenesse of persecutions. **1642** Bridge *Serm. Norfolk Volunteers* 9 He is a stout man whom adversity doth not quaile. **1719** D'Urfey *Pills* (1872) III. 23 You Roaring Boys, who everyone quails. **1816** J. Wilson *City of Plague* iii. i. 49 As thunder quails Th' inferior creatures of the air and earth. **1833** M. Scott *Tom Cringle* ii. (1859) 55 Splinter did not like it, I saw, and that quailed me.

b. To daunt, depress (the heart, courage) with fear or dejection.

1567 Turberv. *Rayling Route* 26 My courage is not quailde by cruell Fo. **1600** Holland *Livy* xcv. 1253 Ouerthrowes in warre and misfortunes..at sea, wherewith his heart was quailed. **1663** Butler *Hud.* i. iii. 204 Am not I here to take thy part? Then what has quail'd thy stubborn heart? **1706** in Phillips (ed. Kersey). **1844** Disraeli *Coningsby* v. ii, It..quailed the heart of Taper, crushed all the rising hopes.

Hence **'quailer**, one who, or that which, quails.

1599 Sandys *Europæ Spec.* (1632) 193 Avarice..the quailer of all manly executions.

quail, *v.*[2] *Obs.* exc. *dial.* Forms: 5–6 quayle, 7 quaile. [a. OF. *quailler* (F. *cailler* = It. *quagliare*, Pg. *coalhar*, Sp. *cuajar*):—L. *coāgulāre* to coagulate.]

1. *intr.* To curdle, coagulate.

c **1430** *Two Cookery-bks.* 27 Caste on whyte Wyne or Venegre, & make it quayle. *c* **1440** *Promp. Parv.* 418/2 Quaylyn, as mylke, and other lycowre, *coagulo.* **1530** Palsgr. 676/2, I quayle, as mylke dothe, *je quaillebotte.* **1601** Holland *Pliny* II. 323 It is no better than poison, especially the first beestings, if it quaile and cruddle in the stomacke. **1706** in Phillips (ed. Kersey). **1881** *Leicest. Gloss.*, *Quail*, to 'turn' or curdle; go flat or sour.

b. *to be quailed*, to be curdled.

1530 Palsgr. 676/2 This mylke is quayled. **1809** Batchelor *Orthoep. Anal.* 140 The cream is said to be quailed, when the butter begins to appear in the process of churning.

2. *trans.* To cause to curdle. *rare*[−1].

1398 Trevisa *Barth. De P.R.* iv. iv. (1495) 83 The more boystous..partyes of the grayne the erth takyth..and quaylyth theym by heete.

Hence **quailed** *ppl. a.*, curdled. *Obs.*

c **1440** *Promp. Parv.* 418/1 Quaylyd, as mylke, and oþer lyke, *coagulatus.* **1541** R. Copland *Guydon's Quest. Chirurg.*, etc., þe lyuer..is the substaunce of flesshe, and red as quaylled blode. **1601** Holland *Pliny* II. 134 Such as haue ..drunk quailed milke, that is cluttered within their stomack.

'quailery. [f. quail *sb.* + -ery.] A place where quails are kept, esp. to be fattened for food.

1894 *Blackw. Mag.* Sept. 387/2 The native caught the birds alive for the quaileries of Anglo-Indians.

quailing ('kweɪlɪŋ), *vbl. sb.*[1] [f. quail *v.*[1] + -ing[1].] The action of giving way, failing, losing heart, etc.

1549 Coverdale, etc. *Erasm. Par. Tim.* Ded. 1 Seyng Paule was so afrayed of their quayling, whome he had instructed. **1596** Shaks. *1 Hen. IV*, iv. i. 39 There is no quailing now, Because the King is certainely possest Of all our purposes. **1627** G. Hakewill *Power & Prov. God* ii. i. §1. 65 The quailing and withering of all things by the recesse of the Sunne. **1642** Rogers *Naaman* 557 So farre from quailing of judgement. *a* **1700** B. E. *Dict. Cant. Crew* *Quailing of the Stomack*, beginning to be qualmish or uneasy. **1848** C. Bronte *J. Eyre* (1857) 245, I bore with her feeble minded quailings.

†**'quailing**, *vbl. sb.*[2] *Obs.* [f. quail *v.*[2]] Curdling, coagulation.

c **1440** *Promp. Parv.* 418/2 Quaylynge, of lycoure, *coagulacio.* **1600** Surflet *Countrie Farme* ii. xlix. 310 To stay the quailing of the milke in their stomackes.

quailing ('kweɪlɪŋ), *ppl. a.* [f. quail *v.*[1] + -ing[2].] Diminishing, becoming weak; losing hope or courage, etc.

1565 Golding *Ovid's Met.* ix. (1593) 215 To quicken up the quailing love. **1586** Warner *Alb. Eng.* iv. xxi[i]. (1612) 105 Did quicken Englands quailing plowes. **1880** G. Meredith *Trag. Com.* (1881) 158 Her father's unwonted harshness suggested the question to her quailing nature. **1894** Sir E. Sullivan *Woman* 34 Shrinking, quailing, agonised victims.

quail-pipe. [f. quail *sb.* + pipe.]

1. A pipe or whistle on which the note of the quail (usually the female) can be imitated, in order to lure the birds into a net; a quail-call. Also used allusively, or *fig.*

For a full description of the calls used to imitate the notes of the cock and hen, see *Encycl. Brit.* (1797) XV. 733/2.

? *a* **1400** Lydg. *Chorle & Byrde* (Roxb.) 9 The quayle pype can most falsely calle Tyl the quayle under the nette doth crepe. *c* **1400** *Rom. Rose* 7261 High shoos knopped with dagges, That frouncen lyke a quaile pipe. **1611** R. Fenton *Usury* iii. i. 110 Those Echoes and quailpipes amongst vs, who catch friends by imitating their voice. **1711** Addison *Spect.* No. 108 ¶5, A late Invention of Will's for improving the Quail-pipe. **1821** Scott *Kenilw.* vii, Master Varney, you can sound the quailpipe most daintily to wile wantons into his nets. **1884** *St. James's Gaz.* 28 Apr. 6/2 In France they are commonly captured on the ground; a 'quail-pipe'.. being employed.

attrib. **1602** Middleton *Blurt, Master-Constable* ii. i. 17 A gallant that hides his small-timbered legs with a quail-pipe boot. **1603** Dekker *Wonderfull Yeare* F iij b, He.. cryed out in that quaile-pipe voice.

†**2.** *transf.* The throat or vocal organs. *Obs.*

1693 Dryden *Juvenal* vi. (1697) 120 The Rich to Buy him, will refuse no Price; And stretch his Quail-pipe till they crack his Voice. *a* **1700** B. E. *Dict. Cant. Crew*, *Quail-pipe*, a Woman's Tongue. **1748** Richardson *Clarissa* (1811) VI. 383 Squeaking inwardly..from contracted quail-pipes.

Hence **'quailpiping** *vbl. sb.*

1661 R. L'Estrange *State Divinity* 14 To give over.. their Quailpiping in a Pulpit to catch silly women.

quaime, obs. form of qualm *sb.*

†**quain**, *v.* *Obs. rare.* [a. ON. *kveina* = OE. *cwánian*, Goth. *qainôn*: an ablaut-var. appears in MDu. and MLG. *quînen* (Du. *kwijnen*) to complain, be ill (cf. MHG. *verquînen*, OE. *ácwínan* to waste away).] *intr.* (also *refl.*) and *trans.* To lament, bewail, bemoan. Hence **quaining** *vbl. sb.*

a **1300** *Cursor M.* 10488 Sco quainid eft on þis maner, Oft sco said, 'allas! allas!' *Ibid.* 10495 To quils sco quainid þus hir care. *Ibid.* 12495 Quen iesus herd þis quaining gret. *Ibid.* 21886 þarof him quaines iesu crist. [A possible instance of *quain* sb. (cf. ON. *kvein*) occurs in line 11577.]

quain (kweɪn), *sb.* [Prob. var. of quoin *sb.*] In the poetical terminology of G. M. Hopkins: an angle, a wedge-like corner; angularity. Hence **quain** *v.*[2], **'quaining** *vbl. sb.*[2]

1868 G. M. Hopkins *Jrnls. & Papers* (1959) 170 Swiss trees are, like English, well inscaped—in quains. *Ibid.*, Before sunrise..saw a noble scape of stars—..Cassiopeïa on end with her bright quains pointing to the right. *Ibid.* 171 The straight quains and planing of the Alps were only too clear. *Ibid.* 176 Sycomores grew on the slopes of the valley, scantily leaved, sharply quained and accidented by perhaps the valley winds. **1871** *Ibid.* 205 And if you look well at big pack-clouds overhead you will soon find a strong large quaining and squaring in them which makes each pack impressive and whole. *Ibid.* 206 Below it [*sc.* the bud]..is a half-moon-shaped sill as if once chipped from the wood and this gives the twig its quaining in the outline. *a* **1889** *Ibid.* 290 The figure may be repeated runningly, continuously, as in rhythm (ABABAB) or intermittently, as in alliteration and rhyme (ABCDABEFABGH). The former gives more tone, *candorem*, style, chasteness; the latter more brilliancy, starriness, quain, margaretting. **1953** W. H. Gardener in G. M. Hopkins *Poetry & Prose* 114 In July the principal stars of this constellation form a sort of flattened W on end —its two base angles ('quains') pointing to the right.

quain, obs. variant of QUOIN *sb.*

† **quaint**, *sb.*[1] *Obs. rare.* Also 4 queynt(e. [? f. the adj.] (See quot. 1598.)

c **1320** *Sir Tristr.* 2254 Hir queynt abouen hir kne Naked þe kniȝtes knewe. *c* **1386** CHAUCER *Miller's T.* 90 Pryvely he caught hir by the queynte. **1598** FLORIO, *Becchina*, a womans quaint or priuities.

quaint, *sb.*[2] [f. the adj.] An odd, unusual, or strange person.

1939 J. CARY *Mr. Johnson* 112 'He's a comic, isn't he?' 'A perfect quaint.' **1959** B. ALDISS *Canopy of Time* 164 What's it matter what a broken-down quaint like Stayker said or didn't say?

quaint (kweɪnt), *a.* (*adv.*) Forms: α. 3-4 cointe, (3 kointe, 4 coint(t, coynte, koynt(e), quoynte, (3 cwointe, 4 quointe, quoynt), 4-5 coynt, quynte, (4 quinte, 6 quyent). β. 3-6 queynte, (4 qweynt(e), 4-6 queynt, queinte, 4-8 queint, 6 quent, qwent; 4-5 quaynt, (4 qwaynt, qwaint), quante, (5 qwantte), 4-6 quaynte, (5 qwaynte), quainte, 4- quaint. γ. 4-5 waynt, 5 wheynte, quhaynte, whaynt(e; *dial.* 7 wheint, 8-9 whaint, whent, 9 wheant. [a. OF. *cointe* (*quointe*, *cuinte*, etc.), *queinte*:—L. *cognitum* known, pa. pple. of *cognoscĕre* to ascertain. The development of the main senses took place in OF., and is not free from obscurity (cf., however, COUTH and KNOWN).

In its older senses the Eng. word seems to have been in ordinary use down to the 17th c., though in many 16–17th c. examples the exact meaning is difficult to determine. After 1700 it occurs more sparingly (chiefly in sense 6), until its revival in sense 8, which is very frequent after 1800.]

A. *adj.*

I. †**1.** Of persons: Wise, knowing; skilled, clever, ingenious. In later use chiefly with ref. to the employment of fine language (cf. sense 6). *Obs.*

a **1250** *Leg. Kath.* 580 (Cott. MS.) Hei! hwuch wis read Of se cointe [*v.r.* icudd] keiser. *c* **1290** *S. Eng. Leg.* I. 381/165 Þe beste Carpenter And þe quoynteste þat ich euere i-knev. *a* **1325** *Prose Psalter* cxviii. 98 Thou madest me quainte [L. *prudentem*] vp myn enemis to þi comaundement. *c* **1400** *Destr. Troy* 1531 Wise wrightis to wale.. qwaint men of wit. **1501** DOUGLAS *Pal. Hon.* I. lxv, Ȝit clerkis bene in subtell wordis quent, And in the deid als schairp as ony snaillis. **1593** SHAKS. *2 Hen. VI*, III. ii. 274 To shew how queint an Orator you are. **1596** —— *Tam. Shr.* III. ii. 149 Wee'll ouerreach.. The quaint Musician. *a* **1628** PRESTON *New Covt.* (1634) 273 If you would preach as other men do, and be curious and quaint of Oratory. **1697** DRYDEN *Æneid* XI. 698 Talk on ye quaint Haranguers of the Crowd. **1728** MORGAN *Algiers* I. vi. 176 The Arabs in general are quaint, bold, hospitable, and generous, excessive Lovers of Eloquence and Poesy.

†**b.** In bad sense: Cunning, crafty, given to scheming or plotting. *Obs.*

a **1225** *Ancr. R.* 328 Þeos kointe harloz þet scheaweð forð hore gutefestre. *c* **1340** *Cursor M.* 739 (Fairf.) Þe nedder þat ys so quaynt of gyle. *c* **1394** *P. Pl. Crede* 482 'Dere broþer' quaþ Peres 'þe devell is ful queynte'. **1402** HOCCLEVE *Letter of Cupid* 152 Sly, queynt, and fals in al vnthrift coupable. **1513** DOUGLAS *Æneis* II. i. 59 Knaw ȝe nocht bettir the quent Vlexes slycht? **1674-91** RAY *N.-C. Words* (E.D.S.), 'A wheint lad', q. queint; a find lad: *ironice dictum*. Also, cunning, subtle. **1680** OTWAY *Orphan* III. iv. 864 The quaint smooth Rogue, that sins against his Reason.

2. Of actions, schemes, devices, etc.: Marked by ingenuity, cleverness, or cunning. Now *arch.*

a **1225** *Ancr. R.* 294 Ure Louerd.. brouhte so to grunde his kointe kuluertschipe. *c* **1330** *Arth. & Merl.* 4447 (Kölbing) Morgein.. þat wiþ hir queint gin Bigiled þe gode clerk Merlin. **1387** TREVISA *Higden* (Rolls) IV. 429 Iosephus .. fonde up a queynte craft, and heng wete cloþes uppon þe toun walles. *c* **1460** *Towneley Myst.* xiii. 593 This was a qwantte gawde, and a far cast, It was a hee frawde. **1522** *World & Child* in Hazl. *Dodsley* I. 245, I can many a quaint game. **1598** ROWLANDS *Betray. Christ* 10 When traitor meets, these quaint deceits he had. **1641** BROME *Jovial Crew* II. Wks. 1873 III. 378, I.. over-heard you in your queint designe, to new create your selves. **1742** W. SHENSTONE *Schoolmistress* XII, With quaint arts the giddy crowd she sways. **1889** 'MARK TWAIN' *Yankee* iv. 37 This quaint lie was most simply and beautifully told. **1970** C. HAMPTON *Philanthropist* i. 13 *John* puts the revolver into his mouth and presses the trigger. Loud explosion. By some quaint device, gobs of brain and bright blood appear on the whitewashed wall.

†**3.** Of things: Ingeniously or cunningly designed or contrived; made with skill or art; elaborate. *Obs.*

c **1290** *S. Eng. Leg.* I. 88/62 He liet heom makien a quoynte schip. **1297** R. GLOUC. (Rolls) 1555 Hii ȝeue him an quointe [*v.r.* koynte] drench, mid childe vor to be. *c* **1384** CHAUCER *H. Fame* III. 835 And evermo.. This queynte hous aboute wente, That never-mo hit stille stente. *a* **1400-50** *Alexander* 4275 Have we no cures of courte ne na cointe sewes. **1627** DRAYTON *Nymphidia* lxix, He told the arming of each joint, In every piece how neat and quaint. **1631** SHIRLEY *Traitor* IV. ii, Who knows But he may marry her, and discharge his Duchess With a quaint salad?

†**4.** Of things: Skilfully made, so as to have a good appearance; hence, beautiful, pretty, fine, dainty. *Obs.*

13.. *E.E. Allit. P.* B. 1382 With koynt carneles aboue, coruen ful clene. **13..** *Gaw. & Gr. Knt.* 877 Whyssynes vpon queldepoyntes, þat koynt wer boþe. ? *a* **1366** CHAUCER *Rom. Rose* 98 A sylvre nedle forth I droughe, Out of an aguler queynt ynoughe. *c* **1400** *Destr. Troy* 777 An ymage full nobill.. þat qwaint was & qwem, all of white siluer. **1596** SPENSER *F.Q.* IV. x. 22 Nor hart could wish for any queint device, But there it present was, and did fraile sense entice. **1671** MILTON *Samson* 1303 In his hand A Scepter or quaint staff he bears.

†**b.** Of dress: Fine, fashionable, elegant. *Obs.*

? *a* **1366** CHAUCER *Rom. Rose* 65 The ground.. maketh so queynt his robe and fayr That it hath hewes an hundred payr. **1380** *Lay Folks Catech.* (Lamb. MS.) 1221 Ne worschipe not men for here fayre cloþes, ne for here qweynte schappis þat sum men usen. **1501** DOUGLAS *Pal. Hon.* I. xlvi, In vestures quent of mony sindrie gyse. **1592** GREENE *Upst. Courtier* in *Harl. Misc.* (Malh.) II. 223 Costly attire, curious and quaint apparell is the spur that pricks them forward. **1627** FLETCHER *Locusts* I. xiii, All lovely drest In beauties livery, and quaint devise.

†**5.** Of persons: Beautiful or handsome in appearance; finely or fashionably dressed; elegant, foppish. *Obs.*

a **1300** *Cursor M.* 28015 Yee leuedis.. studis.. hu to mak yow semle and quaint. *a* **1310** in Wright *Lyric P.* 26 Coynte ase columbine, such hire cunde ys. **1362** LANGL. *P. Pl.* A. II. 14 A wommon wonderliche clothed.. Ther nis no qweene qweyntore. *a* **1450** *Knt. de la Tour* (1868) 40 Folke shulde not have thaire herte on the worlde, nor make hem queint, to plese it. **1590** GREENE *Never Too Late* Wks. 1882 VIII. 82 He made himselfe as neate and quaint as might be. **1598** SHAKS. *Merry W.* IV. vi. 41 Quaint in greene, she shall be loose en-roab'd. **1610** —— *Temp.* I. ii. 317 Fine apparision: my queint Ariel, Hearke in thine eare. **1784** COWPER *Task* II. 461 A body so fantastic, trim, And queint in its deportment and attire.

†**6.** Of speech, language, modes of expression, etc.: Carefully or ingeniously elaborated; highly elegant or refined; clever, smart; full of fancies or conceits; affected. *Obs.* (now merged in 8).

13.. *Guy Warw.* (A.) 346 To hir he spac.. Wiþ a wel queynt steuen. *c* **1386** CHAUCER *Can. Yeom. Prol. & T.* 199 We semen wonder wise, Oure termes been so clergial and so queynte. **1513** DOUGLAS *Æneis* I. Prol. 255 The quent and curious castis poeticall. *c* **1570** *Pride & Lowl.* (1841) 807 Pleasaunt songes.. To queynt and hard for me to understand. **1655** E. TERRY *Voy. E. Ind.* XII. 232 The Persian there is spoken as their more quaint and Court-tongue. **1676** MARVELL *Mr. Smirke* K iv, A good life is a Clergy man's best Syllogism, and the quaintest Oratory. **1712** STEELE *Spect.* No. 450 ¶1 A new Thought or Conceit dressed up in smooth quaint Language. **1783** BURKE *Rep. Aff. India* Wks. 1842 II. 76 A style,.. full of quaint terms and idiomatick phrases, which strongly bespeak English habits in the way of thinking.

†**7.** Strange, unusual, unfamiliar, odd, curious (in character or appearance). *Obs.* (now merged in 8).

13.. *Coer de L.* 216 Thou schalt se a queynte brayd. *c* **1369** CHAUCER *Dethe Blaunche* 1330 This is so queynt a sweuyn. *c* **1400** *Destr. Troy* 7715 There come with this kyng a coynt mon of shappe. *c* **1440** *Ipomydon* 1637 Right vnsemely on queynte manere He hym dight. **1513** DOUGLAS *Æneis* III. Prol. 12 Now moist I write.. Wyld auentouris, monstreis and qwent affrayis. **1579** SPENSER *Sheph. Cal.* Oct. 114 With queint Bellona in her equipage. **1629** MILTON *Nativity* 194 A drear, and dying sound Affrights the Flamins at their service quaint. **1714** POPE *Wife of Bath* 259 How quaint an appetite in woman reigns! Free gifts we scorn, and love what costs us pains. **1808** SCOTT *Marm.* III. xx, Came forth—a quaint and fearful sight.

8. Unusual or uncommon in character or appearance, but at the same time having some attractive or agreeable feature, esp., having an old-fashioned prettiness or daintiness.

1795 SOUTHEY *Joan of Arc* VIII. 234 He for the wintry hour Knew many a merry ballad and quaint tale. **1808** SCOTT *Marm.* II. iii, For this, with carving rare and quaint, She decked the chapel of the saint. **1824** W. IRVING *T. Trav.* I. 91 The streaks of light and shadow thrown among the quaint articles of furniture. **1862** STANLEY *Jew. Ch.* (1877) I. x. 202 The device is full of a quaint humour which marks its antiquity. **1884** J. T. BENT in *Macm. Mag.* Oct. 434/2 The herdsmen were much quainter and more entertaining than our city-born muleteers.

b. Of furniture: designed in the style of *art nouveau*.

1897 *Furnit. & Decoration* XXXIV. 197/1 That new style called 'Quaint', which seems to be carcase without the spirit of the new style promulgated by the Arts and Crafts and other societies. **1952** J. GLOAG *Short Dict. Furnit.* 377 A fashion in furniture design, corresponding with the New Art movement at the end of the 19th and the opening of the present century, was known as the quaint style. **1975** *Country Life* 2 Oct. 852/3 The spindly chairs and tables of the 'quaint' vogue.

II. †**9.** Proud, haughty. *Obs. rare.*

a **1225** *Ancr. R.* 140 Þet fleshs is her et home.. ant for þui hit is cwointe & cwiuer. **1340** *Ayenb.* 89 Þo þet makeþ ham zuo quaynte of þe ilke poure noblesse þet hi habbeþ of hare moder þe erþe. *c* **1430** *Pilgr. Lyf Manhode* II. cvii. 115, I hatte orgoill, the queynte [F. *la bobanciere*], the feerce hornede beste. [**1610** G. FLETCHER *Christ's Vict.* II. liv, Queint Pride Hath taught her sonnes to wound their mother's side.]

†**10.** Dainty, fastidious, nice; prim. *Obs.*

1483 CAXTON *Gold. Leg.* 128 b/1 She chastyssed them that were nyce and queynte. **1579** G. HARVEY *Letter-bk.* (Camden) 73 The rest in a manner ar.. overstale for so queynte and queasye a worlde. **1590** SPENSER *F.Q.* III. vii. 10 She nothing quaint Nor 'sdeignfull of so homely fashion. **1640** BROME *Sparagus Gard.* III. vii. Wks. 1873 III. 167 Your new infusion of pure blood, by your queint feeding on delicate meates and drinks. **1678** R. L'ESTRANGE *Seneca's Mor.* To Rdr., Fabius.. taxes him.. for being too Queint and Finical in his Expressions.

†**11.** *to make it quaint*, to act quaintly, in various senses, *esp.* to behave proudly, disdainfully, or deceitfully. *Obs.*

c **1369** CHAUCER *Dethe Blaunche* 531 Lo! how goodly spak this knight.. He made hyt nouther tough ne queynte. **1390** GOWER *Conf.* v. 4623 (II. 282) O traiteresse.. Thou hast gret peine wel deserved, That thou canst maken it so queinte. *c* **1400** *Rom. Rose* 2038, I.. kneled doun with hondis Ioynt, And made it in my port ful queynt. *c* **1422** HOCCLEVE *Jonathas* 642 He thoghte not to make it qweynte and tow. *c* **1430** *Pilgr. Lyf Manhode* II. cvi. (1869) 115 With alle myne joyntes stiryinge and with alle my sinewes I make it queynte [F. *je marche si fierement.*]

†**B.** *adv.* Skilfully, cunningly. *Obs. rare.*

c **1340** *Cursor M.* 5511 (Fairf.) Ȝou be-houys to wirke ful quaynte and in þaire dedis ham attaynt. *c* **1384** CHAUCER *H. Fame* I. 245 What shulde I speke more queynte, Or peyne me my wordes peynte? **1552** LYNDESAY *Monarche* 180 Fresche flora spred furth hir tapestrie, Wrocht be dame Nature quent and curiouslie.

C. *Comb.*, as ***quaint-carved, -eyed, -felt, -looking, -mouthed, -shaped, -sounding, -stomached, -witty, -worded*** adjs.

1575 G. HARVEY *Letter-bk.* (Camden) 91 Thou arte so queyntefelt In thy rondelett. **1598** MARSTON *Pygmal.* I. 140 Like no quaint stomack't man [he] Eates vp his armes. **1603** FLORIO *Montaigne* I. xxxvi. (1632) 115 A quaint-wittie, and loftie conceit. **1744** AKENSIDE *Pleas. Imag.* III. 250 Where'er the pow'r of ridicule displays Her quaint-ey'd visage. **1838** J. R. LOWELL *Class Poem* IX. 11 What quaint-mouthed sentences! and how profound! **1853** JAMES *Agnes Sorrel* (1860) I. 2 This tall quaint-shaped window. **1859** J. G. WHITTIER *On Prayer Bk.* in *Independent* (N.Y.) 15 Sept. 1/1 The quaint-carved, Gothic door. **1863** GROSART *Small Sins* (ed. 2) 17 Their quaint-worded dispositions and distinctions. **1922** R. LEIGHTON *Compl. Bk. Dog* xii. 178 Most people are well acquainted with the personal appearance of this quaint-looking dog. **1957** A. N. PRIOR *Time & Modality* 55 'The True' and 'The False' are certainly quaint-sounding objects to be named by phrases like 'The conquest of Gaul by Caesar'.

quaint, *v.*[1] *Obs.* exc. *dial.* Also 4 coynt, 4-6 quaynt. [See ACQUAINT *v.*, and cf. OF. *cointier* in Godef.] = To acquaint, in various uses.

a **1300** *Cursor M.* 5707 (Gött.) Quen þai war quaintid .. þis moyses and sir Raguell [etc.]. *c* **1330** [see ACQUAINT *v.* 3]. *c* **1350** *Will. Palerne* 4644 He coynted him queyntli with þo tvo ladies. *a* **1400-50** *Alexander* 213 Now sall ȝe here How he.. quayntid him with ladis. **1509** BARCLAY *Shyp of Folys* (1570) 81 Spede your pace, To quaynt your selfe and company with grace. **1591** NASHE *Prognost.* 1 To quaint my selfe with the art of Nauigation. **1606** WARNER *Alb. Eng.* XV. xciv. (1612) 378 God quaints not with Baal. **1886** ELWORTHY *W. Somerset Word-bk.*, *Quaint*, to acquaint, inform.

Hence †'**quainted** *ppl. a.*[1], familiar. *Obs.*

1586 W. WEBBE *Eng. Poetrie* (Arb.) 75 Heere by the quainted floodes and springs most holie remaining.

†**quaint**, *v.*[2] *Obs.* Also 5 coynt(e. [In sense 1, a. OF. *cointier*, *cointer*, f. *cointe* quaint; in sense 2, f. QUAINT *a.* 10.]

1. *trans.* To adorn, to make fine or beautiful.

1483 CAXTON *G. de la Tour* (1868) 167 Thus loste.. theldest doughter her maryage bycause she coynted her self. *Ibid.* 168 He thenne hadde.. coynted hym self of a scarlatte gowne.

2. *to quaint it*, to assume a prim air.

c **1585** *Faire Em.* III. 1281 Let Mistress nice go saint it where she list, And coyly quaint it with dissembling face.

Hence †'**quainted** *ppl. a.*[2] (in 5 coynted).

c **1500** *Melusine* 315 In an euyl heure sawe I euer thy coynted body, thy facion, & thy fayre fygure.

†'**quaintance**. *Obs.* In 4 quoynt-, 4-6 queynt-, (5 qw-), 6 quaynta(u)nce; 5-7 *Sc.* quentance, (5 quyntans). [Cf. QUAINT *v.*[1]] = ACQUAINTANCE, q.v.

c **1300** [see ACQUAINTANCE 2]. *c* **1375** *Sc. Leg. Saints* XXX. (*Theodera*) 85 He come to þis theodera & mad his quyntans .. with hyr. *c* **1489** CAXTON *Blanchardyn* xx. 67 Sore harde was his queyntaunce to her. *a* **1533** LD. BERNERS *Huon* XXX. 92 One toke queyntance of an other. **1567** *Satir. Poems Reform.* viii. 28 For all þi quentance with þe quene. **1603** [see ACQUAINTANCE 2].

†**quaintise**, *sb. Obs.* Forms: α. 4 koint-, quointise, quoyntis(e, quint-, quynt-, qwyntis(e, 4-5 coyntise, koyntis. β. 4 qwayntyse, qwaintis, 4-5 quayntyse, quantyse, qwantis(e; queintise, queyntyse, qweyntise, 4-6 quentise (+ variations of suffix, as -ice, -ese, -yze, etc.). [a. OF. *cointise*, *cuint-*, *quentise*, etc., f. *cointe*, *queinte*: see QUAINT *a.* and -ISE[2].]

1. Wisdom, cleverness, skill, ingenuity.

1297 R. GLOUC. (Rolls) 1872 He ladde is kinedom Riȝtuolliche & suþe wel wiþ quoyntise & wisdom. *c* **1330** *Spec. Gy Warw.* 303 Þere is euere ioye inouh.. Wit and kunning and kointise. *a* **1340** HAMPOLE *Psalter, Cant.* 519 Genge withouten counsayl it is and withouten quayntis. *c* **1425** *Seven Sag.* (P.) 378 Fondys.. For to holde my lyf a day With qweyntys of clergye.

b. Cunning, craft, underhand dealing.

a **1300** *Cursor M.* 740 (Gött.) Þe nedder þat es of suilk a schaft, Mast of quantise es in [*v.r.* and of] craft. **1390** GOWER *Conf.* I. 72 This ypocrite of his queintise Awaiteth evere til she slepte. *c* **1450** *St. Cuthbert* (Surtees) 1847 Þe deuel with his quayntys Will be aboute ȝow to suppryse. **1480** CAXTON *Chron. Eng.* liii. 37 Vortiger.. thought priuely in his herte thurgh queyntyse to bee kyng.

2. An instance of cleverness, cunning, or craft; a device, stratagem, trick.

1297 R. GLOUC. (Rolls) 445 Brut & Corineus an quointise hom bi-þouȝte. *c* **1320** *Seuyn Sag.* (W.) 2769 Thai ne might hit no lenger defende, But ase thai dede a fair queintise. *c* **1440** *Ipomydon* 359 She hyr bythought on a queyntyse,.. To wete, where of he were come. **1483** CAXTON *G. de la Tour*

D viij, Such coyntyses..were to compare to the Copspin that made his nette to take the flyes.

3. Cunning or skilful construction. *rare.*

c **1330** *Arth. & Merl.* 3566 (Kölbing) þere þo men miȝt yhere þe queintise of þe spere, Of þe sonne, of mone & ster.

4. Fine or curious dress; fineness, elegance, or fancifulness in dress.

13.. *K. Alis.* 173 Ladies, and damoselis, Maken heom redy..In faire atire, in divers coyntise. **13..** *E.E. Allit. P.* B. 54 Þay..schulde..in comly quoyntis to com to his feste. *c* **1400** *Rom. Rose* 2250 He that loveth trewely Shulde..him disgysen in queyntyse. *a* **1450** *Knt. de la Tour* (1868) 146 The queintise, the plesaunt folyes, and the foule delytis that haue be used for..worldely plesaunce. [**1570** Levins *Manip.* 148/10 A Quentise, *modus, mos insolitus.*]

5. A device, cognizance, badge, armorial bearing; a coat of arms, or any cloth bearing a heraldic device. Cf. cointise.

13.. *Coer de L.* 5657 A queyntyse off the kynges owen, Upon hys hors was i-throwen. *c* **1330** *Arth. & Merl.* 8671 (Kölbing) þai [the helmets] hadde aboue riche queintise Of beten gold. **1375** Barbour *Bruce* xiii. 183 Armoris and quyntis that thai bare.

†quaintise, *v. Obs.* Forms: 4 queintise, 5 queyntise, coyntise. [? f. prec., or a. OF. *cointiss-*, lengthened stem of *cointir.*] *trans.* To beautify, adorn, dress finely.

1390 Gower *Conf.* III. 358 Sondri thinges wel devised, I sih, wherof thei ben queintised. *c* **1430** *Pilgr. Lyf Manhode* II. iii. (1869) 77 He weeneth he be now wel arayed and queyntised! **1483** Caxton *G. de la Tour* C iij, They haue so many gownes wherof they coyntyse and araye their bodyes.

Hence **†quaintising** *vbl. sb.*, adornment, decoration. *Obs.*

c **1430** *Pilgr. Lyf Manhode* II. civ. (1869) 113 Garnementes of velewet beten with gold and siluer and oothere queyntisinges.

quaintish (ˈkweɪntɪʃ), *a.* [f. quaint *a.* + -ish¹.] Somewhat quaint.

1594 Willobie *Avisa* (1880) 53 Your quaintish quirkes can want no mate. **1796** Lamb *Let. to Coleridge* in *Final Mem.* i. 195 The concluding simile is far-fetched—'tempest-honoured' is a quaintish phrase. **1862** Shirley *Nugæ Crit.* xi. 449 The laureate has alluded to the present effect..in some happy but quaintish lines.

So ˈ**quaintlike** *a.*

1844 *Blackw. Mag.* LVI. 159 Good and quaintlike old gentle rhymes they are.

quaintly (ˈkweɪntlɪ), *adv.* Forms: as quaint *a.* + 3–5 -lich(e, -lych(e, -li, 4–6 -lye, 4– -ly. *Comp.* 4 queyntlyer, 7 quaintlier. *Sup.* 4 queyntlokest, quoyntelucst. [f. quaint *a.* + -ly².]

†1. Skilfully, cleverly, ingeniously, so as to accomplish some act or attain some end. *Obs.*

1297 R. Glouc. (Rolls) 2324 þo biþoȝte vortiger..hou he miȝte do quoyntelucst [*v.r.* queyntlokest] þat he him sulf were king. *c* **1330** R. Brunne *Chron. Wace* (Rolls) 1128 þe kynges brother & y Ar skaped out fol queyntely. *c* **1400** *Destr. Troy* 164 Thus coyntly it kept was all with clene art. **1422** tr. *Secreta Secret., Priv. Priv.* 167 A newe Payne he founde, by the whyche fals Iuges queyntly he chastid. **1513** Douglas *Æneis* x. xi. *heading*, Juno rycht quayntly causis Turnus to flee. **1593** R. Harvey *Philad.* 21 He and his surveyed it quantitatively and queintly to the purpose. **1612** Dekker *Lond. Triumph.* Wks. 1873 III. 253 A song is heard; the musicke being queintly conueyed in a priuate room, and not a person discouered. ? **1708** Prior *Turtle & Sparrow* 263 Those points, indeed, you quaintly prove, But logic is no friend to love. **1714** Gay *Sheph. Week* I. 79, I queintly stole a kiss.

†b. Cunningly, craftily. *Obs.*

a **1300** *Cursor M.* 741 (Gött.) Quaintli taght he him þe ginne, Hu he suld at þe wijf bigine. **1387** Trevisa *Higden* (Rolls) VII. 137 Some men tolde þat þis Harold was a sowter sone, and queyntly [*L. dolose*] underput by þe forseide Elgiue. *c* **1400** *Destr. Troy* 11228 Cast is hit cointly by thies kene traytours..pryam to lose.

†2. With ingenious art, so as to produce something artistic, curious, or elaborate. *Obs.*

c **1300** *Leg. Rood* (1871) 30 (Ashm.) Salomon it let velle and hewe as queinteliche as he miȝte. **13..** *Coer de L.* 1387 He leet mak a tour ful strong, That queyntly engynours made. *c* **1384** Chaucer *H. Fame* III. 833 Domus Dedali.. Nas maad so wonderliche, y-wis, Ne half so queynteliche y-wrought. *c* **1440** *Ipomydon* 1641 He..shove hym bothe byhynd & byfore, Queyntly endentyd oute and in. **1513** Douglas *Æneis* v. vi. 125 A riche schield, wrocht quentlie. **1593** Shaks. *3 Hen VI*, II. v. 24 To carue out Dialls queintly, point by point. **1653** Urquhart *Rabelais* I. lvii. I. 248 They could speak five or sixe several languages, and compose in them all very quaintly.

†3. Finely, elegantly; in a pretty and attractive manner. *Obs.*

1340 *Ayenb.* 47 Hy sseaweþ and diȝteþ ham þe more quaynteliche..uor to maki musi þe foles to ham. ? *a* **1366** Chaucer *Rom. Rose* 783 Her-of lyth no remembraunce, How that they daunced queyntely. *c* **1430** *Pilgr. Lyf Manhode* I. cxxxix. (1869) 72 She hadde now arayed me queyntliche and nobleche. **1490** Caxton *Eneydos* x. 40 Wyth the ladyes he byhaued him soo queyntli swete..and curtoys. **1592** Greene *Upst. Courtier* in *Harl. Misc.* (Malh.) II. 247 A murrey cloth gowne..which he quaintly bare vp, to shew his white taffata hose. *c* **1610** Rowlands *Terrible Battell* 31 The quaintly suted Courtier in attyre.

4. In a curious, odd, or old-fashioned, but pleasing or attractive manner.

1782 Cowper *Lett.* 18 Nov., A tale ridiculous in itself and quaintly told. **1816** J. Wilson *City of Plague* I. iii. 176 One quaintly apparell'd like a surpliced priest Led the procession. **1855** Prescott *Philip II*, I. I. ix. 129 His anger, as his secretary quaintly remarks, was more than was good for his health. **1867** Trollope *Chron. Barset* II. xlv. 11 She had added the date in quaintly formed figures. **1870** Lubbock *Orig. Civiliz.* iv. (1875) 178 A father's sister, quaintly enough, is called father.

quaintness (ˈkweɪntnɪs). Also 4 **queyntness,** 5 **qwhayntnes,** 6 **queint-, queyntnesse.** [f. quaint *a.* + -ness.] The quality or condition of being quaint, in various senses of the adj.

13.. *Coer de L.* 1836 Al we should us venge fond, With queyntness and with strength of hond. **1483** *Cath. Angl.* 296/1 A Qwhayntnes; *vbi* wylynes. **1593** Drayton *Eclogues* ix. 133 The easie turnes and queyntnesse of the Song. **1603** Florio *Montaigne* I. xxv. (1632) 80 All niceness and quaintnesse in clothing. **1620** T. V. tr. *Serm. du Moulin* 11 A vulgar stile, destitute of quaintnesse and eloquence. **1702** *Engl. Theophrast.* 234 Some make the quaintness of their wit, to consist in employing bad Instruments. **1765** Blackstone *Comm.* I. 72 Coke; a man of infinite learning.. though not a little infected with the pedantry and quaintness of the times he lived in. **1866** Geo. Eliot *F. Holt* II. xxiii. 122 There's a simplicity and quaintness about the letter which rather pleases me.

b. A particular instance of this.

1642 Milton *Apol. Smect.* xi. Wks. (1851) 313 Which.. must needs be a strange quaintnesse in ordinary prayer. **1830** H. N. Coleridge *Grk. Poets* (1834) 90 The indecorums and quaintnesses with which Homer may be reproached. **1832** L. Hunt *Poems* Pref. 15 The occasional quaintnesses..which formerly disfigured the story of Rimini.

†quaintrelle. *Obs. rare*⁻¹. In 5 queynt-. [a. OF. (**queint-*) *cointerelle* fem. of *cointerel* beau, fop, f. *cointe* quaint *a.*] A finely-dressed woman.

c **1430** *Pilgr. Lyf Manhode* III. xlvii. (1869) 160 It folweth nouht that thouh j be thus wel kembt, and a litel make the queyntrelle [F. *me monstre cointerelle*] that for swich cause j am fair.

†ˈquaintry. *Obs. rare*⁻¹. In 5 queynterye. [a. OF. *queint-, cointerie* f. as prec.] Finery.

1483 Caxton *G. de la Tour* C iv, The tenthe parte of your queynteryes and noblesses myght refresshe..moo than xl persones ageynst the cold.

quair(e, obs. form of quire *sb.*, where *adv.*

quaire, variant of quarry *a.*

quairn, dial. variant of quern.

quaisie, quaisy, obs. forms of queasy.

‖**quaiss kitir** (kwaɪs kɪˈtɪə(r)), *int. Mil. slang.* Also **kwais ketir, quash kateer, quies kiteer,** etc. [ad. Egyptian Arab. *kway·yis*, dim. cl. Arab. *kayyis* fine + *kətīr*, f. cl. Arab. *kaṯīran* very.] Very good! Very well! O.K.! Also **quies, quash, quois** *a.*, good, nice, satisfactory.

1898 G. W. Steevens *With Kitchener to Khartoum* ii. 13 When the recruit made a bull..the white sergeant, standing behind him with a paper, cried '*Quaiss kitir*'—'Very good'. **1919** W. H. Downing *Digger Dial.* 40 *Quies* (Arab.), good. *Quies-kiteer* (Arab.), very good. **1925** Fraser & Gibbons *Soldier & Sailor Words* 233 *Quash*, good; nice. An Arabic word (khwush) in use colloquially on Eastern Fronts. *Quash kateer*, very good. **1947** D. M. Davin *Gorse blooms Pale* 199 Our outfit was parked in a cornfield off the track and very quois it was too. We used to go swimming in the Liri every day. **1965** Brophy & Partridge *Long Trail* 168 *Quaies kateah*, very good. Arabic. Very common with troops in Egypt or with Regulars that had been there. **1967** W. H. Canaway *Mules of Borgo San Marco* ix. 101 'They'll take us off to Germany and make us have nowt but sausages and beer.' Sergeant Entwistle said, 'Sausages and beer, kwais ketir, I wish I had some now instead of this muck.' **1967** *Sunday Times* (Colour Suppl.) 10 Sept. 46/4 *Quiess*, good!, capital! 'Quiess kateer' = very well, the answer to the question 'enta quiess?', you well?

†quait, *v. Obs. rare.* In 5 qwaite. [Of obscure origin: the *qw-* may represent *wh-*.] ? To wait, await.

a **1400–50** *Alexander* 1109 Quen ne in quat time sal qwaite [*Dubl. MS.* falle] þe þis aunter Enquire me noȝt þat question. *c* **1400** *Destr. Troy* 13245 There the qwene with hir qwaintis qwaitid me to cacche.

quait, dial. var. quiet *a.*; obs. f. quoit *sb.* and *v.*

quaite (kweɪt), a representation of an affected pronunc. of quite *adv.* Also quate.

1929 [see cultured *ppl. a.* 2]. **1933** W. S. Maugham *Sheppey* I. 28, I always say I quaite understand. Noblesse oblige if you know what I mean. **1962** Wodehouse *Service with Smile* v. 77 'Do you mean no *beer*?' 'Quate. I shall be keeping an eye on you.' **1965** K. Giles *Some Beasts no More* i. 6 'So you're one of those funny little men who slide about big offices as if they didn't quaite belong there.' Hell, yes, she'd said *quaite*. **1979** G. Petrie *Hand of Glory* iii. 37 She is quaite raight... Ay would not wish to seem *grotesque*.

quaives, pl. of *quaif*, obs. var. coif.

quake (kweɪk), *sb.* [f. the vb.]

1. a. The act of quaking or trembling; *spec.* in mod. use, an earthquake.

Rare as an independent sb., except in very recent use, but not infrequent as the second element in combs., as *church-, house-, ice-, kingdom-, state-quake,* earth-quake. Now apprehended as a colloq. abbrev. of *earthquake*, and occas. written *'quake.*

a **1300** *Cursor M.* 27362 þe dai o wreth, o quak, and soru. *c* **1340** *Ibid.* 927 (Trin.) Til þou turne aȝeyn in quake To þat erþe þou were of take. **1627–77** Feltham *Resolves* I. ii. 2 The quakes and shakes of Fortune. *a* **1643** Suckling *Love's World* in *Fragm. Aurea* (1648) 11 As the Earth may sometimes shake, (For winds shut up will cause a quake). **1812** Lady Granville *Lett.* (1894) I. 35, I have some quakes for the poor country. **1881** *Nature* XXIV. 362 The great shock consisted of two quakes and several smaller, but distinct, vibrations. **1905** *Westm. Gaz.* 14 Nov. 2/1 Even the most violent quakes in the vicinity of Mount Etna are rarely felt with any force across the straits. **1956** R. St. B. Baker *Dance of Trees* vii. 96 It was a serious 'quake though few people lost their lives. **1973** *Express* (Trinidad & Tobago) 1 Feb. 5/1 The quake shook Mexico City and nearby provinces. **1973** 'D. Shannon' *No Holiday for Crime* (1974) v. 83 Glasser's Ford had been demolished by the quake last August. **1976** *Nigerian Chron.* 18 Aug. 1/2 The epicentre of the quake appeared to be in the Celebes Sea, South-West of Mindanao. **1977** *Time* 3 Jan. 27 (*caption*) In May, a quake centered in the Northeastern Italian region of Friuli killed nearly 1,000.

b. *attrib.* and *Comb.*

1931 *Daily Express* 21 Sept. 2/4 (*heading*) More 'quake shocks in Baluchistan. **1937** *Discovery* Feb. 63/1 Quake-proof reservoirs of water. **1960** *Daily Tel.* 27 May 14 Apparently the depth of the Pacific Ocean makes it specially liable to serve as a vehicle for these 'quake waves'. **1973** *Daily Colonist* (Victoria, B.C.) 21 Oct. 5/5 A 36-year-old business executive built a concrete quake-proof shelter in his yard.

2. A stretch of quake-ooze.

1896 *Blackw. Mag.* May 770 They rose in a body and made for the quakes.

quake (kweɪk), *v.*¹ Forms: *Inf.* 1 cwacian, (cwaec-, cuaec-), 2–3 quakie(n, (2 kwak-, 3 cwak-, 4 quakiȝen, 4 quaky), 4–5 quaken, (5 qvakyn, whakyn), 4–6 qwake, 4– quake, (4 quak, quack, 5 qvake, 5– *north.* whake, 5–6 *Sc.* quaik, 9 *Sc.* quack, quauk). *Pa. t.* 1 cwęcede, cwaecade, cwacode, 3 cwakede, 3–4 quakede, 4– quaked, (4 -id, 6 *Sc.* -et); also *north.* 4–5 quok, (4 qwok, quock), 4–6 quoke, quook, qwooke, 5 *Sc.* quouk, quowke, 6 quooke, *Sc.* qu(h)oik, quuik, 7 *dial.* whook't. [OE. *cwacian*, not found in the cognate langs.; the stem *cwac-* is also the base of OE. *cweccan* quetch, and the same initial combination occurs in other words implying agitation or instability, as *quave, quap, quag* (cf. note to quagmire). The strong form of the pa. t. in northern dialects is on anal. of *shake, shook.*]

1. *intr.* Of things: To shake, tremble, be agitated, as the result of external shock, internal convulsion, or natural instability.

Most frequently used, from the earliest period, with ref. to the earth (cf. earthquake), and now somewhat rare even in this connexion.

c **825** *Vesp. Psalter* ciii. 32 Se ȝelocað in eorðan & doeð hie cwaecian. *c* **893** K. Ælfred *Oros.* II. vi. § 3 Ofer eall Romana rice seo eorþe wæs cwaciende & berstende. *c* **1175** *Lamb. Hom.* 143 Eorþe scal kwakien on his ecsene. *c* **1205** Lay. 27111 þa wal of stanen [sculden] quakien and fallen. *a* **1300** *Cursor M.* 7260 He it scok, Sua fast þat al þe hus quok. **1398** Trevisa *Barth. De P.R.* xvii. clix. (1495) 708 The Byrche.. meuyth and quakith wyth a ryght softe blaste of wynde. **1412–20** Lydg. *Chron. Troy* II. x. (1513) E v, I fele also My penne quake, and tremble in my honde. **1513** Douglas *Æneis* III. x. 34 The land all haill of Itaile trumbillit and quhoik. **1596** Dalrymple tr. *Leslie's Hist. Scot.* VIII. 129 Erdquakes..war hard, kirkes quaket and trimblet vehementlie. **1810** Scott *Lady of L.* I. xii, With boughs that quaked at every breath, Grey birch and aspen wept beneath. **1871** Rossetti *Love's Nocturn* vii, Quakes the pall, And the funeral goes by.

2. Of persons or animals, or parts of the body: To shake, tremble. **a.** By reason of cold or other physical cause. Now *rare.*

c **1000** Ælfric *Hom.* I. 132 Ða teð cwaciað on swiðlicum cyle. *Ibid.* II. 312 Ic..cwacode eal on fefore. *a* **1225** *Juliana* 21 [He] inwið bearnde of brune..& cwakede as of calde. *a* **1300** *Cursor M.* 5196 Israel wit þis vplepp..þat quak [*v.r.* quake] wit ilka lim was won. **1362** Langl. *P. Pl.* A. xi. 46 Carful mon may crien..Bothe of hungur and of thurst, and for chele quake. *c* **1460** *Towneley Myst.* xxviii. 70 When I for care and colde qwoke by a fyre burnyng full bright. **1501** Douglas *Pal. Hon.* I. lviii. Skrymmorie fery gaue me mony a clowre For Chyppynutie ful oft my chaftis quuik. **1555** Eden *Decades* 12 Suche as inhabyte the mountaynes, syt quakynge for coulde in the wynter season. **1611** Shaks. *Cymb.* II. iv. 5, [I] quake in the present winters state, and wish That warmer dayes would come. **1784** Cowper *Task* IV. 385 [She] Retires, content to quake so they be warm'd. **1853** Kane *Grinnell Exp.* xxxvii. (1856) 338 Came back again, dinnerless, with legs quaking.

b. Through fear. Freq. *to quake for fear* or *dread*; also *to quake at*, †*for* (the object of dread), and *for* (a thing or person in danger).

a **900** Cynewulf *Crist* 797 þonne cene cwacaþ, ȝehyreð cyning mæðlan. *c* **950** *Lindisf. Gosp.* Luke viii. 47 þæt wif.. cuaccende [*Rushw.* cwacende] cuom, & ȝefeall fore fotum his. *a* **1225** *Leg. Kath.* 1534 þe king..bigon to cwakien & nuste hwet seggen. *a* **1300** *Cursor M.* 12837 For drednes ilk lim him quok. *c* **1330** R. Brunne *Chron. Wace* (Rolls) 10726 Tounes, castels, for hym þey quok. *c* **1386** Chaucer *Frankl. T.* 132 For verray feere so wolde hir herte quake That on hire feet she myghte hire noght sustene. *c* **1460** *Towneley Myst.* vii. 182 Euery man shall whake and gryse Agans that ilk dome. **1558** Knox *First Blast* (Arb.) 32 They reuerence them, and qwake at their presence. **1582** Stanyhurst *Æneis* II. (Arb.) 68 Yoong children..With cold hert moothers, for Greekish victorye quaking. **1603** Drayton *Bar. Wars* VI. lxxxvii, That ne'er quayles me, at which your greatest quake. **1641** Hinde *J. Bruen* xlvii. 154 At which time..the Devill will quake, yea he doth quake for feare now. **1711** Addison *Spect.* No. 44 ¶1 The sounding of the Clock in *Venice Preserved*, makes the Hearts of the whole Audience quake. **1759** Robertson *Hist. Scot.* VIII. Wks. 1813 II. 52 The fellow in the study stood quaking and trembling. **1800**

WELLINGTON *Let. to Lieut. Col. Close* in Gurw. *Desp.* (1837) I. 103, I quake for the fort at Munserabad. 1847 J. WILSON *Chr. North* (1857) II. 22 Our heart quaked too desperately to suffer us to shriek. 1882 OUIDA *Maremma* I. 18 His name was a terror that made the dead quake in their graves.
refl. a1300 *Cursor M.* 19633 (Gött.) Saul him quok, sua was he rad.

†c. With anger. *Obs. rare.*
c1330 R. BRUNNE *Chron.* (1810) 292 Þe kyng his wordes toke wraþefully tille herte, For ire nere he quoke. c1374 CHAUCER *Boeth.* IV. pr. iii. 94 (Camb. MS.) Yif he be distempre and quakith for Ire, men shal weene þat he bereþ the corage of a lyon.

†3. *trans.* To cause to quake. *Obs.*
1398 TREVISA *Barth. De P.R.* X. v. (1495) 377 A full lytyll puffynge of wynde quakyth and styryth flamme. 1607 SHAKS. *Cor.* I. ix. 6 Where ladies shall be frighted, And gladly quak'd, heare more. 1614 H. GREENWOOD *Jayle Deliv.* 468 The property of the Law is to humble and quake us for our sins. 1639 HEYWOOD *Lond. peaceable Est.* Wks. 1874 V. 372 Cannon..Quaking the bellowing Ayre.

4. *Comb.*, as †**quake-belly**, a fat-bellied person; †**quake-breech, -buttock**, one wanting in courage; †**quakeful** *a.*, causing fear or quaking; **quake grass** = QUAKING-GRASS; †**quake-mire**, a quagmire; also as *vb.*, to quagmire; **quake-ooze**, soft trembling ooze; **quake-tail** *Ornith.* (see quot. 1894).
1622 MABBE tr. *Aleman's Guzman d'Alf.* 223 They will all forsooth be alike, the tall man as the short, the *Quack-belly as the Scranio. c1590 in Drake *Secr. Mem. Earl Leicester* (1706) 118, I shall surely be *Quack-breech and think every Bush a Boggle. 1616 WITHALS *Dict.* 400 *Excors*,..a faint hearted fellow, a quake-breech. a1616 BEAUM. & FL. *Wit at Sev. Weap.* I. i, Stand putting in one foot, and shiver,..like a *quake-buttock. 1609 HEYWOOD *Brit. Troy* XIII. xxxii, All imbrude in fight, His *Quakefull hand and sword so often rearing. 1814 O. RICH *Synopsis Genera Amer. Plants* 10 Briza..*Quake Grass. 1909 *Daily Chron.* 25 June 7/2 We used to call 'em 'quake grass', and 'cats' tail'. 1577 STANYHURST *Descr. Irel.* in *Holinshed* (1807–8) VI. 21 He was forced to fasten the *quakemire with hurdels, and upon them to build the citie. 1583 STOCKER *Civ. Warres Lowe C.* II. 70a, His horse was gotten into a quackmyre. 1599 CHAPMAN *Hum. dayes Myrth* Plays 1873 I. 73 Howe nowe my liege! what, quackemyred in Philosophie. 1898 *Daily News* 23 Nov. 6/2 Over a lot of *quake-ooze flats, where a boat could not get. 1855 OGILVIE *Imp. Dict.* Suppl. *Quake-tail. 1894 NEWTON *Dict. Birds*, *Quake-tail*, a book-name invented for the Yellow Wagtail and its allies, after they had been generically separated from *Motacilla* as *Budytes*.

†**quake**, *int.* and *v.*² *Obs.* Also *Sc.* 6 quaik, 8 -ck. [Imitative: see QUACK, and cf. Du. *kwaken*, G. *quaken* to croak, quack.] = QUACK *int.* and *v.*
a1529 SKELTON *E. Rummyng* 506 Quake, quake, sayd the duck. 1549 *Compl. Scot.* vi. 39 The dukis cryit quaik. 1567 HARMAN *Caveat* (1869) 83 A quakinge chete or a red shanke, a drake or ducke. 1785 BURNS *Addr. Deil* viii, An eldritch, stoor quaick, quaick.

quaker ('kweɪkə(r)). [f. QUAKE *v.*¹ + -ER¹.] One who, or that which, quakes.

1. *pl.* = QUAKING-GRASS. *Midl. dial.*
1597 GERARDE *Herbal* I. lvii. 81 *Phalaris pratensis* is called in Cheshire about Namptwich, Quakers and Shakers. 1611 COTGR., *Amourettes*, the grasse tearmed, Quakers, and Shakers, or quaking grasse. 1617 MINSHEU *Ductor*, Quackers, or quaking grasse. 1882 *W. Worc. Gloss.* 1890 *Glouc. Gloss.*

2. With capital Q: A member of the Religious Society of Friends, founded by George Fox in 1648–50, distinguished by its stress on the 'Inner Light' and rejection of sacraments, ordained ministry and set forms of worship; noted also for pacifist principles and simplicity of life, formerly in particular for plainness of dress and speech.
Acc. to Fox (*Jrnl.* I. 38) the name was first given to himself and his followers by Justice Bennet at Derby in 1650, 'because I bid them, Tremble at the Word of the Lord'. It appears, however, from a letter of intelligence, written at London on Oct. 14, 1647, that the name had previously been applied to the members of some foreign religious sect: 'I heare of a Sect of woemen (they are at Southworke) come from beyond Sea, called Quakers, and these swell, shiver, and shake, and when they come to themselves (for in all this fitt Mahomett's holy-ghost hath bin conversing with them) they begin to preache what hath bin delivered to them by the Spiritt' (*Clarendon MSS.* No. 2624). It thus seems probable that Bennet merely employed a term already familiar, and quite appropriate as descriptive of Fox's earlier adherents (cf. quots. 1654, 1694, and see QUAKING *vbl. sb.* and *ppl. a.* 2). The name has never been adopted by the Friends themselves, but is not now regarded as a term of reproach.
1651 T. HALL *Pulpit Guarded* 15 We have many Sects now abroad; Ranters, Seekers, Shakers, Quakers, and now Creepers. *Ibid.* 29 A Bastard-brood of Arrians, Arminians, ..Quakers, Ranters. 1653 H. R. (*title*) A Brief Relation of the Irreligion of the Northern Quakers. 1654 E. TERRILL in R. Barclay's *Inner Life* (1876) 317 Thus, they coming as foretold, they were not known, but afterwards they were called by the name of 'Quakers', from people's shaking and quaking that received them and their doctrine. 1656 EVELYN *Mem.* (1857) I. 332, I had the curiosity to visit some Quakers here in prison: a new fanatic sect, of dangerous principles, who shew no respect to any man, magistrate, or other. 1679 *Trial of Langhorn* 53 He is no Quaker, for he hath got a Perriwig on. 1694 DE LA PRYME *Diary* (Surtees) 53 The Quakers..do not now quake, and howl, and foam with their mouths, as they did formerly. 1731 *Gentl. Mag.* I. 60 The practice of the people called Quakers, who maintain none of their poor in idleness that are able to work. 1771 SMOLLETT *Humph. Cl.* 26 June, By his garb, one would have taken him for a quaker, but he had none of the stiffness of that sect. 1837 W. IRVING *Capt. Bonneville* I. 183 In one respect, their religion partakes of the pacific doctrines of the Quakers. 1876 BANCROFT *Hist. U.S.* I. x. 363 The early Quakers in New England displayed little of the mild philosophy..of Penn. 1924 G. B. SHAW *Saint Joan* p. xlvi, In war, for instance, we suppress the gospels and put Quakers in prison, muzzle the newspapers, [etc.]. 1930 —— *You never can Tell* in *Wks.* VIII. 208 She is too militant an Agnostic to care to be mistaken for a Quaker. She therefore dresses in as business-like a way as she can. 1941 A. HUXLEY *Let.* 17 Nov. (1969) 470 England and America owe an incalculable debt to the Quakers for the way in which they have educated successive generations of rulers to realize that a theocentric opposition is a thing of enormous value to the society containing it. 1972 J. G. DAVIES *Dict. Liturgy & Worship* 329/1 For Quakers the difference between cleric and layman is irrelevant. 1978 J. A. MICHENER *Chesapeake* 380 In the name of God and Jesus Christ they must be set free, and no man dare call himself a Quaker and a slave-holder, too.

b. *transf.* Applied to various plain-coloured birds and moths, with allusion to the colour of the dress usually worn by Quakers.
(*a*) A small bird of the Falkland Islands. (*b*) The sooty albatross. (*c*) The nankeen-bird, or Australian night-heron. (*d*) One of several European, grey or brown, noctuid moths belonging to the genera *Orthosia* or *Agrochola*, esp. *O. stabilis*, the common quaker, or *O. cruda*, the small quaker.
1775 CLAYTON *Falkland Islands* in *Phil. Trans.* LXVI. 105 Of small birds there are several sorts; the red breast,..the white throat; the quaker, from its plumage being of the colour those people wear. 1775 M. HARRIS *Eng. Lepidoptera* 41 Quaker... Of a plain brown colour, having a small ring in the middle, and a whitish line near the edge. 1894 NEWTON *Dict. Birds*, *Quaker*, a sailor's name for the Dusky Albatross, *Phœbetria fuliginosa*. 1907 R. SOUTH *Moths. Brit. Isles* 1st Ser. 328 The Small Quaker... Most specimens of this species have the fore wings pale greyish ochreous. *Ibid.*, (*heading*) The Common Quaker. 1948 W. J. STOKOE *Caterpillars Brit. Moths* I. 312 The Small Quaker..appears to be common throughout England and Wales. *Ibid.* 313 The Common Quaker..is on the wing during March and April. 1968 *Oxf. Bk. Insects* 74/2 Small Quaker... Dingy, undistinguished little moths, usually with a dusky spot on each forewing. *Ibid.*, Common Quakers visit sallow blossoms. *Ibid.* 78/2 Red-line Quaker (*Agrochola lota*). All four wings of this moth are a dingy blackish-grey colour.

c. *ellipt.* for *quaker-colour, -gun, -hat*, etc.
c1754 GARRICK *Epil. to Fielding's Fathers*, The high-cocked, half-cocked quaker, and the slouch, Have at ye all! 1829 J. SHIPP *Mem.* ix. (1890) 139 The man of authority in size not much larger than a quaker. 1840 R. H. DANA *Bef. Mast* xxvii. 88 A Russian government bark,..mounting eight guns (four of which we found to be quakers). 1923 *Daily Mail* 21 Feb. 14 (Advt.), In Black, Nigger, Putty, Fawn, Quaker.

3. *attrib.* and *Comb.* (from sense 2). a. simple attrib.: Of or pertaining to the Society of Friends or its members; as ***quaker*** (or ***Quaker***) ***bonnet, cap, doctrine, dress, meditation, pride***, etc.; also designating various subdued colours, as ***quaker-brown, -green, -grey***. b. similative, as ***quaker-like*** adj. and adv., ***-looking*** adj. c. special combs.: **quaker-bird**, the sooty albatross; **quaker-buttons** (*U.S.*), the seeds of nux vomica; **Quaker City**, Philadelphia, U.S.A.; **Quaker collar** (see quot. 1957); **quaker-colour**, a drab or grey colour; so ***quaker-coloured*** adj.; **quaker-grass**, quaking-grass (Halliwell); **quaker gun** (*U.S.*), a dummy gun in a ship or fort; **quaker-ladies** (*U.S.*), the small pale-blue flowers of the American plant *Houstonia cærulea*; **quaker-linen** (see quot. 1788); **Quaker-meeting** (also **Quakers'**), a religious meeting of the Society of Friends; *transf.* a silent meeting (alluding to the Friends' custom of remaining silent until moved by the spirit); **quaker moth** (see 2 b); **Quaker Oats**, a proprietary brand of oats used esp. for making porridge as a breakfast food; **Quaker state**, Pennsylvania; **quaker string**, a form of string for a stair.
1859 GEO. ELIOT *A. Bede* iii, Dinah had taken off her little *quaker bonnet again. 1851 MRS. GASKELL *Let.* c 28 Mar. (1966) 147, I have got a new silk gown, *quaker-brown coloured. 1822 M. EDGEWORTH *Let.* 16 Mar (1971) 373 Enter Mrs. Fry in drab colored silk cloak and plain borderless *quaker cap. 1851 MRS. STOWE *Uncle Tom's Cabin* (1852) I. xiii. 198 'Nicely,' said Ruth, taking off her little drab bonnet, and..displaying..a round little head, on which the Quaker cap sat with a sort of jaunty air. 1856 M. J. HOLMES *Homestead* IV. viii. 220 Grandma, in rich black silk and plain Quaker cap, was hovering near her favorite child. 1836 T. POWER *Impressions Amer.* i. 51 It was night before we gained the *Quaker city. 1903 *Critic* Aug. 190 Sketches of Philadelphia life and society by a New York woman who..does not find the Quaker city so 'slow' as is generally represented. 1975 *Country Life* 2 Jan. 44/1 The First Troop, Philadelphia City Cavalry,..celebrated its 200th anniversary on November 15, 1974, the night we flew into the 'Quaker City'. 1957 M. B. PICKEN *Fashion Dict.* 267/2 **Quaker collar*, broad flat collar, similar to Puritan collar. 1974 M. HIGGINS *Changeling* ii. 8 Dark dress with wide Quaker collar. 1818 *Blackw. Mag.* III. 406 Solemn suits Of customary snuff or *quaker-colour. c1770 T. ERSKINE *Barber* in *Poet. Reg.* (1810) 331 Simplicity..Waves in the eye of Heav'n her *Quaker-colour'd wings. 1856 R. A. VAUGHAN *Mystics* (1860) II. XI. ii. 222 The *Quaker doctrine concerning stillness and quiet. 1812 CRABBE *Tales* ix. Wks. (1834) V. 13 Young Zelinda, in her *quaker-dress. 1869 *Bradshaw's Railway Man.* 460/3 (Advt.), Greens. Brunswk. Greens, all shades. *Quaker ditto. Emerald Green. 1880 *Harper's Mag.* Nov. 906/1 The powders are most deceptive in color;..black appears a purplish-gray; Vandyck brown, *Quaker gray. 1922 JOYCE *Ulysses* 498 In quakergrey kneebreeches and broadbrimmed hat. 1953 'N. BLAKE' *Dreadful Hollow* 27 The modest Quaker-grey of the house. 1809 W. IRVING *Knickerb.* iii. (1820) 240 A formidable battery of *quaker guns. 1871 *Scribner's Monthly* II. 102 In yonder woods, where hepatica, and May-blossoms, and *Quaker-ladies twinkle into life. 1946 D. C. PEATTIE *Road of Naturalist* v. 58 There are bluets around Stonybrook in Jersey..called also 'innocence' and 'Quaker ladies'. 1954 Quaker-ladies [see INNOCENCE 6]. 1680 R. WARE *Foxes & Firebrands* II. (1682) 103 He..*Quaker-like, thou'd and thee'd Oliver. 1818 SCOTT *Hrt. Midl.* xxvii, Her love of and veneration for truth was almost quaker-like. 1838 LYTTON *Alice* I. i, A stiff cap of quaker-like simplicity. 1788 WESLEY *Wks.* (1872) VII. 24 Let there be no *Quaker-linen,—proverbially so called, for their exquisite fineness. 1792 WOLCOTT (P. Pindar) *Ode to Irony* Wks. 1812 III. 39 Who laughest not, thou *Quaker-looking wight. 1835 WILLIS *Pencillings* II. l. 95 After sitting awhile in *quaker meditation. 1659 in *Compact with Charter & Laws of Colony of New Plymouth* (1836) II. 125 Others thinke it meet to p[er]mitt some p[er]sons to frequent the *Quaker meetings to endeavor to reduce them form [*sic*] the error of theire wayes. 1704 S. SEWALL *Diary* 23 May (1879) II. 102 Convers'd with Mr. Noyes, told him of the Quaker Meeting at Sam. Sawyers. 1751 J. BROWN *Shaftesb. Charac.* 32 The finest speaker..would in vain point the thunder of his eloquence on a quaker-meeting. 1821 [see QUAKERESS]. 1848 J. F. COOPER *Oak Openings* II. i. 9 The silence resembled that of a Quaker meeting. 1861 HUGHES *Tom Brown at Oxf.* xxvi, Isn't it very ridiculous..that we four should be standing here in a sort of Quakers' meeting. 1974 *Encycl. Brit. Macropædia* VII. 743/2 Friends were hounded by penal laws for not swearing oaths,..for going to Quaker meetings, and for refusing tithes. 1819 G. SAMOUELLE *Entomol. Compend.* 363 *Quaker moth. 1894 *Trade Marks Jrnl.* 5 Dec. 984 Pure *Quaker Oats... Rolled white oats for use as food. The American Cereal Company,..Chicago, Illinois. 1901 B. S. ROWNTREE *Poverty* viii. 285/2, 2 lbs. Quaker oats, 5½d. 1921 R. MACAULAY *Dangerous Ages* i. 11 The annoyances and disappointments..such as quaker oats because the grape-nuts had come to an end. 1980 G. GREENE *Dr. Fischer* iv. 28 Do you happen to know anything about porridge? Real porridge I mean. Not Quaker Oats. 176. WILKES *Corr.* (1805) III. 77 That *quaker pride, which is the most disgusting thing in the world. 1896 *Peterson Mag.* Mar. 309/2 It [*sc.* Pennsylvania] has been long and favorably known as 'The *Quaker State', in honor of the Society of Friends. 1934 G. E. SHANKLE *State Names* ii. 142 Five nicknames are given to the State of Pennsylvania; namely, the *Coal State*, the *Keystone State*, the *Oil State*, the *Quaker State*, and the *Steel State*. 1948 MENCKEN *Amer. Lang.* Suppl. II. 598 State nicknames..of Pennsylvania... *Quaker State*. 1825 J. NICHOLSON *Operat. Mechanic* 598 Sometimes the risers are mitred to the brackets, and sometimes mitred with *quaker-strings.

Hence **'Quakerdom**, Quakers as a class, Quakerism. **Qua'kerian, Quakeric**, †**Quake'ristical** *adjs.*, Quakerly, Quakerish. **Quakeri'zation**, the action of Quakerizing. **'Quakerize** *v.*, to convert into a Quaker; to affect with qualities characteristic of a Quaker. **'Quakership**, the condition of being a Quaker. †**'Quakery**, Quakerism.
1824 R. SOUTHEY *Let.* 3 Apr. in *N. & Q.* (1975) Sept. 403/2 My designs upon George Fox have, as you may suppose, excited a stir throughout all *Quakerdom. 1839 CAROLINE FOX *Jrnls.* (1882) 42 He spoke very civilly of modern Quakerdom. 1855 *Tait's Mag.* XXII. 445 Ellwood was a convert to Quakerdom. 1827 HARE *Guesses* (1867) 132 The Jacobinical metonomatosis of the months..might be lookt upon as a parody of the *Quakerian. 1847 MACAULAY in Trevelyan *Life* II. 215 Translate the following passage into the *Quakeric dialect. 1685 *Answ. Dk. Buckhm. on Lib. Consc.* 12, I should suspect the Pensilvanian had Tutor'd him with this *Quakeristical Divinity. 1864 SALA in *Daily Tel.* 5 Dec., No amount of *quakerisation could render the car uncomfortable. 1825 MISS MITFORD in L'Estrange *Life* (1870) II. 198 She is all over *Quakerized, as you of course know. 1826 B. BARTON *Select.*, etc. (1849) 6 'Twould be cook-ship versus *Quaker-ship. 1673 HALLYWELL *Acc. Familism* iv. 75 *Quakery, though it pretend high, is mere Sadducism at the Bottom. 1688 BUNYAN *Heavenly Footman* (1886) 156 Thou may'st stumble and fall,..both in ranting and quakery.

Quakeress ('kweɪkərɪs). [f. QUAKER + -ESS.] A female Quaker.
1721 *New-England Hist. & Geneal. Reg.* (1876) XXX. 61 [Baptism of] John Rennolds, the little child of John Rennolds, his wife a Quakeress, not consenting. 1764 STEWARDSON (*title*) Spiritual Courtship, or, The Rival Quakeresses. 1821 LAMB *Elia* Ser. I. *Quakers' Meeting*, Every Quakeress is a lily. 1827 HONE *Every-day Bk.* II. 110 Three young quakeresses had a sort of semi-bathing. 1852 MRS. STOWE *Uncle Tom's C.* xiii. 116 A burst of joy from the little Quakeress interrupted the speech.

Quakerish ('kweɪkərɪʃ), *a.* [f. as prec. + -ISH.] a. Of persons: Resembling Quakers in character or manners. b. Of things: Characteristic of, appropriate to, Quakers.
1743 in F. Chase *Hist. Dartmouth Coll.* (1891) i. 5 [He] made a great show of sanctity, by means whereof he was under advantage to propagate his Quakerish notions. 1787 M. CUTLER in *Life, Jrnls. & Corr.* (1888) I. 210 We were very Quakerish, every man attending close to the business of eating, without uttering scarcely a word. 1822 LAMB *Lett., to Bernard Barton* xii. 113 Your plain Quakerish beauty has captivated me. 1847 C. BRONTË *J. Eyre* xxiv, I am your plain, Quakerish governess. 1876 GEO. ELIOT *Dan. Der.* I. 354 A motherly figure of quakerish neatness.

Hence **'Quakerishly** *adv.*, **'Quakerishness**.
1785 G. A. BELLAMY *Apology for Life* (ed. 2) I. xiv. 80 Deceived..by the Quakerishness of my dress, (excuse the new coined word). 1886 G. ALLEN *Maimie's Sake* xxxiii, So quaintly and quakerishly pretty.

Quakerism ('kweɪkərɪzm). [f. as prec. + -ISM.] The principles or practice of the Quakers or Society of Friends.
1656 in Brand *Hist. Newcastle* (1789) II. 235 A great apostacy..to popery, quakerisme and all manner of heresy.

1751 CHESTERF. *Lett.* ccxxxi, Plainness, simplicity, and Quakerism, either in dress or manners. **1776–91** PAINE *Com. Sense* App. *Addr. Quakers* 81 The love and desire of peace is not confined to Quakerism. **1856** R. A. VAUGHAN *Mystics* (1860) II. XI. i. 214 The elements of Quakerism lie all complete in the personal history of Fox.

Quakerly ('kweɪkəlɪ), *a.* [f. as prec. + -LY[1].] Like a Quaker; befitting a Quaker.

1684 GOODMAN *Old Relig.* (1848) 247 A malapert quakerly humour. **1797** LOUISA GURNEY *Diary* in A. J. C. Hare *Gurneys of Earlham* (1895) I. 66, I am quite sorry to see him grow so Quakerly. **1829** MACAULAY *Misc. Writ.* (1860) I. 284 They therefore affect a quakerly plainness. **1842** DICKENS *Amer. Notes* I. vii. 235 Philadelphia,..is a handsome city, but distractingly regular. After walking about it for an hour or two,..I would have given the world for a crooked street. The collar of my coat appeared to stiffen, and the brim of my hat to expand, beneath its quakerly influence. **1879** *Church Times* 21 Mar. 187/2 The Quakerly 'simplicity' which the Persecution Company is seeking to force upon so comparatively insignificant a matter as the Worship of the King of Kings. **1958** J. SYKES *Quakers* I. ii. 49 This is the basis of Quakerly action.

Quakerly ('kweɪkəlɪ), *adv.* [f. as prec. + -LY[2].] After the fashion of a Quaker.

1696 C. LESLIE *Snake in Grass* (1697) 368 What Quaker, or Quakerly-Affected Council drew up this Answer for him? **1826** LAMB *Let. to B. Barton* in *Final Mem.* viii. 259 Do I write quakerly and simply, 'tis my..intention to do it. **1847** MRS. CARLYLE *Lett.* II. 6 If 'you feel a stop' (Quakerly speaking), best to let it have way.

Quakery: see under QUAKER.

'quakiness. [f. QUAKY *a.*] The condition of being quaky (Webster, 1864).

quaking ('kweɪkɪŋ), *vbl. sb.* [f. QUAKE *v.*[1] + -ING[1].]

1. The action of the vb. QUAKE in various senses.

c **825** *Vesp. Psalter* liv. 6 Eȝe & cwaecung cwomun ofer mec. *c* **1000** ÆLFRIC *Hom.* I. 504 Wæs se munt Garganus bifiȝende mid ormætre cwacunge. **1297** R. GLOUC. (Rolls) 6894 þat heo..steppe mid folle vot wiþoute quakinge. *c* **1374** CHAUCER *Anel. & Arc.* 214 Turnid is in quakynge all my daunce. *c* **1450** LYDG. & BURGH *Secrees* 1652 Rennyng afftir mete and also rydyng,..cause wyl a seknesse callyd quakyng. *a* **1548** HALL *Chron., Hen. VIII* (1550) 199 b, He and the Quene, and the Ladyes, fled out of their Palace.. and sodeinly the quakyng seassed. **1656** RIDGLEY *Pract. Physick* 136 The Symptoms, as quaking, nauseating, do shew..new matter is recollected. **1855** BAIN *Sens. & Int.* II. iv. §18 (1864) 285 A tremulous quaking is the characteristic of Fear. **1875** LYELL *Princ. Geol.* II. II. xxviii. 107 The incessant quaking of the ground for several successive months.

†**2.** *spec.* with ref. to the behaviour of the early Quakers; hence, Quakerism. *Obs.*

1653 H. R. *Brief Rel. Irrelig. North. Quakers* 17 Their Quakings are very like the Fits of that Child mentioned, *Mark* 9. **1669** (*title*) Truth Triumphant, in a Dialogue between a Papist and a Quaker..Wherein (I suppose) is made Manifest that Quaking is the Off-Spring of Popery. **1671** R. HEAD *Eng. Rogue* II. xxxii. 307 Falling from Ranting to Quaking.

quaking ('kweɪkɪŋ), *ppl. a.* [f. as prec. + -ING[2].]

1. a. That quakes, in senses of the vb.

c **1000** ÆLFRIC *Hom.* II. 32 Seo cwaciȝende swustor. *c* **1375** *Sc. Leg. Saints* xxvii. (*Machor*) 1018 Ȝeit þan with quaquand voice said he [etc.]. *c* **1440** LYDG. *Secrees* 334 With quakyng penne my consceyt to expresse. **1508** DUNBAR *Goldyn Targe* 156 Schamefull Abaising, And quaking Drede. **1586** WARNER *Alb. Eng.* I. v. (1612) 16 The queaking heards-man scarce had said thus much. **1728** POPE *Dunc.* II. 292 Slow circles dimpled o'er The quaking mud, that clos'd, and op'd no more. **1842** BRANDE *Dict. Science* 1008 *Quaking bog*, peat bog..so saturated with water that a considerable extent of surface will quake or shake, when pressed on by the foot. **1875** LYELL *Princ. Geol.* II. III. xliv. 510 Cattle venturing on a 'quaking moss' are often mired.

b. ***quaking pudding*** (see quot. 1971), ***tart***.

1628 Quaking tart [see CUSTARD 1]. **1709** W. KING tr. J. H. van Slonenbergh in *Useful Trans. Philos.* III. 52 White Bread and Butter and Quaking-pudding. **1747** H. GLASSE *Art of Cookery* ix. 112 Quaking Pudding..Cream..Eggs.. Flour..boil it. **1971** R. HOWE *Mrs Groundes-Peace's Old Cookery Notebk.* 119 *Quaking pudding*, a pudding made of breadcrumbs, cream, eggs and spices.

†**2.** That is, or befits, a Quaker; Quaker-. *Obs.*

1654 BURROUGH & HOWGIL *Answ. Queries* in Farmer *Myst. Godl. & Ungodl.* 37 A paper which was directed to Rich. Roper, and to his Quaking friend [etc.]. **1673** HALLYWELL *Acc. Familism* v. 94 If the Quaking Generation shall object and say, that this was under the Law. **1717** MRS. CENTLIVRE *Bold Stroke for a Wife* Dram. Pers., Simon Pure, a quaking preacher. **1720** DE FOE *Capt. Singleton* xi. (1840) 191 He..put it off with some quaking quibble. **1755** J. SHEBBEARE *Lydia* (1769) I. 310 Lydia's misfortunes commence from the source of quaking probity.

quaking asp(en. *U.S.* Also quakenasp. The North American aspen, *Populus tremuloides*, a tall tree belonging to the family Salicaceæ; also, the soft white wood of this tree.

1822 J. FOWLER *Jrnl.* 1 June (1898) 143 The timber on the mountains Heare is Pitch Pine Spruce Pine Hemlock and quakenasp. **1825** W. H. ASHLEY in H. C. Dale *Ashley-Smith Explorations* (1918) 152 This range of mountains is..closely timbered with pine, cedar, quaking-asp. **1845** J. PALMER *Jrnl.* 30 July in *Jrnl. Trav. Rocky Mts.* (1847) 36 Occasionally there is a grove of quaking aspen. **1848** [see ASP[1] 1]. **1878** J. H. BEADLE *Western Wilds* xi. 168 The town is in a grove of quaking asp. **1902** O. WISTER *Virginian* iv. 55 They took us..through a thicket of quaking asps. **1905** *N.Y. Even. Post* 2 Sept. (Sat. Suppl.) 1/6 Have seen quakenasp groves on the summer range. **1919** E. HOUGH *Sagebrusher* 4 A few quaking asps standing near the cabin door likewise gave motion and brightness to the scene. **1947** J. J. ROWLANDS *Cache Lake Country* 19 Up on the sandy ridge the quaking aspen grows. **1963** S. A. GRAHAM et al. *Aspens* i. 2 Two species of aspen trees are indigenous to..the so-called Lake States. These are the trembling (quaking) aspen..and the bigtooth (large-toothed) aspen.

'quaking-,grass. [f. QUAKING *ppl. a.*] A popular name for grasses of the genus *Briza*, esp. *B. media*.

1597 GERARDE *Herbal* I. lvii. 80 Shakers, or quaking grasse, groweth to the height of halfe a foote. **1785** MARTYN *Rousseau's Bot.* xiii. (1794) 136 A loose panicle, the footstalks of which are so slender as to be moved by every wind; whence they have obtained the name of Quaking-grasses. **1848** C. A. JOHNS *Week at Lizard* 294 *Briza minor*, Small Quaking-grass, is one of the most elegant of the British grasses. **1882** *Garden* 14 Jan. 28/3 Briza maxima and gracilis are two of the best of the Quaking grasses.

quakingly ('kweɪkɪŋlɪ), *adv.* [f. as prec. + -LY[2].] Tremblingly; with quaking or fear.

1566 DRANT *Horace, Sat.* I. i. A iij, What vayles it the so quakinglye to grubbe and grip the moulde. *a* **1586** SIDNEY *Arcadia* (1622) 232 Neuer pen did more quakingly performe his office. **1868** HOLME LEE *B. Godfrey* xii. 63 Joan went rather quakingly..to prefer her petition.

quakke: see QUACK *sb.*[3]

quaky ('kweɪkɪ), *a.* [f. QUAKE *v.*[1] + -Y[1].] Inclined to quake; of the nature of quaking.

1864 in WEBSTER. **1865** *Morn. Star* 5 July, *King Pam.* I feel quite quaky. *Brand.* Nay, my good lord, be not at shadows shaky. **1869** THACKERAY *Round. Papers* xxix. 326 So old and toothless and quaky that she can't sing a bit. **1884** H. COLLINGWOOD *Under Meteor Flag* 88 A curious quaky sensation which had for a moment oppressed me.

qual, obs. form of WHALE *sb.*

†**quale**[1]. *Obs.* [OE. *cwalu* = ON. *kvǫl* (stem *kval-*) torment, torture, f. **kwal-* ablaut-var. of **kwel-*: see QUELE, QUELL. The vowel is long in OS. *quâla* (MDu. *quâle*, Du. *kwaal*, LG. *quaal*), OHG. *quâla*, *chwâla*, etc. (MHG. *quâle*, *quâl*, etc., G. *qual*).] Death, destruction, mortality.

c **900** tr. *Bæda's Hist.* II. xi. [xiv.] (1890) 138 Se cyning mid arleasre cwale of sleȝen wæs. *c* **1000** *Ags. Ps.* (Th.) xxix. 8 Drihten, hu nyt is þe min slæȝe, oþþe min cwalu. *c* **1175** *Lamb. Hom.* 121 God ne sparede na his aȝene berne; ac ȝef hine to cwale for us alle. *c* **1205** LAY. 31807 þat quale com on orue vnimete swiðe.

b. *Comb.*, as **quale-house**, house of torture; **quale-sithe**, death from pestilence.

c **1205** LAY. 727 Vt of þon quarterne, of þan quale-huse [*c* **1275** cwal-huse]. *Ibid.* 3769. *Ibid.* 31900 Heo..cudden heore cunne of heore quale-siðe.

‖**quale**[2] ('kweɪliː). [L., neut. sing. of *quālis* of what kind.] The quality of a thing; a thing having certain qualities.

1675 [BP. CROFT] *Naked Truth* 25 The *quid*, the *quale*, the *quantum*, and such-like quacksalving forms. *a* **1679** T. GOODWIN *Govt. Ch. Christ* xi. Wks. 1697 IV. 94 The Quale, or what sort of Bodies..Christ hath instituted, is to be afterward discussed. **1768–74** TUCKER *Lt. Nat.* (1834) II. 462 Qualities..cannot actually subsist, though they may be thought of, without a quale to possess them. **1875** JOWETT *Plato* (ed. 2) I. 270 When I do not know the 'quid' of anything how can I know the 'quale'?

quale, obs. f. QUAIL *sb.* and *v.*, WHALE *sb.*

qualifiable, *a. rare.* [f. QUALIFY *v.* + -ABLE.] That may be qualified or modified.

1611 COTGR., *Modifiable*, modifiable, qualifiable. *a* **1677** BARROW *Serm.* Wks. 1716 III. 296 As to that..Excision of the Canaanites..we may find it qualifiable, if we consider.. the Trespasses which procured it.

qualification (,kwɒlɪfɪ'keɪʃən). [ad. med.L. *quālificātio*, n. of action from *quālificāre*: see QUALIFY and -ATION, and cf. F. *qualification* (1573 in Godef. *Compl.*).] The action of qualifying; the condition or fact of being qualified; that which qualifies.

1. Modification, limitation, restriction; a modifying or limiting element or circumstance.

1543–4 *Act 35 Hen. VIII*, c. 5 (*Title*) An acte concerning the qualification of the statute of the syxe articles. **1651** BAXTER *Inf. Bapt.* 190 There can be no true closing with Christ in a promise that hath a qualification or condition expressed. **1756** BURKE *Subl. & B.* I. iv, The removal or qualification of pleasure has no resemblance to positive pain. **1845** *Encycl. Metrop.* X. 776 There is however some qualification to be admitted in this general statement. **1891** *Law Times Rep.* LXIII. 765/1 The defendants were liable as principals, as they had contracted in their own names without any qualification.

†**2.** The determining or distinctive quality *of* a person or thing; condition, character, nature. *Obs.*

1604 SHAKS. *Oth.* II. i. 282 Out of that will I cause these of Cyprus to Mutiny. Whose qualification shall come into no true taste againe, but by the displanting of Cassio. *a* **1674** CLARENDON *Hist. Reb.* XII. §11 The commissioners.. notwithstanding their qualification..were imprisoned by the Parliament. **1745** *De Foe's Eng. Tradesman* Introd. (1841) I. 3 Having thus described..the English Tradesman, it is needful to inquire into his qualification.

†**3. a.** A quality, attribute, or property (*of*). *Obs.*

1669 GALE *Crt. Gentiles* I. III. x. 107 Plato laies down as qualifications of true Oratorie [etc.]. **1712** ADDISON *Spect.* No. 435 ¶7 Liveliness and Assurance are..the Qualifications of the French Nation. **1719** LONDON & WISE *Compl. Gard.* 118 The useless Branches, whether it be because they are worn or spent, or because they have no good Qualifications. **1799** I. MILNER in *Life* xi. §18 (1842) 194 Whatever may be their views of justifying faith, that is, whether they think it consists in qualifications or in appropriation.

b. An accomplishment. *Obs.*

1715 SIR J. CLERK *Mem.* (1895) 87, I thought it would be an additional Qualification to him that he understood the English Language. **1785** PALEY *Mor. Philos.* (1818) I. 70 The pleasures of grown persons..founded like music, painting, &c. upon any qualification of their own acquiring. **1796** JANE AUSTEN *Sense & Sens.* (1849) 161 Every qualification is raised at times..to more than its real value; and she was sometimes worried down..to rate good-breeding as more indispensable to comfort than good-nature.

†**4.** The action of qualifying, or process of being qualified (for a position, etc.); also, the result of this action or process. *Obs.*

1589–92 in *Wodrow Soc. Misc.* (1844) 535 Being informit of the qualification, literature, and gude conversation of.. N. **1659** PEARSON *Creed* (1839) 308 The death of Christ [was] necessary..in reference to the Priest himself..both in regard of the qualification of himself, and consummation of his office. **1665** BUNYAN *Holy Citie* 6, I must speak a word or two concerning John's qualification, whereby he was enabled to behold..this City.

5. a. A quality, accomplishment, etc., which qualifies or fits a person *for* some office or function.

1669 DK. YORK in *Pepys' Diary* (1879) VI. 111 Besides his general qualifications for that trust. **1765** FOOTE *Commissary* I. Wks. 1799 II. 15 A qualification for a canon of Strasbourg. **1779** BURKE *Corr.* (1844) II. 276 Even a failure in it [law] stands almost as a sort of qualification for other things. **1855** MACAULAY *Hist. Eng.* xii. III. 242 This vehement hatred of Popery was..the first of all qualifications for command. **1873** HAMERTON *Intell. Life* I. vii. (1875) 37 Even to taste and smell properly, are most important qualifications for the pursuit of literature, art, and science.

b. *absol.*

1818 CRUISE *Digest* (ed. 2) III. 27 The bishops are still in law the judges of the qualifications of those who are presented to them. **1861** M. PATTISON *Ess.* (1889) I. 37 The preceptor..whatever his other qualifications may have been, had not earned his promotion by his Latin style. **1882** MISS BRADDON *Mt. Royal* I. i. 29 A sturdy truthfulness was one of her best qualifications.

6. a. A necessary condition, imposed by law or custom, which must be fulfilled or complied with before a certain right can be acquired or exercised, an office held, or the like.

1723 *Act of Pennsylvania*, Every brewer..shall be qualified by oath..which said qualification shall be taken by all persons who brew..for sale. **1765** BLACKSTONE *Comm.* I. ii. 171 The true reason of requiring any qualification, with regard to property, in voters. **1819** MACKINTOSH *Parl. Suffrage* Wks. 1846 III. 215 A representative assembly, elected by a low uniform qualification. **1875** JOWETT *Plato* (ed. 2) III. 440 A law which fixes a sum of money as the qualification of citizenship.

b. A document attesting that a person is qualified.

1748 SMOLLETT *Rod. Rand.* xviii, I carry my qualification to the Navy-office. [*Ibid.*, We must deliver our letters of qualification at the Navy-office before one a-clock.] **1789** J. WOODFORDE *Diary* 26 Sept. (1927) III. 143 Ben returned by Dinner, brought..a Qualification for my sporting this year for which I am to pay 2 Guineas and 1 Shilling.

7. The act of determining the quality or nature of a thing; *spec.* **a.** The determining whether a book or proposition merits theological censure as heretical. Cf. QUALIFICATOR.

1826 *Blackw. Mag.* XX. 336 His Catechism and other works were submitted for qualification to Melchior Cano, his denouncer.

b. *Logic.* The expression of quality, or the distinction of affirmative and negative, in a proposition. (*Cent. Dict.* 1891.)

8. *attrib.* and *Comb.*, as ***qualification-ticket***; **qualification shares**, shares which one must hold in order to be qualified for a directorship of a company.

1797 *Sporting Mag.* IX. 100 A gentleman..applied..for a qualification-ticket. **1899** *Daily News* 28 Mar. 8/3 The money had been given on account of that gentleman's qualification shares.

Hence **,qualifi'cationless** *a.*, having no qualification.

1898 *Westm. Gaz.* 16 Dec. 8/3 The new Bill evidently contemplated the possibility of qualificationless directors.

qualificative ('kwɒlɪfɪkeɪtɪv), *a.* and *sb. rare.* [f. QUALIFY *v.*: see prec. and -ATIVE. Cf. F. *qualificatif, -ive* (18th c.).] **a.** *adj.* Qualifying; denoting some quality. **b.** *sb.* A qualifying word or phrase.

a **1661** FULLER *Worthies* I. (1662) 59 An Apology for Qualificatives used, and Blanks left in this History. **1860** F. WINSLOW *Obscure Dis. Brain* 361 Adjectives or qualificatives disappear last. **1862** RAWLINSON *Anc. Mon.* I. vii. 148 His name..is usually followed by a qualificative adjunct.

qualificator ('kwɒlɪfɪkeɪtə(r)). [a. med.L. agent-n. from *quālificāre* to QUALIFY.] One of a board of theologians attached to the Holy Office, who report on the character (heretical or otherwise) of propositions submitted to them. Cf. QUALIFIER 3.

1688 Burnet *Lett. St. Italy* 20 One of the Qualificators of the Inquisition. **1736** Chandler *Hist. Persec.* 178 The decision in such affairs belongs to the Divines, who are thence called Qualificators. **1826** *Blackw. Mag.* XX. 76 The whole..is then transferred by the Inquisitors to Theologians, Qualificators of the Holy Office.

qualificatory ('kwɒlɪfɪˌkeɪtərɪ), *a.* [ad. L. type **quālificātōri-us*: cf. prec. and -ORY.]

1. Having the character of qualifying, modifying, or limiting; tending to qualify.

1805 W. Taylor in *Ann. Rev.* III. 651 That evasive, Jesuitic, qualificatory extenuation. **1830** James *De L'Orme* xlvi. 319 The Count would hardly hear of any qualificatory measures. **1868** Visct. Strangford *Selections*, etc. (1869) II. 247 A qualificatory commonplace.

2. Such as to confer a qualification: (sense 6).

1889 *Academy* 12 Oct. 233/2 Some teachers urge..that examinations should be solely qualificatory.

qualified ('kwɒlɪfaɪd), *ppl. a.* (and *sb.*) [f. QUALIFY *v.* + -ED[1].]

A. *ppl. a.* **I.** †**1. a.** In predicative use: Furnished with, possessed of (certain) qualities. *Obs.*

1596 Shaks. *Tam. Shr.* IV. v. 66 She is..so qualified as may beseeme The Spouse of any noble Gentleman. **1603** Knolles *Hist. Turks* (1638) 158 A certaine Gentlewoman.. more honourably borne, than honestly qualified. **1665** J. Webb *Stone-Heng* (1725) 45 All Stones are not Qualified alike; some are hard..some soft. **1681** Dryden *Abs. & Achit.* 75 The moderate sort of men, thus qualified, Inclined the balance to the better side.

†**b.** Attributively: Possessed of good qualities; accomplished, perfect. *Obs.*

1592 Nashe *P. Penilesse* (ed. 2) 25 b, The fine qualified Gentleman..should carie it clean away from the lazie clownish droane. **1598** R. Bernard tr. *Terence* 286 Such a qualified yong gentleman. **1656** Finett *For. Ambass.* 238 Reverenced amongst them for his..descent from a race of qualified saints. *a* **1700** B. E. *Dict. Cant. Crew, Qualified*, Accomplisht Statesman, Soldier, Scholar.

2. Endowed with qualities, or possessed of accomplishments, which fit one for a certain end, office, or function; fit, competent.

a. In predicative use: const. *for* (†*in*), or *to* with inf.

1589–92 in *Wodrow Soc. Misc.* (1844) 535 Gif he beis fundin hable, meit, and sufficientlie qualifeit thairfoir. **1605** Shaks. *Lear* I. iv. 37 That which ordinary men are fit for, I am qualified in. **1665** Boyle *Occas. Refl.* I. vii. (1848) 89 Him that is qualify'd for such Employments. **1719** De Foe *Crusoe* II. xiii. (1840) 274 A government qualified only to rule such a people. **1755** J. Mills tr. *Crevier's Rom. Emp.* I. 107 That great man, equally qualified for war or peace. **1845** S. Austin *Ranke's Hist. Ref.* III. 83 A commune was not qualified to dispute concerning things of this kind. **1863** Lyell *Antiq. Man* 33 In every way highly qualified for the task.

b. Used attributively.

1558 Q. Kennedy in *Wodrow Soc. Misc.* (1844) 152 Than sulde be qualifeit men in all the estaitis of the kirk. **1693** Capt. G. St. Lo (*title*) England's Safety..proposing a sure method for..raising qualified Seamen, for manning their Majesties Fleet. **1849** Cobden *Speeches* 86, I have heard qualified persons say, that the..police there, are the finest armed and drilled men in Ireland. **1865** Lightfoot *Galatians* (1874) 72, I am..a qualified witness of his resurrection. **1880** C. R. Markham *Peruv. Bark* 93 The plan..was to make a collection of plants and seeds.. through the instrumentality of qualified agents.

3. a. Legally, properly, or by custom, capable of doing or being something specified or implied.

1559 Q. Kennedy in *Wodrow Soc. Misc.* (1844) 267 That I was nocht qualifiet to ressone with Willok, because..I wes bot ane meyne man in our estait. **1656** in Gross *Gild Merch.* (1890) II. 267 Sundry Persons not being qualified according to the said Custome. **1702** *Lond. Gaz.* No. 3839/4 The next winning Horse that is duly qualified to run for this Plate. **1777** Sheridan *Sch. Scand.* II. ii, No person should be permitted to kill characters..but qualified old maids. **1849** Macaulay *Hist. Eng.* viii. II. 292 The king..had no right to force on them even a qualified candidate.

b. *Eccl.* Entitled to hold two benefices at once (Minsheu *Ductor* 1617: cf. QUALIFY *v.* 4, quot. 1667).

4. Belonging to the upper classes of society; 'of quality'. *Obs.* exc. *dial.*

1604 E. G[rimstone] *D'Acosta's Hist. Indies* v. xix. 380 If any Indian qualified, or of the common sorte were sicke. **1608** Willet *Hexapla Exod.* 481 These personall wrongs are ..of persons not qualified but of common and ordinarie persons. **1703** *Rules of Civility* 116 If..you be behind, and must pass after the qualify'd Person. **1886** *Cheshire Gloss.*, *Qualified*, in good circumstances. A rich man would be said to be *qualified*.

II. 5. a. Limited, modified, or restricted in some respect; *spec.* in ***qualified acceptance, endorsement, estate, fee*** (see quot. 1818), ***negative, oath, privilege, property***.

1599 *Life More* in Wordsw. *Eccl. Biog.* (1853) II. 130 Delivering this qualified answer to the Kinge. **1635** Swan *Spec. M.* vi. §2 (1643) 196 If it be taken in a qualified sense, it is not much amisse. **1746** Hervey *Medit.* (1818) 211 Every object, a little while ago, glared with light, but now all appears under a more qualified lustre. **1769** Blackstone *Comm.* IV. 235 Animals, in which there is no property either absolute or qualified. **1818** Cruise *Digest* (ed. 2) I. 79 Where an estate limited to a person and his heirs has a qualification annexed to it, by which it is provided that it must determine whenever that qualification is at an end; it is then called a qualified or base fee. **1860** Mill *Repr. Govt.* (1865) 1/2 Unfit for more than a limited and qualified freedom. **1891** E. Peacock *N. Brendon* II. 432 Narcissa gave a qualified reply. **1972** *Times* 16 Mar. 9/7 The defence was a denial of the words in the statement of claim, a plea of qualified privilege, a plea of absolute privilege, and also a plea of justification. **1973** *Scotsman* 21 Feb. 10/3 The occasion on which the alleged remarks were made was in his view clearly one where qualified privilege applied.

b. *euphem.* for 'bloody', 'damned', etc. *slang.*

1886 Kipling *Plain Tales from Hills* (1888) 121 He was.. told not to make a (qualified) fool of himself. **1932** D. L. Sayers *Have his Carcase* xxvi. 353 'I wish we'd never come up against this qualified case,' added the Superintendent bitterly. **1949** 'E. C. R. Lorac' *Still Waters* iii. 39, I.. knocked my head on those qualified rocks.

B. *ellipt.* as *sb.* One who is or those who are eligible for a position, military service, etc.; one who possesses a professional qualification.

1910 *Westm. Gaz.* 22 Apr. 14/1 In 1908 of 443,385 persons fully qualified for service the [German] State took only 221,852; and it is estimated that in 1911 the State will take only about 39 per cent. of the qualified. **1972** *Accountant* 12 Oct. 12/1 (Advt.), Newly qualifieds—Birmingham.

Hence '**qualifiedly** *adv.*, in a qualified fashion; '**qualifiedness**, the state of being qualified.

1675 J. Smith *Chr. Relig. App.* I. 23 Cæsar had nothing to commend him to the Electors, but his qualifiedness for that function, by the worth of his parts. **1858** Bushnell *Serm. New Life* 308 A force independent and qualifiedly sovereign. **1865** J. Grote *Treat. Mor. Ideas* vii. (1876) 98 We cannot be truthful as we may be benevolent, less or more, or qualifiedly.

qualifier ('kwɒlɪfaɪə(r)). [f. QUALIFY + -ER[1].]

1. One who, or that which, qualifies, in various senses of the vb. Also, one who makes himself eligible for a tournament, or for the final rounds of a tournament, as in golf or lawn tennis; *transf.*, a preliminary round of a competition. Also *attrib.*

1561 T. Norton *Calvin's Inst.* IV. xix. (1634) 719 Away with these qualifiers, that cover one sacriledge with so many sacriledges. **1576** Newton *Lemnie's Complex.* (1633) 79 Qualifiers and alayers of the heat of blood. **1638** R. Younge *Drunkard's Character* 269 Tobacco, being hot and dry, must have a qualifier of cold and moist from the pot. **1754** Richardson *Grandison* (1781) I. xxvi. 183 Sir Charles is no qualifier, Sir, when he stakes his honour. **1796** Lamb *Lett.* (1837) I. 55, I was unwilling to let my last night's letter go off without this qualifier. **1887** *Pall Mall G.* 9 Mar. 5/1 Our qualifiers of beer have recently been [catching it]. **1909** *Daily Chron.* 7 May 8/4 Out in 36, he came home in a good 73, and..made certain of a place among the qualifiers. **1920** *Glasgow Herald* 15 July 8 [Rifle shooting] Along with the Prince of Wales's tie were decided the ties in the Qualifier competition. **1951** *Sport* 16–22 Mar. 20/3 Although there are still quite a few more qualifying races due between now and April 7th it looks doubtful that we shall get a better qualifier. **1976** *Tennis Today* Aug. 8/1 Representing our shores was a total of sixteen players including the sole British qualifier Corinne Molesworth. **1976** *Western Mail* (Cardiff) 22 Nov. 16/2 Irish jumping star Bannow Rambler will be sent to Chepstow for an Embassy 'Chase qualifier next Saturday week. **1977** *Daily Express* 29 Mar. 32/4 England put nine goals past Luxemburg 16 years ago in the away leg of a World Cup qualifier.

2. *Gram.* A word, as an adjective or adverb, attached to another word to qualify it. Also, a qualifying phrase or subordinate clause.

The specialized applications in quots. 1892, 1965, and 1972 are not in general use.

1589 Puttenham *Eng. Poesie* III. xvii. (Arb.) 193 Your Epitheton or qualifier..must be apt and proper for the thing he is added vnto. **1765** J. Elphinston *Princ. Eng. Lang. Digested* II. viii. 183 Instead of a definition or picture, a name or *noun* was invented; instead of its specification, the qualifier or adjective. *Ibid.* 186 A sentence may also be complex and compound. Complex it becomes, when the subject or object has a qualifier joined. **1875** Whitney *Life Lang.* vi. 103 Formal correspondence between a substantive and its qualifier or representative. **1892** H. Sweet *New Eng. Gram.* I. §34. 13 When we distinguish between *many men, all men,* and *some men* or *few men*, we cannot say that *many, all, some, few* are attribute-words; they are only *qualifiers*. **1925** Grattan & Gurrey *Our Living Lang.* xvii. 104 A Qualifier may be a Substantive or a Case-Phrase, or even a Sentence. **1933** O. Jespersen *Essent. Eng. Gram.* vii. 67 *Little* is sometimes a qualifier (*a little girl*), sometimes a quantifier (*a little bread*). **1965** N. C. Stageberg *Introd. Eng. Gram.* xv. 226 The fourth structure-class contains the qualifiers. The qualifier position is the one just before an adjectival or an adverbial. *Ibid.*, It is evident that uninflected words like *very, quite,* and *rather* can be called qualifiers; and when an inflected word like *pretty* and *mighty* appears in the same position, consider it a qualifier by position. **1972** J. Muir *Mod. Approach Eng. Gram.* i. 5 An element of structure may precede the head element: this is called the modifier; and an element of structure may follow the head element: this is called the qualifier. Thus: *..the big boy with red hair* is a nominal group with three elements of structure, an *m* element (*the big*), an *h* element (*boy*) and a *q* element (*with red hair*) giving the structure *mhq*.

3. *R.C. Ch.* = QUALIFICATOR.

a **1843** Southey *Comm.-pl. Bk.* (1851) IV. 670 Approved and licensed by Qualifiers. **1888** G. Salmon *Infall. Church* xiv. 235 The question of law is referred to a special Board of skilled theologians, under the title of Qualifiers.

qualify ('kwɒlɪfaɪ), *v.* Also 6 qualyfy, -fie, (6–7 qualle-, qualli-, quale-, -fye, -fie), 6–8 qualifie. [a. F. *qualifi-er* (15th c.), or ad. med.L. *quālificāre* to attribute a quality to, f. *quālis* of such a kind + *-ficāre*: see -FY.]

I. To invest with a quality or qualities.

1. *trans.* To attribute a certain quality or qualities to. **a.** To describe or designate in a particular way; to characterize, entitle, name. (†Const. *with.*)

1549 Latimer *4th Serm. bef. Edw. VI* (Arb.) 107 S. Paule in hys epistle qualifyeth a bishop, and saith that he must be ..apte to teache and to confute all maner of false doctryne. **1653** H. Cogan tr. *Pinto's Trav.* xii. 37, I will favor thee as a Vassal, and not as a brother, as thou qualifiest thyself. **1684** J. Peter *Siege Vienna* 21 Two of the Eldest Colonels were qualified with a Title between a Major General and a Colonel. **1823** Byron *Juan* x. lxxxi, The 'Devil's drawing-room', As some have qualified that wondrous place. **1826** *Blackw. Mag.* XX. 77 The propositions referred to the theologians have been qualified as heretical. **1873** Browning *Red Cott. Nt.-cap* 253 Madame Muhlhausen, —whom good taste forbids We qualify as do these documents.

b. *Gram.* Of an adj.: To express some quality belonging to (a noun). Of an adv.: To modify. Also used of attributive nouns, qualifying phrases, or subordinate clauses.

[**1589** Puttenham *Eng. Poesie* III. xvii. (Arb.) 193 Sometimes wordes suffered to go single, do giue greater sence and grace then words quallified by attributions do.] **1837** M. Green *Engl. Gramm.* 14 [Adjectives] are added to nouns to define, qualify, describe, or limit the signification of the noun. **1887** Roget *Introd. Old French* 176 [The Adjective] qualifying two or more Substantives. **1888** H. A. Strong tr. *Paul's Princ. Hist. Lang.* 424 [The adjective] bears the same relation to the substantive as an adverb to the adjective which it qualifies. **1892** H. Sweet *New Eng. Gram.* I. §34. 14 Thus *very* in *a very strong man* qualifies the attribute-word *strong*. Qualifiers themselves may be qualified, as in *very many Englishmen*. **1924** O. Jespersen *Philos. Gram.* vii. 96 In any composite denomination of a thing or person.., we always find that there is one word of supreme importance to which the others are joined as subordinates. This chief word is defined (qualified, modified) by another word, which in its turn may be defined (qualified, modified) by a third word, etc. **1939** G. H. McKnight et al. *Gram. Living Eng.* x. 102 By far the largest class of adjectives is that used in qualifying nouns. **1947** A. M. Clark *Spoken Eng.* (ed. 2) iv. 81 Frequently..noun-adjectives are joined to the nouns they qualify by hyphens:—*bird-cage, book-review*, etc. **1959** S. H. Burton *Handbk. Eng. Pract.* II. 127 Add to each of the following sentences one phrase to qualify the subject word, one phrase to qualify the object word, and one phrase to modify the verb. **1972** M. L. Samuels *Linguistic Evol.* v. 68 *Son* is usually either modified by *my/his/her*, etc. or qualified by an *of*-group, whereas *sun* is normally preceded by the definite article. **1975** [see QUALIFYING *ppl. a.*].

†**2. a.** To impart a certain quality to (a thing); to make (a thing) what it is. *Obs.*

1592 Greene *Upst. Courtier* in *Harl. Misc.* (Malh.) II. 221 Is..not rather true nobility a minde excellently qualified with rare vertues? **1609** Bible (Douay) *Gen.* Comm., Then shal the bodies be qualified according to the state of the soules, happie or miserable for ever. **1645** Quarles *Sol. Recant.* III. 71 But thou hast tainted that immortall breath, Which qualifi'd thy life, and made thee free Of heav'n and earth. *a* **1677** Hale *Prim. Orig. Man.* IV. vi. 344 The Divine Will, determined or qualified (if we may use that improper word) with the highest..Wisdom and Power.

b. *absol.* To bring it about *that*. *Obs.*

a **1670** Hacket *Abp. Williams* I. (1692) 60 It qualified also, that no detection could be made..that he bought this greatness.

3. a. To invest (a person) with proper or essential qualities or accomplishments (*for* being something). Also *refl.*

1581 Mulcaster *Positions* xxxvi. (1887) 134 Set to schoole, to qualifie themselues, to learne how to be religious. **1683** Moxon *Mech. Exerc., Printing* i, A Typographer ought to be equally qualified with all the Sciences that becomes an Architect. **1711** W. Sutherland *Shipbuild. Assist.* 22 Those Properties..will qualify a Man for a compleat Architect. ? **1782** Cowper *Parrot* 11 To qualify him more at large, And make him quite a wit.

b. To make fit or competent *for* doing (or *to do*) something, or *for* some sphere of action, existence, etc. Chiefly *refl.*

1665 Boyle *Occas. Refl.* VI. iv. (1848) 353 He whose parts are too mean to qualifie him to govern others. **1712** *Spect.* No. 524 ⁋5 To refresh and otherwise qualify themselves for their journey. **1749** Fielding *Tom Jones* VI. iii, Moderation ..can qualify us to taste many pleasures. **1817** Scott *Rob Roy* xii, Qualifying myself for my new calling. **1852** Dickens *Bleak Ho.* xxxviii, I am qualifying myself to give lessons. **1873** Hamerton *Intell. Life* III. i. (1875) 77 Men are qualified for their work by knowledge.

absol. **1742** Young *Nt. Th.* IX. 575 That strength, Which best may qualify for final joy.

4. a. To make legally capable; to endow with legal power or capacity; to give a recognized status to (a person).

1583 Stubbes *Anat. Abus.* II. (1882) 113 Would God all Ecclesiastical persons..would nowe..quallifie themselues, shewe obedience to Princes lawes. **1667** Pepys *Diary* (1879) IV. 350 Is made one of the Duke's Chaplains, which qualifies him for two livings. **1767** Blackstone *Comm.* II. 418 These game laws..do indeed qualify nobody, except.. a game-keeper, to kill game. **1862** Merivale *Rom. Emp.* (1865) IV. xxxvii. 291 He qualified others, by adding to their fortunes from his own bounty. **1889** *Pall Mall G.* 27 June 5/1 A Royal Charter enabling it to 'qualify' nurses as doctors are 'qualified'.

b. *spec.* by the administration of an oath. *U.S.*

[**1723** *Act of Pennsylvania*, Every brewer..shall be qualified by oath..that he will not use any molasses, etc.] **1798** in Dallas *Amer. Law Rep.* II. 100 The court said they would order the jury to be qualified. **1800** M. Cutler in

Life, etc. (1888) II. 37 He [the Governor of Mass.] met the two Houses at 12, and was qualified.

5. *intr.* (for *refl.*) To make oneself competent *for* something, or capable of holding some office, exercising some function, etc., *by* fulfilling some necessary condition; *spec.* by taking an oath, and hence *U.S.*: To make oath, to swear *to* something (Bartlett, 1848). Also, to become eligible for an old-age pension.

a **1588** TARLTON *Jests* (1844) p. xxv, Presently he can Qualifie for a mule or a mare, Or for an Alderman. **1790** BURKE *Fr. Rev.* Wks. V. 384 All the ministers of state must qualify, and take this test. **1825** C. R. H. in Hone *Everyday Bk.* I. 1334 His lordship goes to church to qualify. **1849** MACAULAY *Hist. Eng.* vi. II. 27 He could not legally continue to employ officers who refused to qualify. **1891** *Law Reports*, Weekly Notes 118/1 It was his duty to qualify for the office of director by taking forty shares. **1911** *Rep. Labour & Social Conditions in Germany* (Tariff Reform League) III. 92 The man cannot draw his pension until he is 70 years of age, except through invalidity; he qualifies after one year's payment. **1927** W. E. COLLINSON *Contemp. Eng.* 83 The Old Age Pensions Act (1908) supplied the language with at least one phrase: *to qualify for the pension* (to be getting on in years).

†**6.** *trans. Sc. Law.* To establish by evidence. *Obs.*

a **1639** SPOTTISWOOD *Hist. Ch. Scot.* VI. (1677) 333 Hay compeired, and nothing being qualified against him, was upon suspicion confined. *a* **1670** SPALDING *Troub.* (1850) I. 358 The vther half [of the forfeited goods] to be givin to him who dilates the recepteris, and qualefeis the samen. **1776** LD. THURLOW in *Boswell's Johnson* (1848) App. 817/2 If the individual could qualify a wrong, and a damage arising from it. **1946** A. D. GIBB *Students' Gloss. Scottish Legal Terms* 71 *Qualify*, to make out or establish, as in the expression, *to qualify a title.*

II. To modify in some respect.

7. To modify (a statement, opinion, etc.) by any limitation or reservation; to make less strong or positive.

1533 MORE *Apol.* xxvii. Wks. 893/2 He hathe circumspectly..qualyfyed and modered hys tale wyth thys woord (all). **1551** PRINCESS MARY in Ellis *Orig. Lett.* Ser. I. II. 177 The promise made..by your Majesties counsell..although they seeme now to quallefye and deny the thing. *a* **1661** FULLER *Worthies* (1840) III. 8 Whilst a prince he was undutiful to his father; or to qualify the matter, over dutiful to his mother, whose domestic quarrels he always espoused. *a* **1731** ATTERBURY (J.), My proposition I have qualified with the word, often; thereby making allowance [etc.]. **1790** BURKE *Fr. Rev.* Wks. V. 296 To observe whether..I might not find reasons to change or to qualify some of my first sentiments. **1855** PRESCOTT *Philip II*, I. viii. (1857) 146 Elizabeth received the offer of Philip's hand, qualified as it was, in the most gracious manner. **1883** *Contemp. Rev.* XLIII. 49 An avowal, which he qualifies by a subtle afterthought.

absol. **1838** LYTTON *Alice* XI. v, The surgeon..began to apologize—to qualify.

8. a. To moderate or mitigate, so as to reduce to a more satisfactory or normal condition; *esp.* to render less violent, severe or unpleasant; to lessen the force or effect of (something disagreeable).

Extremely common in the 16–17th c., with a great variety of objects; now somewhat rare in comparison with 12 b.

1543–4 *Act 35 Hen. VIII*, c. 5 The greate peril and dangier of the kynges maiesties subiectes, if the same statute shulde not..be tempered qualified or refourmed. **1547** BOORDE *Brev. Health* §170 Qualyfie the heate of the Lyuer ..with the confection of Acetose. **1578** T. N. tr. *Conq. W. India* 229 Our men stoode in great perill..if this war and mutenie had not soone bene qualified. **1608** WILLET *Hexapla Exod.* 688 The incense was..burned..to qualifie the smell..from the sacrifices of flesh. **1648** MARKHAM *Housew. Gard.* III. viii. (1668) 68 Camomile..is sweet smelling, qualifying head-ach. **1664** H. POWER *Exp. Philos.* III. 188 Something..that will abate and qualifie the rigour of this Conception. **1702** W. J. *Bruyn's Voy. Levant* xi. 51 This Civility of the Turks does in some measure qualify the Hardship of those who are confin'd Prisoners in that Castle. **1767** BLACKSTONE *Comm.* II. 147 Though they still are held at the will of the lord,..yet that will is qualified, restrained, and limited. **1827** SCOTT *Highl. Widow* v, A voice in which the authority of the mother was qualified by her tenderness. **1839** BAILEY *Festus* v, Qualifying every line which vice..writes on the brow. **1856** R. A. VAUGHAN *Mystics* (1860) I. v. i. 116 His sincere piety, his large heart,..always qualify, and seem sometimes to redeem, his errors.

†**b.** To make less wrong or reprehensible. *Obs.*

1749 FIELDING *Tom Jones* XIII. xii, The frame of her mind was too delicate to bear the thought of having been guilty of a falsehood, however qualified by circumstances. **1776** PAINE *Com. Sense* 76 It is..the invasion of our country..which conscientiously qualifies the use of arms.

†**c.** To make proportionate *to*; to reduce *to*. *Obs. rare.*

1548 UDALL, etc. *Erasm. Par. Luke* i. (R.), The Highest..tempering and qualifying his infinite power and vertue to the measure and capacitie of mannes nature. **1604** *Nottingham Rec.* IV. 272, 20 li. fyne was ymposed..which fyne was afterwardes..qualefied to iiij li. **1641** MILTON *Reform.* ii. 43 How to qualifie, and mould the sufferance and subjection of the people to the length of that foot that is to tread on their necks.

†**9.** To appease, calm, pacify (a person). *Obs.*

c **1540** tr. *Pol. Verg. Eng. Hist.* (Camden No. 29) 210 Withowt much adoe they began to mollyfy hir..When the quene was thus qualyfyed [etc.]. **1579–80** NORTH *Plutarch* (1676) 488 Sertorius..did qualifie him the best he could, and made him more mild and tractable. **1617** MIDDLETON & ROWLEY *Fair Quarrel* IV. i, When you have left him in a chafe, then I'll qualify the rascal. **1679** *Trials Green, Berry, &c.* 16 You being a Justice of the Peace may qualifie them [two men fighting].

†**10.** To bring into, or keep in, a proper condition; to control, regulate, modulate. *Obs.*

1579 LANGHAM *Gard. Health* (1633) 624 The decoction of the roots..doth qualifie the Liuer. **1606** SHAKS. *Tr. & Cr.* II. ii. 118 Is your blood So madly hot, that no discourse of reason..Can qualifie the same? **1647** N. BACON *Disc. Govt. Eng.* I. xvi. (1739) 30 This Election was qualified under a stipulation or covenant. **1688** PENTON *Guardian's Instruct.* (1897) 15 The practice of these Rules will help qualifie a Life of Action such as yours must be.

11. To modify the strength or flavour of (a liquid).

1591 NASHE *Prognostication* Wks. 1883–4 II. 152 A Cuppe of Sack,..so qualified with Suger, that they proue not rewmatick. **1633** T. ADAMS *Exp. 2 Peter* ii. 13 Poison may be qualified, and become medicinal. **1671** tr. *Frejus' Voy. Mauritania* 43 Having tasted the water,..we mixed it with a little Aqua vitæ, which we had brought with us instead of Wine, to qualifie it. **1748** SMOLLETT *Rod. Rand.* lvi, The Squire..called for his tea, which he drank..qualified with brandy. **1821** BYRON *Juan* IV. liii, Tea and coffee leave us much more serious, Unless when qualified with thee, Cogniac! **1840** DICKENS *Barn. Rudge* xlv, [He] qualified his mug of water with a plentiful infusion of the liquor.

fig. **1697** DRYDEN *Ess. Georgics* in *Virgil* (1721) I. 199 Greek..rightly mixt and qualified with the Doric Dialect.

12. †**a.** To affect (a person or thing) injuriously. Const. *with*. *Obs.* **b.** To abate or diminish (something good); to make less perfect or complete.

1584 R. SCOT *Discov. Witchcr.* III. xv. (1886) 50 Foure old witches, who with their charms so qualified the Danes as they were thereby disabled. **1602** SHAKS. *Ham.* IV. vii. 114 Loue is begun by Time: And..Time qualifies the sparke and fire of it. **1639** FULLER *Holy War* II. xvii. (1840) 72 To qualify the Christians' joy for this good success, Joceline..was conquered and taken prisoner. **1644** BULWER *Chiron.* 52 The standers by heartily wish their Hands qualified with some Chiragracall prohibition. **1860** TYNDALL *Glac.* I. xxvii. 209 Thoughts which tended to qualify the pleasure. **1870** DICKENS *E. Drood* viii, We had better not qualify our good understanding.

†**13.** *intr. to qualify on*, to submit quietly to. *to qualify with*, to come to terms with. *Obs.*

1754 RICHARDSON *Grandison* I. xxxiii. 230 What a slave had I been in spirit, could I have qualified on such villainous treatment. **1797–1805** S. & HT. LEE *Canterb. T.* V. 494 He ..qualifies with any passion which it is vicious to indulge.

qualifying (ˈkwɒlɪfaɪɪŋ), *vbl. sb.* [f. prec. + -ING[1].] The action of the vb. QUALIFY, in various senses.

1574 R. SCOT *Hop Gard.* (1578) Epistle, To deuise argument of priuate profit, to the qualifying of your charges. **1610** GUILLIM *Heraldry* III. vii. (1660) 135 The qualifying and allaying of the scorching heat of burning Agues. **1748** RICHARDSON *Clarissa* (1811) I. 124, I once thought a little qualifying among such violent spirits was not amiss. **1794** J. HUTTON *Philos. Light*, etc. 14 To suppose us knowing heat by any other means, besides its effect in the qualifying of bodies.

qualifying (ˈkwɒlɪfaɪɪŋ), *ppl. a.* [f. as prec. + -ING[2].] That qualifies, in senses of the vb.

1606 SHAKS. *Tr. & Cr.* IV. iv. 9 My loue admits no qualifying crosse [*usu. emend.* dross]. **1704** NORRIS *Ideal World* II. iii. 192 Something..so peculiarly qualifying and distinguishing. **1769** *Junius Lett.* xxxv. 160 A qualifying measure would not be accepted. **1812** SCOTT *Fam. Lett.* (1894) I. viii. 241 The good we meet with..is always blended with qualifying bitterness. **1890** *Athenæum* 26 Apr. 525/3 To pass a qualifying examination and to become a teacher. **1892** H. SWEET *New Eng. Gram.* I. §36. 15 When attribute-words are used in this way [*sc.* as in *give me that red book, not the blue one*], we call them *qualifying attribute-words.* **1924** O. JESPERSEN *Philos. Gram.* viii. 108 The most important of these [classes of adjuncts] undoubtedly is the one composed of what may be called *restrictive* or *qualifying adjuncts.* **1925** GRATTAN & GURREY *Our Living Lang.* xvii. 103 But it is not only variety of gender which distinguishes these qualifying nouns from Substantives. In many languages some of them have special distinguishing suffixes. *Ibid.* xli. 261 *Expansion in the Subject:*—..(*b*) Qualifying Phrases. **1939** G. H. MCKNIGHT et al. *Gram. Living Eng.* x. 102 By the use of qualifying words, the common noun *man* ..might be so narrowed in meaning as to refer to one definite individual. **1975** R. A. CLOSE *Ref. Gram.* ii. 66 *Qualifying clauses*..These qualify the main clause, in the sense of limiting its application to specific cases.

Hence ˈ**qualifyingly** *adv.*

1831 BLAKEY *Free-will* 109 They qualifyingly admit its force, by calling it a difficulty.

†**qualimeter** (kwɒˈlɪmɪtə(r)). *Radiology. Obs.* [f. QUALI(TY *sb.* + -METER.] An apparatus for measuring the penetrating power of a beam of X-rays.

1911 H. BAUER in *Arch. Roentgen Ray* XV. 308 Whether this Roentgen Qualimeter, as we may call it, has all the requisites for the standard measure of hardness so much sought for by every Roentgenologist is a question which I must leave for others. **1915** R. KNOX *Radiography* 58 It is here that the qualimeter is particularly useful, since different degrees of hardness are required for the production of good pictures of various parts of the body. **1926** P. K. BOWES *X-Ray Apparatus* x. 96 This qualimeter can only be used with any degree of success with one installation, using the same X-ray tube all the time, and never altering the rate of interruptions.

qualisign (ˈkwɒlɪsaɪn). *Philos.* [f. QUALI(TY + SIGN *sb.*] A term originally used by C. S. Peirce in his theory of signs (see quot. *c* 1903).

c **1903** C. S. PEIRCE *Coll. Papers* (1932) II. 142 Signs are divisible by three trichotomies; first, according as the sign itself is a mere quality, is an actual existent, or is a general law... A sign may be termed a *Qualisign*, a *Sinsign*, or a *Legisign*... A Qualisign is a quality which is a Sign. It cannot actually act as a sign until it is embodied; but the embodiment has nothing to do with its character as a sign. **1934** *Mind* XLIII. 496 The specific quality of voice by which I recognise a friend (a qualisign) must be embodied in some particular event. **1936** *Jrnl. Philos.* 17 Dec. 702 It is pretty plain that Miss Stebbing means by 'type-word' what we call a 'word' and she does not recognize our category of 'word-type' or Peirce's 'qualisign'. **1966** J. J. FITZGERALD *Peirce's Theory of Signs* iii. 65 The division into Qualisign, Sinsign, and Legisign, is based on the mode of existence of the sign vehicle, not on any relationship within the triad.

ˈ**qualitated,** *pa. pple. rare.* [f. L. type **quālitāt-us* + -ED[1].] = QUALITIED.

1662 J. CHANDLER *Van Helmont's Oriat.* 167 Moystness, and dryness are rather very Bodies themselves qualitated or endowed with qualities. **1949** *Mind* LVIII. 54 The succession of somatic fields which go to constitute a single somatic sense-history may be..uniformly qualitated.

qualitative (ˈkwɒlɪtətɪv), *a.* [ad. late L. *quālitātīv-us* (Cassiodorus): see QUALITY and -IVE. Cf. F. *qualitatif, -ive* (15th c.).]

a. Relating to, connected or concerned with, quality or qualities. Now usually in implied or expressed opposition to QUANTITATIVE.

1607 COLLINS *Serm.* (1608) 5 Fourthly, qualitative, from the dispositions of the persons themselves. **1652** GAULE *Magastrom.* 49 What have the qualitative influxes of the planets..there to doe? *a* **1703** BURKITT *On N.T.* Rom. xii. 2 This conversion and renovation is not a substantial, but a qualitative change. **1881** WESTCOTT & HORT *Grk. N.T.* II. 44 A numerical preponderance may have rightly to yield to a qualitative preponderance.

b. *Chem. qualitative analysis*, identification of the constituents (as elements, ions, or functional groups, etc.) present in a substance. Cf. *quantitative analysis* s.v. QUANTITATIVE *a.* 3 b.

1842 PARNELL *Chem. Anal.* (1845) 2 An examination..which does not develope more than the nature or quality of the constituents, is termed a qualitative analysis. **1923** R. M. CAVEN *Quantitative Chem. Anal.* I. 19 Often the methods of qualitative analysis are available for the quantitative separation of metals in solution. **1953** E. C. PIGOTT *Ferrous Anal.* (ed. 2) 13 The spectrograph is reliable, not merely for the rapid identification of materials, but also for a preliminary qualitative analysis, including trace elements. **1956** SIGGIA & STOLTEN *Introd. Mod. Org. Anal.* iii. 51 In the classical scheme of organic qualitative analysis, the derivatives prepared were characterized by their melting points and the identification was complete when a satisfactory mixed melting point was obtained with the derivative of a known material. **1964** CHERONIS & MA *Org. Functional Group Anal.* i. 3 Qualitative organic analysis aims to identify one or more organic compounds present in an unknown.

Hence ˈ**qualitatively** *adv.*, in respect of quality.

1681 FLAVEL *Meth. Grace* vi. 128 Faith may be considered qualitatively, as a saving grace. **1845** G. E. DAY tr. *Simon's Anim. Chem.* I. 321 The composition of the blood is here qualitatively changed. **1862** H. SPENCER *First Princ.* I. iv. §26 (1875) 90 In consciousness the Unlimited and the Indivisible are qualitatively distinct.

qualitied (ˈkwɒlɪtɪd), *a.* or *ppl. a.* Also 6–7 **qualited.** [f. QUALITY *sb.* or *v.* + -ED.] Furnished with a quality or qualities, in various senses of the sb. (Freq. in 17th c.; chiefly as predicate, and with qualifying adv.).

1600 HAKLUYT *Voy.* II. ii. 194 They were so well qualited in courage, experience, and discretion. **1616** T. SCOTT *Christs Politician* 11 Those men..are conditioned and qualited like sheepe, innocent, harmelesse, simple. **1656** STANLEY *Hist. Philos.* I. VIII. 112 In things properly qualited there is augmentation and diminution. **1728** MORGAN *Algiers* II. iv. 286 The mildest, the best qualitied..Prince that ever existed. **1783** JOHNSON in *Boswell* 23 Mar., Lord Southwell was the highest-bred man..the most qualitied I ever saw. **1865** J. GROTE *Moral Ideals* (1876) 187 The mind is a qualitied unity. **1889** *Harper's Mag.* Jan. 184/2 A dainty hand, and small,..and qualitied Divinely.

Hence ˈ**qualitiedness.** *rare.*

1865 J. GROTE *Explor. Philos.* I. 110 Form of the higher description..quality or qualitiedness. **1940** *Mind* XLIX. 321 My present treatment is thus concerned rather with 'qualitiedness' than with 'quality'.

qualitive, erron. f. QUALITATIVE. *rare*[−1].

1846 J. BAXTER *Libr. Pract. Agric.* (ed. 4) I. 48 The one is called qualitive,..The other is quantitive.

quality (ˈkwɒlɪtɪ), *sb.* Forms: 4–7 **-ite**, 4–5 **-itee**, 6 **-yte**, **-itye**, 6–7 **-itie**, 7 **quall-**, 6– **quality.** [ME. *qualite*, a. F. *qualité* (12th c.), ad. L. *quālitāt-em* (formed by Cicero to render Gr. ποιότης), f. *quālis* of what kind: see -ITY.]

I. Of persons (in 1 and 2 occas. of animals).

1. a. Character, disposition, nature. Now *rare*.

c **1290** *S. Eng. Leg.* I. 312/433 Þe planetes..ȝiuen him also qualite to don so and so. *Ibid.* 435 Swuch qualite..to beon lechor oþur schrewe. **1390** GOWER *Conf.* I. Prol. 35 Thus of his propre qualite The man..Is as a world. **1535** LYNDESAY *Satyre* 247, I knaw, be ȝour qualitie ȝe want the gift of chastitie. **1553** BRENDE *Q. Curtius* 25 He vsed to euery nacion sondry exhortacions as he thought mete for their disposicions and qualitie. *a* **1578** LINDESAY (Pitscottie) *Chron. Scot.* (S.T.S.) I. 10 Knawin[g] of women..That thay are not constant in thair quallitie. **1632** LITHGOW *Trav.* VI. 298 A Dromidore, and Camel differ much in quality. **1639** FORD *Lady's Trial* III. iii, He deserves no wife Of worthy quality, who dares not trust Her virtue in..any danger. **1847** EMERSON *Poems* (1857) 94 They her heralds be, Steeped in her quality. **1873** BROWNING *Red Cott. Nt.-*

cap 268 Her quality was, caterpillar-like, To..select a leaf And..feed her fill.

b. Capacity, ability, or skill, in some respect.

In mod. use as an echo of Shaks., who prob. intended the word in sense 5.

[**1602** Shaks. *Ham.* II. ii. 452 Come giue vs a tast of your quality: come, a passionate speech.] **1856** Kane *Arct. Expl.* I. ii. 24 Hans had given me a touch of his quality by spearing a bird on the wing. **1863** Doran *Ann. Stage* 369 Thomas.. gave the stranger a hearty welcome,..asked for a taste of his quality. **1871** Browning *Pr. Hohenst.* 1165 Can't you contrive to operate at once,..to shew Your quality i' the world.

c. Without article or poss. pron.: Excellence of disposition; good natural gifts. (Cf. 9 c.)

1606 Shaks. *Tr. & Cr.* IV. iv. 78 The Grecian youths are full of qualitie, Their louing well compos'd, with guift of nature. **1607** Heywood *Wom. Killed* II. i, O, sir, disparage not your worth too much; You are full of quality and faire desert. **1889** Tyrwhitt in *Universal Rev.* 15 Feb. 251 One sharp temptation well resisted..shows real moral quality. **1894** Sir Ev. Wood in *Daily News* 1 Oct. 6/2 [Capt. Peel] had a singularly striking appearance, showing both in face and figure what is termed, in describing well-bred horses, as 'quality'.

2. a. A mental or moral attribute, trait, or characteristic; a feature of one's character; †a habit.

1533 Frith *Answ. More* To Rdr., Wks. (1573) 4 A frende beholdeth all qualities and circumstaunces, his byrth, bringyng vp, and what feates hee hath done all hys lyfe long. **1551** R. Robinson tr. *More's Utop.* Ep. Cecil (Arb.) 15 Youre godlye dysposytyon, and vertuous qualytyes. **1602** Marston *Ant. & Mel.* III. Wks. 1856 I. 43, I hate not man, but man's lewd qualities. **1689–90** Temple *Ess. Heroic Virtue* Wks. 1731 I. 208 Particular Qualities have been observed..in the same Families for several hundred Years, as Goodness, Clemency [etc.]. **1783** Cowper *Valediction* 31 In thee some virtuous qualities combine To fit thee for a nobler part. **1849** Macaulay *Hist. Eng.* vii. II. 163 Nature had largely endowed William with the qualities of a great ruler. **1853** J. H. Newman *Hist. Sk.* (1876) I. [II.] I. i. 30 The subtlety and perfidy, which..were the qualities of his ..countrymen.

b. An accomplishment or attainment.

1584 Lyly *Campaspe* v. i, *Diog.* What can thy sons do? *Syl.* You shall see their qualities. Dance, sirrah! **1607** Shaks. *Timon* I. i. 125, I haue bred her at my deerest cost In Qualities of the best. *a* **1674** Clarendon (J.), He had those qualities of horsemanship, dancing and fencing which accompany a good breeding. **1780** Cowper *Progr. Err.* 423 A just deportment, manners graced with ease,..Are qualities that seem to comprehend [etc.]. **1882** *Daily Tel.* 17 May, The fielding..justified the high reputation for this quality which the..colonial teams..have enjoyed.

c. *Law.* A special or characteristic feature.

1818 Cruise *Digest* (ed. 2) I. 155 A tenant in tail..has eight qualities or privileges.

3. a. Rank or position in (a) society. Now *rare.*

a **1400–50** *Alexander* 3303 Lo! so þe quele of qwitsumnes my qualite has changid. **1456** Sir G. Haye *Law Arms* (S.T.S.) 162 To consider..the state and the qualitee of the persouns. **1571** G. Buchanan *Admonition* (S.T.S.) 21 It may seame..that I..pas myne estait, being of sa meane qualitie. **1604** E. G[rimstone] *D'Acosta's Hist. Indies* v. viii. 350 Sometimes this minister had other different habites, according to the quallitie of the dead. **1676** Hobbes *Iliad* Pref. (1686) 2, Readers of Poesie (which are commonly Persons of the best Quality). **1726** De Foe *Hist. Devil* II. v. (1840) 235 The priests of Apollo were sometimes of no mean quality. **1823** Scott *Peveril* i, A gentleman of middling quality. **1873** Browning *Red Cott. Nt.-cap* 1528 What quality, what style and title, eh?

fig. **1791** Wolcott (P. Pindar) *Remonstrance* Wks. 1812 II. 453 Hunger..Is reckon'd now a fellow of bad quality: Not deem'd a gentleman.

†b. *concr.* A body of persons of a certain rank. *Obs. rare*⁻¹.

1636 E. Dacres tr. *Machiavel's Disc. Livy* I. 16 It was compos'd only of two of these forenamed qualities, that is to say, of the Principality and Nobility.

4. a. Nobility, high birth or rank, good social position; chiefly in phr. ***man, woman, gentleman, lady, person, people of quality.*** Now *arch.*

1579–80 North *Plutarch* (1595) 875 He had all the men of qualitie his sworne enemies. **1625** Bacon *Ess., Trav.* (Arb.) 523 Let him..procure Recommendation, to some person of Quality. **1671** Lady Mary Bertie in *12th Rep. Hist. MSS. Comm.* App. v. 22 There are no men of quality but the Duke of Monmouth; all the rest are gentlemen. **1699** M. Lister *Journey to Paris* 180 A Lady of Quality, Madam M——.. askt me, What I had seen in Paris that most pleased me. **1712** [see people *sb.* 6 b]. **1722** De Foe *Col. Jack* (1840) 18 My new friend was a thief of quality, and a pickpocket above the ordinary rank. **1771** Mackenzie *Man. Feel.* xl. (1803) 85 The count, for he was of quality, was solicitous to return the obligation. **1849** Macaulay *Hist. Eng.* viii. II. 273 Many persons of quality sate the whole day in their carriages. **1871** Morley *Vauvenargues* in *Crit. Misc.* Ser. I. (1878) 9 High enough to command the admiration of people of quality. **1922** M. Arlen *Piracy* II. i. 69 I'd forgotten that such a phrase was ever made by fine men for fine women—a woman of quality!

b. *concr.* People of good social position. Now *dial.* or rather *arch.*

1693 *Humours Town* 114 Walk Bare-headed to his Master's Daughter, in imitation of Quality. **1706** Estcourt *Fair Examp.* v. i, Did not you tell me..that you was acquainted with all the Quality. **1712** P. Metcalf *Life St. Winefride* (1917) 82 He and his Son..received the Holy Sacrament of Baptism, at which the greatest Quality of that County were pleased to stand *Patrines.* **1753** Richardson *Sir C. Grandison* III. ii. (1781) 15, I have looked out among the quality for a future husband for her. **1769** Wesley in *Wks.* 1872 III. 370 A large company of Quality (as they called them) came. **1824** Byron *Juan* XVI. lxiv, She was country born and bred And knew no better..Than to wax white—for blushes are for quality. **1843** Lever *J. Hinton* xl, I was standing..among all the grand generals and the quality. **1853** Mrs. Gaskell *Cranford* xiv. 270 He's dazed at being called on to speak before quality. **1889** *John Bull* 2 Mar. 142/2 He was fond of quality, and quality was very fond o' him. **1894** 'Mark Twain' in *Century Mag.* Feb. 550 He wuz the highest quality in dis whole town—ole Virginny stock. Fust famblies, he wuz. **1904** M. Corelli *God's Good Man* (ed. 2) xxii. 415 The quality don't seem to care for no one 'cept theirselves. **1961** *Times* 25 Apr. 20/1 In the period of his second marriage Opie..never lacked sitters among the 'quality'. **1978** M. Kenyon *Deep Pocket* xiv. 184 A grouse-shoot, lad... It's a country sport for the quality.

†5. a. Profession, occupation, business, *esp.* that of an actor. **b.** Fraternity; those of the same profession; *esp.* actors as a body. *Obs.*

1500–20 Dunbar *Poems* xxxiv. 88 The rest of craftis gryt aithis swair..Ilk ane into thair qualitie. **1591** Shaks. *Two Gent.* IV. i. 58 A Linguist, and a man of such perfection, As we doe in our quality much want. **1603** J. Davies *Microcosmos* 215 Players, I love yee, and your Qualitie. **1625** Fletcher *Fair Maid of Inn* v. ii, I am weary of this trade of fortune-telling,..it is a very ticklish quality. **1626** Massinger *Rom. Actor* I. iii, In thee, as being the chief of thy profession, I do accuse the quality of treason. **1633** in A. W. Ward *Hist. Dram. Lit.* II. 324 It may serve..for the improvement of the quality, which hath received some brushings of late.

c. Party, side. *Obs. rare*⁻¹.

1596 Shaks. *1 Hen. IV*, IV. iii. 36 Because you are not of our qualitie, But stand against vs like an Enemie.

6. a. Title, description, character, capacity. Freq. in phr. ***in (the) quality of.*** Now *rare.*

a **1300** *Cursor M.* 26682 Man agh to telle hir qualite, sib or freind or quat sco be. *a* **1626** Bacon *Advice to Villiers* (J.), The attorney of the dutchy of Lancaster partakes of both qualities, partly of a judge..and partly of an attorney general. *a* **1648** Ld. Herbert *Hen. VIII* (1683) 38 Maximilian..came to the King, in the quality of his Soldier. **1664** Butler *Hud.* II. iii. 338 He serv'd his Master In quality of Poetaster. **1711** Addison *Spect.* No. 127 ¶1 Such Packets as I receive under the Quality of Spectator. **1734** tr. *Rollin's Anc. Hist.* (1827) IX. 66 They paid respect to his quality of deputy. **1821** Scott *Kenilw.* xxx, Leicester..rode on her Majesty's right hand..in quality of her host. **1864** D. G. Mitchell *Sev. Stor.* 82 To understand that I had come in the professed quality of Consul.

†b. A part or character (acted). *Obs. rare*⁻¹.

1566 Adlington *Apuleius* 109 When the people was desirous to see me play qualities, they caused the gates to be shutte, and such as entred in shoulde pay.

II. Of things.

7. a. An attribute, property, special feature or characteristic. ***primary, secondary,*** etc. ***qualities:*** see the adjs. Of a ship: (see quot. 1867).

1340 *Ayenb.* 153 To þe bodye of man comeþ alle eueles uor þe destempringe of þise uour qualites oþer of þise uour humours. **1533** Elyot *Cast. Helthe* (1539) 33 a, But nowe to the qualities of water. **1551** Turner *Herbal* I. A iv b, The qualites of it answer nothing unto the qualyties of wormwode pontyke in Galene. **1604** E. G[rimstone] *D'Acosta's Hist. Indies* vi. xiii. 459 According to the qualities and wealth of the Countrie. **1671** R. Bohun *Wind* 165 The judgment to be made concerning the Qualitys of Winds..is very various and fallible. **1725** Watts *Logic* I. iii. §4 Ideas, with Regard to their Qualities,..are either clear and distinct, or obscure and confused [etc.]. **1854** L. Lloyd *Scandinavian Adv.* I. 231 The eatable qualities of the Bothnian salmon. **1867** Smyth *Sailor's Word-bk., Qualities,* the register of the ship's trim, sailing, stowage, &c., all of which are necessary to her *behaviour.* **1872** Ruskin *Eagle's N.* §236 Every high quality of art consists either in some expression of what is decent..or of what is bright.

†b. A manner, style. (Cf. 9 b.) *Obs. rare.*

1596 Shaks. *Merch. V.* III. ii. 6 Hate counsailes not in such a qualitie. **1651** *Fuller's Abel Rediv., Cowper* (1867) II. 307 The parishioners..built and adorned the church in as good a quality as any round about it.

†c. A habit; a power or faculty. *Obs. rare.*

1647 Fuller *Good Th. in Worse T.* (1841) 98 Jordan had a quality in the first month to overflow all his banks. **1663** Gerbier *Counsel* b iij a, If it had a speaking quality, your Grace would hear its..Alembick sing the Gold its joy.

†d. Concretely: A substance of a certain nature; an essence. *Obs. rare.*

1704 Swift *Batt. Bk.* Misc. (1711) 257 An atramentous Quality, of most malignant Nature, was seen to distil from his Lips. **1823** J. Badcock *Dom. Amusem.* 21 The wood.. throws out its volatile qualities, aquæous and acidulous, into the respective tubes.

8. a. The nature, kind, or character (*of* something). Now restricted to cases in which there is comparison (expressed or implied) with other things of the same kind; hence, the degree or grade of excellence, etc. possessed by a thing. †***in the quality of:*** (cf. 6). *spec.* in phr. ***the quality of life.***

c **1374** Chaucer *Troylus* III. Prol. 31 Ye knowe al þilke couered qualite Of þing which þat folk on wondren so. *c* **1400** Maundev. (Roxb.) xiii. 59 A man may gyffe no couenable penaunce bot if he knawe þe qualitee and þe quantitee of þe synne. **1509** Hawes *Past. Pleas.* XXIII. (Percy Soc.) 106 After the qualyte it doth take effecte. **1570** Dee *Math. Pref.* 8 An other liquid Medicine I haue: whose Qualitie is heate, in the first degree. **1650** Baxter *Saints' R.* I. iv. (1662) 22 It is so little I know of mine own soul, either its quiddity or quality. **1697** Dryden *Virg. Georg.* III. 237 This flying Plague (to mark its quality;) Oestros the Grecians call. **1794** J. Hutton *Philos. Light,* etc. 272 This principle of fire moves, in the quality of light, with the most amazing velocity. **1841–4** Emerson *Ess., Prudence* Wks. (Bohn) I. 95 There is more difference in the quality of our pleasures than in the amount. **1842** Miss Mitford in L'Estrange *Life* (1870) III. ix. 142 The perfection of cunning is to conceal its own quality. **1879** Harlan *Eyesight* viii. 114 It is on account of the quality, rather than the size, of English print, that it is usually so much pleasanter to read than American. **1943** J. B. Priestley *Daylight on Saturday* xxxi. 253 The plans already..maturing that would give all our citizens more security, better opportunities, and a nobler quality of life. **1955** E. Sevareid *Newsmakers* (CBS Radio broadcast script) 30 Nov. (Sevareid MS. Collection, Library of Congress) 6 He [*sc.* Adlai Stevenson] seems disturbed about the *quality* of American life, when most politicians measure it only in quantity. [**1955** A. Stevenson *Let.* 13 Dec. (Sevareid MS. Collection, Library of Congress), I have..read Sevareid Newsmakers CBS Radio, November 30, 1955... Your summarization of my anxieties about America and its *quality* was the tonic I needed for some more utterances along that line.] **1956** A. Schlesinger in *N.Y. Times Mag.* 4 Mar. 60/3 The liberal's belief in working for change does..mean that he feels history can never stand still, that social change can better the quality of people's lives and happiness, and that the margin of change, however limited, is worth the effort. **1969** *Guardian* 5 Aug. 8/1 A Government which says it concerns itself with the quality of life..cannot be without a broadcasting policy. **1972** J. Mann *Mrs Knox's Profession* ii. 7 Vic was going to make a corner in housing, and the quality of life, which he had..worked out would be closest to the hearts of his constituents. **1977** M. Edelman *Polit. Lang.* viii. 151 The consequence is a decline in the quality of life, springing from a lowering of real income. **1979** *Nature* 24 May 311/2 Monitoring of trace constituents of the atmosphere is becoming increasingly important because of the implications on the quality of life of growing concentrations of several compounds which, after industrial use, are released to the atmosphere.

†b. Nature, with reference to origin; hence, cause, occasion. *Obs. rare.*

1606 Shaks. *Tr. & Cr.* IV. i. 44 Giue him note of our approach, With the whole quality whereof, I feare We shall be much vnwelcome. **1607** —— *Timon* III. vi. 117 Know you the quality of Lord Timons fury?

c. *ellipt.* for ***quality newspaper*** (see sense 13 below).

1970 *Guardian Weekly* 25 July 11 The 'qualities'..need to earn a greater percentage of their income from advertising than the 'populars', which rely more heavily on mass sales. **1976** *Times* 18 Mar. 4/1 The 'qualities' are the *Daily* and *Sunday Telegraph, Financial Times, Guardian, Observer, The Times* and *Sunday Times.* **1977** *Vole* I. 26/2 Many of the qualities' journalists are good writers.

9. Without article: **a.** That aspect of things under which they are considered in thinking or speaking of their nature, condition, or properties.

The notion of quality includes all the attributes of a thing, except those of relation and quantity. 'Quality' is the third of the Aristotelian categories.

1533 Elyot *Cast. Helthe* (1539) 16 b, Qualitie..is the state thereof, as Hotte or cold, moist or dry. **1656** Stanley *Hist. Philos.* I. v. 70 If quality be void of matter, it must likewise be void of corporeity. **1727** Chambers *Cycl.* s.v., The antient school-philosophers distinguish quality in the general..into essential and accidental. **1829** Jas. Mill *Hum. Mind* (1869) II. xiv. II. 60 Quality is used as the generical name of every thing in objects, for which a separate notation is required. **1884** tr. *Lotze's Metaph.* 45 The question is renewed as to the actual essence which..lies behind this surface of Quality.

b. *Gram.* Manner of action (cf. 7 b), as denoted by an adverb; chiefly in phr. ***adverb of quality.***

1530 Palsgr. Introd. 38 The frenche men..forme theyr adverbes of qualite by addynge to of *ment. Ibid.* 144 Some [adverbs] betoken qualite, and serve to declare..howe a dede is done. *a* **1637** B. Jonson *Eng. Gram.* I. xxi, All adverbs of quality..being formed from nouns, for the most part, by adding *ly.* **1845** Stoddart in *Encycl. Metrop.* (1847) I. 122/1 There is no difference in grammatical use between ..an adverb of quantity, and an adverb of quality. **1872** Morris *Engl. Accid.* xiv. 193.

c. Peculiar excellence or superiority. (Cf. 1 c.)

1874 Tyrwhitt *Sketch. Club* 255 Quality of colour means purity or truth of hue. **1891** *Speaker* 2 May 533/1 The book ..has..more quality and distinction than four-fifths of the novels which come under our notice.

10. In special uses (of senses 8 and 9).

a. *Logic.* Of propositions: The condition of being affirmative or negative. Of concepts: Comparative clearness or distinctness.

1594 Blundevil *Arte Logicke* III. i. (Cent.), How is a simple proposition divided according to qualitie? Into an affirmative and negative proposition. **1697** tr. *Burgersdicius his Logic* I. xxx. 117 In Regard of Quality, it is that an Enunciation is divided..into Affirming and Denying. **1725** Watts *Logic* (1726) 156 If two Universals differ in Quality they are Contraries. **1837–8** Sir W. Hamilton *Lect. Logic* ix. (1860) I. 158 It is this perfection or imperfection which constitutes the logical Quality of a concept. **1843** Mill *Logic* II. ii. §1 (1856) 189 What are called the quantity and quality of the propositions. **1864** Bowen *Logic* v. 120 We thus ascertain the Quality of the Judgment, or whether it is affirmative or negative.

b. *Law.* Of an estate: The manner in which it is to be held or enjoyed.

1818 Cruise *Digest* (ed. 2) II. 354 The alteration in the particular estate, which would destroy a contingent remainder, must amount to an alteration in its quantity, and not in its quality. **1841** *Penny Cycl.* XIX. 46/1.

c. *Physics.* That which distinguishes sounds quantitatively the same; timbre.

1865 *Q. Jrnl. Sc.* 592 Though [certain sounds are] the same for musical purposes, in all other respects the quality is different. **1872** Huxley *Phys.* vii. 183 The quality of a voice—treble, bass, tenor, &c. **1881** Broadhouse *Mus. Acoustics* 77 The most uncultivated ear would perceive a difference of quality.

d. *Engin.* The proportion by weight of vapour in a mixture of vapour and the parent liquid.

1898 H. A. GOLDING *Theta-Phi Diagram* iv. 52 (*in figure*) Dryness fraction or quality curve. **1937** CROFT & PURDY *Steam Boilers* (ed. 2) iii. 24 The quality of steam in average practice is..from about 97 to 99 per cent. **1977** G. F. HEWITT in Butterworth & Hewitt *Two-Phase Flow & Heat Transfer* ii. 24 Data on flow patterns for a particular geometry and fluid pair can be plotted directly in terms of the velocities, flow rates, etc. of the phases. Alternatively, it is often convenient for a single-component fluid to plot the results in terms of mass flux *G* and quality *x*.

e. *Radiology*. The penetrating power of a beam of X-rays.

1903 PUSEY & CALDWELL *Pract. Applic. Röntgen Rays* II. v. 309 The quality of the rays and their intensity vary greatly. **1928** B. J. LEGGETT *Theory & Pract. Radiol.* II. vi. 162 The more or less exact measurement of the quality of X-radiation is of importance in all branches of radiotherapy. **1968** M. B. HOLLANDER *Ultrasoft X Rays* i. 3 Most articles published since about 1940 have stated quality in terms of half-value layer. **1972** BARNES & REES *Conc. Textbk. Radiotherapy* vii. 154 The choice of the radiation quality is determined by the site and the size of the lesion.

f. The degree to which reproduced sound resembles the original; fidelity.

1913 G. F. ROWELL *Hints about Gramophone* 9 He revels in the loudest records he can buy, and so long as the noise is satisfactory the musical quality does not trouble him in the least. **1938** A. E. GREENLEES *Amplification & Distribution of Sound* xvi. 230 The sales literature of manufacturers will provide much useful information as to what may be expected in the way of quality of reproduction. **1971** J. EARL *Pickups & Loudspeakers* i. 9 The tape element involved in the production of a disc record detracts very little from the overall quality these days.

11. A particular class, kind, or grade of anything, as determined by its quality.

1835 URE *Philos. Manuf.* 324, 2*s.* 5*d.* for spinning the same quality. **1866** G. MACDONALD *Ann. Q. Neighb.* xiii. (1878) 253 A quality of dialogue which indicated thought.

III. †12. = QUALIFICATION 1. *Sc. Obs. rare.*

1622 *Burgh Rec. Aberdeen* (Spald. Cl.) II. 375 The said Mr. James Ross..acceptit of the said stipend with the qualitie and conditioun aboue mentioned. **1714** W. FORBES *Jrnl. Sess.* Pref. 7 Advocates admitted with a quality that they should not take in hand to plead in any..difficult cause without..assistance.

IV. 13. a. *attrib.* and *Comb.* (chiefly sense 4), as ***quality-acquaintance, -air, -blood, -end, -friend, gentleman, horse, lady, living, -pride, -white***, etc.; ***quality-like, -mad***, adjs.; (sense 8) ***quality mark***; ***quality-tested*** adj.; (sense 9 c) ***quality audience, food, note, producer***; *spec.* = of a high cultural standard, esp. of newspapers, as ***quality magazine, newspaper, paper, press, programme, publisher, Sunday***, etc.; **quality-binding**, a kind of worsted tape for binding carpets (Jam. 1808); **quality circle**, a group of employees (orig. in Japanese industry) who meet to consider ways of resolving problems and improving production in their organization; **quality control**, the maintenance of the desired quality in a manufactured product, esp. by means of critical examination of a proportion of the output and its comparison with the specification; also *transf.*; freq. *attrib.*; hence **quality controller**, one whose responsibility this is; **quality factor** = Q III. 3.

1751 SMOLLETT *Per. Pic.* (1779) III. lxxxii. 274 Peregrine found some ladies of his quality-acquaintance. **1701** FARQUHAR *Sir H. Wildair* II. i. Wks. (Rtldg.) 545, I thought something was the matter; I wanted of quality-air. **1938** *Time* 10 Oct. 43/1 It has a fairly large and very vociferous 'quality' audience. **1837** CARLYLE *Fr. Rev.* II. II. ii, Young ..men, with quality-blood in them, poisoned with quality-pride. **1980** *Time* 28 Jan. 65/2 On the premise that the workers often know best, the firms are forming 'quality circles'. These are groups of five to 13 employees who volunteer to gather for perhaps an hour each week, on company time, in brainstorming sessions that focus on what can be done to improve output per hour worked. **1984** *Listener* 21 June 13/2 The current vogue for 'quality circles' *à la japonaise* is no more than recognition of the need..for harnessing the creativity, commitment and energy of ordinary managers and workers. **1935** E. S. PEARSON (*title*) The application of statistical methods to industrial standardisation and quality control. **1943** R. E. WAREHAM in J. F. Young *Materials & Processes* xviii. 589 Quality control methods are based on the laws of probability and statistics. **1968** *Brit. Med. Bull.* XXIV. 220/1 Examination of the batch mean has proved to be one of the most valuable quality-control measures available. **1971** *Physics Bull.* July 383/3 Specialist papers were less favoured for the conference and there appeared to be a need for better 'quality control' of these. **1977** P. JOHNSON *Enemies of Society* xi. 158 This forced academic growth leads to an inevitable collapse of quality-control. **1978** *Jrnl. R. Soc. Arts.* CXXVI. 670/2 The result was anarchism, disorder, inadequate production planning, cost and quality control and performance rating. **1972** M. JONES *Life on Dole* II. vii. 126 His next employer was Hoover... He became a quality controller. **1819** *Metropolis* III. 149 The quality-end of the town. **1947** *Electronic Circuits & Tubes* i. 17 The ratio of the series reactance to the series resistance of a reactor is defined as *Q*, its quality factor. **1967** CONDON & ODISHAW *Handbk. Physics* (ed. 2) IV. vii. 108/1 Frequently the inverse of the loss tangent, the quality factor *Q* of the dielectric,..serves as the figure of merit, especially in waveguide problems. **1971** *Nature* 24 Dec. 461/1 Recent measurements of the quality factor, *Q*, for mechanical vibrations generated by dropping parts of the Apollo lunar module and by moonquakes indicate that the *Q* of the Moon for these vibrations is of the order of 3,000. **1961** *Wine & Food* Winter 240 Shoppers should..be well aware of the quality food that comes from their own farmers and growers. **1751** SMOLLETT *Per. Pic.* (1779) II. lxviii. 238 The influence of Peregrine's new quality-friends. **1908** J. M. SULLIVAN *Criminal Slang* 1 *A quality gentleman*, a gentleman by birth and education. **1891** *Field* 7 Mar. 334/2 Quite a quality horse is Gratian. **1706** ESTCOURT *Fair Examp.* I. i. 10 Your Quality Lady, when she speaks, 'tis thus. **1594** CAREW *Huarte's Exam. Wits* vi. (1596) 77 Neither the vnderstanding, nor any other accident, can be qualiti-like. **1784** R. BAGE *Barham Downs* I. 233 My Lady's passion for quality living. **1768** *Woman of Honor* I. 134 She is so stark quality-mad. **1941** *Times* 22 May (Advt.), Issued by The National Magazine Company Limited..who publish such quality magazines as 'Good Housekeeping', 'Harper's Bazaar', 'Connoisseur', etc. **1954** W. FAULKNER *Fable* 352 The quality-mark and warrant of man's immortality: his deathless folly. **1959** *New Statesman* 14 Mar. 362/3 Independent consumer guidance—i.e., journals, quality marks, labelling, etc.—is, they say, unnecessary because advertising already provides adequate information about goods. **1971** *Gloss. Terms Materials Handling* (*B.S.I.*) v. 32 *Quality mark*, a mark which appears on some of the links of higher tensile or alloy steel chain, defining its grade. **1956** *English* Summer 48 Quality newspapers decline alarmingly, serious journals go bankrupt. **1961** *Punch* 11 Jan. 88/2 Whitbreads, for example, is the beer most favoured by forward-looking Pops [i.e. Pop People]. The advertising strikes a 'quality' note. **1962** *Listener* 11 Oct. 569/2 You can see such reporting even in the so-called quality papers. **1960** Quality press [see *quality programme* below]. **1837** Quality pride [see *quality blood* above]. **1936** *Economist* 8 Feb. 314/1 Firms in.. country towns—whose recent progress has been based on lower wage scales than those paid by the 'quality' producers in the leading centres. **1960** *Guardian* 9 Dec. 12/6 Ideally.. the union would like to see..'quality' programmes analogous to the 'quality' press. **1961** *Ibid.* 20 Oct. 11/4 The struggle between the commercial and the quality publisher is fierce. **1961** *Punch* 11 Jan. 86/3 When may a young man be said to have arrived?.. Having his name used as a pun in a quality Sunday paper's erudite crossword puzzle. **1974** *Times* 22 May 20/6 The quality dailies have done rather better than the popular journals... Quality Sundays are up 23 per cent. **1938** *Encycl. Brit. Bk. of Year* 636/2 Guaranteed quality-tested rayon fabrics. **1974** *Times* 15 Aug. (India Suppl.) p. viii/3 (Advt.), India's cottons..are quality tested. **1966** K. L. MORGAN in A. Dundes *Mother Wit* (1973) 603/1, I never questioned the implication that.. my white ancestors were 'quality' whites.

b. Passing into *adj.*

1962 R. WILLIAMS *Brit. in Sixties: Communications* iii. 29 The division of space between advertising and editorial material is not, then, governed by whether a paper is 'quality' or 'popular'. **1972** *Britain 1972* (Central Office of Information) xviii. 429 The national newspapers..fall into two categories: popular and quality.

Hence **'qualityless** *a.*, having no quality or qualities; **'qualityship**, social position (*nonce-wd.*).

1859 MOZLEY *Ess., Indian Convers.* (1878) II. 313 Brahm is a motionless, characterless, qualityless, colourless essence. **1865** *Dublin University Mag.* I. 6 He dressed with regard to his qualityship. **1893** J. ORR *Chr. View God & W.* iv. 146 An absolutely qualityless matter..is unthinkable.

quality, *v. rare.* Also 6 qualit-. [f. prec.] *trans.* **†a.** To furnish with a quality or qualities. *Obs.* **b.** To rate at a certain quality or value.

1579 J. JONES *Preserv. Bodie & Soule* Ep. Ded. 2 By these three they be all qualited. Motion ingendreth, Light shapeth and sheweth, Influence disposeth or qualiteth. **1813** BATCHELOR *Agric. Surv. Bedfordsh.* 236 The warren contained 878 acres, much of which was qualitied at 9*s.* to 10*s.* per acre.

qualiver, -vre, qualliver, obs. ff. CALIVER.

quall(e, obs. forms of WHALE.

quallefy, -ify, obs. forms of QUALIFY.

†quallmire = QUAGMIRE (q.v.). *Obs. rare*$^{-1}$.

1553 BALE *Gardiner's De Vera Obed.* B viij b, Who so euer ..goeth about to fette it [truth] out of mennes puddles and quallmyres [*v.r.* qualmires].

†'qually, *a. Obs. rare.* [Of obscure origin.] Of wine: Turbid, cloudy.

a **1700** B. E. *Dict. Cant. Crew*, *Qually-Wines*, Turbulent and Foul. **1703** *Art & Myst. Vintners* 22 Without good Fermentation, they become Qually, (i.e. Cloudy).

†qualm, *sb.*^{1} *Obs.* Forms: 1-2 **cwealm**, 2-3 **cwalm**, (3 cu-), 2-4 **qualm**, 3 **quelme**, 4 **qw-**, **qualme**, 6 *Sc.* **quhalm**, **qualim**. [OE. *cwealm* death, slaughter, pestilence, = OS. *qualm*, OHG. *qu-*, *chualm* (MHG. *qualm* anguish); f. **kwal-*, ablaut-var. of **kwel-* to die: see QUELE, QUELL.]

1. General or widespread mortality of men or animals; plague, pestilence.

In OE. also used of the (violent) death of a single person.

c **1000** ÆLFRIC *Hom.* II. 122 Micel cwealm wearð þæs folces. *Ibid.* 192 Cwealm on heora orfe. *c* **1125** *O.E. Chron.* (Laud MS.) an. 1125 Hunger & cwealm on men & on erue. *c* **1205** LAY. 31877 þe qualm muchele þe wes on moncunne. *a* **1250** *Owl & Night.* 1155 Thu bodest cualm of orwe. *a* **1340** HAMPOLE *Psalter* cv. 29 And finees stode & quemyd & þe qualm left. *c* **1386** CHAUCER *Knt.'s T.* 1156 A thousand slayn and nat oon of qualm ystorue.

b. Loss or damage.

? *a* **1366** CHAUCER *Rom. Rose* 357 Ywys, great qualme [F. *grant morie*] ne were it noon, Ne synne, although her lyf were gon. **1513** DOUGLAS *Æneis* x. i. 31 Quhen the fers burgh of Cartage To Romys boundis..Ane huge myscheif and gret quhalm [*ed.* 1553 qualim] send sall.

2. *attrib.*, as ***qualm-house, -stow***.

c **725** *Corpus Gloss.* 2 *Calvariae locus*, cualmstou. *c* **1000** ÆLFRIC *Hom.* II. 254 Ða cempan hine ʒelæddon to ðære cwealm-stowe. *a* **1225** *Ancr. R.* 106 Þe munt of Caluarie.. was þe cwalmsteou. *Ibid.* 140 Iput in one prisune, & bitund ase in one cwalm huse.

†qualm, *sb.*^{2} *Obs. rare*$^{-1}$. [App. imitative; cf. G. *galm* sound, noise.] Croak.

c **1374** CHAUCER *Troylus* v. 382 Augurye of thise foweles.. As ravenes qualm, or schrychynge of thise owles.

qualm (kwɑːm, kwɔːm), *sb.*^{3} Forms: 6 **quamme** (? calme), 6-7 **qualme, quaume, qua(i)me**, 7 **quawme, quaem**, 6- **qualm**. [Of obscure origin: in form and sense identical with Da. *kvalme*, †*kvalm*, Sw. *qvalm*, but these are app. not native words. Cf. G. (now dial.) *qualm* (*kalm*) swoon, faint, unconscious state (:—MHG. *twalm*: see DWALM *sb.*), and G. *qualm* (whence Da. *kvalm*, Sw. *qvalm*) vapour, steam, close air.

OE. *cwealm* QUALM *sb.*^{1} had the sense 'pain', 'torment', (see quots. in Bosw.-Toller), and some instances of *qualm* in 16-17th c. use might conceivably mean 'pain', 'pang'; but historical evidence of connexion is wanting, and the sense of 'sick fit', 'sickness' is possible in all the cases.]

1. A (sudden) feeling or fit of faintness, illness, or sickness. (Now restricted to cases in which the seat of the disorder is in the stomach, but formerly in somewhat wider use.)

c **1530** R. COPLAND *Jyl of Brentfords Test.* 233 With qualmes & stytches it doth me torment, That all my body is torne and rent. **1565** JEWEL *Repl. Harding* (1611) 52 If any quame or sicknesse happen to fall vpon him. **1594** T. B. *La Primaud. Fr. Acad.* II. 139 Such as haue some quaume about their heart, so that they faint and sowne. **1683** TRYON *Way to Health* 27 It makes the Stomach sick..and sickish Qualms to arise. **1740** SOMERVILLE *Hobbinol* III. 219 The sickly Qualms That grieve her Soul. **1829** LYTTON *Devereux* II. v, Has the bottle bequeathed thee a qualm or a head-ache. **1874** BURNAND *My time* xxxii. 326 Breeze enough for sailing, ..no qualms to interfere with appetite.

2. *transf.* **a.** A fit of sickening fear, misgiving, or depression; a sudden sinking or faintness of heart. Now *rare*.

a **1555** RIDLEY in Foxe *A. & M.* III. (1596) 446 The weake manne of God..will have now and then such thoughtes and quaumes (as they call them) to runne ouer his hart. **1624** LD. KEEPER WILLIAMS in *Fortesc. Papers* (Camden) 203 A certayne qualme came over his stomacke to be of a Judge noe Judge. **1712** ARBUTHNOT *John Bull* III. iii, Many a doubt, many a qualm, overspread his clouded imagination. **1792** MARY WOLLSTONECR. *Rights Wom.* v. 236, [I] soon heard, with the sickly qualm of disappointed hope..that she was no more. **1861** *Sat. Rev.* 21 Dec. 636 Apt to leave qualms and misgivings on the sensitive..temperament.

b. A strong scruple of conscience; a painful doubt or consciousness of acting wrongly.

1649 MILTON *Eikon.* xxviii. 240 Unedified consciences apt to engage their Leaders in great affaires and then, upon a sudden qualm and swimming of their conscience, betray them. **1687** T. BROWN *Saints in Uproar* Wks. 1730 I. 77 So strangely troubled with qualms of conscience. **1749** FIELDING *Tom Jones* VI. xiii, It was absurd..to affect any qualms about this trifle. **1806** JEFFERSON *Writ.* (1830) IV. 55 One qualm of principle..I do feel. **1863** KINGLAKE *Crimea* (1877) II. xiv. 241 It was natural that some of the members of the Government should have qualms.

c. A fit or sudden access *of* some quality, principle, etc. (Now only with suggestion of prec.)

a **1626** BP. ANDREWES *Serm., Repent. & Fasting* (1661) 170, I doubt ours hath been rather a flash, a qualme, a brunt than otherwise. **1655** FULLER *Ch. Hist.* III. v. §55 Although this qualm of Loyalty took this Church for the present. **1655** JER. TAYLOR *Guide Devot.* (1719) 125 If the Fit or Qualm of my Devotion holds out longer. **1820** W. IRVING *Sketch Bk.* II. 282 Immediately after one of these fits of extravagance, he will be taken with violent qualms of economy. **1873** BROWNING *Red Cott. Nt.-cap* 269 Had he a devotion-fit? Clara grew serious with like qualm.

3. *Comb.*, as ***qualm-sick*** adj.

1718 *Entertainer* No. 30. 202 [They] grew qualm-sick at the Common Prayer. **1758** *Mickmakis & Maricheets* 55 She ..blows the smoak towards his nostrils, even sometimes so violently, as to make him qualm-sick. **1880** BURTON *Queen Anne* II. xi. 189 Qualm-sick stomachs of..self-conceited hypocrites.

†qualm, *sb.*^{4} *Obs. rare*$^{-1}$. [var. of WALM, perh. after G. *qualm* steam.] The act of boiling.

1599 A. M. tr. *Gabelhouer's Bk. Physicke* 4/1 Let it seeth on the fyer one qualme or two.

qualm, *v.*^{1} [Connected with QUALM *sb.*^{3} Cf. Da. *kvalme* to have a qualm, and G. (now dial.) *qualmen* (*kalmen*) to swoon, be unconscious.]

†1. *intr.* To have a qualm or qualms. (Cf. QUALMING *vbl. sb.* and *ppl. a.*) *Obs.*

1565 COOPER *Thesaurus*, *Deficere*, I faynte, sounde, or qualme for heate. **1603** FLORIO tr. *Montaigne* III. xiii. (1897) VI. 253 My stomacke begins to qualme, my head feeleth a violent aking.

2. a. *trans.* To make sick. **b.** *absol.* To induce qualms. *rare*.

1611 BEAUM. & FL. *Scornful Lady* IV. i, How I grew qualm'd in love. **1713** *Gentleman Instructed* III. viii. 434 Envy qualms on his Bowels, Prodigality on his Purse. **1884** G. H. BOUGHTON in *Harper's Mag.* Oct. 701/1 If one is.. qualmed by the show of..confectionery.

†qualm, *v.*^{2} *Obs. rare*$^{-1}$. [var. of WALM, perh. after G. *qualmen* to steam.] To boil.

1599 A. M. tr. *Gabelhouer's Bk. Physicke* 8/2 Take thre quartes of Lye..and let it qualme a little on the fyer.

'qualminess. [f. QUALMY + -NESS.] The condition of being qualmy; nausea.

1778 J. ADAMS *Diary* 19 Feb., Wks. 1851 III. 98 The smell of the ship..or any other offensive smell will increase the qualminess. **1884** MISS DILLWYN *Jill* II. xi. 181 The swell made my qualminess increase.

†'qualming, *vbl. sb. Obs. rare.* [f. QUALM *v.*[1]] The fact of having a qualm or qualms.

1565 COOPER *Thesaurus, Defectio,*..the quaulmyng or sownyng of women after conception. **1596** BARROUGH *Meth. Physick* 450 It taketh away qwalming and ouercasting of the hart.

'qualming, *ppl. a.* [f. as prec.] **a.** That has a qualm or qualms. **b.** Of the nature of a fit or sudden access (cf. QUALM *sb.*[3] 2 c).

1576 FLEMING tr. *Caius' Dogs* in Arb. *Garner* III. 267 To succour and strengthen quailing and qualming stomachs. **1635** QUARLES *Embl.* v. ii. 36 Let Iesses sov'raigne Flow'r perfume my qualming brest. **1643** MILTON *Divorce* Introd. (1851) 6 Till they get a little cordial sobriety to settle their qualming zeal. **1952** AUDEN *Nones* 40 How will you answer when from their qualming spring The immortal nymphs fly shrieking.

qualmire: see QUALLMIRE.

qualmish ('kwɑːmɪʃ, 'kwɔːmɪʃ), *a.* [f. QUALM *sb.*[3] + -ISH[1].]

1. Of persons: Affected with a qualm or qualms; tending, or liable, to be so affected.

1548 UDALL *Erasm. Par. Luke* Pref. 3 Our soule is qualmishe ouer this meate. **1599** SHAKS. *Hen. V*, v. i. 22, I am qualmish at the smell of Leeke. **1670** DRYDEN *Tyran. Love* IV. i, Qualmish and loathing all you had before: Yet with a sickly Appetite to more. **1748** SMOLLETT *Rod. Rand.* lxix, My dear angel has been qualmish of late. **1816** SCOTT *Fam. Lett.* 25 Dec. (1894) I. xii. 388 The..dog arrived..a little lean and qualmish however after his sea voyage. **1860** MOTLEY *Netherl.* (1868) I. viii. 521 Elizabeth was not desirous of peace..she was qualmish at the very suggestion.

2. Of feelings, etc.: Of the nature of a qualm.

1798 *Sporting Mag.* XII. 195, I began to feel some very qualmish symptoms. **1860** T. MARTIN *Horace* 217 Our qualmish sickness drown In Caecuban divine!

3. Of things: Apt to produce qualms. *rare.*

1826 DISRAELI *Viv. Grey* VI. i, It is like a qualmish liqueur in the midst of a bottle of wine.

Hence **'qualmishly** *adv.*; **'qualmishness.**

a **1650** MAY *Satir. Puppy* (1657) 105 She would be as leacherous as the Mountaine-Goate, had not Natures qualmishnesse proved a strong contradiction to her desire. **1844** ALB. SMITH *Adv. Mr. Ledbury* ii. (1886) 8 On approaching the Foreland the first sensations of qualmishness became apparent. **1845** W. CORY *Lett. & Jrnls.* (1897) 32 Thinking about it keenly and qualmishly.

qualmless ('kwɑːmlɪs, 'kwɔːm-), *a.* [f. QUALM *sb.*[3] + -LESS.] Having or feeling no qualms. So **'qualmlessness.**

1849 T. ARNOLD *Let.* 22 Nov. in *N.Z. Lett.* (1966) 158 The beautiful scenery of the Sound did not appear to advantage in this tempestuous weather, nor to tell the truth, was I in that state of quietude and qualmlessness as to my internals, which would allow me to enjoy it. **1905** *Westm. Gaz.* 4 Mar. 5/2 Picture of Ronald absolutely qualmless facing charging rhinoceros. **1927** W. DEEPING *Kitty* xix. 244 Any qualms that she may have suffered in the beginning disappeared... By the end of January she was qualmless.

qualmy ('kwɑːmɪ, 'kwɔːmɪ), *a.* Also 6 **quamie.** [f. QUALM *sb.*[3] + -Y.] = QUALMISH.

1562 LEIGH *Armorie* (1597) 129 Neyther abounding in hote desire, neither oppressed with quamie colde. **1600** S. NICHOLSON *Acolastus* (1876) 38 Astonisht in a qualmy traunce. **1846** LANDOR *Exam. Shaks.* Wks. II. 274, I myself did feel queerish and qualmy. **1884** MISS DILLWYN *Jill* II. xi. 178 The mere smell of it makes one feel qualmy.

Hence **'qualmyish** *a.*, somewhat qualmy.

1831 *Blackw. Mag.* XXX. 975 With a queerish and qualmyish feeling.

‖**qualtagh** ('kwɑːltəx). [Manx, also written *quaaltagh*, f. *quaail* (= Ir. and Gael. *comhdháil*) meeting.] The first person one meets after leaving home on some special occasion; also, the first person entering a house on New Year's Day, the first-foot.

1891 MOORE *Folk-lore Isle of Man* 103 It was considered fortunate if the *qualtagh* were a person..of dark complexion. **1894** HALL CAINE *Manxman* 59, I should be first-foot here, only I'm no use as a qualtagh.

qualup ('kwæləp). The name of an estate in Western Australia, used *attrib.* in **qualup bell** to designate a local shrub, *Pimelea physodes* (cf. PIMELEA), which has greyish-green leaves and reddish-yellow bracts forming bells round the flowers.

1921 E. H. PELLOE *Wildflowers W. Austral* 50 'Qualup Bell'... An erect shrub of about 3 ft., glabrous except the flowers. **1934** *Bulletin* (Sydney) 25 July 26/2 What is the qualup bell?.. It is a native of Australia..and carries bell flowers which are tinged with yellow, green and purple. **1966** *Times* 11 Nov. (W. Austral. Suppl.) p. iv/2 The lovely qualup and mountain bells; the hoveas, the myrtles.

quam, obs. form of WHOM.

quamash (kwə'mæʃ, 'kwɒmæʃ). See also CAMAS. [N. American Indian.] A North American liliaceous plant (*Camassia esculenta*), the bulbs of which are used for food by the American Indians. ***eastern quamash*** (see quot. 1868).

1814 *Lewis & Clarke's Exp.* (1893) 958 The Chopunnish are now dispersed in villages..for the purpose of collecting quamash. **1868** *Rep. U.S. Commissioner Agric.* (1869) 452 The plant [Camus] is otherwise known as the eastern quamash, or wild hyacinth, and in botanical nomenclature is *Scilla Fraseri.* **1882** *Garden* 13 May 323/3 The white Camassia..[is] not nearly so showy as the blue Quamash.

quame, var. of QUEME, *v.*; obs. f. QUALM *sb.*

†quamire. *Obs.* Also 6 **-myre, -mier,** 8 *dial.* **whamire.** [? var. of *quall-* or *quavemire*: see QUAGMIRE, and cf. Sc. *quaw-mire* s.v. QUAW.] A quagmire, bog. Also *fig.*

1555 EDEN *Decades* 99 Muddy marysshes full of suche quamyres that men are oftentymes swalowed vp in them. **1573** TUSSER *Husb.* (1878) 75 For quamier get bootes. **1587** GOLDING *De Mornay* iii. 32 If we wil get out of the Quamyre of our sinnes. *Ibid.* xix. 302 Orpheus..as for the wicked..burieth them in a quamire. **1703** THORESBY *Let. to Ray* 27 Apr. (E.D.S.), *Whamire*, a quagmire.

quamoclit ('kwæməklɪt). [Corruption of Mexican *qua'mochitl* (*ch* = tʃ), f. *qua-*, comb. form of *quaiutl* tree, + *-mochitl*, of unknown meaning.

The erroneous form *quamoclit*, found as early as 1689 in Tournefort's *Schola Botanica*, is the basis of imaginary etymologies from Greek and Sanskrit.]

A sub-genus of climbing plants with brilliant flowers found in the tropical parts of America and Asia, belonging to the genus *Ipomœa.* (Formerly regarded as a distinct genus.)

1731 MILLER *Gard. Dict.* s.v., Quamoclit with very fine, cut, winged Leaves,..called in Barbadoes Sweet-William. **1753** CHAMBERS *Cycl. Supp.*, The species of quamoclit, enumerated by Mr. Tournefort, are these [etc.]. *Ibid.*, Quamoclit differs from bindweed, or convolvulus, in the shape of the flower. **1755** *Gentl. Mag.* XXV. 408 As to specimens I sent you of the bastard quamoclit [*printed* quarnoclif]. **1841** *Penny Cycl.* XIX. 193/1 Quamoclit..vulgaris is common in every part of India. **1892** BENTHAM & HOOKER *Brit. Flora* (ed. 6) 305 The exotic genus Ipomœa, including *Pharbitis* and *Quamoclit*..supplies some of our most beautiful greenhouse and hothouse climbers.

quan, obs. form of GUAN, WHEN.

quandary ('kwɒndərɪ, formerly kwən'dɛərɪ), *sb.* Also 6 **quandare, -arye,** 6–7 **-arie,** 8–9 **quondary.** [Of unknown origin; in common use from *c* 1580.

Possibly a corruption of some term of scholastic Latin. The suggestions that it is ad. F. *qu'en dirai-je* 'what shall I say of it?' that it represents ME. *wandreth*, or is an abbrev. of *hypochondry*, are (apart from other considerations) condemned by the fact that the original stressing is *quan'dary.* The usual pronunc. is now '*quandary*, given by Johnson (who calls it 'a low word') and Webster, but not accepted by Sheridan, Walker, or Smart.]

A state of extreme perplexity or uncertainty; a dilemma causing (great) mental agitation or distress; †a ticklish plight. Freq. in phr. ***in a (great, sad,*** etc.) ***quandary.***

1579 LYLY *Euphues* (Arb.) 45 Euphues..departed, leaving this olde gentleman in a great quandarie. **1582** STANYHURST *Æneis* IV. (Arb.) 94 The Queene in meane while with carks quandare deepe anguisht [etc.]. **1611** BEAUM. & FL. *Knt. Burn. Pestle* I. i, Much I fear, forsaking of my diet, Will bring me presently to that quandary, I shall bid all adieu. **1652** C. B. STAPYLTON *Herodian* xvi. 135 The Nobles, Gentry, Souldiers in quandaries..To Turret tops he fetches more Vagaries. *a* **1720** SHEFFIELD (Dk. Buckhm.) *Wks.* (1729) 201 Apollo now driv'n to a cursed Quandary was wishing for Swift, or for fam'd Lady Mary. **1751** SMOLLETT *Per. Pic.* (1779) I. ii. 9 Thof he be sometimes thrown into perilous passions and quandaries. **1847** DISRAELI *Tancred* II. iv, All his quandaries terminated in the same catastrophe; a compromise. **1875** JOWETT *Plato* (ed. 2) I. 229 Now I was in a great quandary at having to answer this question.

†quandary, *v. Obs. rare.* [f. prec.] **a.** *trans.* To perplex, put in a quandary. **b.** *intr.* To be in a quandary.

1616 T. ADAMS *Soul's Sickness* Wks. 1861 I. 505 He quandaries, whether to goe forward to God, or, with Demas, to turne backe to the world. **1681** OTWAY *Soldier's Fort.* III. i, Methinks I am quandary'd like one going with a Party to discover the Enemy's Camp, but had lost his Guide upon the Mountains. **1794** W. B. STEVENS *Let.* 19 Nov. in *Jrnl.* (1965) 206 Your Grandfather's sentiments are so far come round that he seems to be quandaryed (that's not a dictionary word I believe) and wishes for Peace.

‖**quand même** (kɑ̃ mɛm). [Fr., lit. 'when the same'.] All the same, even so, nevertheless.

1825 H. WILSON *Mem.* III. 179 She was however dreadfully agitated, quand même. **1854** GEO. ELIOT *Let.* 21 Apr. (1954) II. 151, I shall always love her *quand même.* **1884** W. JAMES *Will to Believe* (1897) 162 An optimism *quand même*, a systematic and infatuated optimism like that ridiculed by Voltaire in his Candide, is one of the possible ideal ways in which a man may train himself to look on life. **1909** —— *Pluralistic Universe* ii. 71 First we hear Mr. Bradley convicting things of absurdity; next, calling on the absolute to vouch for them *quand même.* **1952** W. STEVENS *Let.* 26 June (1967) 756 We have no plans..for a holiday. We shall have a good time quand même.

quandong ('kwændɒŋ, 'kwɒn-). Also **quandang, -dung, quon(g)dong, quantong.** [Aboriginal Australian.] **1. a.** A small Australian tree, *Santalum acuminatum*, belonging to the family Santalaceæ, and bearing racemes of small greenish-white flowers; also the globular red fruit of this tree. **b.** A forest tree found in northeastern Australia, *Elæocarpus grandis*, belonging to the family Elæocarpaceæ, and distinguished by grey bark and axillary racemes of bell-shaped, greenish-white flowers; also, the blue berries of this tree. Also *attrib.*

1839 T. L. MITCHELL *3 Exped.* 135 (Morris) In all these scrubs on the Murray the *Fusanus acuminatus* is common, and produces the quandang nut. **1850** CLUTTERBUCK *Port Phillip* II. 30 The indigenous Quandang..is the only really palatable fruit that grows in the wilds of Port Phillip. **1857** W. HOWITT *Tallangetta* I. 41 (Morris) Abundance of fig..trees, cherries, loquots, quondongs. **1859** H. KINGSLEY *G. Hamlyn* xxx. (1894) 279 Such quantongs, such raspberries, surpassing imagination. **1862** R. HENNING *Let.* 2 Nov. (1966) 114 He [*sc.* an emu] also eats quandongs, a sort of wild plum that grows in the bush. They look very like the common black plums you preserve, but they are sour and bitter and harsh to an untold degree. **1887** FARRELL *How he Died* 20 Where barren fig-tree and..quandong Bloom on lone roads. **1903** 'T. COLLINS' *Such is Life* ii. 74 She had watched the deepening crimson of the quandong, amidst its thick contexture of Nile-green leaves. **1908** E. J. BANFIELD *Confessions of Beachcomber* I. i. 22 The shiny blue quandong (*Elæocarpus grandis*), misleading and insipid. **1935** H. H. FINLAYSON *Red Centre* viii. 84 Of the sweet fruits, the quondong and plum are first favourites. **1936** F. CLUNE *Roaming round Darling* xvii. 162 Then there is the quondong-tree, which has a small fruit with a nut inside like a marble. **1945** *Coast to Coast 1944* 88 Give me your quandong stones and your two tortoise-shells. **1953** M. E. PATCHETT in I. Bevan *Sunburnt Country* II. iv. 117 Here are quandong trees with their thick, leathery leaves and red globes of fruit that make delicious jams and jellies. **1965** *Austral. Encycl.* III. 365/1 *E*[*læocarpus*] *grandis* (the blue, white, or silver quandong)..has large blue drupes known to children as blue figs, and sometimes, but incorrectly, as quandongs. **1967** [see NATIVE *a.* 13 d]. **1978** *Observer* (Colour Suppl.) 1 Jan. 24/4 Yatungka..had gone east a great distance to gather the fruit of the quandong tree. *Ibid.*, Yatungka arrived at the camp about midday, carrying a dish full of quandongs.

2. *Austral. slang.* A disreputable person who lives by his wits (see also quot. 1977).

1939 K. TENNANT *Foveaux* 311 In this crowd of low heels, quandongs and ripperty men, she looked at her ease and yet not of them. **1973** F. HUELIN *Keep Moving* 178 *Quandong*, hobo who bludges or imposes on another. **1977** J. RAMSAY *Cop it Sweet* 75 *Quandong*, female who makes a practice of remaining virtuous after being wined and dined.

quango ('kwæŋgəʊ). Also with capital initial and in form **QUANGO.** Pl. **quangos.** [Acronym f. the initial letters of *qua*si *n*on-*go*vernment(al) *o*rganization: see note below.] A semi-public administrative body outside the civil service but financed by the exchequer and having members appointed by the government. Also *attrib.*

The expansion given above appears in the evidence set out below from 1967. The expansion '*qua*si-*a*utonomous *n*ational *go*vernment(al) *o*rganization' and its variants (now common) are first attested in 1976.

[**1967** A. PIFER in *Ann. Rep. Carnegie Corp. N.Y.* 3 In recent years there has appeared on the American scene a new genus of organization which represents a noteworthy experiment in the art of government... We may call it the *quasi nongovernmental organization.*] **1973** C. HOOD in *New Society* 16 Aug. 386/1 It was the Americans who first drew attention to the importance of what they have labelled the 'grants economy', the 'contract state' and the 'quasi-non-government organisation' (Quango). **1975** *Listener* 2 Oct. 433/1 What our American cousins describe as 'quangos', which..are the quasi non-governmental organisations..from the University Grants Committee to the British Tourist Authority. **1976** *Observer* 2 May 1/2 A new species of animal is multiplying in the undergrowth of Britain—the QUANGO, or Quasi Autonomous National Governmental Organisation. **1976** *Daily Tel.* 8 Sept. 8/7 While millions of workers have their pay limits rigidly fixed, their union bosses are able to increase their incomes by becoming members of 'quangos'. The word, newly-coined, stands for Quasi Autonomous National Governmental Organisations. **1977** *New Society* 17 Mar. 531/1 Now sits in the House of Lords and has an array of quango jobs. **1978** *Economist* 5 Aug. 20 A quango covers just about everything from the Price Commission to the Police Complaints Board and the British Waterways Board. **1978** *Daily Tel.* 15 Nov. 18 Baroness Young will be declaring a personal interest when she opens a timely debate in the Lords today on the growth of Quangos, Quasi-Autonomous Non-Governmental Organisations. **1979** *Daily Tel.* 8 Aug. 14 Anthony Barker of Essex University, describes the gathering as his act of atonement for having, he claims, invented the word quango..10 years ago. **1980** *Times* 1 Feb. 15/5 It seems impossible to believe that any government, however intent upon abolishing 'Quangos' (Quasi-Autonomous Non-Governmental Organizations),..would kill off the Advisory Council on the Penal System. **1980** T. SHARPE *Ancestral Vices* ix. 70 He's some sort of personal Quango... A Quasi Autonomous Non-Governmental Organization, as you very well know.

Hence **quan'gocracy,** quangos regarded collectively; the power or influence attributed to quangos; **'quangocrat,** a member of a quango regarded (usu. unfavourably) in terms of his authority.

1979 *Daily Tel.* 17 Apr. 18/1 Mr Callaghan's quangocrats were chosen to perform socialist functions, so were most of their institutions. **1979** *Observer* 23 Sept. 5/2 The sacked quangocrats are almost all unpaid. *Ibid.* 9/6 The original attack of the Conservatives conjured up bogies..of 'union hierarchies which interlock with quangocracy'. **1980** *Times* 12 Jan. 3/2 Those great beneficiaries of quangocracy, the trade unions and the academics of the left, are beginning to fight back.

quank (kwɒŋk), *sb.* [Echoic.] A representation of sounds made by animals and birds. Hence as *v. intr.*, to utter such a sound. Also **'quanking** *vbl. sb.*

1921 *Chambers's Jrnl.* Mar. 178/1 He could even hear the nasal laugh of the zebra, the resonant 'Quank' of the gnus, the rattle of horn against horn as the bucks made play. **1965** E. RICHARDSON *Living Island* 215 Oftener we hear quanking among the tidal pools..as males beat their way to the enticing sounds—for it is the female [duck] which quanks.

quann(e, obs. forms of WHEN.

quannet ('kwɒnɪt). Also quonet. [Of obscure origin.] A flat file set in a frame, and used as a plane in filing flat surfaces, as in comb-making.

1842 WHITTOCK *Complete Book of Trades* 225 The comb-makers use a tool..called a quonet, having coarse single teeth, to the number of about seven or eight to an inch. **1875** KNIGHT *Dict. Mech.* 1842/1 *Quannet.*

quanon, variant of KANOON.

quanset, var. QUONSET, QUONSET.

quant (kwænt, kwɒnt), *sb.*[1] Also 5 quante, (qv-), whante, 9 quont. [? ad. L. *contus* (Gr. κοντός) boat-pole. Current in E. Anglia and Kent (in the latter also 'a young oak-sapling, a walking-stick'): the northern equivalent is KENT *sb.*[1]]

1. A pole for propelling a barge, esp. one with a cap at the top and a prong at the bottom to prevent it from sinking in mud. Also *attrib.*, as ***quant-pole***.

c **1440** *Promp. Parv.* 418/2 Quante, or sprete, rodde.., *contus. Ibid.* 523/2 Whante, or qvante. **1687** SHADWELL *Juvenal* 38 *Contus* signifies a Quant or Sprett, with which they shove Boats. **1847–78** in HALLIWELL. **1883** G. C. DAVIES *Norfolk Broads* iv. 25 When the wind fails, the men betake themselves to the 'quant', which is a long slender pole with a knob at one end and a spike and shoulder at the other. **1893** DOUGHTY *Wherry in Wend. Lands* 167 To get all sail off her, and undertake a tough job with the quants. **1901** *Academy* 26 Oct. 389/1 There..lay a large family-boat immovable... A quant-pole stood rigidly upright beside it. **1974** *Oxf. Jun. Encycl.* (rev. ed.) IX. 389/1 On the Norfolk Broads,..boatmen often propel their 'wherries' (sailing barges) for short distances by 'quanting' with very long, heavy poles called 'quant-poles'.

2. In a windmill: (see quots. 1936 and 1945). Also *Comb.*

1924 *Trans. Newcomen Soc.* III. 42 All the framing and gearing of these mills are of wood, the only important parts of iron being the wrought iron gudgeons upon which the shafts revolve, and perhaps the 'quants' or spindles which drove the runner stones. **1936** P. HEMMING *Windmills in Sussex* ii. 9 The drive from above is called 'quant-drive' and is the more usual drive in a windmill. *Ibid.*, This chute vibrates against the lower part of the stone-shaft, which is called the 'quant' and which is not circular, but ribbed. **1945** *Archit. Rev.* XCVIII. 78/1 When the stones are overdriven the nuts are mounted on vertical spindles or 'quants' which drive the 'runner stones' from above. **1957** S. FREESE *Windmills & Millwrighting* iii. 48 This forked shaft is called a 'crutch-pole' or 'quant', because it oscillates like a quant-pole when freed from its upper bearing (the glut-box) in order to disengage the stone-nut.

† **quant** (kwɒnt), *sb.*[2] Used for QUANTUM 5. *Obs.*

1918 *Phil. Mag.* XXXV. 294 Sommerfeld gave a generalization of the quant-conditions which proved to be of very great importance. *Ibid.* 307 The assumption that the recombining electron comes from one other ring with a higher quant number leads to an equation of the right type. **1926** *Nature* 18 Dec. 874/1 It would seem inappropriate to speak of one of these hypothetical entities as..a corpuscle of light, a light quantum or a light quant, if we are to assume that it spends only a minute fraction of its existence as a carrier of radiant energy. **1932** STILES & WALSH tr. *Castelfranchi's Rec. Adv. Atomic Physics* II. v. 167 The light energy..always remains concentrated in the form of 'light quants', or grains, the magnitude of which depends solely on the *colour*.

quant (kwænt, kwɒnt), *v.* [f. QUANT *sb.*[1]]

a. *trans.* To propel (a boat) with a quant. Also *absol.* **b.** *intr.* Of a boat: To be propelled with a quant.

1865 [implied in QUANTING *vbl. sb.*]. **1883** G. C. DAVIES *Norfolk Broads* v. 37 The water was too deep for us to quant our punt. **1887** W. RYE *Norfolk Broads* p. ii, Great disinclinations to quant or scull. **1893** *Toynbee Rec.* 90 Now her stern, now a broadside, is toward us..as she quants against the breeze.

Hence **'quanting** *vbl. sb.* (also *attrib.*)

1865 W. WHITE *East. Eng.* I. 84 Wherry men, to whom the operation of 'quanting' is very familiar. **1883** G. C. DAVIES *Norfolk Broads* x. 77 There may be a quanting-match. **1887** W. RYE *Norfolk Broads* 39 We and the wherry, by dint of very hard quanting, managed..to get as far as the ruins.

quanta, pl. of QUANTUM.

'quantal, *a.* [Orig. f. as QUANTATIVE *a.* + -AL[1]. Later f. QUANTUM.]

†**1.** = ALIQUANT. *Obs. rare*$^{-1}$.

a **1696** SCARBURGH *Euclid* (1705) 177 A Quantal part measures not the whole: but repeated is either less or greater than it.

2. a. Composed of discrete units; varying in steps, not continuously.

1917 F. H. PRATT in *Amer. Jrnl. Physiol.* XLIV. 518 Regarding the effective energy content of a biological system discharging always to full capacity as a physiological quantum, I purpose to use the derivative *quantal* to express ..the conception of structural carriers of such integers of energy in effects discontinuously graded. *Ibid.*, A series of responsive values would be quantal when composed of discontinuous steps. **1919** *Ibid.* XLIX. 38 That tetanic contractions are quantal is shown even more clearly in figure 15. **1958** *Oxf. Univ. Gaz.* 2 Oct. 84/1 Three problems arising in the analysis of quantal data. **1964** *Language* XL. 206 The most salient characteristic of these linguistic primes ..is their discreteness, their discontinuity... It is obviously their quantal attributes which distinguish linguistic primes from the species units of other behavioural sciences, e.g. the 'culture trait' of anthropology.

b. *Biol.* and *Med.* Of an effect or response (see quots.).

1933 J. H. GADDUM in *Med. Res. Council Special Rep. Ser.* No. 183. 5 The term 'quantal response' is used in this paper for any 'all-or-none' biological reaction, i.e. a reaction of such a type, or observed under such conditions, that only the bare fact of its presence or absence in each animal is recorded. **1954** *Proc. R. Soc. Med.* XLVII. 203 The third kind of method used..to assay drugs depends upon quantal effects. These effects are not measured but recorded as positive or absent and the number of positive effects is counted. **1974** M. C. GERALD *Pharmacol.* iii. 58 Does the rat die at a given dose of poison or not? Let us assume that this quantal (all-or-none) response follows a normal distribution.

c. *Physics.* Of, pertaining to, or being a quantum or the quantum theory.

1936 C. G. DARWIN in *Nature* 28 Nov. 909/1 One may not infrequently see in learned journals such a phrase as 'This may be proved by quantum theoretical methods.'.. The proper English form would be *quantum theory methods*, though even that is very clumsy, and *quantum methods* is quite good enough... The right procedure is to coin the adjective *quantal*. To justify its adequacy it is only necessary to notice the impossibility of finding anything that would be *quantally* right, but *quantum-mechanically* wrong. **1951** E. M. CORSON *Perturbation Methods* iii. 36 If **q**, **p** are to be canonically conjugate in the quantal sense. **1954** *Jrnl. Physiol.* CXXIV. 571 The number of quantal units responding to a nerve impulse fluctuates in a random manner. **1975** *Physics Bull.* Dec. 545/3 Anybody who wishes to learn the mathematics of coherence, classical and quantal, of light fields and their interaction with atoms can do no better than turn to this book. **1978** *Nature* 12 Jan. 191/1 The transmitter, synthesised and packaged on the spot, is released in quantal, countable packets.

Hence **'quantally** *adv.*

1936 [see 2 c above]. **1957** *Psychol. Rev.* LXIV. 137/1 Such preactivation can be produced by gradual learning or quantally by instruction. **1970** *Nature* 5 Sept. 1006/2 Vesicles slotted between dense projections are thought to release transmitter quantally by exocytosis through the membrane into the cleft. **1978** *Ibid.* 13 July 136/1 The small standard error in each case shows clearly that the V_2 change is quantal and, hence, that the junctional conductance itself changes quantally.

quantasome ('kwɒntəsəʊm). *Bot.* [f. *quanta*, pl. of QUANTUM + -SOME[4]. (The quantasome was believed to be the fundamental body capable of photosynthesis.)] One of numerous small proteinaceous particles found in chloroplasts.

Quot. 1962 is only the earliest of several such seeming coinages, all in papers by Professor R. B. Park and his colleagues at the Lawrence Radiation Laboratory and Botany Department, Berkeley, California.

1962 M. CALVIN in *Science* 16 Mar. 889/1 Here we can see the lamellae on its flat side showing a granular structure, made up of fairly uniform oblate spheroids which we have called quantasomes. **1964** *Science* 22 May 1009/1 The quantasome as seen in a two-dimensional crystalline array is 185 Å long, 155 Å wide, and 100 Å thick. The surface of the quantasome appears to contain four or more subunits. The molecular weight.. is 2 × 10⁶. This..corresponds to a chlorophyll content of 230 chlorophyll molecules per quantasome. **1968** R. RIEGER et al. *Gloss. Genetics & Cytogenetics* 370 According to recent evidence, the quantasomes do not participate in photoreduction reactions but show Ca^{++} -dependent ATPase activities. **1976** COOMBS & GREENWOOD in J. Barber *Intact Chloroplast* i. 12 The concept of a quantasome as the structural counterpart of a functional photosynthetic unit in the full classical sense of this term is in doubt.

† **quantative**, *a. Obs. rare.* [For *quantitative*, as if f. L. *quant-us* + -ATIVE: cf. QUANTITIVE. (But perh. a misprint in both quots.)] = QUANTITATIVE.

1644 DIGBY *Nat. Bodies* iii. 30 In compounding and diuiding of bodies according to quantatiue [**1669** quantitive] partes. **1661** GLANVILL *Van. Dogm.* 29 Motion cannot be received but by quantative dimension.

quantic ('kwɒntɪk). *Math.* [f. L. *quant-us* how much + -IC.] A rational, integral, homogeneous function of two or more variables.

A quantic according to its dimensions is a quadric, cubic, quartic, etc. according as it is of the 2nd, 3rd, 4th, etc. degree; and is binary, ternary, quaternary, etc. according as it has two, three, four, etc. variables.

1854 A. CAYLEY *Wks.* (1887) II. 224 We may instead of a single quantic consider two or more quantics. **1881** BURNSIDE & PANTON *Th. Equat.* Introd. p. 4 A polynomial is sometimes called a quantic. **1896** E. B. ELLIOTT (*title*) An Introduction to the Algebra of Quantics.

Hence **'quantical** *a.*, relating to quantics.

quantifiable ('kwɒntɪˌfaɪəb(ə)l), *a.* [f. QUANTIFY *v.* + -ABLE.] That may be conceived or treated as a quantity; that may be measured with regard to quantity.

1883 A. BARRATT *Phys. Metempiric* p. xxv, Those mutual relations of conscious centres which are measurable and quantifiable. **1893** *Athenæum* 11 Nov. 667/2 It is the latter kind only [of feeling] which is immediately and necessarily quantifiable. **1953** D. RIESMAN in *Amer. Scholar* XXIII. 24 The quantifiable measure of longevity. **1966** J. ELLIS in C. E. Bazell *In Memory of J. R. Firth* 80 Both phonological and formal meaning correspond to the information of information theory in being dependent on, and quantifiable in terms of, the number of oppositions in the given system. **1967** *Times Rev. Industry* July 29/1 A first-class service with quantifiable savings in the company's own accounts department is the best possible selling point. **1972** *Daily Tel.* 6 Apr. 21/4 What we wanted were not quantifiable results but actual feelings. **1974** *Sci. Amer.* May 43/1 Reconstruction, redevelopment and the redesign of approach roads and internal streets are destroying the evidence of the city's past at a quantifiable rate.

'quantifiable, *sb. Linguistics.* [f. the adj.] = *mass noun* s.v. MASS *sb.*[2] 10 d.

1957 *College English* XVIII. 351/1 These are the quantifiables, such as *furniture* and *milk* and *news*. **1961** R. B. LONG *Sentence & its Parts* ii. 39 Quantifiables such as *courage, fun, pneumonia, milk, spaghetti, machinery*, and *furniture* are not made plural, though it is true that some quantifiables have pluralizer status also.

quantification (ˌkwɒntɪfɪ'keɪʃən). [f. QUANTIFY *v.*: see -FICATION.] The action of quantifying. Esp. in *Logic*, as ***quantification theory***: theory concerned with quantifiers or with giving formal expression to the scope of variables in general propositions. Cf. QUANTIFIER.

quantification of the predicate: the expression of the logical quantity of the predicate of a proposition, by applying to the predicate the sign *all*, or *some*, or an equivalent; a device introduced chiefly by Sir W. Hamilton, and intended to simplify logical processes.

c **1840** SIR W. HAMILTON *Logic* (1866) II. 297 Because the universal quantification of the predicate is, in this instance, materially false, is such quantification, therefore, always formally illegal? **1864** BOWEN *Logic* vii. 181 It is enough that the quantifications of the Middle Term in both Premises, added together, should exceed unity. **1882** PIAZZI SMITH in *Nature* XXVI. 552 All that we require for the.. quantification of watery vapour. **1918** C. I. LEWIS *Survey of Symbolic Logic* i. 24 He [*sc.* Lambert] reconstructs the whole of Aristotelian logic by the quantification of the predicate. **1940** *Brit. Jrnl. Psychol.* Jan. 233 Quantification pertains to a statistical population of persons, assessed or measured for amounts of that particular quality. **1940** W. V. QUINE *Math. Logic* p. vi, Quantification theory, like the preceding part of logic, is expounded within the medium of metamathematics; its presentation in any other medium appears disadvantageous, indeed, because of subtleties having to do with the so-called bound and free occurrences of variables. **1949** R. K. MERTON *Social Theory* iii. 109 What appears as a tendency in research for quantification (through the development of scales) can thus be seen as a special case of attempting to clarify concepts sufficiently to permit the conduct of empirical investigation. **1950** W. V. QUINE *Methods of Logic* (1952) §28. 166 Quantification theory was founded by Frege in 1879. **1962** E. W. BETH *Formal Methods* iii. 50 If a semantic tableau for the sequent Ø/*Z* is closed, then the formula *Z* will be called a tautology (of quantification theory). **1966** A. D. BIDERMAN in R. Bauer *Social Indicators* ii. 75 Quantification was not until fairly recently an essential element of the definition of statistics. **1969** N. I. STYAZHKIN *Hist. Math. Logic Leibniz to Peano* iii. 123 It would not be an exaggeration to say that Lambert's theory of quantification actually contains all the basic results of the studies in quantification made by W. Hamilton in the nineteenth century. **1971** *World Archaeol.* III. 122 Groups of granaries..do not permit quantification of men by compound. **1973** J. HINTIKKA *Logic, Language-Games & Information* iii. 53 Quantification theory may be characterized from this point of view as the study of the phrases 'there is', and 'for every' over and above the study of the words 'not', and 'or', which are already studied in propositional logic plus whatever terms are required to express predication. **1974** H. WANG *From Math. to Philos.* 143 The many attractive properties of the first order or restricted predicate calculus (quantification theory) have suggested the convenient identification of it with first order logic, pure logic, or just logic. **1979** *Amer. Speech* LIV. 9 Scholars have criticized, sometimes effectively, the validity of the prescriptivists' quantifications. **1979** *Dædalus* Summer 77 A quantification of love that would be comic were it not that its effects are so awful.

quantificational (kwɒntɪfɪ'keɪʃənəl), *a.* [f. QUANTIFICATION + -AL.] Of, pertaining to, or relating to quantification. Hence **quantifi'cationally** *adv.*

1940 W. V. QUINE *Math. Logic.* ii. 89 We avoid the labor of writing out specific sequences of quantificational axioms and ponentials. **1951** —— *Ibid.* (rev. ed.) ii. 81 The advent of quantification opens up a wider class of logical truths: statements which are true by virtue of their structure in terms of joint denial and quantification. These may be *quantificationally* true. **1955** *Jrnl. Philos.* LII. 753 Sententially and quantificationally valid schemata are presented. **1957** N. CHOMSKY in Saporta & Bastian *Psycholinguistics* (1961) 266/2 A 'quantificational' sentence such as 'everyone in the room knows at least two languages'. **1966** *Jrnl. Philos.* LXIII. 699 The first-order quantificational calculus with identity. **1975** *Times Lit. Suppl.* 5 Dec. 1466/3 He is equally curt with some of the most familiar arguments in favour of God's existence: Aquinas's third way is guilty of an elementary quantificational fallacy.

'quantified, *ppl. a.* [f. QUANTIFY *v.* + -ED[1].] Possessing or endowed with quantity; measured or determined with respect to quantity; resulting from quantification or the use of quantifiers.

1589 R. BRUCE *Serm.* (1843) 87 To make it, at ane time,.. a bodie and not a bodie, quantified and not quantified. *c* **1840** SIR W. HAMILTON *Logic* App. (1866) II. 259 The real terms compared in the Convertend..are not the naked, but the quantified. **1847** LEWES *Hist. Philos.* (1867) II. 481 The discovery of precise quantities proves the objectivity of something quantified. **1870** JEVONS *Logic* 186 Immediate inference by added determinant..can also be applied..to quantified propositions. **1951** J. ŁUKASIEWICZ *Aristotle's Syllogistic* iv. 84 Every quantified expression..consists of three parts. **1972** P. T. GEACH *Logic Matters* ii. 69 The wrong idea that a universally quantified subject-term stands for the whole class of Ss^2 *can* be put across. **1974** H. WANG *From Math. to Philos.* iii. 113 The idea that truth functions governing quantified expressions must be explained in terms of propositions in which truth functions do not govern quantified expressions.

quantifier (ˈkwɒntɪfaɪə(r)). [f. QUANTIFY *v.* + -ER[1].] **1. a.** *Logic.* Something which quantifies, esp. an expression (such as 'all' or 'some') that indicates the scope of a term to which it is attached; ***existential quantifier***, a quantifier that asserts that there exists something for which the proposition following it is true or valid. Also *attrib.*

In quot. 1876 'a person who quantifies'.

1876 *Mind* I. 213 Quantifiers of the predicate insert the word *some*, and Boole uses a special symbol V, to mark the partial character of the identity. **1885** C. S. PEIRCE *Coll. Papers* (1933) III. xiii. 232 If the quantifying part, or Quantifier, contains Σ_x, and we wish to replace the *x* by a new index *i*, not already in the Quantifier, and such that every *x* is an *i*, we can do so at once by simply multiplying every letter of the Boolian having *x* as an index by x_i. **1896** —— in *Monist* VII. 32 My general algebra of logic..consists in simply attaching indices to the letters of an expression in the Boolian algebra, making what I term a Boolian, and prefixing to this a series of 'quantifiers', which are the letters Π and Σ, each with an index attached to it. **1940** W. V. QUINE *Math. Logic* ii. 106 Distribution of a universal quantifier through an alternation is not valid, nor is distribution of an existential quantifier through a conjunction. *Ibid.* 110 The last occurrence of '*y*' in (5) refers back to the last quantifier occurrence in (5). **1951** J. ŁUKASIEWICZ *Aristotle's Syllogistic* iv. 84, I denote quantifiers by Greek capitals, the universal quantifier by Π, and the particular or existential quantifier by Σ. Π may be read 'for all', and Σ 'for some' or 'there exists'. **1956** A. CHURCH *Introd. Math. Logic* iv. 288 The notion of propositional function and the use of quantifiers, originated with Frege in his Begriffsschrift of 1879... The terms 'quantifier' and 'quantification' are Peirce's. **1963** O. WOJTASIEWICZ tr. *Łukasiewicz's Elem. Math. Logic* 95 Detachment..is the same as in the quantifier-free sentential calculus. **1965** B. MATES *Elem. Logic* x. 159 A string of universal quantifiers containing *n* quantifier-occurrences. **1971** *Sci. Amer.* Aug. 96/3 Perhaps the only detail in our plan..that requires special comment is the treatment of the quantifiers ∀ (meaning 'for all') and ∃ ('there exists'). **1976** J. S. GRUBER *Lexical Struct. Syntax & Semantics* I. iii. 63 This kind of relationship with *not*, interestingly, is the same that occurs relating the universal and existential quantifiers.

b. *Linguistics.* A word or phrase indicative of quantity. Also *attrib.* and *Comb.*

1924 O. JESPERSEN *Philos. Gram.* vi. 85 All these quantifiers, as they might be called, differ from ordinary qualifying adjectives in being capable of standing alone..as when we say 'some (many, all, both, two) were absent'. **1933** —— *Essent. Eng. Gram.* vii. 67 *Little* is sometimes a qualifier (*a little girl*), sometimes a quantifier (*a little bread*). **1951** S. F. NADEL *Found. Social Anthropol.* 43 Thus I am not considering the 'formal' parts of language (conjunctions, prepositions, 'quantifiers', etc.). **1969** W. A. COOK *Introd. Tagmemic Analysis* iv. 107 *Quantifier tagmeme*, filled by numerals (num) such as: *one, two, first, second*; or quantitative adjectives. **1970** G. CARDEN in *Linguistic Inquiry* I. 287 The higher-S analysis requires an as-yet unspecified rule of Quantifier Lowering (QL) to move the quantifier from the high-S down to its surface-structure position. **1972** J. J. LAMBERTS *Short Introd. Eng. Usage* vii. 137 These are generally taken as plural unless a 'quantifier' like *a pair of* precedes the noun. **1977** *Word 1972* XXVIII. 88 If compared adjectives are to be analyzed as containing underlying quantifier-NPs in sentences such as 1 f and 1 g, then, ideally, we would expect them to be so analyzed elsewhere as well. **1978** *Language* LIV. 83 Certain quantifier constructions in Japanese were shown above to be exceptions.

2. *gen.* One who quantifies.

1963 *Economist* 9 Feb. 513/2 All that can be asked of the quantifiers is that they explore the sources thoroughly. **1970** *Computers & Humanities* V. 1 'Quantifiers' assemble in conferences, workshops and symposia to thrash out common problems and share research methods and findings.

quantify (ˈkwɒntɪfaɪ), *v.* [ad. med.L. *quantificāre* (Du Cange), f. *quant-us* how great: see QUANTITY and -FY.]

1. *Logic.* To make explicit the extent to which a term is referred to in a proposition, by prefixing *all* or *some* or an equivalent word to the term.

c **1840** SIR W. HAMILTON *Logic* App. (1866) II. 261 Ordinary language quantifies the Predicate so often as this determination becomes of the smallest import. *Ibid.* 272 Let us..overtly quantify the subject..and say, *All men are animals.* **1864** BOWEN *Logic* v. 127 They further maintain, that the Predicate is never quantified particularly in a Negative Judgment. **1887** [see INDEFINITE *a.* 4].

2. To determine the quantity of, to measure.

1878 LOCKYER *Stargazing* 152 The magnification..of space, which enables minute portions of it to be most accurately quantified. **1882** PIAZZI SMITH in *Nature* XXVI. 551 A meteorological spectroscope..may also..be able to quantify..the proportions of such aërial supply of water-gas. **1949** *Cape Argus* 5 Nov. 5/4 It pleased them immensely ..to hear him [*sc.* Winston Churchill] fall on Sir Stafford Cripps for having recently used the word 'quantify'. **1962** *Times Lit. Suppl.* 16 Nov. 875/1 Though we can list all these factors, we cannot quantify them. **1971** I. G. GASS et al. *Understanding Earth* 40 Studies using the law of superposition and fossil faunas and floras could only produce a *relative* time scale, and efforts were made during the 19th and early 20th centuries to quantify it. **1971** *Country Life* 3 June 1350/1 What is so often missing from the survey equation is..an adequate technique for quantifying the results. **1977** *Modern Railways* Dec. 472/3 Railfreight's performance in chemicals transport is hard to quantify in terms of market share. **1979** *Dædalus* Summer 76 Lear is quantifying love, confusing it with other things that can be measured.

Hence **ˈquantifying** *ppl. a.*

1847 SIR W. HAMILTON *Let. to A. de Morgan* 43 Logicians ..have referred the quantifying predesignations *plurimi*, and the like, to the most opposite heads. **1955** A. N. PRIOR *Formal Logic* 210 The presence..of..a quantifying element. **1976** *Times Lit. Suppl.* 30 Jan. 104/4 Those who would expect the author..to have little regard for received wisdoms or sacred cows (or even quantifying historians) will not be disappointed.

quantile (ˈkwɒntaɪl). *Statistics.* [f. L. *quant-us* how much, how great: see -IL, -ILE 2.] Each of any set of values of a variate which divide a frequency distribution into equal groups, each containing the same fraction of the total population; also, any one of the groups so produced, e.g. a quartile, decile, or percentile.

1940 *Suppl. to Jrnl. R. Statistical Soc.* VII. 83 It is not shown that the distribution of a quantile tends to normality in large samples. **1961** KENDALL & STUART *Adv. Theory Statistics* (ed. 2) II. xxxii. 513 X_p is the *p*-quantile of the distribution, i.e. the value below which 100_p per cent of the distribution lies. **1961** L. G. PARRATT *Probability & Exper. Errors in Sci.* ii. 79 If there are *M* intervals, each interval is called a quantile or an *M*-tile, or sometimes a fractile.

† quantimeter (kwɒnˈtɪmɪtə(r)). *Radiology. Obs.* [f. QUANTI(TY + -METER.] An apparatus for measuring the quantity of X-rays administered. Hence **quantiˈmetric** *a.*

1906 R. KIENBÖCK in *Arch. Roentgen Ray* XI. 17/2 In 1905, at the Roentgen Congress at Berlin, I introduced the new method of direct dosimetry—the 'quantimetric method'. *Ibid.*, My quantimeter consists essentially of..a strip of photographic paper..and a normal scale of graduated tints, with which it is to be compared. **1915** R. KNOX *Radiography* 282 The Kienböck Quantimeter.—This method is based on the discoloration of bromide of silver under the influence of X-rays. **1926** P. K. BOWES *X-Ray Apparatus* x. 95 (*heading*) Kienböck's quantimeter.

quantitate (ˈkwɒntɪteɪt), *v. Med.* [f. QUANTIT(Y + -ATE[3].] *trans.* To ascertain the quantity or extent of.

1960 *Anat. Rec.* CXXXVIII. 395/1 Because their appearance is sudden the time required for development can be measured and used to quantitate the rate of metabolic change produced by glucose. **1962** BURCHFIELD & STORRS *Biochem. Appl. Gas Chromatogr.* i. 117 All the components of the mixture are converted to the same substance and can be quantitated from a single curve relating detector response to amount of CO_2 or methane. **1969** *Adv. Appl. Microbiol.* XI. 51 The susceptibility of a penicillin to β-lactamases is usually quantitated by measuring its rate of hydrolysis to penicilloic acid. **1976** *Nature* 22 Jan. 236/1 Vitamin E content of the filtrate was quantitated by absorbancy at 292 nm. **1978** *Dædalus* Spring 27 If there is a danger, quantitate it.

So **quantiˈtation**, the action or process of quantitating.

1959 *Jrnl. Lipid Res.* I. 76/2 The separation and quantitation of the shorter acids could have been improved by use of a lower temperature and longer column. **1964** *Analytical Biochem.* VII. 295 Quantitation of each peak was made by triangulating the peak, cutting out, and weighing on an analytical balance. **1975** *Nature* 30 Oct. 828/1 Quantitation of the spectra was aided by the use of a Nicolet 1020A signal averager.

quantitative (ˈkwɒntɪtətɪv), *a.* and *sb.* [ad. med.L. *quantitātīvus*: see QUANTITY and -IVE. Cf. F. *quantitatif* (1586 in Godef. *Compl.*).]

A. *adj.* **1.** Possessing quantity, magnitude, or spatial extent. Now *rare.*

1581 MARBECK *Bk. of Notes* 40 [Angels occupy] no bodilie place, no severall nor quantitative place. **1634** JACKSON *Creed* VII. xxvi. §5 The world in the original doth not signify this visible or quantitative world. **1697** J. SERGEANT *Solid Philos.* 22 The Body, only which (and not the Soul) is Quantitative. **1847** LEWES *Hist. Philos.* (1867) II. 481 The fact that we discover quantitative space and time.

2. That is, or may be, considered with respect to the quantity or quantities involved; estimated or estimable by quantity.

1656 *Artif. Handsom.* 44 This Quantitative Adultery, which..makes far more grosse alterations, & substantiall changes of nature. **1661** GLANVILL *Van. Dogm.* 221 The colour of mens eyes is various, nor is there less diversity in their quantitative proportions. **1842** GROVE *Corr. Phys. For.* (ed. 6) 142 An invariable quantitative relation to each other. **1858** J. MARTINEAU *Stud. Chr.* 160 Not as its quantitative equal..but as a moral equivalent. **1879** FARRAR *St. Paul* (1883) 43 The enormous error that man..can win by quantitative goodness his entrance into the Kingdom of God.

3. a. Relating to, concerned with, quantity or its measurement; ascertaining or expressing quantity.

1668 WILKINS *Real Char.* III. vii. 325 Relative and Quantitative Pronouns. **1830** HERSCHEL *Stud. Nat. Phil.* 123 It is a character of all the higher laws of nature to assume the form of precise quantitative statement. **1882** FARRAR *Early Chr.* I. 125 The quantitative conceptions of Jewish formalism.

b. *Chem.* ***quantitative analysis***, measurement of the amounts of constituents present in a substance. Cf. *qualitative analysis.*

1849 D. CAMPBELL *Inorg. Chem.* Pref. 4 Tables for assisting in the calculations of quantitative analysis. **1913** CUMMING & KAY *Quantitative Chem. Analysis* 109 One of the most difficult problems met with in quantitative analysis is the selection of good methods of separation. **1961** D. & B. A. AMBROSE *Gas Chromatogr.* x. 161 With the integral detectors described..quantitative analysis is simple: the detector response is directly proportional to the mass of material, and the step height permits the analysis to be calculated in accordance with the property being determined (e.g. titre or volume).

4. Pertaining to, based on, vowel-quantity.

1799 *Monthly Rev.* XXIX. 49 The quantitative accent, as it may be called, follows the analogy of the Latin. **1871** LOWELL *Study Wind.* (1886) 241 The best quantitative verses in our language are to be found in Mother Goose. **1933** C. D. BUCK *Compar. Gram. Greek & Latin* 93 Long vowels are shortened before other vowels in various dialects. .. When the second vowel is short it may be lengthened, resulting in what is known as 'quantitative metathesis'... Homer often shows the older forms.., but also in many cases the shortening and quantitative metathesis. **1973** A. H. SOMMERSTEIN *Sound Pattern Anc. Greek* ii. 69 Quantitative Metathesis. The need for this rule arises chiefly from the vocalism and accentuation of certain third-declension genitive case forms. **1978** *Language* LIV. 441 Thus the order of the rules required by this analysis is Pre-German Accentuation followed by Quantitative Ablaut followed by Germanic Accentuation.

5. *Chem.* Of a procedure or a reaction: acting on the whole quantity of a particular substance or species; having an efficiency or a yield of 100 per cent. Hence also used of the yield or product of such a process.

1905 *Proc. R. Soc.* A. LXXVI. 116 Its [*sc.* a possible new element] quantitative extraction from thorium salts has not yet been investigated. **1907** *Chem. Abstr.* I. 1539 The yield is almost quantitative and the product very pure. **1923** [see QUALITATIVE *a.* b]. **1930** W. T. HALL *Textbk. Quantitative Analysis* xi. 140 For practical purposes, a reaction is complete or quantitative, as we often say, when less than 0·1 mg. remains in solution. **1962** COTTON & WILKINSON *Adv. Inorg. Chem.* x. 194 Diborane..is obtained in essentially quantitative yields by reaction of metal hydrides with boron trifluoride. **1964** N. G. CLARK *Mod. Org. Chem.* xi. 204 On careful combustion there remains a quantitative residue of metallic silver.

B. *sb.* **† a.** A sign that indicates quantity. *Obs.* **b.** That which possesses or involves quantity.

1668 WILKINS *Real Char.* III. ii. 305 Of all which [pronouns] it is to be observed, that they are in some kind or other, Quantitatives. **1846** SABINE tr. *Humboldt's Cosmos* (1847) I. 179 An effort..to investigate the quantitative in the laws of one of the great phænomena of nature.

c. = QUANTIFIER 1 b.

1924 H. E. PALMER *Gram. Spoken Eng.* 45 Quantitatives and Numericals (mʌtʃ), (meni), (faiv).., etc.

ˈquantitatively, *adv.* [f. prec. + -LY[2].]

a. In a quantitative manner; in respect of quantity.

1593 R. HARVEY *Philad.* 21 He and his surveyed it quantitatively. **1624** GATAKER *Transubst.* 115 With quantitie, but not quantitatively. **1644** DIGBY *Of Man's Soul* x. 423 One pure simple substance, peraduenture Metaphysically, or formally diuisible;..but not quantitatiuely. **1845** G. E. DAY tr. *Simon's Anim. Chem.* I. 347 The magnesia and silica were not determined quantitatively. **1870** ROLLESTON *Anim. Life* Introd. 49 The brain holds a more favorable relation quantitatively to the body and to the spinal cord.

b. *Chem.* Completely, entirely; with a yield of 100 per cent.

1911 F. SODDY *Chem. Radio-Elements* I. 26 The radium may be precipitated quantitatively by sulphuric acid. **1950** *Thorpe's Dict. Appl. Chem.* (ed. 4) X. 447/1 An equal quantity of barium chloride is added to ensure that the radium is carried quantitatively with the insoluble residue. **1974** *Nature* 1 Feb. 291/1 Prephenate is quantitatively converted to phenylpyruvate in 10 min at acid *p*H (0·1 N HCl).

So **ˈquantitativeness**, the quality or condition of being quantitative.

1858 H. SPENCER *Ess.* I. 225 The more specific characteristic of scientific previsions..their quantitativeness. **1873** —— *Stud. Sociol.* (1882) 45 Where they are quantitative, their quantitativeness..is mostly very indefinite.

quantitativist (kwɒntɪˈteɪtɪvɪst), *sb.* and *a.* [f. QUANTITATIV(E *a.* + -IST.] **a.** *sb.* A person for whom quantity is a criterion of value. **b.** *adj.* Resulting from an evaluation of quantity.

1957 R. K. MERTON *Social Theory* (rev. ed.) x. 396 The local influential is typically concerned with knowing *as many* people as possible. He is a quantitativist in the sphere of social contacts. **1972** *Human World* Feb. 21 The.. quantitativist illusion that the level of enlightenment must correspond to the amount of time spent between the school walls. **1974** B. PEARCE tr. *Amin's Accumulation on World Scale* II. iii. 452 It is by means of concrete historical explanation that we must account for each period of price increase in the nineteenth century, and not by means of a general quantitativist explanation.

‖ **quantité négligeable** (kɑ̃tite negliʒabl). [Fr., lit. 'negligible quantity'.] A factor of no account, something insignificant.

1886 T. P. WHITE *Ordnance Survey U.K.* vi. 98 It is certain that among the details which would not be a *quantité négligeable*, would figure the trees of any particular district or country. **1913** S. SHAW *William of Germany* viii. 151 The resolve that as Emperor he would not allow Germany to be overlooked, to be treated as a *quantité négligeable*, in the discussion or decision of international affairs. **1921** BARON VON MARGUTTI *Emp. Francis Joseph & his Times* viii. 205 The old Sovereign apparently still regarded the Slavs as a *quantité négligeable*, as they had been at the beginning of his reign. **1973** E. OSERS tr. *Waldheim's Austrian Example* 7 The geopolitical position of Austria within the contact zone or testing ground of the great ideological power-groups of our time has given this small country a meaning that is far from that of a *quantité négligeable*.

† **'quantitied**, *a.* *Obs.* [f. QUANTITY + -ED².] Endowed with quantity or spatial magnitude.

1605 SYLVESTER *Du Bartas* II. iii. I. *Abraham* 1115 Alwaies in some place are Angels..selfly limited, And joyn'd to place, yet not as quantiti'd.

quantitive ('kwɒntɪtɪv), *a.* [f. QUANTITY + -IVE: cf. *qualitive*.] = QUANTITATIVE.

1656 STANLEY *Hist. Philos.* v. (1701) 159/2 Neither equal, nor certain, nor quantitive, nor qualitative. **1669** [see QUANTATIVE]. **1827** G. S. FABER *Expiat. Sacrif.* 148 By what intelligible process can we estimate the quantitive proportions of two dissimilar oblations? **1882–3** SCHAFF *Encycl. Relig. Knowl.* II. 1553 He can make no other distinction between them..than a quantitive one. **1958** T. G. E. POWELL *Celts* 182 It cannot be argued here whether it was prestige, or quantitive representation, that won for it eventually an exclusive position. **1959** *Times* 9 Sept. 16/7 The Four No Trump bid is regarded more often than not as quantitive.

Hence **'quantitively** *adv.* = QUANTITATIVELY.

1827 G. S. FABER *Expiat. Sacrif.* 149 The only mode..in which things dissimilar can be quantitively compared. **1871** B. STEWART *Heat* §402 To estimate either temperature or hardness quantitively.

quantity ('kwɒntɪtɪ). Forms: 4–6 **quantite, -yte,** (4 **-itee, -ytee,** 5 **whantite**), 6 **quauntit,** 6–7 **quantitie,** (6 **-etie**), 6– **quantity.** [a. OF. *quantité*, ad. L. *quantitās, -ātem*, f. *quant-us* how much, how great: see -ITY.]

I. 1. a. Size, magnitude, dimensions. In widest sense implying magnitude in three dimensions, but sometimes contextually limited to (*a*) thickness or stoutness, (*b*) extent of surface, area, (*c*) linear extension, length, height. *Obs.* exc. *Math.*

1387 TREVISA *Higden* (Rolls) I. 49 Asia is most in quantite, Europa is lasse. *c* **1400** MAUNDEV. (Roxb.) xxi. 96 Þare er oþer also of less quantitee, as it ware of þe mykill of a mannes thee. **1426** LYDG. *De Guil. Pilgr.* 5845 Sawh thow euere.. Off manhys herte the quantyte? **1470–85** MALORY *Arthur* v. viii, A grete gyaunt..whiche was a man of an huge quantyte and heyghte. **1578** LYTE *Dodoens* I. lxix. 102 The roote is long, of the quantite of one's fingar. *Ibid.* II. v. 153 White huskes..of the quantitie of a groote, or Testerne. **1632** LITHGOW *Trav.* VI. 298 A Dromidore, and Camel differ.. not in quantity, being of one height, bredth, and length. **1669** STURMY *Mariner's Mag.* v. 17 How to find the just Quantity or Content of any Piece of Ground. **1682** R. BURTON *Admir. Curios.* (1684) 30 Diamonds are found in many places,..their quantity is from a Pease to a Walnut. **1830** KATER & LARDNER *Mech.* i. 4 The quantity of a surface is called its area; and the quantity of a line..its length.

† **b.** A dimension. *Obs. rare*⁻¹.

1590 STOCKWOOD *Rules Constr.* 48 Whether the word of measure do signifie the depth, height, length, thicknes, or any such quantitie of a thing.

† **c.** An amount equal to the volume *of*. *Obs.*

1610 B. JONSON *Alch.* II. i, Taking..on a knife's point, The quantity of a grain of mustard. **1694** SALMON *Bate's Dispens.* (1713) 151/1 Of this Balsam..the Patient may take the Quantity of a pretty large Chestnut.

d. In surveying, ***bill of quantity*** (or ***quantities***) (see quot. 1964).

1877 B. FLETCHER *Quantities* i. 5 The operations necessary to produce the schedule, or bills of quantities, from which builders make up their tenders, are: [etc.]. **1964** J. S. SCOTT *Dict. Building* 32 *Bill of quantities*, a list of numbered items, each of which describes the work to be done in a civil engineering or building contract. Each item shows the quantity of work involved... Those contractors who wish to do the work return the bill, with an extended price opposite each item. **1972** *Guardian* 20 June 10/6 When the architect and engineer have produced drawings, the quantity surveyor can begin 'taking off' (which really means reading the drawings) and 'working up' (which means determining the total quantities of the materials and labour requirements)... He can then produce his 'Bills of Quantity'.

2. Amount, sum. **a.** Of material things not subject to, or not usually estimated by, spatial measurement.

c **1400** MAUNDEV. (Roxb.) xxxi. 142 Of þaim þai gader boumbe in grete quantitee. **1533** ELYOT *Cast. Helthe* (1539) 36 a, Ale and bere..do ingender more grosse vapours, and corrupt humors, than wine doth, beinge drunke in lyke excesse of quantitie. **1683** TRYON *Way to Health* (1697) 205 Of the Quantity of Children's Food. **1769** *De Foe's Tour Gt. Brit.* (ed. 7) II. 64 Fern, which formerly grew in great Quantity there. **1849** NOAD *Electricity* 188 The quantity of the Electric current bears a relation to the size of the plates.

b. Of immaterial things.

c **1375** *Sc. Leg. Saints* x. (*Matthew*) 576 Nothire for þe ennormyte of þe syne, na þe quantyte. *c* **1400** tr. *Secreta Secret., Gov. Lordsh.* 106 Chese a sotell man..to shewe þe quantyte of þy hynes. **1432** *Rolls of Parlt.* IV. 403/1 There should no man ben amerced bote after the quantite of his trespas. *c* **1485** *Digby Myst.* IV. 621 After the whantite of sorofull remembrance. **1611** SHAKS. *Cymb.* IV. ii. 17, I loue thee..How much the quantity, the waight as much, As I do loue my Father. **1647** N. BACON *Disc. Govt. Eng.* I. liii. (1739) 94 Fine and Pledges shall be according to the quantity of the offence. **1780** BENTHAM *Princ. Legisl.* xvii. §15 Any punishment is subservient to reformation in proportion to its quantity. **1827** POLLOK *Course T.* VIII, He prayed by quantity.

† **c.** Of money, payment, etc. *Obs.*

c **1460** FORTESCUE *Abs. & Lim. Mon.* vi. (1885) 121 The iiij^th or the vth parte of the quantite of his expenses. **1528** *Galway Arch.* in *10th Rep. Hist. MSS. Comm.* App. v. 403 That some or quauntit of such monye as they playe for. *a* **1548** HALL *Chron., Edw. IV* 223 b, The fees of canonizyng of a kyng, wer of so great a quantitie at Rome [etc.]. **1600** HAMILTON in *Cath. Tract.* (S.T.S.) 219 The qualitie and quantitie of the oblation. **1714** FORTESCUE-ALAND *Pref. Fortescue's Abs. & Lim. Mon.* 48 The Lord was to forfeit 30*s.* which was then near as much in Quantity as 5*l.* now. **1775** JOHNSON *Tax. no Tyr.* 15 The quantity of this payment.

† **d.** Number, numbers. (Cf. 9.) *Obs. rare.*

1456 SIR G. HAYE *Law Arms* (S.T.S.) 10 The cristin men ..war all persewit and put to dede in grete quantitee. **1581** N. BURNE in *Cath. Tract.* (S.T.S.) 135 To mak Chalices of gold and siluer in mair quantitie and aboundance nor befoir.

3. a. Length or duration in time. Now only in the legal phrase ***quantity of estate***, the length of time during which the right of enjoyment of an estate is to continue.

c **1391** CHAUCER *Astrol.* II. §7 Rekne thanne the quantite of tyme in the bordure by-twixe bothe prikkes. *Ibid.* §9 To knowe the quantite of the day vulgare. **1588** A. KING tr. *Canisius* G vij, According to the quantitie of the yere, obserueit in that age to contene 304 dayes. **1818** CRUISE *Digest* (ed. 2) II. 354 The alteration in the particular estate ..must amount to an alteration in its quantity. **1841** *Penny Cycl.* XIX. 46/1 Where the word Estate is used in its technical sense, it..[means] the quantity and quality of enjoyment of the thing.

b. *Pros.* Length or shortness of sounds or syllables, determined by the time required to pronounce them. Chiefly used with reference to Greek and Latin verse, in which the metres are based on quantity. ***false quantity***: see FALSE *a.* 2.

1563–7 BUCHANAN *Reform. St. Andros* Wks. (1892) 9 Thys classe sal reid..sum buik of Ouide, and the quantiteis of syllabes. **1586** W. WEBBE *Eng. Poetrie* (Arb.) 69 As for the quantity of our wordes, therein lyeth great difficultye. *a* **1637** B. JONSON *Eng. Gram.* iii, All our vowels are..In quantity (which is time) long or short. **1727–41** CHAMBERS *Cycl.* s.v., The quantity of the syllables is but little fixed in the modern tongues. **1774** WARTON *Hist. Eng. Poetry* (1840) I. Diss. ii. 108 King Chilperic..wrote two books of Latin verses..without any idea of the common quantities. **1859** THACKERAY *Virgin.* v, George knew much more Latin.. than his master, and caught him in perpetual..false quantities. **1887** RUSKIN *Præterita* II. 275 A rightly bred scholar who knew his grammar and his quantities.

c. *Mus.* Length or duration of notes.

1597 MORLEY *Introd. Mus.* 9 The quantitie of euery note and rest in the song. **1674** PLAYFORD *Skill Mus.* I. vii. 24 Measure in this Science is a Quantity of the length and shortness of Time. **1811** BUSBY *Dict. Mus.* s.v., Quantity, in music..does not signify the number of notes, or syllables, but their relative duration.

4. In the most abstract sense, *esp.* as the subject of mathematics: That property of things which is involved in the questions 'how great?' or 'how much?' and is determinable, or regarded as being so, by measurement of some kind.

In this sense ***continuous*** and ***discrete quantity*** are distinguished: see DISCRETE 2. 'Quantity' is the second of the ten Aristotelian categories.

1530 PALSGR. Introd. 144 Some [adverbs] betoken quantite. **1570, 1687,** etc. [see DISCRETE]. **1690** LOCKE *Hum. Und.* IV. iii. (1695) 314 The Ideas of Quantity are not those alone that are capable of Demonstration and Knowledge. **1756** BURKE *Subl. & B.* III. ii, All proportions, every arrangement of quantity, is alike to the understanding. **1797** *Encycl. Brit.* (ed. 3) XV. 741/1 Mathematics is..employed in discovering and stating many relations of quantity. **1864** BOWEN *Logic* vii. 185 Mathematics is the science of pure quantity.

5. *Logic.* **a.** The extension or intension of a term, distinguished as ***extensive*** and ***intensive quantity*** (see the adjs.). **b.** The degree of extension which a proposition gives to the term forming its subject, and according to which it is said to be ***universal***, ***particular***, ***singular***, and ***indefinite*** or ***indeterminate*** (see these words).

1668 WILKINS *Real Char.* III. i. 306 Another, A certain one, Some one, are for their Quantities, Singulars or Particulars indeterminate. **1697** tr. *Burgersdicius' Logic* I. xxix. 115 In Respect to Quantity, an Enunciation is divided into Universal, Particular, Indefinite, and Singular. **1725** WATTS *Logic* (1726) 160 Both particular and universal Propositions which agree in Quality but not in Quantity are call'd Subaltern. **1836–8** [see INTENSION 5, EXTENSIVE 5]. **1843** MILL *Logic* I. II. ii. §1 According to what are called the quantity and quality of propositions. **1864** BOWEN *Logic* v. 120 We may inquire concerning the number of objects about which we judge, and thus determine the Quantity, or Extension, of the Judgment. [See also EXTENSION 8 b.]

† **6.** Relative or proportional size or amount, proportion. *Obs. rare.*

1551 RECORDE *Cast. Knowl.* (1556) 146 Euery darke body giueth shadowe accordinge to the quantitie that it beareth to that shyning body, which giueth the light. **1602** SHAKS. *Ham.* III. ii. 177 For womens Feare and Loue, holds quantitie, In neither ought, or in extremity:..And as my Loue is siz'd, my Feare is so.

7. Great or considerable amount or bulk.

1753 HOGARTH *Anal. Beauty* vi. 29 Windsor castle is a noble instance of the effect of quantity. **1877** RAYMOND *Statist. Mines & Mining* 175 Only the smelting-ores have been extracted in quantity.

II. 8. a. A (specified) portion or amount *of* an article or commodity. Also *transf.* of immaterial things. (Cf. 2 above.)

c **1325** *Poem times Edw. II* (Percy) xlii, Give the goodman to drink A gode quantite. *c* **1400** MAUNDEV. (Roxb.) viii. 31 Of þis liquour þai giffe a lytill quantitee til pilgrimes. **1484** CAXTON *Fables of Alfonce* xi, A grete dele or quantite of mostard. **1526** *Pilgr. Perf.* (W. de W. 1531) 64 A lytell quantite of sande in an other lytell bagge. **1602** SHAKS. *Ham.* V. i. 293 Fortie thousand Brothers Could not (with all there quantitie of Loue) Make up my summe. **1696** LUTTRELL *Brief Rel.* (1857) IV. 4 Having received great quantities of broad money from Exeter in order to clip it. **1752** JOHNSON *Rambler* No. 203 ¶10 A certain quantity or measure of renown. **1793** BEDDOES *Calculus* 223 A small quantity of azotic air. **1825** LAMB *Elia* Ser. II. *Stage Illusion*, A sufficient quantity of illusion for the purposes of dramatic interest. **1863** *Q. Rev.* July 78 A certain quantity of snow.

b. An indefinite (usually a fair or considerable) portion or amount; †a small piece, fragment.

c **1325** *Song of Yesterday* in *E.E.P.* (1862) 134 Of his strengþe he leost a quantite. *c* **1400** *Song Roland* 585 Offred them every chon a quantite of gold. **1486** *Bk. St. Albans* C vij, Take a quantyte of poorke..and butter. **1535** COVERDALE *1 Sam.* xxx. 12 They..gaue him a quantite of fygges, & two quantities of rasyns. **1596** SHAKS. *Tam. Shr.* IV. iii. 112 Away thou Ragge, thou quantitie, thou remnant. **1597** —— *2 Hen. IV*, v. i. 77 If I were saw'de into Quantities I should make foure dozen of such bearded Hermites staues. **1731** ARBUTHNOT *Aliments* VI. vii. §2 (1735) 182 Warm antiscorbutical Plants taken in Quantities will occasion stinking Breath. **1852** MRS. STOWE *Uncle Tom's C.* xxxiii. 299 Taking a quantity of cotton from her basket, she placed it in his. **1883** *Manch. Guard.* 18 Oct. 4/7 Yesterday..a quantity of wreckage was cast up at Southport.

c. With def. article: The portion or amount (*of* something) present in a particular thing or instance.

1611 BIBLE *2 Esdras* iv. 50 As the fire is greater then the smoke..so the quantity which is past, did more exceede. **1719** DE FOE *Crusoe* I. ix, I resolv'd to sow just the same Quantity every Year. **1780** BENTHAM *Princ. Legisl.* xviii. §44 The quantity of sensible heat in a human body. **1837** *Penny Cycl.* IX. 343 The total quantity of electricity in the charge of an electrised body. **1876** PREECE & SIVEWRIGHT *Telegraphy* 2 We can speak of the quantity of sound caused by the explosion of a cannon. *Ibid.*, The force of attraction is found to increase with the quantity of electricity present.

9. A specified, or indefinite (= fair, considerable), number of persons or things.

1375 BARBOUR *Bruce* VI. 235 [He] slew of thame a quantite. **14..** *Pol. Rel. & L. Poems* 36 Gadyr a good quantyte of snayles. **1456** SIR G. HAYE *Law Arms* (S.T.S.) 57 Almaist mycht nane persave that ony quantitee of peple eschapit fra the bataill. **1485** CAXTON *Chas. Gt.* 3 The moost quantyte of the people vnderstonde not latyn. **1611** CORYAT *Crudities* 169 There is a farre greater quantity of buildings in this [the Rialto] then in ours. **1750** BEAWES *Lex Mercat.* (1752) 8 A quantity of small marshy isles. **1852** MRS. CARLYLE *Lett.* II. 198 Four chairs and a quantity of pillows. **1897** MARY KINGSLEY *W. Africa* 241, I..find in it a quantity of pools.

10. A certain space or surface; a portion *of* something having superficial extent. Now *rare*.

c **1391** CHAUCER *Astrol.* II. §30 Swych a quantite of latitude as [sheweth] by thyn Almykanteras. **1464** *Rolls Parlt.* V. 519/2 A Graunte..of a pece or a quantite of Lande. **1611** COTGR., *Quartellée*, a certaine quantitie of, or measure for, ground. **1758** S. HAYWARD *Serm.* xiv. 408 In a race there is a quantity of ground laid out. **1792** BURKE *Let. to R. Burke* Corr. IV. 26 You would make them a grant of a sufficient quantity of your land. **1812–6** PLAYFAIR *Nat. Phil.* (1819) II. 214 A fixed star..occupies exactly the same place..within a quantity so small as to be hardly measurable.

† **11.** In adverbial phrases: ***great quantity***, by or to a large amount or extent; to a great distance. ***a quantity***, to some extent, considerably. ***a little quantity***, a little way. *Obs.*

a **1300** *Cursor M.* 8816 Vp þai lifted oft-sith þe tre, It was to scort gret quantite. **1375** BARBOUR *Bruce* VI. 76 Endlang the vattir than ȝeid he On aithir syde gret quantite. **1377** LANGL. *P. Pl.* B. XIX. 372 Þere nas no crystene creature þat kynde witte hadde,..That he ne halpe a quantite holynesse to wexe. *c* **1400** MAUNDEV. (1839) xxiii. 253 Thei leyn upon the hors gold and silver gret quantytee. *c* **1420** *Pallad. on Husb.* XI. 157 Ek lyfte her plaunte a litel quantite.

12. *Math.* A thing having quantity (see 4 above); a figure or symbol standing for such a thing. ***imaginary quantity***: see the adj. 1 c.

1570 BILLINGSLEY *Euclid* XI. def. i. 312 A superficies is a quantitie of greater perfection then is a line. **1581** SIDNEY *Apol. Poetrie* (Arb.) 24 So doe the Geometrician, and Arithmetician, in their diverse sorts of quantities. **1700** MOXON *Math. Dict.* 133 Those Quantities are said to be commensurable, which have one Aliquot part..but Incommensurable Quantities have no Aliquot parts. **1806** HUTTON *Course Math.* I. 201 Range the quantities according to the dimensions of some letter. **1831** BREWSTER *Newton* (1855) II. xiv. 11 He considered quantities not as composed of indivisibles, but as generated by motion. **1881** MAXWELL *Electr. & Magn.* I. 11 There are certain cases in which a quantity may be measured with reference to a line as well as with reference to an area.

transf. **1864** CARLYLE *Fredk. Gt.* XII. xi. (1872) IV. 245 This Holy Romish Reich..has been more and ever more becoming an imaginary quantity. **1870** ROGERS *Hist. Gleanings* Ser. II. 9 Such a monarchy was a mere geographical quantity. **1883** STEVENSON *Silverado Squatters* 134 Her husband was an unknown quantity.

III. 13. *attrib.* and *Comb.*, chiefly in terms relating to quantity of electricity, as ***quantity armature, battery, effect, fuse, galvanometer, inductor***; (sense 8) ***quantity output, production***; also **quantity-mark**, a mark indicating the quantity of a vowel or syllable; **quantity surveyor**, a surveyor who estimates the quantities of labour and materials required for building and engineering work; **quantity theory (of money)** the hypothesis that prices correspond to changes in the monetary supply; so ***quantity theorist***.

1838 *Morn. Chron.* in Noad's *Electricity* (1849) 401 The decomposing power of the quantity inductor. **1849** NOAD *Electricity* 397 One..is used for quantity effects, such as igniting platinum wire. *Ibid.* 399 The quantity armature is constructed of stout iron. **1883** JENKIN *Electr. & Magn.* (ed. 7) 190 The term..'quantity galvanometer' [is used to signify] an instrument with few turns of thick wire [in its coil]. **1884** H. SWEET *13th Pres. Addr. Philol. Soc.* 93 When ..quantity and accent-marks are neglected. **1888** M. FREWEN *Econ. Crisis* i. 5 More emphatic still is John Stuart Mill's statement of the 'quantity theory'. 'That an increase of the quantity of money', wrote Mill, 'raises prices, and a diminution lowers them, is the most elementary proposition in the theory of currency.' **1895** *Econ. Jrnl.* V. 103 So far as concerns the possible causes on the side of *money* for the fall in prices, Lex denies that the 'quantity theory' affords any ground for speaking of an appreciation of gold. **1896** *Daily News* 5 Aug. 9/5 The plans of the buildings..will be now submitted to the quantity surveyor, with a view to the quantities being taken out. **1903** J. L. LAUGHLIN *Princ. Money* vii. 225 (*heading*) History and literature of the quantity theory of money. **1908** *Westm. Gaz.* 8 May 8/3 Bills which had been through the hands of the quantity surveyor and architect. **1912** I. FISHER *Purchasing Power of Money* p. vii, The main contentions of this book are at bottom simply a restatement and complification of the old 'quantity theory' of money. **1919** *Brit. Manufacturer* Nov. 42/1 Quantity output may mean cheap production, but the manufacture of more modest quantities need not be much inferior in this aspect. *Ibid.*, An immense home market..has encouraged him to undertake big quantity production. **1928** E. O'NEILL *Strange Interlude* v. 159 The room is a typical sitting room of the quantity-production bungalow type. **1931** *Times Lit. Suppl.* 19 Feb. 124/2 The quantity theorists have always been baffled by variations in the public's habits and other factors. **1968** *Internat. Encycl. Social Sci.* X. 433 In its most rigid and unqualified form the quantity theory asserts strict proportionality between the quantity of what is regarded as money and the level of prices. **1972** Quantity surveyor [see 1 d above]. **1979** *Jrnl. R. Soc. Arts.* CXXVII. 445/1 The quantity surveyor's functions in the construction process may be described as cost planning, cost control, and the attainment of value for money expended.

quantivalence (kwən'tɪvələns). [f. L. *quanti-* comb. form of *quantum* how much + *-valence* after *equi-valence*.]

1. Of a chemical element: The extent to which one of its atoms can hold other atoms in combination; valence; atomicity.

1871 ROSCOE *Elem. Chem.* 172 This difference of combining power is termed Quantivalence of the elements. **1882** STALLO *Concepts Mod. Phys.* 36 Dyads..and other elements of still higher quantivalence.

2. Mechanical equivalence.

1890 *Brit. Med. Jrnl.* 9 Aug. 319/2 It shows that the quantivalence of nerve force is exceedingly small.

So **quan'tivalency** = prec.; **quan'tivalent** *a.* pertaining or relating to quantivalence.

quantizable ('kwɒntaɪzəb(ə)l), *a. Physics.* [f. as next + -ABLE.] Capable of being quantized.

1935 J. DOUGALL tr. *Born's Atomic Physics* v. 101 Certain quantities can only take values which are whole numbers —they are called quantisable quantities. **1946** *Nature* 31 Aug. 309/1 Our solar system is quantizable according to the equation: $n \times 137^k$ = orbital impulse/(2 × planetary spin).

quantization (kwɒntaɪ'zeɪʃən). [f. next + -ATION.] The action of quantizing; the fact or state of being quantized. **a.** *Physics.* Cf. QUANTIZE *v.* 1.

1922 *Rep. Brit. Assoc. Adv. Sci. 1921* 473 In some cases.. the quantisation can be done in several ways and each leads to a different set of permissible orbits, but the energy of each has the same set of values and so they give the same spectrum. **1922** *Proc. Cambr. Philos. Soc.* XXI. 80 (*heading*) A general condition for the quantisation of the conditionally periodic motions with an application for the Bohr atom. **1925** *Nature* 5 Dec. 849/1 It seemed possible to formulate certain general laws, the so-called rules of 'quantisation', by means of which the stationary states were to be chosen from the continuous manifold of such motions. **1940** GLASSTONE *Text-bk. Physical Chem.* i. 63 The existence of $2j + 1$ magnetic quantum numbers for each value of j implies that the electrons can take up $2j + 1$ different orientations in a magnetic field..: in other words, there should be a quantization of electron orbits. **1975** *Physics Bull.* July 311/1 To see the departure of the specific heat of solids from the classical Dulong Petit law due to quantization of lattice vibration energies we often need to go to temperatures of the order of 100 K.

b. *Telecommunications.* Cf. QUANTIZE *v.* 2. Usu. *attrib.*, as ***quantization distortion***, ***level***, ***noise***.

1947 *Bell Syst. Techn. Jrnl.* XXVI. 395 PCM involves the application of two basic concepts. These concepts are..the time-division principle and the amplitude quantization principle. **1948** *Proc. IRE* XXXVI. 1324/2 Representing the signal by certain discrete allowed levels only is called quantizing. It inherently introduces an initial error in the magnitude of the samples, giving rise to quantization noise. **1951** *Ibid.* XXXIX. 44 (*heading*) Quantization distortion in pulse-count modulation with nonuniform spacing of levels. **1953** A. T. STARR *Radio & Radar Technique* i. 32 Quantization could be used with any known system of modulation, e.g. the signal wave could be quantized and then used to modulate the amplitude or frequency of a carrier. **1975** D. G. FINK *Electronics Engineers' Handbk.* IV. 44 A quantization noise..is inevitably associated with all quantized signals. This noise can be made as small as desired by choosing enough quantization levels or, equivalently, making each quantization level small enough.

quantize ('kwɒntaɪz), *v.* [f. QUANTUM + -IZE.]

1. *trans. Physics.* To apply quantum theory to; *esp.* to restrict the number of possible values of (a quantity) or states of (a physical entity or system) so that certain variables can assume only certain discrete magnitudes that are integral multiples of a common factor.

1922 *Rep. Brit. Assoc. Adv. Sci. 1921* 473 For the specific heats of gases..it is necessary to 'quantise' rotations instead of vibrations. **1958** *New Scientist* 27 Feb. 29/1 Yukawa had been very impressed by the success of quantum mechanics ..in explaining phenomena connected with the ordinary electromagnetic field. Such a field can be 'quantised' into photons—discrete packets of light waves. **1973** *Physics Bull.* Nov. 656/2 This amplification of gravity produces a theory which cannot be quantized by standard methods, however. **1975** *Nature* 17 Apr. 560/2 The problem of quantising gravity is a pressing one if a unified theory of all the forces of nature is to be obtained.

2. *trans. Telecommunications.* To approximate (a signal varying continuously in amplitude) by one whose amplitude is restricted to a prescribed set of discrete values.

1947 *Bell Syst. Techn. Jrnl.* XXVI. 409 Over and above these effects,..the background noise which is present to a greater or lesser extent in all communication circuits, is quantized by the PCM system. **1953** *Electronic Engin.* XXV. 148/1 If the signal is sampled before being quantized, harmonics (including the first) of the pulse repetition frequency will be present. **1953** [see QUANTIZATION b]. **1972** *Physics Bull.* Jan. 44/1 In the new technique the signals from the eddy current probes are quantized by digital means. **1977** F. G. STREMLER *Introd. Communication Syst.* vii. 356 Suppose..we wish to quantize one-half a cycle of a one-volt (peak) sinusoid using eight discrete levels.

3. *transf.* and *fig.*

1956 *Kenyon Rev.* XVIII. 412 The sounds..are then quantized into their phonemes. **1965** *Revue Internat. de la Documentation* XXXII. 21/2 To do this it is necessary to quantize the texts by dividing them into convenient units. **1969** *Language* XLIV. 14 As Hoenigswald..remarked, 'The doctrine of gradual phonetic change may turn out to be a remnant from pre-phonemic days,' when the multi-dimensional continua of speech had not yet been successfully quantized. **1974** *Sci. Amer.* Dec. 132/2 Because curves can be coded to any desired precision by numbers, a symphony, like a painting or a poem, can be quantized and expressed by a number chain.

Hence **'quantizing** *vbl. sb.* and *ppl. a.*

1923 E. N. DA C. ANDRADE *Structure of Atom* ix. 147 The principle laid down for the quantising of angular momentum gives $mvr = nh/2\pi$, where n is a whole number. **1948** *Bell Syst. Techn. Jrnl.* XXVII. 456 Since quantizing noise is uniformly distributed throughout the signal band, its interfering effect..is probably similar to that of thermal noise with the same mean power. **1973** *Appl. Physics Lett.* XXIII. 41/1 Because of the quantizing longitudinal magnetic field, the conduction band is split into Landau levels. **1975** D. G. FINK *Electronics Engineers' Handbk.* IV. 44 The process of quantizing is irreversible since regardless of how small the quantization level Q is taken to be, an unresolvable uncertainty of $\pm Q/2$ is associated after quantizing with each amplitude value.

quantized ('kwɒntaɪzd), *ppl. a.* [f. prec. + -ED[1].] Subject to the restrictions imposed by quantization; able to occur with certain discrete values only.

1923 H. L. BROSE tr. *Sommerfeld's Atomic Struct. & Spectral Lines* iv. 212 Both [conditions] together demand that the electron move only in certain 'quantised' circles. **1937** G. GAMOW *Struct. Atomic Nuclei* iv. 67 The atomic nucleus, being a quantized system, is in general capable of existence in any one of a number of states of different energy. **1939** V. ROJANSKY *Introd. Quantum Mech.* iv. 145 The energy of a free particle is not quantized. **1966** C. KITTEL *Introd. Solid State Physics* (ed. 3) v. 134 The lattice contribution to the heat capacity of solids..approaches zero as the temperature approaches zero; this can be explained only if the lattice vibrations are quantized. **1973** *Physics Bull.* Dec. 715/3 The flux which is trapped in a superconducting loop is quantized in units of $h/2e$.

quantizer ('kwɒntaɪzə(r)). *Electronics.* [f. as prec. + -ER[1].] A device that quantizes a signal applied to it.

1948 *Bell Syst. Techn. Jrnl.* XXVII. 450 An actual quantizer (staircase transducer) has a finite overload value which must not be exceeded and hence can have only a finite number of steps. **1953** *Electronic Engin.* XXV. 146/2 The channel modulators of a pulse-length modulated T.D.M. system feed a common quantizer and coder. **1967** *Electronics* 6 Mar. 127/2 Sierra also offers a 'quantizer' that puts thermal contours..on the scope. **1975** C. L. & J. W. S. LIU *Linear Systems Analysis* ii. 48 Consider a discrete quantizer whose output $y(n)$ at any instant n is equal to the integral part of the input $x(n)$ if the fractional part of $x(n)$ is less than 0·5.

Quantometer (kwɒn'tɒmɪtə(r)). Also **quantometer**. [f. QUANT(ITY + -OMETER.] A type of automatic spectrograph, used esp. for the analysis of alloys.

Formerly a proprietary term in the U.S.

1927 *Official Gaz.* (U.S. Patent Office) 3 May 12/1 Francis Cutler Ellis..Chicago, Ill...*Quantometer*... Instrument for diagnosis and food and remedy testing by analysis of radiant energies. Claims use since Sept. 1, 1926. **1947** *Jrnl. Iron & Steel Inst.* CLVI. 78 A commercial model, the Quantometer, consists of source, dispersing, and recording units operating as one instrument. **1958** *Engineering* 21 Feb. 61/2 (Advt.), To meet the need for still greater speed there is now in use at Corby an automatic direct-reading spectrographic analyser known as a Quantometer. **1974** J. H. DIXON tr. *Torasov's Spectroscope* i. 6 The quantometer is used for the simultaneous quantitative emission analysis of several elements in steels or alloys.

quantong, variant of QUANDONG.

quantophrenia (kwɒntəʊ'friːnɪə). [f. QUANT(ITATIVE *a.* + -O + *-phrenia* as in *hebephrenia*.] A term used for an obsession with and exaggerated reliance upon mathematical methods or results, esp. in research connected with the social sciences. So **quanto'phrenic** *a.*

1956 P. A. SOROKIN *Fads & Foibles in Mod. Sociol.* (1958) vii. 103 When the true quantitative method is replaced by pseudomathematical imitations; when the method is misused and abused in various ways; when it is applied to phenomena which, so far, do not lend themselves to quantification..then the approach misfires. Under these conditions, use of mathematical method becomes a mere quantophrenic preoccupation having nothing in common with mathematics and giving no cognition of the psycho-social world... The tidal wave is at present so high that the contemporary stage of the psychosocial sciences can be properly called *the age of quantophrenia and numerology*. **1964** *Encounter* Sept. 72 There is quantophrenia—an obsession with statistics as the sole ground of certitude in a changing world. **1975** *Times Lit. Suppl.* 14 Feb. 162/5 Lundberg remains a sociologist honest and reflective enough to have tried to give 'quantophrenia' and testability ..a firm intellectual base.

quant. suff., abbrev. of QUANTUM SUFFICIT.

†**'quantulate**, *v. Obs. rare*$^{-1}$. [f. L. *quantus* how great (? after *calculate*).] *trans.* To calculate the magnitude of.

1610 W. FOLKINGHAM *Art of Survey* II. iv. 53 Quantulate the angle betwixt the marke and second station.

‖**quantulum** ('kwɒntjʊləm). [L., neut. of *quantulus* how small.] A small quantum.

1824 SOUTHEY *Sir T. More* (1831) II. 260 The quantulum at which Oxenstern admired would be a large allowance now.

quantum ('kwɒntəm). Pl. **quanta** (*rare* except in senses 5 and 6), †**quantums** (sense 5 only). [L., neut. of *quantus* how much, how great.]

1. a. Sum, amount; = QUANTITY 2; *spec.* in *Law*, an amount, a sum (*of* money payable in damages, etc.).

1619 PURCHAS *Microcosmus* xxxii. 302 To set The true *Quantum*, the true poize and price vpon himselfe. **1738** *Hist. Crt. Excheq.* iii. 43 To vote in the first Place, that the King should be supplied; in the next Place, the Quantum of the Supply. **1791** NEWTE *Tour Eng. & Scot.* 179 The momentum of bodies depends on the quantum of their velocity multiplied into that of their matter. **1818** CRUISE *Digest* (ed. 2) I. 427 If the union and accession of the two estates were the cause of the merger, the quantum of the thing granted would be the measure of that merger. **1898** in *Southern Reporter* XXIII. 718/2 The quantum of damages as fixed by the lower court is, we think, too low. **1912** *Law Rep.* (House of Lords Appeal Cases) 688 The quantum of damage is a question of fact, and the only guidance the law can give is to lay down general principles. **1945** *Tulane Law Rev.* XIX. 626 In a large majority of jurisdictions the pecuniary condition of the defendant has no bearing on the *quantum* of compensatory damages awarded the plaintiff in an action for personal injuries. **1951** *Scots Law Times* 11 Aug. 181/1 There can never be any binding precedents on quantum of damages because a sum reasonable in the circumstances of case A might be grossly unreasonable in case B. *Ibid.*, Quantum must be considered afresh in every case having regard to the particular circumstances of that case. **1970** *Internat. & Compar. Law Q.* XIX. 126 Strict liability with an unbreakable limit should confine litigation to questions of quantum. **1974** *Times* 6 Feb. 7/1 The Court of Appeal dismissed an appeal on quantum of damages by Horizon Holidays Ltd.

b. = QUANTITY 7.

1815 W. H. IRELAND *Scribbleomania* 33 His study has not been for quantum to strive, But with beauties to keep the attention alive.

2. = QUANTITY 12.

1647 H. MORE *Song of Soul* II. i. II. lv, Each quantum's infinite, straight will be said. **1678** CUDWORTH *Intell. Syst.* I. v. 783 Though it be an Absolute Contradiction, for a Body, or Quantum, to be..All of it in every Part of that Space, which the Whole is in. **1877** E. CAIRD *Philos. Kant* II. xi. 442 All phenomena, as perceived, are extensive quanta.

3. One's share or portion.

1649 JER. TAYLOR *Gt. Exemp.* II. xii. 94 Poverty is her portion, and her quantum is but food and raiment. **1724** SWIFT *Drapier's Lett.* Wks. 1755 V. II. 60 He will double his present quantum by stealth as soon as he can. **1818** BENTHAM *Ch. Eng.* 421 A Parish, in which the quantum of this soul-saving Mammon rises as high as 12,000*l.* a year. **1897** F. T. BULLEN *Cruise 'Cachalot'* 167 Having completed our quantum of wood, water, and fresh provisions.

4. a. A (specified) amount. = QUANTITY 8.

1789 BELSHAM *Ess.* I. ii. 19 Is there not a sufficient quantum of distress and misfortune? **1829** CARLYLE *Misc.* (1857) II. 113 Some smaller quantum of earthly enjoyment. **1852** JERDAN *Autobiog.* II. xii. 137 Imbued with a moderate quantum of worldly wisdom.

b. = QUANTITY 8 c.

1735 BERKELEY *Querist* I. §215 Such a bank..was faulty in not limiting the quantum of bills. **1828** J. BALLANTYNE *Exam. Hum. Mind* II. 69 The mind..has always a tendency to possess the same quantum of ideas. **1879** E. R. LANKESTER *Advancem. Sc.* (1890) 14 A struggle among all those born for the possession of the small quantum of food.

5. *Physics.* A minimum amount of a physical quantity which can exist and by multiples of which changes in the quantity occur.

This use of *quantum* originated in Ger. in two classic papers by Planck and by Einstein. Planck introduced the concept of a quantum in *Verh. d. Deutsch. Physik. Ges.* (1900) II. 237ff. In that paper he assumed that the energy of an oscillator is always an integral multiple of an 'energy

element' (*G. energieelement*, p. 242), i.e. a quantum (sense 5 a), but he did not call it a quantum; however he did use the word in a passing reference to the electronic charge ('das Elementarquantum der Elektricität', p. 245: = sense 5 b).
Einstein, in *Ann. d. Physik* (1905) XVII. 132ff., assumed that light is radiated in the form of what he called 'energy quanta' (*G. energiequanta*, p. 133: = sense 5 a).
The affinities of the following isolated use are not clear; it seems not to be related to Planck's use, and may derive rather from senses 1–4.

1902 LD. KELVIN in *Phil. Mag.* III. 257 According to the well-known doctrine of Aepinus, .. positive and negative electrifications consist in excess above, and deficiency below, a natural quantum of a fluid, called the electric fluid, permeating among the atoms of ponderable matter. *Ibid.* 259 The neutralizing quantum of electrons [= 'atoms of resinous electricity'] for any atom or group of atoms has exactly the same quantity of electricity of one kind as the atom or group of atoms has of electricity of the opposite kind. The quantum for any single atom may be one or two or three or any integral number, and need not be the same for all atoms... The differences of quality of the atoms of different substances may be partially due to the quantum-numbers of their electrons being different.

a. A discrete quantity of electromagnetic energy proportional in magnitude to the frequency of the radiation it represents.

1910 *Sci. Abstr.* A. XIII. 556 The absorption of the corresponding light-quantum. **1913** *Rep. Brit. Assoc. Adv. Sci. 1912* 407 Assuming that an oscillator can only emit definite, discontinuous quantums of energy, Planck showed that their magnitude is proportional to the frequency. **1913** *Phil. Mag.* XXVI. 19 These calculations strongly suggest that an electron of great velocity in passing through an atom and colliding with the electrons bound will loose energy in distinct finite quanta. **1929** D. H. LAWRENCE *Pansies* 28 Look then Where the father of all things swims in a mist of atoms Electrons and energies, quantums and relativities. **1934** A. J. MEE *Physical Chem.* xix. 721 We can, in a few cases, induce fluorescence of shorter wavelength than that of the absorbed light, since the energy emitted is not only that of the absorbed quantum, but also that inherent in the system before the absorption. **1965** *Physical Rev. Lett.* XV. 1013/1 He^+ ions decaying spontaneously from the $3S$ state do so via the $2P$ levels in $\sim 1 \times 10^{-8}$ seconds with the emission of a 1640Å quantum followed by a 303Å quantum. **1978** *Sci. Amer.* June 69/2 Conversely, when the atom or molecule is de-excited, it drops back one full step or more and the energy difference is either radiated away as a quantum of electromagnetic energy or transferred directly, through a collision, to another atom or molecule.

b. An analogous discrete amount of any other physical quantity (as momentum, electric charge).

1914 *Chem. Abstr.* VIII. 1050 (*heading*) Existence of quantities of electricity which are smaller than the charge of the elementary quantum or the electron. **1923** H. L. BROSE tr. *Sommerfeld's Atomic Struct. & Spectral Lines* iv. 199 We see that the rotator is to be quantised not in energy quanta but in quanta of moment of momentum... The moment of momentum must be a whole multiple of $h/2\pi$. **1931** H. P. ROBERTSON tr. *Weyl's Theory of Groups* i. 43 The constant of proportionality was equal to the quotient of the *h* obtained by Planck from black body radiation and the elementary quantum of electric charge *e*. **1958** *Nature* 31 May 1524/1 (*heading*) Detection of single quanta of circulation in rotating helium II. **1969** *Sci. Jrnl.* Jan. 87/2 There is a possibility that one day a minimum absolute quantum of length may also be found in the universe. **1973** *Sci. Amer.* Jan. 88/3 Waves of elastic crystal vibrations generate quanta of sound called phonons.

c. More fully ***quantum of action***. = *Planck's constant*.

1913 *Phil. Mag.* XXVI. 2 Whatever the alteration in the laws of motion of the electrons may be, it seems necessary to introduce .. a quantity foreign to the classical electrodynamics, *i.e.* Planck's constant, or as it often is called the elementary quantum of action. **1922** *Rep. Brit. Assoc. Adv. Sci. 1921* 473 The essential feature of the [quantum] theory is the existence of a universal constant, the quantum $h = 6{\cdot}55 \times 10^{-27}$ erg sec., which in some way .. controls exchanges of energy. **1923** B. RUSSELL *ABC of Atoms* vi. 80 The quantity *h*, Planck's quantum, has been found to be involved in all the very minute phenomena that can be adequately studied. **1933** *Nature* 25 Mar. 422/2 A causal description in the classical sense is possible only in such cases where the action involved is large compared with the quantum of action. **1956** E. H. HUTTEN *Lang. Mod. Physics* v. 179 We can measure simultaneous values of both parameters only in such a way that the numerical product of their inaccuracies is, at best, equal to the quantum of action h.

d. *fig.*

1960 R. W. MARKS *Dymaxion World of B. Fuller* 10/1 Fuller regards all human experiences as energy events finite in extent. All experiments performed, books written, thoughts expressed, and structures completed, are finite energy events. Together they form a totality, a cornucopia of patterned quanta. **1962** P. STREVENS *Papers in Lang.* (1965) v. 67 Teaching takes place by *quanta*. Whether the teacher realizes it or not, he can teach only in steps, though these vary in size. **1969** *Daily Tel.* (Colour Suppl.) 10 Jan. 32/2 Generalisations serve a purpose, but true understanding is made up of many discrete *quanta*. I can describe the Atlantic littoral thus and so; but I *know* it—thus: [etc.]. **1977** *Times* 4 Aug. 8/6 A fine quantum of derring-do ranging from icy Sweden to a storm-threatened Scottish islet.

6. *Physiol.* Orig. a small voltage of which integral multiples go to make up the end-plate potential measured at a neuromuscular junction; hence, the unit quantity of acetylcholine corresponding to this, multiples of which are released to transmit a nerve impulse across the junction.

1952 FATT & KATZ in *Jrnl. Physiol.* CXVII. 120 The experiment throws some new light on the action of calcium at the nerve-muscle junction: lack of calcium apparently reduces the e.p.p. in definite 'quanta'. **1954** DEL CASTILLO & KATZ in *Ibid.* CXXIV. 560 It has been suggested that the end-plate potential (e.p.p.) at a single nerve-muscle junction is built up statistically of small all-or-none units... A convenient picture of how hundreds of such quanta .. can build up an e.p.p. of, say, 70–80 mV is provided by the hypothesis that separate parcels of acetylcholine (ACh), released from discrete spots of the nerve endings, short-circuit the muscle membrane. *Ibid.* 574 Recent evidence indicating that ACh release occurs in discrete quanta. **1970** J. W. PHILLIS *Pharmacol. of Synapses* ii. 17 In addition to being released by stimulation, individual quanta are released from the terminal spontaneously... At the neuromuscular junction, the number of quanta available for immediate release is probably of the order of 1000. **1978** *Nature* 9 Feb. 561/1 Acetyl-choline .. is released from stimulated nerve terminals in packets or quanta, each containing roughly 10,000 molecules.

7. a. *attrib.* and *Comb.* (in sense 5), as ***quantum energy***, ***hypothesis***, ***law***, ***physics*** (hence ***quantum physicist***), ***property***; **quantum advance** = *quantum leap*; **quantum chemistry**, the branch of physical chemistry concerned with the explanation of chemical phenomena in terms of quantum mechanics; so **quantum chemist**, an expert or specialist in this; **quantum-chemical** *a.*; **quantum chromodynamics** [CHROMO-, after *quantum electrodynamics*], a quantum field theory in which the strong interaction is described in terms of an interaction between quarks that is mediated by gluons, both kinds of particle being assigned a quantum number called 'colour'; abbrev. *QCD*; **quantum condition**, a condition resulting from, or forming part of, the application of quantum theory to a system; a condition that selects from the states allowed by classical physics those that are consistent with quantum theory; **quantum defect**, a number representing the degree to which an energy level of an atom with a single valence electron is displaced from the corresponding level of the hydrogen atom, being the amount by which the true principal quantum number of the level exceeds the effective value of the number; **quantum dynamics** = QUANTUM MECHANICS; hence **quantum-dynamical** *a.*; **quantum effect**, a physical effect attributed to the existence of quanta; **quantum efficiency**, the proportion of incident photons that are effective in causing the decomposition of a molecule, the emission of a photoelectron, or similar photo-effect; **quantum electrodynamics**, the part of quantum field theory concerned with the electromagnetic field and its interaction with electrically charged particles; so **quantum-electrodynamic, -dynamical** *adjs.*; abbrev. *QED*; **quantum electronics**, the branch of physics concerned with the practical consequences of the quantization of energy states and their interaction with electromagnetic radiation; so **quantum-electronic** *a.*; **quantum field theory**, a field theory that incorporates quantum mechanics and the principles of the theory of relativity; **quantum increase**, a sudden large increase; cf. *quantum jump*; **quantum jump**, an abrupt transition between one stationary state of a quantized system and another, with the absorption or emission of a quantum; also *transf.*, a sudden large increase or advance; **quantum leap**, a sudden large advance; cf. *quantum jump*; **quantum level**, an energy level in a quantized system; **quantum liquid**, a liquid that exhibits quantum effects on the macroscopic scale; **quantum number**, a number which enters into the expression for the value of some quantized property of a system (usu. a particle, atom, or molecule) and can assume only certain integral and sometimes half-integral values; also *transf.*, the property so characterized; **quantum orbit**, an orbit (of an electron in an atom) defined by a set of quantum numbers; **quantum solid**, a solid that exhibits quantum effects on the macroscopic scale; **quantum state**, a state of physical (esp. atomic) system that is defined by a set of quantum numbers; a quantized state; **quantum statistics**, the statistics of the energy distribution of particles when the quantization of energy is taken into account; cf. *Bose-Einstein statistics*, *Fermi-Dirac statistics*; hence **quantum-statistical** *a.*; **quantum transition** = *quantum jump* (*lit.* sense); **quantum yield** = *quantum efficiency*. Also QUANTUM MECHANICS, QUANTUM THEORY.

1974 *Sci. Amer.* June 105/3 When these inferences are taken together with the differences between the two material cultures .. one is led to conclude that the Upper Paleolithic represents a *quantum advance in human cultural evolution. **1960** *McGraw-Hill Encycl. Sci. & Technol.* XI. 145/2 The most useful of these methods, the variation method, has produced most of the important *quantum-chemical concepts. *Ibid.* 146/1 The success of this method depends .. on the ability of the *quantum chemist to guess at trial functions which are good approximations and at the same time contain parameters in such a form that *W* can be minimized without undue labor. **1970** *Sci. Amer.* Apr. 54/1 Since the introduction of the fundamental wave equation of quantum mechanics by Erwin Schrödinger in 1926, much of the work of quantum chemists has been focused on its solution for specific chemical systems. **1944** H. EYRING et al. (*title*) *Quantum chemistry. **1963** *New Scientist* 14 Mar. 582/3 After a rather long incubation period, the new subject of 'quantum chemistry' has got into its stride and is gaining rapidly in strength. **1975** H. FRITZSCH et al. in *Phys. Lett.* B. LIX. 256/1 A good name for this theory is *quantum chromodynamics (QCD). **1976** *Nature* 12 Aug. 538/1 The 'gauge field theories' are underlying not only weak electromagnetic but perhaps also strong interactions (the new jargon here being quantum chromo-dynamics, or QCD, analogous to quantum electro-dynamics). **1979** *Sci. Amer.* Aug. 157/2 No one has yet been able to derive the confinement of quarks from the underlying theory of quantum chromodynamics. **1923** *Physical Rev.* XXII. 547 This variation principle includes formally in a single equation the results of classical dynamics and the Sommerfeld *quantum conditions. **1955** O. KLEIN in W. Pauli *Niels Bohr* 99 The importance of transformation groups for the formulation of quantum conditions in field theories .. has been strongly emphasized. **1974** G. REECE tr. *Hund's Hist. Quantum Theory* vi. 89 The 'stationary states' were selected from the possible classical motions by 'quantum conditions' $I_k = hn_k$. **1930** RUARK & UREY *Atoms, Molecules & Quanta* vii. 194 The *quantum defect is a measure of the departure of the spectral term from the hydrogenic term having the same total quantum number. **1970** G. K. WOODGATE *Elem. Atomic Struct.* vi. 103 We consider the sequence iso-electronic with sodium... The ionization potentials for this sequence, .. together with the quantum defect $\delta(s)$ .. are given below. **1932** *Physical Rev.* XL. 406 In solving the wave mechanical perturbation problem the distance between the interacting structures has been treated as a fixed parameter. Then *quantum dynamical reasoning has been abandoned, and the remainder of the problem has been solved by the method of classical statistics. **1927** *Proc. R. Soc.* A. CXIII. 621 (*heading*) The physical interpretation of the *quantum dynamics. **1967** CONDON & ODISHAW *Handbk. Physics* (ed. 2) VII. i. 3/1 These laws of quantum dynamics must involve the universal Planck constant .. in an essential way; and the quantum laws must go over asymptotically into the classical laws, not involving *h*, as the scale of the phenomena is increased. **1914** *Chem. Abstr.* VIII. 3141 E. detd. the at. ht. of highly compressed He at temps. from 18° to 32° abs... A small *quantum effect is apparent. **1946** *Physical Rev.* LXIX. 195 (*heading*) Quantum effects in the interaction of electrons with high frequency fields and the transition to classical theory. **1975** *McGraw-Hill Yearbk. Sci. & Technol.* 114/2 The interaction between two charged particles, classically treated, is given .. by Maxwell's electrodynamic equations, if the particles are in relative motion. The inclusion of quantum effects has led to a more general theory, called quantum electrodynamics. **1926** *Trans. Faraday Soc.* XXI. 453 In the photochemical isomeric change of maleic and fumaric acid, the *quantum efficiency was found to be much smaller than unity. **1940** GLASSTONE *Textbk. Physical Chem.* xiii. 1135 According to the law of the photo-chemical equivalent one mol of absorbing substance should decompose for every $2{\cdot}854 \times 10^5/\lambda$ kg.-cal. of radiation absorbed... This relationship .. permits the law to be tested experimentally. The results are expressed in terms of the quantum efficiency. **1978** *Nature* 16 Mar. p. xiv/3 Two versions of the new EMI photo-multiplier tube .. are available with .. typical peak quantum efficiency of about 22%. **1965** *Physical Rev. Lett.* XV. 1013 (*heading*) Measurement of the *quantum-electrodynamic level shift in the $n = 3$ state of (He^4). **1956** *Physical Rev.* CI. 1410 The *quantum-electro-dynamical fourth-order corrections for the intervals of the triplet fine structure of helium are calculated. **1927** *Proc. R. Soc.* A. CXIV. 243 Hardly anything has been done up to the present on *quantum electrodynamics. **1955** L. ROSENFELD in W. Pauli *Niels Bohr* 70 They questioned the logical consistency of quantum electro-dynamics by contending that the very concept of electro-magnetic field is not susceptible, in quantum theory, to any physical determination by means of measurements. The measurement of a field component requires determinations of the momentum of a charged test-body; and the reaction of the field radiated by the test-body in the course of these operations would .. lead to a limitation of the accuracy of the field measurement, entirely at variance with the premises of the theory. **1971** *Sci. Amer.* June 64/3 The laws of electricity and magnetism as they are now embodied in the equations of quantum electrodynamics represent the one and only area in physics where a single quantitative description has proved valid over the entire range of experiments for which it has been tested, from cosmic dimensions down to 10^{-15} centimeter. **1976** B. BOVA *Multiple Man* (1977) i. 11 The President .. was protected by an invisible laser-activated shield... Fool-proof *quantum-electronic security. **1959** *Jrnl. Appl. Physics* XXX. 956/1 An international conference on *Quantum Electronics—Resonance Phenomena will be held .. on September 14–16, 1959. The conference will consider basic problems in physics and electronics which are important to the increasing use of molecular and atomic resonance in masers, atomic clocks, and related devices. **1965** *Wireless World* Aug. 386/2 The film .. covers a wide range of applications including quantum electronics in transistors, lasers and masers. **1972** *Physics Bull.* Sept. 562/1 Quantum electronics as a field of study dates from the use of stimulated emission for microwave amplification in 1954. **1921** *Discovery* Sept. 227/2 When the *quantum energy of the exciting radiation exceeds this amount the whole K series [of X-rays] is excited. **1948** *Physical Rev.* LXXIV. 224/1 (*heading*) On infinite field reactions in *quantum field theory. **1956** H. UMEZAWA *Quantum Field Theory* i. 11 The present quantum field theory was formulated (Heisenberg and Pauli (1929)) by extending quantum mechanics so as to satisfy the relativity requirements and to treat the various transmutations [of particles into one another]. **1978** *Sci. Amer.* Feb. 128/1 (*caption*) The creation and annihilation of particles and antiparticles is the characteristic process that distinguishes quantum field theories from 'classical' field theories such as Maxwell's or Einstein's. **1914** *Rep. Brit. Assoc. Adv. Sci. 1913* 378 The quite definite result is obtained that.. the exchange of energy between matter and ether must take place by finite jumps of amount.. $\epsilon = h\nu$. This is, of course, the hypothesis, spoken of briefly as the *quantum-hypothesis, which was first suggested by Planck. **1968** F. L. Pilar *Elem. Quantum Chem.* i. 8 Planck's own feeling, which persisted for many years, was that the quantum hypothesis itself could have no basic significance but rather was an artificiality which would eventually be replaced with a more reasonable alternative. **1973** *Sci. Amer.* May 8/2 Intellectual and other exchanges with China appear to be on the verge of a *quantum increase. **1974** *Daily Tel.* (Colour Suppl.) 16 Aug. 17 Throughout this enormous area.. people have been dying of diseases aggravated by malnutrition, just as they have died every year since man first inhabited the Sahel, but so far there has been no *quantum* increase in human mortality as a result of the lengthy drought. **1927** N. V. Sidgwick *Electronic Theory of Valency* ii. 18 Bohr's theory is based on two fundamental postulates... The second.. is that the electron radiates energy.. only when it passes in a '*quantum jump' from one of these stationary states to another of smaller energy. **1937** E. C. Kemble *Fund. Princ. Quantum Mech.* viii. 290 The variation in the distribution function thus defined.. is commonly interpreted as due to 'quantum jumps' from one energy level to the other caused by the radiation. **1955** *Sci. News Let.* 19 Feb. 116/2 Radioactive fall-out is the 'third quantum jump' in the history of modern weapons. The first quantum jump, Dr. Lapp explained, was the A-bomb that shattered Hiroshima. **1961** *Flight* LXXX. 907/1 On the subject of launch operations, Mr Debus claimed that a 'quantum jump' was necessary to meet the challenge of the lunar programme. **1966** *Guardian* 1 Jan. 8/1 This new escalation (or 'quantum jump', to use the latest addition to the bewildering mixture of metaphors) would look better if it were preceded by another bombing pause. **1974** G. Reece tr. *Hund's Hist. Quantum Theory* x. 129 While the emission and absorption of light seemed to be connected with a quantum jump, its dispersion did not. **1975** *Chinese Econ. Stud.* VIII. iv. 52 In old China, the issue of legal tender reached astronomical figures, leading to galloping inflation and quantum jumps in prices. **1916** *Chem. Abstr.* X. 1722 (*heading*) The *quantum law and the structure of the hydrogen atom. **1967** Quantum law [see *quantum dynamics*]. **1970** *New Scientist* 3 Dec. 372/1 The ability of marine technology to take '*quantum' leaps in innovation means that a laissez-faire approach to the ocean mineral resources can no longer be tolerated. **1973** *Daily Tel.* (Colour Suppl.) 2 Nov. 27/2 Hovercraft, like many inventions of modern technology, are supposed to progress in quantum leaps. **1977** *New Yorker* 13 June 108/2 The imperial Presidency did not begin with Richard Nixon although under him abuses of the office took a quantum leap. **1931** G. Gamow *Constitution of Atomic Nuclei* iii. 63 Some elements have rather complicated γ-ray spectra, while others have only a few lines... These facts are evidently connected with the strength of the initial excitation and the relative position of the *quantum-levels in the different nuclei. **1960** Chalmers & Quarrell *Physical Examination of Metals* (ed. 2) xvi. 751 Above the true quantum levels there are further, 'empty' levels, representing states in which nuclei may exist momentarily before disintegrating. **1950** F. London *Superfluids* I. 1 The 'superfluids' or '*quantum liquids' probably exhibit the most conspicuous phenomena of macroscopic physics which have not yet been integrated into molecular theory. **1967** [see *quantum solid* below]. **1975** *Physics Bull.* July 311/3 The electrons in a metal constitute a quantum liquid in this sense at all temperatures up to the melting temperature. [**1902** Quantum-number: see sense 5 above]. **1920, 1922** *Quantum number [see N I. 4b]. **1926**, etc. [see L 7 b]. **1939** G. Herzberg *Molecular Spectra & Molecular Struct.* I. i. 15 The azimuthal quantum number l gives us therefore the orbital angular momentum of the electron in units $h/2\pi$. *Ibid.* 18 In a magnetic or electric field, a precession of the angular momentum of an atom takes place... While classically the precession could take place at any angle to the field direction, according to quantum theory, only those angles are possible for which the components of the angular momentum in the direction of the field have the discrete values $m_l(h/2\pi)$, where $m_l = l, (l-1), (l-2), \ldots, -l$... m_l is called the magnetic quantum number of the electron. **1967** W. R. Hindmarsh *Atomic Spectra* vi. 70 If the magnetic field is so strong that its interaction with the magnetic moment of the atom is much stronger than the spin-orbit interaction, the orbital and spin angular momenta are no longer even approximately conserved, so that L and S are not well-defined quantum numbers. **1968** J. Bernstein *Elementary Particles & their Currents* xiii. 211 The strong interactions of the strange particles are characterized by a new conserved quantum number in addition to the isotopic spin. This quantum number is the 'strangeness', S, or, equivalently, the 'hypercharge' Y. **1976** *Sci. Amer.* Jan. 45/1 Some quantum numbers, such as spin angular momentum and electric charge, are invariably conserved. **1923** H. L. Brose tr. *Sommerfeld's Atomic Struct. & Spectral Lines* ii. 67 The quantum theory asserts that all these *quantum orbits are stationary states of motion, that is they are traversed without radiation being emitted. **1928** Quantum orbit [see packet *sb.* 1 h]. **1946** *Mind* LV. 161 The philosopher finds support in the *quantum physicist's principle of complementarity. **1964** M. McLuhan *Understanding Media* (1967) vii. 73 Werner Heisenberg.. is an example of the new quantum physicist whose over-all awareness of forms suggests to him that we would do well to stand aside from most of them. **1931** H. Johnston tr. *Planck's Universe in Light of Mod. Physics* 22 The Principle of Relativity.. has proved itself a reliable and eloquent guide in the new regions of *Quantum Physics. **1971** *Sci. Amer.* Mar. 75 Quantum physics normally deals with natural phenomena on a submicroscopic scale. **1978** *Ibid.* Dec. 128/3 Quantum physics predicts that captured electrons can have only discrete energies, corresponding to the atomic energy levels described above. **1927** A. S. Eddington *Stars & Atoms* 68 The property here referred to (the *quantum property) is the deepest mystery of light. **1978** *Nature* 16 Mar. 291/3 The quantum properties of electromagnetic radiation. **1967** *Sci. Amer.* Aug. 85/2 Solid helium.. is the only known example of a '*quantum solid', just as liquid helium is the only known example of a 'quantum liquid'. **1921** *Chem. Abstr.* XV. 1843 Schottky discusses.. the Nernst heat theorem from the point of view of the internal '*quantum state' of the mols. composing the system under discussion. **1946** [see polaron]. **1972** *Sci. Amer.* Oct. 101/1 The individual nucleons move in discrete quantum states just as the electrons in the atom exist in discrete quantum states. **1958** *Physical Rev.* CXI. 1460 (*heading*) *Quantum statistical theory of electron correlation. **1932** *Jrnl. Chem. Soc.* 373 We shall.. discuss the important conclusions which can be drawn from the interpretation of molecular spectra regarding the so-called *quantum statistics in their relation to the nuclei. **1935** Pauling & Wilson *Introd. Statistical Mech.* viii. 219 The quantum statistics resulting from the acceptance of only antisymmetric wave functions is considerably different. **1972** *Physics Bull.* Dec. 709/1 It is our great good fortune that the only two substances that remain liquid down to the absolute zero obey different statistics (^{3}He: Fermi–Dirac, ^{4}He: Bose–Einstein) and thus allow us to study the differing effects of quantum statistics on condensed matter. **1924** *Physical Rev.* XXIV. 330 The term to be retained is.. the combination overtone asymptotically connected to the particular *quantum transition under consideration. **1927** Fisher & Hartree tr. *Born's Mech. of Atom* ii. 54 Quantum transitions can be caused by light and by molecular impacts. **1927** *Jrnl. Amer. Chem. Soc.* XLIX. 2451 These new facts make possible a better conception of the mechanism of the photochemical decomposition of ammonia... Warburg measured the *quantum yield and found it to be 4 quanta per molecule for light of wave length 2025–2140 Å. **1971** *Jrnl. Appl. Physics* XLII. 567/2 The quantum yield of the Ag–O–Cs cathode for visible light is less than 5×10^{-3} electron per photon.

b. Passing into adj. (cf. quantal *a.*).

1922 *Rep. Brit. Assoc. Adv. Sci. 1921* 474 This suggests that many phenomena which at present are thought to be satisfactorily explained by dynamics are really quantum phenomena. **1924** *Physical Rev.* XXIV. 340 This connection of the classical and quantum differential absorption we shall term the correspondence principle for absorption. **1951** *Ibid.* LXXXII. 116/2 The quantum nature of the exchange of energy between free electrons and electromagnetic fields. **1967** *Sci. Amer.* Aug. 85/2 Perhaps the most perplexing characteristic of solid helium.. is the fact that in spite of its unique quantum nature solid helium behaves in so many respects as a purely classical, or nonquantum, solid. **1975** *Nature* 20 Mar. 223/3 The book is concerned mainly with electro-dynamics (both classical and quantum).

quantum me'chanics. *Physics.* [f. quantum + mechanics.] A mathematical theory of the motion and interaction of (esp. sub-atomic) particles that was developed from the old quantum theory and incorporates the concept of wave-particle duality, the uncertainty principle, and the correspondence principle; cf. *matrix mechanics, wave mechanics.*

This is not quite the sense in quot. 1922.

1922 *Rep. Brit. Assoc. Adv. Sci. 1921* 473 The spectrum theory is far the most important branch of the quantum theory, as it has led and is still leading to extensions of quantum mechanics. **1925** *Proc. R. Soc.* A. CIX. 642 (*heading*) The fundamental equations of quantum mechanics. **1935** B. Russell *Relig. & Sci.* vi. 151 The challenge has come through the study of the atom by the new methods of quantum mechanics. **1956** E. H. Hutten *Lang. Mod. Physics* v. 179 The mathematical formulae of quantum mechanics permit us to predict future events only within a certain margin of error. **1956** H. Umezawa *Quantum Field Theory* i. 1 Quantum mechanics and relativity are respectively characterised by the constants h and C and, when h and $(1/C)$ are taken as vanishingly small, the results of these theories are identical with those of Newtonian mechanics. **1974** G. Reece tr. *Hund's Hist. Quantum Theory* x. 132 The first strictly valid version of quantum mechanics that was both logical and capable of generalization was provided by Heisenberg's paper of July 1925. **1978** *Sci. Amer.* Feb. 126/3 There is no workable theory of gravitation that is consistent with the principles of quantum mechanics. *Ibid.* 131/1 The present understanding of the fundamental laws of nature arose from three principles: special relativity, general relativity and quantum mechanics.

Hence **quantum-mechanical** *a.*, **quantum-mechanically** *adv.*

1927 *Proc. R. Soc.* A. CXIV. 715 One can obtain the result .. by using a quantum-mechanical argument. **1936** Quantum-mechanically [see quantal *a.* 2c]. **1949** Koestler *Insight & Outlook* xi. 156 Quantum-mechanical concepts slowly permeate all spheres of physics, chemistry, and.. biology. **1963** G. Troup *Masers & Lasers* (ed. 2) iv. 58 It can be shown quantum-mechanically.. that there is a definite probability that A will make the transition $1 \to 2$ while B makes the transition $3 \to 1$. **1968** G. Ludwig *Wave Mech.* i. ii. 9 These equations.. are the basis even today for the construction of modern accelerators, since quantum-mechanical effects are not involved in the motion of the particles in these devices. **1971** *Nature* 15 Jan. 158/2 The existence of such a low-lying σ transition would be a surprise to theoreticians, but quantum-mechanically it is not entirely out of the question.

‖**quantum meruit** ('kwɒntəm 'mɛruːɪt). *Law.* [L., 'as much as he has deserved'.] A reasonable sum of money to be paid for services rendered or work done, when the amount due is not determined by any provision constituting, or forming part of, a legally enforceable contract (see also quot. 1959). Also *attrib.* and as quasi-*adv.*

1657 H. Grimston tr. *G. Croke's Rep.* (Charles I) 77 It is the usuall way to lay down in certainty, *viz.* That he should pay for it *tantum quantum meruit, &c.*, and then to averre what it was reasonably worth, which being the common course and alwaies allowed, Judgment was therefore affirmed. **1659** in E. Bulstrode *Rep.* III. 86 How shall a Taylor be paid upon a *quantum meruit?* **1685** J. Keble *Rep.* I. 422 In action by executors on *indebitatus* for wares sold to pay *quantum meruit*, not shewing what the particulars were. **1718** W. Salkeld *Rep.* II. 557 *Quantum meruit* for meat, drink, &c. **1729** G. Jacob *New Law-Dict.* sig. Hhhh2, *Quantum meruit*, i.e. how much he has deserved, is a Man's Action of the Case,.. grounded upon the Promise of another, to pay him for doing any Thing so much as he should deserve or *merit*. If a man retains any person to do work or other thing for him.. without any certain agreement; in such case the law implies that he shall pay for the same, as much as they are worth, and shall be reasonably demanded; for which *Quantum meruit* may be brought. **1832** in P. Bingham *Rep.* VIII. 16, I agree that, when a special contract is in existence and open, the plaintiff cannot sue on a *quantum meruit*. **1904** *Law Rep. King's Bench Div.* II. 329 Remuneration upon the basis of a quantum meruit in respect of work and labour done for the company at its request. **1919** *Brit. Manufacturer* Nov. 36/2 The owners could, therefore, sue under the old contract (the charter party) for 23s., the agreed freight, on each of the 1208 tons of steel billets; and, in addition, could sue on the new implied contract for a *Quantum Meruit* in respect of the 987 tons of general cargo. So the only question is the rate per ton at which their *Quantum Meruit* should be calculated. **1959** Jowitt *Dict. Eng. Law* II. 1452/2 Where the failure to complete performance of the contract is due to the fault of the other party, the party not in default has the right to sue on a *quantum meruit* for the services which he has done under it. In its early history the action for *quantum meruit* was, no doubt, a genuine action in contract... In many cases the action is now founded on what is known as 'quasi-contract'. **1962** A. Turner *Law of Trade Secrets* iv. iv. 346 Other expressions, like 'unjust enrichment', some-times used by the courts are recovery in *quantum meruit* and recovery under 'quasi contracts', 'constructive contracts', or, contracts 'implied-in-law'. **1964** *Mod. Law Rev.* XXVIII. 353 The carrier deserves remuneration under the *quantum meruit* rule. **1973** *N.Y. Law Jrnl.* 1 Aug. 13/3 However, since the former attorneys have the right to elect whether they will accept their compensation on the basis of a presently fixed dollar amount quantum meruit or whether, still on the basis of quantum meruit, they will accept a contingent percentage instead [etc.]. **1975** S. J. Stoljar *Hist. Contract at Common Law* ix. 109 If, as often happened, the work was undertaken at no specified price, the plaintiff could turn to another count in assumpsit becoming known as the *quantum meruit*, a claim not for a fixed but for a reasonable amount: what the work merited or was worth.

‖**quantum sufficit** ('kwɒntəm 'sʌfɪsɪt). Also abbrev. **quantum suff., quant. suff. (suf.).** [L., a formula used in medical prescriptions.]

a. 'As much as suffices'; hence, a sufficient quantity, a sufficiency; to a sufficient extent, etc.

1699 *Honour of Gout* in *Harl. Misc.* (1809) II. 45 We lead sedentary lives, feed heartily, drink *quantum sufficit*, but sleep immoderately. **1775** J. Adams in *Fam. Lett.* (1876) 58 Scolding at me quantum sufficit for not taking his advice. **1806-7** J. Beresford *Miseries Hum. Life* (ed. 5) II. 238 With numbers though rough, Yet with rage *quantum suff.* **1837** Lockhart *Scott.* (1839) VII. 405 Cabinets china and mirrors *quantum suff.*, and some portraits. **1840** Barham *Patty Morgan* in *Ingol. Leg.* 1st Ser. 60 One glance was enough, Completely '*Quant. suff.*' As the doctors write down when they send you their 'stuff'. **1881** Abney *Photogr.* 69 The amount of alcohol required is invariably shown as 'quant. suf.' **1907** G. B. Shaw *John Bull's Other Island* p. xxv, It was hardly reasonable to ask Parnell to shed blood *quant. suff.* in Egypt.. and then to expect him to become a Tolstoyan or an O'Connellite in regard to his own country. **1964** C. S. Lewis *Discarded Image* i. 9 Popular iconography .. wishing to summon up the idea of the Medieval, draws a knight errant with castles, distressed damsels, and dragons *quant. suff.* in the background.

b. With article or possessive pron.

1747 *Scheme Equip. Men of War* 23 To provide them a *Quantum sufficit* before they enter into that Service. **1795** Burke *Regic. Peace* iv. Wks. IX. 20 What dose is to be the *quantum sufficit?* *a* **1817** T. Dwight *Trav. New Eng.*, etc. (1821) I. 515 They have always a quantum sufficit of money. **1843** Darwin *Let. to Henslow* 25 Jan., My Coral Volume.. has received its quant: suff: of praise. **1863** *Fraser's Mag.* Feb. 156/2 A *quant. suff.* is beaten up with water, which is strained off after standing half an hour.

quantum theory. *Physics.* [f. quantum + theory[1].] A theory of matter and energy based on the concept of quanta (sense 5); *spec.* the branch of physics that was developed from the ideas in Planck's paper of 1900 and Einstein's of 1905 (see quantum 5), was extended by Bohr (1913) in relation to atomic structure, and later evolved into quantum mechanics and quantum field theory; ***old quantum theory***, the early form of the theory, based on classical mechanics, prior to the development of wave mechanics and matrix mechanics in the mid-1920s.

[**1911** *Sci. Abstr.* A. XIV. 1702 The quanta theory of Planck and Einstein must be modified considerably to give a quantitative interpretation of the results obtained.] **1912** *Monthly Notices R. Astron. Soc.* LXXII. 677 The constant of nature in terms of which these spectra can be expressed appears to be that of Planck in his recent quantum theory of energy. **1926** *Times Lit. Suppl.* 19 Aug. 544/3 Relativity theory and quantum theory have not yet been properly assimilated. **1927** *Proc. R. Soc.* A. CXIV. 181 This equation .. was obtained orginally by Sommerfeld from relativistic considerations with the old quantum theory. *Ibid.* 243 The new quantum theory, based on the assumption that the dynamical variables do not obey the commutative law of multiplication, has by now been developed sufficiently to form a fairly complete theory of dynamics. **1958** W. Heisenberg *Physics & Philos.* vi. 106 Quantum theory does not allow a completely objective description of nature. **1970** G. K. Woodgate *Elem. Atomic Struct.* vi. 103 For small l the electron orbit is highly eccentric (to use the language of the old quantum theory). **1972** *Physics Bull.* Sept. 548/1 This book consists of five short chapters, on classical mechanics and the old quantum theory, the new quantum theory, many particle systems, valence theory and quantum theory of chemical reactivity. **1978** *Sci. Amer.* Feb. 132/3 Quantum theories of the gravitational force still have serious difficulties with infinities.

Hence **quantum-theoretical** *a.*, **quantum-theoretically** *adv.*; **quantum theorist**, an expert or specialist in quantum theory.

1920 *Chem. Abstr.* XIV. 1637 (*heading*) Quantum theoretical principles of photochemistry. **1931** *Physical Rev.* XXXVIII. 1787/1 No quantum theoretical calculations have been made for particles of very high energy. **1935** *Amer. Jrnl. Math.* LVII. 429 The algebra II is known to the quantum theorist from the process of 'superquantizing'. **1939** G. HERZBERG *Molecular Spectra & Molecular Struct.* I. iii. 84 Quantum theoretically, emission of radiation takes place as a result of a transition of the oscillator from a higher to a lower state. **1959** K. R. POPPER *Logic of Sci. Discovery* ix. 222 In his derivation of the uncertainty relations, Heisenberg follows Bohr in making use of the idea that atomic processes can be just as well represented by the 'quantum-theoretical image of a particle' as by the 'quantum-theoretical image of a wave'. **1968** G. LUDWIG *Wave Mech.* I. ii. 19 These classical results were transformed by Bohr into quantum-theoretical results. **1976** *Nature* 1 July 17/1 General Electric advertised for a quantum theorist to look into the fundamental quantum processes involved in fluorescence.

quantuplicity (kwɒntjuːˈplɪsɪtɪ). [f. L. *quantus* how much, on anal. of *quadruplicity*, etc.] The relative magnitude of a quantity.

1836 DE MORGAN *Diff. & Int. Calc.* Introd. 17 The proportions of figures..depend..upon what Euclid terms the ratio..which he says is (if we may coin such an English word) the number-of-times-ness or quantuplicity of one quantity, considered with respect to another.

† **quap**, *sb. Obs. rare*⁻¹. ? variant of QUAB *sb.*¹

1598 FLORIO, *Gò, goi*, a fish called a quap [**1611** a quap-fish], which is poison to man, and man to him.

† **quap**, *v. Obs.* Forms: 4–6 quappe, 5 qwappe, (7 quapp). See also QUOP. [Imitative; cf. G. *quappen* to flop, *quappeln* to quiver. A later form is QUAB *v.*] *intr.* To beat, throb, palpitate, quiver.

c **1374** CHAUCER *Troylus* III. 8 (57) And lord how þat his herte gan to quappe, Heryng her come. **1382** WYCLIF *Tobit* vi. 4 He droȝ it [the fish] in to the drie, and it began to quappe befor his feet. *c* **1440** *Partonope* 5938 His hert gan qwappe, his coloure gan change. **1567** TURBERV. tr. *Ovid's Ep.* 67 Even as the sea doth shake and trembling quappe, When with a gentle gale it is enforst. [*a* **1643** W. CARTWRIGHT *Ordinary* II. ii, My heart gan quapp full oft.]

Hence † **ˈquapping** *vbl. sb.* and *ppl. a.*

1398 TREVISA *Barth. De P.R.* VII. lix. (1495) 273 The tokens of a Flegmon or postume..ben..quappynge and lepynge of ventosytee. **1572** J. JONES *Bathes of Bath* I. 7 Beating, or quapping [paine] cometh of a hot Aposteme.

quap, obs. form of WHAP *v.*

† **quaquadrate**. *Math. Obs. rare*⁻¹. [f. QUA(DRI-) + QUADRATE.] A sixteenth power.

1674 JEAKE *Arith.* (1696) 273 Some to shorten..the long Names of..Higher Powers,..call 33 a Biquadrate,..3333 a Quaquadrate, 33333 a Quinquadrate [etc.].

quaquaversal (kweɪkwəˈvɜːsəl), *a.* Also **quâquâ-**, **quâ-quâ-versal**. [f. late L. *quāquāversus*, *-versum*, f. *quāquā* where-, whithersoever + *versus* towards.] Turned or pointing in every direction; chiefly *Geol.* in phr. ***quaquaversal dip*** (see quot. 1877).

1728 NICHOLLS in *Phil. Trans.* XXXV. 442 The quaquaversal Pressure of the Blood will be controll'd by the Pressure on the Artery. **1830** LYELL *Princ. Geol.* I. 394 The slope and quâquâ-versal dip of the beds. **1862** LATHAM *Elem. Comp. Philol.* 126 The affinities of the Lap are one-sided, those of the Turk (to borrow an expression from the geologists) quaquaversal. **1877** A. H. GREEN *Phys. Geol.* ix. §3. 347 If the beds dip away in all directions from a centre they are said to have a quaquaversal dip.

Hence **quaquaˈversally** *adv.*

1875 R. F. BURTON *Ultima Thule* I. 38 The strata all incline gradually and quaquaversally..towards the centre of the island. **1883** BURTON & CAMERON *Gold Coast* I. iii. 76 A central boss..with lines radiating quaquaversally.

quaquiner, erron. form of QUAVIVER.

† **quar**, *sb.*¹, abbrev. of QUARRY *sb.*¹ *Obs.*

1562 PHAER *Æneid* IX. Ee ij, What murthring quarres of men, what heapes downe throwne,..king Turnus then did giue. **1605** SYLVESTER *Du Bartas* II. iii. III. (*Lawe*) 643 The Falcon..shall strike; And with the stroke make on the senseless ground The gut-less Quar..re-bound.

quar, *sb.*² *Obs.* exc. *dial.* Also 6–7 quarre, 7 quarr, 8 quaar. [Abbrev. of QUARRY *sb.*²; still current in W. Midland and S.W. dialects.] A stone-quarry.

a **1485** *Promp. Parv.* 419/1 Quarere (*S.* quar), *lapidicina*. **1529** RASTELL *Pastyme, Hist. Brit.* (1811) 105 Stonys owte of anny quarre, or rokk. **1566** STAPLETON *Ret. Untr. Jewel* IV. 61 Stedfaster than any Rocke or Quarre of what euer stone it be. **1622** DRAYTON *Poly-olb.* xxvi. (1748) 372 She millstones from the quarr with sharpen'd picks could get. **1672** W. S. *Poems B. Johnson Jr.*, To Ld. Aston. Aston, a Stone cut from the marble Quar. *a* **1800** *Song* in *Glouc. Gloss.* (1890) 203 The stwons that built George Ridler's Oven..keum from the Bleakeney's Quaar.

b. *attrib.* and *Comb.*, as ***quarman***, ***-pit***; **quar-martin**, the sand-martin. *dial.*

1606 SYLVESTER *Du Bartas* II. iv. II. (*Magnificence*) 1110 The sturdy Quar-man with steel-headed Cones And massie Sledges slenteth out the stones. **1879** JEFFERIES *Wild Life in S.C.* 169 These birds are called by the labourers 'quar-martins', because they breed in holes drilled in the face of the sandy precipices of quarries. **1886** ELWORTHY *W. Somerset Word-bk.*, *Quar-man*, labourer in a quarry; also the proprietor or lessee of a quarry. *Quar-pit*, a quarry, usually a small one.

† **quar**, *sb.*³, abbrev. of QUARRY *sb.*³ *Obs. rare.*

1600 SYLVESTER *Du Bartas* II. iv. II. (*Magnificence*) 1149 What mightie Rowlers, and what massie Cars Could bring so far so many monstrous Quars? [F. *quarreaux*]. *Ibid.* 1158 The whole, a whole Quar [F. *quarreau*] one might rightly tearm. **1617** *Vestry Bks.* (Surtees) 73 Item xix quarres mendid in the other windowes.

quar, *v.*¹ *Obs.* exc. *dial.* Also 6 querre, 7 quarre. [Of obscure origin: ? cf. OE. *á-cweorran* to glut.]

a. *trans.* To choke or block up (a channel or passage). **b.** *intr.* Of a channel: To silt or fill up. Hence **ˈquarring** *vbl. sb.*

1542-3 *Act 34 & 35 Hen. VIII*, c. 9 §1 The mouth and hole channell of the saide hauen is so heaped and quarred with stones and robull of balastes of the shippes. **1584-5** *Act 27 Eliz.* c. 20 §1 Where also the said hauen of Plymmouth..doth dayly querre and fill with the sand of the Tinne-workes and Mynes. **1628** SIR R. BOYLE *Diary* in *Lismore Papers* (1886) II. 257 Provided..he do nothing to the preiudice of my yron worcks, or stopping or quarreing vp of the River.

quar, *v.*² *Obs.* exc. *dial.* [Of unknown origin: cf. QUARL *v.*] *intr.* To curdle, coagulate.

1578 LYTE *Dodoens* II. lxxiv. 246 It..keepeth the mylke from quarring and crudding in the brest. **1591** PERCIVALL *Sp. Dict.*, *Engrumecer*, to clot, to quar like cold blood.

quar, obs. north. f. WHERE and *were* (see BE *v.*).

quarancy: see QUARANTY.

† **quarantain**. *Obs.* Also 7 -aine, 8 -ane. [ad. F. *quarantaine* (= It. *quarantana*), f. *quarante* forty: see next.]

1. A set of forty (nights). *rare*⁻¹.

1653 URQUHART *Rabelais* II. i. 1 It is above fourty quarantaines, or fourty times fourty nights, according to the supputation of the ancient Druids.

2. = QUARANTINE 2.

1669 R. MONTAGU in *Buccleuch MSS.* (Hist. MSS. Comm.) I. 452 After having made their quarantaine and aired their goods. **1687** *Lond. Gaz.* No. 2211/1 The Prince of Brunswicke keeps his Quarantain in the Island Lazaro. **1702** W. J. *Bruyn's Voy. Levant* xi. 47 Those who come from infected Places, there to pass their Quarantain.

attrib. **1755** MAGENS *Insurances* II. 236 Anchorage, ordinary Quarantain Charges, and such like.

b. *fig.* = QUARANTINE 2 b.

1666-7 DENHAM *Direct. Paint.* I. xvii, There let him languish a long Quarantain. **1714** *Let. fr. Layman* (ed. 2) 23 This Crime..is never to be purged away; no not by performing a Quarantain for a Twelve-month in the Church. **1741** WARBURTON *Div. Legat.* II. Pref. p. xiv, The Calumnies of his Enemies obliged him to a kind of Quarantane.

3. ***King's quarantain*** (tr. F. *quarantaine du roi*): see quots.

1727-41 CHAMBERS *Cycl.*, *Quarantain of the King*, in France, denotes a truce of forty days appointed by St. Louis, during which it was expresly forbid to take any revenge [etc.]. **1818** A. RANKEN *Hist. France* IV. III. i. 233 Forty days, called the King's quarantain, were allowed the friends or relations of a principal in a private war to grant or find security.

† **quarante**, var. COURANTE, a kind of dance. *Obs.*

1598 R. DALLINGTON *Meth. Trav.* V ij, Euery poore draggletayle can Dance all your Quarantes, Leualties, Bransles, and other Dances.

quarantinable, *a.* [f. QUARANTINE *v.* + -ABLE.] Subject or liable to quarantine.

1863 *Laws N.Y. State* ccclviii. 576 With existing quarantinable disease on board,..merchandise of the first class shall be landed at the quarantine warehouse. **1894** *Harper's Weekly* 7 Apr. 315 The protection against cholera and other quarantinable diseases..is secured. **1906** *Daily Colonist* (Victoria, B.C.) 25 Jan. 8/1 Foreign coasting vessels touching at Victoria to the number of 947 required inspection. No quarantinable disease occurred. **1961** *Times* 25 Aug. 12/2 There are six quarantinable diseases.

quarantine (ˈkwɒrəntiːn), *sb.* Also 7 **quarantene**, 8 **-in**, 7–8 **quarentine**. [In sense 1 ad. med.L. *quarentēna*; in sense 2 prob. ad. It. *quarant-*, *quarentina*, f. *quaranta* forty.

The source of the *-ine* spelling in sense 1 is not clear: in the *Stasyons of Jerusalem* (Horstm. *Altengl. Leg.* Neue F., 365) the form *Quaryntyne* (riming with *wyne*) is used to render med.L. *Quarentena*, the name given to the desert where Christ fasted for forty days. In sense 1 the prevailing form in 17–18th c. was *quarentine*, while *quarantine* has always been the usual form in sense 2.]

1. *Law.* A period of forty days during which a widow, entitled to dower, had the right to remain in the chief mansion-house of her deceased husband; hence, the right of a widow to remain in the house during this period.

1609 SKENE *Reg. Maj.* 56 (*Acts Robt. III*, c. 20) Anent widowes, quha..can not haue their quarentene without pley. **1628** COKE *On Litt.* 32 b, If she marry within the forty days she loseth her quarentine. **1767** BLACKSTONE *Comm.* II. 135 These forty days are called the widow's quarentine. **1865** NICHOLS *Britton* II. 247 Some other decent house shall be provided for their dwelling, where they may keep their quarantine.

2. a. A period (orig. of forty days) during which persons who might serve to spread a contagious disease are kept isolated from the rest of the community; *esp.* a period of detention imposed on travellers or voyagers before they are allowed to enter a country or town, and mix with the inhabitants; commonly, the period during which a ship, capable of carrying contagion, is kept isolated on its arrival at a port. Also, a period of seclusion or isolation after exposure to infection from a contagious disease; *transf.*, (a period of) isolation imposed in a similar way on an animal or thing. Hence, the fact or practice of isolating or of being isolated in this way. Freq. in phr. ***in quarantine***. Also *fig.*

1663 PEPYS *Diary* 26 Nov., Making of all ships coming from thence..to perform their 'quarantine for thirty days', as Sir Richard Browne expressed it..contrary to the import of the word (though, in the general acceptation, it signifies now the thing, not the time spent in doing it). **1691** LUTTRELL *Brief Rel.* (1857) II. 185 Those that come from Naples..are obliged to perform a quarantine before they come to Rome, because of the plague in that Kingdom. **1722** DE FOE *Plague* (1884) 204 The Family were oblig'd to begin their Quarantine anew. **1799** E. STANLEY in A. Duncan *Nelson* (1806) 112 Having finished their quarantine of thirteen days. **1836** MARRYAT *Midsh. Easy* xlii, As soon as their quarantine at the Mother-bank was over, they disembarked. **1855** [see ASK *v.* 4 c]. **1859** JEPHSON *Brittany* vi. 77 The lepers often sought a voluntary death as the only escape from their perpetual quarantine. **1867** *Even. Standard* 6 Aug. 6 A Royal order has been issued imposing forty days' quarantine upon all arrivals in Spanish ports from Algeria, Morocco, and the Roman States. **1879** *Investigation of Diseases of Swine* (Special Rep. No. 12, U.S. Dept. Agric.) 151 All strange hogs must be kept in quarantine for fourteen days before being allowed to run with healthy herds. **1891** *Boston Jrnl.* 7 Jan. 2/3 A rigid quarantine against fire-arms and firewater on the reservations of the Northwest is one of the prime requirements of the Indian problem. **1913-14** *Wellcome's Nurse's Diary* 209 Isolation required after exposure to: Asiatic Cholera..12 days' quarantine. **1922** *Encycl. Brit.* XXX. 925/2 Formerly great stress was laid on the value of quarantine; all plant imports were grown in a quarantine ground under the supervision of a Government botanist until it was certain that they had no disease. **1952** *Oxf. Jun. Encycl.* X. 357/2 All dogs..have to be isolated in quarantine for 6 months in case they may be carrying rabies. **1971** *Sci. Amer.* Oct. 49/2 To guard against the possibility..of introducing pathogenic organisms from the moon, the lunar samples were placed in quarantine for seven weeks. **1978** W. GARNER *Möbius Trip* (1979) ii. 60 Putting him in emotional quarantine.

b. *fig.* Any period, instance, etc., of detention or seclusion compared to the above; *spec.* in international politics, a blockade, boycott, or severance of diplomatic relations intended to isolate a nation, or the isolation caused by such action. †***free quarantine***, exemption from quarantine.

The specific use arose from a speech by F. D. Roosevelt, President of the U.S. (see quots. 1937).

a **1680** BUTLER *Rem.* (1759) I. 209 Where she denies Admission, to intrude..Unless they have free Quarentine from her. **1742** YOUNG *Nt. Th.* VII. 1046 Deists! perform your quarentine; and then Fall prostrate, ere you touch it, lest you die. **1855** MOTLEY *Dutch Rep.* II. i. (1866) 132 Nor could bigotry devise an effective quarantine to exclude the religious pest which lurked in every bale of merchandise. **1937** *N.Y. Herald Tribune* 6 Oct. 1/5 (*heading*) President calls for 'quarantine' of aggressors. *Ibid.* 1/8 President Roosevelt today challenged the effectiveness of a policy of neutrality in keeping the United States at peace and advocated instead a collective 'quarantine' of aggressor nations. **1938** *Sun* (Baltimore) 16 Nov. 1/8 Ambassador Wilson will not return soon to his post... It may even imply a 'quarantine' or an effort to quarantine Germany. **1945** *Richmond* (Va.) *News-Leader* 4 Oct. 2/7 (*heading*) Argentina faces diplomatic 'quarantine' by Pan-America. **1962** *Daily Tel.* 23 Oct. 1/2 Mr. Kennedy announced the following actions in response to the military build-up in Cuba. The blockade against delivery of offensive weapons. The 'quarantine' would be extended if necessary, to other types of cargo and carriers. **1975** *Ibid.* 1 Oct. 1/7 A call by the International Transport Workers' Federation..for a 48-hour quarantine of services to and from Spain.

c. A place where quarantine is kept or enforced.

1847 EMERSON *Poems, Monadnoc* Wks. (Bohn) I. 435 His quarantines and grottos, where He slowly cures decrepit flesh. **1892** STEVENSON *Across the Plains* 171 Somnolent Inverkeithing, once the quarantine of Leith.

3. A period of forty days, in other connexions than the above; a set of forty (days).

1639 FULLER *Holy War* III. xxii. 147 When their quarantine, or fourty dayes service, was expired. **1722** DE FOE *Plague* (1756) 235 Not a Quarentine of Days only, but Soixantine, not only 40 Days but 60 Days or longer. **1883-97** *Catholic Dict.* 772/1 Indulgences of seven years and seven quarantines are often granted for certain devotions.

4. *attrib.* (sense 2), as ***quarantine camp***, ***flag***, ***-ground***, ***hospital***, ***kennel***, ***law***, ***officer***, ***regulation***, ***station***, etc.; ***quarantine-breaking*** adj.

1805 *Med. Jrnl.* XVII. 507 The recent extension of the quarantine laws. **1808** *Deb. Congress U.S.* 9 Mar. (1852) 1753 The ship arrived at the quarantine ground, near the harbor of Boston. **1835** J. E. ALEXANDER *Sk. Portugal* xi. 265 After some delay before we could get our yellow quarantine-flag struck, we were allowed to land. **1841** *Penny Cycl.* XIX. 193/2 The most important disease, with reference to quarantine regulations, is the plague of the Levant. *Ibid.* 195/1 A quarantine station on a land-frontier. **1852** G.

COGGESHALL *Second Series of Voyages* xiii. 82 We were requested to proceed immediately to the quarantine ground. **1861-2** G. A. SPOTTISWOODE in *Vac. Tour.* 87 Accommodation..for the director or quarantine-officer. **1867** 'MARK TWAIN' in *Daily Alta California* (San Francisco) 18 Oct. 1/4 This kind of conversation did no good, further than to give a sort of dismal interest to our quarantine-breaking expedition, and so we dropped it. **1871** TYNDALL *Fragm. Sc.* (1879) I. vi. 200 The yellow quarantine flag was hoisted. **1942** E. E. DALE *Cow Country* 203 Wide strips were left for trails across the Outlet and lands were also set aside for quarantine grounds. **1976** T. HEALD *Let Sleeping Dogs Die* i. 11 To prevent it [*sc.* rabies] being imported all dogs coming in to Britain had to spend six months in quarantine kennels. **1977** *Hongkong Standard* 14 Apr. 8/5 A friend visited the Government Quarantine Kennels at Shatin recently and was distressed and appalled at the neglect of the poor animals awaiting their death, particularly the puppies.

quarantine ('kwɒrəntiːn), *v.* Also 9 quaranteen. [f. the sb.]

1. a. *trans.* To put in quarantine. Also *transf.* and *fig.*; *spec.* in sense 2 b of the *sb.*

1804 W. IRVING in *Life & Lett.* (1864) I. v. 89 Where I should be detained, quarantined, smoked, and vinegared. **1860** TROLLOPE *W. Ind.* xxiii. 365 In going to Cuba I had been becalmed..and very nearly quaranteened. **1860** *Harper's Mag.* June 137/2 Duelling had become epidemic among the midshipmen at the Gosport navy-yard. A determined effort was made..to suppress the practice. The entire body of reefers were 'quarantined', i.e. confined to the limits of the yard. **1870** W. M. BAKER *New Timothy* i. 13 The business of these [ministers] is with human nature, and from exactly that are they quarantined for years. **1891** *Cath. News* 2 May 5/3 The Comte de Paris was quarantined for a short time at Southampton. **1937** *N.Y. Times* 6 Oct. 1/8 President Roosevelt today pledged his Administration to a 'concerted effort' with other peace-loving nations to 'quarantine' aggressor nations. **1938** [see NOSE COUNT]. **1938** [see QUARANTINE *sb.* 2 b]. **1945** *Sun* (Baltimore) 28 Sept. 11/2 At school, they find themselves 'quarantined' and they are the butt of jibes and social ostracism. **1953** P. C. BERG *Dict. New Words* 132/1 *Quarantine, v.t.*, to isolate (a nation). **1962** *Listener* 12 Apr. 623/2 They think that, given the Communist Powers' publicly proclaimed hostility to the West, the whole lot of them should be quarantined, as the U.S.A. quarantines China. **1976** *O.E.D. Suppl.* s.v. *L* 7, LRL, Lunar Receiving Laboratory (building where astronauts and lunar samples are quarantined for a period after returning from the moon). **1980** *Early Music* Apr. 255/2 In this setting the melody is not quarantined in the tenor register.

b. To prevent by quarantine. In quot. *fig.*

1850 *Chamb. Jrnl.* XIV. 49 Did any moral taint hang about me that quarantined my entrance into its circle?

c. To isolate (an area) by the imposition of quarantine.

1890 *Stock Grower & Farmer* 24 May 7/3 The state [*sc.* of Nebraska] is strictly quarantined against all cattle from Texas. **1955** *Sci. Amer.* June 82/2 An outbreak of disease may be localized by quarantining the infected area.

2. *intr.* To institute quarantine.

1888 *Harper's Mag.* Oct. 738/1 Only two cases had been reported when every neighboring British colony quarantined against Martinique.

3. *intr.* To go into quarantine.

1928 *Daily News* 7 Aug. 7/3 The Mauretania..is expected to 'quarantine' at New York at 10 a.m. tomorrow.

Hence **'quarantined, 'quarantining** *ppl. adjs.*; also **'quarantiner**, one who puts, or is put, into quarantine.

1831 SCOTT *Jrnl.* II. 444 The guardians, who attend to take care that we quarantiners do not kill the people whom we meet. **1884** *Manch. Exam.* 21 Nov. 5/4 The..block in which the quarantined person is located. **1891** *Lancet* 3 Oct. 777 Egypt..always has been..a quarantining country.

quarantine (apple), variant of QUARRENDEN.

‖**Quarant' Ore** (kwarant 'ore). Also Quarantore. [It., contraction of *quaranta* forty + *ore*, pl. of *ora* hour.] = *forty hours* s.v. FORTY *a.* e.

1623 *Ven. Eng. College, Rome MS. Scritt.* 29.5.1a. f.4, By the church doore, which by chaunce was open by reason that the Quarante Hore were celebrated there at the same tyme. **1839** N. WISEMAN *Let.* in P. Devine *Life Fr. Ignatius of St. Paul* (1866) III. viii. 255 My idea was borrowed from my.. friend, Charles Weld, and consisted in *Quarant' Ore*,.. making the circuit of all England, so that by day and night the Adorable Sacrament might be worshipped through the year. **1859** A. D. HOPE *St. Philip Neri* v. 16 It was also the means of introducing into Rome, A.D. 1548, the devotion of the Quarant' Ore, which had been first practised in Milan A.D. 1534. **1890** GASQUET & BISHOP *Edward VI & Bk. Common Prayer* iv. 54 The devotions known as the benediction of the Blessed Sacrament and the *Quarantore*. **1923** C. MACKENZIE *Parson's Progress* xi. 135 If the authorities remonstrated with him for holding such a service as Creeping to the Cross on Good Friday, he remonstrated with them for allowing such vulgar innovations as the Stations of the Cross or the Devotion of the Quarant'ore. **1974** *Oxf. Dict. Chr. Ch.* (ed. 2) 524/2 *Forty hours' devotion* (also known as the *Quarant' Ore* or *Quarantore*), a modern Catholic devotion in which the Blessed Sacrament is exposed..for for a period of *c.* forty hours, and the faithful pray before it by turns throughout this time.

†**quaranty.** *Obs.* Also -ancy. [ad. It. *quarantia*, f. *quaranta* forty: cf. F. *quarantie.*] A former court of judicature at Venice, consisting of forty members.

1636 E. DACRES tr. *Machiavel's Disc. Livy* I. 198 They have ordained the Quarantie, or counsell of forty. **1659** J. HARRINGTON *Lawgiving* III. i. (1700) 439 After the manner of the Venetian Quarancys. **1707** J. STEVENS tr. *Quevedo's Com. Wks.* (1709) 446 On his Right was one Chief of the Quarantie.

†**quardecu(e**, variants of CARDECU. *Obs.*

1611 COTGR., *Quart d'escu*, a Teston or Quardecue; a siluer peece of coyne worth 18*d.* sterl. **1657** HOWELL *Londinop.* 372 There comes not a Quardecu in every Crown clearly to the Kings Coffers, which is but the fourth part.

quardeel: see CARDEL.

†**quare**, *v. Obs. rare.* [a. OF. *quarer* (F. *carrer*):—L. *quadrāre* QUADRATE *v.*] To square. Hence **quared** *ppl. a.*, **'quaring** *vbl. sb.*

a **1300** *Cursor M.* 1664 (Gött.) A vessel..sal be mad of quarid tre. **1611** *MS. Acc. St. John's Hosp., Canterb.*, Payd for hewing and quaring of the tymber.

quare (kwɛə(r)), *a. dial.* Also quair. [repr. dial. pronunc. of QUEER *a.*[1]] = QUEER *a.*[1] Also, in Ulster English, used as a general intensifier, esp. in phr. ***quare and*** ——, very, extremely. Hence **'quarely** *adv.*

quare fellow = *queer fellow* s.v. QUEER *a.*[1] 1 a.

1805 E. CAVANAGH *Let.* 20 Aug. in *Russ. Jrnls. M. & C. Wilmot* (1934) II. 179 Tis *quair* things I have been seeing! **1805** —— *Let.* 4 Oct. in *Ibid.* II. 185 It was *quairly* made. **1871** E. EGGLESTON *Hoosier Schoolmaster* iii. 32 'What a quare boy Shocky is!' remarked Betsey Short, with a giggle. 'He just likes to wander 'round alone.' **1880** W. H. PATTERSON *Gloss. Words Antrim & Down* 81 Quare, Queer, *adj.* very '*quare* an' nice' = very nice. **1896** J. BARLOW *Mrs. Martin's Company* 13 Sure I know the roof's quare and bad. **1896** M. HAMILTON *Across Ulster Bog* xi. 92 You're mended quarely this last while. **1900** M. O'NEILL *Songs of Glens of Antrim* 17 Now we're quarely betther fixed. **1938** M. K. RAWLINGS *Yearling* vi. 55 Hit's mighty quare you toted a dog along wouldn't be no good to you. **1941** [see JIST]. **1949** C. GRAVES *Ireland Revisited* i. 21 One aged groom said: '.. There's a fine, mettlesome lot of gerrls here today, but they look very quare in thon harness.' **1956** B. BEHAN *Quare Fellow* I. 4 What was the commotion last night round in D. Wing? Did the quare fellow get a reprieve?.. Now which quare fellow do you mean? The fellow beat his wife to death ..was reprieved. *a* **1966** 'M. NA GOPALEEN' *Best of Myles* (1977) 49 I've a quare bit of news for you. The brother's nose is out of order. **1977** G. B. ADAMS in D. Ó Muirithe *Eng. Lang. in Ireland* 67 Mine ye, A was quare an gled tae get anntae ma settle bed thaat naght.

quare, obs. form of QUIRE, WHERE.

quarefour, variant of CARFOUR.

‖**quare impedit** ('kwɛəriː 'ɪmpɪdɪt). *Law.* [L., 'why he impedes or hinders'.] A form of writ issued in cases of disputed presentation to a benefice, requiring the defendant to state why he hinders the plaintiff from making the presentation.

[**1292** BRITTON IV. vi. §2 Si acun, qi ad dreit de presenter ..voille presenter, et autre i mette destourbaunce..adounc tient proprement lu cest bref *Quare impedit*.] **1498-9** *Plumpton Corr.* (Camden) 133 The best remedy for your Incumbent was..to suy a quare Impedit at the comon law. **1548** STAUNFORD *Kinges Prerog.* (1567) 54 b, If his highnes bringe his Quare impedit or accion of trespas. *a* **1670** HACKET *Life Abp. Williams* II. (1693) 79 In matters ecclesiastical, as Advousons, Presentations, Quare-impedits, etc. **1705** BURNET *Own Time* v. (1734) II. 27 The actions of *Quare Impedit*, that they would be liable to, if they did not admit the Clerks presented to them. **1804** BP. OF LINCOLN in G. Rose *Diaries* (1860) II. 88 A *caveat* or a *quare impedit* may be advised. **1875** POSTE *Gaius* IV. (ed. 2) 636 Both parties are said to be equally plaintiffs and equally defendants in the actions..Quare impedit and Replevin.

quarel(e, -ell(e, obs. forms of QUARREL *sb.*

quarelet: see QUARRELET.

quarenden, -der: see QUARRENDEN, QUARRENDER.

†**quarental.** *Obs. rare*[−1]. [f. It. *quaranta* (F. *quarante*) forty, after TRENTAL.] A set of forty requiem masses.

1566 *Pasquine in a Traunce* 89 These false Prophets..that deceyue thy people with Trentals and Quarentals.

'quarenten(e. *Hist. rare.* [ad. med.L. *quarentēna* (AF. *quarenteyne*): see QUARANTINE.] A lineal or square measure containing forty poles; a furlong or rood.

1809 BAWDWEN *Domesday Bk.* 14 Wood pasture four quarentens long and the same broad. **1869** PEARSON *Hist. Maps Eng.* (1870) 51 A wood ten leagues long by six and two quarentenes broad.

quarentine, obs. variant of QUARANTINE.

quarer(e, variants of QUARRER, quarry.

quaresimal (kwə'rɛsɪməl), *a. rare*[−1]. [ad. It. *quaresimale* Lenten.] Of a meal: having the qualities of Lenten fare; meagre, austere.

1923 JOYCE *Let.* 17 Dec. (1966) III. 84 Can we not have a quaresimal dinner somewhere together?

†**quarester**, obs. form of CHORISTER.

1436 *E.E. Wills* 105 To euery secundary & clerc of the chirch iiij[d], and to euery quarester ij[d]. **1450** *Rolls Parlt.* V. 188/1, xii Quaresters, and a maister to teche hem.

quarfe, quarfour, obs. ff. WHARF, CARFOUR.

†**quarfoxe**, obs. form of CARFAX, cross-roads.

1483 CAXTON *Gold. Leg.* 89/2 Whan he cam to the quarfoxe the deuyl caught the chylde.

quarfulle, var. QUARTFUL *a.*

quarie, var. QUARRY *a.*, coagulated.

quarier(e, obs. ff. QUARRIER.

quarilous, var. QUARRELLOUS.

†**quarion**, var. QUARRIER[2], candle. *Obs.*

1512 *Househ. Bk. Dk. Northumbld.* 3 Wax wrought in Quarions j lb. [**1860** *Our Eng. Home* 91 Quarions and morters..for burning in the chambers at night; the former were square lumps of wax with a wick in the centre.]

quark ('kwɔːk), *v.* [Imitative, or a. G. *quarken.*] To croak. Hence **'quarking** *vbl. sb.*

1860 J. F. CAMPBELL *Pop. T.W. Highl.* II. 145 The gurgling and quarking of spring frogs in a pond. **1893** [D. JORDAN] *Forest Tithes*, etc. 186 Rooks..cawing and quarking. *Ibid.* 190 The herons quarked harshly.

quark (kwɔːk, kwɑːk), *sb. Physics.* [Invented word, associated with 'Three quarks for Muster Mark!' (Joyce *Finnegans Wake* (1939) II. iv).

'I employed the sound "quork" for several weeks in 1963 before noticing "quark" in "Finnegans Wake", which I had perused from time to time since it appeared in 1939... The allusion to three quarks seemed perfect... I needed an excuse for retaining the pronunciation quork despite the occurrence of "Mark", "bark", "mark", and so forth in Finnegans Wake. I found that excuse by supposing that one ingredient of the line "Three quarks for Muster Mark" was a cry of "Three quarts for Mister..." heard in H. C. Earwicker's pub.'—M. Gell-Mann, private let. to Ed., 27 June 1978.]

Any of a group of sub-atomic particles (orig. three in number) conceived of as having a fractional electric charge and making up in different combinations the hadrons, but not detected in the free state.

1964 M. GELL-MANN in *Physics Lett.* VIII. 214/2 A simpler and more elegant scheme can be constructed if we allow non-integral values for the charges. We can dispense entirely with the basic baryon b if we assign to the triplet t the following properties: spin $\frac{1}{2}$, $z = -\frac{1}{3}$, and baryon number $\frac{1}{3}$. We then refer to the members $u^{\frac{2}{3}}$, $d^{-\frac{1}{3}}$, and $s^{-\frac{1}{3}}$ of the triplet as quarks q and the members of the anti-triplet as anti-quarks $\bar{q}$. [*Note*] James Joyce, Finnegan's [*sic*] Wake (Viking Press, New York, 1939) p. 383. **1965** *New Scientist* 4 Mar. 575/2 Just as atoms are composed of particles (protons, neutrons and electrons) so may the heavy particles themselves be made up of combinations of simpler entities, called 'quarks'. **1967** *Observer* 23 Apr. 2/6 If quarks exist, they would represent a more fundamental building brick of matter than any yet known. **1972** *Daily Colonist* (Victoria, B.C.) 24 Feb. 5/2 The physicists hope to make the first observation of 'quarks', which many theorists believe are the fundamental building blocks,..by studying the activity of a rare and elusive sub-atomic particle called the omega-minus. **1973** L. J. TASSIE *Physics of Elementary Particles* xi. 146 Mesons have $B = 0$ and are made up of a quark and an antiquark. **1973, 1974** [see PARTON]. **1976** *Sci. Amer.* Nov. 50/1 The *u* quark has a charge of $+2/3$, and the *d* quark and the *s* quark each have a charge of $-1/3$. **1977** *Nature* 21 July 201/1 Quarks..have not been found free in nature; and if present theories are correct they never will be: they are thought to be permanently confined to the interior of the particles they compose. *Ibid.* 204/1 Recently hadrons containing a new, heavier quark—the c-quark (for 'charmed')—have been discovered. The mass of the c-quark is thought to be roughly 1,500 MeV. The old quarks are much lighter: the u- and d-quarks may even be massless while the s-quark's mass is about 300 MeV. **1978** [see PSI 1 b]. **1978** *Sci. Amer.* Oct. 67/1 The upsilon resonances present physics with an embarrassment of riches: an unexpected family of new particles composed of an unexpected fifth quark.

quark, var. QUAWK *sb.*

quarken, variant of QUERKEN, to choke.

quarl, quarle ('kwɔːl), *sb.*[1] [var. of QUARREL *sb.*[1]] A large brick or tile; *esp.* a fire-brick, curved like part of a cylinder, used to form supports for melting-pots, retort-covers, etc.

1875 *Ure's Dict. Arts* III. 67 (s.v. *Lead*) The erection of nine six-ton pots requires..160 feet of quarles. **1883** *Daily News* 19 Sept. 3/2 Making passages below the oven floor, and laying upon these passages perforated quarles or recessed bricks. **1894** *Northumbld. Gloss.* s.v., Under the term 'brick' are included sizes up to twelve inches long by six inches wide. Above this area it is called a quarl or tile.

quarl, *sb.*[2] *rare.* [? ad. G. *qualle*, Du. *kwal.*] The jelly-fish, medusa.

1884 *Harper's Mag.* Dec. 156/1 And momently athwart her track The quarl upreared his island back.

†**quarl**, *v. Obs. rare.* Also 8 quarrel. [Cf. QUAR *v.*[2]] To curdle, ? turn sour. Hence †**quarled** *ppl. a.* (Cf. QUARRED *ppl. a.*)

1607 TOURNEUR *Rev. Trag.* v. Hij, *Moth.* Are you so barbarous to set Iron nipples Vpon the brest that gaue you suck. *Vind.* That brest Is turnd to Quarled poyson. **1703** *Art & Myst. Vintners* 68 Take 2 pennyworth of Rice..and 2 pennyworth of Alum; this will keep your Wine from quarrelling, and make it fine.

quarl(e, quar'le, quarled: see QUARL *sb.*[1], QUARREL *sb.*[1], QUARRELLED *a.*

quar-man, -martin: see QUAR *sb.*[2]

quarn, obs. f. QUERN.

†**quarnell**, *a. Sc. Obs. rare.* Also quernell. [App. var. of QUARREL *sb.*[1] or *sb.*[2] (used *attrib.*),

perh. after CARNEL or CORNEL.] Square, squared. So also **ˈquarnelled** (in 6 **quernallit**).
1533 Bellenden *Livy* I. x. (1901) 62 This virgine horacia was buryit..in ane sepulture of quernallit [*v.r.* quarnell] stanis. 1542 *Inv. R. Wardr.* (1815) 64 Item, ane small chene with thrawin and quernallit linkis. [1808–25 Jamieson, *Quarnelt*, cornered, having angles. *Fife.*]

quarner(e, quarof, quarquenet, quarre, obs. ff. CORNER *sb.*[1], WHEREOF, CARCANET, QUARRY.

quarreaus, obs. pl. of QUARREL *sb.*[1]

ˈquarred, *ppl. a. Obs.* exc. *dial.* [f. QUAR *v.*[2] + -ED[1].] Clotted, curdled; soured.
1599 A. M. tr. *Gabelhouer's Bk. Physicke* 341/1 When we haue fallen, and we feare we haue quarred bloode in our bodye. 1871 Wise *New Forest* in *Hampsh. Gloss.*, Beer is said to be quarred, when it drinks hard or rough.

quarrefour, var. CARFOUR.

quarrel (ˈkwɒrəl), *sb.*[1] Forms: 3 *pl.* **quarreaus, 4–5 quarelle, 4–6 quarel, (4 qwarel, 5 quarele, -eyll, wharle, 6 quar'le), 5–6 quarell, (6 quer-), 6–7 quarrell, (6 -elle), 6– quarrel.** [a. OF. *quarel, quarrel* (*quaral, caral*, etc., pl. *quarriaus, quareus*), later *quarriau, -eau*, mod.F. *carreau*, = Prov. *cairel*, It. *quadrello*, Sp. *cuadrillo*, med.L. *quadrellus*, dim. of Prov. *caire*, It. *quadro*, (Sp. *cu-*), med.L. *quadrus* a square: cf. QUADREL.]

1. A short, heavy, square-headed arrow or bolt, formerly used in shooting with the cross-bow or arbalest.
*a*1225 *Ancr. R.* 62 Þeo hwile þet me mit quarreaus.. asaileð þene castel. 1340 *Ayenb.* 71 Al hit ys ywent wel raþre þan..quarel of arblaste. *c*1400 *Destr. Troy* 4743 The Grekes..Whappet in wharles, whellit the pepull. 1483 Caxton *Gold. Leg.* 314 b/2 A sowne lyke as a quarel had be shotte out of Arbalaste or a crosse bowe. 1540 *Act 33 Hen. VIII*, c. 6 Crossebowes..ready furnished with quarelles. 1590 Spenser *F.Q.* II. xi. 33 Now had the Carle..his hands Discharged of his bow and deadly quar'le. 1750 Carte *Hist. Eng.* II. 463 The Genoese..let fly their quarrels when they imagined themselves to be within a proper distance. 1846 Greener *Sc. Gunnery* 4 It is said of the cross-bow, that a quarrel could be projected from them 200 yards.
attrib. 1412–20 Lydg. *Chron. Troy* II. xi, Dartes daggers ..And quarrelheades sharpe & square yground. 1600 Holland *Livy* XXI. xi. 400 Ordinance of quarell shot, brakes, and other artillerie.
b. *dial.* (See quot.)
1840 Spurdens *East-Anglian Words* (E.D.S.), *Quarrel*, a kind of bird-bolt, with a lozenge-shaped head; now only used by rook-bolters for beating down rooks' nests.
†**2.** A square needle. Also *attrib. Obs. rare.*
1496 *Bk. St. Albans, Fishing* H iij, For smalle fysshe ye shall make your hokes of the smalest quarell nedlys that ye can fynde of stele, & in this wyse. Ye shall put the quarell in a redde charkcole fyre [etc.].
3. A square or (more usually) diamond-shaped pane of glass, of the kind used in making lattice-windows. Now *rare* exc. *dial.* (Cf. QUARRY *sb.*[3] 2.)
1447 in Parker *Gloss. Archit.* (1850) 290 Every windowe conteineth vi lights..Item all the katurs, quarrells, and oylements. 1507 in Gage *Suffolk* 143 Setting vp of white Normandy glas, oon rowe of quarrells white. 1542 Boorde *Dyetary* viii. (1870) 249 Let your skynner cut both..the skynnes in smale peces tryangle wyse, lyke halfe a quarel of a glase wyndow. 1589 Puttenham *Eng. Poesie* (Arb.) 106 The Lozange is..a quadrangle reuerst, with his point vpward like to a quarrell of glasse. 1669 Boyle *Contn. New Exp.* I. (1682) 25 Some plates of glass such as are used for making the Quarrels of Windows. 1711 C. Lockyer *Trade in India* vi. 164 Oyster-shells fixt Diamond-wise in wooden Frames, instead of Glass, which look something like our small, old fashion'd Quarrels. 1828 *Craven Gloss.*, *Quarrel*, a square of glass. 1879 *Cassell's Techn. Educ.* IX. 145/2 The colour..of the quarrels in the original window is a light bluish-green.
attrib. 1820 Scott *Abbot* xxxiv, A quarrel pane of glass in the turret window.
†**4.** A square tile. *Obs. rare.* (Cf. QUARRY *sb.*[3] 3.)
1601 Holland *Pliny* II. 596 The manner of pauing with smal tiles or quarrels ingrauen. 1610 —— *Camden's Brit.* I. 511 The pauements wrought Checker wise with small square quarels.
5. *techn.* **a.** A glazier's diamond (1807 Douce *Illustr. Shaksp.* I. 181). **b.** A four-sided graver (Ogilvie, 1882). **c.** A stonemason's chisel (*ibid.*).

quarrel, *sb.*[2] *Obs.* exc. *north. dial.* Forms: 5 **qwaryle, qvar-, qverelle, qwharrell, 5–6 quarel, (5 -ell), 6 qwarrel,** *Sc.* **querill, querrell, 7, 9 quarrel, 9 wharrel, wharl.** [Alteration of *quarer*, QUARRER, perh. after prec.]
1. A place from which stone, etc., is obtained. = QUARRY *sb.*[2]
14.. *Nom.* in Wr.-Wülcker 737/3 *Hoc saxifragium*, a qwaryle. 1483 *Cath. Angl.* 296/1 A Qvarelle of stone (*A.* Querelle of stane), *lapidicina*. 1500–18 *Acc. Louth Steeple* in *Archæologia* X. 71 Riding to the quarrell for stone. 1513 Douglas *Æneis* I. vii. 22 Wtheris..the huge pillaris greit Out of the querillis can to hew and beit. 1802 *Louth Corpor. Acc.* (1891) 55 That the Market for Sheep and Pigs shall be removed..to some place in the Quarrell. 1828 *Craven Gloss.*, *Quarrel*, a quarry. 1873 *Swaledale Gloss.*, *Wharrel*, a quarry. 1899 *Cumbld. Gloss.*, *Wharl*, a stone quarry; a disused quarry. Seldom heard.

†**b.** *Sc.* The stone or other material obtained by quarrying. Also *pl. Obs.*
1536 Bellenden *Cron. Scot.* (1821) I. 251 He thirllit thaim..to win metteleis, querrellis, and to mak tild. 1661–73 Ld. Fountainhall in M. P. Brown *Suppl. Decis.* (1826) II. 535 (Jam.) To dig, win, work, and carry away coals, limestone, clay, quarrell.
2. *attrib.* as ***quarrel head, hole, man, mell, stone.***
*c*1460 *Towneley Myst.* ii. 367 When I am dede, bery me in gudeboure at the quarell hede. 1472 *Durham Acc. Rolls* (Surtees) 245, j qwharrellmell. 1513 Douglas *Æneis* VIII. iv. 149 All kynd of wapynnis..Wyth branchis rent of treis, and quarrell stanis Of huge wecht. 1535 Lyndesay *Satyre* 3061, I lent my gossop my mear..And he hir drounit into the querrell hollis. *a*1572 Knox *Hist. Ref.* Wks. 1846 I. 379 At the Querrell Hollis, betuix Leyth and Edinburght. 1571 *Wills & Inv. N.C.* (Surtees 1860) 351 John Heworthe of gatisheid..Quarelman.

quarrel (ˈkwɒrəl), *sb.*[3] Forms: **4 querele, 4–5 (6) querel, 5 qwerell(e, 6 querel(l, 6–7** *Sc.* **quer(r)ell; 4–5 quarele, 5 qv-, quarelle, 5–6 quarell, (5 qw-), 5–7 quarel, 6 quarrel, 6–7 -ell).** [a. OF. *querele, -elle*:—L. *querēla, -ella* complaint, f. *querī* to complain. The spelling *quar(r)-* was the prevailing one by Caxton's time; later examples of *quer(r)-* are chiefly Sc.: see also QUERELE.]
†**1.** A complaint; esp. a complaint against a person; hence in *Law*: an accusation or charge; an action or suit. *Obs.*
*c*1374 Chaucer *Boeth.* III. pr. iii. 55 (Camb. MS.) For whennes comyn elles alle thyse foreyne compleyntes or quereles of pletynges [L. *forenses querimoniæ*]. *c*1400 *Destr. Troy* v. *heading*, Of the Qwerell of Kyng Priam for his Fader dethe. 1454 *Rolls Parlt.* V. 258/2 In all maner Actions.. suytes, quereles and demandes. 1483 Caxton *Gold. Leg.* 219/2 They sayd wyth swete and deuout quarelles why she suffred her deuoute seruaunte to dye wythout confessyon. 1535 Coverdale *Acts* xxv. 7 Ye Iewes..broughte vp many and greuous quarels agaynst Paul. 1583 *Exec. for Treason* (1675) 13 None of them have been sought hitherto to be impeached in any point or quarrel of Treason. 1641 *Termes de la Ley* 230 b, Qvarels..extendeth not onely to actions.. but also to the causes of actions & suits.
2. A ground or occasion of complaint against a person, leading to hostile feeling or action; a cause for which one person has unfriendly or unfavourable feelings towards another; also, the state or course of hostility resulting from such ground of complaint. Const. *against*, †*to*, later *with*. Now *rare*. ***to pick a quarrel***: see PICK *v.*
1340 *Ayenb.* 83 Ine oþre quereles huanne me mysnymþ [it may be amended]..ac errour ine batayle ne may naȝt by amended. 1390 Gower *Conf.* III. 303 Love hath mad him a querele Ayein hire youthe friissh and frele. *c*1400 *Destr. Troy* 1763 To qwit claym all querels, & be qweme fryndes. 1489 Caxton *Faytes of A.* I. xviii. 52 What theyre herte sayth of the quarell and what wylle they haue for to fyght. 1526 Tindale *Col.* iii. 13 Forgevynge one another (if eny man have a quarell to a nother). 1603 Knolles *Hist. Turks* (1621) 306 Although they be in number moe than you, yet are they in hope, quarrell and strength, farre inferiour. *a*1633 Austin *Medit.* (1635) 249 The Devill hath the same Quarrell to us Men, that hee had to Christ. 1655 Fuller *Ch. Hist.* II. v. §43 Ethelred..with whom Dunstan had a quarrel from his cradle. 1749 Fielding *Tom Jones* xv. vii, All the quarrel the squire hath to me is for taking your part. 1760–72 H. Brooke *Fool of Qual.* (1809) I. 32, I have no quarrel, I cried, to the high and mighty.
b. With possessive pron., or genitive: One's cause, side, or party in a complaint or contest; †one's claim to a thing.
1380 *Lay Folks Catech.* 1287 Hertely in godes querel to withstonde..in al þat we may. 1390 Gower *Conf.* I. 29 That he wol take the querele Of holy cherche in his defence. *c*1440 *Generydes* 3536 Off all this land I geve vppe my quarell. *c*1489 Caxton *Blanchardyn* xxxiv. 126 He was aduertysed..of the cause & quarelle of Blanchardyn. 1593 Shaks. *2 Hen. VI*, III. ii. 233 Thrice is he arm'd, that hath his Quarrell iust. 1697 Dryden *Virg. Georg.* IV. 318 When their Sov'reign's Quarrel calls 'em out, His Foes to mortal Combat they defie. 1755 Young *Centaur* i. Wks. 1757 IV. 124 The..heart commands the..head, to fight its unjust quarrel, and say it is its own. 1808 Scott *Life Dryden* in *D.'s Wks.* (1882) I. 172 Were a nobleman to have recourse to hired bravoes to avenge his personal quarrel against any one. 1892 Stevenson *Across the Plains* xii. 313 In our own quarrel we can see nothing truly.
c. With adjs., specifying the justice or other aspect of the cause or ground of contention. † ***of great quarrel***: of importance.
*c*1380 Wyclif *Sel. Wks.* III. 323 Alle mysdoeris.. meyntenen a fals quarele aȝenst God and his seyntis. 1456 Sir G. Haye *Law Arms* (S.T.S.) 73 Oft tymes..he that has gude rycht tynis the felde, and the wrang querele wynnis. *a*1533 Ld. Berners *Huon* xlix. 164 By a iust quarell ye may go and make warre vpon hym. 1590 T. Heneage in *Lett. Lit. Men* (Camden) 48 Her Highness dowteth that yt may breed discredyt to dyvers of great quarrell. 1651 Hobbes *Leviath.* II. xix. 97 Sufficient provision being taken, against all just quarrell. 1715–20 Pope *Iliad* III. 309 Perhaps their swords some nobler quarrel draws. *a*1806 K. White *Christmas-Day* 10 Me higher quarrel calls, with loudest song. 1863 Ruskin *Arrows of Chace* (1880) II. 25, I would have the country go to war, with haste, in a good quarrel.
†**d.** *transf.* Cause, reason, ground, plea. *Obs.*
1456 Sir G. Haye *Law Arms* (S.T.S.) 184 The King of France has querele to mak were apon the King of Ungary. 1476 J. Paston in *P. Lett.* III. 164 Then he shold be swer that I shold not be flyttyng, and I had syche a qwarell to kepe me at home. 1545 Ascham *Toxoph.* To Gentlem. Eng. (Arb.) 20 A fletcher hath euen as good a quarell to be angry with an archer. 1607–12 Bacon *Ess., Marriage* (Arb.) 270 So as a Man may have a quarrell to marrye when he will. 1633 Bp. Hall *Hard Texts, N.T.* 142 Judas of Galilee,..upon the quarrell of the Taxes laid by Cæsar..made an insurrection.
†**3.** An objection, opposition, dislike or aversion *to* a thing. *Obs.*
1581 W. Stafford *Exam. Compl.* Pref., I haue indeuoured in fewe wordes to answere certayne quarells and obiections dayly and ordinarily occurrent in the talke of sundry men. 1601 Holland *Pliny* II. 249 In the disease Tinesmus (which is an inordinat quarrell to the stool). 1654–66 Earl Orrery *Parthen.* (1676) 567 It created a general quarrel to Fortune. 1720 Lady Landsdown in *Lett. C'tess Suffolk* (1824) I. 70, I..shall be tempted to have a quarrel to matrimony.
b. Const. *with* (as in 2 and 4).
1726 Swift *Gulliver* III. iv, What quarrel I had with the dress or looks of his domestics?
4. A violent contention or altercation *between* persons, or of one person *with* another; a rupture of friendly relations.
1572 Huloet, Quarell, *controuersia, contentio, jurgium* [etc.]. 1596 Shaks. *Merch. V.* v. i. 238, I am th' vnhappy subiect of these quarrels. —— *Tam. Shr.* I. ii. 27 Rise Grumio rise, we will compound this quarrell. 1639 T. Brugis tr. *Camus' Mor. Relat.* 211 A man very valiant of his hands, but hot brained, he had had many quarrels. 1717 Lady M. W. Montagu *Let. to Pope* 12 Feb., I was very uneasy till they were parted, fearing some quarrel might arise. 1769 Blackstone *Comm.* IV. xiv. 191 If upon a sudden quarrel two persons fight, and one of them kills the other, this is manslaughter. 1818 Scott *Rob Roy* x, He will take care to avoid a quarrel..with any of the natives. 1838 Thirlwall *Greece* V. 265 The quarrels between the Phocians and their Locrian neighbours. 1876 Mozley *Univ. Serm.* x. (1877) 204 People rush into quarrels from simple violence and impetuosity of temper.
†**b.** Quarrelling; quarrelsomeness. *Obs. rare.*
1604 Shaks. *Oth.* II. iii. 52 He'l be as full of Quarrell, and offence As my yong Mistris dogge. 1605 Bacon *Adv. Learn.* I. vii. §2 All beasts..forgetting their severall appetites; some of pray, some of game, some of quarrell.
5. *Comb.* as ***quarrel-breeder.***
1611 Cotgr., *Sursemeur de noises*, a make-bate, firebrand of contention, quarrell-breeder.

quarrel (ˈkwɒrəl), *v.* Forms: **4 querele, 6 -el(l, quarel, 6–7 quar(r)ell, (7** *Sc.* **querrell), 7– quarrel.** [In Gower, a. OF. *quereler* (F. *quereller*), f. *querele* (see prec.): in later use prob. f. the sb.]
1. *intr.* To raise a complaint, protest, or objection; to find fault; to take exception.
a. Const. *with*. Phr. ***to quarrel with one's bread and butter***: to give up a means of livelihood for insufficient reasons.
1390 Gower *Conf.* III. 192 With that word the king quereleth And seith: Non is above me. 1605 Bacon *Adv. Learn.* I. iv. 6 If you take out every axiom..one by one, you may quarrel with them..at your pleasure. 1671 Milton *Samson* 60, I must not quarrel with the will Of highest dispensation. 1752 J. Gill *Trinity* iv. 81, I cannot see why any should quarrel with our translation. 1780 Craig *Mirror* No. 69 ¶1 How did she show superior sense by thus quarrelling with her bread and butter? 1894 H. Drummond *Ascent Man* 265 We cannot quarrel with the principle in.. Nature which condemns to death the worst.
transf. 1830 J. G. Strutt *Sylva Brit.* 82 It [the Chesnut] quarrels with no soil assigned to it.
†**b.** Const. *at*. *Obs.*
1585 W. Lambard in *Camden's Lett.* (1691) 29 This is all that I can quarrel at; and yet have I pried so far as I could. *a*1662 Heylin *Laud* (1668) 142 Which Clause..was now quarrel'd at by the Puritan Faction. 1725 De Foe *Voy. round World* (1840) 26 The whole weight of their resentment seemed to tend to quarrelling at my command.
†**c.** *absol.* or with *that*. *Obs. rare.*
1555 Eden *Decades* 125 For all this were not the enemies satisfyed: querelinge that this thynge was doone by sum slyght. 1563 Foxe *A. & M.* (1684) 865 To thintent to appeale, and..to querell vnder the..moste effectuall way.
2. *intr.* To contend violently, fall out, break off friendly relations, become inimical or hostile. Const. *with* (a person), *over*, *for*, or *about* (a thing).
1530 Palsgr. 676/2, I quarell with one, I pycke a mater to hym to fall out with hym. 1597 Hooker *Eccl. Pol.* v. lxxiv. §1 Those [heretiques] which doe nothing else but quarrell. 1697 Dryden *Virg. Georg.* II. 638 Wine urg'd to lawless Lust the Centaurs Train, Thro' Wine they quarrell'd. 1728 T. Sheridan *Persius* iii. (1739) 41 Quarrel for your Mince-meat, and refuse the Lullaby. 1829 Lytton *Devereux* II. v, She quarrelled with me for supping with St. John. 1868 Mayne Reid *White Squaw* xxviii. 133 Ere long they [*sc.* wolves] could be seen skulking through the enclosure and quarrelling over the corpses. 1875 Jowett *Plato* (ed. 2) V. 48 Having abundance of pasture..they would have nothing to quarrel about. 1883 G. Moore *Mod. Lover* I. xii. 244 Here a group of Cupids quarrelled over some masks and arrows. 1939 G. B. Shaw *In Good King Charles's Golden Days* 24 She has put us to shame for quarrelling over a matter of which we know nothing. 1961 *Middle East Jrnl.* XV. 3 The Istiqlal quarreled over foreign policy, labor politics and economic development.
fig. 1610 Shaks. *Temp.* III. i. 45 Some defect in her Did quarrell with the noblest grace she ow'd.
†**3.** *trans.* To claim contentiously. *Obs. rare.*
1579 Fenton *Guicciard.* 252 Ferdinand..had alwayes secretly quarrelled that title as lawfully apperteining to the crowne of Aragon. 1596 Danett tr. *Comines* (1614) 241 The Emperors daughter was restored vnto him, and the countie of Artois together with all the townes he quarrelled.
†**4.** To dispute, call in question, object to (an act, word, etc.); to challenge the validity or correctness of. *Obs.* (Freq. in 17th c.)
1609 Tourneur *Fun. Poeme Sir F. Vere* 491 If malignant censure quarrels it. 1644 Prynne & Walker *Fiennes's Trial*

4 The Lords Orders being not only quarrelled, but contemned by those who were to bail him. **1699** COLLIER *2nd Def.* (1730) 326 This fine Phrase puts me in mind of his quarrelling a Sentence of mine for want..of Syntax. **1745** RUDDIMAN *Vind. Buchanan* 310 (Jam.), I hope you will not quarrel the words, for they are all Virgil's. **1786** BURNS *On Naething* v, Some quarrel the Presbyter gown, Some quarrel Episcopal graithing.

5. To find fault with (a person); to reprove angrily. *Obs.* exc. *Sc.* (Freq. in 17th c.)

1598 B. JONSON *Ev. Man in Hum.* II. i, I had quarrell'd My brother purposely. **1621** J. REYNOLDS *God's Rev. agst. Murder* I. i. 5 Quarrelling his taylor for the fashion of his clothes. **1688** PENTON *Guard. Instruct.* (1897) 47 Quarrelling the poor man for not coming sooner. **1728** *Wodrow Corr.* (1843) III. 363 He ought not to be quarrelled for his opinions. *c* **1817** HOGG *Tales & Sk.* (1837) III. 344 They might kill a good many without being quarrelled for it. **1897** CROCKETT *Lads' Love* xiii. 140 It was my fault..I quarrelled her, I angered her.

†**6.** With complement: To force or bring by quarrelling. *Obs.*

1610 B. JONSON *Alch.* IV. iv, You must quarrel him out o' the house. **1655** FULLER *Ch. Hist.* III. xi. §2 Many English Bishops..fearing by degrees they should all be quarrelled out of their places..fled into Scotland. **1655** —— *Hist. Camb.* (1840) 159 How easy was it for covetousness, in those ticklish times, to quarrel the College lands into superstition? **1678** *Yng. Mans Call.* 167 There are many..that quarrel themselves carnally to hell.

Hence **'quarrelled** *ppl. a.* Also †**'quarrellable** *a.*, capable of being called in question.

16.. in Peterkin *Rentals Orkney* iii. (1820) 14 (Jam. Suppl.) Quhilk gift is not confirmed..and so his right is most quarrallable. **1673** LD. FOUNTAINHALL in M. P. Brown *Suppl. Decis.* (1826) III. 14 The said act of Parliament appoints these deeds to be quarrellable. **1820** J. BROWN *Hist. Brit. Ch.* II. App. 7 The Antiburghers still continue upon their quarrelled constitution of Synod.

†**'quarrelet.** *Obs. rare*[−1]. In 7 **quarelet.** [f. QUARREL *sb.*[1] 3 or 4 + -ET[1].] A small square.

1648 HERRICK *Hesper., Rock of Rubies* (1869) 32 Some ask'd how pearls did grow, and where? Then spoke I to my girle, To part her lips, and shew'd them there The quarelets of pearl.

quarrelled ('kwɒrəld), *a.* Also **quarled.** [f. QUARREL *sb.*[1] 3 + -ED[2].] **a.** Of windows: Made of quarrels. **b.** Of glass: Formed into quarrels.

1868 J. G. MIALL *Congreg. Yorksh.* 103 The shutters which protected the quarreled windows from injury. **1889** HISSEY *Tour in Phaeton* 26 Mullioned windows, so pleasantly varied by transom and quarrelled glass. **1894** BLACKMORE *Perlycross* 142 The light from a long quarled window.

quarreller ('kwɒrələ(r)). Also 5 **querelour,** 6-7 **quareller,** (7 **-or, -our**). [f. QUARREL *v.* + -ER[1].] One who quarrels, in senses of the vb.

c **1450** *Aristotle's ABC* in *Q. Eliz. Acad.*, etc. 66 Quenche fals querelour; þe quene of heven þe will quite. *a* **1533** LD. BERNERS *Gold. Bk. M. Aurel.* (1546) F vij b, No quarellers, but sufferers. **1566** T. STAPLETON *Ret. Untr. Jewel* ii. 46 Such a wrangler and Childish quareller as you be. **1601** HOLLAND *Pliny* I. 58 No riuer hath lesse liberty..yet he is no quarreller, nor much harm doeth he. *a* **1642** SIR W. MONSON *Wars with Spain* (1682) 3 It were better to keep company with a Coward than a Quarreller. **176.** WESLEY *Husb. & Wives* iii. 6 Wks. 1811 IX. 66 Away then with..this quarreller, suspicion. **1824** SCOTT *St. Ronan's* viii, Quarrellers do not usually live long. **1892** E. REEVES *Homeward Bound* 103 The big albatross..scattering the quarrellers, seizes the tempting morsel for himself.

†**b.** With pun on QUARREL *sb.*[1] 3. *Obs.*

1630 *Conceits, Clinches* etc. (Halliw. 1860) 5 One said it was unfit a glasier should be a constable, because he was a common quareller. **1673** R. HEAD *Canting Acad.* 163 Glasiers..are constant Quarrellers.

quarrelling ('kwɒrəlɪŋ), *vbl. sb.* [f. QUARREL *v.* + -ING[1].] The action of the vb. QUARREL.

1546 BALE *Eng. Votaries* I. 72 They wolde..styll vexe hym with olde quarellynges. **1611** RICH *Honest. Age* (Percy Soc.) 54 The mind is oppressed with idle thoughts which spurreth on the tongue to contentious quarrelling. *a* **1715** BURNET *Own Time* III. (1724) I. 452 Seimour and he had fallen into some quarrellings. **1734** T. WATT *Vocab. Eng. Lat.* 38 You are always making a Quarrelling about nothing. **1866** GEO. ELIOT *F. Holt* (1868) 30 There was no fear of family coolness or quarrelling on this side.

attrib. **1625** MASSINGER *New Way* v. i, Make not My house your quarrelling scene.

'quarrelling, *ppl. a.* [f. as prec. + -ING[2].] That quarrels; quarrelsome.

1589 NASHE *Pref. Greene's Menaphon* (Arb.) 13 That quarrelling kinde of verse. **1593** *Tell-Troth's N.Y. Gift* 30 The quarreling mate shall not complaine. **1670** CLARENDON *Ess.* Tracts (1727) 166 A froward, proud and quarreling conscience. **1822** B. CORNWALL *Two Dreams* 11 The loud quarrelling elements cast out Their sheeted fires.

Hence †**'quarrellingly** *adv. Obs.*

1571 GOLDING *Calvin on Ps.* lxix. 11 They stryve with them quarrellingly, and wythout meeldnesse. **1586** HOLINSHED *Chron. Eng.* III. 20/2 He caused the bishop to be sued, quarelinglie charging him that [etc.].

†**'quarrellous,** *a. Obs.* Forms: 5 **querelous(e, quarelouse,** 6 **quaril-, quarel(l)-,** 6-7 **quarrel-,** 6-7 **quarrellous.** [a. OF. *querelous* (F. *querelleux*): see QUARREL *sb.*[3] and -OUS. In later use perh. a new formation.] **a.** Given to complaining; querulous. **b.** Quarrelsome, contentious; fault-finding. (In common use from about 1560 to 1650.)

c **1400** *Beryn* 2070 They were so querelouse of al myȝt com in mynde Thouȝe it were nevir indede I-do. *c* **1475** *Lerne or be Lewde* in *Babees Bk.* 10 [Be not] To Queynt, to Querelous, and Queme welle thy maistre. **1490** CAXTON *Eneydos* xxii. 80 Grete wepynges and quarellouse plaintes. **1556** ABP. PARKER *Ps.* xxxiv. 84 To scape theyr foes so quarilous. **1610** BP. HALL *Apol. Brownists* 83 His Maiesties speech..might haue staied the course of your quarrelous pen. *a* **1639** SPOTTISWOOD *Hist. Ch. Scot.* II. (1677) 66 This Gentleman had been in former times very quarrellous and turbulent. *a* **1656** HALES *Gold. Rem.* (1688) 113 This quarrellous and fighting humour.

Hence †**'quarrellously** *adv.*

1580 A. MUNDAY in *John a Kent*, etc. (Shaks. Soc.) 78 Everie desperate Dick that can..behave him selfe so quarrelously.

†**quarrel-picker, -piker.** *Obs.* [f. the phr. *to pick a quarrel*: cf. QUARREL *sb.*[3] 2 and PICK *v.*]

1. One who picks quarrels; a quarrelsome person.

1547 COVERDALE *Old Faith* To Rdr. A vij, Then shall we be no Quarrellpykerrs. **1551** T. WILSON *Logike* 46 These quarelpickers, these roysters, and fighters. **1608** TOPSELL *Serpents* (1658) 780 A company of corner-creepers, spider-catchers, fault-finders, and quarrell-pickers.

2. *Slang.* (With pun on QUARREL *sb.*[1] 3; cf. QUARRELLER b.) A glazier.

a **1700** B. E. *Dict. Cant. Crew.*

So **quarrel-picking, -piking** *vbl. sb.* and *ppl. a.*

1557 N.T. (Genev.) *Acts* xvii. 7 *note*, Like quarelpiking they vsed against Christe. **1591** R. TURNBULL *Exp. James* Ep. Ded. A iv b, Reprochfull censure,..without quarrell-picking. **1894** *Westm. Gaz.* 25 Sept. 3/2 A..dining, quarrel-picking, and duelling club.

quarrelsome ('kwɒrəlsəm), *a.* [f. QUARREL *sb.*[3] + -SOME.]

1. Inclined to quarrel; given to, or characterized by, quarrelling. †Const. *at.*

1596 SHAKS. *Tam. Shr.* I. ii. 13 My M[r] is growne quarrelsome. **1616** W. SCLATER *Serm.* 10 Weigh well how..quarrelsome at the liues of magistrates the people are. *a* **1639** W. WHATELEY *Prototypes* I. xvi. (1640) 161 A quarrelsome fellow, still brawling and falling out. **1681** ANNE WYNDHAM *King's Concealm.* 78 This quarrelsom Gossipping was a most seasonable diversion. **1749** FIELDING *Tom Jones* v. ix, Men who are ill-natured and quarrelsome when they are drunk. **1818** SCOTT *Rob Roy* xii, The wine rendered me loquacious, disputatious and quarrelsome. **1879** MRS. SEGUIN *Blk. Forest* viii. 115 The lords of Windeck..were of a specially quarrelsome temper.

2. Offensive, disagreeable. *nonce-use.*

1825 COLERIDGE *Aids Refl.* App. i. (1836) 35 Technical terms, hard to be remembered, and alike quarrelsome to the ear and the tongue.

Hence **'quarrelsomely** *adv.*

1755 in JOHNSON. **1873** MISS BROUGHTON *Nancy* III. 132 In an aggressively loud voice, as if he were quarrelsomely anxious to be overheard. **1880** MRS. PARR *Adam & Eve* II. vii. 147 The crowd grew..quarrelsomely drunk.

'quarrelsomeness. [f. prec. + -NESS.] The condition or character of being quarrelsome; contentious disposition.

1611 DONNE *Serm.* (ed. Alford) V. 32 God giveth not his Children..valour, and then leaveth them to a spirit of Quarrelsomeness. *a* **1656** BP. HALL *Rem.* 77 (T.) The giddiness of some, others' quarrelsomeness. **1780** BENTHAM *Princ. Legisl.* Wks. 1843 I. 76 *note*, Although a man, by his quarrelsomeness, should for once have been engaged in a bad action [etc.]. **1879** R. K. DOUGLAS *Confucianism* iii. 88 In manhood..he avoided quarrelsomeness.

quarrenden, quarrender ('kwɒrənd(ə)n, -də(r)). Also 5 **quaryndo(u)n,** 7, 9 **quarrington,** 9 **quarantine, quarrener, quarendel, -den, -don, -ten.** [Of obscure origin: the L. equivalents given in first quot. seem to be otherwise unknown.] A variety of apple (see quot. 1886) common in Somerset and Devon. Also *attrib.*

14.. *Voc.* in Wr.-Wülcker 574/34 *Conduum*, a Quaryndoun. *Conduus*, a Quaryndon tre. **1676** WORLIDGE *Cyder* (1691) 206 The Devonshire Quarrington is also a very fine early Apple. **1851** R. HOGG *Brit. Pomol.* 67 Devonshire Quarrenden... A very valuable and first-rate dessert apple. **1855** KINGSLEY *Westw. Ho* i, 'Red quarrenders' and mazard cherries. **1869** BLACKMORE *Lorna D.* (1891) 125 As he took the large oxhorn of our quarantine apple cider. **1870** TROLLOPE *Vicar of Bullhampton* vii. 40 The quarantines are rare this year. **1874** T. HARDY *Far fr. Mad. Crowd* I. xxvii. 299 Some tall, gaunt costard, or quarrington. **1886** ELWORTHY *W. Som. Word-bk., Quarrener*,..an oblate shaped, deep red, early apple; also known as suck-apple. **1905** *Westm. Gaz.* 11 Aug. 10/1 One grower in the West of England obtained 20s. a bushel for his Devonshire Quarrendens. **1907** *Ibid.* 31 Aug. 7/2 English apples..are a poor crop, except Worcesters and Quarantines—the latter an early cheap fruit. **1921** *Contemp. Rev.* Oct. 559 The Quarrendens are gone. September saw them out. **1945** H. J. MASSINGHAM *Wisdom of Fields* vii. 133 Red and sweet Quarrendons on the orchard trees. **1969** *Oxf. Bk. Food Plants* 48/1 'Devonshire Quarrendon'. Known before 1650, it was possibly originally French. It has a deep crimson fruit with white juicy flesh.

†**quarrer.** *Obs.* Forms: 4-5 **quarer(e,** 4 **quarrer(e, quariere.** [a. OF. *quarriere* f. (12th c.; mod.F. *carrière*), *quarrier* m. = med.L. *quar(r)er(i)a, quarraria, quadrāria*, f. *quadrāre* to square (stones).] = QUARRY *sb.*[2]

13.. *Metr. Hom.* (Vernon MS.) in Herrig *Archiv* LVII. 259 Ffer fro þe Abbey was a quarere. *c* **1350** *Will. Palerne* 2232 þei saie..a semliche quarrere under an heiȝ hel al holwe newe diked. **1387** TREVISA *Higden* (Rolls) I. 271 In Gallia beþ many good quarers and noble for to digge stoon. *c* **1440** *Promp. Parv.* 419/1 Quarere, or quarere of stone, (*K.* quarer)..*lapidicina.*

†**quarreure.** *Obs. rare.* [a. OF. *quarreure* (*quarrure*, mod.F. *carrure*):—L. *quadrātūra* QUADRATURE.] Quadrature.

c **1400** tr. *Secreta Secret., Gov. Lordsh.* 112 Loke þat þe mone be noght in þe entree of þe way, in þe quarreure of þe sonne, or els yn his contrary.

†**quarreyor.** *Obs. rare*[−1]. [f. QUARRY *v.*[1]] ? A bird proper to be the quarry of a hawk.

1575 TURBERV. *Faulconrie* 130 This you shall doe..vntill your Hawke be well entred and quarreyed and that she knowe a quarreyor sufficiently.

'quarriable, *a. rare.* [f. QUARRY *v.*[2] + -ABLE.] Capable of being quarried.

1856 EMERSON *Eng. Traits* iii. 40 The arable soil, the quarriable rock. **1880** RUSKIN *Fathers Have Told Us* I. i. 16 Quarriable banks above well-watered meadow.

†**'quarried,** *ppl. a.*[1] *Obs.* [f. QUARRY *v.*[1]] *well-quarried*, properly trained to fly at quarry.

1575 TURBERV. *Faulconrie* 154 Then shall you first cast off a well quarried or make Hawke, and let hir stoupe a fowle.

'quarried, *ppl. a.*[2] [f. QUARRY *v.*[2] + -ED[1].]

a. Dug out of, or as out of, a quarry.

1747 H. BROOKE *Fables, Female Seducers* Wks. (1810) 414 He..Of pearl and quarry'd diamond dreams. **1855** O. W. HOLMES *Poems* 35 One leap of Ocean scatters on the sand The quarried bulwarks of the loosening land.

b. *Physical Geogr.* Eroded or broken off by glacial quarrying; = PLUCKED *ppl. a.* 4.

1909 *Jrnl. & Proc. R. Soc. N.S. Wales* XLIII. 265 Moutonnées..if large..appeared to be abraded on the up slope, and heavily quarried on the downslope. **1930** *Prof. Papers U.S. Geol. Survey* No. 160. 90/2 Muir..described long trains of glacially quarried blocks which he had observed in the vicinity of Tenaya Lake.

'quarried, *a.* [f. QUARRY *sb.*[3] + -ED[2].] Of flooring: paved with quarries. Of a window: decorated with quarries.

1842 G. FRANCIS *Dict. Arts* s.v. *Quarry*, Quarried pavements are by no means uncommon in old village churches. **1856** GEO. ELIOT in *Westm. Rev.* X. 56 In those days, the quarried parlour was innocent of a carpet. **1954** M. RICKERT *Painting in Brit.: Middle Ages* 231 *Quarried glass*, window panels divided into squares or diamonds, each containing an ornamental or heraldic motif.

quarrier[1] ('kwɒrɪə(r)). Forms: α. 5 **quarre-, qwari-, qvary-, querrour,** *Sc.* **quereour,** 5-6 **quarriour.** β. **quaryere,** 6 **quarryer,** 7- **quarrier.** [a. OF. *quarreour, -ieur, quarrier* (mod.F. *carrier*), agent-n. to *quarrer* (mod.F. *carrer*):—L. *quadrāre* to square (stones): cf. late L. *quadrātor, quadrātārius*, in same sense, and see QUARRY *sb.*[2]] One who quarries stone; a quarryman.

α. *c* **1375** *Sc. Leg. Saints* xxiii. (*Seven Sleepers*) 212 Quereouris gadryt sone stanis to wyne. *c* **1400** *Destr. Troy* 1531 Masons full mony;..qwariours qweme. **1424** *E.E. Wills* 59 Paied to Fairchild, quarriour, xiijs. and iiijd. for freestone. **1483** *Cath. Angl.* 296/2 A Qvaryour, *lapidicius.* **1590** *Serpent of Devis.* C iij, There was found by quarriours ..a rich tombe of stone.

β. *c* **1440** *Promp. Parv.* 419/1 Quaryere, *lapidicidius.* **1500-18** *Acc. Louth Steeple* in *Archæologia* X. 71 William Bennet, quarryer. **1610** HOLLAND *Camden's Brit.* I. 531 A certaine number of workmen, as Masons and Quarriers. **1673** RAY *Journ. Low C.* 57 Pillars and Galleries made by Quarriers. **1811** PINKERTON *Petral.* I. 498 Where the gypsum once bore a prismatic form, now destroyed by the progress of the quarriers. **1876** T. HARDY *Ethelberta* xxxi, Everybody in the parish who was not a boatman was a quarrier.

fig. **1825** HONE *Every-day Bk.* I. 274 He was the quarrier, and architect, and builder-up of his own greatness.

†**'quarrier**[2]. *Obs.* Forms: 6 **quarier(e,** 6-7 **quarrier,** (6 **-iere, -iour**). [App. an alteration of QUARRY *sb.*[4]; see also QUARION.] A large square candle.

c **1550** *Document* (N.), To cause the groomes to delyver to the groom porter all the remaynes of torches and quarriers. **1581** STYWARD *Mart. Discipl.* I. 24 Their quariers and their cressets being light euerie one by it selfe. **1604** *Househ. Ord.* (1790) 305 Mortores, Torchetts, Torches, Quarrioures. **1659** TORRIANO, *Doppione*, a great torch of wax, which in Court is called a Standard, or a quarrier.

quarring, *vbl. sb.*: see QUAR *v.*[1]

quarrington, variant of QUARRENDEN.

quarrion ('kwɒrɪən). Also **quar(r)ian.** [Prob. Aboriginal name.] An Australian parrot, *Leptolophus hollandicus*, which has grey plumage with white and yellow patches; = COCKATIEL. Also *attrib.*

1901 A. J. CAMPBELL *Nests & Eggs Austral. Birds* 622 The Grey and Yellow Top-knotted Parrot ('Quarrion', native name among bushmen) flies round about water-holes. **1934** *Bulletin* (Sydney) 26 Sept. 21/3 Quarians caught by broken wings on telephone-wires and emus held by the leg in fences are other casualties I've come across. **1938** N. W. CAYLEY

Austral. Parrots 112 The Cockatiel (also called Cockatoo Parrot and Quarrian) was met with during Cook's voyage. **1943** W. HATFIELD *I find Australia* v. 87 Quarrion parrots and ring-necks, rosellas and parakeets, .. and magpies and butcher-birds (singing shrikes) added their morning warbles to the screeching and trilling. **1964** *People* (Austral.) 16 Dec. 38 The quarrians, sometimes known as cockaties or cockatoo parrots, are far from home. **1966** EASTMAN & HUNT *Parrots Austral.* 176 Call-note in flight is distinctive, and is a field mark in indicating the quarrion's presence long before it is sighted.

quarromes, quarron. *Obs.* or *arch. Cant.* Also **quarroms, quarrons.** The body.

1567 HARMAN *Caveat* (1869) 84 Bene Lightmans to thy quarromes .. God morrowe to thy body. **1641** BROME *Jovial Crew* II. Wks. 1873 III. 388 Here's Pannum and Lap, and good Poplars of Yarrum To fill up the Crib and to comfort the Quarron. **1846** *Swell's Night Guide* 128/2 *Quarroms*, a body. **1922** JOYCE *Ulysses* 48 White thy fambles, red thy gan And thy quarrons dainty is. **1932** AUDEN *Orators* III. 105 Salmon draws Its lovely quarrons through the pool.

quarry ('kwɒrɪ), *sb.*^{1} Forms: 4–5 **quirre, quyrre,** 5 **kirre, kyrre, whirry,** 6 **quyrry;** 4–5 **querrye, querre** (also 7), 7 **querry;** 5 **quarre,** 6 **quarie,** 6–7 **quarrie,** (6–7 **-ey**), 6– **quarry.** [a. OF. *cuirée, curée*, f. *cuir* (:—L. *corium*) skin: see sense 1.]

†**1. a.** Certain parts of a deer placed on the hide and given to the hounds as a reward; also, the reward given to a hawk which has killed a bird (see quot. *c* 1350). *Obs.*

c **1320** *Sir Tristr.* 499 Hert, liuer and liȝtes, And blod tille his quirre, Houndes on hyde he diȝtes. *c* **1350** *Parl. Three Ages* 233 [The falconer] puttis owte .. þe maryo [*v.r.* marow] one his gloue And quotes thaym [the hawks] to the querrye [*v.r.* whirry] that quelled hym to þe dethe. *c* **1400** *Master of Game* Prol. (MS. Digby 182), And after whann the hert is spaied and dede, he vndothe hym, and maketh his kirre and enquirreth or rewardeþ his houndes. *c* **1420** *Venery de Twety* in *Rel. Ant.* I. 153 The houndes shal be rewardid with the nekke and with the bewellis .. and thei shal be etyn under the skyn, and therfore it is clepid the quarre. **1486** *Bk. St. Albans* F iv, That callid is Iwis The quyrre, a boue the skyn for it etyn is. **1576** TURBERV. *Venerie* 34 How a man should enter his yong houndes to hunte the Harte, and of the quaries and rewardes that he shall giue them. [**1688** R. HOLME *Armoury* II. 188/1 Quarry .. is a gift or reward given the Hounds, being some part of the thing hunted.]

†**b.** *to blow the quarry*: To sound a horn to call the hounds to the quarry. *Obs. rare*$^{-1}$.

c **1500** *Wyl Bucke's Test.* (Copland) 70, I ma no lenger tarry, I must nedis hense go. I here them blowe the quarry.

†**2. a.** A collection or heap made of the deer killed at a hunting. *Obs.*

13.. *Gaw. & Gr. Knt.* 1324, & quykly of þe quelled dere a querré þay maked. *c* **1400** *Master of Game* xxxv. (MS. Digby 182), Alle þe while that þe huntynge lasteth shulde þe cartes go aboute fro place to place, to brynge deer to þe quirre. *Ibid.*, þen shulde þe maistre of þe game leede þe kynge to þe querre, and shewe it hym. *c* **1500** *Wyl Bucke's Test.* (Copland) 31 He that me helpeth to the quarry bringe I wyll that he haue mi necke, for a shorte repaste. *a* **1550** *Hunting of Cheviot* 8 in Child *Ballads* III. 307 To the quyrry then the Perse went, To se the bryttlynge off the deare. **1590** NASHE *Pasquil's Apol.* I. E, The carkases of the deade, like a quarrie of Deare at a general hunting, [shall be] hurled vppon a heape. **1605** SHAKS. *Macb.* IV. iii. 206 To relate the manner Were on the Quarry of these murther'd Deere To adde the death of you.

†**b.** *transf.* A heap of dead men; a pile of dead bodies. *Obs.*

1589 R. ROBINSON *Gold. Mirr.* (Chetham Soc.) p. xxiii, Till to the quirry, a number out of count, Were brought to reape the iust reward at last. **1603** KNOLLES *Hist. Turks* (1621) 308 All fowly foiled with bloud, and the quarrey of the dead. **1611** SPEED *Hist. Gt. Brit.* VIII. vii. §50. 410 Then went they in haste to the quarry of the dead, but by no meanes could finde the body of the King.

fig. **1633** HERBERT *Temple, Sinner* 30, I finde there quarries of pil'd vanities.

3. a. The bird flown at or killed by a hawk or other bird of prey.

1486 *Bk. St. Albans* D ij, Yowre hawke fleeth to the querre. **1590** SPENSER *F.Q.* II. xi. 43 As when Joue's .. bird from hye Stoupes at a flying heron .. The stone dead quarrey falls. **1695** CONGREVE *Love for L.* v. ii, Hooded like a hawk, to sieze at first sight upon the quarry. **1748** RICHARDSON *Clarissa* (1811) II. xxv. 166 Wrens and sparrows are not too ignoble a quarry for this villanous gos-hawk. **1855** H. SPENCER *Princ. Psychol.* (1872) I. III. viii. 352 A falcon swooping on its quarry. **1878** B. TAYLOR *Deukalion* II. v. 84 There wheels a vulture seeking other quarry.

b. The animal pursued or taken by hounds or hunters (see also quot. 1867).

1612 DRAYTON *Poly-olb.* XIII. 215 No beast shall prove thy Quarries heere, Save those the best of chase. **1665** BOYLE *Occas. Refl., Disc. Occas. Med.* (1848) 22 One [Rabbit] sets him a running, and another proves his Quarry. **1695** TEMPLE *Hist. Eng.* (1699) 180 The Game, which it was their Interest to preserve, both for their Sport and the Quarry. **1808** SCOTT *Marm.* II. Introd., The startled quarry bounds amain, As fast the gallant greyhounds strain. **1867** SMYTH *Sailor's Word-bk.*, *Quarry*, the prey taken by whalers. **1883** E. PENNELL-ELMHIRST *Cream Leicestersh.* 206 The pack pressed their sinking quarry into and through the coverts.

c. *fig.* Any object of chase, aim, or attack; an intended prey or victim.

1615 TOMKINS *Albumazar* v. i. in Hazl. *Dodsley* XI. 404 When they counter Upon one quarry, break that league, as we do. **1693** DRYDEN *Juvenal* Pref. (1697) 61 Folly was the proper Quarry of Horace, and not Vice. **1740** SOMERVILLE *Hobbinol* III. 362 If from some small Creek, A lurking Corsair the rich Quarry Spies. **1837** CARLYLE *Fr. Rev.* I. III. iii, Count Mirabeau .. scents or descries richer quarry from afar. **1883** FROUDE *Short Stud.* IV. I. iii. 29 The archbishop dared not at once strike so large a quarry.

4. The attack or swoop made by a hawk upon a bird; the act of seizing or tearing the quarry.

1607 HEYWOOD *Wom. Killed w. Kindn.* Wks. 1874 II. 99 My Hawke kill'd too. *Char.* I, but 'twas at the querre,—Not at the mount, like mine. **1615** LATHAM *Falconry* (1633) 27 These kindes of Hawkes .. will be presently wonne with two or three quarries. **1667** *Decay Chr. Piety* v. §16 Prometheus's vultur begins her quarry in this life. **1884** T. SPEEDY *Sport* xix. 360 We have not above half-a-dozen times seen the peregrine in the act of making a quarry.

5. *Comb.*, as ***quarry-overtaking***, ***-scorning*** adjs.

1647 FANSHAWE tr. *Pastor Fido* (1676) 7 Within whose Quarry-scorning mind had place The pleasure or the glory of the Chase. **1873** BROWNING *Red. Cott. Nt.-cap* 400 Forward, the firm foot! Onward the quarry-overtaking eye!

quarry ('kwɒrɪ), *sb.*^{2} Forms: 5 **quar(r)ey, querry,** 6 **quarye,** 6–7 **quarrie,** (7 **-ey, quarie**), 6– **quarry,** (9 *dial.* **wharry**). [a. med.L. *quareia* (1266 in Du Cange), var. of *quareria*, etc. QUARRER, q.v. See also QUAR *sb.*^{2}, QUARREL *sb.*^{2}]

1. a. An open-air excavation from which stone for building or other purposes is obtained by cutting, blasting, or the like; a place where the rock has been, or is being, cut away in order to be utilized.

c **1420** *Chron. Vilod.* 3657 W[t] an hors .. He ladde stones from þe quarey to þe chirche. **1458** R. FANNANDE *Inscr. St. Helen's, Abingdon* in Leland *Itin.* (1769) VII. 80 Than crafti men for the querry made crowes of yre. **1480** CAXTON *Descr. Brit.* 5 Quareyes of marble of diuerse maner stones. **1562** *Act. 5 Eliz.* c. 13 §3 The Rubbish or smallest broken Stones of any Quarry. **1577** NORTHBROOKE *Diving* (1843) 135 Let him be punished and cast .. in the quarries to digge stones. **1664** DRYDEN *Rival Ladies* II. i, If thou wouldst offer both the Indies to me, The Eastern Quarries, and the Western Mines. **1728** YOUNG *Love of Fame* I. 168 Belus .. builds himself a name; and, to be great, Sinks in a quarry an immense estate! **1759** JOHNSON *Rasselas* xxxvii, Walls supply stones more easily than quarries. **1838** THIRLWALL *Greece* xv. II. 320 The quarries were filled with these unfortunate captives. **1877** A. B. EDWARDS *Up Nile* vii. 165 An ancient quarry from which the stone has been cut out in smooth masses.

fig. **1647** COWLEY *Mistr., Thraldom* v, Others with sad and tedious art, Labour i' the Quarries of a stony Heart. **1663** SIR G. MACKENZIE *Relig. Stoic* xvii. (1685) 152 Each sentence seems a quarry of rich meditations. **1847** LD. LINDSAY *Chr. Art* I. 60 The whole quarry of legends, ceremonies and superstitions which Rome .. employed in the structure of .. the church of the middle ages.

b. *transf.* Any place from which stones may be obtained as from a quarry.

1838 THIRLWALL *Greece* II. 364 Houses, temples, the monuments of the dead, were the quarries from which they drew. **1858** HAWTHORNE *Fr. & It. Jrnls.* (1872) I. 48 Its walls were a quarry of precious stones. **1871** FREEMAN *Norm. Conq.* (1876) IV. xviii. 220 The ruins of the Roman town still remained as a quarry; where all who would might seek materials for their own buildings.

†**2.** A large mass of stone or rock in its natural state, capable of being quarried. *Obs.*

c **1630** MILTON *Passion* 46 On the softned Quarry would I score My plaining vers. **1670** DRYDEN *2nd Pt. Conq. Granada* v. i, As some huge rock, Rent from its quarry, does the waves divide. **1712** J. JAMES tr. *Le Blond's Gardening* 107 When they meet with Rocks or Quarries, they make use of Gun-powder to blow them up. **1764** *Museum Rust.* II. lxxviii. 272 Where lucern is planted upon a quarry, if the stone hath not many interstices .. the length of the roots will be impeded.

fig. *a* **1625** FLETCHER *Love's Pilgr.* v. iv, Though I am none of those Flinty fathers, yet .. All are not of my quarry.

†**3.** The hard granular part of a pear. *Obs. rare*$^{-1}$. (So F. *carrière*.)

1707 *Curiosities in Husb. & Gard.* 47 Besides these Parts, a Pear has one called the Quarry, which is a little heap of stony Knobs.

4. *attrib.* and *Comb.*, as ***quarry-cart***, ***-district***, ***-face***, ***-ground***, ***-hole***, ***-land***, ***-mason***, ***-master***, ***-owner***, ***-pit***, ***-rid*** (refuse), ***-slave***, ***-stone***, ***-wagon***, etc.; ***quarrylike*** adj.; **quarry-faced** *a.*, rough-faced, as taken from the quarry; **quarry-stone bond**, rubble masonry; **quarry-sap**, **-water**, the moisture contained in newly quarried stone.

1805 R. W. DICKSON *Pract. Agric.* (1807) I. 62 The *quarry-cart, a strong low cart for the loading and carrying of heavy stones. **1893–4** R. O. HESLOP *Northumb. Words* II. 557 *Quarry-fyess*, the *quarry face; its perpendicular side. **1936** *Discovery* Oct. 317/1 The skull .. is thought to be still buried in the quarry-face. **1974** *Environmental Conservation* I. 38/1 Quarry-face risks are by no means confined to high country where population is sparse. **1577** HARRISON *England* II. xxii. (1877) I. 337 Where the rocks and *quarrie grounds are. **1891** G. NEILSON *Per Lineam Valli* 32 Hundreds of *quarry-holes, mere surface pitmarks on the hill sides. **1792** A. YOUNG *Trav. France* 289 Rock and *quarry-land, with sandy gravels, abound there. **1856** MRS. H. B. STOWE *Dred* II. VI. 76 They are *quarry-masters, that quarry out marble enough for a generation to work up. **1579–80** NORTH *Plutarch* (1676) 955 Dionysius .. sent him forthwith to dig in the *Quarry-pit. **1911** J. MASEFIELD *Everlasting Mercy* 4 In the old quarry-pit they say Head-keeper Pike was made away. **1862** *Min. Proc. Inst. C.E.* XXI. 482 Covered with a layer of puddled clay .. '*quarry rid' and broken stone. **1883** *Stonemason* Jan., So that .. the *quarry sap might be thoroughly dried out of them, and the stone .. fit for use. **1813** J. FORSYTH *Rem. Excurs. Italy* 271 An iron crow .. appears to have been left there by some ancient *quarry-slave. **1856** BRYANT *Thanatopsis* 77 Like the quarry-slave at night, Scourged to his dungeon. **1937** BLUNDEN *Elegy* 15 Above the square With plodding *quarry-waggons filled. **1838** C. LYELL *Elements of Geol.* I. iv. 74 It is desirable to shape the stones which are to be used in architecture while they are yet soft and wet, and while they contain their '*quarry-water'. **1878** HUXLEY *Physiogr.* 22 Stone when freshly taken from the quarry usually holds moisture, known to the workman as 'quarry water'.

quarry ('kwɒrɪ), *sb.*^{3} Also 6 **-ey,** 7 **-ie.** [Later form of QUARREL *sb.*^{1}, perh. after QUARRY *a.* or F. *quarré* sb. (see next).]

†**1.** A square-headed arrow. = QUARREL 1. *Obs.*

1600 FAIRFAX *Tasso* III. xlix, The shafts and quarries from their engins flie. **1627** DRAYTON *Agincourt* 20 Out of the Towne come quarries thick as haile.

2. A pane of glass; = QUARREL *sb.*^{1} 3. Also occas. round in shape.

1611 COTGR., *Rhombe*, .. a figure that hath equall sides, and vnequall angles; as a quarrie of glasse, etc. **1652–62** HEYLIN *Cosmogr.* I. (1682) 145 They only open a little quarry of Glass, and presently shut it close again. **1727–41** CHAMBERS *Cycl.* s.v. *Quarry*, Quarries, or quarrels, of glass, are of two kinds: viz. square and long; .. the acute angle being $77^\circ\ 19'$ in the square quarries, and $67^\circ\ 22'$ in the long ones. **1733** NEAL *Hist. Purit.* II. 234 He took down a quarry or two in a quiet and peaceable manner. **1879** MRS. OLIPHANT *Within Precincts* (Tauchn.) I. iv. 62 This window was filled with old painted glass in .. quarries. **1913** F. S. EDEN *Anc. Glass* iv. 82 Round quarries, set close together in rows, are .. formed in lieu of rectangular quarries. **1970** H. BRAUN *Parish Churches* viii. 111 The glass of medieval days was .. set as a mosaic of diamond-shaped 'quarries' fixed together with a network of delicate tooled strips.

attrib. **1703** T. N. *City & C. Purchaser* 158 For taking down Quarry-glass, Scouring it .. and setting up again, the usual Price is 1$\frac{1}{2}$*d.* per Foot. **1899** R. GLAZIER *Man. Hist. Ornament* 98 'Quarry glass', square or diamond in shape, with brown enamel details, was frequently used, where simple masses were desired. **1971** *Country Life* 20 May 1248/1, I have had an estimate made .. for filling all the nave and one chancel window with quarry glass of a very pleasing though simple kind.

3. A square stone, tile, or brick. = QUARREL *sb.*^{1} 4.

1555 EDEN *Decades* 329 Al matters of hard compositions as quarreys and stones. **1664** H. MORE *Myst. Iniq.* 379 Lying not .. as the quarries of a Pavement, but as the scales of Fishes. **1709** STEELE *Tatler* No. 179 ¶8 What Ground remains .. is flagged with large Quarries of white Marble. **1876** GEO. ELIOT *Dan. Der.* II. xvi, Scoured deal, red quarries, and white-wash.

fig. **1593** NASHE *4 Lett. Confut.* 68 In a verse, when a worde of three sillables cannot thrust in but sidelings, to ioynt him euen, we are oftentimes faine to borrowe some lesser quarry of elocution from the Latine.

4. *Comb.*, as ***quarry-layer***; **quarry-tile** (see quot. 1940); also *attrib.*; hence **quarry-tiled** *a.*

1885 *Census Instruct.* 87 Brick-, Tile-maker .. Quarry Layer, Presser, Maker. **1940** *Chambers's Techn. Dict.* 692/2 *Quarry tile*, the common unglazed, machine-made paving tile not less than $\frac{3}{4}$ in. in thickness. **1953** [see *chip-board* s.v. CHIP *sb.*^{1} 9 a]. **1966** *Listener* 28 July 128/2 Rough concrete and quarry-tile floors like a farmhouse kitchen. **1970** G. F. NEWMAN *Sir, You Bastard* 258 He rapped his knuckles against the brown quarry-tiles in frustration. **1976** *Outdoor Living* (N.Z.) I. II. 9/2 You might choose to have concrete, bricks or quarry tiles or it might suit the house more to have a timber surface for your sunny area. **1979** *Arizona Daily Star* 5 Aug. (Advt. Section) 18/9 See this family oriented 3 bedroom home with its quarry tile floors. **1960** *Farmer & Stockbreeder* 22 Mar. 66/3 The covered bullock yard at Drayton has .. a flat quarry-tiled feeding floor edged with a 6 in kerb for silage.

†**quarry**, *sb.*^{4} *Obs. rare*$^{-1}$. [? a. F. *quarré* (now *carré*) a square piece, sb. use of *quarré* QUARRY *a.* See also QUARION, QUARRIER.] A square candle.

1526 *Househ. Ord.* (1790) 157 One of the groomes .. to carry to the chaundrie all the remaine of morters, torches, quarries, pricketts.

†'**quarry**, *a.*^{1} *Obs.* Also 4–5 **quarre,** (4 **-ee, -ey, quare,** ? **quaire**), 6 **quarye,** 7 **quarrie.** [a. OF. *quarré* (mod.F. *carré*):—L. *quadrāt-us* square, QUADRATE *a.*] Square; squarely built, stout.

1297 R. GLOUC. (Rolls) 8527 Quarre [*v.r.* quarry, quare] he was & wel ymad vor to be strong. *c* **1330** R. BRUNNE *Chron. Wace* (Rolls) 10310 þat lough ys here yn þys contre, Cornerd as a cheker quarre. *c* **1380** *Sir Ferumb.* 1072 Brode scholdres had he with-alle; & brustes ful quarree. *c* **1400** tr. *Secreta Secret., Gov. Lordsh.* 92 Anoþer [plant] .. whos braunche is quarre, whos leuys er round. *c* **1440** *Promp. Parv.* 419/1 Quarry, thykk mann, or womann, .. *corpulentus, grossus.* **1575** G. HARVEY *Letter-bk.* (Camden) 93 They are so quarry bigge and righte Babylonian like. **1601** HOLLAND *Pliny* II. 499 To make his images of a quarry and square stature. **1611** COTGR., *Corpulent*, grosse, big-bodied, quarrie, fat.

†'**quarry**, *a.*^{2} *Obs. rare.* In 6–7 **quar(r)ie.** [f. QUAR *v.*^{2} + -Y^{1}.] Clotted, coagulated.

1587 MASCALL *Govt. Cattle, Sheepe* (1627) 241 Put the fine powder of rozen into the cod, and that will dry vp the quarie bloud. **1638** FEATLEY *Transubst.* 76 You touch no soft flesh with your hand, nor quarrie blood with your lips.

quarry ('kwɒrɪ), *v.*^{1} [f. QUARRY *sb.*^{1}]

†**1.** *trans.* **a.** To teach (a hawk) to seize its quarry. **b.** To supply with a quarry (in quot. *fig.*)

1575 TURBERV. *Faulconrie* 121 At the beginning rewarde hir and feede hir well vpon the quarrey... When she is well in bloude, and well quarried, then let hir flee with other hawkes. **1613** BEAUM. & FL. *Captain* III. iii, 'Tis pity Thou shouldst not be well quarred at thy entr'ing Thou art so high flown for him. **1618** LATHAM *2nd Bk. Falconry* (1633) 117

Hauing a good make Hawke, you shall wel quarrie her, and then she will bee worthy the accounting of.

†**2.** *intr.* To pounce or seize *on*, as a hawk on its quarry; to prey or feed *on*. *Obs.*

1627–77 FELTHAM *Resolves* I. xxi. 38 She quarries on the prey she meets withal. *a* **1658** CLEVELAND *Poems, To Protector* (1677) 144 Can your Towring Spirit, which hath quarried upon Kingdoms, make a stoop at us? **1681** T. FLATMAN *Heraclitus Ridens* No. 9 (1713) I. 58 Though Eagles do not quarry upon Flies. **1709** JER. COLLIER *Ess. Mor. Subj.* IV. 39 He has quarryed upon the whole, and master'd the Men, as well as the Money.

3. *trans.* To hunt down or kill (a beast of chase).

1820 BYRON *Mar. Fal.* III. ii. 402 Nor turn aside to strike at such a prey, Till nobler game is quarried.

quarry ('kwɒrɪ), *v.*^{2} [f. QUARRY *sb.*^{2}]

1. a. *trans.* To obtain (stone, etc.) by the processes employed in a quarry. Also with *out*.

1774 GOLDSMITH *Hist. Earth* v, In the mountains of Castravan..they quarry out a white stone. **1811** PINKERTON *Petral.* II. 57 It is quarried at Vulpino, 15 leagues from Milan. **1853** KANE *Grinnell Exp.* xxx. (1856) 258 Now we had to quarry out the blocks [of ice] in flinty, glassy lumps. **1872** YEATS *Growth Comm.* 39 Higher up the river valley were quarried the massive syenite slabs used in the erection of their temples.

b. *fig.* To obtain or extract by laborious methods.

1860 MAURY *Phys. Geog. Sea* x. (Low) §465 Materials which a certain kind of insect quarried from the sea water. **1868** J. H. BLUNT *Ref. Ch. Eng.* I. 361 His only object was to quarry gold and silver out of the monastic treasuries. **1936** R. CAMPBELL *Mithraic Emblems* 57 The gypsies quarried from the gloom, For their carouse a silver hall. **1958** L. DURRELL *Balthazar* vi. 140 Were these words of Pursewarden's quarried from his own experience? **1975** *New Yorker* 29 Apr. 6/1 (Advt.), Dick Wellstood, a subtle and inventive pianist, reproduced the raw materials..that the old-master pianists of the thirties and forties quarried their styles out of.

2. a. To form a quarry in, to cut into (rock, etc.).

1847 EMERSON *Poems, The House*, She ransacks mines and ledges, And quarries every rock. **1866** LIDDON *Bampt. Lect.* i. (1875) 34 The rocky hillside is no longer beautiful when it has been quarried. **1877** A. B. EDWARDS *Up Nile* v. 120 The rocky barrier..quarried here and there in dazzling gaps of snow-white cuttings.

b. *Physical Geogr.* = PLUCK *v.* 1 b.

1874 *Overland Monthly* Aug. 179/1 The size of the blocks, their abundance along the line of dispersal, and the probable rate of motion of the glacier which quarried and transported them, form data by which..the rate of block denudation may be reached. *Ibid.* 180/1 They had been quarried from the base of the ridge. **1909** *Jrnl. & Proc. R. Soc. N.S. Wales* XLIII. 264 Frequently the ice impact had been of such nature that a rock block had been quarried across the dominant joint structure. **1955** LONGWELL & FLINT *Introd. Physical Geol.* xii. 191 The bottom of the glacier breaks off blocks of bedrock and quarries them out, especially from surfaces unsupported on their downstream sides. **1976** J. E. SANDERS et al. *Physical. Geogr.* x. 346 Typically, the remaining mountain rim towers high above the bottom of a cirque because centuries of frost wedging enables the glacier to quarry deeply into the rock.

3. *intr.* To cut or dig in, or as in, a quarry.

1848 KINGSLEY *Saint's Trag.* II. x, Something did strike my heart..Which quarries daily there with dead dull pain. **1874** L. STEPHEN *Hours in Library* (1892) I. x. 345 The industrious will find..waste paper in which they may quarry to their heart's content.

Hence '**quarrying** *vbl. sb.* Also *pl.* and *attrib.*

1823 CRABB, *Quarryings*, pieces that are broken off from the different materials that are wrought in quarries. **1854** H. MILLER *Sch. & Schm.* xiii. (1860) 138 On first commencing our quarrying operations. **1865** SWINBURNE *Poems & Ball., Orchard* 33 No quarrying now the corner-stone is hewn. **1904** *Jrnl. Geol.* XII. 574 The glacier will be efficient as the agent for débris removal; the result, therefore, must be quarrying and excavation, and basal sapping. **1969** D. J. EASTERBROOK *Princ. Geomorphol.* xvi. 314 Storm waves are especially effective where rocks along the shore are highly jointed or bedded, and are thus vulnerable to quarrying.

'**quarry**, *v.*^{3} *rare*$^{-1}$. [f. QUARRY *sb.*^{3} 2 or 3.] *trans.* To glaze or lay with quarries.

1851 TURNER *Dom. Archit.* I. v. 246 To whitewash and quarry the King's chamber.

'**quarryman** ('kwɒrɪmən). [f. QUARRY *sb.*^{2}] One employed in quarrying; one who works in a quarry.

1611 COTGR., *Quarrieur*, a Quarrier, or Quarrey-man. *a* **1728** WOODWARD (J.), The quarryman assured me [it] was flat. **1806** A. DUNCAN *Nelson* 284 His father, a quarryman, ..lived at Rusty Anchor. **1862** ANSTED *Channel Isl.* IV. App. B (ed. 2) 570 In Guernsey, six hundred and fifty-three were quarry men. **1885** *Manch. Exam.* 28 May 5/2 The whole Welsh people, from the aristocracy down to the collier and quarryman, are agreed.

†**quart, quert,** *a.* and *sb.*^{1} *Obs.* Forms: 4–5 **quarte, quert(e, qwert(e,** 5 **qwarte, -tt, whert, whart(e,** 4–6 **quart.** [app. a. ON. **kwert*, neut. of **kwer-r* (of which the recorded forms are Icel. *kyrr*, ONorw. *kvirr*, Da. *qvær*, Sw. *qvar*) quiet, still = MHG. *kürre* (G. *kirre*), Goth. *qairrus* gentle, mild. For the retention of the neuter ending cf. *thwart*. In Engl. the word is chiefly poetic.]

A. *adj.* Healthy; in good condition; whole and sound.

a **1300** *Cursor M.* 26119 (Cott.) Opins to your lauerd your hert, And riues it, to mak it quert. **13..** *Seuyn Sag.* (W.) 771 The cradel turnd up so doun..The stapeles hit upheld al quert. *a* **1400** *Stockh. Med. MS.* i. 146 in *Anglia* XVIII. 298 þis drinke xal..makyn hym hwngry for to ete As a qwert man al maner mete. *a* **1420** HOCCLEVE *De Reg. Princ.* 1061 Be thou riche or poor, or sike or quert. *c* **1450** *Life St. Cuthb.* 4215 On one his eye was hale and whart. **1556** ABP. PARKER *Ps.* lxxiii. 203 Their paunches ful: their helth so quart.

B. *sb.* Health; healthy or sound condition; the state of being alive and well. Chiefly in phr. ***in quart*** (freq. in 14–15th c.).

a **1300** *Cursor M.* 1803 þof þat noe was in quert, He was noght al at es in hert. *c* **1330** R. BRUNNE *Chron. Wace* (Rolls) 9990 Ouer al was wo, & no whar quert. *c* **1400** *Destr. Troy* 6941 [þai] fayn were..þat þai had hym at hond & in holl qwert. *c* **1450** *Life St. Cuthbert* 3958 Bischop Edbart Wex full seke and oute of whart. **1522** MORE *De quat. Nouiss.* Wks. 80/1 Ye would recken your belly not in good quart. **1559** MORWYNG *Evonym.* 149 It preserveth it in good health and in good quart.

b. That which gives health or soundness. *rare.*

a **1300** *Cursor M.* 21354 þe rode..Gains al ur care it es ur quert. *c* **1400** *Ywaine & Gaw.* 1488 My leman swete,..My joy, my comforth, and my quert.

quart (kwɔːt), *sb.*^{2} Forms: 5 **qwh-, qvarte,** 5–7 **quarte,** (7 *dial.* **whart**), 4– **quart.** [a. F. *quarte* fem. (13th c. in sense 1) and *quart* masc. (= It. *quarta, quarto*, Sp. *cuarta, cuarto*), repr. L. *quarta, -tum*, fem. and neut. of *quartus* fourth.]

1. a. An English measure of capacity, one-fourth of a gallon, or two pints.

c **1325** *Poem times Edw. II*, xxix, He wil drawe at a draw3t A gode quart other more Of gode ale. *c* **1386** CHAUCER *Miller's T.* 311 This Carpenter..broghte of myghty Ale a large quart. *c* **1420** *Liber Cocorum* (1862) 26 Of hony a qwharte thou take. **1500–20** DUNBAR *Poems* xl. 27 They drank twa quartis, sowp and sowp. **1555** EDEN *Decades* 197 They take for euery man two or three quartes of water. **1579** in W. H. Turner *Select. Rec. Oxford* 401 An ale quarte for a penye. **1599** HAKLUYT *Voy.* I. 506 Your wines shalbe sold by hogs heads, pipes or buttes, but not by quartes nor pintes. **1709** PRIOR *Yng. Gentlm. in Love* 58 He..brought a Quart of Milk and Tea. **1816** J. SMITH *Panorama Sc. & Art* II. 782 Four ounces of Brazil-wood..in a quart of water. **1896** SIR M. HICKS-BEACH in *Daily News* 23 July 4/3 What he might describe in homely phrase as putting a quart into a pint pot. *fig.* **1797** COLMAN *Heir at Law* III. ii, He can ladle you out Latin by the quart.

b. A vessel holding a quart; a quart-pot or quart-bottle.

c **1450** MYRC *Par. Pr.* 712 False measures, busshelles, galones,..quartes. **1500–20** DUNBAR *Poems* xxvi. 95 Mony fowll drunckart, With can and collep, cop and quart. **1535** LYNDESAY *Satyre* 1373 To fill the Quart I sall rin to the toun. **1596** SHAKS. *Tam. Shr.* Ind. ii. 89 Because she brought stone-Iugs, and no seal'd quarts. **1688** R. HOLME *Armoury* III. 294, 3 Quarts, their lids open,..born by Quaffer. *c* **1800** [see GILL *sb.*^{3} 2]. **1885** H. FINCH-HATTON *Advance Austral.* 111 A tin quart of water is set down by the fire.

c. *attrib.*, as ***quart-ale, bass, bottle, flagon, -measure, retort*** (see quot.). See also QUART-POT.

1454 *Paston Lett.* No. 219 I. 307 To sende hom wyn and ij. quart botelys. **1611** FLORIO, *Quarta*,..a quart measure. *c* **1650** BRATHWAIT *Barnabees Jrnl.* IV. (1818) 167 Thence to Lonesdale, where were at it Boyes that scorned quart-ale by statute. **1764** COLMAN *Prose Sev. Occas.* (1787) II. 51 To see a man get into a Quart Bottle. **1767** WOULFE in *Phil. Trans.* LVII. 521 *note*, What goes by the name of a quart retort holds better than two gallons of water. **1828** SCOTT *F.M. Perth* xvi, He filled a quart flagon.

†**2. a.** [F. *quart* m.] A quarter *of* something. *Obs.*

1454 *Paston Lett.* No. 201 I. 278 Be the space of on qaurte [quarte] of an houre. **1561** HOLLYBUSH *Hom. Apoth.* 9 Take a quarte of an unce.

b. A quarter of a pound. *Obs. rare*$^{-1}$.

1496 *Fysshynge w. angle* (1883) 10 Take..a lytyll iuce of walnot leuys and a quarte of alym.

c. 'Prob., the fourth part of the great tithes' (Jam.). *Obs. rare*$^{-1}$.

1630 GORDON *Hist. Earls Sutherld.* (1813) 32 Ther peculiar landward (or rurall) churches, together with the particular tithes, (crofts, manses, gleibs, and quartes, ar severallie appoynted to everie one of the dignites and channons.

†**3. a.** A quarter of the horizon. **b.** A quarter, region. *Obs. rare.*

1559 W. CUNINGHAM *Cosmogr. Glasse* 154 Betwixt either of these quartes, two other windes brost out. **1590** SPENSER *F.Q.* II. x. 14 Albanact had all the Northerne part..And Camber did possesse the Westerne quart.

†**4.** [ad. Sp. *cuarto.*] A Spanish copper coin, worth four maravedis. *Obs.*

1631 *Celestina* IV. 52, I never wanted..a Quarte, that is the eighth part of sixepence to send for wine. **1777** W. DALRYMPLE *Trav. Sp. & Port.* xxviii, An officer of the customs, demanded a toll, each horse paying three quarts.

5. *Mus.* The interval of a fourth. *rare.*

1890 *Academy* 18 Jan. 51 A succession of parallel quarts, quints, and octaves,..intolerable to modern ears.

attrib. **1976** D. MUNROW *Instruments of Middle Ages & Renaissance* 44/3 Praetorius gives the following sizes of curtals: 1. Quint Bass; 2. Quart Bass. **1977** *Early Music* Oct. 570 (Advt.), [Recorders] The standard range is from Garklein to Bass, the Michael Praetorius range extends to a Quart Bass in C.

quart (kɑːt), *sb.*^{3} [ad. F. *quarte*: see prec.]

1. A position in fencing (see quot. 1692) = QUARTE, CARTE^{2}. ***quart and tierce***, practice between fencers who thrust and parry in quart and tierce alternately; also *fig.*

1692 SIR W. HOPE *Fencing-Master* 4 When a Man holdeth the Nails of his Sword-hand quite upwards, he is said to hold his hand in Quart. **1698** FARQUHAR *Love & Bottle* II. ii, A Frenchman is bounded on the North with Quart, on the South with Tierce. **1727** BOYER *Angl.-Fr. Dict.*, *Quarte*, a Quart, a Pass in Fencing. **1809** MALKIN tr. *Gil Blas* IV. vii. (1881) II. 13 The assassin stab of time was parried by the quart and tierce of art. **1889** TENNYSON *Demeter*, etc. 173 Subtle at tierce and quart of mind with mind.

attrib. **1692** SIR W. HOPE *Fencing-Master* 22 The Quart Parade, or the Parade within the Sword. *Ibid.* 105 Keeping this Quart Guard with a streight point. **1794** *Hope's new Meth. Fencing* 13 Supplying the defect of the Ordinary Quart Guard.

2. A sequence of four cards, in piquet and other card-games. ***quart major***, the sequence of ace, king, queen, knave.

1727 BOYER *Angl.-Fr. Dict.*, *Quarte*, a Quart, or fourth, at Picket. **1746** HOYLE *Whist* (ed. 6) 26 Suppose you have..a Quart from a King;..your Partner has a Quart-major. **1826** MISS MITFORD *Village* Ser. II. (1863) 342 [She] never dealt the right number of cards..did not know a quart from a quint. **1860** *Bohn's Hand-bk. Games* Pref. 12 Lead the highest of a sequence, but if you have a quart..to a King, lead the lowest. *Ibid.* II. 45 A suit of which your partner has a quart-major.

†**quart,** *sb.*^{4}, obs. variant of CARTE^{1}, chart.

1529 RASTELL *Pastyme* Prol. (1811) 5 As they..may well perceyue by the syght of the quart or Mappa mundi.

quart, *a.*: see *sb.*^{1} above.

quart (kɑːt), *v.*^{1} [ad. F. *quarter* (Molière), f. *quarte* QUART *sb.*^{3}] **a.** *intr.* To use the position 'quart' in fencing. **b.** *trans.* To draw back (the head and shoulders) in doing so. Hence '**quarting** *vbl. sb.*

1692 SIR W. HOPE *Fencing-Master* *4 You must give it with your Nails in Quart, and Quart your head well. *Ibid.* 31 The Quarting of your head preserveth you from being hit in the face. *a* **1700** B. E. *Dict. Cant. Crew*, *Quarting upon the streight line*, keeping the Head and Shoulders very much back from the Adversary's Sword, when one thrusts with his own. **1833** *New Monthly Mag.* XXXVIII. 343 He quarts and tierces for twenty minutes.

quart, *v.*^{2}, variant of QUARTER *v.* 11 b. *rare*$^{-1}$.

1812 *Sporting Mag.* XXXIX. 136 The coachman..on quarting out as usual, and finding himself thus borne down upon, poured forth a volley of abuse.

quartal ('kwɔːtəl), *a.* *Mus.* [f. L. *quartus* fourth + -AL.] Of a harmony: based on the interval of the fourth.

1937 *Musical Q.* XXIII. 178 Once we make our choice in favour of quartal harmony, we must be ready to accept all the logical consequences. **1938** J. YASSER *Mediæval Quartal Harmony* III. 87 Unlimited freedom in unison and octave parallelism turned out to be one of the greatest obstacles to completing the rationalization of the quartal harmonic system. **1944** W. APEL *Harvard Dict. Mus.* 619/1 Quartal harmonies have been recommended to replace tertian harmonies in harmonizations of Gregorian chant. **1955** A. HUGHES in *New Oxf. Hist. Mus.* (rev. ed.) II. 329 The two-part version of Brit. Mus. Harl. 524 seems to have been written in 'quartal' harmony, i.e. harmony based on the fourth as the most important interval. **1970** W. APEL *Harvard Dict. Mus.* (ed. 2) 6/2 Attempts have been made to replace this style with..archaic idioms such as quartal harmonies or parallel organum.

quartan ('kwɔːtən), *a.* and *sb.* Forms: 4–7 **quartaine,** 4, 7 **-ain,** 5–6 **-ayn(e;** 4–6 **quarteyn(e,** (4 **-en,** 5 **-ein);** 5–7 **quartane,** (6 **cart-**), 6– **quartan.** See also QUARTERN, *a.* [Orig. a. F. (*fièvre*) *quartaine*, ad. L. (*febris*) *quartāna* fem. of *quartān-us*, f. *quartus* fourth. The mod. form is directly based on the L.]

A. *adj.* **1.** *Path.* Of a fever or ague: Characterized by the occurrence of a paroxysm every fourth (in mod. reckoning, every third) day.

In early use placed after the sb., as in F.

a **1300** *Cursor M.* 11828 He..þar-wit had feuer quartain. *a* **1400** *Stockh. Med. MS.* ii. 954 in *Anglia* XVIII. 330 Ageyn feuerys quarteyn It is medicyn souereyn. **1494** FABYAN *Chron.* VII. 520 The appellaunt..was sore vexyd with a feuer quarteyne. **1547** BOORDE *Brev. Health* cxxxix. 51 A fever quartayne..doth infeste a man every thyrd day, that is to say two dayes whole and one sycke. **1570** GOOGE *Pop. Kingd.* IV. 52 b, The quartan ague and such other sicknesse greate. *a* **1612** HARINGTON *Salerne's Regim.* (1634) 25 Cow flesh, Harts flesh,..doe engender fever Quartaines. **1750** tr. *Leonardus' Mirr. Stones* 73 Taken with wine, it drives away quartan agues. **1852** MISS YONGE *Cameos* (1877) II. xxxiii. 339 Quartan ague had seized on the enfeebled frame of her father. **1875** JOWETT *Plato* (ed. 2) III. 670 A quartan fever, which can with difficulty be shaken off.

†**2.** Belonging to the fourth place or degree. *Obs.*

1794 E. DARWIN *Zoon.* (1801) IV. 185 The tertian or quartan links of associate motions are actuated by direct sympathy.

B. *sb.* A (*or* the) quartan ague or fever.

double quartan, one in which there are two sets of paroxysms, each recurring every fourth (third) day.

1387 TREVISA *Higden* (Rolls) IV. 249 Porcius..slow3 hym self for noye and sorwe of a double quarteyn. **1450–80** tr. *Secreta Secret.* 32 He shalle haue no dowte of flewme..and he shalle haue no quarteyne. *c* **1491** CAXTON *Chast. Goddes Chyld.* 23 Of this quarteyn some men falle in to another feuer that is cleped double quarteın. **1597** GERARDE *Herbal* I. ciii. §2. 170 A roote or two..is a good remedie against old quartaines. **1633** BP. HALL *Occas. Medit.* (1851) 147 The quartan hath of old been justly styled the shame of physicians. **1725** BRADLEY *Fam. Dict.* s.v. *Spider*, The

Spider it self will cure Quartans. **1822–34** *Good's Study Med.* (ed. 4) I. 607 The tertian [has] a longer paroxysm and a shorter interval than the quartan. **1898** P. MANSON *Trop. Diseases* i. 25 In quartans and tertians, but especially in the former, sporulating rosette forms are seen occasionally.

fig. **1590** NASHE *Pasquil's Apol.* I. B iij, He that hath such a dubble quartane of curiositie..will prooue passing treacherous.

quartan: see QUARTERN *sb.*[2] 5.

†quarta'narian = next *sb.* a. *Obs. rare*$^{-1}$.

1680 SIR T. BROWNE *Wks.* (1852) III. 472 Formerly they gave not the cortex to quartanarians, before they had been ill a considerable time.

†'quartanary, *sb.* and *a.* *Obs.* Also 5 quartenare, 7 -ainary. [ad. late L. *quartānāri-us* (in sense A. a): see prec. and -ARY.]

A. *sb.* **a.** One who has a quartan fever or ague. **b.** = QUARTAN *sb. rare.*

c **1440** *Promp. Parv.* 419/1 Quartenare, or þat hathe þe quarteyne. **1684** tr. *Bonet's Merc. Compit.* VI. 223 Quartanaries..gather much crude humours.

B. *adj.* Pertaining to, of the nature of, a quartan fever or ague; characterized by quartans.

1669 BOYLE *Contn. New Exp.* I. 176 An odd Quartainary Distemper, that I slighted so long, as to give it time to take Root. **1679** LOCKE *Jrnl.* 15 Nov. in Bourne *Life* (1876) I. viii. 451 The constitution of this autumn was intermittent and quartanary, though many of the fevers..were continued and several made so by ill management.

quartar(e, obs. forms of QUARTER *sb.*

quartary ('kwɔːtərɪ), *sb.* and *a.* [ad. L. *quartāri-us*, the fourth part of any measure, esp. of a sextarius, f. *quartus*: see QUART *sb.*[2]] **†a.** *sb.* (See quot. 1656.) *Obs.rare*$^{-0}$. **b.** *adj.* Fourth. *rare*$^{-1}$.

1656 BLOUNT *Glossogr.*, *Quartary*, the fourth part of a Sextary; also a quarter of a pound. **1839** J. ROGERS *Antipopopr.* x. ii. 255 Where to go to find the fourth or quartary set of mediators.

quartation (kwɔː'teɪʃən). [f. L. *quart-us* fourth + -ATION.] The operation of combining silver with gold so that the latter metal forms one quarter of the whole; the gold is then separated from the silver, and at the same time freed from its impurities, by means of nitric acid.

1612 WOODALL *Surg. Mate* Wks. (1653) 273 Quartation is the separation of Gold and Silver mixt together, by four unequal parts. **1680** BOYLE *Scept. Chem.* II. 144 That Operation that Refiners call Quartation, which they employ to purifie Gold. **1758** REID tr. *Macquer's Chym.* i. 149 The gold..is frequently alloyed with more or less silver, from which it is to be separated by quartation. **1868** SEYD *Bullion* 219 Fine Gold may also be assayed without Quartation.

‖quarte (kart, kɑːt). [a. F. *quarte*: see QUART *sb.*[3]] A position in fencing. = QUART *sb.*[3] 1.

a **1700** B. E. *Dict. Cant. Crew*, *Quarte*, Nails of the Sword-Hand quite up. *c* **1830** G. ROLAND *Introd. Course Fencing* 16 The parade of quarte is made by offering, with the nails turned upwards, the fort of your blade to the foible of your adversary's. **1885** E. CASTLE *Sch. Fence* 133 A heavy sweep in seconde from a high quarte at arm's length.

fig. **1872** BROWNING *Fifine* xvi, Words urged in vain..You waste your quarte and tierce.

†quarteer, -ier. *Obs. rare.* [? for *quartereer*: see -EER[1], -IER.] = QUARTERMASTER *sb.* 1.

1719 D'URFEY *Pills* III. 305 The Quartier must Cun, Whilst the foremast-man steers. **1727–41** CHAMBERS *Cycl.* s.v. *Quarter-master*, The quarter-master, or quarteer, is also to mind the ship's loading; which is the business he is chiefly employed about.

quartel, var. CUARTEL.

†quartelet. *Obs. rare.* [a. OF. *quartelette*, dim. of *quarte* QUART *sb.*[2]] A small quart.

1453 *Test. Ebor.* (Surtees) II. 191 Item ij pottis quartelettis of siluer couered. **1459** in *Paston Lett.* No. 336 I. 488 Item, .j. quartelet for wine.

quartenare, variant of QUARTANARY.

quarter ('kwɔːtə(r)), *sb.* Also 4 **quartare**, **qwatteer**, 4–6 **quartre**, 5 **quartere**, **-yer**, **wharter**, **qwarter**, 5–6 **quartar**, 6 **qwartter**, (7 coter). [a. OF. *quarter*, *-ier* (12th c. in Littré):— L. *quartār-ius* a fourth part (of a measure), f. *quartus* fourth: see QUART *sb.*[2] and -ER[2] 2.]

I. One of four equal or corresponding parts into which anything is or may be divided.

1. a. Of things generally.

13.. *Guy Warw.* (A.) 1497 Gwichard smot Gij..Opon þe helme..þat a quarter out fleye. *c* **1375** *Sc. Leg. Saints* xl. (*Ninian*) 737 Nere þe quartare of a myl. *c* **1400** *Rom. Rose* 3184 Non herte may thenke..A quarter of my wo and peyne. *c* **1470** HENRY *Wallace* IX. 979 Than off the day thre quartaris was went. **1564** *Child Marriages* 124 About a quarter of a yere ago. **1599** SHAKS. *Hen. V*, I. ii. 215 Diuide your happy England into foure, Whereof, take you one quarter into France. **1650** B. *Discolliminium* 49 And now I am 3 quarters Presbyterian, I keep one quarter still Independent. **1697** DRYDEN *Virg. Georg.* I. 349 The four quarters of the rolling year. **1796** MRS. GLASSE *Cookery* 79 Garnish with a Seville orange cut in quarters. **1841** *Q. Rev.* LXVII. 358 Some quarter of a century ago. **1880** GEIKIE *Phys. Geog.* i. 29 Exactly a quarter of a circle, or 90°.

b. Phr. *a bad* (etc.) ***quarter of an hour*** [tr. F. *un mauvais quart d'heure*], a short but very unpleasant period of time. Cf. MAUVAIS QUART D'HEURE.

[**1717** tr. *Frezier's Voy.* 110 Rablais's Quarter of an Hour, that is, when the Reckoning is to be paid.] [*a* **1851**: see MUSIC *sb.* 11.] **1875** TROLLOPE *Way we live Now* II. lxii. 70 He was prepared..to console himself when the bad quarter of an hour should come with the remembrance that he had garnered up a store. **1887** J. BALL *Nat. in S. Amer.* 338 When I reached the station..I had an unpleasant quarter of an hour. **1897** W. E. NORRIS *Marietta's Marr.* xxxi. 225, I hope he will have a rather nasty quarter of an hour. **1909** *Daily Chron.* 30 Aug. 4/7 The 'bad quarter of an hour' we all know was first given a name by the heartless Louis XIII., who, looking at his watch on the day of the execution of Cinq-Mars, supposed that the poor young fellow 'passait alors un mauvais quart d'heure'. **1922** C. MACKENZIE *Altar Steps* xxi. 233 Mark fancied that it would be the prelate who would have the unpleasant quarter of an hour. **1937** M. SHARP *Nutmeg Tree* xviii. 232 Susan was in for a bad quarter of an hour.

c. Qualifying an adv. or advb. phrase (cf. HALF *adv.* 1 d); † formerly also without *a*.

1522 SIR T. CHEYNE in *State Papers* (1849) VI. 88 He had rather ryde into England..then to ryde a quarter so farre to eny other Prince living. **1545** ASCHAM *Toxoph.* II. (Arb.) 157 Sumtyme ful side wynde, sumtyme quarter with hym and more. **1818** BUSBY *Gramm. Mus.* 69 A quaver is only one quarter as long as a Minim.

d. Const. with sbs. without *of* (cf. HALF *a.* 1 b).

1866 MRS. OLIPHANT *Madonna Mary* (Tauchn.) I. xiv. 184 She had not..a quarter the pleasures you have. **1897** MARY KINGSLEY *W. Africa* 663 There is not one-quarter the amount of drunkenness.

e. *ellipt.* in various contextual uses, as (*a*) † a quarter-barge; (*b*) a 'quarter-note' or crotchet in Music (*U.S.*); (*c*) a quarter-mile race.

1508 *Waterf. Arch.* in *10th Rep. Hist. MSS. Comm.* App. v. 325 Noo boote shal bring woode butt only half barges and quarters... And every quarter to have iiii. men. **1899** *Whitaker's Alm.* 637/1 Harrison also won the 'Quarter' by a foot.

2. a. One of the four parts, each including a leg, into which the carcases of quadrupeds are commonly divided; also of fowls, a part containing a leg or wing. ***fifth quarter***: the hide and fat of a slaughtered animal (*Funk's Stand. Dict.*, 1893). See also FORE 3, HIND *a.*

c **1320** *Sir Tristr.* 453 Bestes þai brac and bare, In quarters þai hem wrouȝt. *c* **1420** *Liber Cocorum* (1862) 8 Hew hom [chickens] in quarteres and lay hom inne. *c* **1430** *Two Cookery-bks.* I. 6 Take fayre beef of þe rybbys of þe fore quarterys. **1563–7** BUCHANAN *Reform. St. Andros* Wks. (1892) 6 Ane quartar of mouton. **1660** PEPYS *Diary* 17 July, They bought a Quarter of Lamb. **1709** STEELE *Tatler* No. 21 ¶13 A Butcher's Daughter..sometimes brings a Quarter of Mutton. **1776** ADAM SMITH *W.N.* I. xi. I. (1869) I. 160 The four quarters of an ox weighing six hundred pounds. **1853** SOYER *Pantroph.* 147 Place a quarter of lamb in a saucepan.

b. *pl.* The four parts, each containing a limb, of a human body similarly divided, as was commonly done in the case of those executed for treason.

1297 R. GLOUC. (Rolls) 10875 A four half engelond is quarters isend were. *c* **1330** R. BRUNNE *Chron.* (1810) 244 His hede þei of smyten..þe quarters wer sent to henge at four citez. *c* **1400** *Destr. Troy* 1971 Brittonet [shuld be] þi body into bare qwarters. **1660** PEPYS *Diary* 15 Oct., This morning Mr. Carew was hanged and quartered..but his quarters..are not to be hanged up. **1773** BRYDONE *Sicily* xxi. (1809) 217 The quarters of a number of robbers were hung up upon hooks. **1855** MACAULAY *Hist. Eng.* xii. III. 207 Their heads and quarters were still rotting on poles.

c. Of a live person or animal, esp. of a horse; also freq. = hind-quarter, haunch.

a **1400** *Morte Arth.* 3389 Abowte scho whirles the whele.. Tille alle my qwarters..ware qwaste. **1590** SPENSER *F.Q.* II. iii. 16 Is not enough fowre quarters of a man, Withouten sword or shield, an hoste to quayle? **1665** BRATHWAIT *Comm. Chaucer* (1901) 84 She had unnimbly rushed down upon her four Quarters, and..done her Reverence. **1678** BUTLER *Hud.* III. i. 1150 They put him to the Cudgel..They stoutly on his Quarters laid. **1806** A. DUNCAN *Nelson's Fun.* 35 Two of his..servants walked at each side of the horse's quarter. **1853** LYTTON *My Novel* I. vi, Down came the staff on the quarters of the donkey.

3. *Her.* **a.** One of the four parts into which a shield is divided by quartering (see QUARTER *v.* 3 b).

The four quarters are: 1 dexter chief; 2 sinister chief; 3 dexter base; 4 sinister base. When one of these is again divided, and the sub-divisions occupied by several coats, it is termed a 'grand quarter'.

1486 *Bk. St. Albans, Her.* D ij b, In the right side of the shelde in the first quarter she bare tharmys of fraunce. **1610** GUILLIM *Heraldry* V. i. 238 Without any charge occupying the quarters of the Escocheon. **1727–41** CHAMBERS *Cycl.*, *Quarter* is also applied to the parts, or members, of the first division of a coat that is quartered, or divided into four quarters. **1797** *Encycl. Brit.* (ed. 3) VIII. 443/1 A perpendicular and horizontal line, which, crossing each other at the centre of the field, divide it into four equal parts called quarters. **1864** BOUTELL *Her. Hist. & Pop.* xv. (ed. 3) 205 The third quarter of his shield. [See also QUARTERLY *adv.* 2 b.] **1893** CUSSANS *Her.* (ed. 4) 165 The second quarter of the Royal Arms of England. *Ibid.* 168 Second and Third grand Quarters, quarterly quartered.

b. A charge occupying one fourth of the shield, placed in chief.

1592 WYRLEY *Armorie, Ld. Chandos* 41 In gold Lord Basset dight Three Rubie piles, a quarter ermins bright. **1610** GUILLIM *Heraldry* II. vi. 61 The Quarter is an Ordinary of like composition with the Canton,..the quarter comprehendeth the full fourth. **1727–41** CHAMBERS *Cycl.* s.v., *Franc-quarter* is a quarter single or alone; which is to possess one-fourth part of the field. This makes one of the honourable ordinaries of a coat. **1838** *Penny Cycl.* XII. 141/2 The Quarter is, as its name imports, the fourth part of the shield, and is always placed in chief. **1893** CUSSANS *Her.* (ed. 4) 66 The Quarter..is formed by two straight lines, drawn in the direction of the Fess and the Pale, and meeting at the Fess-point. Examples of this charge are very rarely to be met with.

c. = QUARTERING *vbl. sb.* 2 b.

1727–41 CHAMBERS *Cycl.* s.v., There are sixteen quarters required to prove nobility, in companies, or orders, where none but nobles are admitted. **1816** SCOTT *Antiq.* xxiv, A baron of sixteen quarters. **1831** CARLYLE *Sart. Res.* (1858) 61 A duke's son that only knew there were two-and-thirty quarters on the family-coach.

II. The fourth part of some usual measure or standard.

4. As a measure of capacity for grain, etc.

a. The British imperial quarter = 8 bushels; the fifth (? originally the fourth) part of a wey or load; also, local variations of this, containing more or less than 8 bushels. † Formerly sometimes const. without *of*.

c **1290** *S. Eng. Leg.* I. 244/130 Ane hondret quarters of þat corn. *c* **1320** *Sir Beues* 1424 A ston gret, þat weȝ seue quarters of whet. *c* **1330** R. BRUNNE *Chron.* (1810) 174 Þe hungre was so grete..þat a quarter whete was at twenty mark. *c* **1386** CHAUCER *Sompn. T.* 255 A! yif that covent half a quarter otes. **1494** FABYAN *Chron.* cxxxvi. 122 A quarter of whete was worth .ii. marks and a halfe. **1523** FITZHERB. *Husb.* §12 Foure London busshelles [of beans] fullye, and that is half a quarter. **1623** *Althorp MS.* in Simpkinson *Washingtons* (1860) App. 48 For 3 coters of rye bought at Harleston. **1663** COWLEY *Ess.*, *Avarice* 129 In thy vast Barns Millions of Quarters store. **1763** *Museum Rust.* I. 74 Wheat will one year sell for 5 l. a load (that is, five quarters). **1845** MCCULLOCH *Taxation* I. i. (1852) 49 A farm which produces 100 quarters of wheat. **1862** ANSTED *Channel Isl.* IV. (ed. 2) App. A. 567 The Jersey quarter (thirty-four gallons and three quarts) [contains] a little more than half an imperial quarter. *Ibid.*, The English imperial quarter is equivalent to about two Guernsey quarters.

b. In the Channel Islands (cf. quot. 1862 in sense a above) used as a unit of value for land.

1682 WARBURTON *Hist. Guernsey* (1822) 94 He that has occasion to take up money on his estate, sells so many quarters. **1694** FALLE *Jersey* ii. 85 The way of reckoning an Estate with us, is not by Pounds, but by Quarters of Wheat. **1862** ANSTED *Channel Isl.* IV. xxiv. (ed. 2) 550 The Guernsey 'quarter of rent' is estimated as worth, on an average, twenty pounds currency.

c. The fourth part of a chaldron.

1434 *E.E. Wills* 101, I bequethe to Iohn Wodrof..v quarteres of coles. **1706** PHILLIPS (ed. Kersey), *Quarter*..In Measure..the fourth part of a Chaldron. **1727–41** CHAMBERS *Cycl.*, *Quarter* is also a dry measure, containing ..of coals the fourth part of a chaldron. **1858** GREENLEAF *National Arithm.* (*U.S.*), cited by Worcester.

†d. The fourth part of a peck. *Obs. rare*$^{-1}$.

1475 *Bk. Noblesse* (Roxb.) 26 The ringis of golde..were.. mesurid to the quantite of mesure of .xij. quarters or more.

†5. The fourth part of a cask or barrel. *Obs.*$^{-1}$

1579 in W. H. Turner *Select Rec. Oxford* (1880) 400 Martine Colepeper..setteth the pryce of a quarter of the best stronge ale at iij^{s} iiij^{d}.

6. As a weight. **a.** The fourth part of a pound.

a **1400** *Stockh. Medical MS.* i. 43 in *Anglia* XVIII. 296 A quarter of vergyn-wax þou take. *a* **1450** *Fysshynge w. Angle* (1883) 9 Take small ale a potell and stamp it with iij handful of walnot levys and a quarter of alom. *c* **1450** *Two Cookery-bks.* 106 Take a quarter of clarefied honey, iij vnces of pouder peper. **1959** I. & P. OPIE *Lore & Lang. Schoolch.* ix. 167 A one-man High-Street confectioner..was found to be offering..*Bassett's Liquorice Allsorts 7d.* per quarter. **1977** *Jackson's of Piccadilly Price List* 2/2 [Ox tongue] £0.48 per qtr [i.e. quarter].

b. The fourth part of a hundredweight = 28 lbs. (*U.S.* commonly 25 lbs.)

Ordinarily used only where the hundredweight is also mentioned, and usually abbreviated 'qr.'

1542 RECORDE *Gr. Artes* (1575) 203 The halfe hundred is 56: the quarter 28 [pounde]. **1588** *Bk. of Charges* in *Dom. St. Papers* CCXV. 88, 4 quille of ropes wayeinge sixe hundred, a quarter, and one pound. **1727–41** CHAMBERS *Cycl.*, *Quarter*, in weights, is a fourth part of the quintal, or hundred weight. The quarter is 28 pounds avoirdupois. **1797** *Encycl. Brit.* (ed. 3) XVII. 410 Iron, 5 cwt. 2 qrs. 24 lb.

†c. 'The fourth part of a Dram' (Phillips, 1706).

7. As a measure of length or area. **a.** The fourth part of a yard: nine inches. Also *fig.*

1433 *Rolls Parlt.* IV. 451/2 Clothe of colour shold conteigne..in brede vi quarters di. *c* **1450** *Bk. Curtasye* 359 in *Babees Bk.*, A stafe, a fyngur gret, two wharters long. **1483** *Act 1 Rich. III*, c. 8 *Preamble*, Some of the same Clothes..ben drawen out..in Brede from .vii. Quarters unto the Brede of .ii. Yerdys. **1596** SHAKS. *Tam. Shr.* IV. iii. 109 Thou yard, three quarters, halfe yard, quarter, naile. **1624** CAPT. SMITH *Virginia* II. 25 His arrowes were fiue quarters long. **1708** J. C. *Compl. Collier* (1845) 16 The 3 Quarter Coal [is] about 3 Quarters thick or more. **1778** *Eng. Gazetteer* (ed. 2) s.v. *Witney*, Blankets..from 10 to 12 quarters wide.

b. *Naut.* The fourth part of a fathom.

1769 FALCONER *Dict. Marine* (1789) Mm iv b, If he judges it to be a quarter..more than any particular number, he calls, 'And a quarter five!' *Ibid.*, At four fathoms and 3-quarters he calls 'A quarter less five!' **1855** *Englishwoman in Russia* 1 'By the quarter seven' sang out..the sailor.. engaged in heaving the lead.

c. An Irish land-measure (tr. Ir. *ceathramhadh*, sometimes anglicized as *carrow*): see quots.

1607 Davies *1st Let. to Ld. Salisbury* (1787) 245 Every ballibetagh is divided into four quarters of lands, and every quarter into four taths. 1683 J. Keogh *Acct. Roscommon* in O'Donovan *Hy Fiachraich* (1844) 453 These countries were subdivided into townlands..which were called Ballys..and each townland was divided again into quarters. *Ibid.*, I have been sometimes perplexed to know how many acres a quarter contains, but I have learned it is an uncertain measure. 1883 Seebohm *Eng. Village Comm.* vii. 223 Annexed is an example of an ancient bally divided into quarters... Two of the quarters, now townlands, still bear the names of 'Cartron' and 'Carrow', or 'Quarter'. 1892 Emily Lawless *Grania* II. 3 Mishmaan possesses but two townlands, containing six quarters each.

d. *U.S.* The fourth part of a mile.

1827 J. F. Cooper *Prairie* I. iv. 56, I can make myself heard a mile in these open fields, and his camp is but a short quarter from us. 1868 H. W. Woodruff *Trotting Horse* vii. 84 What's the use of a horse going a quarter fast? Now, they must go a quarter fast before they can go a mile fast. 1878 J. H. Beadle *Western Wilds* ii. 31 It was weeks before I could walk a quarter.

8. As a measure of time.

a. The fourth part of a year, esp. as divided by the recognized QUARTER-DAYS. Also (esp. in Scotland), the fourth part of the school-year, or of the period during which instruction is usually given, containing about eleven weeks. (See also 11.)

1389 in *Eng. Gilds* (1870) 7 What man is take in to be brother, schal paie..eueri quarter..iij. d. *c*1440 *Ipomydon* 762 My greyhondes ranne not þis quartere. 1536 Boorde *Lett.* in *Introd. Knowl.* (1870) 53 To come to yow ons in a qwartter. 1591 Nashe *Prognost.* Wks. 1883–4 II. 164 The predominant qualities of this quarter [summer] is heate and drynesse. *a*1610 Healey *Theophrastus* (1636) 40 A quarters rent of his house. 1623 *Althorp MS.* in Simpkinson *Washingtons* (1860) App. 41 To the hoggheard for a coter's wages. 1731 Swift *On his Death*, He must..change his comrades once a quarter. 1819 Shelley *Peter Bell* vi. iii, Then *seriatim*, month and quarter, Appeared such mad tirades. 1836 *Penny Cycl.* V. 238 For a commercial education, a guinea a quarter is charged. 1865 Dickens *Mut. Fr.* I. iv, The gentleman proposes to take your apartments by the quarter.

b. A fourth part of the lunar period. Also, the moon's position when between the first and second or third and fourth quarters; quadrature.

*c*1400 Maundev. (Roxb.) xxxiii. 149 Þe moone may noȝt be sene þare, bot in þe secund quartere. 1632 Massinger *Maid of Hon.* I. i, His sheepshearing..Is in every quarter of the moon, and constant. 1694 W. Holder *Time* v. 82 How near she is to her Quarters, Full, or next New-moon. 1728 Pemberton *Newton's Philos.* 201 But..in the quarters the moon..will be made to approach it [the earth]. 1853 Maurice *Proph. & Kings* xi. 189 We sometimes see the moon in her first quarter with one bright luminous border. 1867 Smyth *Sailor's Word-bk.* s.v., When the moon appears exactly as a half-moon, 90° from the sun towards the east, she is in the first quarter.

fig. 1806 Lamb *Let. to Hazlitt* 15 Jan. Wks. 1852. 77/1 Prudentia is in the last quarter of her tutelary shining over me.

c. The fourth part of an hour; the space of fifteen minutes. Also, the moment, as denoted by a mark on the dial, the sound of a bell, etc., at which one quarter of an hour (cf. HOUR 3) ends and the next begins; chiefly used of the quarter after or before an hour, as 'a quarter *past* nine', 'a quarter *to* ten'. Also without article, as ***quarter of an hour***, etc. Also (*Sc.* and *N. Amer.*), 'a quarter *of* (or *till*) (a certain hour)', a quarter to (the hour specified).

[1599 Shaks. *Much Ado* v. ii. 85 An hower in clamour and a quarter in rhewme.] 1617 Moryson *Itin.* I. 31 In the upper part of the clocke are..statuaes, which strike the quarters of the houre. 1659 Mayne *City Match* II. iii. 27 A fellow that turnes upon his toe In a steeple, and strikes quarters. 1727 Bailey vol. II, Quarters [in a *Clock* or *Movement*] are little Bells which sound the Quarters or other Parts of an Hour. 1822 Byron *Vis. Judgm.* lxxxvii, I've scarcely been ten minutes..At least a quarter it can hardly be. 1842 Tennyson *St. Sim. Styl.* 218, I shall die to-night, A quarter before twelve. 1844 Dickens *Mart. Chuz.* xiv, 'The quarter's gone!' cried Mr. Tapley. 1871 *Sci. Amer.* 11 Feb. 102/2 When everything was tightened..and the propellor arranged to cause elevation, it was just quarter of one o'clock. 1894 A. Robertson *Nuggets* 165 His Excellency the Governor wants to see you, detective, at a quarter to eleven sharp. 1912, etc. [see OF *prep.* 4c]. 1913 C. Mackenzie *Sinister St.* I. II. i. 141 In the 'quarter' (as the break was now called) Michael would stand on..the step that led down..into the schoolground. 1920 J. S. Clouston *Carrington's Cases* ix. 135, I found myself sitting in a first-class smoking carriage with nearly quarter of an hour to spare. *Ibid.* xiii. 237 It was then quarter-past eleven. 1933 P. Godfrey *Back-Stage* i. 14 Once more the call-boy appears. 'Shall I call 'the quarter', sir?' 1949 H. Kurath *Word Geogr. Eastern U.S.* ii. 30/2 In the greater part of the Midland ..*quarter till eleven* is current. 1952 M. Laski *Village* vii. 119 If I'm not there by quarter to, you'll know I couldn't make it. 1963 R. I. McDavid *Mencken's Amer. Lang.* 298 Americans may say *quarter to*, *quarter of* or *quarter till*, the last being characteristic of Pennsylvania and its dependencies, including the upland South. 1966 H. Kemelman *Saturday the Rabbi went Hungry* (1969) ii. 21 He said..that traffic would be heaviest between a quarter of and a quarter past seven. 1969 A. Glyn *Dragon Variation* v. 142 He checked the time on his Omega Seamaster. It would be just a quarter of three in New York.

In attrib. phrases. 1849 Mrs. Carlyle *Lett.* II. 77, I was up to leaving..by the quarter-after-eight train. 1857 Hughes *Tom Brown* I. viii. 192 The quarter-to-ten bell..rang.

†**d.** The fourth part of the night, or of the period between two canonical hours. *Obs. rare.*

*c*1369 Chaucer *Dethe Blaunche* 198 Ther-as she lay, Right even a quarter before day. 1412–20 Lydg. *Chron. Troy* I. vi, She..founde a quarter passed after pryme.

e. *Sport.* One of four equal periods of play in a match; also *gen.*, the fourth part of the time taken to play a match.

1911 P. H. Davis *Football* viii. 115 The periods of the game, the halves,..were replaced by quarters. 1922 P. D. Haughton *Football & how to watch It* ix. 191 In contrast to the preceding period this quarter was marked by excellent play. 1954 *New Yorker* 6 Nov. 87/1 The play of the afternoon came in the middle of the final quarter. 1963 *Times* 29 Apr. 4/6 Mellor soon recovered their balance to take a 3–0 lead in the first quarter. 1969 *Sun-Herald* (Sydney) 13 July 48/2 Footscray made a great fight of it in the final quarter. 1972 J. Mosedale *Football* ix. 130 Playing on an 80-yard field the teams were deadlocked near the end of the fourth quarter. 1976 *Eastern Even. News* (Norwich) 9 Dec. 19/8 In the last quarter, Reading gave UEA and their supporters a scare by scoring a well-worked try which was converted. 1979 *Tucson* (Arizona) *Citizen* 20 Sept. 1D/2 The young Warriors battled Sahuaro to a 7–7 draw through three quarters before falling, 16–13, in the season opener.

9. Of coins. †**a.** A farthing. *Obs.*

1389 in *Eng. Gilds* 60 Euery broyer and syster shal offeryn ij. qʳtre and j. qʳ to ye almes. 1641 Best *Farm. Bks.* (Surtees) 140 Harrowers have usually 3*d.*, or 3*d.* two quarters.

b. *U.S.* A silver coin = one fourth of a dollar.

[1799 Washington *Lett.* Writ. 1893 XIV. 150 It ought not to be larger than would cover a quarter of a dollar.] 1856 Olmsted *Slave States* 4 Here's a quarter for you. 1883 *Harper's Mag.* Nov. 950/2 Twenty..oranges for a quarter.

10. *Naut.* †**a.** (See first quot.) *Obs.*

1727–41 Chambers *Cycl.* s.v., A quarter of a point, wind, or rhumb, is the fourth part of a cardinal point, wind, or rhumb; or of the distance between two cardinal points, winds, etc. The quarter contains an arch of 11 degrees 15 minutes. 1796 H. Hunter tr. *St.-Pierre's Stud. Nat.* (1799) I. 156 The highest Tide..set in from east-quarter-north.

b. The fourth part of a point on the compass; 2° 48′ 45″. Also ***quarter-point*** (see 31).

1795 Hutton *Math. Dict.* II. 319.

11. *ellipt.* (from 8 a). A quarterly instalment of an allowance or payment.

1679–88 *Secr. Serv. Money Chas. & Jas.* (Camden) 63 Interest and gratuity for advancing the Dutchess of Portsmouth's quarter when she went into France. 1849 Thackeray *Pendennis* lviii, Pay me down the first quarter now.

III. Senses denoting locality, and transferred uses of these.

12. a. The region lying about or under one of the four principal points of the compass or divisions of the horizon; the point or division itself. Also *spec.* in *Astrol.* (see quot. 1696).

*c*1391 Chaucer *Astrol.* I. §5 The 4 principals plages or quarters of the firmament. 1526 Tindale *Rev.* xx. 8 The people which are in the foure quarters [Gr. γωνίαις] of the erth. 1535 Coverdale *Jer.* xlix. 34 Vpon Elam I wil bringe the foure wyndes from yᵉ foure quarters of heauen. 1611 Bible *1 Chron.* ix. 24 In foure quarters were the Porters: toward the East, West, North, and South. 1696 Phillips, *Quarters of Heaven*..in Astronomy, the [1706 Among Astrologers, certain] Intersections of the Spheres as well in the World as in the Zodiack [1706 of which two are termed Oriental, and counted Masculine; the other two being Occidental and Feminine]. 1748 *Anson's Voy.* II. ii. 136 We espied a sail in the northern quarter. 1826 Scott *Woodst.* ii, Joceline..looked..to the four quarters of the horizon. 1835 Sir J. Ross *Narr. 2nd Voy.* xv. 231 Venus was also seen in the southern quarter. 1860 Dickens *Uncomm. Trav.* iv, The Four Quarters of the World came out of the globe.

transf. 1542 Recorde *Gr. Artes* (1575) 197 The rose..is enuironed on the 4 quarters with 4 floure deluce.

†**b.** Boundary or limit towards one of the cardinal points; side. *Obs.*

1551 Robinson tr. *More's Utop.* II. (Arb.) 78 A drie diche ..goeth about thre sides or quarters of the city. To the fourth side the riuer it selfe serueth for a ditche. 1596 Dalrymple tr. *Leslie's Hist. Scot.* (1885) I. 2, I wil first.. descriue the quarteris and boundes of Scotland. 1611 Bible *Josh.* xviii. 14, 15 This was the West quarter. And the South quarter was from the end of Kiriath-iearim.

c. A direction or point of the compass, when more than four are mentioned or may be implied.

1604 E. G[rimstone] *D'Acosta's Hist. Indies* III. v. 132 They reckon but twoo and thirty quarters of the windes, for that more would confound the memorie. 1664 Evelyn *Sylva* (1679) 16 How speedily they [oaks] spread, and dilate themselves to all quarters. 1674 Grew *Veget. Trunks* vi. §7 Setting down the respect it..hath to any Quarter in the Heavens. 1784 Cowper *Task* I. 373 Winds from all quarters agitate the air. 1806–7 J. Beresford *Miseries Hum. Life* (1826) II. xiii, From every quarter of the compass to which you turn for refuge. 1818 Scott *Rob Roy* viii, 'Whew! sits the wind in that quarter?' enquired the justice.

13. a. Region, district, place, locality.

The pl. is sometimes used in much the same sense as the sing. With the preps. *from*, *in*, *to*, this sense cannot always be clearly distinguished from 12 c.

13.. *K. Alis.* 1902 Sixty citees, in that quarter, Heo forbrente. 1471 E. Paston in *P. Lett.* III. 27, I trow sche be in ȝour quarters. 1534 More *Conf. agst. Trib.* III. Wks. 1214/1 In this quarter here about vs. 1555 W. Watreman *Fardle Facions* II. vii. 157 Suche commodities as the quartre beareth..wher they dwelle. 1667 Milton *P.L.* v. 686 Where we possess The Quarters of the North. 1734 Sale *Koran* Prelim. Disc. §1 (Chandos ed.) 1 In which quarter they dwelt in respect to the Jews. 1765 *Museum Rusticum* IV. 377 There were in that single quarter [of France] above one hundred acres of transplanted cole-seed. 1855 Prescott *Philip II*, II. vi. (1857) 270 The marquis..had left the place on a visit to a distant quarter. 1867 Freeman *Norm. Conq.* (1876) I. v. 383 Troops flocked to him from all quarters.

b. Indicating a certain portion or member of a community, or some thing or things, without reference to actual locality.

1777 Sheridan *Sch. Scand.* I. i, I was hurt..to learn, from the same quarter, that..Sir Peter and Lady Teazle have not agreed lately. 1818 Jas. Mill *Brit. India* II. v. viii. 668 The quarter from which this proposition proceeded..was no secret to him. 1821 J. W. Croker in *Diary* (1884) June 6 This is erroneous in fact,..but T. insisted he had it from a good quarter. 1856 Froude *Hist. Eng.* (1858) I. ii. 136 A suspicion that even in the highest quarters justice had ceased to be much considered. 1886 E. Miller *Textual Guide* 27 This deference to B...leads the two learned Professors to follow it whenever it is supported by only slight testimony from other quarters.

14. a. A particular division or district of a town or city, *esp.* that appropriated to a particular class or race of people, as ***the Jewish quarter***, etc.; *spec.* the Latin Quarter of Paris (see LATIN *sb.* 5).

1526 Tindale *Luke* xiv. 21 Goo out quickly into the stretes and quarters [1611 lanes] of the citie. 1541 *Act 33 Hen. VIII*, c. 15 The said sainctuarymen..enter in euery parte and quarter of the same towne. 1602 *Return fr. Parnass.* v. iv, What newes with you in this quarter of the Citty? 1711 Addison *Spect.* No. 31 ¶1 The several Shows that are exhibited in different Quarters of the Town. 1756–7 tr. *Keysler's Trav.* (1760) II. 467 Rome is divided into fourteen *rioni* or quarters. 1820 W. Irving *Sketch Bk.* I. 121 In the most dark and dingy quarters of the city. 1864 D. G. Mitchell *Sev. Stor.* 214 A narrow court..which leads into a moldering quarter of the city. 1919 W. S. Maugham *Moon & Sixpence* xxvii. 117 Lots of fellows in the Quarter share a studio. 1926 E. Hemingway *Sun also Rises* I. v. 37 'What do you do nights, Jake?'..'Oh, I'm over in the Quarter.' *a*1967 A. Ransome *Autobiogr.* (1976) xii. 120 In those days the Quarter did its best for hard-up students, and I was able to furnish my studio for next to nothing.

†**b.** A particular place or point (in a building, etc.). *Obs.*

*c*1440 *Jacob's Well* 69 Þis wose of pride has viij. corneres, or viij. quarterys. ?1449 *Paston Lett.* No. 67 I. 83 They have made wykets on every quarter of the hwse to schote owte atte. *c*1470 Henry *Wallace* VIII. 1051 At a quartar, quhar fyr had nocht ourtayn, Thai tuk thaim out fra that castell. 1526 *Pilgr. Perf.* (W. de W. 1531) 131 That yᵉ ennemy may fynde in vs no quarter to entre.

†**c.** A part of a gathering or assembly, army, camp, etc. *Obs.*

1591 Shaks. *1 Hen. VI*, II. i. 63 Had all your Quarters been as safely kept As that whereof I had the gouernement, We had not beene..surpriz'd. 1596 *Edward III*, IV. iv. 50 These quarters, squadrons, and these regiments. 1599 Hakluyt *Voy.* II. II. 137 It is a thing almost impossible, at any your Faires or publique assemblies to finde any quarter thereof sober.

†**d.** ***to keep good quarter***: To keep good watch; to preserve good order. *Obs.*

1595 Shaks. *John* v. v. 20 Well: keepe good quarter, & good care to night. 1653 H. More *Antid. Ath.* II. viii. §2 (1712) 63 To have made Man that he might be a Lord over the rest of the Creation and keep good quarter among them.

†**e.** ***to keep a...quarter***: To maintain a (bad) state of things, to behave in a (bad) way; hence, even without adj., to make a noise or disturbance.

1632 Lithgow *Trav.* III. 88 The Souldiers kept a bloody quarter among themselues. *a*1654 Selden *Table-t.* (Arb.) 81 They keep a huge quarter when they carry it into the Cellar. 1659 *Commw. Ball.* (Percy Soc.) 150 For all you kept such a quarter, you are out of the councell of state. 1668 Pepys *Diary* 29 Jan., They had fiddlers, and danced, and kept a quarter, which pleased me though it disturbed me. 1736 Ainsworth *Lat. Dict.*, What a quarter they keep in the market. 1760 Baretti *Engl.-Ital. Dict.*, To keep a heavy quarter, *fare un grande strepito*.

15. a. Place of stay or residence; dwelling-place, lodgings, *esp.* of soldiers. Now usu. in *pl.*

free quarter(s): see FREE-QUARTER. ***head-***, ***home-***, ***out-***, ***summer-***, ***winter-quarters***: see the first element. ***quarters of refreshment*** (see quot. 1702–11). ***to beat up the quarters of***: see BEAT *v.*[1] 28. ***to take up one's quarters***: to establish oneself (in a place).

sing. 1591 *Garrard's Art Warre* 77 Let him remember..to bring backe again into his Quarter those soldiers hee hath led foorth to any enterprise. 1649 G. Daniel *Trinarch., Hen. IV*, lxxxiv, The Lords who must in state Lodge at the Crowne..Defray their Quarter at a Double Rate. 1679 *Establ. Test.* 25 In a place remote from his quarter, he rendevouzes with his fellow adventurers. 1719 De Foe *Crusoe* II. vi, I went from their quarter. 1837 Carlyle *Fr. Rev.* III. I. v, The grate which led to our quarter opened anew. 1897 Hughes *Medit. Fever* ii. 62 The staff-sergeant.. occupied a two-room quarter a few yards away.

pl. 1598 B. Jonson *Ev. Man in Hum.* IV. v, Turnbull, Whitechapel, Shoreditch, which were then my quarters. 1645 W. Browne *Let. to Wood* 9 Sept. in *Wood's Life* (O.H.S.) I. 122 *note*, Our horse from Oxon. fell on the enemies quarters at Thame. 1660 Sancroft *Serm.* 18 Nov. in D'Oyly *Life* (1821) II. 320 God and his church pay their quarters wherever they come. 1702–11 *Milit. & Sea Dict.* (ed. 4) 1, *Quarters of Refreshment*, the Place or Places, where Troops that haue been much harass'd, are put in to recover themselues, during some time of the Summer or Season for the Campaign. 1722 De Foe *Moll Flanders* (1840) 355, I found we must shift our quarters. 1758 Johnson *Idler* No. 21 ¶3, I wandered with the regiment as the quarters were changed. 1807 De Quincey in H. A. Page *Life* (1877) I. vii. 125 Mrs. Koster did me the honour to call at my quarters. 1856 Kane *Arct. Expl.* I. iii. 35 We had a rough time in working to our present quarters. 1881 Besant & Rice *Chapl. of Fleet* I. vi. (1883) 51 Where..robbers of the road had their customary quarters.

†**b.** The compulsory provision by private persons of lodging for troops. *Obs.*

1647 N. Bacon *Disc. Govt. Eng.* I. lxvi. (1739) 142 The Clergy are charged with Quarter, Cart-Service, and Purveying. **1781** Gibbon *Decl. & F.* xvii. II. 45 The most flourishing cities were oppressed by the intolerable weight of quarters.

c. *Hist. U.S.* (South). The cabins in which the Negroes on a plantation lived.

1724 H. Jones *Present State of Virginia* iv. 36 The Negroes live in small Cottages called Quarters. **1760** G. Washington *Diary* 26 Feb. (1925) I. 131 Began Plowing the Field by the Stable and Quarter for Oats and Clover. **1799** I. Weld *Trav. N. Amer.* xi. 84 Their quarters, the name whereby their habitations are called, are usually situated one or two hundred yards from the dwelling house. **1804** *Europ. Mag.* XLV. 19/1, I walked away to the Quarter. [*Note.* The place of abode for the negroes.] **1856** Olmsted *Slave States* 111 Several cabins are placed near together, and they are called 'the quarters'. **1889** *Harper's Mag.* Jan. 253 Let us go out to the quarters, grandpa; they will be dancing by now. **1909** 'O. Henry' *Roads of Destiny* xvii. 282 Almost the entire population of the quarters volunteered their aid. **1916** J. B. Thoburn *Stand. Hist. Oklahoma* I. 261 'The quarters'..formed a picturesque feature of the old time plantation life. **1935** Z. N. Hurston *Mules & Men* I. iv. 85 It sauntered on down the bark-covered road and into the quarters just as if it had really wanted to come. **1949** B. A. Botkin *Treas. S. Folklore* IV. i. 551 The 'South's tradition of good cooking'..belonged originally to the 'big house' rather than to the 'quarters' and the cabin.

d. A place of exercise for dogs.

1844 *Sporting Rev.* XI. 209 If you have sufficient walks or quarters, as they are sometimes called, to enable you to bring your own [hounds], begin with a good stock at first.

16. Assigned or appropriate position. † ***to keep quarter***: to keep one's own place. † ***to hold quarter with***: to remain beside. ***quarter of assembly*** (see quot. 1802). See also close quarters.

1549 *Compl. Scot.* vi. 41 Gunnaris, cum heir and stand by ȝour artailȝee, euyrie gunnar til his auen quartar. **1606** Shaks. *Ant. & Cl.* IV. iii. 22 Follow the noyse so farre as we haue quarter. **1611** Beaum. & Fl. *Philaster* II. ii, Let me hold quarter with you; we'll talk an hour Out quickly. **1612** Bacon *Ess., Love* (Arb.) 446 They doe best that make this affection keepe quarter, and seuer it wholly from their serious affaires. **1667** Milton *P.L.* III. 714 Swift to thir several Quarters hasted then The cumbrous Elements, Earth, Flood, Aire, Fire. **1702–11** *Milit. & Sea Dict.* (ed. 4) I. s.v., A Quarter at a Siege, An Incampment upon any of the principal Avenues of the Place. **1769** Falconer *Dict. Marine* (1780), *Quarters*, a name given, at sea, to the several stations where the officers and crew of the ship of war are posted in action. **1802** James *Milit. Dict.*, *Quarter of Assembly*, the place where the troops meet to march from in body, and is the same as the place of rendezvous. **1836** Marryat *Midsh. Easy* xxvi, 'Call the drummer', said Captain Wilson, 'and let him beat to quarters'.

†**17. a.** Relations with, or conduct towards, another; *esp.* in phr. ***to keep good*** (or ***fair***) ***quarter(s) with***.

1590 Shaks. *Com. Err.* II. i. 108 So he would keepe faire quarter with his bed. **1604** —— *Oth.* II. iii. 180 Friends all ..In Quarter, and in termes like Bride, and Groome. **1625** Bacon *Ess., Cunning* (Arb.) 439 Two, that were Competitors,..yet kept good Quarter betweene themselues. **1637** Rutherford *Lett.* (1862) I. 207, I find it to be hard wrestling to play fair with Christ and to keep good quarters with Him. *a* **1674** Clarendon *Surv. Leviathan* (1676) 153 The two next Kings..kept very fair quarter with Paschal.

b. (Good or fair) treatment or terms. *Obs.* exc. *arch.*

1648 *Eikon Bas.* iv. 25, I never had any thoughts of going from my House at Whitehall, if I could have had but any reasonable fair Quarter. **1699** Bentley *Phal.* 319 Lucian should have no better Quarter from him. **1705** Stanhope *Paraphr.* II. 268 No other Person must expect fair Quarter. **1735** Bolingbroke *On Parties* Ded. (1738) 7 He would deserve certainly much better Quarter [etc.]. **1826** Scott *Woodst.* xxxiii, Neither I nor my fellows will deliver it up but upon good quarter and conditions. *Ibid.*, They will give thee fair quarter.

18. a. Exemption from being immediately put to death, granted to a vanquished opponent by the victor in a battle or fight; clemency or mercy shown in sparing the life of one who surrenders. † Formerly also *pl.* † ***to cry quarter***: to call for quarter.

The precise origin of this sense is obscure, but it may be derived from 17, or even from 15 on the supposition that *to give quarter* originally meant to provide prisoners with quarters. The assertion of De Brieux (1672 *Origines..de plusieurs façons de parler*, 16) that it arose in an agreement between the Dutch and Spaniards, by which the ransom of an officer or private was to be a quarter of his pay, is at variance with the constant sense of the phrases *give* and *receive quarter*.

1611 Cotgr., *Quartier*..Quarter, or faire war, wherein souldiers are taken prisoners and ransomed at a certaine rate. *c* **1645** Howell *Lett.* (1655) I. 231 He suffered Tilly to take that great Town with so much effusion of blood, because they wood receiue no quarter. **1659** B. Harris *Parival's Iron Age* 308 Many were cut down, the Swedes giving no quarter. **1693** *Mem. Ct. Teckely* II. 89 As this was not a War of Quarter, they defended themselves desperately. **1720** De Foe *Capt. Singleton* xi. (1840) 188 The Portuguese cry quarter. **1788** Priestley *Lect. Hist.* v. lxii. 494 Civil wars are also peculiarly bloody, because less quarter is expected in them. **1816** Byron *Siege Cor.* xxiv, Cry For quarter, or for victory. **1841** James *Brigand* iii, Several of them uttered a cry of 'Quarter quarter'. **1865** Kingsley *Herew.* vii, Hereward bid his men give quarter.

pl. *c* **1644** *MS. Hist. Somerville Fam.* in *Scott's Rokeby*, Having refused quarters, every man fell in the same order and ranke wherin he had foughten. **1684** *Scanderbeg Rediv.* iv. 91 There was no Quarters given during the heat of the fight. **1726** Sherlocke *Voy. round World* 129 They instantly came to, and call'd for quarters. **1747** *Gentl. Mag.* 486 Near 7 at night she [the Terrible] called out for quarters. **1769** Falconer *Dict. Marine* (1780) s.v., *Quarters* is also an exclamation to implore mercy from a victorious enemy.

b. *transf.* and *fig.*

1647 Ward *Simp. Cobler* 72 He shewes more true fortitude, that prayes quarter of..Truth. **1684** J. Peter *Siege Vienna* 51 Nor was there any quarter given to the Wine-Cellars of the Emperor's Ministers. **1745** De Foe *Eng. Tradesman* (1841) I. vii. 55 The tradesman can expect no quarter from his creditors. **1762** Kames *Elem. Crit.* xix. (1833) 344 Mere witticisms, which ought to have no quarter. **1817** Shelley *Rev. Islam* Pref., There is no quarter given to Revenge, or Envy, or Prejudice. **1871** Morley *Crit. Misc.* Ser. I. *Vauvenargues* (1878) 25 The Trappist theory of the conditions of virtue found no quarter with him.

IV. Technical uses, in most of which the original sense is much obscured.

19. *Carpentry.* A piece of wood, four inches wide by two or four inches thick (see quot. 1703), used as an upright stud or scantling in partitions and other framing. Chiefly in *pl.*

[**1331** in J. T. Smith *Antiq. Westminister* (1807) 207 Two pieces of timber eight feet long called quarters.] **1497** *Naval Acc. Hen. VII* (1896) 235 Sawyng of tymbre into plankes quarters Bourde and other necessaries. **1565–73** Cooper *Thesaurus, Clostrum*,..a rayle or other like thinge made of quarters. **1617** Minsheu *Ductor*, A quarter, a peece of timber commonly foure square, and foure inches thicke, as it were a quarter or fourth part of a beame. **1665** Pepys *Diary* 21 Sept., The posts and quarters in the walls. **1703** Moxon *Mech. Exerc.* 163 Single Quarters are..two Inches thick, and four Inches broad. The Double Quarters are sawen to Four Inches square. **1811** *Self Instructor* 141 Plastering.. between the quarters in partitioning. **1825** J. Nicholson *Operat. Mechanic* 627 If the workman find materials for rendering between quarters, one-fifth must be added for quarters. **1875** Knight *Dict. Mech.* 1843/2 The English rule is to place the quarters at a distance not exceeding 14 inches.

20. a. *Farriery.* One side of a horse's hoof; one half of the coffin, extending between heel and toe; sometimes, the part of this immediately in front of the heel. ***false quarter***: see false *a.* 7. **b.** The corresponding part of a horse-shoe.

1523 etc. [see false *a.* 7]. **1607** Topsell *Four-f. Beasts* (1658) 309 You shall easily perceive whether his grief be in the inward quarter or in the outward quarter; the quarter is to be understood, from the mid hoof to the heel. **1685** *Lond. Gaz.* No. 2054/4 A Brown Dun Mare..with..a false quarter in one of her fore Feet. **1727** Bradley *Fam. Dict.* s.v. *Cut*, If..the Horse Cuts himself, or interferes, thicken the inner Quarters or Spunges of his Shoes. **1829** *Nat. Philos., Prelim. Treat.* (U.K.S.) 37 The frog coming down in the middle between the quarters, adds greatly to the elasticity. **1875** Knight *Dict. Mech.* 1843/2 *Quarter*,..the rear or heel portion of a horseshoe.

c. That part of a shoe or boot lying immediately in front of the back-line, on either side of the foot; the piece of leather, or other stuff, forming this part of the shoe from the heel to the vamp.

1753 Hanway *Trav.* (1762) I. III. i. 228 They wear slippers like women's shoes, without quarters. **1817** Mar. Edgeworth *Harrington* vi, A slipper, with a heel so high, and a quarter so low. **1834** Planché *Brit. Costume* 315 The shoes were worn with longer quarters and larger buckles. **1885** *Harper's Mag.* Jan. 280/2 The small quarter and button piece are 'closed' on the large quarter.

†**21.** A bed or plot in a garden. *Obs.*

Possibly due, in part at least, to confusion between 'quarter' and 'square' (as in the case of *quadrant, quadrate*): cf. F. *carré*, Sp. *cuadro* square, garden-plot.

1565 Cooper *Thesaurus, Area in hortis*,..a platte or quarter. **1572** Mascall *Plant. & Graff.* (1592) 8 Ye may plant or set all your Nuttes in one square or quarter together. **1688** R. Holme *Armoury* II. 118/1 Statues or Figures cut in Stone [are proper] to be in the quarters of the Garden. **1706** London & Wise *Retir'd Gard'ner* 12 Dig out of the Walks all the good Earth, and wheel or throw it into the Quarters. **1764** *Museum Rusticum* III. xvi. 73 This year they began to attack a large quarter of new-grafted apples.

22. *Naut.* **a.** The upper part of a ship's side between the after part of the main chains and the stern. ***on the quarter***, in a direction about midway between astern and on the beam.

1599 [see after *a.* 4b]. *a* **1618** Raleigh *Royal Navy* 10 Otherwise the bow and quarter will utterly spoile her sayling. **1624** J. Taylor (Water P.) *Brave Sea-fight* Wks. (1630) III. 39/2 To clap the Portugall aboord on the Larboord quarter. **1719** De Foe *Crusoe* I. xiii, All the stern and quarter of her was beaten to pieces with the sea. **1769** Falconer *Dict. Marine* (1780) s.v., If we were to divide the ship's sides into five equal portions..the first, from the stern, would be the quarter. *Ibid.*, s.v. *Bearing*. These bearings..which may be called mechanical, are on the beam,..on the quarter [etc.]. **1805** *Log of H.M.S. Tonnant* 21 Oct. in Nicolas *Disp. Nelson* (1846) VII. 167 *note*, The French Admiral's Ship under our quarter had lost her foremast. **1840** R. H. Dana *Bef. Mast* iv. 8 Leaving the land on our quarter. **1878** *Masque Poets* 120 The sea that came over her quarter.

b. Of a yard: The part between the slings and the yard-arm (see also quot. 1769).

1769 Falconer *Dict. Marine* (1780) s.v. *Yard*, The distance between the slings and the yard-arms on each side is..divided into quarters, which are distinguished into the first, second, third quarters, and yard-arms. *c* **1860** H. Stuart *Seaman's Catech.* 25 The quarter of the mainyard. **1882** Nares *Seamanship* (ed. 6) 41 The truss strop on the quarter of the yard.

23. †**a.** The skirt of a coat or other garment. *Obs.*

1535 Coverdale *Deut.* xxii. 12 Thou shalt make gardes vpon the foure quarters of thy garment. **1591** Percivall *Sp. Dict.*, *Falda*, the lap of a coate, the skirtes, the quarters of a coate. *c* **1658** *Wit Restored* 167 Chill put on my zunday parrell That's lac't about the quarters.

b. Of a saddle: (see quot.).

1753 Chambers *Cycl. Supp.* s.v., Quarters of a saddle are the pieces of leather or stuff made fast to the lower part of the sides of a saddle, and hanging down below the saddle.

24. One of the four parts into which a road is divided by the horse-track and the wheel-ruts.

1767 A. Young *Lett. to People* (1771) I. 445 A road..upon which the tracks may vary, without having quarters a yard high to cross. **1789** *Trans. Soc. Arts* VII. 204 Gravelled roads,..where quarters are formed by carriages following in one continued track. **1805** Dickson *Practical Agric.* I. Plate xxxvii, It is drawn by two horses abreast, the outside horse on the outer quarter, and the other in the path... Thus an inside and outside quarter are taken in going, and the others in returning. **1879** in *Norfolk Arch.* VIII. 172.

25. *dial.* One of the four teats of a cow (cf. quarter-evil 2). ***false quarter*** (see quot. 1797).

1797 J. Billingsley *View Agric. Somerset* 249 This disorder frequently affects the udder, and brings on a false quarter, that is, a deprivation of milk in one teat. **1886** Holland *Cheshire Gloss.* s.v., When a cow..ceases to give milk from one teat, she is said to have lost a quarter.

26. Miscellaneous uses.

a. *Fencing.* Some kind of stroke or blow (cf. *quarter-blow, -stroke* in 31). †**b.** ? A square space. *Obs.* †**c.** ? A square block. *Obs.* †**d.** *Typog.* One of the divisions of a form (see quot.). *Obs.* †**e.** In the manege (see quot.). *Obs.* †**f.** *pl.* In the old style of Rugby football (see quot.). *Obs.* **g.** *Arch.* A portion of a Gothic arch (Knight *Dict. Mech.* 1875). **h.** *Carpentry.* A section of a winding stair (*ibid.*). **i.** A section of a mill-stone dress (*ibid.*). **j.** That part of the side of a cask which lies between the chime and bulge (*ibid.*). **k.** An angular piece of cork, ready for rounding (*ibid.*).

a. *c* **1450** *Fencing w. two handed Sword* in *Rel. Ant.* I. 309 Thy rakys, thy rowndis, thy quarters abowte.

b. **1454** in Dugdale *Antiq. Warwicksh.* 356 Under every principall housing a goodly quarter for a Scutcheon of copper and gilt to be set in.

c. **1601** Holland *Pliny* II. 602 In Portugall..there be found great crystal quarters or masses of a wonderful weight.

d. **1683** Moxon *Mech. Exerc., Printing* 388 Quarto's, Octavo's and Twelves Forms are Imposed in Quarters. They are called Quarters, not from their equal divisions; but because they are Imposed and Lockt up apart. Thus half the Short-Cross in a Twelves Form is called a Quarter, though it be indeed but one Sixth part of the Form.

e. **1727** Bailey vol. II, *To work from Quarter, to Quarter*, is to ride a Horse three Times an End upon the first of the four Lines of a Square, and then changing Hands to ride him three Times upon the second, and so to do upon the third and fourth.

f. **1857** Hughes *Tom Brown* I. v. 114 The captain of quarters..spread his men..half-way between their own goal and the body of their own players-up.

27. In various colloquial shortened and abbreviated forms. **a.** *U.S. Football.* = quarterback *sb.* 2 a.

1893 W. C. Camp *Bk. College Sports* 120 The criss-cross or double pass is another excellent example of a disguised play, the ball being passed by the quarter to one of the backs. **1907** *St. Nicholas* (N.Y.) Sept. 1013/2 A line man could.. take the ball from the quarter. **1914** P. Withington *Bk. Athletics* 58 In handling the team the quarter must have absolute command.

b. (*a*) = *quartermaster-sergeant* s.v. quartermaster 2 c; (*b*) = quartermaster 1 a.

1917 A. G. Empey *Over Top* 304 Quartermaster-Sergeant, or 'Quarter' as he is called. A non-commissioned officer in a company who..takes charge of the company stores. **1963** M. Lowry *Ultramarine* ii. 60 Well, it's your business to get me up, quarter.

c. *pl.* = *quarter-finals* (see sense 31 below).

1978 *Guardian Weekly* 5 Feb. 24/2 The other semi-final was disappointing. Roscoe Tanner..had upset Bjorn Borg in the quarters. **1978** *Times* 4 July 19/3, I had never won a match on grass at Wimbledon and here I am in the quarters.

V. *attrib.* and *Comb.*

28. a. General combs. (sense 1), as ***quarter-barrel, -bottle, century, -ebb, -face, -flood, -hogshead, hour, -inch, litre, -look, -mile, pay, -pint, -rations, -size, truth*** (after half-truth), ***-yard***, etc.; ***quarter-armed, -faced, -hourly, -striking, -witted*** (after half-witted *a.*) adjs.; ***quarter-yearly*** adv.

1881 F. Day *Fishes Gt. Brit. & Ireland* I. 239 *Gasteroteus gymnurus*... The *quarter-armed or smooth-tailed stickleback. **1882** Ouida *Maremma* I. 245 There is a trifle of oil, a *quarter barrel. **1907** *Yesterday's Shopping* (1969) 99/2 *Saumur, sparkling*..In original hampers of 1 Dozen *¼ bots. **1915** H. G. Wells *Boon* ix. 333 One of those quarter-bottles of Perrier Jouet on a tray. **1977** J. R. L. Anderson *Death in City* v. 81, I ordered a quarter bottle of cognac. **1902** *Westm. Gaz.* 21 July 4/1 To put the result in *quarter-century periods. **1920** H. G. Wells *Outl. Hist.* xxix. 265/2 The opening quarter century of the Christian era was troubled by a usurper. **1979** *Bookseller* 23 June 2818/1 The Warsaw Bookfair continues towards its quarter century. *c* **1391** Chaucer *Astrol.* II. §46 Whepir it be..half or *quarter ebbe. **1626** Capt. Smith *Accid. yng. Seamen* 17 A spring tide, ebbe, a quarter ebbe, half ebbe. **1846** McCulloch *Acc. Brit. Empire* (1854) I. 251 Measured from the sea at quarter-ebb tide. **1616** B. Jonson *Forest* xii, Let them still Turn upon scorned verse their *quarter-face. **1833** *Regul. Instr. Cavalry* I. 33 Remain *quarter-faced to the right. *c* **1391** Chaucer *Astrol.* II. §46 Half flode or *quarter flode. **1626** Capt. Smith *Accid. yng. Sea-men* 17 [The sea] flowes quarter floud, high water, or a still water. **1801** Nelson 15 Aug. in Nicolas *Disp.* (1845) IV. 460 At last quarter-flood, at the Pier-head. **1891** T. Hardy *Tess* xxxviii, The washing-tub stood..on the same old *quarter-hogshead. **1883** 'Mark Twain' *Life on Mississippi* xxxvi. 392 My uneasy spirit kept dragging me back at *quarter-hour intervals. **1977** *Detroit Free Press* 11 Dec. 24-A/1 The head of the department [should] have at least..90 quarter hours of criminal justice courses completed. **1929** J. Owen *Shepherd & Child* iv. 46 The church clock.. had a *quarter-hourly chime. **1890** W. J. Gordon *Foundry* 58 Nearly all of them are to a *quarter-inch scale. **1978** J. Sherwood *Limericks of Lachasse* iv. 48 [He] had drunk only a *quarter-litre of light carafe wine. **1636** Massinger *Bashf. Lover* i. i, Observe his posture But with a *quarter-look. **1895** *Westm. Gaz.* 11 Jan. 5/2 A *quarter-mile straight race for professionals. **1691** Luttrell *Brief Rel.* (1857) II. 275 The seamen shall be.. kept in *quarter pay till spring. **1744** Berkeley *Let. to Hanmer* 21 Aug. in Fraser *Life* viii. (1871) 299 You may take this quantity either in half-pint or *quarter-pint glasses. **1856** Lever *Martins of Cro' M.* 201 A shipwrecked crew reduced to *quarter-rations. **1889** *Anthony's Photogr. Bull.* II. 3 A *quarter-size 'detective' camera. **1959** *Times* 6 Mar. 12/5 A Breguet gold and enamelled *quarter-striking, quarter-repeating clock watch. **1977** *Gay News* 7–20 Apr. 22/2 It was such dangerously oversimplified *quarter-truths that led to the vilification of——. **1979** *Daily Tel.* 12 Dec. 16 Mr Timothy Raison's article is a distressing collection of quarter truths and specious arguments. **1864** A. Wallace *Scottish Tales* iii. 38 A *quarter-witted individual from Muthil. **1972** P. Green *Shadow of Parthenon* 128 They vaguely assume their young readers to be either quarter-witted miniature adults or innocent prelapsarian angels. *a* **1400** *Stockh. Med. MS.* ii. 657 in *Anglia* XVIII. 323 His stalke is *quarter 3erde longe. **1795** Hamilton *Wks.* (1886) VII. 95 His allowance is at the rate of 25,000 dollars per annum 6,250 dollars *quarter-yearly.

b. With names of coins, as ***quarter-angel, -dollar, -ducat, -eagle, -florin, -guinea, -noble, -pound, -shekel, -shilling, -sovereign,*** etc.

1866 Crump *Banking* x. 223 *Quarter-angel. **1837** Ht. Martineau *Soc. Amer.* II. 89 The lowest price.. was a *quarter-dollar per acre. **1639** Ford *Lady's Trial* v. i, Pistol a straggler for a *quarter-ducat. **1874** Raymond *6th Rep. Mines* 524 Eagles.. Half-eagles.. *Quarter-eagles. **1707** Fleetwood *Chron. Prec.* 21 The *Quarter Floren he [Fabian] calls a Farthing, val is. viiid. **1776** *Ann. Reg.* 140 *Quarter guineas more deficient in weight than.. 1 dwt. 8 grs. **1803** Hatchett in *Phil. Trans.* XCIII. 137 George I. a quarter-guinea. **1866** Crump *Banking* x. 222 *Quarter-noble. *Ibid.* 223 *Quarter-pound. **1702** R. L'Estrange *Josephus, Antiq.* vi. v. (1733) 136 The Servants told him that he had a *Quarter-Sicle left yet. **1561** *Procl. Abassing Coynes* in Stafford *Exam. Complaints* (1876) 101 The *Quarter shilling That was currant for iij *d* shalbe currant for ij *d.*

†**c.** *Artillery*, denoting small sizes of certain pieces, as ***quarter-cannon, -culverin, -slang, -sling.*** *Obs.* (Cf. half- II. d.)

1549 *Compl. Scot.* vi. 41 Mak reddy 3our.. slangis, & half slangis, quarter slangis. **1570** Drout *Gaulfr. & Barn.* (1844) C 2 Thy roaring cannons.. Yea bases, foulers, quarter-slings. **1611** Florio, *Quarto cannone*, a quarter Cannon, which is but weakely fortifide or mettalled. **1684** J. Peter *Siege Vienna* 111 Quarter Cannon, each 12 pound 306. *Ibid.* 109 Quarter Culverin.. 26.

d. With names of persons, as ***quarter-carrier, -fairy, -ruler, -tyrant.*** Also quartermaster *sb.* 3.

1612 Shaks. & Fl. *Two Noble K.* i. ii. 108 Were he a *quarter carrier of that honour which His enemy comes in. *a* **1634** Randolph *Amyntas* v. 6 They do caper Like *quarter Fairies at the least. **1610** Healey *St. Aug. Citie of God* iv. xi. (1620) 160 A *quarter ruler with his brethren and sisters. *c* **1640** J. Smyth *Lives Berkeleys* (1883) I. 116 The lawes.. as some have written, were as *quarter-tirants.

†**29.** (Sense 8 a) = 'quarter's', 'quarterly', as ***quarter-allowance, -almoner, -feast, -fee, -salary, -sermon, -service, -supper.*** Also quarter-day, -sessions, -waiter.

1727 Boyer *Dict. Fr.-Angl., Quartier*,.. *Quarter-allowance. **1599** Sandys *Europæ Spec.* 9 With an eye perhaps that themselves would be his *quarter Almoners. **1609** B. Jonson *Silent Woman* ii. ii, It is his *quarter-feast, sir. **1615** J. Stephens *Satyr. Ess.* 11 Clearkes and other knaves.. Will take a pention or a *quarter-fee. **1583** Stubbes *Anat. Abus.* ii. (1882) 77 Preaching their *quarter sermons themselues. *a* **1555** Latimer *Serm. & Rem.* (1845) 243 Any services in your churches, either trental, *quarter-service, or other. **1592** in *Acts Priv. Counc.* N.S. XXII. 564 Irysche customes as.. *Quartersupers called Quidraighe.

30. *Naut.* (sense 22 a) as ***quarter-badge, -bitt, -boat, -check, -davits, -fast, -knee*** (knee *sb.* 7 a), ***-netting, -port, -rail, -railing, -stanchions*** (cf. quots.). See also *quarter-board, -cloth, -ladder, -timbers* in 31, and quarter-gallery, -line, -piece, -wind.

1807 Robinson *Archæol. Græca* iv. xiv. 390 To the ἀκροστόλια in the prow answered the ἄφλαστα, *quarter-badges, in the stern. **1867** Smyth *Sailor's Word-bk., Quarter-badge*, artificial galleries; a carved ornament near the stern of those vessels which have no quarter-galleries. **1805** Sir E. Berry 13 Oct. in Nicolas *Disp.* (1846) VII. 118 *note*, I ordered the weather *quarter-boat to be cut away. **1840** R. H. Dana *Bef. Mast* vi. 13 The watch on deck were lowering away the quarter-boat. **1833** Marryat *P. Simple* (1863) 41 Request that he will cast off the *quarter check. **1898** J. Conrad *Nigger of Narcissus* 246 Let go your quarter-checks!.. The ropes splashed heavily, falling in the water. **1867** Smyth *Sailor's Word-bk.*, *Quarter-davits, pieces of iron or timber with sheaves or blocks at their outer ends, projecting from a vessel's quarters, to hoist boats up to. **1846** A. Young *Naut. Dict.* 117 *Fast*, a rope or chain by which a vessel is secured to a wharf or quay. They are called bow, head, *quarter, and stern fasts. **1941** C. O'Brien *Sea-Boats, Oars, & Sails* ii. 22 Breast-hook and *quarter-knees.. connect the gunwales with the stem and transom respectively. **1769** Falconer *Dict. Marine* (1780), **Quarter-Netting*, a sort of net-work, extended along the rails on the upper part of a ship's quarter. **1867** Smyth *Sailor's Word-bk., Quarter-Nettings*, the place alloted on the quarters for the stowage of hammocks. *Ibid.*, **Quarter-ports*, those made in the after side-timbers and especially in round-stern vessels. **1769** Falconer *Dict. Marine* (1780), **Quarter-rails*, are narrow-moulded planks, generally of fir, reaching from the top of the stern to the gangway. *c* **1850** *Rudim. Navig.* (Weale) 139 *Quarter-rails*, rails fixed into stanchions from the stern to the gangway, and serving as a fence. **1809** W. Irving *Knickerb.* (1861) 200 Anthony.. was leaning over the *quarter-railing of the galley. **1860** Longf. *Wayside Inn, Saga K. Olaf* xx, He sat concealed,.. behind the quarter-railing. **1846** A. Young *Naut. Dict.* 243 **Quarter-stanchions*, strong stanchions in the quarters of a square-sterned vessel, one of which forms the outmost boundary of the stern on either side: it connects the main rail with the taffrail; [etc.].

31. Special combs., as **quarter-ail** = quarter-ill; †**quarter-ale**, an 'ale' or festival held by the people of a certain quarter (? or quarterly); **quarter-angled** *a.*, at a quarter of a right angle; also *Her.* = quadrate *a.* 5; **quarter-aspect**, quartile-aspect (Worcester 1860, citing Brande); **quarter-ball** *Billiards*, a ball that strikes another so that a quarter of the one overlaps a quarter of the other; †**quarter-basin**, *Sc.* (?); **quarter-bell**, a bell in a clock which sounds the quarters; **quarter-bend**, a section of pipe bent into a quarter-circle (Knight *Dict. Mech.* Suppl. 1884); **quarter-bill**, *Naut.* (see quot.); **quarter-binding**, a style of bookbinding with narrow leather back and no leather corners; now also, this style of binding using materials other than leather; **quarter-blanket**, a small blanket for a horse's back (Knight); **quarter-block**, *Naut.* a block fitted under the quarter of a yard; **quarter-bloke** *Mil. slang*, a quartermaster(-sergeant); **quarter-blood** *U.S.*, one whose descent is only one fourth derived from the blood of a particular race (esp. Amer. Indian) or breed; also as quasi-*adj.*; †**quarter-blow** (cf. quarter 26 a, and *quarter-stroke*); **quarter-board**, †some kind of board used in carpentry; also *Naut.* in *pl.* (see quot. 1846); **quarter-boat** *U.S.*, a boat containing living quarters for river workmen; †**quarter-book**, ? a book containing quarterly accounts; **quarter-boot**, a leather boot used to protect the heels of a horse's fore-feet from being injured by the hind feet (Knight); **quarter-bound** *a.*, in Bookbinding (see *quarter-binding*); **quarter-boy**, a quarter-jack in the form of a boy; **quarter-bred**, (*a*) of animals: having one fourth good blood (Ogilvie, 1882); (*b*) *N.Z.* = quarterback *sb.* 1; also *attrib.* or as *adj.*; **quarter-breed** *U.S.*, the offspring of a half-breed and a white; a quarter-blood; also *attrib.*; †**quarter-bullet** (see quot.); **quarter-butt**, in Billiards, a cue smaller than the half-butt; **quarter-calf** = *quarter-binding* (in calf); **quarter-cask**, (*a*) a quarter-hogshead; (*b*) a quarter-butt; †**quarter-cast**, *a.* of a horse (see quot.); **quarter-caste** *Austral.* and *N.Z.*, a person of mixed breed, having one-quarter Aboriginal or Maori and three-quarters white descent; also *attrib.*; **quarter-chord** *Aeronaut.*, a quarter of the length of a chord of an aerofoil, *spec.* such a distance measured backwards from the leading edge; freq. *attrib.*, as ***quarter-chord line, point***; **quarter-clock**, a clock that strikes the quarters; **quarter-cloth**, (*a*) *Naut.* (see quot.); (*b*) = *quarter-blanket*; **quarter-coal**, a periodical allowance of coal made to miners (Gresley *Gloss. Coal-mining* 1883); **quarter-column**, *Mil.* (see quots.); †**quarter-cord**, *Mining* (see quot. 1747); **quarter-course**, *U.S.*, a quarter-mile racing-course; **quarter-crack**, a crack on the inner quarter of a horse's fore-hoof (*Syd. Soc. Lex.* 1897); †**quarter-curtsey**, a slight curtsey; **quarter-cut**, plank cut to a quarter of an inch in thickness; **quarter-distance**, *Mil.* a distance intermediate between half and close distance; **quarter-elliptic(al)** *adjs.*, applied to a leaf spring having the profile of a quarter of an ellipse; **quarter-finals** *pl.*, the four matches constituting the round before the semi-finals in a tournament; also *sing.*, one of these four matches; also *attrib.*; **quarter-fishes** [fish *sb.*[2]], *Naut.* 'stout pieces of wood hooped on to a mast to strengthen it' (*Cent. Dict.*); †**quarter-foot** = *quarter-hoof*; †**quarter-four**, (?); **quarter-galley**, *Naut.* 'a Barbary cruiser' (Smyth); **quarter girth measure**, Hoppus measure; **quarter-grain**, the grain of wood in the plane of the medullary fibres and radially from the centre, shown when a log is quartered; †**quarter-ground** (Isle of Man) = quarterland; †**quarter-head**, a brad or flat-nail with a bill or projection at the head; †**quarter-heel** = quarter 20 c; **quarter-hollow**, a concave moulding, having an arc which is approximately a quadrant; also *attrib.*, or *adj.*, as in ***quarter-hollow tool*** (*Cent. Dict.* 1891); †**quarter-hoof**, ? a hoof with one of the quarters cut (cf. *quarter-cast*); **quarter-hoop**, a hoop on the quarter of a cask; also *attrib.*; **quarter-hung** *a.*, of a gun: having trunnions with their axis below the line of bore (Knight); **quarter-in-the-slot** *a. U.S.*, actuated by the fall of a quarter inserted through a slot (in a machine) (cf. *penny-in-the-slot* s.v. penny 12 b); **quarter-iron**, a boom-iron on the quarter of a yard; **quarter-ladder**, *Naut.* (see quots.); **quarter leather** = *quarter-binding* (in leather); **quarter-left**, *Mil.* one quarter of a right-angle towards the left; **quarter-light**, (*a*) a side-window in the body of a close carriage, as distinct from the door-light; (*b*) a small triangular side-window on a motor vehicle for ventilation and the admission of light; also *attrib.*; **quarter-miler**, one who is good at running a quarter-mile race; **quarter-moon**, (*a*) a crescent moon; also *attrib.*; (*b*) = quadrature 4 b; †**quarter-night**, the time when a quarter of the night has passed; **quarter-note**, *Mus.* (*a*) = *quarter-tone*; (*b*) *U.S.* a crochet; also *attrib.* as ***quarter-note rest***; **quarter-pace**, a resting-place or landing on a stair, containing a quadrant or 'quarter-turn'; **quarter-partition**, a partition whose framework is made of quarters; **quarter peal** *Bell-ringing*, a peal comprising one quarter of the number of changes in a full peal; **quarter-pierced** *a.*, *Her.* (see quots.); **quarter-plate**, a photographic plate measuring $3\frac{1}{4} \times 4\frac{1}{4}$ inches; also, a photograph taken on a plate of this size; also *attrib.*; **quarter-ply** *a.* (?); **quarter-point**, *Naut.* = quarter 10 b; **quarter-pointed** *a.*, *Her.* (see quot.); **quarter pole**, *U.S.* a pole marking the quarter-mile on a race-course; **quarter-quibble**, ? a poor or weak quibble; **quarter-race**, *U.S.*, a quarter-mile race; **quarter-racing** *U.S.*, the holding of quarter-races; also *attrib.*; **quarter-rack**, a rack which regulates the striking of the quarters in a clock; †**quarter-ranger**, ? the ranger or keeper of a certain quarter; **quarter-repeater**, a repeater-watch which strikes the quarters; **quarter-rest**, *Mus.* a rest equal in time to a quarter-note, a crotchet-rest (*Cent. Dict.*); **quarter-right**, *Mil.* one quarter of a right angle towards the right; †**quarter-road**, an ordinary road with quarters separated by horse-track and ruts; **quarter-round**, a convex moulding having an outline of a quarter-circle, an ovolo or echinus; also *attrib.*, or *adj.*, as ***quarter-round tool***; †**quarter-sack**, a sack capable of holding a quarter of grain; **quarter-saw** *v. trans.*, to saw (a log) radially into quarters; to produce (a board) by quarter sawing; **quarter-sawed** *a.*, of wood: quartered; **quarter sawing** *vbl. sb.*, the method or action of producing boards by sawing a log radially into quarters and then sawing each quarter into boards so that the growth rings make angles of greater than 45° with the faces of the boards; **quarter-sawn** *ppl. a.*; **quarter-screw**, one of the four screws in a compensation balance by which the watch is regulated; **quarter-seal**, a seal pertaining to the Chancery of Scotland, having the shape and impression of a fourth part of the Great Seal; **quarter-section** (U.S. and Canada), a quarter of a square mile of land, 160 acres; **quarter-sights**, sights engraved on the base-ring of a cannon in quarter degrees (Smyth); **quarter-slings**, *Naut.* (see quot.); **quarter-snail** (see quot.); **quarter-space** = *quarter-pace* (Nicholson, 1823); †**quarter-spells**, some game; **quarter-square**, the fourth part of the square of a number; **quarter stretch** *U.S.*, (a part of) a racecourse that is a quarter of a mile long; **quarter-stroke**, †(*a*) = *quarter-blow*; (*b*) the stroke with which a clock marks the quarters; **quarter-stuff**, (*a*) = *quarter-timber* b; (*b*) = *quarter-cut* (Knight); **quarter-tackle**, *Naut.* (see quot.); †**quarter-tale**, reckoning (grain) by quarters; **quarter-timber**, †(*a*) quartered timber; (*b*) timber in the form of quarters (sense 19); (*c*) *Naut.* in *pl.* (see quot. 1846); **quarter-tonal** *a.*, based on quarter tones; so **quarter-tonality**; **quarter-tone**, *Mus.* one half of a semitone; **quarter-track**, (*a*) = *quarter-course*; (*b*) a track recorded on magnetic tape so that four such tracks can be accommodated side by side; usu. *attrib.*; also as *adv.*, using this width of tape; **quarter-turn**, (*a*) a rifle in which the shot makes a quarter of a revolution in the length of the barrel; (*b*) a bend of a quarter of a circle; also *attrib.*; also as *v. trans.* and *intr.*; also **quarter-turning** *vbl. sb.* (see quot. 1901); **quarter-twist** = prec. a; **quarter-vine**, an American vine (*Bignonia* *capreolata*), the stem of which readily divides into quarters (*Cent. Dict.*); † **quarter-voided** *a.*, *Her.* = *quarter-pierced*; **quarter-watch**, *Naut.* a ship's watch composed of one-fourth of the crew; **quarter-wave** *a. Physics*, having a thickness or a length equal to a quarter of the wavelength transmitted or received; ***quarter-wave plate***, a plate of a birefringent substance cut parallel to the optic axis and of such a thickness that it introduces a time difference of a quarter of a period between ordinary and extraordinary rays passing normally through it; **quarter-wheeling**, turning through a quarter of a circle; † **quarter-wood** = *quarter-timber*.

1797 J. Billingsley *View Agric., Somerset* 249 A disorder provincially called the *quarter-ail, which is a mortification beginning at the hock. 1574 *Proviso in Lease* in Worsley *Hist. Isle Wight* 210 If the Quarter shall need..to make a *Quarter-Ale, or Church-Ale. 1775 Adair *Amer. Ind.* 269 Rushed off with impetuous violence, on a *quarter-angled course. 1873 J. Bennett *Billiards* 34 If the half of one overlaps the half of the other, it is a half ball; and so on for a *quarter ball. Anything less than a quarter ball is called a fine ball. 179. Burns *Lass Ecclefechan* i, A mickle *quarter basin. 1872 Ellacombe *Bells of Ch.* in *Ch. Bells Devon* viii. 393 The four *quarter bells were cast. 1769 Falconer *Dict. Marine* (1780), **Quarter-Bill*, a roll, or list, containing the different stations, to which all the officers and crew of the ship are quartered, in the time of battle, and the names of all the persons appointed to those stations. 1912 Monk & Lawrence *Test Bk. of Stationery Binding* 140 *Quarter binding. 55. 1932 A. F. Collins *Book Crafts for Schools* iii. 27 'Quarter-binding'..has the stronger material..on the back, and the weaker material..on the sides. 1978 A. W. Johnson *Thames & Hudson Man. Bookbinding* 216 *Quarter binding*, an economical covering method in which the spine and part of the sides are covered in one material and a cheaper one is used on the remainder. 1794 *Rigging & Seamanship* I. 157 *Thick-and-thin*, or **Quarter block*, is a double block..used to lead down the topsail-sheets and clue-lines. *c*1860 H. Stuart *Seaman's Catech.* 38 Topsail sheets when made of chain are rove through gins instead of quarter blocks. 1919 *Athenæum* 1 Aug. 695/2 The Q.M.S. (the colour-sergeant or 'Flag' of the Old Army) is always called the '*Quarter Bloke' or 'The Bloke'. 1920 *Punch* 18 Aug. 137/2 It's great.. To eat a daintier kind of grub than quarter-blokes provide. 1944 *Gen* 30 Dec. 55/2 Nickly overstepped the mark when he suggested to the quarter-bloke..that he was flogging the rations. 1950 C. MacInnes *To Victors Spoils* i. 21 I'll drop back there and talk to his quarter-bloke. 1845 *Knickerbocker* Mar. 236 Of this description was a *quarter-blood [*sc.* Indian], of great beauty. 1873 J. H. Beadle *Undevel. West* xix. 355 He had four children, only quarter-blood, but differing very much in shade. 1878 —— *Western Wilds* ii. 26 The straight black hair, and nose just aquiline enough to give piquancy to the countenance, indicated the quarter-blood. 1943 *Sun* (Baltimore) 11 Dec. 11/5 Medium shorn domestic fleeces have had a further small sale, mostly quarter-blood. 1555 W. Watreman *Fardle Facions* II. x. 221 Thei [Tartares] fighte all with a *quarter blow, and neither right downe, ne foyning. 1589 Greene *Menaphon* (Arb.) 85 Breaking a few quarter blowes with such countrey glances as they coulde. 1638 Heywood *Wise Wom.* IV. Wks. 1874 V. 330, I had my wards, and foynes, and quarter-blowes. 1452 in Willis and Clark *Cambridge* (1886) I. 282 The selyng boord..shalbe *quartere borde an inche thyk. 1497 *Naval Acc. Hen. VII* (1896) 296 Sawyng of certeyn tymbre into plankes [&] quarterbordes. 1548 *Privy Council Acts* (1890) II. 174 Quarter boord, iij^{ml}. 1846 A. Young *Naut. Dict.* 242 *Quarter-Boards* or *Top-gallant Quarter-Boards*, a thin bulwark boarding, forming an additional height to the bulwarks at the after part of a vessel. They also get the name of *Topgallant bulwarks*. 1929 *Sun* (Baltimore) 23 Oct. 1/3 The President and his immediate party left Cincinnati..aboard the Greenbrier..and three other light craft—*quarter boats, they are called—for the remaining members of the party. 1962 A. Davison *In Wake of Gemini* 228 A quarterboat is an operational center for the maintenance and repair department of the U.S. Army Corps of Engineers Mississippi River Commission. 1679–88 *Secr. Serv. Money Chas. & Jas.* (Camden) 146 His allowance..for returning the *quarter books to Sr Edmund Turner. 1888 C. T. Jacobi *Printer's Vocab.* 108 **Quarter bound*, books bound with back only in leather. 1929 A. J. Vaughan *Mod. Bookbinding* II. 121 (*caption*) A Quarter Bound Book. *Ibid.* IV. 217 *Quarter Bound*, where the back and some portion of the sides only of the binding consist of one material, and the remainder of the sides of another. 1960 G. A. Glaister *Gloss. Bk.* 338/1 Quarter-bound: a book bound with either leather spine and cloth sides, or cloth spine and paper sides. 1979 *London Rev. Bks.* 25 Oct. 11/2 (Advt.), Quarter-bound in leather. 1826 Southey *Vind. Eccl. Angl.* 260 The machinery..by which his own *quarter-boys in Fleet-street perform their office. 1900 *Academy* 28 Apr. 365/1 The grotesque 'quarter-boys'—corpulent cherubs on either side of the clock—beat the quarters on the dial. 1891 R. Wallace *Rural Econ. Austral. & N.Z.* xviii. 259 In 1890, the better portion of the greasy *quarter-bred wool fetched 1*s.* 2½*d.* *a*1948 L. G. D. Acland *Early Canterbury Runs* (1951) 370 *Comeback*, a sheep three-quarters merino and one quarter long wool..but in New Zealand I think these sheep are often called quarterbreds or quarter-backs. 1826 T. L. McKenney *Sk. Tour to Lakes* (1827) 387 Three were full blood, the remainder half breeds, and *quarter breeds. 1880 *Harper's Mag.* Dec. 31 All four were of mixed blood their mother having been a beautiful French quarter-breed. 1909 *Lady's Realm* Feb. 465/1 El-Soo was a full-blooded Indian, yet she exceeded all the half-breed and quarter-breed girls. She was a treasure. 1627 Capt. Smith *Seaman's Gram.* xiv. 69 *Quarter Bullets is..any bullet quartered in foure or eight parts. 1873 Bennett & Cavendish *Billiards* 27 The cue-butt or *quarter-butt is larger in diameter than the cue, about 5 feet long, and leathered at the bottom. 1956 *Library* XI. 81 The binding has no corner-pieces; and so is properly called '*quarter-calf'. 1711–2 *Advt.* in *Spectator* (1891) 904, 22 Hogsheads and 3 *quarter Casks of new Bene-Carlos Barcelona Wine..at..5*l.* per Hogshead and 25*s.* per Quarter Cask. 1727 Bailey vol. II, **Quarter-cast* (with Horsemen), a Horse is said to cast his Quarter, where for any Disorder in the Coffin, there is a Necessity to cut one of the Quarters of the Hoof. 1948 D. Ballantyne *Cunninghams* I. i. 6 Being up the duff to a young *quarter-caste..was no joke. 1952 R. Finlayson *Schooner came to Atia* x. 51 The crew with the exception of the quartercaste mate were all Maori. 1966 *Times* 28 Mar. (Austral. Suppl.) p. ix/4 Aboriginal people..vary from full-bloods to quarter-castes. 1976 *Times Lit. Suppl.* 9 Apr. 417/1 Prindy, an eight-year-old quarter-caste who sees himself as purely aboriginal, in spite of his fair hair and grey eyes. 1979 *Church Times* 9 Mar. 4/3 Bishop Reeves is a 'quarter-caste' Maori and a graduate of St. Peter's College, Oxford. 1946 *Jrnl. R. Aeronaut. Soc.* L. 436/2 The centre of pressure is at the half-chord instead of approximately at the *quarter-chord point. 1947 C. F. Toms *Introd. Aeronaut.* i. 26 The quarter-point of the mean chords lies very nearly on the quarter-chord line of the wing. 1957 L. L. Beckford *A.B.C. of Aeronaut.* 98/2 This angle, known as Sweep Back, is measured between the lateral axis and a line drawn a quarter-chord back from the leading edges. 1959 J. L. Nayler *Dict. Aeronaut. Engin.* 207 The quarter-chord line is the line joining the quarter points of the chords across the span of the wing. 1967 *Jane's Surface Skimmer Syst. 1967–68* 12/1 Aerofoil section NACA 0009. Sweepback at quarter-chord 30°. 1626 Donne *Serm.* lxxiii. 748 There was never heard *Quarter-clock to strike. 1884 F. J. Britten *Watch & Clockm.* 217 [A] Quarter Clock..[is] a clock that strikes or chimes at the quarter hours. 1769 Falconer *Dict. Marine* (1780), **Quarter-cloths*, long pieces of painted canvas, extended on the outside of the quarter-netting from the upper part of the gallery to the gangway. 1894 *Field* 9 June 828/3 The names of his two horses embroidered on the quarter cloths. 1879 *Cassell's Techn. Educ.* IV. 218/2 The *quarter-column is the formation..most employed when large bodies of troops are working together. 1884 *St. James's Gaz.* 21 Aug. 5/2 A battalion of eight companies in quarter-column, that is, in column of companies one behind the other. 1747 Hooson *Miner's Dict.* Q ij b, **Quartercord* [is] a Measure used in laying out of Flats, 'tis a superficial Measure, and one fourth part of a Mear; it is a Square, each side being seven Yards and one Quarter long. 1851 Tapping *Gloss. Mining Terms* (E.D.S.), s.v., So long as a mine is wrought..everything upon the quarter cord belongs to the miner. 1885 *Century Mag.* XXX. 397/2 '*Quarter-courses' usually consisted of two parallel paths, and were run by two horses at a time. 1753 Smollett *Ct. Fathom* (1784) 147/1 A *quarter curtsey, or slight inclination of the head. 1895 *Westm. Gaz.* 30 Mar. 3/1 The skin of..all kinds of racing eights, is known as '*quarter cut'. 1796 *Instr. & Reg. Cavalry* (1813) 164 The rear ..[divisions] quicken their march, and close up to *quarter distance. 1842 Alison *Hist. Europe* (1849–50) XIV. xciv. §7. 7 They were drawn up in two lines, but the enemy chiefly in quarter-distance columns. 1926 C. T. B. Donkin *Elem. Motor Vehicle Design* xviii. 253 The bending moment in the chassis frame set up by the reactions of a *quarter-elliptic spring is very considerable, and the type is seldom used for heavy cars except in the form of a short subsidiary spring. 1963 Bird & Hutton-Stott *Veteran Motor Car* 53 The characteristic reversed quarter-elliptic rear springs appear on the 5-litre model. 1909 R. W. A. Brewer *Motor Car* xiv. 140 When *quarter-elliptical springs are used they may be either shackled to the side springs or pinned to them direct. 1927 *Daily Express* 28 July 1/5 Miss Helen Jacobs..scored a signal success in the *quarter-finals of the Essex County Invitation Tournament. 1932 *News Chron.* 23 Sept. 2/4 The quarter-finals of the Canadian Women's Open Golf Championship. 1941 G. Marx *Let.* 23 June (1967) 27 Art plays Frank Parker in the quarterfinals of the 55th Annual Los Angeles Tournament. 1976 *Lancs. Even. Post* 7 Dec. 15/5 Morecambe's quarter final game at Runcorn is a vital one. 1977 *Whitaker's Almanack 1978* 583/2 Newcastle United were fined £4000..for fielding a weakened team in the quarter-final of the Anglo-Scottish Cup. 1711 *Lond. Gaz.* No. 4888/4 A *quarter Foot the near Foot behind. 1776 G. Semple *Building in Water* 66 A nine Foot Pantile-lath or a *Quarter-four. 1745 P. Thomas *Voy. S. Seas* 58 We found here in the Road..two *Quarter Galleys. 1867 [see half-galley]. [1894 W. Stevenson *Wood* 194 The Hoppus measure by string, quarter girth..on round timber, is an overmeasure in favour of the buyer.] 1924 *Quarter girth [see Hoppus]. 1954 W. E. Hiley *Woodland Managem.* ix. 127 Quarter girth or 'hoppus' measure. The volume of a felled log is determined by its length and the area of the cross section half way along it. The length is measured by a long tape,..and the middle girth by a specially marked short tape, known as a quarter-girth tape. 1703 T. N. *City & C. Purchaser* 187 The *Quarter-grain..is that Grain which is seen to run in straight Lines towards the Pitch. 1825 J. Nicholson *Operat. Mechanic* 612 Clear them [laths] into thicknesses by the quarter grain. 1593 *Statutes Isle Man* (1821) 76 To pay for every *Quarter Ground in respect of their..Custom Turves. 1703 T. N. *City & C. Purchaser* 35 *Quarter-heads, or Bill-brads for soft Wood-floors. 1727 A. Hamilton *New Acc. E. Ind.* I. vii. 67 Their Shoes..very low and stiff at the *Quarter-heels. 1713 *Lond. Gaz.* No. 5148/12 A *Quarter-hoof on one of his hind Feet. 1885 *Census Instruct.*, *Quarter Hoop Maker, Bender, Shaver. 1903 R. L. McCardell *Conversat. Chorus Girl* 80 Mama de Branscombe had a *quarter-in-the slot gas meter put in. *c*1860 H. Stuart *Seaman's Catech.* 75 On each quarter is a *quarter-iron that opens with a hinge to allow the topmast studding sail booms to be raised or lowered. 1769 Falconer *Dict. Marine* (1789), **Quarter-Ladders*, two ladders of rope, depending from the right and left side of a ship's stern. 1867 Smyth *Sailor's Word-bk.*, *Quarter-Ladder*, from the quarter-deck to the poop. 1938 L. M. Harrod *Librarians' Gloss.* 124 *Quarter leather. A term used to describe a book with a leather spine and cloth sides. 1963 B. C. Middleton *Hist. Eng. Craft Bookbinding Technique* xi. 160 It was not uncommon on the Continent in the Middle Ages for books to be bound in quarter-leather. 1832 *Regul. Instr. Cavalry* III. 93 The..command will be given, Squadrons..*Quarter or Half Left. 1881 *Daily News* 15 Sept. 3/2 The engine.. struck the side of the three last carriages..smashed a number of the '*quarter lights'. 1890 W. J. Gordon *Foundry* 157 The thick glass in the quarter-lights, the thinner plate in the door-lights, are not bought for nothing. 1938 *Times* 13 Oct. 8/4 The quarter lights are taken as far aft as possible. 1972 *Police Rev.* 8 Dec. 1588/2 The campaign includes 200,000 posters, 1½ million car quarter-light stickers, and 250,000 shop-window stickers. 1976 'Z. Stone' *Modigliani Scandal* III. i. 113 He..[was] driving with the quarter-light open and enjoying the fresh air. 1899 *Daily News* 19 July 6/5 The *quarter-miler was only just leading. 1601 Holland *Pliny* I. 121 With horned points like to a *quarter moone. 1665–6 *Phil. Trans.* I. 55 The Course of irregular Tides about the Quartermoons. 1947 L. P. Hartley *Eustace & Hilda* v. 91 The quarter-moon was resting on the roofs. 1977 A. Desai in P. Collenette *Winter's Tales 23* 19 He..went about dividing the melon into quarter-moon portions. *c*1386 Chaucer *Miller's T.* 330 A Monday next, at *quarter-night, Shall fall a reyn. 1763 J. Brown *Poetry & Mus.* v. 63 *Quarter-Notes;..an Interval which no human Ear can precisely distinguish. 1773 Barrington *Singing of Birds* in *Phil. Trans.* LXIII. 264 Such a minute interval..when a quarter-note for example might be required. 1958 Quarter note [see eighth *a.* 3]. 1959 Westrup & Harrison *Collins Music Encycl.* 524/1 *Quarter-note*, American for 'crotchet'. 1825 J. Nicholson *Operat. Mechanic* 594 Where the height of a story is considerable, resting places are necessary, which go under the name of *quarter-paces, and half-paces, according as the passenger..has to describe a quadrant or semi-circle. 1858 *Skyring's Builders' Prices* (ed. 48) 13 The Plates and Braces in *Quarter Partitions must be added. 1842–59 Gwilt *Archit.* (ed. 4) §2024 The scantlings of the timbers of a quarter partition should vary according to the extent of bearing. 1888 A. P. Heywood *Treat. on 'Duffield'* vii. 53 (*heading*) (1296) *Quarter peal. 1931 E. Morris *Hist. & Art Change-Ringing* iii. 53 The above twice repeated will come round at the quarter peal end. 1980 *Times* 7 Apr. 3/1 Bellringers at the parish church rang a quarter peal. 1678 Phillips (ed. 4), **Quarter Pierced*, in Heraldry is when there is a hole of a square form made in the middle of a Cross. 1893 Cussans *Her.* (ed. 4) 63 The Cross..If..that part where the limbs are conjoined be removed, it is termed Quarterly-pierced. A Cross with a square aperture in its centre, smaller than the last example, is Quarter-pierced. 1890 *Anthony's Photogr. Bull.* III. 273 A 'half-plate' or a '*quarter-plate' lens. *Ibid.*, A beginner buying his first quarter-plate outfit. 1856 Olmsted *Slave States* 3 Three yards of ragged and faded *quarter-ply carpeting. 1727–41 Chambers *Cycl.* s.v. *Point*, Half of that, or 2° 48′ ¾, [is] a *quarter point. 1769 Falconer *Dict. Marine* (1789), The quarter-points of the Compass..are distinguished..by the word *by*. 1840 Marryat *Olla Podr.* III. 26 How was it possible that a man could navigate a ship with only one quarter point of the compass in his head? 1825–9 W. Berry *Encycl. Her.*, **Quarter-pointed*,..extending from dexter chief towards the base, and terminated in the fesse point. It ..is just one-fourth part of a partition per saltier. 1857 *Quarter pole [see *peanut boy* s.v. peanut 3 a]. 1868 H. Woodruff *Trotting Horse* xxxi. 259 At the quarter-pole she had recovered her stroke. 1894 *Outing* (U.S.) XXIV. 142/2 Held his place until the quarter-pole was reached. 1975 *New Yorker* 3 Mar. 73/1 Susan's Girl..led past the quarter pole. 1663 Dryden *Wild Gallant* I. i. Wks. 1882 II. 35 A bare clinch will serve the turn; a carwichet, a *quarter-quibble, or a pun. 1729 T. Cooke *Tales*, etc. 96 Quarter-quibbles made his Heart right glad. 1792 *Descr. Kentucky* 12 His time is employed in *quarter-races, cock-fights. 1885 *Century Mag.* XXX. 397/2 In North Carolina..quarter-races were much esteemed. 1784 J. F. D. Smyth *Tour in U.S.* I. ii. 22 In the southern part of the colony and in North Carolina, they are much attached to **Quarter racing*, which is always a match between two horses, to run one quarter of a mile streight [*sic*] out. 1889 *Harper's Mag.* Sept. 554/1 Foot-racing for the men and quarter-racing for the horses. 1974 *New Yorker* 29 Apr. 83/2 His journey into the center of the quarter-racing world. 1884 F. J. Britten *Watch & Clockm.* 219 The *quarter rack..falls against the bent arm of the hour rack hook. *a*1613 Overbury *Characters, Sargeant* Wks. (1856) 163 The gallowes are his purlues, in which the hangman and hee are the *Quarter-rangers. 1884 F. J. Britten *Watch & Clockm.* 224 In a *quarter repeater the last hour is struck, and afterwards the number of quarters that have elapsed since. 1832 *Regul. Instr. Cavalry* II. 72 The Troops..wheel *quarter right. *Ibid.* 90 The previous command is given, Squadrons quarter or half-right. 1767 A. Young *Lett. to People* 282 A broad-wheel waggon will go in any *quarter-road. 1706 Phillips (ed. Kersey), *Echinus*..is termed.. Ovolo by the Italians; but the English Workmen commonly call it the *Quarter-round. 1753 Hogarth *Anal. Beauty* xii. 171 Let us observe the 'ovolo', or quarter-round, in a cornice. 1851 Turner *Dom. Archit.* II. vi. 272 The arches and purlins are well moulded, with the quarter round and fillet. 1963 C. R. Cowell et al. *Inlays, Crowns, & Bridges* iii. 23 A quarter-round bur for contra-angle handpieces is used to cut 2-mm. pinholes. 1975 *New Yorker* 24 Feb. 56/3 He.. addressed the axe to the quarter-round log. 15.. *Merie Tales of Skelton* S.'s Wks. 1843 I. p. lxx, The miller hauying a great *quarter sacke. *a*1661 Fuller *Worthies, Cambridge* I. (1662) 156 Quarter-sacks were here first used, men commonly carrying..eight bushels of Barly. 1898 S. B. Green *Forestry in Minnesota* 299 *Quarter-sawing... The log is first quartered and then sawed into boards, cutting then alternately from each face of the quarter of the log. 1907 Webster, Quarter-saw, *v.t.*; -sawed or -sawn. 1931 *Harper's Mag.* June 62/1 No one rived the beams for his ceiling, or quarter-sawed oak for his chairs. 1934 *Archit. Rev.* LXXVI. 64/1 When logs are riven or quarter-sawn the large rays which form the silver grain are revealed to the fullest extent. 1966 A. W. Lewis *Gloss. Woodworking Terms* 74 Quarter-sawn boards shrink less and are less liable to warp than other boards. 1968 Quarter sawing [see *rift sawing* s.v. rift *sb.*² 4]. 1974 *Islander* (Victoria, B.C.) 29 Dec. 15/2 When the logs have reached the proper degree of dryness staves will be quarter sawn from them. That is, the flat boards will radiate out from the centre of the log like segments of an orange. 1884 F. J. Britten *Watch & Clockm.* 25 Drawing out the *quarter screws of the balance nearest the fast position..and setting in the ones nearest to slow position. 1706 *Act 6 Anne* c. 11 Art. xxiv, The privy seal..*quarter seal and seals of Courts now used in Scotland. 1806 *Deb. Congress U.S.* (1852) 9th Congress 2 Sess., App. 1032 The public lands are now sold in sections, half sections, and *quarter sections. 1879 Ld. Beaconsfield *Sp.* 18 Sept. 2/3 Every man of fair character who comes to Canada, has a right..to obtain what is called a quarter-section of land. 1882 *Contemp. Rev.* Aug. 233 Each township, section, and quarter-section..marked off by mounds and posts. 1876 Voyle & Stevenson *Milit. Dict.* 385/2 In smooth-bore guns, *quarter-sights are cut on the upper quarter of the base ring, and numbered up to 3°. 1867

Smyth *Sailor's Word-bk.*, **Quarter-Slings*, are supports attached to a yard or other spar at one or both sides of (but not in) its centre. **1884** F. J. Britten *Watch & Clockm.* 219 [The] *Quarter Snail..[is] the snail used in the quarter part of clocks and repeating watches. **1448** in Bacon *Ann. Ipswich* 105 John Lackford accused for cheating at Games called Whistilds, Prelleds, and *Quarter spells. **1841** *Penny Cycl.* XIX. 199/2 A table which gives the squares of the halves of numbers will, by the addition of the squares of the halves or *quarter-squares, give the product. **1834** *Southern Lit. Messenger* I. 182/1, I pulled and pulled till I got out of sight, and turned down the *quarter stretch. **1883** H. Watterson *Oddities Southern Life* 439 He ran a quarter stretch down the low grounds of the base. **1559** Aylmer *Harborowe* H, They must know their *quarter strookes, and the waye how to defende their head. **1589** *Marprel. Epit.* D ij, Such a precher..as this, would quickly with his quarter strokes, ouerturne al religion. **1780** Cowper *Table Talk* 531 The clock-work tintinnabulum of rhyme,..such mere quarter-strokes are not for me. **1712** J. James tr. *Le Blond's Gardening* 71 They make use..of *Quarter-Stuff for large Plinths and Facias. **1799** *Naval Chron.* II. 389 Timber.., blocks, quarterstuff, candles. **1815** *Falconer's Mar. Dict.* (ed. Burney), **Quarter-tackle*, a strong tackle fixed occasionally upon the quarter of the main- or fore-yard, to hoist boats and heavy packages into and out of the ship. **1641** Best *Farm. Bks.* (Surtees) 132 For burying of Corne by *Quarter-tayle..to have 6*d.* a quarter for barley, 4*d.* a quarter for oates. **1601** Holland *Pliny* I. 488 The *quarter timber, or that which runneth with foure grains, is simply the best. **1846** A. Young *Naut. Dict.* 243 *Quarter-timbers*, the framing timbers in a vessel's quarter. **1934** S. R. Nelson *All about Jazz* i. 13 Maddening is that persistent beat of the tom-toms and these *quarter-tonal intervals gradually rising to an overwhelming climax. **1930** *Proc. Musical Assoc.* Apr. 92 We are dogged by such words as tonality, ..*quartertonality, modality. **1947** *Penguin Music Mag.* Sept. 11 The romantic composers of the nineteenth century ..needed a new instrument—neo-modality, atonality, polytonality, quarter-tonality. **1776** Burney *Hist. Mus.* (1789) I. ii. 23 A Diesis or *Quarter-tone. **1811** Busby *Dict. Mus.* s.v., The Quarter-tone is of two kinds, viz. the major-enharmonic..and the enharmonic minor. **1866** Engel *Nat. Mus.* ii. 45 The seven intervals of the Hindu Scale..are subdivided into twenty-two *srooti*, corresponding to quarter-tones. **1891** C. R. Day *Music & Mus. Instruments S. India & Deccan* ii. 20 The quarter-tone system used in Syria. **1934** C. Lambert *Music Ho!* v. 311 The quarter-tone quartets of Aloys Haba..differ from the quartets of Brahms only through being written in the quarter-tone scale. **1959** Westrup & Harrison *Collins Music Encycl.* 524/1 Alois Hába has written a number of compositions..for quarter-tone piano, and for quarter-tone harmonium. **1978** P. Griffiths *Conc. Hist. Mod. Music* v. 53 Ives had explored atonality, free rhythm, quarter-tone harmony. **1888** J. C. Harris *Free Joe*, etc. 10 There was a *quarter-track,..if he chose..horse-racing. **1962** R. E. B. Hickman *Magnetic Recording Handbk.* (ed. 3) iii. 29 Present day domestic magnetic tape recorders normally employ dual track (half-track) recording on ¼ in. tape, although four track (quarter track) recording, with alternate tracks recorded in the same direction, is also common practice. **1962** A. Nisbett *Technique Sound Studio* iv. 82 Correction can be made by.. replaying only part of the full recorded track: e.g. replaying ..a half-track recording quarter-track. **1967** P. Spring *Tape Recorders* iv. 41 A correct head alignment is very much more important than in the case of a quarter-track tape recorder. **1975** G. J. King *Audio Handbk.* x. 226 (*caption*) A mono recorder lays one track on each half of the tape, the track then having approximately the width of two quarter tracks. **1810** *Sporting Mag.* XXXVI. 272 A *quarter turn, which is the kind of rifle the line uses. **1934** D. L. Sayers *Nine Tailors* II. i. 73 Rector was saying the other day as she [*sc.* a bell] did soon ought ter be *quarter-turned. **1954** W. Faulkner *Fable* 303 It made a rigid quarter-turn. *Ibid.* 384 Some twenty men with a sergeant, who halted and quarter-turned and stood them at ease. **1964** G. C. Kunzle *Parallel Bars* ix. 403 Quarter turn into handstand on one bar, squat off with straight legs dismount. **1901** H. E. Bulwer *Gloss. Technical Terms Bells* 3 **Quarter-turning*, re-attaching a bell to its 'stock' at right angles (or less) to its former position with reference to the latter, in order that the 'clapper' may strike on a fresh segment of the 'sound-bow'. **1979** *Church Times* 5 Oct. 5/1 The bells [were] unsafe as they were. The bell-founders had recommended quarter-turning. **1661** Morgan *Sph. Gentry* II. iii. 29 Or..a Crosse *quarter-voided azure. **1702–11** *Milit. & Sea Dict.* (ed. 4) II, **Quarter-Watch* is when a Quarter of the Ship's Company watches, which is us'd in Harbour, when there is no Danger. **1769** Falconer *Dict. Marine* (1789), *Faire la petite Bordee*, to set the quarter-watch. **1887** G. B. Goode *Fisheries U.S.* V. ii. 229 On the whaling ground..they stand 'quarter-watches'. **1882** L. Wright *Light* xiv. 298 This then is our '*quarter-wave' plate, which should be at once mounted between two glasses in balsam, and its working planes marked on the edges by scratching with a diamond, or quartz crystal. **1937** Jenkins & White *Fund. Physical Optics* xvi. 357 When a quarter-wave plate is oriented at an angle of 45° with the plane of the incident polarized light the emerging light is circularly polarized. **1943** C. L. Boltz *Basic Radio* xvii. 265 The ¼λ aerial is in two halves... From the centre ends hang two wires ¼λ long. The feeder is then tapped to the quarter-wave line by moving the contacts up or down until the correct impedance is found. **1970** D. W. Tenquist et al. *University Optics* II. iii. 109 Quarter-wave plates are usually made of quartz or of mica (sandwiched between glass plates). **1977** S. W. Amos *Radio, TV & Audio Techn. Ref. Bk.* xxi. 28 It is sometimes necessary to be able to change the input impedance of a λ/2 dipole from its normal value of 73Ω without inserting a separate quarter-wave transformer. **1727–41** Chambers *Cycl.*, **Quarter-wheeling*..in the military art, is a motion whereby the front of a body of men is turned round to where the flank was. **1611** in *Cheshire Gloss.* 275 *Quarter wood att the wiche howses.

quarter ('kwɔːtə(r)), *v.* Also 4–6 quartre. [f. Quarter *sb.* AF. *quarteré* is found *c* 1350.]

1. *trans.* To cut into quarters; to divide into four equal or equivalent parts. Also with *out* (cf. 2 b). **a.** things in general.

c **1430** *Two Cookery-bks.* 18 Take a Capoun..quarter hym. *c* **1500** in *Prymer* (E.E.T.S.) 171 Take a penyworthe of hyt, and quarter hyt in fowre. *c* **1590** Marlowe *Faust.* vii, The streets..Quarter the town in four Equivalents. **1646** Sir T. Browne *Pseud. Ep.* 284 As for the divisions of the yeare, and the quartering out this remarkable standard of time [etc.]. **1735** Pope *Donne Sat.* iv. 136 He knows.. Whose place is quarter'd out, three parts in four. **1796** Mrs. Glasse *Cookery* xiv. 260 Pare and quarter your apples and take out the cores. **1860** Reade *Cloister & H.* lvi, So [to] halve their land instead of quartering it.

b. the body of a person, *esp.* of a traitor or criminal. (Cf. quots. for Hang *v.* 3, Draw *v.* 4.)

1387 Trevisa *Higden* (Rolls) VIII. 291 His body was i-quartred and i-sent into dyvers places of Engelonde. **1440** J. Shirley *Dethe K. James* 23 The said hongman smot of thare hedes, and there quartard hem. **1508** Kennedie *Flyting w. Dunbar* 416 Hang Dunbar, Quarter and draw. **1601** Shaks. *Jul. C.* III. i. 268 Infants quartered with the hands of Warre. **1723** De Foe *Col. Jack* (1840) 292 Being discovered, betrayed,..hanged, quartered, &c. **1849** Macaulay *Hist. Eng.* v. I. 614 A few..were set apart for the hideous office of quartering the captives.

transf. and *fig.* **1595** Shaks. *John* II. i. 506 Hang'd in the frowning wrinkle of her brow!—And quarter'd in her heart. **1632** Lithgow *Trav.* I. 2 The very Gospell it selfe,..is quartered, mangled, and reiected. **1824–8** Landor *Imag. Conv.* Wks. 1846 I. 259 At present the one hangs property, the other quarters it.

c. *Mech.* To fix cranks on (a shaft), to make wrist-pin holes in (a driving-wheel), a quarter of a circle apart (Knight *Dict. Mech.* 1875).

2. a. To divide into parts fewer or more than four. Also with *out*.

14.. *Sir Beues* (M.) 4239 Dede bodyes quarterrid in thre. **1552** Huloet, Quarter or trymme a garden, *deformare aream.* **1596** Spenser *F.Q.* VI. ii. 44 Clad all in gilden armes, with azure band Quartred athwart. **1599** T. M[oufet] *Silkwormes* 55 Send Witte the knife to quarter out their meate as need requires. **1627** Capt. Smith *Seaman's Gram.* xiv. 69 Quarter Bullets is..any bullet quartered in foure or eight parts. **1634** Milton *Comus* 29 This Ile..He quarters to his blu-hair'd deities. *a* **1800** *K. Malcolm & Sir Colvin* in Child *Ballads* II. 62/2 Here is a sword..Will quarter you in three.

†**b.** *to quarter out*: To mark out, outline. *Obs.*

1600 Surflet *Countrie Farme* III. xxvii. 484 The iuice [of the fig] doth constraine the skin to fall into wreathes and to quarter out a thousand shapes. **1616** Surfl. & Markh. *Country Farme* 158 You shall quarter out a bed for Leekes.

3. *Her.* **a.** To place or bear (charges or coats of arms) quarterly upon a shield; to add (another's coat) to one's hereditary arms; to place in alternate quarters *with*.

14.. *Tournam. Tottenham* 153 in Hazl. *E.P.P.* III. 89 The chefe was of a ploo mell,..Quartered with the mone liȝt. **1571** Gascoigne *Deuise of Maske* Wks. (Roxb.) I. 85 Confessing that he..bare the selfe same armes that I dyd quarter in my Scute. **1605** Camden *Rem., Rythmes* 25 King Edward the third when he first quartered the Armes of France with England. **1628** Coke *On Litt.* Pref., This faire descended Family de Littleton,..quartereth many faire Coates. **1762–71** H. Walpole *Vertue's Anecd. Paint.* (1786) I. 152 [Henry's] sacrificing the gallant earl of Surrey for quartering the arms of England, as he undoubtedly had a right to quarter them. **1854** Hawthorne *Eng. Note-bks.* (1883) I. 493 The royal banner of England, quartering the lion, the leopard, and the harp. **1880** Dixon *Windsor* III. ix. 89 Norfolk..had quartered his wife's arms.

absol. **1727–41** Chambers *Cycl.* s.v. *Quartering*, The King of Great Britain quarters with Great Britain, France, Ireland, Brunswick, &c. **1893** Cussans *Heraldry* (ed. 4) 171 Neither would their issue—being unable to quarter—be permitted to bear their maternal coat.

b. To divide (a shield) into quarters, or into any number of divisions formed by vertical and horizontal lines.

1590 Spenser *F.Q.* II. i. 18 In his silver shield He bore a bloodie Crosse that quartred all the field. **1727–41** Chambers *Cycl.*, *Counter-quartered*..denotes the escutcheon, after being quartered, to have each quarter divided again into two. **1868** Browning *Ring & Bk.* VI. 237 Our arms are those of Fiesole itself, The shield quartered with white and red.

4. a. To put (soldiers or others) into quarters; to station, place or lodge in a particular place. Also *pass.* = to have one's abode, lodging, etc.

1594 Shaks. *Rich. III*, v. iii. 34 Where is Lord Stanley quarter'd, do you know? **1665** Manley *Grotius' Low C. Warres* 221 The Duke of Parma all this Winter, quarter'd his men in the village of Brabant. **1723** De Foe *Col. Jack* (1840) 233 After this campaign I was quartered at Cremona. **1795** Wellington in Gurw. *Desp.* (1837) I. 2 The 33rd Regiment was landed and quartered at Poole. **1822** W. Irving *Braceb. Hall* i. 4, I am again quartered in the panelled chamber. **1882** B. D. W. Ramsay *Recoll. Mil. Serv.* I. i. 5 He was then quartered in Edinburgh as a lieutenant.

b. With *on*, *upon*: To impose (soldiers) upon (a householder, town, etc.), to be lodged and fed.

1683 *Apol. Prot. France* ii. 29 He quartered his Men upon those of the Protestant Religion. **1815** J. W. Croker in *C. Papers* 14 July (1884), Blucher has quartered a guard of Prussians on him. **1874** Green *Short Hist.* viii. §3. 485 Soldiers were quartered on recalcitrant boroughs.

transf. and *fig.* **1663** Butler *Hud.* I. ii. 274 He'd suck his Claws And quarter himself upon his Paws. **1714** *Spect.* No. 595 ¶6 You have Quartered all the foul Language upon me, that could be raked out of the Air of Billingsgate. **1812** L. Hunt in *Examiner* 24 Aug. 531/1 Those upon whom the Attorney-General is pleased to quarter his attentions. **1874** Green *Short Hist.* iii. §5. 139 Italian clergy were quartered on the best livings of the Church.

5. a. *intr.* To take up (one's) quarters; to stay, reside, lodge. (Freq. in 17th c.)

1581 Savile *Tacitus, Hist.* II. lxvi. (1591) 91 That they and the cohorts of Batauians should quarter together. **1624** Capt. Smith *Virginia* III. ii. 49 That night they quarterd in the woods. **1670** R. Montagu in *Buccleuch MSS.* (Hist. MSS. Comm.) I. 482 The whole army..will quarter there for some time. **1723** De Foe *Col. Jack* (1840) 240 The man in whose house I quartered was exceedingly civil to me. **1781** Hamilton *Wks.* (1886) VIII. 44, I quarter, at present, by a..warm invitation, with General Lincoln. **1863** Cowden Clarke *Shaks. Char.* x. 262 An atmosphere of manner belonging to those who have quartered in various countries.

transf. **1668** Culpepper & Cole *Barthol. Anat.* Manual I. v. 312 A remarkable Vein about the Heart..quartering on the one side, without another on the other side.

b. With *on* or *upon*. (Cf. 4 b.) ? *Obs.*

1650 Fuller *Pisgah* II. v. 122 The Canaanites quartered ..hard on the men of Asher. **1681** *Lond. Gaz.* No. 1583/4 A body of men should be sent to quarter upon the Country.

6. To give quarters to; to furnish with quarters or lodgings. ? *Obs.*

1681 W. Robertson *Phraseol. Gen.* (1693) 1040 To quarter, *hospitio accipere.* **1682** Bunyan *Holy War* (Cassell) 177 They had called his soldiers into the town [and] coveted who should quarter the most of them.

absol. **1667** *Ormonde MSS.* in *10th Rep. Hist. MSS. Comm.* App. v. 56 [Certain] inhabitants of the said towne, refuse to quarter or pay the allowances for quartering.

7. *Naut.* To assign (men) to a particular quarter on board ship; to place or station for action.

1695 T. Smith *Voy. Constantinople* in *Misc. Cur.* (1708) III. 6 The Captain quartered his Men, and the Decks were cleared. **1748** *Anson's Voy.* III. viii. 378 He had not hands enough remaining to quarter a sufficient number to each great gun. **1769** Falconer *Dict. Marine* (1780) G g ij, The marines are generally quartered on the poop and forecastle. **1809** J. Dale in *Naval Chron.* XXIV. 78 The Europeans.. had been quartered to the upper deck guns.

8. *Naut.* **a.** *intr.* To sail with the wind on the quarter, *i.e.* between beam and stern.

1627 Capt. Smith *Seaman's Gram.* vii. 31 When you goe before the wind, or quartering. **1628** Digby *Voy. Medit.* (1868) 83 Quartering with one tacke abord till you gett your chace vpon your beame. **1725** De Saumarez in *Phil. Trans.* XXXIII. 424 Sometimes sailing right before the Wind, then quartering.

b. *intr.* Of wind: To blow on a ship's quarter.

1720 De Foe *Capt. Singleton* xi. (1840) 192 She came down upon us with the wind quartering.

c. Of a sea: To strike (a ship) on the quarter.

1890 Clark Russell *Ocean Trag.* I. v. 94 The sea had quartered her and swept..along her lustrous bends.

9. *Build.* To construct (a wall or partition) with quarters of wood.

1703 T. N. *City & C. Purchaser* 278 The Walls being quarter'd and Lathed between the Timber. **1848** *Jrnl. R. Agric. Soc.* IX. II. 570 The former [circle] above the brickwork being quartered and plastered.

10. a. To range or traverse (ground, etc.) in every direction. Said esp. of dogs in search of game and of birds of prey flying over their hunting grounds.

1700 J. Collier *2nd Def. Short View* 118 He has rang'd over a great deal of Ground, and Quarter'd the Fields of Greece and Italy. **1760–72** H. Brooke *Fool of Qual.* (1809) IV. 139 They crossed and quartered the country at pleasure. **1766** Pennant *Brit. Zool.* (1768) II. 235 Who pass over the fields and quarter the ground as a setting dog. **1788** Wolcott (P. Pindar) *Sir J. Banks & Emp. of Morocco* Wks. 1812 II. 94 Just like a Pointer quartering well his ground. **1873** Tristram *Moab* viii. 143 To traverse and quarter these ruins is a good day's work. **1888** *Antipod. Notes* 6 Two boats are..quartering the sea, as a..pointer quarters a turnip-field. **1919** T. A. Coward *Birds Brit. Isles* I. 309 Sharing with other Harriers the habit of closely and diligently quartering the ground with buoyant easy flight, the Hen-Harrier more frequently interrupts its progress by hovering. **1946** D. C. Peattie *Road of Naturalist* iii. 39 The hawks and the falcons quartered the dazzling playa. **1976** L. Brown *Brit. Birds of Prey* x. 121 When returning to the roost in the evening they [*sc.* Montagu's harriers] often travel straight and quarter the ground much less than they would when hunting.

b. *intr.* To range to and fro; to shift from point to point.

1857 Hughes *Tom Brown* II. v, They quarter over the ground again and again, Tom always on the defensive. **1873** G. C. Davies *Mount. & Mere* x. 76 The hounds quartered to and fro.

c. *intr.* To drive from side to side of the road.

In quot. 1834 app. a misinterpretation of sense 11.

1834 De Quincey *Autob. Sk.* Wks. 1862 XIV. 296 The postillion..was employed..eternally, in *quartering, i.e.*, in crossing from side to side, according to the casualties of the ground. **1886** Elworthy *W. Somerset Word-bk.*, *Quarter* to drive uphill in such a way that the horse crosses the road backwards and forwards so as to diminish the gradient.

d. *intr.* To move in a slanting direction.

1883 'Mark Twain' *Life on Mississippi* iii. 51, I see a black something floating on the water away off to stabboard [*sic*] and quartering behind us. **1894** *Outing* (U.S.) XXIV. 387/1 The bird quartered past the Judge who had only cut a bunch of feathers from it. **1895** *Ibid.* XXVI. 401/1 We..changed our direction so as to 'quarter' by them. **1938** M. K. Rawlings *Yearling* xx. 260 His bear was quartering from him, but he was able to draw a bead on the left cheek from the rear.

11. a. *intr.* To drive a cart or carriage so that the right and left wheels are on (two of) the quarters of a road, with a rut between. Also, of a horse: To walk with the feet thus placed; hence, to walk in front of the wheel. Also *fig.*

This is also the sense of F. *cartayer*, Walloon *quateler* (Littré), which are etymologically related to the Engl. word.

1800 Tuke *Agric.* 300 Two-horse carts should be drawn by the horses abreast..by which means they would be enabled to quarter or stride the ruts. **1806–7** J. Beresford

Miseries Hum. Life (1826) II. xxvii, A rugged narrow lane in which the ruts refuse to fit your wheels and yet there is no room to quarter. **1824** C. A. Bowles *Let.* 24 Jan. in E. Dowden *Corr. Southey* (1881) 48, I keep quartering, or trying to quarter, for a yard or so, and then down goes the wheel into the old groove. I cannot keep out of blank verse. **1847** *Jrnl. R. Agric. Soc.* VIII. II. 277 The carting off the cabbages..is done with a quarter-cart, as it is termed in Suffolk, having the shafts so placed that the horse walks before the right hand wheel; in other words, it 'quarters'. **1859** Mrs. Gaskell *Round the Sofa* 20 We had to quarter, as Randal called it, nearly all the way along the deep-rutted miry lanes. **1879-** In dialect glossaries (Shropsh., Chesh., etc.).

b. *intr.* To drive to the side in order to allow another vehicle to pass. (Cf. QUART *v.*[2])

1849 De Quincey *Eng. Mail Coach* Wks. 1862 IV. 334 Every creature that met us would rely upon us for quartering. **1866** Geo. Eliot *F. Holt* I Elderly gentlemen in pony-chaises, quartering nervously to make way [etc.].

c. To set (the shafts of a cart) so that the horse walks in front of one of the wheels.

1847 *Jrnl. R. Agric. Soc.* VIII. II. 268 The shafts are quartered, so that the horses (usually two) walk in the furrow followed by one wheel.

12. *intr.* Of the moon: To begin a fresh quarter. Also with *in*.

1789 G. Keate *Pelew Isl.* 227 They would have bad weather until the moon quartered. **1833** Marryat *P. Simple* (1863) 157 The new moon's quartered in with foul weather.

quarterage ('kwɔːtərɪdʒ). Also 4 qwarter-, 5 quater-, 6 quartrage, -errage, querterage, 6-8 quartridge, (6 -redge), 7-8 -eridge, (7 -eridg, 8 -erridge). [f. QUARTER *sb.* + -AGE; perh. a. OF. *quarterage* (Godef.).]

1. A contribution, subscription, tax, or other charge paid by a person every quarter; a quarterly payment made by one.

1389 in *Eng. Gilds* (1870) 3 Which wardeins schul gadere þe qwarterage of bretheren & sustren. **1452** in Gross *Gild Merch.* II. 69 All maner fynnys, amercyments & quarteragys. **1529** in *Vicary's Anat.* (1888) App. xiv. 251 So Alweys that the sayde quarterage be lawfullye demaunded. **1602** Dekker *Satirom.* Wks. 1873 I. 262 You shall not brag that your Vizeroyes or Tributorie kings have done homage to you, or paide quarterage. **1708** *Brit. Apollo* No. 42. I Most of our subscribers having paid their Quarterridges [etc.]. **1795** Burke *Tracts Popery Laws* Wks. 1842 II. 434 They trade and work in their own native towns as aliens, paying, as such, quarterage, and other charges and impositions. **1887** *Times* 20 Jan. 4/3 The plaintiff had not paid his quarterages.

2. A sum paid to, or received by, a person every quarter; a quarter's wages, allowance, pension, etc.

1423 *Leet Bk.* in Sharp *Cov. Myst.* (1825) 207 Thei shall have ij men of every ward, every quarter, to help them to gather per Quarterage. *c* **1515** *Cocke Lorell's B.* 4 Than came a pardoner with his boke, His quarterage of euery man he toke. **1590** Tarlton *News Purgat.* (1844) 82 He, being then bare of pence, because his quarterage was not come in. **1666** Pepys *Diary* 8 Jan., My uncle Thomas with me to receive his quarterage. **1727** Swift *Richmond Lodge & Marble Hill*, An idle Rogue, who spends his Quartridge In tippling at the Dog and Partridge. **1830** D'Israeli *Chas. I*, III. xvii. 370 A half-starved Clerk, eked out his lean quarterage, by these merry perquisites. **1892** *Cornh. Mag.* July 27 He must wait till his new quarterage came before he could pay.

3. Quarters, place of abode; quartering of troops, or the expense of this. *rare.*

1577 Holinshed *Chron., Scot.* I. 485 The Scots that lay in Kelso, and other places keeping their quarterage on the bordures. **1647** in Picton *L'pool Munic. Rec.* (1883) I. 143 Agreed that a Ley..be imposed upon the Towne for payeing of the Quarterage of the horse. *Ibid.*, These burdens of quarterage. **1841** *Tait's Mag.* VIII. 562 Common sense is driven out of her native quarterage in the brain. **1873** O'Curry *Lect. Ancient Irish* I. xvi. 336 Any noble residence at which they [great stewards] intended to claim the free quarterage due to their official dignity.

4. *attrib.*, as *quarterage-bill*, *-book*, *-day*, *-fee*.

1533 in Sharp *Cov. Myst.* (1825) 214 Paid to the mynstrell at quarterage day..viijd. **1692** *Lond. Gaz.* No. 2799/4 A large Folio Book..called the Carmens Quarteridg-Book. **1771-2** *Ess. fr. Batchelor* (1773) II. 192 The Quarterage-bill, like all others, must pass through both houses of parliament. **1894** *Times* 19 Oct. 6/2 The 'quarterage' fees of 4*s.* per annum per member.

'quarterback, *sb.* **1.** *Austral.* and *N.Z.* (See quots.)

1891 [see COME-BACK *sb.*[2] 4]. **1940** E. C. Studholme *Te Waimate* 96 Using Merino rams on the cross-bred ewes, the progeny being known as Quarter Backs.

2. *U.S. Football.* **a.** A player stationed between the forwards and half-backs by whom the team's play is usu. co-ordinated and directed. Usu. in modern practice, a player lining up behind the centre of an offensive team, who calls the signal to initiate a play and receives the ball when it is snapped back by the centre. (See also quot. 1895).

1895 *Westm. Gaz.* 8 Nov. 2/1 Your 'quarter-backs', as half-backs were then called, waited for the ball to roll out. **1899** W. Camp in Badminton *Football* xxii. 286 Seven rushers or forwards,..a quarter-back, who stands just behind this line; two half-backs [etc.]. **1947** *Sun* (Baltimore) 15 Aug. 12/6 He is a stocky man who..has the build of a quarterback. **1979** *Arizona Daily Star* 5 Aug. c. 9/1 Oakland quarterback Ken Stabler..played the first quarter and part of the second.

b. *transf.* A supporter or critic of a football team. Also ***downtown quarterback***, an interested supporter of the home team; ***grandstand quarterback*** (in quot. *fig.*); ***Monday morning quarterback***, one who engages in reductive 'post-mortem' criticism of a game; also *fig.*

1932 B. Wood *What Price Football* vi. 100 A kind of sportswriter known to football players and coaches as a 'Monday morning quarterback'... Not content with reporting the game..the writer must analyze it. **1947** *Collier's* 15 Nov. 17 (*heading*) Penn's downtown quarterbacks were a gloomy lot when George Munger became grid coach. **1949** *Ibid.* 19 Nov. 18/3 The quarterbacks in the stands consider Pop Warner's system.. obsolete. **1976** President Ford in *Sunday Sun* (Baltimore) 10 Oct. K. 4/4 Somebody who sits in Washington D.C., 18 months after the Mayaguez incident, can be a very good grandstand quarterback.

c. *fig.* One who directs or masterminds an operation; a leader.

1961 in Webster. **1968** *Globe & Mail* (Toronto) 10 July 27/5 Van Burkleo is an original-thinking quarterback who can run his own show. **1971** *Sci. Amer.* Aug. 38/1 It was my privilege to be working in Colombia as 'quarterback' of a team of investigators. **1978** *Guardian Weekly* 1 Jan. 18/1 King Juan Carlos I, Franco's 39-year-old successor, and Premier Adolfo Suarez, the monarch's 44-year-old political quarterback.

3. *attrib.* and *Comb.* (sense 2), as **quarterback club**, an association of supporters actively interested in promoting their team's success; **quarterback sack** = SACK *sb.*[1] 1 j; **quarterback sneak** (see quot. 1966).

1948 *Life* 1 Nov. 110/2 Factory workers as well as merchant princes belong to the Quarterback Club, an organization of last-ditch rooters who gather..to put questions to the Ohio State head coach..and to see movies of the team's latest games. **1951** *Sun* (Baltimore) 9 Oct. 21/1 Special funds contributed by..downtown quarterback clubs. **1974** *Plain Dealer* (Cleveland, Ohio) 26 Oct. 6-D/2 Alzado..leads the defense in quarterback sacks with four. **1923** J. Wilce *Football* viii. 105 *Quarterback sneak*,..R. takes the ball from centre directly, pauses a moment as the line charges forward, then sneaks through any opening that may appear between the guards. **1947** *Time* 3 Nov. 74/3 The story Bob liked best was Dad's quarterback sneak. **1966** J. R. Winter *Lang. Pro Football* 132 *Quarterback sneak*, play where quarterback moves straight ahead into line behind charge of his center and guards immediately after taking snap.

'quarterback, *v. U.S. Football.* [f. the sb.] *trans.* **a.** To play quarterback for (a team); to direct as quarterback.

1948 *Sun* (Baltimore) 13 Jan. 13/5 McCann..has 'quarterbacked' the LaSalle team to nine consecutive victories. **1950** *Life* 9 Oct. 66/2 Bob calmly quarterbacked the team to its first victory. **1972** J. Mosedale *Football* v. 62 Detroit, coached by Buddy Parker and quarterbacked by Bobby Layne, exhibited a strange mastery. **1979** *Tucson* (Arizona) *Citizen* 20 Sept. 11 D/1 He used to..quarterback the Sun Devils from 1974 to 1977.

b. *fig.* To direct or co-ordinate (an operation).

1952 *Britannica Bk. of Year* 666/2 *Quarterback*, ..(extension of *n.* in U.S. football terminology). To direct (1945). **1971** *Daily Colonist* (Victoria, B.C.) 26 Oct. 1/7 Bush..quarterbacked what UN observers regarded as Washington's worst diplomatic defeat. **1976** *Guardian Weekly* 7 Mar. 18/3 Relations were particularly strained after the 1972 election success, which Wehner felt he had quarterbacked without credit.

So **'quarterbacking** *vbl. sb.*, the action of playing or directing as quarterback; also *fig.*, esp. ***Monday morning quarterbacking*** (see QUARTERBACK *sb.* 2 b).

1947 *Time* 17 Nov. 75/2 (*heading*) Quarterbacking by telephone. **1948** *Sat. Even. Post* 18 Sept. 24/3 There also should be less of the Western Union quarterbacking from the bench, which frequently backfired in the face of the masterminds. **1950** *Sport Life* Feb. 9/1 Royal, nominated by the coach to take over for Mitchell at the quarterbacking post. **1960** *Guardian* 9 May 6/6 The realities of sheer, hard political quarter-backing. **1966** 'H. B. Taylor' *Triumvirate* iv. 30 There was the usual Thursday morning quarterbacking over what I had put in the paper and how I'd put it in. **1972** *Science* 9 June 1083/2 But Monday-morning quarterbacking is an easy sport. **1977** *N.Y. Rev. Bks.* 13 Oct. 14/3 Despite President Ford's admonition against 'Monday morning quarterbacking' about presidential responsibility for assassination plots, Rockefeller has said.. that there was 'White House knowledge and/or approval of all major undertakings'.

quarter-cart: see QUARTER *v.* 11 (quot. 1847).

quarter-cleft, *a.* and *sb.* Chiefly *dial.* Also 7 -cliff, 9 -clift. [See CLEFT *sb.* and *ppl. a.*]

A. *adj.* (See quots.) *rare*[−0].

1850 Ogilvie, *Quarter-cleft Rod*, a rod cleft at one end, the cleft extending to one-fourth of its length. **1882** *Ibid.*, *Quarter-cleft*, said of timber cut from the centre to the circumference.

B. *sb.* **1.** Wood cleft in four; quartered wood; also, one of the pieces produced by cleaving in four.

1641 Best *Farm. Bks.* (Surtees) 15 Wee gette the biggest of [the willows] riven with iron wedges into quarter-cliffe. *Ibid.*, Shorte forke-shaftes, made of seasoned ashe, and quarter cliffe. **1887** *Scott. Leader* 21 Sept. 6 A large stick known in Tipperary as a 'quarter-clift'.

2. A slightly-crazed or 'half-cracked' person.

1831 *Fraser's Mag.* IV. 327 A mere nincompoop, or quarter-cliff or what else you will that implies feebleness of intellect. **1856** *Chambers's Jrnl.* V. 139 (*Ulster Proverbs*, etc.) An eccentric person..is said..to 'want a square of being round'. The next degree of aberration constitutes a 'quarter clift'. **1880** *Antrim & Down Gloss.*, *Quarter cleft*, a crazy person.

quarter-co(u)sen, -cozin, corrupt varr. of CATER-COUSIN.

1656 in Blount *Glossogr.* **1681** in W. Robertson *Phraseol. General* (1693) 1040.

quarter-day. [QUARTER *sb.* 8 a.] One of the four days fixed by custom as marking off the quarters of the year, on which tenancy of houses usually begins and ends, and the payment of rent and other quarterly charges falls due.

In England and Ireland the quarter-days are Lady Day (March 25), Midsummer Day (June 24), Michaelmas (Sept. 29), and Christmas (Dec. 25). The name is also sometimes applied to the Scottish terms of Candlemas (Feb. 2), Whitsunday (May 15), Lammas (Aug. 1), and Martinmas (Nov. 11).

1480 in *Eng. Gilds* 315 Ther shall be iiij quarter dayys that euery Brother..shall assemble at oure comen hall. **1566** Haryngton in *Leisure H.* (1884) 630/2 All which sommes shal be duly paide each quarter-day. **1596** *Edw. III*, III. ii, What, is it quarter-day, that you remove, And carry bag and baggage too? **1660** Fuller *Mixt Contempl.* (1841) 197 A gentleman had two tenants, whereof one,..repaired to his landlord on the quarter-day. **1767** Blackstone *Comm.* II. 124 Rent..for the occupation of the land since the last quarter day. **1805** Southey *Ball. & Metr. T.* Poet. Wks. VI. 80, I was idle, and quarter-day came on, And I had not the rent in store. **1840** Dickens *Barn. Rudge* xiii, The twenty-fifth of March,..one of those unpleasant epochs termed quarter-days.

fig. **1641** Brome *Joviall Crew* II. Wks. 1873 III. 382 If ever any just or charitable Steward was commended, sure thou shalt be at the last Quarter-day. **1851** Thackeray *Eng. Hum.* ii. (1876) 174 [They] had..a happy quarter-day coming round for them.

'quarter-deck, *sb. Naut.* †**a.** Originally, a smaller deck situated above the HALF-DECK (q.v.), covering about a quarter of the vessel. *Obs.* **b.** In later use: That part of the upper or spar-deck which extends between the stern and after-mast, and is used as a promenade by the superior officers or cabin-passengers. Also *transf.*

1627 Capt. Smith *Seaman's Gram.* ii. 6 The halfe Decke is from the maine mast to the steareage, and the quarter Decke from that to the Masters Cabin called the round house, w[ch] is the vtmost of all. **1667** Denham *Direct. Paint.* I. 55 Each Captain from his Quarter-deck commands. **1748** *Anson's Voy.* I. iii. 29 Many of the principal Officers were on the quarter-deck, indulging in the freshness of the night air. **1840** R. H. Dana *Bef. Mast* xxiii. 67 The chief mate walking the quarter-deck, and keeping a general supervision. **1884** Pae *Eustace* 67 I'd have you to remember that you are not on the quarter-deck just now. **1976** *National Trust* Autumn 17/3 Still unchanged are the 'quarter-deck', a path laid so that the children could reach the river without getting muddy [etc.].

fig. **1853** Lytton *My Novel* I. x, Too old a sailor to think that the State..should admit Jack upon quarterdeck.

attrib. **1712** E. Cooke *Voy. S. Sea* 167 Each Ship is to answer the other with a Quarter-Deck Gun. **1797** Nelson in A. Duncan *Life* (1806) 42 A Spanish officer looked over the quarter-deck rail. **1828** P. Cunningham *N.S. Wales* (ed. 3) II. 299 When surgeon of a brig of war, my quarter-deck promenade was confined to eight paces. **1840** R. H. Dana *Bef. Mast* ix. 19 The quarter-deck dignity and eloquence of the captain. **1850** H. Melville *White-Jacket* xxiii. 117 See, White Jacket, all round they have *shipped their quarter-deck faces again*... I afterward learned that this was an old man-of-war's-man's phrase, expressive of the facility with which a sea-officer falls back upon all the severity of his dignity, after a temporary suspension of it. **1893** W. C. Russell *Emigrant Ship* I. iv. 53, I saluted him with a quarter-deck flourish. **1927** H. D. Capper *Aft —— from Hawsehole* p. xii, There are close upon three thousand naval officers of 'hawsehole origin'..who are, or have been, performing fine quarter-deck service for their country.

Hence **'quarter-decker, -deckish** (see quots.).

1867 Smyth *Sailors' Word-bk.*, *Quarter-Deckers*, those officers more remarkable for etiquette than for a knowledge of seamanship. *Ibid.*, *Quarter-Deckish*, punctilious, severe. **1889** A. Conan Doyle *Micah Clarke* 244 It's your blue-coated, gold-braided..quarter-deckers that talk of canes.

'quarter-deck, *v.* [f. the sb.] *intr.* To walk up and down as on a quarter-deck. So **'quarter-decking** *vbl. sb.*

1901 E. F. Benson *Luck of Vails* xviii. 207 He continued quarter-decking about the room for a few times in silence. **1913** Mrs. H. Ward *Coryston Family* viii. 164 The quarter-decking began again; and Lester waited patiently on a slowly subsiding frenzy. **1924** Kipling *Debits & Credits* 87 There was Potiphar..quarter-decking serenely below the Pebble-ridge. **1954** 'M. Coles' *Not for Export* i. 20 'This it is', said Spelmann, swinging round at each turn of his quarter-decking..'to work hard and be successful.'

quartere, obs. form of QUARTER *sb.*

quartered ('kwɔːtəd), *ppl. a.* [f. QUARTER *v.*]

1. Cut into quarters; divided in four; *spec.* of quarter-cleft timber, which being afterwards cut into planks shows the grain to advantage.

1502 *Priv. Purse Exp. Eliz. of York* (1830) 74 For two quartred bourdes with vysys. **1601** Yarington *Two Lament. Traj.* IV. iii. in Bullen *O. Pl.* IV, Bull always strips all quartered traitors quite. **1626** Capt. Smith *Accid. Yng. Sea-men* 32 Musquet shot, Colyuer shot, quartred shot. **1719** London & Wise *Compl. Gard.* 187 The most convenient..is a Lattice of quarter'd Wood, or Heart of Oak. **1805** Wordsworth *Prelude* II. 83 Through three divisions of the quartered year. **1854** P. B. St. John *Amy Moss* 21 These palisades were formed of quartered oak.

b. *Her.* Of a shield or arms: Divided or arranged quarterly. Of a cross: Quarterly-pierced.

1486 *Bk. St. Albans, Her.* D ij b, Certan armys ther be quarterit and irrasit as here apperis, the Wich..ar called quarterit armys irrasit. **1864** BOUTELL *Her. Hist. & Pop.* xvi. 235 He assumed the quartered arms on his accession to the ducal dignity. **1893** CUSSANS *Heraldry* (ed. 4) 166 The earliest known example of a quartered shield occurs on the monument of Eleanor..wife of Edward the First.

†**c.** Of a building: Cruciform. *Obs. rare*$^{-1}$.

1591 PERCIVALL *Sp. Dict., Cruzero en edeficio*, a kinde of quartered building, *Structura quadrivialis.*

2. *Mil.* Lodged in or belonging to quarters.

1611 SHAKS. *Cymb.* IV. iv. 18 When they heare their Roman horses neigh, Behold their quarter'd Fires. **1824** WIFFEN *Tasso* I. vi, To breme winter's wing The quartered hosts give place.

3. Belonging to a quarter or part of the horizon.

1671 MILTON *P.R.* IV. 202 And on the earth Nations besides from all the quarter'd winds.

4. Having quarters of a specified character.

The sense in first quot. is not clear: the F. orig. has *quarrez* 'square'.

[**1481** CAXTON *Godefroy* 286 His armes grete and wel quartred.] **1641** BEST *Farm Bks.* (Surtees) 5 The lambes that forbeare grasse the longest prove..the straightest, and best quartered. **1891** *Cent. Dict.* s.v., A short-quartered horse. *Ibid.*, Low-quartered shoes.

5. *Carpentry.* Made of quarters.

1842–59 GWILT *Archit.* (ed. 4) §2024 The framework of timber used for dividing the internal parts of a house into rooms is called a partition or quartered partition.

quarterer (ˈkwɔːtərə(r)). [f. QUARTER *v.* + -ER[1].] One who quarters, in various senses of the verb; *esp.* one who takes up quarters, a lodger. Also, a quartering bird (sense 10 d of QUARTER *v.*).

1648 C. WALKER *Hist. Independ.* I. 66 If these quarterers offer violence..they are protected. **1681** W. ROBERTSON *Phraseol. Gen.* (1693) 1040 A quarterer or hang-man. *a* **1802** *Dk. Athole's Nurse* ix. in Child *Ballads* IV. 152 Had you a quarterer here last night,..We are come to clear his lawing. **1881** GREGOR *Folk-lore* 57 Now and again there was a quarterer [a class of beggar] in the family. **1892** W. W. GREENER *Breech-Loader* vii. 209 When the shooter facing No. 2 trap gets a quarterer to the left from No. 5.

†**ˈquarteret.** *Obs. rare.* [f. QUARTER *sb.* 14 or 15 + -ET[1].] A small quarter or allotted space.

1598 BARRET *Theor. Warres* V. iv, The 3000 launciers are deuided and allodged into 6 quarterets. *Ibid.* Gloss. 252 *Quarteret*, is the diminutiue of quarter.

quarter-evil. 1. = QUARTER-ILL.

a **1722** LISLE *Observ. Husb.* (1757) 290 The joint-murrain in calves..by others is called the quarter-evil. **1800** TUKE *Agric.* 259 A complaint very prevalent amongst calves, when a year old, is called the..quarter evil..The calves are first seized in one quarter, and are lame. **1841** DICK *Man. Vet. Science* (1862) 148 In two or three hours the animal is dead, from the Quarter-evil. **1896** *Allbutt's Syst. Med.* I. 548 Rabbits, which are relatively refractory to quarter-evil.

2. [QUARTER *sb.* 25.] An inflammation of part of the udder (*Syd. Soc. Lex.* 1897).

quarterfoil, †**-foyle,** erron. ff. QUATREFOIL.

quarter-gallery. *Naut.* [QUARTER *sb.* 22.]

1. A kind of balcony with windows, projecting from the quarter of a large vessel; cf. GALLERY 2 d.

1769 in FALCONER *Dict. Marine* (1789) D ij. **1796** NELSON 10 Mar. in Nicolas *Disp.* (1846) VII. xxxvii, The very heavy gales..carried away the starboard quarter-gallery. **1830** SCOTT *Demonol.* x. 363 He saw that the captain had thrown himself into the sea from the quarter-gallery. **1836** MARRYAT *Midsh. Easy* xiii, Pulled them out of the quarter gallery. **1867** [see *quarter-badge*, in QUARTER *sb.* 30].

attrib. **1797** NELSON Feb. in Nicolas *Disp.* (1845) II. 342 A soldier..having broke the upper quarter-gallery window.

2. A small projection on the quarter of a ship, containing lavatory accommodation (*Cent. Dict.*).

quarter-guard. *Mil.* [QUARTER *sb.* 14 c.] A small guard mounted in front of each battalion in a camp, at about eighty paces distant.

1741 S. SPEED in *Buccleuch MSS.* (Hist. MSS. Comm.) I. 399 Col. Cockran's and Brigadier Lowther's Regiments..were not able to give more than nine men for their quarter-guard. **1758** WATSON *Milit. Dict.* (ed. 5) s.v. *Guard*, Quarter Guards are more for preserving the Peace and Tranquillity within the Regiment..than for a Security against the Enemy. **1844** *Regul. & Ord. Army* 32 On these occasions, the Tents of the Quarter Guards are to be struck. **1892** R. KIPLING *Ball., East & West* 89 When they drew to the Quarter-Guard, full twenty swords flew clear.

quarter-gunner. *Naut.* An officer subordinate to the gunner, whom he assists in all departments of his work (cf. quots. 1769, 1846).

1627 CAPT. SMITH *Sea-man's Gram.* viii. 35 The Master Gunner hath charge of the ordnance..the rest of the Gunners, or quarter Gunners to receive their charge from him. **1702** *Royal Declar.* 1 June in *Lond. Gaz.* No. 3815/2 The Trumpeter, Quarter Gunners, Carpenters Crew [etc.]. **1769** FALCONER *Dict. Marine* (1780) s.v., The number of quarter-gunners in any ship is always in proportion to the number of her artillery, one quarter-gunner being allowed to every four cannon. **1804** *Med. Jrnl.* XII. 476 One of his Majesty's frigates, on board of which her husband served in the quality of a quarter-gunner. **1846** A. YOUNG *Naut. Dict.* 242 *Quarter-Gunner*, in a ship of war, an able seaman, generally one of the gunner's crew, appointed to act as his assistant under the gunner's mates.

quarter-horse. *U.S.* A small stocky horse belonging to a variety recognized as a breed in 1941 and noted for agility and speed over short distances. Also *attrib.*

1839 *Spirit of Times* 11 May 114/3 *Martha Malone*..was evidently short of work, not fine enough drawn, and too much on the quarter-horse order for a hard race under a hot sun and over a dusty track. **1845** T. J. GREEN *Jrnl. Texian Exped.* x. 136 Nausea which caused me to break for the door like a quarter-horse to relieve my distress. **1887** *Outing* May 115/1 You would not think him a quarter-horse for he looks like a clumsy sleepy old plug. **1907** S. E. WHITE *Arizona Nights* I. i. 11 A quarter-hoss couldn't have beat me to that shack. **1944** *Sun* (Baltimore) 16 May 15/3 Cross-breeding..has developed a new type of quarter horse with a thoroughbred strain. **1954** *Ibid.* 4 Jan. 16/4 An honest to goodness cowboy who runs with a football like a quarterhorse chasing a steer. **1970** *Telegraph* (Brisbane) 17 Dec. 12/3 In America..quarter horse racing is a popular sport. **1973** 'I. DRUMMOND' *Jaws of Watchdog* xvi. 211 Holman Walker was a quarter-horse man and bred Appaloosa ponies..on his ranch. **1979** *Sunset* Apr. 6/2 The horse that helped tame the West—the quarterhorse—is still popular for its versatility and beauty.

quarter-ill. An inflammatory disease of cattle and sheep (*symptomatic anthrax*), causing putrefaction in one or more of the quarters. Called also *quarter-evil, black quarter*, etc.

1797 BAILEY & GULLEY *View Agric. Northumb.* 130 The loss of lambs is sometimes very considerable..from..the 'quarter-ill'. **1834** YOUATT *Cattle* 362 The first symptoms are those of quarter ill. **1855** STEPHENS *Book Farm* (ed. 2) II. 185 Another effect of the same febrile affection in calves in autumn is the quarter ill or evil. **1881** GREGOR *Folk-lore* 186 When the quarter-ill made its appearance [etc.].

quartering (ˈkwɔːtərɪŋ), *vbl. sb.* [f. QUARTER *v.* + -ING[1].] The action of the verb.

1. Division into four equal parts; also, division in general.

1610 W. FOLKINGHAM *Art of Survey* I. ix. 23 The quartering of the sweard of Ant-hils, casting their ballas't, and playning their Plots for pasture. **1694** *Phil. Trans.* XVIII. 70 The halving, trisecting, quartering, &c. is performed by extracting the Square Root,..&c. of the Terms. **1727–41** [see QUARTERIZATION]. **1895** *Pall Mall Gaz.* 18 Jan. 10/3 Even in 'quartering'—the term for breaking up the great nodules of flint—it is not muscle, but eye, that tells.

2. *Her.* The dividing of a shield into quarters; the marshalling or bringing in of various coats upon one shield, to denote the alliances of one family with the heiresses of others.

1592 WYRLEY *Armorie* 4 An other thing that is amisse..is the quartering of many marks in one shield, coate, or banner. **1595** *Blanchardyn* ii. (1890) 15 Then questioned he with his Master, of the blazonry of armes, and yᵉ quartering of these coates. **1605** CAMDEN *Rem.* (1636) 225 Quartering of Coates, beganne, first..in Spaine in the Armes of Castile and Leon. **1727–41** CHAMBERS *Cycl.* s.v., Quartering, in heraldry, the act of dividing a coat into four or more quarters..by parting, couping, &c. *Ibid.*, Colombiere reckons twelve sorts of quarterings. **1893** CUSSANS *Her.* (ed. 3) 166 Quartering..was not generally adopted until the end of the Fourteenth Century. The manner in which various coats are brought in, and marshalled by Quartering [etc.].

b. *pl.* The various coats marshalled upon a shield; rarely *sing.*, one of these coats.

1719 ASHMOLE *Berkshire* II. 214 A Surcoat..of the Quarterings impaled with Fetiplace. **1763** C. JOHNSTON *Reverie* II. 55, I have nine quarterings more than he. **1826** DISRAELI *Viv. Grey* VI. iv, He did nothing but..think of the quarterings of his immaculate shield. **1879** GEO. ELIOT *Theo. Such* ii. 42 Some of them..belong to families with many quarterings.

transf. **1833** MARRYAT *P. Simple* (1863) 229 The pride of colour is very great in the West Indies, and they have as many quarterings as a German prince in his coat of arms.

3. The assigning of quarters to a person; the action of taking up quarters; †a place in which one is or may be quartered.

1625 BP. MOUNTAGU *App. Cæsar* xviii. 236 Heaven..is not..so narrowed..that there cannot bee divers Designations, Regions, Habitations, Mansions, or Quarterings there. **1747** H. WALPOLE *Lett.* (1846) II. 177 A motion for inquiring into useless places and quarterings.

b. *spec.* The billeting of soldiers; the fact of having soldiers quartered upon one; the provision of quarters for soldiers.

1646 SIR E. NICHOLAS in *N. Papers* (Camden) 68 Your Honours frends at Winterborne are well, but much oppressed with quarteringe. **1667** *Ormonde MSS.* in *10th Rep. Hist. MSS. Comm.* App. v. 58 Your petitioner was heretofore charged with the quartering of two private souldiers. **1705** *Lond. Gaz.* No. 4098/2 The Inhabitants..much impoverished by the Quartering of Soldiers. **1867** SMILES *Huguenots Eng.* xii. (1880) 205 In anticipation of the quartering of the dragoons on the family, his wife had gone into concealment.

4. *Build.* **a.** The placing or using of quarters in construction. **b.** Work formed of quarters. **c.** Wood in the form, or of the size, of quarters.

1703 T. N. *City & C. Purchaser* 232 Quartering..signifies the putting in of Quarters. Sometimes 'tis us'd to signifie the Quarters themselves. **1825** J. NICHOLSON *Operat. Mechanic* 580 The braces should be rated..at a superior price to that of the quarterings. **1854** *Jrnl. R. Agric. Soc.* XV. 255 Farms..built of quartering and weather boarding.

5. Driving on the quarters of a road.

1815 SCOTT *Paul's Lett.* (1839) 207 The French postilions ..contrived, by dint of quartering and tugging, to drag us safe through. **1825** C. M. WESTMACOTT *Eng. Spy* I. 313 No ruts or quarterings now.

6. The moon's passage from one quarter to another; also = QUARTER 8 b.

1854 L. TOMLINSON tr. *Arago's Astron.* 67 Changes of weather are not more frequent at the moon's quarterings than at any other period. **1880** L. WALLACE *Ben-Hur* 234 Before the new moon..passes into its next quartering.

7. *attrib.* and *Comb.*, as ***quartering-block, -knife***; **quartering-belt**, a belt connecting pulleys which have their axles at right angles to each other (Knight *Dict. Mech.* 1875); **quartering-hammer**, a steel-hammer with which the rough masses of flint are shaped for flaking (*ibid.*); **quartering-machine**, a machine for boring the wrist-pin holes in driving-wheels a quarter of a circle apart (*ibid.*); †**quartering-money**, money paid in lieu of giving quarters to soldiers.

1688 in Wodrow *Hist. Ch. Scot.* (1721) I. 283 Exacting Cess or Quartering-money for more Soldiers than were actually present. **1818** COBBETT *Pol. Reg.* XXXIII. 425 Why do they..resort to gags, dungeons, halters, axes, and quartering-knives? **1855** MACAULAY *Hist. Eng.* xii. III. 218 Those who were doomed to the gallows and the quartering block.

quartering (ˈkwɔːtərɪŋ), *ppl. a.* [f. QUARTER *v.* + -ING[2].] That quarters, in senses of the vb.

1591 SHAKS. *1 Hen. VI*, IV. ii. 11 You tempt the fury of my three attendants, Leane Famine, quartering Steele, and climbing Fire. **1692** *Capt. Smith's Seaman's Gram.* I. xvi. 76 *The Ship goes Lasking, Quartering, Veering, or Large*; are terms of the same signification, viz. that she neither goes by a Wind nor before the Wind, but betwixt both. **1702–11** *Milit. & Sea Dict.* (ed. 4) 11, *Quartering*, is when a Gun lies so, and may be so travers'd, that it will shoot on the same Line, or Point of the Compass as the Quarter bears. **1765** *Museum Rusticum* IV. 341 The track was just of a proper breadth for post-chaises and all quartering carriages to run in. **1769** FALCONER *Dict. Marine* (1789), *Vent Largue*, a large, or quartering wind. **1860** MAURY *Phys. Geog. Sea* (Low) xx. §815 Through the former [ocean] the wind is aft; through the latter quartering. **1893** *Times* 13 June 12/1 Sheets trimmed for a quartering breeze.

†**quarteriˈzation.** *Obs. rare*$^{-0}$. (See quot.)

1727–41 CHAMBERS *Cycl., Quarterization, Quartering*, part of the punishment of a traitor, by dividing his body into four quarters.

quarter-jack.

1. [JACK *sb.*[1] 6.] A jack of the clock which strikes the quarters.

1604 MIDDLETON *Father Hubbard's T.* Wks. (Bullen) VIII. 54 The quarter-jacks in Paul's, that are up with their elbows four times an hour. **1771** [see JACK *sb.*[1] 6]. **1874** T. HARDY *Far fr. Mad. Crowd* I. xvi. 190 A little canopy with a quarter-jack and small bell beneath it. **1971** *Country Life* 10 June 1444/3, I was fortunate in being on the spot to take this photograph when the Quarter Jack was brought down ..for repairs.

2. [JACK *sb.*[7]] A jack-boot cut down.

1809 A. *Sir Frantic the Reformer* 75 His first born Long with these boots did's shanks adorn, Until..He made them into quarter-jacks.

3. [JACK *sb.*[1]] *Mil. slang.* = QUARTERMASTER 2 a.

1930 G. MCMUNN *Behind Scenes in Many Wars* xiv. 300 Fresh caviare..annoyed our men when they got a ration of it and complained of 'that black jam, what the quarter-jack had said was fish'.

ˈquarterland. A certain division of land in the Isle of Man, originally the fourth part of a *treen* or *balla*; also the class of lands included in such divisions.

Called 'Quarter of Land' in 1593 (*Statutes* 78); see also *quarter-ground* s.v. QUARTER *sb.* 31.

1645 *Statutes Isle Man* (1821) 107 Lands and Tenements in the said Island called Farme Lands or Quarter Lands. **1798** J. FELTHAM *Tour Isl. Mann* iv. 46 Divisions of land prevail here, termed Quarterlands. It is uncertain how they obtained the name. **1845** TRAIN *Isle Man* I. 51 For each four quarterlands he made a chapel. **1865** *Notes & Queries* Ser. 3 VIII. 310/2 Treens..usually contain from three to four quarterlands. *Ibid.*, Quarterlands, which are estates of inheritance, vary in size, and contain from 120 to 140 acres. **1890** A. W. MOORE *Surnames Isle Man* 211 The lowlands about the church are still intack, not quarterland. **1900** —— *Hist. Isle Man* II. vii. 873.

quarter-line. *Naut.*

1. The position of ships in a column when each successive vessel has its bows abaft the beam of the one in front, and a little to one side.

1875 BEDFORD *Sailor's Pocket Bk.* i. (ed. 2) 22 A Column is said to be in Quarter Line when the ships are ranged in one line abaft each others' beam, but not right astern.

2. a. A line from a vessel's quarter.

1886 R. C. LESLIE *Sea-painter's Log* vii. 146 The quarter-line is cast overboard.

b. An additional line fastened to the underside of a seine to assist in drawing it in (*Cent. Dict.*).

quarterly (ˈkwɔːtəlɪ), *a.* and *sb.* Also 6 -lie. [f. QUARTER *sb.* + -LY[1].] **A.** *adj.*

1. That takes place, is done, etc., every quarter of a year; relating to, or covering, a quarter of a year. †***quarterly waiter*** = QUARTER-WAITER.

1563 in *Maitl. Club Misc.* (1833) 32 Takand ilk quarter 225*ol.* As the capitane of the said Gardis quarterlie acquittances proportis. **1688** MIEGE s.v., The quarterly Seasons of Devotion, called the Ember-weeks. **1727** BOYER

Fr.-Angl. Dict. s.v. *Quartier, Officier de Quartier*, a quarterly Waiter. **1750** WESLEY *Wks.* (1872) II. 205 We had a Quarterly Meeting. **1802** MISS EDGEWORTH *Moral T.* (1816) I. xix. 158 Quarterly and half-yearly payments. **1862** SALA *Ship-chandler* 37 Mine is a quarterly hiring, and my quarter is out to-morrow. **1885** *Law Times* LXXIX. 191/1 The necessity of having a quarterly gaol delivery.

transf. **1694** W. HOLDER *On Time* i. 22 The Moon..makes also four Quarterly Seasons within her little Year.

2. Pertaining or relating to a quarter (in other senses). †***quarterly book***: (see quot. 1776). ***quarterly wind***, a wind on the quarter.

1769 FALCONER *Dict. Marine* (1789), *Vent de quartier*, a quarterly, or quartering wind. **1776** JOHNSON *Let. to Wetherell* 12 Mar. in *Boswell* II. 14 We must..superadd what is called the quarterly-book, or for every hundred books so charged we must deliver an hundred and four. **1889** *Standard* 16 Mar. 3/8 The wind..was..quarterly.

3. Special combinations, as ***quarterly-meeting***, (*a*) in the Society of Friends (Quakers): a general meeting of all the local monthly meetings of a district; (*b*) in the Methodist Church: an administrative meeting of society officials within a circuit.

(*a*) **1675** in *Extracts Minutes Yearly Meeting of Friends, London* (1783) 63 Advised that the church's testimonies and judgments against disorderly and scandalous walkers..be recorded in the respective monthly and quarterly meetings. **1675–7** G. FOX *Jrnl.* (1911) I. 267 About this time [*sc.* 1656] I was moved to sett uppe ye mens Quarterly meetinges throughout ye nation though in ye north they was setled before. **1837** J. J. GURNEY *Autobiogr.* in J. B. Braithwaite *Mem.* (1854) I. v. 85, I well remember insisting in our Quarterly Meeting, on the reading of the advice.. respecting what ought to be the character of representatives. **1869** BECK & BALL *London Friends' Meetings* vii. 69 In most parts of the country, the origin of Quarterly Meetings may be traced to those periodical gatherings of Friends from different but adjoining counties, known as *General Meetings*, and held at intervals with more or less regularity in different places. **1912** W. C. BRAITHWAITE *Beginnings of Quakerism* xiii. 336 By Quarterly Meetings we must, I think, understand General business meetings for a district. **1965** *Friend* 19 Nov. 1393/2 We welcome the proposals of the Revision Committee that..the name Quarterly Meeting be changed to General Meeting [etc.]. **1974** G. HUBBARD *Quaker by Convincement* iv. i. 181 General Meetings were until recently Quarterly Meetings, but they now occur as necessary. They..offer an opportunity for Friends from a wide area to meet and discuss matters of common interest. (*b*) **1750** J. WESLEY *Jrnl.* 22 Aug. (1756) 61 We had a Quarterly Meeting, at which were present the Stewards of all the Cornish Societies. **1807** J. NIGHTINGALE *Portraiture of Methodism* xxix. 303 The *Quarterly-meetings* are composed of all the travelling-preachers in the circuit where such meetings are held; of the leaders and stewards of the society; and of such of the local-preachers and members as may be invited by any of the travelling-preachers or stewards. **1898** B. GREGORY *Side Lights on Conflicts of Methodism* x. 501 Take..the essential part of our economy which, next to the Class meeting, the Conference, and the Circuit, is the oldest and most central part of our economy —the Quarterly Meeting. **1963** R. E. DAVIES *Methodism* App. i. 173 The Circuit consists of a group of Societies in a neighbourhood (some contain as many as fifty, others as few as five or even less); its affairs are directed by the Quarterly Meeting, consisting of the ministers, deaconesses, and local preachers of the Circuit, and the leaders and trustees of each Society. **1972** *Methodist Recorder* 6 July 16/1 A number of familiar names in the life of the churches will be changed if the proposals are accepted: circuit quarterly meeting becomes *circuit meeting*.

B. *sb.* A quarterly review, magazine, etc. Also, lesson notes for Sunday schools, issued every three months.

1830 W. SEWALL *Diary* 15 May (1930) 131/1 Methodist quarterly commenced. **1857** [see *Christmas number* s.v. CHRISTMAS *sb.* 4]. **1871** BESANT & RICE *Ready-money Mort.* iv, He had written papers for what were vaguely called the Quarterlies. **1882** MISS BRADDON *Mt. Royal* III. i. 10 'Oh, there are the new Quarterlies', seeing a package on the table. **1908** L. M. MONTGOMERY *Anne of Green Gables* xi. 110, I got a quarterly from Mr. Bell for you and you'll go to Sunday School to-morrow.

quarterly (ˈkwɔːtəlɪ), *adv.* (*a.*, *sb.*) [-LY[2].]

1. Every quarter of a year; once in a quarter.

1458 in Sharp *Cov. Myst.* (1825) 208 To go with þe wayts to gader their wages quarterly. **1529** *Act 21 Hen. VIII* c. 13 §28 Chaplains..daily or quarterly attending. **1581** MULCASTER *Positions* xli. (1887) 234 That there were no admission into schooles, but foure times in the yeare quarterly. *a* **1633** AUSTIN *Medit.* (1635) 254 They be Times that Quarterly bring us in Revenew for our temporall profit. **1712** ADDISON *Spect.* No. 295 ¶1 She should have 400*l.* a Year for Pin-money, which I obliged my self to pay Quarterly. **1878** JEVONS *Prim. Pol. Econ.* 53 Managers, officers, secretaries, and others, are paid quarterly, or sometimes half-yearly.

2. *Her.* In the four divisions of a shield formed by a vertical and a horizontal line drawn through the fess point; usu. with reference to two tinctures, charges, or coats of arms, placed in the diagonally opposite quarters.

c **1450** HOLLAND *Howlat* 591 He bare quarterly..the armes of the Dowglass. **1525** LD. BERNERS *Froiss.* II. clxviii. 192 He bare syluer and sables quarterly. **1592** WYRLEY *Armorie* 91 Sir Neal Loring, who fairly Arms put on Quarterly white and red. **1684** *Lond. Gaz.* No. 1952/4 The Arms of the said Count, being in an Eschutcheon Four Coats quarterly. **1765** H. WALPOLE *Otranto* iii. (1798) 51 A banner with the arms of Vicenza and Otranto quarterly. **1824** SCOTT *St. Ronan's* xviii, A white lion for Mowbray, to be borne quarterly, with three stunted or scrog-bushes for Scrogie. **1893** CUSSANS *Her.* (ed. 3) 168 Their daughter..is entitled to bear both her Father's and her Mother's Arms quarterly.

b. With ref. to the division of the shield into quarters, or to blazoning it by quarters. ***quarterly-quartered***, having one or more quarters divided in four; so ***quarterly-quartering***.

1610 GUILLIM *Heraldry* v. i. (1611) 238 If they be charged, then I hold it best blazoned quarterly. **1705** HEARNE *Collect.* 21 Dec. (O.H.S.) I. 136 His Arms, quarte[r]ly parted per Cross. **1709** STRYPE *Ann. Ref.* Introd. i. 8 This [shield] impaled quarterly, 1. The arms of Scotland. 2. The arms of England. The third as the second. The fourth as the first. **1864** BOUTELL *Her. Hist. & Pop.* iii. (ed. 3) 16 The Grand Quarters of which the first and the fourth..are Quarterly-quartered. *Ibid.* xiv. 142 The Marshalling now proceeds by Quarterly Quartering.

c. *ellipt.* as *adj.* = divided quarterly, or (by extension) into any number of parts by lines at right angles to each other, as *quarterly of eight*; also as *sb.* = a shield divided or charged quarterly.

1869 W. S. ELLIS *Antiq. Her.* x. 228 Aubrey de Vere.. transmitted his..coat of Quarterly to his descendants.

d. ***quarterly-pierced***: (see quots.).

1780 EDMONDSON *Body Her., Gloss.* II, Quarterly Pierced, is used to express a square hole in a saltire, a cross millrine, &c. through which aperture the field is seen. **1893** CUSSANS *Her.* (ed. 3) 63 If..that part where the limbs [of the cross] are conjoined be removed, it is termed Quarterly-pierced.

†**3. a.** Into four parts. **b.** At four equidisant points on a circle. **c.** Through each quarter of a town. *Obs. rare.*

a. **1576** GASCOIGNE *Philomene* (Arb.) 107 They tore in peces quarterly The corps.

b. **1605** CAMDEN *Rem.* (1637) 167 A Wing with these foure Letters, *F.E.L.D.* quarterly about it.

c. *a* **1670** SPALDING *Troub.* (1828) I. 199 The baillies went quarterly about, to cause ilk inhabitant subscrive.

ˈquarterman.

†**1.** ? One of the quarter-guard. *Obs. rare*$^{-1}$.

1599 in *Harington's Nugæ Antiquæ* (ed. Park 1804) I. 274 The deathes of our captaines were revenged by our quartermen and scoutemen, who..slewe 7 of the rebells, whiche assaied to force the quarter.

2. A foreman-shipwright.

1793 SMEATON *Edystone L.* §62 That species of foreman shipwright, called a Quarter-man in Plymouth dock. **1803** R. PERING in *Naval Chron.* XV. 155 The quartermen..give an account of the work performed to the job office. *Ibid.* 157 Quartermen of shipwrights and caulkers..have apprentices. **1861** SMILES *Engineers* II. 30 [He] was then a fore-man of shipwrights, called a quarterman, in Plymouth Dock.

quartermaster (ˈkwɔːtəˌmɑːstə(r), -æ-), *sb.* [In sense 1 app. from QUARTER *sb.*[1] 16; sense 2 (from QUARTER *sb.* 15) is app. the original meaning of F. *quartier-maître*, Du. *kwartier-meester*, G. *quartier-meister*, etc., and may have been adopted from one or other of these languages.]

1. *Naut.* **a.** A petty officer who attends to the steering of the ship, the binnacle, signals, stowing of the hold, etc.

1442 *Rolls Parlt.* V. 60/1 The Maisters of the Shippes, Quarter Maisters, Shipmen and Soudeours. **1509** BARCLAY *Shyp of Folys* (1570) ¶¶iij, Purser and Captayne, Quarter master, Lodesman. **1549** *Compl. Scot.* vi. 41 Euery quartar master til his auen quartar. **1626** CAPT. SMITH *Accid. Yng. Seamen* 5 The *quarter Maisters* hath the charge of the hold for stowage, rommageing, and trimming the shippe; and of their squadrons for their watch. **1643** *Declar. Commons, Reb. Irel.* 50 He is one of the Quarter-masters of the Dunkirke Frigot. **1708** *Royal Proclam.* 20 May in *Lond. Gaz.* No. 4440/1 The Midshipmen,..Quarter-Master, Quarter-Masters Mates,..and Serjeants of Marines. **1836** MARRYAT *Midsh. Easy* xxvi, Up with the helm, quarter-master.

b. *transf.* Steering-gear.

1882 *Standard* 26 Dec. 2/2 She will have a brigantine rig, ..and [be] steered by a steam 'quartermaster'. **1899** F. T. BULLEN *Way Navy* 37 Like everything else in this giant vessel, the steam quartermaster is on an immense scale.

2. *Mil.* **a.** An officer, ranking as lieutenant, attached to each regiment, with the duties of providing quarters for the soldiers, laying out the camp, and looking after the rations, ammunition and other supplies of the regiment.

1600 DYMMOK *Ireland* (1843) 33 The small losse we sustayned..was multiplied upon the rebell by our quarter and skoutmasters. *a* **1653** GOUGE *Comm. Heb.* vi. 18 A quarter-master, who goeth before hand to prepare quarters for souldiers. **1721** DE FOE *Mem. Cavalier* (1840) 97 The king..made him a quarter-master to a troop of Cuirassiers. **1803** WELLINGTON *Let. to Col. Stevenson* 16 Sept. in Gurw. *Desp.* (1837) II. 308, I rather believe that your Quarter Masters have 1000 bullocks for each regiment. **1893** FORBES-MITCHELL *Remin. Gt. Mutiny* 150 Our quartermaster divided among us a lot of shirts and underclothing.

b. quartermaster-general, a staff-officer who is chief of the department exercising control over all matters relating to the quartering, encamping, marching and equipment of troops.

1701 *Lond. Gaz.* No. 3732/1 The said Quartermaster-General and Adjutant-General Baron Riedt were sent out to view the Ground. **1813** WELLINGTON *Let. to Sir G. Collier* 19 Aug. in Gurw. *Desp.* (1838) XI. 15, I enclose a letter to the Quarter Master General directing that the Infantry now in the horse ships at Bilbao may be removed. **1876** BANCROFT *Hist. U.S.* V. xliv. 35 Mifflin, who in August had been appointed quartermaster-general.

c. quartermaster-sergeant, a non-commissioned officer, ranking as a staff-sergeant, who assists the quartermaster in his duties.

1869 E. A. PARKES *Pract. Hygiene* (ed. 3) 309 The Serjeant-major and Quarter-master-serjeant are entitled to two rooms and a kitchen.

d. quartermaster captain, an officer in the U.S. army with the rank of captain having duties similar to those of a quartermaster.

1907 *N.Y. Even. Post* (Semi-Weekly ed.) 13 May 6 The person enjoying the title of quartermaster captain (a rank that causes our British cousins to smile).

†**3.** One who shares authority with another to the extent of a fourth. *Obs.*

Prob. *transf.* from sense 1, with pun on *quarter* = one fourth; cf. QUARTER *sb.* 28 d.

1550 LATIMER *Last Serm. bef. Edw. VI* 111 They do it, because they will be quarter maister with their husbandes: Quarter maister? nay halfe maisters: yea some of them will be whole maisters. **1617** COLLINS *Def. Bp. Ely* I. i. 7 Discerne you no better betweene Popes and Councels, which are the Church in effect? or shall these play quarter-masters with the Pope? **1685** R. BURTON *Eng. Emp. Amer.* ii. 28 The English Nation..might have made themselves Quarter-Masters, at least with the Spaniards.

†**4.** A gild-official, having charge of the gildsmen in a quarter of the town. *Obs.*

1646 in G. Tate *Alnwick* II. xvii. 338 It is agreed that none of the wood shall be sould but with the consent of the four quartermaisters. [**1868–9** G. TATE *Alnwick* II. xvii. 338 Wood and bark were therefore bought for the whole company, by officers called quartermasters, who allotted to each tanner a proportional share of every purchase.]

Hence **ˈquarterˌmaster** *v.*, to perform the duties of a quartermaster (hence ***quartermastering*** vbl. sb.); **quartermasteriveness**, the qualities of a quartermaster (*nonce-wd.*); **quartermastership**, the office of quartermaster (so called ***quartermaster-generalship***).

1745 *Observ. Conc. Navy* 44 Sales of Ensignships, Adjutancies, Quarter-Master-ships, &c. **1824** MCCULLOCH *Scotland* I. 370 His organ of quarter-masteriveness must have been woefully in arrear. **1862** *Times* 8 Jan. 8/6 Questions of massing, manœuvring, or quartermastering. **1870** *Daily News* 3 Nov., The quartermastership..of the district around Metz. **1876** BANCROFT *Hist. U.S.* VI. Index 553 [Greene] resigns [the] quartermaster-generalship abruptly. **1936** W. JAMES *Gangways & Corridors* i. 10 He had quarter-mastered in Cuba during the Spanish American war.

ˈquartermistress. [f. after QUARTERMASTER.] An officer in the W.A.A.C. having the duties of a quartermaster.

1917 *Times* 13 Aug. 3/1 The W.A.A.C. will be controlled by a Chief Controller, and the following appointments are authorized:—..Quarter mistress Class I. Attached to Depôt. 2 roses.

†**quartern**, *sb.*[1] *Obs.* Forms: 1 cweartern, -en, cwert-, cwiertern, 1–2 cwart-, quartern, 3 cwarrt-, quarrterrne, cwart-, quarterne. [Of obscure origin, poss. an alteration of OE. *carcærn, carcern*, ad. L. *carcer*.] A prison.

c **975** *Rushw. Gosp.* Matt. xxv. 39 Hwonne we þe segun untrymne oþðe in quartern? *c* **1000** ÆLFRIC *Exod.* xl. 3 þa dyde hiȝ man on cweartern..and þæs cweairternes hirde betæhte hiȝ Iosepe. *c* **1154** *O.E. Chron.* an. 1137 Hi dyden heom in quarterne. *c* **1200** ORMIN 6168 Himm þatt i cwarrterrne liþ Forrbundenn. *Ibid.* 18187 Inntill quarrterrne worrpenn. *c* **1205** [see QUALE[1] b]. *a* **1225** *Leg. Kath.* 670 Al þe cwarterne of his cume leitede o leie.

quartern (ˈkwɔːtən), *sb.*[2] Forms: 3–7 quartron, (4 -run, -roun, -eroun, quaterone, 6 -eren), 5–7 quarteron, (5 -eren, -rone), 6–7 quarterne, (7 coterne), 7–9 *Ir.* cartron, 9 quartan, *dial.* wartern, 6– quartern. [a. AF. *quartrun*, OF. *quart(e)ron, quat(te)ron*, used in most of the senses of the E. word (see Godef.) f. *quart(e*, fourth, fourth part.]

1. A quarter *of* anything. *Obs.* exc. *dial.*

c **1290** *S. Eng. Leg.* I. 476/510 With-inne a quartron of þe ȝere huy comen to Marcilie. *c* **1440** *Anc. Cookery* in *Househ. Ord.* (1790) 455 A quartrone of a pounde of pynes. **1547** BOORDE *Brev. Health* 20 Take of..greate reasons..a quartron of a pounde. **1587** HARRISON *England* II. vi. (1877) I. 159 She raddeth..halfe a quarterne of an ounce of baiberries. **1607** TOPSELL *Four-f. Beasts* (1658) 287 Take of Hony a quartern of a pinte. **1647** *Will of John Clarke of Scawthorpe* (N. W. Linc. Gloss.), Three quatrans of one oxgange of land. *a* **1796** in PEGGE *Derbicisms*. **1877** *N.W. Linc. Gloss.*, *Quartern*, a quarter of anything.

†**2.** *ellipt.* A quarter of something (*esp.* a weight or measure) already specified. *Obs.* Cf. 3.

1362 LANGL. *P. Pl.* A. v. 131 The pound that heo peysede by peisede a quartrun [*v.r.* quarteroun] more then myn auncel dude. *c* **1400** MAUNDEV. (1839) xxx. 301 There is not the Mone seyn in alle the Lunacioun, saf only the seconde quarteroun. **1480** *Wardr. Acc. Edw. IV* (1830) 130 Sylk j lb. an unce and j quarteron. **1496** *Naval Acc. Hen. VII* (1896) 174 A Chalder and a quarteron of Smythes Coles. **1623** *Althorp MS.* in Simpkinson *The Washingtons* (1860) App. 42, 2 barrells of neates tongues weight 100 and a coterne. *Ibid.* 45 For 3 pintes wanting di.a coterne of aquavitæ. **1653** URQUHART *Rabelais* II. xxix. 187 Weighing nine thousand seven hundred kintals and two quarterons.

3. A quarter of various weights and measures.

a. of a pound. Now *rare*. **b.** of an ounce. **c.** of a chalder, hundredweight, etc. Now only *dial.* †**d.** = QUARTER 4 a. **e.** of a stone or peck. †**f.** of some measure of land; in Ireland = QUARTER 7 c, or the fourth part of this. **g.** of a pint.

a. [**1326** *Durham Acc. Rolls* (Surtees) 15 In uno quarteroun croci, 16½*d.*] *c* **1400** *Master of Game* xii. (MS. Digby 182), Take ye vi poundes of hony, and a quartron of vertgrece. c **1450** *ME. Med. Bk.* (Heinrich) 173 Tak þre quarterons of clene rosyn, & a quateron of good perrosyn, & half a pounde of good oile de olyue. **1520** WHITINTON *Vulg.* (1527) 12 b, Bye me a halfe pounde of saffron, a quarteren of cynamon. **1754-6** *Connoisseur* No. 76 At every petty Chandler's shop in town, while the half quarterns of tea are weighed out. **1836-9** DICKENS *Sk. Boz, Tales* iv, He dispensed tea and coffee by the quartern, retailed sugar by the ounce. **1878** *Cumbld. Gloss.* Suppl., *Quartern*, a quarter of a pound of flax ready for being spun.

b. 1607 T. COCKS *Diary* (1901) 5/6 Paide for a quartern of sylke 4*d.* **1862** MRS. H. WOOD *Mrs. Hallib.* (1864) II. viii. 193 That surly old foreman says.. 'What d'ye leave for silk? .. There's two quarterns down'.

c. 1497 *Naval Acc. Hen. VII* (1896) 230, iiij quarterons salte. **1590** RECORDE, etc. *Gr. Arts* (1646) 134 There bee greater weights, which are called a hundred, halfe a hundred, and a quarterne, and also a halfe quarterne. **1883** *Almondb. & Huddersf. Gloss., Wartern*, i.e. a quartern, a weight of woolen warp which is, when complete, twenty-four or twenty-five pounds.

d. 1583 in *Collect.* (O.H.S.) I. 234, 53 quarterns, 3 bushells of malt.

e. 1836-9 DICKENS *Sk. Boz, Tales* iv, Applicants for.. half-quarterns of bread.

f. 1679 BLOUNT *Anc. Tenures* 3 Each [bondman] held one Messuage, and one Quartron of Land. **1683** J. KEOGH *Acc. Roscommon* in O'Donovan *Tribes Hy-Fiachraich* (1844) 454 The lands here are generally set and let..by the name of quarters, cartrons, and gnieves, a quarter being the fourth part of a townland..and a cartron..the fourth part of a quarter. **1883** [see QUARTER 7 c].

g. 1706 PHILLIPS (ed. Kersey), *Quartern*, a sort of Measure, the fourth part of a Pint. **1762** SMOLLETT *Launcelot Greaves* (1793) II. xvii. 90 The waiter..returned with a quartern of brandy. **1835** MARRYAT *Jac. Faithf.* xxii, There is my mother with a quartern of gin before her. **1839** CARLYLE *Chartism* iv. 132 Liquid Madness [Gin] sold at ten-pence the quartern.

†**4.** A quarter of a hundred; twenty-five. ***quartern-book***: (see quot. 1584). *Obs.*

1472-3 *Rolls Parlt.* VI. 37/2 Item, C of Milwell and Lyng drye; Item, a quartern of Mersaunte Lyng. **1561** AWDELAY *Frat. Vacab.* 12 The xxv orders of Knaves, other-wise called a quarterne of Knaves. **1584** *Star Chamb. Decree* (1863) 15 Any Stationer that shall bye a quarterne at ones or more; which quartern is xxv bokes, in which case the byer hath alwaie a quarterne boke given him freely, that is to saie, one boke for everie xxv that he byeth. **1630** J. TAYLOR (Water P.) *T.'s Water worke* Ded., A Quarterne of new-catcht Epigrams caught the last Fishing-tide. **1650** TRAPP *Comm. Deut.* xvii. 4 The Catholikes follow the Bible (saith Hill, in his quartern of Reasons).

5. A quarter of a sheet of paper.

1821 SOUTHEY *Lett.* (1856) III. 249 During the last year.. at Westminster, one imposition served me:..it lasted till the appearance of the quartan might have betrayed its history. **1874** DASENT *Half a Life* 232 This message, written on a 'quartern', that is, on a quarter of a sheet of ruled paper, on which we wrote our exercises.

6. A quartern-loaf.

1844 DICKENS *Mart. Chuz.* viii, That..loaf which is known to housekeepers as a slack-baked crummy quartern.

7. *Comb.*, as †**quartern-book** (see 4); **quartern-loaf**, a loaf made of a quartern of flour, a four-pound loaf; †**quartern-wind**, a quarter-wind.

1592 GREENE *Disput.* 1 Thinke you a quarterne winde cannot make a quicke saile. **1812** *Examiner* 24 Aug. 531/1 The price of the Quartern Loaf still continues at 1*s.* 8*d.* **1887** JESSOPP *Arcady* vi. 176 Ben has been seen to eat two quartern loaves at a sitting.

†**quartern(e** *a.*, erron. forms of QUARTAN, through assimilation to prec. *Obs.*

1548 HOOPER *Ten Commandm.* ix. Wks. (Parker Soc.) 373 Those..that bid the pestilence, the fever quartern,..or such other execrations. **1588** J. READ *Compend. Meth.* 64 b, The dropsie, quarterne fluxes and strangurie.

quarteron, -oon, variants of QUADROON.

quarter-piece.

†**1.** A quarter of a standard coin. *Obs. rare*⁻¹.

1650 FULLER *Pisgah* I. xii. 38 Some English coines, being quarter-peices, cannot be put away in payment without loss, except four of them be joyned together.

2. *Naut.* †**a.** A piece of ordnance placed on the quarter of a vessel. *Obs. rare*⁻¹.

1626 CAPT. SMITH *Accid. yng. Sea-men* 31 The peeces in the prow,..in the sterne, the quarter peeces [etc.].

b. (See quots.)

1711 W. SUTHERLAND *Shipbuild. Assist.* 162 Quarter-pieces; large carved Pieces fixed to terminate the Quarter with the Stern. **1769** FALCONER *Dict. Marine* (1780) G g, The quarter-pieces, which limit and form the outlines of the stern. **1797** *Encycl. Brit.* XVII. 408/2 The taffarel and quarter pieces, which terminate the ship abaft, the former above and the latter on each side. **1846** A. YOUNG *Naut. Dict.* 243 If there be a quarter-gallery, the quarter-piece forms its after end.

c. 'Projections beyond the quarters of a ship for additional cabin accommodation' (*Cent. Dict.*).

†**3.** = QUARTER 27 and 20 c. *Obs. rare*⁻⁰.

1688 MIEGE *Grt. Fr. Dict.* II, Quarter-piece, *quartier.* The two Quarter-pieces of a Shoe. **1736** AINSWORTH *Lat. Dict.*, A double quarter piece, *trabs crassior.*

quarter sessions. Also with hyphen. [QUARTER *sb.* 8 a.]

1. In England and Ireland: A court of limited criminal and civil jurisdiction, and of appeal, held quarterly by the justices of peace in the counties (in Ireland by county-court judges), and by the recorder in boroughs; ***court of quarter sessions***, a court of record held quarterly before two or more justices of the peace in counties and before a recorder in certain boroughs.

Quarter sessions were abolished in England on 1 Jan. 1972 by the Courts Act, 1971, and their duties largely passed to the newly-instituted Crown Court.

1577 HARRISON *England* II. iv. (1877) I. 100 They haue finallie their quarter sessions, wherein they are assisted by the justices and gentlemen of the countrie. **1660** R. COKE *Power & Subj.* 233 Justices of Peace in their Quarter-sessions, have power to hear and determine the offences aforesaid. **1711** ADDISON *Spect.* No. 122 ¶4 There is not one in the Town where he lives that he has not sued at a Quarter-Sessions. **1844** LD. BROUGHAM *Brit. Const.* xix. §6 (1862) 375 Much of the criminal business of England is transacted by the quarter-sessions. **1889** *Act 52 & 53 Vict.* c. 63. sect. 13 §14 The expression 'court of quarter sessions' shall mean the justices of any county, riding, parts, division, or liberty of a county, or of any county of a city, or county of a town, in general or quarter sessions assembled, and shall include the court of the recorder of a municipal borough having a separate court of quarter sessions. **1901** L. COURTNEY *Working Const. U.K.* II. 248 Prisoners apprehended under charge of crime are..committed for trial at the Assizes or Quarter Sessions. **1916** *Act 6 & 7 Geo. V* c. 50 §38 A justice of the peace in England when committing for trial a person charged with burglary shall commit him for trial before a court of assize unless,..he thinks it expedient in the interest of justice to commit him for trial before a court of quarter sessions. **1967** *Act 15 & 16 Eliz. II* c. 58 §8 A court of quarter sessions shall not have jurisdiction to try an indictment for any offence for which a person may be sentenced to death. **1972** *Daily Tel.* 1 Jan. 2 The ancient legal structure of assizes and quarter sessions disappears today.

attrib. **1847** TENNYSON *Princ.* Concl. 90 A quarter-sessions chairman, abler none.

2. In Scotland: A court of review and appeal held quarterly by the Justices of the Peace on days appointed by statute (1661).

1661 *Sc. Acts Parl.* c. xxxviii. (1681), The Justices of Peace..shall appoint at the Quarter Sessions..the ordinary Hire and Wages of Labourers. **1679** in Wodrow *Hist. Ch. Scot.* (1722) II. 17 With Power..to call the remanent Justices of Peace to the Quarter-sessions. **1773** J. ERSKINE *Inst. Laws Scot.* I. iv. 60 Constables..are appointed by them in their quarter-sessions. **1898** *Green's Encycl. Law Scot.* VII. 268 A judgment in Quarter Sessions cannot be reviewed by a later Quarter Sessions.

3. *Comb.* **quarter-sessions rose**, var. of Quatre Saisons, the name of a variety of perpetual rose, *Rosa damascena* var. *bifera*, bearing pink or white flowers.

1892 C. M. YONGE *Old Woman's Outlook* vi. 137 The *Quatre Saisons* rose might very fairly become the Quarter Sessions rose. **1937** PARTRIDGE *Dict. Slang* 676/1 Quarter-sessions rose. A 'perpetual' rose.

'quarterstaff. **1.** A stout pole, from six to eight feet long and tipped with iron, formerly used as a weapon by the English peasantry.

The exact sense of *quarter* is not clear: quot. 1589 suggests that the staff may have been made from a tree of a certain size cleft in four; cf. QUARTER-CLEFT B. 1.

a **1550** *Play of Robin Hood* 7 in Child *Ballads* III. 127 With a stout frere I met, And a quarter-staffe in his hande. **1589** R. HARVEY *Pl. Perc.* (1860) 3 Plodding through Aldersgate, all armed as I was, with a quarter Ashe staffe on my shoulder. *c* **1626** *Dick of Devon* IV. iii. in Bullen *Old Pl.* II. 81 My owne Country weapon. What? A Quarter staffe. **1700** DRYDEN *Cymon & Iph.* 82 His quarter-staff..Hung half before and half behind his back. **1725** DE FOE *Voy. round World* (1840) 121 A cane about eight foot long and an inch and a half in diameter much like a quarter-staff. **1821** SCOTT *Kenilw.* xxv, Their rude drivers..began to debate precedence with their waggon-whips and quarter-staves. **1887** BESANT *The World went* xv. 128 [He] took the quarterstaff,..poised it in his hands, and turned a smiling face to his adversary.

attrib. **1890** *Daily News* 19 June 6/4 Dumb-bell and quarter-staff drill.

2. Fighting or exercise with the quarterstaff.

1712 ARBUTHNOT *John Bull* I. ii, He had acquir'd immense Riches, which he used to squander away at Back-Sword, Quarter-Staff, and Cudgell-Play. **1775** SHERIDAN *Rivals* IV. i, If you wanted a bout at boxing, quarter staff, or short-staff. **1849** MACAULAY *Hist. Eng.* ii. I. 252 He..wrestled, played at quarterstaff, and won footraces.

Hence **'quarterstaff** *v.*, to beat with a quarterstaff.

1709 STEELE *Tatler* No. 31 ¶5, 400 Senators..thought it an Honour to be cudgelled and quarterstaffed.

quarter-tense, corrupt f. QUATER-TEMPS (q.v.).

1869 T. ARNOLD in *Wyclif's Sel. Wks.* I. 377 'Quatuor Tempora', or, as it is called in Ireland, Quarter Tense.

†**'quarterth**, *a. Obs.* [f. QUARTER *sb.* + -TH¹.] Fourth (part).

1658 *Capel's Rem.* To Rdr., His recipees amounted not to the half nor quarterth part of a common Apothecaries Bill.

quarter-waiter. [QUARTER *sb.* 8 a.] One belonging to the lower class of Gentlemen-Ushers, who remained in waiting for a quarter of a year.

a **1522** in *Rutland Papers* (Camd.) 102 Gentilmen ushers quarter wayters. *c* **1600** SIR J. DAVIES *Dialogue* (Tanner MS. 79 lf. 15), *Gentleman Usher.* I should know something that have beene a quarter-wayter these 15 yeares. **1610** *Househ. Ord.* (1790) 338 The gentlemen ushers, daily waiters, and quarter waiters. **1656** FINETT *For. Ambass.* 225 They gave to the hand of a Gentleman Usher Quarter-waiter 10 Peeces. **1731** *Gentl. Mag.* I. 126 One of the..Quarter-waiters in ordinary to his Majesty.

quarter-wind. **a.** A wind blowing on a vessel's quarter. †**b.** A wind from one of the cardinal points. *Obs.*

a. 1591 PERCIVALL *Sp. Dict.*, *Aorça*, with a quarter winde. **1627** CAPT. SMITH *Seaman's Gram.* vii. 32 Few ships will steare vpon quarter winds with one saile. **1692** *Ibid.* I. xvi. 80 *Quarter Winds*, are when the Wind comes in abaft the main-mast-shrouds even with the Quarter. **1727-41** CHAMBERS *Cycl.* s.v., The quarter-wind is the best of all winds, as bearing into all the sails. **1846** A. YOUNG *Naut. Dict.* 243.

b. 1598 FLORIO, *Quarta*,..a quarter winde of the compasse.

†**quartessence.** *Obs. rare*⁻¹. [f. L. *quarta* fourth, after QUINTESSENCE.] An essence one degree less pure than a quintessence.

1605 TIMME *Quersit.* I. xi. 48 It is called a quintessence, but more truly and properly a quartessence.

quartet, quartette (kwɔːˈtɛt). Also 9 -tett. [a. F. *quartette*, ad. It. *quartetto*: see next.]

1. a. *Mus.* A composition for four voices or instruments, *esp.* one for four stringed instruments.

1773 C. BURNEY *Present State of Music in Germany* I. 313 [Hasse] added, that..his trios, quartets and concertos for instruments, were so numerous that he should not know many of them again if he was either to see or hear them. **1790** COLERIDGE *Inside the Coach*, We snore quartettes in ecstasy of nose. **1845** E. HOLMES *Mozart* 245 A single quartet for stringed instruments. **1867** MACFARREN *Harmony* i. 14 Beethoven's Quartet in A, &c.

attrib. **1872** BROWNING *Fifine* cxvi, Inspect this quartett-score!

fig. **1838** DICKENS *O. Twist* xxxix, A quartette of 'Shameful!' with which the Dianas concluded.

b. *transf.* (See quot. 1965.)

1943 T. S. ELIOT (*title*) Four quartets. **1965** *New Statesman* 21 May 802/3, I asked what the four of his Quartets were four of, and he [*sc.* T. S. Eliot] answered that ..'quartet' suggested Chamber Music composed for close attention by a small audience who had a fair understanding of what they were listening to.

2. a. *Mus.* A set of four singers or players who render a quartet. **b.** *transf.* A set of four persons.

1814 SIR R. WILSON *Priv. Diary* II. 304 We are a quartett of miserables. **1849** THACKERAY *Pendennis* I. 294 The parties are arranged in messes of four, each of which quartets has its piece of beef. **1876** GEO. ELIOT *Dan. Der.* II. xv, When the quartette of gentlemen..met on the terrace.

3. A set of four things; e.g., of lines in a sonnet, of runs at cricket, etc.

1837-9 HALLAM *Hist. Lit.* II. II. v. §44. 208 The first lines or quartets of the sonnet excite a soft expectation, which is harmoniously filled by the tercets, or last six lines. **1882** *Daily Tel.* 17 May, Shaw, letting out at that bowler's next delivery, drove it to the boundary for a quartette. **1889** GROVE *Dict. Mus.* IV. 341 A glass case containing two quartets of stringed instruments.

4. *Comb.*, as **quartette table** *Obs.* exc. *Hist.*, = *quartetto table* s.v. QUARTETTO 3.

1856 F. S. COZZENS *Sparrowgrass Papers* vii. 89 In one door-way stood a tray of delicate confections, upon two slender quartette tables. **1857** *Harper's Mag.* Mar. 453/1 On this quartette-table we will lay the portfolio. **1925** PENDEREL-BRODHURST & LAYTON *Gloss. Eng. Furnit.* 133 *Quartette Tables*, nests of four small tables of light make and diminishing size enclosed within each other and made to draw out. Sheraton, who may have been the first to devise them, called them 'Quartetto tables'.

‖**quartetto** (kwɔːˈtɛtəʊ). [a. It. *quartetto*, f. *quarto* fourth: see prec.]

1. *Mus.* = QUARTET 1. ? *Obs.*

1775 in ASH *Suppl.* **1789** BURNEY *Hist. Mus.* III. Introd. 9 In 1752, Quantz classed Quartettos at the head of Instrumental Music. **1806-7** J. BERESFORD *Miseries Hum. Life* (1826) XVI. ii. 89 Playing the solo part for the flute in a quartetto. **1835** L. RITCHIE *Wand. by Seine* 201 Every song was at least a quartetto.

2. = QUARTET 2 and 3. ? *Obs.*

1790 COWPER *Lett.* Wks. 1836 VI. 340 Wishing much that you could change our trio into a quartetto. **1807** SIR R. C. HOARE *Tour Irel.* 235 Potatoes, oats, flax, and bog, the almost inseparable quartetto. **1819** T. HOPE *Anastasius* III. xiv. (1820) 362 The quartetto..consisted of a poet, a scene-painter, a musical composer and a ballet-master.

3. *Comb.*, as **quartetto table** *Obs.* exc. *Hist.*, one of a nest of four small tables.

1802 T. SHERATON *Cabinet-Maker's & Upholsterer's Drawing-Bk.* (ed. 3) in J. M. Bell *Chippendale, Sheraton & Hepplewhite Furnit. Designs* (1900) 148 (*caption*) Cabinet and Quartetto Table. **1803** —— *Cabinet Dict.* 293 *Quartetto table*, a kind of small work table made to draw out of each other, and may be used separately. **1842** MRS. BROWNING *Grk. Chr. Poets* 173 A large soul..containing sundry Queen Anne's men, one within another, like quartetto tables. **1944** C. W. DREPPERD *Primer Amer. Antiques* 248/2 Quartetto Tables. Sets of tables..resting in and under largest one. **1975** [see NEST *sb.* 6].

[**quarteus**, an error for CERCEAUS, q.v.

1340 *Ayenb.* 159 Yef þe onderstondinge..wyþwent ayen ase deþ þe quarteus, al þe inwyt ssel by þyestre.]

quarteyn, obs. form of QUARTAN.

'quartful, *sb. rare.* [f. QUART *sb.*² + -FUL.] As much as a quart-vessel will hold.

1745 SWIFT *Direct. to Servants* Wks. (1869) 571/1 Carry two quartful [of ale] to the stable.

†**'quartful**, *a. Obs.* Also 5 qwar(t)-, quarfulle, quarty-, 5-6 whart-. [f. QUART *sb.*¹ + -FUL.] Sound, healthy; safe, prosperous.

c **1460** *Towneley Myst.* vi. 29 Whartfull shall I make thi gate, I shal the help erly and late. **1483** *Cath. Angl.* 296/2

Quartyfulle (*A.* Qwartfulle), *compos, prosper, sospes. Ibid.* 297/1 To make Quarfulle, *prosperare.* **1530** *Test. Ebor.* (Surtees) V. 290 Whartfull the mynd, and compleit in remembrance. **1537** *Will of Agnes Bell* (Somerset Ho.), Heyll and quartfull in mynde.

Hence †**quar(t)fulness**, health, prosperity. *Obs.*

1483 *Cath. Angl.* 297/1 A Quarfullnes, *prosperitas.*

quartic ('kwɔːtɪk), *a.* and *sb. Math.* [f. L. *quart-us* fourth + -IC.] **A.** *adj.* **1.** *Math.* Of the fourth degree.

1905 R. W. H. T. HUDSON (*title*) Kummer's quartic surface.

2. Applied to a steering wheel shaped like a rectangle with rounded corners.

1973 *Country Life* 17 May 1417/2 A 'quartic' steering-wheel..is a two-spoke design shaped rather like a television screen. **1974** *Daily Tel.* 17 Sept. 6/5 With two other sporting 1750cc versions also announced today, it becomes the first Allegro to abandon the controversial squared-off 'quartic' steering wheel in favour of a conventional round wheel.

B. *sb. Math.* A quantic, curve, or surface of the fourth degree.

1856 CAYLEY *Wks.* (1889) II. 263 We have for the quartic the following irreducible covariants, viz. the quartic itself *U*[etc.]. **1885** SALMON *Mod. Higher Algebra* 345 Sylvester proved that every invariant of a quartic is a rational function of *S* and *T*.

‖**quartier** (kartje). [Fr.: cf. QUARTER *sb.* 14 a.] **1.** In France: a neighbourhood, district. Also *transf.* Also *ellipt.* = *Quartier Latin* below.

1828 LYTTON *Pelham* I. xxiii. 192, I love that *quartier*—if ever I went to Paris again I should reside there. **1850** THACKERAY *Pendennis* II. vii. 73 I'm thinking of becoming a moral man..with a good reputation in my *quartier.* **1864** MRS GASKELL *French Life* in *Fraser's Mag.* Apr.–June 435/1 The new Boulevard..making a clear passage..through the densely populated *quartier.* **1896** E. DOWSON *Let.* 19 Mar. (1967) 346 It is a refreshing change after Paris and the Quartier. **1967** J. PORTER *Chinks in Curtain* 190 The nuns have a mission in Montmartre. The Princess will work there among the—er—ladies of the quartier. **1976** *Times* 31 July 12/5 A collection of *quartiers* each expressing its own set of neighbourhood loyalties and prejudices.

2. Quartier Latin (kartje latɛ̃), the Latin Quarter (of Paris). Also *attrib.*

1857 C. KINGSLEY *Two Yrs. Ago* I. i. 17 Tom Thurnall went to Paris, and became the best pistol-shot..in the Quartier Latin. **1861** in D. du Maurier *Young George du Maurier* (1951) 92 Physical prowess & muscular development—the natural antidotes to morbid Quartier-latin Romance. **1903** CHESTERTON *Robert Browning* v. 111 The thieves' kitchens and the studios of the Quartier Latin. **1936** C. DAY LEWIS *Friendly Tree* viii. 112 If everyone who comes out of the King's Head is a Bohemian, Kings Ampnett will soon rival the Quartier Latin. **1979** *Guardian* 30 Apr. 10/6 The authentic atmosphere of Paris's Quartier Latin in the late 1950s.

quartier, variant of QUARTEER.

‖**quartiere** (,kwarti'ere). [It.; cf. prec.] In Italy: a district or area (of a city). (In quot. 1888 *transf.*)

1888 H. JAMES *Aspern Papers* I. iii. 52 We walked together along the sala... I was afraid it would not form part of my *quartiere.* **1967** P. E. H. DURSTON *Mortissimo* (1968) xii. 95 Ran into them in a little antique shop. Down in your *quartiere.* **1979** 'C. BRAND' *Rose in Darkness* xi. 140 This is the quartiere of the thieves.

quartile ('kwɔːtɪl; *in sense* B. 2 -taɪl), *a.* and *sb.* [ad. med.L. *quartīlis*, f. *quartus* fourth: cf. *quintile, sextile.*]

A. *adj. Astr.* and *Astrol.* **a.** ***quartile aspect***, the aspect of two heavenly bodies which are 90° distant from each other. (Cf. QUADRATE *a.* 2.) **b.** Connected with, relating to, a quartile aspect.

1585 LUPTON *Thous. Notable Th.* VIII. §43 (1660) 201 If the Aspect be..by a Quartile or Opposite Aspect, he shall get it with tediousness. **1647** LILLY *Chr. Astrol.* i. 26 When two Planets are ninety degrees distant one from another, wee call that Aspect a Quartile Aspect, and write it thus, □. **1768** SMEATON in *Phil. Trans.* LVIII. 166 If the quartile observations are made when the planets are considerably to the east or west of the meridian. **1856** R. A. VAUGHAN *Mystics* (1860) II. 51 To think that he must toil in obscurity like a gnome, calculating aspects, sextile and quartile.

B. *sb.* **1.** *Astr.* and *Astrol.* A quartile aspect; a quadrature.

1509 HAWES *Past. Pleas.* XXXVI. (Percy Soc.) 188 When fyve bodies above on the heaven Wente retrograde..With divers quartils. **1621** BURTON *Anat. Mel.* I. i. I. i, The Heauens threaten vs with their..oppositions, quartiles, and such vnfriendly aspects. **1686** GOAD *Celest. Bodies* I. vi. 22 The Full Moon, the Interlunia, and the Quartiles. **1768** SMEATON in *Phil. Trans.* LVIII. 163 Let the place of Mars be observed when the Moon is nearest her quartile with Mars. **1839** BAILEY *Festus* ix. (1852) 121 Your partite quartiles, and your plastic trines, And all your Heavenly houses and effects.

2. *Statistics.* **a.** The first and third of the three values of a variate which divide a frequency distribution into four groups, each containing one quarter of the total population (the second value of the three, the mean, is sometimes also included); also, any of the four groups so produced.

1879 D. MCALISTER in *Proc. R. Soc.* XXIX. 374 As these two measures, with the mean, divide the curve of facility into four equal parts, I propose to call them the 'higher quartile' and the 'lower quartile' respectively. It will be seen that they correspond to the ill-named 'probable errors' of the ordinary theory. **1931** *Biometrika* XXIII. 360 The distribution of the quartile is not so closely normal as that of the median. **1957** W. MARTIN in R. K. Merton *Student-Physician* III. 203 Among students in the top quartile, 28 per cent have high estimations of their ability to perform as a doctor should. **1964** BRUNER & POTTER in J. S. Bruner *Beyond Information Given* (1974) v. 85 For each picture, the point at which it was first recognized by any subject was obtained.., and likewise the point at which a quarter of the subjects recognized the objects (first quartile). **1977** *N.Y. Times* 4 Apr. 60 (Advt.), The top income half of the nation (those households with incomes above the national median) controls about three-fourths of total income... The top quartile always controls about 48%.

b. quartile deviation, the semi-interquartile range.

1911, etc. [see *semi-interquartile range* s.v. SEMI- 6 a]. **1972** *Jrnl. Social Psychol.* LXXXII. 209 Table 1 shows the medians, quartile deviations, and composite ranks.

quartine ('kwɔːtaɪn). *rare.* [f. L. *quart-us* fourth + -INE[4] and [5].]

1. *Bot.* Mirbel's name for a fourth integument supposed by him to occur in some ovules.

1832 LINDLEY *Introd. Bot.* 158 [Quoting Mirbel], I have only discovered the quartine in ovula of which the tercine is incorporated at an early period with the secondine.

2. *Chem.* (See quot.)

1873 RALFE *Phys. Chem.* p. xviii, Triads. Glycerin Series. Quartine or Crotonylene C_4H_6.

quartin'variant. *Math.* [f. as prec. + INVARIANT.] An invariant of the fourth degree.

1884 W. R. W. ROBERTS in *Hermathena* X. 182 The evectants of the quartinvariants of the quantics. **1885** SALMON *Mod. Higher Algebra* Index, Quartinvariant of odd quantic.

†**quartlé**, *a. Obs. rare.* [a. OF. *quartelé*, pa. pple. of *quart-*, *carteler* to quarter.] Quartered.

c **1420** *Liber Cocorum* (1862) 37 Take fyggus quartle, and raysyns, tho Hole dates, almondes. *c* **1440** *Promp. Parv.* 419/2 Quartle (*S.* quarteryd), *quadripartitus.*

So †**quartled**, *Her.* quartered. *Obs.*

1480 CAXTON *Chron. Eng.* ccxxv. 231 The kynges armes of fraunce quartled with the armes of englond.

quart-major: see QUART *sb.*[3] 2.

quarto ('kwɔːtəʊ). Also written 4to, 4°. [L. (*in*) *quarto*, (in) the fourth (of a sheet), abl. sing. of *quartus* fourth.]

1. The size of paper obtained by folding a whole sheet twice, so as to form four leaves, in which as a rule the height is not markedly in excess of the breadth. Orig. and chiefly in phr. ***in quarto.***

Quarto-sizes range from 15 × 11 inches (***imperial quarto***) to 7⅝ × 6⅜ (***pot quarto***), according to the size of the original sheet.

1589 *Pappe w. Hatchet* B iij, All his works bound close, are at least sixe sheetes in quarto. **1633** PRYNNE *Histrio-m.* To Chr. Rdr., Some Play-books..are growne from Quarto into Folio. **1679** [see FOLIO 5]. **1720** *Lond. Gaz.* No. 5851/4 Sets of his Homer in..large or small Paper, or Quarto Royal may be had. **1793** BOSWELL *Johnson* Pref. 2nd ed., These I have ordered to be printed separately in quarto. **1837–9** HALLAM *Hist. Lit.* I. I. iii. §148. 250 The Psalter of 1457, and the Donatus of the same year, are in quarto. **1898** S. LEE *Life Shaks.* xix. (ed. 3) 299 In 1616 there had been printed in quarto seven editions of his 'Venus and Adonis'.

attrib. **1868** BROWNING *Ring & Bk.* I. 85 Small-quarto size, part print part manuscript.

fig. **1640** GLAPTHORNE *Wit in Constable* II. Wks. 1874 I. 195 The rest were made But fooles in Quarto, but I finde myselfe An asse in Folio.

2. A book composed of paper in this form; a quarto-volume.

1642 FULLER *Holy & Prof. St.* III. xxv. 228 Those which they bought in Folio shrink quickly into Quarto's. **1728** POPE *Dunc.* I. 141 Quarto's, octavo's, shape the less'ning pyre. **1769** *Junius Lett.* xx. 90 The form and magnitude of a quarto imposes upon the mind. **1839** YEOWELL *Anc. Brit. Ch.* Pref. (1847) 7 His writings..contain more matter than would be comprised in twenty modern quartos. **1898** S. LEE *Life Shaks.* xix. (ed. 3) 301 These sixteen quartos were publisher's ventures.

Comb. **1814** COLERIDGE *Lett.* (1895) II. 638 Of all scribblers these agricultural quarto-mongers are the vilest.

3. *attrib.* or as *adj.* Of paper: Folded so as to form four leaves out of the original sheet; having the size or shape of a quarter-sheet. Of books: Printed on paper thus folded or having this form. Of works: Published in quarto.

1633 PRYNNE *Histrio-m.* To Chr. Rdr. 1 b, Farre better paper than most Octavo or Quarto Bibles. *a* **1658** CLEVELAND *Wks.* (1687) 248 Where others go before In..Quarto Pages. **1711** HEARNE *Collect.* (O.H.S.) III. 131 These verses I have transcrib'd in a Q[to]. paper... He has also lent me a Quarto Vol. **1789** DK. LEEDS *Polit. Mem.* (1884) 137 It consisted of three sheets of Quarto Paper. **1807** *Life Fielding* in *Tom Jones*, Every thing..in the London quarto edition..is included in this new edition. **1821** BYRON *Juan* III. lxxxvi, He would write..a six canto quarto tale.

Quartodeciman (,kwɔːtəʊ'desɪmən), *sb.* and *a.* Also 7 **-decuman.** [ad. med.L. *quarta-*, *quartodecimān-us*, f. *quartus decimus* fourteenth.]

A. *sb.* One of those early Christians who celebrated Easter on the day of the Jewish Passover (the 14th of Nisan), whether this was a Sunday or not.

The practice (chiefly observed in Proconsular Asia) was condemned by the Council of Nice, A.D. 325.

1624 DARCIE *Birth of Heresies* viii. 31 The Phrygian Montanists condemne the Quartodecumans. **1642** HALES *Schism* 7 Why might not it be lawful..to celebrate Easter with the Quartodeciman. **1709** J. JOHNSON *Clergym. Vade M.* II. p. cxv, When Austin came first to this island, the Christians he found here were Quartodecimans. **1833** J. H. NEWMAN *Arians* I. i. (1876) 13. **1883** P. SCHAFF *Hist. Church* II. XII. lxxxiii. 706 There is no evidence at all that the apostle John celebrated Easter with the Quarto-decimans.

B. *adj.* Of or relating to the Quartodecimans, or their method of observing Easter.

1702 ECHARD *Eccl. Hist.* (1710) 478 The Quartodeciman controversie..between the Eastern and Western churches. **1761** HUME *Hist. Eng.* I. i. 38 The quartodeciman schism as it was called. **1833** J. H. NEWMAN *Arians* I. i. (1876) 13 Polycrates, who was primate of the Quarto-deciman churches. **1879** MACLEAR *Celts* xi. 180 The quarto-deciman view of the earlier Asiatics of Asia Minor.

Hence **Quarto'decimanism**, the views or practice of the Quartodecimans. Also †**Quartodecimarian** *a. Obs. rare*[−1].

1880 *Athenæum* 9 Oct. 463/2 The *quartodecimanism of John. **1885** G. SALMON in *Academy* 5 Dec. 367/2 The Ignatian letters have not a word about Quartodecimanism. **1666** BP. SAM. PARKER *Free Censure* 90 That early and unhappy *Quartodecimarian Schism.

quart-pot. **a.** A pot capable of containing the measure of a quart. Also *Austral.*, a billy-can of this measure for boiling tea-water, etc.

1422–2 *Abingdon Acc.* (1892) 94 Item j quartpot. **1463** *Bury Wills* (Camden) 23 A quart pot of pewter. **1550** CROWLEY *Epigr.* 363 Go fyll me thys quarte pot. **1593** SHAKS. *2 Hen. VI*, IV. x. 16 Many a time..it hath seru'd me insteede of a quart pot to drinke in. **1613** WITHER *Abuses Stript* I. v. 240 Sometime in reuenge the quart-pot flies. **1711** STEELE *Spect.* No. 22 ¶5, I came in with a Tub about me, that Tub hung with Quart-pots. **1838** DICKENS *O. Twist* xxv, A quart-pot..filled with gin and water. **1838** H. CAPPER *South Australia* (ed. 2) 71 List of other articles provided for the passengers.—One wooden mess bowl, one ditto platter, one mess bread basket, one tin quart-pot, two three-gallon hawse buckets.—For each mess of six passengers. **1863** [see sense b below]. **1870** LOWELL *Study Wind.* 47 Quartpots are for muddier liquor than nectar. **1881** A. C. GRANT *Bush Life in Queensland* I. v. 43 One of the quart-pots..was boiling madly. **1901** M. FRANKLIN *My Brilliant Career* i. 4, I refilled the quart-pot in which we had boiled our tea with water from the creek. **1936** A. RUSSELL *Gone Nomad* iii. 20 We had boiled the quartpots at a waterhole a mile or so back and were continuing on our way. **1941** *Coast to Coast* 155 He was a swaggie all right, with his roll of old blue blanket across his shoulders and his quart pot dangling from it.

b. *attrib.*, as **quart-pot tea**, *Austral.* (see quot. 1885).

1863 R. HENNING *Let.* 29 June (1966) 131 We..then made a fire, boiled some 'quart-pot tea', and sat down..to enjoy our dinner. **1878** MRS. H. JONES *Long Years in Australia* 87 Taking a long draught of the quart-pot tea. **1885** H. FINCH-HATTON *Advance Austral.* 111 'Quart-pot tea', as tea made in the Bush is always called... A tin quart of water is set down by the fire, and when it is boiling hard a handful of tea is thrown in.

quartre, quartrage, -redge, -ridge, quartron(e, -r(o)un, obs. ff. QUARTER *sb.* and *v.*, QUARTERAGE, QUARTERN.

†**quart-saw.** *Obs. rare*[−1]. (?)

1577 *Wills & Inv. N.C.* (Surtees 1835) 414 In the Ireon Seller. Eighte qwarte sawes xvj[s].—thre whope sawes xx[s].

quar'tumvirate. *rare*[−1]. [Cf. QUADRUM-, QUATRUMVIRATE.] = QUATUORVIRATE.

1819 SYD. SMITH *Wks.* (1859) I. 282/1 The noble quartumvirate, in all matters of foreign policy, have a veto on the king's decisions.

quartyer, obs. form of QUARTER *sb.*

quartz (kwɔːts). *Min.* [a. G. *quarz* (first in MHG.) of uncertain origin: hence also Du. *kwarts*, F. *quartz*, It. *quarzo.*]

1. A widely diffused mineral, massive or crystallizing in hexagonal prisms; in a pure form consisting of silica or silicon dioxide (SiO_2), but varying greatly in colour, lustre, etc., according to the different impurities it contains.

Quartz forms the rocks quartzite and sandstone, and is an important constituent in granite, gneiss, and other rocks. It frequently contains gold, and is largely mined and crushed for the purpose of extracting this metal (cf. quots. in 2). The numerous varieties are chiefly denoted by adjs. descriptive of their structure or colour, as (1) *amorphous, asteriated* (star-quartz), *capped, cavernous, compact,* (*crypto-*) *crystalline, fibrous, grained, radiated, sagenitic, sparry,* etc., (2) *blue* (siderite or sapphire-quartz), *brown* or *smoky* (cairngorm, morion), *green* (chrysoprase, prase), *milky* (milk-quartz), *purple* (amethyst), *red, rose, yellow* (citrine), etc.; also ***Babel*** or ***Babylonian quartz***, found in Devonshire, showing on its under-surface the impression of the crystals of fluor-spar on which it was deposited. The colourless crystalline variety is known as ROCK-CRYSTAL.

1756 *Observ. Isl. Scilly* 71 White debas'd Crystal (which the Germans call Quartz). **1772** tr. *Cronstedt's Min.* 57, I shall adopt this name of quartz in English as it has already gained access into other European languages. **1831** BREWSTER *Optics* xvii. §94. 151/2 Among the crystals best fitted for exhibiting the phenomena of positive double refraction is rock crystal or quartz. **1859** R. F. BURTON *Centr. Afr.* in *Jrnl. Geog. Soc.* XXIX. 107 Boulders of primitive formation, streaked with snow-white quartz. **1879** RUTLEY *Stud. Rocks* x. 150 Quartz is infusible before the blowpipe, insoluble in all acids except fluoric acid.

2. *attrib.* and *Comb.*

a. attrib. in sense 'consisting of quartz', or 'containing quartz', as ***quartz-boil*** (see quot. 1869), ***-crystal*** (cf. *quartz clock, watch* in sense c), ***dolerite***, ***-fret*** (poet.) [FRET *sb.*^{1}], ***-gritstone***, ***lead*** [LEAD *sb.*^{2} 6 a], ***leader*** [LEADER^{1} 13 c], ***-lode***, ***-pebble***, ***-porphyry***, ***-reef***, ***-rock***, ***-sand***, ***-schist***, ***-slate***, ***-vein***, etc.; **quartz glass**, a glass consisting almost entirely of silica; = *silica glass*.

1869 R. B. SMYTH *Gold Fields Victoria* 618 Quartz-boil, an outcrop of a quartz reef on the surface, or an outburst or extension in width of the reef beneath it. **1802** PLAYFAIR *Illustr. Hutton. Th.* 326 Granites containing quartz-crystals. **1933** K. HENNEY *Radio Engin. Handbk.* VII. 167 Piezo-electric quartz crystals provide standards of frequency, when permanently connected into suitable vacuum-tube circuits and allowed to oscillate continuously. **1959** R. H. BAKER *Astron.* (ed. 7) iii. 77 In the quartz-crystal clock now in use in observatories, a quartz crystal controls the frequency of an electronic oscillator, imposing its natural frequency of vibration on the current. **1970** *Observer* (Colour Suppl.) 3 May 27/1 The quartz crystal clock; most accurate domestic time-piece of all. **1977** T. ALLBEURY *Man with President's Mind* vii. 66 It was a small quartz-crystal watch. **1911** G. W. GRABHAM in C. T. Clough et al. *Geol. Glasgow District* iv. 146 A very interesting feature of the quartz dolerites is their instability at temperatures slightly above the consolidation point. **1970** R. J. SMALL *Study of Landforms* iii. 73 Among the more important of these are.. quartz-dolerite sills of the areas inland from Dippin Head. **1883** G. M. HOPKINS *Poems* (1967) 96 All The thick stars round him roll Flashing like flecks of coal, Quartz-fret, or sparks of salt, In grimy vasty vault. **1903** *Amer. Jrnl. Sci.* CLXVI. 469 Quartz glass.—A very full account of the behaviour of this material has been given by H. Heraeus. **1912** J. W. MELLOR *Mod. Inorg. Chem.* xl. 773 Quartz glass is used for the manufacture of elastic threads to suspend the delicate parts of electrical instruments. **1941** *Thorpe's Dict. Appl. Chem.* (ed. 4) V. 606/1 Quartz glass has an extremely small coefficient of linear thermal expansion,..and articles made from it can be heated to redness and quenched in cold water without fracture. **1965** PHILLIPS & WILLIAMS *Inorg. Chem.* I. xiv. 553 Soda-glass is conveniently worked at a lower temperature than borosilicate glass, and the latter at a lower temperature than quartz glass. **1789** SAUNDERS in *Phil. Trans.* LXXIX. 82 It is known to mineralists in that state by the name of quartz gritstone. **1866** 'MARK TWAIN' *Lett. from Hawaii* (1967) 272 There are hundreds of men in California who are sitting on their quartz leads..and hoping for the day when they will pay. **1884** R. C. REID *Rambles on Golden Coast N.Z.* x. 105 A slate face in which there are numerous quartz-leaders. **1877** RAYMOND *Statist. Mines & Mining* 218 Very little work has been done..on quartz-lodes. **1869** R. B. SMYTH *Gold Fields Victoria* 283 Quartz reefs are richer as they increase in depth. **1833** LYELL *Princ. Geol.* III. 367 Beds of pure quartz rock. **1843** PORTLOCK *Geol.* 170 Mica slate passing into quartz slate. **1802** PLAYFAIR *Illustr. Hutton. Th.* 167 Vertical strata much intersected by quartz veins.

b. attrib. in other senses, obj., and obj. gen., chiefly in terms relating to the extraction of gold from quartz, as ***quartz-battery***, ***-crusher***, ***-crushing*** adj., ***-gold*** (see quot. 1874), ***-mill***, ***-mining***, ***-prospecting***, ***-reefing*** (= mining), etc.

1860 H. J. HAWLEY *Jrnl.* 22 May in *Wisconsin Mag. of Hist.* (1936) XIX. 341 There are a Quarts Mills runing which crush the quarts that are raised from the Lodes. **1861** MRS. MEREDITH *Over the Straits* iv. 133 Quartz-reefin's the payinest game, now. **1872** RAYMOND *Statist. Mines & Mining* 17 Some gold quartz-mining enterprises have been in operation. **1874** *Ibid.* 317 It is largely 'quartz gold', that is, not rounded and water-worn, but irregular and frequently twisted in form, usually very bright, and always of fine quality, as is the gold of the quartz-veins. **1877** *Ibid.* 220 The discovery..of quartz-claims in the district. This action gave an impetus to quartz-prospecting. **1882** *Rep. to Ho. Repr. Prec. Met. U.S.* 596 Quartz-crushing machines yet to be invented. **1908** *Chambers's Jrnl.* Sept. 640/2 Natthey..had started a little quartz-mill on his claim.

c. Used *attrib.* to designate devices in which use is made of quartz, usu. for its optical or its piezo-electric properties; as ***quartz oscillator***, ***spectrograph***, ***temperature sensor***; **quartz clock**, a clock in which great accuracy is achieved by employing a vibrating quartz crystal in an oscillatory electric circuit to determine the frequency of the current; **quartz-halogen** *a.*, applied to electric light bulbs which have a quartz envelope and contain the vapour of a halogen (usu. iodine) in order to prevent deposition on the envelope of tungsten from the filament; so **quartz-iodine** *a.*; **quartz lamp**, a lamp in which the envelope is of quartz rather than glass, so that ultraviolet light will pass through it; **quartz-locked** *a.*, maintained at a constant speed of rotation by means of a quartz crystal, employed as in a quartz clock; **quartz watch**, a watch in which a quartz crystal is employed as in a quartz clock.

1937 *Ann. Reg. 1936* 63 Scheibe and Adelsberger (*Phys. Zeit.*) described the comparison of three 'quartz' clocks with the mean astronomical time obtained from three observatories during the 30 months ending June, 1935. **1976** R. CONDON *Whisper of Axe* I. xxii. 144 A collection was taken up to present him with a quartz clock. **1968** *Listener* 21 Mar. 391/3 Headlights..should make use of the extra brightness of the new quartz-halogen lamps. **1970** *AA Bk. of Car* 163/4 Quartz-halogen bulbs do not suffer from blackening as ordinary bulbs do. **1979** *Arizona Daily Star* 5 Aug. C5/3 (Advt.), Quartz-halogen fog light kit. Two fog lights and wiring kit. **1965** *Economist* 27 Feb. 929/2 The new quartz-iodine bulbs are being imported to Britain in growing though limited numbers... In France, quartz-iodine headlamps are now standard equipment for the Citroen Pallas. **1973** D. KYLE *Raft of Swords* (1974) xii. 122 'Lights, please.' He switched them on, pivoting the 1,000-watt quartz-iodine beams downward. **1922** *Brit. Med. Jrnl.* 4 Nov. 852/1 The recognition of the antirachitic action of sunlight..is the outcome of Huldschinsky's observations of the curative effect on rickets exerted by the ultra-violet rays emitted by the mercury-vapour quartz lamp. **1933** *Burlington Mag.* Sept. 139/1 If it [*sc.* the painting] could be closely studied with all the resources of the quartz-lamp and the microscope it seems hardly possible that it should not betray its later date. **1977** MCGUINNESS & STEIN *Building Technol.* xiv. 406/1 The quartz lamp has about three to four times the life of a normal incandescent. **1977** *Time* 14 Nov. 7 (Advt.), First they designed an all-direct-drive-motor-system. Using one motor for each reel and another quartz-locked motor for the tape capstan. **1938** *Proc. Physical Soc.* L. 413 The quartz oscillator not only is widely used for stabilizing the frequency of transmitting stations but also constitutes the most accurate means of recording the passage of time. **1905** *Astrophysical Jrnl.* XXII. 129 From negative by Professor R. W. Wood with quartz spectrograph of the Johns Hopkins University. **1966** *McGraw-Hill Encycl. Sci. & Technol.* XII. 590/1 Two types of quartz spectrographs are in common use for recording ultraviolet and visible spectra. **1978** *Sci. Amer.* Mar. 144/1 (Advt.), The HP 2804 digital thermometer achieves exceptional accuracy because HP calibrates each quartz temperature sensor. **1974** *Country Life* 5 Dec. 1763 (Advt.), Seiko sold the first quartz watch. **1976** *Times* 5 Feb. 17/5 The quartz watches now being produced fall into two groups..the traditional watch face..and digital watches.

quartziferous (kwɔːtˈsɪfərəs), *a.* [f. prec. + -(I)FEROUS.] Bearing or containing quartz.

1832 DE LA BECHE *Geol. Man.* (ed. 2) 403 The pieces of quartziferous porphyry..have better resisted attrition. **1872** W. S. SYMONDS *Rec. Rocks* iii. 49 The Quartziferous breccias..of the Caernarvon peninsula. **1879** RUTLEY *Stud. Rocks* xii. 242 A..number of diorites are quartziferous.

ˈquartzine, *a.* *rare*$^{-1}$. [f. as prec. + -INE^{1}.] Quartzose, quartzy.

1853 KANE *Grinnell Exp.* v. 40 Gneiss..was the basis material, the quartzine element greatly predominating.

quartzite (ˈkwɔːtsaɪt). *Min.* Also **-yte**. [f. as prec. + -ITE.] An extremely compact, granular rock, consisting essentially of quartz.

1849 MURCHISON *Siluria* viii. 167 The quartzites of the west are manifestly altered sandstones. **1873** J. GEIKIE *Gt. Ice Age* App. 479 A boulder of quartzite..was found embedded in a seam of coal.

attrib. **1870** *Pall Mall G.* 17 Nov. 4 The stag is formed of white quartzite stones. **1880** DAWKINS *Early Man* vii. 181 There were also quartzite flakes and implements.

Hence **quartˈzitic** *a.*, of the nature of quartzite.

1872 W. S. SYMONDS *Rec. Rocks* vi. 191 This remarkable yellowish and quartzitic conglomerate. **1876** PAGE *Adv. Text-bk. Geol.* viii. 157 Bands of quartzitic rock.

ˈquartzless, *a.* [f. as prec. + -LESS.] Destitute of quartz.

1879 RUTLEY *Stud. Rocks* xii. 235 Some of these rocks are very poor in quartz, and they then pass into the quartzless hornblende-andesites. **1892** *Nation* (N.Y.) 28 July 73/2 This widely distributed andesite is highly basic, in many cases being almost quartzless.

ˌquartzofeldˈspathic, *a.* *Petrol.* Also **-fels-**. [f. QUARTZ + -O + FELDSPATHIC, FELSPATHIC *a.*] Containing a high proportion of quartz and feldspar.

1839 H. T. DE LA BECHE *Rep. Geol. Cornwall, Devon & W. Somerset* vi. 175 It has chiefly a quartzo-felspathic base with crystals of felspar. **1973** *Nature* 11 May 62/2 The oldest known rocks in the world are quartzofeldspathic gneisses (the Amîtsoq gneisses) from the Godthaab area of West Greenland.

ˈquartzoid. [f. as QUARTZ + -OID.] A crystal having the form of a double six-sided pyramid.

1864 WEBSTER cites DANA. **1882** DANA *Man. Min.* (ed. 4) 47.

quartzose (ˈkwɔːtsəʊs), *a.* [f. as prec. + -OSE.] Mainly or entirely composed of quartz; of the nature of quartz.

1757 DA COSTA *Fossils* 275 Pellucid quartzose grains it has none. **1857** BIRCH *Anc. Pottery* (1858) II. 332 Some varieties of this ware are filled with quartzose sand. **1878** A. H. GREEN, etc. *Coal* ii. 47 Thick masses of very coarse quartzose conglomerate.

So †**ˈquartzous** *a.* *Obs.*

1790 *Monthly Rev.* III. 547 It appears, that hard quartzous and silicious stones give a reddish light. **1815** *Chron.* in *Ann. Reg.* 540 The sand..is quartzous.

quartzy (ˈkwɔːtsɪ), *a.* [f. as prec. + -Y^{1}.] Of the nature of quartz; resembling quartz.

1774 PENNANT *Tour Scotl. in 1772*, 218 The stones of this mountain are white—quartzy and composed of small grains. **1836** MACGILLIVRAY tr. *Humboldt's Trav.* xviii. 256 The bottom, which consists of white quartzy sand, is usually visible. **1880** BIRDWOOD *Ind. Art* II. 4 The iron ore is.. separated from its granitic or quartzy matrix by washing.

fig. **1864** ROGERS *New Rush* II. 42 He..avows his inability to find Another lyric in his quartzy mind.

quarved, ? error for *quarred*: see QUAR *v.*^{1}

1627 JACKSON *Creed* VI. xii. §9 This..current of life..the more it is dammed or quarued by opposition of the sonnes of darknesse, the more plentifully it overflowes the sons of light.

†**ˈquary.** *Obs.*$^{-1}$. [? ad. L. *quārē* wherefore.]

a **1550** *Image Hypocr.* in *Skelton's Wks.* (1843) II. 427 With quibes and quaryes Of inventataries.

quaryndo(u)n, obs. forms of QUARRENDEN.

quas, variant of KVASS.

quas(e, obs. northern forms of WHOSE.

quasar (ˈkweɪsɑː(r), -zɑː(r)). *Astr.* [f. QUAS(ISTELL)AR *a.*] Any of a class of celestial objects that give a star-like (i.e. unresolved) image on a photograph and have a spectrum showing a large red shift, usu. taken to indicate great remoteness and immense power.

1964 H.-Y. CHIU in *Physics Today* May 21/2 So far, the clumsily long name 'quasi-stellar radio sources' is used to describe these objects. Because the nature of these objects is entirely unknown, it is hard to prepare a short, appropriate nomenclature for them so that their essential properties are obvious from their name. For convenience, the abbreviated form 'quasar' will be used throughout this paper. **1964** *Observer* 14 June 1/1 For the past twelve months, astronomers have been obsessed with these 'quasars' or 'quasi-stars' as they are now called. **1968** L. DURRELL *Tunc* i. 18 Here was Vibart persuading poor Felix to quit quasars and debouch into memoirs. **1968** *Times* 13 Nov. 16/2 One view is that the red-shift comes about because quasars are remarkably distant at the boundaries of the known universe. The other..is that quasars are extremely massive objects, and that the light from them is reddened by gravitational effects. **1971** *Sci. Amer.* May 55/2 The term quasar..was originally applied only to the starlike counterparts of certain strong radio sources whose optical spectra exhibit red shifts much larger than those of galaxies. Before long, however, a class of quasi-stellar objects was discovered with large red shifts that have little or no emission at radio wave-lengths. 'Quasar' is now commonly applied to starlike objects with large red shifts regardless of their radio emissivity. *Ibid.* 56/2 Assuming that they are at cosmological distances, one can easily show that many quasars are from 50 to 100 times brighter than entire galaxies containing hundreds of billions of stars. **1973** *Nature* 6 July 19/2 Two neutral-coloured stellar objects..have been shown to be QSOs with redshifts of 3·40 and 3·53 respectively. This has stimulated interest in other radio sources identified with stellar objects which lack the ultraviolet or blue colour excesses normally associated with quasars. **1978** *Daily Tel.* 8 June 2/5 The nearest known quasar in space, an object the size of the solar system but emitting the energy of 100 galaxies, has been discovered by an X-ray experiment aboard an American satellite. **1978** PASACHOFF & KUTNER *University Astron.* xxviii. 713 We now use the term quasar to include both quasi-stellar radio sources and quasi-stellar objects.

quash, *sb.*^{1} *rare.* A squash or pumpkin.

1687 MIEGE *Grt. Fr. Dict.* II. Quash. *See* Pompion. **1736** AINSWORTH *Lat. Dict.*, A quash, or pompion, *pepo.* [Hence in JOHNSON and later Dicts.] **1823** T. ROUGHLEY *Jamaica Planter's Guide* 74 The Indian kale, ochro, quash, peppers, akys, and a variety of pulse, being natural to the climate.

quash, *sb.*^{2} *rare*$^{-1}$. [Cf. WASH.] ? A stretch of shallow water.

1790 BEATSON *Nav. & Mil. Mem.* I. 69 From the report made by those who sounded the quash opposite the town.. there was not found water sufficient to enable them to undertake the enterprize.

quash (kwɒʃ), *v.* Forms: 4–5 **quasse**, (5 **qwas-**), 4 **quasche**, 5 **qv-**, **quaschyn**, **quassh-**, **quaysch-**, 6– **quash**. [In branch I, ad. OF. *quasser* = *casser* to annul, ad. late L. *cassāre* (med.L. also *quassāre*), f. *cassus* null, void; in branch II, ad. OF. *quasser*, *casser* to break, smash, etc.:—L. *quassāre*, freq. of *quatĕre* to shake. In later F. the form in all senses is *casser*. Senses 2 and 3 may be partly derived from 4, and the later examples in 5 may be partly of onomatopœic origin. Cf. SQUASH *v.*]

I. 1. *trans.* To annul, to make null or void (a law, decision, election, etc.); to throw out or reject (a writ, indictment, etc.) as invalid; to put an end to, stop completely (legal proceedings). †Also with *down*.

c **1330** R. BRUNNE *Chron.* (1810) 209 Þe pape at his dome þer Elites quassed doun. *Ibid.* 217 Þe purueiance..He quassed it ilk dele þorgh jugement. *c* **1430** *Pilgr. Lyf Manhode* I. lxxvi. (1869) 44 Michel it displeseth hire that ye quassen thus hire ordinaunces. **1589** WARNER *Alb. Eng.* VI. xxx. (1612) 151 Phœbus his plainte did quash. **1671** F. PHILLIPS *Reg. Necess.* 521 All the then Judges did agree, that if a Writ of that Form should be brought unto them..they would immediately quash it. **1768** BLACKSTONE *Comm.* III. 303 Praying 'judgment of the writ, or declaration, and that the same may be quashed', *cassetur*, made void, or abated. **1829** SCOTT *Demonol.* ix. 335 The Lord Advocate..quashed all farther procedure. **1882** SERJT. BALLANTINE *Exper.* iv. 43 My clients were completely exonerated and the conviction was quashed.

b. Used adverbially with *go* (suggesting sense 4).

1802–12 BENTHAM *Ration. Judic. Evid.* (1827) IV. 406 Down comes the money, quash goes the conviction, like a snail under our feet.

2. To bring to nothing; to crush or destroy; to put down or suppress completely; to stifle (*esp.* a feeling, idea, scheme, undertaking, proceeding, etc.). Also with *down*.

1609 BIBLE (Douay) *Ecclus.* vi. 2 Extol not thyself..lest perhaps thy strength be quashed. **1646** P. BULKELEY *Gospel Covt.* v. 366 Balaam had faire hopes before him..but all was quasht in a moment. **1717** TABOR in *Phil. Trans.* XXX. 552 When the Ground about the Pavement was dug, all these Suppositions were quash'd. **1774** GOLDSM. *Nat. Hist.* (1862) I. 34 The sound seemed at last quashed in a bed of water. **1834** PRINGLE *Afr. Sk.* 316 Every such attempt had heretofore been..quashed by the..authorities. **1857** MRS. CARLYLE *Lett.* II. 313, I wanted to scream, but the physical weariness had quashed down that nonsense. **1879** FROUDE *Cæsar* xviii. 305 The preparations for the election were quashed.

3. To crush, quell, or utterly subdue (a person); to squash. Now *rare*.

1639 G. DANIEL *Ecclus.* xxxv. 50 His Arme Shall Quash the Cruell, and prevent their harme. **1643** BURROUGHES *Exp. Hosea* I. v. 128 They did not stay the building of the wall of Jerusalem, till all their adversaries were quashed. **1753** HANWAY *Trav.* (1762) II. VII. ii. 168 This..resolution.. would in all probability have quashed their enemies. **1876** BLACKIE *Songs Relig. & Life* 182 When, by Logic's iron rule, I've quashed each briskly babbling fool.

II. †4. To break or dash in pieces; to smash; also, to crush, squeeze, squash. *Obs.*

1387 TREVISA *Higden* (Rolls) IV 439 þanne þe secounde wal was i-quasched [*v.r.* yquaysched]. ? *a* **1400** *Morte Arth.* 3389 Abowte scho whirles the whele..Tille alle my qwarters..ware qwaste al to peces. **1563–87** FOXE *A. & M.* (1596) 310/2 A mightie stone..able to haue quashed him in peeces. **1608** TOPSELL *Serpents* (1658) 628 Then, shepheard, take both stone in hand, and blade, To quash his swelling neck. **1650** BULWER *Anthropomet.* 12 The Fathers and Mothers never faile to quash, or flat down that part of the face which is between the eyes and mouth. **1750** W. ELLIS *Mod. Husbandm.* IV. iii. 85 (E.D.S.) [Boys] rejoice when they find a nest of eggs to quash with their feet.

†b. To dash or smash *on* or *against* something.

1548 UDALL *Erasm. Par. Luke* ix. 99 The eiuill spirit that was in hym tooke hym, quashyng the chylde on the grounde. **1620** WILKINSON *Coroners & Sherifes* 19 A man falleth from his horse and quasheth his head against a blocke. *c* **1645** WALLER *Batt. Summer-Isl.* II. 25 The whales Against sharp rocks, like reeling vessels quash'd..are in pieces dash'd.

†5. *intr.* To shake; to splash, to make a splashing noise. *Obs.*

1393 LANGL. *P. Pl.* C. XXI. 64 The erthe quook and quashte as hit quyke were. **1691** RAY *Creation* II. (1692) 12 A thin and fine Membrane strait and closely adhering to keep it [the brain] from quashing and shaking. **1739** SHARP *Surg.* xxiv. 122 The water by a sudden Jirk may be heard to quash. **1750** W. ELLIS *Mod. Husbandm.* III. i. 130 (E.D.S.) When the butter is come, which you may know by its quashing.

Hence **quashed** (kwɒʃt) *ppl. a.*; **'quashing** *vbl. sb.* and *ppl. a.*

a **1665** J. GOODWIN *Filled w. the Spirit* (1867) 107 A notion ..of a dangerous and quashing import to the spirit of all signal excellency. **1802–12** BENTHAM *Ration. Judic. Evid.* (1827) IV. 408 A rare trade, this quashing trade. **1816** W. TAYLOR in *Monthly Mag.* XLII. 35 These are called stratous clouds from their sinking quashed appearance. **1846** J. HAMILTON *Mt. of Olives* viii. 196 With quashed delight and bitter fancies. **1859** I. TAYLOR *Logic in Theol.* 270 A factitious quashing of any sensibility.

quash, obs. variant of KVASS.

Quashee ('kwɒʃiː), **Quashie** ('kwɒʃɪ). Also 8 **Quashy**, 9 **Quashi**. [Ashantee or Fantee *Kwasi*, a name commonly given to a child born on Sunday.] A Negro personal name, adopted as a general name for any Black.

1778 P. THICKNESSE *Year's Journey* (ed. 2) II. xlv. 104 When Quashy, found the physicians had given his master over, he stole his breeches..and went off with them... The indignant master..never recovered his *faithful* black, nor his *departed* breeches. **1825** C. WATERTON *Wanderings* iv. 279 Quashi's fiddle was silent. **1833** M. SCOTT *Tom Cringle* (1862) 246 Then Quashie himself, or a company of free blacks. **1850** MRS. CARLYLE *Lett.* II. 122 A certain sympathy with Quashee! **1889** CLARK RUSSELL *Marooned* (1890) 275 The same Quashee whom I had supposed dead. **1960** *Tamarack Rev.* XIV. 7 'Can't catch Quashie, catch his shirt' is a West Indian proverb, so the occupiers turned to gold of another colour: brown gold, sugar.

quashey. *rare*$^{-1}$. (See quot. and cf. QUASH *sb.*^{1})

1823 SOUTHEY *Lett.* (1856) III. 391 With regard to these said quasheys (which, I believe, is their name,—first cousins to the squash pumpkin).

quasi ('kweɪsaɪ, -zaɪ, 'kwaːzɪ), *adv.* and *pref.* [L. *quasi* as if, as it were, almost.]

I. In limiting sense.

1. Used parenthetically = 'as it were', 'almost', 'virtually'. *rare.*

In Caxton after F. *quasi* (15th c., from It. or L.).

1485 CAXTON *Paris & V.* (1868) 30 Whereof he was moche angry, and quasi half in despair. —— *Chas. Gt.* 204 After that charles had the domynacyon quasi in al espayne. **1692** T. WATSON *Body of Div.* 97 Men come quasi armed in Coat of Male, that the Sword of the Word will not enter. **1818** CRUISE *Digest* (ed. 2) V. 184 This devolution..is *quasi* a descent *per formam doni*.

2. In close connexion with the word following; hence usually treated as a prefix and hyphened.

a. With sbs.: (A) kind of; resembling or simulating, but not really the same as, that properly so termed. ***quasi-art***, ***-belief***, ***-continuum***, ***-copula***, ***-crime***, ***-definition***, ***-dereliction***, ***-dying***, ***-emperor***, ***-equilibrium***, ***-existence***, ***-implication***, ***-jazz***, ***-marriage***, ***-miracle***, ***-modal***, ***-molecule***, ***-monopoly***, ***-neutrality***, ***-nuptial***, ***-object***, ***-partner***, ***-quotation***, ***-quote***, ***-religion***, ***-science***, ***-semi***, ***-sensation***, ***-statement***, ***-substance***, ***-totality***, ***-universal***, ***-vacuity***, ***-verb***, ***-war***.

1837 CARLYLE *Fr. Rev.* I. VI. iv, The art, or quasi-art, of standing in tail. **1925** C. D. BROAD *Mind & its Place in Nature* iv. 217 The quasi-belief which is an essential factor in all perceptual situations. **1942** *Mind* LI. 245 When I read about Captain Costigan or about Mr. Micawber I knew perfectly well and all the time that there were no such persons. There is no temporary quasi-belief or make-believe..as there is in the case of the mirage. **1966** D. G. BRANDON *Mod. Techniques Metallogr.* 179 The conduction electrons in a metal occupy a quasi-continuum of energy levels. **1979** *Sci. Amer.* May 108/1 In this region, known as the quasi-continuum, the additional rotational and translational states provide all the 'fine tuning' necessary to match the photon frequency with the quantum gap between vibrational levels. **1934** WEBSTER, Quasi copula. **1963** F. T. VISSER *Hist. Syntax Eng. Lang.* I. ii. 153 We have a similar complete change of status when verbs of this kind function as quasi-copulas, as in 'this meat eats tough'. **1966** *Eng. Stud.* XLVII. 51 An interesting..problem arises with quasi-copulas i.e. border-line cases where the verb may stand between 'copula' and 'full verb'. **1727–41** CHAMBERS *Cycl.* s.v. *Quasi-contract*, The reparation of quasi-crimes. **1927** C. R. S. HARRIS *Duns Scotus* II. vi. 188 We are..able to arrive at a quasi-definition in which we can describe it [*sc.* the divine essence] more perfectly than by means of any of its other attributes. **1939** *Mind* XLVIII. 541 And this he does by discerning (between the lines) the frequent interpolations of new quasi-definitions demarcating new distinctions of meaning of the terms involved. **1978** *Dædalus* Summer 28 Let us note three elements. First, a quasidefinition of the marginal man. **1950** D. GASCOYNE *Vagrant* 8, I stand still in my quasi-dereliction. **1676** R. DIXON *Two Testaments* 30 The reason why God confirmed his Testament..is, because this was an act of his Quasi-dying. **1864** KINGSLEY *Rom. & Teut.* iii. (1875) 91 Romans, with Greek names who become quasi-emperors. **1905** *Jrnl. Geol.* XIII. 393 The surface ever wearing down, the waste.. continually exported by the winds, a nearly level rock-floor, ..everywhere slowly lowering at the rate of sand and dust exportation, is developed over a larger and larger area; and such is the condition of quasi-equilibrium for old age. **1964** *Amer. Jrnl. Sci.* CCLXII. 793 As the landscape slowly degrades..rivers have a tendency to remain in quasi-equilibrium. **1978** *Dædalus* Spring 25 Most states of nature are quasiequilibria, the outcome of competing forces. **1909** W. M. URBAN *Valuation* v. 127 An aspect..is given a quasi-existence. **1944** M. BLACK in P. A. Schilpp *Philos. B. Russell* 241 Hamlet and the Snark, the philosopher's stone and the round square, being all characterised by predicates, must all, in some versions of this position, have their being in a multiplicity of distinct limbos, realms of *Sosein*, *Aussersein* and *Quasisein* in which to enjoy their ambiguous status of partial or quasi-existence. **1951** *Mind* LX. 355 The truth-table for 'quasi-implication' in Professor Reichenbach's three-valued logic. **1973** J. J. ZEMAN *Modal Logic* ii. 21 We may refer to such formulas as 'quasi-implications'. **1947** R. DE TOLEDANO *Frontiers of Jazz* 70 Hundreds of musicians, playing in all the jazz and quasi-jazz styles. **1977** *Time Out* 28 Jan. 47 (*caption*) The already expansive Runt canvas—everything from Philly soul harmonies through wittily timeless psychedelia and inspiring quasi-jazz—has added two more excellent albums. **1926** W. J. LOCKE *Stories Near & Far* 166 Quasi-marriage bond. **1976** *National Observer* (U.S.) 4 Sept. 13/3 'What does it matter what we think?' says a friend of mine, three of whose sons have opted for quasi marriage. **1893** *Mind* II. 210 That seems to me but an excessively clumsy way of stating in terms of a *quasi*-miracle the very truth which Stumpf and I express by saying that likeness is an immediately ascertained relation. **1971** J. ANDERSON in A. J. Aitken et al. *Edin. Stud. Eng. & Scots* 71 Certain 'quasi-modals', which satisfy some but not all of the criteria. **1972** W. LABOV *Lang. in Inner City* ix. 376 The quasimodals produce many problems which are not fully resolved. **1968** C. G. KUPER *Introd. Theory Superconductivity* xi. 181 A pair of electrons in the immediate vicinity of the Fermi surface can form a bound quasimolecule. **1975** *McGraw-Hill Yearbk. Sci. & Technol.* 115/2 Electron ejection from an atom or a quasimolecule is due to the time-varying electric field acting on the electron as the collision partners pass each other. **1934** *Planning* II. XL. 6 Where monopoly or quasi-monopoly powers are taken there shall be an independent chairman and other independent members of the Industry Board administering the scheme. **1980** *Jrnl. R. Soc. Arts* Mar. 207/1 Once a housebuilder has bid successfully for what little land is available..a quasi-monopoly situation is created. **1934** WEBSTER, Quasi neutrality. **1962** W. B. THOMPSON *Introd. Plasma Physics* ii. 9 Because of their inertia, the electrons will oscillate about the initially charged region but with a very high frequency, so that quasi-neutrality is preserved in the mean. **1889** SWINBURNE *Stud. Jonson* 47 The epithalamium of these quasi-nuptials is fine. **1963** F. T. VISSER *Hist. Syntax Eng. Lang.* I. iv. 453 With verbs that do not usually take a direct object..the construction with indefinite *it* as quasi-object is also frequently met with. **1967** Quasi object [see INCOMPLETE *a.* 2]. **1848** BOUVIER *Law Dict.* (ed. 3) II. 401 *Quasi partners*, partners of lands, goods, or chattels, who are not actual partners, are sometimes so called. **1930** M. CLARK *Home Trade* 3 Quasi-partners are those who have played, but no longer play, an active part. **1867** G. M. HOPKINS *Let.* 15 Aug. (1956) 41 There are quotations or quasi-quotations fr. the Bible in it. **1943** *Mind* LII. 267 It may be doubted..whether the additional typographical complexity of the device of 'quasi-quotation' is worth the bother. **1937** W. V. QUINE in *Jrnl. Symbolic Logic* II. 146 An expression beginning and ending in corners is to denote the expression which we obtain, from the expression between the corners, by replacing all Greek letters by the expressions which those Greek letters are intended to denote. The corners may thus be viewed as 'quasi-quotes'; but they must not be confused with ordinary quotation marks. **1949** *Mind* LVIII. 524 The quasi-quotes would not be needed if '⊃' and '~' were being used autonymously. **1934** WEBSTER, Quasi religion. **1952** C. P. BLACKER *Eugenics* 112 Once the importance of eugenics was grasped, once its principles had 'been accepted as a quasi-religion, the result will be manifested in sundry and very effective modes of action which are as yet untried, and many of them unforeseen'. **1977** P. JOHNSON *Enemies of Society* xiv. 193 Pseudo-sciences, irrational quasi-religions, and phantasmagoric utopias. **1874** W. WALLACE tr. *Hegel's Logic* 21 The quasi-sciences..are founded on an act of arbitrary will alone, such as Heraldry. **1924** W. B. SELBIE *Psychol. Relig.* ii. 33 Frazer also regards it [*sc.* magic] as a quasi-science, in fundamental opposition to religion. **1976** *Word 1971* XXVII. 77 To me this is quasiscience, if not pseudoscience. **1974** P. WRIGHT *Lang. Brit. Industry* xvii. 162 *Quasi-semis*, joined by their garages, certainly act as *semis*, though their Latin *quasi* sounds so foreign to English speech. **1979** *W. Lancs. Even. Gaz.* 23 Feb. 17 (Advt.), Quasi semi conveniently situated to all schools. **1922** JOYCE *Ulysses* 674 What were Stephen's and Bloom's quasisimultaneous volitional quasisensations of concealed identities? **1948** *Mind* LVII. 194 Necessary statements, then, might be called 'quasi-statements', to indicate that they neither *mention* the expressions of which they are composed, nor *use* them to talk about the non-linguistic world. **1972** *Jrnl. Symbolic Logic* XXXVII. 421 A quasi-statement is a statement or a question. **1925** C. D. BROAD *Mind & its Place* iii. 99 Even so extreme a dualist about Mind and Matter as Descartes occasionally suggests that a mind and its body together form a quasi-substance. **1943** *Mind* LII. 336 'Space' is the name of an entity, a quasi-substance, though according to Kant a mind-dependent one. **1941** *Mind* L. 389 A mechanism in the modern sense of the term, *viz.*, as a quasi-totality of serial and reciprocating temporal causes. **1977** *Dædalus* Fall 141 History is also connected more generally, more largely to the quasi-totality of the social sciences. **1890** W. JAMES *Princ. Psychol.* I. xii. 475 The nominalists, on their side, admit a *quasi*-universal, something which we think *as if it were* universal, though it is not. **1643** SIR T. BROWNE *Relig. Med.* I. §49 An Empyriall Heaven, a *quasi vacuitie*. **1957** *Publ. Amer. Dial. Soc.* XXVIII. 31 The affirmative quasi-verb *better*. **1972** *Language* XLVIII. 466 Quasi-verbs..constitute an inflectional category which is rare, or possibly unique, among Indo-European languages. **1815** J. ADAMS *Wks.* (1856) X. 151 A ..plot..to draw me into a decided instead of a quasi war with France.

b. With adjs., more rarely with advbs. or vbs.: Seemingly, or in appearance, but not really; almost, nearly, virtually. ***quasi-æsthetic***, ***-arithmetical***, ***-automatic*** (hence ***-automatically***), ***-classic***, ***-colloquial***, ***-continuous***, ***-crystalline***, ***-deify*** vb., ***-divine***, ***-elastic***, ***-Episcopal***, ***-eternal***, ***-ethical*** (hence ***-ethically***), ***-Fascist***, ***-feudal***, ***-general***, ***-governmental***, ***-grammatical***, ***-hallucinatory***, ***-historical***, ***-horizontal***, ***-independent***, ***-instantaneous***, ***-judicial***, ***-legal***, ***-logical***, ***-marital***, ***-material***, ***-mathematical***, ***-mechanical***, ***-mechanistic***, ***-metallic***, ***-metaphysical***, ***-military***, ***-miraculous***, ***-molecular***, ***-monastic***, ***-mythical***, ***-neutral***, ***-normal***, ***-official***, ***-optical***, ***-ossianic***, ***-periodic***, ***-permanent***, ***-personal***, ***-philosophical***, ***-physical***, ***-public***, ***-purposive***, ***-religious***, ***-scientific***, ***-simultaneous*** (hence ***-simultaneously***), ***-stationary***, ***-technical***, ***-thermodynamic***, ***-totalitarian***, ***-transitive***, ***-universal***.

1909 W. M. URBAN *Valuation* vi. 152 In certain quasi-aesthetic combinations of utilities—as in a festal meal..—a detail..may acquire an extraordinary value. **1963** R. M. HARE *Freedom & Reason* ix. 174 The universal, quasi-aesthetic ideal of not having addicts about the place. **1944** *Mind* LIII. 242 One could of course use as M a quasi-arithmetical calculus whose integers are construed as particulars. **1965** *Language* XLI. 490 A quasi-arithmetical notation for syntactic description. **1890** W. JAMES *Princ. Psychol.* II. xxvi. 523 The intermediary terms of an habitual series of acts leading to an end are apt to be of this *quasi*-automatic sort. **1963** F. T. VISSER *Hist. Syntax* I. ii. 152 Intransitive verbs used to represent the action—as quasi-automatic, or self-originated. *Ibid.* 159 An interesting sequence of intransitive verbs and 'transitive' verbs used quasi-automatically. **1905** O. JESPERSEN *Growth & Struct. Eng. Lang.* vi. 123 Authors sometimes coin quasi-classic words without finding anybody to pass them on, as when Milton writes 'our *inquisiturient* Bishops' (Areop. 13). **1802–12** BENTHAM *Ration. Judic. Evid.* (1827) I. 149 Falsehood in this quasi-colloquial shape, as well as in the shape of ordinary discourse. **1890** W. JAMES *Princ. Psychol.* I. xiii. 531 The jingling of the bells on the horses of a horse-car passing the door..and the rumbling of the vehicle itself, ..to our ordinary hearing merge together very readily into a *quasi*-continuous body of sound. **1973** *Jrnl. Amer. Chem. Soc.* XCV. 8301/1 The Raman spectrum of titanium tetraiodide in solution has been obtained previously..by use of 694·3 nm excitation of a quasicontinuous ruby laser. **1946** *Nature* 31 Aug. 297/2 Such scattering [of sound waves] has been ascribed either to the quasi-crystalline structure of a liquid. **1964** G. H. HAGGIS et al. *Introd. Molecular Biol.* ix. 220 Wilkins, Franklin and others.., by drawing out threads from concentrated DNA solutions with careful control of humidity, have been able to get the molecules into a highly-orientated quasi-crystalline form and to obtain in this way more detailed diffraction patterns. **1826** SOUTHEY *Vind. Eccl. Angl.* 394 We neither deify nor quasi-deify the head of our Church. **1941** WYNDHAM LEWIS *Let.* 21 Oct. (1963) 302 The 'Royal Academy' seems to them a quasi-divine institution. **1955** R. GRAVES *Crowning Privilege* 113 The living poet hero is a modernism; I think I am right in saying that Petrarch was the first poet to receive quasi-divine honours during his lifetime. **1899** *Phil. Mag.* XLVIII. 80 The destructive effects of earthquakes are..due to the propagation of quasi-elastic disturbances. **1972** *Sci. Amer.* Oct. 103/3 The observation of pairs of alpha particles with this unique signature emerging from heavy nuclei was taken to indicate the presence of essentially free alpha particles at the nuclear surface. Such scattering is called quasi-elastic because the particles are not totally free but are somewhat bound to the target nucleus. **1976** *Nature* 15 July 177/1 In these plots, the vertical lines around $A = 32$ correspond to the incident ^{32}S ions that have undergone peripheral elastic or quasielastic interactions with the loss or gain of a few nucleons. **1861** KINGSLEY *Lett.* (1878) II. 80 The independent and quasi-Episcopal position of the rector. **1895** *Psychol. Rev.* II. 124 [Parts of mental contents do not] have an eternal or quasi-eternal individual existence, like the parts of objects. **1932** H. H. PRICE *Perception* viii. 223 We must not..think that nearness is always an 'advantage' (if we may go on using this quasi-ethical language). **1949** *Mind*

LVIII. 203 The deductions which welfare economists make are quasi-ethical. **1909** W. M. Urban *Valuation* vii. 214 The feeling . . is quasi-ethically qualified. **1938** *Political Q.* IX. i. 133 The new Germany, imperialist Japan and quasi-Fascist Poland must all, at the least, be democratised. **1954** Koestler *Invis. Writing* iv. xxxv. 376 Greece, too, lived under a quasi-Fascist dictatorship. **1960** —— *Lotus & Robot* ii. x. 228 Japan was able to . . build a quasi-capitalistic state on a quasi-feudal foundation. **1977** *Dædalus* Summer 50 The straitjackets of public regulations, quasi-feudal traditions, financial dependence, and intellectual routine which have so often paralyzed the universities of postwar Europe. **1896** W. Caldwell *Schopenhauer's Syst.* ix. 47 This fact . . warrants us in calling his whole philosophy a *quasi* general overturning of the philosophy of the idea. **1948** *Mind* LVII. 50 If 'If Nero had been Seneca' means anything at all, it is a quasi-general proposition which can be analysed either as 'If Nero had had the character of Seneca' or 'If Seneca had been emperor' or in some similar fashion. **1961** *Ethical Outlook* May–June 93/2 If corporations are not to run away with us, they must become quasi-governmental institutions. **1977** P. Johnson *Enemies of Society* xii. 167 The University Grants Committee, the quasi-governmental body which distributes state cash. **1953** H. A. Hatzfeld *Crit. Bibliogr. New Stylistics* i A theoretical, communicable, analytical, quasi-grammatical language of the critic. **1955** J. L. Austin *How to do Things with Words* (1962) vi. 68 'I state that' seems to conform to our grammatical or quasi-grammatical requirements. **1890** W. James *Princ. Psychol.* ii. xx. 220 *Optical objects not actually present* . . being imagined now with a quasi-hallucinatory strength. **1979** C. E. Schorske *Fin-de-Siècle Vienna* vii. 330 A quasi-hallucinatory, erotic dream experience. **1880** A. H. Sayce *Introd. Sci. Lang.* ii. vii. 98 Many of the ballads are quasi-historical. **1933** *Mind* XLII. 396 Objective Spirits . . *regulate* individual personality, making personality, by participation, a quasi-historical thing, or, as I should perhaps have said, a sui-thing. **1956** *Nature* 21 Jan. 113/2 The salient place in theory taken by horizontal wind divergence . . was stressed by showing its relation . . with the development of circulations, cyclonic and anti-cyclonic, through the vorticity equation applied to quasi-horizontal motions on a rotating Earth. **1967** *Oceanogr. & Marine Biol.* V. 82 The analysis of the water masses of the southwest Pacific show them to be very clearly stratified, . . with the different water masses lying in quasi-horizontal layers. **1933** *Mind* XLII. 385 There is . . no point in '*reifying*' the system, and then treating it as something quasi-independent of its parts, because, in these cases its behaviour is inferable from a knowledge of the parts. **1966** S. Beer *Decision & Control* xv. 381 Cybernetic insights show, in particular, that the totality of the organization ought to be made up of building-blocks that will be called quasi-independent domains. **1958** *Bull. Geol. Soc. Amer.* LXIX. 111/2 In geologic writing . . the standards for contemporaneity and instantaneousness are more flexible. Perhaps, H. and G. Termier's (1956) expression quasi-instantaneous (*quasi-instantané*) could be recommended as a convenient term to indicate instantaneousness in the geologic sense. **1960** C. S. Lewis *Studies in Words* 214 The words in a great poet's phrase . . strike the mind as a quasi-instantaneous chord, yet, strictly speaking, each word must be read or heard before the next. **1836** Sir H. Taylor *Statesman* viii. 50 His functions in these cases are quasi-judicial. **1911** Webster, Quasi legal. **1951** E. E. Evans-Pritchard *Social Anthropol.* i. 14 The sample includes studies of . . quasi-legal institutions . . and of the entire social organization . . of one or other people. **1965** H. Kahn *On Escalation* ix. 172 The declaration of war is just one of a series of legal and quasi-legal measures . . which have a role in escalation situations. **1902** W. James *Var. Relig. Exper.* iv. 106 Philosophers usually profess to give a quasi-logical explanation of the existence of evil. **1960** *New Biol.* XXXI. 135 They form part of an entrancing quasi-logical world, but it has little in common with the pedestrian, irrational world of the empiric. **1959** G. D. Mitchell *Sociol.* 64 His wife's sisters are, therefore, in a relationship to him which Radcliffe-Brown has described as quasi-marital. **1978** *Times Lit. Suppl.* 1 Dec. 1391/4 The eighty-six men assigned to the 'dysfunctional' group also lacked any quasi-marital partnership and often expressed regret about their homosexuality, but they were sexually more active and promiscuous. **1876** *Nation* 8 June 369/1 It [*sc.* liberty] and necessity being alike indemonstrable by any quasi-material process, must be *postulated* if taken at all. **1924** W. B. Selbie *Psychol. Relig.* xiv. 269 This 'soul' was regarded as similar to the body in form and nature, and as having a quasi-material existence of its own. **1870** W. S. Jevons in *Phil. Trans. R. Soc.* CLX. 516 In Boole's system the same groups are indicated by certain quasi-mathematical symbols as follows. **1957** C. Vereker *Devel. Polit. Theory* iv. 147 Men . . pursued their own happiness . . by a comparison of their experienced and expected pleasures and pains in this quasi-mathematical manner. **1920** W. R. Sorley *Hist. Eng. Philos.* xii. 265 He had started in his thinking with the quasi-mechanical view of a fixed norm of belief existing in the past. **1942** *Mind* LI. 166 The 'quasi-mechanical' reproductive and associative processes. **1923** T. P. Nunn *Education* xi. 136 Quasi-mechanistic theory, leading us to think of a man's self as built up of instincts much as a machine is built up of wheels. **1961** *Chicago Rev.* XV. i. 94 Sub-human and quasi-mechanistic powers. **1858** Carlyle *Fredk. Gt.* I. iv. iv. 417 The voice . . was of clangorous and penetrating, quasi-metallic nature. **1968** C. G. Kuper *Introd. Theory Superconductivity* xv. 260 One electron per spine atom is in a π-state, and exhibits quasimetallic properties in one dimension. **1890** W. James *Princ. Psychol.* I. v. 138 To urge the automaton-theory upon us . . on purely *a priori* and *quasi*-metaphysical grounds, is an *unwarrantable impertinence in the present state of psychology.* **1959** *New Biol.* XXX. 59 So impressive is this 'organic unity' that its existence has been claimed to set living matter apart from non-living and has more than once been elevated into a quasi-metaphysical postulate. **1895** M. Pemberton *Impregnable City* xvii. 126 Men in quasi-military uniforms . . contributed to the impression of the scene. **1964** Dentler & Cutright in I. L. Horowitz *New Sociol.* 425 Undemocratic leadership by a quasi-military elite. **1974** tr. *Wertheim's Evolution & Revolution* 127 It is clear that the term 'mutiny' mostly refers to an insurrection within a military or quasi-military apparatus. **1890** W. James *Princ. Psychol.* I. xii. 474 They invent . . as the vehicle of the knowledge of universals . . an Ego, whose function is treated as quasi-miraculous. **1904** *Jrnl. Philos.* I. 541 An experience that knows another can figure as its *representative*, not in any quasi-miraculous 'epistemological' sense, but in the definite practical sense of being its *substitute* in various operations. **1968** C. G. Kuper *Introd. Theory Superconductivity* i. 2 In 1951 Onsager conjectured that conduction electrons might form quasi-molecular pairs bound by the Fröhlich interaction. **1974** *Physics. Bull.* Oct. 467/1 Fernandez . . gave a review of the radiative and other properties of resonant states observed in heavy ion collisions. Usually known as quasimolecular states, these resonances represent states at approximately 30 MeV excitation in the compound system. **1979** *Sci. Amer.* Dec. 125/3 The resulting structure is called a quasi-molecular state. **1938** *Ann. Reg. 1937* 241 President Azaña emerged from his quasi-monastic retirement in a villa near Gerona to appoint a new Government. **1964** P. F. Anson *Bishops at Large* iv. 95 The quasi-monastic character of the life. **1890** W. James *Princ. Psychol.* II. xx. 211 Difficulties arise which have made psychologists appeal to new and *quasi*-mythical mental powers. **1963** M. H. Abrams in N. Frye *Romanticism Reconsidered* 53 Quasi-mythical agents tend to recur. **1905** *Daily Chron.* 11 May 5/1 The Admiral asserts that he is not the only one who has provisioned in neutral or quasi-neutral waters. **1962** W. B. Thompson *Introd. Plasma Physics* iv. 45 Also, from the extremely small value . . it is clear that a conductor resembles a plasma in remaining quasi-neutral. **1909** O. Lodge *Survival of Man* i. 4 Actually more inventive sometimes of other and quasi-normal methods of explaining inexplicable facts. **1965** *Math. in Biol. & Med.* (*Med. Res. Council*) v. 228 The form of this distribution (Figure 2) is negatively exponential, high on the left and tapering away to the right quite unlike the normal and quasi-normal distributions with which we deal intuitively in most everyday situations. **1882** *Mind* VII. 186 Hegel's philosophy . . must, now that it has become quasi-official, make ready to defend itself as well as to attack others. **1965** H. Kahn *On Escalation* ii. 44 A quasi-official move ordered by a government. **1940** *Chambers's Techn. Dict.* 693/2 *Quasi-optical waves* (Radio), electromagnetic waves of such short wavelength that their laws of propagation are similar to those of visible light. **1965** *B.B.C. Handbk.* 115 The signals which carry domestic broadcasting programmes are usually designed to be received by ground-wave on medium and long waves and within a quasi-optical range for television and VHF sound broadcasting. **1956** Auden in *Listener* 26 Jan. 137/1 The Paid Announcer . . with his quasi-ossianic prose Cuts in upon the lovers, halts the band, To name a sponsor or to praise a brand. **1895** *Funk's Stand. Dict.*, *Quasi-periodic*, noting a function in which the increase of the variable by a fixed amount is equivalent to the multiplication of the whole function by another function. **1923** *Proc. R. Soc.* A. CIII. 97 These quasi-periodic atmospherics showed considerable diversity of form, the most frequently recurring form was . . similar to a uniformly damped sinusoid. **1962** W. B. Thompson *Introd. Plasma Physics* vii. 164 In such situations, the orbit of particles along the magnetic field lines is also quasi-periodic, and again an adiabatic invariant may be formed. **1927** B. Russell *Outl. Philos.* iv. 50 The act of writing produces quasi-permanent material structures. **1967** *Oceanogr. & Marine Biol.* V. 77 The Solomon Divergence is a quasi-permanent phenomenon of the Coral Sea. **1909** W. M. Urban *Valuation* xii. 354 Quasi-personal constructions of the group or the nation. **1934** Webster, Quasi-philosophical. **1943** *Mind* LII. 100 If 'practical' means 'relevant to human happiness and misery' there is hardly anything more practically important than have been certain philosophical or quasi-philosophical ideas. **1960** *Spectator* 22 July 137 Vast quasi-philosophical works of great power. **1881** W. James *Let.* 18 Dec. in R. B. Perry *Tht. & Char. W. James* (1935) I. 620 One gains an aesthetic pleasure in what you write that is of a *quasi* physical order. **1953** G. E. M. Anscombe tr. *Wittgenstein's Philos. Investigations* i. 121 You interpret a grammatical movement made by yourself as a quasi-physical phenomenon which you are observing. **1964** E. Palmer tr. *Martinet's Elem. Gen. Linguistics* iv. 131 French has a class of 'adjectives' characterized by uses which are quasi-predicative. **1888** Bryce *Amer. Commw.* II. iii. lxxiv. 610 Public or quasi-public organisms. **1907** H. Rashdall *Theory of Good & Evil* II. iii. iv. 373 Biology now finds that it cannot get on without the idea of 'quasi-purposive' behaviour in accounting for the growth of the individual organisms. **1943** *Mind* LII. 346 A rationalist may be one who, admitting a hierarchy of being and value, seeks to explain the universe as exemplifying the highest degree of quasi-purposive significance, or he may be one who, like the Positivists [etc.]. **1838** J. W. Semple *Kant's Relig. within Boundary of Pure Reason* p. ix, That it concerns us islanders *to know* the religious or quasi-religious opinions entertained by our next-door neighbours on the Continent, no sane man, I apprehend, can doubt. **1906** W. James *Coll. Ess. & Rev.* (1920) 465 In the writings of this youthful Italian [*sc.* Papini] . . I find . . a tone of feeling well fitted to rally devotees and to make of pragmatism a new militant form of religious or quasi-religious philosophy. **1964** P. F. Anson *Bishops at Large* xi. 505 A quasi-religious community known as 'The Clerks Secular of St. Basil'. **1977** P. Johnson *Enemies of Society* xii. 169 Marxism is a system of quasi-religious prophecy. **1979** *Dædalus* Summer 156 The Ford scheme aroused Dewey's intense and quasi-religious sense of his mission to the democracy. *a* **1873** Mill *Three Ess. Relig.* (1874) 204 It is sometimes . . wrapt up in a quasi-scientific language. **1970** G. E. Evans *Where Beards wag All* xx. 230 Many archaeologists appear purposefully to avoid the kind of folk-life material discussed here because they see in it some threat to their lately acquired quasi-scientific respectability. **1977** *Listener* 15 Dec. 782/3 Meanwhile, the mis-spelling of the quasi-scientific term *minuscule*, as *miniscule* is now so common it is close to becoming accepted English. **1922** Quasi-simultaneous [see *quasi-sensation*]. **1946** F. E. Zeuner *Dating Past* xii. 353 Another instance of quasi-simultaneous evolution of classes and orders is provided by primitive vertebrates. **1956** *Nature* 28 Jan. 178/1 It [*sc.* the radio telescope] may be used to scan through a small angle in the meridian plane, recording five separate declinations quasi-simultaneously. **1930** *Physical Rev.* XXXV. 944 For the occurrence of raditionless transitions it is essential that the material system . . be in a quasistationary state of an energy equal to the energy of some aperiodic motion of the system. **1967** *Oceanogr. & Marine Biol.* V. 38 The method first determines the wind-induced elevations of sea-level at a particular place assuming that the changing wind conditions over the North Sea and the English Channel are quasi-stationary. **1906** *Spectator* 7 Apr. 545/1 When metaphysics begin we flounder among quasi-technical platitudes. **1961** R. B. Long *Sentence & its Parts* ix. 224 This kind of thing is commoner in quasi-technical use than in general use. **1956** *Nature* 25 Feb. 369/1 Thermodynamic, quasi-thermodynamic and non-thermodynamic methods of investigating the electrochemistry of clays. **1965** Phillips & Williams *Inorg. Chem.* I. vii. 235 We shall show how by investigation of the mechanisms of chemical reactions it is possible to break them down into a series of elementary reactions, each of which may be treated by a quasi-thermodynamic approach. **1946** W. S. Churchill *Victory* 80 Controls under the pretext of war or its aftermath which are in fact designed to favour the accomplishment of quasi-totalitarian systems . . are a fraud which should be mercilessly exposed to the British public. **1953** M. Lowry *Sel. Lett.* (1967) 337 B.C. at the moment has no government at all, though both of them are totalitarian... Or quasi-totalitarian. **1927** B. Russell *Analysis of Matter* xii. 118 In the case of similarity, we have a relation which is capable of degrees, and may be called 'quasi-transitive'—*i.e.* if *A* is very like *B*, and *B* is very like *C*, then *A* must be rather like *C*. **1963** F. T. Visser *Hist. Syntax* I. ii. 135 (*heading*) Quasi-transitive verbs. **1974** tr. *Wertheim's Evolution & Revolution* 177 Brinton's unsuccessful attempt to introduce a quasi-universal, cyclical model of revolution . . is symptomatic of the danger of any attempt to deal with the genesis and process of revolutions in general. **1977** *Jrnl. R. Soc. Arts* CXXV. 579/1 Most significant of all is the emergence and quasi-universal adoption of the full-fledged *nagara śikhara*.

c. [through It.] With pronunc. (ˈkwɑːziː). Used in musical directions: as if, almost, as ***quasi-parlando***, ***parlato*** [It., 'speaking', 'spoken'] sb. and advb.

1908 R. Dunstan *Cyclopaedic Dict. Music* 325/1 *Quasi parlato*, as if spoken. **1945** Britten & Slater *Peter Grimes* ii. i. 183 Ellen *semplice* (*quasi parlato*) Nothing to tell me, nothing to say. **1959** *Listener* 5 Mar. 432/3 The *quasi-parlando* which Puccini uses so effectively as a stage language seems on the screen so desperately sluggish in effect . . that [etc.]. **1972** V. C. Clinton-Baddeley *To study Long Silence* i. 45 A fine girl . . twirling a malacca cane, and singing, *quasi parlando*, in a fruity baritone. **1975** *Country Life* 13 Nov. 1312/2 Singers do not *have* to be provided with tunes—in *Tristan* . . they get by with almost continuous *quasi parlando*.

II. 3. Introducing an etymological explanation or a word: 'As if it were'. (Abbreviated *q.*, *qu.*: see Q. II. 1.)

1588 Shaks. *L.L.L.* iv. ii. 85 Master person, *quasi* Person. *c* **1630** Risdon *Surv. Devon* §82 (1810) 81 *Culme*, so called, as some say, *quasi* Calme. **1686** Plot *Staffordsh.* 419 They are more properly call'd Almanacks, quasi Almonaght. **1826** Scott *Woodstock* Note 3 Rere-suppers (*quasi arrière*) belonged to a species of luxury [etc.]. **1866** Lowell *Biglow P.* Wks. (1880) 181/2 The Earls of Wilbraham (*quasi* wild boar ham).

quasi, quasie, quass, obs. ff. QUASSIA, QUEASY, KVASS.

ˈ**quasi-ˌcontract.** *Law.* [QUASI *adv.* and *pref.*] (See quot. 1959[1].) Hence ˌ**quasi-conˈtractual** *a.*

[**1618** in *Eng. Reports* (1907) LXXX. 353 For though there was no actual contract, yet there was a kind of contract in law, so it is ex quasi contractu.] **1727–41** Chambers *Cycl.* s.v., In a quasi-contract, one party may be bound . . without having given his consent. **1806** W. D. Evans tr. *Pothier's Treat. Law of Obligations, or Contracts* I. i. i. 69 A Quasi contract is the act of a person permitted by the law which obliges him in favour of another, without any agreement intervening between them. **1847** *Louisiana Supreme Court Ann. Rep. 1846* I. 380 The act of a party in taking as security for a loan of money made to an agent for his private use, a pledge of claim against a third person, known by the lender to belong to the principal of that agent, forms a quasi-contract. **1893** W. A. Keener *Treat. Law of Quasi-Contracts* i. 16 A statutory obligation which does not rest upon the consent of the parties, is clearly quasi-contractual in its nature. **1936** R. M. Jackson *Hist. Quasi-Contract in Eng. Law* II. 127 The name 'quasi-contract' has become the general jurisprudential term for obligations which do not fall into the categories of contract or tort. **1959** Jowitt *Dict. Eng. Law* II. 1456/2 *Quasi-contract*, liability, not exclusively referable to any other head of law, imposed upon a particular person to pay money to another particular person on the ground that non-payment of it would confer on the former an unjust benefit. *Ibid.*, The main heads of quasi-contractual liability are: (1) money paid by the plaintiff at the request of the defendant, including payment by sureties and contribution between joint contractors; [etc.]. **1962** A. Turner *Law of Trade Secrets* iv. iv. 348 We may consider relief under quasi-contract and relief for unjust enrichment to be for practical purposes the same.

ˈ**quasiˌfission.** *Nuclear Physics.* [f. QUASI *adv.* and *pref.* + FISSION.] A type of interaction between heavy ions in which the reaction products have kinetic energies similar to those expected for fission of a compound nucleus but an angular distribution that is quite different.

1974 F. Hanappe et al. in *Physical Rev. Lett.* XXXII. 738/1 A new kind of reaction was observed, which seems to occur instead of complete fusion; therefore we called it 'incomplete fusion', but the name 'quasifission' is perhaps better. **1976** *McGraw-Hill Yearbk. Sci. & Technol.* 297/1 It is now believed that for these quasifission heavy-ion projectile reactions, nuclear encounters which achieve an initial distance of approach or sufficient overlap . . lead to the situation where the projectile's kinetic energy is essentially dissipated, and the nuclei remain in contact for a brief period of time, exchanging large numbers of nucleons, and then begin to separate.

‖**quasi in rem** (ˈkweɪsaɪ ɪn rɛm), *adv. phr. U.S. Law.* [L., 'as if against a thing'.] Used of proceedings in a court with limited jurisdiction, having no power over a defendant's person (see quots.). Also *attrib.*

1887 *U.S. Reports* CXIX. 187 There is, however, a large class of cases which are not strictly actions *in rem*, but are frequently spoken of as actions *quasi in rem*, because, though brought against persons, they only seek to subject certain property of those persons to the discharge of the claims asserted. **1904** *Atlantic Reporter* LVII. 555/2 In suits quasi in rem, that is, where the suit is against the person in respect of the res—where, for example, it has for its object partition or the sale or other disposition of defendant's property within the jurisdiction to satisfy plaintiff's demand by enforcing a lien upon it—personal service within the jurisdiction or appearance is not necessary. **1910** H. C. BLACK *Law Dict.* (ed. 2) 608/1 *Quasi in rem.* A term applied to proceedings which are not strictly and purely *in rem*, but are brought against the defendant personally, though the real object is to deal with particular property or subject property to the discharge of claims asserted. **1963** C. A. WRIGHT *Handbk. Law of Federal Courts* x. 236/2 State statutes which commonly permit so-called 'quasi-in-rem' actions, which are commenced by attachment or garnishment of property within the state, with notice to the person outside the state against whom the claim is asserted. **1970** *Internat. & Compar. Law Q.* XIX. 181 One finds an interesting description..[of] the American *quasi in rem* jurisdiction. **1972** *N.Y. Law Jrnl.* 22 Aug. 12/5 The court is mindful of the quasi in rem judgment granting replevin to plaintiff by a Florida court of competent jurisdiction.

Quasimodo (ˌkwɑːzɪˈməʊdəʊ). Also (*erron.*) Quasimoto, and with small initial. [f. the name of the hunchback in Victor Hugo's novel *Notre-Dame de Paris.*] A surfing feat performed in a crouching position (see quots. 1962 and 1963).

1962 *Austral. Women's Weekly* 24 Oct. (Suppl.) 3/3 *Quasimodo*, trick riding, with body bent nearly double, with one hand stretched out in front and the other behind. **1963** *Surfing Yearbk.* 43/1 *Quasimoto*, riding on the nose of the board in a crouched position, with one arm forward and one arm back. **1965** J. POLLARD *Surfrider* ii. 18 If you are a 'hot dogger', you're an expert, you can perform quick turns, head dips, quasimodos. **1970** *Studies in English* (Univ. Cape Town) I. 31 Another form of crouch is the *Quasimodo*.

ˈquasiˌparticle. *Physics.* [f. QUASI *adv.* and *pref.* + PARTICLE *sb.*] An excitation of a many-body system that has some of the properties of a free particle, such as momentum and position.

1957 R. T. BEYER tr. L. D. Landau in *Soviet Physics: JETP* III. 921/1 The role of the gas particles in this classification is assumed by the 'elementary excitations' (quasi-particles), each of which possesses a definite momentum. **1968** C. G. KUPER *Introd. Theory Superconductivity* xii. 193 As the idea of quasiparticles has developed, it has come to permeate the whole of solid-state theory. Thus, for example, the Debye theory of specific heat can be regarded as a quasiparticle theory in which the quasiparticles are phonons. **1968** [see EXCITON]. **1974** D. M. ADAMS *Inorg. Solids* ix. 283 Phonons are the quasiparticles of energy associated with excitation of one of the modes of vibration of the perfect crystal.

ˌquasi-ˈstellar, *a. Astr.* [f. QUASI *adv.* and *pref.* + STELLAR *a.*] Giving a star-like (i.e. unresolved) image on a photograph but believed not to be a star; chiefly in ***quasi-stellar object*** (= QUASAR), (*radio*) *source*.

1963 *Sci. Amer.* Dec. 54/1 In recognition of their small size, and for lack of a better name, they are called quasi-stellar radio sources. **1964** *New Scientist* 28 May 532/1 The highly enigmatic 'quasi-stellar objects' whose discovery over the past year or so has been of considerable excitement to astronomers. **1964** *Listener* 20 Aug. 266/1 Radio astronomy has already revealed to us an entirely new universe... But the record for excitement and unexpectedness must surely go to the discovery within the last year of the quasi-stellar radio sources. **1973** *Nature* 23 Nov. 185/1 The physical nature of quasistellar objects is as puzzling now as it was 10 years ago when their large redshifts were first discovered. **1973** SMITH & JACOBS *Introd. Astron. & Astrophysics* xix. 493 Some QSOs are strong radio sources; indeed, optical identification of such quasi-stellar sources (QSS) first drew attention to the QSOs. The majority of QSOs, however, are weak radio sources or altogether radio-quiet. **1977** J. NARLIKAR *Struct. Universe* vii. 215 When quasi-stellar objects were first discovered, some with red-shifts close to $z = 2$, it was hoped that they would settle the cosmological issue once for all... Unfortunately QSOs have made the issue more complicated than before. **1978** PASACHOFF & KUTNER *University Astron.* xxviii. 713 Sources in this new class resembled the quasi-stellar radio sources in being quasi-stellar and in having large redshifts but did not emit any detectable radio radiation. These were called quasi-stellar objects (QSO's).

†**quass,** *v. Obs.* Also 6–7 quasse. [a. MLG. *quassen* (*quasen*, *quatzen*: see Grimm) to eat or drink immoderately: prob. of onomatopœic origin.] *intr.* To drink copiously or in excess; to quaff. Hence †ˈ**quassing** *vbl. sb.*

1549 CHALONER *Erasm. on Folly* E iv, Remembre the law of quassyng, 'Other drinke thy drinke, or rise, and goe thy waie'. *c* **1572** GASCOIGNE *Fruites Warre* lxxxvii, Hope brings the boll wherein they all must quasse [*rime* passe]. **1607** MARSTON *What You Will* II. i, Sing, sing, or stay weele quasse or any thing.

quaˈssation. *rare.* [ad. L. *quassātiōn-em*, n. of action f. *quassāre* to shake: see QUASH *v.*] A shaking, beating, pounding.

1654 GAYTON *Pleas. Notes* III. i. 68 Solidated by continual contusions, threshings, and quassations. **1683** PETTUS *Fleta Min.* II. 15 By quassation and constant compressure of such flexible grounds. **1897** *Syd. Soc. Lex.*, *Quassation*,..in *Pharmacy*,..reducing roots and tough bark to pieces, to facilitate the extraction of their chief active principles.

†**quassative,** *a. Obs. rare*$^{-1}$. [f. ppl. stem of L. *quassāre* (see prec.) + -IVE.] Inclined to shake.

1626 MIDDLETON *Anything for Quiet Life* III. ii, A Frenchman's heart is more quassative and subject to tremor than an Englishman's.

quassia (ˈkwæsɪə, ˈkwæʃ-, ˈkwɒʃɪə). Also 8 quassi, quassy, quasi, (quaciæ). [Named by Linnæus, about 1761, after a Surinam Negro, Graman (= grand man) Quassi or Quacy (= QUASHEE), who discovered the virtues of the root in 1730.

Quassi communicated his discovery to C. G. Dahlberg, by whom it was made known to Linnæus: see C. M. Blom in *C. Linnæi Amœnitates Academicæ* VI. (1764) 420, and Stedman *Surinam* II. xxix.]

1. a. The wood, bark, or root of a South American tree (*Quassia amara*), found esp. in Surinam, and of some other trees, esp. the bitter ash (*Picræna excelsa*) of Jamaica, and the bitter damson (*Simaruba amara*) of the West Indies and S. America. **b.** The bitter decoction prepared from this, used for medicinal and other purposes.

The quassia now in use is chiefly that obtained from the bitter ash, commonly sold in the form of chips.

1765 [cf. 3]. **1770** *Gentl. Mag.* XL. 227 The quasi was administered in decoction. **1803** DAVY in *Phil. Trans.* XCIII. 268 The infusions of quassia..are scarcely affected by muriate of tin. **1830** HERSCHEL *Stud. Nat. Phil.* 86 An intense and pure bitter like quassia. **1878** T. BRYANT *Pract. Surg.* (1879) II. 59 An enema of some bitter vegetable infusion, such as quassia.

2. Any of the trees yielding quassia, esp. the *Quassia amara* of Surinam.

1766 [cf. 3]. **1797** *Encycl. Brit.* XV. 753/1 Dr. Wright found this tree to be a species of quassia. **1859** *All Year Round* No. 32. 127 Why not..cultivate..quassia, which is such a handsome shrub? **1876** HARLEY *Mat. Med.* (ed. 6) 673 Quassia bears some resemblance to the common ash, attains a height of 50, 60, or even 100 feet.

3. *attrib.*, as ***quassia-bark, -chips, extract, -root, -tree, -wood***; **quassia cup**, a drinking cup made of quassia wood, a 'bitter cup'.

1765 *Ann. Reg.* 114 Linnaeus..has lately recommended ..a new medicine, called quassi-wood. **1766** *Ibid.* 76 They write from Pensacola that the true Quassi medicinal tree has lately been discovered in the western parts of that province. **1767** HARLEY in *Phil. Trans.* LVIII. 81 At last I tryed the Quassi Root. **1834** T. J. GRAHAM *Dom. Med.* (ed. 6) 70 Quassia wood comes from Jamaica and the Caribbean islands. **1860** PIESSE *Lab. Chem. Wonders* 171 The purest bitter principle is yielded by the quassia tree. **1884** A. J. E. WILSON *Vashti* xxiv. 237, I have been forced to drink out of quassia-cups until my whole being has imbibed the bitter. **1900** G. S. SAUNDERS in E. T. Cook *Century Bk. Gardening* 508 Quassia chips should be soaked..and then boiled. *Ibid.* 509 Quassia extract may be bought... This is a very useful insecticide. **1926** *Army & Navy Stores Catal.* 479/2 Quassia Chips -lb. -/5. **1965** M. THOMAS *Grannies' Remedies* 14 A ½ oz. of quassia chips boiled in a pint of water and mixed with 4 oz. of treacle draws flies and kills them. **1969** E. H. PINTO *Treen* 39 Quassia chips were formerly used for washing lousy heads.

quassin (ˈkwæsɪn). [f. QUASS-IA + -IN¹.] The bitter principle of quassia.

1819 in J. G. Children *Chem. Anal.* 288. **1845** *Penny Cycl.* Suppl. I. 349/2 Quassin dissolves readily in alcohol and in æther. **1876** HARLEY *Mat. Med.* (ed. 6) 675 A neutral, odourless, crystallisable principle, termed quassin.

Also ˈ**quassite**, in same sense.

1838 T. THOMSON *Chem. Org. Bodies* 705 Quassite has been given by Wiggers to the bitter principle of the *quassia amara* and *excelsa*. **1842** *Penny Cycl.* XXII. 26/1 Its chief constituents are quassite, resin [etc.].

quassing, *vbl. sb.*: see QUASS *v.*

qua-sum, north. variant of WHO-SOME.

quasy, obs. form of QUEASY.

quat (kwɒt), *sb.*¹ *Obs.* exc. *dial.* Also 8–9 quot. [Of obscure origin.]

1. A pimple or pustule; a small boil; a stye.

1579 LANGHAM *Gard. Health* 153 Inflammations and soft swellings, burnings and impostumes, and choleric sores or quats. **1752–3** A. MURPHY *Gray's Inn Jrnl.* No. 15 A Quat, or Quot, being a small Heat or Pimple. **1848** A. B. EVANS *Leicestersh. Words* s.v., He was rubbing his throat, and he broke the head of his quot. **1896** *Warwick Gloss.*, *Quat*, a sty or poke.

†**2.** *transf.* Applied contemptuously to a (young) person. *Obs.*

1604 SHAKS. *Oth.* v. i. 11, I haue rub'd this yong Quat almost to the sense, And he growes angry. **1609** DEKKER *Gvlls Horne-bk.* 151 Whether he be a young quat of the first year's revenue, or some austere and sullen-faced steward. **1623** WEBSTER *Devil's Law-Case* II. i, O young quat, incontinence is plagu'd In all the creatures of the world.

†**quat,** *sb.*² *Obs. rare.* Also 7 quatte. [f. QUAT *v.*¹] The act or state of squatting.

1602 *Narcissus* (1893) 475 The doggs have putt the hare from quatte. **1612** WEBSTER *White Devil* Wks. (Rtldg.) 31/2 A full cry for a quarter of an hour, And then..put to the dead quat.

quat (kwɒt), *a. Obs.* exc. *dial.* Also 9 quot. [Related to prec. and next: cf. SQUAT *a.*, and It. *quatto* 'squatting, cowering, quiet, still' (Baretti).]

1. Squatted, close, still, quiet, in hiding.

c **1450** *Merlin* xxv. 463 The x traitoris that were quatte in the gardin vnder an ympe. *Ibid.*, Bretell and Vlfin..weren quat vnder the steyres. **1682** BUNYAN *Holy War* 310 The rest lay so quat and close that they could not be apprehended. **1685** —— *Bk. Boys & Girls* 21 My lying quat, until the Fly is catcht Shews [etc.]. **1879** MISS JACKSON *Shropsh. Word-bk.*, *Quat*, close, still, as a hare on her form. **1886** in ELWORTHY *W. Som. Wd.-bk.*

2. Low and broad; squat.

1863 BARNES *Dorset Gloss.*, 'There's a little quot rick'.

quat (kwɒt), *v.*¹ *Obs.* exc. *dial.* Also 5 qwat(te, 8 quatt, 9 quot. [a. OF. *quaitir*, *quatir* to beat or press down, to force in, to hide (mod.F. *catir* to press), f. OF. **quait*, Prov. *quait*, It. *quatto* (see prec.):—L. *coactus* pressed together, COACT.]

1. *trans.* To beat or press down; to squash, flatten, extinguish. Also *absol.*

c **1400–50** *Alexander* 560 All flames þe flode..And þan ouer-qwelmys in a qwirre & qwatis euer e-like. **1589** GREENE *Tullies Love* (1609) F iij, Her resolution..quatted the conceit of his former hope. **1590** —— *Never too late* (1600) K 4 The renowne of her chastity..almost quatted those sparks that heated him on to such lawlesse affection. **1893** *Wiltsh. Gloss.*, *Quat*, *qwot*,..to flatten, to squash flat.

b. To load, sate, glut (the stomach). See also QUOT. *pa. pple.*

1579 LYLY *Euphues* (Arb.) 44 To the stomack quatted with dainties, al delicates seeme queasie. **1606** J. HYND *Eliosto Libid.* 58 Amazias having quatted the quesy stomaks of the rebels..returned with safety to Famagosta.

2. *intr.* To crouch down or lie close, as an animal in hiding; to squat. (= OF. *se quatir*.)

c **1400** *Master of Game* ii. (MS. Digby 182), þen he shall ruse oute of þe wey for to stalle or qwatte to rest hym. **1602–12** [implied in QUAT *sb.*²]. **1757** FOOTE *Author* II. Wks. 1799 I. 149 You grow tir'd at last and quat, Then I catch you. **1781** W. BLANE *Ess. Hunt.* (1788) 125 She will only leap off a few rods, and quat. **1879** JEFFERIES *Wild Life in S.C.* 222 The crake..will then..if still hunted, 'quat' in the thickest bunch of grass or weeds he can find.

†**b.** To sink, subside. *Obs. rare.*

a **1722** LISLE *Husb.* (1752) 118 If rain in the interim should come, such ground will quatt, and the furrow will fill up.

Hence ˈ**quatting** *vbl. sb.*

1757 FOOTE *Author* II. Wks. 1799 I. 149 Begin and start me, that I may come the sooner to quatting.

quat, *v.*² Sc. var. (also pa. t. and pa. pple) of QUIT *v.* (Cf. QUATED.)

1573 *Satir. Poems Reform.* xxxix. 54 So had the cause bene quat, wer not for shame. **1597** MONTGOMERIE *Cherrie & Slae* 1179 Thou..Gars courage quat them. **1637–50** J. ROW *Hist. Kirk Scotl.* (1842) 254 So he quat his ministrie. **1714** RAMSAY *Elegy John Cowper* xii. (1877) I. 168 To quat the grip he was right laith. **1786** BURNS *To James Smith* xxix, I shall say nae mair, But quat my sang. **1836** M. MACINTOSH *Cottager's Daughter* 49 For your threats ae truth I winna quat.

quat, obs. f. QUOTH, WHAT; Sc. var. QUIT *a.*

quata, var. of COAITA.

†**quatch**¹. *Obs.* [f. *quatch*, var. QUETCH *v.*: cf. QUINCH *sb.*] A word, a sound.

a **1635** BP. CORBET *Poems* (1807) 114 Noe; not a quatch, sad poets; doubt you, There is not greife enough without you? **1783** NICHOLS *Bibl. Top.* (1790) IV. 57 (*Berks*) A quatch is a word. (Hence in GROSE and HALLIWELL.)

†**quatch**². *Obs. rare*$^{-1}$. (Meaning uncertain.)

1601 SHAKS. *All's Well* II. ii. 18 A Barber's chaire, that fits all buttockes, the pin buttocke, the quatch-buttocke [etc.].

quatch, variant of QUETCH.

quate, variant of WHATE, fortune. *Obs.*

quate, var. QUAITE.

quated, obs. Sc. var. *quited*: see QUIT *v.*

a **1605** MONTGOMERIE *Misc. Poems* xlv. 27 Alace! suld my treu service thus be quated? [*rime* hated].

‖**quatenus** (ˈkweɪtɪnəs), *adv.* [L., 'how far', 'to what extent', f. *quā* where + *tenus* up to.] In so far as; in the quality or capacity of; QUA.

1652 N. CULVERWEL *Lt. Nature* xi. (1661) 78 An innate power of the Soul, that is fitted, and fashioned for the receiving of spirituals, *quatenus* Spirituals. **1664** BUTLER *Hud.* II. ii. 277 A broken Oath is, quat'nus Oath, As sound t' all purposes of Troth. **1673** WOOD *Life* (O.H.S.) II. 274 That every canon of Ch. Ch. should (quatenus as a member of the university) preach at St. Marie's, and (quatenus canon) at Ch. Ch. **1697** J. DENNIS *Plot and no Plot* 52 Tho the Viscount be my superiour, quatenus Viscount, yet he does esteem himself my equal.

quater, obs. form of QUATRE.

quater-centenary (ˌkwætəsɛnˈtiːnərɪ, ˌkweɪtə-), *sb.* (and *a.*) [f. L. *quater* four times; cf. *tercentenary*.] A four-hundredth anniversary, or the celebration of this.

1883 *Harper's Mag.* Aug. 479/1 The forthcoming celebration of the Luther quater-centenary. **1904** J. STALKER *John Knox* p. v, In 1905 not only Scotland..will be celebrating..the Quatercentenary of the birth of the greatest of Scotsmen. **1906** *Daily Chron.* 25 Sept. 4/4 That is why the Quatercentenary of the University [of Aberdeen] has created an unparalleled amount of interest in the North. **1955** *Times* 13 July 9/4 The recent quater-centenary celebrations of Queen Mary's School, Walsall. **1971** *Oxford Times* 4 July 28/5 The Jesus College quatercentenary celebrations included a concert of rarities. **1977** *Times* 31 Mar. 14/3 The Jews fled to nearby Cochin... There, in 1567, they built Jewtown and in the following year completed their Synagogue... Its quater-centenary was celebrated..in 1968.

quatercentennial (ˌkwætəsɛnˈtɛnɪəl, ˌkweɪtə-), *a.* [f. L. *quater* four times + CENTENNIAL *a.* (*sb.*).] Pertaining to a four-hundredth anniversary or celebration.

1964 *Listener* 30 Apr. 730/3 Scholars don't regard their function this quater-centennial year as involving.. scratching pocky boils.

quater-co(u)sin, obs. ff. of CATER-COUSIN.

1656 in BLOUNT *Glossogr.* **1755-** in JOHNSON, etc.

quaterime: see QUATREME.

quaˈtern, *sb. rare.* [a. F. *quaterne* set of four numbers, †quire (Godef.), ad. L. *quaternus*: see QUATERNION and QUIRE.]

†**1.** *Sc.* A quire of paper. *Obs.*

1578 in *Maitl. Cl. Misc.* (1840) I. 12 Tuentie fyve countis and quaternis of the Q. and Q. regent.

2. A set of four numbers in a lottery.

1868 BROWNING *Ring & Bk.* XII. 158 But that he forbid The Lottery, why, Twelve were Tern Quatern!

†**quaˈtern**, *a. Bot. Obs. rare*$^{-1}$. [ad. L. *quaternī* four together, by fours.] Arranged in fours.

1760 J. LEE *Introd. Bot.* III. xxiii. (1765) 235 In respect to Opposition, opposite Leaves will sometimes become tern, quatern or quine, growing by Threes, Fours, or Fives.

quaˈternal, *a. rare.* [f. as prec. + -AL[1].]

a. = QUATERNARY *a.* 1. **b.** *erron.* = QUADRENNIAL.

1616 R. C. *Times' Whistle* Cert. Poems (1871) 150 His first Advent yeilds a quaternall section, His birth, his life, his death, his resurrection. **1655** MOUFET & BENNET *Health's Improv.* (1746) 161 The Carthaginians, whose famous quaternal Feast consisted only of four Dishes. **1813** J. C. HOBHOUSE *Journey* (ed. 2) 581 Prizes distributed at each quaternal celebration of the Olympian games.

quaterˈnarian, *a. rare.* [f. as next + -AN.] = QUATERNARY *a.* 1.

1647 M. HUDSON *Div. Right Govt.* I. vi. 55 A quaternarian number, as four beasts, and four wheels. **1856–8** W. CLARK *Van der Hoeven's Zool.* I. 108 Arrangement of parts usually quaternarian.

quaternary (kwəˈtɜːnərɪ), *a.* and *sb.* [ad. L. *quaternāri-us*, f. *quaternī* four together, by fours. Cf. F. *quaternaire* (1515).]

A. *adj.* **1. a.** Consisting of four things or parts; characterized by the number four; † ***quaternary compound***, a combination of four chemical elements or radicals. (This sense is now *Obs.* in *Chem.*)

quaternary number, usually = 4, but sometimes taken as = 10 (see B).

1605 TIMME *Quersit.* I. xi. 45 To appoynt a quaternarie number of elements, out of the quaternary number of the fower qualities. **1695** F. GREGORY *Doctr. Trin.* 63 We read what great respect Pythagoras and his sect had for their quaternary number. **1825** T. THOMSON *1st Princ. Chem.* I. 37 Ammonia is a quaternary compound, consisting of 1 atom azote and 3 atoms hydrogen. **1830** LINDLEY *Nat. Syst. Bot.* 14 The quaternary number of the divisions of the flower. **1872** OLIVER *Elem. Bot.* I. ii. 17 The nitrogen occurs combined with the same three elements, forming a quaternary compound.

b. *Chem.* Of ammonium and phosphonium ions and salts: in which the central atom forms four bonds to organic radicals; also applied to the central atom, and extended to analogous compounds of other elements. Of a carbon atom: bonded to four other carbon atoms.

1871 *Jrnl. Chem. Soc.* XXIV. 570 Hofmann considers that Drechsel and Finkelstein had tertiary and quaternary phosphonium salts under examination, and not a salt of the primary phosphine. **1871** *Chem. News* 9 June 275/1 Quaternary substitution. **1903** A. J. WALKER tr. *Holleman's Text-bk. Org. Chem.* I. 46 A carbon atom which is only linked to one other carbon atom is called primary... If it is linked..to four, quaternary. **1910** N. V. SIDGWICK *Org. Chem. Nitrogen* ii. 22 The quaternary hydroxides are strong bases. **1951** I. L. FINAR *Org. Chem.* I. xxx. 622 Pyridine forms quaternary salts when heated with alkyl halides, *e.g.*, pyridine methiodide or *N*-methyl-pyridinium iodide, $C_5H_5N^+\cdot CH_3\}I^-$. **1955** J. G. DAVIS *Dict. Dairying* (ed. 2) 879 Quaternary ammonium germicides have received considerable attention in the past 10 years in relation to their use as sterilising compounds. **1972** COTTON & WILKINSON *Adv. Inorg. Chem.* (ed. 3) xiii. 390 The stibonium compounds are the most difficult to prepare and are the least common. These quaternary salts, excepting the hydroxides, ..are white crystalline compounds. **1972** *Materials & Technol.* V. x. 304 Among the more complex quaternary surfactants are some which include two quaternary nitrogen atoms. **1975** GUTSCHE & PASTO *Fund. Org. Chem.* iii. 61 If it carries no hydrogen but is attached to four carbons it is called a 'quaternary carbon'.

2. *Geol.* Used, with the sense of 'fourth in order', as an epithet of the most recent of the geological periods (following on the Tertiary), and of the deposits, animals, etc., belonging to it. Also *absol.*

1843 W. HUMBLE *Dict. Geol.* 216 Quaternary formations. **1865** TYLOR *Early Hist. Man.* viii. 198 The instruments of the Drift, or Quaternary deposits. **1871** DARWIN *Desc. Man* I. vii. 237 The quaternary race of the caverns of Belgium. **1880** A. R. WALLACE *Isl. Life* xxi. 448 Deposits which may be of Quaternary or even of Pliocene age. **1910** *Encycl. Brit.* II. 344/2 The beginning of archaeology..may be broadly held to follow on the last of the geological periods, viz., the Quaternary. **1946** L. D. STAMP *Britain's Struct. & Scenery* ii. 16 The Quaternary is not really comparable in duration or importance with the other great eras. **1977** A. HALLAM *Understanding Earth* 234 The Pleistocene is a subdivision embracing the period from the beginning of the Quaternary until 10,000 years ago.

3. a. Of or belonging to the fourth order or rank; fourth in a series. Also *spec.* (see quot. 1961).

1874 H. W. BEECHER *Plymouth Pulpit* II. 486 The first comprehensive determination breaks itself up into subsidiary determinations, so that the primary will becomes secondary, the secondary becomes tertiary, and the tertiary quaternary. **1924** O. JESPERSEN *Philos. Gram.* vii. 96 A tertiary word may be further defined by a (quaternary) word, and this again by a (quinary) word. *Ibid.* 97 Quaternary words..may be termed *sub-subjuncts*. **1961** J. GOTTMAN *Megalopolis* xi. 576 One wonders whether a new distinction should not be introduced in all the mass of nonproduction employment: a differentiation between *tertiary* services—transportation, trade in the simpler sense of direct sales, maintenance, and personal services—and a new and distinct *quaternary* family of economic activities—services that involve transactions, analysis, research, or decision-making, and also education and government. Such quaternary types require more intellectual training and responsibility. **1973** *New Society* 15 Nov. 386/3 The 'tertiary' sector contains at least three divisions—'tertiary' proper..; 'quaternary' (information exchange and decision-making); and 'quinary' (research, development and education). **1975** J. B. GODDARD *Office Location in Urban & Regional Devel.* ii. 11 The intra-urban location of head office functions and of independent firms in the quaternary sector.

b. Biochem. ***quaternary structure***, the relative configuration of polypeptide sub-units in a protein molecule, being structure of an order higher than the tertiary.

1958 J. D. BERNAL in *Discussions Faraday Soc.* XXV. 14 (*caption*) Hierarchy of polymer complexes:..(*d*) quaternary structure (homogeneous type), linked groups of tertiary molecules, haemoglobin structure..; (*e*) quaternary structure (heterogeneous type)—linking of different types of ternary protein and primary ribonuclease, tobacco mosaic virus. **1964** G. H. HAGGIS et al. *Introd. Molecular Biol.* iv. 81 The presence of the nucleic acid chain apparently increases the cohesion between sub-units in successive turns of the helical quaternary structure. **1977** *Lancet* 26 Nov. 1116/1 The four glycoprotein hormones..possess a common quaternary structure characterised by two dissimilar polypeptide chains called the α and β subunits.

B. *sb.* **1.** A set of four (things); the number four.

quaternary of numbers, the Pythagorean τετρακτύς, or 1 + 2 + 3 + 4 = 10.

c **1430** *Art of Nombrynge* (E.E.T.S.) 8 Withdraw ther-for the quaternary, of the article of his denominacion twies, of .40., And ther remaynethe .32. **1603** HOLLAND *Plutarch's Mor.* 1310 The quaternarie is the first square or quadrate number. *a* **1638** MEDE *Wks.* (1672) 654 In which Quaternary of Kingdoms..the Roman, being the Last of the Four, is the Last Kingdom. **1661** LOVELL *Hist. Anim. & Min.* 438 According to quaternaries, or septenaries [of days] after the nature of the disease. **1809** W. IRVING *Knickerb.* (1861) 44 They are regarded with as much veneration as were the disciples of Pythagoras..when initiated into the sacred quaternary of numbers. **1845** DAY *An. Chem.* I. 141 Thus quaternary compounds may be split into several quaternaries with the same or a different radical.

2. *Gram.* In Jespersen's terminology: a word or phrase that belongs to the fourth order or rank.

1937 O. JESPERSEN *Analytic Syntax* 121 The possibility of having quaternaries, quinaries, and so forth. **1946** —— *Mod. Eng. Gram.* V. i. 3 In other combinations we may have quaternaries or quinaries, e.g. *a not* (5) *particularly* (4) *well* (3) *constructed* (2) plot (1).

3. *Chem.* A quaternary ammonium compound.

1947 *Ann. Rev. Microbiol.* I. 173 Jacobs and associates.. studied the relation between structure and bactericidal effects in the hexamethylene tetramine groups. This was followed in 1928 by Hartmann & Kägi's work..with other quaternaries. **1955** J. G. DAVIS *Dict. Dairying* (ed. 2) 880 The degree to which complexes of this kind will be found depends upon the particular quaternary used. **1968** KIRK & OTHMER *Encycl. Chem. Technol.* (ed. 2) XVI. 860 Some quaternaries form hydrates or other solvates.

quaternate (kwəˈtɜːnət), *a.* [f. as prec. + -ATE[2]: cf. F. *quaterné*.] Arranged in, or forming, a set or sets of four; composed of four parts.

1753 CHAMBERS *Cycl. Supp.* s.v. *Leaf*. **1867** J. HOGG *Microsc.* II. i. 295 The *Sarcina ventriculi*, with its remarkable-looking quaternate spores. **1875** BENNETT & DYER tr. *Sachs' Bot.* 391 With a long stalk and a quaternate lamina. **1908** *Scott's Autumn List, Lady Beauclerc and Socialism* is the title of the last book of the Rev. H. T. Perfect's quaternate work on Lady Beauclerc's life.

Comb. **1829** LOUDON *Encycl. Plants* Gloss. 1103/2 *Quaternate-pinnate*, pinnate, the pinnæ being arranged in fours.

‖**quaˈternio.** *rare.* = next.

1678 CUDWORTH *Intell. Syst.* I. iii. §9. 111 Aristotle in his Metaphysicks, speaking of the Quaternio of Causes [etc.]. **1681** H. MORE *Exp. Dan.* ii. 25 These are the Four Winds of Heaven, The Quaternio of the Angelical Ministers of Divine Providence. **1872** D. BROWN *Life John Duncan* v. 87 Watson broke up the quaternio by going to Edinburgh.

quaternion (kwəˈtɜːnɪən). [ad. late L. *quaternio, -iōn-em*, f. *quaternī* four together: cf. obs. F. *quaternion* (Godef.).]

1. a. A group or set of four persons or things; *spec.* a set of four poems.

1382 WYCLIF *Acts* xii. 4 Bitakinge [him] to foure quaternyouns of Knyȝtis..for to kepe him. [TINDALE *and later versions*, quaternions of soudiers (souldiers).] **1599** B. JONSON *Cynthia's Rev.* v. iii. (Masque i), The fitter to conduct this quaternion [= these four fair virgins]. **1648** JENKYN *Blind Guide* Pref. A iij, He puts his whole Booke under a quaternion of topicks. **1695** TRYON *Dreams & Vis.* x. 185 This..Elementary Quaternion of Earth, Air, Water and Fire. **1745** tr. *Columella's Husb.* III. xx, So let us be content with a certain Quaternion as it were of chosen vines. **1815** SCOTT *Guy M.* III. iii. 42 A species of florid elocution, which often became ridiculous from his misarranging the triads and quaternions with which he loaded his sentences. **1868** MILMAN *St. Paul's* xii. 329 His great quaternion of English writers, Shakspeare, Hooker, Bacon, Jeremy Taylor. **1964** C. S. LEWIS *Discarded Image* iv. 68 He accepts the classical quaternion of virtues, Prudence, Temperance, Fortitude and Justice. **1967** J. HENSLEY *Wks. Anne Bradstreet* p. xxiv, The Quaternions follow the structure of Thomas Dudley's own 'On the Four Parts of the World', now lost. **1976** *Times Lit. Suppl.* 27 Aug. 1049/1 The formal elegies and quaternions she [*sc.* Anne Bradstreet] laboured over in imitation of Du Bartas.

b. A quatrain. *rare*$^{-1}$.

1846 LANDOR *Pentam.* iv. Wks. 1876 III. 517 You have given me a noble quaternion.

2. Of paper or parchment: **a.** A quire of four sheets folded in two. †**b.** A sheet folded twice.

1625 USSHER *Answ. Jesuit* 398 The quaternion..in which I transcribed these things out of my table-booke. **1656** BLOUNT *Glossogr.*, *Quaternion*,..a Quire with four sheets, or a sheet foulded into four parts. **1816** SINGER *Hist. Cards* 167 Before they had completed the third quaternion (or gathering of four sheets) 4000 florins were expended. **1882–3** SCHAFF *Encycl. Relig. Knowl.* I. 268 The books were mostly made up of quaternions, i.e. quires of four sheets, doubled so as to make sixteen pages.

3. The number 4 or 10 (cf. QUATERNARY).

1637 HEYWOOD *Lond. Spec.* Wks. 1874 IV. 310 The Pythagoreans expresse their holy oath in the quaternion. **1768–74** TUCKER *Lt. Nat.* (1834) I. 462 Adore the sacred quaternion: the quaternion containeth under it one, two, and three... The quaternion four alone is one and uncompounded.

4. *Math.* **a.** The quotient of two vectors, or the operator which changes one vector into another, so called as depending on four geometrical elements, and capable of being expressed by the quadrinomial formula $w + xi + yj + zk$, in which w, x, y, z are scalars, and i, j, k are mutually perpendicular vectors whose squares are -1. **b.** *pl.* That form of the calculus of vectors in which this operator is employed, invented by Sir W. R. Hamilton in 1843.

1843 SIR W. R. HAMILTON *Let.* in *Philos. Mag.* XXV. 493 We have, then, this first law for the multiplication of two quaternions together. **1858** —— *Let.* 15 Oct. *ibid.* 436 To-morrow will be the 15th birthday of the Quaternions. They started into life, or light, full grown on the 16th of October, 1843. **1866** —— (*Title*) Elements of Quaternions. **1873** H. SPENCER *Stud. Sociol.* (1882) 7 The value of Quaternions for pursuing researches in physics.

c. quaternion group, the group which is generated by multiplication of the unit quaternions, i, j, and k.

1911 W. BURNSIDE *Theory of Groups of Finite Order* (ed. 2) viii. 132 The group defined by these relations is known as the quaternion-group. **1949** H. ZASSENHAUS *Theory of Groups* iv. 116 We wish to find non-abelian groups of order p^n which contain only one subgroup of order p. An example is the quaternion group. By the theorem of Hölder it is defined by the relations $A^4 = 1$, $BAB^{-1} = A^{-1}$, $B^2 = A^2$. **1972** F. J. BUDDEN *Fascination of Groups* xv. 245 The simplest group in this class is Q_4 of order 8 ($n = 4$), and this is usually known as the quaternion group, though in fact all the dicyclic groups may be realised as groups of quaternions.

5. *attrib.* or as *adj.* Consisting of four persons, things, or parts.

1814 CARY *Dante, Purgatory* XXXIII. 3 The trinal now, and now the virgin band Quaternion, their sweet psalmody began. **1849** TICKNOR *Span. Lit.* I. 27 When and where this quaternion rhyme, as it is used by Berceo, was first introduced, cannot be determined.

Hence †**quaˈternion** *v.*, to arrange in quaternions (only in *pa. pple.* **quaˈternioned**); **quaterniˈonic** *a.*, pertaining to quaternions; **quaˈternionist**, one who studies quaternions.

1641 MILTON *Ch. Govt.* I. i, Yea, the Angels themselves.. are distinguish'd and quaternion'd into their Celestial Princedoms, and Satrapies. **1873** TAIT *Quaternions* (ed. 2) 266 It would be easy to give this a more strictly quaternionic form. **1881** J. VENN *Symbolic Logic* 91 Do we depart wider from the primary traditions of arithmetic than the Quaternionist does?

Quaˌterniˈtarian. *rare.* [f. next, after *uni-*, *trinitarian*.] One who believes that there are four persons in the Godhead.

1829 GEN. P. THOMPSON *Exerc.* (1842) I. 72 We should all have been Quaternitarians, and Quaternitarians would have been the orthodox. **1865** M. ARNOLD *Ess. Crit.* viii. (1875) 328 The Jansenists..are, without thinking or intending it, Quaternitarians.

quaternity (kwəˈtɜːnɪtɪ). [ad. late L. *quaternitās* (Augustine, etc.), f. *quaternī* four together: see -TY. Cf. F. *quaternité*.]

1. A set of four persons (*esp.* in the Godhead, in contrast to the Trinity) or of four things.

1529 MORE *Dyaloge* I. Wks. 145/1 He is bounden to beleue in yᵉ trinite. And yᵉ felowe beleueth in a quaternitie. **1603** SIR C. HEYDON *Jud. Astrol.* xx. 405 Antiquitie did deuide the elements into a treble quaternitie. **1678** CUDWORTH *Intell. Syst.* I. iv. §36. 557 Not a Trinity, but a Quaternity, or Four Ranks and Degrees of Beings. **1702** ECHARD *Eccl. Hist.* 349 [The Marcosians] instead of a Trinity..held a Quaternity composed of Ineffability, of Silence, of the Father, and of the Truth. **1830** J. DOUGLAS *Truths Relig.* iv. (1832) 185 Plato may be argued to have held either a trinity or a quaternity. **1889** *Sat. Rev.* 26 Oct. 475/1 A remarkable quaternity of great-grandmamma, grandmamma, mamma, and little daughter.

2. The fact or condition of being four in number, or an aggregate of four.

1839 BAILEY *Festus* xix. (1852) 287 Some [held] that in mystical quaternity all Deity existed.

†**3.** *erron.* A quarter. *Obs. rare*⁻¹.

1633 P. FLETCHER *Purple Isl.* v. xii, The first with divers ..turnings writes, Cutting the town in four quaternities.

quaternize (ˈkwɒtənaɪz), *v.* *Chem.* [f. QUATERN(ARY *a.* + -IZE.] **a.** *trans.* To convert (a tertiary compound, esp. an amine, or an atom) into a quaternary form. **b.** *intr.* To undergo this process.

1951 *Jrnl. Polymer Sci.* VI. 513 This observation suggests that some of the reluctance of 2-pyridyl ethers to quaternize may also be due to steric effects. *Ibid.*, We may consider the butyl salt to be a chain polymer with approximately every other pyridine quaternized. **1965** *Jrnl. Chem. Soc.* 6831 A specimen obtained on quaternising (−)-6-methoxytropan-3α-ol. **1969** *Encycl. Polymer Sci. & Technol.* XI. 333 By copolymerizing vinylpyridine with styrene, quaternizing the nitrogen atoms in the pyridine rings of the resulting copolymer, and..reacting with Li^+TCNQ^- and TCNQ a product is obtained that can be cast from solution into a film with a conductivity of 10^{-3} ohm⁻¹-cm⁻¹. **1970** J. WILLIAMSON in H. W. Mulligan *Afr. Trypanosomiases* vii. 167 The dimethylated diamino dye, Acridinium Yellow, in which the ring N atom was quaternized. **1973** *Nature* 27 Apr. 605/2 A similar reaction of nicotinamides quaternized with alkyl groups was also.. investigated.

So **ˈquaternized** *ppl. a.* Also **quaterniˈzation**, the process of quaternizing a compound or atom.

1949 *Jrnl. Polymer Sci.* IV. 103 An excess of butyl bromide over pyridine content was always used, so that the irreversible quaternization reaction would prevail. **1951** *Ibid.* VI. 523 Quaternized copolymers of styrene and 4-vinylpyridine. **1965** PHILLIPS & WILLIAMS *Inorg. Chem.* I. xv. 556 The quaternization reaction EtI + $Et_3N \rightarrow [Et_4N]^+I^-$ is, at 100°, 80 times faster in benzene..than in hexane. **1966** *Trans. Amer. Soc. Artific. Internal Organs* XII. 151 Simple contact of such a quaternized surface with aqueous sodium heparinate is sufficient to yield a heparinized surface. **1976** *Nature* 15 July 221/2 Quaternisation of the nitrogen atom generally caused a marked decrease in ixodicidal activity.

quateron, obs. variant of QUADROON.

†**quaterpetal.** *Obs. rare*⁻¹. [f. L. *quater* four times.] A plant whose flowers have four petals.

1715 J. PETIVER in *Phil. Trans.* XXIX. 274 *Herbæ Tetrapetalæ*, Quaterpetals.

†**quater-pierced.** *Her.* Var. of *quarter-pierced*: see QUARTER *sb.* 31. *Obs.*

1610 GUILLIM *Heraldry* II. vii. (1611) 71 He beareth azure a crosse moline, Quater-pierced, or... This is termed Quater-pierced, quasi Quadrate pierced, for that the piercing is square as a Trencher.

†**quater-temper, -temps.** *Obs. rare.* [a. OF. *quatior-*, *quatuortempre* (ad. L. *quatuor tempora*) and *quatretemps*, f. *quatre* four + *temps* time. Cf. QUARTER-TENSE.] The four fasting-periods of the year: see EMBER².

1535 in Weaver *Wells Wills* (1890) 205 All crysten sowles contynually remembryd in the fraternyte of yᵉ quater temps of yᵉ same. **1550** BALE *Eng. Votaries* II. 53 They appoynted the laye people to fast yᵉ Lent,..aduent, rogacyon dayes, and quatertemper.

†**quatervois.** *Obs. rare.* Also 7 quatrefois. [Refashioning of CARFAX, after F. *quatre* four + *voie* way.] A place where four ways meet.

1646 J. GREGORY *Notes & Obs.* (1650) 108 In the Tetrampodus or Quatrefois of that City..there stood a marble statue of Venus. **1687** WOOD *Life* Sept. (O.H.S.) III. 230 When he came to Quatervois he was entertaind with the wind musick or waits belonging to the city and Universitie.

quateryme: see QUATREME.

quath(e, obs. variants of QUOTH.

†**ˈquathrigan.** *Obs. rare.* [ad. L. *quadrīga.*] = QUADRIGA (by Ormin supposed to be a four-*wheeled* chariot); also *fig.* the four gospels.

c **1200** ORMIN Pref. 3 þiss boc..iss wrohht off quaþþrigan, Off goddspell bokess fowwre. *Ibid.* 21þatt wa33n iss nemmnedd quaþþrigan þat hafeþþ fowwre wheless.

quatkin, obs. form of WHATKIN.

quatorzain (ˈkætəzeɪn). Also 6 quaterzayn, 7 quatorzen, 9 quatuorzain. See also QUATORZIEM. [a. F. *quatorzaine* a set of fourteen (persons, days, etc.), f. *quatorze*: see next.] A piece of verse consisting of fourteen lines; a sonnet. In mod. use *spec.* A poem of fourteen lines resembling a sonnet, but without strict observance of sonnet-rules.

1583 G. BUCKE *Commend. Verses* in *T. Watson's Centurie of Loue* (Arb.) 33 The Thuscan's poesie, Who skald [= scaled] the skies in lofty Quatorzain. **1591** NASHE *Pref. Sidney's Astr. & Stella*, Put out your rush candles you poets and rimers and bequeath your quaterzayns to chandlers. **1605** CHAPMAN *All Fooles* II. i. 174 Sonnets in Doozens or your Quatorzaines [*printed* -anies]. **1812** LOFFT (*title*) Laura: or, an Anthology of Sonnets (on the Petrarcan model), and Elegiac Quatuorzains. **1836** H. F. CHORLEY *Mrs. Hemans* (1837) II. 276 This volume..contains also many beautiful sonnets, or more strictly speaking, quatuorzains. **1880** *Sat. Rev.* 27 Mar. 421 The sonnet became..as incorrect as in..Cowper's exquisite quatorzain to Mrs. Unwin.

‖**quatorze** (kəˈtɔːz). [F. *quatorze*:—L. *quatuordecim* fourteen.] In piquet, a set of four similar cards (either aces, kings, queens, knaves, or tens) held by one player, which count as fourteen.

1701 FARQUHAR *Sir H. Wildair* v. iv, Show for it, my lord! I showed quint and quatorze for it. **1778** C. JONES *Hoyle's Games Impr.* 127 Let us suppose the Younger-hand to have two Quatorze against him. **1821** LAMB *Elia* Ser. I. *Mrs. Battle on Whist*, I love to get a tierce or a quatorze, though they mean nothing. **1868** PARDON *Card Player* 51 You are to call a quatorze preferably to three aces.

‖**Quatorze Juillet** (katɔrz ʒɥijɛ). Also quatorze juillet and *ellipt.* quatorze. [Fr., lit. fourteenth of July.] In France, the anniversary of the fall of the Bastille (see BASTILLE *sb.* 3) on 14 July 1789, observed as a national holiday. Also *attrib.*

1934 WEBSTER, Quatorze juillet or (le) quatorze. **1951** R. SENHOUSE tr. *Colette's Last of Chéri* 196 One day, not long before the Quatorze Juillet, Charlotte Peloux was lunching with them. **1955** *Times* 18 July 6/1 *Le Quatorze Juillet*—never referred to by French people under any other name, although its official title is *fête nationale* and its most common English name, more explicitly, 'Bastille Day'—has come and gone, as in other years, in a flurry of military parades, undisciplined queues for free matinées at State theatres, firework displays, and ubiquitous *bals populaires* in the streets. **1966** H. YOXALL *Fashion of Life* xxiv. 233 A firework display..far more lavish than anything I'd seen in Paris on the *Quatorze Juillet*. **1971** *Guardian* 15 July 13/4 The 'quatorze' is..the type of public jamboree which carries no obligations. **1977** E. AMBLER *Send no more Roses* viii. 175 It's the Quatorze today. The servants want to..go to the local fête. *Ibid.* x. 214 We had eaten simply..so that the servants could get off early to their local Quatorze juillet fête.

quatorziem, -sime, obs. Sc. varr. QUATORZAIN.

For the change of ending, cf. QUINZIEME 2.

1615 in *Montgomerie's Poems* (S.T.S.) Introd. 51 The Cherrie and the Slae..Newly altered, perfyted and divided into 114 Quatorziems. [*c* **1724** RAMSAY *Some Contents Evergreen* ix, Montgomery's quatorsimes sall evir pleis.]

quatrain (ˈkwɒtreɪn). Also 6 quadrain, -rein(e, -reyne, 7 -ren, -rin, -ran. [a. F. *quatrain*, †*quadrain* (Cotgr.), f. *quatre* four.]

1. A stanza of four lines, usually with alternate rimes; four lines of verse.

α. **1585** JAS. I *Ess. Poesie* (Arb.) 13 Ane qvadrain of Alexandrin verse. **1589** PUTTENHAM *Eng. Poesie* II. ii. (Arb.) 81 It is not a huitane or a staffe of eight, but two quadreins. **1611** FLORIO, *Quartetto*,..a quadren of a Sonnet, or staffe of foure verses. **1651** DELAUNE (*title*) A Legacie to his Sonnes. Digested into Quadrins.

β. **1666** DRYDEN *Pref. Ann. Mirab.* Wks. (Globe) 38, I have chosen to write my poem in quatrains or stanzas of four in alternate rhyme. **1683** TEMPLE *Mem.* Wks. 1731 I. 478 A Quatrain recited out of *Nostredamus*. **1823** ROSCOE tr. *Sismondi's Lit. Eur.* (1846) I. iv. 102 The beautiful stanza of ten lines, in one quatrain and two tercets. **1856** R. A. VAUGHAN *Mystics* (1860) II. 7 There are many terse and happy couplets and quatrains in the Wanderer.

b. A set of four persons. *nonce-use.*

1862 S. LUCAS *Secularia* 289 There were four English men of letters..of this stately quatrain Swift and Dryden are the only two he has encountered in his history.

2. = QUARTERN 5. *rare*⁻¹.

1819 SOUTHEY *Lett.* (1856) III. 120 Did I send you the opening of 'Oliver Newman', in a small square size..or in half quatrain form?

‖**quatre** (katr, ˈkɑːtə(r)). Also 6 quatter, 6, 8 quater. [F. *quatre* four.] The number four; the four in dice. = CATER *sb.*²

a **1550** *Image Hypocr.* iv. in *Skelton's Wks.* II. 442/1 Swordemen and knightes, That for the faith fightes With sise, sinke, and quatter. *c* **1570** *Pride & Lowl.* (1841) 75 All for a matter deer of quater ase. **1611** FLORIO, *Quaderni*, two quaters or foures at dice. **1694** MOTTEUX *Rabelais* v. x. (1737) 37 Cinques, Quaters, Treys. **1772** FOOTE *Nabob* II. Wks. 1799 II. 301 Cinque and quater: you're out. **1814** CARY *Dante, Paradise* v. 59 Included, as the quatre in the sise. **1850** *Bohn's Hand-bk. Games* 383 Should two quatres be thrown, any of the following moves may be played.

Hence **quatre-crested** *a.*, having four crests.

1791 COWPER *Iliad* II. 48 His helmet quatre-crested. [*Note.* Quâtre-crested. So I have rendered τετραφάληρον.]

†**quatreble**, *a.* and *sb. Obs.* Also 5 -trebil, -tribill, 6 -treple, quadreble, -ible. [Alteration of F. *quadruple* on anal. of *trible* TREBLE.]

A. *adj.* = QUADRUPLE.

1398 TREVISA *Barth. De P.R.* XIX. cxxv. (1495) 925 Thre is treble to one; and fowre is quatreble to one. [See also QUINIBLE.] *c* **1400** tr. *Secreta Secret., Gov. Lordsh.* 82 Treble or quatreblee [odours]. **1454** *Rolls Parlt.* V. 273 The quatreble value of Wolles..so shippid. **1489** *Barbour's Bruce* (Edinb. MS.) XVIII. 30 He suld fecht that day Thocht tribill and quatribill war thai. **1553** *Respublica* (Brandl) II. iii. 4 Ye, double knave youe, will ye never be other?.. Ye, quadrible knave [etc.]. **1556** J. HEYWOOD *Spider & F.* xcvi. 8 Double or treble (yea quatreble) cause. [**1735** W. HAWKINS *Stat. at Large* I. 425 The same Hostler shall incur the quatreble Value of that which he hath taken.]

B. *sb.* **1.** A fourfold amount.

14.. *Lansdowne MS.* 763 in *N. & Q.* 4th Ser. (1870) VI. 117/1 The same proportion that is betwene twoe small numberis, the same is betwene doubles and treblis, and quatrebils and quiniblis. **1429** *Rolls Parlt.* IV. 349/1 Ye parte pleynyng shal have ye quatreble of his damages. **1540-1** ELYOT *Image Gov.* 51 If they had dooen euill, they shuld paie the quatreple or foure tymes so much as they receiued.

2. *Mus.* A note higher than the treble, being an octave above the mean. (Cf. QUINIBLE.)

1528 [see next quot.]. **1855-7** W. CHAPPELL *Pop. Mus. Olden Time* I. 34 To sing a 'quatrible' [means] to descant by fourths. The..term is used by Cornish in his Treatise between Trowthe and Enformacion, 1528. **1870** —— in *N. & Q.* 4th Ser. VI. 117/1 The quatreble began and ended a twelfth above [the plain song] and the quinible a fifteenth.

Hence †**quatreble (quadrible)** *v.*, to quadruple; also *Mus.*, to sing a quatreble.

1398 TREVISA *Barth. De P.R.* XVIII. ix. (1495) 759 Some serpentes haue many hedys, for some ben dowble and some treblyd and some quatrebled. *c* **1500** *Prov.* in *Antiq. Rep.* (1809) IV. 406 He that quadribilithe to hy, his voice is variable. **1607** J. NORDEN *Surv. Dial.* II. 67 The profite was twice quadrebled.

‖**quatre-couleur** (katrkulœr), *a.* [Fr., f. *quatre* four + *couleur* colour.] Of objets d'art: made of or decorated with carved gold of several (esp. four) different colours. Hence **quatrecouleurs** *sb. pl.*

1959 *Times* 19 Dec. 9/4 The one [thimble] on the left has fruit and flowers in *quatre-couleur* work round the band. **1960** H. HAYWARD *Antique Coll.* 231/2 *Quatre-couleurs*, the art of combining various colours of carved gold in a decorative scheme. The colour of gold is determined by the nature of the alloy. **1967** *Times* 7 Mar. 21/4 (Advt.), A quatre-couleur gold box..by Barrière, 1768. **1975** *Catal. Important Gold Boxes & Objects of Vertu* (Sotheby, Monaco) 66 A rectangular quatre-couleur gold and enamel snuff-box. **1978** *Times* 5 Aug. 9/1 Snuff-boxes..in imitation of gold boxes with..'quatre-couleurs' decoration.

quatrefoil (ˈkætəfɔɪl), *sb.* and *a.* Forms: 5 quaterfoile, -foyl(e, katir-, katerfoil, quarterfoyle, (9 -foil), 6 quaterfoille, -foyle, -fold, caterfoyle, 7 -foile, 8- quadre-, quatrefoil, (9 -feuil-le). [a. OF. type **quatrefoil*, f. *quatre* four + *foil* leaf, FOIL *sb.*¹ Cf. CINQUEFOIL.]

†**A.** *adj.* Having four leaves. *Obs. rare.*

c **1420** *Pallad. on Husb.* II. 57 Whan whete is quaterfoyle [L. *quatuor foliorum*] and barley fyue..hit is to wede hem. *Ibid.* XI. 118 And katerfoil, when thai beth vp yspronge, Transplaunte hem.

B. *sb.* †**1.** A set of four leaves. *Obs. rare*⁻¹.

c **1420** *Pallad. on Husb.* III. 623 Let grounden glas go syfte on hem..When theyr trefoyl or quaterfoyl is owte.

2. A compound leaf or flower consisting of four (usually rounded) leaflets or petals radiating from a common centre; also, a representation or conventional imitation of this, *esp.* as a charge in Heraldry. **b.** *Arch.* An opening or ornament, having its outline so divided by cusps as to give it the appearance of four radiating leaflets or petals.

double quatrefoil, an ornament, etc., having eight divisions similarly disposed.

1494 FABYAN *Chron.* VII. 600 Quynces in compost. Blaund Iure, powderyd with quarter foyles gylt. **1520** in *Archæologia* LIII. 19 A crosse sylver and gylte like a quaterfold. **1562** LEIGH *Armorie* (1597) 110 b, He beareth.. a double Caterfoyle... He beareth the quaterfoyle double.. because he is the viij from the heire. **1610** GUILLIM *Heraldry* I. vi. (1611) 26 The Crosse Moline, and the Double Caterfoile. **1771** *Antiq. Sarisb.* 191 A little cross..like a quaterfoille. **1805** SCOTT *Last Minstr.* II. ix, The key-stone, that lock'd each ribbed aisle, Was a fleur-de-lys, or a quatre-feuille. **1849** FREEMAN *Archit.* 360 We..find in Early Gothic the head of a couplet filled with a circle, a quatrefoil [etc.].

Hence **ˈquatrefoiled** *a.*, having the form of a quatrefoil, divided into four parts by cusps.

1848 B. WEBB *Cont. Ecclesiol.* 62 The side lights having quatrefoiled circles in their heads. **1855** *Ecclesiologist* XVI. 295 A taller column, quatrefoiled in section. **1881** *N. & Q.* 6th Ser. III. 133/1 A brass seal with a quatrefoiled handle.

So **quatreˈfoliated** *a.*

1850 T. INKERSLEY *Inq. Rom. & Pointed Archit. France* 309 Sustaining two quatrefoliated circles.

quatrefois, variant of QUATERVOIS.

†**quatreme, -ime.** *Obs. rare.* In 5 quaterime, -(e)ryme, katereme. [a. OF. *quatrieme*, *-esme* (14th c. in Godef.), subst. use of *quatrième* fourth.] A duty or tax of a fourth part levied on certain commodities.

c **1460** FORTESCUE *Abs. & Lim. Mon.* x. (1885) 131 The gabell off the salt, and the quaterimes of the wynes, were graunted to the kynge by the iij estates of France. *c* **1465** *Eng. Chron.* (Camden 1856) 48 Alle maner custumez, fe fermez, and quatrymez. **1480** CAXTON *Chron. Eng.* VII. (1520) 149/2 All maner customes and fee fermes and kateremes.

quatreple, -trible, variants of QUATREBLE.

†**qua'tridual**, *a. Obs. rare*⁻¹. [f. L. *quatriduum* + -AL¹.] Lasting for four days.
1646 R. BAILLIE *Anabaptism* (1647) 34 This is the fruit of their quatridual fastings.

'quatrin. Now *rare*. Also 5 katereyn, 6 -in, -yn, 6–7 quatrine. [a. OF. *quatrin, quadrin* (Godef.), or It. *quattrino*, f. *quattro* four.] A small piece of money; a farthing. Cf. QUADRINE¹.
c **1400** *Apol. Loll.* 12 þou schalt ȝeue me foure floreynis... And he ansuerid, Soþli, I haue but foure katereynis. **1547** BOORDE *Introd. Knowl.* xxiii. (1870) 179 (Italy) In bras they haue kateryns, and byokes, and denares. **1582** MUNDAY *Eng. Rom. Life* in *Harl. Misc.* (Malh.) II. 202 Supping so well as I coulde, with two quatrines woorth of leekes. **1617** MORYSON *Itin.* I. 92 From hence [Bologna] we hired a boat for foure bolinei and foure quatrines. **1888** *Pall Mall G.* 17 Nov. 2/2 Does it refer to the Pope who had not a quatrin, or to St. Martin?

quatriplate, quatrivial, varr. or obs. ff. QUADRUPLATE, QUADRIVIAL.

quatro ('kwætrəʊ). *W. Indies.* Also cuatro. [ad. Sp. *cuatro*, lit. four.] A small four-stringed guitar, of a kind originating in Latin America.
1955 *Caribbean Q.* IV. II. 101 The band includes a home-made banjo, a cuatro (small 4-stringed Spanish guitar).. and shac-shacs. **1958** E. BORNEMAN in P. Gammond *Decca Bk. Jazz* xxi. 261 The instruments used were..guitar, quatro, conga drum, bongos, maraccas, cencerro. **1965** 'LAUCHMONEN' *Old Thom's Harvest* v. 59 His guitar-pickney quatro hung over his shoulder and across his back. **1968** E. LOVELACE *Schoolmaster* i. 8 There is the orchestra.. with the fiddle, and the quatros and flute and tambourines. **1974** *Sunday Advocate-News* (Barbados) 3 Feb. 13/7 The programme is dedicated to the composers of the early tent brigade; men who made music with 'Cuatro, bottle and spoon'. **1975** S. MARCUSE *Dict. Mus. Instruments* 135/2 *Cuatro*.., 1. guitar of Puerto Rico, with 5 courses of strings, 4 pairs and a single chanterelle, played with a plectrum; 2. a small guitar of Venezuela, with 4 strings.

quatron(e, quatroon, varr. or obs. ff. QUARTERN, QUADROON.

†**quatrumvirate.** *Obs.*⁻¹ = QUATUORVIRATE.
1684 T. GODDARD *Plato's Demon* 53 The whole Triumvirate, or if you will, Quatrumvirate are included.

‖**quatsch** (kvatʃ). Also quatch. [Ger.] Nonsense, rubbish. Freq. as *int.*
1907 M. A. VON ARNIM *Fräulein Schmidt* liv. 218 '*Quatsch*,' said Onkel Heinrich, with sudden and explosive bitterness. *Ibid.* 219 *Quatsch* is German for silly, or nonsense, and..is more rude than either. **1915** WYNDHAM LEWIS *Lett.* (1963) 72, I never did nor ever shall, as you probably devine, despite 'quatch' about malevolence. **1939** JOYCE *Finnegans Wake* (1964) 520 Quatsch! What hill ar yu fluking about, ye lamelookond fyats! **1947** D. M. DAVIN *Gorse blooms Pale* 165, I notice he commits himself to nothing about Zionism. A lot of quatsch and schmaltz, if you ask me. **1962** K. O'HARA *Double Cross Purposes* iii. 31 'I'm rusty in my law after two years...' '*Quatsch*. You're worse than rusty.' **1976** *Times Lit. Suppl.* 4 June 671/2 Fantasy masquerading as history, pure *quatsch* dressed in purple kitsch. **1979** N. FREELING *Widow* vii. 42 'Oh Quatsch,' she said. 'I..know how to look after myself.'

quat-so-(euer), quatt, obs. ff. WHAT-SO-(EVER), WHAT.

quatter, obs. f. QUATRE.

quattie ('kwɒtı). *W. Indies.* [Corruption of QUARTER *sb.*] A penny halfpenny; money or a coin of the value of 1½d (0.625p).
1859 TROLLOPE *West Indies & Spanish Main* ii. 20 'And now de two quatties,' he said. I knew nothing of quatties then, but I gave him the sixpence. **1873** C. J. G. RAMPINI *Lett. from Jamaica* ix. 94 'Quattie', a penny-half-penny—the 'quarter' of sixpence. **1893** R. BITHELL *Counting-House Dict.* (rev. ed.) 254 *Quattie*, a small silver coin used in the West Indies, worth about 1½d. English. **1961** F. G. CASSIDY *Jamaica Talk* ix. 209 The *tup*, of course, is an abbreviation of *twopence*, but nowadays means the same as *quattie*: 1½d. **1971** *Jamaican Weekly Gleaner* 3 Nov. 25/2 Pound' wort' a fret nebber pay quattie wort' a debt. **1975** *New Yorker* 12 May 37/1 He put every penny, every quattie of what we had into a small herd and a prize black bull.

quattro'centism. [f. QUATTROCENT(O + -ISM.] The fifteenth-century style in Italian art.
1905 W. H. HUNT *Pre-Raphaelitism* II. xiii. 367 It was pointed out to them that our pictures had never attempted quattrocentism.

‖**quattrocento** (kwattro'tʃɛnto), *sb.* (and *a.*) [It., lit. 'four hundred', but used for 'fourteen hundred': cf. CINQUECENTO.] The fifteenth century (14..), as a period of Italian art, architecture, etc. Also *attrib.* or as *adj.*
1875 POLLEN *Anc. & Mod. Furn.* 61 The better known Italian furniture of the quattrocento..is gilt and painted. **1882–3** J. L. CORNING in Schaff *Encycl. Relig. Knowl.* III. 2139 We may include both of these—the quatrocento [*sic*] and the cinquecento—in the third great period of Christian sculpture. **1921** A. HUXLEY *Let.* 31 May (1969) 197 For my taste, at least, Florence is too tre- and quattrocento. **1955** *Times* 20 May 3/7 The settings [in a film] were purely *quattrocento*, very scholarly, and very pretty. **1965** F. RAPHAEL *Darling* xxvi. 131 The pictures started with quattrocento pieces. **1977** *N.Y. Rev. Bks.* 24 Nov. 36/4 The charming *cassone* fronts of a minor painter called Apollonio di Giovannie, which look to us like decorative charades in *quattrocento* costume. **1979** *Jrnl. R. Soc. Arts* CXXVII. 627/2 We know virtually everything we could hope to know about the decoration of a quattrocento chapel.

Hence **quattro'centist**, ‖**-cen'tista** (It., with pl. **-isti**), **-centiste** (F.), an Italian artist, author, etc. of the 15th c.; also *attrib.* or as *adj.*
1855 MOTLEY *Corr.* (1889) I. vi. 182 The wonderful Quattro Centisti of Florence, the painters, I mean, of the fifteenth century. **1873** OUIDA *Pascarel* I. 66 He would bring out from its corner his little old quattrocentiste viol. **1886** HOLMAN HUNT in *Contemp. Rev.* XLIX. 476, I began to trace the purity of work in the quattrocentists, to this drilling of undeviating manipulation. *Ibid.* 477 The quattrocentist work..became dearer to me as I progressed.

'quatuor. *Mus.* [L. 'four'.] = QUARTET 1.
The current term in Fr., but not now in Eng. use.
1726 BAILEY, *Quatuor* (in Musick Books) signifies Musick composed for 4 Voices. **1811** in BUSBY *Dict. Mus.* (ed. 3).

†**quatuordecangle.** *Obs. rare*⁻¹. [f. L. *quatuor* four + *dec-em* ten + ANGLE.] A figure having fourteen angles.
1667 COLLINS in Rigaud *Corr. Sci. Men* (1841) I. 128 The side of a regular quatuordecangle inscribed in a circle.

quatu'orvirate. *rare*⁻¹. [ad. L. *quatuorvirātus*, f. *quatuor* four + *vir* man. Cf. QUADRUM-, QUARTUM-, QUATRUMVIRATE.] A body of four men.
1856 W. C. LAKE in *Life* (1901) 195 Lending his religious influence to the Triumvirate or Quatuorvirate.

†**quaught**, *v. Obs. rare*⁻⁰. [var. of *quaft*, QUAFF *v.* or of Sc. WAUCHT.] To drink deeply.
1530 PALSGR. 676/2, I quaught, I drinke all out. *Je boys dautant.* Wyll you quawght with me?

quauk, Sc. form of QUAKE *v.*

†**quave**, *sb. Obs.* [f. next.] A shake, tremble.
1382, etc. [see EARTH-QUAVE]. *c* **1440** *Promp. Parv.* 419/2 Quaue, of a myre (*K., P.* quaue, as of a myre), *labina.* **1635** SWAN *Spec. M.* (1670) 196 A quave of the earth swallowed a middle part of the city Misia.

†**quave**, *v. Obs.* Also 3 cwauien, 4, 6 quaue, 5 qvavyn, 6 queaue. [Early ME. *cwavien*, prob. repr. an OE. **cwafian*, of parallel formation to *cwacian* QUAKE; for the stem cf. QUIVER *v.*]
1. *intr.* To quake, shake, tremble.
a **1225** *St. Marher.* 19 Al þe eorðe..bigon to cwakien [*B.* ant to cwauien]. **1377** LANGL. *P. Pl.* B. XVIII. 61 The wal wagged and clef, and al the worlde quaued. **1382** WYCLIF *1 Sam.* xxviii. 5 And Saul..dradde, and his herte quauyde ful myche. *c* **1440** *Promp. Parv.* 419/2 Qvavyn, as myre, *tremo.* **1481** CAXTON *Myrr.* II. c. 22 Now vnderstande ye..how the erthe quaueth and shaketh. **1509** *Parl. Devylles* lvi, The erthe quaued..Valeys and stones brest asonder. **1687** MIEGE *Grt. Fr. Dict.* II, To Quave. As to quave with fat. [**1825** see *quaving* ppl. a.]
2. *intr.* To beat, palpitate; to throb with life.
1387 TREVISA *Higden* (Rolls) VII. 37 þe place at Schaftesbury þere his longes ȝit quaveþ al fresche and sound. **1589** PUTTENHAM *Eng. Poesie* III. xix. (Arb.) 223 Is he aliue, Is he as I left him queauing and quick.
Hence †**'quaving** *vbl. sb.* and *ppl. a.*
13.. *E.E. Allit. P.* B. 324, I schal..quelle alle þat is quik with quauende flodez. **1382** WYCLIF *1 Kings* xix. 11 After the wynde, quauynge; not in the quauyng the Lord. **1533** ELYOT *Cast. Helth* I. ii, That body is called fleumatike, wherein water hath pre-eminence, and is perceiued by these signes: fatnesse, quaving, and soft. **1610** HOLLAND *Camden's Brit.* I. 530 So quaving soft and moist the Bases were. **1825** BRITTON *Beauties Wilts* III. 8 In the valley..are some quagmires, called by the inhabitants quaving-gogs.

†**'quavemire.** *Obs.* [f. QUAVE *v.* + MIRE.] = QUAGMIRE (q.v.).
1530 PALSGR., Quave myre, *foundriere, crouliere.* **1565** JEWEL *Def. Apol.* (1611) 404 Pooles, Marishes,..and Quauemires. **1601** HOLLAND *Pliny* I. 221 Dyonisius was forced to leaue his horse sticking fast in a quaue-mire. **1610** —— *Camden's Brit.* 529 The Lower [part] hath in it foule and slabby quave mires, yea and most troublesome fennes.
fig. **1581** J. BELL *Haddon's Answ. Osor.* 206 They do winne nothing by thys distinction: seeing that they fall back into the same quavemire.

quaver ('kweıvə(r)), *sb.* [f. the vb.]
1. *Mus.* A note, equal in length to half a crotchet or one-eighth of a semibreve. Also *Comb.*
1570 LEVINS *Manip.* 76/18 A Quauer, *octaua pars mensuræ.* **1597** MORLEY *Introd. Mus.* Annot., Who inuented the Crotchet, Quauer and Semiquauer is vncertaine. **1659** LEAK *Waterwks.* 31 Demi-crochets or Quavers, whereof there are sixteen in one measure. **1706** A. BEDFORD *Temple Mus.* viii. 165 The greatest Part..is sung in Short Notes.. and are Prickt with Quavers. **1728** CHAMBERS *Cycl.* s.v. *Rest*, The Quaver-Rest of common time. **1789** E. DARWIN *Bot. Gard.* II. (1791) 60 And then the third on four concordant lines, Prints the lone crotchet, and the quaver joins. **1866** ENGEL *Nat. Mus.* iii. 90 A slight alteration of the melody.. such as a substitution of two quavers for a crotchet.
fig. *a* **1619** FOTHERBY *Atheom.* II. xii. § 1 (1622) 327, I will not strictly examine euery crochet and quauer.
2. *Mus.* **a.** A shake or trill in singing.
1611 CORYAT *Crudities* 27, I heard a certaine French man who sung very melodiously with curious quauers. **1711** ADDISON *Spect.* No. 29 ¶11 A Voice so full of Shakes and Quavers, that I should have thought the Murmurs of a Country Brook the much more agreeable Musick. **1768–74** TUCKER *Lt. Nat.* (1834) II. 443 The people..attend solely to their quavers, without heeding the substance of what they sing. **1817** BYRON *Beppo* ii, There are songs and quavers, roaring, humming. **1883** STEVENSON *Treas. Isl.* v. xxiii, A.. sailor's song, with a droop and a quaver at the end of every verse.
b. in instrumental music. *rare.*
1627–77 FELTHAM *Resolves* II. xxxvii. 234 Unlike a quaver on an Instrument, it is not there a grace, but a jar in Music. **1712** ADDISON *Spect.* No. 361 ¶6 Whether we consider the Instrument [the Cat-call] itself, or those several Quavers and Graces which are thrown into the playing of it.
3. A shake or tremble in the voice; a tremulous voice or cry.
1748 RICHARDSON *Clarissa* (1811) III. xiii. 86 [She] drew a sigh into two or three but just audible quavers. **1833** HT. MARTINEAU *Tale of Tyme* iii. 53 There was..a quaver of the voice which belied what he said. **1882** STEVENSON *New Arab. Nts.* (1884) 63 Silas, with a quaver, admitted that he had done so.
4. A quivering or tremulous movement. Also *fig.*
1736 H. BROOKE *Univ. Beauty* v. 136 Tissu'd wing its folded membrane frees, And with blithe quavers fans the gath'ring breeze. **1881** STEVENSON *Virg. Puerisque, Eng. Admirals* 208 The worth of such actions is not a thing to be decided in a quaver of sensibility.

quaver ('kweıvə(r)), *v.* Also 5 qwaver. [f. QUAVE *v.* + -ER⁵. Cf. QUIVER *v.*]
1. a. *intr.* To vibrate, tremble, quiver. Also, with *adv.*, to go with a tremulous or quivering movement.
1430–40 LYDG. *Bochas* VIII. viii. (1558) fol. vi, Whose double whele quauereth euer in dout. **1477** SIR J. PASTON in *P. Lett.* III. 174 It semythe that the worlde is alle qwaveryng. **1590** MARLOWE *2nd Pt. Tamburl.* I. iii, Their fingers made to quaver on a lute. **1629** GAULE *Holy Madn.* 206 Tongue stammers, lips quauer. **1692** LUTTRELL *Brief Rel.* (1857) II. 571 The earthquake was so severe..that the streets quavered like the waves of the sea. **1839** BAILEY *Festus* ix. (1852) 125 Like rivers over reeds Which quaver in the current. **1887** STEVENSON *Misadv. J. Nicholson* ii. 4 The breeze..set the flames of the street-lamps quavering. **1943** A. RANSOME *Picts & Martyrs* xv. 144 The three-cornered white flag..quavered up to the masthead. **1953** C. MACKENZIE *Passionate Elopement* xxx. 270 Old Tabrum would quaver in from time to time to survey the comfort of his guests, regaling them with some particularly choice floral anecdote.
b. Of the voice: To shake, tremble.
1741 RICHARDSON *Pamela* II. 43 That melodious Voice praying for me..still hangs upon my Ears, and quavers upon my Memory. **1825** J. NEAL *Bro. Jonathan* I. 401 His fine voice quavered. **1866** G. MACDONALD *Ann. Q. Neighb.* i. (1878) 2 When my voice quavers.
2. *intr.* To use trills or shakes in singing.
1538 ELYOT, *Vibrisso*, To quauer in syngynge. *a* **1592** H. SMITH in Spurgeon *Treas. Dav.* Ps. cxxxvi. 1 Like a nightingale, which..quavers and capers, and trebles upon it. **1665** BRATHWAIT *Comm. 2 Tales* 23 He quavers in his musical Aires melodiously. **1684** tr. *Agrippa's Van. Arts* liv. 147 In Singing also the Italians Bleat, the Spaniards Whine, the Germans Howl, and the French Quaver. **1708** J. PHILIPS *Cyder* ii. 413 Now sportive Youth Carol incondite Rhythms with suiting Notes, And quaver unharmonious. **1806–7** J. BERESFORD *Miseries Hum. Life* (1826) v. xii, One poor singer quavering like Orpheus of old to the trees. **1854** H. MILLER *Sch. & Schm.* (1858) 403 Jock laboured hard to keep up with his guide; quavering and semi-quavering, as his breath served.
3. a. *trans.* To sing (a note, song, etc.) with trills or quavers. Also with *forth, out.*
1570 LEVINS *Manip.* 78/43 To Quauer a note, *vibrare.* **1596** DRAYTON *Legends* i. 43 The Larke..Quaver'd her cleare Notes in the quiet Ayre. **1651** CLEVELAND *Poems* 49 Can a groan Be quaver'd out by soft division? **1757** DYER *Fleece* (1807) 94 Th' am'rous youth..Quavers the choicest of his sonnets. **1820** W. IRVING *Sketch Bk.* (1859) 150 He quavered forth a quaint old ditty. **1856** R. W. PROCTER *Barber's Shop* xiv. (1883) 118 The song which Jack..liked most to quaver was Alice Gray.
b. *trans.* To utter with a quaver or in a quavering tone.
1872 A. C. STEELE *Broken Toys* I. vii. 102 'Oh, yes, I was the upper-housemaid,' the old woman quavered. **1897** W. W. JACOBS *Skipper's Wooing* iii. 36 'I'd rather you stayed,' he quavered. 'I would indeed.' **1912** *Red Mag.* 1 Mar. 513/2 'Gus!' she quavers. 'Oh, Gus!' **1947** *Punch* 5 Mar. 206/2 'Thank heavens you're here!' he quavered as I went up to him. **1972** 'J. HERRIOT' *It shouldn't happen to Vet* xv. 105 'Have you got a drop o' whisky handy, Jim?' he quavered.
4. *trans.* To drive *away* by playing quavers.
1780 COWPER *Progr. Err.* 127 With wire and catgut.. Quavering and semiquavering care away.
Hence **'quavered** *ppl. a.* Also **'quaverer**, one who quavers.
1611 COTGR., *Gringuenoteur*, A warbler, shaker, quauerer. **1762** SIR W. JONES *Arcadia* 164 His tune so various and uncouth he made, That..not a nymph [could] the quaver'd notes approve. **1802** in *Spirit Pub. Jrnls.* VI. 222 Italia sends us home Three quaverers together.

quaver, obs. Sc. form of QUIVER *sb.*¹

quavering ('kweıvərıŋ), *vbl. sb.* [f. QUAVER *v.* + -ING¹.] The action of the vb., in various senses.
1552 HULOET, Quauerynge, *vibratio.* **1577** tr. *Bullinger's Decades* (1592) 932 A Hymne..may bee humblie vttered without quauering of the voice. **1634** WITHER *Embl.* 82 T'will cause a thousand quaverings in your breast. **1706** A. BEDFORD *Temple Mus.* vii. 158 *Tebhir*..may denote a Shake or Quavering of the Voice. **1826** SCOTT *Woodst.* i, The.. Mayor then interrupted the quavering of..the clerk. **1892** E. REEVES *Homeward Bound* 222 A buzzing, humming sound..with quaverings on its sharp and flat.

quavering ('kweıvərıŋ), *ppl. a.* [f. as prec. + -ING².] That quavers, in senses of the vb.
1430–40 LYDG. *Bochas* IV. xx. (1554) 119 In al such quauering perseuerance Thinke on Lisymachus. **1561**

HOLLYBUSH *Hom. Apoth.* 22 S. Ihons beries..be good for the quauering harte. **1607** TOPSELL *Four-f. Beasts* (1658) 272 Such passing sweet musick as that his fine quavering hand could sometime make. **1725** POPE *Odyss.* XX. 222 With quavering cries the vaulted roofs resound. **1873** HOLLAND *A. Bonnic.* xxi. 340 A voice quite unnatural in its quavering sharpness.

Hence **'quaveringly** *adv.*, in a quavering manner; with a quaver in the voice.

1594 NASHE *Unfort. Trav.* Wks. 1883–4 V. 185 Iarring on them quaueringly with his hammer. **1882** J. HAWTHORNE *Fort. Fool* I. xiii, 'I don't want to have you go, Jack!' said she, quaveringly.

quaverous ('kweɪvərəs), *a.* [f. QUAVER *v.* + -OUS.] Tremulous, quavering.

1918 J. F. BRIDGE *Westm. Pilgrim* xi. 146, I can still see two of these old gentlemen..with hardly a quaverous note to mark their years, valiantly voicing 'I saw lovely Phyllis'.

quavery ('kweɪvərɪ), *a.* [f. as QUAVERING *ppl. a.* + -Y[1].] Apt to quaver; somewhat quavering.

1519 HORMAN *Vulg.* 240 A quauery or maris and vnstable foundacion, must be holpe with great pylys of alder rammed downe. **1866** MISS BRADDON *Lady's Mile* 35 Quavery old sextons. **1890** HALL CAINE *Bondman* III. iv, He began to sing ..in his hoarse and quavery voice. **1965** HOUSE & STOREY *Lett. C. Dickens* I. 557 A quavery line is drawn under 'Ill! *He* ill!', and another under 'Any time while the—'. The writing of the last three lines gets progressively more shaky. **1975** *Daily Tel.* 10 Nov. 2/6 A woman's voice in the crowd soared above the others, quavery but sweet.

So **'quavery-'mavery**, in an uncertain or precarious condition. *rare.*

1809 MALKIN *Gil Blas* x. ii. ¶3 Your father..is standing, as a body may say, quavery-mavery between life and death. *a* **1825** FORBY *Voc. E. Anglia, Quavery-mavery*, undecided; and hesitating how to decide.

quaving, *vbl. sb.* and *ppl. a.*: see QUAVE *v.*

†**quaviver.** *Obs.* Also 7 quaui(u)er, quawiuer. [app. f. VIVER; the first element is obscure.] The fish called sea-dragon or dragonet.

1589 RIDER *Bibl. Scholast.* 1723 A quaviuer, a kind of sea fish, *araneus dracæna*. **1611** COTGR., *Traigne*, the sea Dragon, Viuer, Quauiuer. **1655** MOUFET & BENNET *Health's Improv.* (1746) 258 Quawiuers, for so the Scots and Northern English term them, are very subtile and crafty Fishes. **1725** BRADLEY *Fam. Dict.* s.v. *Fish*, Your Quavivers or Perches must be boiled in Water with Salt. **1783** AINSWORTH *Lat. Dict.* (Morell) II, *Draco*,..a fish called a quaviver.

†**'quavy**, *a. Obs. rare.* Also 5 quauie, qwauy. [f. QUAVE *v.* + -Y[1].] Soft, flabby.

1398 TREVISA *Barth. De P.R.* IV. ix. (Tollem. MS.), Dull of witte..nesche of flesche and quauy. *Ibid.* VI. iv. (1495) 191 The chyldes flesshe that is newe borne is tendre, nesshe, qwauy and vnsadde.

quavyr, obs. Sc. var. of QUIVER *sb.*[1]

quaw (kwɔː). *Sc.* Also 9 qua(a, quah. [Of obscure origin, poss. repr. an earlier **quall*: cf. *quallmire* and the forms cited s.v. QUAGMIRE.] A quag, quagmire. Also **quawmire**.

1535 LYNDESAY *Satyre* 837 (Laing) Lyk ane quaw myre. **1595** DUNCAN *App. Etym.* (E.D.S.), *Vorago*, a gulfe, or quaw-myre. **1824** MACTAGGART *Gallovid. Encycl.*, *Quakinquaws*—or *Quaws*, or moving quagmire bogs. **1880** *Antrim & Down Gloss.*, *Quaa, quah*, a marsh; a quagmire, or shaking bog. **1894** CROCKETT *Raiders* 167 Green, deceitful 'quakkin-qua's', covered with a scum that looked like tender young grass.

quaw-bird, variant of QUA-BIRD.

quawght, variant of QUAUGHT. *Obs.*

quawk (kwɔːk), *sb. U.S.* Also **quark, quauk, quock.** [Imitative; cf. QUAWK *v.* and SQUAWK *sb.*]

1. The black-crowned night-heron, *Nycticorax nycticorax*, which is widely distributed in temperate and tropical regions; = QUA-BIRD.

1844 J. E. DEKAY *Zool. N.Y.* II. 227 The Black-crowned Night Heron, or Quawk,..derives its popular name from the deep gutteral cry. **1867** *Amer. Naturalist* I. 344 Many.. were all agog to cover themselves with glory by shooting a quawk. **1877** W. WHITMAN *Specimen Days* (1882–3) 100, I find [in New Jersey]..Cheewinks, Quawks, Ground robins. **1895** F. M. CHAPMAN *Handbk. Birds Eastern N. Amer.* 136 Black-crowned Night Heron; Quawk. **1926** A. C. BENT *Life Hist. N. Amer. Marsh Birds* 197 The familiar night heron or 'quawk' is one of the best known and most widely distributed of our herons. **1962** R. S. PALMER *Handbk. N. Amer. Birds* I. 475 Characteristic *quock* of this heron has been widely used as a vernacular name: 'squawk', 'quock', etc. **1968** *Times* 28 Feb. 11/7 During a recent expedition to the Falkland Islands I was lucky enough to see and hear.. the Quark. They are birds of great beauty, heron-like in appearance.

2. The cry of a duck or night-heron; = QUACK *sb.*[2]

1863 'G. HAMILTON' *Gala-Days* 73 For the heavy booming of cannon rose the 'quauk!' of ducks. **1895** F. M. CHAPMAN *Handbk. Birds Eastern N. Amer.* 137 Occasionally they [*sc.* black-crowned night herons] utter a loud, hoarse *quawk*, the origin of their common name. **1962** R. S. PALMER *Handbk. N. Amer. Birds* I. 476 The Black-crown's note can be expressed as *quock*.

quawk (kwɔːk), *v. dial.* [Imitative; cf. CAWK *sb.*[2]] *intr.* To caw. Hence **quawking** *vbl. sb.*

1821 CLARE *Vill. Minstr.* I. 24 Rous'd by quawking of the flopping crows. *Ibid.* II. 121 The rooks..Quawk clamorous to the spring's approach. **1879–** In dial. glossaries (Leic., Shropsh., etc.).

†**quax**, *v. Obs.*[−1] [? var. QUASS *v.*] To quaff.

1509 BARCLAY *Shyp of Folys* (1874) II. 261 Some drynkes: some quaxes the canykyn halfe full.

quay (kiː), *sb.* [Later spelling of *kay*, KEY *sb.*[2], after F. *quai*. The pron. is that of *key*; cf. however quots. 1723 and 1850.] **a.** An artificial bank or landing-place, built of stone or other solid material, lying along or projecting into a navigable water for convenience of loading and unloading ships.

1696 PHILLIPS (ed. 5), *Quay* or *Kay*, a broad Space pav'd upon the Shore of a River, Haven or Port, for the loading and unloading of Goods. **1723** SWIFT *Stella at Wood-Park* 46 But now arrives the dismal day, She must return to Ormond-quay. **1756–7** tr. *Keysler's Trav.* (1760) II. 382 Repairs and improvement of the ancient quay. **1800** COLQUHOUN *Comm. & Pol. Thames* i. 26 The small Vessels land their Goods at the Quays. **1850** TENNYSON *In Mem.* xiv, If..I went down unto the quay [*rime* to-day], And found thee lying in the port. **1884** PAE *Eustace* xviii. 233 A small quay ran along the north of the little harbour.

b. *attrib.* and *Comb.*, as *quay-berth, -charges, -dues, -edge, -head, -holder, -labourer, -like* adj., *-man, -master, -rail, -room, -side* (hence *-sider*), *-space, -stone, -wall*, etc.; **quay crane** = *wharf crane*; **quay-punt** (in full, **Falmouth quay-punt**), a small fore-and-aft-rigged half-decked two-masted sailing boat, orig. used on the river Fal for transporting stores between ship and shore.

1969 *Jane's Freight Containers 1968–69* 286/3 Stevedoring companies who already have modern mechanised equipment at their disposal (quay-cranes, pontoon-cranes, trucks and elevators). **1977** *Hongkong Standard* 12 Apr. (Business Suppl.) 4/5 The group has a total of seven quay cranes. **1889** P. H. EMERSON *Eng. Idyls* 128 Paddling to a quay-head, they landed. **1798** R. DODD *Port Lond.* 9 The legal quay-holders and wharfingers. *c* **1820** S. ROGERS *Italy, Como* 28 A quay-like scene, glittering and full of life. **1886** D. KEMP *Man. Yacht & Boat Sailing* (ed. 5) 341 Table of offsets (Falmouth quay punt). **1925** *Yachting Monthly* XXXIX. 39/2 A quay punt before the war cost about £120 to build. **1971** *Country Life* 20 May 1224/1 They were the bum boats of the western world and ranged from such rugged deep-keel craft as the Quay Punts of Falmouth to the graceful Deal galleys. **1936** DYLAN THOMAS in *Contemp. Poetry & Prose* 53 Let the first Peter from a rainbow's quayrail Ask the tall fish. **1862** ANSTED *Channel Isl.* I. iii. (ed. 2) 40 The quay-room was extremely narrow and restricted. **1903** *Westm. Gaz.* 31 Dec. 5/3 He saw another man climbing up the quayside ladder. **1928** *Daily Tel.* 7 Feb. 14/1 The foundations..rested in the rock found 70 ft. under the two quaysides. **1974** *Times* 12 Nov. 3/1 Quayside fish merchants at Hull. **1979** *Jrnl. R. Soc. Arts* CXXVII. 663/1 Local fishermen..used to sell their hake, cod and herring on the quayside. **1820** KEATS *Lamia* I. 224 His galley now Grated the quay-stones. **1938** DYLAN THOMAS in *20th Cent. Verse* Jan./Feb. 3, I make this in a warring absence when Each ancient, stone-necked minute of love's season Harbours my anchored tongue, slips the quaystone. **1798** R. DODD *Port Lond.* 7 Regular quay-walls on both sides the river.

Hence **quay** *v.*[1] *trans.*, to provide with a quay. Also **quayed** (kiːd) *ppl. a.*

1799 W. TOOKE *View Russian Emp.* I. 256 The whole extent of the left-hand bank, Catharine the second caused to be quayed with granite. **1807** J. BARLOW *Columb.* iv. 592 Quay the calm ports and dike the lawns I lave. **1857** *Ecclesiologist* XVIII. 175 The quayed and purified Thames.

†**quay**, *v.*[2] *Obs. rare*[−1]. [? Alteration of QUAIL *v.*] *trans.* To depress, subdue, daunt.

1590 SPENSER *F.Q.* I. viii. 14 Therewith his sturdie corage soon was quayd, And all his sences were with suddein dread dismayd.

quay, obs. form of WHEY.

quayage ('kiːɪdʒ). [In sense 1 for earlier *kay-*, KEYAGE, q.v.; in sense 2 f. QUAY *sb.* + -AGE.]

1. Dues levied on goods landed or shipped at a quay, or on ships using the quay.

1756 in ROLT *Dict. Trade.* **1778** *Engl. Gazetteer* (ed. 2) s.v. *Truro*, The quayage of goods laden or unladen there. **1894** J. H. WYLIE *Hist. Eng. Hen. IV*, II. 475 A quayage of 6*d.* was levied on every ship bringing articles alongside.

2. Quay-room, quay-space.

1840 *Evid. Hull Docks Comm.* 29 You have allotted considerable room for quayage. **1881** W. WILKINS *Songs of Study* 32 We strolled by the quayage and bridges. **1888** *Spectator* 30 June 891/2 A hundred years ago, the quayage of the harbour [Glasgow] measured 382 yards.

quayer(e, obs. forms of QUIRE *sb.*[1]

†**quayf(e, quaff**, obs. ff. COIF. (In quots. = 'omentum'; cf. COIF 6, and Cotgr. s.v. *Coiffe.*)

1597 LOWE *Chirurg.* (1634) 223 The cure [of tumor in the Navel] is..reduce the pudding and Quaffe [etc.]. **1622** J. REYNOLDS *God's Revenge* II. 195 On his right side; but it touch't neither his bowels nor quayfe.

'quayful. [f. QUAY *sb.* + -FUL.] A quantity sufficient to fill a quay.

1856 KANE *Arct. Expl.* II. xvii. 181 Much like a gang of stevedores going to work over a quayful of broken cargo.

quayl(e, quaym, obs. ff. QUAIL *sb.* and *v.*, WHOM.

quaynt(e, obs. f. QUAINT *a.*; obs. pa. pple. of QUENCH *v.*

quayntance: see QUAINTANCE.

quayre, quays, obs. ff. QUIRE, WHOSE.

que, obs. f. CUE *sb.*[1] and *sb.*[2], QUEY.

queach (kwiːtʃ). *Obs.* exc. *dial.* Also 5 quech(e, 7 queich. [Of obscure etym.] A dense growth of bushes; a thicket (see also quot. 1825).

c **1450** *Merlin* xxvii. 540 Thei rode so longe till thei com in to a thikke queche in a depe valey. **1486** *Bk. St. Albans* D j, When ye come to a wode or a quech of bushus. **1565** GOLDING *Ovid's Met.* I. (1593) 4 Their houses were the thicks, And bushie queaches. **1653** SIR W. DENNY *Pelecanicidium* III. ix. 7 Through furzie Queaches thou must goe. *a* **1825** FORBY *Voc. E. Anglia, Queach*, a plat of ground adjoining arable land, and left unploughed, because full of bushes or roots of trees. **1832** L. HUNT *Poems* 198 Wood, copse, or queach.

queachy ('kwiːtʃɪ), *a. Obs.* exc. *dial.* Also 6–7 quechy, 9 (*dial.*) queechy. [f. prec. + -Y[2]. For the connexion between senses 1 and 2, cf. CARR[2].]

†**1.** Forming a dense growth or thicket. *Obs.*

1565 GOLDING *Ovid's Met.* To Rdr. (1593) 1 Eche queachie grove, eche cragged cliffe, the name of Godhead tooke. **1586** W. WEBBE *Eng. Poetrie* (Arb.) 76 Neuer agaíne shall I..See ye in queachie briers..clambring on a high hill.

2. Of ground: Swampy, boggy. *Obs.* exc. *dial.*

1593 PEELE *Edw. I* E iv, The dampes that rise from out the quechy [1599 quesie] plots. **1613** HEYWOOD *Braz. Age* II. ii. Wks. 1874 III. 190 Aime them at yon fiend, Den'd in the quechy bogge. **1631** CHETTLE *Hoffmann* I b, Nor doth the sun sucke from the queachy plot The ranknes..of the Earth. **1886** ELWORTHY *W. Som. Word-bk.*, *Queechy*,..Applied to land—wet; sodden; swampy.

3. *dial.* Feeble, weak, small.

1859 GEO. ELIOT *A. Bede* x, They're poor queechy things, gells is. **1886** ELWORTHY *W. Som. Word-bk.*, *Queechy*, sickly, feeble, queasy.

quead, variant of QUED, bad. *Obs.*

queal, queel (kwiːl), *v. Obs.* exc. *dial.* [Later form of QUAIL *v.*; for the change of vowel, cf. QUEASY.] *intr.* and *trans.* = QUAIL *v.*

1515 BARCLAY *Egloges* ii. (1570) B v, Their matters quealeth, for solde is all Justice. **1550** HOOPER *Serm. Jonas* vii. Wks. (Parker Soc.) 552 He bringeth forth a young tree. .. But the Lord queeleth it again straightway. **1622** W. YONGE *Diary* 19 Aug. (Camden) 63 The wind..quealed all hedges towards the south. **1847–78** HALLIWELL, *Queal*, to faint away. *Devon. Ibid.*, *Queel*, to grow flabby. *Devon.* **1848** A. B. EVANS *Leicestersh. Words, Queel*, to extinguish: 'He could not queel the fire'.

queale, obs. form of WHEAL.

quealy (?), *a.*: see QUEASY 2 c, quot. 1649.

quean (kwiːn). Forms: 1, 3 **cwene**, (1 **cwyne**), 3–6 **quene**, (5 **qw-**), 4–5 **quen, queyne**, 5 **qw-**, **queyn**, 4–6 **queine**, 7 **queene**, 7–8 **queen**, (8 *north.* **whein**); 6–7 **queane**, (8 **quane**, 8–9 *north.* **whean**), 6– **quean**; 8–9 *Sc.* **quine**. [OE. *cwene* wk. fem. = OS. *quena* (MDu. *quene*, Du. *kween* a barren cow), OHG. *quina, quena, ch(w)ena*, ON. *kvenna, kvinna* (gen. pl.), Goth. *qino* woman:—OTeut. **kwenōn-*, a lengthened form of the stem which appears in Zend *genā*, Gr. γυνή, OSl. and Russ. *žená*, OIr. *ben*, repr. a common Aryan type *g^{w}*enā*: cf. QUEEN.

In ME. the word was distinguished from QUEEN by its open *e*, which in the 14–15th c. was sometimes denoted by the spelling with *ei* or *ey*, and later (as in other words of the class) by *ea*.]

1. A woman, a female; from early ME. a term of disparagement or abuse, hence: A bold, impudent, or ill-behaved woman; a jade, hussy; and *spec.* a harlot, strumpet (esp. in 16–17th c.). Now *arch.*

a **1000** *Riddles* lxxiii. (lxxiv.) 1 Ic wæs fæmne ȝeong, feaxhar cwene. *a* **1023** WULFSTAN *Hom.* xxiii. (1883) 161 *note*, þæt..ane cwenan ȝemænum ceape bicȝað..and wið þa ane fylðe adreoȝað. *c* **1205** LAY. 12872 Whær swa heo funden æine mon..þa quenen [*c* 1275 cwenes] lude loȝen. *c* **1290** *S. Eng. Leg.* I. 194/6 An old quene þare was biside, strong hore and baudestrote. **1393** LANGL. *P. Pl.* C. IX. 46 At churche in the charnel cheorles aren vuel to knowe..other a queyne fro a queene. **1481** CAXTON *Reynard* (Arb.) 95 The fowle olde quenes wold fayne haue beten vs. **1532** MORE *Confut. Tindale* Wks. 618/1 Tyll he..catch him a queane & cal her his wife. **1589** NASHE *Almond for Parrat* 17 b, All spent in a Tauerne amongst a consort of queanes and fidlers. **1627** HAKEWILL *Apol.* (1630) 361 The common queanes, which got their maintenance by that trade. **1670** G. H. *Hist. Cardinals* I. III. 98 A certain paultry Queen in mans apparel, that would pass for a Lady. **1777** SHERIDAN *Sch. Scand.* III. ii, Here's to the flaunting extravagant quean And here's to the housewife that's thrifty. **1823** BYRON *Juan* VI. xcvi, This martial scold, This modern Amazon and queen of queans. **1880** WEBB *Goethe's Faust* III. ii. 190 The dame's a most commodious quean, A gypsy born and go-between! **1924** E. SITWELL *Sleeping Beauty* xiv. 47 My eyes are dim,—I yet can see You, lazy quean! Go work! **1969** *Listener* 10 Apr. 503/3 Nora (an old quean who thinks she's an old queen).

transf. *a* **1845** HOOD *Flowers* i, The tulip is a courtly quean, whom, therefore, I will shun.

2. *Sc.* A young woman, girl, lass; usually denoting one of a healthy and robust appearance.

c **1470** HENRY *Wallace* IV. 782 A stalwart queyne, forsuth, yon semys to be. **1728** W. STARRAT *Ep. to Ramsay* 13 Blaw up my heart-strings, ye Pierian quines. **1787** BURNS

Guidwife Wauchope iii, I see her yet, the sonsie quean, That lighted up my jingle. **1818** SCOTT *Rob Roy* xxvii, It shews a kind heart..in sae young a quean; Mattie's a carefu' lass. **1871** W. ALEXANDER *Johnny Gibb* (1873) 215, I notices brawly that the quine hed been greetin.

3. *slang.* A male homosexual of effeminate appearance. Cf. QUEEN *sb.* 12.

1935 D. LAMSON *We who are about to Die* xv. 294 We did hear startling tales..of 'family' life, of marriage ceremonies, of fights with knives for the favor of some 'quean', as the perverts are called in prison. **1937** PARTRIDGE *Dict. Slang* 676/1 *Quean*; incorrectly *queen*, a homosexual, esp. one with girlish manners and carriage; low: late C. 19–20; ob. except in Australia. **1968** J. R. ACKERLEY *My Father & Myself* xii. 127, I did not want him to think me 'queer' and himself a part of homosexuality, a term I disliked since it included prostitutes, pansies, pouffs and queans.

Hence †'**queaning**, associating with immodest women; †'**queanish** *a.*, of the nature of, characteristic of, a quean; †'**queanry** = *queaning*.

c **1560** A. SCOTT *Poems* (S.T.S.) xxxiv. 124 Quhair hurdome ay vnhappis, With quenry, canis, and coppis. **1569** J. SANFORD tr. *Agrippa's Van. Artes* 119 b, In feastinge, queaninge, huntinge, fowlinge and attiringe. **1596** COLSE *Penelope* (1880) 167 Thy giggish tricke, thy queanish trade, A thousand Bridewel birds hath made. **1618** ROWLANDS *Night Raven* (1620) 25 If she would seeke to mend her queanish life. *a* **1693** MOTTEUX *Rabelais* III. xxxiv. 284 Queanish flurting Harlots.

queare, obs. form of CHOIR *sb.*

†**quease**, *v.*[1] *Obs. rare.* Also 5 qveyse, 6 queash. [See SQUEEZE *v.*] To press, squeeze.

c **1450** *Bk. Hawking* in *Rel. Ant.* I. 302 Take mellfoyle and stamp it..then after take al togedere, and put in a lynnyn cloth, and qveyse out the jus. *c* **1550** LLOYD *Treas. Health* (1585) E iij, Presse the holowe ulcere, so that the rottenness may be queashed or crushed out. **1601** R. JOHNSON *Kingd. & Commw.* (1603) 168 Their chiefest sustenance is milke dried in the sunne after the butter is queased out.

†**quease**, *v.*[2] *Obs. rare*$^{-1}$. In 5 qwease. (Of obscure origin and meaning.)

c **1460** *Towneley Myst.* xiii. 487, I may not well qwease. Ich fote that ye trede goys thorow my nese.

'**queasily**, *adv.* [f. as next + -LY[2].] In a queasy manner. (In quot. 1845 used as adj.; cf. *badly*.)

1845 BROWNING *Flight Duchess* xii. Wks. (1896) I. 416/2 Since, before breakfast, a man feels but queasily. **1973** *Times Lit. Suppl.* 2 Feb. 118/2 We are growing somewhat queasily disillusioned with the achievements of our post-Renaissance civilization. **1976** *New Society* 4 Mar. 502/2 *Super Natural Cookery*, a typically camp title, written in the queasily flirtatious style which seems to afflict all Aquarian cookery books.

queasiness ('kwiːzɪnɪs). Also 6 quesi-, 7 queisi-, que(e)zi-. [f. QUEASY *a.* + -NESS.] The state or condition of being queasy (*lit.* and *fig.*).

1579 LYLY *Euphues* (Arb.) 116 Their slibber sawces, whiche bring quesinesse to the stomacke. **1632** tr. *Bruel's Praxis Med.* 44 Then queisinesse and gnawing of the stomacke doth very much trouble him. **1660** H. MORE *Myst. Godl.* To Rdr. 29 A pretended queziness of Conscience. **1710** T. FULLER *Pharm. Extemp.* 120 It is prevalent against ..Queasiness. **1851** D. JERROLD *St. Giles* viii. 78 [He] felt an odd queasiness in his throat, and could say nothing. **1898** STEVENSON *St. Ives* xxxiv, Captain Colenso perceived my queasiness, and advised me to seek my berth and lie down.

'**queasom**, *v. Obs.* exc. *dial.* Also 6 quesomen, queazen, 9 *dial.* quessom, quezzen. [Of obscure origin.] **a.** *trans.* To choke, stifle. **b.** *intr.* To be choked or smothered.

1561 DAUS tr. *Bullinger on Apoc.* (1573) 99 Without breathing and cooling, men must needes wither and be quesomened and choked vp. **1599** NASHE *Lenten Stuffe* 57 The spirable odor and pestilent steame..would haue queazened him. **1616** HAYWARD *Sanct. Troub. Soul* I. iii. (1620) 46 Behold (O Lord) how my conscience lyeth queasomed vnder the multitude of my offences. *a* **1825** FORBY *Voc. E. Anglia*, *Quezzen*, (1) To suffocate with noxious vapour. (2) To smother away without flame. If the fuel be damp, the fire quezzens out.

queasy ('kwiːzɪ), *a.* Forms: 5–6 **coisy, coysy**; 5 **qweysye**, 5–6 **queysy**, (6 **-se, -sie**), 6 **quaisie, -sy**, 6–7 **queisie**; 5–6 **quasy**, (6 **-ie, -ye**); 5 **qwesye**, 6 **quesie, -y(e**, 6–7 **queasie**, (6 **-ye**), **queazie**, 7– **queasy**, 6–7, 20- **queazy**. [Of obscure history.

The early forms *coisy* and *queisy* prob. indicate a F. origin, and connexion with OF. *coisier* to hurt, wound (Godef.), seems possible, if the original sense was 'wounded', 'bruised' and hence 'tender', 'uneasy', but of this there is no clear evidence. A similar development of sense is implied in the usual etym. from ON. *kveisa* boil (see CWEISE), whence perh. Icel. *kveistinn* tender, touchy, but there is little evidence for this as an Eng. word, and the form *coisy* would remain unexplained. The change from *queisy* or *quaisy* to *queasy* is parallel to *quail*: *queal* and *quair*: *quear*, QUIRE.]

†**1. a.** Of the times or state of affairs: Unsettled, troublous, ticklish. *Obs.* (Cf. also 5 b.)

1459 *Paston Lett.* I. 497 Be my feyth, here is a coysy werd. **1471** SIR J. PASTON *ibid.* III. 4 The worlde I ensur yow is ryght qwesye. *c* **1563** *Jack Juggler* I. 66 The time is so quesie That he that speaketh best, is lest thanke worthie. **1586** J. HOOKER *Hist. Irel.* in *Holinshed* II. 136/2 So manie of hir maiesties priuie councell, as could in that quesie time be assembled. **1611** SPEED *Hist. Gr. Brit.* IX. xx. §47. 965 The times being queasie, the King wisely forbare to take any seuere reuenge. **1906** C. M. DOUGHTY *Dawn in Brit.* VI. 64 Proud queazy, faltering-kneed, Men, fat of the lean people's gifts. **1912** GALSWORTHY *Inn of Tranquility* 187, I would think, Sirs, that you should rather blame the queazy state of Pranza's stomach.

†**b.** Of a matter: Uncertain, hazardous. *Obs.*

1589 COOPER *Admon.* 203, I must..protest it is a queisie & dangerous matter. **1605** SHAKS. *Lear* II. i. 19, I haue one thing of a queazie question Which I must act.

2. a. Of articles of diet: Unsettling the stomach or health; causing sickness or nausea. Now *rare.*

1496 *Fysshynge w. Angle* (1883) 24 The barbyll..is a quasy meete & a peryllous for mannys body. **15..** *Piers of Fullham* 19 in Hazl. *E.P.P.* II. 3 Kodlynges, konger, or suche queyse [*v.r.* coisy] fysche. **1544** PHAER *Pestilence* (1553) N viij b, In this disease ye maye eate no queasie meates, as eles, gese, duckes. **1579** LYLY *Euphues* (Arb.) 44 To the stomacke sated with dainties, all delicates seeme queasie. **1653** MANTON *Exp. James* i. 21 Like a hot morsel or queasy bit, it was soon given up again. **1661** LOVELL *Hist. Anim. & Min.* 225 Their flesh is queasy, corruptible, and aguish. **1876** G. MEREDITH *Beauch. Career* I. xiv. 210 The ..queasy brew..which she calls by the innocent name of tea.

†**b.** Of seasons: Unhealthy; in which sickness is prevalent. Also of days of ill-health. *Obs.*

1510–20 *Compl. them that ben to late maryed* (Collier 1862) 16, I haue passed full many quasy dayes. **1603** KNOLLES *Hist. Turks* (1621) 732 Infection taken in the campe in strange aire, and a most queasie time of the yeare.

†**c.** Of land: Unfavourable to growth. *Obs. rare.*

1599 [see QUEACHY 2]. **1649** BLITHE *Eng. Improv.* xiv. 80 It was great Lands..full of your soft Rushes..and lay very wet ..it was so Weake and Barren, so cold and queasy. [Cf. *ibid.* xxiv. 149 The coldest and most quealiest (? *misprint*) parts of thy Lands.]

3. a. Of the stomach: Easily upset; unable to digest strong food; inclined to sickness or nausea. (In 16–17th c. freq. *fig.* and in fig. context.) Hence of the body, heart, health, etc.

1545 RAYNOLD *Byrth Mankynde* fol. 142 She shall better digest and lyke her meate; her stomacke nothyng so quesy ne feable. **1574** NEWTON *Health Mag.* 26 It is better for.. stronge Stomackes then for Quasie and weake bodies. **1604** DEKKER *Honest Wh.* Wks. 1873 II. 46 Ile gird it close, As if my health were queazy. *a* **1652** J. SMITH *Sel. Disc.* ix. 468 A divine philosophy; which..as men grew worse, their queasy stomachs began to loathe it. *a* **1684** LEIGHTON *Wks.* (1830) I. 42 A full table, but a sickly body and queasy stomach. **1839** J. FUME '*Paper on Tobacco*' 70 Not digested without grumbling by certain queasy stomachs. **1889** C. KEENE *Let.* in *Life* xiii. (1892) 409 My stomach is in such a queasy state, that a gram in excess puts me all wrong.

†**b.** *transf.* Of the mind, feelings, etc.: Delicate, fastidious, nice. *Obs.*

1545 ASCHAM *Toxoph.* I. (Arb.) 40 These Instrumentes make a mannes wit..so tender and quaisie that they be lesse able to brooke strong and tough studie. *c* **1590** GREENE *Fr. Bacon* x. 130 Eyes are dissemblers, and fancy is but queasy. **1642** ROGERS *Naaman* 565 Beware then of a sullen, queazy, coy and proud heart. **1659** EEDES *Wisdom's Justif.* 40 The queasie soul that receives not the Word.

c. Of conscience, etc.: Tender, scrupulous.

1579 G. HARVEY *Letter-bk.* (Camden) 76 The thinges themselves..ar not so offensive to quesy consciences. **1646** SIR T. BROWNE *Pseud. Ep.* 374 The ambition of Boniface made no scruple thereof; nor of more queasie resolutions have been their Successors ever since. **1781** COWPER *Charity* 447 When queasy conscience has its qualms. **1886** SYMONDS *Renaiss. It., Cath. React.* (1898) I. iv. 223 Ignatius recommended fishers of souls to humour queasy consciences.

4. Of pains, etc.: Of the nature of sickness; uneasy, uncomfortable.

1589 *Pappe w. Hatchet* (1844) 13 O what queasie girds were they towards the fall of the leafe. **1650** BULWER *Anthropomet.* 158 To return by Art their queasie paine upon women, to the great reproach of Nature. **1878** STEVENSON *Inland Voy.* 114, I had a queasy sense that I wore my last dry clothes upon my body.

5. a. Of persons: Having a queasy stomach; liable to turn sick; subject to, or affected with, nausea. Also *fig.*

1606 SHAKS. *Ant. & Cl.* III. vi. 20 [The Romans] queazie with his insolence already, Will their good thoughts call from him. **1622** FLETCHER *Span. Cur.* III. ii, Your queazie young wiues That perish undelivered, I am vext with. **1682** N. O. *Boileau's Lutrin.* I. Argt., Thus Queasie Madams meat forbear Untill they read, The Bill of Fare. **1816** T. L. PEACOCK *Headlong Hall* vii, The Reverend Doctor Gaster found himself rather queasy in the morning. **1855** BROWNING *Grammar. Funeral* 64 Even to the crumbs I'd fain eat up the feast, Ay, nor feel queasy.

b. *transf.* (with earlier quots. cf. sense 1).

1579 G. HARVEY *Letter-bk.* (Camden) 73 Over-stale for so queynte and queasye a worlde. **1602** MARSTON *Ant. & Mel.* II. Wks. 1856 I. 22 O that the stomack of this queasie age Digestes, or brookes such raw unseasoned gobs. **1641** S. MARSHALL *Fast Serm. bef. Ho. Comm.* Ep. Ded. 3 A time so queasie and distempered as can hardly beare that Food or Physicke which is needfull. **1869** BROWNING *Ring & Bk.* x. 113 The queasy river could not hold Its swallowed Jonas, but discharged the meal.

6. *Comb.* **queasy-stomached** *a.* (see sense 3).

1579–80 NORTH *Plutarch* (1676) 757 Antonius..being queasie stomacked with his Surfeit. **1608** ARMIN *Nest Ninn.* (1842) 6 The World, queasie stomackt as one fed with the earth's nectar, and delicates. **1635** QUARLES *Embl.* III. xiv. (1718) 181 Look, sister, how the queazy-stomach'd graves Vomit their dead. **1802** W. GIFFORD tr. *Juvenal's Satires* vi. 292 Why waste the wine and cakes The queasy-stomach'd guest, at parting, takes?

queat(e, queatch(e, queave, queazen: see QUIET, WHEAT, QUETCH, QUAVE, QUEASOM.

†**quebas.** *Obs. rare*$^{-1}$. Some kind of a game.

1668 ETHEREDGE *She wou'd if she cou'd* III. iii, Did I associate myself with the Gaming Madams, and were every afternoon at my Lady Briefes..at Umbre and Quebas.

Quebec (kwə'bɛk, kə-). The name of the city and province in eastern Canada, used *attrib.* in ***Quebec heater***, a kind of solid-fuel, domestic heating stove with a tall, cylindrical fire-box.

1918–19 *T. Eaton & Co. Catal.* Fall & Winter 461 The new Quebec heaters. Built on the popular 'Quebec Idea' pattern..burn coal, coke and any kind of wood fuel. **1927** *Toronto Daily Star* 8 Oct. 2 Dominion Circulation 'Quebec' Heater..gets the heat into every corner of the house. **1948** H. MACLENNAN *Precipice* (1949) i. 20 In the winters there had been a Quebec heater in the pavilion. **1968** E. A. MCCOURT *Saskatchewan* iii. 42 The long glorious winter evenings we spent huddled behind the old Quebec heater.

Quebecker (kwə'bɛkə(r), kə-). Also **Quebecer**. [f. prec. + -ER[1].] = QUÉBECOIS *sb.* a.

1836 *Bytown* (Ottawa) *Independent* 24 Feb. 3/2 We think the Quebecers are not such flats as to pay for measuring timber, merely because they receive it. **1837** *Montreal Transcript* 14 Jan. 2/2 The match..was played on Tuesday last, at Three Rivers, when the Quebeckers proved victorious. **1890** [see NEW *a.* 5 d]. **1946** H. CROOME *Faithless Mirror* xiv. 153 Other Canadians go overseas..the Quebeckers stay at home. **1957** *Listener* 17 Oct. 593/1 The typical Quebecer is still a Royalist, a Conservative, even if he votes Liberal. **1963** *Times* 25 Feb. (Canada Suppl.) p. vii/3 We've got to keep control of new industries in Quebec for Quebecers. **1973** *Times Lit. Suppl.* 26 Oct. 1295/2 The backward, Church-controlled, inferiority-complex-ridden Quebecker of yesteryear. **1977** *Time* 7 Feb. 21/1 The man who wants to lead 6 million Quebeckers out of Canadian confederation. **1979** *Amer. N. & Q.* Mar. 119/2 Radwanski believes that Trudeau is the man best equipped to meet Lévesque's challenge. Most Quebecers appear to think that, too.

‖**Québecois** (kebɛkwa), *sb.* and *a.* Also **Québecquois.** [Fr., f. QUEBEC.]

A. *sb.* **a.** A native or inhabitant of the city or province of Quebec, esp. one who is a French-Canadian. **b.** The French spoken in Quebec. **B.** *adj.* Of or pertaining to Quebec or its inhabitants.

1873 J. M. LEMOINE *Maple Leaves* 171 The County and town of Joliette preserve the name of another distinguished Canadian, a Québecquois, Louis Joliette. **1954** T. H. RADDALL *Muster of Arms* 135 She was speaking in English but the mind behind the tongue was Quebecois. **1960** *Times* 21 Nov. (Canada Suppl.) p. ii/7 Mr. Dorion is the most typically Quebecois of the French-Canadian ministers. **1962** *Maclean's Mag.* 17 Nov. 4/1 Editors of French language newspapers who had wailed about the 'stupidity' of rural Québecois in the last federal election. **1963** *Ibid.* 6 Apr. 23/1 Her French sounds more Parisian than what we who don't speak French well call Quebecois. **1970** *Globe Mag.* (Toronto) 26 Sept. 17/1 The manuscripts of Pauline Archange is a first-person story of a Quebecois slum child. **1974** *Times Lit. Suppl.* 14 June 634/2 Her little book assembles..comments by prominent Québécois. *Ibid.* 634/3 M Ėtheir-Blais is a Franco-Ontarian, not a Québécois. **1977** H. GILES *Lang., Ethnicity & Intergroup Relations* 2 Québécois air controllers engaged in industrial action for a refusal at their not being allowed to use French as a medium of air communications. **1977** *Listener* 23 June 808/2 The beleaguered English-speaking Québécois. **1978** *Maledicta* II. 61 For the most part, Québecois imprecations flourished on the spot in response to the needs of a people living in conditions of moral and material misery.

‖**quebracho** (ke'bratʃo). Also **quiebrahacha.** [Sp. *quebracho*, also *quiebra-hacha*, f. *quebrar* to break + *hacha* axe.] **a.** The name of several American trees, having extremely hard timber and medicinal bark; esp. the white quebracho of S. America (*Aspidosperma Quebracho*) and the red quebracho of Mexico (*Schinopsis Lorentzii*). Also, the timber of these trees. Also *attrib.* as ***quebracho bark, gum***. **b.** = Quebracho-bark. Hence **que'brachamine, que'brachine**, alkaloids found in quebracho-bark.

1881 WATTS *Dict. Chem.* 3rd Suppl. 916, 1731. **1889** G. S. BOULGER *Uses of Plants* v. 159 Red Quebracho..is a hard wood from the River Plate... Other Quebrachos..are also used in South America. **1891** W. MARTINDALE *Extra Pharmacop.* (ed. 6) 325 White Quebracho Bark..imported from the Argentine Republic. *Ibid.*, Quebracho contains six alkaloids,..Quebrachine, Quebrachamine [etc.]. **1897** *Syd. Soc. Lex.* s.v., Quebracho is a valuable remedy for dyspnœa. **1908** W. R. FISHER *Schlich's Man. Forestry* (ed. 2) V. I. viii. 572 Experimental use is also made of pitch pine and quebracho wood [for railway sleepers]. **1913** *Chambers's Jrnl.* 28 June 480/2 Quebracho ('break-axe'), one of the hardest, heaviest, and most durable woods known. **1923** *Nature* 8 Sept. 376/2 The principal sources of this [*sc.* tannin] are oak galls and bark, mangrove bark, Myrobalans, Quebracho, and *Acacia decurrens*. **1924** RECORD & MELL *Timbers Trop. Amer.* II. 508 White quebracho is the name most commonly applied to *Aspidosperma quebracho-blanco* ..of Argentina, Paraguay, and south-western Brazil. **1933** H. ALLEN *Anthony Adverse* v. xxix. 409 It was full of a thousand lush and exotic odours from..juniper and lantana; the fragrant quiebrahacha, tamarind and rotting mastic leaves. **1955** *Times* 30 June 18/2 The production of Quebracho extract during the year amounted to 81,644 tons. **1969** T. C. THORSTENSEN *Pract. Leather Technol.* ix. 140 Quebracho extract is used in the manufacture of heavy leathers and in the vegetable re-tanning of chrome tanned upper leathers. **1974** D. MEIRING *President Plan* ix. 74 A big fire of *quebracho* glowed and flickered.

‖**quebrada** (ke'brada). [Sp., fem. of *quebrado*, pa. pple. of *quebrar* to break.] **1.** A mountain stream in S. America.

1833 *Blackw. Mag.* Aug. 144/2 Next morning I rode out on my mule, to take my last dip in the *Quebrada* of the *Loseria*, which was a rapid in a beautiful little rivulet, distant from Panama about three miles. **1920** *Chambers's Jrnl.* Dec. 979 The many quebradas which flow down the mountain ravines. **1973** K. BENTON *Craig & Jaguar* v. 45 The Chasco [river] was fed by the *quebradas* that brought down meltwater from the high ranges.

2. A ravine in S. America.

1845 *Encycl. Metrop.* XIV. 565/1 Abrupt precipices.. occur in every part of the parent chain of the Andes near the equator, and diversify its appearance with the most horrid chasms, or rents, here called Quebradas, varying from 100 feet to 4 or 5,000 feet in depth. **1860** MAYNE REID *Odd People* 456 The stupendous ravines termed 'barrancas' & 'quebradas', which intersect the Cordilleras of the Andes in other parts of South America. **1927** *Blackw. Mag.* Aug. 229/2 We will build another house in the quebrada at Palalle Grande. **1949** *Américas* Sept. 17 The men wore rags and undoubtedly lived in one-room shanties in the quebradas. **1974** *Encycl. Brit. Macropædia* I. 1135/1 To the west are the Salto-Jujeña, cut by canyons called *quebradas* through which run small rivers.

quecchen, quech(e, obs. forms of QUETCH.

quech(e, obs. forms of QUEACH, WHICH.

Quechua ('kɛtʃwə), *sb.* and *a.* Also **Quichua, Kechua,** and other varr. [Sp., ad. Quechua *k'echua*, *k'eshua*, plunderer, despoiler.]

A. *sb.* **a.** An Indian people of Peru and neighbouring parts of Bolivia, Chile, Colombia, and Ecuador; a member of this people. **b.** The language (actually a group of related languages) spoken by this people. **B.** *adj.* Of or pertaining to this people or their language.

1840 *Penny Cycl.* XVIII. 6/2 They [*sc.* the Peruvian Indians] speak the Quichua language, which is generally called the language of the Incas, and which is used by all the natives of South America, from Quito near the equator, to Tucuman in La Plata, 27° S. lat. *Ibid.* 9/2 As the aborigines who inhabit this extensive country speak one language, the Quichua, it must be supposed that they belong to one race. **1843** J. C. PRICHARD *Nat. Hist. Man* xlv. 431 Among the Peruvian nations, the dominant race were the Quichuas, or Incas, distinguished by their language, which is the Quichuan. **1860** [see AYMARA]. **1877** [see CHIBCHA]. **1891** D. G. BRINTON *Amer. Race* II. i. 203 The Kechua.. was spoken by an unbroken chain of tribes for nearly two thousand miles from north to south. **1908** [see CHOLO, CHOLO]. **1921** [see AYMARA]. **1926** *South Amer.* Sept. 71/2 We take with us a native helper who can speak Quechua. **1937** R. H. LOWIE *Hist. Ethnol. Theory* xiv. 258 The absence of hoes from all of South America would be of real interest were it not that their undoubted use among the Quichua, past and present, eliminates the problems otherwise raised. **1948** A. L. KROEBER *Anthropol.* (ed. 2) x. 431 The Aztec, Otomí, Maya, Quechua, or Aymará Indians were economically oppressed by their conquest. **1950** J. A. MASON in J. H. Steward *Handbk. S. Amer. Indians* VI. 197 Quechua (Kechua, Quichua, Keshwa, etc.) is the South American analogue of Aztec. *Ibid.*, Today probably several millions of Indians in Perú, southwestern Ecuador, western Bolivia, and northwestern Argentina speak Quechua, and most of them nothing else. **1952** *Language* XXVIII. 366 (*title*) Semantic components in Kechua person morphemes. **1966** *Chambers's Encycl.* VIII. 366/2 Quechumaran comprises two branches..the Quechuan branch, spoken from Colombia to Chile, has as its main member Quechua, of Peru, Ecuador and Bolivia. This is by far the most important native language of South America. **1973** [see PICK *v.*[1] 21 i]. **1974** *Times* 6 Dec. 15/7 The Quechua Indian women of Southern Peru. *Ibid.* 15/8 The Quechua hitherto have lived in inconveniently scattered farmholdings. **1977** C. F. & F. M. VOEGELIN *Classification & Index of World's Languages* 21 Quechua and Aymara were said to be genetically related as early as Steinthal (1890).

Quechuan ('kɛtʃwən), *a.* Also **Quichuan, Kechuan.** [f. prec. + -AN.] = prec. B. Also as *sb.*

1843 [see prec.]. **1853** F. L. HAWKS tr. *Rivero & Tschudi's Peruvian Antiquities* v. 93 We here present a short review.. of the character of the Quichuan or Peruvian tongue. **1862** R. G. LATHAM *Compar. Philol.* 482 The capital Cuzco, Quichuan as it is in many respects, is a town upon Aymara ground. **1901** A. H. KEANE *Central & S. Amer.* 207 The Incas were originally a tribe of Quichuan stock. **1931** W. A. READ *Louisiana-French* 142 A French adaptation of Spanish *ñapa*, which is taken in turn from Kechuan *yapa*, 'a present made to a customer'. **1933** L. BLOOMFIELD *Language* iv. 73 *Kechuan*, the language of the Inca civilization. **1966** [see prec.]. **1972** W. B. LOCKWOOD *Panorama Indo-Europ. Lang.* iii. 35 A large majority of Aymarans and Quechuans are monoglots. **1973** K. BENTON *Craig & Jaguar* xii. 190 The men, under Huaman's directions, spiced with obscene Quechuan oaths, lowered it.

†**queck,** *sb. Obs. rare*[−1]. ? A knock, whack.

1554 *Enterl. Youth* A ij, If I fal I catche a quecke, I may fortune to breke my necke.

†**queck** *v.*[1] *Obs.* Also 4–5 quek. [Imitative: cf. Du. *kwekken*, and see QUACK *v.*[2]] *intr.* To quack, as a duck. Hence '**quecking** *vbl. sb.*

c **1325** *Gloss. W. de Bibbesw.* in *Rel. Ant.* II. 79 [The gander] quekez, *taroile.* Quekine, *taroil.* **1492** in *Archiv Stud. neu. Spr.* LXXXIX. 285 He toke a gose fast by the nek, And the goose thoo began to quek. **1573** TWYNE *Æneid* x. D d iv, Whom stars of heauen obeyen at beck..and chattring birds with tong that queck. *a* **1693** MOTTEUX *Rabelais* III. xiii. 107 The..pioling of Pelicanes, quecking of Ducks,..and wailing of Turtles.

†**queck,** *v.*[2] *Obs. rare*[−1]. ? = QUETCH *v.*

a **1550** *Image Hypocr.* III. in *Skelton's Wks.* (1843) II. 436/2 Not for his life to quecke [*rime* necke] But stande vpp, like a bosse. [**1755** in JOHNSON (and hence in some later dicts.), with quot. from Bacon *Ess.*, in which however the correct reading is *queching*.]

queck: see QUEK(E.

Queckenstedt ('kwɛkənstɛt). *Med.* The name of Hans Heinrich *Queckenstedt* (1876–1918), German physician, used *attrib.* and in the possessive to denote the procedure proposed by him (*Deutsch. Zeitschr. f. Nervenheilk.* (1916) LV. 326) of compressing a patient's jugular veins while observing the pressure of the cerebrospinal fluid (the absence of a marked increase in this indicating obstruction of the subarachnoid space).

1928 R. J. E. SCOTT *Gould's Med. Dict.* (ed. 2) 1175/2 *Queckenstedt's test*, in healthy persons pressure on the veins of the neck causes a prompt rise in the pressure of the cerebrospinal fluid, which disappears on release of the pressure on the veins. **1934** D. MUNRO in *Practitioners Library of Med. & Surg.* V. xi. 803 If..the Queckenstedt test is positive, that is, if flow of cerebrospinal fluid is partly or completely interfered with by a block in the subarachnoid space, the rise on jugular compression will be totally absent if the block is complete, or greatly slowed and diminished in height if the block is incomplete. **1968** PASSMORE & ROBSON *Compan. Med. Stud.* I. xxiv. 76/2 In performing Queckenstedt's test, it is as well not to squeeze or even seem to squeeze the trachea. **1970** R. G. FELDMAN in Keefer & Wilkins *Medicine* xiii. 957 Compression of the jugular vein (Queckenstedt maneuver) has been used to observe the response of intracranial pressure to a change in venous pressure.

†**qued, quede,** *a.* and *sb. Obs.* Forms: 3 **cwead,** 3–4 **quead,** 4 **kuead;** 3 **cwed,** 3–5 **qued, quede,** 4 **kued, quet,** 4–6 **queed,** (5 **qw-**), 5 **queyd, quethe, qweþe;** 3–4 (6 *Sc.*) **quad,** 4 (6 *Sc.*) 7 **quade,** 6 *Sc.* **quaid.** [Early ME. *cwead*, *cwed*, *cwad* = OFris. *quad* (mod.Fris. *quaad*, *quae*'), MDu. *quaet*, *quaed-* (Du. *kwaad*), MLG. *quât*, *quâd-*, of uncertain origin. OHG. *quât* (MHG. *quât*, *kât*, *kôt*, G. *kot*, *koth*), filth, is usually regarded as a subst. use of the same adj., but the vowel of the corresp. OE. *cwéad* presents difficulties.]

A. *adj.* Evil, wicked, bad.

c **1205–25** [implied in QUEDSHIP]. *c* **1250** *Gen. & Ex.* 536 Wapmen bigunnen quad mester. *a* **1300** *Vox & Wolf* 200 in Hazl. *E.P.P.* (1864) I. 64 Ich habbe ben qued al mi lif-daie. *c* **1330** *Arth. & Merl.* 1498 (Kölbing) þat oþer dragoun.. clowes he hadde qued. **1340** *Ayenb.* 17 Þe uerste is kuead, þo oþer worse, þe þridde alþerworst. *c* **1386** CHAUCER *Prioress' Prol.* 4 God yeue this monk a thousand last quade yeer. *c* **1420** *Liber Cocorum* (1862) 37 Þou take gode ale, þat is not quede. **1501** DOUGLAS *Pal. Hon.* I. lxii, This inordinate court, and proces quaid [*rime* braid, laid] I will obiect. **1560** ROLLAND *Crt. Venus* II. 161 The quader was his weird. *Ibid.* 333 Quad knaif, thow was ouir negligent. **1669** STURMY *Mariner's Mag.* I. ii. 18 'How Wind you?' 'East'. A bad quade Wind.

b. Hostile, inimical *to. rare.*

a **1300** *Cursor M.* 8535 (Gött.) Þe cyte of cartage, þat to Rome was euer quede. **1418–20** *Siege Rouen* in *Archæologia* XXI. 65 Owre men gaff ham sum off here brede, Thow thay to us ware now so quede.

B. *sb.* **1.** A bad or wicked person.

c **1250** *Gen. & Ex.* 295 Ðowgte ðis quead, 'hu ma it ben [etc.]'. *Ibid.* 4063 Balaam, ðat ille quad [*rime* dead]. *c* **1300** *Prov. Hending* xxvi. in Kemble *Salomon & Sat.* (1848) 277 Ant himself is þe meste qued þat may breke eny bred. *c* **1330** R. BRUNNE *Chron. Wace* (Rolls) 8596 Kyng of Amalek was that qued, A ful fers kyng. *a* **1400** *Minor Poems fr. Vernon MS.* (E.E.T.S.) 589/440 Kep, and saue þi gode los, And beo I-holden no qued. *c* **1460** *Towneley Myst.* ix. 117, I am fulle bowne To spyr and spy..After that wykkyd queyd.

b. *spec.* The evil one; the Devil.

c **1250** *Death* 246 in *O.E. Misc.* 182 Ne mai no tunge telle hu lodlich is þe cwed. **1297** R. GLOUC. (Rolls) 6429 Hii bitoke þe qued hor soule, þe kunde eirs to bitraye. *c* **1325** *Chron. Eng.* 210 in *Ritson*, Tho thes maister was ded, Anon he wende to the qued. **1377** LANGL. *P. Pl.* B. xiv. 189 He shulde take the acquitance..and to the qued schewe it. *c* **1450** LONELICH *Grail* xxxvii. 634 He [Jesus] travailled.. Man-kynde to byen from the qwed.

2. Evil, mischief, harm.

a **1225** *Ancr. R.* 72 Moni mon weneð to don wel þ he deð alto cweade. *a* **1300** *Vox & Wolf* 210 in Hazl. *E.P.P.* (1864) I. 65 Forȝef hit me, Ich habbe ofte sehid qued bi the. *c* **1330** *Arth. & Merl.* 5508 (Kölbing) Com we nouȝt hider for þi qued..ac for þi gode. **1340** *Ayenb.* 28 Þe kueades of oþren he hise moreþ and arereþ be his miȝte. **1387** TREVISA *Higden* (Rolls) I. 417 At Penbrook in a stede Fendes dooþ ofte quede. *a* **1529** SKELTON *Epithaphe* 4 This knaues be deade, Full of myschiefe and queed.

Hence †**quedful** *a.*, full of evil or wickedness; **quedhead** [= OFris. *quadhed*, Du. *kwaadheid*] = *quedship*; **quedly** *adv.* [= OFris. *qua(de)like*], wickedly; **quedness, quedship,** evil, wickedness.

1340 *Ayenb.* 6 Þaȝles þe wone is *kueaduol and may wel wende to zenne dyadliche. **1340–70** *Alex. & Dind.* 541 To quem quedfulle godeis þat quenchen your blisse. *c* **1315** SHOREHAM 151 O justyse..[that] dampneth theves for to ordeyne Peys in londe..Ne for *queadhevede. **1340** *Ayenb.* 101 Þet þou hatye zenne and uoulhedes and kueadhedes. *c* **1300** *E.E. Psalter* xvii. 22 (Harl. MS.), I ȝhemed waies of Laverd wel, Ne *quedlic bare I fra mi God na del. **1340** *Ayenb.* 2 Naȝt kueadliche ake liȝtliche and wyþoute sklaundre. *c* **1300** *E.E. Psalter* x. 6 þat loues *quednes, his saule hates he. **1340** *Ayenb.* 40 Ofte lyese þe guode playntes be hare kueadnesse. *c* **1205** LAY. 5067 Ne sculde na cniht.. on his cuhðe *quedschipe wurchen. *c* **1220** *Bestiary* 587 Fox is hire to name for hire queðsipe. *a* **1225** *Ancr. R.* 422 Al Sodomes cweadschipe com of idelnesse & of ful wombe.

quede, var. QUIDE *sb.*

quee, queece, queech, varr. QUEY, QUEEST, QUETCH.

queed, var. QUED(E *a.*; dial. var. CUD.

queel, var. QUEAL *v.*

queen (kwiːn), *sb.* Forms: 1 **cwœn, cwæn, cwénn,** 1–3 **cwén,** (1 **cu-**), 2–3 **cwene, kwene;** 2–4 **quen,** (3 **quu-,** 4 **qw-**), 2–6 **quene,** (4–6 **qw-,** 5 **qv-**), 3 **quiene, quyene,** 4 **qwhene,** 4–5 **whene, queyn,** 4–6 **queyne,** 4–7 **queene,** 6 **quein(e,** 4– **queen.** [OE. *cwén* str. fem. = OS. *quân* (once in Hel.), ON. *kvæn* (also *kván*), Goth. *qêns* woman:—OTeut. **kwǣni-z* f., an ablaut-var. of the stem represented by OE. *cwene* QUEAN. The gen. sing. *quene* (OE. *cwéne*) is occas. found in ME.]

I. 1. A (king's) wife or consort; a lady who is wife *to* a king.

Even in OE., *cwén* was app. not an ordinary term for 'wife', but was applied only to the wife of a king or (in poetry) some famous person; in later use the only distinction between this sense and 2 a is that here the relationship of the queen to her husband is formally expressed.

c **893** K. ÆLFRED *Oros.* I. ii. §2 Æfter his deaðe Sameramis his cwen [L. *uxor*] fengc..to þæm rice. *a* **1000** *Cædmon's Gen.* 2259 Ða wearð unbliðe Abrahames cwen. *c* **1050** *O.E. Chron.* (Laud MS.) an. 1048 Þa forlet se cyng þa hlæfdian seo wæs ȝehalȝod him to cwene. *a* **1123** *Ibid.* an. 1115 Willelme þe he be his cwene hæfde. *c* **1205** LAY. 43 Ælienor þe wes Henries quene. **13..** *Coer de L.* 1123 Erlys and barouns come hym to, And his quene dede alsoo. **1591** SHAKS. *1 Hen. VI*, v. iii. 117 Ile vndertake to make thee Henries Queene. **1611** —— *Wint. T.* III. ii. 12 Hermione, Queene to the worthy Leontes, King of Sicilia. **1859** TENNYSON *Elaine* 1215 As Arthur's Queen I move and rule.

2. a. The wife or consort of a king. **b.** A woman who is the chief ruler of a state, having the same rank and position as a king.

c **825** *Vesp. Psalter* xliv. 10 Ætstod cwoen [L. *regina*] to swiðran ðire. *c* **1000** ÆLFRIC *Hom.* II. 584 Sum cwen wæs on ðam daȝum on suðdæle, Saba ȝehaten. *c* **1205** LAY. 24555 Þe king..to his mete uerde..þa quene [*c* **1275** cweane] on oðer halue hire hereberwe isohte. *c* **1290** *S. Eng. Leg.* I. 2/41 Bifore þe quyene huy come. **1297** R. GLOUC. (Rolls) 608 Þe quene fader Corineus. **13..** *Gaw. & Gr. Knt.* 2492 Þe kyng kysseȝ þe knyȝt, & þe whene alce. *c* **1400** *Destr. Troy* 3163 Menelai wife, Lady of þis lond..and a gai qwhene. *c* **1420** *Avow. Arth.* xxxiii, Hit is atte the quene wille. **1473** WARKW. *Chron.* (Camden) 9 The Lorde Scales, the Quenes brother, was sent thedere. **1562** WINȜET *Cert. Tractates* Wks. 1888 I. 32 Dew obedience..to kingis, quenis, princes, and prelatis. **1590** SHAKS. *Mids. N.* II. i. 19 The King doth keepe his Reuels here to night, Take heed the Queene come not within his sight. **1628** MILTON *Vacat. Exerc.* 47 Then sing of secret things..And last of Kings and Queens and Hero's old. **1710** SWIFT *Lett.* (1767) III. 29 My memorial which was given to the queen. **1845** S. AUSTIN *Ranke's Hist. Ref.* II. 385 His sister waited in Vittoria..in order to enter France as queen.

c. With additions, as ***queen-consort, -dowager,*** †***-dowrier, -rectrix, -regent, -regnant, -widow:*** see CONSORT, etc.; also QUEEN-MOTHER. **Queen Mum,** colloq. alteration of QUEEN-MOTHER, used with affectionate reference to Queen Elizabeth, the Queen Mother (b. 1900).

1555 [see DOWRIER]. **1622** BACON *Hen. VII*, Mor. & Hist. Wks. (Bohn, 1860) 311 To remain with the queen dowager her mother. **1650** BULWER *Anthropomet.* 198 A late Queen-Rectrix. **1727** DE FOE *Syst. Magic* I. ii. (1840) 42 The queen dowager was with child, and would bring forth a prince. **1765** BLACKSTONE *Comm.* I. iv. 212 The queen of England is either queen regent, queen consort, or queen dowager. **1818** SCOTT *Hrt. Midl.* xxxvii, Since Margaret of Anjou, no queen-consort had exercised such weight in the political affairs of England. **1891** C. CREIGHTON *Hist. Epidem. Brit.* 288 The queen-widow (mother of Edward V) had died of the plague. **1960** L. R. BANKS *L-Shaped Room* ix. 135, I kept it a treat. I could've had the Queen Mum to tea there and not been ashamed. **1965** J. POTTER *Death in Office* x. 101 Mrs Barber..extending a gloved hand from the sitting position: her imitation of the Queen Mum no doubt. **1974** J. GARDNER *Corner Men* xiii. 185 What do you think I do all day..? Play canasta with the Queen Mum and help feed the royal corgis? **1980** *Times* 4 Aug. 4/1 The dear old Queen Mum is..'the best loved lady in the land'.

d. ***Queen and country:*** the objects of allegiance for a patriot whose head of state is a queen.

1706 FARQUHAR *Recruiting Officer* v. 72, I endeavour by the Example of this worthy Gentleman to serve my Queen and Country at home. **1861** C. M. YONGE *Young Step-Mother* xxix. 443 His son got his death fighting for his queen and his country. **1900** *Times* 2 Apr. 7/1 It was a keen joy.. to be allowed to fight for his Queen and country. **1906** W. S. CHURCHILL *Lord Randolph Churchill* (1907) xxi. 792 Night after night he had risen in his place to discharge..his duty—as he would have phrased it—to 'Queen and country'. **1948** F. THOMPSON *Still glides Stream* ii. 41 Thank God he died for his Queen and country! **1966** J. GARDNER *Amber Nine* i. 28 Anyway, got to go. Queen-and-Country as my lovable boss would say. **1977** *Sounds* 9 July 20/6 Step up the beaches and annihilate somebody for Queen and country, get a medal pinned on your chest.

e. *ellipt.* as ***the Queen:*** the national anthem 'God save the Queen'.

1898 J. D. BRAYSHAW *Slum Silhouettes* 37 The curtain fell at last, and the band struck up the 'Queen'. **1916** M. DIVER

Desmond's Daughter IV. iv. 341 They're playing 'The Queen'. I *must* be on the spot to say good-bye to people. **1965** 'W. HAGGARD' *Powder Barrel* ix. 86 The police band.. crashed into The Queen in time in a formal way. **1970** *Daily Tel.* 18 Aug. 13/7 Wherever the Prince was present at a function organised by the association three anthems were played—the Queen, 'Land of My Fathers' and 'God Bless the Prince of Wales'.

3. a. As a title, place immediately before a personal name (†in OE. immediately after it); also *the queen*, before or after the name (now *arch.*). See also QUEEN ANNE.

c **893** K. ÆLFRED *Oros.* I. x. §3 þær wearð Marsepia sio cwen ofslaȝen. *c* **893** *O.E. Chron.* (Parker MS.) an. 888 Æþelswiþ cuen, sio wæs Ælfredes sweostor cyninges. *a* **1121** *Ibid.* (Laud MS.) an. 1097 Malcomes sunu cynges & Margarite þære cwenan. *c* **1205** LAY. 2122 Hit is iceleped Wales for þere quen Galoes. **13..** *Gaw. & Gr. Knt.* 74 Whene Guenore ful gay, grayþed in þe myddes. **1387** TREVISA *Higden* (Rolls) VII. 165 þan þe queene Emme gaf unto seynt Swithyn nyne maneres. **1506** GUYLFORDE *Pylgr.* (1851) 4 Lasheles, where lyethe quene Elyanour of Englonde. **1572** *Memorial* in *Buccleuch MSS.* (Hist. MSS. Comm.) 23 Young Queín Marie. **1673** WYCHERLEY *Gent. Dancing-Master* V. i. 95 You must.. furnish as becomes one of my Quality; for don't you think we'll take up with your old Queen Elizabeth Furniture. *a* **1700** B. E. *Dict. Cant. Crew*, *Queen Elizabeth's Pocket-pistol*, a Brass-Cannon of a prodigious Length at Dover-Castle. **1738** SWIFT *Polite Conv.* i, News? Why, Madam, Queen Elizabeth's dead. **1754** RICHARDSON *Grandison* I. xxxvii. 270 We will leave the modern world to themselves; and be Queen Elizabeth's women. **1847** WORDSW. *Ode Install. Pr. Albert* ad. fin., The pride of the islands, Victoria the Queen. **1884** KNIGHT *Dict. Mech.* Suppl. 733/2 Queen Charlotte's ware, now known by the contracted title [Queensware].

b. ***Queen Mary.*** (*a*) Used *attrib.* in ***Queen Mary hat***, a variety of toque popularized by Queen Mary (1867–1953), wife of King George V, who favoured it because it enabled the public to have a clear view of her face; so ***Queen Mary toque.*** (*b*) A type of long low-loading road trailer (in allusion to the Cunard passenger liner: see below).

(*a*) **1938** L. BEMELMANS *Life Class* II. iii. 140 She is dressed in a trotteur, and wears a hat with a thousand cloth violets, a Queen Mary toque. **1947** *New Yorker* 22 Nov. 38/1 A Queen Mary hat protected her from the autumnal sunlight. **1950** J. D. MACDONALD *Brass Cupcake* (1955) xv. 157 She sold power shovels, sang baritone and wore Queen Mary hats. **1967** L. J. BRAUN *Cat who ate Danish Modern* ix. 76 There was enough blue blood to float a ship... You never saw so many pince-nez and Queen Mary hats. **1977** G. MARKSTEIN *Chance Awakening* x. 25 Golly sat down in the deck chair.. with the grey-haired gentleman.. and the old ladies with Queen Mary toques.

(*b*) **1943** C. H. WARD-JACKSON *It's a Piece of Cake* 50 *Queen Mary*, a type of long, low-loading, articulated vehicle specially designed for the road transportation of airframes. **1949** *Jrnl. R. Aeronaut. Soc.* LIII. 822 The Council wish to acknowledge their appreciation of the 'Queen Mary' which was kindly provided by Hawker Aircraft Ltd. for the transport of some of the aircraft of the Shuttleworth Collection. **1960** *Picture Show Ann. 1961* (Austral.) 151/2 *Queen Mary*, a 60ft. trailer used for moving scenery. **1968** I. LAMBOT *Queen dies First* v. 34 There's a signal in, from the salvage boys. They'll be sending a Queen Mary on Monday to shift it.

c. ***the Queens***: the Cunard passenger liners, 'Queen Mary' and 'Queen Elizabeth'.

1949 P. DUFF *Brit. Ships & Shipping* i. 28 The two *Queens* of the North Atlantic did invaluable service in every theatre of war. **1956** H. GRATTIDGE *Captain of Queens* 291 Both *Queens* had the same 118 foot breadth, but at 1,031 feet the *Elizabeth* eclipsed the *Mary's* length by ten clear feet. **1959** *Daily Tel.* 9 Apr. 1/4 Plans to replace the 'Queens' must be modern and far-reaching. **1968** O. WYND *Sumatra Seven Zero* vi. 85 The first clang of metal sounded like a mid-Atlantic collision between the two Queens. **1970** W. G. ROBERTS *Quest for Oil* xi. 116 This may seem slow compared with the 30 knots of the 'Queens' or even with the 20 to 25 knots of the majority of other passenger liners.

4. With specification of the people, country, etc. ruled over by a queen or by the king her consort, as ***Queen of Scots***, ***of France***. Also ***Queen of Spain*** (see quot. 1866 and FRITILLARY 2). ***Queen of Spain fritillary***, an orange butterfly with black markings, *Argynnis lathonia*, belonging to the family Nymphalidæ and widely distributed in Europe, N. Africa, and parts of Asia.

c **950** *Lindisf. Gosp.* Matt. xii. 42 Cuen suð-dæles arises.. in dom. *c* **1205** LAY. 4570 He þohte to habben Delgan to quene of Denemarke. *c* **1250** *Gen. & Ex.* 296 Hu ma it ben, Adam ben king and eue quuen Of alle ðe ðinge in werlde ben. *c* **1386** CHAUCER *Man of Law's T.* 63, I.. wolde she were of all Europe the queene. *c* **1440** *Generydes* 17 His doughter quene of Inde. **1562** WINȜET *Cert. Tractates* Wks. 1888 I. 2 The maist excellent and gracius Souerane, Marie Quene of Scottis. **1606** SHAKS. *Ant. & Cl.* III. vi. 11 He.. made her Of lower Syria, Cyprus, Lydia, absolute Queene. **1712–4** POPE *Rape Lock* III. 13 One speaks the glory of the British Queen. **1770** *Ann. Reg.* 102 Died lately, at her hut at Norwood, Bridget, the Queen of the Gipseys. **1775** M. HARRIS *Eng. Lepidoptera* 3 Fritillaria, Queen of Spain... Orange brown spotted with black. **1818** CRUISE *Digest* (ed. 2) III. 200 Her Majesty or her successors, kings or queens of the realm. **1866** BLACKMORE *Cradock Nowell* xxx, If by the 'Queen of Spain' you mean that common brown little butterfly. **1866** [see FRITILLARY 2]. **1906** R. SOUTH *Butterflies Brit. Isles* 91 The Queen of Spain Fritillary... This butterfly is not unlike a small example of the Silver-washed Fritillary. **1976** *Country Life* 18 Mar. 680/2 The remaining nine fritillaries include three occasional migrants, the Queen of Spain fritillary, the cardinal and the weaver's fritillary.

5. *transf.* A female whose rank or pre-eminence is comparable to that of a queen.

a. Applied to the Virgin Mary, esp. in phr. as ***Queen of glory***, ***grace***, ***heaven***, ***paradise***, ***women***, etc.

a **900** CYNEWULF *Christ* 276 Seo clæneste cwen ofer eorþan. **971** *Blickl. Hom.* 105 þa ealra fæmnena cwen cende þone soþan scyppend. *a* **1240** *Ureisun* in *Cott. Hom.* 195 Ich ðe bidde holi heouene kwene. *c* **1325** *Song Virg.* 33 in *O.E. Misc.* 195 Leuedi quene of parays. *c* **1375** *Sc. Leg. Saints* xxiv. (*Alexis*) 26 þat he in weding borne was of mary, þe quene of grace. *c* **1410** HOCCLEVE *Mother of God* 2 O blisful queene, of queenes Emperice. *c* **1470** HENRY *Wallace* I. 261 Quhen scho him saw scho thankit hewynnis queyn. **1500–20** DUNBAR *Poems* lxxxv. 37 Haile, qwene serene! Haile, mosteamene! **1604** E. G[RIMSTONE] *D'Acosta's Hist. Indies* VII. xxvii. 582 The favour which the Queene of glorie did to our men. **1798** COLERIDGE *Anc. Mar.* v. i, To Mary-queen the praise be yeven. **1840** I. TAYLOR *Ancient Chr.* (1842) II. ii. 169 Our Queen, though the Queen of heaven as well as of earth [etc.].

b. Applied to the goddesses of ancient religions or mythologies; also in phrases, as ***queen of heaven***, ***love***, ***marriage***, etc.

1382 WYCLIF *Jer.* vii. 18 That thei make sweete cakis to the quen of heuene. **1508** DUNBAR *Gold. Targe* 73 Thare saw I Nature, and [als dame] Venus quene. **1500–20** —— *Poems* xlviii. 63 Haill princes Natur, haill Venus luvis quene. **1592** SHAKS. *Ven. & Ad.* 251 Poor queen of love, in thine own law forlorn! **1608** —— *Per.* II. iii. 30 By Juno, that is queen of marriage. **1629** MILTON *Ode Nativity* 201 Mooned Ashtaroth, Heavn's Queen and Mother both. **1809** in *Spirit Pub. Jrnls.* (1810) XIII. 328 O Venus, Queen of Drury Lane. *a* **1822** SHELLEY *Hom. Venus* 13 Diana, golden-shafted queen.

c. Applied to a woman as a term of endearment and honour.

1588 SHAKS. *L.L.L.* IV. iii. 41 O Queene of Queenes, how farre dost thou excell, No thought can thinke. **1596** —— *Merch. V.* II. i. 12, I would not change this hue, Except to steale your thoughts, my gentle Queene. **1865** RUSKIN *Sesame* 185 Queens you must always be; queens to your lovers; queens to your husbands and your sons.

d. A woman who has pre-eminence or authority in a specified sphere. † ***Queen of the Bean***: see BEAN *sb.* 6 c. ***Queen of Hearts*** (cf. 8 b). ***Queen of the May***: see MAY. See also ***beauty queen*** s.v. BEAUTY *sb.* III b, etc. Also, a woman who has pre-eminence in an unspecified sphere.

1596 SHAKS. *Merch. V.* III. ii. 171, I was the lord of this fair mansion.. Queen o'er myself. **1608** —— *Per.* II. iii. 17 Come, queen o' the feast, For, daughter, so you are. *c* **1645** HOWELL *Lett.* II. xii. (1650) 13 The Lady Elizabeth, which .. is called.. for her winning Princely comportment, the Queen of Hearts. **1652** J. WRIGHT tr. *Camus' Nat. Paradox* III. 53 Shee thought to triumph over all her Competitors and be Queen of the Bean. **1816** KEATS *To my Brother George* 87 Upon a morn in May.. that lovely lass Who chosen is their queen. *a* **1822** SHELLEY *Chas. I*, II. 394 The Twelfth-night Queen of Hearts. **1830** TENNYSON *Isabel* ii, Isabel.. The queen of marriage, a most perfect wife. **1847** C. BRONTË *Jane Eyre* II. i. 14 Most of them.. looked handsome; but Miss Ingram was certainly the queen. **1858** LYTTON *What will He do* I. xiv, Lady Selina Vipont was one of the queens of London. **1958** *Spectator* 22 Aug. 247/1 A robust, jolly-looking person, more like a hockey queen than a film star. **1962** E. LUCIA *Klondike Kate* 9 Rare instances of chivalry and devotion were exhibited by the miners toward this frontier queen. **1979** C. MACLEOD *Family Vault* (1980) xxiv. 213 She decided to become a society queen and married a man who had the cash but not the inclination.

e. *slang.* An attractive woman; a girl-friend, female partner.

1900 *Dialect Notes* II. 53 *Queen*,.. an attractive girl. **1914** 'HIGH JINKS, Jr.' *Choice Slang* 17 *Queen*, a pretty girl. 'A Beauty'. **1937** J. T. FARRELL *Fellow Countrymen* 181 Wouldn't it be luck if a ritzy queen fell for him! **1944** C. HIMES *Black on Black* (1973) 196 My queen 'gan bouncin' out her twelve-dollar dress. **1952** S. SELVON *Brighter Sun* x. 207 Same ting happen wen my old queen was sick. **1955** P. SILLITOE *Cloak without Dagger* xiv. 128 Both gangs used hatchets, swords, and sharpened bicycle chains.. and these were conveyed to the scenes of their battles by their 'queens'. **1975** *Globe & Mail* (Toronto) 11 June 3/7 Since some of the members have no respect for the law, they refuse to enter into a legal marriage. They view it as an unnecessary burden and responsibility. Instead, some Rastafarians have many 'Queens'.

6. Applied to things: **a.** Anything personified as a woman and looked upon as the chief, *esp.* the most excellent or beautiful, of its class.

a **1050** *Liber Scintill.* xvii. (1889) 84 Ealdorlicra leahtra cwen and modor ofermodignyss ys. *a* **1225** *St. Marher.* 19 Meiðhad þe is cwen of alle mihtes. **1340** *Ayenb.* 10 þe kuen of uirtues, dame charite. **1508** DUNBAR *Gold. Targe* 82 There saw I May, of myrthfull monethis quene. **1563** FOXE *A. & M.* 333/2 That noble ground and quene of prouinces. **1604** E. G[RIMSTONE] *D' Acosta's Hist. Indies* II. vi. 93 This river (which in my opinion, deserves well the name of Empresse and Queene of all flouds). *a* **1720** SHEFFIELD (Dk. Buckhm.) *Wks.* (1753) I. 6 Paris, the queen of cities. **1861** S. THOMSON *Wild Fl.* III. (ed. 4) 286 The 'lady fern'.. sometimes called the 'Queen of Ferns'. **1886** E. MILLER *Text. Guide* 75 The Peshito has been called 'The Queen of Versions'.

b. That which in a particular sphere has pre-eminence comparable to that of a queen. ***queen of heaven***, ***night***, ***the tides***, the moon; ***queen of puddings***, a pudding made of breadcrumbs, milk, and other ingredients, freq. with a layer of meringue on top; ***queen-of-the-meadow***(*s*, (*a*) the meadow-sweet, *Filipendula ulmaria*, native to Europe and Asia and naturalized in eastern North America; (*b*) *U.S.* = JOE-PYE WEED; ***queen-of-the-night***, a variety of night-blooming cereus (see NIGHT *sb.* 14), esp. *Selenicereus grandiflorus*, which is native to the West Indies and bears fragrant white flowers; ***queen-of-the-prairie***, a perennial North American herb, *Filipendula rubra*, found in meadows and prairies and bearing clusters of small pink flowers; ***Queen of the West***: Cincinnati, Ohio (cf. *Queen City* in sense 14). Similarly with an *of* phrase to designate other cities.

1552 LYNDESAY *Monarche* Prol. 153 Synthea, the hornit nychtis quene. **1597** GERARDE *Herbal* II. ccccxix. (1633) 1043 Called in English Meadow Sweet and Queene of the Medowes. **1611** SHAKS. *Wint. T.* IV. iv. 146 Each your doing .. Crownes what you are doing.. That all your Actes, are Queenes. **1671** MILTON *P.R.* IV. 45 Great and glorious Rome, Queen of the Earth. **1784** *Mem. Amer. Acad.* I. 451 Queen of the Meadows. Blossoms red or purple. In moist pastures. **1812** BYRON *Ch. Har.* II. lxxx, The Queen of tides on high consenting shone. **1835** C. F. HOFFMAN *Winter in West* I. 130 It is in vain for thriving Pittsburg or flourishing Louisville.. to dispute with Cincinnati her title of 'Queen of the West'. **1838** H. MARTINEAU *Retrospect* II. 254, I should prefer Cincinnati as a residence... The 'Queen of the West' is enthroned in a region of wonderful and inexhaustible beauty. **1840** *Knickerbocker* XVI. 157 In this way we glided in our broad-horn past Cincinnati, the 'Queen of the West' as she is now called. **1840** ALISON *Hist. Europe* li. §52 The Emperor travelled.. to Venice: he there admired the marble palaces of the Queen of the Adriatic. **1851** *San Francisco Picayune* 19 Sept. 2/4 Some person, gifted with a sufficient amount of patience, may undertake to compile the history of San Francisco.. the Queen of the Pacific. **1852** H. R. NOLL *Bot. Class Bk. & Flora Pennsylvania* 100 S[piræa] lobata, Murr. Queen of the Prairie. **1878** BOSW. SMITH *Carthage* 9 Destined.. to become the Queen of the Mediterranean. **1883** G. MACDONALD *Donal Grant* ii. 18 Bushes of meadow-sweet, or queen-of-the-meadow, as it is called in Scotland. **1892** *Amer. Folk-Lore* V. 98 *Eupatorium purpureum*, Queen of the meadow. **1898** C. A. CREEVEY *Flowers of Field, Hill & Swamp* 146 Queen-of-the-prairie... A stately, beautiful plant adorning the meadows and prairies south and west of Pennsylvania. *Ibid.* 484 Meadow-sweet. Queen-of-the-meadows... A slender, reddish-stemmed shrub, 2 to 6 feet high. **1911** Queen-of-the-meadow [see *Indian turnip* s.v. INDIAN *a.* 4 b]. **1917** M. BYRON *Pudding Book* iii. 72 Queen of Puddings... Soak a pint of breadcrumbs in boiling milk, and the yolks of four eggs well beaten. **1920** BRITTON & MILLSPAUGH *Bahama Flora* 294 *Selenicereus grandiflorus*... Queen-of-the-Night. Often cultivated. **1949** H. HORNSBY *Lonesome Valley* xxii. 291 The wind was working among the alder bushes and the willows and queen of the meadow. **1963** M. PATTEN *Puddings & Desserts* (recipe no. 389) Queen of puddings. **1968** PETERSON & MCKENNY *Field Guide to Wildflowers N. Amer.* 284 Queen-of-the-prairie... Flowers deep pink. **1971** *Fashion Panorama* (Ceylon) Apr.–June 21 The Queen of the night was in full bloom outside and its heavy and overpowering scent reached her from the garden. **1972** E. WIGGINTON *Foxfire Bk.* 242 Take one root from a queen-of-the-meadow plant. **1977** H. FAST *Immigrants* I. 30 For almost nine weeks, the shattered city [*sc.* San Francisco], known not only as the 'Queen of the Pacific' but as the 'queen of larceny' as well, entered into a period of benign brotherhood.

7. The perfect female of bees, wasps, or ants.

1609 C. BUTLER *Fem. Mon.* I Of the nature and properties of Bees, and of their Queene. *a* **1711** KEN *Sion* Poet. Wks. 1721 IV. 352 The same Tune.. In which the Bees.. For their Dismission to their Queen entreat. **1724** DERHAM in *Phil. Trans.* XXXIII. 54 The Male Wasps are lesser than the Queens. **1774** GOLDSM. *Nat. Hist.* (1776) VIII. 124 The working ants having.. deposed their queens. **1847** TENNYSON *Princ.* I. 39 Around them both Sweet thoughts would swarm as bees about their queen. **1892** LUBBOCK *Beaut. Nat.* 60 The working Ants and Bees always turn their heads towards the Queen.

8. In games. **a.** In chess: The piece which has greatest freedom of movement, and hence is most effective for defending the king, next to which it is placed at the beginning of the game. Also, the position on the board attained by a pawn when it is queened (see QUEEN *v.* 4).

queen's bishop, ***knight***, ***pawn***, etc.: cf. KING 9 a. ***queen's gambit***: see GAMBIT. † ***to make a queen*** = QUEEN *v.* 4.

c **1440** *Gesta Rom.* xxi. 71 (Harl. MS.) The fifthe [piece] is þe quene, that goth fro blak to blak, or fro white to white, and is yset beside þe kyng. **1474** CAXTON *Chesse* II. ii. B iij b, Thus ought the Quene be maad; She ought to be a fayr lady sittyng in a chayer [etc.]. **1562** ROWBOTHUM *Playe of Cheasts* C v, Thou shalte playe thy queenes Paune one steppe geuing him checke by discouery of thy queenes Bishoppe. **1597** G. B. *Ludus Schacciæ* A 4 When he [the pawn] can.. arrive at the last ranke of his enemies he is chosen and made.. the Queene. *a* **1689** *Yng. Statesmen* vi. in *Coll. Poems Popery* 8/2 So have I seen a King on Chess.. His Queen and Bishops in distress. **1735** BERTIN *Chess* 38 The Queens Gambet, which gives a Pawn with a design to catch her adversary's Queen's Rook. **1761** HOYLE *Chess* 51 The exact Number of Moves, before you can make a Queen. **1773** PHILIDOR *Chess Analysed* 13 The King's Pawn makes a Queen, and wins the Game. **1797** *Encycl. Brit.* (ed. 3) IV. 640 He should take the adversary's pawns, and move the others to queen. **1822** W. LEWIS *Elem. Game Chess* 149 If a Pawn be on a Rook's file it will go to Queen. **1838** LYTTON *Alice* 169, I think I will take the queen's pawn. **1894** J. MASON *Principles Chess* 77 Just as the foremost [Pawn] is but a square from Queen.

b. In ordinary playing-cards: A card bearing the figure of a queen, of which there are four in each pack, ranking next to the kings.

1575 *Gamm. Gurton* II. ii. 29 There is five trumps beside the queene. **1607** HEYWOOD *Wom. Killed w. Kindn.* Wks. 1874 II. 123 This Queene I haue more then my owne.. Giue me the stocke. **1712–4** POPE *Rape of Lock* III. 88 The Knave of Diamonds.. wins.. the Queen of Hearts. **1791** *Gentl. Mag.* 141 The Queen of Clubs is called in Northamptonshire, Queen Bess. **1816** SINGER *Hist. Cards* 39 Like the Italians and Germans, they [the Spaniards] have no Queen in the Pack. **1885** R. A. PROCTOR *Whist* 5, I lead Ace, and follow with Queen of my best suit.

9. Technical uses. **a.** *pl.* One of the classes into which fullers' teasels are sorted (see quot.).

1813 T. RUDGE *Gen. View Agric. Glouc.* 156 The produce of the second and subsequent cuttings are sorted, according to their size, into Queens, which are the best teazles; Middlings.. and Scrubs.

b. A roofing-slate, measuring three feet by two.

1825 J. NICHOLSON *Operat. Mechanic* 622 Slaters class the Welsh slates in the following order: Doubles, Ladies,.. Queens. **1893** J. BROWN *Open. Railw. to Delabole* xxiii, We've countess, duchess, queens and rags.

c. *pl.* A class of apples, the rennets (q.v.).

1836 LOUDON *Encycl. Plants* 426 Apples are classed as pippins or seedlings,.. rennets or queens, specked fruits.

10. a. A small scallop, *Chlamys opercularis*, found off several parts of the coast of north-western Europe; = QUIN.

1803 G. MONTAGU *Testacea Brit.* I. 146 *Pecten opercularis* ..in Devonshire and Cornwall is..known by the name of Frills or Queens. **1883** N. JOLY *Man before Metals* II. i. 200 Several molluscs, especially oysters,..mussels, queens, whelks, and snails. **1901** E. STEP *Shell Life* 84 The Quin or Queen..is more nearly circular in shape, thin and smooth. **1928** RUSSELL & YONGE *Seas* iii. 74 Another animal which can move about is the scallop, especially the smaller 'queen'. **1959** A. C. HARDY *Open Sea* II. vi. 143 The smaller and delicious 'queens'..may occasionally be brought in by trawlers..in sufficient quantities to be marketed. **1971** *Country Life* 21 Oct. 1040/1 Last year nearly 5,000 tons of queens..were brought into Scottish ports.

b. A local name for the smear-dab.

1674 RAY *Coll. Words, Sea Fishes* 100 *Queens*: a Fish thinner than a Plaise. **1884** *St. James's Gaz.* 18 Jan. 6/1 The ..lemon-dab or queen.

11. A female cat. (Cf. *queen-cat* in 14.)

1898 *Bishopsgate Cats* in *Ladies' Field* 6 Aug. 378/1 A few outdoor houses for the queens are used. **1934** P. WADE *Siamese Cat* iv. 45 Not only should the queen herself be excellent, but her pedigree must be above suspicion. **1954** D. HARTLEY *Food in England* 660 You cannot keep a cat on milk only... Nursing queens should be given water to drink and solid food. **1960** *Amer. Speech* XXXV. 300 Cat fanciers use the name queen in speaking of their litter-bearing female cats. **1977** *Proc. R. Soc. Med.* LXX. 3/1 This calcium deficient diet produced..fractures of vertebrae and limb bones in growing kittens and young zoo felids. Calcium deficiency also occurred in lactating queens and their young litters.

12. A male homosexual, esp. the effeminate partner in a homosexual relationship. *slang*. Cf. QUEAN 3.

1924 *Truth* (Sydney) 27 Apr. 6 *Queen*, effeminate person. **1929** M. LIEF *Hangover* vi. 100 'What's those?' 'You know—all those queens.' **1930** E. WAUGH *Vile Bodies* 61 'Now what may *you* want, my Italian queen?' said Lottie as the waiter came in with a tray. **1938** N. MARSH *Artists in Crime* ix. 127 We met the chap that runs the place. One of those die-away queens. **1952** A. WILSON *Hemlock & After* I. v. 88 Anyone would think he was just another routine, harmless old queen. **1962** [see FAGGOT, FAGOT 6b]. **1971** F. FORSYTH *Day of Jackal* xx. 333 He must be..how marvellous! A handsome young butch looking for an old queen to take him home. **1977** *New Yorker* 24 Oct. 64/2 There are only a handful of 'queens' at Green Haven at any one time—men with feminine characteristics they do their best to enhance. The queens are usually given women's nicknames.

II. *attrib.* and *Comb.*

13. General combs. **a.** appositive, as ***queen-bride***, ***-county***, ***-galley***, ***-moon***, ***-rose***, ***-spirit***, ***-spouse***, ***-strumpet***, ***-woman***. **b.** attrib., as ***queen-craft***, ***-features***. **c.** objective, as ***queen-killing***.

1606 *Proc. agst. late Traitors* 105 That King-killing and Queen-killing was not indeed a doctrine of theirs. **1634** FORD *Perk. Warbeck* III. ii, This new queen-bride must henceforth be no more My daughter. *a* **1661** FULLER *Worthies, Kent* (1662) I. 67 She [Q. Elizabeth] was well skilled in the Queen-craft. **1820** KEATS *Ode to Nightingale* 36 Haply the Queen-Moon is on her throne. **1846** BROWNING *Lett.* 16 June (1899) II. 241 You must..add the queen-rose to his garland. **1863** *Atlantic Monthly* Oct. 502 The queen-strumpet of modern history. **1880** HAY *Pike County Ball.* 113 The still queen-features glorious In the dawn of love's first gleams. **1888** TH. WATTS in *Athenæum* 18 Aug. 224/2 See how the four queen-galleys ride. **1904** W. B. YEATS *Stories of Red Hanrahan* 20, I heard under a ragged hollow wood, A queen-woman dressed out in silver, cry.

14. Special combs.: †**queen-apple**, an early variety of apple; **Queen At, A.T.** *Mil. slang* (see quot. 1943); **queen bee**, a fully developed female bee; also *transf.* and *fig.*; *spec.* (*Mil.*) an automatically-controlled aeroplane used as a target in firing practice; **queen-bird**, a swan; **queen-cage**, an apparatus for conveying or transferring a queen-bee to a hive; **queen-cake**, a small currant-cake, usually heart-shaped; **queen cat** = QUEEN 11; **queen-cell**, a cell in a bee-hive, in which the queen is reared; **Queen City** *N. Amer.*, an epithet applied to the chief or pre-eminent city (*of* a region) (cf. sense 6b); **queen closer**, a quarter of a brick, used in building to 'close' the end of a course (see CLOSER[2] 3); **queen conch**, a large marine shell, *Strombus gigas*; **queen-excluder**, a device in a bee-hive to prevent the passage of the queen without excluding the workers; **queen-fish**, (*a*) *U.S.* a small edible fish (*Seriphus politus*) found along the Pacific coast of America; (*b*) a large Australian marine fish, *Scomberoides sanctipetri*, of the family Carangidæ; †**queen-gold**, a former revenue of the king's consort, consisting of one-tenth on certain fines paid to the king; **queen-lily**, a Peruvian ornamental flowering plant of the genus *Phædranassa* (*Cent. Dict.*); **queen olive**, the particularly large fruit of certain varieties of olive; **queen-pigeon** = *queen's pigeon* (Funk's *Stand. Dict.*); **queen-pin** *colloq.*, a woman who controls the (successful) organization of a specified institution or event; (see KING-PIN); **queen pudding** = *queen's pudding*; **queen scallop** = QUEEN *sb.* 10 a; **queen-side** *a. Chess*, of or pertaining to the side of the board in which both queens start the game; **queen-size** *a.*, of an extra large size, though occas. in a series (as of beds), smaller than *king-size*; also ***queen-sized*** adj.; **queen staysail**, a triangular main topmast staysail in a schooner yacht (see quot. 1948); **queen-stitch**, a fancy stitch in embroidery; **queen substance**, a pheromone produced by a queen bee and given to the colony's workers to prevent the production of more queens; †**queen-suit**, a set of cards belonging to one suit, of which the queen is the highest; **queen trigger-fish**, a deep-bodied, blue and yellow marine fish, *Balistes vetula*, found in the Indian and Atlantic Oceans; **queen-truss**, a roof-truss in which there are QUEEN-POSTS; **queen-wasp**, a perfect female wasp; **queenwood**, an Australian evergreen tree, *Daviesia arborea*, of the family Leguminosæ, or its wood.

1579 SPENSER *Sheph. Cal.* June 43 Tho would I seeke for *Queene apples vnrype. **1626** BACON *Sylva* §511 Few Fruits are coloured Red within; The Queen-apple is. **1707** MORTIMER *Husbandry* 537 The Queen Apple, those..of the Summer kind, are good Cyder Apples, mix'd with others. **1943** HUNT & PRINGLE *Service Slang* 54 **Queen At*, a Chief Commander of the A[uxiliary] T[erritorial] S[ervice]. **1947** N. STREATFEILD *Grass in Piccadilly* 33 That queen A.T. of yours must have been a holy terror. **1609** C. BUTLER *Fem. Mon.* i. A3 The *Q[u]eene-bee is a Bee of a comely and stately shape. **1753** CHAMBERS *Cycl. Supp.*, *Queen-bee*, a term given by late writers to what used to be called the *king-bee.* **1807** R. SOUTHEY *Lett. from England* II. xxx. 41 Wherever one of the queen bees of fashion alights, a whole swarm follows her. **1823** BYRON *Juan* XIII. xiii, Sweet Adeline, amidst the gay world's hum, Was the Queen-Bee. **1935** *Sun* (Baltimore) 18 July 2/6 King George today saw the British fleet repel an attack by robot planes. The feature of the war game was the fight between the new aircraft guns on the battleship and the radio-controlled 'queen bee' flying machines. **1938** *Times* 26 Aug. 11/1 'Queen Bees'—pilotless, wireless controlled target machines—were only available at two of the..camps. **1943** C. H. WARD-JACKSON *It's a Piece of Cake* 50 *The Queen Bee*, the Director of the Women's Auxiliary Air Force; or the senior W.A.A.F. officer on a station. **1951** A. CHRISTIE *They came to Baghdad* xv. 139, I thought it was just some female who was coming out to boss things. A kind of Queen Bee. **1956** N. STREATFEILD *Judith* I. 44 Beatrice became a queen bee in London's civil defence force. **1960** P. STANTON *Village of Stars* 63 She walked into the W.R.A.F. sitting-room... There was a little radio in the corner... The Queen Bee had no doubt been wangling the Comforts Fund. **1973** G. BROMLEY *Chance to Poison* v. 79 She's a very dominating character..Queen Bee of the Women's Institute—without her it would collapse. **1978** R. V. JONES *Most Secret War* xxxix. 356 We had in fact evolved our own 'Queen Bee' remote controlled aeroplane for use as an anti-aircraft target in the years before the war. **1830** MISS MITFORD *Village* Ser. IV. (1863) 286 Repeating..as we met the *Queen-birds, 'The swans on fair St. Mary's lake'. **1875** J. HUNTER *Manual Bee-keeping* 82 There are many more *Queen cages in use, and..there is no reason why any Bee-keeper should not make modifications. **1769** MRS. RAFFALD *Eng. Housekpr.* (1778) 271 To make *Queen Cakes. **1840** MRS. F. TROLLOPE *Widow Married* xii, When I've done eating this one queen-cake more. **1894** W. B. YEATS *Land of Heart's Desire* 32, I will have queen cakes when you come to me! **1977** *Radio Times* 12–18 Mar. 16/4 They added a domestic touch by selling their own home produce, little queen cakes and jam. **1691** RAY *N.-C. Words, Wheen-cat*, a *queen-cat. **1893** J. JENNINGS *Domestic or Fancy Cats* iv. 31 At what age should the queen cat breed? **1960** *Amer. Speech* XXXV. 300 Has this name [*sc.* queen] arisen from the often-observed imperious bearing of queen cats? **1843** *Zoologist* I. 158, I had the satisfaction of seeing that one *queen-cell had been commenced. **1838** B. DRAKE (*title*) Tales and sketches from the *Queen City [= Cincinnati]. **1844** in C. Cist *Cincinnati Misc.* (1845) I. 9/1 [Cincinnati] is now familiarly called the Queen City of the West. **1870** *Colorado Gazetteer* 40 Denver, the principal city and capital of Colorado—the Queen City of the Plains— is the county seat of Arapahoe county. **1879** WHITMAN *Specimen Days* (1882) 147 So much for my feeling toward the Queen City of the plains and peaks [= Denver]. **1880** *Harper's Mag.* Dec. 70 Local prejudice.. and proverbial procrastination..unite to keep 'Chinatown' practically a sealed book to the better-class denizens of the Queen City of the Pacific [= San Francisco]. **1943** *Colorado Mag.* Jan. 15 The Queen City of the Plains [= Denver] started in 1878. **1949** *Bull. Hist. & Philos. Soc. Ohio* Apr. 99 That enthusiastic booster for the 'Queen City' [= Cincinnati], Dr. Daniel Drake. **1979** M. G. EBERHART *Bayou Road* v. 47 How *could* the Yankees have injured.. New Orleans, the Queen City, so completely. **1842–59** GWILT *Archit.* (ed. 4) §1896 It becomes necessary near the angles to interpose a quarter brick..called a **queen closer*. **1813** *Sketches Character* (ed. 2) I. 130 That *Queen Conch was anxious only colouring to persuade us it is a real one. **1885** LADY BRASSEY *The Trades* 303 Some years ago the queen-conch (a shell with a delicate pink lining) was in great demand. **1918** *Chambers's Jrnl.* Aug. 541/2 It is the Queen conch my friend has come to buy. **1975** M. HUMFREY *Sea Shells W. Indies* I. 29 The powerful Queen Conch..may weigh more than five pounds. **1881** T. W. COWAN *Brit. Bee-keeper's Guide Bk.* [vii. 33 One of the features of this hive is the possibility of preventing swarming, by confining the queen..by placing a zinc excluder..near the front of the hive.] *Ibid.* 134/1 *Queen-excluder. **1887** F. R. CHESHIRE *Bees & Bee-keeping* II. iii. 74 This [*sc.* the restriction of the queen] is now accomplished by what is called 'excluder-zinc', or 'queen-excluder'. **1930** W. HERROD-HEMPSALL *Bee-keeping* I. ix. 447 The first queen excluder, made from wood, was invented and used in Scotland in 1849. **1976** T. HOOPER *Guide to Bees & Honey* iv. 76 A queen-excluder will be necessary for each [hive]. **1883** J. J. LALOR *Cycl. Political Sci.* II. 217/2 The *queen-fish, the bagre and the roncador are..well known in California. **1905** D. S. JORDAN *Guide to Study of Fishes* II. xx. 354 The queenfish, *Seriphus politus*, of the California coast, is much like the others of this series. .. It is a very choice fish. **1937** Z. GREY *Amer. Angler in Austral.* x. 111 The queen fish, a beautiful silvery dolphin-like leaper, is one of the greatest fish I have caught. **1951** T. C. ROUGHLEY *Fish & Fisheries Austral.* I. 60 The queenfish has a wide distribution from northern New South Wales to the north-west coast of Western Australia, and..is considered to be one of the fastest and most spectacular game-fish. **1965** A. J. MCCLANE *Stand. Fishing Encycl.* 223/1 The queen-fish, *Seriphus politus*, is elongate... Its body is bluish and the fins are yellowish. Growing to about a foot, it occurs from central California to Baja California in shallow water. **1969** *Northern Territory News* (Darwin) *Focus '69* 63/1 The next biggest catch is the threadfin.. followed by the mackerel..and queenfish. **1679** BLOUNT *Anc. Tenures* 36 *Queen-gold is a Royal duty of Ten in the Hundred. **1765** BLACKSTONE *Comm.* I. 221 The queen..is intitled to an antient perquisite called queen-gold or *aurum reginae.* **1875** STUBBS *Const. Hist.* II. xv. 218 *note*, In 1255 the citizens refused to pay queen-gold. **1911** *Daily Colonist* (Victoria, B.C.) 15 Apr. 10/1 (Advt.), Spanish *Queen Olives, bottle, 50c or $1.00..Rowat's Selected Queen Olives, bottle 50c. **1974** Queen olive [see MANZANILLA 2]. **1961** *Guardian* 16 Jan. 4/2 A break for the '*queen-pin'..is utterly essential if you are to keep going. **1972** *Daily Tel.* 21 Jan. 13/1 Welcome to Elaine May..not just as a voice but as the queen-pin—director, author and actress. **1891** T. F. GARRETT *Encycl. Pract. Cookery* II. 267/2 *Queen pudding. **1971** *Jean Bowring Cookbook* 227 Queen pudding. [Recipe follows]. **1959** A. C. HARDY *Open Sea* II. vi. 143 (*caption*) The *queen scallop..showing the swimming action. **1972** *Aquaculture* I. 280 The fish were fed a mixed diet of fresh or frozen chopped herring and queen scallop (*Chlamys opercularis*) meat, at a rate of 750 g twice weekly. **1941** F. REINFELD *Keres' Best Games of Chess* 70/1 Richter prefers to retain the *Queen-side Pawns, even at the cost of exchanging Rooks. **1966** J. R. CAPABLANCA *Last Chess Lectures* (1967) i. 37 His Queen-side majority of Pawns could be converted into a passed Pawn. **1959** *Punch* 28 Oct. 371/1 A motel in Los Angeles advertises *Queen-size beds. **1967** *Boston Sunday Herald* 30 Apr. (Bedding Suppl.) 1/5 Queen size is the answer if a king-size bed doesn't fit your plans... Its 60-by-80-inch innerspring mattress is six inches wider and five inches longer than the old double size. **1973** *Publishers Weekly* 23 July 66/3 An appealing and handsomely produced queen-size book. **1976** *Washington Post* 19 Apr. A9/4 (Advt.), Traditionally styled Queen Size Sleep Sofa and matching love-seat combination. **1979** *Arizona Daily Star* 5 Aug. (Advt. Section) 8/8 It is beautifully designed, complete with queen-size bed. **1955** *Sun* (Baltimore) 19 Mar. 9/4 Mrs Daniel J. Flood, wife of a Democratic Congressman from Pennsylvania, is introducing a new fad here—'*queen-sized' colored cigarettes to match her costume. **1975** A. BERGMAN *Hollywood & Le Vine* (1976) ix. 123 A queen-sized mattress. **1978** *New York* 3 Apr. 74 (Advt.), And for just $50 more, we'll transform the Sofa into a queen-sized sleeper convertible! **1944** H. A. CALLAHAN *Rigging* 130 The late J. Rogers Maxwell introduced a funny little staysail on his famous schooner *Queen* and it has always been known as the *queen staysail. **1948** L. F. HERRESHOFF in *Rudder* Aug. 58 Because previous staysails had to be lowered away in tacking, when my father designed the schooner Queen he did away with the triatic stay and in its place ran a stay called a 'fresh water stay' between the topmast heads. This staysail with which a schooner can tack is called a 'Queen staysail', as it was first used on the schooner Queen. **1631** J. TAYLOR *Needles Excellency* (1634) sig. A2, col. 2, Bred-stitch, Fisher-stitch, Irish-stitch, and *Queen-stitch. **1841** LADY WILTON *Art of Needle-work* (ed. 3) xx. 317 There are..ferne- and queen-stitches. **1882** CAULFEILD & SAWARD *Dict. Needlework* 192 Queen Stitch.—Also known as Double Square. [Description follows.] **1954** C. G. BUTLER in *Trans. R. Entomol. Soc.* CV. 14 It is necessary for the bees to have physical contact with their queen in order to obtain this '*queen substance'. **1972** *Sci. Amer.* Sept. 56/3 The 'queen substances' are outstanding in the complexity and pervasiveness of their role in social organization. **1744** HOYLE *Piquet* 9 The younger-hand is generally to carry Guards to his *Queen-suits. **1778** C. JONES *Hoyle's Games Impr.* 71. **1924** J. T. NICHOLS in J. O. La Gorce *Bk. Fishes* 166/2 The gaudy colors of the *Queen Trigger-fish..are an exception among such forms. **1971** 'D. HALLIDAY' *Dolly & Doctor Bird* xii. 166 Bahamian waters are full of extraordinary fish, from Striped Grunts to Queen Triggerfish. **1724** DERHAM in *Phil. Trans.* XXXIII. 59 The *Queen-Wasps..were weak, and did not buz long. **1827** E. BEVAN *Honey-Bee* 187 The queen-wasps were unusually numerous in the spring of that year. **1882** OGILVIE (citing Weale), **Queen-wood*, a name sometimes given to woods of the greenheart and cocoa-wood character, imported from the Brazils. **1889** J. H. MAIDEN *Useful Native Plants Austral.* 415 *Daviesia arborea*..'Queen-wood'. This wood is hard, close-grained, with beautiful pink streaked lines. **1902** G. S. BOULGER *Wood* II. 300 Queen-wood..North-eastern Australia... Streaked with pink, hard, close-grained, susceptible of a fine polish.

15. Combinations with *queen's*. **a.** In titles or appellations, with the sense of 'belonging to, in the service of, the queen', 'royal' (cf. KING'S), as ***Queen's advocate***, ***bench***, ***counsel***, ***evidence***, ***highway***, ***keys***, ***letter***, ***messenger***, ***pay***, ***peace***,

prison*, *servant*, *speech*, *wardrobe: see these words.

In these terms, as in many of those given under b, the use of *queen's* in place of *king's* is largely or entirely a result of the long reign of Queen Victoria (1837–1901) or that of Queen Elizabeth II (1952–).

b. **queen's allowance** (see quot.); **queen's arm**, a musket; **queen's chair**, a makeshift seat (cf. *queen's cushion*); **queen's cloth** (?); **queen's colours**, one of the pair of colours carried by a regiment, the royal colours; **queen's conch** = *queen conch* (sense 14); **queen's cushion**, a seat (for a girl) made by the crossed hands of two persons (Jamieson, 1825); **Queen's English**, the English language regarded as under the guardianship of the Queen; hence, standard or correct English; †**queen's evil** = king's evil, scrofula; **queen's gambit**: see GAMBIT; **queen's game**: see DOUBLET 3 b; **Queen's Guide**, a holder of the highest award in Guiding, *spec.* during the reign of a queen; **queen's head**, a postage stamp; **queen's metal**, an alloy of tin, antimony, bismuth, and lead; **queen's own**, Government property or provisions (Smyth *Sailor's Word-bk.* 1867); **queen's parade**, the quarter-deck (*ibid.*); **queen's pattern** (see quots. 1910 and 1957); **queen's pigeon**, a large and beautiful crested pigeon of the Papuan region, *Gaura Victoriæ*; **queen's pipe**, a furnace formerly used for destroying smuggled or damaged tobacco; **queen's pudding**, a steamed suet pudding (occas. used for *queen of puddings*, sense 6 b above); **Queen's Scout**, a holder of the highest award in Scouting, *spec.* during the reign of a queen; **queen's shilling**, a shilling formerly given to a recruit when enlisting; also *transf.* and *fig.*; **queen's staysail** = *queen staysail*; **queen's stuff** (?); **queen's taste**: in phr. *to the* or *a queen's taste*, to perfection; **queen's tobacco pipe** = *queen's pipe*; **queen's ware**, (*a*) a cream-coloured kind of Wedgwood ware; (*b*) a kind of stone-ware; **queen's weather**, fine weather; **queen's woman** *slang* (now *Hist.*), a prostitute who received medical attention under the terms of the Contagious Diseases Acts of the 1860s; **queen's yellow**, turpeth mineral, used as a yellow pigment.

1876 Voyle & Stevenson *Milit. Dict.* 320/2 **Queen's allowance*, an allowance in aid of the expenses of the officers' mess. **1848** Lowell *Biglow P.* Ser. I. *The Courtin'*, The ole *queen's-arm that gran'ther Young Fetched back from Concord busted. **1965** S. T. Ollivier *Petticoat Farm* vi. 77 Henry's buggy reins, tied to a cream-can lid, had formed a *queen's chair for Harry. **14..** *Voc.* in Wr.-Wülcker 607/19 *Regilla*, a *Quenyscloth. **1818** M. Edgeworth *Let.* 29 Oct. (1971) 130 Tell me which you prefer the Merino or the Queens cloth... The queens cloth comes to a guinea the dress cheaper. **1812** E. Weeton *Let.* June in *Jrnl. of Governess* (1969) II. 93, I have inquired the price of shells. .. Yours are conch shells; these are called *Queen's conches. **1963** *Times* 27 Apr. 11/2 The pink queen's conch shell from the Caribbean. **1825** J. Jamieson *Suppl. to Etym. Dict. of Scottish Lang.* II. 253/1 **Queen's*, also *king's cushion*, a mode of carriage, whether in sport, or from necessity... Two persons, each of whom grasps his right wrist with his left hand, with the other lays hold of his neighbour's wrist, so as to form a seat of four hands and wrists conjoined. On these the person, who is to be carried, seats himself, or is seated by others, putting both his arms, for greater security, round the necks of the bearers. **1873** C. M. Yonge *Pillars of House* IV. xl. 161 The hands were clasped, queen's-cushion fashion, beneath her, the necks were bent for the arms to be thrown round them. **1592** T. Nashe *Strange Newes* sig. B1ᵛ, He must be running on the letter, and abusing the *Queenes English without pittie or mercie. **1848** [see ON *prep.* 6 a]. **1864** H. Alford *Plea for Queen's Eng.* (ed. 2) 2 The *Queen's English* is not an unmeaning phrase, but one which may serve to teach us some profitable lessons with regard to our language. **1867** F. S. Cozzens *Sayings of Dr. Bushwhacker* 82 In fact, that arbitrary style of speaking which is commonly known as the Queen's English. **1885** *Punch* 4 July 5/2 (*heading*) The Premier's Primer; or Queen's English as she is wrote. **1902** F. Hume *Fever of Life* 146, I! Oh, how can you? I speak the Queen's English. **1975** *Verbatim* Dec. 15/2 One irate caller said, according to the network [NKH], 'How dare you deprive us of our one chance to hear the Queen's English?' **1597** A. M. tr. *Guillemeau's Fr. Chirurg.* 19/2 The curinge of *Queenes evil. **1600** Surflet *Countrie Farme* I. xii. 58 For the Queenes euill [*margin* The Kinges euill]. *c* **1554** *Interlude of Youth* C iij, I can teache you to play at the dice, At the *quenes game and at the Iryshe. *a* **1618** J. Davies *Wittes Pilgr.* (1878) 32 (D.) Here Love at tick-tack plaies, or at Queen's-game, But Irish hates. **1968** M. E. Brimelow *Guide Handbk.* iv. 70 If a Guide has..taken a full and active part including earning badges, in all the Eight Points of the Programme.. she can qualify as a *Queen's Guide. **1976** *Milton Keynes Express* 9 July 5/7 Three North Bucks girls received Queen's Guides awards at Milton Keynes College of Education, Wolverton, on Tuesday evening. **1840** *Chambers's Edin. Jrnl.* 11 July 193/2 The perplexed purchaser immediately devotes a *queen's head, as he most irreverently calls it, to the purpose of asking the editors what he is to do. **1844** Alb. Smith *Adv. Mr. Ledbury* xv. (1886) 45 Notes it would not do to stick a penny Queen's Head upon. **1860** Miss Yonge *Stokesley Secr.* i. (1861) 16, I must have a queen's-head to write to Mamma. **1879** Trollope *John Caldigate* III. x. 132 That stamp, that effigy, that two-penny queen's-head. **1915** *Chambers's Jrnl.* Sept. 599/1 When the new stamp was introduced it was invariably called the 'queen's head'. **1839** Ure *Dict. Arts* 952 *Queen's metal..serves also for teapots and other domestic utensils. **1856** Miller *Inorg. Chem.* II. 930 Another alloy, which is intermediate in properties between pewter and Britannia metal, is called Queen's metal. **1769** *Catal. Worcester Porcelaine* in J. E. Nightingale *Contrib. towards Hist. of Eng. Porcelain* (1881) 95 Twelve fluted handle cups and saucers, 6 coffee cups, and two tea pots plain *Queen's pattern 2*l.* **1910** R. L. Hobson *Worcester Porcelain* vii. 58 The catalogue of a sale of Worcester porcelain at Christie's, in 1769, includes several references to a 'Queen's pattern', which was no doubt the same as the traditional 'Queen Charlotte's pattern' of today. **1928** W. B. Honey *Old Eng. Porcelain* viii. 167 A design in Oriental style long popular at Worcester..consists of vertical or spirally curved panels alternately red on white and white on blue, with gilding... It was variously known as the 'whorl', 'spiral', 'catherine-wheel' and 'Queen's pattern'. **1957** Mankowitz & Haggar *Encycl. Eng. Pottery & Porcelain* 186/1 *Queen's pattern*, a counter-changed pattern consisting of alternate radiating whirling bands of red-on-white and white-on-blue ornament with gilded embellishments used at Worcester from c. 1770 onwards. **1974** K. Royce *Trap Spider* i. 12 The cutlery was mid-Georgian Queen's pattern. **1882** *B'ham Weekly Post* 2 Jan. 8/4 Abolition of the '*Queen's Pipe'. **1884** *Cassell's Dict. Cookery* 675/2 **Queen's Pudding*. [Recipe follows.] **1917** N. Soyer *Standard Cookery* 271 Queen's Pudding. Ingredients.—Eight ounces of finely-chopped suet [etc.]. **1935** G. Greene *Basement Room* 9 It was a pudding he liked, Queen's pudding with a perfect meringue. **1955** *Radio Times* 22 Apr. 14 St. George's Parade of *Queen's Scouts. **1962** L. Deighton *Ipcress File* iii. 24 He picked the limp Raven off the..table like a Queen's scout with a rucksack. **1975** *Scout Handbk.* xxix. 274 Beyond the Membership Badge you'll aim for the Venture Award and the Queen's Scout Award. **1877** G. W. Godfrey (*title*) The *Queen's Shilling. **1882** J. Ashton *Soc. Life Reign Q. Anne* II. 203 The Queen's shilling once being taken..there was no help for the recruit, unless he was bought out. **1975** N. Luard *Travelling Horseman* vi. 161 If you've had enough of the Queen's shilling, try Pat Foley. **1976** *Listener* 1 Apr. 403/2 He took the Queen's shilling and joined the Royal West Kents..as a private soldier. **1926** *Yachting Monthly* XLI. 244/1 Above the mainstay-sail was another triangular sail, commonly known as a '*Queen's' staysail. **1766** W. Gordon *Gen. Counting-ho.* 428, 16 fine brocaded *queens stuffs. **1845** S. Judd *Margaret* II. xi. 358 Rose had on..a queens-stuff habit of the same colour. **1902** W. N. Harben *Abner Daniel* xxxiii. 279 You worked 'im to a *queen's taste—as fine as spilt milk. **1911** R. D. Saunders *Col. Todhunter* ix. 126 It's the best and truest thing I ever saw in my life! They've got you finished off to the Queen's taste. **1843** *Penny Cycl.* XXV. 17 The damaged tobacco thus removed is consumed in a furnace..jocularly termed the '*queen's tobacco-pipe'. **1767** J. Wedgwood *Sel. Lett.* (1965) 58 The demand for this said *Creamcolour*, Alias **Queens Ware*, Alias *Ivory* still increases. **1782** Wedgwood in *Phil. Trans.* LXX. 320 Delft ware is fired by a heat of 40 or 41°; cream-coloured or Queen's ware, by 86°. **1792** A. Young *Trav. France* 79 English goods..hard and queen's ware; cloths and cottons. **1863** W. Chaffers *Marks & Monograms on Pott. & Porc.* 120 The principal inventions of Wedgwood were, 1, the cream-coloured table ware, afterwards called *Queen's ware*; [etc.]. **1872** 'Mark Twain' *Roughing It* lix. 432 By-and-by he went home to his lodgings—an empty queensware hogshead—and employed himself till night trying to make up his mind what to buy with it. **1884** *Health Exhib. Catal.* 49/2 Sanitary appliances in action, and general Queen's Ware. **1897** [see MERCHANT *sb.* 1 d]. **1900** F. Litchfield *Pottery & Porcelain* iii. 32 [Thomas Whieldon's] celebrated cream ware, called 'Queen's ware'. **1906** *Dialect Notes* III. 152 *Queensware*.., ordinary crockery. 'You can get queensware at Hansard's grocery or the ten-cent store.' **1961** *Connoisseur New Guide to Antique Eng. Pottery, Porcelain & Glass* 54 [Wedgwood's] Queensware was copied by most of the potters of his time. **1851** *Illustr. London News* 7 June 512/2 The '*Queen's weather', as it has been styled, did not hold good to-day, for..the rain began to come down. **1893** S. Grand *Heavenly Twins* I. II. iv. 234 'Queen's weather!' he remarked. 'Yes,' she answered, looking out at the sparkling water. **1899** *Johannesburg Star* (weekly ed.) 22 Apr., Although the wind is rather high, Queen's weather prevails. **1937** M. V. Hughes *London Home in Nineties* x. 167 The 'Queen's weather' of glorious sunshine began to work in the early part of the year [1897]. **1979** G. St. Aubyn *Edward VII* v. 251 There could hardly have been a more convincing demonstration of 'Queen's Weather' than on..the day of the Diamond Jubilee... The sun burst through the clouds. **1871** *Rep. R. Comm. Admin. Contag. Dis. Acts* I. 14 in *Parl. Papers* (C. 408) XIX. 1 Some of them are called '*Queen's women'; some exhibit the printed order to attend the periodical examination as a certificate of health. **1981** F. K. Prochaska *Women & Philanthropy* vi. 205 One effect of the [Contagious Diseases] Acts was the creation of an outcast and more professional class of prostitute, 'Queen's women' as they were sometimes called. **1839** Ure *Dict. Arts* 1054 **Queen's Yellow* is an antient name of Turbith Mineral, or yellow subsulphate of mercury. **1851–61** Mayhew *Lond. Labour* II. 70 When canaries are 'a bad colour'..they are re-dyed, by the application of..'Queen's Yellow'.

c. in names of plants, as †**queen's balm**, alyssum; **queen's berry**, the cloudberry, *Rubus Chamæmorus*; **queen's cushion**, cut-leaved saxifrage (*Treas. Bot.* 1866); **queen's delight**, an American euphorbiaceous plant, *Stillingia sylvatica* (*ibid.*); **queen's flower**, an Indian tree (*Lagerstrœmia Flos-Reginæ*) with beautiful rose-coloured flowers (*Cent. Dict.* 1891); **queen's gilliflower** or **July-flower**, dame's violet, *Hesperis Matronalis*; †**queen's herb**, tobacco (see QUEEN-MOTHER 4); **queen's lace** *U.S.*, the wild carrot or Queen Anne's lace, *Daucus carota*; **queen's pincushion**, the flowers of the guelder rose (*Cassell's Encycl. Dict.* 1886); **queen's root** = *queen's delight* (Mayne *Expos. Lex.* 1858); **queen's violet** = *queen's gilliflower*.

1767 Abercrombie *Ev. Man his own Gardener* (1803) 735/1 List of Hardy Annuals..*Alysson*, or mad-wort, **Queen's Balm.* **1861** S. Thomson *Wild Fl.* III. (ed. 4) 221 It is the cloud-berry or *queen's-berry. **1573** Tusser *Husb.* (1878) 96 Herbes, branches, and flowers, for windowes and pots. *Queenes gilleflowers. **1597** Gerarde *Herbal* II. cxxii. (1633) 461 Dames Violets or Queenes Gillofloures. **1760** J. Lee *Introd. Bot.* App. 324 Queen's July-flower. **1577** Frampton *Joyfull Newes* II. lxxvi. 42 Some haue called this Hearbe the *Queenes herbe, because it was firste sente vnto her. [**1894** S. J. Weyman *Man in Black* 60 You take the Queen's herb, you sneeze.] **1906** M. E. W. Freeman *By Light of Soul* 52 The fields..were white and gold with *queen's lace and golden rod. **1947** L. M. Beebe *Mixed Train Daily* 88 This freight train, carrying its passengers in the caboose and wading pleasantly through springtime Arkansas meadows brave with daisies and queen's lace, is the Graysonia, Nashville and Ashdown's morning redball. **1731** Miller *Gard. Dict.* Index (1733), *Queen's Violet, *vide* Hesperis.

queen (kwiːn), *v.* [f. prec.]

1. a. ***to queen it***: To be a queen; to act or rule as queen; to have pre-eminence like a queen.

1611 Shaks. *Wint. T.* IV. iv. 460 Ile Queene it no inch farther, But milke my Ewes, and weepe. **1613** —— *Hen. VIII*, II. iii. 37 A threepence bow'd would hire me Old as I am, to Queene it. **1790** Burns *Prol. Theatre Dumfries* 2 Yon great city That queens it o'er our taste. **1818** Milman *Samor* 7 Her milk-white neck embour'd in arching spray, Queens it along the waters. **1826** Scott *Woodst.* xxvi, The imperious Vashti is left to queen it in solitude. **1894** Mrs. F. Elliot *Roman Gossip* vi. 181 Josephine was queening it at the Tuileries.

b. *absol.* in same sense. *rare.*

1843 Lytton *Last Bar.* IV. ii, 'I can scarce queen while Warwick is minister', said Elizabeth.

2. *trans.* To make (a woman) a queen. Also *fig.*

1843 Lytton *Last Bar.* II. i, This Dame Woodville, whom I queened. **1880** Lady Martin *Shaks. Fem. Char.* 120 That passionate childlike loving queens her in his sight.

3. To rule over as a queen.

1839 Bailey *Festus* xvi. (1852) 182 As the moon doth Queen the night. **1843** E. Jones *Poems, Sens. & Event* 115 His will, a trembling rudder She held to play with, or to queen.

4. *Chess.* **a.** To advance (a pawn) to the opponent's end of the board, where it acquires the power of, and is replaced by, a queen or such other piece as the player may choose. Also *absol.*

1789 Twiss *Chess* II. 155 *Damer le Pion*, literally *to queen the Pawn*, is a French expression. **1797** *Encycl. Brit.* (ed. 3) IV. 640 note, *To queen* is to make a queen. **1808** *Studies Chess* I. 219 The pawn is queened, and wins the game. **1848** H. R. Agnel *Chess* 63 You..queen your Pawn, and instead of claiming a Queen, you take a Knight. **1894** J. Mason *Principles Chess* 88 That the player who Queens first wins is a rule.

b. *intr.* Of a pawn: To reach the position at which it acquires the power of a queen.

1842 *Chess Exemplified* 78 If the pawn have the move—it will queen. **1894** J. Mason *Principles Chess* 61 Attacking the Pawn, and taking it on the next move, whether it queens or not.

5. To supply (a hive) with a queen-bee.

1884 *Bee-keeping* (*Brit. Bee-keepers' Assoc.*) 27 The bees came up..I lifted the card, she was welcomed, and the hive was now queened.

Hence **queened** *ppl. a.*

1860 Staunton *Chess Praxis* iv. 43 White can win the game by converting a 'Queened Pawn' into a Bishop.

Queen Anne. **a.** The Queen of Great Britain and Ireland who reigned from 1702 to 1714.

Queen Anne is dead: a phrase implying stale news (cf. QUEEN 3, quot. 1738). ***Queen Anne's bounty***: see BOUNTY 5 a. ***Queen Anne's free gift***: see quot. 1867.

1840 Barham *Ingol. Leg.* Ser. I. *Acc. New Play*, Lord Brougham, it appears, isn't dead, though Queen Anne is. **1859** Thackeray *Virgin.* lxxiii, On which my lady cried petulantly, 'Oh Lord, Queen Anne's dead, I suppose.' **1867** Smyth *Sailor's Word-bk.*, *Queen Anne's Free Gift*, a sum of money formerly granted to surgeons annually, in addition to their monthly twopences from each man.

b. *attrib.* as an epithet of the style of furniture, buildings, etc., characteristic of Queen Anne's reign, or of things made in this style. Also *absol.*

1863 A. J. Munby *Diary* 12 May (1972) 160 The house.. is noble, having a fine Queen Anne front and elaborate scrollwork gates. **1878** C. L. Eastlake *Hints on Househ. Taste* (ed. 4) i. 25 The recently revived taste for the so-called 'Queen Anne' style..for that domestic type of brick architecture which prevailed..from the Caroline to the Georgian period. **1879** M. E. Braddon *Vixen* I. xiii. 253 The Queen Anne kettle was hissing merrily over its spirit-lamp. **1881** A. Lang *Library* 36 What furniture-dealers indifferently call the 'Queen Anne' or the 'Chippendale' style. **1883** *Harper's Mag.* Sept. 560/2 In all Queen Anne buildings the architecture is *appliqué*. However, to disparage Queen Anne is not to explain its acceptance. **1913** W. J. Locke *Stella Maris* ii. 13 A Queen Anne gem of a tiny house in Kensington. **1936** *Archit. Rev.* LXXIX. 213 (*caption*) This house claims to be the first brick-built house of the 'Queen Anne' Revival; No. 1 Palace Green, Kensington, by Philip Webb. **1964** S. Nowell Smith *Edwardian England* iv. 152 Tudor, Jacobean, Queen Anne, and Chippendale pieces..often jostled each other in the same room. **1977** *Times* 28 May 22/7 The audio and radiogram..designs are in Jacobean, Regency, Queen Anne and Scandinavian contemporary.

c. In the possessive in the names of plants: **Queen Anne's (double) daffodil**, a daffodil, *Narcissus capax plenus*, with pale yellow double flowers; **Queen Anne's (double) jonquil**, a small variety of *Narcissus jonquilla* with clusters of double, yellow, fragrant flowers; **Queen Anne's**

lace, a popular name for various umbelliferous plants bearing clusters of small white flowers, esp., in North America, the wild carrot, *Daucus carota*, and in Britain, cow parsley, *Anthriscus sylvestris*.

1806 *Curtis's Bot. Mag.* XXIV. 934 Varies with very double flowers, and is then called by some Gardeners 'Queen Anne's Jonquil'. **1886** G. NICHOLSON *Illustr. Dict. Gardening* II. 413/1 A double form of this species [sc. *Narcissus jonquilla*] is known as Queen Anne's Jonquil. **1889** *Jrnl. R. Hort. Soc.* XI. 90 Its name of 'Queen Anne's Daffodil' was no doubt originally given in honour of Queen Anne of Austria. **1894** *Amer. Folk-Lore* VII. 89 *Daucus Carota*, Queen Anne's lace, some-what general. **1913** W. P. EATON *Barn Doors & Byways* 273 Wild carrot bears a dainty, flat-topped white bloom sometimes as large as a saucer, and a long bed of them will often appear like a strip of delicate embroidery along the wayside, making their more aristocratic title of Queen Anne's lace entirely applicable. **1926** W. DE LA MARE *Connoisseur* 318 Only the rotting sleepers remained, matted with weeds and bordered with Queen Ann's [*sic*] lace, golden rod and Michaelmas daisy. **1930** F. A. POTTLE *Stretchers* 204 The fields.. are rioting with the delicate blooms of Queen Anne's lace. **1934** E. A. BOWLES *Handbk. Narcissus* viii. 89 *N*[*arcissus*] *eystettensis*,.. otherwise known as capax plenus or Queen Anne's Double Daffodil, is another plant of mysterious origin. *Ibid.* 90 Queen Anne's Daffodil may be a garden hybrid of the sixteenth century. *Ibid.* xiv. 137 Its double form is known as 'Queen Anne's Jonquil'. **1946** D. C. PEATTIE *Road of Naturalist* i. 21 In Maryland the Queen Anne's lace was dancing under the apple trees that made wide pools of shadow. **1951** M. JEFFERSON-BROWN *Daffodil* x. 117 Queen Anne's Double Daffodil is another flower with which this monarch's name is associated. *Ibid.*, Queen Anne's Double Jonquil.. is but six inches high. **1955** W. GADDIS *Recognitions* III. ii. 760, I remember.. tall weeds including Queen Anne's laces. **1961** M. FISH *Cottage Garden Flowers* iii. 29 *N*[*arcissus*] *capax plenus* (Syn. *N. eystettensis*) is the flower that was known as 'Queen Anne's Double Daffodil'. **1961** P. SYNGE *Collins Guide to Bulbs* 236 *N*[*arcissus*] *jonquilla flore pleno* is the double form often known as Queen Anne's Double Jonquil. **1971** P. LARKIN in *Listener* 29 July 144/1 Young-leafed June,.. With hedges snowlike strewn, .. Lost lanes of Queen Anne's lace. **1974** M. INGATE *Sound of Weir* xix. 164 A dragonfly.. settled for a moment among the litter scent of Queen Anne's lace. **1978** *Church Times* 23 June 14/5, I waded into waist-high cow-parsley (or, if you prefer it, Queen Anne's lace, hemlock or bogy's gruel).

Hence **Queen 'Anneified** *a.*, in Queen Anne style; **Queen 'Ann(e)ish** *a.*, suggestive of, or designed in, a Queen Anne style; **Queen 'Anneism**, employment of, or preference for, a Queen Anne style; **Queen 'Anneist, -ite**, one who adopts or favours this style; **Queen 'Annery**, a style (of utterance, etc.) characteristic or reminiscent of the reign of Queen Anne.

a **1878** SIR G. SCOTT *Recoll.* ix. (1879) 375 The Queen-Anne-ites soon threw off this disguise. **1879** *Athenæum* No. 2696. 818 Even Queen-Anne-ism should draw the line somewhere. **1881** G. M. HOPKINS *Let.* 29 Oct. in Hopkins & Dixon *Corr.* (1955) 83 The language is a quaint medley of Middle-Ages and 'QueenAnnery'. **1887** J. C. ROBINSON in *Times* 17 Aug. 5/4 All architects, Gothic, Classic, and Queen Anneists alike. **1889** J. K. JEROME *Idle Thoughts* 43 'Drinking the waters' sounded fashionable and Queen Anneified. **1926** *Spectator* 24 July 154/2 Gradually Queen-Annish cornices began to creep in. **1943** J. LEES-MILNE *Ancestral Voices* (1975) 269 It is a low, rambling, attractive house, Queen Anne-ish but not of architectural distinction. **1975** *Country Life* 9 Oct. 909/1 The Queen Anne-ish windows fill the room with light.

queendom ('kwi:ndəm). [f. QUEEN *sb.* + -DOM.]

1. The country ruled over by a queen. Also *fig.*

1606 G. W[OODCOCKE] *Hist. Ivstine* II. 9 The Queendome was governed by two of the foure Sisters. **1705** HICKERINGILL *Priest-cr.* II. viii. 75 It has been fatal and ruinous to these Queendoms already. **1834** *Fraser's Mag.* IX. 248 Ours is a literary kingdom, or rather, queendom. **1873** RUSKIN *Fors Clav.* xxxiii. (1896) II. 217 She should as seldom leave it [her home] as a queen her queendom.

2. The position of a queen; queenhood.

1657 TRAPP *Comm. Esther* ii. 12 Whereby they might get the Kings favour and attaine to the Queendome. **1844** MRS. BROWNING *Dead Pan* xi, Will thy queendom all lie hid Meekly under either lid? *c* **1861** MRS. CRAIK *Eliz. & Vict.* (1870) 121 Womanhood is higher than queendom. **1877** G. MACDONALD *Marquis of Lossie* xl, [The moon] shone out fair and clear, in conscious queendom of the night.

queenhood ('kwi:nhʊd). [f. as prec. + -HOOD.] The rank or dignity of a queen; queenly estate.

1859 TENNYSON *Enid* 176 She.. with all grace Of womanhood and Queenhood, answered him. **1885** MRS. LYNN LINTON in *Fortn. Rev.* Nov. 629 Her queenhood was not real. **1894** RALPH in *Harper's Mag.* Aug. 338 Thousands of tiny flowers, over which the wood-violet, the strawberry, and the arbutus struggle for queenhood.

queenie ('kwi:nɪ). Also **queeny**. [f. QUEEN *sb.* + -IE, -Y[6].] **1. a.** An effeminate male, a homosexual; used esp. as a term of address. **b.** *Comb.*, as *queenie-fashion* adv.

[*c* **1736** POPE *Poems* (1954) VI. 367 The Motley Race of Hervey queenies [*var. reading* Harvequini's] And Courtly Vices, Beastly Venyes.] **1933** N. ERSINE *Underworld & Prison Slang* 60 *Queenie*.., a homosexual man. **1936** J. CURTIS *Gilt Kid* viii. 79 'You're not a man. You're a pouf.' .. 'I'll show you who's a pouf.' 'Call yourself a man do you this morning, Queenie? Well you wasn't one last night, see. You gets into bed and goes straight off to kip.' **1948** D. BALLANTYNE *Cunninghams* xx. 261 The dark, good-looking kid.. who always had his shirt collar turned up queeny-fashion. **1966** 'L. LANE' *ABZ of Scouse* II. 87 *Queenie*, an effeminate male. **1974** R. BLY tr. *Hamsun's Hunger* I. 41, I felt a hand on my shoulder, and turned: 'Queeny' was saying good morning... The sight of this aimless, painted-up creature somehow enraged me.

2. (With capital initial.) An affectionate informal term for Queen Elizabeth II.

1976 C. STORR *Unnatural Fathers* xiii. 131 'The Queen absolutely refuses.'.. 'So Queenie's turned up trumps, has she? Good for her!' **1979** *Time* 13 Aug. 6/1 When Britain's Queen Elizabeth II arrived in Lusaka,.. she was cheered by Zambians everywhere she went as 'Queenie! Queenie!'.

queening ('kwi:nɪŋ), *sb.* Also 5 **quenyng**, 7 **queenen**. [? f. QUEEN *sb.* + -ING[3].] A variety of apple. Cf. WINTER-QUEENING.

c **1430** LYDG. *Min. Poems* (Percy Soc.) 15 Eke the frutis wiche more comon be, Quenyngez, pechis, costardes, *etiam* wardons. **1635** QUARLES *Embl.* v. ii. (1818) 262 'Tis not the lasting deuzan I require, Nor yet the red-cheeked queening. **1688** R. HOLME *Armoury* II. iii. 48 The Queening, is a fair red striped Apple, and beautiful in its Season, being a kind of Winter Fruit. **1698** M. LISTER *Journ. Paris* (1699) 194 It was the White Queenen (or *Calvil d'Este*) the Stem of the bigness only of my Thumb. **1879** MISS JACKSON *Shropsh. Word-bk.*, *Queening*, a fine-flavoured sweet apple, common in the cider-orchards.

queening ('kwi:nɪŋ), *vbl. sb.* [f. QUEEN *v.* + -ING[1].] The action of queening a pawn in chess. Also *attrib.* in ***queening square***, the square on a chess board on which a particular pawn may be queened.

1860 STAUNTON *Chess Praxis* iv. 41 The spirit of the modern game is to regard the Queening of a Pawn as the highest feat a player can accomplish. **1922** A. EMERY *Elements of Chess* iv. 32 Under no circumstances whatever can a solitary pawn on either rook's file be advanced to the queening square, if it is possible for the adverse king to take up a position in front of it on the same file. **1937** M. EUWE *Strategy & Tactics in Chess* viii. 168 In choosing the queening square Black takes care that, at all cost, the White Rook is standing on the adjacent file. **1966** *New Statesman* 9 Sept. 371/3 The draw is secured either by stalemate or by perpetuating the Black Bishop's command of the queening square. **1969** A. GLYN *Dragon Variation* ii. 58 If he takes your Knight now, you play Pawn on and then Queen it, and his own Pawn protects the queening square from his Bishop.

†**'Queenist.** *Obs. rare.* = QUEENITE (applied to partisans of Mary, Queen of Scots).

1563 WINZET *Four Scoir Thre Quest.* Wks. 1888 I. 59 Thai wold mok ws on lyke manere, and call ws Kingistis and Queneistis. **1584** CALDERWOOD in *Wodrow Soc. Misc.* I. 426 In their places entered.. Queenists, such as employed their witts and force with his Mother against himself.

'Queenite. [f. QUEEN *sb.* + -ITE.] One of the partisans of a queen, *esp.* of Queen Caroline against George IV, or of Queen Isabella of Spain against Don Carlos.

1820 J. JEKYLL *Corr.* iii. (1894) 106 Fourteen at table.. mixed of Queenites and Anti-Queenites. **1837** MAJOR RICHARDSON *Brit. Legion* v. (ed. 2) 132 The inhabitants of Vitoria are infinitely more Carlists than Queenites. **1859** DK. BUCKINGHAM *Mem. Geo. IV*, I. 87 Theodore Hook.. made the respectable portion of the Queenites heartily ashamed of their cause.

attrib. **1839** THACKERAY *Major Gahagan* iii, A troop of the Queenite lancers [in Spain].

'queenless, *a.* [-LESS.] Having no queen.

1858 *Sat. Rev.* VI. 29/1 They may learn what happens to the queenless swarm. **1880** LUBBOCK in *Jrnl. Linn. Soc.* XV. 176, I procured a queen.. and put her with some honey in a queenless nest. **1882** *Harper's Mag.* LXV. 252 Gladis hung the cage for one day in her queenless hive.

Hence **'queenlessness**.

1884 *Bee-keeping* (*Brit. Bee-keepers' Assoc.*) 26 With me queenlessness presents the worst of all difficulties.

'queenlet. [-LET.] A petty queen.

1833 CARLYLE *Diderot* in *Misc. Ess.* (1888) V. 33 The whole North swarms with kinglets and queenlets of the like temper. **1899** *Month* Apr. 429, I thought this queenlet lived among the forest folk.

'queenlike, *a.* [-LIKE.] Like a queen; majestic, haughty, etc., as a queen; queenly.

1612 DRAYTON *Poly-olb.* x. 117 Istrad likewise hies Unto the Queen-like Cluyd. **1670** HANNAH WOLLEY (*title*) The Queen-like Closet; or Rich Cabinet stored with all manner of Rare Receipts. **1828** CARLYLE *Misc.* (1857) I. 200 With queenlike indifference she cast it from her hand. **1871** CARLYLE in *Mrs. C.'s Lett.* II. 310 The most queen-like woman I had ever known.

queenliness ('kwi:nlɪnɪs). [f. QUEENLY *a.* + -NESS.] The condition or quality of being queenly.

1863 GEO. ELIOT *Romola* I. 290 Casting around, as it were, an odour of queenliness. **1874** GREEN *Short Hist.* vii. §8. 446 If she [Elizabeth] once broke the silence, it was with a flash of her old queenliness. **1875** BROWNING *Inn Album* iv, The lady's proud pale queenliness of scorn.

queenly ('kwi:nlɪ), *a.* [f. QUEEN *sb.* + -LY[1]. OE. had *cwénlic* in the sense of 'feminine'.]

1. Belonging to, appropriate to, a queen.

c **1540** CROMWELL *Let. to Hen. VIII* in Burnet *Rec.* (1779) I. III. 193, I answered and said.. that I thought she had a Queenly manner. **1550** BALE *Eng. Votaries* II. Diij, He deprived her of all queenly honour. **1570** FOXE *A. & M.* I. 546 Whether they shal be eyther of regal, quenely, or imperial dignitie. **1849** W. M. W. CULL *Reverberations* ii. 2 Soon Alcestis.. With a queenlier presence.. Stept forth. **1878** GLADSTONE *Prim. Homer* 133 In the *Odyssey* Helen reappears full of queenly dignity.

2. Resembling a queen; queenlike. Also *fig.*

1824 MISS MITFORD *Village* Ser. I. (1863) 87 That queenly flower becomes the water. **1854** DORAN *Habits & Men* 104 Anne of Denmark.. did not look queenly even in Elizabeth's robes. **1869** FREEMAN *Norm. Conq.* (1876) III. xi. 33 It had brought forth its queenly leaves and its kingly fruit.

Comb. **1871** AMY DUTTON *Streets & Lanes* i. 32 A queenly-looking old lady.

3. Characteristic or reminiscent of a male homosexual (see QUEEN *sb.* 12).

1968 *Listener* 11 July 59/3 Paul Scofield.. is using his queenliest *Staircase* manner to play a bisexual script-writer. **1976** *Times* 5 Apr. 6/8 A.. rumour went around that the play was really about homosexuals. Certainly some of the dialogue does have a queenly tinge.

So **'queenly** *adv.*, in the manner of a queen.

a **1851** MOIR *To a wounded Ptarmigan* vi, The wild swan from the lake, Ice-unfetter'd oar'd it queenly. **1864** TENNYSON *Aylmer's Field* 169 Queenly responsive when the loyal hand Rose.. as she past.

queen-'mother. [See QUEEN 2 c.]

1. A queen dowager who is the mother of the reigning sovereign.

1577 FRAMPTON *Joyfull Newes* II. lxxvi. 43 b He.. did sende it to kyng Fraunces the seconde, and to the Queene Mother. **1664–5** PEPYS *Diary* (1879) III. 106 Mr. Povy carried me to Somerset House and showed me the Queene-Mother's Chamber. **1768** H. WALPOLE *Hist. Doubts* 98 Why was not the queen-mother applied to.. for his support and education? **1853** MAURICE *Proph. & Kings* xi. 177 A usurpation by the queen-mother for six years follows.

2. A queen who is a mother. Also applied to a queen-bee, and *fig.*

1602 SHAKS. *Ham.* III. i. 190 Let his Queene Mother all alone intreat him To shew his Greefes. *a* **1658** CLEVELAND *Myrtle-Grove* 9 Clarinda rose.. Like the Queen-mother of the Stars above. **1816** KIRBY & SP. *Entomol.* (1818) II. xviii. 118 The first fruits of the queen-mother's vernal parturition assist her. **1899** *Westm. Gaz.* 24 May 5/1 For more than sixty years the Queen-mother has gone in and out among generations of Windsor people.

3. a. A variety of plum. **b.** A variety of pear.

1664 EVELYN *Kal. Hort.* (1729) 233/2 Plums,.. Saint Julian, Queen Mother. **1767** J. ABERCROMBIE *Ev. Man his own Gardener* (1803) 673 Pears,.. Queen mother, Myrobalan [etc.]. **1770** FOOTE *Lame Lover* III. Wks. 1799 II. 86 A damascen plum.. does pretty well indeed in a tart, but .. to compare it with the queen mother, the padrigons [etc.].

4. *attrib.* as †**queen-mother herb**, 'queen's herb', tobacco (Minsheu *Ductor* 1617). *Obs.*

So called after Catherine de Medici, to whom it was sent by Nicot, then ambassador in Portugal (1559–61).

'queen-post. [Cf. KING-POST.] One of two upright timbers in a roof-truss, which are framed above into the rafters and below into the tie-beam, at points equidistant from its middle or ends.

1823 P. NICHOLSON *Pract. Build.* 127 The use of the queen-posts is similar to that of the king-posts; viz. for furnishing a general support for the principals. **1847** SMEATON *Builder's Man.* 72 When the king-post is not thought to be sufficient to support the pressure.. Queen-posts.. may be used. **1851** TURNER *Dom. Archit.* II. iv. 162 This [roof] is very strong and massive, with tie-beams and queen posts.

attrib. **1836** PARKER *Gloss. Archit.* (1850) 394 A king-post roof has one vertical post in each truss, a queen-post roof has two.

queenright ('kwi:nraɪt), *a.* [f. QUEEN *sb.* + RIGHT *a.*] Of a colony of social insects, esp. bees: provided with a queen. (In quot. 1932, 'relating to the presence of a queen'.)

1932 E. B. WEDMORE *Man. Beekeeping* ii. 38 In the writer's opinion the bees in the portion of the hive in question conclude that the queen is failing, and he calls the impulse [to rear a second queen] 'queenright supersedure'. **1966** LAIDLAW & ECKERT *Queen Rearing* ii. 33 A strong queenright colony can care for 45 grafted cells a day. **1971** E. O. WILSON *Insect Societies* xvii. 333/2 Marchal.. also reported the presence of laying workers in queenright wasp colonies. **1974** *Country Life* 2 May 1041/1 The owner of the colony who hasn't an ear for the contented hum of what apiarists call a 'queenright-hive' waits until his slow wits tell him that tragedy has struck.

Queensberry ('kwi:nzbərɪ). Also (*erron.*) **-bury**. The name of Sir John Sholto Douglas (1844–1900), eighth Marquis of Queensberry, used *attrib.* in ***Queensberry rules***, a code of rules drawn up in 1867 under his supervision to govern the sport of boxing in Great Britain; also, the name by which the present rules of boxing are known; also *transf.*

1895 G. B. SHAW in *Sat. Rev.* 28 Sept. 410/1 There the contest was in the presence of a court, with measured ground and due formality—under Queensberry rules, so to speak. **1899** A. CONAN DOYLE in *Strand Mag.* XVIII. 368/1 It's twenty rounds, two-ounce gloves, Queensberry rules. **1931** *Times Lit. Suppl.* 11 June 472/3 Ever since 1866, when the Queensberry rules were introduced, pugilism has lost much of its romantic interest. **1960** *Observer* 24 Jan. 7/2 You would have thought that the average citizen would be only too anxious to see property being protected and would not worry so much about the Queensberry Rules being observed. **1975** *Oxf. Compan. Sports* 110 Broughton's rules were so sensible that they formed the basis of the London Prize-ring Rules drawn up in 1838.. and even of the Queensberry Rules introduced towards the end of the nineteenth century in London. **1977** *New Yorker* 13 June 121/1 An at last complete love affair with a married woman .. was in the Queensberry rules; she could not object.

queenship ('kwi:nʃɪp). [f. QUEEN *sb.* + -SHIP.]

1. The dignity or office of a queen.

1536 ANNE BOLEYN in Ld. Herbert *Hen. VIII* (1683) 447 Neither did I..forget my self in my exaltation, or received Queenship. **1648** HERRICK *Hesper., to Julia* (1869) 28 For thy queen-ship on thy head is set Of flowers a sweet commingled coronet. **1848** FABER *Spir. Confer.* (1861) 146 What name can we give to a queenship so grand? **1876** J. ELLIS *Cæsar in Egypt* 83 Hast thou not saved my State.. And given me Queenship?

2. The personality of a queen; (her) majesty.

1603 DRAYTON *Heroical Ep.* xiii. 107 Y faith her Queeneship little Rest should take. **1694** MOTTEUX *Rabelais* v. xxii. (1737) 101 We..thank'd her Queenship. **1767** *Woman of Fashion* I. 91 It was my Ladyship, I presume, that put her in mind of Cleopatra, no Disparagement to her Queenship.

Queensland ('kwi:nzlənd). [The name of a state in north-eastern Australia.] **a.** In the names of local trees or their woods, esp. **Queensland kauri**, a tall evergreen tree, *Agathis robusta*, of the family Pinaceæ; **Queensland maple**, either of two evergreen trees, *Flindersia brayleyana* or *F. pimenteliana*, of the family Rutaceæ; **Queensland nut** = MACADAMIA; also, the fruit of this tree; **Queensland walnut**, an evergreen tree, *Endiandra palmerstonii*, of the family Lauraceæ. **b. Queensland blue** = *blue heeler* s.v. BLUE *a.* 12 a; **Queensland sore**, a sore which does not heal readily because of scurvy.

1956 G. CASEY in *Coast to Coast 1955–56* 80 It was a noble animal, a true Queensland-blue, with jaws like an alligator, sagacity in its eye, and limbs like a well-muscled leopard. **1977** C. MCCULLOUGH *Thorn Birds* iv. 80 The big Queensland blue fawning and cringing at Father Ralph's feet. **1889** J. H. MAIDEN *Useful Native Plants Austral.* 414 'Queensland Kauri', or 'Dundathu Pine'. Wood of a light yellow colour..largely used by joiners and cabinet-makers. **1932** R. S. TROUP *Exotic Forest Trees in Brit. Empire* 32 *Agathis robusta*..Queensland kauri. A very large tree attaining 160 ft. in height. **1919** R. T. BAKER *Hardwoods Austral.* II. 33 The soft woods are those most generally found on the market, such as Red Cedar, Red Bean, Queensland Maple, Beech, and Pines. **1928** E. H. F. SWAIN *Timber & Forest Products Queensland* 147 Placed on the Southern markets later under the name of Queensland Maple, the wood has risen to fame under this unsuitable trade appellation. **1967** A. RULE *Forests Austral.* xii. 140 Australia's cabinet timbers—Queensland walnut, Queensland maple, red cedar, silky oak, black bean and so forth—were found to make fine sliced veneers. **1881** *Official Rec. Sydney Internat. Exhib. 1879* 750 Queensland Nut... A small-sized tree with a very dense foliage. **1928** E. H. F. SWAIN *Timbers & Forest Products Queensland* 472 The Queensland Nut is one of the finest edible nuts. **1929** [see MACADAMIA]. **1950** *N.Z. Jrnl. Agric.* Dec. 527/1 A number of Queensland nut trees growing in Northland are producing good crops annually. **1963** A. LUBBOCK *Austral. Roundabout* 93 A great, dark tree, rather like an ilex,..bears the Queensland nut. **1892** G. L. JAMES *Shall I try Australia?* xxiv. 242 'Queensland Sores'..are, I believe, generally attributed to excessive thinness and poverty of the blood, caused by the great heat and an absence of vegetable diet. **1945** BAKER *Austral. Lang.* iii. 62 *Barcoo rot*, *Kennedy rot* or *Queensland sore*, a festering sore difficult to cure under inland conditions—it rapidly disappears when the sufferer eats plenty of fruit or green vegetables. **1919** R. T. BAKER *Hardwoods Austral.* II. 339 'Queensland Walnut'..is a good commercial timber. **1967** Queensland walnut [see *Queensland maple* above].

'**Queenslander**. [f. prec. + -ER^{1}.] A native or inhabitant of the state of Queensland in Australia.

1861 J. D. LANG *Queensland, Australia* viii. 238 A letter addressed to the editor of the 'Moreton Bay Courier',..is signed 'A. Queenslander'. **1883** G. W. RUSDEN *Hist. Australia* III. xvii. 235 The gallant conduct of the 'Queenslander', a well-managed newspaper in Brisbane, enables me to use the words of witnesses or neighbours. **1899** E. W. HORNUNG *Amateur Cracksman* 176 The Queenslander handed it to me. **1924** KIPLING *Debits & Credits* (1926) 316 'An' what about your Queenslander?' the Australian asked. **1963** *Times* 12 Mar. p. vi/3 The wise detective could deduce from such a sign that Queenslanders are easy-going to an incredible degree, that they have a loathing for formality and they live in a warm climate. **1978** R. V. JONES *Most Secret War* xvi. 130 A buccaneering Queenslander, Sidney Cotton, who had been a pilot in the Royal Naval Air Service.

queeny ('kwi:nɪ), *a.* Also **queenie**. [f. QUEEN *sb.* 12 + -Y^{1}.] Effeminate; also as *adv.*, in an effeminate manner.

1936 N. MARSH *Death in Ecstasy* xxiv. 299 Alleyn may talk queeny, but he's doped that out. **1937** —— *Vintage Murder* vii. 72 He talks with a corker sort of voice. Not queeny, but just corker. **1952** *Arena* (N.Z.) XXXI. 2 Up in front would be Slick, the leader [*sc.* a sheepdog], stepping along in a queenie way. **1965** G. MCINNES *Road to Gundagai* xv. 265 Thereafter he said he'd rather play football with the other fellows: reading aloud was a bit 'queeny'. **1977** 'J. LE CARRÉ' *Honourable Schoolboy* i. 19 'So what's happened, Lukie?' whined the dwarf, in his queeny Greenwich Village drawl.

queer (kwɪər), *a.*^{1} Forms: 6 queir, queyr, que(e)re, 7 quer, 7– queer. [Of doubtful origin.

Commonly regarded as a. G. *quer* (MHG. *twer*, see THWART), cross, oblique, squint, perverse, wrongheaded; but the date at which the word appears in Sc. is against this, and the prominent sense does not precisely correspond to any of the uses of G. *quer*. There are few examples prior to 1700.]

1. a. Strange, odd, peculiar, eccentric, in appearance or character. Also, of questionable character, suspicious, dubious. ***queer fellow***, an eccentric person; also used, esp. in Ireland and in nautical contexts, with varying contextual connotations (see quots.) Cf. QUARE *a.*

Possibly some examples illustrate QUEER *a.*^{2}

1508 DUNBAR *Flyting* 218 Heir cumis our awin queir Clerk. **1513** DOUGLAS *Æneis* VIII. Prol. 43 The cadgear.. Calland the colȝear ane knaif and culroun full queyr. **1550** BALE *Eng. Votaries* II. 21 Yᵉ Chronycles..contayne muche more truthe than their quere legendes. **1598** MARSTON *Pygmal.* i. 138 Show thy queere substance, worthlesse, most absurd. **1621** W. YONGE *Diary* 27 Aug. (Camden) 43 The emperor is in that quer case, that he is not able to bid battle. **1663** *Flagellum or O. Cromwell* 109 That the world may see what queer hypocrites his attendants were. **1712** STEELE *Spect.* No. 474 ¶2 Let me be known all at once for a queer Fellow, and avoided. **1742** RICHARDSON *Pamela* III. 224, I have heard of many queer Pranks among my Bedfordshire Neighbours. **1840** DICKENS *Barn. Rudge* xxxix, It was a queer fancy..but he was a queer subject altogether. **1870** H. SMART *Race for Wife* i, In the queer old room with its still queerer attempts at decoration. **1883** J. F. KEANE *On Blue Water* 212 Remembering that incident, the 'queer-fellow's' disappearance didn't alarm me very much. **1910** D. W. BONE *Brassbounder* 64 D'ye think th' queer-fella' is goin' t' pay them prices for 'is kit? **1922** [see *middle leg* s.v. MIDDLE *a.* 6]. **1932** J. W. HARRIS *Days of Endeavour* 17 No matter what ship you serves your time in, you'll find there'll be a queer-feller. **1936** J. CURTIS *Gilt Kid* vi. 60 He'd a good mind to tear over and spoil her lark with the queer fellow. **1939** J. BROPHY *Queer Fellow* 10 When I am 'making up' a story,..I am never my normal self, the man that other people know. Nor dare my normal self return for a moment in the hope of catching the other one, The Queer Fellow, as they say in Ireland, at work. **1958** M. PROCTER *Man in Ambush* xii. 134 Mobsters, queer fellows, bar flies and layabouts. **1961** PARTRIDGE *Dict. Slang* Suppl. 1240/2 *The queer fella*, the person that happens to be in command: Regular Army: late c. 19–20. **1962** GRANVILLE *Dict. Sailors' Slang* 93/2 *Queer fella*, any merchant seaman who does not conform to the average type. A nautical eccentric. **1966** 'L. LANE' *ABZ of Scouse* II. 87 *Whur's ther queer feller*? Where is the boss or foreman whose name I don't know?

absol. **1826** SCOTT *Woodstock* (1894) II. 19 His appearance bordered..upon what is vulgarly called the queer.

b. Of a person (usu. a man): homosexual. Also in phr. ***as queer as a coot*** (cf. COOT *sb.*^{1} 2 b). Hence, of things: pertaining to homosexuals or homosexuality. orig. *U.S.*

1922 *Pract. Value of Scientific Study of Juvenile Delinquents* (Children's Bureau, U.S. Dept. of Labor) 8 A young man, easily ascertainable to be unusually fine in other characteristics, is probably 'queer' in sex tendency. **1931** G. IRWIN *Amer. Tramp & Underworld Slang* 153 *Queer*, crooked; criminal. Also applied to effeminate or degenerate men or boys. **1936** J. G. COZZENS *Men & Brethren* i. 24 'He's not queer, or something, is he?' 'Lord, no! Worse than that. He's a convert.' **1937** *Listener* 10 Mar. (Suppl.) p. vii/2 'Queer', in a specifically sexual sense—a word imported from America. **1939** C. ISHERWOOD *Goodbye to Berlin* 296 Men dressed as *women*?.. Do you mean they're *queer*? **1952** [see CAMP *a.* (and *sb.*^{5})]. **1958** P. MORTIMER *Daddy's gone a-Hunting* xxx. 169, I suppose they're queer as coots. **1960** [see BENT *ppl. a.* 5 c]. **1963** [see GAY *a.* 2 c]. **1974** *Amer. Speech 1971* XLVI. 81 *Female homosexual*, lesbian, screwball, queer, lady-lover, minty. **1975** *Times* 9 July 14/2 *Bombus fragrans*..sprinkles himself..with attar of roses, and..is as queer as a coot. **1976** A. WHITE *Long Silence* i. 10 'I say, Peter, you're not turning *queer* by any chance, are you?' The thought that I might be queer had haunted me.

c. In U.S. colloq. phr. ***to be queer for*** (someone or something): to be fond of or 'keen on'; to be in love with.

1953 W. BURROUGHS *Junkie* ii. 28 She began talking about Jack. 'I'm queer for Jack,' she said. 'He works at being a thief just like any job.' **1956** J. BALDWIN *Giovanni's Room* I. ii. 45 Actually, I'm sort of queer for girls myself. **1957** M. SHULMAN *Rally round Flag, Boys!* iv. 51 When..the cellars were finally snug and dry, Waldo promptly persuaded the homesteaders to fill them with..a huge, gleaming variety of tools. This took no great persuasion, for..the average commuter was queer for tools. **1977** *Time* 28 Mar. 54/2 The sister (Carol Potter) is crazy about him and Francis is queer for her brother (Reed Birney), or so he fears.

2. Not in a normal condition; out of sorts; giddy, faint, or ill: *esp.* in phr. ***to feel*** (or ***look***) ***queer***. Also *slang*: Drunk.

1781 S. CRISP *Let.* 1 Mar. in W. H. Hutton *Burford Papers* (1905) 60, I have been very queer for some time, sleepless and indigestion. **1800** W. B. RHODES *Bomb. Fur.* i (1830) 8 We feel ourselves a little queer. **1826** *Sporting Mag.* XVIII. 285 Galloping..with a rummish team, and himself queer. **1837** [see EARTHQUAKY *a.*]. **1848** DICKENS *Dombey* i, I am so very queer that I must ask you for a glass of wine and a morsel of that cake. **1885** MISS BRADDON *Wyllard's Weird* I. i. 39 That business on the railway was enough to make any man feel queer. **1889** J. K. JEROME *Three Men in Boat* i. 14 So I set my face against the sea trip. Not, as I explained, upon my own account. I was never queer. But I was afraid for George. **1922**, **1938** [see COME *v.* 70 f]. **1952** A. CHRISTIE *Mrs McGinty's Dead* iv. 28 Either the husband's taken queer, or the old mother... With old McGinty, at least it was only she herself who came over queer. **1978** 'F. PARRISH' *Sting of Honeybee* iv. 43 Jake's off queer, wi' a rumblin' stummick.

3. ***Queer Street***: An imaginary street where people in difficulties are supposed to reside; hence, any difficulty, fix, or trouble, bad circumstances, debt, illness, etc. *slang*.

1811 *Lex. Balatron.*, *Queer Street*, wrong, improper, contrary to one's wish. It is queer street, a cant phrase, to signify that it is wrong or different to our wish. **1821** P. EGAN *Real Life in London* I. xi. 186 Limping Billy was also evidently in *queer-street*. **1829** —— *Boxiana* 2nd Ser. II. 503 Gas let fly right and left, give Pope a tremendous blow over his left *ogle*, putting him a little into Queer-street. **1837** LYTTON *E. Maltrav.* IV. vii, You are in the wrong box—planted in Queer Street, as we say in London. **1865** DICKENS *Mut. Fr.* III. i, Queer Street is full of lodgers just at present. **1886** STEVENSON *Dr. Jekyll* i. (ed. 2) 11 The more it looks like Queer Street, the less I ask. **1952** A. WILSON *Hemlock & After* III. i. 208 He enjoys a little flutter..and if he finds himself in Queer Street now and again, I'm sure no one would grudge him his bit of fun. **1963** *Times* 8 May 9/2 He felt that the levy should not be applied so rigidly as to force companies into Queer Street if their costs rose faster than their incomes. **1980** J. WAINWRIGHT *Man of Law* xlvii. 222 If Patsold talks, Webb's in queer street.

4. *Comb.*, as ***queer-looking***, ***-shaped***, ***-tempered***.

1825 J. NEAL *Bro. Jonathan* II. 171 A little, modest, queer-looking brown girl. **1838** DICKENS *Nich. Nick.* x, You are the longest-headed, queerest-tempered, old coiner of gold and silver there ever was. **1876** H. SIDGWICK in A. & E. M. Sidgwick *Henry Sidgwick* (1906) v. 323 Stone hovels that a generation ago were the ordinary houses here: things with a hole in the roof, low, queer-shaped. **1891** T. HARDY *Tess* (1900) 105/1 The queer-shaped flints.

queer, *a.*^{2} and *sb.*^{1} *Thieves' cant.* Forms: 6 quyer, quyre, 6–7 quire, quyre, 7 queere, 9 queer. [Of obscure origin: in later use (from *c* 1700) identified in form with prec., and perh. associated with it in meaning.]

A. *adj.* **a.** Bad; worthless.

The exact sense varies with the sb.; for a list of the commonest phrases, as *queer bird*, *buffer*, *bung*, *cole*, etc. see the *Dict. Cant. Crew* (*a* 1700). Cf. also the sbs., as CUFFIN, CULL, etc. In quot. 1561 there may be an allusion to *quire* choir.

1561 AWDELAY *Frat. Vacab.* (1869) 4 A Quire bird is one that came lately out of prison. **1567** HARMAN *Caveat* (1869) 84 *To cutte quyre whyddes*, to geue euell wordes or euell languages. **1609** DEKKER *Lanth. & Candle Lt.* C iij b, To the quier cuffing we bing. **1641** BROME *Jovial Crew* IV. ii. Wks. 1873 III. 431 The Quire Cove and the Harmanbeck. *a* **1700** B. E. *Dict. Cant. Crew*, *Queere*, base, Roguish, naught. **1812** J. H. VAUX *Flash Dict.*, *Queer-bail*, Persons of no repute, hired to bail a prisoner in any bailable case. [**1865** DICKENS *Mut. Fr.* III. i, Concerning that bill-broking branch of the business... What queer bills are to be bought, and at what prices?]

b. Of coins or banknotes: counterfeit, forged.

1740 *Ordinary of Newgate, his Account* III. 15/1 Instead of returning the good Guinea again, they used to give a *Queer One*. **1812**, etc. [see SCREEN *sb.* 2]. **1848** *Ladies' Repository* Oct. 316/2 *Queer*, counterfeit. *Queer screen*, counterfeit paper money. *Queer wedge*, counterfeited silver money. *Queer ridge*, counterfeited *gold money*. **1877** J. HABBERTON *Jericho Road* xvi. 151 'Let's give him fifty [dollars] to send her.' 'Fifty queer?' asked Mr. Lodge. 'No, fifty straight,' said the little man. **1890** *Buckskin Mose* ii. 34 At the same time he pulled out of his pocket a lot of 'queer' or counterfeit bills. **1941** R. CHANDLER in *Detective Story Mag.* Sept. 52 If it was discovered to be queer money, as you say, it would be very difficult to trace the source of it.

B. *sb.*^{1} **a.** Bad money; base coin. Also (*U.S.*), forged paper currency or bonds. Phr. ***to shove*** (***the***) ***queer***: see SHOVE *v.* 10 a.

1812 in J. H. VAUX *Flash Dict.* **1821** P. EGAN *Life in London* II. i. 154 That admired sort of Life in London, all jostling against each other in the Park... The Duke and the 'Dealer in Queer'—the Lady and her Scullion [etc.]. **1847** *National Police Gaz.* (U.S.) 9 Jan. 137/1 'Bogus' is base coin, 'queer' is counterfeit paper. **1859** [see SHOVE *v.* 10]. **1889** G. GISSING *Nether World* II. xi. 233 'Got any *queer* to put round?'.. 'You know what he meant, Bob?' Bob nodded and became reflective. *Ibid.* III. ii. 38 He opened it, and showed about a dozen pieces of money—in appearance half-crowns and florins... 'The snyde' or the 'queer' is the technical name by which such products are known. **1898** A. M. BINSTEAD *Pink 'Un & Pelican* xi. 240 He hardly ever uttered the spurious coins himself..and, consequently, seldom had any 'queer' about his person. **1926** *Flynn's* 16 Jan. 640/2 After I coughed up an' promised to quit the queer he give me th' gate. **1949** E. L. IREY *Tax Dodgers* v. 112 An alcoholic engraver..turned out the best 'queer' that ever competed with the Bureau of Engraving's product and Lustig took over the distribution of the counterfeit money. **1954** W. R. & F. K. SIMPSON *Hockshop* ix. 232 Eagle-eyed concessionaires..always on the lookout for shovers of the queer. **1981** 'E. LATHEN' *Going for Gold* iii. 37 Nobody's laying off any queer on the Sloan [Bank].

b. ***on the queer***: living dishonestly; *spec.* engaged in the forging of currency.

1905 C. H. DAY *Actress & Clerk* ii. 22 Only just feeling of you to see if you was on the queer. **1909** R. A. WASON *Happy Hawkins* 277 Dick may have been on the queer all right, but he was smooth enough to hide it. **1910** C. E. B. RUSSELL *Young Gaol-birds* x. 150 Convinced that he could get along as well 'on the queer', *i.e.*, by thieving, as he could by keeping straight. **1935** *Amer. Speech* X. 11/1 Boys who are *on the queer* are handsomely equipped to print anything from twenty dollar bills to fake government bonds. **1942** BERREY & VAN DEN BARK *Amer. Thes. Slang* §494/2 Counterfeit; forge,..*be on the green goods,—the queer* or *the spud*(*s*).

queer (kwɪə(r)), *sb.*^{2} *slang.* [f. QUEER *a.*^{1} 1 b.] A (usu. male) homosexual. Also in *Comb.*, as ***queer-bashing*** vbl. sb., the attacking of homosexuals; hence ***queer-basher***.

[**1932** AUDEN in *Rev. Eng. Stud.* (1978) Aug. 294 An underground cottage frequented by the queer.] **1935** *Amer. Speech* X. 19/2 *Queer*... A male homosexual. **1936** L. DUNCAN *Over Wall* xx. 277 There was even a little room.. where the 'fairies', 'pansies', and 'queers' conducted their lewd practices. **1946** E. WAUGH *Jrnl.* 21 Nov. (1976) VI. 663 The headmaster, an old queer. **1952** A. WILSON *Hemlock & After* I. iii. 58, I quite like queers if it comes to that, so long as they're not on the make. **1959** ANON. *Streetwalker* I. i. 18 Jackie, one of the commercial queers..is a tall, gangling boy with long hair..combed into carefully casual curls. **1965** *Spectator* 19 Feb. 239/1 Smith pursues Lulu in Valletta only to discover that she is a queer. **1966** [see FAGGOT, FAGOT *sb.* 6 b]. **1970** *Times* 5 Feb. 2/3 Four of 12 youths said to have taken part in a 'queer bashing' expedition on Wimbledon Common on September 25 were found Guilty of murder. *Ibid.* 25 Nov. 9/5 (*heading*) 'Queer-bashers' lose appeal. **1975** [see PANSY 3 a]. **1977** *New Wave Mag.* No. 7. 6 To fight the National Front, the queer-bashers and any other diseases.

Hence **'queerdom.**

1965 *New Statesman* 9 July 58/1 Its climactic evocation of high Hapsburg queerdom at its annual drag ball. **1977** *Daily Express* 29 Jan. 7/2 This is a groin-directed compound of mime, ballet and freak show which, as a mere heterosexual, I take to be a celebration of the erotic imagery of queerdom.

queer (kwɪə(r)), *v. slang.* [f. QUEER *a.*[1] or *a.*[2]] **1.** *trans.* **a.** To quiz or ridicule; to puzzle. **b.** To impose on, swindle, cheat.

1790 *By-Stander* 343 Young rascals, who are telling you.. how archly they queer attornies. **1797** MRS. M. ROBINSON *Walsingham* II. 299 'You're found out, that's all', replied the turnkey,..'there's no queering the law'. **1812** COLMAN *Br. Grins, Two Parsons* lxviii, A shoulder-knotted puppy, with a grin, Queering the threadbare curate, let him in. **1819** BORROW *Wand. Children* in W. J. Knapp *Life* I. 64 Well, we have tramped the roads, and queered Full many a sharp and flat. **1854** W. HARCOURT *Let.* in A. G. Gardiner *Life W. Harcourt* (1923) I. iv. 76 The American Minister..spat on the floor all dinner-time. I hear he does this to queer the Britishers, and does not practise those manners at home.

2. a. To spoil, put out of order. Also, with a person as object: to spoil the reputation of, to put (a person) in bad odour (with someone); to spoil (a person's) undertaking, chances, etc.

1812 J. H. VAUX *Flash Dict.* **1818** *Sporting Mag.* II. 189 His ogles were queered..and his head was dunned. **1884** G. MOORE *Mummer's Wife* (1887) 190 All they [the chorus] dared do they did to 'queer' her Scene. **1895** J. L. FORD *Bohemia Invaded* 91 Without having you come in and queer me right in the middle of it [*sc.* a story]. **1895** E. W. TOWNSEND *Chimmie Fadden* 38 De Duchess gives me de orders, an' I wasn't goin' to queer meself wid 'er any more. **1904** *N.Y. Tribune* 12 Jan. 2/1 Van Wyck will queer the whole thing. His appearance before the National Committee will recall..things that knocked Tammany out in 1901. **1913** *Dialect Notes* IV. 11 *Queer, v.* To spoil the reputation (or good impression) a person has made or is trying to make. 'That *queered* me with the teacher.' **1919** E. O'NEILL *Moon of Caribbees* 17 *Bella*... Don't talk so loud. .. Think I wants the ole captain to put me off the ship, do you? *Yank.* Yes, nix on hollerin', you! D'yuh wanta queer all of us? **1927** [see HORN *v.* 3 c]. **1941** *Sun* (Baltimore) 25 Aug. 10/1 (*heading*) Queering the oil conservation drive.

b. *to queer the pitch*: to interfere with or spoil the business (of a tradesman or showman) (cf. PITCH *sb.*[2] 11 a); now freq. *to queer one's pitch* (in more general use). Hence in similar phrases, as *to queer the game, the job*, etc.

1846 *Swell's Night Guide* 47 Rule iv... Nanty coming it on a pall, or wid cracking to queer a pitch. **1866** M. MACKINTOSH *Stage Reminisc.* vii. 93 The smoke and fumes of 'blue fire' which had been used to illuminate the fight came up through the chinks of the stage, fit to choke a dozen Macbeths, and—pardon the little bit of professional slang —poor Jamie's 'pitch' was 'queered' with a vengeance. **1875** T. FROST *Circus Life* xvi. 278 The spot they select for their performance is their 'pitch', and any interruption of their feats, such as an accident, or the interference of a policeman, is said to 'queer the pitch'. **1889** E. SAMPSON *Tales of Fancy* 38 They could not understand it when their pitch was queered, and one or two of the gang arrested. **1890** *Punch* 16 Aug. 74/3 Wy, they'd queer the best pitches in life, if they kiboshed the Power of the Quid! **1901** *Windsor Mag.* Dec. 204/1, I think you and I between us have queered the game. **1911** L. MERRICK *Position of Peggy Harper* III. i. 287 'You leave the contract to me...' 'I can do all that's wanted... You'd go asking too much and queering the job for me.' **1919** H. JENKINS *John Dene of Toronto* (1920) i. 17 'Suppose the Germans were able to sink a ship without even showing their periscopes?'.. 'Oh, shucks!' cried John Dene in disgust. It would queer the whole outfit... It would mighty soon finish the war.' **1927** *Observer* 4 Dec. 19/4 It may conceivably queer the pitch of Mr. de Valera, who..is about to approach the American public for a substantial sum. **1934** J. E. NEALE *Queen Eliz. I* xix. 334 Elizabeth..tried to break off... He went on, determined to queer the pitch for Coke and his supporter Burghley. **1973** E. LEMARCHAND *Let or Hindrance* iv. 31 He's a decent lad... He would never have risked queering Wendy's pitch with Eddy. **1977** *Rolling Stone* 5 May 50/1 Since trying to crash a closed Stones party the first night would likely queer the whole deal, I decided to check out El Mocambo with a local reporter.

3. To put (one) out; to make (one) feel queer.

1845 W. CORY *Lett. & Jrnls.* (1897) 34 Hallam was rather queered (it not being in his line to do anything so conspicuous). **1894** *Outing* (U.S.) XXIV. 362/2 It queered me to think what would happen if they were to lose foothold.

Hence **'queerer**, one who queers.

1812 COLMAN *Br. Grins, Two Parsons* lxxxv, These wooden wits, these quizzers, queerers, smokers.

queer, obs. form of *quere* QUÆRE, QUIRE.

queer(e, obs. forms of CHOIR *sb.*

queerie ('kwɪərɪ). *slang.* [f. QUEER *a.*[1] 1 b + -IE.] One who is queer; esp. one who is soft, effeminate, or homosexual.

1938 *Amer. Mercury* Oct. 181/1 Any boy showing interest in [classes] is correctly considered a 'queerie'. **1940** L. L. STANLEY *Men at their Worst* xx. 201 In every prison are many sex perverts. We know them the minute they step through the front gates on their way into prison. They are known as the 'Queens', the 'Fairies', the 'Queeries', and by other names. **1942** BERREY & VAN DEN BARK *Amer. Thes. Slang* §405/1 Effeminate man or masculine woman; homosexual,..*queerie.* **1951** *N.Y. Jrnl.-American* 14 Aug. 3/1 Why then does he want to get his hands on these millions? To pay the wages of a lot of queeries in the State Department? **1972** B. RODGERS *Queen's Vernacular* 165 *Queer,..queerie* ('that little "queerie" is the only one I know who shoots Sal Hepatica').

†**queering**, ? syncopated f. *kevering* COVERING.

1688 R. HOLME *Armoury* III. 261/2 Queering is the covering of a Wall..new built, that Rain drive not into it.

'queeringness. *rare*[−1]. [f. QUEER *v.* + -ING[1] + -NESS.] Aptness to distort or to falsify.

1955 E. BOWEN *World of Love* ii. 49 She mistrusted the past's activity and its queeringness..who did not speak of it either with falsifying piety or with bitterness.

queerish ('kwɪərɪʃ), *a.* Also 8 quear-. [f. QUEER *a.*[1] + -ISH.] Somewhat queer.

1747 *Gentl. Mag.* 191 God knows the cause! but Nan looks quearish. **1775** S. J. PRATT *Liberal Opin.* xlix. (1783) II. 97 Methinks the London ladies are a little queerish. **1819** SHELLEY *Peter Bell* II. vi, He called the ghost..It had a queerish look. **1846** LANDOR *Exam. Shaks.* Wks. II. 274, I myself did feel queerish and qualmy.

Hence **'queerishness.**

1805 RAMSAY *Scotl. & Scotsmen in 18th C.* (Allardyce, 1888) I. 382 The queerishness of his countenance.

queerister, obs. form of CHORISTER.

queerity ('kwɪərɪtɪ). Also 8 que(a)r-. [f. QUEER *a.*[1] + -ITY.] Queerness, oddity.

1711 STEELE *Spect.* No. 17 ¶3 No Person..shall be admitted without a visible Quearity in his Aspect, or peculiar Cast of Countenance. **1720–1** *Lett. fr. Mist's Jrnl.* (1722) II. 303 When I survey the Querity of thy Aspect. *a* **1849** POE *Marginalia* Wks. 1864 III. 555 The pages have now and then a typographical queerity. **1880** BLACKMORE *Mary Anerley* II. 146 York city, teeming..with most delightful queerities.

queerk, obs. form of QUIRK *sb.*

queerly ('kwɪəlɪ), *adv.*[1] [f. QUEER *a.*[1] + -LY[2].] Strangely, oddly.

1707 HEARNE *Collect.* 16 Apr. (O.H.S.) II. 6 [He] liv'd querely. **1714** in Somers *Tracts* (1748) I. 387 The Earl looked queerly. **1790** MAD. D'ARBLAY *Diary* 6 May, A sister-in-law of the queerly celebrated Miss Monckton. **1864** SIR F. PALGRAVE *Norm. & Eng.* IV. 395 Names.. queerly inappropriate.

†**'queerly**, *adv.*[2] *Obs. Cant.* [f. QUEER *a.*[2]] In a bad or rascally manner.

a **1700** B. E. *Dict. Cant. Crew* s.v. *Queere, How Queerely the Cull Touts*, how roguishly the Fellow looks.

queerness ('kwɪənɪs). [f. QUEER *a.*[1] + -NESS.] **1.** Strangeness († reluctance); queer ways, condition, etc. Also, an instance of this.

1687 BP. TRELAWNY in *T. Papers* Camden Misc. (1853) II. 19 There seemed a greate querenesse in them to the signing of it. **1748** RICHARDSON *Clarissa* (1811) IV. 171 Queernesses I could not away with. **1821–30** LD. COCKBURN *Mem.* 54 The boys stared at him for his queerness. **1879** ATCHERLEY *Trip Boërland* 43 Six or eight [oxen] were lying dead, and the whole..were showing unmistakable signs of queerness.

2. Homosexuality. Cf. QUEER *a.*[1] 1 b.

1956 L. MCINTOSH *Oxford Folly* 104 Some of the most brilliant Oxford figures are queers, and the others simply ape their mannerisms without having the courage to imitate their queerness. **1958** *Observer* 4 May 15/5 A play which says more about the simple, non-tragic aspects of queerness than anything our theatre has so far permitted. **1965** *New Statesman* 9 July 58/1 Osborne has taken queerness as his subject precisely as Nabokov took the love of pubescent girls.

queest (kwiːst). Forms: α. 5 quysht(e, quyste, quiste, 7, 9 quist, quoist, (7 coist), 8 quiest, 9 quest, queist, 7– queest. β. 7 quees, quiese, 8–9 queece, 9 queeze, quice, quoice, etc. [ME. *quisht*, ? for **cusht*, var. of CUSHAT (OE. *cuscote, -sceote*) by elision of the second vowel. Still current in western dialects.] The ring-dove, wood-pigeon.

α. *c* **1420** *Pallad. on Husb.* I. 758 So hoot is no donge Of foul as of the dowue, a quyshte out take. *c* **1430** *Two Cookery-bks.* 8 Take quystes, an stoppe hem wyth-in wyth hole peper. **1598** SYLVESTER *Du Bartas* I. v. 713 The grizel Quoist. **1601** HOLLAND *Pliny* I. 342 Coists or Stockdoues. **1611** COTGR., *Phavier*, a Ringdoue, Queest, Coushot, Woodculuer. **1800** *Gentl. Mag.* I. 106 The ring-dove or quiest. **1843** *Zoologist* I. 213 Hiding himself in a barn, waiting for 'queests'. **1860** WHYTE MELVILLE *Holmby House* II. iii. 29 The quest's soft, plaintive lullaby. **1870** M. COLLINS *Vivian* II. iii. 35 As pensive as a quoist.

attrib. **1653** URQUHART *Rabelais* II. xxvii, The hornes of a roebuck..the feet of foure queest-doves.

β. **1688** R. HOLME *Armoury* II. 244/2 The Stock Dove..is also termed by us a Quees or Quiese. **1882** *W. Worc. Gloss.*, *Queece.* **1895** *B'ham Weekly Post* 16 Feb. 4/8 A wood-pigeon, or 'quice', is commonly called.

collect. **1896** *Westm. Gaz.* 12 May 4/1 Sitting with his gun waiting for quoice. The quoice were disappointing.

queet, var. COOT *sb.*[2], ankle-joint.

queethe, var. QUETHE *v.*

queeziness, obs. f. QUEASINESS.

queff, quegh, varr. QUAIGH.

quehen, obs. f. WHEN.

quehte, obs. pa. t. of QUETCH *v.*

queich, var. QUAIGH, QUEACH.

queif, obs. Sc. f. COIF.

queiȝte, obs. pa. t. of QUETCH *v.*

†**'queimish**, *a.* (also 5 qweymows), obs. var. SQUEAMISH, q.v. Hence **'queimishly** *adv.*

a **1485** *Promp. Parv.* 419/2 (MS. S.) Qweymows, *infra in* skeymowse, or sweymows, *abhominativus.* **1594** CHAPMAN *Shadow Night*, Ded. A ij, They queimishlie commende it for a pretie toy.

queine, obs. f. QUEAN, QUEEN.

queint, obs. f. QUAINT *a.*; obs. pa. pple. of QUENCH; var. QUENT *v.*

queintise, etc.: see QUAINT-.

queir, obs. Sc. f. CHOIR.

queist, var. QUEEST.

queit, obs. f. QUOIT *sb.*

queite, obs. pa. t. of QUETCH *v.*

queith: see QUETHE *sb.* and *v.*

†**quek, queke.** *Obs. rare.* [Of obscure origin.] A chequer or chess-board; some game played on this. Also *queke-board.*

[**1376** in Riley *Lond. Mem.* (1868) 395 A pair of tables on the outside of which was painted a chequer-board that is called a 'quek'. The complainants played with the defendant Nicholas at quek.] **1426** LYDG. *De Guil. Pilgr.* 11198 Rede..On thyng that ys nat worth a lek; Pleye at the keylës & the quek. **1477** *Act 17 Edw. IV*, c. 3 Diversez novelx ymaginez jeuez appellez Cloishe Kaylez half kewle Hondyn & Hondoute & Quekeborde. *a* **1500** in Freeman *Exeter* (1887) 161 Yong peple..within the said cloistre have exercised unlawful games as the toppe, queke, penny prykke.

quek, var. of QUECK *v.*[1] *Obs.*

quek(e, obs. forms of QUICK.

†**queke**, *int. Obs. rare*[−1]. [Cf. Du. *kweken* to quack.] An imitation of the note of a goose.

c **1381** CHAUCER *Parl. Foules* (Harl. MS.) 594 ȝa queke yit saide the goos ful wele & faire.

queken, -yn, obs. forms of QUICKEN *v.*

quelch (kwɛlʃ, -tʃ), *v. rare.* Also 7 quelsh. [Related to SQUELCH as *quash, quat* to *squash, squat.*] *intr.* and *trans.* To squelch.

1659 WOOD *Life* 31 July (O.H.S.) I. 280 Some hang swinging on the gallery..and then come quelshing downe on people's heads. **1866** BLACKMORE *Cradock Nowell* xxxvi. (1883) 219 With the water quelching in his boots. **1896** A. J. C. HARE *Life* II. x. 277 Any good opinion of me..was quelched by my want of admiration.

queldepoynte: see QUILTPOINT.

†**quele**, *v. Obs.* [OE. *cwelan* = OS. *quelan* to die a violent death (MDu. *quelen* to suffer, be ill), OHG. *quelen* (MHG. *queln*):—OTeut. **kwelan* from root **kwel-*: see QUELL *v.*] To die.

c **1000** *Saxon Leechd.* III. 272 Swa swa fixas cwelað ȝyf hi of wætere beoð. *c* **1175** *Lamb. Hom.* 111 Ðu gederast mare & mare, & men cwelað on hungre. *c* **1205** LAY. 31815 Morð wes iwurðen; quelen þa eorles, quelen þa beornes [etc.]. *a* **1250** *Prov. Ælfred* 155 in *O.E. Misc.* 112 þat he may..god iqueme er he quele.

quele, obs. north. form of WHEEL.

quelea ('kwiːlɪə). [mod.L., the specific name of *Emberiza quelea* (Linnæus *Systema Naturæ* (ed. 10, 1758) I. 177), perh. f. med.L. *qualea* QUAIL *sb.*; adopted as a generic name by H. G. L. Reichenbach (*Avium Systema Naturale* (1850) pl. lxxvi).] An African weaver-bird of the genus so called, belonging to the family Ploceidæ, esp. the red-billed dioch, *Quelea quelea*, which is an important pest of grain crops; = DIOCH. Also *attrib.*

1930 C. F. BELCHER *Birds Nyasaland* 316 (*heading*) Black-fronted Quelea. **1936** E. L. GILL *First Guide S. Afr. Birds* 26 Southern Pink-billed Weaver, Quelea Finch... The adult male in breeding plumage, with his black face surrounded by a halo of pink, is readily recognizable. **1957** BENSON & WHITE *Check List Birds N. Rhodesia* 123 Red-billed Quelea... Only numerous in drier, more open areas. **1964** [see DIOCH]. **1969** N. W. PIRIE *Food Resources* ii. 67 The weaver bird, or quelea, infests 2m square miles of Africa. **1969** *Sci. Jrnl.* Apr. 15/1 Quelea birds..raid cereal crops in swarms numbered in millions. **1973** *Bokmakierie* XXV. 46/2 Colleagues in Kenya handed Mr. Skead over to the Quelea Control officers. **1975** *Times* 19 Feb. 14/6 Other exhibits [at the Centre for Overseas Pest Research] relate to army-worms, quelea birds, and termites.

†**quelet, quylet(e.** *Obs. rare.* [a. OF. *cueillete, cuillette*, etc.: see CULET[1].] A gathering, collection; congregation.

1382 WYCLIF *Lev.* xxiii. 36 It is forsothe of companye, and of quelet. —— *Deut.* xvi. 8 The quylet of the Lord thi God. **1422** tr. *Secreta Secret. Priv. Priv.* vii. 136 There shall noone quylete of auere, ne no hepe of tresure..make his roialme ayeyne come.

quelk-chose, var. *quelque-chose* KICK-SHAW.

quell (kwɛl), *sb.*[1] *rare.* [f. QUELL *v.*[1]] Slaying, slaughter; power or means to quell.

c **1420** *Anturs of Arth.* 49 (Douce MS.) Withe gret questes and quelles Bothe in frethes and felles. **1543** GRAFTON *Contn. Harding* 518 Through al the tyme of hys vsurped reygne neuer ceased theyre quel, murder, death & slaughter. **1605** SHAKS. *Macb.* I. vii. 72 His spungie Officers..shall beare the guilt Of our great quell. **1818** KEATS *Endym.* II. 537 Awfully he stands, A sovereign quell is in his waving hands.

quell, *sb.*² *rare*⁻¹. [a. G. *quelle* spring: cf. QUELL *v.*²] A spring, fountain.

1894 'G. EGERTON' *Discords* 213 She was..the quell of living waters out of which he drew fresh strength for new lays.

quell (kwɛl), *v.*¹ Forms: 1 cwellan, (cwoellan), 3 cwelle, -enn; 3–4 quellen, (5 qvellyn), 3–5 quelle, 5 qwell(e, whell(e, 4, 6 quel, 4– quell. *Pa. t.* 1 cwealde, 3 qualde, quolde, (*pl.* cwelden, cwaldenn, qualden), 3–4 queld(e; 4– quelled, (4 -id, 6 *Sc.* -it, -yt). *Pa. pple.* 3 i-queld, 4 quelt, 6 queld, 4– quelled, (5 -et). [OE. *cwellan* = OS. *quellian* (MDu. *quellen*, Du. *kwellen*), OHG. *quellen*, *chellen* (MHG. *quellen queln*, etc. G. *quälen*), ON. *kvelja* (Sw. *qvälja*, Da. *kvæle*):—OTeut. **kwaljan*, causative from the root *kwal-*: see QUALE, QUELE.]

1. *trans.* To kill, slay, put to death, destroy (a person or animal). Now *rare* or *Obs.* (in later use associated with sense 3).

c **897** K. ÆLFRED *Gregory's Past.* xlv. 342 Swelce hwa wille blotan ðæm fæder..his agen bearn, & hit ðonne cwelle beforan his eagum. *c* **1000** ÆLFRIC *Exod.* xxix. 16 Þonne þu hine cwelst, þu nymst his blod. *c* **1205** LAY. 1752 Heo qualden [*c* 1275 cwelden] þa Frensce alle þa heo funden. *c* **1250** *Death* 14 in *O.E. Misc.* 168 Þe feond þencheð iwis þe sawle forto cwelle [*v.r.* quelle]. *c* **1350** *Will. Palerne* 179 Briddes & smale bestes wiþ his bow he quelles. *a* **1400–50** *Alexander* 1307 He..Bretens doun all þe bild & þe bernys quellis [*v.r.* whellis]. *c* **1510** BARCLAY *Mirr. Gd. Manners* (1570) D vj, If he be much cruell which doth his body quell Who killeth his owne soule is much more cruell. **1598** HAKLUYT *Voy.* I. 20 Like barbarous miscreants, they quelled virgins vnto death. **1658** J. JONES *Ovid's Ibis* 93 Cassandrus..was by his subjects quelled with earth. **1791** COWPER *Iliad* v. 128 Yet him the dart Quell'd not. **1817** BYRON *Manfred* II. i. 85, I never quell'd An enemy, save in my just defence.

absol. **1297** R. GLOUC. (Rolls) 885 Þis king..bigan berne & quelle. **1590** SHAKS. *Mids. N.* V. i. 292 O Fates..Quaile, crush, conclude, and quell.

†**b.** To dash *out*, knock *down*. (Cf. KILL *v.* 1.) *Obs. rare.*

c **1374** CHAUCER *Troylus* IV. 18 (46) They fyghte..And with here axes out þe braynes quelle. **1535** STEWART *Cron. Scot.* I. 636 With mony knok the Romanes doun tha quell. *a* **1550** *Christis Kirke Gr.* xxi, The carlis with clubbis coud udir quell Quhyle blude at breistis out bokkit.

c. To kill, destroy (a plant). *rare*⁻¹.

1778 [W. MARSHALL] *Minutes Agric.* 6 June 1775 A dry summer, no doubt, quells the roots.

2. To destroy, put an end to, suppress, extinguish, etc. (a thing or state of things, *esp.* a bad or disagreeable one, a feeling, disposition, etc.).

13.. *Gaw. & Gr. Knt.* 751 Þat syre þat..was borne oure baret to quelle. *a* **1400** *Ipotis* 334 in Horstm. *Altengl. Leg.* (1881) 345 He wente to helle, þe fendes pouste for to quelle. **1591** SHAKS. *Two Gent.* IV. ii. 13 All her sodaine quips, The least whereof would quell a louers hope. **1650** FULLER *Pisgah* II. iv. 103 Here some Commentators being not able to quell, never raise this objection. **1678** *Trans. Crt. Spain* 25 This light punishment quelled all the false reports. **1725** DE FOE *Voy. round World* (1840) 342 The captain quelled this mutiny. **1781** GIBBON *Decl. & F.* xxxi. III. 249 An indefatigable ardour, which could neither be quelled by adversity, nor satiated by success. **1832** LANDER *Adv. Niger* II. xii. 181 We soon succeeded in quelling their fears. **1868** FREEMAN *Norm. Conq.* (1876) II. viii. 173 All opposition was quelled by fire and sword.

3. To crush or overcome (a person or thing); to subdue, vanquish, reduce to subjection or submission; †to force down *to*.

1570 *Satir. Poems Reform.* xxiii. 124 Thay did comfort vs, And maid vs fre quhen strangers did vs quell. **1610** HEALEY *St. Aug. City of God* 650 Pompey the great quelled them first, and made them tributaries to Rome. **1645** MILTON *Tetrach.* Wks. (1847) 178/1 (Gen. i. 27) The want of this quells them to a servile sense of their own conscious unworthiness. **1748** GRAY *Alliance* 91 With side-long plough to quell the flinty ground. **1838** THIRLWALL *Greece* IV. xxxiii. 320 It might enable him to quell the revolted Egyptians. **1868** FREEMAN *Norm. Conq.* (1876) II. viii. 297 The energy of William had thus thoroughly quelled all his foes.

absol. **1853** C. BRONTE *Villette* xv, He quelled, he kept down when he could.

†**4.** *intr.* = QUAIL *v.* 2, QUEAL *v. Obs.*

1579 SPENSER *Sheph. Cal.* Mar. 8 Winters wrath beginnes to quell [*gloss.* to abate]. *a* **1599** —— *F.Q.* VII. vii. 42 Then came old January, wrapped well..Yet did he quake and quiver, like to quell. **1616** SURFL. & MARKH. *Country Farme* 114 Where ten thousand haue died for want of this exercise, not one hath quelled which hath beene vsed in this manner.

Hence **quelled** *ppl. a.*

13.. *Gaw. & Gr. Knt.* 1324 Quykly of þe quelled dere a querré þay maked. **1821** JOANNA BAILLIE *Metr. Leg.*, *Wallace* iii, Her quell'd chiefs must tamely bear From braggart pride the taunting jeer.

quell, *v.*² *rare.* [In first quot. app. repr. an OE. **cwellan* = OS., OHG. *quellan*: in second quot. a. G. *quellen.*] *intr.* To well out, flow.

1340 *Ayenb.* 248 Þe welle eurelestinde þet alneway kuelȝ and fayly ne may. **1863** KINGSLEY *Water-Bab.* i, Out of a low cave..the great fountain rose, quelling and bubbling.

‖**Quellenforschung** ('kvɛlən,fɔrʃʊŋ). [Ger., f. *quelle* source + *forschung* research.] The study of the sources of, or influences upon, a literary work.

1958 C. S. LEWIS in *Times Lit. Suppl.* 28 Nov. 689/3, I wonder how much *Quellenforschung* in our studies of older literature seems solid only because those who knew the facts are dead and cannot contradict it? **1966** J. WAIN in *Punch* 27 Apr. 616/2, I hadn't read the book when I wrote *Hurry On Down*, but I had read Orwell's literary and social criticism. .. Conclusion of *Quellenforschung.* **1975** *Times Lit. Suppl.* 29 Aug. 974/4 Inter-textuality would appear to be so universally applicable to medieval literature as to imply, at best a statement of the obvious, at worst *Quellenforschung* in sheep's clothing.

queller ('kwɛlə(r)). [OE. *cwellere* = ON. *kveljari*: see QUELL *v.*¹ and -ER¹.] One who quells, in senses of the vb.

Freq. as a second element in combs., e.g. *boy-*, *child-*, *devil-*, *giant-*, *manqueller*.

c **900** tr. *Bæda's Hist.* I. vii. (1890) 38 Se sylfa cwellere ðe hine slean sceolde. *c* **1000** *Ags. Gosp.* Mark vi. 27 Se cinincg ..sende ænne cwellere. *c* **1290** *S. Eng. Leg.* I. 37/116 [To] Iosie þe quellare he was bi-take. **1388** WYCLIF *Tobit* iii. 9 Thou sleeresse [*v.r.* quellere] of thin hosebondis. *c* **1520** BARCLAY *Jugurtha* (ed. 2) 48 The ioye of the quellars and murderers. **1671** MILTON *P.R.* IV. 633 Hail Son of the most High..Queller of Satan. **1804** W. TAYLOR in *Ann. Rev.* II. 219 The promoters and quellers of the Wexford insurrection. **1881** SEELEY *Bonaparte* in *Macm. Mag.* XLIV. 168/2 The queller of Jacobinism..Bonaparte.

quelling ('kwɛlɪŋ), *vbl. sb.* [f. QUELL *v.*¹ + -ING¹.] The action of the vb. QUELL.

1297 R. GLOUC. (Rolls) 5996 Brenningge & robberye & quellinge. **1513** DOUGLAS *Æneis* XIII. iii. 116 All the fludis walxyn reid..Of mannis quelling. **1603** OWEN *Pembrokeshire* (1891) 91 The fallinge of the earth and the quellinge of the poore people. **1641** HINDE *J. Bruen* xlv. 143 The killing or quelling of many noysome lusts. **1779** HERVEY *Nav. Hist.* II. 97 The quelling of Tyrone's rebellion.

quelling ('kwɛlɪŋ), *ppl. a.* [f. as prec. + -ING².] That quells, in senses of the vb.

1581 T. HOWELL *Deuises* (1879) 211 Through quelling cares that threat my woful wrack. **1602** CAREW *Cornwall* 125 b, The imaginary Prince receiued a quelling wound in his head. **1641** MILTON *Ch. Govt.* II. iii, The heaviest and most quelling tyranny. **1894** MRS. H. WARD *Marcella* I. 124 Lord Maxwell had written him a quelling letter.

†'**quellio.** *Obs.* [ad. Sp. *cuello* neck, collar:—L. *collum* neck.] A Spanish ruff. Also *attrib.*

1632 MASSINGER *City Madam* IV. iv, Your Hungerland bands, and Spanish quellio ruffs. **1633** SHIRLEY *Triumph Peace* 9, I ha' seene..Baboones in Quellios, and so forth. **1638** FORD *Lady's Trial* II. i, Our rich mockado doublet, With our cut cloth-of-gold sleeves, and our quellio.

†**quelm**, *v. Obs.* [OE. *cwelman*, *cwielman* (= OS. *quelmian* once in Hel.), f. *cwealm* QUALM.] *trans.* To torment; to kill, destroy.

c **825** *Vesp. Psalter* xxxvi. 11 Ðenedon bogan his..ðæt hie cwaelmen ða rehtheortan. **971** *Blickl. Hom.* 63 Judas nu is cwylmed..on þæm ecum witum. *a* **1300** *E.E. Psalter* xxxvi. 14 He bent his bowe..þat he..quelm rightwis of hert.

Hence †'**quelmer**, a destroyer. *Obs.*

c **1425** LYDG. *Assembly of Gods* 709 Quelmers of chyldren, with fornycatours.

†**quelme**, obs. variant of WHELM.

1647 H. MORE *Song of Soul* I. I. xxv, So School-boyes do aspire With coppell'd hat to quelme the Bee.

quelp, obs. f. WHELP.

quelque-chose: see KICKSHAW.

quelt, obs. f. KILT *sb.*

DOMI MINA
NVS TIO
ILLV MEA